SUBJECT GUIDE TO

Children's Books In Print®

2018

This edition of

SUBJECT GUIDE TO CHILDREN'S BOOKS IN PRINT® 2018

was prepared by R.R. Bowker's Database Publishing Group
in collaboration with the Information Technology Department.

Kevin Sayar, Senior Vice President & General Manager
Angela D'Agostino, Vice President Business Development
Mark Van Orman, Senior Director Content Operations

International Standard Book Number/Standard Address Number Agency
Beat Barblan, Director Identifier Services
John Purcell, Manager, ISBN Agency
Richard Smith, Product Manager, Identifier Services
Raymond Reynolds, Lisseth Montecinos, Cheryl Russo, Publisher Relations Representatives

Data Services
Lisa Heft, Senior Manager Content Operations
Adrene Allen, Kathleen Cunningham, Managers Content Operations
Ron Butkiewicz, Latonia Hall, Ila Joseph, John Litzenberger,
Rhonda McKendrick, Tom Lucas,
Beverly Palacio, and Cheryl Patrick, Senior Data Analysts QA
Jenny Marie Adams, Supervisor Data Quality
Terry Campesi, E-Content Editor II
Mark Ahmad, Lynda Keller, Rosemary Walker, Profilers

Publisher Relations
Patricia Payton, Senior Manager Publisher Relations & Content Development
Ralph Coviello, Jack Tipping and Suzanne Franks, Publisher Relations Managers
Claire Edwards, Publisher Relations Administrator
Joanne Firca, Assistant Publisher Relations Analyst

Data Services Production
Andy K. Haramasz, Manager Data Distribution & QA

Editorial Systems Group
Mark Heinzelman, Chief Data Architect

Computer Operations Group
Ed Albright, UNIX Administrator
John Nesselt, UNIX Administrator

Bowker®

SUBJECT GUIDE TO

Children's Books In Print®

2018

A Subject Index to Books
for Children and Young Adults

SUBJECT GUIDE

- **Subjects A-Z**
- **Publishers**
- **Wholesalers & Distributors**

GREY HOUSE PUBLISHING

ProQuest LLC
789 E. Eisenhower Parkway
P.O. Box 1346
Ann Arbor, MI 48106-1346
Phone: 734-761-4700
Toll-free: 1-800-521-0600
E-mail: customerservice@proquest.com
URL: http://www.proquest.com

Grey House Publishing, Inc.
4919 Route 22
Amenia, NY 12501
Phone: 518-789-8700
Toll-free: 1-800-562-2139
Fax: 518-789-0545
E-mail: books@greyhouse.com
URL: http://www.greyhouse.com

Subject Guide to Children's Books In Print® 2018 is published by Grey House Publishing, Inc. under exclusive license from ProQuest LLC.

Publishers may update or add to their listings by accessing one of Bowker's online portals: **BowkerLink** for international publishers at http://www.bowkerlink.com and **MyIdentifiers** for USA publishers at http://www.myidentifiers.com.

No payment is either solicited or accepted for the inclusion of entries in this publication.

International Standard Book Numbers

ISBN 13: 978-1-68217-519-4

International Standard Serial Number

0000-0167

Library of Congress Control Number

74-643526

Printed and bound in Canada.

CONTENTS

How To Use
SUBJECT GUIDE TO CHILDREN'S BOOKS IN PRINT®

The 49th edition of R.R. Bowker's ***Subject Guide to Children's Books In Print®*** was produced from the Books In Print database. This volume only includes books published after 2003. Titles listed in ***Children's Books In Print®*** *are included in the Subject Guide edition.* There are approximately 464,000 listings under 10,000 subject categories. These titles are available from approximately 17,000 United States publishers. An index with full contact information for all of the publishers listed in the bibliographic entries is included in this volume, as well as in a separate index to wholesalers and distributors.

RELATED PRODUCTS

In addition to the printed version, the entire Books In Print database (more than 45 million records, including OP/OSI titles, ebooks, audio books and videos) can be searched by customers on Bowker's Web site, *http://www.booksinprint.com*.

The Books In Print database is also available in an array of other formats such as online access through Books In Print site licensing. Database vendors such as OVID Technologies, Inc make the Books In Print database available to their subscribers.

COMPILATION

In order to be useful to subscribers, the information contained in ***Subject Guide to Children's Books In Print®*** must be complete and accurate. Publishers are asked to review and correct their entries prior to each publication, providing current price, publication date, availability status, and ordering information, as well as recently published and forthcoming titles. Tens of thousands of entries are added or updated for each edition.

DATA ACQUISITION

Bowker aggregates bibliographic information via ONIX, Excel & Text data feeds from publishers, national libraries, distributors & wholesalers. Publishers may also add to or update their listings using one of Bowker's online portals: **BowkerLink** for international publishers at http://www.bowkerlink.com and **MyIdentifiers** for USA publishers at http://www.myidentifiers.com.

Larger publishing houses can submit their bibliographic information to the Books In Print database from their own databases. Bowker's system accepts publisher data 24 hours a day, 7 days a week via FTP. The benefits to this method are: no paper intervention, reduced costs, increased timeliness, and less chance of human error that can occur when re-keying information.

To communicate new title information to Books In Print, the quality of the publisher's textual data must be up to—or extremely close to—reference book standards. Publishers interested in setting up a data feed are invited to access the Bowker Title Submission Guide at http://www.bowker.com or contact us at Data.Submission@bowker.com.

Updated information or corrections to the listings in *Books In Print* can now be submitted at any time via email at Data.Submission@bowker.com. Publishers can also submit updates and new titles to ***Children's Books In Print®*** through one of Bowker's online portals: **BowkerLink** for international publishers at http://www.bowkerlink.com and **MyIdentifiers** for USA publishers at http://www.myidentifiers.com.

To ensure the accuracy, timeliness and comprehensiveness of data in ***Children's Books In Print®***, Bowker has initiated discussions with the major publishers. This outreach entails analyzing the quality of all publisher submissions to the Books In Print database and working closely with the publisher to improve the content and timeliness of the information. This outreach also lays the groundwork for incorporating new valuable information into ***Children's Books In Print®***. We are now collecting cover art, descriptive jacket and catalog copy, tables of contents, and contributor biographies, as well as awards won, bestseller listings, and review citations.

Bowker will make this important additional information available to customers who receive *Books In Print* in specific electronic formats and through subscriptions to *http://www.booksinprint.com*.

HOW THE SUBJECT HEADINGS WERE ASSIGNED

R.R. Bowker's ***Subject Guide to Children's Books In Print®*** is based primarily on the Library of Congress Subject Headings. Many headings were consolidated where they seemed too cumbersome for the needs of this *Subject Guide.* Some books have been assigned to a single category, while other books have been assigned two, three, or more headings.

ALPHABETICAL ARRANGEMENT OF SUBJECT CATEGORIES

Headings are filed alphabetically with the following conditions and variations. First, punctuation is not considered:

ART, ANCIENT
ART—FICTION
ART, GREEK

Second, proper nouns precede improper nouns and names of people precede geographical names:

CLEVELAND, GROVER, 1837-1908
CLEVELAND (OHIO)
CLEVELAND BROWNS (FOOTBALL TEAM)

Third, when personal names appear as headings, those without surnames appear first and religious titles precede royal titles:

PETER, THE APOSTLE, SAINT
PETER I, EMPEROR OF RUSSIA, 1672-1725
PETER, SARAH (WORTHINGTON) KING, 1800-1877

ALPHABETICAL ARRANGEMENT OF TITLES WITHIN THE SUBJECT CATEGORIES

Under each subject heading entries are filed alphabetically by contributor's last name if available, and by title when no contributor exists. Please note the following exceptions:

Initial articles of titles in English, French, German, Italian, and Spanish are deleted from both author and title entries.

Numerals, including year dates, are written out in most cases and are filed alphabetically.

U.S., UN, Dr., Mr., and St. are filed in strict alphabetical order unless the author/publisher requests that the title be filed as if it were spelled out.

Proper names beginning with "Mc" and "Mac" are filed in strict alphabetical order. For example, entries for contributor's names such as MacAdam, MacAvory, MacCarthy, MacDonald, and MacLean are located prior to the pages with entries for names such as McAdams, McCarthy, McCoy, and McDermott.

Entries beginning with initial letters (whether authors' given names, or titles) are filed first, e.g., Smith, H. C., comes before Smith, Harold A.; B is for Betsy comes before Babar, etc.

Compound names are listed under the first part of the name, and cross-references appear under the last part of the name.

INFORMATION INCLUDED IN ENTRIES

Entries include the following bibliographic information, when available: author, co-author, editor, co-editor, translator, co-translator, illustrator, co-illustrator, photographer, co-photographer, title, number of volumes, edition, series information, language if other than English, whether or not illustrated, grade range, year of publication, price, International Standard Book Number, publisher's order number, imprint, and publisher abbreviation. Entries new to this edition are indicated by an asterisk (*) before the bolded ISBN. (Information on the International Standard Book Numbering System is available from R.R. Bowker.)

The prices cited are those provided by the publishers and generally refer to either the trade edition or the Publisher's Library Bound edition. The abbreviation "lib. bdg." is used whenever the price cited is for a publisher's library bound edition.

ISBN AGENCY

Each title included in R.R. Bowker's ***Subject Guide to Children's Books In Print®*** has been assigned an International Standard Book Number (ISBN) by the publisher. All ISBNs listed in this directory have been validated by using the check digit control, ensuring accuracy. ISBNs allow order transmission and bibliographic information updating using publishing industry supported EDI formats (e.g., ONIX). Publishers not currently participating in the ISBN system may request the assignment of an ISBN Publisher Prefix from the ISBN Agency by calling 877-310-7333, faxing 908-795-3518, or through the ISBN Agency's web site at **http://www.myidentifiers.com**. Please note: The ISBN prefix 0-615 is for decentralized use by the U.S. ISBN Agency and has been assigned to many publishers. It is not unique to one publisher.

SAN AGENCY

Another listing feature in **Subject Guide to Books In Print®** is the Standard Address Number (SAN), a unique identification number assigned to each address of an organization in or served by the publishing industry; it facilitates communications and transactions with other members of the industry.

The SAN identifies either a bill to or ship to address for purchasing, billing, shipping, receiving, paying, crediting, and refunding, and can be used for any other communication or transaction between participating companies and organizations in the publishing supply chain.

To obtain an application or further information on the SAN system, please email the SAN Agency at **SAN@bowker.com,** or visit **www.myidentifiers.com**

PUBLISHER NAME INDEX

A key to the abbreviated publisher names (e.g., "Middle Atlantic Pr.") used in the bibliographic entries of ***Subject Guide to Children's Books In Print®*** is found after the Subject Index. Entries in this index contain each publisher's abbreviated name, followed by its ISBN prefix(es), business affiliation, (e.g., "Div. of International Publishing") when available, ordering address(es), SAN (Standard Address Number), telephone, fax, and toll-free numbers. Editorial address(es) (and associated contact numbers) follow. Addresses without a specific label are for editorial offices rather than ordering purposes.

Abbreviations used to identify publishers' imprints are followed by the full name of the imprint. E-mail and Web site addresses are then supplied. A listing of distributors associated with the publisher concludes each entry; each distributor name is in bold type and may be found in the Wholesaler & Distributor Name Index (see below).

A dagger preceding an entry and the note "CIP" at the end of the entry both indicate that the publisher participates in the Cataloging in Publication Program of the Library of Congress.

Foreign publishers with U.S. distributors are listed, followed by their three-character ISO (International Standards Organization) country code ("GBR," "CAN," etc.), ISBN prefix(es), when available, and a cross-reference to their U.S. distributor, as shown below:

Atrium (GBR) *(0-9535353) Dist by* **Dufour.**

Publishers with like or similar names are referenced by a "Do not confuse with ... " notation at the end of the entry. In addition, cross-references are provided from imprints and former company names to the new name.

WHOLESALER & DISTRIBUTOR NAME INDEX

Full information on distributors as well as wholesalers is provided in this index. Note that those publishers who also serve as distributors may be listed both here and in the Publisher Name Index.

SAMPLE ENTRY – SUBJECT

1 BEACH EROSION
2 see also Coast Changes; Shore Protection
3 Akyeampong, Emmanuel. 4 Between the Sea & the Lagoon:
5 An Eco-Social History of the Anlo of Southeastern Ghana: c. 1850 to Recent Times
6 2008 7 (Western African Studies). 8 (Illus.). 9 256p. 10 pap. 11 24.95.
12 978-0-8214-1409-5(7). 13 Ohio Univ. Pr.
14 __ 15 Between the Sea & the Lagoon:
16 An Eco-Social History of the Anlo of Southeastern Ghana: c. 1850 to Recent Times
17 2008 18 Tchr's Ed. 19 (Western African Studies). 20 (Illus.). 95 21 256p.
22 34.99 23 978-0-8214-1408-8(9). 24 Ohio Univ. Pr.

BEACH EROSION

see also Coast Changes; Shore Protection

Akyeampong, Emmanuel Kwaku. Between the Sea & the Lagoon : An Eco-Social History of the Anlo of South-eastern Ghana: c. 1850 to Recent Times. 2002. (Western African Studies). (Illus.). 256p. pap. 24.95 978-0-8214-1409-5(7) . Ohio Univ. Pr.

—Between the Sea & the Lagoon : An Eco-Social History of the Anlo of Southeastern Ghana: C. 1850 to Recent Times. 2002. (Western African Studies). (Illus.). 256p. 44.95 978-0-8214-1408-8(9) . Ohio Univ. Pr.

Footnote:
This sample does not include all elements that can be found in an entry.

KEY

1 Subject Heading
2 Subject x-reference information
3 Main Contributor's last name, first, M.I.
4 Title of the Book
5 Subtitle
6 Publication Year
7 Title of the Series
8 Illustration Indicator
9 Total pages
10 Binding - format
11 Price
12 International Standard Book Number - ISBN13 (ISBN10 check digit)
13 Publisher
14 New title under same contributor indicator
15 Title of book
16 Subtitle
17 Publication year
18 Edition Information
19 Title of Series
20 Illustration Indicator
21 Total pages
22 Price
23 International Standard Book Number - ISBN13 (ISBN10 check digit)
24 Publisher

SAMPLE ENTRY
PUBLISHER NAME INDEX

1 † 2 **Mosby, Inc.,** 3 *(0-323; 0-7234; 0-8016; 0-8151; 0-88416; 0-941158; 1-55664; 1-56815),* 4 Div. of Harcourt, Inc., A Harcourt Health Sciences Co., 5 Orders Addr.: 6227 Sea Harbor Dr., Orlando, FL 32887 6 Toll Free Fax: 800-235-0256 7 Toll Free: 800-543-1918 8 Edit Addr.: 11830 Westline Industrial Dr., Saint Louis, MO 63146
9 (SAN 200-2280) 10 Toll Free: 800-325-4177
11 Web site: http://www.mosby.com/
12 Dist(s): ***PennWell Corp.*** 13 *CIP.*

KEY

1 CIP Identifier
2 Publisher Name
3 ISBN Prefixes
4 Division of
5 Orders Address
6 Orders Fax
7 Orders Telephone
8 Editorial Address
9 SAN
10 Toll-Free
11 Web site
12 Distributors
13 Cataloging in Publication

SAMPLE ENTRY
WHOLESALER & DISTRIBUTOR NAME INDEX

1 **New Leaf Distributing Co., Inc.,** 2 *(0-9627209),* 3 Div. of Al-Wali Corp.,
4 401 Thornton Rd., Lithia Springs, GA 30122-1557 5 (SAN 169-1449)
6 Tel: 770-948-7845; 7 Fax: 770-944-2313; 8 Toll Free Fax: 800-326-1066;
9 Toll Free: 800-326-2665
10 Email: NewLeaf-dist.com
11 Web site: http://www.NewLeaf-dist.com

KEY

1 Distributor name
2 ISBN prefix
3 Division of
4 Editorial address
5 SAN
6 Telephone
7 Fax
8 Toll free fax
9 Toll free
10 E-mail
11 Web site

PUBLISHER COUNTRY CODES

Foreign Publishers are listed with the three letter International Standards Organization (ISO) code for their country of domicile. This is the complete list of ISO codes though not all countries may be represented. The codes are mnemonic in most cases. The country names here may be shortened to a more common usage form.

AFG	AFGHANISTAN
AGO	ANGOLA
ALB	ALBANIA
AND	ANDORRA
ANT	NETHERLANDS ANTILLES
ARE	UNITED ARAB EMIRATES
ARG	ARGENTINA
ARM	ARMENIA
ASM	AMERICAN SAMOA
ATA	ANTARCTICA
ATG	ANTIGUA & BARBUDA
AUS	AUSTRALIA
AUT	AUSTRIA
AZE	AZERBAIJAN
BDI	BURUNDI
BEL	BELGIUM
BEN	BENIN
BFA	BURKINA FASO
BGD	BANGLADESH
BGR	BULGARIA
BHR	BAHRAIN
BHS	BAHAMAS
BIH	BOSNIA & HERZEGOVINA
BLR	BELARUS
BLZ	BELIZE
BMU	BERMUDA
BOL	BOLIVIA
BRA	BRAZIL
BRB	BARBADOS
BRN	BRUNEI DARUSSALAM
BTN	BHUTAN
BWA	BOTSWANA
BWI	BRITISH WEST INDIES
CAF	CENTRAL AFRICAN REP
CAN	CANADA
CH2	CHINA
CHE	SWITZERLAND
CHL	CHILE
CHN	CHINA
CIV	IVORY COAST
CMR	CAMEROON
COD	ZAIRE
COG	CONGO (BRAZZAVILLE)
COL	COLOMBIA
COM	COMOROS
CPV	CAPE VERDE
CRI	COSTA RICA
CS	CZECHOSLOVAKIA
CUB	CUBA
CYM	CAYMAN ISLANDS
CYP	CYPRUS
CZE	CZECH REPUBLIC
DEU	GERMANY
DJI	DJIBOUTI
DMA	DOMINICA
DNK	DENMARK
DOM	DOMINICAN REPUBLIC
DZA	ALGERIA
ECU	ECUADOR
EG	East Germany
EGY	EGYPT
EI	EUROPEAN UNION
EN	England
ESP	SPAIN
EST	ESTONIA
ETH	ETHIOPIA
FIN	FINLAND
FJI	FIJI
FLK	FALKLAND ISLANDS
FRA	FRANCE
FRO	FAEROE ISLANDS
FSM	MICRONESIA
GAB	GABON
GBR	UNITED KINGDOM
GEO	GEORGIA
GHA	GHANA
GIB	GIBRALTAR
GIN	GUINEA
GLP	GUADELOUPE
GMB	GAMBIA
GNB	GUINEA-BISSAU
GNQ	EQUATORIAL GUINEA
GRC	GREECE
GRD	GRENADA
GRL	GREENLAND
GTM	GUATEMALA
GUF	FRENCH GUIANA
GUM	GUAM
GUY	GUYANA
HKG	HONG KONG
HND	HONDURAS
HRV	Croatia
HTI	HAITI
HUN	HUNGARY
IDN	INDONESIA
IND	INDIA
IRL	IRELAND
IRN	IRAN
IRQ	IRAQ
ISL	ICELAND
ISR	ISRAEL
ITA	ITALY
JAM	JAMAICA
JOR	JORDAN
JPN	JAPAN
KAZ	KAZAKSTAN
KEN	KENYA
KGZ	KYRGYZSTAN
KHM	CAMBODIA
KNA	ST. KITTS-NEVIS
KO	Korea
KOR	SOUTH KOREA
KOS	KOSOVA
KWT	KUWAIT
LAO	LAOS
LBN	LEBANON
LBR	LIBERIA
LBY	LIBYA
LCA	ST. LUCIA
LIE	LIECHTENSTEIN
LKA	SRI LANKA
LSO	LESOTHO
LTU	LITHUANIA
LUX	LUXEMBOURG
LVA	LATVIA
MAC	MACAO
MAR	MOROCCO
MCO	MONACO
MDA	MOLDOVA
MDG	MALAGASY REPUBLIC
MDV	MALDIVE ISLANDS
MEX	MEXICO
MHL	MARSHALL ISLANDS
MKD	MACEDONIA
MLI	MALI
MLT	MALTA
MMR	UNION OF MYANMAR
MNE	MONTENEGRO
MNG	MONGOLIA
MOZ	MOZAMBIQUE
MRT	MAURITANIA
MSR	MONTESERRAT
MTQ	MARTINIQUE
MUS	MAURITIUS
MWI	MALAWI
MYS	MALAYSIA
NAM	NAMIBIA
NCL	NEW CALEDONIA
NER	NIGER
NGA	NIGERIA
NIC	NICARAGUA
NLD	THE NETHERLANDS
NOR	NORWAY
NPL	NEPAL
NRU	NAURU
NZL	NEW ZEALAND
OMN	SULTANATE OF OMAN
PAK	PAKISTAN
PAN	PANAMA
PER	PERU
PHL	PHILIPPINES
PNG	PAPUA NEW GUINEA
POL	POLAND
PRI	Puerto Rico
PRK	NORTH KOREA
PRT	PORTUGAL
PRY	PARAGUAY
PYF	FRENCH POLYNESIA
REU	REUNION
ROM	RUMANIA
RUS	RUSSIA
RWA	RWANDA
SAU	SAUDI ARABIA
SC	Scotland
SCG	SERBIA & MONTENEGRO
SDN	SUDAN
SEN	SENEGAL
SGP	SINGAPORE
SLB	SOLOMON ISLANDS
SLE	SIERRA LEONE
SLV	EL SALVADOR
SMR	SAN MARINO
SOM	SOMALIA
STP	SAO TOME E PRINCIPE
SU	Soviet Union
SUR	SURINAM

PUBLISHER COUNTRY CODES

SVK	Slovakia
SVN	SLOVENIA
SWE	SWEDEN
SWZ	SWAZILAND
SYC	SEYCHELLES
SYN	SYNDETICS
SYR	SYRIA
TCA	TURKS NDS
TCD	CHAD
TGO	TOGO
THA	THAILAND
TKM	TURKMENISTAN
TON	TONGA
TTO	TRINIDAD AND TOBAGO
TUN	TUNISIA
TUR	TURKEY
TWN	TAIWAN
TZA	TANZANIA
UGA	UGANDA
UI	UNITED KINGDOM
UKR	UKRAINE
UN	UNITED NATIONS
URY	URUGUAY
USA	UNITED STATES
UZB	UZBEKISTAN
VAT	VATICAN CITY
VCT	ST. VINCENT
VEN	VENEZUELA
VGB	BRITISH VIRGIN ISLANDS
VIR	U.S. VIRGIN ISLANDS
VNM	VIETNAM
VUT	VANUATU
WA	Wales
WSM	WESTERN SAMOA
YEM	REPUBLIC OF YEMEN
YUG	YUGOSLAVIA
ZAF	SOUTH AFRICA
ZMB	ZAMBIA
ZWE	ZIMBABWE

COUNTRY SEQUENCE

AFGHANISTAN	AFG
ALBANIA	ALB
ALGERIA	DZA
AMERICAN SAMOA	ASM
ANDORRA	AND
ANGOLA	AGO
ANGUILLA	AIA
ANTARCTICA	ATA
ANTIGUA & BARBUDA	ATG
ARGENTINA	ARG
ARMENIA	ARM
ARUBA	ABW
AUSTRALIA	AUS
AUSTRIA	AUT
AZERBAIJAN	AZE
BAHAMAS	BHS
BAHRAIN	BHR
BANGLADESH	BGD
BARBADOS	BRB
BELARUS	BLR
BELGIUM	BEL
BELIZE	BLZ
BENIN	BEN
BERMUDA	BMU
BHUTAN	BTN
BOLIVIA	BOL
BOSNIA & HERZEGOVINA	BIH
BOTSWANA	BWA
BOUVET ISLAND	BVT
BRAZIL	BRA
BRITISH INDIAN OCEAN TERRITORY	IOT
BRITISH WEST INDIES	BWI
BRUNEI DARUSSALAM	BRN
BULGARIA	BGR
BURKINA FASO	BFA
BURUNDI	BDI
CAMBODIA	KHM
CAMEROON	CMR
CANADA	CAN
CAPE VERDE	CPV
CAYMAN ISLANDS	CYM
CENTRAL AFRICAN REPUBLIC	CAF
CHAD	TCD
CHILE	CHL
CHINA	CHN
CHRISTMAS ISLAND	CXR
COCOS (KEELING) ISLANDS	CCK
COLOMBIA	COL
COMOROS	COM
CONGO	COG
CONGO, THE DEMOCRATIC REPUBLIC OF THE CONGO	COD
COOK ISLANDS	COK
COSTA RICA	CRI
COTE' D' IVOIRE	CIV
CROATIA	HRV
CUBA	CUB
CYPRUS	CYP
CZECH REPUBLIC	CZE
CZECHOSLOVAKIA	CSK
DENMARK	DNK
DJIBOUTI	DJI
DOMINICA	DMA
DOMINICAN REPUBLIC	DOM
EAST TIMOR	TMP
ECUADOR	ECU
EGYPT (ARAB REPUBLIC OF EGYPT)	EGY
EL SALVADOR	SLV
EQUATORIAL GUINEA	GNQ
ERITREA	ERI
ESTONIA	EST
ETHIOPIA	ETH
EAST GERMANY	DDR
FALKLAND ISLANDS	FLK
FAROE ISLANDS	FRO
FEDERATED STATES OF MICRONESIA	FSM
FIJI	FJI
FINLAND	FIN
FRANCE	FRA
FRENCH GUIANA	GUF
FRENCH POLYNESIA	PYF
FRENCH SOUTHERN TERRITORIES	ATF
GABON	GAB
GAMBIA	GMB
GEORGIA	GEO
GERMANY	DEU
GHANA	GHA
GIBRALTAR	GIB
GREECE	GRC
GREENLAND	GRL
GRENADA	GRD
GUADELOUPE	GLP
GUAM	GUM
GUATEMALA	GTM
GUINEA	GIN
GUINEA-BISSAU	GNB
GUYANA	GUY
HAITI	HTI
HEARD ISLAND & MCDONALD ISLANDS	HMD
HONDURAS	HND
HONG KONG	HKG
HUNGARY	HUN
ICELAND	ISL
INDIA	IND
INDONESIA	IDN
IRAN, ISLAMIC REPUBLIC OF	IRN
IRAQ	IRQ
IRELAND	IRL
ISRAEL	ISR
ITALY	ITA
JAMAICA	JAM
JAPAN	JPN
JORDAN	JOR
KAZAKSTAN	KAZ
KENYA	KEN
KIRIBATI	KIR
KOREA, DEMOCRATIC PEOPLE'S REPUBLIC OF	PRK
KOREA, REPUBLIC OF	KOR
KUWAIT	KWT
KYRGYZSTAN	KGZ
KOSOVA	KOS
LAO PEOPLE'S DEMOCRATIC REPUBLIC	LAO
LATVIA	LVA
LEBANON	LBN
LESOTHO	LSO
LIBERIA	LBR
LIBYAN ARAB JAMAHIRIYA	LBY
LIECHTENSTEIN	LIE
LITHUANIA	LTU
LUXEMBOURG	LUX
MACAU	MAC
MACEDONIA, THE FORMER YUGOSLAV REPUBLIC OF	MKD
MADAGASCAR	MDG
MALAWI	MWI
MALAYSIA	MYS
MALDIVE ISLANDS	MDV
MALI	MLI
MALTA	MLT
MARSHALL ISLANDS	MHL
MARTINIQUE	MTQ
MAURITANIA	MRT
MAURITIUS	MUS
MAYOTTE	MYT
MEXICO	MEX
MOLDOVA, REPUBLIC OF	MDA
MONACO	MCO

COUNTRY SEQUENCE

MONGOLIA	MNG
MONTENEGRO	MNE
MONTSERRAT	MSR
MOROCCO	MAR
MOZAMBIQUE	MOZ
MYANMAR	MMR
NAMIBIA	NAM
NAURU	NRU
NEPAL	NPL
NETHERLANDS	NLD
NETHERLANDS ANTILLES	ANT
NEW CALEDONIA	NCL
NEW ZEALAND	NZL
NICARAGUA	NIC
NIGER	NER
NIGERIA	NGA
NIUE	NIU
NORFOLK ISLAND	NFK
NORTHERN MARIANA ISLANDS	MNP
NORWAY	NOR
OMAN	OMN
OCCUPIED PALESTINIAN TERRITORY	PSE
PAKISTAN	PAK
PALAU	PLW
PANAMA	PAN
PAPUA NEW GUINEA	PNG
PARAGUAY	PRY
PERU	PER
PHILIPPINES	PHL
PITCAIRN	PCN
POLAND	POL
PORTUGAL	PRT
PUERTO RICO	PRI
QATAR	QAT
REUNION	REU
ROMANIA	ROM
RUSSIAN FEDERATION	RUS
RWANDA	RWA
SAINT HELENA	SHN
SAINT KITTS & NEVIS	KNA
SAINT PIERRE & MIQUELON	SPM
SAINT VINCENT & THE GRENADINES	VCT
SAMOA	WSM
SAN MARINO	SMR
SAO TOME E PRINCIPE	STP
SAUDI ARABIA	SAU
SENEGAL	SEN
SERBIA	SRB
SERBIA & MONTENEGRO	SCG
SEYCHELLES	SYC
SIERRA LEONE	SLE
SINGAPORE	SGP
SLOVAKIA	SVK
SLOVENIA	SVN
SOLOMON ISLANDS	SLB
SOMALIA	SOM
SOUTH AFRICA	ZAF
SOUTH GEORGIA & THE SANDWICH ISLANDS	SGS
SPAIN	ESP
SRI LANKA	LKA
ST. LUCIA	LCA
SUDAN	SDN
SURINAME	SUR
SVALBARD & JAN MAYEN	SJM
SWAZILAND	SWZ
SWEDEN	SWE
SWITZERLAND	CHE
SYRIAN ARAB REPUBLIC	SYR
TAIWAN, REPUBLIC OF CHINA	TWN
TAJIKISTAN	TJK
TANZANIA, UNITED REPUBLIC OF	TZA
THAILAND	THA
TOGO	TGO
TOKELAU	TKL
TONGA	TON
TRINIDAD & TOBAGO	TTO
TUNISIA	TUN
TURKEY	TUR
TURKMENISTAN	TKM
TURKS & CAICOS ISLANDS	TCA
TUVALU	TUV
U.S.S.R.	SUN
UGANDA	UGA
UKRAINE	UKR
UNITED ARAB EMIRATES	UAE
UNITED KINGDOM	GBR
UNITED STATES	USA
UNITED STATES MINOR OUTLYING ISLANDS	UMI
URUGUAY	URY
UZBEKISTAN	UZB
VANUATU	VUT
VATICAN CITY STATE (HOLY SEE)	VAT
VENEZUELA	VEN
VIET NAM	VNM
VIRGIN ISLANDS, BRITISH	VGB
VIRGIN ISLANDS, U. S.	VIR
WALLIS & FUTUNA	WLF
WESTERN SAHARA	ESH
West Germany	BRD
YEMEN	YEM
YUGOSLAVIA	YUG
ZAMBIA	ZMB
ZIMBABWE	ZWE
ZAIRE	ZAR

LANGUAGE CODES

ACE	Achioli
AFA	Afro-Asiatic
AFR	Afrikaans
AKK	Akkadian
ALB	Albanian
ALE	Aleut
ALG	Algonquin
AMH	Amharic
ANG	Anglo-Saxon
APA	Apache
ARA	Arabic
ARC	Aramaic
ARM	Armenian
ARN	Araucanian
ARP	Arapaho
ARW	Arawak
ASM	Assamese
AVA	Avar
AVE	Avesta
AYM	Aymara
AZE	Azerbaijani
BAK	Bashkir
BAL	Baluchi
BAM	Bambara
BAQ	Basque
BAT	Baltic
BEJ	Beja
BEL	Belorussian
BEM	Bemba
BEN	Bengali
BER	Berber Group
BIH	Bihari
BLA	Blackfoot
BRE	Breton
BUL	Bulgarian
BUR	Burmese
CAD	Caddo
CAI	Central American
CAM	Cambodian
CAR	Carib
CAT	Catalan
CAU	Caucasian
CEL	Celtic Group
CHB	Chibcha
CHE	Chechen
CHI	Chinese
CHN	Chinook
CHO	Choctaw
CHR	Cherokee
CHU	Church Slavic
CHV	Chuvash
CHY	Cheyenne
COP	Coptic
COR	Cornish
CRE	Cree
CRO	Croatian
CRP	Creoles and Pidgins
CUS	Cushitic
CZE	Czech
DAK	Dakota
DAN	Danish
DEL	Delaware
DIN	Dinka
DOI	Dogri
DRA	Dravidian
DUA	Duala
DUT	Dutch
EFI	Efik
EGY	Egyptian
ELX	Elamite
ENG	English
ENM	English, Middle
ESK	Eskimo
RUM	Romanian
RUN	Rundi
RUS	Russian
SAD	Sandawe
SAG	Sango
SAI	South American
SAM	Samaritan
SAN	Sanskrit
SAO	Sampan
SBC	Serbo-Croatian
SCO	Scots
SEL	Selkup
SEM	Semitic
SER	Serbian
SHN	Shan
SHO	Shona
SID	Sidamo
SIO	Siouan Languages
SIT	Sino-Tibetan
SLA	Slavic
SLO	Slovak
SLV	Slovenian
SMO	Samoan
SND	Sindhi
SNH	Singhalese
SOG	Sogdian
SOM	Somali
SON	Songhai
ESP	Esperanto
EST	Estonian
ETH	Ethiopic
EWE	Ewe
FAN	Fang
FAR	Faroese
FEM	French, Middle
FIJ	Fijian
FIN	Finnish
FIU	Finno-Ugrian
FLE	Flemish
FON	Fon
FRE	French
FRI	Frisian
FRO	French, Old
GAA	Ga
GAE	Gaelic
GAG	Gallegan
GAL	Galla
GEC	Greek, Classical
GEH	German, Middle h
GEM	Germanic
GEO	Georgian
GER	German
GLG	Galician
GOH	German, Old High
GON	Gondi
GOT	Gothic
GRE	Greek
GUA	Guarani
GUJ	Gujarati
HAU	Hausa
HAW	Hawaiian
HEB	Hebrew
HER	Herero
HIL	Hiligaynon
HIN	Hindi
HUN	Hungarian
HUP	Hupa
IBA	Iban
IBO	Igbo
ICE	Icelandic
IKU	Inuktitut
ILO	Ilocano
INC	Indic
IND	Indonesian
INE	Indo-European
INT	Interlingua
IRA	Iranian
IRI	Irish
IRO	Iroquois
ITA	Italian
JAV	Javanese
JPN	Japanese
KAA	Karakalpak
KAC	Kachin
KAM	Kamba
KAN	Kannada
KAR	Karen
KAS	Kashmiri
KAU	Kanuri
KAZ	Kazakh
KHA	Khasi
KHM	Khmer, Central
KIK	Kikuyu
KIN	Kinyarwanda
KIR	Kirghiz
KOK	Konkani
KON	Kongo
KOR	Korean
KPE	Kpelle
KRO	Kru
KRU	Kurukh
SOT	Sotho, Southern
SPA	Spanish
SRD	Sardinian
SRR	Serer
SSA	Sub-Saharan
SUK	Sukuma
SUN	Sundanese
SUS	Susu
SUX	Sumerian
SWA	Swahili
SWE	Swedish
SYR	Syriac
TAG	Tagalog
TAJ	Tajik
TAM	Tamil
TAR	Tatar
TEL	Telugu
TEM	Temne
TER	Tereno
THA	Thai
TIB	Tibetan
TIG	Tigre
TIR	Tigrinya
TOG	Tonga, Nyasa

LANGUAGE CODES

TON	Tonga, Tonga
TSI	Tsimshian
TSO	Tsonga
TSW	Tswana
KUA	Kwanyama
KUR	Kurdish
LAD	Ladino
LAH	Lahnda
LAM	Lamba
LAO	Laotian
LAP	Lapp
LAT	Latin
LAV	Latvian
LIN	Lingala
LIT	Lithuanian
LOL	Lolo
LUB	Luba
LUG	Luganda
LUI	Luiseno
MAC	Macedonian
MAI	Maithili
MAL	Malayalam
MAN	Mandingo
MAO	Maori
MAP	Malayo-Polynesian
MAR	Marathi
MAS	Masai
MAY	Malay
MEN	Mende
MIC	Micmac
MIS	Miscellaneous
MLA	Malagasy
MLT	Malteses
MNO	Manobo
MOL	Moldavian
MON	Mongol
MOS	Mossi
MUL	Multiple Languages
MUS	Muskogee
MYN	Mayan
NAI	North American
NAV	Navaho
NBL	Ndebele, Southern
NDE	Ndebele, Northern
NEP	Nepali
NEW	Newari
NIC	Niger-Congo
NNO	Norwegian
NOB	Norwegian Bokmal
NOR	Norwegian
NSO	Sotho, Northern
NUB	Nubian
NYA	Nyanja
NYM	Nyamwezi
NYO	Nyoro Group
OES	Ossetic
OJI	Ojibwa
ORI	Oriya
OSA	Osage
OTO	Otomi
PAA	Papuan-Australian
PAH	Pahari
PAL	Pahlavi
PAN	Panjabi
PEO	Persian, Old
PER	Persian, Modern
PLI	Pali
POL	Polish
POR	Portuguese
PRA	Prakrit
PRO	Provencal
PUS	Pushto
QUE	Quechua
RAJ	Rajasthani
ROA	Romance
ROH	Romanish
ROM	Romany
TUK	Turkmen
TUR	Turkish
TUT	Turko-Tataric
TWI	Twi
UGA	Ugaritic
UIG	Uigur
UKR	Ukrainian
UMB	Umbundu
UND	Undetermined
URD	Urdu
UZB	Uzbek
VIE	Vietnamese
VOT	Votic
WAL	Walamo
WAS	Washo
WEL	Welsh
WEN	Wendic
WOL	Wolof
XHO	Xhosa
YAO	Yao
YID	Yiddish
YOR	Yoruba
ZAP	Zapotec
ZEN	Zenaga
ZUL	Zulu
ZUN	Zuni

LIST OF ABBREVIATIONS

Abr.	abridged
act. bk.	activity book
adapt.	adapted
aft.	afterword
alt.	alternate
Amer.	American
anniv.	anniversary
anno.	annotated by
annot.	annotation(s)
ans.	answer(s)
app.	appendix
Apple II	Apple II disk
approx.	approximately
assn.	association
audio	analog audio cassette
auth.	author
bd.	bound
bdg.	binding
bds.	boards
bibl(s).	bibliography(ies)
bk(s).	book(s)
bklet(s).	booklet(s)
boxed	boxed set, slipcase or caseboard
Bro.	Brother
C	college audience level
co.	company
comm.	commission, committee
comment.	commentaries
comp.	complied
cond.	condensed
contrib.	contributed
corp.	corporation
dept.	department
des	designed
diag(s).	diagram(s)
digital audio	digital audio cassette
dir.	director
disk	software disk or diskette
dist.	distributed
Div.	Division
doz.	dozen
ea.	each
ed.	edited, edition, editor
eds.	editions, editors
educ.	education
elem.	elementary
ency.	encyclopedia
ENG	English
enl.	enlarged
epil.	epilogue
exp.	expanded
expr.	experiments
expurg.	expurgated
fac.	facsimile
fasc.	fascicule
fict.	fiction
fig(s).	figure(s)
flmstrp.	filmstrip
footn.	
for.	foreign
frwd.	foreword
gen.	general
gr.	grade(s)
hndbk.	handbook
illus.	Illustrated, illustration(s), Illustrator(s)
in prep.	in preparation
incl.	includes, including
info.	information
inst.	institute
intro.	introduction
ISBN	International Standard Book Number
ISO	International Standards Organization
ITA	Italian
i.t.a.	initial teaching alphabet
J.	juvenile audience level
JPN	Japanese
Jr.	Junior
jt. auth.	joint author
jt. ed.	joint editor
k	kindergarten audience level
lab	laboratory
lang(s).	language(s)
LC	Library of Congress
lea.	leather
lib.	library
lib. bdg.	library binding
lit.	literature, literary
lp	record, album, long playing
l.t.	large type
ltd.	limited
ltd. ed.	limited edition
mac hd	144M, Mac
mac ld	800K, Mac
mass mkt.	mass market paperbound
math.	mathematics
mic. film	microfilm
mic form	microform
mod.	modern
MS(S)	manuscript(s)
natl.	national
net	net price
no(s).	number(s)
o.p.	out of print
orig.	original text, not a reprint (paperback)
o.s.i.	out of stock indefinitely
p.	pages
pap.	paper
per.	perfect binding
photos	photographer, photographs
pop. ed.	Popular edition
prep.	preparation
probs.	problems
prog. bk.	programmed books
ps.	preschool audience level
pseud.	pseudonym
pt(s).	part(s)
pub.	published, publisher publishing
pubn.	publication
ref(s).	reference(s)
rep.	reprint
reprod(s).	reproduction(s)
ret.	retold by
rev.	revised
rpm.	revolution per minute (phono records)
SAN	Standard Address Number
S&L	signed and limited
sec.	section
sel.	selected
ser.	series
Soc.	society
sols.	solutions
s.p.	school price
Sr. (after given name)	Senior
Sr. (before given name	Sister
St.	Saint
stu.	student manual, study guide, etc.
subs.	subsidiary
subsc.	subscription
suppl.	supplement
tech.	technical
text ed.	text edition
tr.	translated, translation translator
trans.	transparencies
unabr.	unabridged
unexpurg.	unexpurgated
univ.	university
var.	variorum
vdisk	videodisk
VHS	video, VHS format
vol(s).	volume(s)
wkbk.	workbook
YA	Young adult audience level
yrbk.	yearbook
3.5 hd	1.44M, 3.5 disk, DOS
3.5 ld	720, 3.5 Disk, DOS
5.25 hd	1.2M, 5.25 Disk, DOS
5.25 ld	360K, 5.25 Disk, DOS

SUBJECT INDEX

A

A B C BOOKS
see Alphabet Books

A. D. C.
see Child Welfare

AARDVARK

Borgert-Spaniol, Megan. Aardvarks. 2013. (Animal Safari Ser.). (ENG., Illus.). 24p. (J). (gr. k-3). lib. bdg. 25.95 *(978-1-60014-906-1(5)*, Blastoff! Readers) Bellwether Media.

Gibbs, Maddie. Aardvarks. 2011. (Safari Animals Ser.). (Illus.). 24p. (J). 22.60 *(978-1-4488-3187-6(3))*; pap. 8.25 *(978-1-4488-3188-3(1))* Rosen Publishing Group, Inc., The. (PowerKids Pr.).

—Aardvarks: Cerdos Hormigueros. 2011. (Safari Animals / Animales de Safari Ser.). (SPA., Illus.). 24p. (J). (gr. -1-2). lib. bdg. 22.60 *(978-1-4488-3214-9(4))* Rosen Publishing Group, Inc., The.

Gregory, Josh. Aardvarks. 2015. (ENG.). 48p. (J). pap. 6.95 *(978-0-531-21185-4(1)*, Orchard Bks.) Scholastic Library Publishing.

AARDVARK—FICTION

Brown, Marc. Arthur & the 1,001 Dads, Bk. 28. Brown, Marc, illus. 2003. (ENG., Illus.). 64p. (J). (gr. 1-4). pap. 4.25 *(978-0-316-12280-1(7))* Little, Brown Bks. for Young Readers.

—Arthur & the Baby. Brown, Marc, illus. 2011. (Classic Arthur Adventure Ser.). (ENG., Illus.). 32p. (J). (gr. -1-3). pap. 7.99 *(978-0-316-12905-3(4))* Little Brown & Co.

—Arthur & the Bad-Luck Brain. 2003. (Marc Brown Arthur Chapter Bks.). (Illus.). 55p. (gr. 2-4). 14.25 *(978-0-7569-1701-2(8))* Perfection Learning Corp.

—Arthur & the Bad-Luck Brain, Bk. 30. 2003. (ENG., Illus.). 64p. (J). (gr. 1-4). pap. 4.25 *(978-0-316-12377-8(3))* Little, Brown Bks. for Young Readers.

—Arthur & the Lost Diary. (Arthur Chapter Bks.: Bk. 9). 55p. (J). (gr. 3-6). pap. 3.95 *(978-0-8072-1305-6(5)*, Listening Library) Random Hse. Audio Publishing Group.

—Arthur & the Nerves of Steal. 32nd ed. 2004. (ENG., Illus.). 64p. (J). (gr. 1-4). pap. 4.25 *(978-0-316-12618-2(7)*, Tingley, Megan Bks.) Little, Brown Bks. for Young Readers.

—Arthur & the Popularity Test. (Arthur Chapter Bks.: Bk. 12). 58p. (J). (gr. 3-6). pap. 3.95 *(978-0-8072-1308-7(X))*; 2004. (gr. 2-4). pap. 17.00 incl. audio *(978-0-8072-0413-9(7)*, FTR204SP) Random Hse. Audio Publishing Group. (Listening Library).

—Arthur & the School Pet. 2005. (Step into Reading Sticker Bks.). (Illus.). 24p. 14.00 *(978-0-7569-5571-7(8))* Perfection Learning Corp.

—Arthur & the School Pet. 2003. (Step into Reading Ser.). (ENG., Illus.). 24p. (J). (gr. k-3). pap. 3.99 *(978-0-375-81001-5(3)*, Random Hse. Bks. for Young Readers) Random Hse. Children's Bks.

—Arthur & the School Pet. 2003. (Arthur Step into Reading Ser.). (gr. -1-2). lib. bdg. 13.55 *(978-0-613-57492-1(3)*, Turtleback) Turtleback Bks.

—Arthur & the True Francine. (Arthur Adventure Ser.). (J). (gr. k-3). 7.98 incl. audio NewSound, LLC.

—Arthur in New York. 2008. (Step into Reading Ser.). (ENG., Illus.). 24p. (J). (gr. k-3). pap. 3.99 *(978-0-375-82976-5(8)*, Random Hse. Bks. for Young Readers) Random Hse. Children's Bks.

—Arthur Loses His Marbles. 31st ed. 2004. (ENG., Illus.). 64p. (J). (gr. 1-4). pap. 4.25 *(978-0-316-12557-4(1))* Little, Brown Bks. for Young Readers.

—Arthur Lost & Found. 2004. (Arthur Adventure Ser.). (J). (gr. k-3). spiral bd. *(978-0-616-11102-4(9))* Canadian National Institute for the Blind/Institut National Canadien pour les Aveugles.

—Arthur Rocks with Binky. (Arthur Chapter Bks.: Bk. 11). 61p. (J). (gr. 3-6). pap. 3.95 *(978-0-8072-1307-0(1)*, Listening Library) Random Hse. Audio Publishing Group.

—Arthur Turns Green. 2014. (ENG.). 32p. (J). (gr. 1-4). 7.00 *(978-0-316-12923-7(2))* Little Brown & Co.

—Arthur Turns Green. 2014. (Arthur Adventures Ser.). (J). lib. bdg. 17.20 *(978-0-606-34069-4(6)*, Turtleback) Turtleback Bks.

—Arthur Writes a Story. 2004. (Arthur Adventure Ser.). (J). (gr. k-3). spiral bd. *(978-0-616-01604-6(2))*; spiral bd. *(978-0-616-01605-3(0))* Canadian National Institute for the Blind/Institut National Canadien pour les Aveugles.

—Arthur Writes a Story. 2003. (Arthur Adventure Ser.). (Illus.). 14.95 *(978-1-59319-021-7(2))* LeapFrog Enterprises, Inc.

—Arthur's Birthday Surprise. 2004. (ENG., Illus.). 24p. (J). (gr. -1-1). pap. 3.99 *(978-0-316-73379-3(2))* Little, Brown Bks. for Young Readers.

—Arthur's Classroom Fib. 2007. (Arthur Step into Reading Ser.). lib. bdg. 13.55 *(978-1-4177-7281-0(6)*, Turtleback) Turtleback Bks.

—Arthur's Family Vacation. 2004. (Arthur Adventure Ser.). (J). (gr. k-3). spiral bd. *(978-0-616-01601-5(8))*; spiral bd. *(978-0-616-01602-2(6))* Canadian National Institute for the Blind/Institut National Canadien pour les Aveugles.

—Arthur's Jelly Beans. 2004. (ENG., Illus.). 24p. (J). (gr. -1-1). pap. 3.99 *(978-0-316-73382-3(2))* Little, Brown Bks. for Young Readers.

—Arthur's New Puppy. (Arthur Adventure Ser.). (J). (gr. k-3). 7.98 incl. audio NewSound, LLC.

—Arthur's off to School. 2004. (ENG., Illus.). 24p. (J). (gr. -1-1). pap. 3.99 *(978-0-316-73378-6(4))* Little, Brown Bks. for Young Readers.

—Arthur's Pet Business. Brown, Marc, illus. rev. ed. 2007. (ENG., Illus.). 32p. (J). (gr. -1-3). pap. 10.99 *(978-0-316-11863-7(X))* Little, Brown Bks. for Young Readers.

—Arthur's Reading Trick. 2009. (Step into Reading Ser.). (ENG., Illus.). 24p. (J). (gr. k-3). pap. 3.99 *(978-0-375-82977-2(6)*, Random Hse. Bks. for Young Readers) Random Hse. Children's Bks.

—Arthur's Teacher Trouble. 2004. (Arthur Adventure Ser.). (J). (gr. k-3). spiral bd. *(978-0-616-00406-7(0))*; spiral bd. *(978-0-616-01603-9(4))* Canadian National Institute for the Blind/Institut National Canadien pour les Aveugles.

—Arthur's Underwear. 2004. (Arthur Adventure Ser.). (Illus.). (J). (gr. k-3). spiral bd. *(978-0-616-14564-7(0))*; spiral bd. *(978-0-616-14563-0(2))* Canadian National Institute for the Blind/Institut National Canadien pour les Aveugles.

—Arturo y el Misterioso Sobre. Sarfatti, Esther, tr. from ENG. 2006. (Libro de Capitulos de Arturo Ser.). (Illus.). 58p. (J). (gr. 6-8). per. 4.99 *(978-1-930332-93-5(9))* Lectorum Pubns., Inc.

—Buster's Dino Dilemma. (Arthur Chapter Bks.: Bk. 7). 58p. (J). (gr. 3-6). pap. 3.95 *(978-0-8072-1303-2(9)*, Listening Library) Random Hse. Audio Publishing Group.

—D. W. la Quisquillosa. Sarfatti, Esther, tr. from ENG. 2003.Tr. of D. W. the Picky Eater. (SPA.). (J). (gr. k-2). pap. 6.95 *(978-1-930332-42-3(4))* Lectorum Pubns., Inc.

—D. W.'s Library Card. Brown, Marc, illus. 2003. (ENG., Illus.). 24p. (J). (gr. -1-3). pap. 7.00 *(978-0-316-73820-0(4))* Little, Brown Bks. for Young Readers.

—Marc Brown Arthur: King Arthur; Francine, Believe it or Not; Arthur & the Cootie-Catcher; (Arthur Chapter Bks.: No. 5). 58p. (J). (gr. 3-6). pap. 3.95 *(978-0-8072-1299-8(7)*, Listening Library) Random Hse. Audio Publishing Group.

—Marc Brown's Arthur: Arthur & the Crunch Cereal Contest; Arthur Accused!; Locked in the Library. (Arthur Chapter Bks.: No. 2). 58p. (J). (gr. 3-6). pap. 3.95 *(978-0-8072-1296-7(2)*, Listening Library) Random Hse. Audio Publishing Group.

—Marc Brown's Arthur: Arthur & the Scare-Your-Pants-off Club; Arthur Makes the Team. (Arthur Chapter Bks.: No. 1). 58p. (J). (gr. 3-6). pap. 3.95 *(978-0-8072-1295-0(4)*, Listening Library) Random Hse. Audio Publishing Group.

—Marc Brown's Arthur: Buster's Dino Dilemma; the Mystery of the Stolen Bike; Arthur & the Lost Diary. (Arthur Chapter Bks.: No. 3). 61p. (J). (gr. 3-6). pap. 3.95 *(978-0-8072-1297-4(0))*; pap. 3.95 *(978-0-8072-1298-1(9))* Random Hse. Audio Publishing Group. (Listening Library).

—The Mystery of the Stolen Bike. (Arthur Chapter Bks.: Bk. 8). 59p. (J). (gr. 3-6). pap. 3.95 *(978-0-8072-1304-9(7)*, Listening Library) Random Hse. Audio Publishing Group.

—La Visita del Senor Rataquemada. Sarfatti, Esther, tr. from ENG. 2003.Tr. of Arthur's Teacher Moves In. (SPA.). (J). (gr. k-2). pap. 6.95 *(978-1-930332-41-6(6))* Lectorum Pubns., Inc.

—Who's in Love with Arthur? (Arthur Chapter Bks.: Bk. 10). 57p. (J). (gr. 3-6). pap. 3.95 *(978-0-8072-1306-3(3)*, Listening Library) Random Hse. Audio Publishing Group.

Brown, Marc & Sarfatti, Esther. Arturo y la Navidad. 2004. (SPA.). (J). pap. 6.95 *(978-1-930332-48-5(3))* Lectorum Pubns., Inc.

Gilliland, Tom. The Adventures of Archie Aardvark. 2012. 60p. pap. 10.00 *(978-1-4691-7957-5(1))* Xlibris Corp.

Krensky, Stephen. Arthur & the 1,001 Dads. 2003. (Marc Brown Arthur Chapter Bks.). (Illus.). 57p. (J). (gr. 1-4). 11.90 *(978-0-7569-1600-8(3))* Perfection Learning Corp.

—Locked in the Library! (Arthur Chapter Bks.: Bk. 6). 58p. (J). (gr. 3-6). pap. 3.95 *(978-0-8072-1300-1(4)*, Listening Library) Random Hse. Audio Publishing Group.

Krensky, Stephen & Brown, Marc. Arthur Plays the Blues. 2003. (Marc Brown Arthur Chapter Bks.). (Illus.). 53p. (gr. 2-4). 14.25 *(978-0-7569-1700-5(X))* Perfection Learning Corp.

O'Toole-Freel, Judy. Aardvark, Aardvark, How Do You Do!, 1 vol. 2008. (ENG.). 31p. 24.95 *(978-1-4241-6618-3(7))* America Star Bks.

Sarfatti, Esther, tr. from ENG. Berto Da la Talla. 2006. (Libro de Capitulos de Arturo Ser.). (Illus.). 55p. (J). (gr. 6-8). per. 4.99 *(978-1-930332-94-2(7))* Lectorum Pubns., Inc.

AARON, HANK, 1934-

Golenbock, Peter. Hank Aaron: Brave in Every Way. Lee, Paul, illus. 2005. (ENG.). 32p. (J). (gr. -1-3). reprint ed. pap. 6.99 *(978-0-15-205250-8(X))* Houghton Mifflin Harcourt Publishing Co.

Kappes, Serena. Hank Aaron. 2005. (Sports Heroes & Legends Ser.). (Illus.). 106p. (YA). (gr. 7-12). lib. bdg. 27.93 *(978-0-8225-3069-5(4))* Lerner Publishing Group.

Morrison, Jessica. Hank Aaron: Home Run Hero. 2010. (Crabtree Groundbreaker Biographies Ser.). (ENG., Illus.). 112p. (J). pap. *(978-0-7787-2547-3(2))*; (gr. 5-8). lib. bdg. *(978-0-7787-2538-1(3))* Crabtree Publishing Co.

Poolos, Jamie & Poolos, J. Hank Aaron. 2007. (Baseball Superstars Ser.). (Illus.). 122p. (YA). (gr. 7-12). lib. bdg. 30.00 *(978-0-7910-9536-2(3))* Facts On File, Inc.

Spencer, Lauren. Hank Aaron. (Baseball Hall of Famers Ser.). 112p. (gr. 5-8). 2009. 63.90 *(978-1-61511-509-9(9))* 2003. (Illus.). lib. bdg. 34.60 *(978-0-8239-3600-7(7))* Rosen Publishing Group, Inc., The. (Rosen Reference).

Tavares, Matt. Henry Aaron's Dream. Tavares, Matt, illus. (Candlewick Biographies Ser.). (ENG., Illus.). (J). 2015. 48p. (gr. k-3). 14.99 *(978-0-7636-7653-7(5))* 2012. 40p. (gr. 3-7). pap. 6.99 *(978-0-7636-5820-5(0))* 2010. 40p. (gr. 3-7). 16.99 *(978-0-7636-3224-3(4))* Candlewick Pr.

ABACUS

Murphy, Patricia J. Counting with an Abacus: Learning the Place Values of Ones, Tens, & Hundreds. 2009. (Math for the REAL World Ser.). 16p. (gr. 2-3). pap. 7.05 *(978-0-8239-8880-8(5)*, Rosen Classroom) Rosen Publishing Group, Inc., The.

ABANDONED CHILDREN

Cope Bowley, Tonia. From a Street Kid: Stephen Lungu's Incredible Life Journey. Petropouleas, Niko, illus. 2012. 192p. pap. *(978-1-78003-380-8(X))* Pen Pr. Pubs., Ltd.

Williams, Shirley. Zipper - the Mischievous Kid. 2008. 44p. pap. 20.99 *(978-1-4389-0565-5(3))* AuthorHouse.

ABANDONED CHILDREN—FICTION

Acheson, Alison. The Mud Girl, 1 vol. 2006. (ENG.). 328p. (YA). (gr. 8-12). per. 10.95 *(978-1-55050-354-8(5))* Coteau Bks. CAN. Dist: Orca Bk. Pubs. USA.

Adderson, Caroline. Middle of Nowhere. 2013. 212p. pap. *(978-1-4596-6452-4(3))* ReadHowYouWant.com, Ltd.

Alger, Horatio. The Errand Boy: Or, How Phil Brent Won Success. 271p. reprint ed. pap. 79.00 *(978-1-4047-3566-8(6))* Classic Textbooks.

—The Errand Boy: Or, How Phil Brent Won Success. 2013. (Works of Horatio Alger Jr.). 425p. reprint ed. lthr. 79.00 *(978-0-7812-3566-2(9))* Reprint Services Corp.

Alonso, Manuel L. Rumbo Sur. 2005. *(978-84-263-5948-3(5))* Vives, Luis Editorial (Edelvives).

Baratz-Logsted, Lauren. Jackie's Jokes. 2009. (Sisters Eight Ser.: 4). (ENG., Illus.). 128p. (J). (gr. 1-4). pap. 5.99 *(978-0-547-05328-8(2))* Houghton Mifflin Harcourt Publishing Co.

—Rebecca's Rashness, Bk. 7. 2011. (Sisters Eight Ser.: 7). (ENG., Illus.). 144p. (J). (gr. 1-4). pap. 5.99 *(978-0-547-55434-1(6))* Houghton Mifflin Harcourt Publishing Co.

—Zinnia's Zaniness. 2011. (Sisters Eight Ser.: 8). (ENG., Illus.). 128p. (J). (gr. 1-4). pap. 5.99 *(978-0-547-55439-6(7))* Houghton Mifflin Harcourt Publishing Co.

Baratz-Logsted, Lauren, et al. The Final Battle... for Now Bk. 9. 2012. (Sisters Eight Ser.: 9). (ENG., Illus.). 160p. (J). (gr. 1-4). pap. 6.99 *(978-0-547-55441-9(9))* Houghton Mifflin Harcourt Publishing Co.

Beasley, Kate. Gertie's Leap to Greatness. Tamaki, Jillian, illus. 2016. (ENG.). 256p. (J). 16.99 *(978-0-374-30261-0(8)*, 9780374302610, Farrar, Straus & Giroux (BYR)) Farrar, Straus & Giroux.

Bowsher, Melodie. My Lost & Found Life. 2006. (ENG.). 320p. (YA). (gr. 9-13). 16.95 *(978-1-58234-736-3(0)*, 9781582347363, Bloomsbury USA Childrens) Bloomsbury Publishing USA.

Clay, Ian. Coyote Lake. 2007. 104p. per. 9.95 *(978-0-595-44590-5(X))* iUniverse, Inc.

Cooney, Caroline B. They Never Came Back. 2011. (ENG., Illus.). 208p. (YA). (gr. 7). pap. 7.99 *(978-0-385-73809-5(9)*, Ember) Random Hse. Children's Bks.

Cousins, Dave. 15 Days Without a Head. 2013. (ENG.). 312p. (YA). pap. 9.99 *(978-0-7387-3642-6(2)*, Flux) North Star Editions.

Coville, Bruce. Always October. 2012. (ENG.). 384p. (J). (gr. 3-7). 16.99 *(978-0-06-089095-7(9))* HarperCollins Pubs.

Dessen, Sarah. Lock & Key. 2009. (ENG.). 448p. (YA). (gr. 7-18). 10.99 *(978-0-14-241472-9(7)*, Speak) Penguin Young Readers Group.

—Lock & Key. 2009. lib. bdg. 22.10 *(978-0-606-14396-7(3)*, Turtleback) Turtleback Bks.

Duey, Kathleen. True Heart. Rayyan, Omar, illus. 2004. (Unicorn's Secret Ser.). 75p. (gr. 2-5). 15.00 *(978-0-7569-3385-2(4))* Perfection Learning Corp.

Gagnon, Michelle. Don't Let Go. 2014. (Don't Turn Around Ser.: 3). (ENG.). 352p. (YA). (gr. 8). 17.99 *(978-0-06-210296-6(6))* HarperCollins Pubs.

—Don't Turn Around. 2013. (Don't Turn Around Ser.: 1). (ENG.). 336p. (YA). (gr. 8). pap. 9.99 *(978-0-06-210291-1(5))* HarperCollins Pubs.

George, Elisabeth. The Edge of Nowhere. 2014. (Edge of Nowhere Ser.). (ENG.). 464p. (YA). (gr. 7). pap. 10.99 *(978-0-14-242675-3(X)*, Speak) Penguin Young Readers Group.

—The Edge of the Shadows. 2015. (Edge of Nowhere Ser.). (ENG.). 464p. (YA). (gr. 7). 18.99 *(978-0-670-01298-5(X)*, Viking Books for Young Readers) Penguin Young Readers Group.

—The Edge of the Water. 2014. (Edge of Nowhere Ser.). (ENG.). 448p. (YA). (gr. 7). 18.99 *(978-0-670-01297-8(1)*, Viking Books for Young Readers) Penguin Young Readers Group.

Hill, Kirkpatrick. Bo at Ballard Creek. Pham, LeUyen, illus. 2014. (ENG.). 304p. (J). (gr. 3-7). pap. 7.99 *(978-1-250-04425-9(1)*, 9781250044259) Square Fish.

Horton, Babs. Dandelion Soup. l.t. ed. 2005. (Charnwood Large Print Ser.). (Illus.). 504p. 35.50 *(978-1-84395-621-1(7))* Ulverscroft Large Print Bks. GBR. Dist: Ulverscroft Large Print Bks., Ltd.

Ibbotson, Eva. The Star of Kazan. Hawkes, Kevin, illus. 2006. (ENG.). 416p. (J). (gr. 3-7). reprint ed. 8.99 *(978-0-14-240582-6(5)*, Puffin Books) Penguin Young Readers Group.

Jacobson, Jennifer Richard. Small as an Elephant. 2011. (ENG., Illus.). 288p. (J). (gr. 4-7). 15.99 *(978-0-7636-4155-9(3))* Candlewick Pr.

Kadohata, Cynthia. Half a World Away. 2015. lib. bdg. 18.40 *(978-0-606-37845-1(6))* Turtleback Bks.

LaFleur, Suzanne. Love, Aubrey. 2011. (ENG.). 272p. (J). (gr. 3-7). pap. 7.99 *(978-0-375-85159-9(3)*, Yearling) Random Hse. Children's Bks.

Laird, Elizabeth. The Garbage King. 2016. (ENG., Illus.). 336p. (J). (gr. 4-7). pap. 9.99 *(978-1-5098-0295-1(9))* Pan Macmillan GBR. Dist: Independent Pubs. Group.

The Last Wild Run. 2006. (J). per. 14.95 *(978-1-933791-05-0(5))* Finial Publishing.

Leavitt, Martine. Heck Superhero!, 1 vol. 2005. (ENG.). 144p. pap. 12.95 *(978-0-88995-333-8(3))* Red Deer Pr. CAN. Dist: Ingram Publisher Services.
—Heck, Superhero. 2003. (ENG.). 172p. (J). (gr. 4-7). 16.95 *(978-1-886910-94-2(4)*, Lemniscaat) Boyds Mills Pr.
Lynch, Janet Nichols. Messed Up. 2009. (ENG.). 320p. (YA). (gr. 7-18). 17.95 *(978-0-8234-2185-5(6))* Holiday Hse., Inc.
Marchetta, Melina. Jellicoe Road. (ENG.). 432p. (YA). (gr. 9). 2010. pap. 9.99 *(978-0-06-143185-2(0))* 2008. 17.99 *(978-0-06-143183-8(4))* HarperCollins Pubs. (HarperTeen).
Marsden, Carolyn. Take Me with You. 2010. (ENG., Illus.). 176p. (J). (gr. 5-18). 14.99 *(978-0-7636-3739-2(4))* Candlewick Pr.
McMullan, Margaret. When I Crossed No-Bob. 2009. (ENG.). 224p. (J). (gr. 2-5). pap. 7.99 *(978-0-547-23763-3(4))* Houghton Mifflin Harcourt Publishing Co.
McMurchy-Barber, Gina & Zweig, Eric. Free as a Bird. 2010. (ENG., Illus.). 176p. (YA). (gr. 6-8). pap. 10.99 *(978-1-55488-447-6(0)*, Dundurn Pr.) Dundurn CAN. Dist: Ingram Publisher Services.
Nolan, Han. Born Blue. 2003. (ENG.). 308p. (YA). (gr. 9-12). pap. 7.99 *(978-0-15-204697-2(6))* Houghton Mifflin Harcourt Publishing Co.
Patron, Susan. The Higher Power of Lucky. 2008. (JPN., Illus.). 215p. (J). *(978-4-7515-2209-7(4))* Asunaro Shobo.
—The Higher Power of Lucky. 2009. 9.00 *(978-0-7848-2460-3(6)*, Everbind) Marco Bk. Co.
—The Higher Power of Lucky. 2008. 17.00 *(978-1-60686-088-5(7))* Perfection Learning Corp.
—The Higher Power of Lucky. Phelan, Matt, illus. (ENG.). (J). (gr. 4-6). 2008. 160p. pap. 7.99 *(978-1-4169-7557-1(8)*, Atheneum Bks. for Young Readers) 2006. 144p. 17.99 *(978-1-4169-0194-5(9)*, Atheneum/Richard Jackson Bks.) Simon & Schuster Children's Publishing.
—The Higher Power of Lucky. 2008. lib. bdg. 18.40 *(978-0-606-08934-0(9)*, Turtleback) Turtleback Bks.
—Lucky Breaks. Phelan, Matt, illus. 2010. (ENG.). 208p. (J). (gr. 3-7). pap. 7.99 *(978-1-4169-9772-6(5)*, Atheneum Bks. for Young Readers) Simon & Schuster Children's Publishing.
Stewart, Paul & Riddell, Chris. Beyond the Deepwoods. 2008. (Edge Chronicles Ser.: Bk. 1). (ENG.). 288p. (J). (gr. 3-7). 8.99 *(978-0-440-42087-3(3)*, Bluefire) Random Hse. Children's Bks.
Unsworth, Tania. The One Safe Place. 2014. (ENG.). 304p. (J). (gr. 5-8). 15.95 *(978-1-61620-329-0(3)*, 73329) Algonquin Bks. of Chapel Hill.
Van Draanen, Wendelin. Sammy Keyes & the Search for Snake Eyes. 2008. (Sammy Keyes Ser.: Bk. 7). (J). 64.99 *(978-1-60640-645-8(0))* Findaway World, LLC.
—Sammy Keyes & the Search for Snake Eyes. Van Draanen, Wendelin, illus. 2003. (Sammy Keyes Ser.: Bk. 7). (Illus.). pap. 36.95 incl. audio *(978-1-59112-273-9(2))*; pap. 54.95 incl. audio compact disk *(978-1-59112-281-4(3))* Live Oak Media.
—Sammy Keyes & the Search for Snake Eyes. 2003. (Sammy Keyes Ser.: 7). (ENG.). 320p. (J). (gr. 5-7). 7.99 *(978-0-440-41900-6(X)*, Yearling) Random Hse. Children's Bks.
White, Jennifer. Survival Strategies of the Almost Brave. 2015. (ENG.). 320p. (J). (gr. 3-7). 16.99 *(978-0-374-30084-5(4)*, 9780374300845, Farrar, Straus & Giroux (BYR)) Farrar, Straus & Giroux.
White, Ruth. The Search for Belle Prater. 2007. 169p. (J). (gr. 4-7). 14.15 *(978-0-7569-7274-5(4))* Perfection Learning Corp.

ABANDONED TOWNS

see Extinct Cities

ABDUL-JABBAR, KAREEM, 1947-

Kneib, Martha. Kareem Abdul-Jabbar. 2009. (Basketball Hall of Famers Ser.). 112p. (gr. 5-8). 63.90 *(978-1-61511-533-4(1)*, Rosen Reference) Rosen Publishing Group, Inc., The.

ABERNATHY, TEMPLE, 1904-1987

Jackson, Robert B. The Remarkable Ride of the Abernathy Boys. 2003. (Land We Belong to Is Grand Ser.). (Illus.). 69p. (J). pap. *(978-1-57168-798-2(X)*, Eakin Pr.) Eakin Pr.

ABNORMAL PSYCHOLOGY

see Psychology, Pathological

ABOLITION OF SLAVERY

see Abolitionists

ABOLITIONISTS

Abolitionism. 2010. (Key Concepts in American History Ser.). (Illus.). 128p. (gr. 6-12). 45.00 *(978-1-60413-220-5(5)*, Chelsea Hse.) Facts On File, Inc.
Adler, David A. Enemies of Slavery. Smith, Donald A., illus. 2004. (ENG.). 32p. (J). (gr. k-3). lib. bdg., tchr. ed. 16.95 *(978-0-8234-1596-0(1))* Holiday Hse., Inc.
—Frederick Douglass: A Noble Life. 2010. (ENG., Illus.). 144p. (J). (gr. 5-18). 21.95 *(978-0-8234-2056-8(6))* Holiday Hse., Inc.
—A Picture Book of Frederick Douglass. Byrd, Samuel, illus. unabr. ed. 2005. (Picture Book Readalongs Ser.). (J). (gr. k-4). 25.95 incl. audio *(978-1-59519-373-5(1))*; pap. 28.95 incl. audio compact disk *(978-1-59519-377-3(4))*;Set. pap. 37.95 incl. audio *(978-1-59519-374-2(X))*;Set. pap. 39.95 incl. audio compact disk *(978-1-59519-378-0(2))* Live Oak Media.
—A Picture Book of Harriet Beecher Stowe. Bootman, Colin, illus. 2003. (ENG.). 32p. (J). (gr. k-3). tchr. ed. 17.95 *(978-0-8234-1646-2(1))* Holiday Hse., Inc.
Allen, Nancy. The Underground Railroad. 2015. (ENG.). 32p. (gr. 3-6). 32.79 *(978-1-63430-043-8(2))* Rourke Educational Media.
Altman, Linda Jacobs. The Story of Slavery & Abolition in United States History. 2015. (In United States History Ser.). 96p. (J). (gr. 5-12). 27.94 *(978-0-7660-6330-3(5))*; pap. 10.95 *(978-0-7660-6331-0(3))* Enslow Pubs., Inc.
Beckett, Leslie. Abolitionists & Human Rights: Fighting for Emancipation. 2016. (Spotlight on American History Ser.). 24p. (J). (gr. 6-4). 26.25 *(978-1-5081-4937-8(2)*, PowerKids Pr.) Rosen Publishing Group, Inc., The.
Belmonte, Kevin. A Journey Through the Life of William Wilberforce: The Abolitionist Who Changed the Face of a Nation. 2007. (Illus.). 122p. *(978-0-89221-671-0(9))* New Leaf Pub. Group.
—Travel with William Wilberforce: The Friend of Humanity. 2006. (Travel With... Ser.). (Illus.). 128p. per. 15.00 *(978-1-84625-027-9(7))* DayOne Pubns. GBR. Dist: Send The Light Distribution LLC.
Benge, Janet & Benge, Geoff. William Wilberforce: Take up the Fight. 2015. (ENG.). 201p. (YA). pap. 9.99 *(978-1-62486-057-7(5))* Emerald Bks.
Bernard, Catherine. Sojourner Truth: Women's Rights Activist & Abolitionist. 2016. (Heroes of the Women's Suffrage Movement Ser.). 128p. (gr. 6-6). 37.27 *(978-0-7660-7887-1(6))* Enslow Pubs., Inc.
Berne, Emma. Face of Freedom: How the Photos of Frederick Douglass Celebrated Racial Equality. 2017. (Captured History Ser.). (ENG.). 64p. (gr. 5-7). pap. 9.10 ***(978-0-7565-5619-8(8)***, CPB Grades 4-8) Compass Point Bks.
Berne, Emma Carlson. Face of Freedom: How the Photos of Frederick Douglass Celebrated Racial Equality. 2017. (Captured History Ser.). (ENG.). 64p. (gr. 5-7). lib. bdg. 34.65 ***(978-0-7565-5617-4(1)***, CPB Grades 4-8) Compass Point Bks.
Bodden, Valerie. How to Analyze the Works of Frederick Douglass, 1 vol. 2013. (Essential Critiques Set 4 Ser.). (ENG.). 112p. (J). (gr. 6-12). lib. bdg. 35.64 *(978-1-61783-644-2(3)*, Essential Library) ABDO Publishing Co.
Burchard, Peter. Frederick Douglass: For the Great Family of Man. 2007. (ENG., Illus.). 240p. (YA). (gr. 7). pap. 13.95 *(978-1-4169-6752-1(4)*, Atheneum Bks. for Young Readers) Simon & Schuster Children's Publishing.
Burgan, Michael. The Underground Railroad. Schwarz, Philip, ed. 2006. (Slavery in the Americas Ser.). (Illus.). 112p. (gr. 5-8). 35.00 *(978-0-8160-6137-2(8))* Facts On File, Inc.
Butler, Mary. Sojourner Truth: From Slave to Activist for Freedom. 2009. (Library of American Lives & Times Ser.). 112p. (gr. 5-5). 69.20 *(978-1-60853-505-7(3))* Rosen Publishing Group, Inc., The.
Butler, Mary G. Sojourner Truth: From Slave to Activist for Freedom. 2005. (Library of American Lives & Times). (Illus.). 112p. (YA). (gr. 4-8). lib. bdg. 34.60 *(978-0-8239-5736-1(5))* Rosen Publishing Group, Inc., The.
Cline-Ransome, Lesa. Words Set Me Free: The Story of Young Frederick Douglass. Ransome, James E., illus. 2012. (ENG.). 32p. (J). (gr. k-4). 17.99 *(978-1-4169-5903-8(3)*, Simon & Schuster/Paula Wiseman Bks.) Simon & Schuster/Paula Wiseman Bks.
Clinton, Catherine. When Harriet Met Sojourner. Evans, Shane W., illus. 2007. (ENG.). 32p. (J). (gr. k-2). 16.99 *(978-0-06-050425-0(0)*, Tegen, Katherine Bks) HarperCollins Pubs.
Cloud Tapper, Suzanne. The Abolition of Slavery: Fighting for a Free America. 2006. (American Saga Ser.). (Illus.). 128p. (J). (gr. 5-18). lib. bdg. 33.27 *(978-0-7660-2605-6(1))* Enslow Pubs., Inc.
Collins, Kathleen. Sojourner Truth: Defensora de los derechos Civiles. 2004. (Grandes personajes en la historia de los Estados Unidos Ser.). (SPA.). 32p. (gr. 3-6). pap. 10.00 *(978-0-8239-4239-8(2)*, Rosen Classroom) Rosen Publishing Group, Inc., The.
—Sojourner Truth: Defensora de los derechos civiles (Sojourner Truth: Equal Rights Advocate) 2009. (Grandes personajes en la historia de los Estados Unidos (Famous People in American History) Ser.). (SPA.). 32p. (gr. 2-3). 47.90 *(978-1-61512-808-2(5)*, Editorial Buenas Letras) Rosen Publishing Group, Inc., The.
—Sojourner Truth: Equal Rights Advocate. (Primary Sources of Famous People in American History Ser.). 32p. 2009. (gr. 2-3). 47.90 *(978-1-60851-727-5(6))* 2004. (ENG., Illus.). (gr. 4-8). pap. 10.00 *(978-0-8239-4193-3(0))* Rosen Publishing Group, Inc., The.
—Sojourner Truth: Equal Rights Advocate / Defensora de los derechos Civiles. 2009. (Famous People in American History/Grandes personajes en la historia de los Estados Unidos Ser.). (ENG & SPA.). 32p. (gr. 2-3). 47.90 *(978-1-61512-556-2(6)*, Editorial Buenas Letras) Rosen Publishing Group, Inc., The.
Down, Susan. Theodore Weld: Architect of Abolitionism. 2013. (ENG., Illus.). 64p. (J). *(978-0-7787-1062-2(9))*; pap. *(978-0-7787-1065-3(3))* Crabtree Publishing Co.
Dudley Gold, Susan. The Women's Rights Movement & Abolitionism. 2015. (Primary Sources of the Abolitionist Movement Ser.). (ENG., Illus.). 64p. (J). (gr. 6-6). lib. bdg. 34.21 *(978-1-5026-0536-8(8))* Cavendish Square Publishing.
Edwards, Andrew & Thornton, Fleur. Wilberforce: an Activity Book: 24 Ready to Use Lesson Plans. 2007. (Illus.). 32p. (J). (gr. 3-7). pap. 6.99 *(978-0-89221-672-7(7))* New Leaf Pub. Group.
Edwards, Judith. Abolitionists & Slave Resistance: Breaking the Chains of Slavery. 2004. (Slavery in American History Ser.). (Illus.). 128p. (J). lib. bdg. 27.94 *(978-0-7660-2155-6(6))* Enslow Pubs., Inc.
Elliot, Henry. Frederick Douglass: From Slavery to Statesman. 2009. (Voices for Freedom Ser.). (ENG., Illus.). 64p. (J). (gr. 5-8). pap. *(978-0-7787-4836-6(7))*; lib. bdg. *(978-0-7787-4820-5(0))* Crabtree Publishing Co.
—Harriet Beecher Stowe: The Voice of Humanity in White America. 2009. (Voices for Freedom Ser.). (ENG., Illus.). 64p. (J). (gr. 5-8). pap. *(978-0-7787-4837-3(5))*; lib. bdg. *(978-0-7787-4821-2(9))* Crabtree Publishing Co.
Esty, Amos. The Liberator: The Story of William Lloyd Garrison. 2011. (Civil Rights Leaders Ser.). 144p. 28.95 *(978-1-59935-137-7(4))* Reynolds, Morgan Inc.
Evans, Shane W. Underground: Finding the Light to Freedom. Evans, Shane W., illus. 2011. (ENG., Illus.). 32p. (J). (gr. -1-3). 16.99 *(978-1-59643-538-4(0)*, 9781596435384) Roaring Brook Pr.
Fleming, Alice. Frederick Douglass: From Slave to Statesman. 2009. (Library of American Lives & Times Ser.). 112p. (gr. 5-5). 69.20 *(978-1-60853-482-1(0))* Rosen Publishing Group, Inc., The.
Fleming, Alice Mulcahey. Frederick Douglass: From Slave to Statesman. 2005. (Library of American Lives & Times). (Illus.). 112p. (J). (gr. 4-8). lib. bdg. 34.60 *(978-0-8239-6624-0(0))* Rosen Publishing Group, Inc., The.
Fradin, Dennis B. The Underground Railroad. 2011. (Great Escapes Ser.). 80p. (gr. 6). 34.21 *(978-1-60870-476-7(9))* Marshall Cavendish Corp.
Freedman, Russell. Abraham Lincoln & Frederick Douglass: The Story Behind an American Friendship. 2012. (ENG., Illus.). 128p. (J). (gr. 5-7). 18.99 *(978-0-547-38562-4(5))* Houghton Mifflin Harcourt Publishing Co.
Gregory, Josh. Frederick Douglass. 2015. (ENG., Illus.). 48p. (J). lib. bdg. *(978-0-531-21597-5(0)*, Orchard Bks.) Scholastic, Inc.
Griffiths, Katie. Harriet Beecher Stowe. 2016. (Great American Thinkers Ser.). (ENG.). 128p. (J). (gr. 9-9). 45.64 *(978-1-5026-1930-3(X))* Cavendish Square Publishing.
Griskey, Michele. Harriet Beecher Stowe. 2005. (Classic Storytellers Ser.). (Illus.). 48p. (J). (gr. 4-8). lib. bdg. 29.95 *(978-1-58415-375-7(X))* Mitchell Lane Pubs., Inc.
Haldy, Emma E. Frederick Douglass. Bane, Jeff, illus. 2016. (My Early Library: My Itty-Bitty Bio Ser.). (ENG.). 24p. (J). (gr. k-1). 28.50 *(978-1-63470-479-3(7)*, 207647) Cherry Lake Publishing.
Haugen, Brenda. Harriet Beecher Stowe: The Inspiring Life Story of the Abolition Advocate. 2016. (Inspiring Stories Ser.). (ENG., Illus.). 112p. (gr. 5-7). lib. bdg. 35.99 *(978-0-7565-5164-3(1)*, CPB Grades 4-8) Compass Point Bks.
Hillstrom, Laurie Collier. The Underground Railroad. 2015. (Defining Moments Ser.). (Illus.). 240p. (J). lib. bdg. 55.00 *(978-0-7808-1346-5(4))* Omnigraphics, Inc.
Horn, Geoffrey Michael. John Brown: Putting Actions above Words. 2009. (Voices for Freedom Ser.). (ENG., Illus.). 64p. (J). (gr. 5-8). pap. *(978-0-7787-4839-7(1))*; lib. bdg. *(978-0-7787-4823-6(5))* Crabtree Publishing Co.
Jackson, Constance L. Over the River: Life of Lydia Maria Child, Abolitionist for Freedom, 1802-1880. 2008. (Illus.). 160p. pap. 18.95 *(978-0-9818204-0-8(9))* Permanent Productions Publishing.
Johnson, Claudia Durst. Slavery & Racism in the Narrative Life of Freddrick Douglass. 2014. (Social Issues in Literature Ser.). (ENG., Illus.). 224p. (gr. 7-12). lib. bdg. 46.40 *(978-0-7377-6986-9(6)*, Greenhaven Pr., Inc.) Cengage Gale.
Krass. Sojourner Truth. 2004. (Black Americans of Achievement Ser.). (Illus.). 112p. (gr. 6-12). 35.00 *(978-0-7910-8165-5(6)*, Chelsea Hse.) Facts On File, Inc.
Kudlinski, Kathleen. Sojourner Truth: Voice for Freedom. Wooden, Lenny, illus. 2003. (Childhood of Famous Americans Ser.). (ENG.). 160p. (Orig.). (J). (gr. 3-7). mass mkt. 7.99 *(978-0-689-85274-9(6)*, Simon & Schuster/Paula Wiseman Bks.) Simon & Schuster/Paula Wiseman Bks.
Landau, Elaine. Fleeing to Freedom on the Underground Railroad: The Courageous Slaves, Agents, & Conductors. 2006. (People's History Ser.). (ENG., Illus.). 88p. (gr. 5-12). lib. bdg. 33.26 *(978-0-8225-3490-7(8))* Lerner Publishing Group.
Lantier, Patricia & Michael Horn, Geoffrey. Sojourner Truth: Speaking up for Freedom. 2009. (Voices for Freedom Ser.). (ENG.). 64p. (J). (gr. 5-8). pap. *(978-0-7787-4840-3(5))* Crabtree Publishing Co.
Levin, Judy. A Timeline of the Abolitionist Movement. 2009. (Timelines of American History Ser.). 32p. (gr. 4-4). 47.90 *(978-1-60854-381-6(1)*, Rosen Reference) Rosen Publishing Group, Inc., The.
Maloof, Torrey. Abolitionists: What We Need Is Action (America in The 1800s) 2017. (Primary Source Readers Ser.). (Illus.). 32p. (J). (gr. 4-5). pap. 8.99 ***(978-1-4938-3801-1(6))*** Teacher Created Materials, Inc.
—True Life: Frederick Douglass. 2017. (J). pap. 9.97 ***(978-1-4938-3634-5(X))*** Teacher Created Materials, Inc.
—True Life: Frederick Douglass. 2017. (Time for Kids Nonfiction Readers Ser.). lib. bdg. 20.85 ***(978-0-606-40287-3(X))*** Turtleback Bks.
Marlowe, Sam. Learning about Dedication from the Life of Frederick Douglass. 2009. (Character Building Book Ser.). 24p. (gr. 2-3). 42.50 *(978-1-60854-970-2(4)*, PowerKids Pr.) Rosen Publishing Group, Inc., The.
Marrin, Albert. A Volcano Beneath the Snow: John Brown's War Against Slavery. (ENG., Illus.). 256p. (YA). (gr. 7). 2016. pap. 15.99 *(978-0-307-98154-7(1)*, Ember) 2014. 19.99 *(978-0-307-98152-3(5)*, Knopf Bks. for Young Readers) Random Hse. Children's Bks.
Marsh, Carole. Frederick Douglass. 2003. 12p. (gr. k-4). 2.95 *(978-0-635-02125-0(0))* Gallopade International.
—Harriet Beecher Stowe. 2003. 12p. (gr. k-4). 2.95 *(978-0-635-02356-8(3))* Gallopade International.
—Sojourner Truth. 2003. 12p. (gr. k-4). 2.95 *(978-0-635-02355-1(5))* Gallopade International.
Marsico, Katie. Lucretia Mott: Abolitionist & Women's Rights Leader, 1 vol. 2008. (Essential Lives Set 2 Ser.). (ENG., Illus.). 112p. (J). (gr. 6-12). lib. bdg. 35.64 *(978-1-60453-039-1(1))* ABDO Publishing Co.
Martin, Isabel. Frederick Douglass, 1 vol. 2014. (Great African-Americans Ser.). (ENG., Illus.). 24p. (gr. k-1). pap. 5.95 *(978-1-4914-0507-9(4)*, Pebble Bks.) Capstone Press of Coughlan Cos.
Mattern, Joanne. Sojourner Truth: Early Abolitionist. (Women Who Shaped History Ser.). 24p. 2009. (gr. 2-3). 42.50 *(978-1-60854-821-7(X))* 2003. (Illus.). (J). lib. bdg. 22.60 *(978-0-8239-6502-1(3))* Rosen Publishing Group, Inc., The. (PowerKids Pr.).
Mcdonough, Yona Zeldis. Who Was Sojourner Truth? 2015. (Who Was... ? Ser.). lib. bdg. 16.00 *(978-0-606-37560-3(0))* Turtleback Bks.
McDonough, Yona Zeldis & dePaola, Tomie. Who Was Sojourner Truth? Eldridge, Jim, illus. 2015. (Who Was? Ser.). (ENG.). 112p. (J). (gr. 3-7). 5.99 *(978-0-448-48678-9(4)*, Grosset & Dunlap) Penguin Young Readers Group.
McDougal-Littell Publishing Staff, contrib. by. A Nation Dividing 1800-1860. 2004. (Stories in History Ser.). (Illus.). 176p. (gr. 6-12). 13.32 *(978-0-618-14222-4(3)*, 2-00242) Holt McDougal.
McKissack, Patricia C. & McKissack, Fredrick, Jr. Sojourner Truth: Ain't I a Woman? 2003. (Illus.). 186p. (gr. 4-7). 17.20 *(978-0-7857-2515-2(6)*, Turtleback) Turtleback Bks.
McKissack, Patricia C. & McKissack, Fredrick L. Frederick Douglass: Fighter Against Slavery. 2013. (Famous African Americans Ser.). 24p. (J). (gr. k-3). pap. 7.95 *(978-1-4644-0196-1(9))*; (Illus.). 22.60 *(978-0-7660-4098-4(4))* Enslow Pubs., Inc. (Enslow Elementary).
Metz, Lorijo. The Abolitionist Movement, 1 vol., 1. 2014. (Let's Celebrate Freedom! Ser.). (ENG.). 24p. (J). (gr. 3-6). 23.60 *(978-1-4777-2897-0(X)*, PowerKids Pr.) Rosen Publishing Group, Inc., The.
—El Movimiento Abolicionista / the Abolitionist Movement, 1 vol., 1. Beullens-Maoui, Nathalie, ed. 2014. (¡Celebremos la Libertad! / Let's Celebrate Freedom! Ser.). (SPA & BYN.). 24p. (J). (gr. 3-6). 23.60 *(978-1-4777-3249-6(7)*, PowerKids Pr.) Rosen Publishing Group, Inc., The.
Miller, Barbara Kiely. Frederick Douglass. 2007. (Great Americans Ser.). 24p. (gr. 1-4). pap. 8.15 *(978-0-8368-8322-0(5))*; (SPA.). pap. 8.15 *(978-0-8368-8335-0(7))*; lib. bdg. 22.00 *(978-0-8368-8315-2(2))*; (SPA., Illus.). lib. bdg. 22.00 *(978-0-8368-8328-2(4))* Stevens, Gareth Publishing LLLP. (Weekly Reader Leveled Readers).
Miller, Reagan & Arthur, Martin. Great Leaders of the Civil War. 2011. (ENG.). 48p. (J). pap. *(978-0-7787-5359-9(X))*; lib. bdg. *(978-0-7787-5342-1(5))* Crabtree Publishing Co.
Moore, Barbara R. Sojourner Truth. 2005. (Illus.). 16p. (J). *(978-0-618-56039-4(4))* Houghton Mifflin Harcourt Publishing Co.
Morretta, Alison. Frederick Douglass & William Garrison. 2015. (Primary Sources of the Abolitionist Movement Ser.). (ENG., Illus.). 64p. (J). (gr. 6-6). lib. bdg. 34.21 *(978-1-5026-0532-0(5))* Cavendish Square Publishing.
Myers, Walter Dean. Frederick Douglass: The Lion Who Wrote History. Cooper, Floyd, illus. 2017. 40p. (J). (gr. -1-3). 17.99 *(978-0-06-027709-3(2))* HarperCollins Pubs.
National Geographic Learning, National Geographic Learning & Rossi, Ann. Reading Expeditions - The Anti-Slavery Movement. 2007. (Rise & Shine Ser.). (ENG.). 40p. pap. 19.95 *(978-0-7922-8622-6(7))* National Geographic School Publishing, Inc.
Nelson, Kadir. Heart & Soul: The Story of America & African Americans. 2013. (J). lib. bdg. 19.65 *(978-0-606-35050-1(0)*, Turtleback) Turtleback Bks.
Niver, Heather Moore. Sojourner Truth. 2015. (Heroes of Black History Ser.). (ENG., Illus.). 32p. (J). (gr. 3-4). pap. 10.50 *(978-1-4824-2912-1(8))* Stevens, Gareth Publishing LLLP.
Pace, Lorenzo. Frederick Douglass & the North Star, 1 vol. 2015. (African American Quartet Ser.). (ENG., Illus.). 48p. (J). 30.25 *(978-1-4777-9281-0(3)*, Windmill Bks.) Rosen Publishing Group, Inc., The.
—Harriet Tubman & My Grandmother's Quilts, 1 vol. 2015. (African American Quartet Ser.). (ENG., Illus.). 48p. (J). 30.25 *(978-1-4777-9289-6(9)*, Windmill Bks.) Rosen Publishing Group, Inc., The.
Passaro, John. Frederick Douglass. 2009. (Journey to Freedom Ser.). (ENG., Illus.). 32p. (J). (gr. 4-7). 29.93 *(978-1-60253-122-2(6)*, 200388) Child's World, Inc., The.
Pearce, Q. L. Zach Hunter: Modern-Day Abolitionist. 2008. (Young Heroes Ser.). (ENG., Illus.). 64p. (gr. 4-8). 35.70 *(978-0-7377-4053-0(1)*, Kidhaven) Cengage Gale.
Pierce, Alan. Underground Railroad, 1 vol. 2005. (American Moments Ser.). (ENG., Illus.). 48p. (gr. 4-8). 27.07 *(978-1-59197-942-5(0)*, Abdo & Daughters) ABDO Publishing Co.
Porterfield, Jason. Frederick Douglass: Abolitionist & Fighter for Equality. 2017. (J). ***(978-1-5383-0019-0(2))***; pap. ***(978-1-68048-802-9(3))*** Rosen Publishing Group, Inc., The. (Britannica Educational Publishing).
Prince, April Jones. Who Was Frederick Douglass? Squier, Robert & Harrison, Nancy, illus. 2014. (Who Was? Ser.). (ENG.). 112p. (J). (gr. 3-7). 5.99 *(978-0-448-47911-8(7)*, Grosset & Dunlap) Penguin Young Readers Group.
Rajczak, Michael. The Underground Railroad, Vol. 1. 2014. (What You Didn't Know about History Ser.). (ENG.). 24p. (J). (gr. 2-3). 22.60 *(978-1-4824-0601-6(2))* Stevens, Gareth Publishing LLLP.
Rappaport, Doreen. Frederick's Journey: The Life of Frederick Douglass. Ladd, London, illus. 2015. (Big Words Ser.). (ENG.). 48p. (J). (gr. 1-3). 17.99 *(978-1-4231-1438-3(8))* Disney Pr.
Rau, Dana Meachen. Who Was Harriet Beecher Stowe? 2015. (Who Was... ? Ser.). lib. bdg. 16.00 *(978-0-606-36598-7(2))* Turtleback Bks.
Rau, Dana Meachen & dePaola, Tomie. Who Was Harriet Beecher Stowe? Harrison, Nancy & Copeland, Gregory, illus. 2015. (Who Was? Ser.). (ENG.). 112p. (J). (gr. 3-7). 5.99 *(978-0-448-48301-6(7)*, Grosset & Dunlap) Penguin Young Readers Group.
Rice, Dona Herwick & Housel, Debra. Civil War Hero of Marye's Heights, 1 vol. 2009. (Building Fluency Through Reader's Theater Ser.). (ENG., Illus.). 32p. (J). (gr. 3-5). pap. 7.99 *(978-1-4333-0546-7(1))* Teacher Created Materials, Inc.
Rosen, Daniel. Dred Scott & the Supreme Court: Set Of 6. 2011. (Navigators Ser.). (J). pap. 48.00 net. *(978-1-4108-6258-7(5))* Benchmark Education Co.
Ruffin, Frances E. Her Story, Her Words: The Narrative of Sojourner Truth. (Great Moments in American History Ser.). 32p. 2009. (gr. 3-3). 47.90 *(978-1-61513-144-0(2))* 2004. (Illus.). (gr. 4-8). lib. bdg. 22.50 *(978-0-8239-4387-6(9)*, Rosen Reference) Rosen Publishing Group, Inc., The.
—Sojourner Truth: Early Abolitionist. 2009. (American Legends Ser.). 24p. (gr. 3-3). 42.50 *(978-1-61511-387-3(8)*, PowerKids Pr.) Rosen Publishing Group, Inc., The.
Russell, Sharman Apt. Frederick Douglass: Abolitionist Editor. 2004. (Black Americans of Achievement Ser.). (Illus.). 112p. (gr. 6-12). 35.00 *(978-0-7910-8157-0(5)*, Chelsea Hse.) Facts On File, Inc.
Sanders, Nancy I. Frederick Douglass for Kids: His Life & Times, with 21 Activities. 2012. (For Kids Ser.). (ENG., Illus.). 144p. (J). (gr. 4). pap. 16.95 *(978-1-56976-717-7(3))* Chicago Review Pr., Inc.
Sawyer, Kem Knapp. Harriet Tubman - A Photographic Story of a Life. 2010. (DK Biography Ser.). (ENG.). 128p. (J). (gr. 5-12). 6.99 *(978-0-7566-5806-9(3)*, DK Children) Dorling Kindersley Publishing, Inc.
Schraff, Anne. The Life of Frederick Douglass: Speaking Out Against Slavery. 2014. (Legendary African Americans Ser.). (Illus.). 96p. (J). (gr. 6-12). pap. 10.95 *(978-0-7660-6133-0(7))* Enslow Pubs., Inc.
Schraff, Anne E. John Brown: We Came to Free the Slaves. 2010. (Americans—the Spirit of a Nation Ser.). (Illus.). 128p. (J). lib. bdg. 33.27 *(978-0-7660-3355-9(4))* Enslow Pubs., Inc.

—The Life of Frederick Douglass: Speaking Out Against Slavery. 2014. (Legendary African Americans Ser.). 96p. (J). (gr. 6-12). 27.94 *(978-0-7660-6132-3(9))* Enslow Pubs., Inc.

Schuman, Michael A. Frederick Douglass: Truth Is of No Color. 2009. (Americans—the Spirit of a Nation Ser.). (Illus.). 128p. (J). (gr. 5-12). lib. bdg. 33.27 *(978-0-7660-3025-1(3))* Enslow Pubs., Inc.

Shaffer, Jody Jensen. What's Your Story, Frederick Douglass? 2016. (Cub Reporter Meets Famous Americans Ser.). (ENG., Illus.). 32p. (J). (gr. k-3). pap. 8.99 *(978-1-4677-9647-7(6),* Lerner Pubns.) Lerner Publishing Group.

Shea, Nicole. Frederick Douglass in His Own Words, Vol. 1. 2014. (Eyewitness to History Ser.). 32p. (J). (gr. 4-5). (ENG.). 26.60 *(978-1-4339-9898-0(X))*; pap. 10.50 *(978-1-4824-3288-6(9))* Stevens, Gareth Publishing LLLP.

Slade, Suzanne. Friends for Freedom: The Story of Susan B. Anthony & Frederick Douglass. Tadgell, Nicole, illus. 2014. (ENG.). 40p. (J). (gr. 1-4). 16.95 *(978-1-58089-568-2(9))* Charlesbridge Publishing, Inc.

—Friends for Freedom: The Story of Susan B. Anthony & Frederick Douglass. 2014. (Illus.). 39p. *(978-1-60734-651-7(6))* Charlesbridge Publishing, Inc.

Stanley, George E. Frederick Douglass: Abolitionist Hero. Henderson, Meryl, illus. 2008. (Childhood of Famous Americans Ser.). (ENG.). 208p. (J). (gr. 3-7). pap. 6.99 *(978-1-4169-5547-4(X),* Aladdin) Simon & Schuster Children's Publishing.

Stefoff, Rebecca. John Brown & Armed Resistance to Slavery. 2015. (Primary Sources of the Abolitionist Movement Ser.). (ENG., Illus.). 64p. (J). (gr. 6-6). 34.21 *(978-1-5026-0534-4(1))* Cavendish Square Publishing.

Stein, R. Conrad. Escaping Slavery on the Underground Railroad. 2008. (From Many Cultures, One History Ser.). (Illus.). 128p. (J). (gr. 5-18). lib. bdg. 33.27 *(978-0-7660-2799-2(6))* Enslow Pubs., Inc.

Sutherland, Jonathan. Slavery & the Abolition Movement. 2017. (Civil War Ser.: Vol. 5). (ENG.). (YA). (gr. 7-12). 24.95 ***(978-1-4222-3883-7(0))*** Mason Crest.

Swain, Gwenyth. Sojourner Truth. Archambault, Matthew, illus. 2005. (On My Own Biography Ser.). 48p. (J). (gr. 1-3). pap. 6.95 *(978-1-57505-827-6(8))* Lerner Publishing Group.

—Sojourner Truth. 2005. (On My Own Biography Ser.). (Illus.). 48p. (J). 25.26 *(978-1-57505-651-7(8),* Carolrhoda Bks.) Lerner Publishing Group.

Taylor, Charlotte. Sojourner Truth: Abolitionist & Activist. 2016. (Exceptional African Americans Ser.). (ENG.). 24p. (J). (gr. 3-3). pap. 9.35 *(978-0-7660-7370-8(X))*; (Illus.). 22.60 *(978-0-7660-7372-2(6))* Enslow Pubs., Inc.

Turner, Ann. My Name Is Truth: The Life of Sojourner Truth. Ransome, James, illus. 2015. 40p. (J). (gr. 1-5). (ENG.). 17.99 *(978-0-06-075898-1(8))*; lib. bdg. 18.89 *(978-0-06-075899-8(6))* HarperCollins Pubs.

The Underground Railroad: The Journey to Freedom. 2010. (Milestones in American History Ser.). (Illus.). 152p. (gr. 6-12). 35.00 *(978-1-60413-694-4(4),* Chelsea Hse.) Facts On File, Inc.

Vander Hook, Sue. Frederick Douglass: Fugitive Slave & Abolitionist, 1 vol. 2010. (Essential Lives Set 5 Ser.). (ENG., Illus.). 112p. (J). (gr. 6-12). lib. bdg. 35.64 *(978-1-61613-513-3(1))* ABDO Publishing Co.

Waxman, Laura Hamilton. How Did Slaves Find a Route to Freedom? And Other Questions about the Underground Railroad. 2011. (Six Questions of American History Ser.). (ENG.). 48p. (gr. 4-6). pap. 9.95 *(978-0-7613-7129-8(X))*; pap. 56.72 *(978-0-7613-7641-5(0))*; lib. bdg. 30.60 *(978-0-7613-5229-7(5))* Lerner Publishing Group.

—Sojourner Truth. 2008. pap. 52.95 *(978-0-8225-9396-6(3))*; (ENG., Illus.). 48p. (gr. 3-6). lib. bdg. 27.93 *(978-0-8225-7172-8(2),* Lerner Pubns.) Lerner Publishing Group.

Weidt, Maryann N. & National Geographic Learning Staff. Voice of Freedom: A Story about Frederick Douglass. Reeves, Jeni, illus. 2010. (Rise & Shine Ser.). (ENG.). 64p. (C). (gr. 4-8). pap. 14.95 *(978-1-57505-553-4(8))* National Geographic School Publishing, Inc.

Weiss, Lynne. Frederick Douglass & the Abolitionist Movement. 2013. (Jr. Graphic African American History Ser.). (Illus.). 24p. (J). (gr. 3-6). pap. 63.60 *(978-1-4777-1452-2(9))*; (ENG., pap. 10.60 *(978-1-4777-1451-5(0))*; (ENG., lib. bdg. 25.25 *(978-1-4777-1313-6(1))* Rosen Publishing Group, Inc., The. (PowerKids Pr.).

Welch, Catherine A. Frederick Douglass. 2003. (History Maker Bios Ser.). (Illus.). 48p. (J). (gr. 4-7). pap. 8.95 *(978-0-8225-4802-7(X))*; (gr. 3-5). lib. bdg. 26.60 *(978-0-8225-4672-6(8))* Lerner Publishing Group.

Weymouth Seguin, Marilyn. The Freedom Stairs: The Story of Adam Lowry Rankin, Underground Railroad Conductor. 2004. (Illus.). 93p. (J). (gr. 3-7). per. 12.95 net. *(978-0-8283-2084-9(5))* Branden Bks.

Whiting, Jim. Frederick Douglass. 2010. (Transcending Race in America: Biographies of Biracial Achievers Ser.). (Illus.). 64p. (YA). (gr. 5-18). lib. bdg. 22.95 *(978-1-4222-1611-8(X))* Mason Crest.

Willen, Janet & Gann, Marjorie. Speak a Word for Freedom: Women Against Slavery. 2015. (ENG., Illus.). 208p. (J). (gr. 7). 21.99 *(978-1-77049-651-4(3),* Tundra Bks.) Tundra Bks. CAN. Dist: Penguin Random Hse. LLC.

Wilson, Camilla. Frederick Douglass: A Voice for Freedom in the 1800s. 2003. (Scholastic Biography Ser.). (Illus.). 90p. (J). pap. *(978-0-439-38082-9(0))* Scholastic, Inc.

yancey, diane. The Abolition of Slavery. 2012. (Illus.). 96p. (J). lib. bdg. *(978-1-60152-476-8(5))* ReferencePoint Pr., Inc.

Yomtov, Nel. John Brown: Defending the Innocent or Plotting Terror?, 1 vol. 2013. (Perspectives on History Ser.). (ENG.). 32p. (gr. 3-4). 27.32 *(978-1-4765-0244-1(7))*; pap. 7.95 *(978-1-4765-3408-4(X))* Capstone Press of Coughlan Cos. (Fact Finders).

Yomtov, Nel & Gunderson, Jessica. Perspectives on History. 2013. (Perspectives on History Ser.). (ENG.). 32p. (gr. 3-4). pap. 31.80 *(978-1-4765-3640-8(6))*; lib. bdg. 109.28 *(978-1-4765-0425-4(3))* Capstone Press of Coughlan Cos. (Fact Finders).

ABOLITIONISTS—FICTION

Cooper, Afua. My Name Is Henry Bibb: A Story of Slavery & Freedom. 2009. (ENG., Illus.). 160p. (J). (gr. 5-9). 16.95 *(978-1-55337-813-6(X))* Kids Can Pr., Ltd. CAN. Dist: Hachette Bk. Group.

Engle, Margarita. The Lightning Dreamer: Cuba's Greatest Abolitionist. 2013. (ENG.). 192p. (YA). (gr. 7). 16.99 *(978-0-547-80743-0(0))* Houghton Mifflin Harcourt Publishing Co.

O'Maley, Elizabeth. By Freedom's Light. 2009. 188p. (J). 15.95 *(978-0-87195-273-8(4))*; pap. 7.95 *(978-0-87195-274-5(2))* Indiana Historical Society.

ABORTION

Bacon, Lizzy. Abortion. 2004. (World Issues Ser.). (J). lib. bdg. 28.50 *(978-1-59389-157-2(1))* Chrysalis Education.

Berlatsky, Noah. Abortion. 2010. (Global Viewpoints Ser.). (ENG., Illus.). 160-224p. (J). 40.45 *(978-0-7377-4927-4(X))*; pap. 27.95 *(978-0-7377-4928-1(8))* Cengage Gale. (Greenhaven Pr., Inc.).

Cunningham, Anne C. Critical Perspectives on Abortion. 2017. (Analyzing the Issues Ser.). 208p. (J). (gr. 8-8). lib. bdg. 47.93 ***(978-0-7660-8477-3(9))*** Enslow Pubs., Inc.

Friedman, Lauri S. Abortion. 2008. (Compact Research Ser.). (YA). (gr. 7-12). lib. bdg. 25.95 *(978-1-60152-047-0(6))* ReferencePoint Pr., Inc.

Gay, Kathlyn. Abortion: Understanding the Debate. 2004. (Issues in Focus Ser.). (Illus.). 128p. (J). lib. bdg. 26.60 *(978-0-7660-2162-4(9))* Enslow Pubs., Inc.

Hand, Carol. Abortion: Interpreting the Constitution. 2014. (Understanding the United States Constitution Ser.). 112p. (YA). (gr. 7-12). 35.60 *(978-1-4777-7510-3(2))* Rosen Publishing Group, Inc., The.

Haney, Johannah. The Abortion Debate: Understanding the Issues. 2008. (Issues in Focus Today Ser.). (Illus.). 112p. (J). (gr. k-6). lib. bdg. 33.27 *(978-0-7660-2916-3(6))* Enslow Pubs., Inc.

Herda, D. J. A Woman's Right to an Abortion: Roe V. Wade. 2016. (US Supreme Court Landmark Cases Ser.). (Illus.). 128p. (J). 37.27 *(978-0-7660-8424-7(8))* Enslow Pubs., Inc.

Higgins, Melissa & Dellapenna, Joseph W. Roe v. Wade: Abortion & a Woman's Right to Privacy, 1 vol. 2012. (Landmark Supreme Court Cases Ser.). (ENG., Illus.). 160p. (J). (gr. 6-12). 37.07 *(978-1-61783-476-9(9))* ABDO Publishing Co.

Hitchcock, Susan Tyler. Roe V. Wade: Protecting a Woman's Right to Choose. 2006. (Great Supreme Court Decisions Ser.). (Illus.). 128p. (J). (gr. 5-9). lib. bdg. 32.95 *(978-0-7910-9239-2(9))* Facts On File, Inc.

Juettner, Bonnie. Abortion. 2007. (Ripped from the Headlines Ser.). (YA). (gr. 7-12). 23.95 *(978-1-60217-020-9(7))* Erickson Pr.

Marcovitz, Hal. Abortion. 2008. (Gallup Major Trends & Events Ser.). (Illus.). 111p. (YA). (gr. 7-18). lib. bdg. 22.95 *(978-1-59084-962-0(0),* 1260827) Mason Crest.

Merino, Noël. Abortion. Greenhaven Press Editors & Gale Editors, eds. 2014. (Opposing Viewpoints Ser.). (ENG., Illus.). 224p. (gr. 7-12). pap. 33.80 *(978-0-7377-6940-1(8),* Greenhaven Pr., Inc.) Cengage Gale.

Merino, Noel. Abortion. Greenhaven Press Editors, ed. 2014. (Opposing Viewpoints Ser.). (ENG., Illus.). 224p. (gr. 7-10). lib. bdg. 48.80 *(978-0-7377-6939-5(4),* Greenhaven Pr., Inc.) Cengage Gale.

Merino, No'l, ed. Abortion. 2013. (Teen Rights & Freedoms Ser.). (ENG., Illus.). 176p. (gr. 10-12). lib. bdg. 37.45 *(978-0-7377-6397-3(3),* Greenhaven Pr., Inc.) Cengage Gale.

Naden, Corinne J. Abortion. 2007. (Open for Debate Ser.). (Illus.). 128p. (gr. 7-7). lib. bdg. 42.79 *(978-0-7614-2573-1(X),* Benchmark Bks.) Marshall Cavendish Corp.

Thompson, Tamara. Abortion. Greenhaven Press Staff, ed. 2015. (Current Controversies Ser.). (ENG.). 224p. (gr. 10-12). pap. 32.00 *(978-0-7377-7206-7(9),* Greenhaven Pr., Inc.) Cengage Gale.

Walters, Mike. Critical World Issues: Abortion, Vol. 16. 2016. (Critical World Issues Ser.: Vol. 16). (ENG., Illus.). 112p. (J). (gr. 7-12). 25.95 *(978-1-4222-3646-8(3))* Mason Crest.

Wilcox, Christine. Thinking Critically: Abortion. 2017. (ENG.). 80p. (YA). (gr. 5-12). ***(978-1-68282-261-6(3))*** ReferencePoint Pr., Inc.

Williams, Heidi. Teen Pregnancy. 2009. (Issues That Concern You Ser.). (ENG., Illus.). 144p. (J). 36.95 *(978-0-7377-4498-9(7),* 1330228) Cengage Gale.

ABORTION—FICTION

Calkin, Author & Calkin, Abigail B. The Carolyne Letters: A Story of Birth, Abortion & Adoption. 2013. (ENG., Illus.). 230p. (YA). pap. 14.95 *(978-1-938301-15-5(3))* Familius LLC.

Cohn, Rachel & Wattenberg, Jane. Gingerbread. 2003. (ENG., Illus.). 224p. (YA). (gr. 9). pap. 8.99 *(978-0-689-86020-1(X),* Simon & Schuster Bks. For Young Readers) Simon & Schuster Bks. For Young Readers.

Hamilton, Elizabeth L. Date with Responsibility. 2004. (Character-in-Action Ser.: No. 2). (Illus.). 384p. (YA). per. 19.95 *(978-0-9713749-0-4(2),* Character-in-Action) Quiet Impact, Inc.

Levine, Ellen. In Trouble. 2011. (Carolrhoda YA Ser.). (ENG.). 208p. (YA). (gr. 9-12). 17.95 *(978-0-7613-6558-7(3),* Carolrhoda Lab™) Lerner Publishing Group.

Stevenson, Robin. Under Threat, 1 vol. 2016. (Orca Soundings Ser.). (ENG.). 144p. (YA). (gr. 8-12). pap. 9.95 *(978-1-4598-1131-7(3))* Orca Bk. Pubs. USA.

—Under Threat. 2016. (Orca Soundings Ser.). lib. bdg. 20.80 *(978-0-606-38702-6(1))* Turtleback Bks.

ABRAHAM (BIBLICAL PATRIARCH)

Abraham. (Divertidas Historias Bíblicas para Ninos Ser.). (SPA.). (J). 3.49 *(978-0-7899-0600-7(7),* 496647) Editorial Unilit.

Arthur, Kay & Arndt, Janna. Abraham - God's Brave Explorer: Genesis 11-25. 2003. (ENG.). 208p. (J). pap., wbk. ed. 11.99 *(978-0-7369-0936-5(2),* 6909362) Harvest Hse. Pubs.

Brand, Ruth Redding. Abraham. White, John, Jr. & Tank, Daniel, illus. 2004. (Family Bible Story Ser.). 109p. (J). 19.99 *(978-0-8280-1856-2(1),* 010-570) Review & Herald Publishing Assn.

Dickison, Forrest, illus. The Sword of Abram. 2013. (J). *(978-1-59128-046-0(X))* Canon Pr.

Ganeri, Anita. Hajj Story. 2003. (Festival Stories Ser.). (ENG., Illus.). 24p. (J). pap. 10.99 *(978-0-237-52732-7(4))* Evans Brothers, Ltd. GBR. Dist: Independent Pubs. Group.

Haus, Cari. Father of Many Nations. 2007. (Illus.). 112p. (J). pap. 9.99 *(978-0-8127-0468-6(1))* Autumn Hse. Publishing Co.

Holder, Jennifer. Abraham Trusts God. Julien, Terry, illus. 2015. (Faith That Sticks Bks.). (ENG.). 24p. (J). pap. 3.99 *(978-1-4964-0320-9(7))* Tyndale Hse. Pubs.

Larsen, Carolyn. Abraham, Isaac, & Jacob. 2012. (Standard Bible Storybook Ser.). (ENG., Illus.). 32p. (J). 7.99 *(978-0-7847-3563-3(8))* Standard Publishing.

Racklin-Siegel, Carol, illus. Lech Lecha: The Story of Abraham & Rebecca. 2004. (HEB & ENG.). 32p. (J). per. 10.95 *(978-0-939144-49-5(2))* EKS Publishing Co.

Ravasi, Gianfranco. Abraham: Father of Our Faith. 2015. (ENG., Illus.). 68p. pap. 19.95 *(978-0-8091-6775-3(1))* Paulist Pr.

Shenton, Tim. The Life of Abraham: Faith, Courage, Children, God. 2003. (Daily Readings From Ser.). (Illus.). 76p. (J). (gr. -1-7). per. 7.99 *(978-1-903087-72-5(4))* DayOne Pubns. GBR. Dist: Send The Light Distribution LLC.

White, John, Jr. & Tank, Daniel, illus. Abraham. 2004. (Family Bible Story Ser.). 109p. (J). pap. *(978-0-8280-1857-9(X))* Review & Herald Publishing Assn.

ABSENCE FROM SCHOOL

see School Attendance

ABSTINENCE, SEXUAL

see Sexual Abstinence

ABSTRACT ART

see Art, Abstract

ACADIANS

Bernard, Shane K. Cajuns & Their Acadian Ancestors: A Young Reader's History. 2008. (ENG., Illus.). 104p. (gr. 7-12). 18.00 *(978-1-934110-78-2(7))* Univ. Pr. of Mississippi.

Reneaux, J. J. Cajun Folktales. 2005. (American Storytelling Ser.). (ENG.). 176p. (J). (gr. 4-17). pap. 12.95 *(978-0-87483-282-2(9))* August Hse. Pubs., Inc.

ACCIDENTS

see also Disasters

Aronson, Marc. Trapped: How the World Rescued 33 Miners from 2,000 Feet below the Chilean Desert. 2012. (ENG., Illus.). 144p. (J). pap. 6.99 *(978-1-4424-4025-8(2),* Atheneum Bks. for Young Readers) Simon & Schuster Children's Publishing.

Baxter, Roberta. Challenger Explosion. 2013. (Illus.). 48p. (J). 15.64 *(978-1-62403-019-2(X),* 1360919, Core Library); (ENG., (gr. 3-6). lib. bdg. 32.79 *(978-1-61783-954-2(X),* 1360919) ABDO Publishing Co.

Ford, Jean. Explosives & Arson Investigation. Noziglia, Carla Miller & Siegel, Jay A., eds. 2013. (Solving Crimes with Science: Forensics Ser.: 12). (Illus.). 112p. (J). (gr. 7-18). 22.95 *(978-1-4222-2867-8(3))* Mason Crest.

Goldberg, Jan. James Lovell: The Rescue of Apollo 13. 2009. (Library of Astronaut Biographies Ser.). 112p. (gr. 5-8). 63.90 *(978-1-60853-522-4(3),* Rosen Reference) Rosen Publishing Group, Inc., The.

Greathouse, Lisa. Emergency! Be Prepared, 1 vol. 2011. (Science Readers: a Closer Look Ser.). (ENG., Illus.). 32p. (J). (gr. 2-2). pap. 8.99 *(978-1-4333-3092-6(X))* Teacher Created Materials, Inc.

Holden, Henry M. Danger in Space: Surviving the Apollo 13 Disaster. 2012. (American Space Missions — Astronauts, Exploration, & Discovery Ser.). (Illus.). 48p. (J). (gr. 5-18). 25.27 *(978-0-7660-4072-4(0))* Enslow Pubs., Inc.

Hyland, Tony. Emergency. 2003. (Bookweb Plus Ser.). (Illus.). 32p. (J). (gr. -1-3). pap. *(978-0-7578-8447-4(4),* Rigby) Pearson Education Australia.

Jankowski, Susan & Library. True Ocean Rescue Stories. 2010. (True Rescue Stories Ser.). 48p. (J). lib. bdg. 22.60 *(978-0-7660-3665-9(0))* Enslow Pubs., Inc.

Jeffrey, Gary. Defying Death at Sea. Riley, Terry, illus. 2010. (Graphic Survival Stories Ser.). 48p. (YA). 58.50 *(978-1-61532-897-0(1))*; (ENG.). pap. 14.05 *(978-1-61532-863-5(7))*; (gr. 5-8). 31.95 *(978-1-4358-3530-6(1))* Rosen Publishing Group, Inc., The. (Rosen Reference).

Kate Shelley & the Midnight Express. 9.95 *(978-1-59112-169-5(8))* Live Oak Media.

Kops, Deborah. The Great Molasses Flood. 2015. (ENG.). 112p. (J). (gr. 4-7). pap. 11.95 *(978-1-58089-349-7(X))* Charlesbridge Publishing, Inc.

Lindeen, Mary & Kesselring, Susan. Being Safe on Wheels. McGeehan, Dan & Moore, David, illus. 2011. (Be Safe Ser.). (ENG.). 24p. (J). (gr. k-3). lib. bdg. 27.07 *(978-1-60954-371-6(8),* 200082) Child's World, Inc., The.

Make Believe Ideas, creator. Emergency: Sticker Activity Book. 2006. (Lift Stick & Learn Ser.). (Illus.). 12p. (J). (gr. -1-k). *(978-1-905051-69-4(7))* Make Believe Ideas.

Man-Made Disasters. (Illus.). (J). (gr. 3-6). 103.50 *(978-0-8239-7292-0(5),* Reading Power) Rosen Publishing Group, Inc., The.

Micklos, John, Jr. The Challenger Explosion: Core Events of a Space Tragedy. 2015. (What Went Wrong? Ser.). (ENG.). 32p. (gr. 3-4). lib. bdg. 27.32 *(978-1-4914-2046-1(4))* Capstone Press of Coughlan Cos.

Morris, Neil. Transportation, 1 vol. 2010. (From Fail to Win! Learning from Bad Ideas Ser.). (ENG., Illus.). 56p. (gr. 5-8). 34.65 *(978-1-4109-3911-1(1),* Raintree Freestyle) Heinemann-Raintree.

Naughton, Diane. Rescued. 2014. (ENG., Illus.). 28p. (J). pap. 9.50 *(978-1-107-65519-5(6))* Cambridge Univ. Pr.

Nelson, Robin. Jugar Sin Peligro. Aguirre, Barbara & Fitzpatrick, Julia, trs. 2005. (Libros para Avanzar-La Salud (Pull Ahead Books-Health) Ser.). (SPA & ENG., Illus.). 32p. (gr. k-3). lib. bdg. 22.60 *(978-0-8225-3146-3(1),* Ediciones Lerner) Lerner Publishing Group.

Oxlade, Chris & West, David. The Apollo Missions & Other Adventures in Space. 2011. (Incredible True Adventures Ser.). (ENG., Illus.). 48p. (YA). (gr. 5-8). pap. 11.75 *(978-1-4488-6664-9(2))*; lib. bdg. 29.25 *(978-1-4488-6660-1(X))* Rosen Publishing Group, Inc., The. (Rosen Reference).

Parks, Peggy J. Driving under the Influence. 2007. (Ripped from the Headlines Ser.). (YA). (gr. 7-12). 23.95 *(978-1-60217-013-1(4))* Erickson Pr.

Radomski, Kassandra. The Apollo 13 Mission: Core Events of a Crisis in Space, 1 vol. 2014. (What Went Wrong? Ser.). (ENG.). 32p. (gr. 3-4). lib. bdg. 27.32 *(978-1-4765-4181-5(7))* Capstone Press of Coughlan Cos.

Renaud, Anne. Into the Mist: The Story of the Empress of Ireland. 2010. (ENG., Illus.). 112p. (YA). (gr. 6). pap. 14.99 *(978-1-55488-759-0(3))* Dundurn CAN. Dist: Ingram Publisher Services.

Richards, M. & Creese, S. Carry Me Rough N Tough - Emergency. 2009. 12p. pap. *(978-1-84610-985-0(X))* Make Believe Ideas.

Scherer, Glenn & Library. True Mountain Rescue Stories. 2010. (True Rescue Stories Ser.). 48p. (J). lib. bdg. 22.60 *(978-0-7660-3572-0(7))* Enslow Pubs., Inc.

SchreyerKarmel. TRAGEDY ON THE SLOPES UPPER INTERMEDIATE BOOK WITH ONLINE ACCESS. 2014. (ENG., Illus.). 28p. pap. 9.50 *(978-1-107-62159-6(3))* Cambridge Univ. Pr.

The Science of a Shipwreck. 2014. (21st Century Skills Library: Disaster Science Ser.). (ENG., Illus.). 32p. (J). (gr. 4-8). 28.50 *(978-1-63137-627-6(6),* 205291) Cherry Lake Publishing.

Stone, Adam. The Apollo 13 Mission. 2014. (Disaster Stories Ser.). (ENG., Illus.). 24p. (J). (gr. 3-8). 29.95 *(978-1-62617-149-7(1),* Black Sheep) Bellwether Media.

Walker, Niki. Transportation Disaster Alert! 2005. (Disaster Alert! Ser.). (ENG., Illus.). 32p. (J). (gr. 4-7). pap. *(978-0-7787-1616-7(3))* Crabtree Publishing Co.

Wheeler-Toppen, Jodi. Science Experiments That Explode & Implode: Fun Projects for Curious Kids, 1 vol. 2010. (Kitchen Science Ser.). (ENG.). 32p. (gr. 3-4). lib. bdg. 27.99 *(978-1-4296-5427-2(9),* Edge Bks.) Capstone Press of Coughlan Cos.

When Disaster Strikes! 2005. (Illus.). 48p. (gr. 5-8). lib. bdg. 143.70 *(978-0-8239-3892-6(1))* Rosen Publishing Group, Inc., The.

Woods, Michael & Woods, Mary B. Disasters at Sea. 2008. (Disasters up Close Ser.). (ENG., Illus.). 64p. (gr. 4-8). lib. bdg. 27.93 *(978-0-8225-6773-8(3),* Lerner Pubns.) Lerner Publishing Group.

ACCIDENTS—FICTION

Ackerman, Jill. Uh-Oh! I'm Sorry. Berg, Michelle, illus. 2011. (Little Scholastic Ser.). (ENG.). 10p. (J). (gr. k — 1). bds. 6.99 *(978-0-545-30745-1(7),* Cartwheel Bks.) Scholastic, Inc.

Albrecht, Joshua. Victims of a Tragedy. 2012. 100p. pap. 8.99 *(978-1-937165-28-4(0))* Orange Hat Publishing.

Alcott, Louisa May. Jack & Jill. l.t. ed. 2005. 496p. pap. *(978-1-84637-054-0(X))* Echo Library.

Archer, Dosh. Big Bad Wolf. Archer, Dosh, illus. 2013. (Urgency Emergency! Ser.). (ENG., Illus.). 48p. (J). (gr. -1-3). 12.99 *(978-0-8075-8352-4(9))* Whitman, Albert & Co.

Ballantyne, Robert Michael. My Doggie & I. 2007. 120p. pap. 18.99 *(978-1-4346-3682-9(8))*; (ENG.). 130p. pap. 19.99 *(978-1-4346-3730-7(1))* Creative Media Partners, LLC.

Banks, Kimberly E. Mask Man. Wroe, Dameon K., ed. 2003. 57p. (YA). pap. 9.99 *(978-0-9740685-0-3(0))* Another Ep Publishing.

Barkhouse, Joyce & Barkhouse, Janet. Pit Pony: The Picture Book. Smith, Sydney, illus. 2012. (ENG.). 32p. (J). (gr. -1-2). 14.95 *(978-1-4595-0143-0(8),* 9781459501430) Formac Publishing Co., Ltd. CAN. Dist: Casemate Pubs. & Bk. Distributors, LLC.

Bauer, Marion Dane. On My Honor. 2012. lib. bdg. 18.40 *(978-0-606-24717-7(3),* Turtleback) Turtleback Bks.

Bauer, Tiffany Jamie. Swim Little Swimmy, 1 vol. 2009. 25p. pap. 24.95 *(978-1-60813-520-2(9))* America Star Bks.

Blackwater Mine, 6 Pack. (Bookweb Ser.). 32p. (gr. 6-18). 34.00 *(978-0-7578-0893-7(X))* Rigby Education.

Branning, Debe. The Adventures of Chickolet Pigolet: The Bribe of Frankenbeans. Knold, Nijlon, illus. 2008. 48p. pap. 7.95 *(978-1-935137-40-5(9))* Guardian Angel Publishing, Inc.

Brezenoff, Steve. Lost Island. 2013. (Ravens Pass Ser.). (ENG.). 96p. (gr. 2-3). pap. 35.70 *(978-1-4342-6290-5(1))* Stone Arch Bks.

Brooks, Charlie. Greystone Valley. Grundy, Jessica, illus. 2013. 166p. 17.99 *(978-1-938821-33-2(5))*; 198p. pap. 9.99 *(978-1-938821-41-7(6))* Grey Gecko Pr.

Byous, Shawn. Because I Stubbed My Toe, 1 vol. 2014. (ENG.). 32p. (gr. -1-3). pap. 6.95 *(978-1-4795-3808-9(6),* Fiction Picture Bks.) Picture Window Bks.

Campbell, Todd M. Puppy Dog's New Friend. 2012. 24p. 24.95 *(978-1-4626-6127-5(0))* America Star Bks.

Carithers, Rochelle. The Purple with Pink Polka Dot Ponies. Weber, Caressa, illus. 2010. 102p. pap. 7.95 *(978-1-936107-31-5(7))* Salem Author Services.

Choyce, Lesley. Smoke & Mirrors. 2004. (ENG.). 200p. (YA). (gr. 7). pap. 8.99 *(978-1-55002-534-7(1))* Dundurn CAN. Dist: Ingram Publisher Services.

Clark, Brenda. Spiro Goes West: More Adventures of Spiro the Shooting Star. 2008. 57p. pap. 16.95 *(978-1-60474-770-6(6))* America Star Bks.

Classic Goosebumps & Stine, R. L. Be Careful What You Wish For. 2009. (Classic Goosebumps Ser.: 7). (ENG.). 160p. (J). (gr. 3-7). 6.99 *(978-0-545-03524-8(4),* Scholastic Paperbacks) Scholastic, Inc.

Clover, Peter. Rescue Riders: Race Against Time. l.t. ed. 2007. 88p. per. *(978-1-905665-29-7(6))* Pollinger In Print.

Coolidge, Susan. What Katy Did. 2013. (ENG., Illus.). 200p. (J). 15.00 *(978-1-84135-843-7(6))* Award Pubns. Ltd. GBR. Dist: Parkwest Pubns., Inc.

—What Katy Did. Ledyard, Addie, illus. 2013. 132p. pap. *(978-1-909735-03-3(5))* Aziloth Bks.

—What Katy Did. 2012. 246p. pap. *(978-1-78139-262-1(5))* Benediction Classics.

—What Katy Did. 2012. 300p. pap. 29.75 *(978-1-286-00091-5(2))* 2012. 302p. pap. 29.75 *(978-1-286-07372-8(3))* 2011. 290p. (gr. 3-7). pap. 28.75 *(978-1-179-65265-8(7))* 2010. (ENG.). 300p. pap. 29.75 *(978-1-178-00783-1(9))* 2010. (ENG.). 282p. (gr. 3-7). pap. 28.75 *(978-1-177-27477-7(9))* 2010. 302p. pap. 29.75 *(978-1-145-74830-9(9))* 2008. 164p. (gr. 4-7). 25.99 *(978-0-554-28634-1(3))* 2008. 164p. (gr. 4-7). 22.99 *(978-0-554-37937-1(6))* 2007. (ENG.). 144p. pap. 18.99 *(978-1-4346-5943-9(7))* 2007. (ENG.). 160p. pap. 21.99 *(978-1-4346-5944-6(5))* Creative Media Partners, LLC.

—What Katy Did. 2007. (ENG.). 148p. per. (978-1-4065-1527-5(2)) Dodo Pr.

—What Katy Did. 2006. (Dover Children's Classics Ser.). (ENG., Illus.). 160p. (J). (gr. 3-8). per. 6.95 (978-0-486-44760-5(X)) Dover Pubns., Inc.

—What Katy Did. 2007. (ENG.). 104p. per. (978-1-4068-4855-7(7)) Echo Library.

—What Katy Did. 2010. (Illus.). 92p. (gr. 3-7). pap. 19.99 (978-1-153-74507-9(0)) 2009. 104p. pap. 6.40 (978-0-217-53637-0(9)) General Bks. LLC.

—What Katy Did. 2010. 132p. pap. (978-1-4076-5115-6(3)) HardPr.

—What Katy Did. Ledyard, Addie, illus. 284p. 2010. 35.16 (978-1-163-85079-4(9)) 2010. pap. 23.16 (978-1-163-77965-1(2)) 2007. 43.95 (978-0-548-53870-8(0)) 2007. per. 28.95 (978-0-548-48700-6(6)) Kessinger Publishing, LLC.

—What Katy Did. 2010. (Puffin Classics Ser.). (ENG., Illus.). 240p. (J). (gr. 5-7). pap. 5.99 (978-0-14-132671-9(9), Puffin Books) Penguin Young Readers Group.

—What Katy Did. 2013. (ENG., Illus.). 256p. (J). (gr. 4-7). pap. 12.99 (978-0-09-957312-8(1)) Random Hse. GBR. Dist: Independent Pubs. Group.

—What Katy Did. 2007. (ENG.). 192p. pap. 12.45 (978-1-60424-403-8(8), Book Jungle) Standard Pubns., Inc.

—What Katy Did. 2011. 162p. (gr. 3-7). pap. (978-3-8424-6664-7(1)) Tredition GmbH.

—What Katy Did. 2010. 144p. pap. 4.99 (978-1-61720-100-4(6)) Wilder Pubns., Corp.

Coolidge, Susan & Ledyard, Addie. What Katy Did. 2010. (ENG.). 292p. pap. 28.75 (978-1-172-34659-2(3)) Creative Media Partners, LLC.

Couloumbis, Audrey. Jake. 2011. (ENG.). 176p. (J). (gr. 3-7). pap. 6.99 (978-0-375-85631-0(5), Yearling) Random Hse. Children's Bks.

Crews, Deborah Sue. Broken Slippers. 2013. 92p. pap. 12.00 (978-1-936688-82-1(4), Compass Flower Pr.) AKA:yoLa.

Cronin, Doreen. Cyclone. 2017. (ENG., Illus.). 352p. (J). (gr. 4-8). 16.99 **(978-1-4814-3525-3(6)**, Atheneum/Caitlyn Dlouhy Books) Simon & Schuster Children's Publishing.

Cross, Mimi. Before Goodbye, 0 vols. 2016. (ENG.). 389p. (YA). (gr. 8-12). pap. 9.99 (978-1-5039-4972-0(9), 9781503949720, Skyscape) Amazon Publishing.

Cusick, Richie Tankersley. Summer of Secrets. 2013. (ENG., Illus.). 224p. (YA). (gr. 7). pap. 15.99 (978-1-4814-0160-9(2), Simon Pulse) Simon Pulse.

Cuyler, Margery. That's Good! That's Bad! on Santa's Journey. 2015. (J). lib. bdg. 17.20 (978-0-606-37582-5(1)) Turtleback Bks.

Dillon, Kimberly M. The Ghosts of Wolf Creek. 2008. 73p. pap. 19.95 (978-1-60563-996-3(6)) America Star Bks.

Elston, Ashley. This Is Our Story. 2016. (ENG.). 320p. (YA). (gr. 7-12). 17.99 (978-1-4847-3089-8(5)) Hyperion Bks. for Children.

Emerson, Alice B. Ruth Fielding on Cliff Island: Or the Old Hunter's Treasure Box. 2007. (ENG.). 136p. pap. 18.99 (978-1-4346-2493-2(5)); 148p. pap. 19.99 (978-1-4346-2535-9(4)) Creative Media Partners, LLC.

Everett, Sarah. Everyone We've Been. 2016. (ENG., Illus.). 400p. (YA). (gr. 7). 17.99 (978-0-553-53844-1(6), Knopf Bks. for Young Readers) Random Hse. Children's Bks.

Finney, Ruth. A Prayer for Momma. 2007. 38p. pap. 8.00 (978-0-8059-7483-6(0)) Dorrance Publishing Co., Inc.

Forman, Gayle. If I Stay. 2010. (If I Stay Ser.: BK.1). (YA). lib. bdg. 22.10 (978-0-606-14395-0(5), Turtleback) Turtleback Bks.

Fowley-Doyle, Moira. The Accident Season. 2015. (ENG.). 304p. (YA). (gr. 9). 17.99 (978-0-525-42948-7(4), Kathy Dawson Books) Penguin Young Readers Group.

Frewin Jones, Allan. The Mole & Beverley Miller. l.t. ed. 2007. 232p. per. (978-1-905665-34-1(2)) Pollinger In Print.

Gal, Dakota. Jaffy Gaffy. 2009. 60p. pap. 12.00 (978-1-4389-8336-3(0)) AuthorHouse.

Garvie, Maureen. Amy by Any Other Name. 2009. (ENG.). 256p. (YA). (gr. 7-18). pap. (978-1-55470-142-1(2)) Me to We.

Gillespie, Hollis. We Will Be Crashing Shortly. 2015. (ENG.). 240p. (YA). 17.99 (978-1-4405-6770-4(0), Simon Pulse) Simon Pulse.

Harrell, Deborah A. Pintos Hope. 2003. 124p. (YA). pap. 10.95 (978-0-595-26514-5(6), Writers Club Pr.) iUniverse, Inc.

Hawes, Rachelle. Dan the Rescue Man: Fire at Farmer Dave's. 2013. 24p. pap. 10.95 (978-1-4525-1161-0(6), Balboa Pr.) Author Solutions, Inc.

Heckman, Ashley. The Last Three Words. 2013. 104p. pap. (978-1-77130-651-5(3)) Evernight Publishing.

Henderson, Lauren. Kiss of Death. 2012. (ENG.). 318p. (YA). (gr. 9). pap. 9.99 (978-0-385-73780-7(7), Ember) Random Hse. Children's Bks.

Hengel, Katherine. Wings, 1 vol. unabr. ed. 2011. (District 13 Ser.). (ENG.). 48p. (YA). (gr. 9-12). pap. 7.95 (978-1-61651-280-4(6)) Saddleback Educational Publishing, Inc.

Hensley, Judith Victoria. Terrible Tin. 2008. 136p. pap. 14.95 (978-0-9795103-3-5(3)) Ascended Ideas.

Hesse, Karen. Phoenix Rising. 2009. (ENG.). 208p. (J). (gr. 6-11). pap. 9.99 (978-0-312-53562-9(7), 9780312535629) Square Fish.

Hill, David. Coming Back. 2007. (ENG.). 200p. per. 18.95 (978-0-9542330-2-0(6)) Aurora Metro Pubns. Ltd. GBR. Dist: Consortium Bk. Sales & Distribution.

Hooper, Mary. Down to Earth. Harker, Lesley, illus. 2008. (Two Naughty Angels Ser.). (ENG.). 96p. (J). (gr. 2-4). pap. 11.95 (978-0-7475-9061-3(3)) Bloomsbury Publishing Plc GBR. Dist: Independent Pubs. Group.

Huxman, K. D. Grizzelda Gorilla. l.t. ed. 2007. (Illus.). 24p. (J). 24.99 (978-0-9794660-2-1(4)); per. 12.99 (978-0-9794660-3-8(2)) Dragonfly Publishing, Inc.

Jan Baer: And the Mystery of the Silent Circus. 2005. (J). per. 10.00 (978-1-930052-29-1(4)) Cherokee Bks.

Jones, Elwynn. Frank's Frantic Friday. 2010. 40p. pap. 16.95 (978-1-60911-750-4(6), Eloquent Bks.) Strategic Book Publishing & Rights Agency (SBPRA).

Jones, Frewin. The Seventh Daughter. 2009. (Faerie Path Ser.: 3). (ENG.). 352p. (YA). (gr. 8). pap. 9.99 (978-0-06-087110-9(5), HarperTeen) HarperCollins Pubs.

Kenney, Cindy. Project Precious Paws, Bk. 3. 2009. 86p. (J). pap. 5.99 (978-0-9817159-4-0(X)) Precious Moments, Inc.

Kriszt, Ann Marie. Bestis Friends. 2008. 276p. pap. 27.95 (978-1-60703-154-3(X)) PublishAmerica, Inc.

Lasota, Mary. Kitty Piper Angel Cat: I Almost Lost My Best Friend. 2009. 36p. pap. 16.99 (978-1-4490-2012-5(7)) AuthorHouse.

Leblanc, Louise. Leo's Skiing Surprise. Prud'homme, Jules, illus. 2007. (Formac First Novels Ser.). (ENG.). 64p. (J). (gr. 2-5). 14.95 (978-0-88780-738-1(0), 9780887807381) Formac Publishing Co., Ltd. CAN. Dist: Casemate Pubs. & Bk. Distributors, LLC.

—Leo's Skiing Surprise, 1 vol. Cummins, Sarah, tr. from FRE. Prud'homme, Jules, illus. 2007. (Formac First Novels Ser.). (ENG.). 64p. (J). (gr. 2-5). 4.95 (978-0-88780-736-7(4), 9780887807367) Formac Publishing Co., Ltd. CAN. Dist: Casemate Pubs. & Bk. Distributors, LLC.

Lee, Thomas. The Battle at Otter Lake. 2007. 167p. pap. 24.95 (978-1-60441-488-2(X)) America Star Bks.

Leslie, Emma. For Merrie England: A Tale of the Weavers of Norfolk. Taylor, R., illus. 2010. 168p. 20.95 (978-1-934671-38-2(X)); pap. 10.95 (978-1-934671-39-9(8)) Salem Ridge Press LLC.

Lester, Helen. It Wasn't My Fault. Munsinger, Lynn, illus. alt. ed. 2013. (Laugh-Along Lessons Ser.). (ENG.). 32p. (J). (gr. -1-3). 8.99 (978-0-544-00323-1(3)) Houghton Mifflin Harcourt Publishing Co.

MacDonald, George. The Elect Lady. 2008. 148p. 24.95 (978-1-60664-792-9(X)) Aegypan.

Mass, Wendy. Finally. 2011. (ENG.). 304p. (J). (gr. 3-7). pap. 6.99 (978-0-545-05243-6(2), Scholastic Paperbacks) Scholastic, Inc.

McKinlay, Meg. Below. 2013. (ENG., Illus.). 224p. (J). (gr. 4-7). 15.99 (978-0-7636-6126-7(0)) Candlewick Pr.

McNulty, Faith & Shiffman, Lena. Le Chant des Baleines. (Hello Reader! Ser.). (FRE., Illus.). 40p. (J). pap. 5.99 (978-0-590-16027-8(3)) Scholastic, Inc.

Meddaugh, Susan. Martha Speaks: Good Luck, Martha! (Reader) 2012. (Martha Speaks Ser.). (ENG., Illus.). 24p. (J). (gr. -1-3). 12.99 (978-0-547-57657-2(9)); pap. 3.99 (978-0-547-57658-9(7)) Houghton Mifflin Harcourt Publishing Co.

Mendes, Valerie. The Drowning. 2005. (ENG.). 256p. (J). (gr. 7). per. 8.99 (978-1-4169-0127-3(2)) Simon & Schuster, Ltd. GBR. Dist: Simon & Schuster, Inc.

Mills, Rob. Charlie's Key, 1 vol. 2011. (ENG.). 264p. (J). (gr. 6-12). pap. 9.95 (978-1-55469-872-1(3)) Orca Bk. Pubs. USA.

Newbold, Keva N. The Family's Sorrow. 2009. 44p. pap. 16.99 (978-1-4389-4811-9(5)) AuthorHouse.

Oates, Joyce Carol. After the Wreck, I Picked Myself Up, Spread My Wings, & Flew Away. 2006. (YA). (gr. 9-12). 304p. 16.99 (978-0-06-073525-8(2)); 292p. lib. bdg. 17.89 (978-0-06-073526-5(0)) HarperCollins Pubs. (HarperTeen).

Olson, Cynthia J. Kiera's Cry, 1 vol. 2009. 151p. pap. 24.95 (978-1-60749-280-1(6)) America Star Bks.

Orme, Helen. Horsing Around. 2008. (Siti's Sisters Ser.). (ENG., Illus.). 36p. pap. (978-1-84167-685-2(3)) Ransom Publishing Ltd.

Park, Barbara. Mick Harte Was Here. 88p. (J). (gr. 4-6). pap. 4.99 (978-0-8072-1502-9(3), Listening Library) Random Hse. Audio Publishing Group.

Park, Barbara, ed. Mick Harte Was Here. unabr. ed. 2004. (Middle Grade Cassette Librariestm Ser.). 88p. (J). (gr. 3-7). pap. 29.00 incl. audio (978-0-8072-7797-3(5), S YA 922 SP, Listening Library) Random Hse. Audio Publishing Group.

Pattou, Edith. Ghosting, 0 vols. 2014. (ENG.). 432p. (YA). (gr. 7-12). 16.99 (978-1-4778-4774-9(X), 9781477847749, Skyscape) Amazon Publishing.

Perkins, Lynne Rae. As Easy As Falling off the Face of the Earth. (YA). (gr. 8). 2012. (ENG., Illus.). 384p. pap. 9.99 (978-0-06-187092-7(7)) 2010. (ENG.). 368p. 16.99 (978-0-06-187090-3(0)) 2010. 368p. lib. bdg. 17.89 (978-0-06-187091-0(9)) HarperCollins Pubs. (Greenwillow Bks.).

Perritano, John. Madness of Captain Cyclops, 1 vol. 2014. (Kid Squad Saves the World Ser.). (ENG.). 112p. (J). (gr. 8-12). lib. bdg. 27.07 (978-1-62402-040-7(2), Calico Chapter Bks) Magic Wagon.

Preller, James. Before You Go. 2013. (ENG.). 224p. (YA). (gr. 7-12). pap. 16.99 (978-1-250-03421-2(3), 9781250034212) Square Fish.

Reed, Jaime. Keep Me in Mind. 2016. (ENG.). 336p. (J). (gr. 7). 17.99 (978-0-545-88381-8(4)) Scholastic, Inc.

Ripley's Believe It Or Not! Staff. Running Wild. 2010. (Rbi Ser.: 3). (ENG.). 128p. (J). pap. 4.99 (978-1-893951-55-6(3)) Ripley Entertainment, Inc.

Saddleback Educational Publishing Staff, ed. Crash, 1 vol. unabr. ed. 2011. (Heights Ser.). (ENG.). 49p. (gr. 5-8). pap. 7.95 (978-1-61651-283-5(0)) Saddleback Educational Publishing, Inc.

Scieszka, Jon. Uh-Oh, Max. Shannon, David et al, illus. 2014. (Jon Scieszka's Trucktown Ser.). (ENG.). 24p. (J). (gr. -1-1). 16.99 (978-1-4814-1461-6(5), Simon Spotlight) Simon Spotlight.

S.E.W. The Year at Widows' Creek: The Beginning. 2009. 44p. pap. 17.49 (978-1-4389-5546-9(4)) AuthorHouse.

Shaw, Natalie. Be Careful, Friend! Craig, Karen, illus. 2010. (Yo Gabba Gabba! Ser.). (ENG.). 26p. (J). (gr. -1 — 1). bds. 5.99 (978-1-4169-9534-0(X), Simon Spotlight) Simon Spotlight.

Simone, Kriss. Fairy Forest. 2007. 86p. pap. 7.78 (978-1-84799-156-0(4)) Lulu Pr., Inc.

Slater, Teddy. Emergency, Call 911. Lewis, Anthony, illus. 2010. 16p. (J). (978-0-545-24601-9(6)) Scholastic, Inc.

—Fire Prevention. Lewis, Anthony, illus. 2010. 16p. (J). (978-0-545-24603-3(2)) Scholastic, Inc.

—Home Safe Home. Smith, Jamie, illus. 2010. 16p. (J). (978-0-545-24606-4(7)) Scholastic, Inc.

—Safety in the Bus. Smith, Jamie, illus. 2010. 16p. (J). (978-0-545-24602-6(4)) Scholastic, Inc.

—Stranger Danger. Lewis, Anthony, illus. 2010. 16p. (J). (978-0-545-24605-7(9)) Scholastic, Inc.

—Street Safety. Smith, Jamie, illus. 2010. 16p. (J). (978-0-545-24604-0(0)) Scholastic, Inc.

Smith, Tina. The Secret Love of Lone Wolf & Sarah. 2008. 55p. pap. 13.95 (978-1-4357-4550-6(7)) Lulu Pr., Inc.

Stewart, Barbara. The In-Between. 2013. (ENG.). 256p. (YA). (gr. 9-12). pap. 9.99 (978-1-250-03016-0(1), 9781250030160, St. Martin's Griffin) St. Martin's Pr.

Taekema, Sylvia. Ripple Effect, 1 vol. 2015. (ENG.). 144p. (J). (gr. 4-7). pap. 9.95 (978-1-4598-0872-0(X)) Orca Bk. Pubs. USA.

Tonge, Neil. A Victorian Mine Disaster: A Young Boy's Story. 2017. (Survivors Ser.). (ENG., Illus.). 96p. (J). (gr. 4-6). pap. 9.99 (978-0-7502-9643-4(7), Wayland) Hachette Children's Group GBR. Dist: Hachette Bk. Group.

Tristan, Sarah. Cheat Codes. 2003. 234p. (YA). pap. 15.95 (978-0-595-29670-5(X)) iUniverse, Inc.

Tsurumi, Andrea. Accident! 2017. (ENG., Illus.). 48p. (J). (gr. -1-3). 17.99 **(978-0-544-94480-0(1)**, HMH Books For Young Readers) Houghton Mifflin Harcourt Publishing Co.

Waggener, Anna. Grim. 2012. (ENG.). 320p. (J). (gr. 7-7). 17.99 (978-0-545-38480-3(X), Scholastic Pr.) Scholastic, Inc.

Walsh, Ann. The Ghost of Soda Creek. 2009. (ENG.). 176p. (J). pap. 11.99 (978-1-55002-830-0(8), Sandcastle Bks.) Dundurn CAN. Dist: Ingram Publisher Services.

Walters, Heidi. Hospitals Aren't So Scary. 2010. 24p. pap. 11.49 (978-1-4490-7163-9(5)) AuthorHouse.

Waring, Scott C. West's Time MacHine. 2007. 200p. 24.95 (978-0-595-88775-0(9)); per. 14.95 (978-0-595-41887-9(2)) iUniverse, Inc.

Wasserman, Robin. Torn. 2011. (Cold Awakening Ser.: 3). (ENG.). 384p. (YA). (gr. 9). pap. 9.99 (978-1-4169-3636-7(X), Simon Pulse) Simon Pulse.

Watt, Cliff. Jenny Brown & the Search for Eusebio's Star. 2008. 77p. pap. 19.95 (978-1-60672-169-8(0)) America Star Bks.

Westerfeld, Scott. Horizon. 2017. (Horizon Ser.: 1). (ENG.). 256p. (J). (gr. 4-7). 14.99 (978-0-545-91677-6(1)) Scholastic, Inc.

Westling, Vicki Diane. Hannibal Goes to the Hospital: A Sam & Friends Book. 2011. 32p. pap. 15.99 (978-1-4634-0997-5(4)) AuthorHouse.

Wetterer, Margaret K. The Midnight Adventure of Kate Shelley, Train Rescuer. Trover, Zachary, illus. 2010. (History's Kid Heroes Ser.). (ENG.). 32p. (gr. 3-5). pap. 8.95 (978-0-7613-6192-3(8), Graphic Universe™) Lerner Publishing Group.

Willis, Jeanne. The Cow Tripped over the Moon: a Nursery Rhyme Emergency. Stewart, Joel, illus. 2015. (ENG.). 32p. (J). (gr. -1-2). 15.99 (978-0-7636-7402-1(8)) Candlewick Pr.

Wittman, Kathy A. Raina's Vision Quest, 1 vol. 2010. 78p. pap. 19.95 (978-1-61582-656-8(4)) America Star Bks.

Zephaniah, Benjamin. Face. 2004. (ENG.). 208p. (YA). (gr. 7). reprint ed. pap. 9.99 (978-1-58234-921-3(5), 9781582349213, Bloomsbury USA Childrens) Bloomsbury Publishing USA.

Zhang, Amy. Falling into Place. 2014. (ENG.). 304p. (YA). (gr. 9). 17.99 (978-0-06-229504-0(7), Greenwillow Bks.) HarperCollins Pubs.

ACCIDENTS—PREVENTION

see also Safety Education

Anderson, Judith. Know the Facts about Personal Safety. 2009. (Illus.). 48p. (J). 70.50 (978-1-4358-5465-9(9), 1300674); (ENG., (J). lib. bdg. 29.25 (978-1-4358-5340-9(7), 1300674); (ENG., (YA). pap. 11.75 (978-1-4358-5464-2(0), 1300674) Rosen Publishing Group, Inc., The. (Rosen Reference).

Bair, Carolyn. Fireman Dave Goes to School. 2012. 16p. pap. 13.99 (978-1-4685-4194-6(3)) AuthorHouse.

Bellisario, Gina. Be Aware! My Tips for Personal Safety. Kurilla, Renee, illus. 2014. (Cloverleaf Books — My Healthy Habits Ser.). (ENG.). 24p. (gr. k-2). lib. bdg. 23.93 (978-1-4677-1351-1(1), Millbrook Pr.) Lerner Publishing Group.

Berry, Joy Wilt. A Book about Being Careless. 2005. (Illus.). (J). (978-0-7172-8582-2(0)) Scholastic, Inc.

Desalle, Nicole. Safe at Home. 2011. pap. 39.95 (978-0-7664-3751-7(5)) Abrams & Co. Pubs., Inc.

Don't Stick Sticks up Your Nose! Don't Stuff Stuff in Your Ears! 2013. (Don't Stick Sticks up Your Nose! Don't Stuff Stuff in Your Ears! Ser.). (ENG.). 22p. bds. 5.99 (978-0-9888861-0-0(3), 9780988886100) Dontstickdontstuff.

Gogerly, Liz. Safety. Gordon, Mike, illus. 2008. (Looking after Me Ser.). (ENG.). 32p. (J). (gr. -1-3). pap. (978-0-7787-4120-6(6)); lib. bdg. (978-0-7787-4113-8(3)) Crabtree Publishing Co.

Goldsmith, Mike & Johnson, Jinny. Being Safe. 2009. (Now We Know About... Ser.). (ENG., Illus.). 24p. (J). (gr. k-3). pap. (978-0-7787-4734-5(4)); lib. bdg. (978-0-7787-4717-8(4)) Crabtree Publishing Co.

Goodbody, Slim. Avoiding Injuries. McGinnis, Ben, illus. Pinchbeck, Chris, photos by. 2007. (Slim Goodbody Good Health Guides). 32p. (J). (gr. 2-6). lib. bdg. 26.00 (978-0-8368-7739-7(X), Gareth Stevens Learning Library) Stevens, Gareth Publishing LLLP.

—Keeping Safe. McGinnis, Ben, illus. Pinchbeck, Chris, photos by. 2007. (Slim Goodbody Good Health Guides). 32p. (gr. 2-6). lib. bdg. 26.00 (978-0-8368-7743-4(8), Gareth Stevens Learning Library) Stevens, Gareth Publishing LLLP.

Hardyman, Robyn. Safe & Healthy. 2012. (Healthy & Happy Ser.). (Illus.). 32p. (J). (gr. 1-4). lib. bdg. 26.50 (978-1-4488-5278-9(1)) Rosen Publishing Group, Inc., The.

Harrison, Jean. Safety. 2004. (Children's Rights Ser.). (J). lib. bdg. 27.10 (978-1-58340-422-5(8)) Black Rabbit Bks.

Head, Honor. Being Safe Out & About. 2017. (Keep Yourself Safe Ser.). (ENG., Illus.). 24p. (J). (gr. k-2). 16.99 (978-1-4451-4430-6(1), Franklin Watts) Hachette Children's Group GBR. Dist: Hachette Bk. Group.

Holden, Pam. Keeping Safe. 2015. (ENG., Illus.). 16p. (-2). pap. (978-1-77654-139-3(1), Red Rocket Readers) Flying Start Bks.

Hord, Colleen. My Safe Community. 2011. (ENG., Illus.). 24p. (gr. k-2). pap. 8.95 (978-1-61741-997-3(4)) Rourke Educational Media.

Hunt, Jilly. Safety. 2010. (Being Healthy, Feeling Great Ser.). (ENG.). 32p. (J). pap. 10.60 (978-1-61532-383-8(X), PowerKids Pr.); (YA). (gr. 3-6). lib. bdg. 26.50 (978-1-61532-382-1(1)) Rosen Publishing Group, Inc., The.

Kallio, Jamie. 12 Tips for Staying Safe. 2017. (Illus.). 32p. (J). (978-1-62143-509-9(1)) Pr. Room Editions LLC.

Kallio, Jamie & Ringstad, Arnold. 12 Tips for Staying Safe. 2016. (Healthy Living Ser.). (ENG., Illus.). 32p. (J). pap. 9.95 (978-1-63235-385-6(7)) Pr. Room Editions LLC.

Knowlton, MaryLee. Safety at Home. Andersen, Gregg, photos by. 2008. (Staying Safe Ser.). (ENG., Illus.). 32p. (J). (gr. -1-3). lib. bdg. (978-0-7787-4316-3(0)) Crabtree Publishing Co.

Lindeen, Mary & Kesselring, Susan. Being Safe at Home. McGeehan, Dan & Moore, David, Jr., illus. 2011. (Be Safe Ser.). (ENG.). 24p. (J). (gr. k-3). lib. bdg. 27.07 (978-1-60954-299-3(1), 200079) Child's World, Inc., The.

—Being Safe in Your Neighborhood. McGeehan, Dan & Moore, David, illus. 2011. (Be Safe Ser.). (ENG.). 24p. (J). (gr. k-3). lib. bdg. 27.07 (978-1-60954-370-9(X), 200081) Child's World, Inc., The.

Llewellyn, Claire. Watch Out! at Home. Gordon, Mike, illus. 2006. (Watch Out! Bks.). (ENG.). 32p. (J). (gr. -1-2). pap. 7.99 (978-0-7641-3323-7(3)) Barron's Educational Series, Inc.

—Watch Out! on the Road. Gordon, Mike, illus. 2006. (Watch Out! Bks.). (ENG.). 32p. (J). (gr. -1-2). pap. 7.99 (978-0-7641-3324-4(1)) Barron's Educational Series, Inc.

Mattern, Joanne. Staying Safe at Home. 2007. (Safety First Ser.). (Illus.). 24p. (gr. k-3). pap. 8.15 (978-0-8368-7798-4(5)); (ENG & SPA., pap. 8.15 (978-0-8368-8063-2(3)); lib. bdg. 22.00 (978-0-8368-7791-5(8)) Stevens, Gareth Publishing LLLP. (Weekly Reader Leveled Readers).

—Staying Safe at Home (la Seguridad en Casa) 2007. (Safety First / la Seguridad Es lo Primero Ser.). (ENG & SPA., Illus.). 24p. (gr. k-3). lib. bdg. 22.00 (978-0-8368-8056-4(0), Weekly Reader Leveled Readers) Stevens, Gareth Publishing LLLP.

—Staying Safe on the Street. 2007. (Safety First Ser.). (Illus.). 24p. (gr. k-3). pap. 8.15 (978-0-8368-7803-5(5)); lib. bdg. 22.00 (978-0-8368-7796-0(9)) Stevens, Gareth Publishing LLLP. (Weekly Reader Leveled Readers).

—Staying Safe on the Street (la Seguridad en la Calle) 2007. (Safety First / la Seguridad Es lo Primero Ser.). (SPA & ENG., Illus.). 24p. (gr. k-3). lib. bdg. 22.00 (978-0-8368-8061-8(7), Weekly Reader Leveled Readers) Stevens, Gareth Publishing LLLP.

McKay, Sindy. We Both Read-Being Safe Big Book: Being Safe Big Book Edition. 2005. 44p. (J). (gr. 1-2). 29.95 (978-1-891327-92-6(5)) Treasure Bay, Inc.

Meiners, Cheri J. Be Careful & Stay Safe. Johnson, Meredith, illus. 2006. (Learning to Get Along(r) Ser.). (ENG.). 40p. (J). (gr. -1-3). pap. 10.95 (978-1-57542-211-4(5)) Free Spirit Publishing, Inc.

Nelson, Robin. Playing Safely. 2006. (Pull Ahead Books: Health Ser.). (ENG., Illus.). 32p. (gr. k-3). pap. 7.95 (978-0-8225-2770-1(7)) Lerner Publishing Group.

O'Brien, Cynthia. Innovations in Safety. 2016. (Problem Solved! Your Turn to Think Big Ser.). (ENG., Illus.). 32p. (J). (gr. 3-6). (978-0-7787-2679-1(7)) Crabtree Publishing Co.

Olson, Karen W. Living Safe, Playing Safe. Hamelin, Marie-Micheline, illus. 2005. (Caring for Me Ser.). (ENG.). 20p. (J). pap. 10.95 (978-1-894778-33-6(2)) Theytus Bks., Ltd. CAN. Dist: Univ. of Toronto Pr.

—Living Safe, Playing Safe. George, Leonard, Jr., illus. 2009. (Caring for Me Ser.). (ENG.). 20p. pap. 9.95 (978-1-894778-51-0(0)) Theytus Bks., Ltd. CAN. Dist: Univ. of Toronto Pr.

Oregon Center for Applied Science, creator. Walk Smart: Children's Pedestrian Safety Program. 2005. (J). cd-rom 19.95 (978-1-933898-10-0(0)) Oregon Ctr. for Applied Science, Inc.

Raatma, Lucia. Staying Safe Around Fire. 2011. (Staying Safe Ser.). (ENG.). 24p. (gr. 1-2). pap. 41.70 (978-1-4296-7194-1(7)); lib. bdg. 25.32 (978-1-4296-6820-0(2)) Capstone Press of Coughlan Cos. (First Facts).

Rau, Dana Meachen. Safety at Home: Seguridad en la Casa. 2009. (Bookworms — Bilingual Editions: Safe Kids/Ninos Seguros Ser.). (SPA & ENG.). 32p. (gr. k-2). lib. bdg. 15.95 (978-0-7614-4780-1(6)) Marshall Cavendish Corp.

Rau, Dana Meachen & Meachen Rau, Dana. Safety at Home: Seguridad en la Casa. 2009. (Bookworms: Safe Kids Ser.). (SPA & ENG.). 32p. (gr. k-2). 15.95 (978-0-7614-4089-5(5)) Marshall Cavendish Corp.

Rissman, Rebecca. Should Henry Wear a Helmet? Staying Safe, 1 vol. 2013. (What Would You Do? Ser.). (ENG., Illus.). 24p. (gr. -1-1). pap. 6.29 (978-1-4329-7247-9(2)); lib. bdg. 22.65 (978-1-4329-7241-7(3)) Heinemann-Raintree. (Acorn).

SafeKids 101. . . Preparing Kids to Stay Safe at Home & in the Community! 2003. (J). stu. ed. (978-0-9729706-5-5(7)); (978-0-9729706-4-8(9)) Production 101, Inc.

Safety Always Matters (SAM), Vol. II. 12p. (J). (gr. k-3). 29.50 (978-1-883994-06-8(3)) Safety Always Matters, Inc.

Safety Makes Sense. (J). 29.50 (978-1-883994-11-2(X)); 29.50 (978-1-883994-10-5(1)) Safety Always Matters, Inc.

Salzmann, Mary Elizabeth. Wear a Helmet! Healthy Safety Habits, 1 vol. 2014. (Healthy Habits Ser.). (ENG.). 24p. (J). (gr. -1-3). 24.21 (978-1-62403-533-3(7)) ABDO Publishing Co.

Sanschagrin, Joceline. Caillou, Be Careful! Brignaud, Pierre, illus. 2nd ed. 2013. (Step by Step Ser.). (ENG.). 24p. (J). (gr. -1-k). bds. (978-2-89718-039-3(0)) Filmer Ltd.

Schulz, Kathy. Always Be Safe. 2011. (Rookie Ready to Learn — Out & about: in My Community Ser.). (Illus.). 40p. (J). (gr. -1-k). lib. bdg. 25.00 (978-0-531-27175-9(7), Children's Pr.) Scholastic Library Publishing.

Stranaghan, Crystal J. & Bzymek, Izabela. Safety Superheroes: Preventing Grandparents from Falling. 2010. (978-0-9867103-0-8(X)) Feldman, Fabio.

Weber, Rebecca. Safety Basics. 2012. (Health & Your Body Ser.). (ENG.). 24p. (gr. k-1). pap. 41.70 (978-1-4296-8346-3(5)); lib. bdg. 26.65 (978-1-4296-7694-6(9)) Capstone Press of Coughlan Cos. (Pebble Plus).

ACCLIMATIZATION

see Adaptation (Biology); Human Beings—Effect of Environment on; Plant Introduction

ACCOUNTING

Accounting, 11 vols., Set. 2004. (Illus.). (YA). (gr. 9-12). tchr. ed., stu. ed. 47.95 (978-0-7403-0196-4(9), ES9315, Lifepac) Alpha Omega Pubns., Inc.

Barnard, Marietjie & Gous, M. M. Introduction to Accounting for the Senior Phase Learner's Book (Afrikaans Translation). 2007. 220p. pap. (978-0-521-71064-0(2)) Cambridge Univ. Pr.

Barnard, Marietjie & Gous, M.M. Introduction to Accounting for the Senior Phase Learner's Book. 2007. pap. (978-0-521-71062-6(6)) Cambridge Univ. Pr.
Hinnant, Jamal & Beattie, Amy. Getting a Job in Accounting. 2016. (Job Basics: Getting the Job You Need Ser.). (ENG.). 80p. (J). (gr. 8-8). lib. bdg. 35.75 (978-1-4777-8560-7(4)) Rosen Publishing Group, Inc., The.
Houghton, Gillian. Balancing a Checkbook. 2009. (Invest Kids Ser.). 24p. (J). (gr. 2-5). (ENG., Illus.). pap. 8.25 (978-1-4358-3207-7(8)); lib. bdg. 22.60 (978-1-4358-2772-1(4)) Rosen Publishing Group, Inc., The. (PowerKids Pr.).
Joyce, Tim. VCE Accounting Units 3 & 4. 2015. (Cambridge Checkpoints Ser.). (ENG.). pap. 23.50 (978-1-316-50162-7(0)) Cambridge Univ. Pr.
La Bella, Laura. What Degree Do I Need to Pursue a Career in Bookkeeping & Accounting?, 1 vol. 2015. (ENG.). 80p. (YA). 34.60 (978-1-4777-7861-6(6), Rosen Young Adult) Rosen Publishing Group, Inc., The.
Meyer, Susan. Careers As a Bookkeeper & Auditor. 2013. (Essential Careers Ser.). 80p. (YA). (gr. 7-12). 33.25 (978-1-4777-1792-9(7)) Rosen Publishing Group, Inc., The.
Peterman, Lori. Practical Accounting Fundamentals. 2004. spiral bd. (978-0-9722058-7-0(X)) Insight Technical Education.
Romney, Marshall B. & Schiff, Andrew D. Casebook in Accounting Information Systems. 4th ed. 2003. (ENG.). 90p. (C). pap. 32.95 (978-0-7593-2017-8(9)) Cengage South-Western.

ACCOUNTING MACHINES

see Calculators

ACID RAIN

Acid Rain: Level M, 6 vols. (Wonder Worldtm Ser.). 16p. 34.95 (978-0-7802-2887-0(1)) Wright Group/McGraw-Hill.
Jakubiak, David J. What Can We Do about Acid Rain? 2012. (Illus.). 24p. (J). 49.50 (978-1-4488-5117-1(3), PowerKids Pr.); pap. 8.25 (978-1-4488-5116-4(5), PowerKids Pr.); (gr. 2-5). lib. bdg. 22.60 (978-1-4488-4984-0(5)) Rosen Publishing Group, Inc., The.

ACOUSTICS

see Hearing; Music—Acoustics and Physics; Sound

ACQUIRED IMMUNE DEFICIENCY SYNDROME

see AIDS (Disease)

ACTING

see also Actors and Actresses; Theater

Allen, Laurie. Acting Duets for Young Women: Eight- to ten-minute duo scenes for practice & Competition, 1 vol. 2010. (ENG.). 216p. (J). pap. 17.95 (978-1-56608-172-6(6)) Meriwether Publishing, Ltd.
Bauman, Elizabeth. Private Stories: Monologues for Young Actors Ages 8 to 16 & the Seven Key Questions to Unlock Your Imagination. 2007. (ENG.). 152p. per. 10.95 (978-0-87910-341-5(8), 0879103418, Limelight Editions) Leonard, Hal Corp.
Bolton, Martha. Humorous Monologues. Behr, Joyce, illus. 2003. 128p. (J). (gr. 2-7). 19.00 (978-0-8069-6750-9(1)) Sterling Publishing Co., Inc.
Dabrowski, Kristen. My Second Monologue Book: Famous & Historical People: 100 Monologues for Young Children. 2008. (My First Acting Ser.). (Illus.). 112p. (J). (gr. 1-8). pap. 11.95 (978-1-57525-601-6(0)) Smith & Kraus Pubs., Inc.
—My Third Monologue Book: 100 Monologues about Places near & Far. 2008. 112p. (J). (gr. 1-8). pap. 11.95 (978-1-57525-602-3(9)) Smith & Kraus Pubs., Inc.
—Teens Speak, Girls Ages 13 to 15: Sixty Original Character Monologues. 2005. (Kids Speak Ser.). 80p. pap. 11.95 (978-1-57525-412-8(3)) Smith & Kraus Pubs., Inc.
—The Ultimate Audition Book for Middle School Actors Volume IV: 111 One-Minute Monologues: the Rich, the Famous, the Historical, Vol. 4. 2008. (Young Actors Ser.: Vol. IV). 160p. (J). pap. 11.95 (978-1-57525-579-8(0)) Smith & Kraus Pubs., Inc.
—Volume IV for Kids: 10+ Format Comedy. 2005. (Young Actor Ser.). 240p. 16.95 (978-1-57525-441-8(7)) Smith & Kraus Pubs., Inc.
—Volume V for Kids: 10+ Format Drama. 2005. (Young Actor Ser.: Vol. II). 16.95 (978-1-57525-438-8(7)) Smith & Kraus Pubs., Inc.
—Volume V for Middle School: 10+ Format Comedy. 2005. (Young Actor Ser.: Vol. 3). 16.95 (978-1-57525-442-5(5)) Smith & Kraus Pubs., Inc.
—Volume VII for Middle School: 10+ Format Drama. 2005. (Young Actor Ser.: Vol. IV). 240p. 16.95 (978-1-57525-439-5(5)) Smith & Kraus Pubs., Inc.
—111 One-Minute Monologues: The Ultimate Monologue Book for Middle School Actors, Vol. 3. 2004. (Ultimate Monologue Book for Middle School Actors Ser.: Vol. 1). 136p. (J). pap. 11.95 (978-1-57525-419-7(0)) Smith & Kraus Pubs., Inc.
DonRauf & Vescia, Monique. Virtual Apprentice: Actor. 2009. (Virtual Apprentice Ser.). 64p. (gr. 4-9). pap. 9.95 (978-0-8160-7891-2(2), Checkmark Bks.) Facts On File, Inc.
Evans, Cheryl & Smith, Lucy. Acting & Theatre. Evans, Cheryl, ed. Jude, Conny, illus. Putsman, Helen, photos by. 2008. (Acting & Theatre Ser.). 64p. (J). pap. 8.99 (978-0-7945-2216-2(5), Usborne) EDC Publishing.
Fife, Stephen, et al, eds. One on One: Playing with a Purpose - Monologues for Kids 7-14. 2013. (ENG.). 248p. pap. 16.99 (978-1-55783-841-4(0), 1557838410, Applause Theatre & Cinema) Leonard, Hal Corp.
Fretland VanVoorst, Jenny. Acting. 2016. (Artist's Studio Ser.). 24p. (J). (gr. k-2). lib. bdg. 25.65 (978-1-62031-280-3(8), Bullfrog Bks.) Jump! Inc.
Frick, Sheila M. & Kawar, Mary. Core Concepts in Action. 2004. (Illus.). spiral bd. 34.00 (978-0-9717653-0-6(8)) Vital Links.
Gaddis, Alisha. Kids' Comedic Monologues That Are Actually Funny. 2016. (ENG.). 208p. pap. 14.99 (978-1-4950-1176-4(3), 1495011763, Applause Theatre & Cinema) Leonard, Hal Corp.
—Teen Boys Comedic Monologues That Are Actually Funny. 2015. (ENG.). 216p. pap. 14.99 (978-1-4803-9679-1(6), 1480396796, Applause Theatre & Cinema) Leonard, Hal Corp.
—Teen Girls' Comedic Monologues That Are Actually Funny. 2015. (ENG.). 208p. pap. 14.99 (978-1-4803-9680-7(X), 148039680X) Leonard, Hal Corp.
Gottfried Hollander, Barbara. Participating in Plays, Skits, & Debates with Cool New Digital Tools. 2013. (Way Beyond PowerPoint: Making 21st Century Presentations Ser.). 48p. (J). (gr. 5-8). 29.95 (978-1-4777-1838-4(9)); pap. 11.75 (978-1-4777-1849-0(4)) Rosen Publishing Group, Inc., The. (Rosen Reference).
Harbison, Lawrence. The Best Scenes for Kids Ages 7-15. 2015. (ENG.). 304p. pap. 16.99 (978-1-4950-1179-5(8), 1495011798, Applause Theatre & Cinema) Leonard, Hal Corp.
Horn, Geoffrey M. Movie Acting. 2006. (Making Movies Ser.). (Illus.). 32p. (gr. 5-8). lib. bdg. 26.00 (978-0-8368-6836-4(6)) Stevens, Gareth Publishing LLLP.
Kenney, Karen Latchana. Cool Scripts & Acting: How to Stage Your Very Own Show, 1 vol. 2010. (Cool Performances Ser.). (ENG., Illus.). 32p. (gr. 3-6). 28.50 (978-1-60453-717-8(5), Checkerboard Library) ABDO Publishing Co.
Lamedman, Debbie. The Ultimate Audition Book for Teens Vol. II: 111 Monologues from Classical Theater, 2 Minutes & Under. 2006. 11.95 (978-1-57525-458-6(1)) Smith & Kraus Pubs., Inc.
—The Ultimate Audition Book for Teens Vol. III: 111 Monologues from Classical Literature, 2 Minutes & Under, VIII. 2006. (ENG.). (J). 11.95 (978-1-57525-459-3(X)) Smith & Kraus Pubs., Inc.
—The Ultimate Audition Book for Teens IV: 111 One Minute Monologues. 2003. (Ultimate Audition Book for Teens Ser.: Vol. 4). viii, 117p. (J). 11.95 (978-1-57525-353-4(4)) Smith & Kraus Pubs., Inc.
Laurie, Rona. Auditioning: A Practical Guide for the Would-Be Actor & Drama Student. 2nd ed. 2003. (Illus.). 64p. (YA). (gr. 8-12). pap. 10.00 (978-0-85343-585-3(5)) Miller, J. Garnet Ltd. GBR. Dist: Empire Publishing Service.
Leavitt, Amie Jane. For People Who Love to Entertain. 2016. (Cool Careers Without College Ser.). 00104p. (J). (gr. 7-7). 38.45 (978-1-5081-7274-1(9)) Rosen Publishing Group, Inc., The.
Marcus, Cindy. The Ultimate Young Actor's Guide: Getting the Role & Making It Shine. 2011. (ENG., Illus.). 168p. (J). pap. 19.95 (978-1-56608-179-5(3)) Meriwether Publishing, Ltd.
Martin, Rod. Drama Games & Acting Exercises: 177 Games & Activities. 2009. (ENG.). 120p. (J). pap. 17.95 (978-1-56608-166-5(1)) Meriwether Publishing, Ltd.
McCormick, Kimberly A. Hey, Girlfriend: Seventy-five monologues for Girls, 1 vol. 2009. (ENG.). 160p. (YA). (gr. 9-18). pap. 15.95 (978-1-56608-162-7(9)) Meriwether Publishing, Ltd.
Mercanti, J. V. In Performance: Contemporary Monologues for Teens. 2015. (ENG.). 200p. pap. 16.99 (978-1-4803-9661-6(3), 1480396613, Applause Theatre & Cinema) Leonard, Hal Corp.
Milstein, Janet. Winners Competition Series: Award-Winning, Custom-Made, 90-Second Comic Monologues Ages 13-18, Vol. 3. 2008. 96p. (YA). pap. 14.95 (978-1-57525-614-6(2)) Smith & Kraus Pubs., Inc.
—Winners Competition Series Volume I: Award-winning, Custom-made, 60-Second Comic Monologues Ages 4-12. 2008. 96p. (J). pap. (978-1-57525-612-2(6)) Smith & Kraus Pubs., Inc.
Milstein, Karen Kaufman. Hot Spots for Teens: Cold Readings for Commercial Audition Success. 2006. 112p. 11.95 (978-1-57525-461-6(1)) Smith & Kraus Pubs., Inc.
Muir, Kerry. Childsplay: A Collection of Scenes & Monologues for Children, 1 vol. Johnson, Kris, photos by. 2004. (ENG., Illus.). 260p. (Orig.). (gr. -1-18). pap. 16.99 (978-0-87910-188-6(1), 0879101881, Limelight Editions) Leonard, Hal Corp.
Participating in Plays, Skits, & Debates with Cool New Digital Tools. 2013. (Way Beyond PowerPoint: Making 21st Century Presentations Ser.). 48p. (J). (gr. 5-8). pap. 70.50 (978-1-4777-1850-6(8), Rosen Reference) Rosen Publishing Group, Inc., The.
Polsky, Milton & Gilead, Jack. The Improv Workshop Handbook: Creative Movement & Verbal Interaction for Students K-8: The Object Is Teamwork. Cordero, Chris, ed. Rockwell, Richard, illus. l.t. ed. 2003. 112p. (J). (gr. k-8). pap. 15.00 (978-0-88734-691-0(X)) Players Pr., Inc.
Quinn, Stephanie. Beginning Improv Workshop for Kids. 2008. per. (978-0-9773099-4-8(0)) Quinn Entertainment.
Silverberg, Larry. The 7 Simple Truths of Acting for the Teen Actor. 2007. (Young Actors Ser.). 77p. (YA). (gr. 8-12). pap. 16.95 (978-1-57525-462-3(X)) Smith & Kraus Pubs., Inc.
Somervill, Barbara. Actor. 2011. (21st Century Skills Library: Cool Arts Careers Ser.). (ENG.). 32p. (gr. 4-8). lib. bdg. 28.50 (978-1-61080-129-4(6), 201136) Cherry Lake Publishing.
Stephens, Heather. Cabbage & Other Scenes. 2003. 48p. (Orig.). (J). (gr. 3-9). pap. 12.00 (978-0-88734-656-9(1)) Players Pr., Inc.
Stevens, Chambers. Magnificent Monologues for Kids 2: More Kids' Monologues for Every Occasion! 2008. (Hollywood 101 Ser.). 79p. (J). (gr. k-7). pap. 14.95 (978-1-883995-14-0(0)) Sandcastle Publishing.
—Sensational Scenes for Kids: The Scene Study-Guide for Young Actors! 2003. (Hollywood 101 Ser.: 5). (Illus.). 105p. (J). (gr. 3-7). per. 14.95 (978-1-883995-12-6(4)) Sandcastle Publishing.
—The Ultimate Commercial Book for Kids & Teens: The Young Actors' Commercial Study-guide! Stevens, Chambers, ed. 2005. (Hollywood 101 Ser.: 6). (Illus.). 112p. (J). per. 14.95 (978-1-883995-13-3(2)) Sandcastle Publishing.
Surface, Mary Hall. More Short Scenes & Monologues for Middle School Students: Inspired by Literature, Social Studies, & Real Life. 2007. (Young Actors Ser.). 207p. (J). (gr. 3-7). pap. 11.95 (978-1-57525-560-6(X)) Smith & Kraus Pubs., Inc.
Turnbull, Stephanie. Acting Skills. 2012. (Super Skills Ser.). (Illus.). 32p. (gr. 3-6). lib. bdg. 31.35 (978-1-59920-797-1(4)) Black Rabbit Bks.
—An Actor. 2016. (How to Be... Ser.). 24p. (gr. 2-6). 28.50 (978-1-62588-364-3(1), Smart Apple Media) Black Rabbit Bks.
VanVoorst, Jenny Fretland. La Actuación. 2016. (El Estudio del Artista (Artist's Studio)).Tr. of Acting. 24p. (J). (gr. k-2). lib. bdg. 25.65 (978-1-62031-320-6(0), Bullfrog Bks.) Jump! Inc.
Williamson, Walter. Theater for Young Actors: The Definitive Teen Guide. 2008. (Illus.). 128p. pap. 16.00 (978-0-9814843-9-6(5)) Simon & Brown.
Wyndham, Lee, ed. Acting, Acting, Acting: Stories of Stardust & Grease Paint, of Amateur Striving & Professional Polish. 2011. 222p. 44.95 (978-1-258-06391-7(3)) Literary Licensing, LLC.
Young, Rebecca. 102 Great Monologues: A versatile collection of monologues & duologues for student Actors, 1 vol. 2010. (ENG.). 154p. (J). pap. 16.95 (978-1-56608-171-9(8)) Meriwether Publishing, Ltd.
Zimmerman, Suzi. Introduction to Theatre Arts: An Action Handbook for Middle Grade & High School Students & Teachers. 2007. (ENG., Illus.). 255p. stu. ed., per. 24.95 (978-1-56608-148-1(3)) Meriwether Publishing, Ltd.

ACTING—FICTION

Ain, Beth. Starring Jules (As Herself) 2014. (Starring Jules Ser.: 1). (ENG., Illus.). 160p. (J). (gr. 2-5). pap. 5.99 (978-0-545-44353-1(9), Scholastic Paperbacks) Scholastic, Inc.
—Starring Jules (As Herself) 2014. (Starring Jules Ser.: 1). lib. bdg. 16.00 (978-0-606-35365-6(8)) Turtleback Bks.
—Starring Jules (in Drama-Rama) Higgins, Anne Keenan, illus. 2013. (Starring Jules Ser.: 2). (ENG.). 176p. (J). (gr. 2-5). 14.99 (978-0-545-44354-8(7), Scholastic Pr.) Scholastic, Inc.
Archer, Nick & McDonald, Megan. Rule of Three. 2010. (Sisters Club Ser.: 2). (ENG., Illus.). 240p. (J). (gr. 3-7). pap. 5.99 (978-0-7636-4830-5(2)) Candlewick Pr.
—Rule of Three. Consolazio, Pamela A., illus. 2009. (Sisters Club Ser.: 2). (ENG.). 240p. (J). (gr. 3-7). 15.99 (978-0-7636-4153-5(7)) Candlewick Pr.
Bound, Samantha-Ellen. Broadway Baby. 2016. (Silver Shoes Ser.: 5). (ENG., Illus.). 144p. (J). (gr. 4-7). pap. 8.99 (978-0-85798-903-1(0)) Random Hse. Australia AUS. Dist: Independent Pubs. Group.
Bryant, Ann. School Friends - Drama at Silver Spires. 2013. pap. 5.99 (978-0-7945-3147-8(4), Usborne) EDC Publishing.
Calin, Marisa. Between You & Me. 2012. (ENG.). 256p. (YA). (gr. 7-12). 16.99 (978-1-59990-758-1(5), 9781599907581, Bloomsbury USA Childrens) Bloomsbury Publishing USA.
Caple, Kathy. Starring Hillary. Caple, Kathy, illus. 2003. (Picture Bks.). (Illus.). 28p. (J). (gr. -1-3). 15.95 (978-1-57505-261-8(X), Carolrhoda Bks.) Lerner Publishing Group.
Cherry, Alison. Look Both Ways. 2016. (ENG.). 304p. (YA). (gr. 7). 17.99 (978-0-553-51186-4(6), Delacorte Pr.) Random Hse. Children's Bks.
Costain, Meredith. Stella & the Movie Star. McGowan, Shane, illus. 2015. (Legends in Their Own Lunchbox Ser.). (ENG.). 56p. (gr. 2-3). pap. 7.99 (978-1-4966-0261-9(7), Legends in Their Own Lunchbox) Capstone Classroom.
Cottringer, Anne. Mary Is Scary. Gale, Cathy, illus. 2005. (ENG.). 32p. (J). (gr. -1-3). 19.99 (978-0-7475-6464-5(7)) Bloomsbury Publishing Plc GBR. Dist: Independent Pubs. Group.
Culbertson, Kim. Catch a Falling Star. 2014. (ENG.). 304p. (J). (gr. 7). 17.99 (978-0-545-62704-7(4), Scholastic Pr.) Scholastic, Inc.
Davidson, Jody. Broadway Beginner. 2006. 172p. pap. 10.95 (978-1-59800-494-6(8)) Outskirts Pr., Inc.
Deaver, Julie Reece & Deaver, Julie. Say Goodnight, Gracie. 20th anniv. ed. 2009. (Charlotte Zolotow Bk.). (ENG.). 224p. (YA). (gr. 8-18). pap. 8.99 (978-0-06-447007-0(5), HarperTeen) HarperCollins Pubs.
Dussling, Jennifer A. The Longest Yawn. Sims, Blanche, illus. 2005. (Science Solves It! Ser.). 32p. (J). (gr. -1-3). pap. 5.95 (978-1-57565-160-6(2)) Kane Press, Inc.
Flint, Ann. Charlotte's Curtain Call. 2011. 190p. pap. (978-1-908105-51-6(8)) Grosvenor Hse. Publishing Ltd.
Green, D. L. Zeke Meeks vs the Crummy Class Play, 1 vol. Alves, Josh, illus. 2014. (Zeke Meeks Ser.). (ENG.). 128p. (gr. 2-2). 22.65 (978-1-4795-4827-9(8), Zeke Meeks) Picture Window Bks.
Hamilton, Rachel. Louie Lets Loose! (Unicorn in New York #1) 2017. (Unicorn in New York Ser.: 1). (ENG.). 128p. (J). (gr. 2-5). pap. 4.99 **(978-1-338-05508-5(9)**, Scholastic Paperbacks) Scholastic, Inc.
Hamilton, Sable. Free Spirit. 2015. (Stardust Stables Ser.). (ENG.). 160p. (gr. 3-6). lib. bdg. 22.65 (978-1-4342-9792-1(6)) Stone Arch Bks.
Hill, Grace Brooks. The Corner House Girls in a Play. 2011. (Illus.). 154p. pap. 9.99 (978-1-61203-171-2(4)) Bottom of the Hill Publishing.
Holmes, Sara. Operation Yes. 2009. 234p. (J). pap. (978-0-545-20418-7(6)) Scholastic, Inc.
Holmes, Sara Lewis. Operation Yes. 2009. (ENG.). 256p. (J). (gr. 4-7). 16.99 (978-0-545-10795-2(4), Levine, Arthur A. Bks.) Scholastic, Inc.
Kain, P. G. Famous for Thirty Seconds. 2012. (Commercial Breaks Ser.: 1). (ENG.). 320p. (J). (gr. 4-8). pap. 6.99 (978-1-4169-9786-3(5), Aladdin) Simon & Schuster Children's Publishing.
Katschke, Judy, et al. Bye-Bye Boyfriend, 3 vols. 2003. (ENG., Illus.). 112p. (978-0-00-714467-9(9), HarperCollins Children's Bks.) HarperCollins Pubs. Ltd.
McCowan, Patricia. Upstaged, 1 vol. 2016. (Orca Limelights Ser.). (ENG.). 160p. (J). (gr. 6-9). pap. 9.95 (978-1-4598-1004-4(X)) Orca Bk. Pubs. USA.
McDonald, Megan. Cloudy with a Chance of Boys. (Sisters Club Ser.: 3). (ENG., Illus.). 272p. (J). (gr. 3-7). 2012. pap. 5.99 (978-0-7636-5577-8(5)) 2011. 15.99 (978-0-7636-4615-8(6)) Candlewick Pr.
—The Sisters Club. 2008. (Sisters Club Ser.: 1). (ENG., Illus.). 208p. (J). (gr. 3-7). pap. 5.99 (978-0-7636-3251-9(1)) Candlewick Pr.
—The Sisters Club. 2008. (Sisters Club Ser.: 1). lib. bdg. 16.00 (978-1-4178-1785-6(2), Turtleback) Turtleback Bks.
Murphy, Barbara Beasley & Wolkoff, Judie. Ace Hits Rock Bottom. 2003. (Can't Stop Ace Ser.: No. 2). 204p. (J). pap. 16.95 (978-0-86534-408-2(6)) Sunstone Pr.
Raghbeer, Anjali. A Poster Boy: Indian Cinema Poster Art. 2012. (Art Tales from India Ser.). (ENG., Illus.). 24p. 14.95 (978-81-8328-193-5(1)) Wisdom Tree IND. Dist: SCB Distributors.
Romanek, Trudee. Raising the Stakes, 1 vol. 2015. (Orca Limelights Ser.). (ENG.). 160p. (J). (gr. 6-9). pap. 9.95 (978-1-4598-0779-2(0)) Orca Bk. Pubs. USA.
Scholastic, Inc. Staff & Rusu, Meredith. Lights, Camera, Shopkins! 2016. (Shopkins Ser.: 2). (ENG.). 24p. (J). (gr. -1-3). pap. 4.99 (978-0-545-94041-2(9)) Scholastic, Inc.
Schraff, Anne. Outrunning the Darkness, 1 vol. unabr. ed. 2010. (Urban Underground Ser.). (ENG.). 191p. (YA). (gr. 9-12). pap. 9.95 (978-1-61651-000-8(5)) Saddleback Educational Publishing, Inc.
Sheinmel, Courtney. Superstar. Bell, Jennifer A., illus. 2015. (Stella Batts Ser.). (ENG.). 184p. (J). (gr. 1-3). pap. 5.99 (978-1-58536-856-3(3), 203956) Sleeping Bear Pr.
Shevah, Emma. Dara Palmer's Major Drama. 2016. (ENG.). 288p. (J). (gr. 3-7). 16.99 (978-1-4926-3138-5(3), 9781492631385, Sourcebooks Jabberwocky) Sourcebooks, Inc.
Snyder, Zilpha Keatley. William S. & the Great Escape. (ENG.). (J). (gr. 3-7). 2010. 240p. pap. 7.99 (978-1-4169-6764-4(8)) 2009. 224p. 16.99 (978-1-4169-6763-7(X)) Simon & Schuster Children's Publishing. (Atheneum Bks. for Young Readers).
—William's Midsummer Dreams. (ENG., (J). (gr. 3-7). 2012. Illus.). 240p. pap. 6.99 (978-1-4424-1998-8(9)) 2011. 224p. 16.99 (978-1-4424-1997-1(0)) Simon & Schuster Children's Publishing. (Atheneum Bks. for Young Readers).

ACTING—VOCATIONAL GUIDANCE

Albert, Lisa Rondinelli. So You Want to Be a Film or TV Actor? 2008. (Careers in Film & Television Ser.). (Illus.). 128p. (J). (gr. 3-7). lib. bdg. 33.27 (978-0-7660-2741-1(4)) Enslow Pubs., Inc.
Capaccio, George. Acting in Theater. 2016. (Exploring Theater Ser.). 96p. (J). lib. bdg. 42.79 (978-1-5026-2269-3(6)) Cavendish Square Publishing.
Hodges, Henry & Engel, Margaret. How to Act Like a Kid: Backstage Secrets of a Young Performer. 2013. (ENG., Illus.). 256p. (YA). (gr. 7-17). pap. 16.99 (978-1-4231-6320-6(6), Disney Editions) Disney Pr.
Howey, Bill. The Actor's Menu: A Character Preparation Handbook. 2005. (ENG.). 204p. per. 14.95 (978-0-9753102-2-9(4)) Compass Publishing.
Lamedman, Debbie. A Teen Drama Student's Guide to Laying the Foundation for A. 2006. (ENG.). 192p. 16.95 (978-1-57525-463-0(8)) Smith & Kraus Pubs., Inc.
Mahaney, Ian F. Movie Star, 1 vol. 2015. (ENG., Illus.). 24p. (J). pap. 8.25 (978-1-4994-0116-5(7), PowerKids Pr.) Rosen Publishing Group, Inc., The.
Rauf, Don & Vescia, Monique. Actor. 2009. (Virtual Apprentice Ser.). (Illus.). 64p. (gr. 4-9). 29.95 (978-0-8160-6757-2(0), Ferguson Publishing Co.) Facts On File, Inc.
Regan, Lisa. Broadway Star. 2012. (Stage School Ser.). (ENG., Illus.). 32p. (J). (gr. 3-6). 25.25 (978-1-4488-8092-8(0)); pap. 10.00 (978-1-4488-8151-2(X)) Windmill Bks.
—Movie Star. 2012. (Stage School Ser.). (ENG., Illus.). 32p. (J). (gr. 3-6). pap. 10.00 (978-1-4488-8154-3(4)); lib. bdg. 25.25 (978-1-4488-8095-9(5)) Windmill Bks.

ACTORS AND ACTRESSES

see also Acting; Acting—Vocational Guidance; African American Actors; Motion Pictures—Biography; Theater

Abrams, Dennis. America Ferrera. 2010. (Great Hispanic Heritage Ser.). (Illus.). 112p. (gr. 6-12). 35.00 (978-1-60413-967-9(6), Chelsea Hse.) Facts On File, Inc.
—Angelina Jolie. 2011. (Women of Achievement Ser.). (Illus.). 146p. (gr. 6-12). 35.00 (978-1-60413-909-9(9), Chelsea Hse.) Facts On File, Inc.
Adams, Colleen. Jake Gyllenhaal. (Stars in the Spotlight Ser.). 32p. (gr. 4-4). 2009. 47.90 (978-1-60853-202-5(X), PowerKids Pr.) 2006. (Illus.). (YA). lib. bdg. 25.25 (978-1-4042-3514-4(0)) Rosen Publishing Group, Inc., The.
—Johnny Depp. 2006. (Tony Stead Nonfiction Independent Reading Collection). (ENG.). 24p. (gr. 3-6). pap. 8.85 (978-1-4042-5667-5(9)) Rosen Publishing Group, Inc., The.
—Keira Knightley. (Stars in the Spotlight Ser.). 32p. (gr. 4-4). 2009. 47.90 (978-1-60853-203-2(8), PowerKids Pr.) 2006. (Illus.). (YA). lib. bdg. 25.25 (978-1-4042-3513-7(2)) Rosen Publishing Group, Inc., The.
—Kelly Clarkson. (Stars in the Spotlight Ser.). 32p. (gr. 4-4). 2009. 47.90 (978-1-60853-204-9(6), PowerKids Pr.) 2006. (Illus.). (YA). lib. bdg. 25.25 (978-1-4042-3515-1(9)) Rosen Publishing Group, Inc., The.
—Orlando Bloom. (Stars in the Spotlight Ser.). 32p. (gr. 4-4). 2009. 47.90 (978-1-60853-205-6(4), PowerKids Pr.) 2006. (Illus.). (YA). lib. bdg. 25.25 (978-1-4042-3517-5(5)) Rosen Publishing Group, Inc., The.
Allen, Amy Ruth. Queen Latifah: From Jersey Girl to Superstar. 2012. (USA TODAY Lifeline Biographies Ser.). (ENG., Illus.). 112p. (gr. 6-12). lib. bdg. 34.60 (978-0-7613-4234-2(6)) Lerner Publishing Group.
Allen, Audrey. Jennifer Lawrence. 2013. 32p. (J). (gr. 3-6). 25.25 (978-1-4339-8977-3(8)); pap. 10.50 (978-1-4339-8978-0(6)) Stevens, Gareth Publishing LLLP.
Aloian, Molly. Jennifer Lawrence. 2012. (ENG., Illus.). 32p. (J). (978-0-7787-8051-9(1)); pap. (978-0-7787-8056-4(2)) Crabtree Publishing Co.
—Josh Hutcherson. 2012. (ENG.). 32p. (J). lib. bdg. (978-0-7787-8053-3(8)); (Illus.). pap. (978-0-7787-8058-8(9)) Crabtree Publishing Co.
Alter, Judy. Oprah Winfrey. 2007. (21st Century Skills Library: Life Skills Biographies Ser.). (ENG., Illus.). 48p. (gr. 4-8). lib. bdg. 31.36 (978-1-60279-069-8(8), 200045) Cherry Lake Publishing.
Anderson, Sheila. America Ferrera: Latina Superstar. 2009. (Hot Celebrity Biographies Ser.). (Illus.). 48p. (J). (gr. 5-9). lib. bdg. 25.27 (978-0-7660-3210-1(8)) Enslow Pubs., Inc.
—Miley Cyrus: Music & TV Superstar. 2009. (Hot Celebrity Biographies Ser.). (Illus.). 48p. (J). (gr. 5-9). lib. bdg. 25.27 (978-0-7660-3213-2(2)) Enslow Pubs., Inc.
Apte, Sunita. Christopher Reeve: Don't Lose Hope! 2005. (Defining Moments Ser.). (Illus.). 32p. (J). (gr. 2-5). lib. bdg. 25.27 (978-1-59716-074-2(1)) Bearport Publishing Co., Inc.
—Michael J. Fox: I Can Make a Difference! 2006. (Defining Moments Ser.). (Illus.). 32p. (J). (gr. 2-5). lib. bdg. 25.27 (978-1-59716-269-2(8)) Bearport Publishing Co., Inc.

Asselin, Kristine Carlson. Jennifer Lopez: Actress & Pop Superstar, 1 vol. 2013. (Contemporary Lives Set 2 Ser.). (ENG.). 112p. (J). (gr. 6-12). lib. bdg. 35.64 (978-1-61783-621-3(4), Essential Library) ABDO Publishing Co.

Azzarelli, Ally. Selena Gomez: Latina TV & Music Star. 2011. (Hot Celebrity Biographies Ser.). (Illus.). 48p. (J). (gr. 5-18). pap. 8.95 (978-1-59845-289-1(4)); lib. bdg. 25.27 (978-0-7660-3875-2(0)) Enslow Pubs., Inc.

—Taylor Lautner: Film Superstar. 2011. (Hot Celebrity Biographies Ser.). (Illus.). 48p. (J). (gr. 5-18). pap. 8.95 (978-1-59845-288-4(6)); lib. bdg. 25.27 (978-0-7660-3874-5(2)) Enslow Pubs., Inc.

Bankston, John. Daniel Radcliffe. l.t. ed. 2003. (Blue Banner Biography Ser.). (Illus.). 32p. (J). (gr. 3-8). lib. bdg. 25.70 (978-1-58415-250-7(8)) Mitchell Lane Pubs., Inc.

—Day by Day with Chloe Moretz. 2012. (J). lib. bdg. 25.70 (978-1-61228-328-9(4)) Mitchell Lane Pubs., Inc.

—Shirley Temple. l.t. ed. 2003. (Real-Life Reader Biography Ser.). (Illus.). 32p. (J). (gr. 3-8). lib. bdg. 25.70 (978-1-58415-172-2(2)) Mitchell Lane Pubs., Inc.

—What It's Like to Be Selena Gomez. 2012. (SPA.). (J). lib. bdg. 25.70 (978-1-61228-321-0(7)) Mitchell Lane Pubs., Inc.

Banting, Erinn. Angelina Jolie. 2008. (Remarkable People Ser.). (Illus.). 24p. (J). (gr. 4-6). pap. 8.95 (978-1-59036-987-6(4)); lib. bdg. 24.45 (978-1-59036-986-9(6)) Weigl Pubs., Inc.

—Halle Berry. 2005. (Great African American Women for Kids Ser.). (Illus.). 24p. (J). (gr. 2-3). lib. bdg. 24.45 (978-1-59036-333-1(7)); (gr. 3-7). per. 9.95 (978-1-59036-339-3(6)) Weigl Pubs., Inc.

Beauregarde, Madelyn & Kelly, David M. Jennifer Lawrence: Academy Award-Winning Actress. 2016. (Leading Women Ser.). 112p. (gr. 7-7). 39.93 (978-1-5026-1985-3(7)) Cavendish Square Publishing.

Berman, Ron. The Biz. 2013. (Av2 Audio Chapter Bks.). (ENG., Illus.). 73p. (J). (gr. 4-7). lib. bdg. 27.13 (978-1-62127-992-1(8), AV2 by Weigl) Weigl Pubs., Inc.

Bernard, Jan. Daniel Radcliffe. 2012. (Stars of Today Ser.). (ENG.). 32p. (J). (gr. 2-5). 28.50 (978-1-61473-290-7(6), 205039) Child's World, Inc., The.

Berne, Emma Carlson. Paris & Nicky Hilton. (Pop Culture Ser.). (Illus.). 64p. (YA). (gr. 3-7). 2008. lib. bdg. 22.95 (978-1-4222-0204-3(6)) 2007. pap. 7.95 (978-1-4222-0358-3(1)) Mason Crest.

Betances, Maria. Eva Longoria: Actress & Businesswoman. 2015. (Exceptional Latinos Ser.). (ENG., Illus.). 24p. (J). (gr. 3-4). pap. 9.35 (978-0-7660-6706-6(8), 1392054) Enslow Pubs., Inc.

Bjornlund, Lydia D. Angelina Jolie. 2010. (Modern Role Models Ser.). (Illus.). 64p. (YA). (gr. 7-12). 22.95 (978-1-4222-0504-4(5)) Mason Crest.

Blashfield, Jean F. Oprah Winfrey. 2003. (Trailblazers of the Modern World Ser.). (ENG & SPA., Illus.). 48p. (gr. 5-12). pap. 14.05 (978-0-8368-5247-9(8), Gareth Stevens Secondary Library) Stevens, Gareth Publishing LLLP.

Bodden, Valerie. Kristen Stewart. 2015. (Illus.). 21p. (978-1-60818-496-5(X), Creative Education) Creative Co., The.

—Selena Gomez. 2015. (Illus.). 21p. (J). (978-1-60818-498-9(6), Creative Education) Creative Co., The.

—Taylor Lautner. 2015. (Illus.). 21p. (J). (978-1-60818-499-6(4), Creative Education) Creative Co., The.

Boone, Mary. Corbin Bleu. 2008. (Blue Banner Biography Ser.). (Illus.). 32p. (YA). (gr. 4-7). lib. bdg. 25.70 (978-1-58415-674-1(0)) Mitchell Lane Pubs., Inc.

—Vanessa Anne Hudgens. 2008. (Blue Banner Biography Ser.). (Illus.). 32p. (YA). (gr. 4-7). lib. bdg. 25.70 (978-1-58415-672-7(4)) Mitchell Lane Pubs., Inc.

Boshier, Rosa. Ronald Reagan: 40th US President, 1 vol. 2013. (Essential Lives Set 8 Ser.). (ENG.). 112p. (J). (gr. 6-12). lib. bdg. 35.64 (978-1-61783-895-8(0), Essential Library) ABDO Publishing Co.

Boyd, Christie Brewer. James Franco. Greenhaven Press Staff, ed. 2012. (People in the News Ser.). (ENG., Illus.). 128p. (gr. 7-10). lib. bdg. 39.40 (978-1-4205-0754-6(0), Lucent Bks.) Cengage Gale.

Brooks, Riley. Up Close! [25 of Your Fave Stars Inside!]. 2013. (Illus.). 48p. (J). pap. (978-0-545-54126-8(3)) Scholastic, Inc.

—Willow Smith: Pop's Newest Princess. 2011. (Illus.). 46p. (J). pap. (978-0-545-36887-2(1)) Scholastic, Inc.

Brown, Jonatha A. Oprah Winfrey. 2004. (People We Should Know Ser.). (Illus.). 24p. (gr. 1-4). pap. 8.15 (978-0-8368-4319-4(3)); (ENG & SPA., pap. 8.15 (978-0-8368-4361-3(4)); lib. bdg. 22.00 (978-0-8368-4312-5(6)) Stevens, Gareth Publishing LLLP. (Weekly Reader Leveled Readers).

—Oprah Winfrey. Acosta, Tatiana & Gutierrez, Guillermo, trs. 2004. (Gente Que Hay Que Conocer Ser.). (SPA., Illus.). 24p. (gr. 1-4). lib. bdg. 22.00 (978-0-8368-4354-5(1), Weekly Reader Leveled Readers) Stevens, Gareth Publishing LLLP.

Bryan, Dale-Marie. Anne Hathaway. 2012. (Stars of Today Ser.). (ENG.). 32p. (J). (gr. 2-5). 28.50 (978-1-61473-286-0(8), 205038) Child's World, Inc., The.

—Emma Watson. 2012. (Stars of Today Ser.). (ENG.). 32p. (J). (gr. 2-5). 28.50 (978-1-61473-289-1(2), 205041) Child's World, Inc., The.

—Johnny Depp. 2012. (Stars of Today Ser.). (ENG.). 32p. (J). (gr. 2-5). 28.50 (978-1-61473-288-4(4), 205042) Child's World, Inc., The.

Burgan, Michael. Ronald Reagan. 2011. 128p. pap. 14.99 (978-0-7566-7739-8(4)) Dorling Kindersley Publishing, Inc.

Burlingame, Jeff. Demi! Latina Star Demi Lovato. 2013. (Sizzling Celebrities Ser.). 48p. (J). (gr. 4-9). pap. 8.95 (978-1-4644-0277-7(9)) Enslow Pubs., Inc.

—Jennifer! Film Star Jennifer Lawrence. 2013. (Sizzling Celebrities Ser.). 48p. (J). lib. bdg. 25.27 (978-0-7660-4170-7(0)); (gr. 4-9). pap. 8.95 (978-1-4644-0279-1(5)) Enslow Pubs., Inc.

Cartlidge, Cherese. Anne Hathaway. Greenhaven Press Staff, ed. 2013. (People in the News Ser.). (ENG., Illus.). 128p. (gr. 7-10). lib. bdg. 39.40 (978-1-4205-0751-5(6), Lucent Bks.) Cengage Gale.

—Jane Lynch. Greenhaven Press Editors, ed. 2014. (People in the News Ser.). (ENG., Illus.). 128p. (gr. 7-10). lib. bdg. 39.40 (978-1-4205-0887-1(3), Lucent Bks.) Cengage Gale.

—Jennifer Lopez. Greenhaven Press Staff, ed. 2012. (People in the News Ser.). (ENG., Illus.). 128p. (gr. 7-10). lib. bdg. 39.40 (978-1-4205-0755-3(9), Lucent Bks.) Cengage Gale.

—Neil Patrick Harris. Greenhaven Press Editors, ed. 2012. (People in the News Ser.). (ENG., Illus.). 128p. (gr. 7-10). lib. bdg. 39.40 (978-1-4205-0615-0(3)) Cengage Gale.

—Ryan Gosling. Greenhaven Press Editors, ed. 2014. (People in the News Ser.). (ENG., Illus.). 128p. (J). (gr. 7-10). lib. bdg. 39.40 (978-1-4205-0890-1(3), Lucent Bks.) Cengage Gale.

Ciovacco, Justine. Amy Poehler, 01 vols., 1. 2016. (Giants of Comedy Ser.). (ENG., Illus.). 112p. (J). 35.60 (978-1-4994-6258-6(1), Rosen Young Adult) Rosen Publishing Group, Inc., The.

Clark, Travis. Will Ferrell. 2008. (Pop Culture Ser.). (Illus.). 64p. (YA). (gr. 3-7). lib. bdg. 22.95 (978-1-4222-0202-9(X)) Mason Crest.

Cohn, Jessica & Kuligowski, Stephanie. Fearless! Stunt People, 1 vol. 2nd rev. ed. 2013. (Nonfiction Readers Ser.). (ENG.). 64p. (J). (gr. 5-5). pap. 10.99 (978-1-4333-4941-6(8)) Teacher Created Materials, Inc.

Corporate Contributor. Selena Gomez. 2012. (ENG.). 32p. (J). (978-0-7787-7617-8(4)); pap. (978-0-7787-7630-7(1)) Crabtree Publishing Co.

—Taylor Lautner. 2012. (ENG.). 32p. (J). (978-0-7787-7619-2(0)); pap. (978-0-7787-7632-1(8)) Crabtree Publishing Co.

Corrick, James A. Dwayne "The Rock" Johnson. 2012. (Role Model Entertainers Ser.). 64p. (J). (gr. 7). 22.95 (978-1-4222-2716-9(2)) Mason Crest.

Currie, Cherie & O'Neill, Tony. Neon Angel: A Memoir of a Runaway. 2010. (ENG.). 368p. 24.99 (978-0-06-196135-9(3)) HarperCollins Pubs.

Davidson, Amy. Abigail Breslin. 2012. (Rising Stars Ser.). (Illus.). 32p. (J). (gr. 3-6). 25.25 (978-1-4339-7272-0(7)); pap. 10.50 (978-1-4339-7273-7(5)) Stevens, Gareth Publishing LLLP.

—Darren Criss. 2012. (Rising Stars Ser.). (Illus.). 32p. (gr. 3-6). 25.25 (978-1-4339-7276-8(X)); pap. 10.50 (978-1-4339-7277-5(8)) Stevens, Gareth Publishing LLLP.

—Elle Fanning. 2012. (Rising Stars Ser.). (Illus.). 32p. (J). (gr. 3-6). 25.25 (978-1-4339-7280-5(8)); pap. 10.50 (978-1-4339-7281-2(6)) Stevens, Gareth Publishing LLLP.

—Rico Rodriguez. 2012. (Rising Stars Ser.). (Illus.). 32p. (J). (gr. 3-6). 25.25 (978-1-4339-7292-8(1)); pap. 10.50 (978-1-4339-7293-5(X)) Stevens, Gareth Publishing LLLP.

Davies, Ross. Andre the Giant. 2005. (Wrestling Greats Ser.). (Illus.). 112p. (YA). (gr. 7-12). lib. bdg. 34.60 (978-0-8239-3430-0(6)) Rosen Publishing Group, Inc., The.

Delmar, Pete. Scarlett Johansson. 2016. (Hollywood Action Heroes Ser.). (ENG., Illus.). 32p. (gr. 3-4). lib. bdg. 27.99 (978-1-5157-1097-4(1), Edge Bks.) Capstone Press of Coughlan Cos.

—Zoe Saldana. 2016. (Hollywood Action Heroes Ser.). (ENG., Illus.). 32p. (gr. 3-4). lib. bdg. 27.99 (978-1-5157-0962-6(0), Edge Bks.) Capstone Press of Coughlan Cos.

Demers, Roxanna. The Rusty Bucket Kids, A Behind the Scenes Look at the Rusty Bucket Kids, Lincoln, Journey To 16. Eason, D. M., illus. 2010. (ENG.). 82p. (J). pap. 19.99 (978-1-935711-04-9(0)) Peak City Publishing, LLC.

Deutsch, Stacia & Cohon, Rhody. Martin Lawrence. (Sharing the American Dream Ser.). 64p. (YA). (gr. 7-12). 2009. 22.95 (978-1-4222-0587-7(8)) 2007. pap. 9.95 (978-1-4222-0752-9(8)) Mason Crest.

—Samuel L. Jackson. (Sharing the American Dream Ser.). 64p. (YA). (gr. 7-12). 2009. (Illus.). 22.95 (978-1-4222-0580-8(0)) 2007. pap. 9.95 (978-1-4222-0750-5(1)) Mason Crest.

Diver, Lucas. Ross Lynch: Disney Channel Actor, 1 vol. 2014. (Pop Bios Ser.). (ENG., Illus.). 24p. (J). (gr. 2-4). lib. bdg. 28.50 (978-1-62970-727-3(9)) ABDO Publishing Co.

—Rowan Blanchard: Star of Girl Meets World, 1 vol. 2014. (Pop Bios Ser.). (ENG., Illus.). 24p. (J). (gr. 2-4). lib. bdg. 28.50 (978-1-62970-728-0(7)) ABDO Publishing Co.

—Zendaya: Disney Channel Actress, 1 vol. 2014. (Pop Bios Ser.). (ENG.). 24p. (J). (gr. 2-4). lib. bdg. 28.50 (978-1-62970-729-7(5)) ABDO Publishing Co.

Doeden, Matt. Will Smith. 2007. (Just the Facts Biographies Ser.). (ENG., Illus.). 112p. (gr. 5-12). lib. bdg. 27.93 (978-0-8225-6608-3(7), Lerner Pubns.) Lerner Publishing Group.

—Will Smith: Box Office Superstar. 2009. (USA TODAY Lifeline Biographies Ser.). (ENG., Illus.). 112p. (J). (gr. 6-12). lib. bdg. 34.60 (978-0-7613-4265-6(6), 1299611) Lerner Publishing Group.

Donovan, Sandy. Zoe Kravitz: X-Men's Amazing Angel. 2013. (Pop Culture Bios Ser.). (ENG., Illus.). 32p. (gr. 3-6). pap. 7.95 (978-1-4677-0885-2(2)); lib. bdg. 26.60 (978-1-4677-0747-3(3), Lerner Pubns.) Lerner Publishing Group.

Dougherty, Terri. Ben Stiller. 2007. (People in the News Ser.). (ENG., Illus.). 128p. (J). (gr. 7-12). lib. bdg. 39.40 (978-1-59018-723-4(7), LML02109-221297) Cengage Gale.

—Daniel Radcliffe. 2009. (People in the News Ser.). (ENG.). 128p. (gr. 7-12). 39.40 (978-1-4205-0156-8(9)) Cengage Gale.

—Jennifer Lopez. 2007. (Twentieth Century Most Influential Hispanics Ser.). (ENG., Illus.). 128p. (YA). (gr. 7-12). 34.80 (978-1-4205-0021-9(X)) Cengage Gale.

—Raven-Symoné. (Role Model Entertainers Ser.). (Illus.). 64p. (YA). 2010. (gr. 7-12). 22.95 (978-1-4222-0508-2(8)) 2007. pap. 9.95 (978-1-4222-0795-6(1)) Mason Crest.

—Salma Hayek. 2008. (People in the News Ser.). (ENG., Illus.). 128p. (gr. 7-10). lib. bdg. 39.40 (978-1-4205-0096-7(1), LML02109-242100, Lucent Bks.) Cengage Gale.

—Tobey Maguire. 2010. (Modern Role Models Ser.). (Illus.). 64p. (YA). (gr. 7-12). 22.95 (978-1-4222-0505-1(3)) Mason Crest.

Dzidrums, Christine. Idina Menzel: Broadway Superstar. 2013. 112p. pap. 9.99 (978-1-938438-17-2(5)) Creative Media Publishing.

Edge, Laura B. Hilary Duff: Celebrity with Heart. 2010. (Celebrities with Heart Ser.). (Illus.). 128p. (J). pap. 10.95 (978-1-59845-205-1(3)) Enslow Pubs., Inc.

Edge, Laura Bufano. Hilary Duff: Celebrity with Heart. 2010. (Celebrities with Heart Ser.). (Illus.). 128p. (J). (gr. 7-12). 33.27 (978-0-7660-3404-4(6)) Enslow Pubs., Inc.

Edwards, Karen. Christopher Reeve: A Real-Life Superhero. 2005. (Illus.). 32p. (J). (978-0-669-51411-7(X)) Great Source Education Group, Inc.

Eldridge, Stephen. Logan! Rising Star Logan Lerman. 2013. (Sizzling Celebrities Ser.). 48p. (J). lib. bdg. 25.27 (978-0-7660-4171-4(9)); (gr. 4-9). pap. 8.95 (978-1-4644-0281-4(7)) Enslow Pubs., Inc.

Embacher, Eric. Will Smith: The Funny, Funky, & Confident Fresh Prince. 2003. (High Five Reading - Red Ser.). (ENG., Illus.). 48p. (gr. 3-4). per. 9.00 (978-0-7368-2829-1(X), High Five Reading (RBL)) Capstone Press of Coughlan Cos.

Epstein, Dwayne. Adam Sandler. 2004. (People in the News Ser.). (ENG., Illus.). 112p. (J). 33.45 (978-1-59018-447-9(5), Lucent Bks.) Cengage Gale.

—Denzel Washington. 2009. (People in the News Ser.). (ENG.). (YA). (gr. 7-12). 33.95 (978-1-4205-0157-5(7)) Cengage Gale.

Etingoff, Kim. Jennifer Aniston. 2012. (Illus.). 64p. (J). pap. (978-1-4222-2483-0(X)) Mason Crest.

—Jennifer Aniston: From Friends to Films. 2012. (Extraordinary Success with a High School Diploma or Less Ser.). (Illus.). 64p. (J). (gr. 7-8). 22.95 (978-1-4222-2480-9(5)) Mason Crest.

Feinstein, Stephen. Denzel Washington. 2008. (African-American Heroes Ser.). (Illus.). 24p. (J). (gr. 1-3). lib. bdg. 22.60 (978-0-7660-2895-1(X), Enslow Elementary) Enslow Pubs., Inc.

—Oprah Winfrey. 2007. (African-American Heroes Ser.). (Illus.). 24p. (J). (gr. 1-3). lib. bdg. 22.60 (978-0-7660-2764-0(3), Enslow Elementary) Enslow Pubs., Inc.

—Queen Latifah. 2008. (African-American Heroes Ser.). (Illus.). 24p. (J). (gr. 1-3). lib. bdg. 22.60 (978-0-7660-2896-8(8)) Enslow Pubs., Inc.

—Will Smith. 2007. (African-American Heroes Ser.). (Illus.). 24p. (J). (gr. 1-3). lib. bdg. 22.60 (978-0-7660-2765-7(1), Enslow Elementary) Enslow Pubs., Inc.

Fleischman, Sid. Sir Charlie: Chaplin, the Funniest Man in the World. 2010. (ENG.). 288p. (J). (gr. 4-18). 19.99 (978-0-06-189640-8(3), Greenwillow Bks.) HarperCollins Pubs.

Ford, Carin T. Paul Robeson: I Want to Make Freedom Ring. 2007. (African-American Biography Library). (Illus.). 128p. (J). (gr. 3-7). lib. bdg. 33.27 (978-0-7660-2703-9(1)) Enslow Pubs., Inc.

Forte, Virginia, ed. The 100 Most Influential Entertainers of Stage & Screen, Vol. 1. 2016. (Britannica Guide to the World's Most Influential People Ser.). (ENG.). 224p. (J). (gr. 10-10). 54.00 (978-1-68048-278-2(5), Britannica Educational Publishing) Rosen Publishing Group, Inc., The.

Franks, Katie. Ashley Tisdale. 2009. (Kid Stars! Ser.). 24p. (ENG., Illus.). (J). (gr. 1-6). pap. 9.40 (978-1-4042-4533-4(2), 1284716); (gr. 2-3). 42.50 (978-1-61513-876-0(5)); (Illus.). (J). (gr. 1-6). lib. bdg. 22.60 (978-1-4042-4468-9(9), 1284716) Rosen Publishing Group, Inc., The. (PowerKids Pr.).

—Drake Bell & Josh Peck. 2009. 24p. (gr. 1-6). pap. 9.40 (978-1-4042-4534-1(0), Rosen Classroom); (gr. 2-3). 42.50 (978-1-61513-879-1(X), PowerKids Pr.); (Illus.). (J). (gr. 1-6). lib. bdg. 22.60 (978-1-4042-4463-4(8), PowerKids Pr.) Rosen Publishing Group, Inc., The.

—Dylan & Cole Sprouse. 2009. (Kid Stars! Ser.). 24p. (ENG., Illus.). (gr. 1-6). pap. 9.40 (978-1-4042-4529-7(4)); (gr. 2-3). 42.50 (978-1-61513-882-1(X)); (Illus.). (J). (gr. 1-6). lib. bdg. 22.60 (978-1-4042-4464-1(6)) Rosen Publishing Group, Inc., The. (PowerKids Pr.).

—I Want to Be a Movie Star. 2009. (Dream Jobs Ser.). 24p. (gr. 2-3). 42.50 (978-1-61512-207-3(9), PowerKids Pr.) Rosen Publishing Group, Inc., The.

—Kid Stars!, 6 vols., Set. Incl. Ashley Tisdale. lib. bdg. 22.60 (978-1-4042-4468-9(9), 1284716); Drake Bell & Josh Peck. lib. bdg. 22.60 (978-1-4042-4463-4(8)); Dylan & Cole Sprouse. lib. bdg. 22.60 (978-1-4042-4464-1(6)); Miley Cyrus. lib. bdg. 22.60 (978-1-4042-4467-2(0)); Miranda Cosgrove. lib. bdg. 22.60 (978-1-4042-4466-5(2)); Zac Efron. lib. bdg. 22.60 (978-1-4042-4465-8(4)); (Illus.). 24p. (J). (gr. 1-6). 2009. 2008. Set lib. bdg. 127.50 (978-1-4358-2550-5(0), PowerKids Pr.) Rosen Publishing Group, Inc., The.

—Miley Cyrus. 2009. (Kid Stars! Ser.). 24p. (gr. 2-3). 42.50 (978-1-61513-885-2(4)); (Illus.). (J). (gr. 1-6). lib. bdg. 22.60 (978-1-4042-4467-2(0)) Rosen Publishing Group, Inc., The. (PowerKids Pr.).

—Miranda Cosgrove. 2009. (Kid Stars! Ser.). 24p. (ENG., Illus.). (gr. 1-6). pap. 9.40 (978-1-4042-4531-0(6)); (gr. 2-3). 42.50 (978-1-61513-888-3(9)); (Illus.). (J). (gr. 1-6). lib. bdg. 22.60 (978-1-4042-4466-5(2)) Rosen Publishing Group, Inc., The. (PowerKids Pr.).

—Zac Efron. 2009. (Kid Stars! Ser.). 24p. (ENG., Illus.). (gr. 1-6). pap. 9.40 (978-1-4042-4530-3(8)); (gr. 2-3). 42.50 (978-1-61513-891-3(9)); (Illus.). (J). (gr. 1-6). lib. bdg. 22.60 (978-1-4042-4465-8(4)) Rosen Publishing Group, Inc., The. (PowerKids Pr.).

Gagne, Tammy. Day by Day with Bindi Sue Irwin. 2012. 32p. (J). (gr. -1-2). lib. bdg. 25.70 (978-1-61228-326-5(8)) Mitchell Lane Pubs., Inc.

—Debby Ryan. 2012. (Illus.). 32p. (J). lib. bdg. 25.70 (978-1-61228-332-6(2)) Mitchell Lane Pubs., Inc.

—What It's Like to Be America Ferrara. de la Vega, Eida, tr. from ENG. 2010. (What It's Like to Be/Que se Siente al Ser Ser.). (ENG & SPA., Illus.). 32p. (J). (gr. -1-2). lib. bdg. 25.70 (978-1-58415-854-7(9)) Mitchell Lane Pubs., Inc.

Galaxy of Superstars. 2005. (Galaxy of Superstars Ser.). (gr. 6-12). 375.00 (978-0-7910-9145-6(7), Chelsea Hse.) Facts On File, Inc.

Gibson, Karen. What It's Like to Be George Lopez. de la Vega, Eida, tr. from ENG. 2011. (What It's Like to Be... = Que Se Sienta Al Ser... Ser.). (SPA., Illus.). 32p. (J). (gr. -1-2). lib. bdg. 25.70 (978-1-58415-991-9(X)) Mitchell Lane Pubs., Inc.

—What It's Like to Be Jennifer Lopez. de la Vega, Eida, tr. from ENG. 2011. (What It's Like to Be... = Que Se Sienta Al Ser... Ser.). (SPA., Illus.). 32p. (J). (gr. -1-2). lib. bdg. 25.70 (978-1-58415-990-2(1)) Mitchell Lane Pubs., Inc.

Gigliotti, Jim. Who Was Bruce Lee? Hinderliter, John et al, illus. 2014. (Who Was? Ser.). (ENG.). 112p. (J). (gr. 3-7). 5.99 (978-0-448-47949-1(4), Grosset & Dunlap) Penguin Young Readers Group.

—Who Was Bruce Lee? 2014. (Who Was... ? Ser.). lib. bdg. 16.00 (978-0-606-35689-3(4)) Turtleback Bks.

Gitlin, Martin. Chris Rock: A Biography of a Comic Genius. 2014. (African-American Icons Ser.). 104p. (J). lib. bdg. 27.94 (978-0-7660-4229-2(4)) Enslow Pubs., Inc.

Gogerly, Liz. Film Stars. 2012. (Celebrity Secrets Ser.). (ENG., Illus.). 24p. (J). (gr. 5-8). pap. 8.25 (978-1-4488-7084-4(4)); lib. bdg. 22.60 (978-1-4488-7037-0(2)) Rosen Publishing Group, Inc., The. (PowerKids Pr.).

—Taylor Momsen. 2013. (Illus.). 32p. (J). 28.50 (978-1-59771-418-1(6)) Sea-To-Sea Pubns.

Goldish, Meish. Lights! Camera! Action! 2012. (Discovery Phonics Ser.). (ENG., Illus.). 14p. (J). (gr. 1-3). pap. 10.47 (978-0-8136-1154-9(7)) Modern Curriculum Pr.

Gomez, Selena. Selena Gomez Style Guide. 2010. 14.99 (978-1-4231-2976-9(8)) Hyperion Bks. for Children.

Gordon, Sherri Mabry. Josh! Leading Man Josh Hutcherson. 2013. (Sizzling Celebrities Ser.). 48p. (J). lib. bdg. 25.27 (978-0-7660-4200-1(6)); (gr. 4-9). pap. 8.95 (978-1-4644-0343-9(0)) Enslow Pubs., Inc.

Gorman, Jacqueline Laks. Chris Rock. 2008. (Today's Superstars). 32p. (YA). (gr. 4-7). lib. bdg. 31.95 (978-0-8368-9235-2(6)) Stevens, Gareth Publishing LLLP.

—The Olsen Twins. 2007. (Today's Superstars). (Illus.). 32p. (gr. 5-8). lib. bdg. 31.95 (978-0-8368-8199-8(0)) Stevens, Gareth Publishing LLLP.

Gosman, Gillian. Chris Colfer. 2012. (Kid Stars! Ser.). (ENG., Illus.). 24p. (J). (gr. 1-6). pap. 8.25 (978-1-4488-6347-1(3)); lib. bdg. 22.60 (978-1-4488-6193-4(4)) Rosen Publishing Group, Inc., The. (PowerKids Pr.).

—Jaden Smith. 2012. (Kid Stars! Ser.). (ENG., Illus.). 24p. (J). (gr. 1-6). pap. 8.25 (978-1-4488-6341-9(4)); lib. bdg. 22.60 (978-1-4488-6191-0(8)) Rosen Publishing Group, Inc., The. (PowerKids Pr.).

—Jennifer Lawrence. 2012. (Kid Stars! Ser.). (ENG., Illus.). 24p. (J). (gr. 1-6). pap. 8.25 (978-1-4488-6349-5(X)); lib. bdg. 22.60 (978-1-4488-6194-1(2)) Rosen Publishing Group, Inc., The. (PowerKids Pr.).

—Meaghan Jette Martin. 2012. (Kid Stars! Ser.). (ENG., Illus.). 24p. (J). (gr. 1-6). pap. 8.25 (978-1-4488-6343-3(0)); lib. bdg. 22.60 (978-1-4488-6192-7(6)) Rosen Publishing Group, Inc., The. (PowerKids Pr.).

—Taylor Lautner. 2012. (Kid Stars! Ser.). (ENG., Illus.). 24p. (J). (gr. 1-6). pap. 8.25 (978-1-4488-6345-7(7)); lib. bdg. 22.60 (978-1-4488-6195-8(0)) Rosen Publishing Group, Inc., The. (PowerKids Pr.).

Gravel, Élise. The Great Antonio, Level 3. 2016. (ENG., Illus.). 64p. (J). (gr. -1-4). 12.95 (978-1-943145-08-9(3), 9781943145089) TOON Books / RAW Junior, LLC.

Grayson, Robert. John Cena. 2012. (Role Model Entertainers Ser.). 64p. (J). (gr. 7). 22.95 (978-1-4222-2717-6(0)) Mason Crest.

Greenfield, Eloise. Paul Robeson. Ford, George, illus. 2009. (ENG.). 40p. (J). (gr. 1-6). pap. 10.95 (978-1-60060-262-7(2)) Lee & Low Bks., Inc.

Greenfield, Eloise & Ford, George. Paul Robeson. 2009. (ENG., Illus.). 40p. (J). (gr. 1-6). 10.95 (978-1-60060-256-6(8)) Lee & Low Bks., Inc.

Greenhaven Press Editors. Taylor Lautner. 2012. (People in the News Ser.). (Illus.). 128p. (YA). (gr. 7-12). lib. bdg. 33.95 (978-1-4205-0618-1(8)) Cengage Gale.

Greenhaven Press Editors & Szumski, Bonnie. Stephen Colbert. 2012. (People in the News Ser.). (ENG., Illus.). 128p. (gr. 7-10). lib. bdg. 39.40 (978-1-4205-0617-4(X)) Cengage Gale.

Guzmán, Lila & Guzmán, Rick. George Lopez: Comedian & TV Star. 2006. (Famous Latinos Ser.). (Illus.). 32p. (J). (gr. 3-4). lib. bdg. 23.94 (978-0-7660-2644-5(2), Enslow Elementary) Enslow Pubs., Inc.

—George Lopez: Comediante y Estrella de TV. 2007. (Latinos Famosos Ser.). (Illus.). 32p. (J). (gr. 4-7). lib. bdg. 23.94 (978-0-7660-2680-3(9), Enslow Elementary) Enslow Pubs., Inc.

—George Lopez: Latino King of Comedy. 2008. (Latino Biography Library). (Illus.). 128p. (J). (gr. k-6). lib. bdg. 33.27 (978-0-7660-2968-2(9)) Enslow Pubs., Inc.

Hadley, Joyce M. Dorothy Arnold: Joe Dimaggio's First Wife. 2004. (Illus.). 189p. (YA). per. 16.95 (978-0-9667808-2-6(5)) Chauncey Park Pr.

Hamilton, Toby G. Busta Rhymes. 2009. (Hip Hop (Mason Crest Paperback) Ser.). (Illus.). 64p. (YA). (gr. 4-7). pap. 7.95 (978-1-4222-0333-0(6)); (gr. 7-12). lib. bdg. 22.95 (978-1-4222-0284-5(4)) Mason Crest.

Harris, Lois V. Lotta Crabtree: Gold Rush Fairy Star, 1 vol. 2017. (ENG., Illus.). 80p. (J). (gr. 3-7). 17.99 (978-1-4556-2230-6(3)) Pelican Publishing Co., Inc.

Harrison, Kat. Lin-Manuel Miranda: Composer, Actor, & Creator of Hamilton. 2017. (Influential Lives Ser.). 128p. (J). (gr. 7-8). lib. bdg. 37.27 **(978-0-7660-8505-3(8))** Enslow Pubs., Inc.

Hart, Haley. I (Heart) Zac Efron. 2010. 144p. (YA). (gr. 7-18). pap. 4.95 (978-1-60747-707-5(6), Dove Books and Audio) Phoenix Bks., Inc.

Harte, Harlee. I (Heart) Taylor Lautner. 2009. 144p. (YA). (gr. 7-18). pap. 4.95 (978-1-60747-705-1(X)) Phoenix Bks., Inc.

—I (Heart) Taylor Swift. 2009. (ENG.). 144p. (J). pap. 4.95 (978-1-59777-647-9(5)) Phoenix Bks., Inc.

—The Jonas Brothers. 2009. (I Heart Ser.). (ENG.). 144p. (J). (gr. 4-7). pap. 4.95 (978-1-59777-641-7(6)) Phoenix Bks., Inc.

—Robert Pattinson. 2009. (I Heart Ser.). (ENG.). 144p. (J). pap. 4.95 (978-1-59777-649-3(1)) Phoenix Bks., Inc.

—Selena Gomez. 2009. (I Heart Ser.). (ENG.). 144p. (J). (gr. 4-7). pap. 4.95 (978-1-59777-648-6(3)) Phoenix Bks., Inc.

Hasday, Judy L. Extraordinary People in the Movies. 2003. (Extraordinary People Ser.). (ENG., Illus.). 288p. (J). (gr. 6-18). 40.00 (978-0-516-22348-3(8), Children's Pr.) Scholastic Library Publishing.

Hemingway, Albert. Barack Obama. 2007. (Sharing the American Dream Ser.). 64p. (YA). (gr. 7-18). pap. 9.95 (978-1-4222-0759-8(5)) Mason Crest.

—Chuck Norris. 2009. (Sharing the American Dream Ser.). 64p. (YA). (gr. 7-12). 22.95 *(978-1-4222-0591-4(6))* Mason Crest.

Henricks, Dana. George Clooney. (Sharing the American Dream Ser.). 64p. (YA). (gr. 7-12). 2009. 22.95 *(978-1-4222-0600-3(9))* 2007. pap. 9.95 *(978-1-4222-0741-3(2))* Mason Crest.

Hibbert, Clare. Dakota Fanning. 2012. (Teen Stars Ser.). (ENG., Illus.). 32p. (J). (gr. 3-6). lib. bdg. 28.50 *(978-1-59771-413-6(5))* Sea-To-Sea Pubns.

—Jaden Smith. 2013. (Illus.). 32p. 28.50 *(978-1-59771-414-3(3))* Sea-To-Sea Pubns.

Hibbert, Clare & Hachette Children's Books Staff. Movie Star: Find Out How Your Favorite Movie Stars Made It! 2012. (Celeb Ser.). (Illus.). 32p. (gr. 4-6). lib. bdg. 28.50 *(978-1-59771-332-0(5))* Sea-To-Sea Pubns.

Higgins, Melissa. Jennifer Lawrence: Breakout Actress, 1 vol. 2013. (Contemporary Lives Set 2 Ser.). (ENG.). 112p. (J). (gr. 6-12). lib. bdg. 35.64 *(978-1-61783-620-6(6),* Essential Library) ABDO Publishing Co.

Higgins, Nadia. Bella Thorne: Shaking up the Small Screen. 2013. (Pop Culture Bios Ser.). (ENG., Illus.). 32p. (gr. 3-6). pap. 7.95 *(978-1-4677-1549-2(2));* lib. bdg. 26.60 *(978-1-4677-1308-5(2),* Lerner Pubns.) Lerner Publishing Group.

—Emma Watson: From Wizards to Wallflowers. 2014. (Pop Culture Bios Ser.). (ENG., Illus.). 32p. (gr. 3-6). lib. bdg. 26.60 *(978-1-4677-1442-6(9),* Lerner Pubns.) Lerner Publishing Group.

—Jennifer Lawrence: The Hunger Games' Girl on Fire. 2013. (Pop Culture Bios Ser.). (ENG., Illus.). 32p. (gr. 3-6). pap. 7.95 *(978-1-4677-0881-4(X));* lib. bdg. 26.60 *(978-1-4677-0743-5(0),* Lerner Pubns.) Lerner Publishing Group.

—Logan Lerman: The Perks of Being of an Action Star. 2014. (Pop Culture Bios Ser.). (ENG., Illus.). 32p. (gr. 3-6). lib. bdg. 26.60 *(978-1-4677-1445-7(3),* Lerner Pubns.) Lerner Publishing Group.

—Nicholas Hoult: Beast of the Silver Screen. 2014. (Pop Culture Bios Ser.). (ENG., Illus.). 32p. (gr. 3-6). lib. bdg. 26.60 *(978-1-4677-1444-0(5),* Lerner Pubns.) Lerner Publishing Group.

Hill, Anne E. Kirsten Dunst. 2005. (People in the News Ser.). (ENG., Illus.). 112p. (YA). (gr. 7-10). lib. bdg. 33.45 *(978-1-59018-715-9(6),* Lucent Bks.) Cengage Gale.

Hinds, Maurene J. Halle Berry. (Sharing the American Dream Ser.). 64p. (YA). (gr. 7-12). 2009. 22.95 *(978-1-4222-0596-9(7))* 2007. pap. 9.95 *(978-1-4222-0738-3(2))* Mason Crest.

Hirsch, Jesse. Tina Fey, 01 vols., 1. 2016. (Giants of Comedy Ser.). (ENG.). 112p. (J). 35.60 *(978-1-4994-6256-2(5),* Rosen Young Adult) Rosen Publishing Group, Inc., The.

Holt, Julia. Jackie Chan: The International Man of Action, 6 vols. 2005. (ENG., Illus.). 32p. pap. *(978-0-340-87655-8(7))* Cambridge Univ. Pr.

Hord, Colleen. Michael J. Fox: Little World Biographies. 2013. (ENG.). 24p. (gr. k-3). pap. 8.95 *(978-1-61810-287-4(7))* Rourke Educational Media.

Horn, Geoffrey M. Adam Sandler. 2005. (Today's Superstars). (Illus.). 32p. (gr. 5-8). lib. bdg. 31.95 *(978-0-8368-4234-0(0))* Stevens, Gareth Publishing LLLP.

—Cameron Diaz. 2005. (Today's Superstars). (Illus.). 32p. (gr. 5-8). lib. bdg. 31.95 *(978-0-8368-4231-9(6))* Stevens, Gareth Publishing LLLP.

—Jamie Foxx. 2005. (Today's Superstars). (Illus.). 32p. (gr. 5-8). lib. bdg. 31.95 *(978-0-8368-4232-6(4))* Stevens, Gareth Publishing LLLP.

Howse, Jennifer. Miley Cyrus. 2008. (Remarkable People Ser.). (Illus.). 24p. (J). (gr. 4-6). pap. 8.95 *(978-1-59036-985-2(8));* lib. bdg. 24.45 *(978-1-59036-984-5(X))* Weigl Pubs., Inc.

Hudak, Heather C. Oprah Winfrey. (Remarkable People Ser.). (Illus.). 24p. (J). 2009. (gr. 4-6). pap. 8.95 *(978-1-60596-631-1(2))* 2009. (gr. 4-6). lib. bdg. 24.45 *(978-1-60596-630-4(4))* 2005. (gr. 2-3). lib. bdg. 24.45 *(978-1-59036-335-5(3))* 2005. (gr. 3-7). per. 8.95 *(978-1-59036-341-6(8))* Weigl Pubs., Inc.

Hurst, Heidi. Jennifer Lopez. 2003. (People in the News Ser.). (Illus.). 112p. (J). 32.45 *(978-1-59018-325-0(8),* Lucent Bks.) Cengage Gale.

Isbell, Hannah. Drake: Actor & Rapper. 2017. (Junior Biographies Ser.). 24p. (J). (gr. 3-4). pap. 9.35 ***(978-0-7660-8789-7(1))*** Enslow Pubs., Inc.

Israel, Elaine. Hilary Duff. 2007. (Today's Superstars). (Illus.). 32p. (gr. 5-8). lib. bdg. 31.95 *(978-0-8368-7651-2(2))* Stevens, Gareth Publishing LLLP.

Jackson, Katy. Doodles Movie Star: Sensational, Show-Stopping Pictures to Create & Complete. 2013. (ENG., Illus.). 64p. (J). (gr. k-3). pap. 7.95 *(978-1-62087-530-8(6),* 620530, Sky Pony Pr.) Skyhorse Publishing Co., Inc.

Janic, Susan. Living the Dream: Hannah Montana & Miley Cyrus - The Unofficial Story. 2008. (ENG., Illus.). 144p. (J). (gr. 4-7). pap. *(978-1-55022-848-9(X))* Filmer Ltd.

Jeffery, Marika. Jennifer Garner. (Sharing the American Dream Ser.). 64p. (YA). (gr. 7-12). 2009. (Illus.). 22.95 *(978-1-4222-0598-3(3))* 2007. pap. 9.95 *(978-1-4222-0745-1(5))* Mason Crest.

Jeffrey, Gary. Oprah Winfrey: The Life of a Media Superstar. (Graphic Nonfiction Biographies Ser.). (ENG.). 48p. 2009. (YA). (gr. 4-5). 58.50 *(978-1-61513-024-5(1),* Rosen Reference) 2007. (Illus.). (gr. 5-8). pap. 14.05 *(978-1-4042-0925-1(5))* Rosen Publishing Group, Inc., The.

—Oprah Winfrey: The Life of a Media Superstar. Riley, Terry, illus. 2007. (Graphic Nonfiction Biographies Ser.). (ENG.). 48p. (YA). (gr. 4-7). lib. bdg. 31.95 *(978-1-4042-0862-9(3))* Rosen Publishing Group, Inc., The.

Jennifer Lawrence. 2013. (Rising Stars Ser.). 32p. (J). (gr. 3-6). pap. 63.00 *(978-1-4339-8979-7(4))* Stevens, Gareth Publishing LLLP.

Johns, Michael-Anne. Celeb Fact Files! The 411 on All Your Faves. 2006. (Illus.). 48p. (J). pap. *(978-0-439-87972-9(8))* Scholastic, Inc.

—Hangin' with Lindsay Lohan. 2004. (Illus.). 48p. (J). *(978-0-439-72512-5(7))* Scholastic, Inc.

Johnson, Robin. Kristen Stewart. 2010. (Superstars! Ser.). (ENG.). 32p. (J). (gr. 3-6). lib. bdg. *(978-0-7787-7248-4(9))* Crabtree Publishing Co.

—Robert Pattinson. 2010. (Superstars! Ser.). (ENG., Illus.). 32p. (J). pap. *(978-0-7787-7260-6(8))* Crabtree Publishing Co.

Jones, Jen. Chris Evans. 2016. (Hollywood Action Heroes Ser.). (ENG., Illus.). 32p. (gr. 3-4). lib. bdg. 27.99 *(978-1-5157-1238-1(9),* Edge Bks.) Capstone Press of Coughlan Cos.

—Dwayne Johnson. 2016. (Hollywood Action Heroes Ser.). (ENG., Illus.). 32p. (gr. 3-4). lib. bdg. 27.99 *(978-1-5157-1096-7(3),* Edge Bks.) Capstone Press of Coughlan Cos.

—Oprah Winfrey: Celebrity with Heart. 2010. (Celebrities with Heart Ser.). (Illus.). 128p. (J). pap. 10.95 *(978-1-59845-206-8(1));* (gr. 7-12). 33.27 *(978-0-7660-3406-8(2))* Enslow Pubs., Inc.

Jones, Jen & Delmar, Pete. Hollywood Action Heroes. 2016. (Hollywood Action Heroes Ser.). (ENG.). 32p. (gr. 3-4). 111.96 *(978-1-5157-1307-4(5),* Edge Bks.) Capstone Press of Coughlan Cos.

Kara Higgins. Johnny Depp. 2004. (People in the News Ser.). (ENG., Illus.). 96p. 33.45 *(978-1-59018-538-4(2))* Cengage Gale.

Kauffman, Susan. Kevin Hart: Comedian, Actor, Writer, & Producer. 2017. (Influential Lives Ser.). 128p. (gr. 7-8). lib. bdg. 37.27 ***(978-0-7660-8507-7(4))*** Enslow Pubs., Inc.

Keedle, Jayne. Oprah Winfrey. 2008. (Today's Superstars). (Illus.). 32p. (J). (gr. 4-7). lib. bdg. 31.95 *(978-0-8368-9238-3(0))* Stevens, Gareth Publishing LLLP.

—Zac Efron. 2008. (Today's Superstars). (Illus.). 32p. (J). (gr. 4-7). lib. bdg. 31.95 *(978-0-8368-9239-0(9))* Stevens, Gareth Publishing LLLP.

Kennon, Michou. Queen Latifah. 2011. (Hip-Hop Headliners Ser.). (Illus.). 32p. (J). (gr. 3-8). lib. bdg. 25.25 *(978-1-4339-4808-4(7))* Stevens, Gareth Publishing LLLP.

Kjelle, Marylou Morano. Brittany Murphy. 2006. (Robbie Reader Ser.). (Illus.). 32p. (J). (gr. 2-5). lib. bdg. 25.70 *(978-1-58415-520-1(5))* Mitchell Lane Pubs., Inc.

—Dwayne the Rock Johnson. 2008. (Robbie Reader Ser.). (Illus.). 32p. (YA). (gr. 2-5). lib. bdg. 25.70 *(978-1-58415-722-9(4))* Mitchell Lane Pubs., Inc.

—Hilary Duff. 2004. (Robbie Reader Ser.). (Illus.). 32p. (J). (gr. 1-4). lib. bdg. 25.70 *(978-1-58415-295-8(8))* Mitchell Lane Pubs., Inc.

Klein, Adria F. Arnold Schwarzenegger. 2009. pap. 13.25 *(978-1-60559-054-7(1))* Hameray Publishing Group, Inc.

Klein, Emily. Bindi Irwin's Wild Life. 2016. (ENG.). 48p. (J). (gr. 1-3). pap. 4.99 *(978-1-338-05452-1(X))* Scholastic, Inc.

Knelman, Martin. Mike's World: The Life of Mike Myers. 2003. (ENG., Illus.). 268p. (gr. 5-12). pap. 16.95 *(978-1-55297-661-6(0),* 9781552976616) Firefly Bks., Ltd.

Kramer, Barbara. Michael J. Fox: Courage for Life. 2005. (Awesome Values in Famous Lives Ser.). (Illus.). 48p. (J). (gr. 3-4). lib. bdg. 23.93 *(978-0-7660-2376-5(1),* Enslow Elementary) Enslow Pubs., Inc.

—Oprah Winfrey: Reaching Out to Others. 2005. (Awesome Values in Famous Lives Ser.). (Illus.). 48p. (J). (gr. 3-4). lib. bdg. 25.27 *(978-0-7660-2378-9(8),* Enslow Elementary) Enslow Pubs., Inc.

Krohn, Katherine. Jennifer Lawrence: Star of the Hunger Games. 2012. (Gateway Biographies Ser.). 48p. (gr. 4-8). (J). pap. 51.02 *(978-0-7613-9226-2(2));* (ENG.). pap. 8.95 *(978-0-7613-8665-0(3))* Lerner Publishing Group.

Krohn, Katherine E. Jennifer Lawrence: Star of the Hunger Games. 2012. (Gateway Biographies Ser.). (ENG., Illus.). 48p. (J). (gr. 4-8). lib. bdg. 26.60 *(978-0-7613-8642-1(4))* Lerner Publishing Group.

—Oprah Winfrey. (Just the Facts Biographies Ser.). (Illus.). 112p. 2004. (ENG.). (gr. 5-12). lib. bdg. 27.93 *(978-0-8225-2472-4(4))* 2003. (J). (gr. 6-18). pap. 7.95 *(978-0-8225-5000-6(8))* Lerner Publishing Group.

—Oprah Winfrey: Global Media Leader. 2008. (USA TODAY Lifeline Biographies Ser.). (ENG.). 112p. (gr. 6-12). lib. bdg. 34.60 *(978-1-58013-571-9(4))* Lerner Publishing Group.

—Rosie O'Donnell. 2003. (Biography Ser.). (Illus.). 112p. (YA). (gr. 6-18). 7.95 *(978-0-8225-9681-3(4),* Carolrhoda Bks.) Lerner Publishing Group.

La Bella, Laura. Angelina Jolie: Goodwill Ambassador for the United Nations. 2009. (Celebrity Activists Ser.). 112p. (gr. 8-8). 66.50 *(978-1-61511-827-4(6))* Rosen Publishing Group, Inc., The.

Lajiness, Katie. Adam Sandler, 1 vol. 2016. (Big Buddy Pop Biographies Ser.). (ENG., Illus.). 32p. (J). (gr. 2-5). 28.50 *(978-1-68078-059-8(X))* ABDO Publishing Co.

—Riker Lynch, 1 vol. 2016. (Big Buddy Pop Biographies Ser.). (ENG., Illus.). 32p. (J). (gr. 2-5). 28.50 *(978-1-68078-054-3(9))* ABDO Publishing Co.

Landau, Elaine. Taylor Lautner: Twilight's Fearless Werewolf. 2013. (Pop Culture Bios Ser.). (ENG., Illus.). 32p. (gr. 3-6). pap. 7.95 *(978-1-4677-0884-5(4));* lib. bdg. 26.60 *(978-1-4677-0745-9(7),* Lerner Pubns.) Lerner Publishing Group.

Landau, Jennifer. Jane Lynch, 1 vol. 2015. (ENG.). 112p. (YA). 35.60 *(978-1-4777-7901-9(9),* Rosen Young Adult) Rosen Publishing Group, Inc., The.

Langston-George, Rebecca. The Booth Brothers: Drama, Fame, & the Death of President Lincoln. 2017. (Encounter: Narrative Nonfiction Stories Ser.). (ENG.). 112p. (gr. 3-5). lib. bdg. 30.65 ***(978-1-5157-7338-2(8))*** Encounter Bks.

Latinos in the Limelight. 2005. (Latinos in the Limelight Ser.). (gr. 5-8). 165.00 *(978-0-7910-8728-2(X),* Chelsea Hse.) Facts On File, Inc.

Lawrence, Katherine. Jean-Claude Van Damme. 2009. (Martial Arts Masters Ser.). 112p. (gr. 5-5). 63.90 *(978-1-61514-373-3(4))* Rosen Publishing Group, Inc., The.

Lawrence, Katherine Drobot. Jean-Claude Van Damme. 2005. (Martial Arts Masters Ser.). (Illus.). 112p. (YA). (gr. 7-12). lib. bdg. 34.60 *(978-0-8239-3517-8(5))* Rosen Publishing Group, Inc., The.

Leavitt, Amie. Amanda Bynes. 2007. (Robbie Reader Ser.). (Illus.). 32p. (J). (gr. 2-5). lib. bdg. 25.70 *(978-1-58415-594-2(9))* Mitchell Lane Pubs., Inc.

—Miley Cyrus. 2007. (Robbie Reader Ser.). (Illus.). 32p. (J). (gr. 2-5). lib. bdg. 25.70 *(978-1-58415-590-4(6))* Mitchell Lane Pubs., Inc.

—Raven-Symone. 2007. (Robbie Reader Ser.). (Illus.). 32p. (YA). (gr. 2-5). lib. bdg. 25.70 *(978-1-58415-593-5(0))* Mitchell Lane Pubs., Inc.

Leavitt, Amie Jane. Abigail Breslin. 2009. (Robbie Reader Ser.). (Illus.). 32p. (YA). (gr. 2-5). lib. bdg. 25.70 *(978-1-58415-759-5(3))* Mitchell Lane Pubs., Inc.

—Day by Day with Miley Cyrus. 2010. (Randy's Corner Ser.). (Illus.). 32p. (J). (gr. -1-2). lib. bdg. 25.70 *(978-1-58415-856-1(5))* Mitchell Lane Pubs., Inc.

—Dylan & Cole Sprouse. 2007. (Robbie Reader Ser.). (Illus.). 32p. (YA). (gr. 2-5). lib. bdg. 25.70 *(978-1-58415-591-1(4))* Mitchell Lane Pubs., Inc.

—Miranda Cosgrove. 2008. (Robbie Reader Ser.). (Illus.). 32p. (YA). (gr. 2-5). lib. bdg. 25.70 *(978-1-58415-720-5(8))* Mitchell Lane Pubs., Inc.

—Robert Downey Jr. 2011. (Blue Banner Biography Ser.). (Illus.). 32p. (YA). (gr. 4-7). lib. bdg. 25.70 *(978-1-61228-056-1(0))* Mitchell Lane Pubs., Inc.

—Taylor Lautner. 2010. (Robbie Reader Ser.). (Illus.). 32p. (YA). (gr. 2-5). lib. bdg. 25.70 *(978-1-58415-897-4(2))* Mitchell Lane Pubs., Inc.

—What It's Like to Be Miley Cyrus. Vega, Eida de la, tr. 2009. (What It's Like to Be/Que se Siente al Ser Ser.). (SPA & ENG., Illus.). 32p. (J). (gr. -1-2). lib. bdg. 25.70 *(978-1-58415-841-7(7))* Mitchell Lane Pubs., Inc.

Lee, Sally. Arnold Schwarzenegger: From Superstar to Governor. 2006. (People to Know Today Ser.). (Illus.). 128p. (J). (gr. 6-12). lib. bdg. 33.27 *(978-0-7660-2625-4(6))* Enslow Pubs., Inc.

—Freddie Prinze, Jr: From Shy Guy to Movie Star. 2008. (Latino Biography Library). (Illus.). 128p. (J). (gr. k-6). lib. bdg. 33.27 *(978-0-7660-2965-1(4))* Enslow Pubs., Inc.

Lee, T. S. The Oprah Winfrey Story: The First Oprah Winfrey Comic Biography. 2010. 190p. (J). pap. 14.95 *(978-0-9819542-6-4(X))* DASANBOOKS.

Lemmens, Mary Jo. Jennifer Lopez. 2009. (Hip Hop (Mason Crest Paperback) Ser.). (Illus.). 64p. (YA). (gr. 4-7). pap. 7.95 *(978-1-4222-0347-7(6))* Mason Crest.

Lemmens, Maryjo. Jennifer Lopez. 2009. (Hip-Hop 2 Ser.). (Illus.). 64p. (YA). (gr. 7-12). lib. bdg. 22.95 *(978-1-4222-0296-8(8))* Mason Crest.

Levete, Sarah. David Walliams: A Cosmic Genius. 2016. (ENG., Illus.). 32p. (J). (gr. 4-6). pap. 11.99 *(978-0-7502-9051-7(X),* Wayland) Hachette Children's Group GBR. Dist: Hachette Bk. Group.

Lies, Anne. Oprah Winfrey: Media Mogul, 1 vol. 2011. (Essential Lives Set 6 Ser.). (ENG., Illus.). 112p. (J). (gr. 6-12). lib. bdg. 35.64 *(978-1-61714-786-9(9),* Essential Library) ABDO Publishing Co.

Linde, Barbara M. Daniel Radcliffe. 2010. (Today's Superstars Ser.). (ENG.). 48p. (J). (gr. 5-8). pap. 14.05 *(978-1-4339-3990-7(8));* lib. bdg. 31.95 *(978-1-4339-3989-1(4))* Stevens, Gareth Publishing LLLP.

Llanas, Sheila Griffin. Taylor Lautner. 2012. (Star Biographies Ser.). (ENG.). 32p. (gr. 3-4). pap. 47.70 *(978-1-4296-9467-4(X),* Snap Bks.) Capstone Press of Coughlan Cos.

Lunzer, Lee. Betty Grable Paper Dolls. Lunzer, Lee, illus. 2007. (ENG., Illus.). 16p. pap. 12.00 *(978-0-9790668-7-0(5))* Paper Studio Pr.

Lusted, Marcia Amidon. Booboo Stewart: Twilight's Breakout Idol. 2013. (Pop Culture Bios Ser.). (ENG., Illus.). 32p. (gr. 3-6). (J). lib. bdg. 26.60 *(978-1-4677-0746-6(5),* Lerner Pubns.); pap. 7.95 *(978-1-4677-0880-7(1))* Lerner Publishing Group.

Lynette, Rachel. Jennifer Aniston. 2010. (People in the News Ser.). (Illus.). 128p. (J). 33.95 *(978-1-4205-0235-0(2),* 1304724, Lucent Bks.) Cengage Gale.

Lyons, Shelly. If I Were a Movie Star, 1 vol. Rooney, Ronnie, illus. 2010. (Dream Big! Ser.). (ENG.). 24p. (gr. k-3). lib. bdg. 26.65 *(978-1-4048-6162-6(9))* Picture Window Bks.

Madan, Fredric C. Greer Garson Paper Dolls. Madan, Fredric C. & Ernst, Clara, illus. 2007. (ENG.). 16p. pap. 12.00 *(978-0-9790668-6-3(7))* Paper Studio Pr.

Madison, Taylor. Boys We Love: Today's Top 30 Hottest Stars. 2005. (Illus.). (J). *(978-0-439-74864-3(X))* Scholastic, Inc.

Magid, Jennifer. Miley Cyrus/Hannah Montana. 2008. (Today's Superstars). 32p. (YA). (gr. 4-7). lib. bdg. 31.95 *(978-0-8368-9236-9(4))* Stevens, Gareth Publishing LLLP.

Magnarelli, Margaret. Backstage Pass: Today's Hottest Stars. 2013. (ENG., Illus.). 48p. (J). (gr. 3-7). pap. 4.99 *(978-0-545-59132-4(5))* Scholastic, Inc.

Malley, Alex. Chris Hemsworth. 2013. (Rising Stars Ser.). 32p. (J). (gr. 3-6). 25.25 *(978-1-4339-8969-8(7));* pap. 10.50 *(978-1-4339-8970-4(0));* pap. 63.00 *(978-1-4339-8971-1(9))* Stevens, Gareth Publishing LLLP.

Manzano, Sonia. Becoming Maria: Love & Chaos in the South Bronx. 2015. (ENG.). 272p. (J). (gr. 7). 17.99 *(978-0-545-62184-7(4),* Scholastic Pr.) Scholastic, Inc.

Mara, Wil. Clint Eastwood. 2014. (Great Filmmakers Ser.). 80p. (YA). (gr. 8-11). lib. bdg. 35.64 *(978-1-62712-948-0(0))* Cavendish Square Publishing.

—Oprah Winfrey. 2005. (Rookie Biographies Ser.). (ENG., Illus.). 32p. (J). (gr. 1-2). per. 4.95 *(978-0-516-25819-5(2),* Children's Pr.) Scholastic Library Publishing.

Marcovitz, Hal. Eddie Murphy. 2nd rev. ed. 2011. (Black Americans of Achievement Legacy Edition Ser.). 112p. (gr. 6-12). 35.00 *(978-1-60413-844-3(0))* Facts On File, Inc.

—Lindsay Lohan. 2008. (Pop Culture Ser.). (Illus.). 64p. (YA). (gr. 3-7). lib. bdg. 22.95 *(978-1-4222-0206-7(2))* Mason Crest.

—Owen & Luke Wilson. 2008. (Pop Culture Ser.). (Illus.). 64p. (YA). (gr. 3-7). lib. bdg. 22.95 *(978-1-4222-0210-4(0))* Mason Crest.

Markarian, Margie. Hilary Duff: Life in the Spotlight. 2009. (Hot Celebrity Biographies Ser.). (Illus.). 48p. (J). (gr. 5-9). pap. 8.95 *(978-0-7660-3626-0(X));* lib. bdg. 25.27 *(978-0-7660-3211-8(6))* Enslow Pubs., Inc.

Marx, Christy. Jet Li. (Martial Arts Masters Ser.). 112p. 2009. (gr. 5-5). 63.90 *(978-1-61514-374-0(2))* 2005. (Illus.). (YA). (gr. 7-12). lib. bdg. 34.60 *(978-0-8239-3519-2(1))* Rosen Publishing Group, Inc., The.

Mattern, Joanne. Ashley Tisdale. 2008. (Robbie Reader Ser.). (Illus.). 32p. (YA). (gr. 2-5). lib. bdg. 25.70 *(978-1-58415-719-9(4))* Mitchell Lane Pubs., Inc.

—Blake Lively. 2010. (Blue Banner Biography Ser.). (Illus.). 32p. (YA). (gr. 4-7). lib. bdg. 25.70 *(978-1-58415-909-4(X))* Mitchell Lane Pubs., Inc.

—Dakota Fanning. 2006. (Robbie Reader Ser.). (Illus.). 32p. (J). (gr. 2-5). lib. bdg. 25.70 *(978-1-58415-519-5(1))* Mitchell Lane Pubs., Inc.

—Drake Bell & Josh Peck. 2007. (Robbie Reader Ser.). (Illus.). 32p. (YA). (gr. 2-5). lib. bdg. 25.70 *(978-1-58415-592-8(2))* Mitchell Lane Pubs., Inc.

—Jaden Smith. 2009. (Robbie Reader Ser.). (Illus.). 32p. (YA). (gr. 2-5). lib. bdg. 25.70 *(978-1-58415-757-1(7))* Mitchell Lane Pubs., Inc.

—Jennifer Hudson. 2012. (Illus.). 32p. (gr. 4-8). lib. bdg. 25.70 *(978-1-61228-315-9(2))* Mitchell Lane Pubs., Inc.

—Orlando Bloom. 2008. (Pop Culture Ser.). (Illus.). 64p. (YA). (gr. 3-7). lib. bdg. 22.95 *(978-1-4222-0198-5(8))* Mason Crest.

—Tyler Perry. 2012. (J). lib. bdg. 25.70 *(978-1-61228-334-0(9))* Mitchell Lane Pubs., Inc.

McDowell, Pamela. Selena Gomez. 2012. (J). 27.13 *(978-1-61913-588-8(4));* pap. 13.95 *(978-1-61913-594-9(9))* Weigl Pubs., Inc.

McGowan, Joseph. Will Smith. 2009. (Today's Superstars Ser.). 48p. (J). (gr. 5-8). (ENG.). pap. 14.05 *(978-1-4339-2376-0(9));* lib. bdg. 31.95 *(978-1-4339-2380-7(7))* Stevens, Gareth Publishing LLLP.

McKissack, Patricia C. & McKissack, Fredrick L. Paul Robeson: A Voice for Change. 2013. (Famous African Americans Ser.). 24p. (J). (gr. k-3). pap. 7.95 *(978-1-4644-0205-0(1));* (Illus.). 22.60 *(978-0-7660-4107-3(7))* Enslow Pubs., Inc. (Enslow Elementary).

Meinking, Mary. Demi Lovato, 1 vol. 2012. (Star Biographies Ser.). (ENG., Illus.). 32p. (gr. 3-4). lib. bdg. 27.99 *(978-1-4296-8770-6(3),* Snap Bks.) Capstone Press of Coughlan Cos.

Menard, Valerie. Jennifer Lopez. 2003. (Blue Banner Biography Ser.). (Illus.). 32p. (J). (gr. 3-8). lib. bdg. 25.70 *(978-1-58415-225-5(7))* Mitchell Lane Pubs., Inc.

Michelson, Richard. Fascinating: The Life of Leonard Nimoy. Rodriguez, Edel, illus. 2016. (ENG.). 40p. (J). (gr. -1-3). 17.99 *(978-1-101-93330-5(5),* Knopf Bks. for Young Readers) Random Hse. Children's Bks.

Micklos, John. Jennifer Hudson: A Biography of an American Music Idol. 2014. (African-American Icons Ser.). 104p. (J). lib. bdg. 27.94 *(978-0-7660-4233-9(2))* Enslow Pubs., Inc.

Miller, Kat. I Love Daniel Radcliffe. 2010. (Fan Club Ser.). (ENG.). 24p. (J). (gr. 3-6). lib. bdg. 22.60 *(978-1-61533-054-6(2));* (Illus.). pap. 8.15 *(978-1-61533-055-3(0))* Windmill Bks.

—I Love Kristen Stewart. 2010. (Fan Club Ser.). (ENG.). 24p. (gr. 3-6). lib. bdg. 22.60 *(978-1-61533-060-7(7));* (Illus.). (J). pap. 8.15 *(978-1-61533-061-4(5))* Windmill Bks.

—I Love Miley Cyrus. 2010. (Fan Club Ser.). (ENG.). 24p. (J). (gr. 3-6). lib. bdg. 22.60 *(978-1-61533-045-4(3));* (Illus.). pap. 8.15 *(978-1-61533-046-1(1))* Windmill Bks.

—I Love Robert Pattinson. 2010. (Fan Club Ser.). (ENG.). 24p. (gr. 3-6). lib. bdg. 22.60 *(978-1-61533-057-7(7));* (Illus.). (J). pap. 8.15 *(978-1-61533-058-4(5))* Windmill Bks.

Mingo, Norman. Alice Faye Paper Dolls: Glamorous Movie Star Paper Dolls & Costumes. Mingo, Norman & Ernst, Clara, illus. 2007. 8p. pap. 12.00 *(978-0-9795053-0-0(5))* Paper Studio Pr.

—Bette Davis Paper Dolls. Taliadoros, Jenny, ed. Mingo, Norman & Ernst, Clara, illus. 2007. (ENG.). 16p. pap. 12.00 *(978-0-9790668-2-5(4))* Paper Studio Pr.

—Deanna Durbin Paper Dolls. Mingo, Norman & Ernt, Clara, illus. 2007. 16p. pap. 12.00 *(978-0-9790668-5-6(9))* Paper Studio Pr.

Mitchell, Susan. Will Ferrell. 2009. (Today's Superstars Ser.). 48p. (J). (gr. 5-8). pap. 14.05 *(978-1-4339-2374-6(2));* lib. bdg. 31.95 *(978-1-4339-2378-4(5))* Stevens, Gareth Publishing LLLP.

Mochizuki, Ken & Lee, Dom. Be Water, My Friend: The Early Years of Bruce Lee, 1 vol. 2006. (ENG., Illus.). 32p. (J). 16.95 *(978-1-58430-265-0(8))* Lee & Low Bks., Inc.

Mooney, Carla. The Creators & Cast of Glee. 2012. (People in the News Ser.). (ENG., Illus.). 128p. (gr. 7-10). lib. bdg. 39.40 *(978-1-4205-0789-8(3),* Lucent Bks.) Cengage Gale.

—Vanessa Hudgens. 2007. (Sharing the American Dream Ser.). 64p. (YA). (gr. 7-18). pap. 9.95 *(978-1-4222-0749-9(8))* Mason Crest.

—Vanessa Hudgens/Carla Mooney. 2009. (Sharing the American Dream Ser.). 64p. (YA). (gr. 7-12). 22.95 *(978-1-4222-0583-9(5))* Mason Crest.

Morganelli-Sacco, Adrianna. Liam Hemsworth. 2015. (ENG., Illus.). 32p. (J). *(978-0-7787-8079-3(1))* Crabtree Publishing Co.

Morley, Jacqueline. You Wouldn't Want to Be a Shakespearean Actor! Some Roles You Might Not Want to Play. Antram, David, illus. 2010. (You Wouldn't Want to Ser.). (ENG.). 32p. (J). (gr. 3-18). pap. 9.95 *(978-0-531-22826-5(6))* Scholastic Library Publishing.

Morley, Jacqueline & Salariya, David. You Wouldn't Want to Be a Shakespearean Actor! Some Roles You Might Not Want to Play. Antram, David, illus. 2010. (You Wouldn't Want to Ser.). (ENG.). 32p. (J). 29.00 *(978-0-531-20471-9(5))* Scholastic Library Publishing.

Morreale, Marie. Ansel Elgort. 2016. (Real Bios Ser.). (ENG., Illus.). 48p. (J). lib. bdg. 29.00 *(978-0-531-22377-2(9),* Children's Pr.) Scholastic Library Publishing.

—The Cast of Girl Meets World. 2015. (ENG.). 48p. lib. bdg. *(978-0-531-21572-2(5))* Children's Pr., Ltd.

—Jennifer Lawrence. 2015. (Real Bios Ser.). (ENG.). 48p. (J). lib. bdg. 29.00 *(978-0-531-21375-9(7))* Scholastic Library Publishing.

—Selena Gomez. 2015. (ENG., Illus.). 48p. pap. 7.95 *(978-0-531-21663-7(2),* Orchard Bks.) Scholastic, Inc.

Murphy, Maggie. Johnny Depp. 2011. (Movie Superstars Ser.). (Illus.). 32p. (J). pap. 10.00 *(978-1-4488-2721-3(3));* (gr. 4-6). 25.25 *(978-1-4488-2566-0(0))* Rosen Publishing Group, Inc., The. (PowerKids Pr.).

—Kristen Stewart: Twilight Star. 2010. (Young & Famous Ser.). 24p. (J). (ENG.). (gr. 3-6). lib. bdg. 22.60 *(978-1-4488-0641-6(0));* (Illus.). pap. 8.85 *(978-1-4488-1795-5(1),* PowerKids Pr.) Rosen Publishing Group, Inc., The.

A
B

—Megan Fox. 2011. (Movie Superstars Ser.). (Illus.). 32p. (J). pap. 10.00 (978-1-4488-2723-7(X)); (gr. 4-6). lib. bdg. 25.25 (978-1-4488-2567-7(9)) Rosen Publishing Group, Inc., The. (PowerKids Pr.).

—Miley Cyrus: Rock Star. 2010. (Young & Famous Ser.). 24p. (J). (ENG.). (gr. 3-6). 22.60 (978-1-4488-0643-0(7)); (Illus.). pap. 8.85 (978-1-4488-1799-3(4), PowerKids Pr.) Rosen Publishing Group, Inc., The.

—Reese Witherspoon. 2011. (Movie Superstars Ser.). (Illus.). 32p. (J). pap. 10.00 (978-1-4488-2725-1(6)); (gr. 4-6). lib. bdg. 25.25 (978-1-4488-2568-4(7)) Rosen Publishing Group, Inc., The. (PowerKids Pr.).

—Shia Labeouf. 2011. (Movie Superstars Ser.). (Illus.). 32p. (J). pap. 10.00 (978-1-4488-2715-2(9)); (gr. 4-6). 25.25 (978-1-4488-2563-9(6)) Rosen Publishing Group, Inc., The. (PowerKids Pr.).

—Taylor Lautner. 2011. (Movie Superstars Ser.). (Illus.). 32p. (J). pap. 10.00 (978-1-4488-2717-6(5)); (gr. 4-6). lib. bdg. 25.25 (978-1-4488-2564-6(4)) Rosen Publishing Group, Inc., The. (PowerKids Pr.).

—Taylor Lautner: Twilight Star. 2010. (Young & Famous Ser.). 24p. (ENG.). (YA). (gr. 3-6). lib. bdg. 22.60 (978-1-4488-0642-3(9)); (Illus.). (J). pap. 8.85 (978-1-4488-1797-9(8), PowerKids Pr.) Rosen Publishing Group, Inc., The.

—Zac Efron: Movie Star. 2010. (Young & Famous Ser.). 24p. (J). (ENG.). (gr. 3-6). lib. bdg. 22.60 (978-1-4488-0644-7(5)); (Illus.). pap. 8.85 (978-1-4488-1801-3(X), PowerKids Pr.) Rosen Publishing Group, Inc., The.

—Zoe Saldana. 2011. (Movie Superstars Ser.). (Illus.). 32p. (J). pap. 10.00 (978-1-4488-2719-0(1)); (gr. 4-6). lib. bdg. 25.25 (978-1-4488-2565-3(2)) Rosen Publishing Group, Inc., The. (PowerKids Pr.).

Nagle, Jeanne. Chris Rock, 01 vols., 1. 2016. (Giants of Comedy Ser.). (ENG., Illus.). 112p. (J). 35.60 (978-1-4994-6262-3(X), Rosen Young Adult) Rosen Publishing Group, Inc., The.

—Jennifer Hudson. 2008. (Who's Your Idol? Ser.). (Illus.). 48p. (J). (gr. 3-7). lib. bdg. 29.25 (978-1-4042-1372-2(4)) Rosen Publishing Group, Inc., The.

Nardo, Don, ed. Hugh Jackman. 2011. (People in the News Ser.). (Illus.). 128p. (YA). (gr. 9-12). lib. bdg. 33.45 (978-1-4205-0652-5(8)) Cengage Gale.

Nelson, Maria. Selena Gomez. 2011. (Rising Stars Ser.). 32p. (J). (gr. 3-6). pap. 10.50 (978-1-4339-5904-2(6)); lib. bdg. 25.25 (978-1-4339-5902-8(X)) Stevens, Gareth Publishing LLLP.

—Taylor Lautner. 2011. (Rising Stars Ser.). (Illus.). 32p. (gr. 3-6). 25.25 (978-1-4339-5906-6(2)); pap. 10.50 (978-1-4339-5908-0(9)) Stevens, Gareth Publishing LLLP.

Nelson, Robin. Selena Gomez: Pop Star & Actress. 2012. (Pop Culture Bios Ser.). (ENG., Illus.). 32p. (gr. 3-6). pap. 7.95 (978-1-4677-0238-6(2)); lib. bdg. 26.60 (978-0-7613-4142-0(0), Lerner Pubns.) Lerner Publishing Group.

Niver, Heather Moore. Aziz Ansari, 01 vols., 1. 2016. (Giants of Comedy Ser.). (ENG., Illus.). 112p. (J). 35.60 (978-1-5081-7051-8(7), Rosen Young Adult) Rosen Publishing Group, Inc., The.

Norwich, Grace. Daniel Radcliffe: No Ordinary Wizard. 2008. (ENG.). 128p. (J). (gr. 4-9). pap. 5.99 (978-1-4169-6771-2(0), Simon Spotlight) Simon Spotlight.

Null Petersen, Kathleen C. Theater Actors Then & Now, 1 vol. 2006. (Primary Source Readers Ser.). (ENG.). 32p. (J). (gr. 2-2). pap. 8.99 (978-0-7439-9379-1(9)) Shell Educational Publishing.

Olsen, Mary-Kate & Olsen, Ashley. The Ultimate Guide to Mary-Kate & Ashley. 2004. (Illus.). 93p. (978-0-00-718136-0(1)) HarperCollins Pubs. Australia.

Orr, Tamara. Emily Osment. 2009. (Robbie Reader Ser.). (Illus.). 32p. (YA). (gr. 2-5). lib. bdg. 25.70 (978-1-58415-755-7(0)) Mitchell Lane Pubs., Inc.

Orr, Tamra. AnnaSophia Robb. 2010. (Robbie Reader Ser.). (Illus.). 32p. (YA). (gr. 2-5). lib. bdg. 25.70 (978-1-58415-898-1(0)) Mitchell Lane Pubs., Inc.

—Brenda Song. 2009. (Robbie Reader Ser.). (Illus.). 32p. (YA). (gr. 2-5). lib. bdg. 25.70 (978-1-58415-753-3(4)) Mitchell Lane Pubs., Inc.

—Day by Day with Willow Smith. 2011. (Day by Day with... Ser.). (Illus.). 32p. (J). (gr. -1-2). lib. bdg. 25.70 (978-1-58415-983-4(9)) Mitchell Lane Pubs., Inc.

—Jennifer Lawrence. 2014. (ENG., Illus.). 48p. (J). lib. bdg. 25.70 (978-1-62469-001-3(7)) Purple Toad Publishing, Inc.

—Kristen Stewart. 2009. (Blue Banner Biography Ser.). (Illus.). 32p. (YA). (gr. 4-7). lib. bdg. 25.70 (978-1-58415-773-1(9)) Mitchell Lane Pubs., Inc.

—Shia Labeouf. 2010. (Blue Banner Biography Ser.). (Illus.). 32p. (YA). (gr. 4-7). lib. bdg. 25.70 (978-1-58415-908-7(1)) Mitchell Lane Pubs., Inc.

Orr, Tamra B. Ice Cube. 2006. (Blue Banner Biography Ser.). (Illus.). 32p. (YA). (gr. 4-7). lib. bdg. 25.70 (978-1-58415-517-1(5)) Mitchell Lane Pubs., Inc.

—Orlando Bloom. 2006. (Blue Banner Biography Ser.). (Illus.). 32p. (YA). (gr. 4-7). lib. bdg. 25.70 (978-1-58415-515-7(9)) Mitchell Lane Pubs., Inc.

Paprocki, Sherry Beck. Ellen Degeneres: Entertainer. 2009. (Women of Achievement Ser.). (Illus.). 136p. (gr. 6-12). 35.00 (978-1-60413-082-9(2), Chelsea Hse.) Facts On File, Inc.

Parish, James Robert. Tom Hanks: Actor. 2004. (Ferguson Career Biographies Ser.). (Illus.). 128p. (gr. 6-12). 25.00 (978-0-8160-5542-5(4), Ferguson Publishing Co.) Facts On File, Inc.

Parvis, Sarah. Taylor Lautner. 2010. (ENG.). 80p. 5.99 (978-0-7407-9962-4(2)) Andrews McMeel Publishing.

Passudetti, Christopher. Being Sara. 2013. (Av2 Audio Chapter Bks.). (ENG., Illus.). 81p. (J). (gr. 4-7). lib. bdg. 27.13 (978-1-62127-970-9(7), AV2 by Weigl) Weigl Pubs., Inc.

Pawlak, Debra Ann. Bruce Lee. 2009. (Sharing the American Dream Ser.). 64p. (YA). (gr. 7-12). 22.95 (978-1-4222-0586-0(X)) Mason Crest.

Payment, Simone. Michael J. Fox: Parkinson's Disease Research Advocate (Celebrity Activists) l.t. ed. 2012. 188p. pap. (978-1-4596-3346-9(6)) ReadHowYouWant.com, Ltd.

Peppas, Lynn. Demi Lovato. 2013. (ENG., Illus.). 32p. (J). (978-0-7787-1050-9(5)); pap. (978-0-7787-1054-7(8)) Crabtree Publishing Co.

—Taylor Swift. 2010. (Superstars! Ser.). (ENG.). 32p. (J). pap. (978-0-7787-7261-3(6)) Crabtree Publishing Co.

—Zac Efron. 2010. (Superstars! Ser.). (ENG., Illus.). 32p. (J). pap. (978-0-7787-7263-7(2)); (gr. 3-6). lib. bdg. (978-0-7787-7254-5(3)) Crabtree Publishing Co.

Pettinella, Amy. Queen Latifah: Award-Winning Actress & Hip-Hop Activist. 2014. (Leading Women Ser.). 112p. (J). (gr. 7-11). lib. bdg. 39.93 (978-1-62712-984-8(7)) Cavendish Square Publishing.

Pollack, Pam & Belviso, Meg. Who Were the Three Stooges? 2016. (Who Was? Ser.). (ENG., Illus.). 112p. (J). (gr. 3-7). 5.99 (978-0-448-48866-0(3)); lib. bdg. 15.99 (978-0-399-54244-2(2)) Penguin Young Readers Group. (Grosset & Dunlap).

—Who Were the Three Stooges? 2016. (Who Was... ? Ser.). (ENG.). 112p. (J). (gr. 3-7). 16.00 (978-0-606-39320-1(X)) Turtleback Bks.

Raatma, Lucia. John Cena: Rapping Wrestler with Attitude, 1 vol. 2012. (Pro Wrestling Stars Ser.). (ENG., Illus.). 48p. (gr. 3-4). lib. bdg. 31.99 (978-1-4296-8676-1(6)) Capstone Press of Coughlan Cos.

Rajczak, Kristen. Demi Lovato. 2011. (Rising Stars Ser.). (Illus.). 32p. (J). (gr. 3-6). pap. 10.50 (978-1-4339-5888-5(0)); lib. bdg. 25.25 (978-1-4339-5886-1(4)) Stevens, Gareth Publishing LLLP.

—Jaden Smith. 2011. (Rising Stars Ser.). (Illus.). 32p. (J). (gr. 3-6). pap. 10.50 (978-1-4339-5892-2(9)); lib. bdg. 25.25 (978-1-4339-5890-8(2)) Stevens, Gareth Publishing LLLP.

Rawson, Katherine. Abigail Breslin. (J). 2010. pap. 9.40 (978-1-4358-3412-5(7)) 2009. (Illus.). 24p. lib. bdg. 22.60 (978-1-4042-8146-2(0)) Rosen Publishing Group, Inc., The. (PowerKids Pr.).

—Brenda Song. (J). 2010. pap. 9.40 (978-1-4358-3406-4(2)) 2009. (Illus.). 24p. lib. bdg. 22.60 (978-1-4042-8136-3(3)) Rosen Publishing Group, Inc., The. (PowerKids Pr.).

—Daniel Radcliffe. (J). 2010. pap. 9.40 (978-1-4358-3404-0(6)) 2009. (Illus.). 24p. lib. bdg. 22.60 (978-1-4042-8135-6(5)) Rosen Publishing Group, Inc., The. (PowerKids Pr.).

—Vanessa Hudgens. (Illus.). 24p. (J). 2010. pap. 9.40 (978-1-4358-3408-8(9)) 2009. lib. bdg. 22.60 (978-1-4042-8137-0(1)) Rosen Publishing Group, Inc., The. (PowerKids Pr.).

Reusser, Kayleen. Selena Gomez. 2009. (Robbie Reader Ser.). (Illus.). 32p. (YA). (gr. 2-5). lib. bdg. 25.70 (978-1-58415-752-6(6)) Mitchell Lane Pubs., Inc.

Riddolls, Tom & Wearing, Judy. Zac Efron. 2009. (Remarkable People Ser.). (Illus.). 24p. (J). (gr. 4-6). pap. 8.95 (978-1-60596-629-8(0)); lib. bdg. 24.45 (978-1-60596-628-1(2)) Weigl Pubs., Inc.

Robb, Jackie. Miley Mania! Behind the Scenes with Miley Cyrus. 2008. (Star Scene Ser.). (ENG., Illus.). 48p. (J). (gr. 3-7). pap. 5.99 (978-0-545-08565-6(9)) Scholastic, Inc.

Robbins, Trina. Hedy Lamarr & a Secret Communication System, 1 vol. Martin, Cynthia, illus. 2006. (Inventions & Discovery Ser.). (ENG.). 32p. (gr. 3-4). 8.10 (978-0-7368-9641-2(4), Graphic Library) Capstone Press of Coughlan Cos.

—Hedy Lamarr & a Secret Communication System, 1 vol. Martin, Cynthia & Timmons, Anne, illus. 2006. (Inventions & Discovery Ser.). (ENG.). 32p. (gr. 3-4). 30.65 (978-0-7368-6479-4(2), Graphic Library) Capstone Press of Coughlan Cos.

Roberts, Russell. Sally Field. l.t. ed. 2003. (Billboard Biography Ser.). (Illus.). 32p. (J). (gr. 3-8). lib. bdg. 25.70 (978-1-58415-183-8(8)) Mitchell Lane Pubs., Inc.

Robson, David. Chris Rock. 2010. (Modern Role Models Ser.). (Illus.). 64p. (YA). (gr. 7-12). 22.95 (978-1-4222-0506-8(1)) Mason Crest.

—Miley Cyrus. 2010. (Role Model Entertainers Ser.). (Illus.). 64p. (YA). (gr. 7-12). 22.95 (978-1-4222-0501-3(0)) Mason Crest.

Roensch, Greg. Bruce Lee. (Martial Arts Masters Ser.). 112p. 2009. (gr. 5-5). 63.90 (978-1-61514-371-9(8)) 2005. (Illus.). (YA). (gr. 7-12). lib. bdg. 34.60 (978-0-8239-3515-4(9)) Rosen Publishing Group, Inc., The.

Roza, Autumn & Roza, Greg. Miranda Cosgrove. 2010. (Today's Superstars Ser.). (ENG.). 48p. (J). (gr. 5-8). pap. 14.05 (978-1-4339-3999-0(1)); lib. bdg. 31.95 (978-1-4339-3998-3(3)) Stevens, Gareth Publishing LLLP.

Rueda, Marty. Emma Stone. 2013. 32p. (J). (gr. 3-6). 25.25 (978-1-4339-8973-5(5)); pap. 10.50 (978-1-4339-8974-2(3)); pap. 63.00 (978-1-4339-8975-9(1)) Stevens, Gareth Publishing LLLP.

Rutherford, Lucy. Demi Lovato & Selena Gomez: The Complete Unofficial Story of the BFFs. 2009. (ENG., Illus.). 104p. (J). (gr. 4-7). pap. (978-1-55022-901-1(X)) Filmer Ltd.

Salamoff, Paul. The Cast of Doctor Who. 2012. (ENG., Illus.). 40p. pap. 7.99 (978-1-4507-8451-1(8)) Bluewater Productions, Inc.

Sandler, Michael. The Rock. 2012. (Wrestling's Tough Guys Ser.). 24p. (J). (gr. 1-6). lib. bdg. 23.93 (978-1-61772-574-6(9)) Bearport Publishing Co., Inc.

Sapet, Kerrily. Salma Hayek. (Transcending Race in America Ser.). 64p. (YA). (gr. 5-18). 2010. (Illus.). lib. bdg. 22.95 (978-1-4222-1616-3(0)) 2009. pap. 9.95 (978-1-4222-1630-9(6)) Mason Crest.

Schulte, Mary. Eva Longoria. (Sharing the American Dream Ser.). 64p. (YA). (gr. 7-12). 2009. 22.95 (978-1-4222-0595-2(9)) 2007. pap. 9.95 (978-1-4222-0754-3(4)) Mason Crest.

Schuman, Michael. Margaret Cho: Comedian, Actress, & Activist. 2016. (Influential Asians Ser.). 128p. (J). (gr. 7-6). 37.27 (978-0-7660-7904-5(X)) Enslow Pubs., Inc.

—Will Smith: A Biography of Rapper Turned Movie Star. 2013. (African-American Icons Ser.). 104p. (J). (gr. 6-12). 27.94 (978-0-7660-3994-0(3)) Enslow Pubs., Inc.

Schuman, Michael A. Adam Sandler: Celebrity with Heart. 2010. (Celebrities with Heart Ser.). (Illus.). 128p. (J). pap. 10.95 (978-1-59845-202-0(9)); (gr. 7-12). 33.27 (978-0-7660-3402-0(X)) Enslow Pubs., Inc.

—Angelina Jolie: Celebrity with Heart. 2010. (Celebrities with Heart Ser.). (Illus.). 128p. (J). pap. 10.95 (978-1-59845-203-7(7)); (gr. 7-12). 33.27 (978-0-7660-3403-7(8)) Enslow Pubs., Inc.

—Emma! Amazing Actress Emma Stone. 2013. (Sizzling Celebrities Ser.). 48p. (J). lib. bdg. 25.27 (978-0-7660-4113-4(1)); (gr. 4-9). pap. 8.95 (978-1-4644-0175-6(6)) Enslow Pubs., Inc.

—Halle Berry: A Biography of an Oscar-Winning Actress. 2013. (African-American Icons Ser.). 104p. (J). (gr. 6-12). pap. 10.95 (978-1-59845-396-6(3)) Enslow Pubs., Inc.

—Robert Pattinson: Shining Star. 2011. (Hot Celebrity Biographies Ser.). (Illus.). 48p. (J). (gr. 5-18). pap. 8.95 (978-1-59845-284-6(3)); lib. bdg. 25.27 (978-0-7660-3872-1(6)) Enslow Pubs., Inc.

—Scarlett Johansson: Hollywood Superstar. 2011. (People to Know Today Ser.). (Illus.). 112p. (J). (gr. 7-12). lib. bdg. 33.27 (978-0-7660-3556-0(5)) Enslow Pubs., Inc.

—Will Smith: A Biography of a Rapper Turned Movie Star. 2013. (African-American Icons Ser.). 104p. (J). (gr. 6-12). pap. 10.95 (978-1-59845-397-3(1)) Enslow Pubs., Inc.

—Will Smith: I Like Blending a Message with Comedy. 2006. (African-American Biography Library). (Illus.). 128p. (J). (gr. 6). lib. bdg. 33.27 (978-0-7660-2465-6(2), 1250489) Enslow Pubs., Inc.

Schwaeber, Barbie. Grand Old Flag. Nussbaum, Ben, ed. Pamintuan, Macky & Wang, Qi, illus. 2006. (Smithsonian American Favorites Ser.). (ENG.). 32p. (J). (gr. -1-3). 9.85 (978-1-59249-650-1(4)) Soundprints.

Schwaeber, Barbie H. Grand Old Flag. Nussbaum, Ben, ed. Wang, Qi, illus. 2006. (Smithsonian American Favorites Ser.). (ENG.). 32p. (J). (gr. 3-7). 14.95 (978-1-59249-649-5(0)) Soundprints.

Schwartz, Heather. Ariana Grande: From Actress to Chart-Topping Singer. 2014. (Pop Culture Bios Ser.). (ENG., Illus.). 32p. (gr. 3-6). pap. 7.95 (978-1-4677-4544-4(8)) Lerner Publishing Group.

—Maia Mitchell: Talent from down Under. 2014. (Pop Culture Bios Ser.). (ENG., Illus.). 32p. (gr. 3-6). pap. 7.95 (978-1-4677-4546-8(4)) Lerner Publishing Group.

—Zendaya: Capturing the Stage, Screen, & Modeling Scene. 2014. (Pop Culture Bios Ser.). (ENG., Illus.). 32p. (gr. 3-6). pap. 7.95 (978-1-4677-4548-2(0)) Lerner Publishing Group.

Schwartz, Heather E. Ariana Grande: From Actress to Chart-Topping Singer. 2014. (Pop Culture Bios Ser.). (ENG.). 32p. (gr. 3-6). lib. bdg. 26.60 (978-1-4677-3669-5(4), Lerner Pubns.) Lerner Publishing Group.

—Emma Stone: Star of the Stage, TV, & Film. 2014. (Pop Culture Bios Ser.). (ENG., Illus.). 32p. (gr. 3-6). pap. 7.95 (978-1-4677-2374-9(6)); lib. bdg. 26.60 (978-1-4677-1440-2(2), Lerner Pubns.) Lerner Publishing Group.

—Idina Menzel: Vocal Superpower. 2015. (Pop Culture Bios Ser.). (ENG., Illus.). 32p. (gr. 3-6). pap. 7.95 (978-1-4677-6102-4(8), Lerner Pubns.) Lerner Publishing Group.

—Jaden Smith: Actor, Rapper, & Activist. 2014. (Pop Culture Bios Ser.). (ENG., Illus.). 32p. (gr. 3-6). lib. bdg. 26.60 (978-1-4677-1441-9(0), Lerner Pubns.) Lerner Publishing Group.

—Maia Mitchell: Talent from down Under. 2014. (Pop Culture Bios Ser.). (ENG., Illus.). 32p. (J). (gr. 3-6). lib. bdg. 26.60 (978-1-4677-3672-5(4), Lerner Pubns.) Lerner Publishing Group.

—Miranda Cosgrove. 2012. (Star Biographies Ser.). (ENG.). 32p. (gr. 3-4). pap. 47.70 (978-1-4296-9459-9(9), Snap Bks.) Capstone Press of Coughlan Cos.

—Rebel Wilson: From Stand-Up Laughs to Box-Office Smash. 2014. (Pop Culture Bios Ser.). (ENG., Illus.). 32p. (gr. 3-6). lib. bdg. 26.60 (978-1-4677-1443-3(7), Lerner Pubns.) Lerner Publishing Group.

—Selena Gomez. 2012. (Star Biographies Ser.). (ENG.). 32p. (gr. 3-4). pap. 47.70 (978-1-4296-9465-0(3)); (Illus.). lib. bdg. 27.99 (978-1-4296-4761-8(2)) Capstone Press of Coughlan Cos. (Snap Bks.).

—Shailene Woodley: Divergent's Daring Star. 2015. (Pop Culture Bios Ser.). (ENG., Illus.). 32p. (J). (gr. 3-6). pap. 7.95 (978-1-4677-6097-3(8)); lib. bdg. 26.60 (978-1-4677-5714-0(4)) Lerner Publishing Group. (Lerner Pubns.).

—Zendaya: Capturing the Stage, Screen, & Modeling Scene. 2014. (Pop Culture Bios Ser.). (ENG., Illus.). 32p. (J). (gr. 3-6). lib. bdg. 26.60 (978-1-4677-3673-2(2), Lerner Pubns.) Lerner Publishing Group.

Schwartz, Heather E., et al. Star Biographies. 2012. (Star Biographies Ser.). (ENG.). 32p. (gr. 3-4). pap. 381.60 (978-1-4296-9471-1(8), Snap Bks.) Capstone Press of Coughlan Cos.

Seba, Jaime. Ellen DeGeneres: From Comedy Club to Talk Show. 2012. (Illus.). 64p. (J). pap. (978-1-4222-2308-6(6)); (gr. 7-8). 22.95 (978-1-4222-2297-3(7)) Mason Crest.

Sexton, Colleen A. Arnold Schwarzenegger. 2005. (A&E Biography Ser.). (Illus.). 112p. (J). (gr. 6-12). 29.27 (978-0-8225-1634-7(9)); (ENG & SPA., pap. 7.95 (978-0-8225-5328-1(7)) Lerner Publishing Group.

Shaffer, Jody Jensen. Demi Lovato: Taking Another Chance. 2013. (Pop Culture Bios Ser.). (ENG., Illus.). 32p. (gr. 3-6). pap. 7.95 (978-1-4677-1551-5(4)); lib. bdg. 26.60 (978-1-4677-1310-8(4), Lerner Pubns.) Lerner Publishing Group.

—Josh Hutcherson: The Hunger Games' Hot Hero. 2013. (Pop Culture Bios Ser.). (ENG., Illus.). 32p. (gr. 3-6). pap. 7.95 (978-1-4677-0882-1(8)); lib. bdg. 26.60 (978-1-4677-0744-2(9), Lerner Pubns.) Lerner Publishing Group.

—Lea Michele. 2012. (Stars of Today Ser.). (ENG., Illus.). 32p. (J). (gr. 2-5). 28.50 (978-1-61473-294-5(9), 205045) Child's World, Inc., The.

—Liam Hemsworth. 2013. (Pop Culture Bios Ser.). (ENG., Illus.). 32p. (gr. 3-6). lib. bdg. 26.60 (978-1-4677-0742-8(2), Lerner Pubns.) Lerner Publishing Group.

—Liam Hemsworth: The Hunger Games' Strong Survivor. 2013. (Pop Culture Bios Ser.). (ENG., Illus.). 32p. (gr. 3-6). pap. 7.95 (978-1-4677-0883-8(6)) Lerner Publishing Group.

—Taylor Lautner. 2012. (Stars of Today Ser.). (ENG.). 32p. (J). (gr. 2-5). 28.50 (978-1-61473-296-9(5), 205047) Child's World, Inc., The.

—Victoria Justice: Television's It Girl. 2013. (Pop Culture Bios Ser.). (ENG., Illus.). 32p. (gr. 3-6). pap. 7.95 (978-1-4677-1550-8(6)); lib. bdg. 26.60 (978-1-4677-1309-2(0), Lerner Pubns.) Lerner Publishing Group.

Shea, Abigail. Victoria Justice. 2013. (Rising Stars Ser.). 32p. (J). (gr. 3-6). pap. 10.50 (978-1-4339-8990-2(5)); (ENG., Illus.). lib. bdg. 25.25 (978-1-4339-8989-6(1)) Stevens, Gareth Publishing LLLP.

Shea, Therese. Sharks. 2006. (Big Bad Biters Ser.). (Illus.). 24p. (J). (gr. 3-7). lib. bdg. 22.60 (978-1-4042-3519-9(1)) Rosen Publishing Group, Inc., The.

Sherrard, Valerie. Vanessa Hudgens. 2010. (Superstars! Ser.). (ENG., Illus.). 32p. (J). pap. (978-0-7787-7262-0(4)); (gr. 3-6). lib. bdg. (978-0-7787-7253-8(5)) Crabtree Publishing Co.

Shofner, Melissa Rae & Friedman, Lauri S. Tina Fey: Queen of Comedy. 2017. (People in the News Ser.). 104p. (YA). (gr. 7-7). lib. bdg. 39.40 **(978-1-5345-6033-8(5)**, Lucent Pr.) Greenhaven Publishing LLC.

Sjonger, Rebecca. Shailene Woodley. 2015. (ENG., Illus.). 32p. (J). (978-0-7787-8081-6(3)) Crabtree Publishing Co.

Slavicek, Louise Chipley. Paul Robeson. 2011. (Black Americans of Achievement Legacy Edition Ser.). 120p. (YA). (gr. 6-12). 35.00 (978-1-60413-843-6(2)) Facts On File, Inc.

Smith, Terri Smith. Jessica Simpson. 2004. (J). pap. (978-1-932724-25-7(7), Bios for Kids) Panda Publishing, L.L.C.

Snyder, Gail. Jake Gyllenhaal. 2007. (Popular Culture: A View from the Paparazzi Ser.). (Illus.). 64p. (YA). (gr. 3-7). pap. 7.95 (978-1-4222-0357-6(3)) Mason Crest.

—Queen Latifah. 2008. (Hip-Hop Ser.). (Illus.). 64p. (YA). (gr. 7-12). lib. bdg. 22.95 (978-1-4222-0126-8(0)) Mason Crest.

Sonneborn, Liz. Fantasia Barrino. 2009. (Who's Your Idol? Ser.). 48p. (gr. 5-5). 53.00 (978-1-60854-787-6(6), Rosen Reference) Rosen Publishing Group, Inc., The.

Spence, Kelly. Emma Stone. 2015. (ENG., Illus.). 32p. (J). (978-0-7787-8078-6(3)) Crabtree Publishing Co.

Spencer, Liv. The Miranda Cosgrove & iCarly Spectacular! Unofficial & Unstoppable. 2010. (ENG., Illus.). 142p. (J). (gr. 4-7). pap. (978-1-55022-929-5(X)) Filmer Ltd.

Spielman, Gloria. Marcel Marceau: Master of Mime. Gauthier, Manon, illus. 2011. (Kar-Ben Biographies Ser.). (ENG.). 32p. (J). (gr. 3-5). pap. 7.95 (978-0-7613-3962-5(0)); lib. bdg. 17.95 (978-0-7613-3961-8(2)) Lerner Publishing Group. (Kar-Ben Publishing).

Stewart, Gail B. Jennifer Lawrence. 2015. (People in the News Ser.). (ENG., Illus.). 128p. (gr. 7-10). 39.40 (978-1-4205-1223-6(4), Lucent Bks.) Cengage Gale.

Stone, Amy. Jim Carrey. 2007. (Today's Superstars). (Illus.). 32p. (gr. 5-8). lib. bdg. 31.95 (978-0-8368-8197-4(4)) Stevens, Gareth Publishing LLLP.

Summers, Kimberly Dillon. Miley Cyrus: A Biography, 1 vol. 2009. (Greenwood Biographies Ser.). 156p. (C). 39.00 (978-0-313-37847-8(9), GR7847, Greenwood) ABC-CLIO, LLC.

Szumski, Bonnie. Angelina Jolie. Greenhaven Press Staff, ed. 2013. (People in the News Ser.). (ENG., Illus.). 128p. (gr. 7-10). lib. bdg. 39.40 (978-1-4205-0750-8(8), Lucent Bks.) Cengage Gale.

Tagliaferro, Linda. Bruce Lee. (Biography Ser.). (Illus.). 112p. (gr. 6-12). 2005. lib. bdg. 27.93 (978-0-8225-4948-2(4)) 2003. (YA). pap. 7.95 (978-0-8225-9688-2(1), Carolrhoda Bks.) Lerner Publishing Group.

Taliadoros, Jenny, ed. Doris Day Paper Dolls. 2007. (ENG., Illus.). 16p. pap. 12.00 (978-0-9790668-4-9(0)) Paper Studio Pr.

Thomas, William. Movie Stunt Worker. 2010. (Benchmark Rockets: Dirty & Dangerous Jobs Ser.). 32p. (J). (gr. 3-6). 28.50 (978-1-60870-172-8(7)) Marshall Cavendish Corp.

Tieck, Sarah. Abigail Breslin: Famous Actress, 1 vol. 2009. (Big Buddy Biographies Set 2 Ser.). (ENG., Illus.). 32p. (J). (gr. 2-5). 28.50 (978-1-60453-547-1(4)) ABDO Publishing Co.

—American Idol Host & Judges, 1 vol. 2010. (Big Buddy Biographies Set 4 Ser.). (ENG.). 32p. (J). (gr. 2-5). 28.50 (978-1-60453-969-1(0)) ABDO Publishing Co.

—Ariana Grande: Famous Actress & Singer, 1 vol. 2014. (Big Buddy Biographies Set 12 Ser.). (ENG.). 32p. (J). (gr. 2-5). 28.50 (978-1-62403-568-5(X)) ABDO Publishing Co.

—Chris Colfer: Star of Glee, 1 vol. 2013. (Big Buddy Biographies Set 10 Ser.). (ENG.). 32p. (J). (gr. 2-5). lib. bdg. 28.50 (978-1-61783-857-6(8), Big Buddy Bks.) ABDO Publishing Co.

—Dakota Fanning: Talented Actress, 1 vol. 2010. (Big Buddy Biographies Set 4 Ser.). (ENG.). 32p. (J). (gr. 2-5). 28.50 (978-1-60453-971-4(2)) ABDO Publishing Co.

—Daniel Radcliffe: Harry Potter Star, 1 vol. 2010. (Big Buddy Biographies Set 4 Ser.). (ENG.). 32p. (J). (gr. 2-5). 28.50 (978-1-60453-973-8(9)) ABDO Publishing Co.

—Debby Ryan: Disney TV Star, 1 vol. 2014. (Big Buddy Biographies Set 12 Ser.). (ENG.). 32p. (gr. 2-5). 28.50 (978-1-62403-572-2(8)) ABDO Publishing Co.

—Demi Lovato: Talented Actress & Singer, 1 vol. 2009. (Big Buddy Biographies Set 3 Ser.). (ENG., Illus.). 32p. (J). (gr. 2-5). 28.50 (978-1-60453-711-6(6)) ABDO Publishing Co.

—Drake Bell & Josh Peck: Famous Actors, 1 vol. 2009. (Big Buddy Biographies Set 2 Ser.). (ENG., Illus.). 32p. (J). (gr. 2-5). 28.50 (978-1-60453-546-4(6)) ABDO Publishing Co.

—Emma Stone: Talented Actress, 1 vol. 2013. (Big Buddy Biographies Set 10 Ser.). (ENG.). 32p. (J). (gr. 2-5). lib. bdg. 28.50 (978-1-61783-861-3(6), Big Buddy Bks.) ABDO Publishing Co.

—Emma Watson: Harry Potter Star, 1 vol. 2010. (Big Buddy Biographies Set 4 Ser.). (ENG.). 32p. (J). (gr. 2-5). 28.50 (978-1-60453-974-5(7)) ABDO Publishing Co.

—Jennifer Lawrence: Star of the Hunger Games, 1 vol. 2013. (Big Buddy Biographies Set 9 Ser.). (ENG.). 32p. (J). (gr. 2-5). lib. bdg. 28.50 (978-1-61783-751-7(2), Big Buddy Bks.) ABDO Publishing Co.

—Jennifer Lopez: Famous Entertainer, 1 vol. 2012. (Big Buddy Biographies Ser.). (ENG.). 32p. (J). (gr. 2-5). 28.50 (978-1-61783-225-3(1)) ABDO Publishing Co.

—Johnny Depp: Famous Actor, 1 vol. 2009. (Big Buddy Biographies Set 3 Ser.). (ENG., Illus.). 32p. (J). (gr. 2-5). 28.50 (978-1-60453-707-9(8)) ABDO Publishing Co.

—Kristen Stewart: Twilight Star, 1 vol. 2010. (Big Buddy Bks.). (ENG.). 32p. (J). (gr. 2-5). 28.50 (978-1-61613-977-3(3)) ABDO Publishing Co.

—Kyle Massey: Talented Entertainer, 1 vol. 2011. (Big Buddy Biographies Set 7 Ser.). (ENG., Illus.). 32p. (J). (gr. 2-5). 28.50 (978-1-61783-019-8(4)) ABDO Publishing Co.

—Laura Marano: Famous Actress & Singer, 1 vol. 2014. (Big Buddy Biographies Set 12 Ser.). (ENG.). 32p. (gr. 2-5). 28.50 *(978-1-62403-570-8(1))* ABDO Publishing Co.

—Lea Michele: Star of Glee, 1 vol. 2011. (Big Buddy Biographies Set 6 Ser.). (ENG., Illus.). 32p. (J). (gr. 2-5). 28.50 *(978-1-61714-706-7(0))* ABDO Publishing Co.

—Liam Hemsworth: Star of the Hunger Games, 1 vol. 2013. (Big Buddy Biographies Set 9 Ser.). (ENG.). 32p. (J). (gr. 2-5). lib. bdg. 28.50 *(978-1-61783-749-4(0)*, Big Buddy Bks.) ABDO Publishing Co.

—Miley Cyrus: Singer/Actress/ Star of Hannah Montana, 1 vol. 2008. (Big Buddy Biographies Ser.). (ENG.). 32p. (J). (gr. 2-5). 28.50 *(978-1-60453-119-0(3))* ABDO Publishing Co.

—Miley Cyrus CD & Book. 2010. (Big Buddy Biographies CD+Book Ser.). 32p. (gr. 2-5). audio compact disk 57.00 *(978-1-61613-306-1(6)*, Big Buddy Bks.) ABDO Publishing Co.

—Miley Cyrus Site CD & Book. 2010. (Big Buddy Biographies Site CD+Book Ser.). 32p. (gr. 2-5). cd-rom 85.57 *(978-1-61613-278-1(7)*, Big Buddy Bks.) ABDO Publishing Co.

—Miranda Cosgrove: Famous Actress & Singer, 1 vol. 2010. (Big Buddy Biographies Set 4 Ser.). (ENG.). 32p. (J). (gr. 2-5). 28.50 *(978-1-60453-970-7(4))* ABDO Publishing Co.

—Robert Downey Jr. Star of Iron Man, 1 vol. 2014. (Big Buddy Biographies Set 11 Ser.). (ENG., Illus.). 32p. (gr. 2-5). lib. bdg. 28.50 *(978-1-62403-197-7(8)*, Big Buddy Bks.) ABDO Publishing Co.

—Robert Pattinson: Twilight Star, 1 vol. 2010. (Big Buddy Biographies Set 4 Ser.). (ENG., Illus.). 32p. (J). (gr. 2-5). 28.50 *(978-1-60453-972-1(0)*, 1307642) ABDO Publishing Co.

—Selena Gomez: Star of Wizards of Waverly Place, 1 vol. 2009. (Big Buddy Biographies Set 2 Ser.). (ENG., Illus.). 32p. (J). (gr. 2-5). 28.50 *(978-1-60453-548-8(2))* ABDO Publishing Co.

—Shia Labeouf: Movie Star, 1 vol. 2008. (Big Buddy Biographies Ser.). (ENG.). 32p. (J). (gr. 2-5). 28.50 *(978-1-60453-123-7(1))* ABDO Publishing Co.

—Taylor Lautner: Star of Twilight, 1 vol. 2011. (Big Buddy Biographies Set 6 Ser.). (ENG., Illus.). 32p. (J). (gr. 2-5). 28.50 *(978-1-61714-704-3(4))* ABDO Publishing Co.

—Vanessa Hudgens: High School Musical Star, 1 vol. 2008. (Big Buddy Biographies Ser.). (ENG.). 32p. (J). (gr. 2-5). 28.50 *(978-1-60453-121-3(5))* ABDO Publishing Co.

—Victoria Justice: Famous Actress & Singer, 1 vol. 2013. (Big Buddy Biographies Set 9 Ser.). (ENG.). 32p. (J). (gr. 2-5). lib. bdg. 28.50 *(978-1-61783-750-0(4)*, Big Buddy Bks.) ABDO Publishing Co.

—Zac Efron: High School Musical Star, 1 vol. 2008. (Big Buddy Biographies Ser.). (ENG.). 32p. (J). (gr. 2-5). 28.50 *(978-1-60453-120-6(7))* ABDO Publishing Co.

—Zac Efron CD & Book. 2010. (Big Buddy Biographies CD+Book Ser.). 32p. (gr. 2-5). audio compact disk 57.00 *(978-1-61613-307-8(4)*, Big Buddy Bks.) ABDO Publishing Co.

—Zac Efron Site CD & Book. 2010. (Big Buddy Biographies Site CD+Book Ser.). 32p. (gr. 2-5). cd-rom 85.57 *(978-1-61613-279-8(5)*, Big Buddy Bks.) ABDO Publishing Co.

Todd, Anne M. Jamie Foxx. 2008. (Black Americans of Achievement Ser.). (Illus.). 112p. (gr. 6-12). 35.00 *(978-1-60413-000-3(8)*, Chelsea Hse.) Facts On File, Inc.

Toler, Pamela D. Matt Damon. (Role Model Entertainers Ser.). 64p. (J). (gr. 7). 2012. 22.95 *(978-1-4222-2718-3(9))* 2010. (Illus.). 22.95 *(978-1-4222-0502-0(9))* Mason Crest.

Torres, Jennifer. Ashton Kutcher. 2005. (Blue Banner Biography Ser.). (Illus.). 32p. (J). (gr. 4-8). lib. bdg. 25.70 *(978-1-58415-380-1(6))* Mitchell Lane Pubs., Inc.

—Kate Hudson. 2005. (Blue Banner Biography Ser.). (Illus.). 32p. (J). (gr. 3-8). lib. bdg. 25.70 *(978-1-58415-381-8(4))* Mitchell Lane Pubs., Inc.

—Paris Hilton. 2005. (Blue Banner Biography Ser.). (Illus.). 32p. (J). (gr. 4-8). lib. bdg. 25.70 *(978-1-58415-382-5(2))* Mitchell Lane Pubs., Inc.

—Selena Gomez: Pop Singer & Actress. 2015. (Influential Latinos Ser.). (ENG., Illus.). 128p. (J). (gr. 7-7). 37.27 *(978-0-7660-6999-2(0))* Enslow Pubs., Inc.

Tougas, Shelley. Girls Star! Amazing Tales of Hollywood's Leading Ladies, 1 vol. 2014. (Girls Rock! Ser.). (ENG.). 64p. (gr. 4-5). lib. bdg. 34.65 *(978-1-4765-4057-3(8))* Capstone Press of Coughlan Cos.

Tracy, Kathleen. Aly & AJ. 2007. (Robbie Reader Ser.). (Illus.). 32p. (YA). (gr. 2-5). lib. bdg. 25.70 *(978-1-58415-595-9(7))* Mitchell Lane Pubs., Inc.

—Demi Lovato. 2009. (Robbie Reader Ser.). (Illus.). 32p. (YA). (gr. 2-5). lib. bdg. 25.70 *(978-1-58415-754-0(2))* Mitchell Lane Pubs., Inc.

—Emma Watson. 2010. (Robbie Reader Ser.). (Illus.). 32p. (YA). (gr. 2-5). lib. bdg. 25.70 *(978-1-58415-901-8(4))* Mitchell Lane Pubs., Inc.

—Johnny Depp. 2007. (Blue Banner Biography Ser.). (Illus.). 32p. (J). (gr. 4-7). lib. bdg. 25.70 *(978-1-58415-614-7(7))* Mitchell Lane Pubs., Inc.

—Justin Berfield. 2005. (Blue Banner Biography Ser.). (Illus.). 32p. (J). (gr. 3-8). lib. bdg. 25.70 *(978-1-58415-392-4(X))* Mitchell Lane Pubs., Inc.

—Lindsay Lohan. 2005. (Blue Banner Biography Ser.). (Illus.). 32p. (J). (gr. 3-8). lib. bdg. 25.70 *(978-1-58415-393-1(8))* Mitchell Lane Pubs., Inc.

—Mary-Kate & Ashley Olsen. l.t. ed. 2003. (Blue Banner Biography Ser.). (Illus.). 32p. (J). (gr. 3-8). lib. bdg. 25.70 *(978-1-58415-256-9(7))* Mitchell Lane Pubs., Inc.

—Megan Fox. 2010. (Blue Banner Biography Ser.). (Illus.). 32p. (YA). (gr. 4-7). lib. bdg. 25.70 *(978-1-58415-912-4(X))* Mitchell Lane Pubs., Inc.

—Zac Efron. 2007. (Blue Banner Biography Ser.). (Illus.). 32p. (YA). (gr. 4-7). lib. bdg. 25.70 *(978-1-58415-618-5(X))* Mitchell Lane Pubs., Inc.

Triumph Books Staff. Jennifer Lawrence: Burning Bright. 2013. (ENG.). 96p. (YA). (gr. 7). pap. 9.99 *(978-1-60078-907-6(2))* Triumph Bks.

—Lindsay Lohan: Rising Star. 2004. (Illus.). 80p. (J). 9.95 *(978-1-57243-689-3(1))* Triumph Bks.

Tucker, Rosalyn. Ronald Reagan, 1 vol. 2014. (Presidential Biographies Ser.). (ENG.). 24p. (gr. k-1). lib. bdg. 26.65 *(978-1-4765-9613-6(1)*, Pebble Plus) Capstone Press of Coughlan Cos.

Turnbull, Stephanie. An Actor. 2016. (How to Be... Ser.). 24p. (gr. 2-6). 28.50 *(978-1-62588-364-3(1)*, Smart Apple Media) Black Rabbit Bks.

Uschan, Michael V. Jet Li. 2011. (People in the News Ser.). (ENG., Illus.). 128p. (gr. 7-10). lib. bdg. 39.40 *(978-1-4205-0731-7(1))* Cengage Gale.

Uschan, Michael V., ed. Tyler Perry. 2010. (People in the News Ser.). (ENG.). 96p. (YA). (gr. 7-12). 33.95 *(978-1-4205-0309-8(X))* Cengage Gale.

Uschan, Michael V. & Juettner, Bonnie. Will Smith. 2009. (People in the News Ser.). (ENG., Illus.). 128p. (gr. 7-12). lib. bdg. 39.40 *(978-1-4205-0130-8(5)*, LML02109-245444) Cengage Gale.

Valliant, Regina. Judy Garland Cut-Out Dolls. Valliant, Regina & Lunzer, Lee, illus. 2007. (ENG.). 16p. pap. 12.00 *(978-0-9790668-9-4(1))* Paper Studio Pr.

Vaughan, Jenny. Selena Gomez - Teen Stars. 2013. (Illus.). 32p. (J). 28.50 *(978-1-59771-417-4(8))* Sea-To-Sea Pubns.

Vescia, Monique. Zachary Quinto, 1 vol. 2015. (ENG.). 112p. (YA). 35.60 *(978-1-4777-7893-7(4)*, Rosen Young Adult) Rosen Publishing Group, Inc., The.

Victoria Justice. 2013. (Rising Stars Ser.). 32p. (J). (gr. 3-6). pap. 63.00 *(978-1-4339-8991-9(3))* Stevens, Gareth Publishing LLLP.

Watson, Stephanie. Amy Poehler. Greenhaven Press Editors, ed. 2013. (People in the News Ser.). (ENG., Illus.). 128p. (gr. 7-10). lib. bdg. 39.40 *(978-1-4205-0883-3(0)*, Lucent Bks.) Cengage Gale.

—Daniel Radcliffe: Film & Stage Star. 2009. (Hot Celebrity Biographies Ser.). (Illus.). 48p. (J). (gr. 5-9). lib. bdg. 25.27 *(978-0-7660-3209-5(4))* Enslow Pubs., Inc.

—Heath Ledger: Talented Actor, 1 vol. 2010. (Lives Cut Short Set 1 Ser.). (ENG.). 112p. (J). (gr. 6-12). lib. bdg. 35.64 *(978-1-60453-789-5(2))* ABDO Publishing Co.

—Robert Downey Jr: Blockbuster Movie Star, 1 vol. 2012. (Contemporary Lives Set 1 Ser.). (ENG., Illus.). 112p. (J). (gr. 6-12). lib. bdg. 35.64 *(978-1-61783-322-9(3))* ABDO Publishing Co.

Weber, Terri Smith. Frankie Muniz: Enjoying His Success. 2004. (J). pap. *(978-1-932724-27-1(3))*; lib. bdg. *(978-1-932724-26-4(5))* Panda Publishing, L.L.C. (Bios for Kids).

—Hilary Duff: Branching Out. 2003. (J). pap. *(978-1-932724-03-5(6))*; lib. bdg. *(978-1-932724-02-8(8)*, Bios for Kids) Panda Publishing, L.L.C.

—Jennifer Lopez: Realizando Los Suenos. 2003. (SPA.). (J). pap. *(978-0-9740180-4-1(X))*; lib. bdg. *(978-0-9740180-3-4(1))* Panda Publishing, L.L.C. (Bios for Kids).

—Jessica Simpson. 2004. (J). lib. bdg. *(978-1-932724-24-0(9)*, Bios for Kids) Panda Publishing, L.L.C.

Westen, Robin. Oprah Winfrey: A Biography of a Billionaire Talk Show Host. 2013. (African-American Icons Ser.). 104p. (J). (gr. 6-12). pap. 10.95 *(978-1-59845-394-2(7))* Enslow Pubs., Inc.

—Oprah Winfrey: I Don't Believe in Failure. 2005. (African-American Biography Library). (Illus.). 128p. (J). (gr. 6-12). lib. bdg. 33.27 *(978-0-7660-2462-5(8))* Enslow Pubs., Inc.

Wheeler, Jill C. Brad Pitt. 2003. (Star Tracks Ser.). (Illus.). 64p. (YA). (gr. 4-7). 27.07 *(978-1-57765-769-9(1))* ABDO Publishing Co.

—Denzel Washington. 2003. (Star Tracks Ser.). (Illus.). 64p. (J). (gr. 3-8). lib. bdg. 27.07 *(978-1-57765-772-9(1))* ABDO Publishing Co.

—Jennifer Lopez. 2003. (Star Tracks Ser.). (Illus.). 64p. (J). (gr. 3-8). lib. bdg. 27.07 *(978-1-57765-770-5(5))* ABDO Publishing Co.

—Madonna. 2003. (Star Tracks Ser.). (Illus.). 64p. (gr. 3-8). 27.07 *(978-1-57765-768-2(3)*, Abdo & Daughters) ABDO Publishing Co.

—Mel Gibson. 2003. (Star Tracks Ser.). (Illus.). 64p. (gr. 3-8). 27.07 *(978-1-57765-767-5(5)*, Abdo & Daughters) ABDO Publishing Co.

Whiting, Jim. Hilary Duff. (Pop Culture Ser.). (Illus.). 64p. (YA). (gr. 3-7). 2008. lib. bdg. 22.95 *(978-1-4222-0201-2(1))* 2007. pap. 7.95 *(978-1-4222-0355-2(7))* Mason Crest.

Will Smith: Actor. 2nd rev. ed. 2010. (Black Americans of Achievement Legacy Edition Ser.). (Illus.). 104p. (gr. 6-12). 35.00 *(978-1-60413-713-2(4))* Facts On File, Inc.

Williams, Mel. Robert Pattinson: Fated for Fame. 2009. (ENG.). 48p. (YA). pap. 9.99 *(978-1-4169-8997-4(8)*, Simon Pulse) Simon Pulse.

—Stars in the Arena: Meet the Hotties of the Hunger Games. 2012. (ENG.). 48p. (YA). (gr. 7). pap. 9.99 *(978-1-4424-5363-0(X)*, Simon Pulse) Simon Pulse.

—Taylor Lautner: Overnight Sizzlin' Sensation. 2009. (ENG.). 48p. (YA). pap. 9.99 *(978-1-4424-0368-0(3)*, Simon Pulse) Simon Pulse.

Williams, Zella. America Fererra: Award-Winning Actress. 2010. (Hispanic Headliners Ser.). (ENG.). 24p. (J). pap. 8.25 *(978-1-4488-1478-7(2))*; lib. bdg. 22.60 *(978-1-4488-1473-2(1))* Rosen Publishing Group, Inc., The. (PowerKids Pr.).

—America Fererra: Award-Winning Actress = Estrella de la Pantalla. 2010. (Hispanic Headliners / Hispanos en Las Noticias Ser.). (ENG & SPA.). 24p. (J). (gr. 2-5). lib. bdg. 22.60 *(978-1-4488-0713-0(1))* Rosen Publishing Group, Inc., The.

—Selena Gomez: Actress & Singer. 2010. (Hispanic Headliners Ser.). (ENG.). 24p. (J). pap. 8.25 *(978-1-4488-1482-4(0))*; lib. bdg. 22.60 *(978-1-4488-1458-9(8))* Rosen Publishing Group, Inc., The. (PowerKids Pr.).

—Selena Gomez: Actress & Singer - Actriz y Cantante. 2010. (Hispanic Headliners / Hispanos en Las Noticias Ser.). (ENG & SPA.). 24p. (J). (gr. 2-5). lib. bdg. 22.60 *(978-1-4488-0715-4(8))* Rosen Publishing Group, Inc., The.

Wine, Bill. Johnny Depp. 2009. (Sharing the American Dream Ser.). (Illus.). 64p. (YA). (gr. 7-12). 22.95 *(978-1-4222-0593-8(2))* Mason Crest.

—Salma Hayek. (Sharing the American Dream Ser.). 64p. (YA). (gr. 7-12). 2009. (Illus.). 22.95 *(978-1-4222-0585-3(1))* 2007. pap. 9.95 *(978-1-4222-0748-2(X))* Mason Crest.

Woog, Adam. Jennifer Lopez. 2008. (Great Hispanic Heritage Ser.). (Illus.). 117p. (gr. 6-12). lib. bdg. 35.00 *(978-0-7910-9724-3(2)*, Chelsea Hse.) Facts On File, Inc.

—Oprah Winfrey. 2009. (People in the News Ser.). (ENG., Illus.). 128p. (gr. 7-12). lib. bdg. 39.40 *(978-1-4205-0128-5(3)*, LML02109-245442) Cengage Gale.

Wooten, Sara McIntosh. Denzel Washington: Academy Award-Winning Actor. 2003. (African-American Biographies Ser.). (Illus.). 128p. (J). lib. bdg. 26.60 *(978-0-7660-2131-0(9))* Enslow Pubs., Inc.

Worth, Richard. Eva Longoria: Actress, Activist, & Entrepreneur. 2015. (Influential Latinos Ser.). (ENG., Illus.). 128p. (J). (gr. 7-7). 37.27 *(978-0-7660-6993-0(1))* Enslow Pubs., Inc.

Wright, David K. The Life of Paul Robeson: Actor, Singer, Political Activist. 2014. (Legendary African Americans Ser.). 96p. (J). (gr. 6-12). 27.94 *(978-0-7660-6157-6(4))*; (Illus.). pap. 10.95 *(978-0-7660-6158-3(2))* Enslow Pubs., Inc.

Wukovits, John, ed. George Clooney. 2013. (People in the News Ser.). (ENG., Illus.). 128p. (gr. 7-10). lib. bdg. 33.95 *(978-1-4205-0927-4(6)*, Lucent Bks.) Cengage Gale.

Wybomy, Sheila. Dwayne Johnson. 2009. (People in the News Ser.). (ENG., Illus.). 128p. (YA). (gr. 7-12). lib. bdg. 33.95 *(978-1-4205-0125-4(9)*, LML02109-245439) Cengage Gale.

Yasuda, Anita. Kristen Stewart. 2010. (Remarkable People Ser.). (Illus.). 24p. (J). (gr. 4-6). pap. 11.95 *(978-1-61690-164-6(0))*; lib. bdg. 25.70 *(978-1-61690-163-9(2))* Weigl Pubs., Inc.

—Miranda Cosgrove. 2011. (J). (gr. 4-6). pap. 12.95 *(978-1-61690-673-3(1)*, AV2 by Weigl); (Illus.). 24p. (YA). (gr. 3-6). 27.13 *(978-1-61690-668-9(5))* Weigl Pubs., Inc.

—Robert Pattinson. 2010. (Remarkable People Ser.). (Illus.). 24p. (J). (gr. 4-6). pap. 11.95 *(978-1-61690-155-4(1))*; lib. bdg. 25.70 *(978-1-61690-154-7(3))* Weigl Pubs., Inc.

—Taylor Lautner. 2010. (Remarkable People Ser.). (Illus.). 24p. (J). (gr. 4-6). pap. 11.95 *(978-1-61690-161-5(6))*; lib. bdg. 25.70 *(978-1-61690-160-8(8))* Weigl Pubs., Inc.

Yoo, Paula & Wang, Lin. Shining Star: The Anna May Wong Story. (ENG., Illus.). 32p. (J). (gr. 1-4). 2016. pap. 9.95 *(978-1-62014-257-8(0))* 2009. 17.95 *(978-1-60060-259-7(2))* Lee & Low Bks., Inc.

Young, Jeff C. Arnold Schwarzenegger. 2007. (Political Profiles Ser.). (Illus.). 112p. (YA). (gr. 5-9). 27.95 *(978-1-59935-050-9(5))* Reynolds, Morgan Inc.

Zannos, Susan. Ron Howard. l.t. ed. 2003. (Billboard Biography Ser.). (Illus.). 32p. (J). (gr. 3-8). lib. bdg. 25.70 *(978-1-58415-185-2(4))* Mitchell Lane Pubs., Inc.

ACTORS AND ACTRESSES—FICTION

Ain, Beth. Starring Jules (Third Grade Debut) (Starring Jules Ser.: 4). (ENG.). 176p. (J). (gr. 2-5). 2015. pap. 5.99 *(978-0-545-44359-3(8))* 2014. 14.99 *(978-0-545-44358-6(X))* Scholastic, Inc. (Scholastic Pr.).

Alger, Horatio. Five Hundred Dollars: Or: Jacob Marlowe's Secret. 2007. (ENG.). 192p. per. 19.99 *(978-1-4346-5063-4(4))*; 206p. per. 22.99 *(978-1-4346-5064-1(2))* Creative Media Partners, LLC.

Andrews, Julie & Hamilton, Emma Walton. The Great American Mousical. Walton, Tony, illus. 2006. (Julie Andrews Collection). (J). (gr. k-4). 160p. 15.99 *(978-0-06-057918-0(8)*, Julie Andrews Collection); 147p. lib. bdg. 16.89 *(978-0-06-057919-7(6))* HarperCollins Pubs.

Bentley, Sue. Star of the Show, 4 vols. Swan, Angela & Farley, Andrew, illus. 2009. (Magic Puppy Ser.: 4). (ENG.). 128p. (J). (gr. 1-3). pap. 5.99 *(978-0-448-45047-6(X)*, Grosset & Dunlap) Penguin Young Readers Group.

Blackwood, Gary. Shakespeare's Spy. 2005. 281p. (gr. 5-9). 17.00 *(978-0-7569-5216-7(6))* Perfection Learning Corp.

Blackwood, Gary L. Shakespeare's Spy. 2005. (ENG.). 288p. (J). (gr. 3-7). 6.99 *(978-0-14-240311-2(3)*, Puffin Books) Penguin Young Readers Group.

Block, Francesca Lia. Psyche in a Dress. 2008. (ENG.). 128p. (YA). (gr. 9). pap. 8.99 *(978-0-06-076376-3(0)*, HarperTeen) HarperCollins Pubs.

Blumenthal, Deborah. Charlie Hits It Big. Brunkus, Denise, illus. 2008. 32p. (J). (gr. -1). lib. bdg. 17.89 *(978-0-06-056354-7(0))* HarperCollins Pubs.

Bradman, Tony. Final Cut. 2004. (Illus.). 87p. *(978-0-439-79597-5(4))* Scholastic, Inc.

Brown, Merry. Gold Manor Ghost House. 2013. 328p. pap. 13.99 *(978-0-615-79766-3(0))* YA Bks.

Cabot, Meg. Teen Idol. 2005. (ENG., Illus.). 320p. (YA). (gr. 8-18). reprint ed. pap. 9.99 *(978-0-06-009618-2(7)*, HarperTeen) HarperCollins Pubs.

—Teen Idol. 2005. 291p. (YA). 16.65 *(978-0-7569-5735-3(4))* Perfection Learning Corp.

Calonita, Jen. Family Affairs. 2009. (Secrets of My Hollywood Life Ser.: 3). (ENG.). 352p. (YA). (gr. 7-17). pap. 7.99 *(978-0-316-11800-2(1)*, Poppy) Little, Brown Bks. for Young Readers.

—On Location. 2008. (Secrets of My Hollywood Life Ser.: 2). (ENG.). 256p. (YA). (gr. 7-17). per. 7.99 *(978-0-316-15440-6(7)*, Poppy) Little, Brown Bks. for Young Readers.

—Secrets of My Hollywood Life. 2007. (Secrets of My Hollywood Life Ser.: 1). (ENG.). 256p. (J). (gr. 7-17). per. 19.99 *(978-0-316-15443-7(1)*, Poppy) Little, Brown Bks. for Young Readers.

Cocks, Heather & Morgan, Jessica. Messy. 2013. (ENG.). 368p. (YA). (gr. 7-17). pap. 9.00 *(978-0-316-09828-1(0)*, Poppy) Little, Brown Bks. for Young Readers.

Coleman, Rowan. Film Star. 2011. (ENG., Illus.). 320p. (J). (gr. 6-9). pap. 11.99 *(978-0-00-719039-3(5))* HarperCollins Pubs. Ltd. GBR. Dist: HarperCollins Pubs.

—Hollywood Star. 2011. (ENG.). 320p. (J). (gr. 6-9). pap. 11.99 *(978-0-00-724433-1(9))* HarperCollins Pubs. Ltd. GBR. Dist: HarperCollins Pubs.

—Musical Star. 2011. (ENG., Illus.). 256p. (J). (gr. 6-9). pap. 9.99 *(978-0-00-724434-8(7))* HarperCollins Pubs. Ltd. GBR. Dist: HarperCollins Pubs.

—Shooting Star. 2011. (ENG.). 256p. (J). (gr. 6-9). pap. 9.99 *(978-0-00-725812-3(7))* HarperCollins Pubs. Ltd. GBR. Dist: HarperCollins Pubs.

—Soap Star. 2011. (ENG., Illus.). 240p. (J). pap. 9.99 *(978-0-00-724401-0(0)*, HarperCollins Children's Bks.) HarperCollins Pubs. Ltd. GBR. Dist: HarperCollins Pubs.

Colfer, Chris. Stranger Than Fanfiction. 2017. (ENG.). (J). 304p. (gr. 10-17). 18.99 *(978-0-316-38344-8(9))*; 432p. (gr. 9-17). 20.99 *(978-0-316-39678-3(8))* Little, Brown Bks. for Young Readers.

Conford, Ellen. Annabel the Actress Starring in Camping It Up. Andriani, Renee W., illus. 2005. (Annabel the Actress Ser.). 60p. (J). (gr. 2-5). 11.65 *(978-0-7569-5555-7(6))* Perfection Learning Corp.

—Annabel the Actress Starring in Camping It Up. Andriani, Renee W., illus. 2013. (ENG.). 64p. (J). (gr. 2-5). pap. 13.99 *(978-1-4814-0147-0(5)*, Simon & Schuster Bks. For Young Readers) Simon & Schuster Bks. For Young Readers.

—Annabel the Actress Starring in Just a Little Extra. Andriani, Renee W., illus. 2013. (ENG.). 64p. (J). (gr. 4-6). pap. 13.99 *(978-1-4814-0148-7(3)*, Simon & Schuster Bks. For Young Readers) Simon & Schuster Bks. For Young Readers.

—Annabel the Actress Starring in the Hound of the Barkervilles. Andriani, Renee W., illus. 2004. (Annabel the Actress Ser.). 83p. (gr. 2-5). 14.00 *(978-0-7569-2180-4(5))* Perfection Learning Corp.

Cooke, Marjorie Benton. Bambi. 2004. reprint ed. pap. 27.95 *(978-1-4191-0885-3(9))*; pap. 1.99 *(978-1-4192-0885-0(3))* Kessinger Publishing, LLC.

Costain, Meredith. Stella & the Movie Star. McGowan, Shane, illus. 2015. (Legends in Their Own Lunchbox Ser.). (ENG.). 56p. (gr. 2-3). pap. 7.99 *(978-1-4966-0261-9(7)*, Legends in Their Own Lunchbox) Capstone Classroom.

Cray, Jordan. Shiver. 2009. (Danger. com Ser.: 9). (ENG.). 224p. (YA). (gr. 7). pap. 10.99 *(978-1-4169-9853-2(5)*, Simon Pulse) Simon Pulse.

Culbertson, Kim. Catch a Falling Star. 2014. (ENG.). 304p. (J). (gr. 7). 17.99 *(978-0-545-62704-7(4)*, Scholastic Pr.) Scholastic, Inc.

Cusick, Richie Tankersley. Starstruck. 2013. (ENG., Illus.). 240p. (YA). (gr. 7). pap. 15.99 *(978-1-4814-0161-6(0)*, Simon Pulse) Simon Pulse.

DPWW, ed. High School Musical Actors' Biography. 2007. (J). (gr. 2-7). pap. 6.99 *(978-1-4231-0827-6(2))* Disney Pr.

Finnegan, Amy. Not in the Script. 2014. (If Only... Ser.). (ENG.). 392p. (YA). (gr. 7). 17.99 *(978-1-61963-397-1(3)*, 9781619633971, Bloomsbury USA Childrens) Bloomsbury Publishing USA.

Fisher, Linda C. A Will of Her Own. 2006. (YA). pap. *(978-0-88092-641-6(4))*; lib. bdg. *(978-0-88092-640-9(6))* Royal Fireworks Publishing Co.

Forman, Gayle. Just One Day. 2013. (ENG.). (YA). (gr. 9). 416p. pap. 10.99 *(978-0-14-242295-3(9)*, Speak); 384p. 17.99 *(978-0-525-42591-5(8)*, Dutton Books for Young Readers) Penguin Young Readers Group.

—Just One Day. 2013. lib. bdg. 22.10 *(978-0-606-34405-0(5)*, Turtleback) Turtleback Bks.

—Just One Year. 2013. (ENG.). 336p. (YA). (gr. 9). 17.99 *(978-0-525-42592-2(6)*, Dutton Books for Young Readers) Penguin Young Readers Group.

Gentry, Brad. The Hollywood Princess. 2009. 40p. pap. 20.99 *(978-1-4490-3545-7(0))* AuthorHouse.

Green, Tim. Pinch Hit. (ENG.). (J). (gr. 3-7). 2013. 336p. pap. 6.99 *(978-0-06-201247-0(9))* 2012. 320p. 16.99 *(978-0-06-201246-3(0))* HarperCollins Pubs.

Gutman, Dan. Johnny Hangtime. 2016. 160p. (J). (gr. 3-7). pap. 5.99 *(978-0-06-238574-1(7))* HarperCollins Pubs.

Haddix, Margaret Peterson. Claim to Fame. (ENG.). 272p. (YA). (gr. 7). 2010. pap. 9.99 *(978-1-4169-3918-4(0))* 2009. 16.99 *(978-1-4169-3917-7(2))* Simon & Schuster Bks. For Young Readers. (Simon & Schuster Bks. For Young Readers).

Hantz, Sara. Will the Real Abi Saunders Please Stand Up? 2014. (Entangled Teen Ser.). (ENG.). 320p. (YA). (gr. 7-12). pap. 9.99 *(978-1-62266-262-3(8)*, 9781622662623) Entangled Publishing, LLC.

Hartinger, Brent. Split Screen: Attack of the Soul-Sucking Brain Zombies; Bride of the Soul-Sucking Brain Zombies. 2007. 304p. (YA). (gr. 9-12). lib. bdg. 17.89 *(978-0-06-082409-9(3)*, HarperTeen) HarperCollins Pubs.

Henry, O. One Thousand Dollars & Other Plays, Level 2. Oxford University Press Staff & West, Clare, eds. 2nd ed. 2008. (ENG., Illus.). 64p. 9.38 *(978-0-19-423520-4(3))* Oxford Univ. Pr., Inc.

Henson, Heather. Here's How I See It — Here's How It Is. 2010. (ENG., Illus.). 304p. (J). (gr. 5-9). pap. 6.99 *(978-1-4169-9773-3(3)*, Atheneum Bks. for Young Readers) Simon & Schuster Children's Publishing.

Herzog, Kenny. Phil Pickle. Canby, Kelly, illus. 2016. (J). *(978-1-4413-1933-3(6))* Peter Pauper Pr. Inc.

Hope, Laura Lee. Moving Picture Girls under the Palms. 2006. 26.95 *(978-1-4218-2980-7(0))*; pap. 11.95 *(978-1-4218-3080-3(9))* 1st World Publishing, Inc.

Howie, Betsy. Unscripted by Lainey McBride. Lowery, Mike, illus. 2012. 183p. (J). *(978-0-545-39705-6(7))* Scholastic, Inc.

Howland, Leila. The Forget-Me-Not Summer. Kim, Ji-Hyuk, illus. 2015. (Silver Sisters Ser.: 1). (ENG.). 352p. (J). (gr. 3-7). 16.99 *(978-0-06-231869-5(1))* HarperCollins Pubs.

Howland, Leila. Hello, Sunshine. 2017. (ENG.). 368p. (YA). (gr. 9-17). 17.99 ***(978-1-4847-2545-0(X))*** Hyperion Bks. for Children.

John, Antony. Imposter. 2015. (ENG.). 320p. (YA). (gr. 7). 17.99 *(978-0-8037-4124-9(3)*, Dial Bks) Penguin Young Readers Group.

Johnson, Maureen. Scarlett Fever. (ENG.). 352p. (J). (gr. 7-7). 2011. pap. 9.99 *(978-0-545-09633-1(2))* 2010. 16.99 *(978-0-439-89928-4(1))* Scholastic, Inc.

—Suite Scarlett. 2009. (ENG.). 368p. (J). (gr. 3-7). 8.99 *(978-0-545-09632-4(4))* Scholastic, Inc.

Keenan-Bolger, Andrew, et al. Jack & Louisa - Act 1. Webster, Kyle T., illus. 2015. (Jack & Louisa Ser.: 1). (ENG.). 240p. (J). (gr. 3-7). bds. 16.99 *(978-0-448-47839-5(0)*, Grosset & Dunlap) Penguin Young Readers Group.

Kennedy, Emma. The Case of the Putrid Poison, 2 vols. Marc, Sylvain & Dorman, Brandon, illus. 2011. (Wilma Tenderfoot Ser.: 2). (ENG.). 336p. (J). (gr. 3-7). 16.99 *(978-0-8037-3541-5(3)*, Dial Bks) Penguin Young Readers Group.

King, Trey. Mystery on the Lego Express. Wang, Sean, illus. 2014. (Lego City Ser.). (ENG.). 24p. (J). (gr. -1-3). 3.99 *(978-0-545-60366-9(8))* Scholastic, Inc.

Klise, Kate. Hollywood, Dead Ahead. Klise, M. Sarah, illus. (43 Old Cemetery Road Ser.: 5). (ENG.). 144p. (J). (gr. 2-5). 2014. pap. 6.99 *(978-0-544-33661-2(5)*, HMH Books For

Young Readers) 2013. 15.99 *(978-0-547-85283-6(5))* Houghton Mifflin Harcourt Publishing Co.

Krishnaswami, Uma. The Grand Plan to Fix Everything. Halpin, Abigail, illus. (ENG.). (J). (gr. 3-7). 2013. 288p. pap. 8.99 *(978-1-4169-9590-6(0))* 2011. 272p. 16.99 *(978-1-4169-9589-0(7))* Simon & Schuster Children's Publishing. (Atheneum Bks. for Young Readers).

—The Problem with Being Slightly Heroic. Halpin, Abigail, illus. (ENG.). 288p. (J). (gr. 3-7). 2014. pap. 6.99 *(978-1-4424-2329-9(3)*, Atheneum Bks. for Young Readers) 2013. 16.99 *(978-1-4424-2328-2(5))* Simon & Schuster Children's Publishing.

Krulik, Nancy. Quiet on the Set! John and Wendy Staff, illus. 10th ed. 2003. (Katie Kazoo, Switcheroo Ser.: 10). (ENG.). 80p. (J). (gr. 2-4). pap. 4.99 *(978-0-448-43214-4(5)*, Grosset & Dunlap) Penguin Young Readers Group.

Lazebnik, Claire. The Trouble with Flirting. 2013. (ENG.). 336p. (YA). (gr. 8). pap. 9.99 *(978-0-06-192127-8(0)*, HarperTeen) HarperCollins Pubs.

Lee, Tanith. Piratica: Being a Daring Tale of a Singular Girl's Adventure upon the High Seas. 2006. (ENG.). 304p. (YA). (gr. 7-18). per. 8.99 *(978-0-14-240644-1(9)*, Firebird) Penguin Young Readers Group.

Livingston, Lesley. Wondrous Strange. 2009. (Wondrous Strange Trilogy Ser.: 1). (ENG.). 352p. (YA). (gr. 8). pap. 9.99 *(978-0-06-157539-6(9)*, HarperTeen) HarperCollins Pubs.

Lockhart, E. Dramarama. 2007. (ENG.). 320p. (YA). 24.80 *(978-1-4287-4612-1(9))* Hyperion Pr.

Loewen, Nancy. No Lie, I Acted Like a Beast! The Story of Beauty & the Beast As Told by the Beast, 1 vol. Bernardini, Cristian, illus. 2013. (Other Side of the Story Ser.). (ENG.). 24p. (gr. 2-3). pap. 6.95 *(978-1-4048-8083-2(6))*; lib. bdg. 27.32 *(978-1-4048-7938-6(2))* Picture Window Bks.

Lombardo, Constance. Stunt Cat to the Stars. Lombardo, Constance, illus. 2015. (Mr. Puffball Ser.: 1). (ENG., Illus.). 240p. (J). (gr. 3-7). 12.99 *(978-0-06-232065-0(3))* HarperCollins Pubs.

Macauley, Jo. Inferno, 1 vol. 2014. (Secrets & Spies Ser.). (ENG.). 224p. (gr. 4-7). 26.65 *(978-1-4342-9595-8(8))* Stone Arch Bks.

—New World, 1 vol. 2014. (Secrets & Spies Ser.). (ENG.). 224p. (gr. 4-7). 26.65 *(978-1-4342-9596-5(6))* Stone Arch Bks.

—Plague. 2014. 221p. (J). *(978-1-4342-7945-3(6)*, Capstone Bks.) Capstone Press of Coughlan Cos.

—Plague, 1 vol. 2014. (Secrets & Spies Ser.). (ENG.). 224p. (gr. 4-7). 26.65 *(978-1-4342-7947-7(2))* Stone Arch Bks.

—Treason. 2014. (J). pap. *(978-1-4342-7944-6(8))*; (ENG.). 224p. (gr. 4-7). 26.65 *(978-1-4342-7946-0(4))* Stone Arch Bks.

MacDonald, Bailey. The Secret of the Sealed Room: A Mystery of Young Benjamin Franklin. 2010. (ENG.). 224p. (J). (gr. 3-7). 17.99 *(978-1-4169-9760-3(1)*, Simon & Schuster/Paula Wiseman Bks.) Simon & Schuster/Paula Wiseman Bks.

Mantchev, Lisa. Eyes Like Stars. 2010. (Theatre Illuminata Ser.: 1). (ENG.). 384p. (YA). (gr. 7-12). pap. 11.99 *(978-0-312-60866-8(7)*, 9780312608668) Square Fish.

McDonald, Megan. Cloudy with a Chance of Boys. (Sisters Club Ser.: 3). (ENG., Illus.). 272p. (J). (gr. 3-7). 2012. pap. 5.99 *(978-0-7636-5577-8(5))* 2011. 15.99 *(978-0-7636-4615-8(6))* Candlewick Pr.

—The Sisters Club. 2008. (Sisters Club Ser.: 1). (ENG., Illus.). 208p. (J). (gr. 3-7). pap. 5.99 *(978-0-7636-3251-9(1))* Candlewick Pr.

—The Sisters Club. 2008. (Sisters Club Ser.: 1). lib. bdg. 16.00 *(978-1-4178-1785-6(2)*, Turtleback) Turtleback Bks.

Meyerhoff, Jenny. The Barftastic Life of Louie Burger. 2015. (J). lib. bdg. 17.20 *(978-0-606-37585-6(6))* Turtleback Bks.

Miller, Lauren. Parallel. 2013. (ENG.). 432p. (YA). (gr. 8). 17.99 *(978-0-06-219977-5(3)*, HarperTeen) HarperCollins Pubs.

Moldavsky, Goldy. No Good Deed. 2017. (ENG.). 352p. (J). (gr. 9). 17.99 ***(978-0-545-86751-1(7))*** Scholastic, Inc.

Montgomery, Lewis B. The Case of the Superstar Scam. Wummer, Amy, illus. 2013. (Milo & Jazz Mysteries (r) Ser.). 112p. (J). (gr. 2-5). 22.60 *(978-1-57565-518-5(7))*; (ENG.). pap. 6.95 *(978-1-57565-519-2(5))* Kane Press, Inc.

Morgan, Melissa J. Extra Credit. 2009. (Camp Confidential Ser.: 22). (ENG.). 160p. (J). (gr. 4-7). pap. 4.99 *(978-0-448-45216-6(2)*, Grosset & Dunlap) Penguin Young Readers Group.

Movie Menace. 2011. (Hardy Boys (All New) Undercover Brothers Ser.: 37). (ENG.). 176p. (J). (gr. 3-7). pap. 5.99 *(978-1-4424-0258-4(X)*, Aladdin) Simon & Schuster Children's Publishing.

Pasiadis, Vanessa. Don't Call Me Cookie. Lowenstein, Anna, illus. 2010. 178p. pap. 21.00 *(978-1-60911-470-1(1)*, Strategic Bk. Publishing) Strategic Book Publishing & Rights Agency (SBPRA).

Patterson, Nancy Ruth. A Simple Gift. 2009. 128p. (gr. 3-7). pap. 10.95 *(978-1-4401-1206-5(1))* iUniverse, Inc.

Peñaflor, Lygia Day. Unscripted Joss Byrd. 2016. (ENG.). 224p. (YA). 16.99 *(978-1-62672-369-6(9)*, 9781626723696) Roaring Brook Pr.

Pfeffer, Susan Beth. Revenge of the Aztecs. 2004. 118p. (J). lib. bdg. 16.92 *(978-1-4242-0763-3(0))* Fitzgerald Bks.

Pietsch, Nicole. Sideshow of Merit. 2013. 330p. 22.95 *(978-1-60898-163-2(0))*; pap. 11.95 *(978-1-60898-164-9(9))* namelos llc.

Reisfeld, Randi. Rehab. 2008. (ENG.). 256p. (YA). (gr. 9-18). pap. 8.99 *(978-1-4169-6121-5(6)*, Simon Pulse) Simon Pulse.

Rocheleau, Nicole. Ollie Ollie in Come Free! 2006. 76p. pap. 16.95 *(978-1-4241-0433-8(5))* PublishAmerica, Inc.

Rudnick, Paul. It's All Your Fault. (ENG.). 304p. (J). (gr. 9). 2017. pap. 10.99 *(978-0-545-46429-1(3))* 2016. 19.99 *(978-0-545-46428-4(5)*, Scholastic Pr.) Scholastic, Inc.

Ryals, Lexi. Liv & Maddie: Sisters Forever. 2015. (Liv & Maddie Junior Novel Ser.). (ENG., Illus.). 112p. (J). (gr. 3-7). pap. 5.99 *(978-1-4847-1079-1(7))* Disney Pr.

Scheunemann, Pam. Peacock Fan, 1 vol. Chawla, Neena, illus. 2007. (Critter Chronicles Ser.). (ENG.). 24p. (J). (gr. k-3). lib. bdg. 24.21 *(978-1-59928-460-6(X)*, SandCastle) ABDO Publishing Co.

Selznick, Brian. The Marvels. 2016. (CHI.). (J). ***(978-986-479-039-5(0))*** Commonwealth Publishing Co., Ltd.

—The Marvels. Selznick, Brian, illus. 2015. (ENG., Illus.). 672p. (J). (gr. 5-7). 32.99 *(978-0-545-44868-0(9)*, Scholastic Pr.) Scholastic, Inc.

Serle, Rebecca. Famous in Love. 2014. (ENG.). 336p. (YA). (gr. 7-17). 18.00 *(978-0-316-36632-8(3)*, Poppy) Little, Brown Bks. for Young Readers.

—Truly Madly Famously. 2015. (Famous in Love Ser.: 2). (ENG.). 320p. (YA). (gr. 7-17). 18.00 *(978-0-316-36640-3(4)*, Poppy) Little, Brown Bks. for Young Readers.

Shankman, Adam & Sullivan, Laura L. Murder among the Stars. 2017. (YA). pap. ***(978-1-4814-4791-1(2))***; (ENG., Illus.). 320p. (gr. 9). 17.99 ***(978-1-4814-4790-4(4))*** Simon & Schuster Children's Publishing. (Atheneum Bks. for Young Readers).

Sheldon, Dyan. Confessions of a Teenage Hollywood Star. 2007. (ENG., Illus.). 208p. (YA). (gr. 7-12). per. 7.99 *(978-0-7636-3408-7(5))* Candlewick Pr.

Shukert, Rachel. Starstruck. 2013. (ENG.). 352p. (YA). (gr. 7). 17.99 *(978-0-385-74108-8(1)*, Delacorte Pr.) Random Hse. Children's Bks.

Sones, Sonya. One of Those Hideous Books Where the Mother Dies. (ENG., (YA). (gr. 7). 2013. Illus.). 288p. pap. 9.99 *(978-1-4424-9383-4(6))* 2005. 272p. reprint ed. pap. 7.99 *(978-1-4169-0788-6(2))* Simon & Schuster Bks. For Young Readers. (Simon & Schuster Bks. For Young Readers).

Strasser, Todd. Famous. (ENG.). 272p. (YA). (gr. 7). 2013. pap. 9.99 *(978-1-4424-5418-7(0))* 2011. 15.99 *(978-1-4169-7511-3(X))* Simon & Schuster Bks. For Young Readers. (Simon & Schuster Bks. For Young Readers).

Van Draanen, Wendelin. Sammy Keyes & the Hollywood Mummy. 2008. (Sammy Keyes Ser.: Bk. 6). (J). 64.99 *(978-1-60640-641-0(8))* Findaway World, LLC.

Wasserman, Robin. Life, Starring Me! 2009. (Candy Apple Ser.). 182p. (J). *(978-0-545-19777-9(5))* Scholastic, Inc.

Zucker, Jonny. Stunt Girl. 2009. pap. 1.00 *(978-1-4074-4531-1(6))* Recorded Bks., Inc.

ADAGES

see Proverbs

ADAM (BIBLICAL FIGURE)

Frank, Penny. Adam & Eve. (Illus.). 24p. pap. 2.99 *(978-0-7459-4102-8(8)*, Lion Books) Lion Hudson PLC GBR. Dist: Trafalgar Square Publishing.

Pingry, Patricia A. The Story of Adam & Eve. Thornburgh, Rebecca, illus. 2003. (ENG.). 24p. (J). bds. 6.95 *(978-0-8249-4229-8(9)*, Ideal Pubns.) Worthy Publishing.

Priddy, Roger & Priddy Books Staff. Adam & Eve. 2012. (ENG., Illus.). 10p. (J). (gr. -1 — 1). bds. 4.95 *(978-0-312-51454-9(9)*, 9780312514549, Priddy Bks.) St. Martin's Pr.

Pulley, Kelly & Zondervan Staff. Adan y Eva en el Jardin, 1 vol. Pulley, Kelly, illus. 2009. (I Can Read! / the Beginner's Bible / ¡Yo Sé Leer! Ser.).Tr. of Adam & Eve in the Garden. (SPA & ENG., Illus.). 32p. (J). pap. 3.99 *(978-0-310-71892-5(9))* Zonderkidz.

Ray, Jane. Adam & Eve & the Garden of Eden. Ray, Jane, illus. 2005. (Illus.). 32p. (J). 17.00 *(978-0-8028-5278-6(5))* Eerdmans, William B. Publishing Co.

—Adam & Eve & the Garden of Eden. 2006. (Illus.). 32p. (J). pap. *(978-1-903919-07-1(X)*, Eden Project Books) Transworld Publishers Ltd.

Sasso, Sandy Eisenberg. Adam & Eve's First Sunset: God's New Day. Rothenberg, Joani Keller, illus. 2003. (ENG.). 32p. (gr. -1-3). 17.99 *(978-1-58023-177-0(2)*, 9781580231770, Jewish Lights Publishing) LongHill Partners, Inc.

—Adam & Eve's New Day. Rothenberg, Joani Keller, illus. 2006. (ENG.). 24p. (gr. -1). bds. 7.99 *(978-1-59473-205-8(1)*, 9781594732058, Skylight Paths Publishing) LongHill Partners, Inc.

Smart Kids Publishing Staff, creator. Adam & Eve: A Story about Making the Right Choices. 2006. (I Can Read the Bible Ser.). (ENG., Illus.). 12p. (J). (gr. -1-3). 14.95 *(978-0-8249-6660-7(0)*, Ideal Pubns.) Worthy Publishing.

Smith, Martina. La Historia de la Creacion: Un Relato de la Biblia Chispita. Grosshauser, Peter & Temple, Ed, illus. 2016. (SPA.). (J). *(978-1-5064-2100-1(8))* Augsburg Fortress, Pubs.

Suter, Janine. The Day the World Went Wacky. Gunther, Richard, illus. 2009. 32p. (J). 10.99 *(978-0-89051-575-4(1))* Master Bks.

Thompson, Timothy. Adam & Eve. 2013. 20p. pap. 24.95 *(978-1-63000-641-9(6))* America Star Bks.

Vitale, Raoul & Tank, Daniel, illus. Adam & Eve. 2005. (Family Bible Story Ser.). 93p. (J). pap. *(978-0-8280-1851-7(0))* Review & Herald Publishing Assn.

Wilson, N. D. The Dragon & the Garden. 2007. (Old Stories Ser.). (Illus.). 28p. (J). (gr. 3-7). 14.00 *(978-1-59128-044-6(3))* Canon Pr.

Zondervan Staff. Adam & Eve in the Garden, 1 vol. Pulley, Kelly, illus. 2008. (I Can Read! / the Beginner's Bible Ser.). (ENG.). 32p. (J). (gr. -1-1). pap. 3.99 *(978-0-310-71552-8(0))* Zonderkidz.

ADAMS, ABIGAIL, 1744-1818

Adler, David A. & Adler, Michael S. A Picture Book of John & Abigail Adams. Himler, Ronald, illus. 2010. (ENG.). 32p. (J). (gr. -1-3). 17.95 *(978-0-8234-2007-0(8))* Holiday Hse., Inc.

Ashby, Ruth. John & Abigail Adams. 2005. (Presidents & First Ladies Ser.). (Illus.). 48p. (gr. 5-12). lib. bdg. 31.00 *(978-0-8368-5755-9(0)*, World Almanac Library) Stevens, Gareth Publishing LLLP.

Belton, Blair. Abigail Adams in Her Own Words, Vol. 1. 2014. (Eyewitness to History Ser.). 32p. (J). (gr. 4-5). (ENG.). pap. 10.50 *(978-1-4339-9871-3(8))*; 26.60 *(978-1-4339-9870-6(X))* Stevens, Gareth Publishing LLLP.

Ching, Jacqueline. Abigail Adams: A Revolutionary Woman. 2009. (Library of American Lives & Times Ser.). 112p. (gr. 5-5). 69.20 *(978-1-60853-469-2(3))* Rosen Publishing Group, Inc., The.

Connell, Kate. Servant to Abigail Adams: The Early American Adventures of Hannah Cooper. 2004. (Illus.). 40p. (J). (gr. 4-8). pap. 7.00 *(978-0-7567-8216-0(3))* DIANE Publishing Co.

Connell, Kate & Feresten, Nancy. Servant to Abigail Adams: The Early Colonial Adventures of Hannah Cooper. 2003. (I Am American Ser.). (ENG., Illus.). 40p. (J). (gr. 3-7). pap. 6.99 *(978-0-7922-5828-5(2)*, National Geographic Children's Bks.) National Geographic Society.

Glass, Maya. Abigail Adams: Destacada Primera Dama. 2004. (Grandes personajes en la historia de los Estados Unidos Ser.). (SPA.). 32p. (gr. 5-8). pap. 10.00 *(978-0-8239-4218-3(X)*, Rosen Classroom) Rosen Publishing Group, Inc., The.

—Abigail Adams: Destacada Primera Dama (Abigail Adams: Famous First Lady) 2009. (Grandes personajes en la historia de los Estados Unidos (Famous People in American History) Ser.). (SPA.). 32p. (gr. 2-3). 47.90 *(978-1-61512-787-0(9)*, Editorial Buenas Letras) Rosen Publishing Group, Inc., The.

—Abigail Adams: Famous First Lady. (Primary Sources of Famous People in American History Ser.). 32p. 2009. (gr. 2-3). 47.90 *(978-1-60851-643-8(1))* 2004. (ENG., Illus.). (gr. 4-8). pap. 10.00 *(978-0-8239-4172-8(8))* Rosen Publishing Group, Inc., The.

—Abigail Adams: Famous First Lady / Destacada Primera Dama. 2009. (Famous People in American History/Grandes personajes en la historia de los Estados Unidos Ser.). (ENG & SPA.). 32p. (gr. 2-3). 47.90 *(978-1-61512-535-7(3)*, Editorial Buenas Letras) Rosen Publishing Group, Inc., The.

Hubbard-Brown, Janet. Abigail Adams: First Lady. 2009. (Women of Achievement Ser.). (Illus.). 128p. (gr. 6-12). 35.00 *(978-1-60413-491-9(7)*, Chelsea Hse.) Facts On File, Inc.

Kelley, True. Who Was Abigail Adams? O'brien, John, illus. 2014. (Who Was? Ser.). (ENG.). 112p. (J). (gr. 3-7). 5.99 *(978-0-448-47890-6(0)*, Grosset & Dunlap) Penguin Young Readers Group.

—Who Was Abigail Adams? 2014. (Who Was... ? Ser.). lib. bdg. 16.00 *(978-0-606-34166-0(8)*, Turtleback) Turtleback Bks.

Lakin, Patricia. Abigail Adams: First Lady of the American Revolution. Bandelin, Debra & Dacey, Bob, illus. 2006. 48p. (J). lib. bdg. 15.00 *(978-1-4242-1560-7(9))* Fitzgerald Bks.

—Abigail Adams: First Lady of the American Revolution. Dacey, Bob & Bandelin, Debra, illus. 2006. (Ready-To-read SOFA Ser.). (ENG.). 48p. (J). (gr. 1-3). pap. 3.99 *(978-0-689-87032-3(9)*, Simon Spotlight) Simon Spotlight.

Larkin, Tanya. What Was Cooking in Abigail Adams' White House? 2009. (Cooking Throughout American History Ser.). 24p. (gr. 3-3). 42.50 *(978-1-61511-949-3(3)*, PowerKids Pr.) Rosen Publishing Group, Inc., The.

Maloof, Torrey. Abigail Adams & the Women Who Shaped America. 2016. (Primary Source Readers Ser.). (Illus.). 32p. (J). (gr. 4-5). 8.99 *(978-1-4938-3080-0(5))* Teacher Created Materials, Inc.

Manera, Alexandria. Abigail Adams. 2003. (Women of the Revolution Ser.). (J). pap. *(978-1-58417-086-0(7))*; lib. bdg. *(978-1-58417-023-5(9))* Lake Street Pubs.

Marsh, Carole. Abigail Adams. 2004. 12p. (gr. k-4). 2.95 *(978-0-635-02372-8(5))* Gallopade International.

McPherson, Stephanie. My Dear Husband: Important Letters of Abigail Adams. 2009. (Great Moments in American History Ser.). 32p. (gr. 3-3). 47.90 *(978-1-61513-134-1(5))* Rosen Publishing Group, Inc., The.

Mulhall, Jill K. Abigail Adams, 1 vol. 2004. (Primary Source Readers Ser.). (ENG.). 24p. (J). (gr. 4-4). pap. 8.99 *(978-0-7439-8786-8(1))* Shell Educational Publishing.

Nelson, Maria. The Life of Abigail Adams. 2012. (Famous Lives Ser.). (ENG., Illus.). 24p. (J). (gr. k-3). lib. bdg. 22.60 *(978-1-4339-6337-7(X))*; (gr. 1-4). pap. 8.15 *(978-1-4339-6339-1(6))* Stevens, Gareth Publishing LLLP.

—The Life of Abigail Adams / la Vida de Abigail Adams. 2012. (Famous Lives / Vidas extraordinarias Ser.). (ENG & SPA., Illus.). 24p. (J). (gr. k-3). 22.60 *(978-1-4339-6649-1(2))* Stevens, Gareth Publishing LLLP.

Sabin, Francene & Macken, JoAnn Early. Abigail Adams: Young Patriot. Miyake, Yoshi, illus. 2007. 55p. (J). pap. *(978-0-439-88003-9(3))* Scholastic, Inc.

Sutcliffe, Jane. Abigail Adams. 2006. (History Maker Biographies Ser.). (ENG., Illus.). 48p. (gr. 3-6). lib. bdg. 27.93 *(978-0-8225-5942-9(0)*, Lerner Pubns.) Lerner Publishing Group.

Time for Kids Editors. Abigail Adams: Eyewitness to America's Birth. 2009. (Time for Kids Ser.). (ENG.). 48p. (J). (gr. 2-4). 15.99 *(978-0-06-057629-5(4))*; pap. 3.99 *(978-0-06-057628-8(6)*, Collins) HarperCollins Pubs.

Whiting, Jim. The Life & Times of Abigail Adams. 2007. (Profiles in American History Ser.). (Illus.). 48p. (J). (gr. 4-7). lib. bdg. 29.95 *(978-1-58415-527-0(2))* Mitchell Lane Pubs., Inc.

ADAMS, JOHN, 1735-1826

Adler, David A. & Adler, Michael S. A Picture Book of John & Abigail Adams. Himler, Ronald, illus. 2010. (ENG.). 32p. (J). (gr. -1-3). 17.95 *(978-0-8234-2007-0(8))* Holiday Hse., Inc.

Ashby, Ruth. John & Abigail Adams. 2005. (Presidents & First Ladies Ser.). (Illus.). 48p. (gr. 5-12). lib. bdg. 31.00 *(978-0-8368-5755-9(0)*, World Almanac Library) Stevens, Gareth Publishing LLLP.

Behrman, Carol H. John Adams. 2004. (Presidential Leaders Ser.). (Illus.). 112p. (J). 29.27 *(978-0-8225-0820-5(6)*, Lerner Pubns.) Lerner Publishing Group.

Ching, Jacqueline. Abigail Adams: A Revolutionary Woman. 2009. (Library of American Lives & Times Ser.). 112p. (gr. 5-5). 69.20 *(978-1-60853-469-2(3))* Rosen Publishing Group, Inc., The.

Collard, Sneed B., III. John Adams: Our Second President. 2006. (American Heroes Ser.). (Illus.). 48p. (gr. 3-7). 29.93 *(978-0-7614-2159-7(9)*, Benchmark Bks.) Marshall Cavendish Corp.

Combs, Maggie. How to Analyze the Works of John Adams, 1 vol. 2013. (Essential Critiques Set 4 Ser.). (ENG.). 112p. (J). (gr. 6-12). lib. bdg. 35.64 *(978-1-61783-646-6(X)*, Essential Library) ABDO Publishing Co.

Connell, Kate. Servant to Abigail Adams: The Early American Adventures of Hannah Cooper. 2004. (Illus.). 40p. (J). (gr. 4-8). pap. 7.00 *(978-0-7567-8216-0(3))* DIANE Publishing Co.

Connell, Kate, et al. The Spirit of a New Nation. 2007. (Avenues Ser.). (ENG., Illus.). 40p. (J). pap. 19.95 *(978-0-7922-8684-4(7))* CENGAGE Learning.

Crompton, Samuel Willard. John Adams: American Patriot. 2005. (Leaders of the American Revolution Ser.). (Illus.). 100p. (J). (gr. 5-8). lib. bdg. 30.00 *(978-0-7910-8620-9(8))* Facts On File, Inc.

Daly, Ruth. John Adams. 2015. (Padres Fundadores Ser.). (SPA.). (J). (gr. -1-3). lib. bdg. 27.13 *(978-1-4896-2799-5(5)*, AV2 by Weigl) Weigl Pubs., Inc.

Dunn, Joeming & Espinosa, Rod. John Adams: 2nd U. S. President, 1 vol. 2011. (Presidents of the United States Bio-Graphics Ser.). (ENG., Illus.). 32p. (YA). (gr. 3-6). 28.50 *(978-1-61641-644-7(0))* Magic Wagon.

Elston, Heidi M. D. John Adams, 1 vol. 2009. (United States Presidents Ser.). (ENG., Illus.). 40p. (YA). (gr. 3-6). 27.07 *(978-1-60453-439-9(7))* ABDO Publishing Co.

Gaines, Ann Graham. John Adams. 2008. (Presidents of the U. S. A. Ser.). (ENG., Illus.). 48p. (J). (gr. 3-6). 32.79 *(978-1-60253-031-7(9)*, 200670) Child's World, Inc., The.

Glass, Maya. Abigail Adams: Destacada Primera Dama. 2004. (Grandes personajes en la historia de los Estados Unidos Ser.). (SPA.). 32p. (gr. 5-8). pap. 10.00 *(978-0-8239-4218-3(X)*, Rosen Classroom) Rosen Publishing Group, Inc., The.

—Abigail Adams: Destacada Primera Dama (Abigail Adams: Famous First Lady) 2009. (Grandes personajes en la historia de los Estados Unidos (Famous People in American History) Ser.). (SPA.). 32p. (gr. 2-3). 47.90 *(978-1-61512-787-0(9)*, Editorial Buenas Letras) Rosen Publishing Group, Inc., The.

—Abigail Adams: Famous First Lady. (Primary Sources of Famous People in American History Ser.). 32p. 2009. (gr. 2-3). 47.90 *(978-1-60851-643-8(1))* 2004. (ENG., Illus.). (gr. 4-8). pap. 10.00 *(978-0-8239-4172-8(8))* Rosen Publishing Group, Inc., The.

—Abigail Adams: Famous First Lady / Destacada Primera Dama. 2009. (Famous People in American History/Grandes personajes en la historia de los Estados Unidos Ser.). (ENG & SPA.). 32p. (gr. 2-3). 47.90 *(978-1-61512-535-7(3)*, Editorial Buenas Letras) Rosen Publishing Group, Inc., The.

Gregory, Josh & Bose, Meenekshi. John Adams: The 2nd President. 2015. (First Look at America's Presidents Ser.). (ENG.). 24p. (J). (gr. -1-3). lib. bdg. 23.93 *(978-1-62724-558-6(8))* Bearport Publishing Co., Inc.

Gross, Miriam. John Adams: Patriot, Diplomat, & Statesman. 2009. (Library of American Lives & Times Ser.). 112p. (gr. 5-5). 69.20 *(978-1-60853-489-0(8))* Rosen Publishing Group, Inc., The.

Harness, Cheryl. The Revolutionary John Adams. (ENG., Illus.). 48p. (J). 2006. (gr. 2-4). per. 7.95 *(978-0-7922-5491-1(0))* 2003. (gr. 3-7). 17.95 *(978-0-7922-6970-0(5))* National Geographic Society. (National Geographic Children's Bks.).

Hubbard-Brown, Janet. Abigail Adams: First Lady. 2009. (Women of Achievement Ser.). (Illus.). 128p. (gr. 6-12). 35.00 *(978-1-60413-491-9(7)*, Chelsea Hse.) Facts On File, Inc.

Jeffrey, Gary. John Adams & the Boston Massacre. 2011. (Graphic Heroes of the American Revolution Ser.). (Illus.). 24p. (J). (gr. 3-6). lib. bdg. 23.95 *(978-1-4339-6016-1(8))*; pap. 8.15 *(978-1-4339-6017-8(6)*, Gareth Stevens Learning Library) Stevens, Gareth Publishing LLLP.

John Adams, 6 vols. (gr. 2-5). 36.95 *(978-0-7368-4560-1(7))* Red Brick Learning.

Jurmain, Suzanne Tripp. Worst of Friends: Thomas Jefferson, John Adams, & the True Story of an American Feud. Day, Larry, illus. 2011. (ENG.). 32p. (J). (gr. 1-3). 16.99 *(978-0-525-47903-1(1)*, Dutton Books for Young Readers) Penguin Young Readers Group.

Kelley, True. Who Was Abigail Adams? O'brien, John, illus. 2014. (Who Was? Ser.). (ENG.). 112p. (J). (gr. 3-7). 5.99 *(978-0-448-47890-6(0)*, Grosset & Dunlap) Penguin Young Readers Group.

—Who Was Abigail Adams? 2014. (Who Was... ? Ser.). lib. bdg. 16.00 *(978-0-606-34166-0(8)*, Turtleback) Turtleback Bks.

Kent, Zachary. John Adams: Creating a Nation. 2004. (America's Founding Fathers Ser.). (Illus.). 128p. (J). lib. bdg. 26.60 *(978-0-7660-2183-9(1))* Enslow Pubs., Inc.

Kerley, Barbara. Those Rebels, John & Tom. Fotheringham, Edwin, illus. 2012. (ENG.). 48p. (J). (gr. 2-5). 17.99 *(978-0-545-22268-6(0)*, Scholastic Pr.) Scholastic, Inc.

Lukes, Bonnie L. John Adams: Public Servant. 2004. (Notable Americans Ser.). (Illus.). 128p. (J). (gr. 6-12). 23.95 *(978-1-883846-80-0(3)*, First Biographies) Reynolds, Morgan Inc.

Lusted, Marcia Amidon. Revolution & the New Nation: 1750-Early 1800s. 2007. (Presidents of the United States Ser.). (Illus.). 48p. (J). (gr. 4-7). lib. bdg. 29.05 *(978-1-59036-739-1(1))*; per. 10.95 *(978-1-59036-740-7(5))* Weigl Pubs., Inc.

Mara, Wil. John Adams. 2008. (Presidents & Their Times Ser.). 96p. (gr. 6-18). lib. bdg. 34.21 *(978-0-7614-2840-4(2)*, Benchmark Bks.) Marshall Cavendish Corp.

Marcovitz, Hal. John Adams. 2004. (Childhoods of the Presidents Ser.). (Illus.). 48p. (J). (gr. 4-18). lib. bdg. 17.95 *(978-1-59084-268-3(5))* Mason Crest.

Marsh, Carole. John Adams. 2003. 12p. (gr. k-4). 2.95 *(978-0-635-02357-5(1))* Gallopade International.

McPherson, Stephanie. My Dear Husband: Important Letters of Abigail Adams. 2009. (Great Moments in American History Ser.). 32p. (gr. 3-3). 47.90 *(978-1-61513-134-1(5))* Rosen Publishing Group, Inc., The.

Miller, Chuck. John Adams. 2003. (America's Founders Ser.). (J). pap. *(978-1-58417-082-2(4))*; lib. bdg. *(978-1-58417-019-8(0))* Lake Street Pubs.

Randolph, Ryan P. How to Draw the Life & Times of John Adams. (Kid's Guide to Drawing the Presidents of the United States of America Ser.). 2009. 32p. (gr. 4-4). 50.50 *(978-1-61511-150-3(6)*, PowerKids Pr.) 2006. (YA). (gr. 2-5). 26.50 *(978-1-4042-2979-2(5))* Rosen Publishing Group, Inc., The.

Roxburgh, Ellis. Thomas Jefferson vs. John Adams: Founding Fathers & Political Rivals. 2016. (History's Greatest Rivals Ser.). (ENG., Illus.). 48p. (J). (gr. 6-8). pap. 14.05 *(978-1-4824-4239-7(6))* Stevens, Gareth Publishing LLLP.

Sutcliffe, Jane. John Adams. 2006. (History Maker Biographies Ser.). (ENG., Illus.). 48p. (gr. 3-6). lib. bdg. 27.93 *(978-0-8225-5940-5(4)*, Lerner Pubns.) Lerner Publishing Group.

Whiting, Jim. The Life & Times of John Adams. 2006. (Profiles in American History Ser.). (Illus.). 48p. (J). (gr. 3-7). lib. bdg. 29.95 *(978-1-58415-442-6(X))* Mitchell Lane Pubs., Inc.

ADAMS, JOHN, 1735-1826—FICTION

Gould, Jane H. John Adams. 2012. (Jr. Graphic Founding Fathers Ser.). (ENG., Illus.). 24p. (J). (gr. 3-6). pap. 10.60 *(978-1-4488-7993-9(0))*; lib. bdg. 25.25 *(978-1-4488-7899-4(3))* Rosen Publishing Group, Inc., The. (PowerKids Pr.).

Hopkinson, Deborah. John Adams Speaks for Freedom. Orback, Craig, illus. 2005. 32p. (J). lib. bdg. 15.00 *(978-1-59054-992-6(9))* Fitzgerald Bks.

Limbaugh, Rush H., III & Limbaugh, Kathryn Adams. Rush Revere & the Presidency. 2016. (Rush Revere Ser.: 5). (ENG., Illus.). 272p. (gr. 4-7). 19.99 *(978-1-5011-5689-2(6))*, Threshold Editions) Threshold Editions.

ADAMS, JOHN QUINCY, 1767-1848

Bailey, Diane & Nash, Philip. John Quincy Adams: The 6th President. 2016. (First Look at America's Presidents Ser.). (ENG.). 24p. (J). (gr. -1-3). lib. bdg. 17.95 *(978-1-944102-65-4(5))* Bearport Publishing Co., Inc.

Elish, Dan. John Quincy Adams. 2011. (Presidents & Their Times 5 Ser.). 96p. (gr. 6). 34.21 *(978-1-60870-182-7(4))* Marshall Cavendish Corp.

Elston, Heidi M. D. John Quincy Adams, 1 vol. 2009. (United States Presidents Ser.). (ENG., Illus.). 40p. (YA). (gr. 3-6). 27.07 *(978-1-60453-440-5(0))* ABDO Publishing Co.

Gherman, Beverly. First Son & President: A Story about John Quincy Adams. Bird, Matthew, illus. 2006. (Creative Minds Biographies Ser.). (ENG.). 64p. (gr. 4-8). pap. 8.95 *(978-0-8225-3091-6(0))* Lerner Publishing Group.

Levy, Debbie. John Quincy Adams. 2004. (Presidential Leaders Ser.). (Illus.). 112p. (J). (gr. 3-7). lib. bdg. 29.27 *(978-0-8225-0825-0(7))* Lerner Publishing Group.

Souter, Gerry & Souter, Janet. John Quincy Adams. 2008. (Presidents of the U. S. A. Ser.). (ENG., Illus.). 48p. (J). (gr. 3-6). 32.79 *(978-1-60253-035-5(1)*, 200674) Child's World, Inc., The.

Tecco, Betsy Dru. How to Draw the Life & Times of John Quincy Adams. (Kid's Guide to Drawing the Presidents of the United States of America Ser.). 2009. 32p. (gr. 4-4). 50.50 *(978-1-61511-152-7(2)*, PowerKids Pr.) 2006. (YA). (gr. 2-5). 26.50 *(978-1-4042-2983-9(3))* Rosen Publishing Group, Inc., The.

Venezia, Mike. John Quincy Adams: Sixth President, 1825-1829. Venezia, Mike, illus. 2005. (Getting to Know the U. S. Presidents Ser.). (ENG., Illus.). 32p. (J). (gr. 3-4). pap. 7.95 *(978-0-516-27480-5(5)*, Children's Pr.) Scholastic Library Publishing.

ADAMS, SAMUEL, 1722-1803

Adler, David A. & Adler, Michael S. A Picture Book of Sam Houston. Collins, Matt, illus. 2012. (ENG.). 32p. (J). (gr. -1-3). 17.95 *(978-0-8234-2369-9(7))* Holiday Hse., Inc.

—A Picture Book of Samuel Adams. Himler, Ronald, illus. 2005. (ENG.). 32p. (J). 16.95 *(978-0-8234-1846-6(4))* Holiday Hse., Inc.

Gibson, Karen Bush. Samuel Adams. 2006. (Profiles in American History Ser.). (Illus.). 48p. (J). (gr. 3-7). lib. bdg. 20.95 *(978-1-58415-440-2(3))* Mitchell Lane Pubs., Inc.

Heinrichs, Ann. Samuel Adams: Father of the Revolution. 2004. (Our People Ser.). (ENG., Illus.). 32p. (J). (gr. 3-6). 29.93 *(978-1-59296-177-1(0)*, 200653) Child's World, Inc., The.

Jeffrey, Gary. Samuel Adams & the Boston Tea Party. 2011. (Graphic Heroes of the American Revolution Ser.). 24p. (J). (gr. 3-6). lib. bdg. 23.95 *(978-1-4339-6022-2(2))*; pap. 8.15 *(978-1-4339-6023-9(0)*, Gareth Stevens Learning Library) Stevens, Gareth Publishing LLLP.

Marsh, Carole. Samuel Adams. 2003. 12p. (gr. k-4). 2.95 *(978-0-635-02367-4(9))* Gallopade International.

ADAMS FAMILY

Connell, Kate, et al. The Spirit of a New Nation. 2007. (Avenues Ser.). (ENG., Illus.). 40p. (J). pap. 19.95 *(978-0-7922-8684-4(7))* CENGAGE Learning.

ADAPTATION (BIOLOGY)

see also Human Beings—Effect of Environment on

Amstutz, Lisa J. Thorny Devil Lizards & Other Extreme Reptile Adaptations, 1 vol. 2014. (Extreme Adaptations Ser.). (ENG.). 32p. (gr. 3-4). lib. bdg. 27.32 *(978-1-4914-0168-2(0))* Capstone Press of Coughlan Cos.

Anderson, Sheila. What Can Live in a Lake? 2010. (First Step Nonfiction - Animal Adaptations Ser.). (ENG., Illus.). 24p. (J). (gr. k-2). lib. bdg. 23.93 *(978-0-7613-4573-2(6))* Lerner Publishing Group.

—What Can Live in the Mountains? 2010. (First Step Nonfiction - Animal Adaptations Ser.). (ENG., Illus.). 24p. (J). (gr. k-2). lib. bdg. 23.93 *(978-0-7613-4572-5(8))* Lerner Publishing Group.

—What Can Live in the Ocean? 2010. (First Step Nonfiction - Animal Adaptations Ser.). (ENG., Illus.). 24p. (J). (gr. k-2). lib. bdg. 23.93 *(978-0-7613-4569-5(8))* Lerner Publishing Group.

Beaumont, Holly. Why Do Snails & Other Animals Have Shells? 2015. (Animal Body Coverings Ser.). (ENG., Illus.). 24p. (gr. 1-3). 23.32 *(978-1-4846-2536-1(6))* Heinemann-Raintree.

Benchmark Education Company. Adaptation (Teacher Guide) 2005. *(978-1-4108-4676-1(8))* Benchmark Education Co.

Benchmark Education Company, LLC Staff, compiled by. Watery World & Animal Adaptations. 2005. spiral bd. 225.00 *(978-1-4108-5814-6(6))* Benchmark Education Co.

Bjorklund, Ruth. Migratory & Resident Birds Explained. 2016. (Distinctions in Nature Ser.). 32p. (J). pap. 10.58 *(978-1-5026-2169-6(X))* Cavendish Square Publishing.

Blake, Carly. Why Why Why... Do Fish Bite? 2010. (Why Why Why Ser.). 32p. (J). (gr. 1-3). lib. bdg. 18.95 *(978-1-4222-1585-2(7))* Mason Crest.

Brannon, Barbara. Discover Adaptation. 2005. (J). pap. *(978-1-4108-5122-2(2))* Benchmark Education Co.

Built to Survive: Animal Adaptations. 2007. (Illus.). 32p. (J). pap. *(978-0-545-04074-7(4))* Scholastic, Inc.

Capon, Brian. Plant Survival: Adapting to a Hostile World. Capon, Brian, illus. 2009. (ENG., Illus.). 144p. pap. 15.95 *(978-0-88192-287-5(0)*, 682287) Timber Pr., Inc.

Collins, Terry. Bigfoot & Adaptation, 1 vol. 2011. (Monster Science Ser.). (ENG.). 32p. (gr. 3-4). pap. 8.10 *(978-1-4296-7327-3(3))*; pap. 47.70 *(978-1-4296-7328-0(1))* Capstone Press of Coughlan Cos. (Graphic Library).

—Bigfoot & Adaptation, 1 vol. Mallea, Cristian, illus. 2011. (Monster Science Ser.). (ENG.). 32p. (gr. 3-4). lib. bdg. 30.65 *(978-1-4296-6579-7(3)*, Graphic Library) Capstone Press of Coughlan Cos.

Davies, Monika. Adaptations. 2015. (Science Readers: Content & Literacy Ser.). (ENG., Illus.). 32p. (gr. 4-4). pap. 8.99 *(978-1-4807-4679-4(7))* Teacher Created Materials, Inc.

Davies, Nicola. Extreme Animals: The Toughest Creatures on Earth. Layton, Neal, illus. 2009. (Animal Science Ser.). (ENG.). 64p. (J). (gr. 3-7). pap. 7.99 *(978-0-7636-4127-6(8))* Candlewick Pr.

Dlugos, Jenn & Hatton, Charlie. Crooked Critters. 2016. (Things That Make You Go Yuck! Ser.: 0). (ENG., Illus.). 88p. (J). (gr. 4-7). pap. 7.95 *(978-1-61821-609-0(0)*, 9781618216090) Prufrock Pr.

—Extreme Living. 2016. (Things That Make You Go Yuck! Ser.: 0). (ENG., Illus.). 88p. (J). (gr. 4-7). pap. 7.95 *(978-1-61821-568-0(X)*, 9781618215680) Prufrock Pr.

—Odd Couples. 2016. (Things That Make You Go Yuck! Ser.: 0). (ENG., Illus.). 88p. (J). (gr. 4-7). pap. 7.95 *(978-1-61821-566-6(3)*, 9781618215666) Prufrock Pr.

Fletcher, Patricia. Why Are Ostriches So Big? And Other Curious Bird Adaptations. 2017. (Odd Adaptations Ser.). 32p. (J). (gr. 3-4). pap. 63.00 ***(978-1-5382-0367-5(7))*** Stevens, Gareth Publishing LLLP.

—Why Do Frogs Have Teeth? And Other Curious Amphibian Adaptations. 2017. (Odd Adaptations Ser.). 32p. (J). (gr. 3-4). pap. 10.50 ***(978-1-5382-0389-7(8))*** Stevens, Gareth Publishing LLLP.

—Why Do Mudskippers Walk? And Other Curious Fish Adaptations. 2017. (Odd Adaptations Ser.). 32p. (J). (gr. 3-4). pap. 10.50 ***(978-1-5382-0393-4(6))*** Stevens, Gareth Publishing LLLP.

—Why Do Platypuses Lay Eggs? And Other Curious Mammal Adaptations. 2017. (Odd Adaptations Ser.). 32p. (J). (gr. 3-4). pap. 10.50 ***(978-1-5382-0401-6(0))*** Stevens, Gareth Publishing LLLP.

Ganeri, Anita. Harsh Habitats, 1 vol. 2012. (Extreme Nature Ser.). (ENG.). 32p. (gr. 1-3). pap. 8.29 *(978-1-4109-4702-4(5))*; lib. bdg. 29.99 *(978-1-4109-4697-3(5))* Heinemann-Raintree. (Read Me!).

Garside, Jeff. Extreme Environments: Living on the Edge. 2011. (Second Nature Ser.). 48p. (J). (gr. 5-8). lib. bdg. 26.60 *(978-1-59953-458-9(4))* Norwood Hse. Pr.

George, Gale. Adaptation. 2016. (Spotlight on Ecology & Life Science Ser.). 00024p. (J). (gr. 4-6). pap. 10.00 *(978-1-4994-2552-9(X)*, PowerKids Pr.) Rosen Publishing Group, Inc., The.

Goldsworthy, Steve. Physical Characteristics. 2016. (Illus.). 24p. (J). *(978-1-5105-0933-7(X))* SmartBook Media, Inc.

Gray, Leon. Life in Extreme Places. 2013. (Life Science Stories Ser.). (Illus.). 32p. (gr. 3-5). 26.60 *(978-1-4339-8715-1(5))*; pap. 10.50 *(978-1-4339-8716-8(3))* Stevens, Gareth Publishing LLLP. (Gareth Stevens Learning Library).

Gray, Susan H. Skunks Smell Bad. 2015. (Tell Me Why Library). (ENG., Illus.). 24p. (J). (gr. 2-5). 27.07 *(978-1-63188-999-8(0)*, 205908) Cherry Lake Publishing.

Hall, Katharine. Osos Polares y Pingüinos: Un Libro de Comparación y Contraste. 2014.Tr. of Polar Bears & Penguins: a Compare & Contrast Book. (SPA.). 32p. (J). (gr. -1-3). pap. 9.95 *(978-1-62855-227-0(1))* Arbordale Publishing.

Harrison, David L. Now You See Them, Now You Don't: Creatures That Know How to Hide. Laroche, Giles, illus. 2016. (ENG.). 32p. (J). (gr. k-4). lib. bdg. 17.95 *(978-1-58089-610-8(3))* Charlesbridge Publishing, Inc.

Heos, Bridget. Shell, Beak, Tusk: Shared Traits & the Wonders of Convergent Evolution. 2017. (ENG., Illus.). 32p. (J). (gr. 1-4). 16.99 *(978-0-544-81166-9(6)*, HMH Books For Young Readers) Houghton Mifflin Harcourt Publishing Co.

Higgins, Nadia. Prickly Animals. Fretland VanVoorst, Jenny, ed. 2016. (Back off! Animal Defenses). 24p. (J). (gr. 2-5). lib. bdg. 25.65 *(978-1-62031-311-4(1)*, Pogo) Jump! Inc.

—Slimy Animals. Fretland VanVoorst, Jenny, ed. 2016. (Back off! Animal Defenses). 24p. (J). (gr. 2-5). lib. bdg. 25.65 *(978-1-62031-306-0(5))* Jump! Inc.

—Stinky Animals. Fretland VanVoorst, Jenny, ed. 2016. (Back off! Animal Defenses). 24p. (J). (gr. 2-5). lib. bdg. 25.65 *(978-1-62031-312-1(X)*, Pogo) Jump! Inc.

Hirsch, Rebecca E. Exploding Ants & Other Amazing Defenses. 2017. (Searchlight Books (tm) — Animal Superpowers Ser.). (ENG.). 40p. (J). (gr. 3-5). pap. 9.99 *(978-1-5124-3112-4(5))*; 16.99 ***(978-1-5124-3660-0(7)***, Lerner Pubns.); 46.65 ***(978-1-5124-2819-3(1)***, Lerner Pubns.); 46.65 ***(978-1-5124-3659-4(3)***, Lerner Pubns.); (Illus.). 30.65 *(978-1-5124-2544-4(3))* Lerner Publishing Group.

Hirschmann, Kris. Real Life Zombies. 2013. (Illus.). 32p. (J). *(978-0-545-53563-2(8))* Scholastic, Inc.

Holland, Mary. Patas de Los Animales, 1 vol. 2016. (SPA., Illus.). 32p. (J). (gr. k-3). pap. 9.95 *(978-1-62855-845-6(8))* Arbordale Publishing.

Housel, Debra J. & Rice, Dona. The Right Environment, 1 vol. 2015. (Science Readers: Content & Literacy Ser.). (ENG., Illus.). 32p. (gr. 3-3). pap. 8.99 *(978-1-4807-4641-1(X))* Teacher Created Materials, Inc.

Howell, Sara. Lantern Fish, 1 vol. 2015. (ENG., Illus.). 24p. (J). lib. bdg. 23.60 *(978-1-4994-0147-9(7)*, PowerKids Pr.) Rosen Publishing Group, Inc., The.

Kalman, Bobbie. How & Why Do Animals Change As They Grow? 2014. (ENG., Illus.). 24p. (J). *(978-0-7787-0545-1(5))* Crabtree Publishing Co.

Klepeis, Alicia. Nocturnal & Diurnal Animals Explained. 2016. (Distinctions in Nature Ser.). 32p. (J). pap. 10.58 *(978-1-5026-2173-3(8))* Cavendish Square Publishing.

Klepeis, Alicia Z. Nature's Undead: Snapping Rattlesnakes, Frozen Frogs, & Other Animals That Seem to Rise from the Grave. 2016. (Real-Life Zombies Ser.). (ENG., Illus.). 32p. (gr. 3-4). lib. bdg. 27.99 *(978-1-5157-2481-0(6)*, Edge Bks.) Capstone Press of Coughlan Cos.

LaPlante, Walter. There's a Desert in My Backyard! 2016. (Backyard Biomes Ser.). 00024p. (J). pap. 8.15 *(978-1-4824-5555-7(2))* Stevens, Gareth Publishing LLLP.

Larson, Kirsten W. Super Powers in Nature. 2015. (Freaky Nature Ser.). (ENG., Illus.). 32p. (J). (gr. 2-4). 19.95 *(978-1-60753-781-6(8))* Amicus Publishing.

Marsico, Katie. Chameleons Change Color. 2015. (Tell Me Why Library). (ENG., Illus.). 24p. (J). (gr. 2-5). pap. 12.79 *(978-1-63362-699-7(7)*, 206621) Cherry Lake Publishing.

McDowell, Pamela. Flight. 2015. (Illus.). 24p. (J). *(978-1-4896-3671-3(4))* Weigl Pubs., Inc.

Murphy, Julie. Desert Animal Adaptations. 2011. (Amazing Animal Adaptations Ser.). (ENG.). 32p. (gr. 1-2). pap. 47.70 *(978-1-4296-7035-7(5)*, Aplus Bks.) Capstone Press of Coughlan Cos.

Parker, Steve. Adaptation. 2003. (Life Processes Ser.). (Illus.). 32p. (J). (gr. 4-6). per. 7.50 *(978-1-4034-4071-6(9))* Heinemann-Raintree.

—Survival & Change. (Life Processes Ser.). 32p. pap. 7.50 *(978-1-4034-4076-1(X))* Heinemann-Raintree.

Pearson, Carrie A. A Cool Summer Tail, 1 vol. Wald, Christina, illus. 2014. (ENG.). 32p. (J). (gr. -1-3). 17.95 *(978-1-62855-205-8(0))*; pap. 9.95 *(978-1-62855-214-0(X))* Arbordale Publishing.

—Un Invierno Muy Abrigador, 1 vol. Wald, Christina, illus. 2012. (SPA & ENG.). 32p. (J). (gr. -1-3). 17.95 *(978-1-60718-680-9(2))* Arbordale Publishing.

—A Warm Winter Tail, 1 vol. Wald, Christina, illus. 2012. (SPA & ENG.). 32p. (J). (gr. -1-3). 17.95 *(978-1-60718-529-1(6))*; pap. 9.95 *(978-1-60718-538-3(5))* Arbordale Publishing.

Pearson, Carrie A. & Wald, Christina. Un Fresco Cuento de Verano, 1 vol. Wald, Christina, illus. 2014.Tr. of Cool Summer Tail. (SPA & ENG., Illus.). 32p. (J). (gr. -1-3). pap. 9.95 *(978-1-62855-223-2(9))* Arbordale Publishing.

Rabe, Tish. Out of Sight till Tonight! All about Nocturnal Animals. 2015. (Cat in the Hat's Learning Library). (ENG., Illus.). 48p. (J). (gr. k-3). 9.99 *(978-0-375-87076-7(8)*, Random Hse. Bks. for Young Readers) Random Hse. Children's Bks.

Rajczak, Kristen. How Snakes & Other Animals Taste the Air. 2015. (Superior Animal Senses Ser.). (ENG., Illus.). 24p. (J). (gr. 3-4). pap. 8.25 *(978-1-4994-0995-6(8)*, PowerKids Pr.) Rosen Publishing Group, Inc., The.

Rake, Jody Sullivan. Gross Me Out. 2012. (Gross Me Out Ser.). (ENG.). 24p. (gr. 1-2). pap. 166.80 *(978-1-4296-8381-4(3))*; pap. 21.87 *(978-1-4296-8380-7(5))*; lib. bdg. 101.28 *(978-1-4296-8148-3(9))* Capstone Press of Coughlan Cos. (First Facts).

—Mudskippers & Other Extreme Fish Adaptations, 1 vol. 2014. (Extreme Adaptations Ser.). (ENG.). 32p. (gr. 3-4). lib. bdg. 27.32 *(978-1-4914-0165-1(6))* Capstone Press of Coughlan Cos.

—Star-Nosed Moles & Other Extreme Mammal Adaptations, 1 vol. 2014. (Extreme Adaptations Ser.). (ENG.). 32p. (gr. 3-4). lib. bdg. 27.32 *(978-1-4914-0167-5(2))* Capstone Press of Coughlan Cos.

Rake, Jody Sullivan, et al. Extreme Adaptations, 1 vol. 2014. (Extreme Adaptations Ser.). (ENG.). 32p. (gr. 3-4). pap. 31.80 *(978-1-4914-0178-1(8)*, Fact Finders) Capstone Press of Coughlan Cos.

Really Strange Adaptations. 2016. (Really Strange Adaptations Ser.). 00032p. (J). (gr. 5-5). 157.50 *(978-1-4994-2687-8(9)*, PowerKids Pr.) Rosen Publishing Group, Inc., The.

Rice, Dona. Traits for Survival, 1 vol. 2015. (Science Readers: Content & Literacy Ser.). (ENG., Illus.). 32p. (gr. 3-3). pap. 8.99 *(978-1-4807-4639-8(8))* Teacher Created Materials, Inc.

Riggs, Kate. Camels. 2015. (J). *(978-1-60818-513-9(3)*, Creative Education) Creative Co., The.

—Pandas. 2015. (J). *(978-1-60818-514-6(1)*, Creative Education) Creative Co., The.

—Sea Lions. 2015. (J). *(978-1-60818-516-0(8)*, Creative Education) Creative Co., The.

—Seedlings: Sea Lions. 2015. (Seedlings Ser.). (ENG.). 24p. (J). (gr. -1-1). pap. 7.99 *(978-1-62832-116-6(4)*, Creative Paperbacks) Creative Co., The.

Romero, Libby. Adaptation. 2005. (J). pap. *(978-1-4108-4628-0(8))* Benchmark Education Co.

Rose, Simon. Family Groups. 2015. (Illus.). 24p. (J). *(978-1-4896-3667-6(6))* Weigl Pubs., Inc.

Royston, Angela. Hostile Homes: Extreme Habitats. 2015. (Extreme Biology Ser.). (ENG., Illus.). 48p. (J). (gr. 4-4). lib. bdg. 31.95 *(978-1-4824-2242-9(5))* Stevens, Gareth Publishing LLLP.

Roza, Greg. Tasmanian Devil vs. Hyena. 2015. (Bizarre Beast Battles Ser.). (ENG.). 24p. (J). (gr. 2-3). 22.60 *(978-1-4824-2798-1(2))* Stevens, Gareth Publishing LLLP.

Russell, Margaret. Exploring the Native Plant World: A Life Science Curriculum, 5th-6th Grade: Adaptations in the Native Plant World. Thompson, Maria, illus. 2004. 63p. (J). (gr. 5-6). per. 14.95 *(978-1-57168-851-4(X)*, Eakin Pr.) Eakin Pr.

Ryndak, Rob. Turtle or Tortoise? 2015. (Animal Look-Alikes Ser.). (ENG., Illus.). 24p. (J). (gr. 1-2). pap. 8.15 *(978-1-4824-2728-8(1))* Stevens, Gareth Publishing LLLP.

Salaka, Michael. Animals in Hiding. 2017. (Animals in My World Ser.). 24p. (J). (gr. 4-6). pap. 8.25 ***(978-1-5383-2148-5(3)***, PowerKids Pr.) Rosen Publishing Group, Inc., The.

Shea, Therese. How Dolphins & Other Animals Use Sonar. 2015. (Superior Animal Senses Ser.). (ENG., Illus.). 24p. (J). (gr. 3-4). pap. 8.25 *(978-1-4994-0988-8(5)*, PowerKids Pr.) Rosen Publishing Group, Inc., The.

Silverstein, Alvin, et al. Adaptation. 2007. (Science Concepts, Second Ser.). (ENG., Illus.). 112p. (gr. 6-8). lib. bdg. 31.93 *(978-0-8225-3434-1(7))* Lerner Publishing Group.

Snedden, Robert. Adaptation & Survival, 1 vol. 2012. (Web of Life Ser.). (ENG.). 48p. (gr. 3-3). pap. 9.49 *(978-1-4109-4435-1(2)*, Raintree Freestyle Express); (gr. 3-3). lib. bdg. 34.65 *(978-1-4109-4428-3(X)*, Raintree Freestyle Express); (Illus.). (gr. 6-10). lib. bdg. 34.65 *(978-1-4109-4401-6(8)*, Raintree Freestyle) Heinemann-Raintree.

Spilsbury, Louise. Animal Bodies: Extreme Anatomies. 2015. (Extreme Biology Ser.). (ENG.). 48p. (J). (gr. 4-4). lib. bdg. 31.95 *(978-1-4824-2230-6(1))* Stevens, Gareth Publishing LLLP.

—Kill or Die: Extreme Life Cycles. 2015. (Extreme Biology Ser.). (ENG., Illus.). 48p. (J). (gr. 4-4). lib. bdg. 31.95 *(978-1-4824-2246-7(8))* Stevens, Gareth Publishing LLLP.

—Survival of the Fittest: Extreme Adaptations. 2015. (Extreme Biology Ser.). (ENG., Illus.). 48p. (J). (gr. 4-4). lib. bdg. 31.95 *(978-1-4824-2250-4(6))* Stevens, Gareth Publishing LLLP.

Spilsbury, Richard. Adaptation & Survival. 2010. (Living Processes Ser.). (Illus.). 48p. (J). pap. 11.75 *(978-1-61532-348-7(1))*; (YA). (gr. 5-8). lib. bdg. 29.25 *(978-1-61532-343-2(0))* Rosen Publishing Group, Inc., The. (Rosen Reference).

—Adaptation & Survival. 2013. (Life Science Stories Ser.). (Illus.). 32p. (J). (gr. 3-5). pap. 10.50 *(978-1-4339-8700-7(7))*; lib. bdg. 26.60 *(978-1-4339-8699-4(X))* Stevens, Gareth Publishing LLLP.

Sundance/Newbridge LLC Staff. How Animals Survive. 2004. (Reading PowerWorks Ser.). (gr. 1-3). 37.50 *(978-0-7608-8892-6(2))*; pap. 6.10 *(978-0-7608-8893-3(0))* Sundance/Newbridge Educational Publishing.

Taylor, Barbara. Stinky Skunks & Other Animal Adaptations. 2014. (ENG.). 32p. (J). *(978-0-7787-1420-0(9))* Crabtree Publishing Co.

Waldron, Melanie. Adaptation, 1 vol. 2013. (Essential Life Science Ser.). (ENG.). 48p. (gr. 4-6). 33.32 *(978-1-4329-7805-1(5)*, Heinemann InfoSearch) Heinemann-Raintree.

Waldron, Melanie, et al. Essential Life Science, 1 vol. 2014. (Essential Life Science Ser.). (ENG.). 48p. (gr. 4-6). lib. bdg. 133.28 *(978-1-4329-7814-3(4)*, Heinemann InfoSearch) Heinemann-Raintree.

Waters, Rosa. Surprise & Flexibility. Croft, Cindy, ed. 2014. (Causes & Effects of Emotions Ser.: 13). 64p. (J). (gr. 7-18). 23.95 *(978-1-4222-3080-0(5))* Mason Crest.

Wheeler-Toppen, Jodi. Orchid Mantises & Other Extreme Insect Adaptations, 1 vol. 2014. (Extreme Adaptations Ser.). (ENG.). 32p. (gr. 3-4). pap. 7.95 *(978-1-4914-0171-2(0)*, Fact Finders); lib. bdg. 27.32 *(978-1-4914-0166-8(4))* Capstone Press of Coughlan Cos.

Wheeler-Toppen, Jodi, et al. Extreme Adaptations, 1 vol. 2014. (Extreme Adaptations Ser.). (ENG.). 32p. (gr. 3-4). 109.28 *(978-1-4914-0169-9(9)*, Fact Finders) Capstone Press of Coughlan Cos.

Willis, John. Biological Adaptations. 2016. (Illus.). 32p. (J). *(978-1-5105-1182-8(2))* SmartBook Media, Inc.

Winner, Cherie. Life on the Edge. 2005. (Cool Science Ser.). (ENG., Illus.). 48p. (gr. 4-8). lib. bdg. 27.93 *(978-0-8225-2499-1(6)*, Lerner Pubns.) Lerner Publishing Group.

Worth, Richard & Benchmark Education Co., LLC. Adaptation & Biodiversity. 2013. (PRIME Ser.). (J). (gr. 6-8). pap. *(978-1-4509-9469-9(5))* Benchmark Education Co.

Yardi, Robin. ¡Ellos Ya Saben! Instintos de Los Animales, 1 vol. Klein, Laurie Allen, illus. 2015. (SPA & ENG.). 32p. (J). (gr. k-3). pap. 9.95 *(978-1-62855-644-5(7))* Arbordale Publishing.

—They Just Know: Animal Instincts, 1 vol. Klein, Laurie Allen, illus. 2015. (ENG.). 32p. (J). (gr. k-3). 17.95 *(978-1-62855-634-6(X))* Arbordale Publishing.

ADD (CHILD BEHAVIOR DISORDER)

see Attention-Deficit Hyperactivity Disorder

ADDAMS, JANE, 1860-1935

Caravantes, Peggy. Waging Peace: The Story of Jane Addams. 2004. (Illus.). 144p. (YA). (gr. 6-12). 23.95 *(978-1-931798-40-2(0))* Reynolds, Morgan Inc.

Harvey, Bonnie C. Jane Addams: Social Worker & Nobel Peace Prize Winner. 2015. (Legendary American Biographies Ser.). 96p. (J). (gr. 6-12). pap. 10.95 *(978-0-7660-6461-4(1))* Enslow Pubs., Inc.

Harvey, Bonnie Carman. Jane Addams: Social Worker & Nobel Peace Prize Winner. 2015. (Legendary American Biographies Ser.). 96p. (J). (gr. 6-12). 27.94 *(978-0-7660-6460-7(3))* Enslow Pubs., Inc.

Jane Addams, 34 bks., Set. Incl. Air Pollution. Lopez, Gary. 32p. (gr. 2-12). 1992. lib. bdg. *(978-0-88682-427-3(3))*; Cells. George, Michael. 40p. (gr. 2-7). 1992. lib. bdg. 23.95 *(978-0-88682-437-2(0))*; Clouds. Markert, Jenny. 40p. (gr. 2-12). 1997. lib. bdg. 23.95 *(978-0-88682-435-8(4))*; Coral Reef. George, Michael. 32p. (gr. 2-12). 1992. lib. bdg. *(978-0-88682-430-3(3))*; Deserts. George, Michael. 40p. (gr. 2-12). 1992. lib. bdg. 23.95 *(978-0-88682-434-1(6))*; Earthquakes. George, Michael. 30p. (gr. 2-12). 1997. lib. bdg. 23.95 *(978-0-88682-709-0(4))*; Fungi. Rotter, Charles M. 40p. (gr. 2-12). 1993. lib. bdg. 23.95 *(978-0-88682-593-5(8))*; Galaxies. George, Michael. 40p. (gr. 2-12). 1993. lib. bdg. 23.95 *(978-0-88682-433-4(8))*; Glaciers. George, Michael. 32p. (gr. 2-12). 1992. lib. bdg. *(978-0-88682-401-3(X))*; Life. George, Michael. 32p. (gr. 2-12). 1994. lib. bdg. *(978-0-88682-602-4(0))*; Mars. George, Michael. 32p. (gr. 3-7). 1992. lib. bdg. *(978-0-88682-432-7(X))*; Moon. George, Michael. 40p. (gr. 2-12). 1993. lib. bdg. 23.95 *(978-0-88682-436-5(2))*; Mountains. Rotter, Charles M. 40p. (gr. 2-12). 1994. lib. bdg. 23.95 *(978-0-88682-596-6(2))*; Ocean Resources. Markert, Jenny. 40p. (gr. 2-12). 1994. lib. bdg. 23.95 *(978-0-88682-599-7(7))*; Prairie. Rotter, Charles M. 40p. (gr. 2-12). 1994. lib. bdg. 17.95 *(978-0-88682-598-0(9))*; Rain Forest. George, Michael. 40p. (gr. 2-12). 1992. lib. bdg. 23.95 *(978-0-88682-483-9(4))*; Sequoias. George, Michael. 32p. (gr. 2-12). 1992. lib. bdg. *(978-0-88682-482-2(6))*; Space Exploration. George, Michael. 32p. (gr. 2-12). 1993. lib. bdg. *(978-0-88682-481-5(8))*; Stars. George, Michael. 40p. (gr. 2-12). 1992. lib. bdg. 17.95 *(978-0-88682-400-6(1))*; Sun. George, Michael. 40p. (gr. 2-12). 1992. lib. bdg. 23.95 *(978-0-88682-402-0(8))*; Volcanoes. George, Michael. 32p. (gr. 3-12). 1992. lib. bdg. *(978-0-88682-403-7(6))*; Water. Markert, Jenny. 32p. (gr. 2-12). 1992. lib. bdg. *(978-0-88682-431-0(1))*; (Illus.). (J). (Women of America Ser.). 32p. Set lib. bdg. 576.30 o.p. *(978-0-88682-165-4(7)*, Creative Education) Creative Co., The.

Kishel, Ann-Marie. Jane Addams: A Life of Cooperation. (Pull Ahead Books-Biographies Ser.). 32p. 2007. (ENG.). (gr. k-3). pap. 7.95 *(978-0-8225-6436-2(X))* 2006. (Illus.). (J). (gr. 3-7). lib. bdg. 22.60 *(978-0-8225-6382-2(7)*, Lerner Pubns.) Lerner Publishing Group.

Owens, Tom. Immigrants & Neighbors. 2003. (Illus.). 40p. pap. 8.00 *(978-0-7891-5850-5(7))* Perfection Learning Corp.

Riley, John B. Jane Addams: A Photo Biography. l.t. ed. 2004. (First Biographies Ser.). (Illus.). 24p. (YA). (gr. 5-18). 16.95 *(978-1-883846-61-9(7)*, First Biographies) Reynolds, Morgan Inc.

Slade, Suzanne. Dangerous Jane, 1 vol. Ratterree, Alice, illus. 2017. (ENG.). 40p. (J). (gr. 1-5). 17.95 *(978-1-56145-913-1(5))* Peachtree Pubs.

Slavicek, Louise Chipley. Jane Addams. 2011. (Women of Achievement Ser.). (Illus.). 126p. (gr. 6-12). 35.00 *(978-1-60413-907-5(2),* Chelsea Hse.) Facts On File, Inc.

ADDING MACHINES

see Calculators

ADHD (CHILD BEHAVIOR DISORDER)

see Attention-Deficit Hyperactivity Disorder

ADIRONDACK MOUNTAINS (N.Y.)

Jamieson, Paul F. & Burdick, Neal S. The Adirondack Reader. 3rd ed. 2007. *(978-1-931951-12-8(8));* pap. *(978-1-931951-11-1(X))* Adirondack Mountain Club, Inc.

MacMillan, Dianne M. Life in a Deciduous Forest. 2003. (Ecosystems in Action Ser.). (ENG., Illus.). 72p. (gr. 5-9). 26.60 *(978-0-8225-4684-9(1))* Lerner Publishing Group.

Snavlin, Joyce Burgess. Adirondack ABCs. Reed, Linda Davis, illus. 2009. 32p. (J). 9.95 *(978-1-59531-028-6(2))* North Country Bks., Inc.

Zschock, Martha Day. Hello, Adirondacks! 2013. (Hello! Ser.). (ENG., Illus.). 16p. (gr. -1-k). bds. 9.95 *(978-1-933212-55-5(1),* 9781933212555, Commonwealth Editions) Applewood Bks.

ADIRONDACK MOUNTAINS (N.Y.)—FICTION

The Adirondack. 2006. (YA). per. *(978-1-59872-344-1(8))* Instant Pub.

Altsheler, Joseph A. The French & Indian War Novels: The Rulers of the Lakes & The Masters of the Peaks, Vol. 2. 2008. 416p. (J). reprint ed. *(978-1-84677-588-8(4));* pap. *(978-1-84677-587-1(6))* Leonaur Ltd.

—The Rulers of the Lakes: A Story of George & Champlain. 2006. (French & Indian War Ser.: Vol. 3). 300p. (J). reprint ed. 29.95 *(978-1-4218-1778-1(0));* pap. 14.95 *(978-1-4218-1878-8(7))* 1st World Publishing, Inc. (1st World Library - Literary Society).

—The Rulers of the Lakes: A Story of George & Champlain. (French & Indian War Ser.: Vol. 3). (J). reprint ed. 25.95 *(978-0-8488-0906-5(8))* Amereon Ltd.

—The Rulers of the Lakes: A Story of George & Champlain. 2008. (French & Indian War Ser.: Vol. 3). 272p. (J). 25.99 *(978-0-554-34451-5(3))* 2008. (French & Indian War Ser.: Vol. 3). 272p. (J). 28.99 *(978-0-554-25148-6(5))* 2007. (ENG.). 268p. reprint ed. pap. 23.99 *(978-1-4264-8309-7(0))* 2010. (French & Indian War Ser.: Vol. 3). (ENG.). 370p. (J). (gr. 4-7). reprint ed. pap. 32.75 *(978-1-177-56810-4(1))* Creative Media Partners, LLC.

—The Rulers of the Lakes: A Story of George & Champlain. Henry, J., illus. 2007. (French & Indian War Ser.: Vol. 3). 214p. (J). reprint ed. pap. 20.99 *(978-1-4264-8272-4(8))* Creative Media Partners, LLC.

—The Rulers of the Lakes: A Story of George & Champlain. 2006. (French & Indian War Ser.: Vol. 3). (J). reprint ed. pap. *(978-1-4065-0819-2(5))* Dodo Pr.

—The Rulers of the Lakes: A Story of George & Champlain. 2010. 166p. pap. 24.67 *(978-1-152-80290-2(9));* (French & Indian War Ser.: Vol. 3). (Illus.). 160p. (J). (gr. 4-7). reprint ed. pap. 19.99 *(978-1-153-71979-7(7))* General Bks. LLC.

—The Rulers of the Lakes: A Story of George & Champlain. reprint ed. 2010. 366p. 39.16 *(978-1-163-74095-8(0))* 2010. 366p. pap. 27.16 *(978-1-163-71977-0(3))* 2007. (French & Indian War Ser.: Vol. 3). 368p. (J). 48.95 *(978-0-548-43205-1(8))* 2007. (French & Indian War Ser.: Vol. 3). 368p. (J). pap. 33.95 *(978-0-548-40955-8(2))* Kessinger Publishing, LLC.

—The Rulers of the Lakes: A Story of George & Champlain. 2011. (French & Indian War Ser.: Vol. 3). 272p. (J). (gr. 4-7). reprint ed. pap. *(978-3-8424-7701-8(5))* Tredition GmbH.

Altsheler, Joseph A., ed. The Masters of the Peaks: A Story of the Great North Woods. (French & Indian War Ser.: Vol. 4). 311p. (J). reprint ed. lib. bdg. 24.95 *(978-0-88411-938-8(6))* Amereon Ltd.

—The Masters of the Peaks: A Story of the Great North Woods. 2010. (French & Indian War Ser.: Vol. 4). (Illus.). 144p. (J). (gr. 4-7). reprint ed. pap. *(978-1-4432-2285-3(2))* Books LLC.

—The Masters of the Peaks: A Story of the Great North Woods. l.t. ed. reprint ed. 2007. (French & Indian War Ser.: Vol. 4). (ENG.). 248p. (J). pap. 22.99 *(978-1-4264-4882-9(1))* 2012. 182p. pap. 22.75 *(978-1-276-49474-8(2))* 2010. (French & Indian War Ser.: Vol. 4). 320p. (J). pap. 30.75 *(978-1-142-51783-0(7))* 2008. (French & Indian War Ser.: Vol. 4). 252p. (J). 24.99 *(978-0-554-32953-6(0))* 2008. (French & Indian War Ser.: Vol. 4). 252p. (J). 27.99 *(978-0-554-23650-6(8))* 2007. (French & Indian War Ser.: Vol. 4). (ENG.). 222p. (J). pap. 20.99 *(978-1-4264-4839-3(2))* Creative Media Partners, LLC.

—The Masters of the Peaks: A Story of the Great North Woods. 2006. (French & Indian War Ser.: Vol. 4). (J). reprint ed. pap. *(978-1-4068-0762-2(1))* Echo Library.

—The Masters of the Peaks: A Story of the Great North Woods. 2009. (French & Indian War Ser.: Vol. 4). 162p. (J). reprint ed. pap. 8.85 *(978-1-150-40712-3(3))* General Bks. LLC.

—The Masters of the Peaks: A Story of the Great North Woods. (French & Indian War Ser.: Vol. 4). (J). reprint ed. 2010. 220p. (gr. 4-7). 31.96 *(978-1-169-29283-3(6))* 2010. 220p. (gr. 4-7). pap. 19.96 *(978-1-162-70171-4(4))* 2010. 39.95 *(978-1-161-47035-2(2))* 2004. pap. 24.95 *(978-1-4191-7205-2(0))* 2004. pap. 1.99 *(978-1-4192-7205-9(5))* Kessinger Publishing, LLC.

—The Masters of the Peaks: A Story of the Great North Woods. 2011. (French & Indian War Ser.: Vol. 4). 228p. (J). reprint ed. pap. *(978-3-8424-4394-5(3))* Tredition GmbH.

Auch, M. J. Guitar Boy. 2012. (ENG.). 288p. (J). (gr. 5-9). pap. 14.99 *(978-0-312-64124-5(9),* 9780312641245) Square Fish.

Bauer, Joan. Backwater. 2005. 185p. 18.00 *(978-0-7569-5779-7(6))* Perfection Learning Corp.

Bruchac, Joseph. Bearwalker. Comport, Sally Wern, illus. 2010. (ENG.). 240p. (J). (gr. 5). pap. 6.99 *(978-0-06-112315-3(3))* HarperCollins Pubs.

Donnelly, Jennifer. A Northern Light. 2004. (ENG.). 416p. (YA). (gr. 9-12). reprint ed. pap. 9.99 *(978-0-15-205310-9(7))* Houghton Mifflin Harcourt Publishing Co.

—A Northern Light. 2004. 396p. (gr. 9-12). 20.00 *(978-0-7569-3614-3(4))* Perfection Learning Corp.

Granger, Persis R. Adirondack Gold. 2003. (Illus.). 168p. (J). (gr. 3-6). pap. 9.95 *(978-0-9742085-0-3(7))* Beaver Meadow Publishing.

Heinz, Brian J. A Coming of Winter in the Adirondacks. Healy, Maggie, illus. 2011. 32p. (J). 19.95 *(978-1-59531-038-5(X))* North Country Bks., Inc.

Laughton, Geoff. At the Lake. 2016. (ENG., Illus.). (J). 24.99 **(978-1-63477-937-1(1),** Harmony Ink Pr.) Dreamspinner Pr.

Mahoney, Liana. Forest Green: A Walk Through the Adirondack Seasons. Henry, Maggie, illus. 2014. (J). *(978-1-59531-047-7(9))* North Country Bks., Inc.

Mcghee, Alison. All Rivers Flow to the Sea. 2005. (ENG.). 176p. (YA). (gr. 9-12). 15.99 *(978-0-7636-2591-7(4))* Candlewick Pr.

Mlynowski, Sarah. Spells & Sleeping Bags. 2008. (Magic in Manhattan Ser.: No. 3). (ENG.). 320p. (YA). (gr. 7-12). pap. 8.99 *(978-0-385-73388-5(7),* Delacorte Pr.) Random Hse. Children's Bks.

Payson, Howard. Boy Scouts' Mountain Camp. 2005. (Illus.). pap. 28.95 *(978-1-885529-54-1(6))* Stevens Publishing.

Steiner, Barbara. The Cry of the Loon: A Samantha Mystery. Tibbles, Jean-Paul, illus. (ENG.). 192p. (gr. 4-18). 2009. (YA). pap. 6.95 *(978-1-59369-480-7(6))* 2006. 10.95 *(978-1-59369-479-1(2))* American Girl Publishing, Inc.

Sutliff, Jamie. The Land of Nen-Us-Yok. Blumberg, Christine A., ed. Evans, Kevin C., illus. 2007. 256p. pap. 10.95 *(978-0-9712867-4-0(4));* 26.95 *(978-0-9712867-6-4(0))* Cold River Pubns.

VanRiper, Gary & VanRiper, Justin. Escape from Black Bear Mountain. 2008. (Adirondack Kids Ser.: Vol. 8). 70p. (J). (gr. 2-7). pap. 9.95 *(978-0-9707044-8-1(8))* Adirondack Kids Pr.

—The Final Daze of Summer. 2010. (Adirondack Kids Ser.: Vol. 10). 96p. (J). (gr. 2-7). pap. 9.95 *(978-0-9826250-0-2(6))* Adirondack Kids Pr.

—The Great Train Robbery. 2004. (Adirondack Kids Ser.: Vol. 4). (Illus.). 82p. (J). (gr. 2-7). pap. 9.95 *(978-0-9707044-3-6(7))* Adirondack Kids Pr.

—Islands in the Sky. 2005. (Adirondack Kids Ser.: Vol. 5). 78p. (J). (gr. 2-7). pap. 9.95 *(978-0-9707044-5-0(3))* Adirondack Kids Pr.

—Legend of the Lake Monster. 2009. (Adirondack Kids Ser.: Vol. 9). 96p. (J). (gr. 2-7). pap. 9.95 *(978-0-9707044-9-8(6))* Adirondack Kids Pr.

—Mystery of the Missing Moose. 2007. (Adirondack Kids Ser.: Vol. 7). 77p. (J). (gr. 2-7). pap. 9.95 *(978-0-9707044-7-4(X),* ADK7) Adirondack Kids Pr.

—The Secret of the Skeleton Key. 2006. (Adirondack Kids Ser.: Vol. 6). 71p. (J). (gr. 2-7). pap. 9.95 *(978-0-9707044-6-7(1))* Adirondack Kids Pr.

VanRiper, Justin & VanRiper, Gary. The Fall of Fort Ticonderoga. 2011. (Adirondack Kids Ser.: Vol. 11). 96p. (J). (gr. 2-7). pap. 9.95 *(978-0-9826250-1-9(4))* Adirondack Kids Pr.

—The Lost Lighthouse. Gary, Glenn, illus. 2003. (Adirondack Kids Ser.: Vol. 3). 82p. (J). (gr. 2-7). pap. 9.95 *(978-0-9707044-2-9(9),* ADK3) Adirondack Kids Pr.

—The Pond Hockey Challenge. 2012. (Adirondack Kids Ser.: Vol. 12). (Illus.). 96p. (J). pap. 9.95 *(978-0-9826250-2-6(2))* Adirondack Kids Pr.

Winfield, Arthur M. The Rover Boys in the Mountains. 2005. 27.95 *(978-1-4218-1009-6(3));* 216p. pap. 12.95 *(978-1-4218-1109-3(X))* 1st World Publishing, Inc. (1st World Library - Literary Society).

—The Rover Boys in the Mountains: Or, A Hunt for Fun & Fortune. 2007. 170p. pap. 19.99 *(978-1-4264-7052-3(5))* 2006. (ENG.). 188p. pap. 21.99 *(978-1-4264-7128-5(9))* Creative Media Partners, LLC.

ADJUSTMENT, SOCIAL

see Social Adjustment

ADMINISTRATION

see Civil Service; Management; Political Science; Public Administration

see names of countries, cities, etc. with the subdivision Politics and Government, e.g. U. S.—Politics and Government; etc.

ADMINISTRATION OF JUSTICE

see Justice, Administration of

ADMIRALS

Alphin, Elaine Marie & Alphin, Arthur B. I Have Not Yet Begun to Fight: A Story about John Paul Jones. Casale, Paul, tr. Casale, Paul, illus. 2004. (Creative Minds Biography Ser.). 64p. (J). 22.60 *(978-1-57505-601-2(1),* Carolrhoda Bks.); (ENG.). (gr. 4-8). pap. 8.95 *(978-1-57505-635-7(6))* Lerner Publishing Group.

Bailey, Tom. Raphael Semmes: Commander of the Alabama. 2011. (Illus.). 120p. (J). *(978-1-59421-062-4(4))* Seacoast Publishing, Inc.

Bradford, James C. John Paul Jones & the American Navy. 2009. (Library of American Lives & Times Ser.). 112p. (gr. 5-5). 69.20 *(978-1-60853-490-6(1))* Rosen Publishing Group, Inc., The.

Brager, Bruce L. John Paul Jones: America's Sailor. 2006. (Founders of the Republic Ser.). (Illus.). 160p. (J). (gr. 6-12). lib. bdg. 26.95 *(978-1-931798-84-6(2))* Reynolds, Morgan Inc.

Cawthorne, Nigel. Military Commanders: The 100 Greatest Throughout History. 2004. (Illus.). 208p. 18.95 *(978-1-59270-029-5(2))* Enchanted Lion Bks., LLC.

—Victory: 100 Great Military Commanders. 2012. (Illus.). 208p. (J). *(978-1-4351-4242-8(X))* Metro Bks.

Cooper, Michael L. Hero of the High Seas: John Paul Jones & the American Revolution. 2006. (ENG., Illus.). 128p. (gr. 5-7). 21.95 *(978-0-7922-5547-5(X));* lib. bdg. 32.90 *(978-0-7922-5548-2(8))* National Geographic Society. (National Geographic Children's Bks.).

Crickard, Sarah. John Paul Jones & the Birth of the American Navy. 2015. (Spotlight on American History Ser.). (ENG., Illus.). 24p. (J). (gr. 4-6). pap. 10.00 *(978-1-4994-1759-3(4),* PowerKids Pr.) Rosen Publishing Group, Inc., The.

Crompton, Samuel Willard. Francis Drake & the Oceans of the World. Goetzmann, William H., ed. 2005. (Explorers of New Worlds Ser.). (Illus.). 160p. (J). (gr. 5-8). lib. bdg. 30.00 *(978-0-7910-8615-5(1))* Facts On File, Inc.

Dougherty, Terri. Admiral David Farragut: "Full Speed Ahead!" 2011. (J). *(978-1-59556-041-4(6));* pap. *(978-1-59556-047-6(5))* OTTN Publishing.

Egan, Tracie. John Paul Jones: American Naval Hero. 2009. (Primary Sources of Famous People in American History Ser.). 32p. (gr. 2-3). 47.90 *(978-1-60851-693-3(8))* Rosen Publishing Group, Inc., The.

—John Paul Jones: American Naval Hero / Héroe de la marina Estadounidense. 2009. (Famous People in American History/Grandes personajes en la historia de los Estados Unidos Ser.). (ENG & SPA.). 32p. (gr. 2-3). 47.90 *(978-1-61512-548-7(5),* Editorial Buenas Letras) Rosen Publishing Group, Inc., The.

—John Paul Jones: Héroe de la marina estadounidense (John Paul Jones: American Naval Hero) 2009. (Grandes personajes en la historia de los Estados Unidos (Famous People in American History) Ser.). (SPA.). 32p. (gr. 2-3). 47.90 *(978-1-61512-802-0(6),* Editorial Buenas Letras) Rosen Publishing Group, Inc., The.

Harkins, Susan Sales & Harkins, William H. The Life & Times of John Paul Jones. 2007. (Profiles in American History Ser.). (Illus.). 48p. (J). (gr. 4-8). lib. bdg. 29.95 *(978-1-58415-529-4(9))* Mitchell Lane Pubs., Inc.

Hoogenboom, Lynn. Sir Francis Drake. 2009. (Primary Source Library of Famous Explorers Ser.). 24p. (gr. 4-4). 42.50 *(978-1-60854-131-7(2),* PowerKids Pr.) Rosen Publishing Group, Inc., The.

—Sir Francis Drake: A Primary Source Biography. 2006. (Primary Source Library of Famous Explorers Ser.). (Illus.). 24p. (YA). (gr. 2-5). lib. bdg. 22.60 *(978-1-4042-3035-4(1))* Rosen Publishing Group, Inc., The.

Krasner, Barbara. Sir Francis Drake. 2016. (Spotlight on Explorers & Colonization Ser.). 00048p. (J). (gr. 6-6). pap. 11.75 *(978-1-5081-7218-5(8))* Rosen Publishing Group, Inc., The.

Lace, William W. Sir Francis Drake. 2009. (Great Explorers Ser.). (Illus.). 112p. (gr. 6-12). 30.00 *(978-1-60413-417-9(8),* Chelsea Hse.) Facts On File, Inc.

Mattern, Joanne. Grace Hopper: Computer Pioneer. 2003. (Women Who Shaped History Ser.). (Illus.). 24p. (J). lib. bdg. 22.60 *(978-0-8239-6505-2(8),* PowerKids Pr.) Rosen Publishing Group, Inc., The.

Murphy, Patricia J. Grace Hopper: Computer Pioneer. 2004. (Famous Inventors Ser.). (Illus.). 32p. (J). lib. bdg. 22.60 *(978-0-7660-2273-7(0))* Enslow Pubs., Inc.

Nick, Charles. Sir Francis Drake: Slave Trader & Pirate. 2010. (ENG., Illus.). 128p. (C). (gr. 6-12). pap. 9.95 *(978-0-531-20740-6(4))* National Geographic School Publishing, Inc.

—Sir Francis Drake: Slave Trader & Pirate. 2009. (Wicked History Ser.). (ENG., Illus.). 128p. (J). (gr. 6-12). 31.00 *(978-0-531-21800-6(7),* Watts, Franklin) Scholastic Library Publishing.

Pelleschi, Andrea. Mathematician & Computer Scientist Grace Hopper. 2016. (STEM Trailblazer Bios Ser.). (ENG., Illus.). 32p. (J). (gr. 2-5). 26.65 *(978-1-5124-0785-3(2))* Lerner Publishing Group.

Riley, John B. John Paul Jones: A Photo Biography. l.t. ed. 2004. (First Biographies Ser.). (Illus.). 24p. (YA). (gr. 5-18). 16.95 *(978-1-883846-63-3(3),* First Biographies) Reynolds, Morgan Inc.

Sir Francis Drake. 2013. 56p. 15.95 *(978-0-9897533-0-2(1))* Croce, Pat & Co.

Sonneborn, Liz. John Paul Jones: American Naval Hero. 2005. (Leaders of the American Revolution Ser.). (Illus.). 100p. (gr. 5-8). lib. bdg. 30.00 *(978-0-7910-8621-6(6))* Facts On File, Inc.

Sperry, Armstrong. John Paul Jones: The Pirate Patriot. (Great Leaders & Events Ser.). (ENG.). (J). (gr. 4-8). 2017. lib. bdg. 35.99 **(978-1-942875-42-0(8))** 2016. (Illus.). 168p. pap. 12.99 *(978-0-7603-5230-4(5),* Voyageur Pr.) Quarto Publishing Group USA.

Staley, Erin. Grace Murray Hopper, 01 vols., 1. 2016. (Tech Pioneers Ser.). (ENG.). 112p. (J). 35.60 *(978-1-4994-6288-3(3),* Rosen Young Adult) Rosen Publishing Group, Inc., The.

Stefoff, Rebecca. Redbeard. 2015. (J). lib. bdg. *(978-1-62713-533-7(2));* (ENG.). 48p. (gr. 3-3). 31.36 *(978-1-5026-0199-5(0))* Cavendish Square Publishing.

Sterngass, Jon. John Brown. 2009. (Leaders of the Civil War Era Ser.). (Illus.). 144p. (gr. 6-12). 35.00 *(978-1-60413-305-9(8),* Chelsea Hse.) Facts On File, Inc.

Sutcliffe, Jane & Kodera, Craig. Chester Nimitz & the Sea, 1 vol. 2013. (ENG., Illus.). 32p. (J). (gr. k-3). 16.99 *(978-1-4556-1796-8(2))* Pelican Publishing Co., Inc.

Waldman, Scott. Victory at Sea: John Paul Jones & the Continental Navy. 2009. (Great Moments in American History Ser.). 32p. (gr. 3-3). 47.90 *(978-1-61513-156-3(6))* Rosen Publishing Group, Inc., The.

Wallmark, Laurie. Grace Hopper: Queen of Computer Code. Wu, Katy, illus. 2017. (ENG.). 48p. (J). (gr. k). 16.95 *(978-1-4549-2000-7(9))* Sterling Publishing Co., Inc.

Wittner, David G. Commodore Matthew Perry & the Perry Expedition to Japan. 2009. (Library of American Lives & Times Ser.). 112p. (gr. 5-5). 69.20 *(978-1-60853-474-6(X))* Rosen Publishing Group, Inc., The.

ADOLESCENCE

see also Puberty

Adams, Andrea. If We Were Girlfriends, This Is What I'd Tell You: Straight Talk for Teenage Girls. 2008. (Illus.). 142p. (YA). per. 12.99 *(978-0-9743432-0-4(X))* Panacea Publishing.

Alexander, Kwame, et al. Love & Profanity: A Collection of True, Tortured, Wild, Hilarious, Concise, & Intense Tales of Teenage Life. 2015. (ENG.). 232p. (gr. 8-12). 16.95 *(978-1-63079-012-7(5))* Switch Pr.

Allenbaugh, Kay. Chocolate for a Teen's Dreams: Heartwarming Stories about Making Your Wishes Come True. 2003. (ENG., Illus.). 224p. pap. 16.95 *(978-0-7432-3703-1(X),* Touchstone) Touchstone.

Arthur, Kay, et al. How to Study Your Bible for Teens. 2004. 176p. (YA). pap. 9.99 *(978-0-7369-0965-5(6))* Harvest Hse. Pubs.

Babour Staff & Frazier, April. 3-Minute Devotions for Teen Girls: 180 Encouraging Readings. 2015. (3-Minute Devotions Ser.). (ENG.). 192p. pap. 4.99 *(978-1-63058-856-4(3),* Barbour Bks.) Barbour Publishing, Inc.

Bialik, Mayim. Girling Up, 9 vols. 2017. (ENG.). (YA). 170.91 **(978-0-525-48653-4(4));** 192p. (gr. 7). 18.99 *(978-0-399-54860-4(2))* Penguin Young Readers Group. (Philomel Bks.).

Bickerstaff, Linda. Smart Strategies for Saving & Building Wealth. 2014. (Financial Security & Life Success for Teens Ser.). (Illus.). 80p. (J). (gr. 7-12). pap. 84.90 *(978-1-4777-7629-2(X))* Rosen Publishing Group, Inc., The.

Bradley, Michael J. Yes, Your Parents Are Crazy! A Teen Survival Handbook. Glasbergen, Randy, illus. 2004. (ENG.). 432p. pap. 14.95 *(978-0-936197-48-7(X))* Harbor Pr., Inc.

Brecon, Connah. Tomorrow. 2005. (Illus.). 32p. (J). (gr. -1-7). *(978-0-7344-0730-6(0),* Lothian Children's Bks.) Hachette Australia.

Brown, Marty. Infogirl: A Girl's Guide to the Internet. rev. ed. 2005. (Girls' Guides). (Illus.). 48p. (YA). (gr. 5-8). lib. bdg. 29.25 *(978-0-8239-2984-9(1),* GGINGI) Rosen Publishing Group, Inc., The.

Burgen, Jim. What's the Big Deal about My Parents? Reeves, Dale, ed. 2006. (What's the Big Deal Ser.). 160p. (gr. 7-18). pap. 10.99 *(978-0-7847-1252-8(2),* 23335) Standard Publishing.

Carlson, Dale. The Teen Brain Book: Who & What Are You? Teasdale, Nancy, ed. Nicklaus, Carol, illus. 2004. (ENG.). 230p. (gr. 7-12). pap. 14.95 *(978-1-884158-29-2(3))* Team Kreskin Productions, LLC.

—Understand Your Self: Teen Manual for the Understanding of Oneself. 2013. (ENG., Illus.). 192p. (gr. 9-13). pap. 14.95 *(978-1-884158-36-0(6),* 21540f59-9618-4de6-80e4-f5fe89e31805) Team Kreskin Productions, LLC.

Carlson, Melody & Rue, Nancy N. Dear Nancy: Answers to Letters from Girls Like You, 1 vol. 2008. (Faithgirlz Ser.). (ENG.). 160p. (J). pap. 7.99 *(978-0-310-71496-5(6))* Zonderkidz.

Collins-Donnelly, Kate. Starving the Anxiety Gremlin: A Cognitive Behavioural Therapy Workbook on Anxiety Management for Young People. 2013. (Gremlin & Thief CBT Workbooks Ser.). (ENG., Illus.). 168p. (C). pap. 19.95 *(978-1-84905-341-9(3),* 1990) Kingsley, Jessica Pubs. GBR. Dist: Macmillan Distribution Ltd.

Conner, Kate. 10 Things for Teen Girls. 2014. (ENG.). 208p. (J). (gr. 8-12). pap. 14.99 *(978-1-4336-8291-9(5),* B&H Kids) B&H Publishing Group.

Couwenhoven, Terri. Girls' Guide to Growing Up: Choices & Changes in the Tween Years. 2011. (ENG., Illus.). 62p. pap. 16.95 *(978-1-60613-026-1(9))* Woodbine Hse.

Daldry, Jeremy. Teenage Guy's Survival Guide. 2011. 11.04 *(978-0-7848-3378-0(8),* Everbind) Marco Bk. Co.

Davis, Rachel, creator. A Hero's Stand: An Experience of Self Discovery for Teens. 2004. (YA). spiral bd. 18.00 *(978-0-9741833-1-2(8))* Thumbprint Publishing.

Deak, JoAnn & Deak, Terrence. The Owner's Manual for Driving Your Adolescent Brain. Harrison, Freya, illus. 2013. (ENG.). 72p. (J). (gr. 3-9). pap. 15.95 *(978-1-939775-02-3(7),* 9781939775023) March 4th, Inc.

Diaz, Juan R. Amaneciendo en la Adolescencia: Comprendiendo la Adolescencia 2004. (SPA.). 96p. (J). per. 12.00 *(978-0-9758755-1-3(5))* Alpha Behavior Consultants.

Dobson, Danae. Let's Talk! Good Stuff for Girlfriends about God, Guys, & Growing Up. 2003. (ENG.). 204p. (YA). pap. 12.99 *(978-0-8423-0818-2(0))* Tyndale Hse. Pubs.

Donovan, Sandra. Teen Wise Guide to Time Management. 2012. (USA TODAY Teen Wise Guides: Time, Money, & Relationships Ser.). (ENG.). 64p. (gr. 8-12). lib. bdg. 31.93 *(978-0-7613-7019-2(6))* Lerner Publishing Group.

Dunagan, Cindy. Journaling Toward Moral Excellence Volume Two for Pre-Teens Vol. 2: A Character Building Workbook of 100 Thought-Provoking Questions to Help the Young Discover the Value of Moral Strength. 2004. (Journaling Toward Moral Excellence Ser.: Vol. 2). 107p. (J). (gr. 5-7). 11.95 *(978-0-9759871-1-7(9))* Straight Paths Pr.

Espejo, Roman. Tobacco & Smoking. 2015. (Opposing Viewpoints Ser.). (ENG., Illus.). 224p. (J). (gr. 10-12). 48.80 *(978-0-7377-7294-4(8),* Greenhaven Pr., Inc.) Cengage Gale.

FAQ: Teen Life, 6 vols., Set 6. Incl. Frequently Asked Questions about Drinking & Driving. Cefrey, Holly. lib. bdg. 31.95 *(978-1-4042-1809-3(2));* Frequently Asked Questions about Exercise Addiction. Willett, Edward. lib. bdg. 31.95 *(978-1-4042-1806-2(8));* Frequently Asked Questions about Human Papillomavirus. Gonzalez, Lissette. lib. bdg. 31.95 *(978-1-4042-1813-0(0));* Frequently Asked Questions about Migraines & Headaches. Cobb, Allan B. lib. bdg. 31.95 *(978-1-4042-1814-7(9));* Frequently Asked Questions about Peer Pressure. Juzwiak, Richard. lib. bdg. 31.95 *(978-1-4042-1805-5(X));* Frequently Asked Questions about Suicide. Giddens, Sandra. lib. bdg. 31.95 *(978-1-4042-1811-6(4));* (Illus.). 64p. (YA). (gr. 7-12). 2008. 2008. Set lib. bdg. 175.50 *(978-1-4042-1887-1(4))* Rosen Publishing Group, Inc., The.

Favor, Lesli J. Everything You Need to Know about Growth Spurts & Delayed Growth. 2005. (Need to Know Library). (Illus.). 64p. (YA). (gr. 4-6). lib. bdg. 31.95 *(978-0-8239-3549-9(3))* Rosen Publishing Group, Inc., The.

Favor, Leslie. Everything You Need to Know about Growth Spurts & Delayed Growth. 2009. (Need to Know Library). 64p. (gr. 5-5). 58.50 *(978-1-60854-071-6(5))* Rosen Publishing Group, Inc., The.

Fletcher, Carrie Hope. All I Know Now: Wonderings & Reflections on Growing up Gracefully. 2015. (ENG., Illus.). 352p. (YA). (gr. 8-12). pap. 15.95 *(978-1-61519-294-6(8))* Experiment LLC, The.

Fonda, Jane. Being a Teen: Everything Teen Girls & Boys Should Know about Relationships, Sex, Love, Health, Identity & More. 2014. (ENG., Illus.). 288p. (J). pap. 17.00 *(978-0-8129-7861-2(7),* Random Hse. Trade Paperbacks) Random House Publishing Group.

—Being a Teen: Everything Teen Girls & Boys Should Know about Relationships, Sex, Love, Health, Identity & More. 2014. lib. bdg. 29.40 *(978-0-606-35596-4(0))* Turtleback Bks.

Frankenberger, Elizabeth. Crushes, Creeps & Classmates: A Girl's Guide to Getting along with Boys. rev. ed. 2005. (Girls' Guides). (Illus.). 48p. (YA). (gr. 5-8). lib. bdg. 29.25

(978-0-8239-2980-1(9), GGCRCR) Rosen Publishing Group, Inc., The.

Friedman, Hannah. Everything Sucks: Losing My Mind & Finding Myself in a High School Quest for Cool. 2009. (ENG.). 264p. (YA). (gr. 8-12). pap. 12.95 *(978-0-7573-0775-1(2)*, HCI Teens) Health Communications, Inc.

Frohnapfel-Krueger, Lisa. Teen Pregnancy & Parenting. Gale Editors, ed. 2010. (Current Controversies Ser.). (ENG.). 176240p. (gr. 10-12). 44.10 *(978-0-7377-4923-6(7)*, Greenhaven Pr., Inc.) Cengage Gale.

Guillain, Charlotte. 101 Ways to Be a Great Role Model. 2011. (101 Ser.). (ENG., Illus.). 56p. (gr. 5-9). pap. 9.95 *(978-1-4109-4387-3(9)*, NA-r) Heinemann-Raintree.

Hamilton, Bethany. Body & Soul: A Girl's Guide to a Fit, Fun & Fabulous Life, 1 vol. 2014. (ENG.). 160p. (J). pap. 19.99 *(978-0-310-73105-4(4))* Zondervan.

Harris, Ashley Rae. Girl in the Mirror: Understanding Physical Changes, 1 vol. 2008. (Essential Health: Strong Beautiful Girls Set 1 Ser.). (ENG.). 112p. (J). (gr. 6-12). lib. bdg. 35.64 *(978-1-60453-100-8(2))* ABDO Publishing Co.

Hartman, Davida. The Growing up Guide for Girls: What Girls on the Autism Spectrum Need to Know! Suggs, Margaret Anne, illus. 2015. (Growing Up Ser.). (ENG.). 72p. (J). 16.95 *(978-1-84905-574-1(2)*, 2878) Kingsley, Jessica Pubs. GBR. Dist: Macmillan Distribution Ltd.

Hascall, Glenn & Barbour Publishing Staff. 3-Minute Devotions for Guys: 180 Encouraging Readings for Teens. 2015. (3-Minute Devotions Ser.). (ENG.). 192p. pap. 4.99 *(978-1-63058-857-1(1)*, Barbour Bks.) Barbour Publishing, Inc.

Hidalgo-Robert, Alberto. Fat No More: A Teenager's Victory over Obesity. 2012. (J). pap. 16.95 *(978-1-55885-745-2(1)*, Piñata Books) Arte Publico Pr.

Higgins, Melissa. Teen Self-Injury, 1 vol. 2014. (Essential Issues Set 4 Ser.). (ENG.). 112p. (J). (gr. 6-12). lib. bdg. 35.64 *(978-1-62403-423-7(3)*, Essential Library) ABDO Publishing Co.

Jacobson, Ryan. Get a Job at a Business. Cannell, Jon, illus. 2014. (You're in Business! Ser.). (ENG.). 40p. (gr. 5-9). lib. bdg. 27.93 *(978-1-4677-3838-5(7)*, Lerner Pubns.) Lerner Publishing Group.

Kampakis, Kari. 10 Ultimate Truths Girls Should Know, 1 vol. 2014. (ENG.). 224p. (YA). pap. 14.99 *(978-0-529-11103-6(9))* Nelson, Thomas Inc.

Kershner, Tad. Body Double: Understanding Physical Changes, 1 vol. 2010. (Essential Health: a Guy's Guide Ser.). (ENG.). 112p. (J). (gr. 6-12). lib. bdg. 35.64 *(978-1-61613-538-6(7))* ABDO Publishing Co.

King, Bart. The Pocket Guide to Boy Stuff, 1 vol. 2008. (ENG., Illus.). 272p. (J). (gr. 4-8). pap., instr.'s gde. ed. 9.99 *(978-1-4236-0574-4(8))* Gibbs Smith, Publisher.

—The Pocket Guide to Girl Stuff, 1 vol. 2008. (ENG., Illus.). 272p. (J). (gr. 4-8). pap. 9.99 *(978-1-4236-0573-7(X))* Gibbs Smith, Publisher.

Landau, Jennifer. Teens Talk about Body Image & Eating Disorders. 2017. (J). ***(978-1-5081-7632-9(9)***, Rosen Young Adult) Rosen Publishing Group, Inc., The.

MacAdam, Lea. You & Rules in Your Family. 2009. (Family Matters Ser.). 48p. (gr. 5-8). 53.00 *(978-1-61512-483-1(7)*, Rosen Reference) Rosen Publishing Group, Inc., The.

Madaras, Lynda & Madaras, Area. My Body, My Self for Boys. 2nd rev. ed. 2007. (What's Happening to My Body? Ser.). (ENG., Illus.). 128p. (gr. 4-6). pap. 12.99 *(978-1-55704-767-0(7)*, William Morrow Paperbacks) HarperCollins Pubs.

—My Body, My Self for Girls. 3rd rev. ed. 2007. (What's Happening to My Body? Ser.). (ENG., Illus.). 160p. (gr. 4-6). pap. 12.99 *(978-1-55704-766-3(9)*, William Morrow Paperbacks) HarperCollins Pubs.

—¿Que Pasa en Mi Cuerpo? El Libro para Muchachos: La Guía de Mayor Venta Sobre el Desarrollo, Escrita para Adolescentes y Preadolescentes. 2012. (What's Happening to My Body? Ser.). (SPA., Illus.). 256p. (gr. 4-18). pap. 12.99 *(978-1-55704-940-7(8)*, William Morrow Paperbacks) HarperCollins Pubs.

—¿Que Pasa en Mi Cuerpo? Libro para Muchachas: La Guía de Mayor Venta Sobre el Desarrollo Escrita para Adolescentes y Preadolescentes. 2011. (What's Happening to My Body? Ser.). (SPA & ENG., Illus.). 288p. (gr. 4-18). pap. 12.95 *(978-1-55704-939-1(4)*, William Morrow Paperbacks) HarperCollins Pubs.

Madaras, Lynda, et al. "What's Happening to My Body?" Book for Boys. 3rd rev. ed. 2007. (What's Happening to My Body? Ser.). (ENG., Illus.). 256p. (gr. 5-7). pap. 15.99 *(978-1-55704-765-6(0)*, William Morrow Paperbacks) HarperCollins Pubs.

—"What's Happening to My Body?" Book for Girls. 3rd rev. ed. 2007. (What's Happening to My Body? Ser.). (ENG., Illus.). 288p. (gr. 7-9). pap. 14.99 *(978-1-55704-764-9(2)*, William Morrow Paperbacks) HarperCollins Pubs.

—The "What's Happening to My Body?" Book for Boys. 3rd rev. ed. 2007. (What's Happening to My Body? Ser.). (ENG., Illus.). 256p. (gr. 7-9). 24.99 *(978-1-55704-769-4(3)*, Morrow, William & Co.) HarperCollins Pubs.

Mahoney, Emily & MacKay, Jenny. Dealing with Teen Pregnancy. 2017. (Hot Topics Ser.). 112p. (YA). (gr. 7-7). lib. bdg. 39.40 ***(978-1-5345-6019-2(X)***, Lucent Pr.) Greenhaven Publishing LLC.

Malaspina, Ann. False Images, Deadly Promises: Smoking & the Media. 2007. (Tobacco: the Deadly Drug Ser.). (Illus.). 112p. (YA). pap. 12.95 *(978-1-4222-0812-0(5))* Mason Crest.

Martin, Courtney Autumn, et al, illus. Life in Color: A Coloring Book of Teenage Confusion, Creativity, & Discovery. 2016. (ENG.). 96p. (gr. 9-11). pap. 12.95 *(978-1-63079-059-2(1))* Switch Pr.

McKee, Jonathan. The Guy's Guide to God, Girls, & the Phone in Your Pocket: 101 Real-World Tips for Teenaged Guys. 2014. (ENG.). 224p. pap. 12.99 *(978-1-62416-990-8(2)*, Barbour Bks.) Barbour Publishing, Inc.

Merino, Noël. Teens & Privacy. Gale Editor, ed. 2011. (Current Controversies Ser.). (ENG.). 224p. (gr. 12-12). pap. 32.00 *(978-0-7377-5134-5(7)*, Greenhaven Pr., Inc.) Cengage Gale.

—Teens & Privacy. 2011. (Current Controversies Ser.). 240p. lib. bdg. 40.95 *(978-0-7377-5133-8(9)*, Greenhaven Pr., Inc.) Cengage Gale.

Meyer, Stephanie H., et al. Teen Ink: What Matters. 2003. (Teen Ink Ser.). (ENG., Illus.). 400p. (YA). pap. 17.95 *(978-0-7573-0063-9(4)*, HCI Teens) Health Communications, Inc.

Mihaly, Mary E. Getting Your Own Way: A Guide to Growing up Assertively. 2014. (ENG.). 176p. pap. 12.95 *(978-1-59077-306-2(3))* Evans, M. & Co., Inc.

Morrow, Paula. My Parents Are Divorcing. Now What?, 1 vol. 2015. (ENG.). 112p. (YA). 35.60 *(978-1-4777-7986-6(8)*, Rosen Young Adult) Rosen Publishing Group, Inc., The.

Movsessian, Shushann. Puberty Girl. 2005. (ENG., Illus.). 128p. (J). (gr. 4-7). pap. 19.95 *(978-1-74114-104-7(4))* Allen & Unwin AUS. Dist: Independent Pubs. Group.

Nakaya, Andrea C. Growin up in Japan. 2017. (ENG.). 80p. (YA). (gr. 5-12). ***(978-1-68282-219-7(2))*** ReferencePoint Pr., Inc.

Parents Don't Know Everything: A Teen Freedom of Expression Journal. 2004. spiral bd. 9.50 *(978-0-9749216-1-7(0))* Rivers, Swannee.

Parks, Peggy J. Teens & Cheating. 2015. (ENG., Illus.). 96p. (J). lib. bdg. *(978-1-60152-766-0(7))* ReferencePoint Pr., Inc.

Pingry, Patricia A. The Power of Faith for Teens: True Stories. 2004. (Illus.). 160p. pap. 9.95 *(978-0-8249-4622-7(7)*, Ideal Pubns.) Worthy Publishing.

Plaisted, Caroline. Boy Talk. 2011. (ENG., Illus.). 48p. (J). pap. 11.95 *(978-1-926853-90-1(3))* Saunders Bk. Co. CAN. Dist: RiverStream Publishing.

—Girl Talk: Girl Talk: A Survival Guide to Growing Up. 2011. (ENG., Illus.). 48p. (J). pap. 11.95 *(978-1-926853-91-8(1))* Saunders Bk. Co. CAN. Dist: RiverStream Publishing.

Reber, Deborah. Doable: The Girls' Guide to Accomplishing Just about Anything. 2015. (ENG., Illus.). 208p. (YA). (gr. 7). pap. 12.99 *(978-1-58270-466-1(X)*, Simon Pulse) Simon Pulse.

Rice, Ashley. Girls Rule: A Very Special Book Created Especially for Girls. Rice, Ashley, illus. (Illus.). 64p. (J). pap. 9.95 *(978-0-88396-627-3(1)*, Blue Mountain Pr.) Blue Mountain Arts Inc.

Rissman, Rebecca. Calm Girl: Yoga for Stress Relief. 2015. (Yoga for You Ser.). (ENG.). 64p. (gr. 4-5). lib. bdg. 34.65 *(978-1-4914-2121-5(5))* Capstone Press of Coughlan Cos.

—Fit Girl: Yoga for Fitness & Flexibility. 2015. (Yoga for You Ser.). (ENG.). 64p. (gr. 4-5). lib. bdg. 34.65 *(978-1-4914-2120-8(7))* Capstone Press of Coughlan Cos.

—Smart Girl: Yoga for Brain Power. 2015. (Yoga for You Ser.). (ENG.). 64p. (gr. 4-5). lib. bdg. 34.65 *(978-1-4914-2119-2(3))* Capstone Press of Coughlan Cos.

—Strong Girl: Yoga for Building Strength. 2015. (Yoga for You Ser.). (ENG.). 64p. (gr. 4-5). lib. bdg. 34.65 *(978-1-4914-2122-2(3))* Capstone Press of Coughlan Cos.

—Yoga for Your Mind & Body: A Teenage Practice for a Healthy, Balanced Life. 2015. (ENG., Illus.). 208p. (gr. 4-5). pap. 14.95 *(978-1-63079-013-4(3))* Switch Pr.

Ross, Michael, et al. Dating, Relating, Waiting: God's Word on Purity. 2015. (ENG., Illus.). 192p. (YA). pap. 7.99 *(978-1-63058-369-9(3)*, GoTandem) Barbour Publishing, Inc.

Sanford. Today's Teen. 2010. 58p. pap. 12.96 *(978-0-557-15832-4(X))* Lulu Pr., Inc.

Sharp, Katie John. Teenagers & Tobacco: Nicotine & the Adolescent Brain. (Illus.). 112p. 2008. (J). pap. 26.95 *(978-1-4222-1333-9(1))* 2007. (YA). (gr. 3-7). pap. 12.95 *(978-1-4222-0816-8(8))* Mason Crest.

Shellenberger, Susie & Weber, Kristin. The Smart Girl's Guide to God, Guys, & the Galaxy: Save the Drama! & 100 Other Practical Tips for Teens. 2014. (ENG., Illus.). 224p. pap. 12.99 *(978-1-62416-760-7(8)*, Barbour Bks.) Barbour Publishing, Inc.

Tavolacci, Joyce. Teen Wise Guide to Relationships. 2012. (USA TODAY Teen Wise Guides: Time, Money, & Relationships Ser.). (ENG., Illus.). 64p. (gr. 8-12). lib. bdg. 31.93 *(978-0-7613-7018-5(8))* Lerner Publishing Group.

Thrash, Maggie. Honor Girl: A Graphic Memoir. Thrash, Maggie, illus. 2015. (ENG., Illus.). 272p. (YA). (gr. 9). 19.99 *(978-0-7636-7382-6(X))* Candlewick Pr.

Vermond, Kira. Growing Up. Chin, Carl & Owlkids Books Inc. Staff, illus. 2013. (ENG.). 104p. (J). (gr. 7-7). pap. 11.95 *(978-1-77147-004-9(6)*, Owlkids) Owlkids Bks. Inc. CAN. Dist: Publishers Group West (PGW).

—Growing Up, Inside & Out. 2013. 104p. *(978-1-77147-036-0(4))* Owlkids Bks. Inc.

Willis, Laurie, ed. Teen Parenting. 2011. (Issues That Concern You Ser.). (Illus.). 144p. (YA). (gr. 9-12). 36.95 *(978-0-7377-5700-2(0))* Cengage Gale.

Wilson, Michael R. Frequently Asked Questions about How the Teen Brain Works. 2009. (FAQ: Teen Life Ser.). (Illus.). 64p. (J). (gr. 5-6). lib. bdg. 31.95 *(978-1-4358-5324-9(5))* Rosen Publishing Group, Inc., The.

Winkler, Kathleen. Are You Being Bullied? How to Deal with Taunting, Teasing, & Tormenting. 2014. (Got Issues? Ser.). (Illus.). 112p. (J). (gr. 6-12). 33.27 *(978-0-7660-5953-5(7))* Enslow Pubs., Inc.

The Winners. 2005. (YA). 14.95 *(978-0-9661256-4-1(9))* Youth Communication - New York Center.

Wolny, Philip. Abusing Prescription Drugs. 2009. (Incredibly Disgusting Drugs Ser.). 48p. (gr. 5-8). 53.00 *(978-1-61513-492-2(1)*, Rosen Reference) Rosen Publishing Group, Inc., The.

Zep. What's Going on down There? All the Stuff Your Body Won't Tell You about Sex. Zimmerman, Dwight Jon, ed. 2005. (Illus.). 96p. pap. 14.95 *(978-1-4165-0458-0(3))* ibooks, Inc.

ADOLESCENCE—FICTION

Abrams, Amir. Diva Rules. 2015. (Mcpherson High Ser.). (ENG., Illus.). 300p. (YA). (gr. 9). pap. 9.95 *(978-0-7582-9480-7(8)*, Dafina) Kensington Publishing Corp.

Alegria, Malin. Cruzar el Limite (Crossing the Boundary) 2012. (Border Town (Spanish) Ser.: 1). (SPA.). lib. bdg. 16.00 *(978-0-606-26239-2(3)*, Turtleback) Turtleback Bks.

Alfonsi, Alice, adapted by. Face-off. 2006. (Hannah Montana Ser.). (Illus.). 126p. (J). (gr. 3-7). 12.65 *(978-0-7569-8315-4(0))* Perfection Learning Corp.

Alger, Horatio. Driven from Home: Carl Crawford's Experience. reprint ed. pap. 79.00 *(978-1-4047-3564-4(X))* Classic Textbooks.

—Driven from Home: Carl Crawford's Experience. 2006. pap. *(978-1-4065-0702-7(4))* Dodo Pr.

Almond, David. The Tightrope Walkers. 2015. (ENG.). 336p. (YA). (gr. 9). 17.99 *(978-0-7636-7310-9(2))* Candlewick Pr.

Alsaid, Adi. Let's Get Lost. 2015. (ENG.). 384p. (YA). pap. 9.99 *(978-0-373-21149-4(X)*, Harlequin Teen) Harlequin Enterprises, Ltd. CAN. Dist: HarperCollins Pubs.

—Never Always Sometimes. 2015. (ENG.). 320p. (YA). 17.99 *(978-0-373-21154-8(6)*, Harlequin Teen) Harlequin Enterprises, Ltd. CAN. Dist: HarperCollins Pubs.

Amowitz, Lisa. Vision. 2014. (ENG.). 264p. (YA). (gr. 10-12). pap. 9.95 *(978-1-937053-99-4(7))* Spencer Hill Pr.

Anderson, Holli. Five: Out of the Dark. 2013. 250p. (YA). pap. 15.99 *(978-1-62007-299-8(8))* Curiosity Quills Pr.

Angel, Katharine Ann. Being Forgotten. 2012. (Illus.). 218p. pap. *(978-1-908098-45-0(7))* 2QT, Ltd. (Publishing).

Asch, Sheila. Katy's Time. 2007. 184p. pap. 16.95 *(978-1-84753-333-3(7))* Lulu Pr., Inc.

Auth, Jeannine. Emmy's Question. 2010. 155p. pap. 11.99 *(978-0-9790395-3-9(3))* 2007. 151p. (J). (gr. 4-7). 16.99 *(978-0-9790395-2-2(5))* Morningtide Pr.

Axelrod, Amy. Your Friend in Fashion, Abby Shapiro. 2011. (ENG.). 288p. (J). (gr. 3-7). 17.95 *(978-0-8234-2340-8(9))* Holiday Hse., Inc.

Ayarbe, Heidi. Freeze Frame. 2010. (ENG.). 400p. (YA). (gr. 8). pap. 8.99 *(978-0-06-135175-4(X)*, HarperTeen) HarperCollins Pubs.

Ayers, Michelle. Michael. 2011. 134p. pap. 9.99 *(978-0-557-78630-5(4))* Lulu Pr., Inc.

Bailey, Helen. Life at the Shallow End. 2010. (ENG., Illus.). 304p. (YA). (gr. 7-17). pap. 9.99 *(978-0-340-94538-4(9))* Hodder & Stoughton GBR. Dist: Hachette Bk. Group.

Banks, Anna. Joyride. 2015. (ENG.). 288p. (YA). (gr. 7). 17.99 *(978-1-250-03961-3(4)*, 9781250039613) Feiwel & Friends.

—Of Neptune. 2014. (Syrena Legacy Ser.: 3). (ENG.). 336p. (YA). (gr. 8-12). 17.99 *(978-1-250-03960-6(6)*, 9781250039606) Feiwel & Friends.

Baras, Ronit. Be Special, Be Yourself: For Teenagers. 2005. 171p. (YA). per. *(978-0-9757976-0-0(3))* Be Happy in LIFE.

Barnholdt, Lauren. Four Truths & a Lie. 2008. (Mix Ser.). (ENG.). 272p. (J). (gr. 4-8). pap. 5.99 *(978-1-4169-3504-9(5)*, Aladdin) Simon & Schuster Children's Publishing.

Baskin, Nora Raleigh. Surfacing. 2013. (ENG.). 208p. (YA). (gr. 9). 17.99 *(978-0-7636-4908-1(2))* Candlewick Pr.

Bauer, Joan. Hope Was Here. 2005. (ENG.). 208p. (YA). (gr. 7-7). pap. 7.99 *(978-0-14-240424-9(1)*, Puffin Books) Penguin Young Readers Group.

—Hope Was Here. unabr. ed. 2004. 186p. (J). (gr. 7-18). pap. 36.00 incl. audio *(978-0-8072-1706-1(9)*, S YA 1013 SP, Listening Library) Random Hse. Audio Publishing Group.

Baum, L. Frank & van Dyne, Edith. Mary Louise in the Country. 2011. 188p. 26.95 *(978-1-4638-9605-8(0))* Rodgers, Alan Bks.

Becker Holstein, Barbara. The Truth: I'm a Girl, I'm Smart, & I Know Everything! 2007. (Illus.). 91p. (J). per. 6.95 *(978-0-9798952-0-3(0))* Enchanted Self Pr.

Berard, Robin M. King Tut & the Girl Who Loved Him: The Strange Adventures of Johanna Wilson. 2007. 212p. per. 12.95 *(978-1-58348-477-7(9)*, iUniverse Star) iUniverse, Inc.

Bick, Ilsa J. White Space, Bk. 1. 2015. (Dark Passages Ser.: Bk. 1). (ENG.). 560p. (gr. 9). pap. 9.99 *(978-1-60684-565-3(9)*, Carolrhoda Lab™) Lerner Publishing Group.

Blume, Judy. Then Again, Maybe I Won't. (J). 125p. pap. 3.99 *(978-0-8072-1445-9(0))*; 2004. 164p. (gr. 5-9). pap. 29.00 incl. audio *(978-0-8072-0796-3(9)*, LYA 354 SP) Random Hse. Audio Publishing Group. (Listening Library).

Boggess, Eileen. Mia the Melodramatic. 2008. (MIA Fullerton Ser.). 168p. (J). (gr. 6-13). 19.95 *(978-1-890862-56-5(8))* Bancroft Pr.

Bristow, Catherine. My Strange & Terrible Malady. 2008. (YA). pap. 15.95 *(978-1-934575-19-2(4))* Autism Asperger Publishing Co.

Brooks, Bruce. The Moves Make the Man. (J). pap., stu. ed. *(978-0-13-017518-2(8))*; 3rd ed. pap. 3.95 *(978-0-13-800079-0(4))* Prentice Hall (Schl. Div.).

Brooks, Martha. Being with Henry, 1 vol. (ENG.). 174p. pap. 8.95 *(978-0-88899-502-5(4))* Groundwood Bks. CAN. Dist: Publishers Group West (PGW).

Brothers, Marilee. Shadow Moon. 2011. 230p. (YA). pap. *(978-1-61194-058-9(3))* BelleBks., Inc.

Brouwer, Sigmund. Devil's Pass, 1 vol. 2012. (Seven (the Series) Ser.). (ENG., Illus.). 256p. (J). (gr. 5-10). pap. 9.95 *(978-1-55469-938-4(X))* Orca Bk. Pubs. USA.

Brown, Jaye Robin. Georgia Peaches & Other Forbidden Fruit. 2016. 432p. (YA). (gr. 9). 17.99 *(978-0-06-227098-6(2)*, HarperTeen) HarperCollins Pubs.

Bryant, Annie. Bad News/Good News. 2008. (Beacon Street Girls Ser.: 2). (ENG., Illus.). 256p. (J). (gr. 4-8). pap. 7.99 *(978-1-4169-6425-4(8)*, Aladdin) Simon & Schuster Children's Publishing.

—Charlotte in Paris. 2008. (Beacon Street Girls Ser.: No. 1). (ENG.). 224p. (J). (gr. 5-8). pap. 8.99 *(978-1-4169-6428-5(2)*, Aladdin) Simon & Schuster Children's Publishing.

—Fashion Frenzy. 2006. (Beacon Street Girls Ser.: No. 9). (Illus.). 203p. (J). (gr. 4-8). per. 7.99 *(978-1-933566-02-3(7)*, Beacon Street Girls); *(978-1-4156-9393-3(5))* B*tween Productions, Inc.

—Promises, Promises. 2008. (Beacon Street Girls Ser.: 5). (ENG.). 304p. (J). (gr. 4-8). pap. 8.99 *(978-1-4169-6430-8(4)*, Aladdin) Simon & Schuster Children's Publishing.

Burgess, Melvin. The Hit. 2014. (ENG.). 304p. (J). (gr. 9). 17.99 *(978-0-545-55699-6(6)*, Chicken Hse., The) Scholastic, Inc.

Burkhart, Jessica. Comeback. 2012. (Canterwood Crest Ser.: 15). lib. bdg. 18.40 *(978-0-606-26312-2(8)*, Turtleback) Turtleback Bks.

—Home Sweet Drama. 2010. (Canterwood Crest Ser.: 8). (ENG.). 240p. (J). (gr. 4-8). pap. 7.99 *(978-1-4169-9040-6(2)*, Aladdin) Simon & Schuster Children's Publishing.

Butcher, Andrew. The Time of the Reapers, Bk. 1. 2007. (ENG.). 400p. (gr. 7). pap. 12.95 *(978-1-904233-94-7(5))* Little, Brown Book Group Ltd. GBR. Dist: Hachette Bk. Group.

Callaghan, Cindy. Lost in Paris. 2015. (Mix Ser.). (ENG., Illus.). 192p. (J). (gr. 4-8). pap. 7.99 *(978-1-4814-2601-5(X)*, Aladdin) Simon & Schuster Children's Publishing.

—Lost in Rome. 2015. (ENG., Illus.). 208p. (J). (gr. 4-8). 17.99 *(978-1-4814-4282-4(1)*, Aladdin) Simon & Schuster Children's Publishing.

Carey, Anna. Deadfall: The Sequel to Blackbird. 2015. (Blackbird Ser.: 2). (ENG.). 256p. (YA). (gr. 9). 17.99 *(978-0-06-229976-5(X)*, HarperTeen) HarperCollins Pubs.

Carlson, Melody. Lost in Las Vegas, 1 vol. 2014. (Carter House Girls Ser.). (ENG.). 208p. (YA). pap. 9.99 *(978-0-310-74716-1(3))* Zondervan.

Carroll, Jenny, pseud. Safe House. 2011. (1-800-Where-R-You Ser.: 3). (ENG.). 272p. (YA). (gr. 9). pap. 12.99 *(978-1-4424-3084-6(2)*, Simon Pulse) Simon Pulse.

Carroll, Jenny, pseud & Cabot, Meg. Sanctuary. 2007. (1-800-Where-R-You Ser.: No. 4). (ENG., Illus.). 240p. (YA). (gr. 9-12). mass mkt. 6.99 *(978-1-4169-2707-5(7)*, Simon Pulse) Simon Pulse.

Carter, Aimée. The Goddess Test. 2011. (Goddess Test Ser.: 1). lib. bdg. 20.85 *(978-0-606-26943-8(6)*, Turtleback) Turtleback Bks.

Carthage, Lynn. Haunted. 2015. (Arnaud Legacy Ser.: 1). (ENG.). 288p. (YA). (gr. 9). pap. 9.95 *(978-1-61773-626-1(0))* Kensington Publishing Corp.

Cast, P. C. & Cast, Kristin. Hunted. (House of Night Novels Ser.: 5). (ENG.). 336p. (YA). (gr. 7-12). 2013. mass mkt. 9.99 *(978-1-250-04696-3(3)*, 9781250046963, St. Martin's Paperbacks) 2010. pap. 10.99 *(978-0-312-57799-5(0)*, 9780312577995, St. Martin's Griffin) St. Martin's Pr.

—Hunted. l.t. ed. 2010. (House of Night Ser.: Bk. 5). (ENG.). 548p. 23.95 *(978-1-4104-1951-4(7))* Thorndike Pr.

—Untamed. 2008. (House of Night Novels Ser.: 4). (ENG.). 352p. (YA). (gr. 8-12). pap. 10.99 *(978-0-312-37983-4(8)*, 9780312379834, St. Martin's Griffin) St. Martin's Pr.

—Untamed. l.t. ed. 2009. (House of Night Ser.: Bk. 4). (ENG.). 510p. (YA). 23.95 *(978-1-4104-1965-1(7))* Thorndike Pr.

Charles, Norma. The Girl in the Backseat. 2008. (ENG., Ilus.). 184p. (YA). (gr. 7-18). per. *(978-1-55380-056-9(7))* Ronsdale Pr.

Childs, Tera Lynn. Ten Things Sloane Hates about Tru. 2015. (ENG., Illus.). 240p. (J). pap. 14.99 *(978-1-943892-44-0(X))* Entangled Publishing, LLC.

Choyce, Lesley. Hell's Hotel, 1 vol. rev. ed. 2008. (Lorimer SideStreets Ser.). (ENG.). 224p. (YA). (gr. 9-12). 9.95 *(978-1-55277-022-1(2)*, 9781552770221) Lorimer, James & Co., Ltd., Pubs. CAN. Dist: Casemate Pubs. & Bk. Distributors, LLC.

—Last Chance, 1 vol. 2009. (Lorimer SideStreets Ser.). (ENG.). 152p. (YA). (gr. 9-12). 9.95 *(978-1-55277-444-1(9)*, 9781552774441) Lorimer, James & Co., Ltd., Pubs. CAN. Dist: Casemate Pubs. & Bk. Distributors, LLC.

—Scam, 1 vol. 2016. (Orca Soundings Ser.). (ENG.). 144p. (YA). (gr. 8-12). pap. 9.95 *(978-1-4598-1174-4(7))* Orca Bk. Pubs. USA.

Christy Mahler Mills. No Regrets. 2010. 180p. 23.95 *(978-1-4401-9740-6(7))*; pap. 13.95 *(978-1-4401-9738-3(5))* iUniverse, Inc.

Circle of Blue. 2006. (J). *(978-1-933343-37-2(0)*, PONY) Stabenfeldt Inc.

Clamp Staff, ed. Clover. 2003. (Illus.). (YA). 29.99 *(978-1-59182-592-0(X))* TOKYOPOP, Inc.

Clark, Catherine. Picture Perfect. 2008. (ENG.). 352p. (YA). (gr. 9-18). pap. 5.99 *(978-0-06-137497-5(0)*, HarperTeen) HarperCollins Pubs.

Clark, Wook Jin. Megagogo, Vol. 1. 2014. (ENG., Illus.). 176p. (YA). pap. 19.99 *(978-1-62010-117-9(3)*, 9781620101179) Oni Pr., Inc.

Cleary, Beverly & Cleary, B. Fifteen. 2007. (Avon Camelot Bks.). (ENG., Illus.). 208p. (J). (gr. 5-18). pap. 7.99 *(978-0-380-72804-6(4))* HarperCollins Pubs.

Cleary, Christopher. Writing on the Wall. 2007. 198p. (YA). per. 9.99 *(978-0-9795753-5-8(4))* Immortality Pr.

Cofer, Judith Ortiz. An Island Like You: Stories of the Barrio. 2009. 243p. 17.00 *(978-1-60686-446-3(7))* Perfection Learning Corp.

Cohen, Tish. Inside Out Girl. 2008. (P. S. Ser.). (ENG.). 352p. pap. 14.99 *(978-0-06-145295-6(5)*, Harper Perennial) HarperCollins Pubs.

Combs, Sarah. Breakfast Served Anytime. 2016. (ENG.). 272p. (YA). (gr. 7). pap. 7.99 *(978-0-7636-8752-6(9))* Candlewick Pr.

Cook, Eileen. Used to Be: The Education of Hailey Kendrick & Getting Revenge on Lauren Wood. 2012. (ENG., Illus.). 608p. (YA). (gr. 9). pap. 11.99 *(978-1-4424-7514-4(5)*, Simon Pulse) Simon Pulse.

Cormier, Robert. Fade. 2004. (ENG.). 320p. (YA). (gr. 9-17). pap. 7.99 *(978-0-385-73134-8(5)*, Delacorte Bks. for Young Readers) Random Hse. Children's Bks.

Crow, Matthew. The Brilliant Light of Amber Sunrise. 2015. (ENG., Illus.). 304p. (YA). (gr. 9). 17.99 *(978-1-4814-1873-7(4)*, Simon Pulse) Simon Pulse.

Daddo, Andrew. One Step. 2016. (ENG.). 256p. (YA). (gr. 8). 18.99 ***(978-0-14-357361-6(6))*** Random Hse. Australia AUS. Dist: Independent Pubs. Group.

Dahl, Michael. The Horizontal Man: Finnegan Zwake #1. 2008. (Finnegan Zwake Ser.: 1). (ENG.). 192p. (YA). (gr. 7). *(978-1-4169-8668-3(5)*, Simon Pulse) Simon Pulse.

—The Ruby Raven. 2008. (Finnegan Zwake Ser.: 3). (ENG.). 192p. (YA). (gr. 7). pap. 9.99 *(978-1-4169-8666-9(9)*, Simon Pulse) Simon Pulse.

Dale, Mitzi. The Great & Awful Summer, 1 vol. 2007. (ENG.). 192p. (YA). (gr. 8-12). pap. 9.95 *(978-1-55109-614-8(5))* Nimbus Publishing, Ltd. CAN. Dist: Orca Bk. Pubs. USA.

Daley, James Ryan. Jesus Jackson. 2014. (ENG.). 278p. (YA). pap. 10.95 *(978-1-929345-06-9(2))* Poisoned Pen Pr.

Dalton, Michelle. Sixteenth Summer. 2011. (Sixteenth Summer Ser.). (ENG.). 304p. (YA). (gr. 7-18). pap. 9.99 *(978-1-4424-2344-2(7)*, Simon Pulse) Simon Pulse.

Daly, Maureen. Seventeenth Summer. 2010. (ENG.). 384p. (YA). (gr. 7). pap. 9.99 *(978-1-4169-9463-3(7)*, Simon Pulse) Simon Pulse.

De Goldi, Kate. The 10 PM Question. 2012. (ENG., Illus.). 256p. (YA). (gr. 7). pap. 6.99 *(978-0-7636-5848-9(0))* Candlewick Pr.

De la Cruz, Melissa. The Ashley Project. 2014. (Ashley Project Ser.: 1). (ENG., Illus.). 288p. (J). (gr. 4-8). pap. 6.99

(978-1-4424-9033-8(0), Aladdin) Simon & Schuster Children's Publishing.

—Fresh off the Boat. 2005. (Illus.). 256p. (J). (gr. 7-18). 15.99 (978-0-06-054540-6(2)) HarperCollins Pubs.

—Social Order. 2014. (Ashley Project Ser.: 2). (ENG., Illus.). 288p. (J). (gr. 4-8). 16.99 (978-1-4814-0667-3(1), Simon & Schuster/Paula Wiseman Bks.) Simon & Schuster/Paula Wiseman Bks.

Deaver, Julie Reece & Deaver, Julie. Say Goodnight, Gracie. 20th anniv. ed. 2009. (Charlotte Zolotow Bk.). (ENG.). 224p. (YA). (gr. 8-18). pap. 8.99 (978-0-06-447007-0(5), HarperTeen) HarperCollins Pubs.

DeClements, Barthe. Nothing's Fair in Fifth Grade. 137p. (J). (gr. 3-5). pap. 4.50 (978-0-8072-1413-8(2), Listening Library) Random Hse. Audio Publishing Group.

Dekker, James C. Impact, 1 vol. 2009. (Orca Soundings Ser.). (ENG.). 112p. (YA). (gr. 8-12). 16.95 (978-1-55143-997-6(2)); pap. 9.95 (978-1-55143-995-2(6)) Orca Bk. Pubs. USA.

Denman, K. L. Perfect Revenge, 1 vol. 2009. (Orca Currents Ser.). (ENG.). (J). (gr. 5-9). 112p. 16.95 (978-1-55469-103-6(6)); 128p. pap. 9.95 (978-1-55469-102-9(8)) Orca Bk. Pubs. USA.

—La Revanche Parfaite, 1 vol. 2011. (FRE.). 144p. (J). (gr. 5-9). pap. 9.95 (978-1-55469-853-0(7)) Orca Bk. Pubs. USA.

—Spiral, 1 vol. 2008. (Orca Soundings Ser.). (ENG.). (YA). (gr. 8-12). 112p. 16.95 (978-1-55143-932-7(8)); 128p. pap. 9.95 (978-1-55143-930-3(1)) Orca Bk. Pubs. USA.

Derting, Kimberly. The Replaced. 2015. (Taking Ser.: 2). (ENG.). 368p. (YA). (gr. 9). 17.99 (978-0-06-229363-3(X), HarperTeen) HarperCollins Pubs.

Dessen, Sarah. How to Deal: Someone Like You & That Summer. movie tie-in ed. 2003. (ENG.). 496p. (YA). (gr. 7-7). pap. 8.99 (978-0-14-250103-0(4), Puffin Books) Penguin Young Readers Group.

—The Truth about Forever. 2006. (ENG.). 400p. (YA). (gr. 7-18). reprint ed. 10.99 (978-0-14-240625-0(2), Speak) Penguin Young Readers Group.

—The Truth about Forever. 2007. 374p. (gr. 7-12). 20.00 (978-0-7569-8275-1(8)) Perfection Learning Corp.

—The Truth about Forever. (YA). 2006. 1.25 (978-1-4193-2647-9(3)) 2005. 127.75 (978-1-4193-3880-9(3)) 2005. 107.75 (978-1-4193-2650-9(3)) Recorded Bks., Inc.

Disney Book Group. Girl Meets World Friend Power. No New Art Needed, illus. 2016. (Girl Meets World Junior Novel Ser.). (ENG.). 128p. (J). (gr. 3-7). pap. 5.99 (978-1-4847-6715-3(2)) Disney Pr.

Disney Book Group Staff. Girl Meets World Follow Your Heart. 2015. (Girl Meets World Junior Novel Ser.). (ENG., Illus.). 128p. (J). (gr. 3-7). pap. 5.99 (978-1-4847-2812-3(2)) Disney Pr.

—Pining Away. 2014. (Gravity Falls Ser.: 1). (J). lib. bdg. 14.75 (978-0-606-35287-1(2)) Turtleback Bks.

Divine, L. The Fight. 2008. (Drama High Ser.: Vol. 1). 202p. (gr. 8-12). 19.95 (978-0-7569-8830-2(6)) Perfection Learning Corp.

Donovan, John. I'll Get There. It Better Be Worth the Trip: 40th Anniversary Edition. 40th ed. 2010. (ENG.). 240p. (YA). (gr. 8-18). pap. 11.99 (978-0-7387-2174-7(4), Flux) North Star Editions.

Dower, Laura. Three's a Crowd. 2004. (From the Files of Madison Finn Ser.). (Illus.). 182p. (J). 12.65 (978-0-7569-5263-1(8)) Perfection Learning Corp.

Duncan, Lois. Killing Mr. Griffin. 223p. (YA). (gr. 7-18). pap. 4.50 (978-0-8072-1373-5(X), Listening Library) Random Hse. Audio Publishing Group.

Dunn, Pintip. Forget Tomorrow. 2015. (Forget Tomorrow Ser.: 1). (ENG.). 400p. (YA). 16.99 (978-1-63375-238-2(0), 9781633752382) Entangled Publishing, LLC.

Effie, Sandy. New Comings of What's Next. 2011. 32p. pap. 16.95 (978-1-4626-0708-2(X)) America Star Bks.

Elfgren, Sara B. & Strandberg, Mats. Fire: The Engelsfors Trilogy Book II. 2014. (Engelsfors Trilogy Ser.: 2). (ENG.). 704p. (gr. 9-13). 18.99 (978-1-4683-0672-9(3), 460672) Overlook Pr., The.

Elizabeth, Lauren. Looks of an Angel. 2012. 148p. (-18). pap. 12.00 (978-1-4575-1445-6(1)) Dog Ear Publishing, LLC.

Elkeles, Simone. How to Ruin My Teenage Life. 2007. (How to Ruin a Summer Vacation Novel Ser.: 2). (ENG.). 288p. (YA). (gr. 7-12). per. 11.99 (978-0-7387-1019-8(9), Flux) North Star Editions.

Ellis, Deborah. Parvana's Journey, 1 vol. 2015. (Breadwinner Ser.). (ENG., Illus.). 200p. (J). (gr. 4-9). pap. 9.95 (978-1-55498-770-2(9)) Groundwood Bks. CAN. Dist: Publishers Group West (PGW).

Eulberg, Elizabeth. Better off Friends. 2014. (ENG.). 288p. (J). (gr. 7). 17.99 (978-0-545-55145-8(5)) Scholastic, Inc.

Evans, Leslie, illus. You Have to Be Smart If You're Going to Be Tall/Tienes Que Ser Inteligente Si Vas a Ser Alta. 2006. 46p. (J). (gr. -1-3). per. 16.99 (978-1-59879-217-1(2)) Lifevest Publishing, Inc.

Everett, Sarah. Everyone We've Been. 2016. (ENG., Illus.). 400p. (YA). (gr. 7). 17.99 (978-0-553-53844-1(6), Knopf Bks. for Young Readers) Random Hse. Children's Bks.

Ewing, Deborah. Secret Celebrity. 2009. (Hodder African Readers Ser.). (Illus.). 112p. pap. 12.95 (978-0-340-98420-8(1)) Hodder Education Group GBR. Dist: Trans-Atlantic Pubns., Inc.

Farrant, Natasha. What We Did for Love: Resistance, Heartbreak, Betrayal. 2014. (Illus.). 208p. (YA). (gr. 6-12). pap. 10.95 (978-1-62324-029-5(8)) Enslow Pubs., Inc.

Fifteen. 190p. (YA). (gr. 7-18). pap. 4.99 (978-0-8072-1361-2(6), Listening Library) Random Hse. Audio Publishing Group.

Figueroa, Acton. So Not the Drama. 2005. (Illus.). 79p. (J). (978-1-4156-3929-0(9)) Disney Pr.

Fison, Julie. The Call of the Wild. 2015. (ENG.). 288p. (J). pap. (978-1-61067-388-4(3)) Kane Miller.

Foon, Dennis. Skud, 1 vol. 2004. (ENG.). 176p. (YA). pap. 9.95 (978-0-88899-549-0(0)) Groundwood Bks. CAN. Dist: Publishers Group West (PGW).

Freeman, Shannon. High School High, 1 vol. 2013. (Port City High Ser.). (ENG.). 199p. (YA). (gr. 9-12). pap. 9.95 (978-1-62250-037-6(7)) Saddleback Educational Publishing, Inc.

—Taken, 1 vol. 2013. (Port City High Ser.). (ENG.). 199p. (YA). (gr. 9-12). pap. 9.95 (978-1-62250-038-3(5)) Saddleback Educational Publishing, Inc.

Friesen, Gayle. For Now. 2007. (ENG.). 248p. (J). (gr. 5-9). 7.95 (978-1-55453-133-2(0)) Kids Can Pr., Ltd. CAN. Dist: Hachette Bk. Group.

Frost, Helen. Keesha's House. 2011. 9.46 (978-0-7848-3534-0(9), Everbind) Marco Bk. Co.

Gaertner, Connie. Wake-Up Calls. 2013. 154p. (gr. 10-12). pap. 12.95 (978-1-4759-6646-6(0)) iUniverse, Inc.

Garvie, Maureen. Amy by Any Other Name. 2009. (ENG.). 256p. (YA). (gr. 7-18). pap. (978-1-55470-142-1(2)) Me to We.

Getson, Denise. Dry Souls. 2011. (ENG.). 200p. (YA). (gr. 8-3). pap. 7.95 (978-1-933767-12-3(X)) CBAY Bks.

Giles, Gail. Girls Like Us. 2014. (ENG.). 224p. (YA). (gr. 9). 16.99 (978-0-7636-6267-7(4)) Candlewick Pr.

Gingras, Charlotte. Pieces of Me. Ouriou, Susan, tr. from FRE. 2009. (ENG.). 144p. (J). (gr. 7-9). 8.95 (978-1-55453-432-6(1)) Kids Can Pr., Ltd. CAN. Dist: Hachette Bk. Group.

Godbersen, Anna. Rumors. 2008. (Luxe Ser.: No. 2). (YA). (gr. 9-12). (ENG.). 304p. 17.99 (978-0-06-134569-2(5)); 423p. lib. bdg. 18.89 (978-0-06-134570-8(9)) HarperCollins Pubs. (HarperTeen).

Goldstein, Lori A. Becoming Jinn. 2015. (Becoming Jinn Ser.: 1). (ENG.). 384p. (YA). (gr. 7). 17.99 (978-1-250-05539-2(3), 9781250055392) Feiwel & Friends.

Goobie, Beth. Hello, Groin, 1 vol. 2006. (ENG.). 292p. (YA). (gr. 8-12). 17.95 (978-1-55143-459-9(8)) Orca Bk. Pubs. USA.

Gow, Kailin. Loving Summer. 2012. 250p. (-18). pap. 9.99 (978-1-59748-044-4(4), The Edge) Sparklesoup LLC.

Grant, Vicki. Pigboy. 2007. (Orca Currents Ser.). 101p. (gr. 5). 19.95 (978-0-7569-8067-2(4)) Perfection Learning Corp.

Graziano, Alexandra Marie. The Colors of Rayne. 2012. 140p. pap. 19.99 (978-1-4771-0791-1(6)) Xlibris Corp.

Greenberg, Joanne. I Never Promised You a Rose Garden. 256p. (YA). (gr. 7-18). pap. 5.99 (978-0-8072-1362-9(4), Listening Library) Random Hse. Audio Publishing Group.

Greg, Neri. Yummy: The Last Days of a Southside Shorty. 2014. (ENG.). 94p. (YA). (gr. k-3). 21.20 (978-1-63245-250-4(2)) Lectorum Pubns., Inc.

Griffiths, Corinne Escobar. Corky Eckelsbriar. 2004. (J). pap. 6.95 (978-0-9760271-0-2(0)) Cappella Publishing, A.

Griffiths, Sara. Thrown a Curve. 2007. 151p. (ENG.). (gr. 6-10). pap. 13.99 (978-1-890862-49-7(5)); (J). (gr. 5-13). 16.95 (978-1-890862-48-0(7)) Bancroft Pr.

Grossman, Linda Sky & Toronto Child Abuse Centre Staff. I'M a Great Little Kid, Set. (ENG., Illus.). 1p. 79.95 (978-1-896764-75-7(4)) Second Story Pr. CAN. Dist: Orca Bk. Pubs. USA.

—I'm a Great Little Kid, Set. (ENG., Illus.). 1p. pap. 39.95 (978-1-896764-74-0(6)) Second Story Pr. CAN. Dist: Orca Bk. Pubs. USA.

Gulledge, Laura Lee. Page by Paige. 2011. (ENG., Illus.). 192p. (YA). (gr. 7-17). 18.95 (978-0-8109-9721-9(5)); pap. 9.95 (978-0-8109-9722-6(3)) Abrams, Inc. (Amulet Bks.).

Gutman, Dan. Johnny Hangtime. 2008. (ENG.). 144p. (J). (gr. 3-7). pap. 5.99 (978-0-380-81012-3(3)) HarperCollins Pubs.

Han, Jenny. Always & Forever, Lara Jean. 2017. (To All the Boys I've Loved Before Ser.: 3). (ENG., Illus.). 336p. (YA). (gr. 7). 17.99 (978-1-4814-3048-7(3), Simon & Schuster Bks. For Young Readers) Simon & Schuster Bks. For Young Readers.

Hargrove, Jason. Looking Good, Cody Greer. 2006. 188p. pap. 24.95 (978-1-4241-4013-8(7)) PublishAmerica, Inc.

Harkins, Philip. Knockout. 2011. 250p. 46.95 (978-1-258-08794-4(4)) Literary Licensing, LLC.

Harper, Benjamin & Scieszka, Jon. All Around Trucktown. Shannon, David et al, illus. 2008. (Jon Scieszka's Trucktown Ser.). (ENG.). 32p. (J). (gr. -1-1). 3.99 (978-1-4169-4194-1(0), Simon Scribbles) Simon Scribbles.

Harris, Rachel. A Tale of Two Centuries. 2013. (Entangled Teen Ser.). (ENG.). 320p. (YA). (gr. 7-12). pap. 9.99 (978-1-62266-012-4(9), 9781622660124) Entangled Publishing, LLC.

Harrison, Lisi. P. S. I Loathe You. 2009. (Clique Ser.: 10). (ENG.). 224p. (YA). (gr. 7-17). pap. 9.99 (978-0-316-00681-1(5), Poppy) Little, Brown Bks. for Young Readers.

—P. S. I Loathe You. 2008. (Clique Novels Ser.). 208p. 20.00 (978-1-60686-338-1(X)) Perfection Learning Corp.

Harrison, Lisi, creator. Dylan. 2008. (Clique Ser.). (ENG.). 144p. (YA). (gr. 10-17). pap. 6.99 (978-0-316-03565-1(3), Poppy) Little, Brown Bks. for Young Readers.

Harrison, S. Infinity Rises, 0 vols. 2016. (Infinity Trilogy Ser.: 2). (ENG.). 261p. (YA). (gr. 9-13). pap. 9.99 (978-1-5039-5225-6(8), 9781503952256, Skyscape) Amazon Publishing.

Hartnett, Sonya. Butterfly. (ENG.). 240p. (YA). (gr. 9). 2013. pap. 7.99 (978-0-7636-6334-6(4)) 2010. (Illus.). 16.99 (978-0-7636-4760-5(8)) Candlewick Pr.

Hartt-Sussman, Heather. Nana's Summer Surprise. Graham, Georgia, illus. 2013. (ENG.). 32p. (J). (gr. -1-1). 17.95 (978-1-77049-324-7(7), Tundra Bks.) Tundra Bks. CAN. Dist: Penguin Random Hse. LLC.

Harvey, Sarah N. Three Little Words, 1 vol. 2012. (ENG.). 224p. (YA). (gr. 8-12). pap. 14.95 (978-1-4598-0065-6(6)) Orca Bk. Pubs. USA.

Hasiuk, Brenda. Your Constant Star, 1 vol. 2014. (ENG.). 248p. (YA). (gr. 8-12). pap. 12.95 (978-1-4598-0368-8(X)) Orca Bk. Pubs. USA.

Hautman, Pete. What Boys Really Want. 2012. (ENG.). 304p. (J). (gr. 7). 17.99 (978-0-545-11315-1(6), Scholastic Pr.) Scholastic, Inc.

Hawkins, Karen. The Seduction of Sara. 2009. (ENG.). 384p. pap. 7.99 (978-0-380-81526-5(5), Avon Bks.) HarperCollins Pubs.

Hawthorne, Rachel. Caribbean Cruising. 2004. (ENG.). 336p. (YA). (gr. 9-18). pap. 5.99 (978-0-06-056507-7(1), HarperTeen) HarperCollins Pubs.

—Labor of Love. 2008. (ENG.). 320p. (YA). (gr. 9-18). pap. 5.99 (978-0-06-136384-9(7), HarperTeen) HarperCollins Pubs.

Hayes, Sonia. Eye Candy. 2008. (YA). per. 9.95 (978-0-9777573-2-9(3)) NUA Multimedia.

—Ms. Thang. 2009. (ENG.). 200p. (YA). per. 9.95 (978-0-9777573-0-5(7)) NUA Multimedia.

Heathfield, Lisa. Seed. 2015. (ENG.). 336p. (YA). (gr. 7). 16.95 (978-0-7624-5634-5(5), Running Pr. Kids) Running Pr. Bk. Pubs.

Herman, Carli. Good Graffiti Teen Talk on Tough Issues. 2009. 108p. pap. 10.00 (978-0-578-01524-8(2)) Black Bart Bks.

Herrick, Steven. The Simple Gift. 2004. (ENG.). 192p. (YA). (gr. 9). pap. 9.99 (978-0-689-86867-2(7), Simon Pulse) Simon Pulse.

Higgins, M. G. Falling Out of Place, 1 vol. 2013. (Gravel Road Ser.). (ENG.). 191p. (YA). (gr. 9-12). pap. 9.95 (978-1-62250-021-5(0)) Saddleback Educational Publishing, Inc.

—Falling Out of Place. 2013. (Gravel Road Ser.). (YA). lib. bdg. 20.80 (978-0-606-26963-6(0), Turtleback) Turtleback Bks.

Highley, Kendra C. Finding Perfect. 2015. (ENG., Illus.). 248p. (J). pap. 15.99 (978-1-943892-43-3(1)) Entangled Publishing, LLC.

Hijuelos, Óscar & Óscar, Hijuelos. Dark Dude. Roja, Alberto Jimenez, tr. 2010. (SPA.). 430p. (YA). (gr. 9-18). 19.99 (978-84-441-4316-3(2)) Everest Editora ESP. Dist: Lectorum Pubns., Inc.

Hoffmann, Kerry Cohen. Easy. 2007. (ENG.). 176p. (YA). (gr. 9-12). pap. 6.99 (978-1-4169-1426-6(9), Simon & Schuster Bks. For Young Readers) Simon & Schuster Bks. For Young Readers.

Holman, Felice. Slake's Limbo. unabr. ed. 2004. 117p. (J). (gr. 7-18). pap. 29.00 incl. audio (978-0-8072-8744-6(X), YA254SP, Listening Library) Random Hse. Audio Publishing Group.

Homzie, Hillary. Things Are Gonna Get Ugly. 2009. (Mix Ser.). (ENG.). 272p. (J). (gr. 4-8). pap. 5.99 (978-1-4169-7563-2(2), Aladdin) Simon & Schuster Children's Publishing.

Hopkins, Cathy. Love Lottery. 2012. (Truth or Dare Ser.). (ENG.). 208p. (YA). (gr. 7). pap. 11.99 (978-1-4424-7176-4(X), Simon Pulse) Simon Pulse.

Hopkins, Cathy & Hopkins, Cathy. White Lies & Barefaced Truths. 2005. (Truth or Dare Ser.: No. 1). (ENG.). 176p. (YA). (gr. 7-12). mass mkt. 3.99 (978-1-4169-1152-4(9), Simon Pulse) Simon Pulse.

Hopkins, Ellen. Traffick. (ENG., Illus.). 528p. (YA). (gr. 9). 2017. pap. 10.99 (978-1-4424-8288-3(5)) 2015. 18.99 (978-1-4424-8287-6(7)) McElderry, Margaret K. Bks. (McElderry, Margaret K. Bks.).

—Tricks. (ENG.). (YA). (gr. 9). 2017. 656p. pap. 11.99 (978-1-4814-9824-1(X)) 2009. 640p. 22.99 (978-1-4169-5007-3(9)) McElderry, Margaret K. Bks. (McElderry, Margaret K. Bks.).

—Tricks. 2011. lib. bdg. 24.50 (978-0-606-23290-6(7), Turtleback) Turtleback Bks.

Hornby, Nick. Slam. (ENG.). 320p. (gr. 12). 2009. 16.00 (978-1-59448-471-1(6)) 2008. 15.00 (978-1-59448-345-5(0)) Penguin Publishing Group. (Riverhead Bks. (Hardcover)).

Hourihan, Kelly. 4 to 16 Characters. 2013. 376p. pap. 11.50 (978-0-9897411-0-1(9)) Lemon Sherbet Pr.

Howell, Robert. Third Times the Charm. 2007. (ENG.). 224p. (gr. 4-7). per. 12.95 (978-1-897235-20-1(8)) Thistledown Pr., Ltd. CAN. Dist: Univ. of Toronto Pr.

Hughes, Alison. Lost in the Backyard, 1 vol. 2015. (ENG.). 144p. (J). (gr. 4-7). pap. 9.95 (978-1-4598-0794-5(4)) Orca Bk. Pubs. USA.

Humphries, Jessie. Killing Ruby Rose, 0 vols. 2014. (Ruby Rose Ser.: 1). (ENG.). 304p. (YA). (gr. 9-12). pap. 9.99 (978-1-4778-2006-3(X), 9781477820063, Amazon Children's Publishing) Amazon Publishing.

Jacobs, Evan. Screaming Quietly, 1 vol. 2013. (Gravel Road Ser.). (ENG.). 212p. (YA). (gr. 9-12). pap. 9.95 (978-1-62250-003-1(2)) Saddleback Educational Publishing, Inc.

Johnston, Julie. Hero of Lesser Causes. pap. 6.95 (978-0-7737-5850-6(X)) Stoddart Kids CAN. Dist: Fitzhenry & Whiteside, Ltd.

—Hero of Lesser Causes. 2003. (ENG.). 232p. (J). (gr. 5). pap. 10.95 (978-0-88776-649-7(8), Tundra Bks.) Tundra Bks. CAN. Dist: Penguin Random Hse. LLC.

Jonach, Ingrid. When the World Was Flat (And We Were in Love) 2013. 320p. (J). pap. (978-1-908844-57-6(4), Angry Robot, Limited) Watkins Media Limited.

Jones, Ursula. Star Turn. 2012. (Inside Pocket Single Titles Ser.). (ENG.). 32p. (gr. 5-12). pap. (978-1-908458-16-2(X)) Inside Pocket Publishing, Ltd.

Jonsberg, Barry. Reckoning. 2016. (Pandora Jones Ser.). (ENG.). 336p. (YA). (gr. 8). pap. 12.99 (978-1-74331-813-3(8)) Allen & Unwin AUS. Dist: Independent Pubs. Group.

Joseph, Lynn. The Color of My Words. unabr. ed. 2004. 96p. (J). (gr. 3-7). pap. 29.00 incl. audio (978-0-8072-0659-1(8), Listening Library) Random Hse. Audio Publishing Group.

Juckes, Deborah Sioux. Meesha, Guardian of Grand Mountain: Book One of the Guardian Series. McCleary, Twila, illus. 2005. (Guardian Ser.: Bk. 1). (YA). pap. 12.95 (978-0-9767748-0-8(1)) Red Earth Publishing.

—Meesha, Guardian of Grand Mountain: Book One of the Guardian Series. McCleary, Twila, illus. 2005. (YA). 18.95 (978-0-9767748-1-5(X)) Red Earth Publishing.

Kelley, Ann. The Burying Beetle. 2005. (ENG.). 208p. (gr. 7-9). per. 19.95 (978-1-84282-099-5(0), 9781842820995) Luath Pr. Ltd. GBR. Dist: Midpoint Trade Bks., Inc.

Kenneally, Miranda. Stealing Parker. 2012. (Hundred Oaks Ser.: Bk. 2). (ENG.). 256p. (YA). (gr. 7-12). pap. 10.99 (978-1-4022-7187-8(5)) Sourcebooks, Inc.

Kenny A Portrait of a Prodigy. 2004. per. (978-1-59581-010-6(2)) Brentwood Communications Group.

Kerbel, Deborah. Girl on the Other Side. 2009. (ENG., Illus.). 152p. (YA). (gr. 6-18). pap. 10.99 (978-1-55488-443-8(8), Dundurn Pr.) Dundurn CAN. Dist: Ingram Publisher Services.

King, A. S. I Crawl Through It. 2015. (ENG.). 336p. (YA). (gr. 10-17). 18.00 (978-0-316-33409-9(X)) Little, Brown Bks. for Young Readers.

King, M. C. Truth or Dare. 2nd ed. 2008. (Hannah Montana Ser.). (Illus.). 126p. (gr. 3-7). 15.00 (978-0-7569-8336-9(3)) Perfection Learning Corp.

Kinsella, Sophie, pseud. Finding Audrey. (ENG.). 304p. (YA). (gr. 7). 2016. pap. 9.99 (978-0-553-53653-9(2), Ember) 2015. 18.99 (978-0-553-53651-5(6), Delacorte Pr.) Random Hse. Children's Bks.

—Finding Audrey. 2016. lib. bdg. 20.85 (978-0-606-38874-0(5)) Turtleback Bks.

Knight, Christopher. World Is Black & White. 2008. 459p. (YA). pap. 14.95 (978-1-893699-97-7(8)) AudioCraft Publishing, Inc.

Koertge, Ronald. The Arizona Kid. 2005. (ENG.). 304p. (YA). (gr. 9-18). pap. 6.99 (978-0-7636-2695-2(3)) Candlewick Pr.

—Deadville. 2008. (ENG., Illus.). 224p. (YA). (gr. 9). 16.99 (978-0-7636-3580-0(4)) Candlewick Pr.

Konigsberg, Bill. Openly Straight. 2015. (ENG.). 336p. (J). (gr. 9). pap. 9.99 (978-0-545-79865-5(5), Levine, Arthur A. Bks.) Scholastic, Inc.

Kropp, Paul. The Edge Is Burning. Doherty, Catherine, illus. 2008. 112p. (YA). (gr. 7-18). pap. (978-1-897039-33-5(6)) High Interest Publishing (HIP).

Krulik, Nancy. Puppy Love. 2011. (Romantic Comedies Ser.). (ENG.). 224p. (YA). (gr. 7). pap. 12.99 (978-1-4424-3079-2(6), Simon Pulse) Simon Pulse.

L&ostroke, et al. Omstigning. 2011. 230p. pap. 26.50 (978-87-7114-326-3(2)) Bks. on Demand.

Laflamme, Mark. Guys Named Jack. 2013. 308p. pap. 17.95 (978-1-62646-391-2(3)) Booklocker.com, Inc.

Lambert, Janet. Just Jenifer. 2011. 184p. 42.95 (978-1-258-09133-0(X)) Literary Licensing, LLC.

Lantz, Francess L. Current Affairs. 2004. (Luna Bay Ser.: No. 9). 176p. mass mkt. 4.99 (978-0-06-059521-0(3), Harper Entertainment) HarperCollins Pubs.

—Sea for Yourself. 2004. (Luna Bay Ser.: No. 8). 176p. mass mkt. 4.99 (978-0-06-059520-3(5), Harper Entertainment) HarperCollins Pubs.

Larson, Hope. Chiggers. Larson, Hope, illus. 2008. (ENG., Illus.). 176p. (J). (gr. 5-9). pap. 11.99 (978-1-4169-3587-2(8), Simon & Schuster/Paula Wiseman Bks.) Simon & Schuster Children's Publishing.

Layboume, Emmy. Savage Drift. 2014. (Monument 14 Ser.: 3). (ENG.). 320p. (YA). (gr. 8). 17.99 (978-1-250-03642-1(9), 9781250036421) Feiwel & Friends.

L'Engle, Madeleine. A House Like a Lotus. 2012. (ENG.). 336p. (YA). (gr. 7-12). pap. 11.99 (978-0-312-54798-1(6), 9780312547981) Square Fish.

Lieberman, Leanne. Gravity, 1 vol. 2008. (ENG.). 280p. (YA). (gr. 7-12). pap. 12.95 (978-1-55469-049-7(8)) Orca Bk. Pubs. USA.

Livingston, Lesley. Starling. 2075. (ENG.). 368p. (J). (gr. 8). 9.99 (978-0-06-206308-3(1), HarperTeen) HarperCollins Pubs.

Llewellyn, Tom. The Shadow of Seth: A Seth Anomundy Murder Mystery. 2015. (Seth Anomundy Murder Mysteries Ser.). (ENG.). viii, 174p. (YA). pap. 10.95 (978-1-929345-18-2(6)) Poisoned Pen Pr.

London, Alex. Proxy. 2014. (ENG.). 432p. (YA). (gr. 7). pap. 10.99 (978-0-14-751133-1(X), Speak) Penguin Young Readers Group.

Lost in the Wilderness. 2006. (J). (978-1-933343-39-6(7), PONY) Stabenfeldt Inc.

Luck, Gail. Bumduggle Davis Beats the Boobrats or the Inauguration of the Motherless Club. 2011. 146p. pap. 12.50 (978-1-61204-727-0(0), Strategic Bk. Publishing) Strategic Book Publishing & Rights Agency (SBPRA).

MacIntyre, R. P. Feeding at Nine. 2006. (ENG.). 187p. per. 17.95 (978-1-897235-15-7(1)) Thistledown Pr., Ltd. CAN. Dist: Univ. of Toronto Pr.

Mackler, Carolyn. Vegan Virgin Valentine. 2004. (ENG., Illus.). 240p. (YA). (gr. 9-18). 16.99 (978-0-7636-2155-1(2)) Candlewick Pr.

Malik, S. A. Omari's Flight: The Mercy of Love. 2007. (Illus.). 81p. (YA). per. 7.98 (978-0-9794615-0-7(2)) EDR.

Manaster, Ilana. Doreen. 2016. (ENG.). 336p. (YA). (gr. 2-17). 16.95 (978-0-7624-5962-9(X), Running Pr. Kids) Running Pr. Bk. Pubs.

Manell, Keane. Hall Pass to the Tenth Dimension. 2009. 56p. pap. 10.95 (978-1-4389-7401-9(9)) AuthorHouse.

Manning, Sarra. Guitar Girl. 2003. (ENG.). 256p. (YA). pap. (978-0-340-86071-7(5)) Hodder & Stoughton.

—Guitar Girl. 2005. (ENG.). 240p. (YA). (gr. 7-9). reprint ed. pap. 6.99 (978-0-14-240318-1(0), Speak) Penguin Young Readers Group.

Marien, Donna. Waiting at the Bay: A Young Woman's Reflections on Journeys in the Sea of Life. 2003. 108p. (YA). pap. 10.95 (978-0-595-26304-2(6), Writers Club Pr.) iUniverse, Inc.

Marrone, Amanda. Revealers. 2008. (ENG.). 288p. (YA). (gr. 9-18). pap. 8.99 (978-1-4169-5874-1(6), Simon Pulse) Simon Pulse.

Martinez, Victor. Parrot in the Oven. Scott, Steve, illus. rev. ed. 2004. (ENG.). 240p. (YA). (gr. 8-18). pap. 8.99 (978-0-06-447186-2(1), Rayo) HarperCollins Pubs.

Maruno, Jennifer. Totem, 0 vols. 2014. (ENG.). 168p. (YA). pap. 10.99 (978-1-4597-1934-7(4), 9781459719347) Dundurn CAN. Dist: Ingram Publisher Services.

Mason, Simon. Running Girl. 2016. (ENG.). 432p. (J). (gr. 9). 18.99 (978-1-338-03642-8(4)) Scholastic, Inc.

Maunder, Roger. Mundy Pond. 2006. (ENG.). 195p. per. (978-1-897174-09-8(8), Tuckamore Bks) Creative Bk. Publishing.

May, Judy. Blue Lavender Girl. 2006. (Journals). (ENG., Illus.). 192p. (J). pap. 12.95 (978-0-86278-991-6(5)) O'Brien Pr., Ltd., The IRL. Dist: Dufour Editions, Inc.

—Copper Girl. 2006. (Journals). (ENG., Illus.). 160p. (J). pap. 12.95 (978-0-86278-990-9(7)) O'Brien Pr., Ltd., The IRL. Dist: Dufour Editions, Inc.

Mayhew, Julie. Red Ink. 2016. (ENG.). 320p. (YA). (gr. 9). 16.99 (978-0-7636-7731-2(0)) Candlewick Pr.

McCaffrey, Kate. Crashing Down. 2015. 304p. (YA). (gr. 7). 14.95 (978-1-922089-85-4(0)) Fremantle Pr. AUS. Dist: Independent Pubs. Group.

McClintock, Norah. Bang, 1 vol. 2007. (Orca Soundings Ser.). (ENG.). 112p. (YA). (gr. 8-12). per. 9.95 (978-1-55143-654-8(X)) Orca Bk. Pubs. USA.

McClymer, Kelly. Getting to Third Date. 2006. (Romantic Comedies Ser.). (ENG., Illus.). 304p. (YA). (gr. 9-18). mass mkt. 6.99 (978-1-4169-1479-2(X), Simon Pulse) Simon Pulse.

McCoola, Marika. Baba Yaga's Assistant. 2015. (ENG., Illus.). 136p. (J). (gr. 5). 16.99 (978-0-7636-6961-4(X)) Candlewick Pr.

McCormick, Patricia. Cut. unabr. ed. 2004. 168p. (J). (gr. 7-18). pap. 36.00 incl. audio (978-0-8072-0868-7(X), LYA 320 SP, Listening Library) Random Hse. Audio Publishing Group.

—Cut. 2011. (gr. 7-12). lib. bdg. 19.65 (978-0-613-49394-9(X), Turtleback) Turtleback Bks.

—Sold. 2011. 10.36 (978-0-7848-3420-6(2), Everbind) Marco Bk. Co.

McCredie, Elise. Nowhere Boys. 2016. (ENG.). 314p. (YA). (gr. 7). pap. 12.99 (978-1-76012-016-0(2)) Hardie Grant Egmont Pty, Ltd. AUS. Dist: Independent Pubs. Group.

McGee, Ron. Ryan Quinn & the Rebel's Escape. Samnee, Chris, illus. 2016. (Ryan Quinn Ser.: 1). 368p. (J). (gr. 3-7). 16.99 (978-0-06-242164-7(6)) HarperCollins Pubs.

McGill, Nichole. Girl #3. 2009. (ENG.). 224p. (YA). (gr. 7-18). pap. (978-1-55470-143-8(0)) Me to We.

McGinnis, Mindy. The Female of the Species. (YA). (gr. 9). 2017. 368p. pap. 9.99 **(978-0-06-232090-2(4))** 2016. 352p. 17.99 (978-0-06-232089-6(0)) HarperCollins Pubs. (Tegen, Katherine Bks).

McGowan, Anthony. The Fall. 2012. (Stoke Books Titles Ser.). (ENG.). 64p. (YA). (gr. 8-12). pap. 6.95 (978-1-78112-094-1(3)); lib. bdg. 22.60 (978-1-78112-095-8(1)) Lerner Publishing Group.

McGowan, Sharlene. Macaroni Monday. 2007. 112p. (YA). per. 10.95 (978-0-595-45984-1(6)) iUniverse, Inc.

McNamara, Brian. Breaking up Point. 2015. (ENG.). 36p. (YA). (gr. 9). pap. 11.95 (978-1-62639-430-8(X)) Bold Strokes Bks.

Meaney, Roisin. Don't Even Think about It. 2006. (Journals). (ENG., Illus.). 192p. (J). pap. 12.95 (978-0-86278-984-8(2)) O'Brien Pr., Ltd., The IRL. Dist: Dufour Editions, Inc.

Medina, Nico. Fat Hoochie Prom Queen. 2008. (ENG.). 320p. (YA). (gr. 9-18). pap. 8.99 (978-1-4169-3603-9(3), Simon Pulse) Simon Pulse.

Melcher, Rich. A Work in Progress. 2011. 148p. 29.99 (978-1-4568-5192-7(6)); pap. 15.99 (978-1-4568-5191-0(8)) Xlibris Corp.

Michener, Tara. No Longer Besties: And Other Assorted Teenage Drama. 2011. 192p. (gr. 10-12). pap. 14.99 (978-1-4634-0118-4(3)) AuthorHouse.

Mikaelsen, Ben. Jungle of Bones. 2014. (ENG.). 224p. (J). (gr. 3-7). 16.99 (978-0-545-44287-9(7)) Scholastic, Inc.

Mizutani, Fuka. Love at Fourteen. 2015. (Love at Fourteen Ser.: 3). (ENG., Illus.). 192p. (J). (gr. 8-17). pap. 15.00 (978-0-316-29876-6(X), Yen Pr.) Orbit.

Molnar, Gwen. Hate Cell: A Casey Templeton Mystery. 2009. (Casey Templeton Mystery Ser.: 1). (ENG.). 184p. (YA). (gr. 5). pap. 11.99 (978-1-55002-850-8(2)) Dundurn CAN. Dist: Ingram Publisher Services.

Moore, Stephanie Perry & Moore, Derrick. Golden Heart - Deep Soul, 1 vol. 2013. (Grovehill Giants Ser.: Bk. 2). (ENG.). 320p. (YA). (gr. 9-12). pap. 14.95 (978-1-62250-684-2(7)) Saddleback Educational Publishing, Inc.

Moreira, Carol. Charged, 1 vol. 2008. (Lorimer SideStreets Ser.). (ENG.). 128p. (YA). (gr. 9-12). 9.95 (978-1-55277-006-1(0), 9781552770061); 16.95 (978-1-55277-008-5(7), 9781552770085) Lorimer, James & Co., Ltd., Pubs. CAN. Dist: Casemate Pubs. & Bk. Distributors, LLC.

Morgan, Melissa J. And the Winner Is... 2007. (Camp Confidential Ser.: 18). (ENG.). 160p. (J). (gr. 3-7). pap. 4.99 (978-0-448-44652-3(9), Grosset & Dunlap) Penguin Young Readers Group.

—Suddenly Last Summer. 2008. (Camp Confidential Ser.: 20). (ENG.). 160p. (J). (gr. 3-7). pap. 4.99 (978-0-448-44881-7(5), Grosset & Dunlap) Penguin Young Readers Group.

—Super Special. 2007. (Camp Confidential Ser.: 14). (ENG.). 256p. (J). (gr. 4-7). pap. 5.99 (978-0-448-44452-9(6), Grosset & Dunlap) Penguin Young Readers Group.

—TTYL. 2005. (Camp Confidential Ser.: 5). (ENG.). 160p. (J). (gr. 4-7). pap. 4.99 (978-0-448-43961-7(1), Grosset & Dunlap) Penguin Young Readers Group.

Morris, Taylor. Class Favorite. 2007. (Mix Ser.). (ENG., Illus.). 304p. (J). (gr. 4-8). pap. 5.99 (978-1-4169-3598-8(3), Simon & Schuster/Paula Wiseman Bks.) Simon & Schuster/Paula Wiseman Bks.

Moses, Jennifer Anne. Tales from My Closet. 2014. (ENG.). 304p. (J). (gr. 7-9). 17.99 (978-0-545-51608-2(0), Scholastic Pr.) Scholastic, Inc.

Murphy, Julie. Ramona Blue. (YA). (gr. 8). 2018. (ENG.). 448p. pap. 9.99 **(978-0-06-241836-4(X))** 2017. 432p. 17.99 (978-0-06-241835-7(1)) HarperCollins Pubs.

Myers, Walter Dean. Scorpions. 2013. (Trophy Bk.). (ENG.). 240p. (YA). (gr. 8-18). pap. 8.99 (978-0-06-447066-7(0)); 25th anniv. ed. pap. 9.99 (978-0-06-440623-9(7)) HarperCollins Pubs. (Amistad).

—Scorpions. 2013. 216p. (YA). (gr. 7-12). lib. bdg. 19.65 (978-0-8335-4233-5(8), Turtleback) Turtleback Bks.

Naylor, Phyllis Reynolds. Alice In-Between. 2008. (Alice McKinley Ser.: No. 6). (ENG.). 176p. (J). pap. 5.99 (978-1-4169-6770-5(2), Simon & Schuster/Paula Wiseman Bks.) Simon & Schuster/Paula Wiseman Bks.

—Cricket Man. 2008. (ENG.). 208p. (YA). (gr. 7-18). 16.99 (978-1-4169-4981-7(X), Atheneum Bks. for Young Readers) Simon & Schuster Children's Publishing.

Neilson, G. G. Beogall's Choice - How a Boy & a Bird Rescue Nature. 2012. 320p. (978-1-77097-517-0(9)); pap. (978-1-77097-518-7(7)) FriesenPress.

Nickerson, Sara. The Secrets of Blueberries, Brothers, Moose & Me. 2016. (ENG.). 336p. (J). (gr. 5). 8.99 (978-0-14-751179-9(8), Puffin Books) Penguin Young Readers Group.

Noel Paul, Chrisana B. The Crescent Street Crew: A novel teens & young adults can identify With. 2008. 69p. pap. 8.95 (978-1-4327-2466-5(5)) Outskirts Pr., Inc.

Oates, Joyce Carol. Small Avalanches & Other Stories. 2003. 400p. (YA). 17.89 (978-0-06-001218-2(8), HarperTeen) HarperCollins Pubs.

Oliver, Lauren. Replica. (Replica Ser.: 1). (YA). (gr. 9). 2017. 560p. pap. 12.99 **(978-0-06-239417-0(7))** 2016. 544p. 19.99 (978-0-06-239416-3(9)) HarperCollins Pubs.

—RÉPLICA. 2017. (SPA.). (YA). (gr. 8-12). pap. 21.95 **(978-84-666-6144-7(1))** Ediciones B ESP. Dist: Spanish Pubs., LLC.

Olsen, Mary-Kate & Olsen, Ashley. Camp Rock 'N' Roll. 2005. (ENG.). 112p. (978-0-00-718091-2(8)) HarperCollins Pubs. Australia.

—Twist & Shout. 2005. (ENG., Illus.). 112p. (978-0-00-718092-9(6)) HarperCollins Pubs. Australia.

Orme, Helen. Don't Even Think It. 2008. (Cutting Edge Ser.). (ENG.). 168p. pap. (978-1-84167-698-2(5)) Ransom Publishing Ltd.

O'Shea, M.J. Cold Moon [Library Edition]. 2nd ed. 2014. 180p. pap. 14.99 (978-1-62798-460-7(7), Harmony Ink Pr.) Dreamspinner Pr.

Palatini, Margie. The Zoey Zone. Palatini, Margie, illus. 2008. (ENG., Illus.). 192p. (J). (gr. 3-6). 10.99 (978-0-06-113898-0(3), Tegen, Katherine Bks) HarperCollins Pubs.

Payne, K. E. Because of Her. 2014. (ENG.). 264p. (J). (gr. 7). pap. 11.95 (978-1-62639-049-2(5)) Bold Strokes Bks.

Pearce, Jacqueline. Weeds & Other Stories. 2006. (ENG.). 144p. pap. 10.95 (978-1-894345-64-4(9)) Thistledown Pr., Ltd. CAN. Dist: Univ. of Toronto Pr.

Pearson, Ridley. Power Play. 2012. (Kingdom Keepers Ser.: 4). (J). lib. bdg. 19.65 (978-0-606-23613-3(9), Turtleback) Turtleback Bks.

Peck, Richard. A Long Way from Chicago. unabr. ed. 2004. 176p. (J). (gr. 5-9). pap. 36.00 incl. audio (978-0-8072-8126-0(3), Listening Library) Random Hse. Audio Publishing Group.

—Remembering the Good Times. 181p. (YA). (gr. 7-18). pap. 4.50 (978-0-8072-1380-3(2), Listening Library) Random Hse. Audio Publishing Group.

Peck, Robert Newton. A Day No Pigs Would Die. 139p. (YA). (gr. 7-18). pap. 4.99 (978-0-8072-1357-5(8)); pap. 4.99 (978-0-8072-1384-1(5)) Random Hse. Audio Publishing Group. (Listening Library).

Peet, Mal & Rosoff, Meg. Beck. 2017. (ENG.). 272p. (YA). (gr. 11). 17.99 (978-0-7636-7842-5(2)) Candlewick Pr.

Perreault, Diane Juttner. Breath of the Dragon. 2005. (ENG.). 208p. pap. 16.95 (978-1-894283-54-0(6)) Great Plains Pubns. CAN. Dist: Publishers Group Canada.

Pfitzenmaier, Audrey. Cheating Fate, 1 vol. 2008. (ENG.). 240p. (J). (gr. 8-18). pap. 12.95 (978-1-897235-41-6(0)) Thistledown Pr., Ltd. CAN. Dist: Univ. of Toronto Pr.

Phillips, Dee. Mirror, 1 vol. 2014. (Right Now! Ser.). (ENG.). 48p. (YA). (gr. 9-12). pap. 8.95 (978-1-62250-879-2(3)) Saddleback Educational Publishing, Inc.

Poling, Atarah L. Forbidden Secret: Shadows Behind Locked Doors. 2011. 162p. pap. 24.95 (978-1-4560-5477-9(5)) America Star Bks.

The Pony Winter. 2007. (J). (978-1-933343-42-6(7), PONY) Stabenfeldt Inc.

Poulsen, David A. Last Sam's Cage. rev. ed. 2004. (ENG.). 224p. (YA). pap. 9.95 (978-1-55263-611-4(9)) Keyhole Pr.

Priest, Robert. The Paper Sword. 2014. (Spell Crossed Ser.: 1). (ENG.). 224p. (YA). pap. 12.99 (978-1-4597-0826-6(1), 9781459708266) Dundurn CAN. Dist: Ingram Publisher Services.

Prm, Katherine & Dee, Stacy. The Veil. 2010. 233p. (YA). pap. 15.95 (978-1-59705-540-6(9)) Wings ePress, Inc.

Rainbird, Becky. Taking Notes. 2010. (Lucky Six Ser.: 3). (ENG., Illus.). 160p. (J). (gr. 4-7). pap. 6.99 (978-1-4052-3944-8(1)) Egmont Bks., Ltd. GBR. Dist: Independent Pubs. Group.

Ramsey, Jo. Work Boots & Tees. (YA). 2016. (ENG., Illus.). (gr. 9-12). 24.99 **(978-1-63477-997-5(5)**, Harmony Ink Pr.) 2015. 156p. (978-1-61372-834-5(4)) Dreamspinner Pr.

Ray, Gracie. Falling Slowly. 2012. 270p. (978-1-105-59084-9(4)) Lulu.com.

Reisfeld, Randi. Partiers Preferred. 2007. (Summer Share Ser.). (ENG.). 288p. (YA). (gr. 9-12). pap. 13.99 (978-1-4169-0037-5(3), Simon Pulse) Simon Pulse.

Rennison, Louise. Angus, Thongs & Full-Frontal Snogging. 2006. (Confessions of Georgia Nicolson Ser.: 1). (ENG.). 272p. (YA). (gr. 8-18). pap. 9.99 (978-0-06-447227-2(2), HarperTeen) HarperCollins Pubs.

—Angus, Thongs & Full-Frontal Snogging. 2009. (Confessions of Georgia Nicolson Ser.: No. 1). 10.36 (978-0-7848-1994-4(7), Everbind) Marco Bk. Co.

—Angus, Thongs & Full-Frontal Snogging. (Confessions of Georgia Nicolson Ser.: 1). (J). 2008. 70.49 (978-1-4281-7895-3(3)) 2005. 1.25 (978-1-4193-4293-6(2)) 2004. 68.75 (978-1-4025-9087-0(3)) Recorded Bks., Inc.

Rice, Morgan. Before Dawn (Vampire, Fallen-Book 1) 2016. (ENG., Illus.). 118p. (J). pap. 6.99 (978-1-63291-611-2(8)) Morgan Rice Bks.

Rillera, Catherine. Freedom. 2003. 440p. (YA). pap. 22.95 (978-0-595-27088-0(3), Writers Club Pr.) iUniverse, Inc.

Roat, Sharon Huss. Between the Notes. 2015. (ENG.). 400p. (YA). (gr. 9). 17.99 (978-0-06-229172-1(6), HarperTeen) HarperCollins Pubs.

Roberts, Lisa Brown. Playing the Player. 2015. (ENG., Illus.). 316p. (J). pap. 17.99 (978-1-943892-56-3(3)) Entangled Publishing, LLC.

Robico. My Little Monster 3. 2014. (My Little Monster Ser.). (ENG., Illus.). 176p. (YA). (gr. 9). pap. 10.99 (978-1-61262-599-7(1)) Kodansha America, Inc.

—My Little Monster 4. 2014. (My Little Monster Ser.). (ENG., Illus.). 176p. (YA). pap. 10.99 (978-1-61262-600-0(9)) Kodansha America, Inc.

Robinson, Anitha. Broken Worlds. 2014. (Broken Worlds Ser.). (ENG.). 200p. (YA). (gr. 8-11). pap. 8.95 (978-1-933767-37-6(5)) CBAY Bks.

Roman, Dave. Teen Boat! The Race for Boatlantis. Green, John, illus. 2015. (ENG.). 160p. (YA). (gr. 7). 14.99 (978-0-547-86563-8(5)) Houghton Mifflin Harcourt Publishing Co.

Rooyen, Suzanne Van. The Other Me [Library Edition]. 2014. 216p. pap. 14.99 (978-1-62798-645-8(6), Harmony Ink Pr.) Dreamspinner Pr.

Rud, Jeff. Centerville. 2016. (Orca Sports Ser.). lib. bdg. 20.80 (978-0-606-38688-3(2)) Turtleback Bks.

Rushton, Rosie. I Think I'll Just Curl up & Die. 2005. 176p. (J). pap. 5.99 (978-0-7868-5188-1(0)) Hyperion Bks. for Children.

—Just Don't Make a Scene, Mum! 2005. 224p. (J). pap. 5.99 (978-0-7868-5186-7(4)) Hyperion Bks. for Children.

Russell, Rachel Renée. Tales from a Not-So-Dorky Drama Queen, 3 vols. unabr. ed. 2015. (Dork Diaries: 8). (ENG.). 320p. (gr. 4-8). audio compact disk 14.99 (978-1-4423-7023-4(8)) Simon & Schuster Audio.

—Tales from a Not-So-Dorky Drama Queen. Russell, Rachel Renée, illus. 2015. (Dork Diaries: Bk. 9). (ENG., Illus.). 352p. (J). (gr. 4-8). 13.99 (978-1-4424-8769-7(0), Aladdin Paperbacks) Simon & Schuster Children's Publishing.

Saddleback Educational Publishing Staff, ed. Score, 1 vol. unabr. ed. 2011. (Heights Ser.). (ENG.). 50p. (gr. 5-8). 7.95 (978-1-61651-624-6(0)) Saddleback Educational Publishing, Inc.

Schaeffer, Teresa. The Questions Within. 2008. (Cutting Edge Ser.). (ENG.). 144p. pap. (978-1-84167-700-2(0)) Ransom Publishing Ltd.

Schraff, Anne E. Deliverance, 1 vol. unabr. ed. 2011. (Urban Underground Ser.). (ENG.). 198p. (YA). (gr. 9-12). pap. 9.95 (978-1-61651-587-4(2)) Saddleback Educational Publishing, Inc.

Schuck, Philip. A Ricochet from Circumstance. 2005. (YA). 19.95 (978-0-9764670-0-7(3)) Smithfield Capital Corp.

Scott, Elizabeth. Something, Maybe. 2010. (ENG.). 240p. (YA). (gr. 9). pap. 9.99 (978-1-4169-5356-2(6), Simon Pulse) Simon Pulse.

Scrimger, Richard. Me & Death: An Afterlife Adventure. 2010. (ENG.). 192p. (YA). (gr. 5). pap. 12.95 (978-0-88776-796-8(6), Tundra Bks.) Tundra Bks. CAN. Dist: Penguin Random Hse. LLC.

Sharafeddine, Fatima. The Servant, 1 vol. 2017. (ENG.). 160p. (J). (gr. 6). pap. 9.95 (978-1-55498-308-7(8)) Groundwood Bks. CAN. Dist: Publishers Group West (PGW).

Shaw, J. D. Leave No Footprints. 2011. (ENG.). 276p. (J). (gr. 7). pap. 14.95 (978-0-9845318-6-8(6)) Tiny Stachel Pr.

Sheldon, Dyan. Confessions of a Teenage Drama Queen. braille ed. 2003. (J). (gr. 2). spiral bd. (978-0-616-15873-9(4)) Canadian National Institute for the Blind/Institut National Canadien pour les Aveugles.

Shraya, Vivek. God Loves Hair. Neufeld, Juliana, illus. 2014. (ENG.). 112p. (gr. 6). pap. 18.95 (978-1-55152-543-3(7), 399) Arsenal Pulp Pr. CAN. Dist: Consortium Bk. Sales & Distribution.

Shusterman, Neal. Challenger Deep. 2016. (YA). lib. bdg. 20.85 (978-0-606-38734-7(X)) Turtleback Bks.

Simone, Ni-Ni & Abrams, Amir. Get Ready for War. 2013. (Hollywood High Ser.: 2). 423p. (YA). lib. bdg. 20.80 (978-0-606-27305-3(0), Turtleback) Turtleback Bks.

Slater, Calvin. Game On. 2015. 332p. (YA). (978-1-4806-9396-8(0)) Kensington Publishing Corp.

—Hold Me Down. 2015. (Coleman High Ser.: 2). (ENG., Illus.). 328p. (J). (gr. 9). pap. 9.95 (978-1-61773-134-1(X), Dafina) Kensington Publishing Corp.

Smith, Kirsten. The Geography of Girlhood. 2007. (ENG.). 192p. (YA). (gr. 7-17). per. 7.99 (978-0-316-01735-0(3)) Little, Brown Bks. for Young Readers.

Sobat, Gail Sidonie. Gravity Journal. 2008. (ENG.). 162p. (YA). (gr. 15-18). pap. 14.95 (978-1-894283-78-6(3)) Great Plains Pubns. CAN. Dist: Publishers Group Canada.

Spady, Angie. Catie Conrad: Faith, Friendship & Fashion Disasters. Everidge, Channing, illus. 2014. (Desperate Diva Diaries Ser.). (ENG.). 304p. (gr. 3-7). 12.99 (978-1-4336-8460-9(8), B&H Kids) B&H Publishing Group.

—Catie Conrad: How to Become the Most (un)Popular Girl in Jr. High. Everidge, Channing, illus. 2015. (Desperate Diva Diaries Ser.). (ENG.). 304p. (gr. 3-7). pap. 8.99 (978-1-4336-8461-6(6), B&H Kids) B&H Publishing Group.

Sparks, Megan. Falling Hard, 1 vol. 2013. (Roller Girls Ser.). (ENG.). 256p. (gr. 8-10). 12.95 (978-1-62370-023-2(X)) Capstone Young Readers of Coughlan Cos.

—Hell's Belles, 1 vol. 2013. (Roller Girls Ser.). (ENG.). 256p. (gr. 8-10). 12.95 (978-1-62370-024-9(8)) Capstone Young Readers of Coughlan Cos.

Spears, Rick. Black Metal Volume 3: Darkness Enthroned: Darkness Enthroned. 2014. (ENG., Illus.). 160p. (YA). pap. 11.99 (978-1-934964-82-8(4), 9781934964828) Oni Pr., Inc.

Stanley, Malaika Rose. Dance Dreams. 2013. (ENG., Illus.). 144p. (J). (gr. 3-6). pap. 8.99 (978-1-84853-055-3(2)) Transworld Publishers Ltd. GBR. Dist: Independent Pubs. Group.

Stanton, Angie. Royally Lost. 2014. (ENG.). 336p. (YA). (gr. 8). pap. 9.99 (978-0-06-227258-4(6), HarperTeen) HarperCollins Pubs.

Staunton, Ted. Ace's Basement, 1 vol. 2013. (Orca Currents Ser.). (ENG.). 112p. (J). (gr. 5-9). pap. 9.95 (978-1-4598-0437-1(6)); lib. bdg. 16.95 (978-1-4598-0438-8(4)) Orca Bk. Pubs. USA.

Stevens, R. Bacon Is a Vegetable, Coffee Is a Vitamin, Vol. 2. 2014. (ENG., Illus.). 136p. (YA). pap. 19.99 (978-1-62010-091-2(6), 9781620100912) Oni Pr., Inc.

Stevenson, Robin. Under Threat, 1 vol. 2016. (Orca Soundings Ser.). (ENG.). 144p. (YA). (gr. 8-12). pap. 9.95 (978-1-4598-1131-7(3)) Orca Bk. Pubs. USA.

Stewart, Michael F. Assured Destruction. 2013. 188p. pap. (978-0-9812699-4-8(X)) Non Sequitur Pr.

Stine, R. L. Can You Keep a Secret? 2016. (Fear Street Ser.). (ENG.). 272p. (YA). 18.99 (978-1-250-05894-2(5), 9781250058942, St. Martin's Griffin) St. Martin's Pr.

Stone, Tanya Lee. A Bad Boy Can Be Good for a Girl. 2007. (ENG.). 240p. (YA). (gr. 7-11). per. 8.99 (978-0-553-49509-6(7), Lamb, Wendy Bks.) Random Hse. Children's Bks.

Strasser, Todd. Can't Get There from Here. 2012. (ENG.). 224p. (YA). (gr. 7). pap. 8.99 (978-1-4424-3357-1(4), Simon & Schuster Bks. For Young Readers) Simon & Schuster Bks. For Young Readers.

Stringham, Jean. Balance. 2011. 208p. (J). pap. 14.99 (978-1-59955-518-8(2), Bonneville Bks.) Cedar Fort, Inc./CFI Distribution.

Sugg, Zoe. Girl Online: On Tour. 2016. (ENG.). (Girl Online Book Ser.: 2). 368p. (gr. 7). pap. 11.99 (978-1-5011-0034-5(3), Atria Bks.); (J). pap. 13.00 **(978-1-5011-5958-9(5))** Simon & Schuster.

—Girl Online - On Tour. 2015. (Girl Online Book Ser.: 2). (ENG., Illus.). 352p. (gr. 7-12). 17.99 (978-1-5011-0033-8(5), Atria Bks.) Simon & Schuster.

—Girl Online: 3. 2016. (Girl Online Book Ser.: 3). (ENG., Illus.). 336p. (gr. 7). 17.99 (978-1-5011-6211-4(X), Atria Bks.) Simon & Schuster.

Sugg, Zoe "Zoella". Girl Online. 2014. (ENG.). 352p. 17.99 (978-1-4767-9745-8(5), Atria Bks.) Simon & Schuster.

Suma, Nova Ren. Dani Noir. 2009. (ENG.). 272p. (J). (gr. 4-9). 15.99 (978-1-4169-7564-9(0), Simon & Schuster/Paula Wiseman Bks.) Simon & Schuster/Paula Wiseman Bks.

Summers, Tamara. Never Bite a Boy on the First Date. 2009. (ENG.). 288p. (YA). (gr. 9-18). pap. 5.99 (978-0-06-172154-0(9), HarperTeen) HarperCollins Pubs.

Tamaki, Mariko. This One Summer. Tamaki, Jillian, illus. 2014. (ENG.). 320p. (YA). (gr. 7). 21.99 (978-1-62672-094-7(0), 9781626720947); pap. 18.99 (978-1-59643-774-6(X), 9781596437746) Roaring Brook Pr. (First Second Bks.).

Tea, Michelle. Girl at the Bottom of the Sea. Verwey, Amanda, illus. 2015. (ENG.). 240p. (gr. 6). 19.95 (978-1-940450-00-1(4)) McSweeney's Publishing.

Toliver, Wendy. The Secret Life of a Teenage Siren. 2012. (Romantic Comedies Ser.). (ENG.). 304p. (YA). (gr. 7). pap. 14.99 (978-1-4424-7494-9(7), Simon Pulse) Simon Pulse.

Toon, Paige. I Knew You Were Trouble: A Jessie Jefferson Novel. 2016. (Jessie Jefferson Novels Ser.: 2). (ENG.). 336p. (J). pap. 9.99 (978-1-4711-1880-7(0), Simon & Schuster Children's) Simon & Schuster, Ltd. GBR. Dist: Simon & Schuster, Inc.

Torres, J. Degrassi the Next Generation Extra Credit Suddenly, Last Summer. Northcott, Ed, illus. 2nd ed. 2006. (Degrassi the Next Generation Ser.). (ENG.). 128p. (J). pap. (978-1-55168-320-1(2)) Fenn, H. B. & Co., Ltd.

—Degrassi The Next Generation Extra Credit Turning Japanese. 2006. (Degrassi the Next Generation Ser.). (ENG., Illus.). 120p. (J). pap. (978-1-55168-318-8(0)) Fenn, H. B. & Co., Ltd.

Trottier, Maxine. Three Songs for Courage. 2008. (ENG.). 328p. (YA). (gr. 9). pap. 10.95 (978-0-88776-831-6(8), Tundra Bks.) Tundra Bks. CAN. Dist: Penguin Random Hse. LLC.

Tullson, Diane. Riley Park, 1 vol. 2009. (Orca Soundings Ser.). (ENG.). 128p. (YA). (gr. 8-12). pap. 9.95 (978-1-55469-123-4(0)) Orca Bk. Pubs. USA.

Valentino, Amanda & Stolarz, Laurie Faria. Shattered, Bk. 3. 2011. (Amanda Project Ser.: 3). (ENG.). 272p. (YA). (gr. 8). pap. 8.99 (978-0-06-174217-0(1), HarperTeen) HarperCollins Pubs.

Vestry, Annabelle. The Carlyles, Vol. 1. 2008. (Gossip Girl: the Carlyles Ser.: 1). (ENG.). 256p. (YA). (gr. 10-17). pap. 10.99 (978-0-316-02064-0(8), Poppy) Little, Brown Bks. for Young Readers.

Von Schlichten, David. H-E-Double Hockey Stick. 2011. 124p. pap. 19.95 (978-1-4560-9019-7(4)) America Star Bks.

Walters, Eric. In a Flash, 1 vol. 2008. (Orca Currents Ser.). (ENG.). 112p. (J). (gr. 5-9). pap. 9.95 (978-1-55469-034-3(X)) Orca Bk. Pubs. USA.

Walton, Will. Anything Could Happen. 2015. (ENG.). 288p. (J). (gr. 7). 17.99 (978-0-545-70954-5(7), PUSH) Scholastic, Inc.

Watch Out, Sara! 2006. (J). (978-1-933343-35-8(4), PONY) Stabenfeldt Inc.

Watt, Erin. Broken Prince. 2016. (Royals Ser.: 2). (ENG.). 370p. (gr. 7-12). pap. 14.99 (978-1-68230-503-4(1), EverAfter Romance) Diversion Publishing Corp.

—Twisted Palace. 2016. (Royals Ser.: 3). (ENG.). 370p. (gr. 7-12). pap. 14.99 (978-1-68230-506-5(6), EverAfter Romance) Diversion Publishing Corp.

Watt, Erin & Frederick, Jen. Paper Princess. 2016. (Royals Ser.: 1). (ENG., Illus.). 370p. pap. 14.99 (978-1-68230-456-3(6), EverAfter Romance) Diversion Publishing Corp.

Weeks, Sarah. As Simple as It Seems. 2010. (ENG.). 192p. (J). (gr. 3-7). 15.99 (978-0-06-084663-3(1)) HarperCollins Pubs.

Weitz, Chris. The Revival. 2016. (Young World Ser.: 3). (ENG.). 272p. (YA). (gr. 10-17). 18.99 (978-0-316-22634-9(3)) Little, Brown Bks. for Young Readers.

West, Melissa. Hover. 2013. (Taking Ser.: 2). (ENG.). 352p. (YA). (gr. 7-12). pap. 9.99 (978-1-62266-008-7(0), 9781622660087) Entangled Publishing, LLC.

Weyn, Suzanne. The Bar Code Rebellion. 2012. (ENG.). 272p. (J). (gr. 7). pap. 9.99 (978-0-545-47055-1(2), Scholastic Paperbacks) Scholastic, Inc.

Whitehouse, Howard. The Faceless Fiend: Being the Tale of a Criminal Mastermind, His Masked Minions & a Princess with a Butter Knife, Involving Explosives & a Certain Amount of Pushing & Shoving. Slavin, Bill, illus. 2007. (Mad Misadventures of Emmaline & Rubberbones Ser.). (ENG.). 272p. (J). (gr. 4-7). 7.95 (978-1-55453-180-6(2)) Kids Can Pr., Ltd. CAN. Dist: Hachette Bk. Group.

Wittlinger, Ellen. Lombardo's Law. 2003. (ENG.). 144p. (J). (gr. 5-7). pap. 10.95 (978-0-618-31108-8(4)) Houghton Mifflin Harcourt Publishing Co.

Wolf, Sara. Forget Me Always. 2016. (Lovely Vicious Ser.: 2). (ENG.). 250p. (YA). pap. 9.99 (978-1-63375-317-4(4), 9781633753174) Entangled Publishing, LLC.

Wolff, Virginia Euwer. Make Lemonade. unabr. ed. 2004. (Make Lemonade Trilogy: No. 1). 200p. (J). (gr. 7-18). pap. 36.00 incl. audio (978-0-8072-0793-2(4), S YA 348 SP, Listening Library) Random Hse. Audio Publishing Group.

Wynne-Jones, Tim. Lord of the Fries & Other Stories: Other Stories. pap. 9.95 (978-0-88899-274-1(2)) Groundwood Bks. CAN. Dist: Publishers Group West (PGW).

Young, Janet Ruth. Things I Shouldn't Think. 2012. (ENG., Illus.). 352p. (YA). (gr. 9). pap. 8.99 (978-1-4424-5107-0(6), Atheneum Bks. for Young Readers) Simon & Schuster Children's Publishing.

Ziegesar, Cecily von. Adored. 2009. (It Girl Ser.: 8). (ENG.). 240p. (YA). (gr. 10-17). pap. 9.99 (978-0-316-02509-6(7), Tingley, Megan Bks.) Little, Brown Bks. for Young Readers.

—Because I'm Worth It. 2003. (Gossip Girl Ser.: 4). (ENG.). 256p. (YA). (gr. 10-17). pap. 10.99 (978-0-316-90968-6(8), Poppy) Little, Brown Bks. for Young Readers.

Ziegesar, Cecily von & Turner, Steve. All I Want Is Everything. 2003. (Gossip Girl Ser.: 3). (ENG.). 240p. (YA). (gr. 10-17). pap. 10.99 (978-0-316-91212-9(3), Poppy) Little, Brown Bks. for Young Readers.

ADOPTION

Aldrich, Andrew R. How My Family Came to Be - Daddy, Papa & Me. 2003. (Illus.). 32p. (J). 19.95 (978-0-9742008-0-4(8)) New Family Pr.
Amato, Mary Anne. Where Are My Pictures, Mommy? 2009. 36p. pap. 16.49 (978-1-4490-2672-1(9)) AuthorHouse.
Bowes, Aurette. Someone's Daughter. 2009. 118p. pap. 9.99 (978-1-935383-88-8(4)) Raider Publishing International.
Brierley, Saroo. Lion: A Long Way Home Young Readers' Edition. 2017. (ENG.). 272p. (J). (gr. 5). 8.99 **(978-0-425-29176-4(6)**, Puffin Books) Penguin Young Readers Group.
Cahill, Stacie. My Parents Love Me Too! 2005. (ENG., Illus.). 25p. per. 13.99 (978-1-4134-9527-0(3)) Xlibris Corp.
The Changing Face of Modern Families, 14 vols., Set. Incl. Adoptive Parents. Simons, Rae. (gr. 5-18). lib. bdg. 22.95 (978-1-4222-1502-9(4)); Blended Families. Simons, Rae. (gr. 6-18). 22.95 (978-1-4222-1492-3(3)); Celebrity Families. Stewart, Sheila. (gr. 6-18). lib. bdg. 22.95 (978-1-4222-1503-6(2)); First-Generation Immigrant Families. Fields, Julianna. (gr. 6-18). lib. bdg. 22.95 (978-1-4222-1499-2(0)); Foster Families. Fields, Julianna. (gr. 5-18). lib. bdg. 22.95 (978-1-4222-1497-8(4)); Gay & Lesbian Parents. Fields, Julianna. (gr. 5-18). lib. bdg. 22.95 (978-1-4222-1495-4(8)); Grandparents Raising Kids. Simons, Rae. (gr. 6-18). lib. bdg. 22.95 (978-1-4222-1496-1(6)); Growing up in Religious Communities. Stewart, Sheila. (gr. 6-18). lib. bdg. 22.95 (978-1-4222-1500-5(8)); Kids Growing up Without a Home. Fields, Julianna. (gr. 5-18). lib. bdg. 22.95 (978-1-4222-1498-5(2)); Multiracial Families. Fields, Julianna. (gr. 5-18). lib. bdg. 22.95 (978-1-4222-1494-7(X)); Single Parents. Simons, Rae. (gr. 6-18). 22.95 (978-1-4222-1493-0(1)); Teen Parents. Simons, Rae. (gr. 5-18). lib. bdg. 22.95 (978-1-4222-1491-6(5)); What Is a Family? Stewart, Sheila. (gr. 6-18). lib. bdg. 22.95 (978-1-4222-1528-9(8)); (YA). 2010. (Illus.). 64p. 2010. 321.30 (978-1-4222-1490-9(7)) Mason Crest.
Collins Easy Learning Staff & Clarke, Peter. Addition & Subtraction Ages 5-7. 2015. (Collins Easy Learning Ser.). (ENG.). 32p. (J). (gr. k-2). pap. 6.95 (978-0-00-813428-0(6)) HarperCollins Pubs. Ltd. GBR. Dist: Independent Pubs. Group.
Conn, Peter. Adoption: A Brief Social & Cultural History. 1 vol. 2013. (ENG., Illus.). vi, 161p. 49.00 (978-1-137-33220-2(4), 9781137332202) Palgrave Macmillan Ltd. GBR. Dist: Springer.
Dellinger, Annetta. Adopted & Loved Forever. McDonnell, Janet, illus. 2nd ed. 2009. 32p. (J). 12.99 (978-0-7586-1591-6(4)) Concordia Publishing Hse.
Early, Sandy. Tell Tanner Tales: We're Adopted! 2012. (ENG.). 21p. (J). pap. 18.95 (978-1-4327-9028-8(5)) Outskirts Pr., Inc.
Felix, Rebecca. International Adoption. 1 vol. 2014. (Essential Issues Set 4 Ser.). (ENG., Illus.). 112p. (YA). (gr. 6-12). lib. bdg. 35.64 (978-1-62403-420-6(9), Essential Library) ABDO Publishing Co.
Fisanick, Christina. Issues in Adoption, No. 9. 2009. (Current Controversies Ser.). (ENG.). 240p. (gr. 10-12). 27.50 (978-0-7377-4323-4(9)); pap. 39.70 (978-0-7377-4324-1(7)) Cengage Gale. (Greenhaven Pr., Inc.).
Gorbett, Danea. Adopted Teens Only: A Survival Guide to Adolescence. 2007. 120p. per. 9.95 (978-1-58348-481-4(7), iUniverse Star) iUniverse, Inc.
Greenhaven Press Editors. Adoption. 2012. (Issues That Concern You Ser.). (ENG., Illus.). 144p. (J). (gr. 7-10). lib. bdg. 36.95 (978-0-7377-5688-3(8)) Cengage Gale.
Haerens, Margaret. International Adoptions. 2010. (Opposing Viewpoints Ser.). (ENG.). 224p. (gr. 10-12). 48.80 (978-0-7377-4970-0(9)); 240p. (YA). (gr. 9-18). pap. 29.45 (978-0-7377-4971-7(7)) Cengage Gale. (Greenhaven Pr., Inc.).
Hannula, Kate. Forever, Jewel. 2011. 32p. pap. 13.95 (978-1-4497-2381-1(0), WestBow Pr.) Author Solutions, Inc.
Heegaard, Marge Eaton. Adopted & Wondering: Drawing Out Feelings. 2007. (ENG., Illus.). 40p. per. 9.95 (978-1-57749-166-8(1)) Taylor Trade Publishing.
Henningfeld, Diane Andrews. Adoption. 2013. (Global Viewpoints Ser.). (ENG., Illus.). 224p. (gr. 10-12). pap. 31.70 (978-0-7377-6435-2(X), Greenhaven Pr., Inc.) Cengage Gale.
Henningfeld, Diane Andrews, ed. Adoption. 2013. (Global Viewpoints Ser.). (ENG., Illus.). 224p. (gr. 10-12). lib. bdg. 40.45 (978-0-7377-6259-4(4), Greenhaven Pr., Inc.) Cengage Gale.
Hiber, Amanda. Are Adoption Policies Fair? 2008. (At Issue Ser.). (ENG., Illus.). 80-128p. (YA). (gr. 9-12). pap. 34.45 (978-0-7377-3910-7(X)); (J). (gr. 10-12). 24.45 (978-0-7377-3911-4(8), Greenhaven Pr., Inc.) Cengage Gale.
Langwith, Jacqueline. Adoption. Greenhaven Press Editors & Gale Editors, eds. 2014. (Introducing Issues with Opposing Viewpoints Ser.). (ENG., Illus.). 144p. (gr. 7-10). lib. bdg. 42.00 (978-0-7377-6918-0(1), Greenhaven Pr., Inc.) Cengage Gale.
Lodien, Jennie, des. I Am Chosen: Brights. 2003. 56p. (YA). ring bd. 29.95 (978-0-9746341-0-4(7)) Chin & A Pr.
Lotorto - Soroka, Mary. Catiana Makes a Family. 2009. 30p. pap. 13.99 (978-1-4490-0126-1(2)) AuthorHouse.
McCormick, Patricia. Just Add One Chinese Sister (p) 2010. pap. 10.95 (978-1-59078-772-4(2)) Boyds Mills Pr.
Meese, Ruth Lyn. Family Matters: Adoption & Foster Care in Children's Literature. 1 vol. 2009. 147p. (C). pap. 35.00 (978-1-59158-782-8(4), TIP8782, Libraries Unlimited) ABC-CLIO, LLC.
Meissner, Jacqueline. Why Am I Brown? A Child's View of Multi-cultural Adoption. 1 vol. Stabile, Nicolette, illus. 2009. 22p. pap. 24.95 (978-1-60836-234-9(5)) America Star Bks.
Nemiroff, Marc A. & Annunziata, Jane. All about Adoption: How Families Are Made & How Kids Feel about It. Koeller, Carol, tr. Koeller, Carol, illus. 2003. 48p. (J). (gr. k-3). 14.95 (978-1-59147-058-8(7)); pap. 9.95 (978-1-59147-059-5(5)) American Psychological Assn. (Magination Pr.).
Parr, Todd. We Belong Together: A Book about Adoption & Families. 2007. (ENG., Illus.). 32p. (J). (gr. -1-1). 17.99 (978-0-316-01668-1(3)) Little, Brown Bks. for Young Readers.
Poole, H. W. Multiracial Families, Vol. 12. 2016. (Families Today Ser.). (Illus.). 48p. (J). (gr. 5). 20.95 (978-1-4222-3622-2(6)) Mason Crest.
Poole, Hilary W. Military Families. 2017. (Illus.). 48p. (J). (978-1-4222-3612-3(9)) Mason Crest.
Rice, Beth. I'm Adopted, I'm Special. Podgurski, Sharon, illus. 2008. 32p. pap. 12.95 (978-0-9817572-0-9(0)) Peppertree Pr., The.
Rotner, Shelley & Kelly, Sheila M. I'm Adopted! Rotner, Shelley, photos by. (ENG., Illus.). 32p. (J). 2012. pap. 6.95 (978-0-8234-2430-6(8)) 2011. 16.95 (978-0-8234-2294-4(1)) Holiday Hse., Inc.
Schuette, Sarah L. Adoptive Families. 2010. (My Family Ser.). (ENG.). 24p. (gr. k-1). pap. 35.70 (978-1-4296-5157-8(1)); lib. bdg. 21.99 (978-1-4296-3977-4(6)) Capstone Press of Coughlan Cos. (Pebble Bks.).
Sherman, Aliza. Everything You Need to Know about Placing Your Baby for Adoption. 2009. (Need to Know Library). 64p. (gr. 5-5). 58.50 (978-1-60854-082-2(0)) Rosen Publishing Group, Inc., The.
Simons, Rae. Adoptive Parents. 2010. (Changing Face of Modern Families Ser.). (Illus.). 64p. (YA). (gr. 5-18). lib. bdg. 22.95 (978-1-4222-1502-9(4)) Mason Crest.
Slade, Suzanne Buckingham. Adopted: The Ultimate Teen Guide. Papile, Christopher et al, illus. Washburn, Chris, photos by. 2007. (It Happened to Me Ser.: 20). (ENG.). 272p. (gr. 8-12). 70.00 (978-0-8108-5774-2(X)) Scarecrow Pr., Inc.
Stewart, Kelsey. The Best for You. 2009. 24p. pap. 12.49 (978-1-4490-0832-1(1)) AuthorHouse.
Swift, Gayle H. & Swift, Casey Anne. Abc, Adoption & Me. Griffin, Paul, illus. 2013. 36p. pap. 13.99 (978-0-9856762-8-5(0)) WRB Pub.
Warren, Andrea & National Geographic Learning Staff. Escape from Saigon: How a Vietnam War Orphan Became an American Boy. 2008. (ENG., Illus.). 128p. (J). (gr. 5-9). pap. 12.99 (978-0-374-40023-1(7), 9780374400231) Square Fish.
Watkins, Christine. Are Adoption Policies Fair? 2012. (At Issue Ser.). (ENG.). 128p. (gr. 10-12). pap. 27.80 (978-0-7377-6148-1(2), Greenhaven Pr., Inc.) Cengage Gale.
Watkins, Christine, ed. Are Adoption Policies Fair? 2012. (At Issue Ser.). (ENG.). 128p. (J). (gr. 10-12). lib. bdg. 34.45 (978-0-7377-6147-4(4), Greenhaven Pr., Inc.) Cengage Gale.

ADOPTION—FICTION

see also Foster Home Care—Fiction

Adam, Sally. The Adventures of Rex Adam. 2011. 28p. pap. 14.00 (978-1-4567-1721-6(9)) AuthorHouse.
Adams, Jean Ekman. When Dogs Dream. 2013. 32p. (J). 15.95 (978-1-933855-84-4(3), Rio Nuevo Pubs.) Rio Nuevo Pubs.
Alders, Willa. Leafy Finds a Home. Burns, Sandra, illus. 2013. 24p. pap. 8.99 (978-1-938768-13-2(2)) Gypsy Pubns.
Alger, Horatio & Stratemeyer, Edward. Young Captain Jack: The Son of a Soldier. 2007. (ENG.). 180p. pap. 19.99 (978-1-4346-5115-0(0)); 192p. pap. 21.99 (978-1-4346-5116-7(9)) Creative Media Partners, LLC.
Alsius, Lourdes. Unos Padres Para Aruna. 2005. (SPA.). 32p. (J). 18.95 (978-84-8418-096-8(4)) Zendrera Zariquiey, Editorial ESP. Dist: Iaconi, Mariuccia Bk. Imports.
Altieri, Maria. Mom, Tell Me a Story. 2012. 20p. pap. 24.95 (978-1-62709-702-4(3)) America Star Bks.
Alvarez, Julia. En Busca de Milagros. 2006.Tr. of Finding Miracles. (SPA.). 224p. (YA). (gr. 7). mass mkt. 6.99 (978-0-553-49407-5(4), Laurel Leaf) Random Hse. Children's Bks.
—Finding Miracles. 2006. (ENG.). 288p. (YA). (gr. 7-12). mass mkt. 6.99 (978-0-553-49406-8(6), Laurel Leaf) Random Hse. Children's Bks.
Anderson, John David. Minion. 2014. (ENG.). 288p. (J). (gr. 3-7). 16.99 (978-0-06-213311-3(X), Walden Pond Pr.) HarperCollins Pubs.
Archway Care Sons and Daughters Group & Archway Care Sons And Daughters Group. How Does Jorge Feel ? 2011. 12p. pap. 7.70 (978-1-4467-1645-8(7)) Lulu Pr., Inc.
Auerbach, Annie, adapted by. Despicable Me 2: The Junior Novel. movie tie-in ed. 2013. (ENG.). 144p. (J). (gr. 3-7). pap. 6.99 (978-0-316-23432-0(X)) Little, Brown Bks. for Young Readers.
Ayres, S. C. Finding the Perfect Fit. Steckler, Megan, illus. 2011. 28p. pap. 24.95 (978-1-4560-0912-0(5)) America Star Bks.
Babbitt, Natalie. The Moon over High Street. 2012. (ENG.). 160p. (J). (gr. 5-9). 15.95 (978-0-545-37636-5(X), Di Capua, Michael) Scholastic, Inc.
Baker, David. The Roos, A home for Baby. 2005. 14p. 12.49 (978-1-4116-2290-6(1)) Lulu Pr., Inc.
Ballengee, Fran. Sara Elizabeth, an Adoption Story. 2008. 22p. pap. 24.95 (978-1-60610-557-3(4)) PublishAmerica, Inc.
Banks, Kate. Dillon Dillon. 2005. 149p. (gr. 3-7). 18.00 (978-0-7569-5767-4(2)) Perfection Learning Corp.
Barkley, Callie. Ellie the Flower Girl. Bishop, Tracy, illus. 2016. (Critter Club Ser.: 14). (ENG.). 128p. (J). (gr. k-4). pap. 5.99 (978-1-4814-6718-6(2), Little Simon) Little Simon.
Barna, Beverly. The Daughter of Dreams, a Fable of Destiny. White, David, illus. 2009. 28p. pap. 14.95 (978-1-936051-09-0(5)) Peppertree Pr., The.
Bauer, Joan. Soar. 2016. (ENG.). 304p. (J). (gr. 5). 16.99 (978-0-451-47034-8(6), Viking Books for Young Readers) Penguin Young Readers Group.
Beal, Tracy Lynn. The Puzzle. Cunningham, Charles E., illus. 2008. 17p. pap. 24.95 (978-1-60610-078-3(5)) America Star Bks.
Beheler, Rhonda. They Chose Me: A Story of Grandparent Adoption. 2008. 32p. per. 24.95 (978-1-4241-8616-7(1)) America Star Bks.
Belonie, Shannon. Teaching an Ostrich to Fly. 2008. 16p. pap. 8.74 (978-1-4343-5519-5(5)) AuthorHouse.
Bergren, Lisa T. God Found Us You. Bryant, Laura J., illus. 2009. (J). lib. bdg. 3.99 (978-0-06-113177-6(6)) HarperCollins Pubs.
—God Found Us You. Bryant, Laura J., illus. 2009. (HarperBlessings Ser.). (ENG.). 40p. (J). (gr. -1-2). 10.99 (978-0-06-113176-9(8)) HarperCollins Pubs.
Bernstein, Jonathan. Bridget Wilder: Spy-In-Training. 2016. (Bridget Wilder Ser.: 1). (J). lib. bdg. 17.20 (978-0-606-38746-0(3)) Turtleback Bks.
—Bridget Wilder: Spy-In-Training. 2015. (Bridget Wilder Ser.: 1). (ENG.). 320p. (J). (gr. 3-7). 16.99 (978-0-06-238266-5(7), Tegen, Katherine Bks) HarperCollins Pubs.
Bigler, Ashley Hansen. Once upon a Time: An Adoption Story. Hintz, Amy, illus. 2010. (J). pap. 12.99 (978-1-59955-310-8(4)) Cedar Fort, Inc./CFI Distribution.
Blacker, Terence. The Angel Factory. 2012. (ENG., Illus.). 224p. (J). (gr. 5-9). pap. 10.99 (978-0-689-86413-1(2), Simon & Schuster/Paula Wiseman Bks.) Simon & Schuster/Paula Wiseman Bks.
Blackidge, Barbara. Lucky: My Story. 2010. 24p. (J). pap. 12.95 (978-1-934449-64-6(4)) Legacy Publishing Services, Inc.
Blake, Linda. My Pet Rabbit. 2012. 24p. 24.95 (978-1-4626-6187-9(4)) America Star Bks.
Blevins, Wiley. Rice & Beans. Cerato, Mattia, illus. 2014. (Family Snaps Ser.). (ENG.). 32p. (J). (gr. k-2). pap. 6.95 (978-1-939656-63-6(X)) Red Chair Pr.
Blunt, Julia & Gilbert, Dawn. How Donkey Became GREAT. 2007. 48p. pap. 22.85 (978-0-615-16220-1(7)) Runamuck Publishing.
Bond, Juliet C. Sam's Sister. Majewski, Dawn, illus. 2004. (J). 18.00 (978-0-944934-30-2(7)) Perspectives Pr., Inc.
Bongiorno, Patti Lynn, text. Tangled Hearts. 2004. 288p. (YA). per. 12.95 (978-0-9715819-1-3(6)) Bongiorno Bks.
Breckwoldt. The Story of Craig Winston: An Adopted Bear. 2009. 36p. pap. 21.99 (978-1-4389-9636-3(5)) AuthorHouse.
Brewer, Jo Ann. The Little Girl No One Wanted. 2011. 48p. pap. 15.99 (978-1-4568-6581-8(1)) Xlibris Corp.
Brodzinsky, Anne Braff. The Mulberry Bird: An Adoption Story. 2012. (ENG., Illus.). 48p. 14.95 (978-1-84905-933-6(0), 1852) Kingsley, Jessica Pubs. GBR. Dist: Macmillan Distribution Ltd.
Brown, Betisa Garagozlu. Sister Sun & Sister Moon. 2012. 28p. pap. 13.95 (978-1-4525-4635-3(5)) Balboa Pr.
Bruel, Nick. Bad Kitty Meets the Baby. Bruel, Nick, illus. 2011. (Bad Kitty Ser.). (ENG., Illus.). 144p. (J). (gr. 2-5). 14.99 (978-1-59643-597-1(6), 9781596435971) Roaring Brook Pr.
—Bad Kitty Meets the Baby. Bruel, Nick, illus. 2012. (Bad Kitty Ser.). (ENG., Illus.). 160p. (J). (gr. 2-5). pap. 6.99 (978-0-312-64121-4(4), 9780312641214) Square Fish.
—Bad Kitty Meets the Baby. 2012. (Bad Kitty Chapter Bks.). (J). lib. bdg. 17.20 (978-0-606-23754-3(2), Turtleback) Turtleback Bks.
Brutton, Elizabeth. Tabbies & Tigers in Provence. 2009. (Illus.). 112p. pap. 12.49 (978-1-4490-2104-7(2)) AuthorHouse.
Burg, Ann E. All the Broken Pieces. (ENG.). 240p. (J). 2012. (gr. 7). pap. 6.99 (978-0-545-08093-4(2), Scholastic Paperbacks) 2009. (gr. 5-9). 16.99 (978-0-545-08092-7(4), Scholastic Pr.) Scholastic, Inc.
Byrne, Jennifer. Adopting Ahava. 2013. 44p. (J). pap. 9.99 (978-0-9851067-3-7(5)) Dodi Pr.
Calkin, Author & Calkin, Abigail B. The Carolyne Letters: A Story of Birth, Abortion & Adoption. 2013. (ENG., Illus.). 230p. (YA). pap. 14.95 (978-1-938301-15-5(3)) Familius LLC.
Campbell, H. David. Merribell: A Comforting Story. 2011. 218p. (gr. 2-2). 23.95 (978-1-4620-4477-1(8)); pap. 13.95 (978-1-4620-4476-4(X)) iUniverse, Inc.
Campbell, Howard. A Dog Named Pavlov: Un Perro Llamado Pavlov. McCloskey, Kevin, illus. 2010. 44p. (J). pap. (978-0-9790350-4-3(X)) Star Fire.
Canady, Mary Monica. Why Is My Name Sam? Papeo, Maria Eugenia & Saumell, Marina, illus. 2008. 24p. pap. 24.95 (978-1-60474-028-7(0)) America Star Bks.
Carlson, Melody. Just Ask. 2005. (Diary of a Teenage Girl Ser.: Bk. 10). (ENG.). 256p. (J). (gr. 7-12). per. 14.99 (978-1-59052-321-6(0), Multnomah Bks.) Crown Publishing Group.
Carlson, Nancy. My Family Is Forever. Carlson, Nancy, illus. 2006. (ENG., Illus.). 32p. (J). (gr. -1-k). pap. 5.99 (978-0-14-240561-1(2), Puffin Books) Penguin Young Readers Group.
Cavanaugh, Nancy. Just Like Me. 2016. (ENG.). 256p. (J). (gr. 3-7). 16.99 (978-1-4926-0427-3(5), 9781492604273, Sourcebooks Jabberwocky) Sourcebooks, Inc.
Celcer, Irene. The Gift of Adoption. Gatto, Horacio, illus. 2009. (J). pap. (978-0-9755810-5-6(8)) Graphite Pr.
Chall, Marsha Wilson. Pick a Pup. Henry, Jed, illus. 2011. (ENG.). 32p. (J). (gr. -1-k). 16.99 (978-1-4169-7961-6(1), McElderry, Margaret K. Bks.) McElderry, Margaret K. Bks.
Chen, Shan-Shan & Goodman, Heidi. Mei-Mei's Lucky Birthday Noodles: A Loving Story of Adoption, Chinese Culture & a Special Birthday Treat. 2014. (ENG., Illus.). 32p. (J). (gr. -1-3). 13.95 (978-0-8048-4461-1(5)) Tuttle Publishing.
Cheng, Andrea. The Year of the Baby. Barton, Patrice, illus. 2014. (Anna Wang Novel Ser.: 2). (ENG.). 176p. (J). (gr. 1-4). pap. 5.99 (978-0-544-22525-1(2), HMH Books For Young Readers) Houghton Mifflin Harcourt Publishing Co.
—The Year of the Fortune Cookie. Barton, Patrice, illus. 2014. (Anna Wang Novel Ser.: 3). (ENG.). 176p. (J). (gr. 1-4). 15.99 (978-0-544-10519-5(2), HMH Books For Young Readers) Houghton Mifflin Harcourt Publishing Co.
Ching, Lorilei. He Ping: An Orphan's Destiny. 2013. 32p. pap. 13.95 (978-1-4624-0807-8(9), Inspiring Voices) Author Solutions, Inc.
Chriss, Granddad. The Adventures of Barazaburg. 2011. 54p. 24.99 (978-1-4568-7988-4(X)); pap. 15.99 (978-1-4568-7987-7(1)) Xlibris Corp.
Coffman, Jan. A Common Bond. 2008. 73p. pap. 19.95 (978-1-60672-302-9(2)) America Star Bks.
Columbro, Judy. The Gift of Rainbows. Scottorosano, Deborah, illus. 2011. 24p. pap. 24.95 (978-1-4626-0355-8(6)) PublishAmerica, Inc.
Combs, Jan Marie. The Forever Garden. 2012. 24p. pap. 14.50 (978-1-105-15343-3(6)) Lulu Pr., Inc.
Cook, Eileen. Year of Mistaken Discoveries. 2014. (ENG., Illus.). 272p. (YA). (gr. 9). 17.99 (978-1-4424-4022-7(8), Simon Pulse) Simon Pulse.
Cooney, Caroline B. Three Black Swans. 2012. (ENG.). 288p. (YA). (gr. 7). pap. 9.99 (978-0-385-73868-2(4), Ember) Random Hse. Children's Bks.
Cooper, D. C. Rascal the Baby Squirrel. 2013. 32p. (978-1-4602-2658-2(5)) FriesenPress.
Cray, Jordan. Most Wanted. 2009. (Danger. com Ser.: 7). (ENG.). 240p. (YA). (gr. 7). pap. 11.99 (978-1-4169-9851-8(9), Simon Pulse) Simon Pulse.
Crowder, Melanie. Three Pennies. 2017. (ENG., Illus.). 192p. (J). (gr. 3-7). 16.99 **(978-1-4814-7187-9(2)**, Atheneum Bks. for Young Readers) Simon & Schuster Children's Publishing.
Crutcher, Chris. Whale Talk. 2004. 224p. (J). (gr. 7-18). pap. 38.00 incl. audio (978-0-8072-2289-8(5), Listening Library) Random Hse. Audio Publishing Group.
Czarnota, Jennifer. Blessing Baby & the Heart As Big As the Sky. 2013. 28p. pap. 16.99 (978-1-4808-0238-4(7)) Archway Publishing.
Czekaj, Jef. Austin, Lost in America: A Geography Adventure. Czekaj, Jef, illus. 2015. (ENG., Illus.). 40p. (J). (gr. -1-3). 17.99 (978-0-06-228017-6(1)) HarperCollins Pubs.
Darcy N. Carmichael. Ember's Rising. 2009. 104p. pap. 9.95 (978-1-4401-6368-5(5)) iUniverse, Inc.
David, Erica, adapted by. Hotel for Dogs. movie tie-in novel ed. 2008. (Hotel for Dogs Ser.). (ENG., Illus.). 128p. (J). pap. 5.99 (978-1-4169-7183-2(1), Simon Spotlight) Simon Spotlight.
Davis, Penny. Annabel's Yearnings. 2012. 274p. pap. (978-1-78003-309-9(5)) Pen Pr. Pubs., Ltd.
Davis, Susan. I'm Adopted, You're Adopted: Welcome to God's Family. 2007. (ENG.). 79p. (J). (gr. 1-4). per. 8.99 (978-0-8127-0434-1(7)) Autumn Hse. Publishing Co.
Diersch, Sandra. No Contact. 1 vol. 2008. (Lorimer Sports Stories Ser.). (ENG.). 136p. (J). (gr. 4-8). 16.95 (978-1-55277-025-2(7), 9781552770252); 8.95 (978-1-55277-024-5(9), 9781552770245) Lorimer, James & Co., Ltd., Pubs. CAN. Dist: Casemate Pubs. & Bk. Distributors, LLC.
Dowswell, Paul. The Auslander. 2011. (ENG.). 304p. (YA). 17.99 (978-1-59990-633-1(3), 9781599906331, Bloomsbury USA Childrens) Bloomsbury Publishing USA.
Dukovich, Amanda J. A Star Named Little One (Boy) Pride, Matthew, illus. l.t. ed. 2006. 32p. (J). (gr. -1). 15.99 (978-1-59879-189-1(3)) Lifevest Publishing, Inc.
—A Star Named Little One (Girl) Pride, Matthew, illus. l.t. ed. 2006. 32p. (J). (gr. -1-k). 15.99 (978-1-59879-090-0(0)) Lifevest Publishing, Inc.
Dyckman, Ame. Wolfie the Bunny. OHora, Zachariah, illus. 2015. (ENG.). 40p. (J). (gr. -1-1). 17.99 (978-0-316-22614-1(9)) Little, Brown Bks. for Young Readers.
Easton, Marilyn. New Girl in Town. 2013. (LEGO Friends Chapter Bks.: 1). lib. bdg. 14.75 (978-0-606-31548-7(9), Turtleback) Turtleback Bks.
Eboch, M. M. Walking the Dragon's Back. 2015. (ENG.). 96p. (gr. 3-6). 31.36 (978-1-63430-396-5(2)) Rourke Educational Media.
Edwards, Nicholas & White, Ellen Emerson. The Rescue. 2009. (Dog Whisperer Ser.: 1). (ENG.). 224p. (J). (gr. 3-7). pap. 9.99 (978-0-312-36768-8(6), 9780312367688) Square Fish.
Edwards, Sal A. A Forever Family: Living in the Big House. 2012. 42p. (-18). pap. 17.45 (978-1-4624-0329-5(8), Inspiring Voices) Author Solutions, Inc.
Eldridge, Sherrie. Forever Fingerprints: An Amazing Discovery for Adopted Children. Williams, Rob, illus. 2014. (ENG.). 32p. 15.95 (978-1-84905-778-3(8), 3057) Kingsley, Jessica Pubs. GBR. Dist: Macmillan Distribution Ltd.
Eliot, George. Silas Marner. 2008. (Bring the Classics to Life Ser.). (ENG., Illus.). 72p. (gr. 2-12). pap., act. bk. ed. 10.95 (978-1-55576-356-5(1), EDCTR-209B) EDCON Publishing Group.
Enderlin, Darlene C. Pathways of Hermie. 2008. 48p. pap. 16.95 (978-1-60672-086-8(4)) America Star Bks.
Enriquez, Lucy Rivas. Dj's Lullaby: A Mother's Love Song. 2013. (ENG.). 26p. (J). pap. 12.95 (978-1-4787-1148-3(5)) Outskirts Pr., Inc.
Fan, Nancy Yi. Sword Mountain. 2012. (Swordbird Ser.: 3). (ENG., Illus.). 336p. (J). (gr. 3-7). 16.99 (978-0-06-165108-3(7)) HarperCollins Pubs.
Fennell, Kristen & Petruccelli, Jessica, illus. A World of Hope: Written by Hope's Parents Laurie & Mike. l.t. ed. 2005. 18p. (J). per. 9.99 (978-1-59879-069-6(2)) Lifevest Publishing, Inc.
Ferguson, Alane & Skurzynski, Gloria. Escape from Fear: A Mystery in Virgin Islands National Park. 2008. (Mysteries in Our National Park Ser.). (ENG., Illus.). 160p. (J). (gr. 3-7). mass mkt. 4.99 (978-1-4263-0181-0(2), National Geographic Children's Bks.) National Geographic Society.
Ferguson, J. M. Bubbles the Little Pig. 1 vol. 2008. (ENG.). 44p. 24.95 (978-1-60474-229-9(1)) America Star Bks.
Fernandez, Eugenia. Astria & the Missing Prince. 2009. (Illus.). 39p. (J). 31.99 (978-1-4363-7543-6(6)) Xlibris Corp.
Fisher, C. R. The Adventures of Sam Fisher: It's Ruff to Be A Puppy. 2008. 64p. pap. 19.49 (978-1-4389-2040-5(7)) AuthorHouse.
Fitzgerald, Mary. Samson's Best Friend. 2012. (ENG.). 32p. (J). 22.95 (978-1-4327-9039-4(0)) Outskirts Pr., Inc.
Ford, Martyn. The Imagination Box. 2016. (ENG.). 240p. (J). (gr. 4-7). 16.99 (978-1-101-93627-6(4), Delacorte Pr.) Random Hse. Children's Bks.
Frazier, Sundee T. Cleo Edison Oliver in Persuasion Power. 2017. (ENG.). 256p. (J). (gr. 3-7). 16.99 (978-0-545-82239-8(4), Levine, Arthur A. Bks.) Scholastic, Inc.
Friedman, Darlene. Star of the Week: A Story of Love, Adoption, & Brownies with Sprinkles. Roth, Roger, illus. 2009. (ENG.). 32p. (J). (gr. k-3). 17.99 (978-0-06-114136-2(4)) HarperCollins Pubs.
Frizzell, Sally Parker. The Adventures in the Secret Valley. 2007. 40p. pap. 9.00 (978-0-8059-7615-1(9)) Dorrance Publishing Co., Inc.
Froeb, Lori. I Am Daisy. Lemay, Violet, illus. 2015. (ENG.). 32p. (J). (gr. 1-3). pap. 3.99 (978-0-7944-3311-6(1), Reader's Digest Children's Bks.) Studio Fun International.
—I Am Daisy, Level 2. Lemay, Violet, illus. 2015. (Rescue Readers Ser.: 2). (ENG.). 32p. (J). (gr. k-3). lib. bdg. 16.99 (978-0-7944-3350-5(2)) Reader's Digest Assn., Inc., The.
—I Am McKinley, Level 2. Sakamoto, Miki, illus. 2015. (Rescue Readers Ser.: 1). (ENG.). 32p. (J). (gr. k-3). lib. bdg. 16.99 (978-0-7944-3349-9(9)) Reader's Digest Assn., Inc., The.

Froeb, Lori C. I Am McKinley, Level 2. Sakamoto, Miki, illus. 2015. (Rescue Readers Ser.: 1). (ENG.). 32p. (J). (gr. 1-2). pap. 3.99 (978-0-7944-3310-9(3), Reader's Digest Children's Bks.) Studio Fun International.
Funnell, Pippa. Team Magic. 2016. (Tilly's Horse, Magic Ser.). (ENG.). 128p. (J). (gr. 4-6). 6.99 (978-1-4440-1204-0(5), Orion Children's Bks.) Hachette Children's Group GBR. Dist: Hachette Bk. Group.
Fuqua, Jonathon. Medusa's Daughter. 2012. 144p. (YA). 14.95 (978-0-9848808-0-5(1), Red Giant Entertainment) Active Media Publishing, LLC.
Furrow, Rebecca. You Grew in My Heart: An Adoption Story. 2012. 32p. pap. 16.95 (978-1-4497-6064-9(3), WestBow Pr.) Author Solutions, Inc.
Galindo, Renata. My New Mom & Me. 2016. (ENG., Illus.). 32p. (J). (gr. -1-2). 19.99 (978-0-553-52135-1(7), Schwartz & Wade Bks.) Random Hse. Children's Bks.
Galla, Jessica. Not Just Babies Are Adopted, 1 vol. 2010. 16p. 24.95 (978-1-4512-9358-6(5)) PublishAmerica, Inc.
Gardner, Sally. Operation Bunny. Roberts, David, illus. 2014. (Wings & Co Ser.: 1). (ENG.). 192p. (J). (gr. 2-5). 12.99 (978-0-8050-9892-1(5), 9780805098921, Holt, Henry & Co. Bks. For Young Readers) Holt, Henry & Co.
—Operation Bunny. Roberts, David, illus. 2014. (Wings & Co Ser.: 1). (ENG.). 208p. (J). (gr. 2-5). pap. 6.99 (978-1-250-05053-3(7), 9781250050533) Square Fish.
Garris, Rebekah. Whither Thou Goest, i Will Go. 2005. pap. 24.95 (978-1-4137-8823-5(8)) PublishAmerica, Inc.
George, Kallie. The Enchanted Egg. Boiger, Alexandra, illus. 2015. (Magical Animal Adoption Agency Ser.). (ENG.). 138p. (J). (gr. 3-7). 14.99 (978-1-4231-8383-9(5)) Disney Pr.
—The Enchanted Egg. Boiger, Alexandra, illus. 2016. (Magical Animal Adoption Agency Ser.). (ENG.). 160p. (J). (gr. 2-5). pap. 5.99 (978-1-4847-0146-1(1)) Hyperion Bks. for Children.
—The Enchanted Egg. 2015. (Magical Animal Adoption Agency Ser.: 2). (J). lib. bdg. 26.95 (978-0-606-38337-0(9)) Turtleback Bks.
—The Magical Animal Adoption Agency, Bk. 1. Boiger, Alexandra, illus. 2015. (Magical Animal Adoption Agency Ser.). (ENG.). 152p. (J). (gr. 2-5). pap. 5.99 (978-1-4847-0148-5(8)) Hyperion Bks. for Children.
George, Kallie & Boiger, Alexandra. The Missing Magic. Boiger, Alexandra, illus. 2016. (Magical Animal Adoption Agency Ser.). (ENG., Illus.). 144p. (J). (gr. 2-5). 14.99 (978-1-4231-8384-6(3)) Hyperion Bks. for Children.
Gibaldi, Lauren. Autofocus. 2016. 352p. (YA). (gr. 9). 17.99 (978-0-06-230223-6(X), HarperTeen) HarperCollins Pubs.
Gibney, Shannon. See No Color. 2015. (ENG.). 192p. (YA). (gr. 7-12). 18.99 (978-1-4677-8814-4(7), Carolrhoda Lab™); 18.99 (978-1-4677-7682-0(3)) Lerner Publishing Group.
Giroir, Constance H. Mommy Did You Know... An Adoption Story. Longo, Jason, illus. 2005. 22p. per. 17.32 (978-1-59926-397-7(1)) Xlibris Corp.
Gliori, Debi. Dragon's Extraordinary Egg. 2014. (ENG., Illus.). 32p. (J). (gr. -1-3). 17.99 (978-0-8027-3759-5(5), 9780802737595, Bloomsbury USA Childrens) Bloomsbury Publishing USA.
Golding, Theresa Martin. Niner. 2008. (ENG.). 208p. (J). (gr. 6-9). 16.95 (978-1-59078-549-2(5), Front Street) Boyds Mills Pr.
Goldman Marshall, Lauren. My Beautiful Bow: An Adoption Story. Marschell, Hannah, illus. 2010. 36p. pap. 14.95 (978-1-60844-395-6(7)) Dog Ear Publishing, LLC.
Grab, Daphne. Halftime. 2010. (J). (978-0-385-90693-7(5)); (978-0-385-73783-8(1)) Random House Publishing Group. (Delacorte Pr).
Graham, Frederick. Why Me? 2008. 98p. pap. 13.95 (978-1-4303-1628-2(4)) Lulu Pr., Inc.
Greiner, Linda. Sashi Adopts a Brother. Spicer, Morgan, illus. 2015. (ENG.). 40p. (J). 14.95 net. (978-1-61254-856-2(3)) Brown Books Publishing Group.
Griffin, Paul. When Friendship Followed Me Home. 2016. (ENG.). 256p. (J). (gr. 5-9). 16.99 (978-0-8037-3816-4(1), Dial Bks) Penguin Young Readers Group.
Grossnickle, Mary. A Place in My Heart. Relyea, Alison, illus. 2014. (ENG.). 36p. 15.95 (978-1-84905-771-4(0), 3958) Kingsley, Jessica Pubs. GBR. Dist: Macmillan Distribution Ltd.
Grund, Carol A. Anna Mei, Blessing in Disguise. 2011. 181p. (J). pap. (978-0-8198-0796-0(6)) Pauline Bks. & Media.
—Anna Mei, Cartoon Girl. 2010. 140p. (J). (gr. 4-7). pap. 8.95 (978-0-8198-0788-5(5)) Pauline Bks. & Media.
Haddix, Margaret Peterson. Found. (Missing Ser.: 1). (ENG.). (J). (gr. 3-7). 2009. 336p. pap. 7.99 (978-1-4169-5421-7(X)) 2008. 320p. 17.99 (978-1-4169-5417-0(1)) Simon & Schuster Bks. For Young Readers. (Simon & Schuster Bks. For Young Readers).
Half a World Away. 2014. (ENG., Illus.). 240p. (J). (gr. 5-9). 17.99 (978-1-4424-1275-0(5), Atheneum Bks. for Young Readers) Simon & Schuster Children's Publishing.
Hamilton, Deborah E. Why are You my Mother? A Mother's Response to Her Adopted Daughter. Andrules, Jamie L., illus. 2006. (J). 9.99 net. (978-0-9789202-0-3(1)) Dreams Due Media Group, Inc.
Hapka, Catherine, pseud. ASPCA Pet Rescue Club: the Lonely Pony. 2015. (Pet Rescue Club Ser.: 3). (ENG., Illus.). 128p. (J). (gr. 1-3). lib. bdg. 16.99 (978-0-7944-3454-0(1)) Reader's Digest Assn., Inc., The.
—No Time for Hallie. Regan, Dana, illus. 2015. (Pet Rescue Club Ser.: 2). (ENG.). 128p. (J). (gr. 1-3). lib. bdg. 16.99 (978-0-7944-3352-9(9)) Reader's Digest Assn., Inc., The.
—No Time for Hallie. Regan, Dana, illus. 2015. (Pet Rescue Club Ser.: 2). (ENG.). 128p. (J). (gr. 1-3). pap. 5.99 (978-0-7944-3313-0(8)) Studio Fun International.
Hapka, Cathy, pseud. ASPCA Pet Rescue Club Collection, Bks. 1-3. Regan, Dana, illus. 2016. (Pet Rescue Club Ser.: 5). (ENG.). 384p. (J). (gr. 1-3). pap. 8.99 (978-0-7944-3572-1(6), Reader's Digest Children's Bks.) Studio Fun International.
Harper, Richard. Richie Gets a Dog: A Father & Son Book about Adopting Animals Shelter Dogs & Cats. 2012. 28p. pap. 24.95 (978-1-4626-6549-5(7)) America Star Bks.
Haywood, Carolyn. Here's a Penny. 2005. (ENG., Illus.). 160p. (J). (gr. 1-4). pap. 6.99 (978-0-15-205225-6(9)) Houghton Mifflin Harcourt Publishing Co.
—Penny & Peter. 2005. (ENG., Illus.). 160p. (J). (gr. 1-4). pap. 10.95 (978-0-15-205226-3(7)) Houghton Mifflin Harcourt Publishing Co.
Hecker, Vera, illus. A Home for Rainbow. 2007. 32p. (J). (978-0-9799729-0-4(6)) Banta, Sandra.
Henderson, Barbara. Down in Mr Brown's Garden. 2009. 40p. pap. 14.75 (978-1-60860-703-7(8), Strategic Bk. Publishing) Strategic Book Publishing & Rights Agency (SBPRA).
Henry, Emily. The Love That Split the World. (ENG.). (YA). (gr. 7). 2017. 416p. pap. 9.99 (978-1-59514-851-3(5)) 2016. 400p. 17.99 (978-1-59514-850-6(7)) Penguin Young Readers Group. (Razorbill).
Henson, Andora. Shelby's 'Doption Story. Moody, Julie, illus. 2004. (J). bds. 9.99 (978-1-4183-0013-5(6)) Christ Inspired, Inc.
Heo, Yumi. Ten Days & Nine Nights: An Adoption Story. Heo, Yumi, illus. 2009. (Rise & Shine Ser.). (ENG., Illus.). 40p. (J). (gr. -1-3). 17.99 (978-0-375-84718-9(9), Schwartz & Wade Bks.) Random Hse. Children's Bks.
Hepworth, Emily. Stray Dog. 2009. 39p. pap. 9.81 (978-0-557-21434-1(3)) Lulu Pr., Inc.
Hickman, Kirt. Purple. Olson, Julie, illus. 2012. 32p. pap. 15.99 (978-0-9796330-8-9(7)) Quillrunner Publishing LLC.
Higgins, Heather. The Foal That Doesn't Have a Family. 2007. 24p. 13.95 (978-1-4303-2336-5(1)) Lulu Pr., Inc.
Higgins, Wendy. Sweet Evil. 2012. (Sweet Evil Ser.: 1). (ENG.). 464p. (YA). (gr. 8). pap. 9.99 (978-0-06-208561-0(1), HarperTeen) HarperCollins Pubs.
Hill, Kirkpatrick. Bo at Ballard Creek. Pham, LeUyen, illus. 2013. (ENG.). 288p. (J). (gr. 3-7). 16.99 (978-0-8050-9351-3(6), 9780805093513, Holt, Henry & Co. Bks. For Young Readers) Holt, Henry & Co.
—Bo at Iditarod Creek. Pham, LeUyen, illus. 2014. (ENG.). 288p. (J). (gr. 3-7). 15.99 (978-0-8050-9352-0(4), 9780805093520, Holt, Henry & Co. Bks. For Young Readers) Holt, Henry & Co.
Hills, Jodi. Hope-So. Bjornson, Barbara, illus. 2004. (ENG.). 36p. (J). 16.95 (978-0-9726504-2-7(3)) TRISTAN Publishing, Inc.
Hodge, Deborah. Emma's Story. Zhang, Song Nan, illus. 2003. (ENG.). 24p. (J). (gr. k-3). 17.95 (978-0-88776-632-9(3), Tundra Bks.) Tundra Bks. CAN. Dist: Penguin Random Hse. LLC.
Horatio Alger Jr. The Cash Boy. l.t. ed. 2007. 186p. pap. 19.99 (978-1-4264-7014-1(2)) Creative Media Partners, LLC.
Horsfall, Jacqueline. For the Love of Strangers. Kelly, Mary B., illus. 2011. 292p. (YA). (gr. 6-9). pap. 14.99 (978-1-61603-003-2(8)) Leap Bks.
Horvath, Polly. The Night Garden. 2017. (ENG.). 304p. (J). 16.99 **(978-0-374-30452-2(1)**, 9780374304522, Farrar, Straus & Giroux (BYR)) Farrar, Straus & Giroux.
Howard, J. J. Sit, Stay, Love. 2016. (ENG.). 256p. (J). (gr. 4-7). pap. 6.99 (978-0-545-86157-1(8), Scholastic Paperbacks) Scholastic, Inc.
Hull, Teresa Travous. Love's Complete: A Russian Adoption Journey. 2012. 32p. pap. 15.95 (978-1-4497-5821-9(5), WestBow Pr.) Author Solutions, Inc.
Humphry, Christy. Fire & Water. 2005. 161p. pap. 24.95 (978-1-4137-8740-5(1)) America Star Bks.
Ieronimo, Christine. A Thirst for Home: A Story of Water Across the World. Velasquez, Eric, illus. 2014. (ENG.). 32p. (J). (gr. 1-4). 17.99 (978-0-8027-2307-9(1), 9780802723079, Bloomsbury USA Childrens) Bloomsbury Publishing USA.
Johns, Linda & National Geographic Learning Staff. Hannah West in Deep Water. 2010. (Rise & Shine Ser.). (ENG., Illus.). 160p. (C). (gr. 5-18). 9.95 (978-0-14-240700-4(3)) National Geographic School Publishing, Inc.
Johnson, Angela. Heaven, 3 vols. 2006. (J). 44.75 (978-1-4281-0237-8(X)) Recorded Bks., Inc.
—Heaven. 2010. (ENG.). 160p. (YA). (gr. 7). pap. 9.99 (978-1-4424-0342-0(X), Simon & Schuster Bks. For Young Readers) Simon & Schuster Bks. For Young Readers.
Jones, Sandra. Sasha's Little Red Box: An Adoption Story. 2008. 27p. pap. 24.95 (978-1-60703-187-1(6)) America Star Bks.
Kadohata, Cynthia. Half a World Away. 2015. (ENG., Illus.). 256p. (J). (gr. 5-9). pap. 7.99 (978-1-4424-1276-7(3), Atheneum Bks. for Young Readers) Simon & Schuster Children's Publishing.
—Half a World Away. 2014. 240p. 16.99 (978-1-4814-1806-5(8)) Simon & Schuster, Inc.
—Half a World Away. 2015. lib. bdg. 18.40 (978-0-606-37845-1(6)) Turtleback Bks.
Kane, Kimberly Brougham. Every Time You Call Me Mommy-an Adoption Blessing. 2007. 32p. 16.50 (978-0-615-17610-9(0)) Kane, Kimberly Brougham.
Kearney, Meg. The Girl in the Mirror. 2012. (ENG.). 176p. (YA). (gr. 9-17). pap. 15.00 (978-0-89255-385-3(5), 255385) Persea Bks., Inc.
—Trouper. Lewis, E. B., illus. 2013. (ENG.). 32p. (J). (gr. -1-3). 16.99 (978-0-545-10041-0(0), Scholastic Pr.) Scholastic, Inc.
—When You Never Said Goodbye: An Adoptee's Search for Her Birth Mother. 2017. (ENG.). 224p. (YA). (gr. 9-17). 17.95 (978-0-89255-479-9(7), 255479) Persea Bks., Inc.
Kennedy, Pamela. A Sister for Matthew. 2008. (ENG., Illus.). 32p. (J). (gr. -1-3). 8.95 (978-0-8249-5527-4(7), 1256104, Ideal Pubns.) Worthy Publishing.
Kent, Derek Taylor. El Perro con Sombrero: A Bilingual Doggy Tale. Henry, Jed, illus. 2015. (ENG & SPA.). 40p. (J). (gr. -1-2). 17.99 (978-0-8050-9989-8(1), 9780805099898, Holt, Henry & Co. Bks. For Young Readers) Holt, Henry & Co.
Kent, Rose. Kimchi & Calamari. 2010. (ENG.). 240p. (J). (gr. 3-7). pap. 6.99 (978-0-06-083771-6(3)) HarperCollins Pubs.
Kephart, Beth. Small Damages. 2013. (ENG., Illus.). 304p. (YA). (gr. 9). pap. 8.99 (978-0-14-242641-8(5), Speak) Penguin Young Readers Group.
Kimura, Yasuko. You Look Yummy! 2015. (Tyrannosaurus Ser.). (ENG.). 40p. (J). (gr. k-2). 16.99 (978-1-940842-06-6(9)) Museyon.
Klein, Adria F. Max y la Fiesta de Adopcion, 1 vol. Robledo, Sol, tr. from ENG. Gallagher-Cole, Mernie, illus. 2007. (Read-It! Readers en Español: la Vida de Max Ser.). (SPA.). 24p. (gr. -1-3). lib. bdg. 21.32 (978-1-4048-3793-5(0), Easy Readers) Picture Window Bks.
Krishnaswami, Uma. Bringing Asha Home, 1 vol. Akib, Jamel, illus. 2015. (ENG.). 32p. (J). pap. 9.95 (978-1-62014-225-7(2)) Lee & Low Bks., Inc.
—Bringing Asha Home, 1 vol. Jeyaveeran, Ruth & Akib, Jamel, illus. 2006. (ENG.). 32p. (J). (gr. -1-3). 16.95 (978-1-58430-259-9(3)) Lee & Low Bks., Inc.
Kurtz, Jane. Planet Jupiter. 2017. 288p. (J). (gr. 3-7). 16.99 (978-0-06-056486-5(5), Greenwillow Bks.) HarperCollins Pubs.
Lake, Mary. Piccolo. Collier, Kevin Scott, illus. 2007. (J). (gr. -1-3). 25p. 14.99 (978-1-59879-358-1(6)); per. 10.99 (978-1-59879-253-9(9)) Lifevest Publishing, Inc.
Lambert, Megan Dowd & Daniels, Peter. Real Sisters Pretend, 1 vol. Carmb, Sara Lynn & Tadgell, Nicole, illus. 2016. (ENG.). 32p. (J). (gr. k-5). 17.95 (978-0-88448-441-7(6), 884441) Tilbury Hse. Pubs.
Langstrom, Angela Chapman. And God Said See, I Told You So! A True Story of Faith & Adoption. 2008. 20p. per. 24.95 (978-1-4241-9195-6(5)) America Star Bks.
Lasenby, Jack. Because We Were the Travellers. 160p. (YA). (gr. 8-18). pap. (978-1-877135-02-6(X), Longacre Pr.) Random Hse. New Zealand.
Layne, Steven L. Over Land & Sea: The Story of International Adoption, 1 vol. Bower, Jan, illus. 2005. (ENG.). 32p. (J). (gr. k-3). 16.99 (978-1-58980-182-0(2)) Pelican Publishing Co., Inc.
Leavitt, Caroline. Girls in Trouble: A Novel. 2005. (ENG.). 368p. pap. 22.99 (978-0-312-33973-9(9), 9780312339739, St. Martin's Griffin) St. Martin's Pr.
Lee, Marie Myung-Ok. Somebody's Daughter. 2006. (ENG.). 280p. per. 21.00 (978-0-8070-8389-5(5), Beacon Pr.) Beacon Pr.
Leeuwen, Joke Van & Leeuwen, Joke van. Eep! Leeuwen, Joke van, illus. 2012. (Gecko Press Titles Ser.). (ENG., Illus.). 152p. (J). (gr. 2-5). pap. 7.95 (978-1-877579-07-3(6)) Gecko Pr. NZL. Dist: Lerner Publishing Group.
Levering, Vicki. Postcards from the Pound. 2008. 48p. pap. 23.99 (978-1-4363-1406-0(2)) Xlibris Corp.
Levey, Emma, illus. Hattie Peck. 2016. (ENG.). 32p. (J). (gr. -1-k). 16.99 (978-1-63450-170-5(5), Sky Pony Pr.) Skyhorse Publishing Co., Inc.
Lewin, Terry. God Remembered Us. Gumm, Susan Kathleen, illus. 2006. 36p. (J). per. 19.00 (978-0-9771482-1-9(1), Ithaca Pr.) Authors & Artists Publishers of New York, Inc.
Lin, Grace. The Red Thread: An Adoption Fairy Tale. Lin, Grace, illus. 2007. (ENG., Illus.). 32p. (J). (gr. -1-3). 16.99 (978-0-8075-6922-1(4)) Whitman, Albert & Co.
Ling, Nancy Tupper. The Story I'll Tell, 1 vol. Lanan, Jessica, illus. 2015. (ENG.). 32p. (J). (gr. 3-3). 17.95 (978-1-62014-160-1(4)) Lee & Low Bks., Inc.
Lisle, Janet Taylor. The Crying Rocks. 2017. (ENG., Illus.). 208p. (YA). (gr. 7). pap. 10.99 **(978-1-4814-7976-9(8)**, Atheneum Bks. for Young Readers) Simon & Schuster Children's Publishing.
Little, Jean. Emma's Strange Pet. Plecas, Jennifer, illus. (I Can Read Level 3 Ser.). 64p. (J). (gr. k-3). 2004. (ENG.). pap. 3.99 (978-0-06-444259-6(4)) 2003. 15.99 (978-0-06-028350-6(5)) HarperCollins Pubs.
Lois, Lowry. Son. 2014. (Giver Quartet Ser.: 4). lib. bdg. 20.85 (978-0-606-35979-5(6)) Turtleback Bks.
Lord, Cynthia. Merlin. McGuire, Erin, illus. 2015. (Shelter Pet Squad Ser.: 2). (ENG.). 128p. (J). (gr. 2-5). 16.99 (978-0-545-63599-8(3)) Scholastic, Inc.
Lowe, Natasha. The Marvelous Magic of Miss Mabel. 2016. (Poppy Pendle Ser.). (ENG., Illus.). 288p. (J). (gr. 3-7). 16.99 (978-1-4814-6533-5(3), Simon & Schuster/Paula Wiseman Bks.) Simon & Schuster/Paula Wiseman Bks.
Lupica, Mike. Safe at Home, 1 vol. 2012. (Comeback Kids Ser.). (ENG.). 192p. (J). (gr. 4-8). lib. bdg. 27.07 (978-1-59961-177-8(5)) Spotlight.
MacColl, Michaela & Nichols, Rosemary. Rory's Promise. 2014. (Hidden Histories Ser.). (ENG.). 288p. (J). (gr. 4-7). 16.95 (978-1-62091-623-0(1), Calkins Creek) Boyds Mills Pr.
Mackall, Dandi Daley. Natalie Wants a Puppy, 1 vol. Blakeslee, Lys, illus. 2009. (That's Nat! Ser.). (ENG.). 96p. (J). (gr. 1-4). pap. 4.99 (978-0-310-71571-9(7)) Zonderkidz.
Madrid-Branch, Michelle. The Tummy Mummy. 2004. (Adoption Means Love Ser.). 32p. 14.95 (978-0-9747443-0-8(1)) MMB Enterprises, LLC.
Maguire, Gregory. Missing Sisters. 2009. 192p. (J). 16.99 (978-0-06-123204-6(1)); (ENG.). (gr. 3-7). pap. 6.99 (978-0-06-123203-9(3)) HarperCollins Pubs.
Marquez, Colleen D. C. A Gift for Little Tree. 2014. (ENG.). 32p. (J). (gr. k-2). 16.99 (978-0-9857932-4-1(4)) Cupola Pr.
Marsden, Carolyn. Take Me with You. 2010. (ENG., Illus.). 176p. (J). (gr. 5-18). 14.99 (978-0-7636-3739-2(4)) Candlewick Pr.
Marsh, Katherine. The Door by the Staircase. 2016. (ENG., Illus.). 284p. (J). (gr. 3-7). 16.99 (978-1-4231-3499-2(0)) Disney Pr.
—The Door by the Staircase. Murphy, Kelly, illus. 2017. (ENG.). 288p. (J). (gr. 5-9). pap. 7.99 (978-1-4231-3785-6(X)) Hyperion Bks. for Children.
McKay, Hilary. Saffy's Angel. 2003. (ENG., Illus.). 160p. (J). (gr. 3-7). pap. 7.99 (978-0-689-84934-3(6), McElderry, Margaret K. Bks.) McElderry, Margaret K. Bks.
—Saffy's Angel. 2004. (Casson Family Ser.: Bk. 1). 160p. (J). (gr. 4-7). pap. 36.00 incl. audio (978-0-8072-2098-6(1), Listening Library) Random Hse. Audio Publishing Group.
McKenzie, Paige. The Haunting of Sunshine Girl. (ENG.). 2016. 320p. (gr. 7-10). pap. 9.99 (978-1-60286-302-6(4)) 2015. (Haunting of Sunshine Girl Ser.: Bk. 1). 304p. (YA). 16.00 (978-1-60286-272-2(9)) Perseus Bks. Group. (Weinstein Bks.).
McKimmie, Chris. Lara of Newtown. 2016. (ENG.). 32p. (J). (gr. -1-3). 19.99 (978-1-76011-232-5(1)) Allen & Unwin AUS. Dist: Independent Pubs. Group.
McLaughlin, Lauren. Wonderful You: An Adoption Story. So, Meilo, illus. 2017. (ENG.). (J). (gr. -1-2). 32p. 17.99 (978-0-553-51001-0(0)); 40p. lib. bdg. 20.99 (978-0-553-51003-4(7)) Random Hse. Children's Bks. (Random Hse. Bks. for Young Readers).
McNamara, Joan. Borya & the Burps: An Eastern European Adoption Story. Majewski, Dawn, illus. 2005. 30p. (J). (gr. -1 — 1). 18.00 (978-0-944934-31-9(5)) Perspectives Pr., Inc.
McQuinn, Anna. Lola Gets a Cat. Beardshaw, Rosalind, illus. 2017. (ENG.). 28p. (J). (-k). lib. bdg. 15.99 (978-1-58089-736-5(3)) Charlesbridge Publishing, Inc.
McWherter, Susie. The Search for the Tiny Princess. 2008. (Illus.). 28p. pap. 10.95 (978-0-9791317-7-6(4), RealityIs Bks.) RealityIsBooks.com, Inc.
Meadows, Amy. Emma's American Chinese New Year. 2012. (ENG.). 31p. (J). pap. 12.95 (978-1-4327-8694-6(6)) Outskirts Pr., Inc.
Meckley, Phyllis. Free Puppies. 2008. 56p. pap. 12.95 (978-1-4327-2947-9(0)) Outskirts Pr., Inc.
Meddaugh, Susan. Shelter Dog Blues. 2010. (Martha Speaks Ser.). (ENG., Illus.). 112p. (J). (gr. 1-4). pap. 5.99 (978-0-547-21050-6(7)) Houghton Mifflin Harcourt Publishing Co.
Medler, John, Jr. The Mommy Mole. Wagoner, Kim, illus. 2004. (J). pap. 15.00 (978-0-8059-6664-0(1)) Dorrance Publishing Co., Inc.
Meissner, Jacqueline. I Am a Doctor: A Child's View of Adoption, 1 vol. 2010. 16p. 24.95 (978-1-4489-4617-4(4)) PublishAmerica, Inc.
Michaelis, Antonia. The Secret Room. 2012. (ENG., Illus.). 208p. (J). (gr. 2-7). 14.95 (978-1-61608-960-3(1), 608960, Sky Pony Pr.) Skyhorse Publishing Co., Inc.
Miles, Ellen. Snowball. 2006. (Puppy Place Ser.: 2). (ENG., Illus.). 80p. (J). (gr. 2-5). 4.99 (978-0-439-79380-3(7), Scholastic Paperbacks) Scholastic, Inc.
Milford, Kate. Ghosts of Greenglass House. 2017. (ENG., Illus.). 464p. (J). (gr. 5-7). 17.99 **(978-0-544-99146-0(X)**, Clarion Bks.) Houghton Mifflin Harcourt Trade & Reference Pubs.
Milford, Kate. Greenglass House. 2015. (CHI.). 352p. (J). (gr. 5-7). pap. (978-986-320-886-0(8)) Commonwealth Publishing Co., Ltd.
—Greenglass House. Zollars, Jaime, illus. (ENG.). (J). (gr. 5-7). 2016. 400p. pap. 7.99 (978-0-544-54028-6(X), HMH Books For Young Readers) 2014. 384p. 17.99 (978-0-544-05270-3(6)) Houghton Mifflin Harcourt Publishing Co.
—Greenglass House. 2016. lib. bdg. 18.40 (978-0-606-38908-2(3)) Turtleback Bks.
Mitchell, Christine. Family Day: Celebrating Ethan's Adoption Anniversary. 2009. 32p. pap. 13.95 (978-1-4389-5542-1(1)) AuthorHouse.
Moore, Stephanie. Better Than Picture Perfect. 2014. (Sharp Sisters Ser.: 2). (ENG.). 160p. (YA). (gr. 6-12). pap. 7.95 (978-1-4677-4486-7(7), Darby Creek) Lerner Publishing Group.
Moore, Stephanie Perry. Better Than Picture Perfect. 2014. (Sharp Sisters Ser.: 2). (ENG.). 160p. (YA). (gr. 6-12). lib. bdg. 27.93 (978-1-4677-3725-8(9)) Lerner Publishing Group.
—Icing on the Cake. 2014. (Sharp Sisters Ser.: 5). (ENG.). 160p. (YA). (gr. 6-12). pap. 7.95 (978-1-4677-4487-4(5), Darby Creek); lib. bdg. 27.93 (978-1-4677-3728-9(3)) Lerner Publishing Group.
—Sweet Honesty. 2005. (Carmen Browne Ser.: 2). (ENG.). 160p. (YA). (gr. 3-7). per. 6.99 (978-0-8024-8168-9(X), Lift Every Voice) Moody Pubs.
Morris, Dawn. Concorde the Beautiful Flying Collie. 2012. 32p. pap. 21.99 (978-1-4691-8098-4(7)) Xlibris Corp.
Mueller, Miranda, illus. Mishka: An Adoption Tale. 2007. 32p. (J). 16.95 (978-1-933084-01-5(4)) DRT Pr.
Musselwhite, Harry. Martin - The Guitar. 2012. (ENG.). 32p. 19.99 incl. audio compact disk (978-1-57424-280-5(6), 1574242806) Centerstream Publishing.
Nelson, R. A. Breathe My Name. 2008. (ENG.). 320p. (YA). (gr. 7-18). 9.99 (978-1-59514-186-6(3), Razorbill) Penguin Young Readers Group.
Newman, Lesléa. Felicia's Favorite Story. Romo, Adriana, illus. 2003. 24p. (J). pap. 9.95 (978-0-9674468-5-1(6)) Two Lives Publishing.
Noah, Jennifer. Nala's Magical Mitsiaq: A Story of Inuit Adoption, 1 vol. Leng, Qin, illus. 2013. (ENG.). 32p. (J). (gr. 1-3). 10.95 (978-1-927095-26-3(3)) Inhabit Media Inc. CAN. Dist: Independent Pubs. Group.
Nyikos, Stacy. Waggers. Anegon, Tamara, illus. 2014. (ENG.). 32p. (J). (gr. -1-k). 16.95 (978-1-62914-629-4(3), Sky Pony Pr.) Skyhorse Publishing Co., Inc.
Oelschlager, Vanita. Made in China: A Story of Adoption. Blackwood, Kristin, illus. 2008. (ENG.). 32p. (J). (gr. -1-3). 17.95 (978-0-9800162-3-9(1)) VanitaBooks.
Olson, Denise. Geoff the Green Hippo: A Children's Book about Adoption. 2011. 16p. (gr. -1). pap. 14.99 (978-1-4567-6951-2(0)) AuthorHouse.
Omololu, C. J. The Third Twin. 2015. (ENG.). 336p. (YA). (gr. 7). 20.99 (978-0-375-99171-4(9), Delacorte Pr.) Random Hse. Children's Bks.
Owens, Robert & Owens, Donna. The Misadventures of Our Son Henry. Bollinger, Carol, illus. 2007. 52p. per. 16.95 (978-1-4241-8721-8(4)) America Star Bks.
Palumbo, Mary Lou. Skippy the Dog in the Band. Mikle, Toby, illus. 2009. 48p. pap. 19.49 (978-1-4389-9218-1(1)) AuthorHouse.
Partridge, Elizabeth. Dogtag Summer. (ENG.). 240p. (YA). (gr. 3-12). 2012. pap. 7.99 (978-1-59990-829-8(8), 9781599908298) 2011. 16.99 (978-1-59990-183-1(8), 9781599901831) Bloomsbury Publishing USA. (Bloomsbury USA Childrens).
Patron, Susan. Lucky Breaks. Phelan, Matt, illus. 2010. (ENG.). 208p. (J). (gr. 3-7). pap. 7.99 (978-1-4169-9772-6(5), Atheneum Bks. for Young Readers) Simon & Schuster Children's Publishing.
Pelton, Lisa. Logos & Adoption: Remi's Journey. 2012. 40p. pap. 14.95 (978-1-4497-5378-8(7), WestBow Pr.) Author Solutions, Inc.
Pernikoff, Doug. So What If Im Adopted. 2009. 36p. 11.99 (978-0-9816923-2-6(X)) Cochran, Russ Co., The.
Perry, Sarah Catherine. Clara's Test. 2006. (J). per. (978-1-55452-022-0(3)) Essence Publishing.
Peterson, David. 10 Days Until Forever. 2011. 32p. 14.99 (978-1-59955-266-8(3), Bonneville Bks.) Cedar Fort, Inc./CFI Distribution.
Philipson, Sandra J. Forever Home. Campbell, Jenny, illus. 2007. (ENG.). 89p. (J). (gr. 3-7). bds. 7.95 (978-1-59624-080-3(6)) Cleveland Clinic Pr.
Poe, Roderick. Ben: A Novella from the Heart. 2006. 82p. pap. 16.95 (978-1-4241-3263-8(0)) PublishAmerica, Inc.
Prophet, John M. Body in the Salt Marsh Boatyard: A Casey Miller Mystery. 2004. 162p. (YA). pap. 13.95

(978-0-595-30991-7(7), Mystery & Suspense Pr.) iUniverse, Inc.

Pyatt, K. C. Rebekah As Her Journey Begins. 2008. 60p. pap. 9.95 *(978-1-933912-00-4(6))* Westview Publishing Co., Inc.

Queralt, Elisenda. La Luna Contenta. 2005. (Caballo Alado Series-Al Galope Ser.). (SPA & ENG., Illus.). 24p. (J). (gr. k-2). per. 5.95 *(978-84-7864-886-3(0))* Combel Editorial, S.A. ESP. Dist: Independent Pubs. Group.

Redmon, Jaylyle. Gracie the Lop-Eared Burro. 2008. 17p. pap. 24.95 *(978-1-60672-626-6(9))* America Star Bks.

Reinhardt, Dana. A Brief Chapter in My Impossible Life. 2007. (ENG.). 256p. (YA). (gr. 9-12). pap. 8.99 *(978-0-375-84691-5(3)*, Ember) Random Hse. Children's Bks.

Remza, Freddie. The Journey to Mei. 2007. 164p. (YA). per. 10.95 *(978-1-4327-0459-9(1))* Outskirts Pr., Inc.

Richmond, Marianne R. I Wished for You: An Adoption Story. 2008. (ENG., Illus.). 40p. (J). (gr. -1-3). 15.95 *(978-1-934082-06-5(6)*, Marianne Richmond Studios, Inc.) Sourcebooks, Inc.

Riley, Elliot. Jing's Family. Bassani, Srimalie, illus. 2017. (All Kinds of Families Ser.). (ENG.). (J). (gr. k-1). 28.51 ***(978-1-68342-145-0(0))*** Rourke Educational Media.

Rivers, Karen. Finding Ruby Starling. 2014. (ENG.). 304p. (J). (gr. 4-7). 17.99 *(978-0-545-53479-6(8)*, Levine, Arthur A. Bks.) Scholastic, Inc.

Rizzo, M. Anthony. Sir Bentley the Beginning. 2009. 36p. pap. 14.95 *(978-1-60860-648-1(1)*, Strategic Bk. Publishing) Strategic Book Publishing & Rights Agency (SBPRA).

Robe, Adam D. Moving to Another Foster Home. Robe, Kim A., ed. Gavet, Nathalie, illus. 2009. 16p. pap. 11.99 *(978-0-9817403-4-8(0))* Robe Communications, Inc.

—Robbie's Trail Through Adoption. Robe, Kim A., ed. Gavet, Nathalie, illus. 2010. 44p. pap. 23.99 *(978-1-935831-03-7(8))* Robe Communications, Inc.

—Robbie's Trail Through Open Adoption. Robe, Kim A., ed. Gavet, Nathalie, illus. 2010. 44p. pap. 23.99 *(978-1-935831-06-8(2))* Robe Communications, Inc.

—Wanting to Belong. Robe, Kim A., ed. Gavet, Nathalie, illus. 2009. 16p. pap. 11.99 *(978-0-9817403-6-2(7))* Robe Communications, Inc.

Royster, D. A. Adoption Is... l.t. ed. 2005. (Illus.). 30p. (J). bds. 15.99 *(978-0-9761538-0-1(7))* Unspeakable Joy Pr.

Rylant, Cynthia. The Whale. McDaniels, Preston, illus. 2003. (Lighthouse Family Ser.: 2). (ENG.). 64p. (J). (gr. 1-5). 15.99 *(978-0-689-84881-0(1)*, Simon & Schuster Bks. For Young Readers) Simon & Schuster Bks. For Young Readers.

Sáenz, Benjamin Alire. The Inexplicable Logic of My Life. 2017. (ENG.). 464p. (gr. 7). 17.99 *(978-0-544-58650-5(6))* Houghton Mifflin Harcourt Publishing Co.

Sarta, Jon. Your Adoption Story. 2005. 20p. 9.99 *(978-1-4116-6439-5(6))* Lulu Pr., Inc.

Schaumberg, Rose Mary & Schaumberg, Emily Rose. I'll Miss My Grandma, Wouldn't You? 2008. (Illus.). 40p. pap. 16.99 *(978-1-4389-1335-3(4))* AuthorHouse.

Scheerger, Sarah Lynn. The Opposite of Love. 2014. (ENG.). 272p. (YA). (gr. 8-12). 16.99 *(978-0-8075-6132-4(0))* Whitman, Albert & Co.

Schindler, Holly. Spark. 2016. 304p. (YA). (gr. 8). 17.99 *(978-0-06-222023-3(3)*, HarperTeen) HarperCollins Pubs.

Schroeder, Lisa. Keys to the City. 2017. (ENG.). 240p. (J). (gr. 3-7). 16.99 ***(978-0-545-90738-5(1)***, Scholastic Pr.) Scholastic, Inc.

Scott, Shirley A. The Adventures of Jack & Dobbie: The Beginning. 2009. 32p. pap. 13.95 *(978-1-4389-4840-9(9))* AuthorHouse.

Shemin, Craig. Families Are Forever. McCoy, John, illus. 34p. 2006. (J). (gr. -1-2). 16.95 *(978-0-9728666-8-6(3))* 2004. 9.95 *(978-0-9728666-1-3(2)*, 1) As Simple As That Publishing.

Shevah, Emma. Dara Palmer's Major Drama. 2016. (ENG.). 288p. (J). (gr. 3-7). 16.99 *(978-1-4926-3138-5(8)*, 9781492631385, Sourcebooks Jabberwocky) Sourcebooks, Inc.

Shimokawa, Melanie. A Family for Madison. 2008. 53p. pap. 16.95 *(978-1-60672-701-0(X))* America Star Bks.

Simcox, Lorraine. A Single Red Thread. 2008. (J). 21.99 *(978-1-60131-024-8(2))* Big Tent Bks.

Sims, Lesley. Anne of Green Gables. 2017. (Picture Bks.). (ENG.). 24p. (J). (gr. k). 9.99 ***(978-0-7945-3750-0(2)***, Usborne) EDC Publishing.

Smith, Andrew. The Alex Crow. 2015. (ENG.). 336p. (YA). (gr. 9). 18.99 *(978-0-525-42653-0(1)*, Dutton Books for Young Readers) Penguin Young Readers Group.

—The Alex Crow. 2016. lib. bdg. 22.10 *(978-0-606-38854-2(0))* Turtleback Bks.

Snyder, Zilpha Keatley. William's Midsummer Dreams. (ENG., (J). (gr. 3-7). 2012. Illus.). 240p. pap. 6.99 *(978-1-4424-1998-8(9))* 2011. 224p. 16.99 *(978-1-4424-1997-1(0))* Simon & Schuster Children's Publishing. (Atheneum Bks. for Young Readers).

Sonnichsen, A. L. Red Butterfly. Bates, Amy June, illus. 2015. (ENG.). 400p. (J). (gr. 3-7). 17.99 *(978-1-4814-1109-7(8))* Simon & Schuster, Inc.

Spalding, Amy. Ink Is Thicker Than Water. 2013. (Entangled Teen Ser.). (ENG.). 320p. (YA). (gr. 7-12). pap. 9.99 *(978-1-62266-040-7(4)*, 9781622660407) Entangled Publishing, LLC.

Spangler, Jon. The Sky Princess. 2007. 24p. per. 10.95 *(978-1-4327-1557-1(7))* Outskirts Pr., Inc.

Steedley-Tolan, Chopper. I've Been Picked! Chopper's Tail of Adoption. 2011. 32p. pap. 12.95 *(978-1-4634-3554-7(1))* AuthorHouse.

Steers, Billy. Tractor Mac Family Reunion. 2015. (Tractor Mac Ser.). (ENG., Illus.). 32p. (J). (gr. -1-k). 8.99 *(978-0-374-30109-5(3)*, 9780374301095, Farrar, Straus & Giroux (BYR)) Farrar, Straus & Giroux.

Stewart, Emma. The Adventures of Fillmore the Gerbil. 2008. 24p. pap. 13.50 *(978-1-60693-033-5(8)*, Eloquent Bks.) Strategic Book Publishing & Rights Agency (SBPRA).

Stokes, Paula. Liars, Inc. 2015. (ENG.). 368p. (YA). (gr. 8). 17.99 *(978-0-06-232328-6(8)*, HarperTeen) HarperCollins Pubs.

Stuber, Barbara. Girl in Reverse. 2014. (ENG., Illus.). 336p. (YA). (gr. 7). 17.99 *(978-1-4424-9734-4(3)*, McElderry, Margaret K. Bks.) McElderry, Margaret K. Bks.

Sugarman, Brynn Olenberg. Rebecca's Journey Home. Shapiro, Michelle, illus. (Life Cycle Ser.). 32p. (J). 2014. (ENG.). (gr. k-4). 8.95 *(978-1-4677-4937-4(0))* 2006. (gr. -1-3). lib. bdg. 17.95 *(978-1-58013-157-5(3))* Lerner Publishing Group. (Kar-Ben Publishing).

Taeschner, Jacquelin. Boss. 2005. pap. 32.50 *(978-1-4208-7369-6(5))* AuthorHouse.

Taylor, G. P. The First Escape. 2008. (Dopple Ganger Chronicles Ser.: 1). (ENG., Illus.). 288p. (J). (gr. 3-7). 19.99 *(978-1-4143-1947-6(9)*, SaltRiver) Tyndale Hse. Pubs.

Teal, Val. The Little Woman Wanted Noise. Lawson, Robert, illus. 2013. (ENG.). 48p. (J). (gr. -1-2). 14.95 *(978-1-59017-711-2(8)*, NYR Children's Collection) New York Review of Bks., Inc., The.

Thisdale, Francois. Nini. Thisdale, Francois, illus. 2011. (ENG., Illus.). 40p. (J). (gr. -1-2). 15.95 *(978-1-77049-270-7(4)*, Tundra Bks.) Tundra Bks. CAN. Dist: Penguin Random Hse. LLC.

Thrasher, Jenny & Thrasher, Phil. The Golden Egg: A Story about Adoption. Enroc Illustrations, illus. 2006. (ENG.). 24p. per. 10.95 *(978-1-59800-468-7(9))* Outskirts Pr., Inc.

Throckmorton, Sylvestra. Annie Cabannie's Star Baby. 2004. (Illus.). 23p. (J). per. 11.95 *(978-0-9761723-0-7(5))* Greene, A.S. & Co.

—Star Baby. Throckmorton, Sylvestra et al, illus. 2006. (ENG & RAJ.). 16p. (J). 14.95 *(978-0-9761723-1-4(3))* Greene, A.S. & Co.

Tomey, Ingrid. The Queen of Dreamland. 2004. 179p. (YA). (gr. 6-10). reprint ed. 15.00 *(978-0-7567-7151-5(X))* DIANE Publishing Co.

Uncle Bob. Tobi the Little Puppy Dog. Arnold, Stephen, illus. 2006. (Uncle Bob Ser.). 12p. (J). pap. 3.95 *(978-1-930596-61-0(8))* Amherst Pr.

Van Hamme, Jean. The Heir. Francq, Philippe, illus. 2008. (Largo Winch Ser.: 1). (ENG.). 96p. pap. 19.95 *(978-1-905460-48-9(1))* CineBook GBR. Dist: National Bk. Network.

Viswanath, Shobha. Whose Lovely Child Can You Be? Tappin, Christine, illus. 2013. (ENG.). 32p. (J). (gr. -1). pap. 9.95 *(978-81-8190-304-4(8))* Karadi Tales Co. Pvt, Ltd. IND. Dist: Consortium Bk. Sales & Distribution.

von Klan, Stella and Laurene. Beauty & the Boy. 2009. 32p. 16.98 *(978-0-578-00322-1(8))* von Klan, Laurene.

Wardlaw, Lee. Won Ton & Chopstick. Yelchin, Eugene, illus. 2015. (ENG.). 40p. (J). (gr. -1-3). 17.99 *(978-0-8050-9987-4(5)*, 9780805099874, Holt, Henry & Co. Bks. For Young Readers) Holt, Henry & Co.

Warner, Jodi. Shia's Tail 2. 2012. 24p. pap. 10.95 *(978-1-4624-0369-1(7)*, Inspiring Voices) Author Solutions, Inc.

Waters, Terrance D. I f l Y: A Novel Based on a True Story. 2008. 148p. 26.00 *(978-1-4251-3496-9(3))* Trafford Publishing.

Watson, K. R. Little Gabby Meets Her New Family. 2008. 44p. pap. 17.99 *(978-1-4389-1767-2(8))* AuthorHouse.

Weber, John. Orphan. 2010. 266p. (YA). (gr. 7-18). 16.95 *(978-1-934813-38-6(9))* Westside Bks.

Weeks, Sarah. As Simple as It Seems. (ENG.). 192p. (J). (gr. 3-7). 2011. pap. 5.99 *(978-0-06-084665-7(8))* 2010. 15.99 *(978-0-06-084663-3(1))* HarperCollins Pubs.

Wein, Elizabeth. Black Dove, White Raven. 2015. (ENG.). 368p. (YA). (gr. 7-12). 17.99 *(978-1-4231-8310-5(X))* Hyperion Bks. for Children.

Weiskal, N. j. & Weiskal, N. J. The Skittery Kitten & the Scaredy Cat. Weiskal, N. J., illus. 2009. (Illus.). 36p. pap. 8.00 *(978-1-935125-59-4(1))* Robertson Publishing.

Werner, Teresa Orem. A Quilt of Wishes. Tremlin, Nathan, illus. l.t. ed. 2005. 26p. (J). 16.95 *(978-1-59879-147-1(8))* Lifevest Publishing, Inc.

White, A. Rose. Just the Way I Am. 2012. 16p. pap. 12.99 *(978-1-62230-382-3(2))* Salem Author Services.

Williams, Vera B. Home at Last. Raschka, Chris, illus. 2016. 40p. (J). (gr. -1-3). 17.99 *(978-0-06-134973-7(9)*, Greenwillow Bks.) HarperCollins Pubs.

Williamson, A. M. The Castle of the Shadows. 2007. (ENG.). 164p. pap. 19.99 *(978-1-4346-3410-8(8))* Creative Media Partners, LLC.

Wing, Natasha. The Night Before the New Pet. 2016. (Night Before Ser.). lib. bdg. 14.75 *(978-0-606-38418-6(9))* Turtleback Bks.

Witthaus, A. S. Princess Sach. 2011. 28p. pap. 24.95 *(978-1-4626-4482-7(1))* America Star Bks.

Wittreich, Yvonne M. B. The True Story of Sasha, from Homelessness to Happiness. 2008. 36p. per. 17.95 *(978-1-4327-1502-1(X))* Outskirts Pr., Inc.

Woolley, Barbara B. Freedom West. 2006. 22.99 *(978-1-4257-0124-6(8))*; pap. 15.99 *(978-1-4257-0123-9(X))* Xlibris Corp.

Worley, Michelle. Buster Goes to the White House, 1 vol. 2009. 48p. pap. 16.95 *(978-1-61546-352-7(6))* PublishAmerica, Inc.

Wright, Bill & Wright, Bil. When the Black Girl Sings. 2008. (ENG.). 272p. (YA). (gr. 7-12). 16.99 *(978-1-4169-3995-5(4)*, Simon & Schuster Bks. For Young Readers) Simon & Schuster Bks. For Young Readers.

—When the Black Girl Sings. 2009. (ENG.). 272p. (YA). (gr. 7). mass mkt. 6.99 *(978-1-4169-4003-6(0)*, Simon Pulse) Simon Pulse.

Xinran, Xinran & Mother's Bridge of Love Staff. Motherbridge of Love. Masse, Josée, illus. 2013. (ENG.). 32p. (J). (gr. k-3). 7.99 *(978-1-78285-040-3(6))* Barefoot Bks., Inc.

Ye, Ting-Xing. Throwaway Daughter. 2004. (ENG.). 320p. (J). (gr. 7). mass mkt. 9.99 *(978-0-7704-2921-8(1)*, Seal Bks.) Penguin Random House Canada Young Readers CAN. Dist: Penguin Random Hse. LLC.

Yrjana, Colleen. Carry Me to Kinshasa Our Adoption Journey. Ulrich, Kelly, illus. 2012. 24p. pap. *(978-1-77097-655-9(8))* FriesenPress.

Yukkie the Yorkie, A. K. A. Marilyn J. Sanders. The Adventures of Yukkie the Yorkie: The Beginning. 2008. (Illus.). 32p. (J). 16.00 *(978-0-8059-7606-9(X))* Dorrance Publishing Co., Inc.

Zafrilla, Marta. Little Chick & Mommy Cat. 2012. (ENG., Illus.). 32p. (J). (gr. k-2). *(978-84-15241-96-6(8))* D P & G Military Pubs.

Zarr, Sara. How to Save a Life. 2012. (ENG.). 368p. (YA). (gr. 7-17). pap. 10.99 *(978-0-316-03605-4(6))* Little, Brown Bks. for Young Readers.

Zink, Michelle. Lies I Told. 2015. (Lies I Told Ser.: 1). (ENG.). 352p. (YA). (gr. 8). pap. 9.99 *(978-0-06-232713-0(5)*, HarperTeen); 17.99 *(978-0-06-232712-3(7))* HarperCollins Pubs.

—Promises I Made. 2015. (Lies I Told Ser.: 2). (ENG.). 304p. (YA). (gr. 8). 17.99 *(978-0-06-232715-4(1))* HarperCollins Pubs.

ADULTHOOD

Eirienne, Arielle. The You Behind the Mascara: A Growing-up Guide for Teenage Girls. 2009. 41p. pap. 14.64 *(978-0-557-09624-4(3))* Lulu Pr., Inc.

ADVENTURE AND ADVENTURERS

see also Discoveries in Geography; Escapes; Explorers; Frontier and Pioneer Life; Heroes; Sea Stories; Seafaring Life; Shipwrecks; Underwater Exploration; Voyages and Travels

Adventures in Culture. 2016. (Adventures in Culture Ser.). 00024p. (J). pap. 48.90 ***(978-1-4824-5841-1(1))*** Stevens, Gareth Publishing LLLP.

Alger, Horatio. Joe the Hotel Boy: Or, Winning Out by Pluck. 363p. reprint ed. pap. 79.00 *(978-1-4047-3578-1(X))* Classic Textbooks.

Bingham, Jane. Adventurers. 2011. (20th Century Lives Ser.). (ENG.). 32p. (YA). (gr. 3-6). lib. bdg. 26.50 *(978-1-4488-3291-0(8))* Rosen Publishing Group, Inc., The.

Blasingame, James B. Gary Paulsen, 1 vol. 2007. (Teen Reads: Student Companions to Young Adult Literature Ser.). 184p. (C). (gr. 7). 50.00 *(978-0-313-33532-7(X)*, GR3532, Greenwood) ABC-CLIO, LLC.

Bledsoe, Lucy Jane. How to Survive in Antarctica. 2006. (ENG., Illus.). 96p. (J). (gr. 5-9). 17.95 *(978-0-8234-1890-9(1))* Holiday Hse., Inc.

Blotnick, Elihu. Glimmins: Children of the Western Woods. Blotnick, Elihu, illus. 2009. (Illus.). 72p. (J). (gr. 1-18). pap. 14.50 *(978-0-915090-18-1(X)*, California Street) Firefall Editions.

Bodden, Valerie. Conquistadors. 2013. 24p. pap. *(978-1-60818-467-5(6))* Creative Co., The.

—Great Warriors: Conquistadors. 2014. (Great Warriors Ser.). (ENG.). 24p. (J). (gr. 1-3). pap. 9.99 *(978-1-62832-067-1(2)*, Creative Paperbacks) Creative Co., The.

Boer, Paula. Brumbies. Evans, Rowena, illus. 2011. (ENG.). 148p. pap. 14.99 *(978-0-615-56093-9(8))* IFWG Publishing Inc.

Bremner-Lewis, P. L. My Friend, the Unicorn. 2009. 28p. pap. 12.95 *(978-1-4389-8966-2(0))* AuthorHouse.

The Britannica Guide to Explorers & Adventurers. 2013. (Britannica Guide to Explorers & Adventurers Ser.). (YA). (gr. 9-12). 352.50 *(978-1-62275-065-8(9))*; 176.25 *(978-1-62275-033-7(0))* Rosen Publishing Group, Inc., The.

Broadbent, Paul. Down under Vacation. 2007. (Trackers-Math Ser.). (gr. 2-5). pap. 5.00 *(978-1-59055-940-6(1))* Pacific Learning, Inc.

Brooks, E. s. & Brooks, E. S. Historic Boys. 2013. 208p. pap. *(978-3-95507-947-5(3))* DOGMA. in Europäischer Hochschulverlag GmbH & Co. KG.

Brown, Chris. Shiver Me Timbers: A Fun Book of Pirates, Sailors, & Other Sea-Farers. 2006. (ENG., Illus.). 32p. (J). (gr. 4-7). pap. 8.95 *(978-0-7145-3303-2(3))* Consortium Bk. Sales & Distribution.

Burke Battistini, Maryanne. Lacey's Story: A Little Tale That Wags. 2009. 72p. pap. 24.99 *(978-1-4389-8874-0(5))* AuthorHouse.

Burns, Marie. The Quest for Gold. 2012. 64p. pap. 15.99 *(978-1-4691-4632-4(0))* Xlibris Corp.

Calkhoven, Laurie & Laskey, Shannon. Miles of Smiles: Travel Games & Quizzes to Go. Hunt, Sara, ed. 2007. (ENG., Illus.). 80p. (gr. 4-7). spiral bd. 9.95 *(978-1-59369-170-7(X)*, Pleasant Co.) American Girl Publishing, Inc.

Campbell, Corbin. The Little Blue Man. 2011. 32p. pap. 13.99 *(978-1-257-37707-7(8))* Lulu Pr., Inc.

Caprin, K. F. The Adventures of the Little Savages. 2009. (ENG.). 167p. pap. 16.95 *(978-1-4092-3379-4(0))* Lulu Pr., Inc.

Career Ideas for Kids Who Like Adventure & Travel. 2nd rev. ed. 2007. (Career Ideas for Kids Ser.). (Illus.). 208p. (gr. 4-9). 32.95 *(978-0-8160-6547-9(0)*, Checkmark Bks.) Facts On File, Inc.

Carey-Costa, Denise. A Tale of Three Tails. Sjostrom, Nicole & Iseminger, Jonathon, illus. 2009. 81p. 10.99 *(978-1-4251-8492-6(8))* Trafford Publishing.

Carr, Roger Vaughan & Knapsey, Kath. How to Discover the World. 2007. 96p. (J). pap. *(978-1-4207-0729-8(9))* Sundance/Newbridge Educational Publishing.

Cartee, Mary. Patchwork Princess. 2011. 42p. pap. 16.95 *(978-1-4560-8504-9(2))* America Star Bks.

Catel, Patrick. Surviving Stunts & Other Amazing Feats. 2011. (Extreme Survival Ser.). (ENG.). 56p. (gr. 5-5). pap. 9.49 *(978-1-4109-3976-0(6)*, Raintree Freestyle) Heinemann-Raintree.

Christensen, Gerda. Troll Peter Visits His Uncle, the Bridge Troll & Other Stories. 2011. 36p. pap. *(978-1-4269-5602-7(9))* Trafford Publishing (UK) Ltd.

Christensen, Gerda & Evans, Carol. Troll Peter & His Family Prepare for Winter & Other Stories: Troll Peter's Adventures Book 4. 2011. 40p. pap. *(978-1-4269-7312-3(8))* Trafford Publishing (UK) Ltd.

Chwast, Seymour. Bobo's Smile. Chwast, Seymour, illus. 2012. (ENG., Illus.). 32p. (J). (gr. 1-3). 14.99 *(978-1-56846-221-9(2)*, Creative Editions) Creative Co., The.

Cleare, John. Epic Climbs. 2011. (Illus.). 64p. (J). (gr. 3-6). 19.99 *(978-0-7534-6473-1(X))* Larousse Kingfisher Chambers, Inc.

Coatsworth, Elizabeth Jane. Forgotten Island. Paull, Grace, illus. 2011. 74p. 36.95 *(978-1-258-07461-6(3))* Literary Licensing, LLC.

Connolly, Ryan. Tom's Field Trip. 2012. (InfoMax Readers Ser.). (ENG., Illus.). 16 pp.p. (J). (gr. k-1). pap. 7.00 *(978-1-4488-8971-6(5)*, Rosen Classroom) Rosen Publishing Group, Inc., The.

Cummins, Julie & Cummins, Julia. Women Daredevils: Thrills, Chills, & Frills. Harness, Cheryl, illus. 2008. (ENG.). 48p. (J). (gr. 2-5). 17.99 *(978-0-525-47948-2(1)*, Dutton Books for Young Readers) Penguin Young Readers Group.

Currie, Stephen & National Geographic Learning Staff. Travels to Distant Lands, 1000-1400. 2007. (Nonfiction Reading & Writing Workshops Ser.). (ENG., Illus.). 32p. (J). pap. 17.95 *(978-0-7922-4542-1(3))* CENGAGE Learning.

Dashner, James. The Blade of Shattered Hope. 2010. (13th Reality Ser.: Bk. 3). 432p. (J). 18.99 *(978-1-60641-239-8(6)*, Shadow Mountain) Shadow Mountain Publishing.

Discovery Education. 2013. (Discovery Education Ser.). 32p. (J). (gr. 3-6). 1035.25 *(978-1-4777-1555-0(X))*; pap. 2460.00 *(978-1-4777-2737-9(X))*; pap. 410.00 *(978-1-4777-2736-2(1))* Rosen Publishing Group, Inc., The. (PowerKids Pr.).

d'Lacey, Chris. Alexander's Army. 2015. (UFiles Ser.: 2). (ENG.). 304p. (J). (gr. 3-7). 16.99 *(978-0-545-60880-0(5)*, Scholastic Pr.) Scholastic, Inc.

—The Fire Eternal. 2010. (Last Dragon Chronicles Ser.: 4). (ENG.). 512p. (J). (gr. 3-7). 8.99 *(978-0-545-05164-4(9)*, Orchard Bks.) Scholastic, Inc.

Dorling Kindersley Publishing Staff. The Adventure Guide. 2015. (ENG., Illus.). 96p. (J). (gr. k-4). lib. bdg. 16.99 *(978-1-4654-3623-8(5)*, DK Children) Dorling Kindersley Publishing, Inc.

Dowswell, Paul. True Escape Stories. Tyler, Jenny, ed. 2004. (True Adventure Stories Ser.). (Illus.). 144p. (J). pap. 4.95 *(978-0-7945-0087-0(0)*, Usborne) EDC Publishing.

—True Polar Adventures. Woodcock, John, illus. 2004. (True Adventure Stories Ser.). 144p. (J). pap. 4.95 *(978-0-7945-0404-5(3)*, Usborne) EDC Publishing.

—True Stories of Sea Adventures. 2005. (True Adventure Stories Ser.). 144p. (J). pap. 4.95 *(978-0-7945-0733-6(6)*, Usborne) EDC Publishing.

Dowswell, Paul & Fleming, Fergus. True Adventures Collection. 2007. (True Adventure Stories Ser.). (Illus.). 421p. (J). per. 9.99 *(978-0-7945-1500-3(2)*, Usborne) EDC Publishing.

Duder, Tessa, ed. Down to the Sea Again: True Sea Stories for Young Newzealanders. 2005. 256p. (J). *(978-1-86950-476-2(3))* HarperCollins Pubs. New Zealand NZL. Dist: HarperCollins Pubs. Australia.

Dunn, Joeming & Espinosa, Rod. The Heart: A Graphic Novel Tour, 1 vol. Espinosa, Rod, illus. 2009. (Graphic Body Ser.). (ENG., Illus.). 32p. (J). (gr. 3-6). 28.50 *(978-1-60270-685-9(9))* ABDO Publishing Co.

Dybvik, Tina & Meister, Cari. Take It Outside. Record, Adam, illus. 2013. (Take It Outside Ser.). (ENG.). 24p. (gr. k-2). pap. 31.80 *(978-1-4795-1998-9(7))*; lib. bdg. 109.28 *(978-1-4048-8142-6(5))* Picture Window Bks.

Ebiringa, Chudy. The Adventures of Ella at Bulukutu Stream. 2011. (ENG.). 50p. pap. 11.95 *(978-1-4327-6655-9(4))* Outskirts Pr., Inc.

Egan, Kate. Evil Comes in Pairs. Merkel, Joe F., illus. 2009. (Spider-Man Ser.). 64p. (J). (gr. 2-5). pap. 4.99 *(978-0-06-162625-8(2)*, HarperFestival) HarperCollins Pubs.

Extreme Adventures!, 6 vols. 2010. (Extreme Adventures! Ser.). (ENG.). 32p. (gr. 3-4). lib. bdg. 54.64 *(978-1-4296-4583-6(0)*, Fact Finders) Capstone Press of Coughlan Cos.

Extreme Adventures! [Capstone Sole Source]. 2010. (Extreme Adventures! Ser.). 32p. lib. bdg. 155.94 *(978-1-4296-5855-3(X)*, Fact Finders) Capstone Press of Coughlan Cos.

Facts on File, Inc. Staff. Adventure. 2010. (New Discovering Careers for Your Future Ser.). (Illus.). 128p. (gr. 4-9). 24.95 *(978-0-8160-8043-4(7)*, Ferguson Publishing Co.) Facts On File, Inc.

Felsing, Dean E. New Orleans or Sunk! 2011. 64p. (gr. -1). pap. 13.95 *(978-1-4582-0092-1(2)*, Abbott Pr.) Author Solutions, Inc.

Flynn, Claire E. Running with the Bulls. 2013. (Thrill Seekers Ser.). (Illus.). 32p. (J). (gr. 3-6). pap. 10.50 *(978-1-4824-3294-7(3))* Rosen Publishing Group, Inc., The.

Frino Ph. D., Michael G. Waycool School Takes the Bus. 2011. 40p. pap. *(978-1-4269-9003-8(0))* Trafford Publishing (UK) Ltd.

Gerstein, Mordicai. The Man Who Walked Between the Towers. Gerstein, Mordicai, illus. rev. ed. 2003. (ENG., Illus.). 44p. (J). (gr. k-3). 18.99 *(978-0-7613-1791-3(0)*, 9780761317913) Roaring Brook Pr.

Group/McGraw-Hill, Wright. Aunt Jewel's Ghost, 6 vols. (D-Man Beans Ser.). 47p. (gr. 4-6). 42.50 *(978-0-322-06259-7(4))* Wright Group/McGraw-Hill.

—Possibilities, 6 vols. (D-Man Beans Ser.). 47p. (gr. 4-6). 42.50 *(978-0-322-06264-1(0))* Wright Group/McGraw-Hill.

Guillain, Charlotte. Extreme Athletes: True Stories of Amazing Sporting Adventurers, 1 vol. 2014. (Ultimate Adventurers Ser.). (ENG., Illus.). 48p. (gr. 6-6). lib. bdg. 29.99 *(978-1-4109-5418-3(8))* Heinemann-Raintree.

Hanke, Maureen & Leedham, Jacalyn. Alligator Raggedy-Mouth: Making Music with Poems & Rhymes. (ENG., Illus.). 64p. (J). pap. *(978-0-7136-4281-0(5)*, A&C Black) Bloomsbury Publishing Plc.

Harrison, Paul. Gravity-Defying Stunt Spectaculars. 2010. (Extreme! Ser.). (ENG.). 32p. (gr. 3-4). pap. 47.70 *(978-1-4296-5114-1(8)*, Fact Finders) Capstone Press of Coughlan Cos.

Harvey, Gill. True Desert Adventures. Woodcock, John, illus. 2004. (True Adventure Stories Ser.). 144p. (J). pap. 4.95 *(978-0-7945-0381-9(0)*, Usborne) EDC Publishing.

Harvey, Tom. Top Dog. 2011. 48p. pap. *(978-1-4269-7612-4(7))* Trafford Publishing (UK) Ltd.

Heidtke, John. Family Golf Adventures on Michigan Links. 2010. 242p. (J). pap. 12.95 *(978-1-60920-000-8(4))* Ajoyin Publishing, Inc.

Henry, J. The Big Gray House II: More Adventures of Franklin Meyers. 2011. 112p. (gr. -1-2). pap. 12.06 *(978-1-4269-7337-6(3))* Trafford Publishing.

Heywood, Grand-Mere Geny. Proto: Que faire quand un dinosaure nait dans votre Jardin? Connors, Mary, illus. 2010. 56p. pap. 23.99 *(978-1-4490-5786-2(1))* AuthorHouse.

Honovich, Nancy. Ultimate Explorer Guide: Explore, Discover, & Create Your Own Adventures with Real National Geographic Explorers As Your Guides! 2017. (ENG.). 160p. (J). (gr. 3-7). pap. 14.99 *(978-1-4263-2709-4(9)*, National Geographic Children's Bks.) National Geographic Society.

Hord, Janice. The Walking Stick Adventure. 2007. 52p. per. 19.95 *(978-1-934335-05-5(3))* WordWright.biz, Inc.

Horrigan, David J. The Spark in the Sea: Adventures in Marine Science, 1. 2003. 152p. pap. 24.00 *(978-0-9743712-0-7(3)*, 001) Home Planet Bks.

Howard, Denise. Jameela's Big Adventure. 2009. 84p. pap. 10.49 *(978-1-4490-5355-0(6))* AuthorHouse.
Humphreys, Alastair. The Boy Who Biked the World: On the Road to Africa. Morgan-Jones, Tom, illus. 2012. (Boy Who Biked the World Ser.: 1). (ENG.). 192p. (J). (gr. 4-7). pap. 9.99 *(978-1-903070-75-8(9))* Eye Bks. GBR. Dist: Independent Pubs. Group.
—The Boy Who Biked the World: Riding the Americas. Morgan-Jones, Tom, illus. 2015. (Boy Who Biked the World Ser.: 2). (ENG.). 192p. (J). (gr. 4-7). pap. 9.99 *(978-1-903070-87-1(2))* Eye Bks. GBR. Dist: Independent Pubs. Group.
Incredible True Adventures. 2015. (Incredible True Adventures Ser.). (ENG.). 32p. (J). (gr. 3-4). 159.60 *(978-1-4824-1646-6(8))* Stevens, Gareth Publishing LLLP.
Jensen, Stephanie L. The Purple Watermelon. 2010. 48p. 17.95 *(978-1-4520-1417-3(5))* AuthorHouse.
Johnson, Allen L. Willmore Horseback Adventure: Adventures with Grandchildren 2004. (Illus.). 190p. 15.00 *(978-1-880675-08-3(0))* Creative Enterprises.
Kids Favorite Adventures Audio. 2004. pap. 22.50 *(978-0-01-208207-2(4))* Your Story Hour Recordings.
Kongyin. Sungrass. 2011. 344p. pap. *(978-0-9869858-5-0(6))* Kima Global Pubs.
Kopec, Mary Kate. The Awesome Adventures of Randi Raindrop. 2011. pap. 12.95 *(978-0-7414-6449-1(7))* Infinity Publishing.
Krull, Kathleen. Lives of the Explorers: Discoveries, Disasters (and What the Neighbors Thought) Hewitt, Kathryn, illus. 2014. (ENG.). 96p. (J). (gr. 5-7). 20.99 *(978-0-15-205910-1(5),* HMH Books For Young Readers) Houghton Mifflin Harcourt Publishing Co.
Kuligowski, Stephanie. La Salle: Uno de los Primeros Exploradores de Texas. 2013. (Primary Source Readers Ser.). (SPA.). lib. bdg. 19.65 *(978-0-606-31863-1(1),* Turtleback) Turtleback Bks.
Leone, Anthony. A Great Adventure with a Cub Named Troy. 2011. 32p. pap. 13.99 *(978-1-4634-0212-9(0))* AuthorHouse.
Lesa, Ropeti F. Being a Boy in Samoa in the 1950s. Asuao, Kelcey, illus. 2003. (Polynesian Literature Ser.: Vol. 1). xiii, 197p. (J). pap. 19.95 *(978-0-9728126-3-4(6))* Isles of the Sea Pubs.
lewis, k. s. YELLOW ANGELS DANCING on A RED TOOTHBRUSH: a Charlie Travel Adventure Story. 2009. 36p. pap. 23.90 *(978-0-557-15665-8(3))* Lulu Pr., Inc.
Lewis, Simon. Desperate Escapes. 2009. (Difficult & Dangerous Ser.). (Illus.). 32p. (J). (gr. 4-7). pap. *(978-1-897563-23-6(X))* Saunders Bk. Co.
Lindemann, Lindy. Kicklighter Shadow & the Beeples. White, David, illus. 2009. 24p. pap. 12.95 *(978-0-9822540-9-7(1))* Peppertree Pr., The.
Lively, Deborah Dreher. Walkabout Sam. 2009. 32p. pap. 13.75 *(978-1-60860-740-2(2),* Strategic Bk. Publishing) Strategic Book Publishing & Rights Agency (SBPRA).
Lourie, Peter. Jack London & the Klondike Gold Rush. Minor, Wendell, illus. 2017. (ENG.). 208p. (J). 18.99 *(978-0-8050-9757-3(0),* 9780805097573, Holt, Henry & Co. Bks. For Young Readers) Holt, Henry & Co.
Macdonald, Fiona. Courageous Circumnavigators: True Stories of Around-The-World Adventurers, 1 vol. 2014. (Ultimate Adventurers Ser.). (ENG., Illus.). 48p. (gr. 6-6). lib. bdg. 29.99 *(978-1-4109-5416-9(1))* Heinemann-Raintree.
Macdonald, Fiona, et al. Ultimate Adventurers, 1 vol. 2014. (Ultimate Adventurers Ser.). (ENG.). 48p. (gr. 6-6). lib. bdg. 119.96 *(978-1-4109-6045-0(5))* Heinemann-Raintree.
Macken, JoAnn Early. Gary Paulsen: Voice of Adventure & Survival. 2007. (Authors Teens Love Ser.). (Illus.). 104p. (J). (gr. 8-12). lib. bdg. 33.27 *(978-0-7660-2721-3(X))* Enslow Pubs., Inc.
Madsen, Chris. Undersea Adventure. 2005. (Glow in the Dark Ser.). 24p. (J). *(978-1-902626-76-5(1))* Red Bird Publishing.
Mason, Caroline. The Blacksmith's Cottage: A Pastoral War. 2009. 150p. pap. 13.95 *(978-1-4327-4969-9(2));* 120p. pap. 33.95 *(978-1-4327-2987-5(X))* Outskirts Pr., Inc.
Matheron, Annaliese. Ninja Nan & Sidekick Grandad. 2011. (Illus.). 80p. pap. 8.95 *(978-1-4478-3079-5(2))* Lulu Pr., Inc.
McCracken, Connie. Indigo Boy & Crystalline Girl. Craig, Chris, illus. 2009. 24p. pap. 10.95 *(978-1-4269-0423-3(1))* Trafford Publishing.
McGuinness, Denis E. & Thomson, Sarah L. Gary Paulsen, 01 vols., 1. 2016. (All about the Author Ser.). (ENG., Illus.). 112p. (J). 35.60 *(978-1-4994-6268-5(9),* Rosen Young Adult) Rosen Publishing Group, Inc., The.
Meissner, David & Richardson, Kim. Call of the Klondike: A True Gold Rush Adventure. 2013. (ENG., Illus.). 168p. (J). (gr. 4). 16.95 *(978-1-59078-823-3(0),* Calkins Creek) Boyds Mills Pr.
Michel, June, illus. Going Places: True Tales from Young Travelers. 2003. 160p. (J). (gr. 4-12). pap. *(978-1-58270-070-0(2))* Beyond Words Publishing, Inc.
Modern Publishing, creator. Wildlife Adventures! 2011. (Fisher-Price Luv U Zoo Ser.). (ENG., Illus.). (J). (gr. -1-3). 2.99 *(978-0-7666-3829-7(4))* Modern Publishing.
montell, alicia. Our Friend Oso. 2008. 206p. pap. 24.95 *(978-1-4241-7732-5(4))* America Star Bks.
Moulder, Holly. Eyes of the Calusa. 2007. 111p. (J). pap. 8.95 *(978-0-9790405-0-4(7))* White Pelican Pr.
Muir, John. Stickeen. Buell, Carl Dennis, illus. Date not set. 94p. (J). 16.95 *(978-0-8488-2803-5(8))* Amereon Ltd.
Munsch, Robert. Mortimer. Martchenko, Michael, illus. 10th ed. 2010. (ENG.). 26p. (J). (gr. -1). bds. 7.99 *(978-1-55451-228-7(X),* 9781554512287) Annick Pr., Ltd. CAN. Dist: Publishers Group West (PGW).
Needham, Louise. An Adventure with Katy the Pony. 2009. (Illus.). 36p. pap. 15.49 *(978-1-4490-3972-1(3))* AuthorHouse.
Nichols, Susan. Conquistadors. 2016. (Warriors Around the World Ser.). 00048p. (J). (gr. 5-5). lib. bdg. 26.85 *(978-1-5081-0378-3(X))* Rosen Publishing Group, Inc., The.
Nykko. The Shadow Spies. Bannister, illus. 2009. (Elsewhere Chronicles Ser.: Bk. 2). (ENG.). 48p. (J). (gr. 4-8). pap. 6.95 *(978-0-7613-3964-9(7))* Lerner Publishing Group.
Otoshi, Kathryn. What Emily Saw. Otoshi, Kathryn, illus. 2004. (ENG., Illus.). 36p. (J). (gr. -1-12). 16.95 *(978-0-9723946-0-4(5))* KO Kids Bks.
Oxlade, Chris. Be an Adventurer. Sassin, Eva, illus. 2015. (Go Wild Ser.). (ENG.). 32p. (J). (gr. 3-6). pap. 7.99 *(978-1-4677-7647-9(5),* Lerner Pubns.) Lerner Publishing Group.
Page, Nick. Amazing Academy Survival. 2008. (Illus.). 64p. (J). (gr. 4-7). *(978-1-84610-817-4(9))* Make Believe Ideas.
Parrish, Kat. Micah & the Magic Helment: The Helmet & the Dragon. Milam, C. J., illus. 2011. (ENG.). 32p. (J). (gr. k-7). pap. 8.95 *(978-0-938467-29-8(8),* Headline Kids) Headline Bks., Inc.
Paul, Caroline. The Gutsy Girl: Escapades for Your Life of Epic Adventure. MacNaughton, Wendy, illus. 2016. (ENG.). 160p. (gr. 5-8). 18.00 *(978-1-63286-123-8(2),* 9781632861238) Bloomsbury Publishing USA.
Paulsen, Gary. Woodsong. unabr. ed. 2004. 132p. (J). (gr. 6-18). pap. 29.00 incl. audio *(978-0-8072-0460-3(9),* Listening Library) Random Hse. Audio Publishing Group.
Peers, Jill. Rainbow Cottage. 2011. 24p. pap. 12.96 *(978-1-4490-6199-9(0))* AuthorHouse.
Peters, Gregory N. Daredevils!, 1 vol. 2014. (Real World Adventures Ser.). (ENG.). 48p. (gr. 2-3). 31.99 *(978-1-4765-8466-9(4))* Capstone Press of Coughlan Cos.
Plourde, Lynn. Storytime Stickers: Cowboy Dreams. Kulka, Joe, illus. 2010. (Storytime Stickers Ser.). (ENG.). 16p. (J). (gr. k-2). pap. 5.95 *(978-1-4027-7128-6(2))* Sterling Publishing Co., Inc.
Rath, Tom. Kittencat Adventures for a Special Person. 2012. 40p. pap. *(978-0-9866065-4-0(5))* Wood Islands Prints.
Reinders, Veronica. Adventures at Angels Rest: Maggie Feathers. 2012. 28p. pap. 16.95 *(978-1-4525-0523-7(3))* Balboa Pr.
Reynolds, E. E. Unknown Ways: More Tales of Explorers, Pioneers & Travellers. Tresilian, S., illus. 2011. (ENG.). 126p. pap. 20.99 *(978-1-107-60027-0(8))* Cambridge Univ. Pr.
Ridley, Frances. Stunt Pros. 2009. (ENG., Illus.). 32p. (J). (gr. 4-7). lib. bdg. 19.95 *(978-0-7787-3779-7(9))* Crabtree Publishing Co.
Roddy, Lee. Secret of the Shark Pit. 2006. (Ladd Family Adventure Ser.: Vol. 1). (Illus.). 120p. (Orig.). (J). (gr. 4-7). per. 7.99 *(978-0-88062-250-9(4))* Mott Media.
Rosen, Michael J. Place Hacking: Venturing off Limits. 2015. (Illus.). 72p. (J). *(978-1-4677-6311-0(X))* Twenty First Century Bks.
—Urban Exploration. 2015. (ENG., Illus.). 72p. (J). (gr. 8-12). lib. bdg. 33.32 *(978-1-4677-2515-6(3),* Twenty-First Century Bks.) Lerner Publishing Group.
Ross, Brad. Hocus Pocus Al I Mi Choo. Arnold, Michael, illus. 2012. 62p. pap. 19.95 *(978-0-9834201-0-1(6))* Illusionary Magic LLC.
Rough & Ready. (J). (gr. 5). 42.95 *(978-0-673-72658-2(4),* Scott Foresman) Addison Wesley Schl.
Rumford, James. Traveling Man: The Journey of Ibn Battuta, 1325-1354. 2004. (ENG., Illus.). 40p. (J). (gr. -1-3). pap. 7.99 *(978-0-618-43233-2(7))* Houghton Mifflin Harcourt Publishing Co.
Salant, Dawnelle. Smile. 2009. 112p. pap. 13.35 *(978-1-4251-3268-2(5))* Trafford Publishing.
Seletzky, Valentina. Mosaic: A Child's Recollections of the Russian Revolution. 2003. 132p. (YA). pap. 13.95 *(978-0-595-30408-0(7))* iUniverse, Inc.
Shepherd, Angela. Through the Lens #1: Ava's Big Surprise. 2009. 32p. pap. 14.95 *(978-0-557-23332-8(1))* Lulu Pr., Inc.
Slade, Suzanne. Adventures Outdoors, 6 bks., Set. Incl. Let's Go Camping. lib. bdg. 25.25 *(978-1-4042-3650-9(3));* Let's Go Canoeing & Kayaking. lib. bdg. 25.25 *(978-1-4042-3649-3(X));* Let's Go Fishing. lib. bdg. 25.25 *(978-1-4042-3647-9(3));* Let's Go Hiking. lib. bdg. 25.25 *(978-1-4042-3651-6(1));* Let's Go Snowboarding. lib. bdg. 25.25 *(978-1-4042-3648-6(1));* (Illus.). 32p. (J). (gr. 3-7). 2007. 2007. Set lib. bdg. 143.70 *(978-1-4042-3603-5(1),* PowerKids Pr.) Rosen Publishing Group, Inc., The.
Slamp, Kathy. Little House in the Arctic: An Adventure Story. l.t. ed. 2004. Orig. Title: Our Little House in the Arctic. (Illus.). 228p. pap. 17.95 *(978-0-9713345-3-3(6))* Vessel Ministries.
Stevenson, Sharry. Gibby's Story. 2012. 36p. pap. 18.41 *(978-1-4669-3322-4(4))* Trafford Publishing.
Strom, Laura Layton. Racing on the Wind: Steve Fossett. 2008. (Illus.). 36p. (J). pap. *(978-0-531-15541-7(2))* Children's Pr., Ltd.
—Racing on the Wind: Steve Fossett. 2007. (Shockwave: Life Stories Ser.). (ENG., Illus.). 36p. (J). (gr. 3-5). 25.00 *(978-0-531-17774-7(2),* Children's Pr.) Scholastic Library Publishing.
Studio Mouse, creator. Explore with Little Einsteins. rev. ed. 2007. (ENG., Illus.). 20p. (J). 14.99 *(978-1-59069-563-0(1))* Studio Mouse LLC.
Summers, Barbara, ed. Open the Unusual Door: True Life Stories of Challenge, Adventure, & Success by Black Americans. 2005. (ENG., Illus.). 224p. (YA). (gr. 7-18). pap. 12.99 *(978-0-618-58531-1(1))* Houghton Mifflin Harcourt Publishing Co.
T., Bobby. The Chicalafur. 2011. 40p. pap. 22.65 *(978-1-4134-7115-1(3))* Xlibris Corp.
To the Extreme [Really Good Stuff]. 2010. (To the Extreme Ser.). 32p. pap. 79.50 *(978-1-4296-5362-6(0),* Blazers) Capstone Press of Coughlan Cos.
Treinish, Gregg & Jazynka, Kitson. Danger on the Mountain! True Stories of Extreme Adventures. 2016. (NGK Chapters Ser.). (ENG., Illus.). 112p. (J). (gr. 2-5). pap. 5.99 *(978-1-4263-2565-6(7),* National Geographic Children's Bks.) National Geographic Society.
Turner, Cherie. Adventure Tour Guides: Life on Extreme Outdoor Adventures. 2009. (Extreme Careers Ser.). 64p. (gr. 5-5). 58.50 *(978-1-61512-383-4(0),* Rosen Reference) Rosen Publishing Group, Inc., The.
Turner, Tracey. Hard As Nails Travelers & Explorers. 2015. (Hard As Nails in History Ser.). (ENG., Illus.). 64p. (J). (gr. 3-6). *(978-0-7787-1521-4(3))* Crabtree Publishing Co.
Ventura, Marne & Laughlin, Kara L. 10 Things to Do, 1 vol. 2014. (10 Things to Do Ser.). (ENG.). 32p. (gr. 1-2). 109.28 *(978-1-4765-9902-1(5),* Aplus Bks.) Capstone Press of Coughlan Cos.
Vogel, Carole G. Dangerous Crossings. 2003. (Restless Sea Ser.). (ENG.). 80p. (gr. 5-8). pap. 12.95 *(978-0-531-16679-6(1));* (Illus.). (J). 30.50 *(978-0-531-12325-6(1))* Scholastic Library Publishing. (Watts, Franklin).
West, David. Ten of the Best Adventures in the Jungle. 2015. (Ten of the Best: Stories of Exploration & Adventure Ser.). (ENG., Illus.). 24p. (J). (gr. 3-6). *(978-0-7787-1837-6(9))* Crabtree Publishing Co.
—Ten of the Best Adventures on the Seas. 2015. (Ten of the Best: Stories of Exploration & Adventure Ser.). (ENG., Illus.). 24p. (J). (gr. 3-6). *(978-0-7787-1839-0(5))* Crabtree Publishing Co.
Weston Woods Staff, creator. Man Who Walked Between the Towers. 2011. 18.95 *(978-0-545-14930-3(4));* 38.75 *(978-0-545-14931-0(2))* Weston Woods Studios, Inc.
—The Man Who Walked Between the Towers. 2011. 29.95 *(978-0-439-76703-3(2))* Weston Woods Studios, Inc.
Wilson, W. Shane. Little Monsters. 2009. 99p. pap. 11.96 *(978-0-557-20687-2(1))* Lulu Pr., Inc.
Would You Dare? 2016. (Would You Dare? Ser.). 00032p. (J). pap. 63.00 **(978-1-4824-5843-5(8))** Stevens, Gareth Publishing LLLP.
You Choose: Survival. 2011. (You Choose: Survival Ser.). (ENG.). 112p. (gr. 3-4). 127.96 *(978-1-4296-6590-2(4));* pap. 166.80 *(978-1-4296-7354-9(0));* pap. 27.80 *(978-1-4296-7353-2(2))* Capstone Press of Coughlan Cos. (You Choose Bks.).
Zaunders, Bo. Crocodiles, Camels & Dugout Canoes: Eight Adventurous Episodes. Munro, Roxie, illus. 2006. 48p. (J). (gr. 4-8). reprint ed. 17.00 *(978-1-4223-5397-4(4))* DIANE Publishing Co.
Zhang, Charles Yu. An Adventure into Mediterranean Cultures: Lasting Memories of Our First European Adventure. 2nd num. l.t. ed. 2005. (Illus.). 84p. (YA). 15.98 *(978-1-933361-00-0(X))* Lexington Pubs.
Zullo, Allan. Surviving Sharks & Other Dangerous Creatures. 2006. 151p. (J). *(978-0-439-79207-3(X))* Scholastic, Inc.

ADVENTURE AND ADVENTURERS—FICTION

A, Julie. Roger & the Bum Bubble. 2012. 32p. pap. 22.51 *(978-1-105-62711-8(X))* Lulu Pr., Inc.
A Mother's Pen. The Adventures of Backwards Bear & Baby Curl. 2011. 32p. pap. 16.19 *(978-1-4634-4412-9(5))* AuthorHouse.
Aaron, Chester. Willa's Poppy. 2005. pap. 10.99 *(978-1-55410-282-2(0))* Zumaya Pubns. LLC.
AaronG, Driftin'. Claude Henry, the Iditarod Mouse: The Adventures Begin. 2007. 108p. (J). per. 9.95 *(978-0-595-44990-3(5))* iUniverse, Inc.
Abbey. Señor Manzana & Amigos. 2010. (Illus.). 148p. pap. 37.99 *(978-1-4490-3013-1(0))* AuthorHouse.
Abbott, Charles R. Patches & Leif. 2003. pap. 9.00 *(978-0-8059-6077-8(5))* Dorrance Publishing Co., Inc.
Abbott, Jacob. Ellen Linn a Franconia Story. 2005. pap. 24.95 *(978-1-4179-0056-5(3))* Kessinger Publishing, LLC.
—Rollo at Play. 2008. 124p. (gr. 3-7). 23.95 *(978-1-60664-760-8(1))* Aegypan.
—Rollo at Play. 2009. 148p. pap. 8.95 *(978-1-59915-343-8(2))* Yesterday's Classics.
—Rollo at Work. 2009. 148p. pap. 8.95 *(978-1-59915-342-1(4))* Yesterday's Classics.
—Rollo in Holland. 2008. 108p. 23.95 *(978-1-60664-820-9(9))* Aegypan.
—Rollo in London. 2008. 124p. 23.95 *(978-1-60664-942-8(6));* pap. 10.95 *(978-1-60312-492-8(6))* Aegypan.
—Rollo in Naples. 2008. 108p. 23.95 *(978-1-60664-821-6(7));* pap. 9.95 *(978-1-60664-066-1(6))* Aegypan.
—Rollo in Paris. 2008. 116p. 22.95 *(978-1-60664-943-5(4));* pap. 9.95 *(978-1-60312-493-5(4))* Aegypan.
—Rollo on the Atlantic. 2008. 116p. 23.95 *(978-1-60664-822-3(5));* pap. 9.95 *(978-1-60664-067-8(4))* Aegypan.
Abbott, Tony. Becca & the Prisoner's Cross. 2015. (Copernicus Archives Ser.: 2). (ENG.). 208p. (J). (gr. 3-7). pap. 3.99 *(978-0-06-231474-1(2),* Tegen, Katherine Bks) HarperCollins Pubs.
—The Copernicus Legacy: the Crown of Fire. 2016. (Copernicus Legacy Ser.: 4). 560p. (J). (gr. 3-7). 16.99 *(978-0-06-219452-7(6),* Tegen, Katherine Bks) HarperCollins Pubs.
—The Copernicus Legacy: the Golden Vendetta. 2016. (Copernicus Legacy Ser.: 3). 528p. (J). (gr. 3-7). pap. 6.99 *(978-0-06-219451-0(8),* Tegen, Katherine Bks) HarperCollins Pubs.
—The Forbidden Stone. 2014. (Illus.). 423p. (J). *(978-0-06-232811-3(5))* HarperCollins Pubs.
—The Forbidden Stone. Perkins, Bill, illus. 2014. (Copernicus Legacy Ser.: 1). (ENG.). 432p. (J). (gr. 3-7). 16.99 *(978-0-06-219447-3(X),* Tegen, Katherine Bks) HarperCollins Pubs.
—The Fortress of the Treasure Queen. Merrell, David, illus. 2004. (Secrets of Droon Ser.: No. 23). 115p. (J). lib. bdg. 15.38 *(978-1-4242-0312-3(0))* Fitzgerald Bks.
—The Golden Vendetta. 2015. (Copernicus Legacy Ser.: 3). (ENG.). 528p. (J). (gr. 3-7). 16.99 *(978-0-06-219449-7(6),* Tegen, Katherine Bks) HarperCollins Pubs.
—The Golden Vendetta. 2016. (Copernicus Legacy Ser.: 3). (J). lib. bdg. 17.20 *(978-0-606-38764-4(1))* Turtleback Bks.
—The Ice Dragon. Caparó, Antonio Javier, illus. 2012. (Underworlds Ser.: 4). (ENG.). 128p. (J). (gr. 2-5). pap. 4.99 *(978-0-545-30834-2(8),* Scholastic Paperbacks) Scholastic, Inc.
—The Postcard. 2009. (ENG.). 368p. (J). (gr. 3-7). pap. 8.00 *(978-0-316-01173-0(8))* Little Brown & Co.
—The Serpent's Curse. 2014. (Illus.). 496p. pap. 9.99 *(978-0-06-235159-3(1))* HarperCollins Pubs.
—Wade & the Scorpion's Claw. 2014. (Copernicus Archives Ser.: 1). (ENG.). 224p. (J). (gr. 3-7). pap. 3.99 *(978-0-06-231472-7(6),* Tegen, Katherine Bks) HarperCollins Pubs.
Abdo Publishing. Abby & the Book Bunch, 1 vol. 2013. (Abby & the Book Bunch Ser.: 6). (ENG.). 80p. (J). (gr. 2-5). lib. bdg. 162.42 *(978-1-61641-911-0(3),* Calico Chapter Bks) Magic Wagon.
—Adventures in Extreme Reading, 1 vol. 2013. (Adventures in Extreme Reading Ser.: 6). (ENG.). 112p. (J). (gr. 3-6). lib. bdg. 162.42 *(978-1-61641-918-9(0),* Calico Chapter Bks) Magic Wagon.
ABDO Publishing. Teenage Mutant Ninja Turtles: New Animated Adventures. 2016. (Teenage Mutant Ninja Turtles: New Animated Adventures Ser.: 4). (ENG.). 24p. (J). lib. bdg. 96.84 *(978-1-61479-458-5(8),* Graphic Planet) Magic Wagon.
Abdo Publishing. Up2u Adventures Set 2, 1 vol. 2015. (Up2u Adventures Set 2 Ser.: Vol. 4). (ENG.). 80p. (J). 108.28 *(978-1-62402-091-9(7),* Calico Chapter Bks.) ABDO Publishing Co.
ABDO Publishing Company. Haven't Got a Clue! Set Of 6. 2013. (Haven't Got a Clue! Ser.: 6). 80p. (J). (gr. 3-6). lib. bdg. 162.42 *(978-1-61641-949-3(0),* Calico Chapter Bks) Magic Wagon.
ABDO Publishing Company Staff. Comeback Kids. 2012. (Comeback Kids Ser.: 5). 176-192p. (J). (gr. 4-8). lib. bdg. 135.35 *(978-1-59961-174-7(0))* Spotlight.
—Easy Reader Classics - 8 Titles. 2008. (Easy Reader Classics Ser.: 10). (ENG., Illus.). 32p. lib. bdg. 242.10 *(978-1-59961-333-8(6))* Spotlight.
—Kid Squad Saves the World, 1 vol. 2014. (Kid Squad Saves the World Ser.: 6). (ENG.). 112p. (J). (gr. 8-12). lib. bdg. 162.42 *(978-1-62402-036-0(4),* Calico Chapter Bks) Magic Wagon.
—Mr. & Mrs. Green - 4 Titles. 2007. (Mr. & Mrs. Green Ser.). (ENG., Illus.). 70p. 108.28 *(978-1-59961-299-7(2))* Spotlight.
—Nancy Drew & the Clue Crew - 4 Titles. 2007. (Nancy Drew & the Clue Crew Ser.). (ENG., Illus.). 80p. 96.84 *(978-1-59961-344-4(1))* Spotlight.
—Storm Cliff Stables, 1 vol. 2014. (Storm Cliff Stables Ser.: 4). (ENG.). 112p. (J). (gr. 7-11). lib. bdg. 108.28 *(978-1-62402-048-3(8),* Calico Chapter Bks) Magic Wagon.
—Time Soldiers - 6 Titles. 2006. (Time Soldiers Ser.). (ENG., Illus.). 96p. 121.05 *(978-1-59961-223-2(2))* Spotlight.
Abel, Cheyanne. It's Better by Far, When You Are Who You Are. 2012. 24p. pap. 17.99 *(978-1-4685-7492-0(2))* AuthorHouse.
Ablett, Barry, illus. Great Expectations. 2008. (Usborne Young Reading: Series Three Ser.). 61p. (J). 8.99 *(978-0-7945-1944-5(X),* Usborne) EDC Publishing.
Abner, Jessil. Kingsview Kids Adventures: Internet Friend & Adventure in Africa. 2012. 228p. pap. 16.95 *(978-1-4678-7915-6(0))* AuthorHouse.
About Town with Benny Be. 2005. (J). bds. 15.99 *(978-0-9774752-0-9(4))* Bentley, Trish.
Abrahamson, Ruth Ann. Paris & the Purple Purse: Continuing Adventures of Magic Cookie Bean. 2011. 40p. (gr. 1-2). pap. 13.95 *(978-1-4497-1665-3(2),* WestBow Pr.) Author Solutions, Inc.
Abrams, Amir. Caught Up. 2014. (ENG., Illus.). 336p. (YA). (gr. 13). pap. 9.95 *(978-0-7582-9478-4(6),* K-Teen) Kensington Publishing Corp.
Abshire, Lisa D. Sam's Magical Day. 2006. 48p. pap. 16.95 *(978-1-4241-1484-9(5))* PublishAmerica, Inc.
Abu-Bakr, Sandra. Tales of Lovable Spike: Spike- on the Go! 2008. 72p. pap. 8.95 *(978-0-595-47326-7(1))* iUniverse, Inc.
Abuhamda, Nasser. Short Stories. 2008. 48p. pap. 14.95 *(978-1-59858-581-0(9))* Dog Ear Publishing, LLC.
—6 Tales of Adventure. 2009. 84p. pap. 14.95 *(978-1-59858-833-0(8))* Dog Ear Publishing, LLC.
Accardo, Jus. Tremble. 2013. (Denazen Ser.). (ENG.). 352p. (YA). (gr. 9). pap. 9.99 *(978-1-62061-018-3(3),* 9781620610183) Entangled Publishing, LLC.
Accord Publishing Staff. Trucks: A Mini Animotion Book. 2013. (ENG.). 14p. (J). bds. 5.99 *(978-1-4494-3558-5(0))* Andrews McMeel Publishing.
Accord Publishing Staff & Stone, Kate. One Spooky Night: A Halloween Adventure. 2011. (ENG.). 36p. (J). pap. 11.99 *(978-1-4494-0330-0(1))* Andrews McMeel Publishing.
Acevedo, Jenny. Ginger's Grand Adventure. 2012. 36p. pap. 24.95 *(978-1-4626-2472-0(3))* America Star Bks.
Achampong, Nana S. It Pays to Be Kind. 2010. 78p. pap. 9.99 *(978-0-557-38417-4(6))* Lulu Pr., Inc.
Achatz, Eric. The Adventures of Ryan Alexander: The Great Space Chase. 2010. 52p. pap. 23.50 *(978-1-4269-3763-7(6))* Trafford Publishing.
Achebe, Chinua. Chike & the River. Rodriguez, Edel, illus. 2011. (ENG.). 96p. (YA). pap. 12.00 *(978-0-307-47386-8(4),* Penguin Books) Penguin Publishing Group.
Acker, Rick. The Lost Treasure of Fernando Montoya, Vol. 2. 2003. (Davis Detective Mysteries Ser.). 192p. (J). pap. 7.99 *(978-0-8254-2005-4(9))* Kregel Pubns.
Aclin, Justin. Akaneiro. Marshall, Dave, ed. Lolos, Vasilis & Atiyeh, Michael, illus. 2013. (ENG.). 72p. 14.99 *(978-1-61655-194-0(1))* Dark Horse Comics.
The Acorn Story: An Adventure about Change. 2005. (J). 12.95 *(978-0-9767769-0-1(1))* Rutigliano, Joe.
Acosta, Margarita. The Girl on the Bench. 2013. 38p. pap. 15.95 *(978-1-62550-045-8(9),* Llumina Pr.) Aeon Publishing Inc.
Adair, Dick. The Story of Aloha Bear. Britt, Stephanie, illus. 2008. 24p. (J). 12.95 *(978-1-59700-492-3(8))* Island Heritage Publishing.
Adair Scott, Paula. Blue Button & Red Thread. 2004. (Illus.). 25p. (J). pap. 5.95 *(978-0-9740419-1-9(2))* words4u.
Adam, Paul. Escape from Shadow Island. (ENG.). 304p. (J). (gr. 5). 2011. (Max Cassidy Ser.: Bk. 1). pap. 5.99 *(978-0-06-186325-7(4))* 2010. 16.99 *(978-0-06-186323-3(8))* HarperCollins Pubs. (Walden Pond Pr.).
Adam, Sally. The Cats of Ellis Island. 2009. 28p. pap. 12.50 *(978-1-4389-6012-8(3))* AuthorHouse.
Adams, Andy. The African Ivory Mystery: A Biff Brewster Mystery Adventure. 2011. 184p. 42.95 *(978-1-258-09296-2(4))* Literary Licensing, LLC.
—Mystery of the Mexican Treasure: A Biff Brewster Mystery Adventure. 2011. 192p. 42.95 *(978-1-258-10141-1(6))* Literary Licensing, LLC.
Adams, Denise H. Itchy the Witch. Adams, Denise H., illus. 2007. (Illus.). 32p. (J). (gr. -1-3). 13.99 *(978-1-59879-385-7(3))* Lifevest Publishing, Inc.
Adams, Jackie. Without a Blink. 2008. 40p. (J). 10.99 *(978-0-9800327-0-3(9))* Speranza's Pr.
Adams, Jeanette. Within the Circle, one. 2003. (Camelot Rabbitry Ser.: Two). 108p. (YA). per. 9.95 *(978-0-9672375-2-7(1))* Camelot Tales.
Adams, Jennifer. Arabian Nights Aladdin & the Wonderful Lamp, 1 vol. Oliver, Alison, illus. 2017. (ENG.). 22p. (J). bds. 9.99 *(978-1-4236-4592-4(8))* Gibbs Smith, Publisher.
Adams, Jjt. The Adventures of Junior & Mousey in the Land of Puttin Pow: Don't Talk to Strangers. Adams, Ronald, illus. 2013. 32p. pap. 24.95 *(978-1-63004-457-2(1))* America Star Bks.

A B

Adams, Julie. Kern's Adventures: The Fishing Trip. 2009. 40p. pap. 16.99 (978-1-4389-8458-2(8)) AuthorHouse.

Adams, Keith. The Tales of Henry Tuffin - Henry Goes to School. Hewitt, Geoff, ed. Mawson, Alan, illus. 2013. 20p. pap. (978-1-78222-103-6(4)) Paragon Publishing, Rothersthorpe.

—The Tales of Henry Tuffin - Henry's Christmas. Geoff Hewitt, ed. Mawson, Alan, illus. 2013. 32p. pap. (978-1-78222-172-2(7)) Paragon Publishing, Rothersthorpe.

—The Tales of Henry Tuffin - Henry's Sore Foot & a New Arrival. Hewitt, Geoff, ed. Mawson, illus. 2013. 20p. pap. (978-1-78222-105-0(0)) Paragon Publishing, Rothersthorpe.

—The Tales of Henry Tuffin - the Day the Light Went Out. Hewitt, Geoff, ed. Mawson, Alan, illus. 2013. 20p. pap. (978-1-78222-104-3(2)) Paragon Publishing, Rothersthorpe.

Adams, Michael. The Last Shot. 2017. (Last Trilogy Ser.: 2). (ENG.). 416p. (YA). (gr. 9). pap. 12.99 **(978-1-76029-342-0(3))** Allen & Unwin AUS. Dist: Independent Pubs. Group.

Adams, Najla. The Adventures of Mama Deer. 2012. 48p. pap. 21.99 (978-1-4691-6155-6(9)) Xlibris Corp.

Adams, Nick K. The Uncivil War: Battle in the Classroom. 2010. 84p. pap. 9.99 (978-1-60911-711-5(5), Eloquent Bks.) Strategic Book Publishing & Rights Agency (SBPRA).

Adams, Paul Robert. Buntley's Wing Kit. Oliver, Liana, illus. 2012. 34p. pap. (978-0-9871712-6-9(7)) Fastnet Bks.

Adams, Richard. The Tyger Voyage. Bayley, Nicola, illus. 2013. 32p. (J). 15.95 net. (978-1-56792-491-6(3)) Godine, David R. Pub.

Adams, W. Royce. Raid on Rairarubi. 2008. 148p. (gr. 4-7). pap. 10.95 (978-0-9712206-8-3(9)) Rairarubia Bks.

—Rairarubia Bk. 1: The Rairarubia Tales, 6 vols. 2nd ed. 2004. (Rairarubia Tales Ser.: 1). 138p. (J). pap. 10.95 (978-0-9712206-5-2(4)) Rairarubia Bks.

—Return to Rairarubi. 2008. 148p. (gr. 3-7). pap. 10.95 (978-0-9712206-7-6(0)) Rairarubia Bks.

Adamson, Ged. Shark Dog! Adamson, Ged, illus. 2017. (Illus.). 40p. (J). (gr. -1-3). 17.99 (978-0-06-245713-4(6)) HarperCollins Pubs.

Adamson, Ged, illus. Meet the Mckaws. 2015. (ENG.). 32p. (J). (gr. -1-k). 16.95 (978-1-62914-618-8(8), Sky Pony Pr.) Skyhorse Publishing Co., Inc.

Adappur, Georgekutty. Jack Batson & the Secret in the Manuscript. 2009. 142p. pap. 24.95 (978-1-4489-8439-8(4)) America Star Bks.

Adcock, Kevin J. Adventures with Sir Maxwell. 2016. (ENG.). 76p. (J). pap. 11.95 (978-1-78554-702-7(X), 56406ec7-e1d9-4cf4-ab33-df94d7d00771) Austin, Stan AUS. Dist: Bookmasters Distribution.

Adderson, Caroline. I, Bruno, 1 vol. Flook, Helen, illus. 2007. (Orca Echoes Ser.). (ENG.). 64p. (J). (gr. 2-3). per. 6.95 (978-1-55143-501-5(2)) Orca Bk. Pubs. USA.

Addison, Angelee. Nanny & the Noomies. 2011. (Illus.). 52p. pap. 22.56 (978-1-4567-8916-9(3)) AuthorHouse.

Adkins, Kurt. The Summer of Mucus Mcbain. 2013. 188p. (gr. 4-6). pap. 13.99 (978-1-4582-1138-5(X), Abbott Pr.) Author Solutions, Inc.

Adkinson, Gma Mary. Growing up with Princess Lizzy: Little Life Lessons. 2012. (ENG.). 50p. pap. 16.95 (978-1-4787-1993-9(1)) Outskirts Pr., Inc.

Adler, David A. The Mystery of the Television Dog, 4 vols. Natti, Susanna, illus. 2004. (Cam Jansen Ser.: 4). (ENG.). 64p. (J). (gr. 2-5). 4.99 (978-0-14-240013-5(0), Puffin Books) Penguin Young Readers Group.

—The Mystery of the U. F. O., 2 vols. Natti, Susanna, illus. 2004. (Cam Jansen Ser.: 2). (ENG.). 64p. (J). (gr. 2-5). 4.99 (978-0-14-240011-1(4), Puffin Books) Penguin Young Readers Group.

Adler, Kathy. Wild Waters: The Continuing Adventures of Farley & Breezy. Keith, Doug, illus. 2008. 64p. (J). pap. 5.99 (978-0-9768816-2-9(4)) Beachfront Bks.

Adpot-a-Hulk. 2003. (J). per. (978-1-57657-819-3(4)) Paradise Pr., Inc.

Adventurer Guide: Leader's Handbook. 2004. (Caravan Ser.). 308p. pap. 12.99 (978-0-8341-2117-1(4)) Beacon Hill Pr. of Kansas City.

Adventurer Pathfinder. 2004. (Caravan Ser.). 176p. pap., stu. ed. 9.50 (978-0-8341-2118-8(2)) Beacon Hill Pr. of Kansas City.

Adventurer Trailblazer. 2004. (Caravan Ser.). 168p. pap., stu. ed. 9.50 (978-0-8341-2119-5(0)) Beacon Hill Pr. of Kansas City.

Adventures in the Great Outdoors. 2013. (Adventures in the Great Outdoors Ser.). 32p. (J). (gr. 3-6). 106.00 (978-1-61533-870-2(5)); pap. 47.00 (978-1-61533-872-6(1)); pap. 282.00 (978-1-61533-873-3(X)) Windmill Bks.

Adventures in Yellowstone, 1871-1872, Vol. 1. 2007. (Illus.). 192p. (J). 19.99 (978-0-9798800-0-1(9)) EcoSeekers, The.

The Adventures of Alexandra. 2005. (J). 21.95 (978-0-9761169-0-5(1)) Silhouette Pond Productions.

The Adventures of Chip Green the Forestry Kid l.t. ed. 2005. (Illus.). 34p. (J). per. (978-0-9729753-8-4(1)) Really Big Coloring Bks., Inc.

The Adventures of Little Nina: Nina's First Trip. l.t. ed. 2005. (Illus.). 40p. (J). 16.95 (978-0-9769662-0-3(4)) Strategies Publishing Co.

The Adventures of Marc John Jefferies: The Missing Princess. l.t. ed. 2004. (Illus.). 110p. (YA). per. (978-0-9747218-3-5(2), 100, Young Women Programming) Harper Kids Hse.

The Adventures of Max & Millie: At the Pond. 2003. (Illus.). 32p. (J). 8.95 (978-0-9744427-0-9(4)) Music Bks. & Games.

The Adventures of Mr. Cheesehead: Mr. Cheesehead Goes for A Ride. 2004. Orig. Title: Mr. Cheesehead Goes for A Ride. (J). per. 9.99 (978-0-9764463-0-9(8)) Vertigo Publishing.

The adventures of officer Byrd. 2007. (J). 16.99 (978-0-9787322-0-2(0)) Officer Byrd Publishing Co.

The Adventures of Pinocchio. 2004. 216p. per. 12.95 (978-1-59540-008-6(7)) 1st World Publishing, Inc.

The Adventures of Pinocchio. 2011. 130p. pap. 9.99 (978-1-61203-094-4(7)) Bottom of the Hill Publishing.

The Adventures of Pinocchio. 2004. reprint ed. pap. 1.99 (978-1-4192-5159-7(7)); pap. 21.95 (978-1-4191-5159-0(2)) Kessinger Publishing, LLC.

The Adventures of Pipi & Pearl: Pipi & Pearl Go West. 2003. (J). per. 7.95 (978-0-9747378-0-5(1)) Iverson, Theodore.

The Adventure's of Prissy & Missy "Sleepwalk Affair" 2nd ed. 2009. (Illus.). (J). 15.95 (978-0-615-28905-2(3)) House of the Guilded Scribe.

Adventures of the Robber Pig: Level J, 6 vols. (Leveled Books). 128p. (gr. 2-3). 41.95 (978-0-7699-0987-5(6)) Shortland Pubns. (U. S. A.) Inc.

Adventures with Kat & Dex: The search for the key to Golden Gate Park. l.t. ed. 2004. (Illus.). 32p. (J). lib. bdg. 22.95 (978-0-9754853-0-9(X)) DeAngelis, Anthony.

Afetian, "Uncle Ted". The Adventures of Midas & the Little Red Airplane. 2005. (Illus.). 32p. (J). 16.95i (978-0-9752749-0-3(2)) Snyder-Winston Pr.

Agnew, Kate. Space Saver. Castle, Frances, illus. 2016. (Reading Ladder Ser.). (ENG.). 48p. (J). (gr. k-2). 7.99 (978-1-4052-8213-0(4)) Egmont Bks., Ltd. GBR. Dist: Independent Pubs. Group.

Agro-Melina, Robert Joseph. Joe & the Mysteries of Dream Hall: The Extra Dwarf & the Purloined Parchment. 2012. 152p. pap. 10.99 (978-1-4575-1239-1(4)) Dog Ear Publishing, LLC.

Aguayo, Sal. The Tiny Telepaths: A Continuing Saga, 1 vol. 2010. 62p. pap. 19.95 (978-1-4489-5212-0(3)) America Star Bks.

Aguiar, Nadia. The Great Wave of Tamarind. 2017. (Book of Tamarind Ser.: 3). (ENG.). 384p. (J). 16.99 (978-0-312-38031-1(3), 9780312380311) Feiwel & Friends.

Aguilar, Jose. Jovenes piratas/Youngs Pirates. 2008. 36p. (978-84-934160-7-2(X)) Atalante.

Aguirre, Ann. Vanguard. 2017. (Razorland Trilogy Ser.). (ENG.). 368p. (J). 17.99 (978-1-250-08982-3(4), 9781250089823) Feiwel & Friends.

Ahern, Carolyn L. Tino Turtle Travels to London, England. Burt Sullivan, Neallia, illus. rev. ed. 2008. (ENG.). 32p. (J). 19.95 incl. audio compact disk (978-0-9816297-0-4(9)) Tino Turtle Travels, LLC.

Ahern, Dianne. Break-in at the Basilica: Adventures with Sister Philomena, Special Agent to the Pope. Larson, Katherine, illus. 2006. (J). (978-0-9679437-8-7(7)) Aunt Dee's Attic, Inc.

—Lost in Peter's Tomb: Adventures with Sister Philomena, Special Agent to the Pope. Larson, Katherine, illus. 2006. (J). pap. (978-0-9679437-9-4(5)) Aunt Dee's Attic, Inc.

Ahiers, Sarah. Assassin's Heart. 2016. 432p. (YA). (gr. 9). 17.99 (978-0-06-236378-7(6), HarperTeen) HarperCollins Pubs.

Ahlers, Oly. Following My Magical Dream, 1 vol. 2010. 48p. pap. 16.95 (978-1-61582-758-9(7)) America Star Bks.

Ahlman, Larry. Mittens at Sea, 1. 2004. (Illus.). 200p. (YA). per. 14.95 (978-0-9712906-1-7(X)) Ahlman Publishing.

Ahokangas, Anne Margit. The Adventures of Velvet Series: I Am Who I Am. 2012. 46p. (-18). pap. 20.99 (978-1-4525-6154-7(0)) Balboa Pr.

Ahrens, Albrecht. Simply Out in the Woods: An Inspirational Children's Story. 2013. 232p. pap. (978-1-4602-0688-1(6)) FriesenPress.

Aiken, Joan. Bridle the Wind. 2007. (ENG., Illus.). 352p. (J). (gr. 5-7). pap. 21.95 (978-0-15-206058-9(8)) Houghton Mifflin Harcourt Publishing Co.

—Midwinter Nightingale. 2005. 248p. (J). (gr. 5). 13.65 (978-0-7569-5684-4(6)) Perfection Learning Corp.

—The Teeth of the Gale. 2007. (ENG., Illus.). 352p. (YA). (gr. 7). pap. 18.99 (978-0-15-206070-1(7)) Houghton Mifflin Harcourt Publishing Co.

Aikins, Dave, illus. Bailando Al Rescate. 2005. (Dora la Exploradora Ser.). (SPA.). 24p. (J). pap. 3.99 (978-1-4169-1504-1(4), Libros Para Ninos) Libros Para Ninos.

Ailes, Mark Cusco. The Tree of No Boundaries: Book One. 2009. 196p. 24.95 (978-0-595-63594-8(6)); pap. 14.95 (978-0-595-52834-9(1)) iUniverse, Inc.

Aimard, Gustave. The Indian Scout: a Story of the Aster City. 2006. (ENG.). 464p. per. 37.95 (978-1-4286-1776-6(0)) Kessinger Publishing, LLC.

Aine, Mhari. The Little Children & the Fairies. 2008. 56p. pap. (978-1-84748-375-1(5)) Athena Pr.

Aiosssa, Janet M. Deep in the Woods. Gabel, Deborah Boudreau, illus. l.t. ed. 2005. 24p. (J). lib. bdg. 16.95 (978-0-9769360-0-8(3), 0503) Adam Hill Pubns.

Aira, Luis. Somewhere. 2011. 130p. pap. 14.00 (978-0-557-18746-1(X)) Lulu Pr., Inc.

Aitchison, Jim & Sparks, Marilyn. Tin Pot Puppy. 2013. (Illus.). 76p. pap. 7.50 (978-1-78035-579-5(3), Fastprint Publishing) Upfront Publishing Ltd. GBR. Dist: Printondemand-worldwide.com.

Akatsuki, Natsume. God's Blessing on This Wonderful World! You are Being Summoned Darkness. Mishima, Kurone, illus. 2017. (Konosuba (light Novel) Ser.: 3). (ENG.). 192p. (YA). (gr. 8-17). pap. 14.00 **(978-0-316-46873-2(8)**, Yen Pr.) Orbit.

Akatsuki, Natsume & Steinbach, Kevin. Konosuba, God's Blessing on This Wonderful World! Mishima, Kurone, illus. 2017. (YA). **(978-0-316-46880-0(0)); (978-0-316-46882-4(7)); (978-0-316-46885-5(1))** Yen Pr. LLC.

Aker, Don. The First Stone. 2004. (ENG.). 304p. (J). mass mkt. 6.99 (978-0-00-639286-6(5), Harper Trophy) HarperCollins Pubs.

Akey, Maureen. The Adventures of Molly the Monarch Butterfly & Friends¬Series: Molly. 2009. 28p. pap. 14.99 (978-1-4389-4229-2(X)) AuthorHouse.

Akinje, Wale. The Adventures of Imhotep. Young, Craig, illus. 2006. (J). (978-0-9768485-0-9(3)) Nile Publishing.

Akins, Karen. Loop. 2014. (ENG.). 336p. (YA). (gr. 7-12). 18.99 (978-1-250-03098-6(6), 9781250030986, St. Martin's Griffin) St. Martin's Pr.

—Twist. 2015. (ENG.). 336p. (YA). (gr. 7-12). 18.99 (978-1-250-03100-6(1), 9781250031006, St. Martin's Griffin) St. Martin's Pr.

Akley, Jason. The Candlestick. 2007. 40p. per. 17.95 (978-1-4327-0312-7(9)) Outskirts Pr., Inc.

Al Bahrani, Jawad. The Tales of Bul Bul Adventures. 2014. 128p. pap. 15.77 (978-1-4828-2760-6(3)) Partridge Pub.

Al-Emadi, Hesham. The Savior's Threshold: The Chronicles of Dourren. 2010. 192p. pap. 13.95 (978-1-4502-1846-7(6)) iUniverse, Inc.

—The Savior's Threshold: The Chronicles of Dourren. 2010. 192p. 23.95 (978-1-4502-1848-1(2)) iUniverse, Inc.

Al Mehairi, Maitha. Sally Ride's Adventure: The Dangerous Sea Monster Zelurius. 2013. 24p. pap. 20.21 (978-1-4669-3538-9(3)) Trafford Publishing.

AlaBee. "When Will My Mommy Come?" World & Cross-Cultural Philosophy. 2007. 164p. per. 12.95 (978-1-59800-231-7(7)) Outskirts Pr., Inc.

Albee, Sarah. Kidoozle Kids & the Great Shape Rescue! 2004. (Illus.). 12p. bds. 9.95 (978-1-932915-02-0(8)) Sandvik Publishing.

Albee, Sarah, et al. To the Center of the Earth! 2008. (Backyardigans Ser.). (ENG.). 24p. (J). pap. 3.99 (978-1-4169-7094-1(0), Simon Spotlight/Nickelodeon) Simon Spotlight/Nickelodeon.

Albertalli, Becky. Simon vs. the Homo Sapiens Agenda. 2016. (YA). lib. bdg. 20.85 (978-0-606-38740-8(4)) Turtleback Bks.

Alberto, Daisy. A Horse & a Hero. Random House Disney Staff, illus. 2011. (Step into Reading Ser.). (ENG.). 32p. (J). (gr. k-3). pap. 3.99 (978-0-7364-2746-3(5), RH/Disney) Random Hse. Children's Bks.

Albertson, Bernard. So, You Think There Is No Santa, Bk. 2. 2004. 96p. (J). pap. 7.95 (978-0-87714-744-2(2)) i-5 Publishing LLC.

Albin, Colin. Tom's Tales. 2013. 136p. pap. (978-1-78407-043-4(2)) FeedARead.com.

Albright, David Edward. The Journals of Aiden Hunter: The Marakata Shard. Haight, Joelle, illus. 2012. 262p. 24.99 (978-0-9858325-0-6(9)) Storm Leaf.

Albuquerque, Blossom. Dashing Duke & His Dodgy Adventures. Flinn, Hannah, illus. 2011. 36p. pap. 13.95 (978-1-60911-743-6(3), Strategic Bk. Publishing) Strategic Book Publishing & Rights Agency (SBPRA).

Albuquerque, Jessica. Jessica & the Caramuri. 2012. 32p. pap. 19.99 (978-1-4772-7916-8(4)) AuthorHouse.

Alcántara, Ricardo. El Hijo Del Viento. 2003. (SPA., Illus.). 64p. (978-84-207-6971-4(1), GS2762) Grupo Anaya, S.A. ESP. Dist: Lectorum Pubns., Inc.

Alcott, Louisa May. Little Men. rev. ed. 2006. 352p. 31.95 (978-1-4218-1800-9(0)); pap. 15.95 (978-1-4218-1900-6(7)) 1st World Publishing, Inc. (1st World Library - Literary Society).

Alden-Tirrill, Anna. The Alabaster Jar. 2013. 290p. pap. 14.95 (978-1-885831-07-1(2)) Proclaim Publishing.

—The Promise Box. 2013. 284p. pap. 14.95 (978-1-885831-05-7(6)) Proclaim Publishing.

Aldrich, Sandra D. Trouble in the Park. 2012. 28p. 19.95 (978-1-4626-8818-0(7)) America Star Bks.

—Willie's Lesson. 2012. 28p. 19.95 (978-1-4626-9663-5(5)) America Star Bks.

Aldrich, Thomas Bailey. The Story of a Bad Boy. 2006. pap. (978-1-4065-0613-6(3)) Dodo Pr.

—The Story of a Bad Boy. 2005. pap. 26.95 (978-1-885529-78-7(3)) Stevens Publishing.

Aldrick, Shirley H. F. Gordon, the Great Gobbley Grasshopper. 2011. 32p. pap. 13.00 (978-1-60976-643-6(1), Strategic Bk. Publishing) Strategic Book Publishing & Rights Agency (SBPRA).

Aldridge, Janet. The Meadow-Brook Girls Afloat (Illustrat. 2006. pap. (978-1-4065-0692-1(3)) Dodo Pr.

Alessi, Patty. Rrreggie T Rex's Vacation on Maui, 1 vol. 2009. (ENG.). 90p. pap. 19.95 (978-1-60836-639-2(1)) America Star Bks.

Alexander, Alie. The Wee Boys. 2014. 74p. pap. 9.99 (978-1-60820-911-8(3)) MLR Pr., LLC.

Alexander, Claudia. Windows to Adventure: Windows to the Morning Star. 2012. 68p. pap. 15.99 (978-1-937781-66-8(6)) Blue Pheonix Bks.

Alexander, John. The Adventures of Thunder & Avalanche: Laws of Nature. Alexander, John, illus. 2013. (Illus.). 46p. 18.99 (978-0-9887625-0-3(1)) Mountain Thunder Publishing.

—The Adventures of Thunder & Avalanche: Up & Away. Alexander, John, illus. 2013. (Illus.). 48p. 15.99 (978-0-9887625-1-0(X)) Mountain Thunder Publishing.

Alexander, Lloyd. The Black Cauldron. 2004. (Chronicles of Prydain: Bk. 2). 240p. (J). (gr. 4-7). pap. 38.00 incl. audio (978-1-4000-8636-8(1), Listening Library) Random Hse. Audio Publishing Group.

—The Castle of Llyr. 2004. (Chronicles of Prydain: Bk. 3). 208p. (J). (gr. 4-7). pap. 36.00 incl. audio (978-1-4000-9019-8(9), Listening Library) Random Hse. Audio Publishing Group.

—The Remarkable Journey of Prince Jen. 2004. (ENG., Illus.). 288p. (J). (gr. 3-7). 6.99 (978-0-14-240225-2(7), Puffin Books) Penguin Young Readers Group.

—The Rope Trick. 2004. (ENG.). 208p. (J). (gr. 3-7). reprint ed. pap. 7.99 (978-0-14-240119-4(6), Puffin Books) Penguin Young Readers Group.

—Taran Wanderer. 2006. (Chronicles of Prydain: Bk. 4). 222p. (gr. 3-7). 17.00 (978-0-7569-6815-1(1)) Perfection Learning Corp.

—Taran Wanderer. Wyatt, David, illus. 4th rev. ed. 2006. (Chronicles of Prydain Ser.: 4). (ENG.). 256p. (J). (gr. 3-7). pap. 6.99 (978-0-8050-8051-3(1), 9780805080513) Square Fish.

—The Xanadu Adventure. 2007. (Vesper Holly Ser.). (ENG.). 160p. (J). (gr. 5-18). 5.99 (978-0-14-240786-8(0), Puffin Books) Penguin Young Readers Group.

Alexander, Louise. Legend of Everfree: Save Our Camp! 2016. (ENG.). 24p. (J). (gr. -1-3). pap. 4.99 (978-0-316-39530-4(7)) Little, Brown Bks. for Young Readers.

Alexander, Samantha. Flying Start. 2003. (ENG.). 160p. (J). mass mkt. 6.99 (978-0-330-33639-0(8), Pan) Pan Macmillan GBR. Dist: Trafalgar Square Publishing.

—The Mission. 2003. 128p. (J). pap. 6.99 (978-0-330-34199-8(5), Pan) Pan Macmillan GBR. Dist: Trafalgar Square Publishing.

—Peak Performance, Bk. 3. 3rd ed. (ENG.). 128p. (J). mass mkt. 6.99 (978-0-330-34535-4(4), Pan) Pan Macmillan GBR. Dist: Trafalgar Square Publishing.

—Trapped. 6th ed. 2003. (ENG.). 144p. (J). pap. 6.99 (978-0-330-34200-1(2), Pan) Pan Macmillan GBR. Dist: Trafalgar Square Publishing.

Alexander, Scott L. My Dog Named Whatever. 2007. 68p. per. 10.95 (978-1-4327-1572-4(0)) Outskirts Pr., Inc.

Alexander, Susanne L. Adventures of the Pixies of Penny Brook Village: Reeza's Revenge. 2007. 174p. (J). pap. 12.95 (978-0-7414-4292-5(2)) Infinity Publishing.

Alexander, Troas. A Cat's Tale. Roberts, Ramona, illus. 2007. 36p. per. 14.95 (978-1-59858-371-7(9)) Dog Ear Publishing, LLC.

Alexander, Troas James. Stray's Great Adventure. Mitchell Jr., Leonard, illus. 2010. 40p. pap. 15.95 (978-1-60844-200-3(4)) Dog Ear Publishing, LLC.

Alexander, William. Ambassador. 2015. lib. bdg. 18.40 (978-0-606-37848-2(0)) Turtleback Bks.

Alexander, Yvonne. Adventure in Autou. 2012. 230p. pap. 15.99 (978-1-62230-262-8(1)) Salem Author Services.

Alfano, Doreen D. The Adventures of Hermie the Hermit Crab: Finding a New Shell. 2012. 24p. pap. 14.99 (978-1-4685-5492-2(1)) AuthorHouse.

Alfano, Vicki D. Pound Puppy to Fire Dog. 2011. 28p. (gr. 1-2). pap. 12.95 (978-1-4567-5034-3(8)) AuthorHouse.

Alfaro, Manuel. Griego el Magnifico y la Gotita Verde Golosa Pegajos. Harrington, David, illus. 2007. (SPA.). 36p. per. 15.50 (978-1-59858-337-3(9)) Dog Ear Publishing, LLC.

—Super Griego the Great & the Secret Mission to the Moon. Harrington, David, illus. 2009. 40p. pap. 15.95 (978-1-60844-028-3(1)) Dog Ear Publishing, LLC.

Alfonseca, Manuel. El Rubi del Ganges. (SPA.). 136p. (YA). (gr. 5-8). (978-84-279-3189-3(1), NG3495) Noguer y Caralt Editores, S. A. ESP. Dist: Lectorum Pubns., Inc.

Alford-Craig, Lakiesha. Joe's Dreams of Adventure. 2012. 24p. (-18). pap. 10.00 (978-0-9884237-3-2(1)) CLF Publishing.

Alfred Oscar Valentine: Tales from Spoon Creek. 2005. (J). (978-0-9766894-4-7(8)); (978-0-9766894-3-0(X)); (978-0-9766894-2-3(1)); (978-0-9766894-1-6(3)); (978-0-9766894-0-9(5)) Stanley, Donna Lacy.

Alfred Oscar Valentine: Tales from Spoon Creek: New Beginnings. 2006. (J). 12.00 (978-0-9766894-5-4(6)) Stanley, Donna Lacy.

Alfred Sole. Pandi's Adventures in Afric. Patradol Kitcharoen, illus. 2012. 86p. pap. 23.97 (978-1-61897-493-8(9), Strategic Bk. Publishing) Strategic Book Publishing & Rights Agency (SBPRA).

Alfreda. Story Time Stories Without Rhyme. 2003. 21.95 (978-0-913597-90-3(2)) Prosperity & Profits Unlimited, Distribution Services.

Alger, Horatio. Brave & Bold. 2005. 28.95 (978-1-4218-1452-0(8)); 280p. pap. 13.95 (978-1-4218-1552-7(4)) 1st World Publishing, Inc. (1st World Library - Literary Society).

—Brave & Bold. 2006. 152p. per. 12.95 (978-1-59818-652-9(3)); 24.95 (978-1-59818-570-6(5)) Aegypan.

—Brave & Bold: The Fortunes of Robert Rushton. 2007. (ENG.). 188p. per. 19.99 (978-1-4346-4411-4(1)); 208p. per. 22.99 (978-1-4346-4412-1(X)) Creative Media Partners, LLC.

—Do & Dare: Or, A Brave Boy's Fight for Fortune. 2006. 182p. pap. 19.99 (978-1-4264-0880-9(3)); 170p. pap. 21.99 (978-1-4264-0861-8(7)) Creative Media Partners, LLC.

—Do & Dare: Or, A Brave Boy's Fight for Fortune. 2006. pap. (978-1-4065-0701-0(6)) Dodo Pr.

—The Errand Boy. 2005. 296p. pap. 13.95 (978-1-4218-0455-2(7), 1st World Library - Literary Society) 1st World Publishing, Inc.

—Helping Himself. 2007. (ENG.). 170p. pap. 19.99 (978-1-4264-2793-0(X)) 2006. 190p. pap. 21.99 (978-1-4264-2831-9(6)) Creative Media Partners, LLC.

—Paul the Peddler: Or, The Fortunes of a Young Street Merchant. 2006. pap. (978-1-4065-0718-8(0)) Dodo Pr.

—The Store Boy. 2005. 256p. 28.95 (978-1-4218-0954-0(0), 1st World Library - Literary Society) 1st World Publishing, Inc.

—The Store Boy. 2007. (ENG.). 170p. pap. 19.99 (978-1-4264-4359-6(5)); 182p. pap. 21.99 (978-1-4264-4397-8(8)) Creative Media Partners, LLC.

—The Store Boy. 2006. pap. (978-1-4065-0722-5(9)) Dodo Pr.

—The Store Boy. 2007. 116p. per. (978-1-4068-1617-4(5)) Echo Library.

—Struggling Upward: Or, Luke Larkin's Luck. 2006. pap. (978-1-4065-0723-2(7)) Dodo Pr.

—Struggling Upward; or, Luck Larkin's Luck. 2008. 104p. pap. 7.99 (978-1-4209-3044-3(3)) Digireads.com Publishing.

—Tom Temple's Career. reprint ed. pap. 79.00 (978-1-4047-3611-5(5)) Classic Textbooks.

—Young Acrobat. 2007. 19.95 (978-1-4344-8845-9(4)); pap. 9.95 (978-1-4344-8844-2(6)) Wildside Pr., LLC.

—The Young Musician. reprint ed. pap. 79.00 (978-1-4047-3629-0(8)) Classic Textbooks.

—The Young Musician. 2006. pap. (978-1-4068-0673-1(0)) Echo Library.

Alice Turner Curtis. A Yankee Girl at Fort Sumter. 2007. (ENG.). 128p. per. 18.99 (978-1-4346-3775-8(1)); 140p. per. 19.99 (978-1-4346-3887-8(1)) Creative Media Partners, LLC.

Alimonti, Frederick & Tedesco, Ann. Tommy & the T-Tops: Helping Children Overcome Prejudice. Hazard, John, illus. 2009. (Let's Talk Ser.). (ENG.). 48p. (J). (gr. -1-4). pap. 8.95 (978-0-88282-305-8(1)) New Horizon Pr. Pubs., Inc.

All Aboard! Softi's Adventures. 2003. (J). mass mkt. (978-1-932233-36-0(9)) Aurora Libris Corp.

Allabach, P. R. Dragon & Captain. Turnbloom, Lucas, illus. 2015. (ENG.). 32p. (J). (gr. k-2). 17.95 (978-1-936261-33-8(2)) Flashlight Pr.

Allan, Tony & Dowswell, Paul. True Ghost Stories. 2004. (True Adventure Stories Ser.). (Illus.). 122p. (J). (gr. 5). lib. bdg. 12.95 (978-1-58086-601-9(8)) EDC Publishing.

Allanby, A. C. The Transom Trilogy I: the Adventures of Captain Antonio. 2016. (ENG.). 78p. (J). (gr. 7-9). mass mkt. 11.95 (978-1-78554-330-2(X), 7f0be76a-8027-477c-ba8e-d06ee37f95fb) Austin, Stan AUS. Dist: Bookmasters Distribution.

Allegri, Natasha. Fionna & Cake Mathematical. Allegri, Natasha, illus. 2014. (Adventure Time Ser.: 1). (ENG., Illus.). 192p. (J). (gr. 4). 39.99 (978-1-60886-391-4(3)) Boom! Studios.

Allegri, Natasha, illus. Adventure Time - Fionna & Cake. Allegri, Natasha, . 2013. (ENG.). 176p. (J). (gr. 4). pap. 19.99 (978-1-60886-338-9(7)) Boom! Studios.

Allen, Alejandro & Rountree, Benjamin. El Jirafante Luis: The Giraffephant Luis. 2011. (SPA.). 40p. (gr. 1-2). pap. 18.99 (978-1-4567-3903-4(4)) AuthorHouse.

Allen, Betsy. The Mystery of the Ruby Queens: Connie Blair Mystery Series. 2011. 192p. 42.95 (978-1-258-09539-0(4)) Literary Licensing, LLC.

—The Silver Secret: A Connie Blair Mystery. 2011. 184p. 42.95 (978-1-258-09883-4(0)) Literary Licensing, LLC.

Allen, Christina G. Hippos in the Night: Autobiographical Adventures in Africa. 2003. (Illus.). 144p. (J). 17.89 (978-0-688-17827-7(8)) HarperCollins Pubs.

Allen, Elaine Ann. Olly's Treasure, 1 vol. Nash, Kelli, illus. 2011. (ENG.). 40p. (J). 16.99 (978-0-7643-3772-7(6), 9780764337727, Schiffer Publishing Ltd) Schiffer Publishing, Ltd.

Allen, Eleanor. Mouse Monk in a Christmas Adventure. 2009. 36p. pap. 15.49 (978-1-4490-2197-9(2)) AuthorHouse.

Allen, F. M. Brayhard. 2009. 268p. pap. 30.95 (978-1-4092-7639-5(2)) Lulu Pr., Inc.

Allen, Gregory G. Chicken Boy: The Amazing Adventures of a Super Hero with Autism. Culver, Dennis, illus. 2012. 32p. pap. 9.99 (978-0-9853441-0-8(5)) ASD Publishing.

Allen, J. Kent. Embritt Waters & the Mark of the Rattlesnake. 2006. 229p. (J). pap. 14.95 (978-0-7414-2769-4(9)) Infinity Publishing.

Allen, Justin. The American. 2008. (ENG.). 320p. (gr. 12). 21.95 (978-1-59020-100-8(0)) Overlook Pr., The.

Allen, Michelle. Grandma Nell's Basement. 2009. 24p. pap. 15.00 (978-1-4490-1551-0(4)) AuthorHouse.

Allen, Quinc. The Outdoor Chums. 2006. pap. (978-1-4065-0782-9(2)) Dodo Pr.

—The Outdoor Chums after Big Game (Illust. 2006. pap. (978-1-4065-0780-5(6)) Dodo Pr.

—The Outdoor Chums on the Gulf. 2006. pap. (978-1-4065-0781-2(4)) Dodo Pr.

Allen, Quincy. The Outdoor Chums: The First Tour of the Rod, Gun & Camera Club. l.t. ed. 2006. 160p. pap. 22.99 (978-1-4264-4095-3(2)) Creative Media Partners, LLC.

Allen, Traudi. The Knife & the Fork Go Dancing. 2012. 36p. pap. 16.95 (978-1-4525-0447-6(4)) Balboa Pr.

Allen, Will. Swords for Hire: Two of the Most Unlikely Heroes You'll Ever Meet. Beck, David Michael, illus. 2003. 168p. (gr. 3-18). pap. 6.95 (978-0-9724882-0-4(0)) Centerpunch Pr.

Allende, Isabel. City of the Beasts. 2009. (P. S. Ser.: Bk. 1). (ENG.). 448p. pap. 14.99 (978-0-06-182511-8(5), Harper Perennial) 2005. 464p. (J). (gr. 7-17). pap. 7.99 (978-0-06-077645-9(5), Rayo) HarperCollins Pubs.

—City of the Beasts. Peden, Margaret Sayers, tr. from SPA. 2004. (City of the Beasts Ser.: Bk. 1). (ENG.). 432p. (J). (gr. 5-18). reprint ed. pap. 7.99 (978-0-06-053503-2(2), Rayo) HarperCollins Pubs.

—Forest of the Pygmies. 2009. (City of the Beasts Ser.: Bk. 3).Tr. of Bosque de los Pigmeos. (ENG.). 320p. pap. 14.99 (978-0-06-182510-1(7), Harper Perennial) HarperCollins Pubs.

—Forest of the Pygmies. Peden, Margaret Sayers, tr. from SPA. (City of the Beasts Ser.: Bk. 3).Tr. of Bosque de los Pigmeos. 304p. (J). (gr. 5-12). 2006. (ENG.). pap. 10.99 (978-0-06-076198-1(9)) 2005. 19.99 (978-0-06-076196-7(2)) HarperCollins Pubs. (Rayo).

—Forest of the Pygmies. l.t. ed. 2005. (City of the Beasts Ser.: Bk. 3).Tr. of Bosque de los Pigmeos. 304p. (J). (gr. 5-18). pap. 19.99 (978-0-06-076200-1(4), Rayo) HarperCollins Pubs.

—Kingdom of the Golden Dragon. 2009. (City of the Beasts Ser.: Bk. 2).Tr. of Reino del Dragón de Oro. (ENG.). 480p. pap. 14.99 (978-0-06-182512-5(3), Harper Perennial) HarperCollins Pubs.

—Kingdom of the Golden Dragon. Peden, Margaret Sayers, tr. from SPA. 2005. (City of the Beasts Ser.: Bk. 2).Tr. of Reino del Dragón de Oro. (ENG.). 464p. (J). (gr. 5-12). pap. 10.99 (978-0-06-058944-8(2), Rayo) HarperCollins Pubs.

Allgeier, Steve. Christmas with Norky, the Adventure Begins... 2007. (Illus.). (J). per. 17.99 (978-1-933156-25-5(2), Visikid Bks.) GSVQ Publishing.

Allison, John. Bad Machinery Volume 2: The Case of the Good Boy. 2014. (ENG., Illus.). 136p. (YA). pap. 19.99 (978-1-62010-114-8(9), 9781620101148) Oni Pr., Inc.

Allison, Joseph. Petal Peel & the Ghost Dragon. 2013. 154p. pap. 12.50 (978-1-62857-198-1(5), Strategic Bk. Publishing) Strategic Book Publishing & Rights Agency (SBPRA).

Allison, T. A. Noah's Harbour. 2013. 116p. pap. (978-1-78299-579-1(X)) FeedARead.com.

Alllen, Katherine. Gloves down Under. Alllen, Katherine, illus. 2005. (Illus.). 32p. (J). 15.95 (978-0-9747278-9-9(X)) Diakonia Publishing.

Allman-Varty, Faye. The Kitten Tales of Pumpkin & Parsnip 'Fairy Fields. Knott, Stephen, illus. 2008. 20p. pap. (978-1-905553-28-0(5)) BookPublishingWorld.

Alloway, Kit. Dream Forever: A Novel. 2017. (Dream Walker Trilogy Ser.). (ENG.). 320p. (YA). pap. 19.99 (978-1-250-00125-2(0), 9781250001252, St. Martin's Griffin) St. Martin's Pr.

Allred, Chris Ross. Sir E. Bobbo! 2004. 21p. pap. 24.95 (978-1-4137-2785-2(9)) PublishAmerica, Inc.

Almeida, Jose-Gabriel. Lodiville: Adventure Land. 2008. 52p. pap. 16.95 (978-1-60563-989-5(3)) America Star Bks.

Almekinder, Stephen. Backyardia. 2003. 220p. (YA). pap. 12.95 (978-0-7599-3959-2(4)) Hard Shell Word Factory.

Almhjell, Tone. The Twistrose Key. Schoenherr, Ian, illus. 2014. (ENG.). 384p. (J). (gr. 5). pap. 8.99 (978-0-14-242345-5(9), Puffin Books) Penguin Young Readers Group.

Almond, David. The Boy Who Climbed into the Moon. Dunbar, Polly, illus. 2010. (ENG.). 128p. (J). (gr. 3-7). 15.99 (978-0-7636-4217-4(7)) Candlewick Pr.

—The Boy Who Swam with Piranhas. Jeffers, Oliver, illus. 2013. (ENG.). 256p. (J). (gr. 4-7). 15.99 (978-0-7636-6169-4(4)) Candlewick Pr.

Alonso, Manuel L. Tiempo de Nubes Negras. 4th ed. 2004.Tr. of Time for Black Clouds. (SPA., Illus.). 88p. (J). (gr. 6-8). pap. 12.99 (978-84-207-7770-2(6)) Grupo Anaya, S.A. ESP. Dist: Lectorum Pubns., Inc.

Alpert, Mark. The Silence. 2017. (Six Ser.: 3). (ENG.). 384p. (J). (gr. 6-12). 17.99 (978-1-4926-4896-3(5)) Sourcebooks, Inc.

Alphin, Elaine Marie. Picture Perfect. 2006. (ENG.). 256p. (YA). (gr. 5-12). per. 7.95 (978-0-8225-6468-3(8), First Avenue Editions) Lerner Publishing Group.

Altman, Adam. Lifeshaker: The First Tasmear Novel. 2008. 260p. pap. 16.95 (978-0-595-52623-9(3)) iUniverse, Inc.

Alton, Steve. The Malifex. 2003. (Middle Readers Ser.). (Illus.). 182p. (J). (gr. 3-7). 14.95 (978-0-8225-0959-2(8)) Lerner Publishing Group.

Altsheler, Joseph A. The Border Watch: A Story of the Great Chief's Last Stand. 2008. 320p. pap. (978-1-4099-0579-0(9)) Dodo Pr.

—The Border Watch: A Story of the Great Chief's Last Stand. 2008. 232p. pap. (978-1-84830-132-0(4)) Echo Library.

—The Border Watch: A Story of the Great Chief's Last Stand. 2010. (Young Trailers Ser.: Vol. 8). (Illus.). 206p. (J). (gr. 4-7). reprint ed. pap. 20.31 (978-1-153-78841-0(1)) General Bks. LLC.

—The Border Watch: A Story of the Great Chief's Last Stand. 2012. (Young Trailers Ser.: Vol. 8). 340p. (J). (gr. 4-7). reprint ed. pap. (978-3-8472-2486-0(7)) Tredition GmbH.

—The Colonial Frontier Novels Vol. 1: The Young Trailers & The Forest Runners. 2009. (Young Trailers Ser.). 376p. (J). reprint ed. (978-0-85706-002-0(3)); pap. (978-0-85706-001-3(5)) Leonaur Ltd.

—The Colonial Frontier Novels Vol. 2: The Keepers of the Trail & The Eyes of the Woods. 2009. (Young Trailers Ser.). 400p. (J). reprint ed. (978-0-85706-004-4(X)); pap. (978-0-85706-003-7(1)) Leonaur Ltd.

—The Colonial Frontier Novels Vol. 3: The Free Rangers & The Riflemen of the Ohio. 2009. (Young Trailers Ser.). 468p. (J). reprint ed. (978-0-85706-006-8(6)); pap. (978-0-85706-005-1(8)) Leonaur Ltd.

—The Colonial Frontier Novels Vol. 4: The Scouts of the Valley & The Border Watch. 2009. (Young Trailers Ser.). 536p. (J). reprint ed. (978-0-85706-008-2(2)); pap. (978-0-85706-007-5(4)) Leonaur Ltd.

—The Eyes of the Woods: A Story of the Ancient Wilderness. (Young Trailers Ser.: Vol. 4). (J). reprint ed. 25.95 (978-0-8488-1235-5(2)) Amereon Ltd.

—The Eyes of the Woods: A Story of the Ancient Wilderness. 2009. 284p. reprint ed. pap. (978-1-84902-181-4(3)); (978-1-84902-180-7(5)) Benediction Classics.

—The Eyes of the Woods: A Story of the Ancient Wilderness. Hutchison, D. C., illus. 2008. (Young Trailers Ser.: Vol. 4). 256p. (J). reprint ed. pap. (978-1-4065-4512-8(0)) Dodo Pr.

—The Eyes of the Woods: A Story of the Ancient Wilderness. 2008. (Young Trailers Ser.: Vol. 4). 160p. (J). reprint ed. pap. (978-1-4068-6669-8(5)) Echo Library.

—The Eyes of the Woods: A Story of the Ancient Wilderness. 2010. (Young Trailers Ser.: Vol. 4). (Illus.). 144p. (J). (gr. 4-7). reprint ed. pap. 19.99 (978-1-153-78508-2(0)) General Bks. LLC.

—The Eyes of the Woods: A Story of the Ancient Wilderness. 2012. (Young Trailers Ser.: Vol. 4). 230p. (J). (gr. 4-7). reprint ed. pap. (978-3-8472-2166-1(3)) Tredition GmbH.

—The Free Rangers. 2007. (Young Trailers Ser.: Vol. 5). 244p. reprint ed. per. 14.45 (978-1-60424-038-2(5), Book Jungle) Standard Pubns., Inc.

—The Free Rangers: A Story of the Early Days along the Mississippi. 2005. (Young Trailers Ser.: Vol. 5). (J). reprint ed. 29.95 (978-1-4218-1477-3(3)); 312p. pap. 14.95 (978-1-4218-1577-0(X)) 1st World Publishing, Inc. (1st World Library - Literary Society).

—The Free Rangers: A Story of the Early Days along the Mississippi. 2009. (Young Trailers Ser.: Vol. 4). 294p. (J). reprint ed. 27.99 (978-1-60512-311-0(0)); pap. 14.99 (978-1-60512-411-7(7)) Akasha Publishing, LLC. (Akasha Classics).

—The Free Rangers: A Story of the Early Days along the Mississippi. (Young Trailers Ser.: Vol. 5). (J). reprint ed. 26.95 (978-0-8488-1237-9(9)) Amereon Ltd.

—The Free Rangers: A Story of the Early Days along the Mississippi. (Young Trailers Ser.: Vol. 5). (J). 2008. 280p. 25.99 (978-0-554-36420-9(4)) 2008. 280p. 28.99 (978-0-554-27117-0(6)) 2007. (ENG.). 278p. (gr. 4-7). reprint ed. pap. 23.99 (978-1-4346-2560-1(5)) 2010. (ENG.). 382p. (gr. 4-7). reprint ed. pap. 33.75 (978-1-176-61076-7(7)) 2007. (ENG.). 254p. reprint ed. pap. 21.99 (978-1-4346-2518-2(4)) Creative Media Partners, LLC.

—The Free Rangers: A Story of the Early Days along the Mississippi. 2006. (Young Trailers Ser.: Vol. 5). (J). reprint ed. pap. (978-1-4065-0811-6(X)) Dodo Pr.

—The Free Rangers: A Story of the Early Days along the Mississippi. 2006. (Young Trailers Ser.: Vol. 5). reprint ed. pap. (978-1-4068-0743-1(5)) Echo Library.

—The Free Rangers: A Story of the Early Days along the Mississippi. 2010. (Young Trailers Ser.: Vol. 5). (J). 170p. pap. 13.87 (978-1-152-24703-1(4)); 162p. (gr. 4-7). reprint ed. pap. 19.99 (978-1-4432-1506-0(6)) General Bks. LLC.

—The Free Rangers: A Story of the Early Days along the Mississippi. (Young Trailers Ser.: Vol. 5). (J). 2010. 232p. pap. (978-1-4076-1356-7(1)) 2012. 388p. (gr. 4-7). reprint ed. pap. (978-1-290-66522-3(2)) HardPr.

—The Free Rangers: A Story of the Early Days along the Mississippi. 2012. (Young Trailers Ser.: Vol. 5). 220p. (J). (gr. 4-7). pap. 14.95 (978-1-60444-735-4(4)) IndoEuropeanPublishing.com.

—The Free Rangers: A Story of the Early Days along the Mississippi. (Young Trailers Ser.: Vol. 5). (J). reprint ed. 2010. 248p. (gr. 4-7). 33.56 (978-1-169-30153-5(3)) 2010. 248p. (gr. 4-7). pap. 21.56 (978-1-162-69513-6(7)) 2010. 41.95 (978-1-161-46378-1(X)) 2004. pap. 1.99 (978-1-4192-6302-6(1)) 2004. pap. 26.95 (978-1-4191-6302-9(7)) Kessinger Publishing, LLC.

—The Free Rangers: A Story of the Early Days along the Mississippi. 2012. (Young Trailers Ser.: Vol. 5). 256p. (J). (gr. 4-7). reprint ed. (978-3-8491-6283-2(4)); pap. (978-3-8491-5398-4(3)) Tredition GmbH.

—The Great Sioux Trail: A Story of Mountain & Plain. (Great West Ser.: Vol. 1). (J). reprint ed. 25.95 (978-0-89190-825-8(0)) Amereon Ltd.

—The Great Sioux Trail: A Story of Mountain & Plain. 2008. 360p. 29.99 (978-0-554-43254-0(4)) 2008. 360p. 31.99 (978-0-554-43244-1(7)) 2010. (Great West Ser.: Vol. 1). 366p. (J). (gr. 4-7). reprint ed. pap. 32.75 (978-1-177-69490-2(5)) 2008. 360p. reprint ed. pap. 31.75 (978-0-554-43253-3(6)) 2008. (Great West Ser.: Vol. 1). 360p. (J). reprint ed. pap. 32.75 (978-0-554-43247-2(1)) Creative Media Partners, LLC.

—The Great Sioux Trail: A Story of Mountain & Plain. Wrenn, Charles L., illus. 2009. 258p. (YA). pap. (978-1-4099-7085-9(X)) Dodo Pr.

—The Great Sioux Trail: A Story of Mountain & Plain. 2009. 176p. (J). reprint ed. pap. (978-1-4068-9445-5(1)) Echo Library.

—The Great Sioux Trail: A Story of Mountain & Plain. reprint ed. 2010. 160p. pap. 19.99 (978-1-153-81003-6(4)) 2009. (Great West Ser.: Vol. 1). 182p. (J). pap. 26.81 (978-1-150-71981-3(8)) General Bks. LLC.

—The Great Sioux Trail: A Story of Mountain & Plain. 2012. (Great West Ser.: Vol. 1). 370p. (J). (gr. 4-7). reprint ed. pap. (978-1-290-67583-3(X)) HardPr.

—The Great Sioux Trail: A Story of Mountain & Plain. (Great West Ser.: Vol. 1). (J). reprint ed. 2011. (gr. 4-7). (978-1-164-37592-0(X)) 2010. 362p. (gr. 4-7). pap. 25.56 (978-1-164-19051-6(2)) 2008. 360p. 46.95 (978-1-4366-5490-6(4)) 2008. 360p. pap. 31.95 (978-0-548-90653-8(X)) Kessinger Publishing, LLC.

—The Great Sioux Trail: A Story of Mountain & Plain. 2012. (Great West Ser.: Vol. 1). 258p. (J). pap. (978-3-8472-2260-6(0)) Tredition GmbH.

—The Keepers of the Trail: A Story of the Great Woods. 2010. (Young Trailers Ser.: Vol. 3). (ENG.). 346p. (J). (gr. 4-7). reprint ed. pap. 32.75 (978-1-176-75334-1(7)) Creative Media Partners, LLC.

—The Keepers of the Trail: A Story of the Great Woods. 2012. (Young Trailers Ser.: Vol. 3). 352p. (J). reprint ed. pap. (978-1-290-20366-1(0)) HardPr.

—The Keepers of the Trail: A Story of the Great Woods. 2012. (Young Trailers Ser.: Vol. 3). 240p. (J). reprint ed. pap. (978-3-8472-2195-1(7)) Tredition GmbH.

—The Lost Hunters: A Story of Wild Man & Great Beasts. (Great West Ser.: Vol. 2). 311p. (J). reprint ed. lib. bdg. 27.95 (978-0-88411-949-4(1)) Amereon Ltd.

—The Riflemen of the Ohio: A Story of Early Days along the Beautiful River. (Young Trailers Ser.: Vol. 6). (J). reprint ed. 25.95 (978-0-8488-1239-3(5)) Amereon Ltd.

—The Riflemen of the Ohio: A Story of Early Days along the Beautiful River. 2009. (Young Trailers Ser.: Vol. 6). 312p. (J). reprint ed. pap. (978-1-4099-2567-5(6)) Dodo Pr.

—The Riflemen of the Ohio: A Story of Early Days along the Beautiful River. 2008. (Young Trailers Ser.: Vol. 6). 192p. (J). reprint ed. pap. (978-1-4068-2807-8(6)) Echo Library.

—The Riflemen of the Ohio: A Story of Early Days along the Beautiful River. 2010. (Young Trailers Ser.: Vol. 6). (Illus.). 180p. (J). (gr. 4-7). reprint ed. pap. 19.99 (978-1-153-79466-4(7)) General Bks. LLC.

—The Riflemen of the Ohio: A Story of Early Days along the Beautiful River. 2012. (Young Trailers Ser.: Vol. 6). 340p. (J). (gr. 4-7). pap. (978-3-8472-2473-0(5)) Tredition GmbH.

—The Rock of Chickamauga: A Story of the Western Crisis. 2010. (Civil War Ser.: Vol. 6). 236p. (J). (gr. 4-7). pap. 21.56 (978-1-162-70708-2(9)) Kessinger Publishing, LLC.

—The Scouts of Stonewall: The Story of the Great Valley Campaign. 2006. (Civil War Ser.: Vol. 3). 312p. (J). reprint ed. 29.95 (978-1-4218-1779-8(9)); pap. 14.95 (978-1-4218-1879-5(5)) 1st World Publishing, Inc. (1st World Library - Literary Society).

—The Scouts of Stonewall: The Story of the Great Valley Campaign. l.t. ed. (Civil War Ser.: Vol. 3). (J). reprint ed. 2007. (ENG.). 240p. pap. 22.99 (978-1-4264-1531-9(1)) 2011. 370p. (gr. 4-7). pap. 32.75 (978-1-245-65787-7(9)) 2008. 244p. 27.99 (978-0-554-22030-7(X)) 2008. 244p. 24.99 (978-0-554-31333-7(2)) 2006. 250p. pap. 20.99 (978-1-4264-1498-5(6)) Creative Media Partners, LLC.

—The Scouts of Stonewall: The Story of the Great Valley Campaign. 2006. (Civil War Ser.: Vol. 3). (J). reprint ed. pap. (978-1-4065-0820-8(9)) Dodo Pr.

—The Scouts of Stonewall: The Story of the Great Valley Campaign. 2007. (Civil War Ser.: Vol. 3). 184p. (J). reprint ed. per. (978-1-4068-1684-6(1)) Echo Library.

—The Scouts of Stonewall: The Story of the Great Valley Campaign. 2010. (Civil War Ser.: Vol. 3). (Illus.). 166p. (J). (gr. 4-7). reprint ed. pap. 19.99 (978-1-153-72009-0(4)) General Bks. LLC.

—The Scouts of Stonewall: The Story of the Great Valley Campaign. reprint ed. 2010. (Civil War Ser.: Vol. 3). 252p. (J). (gr. 4-7). 33.56 (978-1-169-30265-5(3)) 2010. (Civil War Ser.: Vol. 3). 252p. (J). (gr. 4-7). pap. 21.56 (978-1-162-70768-6(2)) 2010. (Civil War Ser.: Vol. 3). 252p. (J). 41.95 (978-1-161-47632-3(6)) 2004. pap. 26.95 (978-1-4191-8162-7(9)) 2004. (Civil War Ser.: Vol. 3). (J). pap. 1.99 (978-1-4192-8162-4(3)) Kessinger Publishing, LLC.

—The Scouts of Stonewall: The Story of the Great Valley Campaign. 2011. (Civil War Ser.: Vol. 3). 278p. (J). (gr. 4-7). reprint ed. pap. (978-3-8424-6100-0(3)) Tredition GmbH.

—The Scouts of the Valley. (Young Trailers Ser.: Vol. 7). reprint ed. 2008. 272p. pap. 11.45 (978-1-60597-237-4(1)) 2007. 276p. per. 14.95 (978-1-60424-040-5(7)) Standard Pubns., Inc. (Book Jungle).

—The Scouts of the Valley: A Story of Wyoming & the Chemung. 2005. (Young Trailers Ser.: Vol. 7). (J). reprint ed. 29.95 (978-1-4218-1054-6(9)); 344p. pap. 14.95 (978-1-4218-1154-3(5)) 1st World Publishing, Inc. (1st World Library - Literary Society).

—The Scouts of the Valley: A Story of Wyoming & the Chemung. 2009. (Young Trailers Ser.: Vol. 7). 274p. (J). 27.99 (978-1-60512-310-3(2)); reprint ed. pap. 14.99 (978-1-60512-410-0(9)) Akasha Publishing, LLC. (Akasha Classics).

—The Scouts of the Valley: A Story of Wyoming & the Chemung. (Young Trailers Ser.: Vol. 7). (J). reprint ed. 26.95 (978-0-8488-1241-6(7)) Amereon Ltd.

—The Scouts of the Valley: A Story of Wyoming & the Chemung. (Young Trailers Ser.: Vol. 7). (J). reprint ed. 2008. 320p. 28.99 (978-0-554-35353-1(9)) 2008. 320p. 29.99 (978-0-554-26050-1(6)) 2007. (ENG.). 284p. pap. 21.99 (978-1-4346-0327-2(X)) Creative Media Partners, LLC.

—The Scouts of the Valley: A Story of Wyoming & the Chemung. 2006. (Young Trailers Ser.: Vol. 7). (J). reprint ed. pap. (978-1-4065-0821-5(7)) Dodo Pr.

—The Scouts of the Valley: A Story of Wyoming & the Chemung. 2007. (Young Trailers Ser.: Vol. 7). 208p. (J). reprint ed. per. (978-1-4068-1685-3(X)) Echo Library.

—The Scouts of the Valley: A Story of Wyoming & the Chemung. 2010. (Young Trailers Ser.: Vol. 7). (Illus.). 184p. (J). (gr. 4-7). reprint ed. pap. 19.99 (978-1-153-72010-6(8)) General Bks. LLC.

—The Scouts of the Valley: A Story of Wyoming & the Chemung. 2010. (Young Trailers Ser.: Vol. 7). 250p. (J). pap. (978-1-4076-0985-0(8)) HardPr.

—The Scouts of the Valley: A Story of Wyoming & the Chemung. (Young Trailers Ser.: Vol. 7). (J). reprint ed. 2010. 268p. (gr. 4-7). 34.36 (978-1-169-30757-5(4)) 2010. 268p. (gr. 4-7). pap. 22.36 (978-1-162-70769-3(0)) 2010. 42.95 (978-1-161-47633-0(4)) 2004. pap. 27.95 (978-1-4191-8163-4(7)) 2004. pap. 1.99 (978-1-4192-8163-1(1)) Kessinger Publishing, LLC.

—The Scouts of the Valley (Webster's French Thesaurus Edition) 2008. (Young Trailers Ser.: Vol. 7). (FRE & ENG.). 360p. pap. 28.95 (978-0-497-97888-4(1)) Icon Group International, Inc.

—The Scouts of the Valley (Webster's Korean Thesaurus Edition) 2008. (Young Trailers Ser.: Vol. 7). (KOR & ENG.). 379p. pap. 28.95 (978-0-546-54127-4(5)) Icon Group International, Inc.

—The Texan Scouts. 2007. (Texan Ser.: Vol. 2). 272p. reprint ed. per. 10.45 (978-1-60424-305-5(8), Book Jungle) Standard Pubns., Inc.

—The Texan Scouts: A Story of the Alamo & Goliad. 2006. (Texan Ser.). 352p. (J). reprint ed. pap. 15.95 (978-1-4218-1881-8(7), 1st World Library - Literary Society) 1st World Publishing, Inc.

—The Texan Scouts: A Story of the Alamo & Goliad. l.t. ed. (Texan Ser.: Vol. 2). (J). reprint ed. 2007. (ENG.). 316p. pap. 24.99 (978-1-4264-3365-8(4)) 2010. 376p. (gr. 4-7). pap. 33.75 (978-1-177-24805-1(0)) 2008. 320p. 29.99 (978-0-554-22920-1(X)) 2008. 320p. 28.99 (978-0-554-32223-0(4)) 2007. (ENG.). 282p. pap. 21.99 (978-1-4264-3310-8(7)) Creative Media Partners, LLC.

—The Texan Scouts: A Story of the Alamo & Goliad. 2006. (Texan Ser.: Vol. 2). (J). reprint ed. pap. (978-1-4065-0826-0(8)) Dodo Pr.

—The Texan Scouts: A Story of the Alamo & Goliad. 2007. (Texan Ser.: Vol. 2). 208p. (J). reprint ed. per. (978-1-4068-1691-4(4)) Echo Library.

—The Texan Scouts: A Story of the Alamo & Goliad. 2010. (Texan Ser.: Vol. 2). (Illus.). 184p. (J). (gr. 4-7). reprint ed. pap. 19.99 (978-1-4432-3075-9(8)) General Bks. LLC.

—The Texan Scouts: A Story of the Alamo & Goliad. (Texan Ser.: Vol. 2). (J). reprint ed. 2012. 380p. (gr. 4-7). pap. (978-1-290-32714-5(9)) 2010. 258p. pap. (978-1-4076-1525-7(4)) HardPr.

—The Texan Scouts: A Story of the Alamo & Goliad. (Texan Ser.: Vol. 2). (J). reprint ed. 2011. 362p. (gr. 4-7). 46.95 (978-1-169-83723-2(9)) 2010. 362p. (gr. 4-7). 37.56 (978-1-163-21368-1(3)) 2010. 362p. (gr. 4-7). pap. 25.56 (978-1-162-64067-9(7)) 2004. 360p. 46.95 (978-1-4326-1538-3(6)) 2004. pap. 31.95 (978-1-4179-1479-1(3)) Kessinger Publishing, LLC.

—The Texan Scouts: A Story of the Alamo & Goliad. 2008. (Texan Ser.: Vol. 2). 364p. (J). reprint ed. per. (978-1-4086-5013-4(4)) Read Bks.

—The Texan Scouts: A Story of the Alamo & Goliad. 2011. (Texan Ser.: Vol. 1). 290p. (J). (gr. 4-7). reprint ed. pap. (978-3-8424-7933-3(6)) Tredition GmbH.

—The Texan Star: The Story of a Great Fight for Liberty. 2006. (Texan Ser.: Vol. 1). 364p. (J). reprint ed. 31.95 (978-1-4218-1782-8(9)); pap. 15.95 (978-1-4218-1882-5(5)) 1st World Publishing, Inc. (1st World Library - Literary Society).

—The Texan Star: The Story of a Great Fight for Liberty. (Texan Ser.: Vol. 1). (J). reprint ed. 26.95 (978-0-8488-0729-0(4)) Amereon Ltd.

—The Texan Star: The Story of a Great Fight for Liberty. (Texan Ser.: Vol. 1). (J). 2010. 398p. pap. 33.75 (978-1-145-48797-0(1)) 2007. (ENG.). 328p. pap. 24.99 (978-1-4264-9137-5(9)) 2010. 398p. (gr. 4-7). reprint ed. pap. 33.75 (978-1-177-71810-3(3)) 2008. 332p. reprint ed. 29.99 (978-0-554-25448-7(4)) 2008. 332p. reprint ed. 28.99 (978-0-554-34751-6(2)) 2007. (ENG.). 296p. reprint ed. pap. 21.99 (978-1-4264-9083-5(6)) Creative Media Partners, LLC.

—The Texan Star: The Story of a Great Fight for Liberty. 2006. (Texan Ser.: Vol. 1). (J). reprint ed. pap. (978-1-4065-0827-7(6)) Dodo Pr.

—The Texan Star: The Story of a Great Fight for Liberty. 2007. (Texan Ser.: Vol. 1). 216p. (J). reprint ed. per. (978-1-4068-1692-1(2)) Echo Library.

—The Texan Star: The Story of a Great Fight for Liberty. (Texan Ser.: Vol. 1). (J). reprint ed. 2010. 192p. (gr. 4-7). pap. 19.99 (978-1-4432-0955-7(4)) 2009. 228p. pap. 12.02 (978-1-150-78580-1(2)) General Bks. LLC.

—The Texan Star: The Story of a Great Fight for Liberty. 2010. (Texan Ser.: Vol. 1). 268p. (J). reprint ed. pap. (978-1-4076-1570-7(X)) HardPr.

—The Texan Star: The Story of a Great Fight for Liberty. 2011. (Texan Ser.: Vol. 1). 304p. (J). (gr. 4-7). reprint ed. pap. (978-3-8424-7958-6(1)) Tredition GmbH.

—The Texan Triumph: A Romance of the San Jacinto Campaign. (Texan Ser.: Vol. 3). (J). reprint ed. 24.95 (978-0-8488-0731-3(6)) Amereon Ltd.

—The Young Trailers: A Story of Early Kentucky. 2010. (Young Trailers Ser.: Vol. 1). (J). reprint ed. 180p. (gr. 4-7). 30.36 (978-1-169-27791-5(8)); 180p. (gr. 4-7). pap. 18.36 (978-1-162-71336-6(4)); 37.95 (978-1-161-48200-3(8)) Kessinger Publishing, LLC.

Altsheler, Joseph A., ed. The Masters of the Peaks: A Story of the Great North Woods. (French & Indian War Ser.: Vol. 4). 311p. (J). reprint ed. lib. bdg. 24.95 (978-0-88411-938-8(6)) Amereon Ltd.

—The Masters of the Peaks: A Story of the Great North Woods. 2010. (French & Indian War Ser.: Vol. 4). (Illus.). 144p. (J). (gr. 4-7). reprint ed. pap. (978-1-4432-2285-3(2)) Books LLC.

—The Masters of the Peaks: A Story of the Great North Woods. l.t. ed. reprint ed. 2007. (French & Indian War Ser.: Vol. 4). (ENG.). 248p. (J). pap. 22.99 (978-1-4264-4882-9(1)) 2012. 182p. pap. 22.75 (978-1-276-49474-8(2)) 2010. (French & Indian War Ser.: Vol. 4). 320p. (J). pap. 30.75 (978-1-142-51783-0(7)) 2008. (French & Indian War Ser.: Vol. 4). 252p. (J). 27.99 (978-0-554-23650-6(8)) 2008. (French & Indian War Ser.: Vol. 4). 252p. (J). 24.99 (978-0-554-32953-6(0)) 2007. (French & Indian War Ser.: Vol. 4). (ENG.). 222p. (J). pap.

20.99 *(978-1-4264-4839-3(2))* Creative Media Partners, LLC.

—The Masters of the Peaks: A Story of the Great North Woods. 2006. (French & Indian War Ser.: Vol. 4). (J). reprint ed. pap. *(978-1-4065-0817-8(9))* Dodo Pr.

—The Masters of the Peaks: A Story of the Great North Woods. 2006. (French & Indian War Ser.: Vol. 4). (J). reprint ed. pap. *(978-1-4068-0762-2(1))* Echo Library.

—The Masters of the Peaks: A Story of the Great North Woods. 2009. (French & Indian War Ser.: Vol. 4). 162p. (J). reprint ed. pap. 8.85 *(978-1-150-40712-3(3))* General Bks. LLC.

—The Masters of the Peaks: A Story of the Great North Woods. (French & Indian War Ser.: Vol. 4). (J). reprint ed. 2010. 220p. (gr. 4-7). 31.96 *(978-1-169-29283-3(6))* 2010. 220p. (gr. 4-7). pap. 19.96 *(978-1-162-70171-4(4))* 2010. 39.95 *(978-1-161-47035-2(2))* 2004. pap. 24.95 *(978-1-4191-7205-2(0))* 2004. pap. 1.99 *(978-1-4192-7205-9(5))* Kessinger Publishing, LLC.

—The Masters of the Peaks: A Story of the Great North Woods. 2011. (French & Indian War Ser.: Vol. 4). 228p. (J). reprint ed. pap. *(978-3-8424-4394-5(3))* Tredition GmbH.

Alumbaugh, Michelle. Dream Away. 2009. 28p. pap. 10.75 *(978-1-4490-0663-1(9))* AuthorHouse.

Aluris: The Book of Annua, 1, 4. 2006. (Illus.). 320p. (YA). per. 20.00 *(978-0-9786177-0-7(3))* Michalek, Curtis.

Alvarado, I. J. The Adventures of Saleiah & Emm: Book 1. Zacker, Sandi, illus. 2009. 16p. pap. 11.99 *(978-1-4490-0515-3(2))* AuthorHouse.

Alvarez, Jennifer Lynn. The Guardian Herd: Windborn. McClellan, David, illus. 2017. (Guardian Herd Ser.: 4). 432p. (J). (gr. 3-7). pap. 6.99 ***(978-0-06-228616-1(1))*** HarperCollins Pubs.

—Landfall. 2016. (Guardian Herd Ser.: 3). (Illus.). 352p. (J). (gr. 3-7). 16.99 *(978-0-06-228612-3(9))* HarperCollins Pubs.

—Landfall. 2016. (Guardian Herd Ser.: 3). (J). lib. bdg. 17.20 ***(978-0-606-40049-7(4))*** Turtleback Bks.

—Starfire. (Guardian Herd Ser.: 1). (ENG., Illus.). (J). (gr. 3-7). 2015. 320p. pap. 6.99 *(978-0-06-228607-9(2))* 2014. 272p. 16.99 *(978-0-06-228606-2(4))* HarperCollins Pubs.

—Stormbound. McClellan, David, illus. 2015. (Guardian Herd Ser.: 2). (ENG.). 320p. (J). (gr. 3-7). 16.99 *(978-0-06-228609-3(9))* HarperCollins Pubs.

—Windborn. McClellan, David, illus. 2016. (Guardian Herd Ser.: 4). 368p. (J). (gr. 3-7). 16.99 *(978-0-06-228615-4(3))* HarperCollins Pubs.

—Windborn. McClellan, David, illus. 2017. (Guardian Herd Ser.: 4). (ENG.). (J). (gr. 3-7). lib. bdg. 17.20 ***(978-0-606-40048-0(6))*** Turtleback Bks.

Alvin & the Chipmunks. 2009. 64p. 4.99 *(978-0-06-184568-0(X))* HarperCollins Pubs.

Alvord, Larry. Down by Ol' Chooster's Pond. 2011. 56p. pap. 21.99 *(978-1-4628-7652-5(8))* Xlibris Corp.

Alward, Diane. Pedals & Promises: An Adventure Devotional for Kids. 2013. 86p. pap. 9.95 *(978-1-4908-0512-2(5),* WestBow Pr.) Author Solutions, Inc.

Amanda Rose. Sara James & the Mermaid Tale. 2009. 160p. pap. 11.99 *(978-1-4389-7247-3(4))* AuthorHouse.

Amato, Mary. Good Crooks, Bk. 3. Jenkins, Ward, illus. 2015. (Good Crooks Ser.: Bk. 3). (ENG.). 128p. (gr. 2-4). pap. 4.99 *(978-1-60684-599-8(3),* Darby Creek) Lerner Publishing Group.

Ambau, Getty. Desta & the Winds of Washaa Umera: The Winds of Washaa Umera, vols. 7, vol. 2. 2nd ed. 2013. (ENG., Illus.). 454p. (YA). pap. 15.95 *(978-1-884459-03-0(X))* Falcon Pr. International.

Ambrose, Adrianne. What I Learned from Being a Cheerleader. 2010. 202p. pap. 12.95 *(978-1-935661-94-8(9),* Bell Bridge Bks.) BelleBks., Inc.

AMEET Studio. R2-D2 to the Rescue! 2016. (LEGO Star Wars Chapter Bks.: 4). (ENG.). 64p. (J). (gr. 2-5). lib. bdg. 14.75 *(978-0-606-39152-8(5))* Turtleback Bks.

Ameet Studio Staff. Dragon Adventures. 2016. (LEGO Elves Ser.). (ENG.). 32p. (J). (gr. 2-5). pap. 8.99 *(978-0-545-92539-6(8))* Scholastic, Inc.

—Enter the Dark Knight. 2016. (LEGO DC Super Heroes Ser.). (ENG.). 32p. (J). (gr. 2-5). pap., act. bk. ed. 8.99 *(978-1-338-11411-9(5))* Scholastic, Inc.

—Galactic Freedom Fighters Comics & Activities. 2015. (LEGO Star Wars Ser.). (ENG.). 96p. (J). (gr. 2-5). pap., act. bk. ed. 8.99 *(978-0-545-84237-2(9))* Scholastic, Inc.

—Hack Attack! 2014. (Lego Ninjago Ser.). (ENG.). 16p. (J). (gr. 2-5). act. bk. ed. 6.99 *(978-0-545-68581-8(8))* Scholastic, Inc.

—Quest for the Masks of Power. 2015. (LEGO: Bionicle Ser.). (ENG.). 32p. (J). (gr. 2-5). 8.99 *(978-0-545-87255-3(3))* Scholastic, Inc.

Ameet Studio Staff, illus. The Piece of Resistance. 2013. (ENG.). 32p. (J). (gr. 2-5). pap., act. bk. ed. 8.99 *(978-0-545-62461-9(4))* Scholastic, Inc.

Amelio, Paul. Jack & Zach: The Talk of the Town. 2013. 78p. pap. 10.97 *(978-1-62857-120-2(9),* Strategic Bk. Publishing) Strategic Book Publishing & Rights Agency (SBPRA).

American Sunday School Union. The Allis Family or Scenes of Western Life. 2004. reprint ed. pap. 1.99 *(978-1-4192-5191-7(0));* pap. 15.95 *(978-1-4191-5191-0(6))* Kessinger Publishing, LLC.

Amery, H. & Cartwright, S. The Royal Broomstick. 2004. (First Stories Ser.). 16p. (J). pap. 4.95 *(978-0-7945-0519-6(8))* EDC Publishing.

Ames, Heidi L. Gisselle's Adventures in Color. del Valle, Clara J., photos by. 2010. (Illus.). 36p. pap. 14.95 *(978-1-60844-436-6(8))* Dog Ear Publishing, LLC.

Amico, Sal. Come Back, Zack! 2006. (Neighborhood Readers Ser.). (ENG., Illus.). 16p. (gr. 1-3). pap. 6.50 *(978-1-4042-7256-9(9),* Rosen Classroom) Rosen Publishing Group, Inc., The.

Amma, Jill. The Indaba Tree Odyssey: An African Tale. 2006. 360p. pap. 18.95 *(978-0-7414-3172-1(6))* Infinity Publishing.

Ammann, Michael. Exos. 2003. 108p. (YA). pap. 9.95 *(978-0-595-27121-4(9),* Writers Club Pr.) iUniverse, Inc.

Amon, Ras Ran. Gerald, Fish of the Spirit! A Caribbean Tale of Fortune & Greed. Betiku, Olatukunbo, illus. 2006. Orig. Title: Gerald, Fish of the Spirit! A Caribbean Tale of Fortune & Greed. (ENG.). (J). 7.99 *(978-0-9776603-0-8(3))* One Love Assn. Bks.

Amon, Ras Ran, adapted by. Gerald, Fish of the Spirit! A Caribbean Tale of Fortune & Greed. 2005. Orig. Title: Gerald, Fish of the Spirit! A Caribbean Tale of Fortune & Greed. (J). cd-rom 5.99 *(978-0-9776603-1-5(1))* One Love Assn. Bks.

Amundson, Sandi. Zach & Dougie Dragonfly's Adventure. 2011. 55p. pap. 23.95 *(978-1-4327-3536-4(5))* Outskirts Pr., Inc.

Anders, Lou. Nightborn. 2015. (Thrones & Bones Ser.). (ENG.). 368p. (J). (gr. 3-7). 16.99 *(978-0-385-39036-1(X),* Crown Books For Young Readers) Random Hse. Children's Bks.

Anders, Lou. Skyborn. (Thrones & Bones Ser.: 3). (ENG., Illus.). (J). (gr. 3-7). 2017. 400p. 7.99 ***(978-0-385-39043-9(2),*** Yearling) 2016. 384p. 16.99 *(978-0-385-39040-8(8),* Crown Books For Young Readers) Random Hse. Children's Bks.

Anders, Shirley. The Land of Alphabet: Adventures of Mr. Scribe. 2011. 32p. pap. 21.99 *(978-1-4568-9724-6(1))* Xlibris Corp.

Andersen, Alan Lance. Wizard Academies - Rumpots, Crackpots, & Pooka-Mazed Halfwits. 2008. 174p. pap. 19.96 *(978-0-615-18594-1(0))* Wizard Academies, LLC.

Andersen, D. R. Paul Bunyan Builds a Mighty Mountain. 2005. (J). pap. *(978-1-4108-4205-3(3))* Benchmark Education Co.

Andersen, David W. Tell Us a Story about Flying. 2012. 28p. pap. 24.95 *(978-1-4626-8081-8(X))* America Star Bks.

Andersen, Hans Christian. Snow Queen. 2006. (Illus.). 48p. (J). (gr. -1-3). *(978-1-84732-001-8(5))* Carlton Bks., Ltd.

—The Wild Swans. 2014. (Little Golden Book Ser.). (ENG., Illus.). 24p. (J). (-k). 3.99 *(978-0-375-86430-8(X),* Golden Bks.) Random Hse. Children's Bks.

Andersen, Matthew. Mike & His Marvelous Flying Bike, 1 vol. 2010. 22p. 24.95 *(978-1-4489-4031-8(1))* PublishAmerica, Inc.

Anderson - Hutchison, Laura M. Toby & Talula Trout. 2012. 20p. pap. 17.99 *(978-1-4772-3711-3(9))* AuthorHouse.

Anderson, Al. Adventures with Bingo Borden. Agora Publications Staff, tr. Kurzyca, Krystyna Emilia, illus. 2010. 77p. (J). pap. 9.50 *(978-1-887250-46-7(8))* Agora Pubns., Inc.

Anderson, Brian. The Adventures of Commander Zack Proton & the Red Giant. Holgate, Douglas, illus. 2006. (Adventures of Commander Zack Proton Ser.: 1). (ENG.). 128p. (J). (gr. 2-5). pap. 5.99 *(978-1-4169-1364-1(5),* Simon & Schuster/Paula Wiseman Bks.) Simon & Schuster/Paula Wiseman Bks.

—The Adventures of Commander Zack Proton & the Warlords of Nibblecheese. Holgate, Douglas, illus. 2006. (Adventures of Commander Zack Proton Ser.: 2). (ENG.). 112p. (J). (gr. 2-5). pap. 5.99 *(978-1-4169-1365-8(3),* Aladdin) Simon & Schuster Children's Publishing.

—The Adventures of Commander Zack Proton & the Wrong Planet. Holgate, Douglas, illus. 2007. (Adventures of Commander Zack Proton Ser.: 3). (ENG.). 112p. (J). (gr. 2-5). pap. 6.99 *(978-1-4169-1366-5(1),* Simon & Schuster/Paula Wiseman Bks.) Simon & Schuster/Paula Wiseman Bks.

Anderson, Carolyn. No Counting Sheep, 1 vol. 2010. 34p. 24.95 *(978-1-4489-9078-8(5))* PublishAmerica, Inc.

—Water Queen & the Sea of Kings. 2013. 28p. pap. 24.95 *(978-1-63000-446-0(4))* America Star Bks.

Anderson, Geraldine. Bev's Amazing Adventures Book Ii: The Girl from Peru. 2013. 20p. pap. 24.95 *(978-1-62709-129-9(7))* America Star Bks.

Anderson, Holli. Five: Out of the Dark. 2013. 250p. (YA). pap. 15.99 *(978-1-62007-299-8(8))* Curiosity Quills Pr.

Anderson, James O. Poggy, the Stuffed Donkey. 2006. 16p. 4.95 *(978-1-57258-395-5(9))* TEACH Services, Inc.

Anderson, Jeff. Zack Delacruz 2 (working Title) 2016. (Zack Delacruz Ser.). (ENG., Illus.). 192p. (J). (gr. 5-8). 12.95 *(978-1-4549-2067-0(X))* Sterling Publishing Co., Inc.

Anderson, Jessica. Milkshakes with Maria Mitchell. 2016. (Time Hop Sweets Shop Ser.). (ENG.). 32p. (gr. k-3). 25.65 *(978-1-68191-374-2(7))* Rourke Educational Media.

Anderson, John David. The Dungeoneers. 2015. (ENG.). 448p. (J). (gr. 3-7). 16.99 *(978-0-06-233814-3(5),* Waldon Pond Pr.) HarperCollins Pubs.

—Ms. Bixby's Last Day. 2017. 336p. (J). (gr. 3-7). pap. 6.99 ***(978-0-06-233818-1(8),*** Waldon Pond Pr.) HarperCollins Pubs.

Anderson, John David. Sidekicked. (ENG.). (J). (gr. 3-7). 2014. 400p. pap. 6.99 *(978-0-06-213315-1(2))* 2013. 384p. 16.99 *(978-0-06-213314-4(4))* HarperCollins Pubs. (Waldon Pond Pr.).

Anderson, Km. I Want to Be Like... 2012. 20p. pap. 13.77 *(978-1-4669-6280-4(1))* Trafford Publishing.

Anderson, M. T. Agent Q, or the Smell of Danger! Cyrus, Kurt, illus. (Pals in Peril Tale Ser.). (ENG.). (J). (gr. 5-9). 2011. 320p. pap. 6.99 *(978-1-4424-2640-5(3))* 2010. 304p. 16.99 *(978-1-4169-8640-9(5))* Beach Lane Bks. (Beach Lane Bks.).

—The Chamber in the Sky. 2012. (Norumbegan Quartet Ser.: 4). (ENG.). 288p. (J). (gr. 3-7). 17.99 *(978-0-545-33493-8(4),* Scholastic Pr.) Scholastic, Inc.

—The Empire of Gut & Bone. 2011. (Norumbegan Quartet Ser.: 3). (ENG.). 336p. (J). (gr. 3-7). 17.99 *(978-0-545-13884-0(1),* Scholastic Pr.) Scholastic, Inc.

—He Laughed with His Other Mouths. Cyrus, Kurt, illus. 2014. (Pals in Peril Tale Ser.). (ENG.). 304p. (J). (gr. 5-9). 17.99 *(978-1-4424-5110-0(6),* Beach Lane Bks.) Beach Lane Bks.

—Jasper Dash & the Flame-Pits of Delaware. Cyrus, Kurt, illus. (Pals in Peril Tale Ser.). (ENG.). (J). (gr. 5-9). 2010. 448p. pap. 6.99 *(978-1-4424-0838-8(3))* 2009. 432p. 16.99 *(978-1-4169-8639-3(1))* Beach Lane Bks. (Beach Lane Bks.).

—Whales on Stilts! Cyrus, Kurt, illus. 2010. (Pals in Peril Tale Ser.). (ENG.). (J). (gr. 5-9). 208p. 17.99 *(978-1-4424-0695-7(X));* 224p. pap. 7.99 *(978-1-4424-0701-5(8))* Beach Lane Bks. (Beach Lane Bks.).

—Whales on Stilts! Cyrus, Kurt, illus. 2006. (M. T. Anderson's Thrilling Tales Ser.). 188p. (gr. 5-9). 15.95 *(978-0-7569-7213-4(2))* Perfection Learning Corp.

—Zombie Mommy. Cyrus, Kurt, illus. (Pals in Peril Tale Ser.). (ENG.). 224p. (J). (gr. 5-9). 2012. pap. 6.99 *(978-1-4424-5440-8(7))* 2011. 16.99 *(978-1-4169-8641-6(3))* Beach Lane Bks. (Beach Lane Bks.).

—Zombie Mommy. Cyrus, Kurt, illus. 2011. (M. T. Anderson's Thrilling Tales Ser.). 240p. 16.99 *(978-1-4424-3068-6(0))* Simon & Schuster Children's Publishing.

Anderson, Matt & Hutchins, Eric. White Picket Fences: Double Feature One-shot. 2008. (Illus.). 52p. (YA). pap. 6.95 *(978-0-9801314-9-9(9))* Ape Entertainment.

—White Picket Fences: Red Scare TP: Red Scare TP. 2011. (Illus.). 104p. (J). pap. 12.99 *(978-1-934944-30-1(0))* Ape Entertainment.

Anderson, Max Elliot. Big Rig Rustlers. 2004. 144p. pap. 10.95 *(978-0-9752880-1-6(6))* Baker Trittin Pr.

—Legend of the White Wolf. 2005. (Illus.). 125p. (J). (gr. -1-7). pap. 10.95 *(978-0-9752880-3-0(2))* Baker Trittin Pr.

Anderson, Max Elliott. Secret of Abbott's Cave. 2004. (Tweener Press Adventure Ser.). 127p. (J). (gr. 3). per. 10.95 *(978-0-9752880-0-9(8))* Baker Trittin Pr.

Anderson, Patricia. Tails of a Woodswoman. 2008. 72p. pap. 9.95 *(978-1-4327-2615-7(3))* Outskirts Pr., Inc.

Anderson, Renae. Upon the Heads of the Children. 2009. 236p. 25.75 *(978-1-60860-483-8(7),* Strategic Bk. Publishing) Strategic Book Publishing & Rights Agency (SBPRA).

Anderson, Sara. Noisy Country Day. 2006. (J). bds. 8.95 *(978-1-59354-113-2(9))* Handprint Bks.

—Noisy Country Night. 2006. (J). bds. 8.95 *(978-1-59354-114-9(7))* Handprint Bks.

Anderson, Suzette. Cybertreks: Wildest West. 2004. 196p. pap. 13.95 *(978-0-595-30840-8(6))* iUniverse, Inc.

Anderson, Wayne R. Paula's Perilous Adventure, 1 dvd. 2006. 48p. (YA). 19.95 incl. DVD *(978-0-9773478-2-7(6));* 12.95 *(978-0-9773478-0-3(X))* IMAGECRAFTERS.

Ando, Yuma. Sherlock Bones. 2014. (Sherlock Bones Ser.). (ENG., Illus.). 200p. pap. 10.99 *(978-1-61262-545-4(2))* Kodansha America, Inc.

—Sherlock Bones. Sato, Yuki, illus. (Sherlock Bones Ser.). (ENG.). 200p. Vol. 1. 2013. pap. 10.99 *(978-1-61262-444-0(8))* Vol. 3. 2014. pap. 10.99 *(978-1-61262-446-4(4))* Kodansha America, Inc.

—Sherlock Bones, Vol. 4. 2014. (Sherlock Bones Ser.). (ENG., Illus.). 200p. pap. 10.99 *(978-1-61262-447-1(2))* Kodansha America, Inc.

Andrade, Brigitte. The Adventures of Bibi & Friends: Summer Season in Miami Beach, 17 vols. 7th ed. 2004. Orig. Title: The Adventures of Bibi 7 Friends. (Illus.). 64p. per. 7.95 *(978-0-9754329-0-7(7))* BB International Productions, Inc.

Andre Alice Norton, Alice Norton & Andre Alice Norton. The Time Traders. 2009. 148p. pap. 5.95 *(978-1-60386-204-2(8),* Merchant Bks.) Rough Draft Printing.

Andrea, Karen. The Enchanted Library. 2008. 172p. pap. *(978-1-84923-182-4(6))* YouWriteOn.

Andrea, Leona. El Club de Las Siete Gatas. 2004.Tr. of Seven Kittens Club. (SPA., Illus.). 176p. 13.95 *(978-84-95618-73-3(7),* Umbriel) Ediciones Urano S. A. ESP. Dist: Spanish Pubs., LLC.

Andreae, Giles. Billy Bonkers. Sharratt, Nick, illus. 2006. (ENG.). 128p. (J). (gr. -1-12). pap. 7.99 *(978-1-84616-151-3(7))* Hodder & Stoughton GBR. Dist: Hachette Bk. Group.

—Captain Flinn & the Pirate Dinosaurs. Ayto, Russell, illus. 2005. (Captain Flinn & the Pirate Dinosaurs Ser.). (ENG.). 32p. (J). (gr. -1-1). 17.99 *(978-1-4169-0713-8(0),* McElderry, Margaret K. Bks.) McElderry, Margaret K. Bks.

Andrews, Jane. Each & All: The Seven Little Sisters Prove Their Sisterhood (Yesterday's Classics) 2009. 120p. pap. 8.95 *(978-1-59915-308-7(4))* Yesterday's Classics.

Andrews, Jerome. The Initiation. 2006. 40p. pap. 8.50 *(978-1-4116-9167-4(9))* Lulu Pr., Inc.

Andrews, John. Beck's Missing Shoes. 2013. 28p. pap. 9.95 *(978-1-4787-2524-4(9))* Outskirts Pr., Inc.

Andrews, Julie. The Little Grey Men: A Story for the Young in Heart. Watkins-Pitchford, Denys, illus. 2004. 304p. (J). 17.89 *(978-0-06-055449-1(5),* Julie Andrews Collection) HarperCollins Pubs.

Andrews, Kaare. Spider-Man Legend of the Spider-Clan, 3 vols. Young, Skott, illus. 2003. (Mangaverse Ser.: Vol. 3). 128p. (YA). pap. 11.99 *(978-0-7851-1114-6(X))* Marvel Worldwide, Inc.

Andrews, Neva. Stormy & Stub. 2008. 108p. pap. 10.95 *(978-0-595-52854-7(6),* iUniverse, Inc.) iUniverse, Inc.

Andrews, Roxanna. The Adventures of Super Pig. 2006. (Illus.). 68p. (J). 15.95 *(978-1-59879-232-4(6))* Lifevest Publishing, Inc.

Andrews, Sandy. Best Friends - the Depression Years. 2012. 218p. pap. 12.95 *(978-1-937912-87-1(6))* Cordon Pubns.

Andrisano, Micheal. Harold the High Knight & Princess Megan: Harold & Megan. 2013. (ENG.). 221p. (YA). pap. 16.95 *(978-1-4327-9451-4(5))* Outskirts Pr., Inc.

Angel. Santa Claus's Journey to Texusilver. 2009. 28p. pap. 12.49 *(978-1-4490-2432-1(7))* AuthorHouse.

Angeles: Redemption/Redencion. 2004. (Angeles Ser.).Tr. of Angels. (SPA., Illus.). 48p. pap. 4.99 *(978-0-8054-2839-1(9))* B&H Publishing Group.

Angeles: The Secret/el Secreto. 2004. (Angeles Ser.).Tr. of Angels. (SPA., Illus.). 48p. pap. 4.99 *(978-0-8054-2833-9(X))* B&H Publishing Group.

Angeles: The Sin/el Pecado. 2004. (Angeles Ser.).Tr. of Angels. (SPA., Illus.). 48p. pap. 4.99 *(978-0-8054-2838-4(0))* B&H Publishing Group.

Angelique, Aj. Lady Cy. 2011. 108p. pap. 7.95 *(978-1-4583-5494-5(6))* Lulu Pr., Inc.

Angello, Mary L. The Legend of the Crystal Skull. 2008. 147p. pap. 15.50 *(978-1-4357-3194-3(8))* Lulu Pr., Inc.

Angleberger, Tom. The Rat with the Human Face. 2015. (Qwikpick Papers). (ENG., Illus.). 160p. (J). (gr. 3-7). 12.95 *(978-1-4197-1489-4(9),* Amulet Bks.) Abrams, Inc.

—The Rat with the Human Face: The Qwikpick Papers. 2016. (Qwikpick Papers). (ENG., Illus.). 176p. (J). (gr. 3-7). pap. 6.95 *(978-1-4197-1940-0(8),* Amulet Bks.) Abrams, Inc.

—To Kick a Corpse: The Qwikpick Papers. 2016. (Qwikpick Papers). (ENG., Illus.). 160p. (J). (gr. 3-7). 12.95 *(978-1-4197-1906-6(8),* Amulet Bks.) Abrams, Inc.

Angler, Evan. Spark, 1 vol. 2013. (Swipe Ser.). (ENG.). 272p. (J). pap. 9.99 *(978-1-4003-2198-8(0))* Nelson, Thomas Inc.

Angstrom, Gwen R. The Eemlets & Grandma Eema Stories, Book 1: From Rainbow to Sunshine. 2006. 67p. pap. 16.95 *(978-1-4241-1257-9(5))* PublishAmerica, Inc.

Anita D Martinez. Worm Imposters. 2009. 32p. pap. 14.49 *(978-1-4389-2605-6(7))* AuthorHouse.

Ann, Janice. Kenny Breezes the Clouds. 2013. 24p. pap. 12.45 *(978-1-4525-8206-1(8),* Balboa Pr.) Author Solutions, Inc.

Annie Starks-Johnson, Starks-Johnson & Annie Starks-Johnson. Dottie's Surprise Birthday Party. 2009. 24p. pap. 11.49 *(978-1-4389-4866-9(2))* AuthorHouse.

Anrias, Donnan. Targ - the King of Eagles. 2005. 138p. (YA). per. 23.00 *(978-1-4116-1923-4(4))* Lulu Pr., Inc.

Ant., Mary. The Shiniest Treasure: The Journey with Grammy & Grampa! Part 2. 2012. 38p. pap. 15.10 *(978-1-300-24962-7(5))* Lulu Pr., Inc.

anthony, chance. The Princess of Du'val. 2010. 36p. pap. 7.14 *(978-0-557-03816-9(2))* Lulu Pr., Inc.

Anthony, David & Clasman, Charles David. Heroes A2Z #13: (Heroes a to Z): Monkey Monster Truck. Blakeslee, Lys, illus. 2012. 128p. (J). mass mkt. 4.99 *(978-0-9846528-1-5(7))* Sigil Publishing.

Anthony, Mike. The Adventures of Henry the Patchwork Whale, 1 vol. 2010. 20p. 24.95 *(978-1-60813-076-4(2))* PublishAmerica, Inc.

Anthony, Piers. Key to Chroma. 2003. (ChroMagic Ser.: Bk. 2). 550p. (J). 34.99 *(978-1-59426-017-9(6))* Mundania Pr.

Anthony, Wes. Binger & Stumpy the B D Dawg Series - Book. 2010. 534p. 35.95 *(978-1-60911-088-8(9),* Eloquent Bks.) Strategic Book Publishing & Rights Agency (SBPRA).

Antiporda, Enrico. The Adventures of Jimbo, the Homeless Cat. Antiporda, Enrico, illus. 2013. (Illus.). 66p. pap. 14.95 *(978-0-9672793-5-0(6))* Blue Owl Editions.

Anton, Jackie. Backyard Horse Tales Sox: 2nd Edition. 2012. 124p. pap. 11.99 *(978-1-4575-0949-0(0))* Dog Ear Publishing, LLC.

Antòn, Josef. Deep in the Forest: A Seek-And-Find Adventure. Brunellière, Lucie, illus. 2017. (ENG.). 14p. (J). (gr. -1-k). bds. 17.95 *(978-1-4197-2351-3(0),* Abrams Appleseed) Abrams, Inc.

Anyanwu, Francis Eze. The Awesome Dog: How the Dog Became Man's Best Friend. 2011. 73p. pap. 14.95 *(978-1-4327-5666-6(4))* Outskirts Pr., Inc.

Anyone's Guess Teen Kits: A Murderous Melodrama. 2004. 39.95 *(978-1-932146-26-4(1),* Upstart Bks.) Highsmith Inc.

Anzai, Nobuyuki. Flame of Recca. 2007. (Flame of Recca Ser.: 22). (ENG., Illus.). 192p. pap. 9.99 *(978-1-4215-0893-1(1))* Viz Media.

Anzaldúa, Gloria. Prietita & the Ghost Woman: Prietita y la Llorona. Gonzalez, Maya Christina, illus. 2013. (ENG & SPA.). 32p. (J). (gr. 1-18). pap. 9.95 *(978-0-89239-167-7(7))* Lee & Low Bks., Inc.

Aparici Martin, Irene. Mom Goes to War. 2013. (ENG., Illus.). 24p. (J). (gr. 2-4). 15.95 *(978-84-15503-20-0(2))* Eastern National.

Appel, Julie & Guglielmo, Amy. Find King Henry's Treasure. 2010. (Touch the Art Ser.). (ENG., Illus.). 24p. (J). (gr. -1-1). bds. 12.95 *(978-1-4027-6324-3(7))* Sterling Publishing Co., Inc.

Appello, Lisa K. Zuky's World. 2012. pap. 8.95 *(978-0-7414-7951-8(6))* Infinity Publishing.

Apple, Bonnie. The Karisma Tales. 2013. 142p. (gr. 4-6). 28.99 *(978-1-4525-7296-3(8));* pap. 11.99 *(978-1-4525-7295-6(X))* Author Solutions, Inc. (Balboa Pr.).

Applegate, K. A., pseud. Animorphs #7: the Stranger. 2012. (Animorphs Ser.: 7). (ENG.). 176p. (J). (gr. 3-7). pap. 6.99 *(978-0-545-42414-1(3),* Scholastic Paperbacks) Scholastic, Inc.

Appleton, Nancy. The Rescue: Cecelia's Story. 2012. 24p. 24.95 *(978-1-4626-6713-0(9))* America Star Bks.

Appleton, Victor. The Adventures of Tom Swift. 2007. 456p. per. 19.95 *(978-1-4344-9982-0(0))* Wildside Pr., LLC.

—The Alien Probe. (Tom Swift Ser.). (J). (gr. 3-7). 20.95 *(978-0-88411-464-2(3))* Amereon Ltd.

—The Astral Fortress. (Tom Swift Ser.). (J). (gr. 3-7). 20.95 *(978-0-88411-461-1(9))* Amereon Ltd.

—The City in the Stars. (Tom Swift Ser.). (J). (gr. 3-7). 20.95 *(978-0-88411-463-5(5))* Amereon Ltd.

—The Moving Picture Boys at Panama. 2005. 27.95 *(978-1-4218-1499-5(4));* 208p. pap. 12.95 *(978-1-4218-1599-2(0))* 1st World Publishing, Inc. (1st World Library - Literary Society).

—Moving Picture Boys at Panama. 2006. pap. *(978-1-4065-0890-1(X))* Dodo Pr.

—The Moving Picture Boys at Panama. 2004. reprint ed. pap. 20.95 *(978-1-4191-7472-8(X));* pap. 1.99 *(978-1-4192-7472-5(4))* Kessinger Publishing, LLC.

—The Moving Picture Boys at Panama: Stirring Adventures along the Great Canal. 2007. (ENG.). 140p. pap. 18.99 *(978-1-4346-2170-2(7));* 152p. pap. 21.99 *(978-1-4346-2230-3(4))* Creative Media Partners, LLC.

—Moving Picture Boys on the War Front or. 2006. pap. *(978-1-4065-0891-8(8))* Dodo Pr.

—The Rescue Mission. (Tom Swift Ser.). (J). (gr. 3-7). 20.95 *(978-0-88411-458-1(9))* Amereon Ltd.

—The Space Hotel. 2006. (Tom Swift, Young Inventor Ser.: 3). (ENG.). 160p. (J). (gr. 3-7). pap. 8.99 *(978-1-4169-1751-9(9),* Aladdin) Simon & Schuster Children's Publishing.

—Terror on the Moons of Jupiter. (Tom Swift Ser.). (J). (gr. 3-7). 20.95 *(978-0-88411-460-4(0))* Amereon Ltd.

—Tom Swift among the Diamond Makers. 2005. 26.95 *(978-1-4218-1086-7(7));* 196p. pap. 11.95 *(978-1-4218-1186-4(3))* 1st World Publishing, Inc. (1st World Library - Literary Society).

—Tom Swift among the Diamond Makers. 2007. 224p. 29.95 *(978-1-4344-9458-0(6));* per. 19.95 *(978-1-4344-9457-3(8))* Wildside Pr., LLC.

—Tom Swift among the Diamond Makers or Th. 2006. pap. *(978-1-4065-0892-5(6))* Dodo Pr.

—Tom Swift among the Fire Fighters. 2005. 27.95 *(978-1-4218-1088-1(3));* 204p. pap. 12.95 *(978-1-4218-1188-8(X))* 1st World Publishing, Inc. (1st World Library - Literary Society).

—Tom Swift among the Fire Fighters. 2006. (ENG.). pap. *(978-1-4068-0726-4(5))* Echo Library.

—Tom Swift among the Fire Fighters. 2004. reprint ed. pap. 20.95 *(978-1-4191-9047-6(4));* pap. 1.99 *(978-1-4192-9047-3(9))* Kessinger Publishing, LLC.

—Tom Swift among the Fire Fighters: Or Battling with Flames from the Air. l.t. ed. 2007. (ENG.). 154p. pap. 21.99 *(978-1-4346-1583-1(9))* Creative Media Partners, LLC.
—Tom Swift among the Fire Fighters or Bat. 2006. pap. *(978-1-4065-0893-2(4))* Dodo Pr.
—Tom Swift & His Aerial Warship. 2005. 27.95 *(978-1-4218-1092-8(1))*; 212p. pap. 12.95 *(978-1-4218-1192-5(8))* 1st World Publishing, Inc. (1st World Library - Literary Society).
—Tom Swift & His Aerial Warship. 2004. reprint ed. pap. 1.99 *(978-1-4192-8451-9(7))* Kessinger Publishing, LLC.
—Tom Swift & His Aerial Warship: Or the Naval Terror of the Seas. l.t. ed. 2007. (ENG.). 156p. pap. 21.99 *(978-1-4346-1578-7(2))* Creative Media Partners, LLC.
—Tom Swift & His Aerial Warship or the. 2006. pap. *(978-1-4065-0894-9(2))* Dodo Pr.
—Tom Swift & His Aerial Warship or the Naval Terror of the Seas. 2005. reprint ed. pap. 24.95 *(978-0-7661-9446-5(9))* Kessinger Publishing, LLC.
—Tom Swift & his Air Glider. 2005. 26.95 *(978-1-4218-1500-8(1)*, 1st World Library - Literary Society) 1st World Publishing, Inc.
—Tom Swift & His Air Glider. 2004. reprint ed. pap. 20.95 *(978-1-4191-8452-9(0))*; pap. 1.99 *(978-1-4192-8452-6(5))* Kessinger Publishing, LLC.
—Tom Swift & His Air Glider or Seeking. 2006. pap. *(978-1-4065-0895-6(0))* Dodo Pr.
—Tom Swift & His Air Scout. 2005. 27.95 *(978-1-4218-1091-1(3))*; 208p. pap. 12.95 *(978-1-4218-1191-8(X))* 1st World Publishing, Inc. (1st World Library - Literary Society).
—Tom Swift & His Air Scout. 2004. reprint ed. pap. 1.99 *(978-1-4192-9048-0(7))*; pap. 20.95 *(978-1-4191-9048-3(2))* Kessinger Publishing, LLC.
—Tom Swift & His Air Scout: Or Uncle Sam's Mastery of the Sky. l.t. ed. 2007. (ENG.). 158p. pap. 21.99 *(978-1-4346-1580-0(4))* Creative Media Partners, LLC.
—Tom Swift & His Air Scout or Uncle Sam. 2006. pap. *(978-1-4065-0896-3(9))* Dodo Pr.
—Tom Swift & His Airship. 2005. 27.95 *(978-1-59540-801-3(0))*; 200p. pap. 12.95 *(978-1-59540-806-8(1))* 1st World Publishing, Inc. (1st World Library - Literary Society).
—Tom Swift & His Airship. 2006. pap. *(978-1-4065-0897-0(7))* Dodo Pr.
—Tom Swift & His Airship. 2004. reprint ed. pap. 20.95 *(978-1-4191-8453-6(9))*; pap. 1.99 *(978-1-4192-8453-3(3))* Kessinger Publishing, LLC.
—Tom Swift & His Airship. 2007. 224p. 29.95 *(978-1-4344-9460-3(8))*; per. 19.95 *(978-1-4344-9459-7(4))* Wildside Pr., LLC.
—Tom Swift & His Big Tunnel. 2005. 27.95 *(978-1-4218-1093-5(X))*; 216p. pap. 12.95 *(978-1-4218-1193-2(6))* 1st World Publishing, Inc. (1st World Library - Literary Society).
—Tom Swift & His Big Tunnel. 2004. reprint ed. pap. 20.95 *(978-1-4191-8454-3(7))*; pap. 1.99 *(978-1-4192-8454-0(1))* Kessinger Publishing, LLC.
—Tom Swift & His Big Tunnel or the Hidd. 2006. pap. *(978-1-4065-0898-7(5))* Dodo Pr.
—Tom Swift & His Electric Locomotive. 2005. 27.95 *(978-1-4218-1087-4(5))*; 200p. pap. 12.95 *(978-1-4218-1187-1(1))* 1st World Publishing, Inc. (1st World Library - Literary Society).
—Tom Swift & His Electric Locomotive: Or Two Miles a Minute on the Rails. 2007. (ENG.). 136p. pap. 18.99 *(978-1-4346-1490-2(5))* Creative Media Partners, LLC.
—Tom Swift & His Electric Locomotive or. 2006. pap. *(978-1-4065-0899-4(3))* Dodo Pr.
—Tom Swift & His Electric Rifle. 2005. 26.95 *(978-1-59540-802-0(9))*; 192p. pap. 11.95 *(978-1-59540-807-5(X))* 1st World Publishing, Inc. (1st World Library - Literary Society).
—Tom Swift & His Electric Runabout. 2004. reprint ed. pap. 20.95 *(978-1-4191-8455-0(5))*; pap. 1.99 *(978-1-4192-8455-7(X))* Kessinger Publishing, LLC.
—Tom Swift & His Electric Runabout. 2007. 224p. 29.95 *(978-1-4344-9462-7(4))*; per. 19.95 *(978-1-4344-9461-0(6))* Wildside Pr., LLC.
—Tom Swift & His Electronic Electroscope. (J). (gr. 5-6). 20.95 *(978-0-88411-462-8(7))* Amereon Ltd.
—Tom Swift & His Giant Cannon. 2005. 27.95 *(978-1-4218-1089-8(1))*; 204p. pap. 12.95 *(978-1-4218-1189-5(8))* 1st World Publishing, Inc. (1st World Library - Literary Society).
—Tom Swift & His Giant Cannon. 2004. reprint ed. pap. 20.95 *(978-1-4191-8456-7(3))*; pap. 1.99 *(978-1-4192-8456-4(8))* Kessinger Publishing, LLC.
—Tom Swift & His Giant Cannon or the lo. 2006. pap. *(978-1-4065-0902-1(7))* Dodo Pr.
—Tom Swift & His Great Searchlight. 2005. 204p. pap. 12.95 *(978-1-4218-1190-1(1)*, 1st World Library - Literary Society) 1st World Publishing, Inc.
—Tom Swift & his Great Searchlight. 2005. 27.95 *(978-1-4218-1090-4(5)*, 1st World Library - Literary Society) 1st World Publishing, Inc.
—Tom Swift & His Great Searchlight. 2004. reprint ed. pap. 1.99 *(978-1-4192-8457-1(6))*; pap. 20.95 *(978-1-4191-8457-4(1))* Kessinger Publishing, LLC.
—Tom Swift & His Great Searchlight or O. 2006. pap. *(978-1-4065-0903-8(5))* Dodo Pr.
—Tom Swift & his Motor-Boat. 2005. 26.95 *(978-1-4218-1501-5(X))*; 192p. pap. 11.95 *(978-1-4218-1601-2(6))*; 196p. pap. 11.95 *(978-1-4218-1600-5(8))* 1st World Publishing, Inc. (1st World Library - Literary Society).
—Tom Swift & His Motor-Boat: Or the Rivals of Lake Carlopa. l.t. ed. 2007. (ENG.). 148p. pap. 19.99 *(978-1-4346-1907-5(9))* Creative Media Partners, LLC.
—Tom Swift & his Motor-Cycle. 2005. 26.95 *(978-1-4218-1502-2(8))*; 192p. pap. 11.95 *(978-1-4218-1602-9(4))* 1st World Publishing, Inc. (1st World Library - Literary Society).
—Tom Swift & His Motor Cycle. 2004. reprint ed. pap. 1.99 *(978-1-4192-8459-5(2))* Kessinger Publishing, LLC.
—Tom Swift & His Motor-Cycle, Tom Swift & His Motor-Boat, Tom Swift & His Airship. 2007. 292p. per. 12.99 *(978-1-60459-097-5(1))* Wilder Pubns., Corp.
—Tom Swift & His MotorBoat or the Rival. 2006. pap. *(978-1-4065-0904-5(3))* Dodo Pr.
—Tom Swift & His MotorCycle. 2006. pap. *(978-1-4068-0727-1(3))* Echo Library.
—Tom Swift & His MotorCycle or Fun and. 2006. pap. *(978-1-4065-0905-2(1))* Dodo Pr.
—Tom Swift & His Photo Telephone. 2007. 100p. per. *(978-1-4068-1621-1(3))* Echo Library.
—Tom Swift & his Photo Telephone. 2005. 27.95 *(978-1-4218-1503-9(6))*; 204p. pap. 12.95 *(978-1-4218-1603-6(2))* 1st World Publishing, Inc. (1st World Library - Literary Society).
—Tom Swift & His Photo Telephone or the. 2006. pap. *(978-1-4065-0906-9(X))* Dodo Pr.
—Tom Swift & his Sky Racer. 2005. 26.95 *(978-1-4218-1504-6(4))*; 192p. pap. 11.95 *(978-1-4218-1604-3(0))* 1st World Publishing, Inc. (1st World Library - Literary Society).
—Tom Swift & His Sky Racer. 2004. reprint ed. pap. 1.99 *(978-1-4192-8461-8(4))* Kessinger Publishing, LLC.
—Tom Swift & His Sky Racer or the Quick. 2006. pap. *(978-1-4065-0907-6(8))* Dodo Pr.
—Tom Swift & His Sky Racer or the Quickest Flight on Record. 2005. reprint ed. pap. 24.95 *(978-0-7661-9445-8(0))* Kessinger Publishing, LLC.
—Tom Swift & His Submarine Boat. 2004. reprint ed. pap. 20.95 *(978-1-4191-8462-8(8))*; pap. 1.99 *(978-1-4192-8462-5(2))* Kessinger Publishing, LLC.
—Tom Swift & His Triphibian Atomicar. (Tom Swift Ser.). (J). (gr. 5-6). 20.95 *(978-0-88411-459-8(7))* Amereon Ltd.
—Tom Swift & His Undersea Search. 2007. 228p. 29.95 *(978-1-4344-8363-8(0))*; per. 17.95 *(978-1-4344-8362-1(2))* Wildside Pr., LLC.
—Tom Swift & his War Tank. 2005. 27.95 *(978-1-4218-1505-3(2))*; 212p. pap. 12.95 *(978-1-4218-1605-0(9))* 1st World Publishing, Inc. (1st World Library - Literary Society).
—Tom Swift & His War Tank. 2004. reprint ed. pap. 20.95 *(978-1-4191-9054-4(7))*; pap. 1.99 *(978-1-4192-9054-1(1))* Kessinger Publishing, LLC.
—Tom Swift & His War Tank or Doing His. 2006. pap. *(978-1-4065-0910-6(8))* Dodo Pr.
—Tom Swift & His Wireless Message. 2007. 220p. 24.95 *(978-1-4344-9231-9(1))*; per. 14.95 *(978-1-4344-9137-4(4))* Wildside Pr., LLC.
—Tom Swift & his Wireless Message. 2005. 26.95 *(978-1-4218-1506-0(0))*; 196p. pap. 11.95 *(978-1-4218-1606-7(7))* 1st World Publishing, Inc. (1st World Library - Literary Society).
—Tom Swift & His Wireless Message or Th. 2006. pap. *(978-1-4065-0911-3(6))* Dodo Pr.
—Tom Swift & his Wizard Camera. 2005. 26.95 *(978-1-4218-1507-7(9))*; 196p. pap. 11.95 *(978-1-4218-1607-4(5))* 1st World Publishing, Inc. (1st World Library - Literary Society).
—Tom Swift & His Wizard Camera: Or Thrilling Adventures While Taking Moving Pictu. l.t. ed. 2007. (ENG.). 148p. pap. 19.99 *(978-1-4346-1579-4(0))* Creative Media Partners, LLC.
—Tom Swift & His Wizard Camera or Thril. 2006. pap. *(978-1-4065-0912-0(4))* Dodo Pr.
—Tom Swift & the Visitor from Planet X. 2006. pap. *(978-1-4065-0913-7(2))* Dodo Pr.
—Tom Swift & the Visitor from Planet X. 2006. pap. *(978-1-4068-0728-8(1))* Echo Library.
—Tom Swift Circling the Globe. 2007. 224p. 29.95 *(978-1-4344-9464-1(0))*; per. 19.95 *(978-1-4344-9463-4(2))* Wildside Pr., LLC.
—Tom Swift in Captivity. 2005. 27.95 *(978-1-4218-1508-4(7))*; 200p. pap. 12.95 *(978-1-4218-1608-1(3))* 1st World Publishing, Inc. (1st World Library - Literary Society).
—Tom Swift in Captivity. 2004. reprint ed. pap. 20.95 *(978-1-4191-9056-8(3))*; pap. 1.99 *(978-1-4192-9056-5(8))* Kessinger Publishing, LLC.
—Tom Swift in Captivity or A Daring Escap. 2006. pap. *(978-1-4065-0914-4(0))* Dodo Pr.
—Tom Swift in the Caves of Ice. 2005. 27.95 *(978-1-4218-1509-1(5))*; 204p. pap. 12.95 *(978-1-4218-1609-8(1))* 1st World Publishing, Inc. (1st World Library - Literary Society).
—Tom Swift in the Caves of Ice or the Wre. 2006. pap. *(978-1-4065-0915-1(9))* Dodo Pr.
—Tom Swift in the City of Gold. 2005. 27.95 *(978-1-4218-1510-7(9))*; 204p. pap. 12.95 *(978-1-4218-1610-4(5))* 1st World Publishing, Inc. (1st World Library - Literary Society).
—Tom Swift in the City of Gold or Marvelo. 2006. pap. *(978-1-4065-0916-8(7))* Dodo Pr.
—Tom Swift in the Land of Wonders. 2005. 27.95 *(978-1-4218-1511-4(7))*; 204p. pap. 12.95 *(978-1-4218-1611-1(3))* 1st World Publishing, Inc. (1st World Library - Literary Society).
—Tom Swift in the Land of Wonders. 2004. reprint ed. pap. 1.99 *(978-1-4192-9057-2(6))*; pap. 20.95 *(978-1-4191-9057-5(1))* Kessinger Publishing, LLC.
—Tom Swift in the Land of Wonders or the. 2006. pap. *(978-1-4065-0917-5(5))* Dodo Pr.
—The Tom Swift Omnibus #1: Tom Swift & his Motor-Cycle, Tom Swift & His Motor-Boat, Tom Swift & His Airship. 2007. 292p. 24.95 *(978-1-60459-098-2(X))* Wilder Pubns., Corp.
—The Tom Swift Omnibus #2: Tom Swift & His Submarine Boat, Tom Swift & His Electric Runabout, Tom Swift & His Wireless Message. 2007. 296p. 24.95 *(978-1-60459-100-2(5))*; per. 12.99 *(978-1-60459-099-9(8))* Wilder Pubns., Corp.
—Tom Swift Omnibus #3: Tom Swift among the Diamond Makers, Tom Swift in the Caves of Ice, Tom Swift & His Sky Racer. 2007. 296p. per. 12.99 *(978-1-60459-101-9(3))*; per. 12.99 *(978-1-60459-102-6(1))* Wilder Pubns., Corp.
—Tom Swift Omnibus #4: Tom Swift & His Electric Rifle, Tom Swift in the City of Gold, Tom Swift & His Air Glider. 2007. 304p. 24.95 *(978-1-60459-103-3(X))*; per. 12.99 *(978-1-60459-104-0(8))* Wilder Pubns., Corp.
—Tom Swift Omnibus #5: Tom Swift in Captivity, Tom Swift & His Wizard Camera, Tom Swift & His Great Searchlight. 2007. 312p. 24.95 *(978-1-60459-106-4(4))*; per. 12.99 *(978-1-60459-105-7(6))* Wilder Pubns., Corp.
—The Tom Swift Omnibus #6: Tom Swift & His Giant Cannon, Tom Swift & His Photo Telephone, Tom Swift & His Aerial Warship. 2007. 296p. 24.95 *(978-1-60459-109-5(9))*; per. 12.99 *(978-1-60459-108-8(0))* Wilder Pubns., Corp.
—The Tom Swift Omnibus #7: Tom Swift & His Big Tunnel, Tom Swift in the Land of Wonders, Tom Swift & His War Tank. 2007. 312p. 24.99 *(978-1-60459-111-8(0))*; per. 12.99 *(978-1-60459-110-1(2))* Wilder Pubns., Corp.
—The Tom Swift Omnibus #8: Tom Swift & His Air Scout, Tom Swift & His Undersea Search, Tom Swift among the Fire Fighters, Tom Swift & His Electri. 2007. 420p. per. 14.99 *(978-1-60459-112-5(9))* Wilder Pubns., Corp.
—The Tom Swift Omnibus #8: Tom Swift & His Air Scout, Tom Swift & His Undersea Search, Tom Swift among the Fire Fighters, Tom Swift & His Electric. 2007. 420p. 29.99 *(978-1-60459-113-2(7))* Wilder Pubns., Corp.
—The Tom Swift Treasury. 2007. 540p. per. 29.99 *(978-1-934451-09-0(6))*; 600p. per. 29.99 *(978-1-934451-10-6(X))* Wilder Pubns., Corp.
—The War in Outer Space. (Tom Swift Ser.). (J). (gr. 3-7). 19.95 *(978-0-88411-465-9(1))* Amereon Ltd.
Appleton, Victor & Appleton, Victor, II. Into the Abyss. 2006. (Tom Swift, Young Inventor Ser.: 1). (ENG.). 176p. (J). (gr. 3-7). pap. 4.99 *(978-1-4169-1518-8(4)*, Aladdin) Simon & Schuster Children's Publishing.
Arac de Nyeko, Monica. Children of the Red Fields. 2005. (Illus.). 99p. *(978-9966-47-104-8(9))* Phoenix Pubs., Ltd.
Aranha, Marc. The Queen of Spiders. 2003. 210p. pap. 14.95 *(978-0-595-29275-2(5))* iUniverse, Inc.
Aravena, Cristian. The Adventures of Marmat. 2007. 124p. per. 19.95 *(978-1-4241-6909-2(7))* America Star Bks.
Arce, Andrea. Under the Influence. 2013. 170p. pap. 13.95 *(978-1-4633-6688-9(4))* Palibrio.
Archambault, Douglas J. The Adventures of Little Buddy & Grizz, 1 vol. 2009. 64p. pap. 19.95 *(978-1-60836-159-5(4))* America Star Bks.
Archbold, David M. The Amazing Adventures of Chumley, Robin, Snickers & Mac. 2011. 48p. (gr. 4-6). pap. 19.26 *(978-1-4634-1518-1(4))* AuthorHouse.
Archer, Richard. The Island Home. 2004. reprint ed. pap. 1.99 *(978-1-4192-6772-7(8))*; pap. 27.95 *(978-1-4191-6772-0(3))* Kessinger Publishing, LLC.
Archuleta, Robert B. The Boys' Club: Lost & Found. 2007. 52p. per. 16.95 *(978-1-4241-7372-3(8))* America Star Bks.
Arden, Lynne. Guess What Happened to Me, Auntie Kate! Marino, Natalie, illus. 2008. 52p. pap. 18.95 *(978-1-59858-733-3(1))* Dog Ear Publishing, LLC.
Ardis, C. The Hill: Oh What A Day Series. 2012. 116p. 23.99 *(978-1-4685-3700-0(8))*; pap. 14.95 *(978-1-4685-3701-7(6))* AuthorHouse.
Arenstam, Peter. Nicholas: A New Hampshire Tale. Holman, Karen Busch, illus. 2009. (Nicholas Northeastern Ser.: 3). (ENG.). 144p. (J). (gr. k-7). 14.95 *(978-1-58726-521-1(4)*, Mitten Pr.) Ann Arbor Editions LLC.
—Nicholas: A Vermont Tale. Holman, Karen Busch, illus. 2010. (Nicholas Northeastern Ser.: 4). (ENG.). 144p. (J). (gr. k-7). 14.95 *(978-1-58726-522-8(2)*, Mitten Pr.) Ann Arbor Editions LLC.
—Nicholas, a Maine Tale. Holman, Karen Busch, illus. 2015. (Nicholas Northeastern Ser.: 2). (ENG.). 166p. (J). (gr. k-7). pap. 8.95 *(978-1-938170-67-6(9)*, Mitten Pr.) Ann Arbor Editions LLC.
—Nicholas, a Massachusetts Tale. Holman, Karen Busch, illus. 2015. (Nicholas Northeastern Ser.: 1). (ENG.). 152p. (J). (gr. k-7). pap. 8.95 *(978-1-938170-66-9(0)*, Mitten Pr.) Ann Arbor Editions LLC.
—Nicholas, a New Hampshire Tale. Holman, Karen Busch, illus. 2015. (Nicholas Northeastern Ser.: 3). (ENG.). 158p. (J). (gr. k-7). pap. 8.95 *(978-1-938170-68-3(7)*, Mitten Pr.) Ann Arbor Editions LLC.
—Nicholas, a Vermont Tale. Holman, Karen Busch, illus. 2015. (Nicholas Northeastern Ser.: 4). (ENG.). 156p. (J). (gr. k-7). pap. 8.95 *(978-1-938170-69-0(5)*, Mitten Pr.) Ann Arbor Editions LLC.
Argo, Sandi & Argo, Kaitlyn. Don't You See It? Jungle Edition, 1 vol. Stephens, Sherry & Finnell, Cyndy, illus. 2009. 39p. pap. 19.95 *(978-1-61546-322-0(4))* PublishAmerica, Inc.
Arias, Carlos Ballesteros. The Magic Forest. 2006. (J). pap. 8.00 *(978-0-8059-7022-7(3))* Dorrance Publishing Co., Inc.
Ariga, Hitoshi. Mega Man Gigamix, 2 vols., Vol. 3. 2011. (ENG., Illus.). 224p. (J). pap. 13.95 *(978-1-926778-31-0(6)*, 9781926778310) UDON Entertainment Corp. CAN. Dist: Diamond Comic Distributors, Inc.
Arinola Awokoya. The Adventures of High Jumper. 2009. 112p. pap. 14.99 *(978-1-4269-1792-9(9))* Trafford Publishing.
Arkell, O. E. The Adventures of Munchkin-Patch Tabby: How Munchkin Patch-Tabby Got His Name. 2009. 16p. pap. 15.95 *(978-1-4389-4273-5(7))* AuthorHouse.
Arlon, Penelope. Factastic: A Lego Adventure in the Real World. 2016. (LEGO Nonfiction Ser.). (ENG.). 176p. (J). (gr. 3-7). 19.99 *(978-1-338-03284-0(4))* Scholastic, Inc.
Armstrong, Alan. Raleigh's Page. Jessell, Tim, illus. 2009. (ENG.). 336p. (J). (gr. 3-7). 7.99 *(978-0-375-83320-5(X)*, Yearling) Random Hse. Children's Bks.
Armstrong, Ashley Sage-Taylor. The Adventures of Starlight & Sunny: Book Four in the Adventures of Starlight & Sunny Series, ?Princesses Don't Need a Job !? How to Be an Indepen. 2013. 52p. pap. *(978-1-927863-02-2(3))* Armstrong, Ashley.
—The Adventures of Starlight & Sunny: Building a Dream , How to Focus & Make Your Dreams Come to Life, with Positive Conscious Morals. Picture Boo. 2013. 52p. pap. *(978-1-927863-04-6(X))* Armstrong, Ashley.
—The Adventures of Starlight & Sunny: I Am Me ! Who Are You?, How to Find Good Quality Friends & Stand up for One Another, with Positive Morals, Pi. 2013. 52p. pap. *(978-1-927863-00-8(7))* Armstrong, Ashley.
—The Adventures of Starlight & Sunny: The Secret Valley , Book 2, How to Be Happy, to Find Inner Beauty & Peace, with Positive Conscious Morals, P. 2013. 52p. pap. *(978-0-9919517-9-6(4))* Armstrong, Ashley.
Armstrong, Cindy. Boudreaux & His Buddies. 2006. 98p. pap. 16.95 *(978-1-4241-3906-4(6))* PublishAmerica, Inc.
Armstrong, K. L. & Marr, M. A. Loki's Wolves. (Blackwell Pages Ser.: 1). (ENG.). (J). (gr. 3-7). 2014. 374p. pap. 8.99 *(978-0-316-20497-2(8))* 2013. (Illus.). 358p. 17.00 *(978-0-316-20496-5(X))* Little, Brown Bks. for Young Readers.
—Odin's Ravens. 2014. (Blackwell Pages Ser.: 2). (ENG., Illus.). 342p. (J). (gr. 3-7). 17.00 *(978-0-316-20498-9(6))* Little, Brown Bks. for Young Readers.
Armstrong, Kelley. Empire of Night. 2015. (Age of Legends Trilogy Ser.: 2). 432p. (YA). (gr. 8). 17.99 *(978-0-06-207127-9(0))* HarperCollins Pubs.
—Forest of Ruin. 2016. (Age of Legends Trilogy Ser.: 3). 448p. (YA). (gr. 8). 17.99 *(978-0-06-207130-9(0))* HarperCollins Pubs.
—The Reckoning. 2010. (Darkest Powers Ser.: 3). 400p. (YA). (gr. 8-18). 17.99 *(978-0-06-166283-6(6))* HarperCollins Pubs.
—Sea of Shadows. (gr. 8). 2015. (Age of Legends Trilogy Ser.: 1). 432p. (YA). pap. 9.99 *(978-0-06-207125-5(4))* 2014. (Age of Legends Trilogy: Bk. 1). 416p. (J). 17.99 *(978-0-06-207124-8(6))* HarperCollins Pubs.
—Sea of Shadows. 2015. (Age of Legends Ser.: 1). (YA). lib. bdg. 20.85 *(978-0-606-36511-6(7))* Turtleback Bks.
Armstrong Nhp, Ashley Sage-Taylor. The Adventures of Starlight & Sunny: Book One in, the Adventures of Starlight & Sunny Series, ?the Princess Path?, How to Be True with Good Deeds; 2013. 46p. pap. *(978-0-9919517-7-2(8))* Armstrong, Ashley.
Armstrong, Tiffani. Zach & the Incredible Traveling Hat. 2010. 28p. pap. 13.00 *(978-1-4490-8129-4(0))* AuthorHouse.
Armstrong, Tony. The Water Troll. 2008. (ENG.). 16p. 8.49 *(978-1-4389-1925-6(5))* AuthorHouse.
Armstrong, Z. A. The Origins of Dexter & Stray, Part: The Man Who Knows Everything. 2012. 166p. pap. 9.99 *(978-0-9855731-0-2(4))* Tres Clavas Pr.
Arndt, Rhonda. Mac's Adventure. 2006. 48p. pap. 16.95 *(978-1-4241-1321-7(0))* PublishAmerica, Inc.
Arnett, Dee. Gifted. 2008. 240p. pap. 18.95 *(978-1-4092-0442-8(1))* Lulu Pr., Inc.
Arnoff, Rebecca D. The Trouble with Tooth Fairies: The Adventures of Sam & Angela. 2013. 24p. 22.99 *(978-1-4582-1028-9(6))*; pap. 12.99 *(978-1-4582-1026-5(X))* Author Solutions, Inc. (Abbott Pr.).
Arnold, Audrey. Elkin's Tail. 2012. (Illus.). 52p. pap. 27.45 *(978-1-4772-2180-8(8))* AuthorHouse.
Arnold, George. Los Gatos of the CIA. 2005. (SPA & ENG., Illus.). 225p. pap. 22.95 *(978-1-57168-861-3(7)*, Nortex Pr.) Eakin Pr.
Arnold, George. Pharaohs' Follies: Kits of the CIA Adventures in Egypt. Kablaoui, Rasmia, tr. Eckhardt, Jason C., illus. 2016. (Cats of the CIA Ser.). (ENG.). (YA). (gr. 7-12). pap. 19.95 **(978-1-68179-074-9(2)**, Eakin Pr.) Eakin Pr.
Arnold, Ginger Fudge. Billy's Mountain Adventure, 1 vol. Almeyda, Tonito Avalon, illus. 2010. 32p. pap. 24.95 *(978-1-4489-5582-4(3))* PublishAmerica, Inc.
—Two Tipsy Tots, 1 vol. Crème, Aurora C., illus. 2009. 32p. pap. 24.95 *(978-1-4489-1891-1(X))* America Star Bks.
Arnold, Ginny. The Nomadic Healer, 1 vol. 2010. 86p. pap. 19.95 *(978-1-4489-5359-2(6))* America Star Bks.
Arnold, Michelle Lee. Mathew Sunburst & the Keepers of the Sky. 2003. 141p. (J). pap. 13.95 *(978-0-7414-1575-2(5))* Infinity Publishing.
Arnold, Tedd. Hi! Fly Guy. Arnold, Tedd, illus. 2006. (Scholastic Reader Level 2 Ser.). (ENG., Illus.). 32p. (J). (gr. -1-3). pap. 3.99 *(978-0-439-85311-8(7)*, Cartwheel Bks.) Scholastic, Inc.
Aronskind, Ofer. Escape from Sunday School. 2009. 152p. pap. 12.95 *(978-1-4401-3217-9(8))* iUniverse, Inc.
—That Same Summer. 2008. 156p. pap. 12.95 *(978-0-595-50605-7(4))* iUniverse, Inc.
Aronson, Jeff & Aronson, Miriam. Little Mike & Maddie's Black Hill's Adventure. Aronson, Jeff & Zephyr, Jay, illus. 2007. 33p. (J). 16.00 *(978-0-9795302-1-0(0)*, CrumbGobbler Pr.) Downtown Wetmore Pr.
—Little Mike & Maddie's Christmas Book. Aronson, Jeff & Zephyr, Jay, illus. 2007. 32p. (J). 16.00 *(978-0-9795302-2-7(9)*, CrumbGobbler Pr.) Downtown Wetmore Pr.
—Little Mike & Maddie's First Motorcycle Ride. Aronson, Jeff & Zephyr, Jay, illus. 2007. 32p. (J). 16.00 *(978-0-9795302-0-3(2)*, CrumbGobbler Pr.) Downtown Wetmore Pr.
Aronson, Rosy. A Tale of Serendipity: the Adventure Begins! 2010. 370p. pap. 24.84 *(978-0-557-12641-5(X))* Lulu Pr., Inc.
Arrigan, Mary. Milo & the Raging Chieftains. 2014. (Milo Adventures Ser.: 2). (ENG., Illus.). 176p. (J). pap. 14.00 *(978-1-84717-561-8(9))* O'Brien Pr., Ltd., The. IRL. Dist: Dufour Editions, Inc.
Arrington, R. Region. Billy Buckins & the Pirates Map, 1 vol. 2010. 64p. pap. 19.95 *(978-1-4512-2087-2(1))* America Star Bks.
—The Voyage of Billy Buckins, 1 vol. Harrington, Linda, illus. 2009. 73p. pap. 19.95 *(978-1-4489-2083-9(3))* America Star Bks.
Arroyo, Kritzia. Angel Princess Star. 2008. 18p. 10.28 *(978-1-4303-2776-9(6))* Lulu Pr., Inc.
Arroyo, Raymond. The Relic of Perilous Falls. (Will Wilder Ser.: 1). (ENG.). (J). (gr. 3-7). 2017. 352p. 7.99 *(978-0-553-53962-2(0)*, Yearling) 2016. 336p. lib. bdg. 19.99 *(978-0-553-53960-8(4)*, Crown Books For Young Readers) 2016. 336p. 16.99 *(978-0-553-53959-2(0)*, Crown Books For Young Readers) Random Hse. Children's Bks.
Arruda, Diane. The Ancient One, Book II in the Dream River Adventure. 2009. 56p. pap. 12.95 *(978-1-60860-397-8(0)*, Eloquent Bks.) Strategic Book Publishing & Rights Agency (SBPRA).
—The Undiscovered River: Golden Fish & a True Dream. 2008. 60p. pap. 12.95 *(978-1-60693-399-2(X)*, Eloquent Bks.) Strategic Book Publishing & Rights Agency (SBPRA).
Artibani, Francesco, et al. Donald Duck Adventures, Vol. 19. Clark, John, ed. 2006. (ENG., Illus.). 128p. (YA). pap. 7.95 *(978-1-888472-31-8(6)*, 9781888472318) Gemstone Publishing, Inc.
Artifact Group Staff & Artifact Group, The. Atlantis SquarePantis. 2007. (SpongeBob SquarePants Ser.).

(ENG., Illus.). 24p. (J). (gr. k-3). pap. 3.99 *(978-1-4169-3799-9(4)*, Simon Spotlight/Nickelodeon) Simon Spotlight/Nickelodeon.

Artifact Group, The. The Trash Planet. 2009. (Backyardigans Ser.: 12). (ENG.). 24p. (J). pap. 3.99 *(978-1-4169-6868-9(7)*, Simon Spotlight/Nickelodeon) Simon Spotlight/Nickelodeon.

Artus, William. The King on the Moon. 2008. 32p. pap. 20.95 *(978-1-4092-3044-1(9))* Lulu Pr., Inc.

Aryal, Aimee. Cort Spells It Out. De Angel, Miguel, illus. 2006. (Cort the Sport Adventures Ser.). 24p. (J). (gr. -1-3). per. 5.95 *(978-1-932888-62-1(4)*, 91-101-01) Mascot Bks., Inc.

—Hello Big Jay! Shrestha, Anuj, illus. 2004. 24p. (J). 14.95 *(978-1-932888-41-6(1))* Mascot Bks., Inc.

—Hello Herbie Husker! Shrestha, Anuj, illus. 2004. 24p. (J). 14.95 *(978-1-932888-43-0(8))* Mascot Bks., Inc.

—Hello, Pistol Pete! Craig, Megan, illus. 2007. 24p. (J). lib. bdg. 14.95 *(978-1-932888-38-6(1))* Mascot Bks., Inc.

—Let's Go Irish! Shrestha, Anuj, illus. 2004. 24p. (J). 19.95 *(978-0-9743442-5-6(7))* Mascot Bks., Inc.

Aryal, Aimee & Halligan, Chris. Meet Cort the Sport. 2006. (Cort the Sport Adventures Ser.). (Illus.). 24p. (J). (gr. -1-3). per. 5.95 *(978-1-932888-61-4(6)*, 91-100-01) Mascot Bks., Inc.

Asad, Megan Emily. The Juggler's Journey. 2005. 144p. pap. 9.95 *(978-0-7599-4470-1(9))* Hard Shell Word Factory.

Asai, Carrie. The Book of the Flame. Verhoye, Annabelle & Alarcão, Renato, illus. 2004. (Samurai Girl Ser.: 5). (ENG.). 224p. (YA). (gr. 11). pap. 7.99 *(978-0-689-86713-2(1)*, Simon Pulse) Simon Pulse.

—The Book of the Heart: Heaven's Mission - To Sharpen Her Senses. Alarcao, Renato, illus. 2004. (Samurai Girl Ser.: 6). (ENG.). 240p. (YA). (gr. 11). pap. 11.99 *(978-0-689-86712-5(3)*, Simon Pulse) Simon Pulse.

—The Book of the Pearl. Verhoye, Annabelle & Alarcao, Renato, illus. 2003. (Samurai Girl Ser.: 3). (ENG.). 240p. (YA). (gr. 11). pap. 6.99 *(978-0-689-86432-2(9)*, Simon Pulse) Simon Pulse.

—The Book of the Sword. Verhoye, Annabelle, illus. 2003. (Samurai Girl Ser.: 1). (ENG.). 224p. (YA). (gr. 11). pap. 11.99 *(978-0-689-85948-9(1)*, Simon Pulse) Simon Pulse.

Asai, Carrie & Gray, Mitchel. The Book of the Wind. Verhoye, Annabelle & Alarcão, Renato, illus. 2003. (Samurai Girl Ser.: 4). (ENG.). 224p. (YA). (gr. 11). pap. 6.99 *(978-0-689-86433-9(7)*, Simon Pulse) Simon Pulse.

Aschermann, Kurt. Bj & the Amazing Doctor Directions. 2008. 172p. pap. 11.99 *(978-1-4343-7708-1(3))* AuthorHouse.

ASF, Jerome. Bacca & the Skeleton King: An Unofficial Minecrafter's Adventure. 2016. (ENG.). 224p. (J). (gr. 3). pap. 9.99 *(978-1-5107-0902-7(9)*, Sky Pony Pr.) Skyhorse Publishing Co., Inc.

Ashby, Mandy Anne. Mindy's Adventure with the Pussycat Witches: Playing in the Rain. 2011. (Illus.). 28p. pap. 20.66 *(978-1-4567-8788-2(8))* AuthorHouse.

Ashdown, Rebecca. Bob & Flo Play Hide-And-Seek (Board Book) 2017. (ENG., Illus.). 26p. (J). (— 1). bds. 7.99 *(978-0-544-85959-3(6)*, HMH Books For Young Readers) Houghton Mifflin Harcourt Publishing Co.

Ashe, Gregory. The Imagineer (Fire Eye Edition) A Book of Miracles. Whittaker, Kay, illus. 3rd ed. 2005. 198p. pap. *(978-1-905532-01-8(6))* Humdrumming, Ltd.

—The Imagineer (Snow Scene Edition) A Book of Miracles. Whittaker, Kay, illus. 2nd ed. 2005. 198p. (YA). pap. *(978-1-905532-00-1(8))* Humdrumming, Ltd.

Ashley, John A. The Gathering of the Fairy Horses Series. 2009. 59p. pap. 16.84 *(978-1-4092-0638-5(6))* Lulu Pr., Inc.

Ashta, Lucia. The Perfect Fuzzy-Wuzz. 2010. 48p. pap. 17.45 *(978-1-4525-0041-6(X))* Get Published.

Ashworth, Caspian. Copper Smith & the Battle of the Bands. 2012. (Illus.). 228p. pap. 18.24 *(978-1-4772-5071-6(9))* AuthorHouse.

Askounis, Christina. The Dream of the Stone. 2007. (ENG.). 304p. (YA). (gr. 7). pap. 13.99 *(978-1-4169-1187-6(1)*, Simon Pulse) Simon Pulse.

Asquith, Ros. Trixie Gets the Witch Factor. 2007. (Trixie Ser.). (ENG., Illus.). 176p. (J). (gr. 3-6). pap. 13.95 *(978-0-00-725910-6(7))* HarperCollins Pubs. Ltd. GBR. Dist: Independent Pubs. Group.

Assorted. Treasury of Adventure Stories. 2014. (Storytale Treasuries Ser.). (ENG., Illus.). 144p. (J). (gr. -1-k). 14.99 ***(978-1-78445-035-9(9))*** Top That! Publishing PLC GBR. Dist: Independent Pubs. Group.

Atamer, Billie. Banjo Billy & the River Rat Kids. 2009. 130p. pap. 7.99 *(978-1-61667-004-7(5))* Raider Publishing International.

Atanacio, Frank. Aggravating Factors: From the Nick Barnum Sealed Case File a Nick Barnum Novel II. 2003. 128p. (YA). pap. 10.95 *(978-0-595-26985-3(0)*, Writers Club Pr.) iUniverse, Inc.

Atchison, David. The Adventures of Black Bart: the Lone Stranger. 2009. 84p. pap. 8.95 *(978-0-578-02511-7(6))* Black Bart Bks.

Athens, Sandra & Colarik, Kim. The Adventures of Foxy: The Lonely Lost Dog. 2009. 44p. pap. 18.50 *(978-1-4490-0506-1(3))* AuthorHouse.

Atherton, Isabel. Ruby Moo's Deep-Sea Adventure! Straker, Bethany, illus. 2014. (ENG.). 32p. (J). (gr. -1-k). 14.95 *(978-1-62914-625-6(0)*, Sky Pony Pr.) Skyhorse Publishing Co., Inc.

Atkin, Jean. The Crow House. 2013. 270p. pap. *(978-1-78299-650-7(8))* FeedARead.com.

Atkins, Dan. Tony Transitions, 1 vol. 2009. 82p. pap. 19.95 *(978-1-4489-9668-1(6))* America Star Bks.

Atkinson, Cale. Explorers of the Wild. Atkinson, Cale, illus. 2016. (ENG., Illus.). 40p. (J). (gr. -1-k). 16.99 *(978-1-4847-2340-1(6))* Disney Pr.

Atlas, Lilly. Journey to the Deep Woods. 2008. 36p. pap. 16.99 *(978-1-4389-2596-7(4))* AuthorHouse.

Atmadja, Titin. Liam's Adventure: Liam Meets the King of Java. 2012. 20p. pap. 17.99 *(978-1-4772-6064-7(1))* AuthorHouse.

—Liam's Adventure: Liam's Wild Life at Richard's Cabin. 2012. 24p. pap. 17.99 *(978-1-4772-6066-1(8))* AuthorHouse.

Atwarie, Rossi. The Adventures of Fox Brown. Bachan, Krystal Ann, illus. 2011. 62p. pap. 19.00 *(978-1-60911-845-7(6)*, Eloquent Bks.) Strategic Book Publishing & Rights Agency (SBPRA).

Atwater, Jillene. Small & Sassy. DeBroeck, Sarah, illus. 2011. 36p. pap. 24.95 *(978-1-4489-8374-2(6))* America Star Bks.

Atwood, Margaret. For the Birds. (J). pap. 4.99 *(978-0-88894-825-0(5))* Da Capo Pr., Inc.

Atxaga, Bernardo & Costa, Margaret Jull. The Adventures of Shola. Valverde, Mikel, illus. 2014. (ENG.). 220p. (J). (gr. 4-7). 20.00 *(978-1-78269-009-2(3)*, Pushkin Press) Steerforth Pr.

Auborn, Jodi. Secrets of the North Country: The Hobo's Story. 2012. 210p. pap. 24.95 *(978-1-4626-7898-3(X))* America Star Bks.

Auch, Mary Jane. A Dog on His Own. 2009. (ENG., Illus.). 160p. (J). (gr. 3-7). pap. 7.95 *(978-0-8234-2243-2(7))* Holiday Hse., Inc.

Audibert, Tara. Matthew Loses His Laugh. 2009. 32p. pap. 16.00 *(978-0-557-09385-4(6))* Lulu Pr., Inc.

Auerbach, Annie. Despicable Me. 2010. (Despicable Me Ser.). (ENG., Illus.). 144p. (gr. 3-7). pap. 5.99 *(978-0-316-08380-5(1)*, L,B Kids) Hachette Bk. Group.

—Grosse Adventures - Trouble at Twilight Cave. 2007. (Grosse Adventures Ser.). (Illus.). 96p. per. 4.99 *(978-1-59816-051-2(6))* TOKYOPOP, Inc.

—Scooby-Doo in the Coolsville Contraption Contest, 1 vol. 2016. (Scooby-Doo! Set 3 Ser.). (ENG., Illus.). 32p. (J). (gr. k-4). lib. bdg. 24.21 *(978-1-61479-409-7(X))* Spotlight.

—Scooby-Doo in the Mystery Mansion, 1 vol. 2016. (Scooby-Doo! Set 3 Ser.). (ENG., Illus.). 32p. (J). (gr. k-4). lib. bdg. 24.21 *(978-1-61479-411-0(1)*, 1401187) Spotlight.

—The Squeakquel: Battle of the Bands. 2009. (Alvin & the Chipmunks Ser.). (ENG., Illus.). 24p. (J). (gr. -1-2). pap. 3.99 *(978-0-06-184565-9(5)*, HarperFestival) HarperCollins Pubs.

Auerbach, Annie, adapted by. Despicable Me 2: The Junior Novel. movie tie-in ed. 2013. (ENG.). 144p. (J). (gr. 3-7). pap. 6.99 *(978-0-316-23432-0(X))* Little, Brown Bks. for Young Readers.

Auerbach, Annie & PopCap Games Staff. Brains & the Beanstalk. Grosvenor, Charles & Roberts, Jeremy, illus. 2013. (Plants vs. Zombies Ser.). (ENG.). 24p. (J). (gr. -1-3). pap. 4.99 *(978-0-06-222836-9(6)*, HarperFestival) HarperCollins Pubs.

—The Three Little Pigs Fight Back. Grosvenor, Charles & Roberts, Jeremy, illus. 2013. (Plants vs. Zombies Ser.). (ENG.). 24p. (J). (gr. -1-3). pap. 4.99 *(978-0-06-222838-3(2)*, HarperFestival) HarperCollins Pubs.

Augenstein, Marianne R. The Quest for Kair, 1 vol. 2009. 152p. pap. 24.95 *(978-1-60813-899-9(2))* America Star Bks.

August, Elaine. It Only Snows in Brooklyn. 2012. 30p. 24.95 *(978-1-4626-9438-9(1))*; 32p. pap. 24.95 *(978-1-4626-7588-3(3))* America Star Bks.

August, Elaine Schiller. Southern Mischief. 2005. 78p. pap. 19.95 *(978-1-4137-7893-9(3))* America Star Bks.

August, Rachel. Adventures of Libby Nickel: What's your Mommy's First Name? 2011. 25p. (J). pap. 17.95 *(978-1-4327-6513-2(2))* Outskirts Pr., Inc.

—Adventures of Libby Nickel: Why Are There Colors? 2011. 33p. (J). pap. 19.95 *(978-1-4327-7078-5(0))* Outskirts Pr., Inc.

—Journey of My Untied Shoes. 2010. 28p. pap. 9.95 *(978-1-4327-6214-8(1))* Outskirts Pr., Inc.

Aulton, Frank. The Adventures of Po-Po. 2015. (ENG., Illus.). 98p. (J). (gr. 3-4). pap. 16.95 *(978-1-78455-577-1(0)*, 43a06cbf-bb6d-4489-8363-2202b9e5abcc) Austin, Stan AUS. Dist: Bookmasters Distribution.

Aunt Fezzie. Happy-Feliz & Fatso's Heroic School Adventures: Heroes vs. Bullies. 2013. 32p. pap. 13.99 *(978-1-4808-0134-9(8))* Archway Publishing.

Auntie Annie. Knute: Dreams of Africa. 2013. 32p. pap. 17.25 *(978-1-4669-7519-4(9))* Trafford Publishing.

—Knute: In the Magical Meadow. 2013. 32p. pap. 17.25 *(978-1-4669-9778-3(8))* Trafford Publishing.

—Knute: Meets Mike in the Magical Meadow. 2013. 28p. pap. 16.09 *(978-1-4669-9780-6(X))* Trafford Publishing.

Aureliani, Franco. Dino-Mike! Aureliani, Franco, illus. 2015. (Dino-Mike! Ser.). (ENG., Illus.). 128p. (gr. 1-3). lib. bdg. 101.28 *(978-1-4965-0311-4(2)*, Dino-Mike!) Stone Arch Bks.

—Dino-Mike & the Jurassic Portal. Aureliani, Franco, illus. 2015. (Dino-Mike! Ser.). (ENG., Illus.). 128p. (gr. 1-3). lib. bdg. 25.32 *(978-1-4342-9630-6(X))* Stone Arch Bks.

—Dino-Mike & the Museum Mayhem. Aureliani, Franco, illus. 2015. (Dino-Mike! Ser.). (ENG., Illus.). 128p. (gr. 1-3). lib. bdg. 25.32 *(978-1-4342-9628-3(8)*, Dino-Mike!) Stone Arch Bks.

—Dino-Mike & the T. Rex Attack. Aureliani, Franco, illus. 2015. (Dino-Mike! Ser.). (ENG., Illus.). 128p. (gr. 1-3). lib. bdg. 25.32 *(978-1-4342-9627-6(X))* Stone Arch Bks.

—Dino-Mike & the Underwater Dinosaurs. Aureliani, Franco, illus. 2015. (Dino-Mike! Ser.). (ENG., Illus.). 128p. (gr. 1-3). lib. bdg. 25.32 *(978-1-4342-9629-0(6))* Stone Arch Bks.

Aureliani, Franco, illus. Dino-Mike & the Museum Mayhem. 2015. (J). lib. bdg. *(978-1-4062-9391-3(1))* Stone Arch Bks.

Austin, Jamie Lea-Elizabeth. Reverie. 2012. 312p. 29.95 *(978-1-4626-6734-5(1))* PublishAmerica, Inc.

Austin, Rikey. Cobby Goes for a Swim: Alice's Bear Shop. 2012. 28p. pap. *(978-1-78092-164-8(0))* MX Publishing, Ltd.

—Sandy Paints a Picture: Alice's Bear Shop. 2012. 28p. pap. *(978-1-78092-155-6(1))* MX Publishing, Ltd.

Authement, Louise. Diaries of the Fifth Grade Miseries. 2013. 68p. pap. 10.95 *(978-1-4327-9996-0(7))* Outskirts Pr., Inc.

Auty, Robert C. A Hare's Tale. 2011. (ENG., Illus.). 80p. pap. 9.99 *(978-1-908098-40-5(6))* 2QT, Ltd. (Publishing) GBR. Dist: Printondemand-worldwide.com.

Auxier, Bryan. Three Days & Four Knights. Daniels, Regina, illus. 2004. 66p. (J). pap. 3.95 *(978-0-9719144-2-1(7))* Where? Pr., Inc.

Auxier, Jonathan. Sophie Quire & the Last Storyguard. (ENG.). 464p. (gr. 3-7). 2017. (J). pap. 8.95 *(978-1-4197-2202-8(6))* 2016. (YA). 18.95 *(978-1-4197-1747-5(2))* Abrams, Inc. (Amulet Bks.).

Avanti, Michele. GreeHee the Journey of Five: Tales of Tamoor Book One. 2008. (Illus.). 304p. (J). per. 14.99 *(978-0-9779590-4-4(X))* GreeHee Publishing.

Avasthi, Swati. Chasing Shadows. Phillips, Craig, illus. 2013. (ENG.). 320p. (YA). (gr. 9). 17.99 *(978-0-375-86342-4(7))*; lib. bdg. 20.99 *(978-0-375-96341-4(3))* Random Hse. Children's Bks. (Knopf Bks. for Young Readers).

Avengers Staff, et al. Meet Captain America No. 2. 2011. (Avengers: Earth's Mightiest Heroes! Ser.). (ENG.). 24p. (J). (gr. 1-2). pap. 3.99 *(978-1-4231-4296-6(9))* Marvel Worldwide, Inc.

Averbeck, Jim. A Hitch at the Fairmont. Bertozzi, Nick, illus. (ENG.). 416p. (J). (gr. 3-7). 2015. pap. 7.99 *(978-1-4424-9448-0(4))* 2014. 16.99 *(978-1-4424-9447-3(6)*, Atheneum Bks. for Young Readers) Simon & Schuster Children's Publishing.

Averette, Sonya M. Aunt Ruby's Kisses, 1 vol. Proulx, Denis, illus. 2009. 35p. pap. 24.95 *(978-1-60749-045-6(5))* America Star Bks.

Avery, Tammy. Molly's Kat Tales, 1 vol. 2009. 17p. pap. 24.95 *(978-1-60836-474-9(7))* America Star Bks.

Avery, Tom. In Too Deep. 2014. (ENG., Illus.). 176p. (J). (gr. 3-7). pap. 8.99 *(978-1-84780-389-4(X)*, Frances Lincoln) Quarto Publishing Group UK GBR. Dist: Hachette Bk. Group.

—Too Much Trouble. 2012. (ENG.). 144p. (J). (gr. 7-10). pap. 8.99 *(978-1-84780-234-7(6)*, Frances Lincoln Children's Bks.) Quarto Publishing Group UK GBR. Dist: Hachette Bk. Group.

Aveyard, Victoria. Red Queen Collector's Edition. 2017. (Red Queen Ser.: 1). 416p. (YA). (gr. 8). 22.99 ***(978-0-06-284000-4(2))*** HarperCollins Pubs.

Avi. A Beginning, a Muddle, & an End: The Right Way to Write Writing. Tusa, Tricia, illus. 2008. (ENG.). 176p. (J). (gr. 2-5). 14.95 *(978-0-15-205555-4(X))* Houghton Mifflin Harcourt Publishing Co.

—The End of the Beginning: Being the Adventures of a Small Snail (and an Even Smaller Ant) Tusa, Tricia, illus. 2008. (ENG.). 144p. (J). (gr. 2-5). pap. 6.95 *(978-0-15-205532-5(0))* Houghton Mifflin Harcourt Publishing Co.

—The End of Time, No. 3. 2010. (ENG.). 240p. (J). (gr. 5-18). 16.99 *(978-0-06-174080-0(2))* HarperCollins Pubs.

—Poppy & Ereth. Floca, Brian, illus. 2011. (Poppy Stories Ser.). (ENG.). 224p. (J). (gr. 3-7). pap. 6.99 *(978-0-06-111971-2(7))* HarperCollins Pubs.

—The True Confessions of Charlotte Doyle. (J). pap. *(978-0-13-667429-0(1))*; pap. 23.94 *(978-0-13-667403-0(8))*; 3rd ed. (J). pap. 3.99 *(978-0-13-800012-7(3))* Prentice Hall (Schl. Div.).

—The True Confessions of Charlotte Doyle. 2003. 20.75 *(978-0-8446-7235-9(1))* Smith, Peter Pub., Inc.

Aviles, Donna Nordmark. Fly Little Bird, Fly! 2004. 80p. per. 10.00 *(978-1-932852-07-3(7))* Wasteland Pr.

Avventure Di Pinocchio. pap. 19.95 *(978-88-451-2911-7(X))* Fabbri Editori - RCS Libri ITA. Dist: Distribooks, Inc.

Awad, Shelley. The Greenhouse Kids: Dan Delion's Secret. Zonta, Rose, illus. 2009. 127p. (J). pap. *(978-0-88887-379-8(4))* Borealis Pr.

Award Staff & Award, Anna. Desert Adventure. 2015. (ENG., Illus.). 32p. (J). pap. 9.99 *(978-1-78270-018-0(8))* Award Pubns. Ltd. GBR. Dist: Parkwest Pubns., Inc.

—The Journey Begins. 2015. (ENG., Illus.). 32p. (J). pap. 9.99 *(978-1-78270-017-3(X))* Award Pubns. Ltd. GBR. Dist: Parkwest Pubns., Inc.

—Meerkat Mayhem. 2015. (ENG., Illus.). 32p. (J). pap. 9.99 *(978-1-78270-050-0(1))* Award Pubns. Ltd. GBR. Dist: Parkwest Pubns., Inc.

—The Search for the Rainbow Gem. 2015. (ENG., Illus.). 32p. (J). pap. 9.99 *(978-1-78270-051-7(X))* Award Pubns. Ltd. GBR. Dist: Parkwest Pubns., Inc.

Awdry, W. Story Time Collection. Courtney, Richard & Stubbs, Tommy, illus. 2014. (ENG.). 320p. (J). (gr. -1-2). 15.99 *(978-0-553-49678-9(6)*, Random Hse. Bks. for Young Readers) Random Hse. Children's Bks.

—Thomas' Big Book of Beginner Books. Random House Staff, illus. 2013. (Beginner Books Ser.). (ENG.). 224p. (J). (gr. -1-1). 16.99 *(978-0-449-81643-1(5)*, Random Hse. Bks. for Young Readers) Random Hse. Children's Bks.

Awdry, Wilbert V. Day of the Diesels. Golden Books Staff, illus. 2012. (Little Golden Book Ser.). (ENG.). 24p. (J). (gr. k-k). 4.99 *(978-0-307-92989-1(2)*, Golden Bks.) Random Hse. Children's Bks.

—Full Steam Ahead! Golden Books, illus. 2012. (Color Plus Tattoos Ser.). (ENG.). 48p. (J). (gr. -1-2). pap. 3.99 *(978-0-307-93120-7(X)*, Golden Bks.) Random Hse. Children's Bks.

—The Lost Crown of Sodor. Random House Staff, illus. 2013. (Pictureback Ser.). (ENG.). 24p. (J). (gr. -1-2). 3.99 *(978-0-449-81533-5(1)*, Random Hse. Bks. for Young Readers) Random Hse. Children's Bks.

—Risky Rails! (Thomas & Friends) Random House Staff, illus. 2012. (Pictureback(R) Ser.). (ENG.). 24p. (J). (gr. -1-2). pap. 3.99 *(978-0-307-97674-1(2)*, Random Hse. Bks. for Young Readers) Random Hse. Children's Bks.

—The Secret of the Mine. Durk, Jim, illus. 2013. (Glow-In-the-Dark Sticker Book Ser.). (ENG.). 48p. (J). (gr. -1-2). pap. 3.99 *(978-0-449-81711-7(3)*, Golden Bks.) Random Hse. Children's Bks.

Awdry, Wilbert Were. The Missing Christmas Tree. Stubbs, Tommy, illus. 2013. (Glitter Board Book Ser.). (ENG.). 12p. (J). (— 1). bds. 6.99 *(978-0-449-81713-1(X)*, Golden Bks.) Random Hse. Children's Bks.

Ayasta, Ayasta. Star. 2007. 117p. pap. 17.96 *(978-1-4303-1809-5(0))* Lulu Pr., Inc.

Ayder, Earl. The Longest Shortcut. McGrellis, Cynthia, illus. 2005. 40p. pap. 8.53 *(978-0-7578-9857-0(2))* Rigby Education.

Ayers, Sanda. Tommy Tractor Goes to the City, 1 vol. Young, Sue, illus. 2009. 29p. pap. 19.95 *(978-1-61582-054-2(X))* PublishAmerica, Inc.

Ayton, Shalanna. The Adventures of Missy the Moose. 2009. 68p. pap. 26.99 *(978-1-4389-7827-7(8))* AuthorHouse.

Azevedo, Eric. Why Is Blue Bear So Blue? The Adventures of Blue Bear. 2012. 28p. pap. 16.95 *(978-1-4582-0674-9(2)*, Abbott Pr.) Author Solutions, Inc.

Aziz, Khalif. The Magikh Series: The Black Phoenix Book 1. 2012. 140p. 30.99 *(978-1-4771-2780-3(1))* Xlibris Corp.

Azzopardi, Jeannie. Maricio & the Magic Suitcase. l.t. ed. 2004. (Illus.). 93p. (J). per. 14.00 incl. cd-rom *(978-0-9744391-3-6(4)*, MAR-BKCD-1st, Once Upon A Time in a Classroom) Interactive Media Publishing.

B&H Kids Editorial Staff. Ambushed by the Ambassador of Ignorance/Wiping Out the Whiner Brothers, Flip-Over Book. 2017. (Bibleman Ser.). (ENG.). 32p. (J). (gr. -1-2). pap. 3.99 *(978-1-4336-4941-7(1)*, B&H Kids) B&H Publishing Group.

—Braving the Big Battle with the Baroness / Repelling the Ronin of Wrong, Flip-Over Book. 2016. (Bibleman Ser.). (ENG., Illus.). 32p. (J). (gr. -1-2). pap. 3.99 *(978-1-4336-4573-0(4)*, B&H Kids) B&H Publishing Group.

—Dr. Fear's Almost Perfectly Disastrous Day / Clobbering the Crusher, Flip-Over Book. 2016. (Bibleman Ser.). (ENG., Illus.). 32p. (J). (gr. -1-2). pap. 3.99 *(978-1-4336-4574-7(2)*, B&H Kids) B&H Publishing Group.

—Melting the Master of Mean / the Mayor of Maybe Doles Out Doubt, Flip-Over Book. 2016. (Bibleman Ser.). (ENG., Illus.). 32p. (J). (gr. -1-2). pap. 3.99 *(978-1-4336-4575-4(0)*, B&H Kids) B&H Publishing Group.

—Putting on the Full Armor of God: A Battle Plan Based on Ephesians 6. 2016. (Bibleman Ser.). (ENG., Illus.). 24p. (J). (gr. -1-2). pap. 5.99 *(978-1-4336-4577-8(7)*, B&H Kids) B&H Publishing Group.

Babb, Gina. Zain & Zoe's Zoo Adventures: Numbers & Colors. 2011. 16p. 9.36 *(978-1-4520-5578-7(5))* AuthorHouse.

Babbitt, Natalie. Tuck Everlasting. 2008. (J). 39.99 *(978-0-7393-7111-4(8))* Findaway World, LLC.

Babcock, Lee L. Ghost of Sunday Creek. 2006. (Illus.). 104p. per. 13.95 *(978-1-4251-0162-6(3))* Trafford Publishing.

Babcock, Nona Burroughs. Little Wolf's Adventure: A Medicine Dream & Warrior Ghosts. 2008. 212p. 24.95 *(978-0-595-49087-5(5))*; pap. 14.95 *(978-0-595-46072-4(0))* iUniverse, Inc.

Babinsky, Joseph. The Magical Dream Forest. 2008. 164p. pap. 15.95 *(978-1-4116-3517-3(5))* Lulu Pr., Inc.

Baccalario, P. D. Suitcase of Stars, 1 vol. Bruno, Iacopo, illus. 2014. (Enchanted Emporium Ser.). (ENG.). 240p. (gr. 4-8). pap. 9.25 *(978-1-4342-6519-7(6))* Stone Arch Bks.

—Suitcase of Stars, 1 vol. Perrigotti, Chiara, tr. from ITA. Bruno, Iacopo, illus. 2014. (Enchanted Emporium Ser.). (ENG.). 240p. (gr. 4-8). 26.65 *(978-1-4342-6516-6(1))* Stone Arch Bks.

Baccalario, Pierdomenico. Century #3: City of Wind. Janeczko, Leah D., tr. from ITA. 2012. (Century Ser.: 3). (ENG., Illus.). 336p. (J). (gr. 5-8). 8.99 *(978-0-375-85797-3(4)*, Yearling) Random Hse. Children's Bks.

—Compass of Dreams, 1 vol. Perrigotti, Chiara, tr. from ITA. Bruno, Iacopo, illus. 2014. (Enchanted Emporium Ser.). (ENG.). 240p. (gr. 4-8). 26.65 *(978-1-4342-6517-3(X))* Stone Arch Bks.

—Dragon of Seas. Janeczko, Leah D., tr. from ITA. 2013. (Century Ser.: 4). (ENG.). 320p. (J). (gr. 3-7). 7.99 *(978-0-375-85798-0(2)*, Yearling) Random Hse. Children's Bks.

—Map of the Passages. McGuinness, Nanette, tr. from ITA. Bruno, Iacopo, illus. 2015. (Enchanted Emporium Ser.). (ENG.). 240p. (gr. 4-8). 12.95 *(978-1-62370-204-5(6))* Stone Arch Bks.

—Suitcase of Stars, 1 vol. Bruno, Iacopo, illus. 2014. (Enchanted Emporium Ser.). (ENG.). 240p. (gr. 4-8). 12.95 *(978-1-62370-039-3(6))* Capstone Young Readers of Coughlan Cos.

Baccalario, Pierdomenico & McGuinness, Nanette. The Thief of Mirrors. Perrigotti, Chiara, tr. from ITA. Bruno, Iacopo, illus. 2015. (Enchanted Emporium Ser.). (ENG.). 240p. (gr. 4-8). lib. bdg. 26.65 *(978-1-4965-0516-3(6))* Stone Arch Bks.

Baccellia, Kim. No More Goddesses. 2013. (ENG.). 252p. (YA). (gr. 3-7). pap. 14.99 *(978-1-61271-012-9(3)*, Zumaya Thresholds) Zumaya Pubns. LLC.

Bach, Shelby. Of Enemies & Endings. 2015. (Ever Afters Ser.: 4). (ENG., Illus.). 400p. (J). (gr. 3-7). 16.99 *(978-1-4424-9787-0(4)*, Simon & Schuster Bks. For Young Readers) Simon & Schuster Bks. For Young Readers.

—Of Giants & Ice. Loftis, Cory, illus. 2013. (Ever Afters Ser.: 1). (ENG.). 368p. (J). (gr. 3-7). pap. 7.99 *(978-1-4424-3147-8(4)*, Simon & Schuster Bks. For Young Readers) Simon & Schuster Bks. For Young Readers.

—Of Giants & Ice. 2012. (Ever Afters Ser.: 1). (ENG., Illus.). 352p. (J). (gr. 3-7). 15.99 *(978-1-4424-3146-1(6)*, Simon & Schuster Bks. For Young Readers) Simon & Schuster Bks. For Young Readers.

—Of Sorcery & Snow. 2015. (Ever Afters Ser.: 3). (ENG., Illus.). 352p. (J). (gr. 3-7). pap. 8.99 *(978-1-4424-9785-6(8)*, Simon & Schuster Bks. For Young Readers) Simon & Schuster Bks. For Young Readers.

—Of Witches & Wind. (Ever Afters Ser.: 2). (ENG., Illus.). (J). (gr. 3-7). 2014. 416p. pap. 8.99 *(978-1-4424-3150-8(4))* 2013. 400p. 15.99 *(978-1-4424-3149-2(0))* Simon & Schuster Bks. For Young Readers. (Simon & Schuster Bks. For Young Readers).

Bachalo, Chris, illus. Ultimate War, 6 vols., Vol. 5. 2006. (ENG.). 112p. (YA). (gr. 8-17). pap. 10.99 *(978-0-7851-1129-0(8))* Marvel Worldwide, Inc.

Bachmann, Stefan. The Whatnot. 2013. (Peculiar Ser.: 2). (ENG.). 432p. (J). (gr. 3-7). 16.99 *(978-0-06-219521-0(2)*, Greenwillow Bks.) HarperCollins Pubs.

Bachmann, Stefan, et al. The Cabinet of Curiosities: 36 Tales Brief & Sinister. Jansson, Alexander, illus. 2014. (ENG.). 496p. (J). (gr. 3-7). 16.99 *(978-0-06-233105-2(1))*; pap. 6.99 *(978-0-06-231314-0(2))* HarperCollins Pubs. (Greenwillow Bks.).

Backshall, Steve. Shark Seas: Action, Danger, Adventure. 2016. (Falcon Chronicles Ser.). (ENG.). 224p. (J). (gr. 4-6). 7.99 *(978-1-4440-1090-9(5)*, Orion Children's Bks.) Hachette Children's Group GBR. Dist: Hachette Bk. Group.

Bacon, Lee. Legendtopia Book #2: the Shadow Queen. 2017. (Legendtopia Ser.: 2). (ENG.). 272p. (J). (gr. 4-7). 16.99 ***(978-0-553-53406-1(8)***, Delacorte Bks. for Young Readers) Random Hse. Children's Bks.

Bacon, Lee. The Nameless Hero. 2014. (Joshua Dread Ser.: 2). (ENG., Illus.). 304p. (J). (gr. 4-7). 7.99 *(978-0-307-92997-6(3)*, Yearling) Random Hse. Children's Bks.

Baczynski, Jolanta & Baczynski, Olga. Freddie & Jet. 2013. 36p. pap. *(978-0-9918166-4-4(1))* Flower Pr.

Badeaux, Dewey. Sam & Skully. Ball, Lauren, illus. 2013. 126p. pap. 12.99 *(978-0-9884057-4-5(1))* Alligator Pr.

Bader, Arlys Elaine. The Adventures of Garth & Cloey. 2008. 40p. pap. 16.99 *(978-1-4389-2472-4(0))* AuthorHouse.

Badescu, Ramona. Pomelo's Big Adventure. Chaud, Benjamin, illus. 2014. (Pomelo the Garden Elephant Ser.). (ENG.). 40p. (J). (gr. -1-3). 17.95 *(978-1-59270-158-2(2))* Enchanted Lion Bks., LLC.

Badu. Learning with the Flowerrrs: Vol. -1 Hospital Visit. 2011. 40p. pap. 21.67 *(978-1-4634-1878-6(7))* AuthorHouse.

Bagdanov, Patricia. The Adventures of Charlie & a Dragon Named Trevor. 2013. 26p. pap. 16.95 *(978-1-63004-985-0(9))* PublishAmerica, Inc.

Bagley, Conor. Ziggy McFinster's Nantucket Adventure. Bernard Westcott, Nadine, illus. 2008. (ENG.). 40p. (J). (gr. -1-3). 16.95 *(978-1-56625-315-4(2))* Bonus Bks., Inc.

Bagley, Mark, illus. Public Scrutiny, 5, Vol. 5. 2007. (ENG.). 120p. (J). (gr. 4-17). pap. 11.99 *(978-0-7851-1087-3(9))* Marvel Worldwide, Inc.

Bailey, Carolyn Sherwin. Stories of Great Adventures. Burd, Clara M., illus. 2005. reprint ed. pap. 24.95 *(978-1-4179-0215-6(9))* Kessinger Publishing, LLC.

—Tell Me Another Story: The Book of Story Programs. 2007. (ENG.). 248p. pap. 20.99 *(978-1-4346-3278-4(4))* Creative Media Partners, LLC.

Bailey, Ethel M. T. Lily Pond Village, 1 vol. 2009. 57p. pap. 16.95 *(978-1-60703-379-0(8))* America Star Bks.

Bailey, Kristin. The Silver Gate. 2017. 320p. (J). (gr. 3-7). 16.99 *(978-0-06-239857-4(1)*, Tegen, Katherine Bks) HarperCollins Pubs.

Bailey, Linda. Seven Dead Pirates. 2015. (ENG., Illus.). 300p. (J). (gr. 3-7). 16.99 *(978-1-77049-815-0(X)*, Tundra Bks.) Tundra Bks. CAN. Dist: Penguin Random Hse. LLC.

Bailey, Margaret A. Dragonworld & the Room of Strange Hangings. 2009. 172p. pap. 11.99 *(978-1-4389-8252-6(6))* AuthorHouse.

Bailey, Mary. Vhan Zeely & the Time Prevaricators. 2009. 192p. 25.50 *(978-1-60693-477-7(5)*, Eloquent Bks.) Strategic Book Publishing & Rights Agency (SBPRA).

Bailey, Patricia. The Tragically True Adventures of Kit Donovan. 2017. (ENG.). 304p. (J). (gr. 3-7). 16.99 ***(978-0-8075-8143-8(7))*** Whitman, Albert & Co.

Bailey, Vicki. Catland Adventures. 2009. 32p. pap. 9.96 *(978-0-557-06543-1(7))* Lulu Pr., Inc.

Bailie, Helen. The Azura Stones. 2007. 212p. (YA). per. 18.00 *(978-1-58982-374-7(5)*, Bedside Bks.) American Bk. Publishing Group.

Baillie, Allan. DragonQuest. Harris, Wayne, illus. 2013. (ENG.). 40p. (J). (gr. k-4). 16.99 *(978-0-7636-6617-0(3))* Candlewick Pr.

Bain, Michelle. The Adventures of Thumbs up Johnnie Banker Bill's Guide to Common Cents: Banker Bill's Guide to Common Cents. Lizana, Lorenzo, illus. 2007. (J). 14.95 *(978-0-9761421-9-5(8))* Pixie Stuff LLC.

—The Adventures of Thumbs up Johnnie Jimmy Jam Germ & the Happy Handshake: Jimmy Jam Germ & the Happy Handshake Version 2. Lizana, Lorenzo, illus. 2007. (J). 14.95 *(978-0-9761421-7-1(1))* Pixie Stuff LLC.

—The Adventures of Thumbs up Johnnie Johnnie Finds A Buddy: Johnnie Finds A Buddy Color Version 2. Lizana, Lorenzo, illus. 2007. (J). 14.95 *(978-0-9761421-6-4(3))* Pixie Stuff LLC.

—The Adventures of Thumbs up Johnnie Johnnie's Missing Boot! Johnnie's Missing Boot! Lizana, Lorenzo, illus. 2007. (J). 14.95 *(978-0-9761421-8-8(X))* Pixie Stuff LLC.

—The Adventures of Thumbs up Johnnie Reading Heart to Heart Thumbs up Johnnie, Little Digit & the Special Delivery: Reading Heart to Heart, Coloring & Activity Book. 2006. (Illus.). (J). pap. 7.95 *(978-0-9795832-5-4(X))* Pixie Stuff LLC.

—The Adventures of Thumbs up Johnnie Rules of Thumb for Going Green: Rules of Thumb for Going Green. Lizana, Lorenzo, illus. 2008. 18p. (J). pap. 5.95 *(978-0-9795832-4-7(1))* Pixie Stuff LLC.

—The Adventures of Thumbs up Johnnie Thumbs up to Red, White & Blue! Thumbs up to Red, White & Blue! Lizana, Lorenzo, illus. 2007. 48p. (J). 14.95 *(978-0-9795832-2-3(5))* Pixie Stuff LLC.

—Las aventuras de Juanito el Pulgarcito Juanito encuentra un Compañerito: Juanito encuentra un Compañerito. Lizana, Lorenzo, illus. 2006.Tr. of Johnnie Finds a Buddy. (SPA.). (J). 16.95 *(978-0-9761421-4-0(7))* Pixie Stuff LLC.

—Las aventuras de Juanito el Pulgarcito Zipp, Pequeño Dígito, las señales y las Señas: Zipp, Pequeño Dígito, las señales y las Señas. Lizana, Lorenzo, illus. 2007.Tr. of Zipp, Digit & the Happy Signs! (SPA.). 28p. (J). *(978-0-9795832-3-0(3))* Pixie Stuff LLC.

Baird, Jeri. Tokens & Omens. 2016. (Tokens & Omens Ser.). (ENG.). 284p. (YA). (gr. 8). pap. 16.99 *(978-1-63163-082-8(2)*, Jolly Fish Pr.) North Star Editions.

Baird Wireman, Ginger. If Wishes Had Wings: A Fall Flight of Fancy. 2009. 40p. pap. 16.99 *(978-1-4490-0262-6(5))* AuthorHouse.

Baity, Cameron & Zelkowicz, Benny. The Foundry's Edg. Foster, John, illus. 2014. (Books of Ore Ser.). (ENG.). 448p. (J). (gr. 3-7). 16.99 *(978-1-4231-6227-8(7))* Hyperion Bks. for Children.

—The Second Book of Ore Waybound. 2016. (Books of Ore Ser.). (ENG.). 368p. (J). (gr. 5-9). 16.99 *(978-1-4231-6239-1(0))* Hyperion Bks. for Children.

Bakare, Rebecca. Short Stories by Rebecc. 2012. 54p. pap. 20.00 *(978-1-937911-26-3(8))* Heavenly Realm Publishing.

Baker, Bill. The Butterfly. RUZICKA, Carol, illus. 2012. 46p. pap. 15.00 *(978-0-9859132-0-5(7))* Asbury Heritage Publishing.

Baker, Deirdre. Becca at Sea, 1 vol. 2007. (ENG.). 168p. (J). (gr. 3-7). 16.95 *(978-0-88899-737-1(X))* Groundwood Bks. CAN. Dist: Publishers Group West (PGW).

Baker, E. D. Princess Between Worlds: A Tale of the Wide-Awake Princess. 2017. (Wide-Awake Princess Ser.). (ENG.). 240p. (J). pap. 8.99 *(978-1-68119-279-6(9)*, 9781681192796, Bloomsbury USA Childrens) Bloomsbury Publishing USA.

Baker, Jennifer. The Lying Game. 2014. (ENG., Illus.). 192p. (YA). (gr. 7). pap. 13.99 *(978-1-4814-2878-1(0)*, Simon Pulse) Simon Pulse.

Baker, Kage. The Hotel under the Sand. Law, Stephanie Pui-Mun, illus. 2009. (ENG.). 179p. (J). (gr. 2-7). pap. *(978-1-892391-89-6(9))* Temmen, Edition, Horst Temmen.

Baker, Willard F. The Boy Ranchers among the Indians. 2007. 180p. 25.96 *(978-1-4218-3920-2(2)*, 1st World Library - Literary Society) 1st World Publishing, Inc.

—The Boy Ranchers among the Indians: Or- Trailing the Yaquis. 2007. (ENG.). 140p. pap. 18.99 *(978-1-4346-3478-8(7))*; 154p. pap. 21.99 *(978-1-4346-3479-5(5))* Creative Media Partners, LLC.

Bakewell, Lori. Savannah Adventure: Pirate's Treasure. 2007. 173p. (J). pap. 12.95 *(978-0-9799473-9-1(1))* Tailwind Press.

Bakshi, Kelly. Myth-Busting Columbus. 2012. 24p. 18.95 *(978-1-61633-316-4(2))*; pap. 10.95 *(978-1-61633-317-1(0))* Guardian Angel Publishing, Inc.

Balasubramanian, Lalitha. The Twins at the Ancient Villa, 1 vol. 2009. 48p. pap. 16.95 *(978-1-61582-601-8(7))* America Star Bks.

Baldacci, David. The Finisher. (ENG.). 512p. (J). (gr. 5-9). 2015. (Vega Jane Ser.: Bk. 1). mass mkt. 7.99 *(978-0-545-88854-7(9))* 2015. (Vega Jane Ser.: 1). pap. 9.99 *(978-0-545-65226-1(X))* 2014. 17.99 *(978-0-545-65220-9(0))* Scholastic, Inc. (Scholastic Pr.).

—The Finisher. 2015. (Vega Jane Ser.: 1). lib. bdg. 20.85 *(978-0-606-36740-0(3))* Turtleback Bks.

—The Keeper. 2016. (Vega Jane Ser.: 2). (ENG.). 448p. (J). (gr. 4-7). pap. 9.99 *(978-0-545-83195-6(4))* 2015. (Vega Jane Ser.: 2). (ENG.). 448p. (J). (gr. 5-9). 17.99 *(978-0-545-83194-9(6))* 2015. 428p. (YA). *(978-0-545-88230-9(3))* Scholastic, Inc. (Scholastic Pr.).

—The Keeper. 2016. (Vega Jane Ser.: 2). (ENG.). 428p. (J). (gr. 5-9). 20.85 *(978-0-606-39127-6(4))* Turtleback Bks.

—The Keeper (Vega Jane, Book 2) 2017. (Vega Jane Ser.: 2). (ENG.). 464p. (J). (gr. 4-7). pap. 7.99 *(978-1-338-05360-9(4))* Scholastic, Inc.

—The Width of the World. 2017. (Vega Jane Ser.: 3). (ENG.). 448p. (J). (gr. 5-9). 17.99 *(978-0-545-83196-3(2)*, Scholastic Pr.) Scholastic, Inc.

Baldwin., C. R. Henry the Spider. 2011. (Illus.). 44p. pap. 16.76 *(978-1-4567-8649-6(0))* AuthorHouse.

Baldwin, J. R. The Magic Jammies, 1 vol. 2010. 24p. 24.95 *(978-1-4512-9442-2(5))* PublishAmerica, Inc.

Baldwin, James. The Story of Roland. 2013. pap. 31.93 *(978-1-4400-6789-1(9))* Forgotten Bks.

Baldwin, Kathleen. A School for Unusual Girls: A Stranje House Novel. 2016. (Stranje House Ser.: 1). (ENG.). 352p. (YA). pap. 9.99 *(978-0-7653-7601-5(6)*, 9780765376015, Tor Teen) Doherty, Tom Assocs., LLC.

Baldwin, Kevin. Beetle Dan & the Big Purple Slide: A Beetle Dan Story. 2006. (Beetle Dan Story Ser.). (ENG., Illus.). 32p. (J). (gr. -1-2). 14.99 *(978-1-59185-921-5(2)*, Creation Hse.) Charisma Media.

Ball, Georgia & Disney Editors. Disney Frozen Comics Collection. 2016. (ENG.). 96p. (J). (gr. 4-7). 20.85 *(978-0-606-39075-0(8))* Turtleback Bks.

Ball, Nate. Blast Off! 2014. (Alien in My Pocket Ser.: 1). (J). lib. bdg. 14.75 *(978-0-606-35181-2(7))* Turtleback Bks.

Ball Sr., Frank J. Bryanna Global Warrior: Attack of the Alaska Aerial Wolf Hunters, 1 vol. Pelton, Bonnie L., illus. 2009. 23p. pap. 24.95 *(978-1-61582-587-5(8))* America Star Bks.

Balla, Trace. Rockhopping. 2016. (ENG., Illus.). 80p. (J). (gr. 3-6). 18.99 *(978-1-76011-234-9(8))* Allen & Unwin AUS. Dist: Independent Pubs. Group.

Ballantyne, R. The Coral Island. 2006. 168p. 29.95 *(978-1-55742-673-4(2))*; pap. 14.95 *(978-1-55742-666-6(X))* Wildside Pr., LLC.

Ballantyne, R. M. The Battle & the Breeze. 2004. reprint ed. pap. 15.95 *(978-1-4191-5365-5(X))*; pap. 1.99 *(978-1-4192-5365-2(4))* Kessinger Publishing, LLC.

—Blown to Bits; or, the Lonely Man of Rak. 2006. pap. *(978-1-4065-0515-3(3))* Dodo Pr.

—The Coral Island. 2014. (ENG.). 368p. (J). (gr. 4-7). pap. 14.99 *(978-1-84391-481-5(6))* Hesperus Pr. GBR. Dist: Independent Pubs. Group.

—The Crew of the Water Wagtail. 2011. 146p. pap. 12.95 *(978-1-60664-550-5(1))* Rodgers, Alan Bks.

—The Dog Crusoe. 2006. (Illus.). pap. *(978-1-4065-0529-0(3))* Dodo Pr.

—Fort Desolation. 2004. reprint ed. pap. 15.95 *(978-1-4191-2037-4(9))*; pap. 1.99 *(978-1-4192-2037-1(3))* Kessinger Publishing, LLC.

—Gascoyne, the Sandal-Wood Trader. 2006. pap. *(978-1-4065-0530-6(7))* Dodo Pr.

—The Lighthouse. 2006. pap. *(978-1-4065-0531-3(5))* Dodo Pr.

—The Lighthouse. l.t. ed. 2006. 504p. pap. *(978-1-84702-270-7(7))* Echo Library.

—The Norsemen in the West or America Before Columbus. 2004. reprint ed. pap. 1.99 *(978-1-4192-7571-5(2))* Kessinger Publishing, LLC.

—Red Rooney: Or, the Last of the Crew. 2007. (R. M. Ballantyne Collection). (Illus.). 408p. 22.00 *(978-1-934554-08-1(1))* Vision Forum, Inc., The.

—Saved by the Lifeboat. 2004. reprint ed. pap. 15.95 *(978-1-4191-4624-4(6))*; pap. 1.99 *(978-1-4192-4624-1(0))* Kessinger Publishing, LLC.

—The World of Ice. 2006. (Illus.). pap. *(978-1-4065-0533-7(1))* Dodo Pr.

Ballantyne, Robert Michael. The Battery & the Boiler: Adventures in Laying of Submarine Electric Cables. 2007. 254p. pap. 21.99 *(978-1-4346-3754-3(9))*; (ENG.). 282p. pap. 23.99 *(978-1-4346-3768-0(9))* Creative Media Partners, LLC.

—The Coxswain's Bride: Also Jack Frost & Sons; & A Double Rescue. 2007. (ENG.). 146p. pap. 18.99 *(978-1-4346-3664-5(X))*; 164p. pap. 21.99 *(978-1-4346-3712-3(3))* Creative Media Partners, LLC.

—The Crew of the Water Wagtail. 2007. (ENG.). 174p. pap. 19.99 *(978-1-4346-3665-2(8))*; 188p. pap. 21.99 *(978-1-4346-3713-0(1))* Creative Media Partners, LLC.

—The Garret & the Garden. 2007. (ENG.). 98p. pap. 16.99 *(978-1-4346-3670-6(4))*; 106p. pap. 19.99 *(978-1-4346-3718-5(2))* Creative Media Partners, LLC.

—Red Rooney: The Last of the Crew. 2007. (ENG.). 270p. pap. 21.99 *(978-1-4346-3693-5(3))*; 302p. pap. 24.99 *(978-1-4346-3741-3(7))* Creative Media Partners, LLC.

—The Rover of the Andes: A Tale of Adventure in South America. 2007. (ENG.). 266p. pap. 21.99 *(978-1-4346-3753-6(0))*; 296p. pap. 23.99 *(978-1-4346-3767-3(0))* Creative Media Partners, LLC.

Ballard, George Anne. Read to Me! James, Melody A. & Arelys, Aguilar, illus. 2013. 60p. pap. 10.00 *(978-0-9855312-8-7(2))* Bolton Publishing LLC.

Ballard, John. The Shining Thing, 1 vol. Hume, Jeff, illus. 2009. 35p. pap. 19.95 *(978-1-61546-655-9(X))* PublishAmerica, Inc.

Ballard, Lisa. A Moose for Mackenzie. Doucette, Constance, illus. 2008. 32p. pap. 24.95 *(978-1-60610-123-0(4))* America Star Bks.

Balletta, Janet. The Legend of the Colombian Mermaid. Mejía, Estella, illus. 2013. 36p. (J). pap. 14.95 *(978-0-9856762-9-2(9))* WRB Pub.

Balliett, Blue. The Danger Box. 2010. (ENG.). 320p. (J). (gr. 4-18). 16.99 *(978-0-439-85209-8(9)*, Scholastic Pr.) Scholastic, Inc.

Balloon Dude Travis. A Twisted Adventure in Twisty Town. 2011. 32p. pap. 12.95 *(978-1-935268-80-2(5))* Halo Publishing International.

Balsamello, Melissa. Happy's Adventure at Se: Starring... Happy the Hotdog Dog. 2011. 28p. pap. 15.00 *(978-1-4634-0821-3(8))* AuthorHouse.

Baltazar, Art & Aureliani, Franco. Aw Yeah Comics! and. . Action!, Vol. 1. Baltazar, Art, illus. 2014. (ENG., Illus.). 152p. (J). (gr. 3-7). pap. 12.99 *(978-1-61655-558-0(0))* Dark Horse Comics.

—Patrick Vol. 4: Wolf Boy. 2008. (Patrick the Wolf Boy Ser.). (Illus.). 144p. pap. 12.99 *(978-1-932796-83-4(5))* Devil's Due Publishing, Inc.

Baltz, Kimberly. Frieda Tails: Freida Goes to Town & Freida, Jack, & the Box. 2012. 28p. 24.99 *(978-1-4575-1294-0(7))*; pap. 13.95 *(978-1-4575-1291-9(2))* Dog Ear Publishing, LLC.

Bama. Lucy Ladybug's Backyard Adventure. 2012. (ENG., Illus.). 48p. 14.95 *(978-1-4697-3868-0(6)*, 2f8a90e6-2c3f-4026-aaad-d311543fc12a) iUniverse, Inc.

Bandy, Sheena. Magdlynn in Flames. 2008. 164p. pap. 19.95 *(978-1-4116-7780-7(3))* Lulu Pr., Inc.

Bank Street College. Sacajawea: the Jacabee Readers: The Adventures of Dooley, Abby & Baldy. 2012. (ENG.). 96p. (J). (gr. 1-3). pap. 9.95 *(978-1-59687-879-2(7)*, Milk & Cookies) ibooks, Inc.

Banks, Alex. Jump Boys: Sos. 2013. 200p. pap. *(978-0-9918599-6-2(0))* Novel Ninjutsu.

Banks, Angelica. Finding Serendipity. Lewis, Stevie, illus. 2015. (Tuesday Mcgillycuddy Adventures Ser.). (ENG.). 288p. (J). (gr. 3-7). 16.99 *(978-1-62779-154-0(X)*, 9781627791540, Holt, Henry & Co. Bks. For Young Readers) Holt, Henry & Co.

—Finding Serendipity. Lewis, Stevie, illus. 2016. (Tuesday Mcgillycuddy Adventures Ser.). (ENG.). 304p. (J). pap. 7.99 *(978-1-250-07337-2(5)*, 9781250073372) Square Fish.

—A Week Without Tuesday. Lewis, Stevie, illus. 2016. (Tuesday Mcgillycuddy Adventures Ser.). (ENG.). 384p. (J). 16.99 *(978-1-62779-155-7(8)*, 9781627791557, Holt, Henry & Co. Bks. For Young Readers) Holt, Henry & Co.

Banks, Kate. The Eraserheads. Kulikov, Boris, illus. 2010. (ENG.). 40p. (J). (gr. -1-3). 16.99 *(978-0-374-39920-7(4)*, 9780374399207, Farrar, Straus & Giroux (BYR)) Farrar, Straus & Giroux.

Banks, Lynne Reid. The Adventures of King Midas. 153p. (J). pap. 4.50 *(978-0-8072-1468-8(X)*, Listening Library) Random Hse. Audio Publishing Group.

—The Farthest-Away Mountain. 130p. (J). (gr. 3-5). pap. 4.50 *(978-0-8072-1499-2(X)*, Listening Library) Random Hse. Audio Publishing Group.

—Harry the Poisonous Centipede: A Story to Make You Squirm. 118p. (J). (gr. 1-3). pap. 4.50 *(978-0-8072-1523-4(6)*, Listening Library) Random Hse. Audio Publishing Group.

Banks, Melanee R. Bryana's Biggest Wish: Believe. Give. Imagine. Create. Hope. Love. 2012. 48p. pap. 21.99 *(978-1-4772-4472-2(7))* AuthorHouse.

Banks, Radine. Nochi Come Back. 2006. 112p. per. 12.20 *(978-1-4120-8803-9(8))* Trafford Publishing.

Banks, Robin Washington. Big Boy. Morgan, Vincent, illus. 2011. 20p. pap. 24.95 *(978-1-4560-7068-7(1))* PublishAmerica, Inc.

Banks, Steven. Love Potion. Sasic, Natasha, illus. 2005. (Adventures of Jimmy Neutron Ser.: 7). 24p. (J). lib. bdg. 15.00 *(978-1-59054-784-7(5))* Fitzgerald Bks.

Banks, Tom. The Great Galloon & the Pirate Queen. 2015. (Great Galloon Ser.). (ENG., Illus.). 192p. (J). (gr. 4-7). pap. 9.99 *(978-1-84812-450-9(3))* Bonnier Publishing GBR. Dist: Independent Pubs. Group.

Bannister, Bram. Rupert, the Alien & the Bank Robbery. 2007. 56p. per. 8.95 *(978-0-595-44839-5(9))* iUniverse, Inc.

Bapiraju Gandham. The Wizard of Ants. 2010. 88p. pap. 33.48 *(978-1-4269-1940-4(9))* Trafford Publishing.

Baptiste, Tracey. The Jumbies. 2016. (ENG.). 240p. (J). (gr. 3-7). pap. 6.95 *(978-1-61620-592-8(X))* Algonquin Bks. of Chapel Hill.

Baranda, Maria. Tulia y la Tecla Magica. Marin, Mary Rodriguez, illus. rev. ed. 2006. (Castillo de la Lectura, Serie Naranja). (SPA & ENG.). 160p. (J). (gr. 4-7). pap. 7.95 *(978-970-20-0177-5(3))* Castillo, Ediciones, S. A. de C. V. MEX. Dist: Macmillan.

Barandela, Jeremy. United We Stand. 2007. 376p. per. 20.95 *(978-1-4327-1495-6(3))* Outskirts Pr., Inc.

Baranello, Pat. The Adventures of Bible Buddy. 2004. pap. 15.00 *(978-0-8059-6568-1(8))* Dorrance Publishing Co., Inc.

Baratz-Logsted, Lauren. Annie's Adventures. Weber, Lisa K., illus. 2008. (Sisters Eight Ser.: 1). (ENG.). 144p. (J). (gr. 1-4). pap. 5.99 *(978-0-547-05338-7(X))* Houghton Mifflin Harcourt Publishing Co.

—Georgia's Greatness. 2009. (Sisters Eight Ser.: 3). (ENG., Illus.). 128p. (J). (gr. 1-4). pap. 5.99 *(978-0-547-05340-0(1))*;Bk. 3. 15.00 *(978-0-547-16699-5(0))* Houghton Mifflin Harcourt Publishing Co.

—Petal's Problems. 2010. (Sisters Eight Ser.: 6). (ENG., Illus.). 144p. (J). (gr. 1-4). pap. 5.99 *(978-0-547-33403-5(6))* Houghton Mifflin Harcourt Publishing Co.

Barba, Rick. The Secret of Stoneship Woods. Steccati, Eve, illus. 2006. (Spy Gear Adventures Ser.: 1). (ENG.). 160p. (J). (gr. 3-7). pap. 8.99 *(978-1-4169-0887-6(0)*, Simon & Schuster/Paula Wiseman Bks.) Simon & Schuster/Paula Wiseman Bks.

Barba, Rick & Gratz, Alan. The Assassination Game. 2012. (ENG.). 320p. (YA). (gr. 7). pap. 7.99 *(978-1-4424-2058-8(8)*, Simon Spotlight) Simon Spotlight.

Barba, Theresa. How Talia Met Tanner. 2012. 40p. pap. 20.99 *(978-1-4772-1617-0(0))* AuthorHouse.

Barbari, Nader. Eddy the Elephant. 2010. 32p. pap. 13.99 *(978-1-4490-9430-0(9))* AuthorHouse.

Barbauld, Anna. Little Stories for Children; Being Easy. 2004. reprint ed. pap. 20.95 *(978-0-7661-9037-5(4))* Kessinger Publishing, LLC.

Barbieri, Sandra Birriel. Cristal & the Secret of the Enchanted Forest: Cristal y el Secreto Del Bosque Encantado. 2013. 64p. pap. 23.99 *(978-1-4525-6512-5(0))* Balboa Pr.

Barbo, Maria S. The Rescue Mission. 2016. (Pokemon Reader Ser.: 1). lib. bdg. 13.55 ***(978-0-606-39736-0(1))*** Turtleback Bks.

—Welcome to Alola! 2017. (Pokémon Ser.). (ENG.). 32p. (J). (gr. -1-3). pap. 3.99 ***(978-1-338-14864-0(8))*** Scholastic, Inc.

Barbo, Theresa Mitchell & Webster, W. Russell. The Daring Coast Guard Rescue of the Pendleton Crew. Marshall, Julia, illus. 2013. Orig. Title: The Daring Coast Guard Rescue of the Pendleton Crew. (ENG.). 128p. (J). (gr. 4-7). 14.99 *(978-1-62619-095-5(X)*, History Pr., The) Arcadia Publishing.

Barbour, Ralph Henry. The Adventure Club Afloat. 2006. (Illus.). pap. *(978-1-4065-0774-4(1))* Dodo Pr.

Barchers, Suzanne. The Adventures of Tom Sawyer. rev. ed. 2015. (Great Works). (ENG., Illus.). 72p. (gr. 4-8). pap. 9.99 *(978-1-4258-8973-9(5))* Shell Educational Publishing.

Barclay. Chipmunk Joe Takes a Nap. 2009. 48p. pap. 11.50 *(978-1-60860-445-6(4)*, Eloquent Bks.) Strategic Book Publishing & Rights Agency (SBPRA).

Bardham-Quallen, Sudipta. The Fire Falls. Random House Disney Staff & Gurihiru Staff, illus. 2016. (Stepping Stone Book(TM) Ser.). (ENG.). 128p. (J). (gr. 1-4). 9.99 *(978-0-7364-3291-7(4)*, RH/Disney) Random Hse. Children's Bks.

Bardhan-Quallen, Sudipta. The Fire Falls. Random House Disney Staff & Gurihiru, illus. 2016. (Stepping Stone Book(TM) Ser.). (ENG.). 128p. (J). (gr. 1-4). lib. bdg. 12.99 *(978-0-7364-8249-3(0)*, RH/Disney) Random Hse. Children's Bks.

—The Pirate Princess. McElmurry, Jill, illus. 2012. (ENG.). 40p. (J). (gr. -1-3). 17.99 *(978-0-06-114242-0(5))* HarperCollins Pubs.

Bardwell, Harrison. The Airplane Girls & the Mystery of Seal Islands. 2003. (ENG.). 223p. (J). pap. 13.95 *(978-1-55753-337-1(7)*, cb32f1de-2660-4a6d-a577-d92ff5815b0e) Purdue Univ. Pr.

—Airplane Girls & the Mystery Ship. 2003. (ENG.). 214p. (J). pap. 13.95 *(978-1-55753-338-8(5)*, 6a53b46d-5f0d-48db-85cf-08cacca98bdd) Purdue Univ. Pr.

—The Lurtiss Field Mystery. 2003. (ENG.). 248p. (J). pap. 13.95 *(978-1-55753-336-4(9)*, 70223fe0-55b5-4180-81b6-539028c63301) Purdue Univ. Pr.

—Roberta's Flying Courage. 2003. (ENG.). 248p. pap. 13.95 *(978-1-55753-335-7(0)*, 9e38e2dc-8c18-49c1-8447-1205f9e2b108) Purdue Univ. Pr.

Barham, Lisa. Project Paris. Rim, Sujean, illus. 2007. (Fashion-Forward Adventures of Imogene Ser.). (ENG.). 224p. (YA). (gr. 7-12). pap. 10.99 *(978-1-4169-1444-0(7)*, Simon Pulse) Simon Pulse.

Barham, Paul Richard. The Adventures of Damen the Duck. 2012. 72p. pap. 41.99 *(978-1-4691-5476-3(5))* Xlibris Corp.

Barham, Timothy E. Blonds Blending: The Adventures of Suzy Q & You Too. Barham, Timothy E., illus. 2011. (Illus.). 20p. pap. 24.95 *(978-1-4626-4458-2(9))* America Star Bks.

Barickman, Traci. Cooper's Adventures: Facing Our Fears. 2010. 24p. 11.49 *(978-1-4520-0326-9(2))* AuthorHouse.

Barker, Mary Ann. A Circus Day Adventure for Emma & Jake. 2012. 28p. pap. 18.65 *(978-1-4771-2849-7(2))* Xlibris Corp.

Barkley, Roger C. Johnny Grasshopper. 2006. 52p. pap. 16.95 *(978-1-4241-0221-1(9))* PublishAmerica, Inc.

Barks, Carl, et al. Walt Disney's Vacation Parade Volume 5. Clark, John, ed. 2008. (ENG., Illus.). 80p. pap. 9.95 *(978-1-60360-031-6(0)*, 9781603600316) Gemstone Publishing, Inc.

—Walt Disney's Vacation Parade Volume 6. 2009. 80p. pap. 9.99 *(978-1-60360-096-5(5))* Gemstone Publishing, Inc.

Barlau, Martin. Lenny Was a Leaf: Learning about Life. 2013. 38p. pap. 16.95 *(978-1-4908-1150-5(8)*, WestBow Pr.) Author Solutions, Inc.

Barlone, M. J. A Mouse & Rabbits Tale. 2010. (Illus.). 40p. pap. 16.99 *(978-1-4490-7771-6(4))* AuthorHouse.

Barnard, Irita. Screech Becomes a Hero. 2012. (Illus.). 32p. pap. 16.95 *(978-1-4497-6554-5(8)*, WestBow Pr.) Author Solutions, Inc.

Barnes, Jennifer Lynn. Every Other Day. 2011. (ENG.). 352p. (gr. 7). 17.99 *(978-1-60684-169-3(6))* Lerner Publishing Group.

—Nobody. 2014. (ENG.). 400p. (J). (gr. 7). pap. 9.99 *(978-1-60684-508-0(X)*, Carolrhoda Lab™) Lerner Publishing Group.

Barnes, John L. C. Clara's Abominable Adventure. 2014. (ENG.). 210p. (J). mass mkt. 8.99 *(978-0-9566042-1-7(8))* Five Valleys Publishing GBR. Dist: Lightning Source, Inc.

—Clara's Clever Custard. 2010. (ENG.). 212p. (J). mass mkt. 8.99 *(978-0-9566042-0-0(X))* Five Valleys Publishing GBR. Dist: Lightning Source, Inc.

Barnes, Kenneth Edward. A Children's Story Collection. 2011. 216p. (gr. -1). pap. 15.95 *(978-1-4634-2863-1(4))*; (gr. 1-2). 24.59 *(978-1-4634-2864-8(2))* AuthorHouse.

—Invasion of the Dregs. 2011. 164p. (gr. 10-12). pap. 13.50 *(978-1-4634-0745-2(9))*; (gr. 4-6). 22.23 *(978-1-4634-0726-1(2))* AuthorHouse.

Barnes, Susan. Kelly Karate: Discovers the Ice Princess. 2004. 138p. (J). (gr. 4-8). pap. 5.95 *(978-0-9705777-3-3(7))* McBook Pubs., LLC.

Barnett, Penny. Matilda & Puppy's Beach Adventure. 2012. 24p. pap. 15.99 *(978-1-4797-1106-2(3))* Xlibris Corp.

Barnhill, Kelly. Iron Hearted Violet. Bruno, Iacopo, illus. 2014. (ENG.). 448p. (J). (gr. 3-7). pap. 7.00 *(978-0-316-05675-5(8))* Little, Brown Bks. for Young Readers.

Barnum, P. T. Dick Broadhead: A Story of Perilous Adve. 2006. pap. 30.95 *(978-1-4286-1959-3(3))* Kessinger Publishing, LLC.

—Jack in the Jungle: A Tale of Land & S. 2006. pap. 33.95 *(978-1-4286-0764-4(1))* Kessinger Publishing, LLC.

Barnum, Richard. Mappo the Merry Monkey Illustrated Editi. 2006. (Illus.). pap. *(978-1-4065-0920-5(5))* Dodo Pr.

—Squinty the Comical Pig. 2004. reprint ed. pap. 15.95 (978-1-4191-4865-1(6)); pap. 1.99 (978-1-4192-4865-8(0)) Kessinger Publishing, LLC.

—Squinty the Comical Pig Illustrated Edit. 2006. (Illus.). pap. (978-1-4065-0921-2(3)) Dodo Pr.

Barnum, Vance. Frank & Andy Afloat. 2007. 212p. 27.95 (978-1-4218-3911-0(3), 1st World Library - Literary Society) 1st World Publishing, Inc.

—Joe Strong the Boy Fire-Eater. 2007. 180p. 25.96 (978-1-4218-3912-7(1), 1st World Library - Literary Society) 1st World Publishing, Inc.

Baron, Andrew, illus. The Adventures of Octopus Rex. 2003. (J). per. 17.95 (978-0-9760348-0-3(8)) BaHart Pubns. / Eight Legs Publishing.

Baron, Lindamichelle. The Lion & the Man: A Fable. Huggins, Carl, illus. 2009. 72p. pap. 15.95 (978-0-940938-25-0(1)) Harlin Jacque Pubns.

Barr, Bitsy. Zock's Adventures: Just for Boys ... 2010. 40p. pap. 16.99 (978-1-4490-5880-7(9)) AuthorHouse.

Barr, Lester. Robots Land at Manchester Airport. 2012. (Illus.). 80p. pap. 13.66 (978-1-4772-2248-5(0)) AuthorHouse.

Barr, Mabel. Hamster Huey & the Gooey Kablooie: The Renowned Hero's Most Famous Adventure. l.t. ed. 2004. (Illus.). 8p. (J). 6.95 (978-0-9749090-0-4(9), 214) Hamster Huey Pr.

Barr, Mary. The Adventures of Kippy Schofield & the Fantastical Cat. 2017. (ENG.). 164p. (J). pap. 14.95 **(978-1-78612-334-3(7),** ba6c4268-0a2e-4b60-a9d5-3ae3a18d4bdd) Austin, Stan AUS. Dist: Bookmasters Distribution.

Barr, Robert. The Clue of the Silver Spoons. 2004. reprint ed. pap. 1.99 (978-1-4192-5701-8(3)); pap. 15.95 (978-1-4191-5701-1(9)) Kessinger Publishing, LLC.

—Dr. Barr's Tales: Stories of Katharine. 2007. 88p. per. 19.95 (978-1-4241-7911-4(4)) America Star Bks.

Barradell, Isabel. Even More Tales from the Toyshop. 2008. 380p. pap. 29.95 (978-1-60474-508-5(8)) America Star Bks.

Barrett, Audrey & Vogt, Denis. The Adventures of Audrey the Cat. 2008. 28p. pap. 14.95 (978-1-4389-1228-8(5)) AuthorHouse.

Barrett, Granny Rita. The Adventures on Granny's Fun-Ee Farm: Book 1. 2012. 20p. pap. 14.00 (978-1-4772-8356-1(0)) AuthorHouse.

Barrett, John F. The Stories of Jake. 2008. 64p. pap. 31.99 (978-1-4363-2010-8(0)) Xlibris Corp.

Barrett, Michellene. Englisha & David's Adventurous Vacation. 2009. 86p. (gr. 3-3). pap. 9.95 (978-1-4401-2319-1(5)) iUniverse, Inc.

Barrett, Susanna. Isabella Goes to the City. 2011. 20p. pap. 11.99 (978-1-4634-0203-7(1)) AuthorHouse.

BARRIE / LEFFLER. Peter Pan. 2016. (ENG., Illus.). 176p. 25.00 (978-0-7358-4259-5(0)) North-South Bks., Inc.

Barrie, J. M. The Adventures of Peter Pan. 2004. 220p. pap. 12.95 (978-1-59540-036-9(2), 1st World Library - Literary Society) 1st World Publishing, Inc.

—The Complete Adventures of Peter Pan Includes: The Little White Bird, Peter Pan in Kensington Gardens(Illustrated) & Peter. Rackham, Arthur & Bedford, F. D., illus. 2013. 326p. (978-1-78139-361-1(3)) Benediction Classics.

—Peter Pan. 2003. (Aladdin Classics Ser.). 228p. (gr. 3-7). lib. bdg. 18.40 (978-0-613-86964-5(8), Turtleback) Turtleback Bks.

—Peter Pan: From the Story by J. M. Barrie. Costa, Patricia Castelao et al, illus. 2009. (ENG.). 48p. (J). (gr. 3-7). 12.95 (978-0-7624-3543-2(7), Running Pr. Kids) Running Pr. Bk. Pubs.

—Peter Pan: The Story of Peter & Wendy [Photoplay Edition]. 2007. 244p. (gr. 4-7). 29.95 (978-1-4344-8379-9(7)); per. 17.95 (978-1-4344-8378-2(9)) Wildside Pr., LLC.

—Peter Pan in Kensington Gardens. 2010. 176p. pap. 19.95 (978-0-557-36522-7(8)) Lulu Pr., Inc.

—Peter Pan y Wendy. 2003.Tr. of Peter Pan & Wendy. (SPA.). 64p. (J). 17.95 (978-84-233-2394-4(3)) Ediciones Destino ESP. Dist: Planeta Publishing Corp.

Barrie, J. M. & Attwell, James M. Barrie - Mabel Lucie. Peter Pan y Wendy. (Coleccion Cuentos Universales).Tr. of Peter Pan & Wendy. (SPA.). 190p. (YA). (gr. 4-18). (978-84-261-5584-9(7), JV30117) Juventud, Editorial ESP. Dist: Lectorum Pubns., Inc.

Barrowman, John & Barrowman, Carole E. Hollow Earth. 2012. (Hollow Earth Ser.). (ENG.). 400p. (J). (gr. 3-7). 16.99 (978-1-4424-5852-9(6), Aladdin) Simon & Schuster Children's Publishing.

Barrowman, John & Barrowman, Carole E. Nephilim. 2017. (Orion Chronicles Ser.: 2). (ENG.). 320p. (YA). (gr. 7). 16.99 **(978-1-78185-641-3(9))** Head of Zeus GBR. Dist: Independent Pubs. Group.

Barrows, Annie. Ivy + Bean - What's the Big Idea? Blackall, Sophie, illus. 2011. (ENG.). 132p. (J). (gr. 1-5). pap. 5.99 (978-1-4521-0236-8(8)) Chronicle Bks. LLC.

—Ivy + Bean + Me: A Fill-in-the-Blank Book. Blackall, Sophie, illus. 2014. (ENG.). 104p. (J). (gr. 3-9). 10.99 (978-1-4521-3729-2(3)) Chronicle Bks. LLC.

—Ivy + Bean Paper Doll Play Set. Blackall, Sophie, illus. 2011. (Ivy & Bean Ser.: IVYB). (ENG.). 11p. (J). (gr. k-5). pap. 14.99 (978-1-4521-0279-5(1)) Chronicle Bks. LLC.

Barrows, Robert. Milestones - the Sixth World. 2009. 312p. pap. 16.98 (978-0-557-02589-3(3)) Lulu Pr., Inc.

Barry, Cotter. The Adventures of Morgan Morgan the Rhymester. 2010. 16p. 12.99 (978-1-4520-0116-6(2)) AuthorHouse.

Barry, Dave & Pearson, Ridley. Peter & the Shadow Thieves. Call, Greg & Brown, Roberta, illus. rev. ed. 2007. (Peter & the Starcatchers Ser.). (ENG.). 592p. (J). (gr. 5-9). pap. 9.99 (978-1-4231-0855-9(8), Disney Editions) Disney Pr.

—Peter & the Shadow Thieves. Call, Greg, illus. 2007. (Starcatchers Ser.: Bk. 2). 556p. (gr. 5-9). 19.00 (978-0-7569-8060-3(7)) Perfection Learning Corp.

—Peter & the Sword of Mercy. Call, Greg, illus. 2011. (Peter & the Starcatchers Ser.: Bk. 4). (ENG.). 528p. (J). (gr. 5-9). pap. 9.99 (978-1-4231-3070-3(7)) Hyperion Pr.

Barry, Maureen. Freddie the Frog's Adventure. 2007. (J). pap. 10.00 net. (978-1-60402-177-6(2)) Independent Pub.

Barry, Nick. Escape of the Terra-Cotta Soldiers: An Ethan Sparks Adventure. 2008. 180p. 23.95 (978-0-595-49365-4(3)); pap. 13.95 (978-0-595-45413-6(5)) iUniverse, Inc.

Barry, William J. Forever Awakening. 2014. 242p. pap. 18.50 (978-1-61213-113-9(1)) Writer's Coffee Shop, The.

Barshaw, Ruth McNally. Ellie McDoodle: Have Pen, Will Travel. Barshaw, Ruth McNally, illus. 2nd ed. 2011. (Ellie Mcdoodle Ser.). (ENG., Illus.). 192p. (YA). (gr. 3-6). pap. 7.99 (978-1-59990-715-4(1), 9781599907154, Bloomsbury USA Childrens) Bloomsbury Publishing USA.

—Have Pen, Will Travel. Barshaw, Ruth McNally, illus. 2013. (Ellie Mcdoodle Diaries). (ENG., Illus.). 192p. (YA). (gr. 3-6). 12.99 (978-1-61963-173-1(3), 9781619631731, Bloomsbury USA Childrens) Bloomsbury Publishing USA.

Bart, Kathleen. Town Teddy & Country Bear Go Global. Bart, Kathleen, illus. 2011. (Illus.). (J). (gr. k-3). 16.95 (978-1-932485-60-8(0)) Reverie Publishing Co.

—Town Teddy & Country Bear Tour the USA. Bart, Kathleen, illus. 2008. (Illus.). 32p. (J). (gr. -1-3). pap. 16.95 (978-1-932485-50-9(3)) Reverie Publishing Co.

Bartelme, Elizabeth. Simon Brute & the Western Adventure. 2012. 132p. pap. 12.95 (978-0-9831800-8-1(3)) Hillside Education.

Barth, Kathleen E. The Amazing Adventures of Quigley D Pigley & His Friends. 2009. 16p. pap. 8.49 (978-1-4389-8322-6(0)) AuthorHouse.

Bartha, Alysa. Petal's Wish. 2010. 32p. 14.99 (978-1-4490-7417-3(0)) AuthorHouse.

Bartlett, Adam. The Littlest Giant. 2010. 32p. pap. 19.95 (978-1-4520-9840-1(9)) AuthorHouse.

Bartlett, Lorrie & Bartlett, Helen. Kicker & the Lost Mine: Book Iii. 2013. 28p. pap. 24.95 (978-1-4626-9286-6(9)) America Star Bks.

—Kicker & the Missing Water: Book I. 2013. 28p. pap. 24.95 (978-1-4626-9245-3(1)) America Star Bks.

Barton, Tamra Clum. The Adventures of Lucky the Leaf. 2007. 32p. per. 18.65 (978-1-4257-3026-0(4)) Xlibris Corp.

Barton, Zoe. Always Neverland. 2011. (ENG.). 320p. (J). (gr. 3-7). 16.99 (978-0-06-196325-4(9)) HarperCollins Pubs.

Bartow, Philip. T & the Jello Castle-Book 1. 2013. 252p. (J). pap. 13.30 (978-0-9835176-2-7(2)) Institute For Outdoor Awareness, Inc.

—T & the Jello Castle-Book 2: Bio Bots. 2013. 264p. (J). pap. 13.30 (978-0-9835176-3-4(0)) Institute For Outdoor Awareness, Inc.

Baruch, M. P. Spend the Day with Me. Arscott, Dean, illus. 2009. 20p. pap. 10.95 (978-1-936051-27-4(3)) Peppertree Pr., The.

Barulich-Liederbach, Terri & Liederbach, Tom. The Memory Chair. 2010. 48p. pap. 19.49 (978-1-4520-5672-2(2)) AuthorHouse.

Base, Graeme. Eye to Eye. Base, Graeme, illus. 2015. (ENG., Illus.). 42p. (J). (gr. -1-1). 24.99 **(978-0-670-07859-2(X))** Random Hse. Australia AUS. Dist: Independent Pubs. Group.

Base, Graeme. The Legend of the Golden Snail. 2010. (ENG., Illus.). 48p. (J). (gr. k-2). 21.95 (978-0-8109-8965-8(4), Abrams Bks. for Young Readers) Abrams, Inc.

Basham, Tom. Sailing Home. Calvert, Lissa, illus. 2012. 168p. (978-1-77097-370-1(2)) FriesenPress.

Basham, Tom & Calvert, Lissa. Sailing Home. 2012. 168p. pap. (978-1-77097-371-8(0)) FriesenPress.

Bashe, Kayla. Kitty Cadawell & the Shadowslayers of Fym. 2008. 290p. pap. 16.50 (978-0-557-01916-8(8)) Lulu Pr., Inc.

Bass, Jules. Herb, the Vegetarian Dragon: Book & Bendo Gift Set. Harter, Debbie, illus. 2005. 32p. (J). 14.99 (978-1-905236-43-5(3)) Barefoot Bks., Inc.

Bassett, Madge A. At Bumblebee Farm. Bassett, Madge A., illus. 2009. (Illus.). 20p. pap. 13.46 (978-1-4251-9230-3(0)) Trafford Publishing.

Bassler, Joni. Chee Choo's Adventures, 1 vol. Leonard, Kaycee, illus. 2007. (ENG.). 33p. 24.95 (978-1-4241-8773-7(7)) America Star Bks.

Bast, Michael. Death's Academy. 2014. (J). pap. 14.99 (978-1-4621-1380-4(X), Horizon Pubs.) Cedar Fort, Inc./CFI Distribution.

Basu, Jayinee. HJBRL - A Nonsense Story by Sukumar Ray. 2005. 68p. pap. 10.98 (978-1-4116-3983-6(9)) Lulu Pr., Inc.

Basye, Dale E. Wise Acres: the Seventh Circle of Heck. Dob, Bob, illus. 2014. (Heck Ser.). (ENG.). 448p. (J). (gr. 4-7). 8.99 (978-0-307-98188-2(6), Yearling) Random Hse. Children's Bks.

Bate, Tharah. White Arrow. 2012. 20p. pap. 13.77 (978-1-4669-0991-5(9)) Trafford Publishing.

Bates, Gordon. The Khaki Boys over the Top: Doing & Daring for Uncle Sam. 2006. (ENG.). 140p. pap. 18.99 (978-1-4264-6542-0(4)) Creative Media Partners, LLC.

Bates, Michelle. Ride by Moonlight. 2004. (Sandy Lane Stables Ser.). 108p. (J). (gr. 5). lib. bdg. 12.95 (978-1-58086-634-7(4), Usborne) EDC Publishing.

—Ride by Moonlight. Leigh, Susannah, ed. Woodcock, John, illus. rev. ed. 2004. (Sandy Lane Stables Ser.). (ENG.). 118p. (J). pap. 4.95 (978-0-7945-0547-9(3), Usborne) EDC Publishing.

Bateson, Maggie. My Pirate Adventure: A Pop-up & Play Book. Eaves, Ed, illus. 2008. (ENG.). 20p. (J). (gr. 4-7). 23.50 (978-0-230-53036-2(2), Macmillan) Pan Macmillan GBR. Dist: Trans-Atlantic Pubns., Inc.

Batham, Matthew. Lightsleep. 2006. 167p. pap. (978-1-904623-39-7(5)) WritersPrintShop.

Batson, Susann. Gilly the Seasick Fish. l.t. ed. 2006. (Illus.). (J). 28p. 15.99 (978-1-933090-22-1(7)); 32p. E-Book 5.00 incl. cd-rom (978-1-933090-37-5(5)) Guardian Angel Publishing, Inc.

Batson, Wayne Thomas. The Final Storm, 1 vol. ed. 2007. (Door Within Trilogy: Bk. 3). (ENG.). 384p. (gr. 5-9). pap. 9.99 (978-1-4003-1013-5(X)) Nelson, Thomas Inc.

Battah, Suzan. Basatai: Outside In. 2012. 330p. pap. (978-0-9872632-1-6(8)) Battah, Suzan.

Battiste, Alyse. Super Sally's Fantastic Fun Day. 2007. (Illus.). 68p. (J). pap. 15.97 (978-0-9798217-1-4(1)) Candalyse Publishing.

Batton, Doris. Snicker & Snore, 1 vol. Griffin, Cheri, illus. 2010. 40p. pap. 24.95 (978-1-4489-6113-9(0)) PublishAmerica, Inc.

Bauer, Christina. The Pirate Queen: A Timewalker Journey. 2005. 280p. (YA). 14.99 (978-1-59092-224-8(7)) Blue Forge Pr.

Bauer, Marion Dane. Little Cat's Luck. Bell, Jennifer A., illus. 2016. (ENG.). 224p. (J). (gr. 3-7). 17.99 (978-1-4814-2488-2(2), Simon & Schuster Bks. For Young Readers) Simon & Schuster Bks. For Young Readers.

Bauer, Michael. The Adventures of Steel Wooly: And my Place on the Farm. 2012. (ENG.). 25p. (J). pap. 12.95 (978-1-4327-8568-0(0)) Outskirts Pr., Inc.

Baum, L. Frank. Adventures in Oz: The Patchwork Girl of Oz, Little Wizard Stories of Oz, Tik-Tok of Oz. 2007. 268p. 24.95 (978-1-60459-019-7(X)); per. 12.99 (978-1-60459-018-0(1)) Wilder Pubns., Corp.

—Adventures in Oz: The Tin Woodman of Oz, the Magic of Oz, Glinda of Oz. 2007. 284p. 24.95 (978-1-60459-023-4(8)); per. 12.99 (978-1-60459-022-7(X)) Wilder Pubns., Corp.

—Adventures in Oz: The Wonderful Wizard of Oz, the Marvelous Land of Oz, Ozma of Oz. 2007. 264p. per. 12.99 (978-1-60459-014-2(9)); per. 24.95 (978-1-60459-015-9(7)) Wilder Pubns., Corp.

—The Boy Fortune Hunters in Egypt. 2013. (Dover Children's Classics Ser.). (ENG., Illus.). 304p. (J). (gr. 3-8). pap. 12.99 (978-0-486-49085-4(8)) Dover Pubns., Inc.

—Enchanted Island of Yew. 2006. 268p. pap. 11.45 (978-1-59462-396-7(1), Book Jungle) Standard Pubns., Inc.

—Glinda of Oz. 2007. 108p. 22.95 (978-1-60312-591-8(4)) Aegypan.

—Mary Louise. 2007. 160p. per. (978-1-4065-3668-3(7)) Dodo Pr.

—Michael Foreman's the Wonderful Wizard of Oz. Foreman, Michael, illus. 2010. (ENG.). 160p. (J). (gr. 2-7). 19.99 (978-1-84365-157-4(2), Pavilion Children's Books) Pavilion Bks. GBR. Dist: Independent Pubs. Group.

—La Mirinda Sorchisto de Oz. Broadribb, Donald, tr. Denslow, W. W., illus. 2012. 278p. pap. 24.00 (978-1-59569-245-0(2)) Mondial.

—Sky Island. 2007. 144p. (gr. 4-7). per. 11.95 (978-1-60312-253-5(2)) Aegypan.

—Sky Island. 2004. (Twelve-Point Ser.). lib. bdg. 24.00 (978-1-58287-280-3(5)); lib. bdg. 25.00 (978-1-58287-792-1(0)) North Bks.

—The Woggle-Bug Book. 2008. 52p. pap. 7.95 (978-1-60664-008-1(9)) Aegypan.

—The Woggle-Bug Book. 2011. 52p. 14.95 (978-1-4638-9578-5(X)) Rodgers, Alan Bks.

—7 Books In: L. Frank Baum's Original Oz Series, Volume 1 of 2. the Wonderful Wizard of Oz, the Marvelous Land of Oz, Ozma of Oz, Dorothy & the W. 2008. 820p. (978-1-905921-02-7(0)) Shoes & Ships & Sealing Wax Ltd.

—7 Books In: L. Frank Baum's Oz Series, volume 1 of 2. the Wonderful Wizard of Oz, the Marvelous Land of Oz, Ozma of Oz, Dorothy & the Wizard In. 2008. 824p. pap. (978-1-905921-01-0(2)) Shoes & Ships & Sealing Wax Ltd.

—8 Books In: L. Frank Baum's Original Oz Series, volume 2 of 2. Little Wizard Stories of Oz, Tik-Tok of Oz, the Scarecrow of Oz, Rinkitink in Oz, T. 2008. 764p. (978-1-905921-03-4(9)) Shoes & Ships & Sealing Wax Ltd.

—8 Books In: L. Frank Baum's Oz Series, volume 2 of 2. Little Wizard Stories of Oz, Tik-Tok of Oz, the Scarecrow of Oz, Rinkitink in Oz, the Lost P. 2008. 812p. pap. (978-1-905921-09-6(8)) Shoes & Ships & Sealing Wax Ltd.

Baum, L. Frank & Thompson, Ruth Plumly. The Royal Book of Oz. 2009. 112p. pap. 8.99 (978-1-60459-763-9(1)) Wilder Pubns., Corp.

Bauman, Marty. The Crater Kid Collection. 2004. (Illus.). 144p. pap. 14.99 (978-0-9728585-0-2(4)) Dinoship, Inc.

Baxter, Alice L. Adam's Atomic Adventures. 2007. 76p. per. 8.95 (978-0-595-45616-1(2)) iUniverse, Inc.

Baxter, Anne M. Everybody Needs a Name: The Adventures of Maybe, Book 1. 2009. 40p. pap. 18.49 (978-1-4389-5816-3(1)) AuthorHouse.

—Maybe Wins!, Bk. 1. 2011. 32p. pap. 14.39 (978-1-4389-5843-9(9)) AuthorHouse.

Baxter B. Ballyhoo Rides Again. 2011. 52p. (gr. 1-2). pap. 9.99 (978-1-4634-3088-7(4)) AuthorHouse.

Baxter, Nicola. Catch That Plane! (Giant Size) A First Reading Adventure Book. Glover, Peter, illus. 2016. (ENG.). 24p. (J). (gr. -1-12). pap. 6.99 (978-1-86147-755-2(4), Armadillo) Anness Publishing GBR. Dist: National Bk. Network.

—Classic Folk Tales: 80 Traditional Stories from Around the World. Langton, Roger, illus. 2013. (ENG.). 96p. (J). (gr. 7-12). pap. 9.99 (978-1-84322-855-4(6)) Anness Publishing GBR. Dist: National Bk. Network.

—Follow That Fire Engine! A First Reading Adventure Book. Glover, Peter, illus. 2016. (ENG.). 24p. (J). (gr. -1-12). pap. 6.99 (978-1-86147-757-6(0), Armadillo) Anness Publishing GBR. Dist: National Bk. Network.

—Trouble on the Ice: First Reading Books for 3-5 Year Olds. Ball, Geoff, illus. 2015. (ENG.). 24p. pap. 6.99 (978-1-86147-492-6(X), Armadillo) Anness Publishing GBR. Dist: National Bk. Network.

—Trouble under the Ocean: First Reading Books for 3-5 Year Olds. Ball, Geoff, illus. 2015. (ENG.). 24p. bds. 6.99 (978-1-86147-493-3(8), Armadillo) Anness Publishing GBR. Dist: National Bk. Network.

Baxter, Stephanie. The Adventures of Jack Brown & Friends. 2013. 72p. pap. 17.99 (978-0-9890288-2-0(8)) Mindstir Media.

Bayham, Dalan J. The Loch Ness Monster Incident - Junior Explorers Society Episode 2. 2007. 160p. pap. 12.95 (978-1-4303-2291-7(8)) Lulu Pr., Inc.

Bayle, B. J. Perilous Passage. 2007. (ENG.). 184p. (YA). (gr. k-7). pap. 11.99 (978-1-55002-689-4(5), Sandcastle Bks.) Dundurn CAN. Dist: Ingram Publisher Services.

Bazaldua, Barbara & Bergen, Lara. Rapunzel & the Golden Rule/Jasmine & the Two Tigers (Disney Princess) Studio IBOIX & Disney Storybook Artists Staff, illus. 2011. (Pictureback(R) Ser.). (ENG.). 32p. (J). (gr. -1-2). pap. 4.99 (978-0-7364-2829-3(1), RH/Disney) Random Hse. Children's Bks.

Beach, Charles Amory. Air Service Boys in the Big Battle, or, Silencing the Big Guns. 2007. 144p. per. (978-1-4065-3675-1(X)) Dodo Pr.

—Air Service Boys over the Atlantic, or, the Longest Flight on Record. 2007. 144p. per. (978-1-4065-3676-8(8)) Dodo Pr.

Beach, Linda M. Michael's First Word! Gadtan Jean Louis, Rosley, illus. 2009. 20p. pap. 12.49 (978-1-4389-0766-6(4)) AuthorHouse.

Beachy, Elaine. Biff & Becka's Stupendous Vacation. 2013. 156p. (J). 30.95 (978-1-4497-9069-1(0)); pap. 13.95 (978-1-4497-9070-7(4)) Author Solutions, Inc. (WestBow Pr.).

Beadling, Marilyn. The Apple Pie Pickle. 2008. 52p. pap. 9.95 (978-1-4327-2302-6(2)) Outskirts Pr., Inc.

Beake, Lesley. Rough Luck: Diamonds in the Kalahari. 2009. (Hodder African Readers Ser.). (Illus.). 112p. pap. 12.95 (978-0-340-99028-5(7)) Hodder Education Group GBR. Dist: Trans-Atlantic Pubns., Inc.

Beakman, Onk. The Mask of Power: Eruptor Meets the Nightmare King. Geremia, Daniela, illus. 2016. 157p. (J). **(978-1-5182-2804-9(6)**, Grosset & Dunlap) Penguin Publishing Group.

Beal, T. J. Wash Day: A Teddy Doonamen Adventure. 2012. 24p. pap. 11.95 (978-1-60693-609-2(3), Strategic Bk. Publishing) Strategic Book Publishing & Rights Agency (SBPRA).

Beale, Madeline. Sarah's Great Adventures. Goh, Douglas, illus. 2017. (ENG.). 24p. 10.00 (978-981-4751-86-5(3)) Marshall Cavendish International (Asia) Private Ltd. SGP. Dist: National Bk. Network.

Beall, Linda. Four PAWS & Lucky Little Duke Dog. 2013. 28p. pap. 9.99 (978-1-62697-252-0(4)) Salem Author Services.

—Four Paws & Lucky Little Duke Dog. 2013. 28p. 20.99 (978-1-62697-253-7(2)) Salem Author Services.

Beamer, Cheryl & Beamer, Frank. Yea, It's Hokie Game Day! De Angel, Miguel, illus. 2006. 24p. (J). lib. bdg. 17.95 (978-1-932888-44-7(6)) Mascot Bks., Inc.

Beard, Robert W. A Boy Named Shawn. 2009. (A Shawn Barton Adventure Ser.). 116p. (J). pap. 12.95 (978-1-935083-07-8(4)) CyPress Pubns.

Beam, Emily. The Rose Cottage Tales. 2010. (Tumtum & Nutmeg Ser.: 2). (ENG., Illus.). 416p. (J). (gr. 3-7). 16.99 (978-0-316-08599-1(5)) Little, Brown Bks. for Young Readers.

—Tumtum & Nutmeg: Adventures Beyond Nutmouse Hall. 2011. (Tumtum & Nutmeg Ser.: 1). (ENG., Illus.). 512p. (J). (gr. 3-7). pap. 10.00 (978-0-316-07574-9(4)) Little, Brown Bks. for Young Readers.

—Tumtum & Nutmeg: the Rose Cottage Adventures. Price, Nick, illus. 2013. (Tumtum & Nutmeg Ser.: 2). (ENG.). 416p. (J). (gr. 3-7). pap. 10.99 (978-0-316-08598-4(7)) Little, Brown Bks. for Young Readers.

Beasley, Cheryl. Piano Paradise: My Piano Has a Big Secret. 2006. (ENG.). 52p. per. 16.95 (978-1-4241-4590-4(2)) PublishAmerica, Inc.

Beasley, Linda L. Meltdowns First Adventure. 2010. 28p. 16.95 (978-1-4490-9725-7(1)) AuthorHouse.

—Meltdown's Next Adventure: The White House. 2012. 48p. pap. 21.99 (978-1-4772-6070-8(6)) AuthorHouse.

The Beast. 2003. (J). per. (978-1-57657-864-3(X)) Paradise Pr., Inc.

Beaty, Janice J. Jarod & the Mystery of the Petroglyphs: A National Park Adventure Series Book. Beaty, Lillian C., illus. 2015. 118p. (J). pap. (978-1-63293-071-2(4)) Sunstone Pr.

Beaty, Janice J. & Beaty, Lillian C., illus. Jarod & the Mystery of the Utah Arches: A National Park Adventure Series Book. 2016. 118p. (J). pap. (978-1-63293-122-1(2)) Sunstone Pr.

Beaty, Noel. The Legend of Snowy the Shrew. 2007. 168p. per. (978-0-7552-0295-9(3)) Authors OnLine, Ltd.

Beaudoin, Beau. The Url King. 2010. (Illus.). 56p. (J). per. 15.95 (978-0-9788401-0-5(0)) Red Ink Pr.

Beauty & the Boy: An old man's story for a dying Boy. 2006. (Illus.). 270p. (YA). per. 19.95 (978-0-9759902-0-9(9)) Before Christmas Pr.

Beavington, Ruth. Edward Bear. 2012. (Illus.). 112p. (gr. 1-2). 19.95 (978-1-84624-721-7(7)) Book Guild, Ltd. GBR. Dist: Trans-Atlantic Pubns., Inc.

Because of Walter, 6 Packs. (Action Packs Ser.). 104p. (gr. 3-5). 44.00 (978-0-7635-8402-3(9)) Rigby Education.

Because of Winn Dixie. 2005. (J). (978-1-59564-832-7(1)) Steps To Literacy, LLC.

Beck, A. E. Master-E: Travel into Mystical Dragon Dimensions: Collision of Fantasy, Science Fiction & Physics. 2010. 212p. pap. 49.49 (978-1-4490-3612-6(0)) AuthorHouse.

Beck, Andrea. Elliot's Emergency. 2004. (J). (gr. k-3). spiral bd. (978-0-616-01543-8(7)); spiral bd. (978-0-616-01542-1(9)) Canadian National Institute for the Blind/Institut National Canadien pour les Aveugles.

Beck, Barbara. Bill Every Cloud Has a Silver Lining. 2012. 108p. pap. 19.95 (978-1-4626-9718-2(6)) America Star Bks.

Beck, Bev. The Acorn Nuts. Deweese, Susan, illus. 2011. 32p. pap. 24.95 (978-1-4626-2233-7(X)) America Star Bks.

Beck, Crystall. The Adventures of Carter & Vincent. 2012. 28p. pap. 9.95 (978-1-4787-1662-4(2)) Outskirts Pr., Inc.

Beck, Dewey. A Ledge, a Pie, & Hazel the Fly. 2012. 28p. pap. 19.99 (978-1-4772-9154-2(7)) AuthorHouse.

Beck, Ernie. Skinni Mini & Friends in the Valley of Hope. Beck, Blaze, illus. 2012. 74p. pap. 13.99 (978-0-9858398-5-7(6)) Mindstir Media.

Beck, Patricia. Prince Hasmir's High Seas Adventure. 2011. 24p. pap. 15.99 (978-1-4628-6151-4(2)) Xlibris Corp.

Becker, Aaron. Journey. Becker, Aaron, illus. 2013. (ENG., Illus.). 40p. (J). (gr. -1-3). 15.99 (978-0-7636-6053-6(1)) Candlewick Pr.

—Quest. 2014. (ENG., Illus.). 40p. (J). (gr. -1-3). 15.99 (978-0-7636-6595-1(9)) Candlewick Pr.

—Quest. 2015. (CHI.). 40p. (J). (978-7-5133-1677-4(5)) New Star Publishing Hse.

Becker and Mayer! Books Staff. Hello Kitty Super-Sweet Stencils. Sanrio Company, Ltd. Staff, illus. 2013. (ENG.). 24p. (J). (gr. k-2). spiral bd. 14.95 (978-1-4197-0631-8(4), Abrams Bks. for Young Readers) Abrams, Inc.

Becker, Brooke. The Adventures of Sammy Snowflake, Vol. 1. Gentry, Kyle, illus. 2007. (ENG.). 64p. (gr. 4-7). 19.95 (978-0-9795260-0-8(0)) Courtyard Publishing, LLC.

Becker-Doyle, Eve & Doyle, Evan Brain. Evan Brain's Christmas List & Other Shenanigans: Boy Warrior Fights Evil. Doyle, Evan Brain, illus. 2008. (ENG., Illus.). 64p. pap. 15.95 (978-0-9794716-3-6(X)) BDA Publishing.

Becker, Helaine. Juba This, Juba That. Lightburn, Ron, illus. 2011. (ENG.). 24p. (J). (gr. k-k). 17.95 (978-0-88776-975-7(6), Tundra Bks.) Tundra Bks. CAN. Dist: Penguin Random Hse. LLC.

Beckerman, Menucha. Crankytown. 2004. (My Smiling World Ser.: No. 2). (Illus.). 32p. (J). 11.95 (978-1-931681-52-0(X)) Israel Bookshop Pubns.

Becket, Jim. Inca Gold: Choose Your Own Adventure #20. 2007. (Choose Your Own Adventure Ser.: 20). (Illus.). 144p. (J). per. 6.99 *(978-1-933390-20-8(4))*, CHCL20) Chooseco LLC.
Beckham, David. Charlie Barker & the Secret of the Deep Dark Woods. 2006. 570p. pap. 33.20 *(978-1-4120-9264-7(7))* Trafford Publishing.
Beckley, N. K. The Three-Some: Book 2. 2012. 66p. 24.99 *(978-1-4771-2938-8(3))* Xlibris Corp.
—The Writer's Corner: Book 3. 2012. 90p. 24.99 *(978-1-4797-1241-0(8))*; pap. 15.99 *(978-1-4797-1240-3(X))* Xlibris Corp.
Beckstedt, Cynthia M. The Great Smoky Mountain Skunk Adventure, 1 vol. 2009. 28p. pap. 24.95 *(978-1-60836-034-5(2))* America Star Bks.
Bedford, Annie North & Golden Books Staff. Scamp. Walt Disney Company Staff & Golden Books Staff, illus. 2004. (Little Golden Book Ser.). (ENG.). 24p. (J). (gr. -1-2). 3.99 *(978-0-7364-2311-3(7))*, Golden/Disney) Random Hse. Children's Bks.
Bedford, David. Mole's in Love. Beardshaw, Rosalind, illus. 2009. 32p. (J). (gr. -1-2). 15.95 *(978-1-58925-084-0(2))*; pap. 6.95 *(978-1-58925-417-6(1))* Tiger Tales.
Beech, Sandy. Isle Be Seeing You. Holder, Jimmy, illus. 2005. (Castaways Ser.: 3). (ENG.). 192p. (J). (gr. 3-7). mass mkt. 9.99 *(978-0-689-87598-4(3))*, Aladdin) Simon & Schuster Children's Publishing.
—Worst Class Trip Ever. Holder, Jimmy, illus. 2005. (Castaways Ser.: 1). (ENG.). 176p. (J). (gr. 3-7). pap. 9.99 *(978-0-689-87596-0(7))*, Aladdin) Simon & Schuster Children's Publishing.
Beecroft, Simon. Ackbar's Underwater Army. 2012. (Star Wars: the Clone Wars DK Readers Ser.). lib. bdg. 13.55 *(978-0-606-26457-0(4))*, Turtleback) Turtleback Bks.
—Chewbacca & the Wookiee Warriors. 2012. (Star Wars: the Clone Wars DK Readers Ser.). lib. bdg. 13.55 *(978-0-606-26456-3(6))*, Turtleback) Turtleback Bks.
—Death Star Battles, Level 3. 2010. (DK Readers Ser.). (ENG.). 48p. (J). (gr. 2-4). 3.99 *(978-0-7566-6314-8(8))*, DK Children) Dorling Kindersley Publishing, Inc.
—Epic Battles, Level 4. 2008. (DK Readers Ser.). (ENG., Illus.). 48p. (J). (gr. 3-7). pap. 3.99 *(978-0-7566-3603-6(5))*, DK Children) Dorling Kindersley Publishing, Inc.
—Jedi Adventures. 2009. (Star Wars: the Clone Wars DK Readers Ser.). lib. bdg. 13.55 *(978-0-606-06254-1(8))*, Turtleback) Turtleback Bks.
Beecroft, Simon & Dorling Kindersley Publishing Staff. Ready, Set, Podrace! Level 1. 2007. (DK Readers Ser.). (ENG., Illus.). 32p. (J). (gr. k-4). pap. 3.99 *(978-0-7566-3274-8(9))*, DK Children) Dorling Kindersley Publishing, Inc.
Beekman, Kelley Lee. Sir Eli & the Halloween Dragon: The Legend of the Toasted Marshmallow. 2006. 55p. pap. 16.95 *(978-1-4241-4047-3(1))* PublishAmerica, Inc.
Beemink, Joe. Nowhere Wild. 2016. 304p. (J). pap. 10.50 *(978-1-4434-2244-4(4))*, Harper Trophy) HarperCollins Pubs.
Beeson, Jan. Mysterious World of the Puffins the Treasure Hunt Book 1. 2013. 74p. pap. 19.99 *(978-0-9890482-0-0(9))* Beeson, Jan.
Beh-Rang, Samad. The Little Black Fish. Emam, Ruby, tr. 2008. 32p. pap. 13.25 *(978-1-4389-1399-5(0))* AuthorHouse.
Behl, Colin. Noüm. 2007. 108p. per. 16.95 *(978-1-4241-4518-8(X))* PublishAmerica, Inc.
Behling, Steve. Daring Dino Rescue! (Rusty Rivets) Lovett, Nate, illus. 2017. (Big Golden Book Ser.). (ENG.). 48p. (J). (gr. -1-2). 9.99 ***(978-1-5247-1678-3(2)***, Golden Bks.) Random Hse. Children's Bks.
Behling, Steve & Sotomayor, Chris. Iron Man: Invasion of the Space Phantoms. Pham, Khoi, illus. 2016. (Mighty Marvel Chapter Book Ser.). (ENG.). 128p. (J). (gr. 3-7). pap. 5.99 *(978-1-4847-3269-4(3))*, Marvel Pr.) Disney Publishing Worldwide.
Behn, Rosa & Graham, Dora. The Adventures of Jenny Duck. 2006. 109p. pap. 19.95 *(978-1-4137-9450-2(5))* PublishAmerica, Inc.
Beil, Michael D. The Red Blazer Girls. 2010. (Red Blazer Girls Ser.). (ENG.). 320p. (J). (gr. 3-7). 7.99 *(978-0-375-84303-7(5))*, Yearling) Random Hse. Children's Bks.
Beinstein, Phoebe. ¡A nadar, Boots! (Swim, Boots, Swim!) Roper, Robert, illus. 2009. (Dora la Exploradora Ser.). (SPA.). 24p. (J). pap. 3.99 *(978-1-4169-7939-5(5))*, Libros Para Ninos) Libros Para Ninos.
—Dora & the Stuck Truck. Roper, Robert, illus. 2008. (Dora the Explorer Ser.: 25). (ENG.). 24p. (J). (gr. -1-2). pap. 3.99 *(978-1-4169-4799-8(X))*, Simon Spotlight/Nickelodeon) Simon Spotlight/Nickelodeon.
—Swim, Boots, Swim! Roper, Robert, illus. 2009. (Dora the Explorer Ser.: 29). (ENG.). 24p. (J). (gr. -1-2). pap. 3.99 *(978-1-4169-7195-5(5))*, Simon Spotlight/Nickelodeon) Simon Spotlight/Nickelodeon.
Beinstein, Phoebe, et al. Dora's Stories: A Boxed Set. 2005. (Dora the Explorer Ser.). (ENG.). 56p. (J). bds. 9.99 *(978-1-4169-0035-1(7))*, Simon Spotlight/Nickelodeon) Simon Spotlight/Nickelodeon.
Beiter, Anna M. & Beiter, Elizabeth A. The Story of the Star-Spangled Banner. 2005. (J). pap. 8.00 *(978-0-8059-6727-2(3))* Dorrance Publishing Co., Inc.
Bekis, Joanne. Bubble & Butterfly. 2009. 20p. pap. 10.50 *(978-1-60693-696-2(4))*, Strategic Bk. Publishing) Strategic Book Publishing & Rights Agency (SBPRA).
Belanger, Kathleen. Cooldog's Holiday Adventures. Baker, David, illus. 2012. 48p. 24.95 *(978-1-4626-3045-5(6))* America Star Bks.
—Cooldog's New Adventures. 2013. 78p. pap. 16.95 *(978-1-63004-207-3(2))* America Star Bks.
Belcher, Angie & Belcher, Andy. Swimming with Dolphins. 2005. (Big Cat Ser.). pap. 6.50 *(978-1-60457-102-8(0))* Pacific Learning, Inc.
Belgue, Nancy. The Scream of the Hawk, 1 vol. 2003. (ENG.). 148p. (J). (gr. 4-7). pap. 6.95 *(978-1-55143-257-1(9))* Orca Bk. Pubs. USA.
Bell, A. L. The Adventures of Captain Zero: I'm the Hero (Special Edition Cover) 2005. 45p. 17.00 *(978-1-4116-3732-0(1))* Lulu Pr., Inc.
Bell, Amber Dawn. Cave of Terror. 2008. 280p. pap. 12.95 *(978-0-9818550-3-5(2))* Highland Pr. Publishing.
Bell, David. Dawn Grays Cosmic Adventure 1. 2007. (Dawn Gray Ser.). (ENG., Illus.). 260p. pap. *(978-1-84167-558-9(X))* Ransom Publishing Ltd.
—Pink Alert! 2007. (Dawn Gray Ser.). (ENG.). 260p. pap. *(978-1-84167-581-7(4))* Ransom Publishing Ltd.
—Pyjamas in Space. 2007. (Dawn Gray Ser.). (ENG.). 260p. pap. *(978-1-84167-580-0(6))* Ransom Publishing Ltd.
Bell, Frank. How Slip Slap Slop Got His Name. Seaman, Paul, illus. 2004. 24p. pap. 7.00 *(978-1-84161-069-6(0))* Ravette Publishing, Ltd. GBR. Dist: Parkwest Pubns., Inc.
Bell, Hilari. Crown of Earth. Willis, Drew, illus. 2010. (Shield, Sword, & Crown Ser.: 3). (ENG.). 272p. (J). (gr. 3-7). pap. 5.99 *(978-1-4169-0599-8(5))*, Aladdin) Simon & Schuster Children's Publishing.
—Crown of Earth. Willis, Drew, illus. 2009. (Shield, Sword, & Crown Ser.: 3). (ENG.). 272p. (J). (gr. 3-7). 16.99 *(978-1-4169-0598-1(7))*, Simon & Schuster/Paula Wiseman Bks.) Simon & Schuster/Paula Wiseman Bks.
—Trickster's Girl: The Raven Duet Book #1. 2011. (Raven Duet Ser.). (ENG.). 288p. (YA). (gr. 7). pap. 15.99 *(978-0-547-57724-1(9))* Houghton Mifflin Harcourt Publishing Co.
Bell-Jackson, Sylvia. Bree's Bubble Gum Adventures: The Pajamas from the Bahamas. 2012. 36p. pap. 13.97 *(978-1-61204-299-2(6))*, Strategic Bk. Publishing) Strategic Book Publishing & Rights Agency (SBPRA).
Bell, Lindzi. Sherlock Times Three, 1 vol. 2009. 62p. pap. 19.95 *(978-1-61582-028-3(0))* America Star Bks.
Bell, Michele Ashman. Dragon's Jaw: A Heart-Pounding Adventure. 2005. 241p. (J). *(978-1-59156-880-3(3))* Covenant Communications.
Bell, Nancy Marie. A Step Sideways. 2013. 134p. (J). pap. *(978-1-77127-162-2(0))* MuseItUp Publishing.
Bell, Parker. Tale of the Hundred. 2012. (ENG.). pap. *(978-1-4675-2062-1(4))* Independent Pub.
Bell, Patricia A. Timothy Caterpillar Gets New Shoes. 2012. 24p. 24.95 *(978-1-62709-669-0(8))*; 20p. pap. 24.95 *(978-1-4626-9147-0(1))* America Star Bks.
Bell, Philip. Jack & Boo's Dinosaur Island. Bell, Eleanor, illus. 2013. 32p. pap. *(978-0-9562980-3-4(6))* Beachy Bks.
Bell, Rebecca. Message from Miami: The Adventures of Sharp-Eye, Book 2. Bell, Rebecca, illus. 2005. (Adventures of Sharp-Eye). (Illus.). 30p. (J). 9.95 *(978-1-934138-09-0(6))* Bouncing Ball Bks., Inc.
—A Regular Bug: The Adventures of Sharp-Eye, Book 1. Bell, Rebecca, illus. 2005. (Adventures of Sharp-Eye: Bk. 1). (Illus.). 25p. (J). 9.95 *(978-1-934138-08-3(8))* Bouncing Ball Bks., Inc.
Bell, Sophie. Lilac Attack! 2014. (Ultra Violets Ser.: 3). (ENG., Illus.). 304p. (J). (gr. 3-7). 12.99 *(978-1-59514-648-9(2))*, Razorbill) Penguin Young Readers Group.
—Power to the Purple! Battle, Christina, illus. 2013. (Ultra Violets Ser.: 2). (ENG.). 336p. (J). (gr. 3-7). 12.99 *(978-1-59514-647-2(4))*, Razorbill) Penguin Young Readers Group.
Bell, Ted. Nick of Time. 2009. (Nick McIver Adventures Through Time Ser.: 1). (ENG., Illus.). 464p. (J). (gr. 5-9). pap. 8.99 *(978-0-312-58143-5(2))*, 9780312581435) Square Fish.
—The Time Pirate. 2011. (Nick McIver Adventures Through Time Ser.: 2). (ENG., Illus.). 480p. (J). (gr. 5-9). pap. 10.99 *(978-0-312-66549-4(0))*, 9780312665494) Square Fish.
Belle, Magnolia. Teen Titans Go! - Read at Your Own Risk. 2015. (ENG., Illus.). 24p. (J). (gr. -1-3). pap. 3.99 *(978-0-316-37725-6(2))* Little, Brown Bks. for Young Readers.
—Teen Titans Go! (TM): Silkie Time. 2017. (Passport to Reading Level 2 Ser.). (ENG., Illus.). 32p. (J). (gr. -1-3). pap. 3.99 *(978-0-316-31580-7(X))* Little, Brown Bks. for Young Readers.
Bellis, Jill. The Magnificent Six. Farmer, Zoe, illus. 2007. 52p. pap. *(978-1-904959-47-2(4))* Mould, Paul Publishing.
—The Return of the Magnificent Six: A Christmas Adventure. Farmer, Zoe, illus. 2008. (The Magnificent Six: Vol. 2). 62p. pap. 14.00 *(978-1-58690-073-1(0))* Players Pr., Inc.
Bellisario, Gina. Ellie Ultra. von Innerebner, Jessika, illus. 2017. (Ellie Ultra Ser.). (ENG.). 128p. (gr. 2-3). pap. 27.80 ***(978-1-4965-5345-4(4))*** Stone Arch Bks.
Belmudes, Bonnie. The Adventures of Gus & Gunther: How They Met. 2012. 44p. pap. 21.99 *(978-1-4772-5350-2(5))* AuthorHouse.
Belt, Christopher R. The Adventures of Nate the Gnat. 2009. 32p. pap. 15.00 *(978-1-4389-6427-0(7))* AuthorHouse.
Bemelmans, Ludwig. Ludwig Bemelmans' Favorite Stories: Hansi, Rosebud & the Castle No. 9. 2016. (Dover Children's Classics Ser.). (ENG., Illus.). 144p. (J). (gr. 1-5). pap. 14.99 *(978-0-486-80718-8(5))* Dover Pubns., Inc.
—A Madeline Treasury: The Original Stories by Ludwig Bemelmans. 2014. (ENG., Illus.). 320p. (J). 35.00 *(978-0-451-47051-5(6))*, Viking Books for Young Readers) Penguin Young Readers Group.
Bender, Carol. The Doctor's Little Stowaway. 2009. 28p. pap. 13.99 *(978-1-4490-3711-6(9))* AuthorHouse.
Bendis, Brian Michael, et al. What If... ? Why Not?, Vol. 1. 2005. (Marvel Heroes Ser.). (Illus.). 152p. pap. 16.99 *(978-0-7851-1593-9(5))* Marvel Worldwide, Inc.
Beneath the Stone Forest. 2014. (Kingdom of Wrenly Ser.: 6). (ENG., Illus.). 128p. (J). (gr. k-4). pap. 5.99 *(978-1-4814-1391-6(0))*, Little Simon) Little Simon.
Benedict, Nicholas & Benedict, Janet. My Mommy Is a Zombie. 2013. 36p. 17.99 *(978-0-9883938-3-7(2))* Janik Pr.
Benintendi, Stephen F. PowerMark Seeker Series Issue 4: Redemption. 2003. (ENG & SPA.). (J). 1.75 *(978-0-9729135-4-6(8))* PowerMark Productions.
—PowerMark Seeker Series Issue 5: Transformation. 2003. (ENG & SPA.). (J). 1.75 *(978-0-9729135-5-3(6))* PowerMark Productions.
—PowerMark Seeker Series Issue 6: The Pathway. 2003. (ENG & SPA.). (J). 1.75 *(978-0-9729135-6-0(4))* PowerMark Productions.
—PowerMark Series One Autographed Box Set: Issues 1-12. aut. ed. 2003. 50.00 *(978-0-9717876-4-3(6))* PowerMark Productions.
Benintendi, Steve. Break Out: Operation: Ascent Part 3 Of 12. 2003. (Powermark Ser.). (Illus.). 32p. (J). pap. 2.95 *(978-0-9713412-4-1(9))* PowerMark Productions.
—PM Seeker Series # 7 Masquerade: Halloween Edition. 2005. (Illus.). 20p. (J). pap. 7.25 *(978-0-9749339-1-7(0))* PowerMark Productions.
—Redemption. 2003. (Powermark Comics Ser.). (Illus.). 32p. (J). pap. 2.95 *(978-0-9713412-1-0(4))* PowerMark Productions.
—Sacrifice: Operation: Ascent Part 4 Of 12. 2003. (Powermark Ser.). (Illus.). 32p. (J). pap. 2.95 *(978-0-9713412-5-8(7))* PowerMark Productions.
—Sinister Plans: Operation: Ascent Part 2 Of 12. 2003. (Powermark Comics Ser.). (Illus.). 32p. (J). pap. 2.95 *(978-0-9713412-3-4(0))* PowerMark Productions.
—Standing Tall: Operation: Ascent Part 1 Of 12. 2003. (Powermark Comics Ser.). (Illus.). 32p. (J). pap. 2.95 *(978-0-9713412-2-7(2))* PowerMark Productions.
—Trojan Horse. 2003. (Powermark Ser.). (Illus.). 32p. (J). pap. 2.95 *(978-0-9713412-0-3(6))* PowerMark Productions.
Benitez, Sofi. Not Your Valentine, no. 2. 2017. (ENG., Illus.). 192p. (J). 14.99 *(978-1-943785-08-7(2))*, 9781943785087) Rabbit Pubs.
Benitez, Sofi & Magnin, Joyce. Dog Daze. 2017. (ENG., Illus.). 240p. (J). 16.99 ***(978-1-943785-19-3(8)***, 9781943785193) Rabbit Pubs.
Benjamin, Matthew C. Andy's Discovery. del Conte, Mia, illus. 2003. 78p. (J). per. 8.95 *(978-0-9744672-0-7(0))* Adventure & Discovery Pr.
—Ricky's Adventure. del Conte, Mia, illus. 2003. 94p. (J). per. 8.95 *(978-0-9744672-1-4(9))* Adventure & Discovery Pr.
Benjamin, Paul. Monsters, Inc: Laugh Factory. Mebberson, Amy, illus. 2010. (ENG.). 112p. (J). pap. 9.99 *(978-1-60886-508-6(8))* Boom! Studios.
Benjamin, Paul & Rosa, Don. Monsters, Inc: Laugh Factory. Mebberson, Amy & Rosa, Don, illus. 2010. (ENG.). 112p. (J). 24.99 *(978-1-60886-533-8(9))* Boom! Studios.
Benn, Iris H. Penelope's New Friends: Early Childhood Life Lesson. 2013. 32p. 29.95 *(978-1-4787-1210-7(4))* Outskirts Pr., Inc.
Bennett, Bonnie. Howard the Worm. 2011. 28p. pap. 16.95 *(978-1-4626-0004-5(2))* America Star Bks.
Bennett, Deborah. The Christmas Star. 2013. 24p. pap. 24.95 *(978-1-63000-934-2(2))* America Star Bks.
Bennett, Debra J. Hip, Hop & Flop's Many Adventures. 2007. (ENG.). 60p. per. 16.95 *(978-1-4241-6564-3(4))* America Star Bks.
Bennett, Holly. The Bonemender's Choice, 1 vol. 2007. (Bonemender Ser.: 3). (ENG.). 234p. (YA). (gr. 7-12). per. 13.00 *(978-1-55143-718-7(X))* Orca Bk. Pubs. USA.
—The Warrior's Daughter, 1 vol. 2007. (ENG., Illus.). 240p. (YA). (gr. 8-12). per. 9.95 *(978-1-55143-607-4(8))* Orca Bk. Pubs. USA.
Bennett, Jeffrey. Max Goes to the Moon: A Science Adventure with Max the Dog. Okamoto, Alan, illus. 2nd ed. 2012. (Science Adventures with Max the Dog Ser.). (ENG.). 32p. (J). (gr. 2-4). 15.00 *(978-1-937548-20-9(1))* Big Kid Science.
Bennett, Larry. Attack of the Giant Stink Bugs. Tov, Basia, illus. 2015. (Ru-Lan Ser.: 2). (ENG.). 56p. (J). (gr. -1-3). pap. 10.95 *(978-1-940242-73-6(8))* Heritage Builders, LLC.
Bennett, Marilyn J. The Poinsettia Adventure. 2010. 60p. pap. 21.99 *(978-1-4490-7108-0(2))* AuthorHouse.
Bennett, Steven. The Adventures of Super Dad: Colossal Encounters (Book #1) 2005. 98p. pap. 10.49 *(978-1-4116-5947-6(3))* Lulu Pr., Inc.
Bennett, W. J., Jr. Sydney & Garrett's Great Arkansas Adventury. 2005. (J). pap. *(978-0-9794044-6-7(0))* Archeological Assessments, Inc.
Bennicke, Rune Brandt. The Mystery Hat. Jensen, Jakob Hjort, illus. 2014. (ENG.). 32p. (J). (gr. -1-k). 16.95 *(978-1-62914-621-8(8))*, Sky Pony Pr.) Skyhorse Publishing Co., Inc.
Benoit, Brian. Crustacean Vacation, 1 vol. Kelley, Marty, illus. 2012. (ENG.). 36p. (J). 17.95 *(978-1-934031-95-7(X))*, 14581bf9-2b61-42b1-8413-13cac209cd63) Islandport Pr., Inc.
Benoit, Charles. Snow Job. 2016. (ENG.). 288p. (YA). (gr. 7). 17.99 *(978-0-544-31886-1(2))* Houghton Mifflin Harcourt Publishing Co.
Benson, Donna. Spotlight on the Cupcakes: The Cupcakes Club #3. 2008. (ENG.). 115p. (J). pap. 7.95 *(978-0-9799159-2-5(9))* Pink Lemonade, LLC.
Benson, E. F. The Confession of Charles Linkworth. 2004. reprint ed. pap. 1.99 *(978-1-4192-5738-4(2))* Kessinger Publishing, LLC.
Benson, Glenda. The Adventures of Pepe & Gracie: Trouble in the Park. 2012. 20p. pap. 13.77 *(978-1-4669-0840-6(8))* Trafford Publishing.
Benson, Jeffrey. The Adventures of Avortit & Rooney. 2005. pap. *(978-1-84401-490-3(8))* Athena Pr.
Benson, Ken. Leela's Great Life. 2012. 28p. pap. 15.99 *(978-1-4771-2713-1(5))* Xlibris Corp.
Benson, Sherry. Introducing Jelly Bean. 2008. 27p. pap. 24.95 *(978-1-60672-427-9(4))* America Star Bks.
Bentley, Bernard E. Little Ben's Pledge. 2013. (ENG.). 33p. pap. 9.95 *(978-1-4787-1737-9(8))* Outskirts Pr., Inc.
Bentley, Douglas W. What Will It Take for a Toad to Kiss a Monkey: The Adventures of Princess Gracie & Prince Wallaby. Bentley, Julia Faye, illus. 2008. 52p. per. 24.95 *(978-1-4137-8849-5(1))* America Star Bks.
Bentley, Tadgh. Little Penguin & the Lollipop. Bentley, Tadgh, illus. 2017. (Illus.). 40p. (J). (gr. -1-3). 17.99 ***(978-0-06-256078-0(6))*** HarperCollins Pubs.
Bently, Peter. Captain Jack & the Pirates. Oxenbury, Helen, illus. 2016. (ENG.). 32p. (J). (-k). 17.99 *(978-0-525-42950-0(6))*, Dial Bks) Penguin Young Readers Group.
—Those Magnificent Sheep in Their Flying Machine. Bently, Peter, illus. 2014. (ENG., Illus.). 32p. (J). (gr. -1-3). 16.95 *(978-1-4677-4935-0(4))* Lerner Publishing Group.
Benton, Jim. The Complete Franny K. Stein, Mad Scientist: Lunch Walks among Us; Attack of the 50-Ft. Cupid - The Invisible Fra - The Fran That Time Forgot - Frantastic Voyage - The Fran with Four Brains - The Franidate. Benton, Jim, illus. 2012. (Franny K. Stein, Mad Scientist Ser.). (ENG., Illus.). 784p. (J). (gr. 2-5). pap. 41.99 *(978-1-4424-7424-6(6))*, Simon & Schuster Bks. For Young Readers) Simon & Schuster Bks. For Young Readers.
—Crate of Danger. Benton, Jim, illus. 2005. (Franny K. Stein, Mad Scientist Ser.). (ENG., Illus.). 448p. (J). (gr. 2-5). pap. 23.99 *(978-1-4169-1402-0(1))*, Simon & Schuster Bks. For Young Readers) Simon & Schuster Bks. For Young Readers.
—The Fran with Four Brains. Benton, Jim, illus. 2006. (Franny K. Stein, Mad Scientist Ser.: 6). (ENG., Illus.). 112p. (J). (gr. 2-5). 17.99 *(978-1-4169-0231-7(7))*, Simon & Schuster Bks. For Young Readers) Simon & Schuster Bks. For Young Readers.
—Frantastic Voyage. Benton, Jim, illus. 2006. (Franny K. Stein, Mad Scientist Ser.: 5). (ENG., Illus.). 112p. (J). (gr. 2-5). pap. 5.99 *(978-1-4169-0230-0(9))*; 15.99 *(978-1-4169-0229-4(5))* Simon & Schuster Bks. For Young Readers. (Simon & Schuster Bks. For Young Readers).
—The Invisible Fran. Benton, Jim, illus. (Franny K. Stein, Mad Scientist Ser.: 3). (ENG., Illus.). 112p. (J). (gr. 2-5). 2005. pap. 6.99 *(978-0-689-86297-7(0))* 2004. 17.99 *(978-0-689-86293-9(8))* Simon & Schuster Bks. For Young Readers. (Simon & Schuster Bks. For Young Readers).
Benton, Lynne. Chariot Race/La Carrera de Carrozas. Ursell, Martin, illus. 2009. (Let's Read! Bks.). (FRE & ENG.). 32p. (J). (gr. 3-7). pap. 4.99 *(978-0-7641-4363-2(8))* Barron's Educational Series, Inc.
Bentorah, Chaim. Biblical Truths from Uncle Otto's Farm. 2012. 108p. 28.95 *(978-1-4497-6170-7(4))*; pap. 11.95 *(978-1-4497-6168-4(2))* Author Solutions, Inc. (WestBow Pr.).
Benz, Derek & Lewis, J. S. The Brimstone Key. 2011. (Grey Griffins: the Clockwork Chronicles Ser.: 1). (ENG.). 400p. (J). (gr. 3-7). pap. 22.99 *(978-0-316-04521-6(7))* Little, Brown Bks. for Young Readers.
—The Brimstone Key Bk. 1. 2010. (Grey Griffins: the Clockwork Chronicles Ser.: 1). (ENG., Illus.). 384p. (J). (gr. 3-7). 15.99 *(978-0-316-04522-3(5))* Little, Brown Bks. for Young Readers.
—The Paragon Prison. 2013. (Grey Griffins: the Clockwork Chronicles Ser.: 3). (ENG.). 368p. (J). (gr. 3-7). pap. 7.99 *(978-0-316-04523-0(3))* Little, Brown Bks. for Young Readers.
—The Relic Hunters: Even Heroes Have to Go to School. 2012. (Grey Griffins: the Clockwork Chronicles Ser.: 2). (ENG.). 384p. (J). (gr. 3-7). pap. 7.99 *(978-0-316-04520-9(9))* Little, Brown Bks. for Young Readers.
—The Revenge of the Shadow King. 2006. (Grey Griffins Ser.: 1). (ENG.). (J). (gr. 3-7). audio compact disk 84.95 *(978-0-439-87913-2(2))* Scholastic, Inc.
BEOBI & the Magic Coloring Book Our First Adventure. 2005. (J). cd-rom 15.99 *(978-0-9743847-9-5(8))* Cohn, Tricia.
Beobi & the Magic Coloring Book Our First Adventure. 2005. (J). 3.99 *(978-0-9743847-2-6(0))* Cohn, Tricia.
ber, Gail. Time of the Cats. 2013. 132p. pap. 11.99 *(978-1-4582-1232-0(7))*, Abbott Pr.) Author Solutions, Inc.
Beraducci, Deborah. Tyler's Halloween Horror, 1 vol. Eyre, Jane, illus. 2009. 22p. pap. 24.95 *(978-1-4489-2133-1(3))* America Star Bks.
Beranek, Malinda. Rocky, the Country Squirrel. 2008. 12p. pap. 24.95 *(978-1-60563-018-2(7))* America Star Bks.
Berard, Robin M. King Tut & the Girl Who Loved Him: The Strange Adventures of Johanna Wilson. 2007. 212p. per. 12.95 *(978-1-58348-477-7(9))*, iUniverse Star) iUniverse, Inc.
Berenstain, Jan & Berenstain, Mike. The Berenstain Bears Take-Along Storybook Set. Berenstain, Mike, illus. 2016. (Berenstain Bears Ser.). (Illus.). 120p. (J). (gr. -1-3). pap. 11.99 *(978-0-06-241155-6(1))*, HarperFestival) HarperCollins Pubs.
Berenstain, Mike. The Berenstain Bears: Gone Fishin'! Berenstain, Mike, illus. 2014. (I Can Read Level 1 Ser.). (ENG., Illus.). 32p. (J). (gr. -1-3). pap. 3.99 *(978-0-06-207559-8(4))* HarperCollins Pubs.
—The Berenstain Bears - Gone Fishin'! Berenstain, Mike, illus. 2014. (I Can Read Level 1 Ser.). (ENG., Illus.). 32p. (J). (gr. -1-3). 16.99 *(978-0-06-207560-4(8))* HarperCollins Pubs.
—The Berenstain Bears' Easter Parade. Berenstain, Mike, illus. 2014. (Berenstain Bears Ser.). (ENG., Illus.). 24p. (J). (gr. -1-3). pap. 3.99 *(978-0-06-207554-3(3))*, HarperFestival) HarperCollins Pubs.
—The Berenstain Bears' Graduation Day. Berenstain, Mike, illus. 2014. (Berenstain Bears Ser.). (ENG., Illus.). 24p. (J). (gr. -1-3). pap. 3.99 *(978-0-06-207555-0(1))*, HarperFestival) HarperCollins Pubs.
—The Berenstain Bears' Lemonade Stand. Berenstain, Mike, illus. 2014. (I Can Read Level 1 Ser.). (ENG., Illus.). 32p. (J). (gr. -1-3). 16.99 *(978-0-06-207545-1(4))*; pap. 3.99 *(978-0-06-207544-4(6))* HarperCollins Pubs.
—The Berenstain Bears' Pirate Adventure. Berenstain, Mike, illus. 2016. (Berenstain Bears Ser.). (Illus.). 24p. (J). (gr. -1-3). pap. 3.99 *(978-0-06-235021-3(8))*, HarperFestival) HarperCollins Pubs.
—The Berenstain Bears' Show-And-tell. 2017. (Berenstain Bears Ser.). lib. bdg. 13.55 ***(978-0-606-40060-2(5))*** Turtleback Bks.
—The Berenstain Bears under the Sea. Berenstain, Mike, illus. 2016. (Berenstain Bears Ser.). (Illus.). 24p. (J). (gr. -1-3). pap. 3.99 *(978-0-06-235011-4(0))*, HarperFestival) HarperCollins Pubs.
—The Berenstain Bears Visit the Firehouse. Berenstain, Mike, illus. 2016. (Berenstain Bears Ser.). (Illus.). 24p. (J). (gr. -1-3). pap. 3.99 *(978-0-06-235016-9(1))*, HarperFestival) HarperCollins Pubs.
Berenstain, Mike, et al. 5-Minute Berenstain Bears Stories. Berenstain, Mike, illus. 2015. (Berenstain Bears Ser.). (ENG., Illus.). 192p. (J). (gr. -1-3). 12.99 *(978-0-06-236018-2(3))*, HarperFestival) HarperCollins Pubs.
Beres, Lisa. My Body My House. 2006. (Illus.). 40p. 16.95 *(978-0-9772392-0-7(9))* Green Nest LLC.
Berg, Deva Jean. A Tail of Two Sisters. Berg, Deva Jean, illus. 2013. (Illus.). 26p. pap. 9.95 *(978-1-939790-07-1(7))* Lorian Assn., The.
Bergen, Lara. Sophie the Hero. Tallardy, Laura, illus. 2010. (Sophie Ser.: 2). (ENG.). 112p. (J). (gr. 2-5). pap. 4.99 *(978-0-545-14605-0(4))*, Scholastic Paperbacks) Scholastic, Inc.
Bergen, Lara Rice. Phonics Comics: the Fearless Four - Level 2. Semple, Dave, illus. 2007. (ENG.). 24p. (J). (gr. 1-17). per. 3.99 *(978-1-58476-564-6(X))* Innovative Kids.
Bergens, Teri. Problemas de Barro. 2012. 34p. pap. 11.99 *(978-1-4575-1243-8(2))* Dog Ear Publishing, LLC.

A B

Berger, Glenn. Princess Chantik & the Outside World. 2012. 92p. pap. 39.99 (978-0-615-61495-3(7)) Marcabru Publishing.

Berger, Samantha. Pirate Potty. Cartwright, Amy, illus. 2010. (ENG.). 24p. (J). (gr. -1 — 1). pap. 5.99 (978-0-545-17295-0(0), Cartwheel Bks.) Scholastic, Inc.

Bergin, Jennifer J. Jungle Jim & Jungle Jen in the African Savannahs. 2012. 68p. pap. 8.99 (978-1-4525-5314-6(9)) Balboa Pr.

Bergner, Bobby. Why kitty Is afraid of Poo: A cautionary Tale. Bergner, Bobby, illus. 2008. (Illus.). 20p. 12.99 (978-0-615-21301-9(4)) Bergner, Bobby.

Bergren, Lisa T. God Gave Us So Much: A Limited-Edition Three-Book Treasury. Bryant, Laura J., illus. 2010. (ENG.). 112p. 19.99 (978-0-307-44629-9(8), WaterBrook Pr.) Crown Publishing Group.

—Season of Fire, 1 vol. 2015. (Remnants Novel Ser.: Bk. 2). (ENG.). 384p. (YA). 16.99 (978-0-310-73565-6(3)) Blink.

Bergstrom, Scott. The Cruelty. 2017. (Cruelty Ser.). (ENG.). 384p. (YA). 18.99 (978-1-250-10818-0(7), 9781250108180) Feiwel & Friends.

Berk, Josh. Guy Langman, Crime Scene Procrastinator. 2013. (ENG.). 240p. (YA). (gr. 7). pap. 8.99 (978-0-375-84627-4(1), Ember) Random Hse. Children's Bks.

Berkeley, Jon. Between the Light. Dorman, Brandon, illus. 2008. (Julie Andrews Collection). (J). lib. bdg. 17.89 (978-0-06-075514-0(8)) HarperCollins Pubs.

—The Palace of Laughter. Dorman, Brandon, illus. (Wednesday Tales Ser.: No. 1). (J). (gr. 3-7). 2007. (ENG.). 464p. pap. 8.99 (978-0-06-075509-6(1)) 2006. 427p. 16.99 (978-0-06-075507-2(5), Julie Andrews Collection) HarperCollins Pubs.

—The Tiger's Egg. Dorman, Brandon, illus. (Wednesday Tales Ser.: No. 2). (J). 2009. (ENG.). 432p. pap. 7.99 (978-0-06-075512-6(1), Harper Trophy) 2007. 416p. (gr. 3-7). 16.99 (978-0-06-075510-2(5), Julie Andrews Collection) HarperCollins Pubs.

Bern, Dave. Best Friends. 2006. 28p. pap. 9.95 (978-1-4327-0036-2(7)) Outskirts Pr., Inc.

Bernadine, Joyce. The Teeth Keepers. 2008. 73p. pap. 19.95 (978-1-60563-848-5(X)) America Star Bks.

Bernard, Greg. Alpha Summer. 2005. (YA). per. 12.95 (978-0-926147-21-8(8)) Loonfeather Pr.

Bernard, Romily. Remember Me. 2016. (Find Me Ser.: 2). 384p. (YA). (gr. 8). pap. 9.99 (978-0-06-222907-6(9), HarperTeen) HarperCollins Pubs.

Bernstein, Danielle V. The Magic in a Mermaid's Tear. 2013. 28p. pap. 24.95 (978-1-62709-604-1(3)) America Star Bks.

Bernstein, Jonathan. Bridget Wilder #2: Spy to the Rescue. 2017. (Bridget Wilder Ser.: 2). 320p. (J). (gr. 3-7). pap. 6.99 (978-0-06-238270-2(5), Tegen, Katherine Bks) HarperCollins Pubs.

—Bridget Wilder #3: Live Free, Spy Hard. 2017. (Bridget Wilder Ser.: 3). 368p. (J). (gr. 3-7). 16.99 (978-0-06-238272-6(1), Tegen, Katherine Bks) HarperCollins Pubs.

—Spy to the Rescue. 2016. (Bridget Wilder Ser.: 2). 320p. (J). (gr. 3-7). 16.99 (978-0-06-238269-6(1), Tegen, Katherine Bks) HarperCollins Pubs.

Berridge-Burley, Niamh. The Shoes That Couldn't Stop Dancing. 2010. 28p. pap. 15.99 (978-1-4535-1415-3(5)) Xlibris Corp.

Berrios, Frank. Bad Weather! (DC Super Friends) Beavers, Ethen, illus. 2014. (Little Golden Book Ser.). (ENG.). 24p. (J). (-k). 4.99 (978-0-385-38440-7(8), Golden Bks.) Random Hse. Children's Bks.

Berrios, Frank. Night of the Vulture! (Marvel: Spider-Man) Legramandi, Francesco & Scolari, Silvano, illus. 2017. (Little Golden Book Ser.). (ENG.). 24p. (J). (-k). 4.99 **(978-1-5247-1728-5(2)**, Golden Bks.) Random Hse. Children's Bks.

Berrios, Frank & Wrecks, Billy. Marvel Spider-Man, Vol. 2. 2016. (Little Golden Book Favorites Ser.). (ENG., Illus.). 80p. (J). (-k). 7.99 (978-0-307-97659-8(9), Golden Bks.) Random Hse. Children's Bks.

Berrow, G. M. Lyra & Bon Bon & the Mares from S. M. I. L. E. 2016. (My Little Pony Chapter Bks.). (J). lib. bdg. 16.00 (978-0-606-38301-1(8)) Turtleback Bks.

—My Little Pony: Daring Do & the Eternal Flower. 2016. (Daring Do Adventure Collection). (ENG.). 208p. (J). (gr. 5-7). 9.99 (978-0-316-38934-1(X)) Little, Brown Bks. for Young Readers.

—My Little Pony: Pinkie Pie & the Rockin' Ponypalooza Party! 2013. (ENG.). 160p. (J). (gr. 3-7). pap. 5.99 (978-0-316-22818-3(4)) Little, Brown Bks. for Young Readers.

—Trixie & the Razzle-Dazzle Ruse. 2017. (ENG.). 144p. (J). (gr. 3-7). pap. 5.99 (978-0-316-30163-3(9)) Little, Brown Bks. for Young Readers.

Berry, Diane Lambright. Port City Pirates. 2008. 128p. pap. 12.95 (978-0-9815763-0-5(3)) Alabaster Bk. Pub.

Berry, Erick. The Winged Girl of Knossos. 2017. (ENG., Illus.). 220p. (J). (gr. 3-7). pap. 11.95 (978-1-58988-120-4(6)) Dry, Paul Bks., Inc.

Berry, Julie. The Emperor's Ostrich. 2017. (ENG.). 288p. (J). 16.99 (978-1-59643-958-0(0), 9781596439580) Roaring Brook Pr.

Berry, R. A. Buddy's Blue Day. 2010. 16p. 10.99 (978-1-4520-2413-4(8)) AuthorHouse.

Berry, Ron. The Silly Safari Bus! Sharp, Chris, illus. 2008. (ENG.). 12p. (J). bds. 12.99 (978-0-8249-6736-9(4), Ideal Pubns.) Worthy Publishing.

—Where Is Daddy? Smart Kids Publishing Staff, ed. 2009. (ENG.). 20p. (J). bds. 7.99 (978-0-8249-1405-9(8), Ideal Pubns.) Worthy Publishing.

—Where Is Mommy? Smart Kids Publishing Staff, ed. 2009. (ENG.). 20p. (J). bds. 7.99 (978-0-8249-1404-2(X), Ideal Pubns.) Worthy Publishing.

Berryhill, Shane. Dragon Island. 2013. 216p. pap. 9.99 (978-1-937530-23-5(X)) Crossroad Pr.

Berryman, Chelsea. Missing Pages. 2007. 77p. pap. 19.95 (978-1-60441-747-0(1)) America Star Bks.

Bertha Bantam. 2003. (J). 9.99 (978-0-9740847-7-0(8)) GiGi Bks.

Beskow, Elsa. Peter & Lotta's Adventure, 1 vol. 2003. (ENG., Illus.). 32p. (J). 17.95 (978-0-86315-398-3(4)) Floris Bks. GBR. Dist: SteinerBooks, Inc.

—Peter in Blueberry Land Mini, 1 vol. gif. ed. 2005. (ENG., Illus.). 32p. (J). (gr. -1-1). (978-0-86315-498-0(0)) Floris Bks.

Bessen, Luc. Arthur & the Minimoys. Sowchek, Ellen, tr. from FRE. 2005. (ENG.). 240p. (J). 15.99 (978-0-06-059623-1(6)) HarperCollins Pubs.

Bessey, Siân Ann. Escape from Germany. 2004. 183p. (J). (978-1-59156-436-2(0)) Covenant Communications.

—Uprising in Samoa: A Novel. 2004. 178p. (J). (978-1-59156-890-2(0)) Covenant Communications.

Bessler, edward. A Smile for Billy. 2008. 175p. pap. 13.95 (978-1-4357-4439-4(X)) Lulu Pr., Inc.

Besson, Luc. Arthur & the Forbidden City. Sowchek, Ellen, tr. 2006. (ENG., Illus.). 192p. (J). (gr. 3-7). pap., pap. 5.99 (978-0-06-059628-6(7), Harper Trophy) HarperCollins Pubs.

—Arthur & the Forbidden City. 2005. (ENG., Illus.). 192p. (J). 15.99 (978-0-06-059626-2(0)) HarperCollins Pubs.

—Arthur & the Minimoys. 2005. (Illus.). 240p. (J). lib. bdg. 16.89 (978-0-06-059624-8(4)) HarperCollins Pubs.

Bethel, Ellie. Michael Recycle. Colombo, Alexandra, illus. 2008. (Michael Recycle Ser.). (ENG.). 28p. (J). (gr. 2-5). 15.99 (978-1-60010-224-0(7), 9781600102240) Idea & Design Works, LLC.

Bethell, Zillah. A Whisper of Horses. 2017. (ENG.). 352p. (J). 16.99 (978-1-250-09394-3(5), 9781250093943) Feiwel & Friends.

Bethune, Helen. A Road Trip to Yosemite, 1 vol. 2013. (Fiction Readers Ser.). (ENG., Illus.). 28p. (J). (gr. 2-2). pap. 6.99 (978-1-4333-5569-1(8)) Shell Educational Publishing.

Bets, Emily. The Shirt. 2012. 24p. pap. 14.93 (978-1-4669-0183-4(7)) Trafford Publishing.

Betterton, Jerry W. The Adventures of Hot Rolls. 2013. 44p. pap. 24.99 (978-1-4797-8184-3(3)) Xlibris Corp.

Bettino, Teresa Adele. The Adventures of Sugarbabe & Thunder. 2013. 34p. pap. 12.00 (978-0-9742842-0-0(3)) Bettino, Teresa Adele.

Bettoni, Angela. More Adventures of Edmund & Martha. 2013. 194p. pap. (978-0-9566421-1-0(X)) Angela Bettoni Publishing.

Betts, Betty. Dylan's Adventure. 2005. 60p. pap. 11.95 (978-1-4208-2293-9(4)) AuthorHouse.

Betts, McKenzie Leigh. Blue Bear Finds a Rainbow. Abbott, Candy, ed. Desautels, Stacie, illus. 2011. 24p. (J). 15.00 (978-1-886068-51-3(8)) Fruitbearer Publishing, LLC.

Bey, Angelique. Jammin' Jerone! The lamb who played the Saxaphone. Gilbert, Cecilia, illus. 2008. (ENG.). 34p. pap. 12.99 (978-1-4196-8093-9(5)) CreateSpace Independent Publishing Platform.

Beyers, Andrea. Johnny Joins the Army. LeTourneau, Anthony Alex, illus. 2008. (Flower Kingdom Ser.: Vol. 2). 40p. (J). 16.95 (978-0-9800754-1-0(6)) RockTuff.

Bhagwat, B. R. Faster Fenay at Fort Pratapgad. Modak, Tejas, tr. 2013. 120p. 10.00 (978-0-14-333201-5(5)) Penguin Group India IND. Dist: Penguin Publishing Group.

Bhakta, Sanjini. The Chocolate Pony. 2010. 28p. pap. 12.99 (978-1-4490-9761-5(8)) AuthorHouse.

—My Life as a Dollar Bill. 2010. 28p. pap. 12.95 (978-1-4520-6152-8(1)) AuthorHouse.

Bhandari, D. Growing Wings: Parrot's Day Out. 2010. 28p. 17.99 (978-1-4520-1102-8(8)) AuthorHouse.

Bickta, Brenda L. Tad's Life in the Lily Pond. 2008. 74p. pap. 19.95 (978-1-60672-647-1(1)) America Star Bks.

Bidoli, Katie. Karate Adventures of Kisho, Hana, & Nobu: Karate Is for Everyone! 2006. (Illus.). 16p. (J). 10.00 (978-1-60243-029-7(2)) Keen's Martial Arts Academy.

Bidwell, Dafne. Danger Unlimited: Action, Mystery & Adventure. 2007. 244p. pap. 15.50 (978-1-921064-89-0(7)) Fremantle Pr. AUS. Dist: Independent Pubs. Group.

Bidzilya, Kristin. Two Girls Dreams Come True. 2007. 64p. per. 9.95 (978-1-934246-87-0(5)) Peppertree Pr., The.

Biegel, Paul. El Pais de las Siete Torres.Tr. of Land of Seven Towers. (SPA.). 120p. (YA). (gr. 5). (978-84-279-3248-7(0), NG0325) Noguer y Caralt Editores, S. A. ESP. Dist: Lectorum Pubns., Inc.

Big Idea Entertainment, LLC. The Ballad of Little Joe. Jones, Cory, illus. 2016. (VeggieTales Ser.). (ENG.). 32p. (J). (gr. -1-3). pap. 3.99 (978-1-4336-4349-1(9), B&H Kids) B&H Publishing Group.

—King George & the Ducky. Jones, Cory, illus. 2016. (VeggieTales Ser.). (ENG.). 32p. (J). (gr. -1-3). pap. 3.99 (978-1-4336-4339-2(1), B&H Kids) B&H Publishing Group.

—LarryBoy & the Foolish Fig from Faraway. Jones, Cory, illus. 2016. (VeggieTales Ser.). (ENG.). 32p. (J). (gr. -1-3). pap. 3.99 (978-1-4336-4340-8(5), B&H Kids) B&H Publishing Group.

—Rack, Shack, & Benny. Jones, Cory, illus. 2016. (VeggieTales Ser.). (ENG.). 32p. (J). (gr. -1-3). pap. 3.99 (978-1-4336-4348-4(0), B&H Kids) B&H Publishing Group.

—Where's God When I'm S-Scared? Jones, Cory, illus. 2016. (VeggieTales Ser.). (ENG.). 32p. (J). (gr. -1-3). pap. 3.99 (978-1-4336-4353-8(7), B&H Kids) B&H Publishing Group.

Biggs, Pauline. A Wild Ride. Mayne, Michael, illus. 2004. 20p. (J). per. 12.95 (978-0-9760129-0-0(1)) The Publishing Place LLC.

Biggs, Stephen. The Time Barrel. 2009. 152p. pap. (978-1-84923-434-4(5)) YouWriteOn.

Bigler, Stephanie, et al. Sir Francis Bacon & the Wolves of Isle Royale: A Little Pig's Big Adventure. 2008. 24p. pap. 13.99 (978-1-4389-1524-1(1)) AuthorHouse.

Bilichniansky, Theodore. The Adventures of Little Tommy Cabin. 2012. 24p. pap. 15.99 (978-1-4797-0725-6(2)) Xlibris Corp.

—The Adventures of Little Tommy Cabin Part Ii: Tom Cabin Meets Mittens. 2012. (Illus.). 40p. pap. 21.99 (978-1-4797-5374-1(2)) Xlibris Corp.

Bill Henry Edge. Blip & the Seat of Arthur. 2009. 500p. pap. 24.99 (978-1-4389-5971-9(0)) AuthorHouse.

Bill, Poppa. The Adventures of Huggyman & Wiggly Worm: The Explorers meet Mr. Moley. 2011. (Illus.). 28p. pap. 14.09 (978-1-4567-7295-6(3)) AuthorHouse.

Billie's World. 2005. (J). pap. 8.99 (978-0-9766295-0-4(X)) My Journey Bks.

Billiot, Wendy Wilson. Before the Saltwater Came. I.t. ed. 2005. (Illus.). 32p. (J). 19.95 (978-0-9762592-0-6(6)) Billiot, Wendy Wilson.

Billows, Denis. The Cranmead Tales. 2010. 88p. pap. 14.09 (978-1-4520-4312-8(4)) AuthorHouse.

—Down in Bluebell Wood. 2010. 164p. pap. 11.99 (978-1-4490-8822-4(8)) AuthorHouse.

Bills, Randall N. Detective Mysteries. 2008. 92p. pap. 6.95 (978-0-9796392-1-0(2)) Adventure Boys Inc.

Bills, Sherry. Flippy the Frog. 2008. 16p. per. 24.95 (978-1-60441-578-0(9)) America Star Bks.

Billups, Ruth A. No Place for a Horse. 2008. 48p. pap. 16.95 (978-1-60703-118-5(3)) America Star Bks.

Billy & Baxter All Around Town, 4 vols. 2005. (Illus.). 24p. (J). (gr. -1 — 1). 8.95 (978-1-58087-098-6(8)) Stampley, C. D. Enterprises, Inc.

Billy & Baxter at the Airport, 4 vols. 2005. (Illus.). 24p. (J). (gr. -1-7). 8.95 (978-1-58087-100-6(3)) Stampley, C. D. Enterprises, Inc.

Binaohan, Simon. Model President, No. 2. 2003. 160p. (J). 17.89 (978-0-06-073915-7(0)) HarperCollins Pubs.

Binder, Mark. Genies, Giants & a Walrus. 2012. 132p. pap. 14.99 (978-0-9824707-9-4(7)) Light Pubns.

Binks. Don't Be a Chicken. Begonia, Ruby, illus. 2013. 32p. 15.95 (978-1-935448-22-8(6)) Lost Coast Pr.

Binns, Paul J. Paul & the Porch Gnome. 2011. 24p. pap. 12.99 (978-1-4634-3226-3(7)) AuthorHouse.

Birchfield, Elaine. Wilbur Two the Woodland Road. 2012. pap. 12.95 (978-1-4675-2830-6(7)) Independent Pub.

Bird, Benjamin. The Amazing Adventures of Superman!, 4 vols. Levins, Tim, illus. 2015. (Amazing Adventures of Superman! Ser.). (ENG.). 32p. (gr. k-2). 101.28 (978-1-4795-8002-6(3)) Picture Window Bks.

Bird, J. K. Shadow the Dog. 2010. 28p. 13.99 (978-1-4520-3476-8(1)) AuthorHouse.

Bird, Linda. Charlie Bird: The Best Bird Ever. 2007. 32p. per. 12.95 (978-1-4327-0489-6(3)) Outskirts Pr., Inc.

Birdseye, Tom. Storm Mountain. 2010. (ENG.). 256p. (J). (gr. 3-7). 16.95 (978-0-8234-2130-5(9)) Holiday Hse., Inc.

Birney, Betty G. Humphrey's Creepy-Crawly Camping Adventure. 2015. (Humphrey's Tiny Tales Ser.: 3). lib. bdg. 14.75 (978-0-606-36772-1(1)) Turtleback Bks.

—Secrets According to Humphrey. 2014. (Humphrey Ser.: 10). (ENG.). 144p. (J). (gr. 3-7). 15.99 (978-0-399-25796-4(9), G.P. Putnam's Sons Books for Young Readers) Penguin Young Readers Group.

Birt, Michael. Kody the Conservation Pup: Helps Tori Cross the Road. Trammell, Brandon, illus. 2012. 58p. 27.95 (978-0-578-11315-9(5)); pap. 19.95 (978-0-578-11306-7(6)) Birt Hse. Publishing.

Bishop, Debbie. Black Tide: Enter the Game. 2003. (Black Tide Rising Ser.: Vol. 1). (ENG., Illus.). 157p. (J). (gr. -1-12). pap. 7.95 (978-0-9664737-3-5(6)) Left Field,Angel Gate.

—MYST of the Lost Shadow Boys. 2008. (ENG.). 228p. (J). (gr. 4-9). pap. 6.99 (978-1-932431-79-7(9)) Left Field,Angel Gate.

Bishop, Desmond. The Wizard of Zee. 2012. 194p. pap. 14.95 (978-1-61897-447-1(5), Strategic Bk. Publishing) Strategic Book Publishing & Rights Agency (SBPRA).

Bishop, Jennie. The Squire & the Scroll: A Tale of the Rewards of a Pure Heart. McDaniels, Preston, illus. 2009. (ENG.). 32p. (J). 15.99 (978-1-59317-382-1(2)) Warner Pr., Inc.

Bishop, Karen C. The Christmas Lantern. Donahue, Jim, illus. 2008. 32p. (J). (978-0-615-20131-3(8)) Three River Rambler.

Biskup, Agnieszka. Graphic Expeditions. Stewart, Roger, illus. 2012. (Graphic Expeditions Ser.). (ENG.). 32p. (gr. 3-4). pap. 667.80 (978-1-4296-8474-3(7)); lib. bdg. 61.30 (978-1-4296-8174-2(8)) Capstone Press of Coughlan Cos. (Graphic Library).

Bittmann, Suzy. Life with Molly Mcgee - Sports Chick: Caught in a Pickle. 2010. 211p. pap. 15.99 (978-0-557-46339-8(4)) Lulu Pr., Inc.

Bixley, Donovan. Dogfight. 2016. (Flying Furballs Ser.: 1). (ENG., Illus.). 112p. (J). (gr. 2-4). pap. 8.99 (978-1-927262-53-5(4)) Upstart Pr. NZL. Dist: Independent Pubs. Group.

Bixley, Donovan. Hot Air. Bixley, Donovan, illus. 2017. (Flying Furballs Ser.: 2). (ENG., Illus.). 112p. (J). (gr. 2-4). pap. 8.99 **(978-1-927262-54-2(2))** Upstart Pr. NZL. Dist: Independent Pubs. Group.

Biz, Jen. The Terrible Noise. 2012. 16p. pap. 24.95 (978-1-4626-9619-2(8)) America Star Bks.

Bjork, Linda. Salmon Cavern. 2006. 92p. pap. 10.95 (978-1-59800-546-2(4)) Outskirts Pr., Inc.

Bjornson, Nancy. Mustangs, Fires & Snakes. 2007. (J). (978-1-930596-84-9(7)) Amherst Pr.

—Sleds, Skins & Snow. 2007. (J). (978-1-930596-83-2(9)) Amherst Pr.

Blabey, Aaron. The Furball Strikes Back. 2017. (Bad Guys Ser.: 3). lib. bdg. 16.00 **(978-0-606-40184-5(9))** Turtleback Bks.

Black, Chuck. Kingdom's Dawn. 2006. (Kingdom Ser.: 1). (ENG., Illus.). 160p. (J). (gr. 4-7). per. 9.99 (978-1-59052-679-8(1), Multnomah) Doubleday Religious Publishing Group, The.

—Kingdom's Reign, 4 bks. Black, Andrea & Black, Brittney, eds. Johnson, Marcella, illus. 2004. 160p. (YA). per. 9.95 (978-0-9679240-3-8(0)) Perfect Praise Publishing.

—The Light of the Last, Bk. 3. 2016. (Wars of the Realm Ser.). (ENG.). 368p. (YA). (gr. 7). pap. 11.99 (978-1-60142-506-5(6), Multnomah Bks.) Crown Publishing Group.

—Rise of the Fallen: Wars of the Realm, Book 2. 2015. (Wars of the Realm Ser.). (ENG.). 320p. (YA). (gr. 7). pap. 11.99 (978-1-60142-504-1(X), Multnomah Bks.) Crown Publishing Group.

—Sir Bentley & Holbrook Court. 2009. (Knights of Arrethtrae Ser.). (ENG., Illus.). 208p. (YA). (gr. 5-7). pap. 9.99 (978-1-60142-125-8(7), Multnomah Bks.) Crown Publishing Group.

—Sir Kendrick & the Castle of Bel Lione. 2008. (Knights of Arrethtrae Ser.). (ENG., Illus.). 208p. (YA). (gr. 7-7). pap. 9.99 (978-1-60142-124-1(9), Multnomah Bks.) Crown Publishing Group.

—Sir Rowan & the Camerian Conquest. 2010. (Knights of Arrethtrae Ser.). (ENG., Illus.). 192p. (J). (gr. 4-7). pap. 9.99 (978-1-60142-129-6(X), Multnomah Bks.) Crown Publishing Group.

Black Friday. 2014. (ENG.). 400p. (gr. 7). 10.99 (978-0-340-99924-0(1)) Hodder & Stoughton GBR. Dist: Hachette Bk. Group.

Black, Holly. Doll Bones. Wheeler, Eliza, illus. 2013. (ENG.). 256p. (J). (gr. 5-9). 18.99 (978-1-4169-6398-1(7), McElderry, Margaret K. Bks.) McElderry, Margaret K. Bks.

—Doll Bones. 2015. lib. bdg. 18.40 (978-0-606-36308-2(4)) Turtleback Bks.

—The Iron Trial. 2014. (Magisterium Ser.: Bk. 1). pap. (978-0-545-84067-5(8), Scholastic Pr.) Scholastic, Inc.

Black, Holly & Clare, Cassandra. The Bronze Key. 2016. (Magisterium Ser.: 3). (ENG., Illus.). 256p. (J). (gr. 3-7). 17.99 (978-0-545-52231-1(5), Scholastic Pr.) Scholastic, Inc.

—The Copper Gauntlet. (Magisterium Ser.: 2). (ENG.). 272p. (J). 2016. (gr. 4-7). pap. 7.99 (978-0-545-52229-8(3)) 2015. (gr. 3-7). 17.99 (978-0-545-52228-1(5), Scholastic Pr.) Scholastic, Inc.

—The Copper Gauntlet. 2016. (Magisterium Ser.). (ENG.). (J). (gr. 4-7). lib. bdg. 18.40 **(978-0-606-38811-5(7))** Turtleback Bks.

—The Iron Trial. (ENG.). (J). 2015. (Magisterium Ser.: 1). 304p. (gr. 3-7). pap. 7.99 (978-0-545-52226-7(9)) 2014. (Magisterium Ser.: 1). (Illus.). 304p. (gr. 3-7). 17.99 (978-0-545-52225-0(0)) 2014. (Illus.). 320p. (978-0-85753-250-3(2)) Scholastic, Inc. (Scholastic Pr.).

—The Iron Trial. 2015. (Magisterium Ser.: 1). lib. bdg. 18.40 (978-0-606-37028-8(5)) Turtleback Bks.

—Magisterium. la Prueba de Hierro. 2015. (SPA & ENG.). 304p. (J). (gr. 8). pap. 13.95 (978-607-07-2604-0(9)) Editorial Planeta, S. A. ESP. Dist: Two Rivers Distribution.

Black, Holly & DiTerlizzi, Tony. Arthur Spiderwick's Field Guide to the Fantastical World Around You. DiTerlizzi, Tony, illus. movie tie-in ed. 2008. (Spiderwick Chronicles Ser.). (ENG., Illus.). 142p. (J). (gr. 3-7). 24.99 (978-1-4169-6095-9(3), Simon & Schuster Bks. For Young Readers) Simon & Schuster Bks. For Young Readers.

—A Giant Problem. DiTerlizzi, Tony, illus. 2008. (Beyond the Spiderwick Chronicles Ser.: 2). (ENG., Illus.). 176p. (J). (gr. 2-5). 12.99 (978-0-689-87132-0(5), Simon & Schuster Bks. For Young Readers) Simon & Schuster Bks. For Young Readers.

—The Wrath of Mulgarath. 5th ed. 2004. (Spiderwick Chronicles Ser.: 5). (ENG., Illus.). 160p. (J). (gr. 2-6). 10.99 (978-0-689-85940-3(6), Simon & Schuster Bks. For Young Readers) Simon & Schuster Bks. For Young Readers.

Black, Kat. A Templar's Apprentice. 2009. (Book of Tormod Ser.: 1). (ENG.). 288p. (J). (gr. 7-18). 17.99 (978-0-545-05654-0(3)) Scholastic, Inc.

—A Templar's Destiny. 2012. (Book of Tormod Ser.). (ENG.). 256p. (J). (gr. 7-7). 17.99 (978-0-545-05677-9(2), Scholastic Pr.) Scholastic, Inc.

—A Templar's Gifts. 2011. (Book of Tormod Ser.: 2). (ENG.). 272p. (J). (gr. 7-7). 17.99 (978-0-545-05675-5(6), Scholastic Pr.) Scholastic, Inc.

Black, Pam, illus. Candee Bar. 42p. (J). 2007. spiral bd. (978-0-9800791-2-8(8)) 2nd rev. ed. 2008. spiral bd. 18.95 (978-0-9800791-3-5(6)) Moore Publishing.

Black, Peter Jay. Blackout. 2015. (Urban Outlaws Ser.: 2). (ENG.). 304p. (YA). (gr. 5-8). 16.99 (978-1-61963-592-0(5), 9781619635920, Bloomsbury USA Childrens) Bloomsbury Publishing USA.

—Urban Outlaws. (Urban Outlaws Ser.: 1). (ENG.). (gr. 5-8). 2015. 304p. (YA). pap. 7.99 (978-1-61963-572-2(0), 9781619635722) 2014. (Illus.). 288p. (J). 16.99 (978-1-61963-400-8(7), 9781619634008) Bloomsbury Publishing USA. (Bloomsbury USA Childrens).

Black, Sean. Extolziby Gruff & the 39th College. 2013. 236p. pap. (978-1-909062-25-2(1)) Sean Black Digital.

Black, Wills W. Touch the Moon & Other Adventures of the Fliff Family. 2010. (J). pap. 14.95 (978-0-7414-5885-8(3)) Infinity Publishing.

Blackburn, Sheila M. Stewie Scraps & the Easy Rider. 2008. 72p. pap. (978-1-903853-85-6(0)) Brilliant Pubns.

—Stewie Scraps & the Star Rocket. 2008. 76p. pap. (978-1-903853-87-0(7)) Brilliant Pubns.

Blackburne, Livia. Daughter of Dusk. 2016. (ENG., Illus.). 384p. (YA). (gr. 7-12). pap. 9.99 (978-1-4847-2366-1(X)) Hyperion Bks. for Children.

Blackford, Ami. Quest for the Elfin Elixir: A Duncan Family Adventure Book 2. Blackford, Ami, illus. 2007. (Illus.). 79p. (J). (gr. 3-7). 16.95 (978-1-60108-021-9(2)) Red Cygnet Pr.

Blackman, Dorothy L. New York Patriots. Gulley, Martha, illus. 2007. (J). (978-1-59531-020-0(7)) North Country Bks., Inc.

Blackman, Jizelle. Buddy & Fred: The Adventurous Chronicles. 2012. 28p. pap. 19.99 (978-1-4772-1276-9(0)) AuthorHouse.

Blackstone, Stella. Bear about Town / Ours en Ville. Harter, Debbie, illus. rev. ed. 2017. (ENG & FRE.). 24p. (J). (gr. -1-1). pap. 6.99 **(978-1-78285-329-9(4))** Barefoot Bks., Inc.

Blackstone, Stella. I Spy the Sun in the Sky. 2009. (ENG., Illus.). (J). 14.99 (978-1-84686-276-2(0)) Barefoot Bks., Inc.

Blackwell, Paul. Undercurrent. 2014. 320p. (YA). (gr. 9). pap. 9.99 (978-0-06-212352-7(1), HarperTeen) HarperCollins Pubs.

Blackwood, Gary. Around the World in 100 Days. 2011. (ENG.). 368p. (J). (gr. 5-18). 7.99 (978-0-14-241963-2(X), Puffin Books) Penguin Young Readers Group.

Blade, Adam. Brutus: The Hound of Horror. 2014. (Beast Quest Ser.: 63). (ENG., Illus.). 144p. (J). (gr. 2-4). pap. 5.99 (978-1-4083-1843-0(1)) Hodder & Stoughton GBR. Dist: Hachette Bk. Group.

—The Chronicles of Avantia #3: Call to War. 2012. (Chronicles of Avantia Ser.: 3). (ENG.). 176p. (J). (gr. 3-7). 15.99 (978-0-545-36156-9(7), Scholastic Pr.) Scholastic, Inc.

—Elko: Lord of the Sea. 2014. (Beast Quest Ser.: 61). (ENG., Illus.). 128p. (J). (gr. 2-4). 5.99 (978-1-4083-1841-6(5)) Hodder & Stoughton GBR. Dist: Hachette Bk. Group.

—Flaymar: The Scorched Blaze. 2014. (Beast Quest Ser.: 64). (ENG., Illus.). 144p. (J). (gr. 2-4). pap. 5.99 (978-1-4083-1844-7(X)) Hodder & Stoughton GBR. Dist: Hachette Bk. Group.

—Sepron vs Narga. 2015. (Beast Quest Ser.: 3). (ENG., Illus.). 192p. (J). (gr. 2-4). pap. 5.99 (978-1-4083-2409-7(1)) Hodder & Stoughton GBR. Dist: Hachette Bk. Group.

—Serpio: The Slithering Shadow. 2014. (Beast Quest Ser.: 65). (ENG., Illus.). 144p. (J). (gr. 2-4). pap. 5.99 (978-1-4083-1845-4(8)) Hodder & Stoughton GBR. Dist: Hachette Bk. Group.

—Tarrok the Blood Spike. 2014. (Beast Quest Ser.: 62). (ENG., Illus.). 144p. (J). (gr. 2-4). pap. 5.99

(978-1-4083-1842-3(3)) Hodder & Stoughton GBR. Dist: Hachette Bk. Group.
—Tauron: The Pounding Fury. 2014. (Beast Quest Ser.: 66). (ENG., Illus.). 144p. (J). (gr. 2-4). pap. 5.99 (978-1-4083-1846-1(6)) Hodder & Stoughton GBR. Dist: Hachette Bk. Group.
Blaha-Black, Caroline. Anika & the Magic Top. 2008. 60p. pap. 11.95 (978-1-4357-1194-5(7)) Lulu Pr., Inc.
Blaine, Jack. The Nightworld. 2012. (ENG.). 240p. (YA). (gr. 9). pap. 8.99 (978-0-06-213380-9(2)) HarperCollins Pubs.
Blaine, John. The Boy Scouts on a Submarine. 2007. 112p. pap. 18.99 (978-1-4346-3960-8(6)); 124p. pap. 19.99 (978-1-4346-3961-5(4)) Creative Media Partners, LLC.
—The Electronic Mind Reader: A Rick Brant Science Adventure Story. 2011. 224p. 44.95 (978-1-258-09692-2(7)) Literary Licensing, LLC.
—The Flaming Mountain: A Rick Brant Science Adventure Story. 2011. 188p. 42.95 (978-1-258-09489-8(4)) Literary Licensing, LLC.
—The Pirates of Shan: A Rick Brant Science Adventure Story. 2011. 190p. 42.95 (978-1-258-10086-5(X)) Literary Licensing, LLC.
—The Scarlet Lake Mystery: A Rick Brant Science Adventure Story. 2011. 192p. 42.95 (978-1-258-09823-0(7)) Literary Licensing, LLC.
Blair, Eric. Annie Oakley, 1 vol. Silverman, Dianne, illus. 2013. (My First Classic Story Ser.). (ENG.). 32p. (gr. k-3). pap. 7.10 (978-1-4795-1846-3(8), My First Classic Story) Picture Window Bks.
—Pecos Bill, 1 vol. Robledo, Sol, tr. from ENG. Chambers-Goldberg, Micah, illus. 2006. (Read-It! Readers en Español: Cuentos Exagerados Ser.).Tr. of Pecos Bill. (SPA.). 32p. (gr. k-3). 21.32 (978-1-4048-1658-9(5), Easy Readers) Picture Window Bks.
—Tom Thumb: A Retelling of the Grimm's Fairy Tale, 1 vol. Ouren, Todd, illus. 2013. (My First Classic Story Ser.). (ENG.). 32p. (gr. k-3). pap. 7.10 (978-1-4795-1847-0(6), My First Classic Story) Picture Window Bks.
Blair, Monica. The Adventures of Mary Ellen: Mary Ellen goes to Day Care. 2011. 24p. pap. 12.79 (978-1-4634-2696-5(8)) AuthorHouse.
Blair, Thomas L. The Sabatini Prophecy. 2006. 469p. 22.95 (978-0-9760237-1-5(7)) Axiom Hse.
Blaisdell, Patty. The Haunted Shed, 1 vol. 2009. 32p. pap. 24.95 (978-1-60836-674-3(X)) America Star Bks.
Blake. The Adventures of Libby the Leaping Learner. 2011. 92p. (gr. -1). pap. 13.95 (978-1-4620-1499-6(2)) iUniverse, Inc.
Blake, Chris. Aztec Attack. 2014. (Time Hunters Ser.: 12). (ENG., Illus.). 176p. (J). 5.99 (978-0-00-755004-3(9), HarperCollins Children's Bks.) HarperCollins Pubs. Ltd. GBR. Dist: HarperCollins Pubs.
—Cowboy Showdown. 2014. (Time Hunters Ser.: 7). (ENG., Illus.). 176p. (J). 5.99 (978-0-00-755007-4(3), HarperCollins Children's Bks.) HarperCollins Pubs. Ltd. GBR. Dist: HarperCollins Pubs.
—Egyptian Curse. 2014. (Time Hunters Ser.: 6). (ENG., Illus.). 176p. (J). 5.99 (978-0-00-751408-3(5), HarperCollins Children's Bks.) HarperCollins Pubs. Ltd. GBR. Dist: HarperCollins Pubs.
—Greek Warriors, 4. 2013. (Time Hunters Ser.: 4). (ENG., Illus.). 176p. (J). 5.99 (978-0-00-751404-5(2), HarperCollins Children's Bks.) HarperCollins Pubs. Ltd. GBR. Dist: HarperCollins Pubs.
—Mohican Brave. 2014. (Time Hunters Ser.: 11). (ENG., Illus.). 176p. (J). 5.99 (978-0-00-755002-9(2), HarperCollins Children's Bks.) HarperCollins Pubs. Ltd. GBR. Dist: HarperCollins Pubs.
—Outback Outlaw. 2014. (Time Hunters Ser.: 9). (ENG., Illus.). 176p. (J). 5.99 (978-0-00-754998-6(9), HarperCollins Children's Bks.) HarperCollins Pubs. Ltd. GBR. Dist: HarperCollins Pubs.
—Pirate Mutiny, 5. 2014. (Time Hunters Ser.: 5). (ENG., Illus.). 176p. (J). 5.99 (978-0-00-751406-9(9), HarperCollins Children's Bks.) HarperCollins Pubs. Ltd. GBR. Dist: HarperCollins Pubs.
—Samurai Assassin. 2014. (Time Hunters Ser.: 8). (ENG., Illus.). 176p. (J). 5.99 (978-0-00-754996-2(2), HarperCollins Children's Bks.) HarperCollins Pubs. Ltd. GBR. Dist: HarperCollins Pubs.
—Stone Age Rampage. 2014. (Time Hunters Ser.: 10). (ENG., Illus.). 176p. (J). 5.99 (978-0-00-755000-5(6), HarperCollins Children's Bks.) HarperCollins Pubs. Ltd. GBR. Dist: HarperCollins Pubs.
Blake, Drew. Engineer's Spell. 2007. 380p. per. 21.95 (978-0-595-45249-1(3)) iUniverse, Inc.
Blake-Garrett, Andrea. The Adventures of Izzy & Juju: Twin Detective Investigators (T. D. I.) 2012. 28p. pap. 19.99 (978-1-4685-0683-9(8)) AuthorHouse.
—Las Aventuras de Izzy y Juju: Gemelos Detectives Investigadores (G. D. I.) 2012. 28p. pap. 19.99 (978-1-4772-2523-3(4)) AuthorHouse.
Blake, Kendare. Antigoddess. (Goddess War Ser.: 1). (ENG.). (YA). (gr. 7-12). 2014. 352p. pap. 9.99 (978-0-7653-3446-6(1), 9780765334466) 2013. 336p. 17.99 (978-0-7653-3443-5(7), 9780765334435) Doherty, Tom Assocs., LLC. (Tor Teen).
—Mortal Gods. 2014. (Goddess War Ser.: 2). (ENG.). 352p. (YA). (gr. 7-12). 17.99 (978-0-7653-3444-2(5), 9780765334442, Tor Teen) Doherty, Tom Assocs., LLC.
Blake, Quentin. Jack & Nancy. 2013. (ENG., Illus.). 32p. (J). (gr. -1-k). pap. 14.99 (978-1-84941-689-4(3), Red Fox) Random House Children's Books GBR. Dist: Independent Pubs. Group.
Blake, Quentin, illus. Quentin Blake's the Seven Voyages of Sinbad the Sailor. 2012. (ENG.). 120p. (J). (gr. 2-4). 19.99 (978-1-84365-129-1(7), Pavilion) Pavilion Bks. GBR. Dist: Independent Pubs. Group.
Blakeney, Crystal Denise. Sharing with Paradise & Cove. 2012. 16p. pap. 15.99 (978-1-4772-9785-8(5)) AuthorHouse.
Blanchard, Daniel. Granddaddy's Secrets: Feeling Good. 2012. 114p. 19.95 (978-1-4626-6150-3(5)) PublishAmerica, Inc.
Blanchet, Deborah A. The Hat. 2009. 122p. 29.99 (978-1-4415-4624-1(3)); pap. 19.99 (978-1-4415-4623-4(5)) Xlibris Corp.
Blanks, Morgan Georgia. The Desert Island. 2008. 52p. pap. 20.49 (978-1-4343-9006-6(3)) AuthorHouse.
Blas, Larry. The Adventures of Island Stickman & His Dog Name Pearl. 2013. 28p. pap. 24.95 (978-1-4626-9943-8(X)) America Star Bks.
Blasing, George. Dinosaur George Prehistoric Safari: Raptor Island. Ramirez, Alberto, illus. 2007. (J). 4.95 (978-0-9797304-2-9(2)) Raining Popcorn Media.
Blaxill, Gina. Saving Silence, 4. 2014. (ENG.). 304p. (YA). (gr. 7). pap. 9.99 (978-1-4472-0884-6(6)) Pan Macmillan GBR. Dist: Independent Pubs. Group.
Blaylock, Kathy. Adventures of Buddy Fairy & Friends. 2007. 48p. 16.95 (978-1-4137-9195-2(6)) America Star Bks.
Bledsoe Jr, Reuben Booo. Bullybuster. 2013. (ENG.). 98p. (J). pap. 14.95 (978-1-4787-1215-2(5)) Outskirts Pr., Inc.
Bliss, Bob, illus. The Hardest Lessons: The Lost Babies Series #3. 2007. 118p. (J). per. 5.99 (978-0-9792499-2-1(9)) Eagle Tree Pr.
—The Ruby Hind: The Lost Babies Series #1. 2007. 116p. (J). per. 5.99 (978-0-9792499-0-7(2)) Eagle Tree Pr.
—Too Many Parents: The Lost Babies Series #2. 2007. 109p. (J). per. 5.99 (978-0-9792499-1-4(0)) Eagle Tree Pr.
Bliven, Jeremy. Captain Stumpy the Pirate Cat. 2004. (ENG., Illus.). 44p. (J). pap. (978-0-9713890-8-3(X)) Outer Banks Pr.
Bloch, Joanne. A Few Little Lies. 2009. (Hodder African Readers Ser.). (Illus.). 96p. pap. 12.95 (978-0-340-98415-4(5)) Hodder Education Group GBR. Dist: Trans-Atlantic Pubns., Inc.
Bloomfield, Charlotte. Corridor of Doors. 2013. 130p. pap. (978-1-909411-28-9(0)) Mauve Square Publishing.
Bloomfield, Glynis. Jake & the Pb's. 2013. 228p. pap. 16.00 (978-1-62212-443-5(X), Strategic Bk. Publishing) Strategic Book Publishing & Rights Agency (SBPRA).
—Jake's Secret. 2011. 194p. pap. 13.95 (978-1-60976-615-3(6), Strategic Bk. Publishing) Strategic Book Publishing & Rights Agency (SBPRA).
Bloomfield, Kevin. Mr. Biggs at the Circus. 2012. (ENG.). 32p. 16.95 (978-1-936299-99-7(2), Raven Tree Pr.,Csi) Continental Sales, Inc.
—Mr. Biggs at the Circus / el Sr. Grande en el Circo. 2012. (ENG.). 32p. 16.95 (978-1-936299-98-0(4), Raven Tree Pr.,Csi) Continental Sales, Inc.
Bloomfield, Susanne George & Reed, Eric Melvin, eds. Adventures in the West: Stories for Young Readers. 2007. (ENG., Illus.). 302p. (gr. 3-7). pap. 19.95 (978-0-8032-5974-4(3), Bison Bks.) Univ. of Nebraska Pr.
Blossom, F. Blossom Kingdom: The Adventures of Emily. 2005. 189p. pap. 24.95 (978-1-4241-1112-1(9)) PublishAmerica, Inc.
Bloumis, Joy. An Adventure in Fairyland. 2013. 84p. pap. 10.50 (978-1-62212-835-8(4), Strategic Bk. Publishing) Strategic Book Publishing & Rights Agency (SBPRA).
Blu De Golyer. The Adventures of Captain Greenspud. 2009. 28p. pap. 13.99 (978-1-4389-6582-6(6)) AuthorHouse.
Blue, Sebastien. Liquid Diamond. 2013. 176p. pap. (978-1-4602-3346-7(8)) FriesenPress.
Blum, Paul. Atlanta. 2007. (Extraordinary Files Ser.). (ENG., Illus.). 48p. (J). (gr. 4-7). pap. 11.99 (978-1-84680-179-2(6)) Evans Brothers, Ltd. GBR. Dist: Independent Pubs. Group.
—Headless Ghost. 2007. (Extraordinary Files Ser.). (ENG., Illus.). 48p. (J). (gr. 4-7). pap. 10.99 (978-1-84680-173-0(7)) Evans Brothers, Ltd. GBR. Dist: Independent Pubs. Group.
Blumenstock, Jacqueline & Pool, David. Making New Friends. 2nd ed. 2005. (Illus.). 32p. (J). per. 5.95 (978-0-9764647-0-9(5)) Big Brown Box, Inc., The.
—Making New Friends. Madden, Colleen, illus. 2nd ed. 2005. 32p. (J). lib. bdg. 14.95 (978-0-9764647-1-6(3)) Big Brown Box, Inc., The.
Blumer, J. Michael. The Book of Broken Promises, Vol. 2. 2007. 280p. (YA). pap. 15.99 (978-1-59092-540-9(8)) Blue Forge Pr.
—The Book of Second Chances, Bk. 1. 2006. (Secret Books of Gabendoor Ser.). 284p. per. 14.99 (978-1-59092-317-7(0)) Blue Forge Pr.
Blumstein, Amy Beth. Jamie & Tallulah. 2009. 16p. pap. 12.00 (978-1-4389-3997-1(3)) AuthorHouse.
Blundell, Gerald Lee. Bunkalunken Goes to Washington & Other Stories, 1 vol. 2010. 138p. pap. 24.95 (978-1-4489-5234-2(4)) America Star Bks.
Blunden, Alan. Tommy & the Garden Shed. 2008. 104p. pap. (978-1-84923-111-4(7)) YouWriteOn.
Blunt, Patricia. George the Jackdaw. 2005. (Illus.). 52p. pap. (978-1-84401-540-5(8)) Athena Pr.
Bly, Leon. Jenny Turnbull Vol. 2: Kurdistan Mission. 180p. (YA). pap. 9.00 (978-0-9621505-4-8(1)) Schwarz Pauper Pr.
Bly, Stephen A. The Secret of the Old Rifle. 2004. (Lewis & Clark Squad Adventure Ser.: No. 2). 160p. (gr. 4-9). 4.99 (978-0-89107-940-8(8)) Crossway.
—Treachery at the River Canyon. 2004. (Lewis & Clark Squad Adventure Ser.: No. 3). 160p. (YA). (gr. 4-9). 4.99 (978-0-89107-941-5(6)) Crossway.
Blyton, Enid. The Adventure of the Secret Necklace. (ENG., Illus.). 84p. (J). pap. 7.99 (978-0-7475-3211-8(7)) Bloomsbury Publishing Plc GBR. Dist: Trafalgar Square Publishing.
—The Adventures of Binkle & Flip. (ENG., Illus.). 137p. (J). pap. 5.95 (978-0-7475-3221-7(4)) Bloomsbury Publishing Plc GBR. Dist: Trafalgar Square Publishing.
—The Adventures of Mr. Pinkwhistle. (ENG., Illus.). 121p. (J). pap. 6.95 (978-0-7475-3219-4(2)) Bloomsbury Publishing Plc GBR. Dist: Trafalgar Square Publishing.
—Adventures of the Six Cousins. Pape, Jane, illus. 2013. (ENG.). 330p. (J). 16.50 (978-1-84135-589-4(5)) Award Pubns. Ltd. GBR. Dist: Parkwest Pubns., Inc.
—The Boy Who Wanted a Dog. (ENG., Illus.). 91p. (J). pap. 7.99 (978-0-7475-3213-2(3)) Bloomsbury Publishing Plc GBR. Dist: Trafalgar Square Publishing.
—The Castle of Adventure. Cobb, Rebecca, illus. unabr. ed. 2014. (Adventure Ser.: 2). (ENG.). 272p. (J). (gr. 4-7). pap. 9.99 (978-1-4472-6275-6(1)) Pan Macmillan GBR. Dist: Independent Pubs. Group.
—Children of Green Meadows. 2013. (ENG.). 240p. (J). pap. 9.99 (978-1-84135-645-7(X)) Award Pubns. Ltd. GBR. Dist: Parkwest Pubns., Inc.
—The Children of St. Kidillin. (ENG., Illus.). 110p. (J). pap. 7.99 (978-0-7475-3216-3(8)) Bloomsbury Publishing Plc GBR. Dist: Trafalgar Square Publishing.
—The Circus of Adventure. Cobb, Rebecca, illus. unabr. ed. 2014. (Adventure Ser.: 7). (ENG.). 272p. (J). (gr. 4-7). pap. 9.99 (978-1-4472-6281-7(6)) Pan Macmillan GBR. Dist: Independent Pubs. Group.
—Enid Blyton Adventure Omnibus. (Illus.). 136p. (J). 8.95 (978-0-09-921981-1(6)) Random Hse. GBR. Dist: Trafalgar Square Publishing.
—Family at Red-Roofs. 2013. (ENG.). 256p. (J). pap. 9.99 (978-1-84135-648-8(4)) Award Pubns. Ltd. GBR. Dist: Parkwest Pubns., Inc.
—Famous Five. 70th deluxe anniv. ed. 2012. pap. (978-1-4449-1248-7(8)) Hachette Children's Group.
—Five on a Treasure Island. l.t. ed. 2015. (ENG., Illus.). 112p. pap. 9.00 (978-1-927558-54-6(9)) Birch Tree Publishing.
—Hedgerow Tales. (Illus.). 128p. (J). pap. 5.95 (978-0-09-973580-9(6)) Random Hse. GBR. Dist: Trafalgar Square Publishing.
—Hello Mr Twiddle. (ENG., Illus.). 118p. (J). pap. 7.99 (978-0-7475-3218-7(4)) Bloomsbury Publishing Plc GBR. Dist: Trafalgar Square Publishing.
—House at the Corner: Family Adventure. 2013. (ENG.). 271p. (J). pap. 9.99 (978-1-84135-647-1(6)) Award Pubns. Ltd. GBR. Dist: Parkwest Pubns., Inc.
—The Island of Adventure. Cobb, Rebecca, illus. unabr. ed. 2014. (Adventure Ser.: 1). (ENG.). 288p. (J). (gr. 4-7). pap. 9.99 (978-1-4472-6277-0(8)) Pan Macmillan GBR. Dist: Independent Pubs. Group.
—The Island of Adventure. Tresilian, Stuart, illus. 70th anniv. unabr. ed. 2014. (Adventure Ser.: 1). (ENG.). 400p. (J). (gr. 4-7). 16.99 (978-0-230-77070-6(3)) Pan Macmillan GBR. Dist: Independent Pubs. Group.
—Magic Snow Bird: And Other Stories. Hamilton, Dorothy, illus. 2013. (ENG.). 192p. (J). 9.95 (978-1-84135-420-0(1)) Award Pubns. Ltd. GBR. Dist: Parkwest Pubns., Inc.
—More Hedgerow Tales. (Illus.). 112p. (J). pap. 5.95 (978-0-09-980880-0(3)) Random Hse. GBR. Dist: Trafalgar Square Publishing.
—The Mountain of Adventure. rev. ed. 2003. (ENG.). 187p. (J). 6.95 (978-0-333-73272-4(3)) Macmillan Pubs., Ltd. GBR. Dist: Trafalgar Square Publishing.
—The Mountain of Adventure. Cobb, Rebecca, illus. unabr. ed. 2014. (Adventure Ser.: 5). (ENG.). 288p. (J). (gr. 4-7). pap. 9.99 (978-1-4472-6279-4(4)) Pan Macmillan GBR. Dist: Independent Pubs. Group.
—Put-Em-Rights: Family Adventures. 2013. (ENG.). 254p. (J). pap. 9.99 (978-1-84135-649-5(2)) Award Pubns. Ltd. GBR. Dist: Parkwest Pubns., Inc.
—The Rat-a-Tat Mystery. 2013. (ENG.). 220p. (J). pap. 9.99 (978-1-84135-732-4(4)) Award Pubns. Ltd. GBR. Dist: Parkwest Pubns., Inc.
—The River of Adventure. Cobb, Rebecca, illus. unabr. ed. 2014. (Adventure Ser.: 8). (ENG.). 272p. (J). (gr. 4-7). pap. 9.99 (978-1-4472-6282-4(4)) Pan Macmillan GBR. Dist: Independent Pubs. Group.
—The Sea of Adventure. Cobb, Rebecca, illus. unabr. ed. 2014. (Adventure Ser.: 4). (ENG.). 272p. (J). (gr. 4-7). pap. 9.99 (978-1-4472-6278-7(6)) Pan Macmillan GBR. Dist: Independent Pubs. Group.
—The Secret of Cliff Castle. (ENG., Illus.). 117p. (J). pap. 7.99 (978-0-7475-3214-9(1)) Bloomsbury Publishing Plc GBR. Dist: Trafalgar Square Publishing.
—The Secret of Cliff Castle: 3 Great Adventure Stories. Downer, Maggie, illus. 2013. (ENG.). 288p. (J). 16.50 (978-1-84135-588-7(7)) Award Pubns. Ltd. GBR. Dist: Parkwest Pubns., Inc.
—The Secret of the Lost Necklace: 3 Great Adventure Stories. Biro, Val, illus. 2013. (ENG.). 272p. (J). 16.50 (978-1-84135-587-0(9)) Award Pubns. Ltd. GBR. Dist: Parkwest Pubns., Inc.
—Secret Seven. 2013. (ENG., Illus.). 144p. (J). (gr. 4-6). pap. **(978-1-4449-1343-9(3))** Hachette Children's Group GBR. Dist: Hachette Bk. Group.
—The Ship of Adventure. Cobb, Rebecca, illus. unabr. ed. 2014. (Adventure Ser.: 6). (ENG.). 288p. (J). (gr. 4-7). pap. 9.99 (978-1-4472-6280-0(8)) Pan Macmillan GBR. Dist: Independent Pubs. Group.
—Six Bad Boys. 2013. (ENG.). 223p. (J). pap. 9.99 (978-1-84135-650-1(6)) Award Pubns. Ltd. GBR. Dist: Parkwest Pubns., Inc.
—The Valley of Adventure. Cobb, Rebecca, illus. unabr. ed. 2014. (Adventure Ser.: 3). (ENG.). 288p. (J). (gr. 4-7). pap. 9.99 (978-1-4472-6276-3(X)) Pan Macmillan GBR. Dist: Independent Pubs. Group.
Blyton, Enid & Biro, Val. The Secret Valley. 2013. (ENG., Illus.). 204p. (J). pap. 9.99 (978-1-84135-678-5(6)) Award Pubns. Ltd. GBR. Dist: Parkwest Pubns., Inc.
BMI Staff, compiled by. Fear Street Collection - Set, 98 vols. 2009. (YA). 114.81 (978-1-60884-415-9(3)) BMI Educational Services.
Boazu, Elena & Balestrieri, Mauro. Lila's Quest. 2007. 48p. per. 13.95 (978-1-4327-0985-3(2)) Outskirts Pr., Inc.
Bobeck, Jade. Paxton's Adventures: A Day on Grandpa's Farm. 2012. 24p. pap. 15.99 (978-1-4797-4415-2(8)) Xlibris Corp.
Bodeen, S. A. Found. 2017. (Shipwreck Island Ser.: 4). (ENG.). 160p. (J). 16.99 (978-1-250-02783-2(7), 9781250027832) Feiwel & Friends.
—Shipwreck Island. 2014. (Shipwreck Island Ser.: 1). (ENG.). 192p. (J). (gr. 5-8). 16.99 (978-1-250-02777-1(2), 9781250027771) Feiwel & Friends.
Bodie, Karen. Will You Play Ball with Me? 2011. 28p. pap. 18.50 (978-1-4583-2023-0(5)) Lulu Pr., Inc.
Bogart, Jo Ellen & Bogart, Jill. Out & about with the Big Tree Gang, 1 vol. Griffiths, Dean, illus. 2006. (Orca Echoes Ser.). (ENG.). 64p. (J). (gr. 2-3). per. 4.99 (978-1-55143-603-6(5)) Orca Bk. Pubs. USA.
Bogumill, Mark P. KingMaker: The Swamp Crusade, 4 vols. 2003. 310p. (YA). bds. 25.00 (978-0-9744870-0-7(7)) KingMaker Bks. LLC.
Bohn, Kendall. Fantasy Adventure. 2008. (Kaleidoscopia Coloring Book Ser.). (Illus.). 56p. (J). (gr. -1-7). 8.95 (978-0-929636-83-2(X)) Syren Bk. Co.
Boland, Shalini. A Shirtful of Frogs. 2012. 244p. pap. (978-0-9569985-4-5(2)) Adrenalin Bks.
Boles, Jim. Ivan the Invacar & the Cave. Cunningham, Bob, illus. 2013. 52p. pap. 19.95 (978-0-9858052-2-7(6)) People Ink Pr.
—Ivan the Invacar Helps Big Dog. Cunningham, Bob, illus. 2012. 56p. pap. 19.95 (978-0-9845983-5-9(9)) People Ink Pr.
Bolger, Z. C. Danny Calloway & the Puzzle House. Robinson, Garrett, ed. Tallent, Alyssa, illus. 2013. 346p. 24.99 (978-1-939898-01-2(3)) Story Road Publishing, Inc.
Bolivar, III, Commander S. T. Munchem Academy, Book 1 the Boy Who Knew Too Much. 2017. (Munchem Academy Ser.). (ENG.). 320p. (J). (gr. 3-7). pap. 7.99 **(978-1-4847-7860-9(X))** Hyperion Bks. for Children.
Bolles, Joshua. Little Kitty in the City. 2008. 36p. 19.99 (978-0-578-00257-6(4)) Daven, Christian Publishing.
Bolling, Ruben. Ghostly Thief of Time: An EMU Club Adventure. 2015. (ENG., Illus.). 144p. (J). 12.99 (978-1-4494-5710-5(X)) Andrews McMeel Publishing.
Bolo the Balloon. Bolo the Balloon. 2007. (Illus.). 22p. (J). per. 10.00 (978-0-9797549-0-6(9)) DeKruyff, Ruth.
Bolton, Chris A. Smash: Trial by Fire. Bolton, Kyle, illus. 2013. (ENG.). 160p. (J). (gr. 4-7). 18.99 (978-0-7636-5596-9(1)) Candlewick Pr.
Bolton, Nicola Joanne. The WeatherGens. 2010. (ENG.). 89p. pap. 10.50 (978-1-4452-7936-7(3)) Lulu Pr., Inc.
Bolton, Violet. Heidi & Huber the Adventures Begin. 2011. (Illus.). 60p. pap. (978-1-908447-90-6(7)) Grosvenor Hse. Publishing Ltd.
Boltonwood-Castle, Tony. Ben,Jay & Ricardo Karate Adventure: The Night the Thieves Came Calling. 2010. 80p. pap. 10.49 (978-1-4520-8114-4(X)) AuthorHouse.
Bomgaars, Sharon. The Best Clubhouse Ever. 2009. 232p. 24.99 (978-1-4259-9307-8(9)); pap. 14.49 (978-1-4259-9306-1(0)) AuthorHouse.
Bon, Kimberly. Mitchie's Amazing Adventures: Good Bye to Pluto. 2012. 48p. pap. 21.99 (978-1-4685-5133-4(7)) AuthorHouse.
Bonasia, Steve. Dominic & the Secret Ingredient. Van Norstrand, Kain, illus. 2012. (ENG.). 39p. (J). pap. 24.95 (978-1-4327-9805-5(7)) Outskirts Pr., Inc.
Bond, Juliana. Salad Cream. 2005. 31p. spiral bd. 12.28 (978-1-4116-6047-2(1)) Lulu Pr., Inc.
Bond, Michael. Paddington. Alley, R. W., illus. 2014. (Paddington Ser.). (ENG.). 32p. (J). (gr. -1-3). 17.99 (978-0-06-231719-3(9)) HarperCollins Pubs.
—Paddington Helps Out. Fortnum, Peggy, illus. 2015. (Paddington Ser.). 160p. (J). (gr. 3-7). 9.99 (978-0-06-231230-3(8)) HarperCollins Pubs.
—Paddington Marches On. Fortnum, Peggy, illus. 2016. (Paddington Ser.). 176p. (J). (gr. 3-7). 9.99 (978-0-06-231232-7(4)) HarperCollins Pubs.
—Paddington Sets Sail. Alley, R. W., illus. 2016. (I Can Read Level 1 Ser.). 32p. (J). (gr. -1-3). pap. 3.99 (978-0-06-243064-9(5)) HarperCollins Pubs.
—Paddington's Day Off. 2017. (Paddington — I Can Read Ser.). (J). lib. bdg. 13.55 **(978-0-606-39636-3(5))** Turtleback Bks.
Bond, Michael. Paddington's Prize Picture. Alley, R. W., illus. 2017. (I Can Read Level 1 Ser.). 32p. (J). (gr. -1-3). pap. 3.99 (978-0-06-243076-2(9)) HarperCollins Pubs.
Bond, Rebecca. Escape from Baxters' Barn. Bond, Rebecca, illus. 2017. (ENG., Illus.). 256p. (J). (gr. 2-5). pap. 7.99 **(978-1-328-74093-9(5)**, HMH Books For Young Readers) Houghton Mifflin Harcourt Publishing Co.
—Escape from Baxters' Barn. 2015. (ENG., Illus.). 256p. (J). (gr. 2-5). 16.99 (978-0-544-33217-1(2), HMH Books For Young Readers) Houghton Mifflin Harcourt Publishing Co.
Bond, Thomas A. The Mill Creek Kids. 2008. 124p. pap. 11.99 (978-1-60647-947-6(4)) Salem Author Services.
—Mill Creek Kids. 2009. 132p. pap. 14.99 (978-1-60791-634-5(7)) Salem Author Services.
Bondor-Stone, Annabeth & White, Connor. The Shivering. Holden, Anthony, illus. 2016. (Shivers! Ser.: 2). 208p. (J). (gr. 3-7). 12.99 (978-0-06-231389-8(4)) HarperCollins Pubs.
—Shivers! - The Pirate Who's Afraid of Everything. Holden, Anthony, illus. 2015. (Shivers! Ser.: 1). (ENG.). 192p. (J). (gr. 3-7). 12.99 (978-0-06-231387-4(8)) HarperCollins Pubs.
Bondoux, Anne-Laure. The Princetta. Bell, Anthea, tr. 2008. (ENG.). 448p. (YA). (gr. 6-12). pap. 10.99 (978-1-59990-098-8(X), 9781599900988, Bloomsbury USA Childrens) Bloomsbury Publishing USA.
Bonehill, Ralph. Guns & Snowshoes. 2006. 27.95 (978-1-4218-3002-5(7)); pap. 12.95 (978-1-4218-3102-2(3)) 1st World Publishing, Inc.
—Guns & Snowshoes. 2006. (ENG., Illus.). 252p. (J). (gr. 4-7). per. 14.95 (978-1-55753-391-3(1), 2f8c1036-e56c-4807-8d17-aadfdcae6e7c) Purdue Univ. Pr.
—Out with Gun & Camera. 2006. (ENG., Illus.). 264p. (J). (gr. 4-7). per. 14.95 (978-1-55753-392-0(X), bd49c68d-0f66-4e9a-aa91-d982014892eb) Purdue Univ. Pr.
Bonham, Frank. Durango Street. 187p. (YA). (gr. 7-18). pap. 4.99 (978-0-8072-1549-4(X), Listening Library) Random Hse. Audio Publishing Group.
Bonilla, Barbara Ann. The Wacky World of Wendy White! A Whopper of a Tale. 2013. (ENG.). 47p. (J). pap. 12.95 (978-1-4787-1543-6(X)) Outskirts Pr., Inc.
Bonner, Sally. Millie's Daydream. 2010. 32p. 12.99 (978-1-4520-8101-4(8)) AuthorHouse.
The Boogly, 6 pack. (Literatura 2000 Ser.). (gr. k-1). 28.00 (978-0-7635-0045-0(3)) Rigby Education.
Book Company Staff. Hoppity Hop. 2003. (Novelty Bks.). (Illus.). (J). 15.95 (978-1-74047-233-3(0)) Book Co. Publishing Pty, Ltd., The AUS. Dist: Penton Overseas, Inc.
Book, Jennie Hale. Baby Dog Beans Comes Home: A Paul & Beans Adventure. 2005. (J). per. 13.95 (978-0-9767514-2-7(9), 2000) Abbott Avenue Pr.
The Book of Enterprise & Adventure. 2004. reprint ed. pap. 1.99 (978-1-4192-5453-6(7)); pap. 15.95 (978-1-4191-5453-9(2)) Kessinger Publishing, LLC.
Books, Appleknobb. Charlie's Monster. Books, Appleknobb, illus. 2013. (Illus.). 26p. (J). pap. 13.95 (978-0-9890903-0-8(2)) Happy Apple Bks.
Boos, Ben. Fantasy: An Artist's Realm. Boos, Ben, illus. 2010. (ENG., Illus.). 96p. (J). (gr. 5-9). 19.99 (978-0-7636-4056-9(5)) Candlewick Pr.
Boot Seeds. 2005. (J). 15.00 (978-0-9771015-2-8(5)) Let's Learn Library of Knowledge Series.
Booth, Sara. Poppy. Horne, Nathan, illus. 2012. 28p. pap. 12.50 (978-1-61897-666-6(4), Strategic Bk. Publishing) Strategic Book Publishing & Rights Agency (SBPRA).

Booton, F. F. The Adventures of Elk. 2011. (Illus.). 180p. pap. 17.09 *(978-1-4567-7517-9(0))* AuthorHouse.

Bordiglioni, Stephen & Bordiglioni, Stefano. Desert Adventure. Bertolucci, Federico, illus. 2009. (Dinodino's Dinosaur Adventures Ser.). 56p. (J). (gr. k-4). 27.95 *(978-1-60754-714-3(7))*; pap. 12.85 *(978-1-60754-721-1(X))* Windmill Bks.

—Earthquake! Bertolucci, Federico, illus. 2009. (Dinodino's Dinosaur Adventures Ser.). 56p. (J). (gr. k-4). 27.95 *(978-1-60754-713-6(9))*; pap. 12.85 *(978-1-60754-719-8(8))* Windmill Bks.

Borgeas, Ted. Grandma Is a Giggle, 5 bks. 2005. 100p. *(978-0-9764475-9-7(2))* Cameltrotters Publishing.

Borgenicht, David & Khan, Hena. Mars: You Decide How to Survive! Labat, Yancey, illus. 2011. (Worst Case Scenario Ser.: WORS). (ENG.). 208p. (J). (gr. 4-7). 12.99 *(978-0-8118-7124-2(X))* Chronicle Bks. LLC.

Borgia, Mary. Tales of the Texas Mermaid: The Boot. 2006. (Illus.). 47p. (J). 17.95 *(978-0-9778451-0-1(9))* Goretti Publishing.

Boricchio, Frances. The Adventure of Rodney & Diane. 2012. 26p. pap. 17.99 *(978-1-4685-6445-7(5))* AuthorHouse.

Borland, Jerre Shadrick. Ferdinand the Frog. Bayard, Janie Domengeaux, illus. 2011. 32p. pap. 24.95 *(978-1-4560-6116-6(X))* America Star Bks.

Borsky, Mary. Benny Bensky & the Parrot-Napper. Hendry, Linda, illus. 2008. (ENG.). 128p. (J). (gr. 4-7). pap. 9.95 *(978-0-88776-840-8(7)*, Tundra Bks.) Tundra Bks. CAN. Dist: Penguin Random Hse. LLC.

Bosch, Pseudonymous. If You're Reading This, It's Too Late. 2009. (Secret Ser.: 2). (ENG.). 400p. (J). (gr. 3-7). pap. 8.99 *(978-0-316-11368-7(9))* Little, Brown Bks. for Young Readers.

—The Name of This Book Is Secret. (Secret Ser.: 1). (ENG.). 400p. (J). (gr. 3-7). 2008. pap. 8.99 *(978-0-316-11369-4(7))* 2015. 12.99 *(978-0-316-26502-7(0))* Little, Brown Bks. for Young Readers.

—The Name of This Book Is Secret. Ford, Gilbert, illus. rev. ed. 2007. (Secret Ser.: 1). (ENG.). 384p. (J). (gr. 3-7). 17.99 *(978-0-316-11366-3(2))* Little, Brown Bks. for Young Readers.

—The Name of This Book Is Secret. 2009. 18.00 *(978-1-60686-518-7(8))* Perfection Learning Corp.

—The Name of This Book Is Secret. 2008. (Secret Ser.: 1). (J). lib. bdg. 19.65 *(978-1-4178-2975-0(3)*, Turtleback) Turtleback Bks.

—The Secret Series Complete Collection. 2012. (ENG.). 2016p. (J). (gr. 3-7). pap. 38.99 *(978-0-316-21981-5(9))* Little, Brown Bks. for Young Readers.

—This Book Is Not Good for You. (Secret Ser.: 3). (ENG.). (J). (gr. 3-7). 2010. 416p. pap. 8.99 *(978-0-316-04085-3(1))* 2009. 400p. 17.99 *(978-0-316-04086-0(X))* Little, Brown Bks. for Young Readers.

—This Isn't What It Looks Like. (Secret Ser.: 4). (ENG.). (J). (gr. 3-7). 2011. 448p. pap. 8.99 *(978-0-316-07624-1(4))* 2010. 432p. 17.00 *(978-0-316-07625-8(2))* Little, Brown Bks. for Young Readers.

—You Have to Stop This. (Secret Ser.: 5). (ENG.). (J). (gr. 3-7). 2012. 368p. pap. 8.99 *(978-0-316-07627-2(9))* 2011. 352p. 16.99 *(978-0-316-07626-5(0))* Little, Brown Bks. for Young Readers.

—You Have to Stop This. 2012. (Secret Ser.: 5). (J). lib. bdg. 18.45 *(978-0-606-26695-6(X)*, Turtleback) Turtleback Bks.

Boss, Nicco. Message to Badabu. 2013. 356p. pap. 12.99 *(978-0-9891635-1-4(2))* Nicco Boss, LLC.

Bossley, Michele Martin. Jumper, 1 vol. 2006. (Orca Sports Ser.). (ENG.). 160p. (YA). (gr. 6-10). per. 9.95 *(978-1-55143-620-3(5))* Orca Bk. Pubs. USA.

Bostick, B. k. Huber Hill & the Brotherhood of Coronado. 2012. 14.99 *(978-1-59955-981-0(1))* Cedar Fort, Inc./CFI Distribution.

—Huber Hill & the Dead Man's Treasure. 2011. (J). *(978-1-59955-911-7(0)*, Bonneville Bks.) Cedar Fort, Inc./CFI Distribution.

—Huber Hill & the Golden Staff of Cibola. 2013. (J). pap. 14.99 *(978-1-4621-1098-8(3)*, Horizon Pubs.) Cedar Fort, Inc./CFI Distribution.

Boston, Ruth. Super Hero for A Day. 2007. 152p. per. 13.95 *(978-1-4327-1427-7(9))* Outskirts Pr., Inc.

Botelho, R. J. G. A. R. T. H. Book IV: A Whale of a Tale. 2007. 104p. per. 19.95 *(978-1-4241-8799-7(0))* America Star Bks.

Botha, Ingrid. Chikin & Scrub. 2011. 108p. pap. 10.50 *(978-1-60976-295-7(9)*, Strategic Bk. Publishing) Strategic Book Publishing & Rights Agency (SBPRA).

Botha, Si. Goosala Goop. 2009. 48p. pap. 16.50 *(978-1-60860-124-0(2)*, Strategic Bk. Publishing) Strategic Book Publishing & Rights Agency (SBPRA).

Botsford, Matthew. Johnny Rocket & His Comrades in Faith. 2005. (ENG.). 160p. pap. 11.99 *(978-88-89127-07-0(4))* Destiny Image Europe ITA. Dist: Send The Light Distribution LLC.

Bouncy & the Bully: Book One of Bouncy's Adventures. 2013. 28p. pap. 13.95 *(978-1-4624-0788-0(9)*, Inspiring Voices) Author Solutions, Inc.

Boutavant, Marc, illus. Around the World with Mouk. 2009. (ENG.). 32p. (J). (gr. 3-17). 17.99 *(978-0-8118-6926-3(1))* Chronicle Bks. LLC.

Bouwman, H. M. A Crack in the Sea. 2017. (ENG., Illus.). 368p. (J). (gr. 5). 16.99 *(978-0-399-54519-1(0)*, G.P. Putnam's Sons Books for Young Readers) Penguin Young Readers Group.

Bova, Della L. The Adventures of Pono: A Puppy Dog's Tale. 2011. 24p. pap. 11.49 *(978-1-4490-7354-1(9))* AuthorHouse.

Bover, Annie. Mooncorn. 2013. (Illus.). 20p. pap. *(978-1-909465-18-3(6))* Cloister Hse. Pr., The.

Bow, Patricia. The Ruby Kingdom. 2007. (Passage to Mythrin Ser.: 1). (ENG.). 256p. (YA). (gr. 7). pap. 12.99 *(978-1-55002-667-2(4)*, Boardwalk Bks.) Dundurn CAN. Dist: Ingram Publisher Services.

Bowden, Poona. Juno Wonders. 2009. (Illus.). (J). 15.99 *(978-0-9821737-0-1(9))* Elotos Pr., LLC.

—Juno¡ s Dromen. 2009. (DUT., Illus.). (J). 15.99 *(978-0-9821737-1-8(7))* Elotos Pr., LLC.

Bowden, Roger. Tales from Wild Westernville. 2007. 52p. per. 16.95 *(978-1-4241-6923-8(2))* America Star Bks.

Bowen, Carl & Fuentes, Benny. Critical Strike. Tortosa, Wilson, illus. 2014. (Shadow Squadron Ser.). (ENG.). 224p. (gr. 4-8). pap. 8.95 *(978-1-62370-109-3(0))* Capstone Young Readers of Coughlan Cos.

—Rogue Agent. Tortosa, Wilson, illus. 2015. (Shadow Squadron Ser.). (ENG.). 224p. (gr. 4-8). pap. 8.95 *(978-1-62370-296-0(8))* Capstone Young Readers of Coughlan Cos.

—Steel Hammer. Tortosa, Wilson, illus. 2015. (Shadow Squadron Ser.). (ENG.). 112p. (gr. 4-8). lib. bdg. 26.65 *(978-1-4965-0385-5(6))* Stone Arch Bks.

Bowen, Marvin. Adventures of the Fluffytail Mouse. 2011. 52p. (gr. -1). pap. 12.99 *(978-1-4670-3879-9(2))* AuthorHouse.

Bower, Kevin. Gilbert Grumble. 2009. (Illus.). 28p. pap. 13.99 *(978-1-4490-3841-0(7))* AuthorHouse.

Bowers, Chuck. Leprechaun Legacy. 2009. 156p. pap. 12.95 *(978-1-4401-2248-4(2))* iUniverse, Inc.

Bowers, Renata. Frieda B. & the Zillabeast. Chesworth, Michael, illus. 2013. 32p. (J). lib. bdg. 15.00 *(978-0-9843862-0-8(3))* Frieda B.

Bowes, Kyle J. The Crossroads of the Other World. 2013. 240p. pap. *(978-1-4602-1892-1(2))* FriesenPress.

Bowler, Ann Martin & Tay-Audouard, Lak-Khee. Adventures of the Treasure Fleet: China Discovers the World. 2006. (ENG., Illus.). 32p. (J). (gr. 3-6). 19.95 *(978-0-8048-3673-9(6))* Tuttle Publishing.

Bowlin, Serina. Wandering Sam. Thrasher, Brian, illus. 2011. 20p. pap. 9.97 *(978-1-61204-280-0(5)*, Eloquent Bks.) Strategic Book Publishing & Rights Agency (SBPRA).

Bowman, Erin. Forged. 2015. (Taken Ser.: 3). (ENG.). 384p. (YA). (gr. 8). 17.99 *(978-0-06-211732-8(7)*, HarperTeen) HarperCollins Pubs.

—Frozen. (Taken Ser.). (ENG.). (YA). (gr. 8). 2015. 384p. pap. 9.99 *(978-0-06-211730-4(0))* 2014. 368p. 17.99 *(978-0-06-211729-8(7))* HarperCollins Pubs. (HarperTeen).

—Taken. 2013. (Taken Ser.: 1). (ENG.). 368p. (YA). (gr. 8). 17.99 *(978-0-06-211726-7(2)*, HarperTeen) HarperCollins Pubs.

Bowman, Robert. The Three Vests: The New Brilliants. 2003. 224p. (J). pap. 7.95 *(978-0-9713530-2-2(6))* Smart & Smarter Publishing.

Bowman, Vicki. Julie Through the Looking Glass. 2005. 55p. pap. 16.95 *(978-1-4137-4679-2(9))* America Star Bks.

Bowness, Kim. The Brave Engineers. 2007. (Illus.). 30p. (J). lib. bdg. 19.95 *(978-1-933732-36-7(9))* Big Ransom Studio.

Bowser, D. M. The Enchanting Tales of Lilith. 2011. 54p. pap. 16.95 *(978-1-4560-9570-3(6))* America Star Bks.

Bowser, Kimberly M. The Circus Dogs. 2012. 20p. pap. 24.95 *(978-1-4626-6524-2(1))* America Star Bks.

Bowyer, Clifford B. The Apprentice of Zoldex: The Imperium Saga: the Adventures of Kyria, 12 vols., Vol. 8. Brigman, June, illus. 2008. (Imperium Saga: 8). (ENG.). 208p. (J). 5.99 *(978-0-9787782-2-4(7)*, BK0023) Silver Leaf Bks., LLC.

—The Awakening: The Imperium Saga: the Adventures of Kyria, 12 vols., Vol. 2. Brigman, June, illus. 2004. (Imperium Saga: 2). (ENG.). 182p. (J). 5.99 *(978-0-9744354-1-1(4)*, BK0004) Silver Leaf Bks., LLC.

—Quest for the Shard: The Imperium Saga: the Adventures of Kyria, 12 vols., Vol. 6. Brigman, June, illus. 2007. (Imperium Saga: 6). (ENG.). 166p. (J). 5.99 *(978-0-9744354-8-0(1)*, BK0020) Silver Leaf Bks., LLC.

—The Shard of Time: The Imperium Saga: the Adventures of Kyria, 12 vols., Vol. 4. Brigman, June, illus. 2005. (Imperium Saga: 4). (ENG.). 182p. (J). 5.99 *(978-0-9744354-3-5(0)*, BK0007) Silver Leaf Bks., LLC.

—The Spread of Darkness: The Imperium Saga: the Adventures of Kyria, 12 vols., Vol. 7. Brigman, June, illus. 2007. (Imperium Saga: 7). (ENG.). 158p. (J). 5.99 *(978-0-9787782-1-7(9)*, BK0022) Silver Leaf Bks., LLC.

—Trapped in Time: The Imperium Saga: the Adventures of Kyria, 12 vols., Vol. 5. Brigman, June, illus. 2006. (Imperium Saga: 5). (ENG.). 150p. (J). 5.99 *(978-0-9744354-7-3(3)*, BK0008) Silver Leaf Bks., LLC.

The Boy Who Tricked the Ghosts. 2003. (J). 14.95 *(978-0-89610-769-4(8))* Island Heritage Publishing.

Boyce, Catherine & Boyce, Peter. A Royal Tea. Sibert, Stephanie Grace, illus. 2006. 32p. (J). per. 16.95 *(978-0-9778420-1-8(0))* Semper Studio.

Boyce, Frank Cottrell. The Astounding Broccoli Boy. (J). (gr. 3-7). 2017. 400p. pap. 6.99 *(978-0-06-240019-2(3))* 2015. 384p. 16.99 *(978-0-06-240017-8(7))* HarperCollins Pubs. (Walden Pond Pr.).

—Chitty Chitty Bang Bang & the Race Against Time. Berger, Joe, illus. (Chitty Chitty Bang Bang Ser.). (ENG.). 240p. (J). (gr. 4-7). 2014. pap. 6.99 *(978-0-7636-6931-7(8))* 2013. 15.99 *(978-0-7636-5982-0(7))* Candlewick Pr.

—Chitty Chitty Bang Bang Flies Again. Berger, Joe, illus. 2013. (Chitty Chitty Bang Bang Ser.). (ENG.). 224p. (J). (gr. 4-7). pap. 6.99 *(978-0-7636-6353-7(0))* Candlewick Pr.

—Chitty Chitty Bang Bang over the Moon. Berger, Joe, illus. 2015. (Chitty Chitty Bang Bang Ser.). (ENG.). 304p. (J). (gr. 4-7). pap. 6.99 *(978-0-7636-7666-7(7))* Candlewick Pr.

Boyce, Frank Cottrell & Boyce, Frank Cottrell. Millions. (J). (gr. 3-18). 2004. (Illus.). 256p. 15.99 *(978-0-06-073330-8(6))* 2004. (Illus.). 256p. lib. bdg. 16.89 *(978-0-06-073331-5(4))* 2005. 272p. reprint ed. pap. 8.99 *(978-0-06-073332-2(2))* HarperCollins Pubs.

Boyd, Benjamin. The Adventures of Kid Humpty Dumpty. 2009. 60p. pap. 19.50 *(978-1-60693-265-0(9)*, Eloquent Bks.) Strategic Book Publishing & Rights Agency (SBPRA).

Boyd, Cathy. The Little Snowman's New Hat. 2011. 28p. pap. 24.95 *(978-1-4560-2751-3(4))* PublishAmerica, Inc.

Boyd, Kate & Brixton, Iris. The Quercus Quest. 2006. 159p. pap. 12.72 *(978-1-4116-8843-8(0))* Lulu Pr., Inc.

Boyd, Sonya. I Have What It Takes. 2011. 28p. pap. 9.95 *(978-1-4327-7975-7(3))* Outskirts Pr., Inc.

Boyden, Linda. Boy & Poi Poi Puppy. Boyden, Linda, illus. 2013. (Illus.). 40p. (J). (gr. -1-2). pap. 11.95 *(978-0-9888568-2-0(4))* Rising Phoenix Pr.

Boykins, Corinthia. Too Big for the Tub. 2008. 36p. per. 14.95 *(978-1-4327-1456-7(2))* Outskirts Pr., Inc.

Boyne, John. Noah Barleywater Runs Away. Jeffers, Oliver, illus. 2011. (ENG.). 240p. (J). (gr. 3-7). 16.99 *(978-0-385-75246-6(6))* Fickling, David Bks. GBR. Dist: Penguin Random Hse. LLC.

—Noah Barleywater Runs Away. Jeffers, Oliver, illus. 2012. (ENG.). 240p. (J). (gr. 3-7). 7.99 *(978-0-385-75264-0(4)*, Yearling) Random Hse. Children's Bks.

—The Terrible Thing That Happened to Barnaby Brocket. Jeffers, Oliver, illus. 2014. (ENG.). 288p. (J). (gr. 3-7). 6.99 *(978-0-307-97765-6(X)*, Yearling) Random Hse. Children's Bks.

Bozarth, Jan. The Fairy Godmother Academy #6: Trinity's Book. 2013. (Fairy Godmother Academy Ser.). (ENG., Illus.). 240p. (J). (gr. 3-7). 6.99 *(978-0-375-86576-3(4)*, Yearling) Random Hse. Children's Bks.

Bracken- Murphy, Julie. Sammy's Summer Vacation. 2007. 52p. per. 13.95 *(978-1-4327-0615-9(2))* Outskirts Pr., Inc.

Bracken, Alexandra. Passenger. 2016. (Passenger Ser.). (ENG.). 512p. (YA). (gr. 9-17). pap. 9.99 *(978-1-4847-3279-3(0))* Disney Pr.

—Passenger. 2016. (Passenger Ser.). (ENG.). 496p. (YA). (gr. 9-12). 17.99 *(978-1-4847-1577-2(2))* Hyperion Bks. for Children.

—Wayfarer. 2017. (Passenger Ser.). (ENG.). 544p. (YA). (gr. 9-17). 17.99 *(978-1-4847-1576-5(4))* Hyperion Bks. for Children.

Brackett, Michael. The Adventures of Bunny & Hare. 2010. 138p. pap. 11.00 *(978-1-60911-296-7(2)*, Eloquent Bks.) Strategic Book Publishing & Rights Agency (SBPRA).

Braddock, Paige. Jane's World, Vol. 4. 2006. (ENG., Illus.). 160p. pap. 15.00 *(978-0-9766707-3-5(9)*, 9780976670735) Girl Twirl Comics.

Braddock, Pauline. The long way Home. 2010. 156p. pap. 9.17 *(978-1-4452-9248-9(3))* Lulu Pr., Inc.

Bradford, Chris. Hostage, Bk. 2. 2017. (Bodyguard Ser.). (ENG.). 224p. (J). (gr. 5). pap. 8.99 *(978-1-5247-3699-6(6)*, Philomel Bks.) Penguin Young Readers Group.

—Ninja: First Mission. 2012. (Stoke Books Titles Ser.). 64p. (J). (gr. 5-8). pap. 45.32 *(978-0-7613-9221-7(1))*; pap. 7.95 *(978-1-78112-022-4(6))*; lib. bdg. 22.60 *(978-1-78112-021-7(8))* Stoke Bks.

—Recruit, Bk. 1. 2017. (Bodyguard Ser.). (ENG.). 272p. (J). (gr. 5). pap. 8.99 *(978-1-5247-3697-2(X)*, Philomel Bks.) Penguin Young Readers Group.

—The Ring of Earth. 4th ed. 2010. (Young Samurai Ser.: 4). (ENG., Illus.). 336p. (YA). (gr. 7). pap. 8.99 *(978-0-14-133253-6(0)*, Penguin Global) Penguin Publishing Group.

—The Ring of Fire. 6th ed. 2011. (Young Samurai Ser.: 6). (ENG., Illus.). 352p. (YA). (gr. 7). pap. 10.95 *(978-0-14-133255-0(7))* Penguin Bks., Ltd. GBR. Dist: Independent Pubs. Group.

—The Ring of Sky. 8th ed. 2012. (Young Samurai Ser.: 8). (ENG., Illus.). 384p. (YA). (gr. 7). pap. 10.95 *(978-0-14-133972-6(1))* Penguin Bks., Ltd. GBR. Dist: Independent Pubs. Group.

—The Ring of Water. 5th ed. 2011. (Young Samurai Ser.: 5). (ENG., Illus.). 320p. (YA). (gr. 7). pap. 8.99 *(978-0-14-133254-3(9))* Penguin Bks., Ltd. GBR. Dist: Independent Pubs. Group.

—The Ring of Wind. 7th ed. 2012. (Young Samurai Ser.: 7). (ENG., Illus.). 368p. (YA). (gr. 7). 8.99 *(978-0-14-133971-9(3)*, Penguin Global) Penguin Publishing Group.

—The Way of the Warrior, Bk. 1. 2008. (Young Samurai Ser.: 1). (ENG., Illus.). 352p. (J). (gr. 6-10). pap. 12.99 ***(978-0-14-132430-2(9))*** Penguin Bks., Ltd. GBR. Dist: Independent Pubs. Group.

—Young Samurai the Way of the Dragon. l.t. ed. 2012. (Young Samurai Ser.). (ENG.). 644p. (J). (gr. 9-12). 23.99 *(978-1-4104-4466-0(X))* Thorndike Pr.

—Young Samurai: the Way of the Sword. 2011. 448p. pap. 7.99 *(978-1-4231-2937-0(7))* Hyperion Pr.

—Young Samurai the Way of the Sword. l.t. ed. 2012. (Young Samurai Ser.). (ENG.). 547p. (J). (gr. 6-9). 23.99 *(978-1-4104-4404-2(X))* Thorndike Pr.

Bradford, Danette J. Eric & Wrinkles Meet the Snacker Sneakers. 2013. 24p. pap. 24.95 *(978-1-4626-9990-2(1))* America Star Bks.

Bradley, A. M. Finnegan's Magic Sunglasses. 2013. 24p. pap. 24.95 *(978-1-62709-814-4(3))* America Star Bks.

Bradley, Adrian. The Faraway Kingdom of Oop Loop la Pink. Laurente, Lourdes, illus. 2013. 36p. pap. 10.95 *(978-0-9910180-0-0(1))* Someday Ranch.

Bradley, F. T. The Alias Men. 2015. (Double Vision Ser.: 3). (ENG.). 256p. (J). (gr. 3-7). pap. 6.99 *(978-0-06-210444-1(6))* HarperCollins Pubs.

—Double Vision. (Double Vision Ser.: 1). (ENG.). (J). (gr. 3-7). 2013. 272p. pap. 6.99 *(978-0-06-210438-0(1))* 2012. (Illus.). 256p. 16.99 *(978-0-06-210437-3(3))* HarperCollins Pubs.

—Double Vision: The Alias Men. 2014. (Double Vision Ser.: 3). (ENG.). 256p. (J). (gr. 3-7). 16.99 *(978-0-06-210443-4(8))* HarperCollins Pubs.

—Double Vision - Code Name 711. 2013. (Double Vision Ser.: 2). (ENG.). 256p. (J). (gr. 3-7). 16.99 *(978-0-06-210440-3(3))* HarperCollins Pubs.

Bradman, Tom. King Fox Purple Band. Bernstein, Galia, illus. 2016. (Cambridge Reading Adventures Ser.). (ENG.). 24p. pap. 7.19 *(978-1-107-56215-8(5))* Cambridge Univ. Pr.

Bradman, Tony. Goldilocks & the Just Right Club. Warburton, Sarah, illus. 2014. (After Happily Ever After Ser.). (ENG.). 56p. (gr. 2-3). pap. 5.05 *(978-1-4342-7963-7(4)*, After Happily Ever After) Stone Arch Bks.

—Polly & the Pirates. Davies, James, illus. 2nd ed. 2016. (Reading Ladder Ser.). (ENG.). 48p. (J). (gr. k-2). 7.99 *(978-1-4052-8249-9(5))* Egmont Bks., Ltd. GBR. Dist: Independent Pubs. Group.

Bradmon, Karen. Goldie: A Fishtale of Adventure. 2008. 22p. pap. 24.95 *(978-1-60672-472-9(X))* America Star Bks.

Bradshaw-White, Karl. The Adventures of Flossy. 2015. (ENG.). 44p. (J). (gr. 1-2). mass mkt. 13.95 *(978-1-78455-971-7(7)*, 51c20d50-dd7c-4585-945d-24d3c8fd00ab) Austin, Stan AUS. Dist: Bookmasters Distribution.

Brady, Carolyn. The Adventures of Pelican Mcfeet: The Big Lumpy Green Monster. Phillips, Deborah, illus. 2008. 32p. pap. 16.95 *(978-1-4389-3539-3(0))* AuthorHouse.

Brady, Laurel. Bronson Row. Date not set. 144p. (YA). (gr. 5-18). 14.99 *(978-0-06-029234-8(2))*; lib. bdg. 15.89 *(978-0-06-029235-5(0))*; mass mkt. 4.99 *(978-0-06-440949-0(X))* HarperCollins Pubs.

Brafman, Joshua. Death Bunny! 2008. 248p. 26.95 *(978-0-595-51446-5(4))*; pap. 16.95 *(978-0-595-52098-5(7))* iUniverse, Inc.

Bragg, Jane. Teddy Bears Christmas Miracle. 2009. 49p. pap. 18.70 *(978-0-557-22087-8(4))* Lulu Pr., Inc.

Brahney, Jenny. Spotty, 1 vol. 2010. 30p. pap. 24.95 *(978-1-4489-8497-8(1))* PublishAmerica, Inc.

Brain, Helen. No More Secrets. 2009. (Hodder African Readers Ser.). (Illus.). 144p. pap. 12.95 *(978-0-340-98419-2(8))* Hodder Education Group GBR. Dist: Trans-Atlantic Pubns., Inc.

Braithwaite, Lisa. Lucy Goes into the Wild. 2012. 28p. pap. 15.99 *(978-1-4771-4341-4(6))* Xlibris Corp.

Brallier, Max. Galactic Hot Dogs 2: The Wiener Strikes Back. Maguire, Rachel & Kelley, Nichole, illus. 2016. (Galactic Hot Dogs Ser.: 2). (ENG.). 288p. (J). (gr. 3-7). 13.99 *(978-1-4814-2496-7(3)*, Aladdin) Simon & Schuster Children's Publishing.

Bramble bear; the Missing Necklace. 2006. (J). per. 3.99 *(978-1-934004-12-8(X))* Byeway Bks.

Bramlett, Timothy A. Sharkey Explores the Unknown. 2007. pap. 14.95 *(978-0-9796444-0-5(2))* Azuria Bks.

—A Visit to Skytropolis. 2012. 24p. pap. 17.99 *(978-1-4772-1173-1(X))* AuthorHouse.

Bramucci, Stephen. The Danger Gang & the Pirates of Borneo! Chung, Arree, illus. 2017. (ENG.). 384p. (J). 16.99 *(978-1-61963-692-7(1)*, 9781619636927, Bloomsbury USA Childrens) Bloomsbury Publishing USA.

Branca, James. The Adventures of General Azù " Azù Explores the World. 2010. 44p. pap. 18.49 *(978-1-4520-2218-5(6))* AuthorHouse.

Branch, Beverly, illus. Thumbelina: A Tale about Being Nice. 2006. (J). 6.99 *(978-1-59939-024-6(8))* Cornerstone Pr.

Branch, Keith. Forest Elves: Protectors of the Rainforest. 2013. (ENG.). 42p. (J). pap. 8.95 *(978-1-4787-0650-2(3))* Outskirts Pr., Inc.

Brand, Mary. Aspen Cat: Adventurer Extraordinaire. Roberts, Tempie, illus. 2009. 44p. pap. 24.95 *(978-1-60749-165-1(6))* America Star Bks.

Brand New Vagabond. Date not set. (J). pap. 140.40 *(978-0-590-39633-2(1))* Scholastic, Inc.

Brandeis, Madeline. Shaun O'Day of Ireland. 2004. reprint ed. pap. 22.95 *(978-1-4179-2725-8(9))* Kessinger Publishing, LLC.

Brandt, Linda M. Henry's Life As a Tulip Bulb: Developing an Attitude of Gratitude (Book 1) Brandt, Linda M., illus. 2013. (Illus.). 24p. pap. 15.95 *(978-1-61314-084-0(3))* Innovo Publishing, LLC.

Branford, Anna. Violet Mackerel's Outside-the-Box Set: Violet Mackerel's Brilliant Plot; Violet Mackerel's Remarkable Recovery; Violet Mackerel's Natural Habita; Violet Mackerel's Personal Space. Allen, Elanna, illus. 2013. (Violet Mackerel Ser.). (ENG.). 464p. (J). (gr. 1-5). pap. 23.99 *(978-1-4424-8859-5(X)*, Atheneum Bks. for Young Readers) Simon & Schuster Children's Publishing.

Brannon, Tom, illus. Where Are You Going, Charlie Brown? 2014. (Peanuts Great American Adventure Ser.). (ENG.). 40p. (J). (gr. -1). 16.99 *(978-1-62157-258-9(7)*, Little Patriot Pr.) Regnery Publishing, Inc., An Eagle Publishing Co.

Branson, Eve. Sarky Puddleboat. Lowe, Wes, illus. 2011. 44p. (J). 14.99 *(978-1-4520-9754-1(2))* AuthorHouse.

Brant, Dennis, Jr. No Andy No! Sciulli, Erika, illus. 2008. 18p. pap. 24.95 *(978-1-60703-203-8(1))* America Star Bks.

Brantley, Meg. Love Family Adventures. 2009. 116p. pap. 11.99 *(978-1-60791-786-1(6))* Salem Author Services.

Brashear Hopper, Celia. The Merry Adventures of Blade & Friends. 2007. (YA). lib. bdg. 26.95 *(978-0-9795460-1-3(X))* Creative Bk. Pubs.

Braswell, Liz. Once upon a Dream: A Twisted Tale. 2017. (Twisted Tale Ser.). (ENG.). 464p. (YA). (gr. 7-17). pap. 9.99 *(978-1-4847-0730-2(3))* Disney Pr.

Braswell, Robert William. Jeffrey: Out from the Depths of Innocence. 2003. 358p. (YA). pap. 19.95 *(978-0-595-26734-7(3)*, Writers Club Pr.) iUniverse, Inc.

Braun, Eric. Goldilocks & the Three Bears: An Interactive Fairy Tale Adventure. Lopez, Alex, illus. 2015. (You Choose: Fractured Fairy Tales Ser.). (ENG.). 112p. (gr. 3-4). lib. bdg. 31.99 *(978-1-4914-5855-6(0)*, You Choose Bks.) Capstone Press of Coughlan Cos.

Brauner, Susan. The Adventures of Sohi: Mystery of Moon Island. 2011. 207p. 28.95 *(978-1-4327-6752-5(6))*; pap. 15.95 *(978-1-4327-6536-1(1))* Outskirts Pr., Inc.

Bray, Adam. Lego Star Wars: Into Battle! 2015. (DK Adventures Ser.). lib. bdg. 16.00 *(978-0-606-36923-7(6))* Turtleback Bks.

Bray, Sorcha. The Adventures of Powerpup & Wonderboy & the Case of the Wicked Chickens. 2010. 48p. pap. 19.75 *(978-1-4490-7133-2(3))* AuthorHouse.

Braymer, Donna. The Adventures of Rowdy Raccoon. 2006. (J). audio compact disk 5.99 *(978-0-9766823-8-7(9))* Sable Creek Pr. LLC.

Brazier, Vaughan. Zach Zephyr & the Coral Gold. 2013. 204p. pap. *(978-1-925086-17-1(8))* Vivid Publishing.

Brazier, Yvonne. Princess Jordan Saves Golden Tree. 2008. 20p. pap. 12.49 *(978-1-4389-3591-1(9))* AuthorHouse.

Brazil, Angela. Monitress Merle. 2004. reprint ed. pap. 1.99 *(978-1-4192-3491-0(9))* Kessinger Publishing, LLC.

Breen, Krista Michelle. Quicksand: The Mysterious Disappearance of Dakotaroo. 2012. pap. *(978-0-9735241-0-9(3))* Groundskeeper's Cottage.

Brege, K. B. Grudge of the Gremlins. 2007. (Mick Morris Myth Solver Ser.: No. 4). pap. 6.99 *(978-0-9774119-3-1(1))* Team B Creative LLC.

Brehm, David L. Willy Nilly Volume 1. Claerhout, Paul, illus. 2013. 94p. (J). pap. 19.95 *(978-0-9860669-0-0(7))* Blue Logic Publishing.

Bremauntz, M. The Adventures of Marcela & Little Joey: Little Joey Loves Bugs. 2010. 32p. 17.25 *(978-1-4269-4417-8(9))* Trafford Publishing.

Brenchley, Chaz & Doyle, Arthur Conan. The Lost World. Bennett, Felix, illus. 2009. (Real Reads Ser.). 64p. (J). (gr. 4-8). pap. 13.55 *(978-1-60754-395-4(8))*; lib. bdg. 29.25 *(978-1-60754-394-7(X))* Windmill Bks.

Brenes, Carlos A. Private Billy. 2011. 32p. pap. 16.95 *(978-1-4560-9096-8(8))* America Star Bks.

Brennan, Herbie. Faerie Wars, Vol. 1. 2004. (Faerie Wars Chronicles Ser.). (ENG.). 384p. (YA). reprint ed. pap. 8.99 *(978-1-58234-943-5(6)*, 9781582349435, Bloomsbury USA Childrens) Bloomsbury Publishing USA.

—El Monstruo del Pantano. (Raton de Biblioteca Coleccion). (SPA.). 128p. (J). (gr. 3). 7.95 *(978-84-88061-87-4(0))* Serres, Ediciones, S. L. ESP. Dist: Lectorum Pubns., Inc.

—The Secret Prophecy. 2012. (ENG.). 368p. (J). (gr. 3-7). 16.99 *(978-0-06-207180-4(7))* HarperCollins Pubs.

Brenner, Barbara, et al. Bunny Tails. Munsinger, Lynn, illus. 2005. 32p. 15.95 *(978-0-689-03925-6(5),* Milk & Cookies) ibooks, Inc.

Brent, Alexander Michael. Play Date with T-Rex: The Adventures of Jake & Sammy Wiggles. 2010. 52p. pap. 19.50 *(978-1-4520-7531-0(X))* AuthorHouse.

Breshears, Alyce Park. Run, Girl, Run! Boyd, Shelby, illus. 2013. 36p. pap. 7.95 *(978-1-60414-742-1(3))* Fideli Publishing, Inc.

Breslin, Jayne. The Princess Jelly Tutu Adventures. 2011. (Illus.). 28p. (gr. -1). pap. 14.09 *(978-1-4567-7611-4(8))* AuthorHouse.

Brewer, Janey. Mist & Moonlight. 2007. 76p. per. 19.95 *(978-1-4241-9525-1(X))* America Star Bks.

Brewer, Sarah. Our New Garden. Brewer, Sarah & Brewer, Dean, illus. 2013. 20p. pap. 24.95 *(978-1-63004-768-9(6))* America Star Bks.

Brewin, Barbara. Sidney Snail's Wonderful World of Adventure. 2009. (Illus.). 32p. pap. 14.49 *(978-1-4389-4100-4(5))* AuthorHouse.

Brewster, James Burd. Uncle Rocky, Fireman: Fire! Barley-Cohrs, Dayna, illus. 2013. 34p. pap. 11.49 *(978-0-9911994-1-9(3))* J2B Publishing LLC.

—Uncle Rocky, Fireman: Something's Missing. Barley-Cohrs, Dayna, illus. 2013. 34p. pap. 11.49 *(978-0-9911994-2-6(1))* J2B Publishing LLC.

Brezenoff, Steve. I Dare You! Hilliker, Phillip, illus. 2008. (Vortex Bks.). (ENG.). 112p. (gr. 2-3). 26.65 *(978-1-4342-0798-2(6),* Vortex Bks.) Stone Arch Bks.

—Time Voyage, 1 vol. Murphy, Scott, illus. 2012. (Return to Titanic Ser.). (ENG.). 112p. (gr. 2-3). pap. 6.95 *(978-1-4342-3909-9(8))*; lib. bdg. 25.32 *(978-1-4342-3299-1(9))* Stone Arch Bks. (Return to Titanic).

—An Unsinkable Ship, 1 vol. Murphy, Scott, illus. 2012. (Return to Titanic Ser.). (ENG.). 112p. (gr. 2-3). pap. 6.95 *(978-1-4342-3911-2(X),* Return to Titanic) Stone Arch Bks.

Brezina, Thomas & Sartin, Laurence. Who Will Find Vincent's Treasury of Colors? 2005. (Illus.). 96p. pap. 16.95 *(978-3-7913-3433-2(6))* Prestel Publishing.

Brianna, et al. The Adventures of Sam Spike. 2012. 50p. pap. 11.95 *(978-0-9711774-0-6(6))* AnEx Pubns.

Brice, Gary. The Birds, Their Carols Raise. 2017. (ENG.). 140p. pap. 14.00 ***(978-1-62288-162-8(1))*** Austin, Stephen F. State Univ. Pr.

Briceno, Carole. Turtle's Journey, 1 vol. White, Tina Jorgenson, illus. 2009. 28p. pap. 24.95 *(978-1-60813-934-7(4))* America Star Bks.

Bricker, Chris. The Leaping Frogs of Calameris County. 2006. 48p. pap. 16.95 *(978-1-4241-2408-4(5))* PublishAmerica, Inc.

Bridges, Eunice. A Day Like Mine. Goodwin, Adrienne Annette, illus. 2011. 32p. pap. 24.95 *(978-1-4560-5766-4(9))* America Star Bks.

Bridges, Robin. The Katerina Trilogy, Vol. II: the Unfailing Light. 2013. (ENG.). 320p. (YA). (gr. 7). pap. 9.99 *(978-0-385-74025-8(5),* Ember) Random Hse. Children's Bks.

Bridgman, Rae. Kingdom of Trolls: A Middlegate Book. 2010. (Illus.). 287p. (J). pap. 15.00 *(978-0-9864974-1-4(X))* Sybertooth, Inc. CAN. Dist: Lightning Source, Inc.

Bridwell, Norman & Scholastic, Inc. Staff. Clifford's Bedtime Story Box. Bridwell, Norman, illus. 2013. (ENG., Illus.). (J). (gr. -1-k). pap. 10.99 *(978-0-545-61521-1(6))* Scholastic, Inc.

Briggs, Andy. Council of Evil. 2009. 1.00 *(978-1-4074-4313-3(5))* Recorded Bks., Inc.

—The Jungle Warrior. 2012. (Tarzan Ser.). (ENG.). 206p. (J). (gr. 3-6). pap. 12.99 *(978-1-4532-7108-7(2),* Open Road Media E-riginal) Open Road Integrated Media, Inc.

—Rise of the Heroes. 2009. 1.00 *(978-1-4074-4312-6(7))* Recorded Bks., Inc.

—Tarzan: The Greystoke Legacy. 2011. (ENG.). 304p. pap. *(978-0-571-27238-9(X))* Faber & Faber, Ltd.

Briggs, Mark T. Jermaine Peterman & the Encounter in the Forest. 2012. 44p. pap. 16.95 *(978-1-4626-8431-1(9))* America Star Bks.

Briggs, Meredith. Polka-Dot Parade. 2007. 52p. per. 16.95 *(978-1-4241-8366-1(9))* America Star Bks.

Briggs, Molly Anne. Momma's Favorite Rock. 2006. (J). pap. 8.00 *(978-0-8059-7070-8(3))* Dorrance Publishing Co., Inc.

Bright, J. E. Best Friends - Continental Drift. 2012. (I Can Read Level 2 Ser.). (ENG.). 32p. (J). (gr. k-3). pap. 3.99 *(978-0-06-210483-0(7))* HarperCollins Pubs.

—Brain Freeze! 2010. (Step into Reading Level 2 Ser.). lib. bdg. 13.55 *(978-0-606-14651-7(2),* Turtleback) Turtleback Bks.

—The Case of the Cheese Thief, 1 vol. Neely, Scott, illus. 2014. (You Choose Stories: Scooby-Doo Ser.). (ENG.). 112p. (gr. 2-3). pap. 6.95 *(978-1-4342-7927-9(8),* You Choose Bks.) Capstone Press of Coughlan Cos.

—Continental Drift: Manny's Big Adventure. 2012. (I Can Read Level 2 Ser.). (ENG.). 32p. (J). (gr. k-3). pap. 3.99 *(978-0-06-210481-6(0))* HarperCollins Pubs.

—Cosmic Clash. 2016. (LEGO DC Super Heroes Chapter Book Ser.). (ENG.). 64p. (J). (gr. -1-3). 14.75 *(978-0-606-39150-4(9))* Turtleback Bks.

—Super Hero Adventures: the Amazing Chase: A Move-Along Adventure. Laufman, Derek, illus. 2017. (ENG.). 12p. (J). (gr. -1-k). bds. 8.99 ***(978-1-4847-8886-8(9),*** Marvel Pr.) Disney Publishing Worldwide.

Bright, J. E. Walking with Dinosaurs: Patchi's Big Adventure. 2013. (Walking with Dinosaurs Ser.). (ENG.). 24p. (J). (gr. -1-3). pap. 4.99 *(978-0-06-223275-5(4),* HarperFestival) HarperCollins Pubs.

Bright, J. E. & West, Alexandra. Super Hero Adventures: Save the Day! Laufman, Derek, illus. 2017. (ENG.). 14p. (J). (gr. -1-k). bds. 10.99 ***(978-1-4847-8859-2(1),*** Marvel Pr.) Disney Publishing Worldwide.

Bright, Phoebe. Lucky Stars #1: Wish upon a Friend. 2012. (Lucky Stars Ser.). (ENG.). 96p. (J). (gr. 2-5). pap. 5.99 *(978-0-545-41998-7(0),* Scholastic Paperbacks) Scholastic, Inc.

—Wish upon a Gift. 2012. (Lucky Stars Ser.: 6). (ENG.). 96p. (J). (gr. 2-5). pap. 5.99 *(978-0-545-42003-7(2),* Scholastic Paperbacks) Scholastic, Inc.

Brightman, Michelle. If I Were. 2012. 24p. pap. 15.99 *(978-1-4771-3385-9(2))* Xlibris Corp.

Brightwood, Laura, illus. Mousanga Bira Mousa. Brightwood, Laura, . 2006. (J). *(978-0-9789871-1-4(X))* 3-C Institute for Social Development.

Briley, Randy. Mr Underneath. 2013. 134p. pap. 12.99 *(978-0-9896269-0-3(3))* Raven Mad Studios.

Brill, Marlene Targ. The Rough-Riding Adventure of Bronco Charlie, Pony Express Rider. 2010. pap. 51.02 *(978-0-7613-6920-2(1))* Lerner Publishing Group.

—The Rough-Riding Adventure of Bronco Charlie, Pony Express Rider. Trover, Zachary, illus. 2010. (History's Kid Heroes Ser.). (ENG.). 32p. (gr. 3-5). pap. 8.95 *(978-0-7613-6195-4(2),* Graphic Universe™); lib. bdg. 26.60 *(978-0-7613-6176-3(6))* Lerner Publishing Group.

Brimmer, Debi & Coleson, Julie. How Six Little Ipu Got Their Names. Coleson, Julie, illus. 2005. (Illus.). 30p. (J). 9.95 incl. audio compact disk *(978-1-57306-186-5(7))* Bess Pr., Inc.

Brin, Susannah. The Climb. Miller, Fujiko, illus. rev. ed. 2004. (Take Ten Ser.). 61p. (J). (gr. 4-12). pap. 4.95 *(978-1-58659-042-0(1))* Artesian Pr.

—Search & Rescue. Miller, Fujiko, illus. rev. ed. 2004. (Take Ten Ser.). 62p. (J). (gr. 4-12). pap. 4.95 *(978-1-58659-043-7(X))* Artesian Pr.

—Tough Guy. Miller, Fujiko, illus. rev. ed. 2004. (Take Ten Ser.). 62p. (J). (gr. 4-12). pap. 4.95 *(978-1-58659-045-1(6))* Artesian Pr.

Bringsvaerd, Tor Age. Ruffen: The Escape to Loch Ness. Hansen, Thore, illus. 2009. (Ruffen Ser.). 72p. (J). (gr. 1-4). 16.95 *(978-0-9815761-2-1(5))* Mackenzie Smiles, LLC.

Brinley, Bertrand R. The Mad Scientists' Club Complete Collection. Geer, Charles, illus. 2010. 619p. (YA). pap. 29.99 *(978-1-930900-51-6(1))* Purple Hse. Pr.

Brinson, Heather. The Adventure of the Poisoned Drink. 2005. 59p. pap. 16.95 *(978-1-4137-9239-3(1))* PublishAmerica, Inc.

Britland, Jan. The Adventures of Rodger Dodger Dog. Swaim, Michael, illus. 2009. 40p. pap. 15.95 *(978-1-936051-23-6(0))* Peppertree Pr., The.

—The Adventures of Rodger Dodger Dog: A Christmas Story. Swaim, Michael, illus. 2009. 52p. pap. 18.95 *(978-1-936051-48-9(6))* Peppertree Pr., The.

Broach, Elise. Gumption! Egielski, Richard, illus. 2010. (ENG.). 40p. (J). (gr. k-3). 18.99 *(978-1-4169-1628-4(8),* Atheneum Bks. for Young Readers) Simon & Schuster Children's Publishing.

Broach, Elise. James to the Rescue. 2017. (Masterpiece Adventures Ser.: 2). (J). lib. bdg. 16.00 ***(978-0-606-39583-0(0))*** Turtleback Bks.

Broadbent, Tom & Kosmo, Lisa. Henrietta. 2009. pap. *(978-1-61623-033-3(9))* Independent Pub.

Broadhurst, Sherree. Bella Finds the Hidden Treasure. 2009. 28p. pap. 12.25 *(978-1-60693-815-7(0),* Eloquent Bks.) Strategic Book Publishing & Rights Agency (SBPRA).

—Bella's Adventures: Bella in the City. Broadhurst, Colin, illus. 2010. 38p. pap. 14.50 *(978-1-60976-179-0(0),* Eloquent Bks.) Strategic Book Publishing & Rights Agency (SBPRA).

—Bella's Adventures: Bella Rescues Gumleaf the Joey. 2010. 46p. pap. 16.50 *(978-1-60911-068-0(4),* Eloquent Bks.) Strategic Book Publishing & Rights Agency (SBPRA).

Broadribb, Donald. Marcia. 2009. 423p. 39.47 *(978-1-4092-6754-6(7))* Lulu Pr., Inc.

Brock, J. Judd. Ima Toothlusa Is My Name. 2007. (Illus.). 38p. (J). (gr. -1-3). per. 11.99 *(978-1-59879-247-8(4))* Lifevest Publishing, Inc.

Brockington, Drew. CatStronauts: Mission Moon. 2017. (CatStronauts Ser.: 1). (J). lib. bdg. 18.40 ***(978-0-606-39900-5(3))*** Turtleback Bks.

—CatStronauts: Race to Mars. 2017. (CatStronauts Ser.: 2). (J). lib. bdg. 18.40 ***(978-0-606-39901-2(1))*** Turtleback Bks.

Brockman, Craig. Marty & the Far Woodchuck. 2007. 116p. pap. 11.95 *(978-1-4357-0273-8(5))* Lulu Pr., Inc.

Brockmann, Suzanne & Brockmann, Melanie. Night Sky. 2014. (Night Sky Ser.: 1). (ENG.). 496p. (YA). (gr. 8-12). 16.99 *(978-1-4926-0144-9(6))* Sourcebooks, Inc.

—Wild Sky: A Night Sky Novel. 2015. (Night Sky Ser.: 2). (ENG.). 448p. (YA). (gr. 8-12). 16.99 *(978-1-4926-0484-6(4))*; pap. 9.99 *(978-1-4926-2314-4(8))* Sourcebooks, Inc.

Brockway, Bettina Chevalier. Muff & the Mushroom Forest. 2010. 32p. pap. 23.50 *(978-1-4520-7426-9(7))* AuthorHouse.

Brodhead, Kimberly. Gaden's Tower: Book One. 2007. 164p. per. 24.95 *(978-1-60441-038-9(8))* America Star Bks.

Brodien-Jones, Chris. The Glass Puzzle. 2013. (Illus.). 319p. (J). *(978-0-385-74298-6(3),* Delacorte Pr) Random House Publishing Group.

Brodien-Jones, Christine. The Glass Puzzle. 2013. (ENG., Illus.). 336p. (J). (gr. 4-7). 16.99 *(978-0-385-74297-9(5),* Delacorte Bks. for Young Readers) Random Hse. Children's Bks.

—The Scorpions of Zahir. Murphy, Kelly, illus. 2012. (ENG.). 384p. (J). (gr. 5). 17.99 *(978-0-385-73933-7(8),* Delacorte Bks. for Young Readers) Random Hse. Children's Bks.

Brodnax, Stephan. Dillwyn & the Purple Picnic Pack, 1 vol. 2009. 19p. pap. 24.95 *(978-1-4241-9593-0(4))* America Star Bks.

Brodsky, Irene. The Adventures of Silly Kitty, Princess Jasmine & First Puppy. 2010. (Illus.). 44p. (J). pap. 23.95 *(978-1-4327-5552-2(8))* Outskirts Pr., Inc.

Brody, Jennifer. Return of the Continuums. 2016. (Continuum Trilogy Ser.: 2). (ENG.). 432p. (YA). 36.95 *(978-1-68162-259-0(9))*; pap. 14.95 *(978-1-68162-258-3(0))* Turner Publishing Co.

Brody, Jessica. Disney Descendants School of Secrets, Bk. 3. No New Art Needed & Disney Storybook Art Team, illus. 2017. (School of Secrets Ser.: 3). (ENG.). 192p. (J). (gr. 3-7). bds. 9.99 *(978-1-4847-7866-1(9))* Disney Pr.

Brogle, Jennifer. The Adventures of Jennifer & Sherry: Summertime. 2013. 60p. pap. 25.36 *(978-1-4669-7560-6(1))* Trafford Publishing.

Brontë, Charlotte. Tales of the Islanders. 2011. (Hesperus Classics Ser.). (ENG., Illus.). 92p. pap. 12.95 *(978-1-84391-201-9(5))* Hesperus Pr. GBR. Dist: Independent Pubs. Group.

Bronte, Jules & Oapos, Jem, illus. The Castle Adventure. 2013. 171p. pap. *(978-1-908804-08-2(4))* Bingham Mayne & Smith, Ltd.

Brook, Harry, retold by. Kidnapped. 2004. (Paperback Classics Ser.). 144p. (J). lib. bdg. 12.95 *(978-1-58086-640-8(9),* Usborne) EDC Publishing.

Brook, Henry, retold by. Tom Sawyer. 2008. (Usborne Classics Retold Ser.). 160p. (J). pap. 4.99 *(978-0-7945-2063-2(4),* Usborne) EDC Publishing.

Brooke, S. The Snow Diamond: the Fourth Journey, 1 vol. 2010. 180p. pap. 24.95 *(978-1-4512-1383-6(2))* America Star Bks.

Brooke, Samantha. Unikitty: A Cuckoo Adventure. 2014. lib. bdg. 13.55 *(978-0-606-36365-5(3))* Turtleback Bks.

—Unikitty - A Cuckoo Adventure. 2014. (LEGO: the LEGO Movie Ser.). (ENG., Illus.). 24p. (J). (gr. -1-3). pap. 3.99 *(978-0-545-79541-8(9))* Scholastic, Inc.

Brookover, Brian D. Neddy & Little Roy Go to Town. 2013. 40p. pap. 20.99 *(978-1-4817-1185-2(7))* AuthorHouse.

Brooks, Dominic, illus. Is It My Turn Yet? 2008. 30p. (J). per. *(978-0-9795768-2-9(2))* Better Tomorrow Publishing, A.

Brooks, Donna. The Golden Spindle. 2010. 112p. pap. 30.00 *(978-1-60860-852-2(2),* Eloquent Bks.) Strategic Book Publishing & Rights Agency (SBPRA).

Brooks, Estell. Magic Farm: A Day of Fun & Adventure. 2004. 96p. (gr. 2-2). pap. 9.95 *(978-0-595-32321-0(9))* iUniverse, Inc.

Brooks, Felicity. Jason & the Argonauts. Humphreys, Graham, illus. 2005. 144p. (J). pap. 4.95 *(978-0-7945-0275-1(X),* Usborne) EDC Publishing.

Brooks, G. Alan & Grandchildren. The Adventures of Zumba & Rumb: Book One - the Separation. 2012. 164p. 29.99 *(978-1-4691-9820-0(7))* Xlibris Corp.

Brooks, Linda Sue. Meet Toado & Friends. Mills, Lori, illus. l.t. ed. 2008. (Toado & Friends Ser.). (ENG.). 30p. (J). (gr. -1-3). per. 11.99 *(978-1-59879-314-7(4),* Lifevest) Lifevest Publishing, Inc.

Brooks-Scrivanich, Olivia. Fiscal Pear & Shimmer in the Call of River Whale. 2008. (ENG.). 92p. pap. 14.99 *(978-1-4196-9589-6(4))* CreateSpace Independent Publishing Platform.

Brooks, Walt. Walter's Pet Bee. 2011. 36p. pap. 16.86 *(978-1-4634-4919-3(4))* AuthorHouse.

Brooks, Walter R. Freddy & the Perilous Adventure. Wiese, Kurt, illus. 2012. (ENG.). 256p. 10.99 *(978-1-59020-742-0(4),* 902742) Overlook Pr., The.

Bross, Lee. Tangled Webs. 2016. (Tangled Webs Ser.). (ENG., Illus.). 400p. (YA). (gr. 9-17). pap. 9.99 *(978-1-4231-9467-5(5))* Hyperion Bks. for Children.

Brost, April. Luckyduck Luckyduck. 2013. 24p. pap. 24.95 *(978-1-63004-104-5(1))* America Star Bks.

Brost, Diane. Courage at Crow Wing River, 1 vol. 2010. 36p. 24.95 *(978-1-4512-1254-9(2))* PublishAmerica, Inc.

Brother, Ernest. Dick of Copper Gap. 2005. pap. 24.95 *(978-1-4179-8824-2(X))* Kessinger Publishing, LLC.

Brothers Grimm. Snow White & Rose Red: A Grimms' Fairy Tale. Marshall, Denise, illus. 2008. 28p. (J). 17.95 *(978-0-88010-591-0(7),* Bell Pond Bks.) SteinerBooks, Inc.

Brouillette, Kathy. What Makes me Smile. 2010. 16p. 8.99 *(978-1-4520-1112-7(5))* AuthorHouse.

Brouwer, Sigmund. Devil's Pass, 1 vol. 2012. (Seven (the Series) Ser.). (ENG., Illus.). 256p. (J). (gr. 5-10). pap. 9.95 *(978-1-55469-938-4(X))* Orca Bk. Pubs. USA.

—Justine Mckeen & the Bird Nerd, 1 vol. Whamond, Dave, illus. 2013. (Orca Echoes Ser.). (ENG.). 64p. (J). (gr. 2-3). pap. 6.95 *(978-1-4598-0394-7(9))* Orca Bk. Pubs. USA.

—Justine Mckeen, Eat Your Beets, 1 vol. Whamond, Dave, illus. 2013. (Orca Echoes Ser.). (ENG.). 64p. (J). (gr. 2-3). pap. 6.95 *(978-1-55469-933-9(9))* Orca Bk. Pubs. USA.

—Wired, 1 vol. 2005. (Orca Currents Ser.). (ENG.). 128p. (J). (gr. 5-9). per. 9.95 *(978-1-55143-478-0(4))* Orca Bk. Pubs. USA.

Brouwer, Sigmund & Gingras, Gaston. La Revanche des Loups Gris, 1 vol. Griffiths, Dean, illus. 2011. (Loups Gris Ser.). (FRE.). 72p. (J). (gr. 2-3). pap. 6.95 *(978-1-4598-0011-3(7))* Orca Bk. Pubs. USA.

Brown, Abbie Farwell. Tales of the Red Children. 2006. pap. 20.95 *(978-1-4286-1602-8(0))* Kessinger Publishing, LLC.

Brown, Adam. The Adventures of Wormie Wormington Book Three: Wormie & the Snowball. Smart, Andy, illus. 2013. 48p. pap. *(978-0-9919196-3-5(7))* Beckon Creative.

—The Adventures of Wormie Wormington Book Two: Wormie & the Kite. Smart, Andy, illus. 2013. 48p. pap. *(978-0-9919196-2-8(9))* Beckon Creative.

Brown, Adam & Smart, Andy. The Adventures of Wormie Wormington Book One: Wormie & the Fish. Smart, Andy, illus. 2013. (Illus.). 50p. pap. *(978-0-9919196-0-4(2))* Beckon Creative.

Brown, Alan James. Michael & the Monkey King. 2008. 180p. pap. 16.95 *(978-1-4092-0241-7(0))* Lulu Pr., Inc.

Brown, Anne. The Dumari Chronicles: Year One: Year One. 2007. 376p. (YA). per. 20.95 *(978-0-595-45725-0(8))* iUniverse, Inc.

Brown, Barbara. The Adventures of Captain Crick, Super Hero. 2011. 28p. pap. 21.99 *(978-1-4568-5005-0(9))* Xlibris Corp.

Brown, Brooklyn. Kifaru Tries Something New. 2012. 32p. (-18). pap. 16.95 *(978-1-4575-1470-8(2))* Dog Ear Publishing, LLC.

Brown, Bruce. Mwumba. O'Reilly, Sean Patrick, ed. 2011. (Illus.). 48p. (J). pap. 7.95 *(978-1-897548-03-5(6))* Arcana Studio, Inc.

Brown, Corinne. Let's Keep This Secret. 2004. (J). per. 5.95 *(978-0-9745951-5-3(2))* All For One Pr.

Brown, Cornelia. Constance the Little Angel Wants Curls. 2009. 28p. pap. 15.99 *(978-1-4490-3962-2(6))* AuthorHouse.

Brown, Courtney Allison. BJ Goes to School. 2008. 36p. per. 24.95 *(978-1-4241-9724-8(4))* America Star Bks.

Brown, Daniel. Chipper Learns a Lesson. 2013. 28p. pap. 5.99 *(978-0-9897549-1-4(4))* Story and Logic Media Group.

Brown, Ian L. Clement & Oscar's American Adventure. Launos, Nina, illus. 2017. (ENG.). 84p. (J). pap. 16.95 ***(978-1-78629-995-6(X),*** 80b9564b-3043-4c5f-b05c-8b40dac9ad8a) Austin, Stan AUS. Dist: Bookmasters Distribution.

Brown, Janet. The Three Billy Goats Gruff (Floor Book) Morton, Ken, illus. 2015. (ENG.). 24p. (J). (gr. -1-1). pap. 6.99 *(978-1-86147-397-4(4),* Armadillo) Anness Publishing GBR. Dist: National Bk. Network.

Brown, Jeff. The African Safari Discovery. Pamintuan, Macky, illus. 2010. (Flat Stanley's Worldwide Adventures Ser.: 6). (ENG.). 112p. (J). (gr. 2-5). pap. 4.99 *(978-0-06-143000-8(5))*;No. 6. 15.99 *(978-0-06-143001-5(3))* HarperCollins Pubs.

—The Amazing Mexican Secret. Pamintuan, Macky, illus. 2010. (Flat Stanley's Worldwide Adventures Ser.: 5). (ENG.). 112p. (J). (gr. 2-5). pap. 4.99 *(978-0-06-142998-9(8))*;No. 5. 15.99 *(978-0-06-142999-6(6))* HarperCollins Pubs.

—The Australian Boomerang Bonanza. Pamintuan, Macky, illus. 2011. (Flat Stanley's Worldwide Adventures Ser.: 8). (ENG.). 112p. (J). (gr. 2-5). 15.99 *(978-0-06-157435-1(X))* HarperCollins Pubs.

—The Australian Boomerang Bonanza No. 8. Pamintuan, Macky, illus. 2011. (Flat Stanley's Worldwide Adventures Ser.: 8). (ENG.). 112p. (J). (gr. 2-5). pap. 4.99 *(978-0-06-143018-3(8))* HarperCollins Pubs.

—Flat Stanley - On Ice. Pamintuan, Macky, illus. 2015. (I Can Read Level 2 Ser.). (ENG.). 32p. (J). (gr. -1-3). pap. 3.99 *(978-0-06-218981-3(6))* HarperCollins Pubs.

—Flat Stanley & the Haunted House. Pamintuan, Macky, illus. 2010. (I Can Read Level 2 Ser.). (ENG.). 32p. (J). (gr. -1-3). 16.99 *(978-0-06-143004-6(8))* HarperCollins Pubs.

—Flat Stanley & the Lost Treasure. Pamintuan, Macky, illus. 2016. (I Can Read Level 2 Ser.). 32p. (J). (gr. -1-3). pap. 3.99 *(978-0-06-236595-8(9))* HarperCollins Pubs.

—Flat Stanley & the Lost Treasure. 2016. (Flat Stanley: I Can Read Ser.). (J). lib. bdg. 13.55 *(978-0-606-38757-6(9))* Turtleback Bks.

—Flat Stanley Goes Camping. Pamintuan, Macky, illus. 2013. (I Can Read Level 2 Ser.). (ENG.). 32p. (J). (gr. -1-3). 16.99 *(978-0-06-143013-8(7))*; pap. 3.99 *(978-0-06-143015-2(3))* HarperCollins Pubs.

—Flat Stanley's Worldwide Adventures #12: Escape to California. Pamintuan, Macky, illus. 2014. (Flat Stanley's Worldwide Adventures Ser.: 12). (ENG.). 128p. (J). (gr. 1-5). pap. 4.99 *(978-0-06-218990-5(5))* HarperCollins Pubs.

—The Intrepid Canadian Expedition. Pamintuan, Macky, illus. 2009. (Flat Stanley's Worldwide Adventures Ser.: 4). (ENG.). 112p. (J). (gr. 2-5). 15.99 *(978-0-06-142997-2(X))* HarperCollins Pubs.

—The Intrepid Canadian Expedition. 2009. (Flat Stanley's Worldwide Adventures Ser.: 4). (J). lib. bdg. 14.75 *(978-0-606-10068-7(7),* Turtleback) Turtleback Bks.

—The Intrepid Canadian Expedition Vol. 4. Pamintuan, Macky, illus. 2009. (Flat Stanley's Worldwide Adventures Ser.: 4). (ENG.). 112p. (J). (gr. 2-5). pap. 4.99 *(978-0-06-142996-5(1))* HarperCollins Pubs.

—The Mount Rushmore Calamity. Pamintuan, Macky, illus. 2009. (Flat Stanley's Worldwide Adventures Ser.: 1). (ENG.). 96p. (J). (gr. 2-5). 15.99 *(978-0-06-142991-0(0))*; pap. 4.99 *(978-0-06-142990-3(2))* HarperCollins Pubs.

Brown, Jeffrey. Jedi Academy. Brown, Jeffrey, illus. 2013. (Star Wars Jedi Academy Ser.: Bk. 1). (Illus.). 160p. (J). (ENG.). (gr. 3-7). 12.99 *(978-0-545-50517-8(8))*; pap. *(978-0-545-60999-9(2))* Scholastic, Inc.

—The Phantom Bully. 2015. (Star Wars: Jedi Academy Ser.: 3). (ENG., Illus.). 176p. (J). (gr. 3-7). 12.99 *(978-0-545-62126-7(7))* Scholastic, Inc.

—Return of the Padawan. Brown, Jeffrey, illus. 2014. (Star Wars Jedi Academy Ser.: Bk. 2). (ENG., Illus.). 176p. (J). (gr. 3-7). 12.99 *(978-0-545-62125-0(9))* Scholastic, Inc.

Brown, Jocelyn. Mitochondrial Curiosities of Marcels 1 to 19. 2004. (ENG., Illus.). 180p. (J). (gr. 7-18). pap. 13.95 *(978-1-55245-209-7(3))* Coach Hse. Bks. CAN. Dist: Consortium Bk. Sales & Distribution.

Brown, K. T. The Adventures of Peter Tucker: Introduction of the Tiger. 2011. 82p. pap. 15.99 *(978-1-4628-7856-7(3))* Xlibris Corp.

Brown, Kathryn. Adventures at Aaron Loch Farm. 2009. 50p. pap. 23.50 *(978-1-4092-6961-8(2))* Lulu Pr., Inc.

Brown, Kevin. In a Field of Sunflowers. 2006. pap. 9.00 *(978-0-8059-6921-4(7))* Dorrance Publishing Co., Inc.

Brown, Kimberly. Autumn Castles. 2012. 28p. pap. 12.50 *(978-1-61897-032-9(1),* Strategic Bk. Publishing) Strategic Book Publishing & Rights Agency (SBPRA).

Brown, Leonard. The Adventure of Paul & Page in Colorado: (Idennital Twins) l.t. ed. 2011. (ENG.). 32p. pap. 12.50 *(978-1-4635-6139-0(3))* CreateSpace Independent Publishing Platform.

—The Adventure of Paul & Page in Hawaii (the Big Island) (Identical Twins) l.t. ed. 2011. (ENG.). 50p. pap. 12.50 *(978-1-4635-6162-8(8))* CreateSpace Independent Publishing Platform.

Brown, Marc. Arthur to the Rescue. 13th ed. 2006. (ENG., Illus.). 24p. (J). (gr. -1-1). pap. 3.99 *(978-0-316-05773-8(8))* Little, Brown Bks. for Young Readers.

Brown, Margaret Wise. The Little Scarecrow Boy. Diaz, David, illus. 2005. (ENG.). 40p. (J). (gr. -1-2). reprint ed. pap. 6.99 *(978-0-06-077891-0(1))* HarperCollins Pubs.

—The Quiet Noisy Book Board Book. Weisgard, Leonard, illus. 2017. 34p. (J). (gr. -1 — 1). bds. 7.99 ***(978-0-06-248466-6(4),*** HarperFestival) HarperCollins Pubs.

Brown, Margaret Wise. Sneakers, the Seaside Cat. Mortimer, Anne, illus. 2005. (ENG.). 32p. (J). (gr. -1-3). pap. 6.99 *(978-0-06-443622-9(5))* HarperCollins Pubs.

Brown, Maureen E. Tanker's Adventures in Monterey. Brown, Michael D., illus. 2007. 24p. (J). 13.95 *(978-0-615-16200-3(2))* TankerToys.

Brown, Mia. Goodnight Joy! Abdullah, Tariq, illus. 2010. 20p. 12.49 *(978-1-4520-1492-0(2))* AuthorHouse.

Brown, Monica. Chavela's Magic Chicle. Morales, Magaly, illus. 2008. (ENG & SPA.). (J). 15.95 *(978-0-87358-918-5(1),* Luna Rising) Northland Publishing.

—Lola Levine & the Vacation Dream. 2017. (Lola Levine Ser.: 5). (J). lib. bdg. 16.00 ***(978-0-606-40222-4(5))*** Turtleback Bks.

—Lola Levine Meets Jelly & Bean. 2017. (Lola Levine Ser.: 4). (ENG., Illus.). 96p. (J). (gr. 1-5). pap. 5.99 *(978-0-316-25850-0(4))* Little, Brown Bks. for Young Readers.

—Lola Levine Meets Jelly & Bean. 2017. (Lola Levine Ser.: 4). (J). lib. bdg. 16.00 **(978-0-606-40221-7(7))** Turtleback Bks.
Brown, Monica. Waiting for the Biblioburro/Esperando el Biblioburro: (Spanish-English Bilingual Edition) Dominguez, Adriana, tr. Parra, John, illus. 2016. (ENG.). 32p. (J). (gr. k-3). lib. bdg. 19.99 *(978-0-553-53894-6(2),* Tricycle Pr.) Random Hse. Children's Bks.
Brown, Palmer. Beyond the Pawpaw Trees. Brown, Palmer, illus. 2011. (ENG., Illus.). 136p. (J). (gr. k-4). 14.95 *(978-1-59017-461-6(5),* NYR Children's Collection) New York Review of Bks., Inc., The.
—Cheerful. 2012. (ENG., Illus.). 72p. (J). (gr. -1-2). 12.95 *(978-1-59017-501-9(8),* NYR Children's Collection) New York Review of Bks., Inc., The.
Brown, Philip. Franky Franklyn's Philadelphia Adventure. 2011. 108p. 21.99 *(978-1-4567-5423-5(8));* pap. 10.99 *(978-1-4567-1269-3(1))* AuthorHouse.
Brown, Rachael. Faerie Wings. 2008. 58p. pap. 10.50 *(978-1-4092-0908-9(3))* Lulu Pr., Inc.
Brown, Riley S. Edward & the Enfeebled: Book Two of the Wunderlannd Novels. 2013. 280p. pap. 14.99 *(978-0-9893166-1-3(0))* Wunderlannd Pr.
Brown, Skila. To Stay Alive: Mary Ann Graves & the Tragic Journey of the Donner Party. 2016. (ENG., Illus.). 304p. (J). (gr. 5-9). 17.99 *(978-0-7636-7811-1(2))* Candlewick Pr.
Brown Sr., David F. Tabby Goes to School: The First in the Tabatha Adventures Series, 1 vol. Brown Jr., David F., illus. 2009. 20p. pap. 24.95 *(978-1-60836-181-6(0))* America Star Bks.
Brown, Tara. First Kiss. 2013. 264p. pap. *(978-1-927866-05-4(7))* Brown, Tara Publishing.
Brown, Wanda E. The Great Escape (from Loneliness) A Dragon Safe Ending Book. 2003. 24p. (J). per. 39.95 *(978-1-59196-272-4(2))* Instant Pub.
Browne, Susan Chalker. Freddy's Day at the Races, 1 vol. Rose, Hilda, illus. 2008. (ENG.). 32p. (J). (gr. 1-8). 10.95 *(978-1-897174-36-4(5))* Creative Bk. Publishing CAN. Dist: Orca Bk. Pubs. USA.
Brownlow, Brooke. The Magic of Old Oak Hill. 2005. 48p. pap. 16.95 *(978-1-4241-0223-5(5))* PublishAmerica, Inc.
Brubacher, Melody. The Adventures of Princess Penelope. 2012. 68p. pap. 31.99 *(978-1-4691-9274-1(8))* Xlibris Corp.
Bruce, Karl. Annie Apple & the Teleportation Phantoms from Outer Space. 2006. (YA). pap. 16.00 *(978-0-8059-7156-9(4))* Dorrance Publishing Co., Inc.
Bruel, Nick. Bad Kitty School Daze. 2014. (Bad Kitty Chapter Bks.). (J). lib. bdg. 17.20 *(978-0-606-34010-6(6),* Turtleback) Turtleback Bks.
Brumbach, Andrew. The Eye of Midnight. 2016. (ENG.). 256p. (J). (gr. 4-7). 16.99 *(978-0-385-74461-4(7));* lib. bdg. 19.99 *(978-0-375-99176-9(X))* Random Hse. Children's Bks. (Delacorte Bks. for Young Readers).
Brundage, Jerome. The Princess & the Bear: Book I: the Battle for Aradam. 2007. 148p. per. 24.95 *(978-1-4241-6346-5(3))* America Star Bks.
Bruneau, Clotilde, et al. The Planet of the Snake. Nautilus Studio Staff, illus. 2015. (ENG.). 48p. (J). (gr. 4-8). pap. 7.95 *(978-1-4677-6027-0(7),* Graphic Universe™) Lerner Publishing Group.
Brunn Emanuele, Susan. Brooms Are Out! 2009. 24p. pap. 12.99 *(978-1-4490-2227-3(8))* AuthorHouse.
Brunner, Kym. Wanted - Dead or in Love. 2014. (ENG.). 288p. (YA). 17.99 *(978-1-4405-7057-5(4),* Simon Pulse) Simon Pulse.
Bruno, Cristina. The Mother Store. 2009. 52p. pap. 30.00 *(978-1-4389-2875-3(0))* AuthorHouse.
Bruno, Debra. Petey's Tale: A Story of Survival Inspired by Actual Events. 2010. 28p. pap. 12.49 *(978-1-4490-6597-3(X))* AuthorHouse.
Bruno, Linette Arthurton. Three's No Crowd: Two's Company. 2011. 33p. (J). pap. 15.95 *(978-1-4327-7125-6(6))* Outskirts Pr., Inc.
Brunson, Marya. The Light of Rigel. 2013. 178p. pap. 9.95 *(978-0-9801414-2-9(7))* Lotus Blossom Bks.
Bruss, Deborah. Big Box for Ben, 1 vol. Bogacki, Tomek, illus. 2011. (ENG.). 16p. (J). (gr. -1-k). bds. 6.95 *(978-1-59572-265-2(3))* Star Bright Bks., Inc.
Bruton, Georgia. Escape. 2012. 210p. pap. 11.95 *(978-1-936083-10-5(5))* Silver Knight Publishing, LLC.
Brutton, Elizabeth. Tabbies & Tigers in Provence. 2009. (Illus.). 112p. pap. 12.49 *(978-1-4490-2104-7(2))* AuthorHouse.
Bryan, Jennifer Liu. The Different Dragon. Hosler, Danamarie, illus. 2006. (J). pap. 12.95 *(978-0-9674468-6-8(4))* Two Lives Publishing.
Bryan, Sean. The Juggling Pug. Murphy, Tom, illus. 2014. (ENG.). 32p. (J). (-k). 12.95 *(978-1-62873-596-3(1),* Sky Pony Pr.) Skyhorse Publishing Co., Inc.
Bryant, Annie. Freaked Out. 2006. (Beacon Street Girls Ser.: No. 7). (Illus.). 226p. (J). (gr. 4-8). per. 7.99 *(978-0-9758511-7-3(9))* B*tween Productions, Inc.
—Freestyle with Avery. 2007. (Beacon Street Girls Special Adventure Ser.: No. 2). 240p. (J). (gr. 4-8). pap. 7.99 *(978-1-933566-01-6(9))* B*tween Productions, Inc.
—Green Algae & Bubble Gum Wars. 2007. (Beacon Street Girls Ser.: No. 13). 240p. (J). pap. 7.99 *(978-0-9758511-8-0(7))* B*tween Productions, Inc.
—Isabel's Texas Two-Step. 2008. (Beacon Street Girls Ser.: No. 5). (ENG.). 256p. (J). (gr. 4-8). pap. 7.99 *(978-1-4169-6423-0(1),* Aladdin) Simon & Schuster Children's Publishing.
—Maeve on the Red Carpet. 2007. (Beacon Street Girls Special Adventure Ser.: No. 3). 221p. (J). (gr. 4-7). per. 7.10 *(978-1-933566-08-5(6))* B*tween Productions, Inc.
—Ready! Set! Hawaii! 2009. (Beacon Street Girls Ser.: No. 7). (ENG.). 304p. (J). (gr. 4-8). pap. 8.99 *(978-1-4169-6436-0(3),* Aladdin) Simon & Schuster Children's Publishing.
—Time's Up. 2008. (Beacon Street Girls Ser.: No. 12). 240p. 7.99 *(978-1-933566-10-8(8))* B*tween Productions, Inc.
Bryant, Megan. Merida: The Legend of the Emeralds. 2014. (Disney Princess Early Chapter Bks.). (J). lib. bdg. 14.75 *(978-0-606-31755-9(4),* Turtleback) Turtleback Bks.
Bryant, Megan & Disney Book Group Staff. Merida: Legend of the Emeralds. Disney Storybook Art Team, illus. 2014. (ENG.). 96p. (J). (gr. 1-3). pap. 4.99 *(978-1-4231-6890-4(9))* Disney Pr.
Bryant, Samantha. Innocent Child. 2012. pap. 15.95 *(978-0-7414-7874-0(9))* Infinity Publishing.
Bryce, Conor. Wesco P. Mcsnaffle & the Great Brave Quest. 2008. 127p. pap. 22.50 *(978-1-4092-1273-7(4))* Lulu Pr., Inc.
Bryson, Brenda. The Adventures of Roo & Winston. 2007. 78p. pap. 12.95 *(978-1-4357-0145-8(3))* Lulu Pr., Inc.
—The Adventures of Roo & Winston - Crop Circles. 2009. 64p. pap. 12.43 *(978-0-557-17564-2(X))* Lulu Pr., Inc.
Bryson, Ernest. Smudgie New Adventure. 2012. 44p. pap. 21.99 *(978-1-4653-0848-1(2))* Xlibris Corp.
Bryson, Karen Mueller. The Incredibly Awesome Adventures of Puggie Liddel, the Graphic Novel. Tisdel, L. L, illus. 2013. 108p. pap. *(978-1-927384-09-1(5))* Zeta Comics.
Buchholz, Quint. Duerme Bien, Pequeño Oso. 2nd ed. 2003. (Rosa y Manzana Ser.). (SPA., Illus.). 208p. 15.16 *(978-84-89804-10-4(9))* Lóguez Ediciones ESP. Dist: Lectorum Pubns., Inc.
Buchwald, Claire. Max Talks to Me. Ritz, Karen, illus. 2007. (Sit! Stay! Read! Ser.). (ENG.). 24p. (J). (gr. k-2). 16.95 *(978-0-940719-03-3(7))* Gryphon Pr., The.
Buck, Alicia. Out of the Ashes. 2015. 281p. (YA). pap. 17.99 *(978-1-4621-1727-7(9))* Cedar Fort, Inc./CFI Distribution.
Buckbee, Johnny. The Adventures of Bumble Bee. 2010. 24p. pap. 12.99 *(978-1-4490-6935-3(5))* AuthorHouse.
Buckeridge, Anthony. Jennings in Particular. 2008. (Jennings Ser.: 17). (ENG.). 164p. (J). (gr. -1-12). pap. 12.95 *(978-0-7551-0160-3(X))* House of Stratus, Inc. GBR. Dist: Gardners Bks. Ltd.
Buckingham, Matt. Bright Stanley. 2006. (Illus.). 32p. (J). (gr. -1-3). 15.95 *(978-1-58925-059-8(1))* Tiger Tales.
Buckingham, Royce Scott. The Terminals. 2014. (ENG.). 288p. (YA). (gr. 9). 18.99 *(978-1-250-01155-8(8),* 9781250011558, Dunne, Thomas Bks.) St. Martin's Pr.
Bucklaschuk, Angela. Movember with My Doggy. Gillen, Rosemarie, illus. 2013. 32p. pap. 11.95 *(978-1-61286-188-3(1))* Avid Readers Publishing Group.
Buckley, Michael. The Council of Mirrors. Ferguson, Peter, illus. 2013. (Sisters Grimm Ser.). (ENG.). 352p. (YA). (gr. 3-7). pap. 7.95 *(978-1-4197-0538-0(5),* Amulet Bks.) Abrams, Inc.
—The Everafter War. Ferguson, Peter, illus. 2010. (Sisters Grimm Ser.: Bk. 7). (ENG.). 336p. (J). (gr. 3-7). pap. 8.95 *(978-0-8109-8429-5(6),* Amulet Bks.) Abrams, Inc.
—M Is for Mama's Boy. Beavers, Ethen, illus. 2010. (ENG.). 288p. (J). (gr. 3-7). pap. 6.95 *(978-0-8109-9674-8(X),* Amulet Bks.) Abrams, Inc.
—The Villain Virus. 2012. (Nerds Ser.). (ENG., Illus.). 288p. (J). (gr. 3-7). 16.95 *(978-1-4197-0415-4(X),* Amulet Bks.) Abrams, Inc.
Buckmaster, Heath L. Box of Hair: A Fairy Tale, 3 bks., Bk. 1. (Illus.). (YA). 2007. 102p. pap. 12.99 *(978-0-9771802-5-7(5))* 2008. 108p. lib. bdg. 25.00 *(978-0-9771802-4-0(7))* Transaltar Publishing.
—Box of Hair: A Fairy Tale. 2008. 104p. pap. 12.50 *(978-1-4357-2690-1(1))* Lulu Pr., Inc.
—The Dragons of Tarnack. 2008. 142p. pap. 13.99 *(978-1-4357-4624-4(4))* Lulu Pr., Inc.
—The Venus Diary. 2008. 136p. pap. 13.50 *(978-0-615-20678-3(6));*Bk. 2. 132p. (YA). lib. bdg. 19.95 *(978-0-9771802-6-4(3))* Transaltar Publishing.
Bucky Badger a Children's Story: The Storm. 2005. (J). 9.99 *(978-0-9765510-3-4(9))* Badgerland Bks. LLC.
Bucky Badger A Children's Story: Treasure. 2005. (J). 9.99 *(978-0-9765510-2-7(0))* Badgerland Bks. LLC.
Bucky Badger A Children's Story: Yard Sale. 2005. (J). 9.99 *(978-0-9765510-1-0(2))* Badgerland Bks. LLC.
Budge, Robyn E. Whoda Thunkit: Rhyming Tales for the Young & Not So. 2013. 180p. pap. 15.95 *(978-1-4787-2097-3(2))* Outskirts Pr., Inc.
Budig, Greg. I Hear the Wind. unabr. ed. 2005. (Illus.). 34p. (J). 18.95 *(978-0-88045-164-2(5))* Stemmer Hse. Pubs.
Buehner, Caralyn. Goldilocks & the Three Bears. Buehner, Mark, illus. 2009. (ENG.). 32p. (J). (gr. -1-k). pap. 6.99 *(978-0-14-241275-6(9),* Puffin Books) Penguin Young Readers Group.
Buffalo, Tom And Tracey. Loganæs Big Night Out. 2008. 24p. pap. 11.99 *(978-1-4389-1893-8(3))* AuthorHouse.
Bugbee, M. Howe. Beyond the Road: Mayhaven Award for Children's Fiction. 2006. 288p. (YA). 23.95 *(978-1-932278-08-8(7))* Mayhaven Publishing, Inc.
Bugg, Ann T. Into the Forest & down the Tower. Kramin, Valerie, illus. 2012. 136p. pap. *(978-1-927044-24-7(3))* Writers AMuse Me.
Bukiet, Melvin Jules. Undertown. 2013. (ENG.). 304p. (J). (gr. 3-7). 17.95 *(978-1-4197-0589-2(X),* Amulet Bks.) Abrams, Inc.
Buklis, Lawrence S. Mysteries from the Yukon: Three Fisheries Adventures for Students. 2003. 217p. (J). pap. 21.00 *(978-1-888569-52-0(2))* American Fisheries Society.
Buller, Laura. DK Readers L1: Star Wars: What Is a Wookiee? Star Wars: What Is a Wookiee? 2015. (DK Readers Ser.). (ENG., Illus.). 48p. (J). (gr. k-4). 14.99 *(978-1-4654-3385-5(6),* DK Children) Dorling Kindersley Publishing, Inc.
Bullis, J. Noah Peepkin - a Small Adventure. 2003. (Illus.). 20p. (J). per. 12.00 *(978-0-9747878-6-2(8))* Jeremy's Things.
Bullock, Cecile Boyd. Grands Visit the Stars: A Trip to the Planetarium. 2013. 36p. pap. 18.41 *(978-1-4669-8856-9(8))* Trafford Publishing.
Bullock, Harold B. The Battle for the Worlds. Anderson, Jean, ed. 2nd rev. ed. Date not set. (Tarlian Adventures Ser.: Vol. 1). 120p. (J). (gr. 2-5). reprint ed. pap. *(978-1-929248-00-1(8))* Golden Oak Pubs. L.P.
Bullock, Rob. Noah Ramsbottom & the Cave Elves. 2009. 48p. pap. 12.25 *(978-1-60860-335-0(0),* Strategic Bk. Publishing) Strategic Book Publishing & Rights Agency (SBPRA).
Bullock, Robert. Sam Marsh & the Battle of the Cloudships: The Sam Marsh Stories - Part 2. 2012. 224p. pap. 13.97 *(978-1-61897-348-1(7),* Strategic Bk. Publishing) Strategic Book Publishing & Rights Agency (SBPRA).
Bullock, Robert John. Jacob's War. 2013. 246p. pap. 13.97 *(978-1-62212-582-1(7),* Strategic Bk. Publishing) Strategic Book Publishing & Rights Agency (SBPRA).
Bully Busters in the Adventures of Wooly Bully. 2003. (Illus.). 100p. (J). per. 8.95 *(978-0-9770294-0-2(9))* Better Me Bks., Inc.
Bulwer-Lytton, Edward. Los Ultimos Dias de Pompeya. (SPA., Illus.). 168p. (YA). 14.95 *(978-84-7281-129-4(8),* AF1129) Auriga, Ediciones S.A. ESP. Dist: Continental Bk. Co., Inc.
Bunce, Margaret. Adventures with Nature: A Story about Olivia & Her Little Dog, Jake. 2011. 24p. pap. 12.95 *(978-1-4567-2497-9(5))* AuthorHouse.
Bunting, Eve. Emma's Turtle. Winborn, Marsha, illus. (ENG.). 32p. (J). 2014. (gr. -1-2). pap. 6.95 *(978-1-62091-735-0(1))* 2007. (gr. 2-4). 15.95 *(978-1-59078-350-4(6))* Boyds Mills Pr.
—Frog & Friends. 2012. (I AM a READER! Frog & Friends Ser.: 4). (ENG., Illus.). 48p. (J). (gr. 1-3). pap. 3.99 *(978-1-58536-806-8(7))* Sleeping Bear Pr.
—Frog & Friends: Frog's Flying Adventure. 2012. (I AM a READER! Frog & Friends Ser.: 4). (ENG., Illus.). 48p. (J). (gr. 1-3). 9.95 *(978-1-58536-805-1(9))* Sleeping Bear Pr.
—The Pirate Captain's Daughter. 2012. (Pirate Captain's Daughter Ser.). (ENG.). 192p. (J). pap. 8.95 *(978-1-58536-790-0(7));* lib. bdg. 15.95 *(978-1-58536-789-4(3))* Sleeping Bear Pr.
Bunyan, Noah F. Lightning Man #1. 2011. 28p. pap. 21.99 *(978-1-4653-3628-6(1))* Xlibris Corp.
Burach, Ross. Pine & Boof: the Lucky Leaf. Burach, Ross, illus. 2017. (Illus.). 40p. (J). (gr. -1-3). 17.99 **(978-0-06-241850-0(5))** HarperCollins Pubs.
Burch, Minnie Kirby. The Adventures of Squir Squirrel: A Story of Love & Trust. 2012. 64p. pap. 31.99 *(978-1-4771-2043-9(2))* Xlibris Corp.
Burch, Sharon. Freddie the Frog & the Bass Clef Monster. Harris, Tiffany, illus. 2010. (ENG.). 44p. (gr. -1-4). 24.99 incl. audio compact disk *(978-0-9747454-8-0(0),* 0974745480) Mystic Publishing.
—Freddie the Frog & the Thump in the Night: 1st Adventure - Treble Clef Island. 2010. (ENG., Illus.). 46p. 24.99 incl. audio compact disk *(978-0-9747454-9-7(9),* 0974745499) Mystic Publishing.
Burchell, Graham. The Ice Spells of Krollinad. 2005. 213p. pap. 11.99 *(978-1-4116-5258-3(4))* Lulu Pr., Inc.
Burchett, Jan & Vogler, Sara. Avalanche Alert, 1 vol. Le Feyer, Diane, illus. (Wild Rescue Ser.). (ENG.). 152p. (gr. 3-6). 2013. 9.95 *(978-1-4342-4893-0(3))* 2012. 25.32 *(978-1-4342-3772-9(9))* Stone Arch Bks.
—Dead Man's Hand. Hartas, Leo, illus. 2014. (ENG.). 128p. (J). (gr. 2-4). pap. 7.99 *(978-1-4440-0770-1(X),* Orion Children's Bks.) Hachette Children's Group GBR. Dist: Hachette Bk. Group.
—Desert Danger, 1 vol. Le Feyer, Diane, illus. 2013. (Wild Rescue Ser.). (ENG.). 152p. (gr. 3-6). 9.95 *(978-1-4342-4892-3(5))* Stone Arch Bks.
—Desert Danger, 1 vol. Le Feyer, Diane & Kennedy, Sam, illus. 2012. (Wild Rescue Ser.). (ENG.). 152p. (gr. 3-6). lib. bdg. 25.32 *(978-1-4342-3773-6(7))* Stone Arch Bks.
—Earthquake Escape, 1 vol. Le Feyer, Diane, illus. 2012. (Wild Rescue Ser.). (ENG.). 152p. (gr. 3-6). lib. bdg. 25.32 *(978-1-4048-6891-5(7))* Picture Window Bks.
—The Ghost Ship. Hartas, Leo, illus. 2012. (ENG.). 128p. (J). (gr. 2-4). 7.99 *(978-1-4440-0585-1(5),* Orion Children's Bks.) Hachette Children's Group GBR. Dist: Hachette Bk. Group.
—Kidnapped. Hartas, Leo, illus. 2012. (ENG.). 128p. (J). (gr. 2-4). pap. 7.99 *(978-1-4440-0586-8(3),* Orion Children's Bks.) Hachette Children's Group GBR. Dist: Hachette Bk. Group.
—Ocean S. O. S. Le Feyer, Diane, illus. 2013. (Wild Rescue Ser.). (ENG.). 152p. (gr. 3-6). 9.95 *(978-1-4342-4891-6(7))* Stone Arch Bks.
—Ocean S. O. S. Le Feyer, Diane & Kennedy, Sam, illus. 2012. (Wild Rescue Ser.). (ENG.). 152p. (gr. 3-6). lib. bdg. 25.32 *(978-1-4342-3771-2(0))* Stone Arch Bks.
—Poacher Panic, 1 vol. Le Feyer, Diane, illus. 2012. (Wild Rescue Ser.). (ENG.). 152p. (gr. 3-6). 9.95 *(978-1-4342-4593-9(4));* lib. bdg. 25.32 *(978-1-4342-3286-1(7))* Stone Arch Bks.
—Polar Meltdown, 1 vol. Le Feyer, Diane, illus. 2012. (Wild Rescue Ser.). (ENG.). 152p. (gr. 3-6). 9.95 *(978-1-4342-4594-6(2));* lib. bdg. 25.32 *(978-1-4342-3769-9(9))* Stone Arch Bks.
—Rainforest Rescue, 1 vol. Le Feyer, Diane, illus. 2012. (Wild Rescue Ser.). (ENG.). 152p. (gr. 3-6). 9.95 *(978-1-4342-4595-3(0));* lib. bdg. 25.32 *(978-1-4342-3768-2(0))* Stone Arch Bks.
—Safari Survival, 1 vol. Le Feyer, Diane, illus. 2013. (Wild Rescue Ser.). (ENG.). 152p. (gr. 3-6). 9.95 *(978-1-4342-4890-9(9))* Stone Arch Bks.
—Safari Survival, 1 vol. Le Feyer, Diane & Kennedy, Sam, illus. 2012. (Wild Rescue Ser.). (ENG.). 152p. (gr. 3-6). lib. bdg. 25.32 *(978-1-4342-3770-5(2))* Stone Arch Bks.
—The Sea Monster. Hartas, Leo, illus. 2013. (ENG.). 128p. (J). (gr. 2-4). pap. 8.99 *(978-1-4440-0769-5(6),* Orion Children's Bks.) Hachette Children's Group GBR. Dist: Hachette Bk. Group.
—Skeleton Island. Hartas, Leo, illus. 2012. (ENG.). 128p. (J). (gr. 2-4). pap. 7.99 *(978-1-4440-0584-4(7),* Orion Children's Bks.) Hachette Children's Group GBR. Dist: Hachette Bk. Group.
—The Treasure Map. Hartas, Leo, illus. 2013. (ENG.). 128p. (J). (gr. 2-4). pap. 7.99 *(978-1-4440-0764-0(5),* Orion Children's Bks.) Hachette Children's Group GBR. Dist: Hachette Bk. Group.
Burchett, Loni R. Bear & Katie in a Day at Nestlenook Farm. lt. ed. 2004. (Illus.). 76p. (J). per. 11.95 *(978-0-9742815-1-3(4))* Black Lab Publishing LLC.
Burden, Meg. The King Commands. 2010. (Tales of the Borderlands Ser.: Bk. 2). 312p. (YA). (gr. 7-18). pap. 8.95 *(978-0-9798824-1-8(9))* Brown Barn Bks.
Burden, Sara. Tom's Wheels. 2003. 16p. (J). per. 12.95 *(978-1-56167-755-9(8))* American Literary Pr.
Burgan, Michael. Hot Iron: The Adventures of a Civil War Powder Boy. Rodriquez, Pedro, illus. 2007. (Historical Fiction Ser.). (ENG.). 56p. (gr. 2-3). pap. 6.25 *(978-1-59889-406-6(4),* Graphic Flash) Stone Arch Bks.
Burger, Hamilton C. No Exit: The Apple Grove Gang #1. 2012. (ENG.). (J). pap. *(978-1-4675-3409-3(9))* Independent Pub.
Burger, Kyle. The Adventures of Buddy the Motocross Bike: Buddy Learns about Confidence. 2012. 32p. pap. 19.99 *(978-1-4685-0609-9(9))* AuthorHouse.
Burgess, Jennifer. Dj Daring & the Dangerous Dragon. 2013. 20p. pap. 11.97 *(978-1-61204-287-9(2),* Strategic Bk. Publishing) Strategic Book Publishing & Rights Agency (SBPRA).
Burgess, Karin Whiting. It's Always a Good Day for Crabbing. 2005. (J). 16.95 *(978-0-9718303-4-9(7))* Flat Hammock Pr.
Burgess, Lisa Maria. Juma on Safari. Gugu, Abdul M., illus. 2013. 32p. 19.95 *(978-1-939604-07-1(9));* pap. 9.99 *(978-1-939604-03-3(6))* Barranca Pr.
Burgess, Melvin. Bloodsong. 2007. (ENG.). 384p. (YA). (gr. 9-18). pap. 16.99 *(978-1-4169-3616-9(5),* Simon Pulse) Simon Pulse.
Burgess, Pauline. Pony Palace Camp. 2014. (Pony Friends Forever Ser.). (ENG., Illus.). 128p. (J). pap. 12.00 *(978-0-85640-923-3(5))* Blackstaff Pr., Ltd. GBR. Dist: Dufour Editions, Inc.
—Pony Surprise. 2014. (Pony Friends Forever Ser.). (ENG., Illus.). 93p. (J). pap. 12.00 *(978-0-85640-936-3(7))* Blackstaff Pr., Ltd. GBR. Dist: Dufour Editions, Inc.
Burgess, Sushila. Jasmine's Unicorn. 2010. 115p. pap. 18.95 *(978-1-4452-5662-7(2))* Lulu Pr., Inc.
Burgess, Thornton W. The Adventures of Buster Bear. 2008. 108p. (gr. 4-7). 22.95 *(978-1-60664-950-3(7));* per. 9.95 *(978-1-60312-500-0(0))* Aegypan.
—The Adventures of Buster Bear. 2007. 192p. (gr. 4-7). 29.95 *(978-1-4344-8855-8(1));* per. 14.95 *(978-1-4344-8854-1(3))* Wildside Pr., LLC.
—The Adventures of Grandfather Frog. 2007. 108p. (gr. -1-3). per. 9.95 *(978-1-60312-154-5(4))* Aegypan.
—The Adventures of Jerry Muskrat. 2007. 108p. (gr. 2-5). per. 9.95 *(978-1-60312-336-5(9));* 22.95 *(978-1-60312-674-8(0))* Aegypan.
—The Adventures of Jimmy Skunk. 112p. 2008. per. 9.95 *(978-1-60312-416-4(0))* 2007. 22.95 *(978-1-60312-594-9(9))* Aegypan.
—The Adventures of Johnny Chuck. 2007. 108p. (gr. 2-5). per. 9.95 *(978-1-60312-257-3(5))* Aegypan.
—The Adventures of Lightfoot the Deer. 2008. 108p. (gr. -1-3). 22.95 *(978-1-60664-951-0(5));* 104p. per. 9.95 *(978-1-60312-501-7(9))* Aegypan.
—The Adventures of Mr Mocker. 2007. 108p. per. 9.95 *(978-1-60312-296-2(6));* (gr. 4-7). 22.95 *(978-1-60312-714-1(3))* Aegypan.
—The Adventures of Old Mr. Buzzard. Cady, Harrison, illus. 2013. (Dover Children's Classics Ser.). (ENG.). 96p. (J). (gr. 1-4). pap. 3.00 *(978-0-486-49726-6(7))* Dover Pubns., Inc.
—The Adventures of Old Mr Toad. 2007. 140p. (gr. 4-7). 24.95 *(978-1-60312-637-3(6));* per. 11.95 *(978-1-60312-379-2(2))* Aegypan.
—The Adventures of Paddy the Beaver. 2008. 108p. (gr. 4-7). 22.95 *(978-1-60664-952-7(3));* per. 9.95 *(978-1-60312-502-4(7))* Aegypan.
—The Adventures of Peter Cottontail. 2017. (Thornton Burgess Library). (ENG., Illus.). 128p. (J). (gr. -1-2). pap. 9.95 *(978-1-63322-292-2(6),* Seagrass) Quarto Publishing Group USA.
—The Adventures of Poor Mrs Quack. 124p. 2008. (gr. 4-7). per. 10.95 *(978-1-60312-417-1(9))* 2007. 23.95 *(978-1-60312-595-6(7))* Aegypan.
—The Adventures of Reddy Fox. 2005. 26.95 *(978-1-4218-0995-3(8),* 1st World Library - Literary Society) 1st World Publishing, Inc.
—The Adventures of Sammy Jay. Cady, Harrison, illus. 2006. (Dover Children's Thrift Classics Ser.). (ENG.). 96p. (J). (gr. 3-8). per. 3.00 *(978-0-486-44946-3(7))* Dover Pubns., Inc.
—The Adventures of Unc' Billy Possum. 2007. 140p. (gr. 4-7). per. 13.95 *(978-1-60312-337-2(7));* 24.95 *(978-1-60312-675-5(9))* Aegypan.
—Bowser the Hound. 2011. 128p. 24.95 *(978-1-4638-9566-2(6))* Rodgers, Alan Bks.
—Mother West Wind 'How' Stories. 2008. 108p. (gr. -1-3). 22.95 *(978-1-60664-893-3(4));* pap. 9.95 *(978-1-60664-012-8(7))* Aegypan.
Burgess, Thornton W. & Cady, Harrison. The Adventures of Peter Cottontail & His Green Forest Friends. 2014. (ENG., Illus.). 304p. (J). (gr. 1-5). 20.00 *(978-0-486-49209-4(5))* Dover Pubns., Inc.
Burghard, Marie. Captain's Best Imbecile: A Young Pirate's Story: Collector's Edition. 2008. 184p. 29.99 *(978-1-4357-4521-6(3))* Lulu Pr., Inc.
Burke, Anjalena. Siren: Book 3 of the Dead End Series, 1 vol. 2010. 66p. pap. 19.95 *(978-1-4489-5795-8(8))* America Star Bks.
Burke, Kurt. Johnny Action. 2011. 44p. pap. 17.95 *(978-1-4575-0499-0(5))* Dog Ear Publishing, LLC.
Burke, Ruth. Gowandale Adventure: And other stories for Boys. 2007. (Illus.). 96p. 9.00 *(978-1-84625-070-5(6))* DayOne Pubns. GBR. Dist: Send The Light Distribution LLC.
Burket, Shelia. Silver & Gold: Sissy Stringbean Meets Morris Norris. 2012. 28p. 24.95 *(978-1-4626-3591-7(1))* America Star Bks.
Burkhart, Jessica. Chasing Blue. 2009. (Canterwood Crest Ser.: 2). (ENG.). 272p. (J). (gr. 4-8). pap. 7.99 *(978-1-4169-5841-3(X),* Aladdin) Simon & Schuster Children's Publishing.
Burks, James. Bird & Squirrel on Fire. 2017. (Bird & Squirrel Ser.). (ENG.). 192p. (J). (gr. 2-5). 18.99 *(978-0-545-80429-5(9),* Graphix) Scholastic, Inc.
—Bird & Squirrel on the Run! 2012. (Bird & Squirrel Ser.). (ENG., Illus.). 128p. (J). (gr. 2-5). pap. 8.99 *(978-0-545-31283-7(3),* Graphix) Scholastic, Inc.
Burnett, Frances Hodgson. The Lost Prince. (J). 25.95 *(978-0-8488-0691-0(3))* Amereon Ltd.
Burnett, Roger J. & Burnett, Wilma J. Short Stories & Tall Tales. 2012. 104p. pap. 9.95 *(978-1-4759-5168-4(X))* iUniverse, Inc.
Burnette, Leon P. Peeka-Boo Fables: Land of the Golems. 2012. 24p. pap. 15.99 *(978-1-4797-4616-3(9))* Xlibris Corp.
Bumford, Sheila. The Incredible Journey. 148p. (J). pap. 4.99 *(978-0-8072-8323-3(1),* Listening Library) Random Hse. Audio Publishing Group.
Burnham, Erik. Teenage Mutant Ninja Turtles: New Animated Adventures: Volume 4, 1 vol. 2016. (Teenage Mutant Ninja Turtles: New Animated Adventures Ser.). (ENG.). 24p. (J). lib. bdg. 24.21 *(978-1-61479-462-2(6),* Graphic Planet) Magic Wagon.
Burningham, John. It's a Secret! Burningham, John, illus. 2009. (ENG., Illus.). 56p. (J). (gr. -1-2). 16.99 *(978-0-7636-4275-4(4))* Candlewick Pr.

—John Burningham. Burningham, John, illus. ltd. ed. 2009. (ENG., Illus.). 224p. (gr. k-12). 70.00 *(978-0-7636-4434-5(X))* Candlewick Pr.

Burns, Brian. My Blankey & Me. 2004. 20p. pap. 24.95 *(978-1-4137-3675-5(0))* PublishAmerica, Inc.

Burns, Emily. Manitou Art Caper. 2003. (Rocky Mountain Mysteries Ser.: 2). 128p. (J). per. 4.95 *(978-0-9723259-1-2(3)*, RMM2) Covered Wagon Publishing LLC.

Burns, Jennifer N. Magic in Time: Fairy Tale Stories. 2012. 198p. 24.95 *(978-1-4759-3965-1(5))*; pap. 14.95 *(978-1-4759-3964-4(7))* iUniverse, Inc.

Burns, John. The Many Adventures of Pengey Penguin. Coles, James, illus. 2005. 207p. (J). per. 17.95 *(978-0-9774227-0-8(4))* San Francisco Story Works.

Burns, Laura J. Magic Below. 2016. (Bewitched in Oz Ser.). (ENG.). 240p. (gr. 4-8). lib. bdg. 30.65 *(978-1-4965-2603-8(1))* Stone Arch Bks.

Burris, Shana Renee. Bailey the Bear: Sees Stars Everywhere! 2012. (ENG.). 31p. (J). pap. 12.95 *(978-1-4327-9011-0(0))* Outskirts Pr., Inc.

Burroughs, Caleb. Dora the Explorer to the Moon. Miller, Victoria, illus. 2007. (Play a Tune Tale Ser.). 16p. (J). (gr. -1-3). 12.98 *(978-1-4127-8830-4(7))* Publications International, Ltd.

Burroughs, Scott, illus. The Missing Mitt. 2010. (Hardy Boys: the Secret Files Ser.: 2). (ENG.). 112p. (J). (gr. 1-4). pap. 5.99 *(978-1-4169-9394-0(0)*, Aladdin) Simon & Schuster Children's Publishing.

—A Monster of a Mystery. 2011. (Hardy Boys: the Secret Files Ser.: 5). (ENG.). 96p. (J). (gr. 1-4). pap. 4.99 *(978-1-4169-9166-3(2)*, Aladdin) Simon & Schuster Children's Publishing.

—Trouble at the Arcade. 2010. (Hardy Boys: the Secret Files Ser.: 1). (ENG.). 96p. (J). (gr. 1-4). pap. 5.99 *(978-1-4169-9164-9(6)*, Aladdin) Simon & Schuster Children's Publishing.

Burshek, Edward & Burshek, Tonja. Explorers of the Word: Episode 1: the Creation. Peterson, Melanie, illus. 2007. (ENG.). 76p. per. 19.95 *(978-1-4241-6691-6(8))* America Star Bks.

Burt, Marissa. A Sliver of Stardust. 2016. 400p. (J). (gr. 3-7). pap. 7.99 *(978-0-06-229156-1(4))* HarperCollins Pubs.

—Story's End. 2013. (Storybound Ser.: 2). (ENG.). 368p. (J). (gr. 3-7). 16.99 *(978-0-06-202054-3(4))* HarperCollins Pubs.

Burt, Vickie. Alvin the Proud Prankster. Thompson, Jessica, illus. 2011. 24p. pap. 13.99 *(978-1-937129-10-1(1))* Faithful Life Pubs.

—Hot Dog or Egg Sandwich? Lindsey, Jessica, illus. 2013. 28p. pap. 13.99 *(978-1-937129-87-3(X))* Faithful Life Pubs.

Burt, Vicky. Eager Beavers. Lindsey, Jessica, illus. 2012. 28p. pap. 13.99 *(978-1-937129-39-2(X))* Faithful Life Pubs.

Burton, Bria & burton, brain. Lance & Ringo Tails: The Wild Adventures of a Dog & a Cat As Told by Their Human. 2013. 134p. pap. 9.99 *(978-1-939181-45-9(3))* Soul Attitude Press.

Burton, Gina. The Adventures of Bill the Seagull. 2009. (Illus.). 52p. pap. *(978-1-84748-636-3(3))* Athena Pr.

Burton, Lynne. The Adventures on Ken's Canal: Volume 1. 2011. 32p. pap. 13.75 *(978-1-61204-511-5(1)*, Eloquent Bks.) Strategic Book Publishing & Rights Agency (SBPRA).

—The Adventures on Ken's Canal: Volume 2. 2011. 32p. pap. 13.75 *(978-1-61204-510-8(3)*, Eloquent Bks.) Strategic Book Publishing & Rights Agency (SBPRA).

—The Adventures on Ken's Canal: Volume 3. 2011. 30p. pap. 13.75 *(978-1-61204-509-2(X)*, Eloquent Bks.) Strategic Book Publishing & Rights Agency (SBPRA).

Burton M.Sc., Kathryn Mac. Diarmid. Haley Honeybee: Finds the Magic Rose. Cox, Glendyne Dewhurst, illus. 2013. 50p. pap. *(978-0-9917941-0-2(9))* Burton, K. Publishing.

Burton, Robert. Wally A. Bow 21st Century Abow. 2010. 48p. 19.49 *(978-1-4520-8046-8(1))* AuthorHouse.

Burton, Thomas. Bluey & Dingo's Outback Adventure. 2011. 40p. 15.66 *(978-1-4567-7006-8(3))* AuthorHouse.

Burton, Virginia Lee. Choo Choo (with Full-Color Art) 2017. (ENG., Illus.). 48p. (J). (gr. -1-3). 17.99 ***(978-0-544-74984-9(7)***, HMH Books For Young Readers) Houghton Mifflin Harcourt Publishing Co.

Bush, Emilie P. Steamduck Learns to Fly! Petty, William Kevin, illus. 2012. 36p. pap. 11.95 *(978-0-9849028-1-1(3))* Coal City Stories.

Bush, Ty. Marcus Jones & the Mastery of the Scripture Balls. 2011. 270p. pap. 27.95 *(978-1-4626-0461-6(7))* America Star Bks.

Bushell, Sharon. Bernie Jones & the Blazing Bandits. 2005. (Illus.). 152p. (J). per. 6.99 *(978-0-9721725-5-4(6))* Road Tunes Media.

—The Trouble with Bernie. 2004. (Illus.). 160p. (J). per. 6.99 *(978-0-9721725-2-3(1))* Road Tunes Media.

Bushnell, Steven G. The Big Adventures of Little Church Mouse: The Parables of Jesus. 2009. 96p. pap. 31.99 *(978-1-4490-0620-4(5))* AuthorHouse.

Bustani, Juma. Adventure in Nairobi. 2005. 72p. pap. *(978-9966-46-842-0(0))* Heinemann Kenya, Limited (East African Educational Publishers Ltd E.A.E.P.) KEN. Dist: Michigan State Univ. Pr.

Busteed, Kerri J. Will's Bow Hunting Adventure. Byers, Leon, illus. 2012. 108p. pap. 30.00 *(978-1-61897-207-1(3)*, Strategic Bk. Publishing) Strategic Book Publishing & Rights Agency (SBPRA).

Busy Builders. (Flip Flap Fun Book Ser.). 10p. (J). bds. *(978-2-7643-0138-8(3))* Phidal Publishing, Inc./Editions Phidal, Inc.

Busy City. (Flip Flap Fun Book Ser.). 10p. (J). bds. *(978-2-89393-820-2(5))* Phidal Publishing, Inc./Editions Phidal, Inc.

Butcher, A. J. The Serpent Scenario. 2004. (ENG.). 224p. (J). (gr. 5-8). pap. 18.99 *(978-0-316-73766-1(6))* Little, Brown Bks. for Young Readers.

Butcher, Derek. Max the ed up Dog: Max & Matts Adventures. 2009. 56p. pap. 10.49 *(978-1-4389-6551-2(6))* AuthorHouse.

Butcher, Nancy, et al. It's Snow Problem, 3 vols. 2003. (ENG., Illus.). 112p. *(978-0-00-714466-2(0)*, HarperCollins Children's Bks.) HarperCollins Pubs. Ltd.

Butcher, Nicholas. The Hand above the Gate. 2008. 204p. pap. *(978-1-84923-348-4(9))* YouWriteOn.

Butineau, W. Turning Thirteen. 2005. 165p. pap. 24.95 *(978-1-4137-5817-7(7))* America Star Bks.

Butler, Berwyn. Dinky the Doorknob: The Adventures of Sir Dinkum Wilhelm, the Third Earl of Surridge. 2005. (J). per. 11.95 *(978-1-933732-02-2(4))* Big Ransom Studio.

Butler, Berwyn & McClean, Shorty. Dinky the Doorknob. 2006. (J). lib. bdg. 21.95 *(978-1-933732-04-6(0))* Big Ransom Studio.

Butler, Dave. The Kidnap Plot. 2016. (Extraordinary Journeys of Clockwork Charlie Ser.). (ENG.). 336p. (J). (gr. 3-7). 16.99 *(978-0-553-51295-3(1)*, Knopf Bks. for Young Readers) Random Hse. Children's Bks.

Butler, Heather. The Milkshake Detectives. 2017. (ENG.). 208p. (J). (gr. 4-6). pap. 7.99 *(978-0-349-12410-0(8))* Little, Brown Bks. for Young Readers.

Butler, Jalen. Helping Man: The Beginning. 2012. (ENG.). (J). pap. 12.95 *(978-1-4675-2359-2(3))* Independent Pub.

Butler, Shirley. The First-Class Adventure of Flat Freddie. 2008. 60p. pap. 19.95 *(978-1-60672-882-6(2))* America Star Bks.

Butler, T. Lee. The Ghost on Tanner's Mountain. 2008. 96p. pap. 11.94 *(978-1-4357-5963-3(X))* Lulu Pr., Inc.

Butler, Tammi. I Am a Ward of the Court. 2003. (YA). pap. *(978-0-9729847-0-6(4))* Sundance Entertainment.

Butler, William S. Scraper Jones: Treasure Hunter. 2007. 320p. pap. 19.95 *(978-1-59663-770-2(6)*, Castle Keep Pr.) Rock, James A. & Co. Pubs.

The Butterfly Pyramid, 6 vols. (Multicultural Programs Ser.). 16p. (gr. 1-6). 42.50 *(978-0-7802-8326-8(0))* Wright Group/McGraw-Hill.

Butterman, Stephen. Rootbeer Beard. 2012. 74p. pap. 8.95 *(978-1-61477-055-8(7))* Bellissima Publishing, LLC.

Buzzeo, Toni. Adventure Annie Goes to Kindergarten. Wummer, Amy, illus. 2013. (ENG.). 32p. (J). (gr. -1-k). mass mkt. 7.99 *(978-0-14-242695-1(4)*, Puffin Books) Penguin Young Readers Group.

Byars, Betsy. The Dark Stairs. 2006. (Herculeah Jones Mystery Ser.). 130p. (gr. 3-7). 16.00 *(978-0-7569-6736-9(8))* Perfection Learning Corp.

Byerly, Kenny. Teenage Mutant Ninja Turtles: New Animated Adventures: Volume 2, 1 vol. 2016. (Teenage Mutant Ninja Turtles: New Animated Adventures Ser.). (ENG.). 24p. (J). lib. bdg. 24.21 *(978-1-61479-460-8(X)*, Graphic Planet) Magic Wagon.

Byers, Edward. Connie & Her Bubble Gum Adventure. 2010. 32p. (J). 13.50 *(978-1-4490-9406-5(6))* AuthorHouse.

Byers, James. One Nutty Family. Collier, Kevin, illus. 2012. 16p. pap. 9.95 *(978-1-61633-200-6(X))* Guardian Angel Publishing, Inc.

Byers, Letha. Tesa, the Adopted Cow-bird. 2007. pap. 9.00 *(978-0-8059-8438-5(0))* Dorrance Publishing Co., Inc.

Byers, Marcella. Mitsy & Marty Mouse Visit Grandpa. Grant, Cheryl, illus. 2014. (ENG.). 32p. (gr. -1-2). pap. 8.95 *(978-1-61448-740-1(5)*, 9781614487401) Morgan James Publishing.

Byrd, Cari Grigsby. Where Did Pop Pop Go? 2013. 24p. pap. 24.95 *(978-1-62709-967-7(0))* America Star Bks.

Byrd, Debbie. Ayla by the Sea. 2010. 28p. pap. 13.99 *(978-1-4520-6454-3(7))* AuthorHouse.

Byrd, Michael. The Adventures of Banter & Jafar: Spoiled Rotten, 1 vol. Bai, Jenny, illus. 2009. 36p. pap. 24.95 *(978-1-60836-131-1(4))* America Star Bks.

Byrne, Lex. Ever Met the Hooferjackal? 2009. 32p. pap. 14.95 *(978-1-4490-4630-9(4))* AuthorHouse.

Bywaters, Mayer. Tempest. (J). 16.95 *(978-1-58717-206-9(2)*, SeaStar Bks.) Chronicle Bks. LLC.

C D Stampley Enterprises, creator. Billy & Baxter Learn to Build, 4 vols. 2005. (Illus.). 24p. (J). (gr. -1 — 1). 8.95 *(978-1-58087-099-3(6))* Stampley, C. D. Enterprises, Inc.

—Billy & Baxter on City Streets, 4 vols. 2005. (Illus.). 24p. (J). (gr. -1 — 1). 8.95 *(978-1-58087-101-3(1))* Stampley, C. D. Enterprises, Inc.

C. Larene Hall. Martha's Freedom Train. 2009. 100p. pap. 10.49 *(978-1-4389-7977-9(0))* AuthorHouse.

Cabell, James Branch. The Jewel Merchants. 2004. reprint ed. pap. 15.95 *(978-1-4191-6788-1(X))*; pap. 1.99 *(978-1-4192-6788-8(4))* Kessinger Publishing, LLC.

Cabell, Robert W. The Mermaid Adventures of Princess Miranda: Volume One. Cabell, Robert W., illus. 2013. (Illus.). 128p. pap. 7.95 *(978-0-9890974-3-7(9)*, Oceanus Bks.) Warrington Pubns.

Cable, Ken. Track of the Hunter. 2013. 192p. pap. 10.95 *(978-0-9837873-3-4(6))* Reader Publishing Group.

Cabot, Meg. Hunter's Moon. Coronado, Jinky, illus. 2009. (Avalon High Coronation Ser.: Bk. 3). (ENG.). 160p. (YA). (gr. 8-18). pap. 9.99 *(978-0-06-117710-1(5))* HarperCollins Pubs.

—Missing You. 2006. (1-800-Where-R-You Ser.: 5). (ENG.). 288p. (YA). (gr. 8-12). pap. 6.99 *(978-0-06-087430-8(9)*, HarperTeen) HarperCollins Pubs.

—Remembrance. 2016. (Mediator Ser.: 7). 400p. pap. 15.99 *(978-0-06-237902-3(X)*, William Morrow Paperbacks) HarperCollins Pubs.

Cadet, John. The Kangaroo's Adventure. 2012. 24p. pap. 24.95 *(978-1-4560-2861-9(8))* America Star Bks.

Cadman, Mistie. Sophie's Summer Sombrero Adventure. 2012. 32p. pap. 24.95 *(978-1-62709-289-0(7))* America Star Bks.

Cadose, Linda A. The Hidden Chamber in the Great Sphinx. 2012. 110p. (gr. 4-6). 23.99 *(978-1-4685-0806-2(7))*; pap. 14.95 *(978-1-4685-0807-9(5))* AuthorHouse.

Cadwallader, Doris Jensen. Little Pine's Christmas Story. 2011. 24p. pap. 12.74 *(978-1-4634-1358-3(0))* AuthorHouse.

Cafaro, Phyllis. Captain Mcfinn & Friends Meet Coral Rose. 2012. (ENG.). 24p. (J). 19.99 *(978-0-9799283-5-2(4)*, 9780979928352) Cold River Pubns.

Cafiero, Crystal. Gone Fishing, Just Daddy & Me. 2013. 24p. pap. 24.95 *(978-1-4241-1532-7(9))* America Star Bks.

Cage, Elizabeth. License to Thrill. 2013. (Spy Girls Ser.: 1). (ENG., Illus.). 192p. (YA). (gr. 7). pap. 13.99 *(978-1-4814-2078-5(X)*, Simon Pulse) Simon Pulse.

—Live & Let Spy. 2013. (Spy Girls Ser.: 2). (ENG., Illus.). 192p. (YA). (gr. 7). pap. 13.99 *(978-1-4814-2079-2(8)*, Simon Pulse) Simon Pulse.

—Nobody Does It Better. 2013. (Spy Girls Ser.: 3). (ENG., Illus.). 192p. (YA). (gr. 7). pap. 13.99 *(978-1-4814-2080-8(1)*, Simon Pulse) Simon Pulse.

—Spy Girls Are Forever. 2013. (Spy Girls Ser.: 4). (ENG., Illus.). 192p. (YA). (gr. 7). pap. 13.99 *(978-1-4814-2082-2(8)*, Simon Pulse) Simon Pulse.

Cain. Tommy Tan & the Bowl of Time. 2011. (ENG.). 150p. (gr. 3-9). pap. 11.95 *(978-988-18094-3-8(6))* Haven Bks.

Caine, Paul. Jake's Journey. 2010. 68p. pap. 10.49 *(978-1-4520-0508-9(7))* AuthorHouse.

Caine, Rachel, pseud. The Morganville Vampires. 2009. (Morganville Vampires Ser.: Bks. 1-2). (ENG.). 480p. (YA). (gr. 9-18). 9.99 *(978-0-451-23054-6(X)*, Berkley) Penguin Publishing Group.

Caird, Frankie Telfer. The Secret of Ellis Meadow. 2013. 160p. pap. 12.95 *(978-1-60911-616-3(X)*, Strategic Bk. Publishing) Strategic Book Publishing & Rights Agency (SBPRA).

Cairns, Barbara. Gatsby's Grand Adventures: Book 1 Winslow Homer's Snap the Whip. Ruble, Eugene, illus. 2012. 16p. pap. 9.95 *(978-1-61633-350-8(2))* Guardian Angel Publishing, Inc.

Caldas, Iara. The Fisherman Collection: The Fishery. 2013. (ENG.). 35p. (J). pap. 13.95 *(978-1-4327-9406-4(X))* Outskirts Pr., Inc.

Caldwell, Bruce. Sidecar Scooter. Hawyard, Charlie O., illus. 2008. 32p. (J). pap. 9.95 *(978-0-9792612-9-9(5))* Blue Gate Bks.

Calero, Dennis. You're Not the Captain of Me! 2011. (ENG.). 272p. (J). (gr. 4-7). pap. 9.95 *(978-1-59687-375-9(2))* IBks., Inc.

Calhoun, Megan. Oscar the Pig: Mommy Goes to Work. 2008. 32p. 18.50 *(978-0-615-25193-6(5))* Silly String Media.

Calkhoven, Laurie. Fork in the Trail. Studios, Arcana, illus. 2010. (ENG.). 120p. (J). (gr. 3-18). pap. 8.95 *(978-1-59369-758-7(9))* American Girl Publishing, Inc.

The Call of the Wild Guide. 16.47 *(978-0-13-425968-0(8))* Prentice Hall PTR.

Callen, Sharon. Anna Goes to Zambia, 1 vol. rev. ed. 2013. (Fiction Readers Ser.). (ENG., Illus.). 20p. (J). (gr. 1-1). pap. 15.96 *(978-1-4807-1151-8(9))*; pap. 4.99 *(978-1-4333-5495-3(0))* Shell Educational Publishing.

—Seb's Train, 1 vol. rev. ed. 2013. (Fiction Readers Ser.). (ENG., Illus.). 12p. (J). (gr. 1-1). pap. 4.99 *(978-1-4333-5446-5(2))*; pap. 12.96 *(978-1-4807-1125-9(X))* Shell Educational Publishing.

—Splash Down!, 1 vol. rev. ed. 2013. (Fiction Readers Ser.). (ENG., Illus.). 12p. (J). (gr. 1-1). pap. 4.99 *(978-1-4333-5456-4(X))*; pap. 12.96 *(978-1-4807-1135-8(7))* Shell Educational Publishing.

—What Can You See?, 1 vol. rev. ed. 2013. (Fiction Readers Ser.). (ENG., Illus.). 20p. (J). (gr. 1-1). pap. 4.99 *(978-1-4333-5490-8(X))*; pap. 15.96 *(978-1-4807-1146-4(2))* Shell Educational Publishing.

Calloway, Nathaniel. The Missing Tape Recorder: An Original Child's Tale. 2013. 12p. pap. 12.68 *(978-1-4669-6423-5(5))* Trafford Publishing.

Callsen, Terri. The Outdoor Adventures of Charlie & Kaylee: Hunting Fear (book 1) Lignor, Amy, ed. Blondahl, Samuel, illus. 2012. 156p. pap. 9.85 *(978-1-938634-10-9(1))* Freedom of Speech Publishing, Inc.

Calmenson, Stephanie. There Are No Moose on This Island, 1 vol. Thermes, Jennifer, illus. 2013. (ENG.). 32p. (J). 17.95 *(978-1-934031-34-6(8)*, a2b39bfc-ad16-4e21-bc2e-5db5168164a8) Islandport Pr., Inc.

Calonita, Jen. The Real Z. 2017. (American Girl: Z Yang Ser.: 1). (ENG.). 176p. (J). (gr. 3-7). pap. 9.99 ***(978-1-338-13705-7(0))*** Scholastic, Inc.

Calopisis, Dennis. The Lonely Little Donkey. 2010. 26p. 14.98 *(978-0-557-20849-4(1))* Lulu Pr., Inc.

Calu, John & Hart, Dave. The Treasure of Tucker's Island. 2003. 80p. (YA). pap. 8.95 *(978-0-595-27953-1(8))* iUniverse, Inc.

Calucag, Angela. Little Freddy S Journey. 2012. 32p. pap. 17.99 *(978-1-62419-840-3(6))* Salem Author Services.

Calumus, Bic-. The Tale of Peter Rabbit, the Original Latin Version, C 777 B C Faithfully Translated by Bic-Calamus. 2009. 48p. pap. 9.95 *(978-1-60693-626-9(3)*, Eloquent Bks.) Strategic Book Publishing & Rights Agency (SBPRA).

Cameron, Anne. The Lightning Catcher. Jamieson, Victoria, illus. 2013. (Lightning Catcher Ser.: 1). (ENG.). 432p. (J). (gr. 3-7). 16.99 *(978-0-06-211276-7(7)*, Greenwillow Bks.) HarperCollins Pubs.

—Secrets of the Storm Vortex. Jamieson, Victoria, illus. 2015. (Lightning Catcher Ser.: 3). (ENG.). 464p. (J). (gr. 3-7). 16.99 *(978-0-06-211283-5(X)*, Greenwillow Bks.) HarperCollins Pubs.

—The Storm Tower Thief. Jamieson, Victoria, illus. 2014. (Lightning Catcher Ser.: 2). (ENG.). 432p. (J). (gr. 3-7). 16.99 *(978-0-06-211279-8(1)*, Greenwillow Bks.) HarperCollins Pubs.

Cameron, Ian. Stirling Bridge. (Illus.). 32p. pap. 6.95 *(978-1-899827-07-7(2))* Scottish Children's Pr. GBR. Dist: Wilson & Assocs.

Cameron, Kristy. The Adventures of Herb the Wild Turkey - Herb Goes Camping. Shickle, Ian, illus. 2012. 38p. pap. *(978-0-9859790-0-3(3))* LP Publishing.

—The Other Side of the Window. Ian, Shickle, illus. 2013. 28p. pap. *(978-0-9859790-2-7(X))* LP Publishing.

Cameron, Sam. The Missing Juliet: a Fisher Key Adventure. 2013. (ENG.). 264p. (gr. 7). pap. 11.95 *(978-1-60282-959-6(4))* Bold Strokes Bks.

Cameron, Sharon. Rook. (ENG.). 464p. (J). (gr. 7). 2016. pap. 9.99 *(978-1-338-03246-8(1))* 2015. 17.99 *(978-0-545-67599-4(5))* Scholastic, Inc. (Scholastic Pr.).

Cameron, Thomas "Tom". Freddy's Adventure on the Safari River. 2012. 36p. pap. 24.95 *(978-1-4626-7436-7(4))* America Star Bks.

—Freddy's Mick Mock Ridge Adventure. 2012. 28p. pap. 24.95 *(978-1-4626-7435-0(6))* America Star Bks.

Caminada, Janet Barnett. Yoga, the Kid & the Cricket: A fun & easy illustrated guide to beginner's yoga. A complete yoga workout that follows along with the story. Written. 2011. 36p. pap. 22.88 *(978-1-4634-4478-5(8))* AuthorHouse.

Cammuso, Frank. Cookie Catastrophe, Bk. 3. 2014. (Misadventures of Salem Hyde Ser.). (ENG., Illus.). 96p. (J). (gr. 1-4). pap. 6.95 *(978-1-4197-1199-2(7)*, Amulet Bks.) Abrams, Inc.

—Dinosaur Dilemma. 2015. (Misadventures of Salem Hyde Ser.: 4). (J). lib. bdg. 17.15 *(978-0-606-37241-1(5))* Turtleback Bks.

—The Misadventures of Salem Hyde, Bk. 5. 2015. (Misadventures of Salem Hyde Ser.: 5). (ENG., Illus.). 96p. (J). (gr. 2-4). 14.95 *(978-1-4197-1651-5(4)*, Amulet Bks.) Abrams, Inc.

—Spelling Trouble. 2013. (Misadventures of Salem Hyde Ser.). (ENG., Illus.). 96p. (J). (gr. 1-3). 14.95 *(978-1-4197-0803-9(1))*; pap. 6.95 *(978-1-4197-0804-6(X))* Abrams, Inc. (Amulet Bks.).

Campbell, D. Andrew. Catharsis. 2013. 340p. pap. 12.50 *(978-0-9897522-0-6(8))* Broviak Publishing.

Campbell, H. David. The Adventurous Jill: And Her Friend Jack. 2012. 112p. pap. 13.95 *(978-1-4772-7241-1(0))* AuthorHouse.

Campbell, Hannah. Skylanders Universe: Take Flight & Fight! 2015. lib. bdg. 14.75 *(978-0-606-36801-8(9))* Turtleback Bks.

Campbell, Isaiah. The Struggles of Johnny Cannon. 2015. 322p. (J). pap. 7.99 *(978-1-4814-2632-9(X)*, Simon & Schuster Bks. For Young Readers) Simon & Schuster Bks. For Young Readers.

Campbell, Lori. The Adventures of Tinkerbelle & Peanut. 2012. 36p. pap. 21.99 *(978-1-4771-4835-8(3))* Xlibris Corp.

Campbell, Mari. Maggiemoosetracks: Making Friends. Katsumoto, Sayaka, tr. Jennings, Randy, illus. 2013. 108p. pap. 21.99 *(978-0-9895205-6-0(0))* MaggieMooseTracks.

—Maggiemoosetracks: Wolf Pack. Jennings, Randy, illus. 2013. 106p. pap. 21.00 *(978-0-9895205-5-3(2))* MaggieMooseTracks.

Campbell, Matt. Unlocked. 2012. 82p. pap. *(978-1-909395-06-0(4))* Legend Pr.

Campbell, R. W. Merrick Tumbledorf: The Last Talcomite Dragon. 2013. (ENG.). 250p. (YA). pap. 15.95 *(978-1-4787-1312-8(7))* Outskirts Pr., Inc.

Campbell, Suzy. The Hidden Graveyard. 2011. 62p. pap. 19.95 *(978-1-4560-4265-3(3))* America Star Bks.

Campbell, Wanda Gail. Little Buckets Full of Big Love. 2008. (Illus.). 48p. pap. 19.49 *(978-1-4389-0688-1(9))* AuthorHouse.

Campi, Alex de. Kat & Mouse, Vol. 1. 2017. (ENG., Illus.). 96p. (YA). pap. 5.99 *(978-1-59816-548-7(8)*, 9781598165487) TOKYOPOP, Inc.

Campos, Jacqueline. The Adventures of Lil' Wolf, Twinkie, to. 2005. 63p. pap. 16.95 *(978-1-4137-8494-7(1))* PublishAmerica, Inc.

Campos, Llanos & Campos Martinez, Llanos. The Treasure of Barracuda. Sardà, Júlia, illus. 2016. (ENG.). 156p. (J). (gr. 3-7). 15.95 *(978-1-939775-14-6(0))* March 4th, Inc.

Campus Confessions Sample Set: XO Ronette/Frenemies/Choices/Crush. 2013. (ENG.). (YA). (gr. 8-12). pap. 39.80 *(978-1-62250-787-0(8))* Saddleback Educational Publishing, Inc.

Canavan, Charles Patrick. Rocky's Road to Sunshine. 2013. (ENG., Illus.). 30p. (J). pap. 19.95 *(978-1-4787-1251-0(1))* Outskirts Pr., Inc.

Cane, Rachel. Soy. 2013. 32p. (J). pap. 10.99 *(978-987-612-530-7(3))* V&R Editoras.

Caniff, Milton. The Complete Terry & the Pirates, 1934-1936, 6 vols., Vol. 1. 2007. (Terry & the Pirates Ser.: 1). (ENG., Illus.). 368p. 49.99 *(978-1-60010-100-7(3)*, 9781600101007) Idea & Design Works, LLC.

Cannella, Marco & Marron, Jose Luis, illus. Tattoo of Death. 2007. (Choose Your Own Adventure Ser.: No. 22). 113p. (J). (gr. 4-7). pap. 6.99 *(978-1-933390-22-2(0))* Chooseco LLC.

Cannon, Deborah. The Pirate Vortex: Elizabeth Latimer, Pirate Hunter. 260p. 2010. 30.03 *(978-1-4269-2683-9(9))* 2009. pap. 20.00 *(978-1-4269-0532-2(7))* Trafford Publishing.

Cannon, Jonathan. Greetings from Scurf Bay: Wish We Weren't Here! 2005. 178p. 23.95 *(978-0-595-67010-9(5))* iUniverse, Inc.

Cannon, Sherrill S. Peter & the Whimper-Whineys. 2010. 30p. pap. 13.00 *(978-1-60911-517-3(1)*, Strategic Bk. Publishing) Strategic Book Publishing & Rights Agency (SBPRA).

—Santa's Birthday Gift. 2009. 24p. pap. 11.50 *(978-1-60860-824-9(7)*, Eloquent Bks.) Strategic Book Publishing & Rights Agency (SBPRA).

Cantu, Sarah. The Dogs that Follow their Detective Dreams. Adventure No. 1: Find a New Home. 2008. 48p. pap. 20.95 *(978-0-615-18600-9(9))* Cantu, Ricardo.

Capdevila, Roser & Vendrell, Maria Martinez. Cambios y Distancias. 97th ed. 2003.Tr. of Changes & Distances. (SPA.). 24p. pap. 22.30 *(978-84-233-1625-0(4))* Harcourt Schl. Pubs.

—Como Duele... 2003.Tr. of Does It Hurt.... (SPA.). 24p. (J). 7.95 *(978-84-233-1566-6(5))* Ediciones Destino ESP. Dist: Planeta Publishing Corp.

— Uno Mas.Tr. of One More. (SPA., Illus.). 24p. (J). 7.95 *(978-84-233-1508-6(8))* Ediciones Destino ESP. Dist: Planeta Publishing Corp.

Capeci, Anne. Danger! Dynamite!, 1 vol. Casale, Paul, illus. 2003. (Cascade Moutain Railroad Mystery Ser.: No. 1). (ENG.). 144p. (J). (gr. 2-5). 12.95 *(978-1-56145-288-0(2))* Peachtree Pubs.

—Daredevils, 1 vol. Casale, Paul, illus. 2004. (Cascade Mountain Railroad Mysteries Ser.). (ENG.). 144p. (J). (gr. 2-5). 12.95 *(978-1-56145-307-8(2))* Peachtree Pubs.

—The Magic School Bus Chapter Book No.17: Food Chain Frenzy. 2004. (Magic School Bus Chapter Bks.: 17). (gr. 3-6). lib. bdg. 14.75 *(978-0-613-87596-7(6)*, Turtleback) Turtleback Bks.

Capehart, Staci. Furry Tails: The Adventures of Mr. Mackie. 2009. 40p. pap. 16.99 *(978-1-4343-6974-1(9))* AuthorHouse.

Capetta, Amy Rose. Entangled. (ENG.). (YA). (gr. 9). 2014. 352p. pap. 9.99 *(978-0-544-33624-7(0)*, HMH Books For Young Readers) 2013. 336p. 17.99 *(978-0-544-08744-6(5))* Houghton Mifflin Harcourt Publishing Co.

Capotosto, Anthony. No Shoes Required. 2005. 49p. pap. 8.00 *(978-1-4116-2523-5(4))* Lulu Pr., Inc.

Capozzi, Suzy & Finnegan, Delphine. Lady & the Tramp. Random House Disney Staff, illus. 2012. (Step into Reading Ser.). (ENG.). 32p. (J). (gr. -1-1). pap. 3.99 *(978-0-7364-3026-5(1)*, RH/Disney) Random Hse. Children's Bks.

Captain America. 2003. (J). per. *(978-1-57657-906-0(9))* Paradise Pr., Inc.

Capucilli, Alyssa Satin. Biscuit Take-Along Storybook Set: Biscuit's Birthday; Meet Biscuit!; Biscuit's Show & Share Day; Mind Your Manners, Biscuit!; Biscuit Visits the Doctor. Schories, Pat, illus. 2017. (Biscuit Ser.). 120p. (J). (gr. -1-3). pap. 11.99 *(978-0-06-162516-9(7),* HarperFestival) HarperCollins Pubs.

—Katy Duck, Dance Star/Katy Duck, Center Stage. Cole, Henry, illus. 2009. (Katy Duck Ser.). (ENG.). 24p. (J). (gr. -1-k). pap. 3.99 *(978-1-4169-8279-1(5),* Little Simon) Little Simon.

—Katy Duck Ready-To-Read Value Pack: Starring Katy Duck; Katy Duck Makes a Friend; Katy Duck Meets the Babysitter; Katy Duck & the Tip-Tip Tap Shoes; Katy Duck, Flower Girl; Katy Duck Goes to Work. Cole, Henry, illus. 2014. (Katy Duck Ser.). (ENG.). 144p. (J). (gr. -1-1). pap. 15.96 *(978-1-4814-2600-8(1),* Simon Spotlight) Simon Spotlight.

—Tulip Loves Rex. Massini, Sarah, illus. 2013. (ENG.). 32p. (J). (gr. -1-3). 17.99 *(978-0-06-209413-1(0),* Tegen, Katherine Bks) HarperCollins Pubs.

Caputo, Frank. The Adventures of Jimmy Farrell & the Magic Red Ring. 2012. 166p. 22.95 *(978-1-4759-4183-8(8));* pap. 12.95 *(978-1-4759-4182-1(X))* iUniverse, Inc.

Caputo, Kenneth. The Adventures of Jay & Tay: Our First Karate Class. 2011. 32p. pap. 14.99 *(978-1-4567-1999-9(8))* AuthorHouse.

Caravan. 2007. (Choose Your Own Adventure - Dragonlarks Ser.). (Illus.). 64p. (J). (gr. 4-7). pap. 7.99 *(978-1-933390-54-3(9))* Chooseco LLC.

Carbone, Courtney. High-Stakes Heist! Atiyeh, Michael & Borkowski, Michael, illus. 2016. (Little Golden Book Ser.). (ENG.). 24p. (J). (-k). 4.99 *(978-0-385-37426-2(7),* Golden Bks.) Random Hse. Children's Bks.

—The Ice Box. Random House Disney Staff, illus. 2014. (Friendship Box Ser.). (ENG.). 48p. (J). (-k). bds. 10.99 *(978-0-7364-3128-6(4),* RH/Disney) Random Hse. Children's Bks.

—Supergirl Takes Off! 2016. (Step into Reading Level 2 Ser.). lib. bdg. 14.75 *(978-0-606-38887-0(7))* Turtleback Bks.

—Supergirl Takes off! (DC Super Friends) Random House Editors & Doescher, Erik, illus. 2016. (Step into Reading Ser.). (ENG.). 24p. (J). (gr. -1-1). 4.99 *(978-0-399-55344-8(4),* Random Hse. Bks. for Young Readers) Random Hse. Children's Bks.

Cardarelli, Mario. Bunny, an Orphan's Story. 2008. 44p. pap. 18.99 *(978-1-4389-1597-5(7))* AuthorHouse.

—Kid Jack Adventures: Prevent Bullying. 2011. 48p. pap. 15.49 *(978-1-4567-2296-8(4))* AuthorHouse.

Cardin, Beth W. Little Red Leaf. 2010. 24p. 12.99 *(978-1-4520-7414-6(3))* AuthorHouse.

Cardoso, Kelly. Thomas & the Toad King. DeBroeck, Sarah, illus. 2011. 28p. pap. 24.95 *(978-1-4560-0956-4(7))* America Star Bks.

Cardoza, Kristina. Pinky Bunny's First Day of Kindergarten. 2011. 16p. pap. 8.75 *(978-1-4634-8753-9(3))* AuthorHouse.

Carey, Anna. Blackbird. 2014. (Blackbird Ser.: 1). (ENG.). 256p. (YA). (gr. 9). 17.99 *(978-0-06-229973-4(5),* HarperTeen) HarperCollins Pubs.

—Blackbird. 2015. (SPA.). 240p. (YA). (gr. 9-12). pap. 17.99 *(978-987-612-909-1(0))* Lectorum Pubns., Inc.

—Deadfall. 2016. (Blackbird Ser.: 2). 272p. (YA). (gr. 9). pap. 9.99 *(978-0-06-229977-2(8),* HarperTeen) HarperCollins Pubs.

Carey, Cassandra L. The Adventures of Uncle Joe: Uncle Joe & His Bear. 2012. 30p. 24.95 *(978-1-4626-5563-2(7))* America Star Bks.

Carey, John. Cook Spies. 2005. 34p. (J). per. *(978-0-9773723-2-4(4))* Trent's Prints.

Carey, Kathleen. Jack Kat Had a Day, 1 vol. Carey, Joseph, illus. 2009. 21p. pap. 24.95 *(978-1-60836-314-8(7))* America Star Bks.

Carigiet, Alois, illus. A Bell for Ursli: A Story from the Engadine in Switzerland. 2007. 44p. (J). *(978-0-86315-614-4(2))* Floris Bks.

Carithers, Rochelle. The Purple with Pink Polka Dot Ponies. Weber, Caressa, illus. 2010. 102p. pap. 7.95 *(978-1-936107-31-5(7))* Salem Author Services.

Carkhuff Jr., Sam. The Ranch Race. Crow, Katie, illus. 2012. 36p. 16.99 *(978-1-939054-03-6(6));* pap. 11.99 *(978-1-939054-02-9(8))* Rowe Publishing and Design.

Carle, Eric. The Eric Carle Ready-To-Read Collection: Have You Seen My Cat?; the Greedy Python; Pancakes, Pancakes!; Rooster Is off to See the World; a House for Hermit Crab; Walter the Baker. Carle, Eric, illus. 2014. (World of Eric Carle Ser.). (ENG., Illus.). 160p. (J). (gr. -1-2). pap. 15.99 *(978-1-4814-1632-0(4),* Simon Spotlight) Simon Spotlight.

—From Head to Toe Soft Book. 2005. (J). 20.00 *(978-0-9774677-2-3(4))* Small World Toys.

—The Tiny Seed. Carle, Eric, illus. 2009. (World of Eric Carle Ser.). (ENG., Illus.). 36p. (J). (gr. -1). 7.99 *(978-1-4169-7917-3(4),* Little Simon) Little Simon.

Carlson, Amanda. Sultenfuss Moose's Lost Slipper. 2006. 26p. 18.03 *(978-1-4116-7729-6(3))* Lulu Pr., Inc.

Carlson, Bert H. The Perilous African Adventures of Sir Bert & Sir Gilbert. 2013. 106p. pap. 32.10 *(978-1-4669-8744-9(8))* Trafford Publishing.

Carlson, Caroline. The Buccaneers' Code. (Very Nearly Honorable League of Pirates Ser.: 3). 320p. (J). (gr. 3-7). 2016. pap. 6.99 *(978-0-06-219440-4(2))* 2015. (ENG.). 16.99 *(978-0-06-219439-8(9))* HarperCollins Pubs.

—Magic Marks the Spot. Phillips, Dave, illus. 2013. (ENG.). 368p. (J). pap. *(978-0-06-231467-3(X))* Harper & Row Ltd.

—Magic Marks the Spot. Phillips, Dave, illus. (Very Nearly Honorable League of Pirates Ser.: 1). (ENG.). (J). (gr. 3-7). 2014. 384p. pap. 6.99 *(978-0-06-219435-0(6))* 2013. 368p. 16.99 *(978-0-06-219434-3(8))* HarperCollins Pubs.

—The Terror of the Southlands. Phillips, Dave, illus. 2014. (ENG.). 336p. (J). pap. *(978-0-06-236178-3(3))* Harper & Row Ltd.

—The Very Nearly Honorable League of Pirates - The Terror of the Southlands. Phillips, Dave, illus. 2014. (Very Nearly Honorable League of Pirates Ser.: 2). (ENG.). 336p. (J). (gr. 3-7). 16.99 *(978-0-06-219436-7(4))* HarperCollins Pubs.

Carman, Patrick. The Black Circle. 2009. (Playaway Children Ser.: Bk. 5). (J). 49.99 *(978-1-61545-995-7(2))* Findaway World, LLC.

—The Black Circle. 2009. (J). (39 Clues Ser.: 5). (ENG.). 176p. (gr. 3-7). 12.99 *(978-0-545-06045-5(1),* Scholastic Pr.); 160p. *(978-0-545-15291-4(7))* Scholastic, Inc.

—The Dark Planet. 2010. (Atherton Ser.: 3). (ENG., Illus.). 368p. (J). (gr. 3-7). pap. 9.99 *(978-0-316-16675-1(8))* Little, Brown Bks. for Young Readers.

—Floors #3: the Field of Wacky Inventions. 2015. (Floors Ser.: 3). (ENG.). 224p. (J). (gr. 3-7). pap. 6.99 *(978-0-545-79859-4(0),* Scholastic Paperbacks) Scholastic, Inc.

Carman, Patrick & Scholastic, Inc. Staff. The Black Circle. 2009. (39 Clues Ser.: 5). (ENG., Illus.). 176p. (J). (gr. 3-7). 12.99 *(978-0-545-09063-6(6),* Scholastic Pr.) Scholastic, Inc.

Carman, Patrick & Studios, P. c. The Crossbones. 2010. (Skeleton Creek Ser.: 3). (ENG.). 224p. (J). (gr. 3-7). 14.99 *(978-0-545-24994-2(5))* Scholastic, Inc.

Carmen Luisa. The Adventures of Cotin Mirel: Three Short Stories. 2012. 20p. pap. 10.95 *(978-1-4525-5161-6(8))* Balboa Pr.

Carmine's Big Race. 2009. (ENG.). 24p. pap. 3.99 *(978-1-4231-1688-2(7))* Disney Pr.

Carmitchel, Andrew. A Wizard on Oak Street. 2007. 68p. per. 8.95 *(978-0-595-47849-1(2))* iUniverse, Inc.

Carmody, Isobelle. A Fox Called Sorrow. 2008. (Little Fur Ser.: Bk. 2). (ENG., Illus.). 272p. (J). (gr. 3-7). 5.99 *(978-0-375-83857-6(0),* Yearling) Random Hse. Children's Bks.

—A Mystery of Wolves. 2009. (Little Fur Ser.: Bk. 3). (ENG., Illus.). 256p. (J). (gr. 3-7). 6.99 *(978-0-375-83859-0(7),* Yearling) Random Hse. Children's Bks.

—A Riddle of Green. 2009. (Little Fur Ser.: Bk. 4). (J). *(978-0-375-83860-6(0))* Random House Children's Books.

Carney, John & Carney, Veta. Teddy's Journey. 2009. 37p. pap. 15.98 *(978-0-557-15269-8(0))* Lulu Pr., Inc.

Carney, Larry, adapted by. Silly Book/CD - Silly Zoo. 2010. (Illus.). 24p. (J). pap. 6.95 incl. cd-rom *(978-1-60072-155-7(9))* PC Treasures, Inc.

—Silly Farm. 2010. (ENG., Illus.). 24p. (J). pap. 6.95 *(978-1-60072-156-4(7))* PC Treasures, Inc.

—Silly Friends. 2010. (ENG., Illus.). 24p. (J). pap. 6.95 *(978-1-60072-158-8(3))* PC Treasures, Inc.

—Silly Neighborhood. 2010. (ENG., Illus.). 24p. (J). pap. 6.95 *(978-1-60072-157-1(5))* PC Treasures, Inc.

Carney, Riley. The Final Alliance: Book Five of the Reign of the Elements. 2012. (Reign of the Elements Ser.: Bk. 5). (Illus.). 312p. (J). 20.95 *(978-0-9841307-9-5(9))* BookLight Pr.

Carol, Darlene. A Puppy Called Runt: The Adventure Begins. 2008. 224p. pap. 12.95 *(978-1-935105-00-8(0))* Avid Readers Publishing Group.

Carolan, Debra. Puppets No Strings Attached. 2012. 58p. (-18). pap. 16.95 *(978-1-4626-8906-4(X))* America Star Bks.

Carolan, Jill. Sadie's Bargain. 2008. 148p. pap. 10.94 *(978-0-615-26231-4(7))* Never Quit Productions, Inc.

Caroll, Robin. Samantha Sanderson off the Record, 1 vol. 2015. (FaithGirlz / Samantha Sanderson Ser.). (ENG.). 240p. (J). pap. 8.99 *(978-0-310-74249-4(8))* Zonderkidz.

Caron, Eleonore. Gizmo & Ellen Mysteries: The Case of the Missing Boy. 2012. 24p. pap. 24.95 *(978-1-4626-6747-5(3))* America Star Bks.

Carpenter, Angie. Digewi Deer: The Tale of a Blind Deer. Berner Coble, Lynn, ed. 2013. 82p. (J). pap. 8.99 *(978-0-9846724-3-1(5))* Paws and Claws Publishing, LLC.

Carr, Bernie. Jake & Miller's Big Adventure: A Prepper's Book for Kids. Wells, Aja & Mulford, Aja, illus. 2014. (ENG.). 32p. (J). (gr. -1). 15.95 *(978-1-61243-271-7(9))* Ulysses Pr.

Carr, C. Hanna's Way. 2011. (Illus.). 112p. 28.31 *(978-1-4567-8179-8(0));* pap. 14.11 *(978-1-4567-8178-1(2))* AuthorHouse.

Carr, Debra. Misty Is Missing. Carr, Stephen, illus. 2008. 52p. pap. 8.95 *(978-0-9816172-7-5(1))* Westview Publishing Co., Inc.

Carr, Fran. Wilbur Runs Away. 2004. (Illus.). 80p. pap. *(978-1-84401-304-3(9))* Athena Pr.

Carr, Paul C. The Adventures of Three Cousins. 2006. 24.00 *(978-0-8059-9032-4(1))* Dorrance Publishing Co., Inc.

Carr, Roger Vaughan. The Climb. 2007. 96p. (J). pap. *(978-1-4207-0730-4(2))* Sundance/Newbridge Educational Publishing.

Carr, Sharleen. Watch for Fallen Rock. 2007. 68p. per. 19.95 *(978-1-4241-6704-3(3))* America Star Bks.

Carrero, Jorge & Cody, William. Buffalo Bill. 2003. (Timeless Classics Ser.). (SPA., Illus.). 92p. (J). (gr. 5-8). pap. 12.95 *(978-84-204-5778-9(7))* Santillana USA Publishing Co., Inc.

Carrington, Jim. Sang Kancil & Crocodile Orange Band. Oliver, Juanbjuan, illus. 2016. (Cambridge Reading Adventures Ser.). (ENG.). 16p. pap. 6.56 *(978-1-107-57604-9(0))* Cambridge Univ. Pr.

Carroll, Claudia. Missy Mouse & the Rocket Ship. 2008. 65p. pap. 9.95 *(978-0-557-01769-0(6))* Lulu Pr., Inc.

Carroll, D. L. Sir Licksalot & the Island Fools. 2012. 120p. pap. 19.95 *(978-1-4626-8092-4(5))* America Star Bks.

Carroll, Jody. Mitsy Morgan: Six Monkeys Past Midnight. 2010. 44p. pap. 18.75 *(978-1-4520-0796-0(9))* AuthorHouse.

Carroll, Lewis, pseud. Alice in Wonderland Made Simple for Kids. Sloan, Peter, illus. 2007. 126p. (J). per. 19.95 net. *(978-0-923891-91-6(9))* Ishi Pr. International.

—Alice's Adventures in Wonderland. 2010. 208p. pap. 24.95 *(978-0-557-01173-5(6))* Lulu Pr., Inc.

—Alice's Adventures in Wonderland. 2008. (Puffin Classics Ser.). (gr. 5-8). lib. bdg. 16.00 *(978-0-613-63916-3(2),* Turtleback) Turtleback Bks.

—Alice's Adventures in Wonderland, & Through the Looking Glass, 1bk. Bachelier, Anne, illus. 2005. (J). *(978-0-9728620-8-0(0)); (978-0-9769071-0-7(0));* per. *(978-0-9769071-1-4(9));* im. lthr. *(978-0-9728620-9-7(9))* CFM.

—Alice's Adventures in Wonderland & Through the Looking Glass. 2010. (Enriched Classics Ser.). (ENG.). 336p. mass mkt. 5.99 *(978-1-4391-6947-6(0))* Simon & Schuster.

—The Story of Sylvie & Bruno. 2005. pap. 31.95 *(978-0-7661-9697-1(6))* Kessinger Publishing, LLC.

—Through the Looking Glass. 2010. 84p. pap. 9.95 *(978-1-59594-837-3(6),* Wingspan Pr.) WingSpan Publishing.

—Through the Looking-Glass. 140p. 2005. 26.95 *(978-1-4218-0656-3(8))* 2004. pap. 10.95 *(978-1-59540-106-9(7))* 1st World Publishing, Inc. (1st World Library - Literary Society).

Carroll, Michael. The Awakening, No. 1. 2008. (Quantum Prophecy Ser.: 1). (ENG.). 288p. (J). (gr. 5-6). 8.99 *(978-0-14-241179-7(5),* Puffin Books) Penguin Young Readers Group.

—Stronger: A Super Human Clash. 3rd ed. 2013. (Super Human Ser.: 3). (ENG.). 400p. (YA). (gr. 7). pap. 9.99 *(978-0-14-242634-0(2),* Speak) Penguin Young Readers Group.

Carroll, Ruth & Carroll, Latrobe. Beanie & Tough Enough. 2015. (ENG., Illus.). 192p. (J). (gr. 3-6). pap. 14.99 *(978-0-486-80223-7(X))* Dover Pubns., Inc.

Carryl, Charles E. Davy & the Goblin: Or, What Followed Reading 'Alice's Adventures in Wonderland' 2011. (Illus.). 128p. pap. *(978-1-904808-65-7(4))* Evertype.

Cars & Disney Book Group Staff. Cars. 2010. (Read-Along Storybook & CD Ser.). (ENG.). 32p. (J). (gr. -1 — 1). pap. 6.99 *(978-1-4231-3332-2(3))* Disney Pr.

Carson, Donna Wren. The Mystery of Grimly Manor. 2012. 114p. 29.99 *(978-1-4771-5508-0(2));* pap. 19.99 *(978-1-4771-5507-3(4))* Xlibris Corp.

Carson, Jack. Academy Attack. 2013. (ENG., Illus.). 144p. (J). pap. 5.99 *(978-0-85707-559-8(4),* Simon & Schuster Children's) Simon & Schuster, Ltd. GBR. Dist: Simon & Schuster, Inc.

—Canyon Clash. 2013. (ENG., Illus.). 128p. (J). pap. 5.99 *(978-0-85707-561-1(6),* Simon & Schuster Children's) Simon & Schuster, Ltd. GBR. Dist: Simon & Schuster, Inc.

—Terminal Takedown. 2014. (ENG., Illus.). 144p. (J). pap. 6.99 *(978-0-85707-565-9(9),* Simon & Schuster Children's) Simon & Schuster, Ltd. GBR. Dist: Simon & Schuster, Inc.

Carson, James. The Saddle Boys of the Rockies. 2007. 104p. per. *(978-1-4068-4406-1(3))* Echo Library.

Carson, John & Carson, Marlene. Ramblin' Rose: The Chinese Fortune Cookie. 2008. 291p. pap. 8.99 *(978-0-9800034-1-3(5))* BBM Bks.

Carson, John E. & Carson, Marlene R. Ramblin' Rose: The Porcelain Mines in Russia. 2007. (Ramblin' Rose Ser.). 191p. (J). (gr. 8-12). per. 8.99 *(978-0-9776043-7-1(3))* Beast Stew.

—The Wire Forest of Peru. 2007. (Ramblin' Rose Ser.). 205p. (YA). (gr. 8-12). per. 8.99 *(978-0-9776043-9-5(X))* Aspirations Media, Inc.

Carson, Marlene R. & Carson, John E. Ramblin' Rose: The Secret in the Arctic Ice. 2008. 136p. pap. 8.99 *(978-0-9800034-0-6(7))* BBM Bks.

Carter, Aimée. Simon Thorn & the Viper's Pit. 2017. (Simon Thorn Ser.). (ENG.). 304p. (J). 16.99 *(978-1-61963-715-3(4),* 9781619637153, Bloomsbury USA Childrens) Bloomsbury Publishing USA.

—Simon Thorn & the Wolf's Den. 2016. (Simon Thorn Ser.). (ENG.). 320p. (YA). (gr. 3-6). 16.99 *(978-1-61963-704-7(9),* 9781619637047, Bloomsbury USA Childrens) Bloomsbury Publishing USA.

Carter, Ally. Don't Judge a Girl by Her Cover. 2016. (Gallagher Girls Ser.: 3). (J). lib. bdg. 20.85 *(978-0-606-38297-7(6))* Turtleback Bks.

—See How They Run (Embassy Row, Book 2) 2015. (Embassy Row Ser.: 2). (ENG.). 336p. (J). (gr. 7). 17.99 *(978-0-545-65484-5(X),* Scholastic Pr.) Scholastic, Inc.

—Take the Key & Lock Her Up. 2016. (Embassy Row Ser.: 3). (ENG.). 336p. (J). (gr. 7). 17.99 *(978-0-545-65495-1(5),* Scholastic Pr.) Scholastic, Inc.

—United We Spy. 2013. (Gallagher Girls Ser.: Bk. 6). (ENG.). 296p. (YA). (gr. 7-17). 17.99 *(978-1-4231-6599-6(3))* Hyperion Pr.

Carter, Brei. Delia Goes to Dreamland. 2011. 36p. pap. 18.99 *(978-1-4520-5001-0(5))* AuthorHouse.

Carter, David. The Nutters of Pendle Forest - Part 1 the Enchanted Valley. 2012. (Illus.). 222p. pap. *(978-1-908098-54-2(6))* 2QT, Ltd. (Publishing).

Carter, Herbert. The Boy Scouts' First Camp Fire: Or Scouting with the Silver Fox Patrol. 2007. (ENG.). 176p. pap. 19.99 *(978-1-4346-6046-6(X));* 190p. pap. 21.99 *(978-1-4346-6047-3(8))* Creative Media Partners, LLC.

—The Boy Scouts on Sturgeon Island. 2004. reprint ed. pap. 21.95 *(978-1-4191-5507-9(5));* pap. 1.99 *(978-1-4192-5507-6(X))* Kessinger Publishing, LLC.

Carter, Jay. The Bully Caterpillar: An Adventurous Journey of the Inner Child. l.t. ed. 2003. (Illus.). 48p. reprint ed. pap. 7.95 *(978-0-937004-17-3(0))* Unicorn Pr.

Carter, Keisha. Maloni's Shoes. 2013. 28p. pap. 9.95 *(978-1-4327-9958-8(4))* Outskirts Pr., Inc.

Carter, Larry. The Red Wallet. 2013. 28p. pap. 24.95 *(978-1-4626-9667-3(8))* America Star Bks.

Carter, Liane. The Chronicles of Joy. 2008. 244p. pap. *(978-1-84923-001-8(3))* YouWriteOn.

carter, robert bob. The Magic Eye. 2009. 106p. pap. 12.95 *(978-0-557-05597-5(0))* Lulu Pr., Inc.

Carter-Stephenson, C. J. The Crystal Ship. 2010. (Illus.). 120p. pap. 12.95 *(978-1-4457-1369-4(1))* Lulu Pr., Inc.

Carter, Wade. The Adventures of Ernie & Ike: Lessons in Life Series. 2008. 44p. pap. 16.99 *(978-1-4343-9087-5(X))* AuthorHouse.

Cartoon Network Books. Learn to Draw Adventure Time. 2015. lib. bdg. 20.85 *(978-0-606-36802-5(7))* Turtleback Bks.

Cartwheel: A Sequel to Double Eagle. 2013. (ENG.). 252p. (YA). 17.00 *(978-0-9844460-3-2(6))* Bucking Horse Bks.

Cartwright, Nancy & Jones, Joanna. Henry's Adventure at the Franklin Hotel. Feterl, Bill, illus. 2011. (YA). lib. bdg. *(978-0-913062-44-9(8))* Fenwyn Pr.

Cartwright, Stephen, illus. Hercules. 2004. (Young Reading Series Two Ser.). 64p. (J). (gr. 2-18). pap. 5.95 *(978-0-7945-0453-3(1),* Usborne) EDC Publishing.

—Jason & the Golden Fleece. 2004. (Young Reading Series Two Ser.). 64p. (J). (gr. 2-18). pap. 5.95 *(978-0-7945-0451-9(5),* Usborne) EDC Publishing.

—Ulysses. 2004. (Young Reading Series Two Ser.). 64p. (J). (gr. 2-18). pap. 5.95 *(978-0-7945-0452-6(3),* Usborne) EDC Publishing.

Caruso, D. A. The Burning House. 2005. pap. 14.99 *(978-0-9765953-1-1(1))* Mighty Kids Media.

—Cool by the Pool. 2005. pap. 19.99 *(978-0-9765953-0-4(3))* Mighty Kids Media.

Caruso, Paul. The Lonely Nail. 2010. (Illus.). 26p. (J). pap. 17.95 *(978-1-4327-5646-8(X))* Outskirts Pr., Inc.

Carver, David. Leafy Leafs Where Is Lester?, 1 vol. Carver, Erin, illus. 2010. 34p. 24.95 *(978-1-4512-1069-9(8))* PublishAmerica, Inc.

—Lester Returns Home with His New Friend La'doo, 1 vol. Carver, Erin, illus. 2010. 28p. 24.95 *(978-1-4489-6340-9(0))* PublishAmerica, Inc.

Casad, Mary Brooke. Bluebonnet at the Alamo, 1 vol. Vincent, Benjamin, illus. 2013. (ENG.). 32p. (J). (gr. k-3). 16.99 *(978-1-4556-1806-4(3))* Pelican Publishing Co., Inc.

Casad, Patricia E. Bubbykins: (Life on the Farm) 2008. 46p. pap. 24.95 *(978-1-4241-9140-6(8))* America Star Bks.

Casaluci, Stacy Manning. Miracles Love a Believer. 2011. 32p. pap. 13.00 *(978-1-61204-094-3(2),* Eloquent Bks.) Strategic Book Publishing & Rights Agency (SBPRA).

Casanova, Mary. Danger at Snow Hill. Rayyan, Omar, illus. 2006. (Dog Watch Ser.: 3). (ENG.). 128p. (J). (gr. 3-7). pap. 4.99 *(978-0-689-86812-2(X),* Simon & Schuster/Paula Wiseman Bks.) Simon & Schuster/Paula Wiseman Bks.

—Dog-Napped! Rayyan, Omar, illus. 2006. (Dog Watch Ser.: 2). (ENG.). 144p. (J). (gr. 3-7). pap. 8.99 *(978-0-689-86811-5(1),* Simon & Schuster/Paula Wiseman Bks.) Simon & Schuster/Paula Wiseman Bks.

—To Catch a Burglar. Rayyan, Omar, illus. 2007. (Dog Watch Ser.: 4). (ENG.). 144p. (J). (gr. 3-7). pap. 4.99 *(978-0-689-86813-9(8),* Simon & Schuster/Paula Wiseman Bks.) Simon & Schuster/Paula Wiseman Bks.

Case, Linda. Brigits Day of Fun. 2006. 28p. pap. 9.95 *(978-1-4327-0001-0(4))* Outskirts Pr., Inc.

Casello-Atassi, Rosemarie. Camel's Tales: The Journey to Bethlehem. 2013. 86p. pap. 15.99 *(978-1-4797-7565-1(7))* Xlibris Corp.

Casey, Dawn. The Great Race: The Story of the Chinese Zodiac. Wilson, Anne, illus. 2008. (ENG.). 32p. (J). (gr. -1-2). 8.99 *(978-1-84686-202-1(7))* Barefoot Bks., Inc.

Casey, Grandpa. The Trilogy: Three adventures of the Müsh-Mice. Brennan, Lisa, illus. 2011. 48p. pap. 24.95 *(978-1-4626-2095-1(7))* America Star Bks.

Casey, Mark. An African Princess: Deasha's Wild Adventure. 2010. (Illus.). 54p. pap. 11.95 *(978-1-4327-3864-8(X))* Outskirts Pr., Inc.

Cash, Lea Michelle. The Strawberry Pot. 2013. (ENG.). 58p. (YA). pap. 11.95 *(978-1-4787-1625-9(8))* Outskirts Pr., Inc.

Cason, Anjanette. Praise Puppy's Adventure in Praise. 2007. (J). *(978-0-9755234-7-6(3))* DOMINIONHOUSE Publishing & Design.

Casper, Gina R. Corky Beagle. 2011. 32p. pap. *(978-1-77067-348-9(2))* FriesenPress.

Cassano, Carol E. A Journey to the Bottom of the Ocean: Heavenly Adventures Volume 2. 2011. 20p. pap. *(978-1-4269-7335-2(7))* Trafford Publishing (UK) Ltd.

Castaneda, Huguette. Mariella y Los Obsequios Del Mar. 2012. 56p. pap. 20.99 *(978-1-4525-6215-5(6))* Balboa Pr.

—Mariella's Gifts from the Se. 2012. 56p. pap. 20.95 *(978-1-4525-5865-3(5))* Balboa Pr.

Castanga, Felicity. The Incredible Here & Now. l.t. ed. 2013. 212p. pap. *(978-1-4596-7083-9(3))* ReadHowYouWant.com, Ltd.

Castellan, Andrea "Casty". Mickey Mouse & the World to Come. Castellan, Andrea "Casty" & Mazzon, Michelle, illus. 2010. (ENG.). 112p. (J). (gr. 3-6). pap. 9.99 *(978-1-60886-562-8(2))* Boom! Studios.

Castenetto, Christiana. Dante's Journey. Ceva, Aline Cantono di, illus. 2009. (ENG.). 28p. (J). (gr. 4-7). 15.00 *(978-88-7461-113-3(7))* Mandragora ITA. Dist: National Bk. Network.

Castillo, Elizabeth. Jaden Christian. 2012. 24p. pap. 24.95 *(978-1-4626-7624-8(3))* America Star Bks.

Castillo, Ina. Red the Super Wiener. 2008. 24p. pap. 24.95 *(978-1-60474-897-0(4))* America Star Bks.

Castle, M. E. Fakespeare: Something Stinks in Hamlet. Jennewein, Daniel, illus. 2017. (J). pap. ***(978-1-250-10157-0(3))*** St. Martin's Pr.

—Fakespeare: Starcrossed in Romeo & Juliet. Jennewein, Daniel, illus. 2017. (J). pap. ***(978-1-250-10160-0(3))*** St. Martin's Pr.

—Fakespeare: Something Stinks in Hamlet. Jennewein, Daniel, illus. 2017. (Fakespeare Ser.: 1). (ENG.). 272p. (J). 13.99 *(978-1-250-10159-4(X),* 9781250101594) Imprint IND. Dist: Macmillan.

—Starcrossed in Romeo & Juliet. Jennewein, Daniel, illus. 2017. (Fakespeare Ser.: 2). (ENG.). 304p. (J). 13.99 *(978-1-250-10162-4(X),* 9781250101624) Imprint IND. Dist: Macmillan.

Castleberry, Stephen B., Sr. & Castleberry, Susie L. Weighty Matters. 2003. (Farm Mystery Ser.). 155p. (YA). per. 8.50 *(978-1-891907-13-5(1))* Castleberry Farms Pr.

Castlemon, Harry. The Boy Trapper. 2006. (Illus.). pap. *(978-1-4065-1308-0(3))* Dodo Pr.

—The Boy Trapper. 2007. 124p. (gr. 4-7). per. *(978-1-4068-4421-4(7))* Echo Library.

—Go-Ahead; or, the Fisher-Boy's Motto, by Harry Castlemon [Pseud]. 2006. 308p. per. 23.99 *(978-1-4255-2946-8(1))* Michigan Publishing.

—No Moss; or, the Career of a Rolling Stone, by Harry Castlemon [Pseud]. 2006. 328p. per. 23.99 *(978-1-4255-3290-1(X))* Michigan Publishing.

Castleton, Chaffee. Runty's Adventure: A Story of Love. Queen, Dana, illus. 2010. 97p. (J). pap. 17.95 *(978-0-578-06109-2(0))* Castleton, Julia J.

Castro, Adam-Troy. Gustav Gloom & the Cryptic Carousel #4. Margiotta, Kristen, illus. 2014. (Gustav Gloom Ser.: 4). (ENG.). 248p. (J). (gr. 3-7). 12.99 *(978-0-448-45836-6(5),* Grosset & Dunlap) Penguin Young Readers Group.

—Gustav Gloom & the Four Terrors #3. Margiotta, Kristen, illus. 2014. (Gustav Gloom Ser.: 3). (ENG.). 248p. (J). (gr. 3-7). 7.99 *(978-0-448-48330-6(0),* Grosset & Dunlap) Penguin Young Readers Group.

—Gustav Gloom & the People Taker #1. Margiotta, Kristen, illus. 2014. (Gustav Gloom Ser.: 1). (ENG.). 248p. (J). (gr. 3-7). 7.99 *(978-0-448-48328-3(9),* Grosset & Dunlap) Penguin Young Readers Group.

Castro-Bran, Rose. The Adventures of Port Herman Lighthouse. 2008. 32p. pap. 14.95 *(978-1-4343-6547-7(6))* AuthorHouse.

Castro, Edmund Lee. Crystal & Her Flying Adventure. 2010. 44p. 16.99 *(978-1-4490-6867-7(7))* AuthorHouse.

Castro, Nachie. The Man in the Ant Hill, 1 vol. Marvel Illustrators, illus. 2012. (Avengers: Earth's Mightiest Heroes! Ser.). (ENG.). 24p. (J). (gr. -1-4). lib. bdg. 24.21 *(978-1-61479-004-4(3))* Spotlight.

Catalano, Nikki. Mitsu: The Dark Witch & the Dream Wilderness. 2010. 88p. pap. 25.13 *(978-1-4251-7411-8(6))* Trafford Publishing.

Catanese, P. W. The Brave Apprentice. 2005. (ENG.). 240p. (J). (gr. 4-7). pap. 6.99 *(978-0-689-87174-0(0),* Aladdin) Simon & Schuster Children's Publishing.

—Dragon Games. Ho, David, illus. (Books of Umber Ser.: 2). (ENG.). (J). (gr. 3-7). 2011. 400p. pap. 7.99 *(978-1-4169-5383-8(3))* 2010. 384p. 17.99 *(978-1-4169-7521-2(7))* Simon & Schuster Children's Publishing. (Aladdin).

—The End of Time. Ho, David, illus. 2012. (Books of Umber Ser.: 3). (ENG.). 432p. (J). (gr. 3-7). pap. 6.99 *(978-1-4169-5384-5(1),* Aladdin) Simon & Schuster Children's Publishing.

—The End of Time. Ho, David, illus. 2011. (Books of Umber Ser.: 3). (ENG.). 432p. (J). (gr. 3-7). 16.99 *(978-1-4169-7520-5(9),* Simon & Schuster/Paula Wiseman Bks.) Simon & Schuster/Paula Wiseman Bks.

—The Eye of the Warlock: A Further Tales Adventure. 2005. (ENG.). 256p. (J). (gr. 5-9). pap. 6.99 *(978-0-689-87175-7(9),* Aladdin) Simon & Schuster Children's Publishing.

—Happenstance Found, No. 1. 2009. (Books of Umber Ser.: 1). (ENG.). 368p. (J). (gr. 3-7). pap. 6.99 *(978-1-4169-5382-1(5),* Aladdin) Simon & Schuster Children's Publishing.

—The Riddle of the Gnome: A Further Tale Adventure. 2007. (ENG.). 256p. (J). (gr. 5-9). pap. 5.99 *(978-1-4169-1252-1(5),* Aladdin) Simon & Schuster Children's Publishing.

Caterer, Claire M. The Key & the Flame. (ENG.). (J). (gr. 3-7). 2015. 496p. pap. 7.99 *(978-1-4424-5742-3(2))* 2013. 480p. 17.99 *(978-1-4424-5741-6(4))* McElderry, Margaret K. Bks. (McElderry, Margaret K. Bks.).

Cathcart Jr., George R. Ernie Goes to Kindergarten. 2013. 24p. pap. 24.95 *(978-1-4626-9628-4(7))* America Star Bks.

Catherall, Arthur. The Strange Intruder. 2006. (Adventure Library). 151p. (YA). (gr. 10). pap. 11.95 *(978-1-883937-97-3(3))* Bethlehem Bks.

Cathie & Jessie's Noisy New England Adventure. 2006. (Illus.). 32p. (J). cd-rom 12.99 *(978-0-9773526-1-6(7))* Diversified A+ Pubns.

Catmull, Katherine. Summer & Bird. 2014. (ENG.). 352p. (J). (gr. 5). pap. 8.99 *(978-0-14-242505-3(2),* Puffin Books) Penguin Young Readers Group.

Caton, Peter. Josh: Hero. 2012. 114p. pap. *(978-1-908128-40-9(2))* Spiderwize.

Cauley, Phil. The Adventures of Io, the Little Angel: Sticks & Stones. 2012. 52p. pap. 20.95 *(978-1-4497-3614-9(9),* WestBow Pr.) Author Solutions, Inc.

Cavaliere, Wanda. Don't Be Afraid of the Dark: Nicky Moonbeam Saves Christmas. 2012. 24p. pap. 14.93 *(978-1-4669-0656-3(1))* Trafford Publishing.

Cavallaro, Brittany. The Last of August. (Charlotte Holmes Novel Ser.: 2). (YA). (gr. 8). 2018. 352p. pap. 9.99 ***(978-0-06-239895-6(4))*** 2017. (Illus.). 336p. 17.99 *(978-0-06-239894-9(6))* HarperCollins Pubs. (Tegen, Katherine Bks).

Cavender, Barbara. B Is for Ben. 2009. 84p. (J). pap. 12.95 *(978-1-4327-3513-5(6))* Outskirts Pr., Inc.

Caveney, Philip. Space Blasters. 2013. (ENG.). 256p. (J). (gr. 4-6). pap. 10.99 *(978-1-84939-572-4(1))* Andersen Pr. GBR. Dist: Independent Pubs. Group.

Cayce, Jw & Guy, K. T. Miss Milli's Adventure: Garden Adventure Series. Moore, Elyse, illus. 2011. 26p. pap. 13.95 *(978-1-4575-0002-2(7))* Dog Ear Publishing, LLC.

Caygill, Ronald. Scrope Hall. 2009. 48p. pap. 11.49 *(978-1-4490-5078-8(6))* AuthorHouse.

Cazet, Denys. Minnie & Moo Adventure Series. Cazet, Denys, illus. 2004. (Illus.). pap. 51.95 incl. audio compact disk *(978-1-59112-850-2(1));* pap. 45.95 incl. audio *(978-1-59112-849-6(8))* Live Oak Media.

Ceballos, Victor M. Mundo Increible. 2009. (SPA.). 104p. pap. 11.50 *(978-1-4251-8651-7(3))* Trafford Publishing.

Cecil, Kimberly. The Adventures of Hebear, 1 vol. 2010. 24p. pap. 24.95 *(978-1-60749-915-2(0))* PublishAmerica, Inc.

Celee. The Adventures of Remmy Raindrop: Book I. 2009. 16p. pap. 8.49 *(978-1-4389-3623-9(0))* AuthorHouse.

Cento, Nucci. Maverick & Miss Murphy at Rascal's Rescue Ranch. 2009. 48p. pap. 12.50 *(978-1-60860-388-6(1),* Eloquent Bks.) Strategic Book Publishing & Rights Agency (SBPRA).

Cerny, Michele. No More Rules! A Boy's Discovery of What Life is Like Without Rules. Cable, Annette, illus. 2013. 32p. (J). *(978-0-9860405-0-4(9))* Hat Trick Publishing.

Cerone, Diane. Lucy & the Red-Tailed Hawk. Auer, Lois, illus. 2007. 32p. (J). pap. 17.00 *(978-0-8059-7565-9(9))* Dorrance Publishing Co., Inc.

Cerpok, M. L. The Mobile Monk: A Zen Tale. Wagner, Gavin, illus. 2008. 73p. pap. 19.95 *(978-1-60610-138-4(2))* America Star Bks.

Cerulli, Claudia. Ottavia e I Gatti Di Roma - Octavia & the Cats of Rome: A Bilingual Picture Book in Italian & English. Lätti, Leo, illus. 2013. 40p. pap. *(978-1-938712-11-1(0))* Roxby Media Ltd.

Cerullo, Claudio V. Isabella Goes to Kindergarden, 1 vol. 2010. 24p. 24.95 *(978-1-4489-2455-4(3))* PublishAmerica, Inc.

—Isabella's Rainy Day with Her Friends. 2011. 16p. pap. 24.95 *(978-1-4626-2463-8(4))* America Star Bks.

Chabot, Jacob. Hello Kitty: Work of Art. McGinty, Ian et al, illus. 2014. (ENG.). 64p. (J). pap. 7.99 *(978-1-4215-7542-1(6))* Viz Media.

Chabot, Jacob & Monlongo, Jorge. Hello Kitty: Here We Go! 2013. (ENG., Illus.). 64p. (J). pap. 7.99 *(978-1-4215-5878-3(5))* Viz Media.

Chachas, George & Wojtak, James. The Adventures of Dynamic Doolittle: The Problem with Paulie Python. De Soto, Ben, illus. 2011. 31p. (J). pap. 9.95 *(978-0-9793144-1-4(0))* Double Dap Bks.

—The Story of Doolittle: An Exceptional Young Gorilla. De Soto, Ben, illus. 2011. 32p. (J). pap. 9.95 *(978-0-9793144-0-7(2))* Dragonetti.

Chacko, Miss Hannah. The Lie. 2009. 372p. pap. 25.50 *(978-0-557-06829-6(0))* Lulu Pr., Inc.

Chad Borrows Money. l.t. ed. 2003. (Illus.). 16p. (J). ring bd. 15.95 *(978-0-9722829-6-3(3))* Red Carpet Publishing.

Chad, Jon. Leo Geo & His Miraculous Journey Through the Center of the Earth. Chad, Jon, illus. 2012. (ENG., Illus.). 36p. (J). (gr. 2-5). 15.99 *(978-1-59643-661-9(1),* 9781596436619) Roaring Brook Pr.

—Leo Geo & the Cosmic Crisis. Chad, Jon, illus. 2013. (ENG., Illus.). 40p. (J). (gr. 2-6). 16.99 *(978-1-59643-822-4(3),* 9781596438224) Roaring Brook Pr.

Chadda, Sarwat. Mission Atomic. 2016. (39 Clues: Doublecross Ser.: 4). (ENG.). 256p. (J). (gr. 3-7). 12.99 *(978-0-545-76751-4(2))* Scholastic, Inc.

Chadwick, Cheryl. The Adventures of Skinny Little Timmy. 2012. 28p. pap. 22.00 *(978-1-4669-2834-3(4))* Trafford Publishing.

Chadwick, Jennie. The Peach Tree Kids: Jaws of Dragon. 2010. 52p. pap. 9.99 *(978-1-60911-991-1(6),* Eloquent Bks.) Strategic Book Publishing & Rights Agency (SBPRA).

Chadwick, Robert. Vengeful Impulse. 2003. 70p. pap. 8.95 *(978-0-595-27876-3(0))* iUniverse, Inc.

Chaffey, Tim & Westbrook, Joe. The Truth Chronicles: The Ark. 2013. 146p. pap. *(978-1-936835-15-7(0))* Roxby Media Ltd.

Chaikin, Miriam. Hardlucky: The Story of a Boy Who Learns How to Think Before He Acts. Lisowski, Gabriel, illus. 2012. (ENG.). 40p. (J). (gr. -1-3). 16.95 *(978-1-61608-963-6(6),* 608963, Sky Pony Pr.) Skyhorse Publishing Co., Inc.

Chaikin, Stacey & Feltes Taylor, Kimberly. Fran & Gran. 2012. (Illus.). 32p. (J). 15.95 *(978-1-60131-100-9(1))* Big Tent Bks.

Chaisson, Kristen. Dreamland. 2013. 28p. pap. 24.95 *(978-1-63000-664-8(5))* America Star Bks.

Chalfoun, Michelle. The Treasure of Maria Mamoun. 2016. (ENG.). 352p. (J). 16.99 *(978-0-374-30340-2(1),* 9780374303402, Farrar, Straus & Giroux (BYR)) Farrar, Straus & Giroux.

Chall, Marsha Wilson. The Secret Life of Figgy Mustardo. Friend, Alison, illus. 2016. 40p. (J). (gr. -1-3). 17.99 *(978-0-06-228582-9(3),* Tegen, Katherine Bks) HarperCollins Pubs.

Chamberlain, Karen, et al. A Feather for the Queen. 2009. 28p. pap. 13.95 *(978-1-4490-3903-5(0))* AuthorHouse.

Chamberlain, Nick. The Adventures of Papillon. 2008. 176p. pap. 15.95 *(978-1-60290-092-9(2))* OakTara Publishing Group LLC.

Chambers, Aidan. Breaktime. 2008. (ENG.). 192p. (YA). (gr. 9-17). pap. 9.95 *(978-0-8109-7262-9(X),* Amulet Bks.) Abrams, Inc.

Chambliss Bertman, Jennifer. Book Scavenger. 2015. (Book Scavenger Ser.). (ENG., Illus.). 368p. (J). (gr. 4-9). 16.99 *(978-1-62779-115-1(9),* 9781627791151, Holt, Henry & Co. Bks. For Young Readers) Holt, Henry & Co.

—Book Scavenger. 2016. (Book Scavenger Ser.). (ENG.). 368p. (J). pap. 7.99 *(978-1-250-07980-0(2),* 9781250079800) Square Fish.

Chan, Marty. Barnabas Bigfoot: a Hairy Tangle. 2012. (ENG.). 104p. (gr. 4-6). 9.95 *(978-1-927068-05-2(3))* Thistledown Pr., Ltd. CAN. Dist: Univ. of Toronto Pr.

Chananie, Gloria. Fearful Frannie & Her Fateful Trip to Maui. 2003. 57p. 16.95 *(978-1-4137-0162-3(0))* America Star Bks.

—Fearful Frannie's African Safari. 2006. 95p. pap. 16.95 *(978-1-4241-2617-0(7))* PublishAmerica, Inc.

Chance, Robyn. Ewela's Unbaalievable Journey. 2012. 46p. (-18). 23.95 *(978-1-936850-87-7(7))* Rhemalda Publishing.

Chand, Emlyn. Davey the Detective: A Bird Brain Book. Shaw, Sarah, illus. l.t. ed. 2012. (ENG.). 42p. (gr. k-1). pap. 10.95 *(978-1-62253-119-6(1));* 21.95 *(978-1-62253-107-3(8))* Evolved Publishing.

—Honey the Hero: A Bird Brain Book. Shaw, Sarah, illus. ed. 2012. (ENG.). 44p. (gr. k-1). (J). 21.95 *(978-1-62253-106-6(X));* pap. 10.95 *(978-1-62253-118-9(3))* Evolved Publishing.

—Izzy the Inventor: A Bird Brain Book. Giffin, Noelle, illus. l.t. ed. 2013. 7. (ENG.). 56p. (gr. k-3). 21.95 *(978-1-62253-123-3(X));* pap. 10.95 *(978-1-62253-122-6(1))* Evolved Publishing.

—Poppy the Proud: A Bird Brain Book. Shaw, Sarah, illus. ed. 2012. 3. (ENG.). 44p. (gr. k-3). 21.95 *(978-1-62253-108-0(6));* pap. 10.95 *(978-1-62253-120-2(5))* Evolved Publishing.

Chandler, Andrew & Chandler, Amanda. Gertrude & Abigail: The Adventures Thereof. 2006. 35p. (J). 18.90 *(978-1-4116-7572-8(X))* Lulu Pr., Inc.

Chandler, Elizabeth. Kissed by an Angel: Kissed by an Angel; the Power of Love; Soulmates. 2008. (Kissed by an Angel Ser.: Bks. 1-3). (ENG.). 704p. (YA). (gr. 9). pap. 12.99 *(978-1-4169-7883-1(6),* Simon Pulse) Simon Pulse.

—Monsters Are We. 2011. 28p. pap. 15.99 *(978-1-4628-8485-8(7))* Xlibris Corp.

Chandler, Jean. The Adventures of Molly: Molly Visits the Farm. 2012. 28p. pap. 13.55 *(978-1-4669-1380-6(0))* Trafford Publishing.

—The Adventures of Molly: No Dogs Allowed. 2012. 48p. pap. 18.40 *(978-1-4669-1378-3(9))* Trafford Publishing.

Chandler, Jeff. The New Kitten: A Story about a Foster Puppy, 1 vol. 2009. 48p. pap. 24.95 *(978-1-61546-176-9(0))* America Star Bks.

Chantler, Scott. The Sign of the Black Rock. Chantler, Scott, illus. 2011. (Three Thieves Ser.: 2). (ENG., Illus.). 112p. (J). (gr. 4-7). pap. 7.95 *(978-1-55453-417-3(8))* Kids Can Pr., Ltd. CAN. Dist: Hachette Bk. Group.

Chapman, Allen. Bart Stirlings Road to Success or the Yo. 2007. pap. *(978-1-4065-1430-8(6))* Dodo Pr.

—Bart Stirling's Road to Success; or, the Young Express Agent. 2007. 112p. per. *(978-1-4068-4512-9(4))* Echo Library.

—Frank Roscoe's Secret; or, the Darewell Chums in the Woods. 2007. 108p. per. *(978-1-4068-4514-3(0))* Echo Library.

—The Radio Boys' First Wireless: The Radio Boys' First Wireless. 2007. (ENG.). 136p. pap. 18.99 *(978-1-4346-1467-4(0))* Creative Media Partners, LLC.

—Radio Boys First Wireless or Winning the. 2007. pap. *(978-1-4065-1432-2(2))* Dodo Pr.

Chapman, Bob. Visitors. 2006. 304p. pap. *(978-1-84401-693-8(5))* Athena Pr.

Chapman, Brenda. Where Trouble Leads. 2007. (Jennifer Bannon Mystery Ser.: 3). (ENG., Illus.). 136p. (YA). (gr. 5-18). per. 9.95 *(978-1-894917-44-5(8),* Napoleon & Co.) Dundurn CAN. Dist: Ingram Publisher Services.

Chapman, Bunny. Shanu the Watcher. 2013. 138p. pap. 9.99 *(978-0-9855008-4-9(0))* Champlain Avenue Bks., Inc.

Chapman, Carlene. Jackson Goes to the Beach. 2010. 24p. pap. 11.95 *(978-1-4490-9768-4(5))* AuthorHouse.

Chapman, Charlotte. The Adventures of Little Payton. 2008. 24p. pap. 14.49 *(978-1-4343-9598-6(7))* AuthorHouse.

Chapman, Karean. The Adventures of Northern the Moose & a Dragon Named Zeus. Ciesinka, Izabela, illus. 2010. 38p. pap. 12.95 *(978-1-935268-44-4(9))* Halo Publishing International.

Chapman, Linda & Cole, Steve. The Last Phoenix. 2010. (ENG.). 288p. (J). (gr. 3-7). 16.99 *(978-0-06-125222-8(0))* HarperCollins Pubs.

Chapman, Megan Joy. Lion Heart & Alessio Book 2: Mission, Peace, Patience, Kindness. 2014. (ENG.). 192p. (J). (gr. 3-7). pap. 11.99 *(978-1-62136-755-0(X),* Creation Hse.) Charisma Media.

Charbonneau, Joelle. Graduation Day. (ENG.). 304p. (gr. 7). 2015. (Testing Ser.: 3). (YA). pap. 9.99 *(978-0-544-54120-7(0))* 2014. (Testing Trilogy: Bk. 3). (J). 17.99 *(978-0-547-95921-4(4))* Houghton Mifflin Harcourt Publishing Co. (HMH Books For Young Readers).

Charles, Faustin. The Selfish Crocodile Book of Words. Terry, Michael, illus. 2012. (Selfish Crocodile Ser.). (ENG.). 12p. (J). (gr. -1-k). bds. 10.99 *(978-1-4088-1452-9(8),* 9781408814529, Bloomsbury USA Childrens) Bloomsbury Publishing USA.

Charles L. Wilson. The Search Is On: The Wild Adventures of Lester & Dora. 2009. 200p. 24.99 *(978-1-4269-1813-1(5));* pap. 14.99 *(978-1-4269-1812-4(7))* Trafford Publishing.

Charles, Mae. Pecos Meets Bad Bart. 2010. (Illus.). 15p. (J). *(978-1-907179-96-9(8))* Original Writing Ltd.

Charles, Valerie. The Dancing Light. 2013. 118p. pap. *(978-1-84944-167-4(7))* UKUnpublished.

Charlie & the Kitten. 2006. (Charlie's Great Adventures: 5). (Illus.). 96p. (J). per. 5.95 *(978-0-9702546-6-5(0))* GoodyGoody Bks.

Charnee, David. P T Mudd in the Land of Lies: A Novel for Children of All Ages. 2007. 196p. 23.95 *(978-0-595-70152-0(3));* per. 13.95 *(978-0-595-46307-7(X))* iUniverse, Inc.

Chase, Anita, et al. Tundra Adventures. Chase, Anita et al, illus. 2006. (Adventure Story Collection Ser.). 28p. (J). (gr. 2-6). pap. 10.00 *(978-1-58084-254-9(2))* Lower Kuskokwim Schl. District.

Chase, Jeffrey Scott. Andy the Alien Visits the Outer Planets. 2007. (J). pap. 17.00 *(978-0-8059-7488-1(1))* Dorrance Publishing Co., Inc.

Chase, Mary. Loretta Mason Potts. Berson, Harold, illus. 2014. (ENG.). 224p. (J). (gr. 3-7). 16.95 *(978-1-59017-757-0(6),* NYR Children's Collection) New York Review of Bks., Inc., The.

Chase, Max. Alien Attack. 2012. (Star Fighters Ser.). (ENG., Illus.). 128p. (YA). pap. 5.99 *(978-1-59990-850-2(6),* 9781599908502, Bloomsbury USA Childrens) Bloomsbury Publishing USA.

—Deadly Mission. 2012. (Star Fighters Ser.). (ENG., Illus.). 128p. (YA). pap. 5.99 *(978-1-59990-851-9(4),* 9781599908519, Bloomsbury USA Childrens) Bloomsbury Publishing USA.

Chasing Gold. 2014. (Marguerite Henry's Ponies of Chincoteague Ser.: 3). (ENG., Illus.). 192p. (J). (gr. 3-7). pap. 6.99 *(978-1-4814-0342-9(7),* Aladdin) Simon & Schuster Children's Publishing.

Chatel, Kim. Burgher & the Woebegone. Bell, Samantha, illus. 2010. 102p. pap. 8.95 *(978-1-61633-061-3(9))* Guardian Angel Publishing, Inc.

Chatterton, Martin. The Brain Finds a Leg. 2007. 207p. *(978-1-921049-79-8(0))* Little Hare Bks. AUS. Dist: HarperCollins Pubs. Australia.

—The Brain Finds a Leg, 1 vol. 2009. (ENG.). 224p. (YA). (gr. 5-9). 16.95 *(978-1-56145-503-4(2))* Peachtree Pubs.

—Brain Full of Holes. 2008. 208p. *(978-1-921272-28-8(7))* Little Hare Bks. AUS. Dist: HarperCollins Pubs. Australia.

Chaucer, Geoffrey. The Canterbury Tales - Literary Touchstone Edition. 2005. 128p. (YA). per. 3.99 *(978-1-58049-396-3(3),* PWH3963) Prestwick Hse., Inc.

Chauvin, Belinda N. Megan... A Child of God I Am. Sun Star, Elan & Snyder, Diana, illus. 2008. 40p. (J). 14.75 *(978-0-9801675-2-8(3))* Robertson Publishing.

Chebatte, Helen. Bro. 2016. (ENG.). 240p. (YA). (gr. 7). pap. 14.99 ***(978-1-76012-550-9(4))*** Hardie Grant Egmont Pty. Ltd. AUS. Dist: Independent Pubs. Group.

Chee, Traci. The Reader. (Sea of Ink & Gold Ser.: 1). (ENG.). 464p. (YA). (gr. 7). 2017. pap. 10.99 ***(978-0-14-751805-7(9),*** Speak)Bk. 1. 2016. 19.99 *(978-0-399-17677-7(2),* G.P. Putnam's Sons Books for Young Readers) Penguin Young Readers Group.

—The Reader. 2017. (Sea of Ink & Gold Ser.: 1). lib. bdg. 22.10 ***(978-0-606-40001-5(X))*** Turtleback Bks.

Cheeseboro, Tyrese. Why Did Ronald Break the Rules? Rules at Home & Rules at School! 2010. 28p. 12.49 *(978-1-4490-8871-2(6))* AuthorHouse.

Chen, Da. Sword. 2008. 240p. (J). (gr. 4-7). lib. bdg. 17.89 *(978-0-06-144759-4(5),* Geringer, Laura Book) HarperCollins Pubs.

Chen, Justina. A Blind Spot for Boys. 2014. (ENG.). 336p. (YA). (gr. 7-17). 18.00 *(978-0-316-10253-7(9))* Little, Brown Bks. for Young Readers.

Chen, Wei Dong. Monkey King: Birth of the Stone Monkey. Peng, Chao, illus. 2012. (Monkey King Ser.: 1). (ENG.). 176p. (gr. 5-8). lib. bdg. 29.27 *(978-89-94208-69-5(0))* JR Comics KOR. Dist: Lerner Publishing Group.

—Monkey King: Enemies & a New Friend. Peng, Chao, illus. 2012. (Monkey King Ser.: 4). (ENG.). 176p. (gr. 5-8). lib. bdg. 29.27 *(978-89-94208-72-5(0))* JR Comics KOR. Dist: Lerner Publishing Group.

—Monkey King: Journey to the West. Peng, Chao, illus. 2012. (Monkey King Ser.: 3). (ENG.). 176p. (gr. 5-8). lib. bdg. 29.27 *(978-89-94208-71-8(2))* JR Comics KOR. Dist: Lerner Publishing Group.

—Monkey King: The Bane of Heaven. Peng, Chao, illus. 2012. (Monkey King Ser.: 2). (ENG.). 176p. (gr. 5-8). lib. bdg. 29.27 *(978-89-94208-70-1(4))* JR Comics KOR. Dist: Lerner Publishing Group.

—Monkey King: The Sacred Tree. Peng, Chao, illus. 2012. (Monkey King Ser.: 6). (ENG.). 176p. (gr. 5-8). lib. bdg. 29.27 *(978-89-94208-74-9(7))* JR Comics KOR. Dist: Lerner Publishing Group.

—Monkey King: Three Trials. Peng, Chao, illus. 2012. (Monkey King Ser.: 5). (ENG.). 176p. (gr. 5-8). lib. bdg. 29.27 *(978-89-94208-73-2(9))* JR Comics KOR. Dist: Lerner Publishing Group.

Chenette, Roseanne V. Shellaby Willowbee. 2008. 13p. pap. 24.95 *(978-1-60672-137-7(2))* America Star Bks.

Chenous, Brad. Stories from Farmer Ready's. 2011. 52p. (gr. 4-6). pap. 9.99 *(978-1-4634-0001-9(2))* AuthorHouse.

Cherobin. Zoomy Boomy & the Moon: Zoomy & the Moon Learn the Strength of Love. 2009. 24p. pap. 14.99 *(978-1-4490-2069-9(0))* AuthorHouse.

—Zoomy Boomy, the Moon, & the Earth: All in its Season, & Seasons Change. 2010. 24p. pap. 14.99 *(978-1-4490-2658-5(3))* AuthorHouse.

Cherobin & Cherobin. Zoomy Boomy Lights the Night: Zoomy Conquers Shyness. 2009. 24p. pap. 14.49 *(978-1-4490-2068-2(2))* AuthorHouse.

Cherry, Alison. For Real. 2016. (ENG.). 304p. (YA). (gr. 7). pap. 9.99 *(978-0-385-74296-2(7),* Ember) Random Hse. Children's Bks.

Cherub - Lone Wolf. 2014. (ENG.). 352p. (YA). (gr. 7). 12.99 *(978-1-4449-1409-2(X))* Hodder & Stoughton GBR. Dist: Hachette Bk. Group.

Cherubini, E. Pinocchio in Africa. 2007. pap. *(978-1-4065-1442-1(X))* Dodo Pr.

Cheshire, Simon. The Boy with Wings. Coburn, Dylan, illus. 2015. (Collins Big Cat Ser.). (ENG.). 24p. (J). (gr. 2-2). pap. 7.95 *(978-0-00-759118-3(7))* HarperCollins Pubs. Ltd. GBR. Dist: Independent Pubs. Group.

Chester, Laura. Hiding Glory. Lippincott, Gary A., illus. 2007. (ENG.). 160p. (J). (gr. 3-7). 18.95 *(978-1-59543-616-0(2))* Willow Creek Pr., Inc.

—Marvel the Marvelous. Lippincott, Gary A., illus. 2008. (ENG.). 176p. (J). 18.95 *(978-1-59543-841-6(6))* Willow Creek Pr., Inc.

Chetkowski, Emily. Mabel Takes the Ferry, 1 vol. Peterson, Dawn, illus. 2nd ed. 2012. (ENG.). 32p. (J). pap. 12.95 *(978-1-934031-99-5(2),* 0da48001-1b7b-4d70-849d-d13163dabbc6) Islandport Pr., Inc.

Cheverton, Mark. Attack of the Shadow-Crafters: The Birth of Herobrine Book Two: a Gameknight999 Adventure: an Unofficial Minecrafter's Adventure. 2016. (Gameknight999 Ser.). (ENG.). 264p. (J). (gr. 3). pap. 9.99 *(978-1-5107-0995-9(9),* Sky Pony Pr.) Skyhorse Publishing Co., Inc.

—Battle for the Nether. 2014. (Gameknight999 Ser.: Bk. 2). (ENG.). 336p. (J). (gr. 3). pap. 9.99 *(978-1-63220-712-8(5),* Sky Pony Pr.) Skyhorse Publishing Co., Inc.

—Confronting the Dragon. 2014. (ENG., Illus.). 352p. (J). (gr. 3). pap. 9.99 *(978-1-63450-046-3(6),* Sky Pony Pr.) Skyhorse Publishing Co., Inc.

—Gameknight999 vs. Herobrine. 2016. (ENG.). 240p. (J). (gr. 3). pap. 9.99 *(978-1-5107-0010-9(2),* Sky Pony Pr.) Skyhorse Publishing Co., Inc.

—The Gameknight999 vs. Herobrine Box Set: Six Unofficial Minecrafter's Adventures. 2016. (Gameknight999 Ser.). (ENG.). 1488p. (J). (gr. 3). 29.99 *(978-1-5107-0993-5(2),* Sky Pony Pr.) Skyhorse Publishing Co., Inc.

—The Great Zombie Invasion: The Birth of Herobrine Book One: a Gameknight999 Adventure: an Unofficial Minecrafter's Adventure. 2016. (Gameknight999 Ser.). (ENG.). 248p. (J). (gr. 3). pap. 9.99 *(978-1-5107-0994-2(0),* Sky Pony Pr.) Skyhorse Publishing Co., Inc.

—Herobrine's War. 2017. (Birth of Herobrine Ser.: 3). lib. bdg. 20.85 ***(978-0-606-40305-4(1))*** Turtleback Bks.

—Herobrine's War: The Birth of Herobrine Book Three: a Gameknight999 Adventure: an Unofficial Minecrafter's Adventure. 2017. (Gameknight999 Ser.). (ENG.). 272p. (J). (gr. 3). pap. 9.99 *(978-1-5107-0996-6(7),* Sky Pony Pr.) Skyhorse Publishing Co., Inc.

—Invasion of the Overworld. 2013. (Gameknight999 Ser.: Bk. 1). (ENG.). 172p. pap. 7.99 *(978-1-4909-3083-1(3))* CreateSpace Independent Publishing Platform.

—Invasion of the Overworld. 2014. (Gameknight999 Ser.: Bk. 1). (ENG.). 208p. (J). (gr. 3). pap. 9.99 *(978-1-63220-711-1(7),* Sky Pony Pr.) Skyhorse Publishing Co., Inc.

—The Jungle Temple Oracle. 2015. (Mystery of Herobrine Ser.: Bk. 2). (ENG.). 256p. (J). (gr. 3). pap. 9.99 *(978-1-63450-096-8(2),* Sky Pony Pr.) Skyhorse Publishing Co., Inc.

—Last Stand on the Ocean Shore. 2015. (ENG.). 272p. (J). (gr. 3). pap. 9.99 *(978-1-63450-098-2(9),* Sky Pony Pr.) Skyhorse Publishing Co., Inc.

—Overworld in Flames. 2016. (Gameknight999 Ser.: Bk. 2). (ENG.). 256p. (J). (gr. 3). pap. 9.99 *(978-1-5107-0681-1(X),* Sky Pony Pr.) Skyhorse Publishing Co., Inc.

—The Phantom Virus. 2016. (Gameknight999 Ser.: Bk. 1). (ENG.). 240p. (J). (gr. 3). pap. 9.99 *(978-1-5107-0683-5(6),* Sky Pony Pr.) Skyhorse Publishing Co., Inc.

—System Overload. 2016. (Gameknight999 Ser.: Bk. 3). (ENG.). 272p. (J). (gr. 3). pap. 9.99 *(978-1-5107-0682-8(8),* Sky Pony Pr.) Skyhorse Publishing Co., Inc.

—Terrors of the Forest. 2017. (Mystery of Entity303 Ser.: 1). lib. bdg. 20.85 ***(978-0-606-40312-2(4))*** Turtleback Bks.

Cheverton, Mark. Trouble in Zombie-Town. 2015. (Mystery of Herobrine Ser.: Bk. 1). (ENG.). 288p. (J). (gr. 3). pap. 9.99 *(978-1-63450-094-4(6),* Sky Pony Pr.) Skyhorse Publishing Co., Inc.

Chiaramonti, Gregory. Probie: the Space Probe, Mission One: the Ocean of Europa. 2007. 32p. (J). 16.72 *(978-0-615-13848-0(9))* Chiaramonti, Gregory.

Chiarini, Chynna. Hippy Potto's Travel Adventure. 2010. 48p. pap. 11.99 *(978-1-4520-3447-8(8))* AuthorHouse.

Chichester Clark, Emma. Friends for Life. Chichester Clark, Emma, illus. 2006. (Melrose & Croc Ser.). (ENG., Illus.). 32p. (J). (gr. -1-2). pap. 8.95 *(978-0-00-718242-8(2),* HarperCollins Children's Bks.) HarperCollins Pubs. Ltd. GBR. Dist: HarperCollins Pubs.

A B

Chick, Bryan. Riddles & Danger. 2012. (Secret Zoo Ser.: 3). (ENG.). 304p. (J). (gr. 3-7). pap. 6.99 (978-0-06-198928-5(2), Greenwillow Bks.) HarperCollins Pubs.

—The Secret Zoo. 2010. (Secret Zoo Ser.: 1). (ENG.). 304p. (J). (gr. 3-7). 16.99 (978-0-06-198750-2(6), Greenwillow Bks.) HarperCollins Pubs.

—The Secret Zoo: Traps & Specters. 2012. (Secret Zoo Ser.: 4). (ENG.). 320p. (J). (gr. 3-7). 16.99 (978-0-06-219222-6(1), Greenwillow Bks.) HarperCollins Pubs.

—The Secret Zoo: Raids & Rescues. 2013. (Secret Zoo Ser.: 5). (ENG.). 272p. (J). (gr. 3-7). 16.99 (978-0-06-219228-8(0), Greenwillow Bks.) HarperCollins Pubs.

—Traps & Specters. 2013. (Secret Zoo Ser.: 4). (ENG.). 320p. (J). (gr. 3-7). pap. 6.99 (978-0-06-219223-3(X), Greenwillow Bks.) HarperCollins Pubs.

Chickasaw Adventures: More than Warriors. 2005. (J). (978-1-4265-0002-2(5)) Layne Morgan Media, Inc.

Chickasaw Adventures: Tears at Fort Coffee. 2004. (J). (978-0-9762904-2-1(1)) Layne Morgan Media, Inc.

Chickasaw Adventures: The Battle of Akia. 2004. (J). (978-0-9762904-1-4(3)) Layne Morgan Media, Inc.

Chickasaw Adventures: The Civil War. 2005. (J). (978-1-4265-0000-8(9)) Layne Morgan Media, Inc.

Chickasaw Adventures: The Making of a Storyteller. 2004. (J). (978-0-9762904-3-8(X)) Layne Morgan Media, Inc.

Chickasaw Adventures: War with the Creeks. 2005. (J). (978-1-4265-0001-5(7)) Layne Morgan Media, Inc.

Chickasaw Adventures No. 1: The Journey Begins. 2004. (J). (978-0-9762904-0-7(5)) Layne Morgan Media, Inc.

Chidebelu-Eze / Dove Publishing, Chibueze Obi. The Lion That Finally Roared: Inspirational Story of Purpose & Destiny. Newborne, David / F., illus. 2008. 80p. (J). 17.99 (978-0-9766578-5-9(6)); pap. 11.99 (978-0-9766578-6-6(4)) Dove Publishing, Inc.

Chihak, Sheena. Kung Fu Panda 3-D Puzzle Book. Salesse, Alain, illus. 2008. 10p. (J). 9.99 (978-0-696-23485-9(8)) Meredith Bks.

—Kung Fu Panda: Paws of Power Activity Kit. 2008. (Illus.). 32p. (J). 14.99 (978-0-696-23483-5(1)) Meredith Bks.

Chihak, Sheena & Loki. Kung Fu Panda. Mada Design Inc, illus. 2008. (I Can Find It Ser.). 22p. (J). 7.99 (978-0-696-23484-2(X)) Meredith Bks.

Child, Lauren. Maude: The Not-So-Noticeable Shrimpton. Krauss, Trisha, illus. 2013. (ENG.). 32p. (J). (gr. k-3). 16.99 (978-0-7636-6515-9(0)) Candlewick Pr.

—Quién Teme al Libro Feroz? 2004. (SPA., Illus.). 32p. (J). 17.99 (978-84-8488-075-2(3)) Serres, Ediciones, S. L. ESP. Dist: Lectorum Pubns., Inc.

—Ruby Redfort Catch Your Death (Book #3) Child, Lauren, illus. 2015. (Ruby Redfort Ser.: 3). (ENG., Illus.). 432p. (J). (gr. 5-9). 17.99 (978-0-7636-5469-6(8)) Candlewick Pr.

—Ruby Redfort Look into My Eyes. Child, Lauren, illus. 2013. (Ruby Redfort Ser.: 1). (ENG., Illus.). 400p. (J). (gr. 5-9). pap. 7.99 (978-0-7636-6257-8(7)) Candlewick Pr.

—Ruby Redfort Pick Your Poison. Child, Lauren, illus. 2017. (Ruby Redfort Ser.: 5). (ENG., Illus.). 528p. (J). (gr. 5-9). 16.99 (978-0-7636-5471-9(X)) Candlewick Pr.

—Ruby Redfort Take Your Last Breath. Child, Lauren, illus. 2013. (Ruby Redfort Ser.: 2). (ENG., Illus.). 432p. (J). (gr. 5-9). 16.99 (978-0-7636-5468-9(X)) Candlewick Pr.

Child, Neil. The Creek. 2012. 82p. pap. 19.95 (978-1-4626-6027-8(4)) America Star Bks.

Childress, Jamie. Galactic Treasure Hunt: Lost City of Atlantis. Braun, Chris, illus. 2015. (ENG.). 100p. (J). pap. 4.99 (978-1-931882-62-0(2)) Adventures Unlimited Pr.

—Galactic Treasure Hunt: Lost City of the Moon. Braun, Chris, illus. 2015. (ENG.). 100p. (J). (gr. -1-7). per. 4.99 (978-1-931882-45-3(2)) Adventures Unlimited Pr.

—Galactic Treasure Hunt #4: Lost in Time. Braun, Chris, illus. 2008. (Galactic Treasure Hunt Ser.). (ENG.). 176p. (J). pap. 5.99 (978-1-931882-89-7(4)) Adventures Unlimited Pr.

—Galactic Treasure Hunt 5: Lost Fortress of Light. Braun, Chris, illus. 2010. (Galactic Treasure Hunt Ser.). (ENG.). 230p. pap. 6.99 (978-1-935487-06-7(X)) Adventures Unlimited Pr.

—Lost Universe. Braun, Chris, illus. 2015. (ENG.). 100p. (J). (gr. 4-7). per. 4.99 (978-1-931882-74-3(6)) Adventures Unlimited Pr.

Childs, Tera Lynn & Deebs, Tracy. Relentless. 2016. (Hero Agenda Ser.: 2). (ENG.). 288p. (YA). (gr. 7-12). 17.99 (978-1-4926-1661-0(3), 9781492616610) Sourcebooks, Inc.

Chima, Ahiru & Misu, Max. Ellenā__- Ellen meets Frog King - 2005. 32p. pap. 14.99 (978-1-4116-4050-4(0)) Lulu Pr., Inc.

Chima, Cinda Williams. The Seven Realms Box Set. 2013. (Seven Realms Novel Ser.). (ENG.). 2272p. (YA). (gr. 7-12). pap. 37.99 (978-1-4231-9961-8(8)) Hyperion Bks. for Children.

Chin, Jason. Redwoods. Chin, Jason, illus. 2009. (ENG., Illus.). 40p. (J). (gr. -1-3). 18.99 (978-1-59643-430-1(9), 9781596434301) Roaring Brook Pr.

Chin, Oliver Clyde. The Adventures of Wonderbaby: From A to Z. Chiodo, Joe, illus. 2005. (ENG.). 32p. (J). bds. 8.95 (978-1-59702-001-5(X)) Immedium.

Chipley, John. The Secret Place: A Boy's Journey into the Woods. 2011. 92p. (gr. 1-1). pap. 13.95 (978-1-4567-4593-6(X)) AuthorHouse.

Chisel Hedgehog Crazy Great Summer, 1. 2008. (Illus.). 256p. (J). per. 18.95 (978-0-9794191-7-1(4)) McKellen-Caffey.

Chisman, James Ph. D. Bullette & Jessic. 2011. 74p. 24.99 (978-1-4628-8880-1(1)); pap. 15.99 (978-1-4628-8881-8(X)) Xlibris Corp.

Chlebowski, Rachel. Magical Misadventures! (Shimmer & Shine) Golden Books, illus. 2017. (Color Plus 1,000 Stickers Ser.). (ENG.). 64p. (J). (gr. -1-2). pap. 9.99 (978-0-399-55890-0(X), Golden Bks.) Random Hse. Children's Bks.

Cho, Charles. Age of Ultron: The Reusable Sticker Book. 2015. (ENG., Illus.). 12p. (J). (gr. -1-1). pap. 6.99 (978-0-316-25642-1(0)) Little, Brown Bks. for Young Readers.

—Ant-Man: The Amazing Adventures of Ant-Man. 2015. (J). lib. bdg. 14.75 (978-0-606-37218-3(0)) Turtleback Bks.

Chokshi, Roshani. A Crown of Wishes. 2017. (Star-Touched Ser.). (ENG.). 384p. (YA). 18.99 (978-1-250-08549-8(7), 9781250085498, St. Martin's Griffin) St. Martin's Pr.

Chooseco, creator. Choose Your Own Adventure 4 Book Boxed Set #1: The Abominable Snowman/Journey under the Sea/Space & Beyond/the Lost Jewels of Nabooti. 2006. (ENG., Illus.). 576p. (J). (gr. 2-9). pap. 22.99 (978-1-933390-94-9(8)) Chooseco LLC.

—Choose Your Own Adventure 4 Book Boxed Set #2: Mystery of the Maya/House of Danger/Race Forever/Escape. 2006. (ENG., Illus.). 144p. (J). pap. 22.99 (978-1-933390-95-6(6)) Chooseco LLC.

Chowdary, Daddala Vineesha. The Locket of Moonstone. 2013. 120p. (gr. 10-12). 30.95 (978-1-4828-1234-3(7)); pap. 11.95 (978-1-4828-1235-0(5)) Author Solutions, Inc. (PartridgeIndia).

Chowning, Judy. Jacki & Jo's Grand Canyon Adventure. 2011. 24p. pap. 15.99 (978-1-4628-9637-0(5)) Xlibris Corp.

Chriss, Granddad. The Adventures of Barazaburg. 2011. 54p. 24.99 (978-1-4568-7988-4(X)); pap. 15.99 (978-1-4568-7987-7(1)) Xlibris Corp.

Christen, Dennis H. Lundon Bridge wa seagae wa Yolsae. Lee, Kathryn, tr. 2008.Tr. of Lundon Bridge wa seagae wa Yolsae. (KOR., Illus.). 280p. (J). pap. 12.95 (978-0-9718151-4-8(3)) C-It Entertainment Group, LLC.

—Lundon's Bridge & the Three Keys. 2008. 221p. (J). pap. 12.95 (978-0-9718151-5-5(1)) 2005. (YA). lib. bdg., act. bk. ed. 24.95 (978-0-9718151-3-1(5)) 2006. (ENG.). (J). per. 12.95 (978-0-9718151-2-4(7)) C-It Entertainment Group, LLC.

Christensen, Bob. Gaylord Goose. Marsh, Bobbi, illus. 2011. 28p. pap. 12.95 (978-1-61493-014-3(7)) Peppertree Pr., The.

Christensen, Gerda. Troll Peter Discovers the Bog-Woman's Secret & Other Stories. 2010. 40p. pap. 18.27 (978-1-4251-8822-1(2)) Trafford Publishing.

—Troll Peter Finds A Treasure at the End of the Rainbow & Other Stories: Troll Peter's Adventures, Book 2. 2010. 36p. pap. 18.41 (978-1-4269-3697-5(4)) Trafford Publishing.

Christenson, Deanna. Best Friends! 2011. 44p. pap. 21.99 (978-1-4568-6560-3(9)) Xlibris Corp.

Christianson, Leslie Rose. Adventures of Peter & Paul. 2010. 28p. 12.99 (978-1-4490-5881-4(7)) AuthorHouse.

—Malinda Matters: And Priscilla the Praying Mantis. 2010. 36p. pap. 15.49 (978-1-4490-6914-8(2)) AuthorHouse.

—Malinda Matters: Malinda's Halloween Adventure. 2010. 32p. 12.99 (978-1-4490-5186-0(3)) AuthorHouse.

Christie, Ed. The Sweet Smell of Rotten Eggs: Volume Two, the Dude Ranch Rangers. 2009. 108p. pap. 10.95 (978-1-4401-3764-8(1)) iUniverse, Inc.

Christie, Jackie. Wacky WaterSlide Wipeout. 2011. 28p. (gr. -1). pap. 16.09 (978-1-4269-5821-2(8)) Trafford Publishing.

Christopher, Kathleen. Janie's First Day of School. 2012. 32p. pap. 24.95 (978-1-62709-914-1(X)) America Star Bks.

Christopher, Lucy. Stolen. (ENG.). (J). 2012. 320p. (gr. 9). pap. 9.99 (978-0-545-17094-9(X)) 2010. 304p. (gr. 7-18). 17.99 (978-0-545-17093-2(1)) Scholastic, Inc. (Chicken Hse., The).

—Stolen. 2012. lib. bdg. 20.85 (978-0-606-23955-4(3), Turtleback) Turtleback Bks.

Christopher, Matt. Lacrosse Firestorm. 2008. (ENG.). 144p. (J). (gr. 3-7). pap. 5.99 (978-0-316-01631-5(4)) Little, Brown Bks. for Young Readers.

—Tough to Tackle. 139p. (J). (gr. 3-5). pap. 3.95 (978-0-8072-1463-3(9), Listening Library) Random Hse. Audio Publishing Group.

Christopherson, Keven. Adventures of the Sky Kids: Lost Treasure of Kolob Canyon. 2005. 58p. pap. 16.95 (978-1-4137-6514-4(9)) America Star Bks.

Chronicle Books Editors & Player, Micah. Lately Lily ABC Travel Flash Cards. 2014. (ENG., Illus.). 26p. (J). (gr. -1-17). 14.99 (978-1-4521-1524-5(9)) Chronicle Bks. LLC.

Chronicle Books Staff & Frank, Paul. Wild West Bananza. 2008. (ENG., Illus.). 36p. (J). (gr. -1-2). 12.99 (978-0-8118-6026-0(4)) Chronicle Bks. LLC.

Chuks-Samuel, Mary. Captain Rainbow & the Agents: Value My Vote. 2012. (Illus.). 24p. pap. 19.82 (978-1-4772-1787-0(8)) AuthorHouse.

Church, Alfred J. The Aeneid for Boys & Girls. 2008. 100p. pap. 9.05 (978-1-60459-519-2(1)) Wilder Pubns., Corp.

Church, Bryan. The Dreamcatcher Bowl. 2009. 54p. pap. 9.99 (978-0-557-07517-1(3)) Lulu Pr., Inc.

Church, Peggy Pond. The Burro of Angelitos. 2013. 52p. pap. 18.95 (978-0-86534-965-0(7)) Sunstone Pr.

—The Pancake Stories: Cuentos Del Panqueque. Chilton, Noel, tr. Church, Elizabeth Comfort, illus. 2013. (ENG & SPA.). 96p. (J). 12.95 (978-0-8263-5387-0(8)) Univ. of New Mexico Pr.

Ciccarelli, Kristen. The Last Namsara. 2017. (Iskari Ser.: 1). 432p. (YA). (gr. 8). 17.99 **(978-0-06-256798-7(5)**, HarperTeen) HarperCollins Pubs.

Cicierega, Emmy. Gravity Falls Don't Color This Book! A Cursed Coloring Book. Ramirez, Stephanie, illus. 2017. (ENG.). 64p. pap. 12.99 **(978-1-368-00899-0(2))** Disney Pr.

El Cid. (SPA., Illus.). 128p. (J). 11.95 (978-84-7281-098-3(4), AF1098) Auriga, Ediciones S.A. ESP. Dist: Continental Bk. Co., Inc.

Cima, Alessandro V. Pirate Jack. 2007. 180p. pap. 11.95 (978-0-615-14024-7(6)) Candlelight Stories, Inc.

Ciminera, Siobhan & Testa, Maggie. So Yummy! So Yummy! Yoe! Studio Staff, illus. 2009. (Yo Gabba Gabba! Ser.). (ENG.). 32p. (J). (gr. -1-1). 4.99 (978-1-4169-8494-8(1), Simon Scribbles) Simon Scribbles.

Cioffi, Erin. The Lost Carrot. 2012. 16p. pap. 15.99 (978-1-4772-2078-8(X)) AuthorHouse.

Cipriano, Sal. Adventures of Bio Boy: The Best of Season One. 2006. (Illus.). 128p. (YA). pap. 12.99 (978-0-9738388-4-8(1)) Speakeasy Comics CAN. Dist: Diamond Bk. Distributors.

Circus Fever. 2008. (Illus.). 32p. (J). 14.95 (978-0-9796380-0-8(3)) Three Wishes Publishing Co.

Citak, Michael J. The Adventures of Leo- & the Curse of the Dreaded Doors. 2008. 51p. pap. 22.95 (978-1-4357-5271-9(6)) Lulu Pr., Inc.

—The Adventures of Leo- & the Treasure Cave. 2009. 51p. pap. 22.95 (978-0-557-02994-5(5)) Lulu Pr., Inc.

Claiborn, Trevor M. The Monkey & the Forbidden Fruit. 2012. 112p. pap. 34.99 (978-1-4772-0987-5(5)) AuthorHouse.

Clamp, Janet. The Adventures of Lilly the Bloodhound & Her Friends: Lilly Gets a New Home & Family. 2013. 20p. pap. 17.99 (978-1-4817-0057-3(X)) AuthorHouse.

Clampitt, Ed & Fortier, Robert. Team Dawg Stranger Danger. 2005. (Illus.). 30p. (J). per. 14.99 (978-0-9749378-1-6(9)) Team Dawg Productions, Inc.

Clarizio, Laura. If I Had a Magic Carpet III: Haunted Holidays. 2008. 73p. pap. 19.95 (978-1-60563-240-7(6)) America Star Bks.

—Traveling Through Time: If I Had a Magic Carpet IV. 2012. 100p. 21.95 (978-1-4489-3229-0(7)) 2010. 98p. pap. 16.95 (978-1-4489-5428-5(2)) America Star Bks.

Clark, Andy S. Heavenly Magic: The Unforgettable Journey of Cassidy, the Valiant. 2013. 64p. pap. 23.95 (978-1-4497-9874-1(8), WestBow Pr.) Author Solutions, Inc.

Clark, Betsy Huhn. Lizzie's Extraordinary Adventure. 2006. (Illus.). 24p. (J). 9.99 (978-1-4276-0116-2(X)) Aardvark Global Publishing.

Clark, Brenda. Spiro & Zinger Rescue the Orphans: Spiro the Shooting Star - Book Three, 1 vol. 2010. 70p. pap. 19.95 (978-1-4489-3992-3(5)) America Star Bks.

Clark, Catherine. Icing on the Lake. 2005. (ENG.). 368p. (YA). (gr. 9-12). pap. 5.99 (978-0-06-081534-9(5), HarperTeen) HarperCollins Pubs.

Clark, Eleanor Linton, et al. Dodo's Dream Boat or the Voyage of the Seven Seas. 2008. (Illus.). 45p. (J). (978-0-9816873-2-2(6)) West Barnstable Pr.

Clark, Gloria. The Little Candy Breathing Dragons. 2008. 36p. per. 12.95 (978-1-4327-1510-6(0)) Outskirts Pr., Inc.

Clark, Isabelle. The Enchanted Forest of Hope. 2009. 44p. pap. 18.50 (978-1-4389-7781-2(6)) AuthorHouse.

Clark, John, ed. Mickey Mouse Adventures, Vol. 5. 2005. (ENG., Illus.). 128p. (YA). pap. 7.95 (978-0-911903-70-6(4), 9780911903706) Gemstone Publishing, Inc.

—Mystery of the Old Mansion, Vol. 6. 2005. (ENG., Illus.). 128p. (YA). pap. 7.95 (978-0-911903-71-3(2), 9780911903713) Gemstone Publishing, Inc.

Clark, Jr. Metrognomes. 2007. 292p. per. 17.95 (978-0-595-42973-8(4)) iUniverse, Inc.

Clark, Kent & Snider, Brandon T. Peter Powers & His Not-So-Super Powers. Bardin, Dave, illus. 2017. (Peter Powers Ser.: 1). (ENG.). 128p. (J). (gr. 1-5). pap. 5.99 (978-0-316-35934-4(3)) Little, Brown Bks. for Young Readers.

—Peter Powers & the Itchy Insect Invasion! Bardin, Dave, illus. 2017. (Peter Powers Ser.: 3). (ENG.). 128p. (J). (gr. 1-5). 15.99 (978-0-316-35947-4(5)) Little, Brown Bks. for Young Readers.

Clark, Kristina. The Great Adventures of Ella: The Magic Desk. 2010. 28p. 12.95 (978-1-4520-2412-7(X)) AuthorHouse.

Clark, Malcolm. Bounty's Cave. 2007. (ENG.). 156p. per. 19.95 (978-1-932762-82-2(5)) Elderberry Press, Inc.

Clark, Platte F. Bad Unicorn. (Bad Unicorn Trilogy Ser.: 1). (ENG., Illus.). (J). (gr. 3-7). 2014. 448p. pap. 7.99 (978-1-4424-5013-4(4)) 2013. 432p. 15.99 (978-1-4424-5012-7(6)) Simon & Schuster Children's Publishing. (Aladdin).

—Good Ogre. 2015. (Bad Unicorn Trilogy Ser.: 3). (ENG., Illus.). 384p. (J). (gr. 3-7). 17.99 (978-1-4424-5018-9(5), Aladdin) Simon & Schuster Children's Publishing.

Clark, Ruth. Airport Mouse Explores on Opening Day. 2008. (ENG.). 32p. (J). 15.95 (978-0-9792963-4-5(X)) Huntington Ludlow Media Group.

—Airport Mouse Works the Nightshift. 2008. (ENG.). 32p. (J). 15.95 (978-0-9792963-3-8(1)) Hollywood Operating System.

Clark, Ruth E. Airport Mouse Activity Fun Book 1. Jones, Phil, illus. 2010. 16p. (J). pap. 5.99 (978-0-9792963-6-9(6)) Huntington Ludlow Media Group.

—Airport Mouse Becomes a VIP/VIM World Traveler. Jones, Phil, illus. 2009. 32p. (J). 15.95 (978-0-9792963-5-2(8)) Kimball, Jane A.

—Airport Mouse Becomes a VIP/VIM World Traveler Activity Fun Book 4. Jones, Phil, illus. 2010. 16p. (J). pap. 5.99 (978-0-9792963-9-0(0)) Huntington Ludlow Media Group.

—Airport Mouse Explores on Opening Day Activity Fun Book 3. Jones, Phil, illus. 2010. 16p. (J). pap. 5.99 (978-0-9792963-8-3(2)) Kimball, Jane A.

—Airport Mouse Works the Night Shift Activity Fun Book 2. Jones, Phil, illus. 2010. 16p. (J). pap. 5.99 (978-0-9792963-7-6(4)) Huntington Ludlow Media Group.

Clark, Wendy S. The Troubles with Bubbles. 2010. 32p. pap. 13.00 (978-1-60911-658-3(5), Eloquent Bks.) Strategic Book Publishing & Rights Agency (SBPRA).

Clarke, Angelique. Boomer Explores Annapolis, 1 vol. Hunt, Jim, illus. 2012. (ENG.). 32p. (J). 12.99 (978-0-7643-4008-6(5), 9780764340086) Schiffer Publishing, Ltd.

Clarke, E. J. Oakwing: A Fairy's Tale. 2017. (Oakwing Ser.: 1). (ENG., Illus.). 192p. (J). (gr. 2-6). 16.99 **(978-1-4814-8191-5(6)**, Aladdin) Simon & Schuster Children's Publishing.

—Oakwing: A Fairy's Tale. 2017. (J). pap. **(978-1-4814-8190-8(8)**, Simon & Schuster/Paula Wiseman Bks.) Simon & Schuster/Paula Wiseman Bks.

Clarke, Ella. When I Grow Up, 1 vol. rev. ed. 2013. (Fiction Readers Ser.). (ENG., Illus.). 12p. (J). (gr. 1-1). pap. 4.99 (978-1-4333-5448-9(9)); pap. 12.96 (978-1-4807-1127-3(6)) Shell Educational Publishing.

Clarke, Lizzy. The Spirit of the Jaguar. 2013. 92p. pap. 11.38 (978-1-4907-0600-9(3)); (gr. -1). 21.38 (978-1-4907-0602-3(X)) Trafford Publishing.

Clarke, Tom E. The Puddle Jumper: The Adventures of A Young Flyer in Alaska. 2011. 190p. 42.95 (978-1-258-05006-1(4)) Literary Licensing, LLC.

Clasicos de Adventura. (Clasicos Juveniles Coleccion). (SPA.). (YA). (gr. 5-8). pap. (978-950-11-1300-6(0), SG4723) Sigmar ARG. Dist: Lectorum Pubns., Inc.

Claudine Sherels Johnson. Nire Goes to the Color Books Bookstore: Featuring God Is Awesome & Pink Carnation. 2009. 84p. pap. 10.49 (978-1-4389-5952-8(4)) AuthorHouse.

Clausen, Kristin. Hank & Frank Encounter the Creatures from Hedgeton. 2012. 16p. pap. 12.00 (978-1-105-81630-7(3)) Lulu Pr., Inc.

Claybourne, Anna. Adventures of Ulysses. 2005. 144p. (J). pap. 4.95 (978-0-7945-0322-2(5), Usborne) EDC Publishing.

Claydon, Darlene. A Most Unusual Whale Tale: The Adventure Begins. 2012. 44p. pap. 24.95 (978-1-4626-8806-7(3)) America Star Bks.

Clayton, E. Pearl. The Adventures of My Heart. 2008. 24p. pap. 19.95 (978-1-4327-3808-2(9)) Outskirts Pr., Inc.

Clayton, Emily. If my Parents Only Knew... 2011. (Illus.). 28p. (gr. -1). pap. 14.09 (978-1-4567-7405-9(0)) AuthorHouse.

CLE, Troy. The Marvelous Effect. 2008. (Marvelous World Ser.: 1). (ENG.). 384p. (J). (gr. 5-9). pap. 8.99 (978-1-4169-4215-3(7), Simon & Schuster Bks. For Young Readers) Simon & Schuster Bks. For Young Readers.

Cle, Troy. Olivion's Favorites. 2009. (Marvelous World Ser.: 2). (ENG.). 352p. (J). (gr. 5-9). 14.99 (978-1-4169-4216-0(5), Simon & Schuster Bks. For Young Readers) Simon & Schuster Bks. For Young Readers.

Cle, Troy & CLE, Troy. The Marvelous Effect. 2007. (Marvelous World Ser.: 1). (ENG., Illus.). 384p. (J). (gr. 5-9). 14.99 (978-1-4169-3958-0(X), Simon & Schuster Bks. For Young Readers) Simon & Schuster Bks. For Young Readers.

Cleaning House. 2003. (J). per. (978-1-57657-964-0(6)) Paradise Pr., Inc.

Cleary, Beverly. The Mouse & the Motorcycle: a Harper Classic. Rogers, Jacqueline, illus. 2017. (Harper Classic Ser.). 224p. (J). (gr. 3-7). 16.99 **(978-0-06-265798-5(4))** HarperCollins Pubs.

Clement-Davies, David. Fell. 2009. (ENG.). 544p. (YA). (gr. 7-11). pap. 10.95 (978-0-8109-7266-7(2), Amulet Bks.) Abrams, Inc.

—The Telling Pool. Huebsch, Rand, illus. 2007. (ENG.). 382p. (YA). (gr. 7-17). per. 8.95 (978-0-8109-9257-3(4)) Abrams, Inc.

—The Telling Pool. 2005. (ENG., Illus.). 376p. (J). (gr. 7-17). 19.95 (978-0-8109-5758-9(2), Abrams Bks. for Young Readers) Abrams, Inc.

—The Telling Pool. 2006. 1.00 (978-1-4237-6417-5(X)) Recorded Bks., Inc.

Clement, Emily Gillespie. Bea & the Smart Kids. 2012. 188p. pap. (978-1-105-50303-0(8)) Lulu.com.

Clements, Becky. A Picnic with Friends: Alaska Adventure Bears. 2003. (Alaska Adventure Bears Ser.). 16p. (J). pap. 9.95 (978-1-888125-87-0(X)) Publication Consultants.

Cleveland, Marie. Prowlers in Peril: A Storybook Land Adventure, 1 vol. 2010. 52p. pap. 16.95 (978-1-4489-5204-5(2)) America Star Bks.

CleverKits, creator. Safari Adventure. 2006. (J). (gr. -1-2). audio compact disk 19.95 (978-0-9778771-1-9(6)) CleverKits,LLC.

—Under the Sea. 2006. (J). (gr. -1-2). audio compact disk 19.95 (978-0-9778771-0-2(8)) CleverKits,LLC.

Cliff, Tony. Delilah Dirk & the King's Shilling. 2016. (ENG., Illus.). 272p. (YA). pap. 17.99 (978-1-62672-155-5(6), 9781626721555, First Second Bks.) Roaring Brook Pr.

Cliffe, Kara. Jeff & His Magic Hot Air Balloon. Campbell, Ken, illus. 2013. 44p. pap. 15.50 (978-1-62212-186-1(4), Strategic Bk. Publishing) Strategic Book Publishing & Rights Agency (SBPRA).

Clifford, Eth. Help! I'm a Prisoner in the Library. Hughes, George, illus. 2004. (Jo-Beth & Mary Rose Mystery Ser.). (ENG.). 112p. (J). (gr. 2-5). pap. 6.99 (978-0-618-49482-8(0)) Houghton Mifflin Harcourt Publishing Co.

Clifford, Ross. The Shiddakovich Adventure. 2009. 122p. pap. 12.88 (978-1-4092-3520-0(3)) Lulu Pr., Inc.

Climent, Paco. El Tesoro del Capitan Nemo. 2003. (SPA.). 128p. (978-84-279-3246-3(4), NG3561) Noguer y Caralt Editores, S. A. ESP. Dist: Lectorum Pubns., Inc.

—El Tesoror del Capitan Nemo.Tr. of Captain Nemo's Treasure. (SPA.). 123p. (YA). (gr. 5-8). 6.80 (978-84-279-3164-0(6)) Noguer y Caralt Editores, S. A. ESP. Dist: Lectorum Pubns., Inc.

Climo, Liz. Rory the Dinosaur: Me & My Dad. 2015. (ENG., Illus.). 40p. (J). (gr. -1-3). 17.00 (978-0-316-27728-0(2)) Little Brown & Co.

Climo, Shirley. Pandora's Gift. Date not set. 64p. (J). pap. 3.99 (978-0-06-444271-8(3)) HarperCollins Pubs.

Cline, Barbara Jean. Seth's' Journey. 2012. 44p. pap. 21.99 (978-1-4685-6313-9(0)) AuthorHouse.

Cline, H. R. Baxter's Backyard Adventures. 2009. 32p. pap. 13.99 (978-1-4389-5939-9(7)) AuthorHouse.

Clocktowerhill Research & Publishing Group. Loyd & Boyd & the Slug Monster of Webster County. 2011. (ENG., Illus.). 104p. (J). 12.99 (978-0-9832130-0-0(3), Lucas Violet) Clocktower Hill Research & Publishing Group, LLC.

Cloke, Rene, illus. The Adventures of Tom Thumb. 2012. (ENG.). 24p. (J). pap. 6.50 (978-1-84135-545-0(3)) Award Pubns. Ltd. GBR. Dist: Parkwest Pubns., Inc.

Clout, Susan. The Six Week Road Trip. 2011. 36p. pap. (978-1-4269-9459-3(1)) Trafford Publishing (UK) Ltd.

Clover, Louise. Bullring Kid & Country Cowboy Level 4 Intermediate. 2009. (ENG., Illus.). 96p. pap. 12.75 (978-84-8323-495-2(5)) Cambridge Univ. Pr.

Clover, Peter. Rescue Riders: Fire Alert. l.t. ed. 2007. 108p. per. (978-1-905665-30-3(X)) Pollinger In Print.

Cloyd, Suzy. Pippi's Silent Message: Adventures of Suzy Q & You Too. Barham, Timothy E., illus. 2012. 24p. 24.95 (978-1-4512-7832-3(2)) America Star Bks.

Clugston-Flores, Chynna. Lumberjanes/Gotham Academy. 2017. lib. bdg. 33.05 **(978-0-606-39766-7(3))** Turtleback Bks.

C.M.M. A Life of Many Forms. 2012. 52p. pap. 16.95 (978-1-62709-318-7(4)) America Star Bks.

Coates, Theresa. Imaginary Time of Life. 2007. 102p. pap. 10.95 (978-0-7414-4067-9(9)) Infinity Publishing.

Coatsworth, Elizabeth. The Wonderful Day. Sewell, Helen, illus. 2006. (Sally (Bethlehem Books) Ser.). 139p. (J). (gr. -1). pap. 11.95 (978-1-883937-87-4(6)) Bethlehem Bks.

Cobb, Daryl K. Do Pirates Go to School. 2010. pap. 11.99 (978-0-578-05535-0(X)) 10 To 2 Children's Bks.

Cobb, Debbie. Gracie's Big Adventure... with Augustine the Beaver. Ferchaud, Steve, illus. 2006. (J). per. 10.95 (978-0-9787376-0-3(1)) Laurob Pr.

Coben, Harlan. Found. 2014. (Mickey Bolitar Novel Ser.: 3). (ENG.). 336p. (YA). (gr. 7). 18.99 (978-0-399-25652-3(0), G.P. Putnam's Sons Books for Young Readers) Penguin Young Readers Group.

—The Magical Fanstastical Fridge. Tinari, Leah, illus. 2016. (ENG.). 48p. (J). (gr. -1-3). 17.99 (978-0-525-42803-9(8), Dial Bks) Penguin Young Readers Group.

—Seconds Away. (Mickey Bolitar Novel Ser.: 2). (ENG.). (YA). (gr. 7). 2012. 352p. 18.99 (978-0-399-25651-6(2), G.P. Putnam's Sons Books for Young Readers)Bk. 2. 2013. 368p. pap. 9.99 (978-0-14-242635-7(0), Speak) Penguin Young Readers Group.

—Seconds Away. l.t. ed. 2012. (Mickey Bolitar Ser.: 2). (ENG.). 396p. 23.99 (978-1-4104-5348-8(0)) Thorndike Pr.

—Seconds Away. 2013. (Mickey Bolitar Ser.: 2). lib. bdg. 20.85 (978-0-606-32141-9(1), Turtleback) Turtleback Bks.

Coburn, Ann. Alex & the Winter Star. 2009. pap. 18.95 (978-1-84002-894-2(7)) Theatre Communications Group, Inc.

—Glint. (J). 2007. 423p. (gr. 4-7). 17.99 (978-0-06-084723-4(9)) 2005. 336p. pap. 6.99 (978-0-06-084725-8(5)) HarperCollins Pubs.

Coccia. The Adventures of Itsy Bitsy Franny Frog: I Like What I Can Do When I Try! 2012. 34p. pap. 14.95 (978-1-4575-0946-9(6)) Dog Ear Publishing, LLC.

Coccia, Mina. Mother Nature & Mz Bee. 2012. 36p. pap. 14.95 (978-1-4575-0709-0(9)) Dog Ear Publishing, LLC.

Cochran, Cheryl. The Mini Message Man & the Great Candy Caper. Cochran, Christina, illus. 2011. 40p. pap. 24.95 (978-1-4560-7565-1(9)) America Star Bks.

Cochran, Randy. Critter Golf: The Adventures at Owl's Nest. 2013. (ENG.). 84p. (YA). pap. 8.95 (978-1-4787-1263-3(5)) Outskirts Pr., Inc.

—Critter Golf Iii: The Storm. 2013. 140p. pap. 10.95 (978-1-4787-1610-5(X)) Outskirts Pr., Inc.

Cody, Matthew. The Dead Gentleman. 2012. (ENG.). 288p. (J). (gr. 5). 6.99 (978-0-375-84490-4(2), Yearling) Random Hse. Children's Bks.

—The Secrets of the Pied Piper 1: the Peddler's Road. 2016. (Secrets of the Pied Piper Ser.: 1). (ENG.). 384p. (J). (gr. 3-7). 7.99 (978-0-385-75525-2(2), Yearling) Random Hse. Children's Bks.

Coelho, Paulo. Warrior of the Light: A Manual. 2004. (ENG.). 160p. pap. 15.99 (978-0-06-052798-3(6), HarperOne) HarperCollins Pubs.

Coerr, Eleanor. Mieko & the Fifth Treasure. 2003. (ENG., Illus.). 80p. (J). (gr. 4-7). 5.99 (978-0-698-11990-1(8), Puffin Books) Penguin Young Readers Group.

Cofer, Amadeus. Aloha Adventure: The Magic of Imagination on a Rainy Day. l.t. ed. 2004. (Illus.). 36p. (J). 14.00 (978-1-932957-01-3(4)) Legacy Pubs.

Coffey, Stephen. Rosemary Herbb & the Zodiac Ghosts. 2009. 148p. pap. 14.50 (978-1-4092-9751-2(9)) Lulu Pr., Inc.

Coffman, Jan. A Common Bond. 2008. 73p. pap. 19.95 (978-1-60672-302-9(2)) America Star Bks.

Cogar, Tubal U., et al. The Journeys of Wobblefoot the Beginning. Cogar, Karen S., ed. O'Connor, Tim, illus. 2003. (J). pap. 17.50 (978-0-9747149-0-5(9)) Wobblefoot Ltd.

Cohen, Lawrence J. The Dragon's Familiar. 2008. 236p. (YA). pap. 15.95 (978-0-595-51413-7(8)) iUniverse, Inc.

Cohen, Lee. Find the Magic: A Rip Squeak Book. 2008. (Illus.). 32p. (J). 16.95 (978-0-9747825-2-2(1), Rip Squeak Pr.) Rip Squeak, Inc.

Cohen, Marina. Ghost Ride. 2009. (ENG.). 184p. (YA). (gr. 6-18). pap. 12.99 (978-1-55488-438-4(1), Dundurn Pr.) Dundurn CAN. Dist: Ingram Publisher Services.

Cohen, Pamela. Ashie: Lost in a Hurricane, 1 vol. 2010. 40p. 24.95 (978-1-4512-1169-6(4)) PublishAmerica, Inc.

Cohen, Pamela June. Ashie: Lost in the Hurricane. Lang, Allison, illus. 2008. 40p. pap. 24.95 (978-1-60474-961-8(X)) America Star Bks.

Cohen, Rich. Alex & the Amazing Time Machine. Murphy, Kelly, illus. 2013. (ENG.). 176p. (J). (gr. 3-7). pap. 6.99 (978-1-250-02729-0(2), 9781250027290) Square Fish.

Cohen, Santiago, illus. The Yiddish Fish. 2014. (ENG.). 32p. (J). (gr. -1-k). 16.95 (978-1-62914-633-1(1), Sky Pony Pr.) Skyhorse Publishing Co., Inc.

Cohen-Spence, Susan. An Amazing Adventure Back in Time. Scott, Susan, illus. 2013. 32p. pap. 14.99 (978-0-9886360-4-0(2)) Kids At Heart Publishing, LLC.

Cohn, Ariel. The Zoo Box. Steinke, Aron Nels, illus. 2014. (ENG.). 48p. (J). (gr. k-2). 17.99 (978-1-62672-052-7(5), 9781626720527, First Second Bks.) Roaring Brook Pr.

Cohn, Karen & Cohn, Brian. The Polar Bear Who Couldn't, Wouldn't Swim. 2013. (J). 14.95 (978-1-62086-335-0(9)) Mascot Bks., Inc.

Coia, Kristina. Lymeria. 2007. 120p. (YA). 20.95 (978-0-595-69347-4(4)); per. 10.95 (978-0-595-45268-2(X)) iUniverse, Inc.

Cola, Arthur. Papa & the Gingerbread Man. 2006. 14.95 (978-0-9789423-0-4(2)) Cola, Arthur.

Colandro, Lucille. There Was an Old Lady Who Swallowed a Sticker Book! Lee, Jared D., illus. 2014. (ENG.). 16p. (J). (gr. -1-k). 6.99 (978-0-545-61308-8(6), Cartwheel Bks.) Scholastic, Inc.

Colbert, Cory. Sammy the Sea Otter Makes New Friends: Adventures of Sammy the Sea Otter. 2011. 18p. pap. 11.95 (978-1-4327-7648-0(7)) Outskirts Pr., Inc.

Colby, J. Z. Trilogy One. Colby, J. Z. et al, illus. 2010. (Nebador Ser.: Books One, Two, and Three). (ENG.). 641p. (YA). pupil's gde. ed. 49.95 (978-1-936253-17-3(8)) Nebador Archives.

Colby, J. Z. & Persons, Katelynn. Flight Training, Kibi & the Search for Happiness. Colby, J. Z. & Powers, Mireille Xioulan, illus. 2011. (Nebador Ser.: Book Four). 178p. (YA). pap. 10.95 (978-1-936253-27-2(5)) Nebador Archives.

Colby's Egypt Adventures. 2005. (J). kivar 17.95 (978-0-9746810-4-7(0)) Versait Pr. LLC.

Cole, Bud. The Mystery of Little Bear. 2012. pap. 12.95 (978-0-7414-8106-1(5)) Infinity Publishing.

Cole, Cathleen. The Night Mare of Four Seasons Stables. 2008. 76p. pap. 19.95 (978-1-60703-860-3(9)) America Star Bks.

Cole, Charmaine W. Barky, a Very Special Beaver. 2012. 28p. (-18). pap. 24.95 (978-1-4626-9528-7(0)) America Star Bks.

Cole, Diedra. The Adventures of Chris & Abby: First Day of School. 2012. (ENG.). 34p. (J). pap. 14.95 (978-1-4327-8170-5(7)) Outskirts Pr., Inc.

Cole, Dina. Are There Alligators at the Equator? An Eddie the Equator Adventure. 2012. 40p. pap. 20.99 (978-1-4772-6819-3(7)) AuthorHouse.

Cole, Dylan. The Other Worldly Adventures of Tyler Washburn: the New Kid. 2012. (ENG., Illus.). 48p. (J). (gr. -1). 19.95 (978-1-933492-77-3(5)) Design Studio Pr.

Cole, Frank. The World's Greatest Adventure Machine. 2017. (J). **(978-0-399-55284-7(7))** Penguin Publishing Group.

Cole, Frank L. The Guardians of the Finisher's Fury (Guardians 3) 2013. pap. 16.99 (978-1-4621-1221-0(8), Horizon Pubs.) Cedar Fort, Inc./CFI Distribution.

—Hashbrown Winters & Whiz-Tastrophe. 2013. pap. 14.99 (978-1-4621-1056-8(8), Bonneville Bks.) Cedar Fort, Inc./CFI Distribution.

Cole, Frank L. The World's Greatest Adventure Machine. 2017. (ENG.). 320p. (J). (gr. 4-7). 16.99 **(978-0-399-55282-3(0)**, Delacorte Bks. for Young Readers) Random Hse. Children's Bks.

Cole, Joanna, et al. The Giant Germ. Degen, Bruce et al, illus. 2010. (Rise & Shine Ser.: 6). (ENG.). 80p. (C). (gr. 2-5). pap. 8.95 (978-0-439-20420-0(8)) National Geographic School Publishing, Inc.

Cole, Stephen. Thieves Like Us. 2007. (ENG., Illus.). 368p. (YA). (gr. 7). per. 8.99 (978-1-59990-041-4(6), 9781599900414, Bloomsbury USA Childrens) Bloomsbury Publishing USA.

Colebourn, Craig. The Knights of Videnland: Passing the Torch. 2007. 428p. per. 23.95 (978-0-595-46989-5(2)) iUniverse, Inc.

Coleman, Tamala J. Donovan's Shoes. 2010. 28p. pap. 9.95 (978-1-4327-5801-1(2)) Outskirts Pr., Inc.

Coleman-Veach, Marti. Balloons in Heaven. 2013. 32p. pap. (978-1-4602-1826-6(4)) FriesenPress.

Colfer, Chris. An Author's Odyssey. 2016. (Land of Stories Ser.: 5). (ENG.). (J). (gr. 3-7). 496p. pap. 11.99 (978-0-316-27214-8(0)); (Illus.). 464p. 19.99 (978-0-316-38329-5(5)) Little, Brown Bks. for Young Readers.

—The Land of Stories: an Author's Odyssey. 2017. (Land of Stories Ser.: 5). (ENG., Illus.). 464p. (J). (gr. 3-7). pap. 9.99 **(978-0-316-38321-9(X))** Little, Brown Bks. for Young Readers.

Colfer, Chris. The Mother Goose Diaries. 2017. (ENG.). 128p. (J). (gr. 3-7). 10.99 (978-0-316-38334-9(1)) Little Brown & Co.

Colfer, Eoin. Airman. 2009. (ENG.). 416p. (J). (gr. 5-9). pap. 8.99 (978-1-4231-0751-4(9)) Hyperion Pr.

—Airman. 2009. (J). lib. bdg. 19.65 (978-0-606-12534-5(5), Turtleback) Turtleback Bks.

—Artemis Fowl & the Atlantis Complex. 2012. (ENG.). 384p. (J). (gr. 5-9). pap. 8.99 (978-1-4231-2972-1(5)) Hyperion Pr.

—The Atlantis Complex. 2010. (Artemis Fowl Ser.: 7). (ENG.). 368p. (J). (gr. 5-9). 17.99 (978-1-4231-2819-9(2)) Hyperion Pr.

—The Atlantis Complex. 2012. (Artemis Fowl Ser.: 7). (J). lib. bdg. 19.65 (978-0-606-23614-0(7), Turtleback) Turtleback Bks.

—Benny & Omar. 2003. 240p. (YA). (gr. 5-18). pap. 7.95 (978-0-86278-567-3(7)) O'Brien Pr., Ltd., The IRL. Dist: Independent Pubs. Group.

—The Eternity Code. rev. ed. 2009. (Artemis Fowl Ser.). (ENG.). 336p. (J). (gr. 5-9). pap. 8.99 (978-1-4231-2453-5(7)) Hyperion Pr.

—The Last Guardian. 2012. (Artemis Fowl Ser.). (ENG.). 336p. (J). (gr. 5-9). 18.99 (978-1-4231-6161-5(0)) Hyperion Pr.

—The Last Guardian. 2014. (Artemis Fowl Ser.: 8). (J). lib. bdg. 19.65 (978-0-606-32288-1(4), Turtleback) Turtleback Bks.

—The Lost Colony. rev. ed. 2009. (Artemis Fowl Ser.). (ENG.). 432p. (J). (gr. 5-9). pap. 8.99 (978-1-4231-2494-8(4)) Hyperion Pr.

—The Opal Deception. 2006. (Artemis Fowl Ser.: Bk. 4). 17.10 (978-0-7569-6828-1(3)) Disney Pr.

—The Opal Deception. rev. ed. 2009. (Artemis Fowl Ser.). (ENG.). 368p. (J). (gr. 5-9). pap. 8.99 (978-1-4231-2455-9(3)) Hyperion Pr.

—The Opal Deception. (Artemis Fowl Ser.: 4). (J). 2007. 1.25 (978-1-4193-6041-1(8)) 2006. 72.75 (978-1-4193-6045-9(0)) 2006. 69.75 (978-1-4193-6047-3(7)) Recorded Bks., Inc.

—The Time Paradox. 2009. (Artemis Fowl Ser.). (ENG.). 448p. (J). (gr. 5-9). pap. 8.99 (978-1-4231-0837-5(X)) Hyperion Pr.

—The Time Paradox. 2009. (Artemis Fowl Ser.: 6). (J). lib. bdg. 19.65 (978-0-606-10579-8(4), Turtleback) Turtleback Bks.

Colfer, Eoin & Donkin, Andrew. Artemis Fowl the Opal Deception Graphic Novel. Rigano, Giovanni & Lamanna, Paolo, illus. 2014. (Artemis Fowl Ser.: 4). (ENG.). 112p. (J). (gr. 5-9). pap. 12.99 (978-1-4231-4549-3(6)) Hyperion Bks. for Children.

—Eternity Code. Rigano, Giovanni & Lamanna, Paolo, illus. 2013. (Artemis Fowl Ser.: 3). (ENG.). 112p. (J). (gr. 5-9). pap. 12.99 (978-1-4231-4577-6(1)) Hyperion Pr.

Colhoun, Sheelah. Elric's Florida Holiday. Cotton, Sue Lynn, illus. 2012. 20p. pap. 13.95 (978-1-61493-110-2(0)) Peppertree Pr., The.

—It's Fun to Feed the Little Lambs. Cotton, Sue Lynn, illus. 2013. 32p. pap. 14.95 (978-1-61493-185-0(2)) Peppertree Pr., The.

Coll, Ivar Da. Bien Vestidos. (SPA.). (J). bds. (978-958-04-4911-9(2)) Norma S.A. COL. Dist: Lectorum Pubns., Inc.

Coll, L. & Coll, C. Beware the Unknown: The Landing. 2003. (Illus.). 144p. (J). per. 12.95 (978-0-9729965-0-1(8)) White Line Productions Inc.

Collar, Orpheus & Riordan, Rick. The Throne of Fire. Collar, Orpheus, illus. 2015. (Kane Chronicles Ser.). (ENG., Illus.). 160p. (J). (gr. 5-9). 21.99 (978-1-4847-1490-4(3)) Hyperion Bks. for Children.

Colledge, Anne. Falling into Fear. 2004. 92p. per. (978-1-904529-12-5(7), Back to Front) Solidus.

Collicutt, Paul. Rust Attack! Collicutt, Paul, illus. 2009. (Robot City Ser.: 2). (ENG., Illus.). 48p. (J). (gr. 3-7). pap. 8.99 (978-0-7636-4594-6(X), Templar) Candlewick Pr.

Collier, Christine. Adventure on Apple Orchard Road. 2003. 50p. pap. 8.95 (978-0-595-27725-4(X), Mystery & Suspense Pr.) iUniverse, Inc.

Collier, Kevin Scott. Professor Horace, Cryptozoologist. Collier, Kevin Scott, illus. 2008. (Illus.). 20p. pap. 9.95 (978-1-935137-14-6(X)) Guardian Angel Publishing, Inc.

Collier, Kristen & Collier, Kevin Scott. The Jumbo Shrimp of Dire Straits. 2008. 20p. pap. 9.95 (978-1-933090-92-4(8)) Guardian Angel Publishing, Inc.

Collier, Talina L. Jacob & the Orange. 2012. 20p. pap. 24.95 (978-1-4626-8046-7(1)) America Star Bks.

—Jacob & the Turtle Race. 2012. 28p. pap. 24.95 (978-1-4626-8045-0(3)) America Star Bks.

Collingwood, Harry. Across the Spanish Main. 204p. 2011. 26.95 (978-1-4638-9643-0(3)) 2009. pap. 14.95 (978-1-60664-390-7(8)) Rodgers, Alan Bks.

—The Castaways. 2008. 172p. 25.95 (978-1-60664-710-3(5)); pap. 13.95 (978-1-60664-209-2(X)) Rodgers, Alan Bks.

—The Cruise of The 'Esmeralda' 2009. 220p. pap. 15.95 (978-1-60664-391-4(6)) Rodgers, Alan Bks.

—In Search of el Dorado. 2008. 200p. 27.95 (978-1-60664-775-2(X)) Aegypan.

—The Log of a Privateersman. 2008. 216p. 26.95 (978-1-60664-899-5(3)); pap. 15.95 (978-1-60664-018-0(6)) Aegypan.

—The Log of the 'Flying Fish' 2011. 236p. 26.95 (978-1-4638-9645-4(X)) Rodgers, Alan Bks.

—The Strange Adventures of Eric Blackburn. 2008. 164p. 25.95 (978-1-60664-711-0(3)); pap. 13.95 (978-1-60664-210-8(3)) Rodgers, Alan Bks.

—Under the Chilean Flag. 2009. 184p. 26.95 (978-1-60664-598-7(6)); pap. 13.95 (978-1-60664-330-3(4)) Rodgers, Alan Bks.

Collins, Amanda. Bff!!! or Not??? 2007. 168p. per. 20.99 (978-1-4257-3370-4(0)) Xlibris Corp.

Collins, Amanda E. Bff!!! or Not??? 2007. 168p. 30.99 (978-1-4257-3371-1(9)) Xlibris Corp.

Collins, Charles. Hover for a Day. Seltzer, Jerry, illus. 2006. (ENG.). 56p. (J). 19.95 (978-1-60131-004-0(8), Castlebridge Bks.) Big Tent Bks.

Collins, Christine. The Knight Meets Ole Dragon. 2009. 100p. pap. 28.95 (978-1-4327-4128-0(4)) Outskirts Pr., Inc.

Collins, Diana Sue. Elfin, the Elf. 2011. 44p. pap. 24.95 (978-1-4560-8493-6(3)) America Star Bks.

Collins, Harper & Harper Collins / LeapFrog. Paddington Bear. 2008. (J). 11.99 (978-1-59319-989-0(9)) LeapFrog Enterprises, Inc.

Collins, Jonathan. The Adventures of Mali & Keela: A Virtues Book for Children. Cooper, Jenny, illus. 2010. (ENG.). 144p. (J). (gr. k-2). pap. 17.95 (978-1-932181-52-4(0)) Personhood Pr.

Collins, Stephan. The Chronicles of Timothy Tabbis. 2009. 45p. pap. 8.55 (978-0-557-09266-6(3)) Lulu Pr., Inc.

Collins, Suzanne. Gregor - The Overlander. 2004. (Underland Chronicles Ser.: 1). (ENG.). 336p. (J). (gr. 3-7). pap. 7.99 (978-0-439-67813-1(7), Scholastic Paperbacks) Scholastic, Inc.

Collins, Terry. Eagle Eye. 2010. 32p. pap. 15.98 (978-0-557-56031-8(4)) Lulu Pr., Inc.

—The World's Greatest Valentine, Vol. 4. 2004. 64p. (J). (gr. 2-5). pap. 17.00 incl. audio (978-0-8072-1989-8(4), Listening Library) Random Hse. Audio Publishing Group.

Collins, Terry & Schulz, Barbara. Escape from Pompeii: An Isabel Soto Archaeology Adventure, 1 vol. 2010. (Graphic Expeditions Ser.). (ENG., Illus.). 32p. (gr. 3-4). pap. 8.10 (978-1-4296-5634-4(4), Graphic Library) Capstone Press of Coughlan Cos.

Collins, Terry, et al. Escape from Pompeii: An Isabel Soto Archaeology Adventure, 1 vol. 2010. (Graphic Expeditions Ser.). (ENG., Illus.). 32p. (gr. 3-4). lib. bdg. 30.65 (978-1-4296-4771-7(X), Graphic Library) Capstone Press of Coughlan Cos.

Collins, Wendy Jane. The Adventure Door: Book 1 'How it all began' & Book 2 'Return to Courtney Bay' 2010. 112p. pap. 10.99 (978-1-4520-4228-2(4)) AuthorHouse.

Collodi, C. The Adventures of Pinocchio. Della Chiesa, Carol, tr. 2007. (ENG.). 160p. per. (978-1-4065-1463-6(2)) Dodo Pr.

Collodi, Carlo. Adventures of Pinocchio. Lucas, Ann Lawson, tr. from ITA. 2009. (Oxford World's Classics Ser.). (ENG., Illus.). 256p. pap. 10.95 (978-0-19-955398-3(X)) Oxford Univ. Pr., Inc.

Colloredo, Sabino. Hercules. Ferrari, Antongionata, illus. 2009. (Hotel Olympus Ser.). 128p. (J). (gr. 3-6). 31.95 (978-1-60754-708-2(2)) Windmill Bks.

Colorado, Papa. Nui & Kiwi's Fantastic Adventures. 2011. 70p. pap. 19.95 (978-1-4626-2806-3(0)) PublishAmerica, Inc.

Colorful Cars. 2017. (Colorful Cars Ser.). 24p. (gr. 4-6). 70.80 **(978-1-5081-6176-9(3)**, PowerKids Pr.) Rosen Publishing Group, Inc., The.

Colossal, Eric. Rutabaga the Adventure Chef: Book 2: Feasts of Fury. 2016. (Rutabaga the Adventure Chef Ser.). (ENG., Illus.). 128p. (J). (gr. 3-7). 16.95 (978-1-4197-1658-4(1), Amulet Bks.) Abrams, Inc.

Colum, Padraic. The Children's Homer: The Adventures of Odysseus & the Tale of Troy. Pogány, Willy, illus. 2004. (ENG.). 256p. (J). (gr. 5-9). pap. 9.99 (978-0-689-86883-2(9), Aladdin) Simon & Schuster Children's Publishing.

—The Golden Fleece: And the Heroes Who Lived Before Achilles. Pogány, Willy, illus. 2004. (ENG.). 320p. (J). (gr. 5-9). pap. 10.99 (978-0-689-86884-9(7), Aladdin) Simon & Schuster Children's Publishing.

Colum, Padraic & Pogány, Willy. The Adventures of Odysseus & the Tale of Troy. 2008. 280p. 42.95 (978-1-4366-0896-1(1)); per. 27.95 (978-0-548-81877-0(0)) Kessinger Publishing, LLC.

Columbus, Chris & Vizzini, Ned. Battle of the Beasts. 2014. (House of Secrets Ser.: 2). (ENG.). 480p. (J). (gr. 3-7). 17.99 (978-0-06-219249-3(3)) HarperCollins Pubs.

—House of Secrets. 2015. (House of Secrets Ser.: Vol. 1). (KOR.). 580p. (J). (978-89-491-7127-2(9)) Biryongso Publishing Co.

—House of Secrets. Call, Greg, illus. (House of Secrets Ser.: 1). (J). 2014. (ENG.). 512p. (gr. 3-7). pap. 7.99 (978-0-06-219247-9(7)) 2013. (ENG.). 496p. (gr. 3-7). 17.99 (978-0-06-219246-2(9)) 2013. 490p. (978-0-06-225964-6(4)) HarperCollins Pubs.

—House of Secrets. 2014. (House of Secrets Ser.: 1). (J). lib. bdg. 18.40 (978-0-606-35070-9(5), Turtleback) Turtleback Bks.

Columbus, Chris, et al. Clash of the Worlds. 2016. (House of Secrets Ser.: 3). 528p. (J). (gr. 3-7). 17.99 (978-0-06-219251-6(5)) HarperCollins Pubs.

—House of Secrets: Clash of the Worlds. 2017. (House of Secrets Ser.: 3). 528p. (J). (gr. 3-7). pap. 7.99 (978-0-06-219254-7(X)) HarperCollins Pubs.

Colvin, Denise Marie. Suzy's Big Dream Comes True. 2007. 61p. pap. 19.95 (978-1-4241-8157-5(7)) America Star Bks.

Comeau, Ceara. Adventures of the Young & Curious. 2008. 136p. pap. 10.94 (978-0-557-00914-5(6)) Lulu Pr., Inc.

Comer, Brigitte Renee. The Little Hopping Frog. 2012. 24p. pap. 24.95 (978-1-4626-8243-0(X)) America Star Bks.

Comfort, Ray. Scratch & Sniff. Hohnstadt, Cedric, illus. 2007. (Creation for Kids Ser.). 24p. (gr. -1-5). 14.99 (978-0-88270-328-2(5)) Bridge-Logos, Inc.

Compagnucci, Veronica M. Emily Finds Her Voice. 2013. 40p. pap. 24.95 (978-1-63004-288-2(9)) America Star Bks.

Comperchio, Shheila. The Club House & the Gang. 2011. 114p. pap. 9.95 (978-0-9837803-0-4(7)) Fiction Publishing, Inc.

Compton, Peggy. Captain Johnnie, 1 vol. 2008. (ENG.). 32p. 24.95 (978-1-60441-693-0(9)) America Star Bks.

Concordia International School Shanghai. Stories from Room 113: International Adventures. 2008. 304p. pap. 18.95 (978-0-595-53090-8(7)) iUniverse, Inc.

Condie, Ally. Reached. 2013. (Matched Trilogy Ser.: 3). lib. bdg. 20.85 (978-0-606-34456-2(X), Turtleback) Turtleback Bks.

Condie, Catherine. Whirl of the Wheel. 2010. 107p. pap. 12.95 (978-1-4452-8648-8(3)) Lulu Pr., Inc.

Conejito Azul: Y la Aventura de Pap Conejo.Tr. of Bunny Rabbit-Father's Adventure. (SPA.). (J). 2.98 (978-970-22-0019-2(9)) Larousse, Ediciones, S. A. de C. V. MEX. Dist: Continental Bk. Co., Inc.

Conford, Ellen. A Case for Jenny Archer. Palmisciano, Diane & Brooks, Erik, illus. 2nd ed. 2006. (ENG.). 64p. (J). (gr. 1-4). per. 13.99 (978-0-316-01486-1(9)) Little, Brown Bks. for Young Readers.

Conforto, Lisa. The Very Compromising Adventures of Thumby Blackstone, 1 vol. 2010. 34p. 24.95 (978-1-4512-0270-0(9)) PublishAmerica, Inc.

Conklin, Wendy. Dos Amigos Planos Viajan por el Mundo, 1 vol. rev. ed. 2007. (Building Fluency Through Reader's Theater Ser.).Tr. of Two Flat Friends Travel the World. (SPA.). 24p. (J). (gr. 3-4). pap. 6.99 (978-1-4333-0022-6(2)) Teacher Created Materials, Inc.

Conley, Cindy Taylor. For Little Louie Someday. 2013. 44p. pap. 24.95 (978-1-63000-044-8(2)) America Star Bks.

Conley, Deane W. Angelino Courage to Fly. 2007. (J). lib. bdg. 19.95 (978-1-933732-27-5(X)) Big Ransom Studio.

—Angelino Flies Again. 2007. (J). lib. bdg. 19.95 (978-1-933732-26-8(1)) Big Ransom Studio.

Conleyosb, Dolores. Bitsy's Strange Adventures: Bitsy Meets Miss Maple & Cassie Bitsy's New Friends. 2012. 44p. pap. 21.99 (978-1-4685-9678-6(0)) AuthorHouse.

Conlin, Laura E. Winston's Wild Journeys: Live Outside Your Shell. 2011. 43p. (J). 18.95 (978-1-4327-6885-0(9)) Outskirts Pr., Inc.

Conly, Jane Leslie. Impetuous R. , Secret Agent. Leick, Bonnie, illus. 2008. (ENG.). 240p. (gr. 3-7). 16.99 (978-1-4231-0418-6(8)) Hyperion Pr.

Connatser, Scott. Excited about Pre-School. 2011. 32p. pap. 12.77 (978-1-4567-6564-4(7)) AuthorHouse.

Connell, Julie. The Adventures of Cutie Pie & Mr. Squishy. 2008. 12p. pap. 24.95 (978-1-60703-826-9(9)) America Star Bks.

Connell, Karen. The Adventures of Katie & Sam: A Day to Fly, 1 vol. 2009. 16p. pap. 24.95 (978-1-60813-702-2(3)) America Star Bks.

—Slow Down: The Adventures of Katie & Sam, 1 vol. 2009. 15p. pap. 24.95 (978-1-61582-420-5(0)) America Star Bks.

—Slow Down: The Adventures of Katie & Sam, 1 vol. 2010. 16p. 24.95 (978-1-4512-2073-5(1)) PublishAmerica, Inc.

Connelly, Peg. If the Forest Is Silent, Beware! 2007. 108p. pap. 19.95 (978-1-60441-548-3(7)) America Star Bks.

—A Madman Hunts for Bigfoot. 2008. 110p. pap. 19.95 (978-1-60672-322-7(7)) America Star Bks.

Connelly, Valerie. Arthur, the Christmas Elf: A Christmas Adventure. 2006. (Illus.). 60p. (J). per. 24.95 (978-1-933449-23-4(3)) Nightengale Pr.

Conner, Guy. Elizabeth & Parr. 2013. 90p. 24.00 (978-0-578-12011-9(9)) GRC Bks.

Conner, Jimmie L. The Adventures of Captain Computerman & His Sidekick Mouseman: The Saving of the Toy Websites. 2005. 77p. pap. 19.95 (978-1-4137-7457-3(1)) America Star Bks.

Conness, Steven A. George Huck, the Founding of Huckville: The Huck Family Chronicles, 1 vol. 2010. 78p. pap. 19.95 (978-1-4489-4471-2(6)) PublishAmerica, Inc.

Connolly, Faye. Puddle Stomp. 2010. 36p. 15.49 (978-1-4520-7202-9(7)) AuthorHouse.

Connolly, Timothy. Joy's Journey Home. Sullivan, Mary, illus. 2012. (ENG.). 92p. (J). 17.95 (978-0-9859986-2-2(8)); pap. 8.95 (978-0-9859986-1-5(X)) Nectar Pubns.

Connor, Naomi. Big Brown Eyes. 2010. 24p. pap. 12.99 (978-1-4490-7331-2(X)) AuthorHouse.

Connor, Patrick M. Tree House. 2011. 312p. pap. 29.95 (978-1-4560-9578-9(1)) America Star Bks.

Connor, Peyton. Humpty Dumpty's Whole Story. 2011. pap. 9.95 (978-0-7414-6734-8(8)) Infinity Publishing.

Conroe, Lindy. Rockafella Jones & the Hidden Treasure. Riette, Susanne, illus. 2011. 108p. (J). pap. 10.95 (978-1-935199-00-7(5)) Blue Mustang Pr.

Conroy, Kathy. Life Through a Dog's Eyes: The Adventures of Ralph. 2008. (ENG.). 44p. pap. 19.69 (978-1-4343-8465-2(9)) AuthorHouse.

Constantinople, Louise T. The Adventures of Ralph Ribbit. 2012. (ENG.). 103p. pap. 8.95 (978-1-4327-8853-7(1)) Outskirts Pr., Inc.

Conway, Celeste. Unlovely. 2015. (ENG.). 256p. (YA). pap. 9.99 (978-1-4405-9225-6(X), Simon Pulse) Simon Pulse.

Conway, Gerry. Crawling with Zombies. 2010. (Hardy Boys the New Case Files Ser.). (ENG., Illus.). 64p. (J). (gr. 3-7). pap. 6.99 (978-1-59707-219-9(2), 9781597072199) Papercutz.

Conway, Portia. Where My Shoes Have Been, 1 vol. 2010. 22p. 24.95 (978-1-4512-9671-6(1)) PublishAmerica, Inc.

Cook, Alison Reeger. The Scholar, the Sphinx & the Shades of Nyx. 2013. (Scholar & the Sphinx Ser.: 1). (ENG.). 296p. (YA). pap. (978-1-908483-87-4(3)) Knox Robinson Pubs.

Cook, Cathy T. The Adventures of Rose Bush. 2010. 64p. pap. 10.49 (978-1-4520-3645-8(4)) AuthorHouse.

Cook, Deena & McIntosh, Cherie. Pinky & Peanut: The Adventure Begins. Scruggs, Trina, illus. 2007. 78p. (J). per. 4.99 (978-0-9797020-0-6(3)) P & P Publishing LLC.

Cook, Diana. Wink Fish: Nate's Missed Adventure. 2011. 72p. pap. 41.99 (978-1-4628-8607-4(8)) Xlibris Corp.

Cook, Eileen. With Malice. 2016. (ENG.). 320p. (YA). (gr. 9). 17.99 (978-0-544-80509-5(7), HMH Books For Young Readers) Houghton Mifflin Harcourt Publishing Co.

Cook, Julia. I Just Want to Do It My Way! De Weerd, Kelsey, illus. 2013. (ENG.). 32p. (J). 16.95 (978-1-934490-44-0(X)) Boys Town Pr.

Cook, Marisa. The Adventures of Ollie & Ronnie: Litter. 2012. 16p. (-18). pap. 12.68 (978-1-4669-6630-7(0)) Trafford Publishing.

Cook, Norman. Sam in the Crimea: A Victorian Adventure Based on the Work of Lord Shaftesbury. 2007. (Illus.). 128p. (J). (gr. 4-7). per. 9.00 (978-1-84625-045-3(5)) DayOne Pubns. GBR. Dist: Send The Light Distribution LLC.

Cook, Sherry & Johnson, Martin. Underwater Utley. 26. Kuhn, Jesse, illus. Lt. ed. 2006. (Quirkles — Exploring Phonics through Science Ser.: 21). 32p. (J). 7.99 (978-1-933815-20-6(5), Quirkles, The) Creative 3, LLC.

Cook, Teri Ann. The Adventures of Mrs. Patsy's Farm: A Gift! Is a Gift! Is a Gift!, 1 vol. 2009. 24p. pap. 24.95 (978-1-60749-549-9(X)) America Star Bks.

Cook, Tina H. Lindsey & the Yellow Masterpiece. 2011. 36p. pap. 15.99 (978-1-4634-0306-5(2)) AuthorHouse.

Cooke, Eunice Perneel. The Awesome Lost & Found Society. 2012. 56p. pap. (978-1-4602-0087-2(X)) FriesenPress.

Cool by the Pool: Coloring/Activity Book. 2005. (Illus.). (J). 2.99 (978-0-9770455-2-5(8)) Mighty Kids Media.

Cool by the Pool: Picture Book (English) 2005. (Illus.). 47p. (J). 5.99 (978-0-9770455-3-2(6)) Mighty Kids Media.

Cooley, Judy. Mom Says I Can. 2008. (Illus.). 32p. (J). (gr. -1-3). lib. bdg. 17.95 (978-1-59038-872-3(0), Shadow Mountain) Shadow Mountain Publishing.

Coomber, Suzanne. The Run Away Persimmon. 2009. 20p. pap. 12.49 (978-1-4490-0911-3(5)) AuthorHouse.

Coon, Dianne. Nerual's Adventures & the Greatness of Agnes. 2010. 68p. pap. 11.49 (978-1-4520-2321-2(2)) AuthorHouse.

Coon, Thomas & Coon, Helene. Two of Our Friends Are Doves. MacMenamin, John, illus. 2003. 64p. (J). per. (978-1-932077-17-9(0)) Athena Pr.

Coonan, Candace N. The Break of Dawn: Tales from Fadreama: Book 3. 2012. 364p. (gr. 4-6). pap. 20.33 (978-1-4669-3567-9(7)) Trafford Publishing.

—The Shattered Souls: Tales from Fadreama: Book 4. 2012. 320p. (gr. 10-12). pap. 19.11 (978-1-4669-3438-2(7)) Trafford Publishing.

—Where Shadows Linger: Tales from Fadreama: Book 2. 2012. 304p. (gr. 2-4). pap. 18.30 (978-1-4669-3541-9(3)) Trafford Publishing.

Cooney, Caroline B. Fatality. 2016. (ENG.). 184p. (J). (gr. 7-12). pap. 11.99 (978-1-5040-3558-3(5)) Open Road Integrated Media, Inc.

—Hush Little Baby. 2016. (ENG.). 198p. (J). (gr. 7-12). pap. 11.99 (978-1-5040-3556-9(9)) Open Road Integrated Media, Inc.

Cooper, Catherine. The Golden Acorn. 2nd rev. ed. 2010. (Adventures of Jack Brenin Ser.). (ENG., Illus.). 376p. pap. 12.34 (978-1-906821-65-4(8)) Infinite Ideas GBR. Dist: Sony Electronics.

Cooper, Chris. Rascal: Facing the Flames. de la Rue, James, illus. 2016. (Rascal Ser.: 4). (ENG.). 160p. (J). (gr. 1-3). pap. 7.99 (978-1-4052-7531-6(6)) Egmont Bks., Ltd. GBR. Dist: Independent Pubs. Group.

—Rascal: Racing Against Time. de la Rue, James, illus. 2017. (Rascal Ser.: 6). (ENG.). 144p. (J). (gr. 1-3). pap. 7.99 (978-1-4052-7533-0(2)) Egmont Bks., Ltd. GBR. Dist: Independent Pubs. Group.

—Rascal: Swept Beneath the Waters. de la Rue, James, illus. 2017. (Rascal Ser.: 5). (ENG.). 160p. (J). (gr. 1-3). pap. 7.99 (978-1-4052-7532-3(4)) Egmont Bks., Ltd. GBR. Dist: Independent Pubs. Group.

Cooper, Constance. Guile. 2017. (ENG.). 384p. (YA). (gr. 7). pap. 9.99 (978-0-544-93691-1(4), HMH Books For Young Readers) Houghton Mifflin Harcourt Publishing Co.

—Guile. 2016. (ENG.). 384p. (YA). (gr. 7). 17.99 (978-0-544-45171-1(6), Clarion Bks.) Houghton Mifflin Harcourt Trade & Reference Pubs.

—Guile. 2017. (ENG.). (YA). (gr. 7). lib. bdg. 20.85 **(978-0-606-39821-3(X))** Turtleback Bks.

Cooper, Gael. Kermeena Kermudgeon Meets Gordon. 2010. 36p. 15.49 (978-1-4490-6735-9(2)) AuthorHouse.

Cooper, Helen S. Historias de Juguetes. (SPA., Illus.). 80p. (J). (gr. k-2). 23.95 (978-84-261-3127-0(1), JV1108) Juventud, Editorial ESP. Dist: Lectorum Pubns., Inc.

Cooper, Helen Wendy. The Vegetarian Vampire: The Lost Fangs. 2013. (Illus.). 50p. pap. 8.50 (978-1-78035-651-8(X), Fastprint Publishing) Upfront Publishing Ltd. GBR. Dist: Printondemand-worldwide.com.

Cooper, James Fenimore. The Last of the Mohicans. Wyeth, N. C., illus. 2013. (Scribner Classics Ser.). (ENG.). 368p. (J). (gr. 5). 24.99 (978-1-4424-8130-5(7), Atheneum Bks. for Young Readers) Simon & Schuster Children's Publishing.

Cooper, Jay. Mutant Rat Attack! 2017. (Spy Next Door Ser.: 1). (ENG.). 144p. (J). (gr. 2-5). 9.99 (978-0-545-93297-4(1), Scholastic Pr.) Scholastic, Inc.

Cooper, Mark A. Revenge: Jason Steed. 2012. (ENG.). 240p. (J). (gr. 4-7). pap. 7.99 (978-1-4022-6429-0(1), Sourcebooks Jabberwocky) Sourcebooks, Inc.

Cooper, Paul Fenimore. Tal, His Marvelous Adventures with Noom-Zor-Noom. Reeves, Ruth, illus. 80th ed. 2009. 305p. (J). pap. 12.95 (978-1-930900-41-7(4)) Purple Hse. Pr.

Cooper, Polly. The Adventures of Sir George & His Friends. 2008. (Illus.). 48p. pap. 17.49 (978-1-4343-4057-3(0)) AuthorHouse.

Cooper, Susan. The Boggart. Rayyan, Omar & Dillon, Julie, illus. 2004. (Boggart Ser.). (ENG.). 224p. (J). (gr. 3-7). pap. 7.99 (978-0-689-86930-3(4), McElderry, Margaret K. Bks.) McElderry, Margaret K. Bks.

—The Boggart. 196p. (YA). (gr. 5-18). pap. 3.95 (978-0-8072-1465-7(5), Listening Library) Random Hse. Audio Publishing Group.

—The Boggart & the Monster. Rayyan, Omar & Dillon, Julie, illus. 2004. (Boggart Ser.). (ENG.). 224p. (J). (gr. 3-7). pap. 7.99 (978-0-689-86931-0(2), McElderry, Margaret K. Bks.) McElderry, Margaret K. Bks.

—The Boggart & the Monster. 185p. (J). (gr. 4-6). pap. 3.95 (978-0-8072-1531-9(7), Listening Library) Random Hse. Audio Publishing Group.

Cooper, William Y. Nakai & the Red Shoes. 2011. 52p. (gr. 4-6). pap. 19.39 (978-1-4269-6048-2(4)) Trafford Publishing.

Coover, Colleen & Tobin, Paul. Adventure Time: The Flip Side. 2014. lib. bdg. 33.05 (978-0-606-36120-0(0)) Turtleback Bks.

Cope, Andrew. Spy Dog & Captured!, 2 bks. in 1. 2014. (Spy Dog Ser.). (ENG., Illus.). 352p. (J). (gr. 2-7). 14.99 (978-0-14-135097-4(0)) Penguin Bks., Ltd. GBR. Dist: Independent Pubs. Group.

—Storm Chaser. 10th ed. 2015. (Spy Dog Ser.: 11). (ENG., Illus.). 160p. (J). (gr. 2-7). pap. 7.99 (978-0-14-135715-7(0)) Penguin Bks., Ltd. GBR. Dist: Independent Pubs. Group.

—Survival Camp. 5th ed. 2015. (Spy Pups Ser.: 5). (ENG., Illus.). 160p. (J). (gr. 2-7). pap. 7.99 (978-0-14-133880-4(6)) Penguin Bks., Ltd. GBR. Dist: Independent Pubs. Group.

Coppard, A. E. Clorinda Walks in Heaven Stories. 2006. 220p. per. (978-1-4067-9414-4(7), Pomona Pr.) Read Bks.

Corbett, Burl N. Coon Tales. 2009. 122p. (gr. 2-2). pap. 19.99 (978-1-4415-3282-4(X)) Xlibris Corp.

Corcoran, Daniel. The Iddly Widdly Fiddly Poo! 2013. 40p. pap. (978-1-74298-340-0(5)) Port Campbell Pr.

Cordone Warner, Debra. A Busy Day for Baby Duck & Little Boy Blue. 2010. 34p. pap. 19.99 (978-0-557-59587-7(8)) Lulu Pr., Inc.

—I Almost Found Some Dinosaur Bones! 2010. 56p. pap. 24.99 (978-0-557-59624-9(6)) Lulu Pr., Inc.

Cordoves, Barbara, pseud & Cordoves, Gladys M. The Legend of Zias. Cordoves, Barbara & Cordoves, Gladys M., illus. (Zias' Adventures Ser.). (Illus.). 44p. (J). pap. 7.99 (978-0-9637252-0-2(3)) Cordoves, Barbara & Gladys M.

Corman, Dick. Fountain of Age. 2006. 185p. (YA). pap. 12.95 (978-0-9655749-2-1(X)) Corman Productions.

Cormier, Robert. I Am the Cheese. Lt. ed. 2005. 255p. pap. 10.95 (978-0-7862-7336-2(4), Large Print Pr.) Thorndike Pr.

Cormier, Shawn P. Necromancer. 2008. 276p. (YA). per. 12.95 (978-0-9740151-4-9(8)) Pine View Pr.

Cornell, Kevin. Go to Sleep, Monster! Cornell, Kevin, illus. 2016. (Illus.). 32p. (J). (gr. -1-3). 17.99 (978-0-06-234915-6(5)) HarperCollins Pubs.

Cornette, Sylvia. The House Across the Lake. 2007. 132p. per. 24.95 (978-1-4241-8247-3(6)) America Star Bks.

Cornfield, Lynda Ellis. Rocks for Clean Oceans. 2009. 28p. pap. 13.99 (978-1-4389-8417-9(0)) AuthorHouse.

Cornwell, Autumn. Carpe Diem. 2009. (ENG.). 368p. (YA). (gr. 7-12). pap. 12.99 (978-0-312-56129-1(6), 9780312561291) Square Fish.

Coronado, Mark & Jackson, Dominic. Swamp Life. 2012. 16p. pap. 15.99 (978-1-4772-1042-0(3)) AuthorHouse.

Correll, Stephanie. Newton's Wildlife Adventures: The Old Mill Pond. Knott, Simon, illus. 2013. 24p. pap. (978-1-910053-64-5(3)) Legend Pr.

Corns, Charles R. Donald Ditz & the Red Tiger, 1 vol. 2010. 64p. pap. 19.95 (978-1-4512-2193-0(2)) America Star Bks.

Corsetto, Danielle. Adventure Time - Seeing Red. 2014. lib. bdg. 23.30 (978-0-606-35465-3(4)) Turtleback Bks.

—Adventure Time Volume 1: Playing with Fire (Color Edition) 2016. lib. bdg. 26.95 (978-0-606-38733-0(1)) Turtleback Bks.

—Pixel Princesses, Vol. 2. Sterling, Zack, illus. 2013. (Adventure Time Ser.: 2). (ENG.). 160p. (J). (gr. 3). pap. 11.99 (978-1-60886-329-7(8)) Boom! Studios.

Cortright, Angel. The Miss Adventure of Animals & Their Short Stories. 2013. 28p. pap. 24.95 (978-1-62709-063-6(0)) America Star Bks.

Corwin, Katherine. The River of Glass. Jasuna, Aija, illus. 2009. 24p. (J). 14.95 (978-1-60131-002-6(1), Castlebridge Bks.) Big Tent Bks.

Corwin, Susan Simon. The Cryptic Cat. Corwin, Stuart, illus. 2006. 99p. (YA). (978-0-9790632-0-6(5)) Lucky Duck Designs.

Cory'S Club Staff. The Adventures of Cory: Lessons in Disobedience. 2010. 48p. pap. 17.49 (978-1-4490-6131-9(1)) AuthorHouse.

Las Cosas de la Cocina. (SPA.). 24p. 7.95 (978-84-488-1107-5(0)) Beascoa, Ediciones S.A. ESP. Dist: Distribooks, Inc.

Cosby, Sam & Metzger, Clancy. Ceruladons: Blue dreams rain to Tears. 2008. 304p. pap. 18.95 (978-0-595-52400-6(1)) iUniverse, Inc.

Cosentino, Ralph. Batman: The Story of the Dark Knight. Cosentino, Ralph, illus. 2008. (ENG., Illus.). 40p. (J). (gr. -1-2). 16.99 (978-0-670-06255-3(3), Viking Books for Young Readers) Penguin Young Readers Group.

Cosper, Andy. The Adventures of Drew Kreeger: Book 1. 2008. 56p. pap. 14.95 (978-1-4327-3320-9(6)) Outskirts Pr., Inc.

Cossi, Olga. Playing Your Heart Out. 2013. 138p. pap. 9.95 (978-1-938083-21-1(0)) Silver Knight Publishing, LLC.

Cosson, M. J. Sherlock Holmes & the Adventure at the Abbey Grange. 2nd rev. ed. 2010. pap. 39.62 (978-0-7613-6957-8(0)) Lerner Publishing Group.

—Sherlock Holmes & the Adventure of the Blue Gem. 3rd rev. ed. 2010. pap. 39.62 (978-0-7613-6959-2(7)) Lerner Publishing Group.

—Sherlock Holmes & the Adventure of the Speckled Band. 5th rev. ed. 2010. pap. 39.62 (978-0-7613-6962-2(7)) Lerner Publishing Group.

—Sherlock Holmes & the Adventure of the Sussex Vampire. 6th rev. ed. 2010. pap. 39.62 (978-0-7613-6963-9(5)) Lerner Publishing Group.

Costantino, Eric. Beeboo Bear Dreamed A Dream. 2004. 31p. pap. 24.95 (978-1-4137-3649-6(1)) PublishAmerica, Inc.

Costelli, Donna Aka: Az-U-C-It. Meet Silly Sammy. 2011. 28p. pap. 24.95 (978-1-4626-4034-8(6)) America Star Bks.

Costello, Judi. Gertrude & the Creature. Bouthyette, Valerie, illus. 2008. 28p. pap. 24.95 (978-1-60672-737-9(0)) America Star Bks.

Costley, Kirk. Custer Brown in Marshmallow Madness. Firpo, Ethan, illus. 2012. 34p. pap. 15.95 (978-1-893075-85-6(0)) Spirit Pr., LLC.

Cote, Denis. Descente Aux Enfers. 2003. (Roman Plus Ser.). (FRE.). 160p. (YA). (gr. 8-18). pap. (978-2-89021-208-4(4)) Diffusion du livre Mirabel (DLM).

—La Foret aux Cent Perils. Poulin, Stephane, tr. 2003. (Roman Jeunesse Ser.). (FRE., Illus.). 96p. (J). (gr. 4-7). pap. (978-2-89021-647-1(0)) Diffusion du livre Mirabel (DLM).

—Un Parfum de Mystere. 2003. (Premier Roman Ser.). (Illus.). 64p. (J). (gr. 2-5). pap. (978-2-89021-352-4(8)) Diffusion du livre Mirabel (DLM).

Cote, Denis & Poulin, Stephane, eds. Les Otages de la Terreur. 2003. (Roman Jeunesse Ser.). (Illus.). 96p. (YA). (gr. 4-7). pap. (978-2-89021-341-8(2)) Diffusion du livre Mirabel (DLM).

Cote, Jenny. The Ark, the Reed & the Fire Cloud: The Amazing Tales of Max & Liz Book One, 2 bks, Bk 1. 2008. (Amazing Tales of Max & Liz Ser.: 1). (ENG., Illus.). 432p. (J). (gr. 5-11). pap. 16.99 (978-0-89957-198-0(0), Living Ink Bks.) AMG Pubs.

Cotler, Amelia. Breakfast with Bigfoot. Swinford, Charles, illus. 2013. 30p. pap. 11.95 (978-1-61876-017-3(3)) Black Oak Media, Inc.

Cotter, Bill. Don't Push the Button! A Christmas Adventure. 2017. (ENG.). 22p. (J). bds. 8.99 **(978-1-4926-5704-0(2))**; bds. 6.99 **(978-1-4926-5705-7(0))** Sourcebooks, Inc. (Sourcebooks Jabberwocky).

Cotton, Peter B. When Jungle Jim Comes to Visit Fred the Snake. Lemaire, Bonnie, illus. 2013. 48p. 24.95 (978-0-9883370-4-6(5)) Fig & The Vine, LLC, The.

Cottrell-Bentley, Lisa M. Wright on Time: Collection 1. Bauerle, Tanja, illus. 2012. 376p. pap. 19.99 (978-1-937848-00-2(0)) Do Life Right, Inc.

—Wright on Time: Minnesota. Bauerle, Tanja, illus. 2012. 126p. pap. 12.99 (978-1-937848-02-6(7)) Do Life Right, Inc.

Couloumbis, Audrey. Maude March on the Run! Or Trouble Is Her Middle Name. 2008. (Maude March Ser.). (ENG., Illus.). 320p. (J). (gr. 3-7). pap. 7.99 (978-0-375-83248-2(3), Yearling) Random Hse. Children's Bks.

—The Misadventures of Maude March: Or Trouble Rides a Fast Horse. 2007. (Illus.). 295p. (gr. 3-7). 18.00 (978-0-7569-7770-2(3)) Perfection Learning Corp.

—The Misadventures of Maude March: Or Trouble Rides a Fast Horse. 2007. (Maude March Ser.). (ENG., Illus.). 320p. (J). (gr. 3-7). 7.99 (978-0-375-83247-5(5), Yearling) Random Hse. Children's Bks.

Coulson-Staak, Louise. Clarisse the Cow: A Circus Adventure. 2012. 28p. pap. 12.50 (978-1-61897-735-9(0), Strategic Bk. Publishing) Strategic Book Publishing & Rights Agency (SBPRA).

Coulton, Mia. Danny Can Sort. Coulton, Mia, photos by. 2003. (ENG., Illus.). pap. 5.35 (978-0-9720295-6-8(7)) Maryruth Bks., Inc.

—Danny's Big Adventure. Coulton, Mia, photos by. 2004. (ENG., Illus.). per. 9.95 (978-0-9746475-0-0(0)) Maryruth Bks., Inc.

—Danny's Timeline. Coulton, Mia, photos by. 2004. (ENG., Illus.). pap. 5.35 (978-0-9746475-2-4(7)) Maryruth Bks., Inc.

Counts, Monika, illus. Alabama Countdown to Touchdown. 2010. (Countdown to Touchdown Ser.). 20p. (J). 14.95 (978-1-61524-080-7(2), Intervisual/Piggy Toes) Bendon, Inc.

—Florida Countdown to Touchdown. 2010. (Countdown to Touchdown Ser.). 20p. 14.95 (978-1-61524-082-1(9), Intervisual/Piggy Toes) Bendon, Inc.

—LSU Countdown to Touchdown. 2010. (Countdown to Touchdown Ser.). 20p. 14.95 (978-1-61524-081-4(0), Intervisual/Piggy Toes) Bendon, Inc.

Courage, Nick. The Loudness: A Novel. 2015. (ENG.). 336p. (J). (gr. 3-7). 15.99 (978-1-63220-414-1(2), Sky Pony Pr.) Skyhorse Publishing Co., Inc.

Courtauld, Sarah. Monkeys Internet-Referenced. 2009. (First Reading Level 3 Ser.). 48p. (J). 6.99 (978-0-7945-2290-2(4), Usborne) EDC Publishing.

Courtenay, L. A. Space Penguins Cosmic Crash! Davies, James, illus. 2015. (Space Penguins Ser.). (ENG.). 112p. (gr. 2-3). lib. bdg. 22.65 (978-1-4342-9785-3(3)) Stone Arch Bks.

—Space Penguins Galaxy Race! Davies, James, illus. 2015. (Space Penguins Ser.). (ENG.). 112p. (gr. 2-3). lib. bdg. 22.65 (978-1-4342-9783-9(7)) Stone Arch Bks.

—Space Penguins Meteor Madness! Davies, James, illus. 2015. (Space Penguins Ser.). (ENG.). 112p. (gr. 2-3). lib. bdg. 22.65 (978-1-4342-9782-2(9)) Stone Arch Bks.

—Space Penguins Star Attack! Davies, James, illus. 2015. (Space Penguins Ser.). (ENG.). 112p. (gr. 2-3). lib. bdg. 22.65 (978-1-4342-9784-6(5)) Stone Arch Bks.

Courtenay, Lucy. Space Penguins. Davies, James, illus. 2015. (Space Penguins Ser.). (ENG.). 112p. (gr. 2-3). 90.60 (978-1-4965-0255-1(8), Space Penguins) Stone Arch Bks.

Courtin, Thierry. Decouvre les contraires Avec. (FRE.). pap. (978-2-09-202276-4(8)) Editions Rouge et Or.

Courtney, Kateri. Welby & the Knobby King. 2003. pap. 14.95 (978-0-9743588-0-2(0)) Castlegate Pr.

Courtney, Suzanne Gene. Florence Flies Alone: An Alliterative Airline Adventure. 2013. 24p. pap. 13.50 (978-1-62212-902-7(4), Strategic Bk. Publishing) Strategic Book Publishing & Rights Agency (SBPRA).

Cousins, Lucy. Maisy Goes to the Movies: A Maisy First Experiences Book. Cousins, Lucy, illus. 2014. (Maisy Ser.). (ENG., Illus.). 32p. (J). (gr. -1-2). 6.99 (978-0-7636-7237-9(8)) Candlewick Pr.

—La Nochebuena de Maisy. 2004.Tr. of Maisy's Christmas Eve. (SPA., Illus.). 32p. (J). 16.99 (978-84-8488-106-3(7)) Serres, Ediciones, S. L. ESP. Dist: Lectorum Pubns., Inc.

—Suenos de Colores. 2004.Tr. of Maisy's Rainbow Dream. (SPA., Illus.). 32p. (J). 18.99 (978-84-8488-108-7(3)) Serres, Ediciones, S. L. ESP. Dist: Lectorum Pubns., Inc.

Coutinho, Lucy M. The Rangers of Andor: The Beginning. 2011. 278p. pap. 27.95 (978-1-4626-1014-3(5)) America Star Bks.

Coveleskie, Sally & Goodrich, Peter. Henry the Steinway Tours the World. Friedman, Laura, illus. 2005. (Henry the Steinway Ser.: 3). 32p. (J). (gr. -1-3). 15.95 (978-0-9729427-8-2(5)) Yorkville Pr.

Coven, Wanda. Heidi Heckelbeck & the Magic Puppy. 2017. (Heidi Heckelbeck Ser.: 20). lib. bdg. 16.00 **(978-0-606-40205-7(5))** Turtleback Bks.

—Heidi Heckelbeck Tries Out for the Team. 2017. (Heidi Heckelbeck Ser.: 19). lib. bdg. 16.00 **(978-0-606-39741-4(8))** Turtleback Bks.

Coverly, Dave. Night of the Living Worms: A Speed Bump & Slingshot Misadventure. Coverly, Dave, illus. 2016. (Speed Bump & Slingshot Misadventure Ser.: 1). (ENG., Illus.). 121p. (J). (gr. 2-5). 16.00 (978-0-606-39299-0(8)) Turtleback Bks.

Covey, Ken. The Adventures of a Little Boy Named Kenny. 2008. 68p. pap. 10.95 (978-1-4327-3110-6(6)) Outskirts Pr., Inc.

Covey, S. K. The Road to Rincon, 1 vol. 2010. 40p. 24.95 (978-1-4489-4929-8(7)) PublishAmerica, Inc.

Coville, Bruce. Always October. 2012. (ENG.). 384p. (J). (gr. 3-7). 16.99 (978-0-06-089095-7(9)) HarperCollins Pubs.

—Cursed. 2016. (Enchanted Files Ser.: 1). lib. bdg. 17.20 (978-0-606-38460-5(X)) Turtleback Bks.

—Diary of a Mad Brownie. 2015. (Enchanted Files Ser.). (ENG., Illus.). 256p. (J). (gr. 3-7). lib. bdg. 19.99 (978-0-385-39248-8(6), Random Hse. Bks. for Young Readers) Random Hse. Children's Bks.

—Goblins on the Prowl. 2015. (ENG., Illus.). 272p. (J). (gr. 3-7). 17.99 (978-1-4169-1440-2(4), Aladdin) Simon & Schuster Children's Publishing.

—My Teacher Fried My Brains. Pierard, John, illus. 2005. (My Teacher Bks.: 2). (ENG.). 176p. (J). (gr. 3-7). pap. 6.99 (978-1-4169-0332-1(1), Aladdin) Simon & Schuster Children's Publishing.

—My Teacher Glows in the Dark. Pierard, John, illus. 2005. (My Teacher Bks.: 3). (ENG.). 144p. (J). (gr. 3-7). pap. 6.99 (978-1-4169-0333-8(X), Aladdin) Simon & Schuster Children's Publishing.

Coville, Bruce. Trolled. Kidby, Paul, illus. 2017. (Enchanted Files Ser.: 3). (ENG.). 288p. (J). (gr. 3-7). 16.99 **(978-0-385-39259-4(1)**, Random Hse. Bks. for Young Readers) Random Hse. Children's Bks.

Cowden, Matt. Emma Mcdougal & the Quest for Father Time. Black, Ilene, illus. 2008. 190p. (J). 24.95 (978-0-9799189-0-2(1)) His Work Christian Publishing.

Cowell, Cressida. How to Break a Dragon's Heart. 2012. (How to Train Your Dragon Ser.: 8). (ENG.). 272p. (J). (gr. 3-7). pap. 8.00 (978-0-316-17617-0(6)) Little, Brown Bks. for Young Readers.

—How to Steal a Dragon's Sword. 2012. (How to Train Your Dragon Ser.: 9). (ENG.). 384p. (J). (gr. 3-7). 12.99 (978-0-316-20571-9(0)) Little, Brown Bks. for Young Readers.

Cowey, James. William Snottengrout - Gangor's Reign. 2006. 104p. per. (978-1-84667-006-0(3)) Derwent Pr., The.

—William Snottengrout - Quapta's Revenge. 2006. 104p. per. (978-1-84667-023-7(3)) Derwent Pr., The.

Cowhard, Patricia Ann. B J 's Underground Adventure. 2011. 28p. pap. 15.99 (978-1-4628-5577-3(6)) Xlibris Corp.

Cowley, Joseph. Alice's Adventures in Wonderland by Lewis Carroll: (Adapted by Joseph Cowley) 2012. 102p. pap. 9.95 (978-1-4759-3276-8(6)) iUniverse, Inc.

Cowsert, Sandra. The Continuing Adventures of Tammi & Her Dragon. 2007. 48p. per. 16.95 (978-1-4241-8313-5(8)) America Star Bks.

Cox, Amy. Odetta the Octopus Teacher. 2013. 28p. pap. 24.95 (978-1-63000-491-0(X)) America Star Bks.

Cox, Buddy. Quicksilver Deep 2004. 401p. per. 19.95 (978-0-9709104-3-1(6)) Hickory Tales Publishing.

Cox, Dorothy Ayling. Children's Stories. 2013. 108p. pap. 11.95 (978-1-4787-0220-7(6)) Outskirts Pr., Inc.

Cox, E. J. The Adventures of Koen & Katie: The Case of the Masked Bandits. 2009. 32p. pap. 14.49 (978-1-4490-0576-4(4)) AuthorHouse.

Cox Gray, Marjorie. Bucky's Adventures. Griffin, Marlin, illus. 2008. 100p. pap. 28.99 (978-1-4389-2645-2(6)) AuthorHouse.

Cox, Jon, illus. Crazy Man & the Plums. 2005. (Wind River Stories Ser.). (ENG & ARP.). 32p. (J). 14.95 (978-0-9759806-1-3(0)) Painted Pony, Inc.

Cox, Joseph J. Grobar & the Mind Control Potion. Becker, Rebecca J., illus. 2005. 168p. (J). per. 9.95 (978-0-9764659-3-5(0)) Suckerfish Bks.

Cox, Judy. The Case of the Purloined Professor, 0 vols. Rayyan, Omar, illus. 2009. (Tails of Frederick & Ishbu Ser.: 0). (ENG.). 256p. (J). (gr. 5-7). 16.99 (978-0-7614-5544-8(2), 9780761455448, Amazon Children's Publishing) Amazon Publishing.

—The Mystery of the Burmese Bandicoot, 1 vol. Rayyan, Omar, illus. 2007. (Tails of frederick & Ishbu Ser.). (ENG.). 224p. (J). (gr. 5-9). lib. bdg. 16.99 (978-0-7614-5376-5(8)) Marshall Cavendish Corp.

—The Mystery of the Burmese Bandicoot. 2012. 254p. (gr. 4-6). pap. 15.95 (978-1-4759-3838-8(1)) iUniverse, Inc.

Cox, M. M. The Condemned. 2016. (ENG., Illus.). 274p. (J). pap. (978-0-908325-23-8(1)) Bluewood Publishing, Ltd.

—Undercover Wiseguy. 2013. 218p. pap. (978-1-927220-28-3(9)) Bluewood Publishing, Ltd.

Cox, Michael. Johnny Catbiscuit & the Stolen Secrets! Dunn, Gary, illus. 2008. (Johnny Catbiscuit Ser.). (ENG.). 160p. (J). (gr. 2-4). pap. 9.95 (978-1-4052-3739-0(2)) Egmont Bks., Ltd. GBR. Dist: Independent Pubs. Group.

Cox, Sarah Webster. The Adventures of Willy & Tilly. 2013. 16p. pap. 12.99 (978-1-4669-7957-4(7)) Trafford Publishing.

Cox, Stephen Angus. The Dare Boys of 1776. 2004. reprint ed. pap. 1.99 (978-1-4192-5856-5(7)); pap. 15.95 (978-1-4191-5856-8(2)) Kessinger Publishing, LLC.

Cox, Steve, illus. Is That You, Monster? Check Inside the Secret Pockets If You Dare! 2013. (ENG.). 22p. (J). (gr. -1-1). 12.99 (978-0-7641-6608-2(5)) Barron's Educational Series, Inc.

Coyle, Carmela Lavigna. Do Princesses & Super Heroes Hit the Trails? A National Park Adventure, Vol. 2016. (ENG., Illus.). 32p. (J). (gr. -1-12). 15.95 (978-1-63076-244-5(X)) Muddy Boots Pr.

Cr. Adventures of Jenni & Jake. 2011. 28p. pap. 12.99 (978-1-4568-8677-6(0)) Xlibris Corp.

Crabbe, Kay. The Pearl-Shell Diver: A Story of Adventure from the Torres Strait. 2016. (ENG.). 192p. (J). (gr. 4-8). 11.99 (978-1-76029-047-4(5)) Allen & Unwin AUS. Dist: Independent Pubs. Group.

Crabtree, Zona Mae. The Travelers. 2004. (Corn Cave Ser.: 2). (Illus.). 155p. (YA). per. 8.00 (978-0-9726826-1-9(9)) Owl Hollow Publishing.

—White Dove. 2005. (Corn Cave Ser.: 3). (ENG., Illus.). (YA). per. 8.00 (978-0-9726826-2-6(7)) Owl Hollow Publishing.

Cracknell, Sharon. Pringles, Visas & a Glow in the Dark Jesus. 2015. (ENG., Illus.). 251p. mass mkt. 13.95 (978-1-78455-747-8(1), b3c2495e-91c0-4b51-905a-caa4b6e9527e) Austin, Stan AUS. Dist: Bookmasters Distribution.

Craig, Bobby & Manifold, Delwyn. The Learning Adventures of Spot. 2011. 28p. pap. 24.95 (978-1-4560-3110-7(4)) America Star Bks.

Craig-Gaddis, Lora. Elsie & Pooka Stories of the Sabbats & Seasons. 2008. 126p. pap. 43.18 (978-0-557-01530-6(8)) Lulu Pr., Inc.

Craig, Joe. Jimmy Coates: Assassin? 2005. 224p. (J). (gr. 5-18). 15.99 *(978-0-06-077263-5(8))* HarperCollins Pubs.
—Jimmy Coates: Killer. 2007. 261p. (J). (gr. 5-9). 15.99 *(978-0-06-077266-6(2))* HarperCollins Pubs.
—Jimmy Coates: Assassin? 2006. 218p. (J). (gr. 5-9). per. 5.99 *(978-0-06-077265-9(4),* Harper Trophy) HarperCollins Pubs.
Craig, Joni. The Fish from the Cherryville Grill. 2013. 30p. pap. 13.95 *(978-1-940224-02-2(0))* Taylor and Seale Publishing, LLC.
—A Shoulder for Oscar. Haddad-Hamwi, Louise, illus. 2013. 40p. pap. 11.95 *(978-0-9887836-6-9(5))* Taylor and Seale Publishing, LLC.
Craik, Maria Dinah. The Little Lame Prince. 2008. 120p. 21.99 *(978-0-554-31012-1(0))* Creative Media Partners, LLC.
Craine, E. J. Airplane Boys at Belize. 2003. (ENG.). 224p. (J). pap. 13.95 *(978-1-55753-323-4(7),* 451f8175-099e-4a08-95b9-2fe962b09c95) Purdue Univ. Pr.
—Airplane Boys at Platinum River. 2003. (ENG.). 200p. (J). pap. 13.95 *(978-1-55753-320-3(2),* b9d659a0-68ba-48a1-a242-99e8f0499774) Purdue Univ. Pr.
—Airplane Boys Discover the Secrets of Cuzco. 2003. (ENG.). 246p. (J). pap. 13.95 *(978-1-55753-318-0(0),* c2a914a5-1d24-4220-b51b-b0f6d6ddfdfe) Purdue Univ. Pr.
—Airplane Boys Flying to Amy-Ran Fastness. 2003. (ENG.). 245p. (J). pap. 13.95 *(978-1-55753-319-7(9),* dace6a4f-5096-44da-9d37-8e4e29b8bd1c) Purdue Univ. Pr.
—Airplane Boys in the Black Woods. 2003. (ENG.). 209p. (J). pap. 13.95 *(978-1-55753-322-7(9),* d34bb521-9c84-4a95-a288-d1a9a2b27b27) Purdue Univ. Pr.
—Airplane Boys on the Border Line. 2003. (ENG.). 246p. (J). pap. 13.95 *(978-1-55753-316-6(4),* d264e88f-e170-4467-b25f-1696b7278137) Purdue Univ. Pr.
—Airplane Boys with the Revolutionists in Bolivia. 2003. (ENG.). 201p. (J). pap. 13.95 *(978-1-55753-321-0(0),* 0bc79ba3-a232-40ec-b30c-db35be518b4d) Purdue Univ. Pr.
Crane, Jordan. Keep Our Secrets. 2012. (ENG., Illus.). 32p. (J). (gr. -1-4). bds. 15.95 *(978-1-936365-52-4(9))* McSweeney's Publishing.
Crane, Phyllis F. Anything but the Most Boring Place on Earth. 2011. 174p. pap. 24.95 *(978-1-4560-6802-8(4))* America Star Bks.
Crane, Venessa. Duck down Under. 2008. 70p. pap. 29.95 *(978-1-4092-2376-4(0))* Lulu Pr., Inc.
Craven, Georgina. Adventures & Rhymes with Grandmother. 2006. (Illus.). 76p. pap. *(978-1-84401-648-8(X))* Athena Pr.
Crawford, Hannah. The Fight for Light by Hannah Crawford. 2012. (Illus.). 86p. pap. 8.50 *(978-1-78035-335-7(9),* Fastprint Publishing) Upfront Publishing Ltd. GBR. Dist: Printondemand-worldwide.com.
—The Fight with Darkness. 2013. (Illus.). 79p. pap. 8.49 *(978-1-78035-586-3(6),* Fastprint Publishing) Upfront Publishing Ltd. GBR. Dist: Printondemand-worldwide.com.
Crawford-Haynes, Debra. Bedtime with Julian. 2010. 32p. 16.99 *(978-1-4520-6943-2(3))* AuthorHouse.
Crawford, John. Life in Honeysuckle Valley the Adventur. 2006. pap. 14.95 *(978-1-4327-0104-8(5))* Outskirts Pr., Inc.
Crawford, K. Michael. The Mystery of Journeys Crowne-an Adventure Drawing Game. Crawford, K. Michael, illus. 2008. (Illus.). 52p. pap. 14.95 *(978-0-9817940-0-6(9))* Virtualbookworm.com Publishing, Inc.
Crawford, Marie. Nutmeg, Ginger & Little Joan. 2012. 24p. pap. 17.99 *(978-1-62230-186-7(2))* Salem Author Services.
Crawford, Ruth. Squirrel Boy & Brad: Solve a Mystery. 2010. 24p. pap. 12.99 *(978-1-4490-1612-8(X))* AuthorHouse.
—Squirrel Boy & Brad Become Friends. 2009. 24p. pap. 12.99 *(978-1-4490-1533-6(6))* AuthorHouse.
Crawford, Tracie. Bart the Blue Bee. 2012. 40p. pap. 19.57 *(978-1-4669-4026-0(3))* Trafford Publishing.
Cray, Jordan. Danger Com 4 Hot Pursuit. 2009. (Danger. com Ser.: 4). (ENG.). 192p. (YA). (gr. 7-7). pap. 9.99 *(978-1-4169-9849-5(7),* Simon Pulse) Simon Pulse.
Cray, Ronda. What's the Matter Cat? 2008. 24p. pap. 24.95 *(978-1-60672-674-7(9))* America Star Bks.
Crayon, Paula. Wrong Dog in the Right Bathroom. 2011. 40p. (gr. -1). pap. 18.50 *(978-1-4567-6344-2(X))* AuthorHouse.
Creal, Nancy & Taylor, Ann Creal. Lydia Ann & Scraggles: The Adventures of a Girl & Her Dog. Taylor, Ann Creal, illus. 2013. (Illus.). 28p. (J). 12.00 *(978-0-9800059-4-3(9))* Taylor, Ann.
Creech, Sharon. Chasing Redbird. 261p. (J). (gr. 4-6). pap. 4.95 *(978-0-8072-1532-6(5),* Listening Library) Random Hse. Audio Publishing Group.
—Chasing Redbird. 2012. (J). (gr. 3-6). lib. bdg. 17.20 *(978-0-613-06536-8(0),* Turtleback) Turtleback Bks.
Creed, Elizabeth. Millie's Merry Christmas. 2011. 26p. (J). pap. 12.95 *(978-1-4327-0580-0(6))* Outskirts Pr., Inc.
Creed, Julie. Danny the Dump Truck. Hastings, Ken, illus. 2003. per. *(978-0-9728181-0-0(3))* Creed, Julie.
Creek, Silent. All the Ice of Afric. 2009. 160p. 22.95 *(978-1-4401-2118-0(4))* iUniverse, Inc.
Cregg, R. J. Batman & Robin's Training Day. 2017. (Batman 8X8 Storybooks Ser.). lib. bdg. 13.55 ***(978-0-606-40217-0(9))*** Turtleback Bks.
Creighton, B. L. Max's Seaworthy Adventure. 2009. 28p. pap. 13.99 *(978-1-4389-7329-6(2))* AuthorHouse.
Creighton, Patricia L. Chirpie the Blue Jay: A True Story. 2008. 13p. pap. 24.95 *(978-1-60610-291-6(5))* America Star Bks.
Cremer, Andrea. The Turncoat's Gambit. 2016. (Inventor's Secret Ser.: 3). (ENG.). 336p. (YA). (gr. 7). 18.99 *(978-0-399-16425-5(1),* Philomel Bks.) Penguin Young Readers Group.
Crenshaw, Glenda. Friends of the Enchanted Forest: How they Save Christmas. 2011. 28p. pap. 15.47 *(978-1-4520-0512-6(5))* AuthorHouse.
Crews, G. S. The Adventures of Mercy Saint. 2011. 258p. pap. 15.00 *(978-0-9795236-5-6(6))* Crews Pubns., LLC.
Crilley, Mark. The Battle for Boach's Keep Vol. 7. 2004. (Illus.). 144p. pap. 14.95 *(978-1-57989-064-3(4))* Sirius Entertainment, Inc.
—Winter. Crilley, Mark, illus. 2008. (Miki Falls Ser.: 4). (ENG., Illus.). 176p. (YA). (gr. 8-12). pap. 8.99 *(978-0-06-084619-0(4))* HarperCollins Pubs.
Crilley, Paul. The Osiris Curse: A Tweed & Nightingale Adventure. 2013. (ENG.). 287p. (J). (gr. 7). 17.99 *(978-1-61614-857-7(8))* Prometheus Bks., Pubs.
Croall, Marie. Ali Baba: Fooling the Forty Thieves [an Arabian Tale]. Hilinski, Clint, illus. 2009. (Graphic Myths & Legends Ser.). (ENG.). 48p. (gr. 4-8). pap. 8.95 *(978-1-58013-887-1(X))* Lerner Publishing Group.
Croce, Warren. Opposite Day. 2007. (ENG.). 28p. per. 14.90 *(978-1-4303-0659-7(9))* Lulu Pr., Inc.
Crocker, Carter & Swift, Jonathan. The Last of the Gullivers. 2012. (ENG.). 224p. (J). (gr. 4-7). 16.99 *(978-0-399-24231-1(7),* Philomel Bks.) Penguin Young Readers Group.
Crockett, Johns. Harold et le crayon Rose. pap. 13.95 *(978-2-266-09592-1(7))* Presses Pocket FRA. Dist: Distribooks, Inc.
Crockett, S. D. After the Snow. 2012. (After the Snow Ser.: 1). (ENG.). 304p. (YA). (gr. 7-12). 16.99 *(978-0-312-64169-6(9))* Feiwel & Friends.
—After the Snow. 2013. (After the Snow Ser.: 1). (ENG.). 320p. (YA). (gr. 7-12). pap. 9.99 *(978-1-250-01676-8(2))* Square Fish.
Crockett, S. R. The Surprising Adventures of Sir Toady L. 2005. pap. 30.95 *(978-1-4179-5884-9(7))* Kessinger Publishing, LLC.
Crofoot, Betty & Arledge, Roo. Battle for the Multiverse - My Genie & Me Series Book 3. 2013. 92p. pap. 8.95 *(978-1-60862-489-8(7))* E-BookTime LLC.
—The Great Celebration Ceremony - My Genie & Me Series Book 2. 2012. 84p. pap. 8.95 *(978-1-60862-430-0(7))* E-BookTime LLC.
Crofoot, Nancy. Sandy & Mitzi: Off to the Zoo. Rawal, Ishita, illus. 2013. 48p. pap. 24.95 *(978-1-62709-868-7(2))* America Star Bks.
—Sandy & Mitzi: Their First Adventure, 1 vol. Rawat, Tania, illus. 2009. 31p. pap. 24.95 *(978-1-60836-707-8(X))* America Star Bks.
Crofoot, Nancy L. Off to the Fair: Another Sandy & Mitzi Adventure. 2011. 24p. pap. 24.95 *(978-1-4560-1027-0(1))* America Star Bks.
Crompton, Paul. Remarkable for Short. 2005. 113p. pap. 19.95 *(978-1-4241-0287-7(1))* PublishAmerica, Inc.
Crompton, Richmal. Just Jimmy Again. Henry, Thomas, illus. 2003. (ENG.). 256p. (J). 16.95 *(978-0-333-71231-3(5))* Macmillan Pubs., Ltd. GBR. Dist: Trafalgar Square Publishing.
—William the Bad. Henry, Thomas & Garbutt, Chris, illus. 2016. (Just William Ser.: 11). (ENG.). 352p. (J). (gr. 4-7). pap. 11.99 *(978-1-5098-0522-8(2))* Pan Macmillan GBR. Dist: Independent Pubs. Group.
Cronin, Bernie. One Step Ahead: An Adventure in Jordan. 2010. (ENG.). 52p. pap. *(978-1-84748-791-9(2))* Athena Pr.
—We're Coming Home. 2004. 56p. pap. *(978-1-84401-253-4(0))* Athena Pr.
Cronin, Doreen. The Chicken Squad: The First Misadventure. 2015. (Chicken Squad Ser.: 1). lib. bdg. 17.20 *(978-0-606-37884-0(7))* Turtleback Bks.
—Into the Wild. 2017. (Chicken Squad Ser.: 3). lib. bdg. 17.20 ***(978-0-606-40204-0(7))*** Turtleback Bks.
Cronin, Doreen. The Legend of Diamond Lil. Cornell, Kevin, illus. 2013. (ENG.). 144p. (J). (gr. 1-5). pap. 5.99 *(978-0-06-177997-8(0))* HarperCollins Pubs.
Cronin, Susan L. Gidget Goes Away. 2006. 54p. pap. 16.95 *(978-1-4137-9878-4(0))* PublishAmerica, Inc.
Crook, Mackenzie. Ragetti's Secret Diary. 2008. (ENG.). 96p. (J). 9.99 *(978-1-4231-0931-0(7))* Disney Pr.
Crosby, Vernon H. The Adventures of Scurry Little: Lost in my Dream. l.t. ed. 2004. 40p. (J). per. 10.95 *(978-1-59196-819-1(4))* Instant Pub.
Croskerry, Frank J. Our Land Is the Sky: The Adventures of Jimmy Fastwing. 2011. 88p. (gr. 4-6). pap. 9.95 *(978-1-4620-2839-9(X))* iUniverse, Inc.
Cross, F. J. Beneath the Banner: Being Narratives of Noble Lives & Brave Deeds. 2007. (ENG.). 170p. per. 19.99 *(978-1-4346-4355-1(7));* 180p. per. 21.99 *(978-1-4346-4356-8(5))* Creative Media Partners, LLC.
Cross, Frances. Boy the Witch & the Blobber 1. 2007. (Blobber Ser.). (Illus.). 98p. pap. *(978-1-84167-560-2(1))* Ransom Publishing Ltd.
—Butternut Blobber & the Blue Jade. 2007. (Blobber Ser.). (ENG.). 84p. pap. *(978-1-84167-561-9(X))* Ransom Publishing Ltd.
—The Mystery of the Green Elephant. 2007. (Blobber Ser.). (ENG.). 84p. (J). per. *(978-1-84167-559-6(8))* Ransom Publishing Ltd.
Cross, Gillian. The Odyssey. Packer, Neil, illus. 2012. (ENG.). 178p. (J). (gr. 3-7). 19.99 *(978-0-7636-4791-9(8))* Candlewick Pr.
Cross, Julie. Timestorm: A Tempest Novel. 2014. (Tempest Trilogy Ser.: 3). (ENG.). 368p. (YA). (gr. 9-12). 18.99 *(978-0-312-56891-7(6),* 9780312568917, St. Martin's Griffin) St. Martin's Pr.
Cross, P. W. The Idea Miners: The Lost Lake Dig. 2009. 288p. (J). pap. 7.99 *(978-0-9662800-8-1(3))* Appalachian Hse.
Cross, Sarah. Tear You Apart. 2015. (ENG.). 384p. (YA). (gr. 9-12). 17.99 *(978-1-5124-0175-2(7),* Carolrhoda Lab™) Lerner Publishing Group.
Crossan, Sarah. Breathe. (Breathe Ser.: 1). (ENG.). (YA). (gr. 9). 2013. 400p. pap. 9.99 *(978-0-06-211870-7(6))* 2012. 384p. 17.99 *(978-0-06-211869-1(2))* HarperCollins Pubs. (Greenwillow Bks.).
Crossley-Holland, Kevin. The Seeing Stone. unabr. ed. 2004. (Young Adult Cassette Librariestm Ser.). 352p. (J). (gr. 6-18). pap. 48.00 incl. audio *(978-0-8072-0999-8(6),* S YA 327 SP, Listening Library) Random Hse. Audio Publishing Group.
Croteau, Marie-Danielle. La Grande Aventure d'un Petit Mouton Noir. 2004. (FRE., Illus.). (J). (gr. -1-3). spiral bd. *(978-0-616-07260-8(0))* Canadian National Institute for the Blind/Institut National Canadien pour les Aveugles.
Crouch, Kathryn L. Nibbly Noshers. 2010. (Illus.). 44p. pap. 16.99 *(978-1-4490-9448-5(1))* AuthorHouse.
Crow, E. J. The Eye Pocket. 2006. (Fantastic Society of Peculiar Adventures Ser.). (ENG., Illus.). 48p. (J). (gr. 2-4). per. *(978-1-933255-17-0(X))* DNA Pr.
Crow, Gary & Crow, Brock. JimJim Meets PosterGuy. 2006. 100p. (J). pap. 14.95 *(978-0-9759621-5-2(9))* Koenisha Pubns.
Crowe, Duane E. Catfish Annie to the Rescue. Ackison, Wendy Wassink, illus. 2004. (Back River Adventures of Catfish Annie Ser.). 48p. (J). (gr. k-5). *(978-0-9672882-0-8(7))* Back River Company, The, LLC.
Crowe, Ellie & Fry, Juliet. HOKU the Stargazer: The Exciting Pirate Adventure! Petosa-Sigel, Kristi, illus. 2009. (ENG.). 28p. (J). *(978-1-59700-601-9(7))* Island Heritage Publishing.
Crowell, Marcia. The Adventures of Little Blackie & Friends. 2009. 36p. pap. 15.99 *(978-1-4389-0386-6(3))* AuthorHouse.
Crowell, Peter Thomas. Haunted Mountain: The Tales of True Adventure, Book Two. 2006. (J). 19.95 *(978-0-9740290-8-5(4))* Crowell, Peter T. Pubns.
Crowley, James. Monsterland. 2017. (ENG.). 384p. (J). (gr. 5). 16.99 *(978-0-399-17589-3(X),* G.P. Putnam's Sons Books for Young Readers) Penguin Young Readers Group.
Crowley, Kieran Mark. Colm & the Lazarus Key. 2009. (ENG., Illus.). 224p. (J). pap. 14.95 *(978-1-85635-646-6(9))* Mercier Pr., Ltd., The IRL. Dist: Dufour Editions, Inc.
Crownberry, Ethan. A Fish with a Wish. 2013. 52p. 17.95 *(978-0-9898533-0-9(6))* Jetpack Publishing.
—Johnny Jetpack. 2013. 52p. 17.95 *(978-0-9898533-1-6(4))* Jetpack Publishing.
—Johnny Jetpack. 2012. 84p. pap. 8.95 *(978-1-300-00783-8(4))* Lulu Pr., Inc.
—The Willies. 2013. 52p. 17.95 *(978-0-9898533-2-3(2))* Jetpack Publishing.
—The Willies. 2012. 80p. pap. 10.95 *(978-0-557-96056-9(8))* Lulu.com GBR. Dist: Lulu Pr., Inc.
Crownover, Rebecca. Texas Farm Girl. Daigle, Brian, illus. 2013. (ENG.). (J). (gr. -1-3). 14.95 *(978-1-62086-265-0(4))* Mascot Bks., Inc.
Cruea, Kim. The Adventures Continue for Summer Falls Junior Rangers, 1 vol. 2009. 75p. pap. 19.95 *(978-1-60749-684-7(4))* America Star Bks.
—Summer Falls Junior Rangers: The First Adventures. 2008. 73p. pap. 19.95 *(978-1-60474-552-8(5))* America Star Bks.
Crum, Karen Boyden. Family Angels. 2012. 32p. pap. 19.99 *(978-1-4772-7502-3(9))* AuthorHouse.
Crum, Sally. Race to Moonrise Rev. Carlson, Eric S., illus. 2006. 12.95 *(978-1-932738-31-5(2))* Western Reflections Publishing Co.
Crumbaugh, David. The Primrose Kids. 2006. 81p. pap. 16.95 *(978-1-4241-3250-8(9))* PublishAmerica, Inc.
Crutcher, Chris. Period 8. 2014. (ENG.). 288p. (YA). (gr. 9). pap. 9.99 *(978-0-06-191482-9(7),* Greenwillow Bks.) HarperCollins Pubs.
—Stotan! 2003. (ENG.). 272p. (YA). (gr. 8). pap. 9.99 *(978-0-06-009492-8(3),* Greenwillow Bks.) HarperCollins Pubs.
Cruz De Jesus, Marta. Chosen: By Nature. 2010. 116p. 21.49 *(978-1-4520-3479-9(6));* pap. 10.99 *(978-1-4520-3480-5(X))* AuthorHouse.
Cruz, Kelly De La. Super Boy's Adventurous Imagination: Let your imagination Flow. 2010. 50p. pap. 26.99 *(978-1-4500-3867-6(0))* Xlibris Corp.
Cruz, Wilfredo. Charlie's Box: A Story about a Boy & His Magical Box. 2013. 24p. pap. 24.95 *(978-1-63000-514-6(2))* America Star Bks.
Cry of the Falcon. 2006. 208p. (J). pap. 9.95 *(978-0-9788541-0-2(1))* m.d. hughes.
Crystow, Charisse. Dainty Dee & Lanky Lee. 2012. (ENG.). 26p. (J). pap. 14.95 *(978-1-59713-120-9(2))* Goose River Pr.
Cuartas, Jennifer M. The Adventures of Delilah Doodle: Mealy Bug Stew. 2012. 24p. pap. 24.95 *(978-1-4626-8147-1(6))* America Star Bks.
—So Many Things. 2012. 28p. 24.95 *(978-1-4626-6328-6(1))* America Star Bks.
Cube Kid, Cube. An Unofficial Minecraft Adventure. 2016. (Diary of an 8-Bit Warrior Ser.: 1). (ENG., Illus.). 256p. (J). (gr. 2-5). pap. 9.99 *(978-1-4494-8005-9(5))* Andrews McMeel Publishing.
—Crafting Alliances: An Unofficial Minecraft Adventure. 2017. (Diary of an 8-Bit Warrior Ser.: 3). (ENG.). 256p. (J). 13.99 ***(978-1-4494-8803-1(X))*** Andrews McMeel Publishing.
—Path of the Diamond: An Unofficial Minecraft Adventure. 2017. (Diary of an 8-Bit Warrior Ser.: 4). (ENG.). 256p. (J). 13.99 ***(978-1-4494-8804-8(8));*** pap. 9.99 *(978-1-4494-8009-7(8))* Andrews McMeel Publishing.
Cue, Ian J. The Renewal: First Encounter. 2003. 192p. (YA). per. 9.95 *(978-0-9741989-0-3(0))* Mill Creek Metro Publishing.
Cuentos de Elfos y Gnomos. 2nd ed. 2004. (SPA., Illus.). 128p. *(978-84-9777-013-2(7))* Ediciones Obelisco.
Cuillain, Adam. Zak's King Arthur Adventure. 2014. (ENG., Illus.). 32p. (J). *(978-0-7787-1315-9(6))* Crabtree Publishing Co.
Culbertson, Jan E. The Legend of the Lost Tiki. 2006. 95p. (YA). pap. 13.95 *(978-1-58909-315-7(1))* Bookstand Publishing.
Culici, Tonia. Kiku Gecko & Rainbow Girl. 2012. 44p. pap. 20.45 *(978-1-4525-0584-8(5))* Balboa Pr.
Cullen, Seán. Hamish X & the Cheese Pirates. 2007. (ENG.). 304p. (J). (gr. 7-18). 9.99 *(978-0-14-305311-8(6),* Penguin Canada) Penguin Canada CAN. Dist: Penguin Random Hse. LLC.
—Hamish X & the Hollow Mountain. 2008. (ENG.). 288p. (J). (gr. 7-18). 9.99 *(978-0-14-305312-5(4),* Puffin Canada) Penguin Random House Canada Young Readers CAN. Dist: Penguin Random Hse. LLC.
Cullingworth, Phillip. Naptime Adventures with Sleepy Slump: The Kings New Fence. 2010. (Illus.). 20p. 10.49 *(978-1-4520-0913-1(9))* AuthorHouse.
Cullison, Martha J. The Adventures of the Culli Bear Boys. 2011. 32p. pap. 21.99 *(978-1-4628-8029-4(0))* Xlibris Corp.
Cullum, A. A. Rugly Puffs: The Bear Detective. 2008. 80p. pap. *(978-1-84923-248-7(2))* YouWriteOn.
Cumberland, Dale. Angel Trap. 2012. 166p. (-18). 22.95 *(978-1-4759-5601-6(0));* pap. 12.95 *(978-1-4759-5599-6(5))* iUniverse, Inc.
Cumberland, Wendy. Inkwelo Mountain: A Child's Adventure in Kwa Zulu, South Africa. 2013. 46p. pap. 10.95 *(978-1-62857-135-6(7),* Strategic Bk. Publishing) Strategic Book Publishing & Rights Agency (SBPRA).
Cumming, Hannah. The Red Boat. Cumming, Hannah, illus. 2012. (Child's Play Library). (ENG., Illus.). 32p. (J). *(978-1-84643-493-8(9))* Child's Play International Ltd.
Cummings, Alicia. The Adventures of Jayda. 2010. 44p. pap. 16.99 *(978-1-4520-2564-3(9))* AuthorHouse.
Cummings, Diana M. Hardy. Trimp II Mystic Island. 2012. (ENG.). 60p. pap. 18.95 *(978-1-4327-8925-1(2))* Outskirts Pr., Inc.
Cummings, Lindsay. The Fires of Calderon. 2014. (Balance Keepers Ser.: 1). (ENG.). 352p. (J). (gr. 3-7). 16.99 *(978-0-06-227518-9(6),* Tegen, Katherine Bks) HarperCollins Pubs.
—The Pillars of Ponderay. (Balance Keepers Ser.: 2). (J). (gr. 3-7). 2016. 400p. pap. 6.99 *(978-0-06-227522-6(4))* 2015. (ENG.). 384p. 16.99 *(978-0-06-227521-9(6))* HarperCollins Pubs. (Tegen, Katherine Bks).
—The Traitor of Belltroll. 2016. (Balance Keepers Ser.: 3). (Illus.). 384p. (J). (gr. 3-7). 16.99 *(978-0-06-227524-0(0),* Tegen, Katherine Bks) HarperCollins Pubs.
Cummings, Mag. Fishplates & Frogs. 2007. 272p. per. *(978-1-905529-99-5(6))* Grosvenor Hse. Publishing Ltd.
Cummings, Quasheba Giri. The World's First Submarine. 2008. 20p. pap. 15.49 *(978-1-4389-1273-8(0))* AuthorHouse.
Cummins, Molly. The Jewel of Fez. 2006. 141p. pap. 24.95 *(978-1-4241-1044-5(0))* PublishAmerica, Inc.
Cumyn, Alan. After Sylvia. 2nd ed. 2008. (ENG.). 200p. (J). (gr. 3-7). pap. 8.95 *(978-0-88899-868-2(6))* Groundwood Bks. CAN. Dist: Publishers Group West (PGW).
Cundiff, Joe. Fly to the Moon on a Witch's Broom. 2013. (ENG.). 34p. (J). pap. 15.95 *(978-1-4787-2306-6(8))* Outskirts Pr., Inc.
Cunningham, Ann. The Adventures of Bossie & the Circus. 2009. 20p. pap. 11.99 *(978-1-4389-3947-6(7))* AuthorHouse.
Cunningham, Darrell. The Adventures of Stan: Book One the Awakening. 2011. (Illus.). 80p. (gr. 4-6). pap. 29.00 *(978-1-4567-7918-4(4))* AuthorHouse.
Cunningham, Kay. Bucky: The Adventures of the Dinosaur Cowboy. Wilson, Mary Ann, illus. 2004. 32p. (J). 18.99 *(978-1-57860-173-8(8))* Clerisy Pr.
Cunningham, Mary. Curse of the Bayou. 2007. (Cynthia's Attic Ser.). 157p. (J). per. 9.99 *(978-1-59080-575-6(5))* Echelon Press Publishing.
—Cynthias Attic Magicians Castle. 2009. 158p. pap. 10.99 *(978-1-59080-656-2(5))* Echelon Press Publishing.
Cupper, Karin. More Adventures from Eidland. 2013. 128p. (J). pap. *(978-1-78148-603-0(4))* Grosvenor Hse. Publishing Ltd.
Cureton-Heifner, Donna Lynn. The Adventures of Itsy & Willy Wabbit: In Search of Lillian the Ladybug. 2012. 16p. pap. 24.95 *(978-1-4626-8547-9(1))* America Star Bks.
Curley, Marianne. Broken. 2014. (Avena Ser.). (ENG.). 384p. (YA). (gr. 7). 17.99 *(978-1-61963-168-7(7),* 9781619631687, Bloomsbury USA Childrens) Bloomsbury Publishing USA.
—The Dark. 2005. (Guardians of Time Ser.). (ENG.). 352p. (YA). (gr. 7-12). per. 8.95 *(978-1-58234-664-9(X),* 9781582346649, Bloomsbury USA Childrens) Bloomsbury Publishing USA.
Curlin, Tera. Pat's Mountain, 1 vol. 2010. 16p. 24.95 *(978-1-4489-4356-2(6))* PublishAmerica, Inc.
Curnin, V. J. Millie's Magic Wellies. 2009. (Illus.). 20p. pap. 10.49 *(978-1-4389-8258-8(5))* AuthorHouse.
Curr, Martin. Sharp Claws Learns to Swim. 2010. 26p. pap. 21.99 *(978-1-4535-1414-6(7))* Xlibris Corp.
Curriculum Corporation. Tai Hao Le! 2005. pap. 79.95 incl. audio compact disk *(978-1-86366-402-8(5))* Education Services Australia Ltd. AUS. Dist: Cheng & Tsui Co.
The Curse of the Nile. 2008. (Looney Tunes 8*8 Ser.). 24p. pap. *(978-1-4075-2639-3(1));* pap. *(978-1-4075-2629-4(4))* Parragon, Inc.
Curtatone, Raffaello. The Adventures of Mr Greenwood from Jamaic. 2011. 50p. (J). pap. 9.99 *(978-0-557-91852-2(9))* Lulu Pr., Inc.
Curtis, Alice. A Little Maid of New Orleans. 2011. (Little Maid Ser.). (ENG.). 236p. pap. 12.95 *(978-1-4290-9746-8(9))* Applewood Bks.
Curtis, Christopher Paul. The Madman of Piney Woods. 2016. (ENG.). 363p. (J). (gr. 3-7). lib. bdg. 18.40 *(978-0-606-38061-4(2))* Turtleback Bks.
Curtis, Jennifer. Scute Salute. 2005. (J). pap. *(978-0-9703021-2-0(6))* Captain Caleb Communications.
Curtis, Kelli. Amber & the Fallen Bridge. 2009. 32p. pap. 13.00 *(978-1-60860-631-3(7),* Strategic Bk. Publishing) Strategic Book Publishing & Rights Agency (SBPRA).
Curtis, Shelly. Shellbear's Adventures. 2012. 56p. pap. *(978-1-4602-0601-0(0))* FriesenPress.
Cusack, Dale. Grace & the Drawl. 2008. (Illus.). 169p. pap. 11.95 *(978-1-4357-0926-3(8))* Lulu Pr., Inc.
—Gwen & the Dragon. 2007. (Illus.). 114p. pap. 9.95 *(978-1-4303-1080-8(4))* Lulu Pr., Inc.
Cusack, Geraldine O'Connell. Wrecker's Cove. 2013. 100p. pap. *(978-1-78407-081-6(5))* FeedARead.com.
Cushman, Karen. Grayling's Song. 2016. (ENG.). 224p. (J). (gr. 5-7). 16.99 *(978-0-544-30180-1(3),* Clarion Bks.) Houghton Mifflin Harcourt Trade & Reference Pubs.
—Matilda Huesos. 2004.Tr. of Matilda Bone. (SPA.). (YA). pap. 7.99 *(978-84-348-9080-0(1))* SM Ediciones ESP. Dist: Lectorum Pubns., Inc.
Cussler, Clive. The Adventures of Vin Fiz. Farnsworth, Bill & W, Farnsworth, illus. 2007. (ENG.). 176p. (J). (gr. 3-7). 6.99 *(978-0-14-240774-5(7),* Puffin Books) Penguin Young Readers Group.
Custureri, Mary C. Meet Happy Anderson. 2nd ed. 2013. 68p. pap. 15.95 *(978-0-9887836-1-4(4))* Taylor and Seale Publishing, LLC.
Cuthbert, Jennifer. The Adventures of Lollipop. 2004. 28p. 4.95 *(978-0-9732053-0-5(X))* Peppermint Publishing CAN. Dist: Hushion Hse. Publishing, Ltd.
Cutler, Betty Jackson. The Flight of SaraJane. 2008. 29p. pap. 24.95 *(978-1-60672-025-7(2))* America Star Bks.
—The Flight of SaraJane, 1 vol. 2010. 30p. 24.95 *(978-1-4512-1018-7(3))* PublishAmerica, Inc.
Cutler-Broyles, Teresa. One Eyed Jack. 2013. 190p. pap. *(978-1-908910-51-6(8))* Crooked Cat Publishing.
Cutri, Julia E. Don't Stir the Tea! 2012. (Illus.). 20p. pap. 18.79 *(978-1-4678-8541-6(X))* AuthorHouse.
Cvetkovic, Judith. Mandy & Star's Sheep Ranch Getaway, 1 vol. 2010. 108p. pap. 19.95 *(978-1-4489-5673-9(0))* America Star Bks.
Cyanne Bandanna Kindergartner always Tell the Truth. 2005. (YA). per. *(978-1-59872-133-1(X))* Instant Pub.

Cypess, Leah. Death Marked. 2016. 400p. (YA). (gr. 8). pap. 9.99 (978-0-06-222125-4(6), Greenwillow Bks.) HarperCollins Pubs.

Cyr, Joe. Shadi, the Shadow Who Wanted to Be Free. Owen, Ramon, illus. 2010. 40p. pap. 14.95 (978-1-936343-08-9(8)) Peppertree Pr., The.

Cyr, Lynne G. Drako's ABC Adventures as an Iguana. 2006. (Illus.). 37p. (J). spiral bd. 21.95 (978-0-9774543-0-3(4)) Cyr Design Publishing.

Czubinski, Robert. The Many Adventures of Pig Batter: A Day at the Park, 1 vol. Czubinski, Amber, illus. 2009. 20p. pap. 24.95 (978-1-61546-495-1(6)) America Star Bks.

D' Almfras, Pauline H. Pisi the Cat & His Adventures. 2009. 16p. pap. 12.95 (978-1-60860-111-0(0), Strategic Bk. Publishing) Strategic Book Publishing & Rights Agency (SBPRA).

Da Coll, Ivar. Jose Tomillo, Maria Juana. Da Coll, Ivar, illus. 2004. (SPA., Illus.). 53p. pap. (978-958-04-7662-7(4)) Norma S.A.

Dabrio-Martinez, Mutzai. The Day the Dinosaurs Came to St. Andrew. 2013. 112p. pap. 10.95 (978-1-4759-6077-8(8)) iUniverse, Inc.

D'Adamo, Francesco. My Brother Johnny. 2008. (ENG.). 200p. pap. 16.95 (978-0-9551566-3-2(7)) Aurora Metro Pubns. Ltd. GBR. Dist: Consortium Bk. Sales & Distribution.

Dadey, Debbie. Treasure in Trident City. Avakyan, Tatevik, illus. 2014. (Mermaid Tales Ser.: 8). (ENG.). 128p. (J). (gr. 1-4). pap. 5.99 (978-1-4424-8266-1(4), Aladdin) Simon & Schuster Children's Publishing.

—A Whale of a Tale. Avakyan, Tatevik, illus. 2012. (Mermaid Tales Ser.: 3). (ENG.). 128p. (J). (gr. 1-4). 14.99 (978-1-4424-5318-0(4)); pap. 5.99 (978-1-4424-2984-0(4)) Simon & Schuster Children's Publishing. (Aladdin).

Dadey, Debby & Dadey, Debbie. Treasure in Trident City, 1 vol., Bk. 8. 2015. (Mermaid Tales Ser.). (ENG.). 120p. (J). (gr. 2-4). 24.21 (978-1-61479-329-8(8), Spotlight) ABDO Publishing Co.

Daher, Anita. Poachers in the Pingos, 1 vol. 2008. (Orca Young Readers Ser.). (ENG.). 128p. (J). (gr. 3-6). pap. 7.95 (978-1-55469-011-4(0)) Orca Bk. Pubs. USA.

Dahl, Lisa. Gorm the Viking: The Lost Voyage. 2013. 282p. (gr. 4-6). 26.95 (978-1-4759-5809-6(9)); pap. 16.95 (978-1-4759-5807-2(2)) iUniverse, Inc.

Dahl, Michael. Dragonblood Spring 2010, 6 vols., Set. 2010. (Dragonblood Ser.). (ENG.). 40p. (gr. 1-3). lib. bdg. 143.94 (978-1-4342-2110-0(5)) Stone Arch Bks.

—The Horizontal Man: Finnegan Zwake #1. 2008. (Finnegan Zwake Ser.: 1). (ENG.). 192p. (YA). (gr. 7). (978-1-4169-8668-3(5), Simon Pulse) Simon Pulse.

—Library of Doom: the Final Chapters. 2015. (Library of Doom: the Final Chapters Ser.). (ENG.). 40p. (gr. 1-3). 95.96 (978-1-4965-0301-5(5), Zone Bks.) Stone Arch Bks.

—Skyfall, 1 vol. Kovar, Ben, illus. 2012. (Troll Hunters Ser.). (ENG.). 112p. (gr. 2-3). lib. bdg. 25.32 (978-1-4342-3307-3(3), Troll Hunters) Stone Arch Bks.

—The Worm Tunnel: Finnegan Zwake #2. 2008. (Finnegan Zwake Ser.: 2). (ENG.). 176p. (YA). (gr. 7). pap. 9.99 (978-1-4169-8667-6(7), Simon Pulse) Simon Pulse.

Dahl, Roald. Charlie y la Fabrica de Chocolate.Tr. of Charlie & the Chocolate Factory. (SPA.). (J). 8.95 (978-968-6026-71-9(1)) Santillana USA Publishing Co., Inc.

—The Complete Adventures of Charlie & Mr. Willy Wonka. Blake, Quentin, illus. 2010. (ENG.). 336p. (J). (gr. 3-7). 10.99 (978-0-14-241740-9(8), Puffin Books) Penguin Young Readers Group.

—James et la Grosse Peche.Tr. of James & the Giant Peach. (FRE.). (J). pap. 17.95 (978-2-07-051374-1(2)) Gallimard, Editions FRA. Dist: Distribooks, Inc.

Dahlstrom, S. J. The Elk Hunt: The Adventure Begins. 2013. (Adventures of Wilder Good Ser.). (ENG., Illus.). 110p. (J). (gr. 3). pap. 8.95 (978-1-58988-087-0(0)) Dry, Paul Bks., Inc.

—Green Colt, No. 4. 2016. (Adventures of Wilder Good Ser.). (ENG.). 162p. (J). (gr. 3). pap. 8.95 (978-1-58988-114-3(1)) Dry, Paul Bks., Inc.

—Wilder & Sunny: the Adventures of Wilder Good #3. 2015. (Adventures of Wilder Good Ser.). (ENG.). 120p. (J). (gr. 3). pap. 7.95 (978-1-58988-100-6(1)) Dry, Paul Bks., Inc.

Daigle, Damien. The Fish That Went Roar. Daigle, Casie, illus. 2011. 28p. pap. 24.95 (978-1-4560-5080-1(X)) America Star Bks.

Dailey, Reid. The Legend of Ross the Reader: A Story of How a Smart Cowboy Saved the Prairie One Book at a Time. Edgerley, Ross, illus. 2007. 32p. per. 15.95 (978-1-59858-483-7(9)) Dog Ear Publishing, LLC.

—Ross the Reader & the Adventure of the Pirate's Treasure. Edgerley, Ross, illus. 2009. 44p. pap. 16.95 (978-1-59858-900-9(8)) Dog Ear Publishing, LLC.

—Ross the Reader & the Great Balloon Race. Stacy, Alan F., illus. 2011. 46p. pap. 13.95 (978-1-4575-0154-8(6)) Dog Ear Publishing, LLC.

Daisley, Liesel F. The Adventures of Lisbeth. 2011. 28p. pap. 13.54 (978-1-4634-4147-0(9)) AuthorHouse.

Dale, Jay. Here I Go, 1 vol. Draycott, MIchelle, illus. 2012. (Wonder Words Ser.). (ENG.). 32p. (gr. k-2). pap. 5.99 (978-1-4296-8892-5(0), Engage Literacy) Capstone Press of Coughlan Cos.

Daley, Debbie. The Harp of Elvyth. 2013. 292p. pap. (978-1-78299-840-2(3)) FeedARead.com.

Daley-Prado, M. The Super Heroes Save Christmas! 2007. 24p. per. 24.95 (978-1-4241-9123-9(8)) America Star Bks.

Daley-Prado, M. J. Baby Duck Gets A New Grandma. 2008. 40p. pap. 17.95 (978-1-4357-1312-3(5)) Lulu Pr., Inc.

—Buzz. 2008. 36p. pap. 17.95 (978-1-4357-1352-9(4)) Lulu Pr., Inc.

Dalhaimer Bartkowski, Anna. Maggie Visits Grandpa: A Coloring Adventure. Dalhaimer Bartkowski, Anna, illus. 2007. (Illus.). 32p. pap. 8.99 (978-0-9790720-1-7(8)) Infinite Adventure.

Dallion 7th, David W. Tales of Tura. 2007. 188p. per. 24.95 (978-1-4241-7131-6(8)) America Star Bks.

Dalmatian Press Staff. A Little Whale Tale. 2008. (ENG.). 8p. bds. 4.95 (978-1-58117-713-8(5), Intervisual/Piggy Toes) Bendon, Inc.

Dalon, Phillip A. Clanwickie: Life High in the Kabalas. 2011. 232p. pap. 24.95 (978-1-4626-4033-1(8)) America Star Bks.

Dalrymple, Farel. The Wrenchies. Dalrymple, Farel, illus. 2014. (ENG., Illus.). 304p. (YA). (gr. 9). pap. 19.99 (978-1-59643-421-9(X), 9781596434219, First Second Bks.) Roaring Brook Pr.

Dalrymple, Jay. The Legend of Tiny O'Liddle. 2012. 42p. (-18). pap. 10.99 (978-0-9883162-1-8(8)) Mindstir Media.

Dalton, Andrew & Boatfield, Jonny. The New Empire of Malplaquet. 2009. (ENG., Illus.). 192p. (gr. 4-7). 35.00 (978-0-7188-3096-0(2)); pap. 17.50 (978-0-7188-3093-9(8)) Lutherworth Pr., The GBR. Dist: Casemate Academic.

—Temples of Malplaquet. 2005. (Malplaquet Trilogy Ser.). (ENG., Illus.). 192p. (978-0-7188-3046-5(6)) Lutherworth Pr., The.

Dalton, Annie. Calling the Shots. 2003. (Angels Unlimited Ser.: No. 4). (ENG., Illus.). 160p. (J). pap. 4.99 (978-0-06-008818-7(4)) HarperCollins Pubs.

—The Divine Collection: Three Amazing Missions in One Book! 2008. (Mel Beeby Agent Angel Ser.). (ENG., Illus.). 608p. (J). (gr. 4-7). pap. 19.95 (978-0-00-719074-4(3)) HarperCollins Pubs. Ltd. GBR. Dist: Independent Pubs. Group.

—The Heavenly Collection: Three Amazing Missions in One Book! 2008. (Mel Beeby Agent Angel Ser.). (ENG.). 400p. (J). (gr. 4-7). pap. 19.95 (978-0-00-723307-6(8)) HarperCollins Pubs. Ltd. GBR. Dist: Independent Pubs. Group.

Dalton, Linda J. The Mystery of the Broomstick Horse. 2012. 116p. 29.99 (978-1-4797-4781-8(5)); pap. 19.99 (978-1-4797-4780-1(7)) Xlibris Corp.

Dalton, Nicola. The Adventurers - the Mystery of the Magical Crystal. 2011. 108p. (gr. -1). 21.23 (978-1-4520-6661-5(2)); pap. 10.99 (978-1-4520-6660-8(4)) AuthorHouse.

Dalton, Susan. The Magic Glasses. 2012. 36p. pap. 19.95 (978-1-4685-2586-1(7)) AuthorHouse.

Daly, Joseph M. Strange Town Volume One: The Woods Behind Trevor Malone's House. 2007. 265p. (YA). pap. 9.99 net. (978-0-9779921-0-2(1)) Wolfs Corner Publishing.

Daly, Kerry. Finding Feldspar. 2005. (Illus.). 22p. (J). per. 8.99 (978-1-932338-91-1(8)) Lifevest Publishing, Inc.

Dames-Johnson, Angela. What's Gerald Done Now? Supermarket Fun. 2009. 24p. pap. 24.95 (978-1-60749-474-4(4)) America Star Bks.

Damian, Gabriela Georgeta. The Chocolate Tree. 2010. 50p. pap. 19.88 (978-0-557-14739-7(5)) Lulu Pr., Inc.

Damiani, AU, Kathleen. Molly O'Brien & the Mark of the Dragon Slayer. 2011. (ENG.). 272p. pap. 15.95 (978-1-936012-55-8(3)) Larson Pubns.

D'Amico, Christine. Higgledy-Piggledy: Mabel's World. Bell-Myers, Darcy, illus. 2005. (ENG.). 32p. (J). 16.95 (978-0-9716631-1-4(4)) Avoomba Group Co.

Damico, Gina. Scorch. 2012. (ENG.). 352p. (YA). (gr. 7). pap. 8.99 (978-0-547-62457-0(3)) Houghton Mifflin Harcourt Publishing Co.

Damiron, Anya. Dreamboy. Pino, Pablo, illus. 2010. (SPA.). 26p. (J). (978-9945-421-42-2(5)) Lucia Stories.

—Inventor Boy. Pino, Pablo, illus. 2010. (SPA.). 26p. (J). (978-9945-00-157-0(4)) Lucia Stories.

—Nino Inventor. Pino, Pablo, illus. 2010. 26p. (J). (978-9945-00-153-2(1)) Lucia Stories.

Dammann, Anke. Chester Crumbleberry Dammann, Anke, illus. 2005. (Illus.). 32p. 15.95 (978-1-893815-11-7(0)) Pie in the Sky Publishing, LLC.

Dammier, Patti. Got Carrots? Rescued Horse: The Winter Vacation. 2012. 142p. 21.95 (978-1-4759-2842-6(4)); pap. 11.95 (978-1-4759-2840-2(8)) iUniverse, Inc.

Damron, Dugan. Further Adventures of Old Shorty: Tales of a Midwest Country Boy, 1 vol. 2010. 112p. pap. 19.95 (978-1-4489-5838-2(5)) America Star Bks.

D'Andra, Anastasia. In the Shadows: Book 2 Rosegrove Series. 2012. 186p. pap. 24.95 (978-1-4626-5920-3(9)) America Star Bks.

Danescary, Pollygeist. Have a Claw-Some Howloween: A Creepy-Cool Activity Book. 2015. (ENG., Illus.). 32p. (J). (gr. 3-7). pap. 7.99 (978-0-316-33742-7(0)) Little, Brown Bks. for Young Readers.

Daneshvari, Gitty. Who's That Ghoulfriend? 2013. Bk. 3. (ENG., Illus.). 272p. (J). (gr. 3-7). 13.00 (978-0-316-22254-9(2)) Little, Brown Bks. for Young Readers.

Danger Alert: Coloring/Activity Book. 2006. (Illus.). (J). 2.99 (978-1-933934-05-1(0)) Mighty Kids Media.

Danger Alert: Picture Book (English) 2006. (Illus.). 47p. (J). 5.99 (978-1-933934-03-7(4)) Mighty Kids Media.

Daniel, Beverly. The Adventures of Madilyn Millicent Middleton-Mew. Daniel, Cindy, ed. Daniel, Beverly, illus. 2013. (Illus.). 64p. pap. 8.95 (978-0-9789429-6-0(5)) Batelier Publishing.

Daniel, Claire. The Chick That Wouldn't Hatch. Ernst, Lisa Campbell, illus. 2003. (Green Light Readers Level 2 Ser.). (ENG.). 24p. (J). (gr. -1-3). pap. 3.95 (978-0-15-204831-0(6)) Houghton Mifflin Harcourt Publishing Co.

Daniel, Liesle. Mittens: A Kitten in Search of Hope. 2011. 48p. pap. 9.95 (978-1-4497-1314-0(9), WestBow Pr.) Author Solutions, Inc.

Daniel, Martha Ann. Mimi Mouse Meets Roger Rat: A Tail of Bullying. 2012. 32p. (-18). pap. 19.99 (978-1-4772-8295-3(5)) AuthorHouse.

Daniell, G. Dusty & Albert's Beaver Tales. 2009. 50p. pap. 24.00 (978-0-557-08541-5(1)) Lulu Pr., Inc.

Daniels, April. Dreadnought. 2017. (Nemesis Ser.: 1). (ENG.). 280p. pap. 14.99 (978-1-68230-068-8(4)) Diversion Publishing Corp.

Daniels, Darla. The Magic Ring: Summer Vacation in London. 2012. 30p. 16.95 (978-1-4626-6252-4(8)) America Star Bks.

Daniels, J. M. The Secret of the Little Dutch Doll. 2009. 68p. pap. 25.49 (978-1-4343-9356-2(9)) AuthorHouse.

Daniels, Katie C. Danny's Adventure in Afric. 2009. 24p. pap. 12.99 (978-1-4389-3404-4(1)) AuthorHouse.

Daniels, Kristine. Floyd & the Irresistible Cookie. 2009. 32p. pap. 18.00 (978-1-60844-276-8(4)) Dog Ear Publishing, LLC.

Daniels, Sterling N., 2nd. Yas. Daniels, Sterling N., 2nd, illus. (Illus.). 36p. (J). (gr. k-3). pap. 4.95 (978-0-9628081-2-8(1)) D. A. W. Enterprise.

Daniels, W. J. The Empress Academy: The Secret of Glittershine. 2009. 144p. pap. 16.95 (978-1-4327-2335-4(9)) Outskirts Pr., Inc.

Danielski, A. The Nick & Austin Chronicles: The Pirate Ship's Magic & a New Home. 2013. 28p. pap. 24.95 (978-1-4626-7709-2(6)) America Star Bks.

Dankyi, Jane Osafoa. Incredible Adventures of Wapi. 2004. (ENG., Illus.). Bk. 1. 60p. pap. (978-9964-70-122-2(5))Bk. 2. 52p. (gr. 3-7). pap. (978-9964-70-123-9(3))Bk. 3. 52p. pap. (978-9964-70-124-6(1)) Afram Pubns. Ghana, Ltd. GHA. Dist: Michigan State Univ. Pr.

Danley, Jerry J. Billy Black Ant's Exciting Adventures. Hilley, Thomas, illus. 2012. 56p. pap. 12.99 (978-0-9885180-5-6(8)) Mindstir Media.

Danna, Minnie. Miss Poppy & Red Jeans: Adventure to Willie Willie's Garden. Danna Sr., Gerald, illus. 2012. 66p. pap. 12.95 (978-0-9852608-0-4(7)) Flower Publishing.

Darby Hall. The Adventures of Tigeret S Meow. 2011. (Illus.). 24p. (gr. -1-3). pap. 15.99 (978-1-4568-9086-5(7)) Xlibris Corp.

Darcy, Kate. Winnie Windmill: The Village Fete. 2012. (Illus.). 52p. pap. 24.40 (978-1-4678-8382-5(4)) AuthorHouse.

Dare, Danni. Jake Jett: Adventures in Space. 2010. 32p. pap. 12.99 (978-1-4520-4981-6(5)) AuthorHouse.

Dare, Will. How to Rope a Giganotosaurus. 2017. (Dino Riders Ser.: 2). lib. bdg. 16.00 **(978-0-606-40352-8(3))** Turtleback Bks.

—How to Tame a Triceratops. 2017. (Dino Riders Ser.: 1). lib. bdg. 16.00 **(978-0-606-40351-1(5))** Turtleback Bks.

Darlington, Edgar. The Circus Boys on the Mississippi. 2007. 116p. per. (978-1-4068-4235-7(4)) Echo Library.

Darlington, Edgar B. P. The Circus Boys Across Continent or Making the Start in the Sawdust Life. 2004. reprint ed. pap. 1.99 (978-1-4192-5679-0(3)); pap. 22.95 (978-1-4191-5679-3(9)) Kessinger Publishing, LLC.

—The Circus Boys in Dixie Land or Winning the Plaudits of the Sunny South. 2004. reprint ed. pap. 1.99 (978-1-4192-5680-6(7)); pap. 22.95 (978-1-4191-5680-9(2)) Kessinger Publishing, LLC.

—The Circus Boys on the Mississippi or Afloat with the Big Show on the Big River. 2004. reprint ed. pap. 22.95 (978-1-4191-5681-6(0)); pap. 1.99 (978-1-4192-5681-3(5)) Kessinger Publishing, LLC.

—The Circus Boys on the Plains or the Young Advance Agents Ahead of the Show. 2004. reprint ed. pap. 1.99 (978-1-4192-5682-0(3)); pap. 22.95 (978-1-4191-5682-3(9)) Kessinger Publishing, LLC.

Darlison, Aleesah. Ellabeth's Light Cancelled. Brailsford, Jill, illus. 2017. (Unicorn Riders Ser.). (ENG.). 112p. (gr. 3-5). pap. 5.95 (978-1-4795-6559-7(8)) Picture Window Bks.

—Ellabeth's Test. Brailsford, Jill, illus. 2016. (Unicorn Riders Ser.). (ENG.). 112p. (gr. 3-5). lib. bdg. 22.65 (978-1-4795-6547-4(4)) Picture Window Bks.

—Ellabeth's Test Cancelled. Brailsford, Jill, illus. 2017. (Unicorn Riders Ser.). (ENG.). 112p. (gr. 3-5). pap. 5.95 (978-1-4795-6555-9(5)) Picture Window Bks.

—Krystal's Charge Cancelled. Brailsford, Jill, illus. 2017. (Unicorn Riders Ser.). (ENG.). 112p. (gr. 3-5). pap. 5.95 (978-1-4795-6558-0(X)) Picture Window Bks.

—Krystal's Choice. Brailsford, Jill, illus. 2016. (Unicorn Riders Ser.). (ENG.). 112p. (gr. 3-5). lib. bdg. 22.65 (978-1-4795-6546-7(6)) Picture Window Bks.

—Krystal's Choice Cancelled. Brailsford, Jill, illus. 2017. (Unicorn Riders Ser.). (ENG.). 112p. (gr. 3-5). pap. 5.95 (978-1-4795-6554-2(7)) Picture Window Bks.

—Quinn's Riddles. Brailsford, Jill, illus. 2016. (Unicorn Riders Ser.). (ENG.). 112p. (gr. 3-5). lib. bdg. 22.65 (978-1-4795-6544-3(X)) Picture Window Bks.

—Quinn's Truth Cancelled. Brailsford, Jill, illus. 2017. (Unicorn Riders Ser.). (ENG.). 112p. (gr. 3-5). pap. 5.95 (978-1-4795-6556-6(3)) Picture Window Bks.

—Willow's Challenge. Brailsford, Jill, illus. 2016. (Unicorn Riders Ser.). (ENG.). 112p. (gr. 3-5). lib. bdg. 22.65 (978-1-4795-6545-0(8)) Picture Window Bks.

—Willow's Victory Cancelled. Brailsford, Jill, illus. 2017. (Unicorn Riders Ser.). (ENG.). 112p. (gr. 3-5). pap. 5.95 (978-1-4795-6557-3(1)) Picture Window Bks.

Darlison, Aleesha. Quinn's Riddles. Brailsford, Jill, illus. 2017. (Unicorn Riders Ser.). (ENG.). 112p. (gr. 3-5). pap. 5.95 (978-1-4795-6552-8(0)) Picture Window Bks.

—Willow's Challenge. Brailsford, Jill, illus. 2017. (Unicorn Riders Ser.). (ENG.). 112p. (gr. 3-5). pap. 5.95 (978-1-4795-6553-5(9)) Picture Window Bks.

Darsana, Nam Aste. Guppie: God's Unified Perfect Plan Inspiring Everyone. 2011. 40p. pap. 21.99 (978-1-4628-4535-4(5)) Xlibris Corp.

Dashner, James. The Blade of Shattered Hope. Dorman, Brandon, illus. 2011. (13th Reality Ser.: 3). (ENG.). 528p. (J). (gr. 3-7). pap. 8.99 (978-1-4424-0871-5(5), Aladdin) Simon & Schuster Children's Publishing.

—The Hunt for Dark Infinity. Beus, Bryan, illus. 2009. (13th Reality Ser.: Bk. 2). 446p. (J). 18.95 (978-1-60641-034-9(2), Shadow Mountain) Shadow Mountain Publishing.

—The Hunt for Dark Infinity. Beus, Bryan, illus. 2010. (13th Reality Ser.: 2). (ENG.). 544p. (J). (gr. 3-7). pap. 8.99 (978-1-4169-9153-3(0), Aladdin) Simon & Schuster Children's Publishing.

—The Iron Empire. 2014. (Infinity Ring Ser.: 7). (ENG., Illus.). 192p. (J). (gr. 3-7). 12.99 (978-0-545-38702-6(7)) Scholastic, Inc.

—A Mutiny in Time. 2015. (Infinity Ring Ser.: 1). lib. bdg. 17.20 (978-0-606-37765-2(4)) Turtleback Bks.

—The Void of Mist & Thunder. Dorman, Brandon, illus. 2013. (13th Reality Ser.: 4). (ENG.). 496p. (J). (gr. 3-7). pap. 8.99 (978-1-4424-0873-9(1), Aladdin) Simon & Schuster Children's Publishing.

—War of the Black Curtain. Phipps, Michael, illus. 2005. (Jimmy Fincher Saga: Bk. 4). per. 14.99 (978-1-55517-879-6(0)) Cedar Fort, Inc./CFI Distribution.

—The 13th Reality: The Blade of Shattered Hope; the Void of Mist & Thunder. Dorman, Brandon, illus. 2015. (13th Reality Ser.). (ENG.). 976p. (YA). (gr. 7-7). pap. 12.99 (978-1-4814-5702-6(0), Simon & Schuster/Paula Wiseman Bks.) Simon & Schuster/Paula Wiseman Bks.

—The 13th Reality: The Journal of Curious Letters; the Hunt for Dark Infinity. Beus, Bryan, illus. 2015. (13th Reality Ser.). (ENG.). 1024p. (YA). (gr. 7-7). pap. 12.99 (978-1-4814-5315-8(7), Simon & Schuster/Paula Wiseman Bks.) Simon & Schuster/Paula Wiseman Bks.

—13th Reality Complete Set: The Journal of Curious Letters; the Hunt for Dark Infinity; the Blade of Shattered Hope; the Void of Mist & Thunder. 2013. (13th Reality Ser.: Bks. 1-4). (ENG., Illus.). 2096p. (J). (gr. 3-7). pap. 35.99 (978-1-4424-8452-8(7), Aladdin) Simon & Schuster Children's Publishing.

Datsiouk, Andrew. Kristo. 2011. 140p. (gr. 4-6). pap. 12.87 (978-1-4269-5083-4(7)) Trafford Publishing.

Dauber, Veronica. Mudslide. 2009. 176p. pap. 13.95 (978-1-4401-6229-9(8)) iUniverse, Inc.

Dauer, Marty. Harvey's Woods: the Royal Adventures. LaRiccia, Mike, illus. 2007. 52p. per. 16.95 (978-1-4241-7924-4(6)) America Star Bks.

D'Aulaire, Edgar Parin & D'Aulaire, Ingri. Ola. 2013. (ENG., Illus.). 56p. 16.95 (978-0-8166-9017-6(0)) Univ. of Minnesota Pr.

D'Aulaire, Ingri & D'Aulaire, Edgar Parin. Too Big. 2008. (New York Review Children's Collection). (ENG., Illus.). 40p. (J). (gr. k-k). 14.95 (978-1-59017-291-9(4), NYR Children's Collection) New York Review of Bks., Inc., The.

Dautel, Daniel. Mission to Mount Everest. 2009. 90p. pap. 9.96 (978-0-557-09695-4(2)) Lulu Pr., Inc.

Dave, Matt. Supercool Snotman, No. 8. Baines, Nigel, illus. (ENG.). 112p. pap. (978-1-84738-288-7(6)) Simon & Schuster, Ltd.

Dave, Safety. Safety Dave & Daisy Ride the Bus. 2011. 16p. 8.95 (978-1-4520-7218-0(3)) AuthorHouse.

Davenport, Eddie. Bunnyburg: The Newcomers. 2013. (ENG.). 30p. (J). pap. 14.95 (978-1-4787-2062-1(X)) Outskirts Pr., Inc.

David, Christopher. Denholme & the Skeleton Mystery. 2006. 274p. pap. 22.52 (978-1-4120-8014-9(2)) Trafford Publishing.

David, Erica. Anna & Elsa No. 7: The Secret Admirer. Random House Disney Staff et al, illus. 2016. (Stepping Stone Book(TM) Ser.: 7). (ENG.). 128p. (J). (gr. 1-4). 9.99 (978-0-7364-3475-1(5), RH/Disney) Random Hse. Children's Bks.

—Anna & Elsa #6: the Arendelle Cup (Disney Frozen) RH Disney Staff et al, illus. 2015. (Stepping Stone Book(TM) Ser.: 6). (ENG.). 128p. (J). (gr. 1-4). 9.99 (978-0-7364-3437-9(2), RH/Disney) Random Hse. Children's Bks.

—Extreme Rescue: Crocodile Mission. McGee, Warner, illus. 2009. (Go, Diego, Go! Ser.). (ENG.). 24p. (J). pap. 3.99 (978-1-4169-8515-0(8), Simon Spotlight/Nickelodeon) Simon Spotlight/Nickelodeon.

—The Great Ice Engine. RH Disney Staff et al, illus. 2015. (Stepping Stone Book(TM) Ser.: 4). (ENG.). 128p. (J). (gr. 1-4). 9.99 (978-0-7364-3431-7(3), RH/Disney) Random Hse. Children's Bks.

—How to Track a Dragon. 2016. (Simon & Schuster Ready-To-Read Level 2 Ser.). lib. bdg. 13.55 (978-0-606-38992-1(X)) Turtleback Bks.

—The Secret Admirer. Random House Disney Staff et al, illus. 2016. (Stepping Stone Book(TM) Ser.: 7). (ENG.). 128p. (J). (gr. 1-4). lib. bdg. 12.99 (978-0-7364-8210-3(5), RH/Disney) Random Hse. Children's Bks.

David, Erica & Foreman, Matthew Sinclair. Disney Frozen - A Year with Elsa & Anna, & Olaf Too! 2016. (Replica Journal Ser.). (ENG.). 96p. (J). (gr. k-3). 9.99 (978-0-7944-3701-5(X), Reader's Digest Children's Bks.) Studio Fun International.

David Iii, Paul. Brave Americans. 2013. 28p. pap. 15.95 (978-0-7414-9638-6(0)) Infinity Publishing.

David, Jamie. Johann Sebastian Humpbach. David, Jamie, illus. 2009. (Illus.). 167p. pap. 14.95 (978-0-615-31840-0(1)) Chai Yo Maui Pr.

David, Keren. Another Life. 2012. (ENG.). 384p. (YA). (gr. 7-10). pap. 8.99 (978-1-84780-286-6(9), Frances Lincoln) Quarto Publishing Group UK GBR. Dist: Hachette Bk. Group.

David, Peter. Nothing to Lose. Cross, Chris, illus. 2003. (Captain Marvel Ser.). 144p. (YA). pap. 12.99 (978-0-7851-1104-7(2)) Marvel Worldwide, Inc.

Davidge, James. The Duchess Ranch of Old John Ware. Prodor, Bob, illus. 2010. (ENG.). 104p. pap. 10.95 (978-1-897411-18-6(9)) Bayeux Arts, Inc. CAN. Dist: Chicago Distribution Ctr.

Davidson, Danica. Down into the Nether: An Unofficial Overworld Adventure, Book Four. 2016. (Unofficial Overworld Adventure Ser.). (ENG., Illus.). 112p. (J). (gr. 1-7). pap. 7.99 (978-1-5107-1220-1(8), Sky Pony Pr.) Skyhorse Publishing Co., Inc.

—Escape from the Overworld. 2015. (Unofficial Overworld Adventure Ser.). (ENG.). 112p. (J). (gr. 1-7). pap. 7.99 (978-1-63450-103-3(9), Sky Pony Pr.) Skyhorse Publishing Co., Inc.

—The Rise of Herobrine: An Unofficial Overworld Adventure, Book Three. 2016. (Unofficial Overworld Adventure Ser.). (ENG.). 112p. (J). (gr. 1-7). pap. 7.99 (978-1-5107-0802-0(2), Sky Pony Pr.) Skyhorse Publishing Co., Inc.

Davidson, Ellen. When the Third Moon Wanes. 2004. 123p. pap. 19.95 (978-1-4137-2233-8(4)) America Star Bks.

Davidson, Halsey. Navy Boys Behind the Big Guns or Sinking the German U-Boats. 2007. 108p. per. (978-1-4068-1847-5(X)) Echo Library.

Davidson, Kayla Shurley. Daddy's Little Squirrel. 2010. 28p. pap. 12.49 (978-1-4490-8474-5(5)) AuthorHouse.

Davidson, Susanna. Stories of Dolls. Wanert, Amandine, illus. 2006. 48p. (J). (gr. 2-5). 8.99 (978-0-7945-1327-6(1), Usborne) EDC Publishing.

—Stories of Mermaids. 2009. (Young Reading 1 Ser.). 48p. (J). (gr. 2). 6.99 (978-0-7945-2589-7(X), Usborne) EDC Publishing.

—Thumbelina. 2009. (First Reading Level 4 Ser.). 48p. (J). (gr. 2). 6.99 (978-0-7945-2280-3(7), Usborne) EDC Publishing.

Davidson, Thomas A. Penny Found in Willowbrooke. 2009. 40p. pap. 14.75 (978-1-60693-774-7(X), Strategic Bk. Publishing) Strategic Book Publishing & Rights Agency (SBPRA).

Davie, Jan. The Nexus Facilitator. 2006. 96p. pap. (978-1-84401-798-0(2)) Athena Pr.

Davies, Christie. Dewi the Dragon. 2006. (ENG.). 96p. (J). pap. 9.95 (978-0-86243-770-1(9)) Y Lolfa GBR. Dist: Dufour Editions, Inc.

Davies, Linda. Longbow Girl. 2016. (ENG.). 336p. (J). (gr. 7). 17.99 *(978-0-545-85345-3(1),* Chicken Hse., The) Scholastic, Inc.

Davies, Nicola. Rubbish Town Hero. 2012. (ENG., Illus.). 256p. (J). (gr. 1-4). pap. 10.99 *(978-0-552-56302-4(1))* Transworld Publishers Ltd. GBR. Dist: Independent Pubs. Group.

Davies, Peter. Molly's Magic Pencil: The Blue Genie. 2011. 28p. (gr. 1-2). 14.99 *(978-1-4567-3018-5(5))* AuthorHouse.

Davies, Robert, adapted by. Lit a Shuck for Texas: Adapted Louis l'Amour Short Stories Series. 2003. (Adapted Louis L'Amour Short Stories Ser.). (Illus.). 56p. (YA). *(978-1-57035-983-5(0),* 233LIT) Cambium Education, Inc.

—Merrano of the Dry Country: Adapted Louis l'Amour Short Story Series. 2003. (Adapted Louis L'Amour Short Stories Ser.). (Illus.). 60p. (J). *(978-1-57035-985-9(7),* 233MERRANO) Cambium Education, Inc.

—A Trail to the West: Adapted Louis l'Amour Short Stories Series. 2003. (Adapted Louis L'Amour Short Stories Ser.). (Illus.). 56p. (J). *(978-1-57035-984-2(9),* 233TRAIL) Cambium Education, Inc.

Davies, Tim. The Crystals. 2013. 176p. pap. *(978-1-78407-202-5(8))* FeedARead.com.

Davis, Adam. Guardians of the Galaxy. 2014. (ENG., Illus.). 24p. (J). (gr. -1-3). pap. 3.99 *(978-0-316-29319-8(9))* Little, Brown Bks. for Young Readers.

—Guardians of the Galaxy: Rocket & Groot Fight Back. 2014. (ENG., Illus.). 24p. (J). (gr. -1-3). pap. 4.99 *(978-0-316-29323-5(7))* Little, Brown Bks. for Young Readers.

Davis, Alan. Killraven. Davis, Alan, illus. 2003. (Spider-Man Ser.). (Illus.). 144p. (YA). pap. 16.99 *(978-0-7851-1083-5(6))* Marvel Worldwide, Inc.

Davis, Andrea Nicek. Rex Polar Bear. 2008. 40p. pap. 24.95 *(978-1-60474-962-5(8))* PublishAmerica, Inc.

Davis, Beneta. My Covers. 2008. 24p. pap. 24.95 *(978-1-60441-584-1(3))* America Star Bks.

Davis, Carol Marie. The Adventures of Moon Spirit, a Girl from Florida's Past. Davis, Carol Marie, illus. 2008. (Illus.). 60p. pap. 8.95 *(978-0-9821654-2-3(0))* Peppertree Pr., The.

Davis, Dana A. Teala & Tony's Adventure to Baby Land. 2008. 16p. pap. 24.95 *(978-1-4241-4459-4(0))* America Star Bks.

Davis, Derek and Nikki. T. E. A. the Ered Adventures Presents Skinny Skelley in: Do the Right Thing. 2009. 59p. pap. 24.99 *(978-1-4357-4184-3(6))* Lulu Pr., Inc.

—T. E. A. the Ered Adventures Presents Skinny Skelley in It's Ok to Be Different. 2009. 49p. pap. 24.99 *(978-1-4357-4183-6(8))* Lulu Pr., Inc.

Davis, Izzy. The Croaks at Roaring River, 1 vol. 2009. 40p. pap. 24.95 *(978-1-60813-245-4(5))* America Star Bks.

Davis, Jacky & Soman, David. Ladybug Girl Dresses Up! Soman, David, illus. 2010. (Ladybug Girl Ser.). (ENG., Illus.). 14p. (J). (gr. -1 — 1). bds. 5.99 *(978-0-448-45373-6(8),* Grosset & Dunlap) Penguin Young Readers Group.

—Ladybug Girl Visits the Farm. Soman, David, illus. 2011. (Ladybug Girl Ser.). (ENG., Illus.). 16p. (J). (gr. -1-k). pap. 6.99 *(978-0-448-45598-3(6),* Grosset & Dunlap) Penguin Young Readers Group.

Davis, Jim & Michiels, Cedric. Unfair Weather. Dargaud Media Staff & Ellipsanime Staff, illus. 2013. (Garfield Show Ser.). (ENG.). 64p. (J). (gr. 1-5). 11.99 *(978-1-59707-433-9(0),* 9781597074339) Papercutz.

Davis, Kent. A Riddle in Ruby. (Riddle in Ruby Ser.: 1). (J). (gr. 3-7). 2016. 448p. pap. 7.99 *(978-0-06-236835-5(4))* 2015. (ENG.). 432p. 17.99 *(978-0-06-236834-8(6))* HarperCollins Pubs. (Greenwillow Bks.).

—Riddle in Ruby - The Changer's Key. 2016. (Riddle in Ruby Ser.: 2). 448p. (J). (gr. 3-7). 17.99 *(978-0-06-236837-9(0),* Greenwillow Bks.) HarperCollins Pubs.

Davis, Kent. A Riddle in Ruby #2: the Changer's Key. 2017. (Riddle in Ruby Ser.: 2). 464p. (J). (gr. 3-7). pap. 7.99 ***(978-0-06-236838-6(9),*** Greenwillow Bks.) HarperCollins Pubs.

Davis, Kesa Royette. The Adventures of Keitly Dee & Geode. 2012. 36p. pap. 20.99 *(978-1-4772-3754-0(2))* AuthorHouse.

Davis, Lynda S. & Weisel, Kaitlyn E. Christopher James Mcabee & the Wonderful Tree. Trone, Melody Karns, illus. 2013. 54p. pap. 6.99 *(978-0-9889907-0-8(9))* Sruvis Publishing.

Davis, Milton J. Amber & the Hidden City. 2013. 220p. pap. 16.95 *(978-0-9800842-7-6(X))* MVmedia.

Davis, Pat. Estelle & the Escape from Mars: A Children's Novel By. 2009. 136p. pap. 10.99 *(978-1-4389-5432-5(8))* AuthorHouse.

Davis, Rhonda L. Faces of Darkness: The Daredevil Friends. 2008. 284p. pap. 14.95 *(978-1-934925-75-1(6),* Eloquent Bks.) Strategic Book Publishing & Rights Agency (SBPRA).

Davis, Samira And Edwina. Nikko & Sierra's Adventures: I Hate Knuckle Sandwiches. 2011. 24p. pap. 11.32 *(978-1-4634-0408-6(5))* AuthorHouse.

Davis, Spencer W. Charlie Chubby Bubble. 2004. 40p. pap. 20.50 *(978-1-4140-3878-0(X))* AuthorHouse.

Davis, Terry. Camping with Dad: The Mystery of Valley Gulch. 2006. (ENG.). 148p. per. 24.95 *(978-1-4241-5659-7(9))* America Star Bks.

Davis, Tim, illus. The Case of the Purple Diamonds. 2011. 88p. pap. 9.95 *(978-1-934606-07-0(3))* TAG Publishing, LLC.

Davis, Toby K. The Ever Part of Always: Keely Tucker's First Adventure. 2012. 208p. (gr. 4-6). 24.95 *(978-1-4697-4592-3(5));* pap. 14.95 *(978-1-4697-4591-6(7))* iUniverse, Inc.

Davis, Trevor. The Adventures of Charley Mcchoochoo: Danny & the Whistling Engine. Davis, Natalie, ed. Anderson, Lochlin, illus. 2012. 34p. pap. 9.99 *(978-0-9853650-5-9(6))* Mindstir Media.

Dawson, Jennifer. Silly Sally Sue. 2013. 24p. pap. 24.95 *(978-1-62709-938-7(7))* America Star Bks.

Dawson, JoAnn S. Lady's Big Surprise. 2004. 288p. pap. 8.95 *(978-0-9746561-6-8(X));* (Illus.). 15.95 *(978-0-9746561-5-1(1))* FT Richards Publishing.

—Star of Wonder. 2005. (Illus.). 268p. pap. 8.95 *(978-0-9746561-4-4(3))* FT Richards Publishing.

Dawson, Patricia. The Adventures of Farmer Bill. 2013. 28p. pap. 19.99 *(978-1-4817-0551-6(2))* AuthorHouse.

Dawson, Piper. The Adventures of Fenway & Becc. 2012. 76p. pap. 8.95 *(978-1-4502-8646-6(1))* iUniverse, Inc.

Day, Alexandra. Carl's Summer Vacation. Day, Alexandra, illus. 2008. (Carl Ser.). (ENG., Illus.). 32p. (J). (gr. -1-1). 15.99 *(978-0-374-31085-1(8),* 9780374310851, Farrar, Straus & Giroux (BYR)) Farrar, Straus & Giroux.

Day, Jan. Pirate Pink & Treasures of the Reef, 1 vol. Mason, Janeen, illus. 2003. (ENG.). 32p. (J). (gr. k-3). 16.99 *(978-1-58980-086-1(9))* Pelican Publishing Co., Inc.

Day, K. The Silver Bullet: Tour of the Universe. 2010. 120p. pap. 12.49 *(978-1-4490-6534-8(1))* AuthorHouse.

Day, Tracy. The Silver Lining: Book the First of the Kadnohkka Grey Series. 2007. 96p. per. 11.95 *(978-1-59858-440-0(5))* Dog Ear Publishing, LLC.

Day, Williamson. The Pretorius Stories. 2011. 96p. pap. 9.99 *(978-1-4634-7430-0(X))* AuthorHouse.

Daynes, Katie, retold by. Pinocchio. 2005. (Young Reading Gift Books Ser.). 64p. (J). (gr. 2-18). 8.95 *(978-0-7945-0887-6(1),* Usborne) EDC Publishing.

Dayton, Dorothy. The Legend of Farmer Will. 2006. 70p. pap. 16.95 *(978-1-4241-0985-2(X))* PublishAmerica, Inc.

Da2. Bb Roc & His Adventurous Days. 2011. 28p. pap. 16.95 *(978-1-4626-2049-4(3))* America Star Bks.

DC Comics Staff. DC Super Friends Workbook ABC 123. 2016. (ENG., Illus.). 56p. (J). spiral bd. 12.99 *(978-0-374-30399-0(1),* 9780374303990, Farrar, Straus & Giroux (BYR)) Farrar, Straus & Giroux.

—Superman. 2013. (Stand-Up Mover Ser.: 1). (ENG.). 10p. (J). bds. 8.99 *(978-0-7944-2839-6(8))* Reader's Digest Assn., Inc., The.

Ddlewis. Adventurers. 2008. 76p. pap. 24.99 *(978-1-4343-6769-3(X))* AuthorHouse.

de Beer, Hans, pseud. Kleiner eisbar wohin fahrst Du. pap. 17.95 *(978-3-423-07954-9(1))* Deutscher Taschenbuch Verlag GmbH & Co KG DEU. Dist: Distribooks, Inc.

de Bree, Alexander. Casting Dragon, 1 vol. 2010. 94p. pap. 19.95 *(978-1-4512-8691-5(0))* America Star Bks.

de Brun, Kieran Christopher. The Talking Llama: la Llama Que Habla. de Brun, Brendan Joseph, illus. 2005. (J). pap. 16.00 *(978-0-8059-6910-8(1))* Dorrance Publishing Co., Inc.

De Fombelle, Timothée. Toby & the Secrets of the Tree. Ardizzone, Sarah, tr. from FRE. Place, Francois, illus. 2010. (ENG.). 432p. (J). (gr. 4-7). 16.99 *(978-0-7636-4655-4(5))* Candlewick Pr.

De Fombelle, Timothee. Vango: Between Sky & Earth. 2016. (Vango Ser.: 1). lib. bdg. 20.85 *(978-0-606-37948-9(7))* Turtleback Bks.

De Gieter, Lucien. Imhotep's Transformation. Spear, Luke, tr. from FRE. 2008. (Papyrus Ser.: 2). (ENG., Illus.). 48p. pap. 11.95 *(978-1-905460-50-2(3))* CineBook GBR. Dist: National Bk. Network.

—The Rameses' Revenge. Spear, Luke, tr. from FRE. 2007. (Papyrus Ser.: 1). (ENG., Illus.). 48p. (J). (gr. 4-7). pap. 11.95 *(978-1-905460-35-9(X))* CineBook GBR. Dist: National Bk. Network.

De Golyer, Blu. The Adventures of Captain Greenspud. 2009. 28p. pap. 14.50 *(978-1-60860-425-8(X),* Eloquent Bks.) Strategic Book Publishing & Rights Agency (SBPRA).

De La Llata, Lorenza. Awaking the Mighty. 2008. 49p. pap. 16.95 *(978-1-60563-689-4(4))* America Star Bks.

De la Peña, Matt. Eternity. 2014. (Infinity Ring Ser.: 8). (ENG.). 192p. (J). (gr. 3-7). lib. bdg. 16.99 *(978-0-545-66770-8(4));* (Illus.). lib. bdg. 12.99 *(978-0-545-66535-3(3))* Scholastic, Inc.

De La Ramee, Louise & Ouida. The Nurnberg Stove. 2009. 64p. pap. 7.95 *(978-1-60664-399-0(1))* Rodgers, Alan Bks.

de Las Casas, Dianne. The Cajun Cornbread Boy, 1 vol. Gentry, Marita, illus. 2008. (ENG.). 32p. (J). (gr. k-3). 16.99 *(978-1-58980-224-7(1))* Pelican Publishing Co., Inc.

De Laurentiis, Giada. Paris!, No. 2. Gambatesa, Francesca, illus. 2013. (Recipe for Adventure Ser.: 2). (ENG.). 144p. (J). (gr. 2-5). 6.99 *(978-0-448-46257-8(5),* Grosset & Dunlap) Penguin Young Readers Group.

—Paris! No. 2. Gambatesa, Francesca, illus. 2013. (Recipe for Adventure Ser.: 2). (ENG.). 144p. (J). (gr. 2-5). 16.99 *(978-0-448-47854-8(4),* Grosset & Dunlap) Penguin Young Readers Group.

De Laurentiis, Giada, et al. Hawaii! #6. Gambatesa, Francesca, illus. 2015. (Recipe for Adventure Ser.: 6). (ENG.). 160p. (J). (gr. 2-4). bds. 6.99 *(978-0-448-48391-7(2),* Grosset & Dunlap) Penguin Young Readers Group.

—Miami! #7. Gambatesa, Francesca, illus. 2015. (Recipe for Adventure Ser.: 7). (ENG.). 160p. (J). (gr. 2-4). bds. 6.99 *(978-0-448-48393-1(9),* Grosset & Dunlap) Penguin Young Readers Group.

—Rio de Janeiro! #5. Gambatesa, Francesca, illus. 2015. (Recipe for Adventure Ser.: 5). (ENG.). 160p. (J). (gr. 2-4). bds. 6.99 *(978-0-448-48204-0(5),* Grosset & Dunlap) Penguin Young Readers Group.

De Lesseps, Ferdinand Zoticus. Oceanology: The True Account of the Voyage of the Nautilus. Steer, Dugald A. & Hawkins, Emily, eds. 2009. (Ologies Ser.: 8). (ENG., Illus.). 32p. (J). (gr. 3-7). 24.99 *(978-0-7636-4290-7(8))* Candlewick Pr.

de Lint, Charles. Wolf Moon. 2004. (ENG., Illus.). 256p. (Orig.). (YA). (gr. 7-18). 6.99 *(978-0-14-240077-7(7),* Firebird) Penguin Young Readers Group.

De Los Heros, Luis & Wilson, Elizabeth. Chifa Chi's Little Adventure in Washington Dc. 2010. 40p. pap. 21.99 *(978-0-557-23085-3(3))* Lulu Pr., Inc.

de los Santos, Marisa & Teague, David. Connect the Stars. 2016. 368p. (J). (gr. 3-7). pap. 6.99 *(978-0-06-227466-3(X))* HarperCollins Pubs.

De Michel. What's an Egg Got to Do with It? A Dozen Adventures with God for Grades 4-6. 2007. 108p. pap. 19.95 *(978-1-4241-8994-6(2))* America Star Bks.

De Munnik, Hema. Bhole: Adventures of a Young Yogi. 2006. (ENG., Illus.). 352p. (J). (gr. 3-7). per. 18.95 *(978-81-88157-37-2(6))* Lotus Pr.

De Pauw, Linda Grant. In Search of Molly Pitcher. 2007. 164p. 30.00 *(978-1-4303-1345-8(5))* Lulu Pr., Inc.

De Saint-Exupéry, Antoine. Le Petit Prince Graphic Novel. Sfar, Joann, illus. 2010. (FRE & ENG.). 112p. (J). (gr. 5-7). 22.00 *(978-0-547-44330-0(7))* Houghton Mifflin Harcourt Publishing Co.

De Saulnier, Gia Volterra. Journey to Jazzland. Zieroth, Emily, illus. 2013. 44p. 14.99 *(978-0-9851492-8-4(0))* Flying Turtle Publishing.

De Sena, Joseph. The Butterfly & the Bunny's Tail. Anfuso, Dennis, illus. 2007. 60p. per. 19.95 *(978-1-4327-0404-9(4))* Outskirts Pr., Inc.

de Silva, Eugenie. The Adventures of Princess Eugenie. 2008. 35p. pap. 24.65 *(978-0-557-01213-8(9))* Lulu Pr., Inc.

De Valor, Diana. The Great Adventures of Sea Worthy with the I Can Crew: The Treasure of Captain Blue Beard. 2011. 32p. pap. 19.95 *(978-1-4269-6627-9(X))* Trafford Publishing.

de Vries, Maggie. Fraser Bear: A Cub's Life. Benoit, Renné, illus. 2012. (ENG.). 48p. (J). (gr. k-4). pap. 10.95 *(978-1-926812-95-3(6))* Greystone Books Ltd. CAN. Dist: Publishers Group West (PGW).

Deacon, Alexis. A Place to Call Home. Schwarz, Viviane, illus. 2011. (ENG.). 40p. (J). (gr. -1-2). 16.99 *(978-0-7636-5360-6(8))* Candlewick Pr.

Deacon, Jools A. Anouska's Adventures. 2017. (ENG.). 16p. (J). pap. 13.95 ***(978-1-78612-891-1(8),*** 8f5d2400-b5da-481a-a90c-2d1ba360d195) Austin, Stan AUS. Dist: Bookmasters Distribution.

Deal, L. Kate, illus. The Boxcar Children. collector's ed. 2009. (Boxcar Children Mysteries Ser.). (ENG.). 168p. (J). (gr. 1-5). 18.99 *(978-0-8075-0850-3(0))* Whitman, Albert & Co.

Deal-Trainor, Carol. Marilee: A Manatee's First Journey to the Springs. 2008. 48p. pap. 16.95 *(978-1-60563-660-3(6))* America Star Bks.

Dean, James. Pete the Cat & the Tip-Top Tree House (backpack Special Edition) Dean, James, illus. 2017. (My First I Can Read Ser.). (Illus.). 32p. (J). (gr. -1-3). 4.50 ***(978-0-06-274847-8(5))*** HarperCollins Pubs.

Dean, James. Sir Pete the Brave. 2016. (Pete the Cat I Can Read Ser.). (J). lib. bdg. 13.55 *(978-0-606-38753-8(6))* Turtleback Bks.

Dean, Natalia. The Dream. 2012. 30p. 24.95 *(978-1-4626-6008-7(8))* America Star Bks.

Dean, Ramsey. Riding on a Beam of Light: Albert Einstein. Hamdan, Noah, illus. 2013. 48p. pap. 10.48 *(978-0-9893372-1-2(9))* Ramsey Dean, Inc.

Deane, Nancy Lou. Meg's Secret. 2011. 148p. (gr. 4-6). pap. 14.69 *(978-1-4567-8884-1(1))* AuthorHouse.

Dearing, Ruth. Tommy & the Hiccups. 2013. 44p. pap. 10.00 *(978-0-9843487-9-4(4))* Painting the Pages Publishing.

Dearle, Anne Crofton. Ginger Cat. 2011. (Illus.). 92p. pap. 12.10 *(978-1-4567-7484-4(0))* AuthorHouse.

DeArville, J. It's Kambri Time! 2007. 28p. per. 9.95 *(978-1-4327-0812-2(0))* Outskirts Pr., Inc.

Debesay, Samson. Cubby, the Lionsheep: Son, you are a lion, live like One! 2011. (Illus.). 24p. pap. 14.89 *(978-1-4567-7899-6(4))* AuthorHouse.

Deborah Strandberg, Rebecca Reynolds and. Trammler Triplet Tales #2 - HIDDEN in TIME. 2007. 116p. pap. 8.94 *(978-1-4303-2097-5(4))* Lulu Pr., Inc.

—Trammler Triplet Tales Advente #4 MYSTERIOUS ABBY. 2007. 113p. pap. 8.90 *(978-1-4357-0651-4(X))* Lulu Pr., Inc.

—Trammler Triplet Tales-Adventure #3 SEEKING the SOURCE. 2007. 175p. pap. 11.38 *(978-1-4303-1197-3(5))* Lulu Pr., Inc.

DeCamp, Alison. My Near-Death Adventures: I Almost Died. Again. 2016. (ENG., Illus.). 288p. (J). (gr. 3-7). 16.99 *(978-0-385-39048-4(3),* Crown Books For Young Readers) Random Hse. Children's Bks.

Décary, Marie. Adam's Tropical Adventure. Cummins, Sarah, tr. from FRE. Beshwaty, Steve, illus. 2005. (Formac First Novels Ser.: 56). (ENG.). 64p. (gr. 2-5). 14.95 *(978-0-88780-687-2(2),* 9780887806872); (J). 4.95 *(978-0-88780-686-5(4),* 9780887806865) Formac Publishing Co., Ltd. CAN. Dist: Casemate Pubs. & Bk. Distributors, LLC.

Decary, Marie. Le Combats des Chocolats. Brignaud, Pierre, illus. 2003. (Roman Jeunesse Ser.). (FRE.). 96p. (J). (gr. 4-7). pap. *(978-2-89021-611-2(X))* Diffusion du livre Mirabel (DLM).

Decker, Wendy. The Bedazzling Bowl. 2006. pap. 13.99 *(978-1-60034-468-8(2))* Salem Author Services.

Decter, Ed. Expedition to Pine Hollow. Yuen, Sammy, Jr. & Yuen Jr., Sammy, illus. 2007. (Outriders Ser.: 3). (ENG.). 240p. (J). (gr. 3-7). pap. 11.99 *(978-1-4169-1307-8(6),* Simon & Schuster/Paula Wiseman Bks.) Simon & Schuster/Paula Wiseman Bks.

Deddens, Rachel Campbell. The Day the Calf Ate the Chocolate Cake. 2016. (ENG., Illus.). 28p. pap. 8.95 *(978-1-63047-607-6(2))* Morgan James Publishing.

DEE and AMA. The Toybox Grannies. Katie & Savannah - Special Edition. 2009. 216p. pap. 21.89 *(978-0-557-04568-6(1))* Lulu Pr., Inc.

Deegan, J. E. When I Was a Little Guy. 2008. 76p. pap. 19.95 *(978-1-60703-120-8(5))* America Star Bks.

Deering, Leta. Patriotic Samáand the Mendez Twins at the Alamo. 2008. 112p. pap. 19.95 *(978-1-60610-689-1(9))* America Star Bks.

DeFelice, Jennie & Landry, Jennifer. The Adventures of Zsa-Zsa & Gabby-Lou: Dangers at the Seashore. DeFelice, Bonnie, illus. 2005. (J). lib. bdg. 19.95 *(978-0-9767072-0-2(9))* Two Dogz.

Defelice, Jennie & Landry, Jennifer. The Adventures of Zsa Zsa & Gabby Lou a Country Harvest. 2006. (J). lib. bdg. 20.00 *(978-0-9767072-2-6(5))* Two Dogz.

—The Adventures of Zsa Zsa & Gabby Lou in New Orleans. Defelice, Bonnie, illus. 2006. (J). lib. bdg. 21.95 *(978-0-9767072-1-9(7))* Two Dogz.

Defitch, Jennifer L. Delia the Dragonfly's Grand Adventures: Delia Goes to Washington D. C. 2012. 28p. (-18). pap. 24.95 *(978-1-62709-290-6(0))* America Star Bks.

Defoe, Daniel. Robinson Crusoe. Cabrera, Eva, illus. 2015. (Graphic Revolve: Common Core Editions Ser.). (ENG.). 72p. (gr. 2-3). lib. bdg. 27.99 *(978-1-4965-0371-8(6))* Stone Arch Bks.

—Robinson Crusoe. 2012. 338p. pap. 10.99 *(978-1-61382-256-2(1))* Simon & Brown.

—Robinson Crusoe. McKowen, Scott, illus. 2011. (Sterling Unabridged Classics Ser.). (ENG.). 288p. (J). 9.95 *(978-1-4027-8406-4(6))* Sterling Publishing Co., Inc.

—Robinson Crusoe. Akib, Jamel, illus. 2006. (Classic Starts(tm) Ser.). (ENG.). 160p. (J). (gr. 2-4). 6.95 *(978-1-4027-2664-4(3))* Sterling Publishing Co., Inc.

—Robinson Crusoe: The Complete Story of Robinson Crusoe. 2004. (SPA., Illus.). 284p. (YA). (gr. -1-7). pap. *(978-958-30-0091-1(4))* Panamericana Editorial.

—Robinson Crusoe: The Complete Story of Robinson Crusoe. 2nd ed. 2003. (Historias de Siempre Ser.). (SPA., Illus.). 92p. (J). (gr. 5-8). pap. 12.95 *(978-84-204-5723-9(X))* Santillana USA Publishing Co., Inc.

Defoe, Daniel, et al. Robinson Crusoe: The Complete Story of Robinson Crusoe. (Classics Illustrated Ser.). (Illus.). 52p. (YA). pap. 4.95 *(978-1-57209-021-7(9))* Classics International Entertainment, Inc.

Deford, Ted. Po & the Gang: In Two Big Adventures. 2005. 49p. pap. 16.95 *(978-1-4137-9068-9(2))* PublishAmerica, Inc.

Defreitas, Henrietta. Henratty Mortimer: The Meerville Myth. (Illus.). 2012. 84p. pap. 32.03 *(978-1-4772-3867-7(0))* 2011. 88p. pap. 28.14 *(978-1-4520-8237-0(5))* AuthorHouse.

Degrado, Louis Paul. The Questors' Adventures: The Round House & the Moaning Walls. 2012. 326p. 29.95 *(978-1-4759-4469-3(1));* pap. 19.95 *(978-1-4759-4470-9(5))* iUniverse, Inc.

Degruy, David. As the Sparks Fly Upward: The Jimmy & Johnny Adventure Stories. 2003. (Illus.). 104p. pap. 12.95 *(978-0-929292-55-7(3),* 800-747-0738) Hannibal Bks.

Dehghanpisheh, Corine. Buddy's Dream. Dehghanpisheh, Corine, illus. 2013. (Illus.). 34p. pap. 12.95 *(978-0-9851930-4-1(2))* Dehghanpisheh, Corine.

Dehoratius. Follow Your Fates Exile of Aeneas. 2010. (Illus.). x, 113p. (J). pap. 12.00 *(978-0-86516-709-4(5))* Bolchazy-Carducci Pubs.

DeHoratius, Ed. The Journey of Odysseus. Delandro Hardison, Brian, illus. 2009. (Follow Your Fates Ser.). 116p. (J). pap. 12.00 *(978-0-86516-710-0(9))* Bolchazy-Carducci Pubs.

—Wrath of Achilles. 2009. 62p. pap. 12.00 *(978-0-86516-708-7(7))* Bolchazy-Carducci Pubs.

Deiser, Donald. Egg Money. 2005. 112p. per. 12.95 *(978-1-931195-76-8(5))* KiwE Publishing, Ltd.

Deisher, Kathleen E. Beyond the Gloesmur: In the Gloesmur Scrolls. Deisher, Kathleen E., illus. 2003. (Gloesmur Scrolls Ser.: Bk. 1). (Illus.). 270p. (J). pap. 13.95 *(978-1-892135-00-1(0))* Lamp Post Publishing, Inc.

Deiss, A. G. & Emi. The Sad Tale of Emmaline Austin, Monkey-Girl. 2005. 23p. 10.67 *(978-1-4116-5439-6(0))* Lulu Pr., Inc.

Del Amo, Montserrat. El Nudo. (SPA.). 94p. (YA). (gr. 5-8). *(978-84-261-1691-8(4),* JV2941) Juventud, Editorial ESP. Dist: Lectorum Pubns., Inc.

Del Rio, Adam. Teo in Palo Verde/Teo en Palo Verde. III, Noel, illus. 2008. (ENG & SPA.). 28p. (J). (gr. k-3). 15.95 *(978-1-60448-000-9(9))* Lectura Bks.

del Rio, Tania. Warren the 13th & the All-Seeing Eye. Staehle, Will, illus. 2015. (Warren The 13th Ser.: 1). (ENG.). 224p. (J). (gr. 5). 16.95 *(978-1-59474-803-5(9))* Quirk Bks.

del Rio, Tania & Staehle, Will. Warren the 13th & the Whispering Woods. 2017. (Warren The 13th Ser.: 2). (ENG., Illus.). 240p. (J). (gr. 5). 16.95 *(978-1-59474-929-2(9))* Quirk Bks.

Delaney, Joseph. I Am Alice, Bk. 12. Arrasmith, Patrick, illus. 2014. (Last Apprentice Ser.: 12). (ENG.). 464p. (YA). (gr. 8). pap. 9.99 *(978-0-06-171515-0(8),* Greenwillow Bks.) HarperCollins Pubs.

—Lure of the Dead, Bk. 10. Arrasmith, Patrick, illus. 2012. (Last Apprentice Ser.: 10). (ENG.). 432p. (YA). (gr. 8). 17.99 *(978-0-06-202760-3(3),* Greenwillow Bks.) HarperCollins Pubs.

Delaney, Michael. Obi, Gerbil on the Loose! 2008. (ENG.). 208p. (J). (gr. 5-18). 16.99 *(978-0-525-47890-4(6),* Dutton Books for Young Readers) Penguin Young Readers Group.

Delashmit, Margaret V. Thief! 2012. 148p. (gr. 4-6). pap. 12.99 *(978-1-4624-0348-6(4),* Inspiring Voices) Author Solutions, Inc.

Delawrence, T. M. Millie: M. C. E. (Mail Carrier Extraordinaire) In. 2012. 28p. pap. 24.95 *(978-1-4626-6057-5(6))* America Star Bks.

Delcoglin, Gwen. Bella's Umbrella. Delcoglin, Nathan, illus. 2007. 28p. (J). (gr. -1-3). per. 10.99 *(978-1-59879-315-4(2))* Lifevest Publishing, Inc.

Delena Deatherage. The Beginning of People's Chicken. Joe Kent, illus. 2009. 40p. pap. 18.95 *(978-1-4208-9094-5(8))* AuthorHouse.

De'Leon, Lunden. Oops Loops. 2006. 28p. pap. 9.95 *(978-1-4327-0114-7(2))* Outskirts Pr., Inc.

Delgado, Josep Francesc. Nima, El Sherpa. 2003. (SPA.). 168p. *(978-84-8453-060-2(4),* PT31196) Ediciones del Bronce ESP. Dist: Lectorum Pubns., Inc.

Delibero, Bob. Petrucchio. 2012. 234p. 24.95 *(978-1-4626-6155-8(6))* America Star Bks.

Dell, Bella. Rosie the Robin. 2013. 24p. pap. 24.95 *(978-1-63000-892-5(3))* America Star Bks.

Dellicurti, Dana. Joey's First Day at School. 2008. 24p. per. 14.95 *(978-1-4327-1408-6(2))* Outskirts Pr., Inc.

Dellolio, Kristina. Penelope's Tea Party Oh No Where's Kangaroo. 2012. 28p. pap. 24.95 *(978-1-4626-9748-9(8))* America Star Bks.

Delmain, Judy. Andy Beane & the Catkins' Tale. 2012. 192p. pap. 12.99 *(978-0-9857420-0-3(3))* Shadow Canyon Graphics.

DeLorge, Jaqueline. Giffinton under the Sea. 2005. (Illus.). 28p. (J). per. 7.99 *(978-1-932338-97-3(7))* Lifevest Publishing, Inc.

Delrusso, Diana. Pages, the Book-Maker Elf. Schwab, Jordan, illus. 2008. 68p. pap. 23.49 *(978-1-4343-9844-4(7))* AuthorHouse.

DeLuise, Dom & Brown, Tim. No Place Like Home. 2007. 240p. pap. 9.95 *(978-0-9769369-1-6(7))* Bacchus Bks.

Delval, Marie-Hélène. Lili et Mistigri jouent a Cache. (FRE.). pap. 14.95 *(978-2-227-75602-1(0))* Bayard Editions FRA. Dist: Distribooks, Inc.

DeMatteis, J. M. Stardust Kid. Ploog, Mike, illus. 2008. (ENG.). 128p. pap. 14.99 *(978-1-934506-04-2(4))* Boom! Studios.

Dembo, Jaiden. Finding Strider. 2010. 52p. pap. 15.54 *(978-0-557-39981-9(5))* Lulu Pr., Inc.

Demers, Karen. The Adventuresome Antics of Taf, Tif, Tobe, Tiggy, Princess & Toby. 2012. 24p. pap. 15.99 *(978-1-4797-0699-0(X))* Xlibris Corp.

Demetrios, Heather. Freedom's Slave. 2017. (Dark Caravan Cycle Ser.: 3). 608p. (YA). (gr. 8). 17.99 *(978-0-06-231862-6(4))* HarperCollins Pubs.

Demi. Marco Polo, 0 vols. 2008. (ENG., Illus.). 56p. (J). (gr. 4-7). 19.99 *(978-0-7614-5433-5(0)*, 9780761454335, Amazon Children's Publishing) Amazon Publishing.
Demi, illus. The Conference of the Birds. 2012. (ENG.). 44p. (J). (gr. -1-3). 19.95 *(978-1-937786-02-1(1))* World Wisdom, Inc.
Deming, Lynette. Day in Matthews Shoes. 2006. 28p. pap. 9.95 *(978-1-4327-0100-0(2))* Outskirts Pr., Inc.
Dennard, Susan. A Darkness Strange & Lovely. 2017. (Something Strange & Deadly Trilogy Ser.: 2). 432p. (YA). (gr. 9). pap. 9.99 *(978-0-06-265816-6(6)*, HarperTeen) HarperCollins Pubs.
Dennett, Kathleen. The 4 Corners Mystery. 2008. 32p. pap. 24.95 *(978-1-4137-2603-9(8))* America Star Bks.
Dennis, Helen. Genesis. 2017. (River of Ink Ser.). (ENG., Illus.). 368p. (J). (gr. 4-7). pap. 7.99 *(978-1-4449-2043-7(X))* Hachette Children's Group GBR. Dist: Hachette Bk. Group.
—Mortal: Will Chasing the Truth Lead Themto Mortal Danger? 2017. (River of Ink Ser.). (ENG., Illus.). 352p. (J). (gr. 4-7). pap. 7.99 *(978-1-4449-2048-2(0))* Hachette Children's Group GBR. Dist: Hachette Bk. Group.
—River of Ink Immortal Bk. 4: The Secret of Eternal Life Is Almost Within Reach... 2017. (River of Ink Ser.). (ENG.). 320p. (J). (gr. 4-6). pap. 11.99 ***(978-1-4449-2049-9(9))*** Hachette Children's Group GBR. Dist: Hachette Bk. Group.
Dennis, Helen. River of Ink Zenith. 2017. (River of Ink Ser.). (ENG., Illus.). 352p. (J). (gr. 4-6). pap. 7.99 *(978-1-4449-2045-1(6))* Hachette Children's Group GBR. Dist: Hachette Bk. Group.
Dennis, Peter, illus. The Adventures of King Arthur. 2003. (Usborne Young Reading: Series Two Ser.). 64p. (J). (gr. k-7). 8.99 *(978-0-7945-1871-4(0)*, Usborne) EDC Publishing.
Denny, Joe. Triune: Jimmy's Escape. 2005. 80p. (J). pap. *(978-0-9772240-0-5(7))* JD Entertainment.
—Triune 2: Journey to the Unknown. 2005. (J). per. 5.95 *(978-0-9772240-1-2(5))* JD Entertainment.
Dent, Jenny. Adventures of Hoppy the Gnome. (Illus.). 16p. (J). (gr. k-3). 1.75 *(978-0-85487-048-6(2))* White Eagle Publishing Trust GBR. Dist: DeVorss & Co.
Dent, Josh. Hot Chips & Sauce. 2011. 40p. pap. 32.70 *(978-1-4628-7132-2(1))* Xlibris Corp.
Denton, Terry. The Minotaur's Maze. 2004. (Storymaze Ser.). (ENG., Illus.). 144p. (J). (gr. 4-8). pap. 24.99 *(978-1-74114-088-0(9))* Allen & Unwin AUS. Dist: Independent Pubs. Group.
—The Obelisk of Eeeno. 2004. (Storymaze Ser.). (ENG., Illus.). 144p. (J). (gr. 4-8). pap. 11.99 *(978-1-74114-089-7(7))* Allen & Unwin AUS. Dist: Independent Pubs. Group.
Depken, Kristen L. All about the Trolls. Random House, illus. 2016. (Step into Reading Ser.). (ENG.). 32p. (J). (gr. -1-2). lib. bdg. 12.99 *(978-0-399-55904-4(3)*, Random Hse. Bks. for Young Readers) Random Hse. Children's Bks.
—Fairytale Magic (Dora the Explorer) Random House & Miller, Victoria, illus. 2014. (Step into Reading Ser.). (ENG.). 24p. (J). (gr. -1-1). 3.99 *(978-0-385-37503-0(4)*, Random Hse. Bks. for Young Readers) Random Hse. Children's Bks.
—Let's Go to the Circus! (Pocoyo) 2014. (Little Golden Book Ser.). (ENG., Illus.). 24p. (J). (-k). 3.99 *(978-0-385-37512-2(3)*, Golden Bks.) Random Hse. Children's Bks.
—A Roaring Adventure (Disney/Pixar Toy Story) RH Disney Staff & Holtsclaw, Josh, illus. 2012. (Little Golden Book Ser.). (ENG.). 24p. (J). (gr. k-k). 4.99 *(978-0-7364-2907-8(7)*, Golden/Disney) Random Hse. Children's Bks.
—Scuffy the Tugboat. 2017. (Step into Reading Ser.). (ENG., Illus.). 32p. (J). (gr. -1-1). 3.99 *(978-1-101-93929-1(X)*, Random Hse. Bks. for Young Readers) Random Hse. Children's Bks.
Depperschmidt, Dustin & Andrea. The Adventures of Dax: The Golden Hammer. 2012. 28p. pap. 13.95 *(978-1-4497-7601-5(9)*, WestBow Pr.) Author Solutions, Inc.
Depucci, Diana M. Lady, 1 vol. Stutz, Chris, illus. 2009. 25p. pap. 24.95 *(978-1-61546-677-1(0))* America Star Bks.
Derdowski, Chad. All Robots Must Die: Nacho-Geddon. 2013. 187p. (J). pap. 7.99 *(978-1-933925-50-9(7)*, Agent of Danger) Komikwerks, LLC.
Derenge, Garett. The Adventures of Iggy the Iguana. 2013. (ENG.). 30p. (J). pap. 13.95 *(978-1-4787-1290-9(2))* Outskirts Pr., Inc.
Derksen, Barbara Ann. Alexis Learns to Trust: Shih-Tzu Puppy Adventures. 2007. (J). 9.99 *(978-1-59872-845-3(8))* Instant Pub.
Derting, Kimberly. The Countdown. 2016. (Taking Ser.: 3). 384p. (YA). (gr. 9). 17.99 *(978-0-06-229366-4(4)*, HarperTeen) HarperCollins Pubs.
—The Taking. 2015. (Taking Ser.: 1). (ENG.). 384p. (YA). (gr. 9). pap. 9.99 *(978-0-06-229361-9(3)*, HarperTeen) HarperCollins Pubs.
Derwent, Lavinia. Return to Sula, 1 vol. Rush, Peter, illus. 2003. (Kelpies Ser.). (ENG.). 128p. 10.00 *(978-0-86315-424-9(7))* Floris Bks. GBR. Dist: SteinerBooks, Inc.
Des Fosses, John. The Cat Lottery. 2013. 148p. pap. *(978-1-61950-071-6(X))* Roxby Media Ltd.
Desch, Sandra Lee. Erika Flowers. Seeds of Grace. Phipps, Catherine Wood, illus. 2013. 80p. pap. 10.00 *(978-1-61170-144-9(9))* Robertson Publishing.
Desclouds, Rick. My Year with the ESL Boys. 2009. 280p. pap. 22.92 *(978-1-4269-0621-3(8))* Trafford Publishing.
Desisti, Sam F. The Paco & Angelina Stories, 1 vol. 2009. 48p. pap. 16.95 *(978-1-61582-604-9(1))* America Star Bks.
Desmond, Elisabeth. God s Little Adventures Destiny & Dillon. 2010. 16p. pap. 15.99 *(978-1-60957-849-7(X))* Salem Author Services.
DeStefano, Lauren. The Peculiar Night of the Blue Heart. 2017. (ENG.). 224p. pap. 7.99 *(978-1-61963-645-3(X)*, 9781619636453, Bloomsbury USA Childrens) Bloomsbury Publishing USA.
Dettman, Eric. Any Day Friends. 2012. 28p. pap. 19.99 *(978-1-4685-4297-4(4))* AuthorHouse.
Deutsch, Barry. Hereville: How Mirka Got Her Sword. 2012. (Hereville Ser.). (ENG., Illus.). 144p. (J). (gr. 3-7). pap. 9.95 *(978-1-4197-0619-6(5)*, Amulet Bks.) Abrams, Inc.
—Hereville: How Mirka Met a Meteorite. 2012. (Hereville Ser.). (ENG., Illus.). 128p. (J). (gr. 3-7). 17.95 *(978-1-4197-0398-0(6)*, Amulet Bks.) Abrams, Inc.
Deutsch, Barry & Hansen Literary Agency Staff. Hereville: How Mirka Got Her Sword. 2010. (Hereville Ser.). (ENG., Illus.). 144p. (J). (gr. 3-7). 17.99 *(978-0-8109-8422-6(9)*, Amulet Bks.) Abrams, Inc.
Deutsch, David. In Search of the Little People. l.t. ed. 2005. (Illus.). 60p. (J). per. 13.95 *(978-1-59879-013-9(7))* Lifevest Publishing, Inc.
Deutsch, Stacia. The Book of Life Movie Novelization. 2014. (Book of Life Ser.). (ENG., Illus.). 144p. (J). (gr. 3-7). pap. 6.99 *(978-1-4814-2351-9(7)*, Simon Spotlight) Simon Spotlight.
—Quest for the Keys. 2015. (LEGO Elves Chapter Book Ser.: 1). lib. bdg. 16.00 *(978-0-606-37769-0(7))* Turtleback Bks.
Deutsch, Stacia & Cohon, Rhody. Bell's Breakthrough. Wenzel, David, illus. 2005. (Blast to the Past Ser.: 3). (ENG.). 112p. (J). (gr. 2-5). pap. 6.99 *(978-0-689-87026-2(4)*, Simon & Schuster/Paula Wiseman Bks.) Simon & Schuster/Paula Wiseman Bks.
—King's Courage. Wenzel, David, illus. 2006. (Blast to the Past Ser.: 4). (ENG.). 112p. (J). (gr. 2-5). pap. 6.99 *(978-1-4169-1269-9(X)*, Simon & Schuster/Paula Wiseman Bks.) Simon & Schuster/Paula Wiseman Bks.
—Lincoln's Legacy. Wenzel, David, illus. 2005. (Blast to the Past Ser.: 1). (ENG.). 112p. (J). (gr. 2-5). pap. 6.99 *(978-0-689-87024-8(8)*, Simon & Schuster/Paula Wiseman Bks.) Simon & Schuster/Paula Wiseman Bks.
—Lincoln's Legacy. Wenzel, David, illus. 2013. (Blast to the Past Ser.: 1). (ENG.). 128p. (J). (gr. 2-5). pap. 6.99 *(978-1-4424-9534-0(0)*, Simon & Schuster/Paula Wiseman Bks.) Simon & Schuster/Paula Wiseman Bks.
—Sacagawea's Strength. Wenzel, David T. & Wenzel, David, illus. 2006. (Blast to the Past Ser.: 5). (ENG.). 128p. (J). (gr. 2-5). pap. 9.99 *(978-1-4169-1270-5(3)*, Simon & Schuster/Paula Wiseman Bks.) Simon & Schuster/Paula Wiseman Bks.
Deutsch/Cohon. Lincoln's Legacy. Wenzel, David, illus. 2005. 104p. (J). lib. bdg. 16.92 *(978-1-4242-1716-8(4))* Fitzgerald Bks.
Devargas, Casey Anthony. The Kindergarten Treasure. 2012. 44p. pap. 7.00 *(978-0-9859042-0-3(8))* CD Publishing.
Deveze, Winky. Hewitch. Neate, Andy, illus. 2006. (J). *(978-0-9787174-0-7(0))* Love Bug Bks.
Devine, Eric. Dare Me. 2013. (ENG.). 336p. (YA). (gr. 3-17). pap. 9.95 *(978-0-7624-5015-2(0)*, Running Pr. Kids) Running Pr. Bk. Pubs.
DeVoe, James E. Daydreamer: The Adventures of Dylan Lawson & His Unbridled Imagination. 2010. 143p. pap. 19.99 *(978-1-4500-8622-6(5))* Xlibris Corp.
DeVogt, Rindia M. Tommy Hare & the Color Purple, 1 vol. Trogdon, Kathryn, illus. 2009. (ENG.). 22p. pap. 24.95 *(978-1-61582-827-2(3))* America Star Bks.
Devol, Laura. To Be a Frog. Boone, Patti, illus. 2010. 20p. pap. 12.95 *(978-1-60910-278-4(9))* Booklocker.com, Inc.
Dewane, Patrick Ryan. What If the Rain Were Bugs? Konecny, John, illus. 2013. 24p. 14.99 *(978-1-937165-39-0(6))* Orange Hat Publishing.
Dewin, Howie & Scholastic Editors. Wacky Word Wedgies & Flushable Fill-Ins. 2017. (Captain Underpants Movie Ser.). (ENG., Illus.). 32p. (J). (gr. -1-3). pap. 4.99 ***(978-1-338-19655-9(3))*** Scholastic, Inc.
Dewitt, Becky. Destiny's Closet. 2010. 64p. pap. 24.00 *(978-1-4490-8970-2(4))* AuthorHouse.
—Destiny's Closet: The Wonder School. 2012. 64p. pap. 24.99 *(978-1-4772-7222-0(4))* AuthorHouse.
Dewolfe, Jeannee'. The Adventures of Billy Chicken Toes & the Wolf: Add Your Own Art Children's Books. 2012. 56p. pap. 11.97 *(978-1-61204-921-2(4)*, Strategic Bk. Publishing) Strategic Book Publishing & Rights Agency (SBPRA).
Di Gregorio, Robert & Schauer, S. Ava the Adventurer: Ava in India. 2014. 36p. pap. 22.50 *(978-1-4828-9662-6(1))* Partridge Pub.
Di-Nsteins, The Albert. No Reading Allowed. 2012. 32p. pap. *(978-1-77093-477-1(4))* Flowerpot Children's Pr. Inc.
di Vries, Maggie. Hunger Journeys. 2014. 240p. (YA). (gr. 8). pap. 8.99 *(978-0-06-231351-5(7))* HarperCollins Pubs.
Diablo - the Bequest. 2006. (J). *(978-1-933343-14-3(1))* Stabenfeldt Inc.
Diablo - the Secret of Echo Lake. 2006. (J). *(978-1-933343-21-1(4))* Stabenfeldt Inc.
Diagana, Susan. Princess Aminata & the Apple Tree. 2013. 40p. pap. 20.99 *(978-1-4772-7910-6(5))* AuthorHouse.
Diamand, Emily. Raiders' Ransom. 2009. (Raiders' Ransom Ser.: 1). (ENG.). 368p. (J). (gr. 3-7). 17.99 *(978-0-545-14297-7(0))* Scholastic, Inc.
Diamond, Kathryn. Rachel's Magic Swing. 2009. 80p. pap. 11.00 *(978-0-557-06497-7(X))* Lulu Pr., Inc.
Diaz, Gloria Cecilia. El Valle de los Cocuyos. (Barco de Vapor). (SPA.). 136p. (YA). (gr. 5-8). *(978-84-348-1939-9(2))* SM Ediciones.
Diaz, Mariano. The Adventures of KCTMJ: Kitty, China, Tina, & Mary Jane. 2006. 125p. pap. 10.50 *(978-1-4116-7620-6(3))* Lulu Pr., Inc.
DiCamillo, Kate. Flora & Ulysses: The Illuminated Adventures. Campbell, K. G., illus. (ENG.). (J). (gr. 3-7). 2016. pap. 6.99 *(978-0-7636-8764-9(2))* 2013. 240p. 17.99 *(978-0-7636-6040-6(X))* Candlewick Pr.
—Flora & Ulysses: The Illuminated Adventures. Campbell, K. G., illus. 2016. (ENG.). 256p. (J). (gr. 3-7). 17.20 *(978-0-606-39100-9(2))* Turtleback Bks.
—Flora & Ulysses: The Illuminated Adventures. 2015. lib. bdg. 19.65 *(978-0-606-36861-2(2))* Turtleback Bks.
—Louise, the Adventures of a Chicken. Bliss, Harry, illus. 2008. (ENG.). 56p. (J). (gr. -1-3). 17.99 *(978-0-06-075554-6(7))* HarperCollins Pubs.
—Louise, the Adventures of a Chicken. Bliss, Harry, illus. 2009. (J). (gr. -1-2). 29.95 incl. audio compact disk *(978-1-4301-0688-3(3))* Live Oak Media.
—The Magician's Elephant. Tanaka, Yoko, illus. (ENG.). (J). (gr. 3-7). 2015. 224p. pap. 7.99 *(978-0-7636-8088-6(5))* 2009. 208p. 16.99 *(978-0-7636-4410-9(2))* Candlewick Pr.
—The Magician's Elephant. l.t. ed. 2010. (ENG.). 242p. 23.95 *(978-1-4104-2493-8(6))* Thorndike Pr.
—The Magician's Elephant. 2015. lib. bdg. 17.20 *(978-0-606-37891-8(X))* 2011. lib. bdg. 17.20 *(978-0-606-15375-1(6)*, Turtleback) Turtleback Bks.
—The Miraculous Journey of Edward Tulane. Ibatoulline, Bagram, illus. (ENG.). (J). 2015. 240p. (gr. 2-5). pap. 7.99 *(978-0-7636-8090-9(7))* 2009. 228p. (gr. 2-5). pap. 11.99 *(978-0-7636-4783-4(7))* 2006. 228p. (gr. 1-4). 19.99 *(978-0-7636-2589-4(2))* Candlewick Pr.
—The Miraculous Journey of Edward Tulane. 2012. 22.00 *(978-1-61383-813-6(1))* Perfection Learning Corp.
—The Miraculous Journey of Edward Tulane. 2015. lib. bdg. 17.20 *(978-0-606-37892-5(8))* Turtleback Bks.
—The Miraculous Journey of Edward Tulane. Ibatoulline, Bagram, illus. 2009. 198p. (gr. 8-12). 23.30 *(978-1-4178-0763-5(6)*, Turtleback) Turtleback Bks.
—Something Wonky This Way Comes. Van Dusen, Chris, illus. 2009. (Mercy Watson Ser.: 6). (ENG.). 96p. (J). (gr. 1-4). 14.99 *(978-0-7636-3644-9(4))* Candlewick Pr.
Dicerto, Mike. The Ghost of Winter Joy. 2013. 196p. pap. 12.99 *(978-1-61271-111-9(1))* Zumaya Pubns. LLC.
Dicicco, Peter & Flynn, Ian. Teenage Mutant Ninja Turtles Amazing Adventures, Volume 2. 2016. (Teenage Mutant Ninja Turtles Amazing Adventures Ser.: 2). lib. bdg. 30.60 *(978-0-606-38731-6(5))* Turtleback Bks.
DiCicco, Sue & Mawhinney, Art, illus. Diego y los Dinosaurios. 2008. (Go, Diego, Go! Ser.). Orig. Title: Diego's Great Dinosaur Rescue. (SPA & ENG.). 24p. (J). (gr. -1-2). pap. 3.99 *(978-1-4169-5871-0(1)*, Libros Para Ninos) Libros Para Ninos.
—Diego's Great Dinosaur Rescue. 2008. (Go, Diego, Go! Ser.). (ENG.). 24p. (J). (gr. -1-2). pap. 3.99 *(978-1-4169-5867-3(3)*, Simon Spotlight/Nickelodeon) Simon Spotlight/Nickelodeon.
Dick, Beth-Ann. Henry the Hart Room Hamster. 2011. 28p. pap. 15.99 *(978-1-4568-6140-7(9))* Xlibris Corp.
Dick, Philip K. The Gun. 2011. 26p. pap. 6.95 *(978-1-60664-563-5(3))* Rodgers, Alan Bks.
Dickens, Monica. House at World's End. 2012. (ENG.). 160p. (YA). pap. 13.99 *(978-1-4482-0309-3(0)*, 9781448203093, Bloomsbury Reader) Bloomsbury Publishing Plc GBR. Dist: Macmillan.
—Spring Comes to World's End. 2012. (ENG.). 170p. (YA). pap. 13.99 *(978-1-4482-0312-3(0)*, 9781448203123, Bloomsbury Reader) Bloomsbury Publishing Plc GBR. Dist: Macmillan.
—Summer at World's End. 2012. (ENG.). 168p. (YA). pap. 13.99 *(978-1-4482-0313-0(9)*, 9781448203130, Bloomsbury Reader) Bloomsbury Publishing Plc GBR. Dist: Macmillan.
—World's End in Winter. 2012. (ENG.). 148p. (YA). pap. 13.99 *(978-1-4482-0111-2(X)*, 9781448201112, Bloomsbury Reader) Bloomsbury Publishing Plc GBR. Dist: Macmillan.
Dickerson, Melanie. The Princess Spy, 1 vol. 2014. (Fairy Tale Romance Ser.). (ENG.). 304p. (YA). pap. 12.99 *(978-0-310-73098-9(8))* Zondervan.
Dickson, Diane. 3 Things That Might Have Happened. 2010. 100p. pap. 15.50 *(978-1-4452-3414-4(9))* Lulu Pr., Inc.
Dickson, Robert. Sam Ferret Mysteries. 2010. 88p. pap. 14.95 *(978-1-4259-2741-7(6))* AuthorHouse.
Dicmas, Courtney. The Great Googly Moogly. Dicmas, Courtney, illus. 2014. (Child's Play Library). (ENG., Illus.). 32p. (J). *(978-1-84643-640-6(0))* Child's Play International Ltd.
—Harold Finds a Voice. Dicmas, Courtney, illus. 2013. (Child's Play Library). (ENG., Illus.). 32p. (J). *(978-1-84643-550-8(1))* Child's Play International Ltd.
Didling, Alisha Anne. Alisha, Her Blankie & the Surprise!, 1 vol. 2009. 20p. pap. 24.95 *(978-1-60836-915-7(3))* America Star Bks.
Diego, Marene. Hyper Spin, 1 vol. 2010. 190p. pap. 24.95 *(978-1-4489-2490-5(1))* America Star Bks.
Diesen, Deborah. Happy Easter, Pout-Pout Fish. Hanna, Dan, illus. 2017. (Pout-Pout Fish Mini Adventure Ser.). (ENG.). 12p. (J). bds. 5.99 *(978-0-374-30400-3(9)*, 9780374304003, Farrar, Straus & Giroux (BYR)) Farrar, Straus & Giroux.
—Trick or Treat, Pout-Pout Fish. Hanna, Dan, illus. 2016. (Pout-Pout Fish Mini Adventure Ser.). (ENG.). 12p. (J). bds. 5.99 *(978-0-374-30191-0(3)*, 9780374301910, Farrar, Straus & Giroux (BYR)) Farrar, Straus & Giroux.
Dietrich, Sean, illus. Hansel & Gretel: The Graphic Novel, 1 vol. 2008. (Graphic Spin Ser.). (ENG.). 40p. (J). (gr. 1-3). 25.32 *(978-1-4342-0767-8(6)*, Graphic Revolve) Stone Arch Bks.
Diffenderfer, David W. The Adventures of Boo & Fred. 2010. 58p. pap. 9.99 *(978-1-60911-966-9(5)*, Eloquent Bks.) Strategic Book Publishing & Rights Agency (SBPRA).
Digby Tracks a Catamount. 2008. (Illus.). 36p. (J). per. *(978-0-9745931-1-1(7))* Vermont Bookworks.
DiGenti, Victor. Windrusher. 2nd ed. 2004. 280p. per. 15.95 *(978-1-59411-098-6(0))* Writers' Collective, The.
Dillingham, Mike. Rivers Book Two: Through the Eyes of a Blind Sled Dog. 2003. (YA). pap. 13.95 *(978-1-59433-004-9(2))* Publication Consultants.
Dillon, Doug. Stepping off a Cliff [the St. Augustine Trilogy: The St. Augustine Trilogy: Book II. 2013. (ENG., Illus.). 394p. (YA). pap. 13.99 *(978-0-9833684-3-4(0))* Old St. Augustine Pubns.
Dillon, Eilis. The Island of Horses. 2004. (New York Review Children's Collection). (ENG.). 224p. (J). (gr. 4-7). 17.95 *(978-1-59017-102-8(0)*, NYR Children's Collection) New York Review of Bks., Inc., The.
—The Lost Island. Kennedy, Richard, illus. 2006. (New York Review Children's Collection). (ENG.). 208p. (J). (gr. 4-7). 17.95 *(978-1-59017-205-6(1)*, NYR Children's Collection) New York Review of Bks., Inc., The.
Dillon, Terence. Aurora, Me & Sardinia. 2015. (ENG.). 126p. mass mkt. 10.95 *(978-1-78554-526-9(4)*, 05c65056-597d-47c5-8d78-24785d971132) Austin, Stan AUS. Dist: Bookmasters Distribution.
DiLorenzo, Michael A. & Julich, Jennifer. Adventures with Jonny: Road Trip to the Parks. 2012. 70p. (J). 17.95 *(978-0-9777210-3-0(5))* Running Moose Publications.
Dilz, Ric. My Dad Could Do Anything! 2008. (J). 14.95 *(978-0-9758704-4-0(0))* Ric Design LLC.
—My Grandma Could Do Anything! 2008. (J). 14.95 *(978-0-9758704-3-3(2))* Ric Design LLC.
—My Grandma Could Do Anything in Hawaii! 2008. (Illus.). 32p. (J). 14.95 *(978-0-9758704-5-7(9))* Ric Design LLC.
Dimarcello, Pete. Panic at the Pool. Harpan, Gaile, ed. Baker, Edmund, illus. 2013. 20p. pap. 12.95 *(978-1-61493-169-0(0))* Peppertree Pr., The.
Dimarco, Tony. The Three Keys. Mallette, Dania, illus. 2010. 146p. pap. 9.95 *(978-0-9818391-2-7(6))* Panoply Pubns.
DiMaulo, Michael A. Maggie's Window, 1 vol. 2010. 48p. pap. 16.95 *(978-1-4489-5288-5(3))* America Star Bks.
Dimpel, Matt. The War of the Serpent Swords. 2011. 230p. pap. 24.95 *(978-1-4626-3169-8(X))* PublishAmerica, Inc.
Ding, Yuhui Andrew. Warrior Soul. 2009. 28p. pap. 15.99 *(978-1-4415-6734-5(8))* Xlibris Corp.
Dingwell, Carson. Rory of Cain's Mountain. 2005. pap. 16.95 *(978-1-4137-8756-6(8))* America Star Bks.
Dini, Paul. The Batman & Robin Adventures Vol. 1. 2016. (ENG., Illus.). 240p. (J). (gr. 2-5). pap. 19.99 *(978-1-4012-6783-4(1))* DC Comics.
Dinsdale, Christopher. Betrayed: The Legend of Oak Island. 2009. (Stories of Canada Ser.). (ENG., Illus.). 304p. (J). (gr. 6-8). pap. 10.95 *(978-1-894917-91-9(X)*, Napoleon & Co.) Dundurn CAN. Dist: Ingram Publisher Services.
—Stolen Away. 2006. (ENG., Illus.). 240p. (J). per. 10.95 *(978-1-894917-20-9(0)*, Napoleon & Co.) Dundurn CAN. Dist: Ingram Publisher Services.
Dion, Elayne. The Brass Button. 2008. 72p. pap. 9.95 *(978-0-557-01210-7(4))* Lulu Pr., Inc.
Dirst, Tracy. The Adventures of Pixie & Pete: They Meet. 2011. 16p. 9.50 *(978-1-4567-1077-4(X))* AuthorHouse.
Disbro, Laura M. Adventures with Miss Lol: The Magic Paper Ride. 2011. 28p. pap. 15.99 *(978-1-4628-9072-9(5))* Xlibris Corp.
Discovering Dinos. (Flip Flap Fun Book Ser.). 10p. (J). bds. *(978-2-7643-0137-1(5))* Phidal Publishing, Inc./Editions Phidal, Inc.
Disney. Big Hero 6 8x8. 2014. lib. bdg. 14.75 *(978-0-606-35995-5(8))* Turtleback Bks.
—Disney Fairies: Pixie Hollow Reading Adventures. 2014. (Passport to Reading Level 1 Ser.). (ENG., Illus.). 160p. (J). (gr. -1-3). 7.99 *(978-0-316-28329-8(0))* Little, Brown Bks. for Young Readers.
—Disney Fairies: Rosetta's Magical Reading Journey. 2016. (ENG.). 160p. (J). (gr. 3-7). pap. 5.99 *(978-0-316-31170-0(7))* Little, Brown Bks. for Young Readers.
—Disney Fairies: Tinker Bell's Fairytastic Reading Adventure. 2016. (ENG.). 160p. (J). (gr. 3-7). pap. 5.99 *(978-0-316-31167-0(7))* Little, Brown Bks. for Young Readers.
—Disney Miles from Tomorrowland: Galactic Explorers! 2016. (ENG.). 24p. (J). (gr. -1-1). 14.99 *(978-0-7944-3790-9(7)*, Reader's Digest Children's Bks.) Studio Fun International.
—Disney Moana: Call of the Ocean. 2016. (ENG.). 12p. (J). (gr. -1-1). 8.99 *(978-0-7944-3797-8(4)*, Reader's Digest Children's Bks.) Studio Fun International.
—Disney Moana: Movie Theater Storybook & Movie Projector. 2016. (ENG.). 32p. (J). (gr. -1-1). 19.99 *(978-0-7944-3794-7(X)*, Reader's Digest Children's Bks.) Studio Fun International.
—Disney Princess: Adventure under the Sea. 2008. (J). 13.99 *(978-1-59319-979-1(1))* LeapFrog Enterprises, Inc.
Disney, ed. Big Learning Superstar: Read & Sing. 2009. (ENG.). 20p. 16.99 *(978-1-59069-835-8(5))* Studio Mouse LLC.
Disney Art Archives Staff. Race & Rescue. 2014. (Movie Theater Ser.). (ENG.). 32p. (J). (gr. -1-1). 19.99 *(978-0-7944-3265-2(4)*, Reader's Digest Children's Bks.) Studio Fun International.
Disney Book Club Staff. Disney Planes Built for Speed. 2013. (ENG.). 24p. (J). (gr. -1). 14.99 *(978-0-7944-3000-9(7))* Reader's Digest Assn., Inc., The.
Disney Book Group. Descendants: Mal's Diary. Disney Storybook Art Team, illus. 2015. (ENG.). 192p. (J). (gr. 3-7). 9.99 *(978-1-4847-2685-3(5))* Disney Pr.
—Descendants: Mal's Spell Book. Disney Storybook Art Team, illus. 2015. (ENG.). 192p. (J). (gr. 3-7). 11.99 *(978-1-4847-2638-9(3))* Disney Pr.
—Finding Dory Middle Grade Novel. 2016. (ENG., Illus.). 128p. (J). (gr. 3-7). 10.99 *(978-1-4847-4871-8(9))* Disney Pr.
—Frozen Arendelle Adventures: Purchase Includes Mobile App for iPone & iPad! Disney Storybook Art Team, illus. 2015. (Read-And-Play Storybook Ser.). (ENG.). 96p. (J). (gr. 1-3). 12.99 *(978-1-4847-2389-0(9))* Disney Pr.
—The Lion Guard Adventures of the Lion Guard: Board Book Box Set. Disney Storybook Art Team, illus. 2017. (ENG.). 40p. (J). (gr. -1-k). 10.99 *(978-1-4847-8250-7(X))* Disney Pr.
—The Lion Guard Read-Along Storybook & CD the Power of the Roar. Disney Storybook Art Team, illus. 2017. (Read-Along Storybook & CD Ser.). (ENG.). 32p. (J). (gr. -1-k). pap. 6.99 *(978-1-4847-2950-2(1))* Disney Pr.
—Rebel Rising. 2017. (ENG.). 416p. (YA). (gr. 7-12). 17.99 *(978-1-4847-8083-1(3)*, Disney Lucasfilm Press) Disney Publishing Worldwide.
—Sheriff Callie's Wild West Callie Saves the Day! Disney Storybook Art Team, illus. 2016. (ENG.). 10p. (J). (gr. -1-k). bds. 8.99 *(978-1-4847-1567-3(5))* Disney Pr.
—Snow White & the Seven Dwarfs: The Story of Snow White. Disney Storybook Art Team, illus. 2016. (ENG.). 112p. (J). (gr. -1-k). 12.99 *(978-1-4847-2726-9(8))* Disney Pr.
—Sofia the First Read-Along Storybook & CD the Tale of Miss Nettle. Disney Storybook Art Team, illus. 2016. (ENG.). 32p. (J). (gr. -1-k). pap. 6.99 *(978-1-4847-3040-9(2))* Disney Pr.
—Trapped in the Death Star! 2016. (Star Wars: World of Reading Ser.). (J). lib. bdg. 14.75 ***(978-0-606-39174-0(6))*** Turtleback Bks.
—Whisker Haven Tales Treasure's Adventures (Storybook Plus Collectible Toy) Five Tiny Tales. Disney Storybook Art Team, illus. 2016. (ENG.). 128p. (J). (gr. 1-3). 14.99 *(978-1-4847-4648-6(1))* Disney Pr.
—World of Reading: Elena of Avalor the Secret Spell Book: Level 2. Disney Storybook Art Team, illus. 2017. (World of Reading Ser.). (ENG.). 32p. (J). (gr. 1-3). pap. 4.99 *(978-1-4847-4793-3(3))* Disney Pr.
—World of Reading Star Wars: Death Star Battle. 2016. (ENG.). 32p. (J). (gr. 1-3). pap. 3.99 *(978-1-4847-3148-2(4)*, Disney Lucasfilm Press) Disney Publishing Worldwide.
—World of Reading Star Wars Chaos at the Castle. 2016. (ENG.). 32p. (J). (gr. 1-3). pap. 3.99 *(978-1-4847-7410-6(8)*, Disney Lucasfilm Press) Disney Publishing Worldwide.
—World of Reading Star Wars Rebels Kanan's Jedi Training: Level 2. 2015. (World of Reading Ser.). (ENG.). 32p. (J). (gr. 1-3). pap. 3.99 *(978-1-4847-0563-6(7)*, Disney Lucasfilm Press) Disney Publishing Worldwide.
—World of Reading Star Wars the Fight in the Forest (Level 2) 2017. (World of Reading Ser.). (ENG.). 32p. (J). (gr. 1-3).

pap. 4.99 *(978-1-4847-0511-7(4),* Disney Lucasfilm Press) Disney Publishing Worldwide.
Disney Book Group & Brody, Jessica. CJ's Treasure Chase. No New Art Needed & Disney Storybook Art Team, illus. 2016. (School of Secrets Ser.: 1). (ENG.). 192p. (J). (gr. 3-7). 9.99 *(978-1-4847-7864-7(2))* Disney Pr.
Disney Book Group & Fry, Jason. Leia & the Great Island Escape. 2016. (ENG.). 24p. (J). (gr. 1-3). pap. 4.99 *(978-1-368-00240-0(4),* Disney Lucasfilm Press) Disney Publishing Worldwide.
Disney Book Group & Glass, Calliope. Star Wars Obi-1,2,3. Cook, Katie, illus. 2017. (ENG.). 48p. (J). (gr. -1-k). 12.99 *(978-1-4847-6812-9(4),* Disney Lucasfilm Press) Disney Publishing Worldwide.
Disney Book Group & Landers, Ace. Lead the Way. Disney Storybook Art Team & Taylor, Garrett, illus. 2017. (ENG.). 40p. (J). (gr. 1-3). 16.99 *(978-1-4847-8127-2(9))* Disney Pr.
Disney Book Group & Olivas, Silvia. Elena of Avalor Elena & Naomi's Big Adventure. Disney Storybook Art Team, illus. 2017. (ENG.). 24p. (J). (gr. 1-3). pap. 3.99 *(978-1-4847-7493-9(0))* Disney Pr.
Disney Book Group & Ritchey, Kate. Mickey & Friends Huey, Dewey, & Louie's Rainy Day. Loter, Inc. Staff, illus. 2014. (World of Reading Ser.). (ENG.). 32p. (J). (gr. 1-3). pap. 3.99 *(978-1-4231-6965-9(4))* Disney Pr.
Disney Book Group & Sutherland, Kari. The Story of Moana Moana: A Tale of Courage & Adventure. 2016. (ENG., Illus.). 304p. (J). (gr. 3-7). 10.99 *(978-1-4847-4358-4(X))* Disney Pr.
Disney Book Group, et al. Northern Lights: Adventure Notebook. Disney Storybook Art Team, illus. 2016. (ENG.). 160p. (J). (gr. 3-7). 12.99 *(978-1-4847-8662-8(9))* Disney Pr.
—Stealing Starlight. Disney Storybook Art Team, illus. 2017. (Star Darlings Ser.: 1). (ENG.). 224p. (J). (gr. 3-7). 12.99 *(978-1-4847-5639-3(8))* Disney Pr.
—World of Reading Star Wars. Rood, Brian, illus. 2015. (World of Reading Ser.). (ENG.). 32p. (J). (gr. 1-3). pap. 3.99 *(978-1-4847-0480-6(0))* Disney Pr.
Disney Book Group Editors. Mickey & the Roadster Racers Race for the Rigatoni Ribbon! 2017. (Mickey Mouse 8x8 Ser.). (J). lib. bdg. 14.75 *(978-0-606-39510-6(5))* Turtleback Bks.
—Mystic Isles. 2017. (Sofia the First Ser.). (J). lib. bdg. 13.55 *(978-0-606-39511-3(3))* Turtleback Bks.
Disney Book Group Staff. Brave. 2012. (Read-Along Storybook & CD Ser.). (ENG.). 32p. (J). (gr. -1-k). pap. 6.99 *(978-1-4231-3770-2(1))* Disney Pr.
—Disney Bedtime Favorites. Disney Storybook Artists Staff & Disney Book Group Staff, illus. 2012. (Storybook Collection). (ENG.). 304p. (J). (gr. -1 — 1). 15.99 *(978-1-4231-6034-2(7))* Disney Pr.
—Elena & the Secret of Avalor. Disney Storybook Art Team & Lee, Grace, illus. 2016. (ENG.). 48p. (J). (gr. 1-3). 15.99 *(978-1-4847-1554-3(3))* Disney Pr.
—Gravity Falls Once upon a Swine. Disney Storybook Artists Staff & No New Art Needed, illus. 2014. (Gravity Falls Chapter Book Ser.: 2). (ENG.). 112p. (J). (gr. 1-3). pap. 4.99 *(978-1-4847-1140-8(8))* Disney Pr.
—Gravity Falls Pining Away. Disney Storybook Artists Staff & Disney Storybook Art Team, illus. 2014. (Gravity Falls Chapter Book Ser.: 1). (ENG.). 112p. (J). (gr. 1-3). pap. 4.99 *(978-1-4847-1139-2(4))* Disney Pr.
—Haunted Clubhouse. 2010. (ENG., Illus.). 12p. (J). (gr. -1-k). bds. 6.99 *(978-1-4231-2832-8(X))* Disney Pr.
—The Inside Scoop. Peake, Marilyn, ed. movie tie-in ed. 2009. (ENG.). 32p. (J). (gr. 1-4). pap. 3.99 *(978-1-4231-1819-0(7))* Disney Pr.
—Mickey Mouse Clubhouse Choo Choo Express. 2009. (ENG.). 16p. (J). (gr. -1-k). pap. 4.99 *(978-1-4231-2230-2(5))* Disney Pr.
—Mickey Saves Santa. Disney Storybook Artists Staff, illus. 2009. (ENG.). 24p. (J). (gr. -1-k). pap. 5.99 *(978-1-4231-1846-6(4))* Disney Pr.
—Peter Pan Read-Along Storybook & CD. Disney Storybook Art Team, illus. 2013. (Read-Along Storybook & CD Ser.). (ENG.). 32p. (J). (gr. -1-k). pap. 6.99 *(978-1-4231-8034-0(8))* Disney Pr.
—Princess Adventure Stories. Disney Storybook Artists Staff, illus. 2013. (Storybook Collection). (ENG.). 304p. (J). (gr. -1 — 1). 15.99 *(978-1-4231-4691-9(3))* Disney Pr.
—Sofia the First Sofia's Princess Adventures: Board Book Boxed Set. Disney Storybook Art Team, illus. 2015. (ENG.). 40p. (J). (gr. -1-k). 10.99 *(978-1-4847-0042-6(2))* Disney Pr.
—Star Wars: Ewoks Join the Fight, Level 1. 2015. (ENG.). 32p. (J). (gr. 1-3). pap. 3.99 *(978-1-4847-0548-3(3),* Disney Lucasfilm Press) Disney Publishing Worldwide.
—Star Wars: Return of the Jedi Read-Along Storybook & CD. 2015. (Read-Along Storybook & CD Ser.). (ENG.). 32p. (J). (gr. 1-3). pap. 6.99 *(978-1-4847-0685-5(4),* Disney Lucasfilm Press) Disney Publishing Worldwide.
—Tangled. Disney Storybook Art Team, illus. 2010. (Read-Along Storybook & CD Ser.). (ENG.). 32p. (J). (gr. -1 — 1). pap. 6.99 *(978-1-4231-3742-9(6))* Disney Pr.
—Teen Beach Movie. 2013. (ENG.). 128p. (J). (gr. 5-9). pap. 5.99 *(978-1-4231-7790-6(8))* Disney Pr.
—World of Reading Avengers Boxed Set: Level 1 - Purchase Includes Marvel EBook! Disney Book Group Staff, illus. 2015. (World of Reading Ser.: 2). (ENG., Illus.). 192p. (J). (gr. 1-3). pap. 12.99 *(978-1-4847-0438-7(X),* Marvel Pr.) Disney Publishing Worldwide.
—World of Reading Star Wars Rescue from Jabba's Palace: Level 2. 2015. (World of Reading Ser.). (ENG., Illus.). 32p. (J). (gr. 1-3). pap. 3.99 *(978-1-4847-0501-8(7),* Disney Lucasfilm Press) Disney Publishing Worldwide.
—5-Minute Disney*Pixar Stories. 2012. (5-Minute Stories Ser.). (ENG.). 192p. (J). (gr. -1-k). 12.99 *(978-1-4231-6520-0(9))* Disney Pr.
—5-Minute Snuggle Stories. Disney Storybook Artists Staff, illus. 2013. (5-Minute Stories Ser.). (ENG.). 192p. (J). (gr. -1 — 1). 12.99 *(978-1-4231-6765-5(1))* Disney Pr.
—5-Minute Spooky Stories. Disney Storybook Artists Staff & Disney Storybook Art Team, illus. 2014. (5-Minute Stories Ser.). (ENG.). 192p. (J). (gr. -1-k). 12.99 *(978-1-4231-8915-2(9))* Disney Pr.
Disney Book Group Staff & DiTerlizzi, Tony. The Adventures of Luke Skywalker, Jedi Knight. McQuarrie, Ralph, illus. 2014. (ENG.). 64p. (J). (gr. 1-3). 19.99 *(978-1-4847-0668-8(4))* Disney Pr.
Disney Book Group Staff & Dworkin, Brooke. This Is Thor. 2014. (Marvel World of Reading Level 1 Ser.). (J). lib. bdg. 13.55 *(978-0-606-35288-8(0))* Turtleback Bks.
Disney Book Group Staff & Green, Rico. Descendants: Junior Novel. Disney Storybook Art Team, illus. 2015. (ENG.). 176p. (J). (gr. 5-9). 10.99 *(978-1-4847-2614-3(6))* Disney Pr.
Disney Book Group Staff & Kogge, Michael. Rise of the Rebels. 2014. (ENG., Illus.). 128p. (J). (gr. 3-7). pap. 5.99 *(978-1-4847-0270-3(0))* Disney Pr.
Disney Book Group Staff & Lewis, Kevin. Hide & Hug Olaf: A Fun Family Experience! Disney Storybook Art Team & Mosqueda, Olga, illus. 2014. (ENG.). 48p. (J). (gr. -1-k). 26.99 *(978-1-4847-2150-6(0))* Disney Pr.
Disney Book Group Staff & Schaefer, Elizabeth A. Chopper Saves the Day. 2014. (ENG.). 24p. (J). (gr. 1-3). pap. 4.99 *(978-1-4847-0273-4(5))* Disney Pr.
Disney Book Group Staff & Siglain, Michael. Star Wars - Use the Force, Level 2. Disney Book Group Staff et al, illus. 2015. (World of Reading Ser.). (ENG.). 32p. (J). (gr. 1-3). pap. 3.99 *(978-1-4847-0464-6(9))* Disney Pr.
Disney Book Group Staff & Thornton, Randy. Star Wars: a New Hope Read-Along Storybook & CD. Rood, Brian, illus. 2015. (Read-Along Storybook & CD Ser.). (ENG.). 32p. (J). (gr. 1-3). pap. 6.99 *(978-1-4847-0667-1(6),* Disney Lucasfilm Press) Disney Publishing Worldwide.
Disney Book Group Staff & Windham, Ryder. Ezra's Gamble. 2014. (ENG.). 160p. (J). (gr. 3-7). pap. 6.99 *(978-1-4847-0272-7(7))* Disney Pr.
Disney Book Group Staff, et al. Star Wars Rebels Always Bet on Chopper: Level 1. 2015. (World of Reading Ser.). (ENG., Illus.). 32p. (J). (gr. 1-3). pap. 3.99 *(978-1-4847-0560-5(2),* Disney Lucasfilm Press) Disney Publishing Worldwide.
—Star Wars the Force Awakens: Before the Awakening. Noto, Phil, illus. 2015. (ENG.). 224p. (J). (gr. 3-7). 12.99 *(978-1-4847-2822-2(X))* Disney Pr.
Disney Editors. Anna's Act of Love. 2013. (Frozen 8X8 Ser.). lib. bdg. 14.75 *(978-0-606-32204-1(3),* Turtleback) Turtleback Bks.
—Beauty & the Beast Novelization. 2017. (J). lib. bdg. 19.65 ***(978-0-606-40201-9(2))*** Turtleback Bks.
—Disney Beauty & the Beast Move Comic. 2016. lib. bdg. 18.40 *(978-0-606-39429-1(X))* Turtleback Bks.
—Disney Descendants: Wicked World Cinestory Comic, Volume 2. 2016. (J). lib. bdg. 20.85 *(978-0-606-39425-3(7))* Turtleback Bks.
—Disney Descendants Cinestory Comic, Volume 1, 1. 2016. (J). lib. bdg. 20.85 *(978-0-606-38727-9(7))* Turtleback Bks.
Disney Editors. Opposites Attract. 2017. (Tales of Rapunzel Ser.: 2). lib. bdg. 16.00 ***(978-0-606-40248-4(9))*** Turtleback Bks.
Disney Enterprises Inc. Staff, creator. Disney Caritas Felices: Simba. 2007. (Illus.). 8p. (J). (gr. -1). *(978-970-718-392-6(6),* Silver Dolphin en Español) Advanced Marketing, S. de R. L. de C. V.
Disney Frozen Staff. Disney Frozen Movie Theater: Storybook & Movie Projector. 2013. (Movie Theater Ser.: 1). (ENG.). 32p. (J). (gr. -1-1). 19.99 *(978-0-7944-2895-2(9))* Reader's Digest Assn., Inc., The.
Disney Planes, Disney. Disney Planes Fire & Rescue to the Rescue: Build 6 Planes That Really Fly! 2014. (Build It Ser.: 3). (ENG.). 24p. (J). (gr. -1-1). 14.99 *(978-0-7944-3139-6(9))* Reader's Digest Assn., Inc., The.
Disney Press. Ant-Man: Small World, Big Problems. 2015. (Mighty Marvel Chapter Bks.). (J). lib. bdg. 16.00 *(978-0-606-36907-7(4))* Turtleback Bks.
—Avengers: Battle with Ultron. 2015. (Marvel World of Reading Level 2 Ser.). (J). lib. bdg. 13.55 *(978-0-606-36904-6(X))* Turtleback Bks.
Disney Press Editors. Star Wars: Escape from Darth Vader. 2014. (Star Wars: World of Reading Ser.). (J). lib. bdg. 13.55 *(978-0-606-35924-5(9))* Turtleback Bks.
—Star Wars Rebels: Always Bet on Chopper. 2015. (Star Wars: World of Reading Ser.). (Illus.). 32p. (J). lib. bdg. 13.55 *(978-0-606-36910-7(4))* Turtleback Bks.
—Star Wars Rebels: Hera's Phantom Flight. 2015. (Star Wars: World of Reading Ser.). (J). lib. bdg. 13.55 *(978-0-606-36909-1(0))* Turtleback Bks.
Disney Press Staff. Once upon a Swine. 2014. (Gravity Falls Ser.: 2). (J). lib. bdg. 14.75 *(978-0-606-35916-0(8))* Turtleback Bks.
Disney Press Staff, ed. Pirates of the Caribbean 3: Swann. 2007. (ENG.). 24p. (J). (gr. -1-2). pap. 3.99 *(978-1-4231-0375-2(0))* Disney Pr.
Disney Press Staff & Disney Book Group Staff. 5-Minute Princess Stories. Disney Storybook Artists Staff, illus. 2011. (5-Minute Stories Ser.). (ENG.). 192p. (J). (gr. -1 — 1). 12.99 *(978-1-4231-4557-5(3))* Disney Pr.
Disney Press Staff & Heddle, Jennifer. Sabine's Art Attack. 2015. (Star Wars: World of Reading Ser.). (J). lib. bdg. 13.55 *(978-0-606-35928-3(1))* Turtleback Bks.
Disney Press Staff & Rusu, Meredith. The Inquisitor's Trap. 2014. (Star Wars Rebels 8x8 Ser.). (J). lib. bdg. 14.75 *(978-0-606-35926-9(5))* Turtleback Bks.
Disney Princess Holiday: Cinderella So This Is Christmas/Beauty & the Beast One Magical Christmas/Ariel's Christmas under the Sea. unabr. ed. 2005. (Disney's Read along Collection Ser.). (J). pap. *(978-0-7634-1146-6(9))* Walt Disney Records.
Disney Staff. Aladdin. (FRE.). 96p. (J). (gr. k-5). pap. 9.95 *(978-0-7859-8852-6(1))* French & European Pubns., Inc.
Disney Storybook Art Team, illus. Legend of the Neverbeast. 2015. (Read-Along Storybook & CD Ser.). (ENG.). 32p. (J). (gr. 1-3). pap. 6.99 *(978-1-4847-1075-3(4))* Disney Pr.
—Snow White & the Seven Dwarfs (Read-Along Storybook & CD) 2016. (Read-Along Storybook & CD Ser.). (ENG.). 32p. (J). (gr. 1-3). pap. 6.99 *(978-1-4847-3049-2(6))* Disney Pr.
Disney Storybook Artists Staff. Tangled, Rapunzel's Adventures: Storybook with Music Player. 2010. (Music Player Storybook Ser.). (ENG., Illus.). 32p. (J). (gr. -1-3). 24.99 *(978-0-7944-2029-1(X))* Reader's Digest Assn., Inc., The.
Disney Storybook Artists Staff, contrib. by. Princess Adventure Stories. 2013. (Illus.). 300p. (J). *(978-1-4231-2661-4(0))* Disney Pr.
Disney Storybook Artists Staff, illus. Disney Mickey Mouse Clubhouse Movie Theater: Storybook & Movie Projector, 2012. (Movie Theater Ser.). (ENG.). 32p. (J). (gr. k-3). 19.99 *(978-0-7944-2587-6(9))* Reader's Digest Assn., Inc., The.
Ditchfield, Lily K. & Zielski, Juile A. The Witches That Saved the Dogs. 2009. 26p. pap. 12.95 *(978-1-60264-494-6(2))* Virtualbookworm.com Publishing, Inc.
DiTerlizzi, Tony. G Is for One Gzonk! An Alpha-Number-Bet Book. DiTerlizzi, Tony, illus. 2006. (ENG., Illus.). 80p. (J). (gr. -1-2). 29.99 *(978-0-689-85290-9(8));* 150.00 *(978-1-4169-2471-5(X))* Simon & Schuster Bks. For Young Readers. (Simon & Schuster Bks. For Young Readers).
DiTerlizzi, Tony & Black, Holly. The Nixie's Song. DiTerlizzi, Tony, illus. 2007. (Beyond the Spiderwick Chronicles Ser.: 1). (ENG., Illus.). 192p. (J). (gr. 2-6). 12.99 *(978-0-689-87131-3(7),* Simon & Schuster Bks. For Young Readers) Simon & Schuster Bks. For Young Readers.
—The Spiderwick Chronicles Vols. 1-5, Set: The Field Guide - The Seeing Stone - Lucinda's Secret - The Ironwood Tree - The Wrath of Mulgrath. DiTerlizzi, Tony & Black, Holly, illus. 2004. (Spiderwick Chronicles Ser.). (ENG., Illus.). 672p. (J). (gr. 2-6). 59.99 *(978-0-689-04034-4(2),* Simon & Schuster Bks. For Young Readers) Simon & Schuster Bks. For Young Readers.
Dittman, Jeffery. Jungle Heroes. 2013. 36p. pap. 15.95 *(978-1-4327-9935-9(5))* Outskirts Pr., Inc.
Divakaruni, Chitra Banerjee. The Conch Bearer. 2005. (ENG.). 272p. (J). (gr. 3-7). reprint ed. pap. 8.99 *(978-0-689-87242-6(9),* Aladdin) Simon & Schuster Children's Publishing.
Divine, J. J. The Light & the Shadow: Adventures in Sacred Geometry. 2011. 252p. pap. 17.76 *(978-1-936780-01-3(1))* Salem Author Services.
Dixon, Chuck. Airboy, Vol. 1. Truman, Timothy et al, illus. 2014. (Airboy Ser.: 1). (ENG.). 308p. pap. 29.99 *(978-1-61377-900-2(3),* 9781613779002) Idea & Design Works, LLC.
Dixon, Franklin W. The Dangerous Transmission. 184th ed. 2004. (Hardy Boys Ser.: 184). (ENG., Illus.). 160p. (J). (gr. 3-7). pap. 5.99 *(978-0-689-86378-3(0),* Aladdin) Simon & Schuster Children's Publishing.
—Deprivation House. 22nd ed. 2008. (Hardy Boys (All New) Undercover Brothers Ser.: 22). (ENG., Illus.). 176p. (J). (gr. 3-7). pap. 5.99 *(978-1-4169-6170-3(4),* Aladdin) Simon & Schuster Children's Publishing.
—Double Jeopardy. 2003. (Hardy Boys Ser.: 181). (ENG.). 160p. (J). (gr. 3-7). pap. 5.99 *(978-0-689-85780-5(2),* Aladdin) Simon & Schuster Children's Publishing.
—Feeding Frenzy. 20th ed. 2008. (Hardy Boys (All New) Undercover Brothers Ser.: 20). (ENG., Illus.). 160p. (J). (gr. 3-7). pap. 7.99 *(978-1-4169-5499-6(6),* Aladdin) Simon & Schuster Children's Publishing.
—A Figure in Hiding, No. 16. Laune, Paul, illus. 2005. (Hardy Boys Ser.). (ENG.). 228p. (J). (gr. 3-9). 17.95 *(978-1-55709-274-8(5))* Applewood Bks.
—Fossil Frenzy. 2014. (Hardy Boys: Secret Files Ser.: 14). lib. bdg. 16.00 *(978-0-606-35434-9(4))* Turtleback Bks.
—Hidden Mountain. 186th ed. 2004. (Hardy Boys Ser.: 186). (ENG., Illus.). 160p. (J). (gr. 3-7). pap. 5.99 *(978-0-689-86737-8(9),* Aladdin) Simon & Schuster Children's Publishing.
—Hurricane Joe. 11th ed. 2006. (Hardy Boys (All New) Undercover Brothers Ser.: 11). (ENG., Illus.). 160p. (J). (gr. 3-7). pap. 5.99 *(978-1-4169-1174-6(X),* Aladdin) Simon & Schuster Children's Publishing.
—Motocross Madness. 190th ed. 2005. (Hardy Boys Ser.: 190). (ENG.). 160p. (J). (gr. 3-7). pap. 5.99 *(978-0-689-87365-2(4),* Aladdin) Simon & Schuster Children's Publishing.
—No Way Out. 187th ed. 2004. (Hardy Boys Ser.: 187). (ENG., Illus.). 160p. (J). (gr. 3-7). pap. 5.99 *(978-0-689-86738-5(7),* Aladdin) Simon & Schuster Children's Publishing.
—Operation: Survival. 7th ed. 2005. (Hardy Boys (All New) Undercover Brothers Ser.: 7). (ENG., Illus.). 160p. (J). (gr. 3-7). pap. 6.99 *(978-1-4169-0067-2(5),* Aladdin) Simon & Schuster Children's Publishing.
—Pushed. 18th ed. 2007. (Hardy Boys (All New) Undercover Brothers Ser.: 18). (ENG., Illus.). 160p. (J). (gr. 3-7). pap. 5.99 *(978-1-4169-4802-5(3),* Aladdin) Simon & Schuster Children's Publishing.
—The Race Is On. 2015. (Hardy Boys: Secret Files Ser.: 19). lib. bdg. 16.00 *(978-0-606-37840-6(5))* Turtleback Bks.
—Rocky Road. 5th ed. 2005. (Hardy Boys (All New) Undercover Brothers Ser.: 5). (ENG., Illus.). 160p. (J). (gr. 3-7). pap. 5.99 *(978-1-4169-0006-1(3),* Aladdin) Simon & Schuster Children's Publishing.
—Running on Fumes, Vol. 2. 2nd ed. 2005. (Hardy Boys (All New) Undercover Brothers Ser.: 2). (ENG.). 160p. (J). (gr. 3-7). pap. 6.99 *(978-1-4169-0003-0(9),* Aladdin) Simon & Schuster Children's Publishing.
—Thrill Ride, Vol. 4. 4th ed. 2005. (Hardy Boys (All New) Undercover Brothers Ser.: 4). (ENG.). 160p. (J). (gr. 3-7). pap. 6.99 *(978-1-4169-0005-4(5),* Aladdin) Simon & Schuster Children's Publishing.
—Wreck & Roll. 185th ed. 2004. (Hardy Boys Ser.: 185). (ENG., Illus.). 160p. (J). (gr. 3-7). pap. 5.99 *(978-0-689-86736-1(0),* Aladdin) Simon & Schuster Children's Publishing.
Dixon, Franklin W. & Keele, Kevin. A con Artist in Paris. 2017. (Hardy Boys Adventures Ser.: 15). (ENG.). 128p. (J). (gr. 3-7). 17.99 ***(978-1-4814-9007-8(9));*** pap. 6.99 ***(978-1-4814-9006-1(0))*** Simon & Schuster Children's Publishing. (Aladdin).
Dixon, Franklin W. & Walker, Jeff. The Secret of the Soldier's Gold. 2003. (Hardy Boys Ser.: 182). (ENG., Illus.). 160p. (J). (gr. 3-7). pap. 5.99 *(978-0-689-85885-7(X),* Aladdin) Simon & Schuster Children's Publishing.
Dixon, Joyce Ann. Katie's Tree House. 2009. 48p. pap. 16.95 *(978-1-60836-626-2(X))* America Star Bks.
Dixon, Ken. Cobweb Jack & the Sacred Khunjar. 2009. 210p. pap. 28.50 *(978-1-4092-8919-7(2))* Lulu Pr., Inc.
Dixon, Ronald. The Adventures of Nip & Dip, on a Dog Named Duffy. 2010. 28p. 13.99 *(978-1-4490-7533-0(9))* AuthorHouse.
Dixon, Sean. The Feathered Cloak. 2009. (Trilogy of the Tree Ser.: Pt. 1). (ENG., Illus.). 200p. (J). (gr. 4-7). pap. *(978-1-55470-119-3(8))* Me to We.
Dixon, Steve. Out of the Shadows. 2003. (Rumours of the King Ser.). 128p. 6.99 *(978-1-85999-671-3(X))* Scripture Union GBR. Dist: Gabriel Resources.
d'Lacey, Chris. A Crown of Dragons. 2016. (UFiles Ser.: 3). (ENG.). 320p. (J). (gr. 3-7). 16.99 *(978-0-545-60883-1(X),* Scholastic Pr.) Scholastic, Inc.
—A Dark Inheritance. 2014. (UFiles Ser.). (ENG.). 304p. (J). (gr. 3-7). 16.99 *(978-0-545-60876-3(7),* Scholastic Pr.) Scholastic, Inc.
—UFiles #1: a Dark Inheritance. 2014. (UFiles Ser.: 1). (ENG.). 304p. (J). (gr. 3-7). pap. 7.99 *(978-0-545-60878-7(3),* Scholastic Paperbacks) Scholastic, Inc.
—The Wearle. 2016. (Erth Dragons Ser.: 1). (ENG.). 320p. (J). (gr. 3-7). 16.99 *(978-0-545-90018-8(2),* Scholastic Pr.) Scholastic, Inc.
Do, Kim-Thu, tr. from ENG. Tang Monk Disciples Monkey King: English/Vietnamese. Ma, Wenhai, illus. 2005. (Adventures of Monkey King Ser.: No. 3). (ENG & VIE.). 32p. (J). 16.95 *(978-1-57227-087-9(X))* Pan Asia Pubns. (USA), Inc.
Doan, Lisa. Jack & the Wild Life. Stevanovic, Ivica, illus. (Berenson Schemes Ser.: 2). (ENG.). 144p. (J). (gr. 4-6). 2015. pap. 6.95 *(978-1-4677-2476-0(9),* Darby Creek) 2014. 17.95 *(978-1-4677-1077-0(6))* Lerner Publishing Group.
—Jack at the Helm. Stevanovic, Ivica, illus. 2015. (J). 9.99 *(978-1-4677-7787-2(0));* (Berenson Schemes Ser.: 3). (ENG.). 152p. (gr. 4-6). 17.95 *(978-1-4677-1078-7(4))* Lerner Publishing Group.
—Jack the Castaway. Stevanovic, Ivica, illus. 2014. (Berenson Schemes Ser.: 1). (ENG.). 152p. (J). (gr. 4-6). 17.95 *(978-1-4677-1076-3(8),* Darby Creek) Lerner Publishing Group.
Doan, Nicholas. Fat Rabbit Farm: Big T's Big Adventure. 2012. (ENG.). pap. 17.95 *(978-1-4675-2918-1(4))* Independent Pub.
Dober, Jim. Hickory Woods Adventures: Waiting for A Bubble. 2010. pap. 14.99 *(978-1-61579-688-5(6))* Salem Author Services.
Dobrina, Elena. The Beaver Kid's Adventures. 2007. (Illus.). 120p. (J). pap. 88.00 *(978-0-8059-7451-5(2))* Dorrance Publishing Co., Inc.
Dobson, Carol Anne. Freedom. 2013. 130p. pap. *(978-0-9558324-3-7(8))* Appledrane Bks.
Dobson, Donna. Timmy's First Adventure. 2012. 28p. pap. 24.95 *(978-1-4626-7945-4(5))* America Star Bks.
Docherty, Thomas. Little Boat. Docherty, Thomas, illus. 2009. (ENG., Illus.). 40p. (J). (gr. -1-2). 15.99 *(978-0-7636-4428-4(5),* Templar) Candlewick Pr.
Dockery, L. D. Michael Monkey Saves the Day. 2012. 30p. pap. 19.99 *(978-1-4772-6898-8(7))* AuthorHouse.
Dodd, Emma, illus. Dog's 123: A Canine Counting Adventure! 2016. (ENG.). 14p. bds. 14.99 *(978-1-86147-698-2(1),* Armadillo) Anness Publishing GBR. Dist: National Bk. Network.
Dodd, Melissa. Santa Sheds, 1 vol. 2009. 17p. pap. 24.95 *(978-1-60749-208-5(3))* America Star Bks.
Dodds, Dayle Ann. The Great Divide: A Mathematical Marathon. Mitchell, Tracy, illus. 2005. (ENG.). 32p. (J). (gr. k-4). reprint ed. pap. 6.99 *(978-0-7636-1592-5(7))* Candlewick Pr.
Dodee & Dodee. That Big Old Round Orange Thing: A Mrs. Tockalocka Adventure. 2006. (Illus.). 60p. (J). per. 9.95 *(978-1-60002-129-9(8),* 3931) Mountain Valley Publishing, LLC.
Doder, Joshua. A Dog Called Grk. 2008. (Grk Bks.). (ENG.). 272p. (J). (gr. 3-7). 6.99 *(978-0-440-42147-4(0),* Yearling) Random Hse. Children's Bks.
—Grk: Operation Tortoise. 2009. 219p. (J). pap. *(978-0-440-42152-8(7),* Delacorte Pr) Random House Publishing Group.
—Grk Smells a Rat. 2009. (J). *(978-0-385-90654-8(4),* Delacorte Pr) Random House Publishing Group.
—Grk Takes Revenge. 2010. (J). *(978-0-385-90655-5(2));* *(978-0-385-73723-4(8))* Random House Publishing Group. (Delacorte Pr).
Dodge, Louis. Everychild: A Story Which the Old May Interpret to the Young A. 2007. (ENG.). 178p. pap. 19.99 *(978-1-4346-1155-0(8));* 192p. pap. 21.99 *(978-1-4346-1226-7(0))* Creative Media Partners, LLC.
Dodge, Mary Mapes. Po No Kah an Indian Tale of Long Ago. 2004. reprint ed. pap. 15.95 *(978-1-4191-4185-0(6))* Kessinger Publishing, LLC.
Dodson, Emma. Speckle the Spider. Dodson, Emma, illus. 2010. (ENG., Illus.). 32p. (J). (gr. -1-2). 14.99 *(978-0-7636-4778-0(0))* Candlewick Pr.
Doe, Cheyenne. Kitty Kats. 2012. 264p. 27.95 *(978-1-4626-7201-1(9))* America Star Bks.
Dogiakis, Helen. Captain Terry the Pirate Cow's Adventure to Italy. 2011. 32p. pap. 14.99 *(978-1-4567-3131-1(9))* AuthorHouse.
Doherty, Gillian. Stories of Wizards. Edwards, Linda, illus. 2008. (Stories for Young Children Ser.). 95p. (J). (gr. 1). 16.99 *(978-0-7945-1915-5(6),* Usborne) EDC Publishing.
Doherty, Glen. Eddie's Christmas Surprise. 2012. 28p. pap. 12.99 *(978-1-4797-0976-2(X))* Xlibris Corp.
Dohlke, Nora. The Wonderful Adventures of Ozzie Sea Otter (Spanish) Stearns, Forest, illus. 2009. (ENG.). 98p. 19.95 *(978-0-9822046-2-7(0))* Bay Publishing.
—The Wonderful Adventures of Ozzie the Sea Otter. Stearns, Forest, illus. 2009. 98p. (J). 19.95 *(978-0-9822046-0-3(4))* Bay Publishing.
—The Wonderful Adventures of Ozzie the Sea Otter (Book & CD) Stearns, Forest, illus. 2009. (ENG.). 98p. 26.95 *(978-0-9822046-1-0(2))* Bay Publishing.
Doi, Kaya, illus. Chirri & Chirra. 2016. (ENG.). 40p. (J). (gr. -1-3). 15.95 *(978-1-59270-199-5(X))* Enchanted Lion Bks., LLC.
Dolenz, Ami. Harold & Agatha: The Mysterious Jewel. 2013. 176p. *(978-1-4602-0520-4(0));* pap. *(978-1-4602-0420-7(4))* FriesenPress.
Dominado, Guia. The Fear of Max. 2013. 40p. pap. 15.95 *(978-1-4908-0971-7(6),* WestBow Pr.) Author Solutions, Inc.
Dominguez, Elaudy. The Mountain Mystery. 2006. (Neighborhood Readers Ser.). (ENG.). 16p. (gr. 1-3). pap. 6.50 *(978-1-4042-7124-1(4),* Rosen Classroom) Rosen Publishing Group, Inc., The.

Dompierre, Judith. Jennie's Search for Colors & Numbers. 2012. 38p. 29.95 *(978-1-4626-9277-4(X))*; 40p. pap. 24.95 *(978-1-4626-6487-0(3))* America Star Bks.

—Little Bear's & Friend's Summer Trip. 32p. 2012. 29.95 *(978-1-4626-9272-9(9))* 2011. pap. 24.95 *(978-1-4512-6624-5(3))* America Star Bks.

Dompierre, Judith E. Jennie's New Adventure Looking for Letters. 2012. 28p. pap. 24.95 *(978-1-4626-9625-3(2))*; pap. 24.95 *(978-1-4626-9330-6(X))*; 24.95 *(978-1-4626-6486-3(5))* America Star Bks.

—Jennie's Search for Colors & Numbers. 2012. 40p. pap. 24.95 *(978-1-4626-9331-3(8))* America Star Bks.

—Little Bear's & Friend's Summer Trip. 2012. 32p. pap. 24.95 *(978-1-4626-9325-2(3))* America Star Bks.

Donaki & Rosenberry, Donald. Spectacular Journey. Rosenberry, Akiko & Rosenberry, Susan, illus. 2006. (J). per. 20.00 *(978-0-9771482-6-4(2)*, Ithaca Pr.) Authors & Artists Publishers of New York, Inc.

Donaldson, Julia. Charlie Cook's Favorite Book. Scheffler, Axel, illus. 2008. (ENG.). 32p. (J). (gr. -1-k). pap. 7.99 *(978-0-14-241138-4(8)*, Puffin Books) Penguin Young Readers Group.

—The Further Adventures of the Owl & the Pussy-Cat. Voake, Charlotte, illus. 2017. (ENG.). 32p. (J). (gr. -1-2). 16.99 *(978-0-7636-9081-6(3))* Candlewick Pr.

—The Gruffalo Theatre, 1. Scheffler, Axel, illus. 2008. (ENG.). 18p. (gr. 2-5). 34.95 *(978-0-230-53179-6(2)*, Macmillan) Pan Macmillan GBR. Dist: Trans-Atlantic Pubns., Inc.

—The Quick Brown Fox Cub. 2006. (Red Bananas Ser.). (ENG., Illus.). 48p. (J). (gr. -1-3). lib. bdg. *(978-0-7787-1080-6(7))* Crabtree Publishing Co.

Donbavand, Tommy. Blood of the Witch. 2009. (Scream Street Ser.: 2). (ENG., Illus.). 128p. (J). (gr. 3-7). pap. 5.99 *(978-0-7636-4607-3(5))* Candlewick Pr.

—Hunger of the Yeti. Donbavand, Tommy, illus. 2015. (Scream Street Ser.: 11). (ENG., Illus.). 128p. (J). (gr. 3-7). pap. 5.99 *(978-0-7636-5763-5(8))* Candlewick Pr.

—Terror of the Nightwatchman. 2014. (Scream Street Ser.: 9). (ENG.). 128p. (J). (gr. 3-7). pap. 5.99 *(978-0-7636-5761-1(1))* Candlewick Pr.

—Wolf. 2012. (Stoke Books Titles Ser.). 64p. (J). (gr. 5-8). pap. 45.32 *(978-0-7613-9225-5(4))* Stoke Bks.

Donfrancesco, Anna. Keepers of the Dream. 2007. (Illus.). 92p. per. *(978-1-84549-238-0(2))* arima publishing.

Dong Chen, Wei & Peng, Chao. Bane of Heaven. 2012. (Monkey King Ser.: 2). (ENG., Illus.). 176p. (gr. 5-8). pap. 9.99 *(978-89-94208-46-6(1))* JR Comics KOR. Dist: Lerner Publishing Group.

—Birth of Stone Monkey. 2012. (Monkey King Ser.: 1). (ENG., Illus.). 176p. (gr. 5-8). pap. 9.99 *(978-89-94208-45-9(3))* JR Comics KOR. Dist: Lerner Publishing Group.

—Enemies & New Friend. 2012. (Monkey King Ser.: 4). (ENG., Illus.). 176p. (gr. 5-8). pap. 9.99 *(978-89-94208-48-0(8))* JR Comics KOR. Dist: Lerner Publishing Group.

—Journey to the West. 2012. (Monkey King Ser.: 3). (ENG., Illus.). 176p. (gr. 5-8). pap. 9.99 *(978-89-94208-47-3(X))* JR Comics KOR. Dist: Lerner Publishing Group.

—Sacred Tree. 2012. (Monkey King Ser.: 6). (ENG., Illus.). 176p. (gr. 5-8). pap. 9.99 *(978-89-94208-50-3(X))* JR Comics KOR. Dist: Lerner Publishing Group.

—Three Trials. 2012. (Monkey King Ser.: 5). (ENG., Illus.). 176p. (gr. 5-8). pap. 9.99 *(978-89-94208-49-7(6))* JR Comics KOR. Dist: Lerner Publishing Group.

Donovan, Dan. Holiday Tails! 2011. 48p. pap. 19.26 *(978-1-4520-9628-5(7))* AuthorHouse.

Donovan, Dawn. Nosey Rosie. 2011. 28p. pap. 14.00 *(978-1-4634-1542-6(7))* AuthorHouse.

Donovan, Kim. St Viper's School for Super Villains. the Big Bank Burglary. Bean, Izzy, illus. 2013. 160p. pap. *(978-0-9571300-2-9(3))* Squawk Bks.

Doodler, Todd H. Rise of the Evil Army. 2017. (Super Fly Ser.: 4). (J). lib. bdg. 17.20 ***(978-0-606-39594-6(6))*** Turtleback Bks.

Dooley, Larry. A Peanut Butter & Monster Sandwich. Grzelak, Kyle, illus. 2013. 24p. pap. 12.95 *(978-1-61493-206-2(9))* Peppertree Pr., The.

Dooley, Sarah. Wilfred & Harold's Dinner Party Disaster . 2004. 35p. pap. 17.95 *(978-1-4137-1585-9(0))* PublishAmerica, Inc.

Dor, George Vincent. Sit. 2012. (Illus.). 112p. 27.45 *(978-1-4678-9732-7(9))*; pap. 15.18 *(978-1-4678-9731-0(0))* AuthorHouse.

Dora the Explorer Publishing Staff. Rockin' Maraca Adventure: Storybook with Maracas. 2013. (ENG.). 32p. (J). (gr. -1-k). 17.99 *(978-0-7944-2918-8(1))* Reader's Digest Assn., Inc., The.

Doran, Colleen. Coda, Vol. 4. ltd. ed. 2007. (Distant Soil Ser.). (Illus.). 164p. (YA). lib. bdg. 29.95 *(978-1-58240-525-4(5))* Image Comics.

Dora's Magical Adventures, Set. 2008. (Dora the Explorer Ser.). (ENG.). 144p. (J). pap. 10.99 *(978-1-4169-7583-0(7)*, Simon Spotlight/Nickelodeon) Simon Spotlight/Nickelodeon.

Dorismond, Joanne R. A Day in New York with Beatrice & Duke. 2010. 37p. pap. 17.95 *(978-0-557-23850-7(1))* Lulu Pr., Inc.

Dorison, Xavier. The Emerald Maze, Vol. 3. Lauffray, Mathieu, illus. 2012. (Long John Silver Ser.: 3). (ENG.). 56p. pap. 13.95 *(978-1-84918-105-1(5))* CineBook GBR. Dist: National Bk. Network.

—Lady Vivian Hastings. Saincantin, Jerome, tr. from FRE. Lauffray, Mathieu, illus. 2011. (Long John Silver Ser.: 1). (ENG.). 56p. pap. 13.95 *(978-1-84918-062-7(8))* CineBook GBR. Dist: National Bk. Network.

—Long John Silver Vol. 4: Guiana-Capac. Lauffray, Mathieu, illus. 2014. (Long John Silver Ser.: 4). (ENG.). 64p. pap. 15.95 *(978-1-84918-175-4(6))* CineBook GBR. Dist: National Bk. Network.

—Neptune Vol. 2: Long John Silver. Lauffray, Mathieu, illus. 2011. (Long John Silver Ser.: 2). (ENG.). 56p. pap. 13.95 *(978-1-84918-072-6(5))* CineBook GBR. Dist: National Bk. Network.

Dorkin, Evan & Dyer, Sarah. Calla Cthulhu. Humiston, Erin & Mudron, Bill, illus. 2017. (ENG.). 136p. (gr. 5-9). pap. 12.99 ***(978-1-5067-0293-3(7))*** Dark Horse Comics.

Dorling Kindersley Publishing Staff. Alice Through the Looking Glass. 2016. (Ultimate Sticker Bks.). (ENG.). 16p. (J). (gr. 3-7). pap. 6.99 *(978-1-4654-5254-2(0)*, DK Children) Dorling Kindersley Publishing, Inc.

—Amazing Battles! 2015. (DK Readers Ser.). (ENG., Illus.). 48p. (J). (gr. 1-3). pap. 3.99 *(978-1-4654-3011-3(3)*, DK Children) Dorling Kindersley Publishing, Inc.

—Batman's Missions. 2015. (DK Readers Ser.). (ENG.). 64p. (J). (gr. 2-4). pap. 3.99 *(978-1-4654-3014-4(8)*, DK Children) Dorling Kindersley Publishing, Inc.

—The Brain Wars. 2013. (DK Reader Level 3 Ser.). lib. bdg. 13.55 *(978-0-606-32114-3(4)*, Turtleback) Turtleback Bks.

—Disney Frozen: the Enchanted Guide. 2015. (ENG., Illus.). 96p. (J). (gr. 1-4). 14.99 *(978-1-4654-4081-5(X)*, DK Children) Dorling Kindersley Publishing, Inc.

—DK Adventures: Star Wars: Jedi Battles: Star Wars: Jedi Battles. 2013. (DK Adventures Ser.). (ENG.). 128p. (J). (gr. 3-7). 16.99 *(978-1-4654-1813-5(X)*, DK Children) Dorling Kindersley Publishing, Inc.

—DK Adventures: Star Wars: Sith Wars: Star Wars: Sith Wars. 2013. (DK Adventures Ser.). (ENG., Illus.). 128p. (J). (gr. 3-7). 16.99 *(978-1-4654-1814-2(8)*, DK Children) Dorling Kindersley Publishing, Inc.

—DK Readers L3: LEGO DC Comics Super Heroes: Batman's Missions: LEGO DC Comics Super Heroes: Batman's Missions. 2015. (DK Readers Ser.). (ENG.). 64p. (J). (gr. 2-4). 14.99 *(978-1-4654-3013-7(X)*, DK Children) Dorling Kindersley Publishing, Inc.

—Jedi Battles. 2013. (DK Adventures Ser.). (ENG., Illus.). 128p. (J). (gr. 3-7). pap. 5.99 *(978-1-4654-1724-4(9)*, DK Children) Dorling Kindersley Publishing, Inc.

—Lego Friends: The Adventure Guide. 2015. (ENG., Illus.). 96p. (J). (gr. k-4). 16.99 *(978-1-4654-3549-1(2)*, DK Children) Dorling Kindersley Publishing, Inc.

—Meet the Rebels. 2014. (DK Readers Ser.). (ENG.). 32p. (J). (gr. 1-3). 14.99 *(978-1-4654-2268-2(4))*; pap. 3.99 *(978-1-4654-2269-9(2))* Dorling Kindersley Publishing, Inc. (DK Children).

—OBI-Wan Kenobi Jedi Knight, Level 3. 2012. (DK Readers Ser.). (ENG.). 48p. (J). (gr. 2-4). pap. 3.99 *(978-0-7566-9810-2(3)*, DK Children) Dorling Kindersley Publishing, Inc.

—Revenge of the Sith. 2013. (LEGO Star Wars DK Reader Ser.). lib. bdg. 13.55 *(978-0-606-32112-9(8)*, Turtleback) Turtleback Bks.

—Secrets of the Rebels. 2015. (Ultimate Sticker Collections). (ENG.). 96p. (J). (gr. 1-4). pap. 12.99 *(978-1-4654-3593-4(X)*, DK Children) Dorling Kindersley Publishing, Inc.

—Sith Wars. 2013. (DK Adventures Ser.). (ENG., Illus.). 128p. (J). (gr. 3-7). pap. 5.99 *(978-1-4654-1725-1(7)*, DK Children) Dorling Kindersley Publishing, Inc.

—Spider-Man: Inside the World of Your Friendly Neighborhood Hero. 2012. (ENG.). 200p. (J). (gr. 3-7). 24.99 *(978-0-7566-9089-2(7)*, DK Children) Dorling Kindersley Publishing, Inc.

—Summer Adventures. 2013. (DK Reader Level 3 Ser.). lib. bdg. 13.55 *(978-0-606-31476-3(8)*, Turtleback) Turtleback Bks.

—Super Heroes - Ready for Action! 2013. (LEGO DC Universe DK Readers Ser.). lib. bdg. 13.55 *(978-0-606-31474-9(1)*, Turtleback) Turtleback Bks.

—Who Saved the Galaxy? 2012. (DK Readers Ser.). (ENG., Illus.). 32p. (J). (gr. k-4). pap. 3.99 *(978-0-7566-9808-9(1)*, DK Children) Dorling Kindersley Publishing, Inc.

Dorling Kindersley Publishing Staff & Beecroft, Simon. Ackbar's Underwater Army, Level 3. 2012. (DK Readers Ser.). (ENG.). 48p. (J). (gr. 2-4). 3.99 *(978-0-7566-9247-6(4)*, DK Children) Dorling Kindersley Publishing, Inc.

—Clone Wars - Jedi Adventures. 2009. (DK Readers Ser.). (ENG.). 48p. (J). (gr. 3-7). pap. 3.99 *(978-0-7566-4527-4(1)*, DK Children) Dorling Kindersley Publishing, Inc.

—Luke Skywalker's Amazing Story. 2008. (DK Readers Ser.). (ENG.). 32p. (J). (gr. k-2). pap. 3.99 *(978-0-7566-4518-2(2)*, DK Children) Dorling Kindersley Publishing, Inc.

Dorling Kindersley Publishing Staff & Fentiman, David. Fight the Empire! 2015. (DK Readers Ser.). (ENG.). 64p. (J). (gr. 2-4). pap. 3.99 *(978-1-4654-1989-7(6)*, DK Children) Dorling Kindersley Publishing, Inc.

—Fight the Empire. 2015. (DK Readers Ser.). (ENG.). 64p. (J). (gr. 2-4). 14.99 *(978-1-4654-1988-0(8)*, DK Children) Dorling Kindersley Publishing, Inc.

Dorling Kindersley Publishing Staff & Hibbert, Clare. Boba Fett Jedi Hunter, Level 2. 2011. (DK Readers Ser.). (ENG.). 32p. (J). (gr. 1-3). 3.99 *(978-0-7566-8281-1(9)*, DK Children) Dorling Kindersley Publishing, Inc.

—Clone Troopers in Action. 2010. (DK Readers Ser.). (ENG.). 32p. (J). (gr. 1-3). 3.99 *(978-0-7566-6691-0(0)*, DK Children) Dorling Kindersley Publishing, Inc.

Dorling Kindersley Publishing Staff & Kent, Lindsay. The Adventures of Han Solo, Level 2. 2011. (DK Readers Ser.). (ENG.). 32p. (J). (gr. -1-1). 3.99 *(978-0-7566-8252-1(5)*, DK Children) Dorling Kindersley Publishing, Inc.

Dorling Kindersley Publishing Staff & Khatreja, Himani. DK Readers L2: LEGO Star Wars: Free the Galaxy. 2015. (DK Readers Ser.). (ENG.). 48p. (J). (gr. k-4). pap. 3.99 *(978-1-4654-3793-8(2)*, DK Children) Dorling Kindersley Publishing, Inc.

Dorling Kindersley Publishing Staff & Last, Shari. The Adventures of C-3PO. 2014. (DK Readers Ser.). (ENG.). 32p. (J). (gr. 1-3). 14.99 *(978-1-4654-1683-4(8)*, DK Children) Dorling Kindersley Publishing, Inc.

Dorling Kindersley Publishing Staff & Scott, Heather. Stand Aside - Bounty Hunters! 2009. (DK Readers Ser.). (ENG.). 32p. (J). (gr. 1-3). 3.99 *(978-0-7566-5775-8(X)*, DK Children) Dorling Kindersley Publishing, Inc.

Dorling Kindersley Publishing Staff, et al. Alice Through the Looking Glass: The Complete Visual Guide. 2016. (ENG., Illus.). 96p. (J). (gr. 3-7). 16.99 *(978-1-4654-5255-9(9)*, DK Children) Dorling Kindersley Publishing, Inc.

—The Clone Wars - Pirates... & Worse! 2009. (DK Readers Ser.). (ENG., Illus.). 32p. (J). (gr. k-2). 3.99 *(978-0-7566-5773-4(3)*, DK Children) Dorling Kindersley Publishing, Inc.

—Star Wars Character Encyclopedia, Updated & Expanded. 2016. (ENG., Illus.). 224p. (J). (gr. 2-5). 16.99 *(978-1-4654-4885-9(3)*, DK Children) Dorling Kindersley Publishing, Inc.

Dorman, Brandon. Hoolie & the Hooligans, Book 1: The Alien That Ate My Socks. Dorman, Brandon, illus. 2016. (Hoolie & the Hooligans Ser.: 1). (ENG., Illus.). 224p. (J). (gr. 2-7). 13.99 *(978-1-62972-222-1(7)*, Shadow Mountain) Shadow Mountain Publishing.

—Pirates of the Sea! Dorman, Brandon, illus. 2011. (ENG., Illus.). 32p. (J). (gr. -1-3). 16.99 *(978-0-06-204068-8(5)*, Greenwillow Bks.) HarperCollins Pubs.

Dorman, Brandon, illus. The Slippery Map. 2007. 288p. (J). (gr. 3-7). lib. bdg. 17.89 *(978-0-06-079109-4(8))* HarperCollins Pubs.

Dorothy, Grandma. Magic, Mystery, Adventure: Wild Animals Talk to Us. 2009. 196p. 24.99 *(978-1-4490-3578-5(7))*; pap. 14.99 *(978-1-4490-3579-2(5))* AuthorHouse.

Dorr, Shay. Khloe Dutch! 2011. 48p. pap. 8.95 *(978-1-4502-8332-8(2))* iUniverse, Inc.

Dorsey, Angela. Autumn of Angels. 2013. 128p. pap. *(978-1-927100-30-1(5))* Enchanted Pony Bks.

—Spring of Secrets. 2012. 122p. pap. *(978-1-927100-26-4(7))* Enchanted Pony Bks.

—Summer of Desperate Races. 2013. 126p. pap. *(978-1-927100-28-8(3))* Enchanted Pony Bks.

—Winter of Sinking Waters. 2012. 130p. pap. *(978-1-927100-25-7(9))* Enchanted Pony Bks.

—Winter of the Whinnies Brigade. 2013. 120p. pap. *(978-1-927100-32-5(1))* Enchanted Pony Bks.

Dorsey, Angela & Miller, Marina. Sun Chaser. 2012. 112p. pap. *(978-1-927100-21-9(6))* Enchanted Pony Bks.

Doscher, E. L. M. S. Emmy Sue & the Blue Moo. Doscher, Susan, illus. 2010. 20p. pap. 9.99 *(978-1-935125-92-1(3))* Robertson Publishing.

Dossantos, Laurie Staples. The Adventures of Stormy. 2009. 34p. pap. 10.50 *(978-1-60693-365-7(5)*, Eloquent Bks.) Strategic Book Publishing & Rights Agency (SBPRA).

Dostoyevsky, Fyodor. Fiodor Mijailovich Dostoievsky. Acosta, Patricia, illus. 2003. (Cajon de Cuentos Ser.). (SPA.). 223p. (J). (gr. 4-7). *(978-958-30-1027-9(8))* Panamericana Editorial.

DOT. My Grandkids Need to Go Home!, 1 vol. 2010. 20p. pap. 24.95 *(978-1-4489-9254-6(0))* PublishAmerica, Inc.

Dotich, Rebecca Kai. Peanut & Pearl's Picnic Adventure. Alley, R. W., illus. 2008. (My First I Can Read Ser.). (ENG.). 32p. (J). (gr. -1 — 1). pap. 3.99 *(978-0-06-054922-0(X))* HarperCollins Pubs.

Doty, Linda. Hydrangea Hill: A New Home for Amy Manchester. 2008. 182p. pap. 24.95 *(978-1-60610-840-6(9))* America Star Bks.

Doucet, Patricia. The Adventures of Blackie & Brownie. 2012. 26p. pap. 19.99 *(978-1-62230-887-3(5))* Salem Author Services.

Doucette, Christina. Gordon's Treasure! A Sparkle Cove Adventure. 2011. 44p. (gr. 1-2). pap. 19.99 *(978-1-4634-0487-1(5))* AuthorHouse.

Dougherty, John. Stinkbomb & Ketchup-Face & the Badness of Badgers. Ricks, Sam, illus. 2017. (Stinkbomb & Ketchup-Face Ser.). (ENG.). 144p. (J). (gr. 3-7). 15.99 *(978-1-101-99662-1(5)*, G.P. Putnam's Sons Books for Young Readers) Penguin Young Readers Group.

Douglas, Alan. Afloat: Or Adventures on Watery Trails. 2007. 120p. pap. 18.99 *(978-1-4346-6016-9(8))*; (ENG.). 134p. pap. 19.99 *(978-1-4346-6017-6(6))* Creative Media Partners, LLC.

Douglas, Atom. Mathew's Space Ship. Douglas, Atom, . 2007. (Illus.). 32p. (J). 6.50 *(978-0-9798316-0-7(1))* JaxPublishing.net.

Douglas, H. I. Voyage to the Stars: David's First Adventure. 2006. 156p. pap. 24.95 *(978-1-4241-1176-3(5))* America Star Bks.

Douglas-Hobbs, Kathy. Kobe & the Rescue Adventure. 2012. 16p. pap. 15.99 *(978-1-4772-0326-2(5))* AuthorHouse.

Douglas, Margaret. Spirit of Meradoon. 2012. 192p. (gr. 2-2). 30.95 *(978-1-4497-6471-5(1))*; pap. 13.95 *(978-1-4497-6470-8(3))* Author Solutions, Inc. (WestBow Pr.).

Douglas, Rich. The Secret of the Dogs. 2008. (ENG.). 266p. pap. 12.50 *(978-1-4196-8783-9(2))* CreateSpace Independent Publishing Platform.

Douglas, Ryke Leigh. Sam's Surprise. 2008. 28p. per. 12.95 *(978-1-4327-0850-4(3))* Outskirts Pr., Inc.

Douglass, E. The Squirrel Friends Adventures: The Monster & the Great Storm. 2013. 100p. 19.95 *(978-1-4759-6640-4(7))*; pap. 9.95 *(978-1-4759-6638-1(5))* iUniverse, Inc.

Doust, Jon & Spillman, Ken. Magwheel Madness. 2005. (Illus.). 128p. (J). pap. 13.50 *(978-1-920731-76-2(8))* Fremantle Pr. AUS. Dist: Independent Pubs. Group.

Douthit, George. Boy Who Slept with Bears. 2005. 60p. pap. 12.95 *(978-0-9700127-3-9(X))* Sweet Success Pr.

Doutrive, Kaleb D. The Funny Chaps. 2012. 24p. pap. 11.00 *(978-0-9851574-1-8(0))* Bran Nue Productions.

Dove, Trudy. The Bunnies. 2016. (ENG.). 119p. (J). pap. 13.95 *(978-1-78554-301-2(6)*, c0670ba6-0dfd-4dc5-aa05-8aea2923e1a3) Austin, Stan AUS. Dist: Bookmasters Distribution.

—Trudy Dove. 2016. (ENG.). 119p. (J). 23.95 *(978-1-78554-302-9(4)*, aad1053f-29f3-47b2-9e68-1fe956b33a80) Austin, Stan AUS. Dist: Bookmasters Distribution.

Dovey, Belinda. Alphabet Adventures. 2012. 136p. pap. 71.99 *(978-1-4653-7250-5(4))* Xlibris Corp.

Downer, Ann. Hatching Magic. 2004. (ENG.). 256p. (J). (gr. 3-7). reprint ed. pap. 15.99 *(978-0-689-87057-6(4)*, Atheneum Bks. for Young Readers) Simon & Schuster Children's Publishing.

Downes, Alice. Lucy & the Magic Loom: A Rainbow Loomer's Adventure Story. 2015. (ENG.). 112p. (gr. k-5). pap. 7.99 *(978-1-63450-137-8(3)*, Sky Pony Pr.) Skyhorse Publishing Co., Inc.

Downest, Madeline. Lucy & the Magic Loom: the Daring Rescue: A Rainbow Loomer's Adventure Story. 2016. (ENG.). 112p. (J). (gr. k-5). pap. 7.99 *(978-1-63450-215-3(9)*, Sky Pony Pr.) Skyhorse Publishing Co., Inc.

Downie, David. David & Jacko. Tatsi, Andreanna, tr. Seroya, Tea, illus. 2012. 52p. pap. *(978-1-922159-24-3(7))*; pap. *(978-1-922159-15-1(8))* Blue Peg Publishing.

—David & Jacko. Ivanova, Kalina, tr. Seroya, Tea, illus. 2012. 52p. pap. *(978-1-922159-01-4(8))* Blue Peg Publishing.

—David & Jacko. Seroya, Tea, illus. 2012. 52p. pap. *(978-1-922159-99-1(9))* Blue Peg Publishing.

Dowson, Jonas. Meteor Man. 2012. 48p. pap. 37.37 *(978-1-4771-3435-1(2))* Xlibris Corp.

Dowswell, Paul. Eleven Eleven. 2012. (ENG., Illus.). 224p. (YA). (gr. 8). pap. 14.99 *(978-1-4088-2623-2(2)*, 9781408826232, Bloomsbury USA Childrens) Bloomsbury Publishing USA.

Dowswell, Paul & Harvey, Gill. True Adventure Stories. 2004. 144p. (YA). (gr. 4-18). lib. bdg. 20.95 *(978-1-58086-703-0(0))* EDC Publishing.

Doyle, Arthur Conan. Adv of the Devils Foot. 2010. (Illus.). 254p. (J). pap. *(978-4-591-11698-2(0))* Fukuinkan Shoten.

—Adventures of Sherlock Holmes. 2008. (Bring the Classics to Life Ser.). (ENG., Illus.). 72p. (gr. 5-12). pap., act. bk. ed. 10.95 *(978-1-55576-064-9(3)*, EDCTR-504B) EDCON Publishing Group.

—Sherlock Holmes & the Adventure of Black Peter. Rohrbach, Sophie & Morrow, J. T., illus. 2012. (On the Case with Holmes & Watson Ser.: 11). (ENG.). 48p. (J). (gr. 4-6). lib. bdg. 27.93 *(978-0-7613-7092-5(7))* Lerner Publishing Group.

—Sherlock Holmes & the Adventure of the Cardboard Box. Rohrbach, Sophie & Morrow, J. T., illus. 2012. (On the Case with Holmes & Watson Ser.: 12). (ENG.). 48p. (J). (gr. 4-6). lib. bdg. 27.93 *(978-0-7613-7090-1(0))* Lerner Publishing Group.

—Sherlock Holmes & the Three Garridebs. Rohrbach, Sophie & Morrow, J. T., illus. 2012. (On the Case with Holmes & Watson Ser.: 13). (ENG.). 48p. (J). (gr. 4-6). lib. bdg. 27.93 *(978-0-7613-7091-8(9))* Lerner Publishing Group.

Doyle, Helen. The Rainbow Pals. 2011. 96p. pap. 39.39 *(978-1-4567-0169-7(X))* AuthorHouse.

Doyle, Malachy & Philpot, Graham. Jack the Giant-Killer. 2009. (Hopscotch Adventures Ser.). (Illus.). 31p. (J). (gr. 1). lib. bdg. 25.65 *(978-1-59771-184-5(5))* Sea-To-Sea Pubns.

Doyle, Patrick H. T. Edgar Font's Hunt for a House to Haunt: Adventure Three: the Flint Island Treehouse. 2008. (Illus.). 300p. (J). per. 7.99 *(978-0-9786132-2-8(8))* Armadillo Bks.

Doyle, Roddy. Brilliant. Hughes, Emily, illus. 2015. (ENG.). 192p. (J). (gr. 3-7). 16.95 *(978-1-4197-1479-5(1)*, Amulet Bks.) Abrams, Inc.

Dragon: Enter the Realm. 2007. (YA). per. *(978-1-934345-43-6(1))* SouthWest Pubns.

Dragon: The Fantasy Continues. 2007. (YA). per. *(978-1-934345-44-3(X))* SouthWest Pubns.

Dragt, Tonke. The Letter for the King. 2015. (ENG., Illus.). 528p. (J). (gr. 7). 18.99 *(978-0-545-81978-7(4))* Scholastic, Inc.

Drake, Christina M. Milo the Monkey. 2013. 88p. *(978-1-4602-2323-9(3))* FriesenPress.

Drake, David. Kidd's Grand Adventure. 2003. 190p. (YA). mass mkt. 13.99 *(978-1-885631-71-8(5))* Hutchison, G.F. Pr.

Drake, Jennifer & Feltham, Sarah. Scotty's Postcards from Rome. 2012. (ENG., Illus.). 27p. (J). pap. 10.95 *(978-0-578-10548-2(9))* Drake Feltham Publishing.

Draper, Adrian. Chili Peppers in Oatmeal. 2012. 30p. 24.95 *(978-1-4626-5553-3(X))* America Star Bks.

Draper, Rohan. Sunny & Mayo. 2012. 146p. 46.72 *(978-1-4771-0446-0(1))*; pap. 28.03 *(978-1-4771-0445-3(3))* Xlibris Corp.

Draper, Sharon M. Stars & Sparks on Stage. Watson, Jesse Joshua, illus. 2007. (Ziggy & the Black Dinosaurs Ser.: 6). (ENG.). 160p. (J). pap. 4.99 *(978-1-4169-0001-6(2)*, Simon & Schuster/Paula Wiseman Bks.) Simon & Schuster/Paula Wiseman Bks.

Drawson, Blair. Flying Dimitri, 1 vol. (ENG., Illus.). 32p. (J). 16.95 *(978-0-88899-284-0(X))* Groundwood Bks. CAN. Dist: Publishers Group West (PGW).

The Dreamer Who Unlocked the Secrets of the Universe... 2004. (Illus.). 126p. (YA). pap. 11.11 *(978-0-9749196-1-4(6))* Don Quixote Publishing Co. Inc.

DreamWorks. Dinotrux - Build It Up! 2016. (ENG.). 12p. (J). (gr. -1-k). bds. 10.99 *(978-0-7944-3806-7(7))* Studio Fun International.

Dreisbach, Kristin Wolf. Winston the Duck & His Big Orange Bill. Dreisbach, Kristin Wolf & Foreman, Austin Lee, illus. 2013. 20p. pap. 13.97 *(978-1-62212-897-6(4)*, Strategic Bk. Publishing) Strategic Book Publishing & Rights Agency (SBPRA).

Drella, Michele. Un Laberinto de Graci. 2012. 26p. pap. 13.95 *(978-1-4497-7191-1(2)*, WestBow Pr.) Author Solutions, Inc.

—A Mazing Grace. 2012. 26p. pap. 13.95 *(978-1-4497-4781-7(7)*, WestBow Pr.) Author Solutions, Inc.

Dressel, Toni Ankeney. Sophie Smiles, 1 vol. 2010. 22p. 24.95 *(978-1-4489-7234-0(5))* PublishAmerica, Inc.

Drew, Alejandrina. Abra Cadabra, Patas de Cabra: A Spanish, English Story for Young Readers. Satcher, David & Ford, Richard, trs. Mora, Mauricio, illus. 41p. (J). pap. 15.95 *(978-1-57168-505-6(7))* Eakin Pr.

Drew, Joyce. Grandma's Adventures with Benjamin. Drew, Benjamin, illus. 2013. 16p. pap. 24.95 *(978-1-63004-098-7(3))* America Star Bks.

Dries, L. M. H. Stella & the Rocks. 2013. 28p. pap. 13.99 *(978-1-4808-0409-8(6))* Archway Publishing.

Driesel, Amy. Why Gretchen Can't Spell. 2009. 28p. pap. 13.99 *(978-1-4343-6166-0(7))* AuthorHouse.

Driftin' Aarong. Claude Henry, the Iditarod Mouse ~3: The Great Castaway Adventure. 2009. 92p. pap. 9.95 *(978-1-4401-1949-1(X))* iUniverse, Inc.

Drischel, Candy L. Restless with the Dark Moon Rising. 2008. 105p. pap. 19.95 *(978-1-60610-421-7(7))* America Star Bks.

Drogo, Susette. Five Blessings. Lukas, Mary, illus. 2008. 24p. (J). pap. 15.00 *(978-0-9800611-8-5(0))* Orr Bks.

The Drums of Legenderry. 2006. (J). per. *(978-0-9776967-0-3(7))* Legenderry.com.

Dube, Tory. A Trixi, a Shmoop & a Monster. Vasilevsky, Marina, illus. 2013. 32p. 19.99 *(978-0-9886193-1-9(8))* Dube, Tory.

Dube, Tory Lee. A Trixi, a Shmoop & a Monster. 2013. 32p. pap. 9.99 *(978-0-9886193-0-2(X))* Dube, Tory.

Dublin, Anne. Stealing Time. 2014. (Jonah Wiley Adventure Ser.: 1). (ENG.). 144p. (J). pap. 9.99 *(978-1-4597-0973-7(X))* Dundurn CAN. Dist: Ingram Publisher Services.

Dubois, Ricardo. Ghost Squirrel. 2007. 99p. pap. 12.49 *(978-0-615-15411-4(5))* Dubois, Ricardo S.

Dubos, Delphine. The Planet of Wind. Burrell, Carol klio, tr. Elyum Studio Staff, illus. 2012. (Little Prince Ser.: 1). (ENG.).

56p. (J). (gr. 4-8). pap. 7.95 *(978-0-8225-9422-2(6)*, Graphic Universe™) Lerner Publishing Group.

Dubrule, Jackie. Kelli, God & New York. Baker, David, illus. 2013. 28p. pap. 24.95 *(978-1-4560-0969-4(9))* America Star Bks.

Dubyn, Bj. The Thrilling & Dynamic Adventures of Barbara Ann, Her Kid Brother, Billy, Jr , & Manfred the Magnificent, Their Parrot. 2008. 104p. pap. 15.99 *(978-1-4363-2652-0(4))* Xlibris Corp.

Duce, Gillian. Magic & Mayhem. 2006. (ENG.). 212p. per. *(978-1-894936-64-4(7))* Saga Bks.

Ducharme, P. J. The Adventures of Jungle Foot Rot, 1 vol. 2009. 17p. pap. 24.95 *(978-1-60813-918-7(2))* America Star Bks.

Duchéne, Mique. The Mystery of Foo & the Great Chasm. 2012. 32p. (-18). pap. 17.99 *(978-1-4772-7211-4(9))* AuthorHouse.

Duckers, John. The Amazing Adventures of the Silly Six. 2013. (Illus.). 188p. pap. *(978-1-78148-626-9(3))* Grosvenor Hse. Publishing Ltd.

Duckett, Brenda. Summit Lane. 2005. 79p. pap. 10.99 *(978-1-4116-3897-6(2))* Lulu Pr., Inc.

Ducote, Billie Seaon. The Adventures of Artie Eco Part One: The Problem with Greed, 2 vols, Vol. 1. Ducote, Billie Seaon, illus. 2007. (ENG., Illus.). 26p. (J). 18.95 *(978-0-9787597-5-9(3))* PureLight Pubns.

—The Adventures of Artie Eco Part Two: The Problem with Greed Artie Eco Goes to Dirtyville, 2 vols., Vol. 2. Ducote, Billie Seaon, illus. 2007. (Illus.). 26p. (J). act. bk. ed. 18.95 *(978-0-9787597-1-1(0))* PureLight Pubns.

Duddle, Jonny. King of Space. Duddle, Jonny, illus. 2013. (ENG., Illus.). 44p. (J). (gr. -1-2). 15.99 *(978-0-7636-6435-0(9)*, Templar) Candlewick Pr.

Dudley, Blanche R. Siggy & the Bullies. 2013. 42p. 22.50 *(978-1-4575-1994-9(1))*; pap. 11.95 *(978-1-4575-1993-2(3))* Dog Ear Publishing, LLC.

Dudley, Maywill. The Story of Little Red Riding Hood. 2005. reprint ed. pap. 15.95 *(978-1-4191-5430-0(3))* Kessinger Publishing, LLC.

Due, Kirsten L. Bearen Bear & the Bunbury Tales. Berends, Jenny, illus. 2013. 194p. pap. *(978-0-9884916-3-2(X))* Roxby Media Ltd.

Duerr, Doug. The Adventures of Jazz & Elliott: Danielle goes to the Magical Land of Roop-E-Doo. 2010. 29p. (J). pap. 17.95 *(978-1-4327-5405-1(X))* Outskirts Pr., Inc.

—The Adventures of Jazz & Elliott: The Love Ness Monster. 2012. (ENG.). 37p. (J). pap. 14.95 *(978-1-4327-7746-3(7))* Outskirts Pr., Inc.

Duey, Kathleen. Arthur. Epstein, Eugene, illus. Gould, Robert, photos by. 2005. (Time Soldiers Ser.: Vol. 4). (ENG.). 96p. (J). (gr. k-2). per. 5.95 *(978-1-929945-56-6(6))* Big Guy Bks., Inc.

—Arthur. Gould, Robert, photos by. 2006. (Time Soldiers Ser.). (ENG., Illus.). 96p. (gr. -1-4). 24.21 *(978-1-59961-224-9(0))* Spotlight.

—Castle Avamir. Rayyan, Omar, illus. 2003. (Unicorn's Secret Ser.: 7). (ENG.). 80p. (J). (gr. 2-5). pap. 5.99 *(978-0-689-85372-2(6)*, Simon & Schuster/Paula Wiseman Bks.) Simon & Schuster/Paula Wiseman Bks.

—Pony Express: Time Soldiers Book #7. 2009. (Time Soldiers Ser.). (ENG., Illus.). (J). (gr. k-2). 48p. 15.95 *(978-1-929945-68-9(X))*; 96p. pap. 5.95 *(978-1-929945-69-6(8))* Big Guy Bks., Inc.

—Rex. Epstein, Eugene, illus. Gould, Robert, photos by. 2003. (Time Soldiers Ser.: Bk. 1). (ENG.). 48p. (J). (gr. k-2). pap. 7.95 *(978-1-929945-20-7(5))* Big Guy Bks., Inc.

—Rex. Epstein, Eugene, illus. Gould, Robert, photos by. 2006. (Time Soldiers Ser.: Bk. 1). (ENG.). 96p. (gr. -1-7). 24.21 *(978-1-59961-226-3(7))* Spotlight.

—Rex. Epstein, Eugene, illus. Epstein, Eugene, photos by. 2006. (Time Soldiers Ser.: Bk. 1). (ENG.). 96p. (gr. 4-7). 24.21 *(978-1-59961-225-6(9))* Spotlight.

—Rex 2. Epstein, Eugene, illus. Gould, Robert, photos by. 2003. (Time Soldiers Ser.: Bk. 2). (ENG.). 48p. (J). (gr. k-2). pap. 8.95 *(978-1-929945-27-6(2))* Big Guy Bks., Inc.

—Samurai. Epstein, Eugene, illus. Gould, Robert, photos by. 2007. (Time Soldiers Ser.). (ENG.). 96p. (gr. k-2). 24.21 *(978-1-59961-229-4(1))* Spotlight.

—The Sunset Gates. Rayyan, Omar, illus. 2005. 76p. (J). lib. bdg. 15.00 *(978-1-59054-918-6(X))* Fitzgerald Bks.

—Time Soldiers, Set. Epstein, Eugene, illus. Gould, Robert, photos by. gif. ed. 2003. (Time Soldiers Ser.). (ENG.). 144p. (J). (gr. k-2). 32.95 *(978-1-929945-23-8(X))* Big Guy Bks., Inc.

—Time Soldiers - Patch. Epstein, Eugene, illus. Gould, Robert, photos by. 2005. (Time Soldiers Ser.: Bk. 3). (ENG.). 96p. (J). (gr. k-2). per. 5.95 *(978-1-929945-55-9(8))* Big Guy Bks., Inc.

—True Heart. Rayyan, Omar, illus. 2003. (Unicorn's Secret Ser.: 6). (ENG.). 80p. (J). (gr. 2-5). pap. 6.99 *(978-0-689-85370-8(X)*, Aladdin) Simon & Schuster Children's Publishing.

Duey, Kathleen & Bale, Karen A. Train Wreck: Kansas 1892. 2016. (Survivors Ser.). (ENG., Illus.). 160p. (J). (gr. 3-7). pap. 6.99 *(978-1-4814-6800-8(6)*, Aladdin) Simon & Schuster Children's Publishing.

Duey, Kathleen, et al. Katie & the Mustang. 2004. (Hoofbeats Ser.: 2). (ENG.). (J). (gr. 3-7). Bk. 2. 2nd ed. 144p. 5.99 *(978-0-14-240091-3(2))*Bk. 3. 3rd ed. 144p. 5.99 *(978-0-14-240092-0(0))*Bk. 4. 4th ed. 140p. 5.99 *(978-0-14-240093-7(9))* Penguin Young Readers Group. (Puffin Books).

Duffield, J. W. Bert Wilson in the Rockies. 2006. 26.95 *(978-1-4218-2964-7(9))*; pap. 11.95 *(978-1-4218-3064-3(7))* 1st World Publishing, Inc.

Duffy, Jacqueline Ann. Dillon the Dog Finds His Family. 2008. 24p. pap. 24.95 *(978-1-60563-331-2(3))* America Star Bks.

Dufresne, Michele. Adventure in the Purple Forest. 2003. (Spaceboy Set 1 Ser.). (ENG., Illus.). (J). pap. 7.33 *(978-1-932570-06-9(3))* Pioneer Valley Bks.

Dugan, David J. The Missing Prince of Distria. 2008. 36p. pap. 24.95 *(978-1-60563-587-3(1))* America Star Bks.

Duguay, Kathleen. Andy Finds a Home. 2012. 24p. pap. 28.03 *(978-1-4691-7390-0(5))* Xlibris Corp.

Duk, Lor. The Firestorm Heart: A Dragon Friend Story. 2010. 236p. pap. 15.95 *(978-1-4401-9474-0(2))* iUniverse, Inc.

Dukes, Martin. Worm Winds of Zanzibar. 2013. 420p. pap. *(978-0-9575679-0-0(1))* Dukes, Martin.

Duley, Wayla C. Strawberry Soup & Other Crazy Things. 2013. 28p. pap. 24.95 *(978-1-63000-952-6(0))* America Star Bks.

Duling, Astrid. The Guinea Pigs Twiggy & Molly. 2012. 134p. pap. *(978-3-8423-1287-6(3))* Books on Demand GmbH.

Dumas, Alexandre. Barbie & the Three Musketeers: A Junior Novelization. Choi, Allan, illus. 2009. 93p. (J). *(978-0-545-09413-9(5))* Scholastic, Inc.

—The Count of Monte Cristo. 2008. (Bring the Classics to Life Ser.). (ENG., Illus.). 72p. (gr. 5-12). pap., act. bk. ed. 10.95 *(978-1-55576-359-6(6)*, EDCTR-509B) EDCON Publishing Group.

—The Count of Monte Cristo, 1 vol. Fisher, Scott, illus. 2011. (Calico Illustrated Classics Ser.). (ENG.). 112p. (YA). (gr. 3-6). 27.07 *(978-1-60270-744-3(8))* Magic Wagon.

—The Man in the Iron Mask. Howell, Troy, illus. 2008. (Classic Starts(tm) Ser.). (ENG.). 160p. (J). (gr. 2-4). 6.95 *(978-1-4027-4579-9(6))* Sterling Publishing Co., Inc.

—The Three Musketeers, 1 vol. Lacey, Mike, illus. 2011. (Calico Illustrated Classics Ser.). (ENG.). 112p. (YA). (gr. 3-6). 27.07 *(978-1-60270-751-1(0))* Magic Wagon.

—The Three Musketeers. Hochman, Eleanor, tr. from FRE. 2006. (ENG., Illus.). 672p. (gr. 12-18). 7.95 *(978-0-451-53003-5(9)*, Signet) Penguin Publishing Group.

—The Three Musketeers. Tayal, Amit, illus. 2011. (Campfire Graphic Novels Ser.). (ENG.). 104p. (YA). (gr. 3-7). pap. 12.99 *(978-93-80028-57-6(1)*, Campfire) Steerforth Pr.

—The Three Musketeers. Dunn, Robert, illus. 2013. 46p. (J). *(978-1-4351-4812-3(6))* Barnes & Noble, Inc.

—The Three Musketeers. Akib, Jamel, illus. 2007. (Classic Starts(tm) Ser.). (ENG.). 160p. (J). (gr. 2-4). 6.95 *(978-1-4027-3695-7(9))* Sterling Publishing Co., Inc.

—The Three Musketeers. Helquist, Brett, illus. 2011. (ENG.). 384p. (J). (gr. 5). pap. 6.99 *(978-0-06-206013-6(9))* HarperCollins Pubs.

—The Three Musketeers. 2004. reprint ed. pap. 1.99 *(978-1-4192-8527-1(0))* Kessinger Publishing, LLC.

—Los Tres Mosqueteros.Tr. of Trois Mousquetaires. (SPA.). (J). 2.49 *(978-968-890-125-0(3))* Edivision Compania Editorial, S.A. de C.V. MEX. Dist: Continental Bk. Co., Inc.

Dumont, Naomi K. Mr. Kitty & the Magical Island. 2005. 39p. pap. 24.95 *(978-1-4137-3294-8(1))* PublishAmerica, Inc.

Duncalf, Joanne. The Zookeeper's Menagerie. 2007. pap. 15.95 *(978-0-9797232-1-6(3))* Twelve Star Pr.

Duncan, Jodi. Happy Flowers. 2009. 24p. pap. 14.50 *(978-1-60693-519-4(4)*, Eloquent Bks.) Strategic Book Publishing & Rights Agency (SBPRA).

Duncan, Lois. Killing Mr. Griffin. 2009. 7.61 *(978-0-7848-3597-5(7)*, Everbind) Marco Bk. Co.

Duncan, Sandy Frances. Gold Rush Orphan. 2005. (ENG., Illus.). 280p. (J). pap. 10.95 *(978-1-55380-012-5(5))* Ronsdale Pr. CAN. Dist: Literary Pr. Group of Canada.

Duncan, Tisha Admire. Myrtle the Blue Eyed Turtle: A My Dirty Cat Mutt Adventure. 2012. 28p. pap. 14.95 *(978-1-4497-5727-4(8)*, WestBow Pr.) Author Solutions, Inc.

Dundon, Adamarie. Niklas Rogers: The Adventure Begins. 2004. 60p. pap. 13.95 *(978-1-4184-4361-0(1))* AuthorHouse.

Dunmore, Helen. The Deep. 2009. (Ingo Ser.: 3). 336p. (YA). (gr. 5-18). 16.99 *(978-0-06-081858-6(1))* HarperCollins Pubs.

—Ingo. 2006. 328p. (J). (gr. 5-9). lib. bdg. 17.89 *(978-0-06-081853-1(0))* HarperCollins Pubs.

Dunn, Edward Grieves. Crinkles Academy for Wizards. 2008. 424p. pap. *(978-1-906210-98-4(5))* Grosvenor Hse. Publishing Ltd.

Dunn, Jill. Littering Is for Losers. Hill, Bodhi, illus. 2012. 64p. (J). 21.99 *(978-0-9852146-2-3(7))* AM Ink Publishing.

Dunn, Joeming. The Eyes: A Graphic Novel Tour, 1 vol. Espinosa, Rod, illus. 2009. (Graphic Body Ser.). (ENG.). 32p. (J). (gr. 3-6). 28.50 *(978-1-60270-684-2(0))* ABDO Publishing Co.

—The Kidneys: A Graphic Novel Tour, 1 vol. Espinosa, Rod, illus. 2009. (Graphic Body Ser.). (ENG.). 32p. (J). (gr. 3-6). 28.50 *(978-1-60270-686-6(7))* ABDO Publishing Co.

—The Lighthouse Mystery. Dunn, Ben, illus. 2010. (Boxcar Children Graphic Novels Ser.: 14). (ENG.). 32p. (J). (gr. 2-5). pap. 6.99 *(978-0-8075-4547-8(3))* Whitman, Albert & Co.

—The Liver: A Graphic Novel Tour, 1 vol. Espinosa, Rod, illus. 2009. (Graphic Body Ser.). (ENG.). 32p. (J). (gr. 3-6). 28.50 *(978-1-60270-687-3(5))* ABDO Publishing Co.

—The Lungs: A Graphic Novel Tour, 1 vol. Espinosa, Rod, illus. 2009. (Graphic Body Ser.). (ENG.). 32p. (J). (gr. 3-6). 28.50 *(978-1-60270-688-0(3))* ABDO Publishing Co.

—Mountain Top Mystery, No. 15. Dunn, Ben, illus. 2010. (Boxcar Children Graphic Novels Ser.: 15). (ENG.). 32p. (J). (gr. 1-5). pap. 6.99 *(978-0-8075-5294-0(1))* Whitman, Albert & Co.

—The Woodshed Mystery. Dunn, Ben, illus. 2010. (Boxcar Children Graphic Novels Ser.: 13). (ENG.). 32p. (J). (gr. 1-5). pap. 6.99 *(978-0-8075-9208-3(0))* Whitman, Albert & Co.

Dunn, Joeming & Espinosa, Rod. The Brain: A Graphic Novel Tour, 1 vol. Espinosa, Rod, illus. 2009. (Graphic Body Ser.). (ENG., Illus.). 32p. (J). (gr. 3-6). 28.50 *(978-1-60270-683-5(2))* ABDO Publishing Co.

Dunn, Matthew. Day One. 2007. 192p. (YA). per. 15.00 *(978-0-9794908-0-4(4))* Onondaga Hill Publishing.

Dunn, Robert, illus. The Littlest Bunny in Michigan: An Easter Adventure. 2015. (ENG.). 32p. (J). (-3). 9.99 *(978-1-4926-1117-2(4)*, Sourcebooks Jabberwocky) Sourcebooks, Inc.

—The Littlest Bunny in Rhode Island: An Easter Adventure. 2015. (ENG.). 32p. (J). (-3). 9.99 *(978-1-4926-1189-9(1)*, Sourcebooks Jabberwocky) Sourcebooks, Inc.

Dunphy, Catherine. Caitlin, 1 vol. 2006. (ENG., Illus.). 184p. (YA). (gr. 5-10). 7.95 *(978-1-55028-923-7(3)*, 9781550289237) Lorimer, James & Co., Ltd., Pubs. CAN. Dist: Casemate Pubs. & Bk. Distributors, LLC.

Dunphy, Lorraine F. An Australian Fairy Tale. 2008. 32p. pap. 14.95 *(978-1-59858-553-7(3))* Dog Ear Publishing, LLC.

Dunrea, Olivier. Gossie & Friends Big Book of Adventures. 2017. (Gossie & Friends Ser.). (ENG., Illus.). 288p. (J). (gr. -1-3). 15.99 *(978-0-544-77980-8(0)*, HMH Books For Young Readers) Houghton Mifflin Harcourt Publishing Co.

Dunsany, Taylor. The Little Witch Who Lost Her Broom & Other Stories. 2008. 48p. pap. 8.95 *(978-0-595-52506-5(7))* iUniverse, Inc.

Dunseith, Peter. Bird of Heaven: The Story of a Swazi Sangoma. 2010. 257p. pap. *(978-0-624-04557-1(9))* NB Pubs. Ltd.

Dupree, J. And S. Cat Tales: The Travel Adventures of Blue Boo & Sambootoo. 2008. 164p. pap. 10.95 *(978-1-4327-3243-1(9))* Outskirts Pr., Inc.

Duran, Teresa. Fabulame un Fabula. Espluga, Maria, illus. 2003. (SPA.). 96p. *(978-84-480-1638-8(6)*, TM30428) Timun Mas, Editorial S.A. ESP. Dist: Lectorum Pubns., Inc.

Durango, Julia. The Leveller. 2015. (ENG.). 256p. (YA). (gr. 8). 17.99 *(978-0-06-231400-0(9)*, HarperTeen) HarperCollins Pubs.

Durbin, William & Durbin, Barbara. Dead Man's Rapids. 2017. (J). pap. ***(978-1-5179-0224-7(X))*** Univ. of Minnesota Pr.

Durham, Paul. Fork-Tongue Charmers. Antonsson, Petur, illus. 2015. (Luck Uglies Ser.: 2). (ENG.). 416p. (J). (gr. 3-7). 16.99 *(978-0-06-227153-2(9))* HarperCollins Pubs.

—The Luck Uglies. Antonsson, Petur, illus. 2014. (Luck Uglies Ser.: 1). (ENG.). 400p. (J). (gr. 3-7). 16.99 *(978-0-06-227150-1(4))* HarperCollins Pubs.

—The Luck Uglies #2: Fork-Tongue Charmers. Antonsson, Petur, illus. 2016. (Luck Uglies Ser.: 2). 432p. (J). (gr. 3-7). pap. 7.99 *(978-0-06-227154-9(7))* HarperCollins Pubs.

—The Luck Uglies #3: Rise of the Ragged Clover. Antonsson, Petur, illus. 2016. (Luck Uglies Ser.: 3). 400p. (J). (gr. 3-7). 16.99 *(978-0-06-227156-3(3))* HarperCollins Pubs.

Durham, Victor G. Submarine Boys & the Spies. 2006. 27.95 *(978-1-4218-3008-7(6))*; pap. 12.95 *(978-1-4218-3108-4(2))* 1st World Publishing, Inc.

—The Submarine Boys & the Spies: Dodging the Sharks of the Deep. 2007. (ENG.). 160p. pap. 19.99 *(978-1-4346-2818-3(3))*; 170p. pap. 21.99 *(978-1-4346-2847-3(7))* Creative Media Partners, LLC.

—Submarine Boys for the Flag. 2006. 27.95 *(978-1-4218-3009-4(4))*; pap. 12.95 *(978-1-4218-3109-1(0))* 1st World Publishing, Inc.

—The Submarine Boys for the Flag: Deeding Their Lives to Uncle Sam. 2007. (ENG.). 158p. pap. 19.99 *(978-1-4346-2849-7(3))*; 174p. pap. 21.99 *(978-1-4346-2884-8(1))* Creative Media Partners, LLC.

—Submarine Boys Lightning Cruise. 2006. 27.95 *(978-1-4218-3010-0(8))*; pap. 12.95 *(978-1-4218-3110-7(4))* 1st World Publishing, Inc.

—The Submarine Boys' Lightning Cruise: The Young Kings of the Deep. 2007. (ENG.). 156p. pap. 19.99 *(978-1-4346-2848-0(5))*; 174p. pap. 21.99 *(978-1-4346-2883-1(3))* Creative Media Partners, LLC.

—Submarine Boys on Duty. 2006. 27.95 *(978-1-4218-3011-7(6))*; pap. 12.95 *(978-1-4218-3111-4(2))* 1st World Publishing, Inc.

—Submarine Boys Trial Trip. 2006. 26.95 *(978-1-4218-3012-4(4))*; pap. 11.95 *(978-1-4218-3112-1(0))* 1st World Publishing, Inc.

Duriez, Marcel Ray. The Many Adventures of Cuddles: Tobey, Pandora & Cuddles. 2012. 30p. 25.95 *(978-1-4327-8806-3(X))* Outskirts Pr., Inc.

Durrant, Geraldine. Pirate Gran. Forshall, Rose, illus. 2009. 32p. (J). 19.95 *(978-0-948065-96-5(6))* National Maritime Museum GBR. Dist: Independent Pubs. Group.

Durst, Sarah Beth. Enchanted Ivy. (ENG.). (YA). (gr. 7). 2011. 336p. pap. 9.99 *(978-1-4169-8646-1(4))* 2010. 320p. 16.99 *(978-1-4169-8645-4(6))* McElderry, Margaret K. Bks. (McElderry, Margaret K. Bks.).

Dussling, Jennifer. Which Way, Wendy? Thornburgh, Rebecca McKillip, illus. 2005. (Social Studies Connects). 32p. (J). pap. 5.95 *(978-1-57565-147-7(5))* Kane Press, Inc.

Duthie, Marion. The Adventures of Pussy Whoosie. 2013. 72p. pap. 21.50 *(978-1-62212-614-9(9)*, Strategic Bk. Publishing) Strategic Book Publishing & Rights Agency (SBPRA).

Dutka, Pamela. Madame Cecil's Swamp. 2005. 48p. pap. 16.95 *(978-1-4137-9701-5(6))* PublishAmerica, Inc.

Dutton, John. Tiger's Island. Dutton, John, illus. unabr. ed. Date not set. (Dreamguard Ser.: Vol. 2). (Illus.). viii, 245p. (J). pap. 12.95 *(978-0-9577556-1-1(9))* Samara Pr.

Dutton, Louise. The Wishing Moon. 2005. pap. 31.95 *(978-1-4191-5933-6(X))* Kessinger Publishing, LLC.

Duvall, Deborah L. Rabbit Goes to Kansas. Jacob, Murv, illus. 2007. (ENG.). 32p. (J). (gr. 1-18). 16.95 *(978-0-8263-4181-5(0))* Univ. of New Mexico Pr.

Duxfield, Philip. Se. 2012. 80p. pap. 41.99 *(978-1-4771-3541-9(3))* Xlibris Corp.

Dvok, Eduard & Dvorák, Eduard. Bobek, the Cat with a Pompon Tail. Dvorák, Jaroslav, illus. 2010. 52p. pap. 17.00 *(978-1-60911-734-4(4)*, Eloquent Bks.) Strategic Book Publishing & Rights Agency (SBPRA).

Dwyer, Mary. Barnyard Bash. Dwyer, Michael, illus. 2006. (J). spiral bd. incl. cd-rom *(978-1-933843-00-1(4))* That's Me Publishing, LLC.

Dyan, Penelope. Ben's Adventures — -Proof Positive That Boys Will Be Boys. Dyan, Penelope, illus. 2008. (Illus.). 44p. pap. 11.95 *(978-1-935118-40-4(4))* Bellissima Publishing, LLC.

—The Carousel. Dyan, Penelope, illus. 2010. (Illus.). 34p. pap. 11.95 *(978-1-935630-26-5(1))* Bellissima Publishing, LLC.

—The Fish That Got Away — -for Boys Only(r). Dyan, Penelope, illus. 2010. (Illus.). 34p. pap. 11.95 *(978-1-935630-29-6(6))* Bellissima Publishing, LLC.

—The Last Mustang. 2013. 94p. pap. 8.95 *(978-1-61477-077-0(8))* Bellissima Publishing, LLC.

—Mikey & Me & the Bees, the Continuing Story of a Girl & Her Dog. Dyan, Penelope, illus. 2010. (Illus.). 48p. pap. 14.95 *(978-1-935118-90-9(0))* Bellissima Publishing, LLC.

—Out of Deepest Africa — -Another of Ben's Big Adventures — -for Boys Only (r). Dyan, Penelope, illus. 2010. (Illus.). 34p. pap. 11.95 *(978-1-935630-13-5(X))* Bellissima Publishing, LLC.

—Summer Surfs the Olympic Trials. 2008. 168p. pap. 11.95 *(978-1-935118-06-0(4))* Bellissima Publishing, LLC.

—Ted E Bearæs Most Unfortunate Experience to Date. Dyan, Penelope, illus. 2009. (Illus.). 44p. pap. 11.95 *(978-1-935118-44-2(7))* Bellissima Publishing, LLC.

Dyan, Penelope, creator. For Love of Pete! The Story of the Boy Who Played the Taps on Iwo Jima. 2005. 292p. (YA). per. 15.95 *(978-0-9768417-9-1(7))* Bellissima Publishing, LLC.

Dyas, Amy. The Robins of St Lawrence Church. 2009. 128p. pap. 29.96 *(978-0-9786567-8-2(4))* Parson Place Pr., LLC.

Dycus, Warren. Monyum Bay - Time Travel. 2010. 24p. 13.99 *(978-0-557-45202-6(3))* Lulu Pr., Inc.

Dye, Troy & Kelesides, Tom. Goblin Chronicles 01A. 2008. (YA). 3.50 *(978-0-9801314-0-6(5))* Ape Entertainment.

—Goblin Chronicles #1B. 2008. (YA). 3.50 *(978-0-9801314-1-3(3))* Ape Entertainment.

—Goblin Chronicles #2A. 2008. (Illus.). 32p. (J). 3.50 *(978-0-9801314-2-0(1))* Ape Entertainment.

—Goblin Chronicles #2B. 2008. (Illus.). 32p. (J). 3.50 *(978-0-9801314-3-7(X))* Ape Entertainment.

Dynyel. Windy the Winged Unicorn. 2004. 140p. 24.95 *(978-1-4184-8615-0(9))* AuthorHouse.

Dyreng, Chelsea Bagley. The Last Messenger of Zitol. 2016. (YA). pap. *(978-1-4621-1896-0(8))* Cedar Fort, Inc./CFI Distribution.

Dyson, Edward. Missing Link. 2006. pap. 11.95 *(978-1-4218-3040-7(X))* 1st World Publishing, Inc.

Dyson, Tony. The Crystal Wand. 2005. 242p. pap. 14.01 *(978-1-4116-5596-6(6))* Lulu Pr., Inc.

Eade, Oliver. The Terminus. 2013. 264p. pap. *(978-1-909411-26-5(4))* Mauve Square Publishing.

Eakins, Bonny Mae. Wonder Island. Eakins, Bonny Mae & Hoffbauer, Wyng, illus. 2nd ed. 2013. 80p. pap. 14.95 *(978-1-893660-26-7(5))* Ravenhawk Bks.

Eames, Brian. The Dagger X. 2013. (Dagger Chronicles Ser.). (ENG.). 368p. (J). (gr. 3-7). 15.99 *(978-1-4424-6855-9(6)*, Simon & Schuster Bks. For Young Readers) Simon & Schuster Bks. For Young Readers.

—The Dagger X. 2013. (Dagger Chronicles Ser.). (ENG., Illus.). 368p. (J). (gr. 3-7). pap. 6.99 *(978-1-4424-6856-6(4)*, Simon & Schuster/Paula Wiseman Bks.) Simon & Schuster/Paula Wiseman Bks.

Earhart, Kristin. Arctic Freeze. 2015. (Race the Wild Ser.: 3). (ENG.). 144p. (J). (gr. 2-5). pap. 4.99 *(978-0-545-77355-3(5)*, Scholastic Paperbacks) Scholastic, Inc.

—Outback All-Stars. 2016. (Race the Wild Ser.: 5). lib. bdg. 14.75 *(978-0-606-38794-1(3))* Turtleback Bks.

—Outback All-Stars (Race the Wild #5) 2016. (Race the Wild Ser.: 5). (ENG., Illus.). 144p. (J). (gr. 2-5). pap. 4.99 *(978-0-545-94064-1(8)*, Scholastic Paperbacks) Scholastic, Inc.

—Race the Wild #2: Great Reef Games. 2015. (Race the Wild Ser.: 2). (ENG.). 144p. (J). (gr. 2-5). pap. 4.99 *(978-0-545-77354-6(7)*, Scholastic Paperbacks) Scholastic, Inc.

Earhart, Kristin. Savanna Showdown. 2016. (Illus.). 138p. (J). ***(978-1-5182-0302-2(7))*** Scholastic, Inc.

—Savanna Showdown. 2015. (Race the Wild Ser.: 4). (ENG., Illus.). 144p. (J). (gr. 2-5). lib. bdg. 14.75 *(978-0-606-38080-5(9))* Turtleback Bks.

Earl, Cheri Pray & Williams, Carol Lynch. The Rescue Begins in Delaware. Oliphant, Manelle, illus. 2013. (Just in Time Ser.: 1). (ENG.). 144p. (J). (gr. 3-7). pap. 9.95 *(978-1-938301-74-2(9))* Familius LLC.

Earls, J S. The Realm Unseen. 2010. 266p. (J). pap. 9.00 *(978-1-60039-155-2(9))* Lamp Post Inc.

—The Realm Unseen: Hard Cover. 2010. 266p. 16.00 *(978-1-60039-156-9(7))* Lamp Post Inc.

Earp-Bridgmon, Krista D. The Adventures of Jim-Bob: A Bearography. 2013. 24p. pap. 10.99 *(978-1-4582-1005-0(7)*, Abbott Pr.) Author Solutions, Inc.

Eason, Sarah. Don't Play Dirty, Gertie: Be Fair. 2013. (You Choose Ser.). 32p. (J). (gr. k-3). pap. 7.95 *(978-1-4644-0559-4(X)*, Enslow Elementary) Enslow Pubs., Inc.

East, Bob. Tommy Cat & the Giant Chickens. East, Matt, illus. 2008. 24p. per. 24.95 *(978-1-4241-9242-7(0))* America Star Bks.

East, Jacqueline, illus. Peter Cottontailss Busy Day. 2009. 10p. 5.95 *(978-1-58117-862-3(X)*, Intervisual/Piggy Toes) Bendon, Inc.

Eastman, Brock D. & Eastman, Brock. Taken. 2011. (Illus.). 315p. (J). pap. *(978-1-59638-245-9(7))* P & R Publishing.

Eastman, Charles A. & Eastman, Elaine Goodale. The Raccoon & the Bee Tree. Susan, Turnbull, illus. 2013. 32p. (J). *(978-0-9860355-4-8(8))* South Dakota State Historical Society Pr.

Easton, Kelly. The Outlandish Adventures of Liberty Aimes. Swearingen, Greg, illus. 2011. (ENG.). 224p. (J). (gr. 3-7). pap. 6.99 *(978-0-375-83772-2(8)*, Yearling) Random Hse. Children's Bks.

Easton, Tom. Seven Second Delay. 2015. (ENG.). 240p. (J). (gr. 7-12). 16.95 *(978-0-8234-3209-7(2))* Holiday Hse., Inc.

Eaton, Kay A. Gleason, the Christmas Giraffe. 2009. 28p. pap. 12.50 *(978-1-4389-3010-7(0))* AuthorHouse.

Eaton, Walter Pricha. Peanut Cub Reporter: A Boy Scout's Life. 2005. pap. 28.95 *(978-1-885529-74-9(0))* Stevens Publishing.

Eaton, Walter Prichard. Boy Scouts in the White Mountains: the Story of a Long Hike. Merrill, Frank T., illus. 2006. (ENG.). 316p. per. 30.95 *(978-1-4286-4117-4(3))* Kessinger Publishing, LLC.

Eaves, G. L. Operation Tiger. 2011. 112p. 20.95 *(978-1-4620-1276-3(0))*; pap. 10.95 *(978-1-4620-1274-9(4))* iUniverse, Inc.

Ebeling, Vicki. The Winners Group. 2007. (J). per. 7.95 *(978-0-9779768-0-5(7))* Ebeling, Vicki.

Ebeltoft, Christine. Koo & Jay in the Rainforest. 2004. 34p. pap. 24.95 *(978-1-4137-3698-4(X))* PublishAmerica, Inc.

Eberhart, Nancy. The Adventures of Granny: Granny Goes to the Zoo. Pyers, Kelsey, illus. 2007. (J). (gr. -1-3). 13.99 *(978-1-59879-373-4(X))* Lifevest Publishing, Inc.

Eboch, Chris. The Ghost on the Stairs. 2009. (Haunted Ser.). (ENG.). 176p. (J). (gr. 3-7). pap. 5.99 *(978-1-4169-7548-9(9)*, Aladdin) Simon & Schuster Children's Publishing.

—The Knight in the Shadows. 2009. (Haunted Ser.). (ENG.). 192p. (J). (gr. 3-7). pap. 5.99 *(978-1-4169-7550-2(0)*, Simon & Schuster/Paula Wiseman Bks.) Simon & Schuster/Paula Wiseman Bks.

—The Riverboat Phantom. 2009. (Haunted Ser.). (ENG.). 192p. (J). (gr. 3-7). pap. 5.99 *(978-1-4169-7549-6(7),* Aladdin) Simon & Schuster Children's Publishing.

Eboch, M. M. Monster Island. 2015. (ENG.). 96p. (gr. 3-6). 31.36 *(978-1-63430-394-1(6))* Rourke Educational Media.

—Walking the Dragon's Back. 2015. (ENG.). 96p. (gr. 3-6). 31.36 *(978-1-63430-396-5(2))* Rourke Educational Media.

Echeverri, Catalina. There's a Dinosaur in My Bathtub. 2014. (ENG., Illus.). 32p. (J). (gr. -1-k). 21.00 *(978-1-4088-3938-6(5),* 9781408839386, Bloomsbury USA Childrens) Bloomsbury Publishing USA.

Ecton, Emily. Night of the Living Lawn Ornaments. 2009. (ENG.). 240p. (J). (gr. 3-7). pap. 5.99 *(978-1-4169-6451-3(7),* Aladdin) Simon & Schuster Children's Publishing.

Edge, A. M. Frankie Feinstein & the Fenworld Thief-Takers. 2013. 156p. (J). pap. *(978-1-78299-419-0(X))* FeedARead.com.

Edgin, Brenda. Little Winston & his Big Adventures in Natchez: Down in the Bayou. 2011. 16p. 12.95 *(978-1-4567-4421-2(6))* AuthorHouse.

—Little Winston & His Big Adventures in Natchez: New Home near the Woods. 2011. 16p. 12.99 *(978-1-4567-3639-2(6))* AuthorHouse.

Edginton, Ian. Assassin's Creed Last Descendants - Locus. Wijngaard, Caspar & Farrell, Triona, illus. 2017. (ENG.). 112p. (gr. 7). pap. 16.99 *(978-1-78276-313-0(9))* Titan Bks. Ltd. GBR. Dist: Penguin Random Hse. LLC.

Edmond, Wally. Cuddles the Chocolate Cow & Friends. Melinda, Sheffler, illus. 2006. 39p. (J). 14.95 *(978-1-59879-108-2(7));* per. 9.99 *(978-1-59879-125-9(7))* Lifevest Publishing, Inc.

Edmonds, Lin. Patric the Pony & the Shining Star. 2010. 36p. pap. 17.49 *(978-1-4520-7389-7(9))* AuthorHouse.

Edmondson, Frank. Mr. Frank's Magic School Bus: Rainbow's End Adventure, 1 vol. Edmondson, Brad, illus. 2010. 20p. 24.95 *(978-1-4512-1042-2(6))* PublishAmerica, Inc.

Educational Adventures, creator. Blazin' Hot: Picture Book (Spanish) 9x9. 2006. (SPA., Illus.). (J). 5.99 *(978-0-9770455-4-9(4))* Mighty Kids Media.

—Poison Patrol: Coloring/Activity Book (Spanish) w/ Snipe. 2006. (Illus.). (J). 2.99 *(978-1-933934-02-0(6))* Mighty Kids Media.

—Poison Patrol: Picture Book (Spanish) 9x9. 2006. (Illus.). (J). 5.99 *(978-1-933934-00-6(X))* Mighty Kids Media.

Edward, J. P. Truckin with Rocky, 1 vol. 2010. 22p. 24.95 *(978-1-4512-9082-0(9))* PublishAmerica, Inc.

Edward Stratemeyer. The Rover Boys on Treasure Isle: Or - the Strange Cruise of the Steam Yacht. Lt. ed. 2007. (ENG.). 202p. pap. 22.99 *(978-1-4264-8951-8(X))* Creative Media Partners, LLC.

Edwards, Amelia. Playground Friends, 1 vol. rev. ed. 2013. (Fiction Readers Ser.). (ENG., Illus.). 12p. (J). (gr. 1-1). 4.99 *(978-1-4333-5449-6(7));* pap. 12.96 *(978-1-4807-1128-0(4))* Shell Educational Publishing.

—The Treasure Hunt, 1 vol. 2013. (Fiction Readers Ser.). (ENG., Illus.). 24p. (J). (gr. 2-2). pap. 6.99 *(978-1-4333-5522-6(1))* Shell Educational Publishing.

Edwards, Carol. Jacy's Search for Jesus Frey, Daniel J., illus. 2005. 31p. (J). (gr. -1-3). 15.95 *(978-0-9755314-0-2(9))* Majestic Publishing, LLC.

Edwards, Cory, et al. Hoodwinked! The True Story of Little Red Riding Hood. 2005. (ENG., Illus.). 32p. (J). (gr. k-2). per. 9.95 *(978-1-57178-188-8(9))* Council Oak Bks.

Edwards, Felicity. The Spider King. 2012. 176p. pap. *(978-1-78176-753-5(X))* FeedARead.com.

Edwards, Garth. Escape from Mercy Hall. 2012. (Thorn Gate Trilogy Ser.). (Illus.). 192p. (J). (gr. 4-6). pap. 7.99 *(978-0-9567122-4-0(X))* Lerner Publishing Group.

—The King of the Castle. Stasyuk, Max, illus. 2011. (Adventures of Titch & Mitch Ser.). (J). pap. *(978-0-9567449-7-5(4))* Inside Pocket Publishing, Ltd.

—The Trolls of Sugar Loaf Wood. Stasyuk, Max, illus. 2011. (Adventures of Titch & Mitch Ser.). (J). pap. *(978-0-9567449-6-8(6))* Inside Pocket Publishing, Ltd.

Edwards, Garth & Stasyuk, Maz. Secrets of Mercy Hall. 2012. (Thorn Gate Trilogy Ser.). (ENG., Illus.). 112p. (gr. 4-6). pap. *(978-0-9567122-5-7(8))* Inside Pocket Publishing, Ltd.

Edwards, Garth & Statyuk, Max. Heroes of Mercy Hall. 2012. (Thorn Gate Trilogy Ser.). (ENG., Illus.). 112p. (gr. 4-6). pap. *(978-0-9567122-6-4(6))* Inside Pocket Publishing, Ltd.

Edwards, Jaimi. Silly Sock. 2011. 24p. 11.99 *(978-1-4567-1412-3(0))* AuthorHouse.

Edwards, Janet. Earth Star. 2014. (ENG.). 287p. (YA). (gr. 7). 17.99 *(978-1-61614-897-3(7),* Pyr Bks.) Prometheus Bks., Pubs.

Edwards, Jean E. Adventure Tales: For Kids Who Want to Become Better Readers. 2012. 102p. 24.99 *(978-1-4771-4118-2(9))* Xlibris Corp.

Edwards, Judith. At the Top of the Mountain: The Adventures of Will Ryan & the Civilian Conservation Corps, 1936-38, Book III. 2013. (ENG., Illus.). 144p. (J). (gr. 3-7). pap. 12.95 *(978-1-884592-63-8(5))* Images from the Past, Inc.

Edwards, Meinir Wyn. Maelgwn, King of Gwynedd. Wade, Gini, illus. 2008. (ENG.). 24p. (J). pap. 4.95 *(978-1-84771-024-6(7))* Y Lolfa GBR. Dist: Dufour Editions, Inc.

Edwards, Nicholas. The Adventures of Santa Paws. 2010. (Santa Paws Ser.). (ENG.). 336p. (J). (gr. 3-7). pap. 7.99 *(978-0-545-22551-9(5),* Scholastic Paperbacks) Scholastic, Inc.

Edwards, Pat & Edwards, LaVell. Hello, Cosmo! De Angel, Miguel, illus. 2006. 24p. (J). lib. bdg. 17.95 *(978-1-932888-45-4(4))* Mascot Bks., Inc.

Edwards, R. G. Eafin Lokdore & the Altar of the Sun Book II. 2007. 264p. pap. 19.96 *(978-0-615-17785-4(9))* Edwards, R. G. Publishing.

Eeles, Alex. Suli's Big Race Blue Band. Rogers, Alan, illus. 2016. (Cambridge Reading Adventures Ser.). (ENG.). 14p. pap. 6.56 *(978-1-316-60086-3(6))* Cambridge Univ. Pr.

Egan, Catherine. Bone, Fog, Ash & Star, 1 vol. 2014. (Last Days of Tian Di Ser.: 3). (ENG.). 320p. (J). (gr. 6-10). pap. 12.95 *(978-1-55050-593-1(9))* Coteau Bks. CAN. Dist: Orca Bk. Pubs. USA.

—Julia Vanishes. 2016. (ENG.). 384p. (YA). (gr. 9). 17.99 *(978-0-553-52484-0(4),* Knopf Bks. for Young Readers) Random Hse. Children's Bks.

Egan, Catherine. Julia Vanishes. 2017. (Witch's Child Ser.: 1). (ENG.). 400p. (YA). (gr. 9). pap. 9.99 ***(978-0-553-52487-1(9),*** Ember) Random Hse. Children's Bks.

Egan, Tim. Dodsworth in New York. 2009. (Dodsworth Book Ser.). (ENG., Illus.). 48p. (J). (gr. 2-5). pap. 3.99 *(978-0-547-24831-8(8))* Houghton Mifflin Harcourt Publishing Co.

—Dodsworth in Paris. Egan, Tim, illus. 2010. (Dodsworth Book Ser.). (ENG., Illus.). 48p. (J). (gr. 1-4). pap. 3.99 *(978-0-547-33192-8(4))* Houghton Mifflin Harcourt Publishing Co.

Ehlin, Gina. Emma & Friends: Emma's Airport Adventure. Ayzenberg, Nina, illus. Lt. ed. 2005. 32p. (J). per. 10.99 *(978-1-59879-014-6(5))* Lifevest Publishing, Inc.

—Emma & Friends; Emma Rescues Cali. Ayzenberg, Nina, illus. Lt. ed. 2006. 24p. (J). per. 10.99 *(978-1-59879-112-9(5))* Lifevest Publishing, Inc.

—Emma's Airport Adventure. Ayesenberg, Nina, illus. Lt. ed. 2005. (Emma & Friends Ser.). 34p. (J). 15.99 *(978-1-59879-015-3(3))* Lifevest Publishing, Inc.

Ehrenhaft, Daniel. Friend Is Not a Verb. 2010. (ENG.). 256p. (YA). (gr. 8-18). 16.99 *(978-0-06-113106-6(7),* HarperTeen) HarperCollins Pubs.

Ehrmantraut, Brenda. Night Catch. Wehrman, Vicki, illus. 2005. 32p. (J). lib. bdg. 15.95 *(978-0-9729833-9-6(2))* Bubble Gum Pr.

Eichler, Ken. Swift Eagle's Dangerous Journey, 1 vol. 2009. 80p. pap. 16.95 *(978-1-61582-289-8(5))* PublishAmerica, Inc.

—Swift Eagle's Vision Quest, 1 vol. 2009. 95p. pap. 19.95 *(978-1-60703-649-4(5))* America Star Bks.

—Swift Eagle's Wagon Train Adventure, 1 vol. 2010. 80p. pap. 19.95 *(978-1-4489-4364-7(7))* America Star Bks.

Eid, Diab. Maido's Story: The Secret of the Engraved Spear. 2011. 114p. pap. 19.95 *(978-1-4560-9669-4(9))* America Star Bks.

Eilers, Roxanne. The Chocolate Brown Coat, 1 vol. 2010. 44p. pap. 24.95 *(978-1-4489-8540-1(4))* PublishAmerica, Inc.

Eilrich, Dinah Kay. Teeny Tessie's Big Baking Adventure. 2009. 28p. pap. 13.99 *(978-1-4490-2277-8(4))* AuthorHouse.

Eisenstein, Ann. Fallen Prey, a Sean Gray Junior Special Agent Mystery. Waugh, Leslie, ed. 2013. 190p. pap. 9.99 *(978-1-935711-31-5(8))* Peak City Publishing, LLC.

Eissler, Trevor. That 17th Hat. de Vries, Marloes, illus. 2012. 32p. (J). 20.00 *(978-0-9835558-1-0(8))* June Bks., LLC.

Elahe. The Story of Earth. 2012. 16p. pap. 12.68 *(978-1-4669-4764-1(0))* Trafford Publishing.

Elaine Vanier. Crystal Lights: Awaken the Power. 2009. 116p. pap. 10.95 *(978-1-4401-8357-7(0))* iUniverse, Inc.

Eldred, Delmer. Cubby & Scotty. 2012. 28p. pap. 19.99 *(978-1-4772-6579-6(1))* AuthorHouse.

Eldridge, Jim. The Invisible Assassin: The Malichea Quest. 2012. (Malichea Quest Ser.). (ENG.). 272p. (YA). (gr. 7). pap. 14.99 *(978-1-4088-1719-3(5),* 9781408817193, Bloomsbury USA Childrens) Bloomsbury Publishing USA.

—The Lethal Target: The Malichea Quest. 2013. (Malichea Quest Ser.). (ENG.). 240p. (YA). (gr. 7). pap. 14.99 *(978-1-4088-1721-6(7),* 9781408817216, Bloomsbury USA Childrens) Bloomsbury Publishing USA.

Eleanor Russell Brown. Mary Warin's Rats: A Time Warp Adventure. 2009. 24p. pap. 12.99 *(978-1-4389-6456-0(0))* AuthorHouse.

Eleniak, Erika. What Do You Do, If You Lose Your Lalabaloo? Monroe, Daniel, illus. 2013. 22p. pap. 9.99 *(978-0-9884468-7-8(1))* AM Ink Publishing.

An Elephant's Tail. 2010. 47p. pap. 6.00 *(978-81-7806-190-0(2))* Unicorn Bks. Pvt Ltd. IND. Dist: Mahal, Pustak Pubs., Booksellers & Order Suppliers.

Elerya. One Step Higher: Piano Paradise Book II, 1 vol. 2009. 79p. pap. 16.95 *(978-1-60749-477-5(9))* PublishAmerica, Inc.

Elfakir, Mahamad Ali. Blueberry Bubble Gum. 2013. 44p. 16.95 *(978-0-578-10978-7(6));* (J). pap. 11.95 *(978-0-578-10974-9(3))* Elfa Bks.

Elgert, C. J. The Elder Brothers & the Dragon's Portal. 2011. 236p. (gr. 4-6). 25.95 *(978-1-4620-1467-5(4));* pap. 15.95 *(978-1-4620-1466-8(6))* iUniverse, Inc.

—The Elder Brothers & the Therian Teacher. 2013. 200p. *(978-1-4602-3567-6(3))* FriesenPress.

Elgin, Wade. Martin's Imagination. 2013. 28p. pap. 9.00 *(978-1-61286-160-9(1))* Avid Readers Publishing Group.

Eliason, Scott. Andy's Magic Marble. 2008. 40p. per. 24.95 *(978-1-4241-8774-4(5))* America Star Bks.

Eliopulos, Nick, et al. Hero Story Collection. 2012. (Step into Reading Level 4 Ser.). lib. bdg. 18.40 *(978-0-606-26791-5(3),* Turtleback) Turtleback Bks.

Eliotte, Lisa J. The Adventures of Derby Doodle. 2009. 640p. pap. 25.99 *(978-1-4389-3058-9(5))* AuthorHouse.

Elizabeth, Julie & Elizabeth, Annelise. Take Care of Our Friend, Baby Dog. 2012. 24p. pap. 13.95 *(978-1-61493-115-7(1))* Peppertree Pr., The.

Elk, Ronit. A Surprise at Dancing Fields. 2009. 76p. pap. 10.49 *(978-1-4490-2064-4(X))* AuthorHouse.

Elkington, John. The Pirates of the Gayoso Bayou. 2012. 24p. pap. 15.99 *(978-1-4797-3940-0(5))* Xlibris Corp.

Elkins, J. Theron. You Are the Pea, & I Am the Carrot. Lemaître, Pascal, illus. 2013. (ENG.). 32p. (J). (gr. k-2). 16.95 *(978-1-4197-0850-3(3),* Abrams Bks. for Young Readers) Abrams, Inc.

Ellcock, Stephen. Stickyscapes Space. Cole, Tom Clohosy & Froese, Tom, illus. 2016. (ENG.). 24p. (J). (gr. 1-5). pap. 14.95 *(978-1-78067-843-6(6))* King, Laurence Publishing GBR. Dist: Hachette Bk. Group.

Ellefson, Benjamin. The Land Without Color. 2015. (ENG.). (J). 16.95 *(978-1-59298-844-0(X))* Beaver's Pond Pr., Inc.

Eller, Sylvia Klope. The Squirrel Who Hitchhiked to Atlanta. 2007. (Illus.). 32p. (J). pap. 8.00 *(978-0-8059-7596-3(9))* Dorrance Publishing Co., Inc.

Ellie. Bengal & Sengal. 2006. (J). pap. 8.00 *(978-0-8059-7273-3(0))* Dorrance Publishing Co., Inc.

Elliott, Alan. Willy the Texas Longhorn, 1 vol. Ford, Stephanie, illus. 2013. (ENG.). 32p. (J). (gr. k-3). 16.99 *(978-1-4556-1870-5(5))* Pelican Publishing Co., Inc.

Elliott, David. Baabwaa & Wooliam: A Tale of Literacy, Dental Hygiene, & Friendship. Sweet, Melissa, illus. 2017. (ENG.). 40p. (J). (gr. -1-3). 16.99 ***(978-0-7636-6074-1(4))*** Candlewick Pr.

—This Orq. (He #1!) Nichols, Lori, illus. 2016. (ENG.). 40p. (J). (gr. -1-2). 16.95 *(978-1-62979-336-8(1))* Boyds Mills Pr.

—What the Grizzly Knows. Grafe, Max, illus. 2008. (ENG.). 32p. (J). (gr. -1-2). 16.99 *(978-0-7636-2778-2(X))* Candlewick Pr.

Elliott, John C. Ri Ra: An Adventure Begins. 2006. 48p. pap. 16.95 *(978-1-4241-2771-9(8))* PublishAmerica, Inc.

Elliott, Laura Malone. Give Me Liberty. 2006. (Illus.). 376p. (J). (gr. 4-7). lib. bdg. 17.89 *(978-0-06-074422-9(7),* Tegen, Katherine Bks) HarperCollins Pubs.

Elliott, Linda. When Little Pinkie Gets Her Wings. Switzer, Bobbi, illus. 2007. 28p. per. 11.95 *(978-1-59800-871-5(4))* Outskirts Pr., Inc.

Elliott, M. G. The Magic Wheel: And the Adventures of Ding-How, Ah-So, & Mi-Tu. 2011. 220p. (gr. 4-6). 33.95 *(978-1-4497-3050-5(7));* pap. 17.95 *(978-1-4497-3049-9(3))* Author Solutions, Inc. (WestBow Pr.).

Elliott, Patricia. The Pale Assassin. 320p. (YA). 2010. (ENG.). (gr. 6-18). pap. 8.95 *(978-0-8234-2312-5(3))* 2009. (gr. 7-18). 17.95 *(978-0-8234-2250-0(X))* Holiday Hse., Inc.

Elliott, Rebecca. Baxter Is Missing. 2017. (Owl Diaries — Branches Ser.: 6). lib. bdg. 14.75 ***(978-0-606-40189-0(X))*** Turtleback Bks.

Elliott, Zetta. Ship of Souls, 0 vols. 2012. (ENG.). 140p. (gr. 7-9). pap. 9.95 *(978-1-61218-268-1(2),* 9781612182681, Amazon Children's Publishing) Amazon Publishing.

ELLIS, B. J. Mrs. Morgan's Adventures with Aliens. 2008. 249p. 29.50 *(978-0-557-00095-1(5))* Lulu Pr., Inc.

Ellis, Edward Sylvester. Two Boys in Wyoming: A Tale of Adventure (Northwest Series No. 3) 2007. (ENG.). 204p. (J). pap. 20.99 *(978-1-4346-3792-5(1));* 228p. pap. 22.99 *(978-1-4346-3793-2(X))* Creative Media Partners, LLC.

Ellis, Jason. The Long Journey to Sincerity. 2013. 268p. pap. *(978-1-906529-52-9(3))* JTT Publishing.

Ellis, Kat. Blackfin Sky. 2014. (ENG.). 304p. (YA). (gr. 2-17). pap. 9.95 *(978-0-7624-5401-3(6),* Running Pr. Kids) Running Pr. Bk. Pubs.

Ellis, Sarah. The Several Lives of Orphan Jack, 1 vol. St-Aubin, Bruno, illus. 2005. (ENG.). 88p. (J). pap. 8.95 *(978-0-88899-618-3(7))* Groundwood Bks. CAN. Dist: Publishers Group West (PGW).

Ellis, Tonya. Sophie Washington: Queen of the Bee. 2013. 100p. pap. 9.99 *(978-1-4575-1754-9(X))* Dog Ear Publishing, LLC.

Elmokadem, Shirley. Serena & The Moor's Last Sigh. 2007. 80p. per. *(978-1-84549-229-6(3))* arima publishing.

Elmore, Amber. Betsy Beansprout Adventure Guide. Short, Kasey, illus. 2011. (J). pap. 15.99 *(978-0-9822632-8-0(7))* ShadeTree Publishing, LLC.

Else, Barbara. The Queen & the Nobody Boy. Broad, Sam, illus. 2013. (Tales of Fontania Ser.). (ENG.). 328p. (J). (gr. 4-7). *(978-1-877579-49-3(1))* Gecko Pr.

—The Traveling Restaurant: Jasper's Voyage in Three Parts. 2012. (Gecko Press Titles Ser.). (ENG.). 304p. (J). (gr. 5-8). 17.95 *(978-1-877579-03-5(3))* Gecko Pr. NZL. Dist: Lerner Publishing Group.

Elson, William H. The Elson Readers, Vol. 5. 2004. reprint ed. pap. 1.99 *(978-1-4192-6079-7(0))* Kessinger Publishing, LLC.

Elston, Ashley. The Rules for Breaking. 2014. (Rules Ser.). (ENG.). 320p. (YA). (gr. 7-12). 16.99 *(978-1-4231-6898-0(4))* Hyperion Bks. for Children.

Eltoukhy, G. N. Fattopia a C: The Tablet Legacy. 2012. 28p. pap. 16.09 *(978-1-4669-3706-2(8))* Trafford Publishing.

Ely, Scott. The Elephant Mountains, 1 vol. 2011. (ENG.). 216p. (J). (gr. 8-12). lib. bdg. 19.95 *(978-1-55469-406-8(X))* Orca Bk. Pubs. USA.

Elys Dayton, Arwen. Traveler. 2016. (Seeker Ser.). (ENG.). 400p. (YA). (gr. 9). lib. bdg. 21.99 *(978-0-375-99149-3(2),* Delacorte Pr.) Random Hse. Children's Bks.

Elzina, Philda. Purple Is the Magic Colour. 2008. 36p. pap. 12.95 *(978-1-4327-1805-3(3))* Outskirts Pr., Inc.

Ember, Julia. Unicorn Tracks. 2016. (ENG., Illus.). (YA). (gr. 8-12). 24.99 ***(978-1-63477-987-6(8));*** 180p. (J). pap. 14.99 *(978-1-63476-878-8(7))* Dreamspinner Pr. (Harmony Ink Pr.).

Emerson, Alice. Betty Gordon in Washington. 2005. pap. 14.95 *(978-1-59605-610-7(X),* Cosimo Classics) Cosimo, Inc.

Emerson, Alice B. Betty Gordon in Washington. 2004. reprint ed. pap. 1.99 *(978-1-4192-0977-2(9));* pap. 20.95 *(978-1-4191-0977-5(4))* Kessinger Publishing, LLC.

—Ruth Fielding on Cliff Island: Or the Old Hunter's Treasure Box. 2007. (ENG.). 136p. pap. 18.99 *(978-1-4346-2493-2(5));* 148p. pap. 19.99 *(978-1-4346-2535-9(4))* Creative Media Partners, LLC.

—Ruth Fielding on the St. Lawrence or the. 2005. pap. 24.95 *(978-0-7661-9911-8(8))* Kessinger Publishing, LLC.

Emerson, Kevin. The Dark Shore. 2014. (Atlanteans Ser.: 2). (ENG.). 496p. (YA). (gr. 8). pap. 9.99 *(978-0-06-206283-3(2),* Tegen, Katherine Bks) HarperCollins Pubs.

—Last Day on Mars. 2017. (Chronicle of the Dark Star Ser.: 1). 336p. (J). (gr. 3-7). 16.99 *(978-0-06-230671-5(5),* Walden Pond Pr.) HarperCollins Pubs.

Emily, Katelyn. The Treasure-Trove Tales at the Gazebo. 2009. 120p. 18.95 *(978-1-59858-940-5(7));* pap. 8.95 *(978-1-59858-855-2(9))* Dog Ear Publishing, LLC.

Emmet, Laura. Julie Trent & the Lightning. 2003. 148p. pap. 11.95 *(978-0-595-27380-5(7),* Writers Club Pr.) iUniverse, Inc.

Ende, Michael & Michael, Ende. El Largo Camino Hacia Santa Cruz. Kehn, Regina, illus. (SPA.). 64p. (J). (gr. 3-5). 6.95 *(978-84-241-3354-2(4),* EV3073) Everest Editora ESP. Dist: Lectorum Pubns., Inc.

Enderlin, Lisa. Dad, There's a Bear in the Pool!!! 2012. 24p. pap. 24.95 *(978-1-4626-8263-8(4))* America Star Bks.

Endicott, Megan. In the Hall of the Mountain King. 2013. 48p. pap. 20.95 *(978-1-4582-0789-0(7),* Abbott Pr.) Author Solutions, Inc.

Endraske, Jackie. Dudley. 2006. 80p. pap. 12.95 *(978-0-9769460-0-7(9))* 2005. (J). lib. bdg. 19.95 net. *(978-0-9769460-1-4(7))* Loma, LLC.

Enge-Grandbois, Kathryn L. Suzy Q. 2008. 48p. pap. 16.95 *(978-1-4241-7650-2(6))* America Star Bks.

Engel, Amy. The Book of Ivy. 2014. (Entangled Teen Ser.). (ENG.). 304p. (YA). (gr. 7-12). pap. 9.99 *(978-1-62266-465-8(5),* 9781622664658) Entangled Publishing, LLC.

—The Book of Ivy. 2014. (YA). lib. bdg. 20.85 *(978-0-606-36239-7(9))* Turtleback Bks.

—The Book of Ivy. 2016. (CHI.). 272p. (YA). (gr. 7-12). pap. *(978-986-133-566-7(8))* Yuan Shen Pr. Co., Ltd.

Engel, Natalie. Marely & Me - Meet Marley. 2008. (I Can Read Level 1 Ser.). (ENG.). 32p. (J). (gr. k-3). pap. 3.99 *(978-0-06-170439-0(3))* HarperCollins Pubs.

Engelbreit, Mary. Mary Engelbreit's Nutcracker. Engelbreit, Mary, illus. 2014. (ENG., Illus.). 40p. (J). (gr. -1-3). 9.99 *(978-0-06-222417-0(4))* HarperCollins Pubs.

England, Don. Old Billy, the Bike. Scardina, Tom, illus. 2011. 24p. pap. 24.95 *(978-1-4560-3049-0(3))* America Star Bks.

England-Lord, Susan. The Adventures of Andrew: Breezy's Day Out. 2004. 23p. pap. 24.95 *(978-1-4137-3285-6(2))* PublishAmerica, Inc.

Engle, Dawn A. Ella's Golden Heart Goes to Camp. 2011. 40p. pap. 14.95 *(978-1-60911-392-6(6),* Eloquent Bks.) Strategic Book Publishing & Rights Agency (SBPRA).

Engle, Janice. Rainbows Stories & Poetry for Children. 2004. 277p. (J). pap. 15.08 *(978-1-4116-8612-0(8))* Lulu Pr., Inc.

Englert, June Scott. My Story by Jake, 1 vol. 2010. 48p. pap. 16.95 *(978-1-4489-5308-0(1))* America Star Bks.

Engram, Teta. Baxter & the Sidewalk Alligator. Holland, Lisa Tomms, illus. 2009. 32p. pap. 12.99 *(978-1-4389-9367-6(6))* AuthorHouse.

Eniwaye, Olu O. Adventures of Jabi-Jabi II: The Return of the King Fly 2nd in the series of adventures of the King Fly Jabi-Jabi. 2011. 48p. pap. 17.30 *(978-1-4634-1974-5(0))* AuthorHouse.

Enna, Bruno. Double Duck. Soffritti, Donald, illus. 2010. (ENG.). 112p. (J). pap. 9.99 *(978-1-60886-545-1(2))* Boom! Studios.

Enos, K. D. The Chronicles of Artici: Children of the Dead. 2012. 324p. 29.95 *(978-1-59330-781-3(0));* pap. 18.95 *(978-1-59330-780-6(2))* Aventine Pr.

Enright, Elizabeth. The Four-Story Mistake. Enright, Elizabeth, illus. 3rd ed. 2008. (Melendy Quartet Ser.: 2). (ENG., Illus.). 208p. (J). (gr. 3-7). per. 8.99 *(978-0-312-37599-7(9),* 9780312375997) Square Fish.

Ensor, Rod. Getting It. 2007. 216p. per. 14.95 *(978-0-595-44800-5(3))* iUniverse, Inc.

Epner, Paul. Herbert Hilligan & His Magical Adventure. Kuon, Vuthy & Nguyen, Duke, illus. 2003. 32p. (J). 15.95 *(978-0-9743335-0-2(6))* Imaginative Publishing, Ltd.

—Herbert Hilligan's Prehistoric Adventure. Kuon, Vuthy & Nguyen, Duke, illus. 2003. 32p. (J). 15.95 *(978-0-9743335-1-9(4))* Imaginative Publishing, Ltd.

—Herbert Hilligan's SeaWorld Adventure. Reed, Bill, illus. 2005. (J). 16.95 *(978-0-9743335-9-5(X))* Imaginative Publishing, Ltd.

Epner, Paul & Kuon, Vuthy. Herbert Hilligan's Prehistoric Adventure. 32p. (J). 15.95 *(978-1-57168-474-5(3))* Eakin Pr.

Epstein, Adam Jay & Jacobson, Andrew. The Familiars. 2011. (Familiars Ser.: 1). (ENG.). 384p. (J). (gr. 3-7). pap. 6.99 *(978-0-06-196110-6(8))* HarperCollins Pubs.

—The Familiars. Chiu, Bobby, illus. 2010. (Familiars Ser.: 1). (ENG.). 368p. (J). (gr. 3-7). 16.99 *(978-0-06-196108-3(6))* HarperCollins Pubs.

—Starbounders. McClellan, David, illus. 2013. (Starbounders Ser.: 1). (ENG.). 320p. (J). (gr. 3-7). 16.99 *(978-0-06-212022-9(0))* HarperCollins Pubs.

—Starbounders Vol. 2: Rebellion. 2014. (Starbounders Ser.: 2). (ENG.). 304p. (J). (gr. 3-7). 16.99 *(978-0-06-212027-4(1))* HarperCollins Pubs.

Epstein, Robin. Growing up Groovy: An Out of This World Adventure. 2005. 60p. (J). *(978-0-439-65795-2(4))* Scholastic, Inc.

Erdrich, Louise. The Porcupine Year. Erdrich, Louise, illus. 2008. (Birchbark House Ser.: 3). (ENG., Illus.). 208p. (J). (gr. 3-7). 16.99 *(978-0-06-029787-9(5))* HarperCollins Pubs.

Erickson, C. J. The Lovet Legend, 1 vol. 2010. 36p. 24.95 *(978-1-4512-1091-0(4))* PublishAmerica, Inc.

Erickson, Mary Ellen. What Happened to the Deer? Peanut Butter Club Mysteries. 2007. 182p. (J). 23.95 *(978-0-595-68396-3(7));* per. 13.95 *(978-0-595-42799-4(5))* iUniverse, Inc.

—Who Jinxed the CG Ranch? 2009. 196p. 24.95 *(978-1-4401-4218-5(1));* pap. 14.95 *(978-1-4401-4216-1(5))* iUniverse, Inc.

Erickson, Robert. Fluke Family Hero: Book Two in the Saga of Maynerd Dumsted. 2003. 276p. 27.95 *(978-0-595-66108-4(4));* pap. 17.95 *(978-0-595-30005-1(7))* iUniverse, Inc.

Eriksen, Craig A. Nollie Gnome & Friends: 1. Return from Holiday. 2008. 52p. pap. 10.50 *(978-1-4092-0497-8(9))* Lulu Pr., Inc.

Eriksen, Valanee. Christmas Bells & Hero's Tails. 2015. (Illus.). vi, 90p. (J). pap. 7.99 *(978-1-4621-1737-6(6))* Cedar Fort, Inc./CFI Distribution.

Erin, K. c. The Carnival. 2009. 60p. pap. 23.99 *(978-1-4389-7048-6(X))* AuthorHouse.

Ering, Timothy Basil. The Almost Fearless Hamilton Squidlegger. Ering, Timothy Basil, illus. 2014. (ENG., Illus.). 48p. (J). (gr. -1-2). 16.99 *(978-0-7636-2357-9(1))* Candlewick Pr.

—Necks Out for Adventure! Ering, Timothy Basil, illus. 2008. (ENG., Illus.). 48p. (J). (gr. -1-3). 16.99 *(978-0-7636-2355-5(5))* Candlewick Pr.

Erkert, Andrea. Islas de Relajacion. (Crecer Jugando Ser.). (SPA.). 94p. *(978-84-95456-83-0(4),* (87901)) Ediciones Oniro S.A.

Erlich, Arty. A Vegie Adventure. 2011. 24p. pap. *(978-1-4269-7427-4(2))* Trafford Publishing (UK) Ltd.

Erskine, Kathryn. The Badger Knight. 2014. (Illus.). (J). 325p. *(978-0-545-66293-2(1));* (ENG., 352p. (gr. 3-7). 17.99 *(978-0-545-46442-0(0))* Scholastic, Inc. (Scholastic Pr.).

Ersoz, Isabella. The Mad Mysterious Mansion: Izzy & Daisy. Ersoz, Sahin, illus. 2013. 40p. pap. 12.95 *(978-0-9912023-4-8(1))* Pep & Olie Publishing.

Ervin, Imogene. Charlie & Chu Chu's Day of Adventure. Ervin, Keith, illus. 2005. (J). 7.00 *(978-0-9771549-0-6(4))* Finer Moments.

Erwin, Kay. A Sheepdog's Christmas. 2008. 56p. pap. 10.99 *(978-1-60647-698-7(X))* Salem Author Services.

Esberger, Trudi. The Boy Who Lost His Bumble. Esberger, Trudi, illus. 2013. (Child's Play Library). (ENG., Illus.). 32p. (J). *(978-1-84643-662-8(1))* Child's Play International Ltd.

Escher, Jill. The Boneyville Dogs - Scuba Dogs. 2011. 24p. 12.79 *(978-1-4567-1908-1(4))* AuthorHouse.

Eschler, Linda. The Strawberry Fairies Save Sandcastle Island. 2007. 52p. per. 16.95 *(978-1-4241-9175-8(0))* America Star Bks.

Escondete y Grita, Vol. II. (Fantasmas de Fear Street Coleccion: No. 1). (SPA.). (J). (gr. 4-7). pap. 7.95 *(978-950-04-1999-4(8)*, EM4474) Emecé Editores S.A. ARG. Dist: Planeta Publishing Corp., Lectorum Pubns., Inc.

Escott, John & Pearson Longman Staff. Hannah & the Hurricane. 2nd ed. 2009. (ENG., Illus.). 20p. pap. 11.99 *(978-1-4058-6947-8(X))* Pearson Education.

Eshbaugh, Julie. Ivory & Bone. 2016. 272p. (YA). (gr. 9). 17.99 *(978-0-06-239925-0(X)*, HarperTeen) HarperCollins Pubs.

Eshed, Tina. The Adventures of Bunzy: The Beginning. 2009. 60p. pap. 24.49 *(978-1-4389-2673-5(1))* AuthorHouse.

Eskye, Tony. The Adventures of Fojo the Frog. 2009. (Illus.). 224p. pap. 14.49 *(978-1-4389-9530-4(X))* AuthorHouse.

Esola, Mike. Diary of a Dinosaur: The Attack of Benny. 2013. (ENG.). 154p. pap. 10.95 *(978-1-4787-1363-0(1))* Outskirts Pr., Inc.

Esperanza, Charles George, illus. Red, Yellow, Blue, & a Dash of White, Too! 2015. (ENG.). 40p. (J). (gr. -1-k). 16.99 *(978-1-62914-624-9(2)*, Sky Pony Pr.) Skyhorse Publishing Co., Inc.

Espinosa, Frank. Rocketo: The Journey to the Hidden Sea. 2006. (Illus.). 200p. (YA). pap. 19.99 *(978-0-9738966-4-0(7))* Speakeasy Comics CAN. Dist: Diamond Bk. Distributors.

Esposito, Tony. The Vagabond Penguin. 2010. 44p. 24.20 *(978-1-4269-4081-1(5))* Trafford Publishing.

Esquivel, Eric. Carnival Capers! 2016. (LEGO DC Super Heroes Ser.). lib. bdg. 13.55 *(978-0-606-38829-0(X))* Turtleback Bks.

Esseltine, Christopher R. Caleb's Quest. 2008. (J). pap. 13.99 *(978-1-59955-104-3(7))* Cedar Fort, Inc./CFI Distribution.

Essence, Angel. The Amazing Adventures of Callie the Cat: The Long Night. 2012. 28p. pap. 19.99 *(978-1-4772-9907-4(6))* AuthorHouse.

Estefan, Gloria & Garland, Michael. Noelle's Treasure Tale: A New Magically Mysterious Adventure. 2006. (SPA & ENG., Illus.). 32p. (gr. -1-3). 17.95 *(978-0-06-112614-7(4)*, Rayo) HarperCollins Pubs.

Estes, Eleanor. The Curious Adventures of Jimmy McGee. O'brien, John, illus. 2005. (ENG.). 224p. (J). (gr. 2-5). pap. 10.95 *(978-0-15-205517-2(7))* Houghton Mifflin Harcourt Publishing Co.

—The Tunnel of Hugsy Goode. Ardizzone, Edward, illus. 2003. (ENG.). 256p. (J). (gr. 2-5). pap. 14.95 *(978-0-15-204916-4(9))* Houghton Mifflin Harcourt Publishing Co.

Estes, Jhon H. Living with Big Foot, 1 vol. 2009. 55p. pap. 16.95 *(978-1-60703-197-0(3))* America Star Bks.

Estrada, E. Gabriela Aguileta. El Espejo en el Agua. De Gante, Guillermo, illus. rev. ed. 2006. (Castillo de la Lectura Naranja Ser.). (SPA & ENG.). 124p. (J). (gr. 4-7). pap. 7.95 *(978-970-20-0131-7(5))* Castillo, Ediciones, S. A. de C. V. MEX. Dist: Macmillan.

Eswar, Smrithi. The Naboola Island. 2013. 44p. pap. 7.99 *(978-1-300-57554-2(9))* Lulu Pr., Inc.

Ettling, Tali. Max's Amazing Adventure. 2011. (Illus.). 32p. 14.09 *(978-1-4567-7251-2(1))* AuthorHouse.

Eugenio, Johnny. Lil' Jordan's 9 Holes of Fear. 2009. (Illus.). 32p. (J). (gr. -1). 16.95 *(978-1-60747-703-7(3))* Phoenix Bks., Inc.

Eulberg, Elizabeth. The Great Shelby Holmes. 2017. (ENG., Illus.). 272p. (J). pap. 7.99 ***(978-1-68119-053-2(2)***, 9781681190532, Bloomsbury USA Childrens) Bloomsbury Publishing USA.

Evangel - the Smallest Angel. 2006. (J). 14.95 *(978-0-9790210-0-8(6))* Evening Star Enterprise, Inc.

Evanovich, Alex & Evanovich, Janet. Troublemaker. Jackson, Dan, illus. 2011. (Alex Barnaby Ser.: Bk. 3). (ENG.). 112p. pap. 16.99 *(978-1-59582-722-7(6))* Dark Horse Comics.

Evans, Ann. Cry Danger. 2012. 114p. pap. *(978-1-907670-27-5(0))* Greenstream Publishing.

—Cry Danger. 2006. 184p. per. *(978-1-904529-31-6(3)*, Back to Front) Solidus.

Evans, Cordelia. Bet on It. Reel FX Inc. Staff, illus. 2014. (Book of Life Ser.). (ENG.). 16p. (J). (gr. -1-3). pap. 5.99 *(978-1-4814-2564-3(1)*, Simon Spotlight) Simon Spotlight.

Evans, D. D. Pixie Eden. 2011. 28p. pap. 12.03 *(978-1-4567-2732-1(X))* AuthorHouse.

Evans, Dan C. The High Peaks Paradigm Shift: A Canine Agent Teabo Adventure, 1 vol. 2010. 362p. pap. 29.95 *(978-1-61582-712-1(9))* America Star Bks.

Evans, Douglas. MVP. Shelley, John, illus. (ENG.). 232p. (J). (gr. 4-6). 2008. pap. 9.95 *(978-1-59078-625-3(4)*, Front Street) 2004. 16.95 *(978-1-932425-13-0(6)*, Lemniscaat) Boyds Mills Pr.

Evans, Jermaine W. The Adventures of Orden: The Sock Bandit. 2011. 24p. (gr. 1-2). pap. 14.99 *(978-1-4634-1479-5(X))* AuthorHouse.

Evans, Joseph. The Trinity Awakening. 2013. 466p. pap. *(978-0-9572912-1-8(3))* Evans, Joseph.

Evans, K. D. Corey, the Little Purple Shopping Cart. 2008. 28p. per. 24.95 *(978-1-4241-8457-6(6))* America Star Bks.

Evans, Leah Beth. A Different Kind of Hero. Gedrich, Colleen, illus. 2007. 40p. (J). per. 14.95 *(978-0-9795045-2-5(X))* Tribute Bks.

Evans, Michelle D. I Don't Belong in the Jungle. 2011. 20p. pap. 24.95 *(978-1-4626-1382-3(9))* America Star Bks.

Evans, Richard. Battle of the Ampere. 2013. (Michael Vey Ser.: No. 3). (ENG., Illus.). 320p. (YA). (gr. 7). 17.99 *(978-1-4424-7511-3(0)*, Simon Pulse/Mercury Ink) Simon Pulse/Mercury Ink.

Evans, Robert J. Dorothy's Mystical Adventures in Oz. 2004. reprint ed. pap. 1.99 *(978-1-4192-1658-9(9))* Kessinger Publishing, LLC.

Evans, Rose-Marie. The Unexpected Adventure at East Haddam High. 2009. 80p. pap. 10.75 *(978-1-60860-182-0(X)*, Strategic Bk. Publishing) Strategic Book Publishing & Rights Agency (SBPRA).

Evans, Shane W. Travelin' Man. 2007. (ENG., Illus.). 32p. 15.99 *(978-0-7868-0679-9(6))* Disney Pr.

Eveleigh, Victoria. Joe & the Hidden Horseshoe. 2013. (ENG., Illus.). 128p. (J). (gr. k-2). pap. 6.99 *(978-1-4440-0591-2(X)*, Orion Children's Bks.) Hachette Children's Group GBR. Dist: Hachette Bk. Group.

—Joe & the Lightning Pony. 2013. (ENG., Illus.). 128p. (J). (gr. k-2). pap. 6.99 *(978-1-4440-0592-9(8)*, Orion Children's Bks.) Hachette Children's Group GBR. Dist: Hachette Bk. Group.

Everest, D. D. Archie Greene & the Magician's Secret. 2016. (Archie Greene Ser.: 1). 336p. (J). (gr. 3-7). pap. 6.99 *(978-0-06-231212-9(X))* HarperCollins Pubs.

Everett, Anita. Abc Adventures Continued: D e F G. 2012. 44p. pap. 21.99 *(978-1-4691-7797-7(8))* Xlibris Corp.

Everett, George W. G. W. Frog & the Haunted House in Misty Meadows. 2010. 44p. 16.95 *(978-1-4497-0752-1(1)*, WestBow Pr.) Author Solutions, Inc.

—G W Frog & the Pickle-Barrel Time MacHine. 2012. 30p. pap. 16.95 *(978-1-4497-4342-0(0)*, WestBow Pr.) Author Solutions, Inc.

Everett Hale, Edward. Last of the Peterkins with Others of the. 2006. pap. *(978-1-4068-1087-5(8))* Echo Library.

Everett, Reese. Monster in the Mangroves. 2015. (ENG.). 48p. (gr. k-3). 27.07 *(978-1-63430-377-4(6))* Rourke Educational Media.

Evers, Alf. Treasure of Watchdog Mountain: The Story of a Mountain in the Catskills. Yanow-Schwartz, Jo & Schwartz, Arthur, eds. 2006. 76p. (J). 16.95 *(978-1-879504-19-6(7))* Woodstocker Books/Arthur Schwartz & Company.

Eversole, Barbara. Adventures of Zorro. 2005. 42p. 14.49 *(978-1-4116-5523-2(0))* Lulu Pr., Inc.

Evert, Lori. The Brave Little Puppy. Breiehagen, Per, illus. 2016. (ENG.). 28p. (J). (-k). bds. 8.99 *(978-0-399-54945-8(5)*, Random Hse. Bks. for Young Readers) Random Hse. Children's Bks.

Evert, Robert. Quests of the Kings: The Quests of the Kings Trilogy - Book One. 2017. (Quest of Kings Trilogy Ser.: 1). (ENG.). 322p. pap. 14.99 *(978-1-68230-699-4(2))* Diversion Publishing Corp.

Ewing, Garen. The Rainbow Orchid, Vol. 1. Ewing, Garen, illus. 2012. (Rainbow Orchid Ser.: 1). (ENG., Illus.). 48p. (J). (gr. 4-7). pap. 10.99 *(978-1-4052-4853-2(X))* Egmont Bks., Ltd. GBR. Dist: Independent Pubs. Group.

Ewing, John. The Adventures of Rennie & Bodger, 1 vol. 2010. 42p. 24.95 *(978-1-4489-5654-8(4))* PublishAmerica, Inc.

Ewing, Juliana Horatia. We & the World. 2007. 276p. per. *(978-1-4065-2536-6(7))* Dodo Pr.

Ewing, Susan. Ten Rowdy Ravens. Zerbetz, Evon, illus. 2005. (ENG.). 32p. (J). (gr. -1-1). per. 11.99 *(978-0-88240-610-7(8)*, Alaska Northwest Bks.) Graphic Arts Ctr. Publishing Co.

The Exciting Adventures of Boo: Ten Tender Lessons. 2008. (Illus.). 144p. (J). 29.95 *(978-0-911752-99-1(4))* Neo-Tech Publishing Co.

Extreme Danger. 2007. 15.00 *(978-0-7569-7603-3(0))* Perfection Learning Corp.

Eyre, David. White Rainbow Black Curse. 2007. 31p. 14.95 *(978-0-87336-117-0(2))* Kamehameha Publishing.

Fabbella, Teresa. Forever Friends. Giaquinta, Maria, illus. 2010. 26p. pap. 9.95 *(978-1-60911-366-7(7)*, Eloquent Bks.) Strategic Book Publishing & Rights Agency (SBPRA).

Facey, Paulet. Tom-Tom & the Punch Bowl of Irish Moss. 2012. 24p. pap. 15.99 *(978-1-4797-3908-0(1))* Xlibris Corp.

Fagan, Cary. Directed by Kaspar Snit. 2007. (ENG.). 160p. (J). (gr. 3-7). per. 9.95 *(978-0-88776-753-1(2)*, Tundra Bks.) Tundra Bks. CAN. Dist: Penguin Random Hse. LLC.

—The Fortress of Kaspar Snit. 2004. (ENG.). 176p. (J). (gr. 3-7). pap. 8.95 *(978-0-88776-665-7(X)*, Tundra Bks.) Tundra Bks. CAN. Dist: Penguin Random Hse. LLC.

—Jacob Two-Two on the High Seas. Petricic, Dusan, illus. 2009. (Jacob Two-Two Ser.). (ENG.). 112p. (J). (gr. 4-7). 10.95 *(978-0-88776-895-8(4)*, Tundra Bks.) Tundra Bks. CAN. Dist: Penguin Random Hse. LLC.

Fair, Chuck. Steven Sockeye Salmon. 2005. 106p. pap. 10.95 *(978-1-4116-4780-0(7))* Lulu Pr., Inc.

Fairbanks, Letitia. Princess April Morning-Glory: What Kind of a World Would You Create, If You Had to Do Three Dood Deeds to Make Ii Home Again? Fairbanks, Letitia, illus. 2013. (ENG., Illus.). 66p. pap. 24.00 *(978-0-9887848-0-2(7))* Sandramantos Publishing.

Faircloth, Sean. The Enchanted Globe. 2016. (ENG., Illus.). 224p. (J). (gr. 4-7). pap. 12.95 *(978-1-63431-101-4(9))* Pitchstone LLC.

Fairlie, Emily. The Lost Treasure of Tuckernuck. Caparo, Antonio Javier, illus. 2013. (Tuckernuck Mysteries Ser.: 1). (ENG.). 320p. (J). (gr. 3-7). pap. 6.99 *(978-0-06-211891-2(9)*, Tegen, Katherine Bks) HarperCollins Pubs.

Fairy Tale- Aladdin. 2005. (J). bds. *(978-1-4194-0037-7(1))* Paradise Pr., Inc.

Falango, Marcy. The Rescue. 2012. 24p. pap. 14.93 *(978-1-4669-7094-6(4))* Trafford Publishing.

Falardeau, Marco. The Adventures of Mega Mini Man. 2011. 28p. pap. 15.49 *(978-1-4567-2995-0(0))* AuthorHouse.

Falcon Press International. Desta & King Solomon's Coin of Magic & Fortune: And king solomon's coinof of magic & Fortune, nos. 7, no. 2. 2nd ed. 2010. (ENG., Illus.). 430p. (YA). pap. 15.95 *(978-1-884459-01-6(3))* Falcon Pr. International.

Falcone, David A. The Adventures of Miss Aiden in Dinoland. 2011. 28p. pap. 15.99 *(978-1-4568-4015-0(0))* Xlibris Corp.

Falcone, L. M. & Wahl, Charis. The Devil, the Banshee & Me. 2006. (ENG.). 192p. (J). (gr. 4-7). 6.95 *(978-1-55337-895-2(4))* Kids Can Pr., Ltd. CAN. Dist: Hachette Bk. Group.

Falconer, Mary. The Spotted Sheep with the Worthless Wool. 2011. 24p. pap. 10.49 *(978-1-4520-9636-0(8))* AuthorHouse.

Falk, Kristi & Falk, Daniel. Eartha Gets Well. Peters, Rob, illus. 2012. (ENG.). 30p. (J). 24.95 *(978-1-937084-27-1(2)*, BQB Publishing) Boutique of Quality Books Publishing Co., Inc.

Falk, Nick. The Battle for the Golden Egg. Flowers, Tony, illus. 2015. (Samurai vs Ninja Ser.: 1). (ENG.). 96p. (J). (gr. 1-3). pap. 7.99 *(978-0-85798-605-4(8))* Random Hse. Australia AUS. Dist: Independent Pubs. Group.

—The Curse of the Oni. Flowers, Tony, illus. 2016. (Samurai vs Ninja Ser.: 4). (ENG.). 96p. (J). (gr. 1-3). pap. 7.99 *(978-0-85798-640-5(6))* Random Hse. Australia AUS. Dist: Independent Pubs. Group.

—The Day of the Undead. Flowers, Tony, illus. 2016. (Samurai vs Ninja Ser.: 3). (ENG.). 96p. (J). (gr. 1-3). pap. 7.99 *(978-0-85798-638-2(4))* Random Hse. Australia AUS. Dist: Independent Pubs. Group.

—The Race for the Shogun's Treasure. Flowers, Tony, illus. 2015. (Samurai vs Ninja Ser.: 2). (ENG.). 96p. (J). (gr. 1-3). pap. 7.99 *(978-0-85798-636-8(8))* Random Hse. Australia AUS. Dist: Independent Pubs. Group.

Falki, Pamela Marie. The Perfect Christmas Tree: Petrie & Toby's Holiday Adventure. 2009. 24p. pap. 11.49 *(978-1-4343-9983-0(4))* AuthorHouse.

Falkner, Brian. The Assault (Recon Team Angel #1) 2013. (Recon Team Angel Ser.: 1). (ENG.). 304p. (YA). (gr. 7). pap. 9.99 *(978-0-375-87190-0(X)*, Ember) Random Hse. Children's Bks.

—Ice War (Recon Team Angel #3) 2014. (Recon Team Angel Ser.). (ENG.). 320p. (YA). (gr. 7). 17.99 *(978-0-449-81303-4(7)*, Random Hse. Bks. for Young Readers) Random Hse. Children's Bks.

—Maddy West & the Tongue Taker, 1 vol. Bixley, Donovan, illus. 2014. (ENG.). 256p. (gr. 4-8). 12.95 *(978-1-62370-084-3(1))* Capstone Young Readers of Coughlan Cos.

—Northwood, 1 vol. Bixley, Donovan, illus. 2014. (ENG.). 272p. (gr. 3-3). 27.93 *(978-1-4342-8667-3(3))* Stone Arch Bks.

—Northwood, 1 vol. 2013. (ENG.). 32p. (J). pap. *(978-1-4342-8666-6(5))* Stone Arch Bks.

—The Project. 2012. (ENG.). 288p. (YA). (gr. 7). pap. 8.99 *(978-0-375-87188-7(8)*, Ember) Random Hse. Children's Bks.

—Task Force. 2013. (Recon Team Angel Ser.). (ENG., Illus.). 288p. (YA). (gr. 7). 17.99 *(978-0-449-81299-0(5)*, Random Hse. Bks. for Young Readers) Random Hse. Children's Bks.

—Task Force (Recon Team Angel #2) 2014. (Recon Team Angel Ser.). (ENG.). 416p. (YA). (gr. 7). pap. 9.99 *(978-0-449-81302-7(9)*, Ember) Random Hse. Children's Bks.

Falkner, John Meade. Moonfleet. l.t. ed. 2004. (Large Print Ser.). 370p. 26.00 *(978-1-58287-658-0(4))* North Bks.

The Fall. 2013. (Cherub Ser.: 7). (ENG., Illus.). 352p. (YA). (gr. 7). 16.99 *(978-1-4424-9945-4(1)*, Simon Pulse) Simon Pulse.

Faller, Regis. The Adventures of Polo. Faller, Regis, illus. 2006. (Adventures of Polo Ser.). (ENG., Illus.). 80p. (J). (gr. -1-3). 19.99 *(978-1-59643-160-7(1)*, 9781596431607) Roaring Brook Pr.

Falligant, Erin. Braving the Lake. Studios, Arcana, illus. 2010. (ENG.). 120p. (YA). (gr. 3-18). pap. 8.95 *(978-1-59369-757-0(0))* American Girl Publishing, Inc.

Fallows, Ralph. Ralphie's after-School Adventure. 2012. 32p. pap. 14.51 *(978-1-4669-2227-3(3))* Trafford Publishing.

Famularo, Joe. Chiara's Bite of the Big Apple: A Happy Book. 2013. 28p. pap. 16.09 *(978-1-4669-5274-4(1))* Trafford Publishing.

Fancher, Joseph. Sydney's Travels Through Dreamland Part. 2006. 48p. pap. 16.95 *(978-1-4241-3690-2(3))* PublishAmerica, Inc.

Fane, Judy B. Paddy the Pelican Survives the Storm. Alden, Carol, illus. 2010. 48p. pap. 16.50 *(978-1-60911-448-0(5)*, Eloquent Bks.) Strategic Book Publishing & Rights Agency (SBPRA).

Fanning, Kieran. The Black Lotus: The Samurai Wars. 2016. (ENG.). 304p. (J). (gr. 3-7). 16.99 *(978-0-545-94028-3(1)*, Chicken Hse., The) Scholastic, Inc.

Fanning, Kim M. Beyond the Island: The Journey of a Boy. 2012. 92p. pap. 10.99 *(978-1-62419-343-9(9))* Salem Author Services.

Fant, Donna. Scotty's Dream: Book & CD. Axford, Elizabeth C., ed. McKeown, David, illus. 2004. (ENG.). 16p. (J). audio compact disk 14.99 *(978-1-931844-17-8(8)*, PP1034) Piano Pr.

Farhat, Michael. Adventures of the Eastside Pigs: Produced by Funnybook Factory. Chan, Carol, ed. 2012. 40p. pap. 19.99 *(978-1-4669-0289-3(2))* Trafford Publishing.

Farkle, Sandy. The Day the Gummies Wrecked: Square Bears Race the Fakers. 2011. 88p. pap. 19.95 *(978-1-4560-4242-4(4))* America Star Bks.

Farley, Brianne. Ike's Incredible Ink. Farley, Brianne, illus. 2013. (ENG., Illus.). 32p. (J). (gr. -1-3). 16.99 *(978-0-7636-6296-7(8))* Candlewick Pr.

Farley, Christina. The Princess & the Page. 2017. (ENG.). 240p. (J). (gr. 3-7). 17.99 *(978-0-545-92409-2(X)*, Scholastic Pr.) Scholastic, Inc.

Farley, Terri. Phantom Stallion Box Set: The Wild One; Mustang Moon; Dark Sunshine. Call, Greg, illus. 2004. (Phantom Stallion Ser.). 704p. (J). (gr. 5-18). pap. 14.99 *(978-0-06-059504-3(3)*, HarperCollins) HarperCollins Pubs.

Farley, Walter. The Black Stallion Adventures!, 4 vols., Set. 2005. (ENG.). 288p. (J). (gr. 3-7). 31.96 *(978-0-375-83406-6(0)*, Yearling) Random Hse. Children's Bks.

Farmer, Tom. Once upon a Daydream: The Story of Patrick & the Clumsy Camel. 2013. 44p. pap. 17.44 *(978-1-4669-6912-4(1))* Trafford Publishing.

Farmyard Tales. 2017. (Farmyard Tales Ser.). 24p. (gr. 4-6). 70.80 ***(978-1-5081-6179-0(8)***, PowerKids Pr.) Rosen Publishing Group, Inc., The.

Farrell, Bill. Walter's Pond: The True Story of Three Brothers Who Went Fishing for Trouble. Julich, Jenniffer, illus. 2008. 16p. 8.95 *(978-0-9797790-0-8(6))* Lower Lane Publishing LLC.

Farrell, Steve. What Do You Do on a Rainy Day? Bendoly, Lynne, illus. 2013. 48p. pap. 24.95 *(978-1-4626-9685-7(6))* America Star Bks.

Farrelly, Linda. Elliot's Amazing Adventures Number 1. Farrelly, Linda & Hopkins, Simon, illus. 2013. 52p. pap. *(978-0-9560331-5-4(6))* Children' Story Pubs.

Farren, Rick. Grandpa & the Pirate. 2007. 49p. (J). per. 9.95 *(978-0-9794863-6-4(X))* Summerland Publishing.

—The Secret of the Lighthouse. 2004. (J). per. 12.95 *(978-0-9748087-3-4(3))* Journey Pubns., LLC.

Farrey, Brian. The Secret of Dreadwillow Carse. 2017. (ENG.). (J). (gr. 4-8). lib. bdg. 17.15 ***(978-0-606-39831-2(7))*** Turtleback Bks.

Farris, Judy. Mr Boo Bear. Farris, Michael, illus. 2009. 24p. pap. 15.49 *(978-1-4389-4553-8(1))* AuthorHouse.

Farrow, George Edward. The Mysterious Shin Shira. Easton, W. G., illus. 2007. 120p. per. *(978-1-4065-1690-6(2))* Dodo Pr.

Farshtey, Greg. Fire & Ice. 2014. (LEGO Legends of Chima Chapter Bks.: 6). lib. bdg. 14.75 *(978-0-606-36069-2(7))* Turtleback Bks.

—Kai - Ninja of Fire, Bk. 1. 2011. (Lego Ninjago Ser.). (ENG.). 80p. (J). (gr. 2-5). pap. 4.99 *(978-0-545-34827-0(7))* Scholastic, Inc.

—Way of the Ninja. 2012. (Lego Ninjago Ser.). (ENG.). 32p. (J). (gr. -1-3). pap. 3.99 *(978-0-545-40113-5(5))* Scholastic, Inc.

Farshtey, Greg & Scholastic, Inc. Staff. Zane - Ninja of Ice. 2011. (Lego Ninjago Ser.). (ENG.). 80p. (J). (gr. 2-5). pap. 4.99 *(978-0-545-34828-7(5))* Scholastic, Inc.

Fastje, Shanaya B. Mystery School: Monday Sleepover Disaster. 2009. 24p. pap. 12.99 *(978-1-4490-0679-2(5))* AuthorHouse.

Fath, Teresa. The Train Track Trolley & the Bell Dogs. 2009. 32p. pap. 21.99 *(978-1-4415-4350-9(3))* Xlibris Corp.

FATUS SOPHIE. My Big Barefoot Book of Spanish & English Words. 2016. (ENG & SPA.). 48p. (J). (gr. -1-1). 19.99 *(978-1-78285-286-5(7))* Barefoot Bks., Inc.

Fawcett, Jack & Rimes, Raleigh. Dinosaurology. 2013. (Ologies Ser.). (ENG.). 30p. (J). (gr. 3-7). 21.99 *(978-0-7636-6739-9(0))* Candlewick Pr.

Fay, Nancy Cartnick. I Wanted a Puppy - Not Fish! 2012. 24p. pap. 15.99 *(978-1-4691-7535-5(5))* Xlibris Corp.

Fay, Nicole. Andy & Armadillio Are Astronauts. 2008. 20p. pap. 10.49 *(978-1-4389-1057-4(6))* AuthorHouse.

Faye. Jazzy Shoes. l.t. ed. 2006. (ENG., Illus.). 28p. per. 9.95 *(978-1-4327-0176-5(2))* Outskirts Pr., Inc.

Faye Morningstar. Little Dream Athe: The Sand Prince. 2012. 20p. pap. 17.99 *(978-1-4772-9540-3(2))* AuthorHouse.

Fayers, Claire. The Voyage to Magical North. 2016. (Accidental Pirates Ser.). (ENG.). 320p. (J). 16.99 *(978-1-62779-420-6(4)*, 9781627794206, Holt, Henry & Co. Bks. For Young Readers) Holt, Henry & Co.

Fears & Phantoms. 2006. (J). *(978-1-933343-20-4(6))* Stabenfeldt Inc.

Feather, Tami Flaming. A Wondrous World of Home. Porter, Tammy, illus. 2012. 24p. pap. 24.95 *(978-1-4626-4544-2(5))* America Star Bks.

Feder, Joel A. Kokomo's Halloween Adventure. 2012. 32p. pap. 15.99 *(978-1-4685-7331-2(4))* AuthorHouse.

Federle, Tim. Better Nate Than Ever. 2014. (ENG., Illus.). 296p. (J). (gr. 4-8). pap. 7.99 *(978-1-4424-4691-5(9)*, Simon & Schuster Bks. For Young Readers) Simon & Schuster Bks. For Young Readers.

Fedorovich, Debbie. The Adventures of Sheila the Therapy Dog. 2007. 36p. per. 13.95 *(978-1-4327-0198-7(3))* Outskirts Pr., Inc.

Fee, J. M. The Amazing Adventures of Phineas Screwdriver. 2012. 64p. pap. 20.95 *(978-1-4497-7236-9(6)*, WestBow Pr.) Author Solutions, Inc.

Feldkamp, Jim And Cate. The Adventures of Tommy & Clara on Mount Catherine. 2008. 32p. pap. 14.49 *(978-1-4389-1366-7(4))* AuthorHouse.

Feldman, Jody. The New Champion. Jamieson, Victoria, illus. 2014. (Gollywhopper Games Ser.: 2). (ENG.). 400p. (J). (gr. 3-7). 16.99 *(978-0-06-221125-5(0)*, Greenwillow Bks.) HarperCollins Pubs.

Feldman, Lowell S. Little Falabella the Magical Horse. 2006. 92p. (gr. 1-1). pap. 31.99 *(978-1-4257-1869-5(8))* Xlibris Corp.

Feldman, Thea. Adventure in the Park. Ward, April, illus. 2006. 20p. (J). *(978-0-696-23234-3(0))* Meredith Bks.

—A Visit to the Farm. Trasler, Janee, illus. 2006. 3p. (J). (gr. -1-3). bds. 5.99 *(978-1-932915-32-7(X))* Sandvik Publishing.

Feliciano, Luis. The Adventures of the Three Angels. 2005. (J). pap. 8.00 *(978-0-8059-6676-3(5))* Dorrance Publishing Co., Inc.

Felipe, Nersys. Cuentos de Guane (Stories of Guane) (SPA.). (J). 4.95 *(978-950-581-518-0(2))* Colihue ARG. Dist: AIMS International Bks., Inc.

Fell, K. The Dragon Stones. 2009. 352p. 30.95 *(978-0-595-51644-5(0))*; pap. 20.95 *(978-0-595-52712-0(4))* iUniverse, Inc.

Felsen, Henry Gregor. Crash Club. Welch, Holly Felsen, ed. 2013. 206p. pap. 15.00 *(978-1-62272-003-3(2))* Felsen Ink.

—Fever Heat. Welch, Holly Felsen, illus. 2013. 230p. pap. 15.00 *(978-1-62272-002-6(4))* Felsen Ink.

—Henry Gregor Felsen Street Rod Collection. Welch, Holly Felsen, illus. 2013. 75.00 *(978-1-62272-005-7(9))* Felsen Ink.

—Rag Top. Felsen, Holly, illus. 2013. 212p. pap. 15.00 *(978-1-62272-001-9(6))* Felsen Ink.

—Road Rocket. 2013. 260p. pap. 15.00 *(978-1-62272-004-0(0))* Felsen Ink.

Fendler, Donn & Plourde, Lynn. Lost Trail: Nine Days Alone in the Wilderness, 1 vol. Bishop, Ben, illus. 2011. (ENG.). 72p. (J). (gr. 4-7). pap. 14.95 *(978-0-89272-945-6(7))* Down East Bks.

Fenn, G. Manville. Brownsmith's Boy. 2008. 260p. 29.95 *(978-1-60664-780-6(6))*; pap. 15.95 *(978-1-60664-154-5(9))* Aegypan.

—The Rajah of Dah. 2011. 194p. 26.95 *(978-1-4638-9697-3(2))* Rodgers, Alan Bks.

Fenn, George. The Rajah of Dah. 2007. 168p. per. 14.95 *(978-1-4344-8187-0(5))* Wildside Pr., LLC.

—Yussuf the Guide or the Mountain Bandits: Being the Strange Story of the Travels in Asia Minor of Burne the Lawyer, Preston the Professor, & Lawren. Schönberg, John, illus. 2007. 424p. 26.95 *(978-0-9776786-6-2(0))* Salem Ridge Press LLC.

Fentiman, David. The Adventures of BB-8. 2016. (Star Wars DK Readers Level 2 Ser.). lib. bdg. 13.55 *(978-0-606-38709-5(9))* Turtleback Bks.

—DK Readers L2: Star Wars: the Adventures of BB-8. 2016. (DK Readers Ser.). (ENG., Illus.). 48p. (J). (gr. k-2). pap. 3.99 *(978-1-4654-5102-6(1)*, DK Children) Dorling Kindersley Publishing, Inc.

—DK Readers L3: Star Wars: Finn's Mission. 2016. (DK Readers Ser.). (ENG., Illus.). 64p. (J). (gr. 2-4). pap. 3.99 *(978-1-4654-5101-9(3)*, DK Children) Dorling Kindersley Publishing, Inc.

—Finn's Mission. 2016. (Star Wars DK Readers Level 3 Ser.). lib. bdg. 13.55 *(978-0-606-38710-1(2))* Turtleback Bks.

—The Lego Movie. 2013. (DK Reader Level 3 Ser.). lib. bdg. 13.55 *(978-0-606-35322-9(4))* Turtleback Bks.

Fenton, Geleta. Joel's Adventure at Sea. Siniard, Ricky, illus. 2013. 50p. (J). mass mkt. 9.95 *(978-0-9824433-2-3(3))* Octopus Publishing Co.

Fenton, Karen B. It's Raining Outside & I'm Gonna Be Bored! Roth, Stacy Schulstrom, illus. 2006. (J). lib. bdg. 16.82 *(978-0-9778196-4-5(7))* Harbour Arts, LLC.

Fenwick, Carol. Jenell & the Berry Thicket Village. 2011. 36p. pap. 15.75 *(978-1-4634-5016-8(8))* AuthorHouse.

—Jennell & the Horse in the Enchanted Valley. 2011. 32p. pap. 12.95 *(978-1-4634-4445-7(1))* AuthorHouse.

Ferdowsi, Rostam: Tales from the Shahnameh. 2007. (ENG., Illus.). 32p. (YA). 5.95 *(978-0-9770213-2-1(7))* Hyperwerks Entertainment.

Fergus, Maureen. Buddy & Earl & the Great Big Baby, 1 vol. Sookocheff, Carey, illus. 2016. (Buddy & Earl Ser.). (ENG.). 32p. (J). (gr. -1-2). 16.95 *(978-1-55498-716-0(4))* Groundwood Bks. CAN. Dist: Publishers Group West (PGW).

Ferguson, Adrian. Hamburger Man: Resurrection. 2008. 155p. pap. 17.95 *(978-1-4092-4500-1(4))* Lulu Pr., Inc.

Ferguson, C.S. A Tale of Two Fairies: The Secret of the Spider's Web. 2013. 268p. pap. 17.95 *(978-0-578-11204-6(3))* Boothroyd & Allnut.

Ferguson, Donald. Chums of Scranton High. 2006. 25.95 *(978-1-4218-2935-7(5))*; pap. 10.95 *(978-1-4218-3035-3(3))* 1st World Publishing, Inc.

—Chums of Scranton High at Ice Hockey. 2006. 25.95 *(978-1-4218-2936-4(3))*; pap. 10.95 *(978-1-4218-3036-0(1))* 1st World Publishing, Inc.

—Chums of Scranton High Out for the Penna. 2006. 25.95 *(978-1-4218-2938-8(X))*; pap. 10.95 *(978-1-4218-3038-4(8))* 1st World Publishing, Inc.

Ferguson, Jamianne. Lost in Past Remembrence. 2010. 265p. pap. 17.25 *(978-0-557-52788-5(0))* Lulu Pr., Inc.

Ferguson, Will. I Was A Teenage Katima-victim. pap. *(978-1-55054-652-1(X))* Dornier Gmbh.

Fernandez, Martina. Jellybean: Jellybean Finds a Home. 2012. 28p. pap. 19.99 *(978-1-4772-7237-4(2))* AuthorHouse.

Ferraiolo, Jack D. The Quick Fix. 2012. (ENG.). 304p. (J). (gr. 3-7). 16.95 *(978-0-8109-9725-7(8))*, Amulet Bks.) Abrams, Inc.

Ferrara-Lester, Lisa. The Sky's the Limit. 2012. 24p. pap. 10.99 *(978-1-937829-60-5(X))*, Total Publishing & Media) Yorkshire Publishing Group.

Ferrari, G. m. Lake, Sky, Dragonfly. 2009. 44p. pap. 16.99 *(978-1-4490-2895-4(0))* AuthorHouse.

Ferrell, Deen. Cryptic Spaces: Book One. 2013. 396p. pap. 16.95 *(978-1-60047-864-2(6))* Wasteland Pr.

Ferri, Jean-Yves. Asterix & the Missing Scroll. Conrad, Didier, illus. 2015. (ENG.). 48p. (J). (gr. 4-6). 17.99 *(978-1-5101-0045-9(8))*, Asterix) Hachette Children's Group GBR. Dist: Hachette Bk. Group.

Ferrier, Charlotte. The Three Little Pigs. 2016. (Fairytale Cottages Ser.). (ENG., Illus.). 12p. (J). (gr. -1-k). bds. 8.99 *(978-0-7641-6819-2(3))* Barron's Educational Series, Inc.

Fettig, Pamela. Leelah at the Lake. Strecker, Darren, illus. 2010. 28p. pap. 9.99 *(978-1-60844-697-1(2))* Dog Ear Publishing, LLC.

Fetty, Margaret & Jasinski, Diane. Three Cheers for August: Prek-K. 2006. (Illus.). 96p. (gr. -1-k). pap. 12.99 *(978-0-7398-9827-7(2))* Steck-Vaughn.

Feuer, Bonnie. Goliaths's Secret. Platt, Sharai, illus. 2013. (ENG.). 38p. (J). 18.50 *(978-0-9825468-8-8(2))* Connecticut Pr., The.

Feutl, Rita. Rescue at Fort Edmonton, 1 vol. 2004. (Disaster Strikes! Ser.: 2). (ENG., Illus.). 176p. (J). (gr. 4-7). pap. 7.95 *(978-1-55050-308-1(1))* Coteau Bks. CAN. Dist: Orca Bk. Pubs. USA.

Few, Valerie. Filbert & Friends. 2008. 56p. pap. *(978-1-84748-346-1(1))* Athena Pr.

Fickey, Brenda. Beckoning Shadows, 1 vol. 2009. (ENG.). 179p. pap. 24.95 *(978-1-61546-330-5(5))* America Star Bks.

—Echoing Silence. 2008. 123p. pap. 19.95 *(978-1-60563-816-4(1))* America Star Bks.

Ficklin, Jonene H. Orinoco Intrigue. 2005. (YA). 14.95 *(978-0-9761188-1-7(5))* Victor's Crown Publishing.

Fiedler, Lisa. Hopper's Destiny. To, Vivienne, illus. 2016. (Mouseheart Ser.: 2). (ENG.). 368p. (J). (gr. 3-7). pap. 7.99 *(978-1-4814-2090-7(9))*, McElderry, Margaret K. Bks.) McElderry, Margaret K. Bks.

—Mouseheart. To, Vivienne, illus. 2015. (Mouseheart Ser.: 1). (ENG.). 336p. (J). (gr. 3-7). pap. 7.99 *(978-1-4424-8783-3(6))*, McElderry, Margaret K. Bks.) McElderry, Margaret K. Bks.

—Mouseheart. 2015. (Mouseheart Ser.: 1). lib. bdg. 18.40 *(978-0-606-37132-2(X))* Turtleback Bks.

—Return of the Forgotten. To, Vivienne, illus. 2015. (Mouseheart Ser.: 3). (ENG.). 320p. (J). (gr. 3-7). 16.99 *(978-1-4814-2092-1(5))*, McElderry, Margaret K. Bks.) McElderry, Margaret K. Bks.

Field, Brett. Screno Magic Medieval Collision. 2007. 52p. per. 10.00 *(978-1-4257-4700-8(0))* Xlibris Corp.

Fielding, Sarah. The Governess, or, the Little Female Academy. 2007. 140p. (gr. 4-7). per. *(978-1-4065-2397-3(6))* Dodo Pr.

Fields, Jan. Chase the Chupacabra, 1 vol. Brundage, Scott, illus. 2014. (Monster Hunters Ser.). (ENG.). 80p. (J). (gr. 8-12). 27.07 *(978-1-62402-044-5(5))* Magic Wagon.

—Hunt for Sewer Gators, 1 vol. Brundage, Scott, illus. 2014. (Monster Hunters Ser.). (ENG.). 80p. (J). (gr. 8-12). 27.07 *(978-1-62402-045-2(3))* Magic Wagon.

—Hunt the Ozark Howler, 1 vol. Brundage, Scott, illus. 2016. (ENG.). 80p. (J). lib. bdg. *(978-1-62402-152-7(2))* Magic Wagon.

—Meet the Mothman, 1 vol. Brundage, Scott, illus. 2016. (ENG.). 80p. (J). lib. bdg. *(978-1-62402-153-4(0))* Magic Wagon.

—Really New School: An Up2U Action Adventure, 1 vol. To, Vivienne, illus. 2013. (Up2U Adventures Ser.). (ENG.). 80p. (J). (gr. 2-5). lib. bdg. 27.07 *(978-1-61641-969-1(5))*, Calico Chapter Bks) Magic Wagon.

—Search for Bigfoot, 1 vol. Brundage, Scott, illus. 2014. (Monster Hunters Ser.). (ENG.). 80p. (J). (gr. 8-12). 27.07 *(978-1-62402-046-9(1))* Magic Wagon.

—Spot the Swamp Lizard Man, 1 vol. Brundage, Scott, illus. 2016. (ENG.). 80p. (J). lib. bdg. *(978-1-62402-154-1(9))* Magic Wagon.

—Tame Tahoe Tessie, 1 vol. Brundage, Scott, illus. 2014. (Monster Hunters Ser.). (ENG.). 80p. (J). (gr. 8-12). 27.07 *(978-1-62402-047-6(X))* Magic Wagon.

—Track the Turtle Lake Monster, 1 vol. Brundage, Scott, illus. 2016. (ENG.). 80p. (J). lib. bdg. *(978-1-62402-155-8(7))* Magic Wagon.

Fienberg, Anna. Wicked's Way. 2016. (ENG., Illus.). 256p. (J). (gr. 3-6). 9.99 *(978-1-74331-990-1(8))* Allen & Unwin AUS. Dist: Independent Pubs. Group.

Fienberg, Anna & Fienberg, Barbara. Tashi Lost in the City. Gamble, Kim, illus. 11th ed. 2007. (Tashi Ser.: 11). (ENG.). 64p. (J). (gr. k-2). pap. 8.99 *(978-1-74114-963-0(0))* Allen & Unwin AUS. Dist: Independent Pubs. Group.

Figueredo, D. H. Un Mundo Nuevo. 2004. (SPA., Illus.). (J). (gr. -1-4). spiral bd. *(978-0-616-07276-9(7))* Canadian National Institute for the Blind/Institut National Canadien pour les Aveugles.

Figurska, A. B. The Island of Harklitt, 1 vol. 2010. 108p. pap. 19.95 *(978-1-4489-4176-6(8))* PublishAmerica, Inc.

The Fijiboat Adventure. 2004. 56p. pap. 6.99 *(978-0-8341-2092-1(5))* Beacon Hill Pr. of Kansas City.

Filali, Lisa. Faith Team 1: Taking Briar Falls. 2007. 84p. per. 19.95 *(978-1-4137-8030-7(X))* America Star Bks.

Filaretos, William. The Potion of Time: A Story of Demetrios. 2006. per. 12.95 *(978-0-9724520-0-7(1))* Filaretos, William.

Filasky, Gail. Mrs. Dishes. 2007. (Illus.). 24p. (J). 8.95 *(978-0-8059-7635-9(3))* Dorrance Publishing Co., Inc.

Filella, Nacho, et al. El Cumpleaños. 2005. (El Juego de Leer Ser.). (SPA.). 6p. 9.95 *(978-84-272-6684-1(7))* Molino, Editorial ESP. Dist: Distribooks, Inc.

Filippello, Michael. In a Place Called Barrontippeny. 2008. 24p. pap. 24.95 *(978-1-60813-295-9(1))* America Star Bks.

Filippello, Mike. Miratambo Moonsong. 2004. 39p. pap. 24.95 *(978-1-4137-2421-9(3))* PublishAmerica, Inc.

Filkins, Allison J. The Amazings. 2007. 484p. per. 25.95 *(978-0-595-47500-1(0))* iUniverse, Inc.

Fillisetti, Celeste. Just a Dream. 2013. 28p. pap. 13.95 *(978-1-4787-1254-1(6))* Outskirts Pr., Inc.

Filmer, Mary, et al. Farmer Frank: Educational Fire Safety, Poetry & Story Colouring Book. 2010. 50p. pap. 9.99 *(978-1-60911-721-4(2))*, Eloquent Bks.) Strategic Book Publishing & Rights Agency (SBPRA).

Filoche, Eric. Hey! We're Talking about Ourselves ! 2013. 68p. pap. *(978-2-9538737-4-0(0))* Koshkindom.

Finch, Donna. The Big Dig: The Continuing Adventures of Brandy the Golden Retriever, 1 vol. 2010. 46p. 24.95 *(978-1-4489-8797-9(0))* PublishAmerica, Inc.

—Brandy & the Rapids, 1 vol. Plante, Beth, illus. 2009. 36p. pap. 24.95 *(978-1-60749-150-7(8))* America Star Bks.

Finding Conway: Seek the Truth. 2006. (YA). *(978-0-9771114-1-1(5))* LIP Publishing LLC.

Finelli, S. Life's Amusement Park: A Whimsical Perspective on the Rides of Life! 2009. 36p. pap. 16.99 *(978-1-4389-3648-2(6))* AuthorHouse.

Finkelstein, Chaim. The Burksfield Bike Club, Book 2: Lost & Found. Jennings, R. W., illus. 2007. 224p. (J). 15.95 *(978-1-932443-69-1(X))*, BBC1H) Judaica Pr., Inc., The.

Finlay, Roger T. The Wonder Island Boys: Exploring the Island. 2007. (Illus.). 216p. per. *(978-1-4065-2409-3(3))* Dodo Pr.

—The Wonder Island Boys: The Mysteries of the Caverns. 2007. (Illus.). 204p. per. *(978-1-4065-2410-9(7))* Dodo Pr.

—The Wonder Island Boys: The Tribesmen. 2007. (Illus.). 204p. per. *(978-1-4065-2411-6(5))* Dodo Pr.

Finlay, Roger Thompson. The Wonder Island Boys: Conquest of the Savages. 2007. (ENG.). 188p. pap. 19.99 *(978-1-4346-5001-6(4))*; 204p. pap. 22.99 *(978-1-4346-5002-3(2))* Creative Media Partners, LLC.

—The Wonder Island Boys: Treasures of the Island. 2007. (ENG.). 180p. pap. 19.99 *(978-1-4346-4905-8(9))*; 198p. pap. 21.99 *(978-1-4346-4906-5(7))* Creative Media Partners, LLC.

Finley, Lou. How to Do Nothin' 2010. 24p. 12.99 *(978-1-4520-8438-1(6))* AuthorHouse.

Finn, Caitlin. Harold the Misfit. 2012. 24p. pap. 14.93 *(978-1-4669-5131-0(1))* Trafford Publishing.

Finn, Perdita. My Little Pony: Equestria Girls: the Legend of Everfree. 2016. (Equestria Girls Ser.: 7). (ENG.). 240p. (J). (gr. 3-7). 10.99 *(978-0-316-39537-3(4))* Little, Brown Bks. for Young Readers.

Finn, Perdita & HarperCollins Publishers Ltd. Staff. Alvin & the Chipmunks - The Squeakuel. 2009. (Alvin & the Chipmunks Ser.). (ENG., Illus.). 144p. (J). (gr. 3-7). pap. 5.99 *(978-0-06-184569-7(8))*, HarperFestival) HarperCollins Pubs.

Finnegan, Delphine. Justice League Classic: Mind Games. Roberts, Jeremy et al, illus. 2016. 24p. (J). (gr. -1-3). pap. 3.99 *(978-0-06-236075-5(2))*, HarperFestival) HarperCollins Pubs.

Finnemore, John. Jack Haydons Quest. 2006. pap. 15.95 *(978-0-8095-0116-8(3))* Wildside Pr., LLC.

Finneron, Karyn A. Susu of the Frufru. Provencher, Annemarie, illus. 2012. 32p. (-18). pap. 9.99 *(978-0-9857362-0-0(8))* Nana's Stories.

Finnish, V. K. The Society's Traitor. Oshida, Tim, illus. 2012. (The Discoveries of Arthur Grey ser.: 1). (ENG.). 298p. (J). (gr. 4-8). 27.99 *(978-0-9852202-0-4(1))* Panama Hat Publishing, Ltd.

Firth, Rachel & Sims, Leslie B. Illustrated Classics for Boys. 2010. (Illustrated Stories Ser.). 383p. (J). (gr. 4-7). 19.99 *(978-0-7945-2439-5(7))*, Usborne) EDC Publishing.

Fischel, Ana. The Twelve Quests - Book 2, a Dragon's Tooth. 2009. 158p. pap. *(978-1-84923-874-8(X))* YouWriteOn.

—The Twelve Quests - Book 3, the Pied Piper's Flute. 2009. 158p. pap. *(978-1-84923-875-5(8))* YouWriteOn.

—The Twelve Quests - Book 4, Rapunzel's Hair. 2009. 158p. pap. *(978-1-84923-876-2(6))* YouWriteOn.

—The Twelve Quests - Book 5, a Firebird's Feather. 2009. 158p. pap. *(978-1-84923-877-9(4))* YouWriteOn.

—The Twelve Quests - Book 6, the Enchanted Harp. 2009. 158p. pap. *(978-1-84923-878-6(2))* YouWriteOn.

—The Twelve Quests - Book 7, a Bottled Genie. 2010. 158p. pap. *(978-1-84923-463-4(9))* YouWriteOn.

Fischer, David. Heir to Oswyn. 2011. 66p. pap. 19.95 *(978-1-4626-2581-9(9))* America Star Bks.

Fiset, Pierre & Ferraro, Damiano. A Gopher's Christmas Adventure. 2012. 70p. pap. *(978-0-9877632-2-8(9))* Flower Pr.

Fishburne, Melody. Three Little Faeries in the Baby Lady Bug Adventure, 1 vol. 2009. 48p. pap. 16.95 *(978-1-4489-8897-6(7))* America Star Bks.

Fishel, Dennis. Russell's Revenge, 1. 2005. (YA). 17.95 *(978-0-9763398-2-3(X))* Dragonon, Inc.

Fisher, C. R. The Adventures of Sam Fisher: It's Ruff to Be A Puppy. 2008. 64p. pap. 19.49 *(978-1-4389-2040-5(7))* AuthorHouse.

Fisher, David & Fisher, David Dayan. Puppy School. 2010. 77p. (J). pap. 5.50 *(978-0-578-06095-8(7))* Sunnyfields Publishing.

Fisher, Edward J. The Little Girl with the Magic Shoes: And Other Delights. 2008. 40p. 31.99 *(978-1-4363-4210-0(4))* Xlibris Corp.

Fisher, James C. Oh No! My Shoe! 2013. 24p. pap. 15.99 *(978-1-4797-8210-9(6))* Xlibris Corp.

Fisher, Leonard Everett. William Tell. Fisher, Leonard Everett, illus. 2006. (Illus.). 32p. (J). reprint ed. 16.00 *(978-0-7567-9880-2(9))* DIANE Publishing Co.

Fisher, Maire & Beautement, Tiah, eds. Follow the Road. 2015. (ENG., Illus.). 154p. (J). pap. *(978-1-920590-98-7(6))* Modajaji Bks.

Fisher, Sandy, illus. The Adventures of CJ & Angel; the Scary Helicopter Ride. 2008. 24p. (J). *(978-0-9779072-1-2(X))* Creative Life Publishing.

Fisher, Suzanne Woods & Kinsinger, Mary Ann. A Surprise for Lily. 2013. (Adventures of Lily Lapp Ser.: 4). (ENG., Illus.). 272p. (J). pap. 13.00 *(978-0-8007-2135-0(7))* Revell.

Fisher, Terri. The Adventures of Grandma Terri: Grandma Terri's Hospital Visit. 2012. 24p. pap. 13.95 *(978-1-4685-4647-7(3))* AuthorHouse.

Fisher, Tina Mollie. Pig's Big Adventure. 2012. 42p. pap. 20.45 *(978-1-4497-5020-6(6))*, WestBow Pr.) Author Solutions, Inc.

Fisk, Scott. Herman the Homeless Hermit Crab. 2004. 17p. 7.99 *(978-1-4116-1770-4(3))* Lulu Pr., Inc.

Fitzgerald, John D. More Adventures of the Great Brain. Mayer, Mercer, illus. 2004. (Great Brain Ser.). (ENG.). 176p. (J). (gr. 3-7). pap. 6.99 *(978-0-14-240065-4(3))*, Puffin Books) Penguin Young Readers Group.

—More Adventures of the Great Brain. 2004. (Great Brain Ser.). 142p. (J). (gr. 3-7). pap., tchr.'s training gde. ed. 36.00 incl. audio *(978-0-8072-0860-1(4))*, Listening Library) Random Hse. Audio Publishing Group.

Fitzgerald, Sarah Moore. Back to Blackbrick. 2013. (ENG., Illus.). 208p. (J). (gr. 5-9). 15.99 *(978-1-4424-8155-8(2))*, McElderry, Margaret K. Bks.) McElderry, Margaret K. Bks.

Fitzhugh, Keese Percy. Roy Blakely- Pathfinder. 2007. (ENG.). 132p. pap. 18.99 *(978-1-4346-3240-1(7))*; 146p. pap. 19.99 *(978-1-4346-3241-8(5))* Creative Media Partners, LLC.

—Roy Blakely, Pathfinder. 2007. 144p. 95.99 *(978-1-4280-7678-5(6))* IndyPublish.com.

—Tom Slade at Temple Camp. 2007. (ENG.). 124p. pap. 18.99 *(978-1-4346-3188-6(5))*; 138p. pap. 19.99 *(978-1-4346-3189-3(3))* Creative Media Partners, LLC.

—Tom Slade's Double Dare. 2007. 140p. pap. 18.99 *(978-1-4346-3202-9(4))*; (ENG.). 150p. pap. 19.99 *(978-1-4346-3203-6(2))* Creative Media Partners, LLC.

Fitzhugh, Percy K. Pee-Wee Harris. 2004. reprint ed. pap. 1.99 *(978-1-4192-4057-7(9))*; pap. 15.95 *(978-1-4191-4057-0(4))* Kessinger Publishing, LLC.

—Roy Blakeley. 2004. reprint ed. pap. 19.95 *(978-1-4191-4560-5(6))*; pap. 1.99 *(978-1-4192-4560-2(0))* Kessinger Publishing, LLC.

—Roy Blakeley's Adventures in Camp. 2004. reprint ed. pap. 20.95 *(978-1-4191-4561-2(4))* Kessinger Publishing, LLC.

—Tom Slade Boy Scout of the Moving Pictur. 2005. pap. 26.95 *(978-1-885529-85-5(6))* Stevens Publishing.

Fitzhugh, Percy Keese. Pee-Wee Harris on the Briny Deep. Barbour, H. S., illus. 2011. 264p. 47.95 *(978-1-258-09985-5(3))* Literary Licensing, LLC.

—Roy Blakeley. 2007. (ENG.). 134p. pap. 18.99 *(978-1-4264-4185-1(1))*; 148p. pap. 19.99 *(978-1-4264-4226-1(2))* Creative Media Partners, LLC.

Flack, Annie. Mysteries of the Lake. 2009. 92p. pap. 10.49 *(978-1-4389-6264-1(9))* AuthorHouse.

Flaker, Tracey. Around the Corner: Gwenever's Quest. 2006. 55p. pap. 16.95 *(978-1-4241-1886-1(7))* PublishAmerica, Inc.

Flambaum, Victor & Flambaum, Andrew. How to Make a Big Bang: A Cosmic Journey. 2012. (ENG.). 226p. (J). (gr. 7-10). pap. 14.95 *(978-1-936782-72-7(3))* Salem Author Services.

Flammer, JoAnn. The Last Wish. 2007. 80p. pap. 10.00 *(978-0-615-16197-6(9))* Flammer, Josephine.

Flanagan, James. Stories Heard Around the Lunchroom. 2010. 96p. pap. 11.49 *(978-1-4490-8443-1(5))* AuthorHouse.

Flanagan, John. The Battle of Hackham Heath. 2016. (Ranger's Apprentice: the Early Years Ser.: 2). (ENG., Illus.). 352p. (J). (gr. 5). 18.99 *(978-0-399-16362-3(X))*, Philomel Bks.) Penguin Young Readers Group.

—The Burning Bridge, 2 vols., Bk. 2. 2006. (Ranger's Apprentice Ser.: 2). (ENG.). 272p. (J). (gr. 5-18). 18.99 *(978-0-399-24455-1(7))*, Philomel Bks.) Penguin Young Readers Group.

—The Ghostfaces. 2016. (Brotherband Chronicles Ser.: 6). (ENG.). 400p. (J). (gr. 5). 18.99 *(978-0-399-16357-9(3))*, Philomel Bks.) Penguin Young Readers Group.

—The Ghostfaces. 2017. (Brotherband Chronicles Ser.: 6). lib. bdg. 19.65 ***(978-0-606-40089-3(3))*** Turtleback Bks.

—The Hunters. (Brotherband Chronicles Ser.: 3). (ENG.). (J). (gr. 5). 2014. 448p. pap. 8.99 *(978-0-14-242664-7(4))*, Puffin Books) 2012. 416p. 18.99 *(978-0-399-25621-9(0))*, Philomel Bks.) Penguin Young Readers Group.

—The Hunters. 2014. (Brotherband Chronicles Ser.: 3). lib. bdg. 19.65 *(978-0-606-35708-1(4))* Turtleback Bks.

—The Invaders. (Brotherband Chronicles Ser.: 2). (ENG.). (J). (gr. 5). 2013. 448p. pap. 8.99 *(978-0-14-242663-0(6))*, Puffin Books) 2012. 432p. 18.99 *(978-0-399-25620-2(2))*, Philomel Bks.) Penguin Young Readers Group.

—The Invaders. 2013. (Brotherband Chronicles Ser.: 2). lib. bdg. 19.65 *(978-0-606-26637-6(2))*, Turtleback) Turtleback Bks.

—The Kings of Clonmel, 8 vols., Bk. 8. 2010. (Ranger's Apprentice Ser.: 8). (ENG.). 368p. (J). (gr. 5-18). 18.99 *(978-0-399-25206-8(1))*, Philomel Bks.) Penguin Young Readers Group.

—The Outcasts. 2011. (Brotherband Chronicles: Bk. 1). (ENG.). (J). (gr. 3-7). 54.99 *(978-1-61657-043-9(1))* Findaway World, LLC.

—The Outcasts. (Brotherband Chronicles Ser.: 1). (ENG.). (J). (gr. 5). 2012. 464p. pap. 8.99 *(978-0-14-242194-9(4))*, Puffin Books) 2011. 448p. 18.99 *(978-0-399-25619-6(9))*, Philomel Bks.) Penguin Young Readers Group.

—The Outcasts. 2012. (Brotherband Chronicles Ser.: 1). lib. bdg. 19.65 *(978-0-606-26636-9(4))*, Turtleback) Turtleback Bks.

—The Ruins of Gorlan, Bk. 1. 2005. (Ranger's Apprentice Ser.: 1). (ENG.). 256p. (J). (gr. 5-18). 18.99 *(978-0-399-24454-4(9))*, Philomel Bks.) Penguin Young Readers Group.

—Scorpion Mountain. 2014. (Brotherband Chronicles Ser.: 5). (ENG., Illus.). 464p. (J). (gr. 5). 18.99 *(978-0-399-16356-2(5))*, Philomel Bks.) Penguin Publishing Group.

—Scorpion Mountain. 2015. (Brotherband Chronicles Ser.: 5). (ENG.). 480p. (J). (gr. 5). 8.99 *(978-0-14-242727-9(6))*, Puffin Books) Penguin Young Readers Group.

—Scorpion Mountain. 2015. (Brotherband Chronicles Ser.: 5). lib. bdg. 19.65 *(978-0-606-37563-4(5))* Turtleback Bks.

—Slaves of Socorro. 2014. (Brotherband Chronicles Ser.: Bk. 4). (ENG., Illus.). 480p. (J). 18.99 *(978-0-399-16355-5(7))*, Philomel Bks.) Penguin Publishing Group.

—Slaves of Socorro. 2015. (Brotherband Chronicles Ser.: 4). (ENG.). 496p. (J). (gr. 5). pap. 8.99 *(978-0-14-242726-2(8))*, Puffin Books) Penguin Young Readers Group.

—Slaves of Socorro. 2015. (Brotherband Chronicles Ser.: 4). lib. bdg. 19.65 *(978-0-606-36771-4(3))* Turtleback Bks.

—The Tournament at Gorlan. 2015. (Ranger's Apprentice: the Early Years Ser.: 1). (ENG., Illus.). 384p. (J). (gr. 5). 18.99 *(978-0-399-16361-6(1))*, Philomel Bks.) Penguin Young Readers Group.

Flanagan, John A. The Tournament at Gorlan. 2016. (Ranger's Apprentice the Early Years Ser.: 1). lib. bdg. 19.65 *(978-0-606-39332-4(3))* Turtleback Bks.

Flat Kid Action Figure. 2004. (J). ring bd. 3.50 *(978-0-9763328-1-7(7))* Smart Smiles Co., The.

Flavin, Teresa. The Blackhope Enigma. 2011. (ENG., Illus.). 304p. (J). (gr. 4-7). 15.99 *(978-0-7636-5694-2(1))*, Templar) Candlewick Pr.

—The Crimson Shard. (ENG.). (J). (gr. 4-7). 2015. 288p. pap. 6.99 *(978-0-7636-7172-3(X))* 2012. (Illus.). 256p. 15.99 *(978-0-7636-6093-2(0))* Candlewick Pr. (Templar).

—The Shadow Lantern. 2014. (ENG., Illus.). 272p. (J). (gr. 4-7). 15.99 *(978-0-7636-6436-7(7))*, Templar) Candlewick Pr.

Fleischer, Barbara R. The Adventures of Scooby, Charlie, & Fluffy. 2011. 64p. pap. 28.95 *(978-1-4567-2496-2(7))* AuthorHouse.

Fleischman, Sid. Disappearing Act. 2004. (ENG.). 144p. (J). (gr. 3-18). reprint ed. pap. 5.99 *(978-0-06-051964-3(9))*, Greenwillow Bks.) HarperCollins Pubs.

—The Whipping Boy. 2011. 7.52 *(978-0-7848-3459-6(8))*, Everbind) Marco Bk. Co.

—The Whipping Boy. 2003. (J). 17.20 *(978-0-613-69320-2(5))*, Turtleback) Turtleback Bks.

Fleming, Celestine. Winkey. 2008. (J). pap. 5.95 *(978-0-9801564-7-8(5))* Kingdom Publishing Group, Inc.

Fleming, Ian. Chitty Chitty Bang Bang. Berger, Joe, illus. 2013. (Chitty Chitty Bang Bang Ser.). (ENG.). 160p. (J). (gr. 4-7). pap. 6.99 *(978-0-7636-6666-8(1))* Candlewick Pr.

Fleming, Sean & Ewald, Jenny, eds. To Catch a Mall Thief. 2004. 85p. (YA). pap. 9.95 *(978-0-7414-2196-8(8))* Infinity Publishing.

Fleming, Theresa. Going Home with Jesus, 1 vol. Fleming, Yvonne B., illus. 2009. 22p. pap. 24.95 *(978-1-60813-703-9(1))* America Star Bks.

Flesher, Brandon. Shattered Dreams in Light. 2014. (J). *(978-1-938237-10-2(2))* Skywater Publishing Co.

Fletcher, Corina. Playbook Pirates. Teckentrup, Britta, illus. 2013. (ENG.). 12p. (J). (gr. -1-2). 24.00 *(978-0-7636-6606-4(8))*, Nosy Crow) Candlewick Pr.

Fleuriel, Allison. Are You Done Sleeping? 2006. (J). pap. 16.00 *(978-0-8059-7115-6(7))* Dorrance Publishing Co., Inc.

Fleury, Barbara. The Runaway Deer. 2008. (Illus.). 36p. (J). pap. 8.95 *(978-0-9728155-9-8(7))* CONVERPAGE.

Flinn, Alex. Breaking Point. 2003. (ENG.). 256p. (YA). (gr. 9). pap. 9.99 *(978-0-06-447371-2(6))*, HarperTeen) HarperCollins Pubs.

Flint, Shamini. The Collected Diaries of a Sporting Superhero: Five Stories in One! 2017. (Diary of A... Ser.). (ENG.). 500p. (J). (gr. 2-6). pap. 14.99 ***(978-1-76029-345-1(8))*** Allen & Unwin AUS. Dist: Independent Pubs. Group.

Flintham, Thomas. Super Rabbit Boy Powers Up! 2017. (Press Start! — Branches Ser.: 2). lib. bdg. 14.75 ***(978-0-606-40188-3(1))*** Turtleback Bks.

Flitcroft, Jean. The Loch Ness Monster. 2010. (Cryptid Files Ser.: No. 1). xii, 176p. (J). pap. *(978-1-84840-940-8(0))* Little Island.

Floen, Douglas. Knowing Noah: The Adventures of a Mouse Who Could Read. 2012. 88p. pap. 13.95 *(978-1-4772-4506-4(5))* AuthorHouse.

Florido, Lorraine. Hugo the Punk. Shami, Susan, ed. Ewing, John, illus. 2013. 108p. (YA). pap. 9.98 *(978-0-9818449-6-1(0))* Thinkus Pubs.

Flower, Graham Jessie. Grace Harlowe's Senior Year at High School. 2006. 156p. pap. 19.99 *(978-1-4264-1912-6(0))* Creative Media Partners, LLC.

—Grace Harlowe's Senior Year at High School. 2004. reprint ed. pap. 1.99 *(978-1-4192-2224-5(4))*; pap. 21.95 *(978-1-4191-2224-8(X))* Kessinger Publishing, LLC.

Flower, Jessie Graham. Grace Harlowe's Return to Overton Campus. 2007. 260p. 29.95 *(978-1-4344-9674-4(0))*; per. 19.95 *(978-1-4344-9673-7(2))* Wildside Pr., LLC.

—Grace Harlowe's Second Year at Overton Campus. 2007. 252p. 29.95 *(978-1-4344-9676-8(7))*; per. 19.95 *(978-1-4344-9675-1(9))* Wildside Pr., LLC.

—Grace Harlowe's Sophomore Year at High School. 2007. 256p. 29.95 *(978-1-4344-9678-2(3))*; per. 19.95 *(978-1-4344-9677-5(5))* Wildside Pr., LLC.

—Grace Harlowe's Third Year at Overton College. 2007. 252p. 29.95 *(978-1-4344-9680-5(5))*; per. 19.95 *(978-1-4344-9679-9(1))* Wildside Pr., LLC.

Floyd, Belinda D. Going to America. 2005. 28p. per. 25.49 *(978-1-4208-8693-1(2))* AuthorHouse.

Floyd, Donyell. The Curious Child. 2008. 16p. per. 11.95 *(978-1-59800-046-7(2))* Outskirts Pr., Inc.
Floyd, Kara. Olivia West vs. Middle School: Round One. 2013. 164p. pap. 11.99 *(978-1-937165-34-5(5))* Orange Hat Publishing.
The Flying Hockey Stick. 2007. (Illus.). 64p. (J). (gr. -1-3). 18.95 *(978-1-930900-31-8(7))* Purple Hse. Pr.
Flynn, Ian & Spaziante, Patrick. Let the Games Begin. 2011. (Mega Man Ser.: 1). (ENG., Illus.). 112p. (gr. 4-7). pap. 11.95 *(978-1-879794-85-6(3),* Archie Comics) Archie Comic Pubns., Inc.
Flynn, S. E. That Night. 2009. 24p. pap. 11.95 *(978-1-4389-6699-1(7))* AuthorHouse.
Fodi, Lee Edward. Kendra Kandlestar & the Crack in Kazah. 2011. (Illus.). 294p. (J). pap. 8.95 *(978-1-61254-019-1(8))* Brown Books Publishing Group.
Fogerty, Ramona. Come to Galapagos at Sea to See. Hayden, Seitu, illus. 2004. (SPA.). (J). pap. 22.95 *(978-0-9759889-1-6(3))* Potenial Psychotherapy Counseling & Remedial Service.
Fogg, K. L. Diamondback Cave: A Novel. 2008. 377p. (J). *(978-1-59811-512-3(X))* Covenant Communications.
—Serpent Tide. 2006. 16.95 *(978-1-59156-861-2(7))* Covenant Communications, Inc.
—Widow's Revenge: A Novel. 2007. 355p. (J). *(978-1-59811-319-8(4))* Covenant Communications.
Fogwill, Joyce Graham. Bubs the Bumblebee & Her Most Unfortunate Fortunate Adventure. 2009. 24p. pap. 12.99 *(978-1-4490-5042-9(5))* AuthorHouse.
Foley, Jonathan. My Very First Adventure. 2007. (ENG.). 20p. per. 24.95 *(978-1-4241-8452-1(5))* America Star Bks.
Foley, Lizzie K. Remarkable. 2013. (ENG.). 336p. (J). (gr. 3-7). pap. 7.99 *(978-0-14-242410-0(2),* Puffin Books) Penguin Young Readers Group.
Follen, Eliza Lee. The Pedler of Dust Sticks. 2004. reprint ed. pap. 15.95 *(978-1-4191-7694-4(3))* Kessinger Publishing, LLC.
—The Talkative Wig. 2004. reprint ed. pap. 15.95 *(978-1-4191-8483-3(0))* Kessinger Publishing, LLC.
Fontenot, Martha Leonard. Grandma Liza's Rainbow Cake. 2009. 28p. pap. 13.99 *(978-1-4490-0772-0(4))* AuthorHouse.
Fontes, Justine. Cheerios Action Park Adventure. 2005. (Picture Clue Math Reader Ser.). (Illus.). 28p. (J). pap. *(978-0-439-70343-7(3))* Scholastic, Inc.
—Showdown in Critterown. 2014. (Cheddar's Tales Ser.). (ENG.). 176p. (J). (gr. 2-4). pap. 5.99 *(978-1-4380-0360-3(9))* Barron's Educational Series, Inc.
Fontes, Justine & Fontes, Ron. The Fifth Musketeer. Meconis, Dylan, illus. 2012. (Twisted Journeys Ser.: 19). (ENG.). 112p. (J). (gr. 4-7). pap. 45.32 *(978-0-7613-9289-7(0));* pap. 7.95 *(978-0-7613-8550-9(9));* lib. bdg. 27.93 *(978-0-7613-4594-7(9))* Lerner Publishing Group. (Graphic Universe™).
Food Fight Frenzy. 2008. (ENG., Illus.). 32p. pap. 15.95 *(978-1-933300-65-8(5))* Wandering Sage Pubns., LLC.
Ford, Christopher. An Epic Doodle, Bk. 1. Ford, Christopher, illus. 2011. (Stickman Odyssey Ser.: 1). (ENG., Illus.). 208p. (J). (gr. 3-7). 12.99 *(978-0-399-25426-0(9),* Philomel Bks.) Penguin Young Readers Group.
—The Wrath of Zozimos, 2 vols., Bk. 2. Ford, Christopher, illus. 2012. (Stickman Odyssey Ser.: 2). (ENG., Illus.). 224p. (J). (gr. 3-7). 12.99 *(978-0-399-25427-7(7),* Philomel Bks.) Penguin Young Readers Group.
Ford, Jayme. The Adventures of Glop-A-Lopikins. 2012. 32p. pap. 24.95 *(978-1-62709-207-4(2))* America Star Bks.
—The Adventures of Glop-A-Lopikins & the Pink Castle. 2013. 28p. pap. 24.95 *(978-1-62709-206-7(4))* America Star Bks.
Ford, John C. & Wells, Rosemary. The Cipher. 2015. (ENG.). 320p. (YA). (gr. 7). bds. 17.99 *(978-0-670-01542-9(3),* Viking Books for Young Readers) Penguin Young Readers Group.
Ford, Laura. Buster Brown & Tige in Misfit Heroes. 2004. (Illus.). 320p. 19.95 *(978-1-881554-28-8(7))* Skyward Publishing Co.
Ford, Martyn. The Imagination Box. 2016. (ENG.). 240p. (J). (gr. 4-7). 16.99 *(978-1-101-93627-6(4),* Delacorte Pr.) Random Hse. Children's Bks.
Ford, Robert. Adventures of Hit the Road Jack. l.t. ed. 2003. (Illus.). 40p. per. 10.00 *(978-1-932338-11-9(X))* Lifevest Publishing, Inc.
Ford, Sandy Lee, illus. Gullah, the Nawleans Cat Meets Katrina. 2007. 32p. (J). *(978-0-9793637-0-2(5))* Hart Street Pubs.
Ford, Sharon Lea. The Pages of Lost Time. 2010. 212p. 24.95 *(978-1-60911-127-4(3),* Eloquent Bks.) Strategic Book Publishing & Rights Agency (SBPRA).
Forde, Catherine. Tug of War. 2008. (ENG.). 320p. (YA). (gr. 7). pap. 9.99 *(978-1-4052-3967-7(0))* Egmont Bks., Ltd. GBR. Dist: Independent Pubs. Group.
Fordham, Walter. Ilian. Krizmanic, Tatjana, illus. 2012. 42p. pap. *(978-0-9813889-5-3(7))* Publish Yourself.
Foreman, Michael. Fortunately, Unfortunately. Foreman, Michael, illus. 2011. (Andersen Press Picture Bks). (ENG., Illus.). 32p. (J). (gr. -1-3). 16.95 *(978-0-7613-7460-2(4))* Lerner Publishing Group.
—Hola, Mundo. 2004.Tr. of Hello, World. (SPA., Illus.). 28p. (J). 19.99 *(978-84-88342-41-6(1))* S.A. Kokinos ESP. Dist: Lectorum Pubns., Inc.
—Newspaper Boy & Origami Girl! 2014. (Origami Girl Ser.). (ENG., Illus.). 32p. (J). (gr. -1-k). pap. 9.99 *(978-1-84939-519-9(5))* Andersen Pr. GBR. Dist: Independent Pubs. Group.
The Forest of the Frendibles. 2006. (J). mass mkt. *(978-0-9791982-0-5(8))* Pine Cone Pr.
Forey, Martin. Maurice Minor's Incredible Adventure: A Children's Book for Grown-Ups. 2010. (Illus.). 256p. pap. 14.49 *(978-1-4490-6875-2(8))* AuthorHouse.
Forgey, Winchester. Chronicle of the Bent Nail. 2004. (J). per. *(978-0-9666572-7-2(6))* Acacia Publishing, Inc.
Forman, Gayle. If I Stay Collection, 2 vols., Set. 2014. (ENG.). 1p. (YA). (gr. 9). pap., pap., pap. 21.98 *(978-0-14-751502-5(5),* Speak) Penguin Young Readers Group.
Forman, M. L. Adventurers Wanted, Book 1: Slathbog's Gold. 2011. 400p. mass mkt. 7.99 *(978-1-60641-681-5(2))* Deseret Bk. Co.
—Adventurers Wanted, Book 2: The Horn of Moran. 2012. (J). pap. 7.99 *(978-1-60908-911-5(1))* 2011. 400p. 39.99 *(978-1-60641-255-8(8))* Deseret Bk. Co.
—Adventurers Wanted, Book 3: Albrek's Tomb. 2013. (Adventurers Wanted Ser.: 3). (ENG.). 504p. (J). (gr. 5). pap. 9.99 *(978-1-60907-339-8(8),* Shadow Mountain) Shadow Mountain Publishing.
—Adventurers Wanted, Book 4: Sands of Nezza. 2013. (Adventurers Wanted Ser.: 4). (ENG.). 400p. (J). (gr. 5). 19.99 *(978-1-60907-329-9(0),* Shadow Mountain) Shadow Mountain Publishing.
—Adventures Wanted, Book 3: Albrek's Tomb. 2012. (YA). 19.99 *(978-1-60908-892-7(1))* Deseret Bk. Co.
Forman, Mark. The Horn of Moran. 2011. 400p. (YA). (gr. 3-18). 18.99 *(978-1-60641-226-8(4),* Shadow Mountain) Shadow Mountain Publishing.
—Slathbog's Gold. 2009. (Adventurers Wanted Ser.: Bk. 1). 432p. (J). 17.95 *(978-1-60641-029-5(6),* Shadow Mountain) Shadow Mountain Publishing.
Forney, Lane. The Super Power Teens. 2009. 140p. pap. 11.95 *(978-0-557-00129-3(3))* Lulu Pr., Inc.
Forsyth, C. A. & Forsyth, Christine. Adrenaline High, 1 vol. 2003. (Lorimer SideStreets Ser.). (ENG.). 128p. (YA). (gr. 9-12). 9.95 *(978-1-55028-792-9(3),* 9781550287929); 16.95 *(978-1-55028-793-6(1),* 9781550287936) Lorimer, James & Co., Ltd., Pubs. CAN. Dist: Casemate Pubs. & Bk. Distributors, LLC.
Forsythe, Amanda J. The Contabulous Adventures of M E. 2012. 28p. 24.95 *(978-1-4626-6531-0(4))* America Star Bks.
El Fortin Musical: Aventura 1: el Viaje a la Coleccion de Liderazgo. 2004. (SPA.). (J). per. 12.95 *(978-0-9727273-6-5(1))* Green Owl, Inc.
Fortunato, Mike. Later Gator, in a While Crocodile. 2013. (ENG.). 40p. (J). pap. 14.95 *(978-1-4787-1285-5(6))* Outskirts Pr., Inc.
Fortune, Emil. Root. 2014. (ENG.). 288p. (J). (gr. 6). pap. 10.99 *(978-0-552-56635-3(7))* Transworld Publishers Ltd. GBR. Dist: Independent Pubs. Group.
Fortune, Tracy. Kaila's Garden. 2009. 32p. pap. 14.98 *(978-0-557-02254-0(1))* Lulu Pr., Inc.
Fosina, Mickie. The Kitten Girls Are Scaredy Cats. 2012. 24p. pap. 15.99 *(978-1-4691-8172-1(X))* Xlibris Corp.
Fosse, Mika. Garage People. 2008. 84p. pap. 9.95 *(978-1-60693-500-2(3),* Eloquent Bks.) Strategic Book Publishing & Rights Agency (SBPRA).
Fossey, Robert. Little Armstrong. 2009. (Illus.). 20p. pap. 12.49 *(978-1-4389-5206-2(6))* AuthorHouse.
Foster, Jo. Chedworth Roman Villa: Discover Roman Britain. Percival, Tom, illus. 2017. (ENG.). 32p. pap. 9.99 **(978-1-911384-38-0(4))** History Pr. Ltd.,The GBR. Dist: Independent Pubs. Group.
Foster, Patricia. Where Did You Come from, Tiny Drop? 2008. 24p. pap. 24.95 *(978-1-60610-224-4(9))* America Star Bks.
Foster, Sheilagh. Mr Coyote Visits the Robson Valley. 2011. 26p. pap. 11.97 *(978-1-61204-439-2(5),* Strategic Bk. Publishing) Strategic Book Publishing & Rights Agency (SBPRA).
Foster, Tim & Foster, Tina. Abap the Ambulance in Happy to Help! 2008. 28p. 18.95 *(978-0-9556910-0-3(1))* Eclipse Solutions (UK) Ltd. GBR. Dist: Lulu Pr., Inc.
Foston, Desirae. The Hawaiian Hiatus of Herkimer Street. Foston, Desirae, illus. 2013. (Illus.). 24p. 24.00 *(978-1-940021-00-3(6))* Bliss Group.
Fournier, Elizabeth. Sailboat Dreams: Monkey Island. 2012. 16p. pap. 15.99 *(978-1-4772-7670-9(X))* AuthorHouse.
Fournier, Martin. The Adventures of Radisson 2: Back to the New World. 2015. (Adventures of Radisson Ser.). (ENG., Illus.). 200p. (YA). (gr. 7). pap. 16.95 *(978-1-77186-026-0(X))* Baraka Bks. CAN. Dist: Independent Pubs. Group.
—The Incredible Escape. McCambridge, Peter, tr. from FRE. 2016. (Adventures of Radisson Ser.). (ENG., Illus.). 200p. (YA). (gr. 7). pap. 16.95 *(978-1-77186-025-3(1))* Baraka Bks. CAN. Dist: Independent Pubs. Group.
Fower, C. A. The Bramblefrost Fairies. 2013. 116p. *(978-1-909740-40-2(3));* pap. *(978-1-909593-96-1(6))* Legend Pr.
Fowler, Frank. The Broncho Rider Boys with Funston at Vera Cruz: Or: Upholding the Honor of the Stars & Stripes. 2007. (ENG.). 190p. pap. 19.99 *(978-1-4346-3206-7(7));* 202p. pap. 22.99 *(978-1-4346-3207-4(5))* Creative Media Partners, LLC.
Fowler, Orval Ray. Wally Gumper & Family Travel & Adventures: In Search of the Stones. 2010. 209p. pap. 71.95 *(978-1-4327-4719-0(3))* Outskirts Pr., Inc.
Fox, Gaines. Go Fly a Kite: A Juvenile Adventure Novel. 2008. 200p. pap. 24.95 *(978-1-60703-573-2(1))* America Star Bks.
Fox, Jennifer. Meet Optimus Prime. 2015. (Passport to Reading Level 1 Ser.). (ENG., Illus.). 32p. (J). (gr. -1-3). pap. 3.99 *(978-0-316-40558-4(2))* Little, Brown Bks. for Young Readers.
—Meet Optimus Prime. 2015. (Transformers Passport to Reading Ser.). (J). lib. bdg. 13.55 *(978-0-606-35938-2(9))* Turtleback Bks.
Fox, Kate & Read, Abigail. Dear Mom: A Journal All about You Written by Me. 2014. (ENG.). 96p. 12.99 *(978-1-84601-469-7(7),* Spruce) Octopus Publishing Group GBR. Dist: Hachette Bk. Group.
Fox, L. B. The Adventures of Marky, Slash & Levy. 2006. (ENG.). 184p. per. 24.95 *(978-1-4241-4992-6(4))* PublishAmerica, Inc.
Fox, Lee White. Toby Erdrich & the Golden Eclipse. Selyov, Trebor E., ed. 2005. 170p. (YA). (gr. 7-12). pap. 11.95 *(978-0-9665055-7-3(3),* 5) Hallmark Emporium.
Fox, Nita. Captain Benjamin Dale. Wallace, Andrea, illus. 2008. 32p. (J). (gr. -1-3). pap. 5.99 *(978-0-9816107-0-2(6))* Fox's Den Publishing.
Fox, Robin C. & Fox, Carol White. The Traveling Adventures of the Robin & the Fox Around the World We Go! A Cruise Through the Mediterranean. 2013. 44p. pap. 20.45 *(978-1-4908-1763-7(8),* WestBow Pr.) Author Solutions, Inc.
Foxe, Steve. Decepticon Island! 2017. (Transformers Passport to Reading Ser.). (J). lib. bdg. 14.75 **(978-0-606-39908-1(9))** Turtleback Bks.
Foxe, Steve. Transformers Robots in Disguise: a New Adventure. 2016. (Passport to Reading Level 2 Ser.). (ENG.). 32p. (J). (gr. -1-3). pap. 4.99 *(978-0-316-27432-6(1))* Little, Brown Bks. for Young Readers.
Foyt, Victoria. The Virtual Life of Lexie Diamond. 2007. 310p. (YA). (gr. 7-12). lib. bdg. 17.89 *(978-0-06-082564-5(2),* HarperTeen) HarperCollins Pubs.
France, Richard. Joshua Stories: Book 1 - New School, New Friends. 2011. (Illus.). 104p. (gr. 4-6). pap. 14.09 *(978-1-4567-7732-6(7))* AuthorHouse.
Frances, Barbara. Lottie's Adventure: A Kidnapping Unraveled. 2007. 180p. pap. 12.95 *(978-0-615-16787-9(X))* Positive Imaging, LLC.
Frances, Janie. Krissy the Littlest Ladybug. 2013. 32p. pap. 8.95 *(978-0-9837403-9-1(9))* JGracia Publishing.
Francia, Giada. Alex & Penny in Egypt Jigsaw Book. 2011. (ENG., Illus.). 14p. 14.95 *(978-88-544-0240-9(0))* White Star ITA. Dist: Random Hse., Inc.
Francia, Giada, ed. Ballooning over Italy: An Extraordinary Voyage Packed with Games & Fantastic Adventures; Special Agents. Ezrin, Amy, tr. Colombo, Angelo, illus. 2007. (Alex & Penny Ser.). (ENG.). 80p. (J). (gr. 2-5). 14.95 *(978-88-544-0160-0(9),* White Star) Rizzoli International Pubns., Inc.
Franciosa, John F. Little Johnny Lion. 2009. 24p. pap. 11.99 *(978-1-4389-8810-8(9))* AuthorHouse.
Francis, Anwen. Siani Shetland. 2008. (ENG.). 84p. (J). pap. 9.95 *(978-1-905762-62-0(3))* Parthian Bks. GBR. Dist: Independent Pubs. Group.
Francis, JennaKay. The Ferry Boat. Woodward II, Ed, illus. 2013. 12p. pap. 8.95 *(978-1-61633-426-0(6))* Guardian Angel Publishing, Inc.
Francis, Nina. Rosemary's Story. 2009. 49p. pap. 7.96 *(978-0-557-03743-8(3))* Lulu Pr., Inc.
Francis, Pauline, retold by. The Count of Monte Cristo. 2010. (Essential Classics - Adventure Ser.). (Illus.). 48p. pap. *(978-0-237-54086-9(X))* Evans Brothers, Ltd.
—Kidnapped. 2010. (Essential Classics - Adventure Ser.). (Illus.). 48p. pap. *(978-0-237-54083-8(5))* Evans Brothers, Ltd.
—Treasure Island. 2010. (Essential Classics - Adventure Ser.). (Illus.). 48p. pap. *(978-0-237-54085-2(1))* Evans Brothers, Ltd.
Francis, Pauline & Verne, Jules. Journey to the Center of the Earth. 2003. (Fast Track Classics Ser.). (Illus.). 48p. (YA). pap. *(978-0-237-52534-7(8))* Evans Brothers, Ltd.
Francis, Suzanne. Let It Glow (Disney Frozen: Northern Lights) The Disney Storybook Art Team, illus. 2017. (Big Golden Book Ser.). (ENG.). 48p. (J). (gr. -1-2). 9.99 **(978-0-7364-3678-6(2),** Golden/Disney) Random Hse. Children's Bks.
Franco, Franco. Dino-Mike! 2016. (Dino-Mike! Ser.). (ENG.). 128p. (gr. 1-3). 151.92 *(978-1-4965-2505-5(1),* Dino-Mike!) Stone Arch Bks.
Franco, Franco & Garcia, Eduardo. Dino-Mike & the Dinosaur Cove. Franco, Franco, illus. 2016. (Dino-Mike! Ser.). (ENG., Illus.). 128p. (gr. 1-3). lib. bdg. 25.32 *(978-1-4965-2490-4(X),* Dino-Mike!) Stone Arch Bks.
—Dino-Mike & the Living Fossils. Franco, Franco, illus. 2016. (Dino-Mike! Ser.). (ENG., Illus.). 128p. (gr. 1-3). lib. bdg. 25.32 *(978-1-4965-2489-8(6),* Dino-Mike!) Stone Arch Bks.
Francoeur, Christine Marie. The Adventures of Jimmy Su: The South Pole. 2008. 16p. pap. 9.95 *(978-1-59858-720-3(X))* Dog Ear Publishing, LLC.
Francois, Rose Darlie. Little Miss Daring Evelynne. 2009. 47p. pap. 19.10 *(978-0-557-07136-4(4))* Lulu Pr., Inc.
Francois, Saragine. The White Gorilla & the Three Chimpanzees a Day from the Zoo. 2011. 28p. pap. 14.99 *(978-1-4520-3190-3(8))* AuthorHouse.
Frangiosa, Simon J. The Adventures of Tom: Tom's First Day. 2013. 16p. pap. 7.95 *(978-1-4525-7820-0(6),* Balboa Pr.) Author Solutions, Inc.
Frank Alvarado Madrigal. Las Increíbles Aventuras Del Pollito Pio Pio: The Incredible Adventures of Pew Pew, the Little Chicken. 2010. 32p. pap. *(978-1-4269-2520-7(4))* Trafford Publishing (UK) Ltd.
Frank Alvarado Madrigal, Alvarado Madrig & Frank Alvarado Madrigal. Las Increíbles Aventuras Del Patito Kuak Kuak: The Incredible Adventures of Kuack Kuack, the Little Duck. 2010. 32p. pap. *(978-1-4269-2540-5(9))* Trafford Publishing (UK) Ltd.
Frank, Church & Barnas, Aloura. The Epic Adventures of Whiz Grass & Poot Berry. 2011. 164p. (gr. -1). 22.99 *(978-1-4634-4525-6(3));* pap. 11.99 *(978-1-4634-4524-9(5))* AuthorHouse.
Frank, Pat. Little Warriors. 2008. 88p. pap. 8.95 *(978-1-60594-158-5(1),* Llumina Pr.) Aeon Publishing Inc.
Frank, Vincent. The Six Pack. 2010. 48p. (J). pap. 18.99 *(978-1-4490-9471-3(6))* AuthorHouse.
Frankel, Jordana. The Ward. (YA). (gr. 8). 2016. 496p. pap. 9.99 *(978-0-06-209535-0(8))* 2013. (ENG.). 480p. 17.99 *(978-0-06-209534-3(X))* HarperCollins Pubs. (Tegen, Katherine Bks).
Frankel, Rachel E., as told by. Twinkle Becomes a Real Tooth Fairy. 2009. (Illus.). 32p. (J). *(978-0-9841188-0-9(2))* Royal Council of the Real Fairyland, LLC.
Franklin, Shawna. Catching Achoo. 2006. (ENG.). 28p. per. 11.95 *(978-1-59800-492-2(1))* Outskirts Pr., Inc.
Franklin, Teii L. Ameelia's Adventures: Ameelia's First Play. 2010. 32p. pap. 16.49 *(978-1-4520-3613-7(6))* AuthorHouse.
Franks, Melissa. Warped! An Adventure Through Time Bk. 1: A What-a-saur? 2008. 96p. pap. 19.95 *(978-1-60703-636-4(3))* America Star Bks.
Frantz, Jennifer. The Lion, the Witch & the Wardrobe: Tea with Mr. Tumnus. Downer, Maggie, illus. 2005. (Festival Reader Ser.). 32p. (J). 14.99 *(978-0-06-079117-9(9))* Zonderkidz.
Franz, Kevin. Into the Hidden Lands: A Castle Rose Adventure. Stigler, Marilyn, illus. 2004. 112p. (J). per. 7.99 *(978-0-9747774-0-5(4))* Starbell Bks.
Fraser, Chelsea Curtis. Around the World in Ten Days. 2007. (ENG.). 192p. pap. 19.99 *(978-1-4346-3412-2(4));* 208p. pap. 22.99 *(978-1-4346-3413-9(2))* Creative Media Partners, LLC.
Fraser, Frank. Bearista: A Grand Adventure. Fraser, Frank, illus. 2003. (Illus.). (J). pap. 14.95 *(978-0-9726394-0-8(3))* Starbucks Coffee Co.
—The Bible Amigos: Five Loaves, Two Fish, & One Big Hat. 2014. (ENG., Illus.). 48p. (J). 7.99 *(978-1-62416-888-8(4))* Barbour Publishing, Inc.
Fraser, Jennifer. Scott the Starfish - an Unexpected Adventure! Eastley, Melanie, illus. 2012. 32p. pap. *(978-0-9868776-4-3(6))* MW Bk. Pubs.
Fraser, P. J. The Mouse with the Torch, 1 vol. 2009. 48p. pap. 16.95 *(978-1-4489-2080-8(9))* America Star Bks.
Frashier, Giva. Bogey the Golf Bug. 2013. 36p. pap. 15.99 *(978-1-4808-0126-4(7))* Archway Publishing.
Fraustino, Lisa Rowe. The Hole in the Wall. 2010. (ENG.). 280p. (J). (gr. 2-7). 16.95 *(978-1-57131-696-7(5))* Milkweed Editions.
Fravel, Gale. Fellsmere the Pirate, Chipley's Adventure. Fravel, Harold, illus. 2011. 28p. pap. 12.95 *(978-1-936343-79-9(7))* Peppertree Pr., The.
Frazier, Angie. The Eternal Sea. 2011. (ENG.). 368p. (J). (gr. 7-7). 17.99 *(978-0-545-11475-2(6),* Scholastic Pr.) Scholastic, Inc.
—Everlasting. 2010. (ENG.). 336p. (J). (gr. 7-18). 17.99 *(978-0-545-11473-8(X),* Scholastic Pr.) Scholastic, Inc.
Fred. Cast Away on the Letter A. Fred, illus. 2013. (Philemon Adventures Ser.). (ENG., Illus.). 48p. (J). (gr. 2-7). 16.95 *(978-1-935179-63-4(2))* TOON Books / RAW Junior, LLC.
Frederick, H. J. Timber Howligan Secret Agent Cat. Wilkins, Wendy H., illus. 2015. (J). pap. 8.99 *(978-0-9964246-9-1(5))* Lionheart Pr.
Frederick, Heather Vogel. Home for the Holidays. 2011. (Mother-Daughter Book Club Ser.). (ENG.). 352p. (J). (gr. 4-7). 18.99 *(978-1-4424-0685-8(2),* Simon & Schuster Bks. For Young Readers) Simon & Schuster Bks. For Young Readers.
Frederick, John. The Flying Hat. 2010. (Illus.). 24p. 12.99 *(978-1-4520-1901-7(0))* AuthorHouse.
Fredericks, Eleanor. The Adventures of Tyler the Dinosaur, 1 vol. Fredericks, Rob, illus. 2009. 31p. pap. 24.95 *(978-1-61546-233-9(3))* America Star Bks.
Free, Zaccai. Mbutu's Mangos. Vasudevan, Vidya, illus. 2006. 24p. (J). per. 12.95 *(978-0-9785326-0-4(0))* Solar Publishing LLC.
Freedman, Claire. Aliens Love Dinopants. Cort, Ben, illus. 2016. (Underpants Bks.). (ENG.). 32p. (J). (gr. -1-2). 17.99 *(978-1-4814-6736-0(0),* Aladdin) Simon & Schuster Children's Publishing.
Freeman, Don. Beady Bear: With the Never-Before-Seen Story Beady's Pillow. 2015. (ENG., Illus.). 96p. (J). (gr. k-4). pap. 12.99 *(978-0-486-79713-7(9))* Dover Pubns., Inc.
Freeman, Meryl. The Voyages of Galley Cat. 2008. 36p. pap. 24.95 *(978-1-60474-632-7(7))* America Star Bks.
Freeman, Shannon. The Accident. 2014. (Port City High Ser.: 5). (YA). lib. bdg. 20.80 *(978-0-606-36617-5(2))* Turtleback Bks.
—A Port in Pieces. 2014. (Port City High Ser.: 8). (YA). lib. bdg. 20.80 *(978-0-606-36620-5(2))* Turtleback Bks.
Freer, Dave. Changeling's Island. 2016. (ENG.). 256p. (YA). (gr. 6). pap. 10.99 *(978-1-4767-8120-4(6))* Baen Bks.
Freestone, Annie. The Little Mars Rovers. 2008. 36p. pap. 13.95 *(978-1-59858-459-2(6))* Dog Ear Publishing, LLC.
French, Allen. The Story of Rolf & the Viking Bow. 2008. 148p. (gr. 7-12). pap. 8.15 *(978-1-60459-522-2(1))* Wilder Pubns., Corp.
French, Moira. The Swingewood Stories. 2009. 36p. pap. 16.99 *(978-1-4490-4777-1(7))* AuthorHouse.
French, Vivian. Alegre Roger y el Tesoro Submarino. Solana, Maria T., tr. Ortega, Damian, illus. 2006. (la Orilla Del Viento Ser.). (SPA.). 125p. (J). pap. 7.50 *(978-968-16-6837-2(5),* 163) Fondo de Cultura Economica USA.
Frey, Hildegard G. The Camp Fire Girls at Camp Keewaydin: Or, Paddles Down. 2007. (ENG.). 156p. pap. 19.99 *(978-1-4264-4283-4(1))* 2006. 174p. pap. 21.99 *(978-1-4264-4347-3(1))* Creative Media Partners, LLC.
—The Camp Fire Girls Go Motoring: Or along the Road That Leads the Way. 2007. (ENG.). 148p. pap. 18.99 *(978-1-4264-5040-2(0));* 166p. pap. 21.99 *(978-1-4264-5341-0(8))* Creative Media Partners, LLC.
—The Camp Fire Girls in the Maine Woods: Or the Winnebagos Go Camping. 2007. (ENG.). 152p. pap. 19.99 *(978-1-4264-9375-1(4));* 168p. pap. 21.99 *(978-1-4264-9756-8(3))* Creative Media Partners, LLC.
Frey, Hildegard Gertrude. The Camp Fire Girls Do Their Bit: Or over the Top with the Winnebagos. 2007. 158p. pap. 19.99 *(978-1-4346-2281-5(9));* (ENG.). 176p. pap. 21.99 *(978-1-4346-2339-3(4))* Creative Media Partners, LLC.
Frey, James. Endgame - The Fugitive Archives. 2017. (Endgame: the Fugitive Archives Ser.). 352p. (YA). (gr. 9). pap. 9.99 *(978-0-06-233278-3(3))* HarperCollins Pubs.
Frey, James & Johnson-Shelton, Nils. Endgame: Rules of the Game. 2017. (Endgame Ser.: 3). 368p. (YA). (gr. 9). pap. 10.99 *(978-0-06-233265-3(1))* HarperCollins Pubs.
—Rules of the Game. 2016. (Endgame Ser.: 3). 352p. (YA). (gr. 9). 19.99 *(978-0-06-233264-6(3))* HarperCollins Pubs.
Freyou, Lerin. The Adventures of Piston the Puppy: A Journey Through the Alphabet as Piston Discovers the World Around Him. 2009. 31p. 15.80 *(978-0-557-12597-5(9))* Lulu Pr., Inc.
Frick, Lisa. "Evie" the Little Jack Russell with Brown Around Her Eyes. 2009. 64p. pap. 31.99 *(978-1-4415-2911-4(X))* Xlibris Corp.
Frid, Colt & Frid, Randy. Demons at the Door. 2009. *(978-0-9811847-1-5(5))* Frid Enterprises, Inc.
Friday, Anita. Twins. Branman, Liz, illus. 2013. 34p. pap. 11.99 *(978-0-9899544-0-2(4))* Two Chicks.
Friday, Kisha. Three Fuzzy Little Bees. 2012. 34p. 24.95 *(978-1-4626-4735-4(9))* America Star Bks.
Friday, Stormy. Signal's Airport Adventure. Saroff, Phyllis, illus. 2006. (J). 14.95 *(978-0-9717047-5-6(9))* Bay Media, Inc.
Fridolfs, Derek. Fort Solitude (DC Comics: Secret Hero Society #2) Nguyen, Dustin, illus. 2016. (DC Comics: Secret Hero Society Ser.: 2). (ENG.). 176p. (J). (gr. 3-7). 12.99 *(978-0-545-87684-1(2))* Scholastic, Inc.
Friedman, D. Dina. Escaping into the Night. 2009. (ENG.). 208p. (J). (gr. 5-9). pap. 9.99 *(978-1-4169-8648-5(0),* Simon & Schuster Bks. For Young Readers) Simon & Schuster Bks. For Young Readers.
Friedman, Mel. The Mystery of the Backlot Banshee: A ClueFinders Mystery Adventure. 2004. (Illus.). 96p. (J). pap. *(978-0-7630-7620-7(1))* Magma.
Friedman, Stanley. I, Dinosaur. 2010. 166p. pap. 11.95 *(978-1-935118-91-6(9))* Bellissima Publishing, LLC.
—Quantum Outlaws. 2010. 210p. pap. 11.95 *(978-1-935630-09-8(1))* Bellissima Publishing, LLC.

—Quantum Prisoner. 2012. 212p. pap. 11.95 (978-1-61477-029-9(8)) Bellissima Publishing, LLC.

Friend, Amanda. Lisa & Laura: African Safari Park Adventure. 2012. (Illus.). 40p. pap. 17.00 (978-1-84426-856-6(X), Fastprint Publishing) Upfront Publishing Ltd. GBR. Dist: Printondemand-worldwide.com.

Friend, Gaythel & Miller, Dalton. The Mystery of the Green Box. 2006. 88p. per. 8.95 (978-1-59824-147-1(8)) E-BookTime LLC.

Friends & Heroes Activity & Coloring Book. 2008. (Friends & Heroes Ser.). (J). pap. (978-1-4143-2157-8(0), Tyndale Entertainment) Tyndale Hse. Pubs.

Friesen, Ray. RQW, Vol. 3. 2003. (YA). 2.95 (978-0-9728177-2-1(7)) Don't Eat Any Bugs Prodns.

Friesner, Esther & Friesner, Esther M. Nobody's Princess. 2008. (Princesses of Myth Ser.). (ENG., Illus.). 336p. (YA). (gr. 7-11). pap. 8.99 (978-0-375-87529-8(8), Ember) Random Hse. Children's Bks.

Fritz, Kevin. The Newf & the Dane. 2003. 108p. (J). pap. 9.95 (978-0-595-27050-7(6), Writers Club Pr.) iUniverse, Inc.

Fritz, Laura. Poodle on a Noodle. 2013. (ENG.). 28p. (J). pap. 9.99 (978-1-936815-88-3(5)) Yawn's Bks. & More, Inc.

Frizzell, Sally Parker. The Adventures in the Secret Valley. 2007. 40p. pap. 9.00 (978-0-8059-7615-1(9)) Dorrance Publishing Co., Inc.

Frommer, Abbey C. A New Fight: (Sequel to the Nix), 1 vol. 2010. 116p. pap. 19.95 (978-1-4489-7959-2(5)) America Star Bks.

Fronte, Kathy. Bella's Bow Tie Bears: Three Magnificent Tales of Adventure, Dreams & Magic. 2006. (Illus.). 36p. (J). pap. 12.95 (978-0-9727725-0-1(2)) Fronte, Kathy.

Frossard, Claire, illus. Emma's Journey. Frossard, Etienne, photos by. 2010. (ENG.). 56p. (J). (gr. -1-3). 17.95 (978-1-59270-099-8(3)) Enchanted Lion Bks., LLC.

Frost, Adam. Run! The Elephant Weighs a Ton! Chambers, Mark, illus. 2012. (ENG.). 128p. (J). (gr. -1-k). pap. 8.99 (978-1-4088-2707-9(7), 9781408827079, Bloomsbury USA Childrens) Bloomsbury Publishing USA.

Fry, Jason. The Jupiter Pirates #2: Curse of the Iris. 2016. (Jupiter Pirates Ser.: 2). 368p. (J). (gr. 3-7). pap. 6.99 (978-0-06-223024-9(7)) HarperCollins Pubs.

—The Jupiter Pirates #3: the Rise of Earth. 2016. (Jupiter Pirates Ser.: 3). (Illus.). 448p. (J). (gr. 3-7). 16.99 (978-0-06-223026-3(3)) HarperCollins Pubs.

Fry, Jason. Leia & the Great Island Escape. 2016. (Star Wars: Force Awakens 8X8 Ser.). (J). lib. bdg. 14.75 **(978-0-606-39934-0(8))** Turtleback Bks.

Fryer, Samantha. A Sorcerer's Tale. 2008. 116p. pap. 14.95 (978-1-84799-366-3(4)) Lulu Pr., Inc.

Fuchs, Menucha. Chatzkel, Mendel & Me: An adventure Story. Daykin, Rachmiel, tr. from HEB. Hechtkopf, H., illus. 2005. Orig. Title: Mah Shekarah Ba'Ayarah. 192p. (J). 15.95 (978-1-932443-39-4(8), CHMH) Judaica Pr., Inc., The.

Fuerst, Jeffrey B. & Benchmark Education Co., LLC. Robert Louis Stevenson's Treasure Island: My Sea Adventure Israel Hands. Hondru, Ovi, illus. 2014. (Text Connections Ser.). (J). (gr. 3). (978-1-4509-9652-5(3)) Benchmark Education Co.

Fujii, Hideaki. LBX Vol. 1: New Dawn Raisers. 2014. (ENG., Illus.). 192p. (J). pap. 9.99 (978-1-4215-7695-4(3)) Viz Media.

—LBX Vol. 2: Artemis Begins. 2014. (ENG., Illus.). 184p. (J). pap. 9.99 (978-1-4215-7696-1(1)) Viz Media.

—LBX: World Battle, Vol. 6. 2015. (ENG., Illus.). 152p. (J). pap. 9.99 (978-1-4215-7700-5(3)) Viz Media.

—LBX: World Changer, Vol. 3. 2015. (ENG., Illus.). 192p. (J). pap. 9.99 (978-1-4215-7697-8(X)) Viz Media.

Fujikawa, Brian. The Adventures of Bibole, Ri: The CURSE of the WEREMOUSE. 2012. 52p. pap. 18.41 (978-1-4669-3547-1(2)) Trafford Publishing.

—The Adventures of Bibole, Rivol & Michelle: The French Fry Caper. 2013. 72p. pap. 24.27 (978-1-4907-0954-3(1)) Trafford Publishing.

Fuller, Audrey. The Twintastic Adventures of TJ & Taylor: TJ Gets a Haircut. 2010. 14p. (J). pap. 13.95 (978-1-4327-5629-1(X)) Outskirts Pr., Inc.

Fultz, Steven D. The Adventures of the Barnyard Detectives: Where's Mr. Peacock, 1 vol. 2009. 79p. pap. 19.95 (978-1-60749-965-7(7)) America Star Bks.

Funaro, Gregory. Alistair Grim's Odd Aquaticum. 2016. (Alistair Grim Ser.). (ENG.). 448p. (J). (gr. 3-7). pap. 7.99 (978-1-4847-0900-9(4)) Hyperion Bks. for Children.

—Alistair Grim's Odd Aquaticum. 2016. (Alistair Grim Ser.). (ENG., Illus.). 448p. (J). (gr. 3-7). 16.99 (978-1-4847-0007-5(4)) Hyperion Pr.

Funk, Michele Housholder. The Adventures of Pete & Max: And the Lost Sock. 2011. (Illus.). 36p. pap. 16.86 (978-1-4567-3724-5(4)) AuthorHouse.

Funk, Rachel. Christabelle in the Museum of Time. 2007. 217p. pap. 14.95 (978-1-4303-2572-7(0)) Lulu Pr., Inc.

Funke, Cornelia. Dragon Rider. 2011.Tr. of Drachenreiter. (ENG.). 560p. (J). (gr. 2-5). pap. 9.99 (978-0-545-31648-4(0), Chicken Hse., The) Scholastic, Inc.

—Emma & the Blue Genie. Latsch, Oliver, tr. from GER. Meyer, Kerstin, illus. 2014. (ENG.). 96p. (J). (gr. 2-5). 9.99 (978-0-385-37540-5(9), Random Hse. Bks. for Young Readers) Random Hse. Children's Bks.

Fuqua, J. Scott. Secrets of the Greaser Hotel. 2014. (ENG., Illus.). 280p. 25.00 (978-1-61088-130-2(3)) Bancroft Pr.

Furgang, Kathy, told to. Paul Bunyan: Set Of 6. 2010. (Early Connections Ser.). (J). pap. 37.00 net. (978-1-4108-1360-2(6)) Benchmark Education Co.

Furlong, C. T. Arctic6Adventures: 6Pack Set. 2012. (Arctic6 Adventure Ser.). 192p. (YA). (gr. 4-6). pap. 136.63 (978-0-7613-9213-2(0)) Lerner Publishing Group.

—Arctic6Adventures: Single Copy Set. 2012. (Arctic6 Adventure Ser.). 192p. (YA). (gr. 4-6). pap. 22.77 (978-0-7613-9212-5(2)) Lerner Publishing Group.

—Killer Star. 2012. (Arctic6 Adventure Ser.). 192p. (YA). (gr. 4-6). pap. 45.54 (978-0-7613-9210-1(6)); pap. 7.99 (978-0-9562315-8-1(6)) Lerner Publishing Group.

—Killer Strangelets. 2011. (Arctic6 Ser.). 208p. (J). pap. (978-0-9562315-6-7(X)) Inside Pocket Publishing, Ltd.

Furlong, Carol T. Killer Genes. 2012. (Arctic6 Adventure Ser.). 192p. (YA). (gr. 4-6). pap. 7.99 (978-0-9562315-7-4(8)) Lerner Publishing Group.

Furman, Ben. Sam's Quest for the Crimson Crystal. 2007. 189p. (J). per. 8.95 (978-0-9778731-8-0(8)) Black Hawk Pr., Inc., The.

Furman, Simon. Revenge of the Fallen, 1 vol. Davis-Hunt, Jon, illus. 2010. (Transformers: Revenge of the Fallen Movie Adaptation Ser.). (ENG.). 24p. (J). (gr. 3-6). Vol. 1. 24.21 (978-1-59961-726-8(9)) Vol. 2. 24.21 (978-1-59961-727-5(7)) Spotlight.

—Revenge of the Fallen, 1 vol., Vol. 3. Milne, Alex, illus. 2010. (Transformers: Revenge of the Fallen Movie Adaptation Ser.). (ENG.). 24p. (J). (gr. 3-6). 24.21 (978-1-59961-728-2(5)) Spotlight.

—Revenge of the Fallen, 1 vol., Vol. 4. Davis-Hunt, Jon, illus. 2010. (Transformers: Revenge of the Fallen Movie Adaptation Ser.). (ENG.). 24p. (J). (gr. 3-6). 24.21 (978-1-59961-729-9(3)) Spotlight.

Fuson, Robin Densmore. Rosita Valdez: And the Giant Sea Turtle. 2012. 108p. 28.99 (978-1-4497-6487-6(8)); pap. 11.99 (978-1-4497-6486-9(X)) Author Solutions, Inc. (WestBow Pr.).

Fuss, Kevin. The Brothers Geek. 2010. 180p. 24.99 (978-1-4490-7366-4(2)); pap. 14.49 (978-1-4490-7365-7(4)) AuthorHouse.

Futers, Kevin P. The Adventures of the Billy Goats Gruff. 2010. 228p. pap. 13.00 (978-1-60911-791-7(3), Eloquent Bks.) Strategic Book Publishing & Rights Agency (SBPRA).

Fyne, Olga. Squirrel Race. 2009. 28p. pap. 13.99 (978-1-4389-3676-5(1)) AuthorHouse.

G-Force Gadget Guide. 2009. 48p. pap. 5.99 (978-1-4231-1805-3(7)) Disney Pr.

Gaetz, Dayle Campbell. Crossbow, 1 vol. 2007. (Orca Currents Ser.). (ENG.). 112p. (J). (gr. 5-9). pap. 9.95 (978-1-55143-841-2(0)); lib. bdg. 14.95 (978-1-55143-843-6(7)) Orca Bk. Pubs. USA.

—Spoiled Rotten, 1 vol. 2005. (Orca Currents Ser.). (ENG.). 128p. (J). (gr. 5-9). per. 9.95 (978-1-55143-474-2(1)) Orca Bk. Pubs. USA.

Gagné, Michel. The Saga of Rex. 2010. (ENG., Illus.). 200p. (J). (gr. 4-7). pap. 17.99 (978-1-60706-322-3(0), 9781607063223) Image Comics.

Gagnon, Michelle. Don't Let Go. 2014. (Don't Turn Around Ser.: 3). (ENG.). 352p. (YA). (gr. 8). 17.99 (978-0-06-210296-6(6)) HarperCollins Pubs.

Gagnon, Michelle & Gangsei, Jan. Zero Day. 2016. (ENG., Illus.). 364p. (YA). (gr. 7-12). 17.99 (978-1-4847-2226-8(4)) Hyperion Bks. for Children.

Gaia, Kerry-Anne. Fairy Love Heart Story Time & Songs: Love Fairies & the Talking Tree. 2013. 24p. pap. 12.99 (978-1-4525-6838-6(3)) Balboa Pr.

Gaiman, NEil. The Dangerous Alphabet. Grimly, Gris, illus. (ENG.). 32p. (J). (gr. k). 2010. pap. 6.99 (978-0-06-078335-8(4)) 2008. 17.99 (978-0-06-078333-4(8)) HarperCollins Pubs.

—Fortunately, the Milk. Young, Skottie, illus. (ENG.). 128p. (J). (gr. 3-7). 2014. pap. 5.99 (978-0-06-222408-8(5)) 2013. 14.99 (978-0-06-222407-1(7)) HarperCollins Pubs.

—Fortunately, the Milk. 2014. (J). lib. bdg. 16.00 (978-0-606-35965-8(6)) Turtleback Bks.

Gainey, Gary. The Bonds. Gillen, Rosemarie, illus. 2012. 150p. pap. 9.99 (978-1-937260-12-5(7)) Sleepytown Pr.

Gajewski, Lois. Benny, the Stubborn Bubble. 2011. 28p. (gr. 1-2). pap. 12.03 (978-1-4567-4703-9(7)) AuthorHouse.

The Galactic Adventures of Team Energy: Episode I: Dr. Slouch & the Candy Factory. 2007. (J). 16.95 (978-0-9778776-1-4(2)) LGE Performance Systems, Inc.

Galbraith, Julie. Stable Ground: The Riding Series #1. 2013. 136p. pap. (978-1-927794-05-0(6)) Lechner Syndications.

Galdone, Paul. The Elves & the Shoemaker. 2015. (Folk Tale Classics Ser.). (ENG., Illus.). 40p. (J). (gr. -1-3). 8.99 (978-0-544-53099-7(3), HMH Books For Young Readers) Houghton Mifflin Harcourt Publishing Co.

Gale, Audra. The Adventures of Buddy & Me. 2007. 32p. (YA). pap. 8.00 (978-0-8059-7277-1(3)) Dorrance Publishing Co., Inc.

Gale, Debra. Halloween Tripper. 2008. 12p. pap. 24.95 (978-1-60441-485-1(5)) America Star Bks.

Gale, Paul. Lisek's Great Adventure. 2012. 28p. pap. 16.09 (978-1-4669-4509-8(5)) Trafford Publishing.

Gales, Rick. Granny Puckerlips: Keepin' It Real with Kindness & Respect. 2013. 108p. (gr. 9-12). pap. 11.95 (978-1-4908-0437-8(4), WestBow Pr.) Author Solutions, Inc.

Galindo, Renata. The Cherry Thief. Galindo, Renata, illus. 2014. (Child's Play Library). (ENG., Illus.). 32p. (J). (978-1-84643-652-9(4)) Child's Play International Ltd.

Gallagher, Michael. X-Men, Scourge of the Savage Land. Severin, Marie, illus. 24p. (YA). (gr. k-18). 12.95 (978-0-9627001-7-0(7)) Futech Educational Products, Inc.

Gallant, Mark D. Christmas at Wildwood Farm. 2010. 140p. 22.49 (978-1-4520-2808-8(7)); pap. 11.99 (978-1-4520-2807-1(9)) AuthorHouse.

Gallard, Bette. Streaks & Cuckoos. 2013. 436p. pap. (978-2-917183-31-1(4)) Nigeria Baptist Convention, Pubns. Dept.

Gallego García, Laura. LAS HIJAS DE TARA. 2004. (SPA.). 272p. (YA). 9.99 (978-84-348-8629-2(4)) SM Ediciones ESP. Dist: Lectorum Pubns., Inc.

Gallegos, Bryan. Ghost Train. 2012. (ENG.). 163p. pap. 12.95 (978-1-4327-7290-1(2)) Outskirts Pr., Inc.

Gallo, Tina. Let's Put on a Show! Style Guide Staff, illus. 2010. (Yo Gabba Gabba! Ser.). (ENG.). 16p. (J). (gr. -1-1). pap. 5.99 (978-1-4169-9535-7(8), Simon Scribbles) Simon Scribbles.

—OLIVIA in the Park. Rose, Drew, illus. 2010. (Olivia TV Tie-In Ser.). (ENG.). 48p. (J). (gr. -1-1). 5.99 (978-1-4169-9887-7(X), Simon Scribbles) Simon Scribbles.

Gallop to the Sea. 2005. (J). (978-1-933343-12-9(5)) Stabenfeldt Inc.

Galloway, Dorian P. Why Pammie's So Small. 2011. 32p. pap. 21.99 (978-1-4568-9508-2(7)) Xlibris Corp.

Galloway, Ruth. Fidgety Fish. Galloway, Ruth, illus. 2017. (Ocean Adventures Ser.). (ENG., Illus.). 32p. (J). (gr. -1-2). 23.99 **(978-1-68010-055-6(6))** Tiger Tales.

Gallup, Zd. Nap Time at the Beach. 2013. 34p. pap. 14.95 (978-1-4575-2129-4(6)) Dog Ear Publishing, LLC.

Galvin, Laura Gates. Ankylosaurus Fights Back. Chesterman, Adrian, illus. 2007. (Smithsonian's Prehistoric Pals Ser.). (ENG.). 36p. (J). 8.95 (978-1-59249-681-5(4)); (J). 14.95 (978-1-59249-679-2(2)); (J). pap. 6.95 (978-1-59249-680-8(6)); (J). (gr. -1-3). 2.95 (978-1-59249-682-2(2)); 9.95 (978-1-59249-683-9(0)) Soundprints.

—Baby Lamb Finds a Friend. 2007. (ENG., Illus.). 16p. (gr. -1-k). 6.95 (978-1-59249-746-1(2)) Soundprints.

—Musical Safari - Little Einsteins. 2009. (Little Einstein Audio Tales). (ENG.). 20p. (J). (gr. -1). 8.99 (978-1-59069-774-0(X)) Studio Mouse LLC.

Gamble, Adam & Jasper, Mark. Good Night Cowboys. Veno, Joe, illus. 2017. (Good Night Our World Ser.). (ENG.). 20p. (J). (— 1). bds. 9.95 (978-1-60219-509-7(9)) Good Night Bks.

Gamble, Adam & Tougias, Michael J. Good Night Coast Guard. Kelly, Cooper, illus. 2017. (Good Night Our World Ser.). (ENG.). 20p. (J). (gr. -1 — 1). bds. 9.95 **(978-1-60219-425-0(4))** Good Night Bks.

Gamble, Paul. The Ministry of S. U. I. T. S. 2016. (Ministry of SUITs Ser.: 1). (ENG.). 384p. (J). 16.99 (978-1-250-07682-3(X), 9781250076823) Feiwel & Friends.

—The Monster's Daughter. 2017. (Ministry of SUITs Ser.: 2). (ENG.). 384p. (J). 16.99 (978-1-250-07683-0(8), 9781250076830) Feiwel & Friends.

Gamble, Rev. Vivian T. I Think All the Time... . Ummm. 2012. 28p. pap. 9.95 (978-1-4787-1359-3(3)) Outskirts Pr., Inc.

—Just to Be Myself. 2012. 28p. pap. 9.95 (978-1-4787-1358-6(5)) Outskirts Pr., Inc.

Game On. 13th ed. 2009. (ENG.). 128p. (J). pap. 4.99 (978-1-4231-0972-3(4)) Disney Pr.

Gangsei, Jan. The Wild Bunch. 2017. (Max Ser.). (ENG., Illus.). 192p. (J). (gr. 4-8). pap. 7.99 **(978-1-4814-6828-2(6)**, Aladdin) Simon & Schuster Children's Publishing.

Gangsei, Jan. Zero Day. 2016. (ENG., Illus.). 368p. (YA). (gr. 7-12). pap. 9.99 (978-1-4847-2548-1(4)) Hyperion Bks. for Children.

Gannett, Ruth Stiles. My Father's Dragon. Gannett, Ruth Chrisman, illus. 2005. (My Father's Dragon Ser.). (ENG.). 96p. (J). (gr. 3-7). 6.99 (978-0-440-42121-4(7), Yearling) Random Hse. Children's Bks.

Ganser, Sara. The Weekend Getaway. 2009. 24p. pap. 15.59 (978-1-4490-2423-9(8)) AuthorHouse.

Gantos, Jack. From Norvelt to Nowhere. 2013. (Norvelt Ser.: 2). (ENG.). 288p. (J). (gr. 5-9). 16.99 (978-0-374-37994-0(7), 9780374379940, Farrar, Straus & Giroux (BYR)) Farrar, Straus & Giroux.

—La Nueva Fuerza de Jack. (Torre de Papel Ser.). (SPA., Illus.). (YA). (gr. 5-8). 8.95 (978-958-04-5636-0(4), NR30644) Norma S.A. COL. Dist: Distribuidora Norma, Inc., Lectorum Pubns., Inc.

Gantt-Smith, Michelle. Little Feet Goes to the Barbershop. 2013. 48p. pap. 12.00 (978-0-9847885-1-4(4)) Gantt Smith Publishing Hse.

Ganzer, Diane & St. Croix, Sammy. Adventures of a Kitten Named Raspberry & Other Tales. 2009. 176p. pap. 9.95 (978-1-935105-30-5(2)) Avid Readers Publishing Group.

—Llama Tails: Ricky's Adventure. Ganzer, Theresa, illus. 2008. 172p. pap. 9.99 (978-0-9801438-7-4(X)) Avid Readers Publishing Group.

Ganzer, Diane & Swanson, Christopher. Called to Serve. 2008. 116p. pap. 9.99 (978-1-935105-10-7(8)) Avid Readers Publishing Group.

Gao, Charlie. Children City & Teacher Town. 2009. 80p. pap. 10.49 (978-1-4389-7547-4(3)) AuthorHouse.

Gapanowicz, Delores. The Finchley House Mystery. 2005. 112p. (J). per. 13.95 (978-1-933449-06-7(3)) Nightengale Pr.

Garant, Andre J. The Elite Eight. 2011. 120p. (gr. 4-6). pap. 10.99 (978-1-4567-4302-4(3)) AuthorHouse.

—Jake's Tree House. 2010. 128p. pap. 10.99 (978-1-4490-8369-4(2)) AuthorHouse.

Garces Iii, Joseph Louis. Garrett the Firefighter. Abercrombie, Bethaney, illus. 2008. 24p. pap. 12.99 (978-1-59858-716-6(1)) Dog Ear Publishing, LLC.

—Tyler the Cowpoke. 2012. 24p. 19.99 (978-1-4575-1724-2(8)); pap. 10.99 (978-1-4575-1609-2(8)) Dog Ear Publishing, LLC.

Garcia, Alice Cook. Bella's Dreams. 2011. 16p. pap. 8.32 (978-1-4634-3485-4(5)) AuthorHouse.

Garcia, Kami & Stohl, Margaret. Beautiful Redemption. 2013. (Beautiful Creatures Ser.: 4). (YA). lib. bdg. 24.50 (978-0-606-32282-9(5), Turtleback) Turtleback Bks.

Garcia, Mia. Even If the Sky Falls. 2016. 304p. (YA). (gr. 9). 17.99 (978-0-06-241180-8(2), Tegen, Katherine Bks) HarperCollins Pubs.

Garcia, R. M. The Steamer Trunk Adventures #1: The Trunk & the Tortoise. 2006. 76p. pap. 16.95 (978-1-4241-0614-1(1)) PublishAmerica, Inc.

Garcia, Randolph. The Steamer Trunk Adventures #2: The Ghosts of Machu Picchu. 2006. (ENG.). 88p. per. 16.95 (978-1-4241-1843-4(3)) PublishAmerica, Inc.

Gard, Don. The Adventures of Beezer. Giancanelli, Candace, illus. 2006. 100p. per. 12.95 (978-1-59858-157-7(0)) Dog Ear Publishing, LLC.

Garden, Nancy. The Case of the Stolen Scarab. 2004. (J). pap. 8.95 (978-0-9674468-7-5(2)) Two Lives Publishing.

Gardener, Amanda & Sealey, Nanlie. Butterfly Pavilion. 2013. 24p. pap. 10.99 (978-1-60820-898-2(2)) MLR Pr., LLC.

—Freddy the White Flamingo. 2013. 28p. pap. 12.99 (978-1-60820-900-2(8)) MLR Pr., LLC.

Gardner, Alecia. Peachy Penelope. 2010. 44p. pap. 19.99 (978-1-4490-0419-4(9)) AuthorHouse.

Gardner, Dianne Lynn. Rubies & Robbers. 2013. (ENG.). 176p. (J). pap. 14.99 (978-0-615-81113-0(2)) Hydra Pubns.

Gardner, Graham. The Santa Beacon. LeBlanc, Nancy, illus. 2012. 40p. (J). 19.95 (978-0-9859358-0-1(4), Belle Isle Bks.) Brandylane Pubs., Inc.

Gardner, Lyn & Asquith, Ros. The Ghastly McNastys Bk. 2: Raiders of the Lost Shark. 2014. (Ghastly Mcnastys Ser.). (ENG., Illus.). 192p. (J). (gr. k-3). pap. 9.99 (978-1-84812-363-2(9)) Bonnier Publishing GBR. Dist: Independent Pubs. Group.

Gardner, Sally. The Red Necklace. 2009. (ENG.). 400p. (YA). (gr. 7-18). 8.99 (978-0-14-241488-0(3), Speak) Penguin Young Readers Group.

—The Red Necklace: A Story of the French Revolution. l.t. ed. 2008. 583p. 23.95 (978-1-4104-1016-0(1)) Thorndike Pr.

—The Silver Blade. 2010. (ENG.). 384p. (YA). (gr. 7-18). 8.99 (978-0-14-241731-7(9), Speak) Penguin Young Readers Group.

Garey, Barbara J. The Adventures of Princess Naomia, 1 vol. 2009. 32p. pap. 24.95 (978-1-61546-090-8(X)) America Star Bks.

Garfield, Henry. The Lost Voyage of John Cabot. 2007. (ENG., Illus.). 320p. (YA). (gr. 7). pap. 16.95 (978-1-4169-5460-6(0), Simon Pulse) Simon Pulse.

Garis, Howard R. Bed Time Stories: Uncle Wiggily's Adventures. Wisa, Louis, illus. 2007. 140p. per. (978-1-4065-2773-5(4)) Dodo Pr.

—The Curlytops & Their Pets. 2009. 120p. 22.95 (978-1-60664-609-0(5)); pap. 10.95 (978-1-60664-341-9(X)) Rodgers, Alan Bks.

—The Curlytops at Silver Lake. 2007. 260p. 29.95 (978-1-4344-9207-4(9)); per. 19.95 (978-1-4344-9113-8(7)) Wildside Pr., LLC.

—The Curlytops on Star Island. 2009. 120p. 22.95 (978-1-60664-611-3(7)); pap. 10.95 (978-1-60664-343-3(6)) Rodgers, Alan Bks.

—Uncle Wiggily & Old Mother Hubbard. 2008. 116p. 22.95 (978-1-60664-970-1(1)); per. 9.95 (978-1-60312-520-8(5)) Aegypan.

—Uncle Wiggily in the Woods. 2008. 132p. 24.95 (978-1-60664-971-8(X)); per. 11.95 (978-1-60312-521-5(3)) Aegypan.

—Uncle Wiggily's Adventures. 2008. 132p. 24.95 (978-1-60664-905-3(1)); pap. 10.95 (978-1-60664-024-1(0)) Aegypan.

—Uncle Wiggily's Travels. 2008. 132p. 24.95 (978-1-60664-906-0(X)); pap. 10.95 (978-1-60664-025-8(9)) Aegypan.

Garis, Howard Roger. The Curlytops at Uncle Frank's Ranch. 2005. 26.95 (978-1-4218-1466-7(8), 1st World Library - Literary Society) 1st World Publishing, Inc.

—The Curlytops at Uncle Frank's Ranch. 2004. reprint ed. pap. 21.95 (978-1-4191-5842-1(2)); pap. 1.99 (978-1-4192-5842-8(7)) Kessinger Publishing, LLC.

—The Curlytops on Star Island. 2005. 26.95 (978-1-4218-1467-4(6)); 192p. pap. 11.95 (978-1-4218-1567-1(2)) 1st World Publishing, Inc. (1st World Library - Literary Society).

—The Curlytops on Star Island. 2004. reprint ed. pap. 1.99 (978-1-4192-5843-5(5)) Kessinger Publishing, LLC.

—Uncle Wiggily's Adventures. 2005. 26.95 (978-1-4218-1468-1(4)); 164p. pap. 11.95 (978-1-4218-1568-8(0)) 1st World Publishing, Inc. (1st World Library - Literary Society).

—Uncle Wiggily's Adventures. Date not set. 192p. (J). 20.95 (978-0-8488-2281-1(1)) Amereon Ltd.

—Uncle Wiggily's Travels. 2005. 26.95 (978-1-4218-1469-8(2)); 164p. pap. 11.95 (978-1-4218-1569-5(9)) 1st World Publishing, Inc. (1st World Library - Literary Society).

Garland, Sarah. Splash! 2006. (ENG., Illus.). 16p. (J). (gr. k — 1). bds. (978-1-84507-345-9(2)) ReiseArt Buchhandlung GmbH.

Garlington, William R. The Great Divide: Coloring & Activity Book. 2004. (Illus.). (J). 5.95 (978-0-9708395-4-1(5)) Legacy Publishing Services, Inc.

—The Great Divide: The Adventures of Billy Bean & Bobby Nut. 2004. (Illus.). 127p. (J). pap. 12.95 (978-0-9708395-2-7(9)) Legacy Publishing Services, Inc.

Garner, Albert. The Adventures of Dimi. 2013. (ENG.). 48p. (J). 24.95 (978-1-4787-1677-8(0)) Outskirts Pr., Inc.

Garner, Phillip. Biff Cardova from Rooster Poot Kansas. 2010. 56p. pap. 21.99 (978-1-4490-7664-1(5)) AuthorHouse.

Garr, Rebecca. Adventures of Baroness of the Arizona Desert. Davisson, Vanessa, illus. 2010. 60p. pap. 18.95 (978-1-60911-958-4(4), Eloquent Bks.) Strategic Book Publishing & Rights Agency (SBPRA).

Garratt, Irene Joyce. Andrew's Activities: Two in One Stories. 2009. (Illus.). 20p. pap. 10.49 (978-1-4389-4235-3(4)) AuthorHouse.

Garretson, Dee. Wildfire Run. 2011. (ENG.). 288p. (J). (gr. 3-7). pap. 6.99 (978-0-06-195350-7(4)) HarperCollins Pubs.

—Wolf Storm. 2011. (ENG.). 288p. (J). (gr. 3-7). 16.99 (978-0-06-200032-3(2)) HarperCollins Pubs.

Garrett, Diane Marie. Buger the Butterfly & the Lion Kitties' First Adventure. Gulley, Hardrick M., illus. 2008. 16p. pap. 24.95 (978-1-60672-237-4(9)) America Star Bks.

Garrett, Kelsey. Lennie's Pennies. Kopler, Joe, illus. 2012. (ENG.). 64p. pap. 19.95 (978-1-4327-9606-8(2)) Outskirts Pr., Inc.

Garrick, Veda. The Place: Jello. 2012. 302p. pap. 19.99 (978-1-4525-5081-7(6)) Balboa Pr.

Garsee, Linmarie. Annabelle's Vacation with Grandma Hayley: A Mountain Quiltfest Adventure. 2012. 50p. pap. 21.99 (978-1-4772-7737-9(4)) AuthorHouse.

Garthwaite, Lynn D. Dirkle Smat Inside Mount Flatbottom. Howarth, Craig, illus. 2006. 48p. (J). pap. 9.95 (978-1-59663-512-8(6), Castle Keep Pr.) Rock, James A. & Co. Pubs.

Garton, Carol. Isabella Barella. 2013. (ENG.). 300p. (YA). 32.95 (978-1-4787-1339-5(9)); pap. 17.95 (978-1-4787-1490-3(5)) Outskirts Pr., Inc.

Garton, Kevan. The Cockleton Mystery. 2006. 68p. pap. (978-1-84401-788-1(5)) Athena Pr.

Garza, Armando N. Itty Bitty Saves the Day. 2007. (Illus.). 22p. (J). (gr. -1-3). 21.99 (978-1-59879-482-5(5)); per. 12.99 (978-1-59879-330-7(6)) Lifevest Publishing, Inc.

Garza, R. Baby Blue Egg's Big Adventure. 2008. 16p. pap. 24.95 (978-1-60441-880-4(X)) America Star Bks.

Garza, Xavier, illus. Maximilian & the Lucha Libre Club. 2016. (ENG & SPA.). 208p. (J). (gr. 2-7). 19.95 (978-1-941026-40-3(0)) Cinco Puntos Pr.

Gashler, Stephen. The Bent Sword. 2010. (YA). pap. 15.99 (978-1-59955-401-3(1)) Cedar Fort, Inc./CFI Distribution.

Gaston County Museum of Art & History, ed. The Secret Adventures of Hamster Sam: Attack of the Evil Boll Weevils! 2008. (Illus.). 32p. (J). 15.95 (978-0-9798445-0-8(9)) DM Creative.

Gates, S. P. The Monster in the Mudball, 1 vol. 2013. (ENG., Illus.). 222p. (J). 16.95 (978-1-62014-141-0(8), Tu Bks.) Lee & Low Bks., Inc.

Gathorne-Hardy, Jonathan. Jane's Adventures: Jane's Adventures in & Out of the Book; Jane's Adventures on the Island of Peeg; Jane's Adventures in a Balloon. Hill, Nicolas, illus. 2006. (ENG.). 588p. (gr. 4-13). 27.95 *(978-1-58567-798-6(1),* 856798) Overlook Pr., The.

Gaudet, M. K. Marley & Me: Marley to the Rescue! 2008. (I Can Read Level 1 Ser.). (ENG.). 32p. (J). (gr. k-3). pap. 3.99 *(978-0-06-170437-6(7))* HarperCollins Pubs.

Gaudissart, Martine. My Blue Lamb. 2012. 140p. pap. 19.95 *(978-0-9677547-2-7(0))* Angie Blue Bks., LLC.

Gaughen, A. C. Lady Thief. 2015. (Scarlet Ser.: No. 2). (ENG.). 336p. (YA). (gr. 7). pap. 9.99 *(978-0-8027-3788-5(9),* 9780802737885, Bloomsbury USA Childrens) Bloomsbury Publishing USA.

—Lion Heart. 2015. (Scarlet Trilogy: No. 3). (ENG.). 352p. (YA). 17.99 *(978-0-8027-3616-1(5),* 9780802736161, Bloomsbury USA Childrens) Bloomsbury Publishing USA.

—Lion Heart: A Scarlet Novel. 2016. (Scarlet Ser.). (ENG.). 352p. (YA). pap. 9.99 *(978-1-61963-928-7(9),* 9781619639287, Bloomsbury USA Childrens) Bloomsbury Publishing USA.

Gault, Linda Fulford. Help Is on the Way: The Adventures of Madame Flutterby Book Iii. 2012. 36p. (-18). pap. 17.46 *(978-1-4772-8746-0(9))* AuthorHouse.

Gauthier, Pamela. The Adventures of Bernie the Moose: Bernie Meets Marla. 2009. 20p. pap. 10.49 *(978-1-4490-3019-3(X))* AuthorHouse.

Gavin, Rebecca Thompson. The Adventures of Oakey Dokey Acorn: Oakey & Ivy. Gavin, Rebecca Thompson, illus. 2003. (Illus.). 64p. (J). *(978-1-57579-255-2(9))* Pine Hill Pr.

Gay, Michel. Una Vez Mas. 2003. (SPA.). 32p. *(978-84-95150-42-4(5))* Corimbo, Editorial S.L.

Gay, Michele. Leoncio's Adventures. 2013. 20p. pap. 17.99 *(978-1-4817-0427-4(3))* AuthorHouse.

Gay, Romney. Conny & Uncle Dick. 2011. 32p. pap. 35.95 *(978-1-258-10120-6(3))* Literary Licensing, LLC.

Gayatri Stein, Mari. Puddle Moon. 2010. (ENG., Illus.). 32p. 17.95 *(978-0-9793840-0-4(1),* Riverwood Bks.) White Cloud Pr.

Gayle, Juliet V. Emily & Beautiful & the Great Strawberry Whipped Cream Pie Mystery. 2011. 24p. pap. 13.95 *(978-1-4520-9744-2(5))* AuthorHouse.

Gayton, Sam. The Adventures of Lettie Peppercorn. Bernatene, Poly, illus. 2016. (ENG.). 304p. (J). (gr. 3-7). 16.99 *(978-1-4814-4769-0(6),* McElderry, Margaret K. Bks.) McElderry, Margaret K. Bks.

Gazdag, Adam. The Non Born Heir. 2010. 313p. pap. 19.27 *(978-0-557-17709-7(X))* Lulu Pr., Inc.

Gebhart, Ryan. There Will Be Bears. 2014. (ENG.). 224p. (J). (gr. 5). 16.99 *(978-0-7636-6521-0(5))* Candlewick Pr.

Gee, Maurice. The Limping Man, 1 vol. 2011. (Salt Trilogy Ser.: 3). (ENG.). 208p. (YA). (gr. 7-12). lib. bdg. 18.00 *(978-1-55469-216-3(4))* Orca Bk. Pubs. USA.

—Salt, 1 vol. 2011. (Salt Trilogy Ser.: 1). (ENG., Illus.). 272p. (J). (gr. 7-12). pap. 12.95 *(978-1-55469-369-6(1))* Orca Bk. Pubs. USA.

Gee, Randi. Smart Cookie. 2010. 32p. pap. 15.50 *(978-0-557-52976-6(X))* Lulu Pr., Inc.

Geiger, A. V. Follow Me Back. 2017. (Follow Me Back Ser.: 1). (ENG.). 368p. (YA). (gr. 8-12). pap. 10.99 *(978-1-4926-4523-8(0))* Sourcebooks, Inc.

Geiger, Eileen. The Adventures of Christina Crankypants. 2010. (ENG.). 80p. pap. 16.95 *(978-1-4452-3771-8(7))* Lulu Pr., Inc.

Gelsey, James. Caper Gets Even. 2011. pap. 10.95 *(978-0-7414-6668-6(6))* Infinity Publishing.

Gendreau, Paula. The Adventures of Lilly Lou: The First Day at Camp Who Who. 2009. 16p. pap. 8.49 *(978-1-4389-5950-4(8))* AuthorHouse.

Geneviève Douyon Flambert. Grace: The Mystical Caribbean Mission. 2009. 152p. 22.95 *(978-0-595-50709-2(3));* pap. 12.95 *(978-0-595-51639-1(4))* iUniverse, Inc.

Gentry, Jennifer Mills. Maria's 4th of July. 2011. 32p. pap. 24.95 *(978-1-4560-7300-8(1))* America Star Bks.

Gentry, Stephen. Journey to the Stars & Back. 2005. 52p. (J). pap. 16.49 *(978-1-4116-5985-8(6))* Lulu Pr., Inc.

George Cary Eggleston. Captain Sam: The Boy Scouts of 1814. 2007. (ENG.). 124p. per. 18.99 *(978-1-4346-3940-0(1));* 132p. per. 19.99 *(978-1-4346-3941-7(X))* Creative Media Partners, LLC.

George, J. A. Camp Aconyte. 2008. 65p. pap. 19.95 *(978-1-60610-631-0(7))* America Star Bks.

George, Jean Craighead. Crowbar. 32p. (J). (gr. -1-17). 15.49 *(978-0-7868-2326-0(7))* Hyperion Bks. for Children.

Georgieva, Zoia. Herman the Earth Worm: Illustrated by Emma C. Van Dyke. 2008. pap. 18.00 *(978-0-8059-8630-3(8))* Dorrance Publishing Co., Inc.

Gerald, Jay. The Adventures of Geo, the Pebble. 2012. 32p. pap. *(978-1-77097-269-8(2))* FriesenPress.

Geraldi, Michele J. The Way to Papou Lake. 2011. 112p. (gr. 2-4). 20.95 *(978-1-4620-3134-4(X));* pap. 10.95 *(978-1-4620-3133-7(1))* iUniverse, Inc.

Geraldine Anderson. Bev's Amazing Adventures: The Kitten. 2012. 28p. pap. 24.95 *(978-1-4626-7386-5(4))* America Star Bks.

Gerard, Justin, illus. Beowulf Bk. 1: Grendel the Ghastly. 2007. 32p. (J). (gr. 4-6). 17.95 *(978-0-9797183-0-4(9))* Portland Studios, Inc.

Gerard, Kevin. Diego's Dragon, Book Three: Battle at Tenochtitlan. Dreadfuls, Penny, ed. Gallegos, Benito, illus. 2013. 298p. pap. 14.99 *(978-0-9859802-3-8(0))* Crying Cougar Pr.

Gerber, Linda. Death by Bikini. 2008. (Death by ... Mysteries Ser.). (ENG.). 272p. (YA). (gr. 7-18). 7.99 *(978-0-14-241117-9(5),* Puffin Books) Penguin Young Readers Group.

—Death by Denim. 2009. (Death by ... Mysteries Ser.). (ENG.). 272p. (YA). (gr. 7-18). pap. 7.99 *(978-0-14-241119-3(1),* Puffin Books) Penguin Young Readers Group.

Gerber, Lisa Ann. Elaina's Sleuthing Days, 1 vol. 2009. 60p. pap. 16.95 *(978-1-60749-623-6(2))* PublishAmerica, Inc.

Gerheim, Su. Bayocor Adventures, the Secret Cave. 2012. 92p. pap. 10.95 *(978-1-61493-034-1(1))* Peppertree Pr., The.

Geringswald, Rita T. The Adventures of Ali Alligator. 2007. (Illus.). 33p. (J). 6.95 *(978-0-9797566-1-0(8))* R & D Publishing of Lakeland, Florida.

Gernhart, Cyndi. The Adventures of Gertrude Mccluck, Chicken in Charge Vol. 4: A Midwinter Light's Dream, 4 vols. Gernhart, Carlie, illus. l.t. ed. 2006. 52p. (J). 8.00 *(978-0-9778240-4-5(7))* Prairie Winds Publishing.

Geron, Eric. Descendants 2 Junior Novel. 2017. (Descendants Junior Novel Ser.). (ENG.). 208p. (J). (gr. 3-7). 10.99 ***(978-1-4847-9970-3(4))*** Disney Pr.

Geronimo Stilton Staff. Sea Monster Surprise. 2016. (Geronimo Stilton Cavemice Ser.: 11). (ENG.). 128p. (J). (gr. 2-5). pap. 6.99 *(978-0-545-87248-5(0),* Scholastic Paperbacks) Scholastic, Inc.

—The Wizard's Wand. 2016. (ENG.). 320p. (J). (gr. 2-5). 14.99 *(978-1-338-03291-8(7),* Scholastic Paperbacks) Scholastic, Inc.

Gerovich, Linda. Preston & the Laundry Chute. 2016. (ENG.). 22p. (J). pap. 14.95 ***(978-1-78612-476-0(9),*** 60278041-f3d5-404c-af8b-b8937f92933e) Austin, Stan AUS. Dist: Bookmasters Distribution.

Gershel, Yolande. Alice. 2007. 32p. (J). pap. 15.00 *(978-0-8059-7613-7(2))* Dorrance Publishing Co., Inc.

Gershon, Neil. The Other Side of the Frame. 2007. 184p. (J). per. 13.95 *(978-0-595-40618-0(1))* iUniverse, Inc.

Gerwitz, Felice & Gerwitz, Christina. Dinosaur Quest at Diamond Peak, 3, Vol. 2. 2nd rev. ed. 2007. (Truth Seeker's Mystery Ser.). 208p. (YA). per. 8.99 *(978-1-931941-11-2(4))* Media Angels, Inc.

—The Missing Link: Found, 3, Vol. 1. 2nd rev. ed. 2004. (Truth Seeker's Mystery Ser.). 208p. (YA). per. 8.99 *(978-1-931941-08-2(4))* Media Angels, Inc.

Gessner, Marina, pseud. The Distance from Me to You. 2015. (ENG.). 352p. (YA). (gr. 7). 16.99 *(978-0-399-17323-3(4),* G.P. Putnam's Sons Books for Young Readers) Penguin Young Readers Group.

Get Ready for Hulk. 2003. (J). per. *(978-1-57657-860-5(7))* Paradise Pr., Inc.

Geye, Susan & Reynolds, Janice. Orca Soundings Resource Guide, 1 vol. 2009. (ENG.). 242p. spiral bd. 45.00 *(978-1-55143-954-9(9))* Orca Bk. Pubs. USA.

Geyer, Clyde. The Awesome Adventures of Chuckie Chopper & Friends. 2012. 52p. pap. 15.95 *(978-1-4575-0741-0(2))* Dog Ear Publishing, LLC.

Ghani, Samna. The Shoe, the Necklace, & the Giant. Williams, Nancy E., ed. Cappoen, Jennifer Tipton, illus. 2012. 48p. (J). pap. 9.95 *(978-1-938526-18-3(X))* Roxby Media Ltd. GBR. Dist: Laurus Co., The.

Ghazi, Suhaib Hamid. Ramadan. Rayyan, Omar, illus. (ENG.). 32p. (J). (gr. k-3). pap. 6.95 *(978-0-8234-1275-4(X))* Holiday Hse., Inc.

Ghent, Rena. The Adventures of Billy the Whale. 2009. 28p. pap. 13.99 *(978-1-4490-3456-6(X))* AuthorHouse.

Giangregorio, Anthony. Only the Young Survive: An Apocalyptic Tale. 2011. 110p. pap. 6.99 *(978-1-935458-89-0(2))* Living Dead Pr.

Giannasi, Maddalena. Bianca & Her Alphabet Soup. 2011. 32p. 18.99 *(978-1-4520-9908-8(1))* AuthorHouse.

Gibbins, Desiree. The Book Keeper's Oracle. 2008. 212p. pap. 14.49 *(978-1-4389-0791-8(5))* AuthorHouse.

Gibbons, Alan. Raining Fire. 2014. (ENG.). 144p. (YA). (gr. 7). 9.99 *(978-1-78062-127-2(2),* Orion Children's Bks.) Hachette Children's Group GBR. Dist: Hachette Bk. Group.

Gibbs, Anna. The Mystery of the Healing Waters. 2005. 55p. pap. 10.00 *(978-1-4134-4533-6(0))* Xlibris Corp.

Gibbs, Gretchen. The Book of Maggie Bradstreet. 2012. (Bradstreet Chronicles). (ENG.). 183p. (YA). pap. 9.99 *(978-0-9852948-0-9(9))* Glenmere Pr.

Gibbs, Stuart. Double Cross. 2013. (Last Musketeer Ser.: 3). (ENG.). 256p. (J). (gr. 3-7). 16.99 *(978-0-06-204844-8(9))* HarperCollins Pubs.

—The Last Musketeer. (Last Musketeer Ser.: 1). (ENG.). (J). (gr. 3-7). 2012. 272p. pap. 6.99 *(978-0-06-204839-4(2))* 2011. 256p. 16.99 *(978-0-06-204838-7(4))* HarperCollins Pubs.

—Traitor's Chase. 2012. (Last Musketeer Ser.: 2). (ENG.). 256p. (J). (gr. 3-7). 16.99 *(978-0-06-204841-7(4))* HarperCollins Pubs.

Gibson, Angela S. The Colors of God. 2012. 34p. 34.99 *(978-1-62419-479-5(6));* (Illus.). pap. 24.99 *(978-1-62419-478-8(8))* Salem Author Services.

Gibson, Narie. Judah the Barracuda. 2013. 42p. pap. 16.95 *(978-1-4908-1495-7(7),* WestBow Pr.) Author Solutions, Inc.

Gibson, Steve. Sparky the Firehouse Dog, 1 vol. Weishampel, Winifred Ann, illus. 2009. 20p. pap. 24.95 *(978-1-60836-254-7(X))* America Star Bks.

Gibson, Sylvia Scott. Ricky the Skating Worm & Friends, 1 vol. Gibson, Gregory V., illus. 2009. 21p. pap. 24.95 *(978-1-60836-473-2(9))* America Star Bks.

Gibson, Tonya. Hiking with Dad. 2008. 12p. pap. 24.95 *(978-1-60703-253-3(8))* America Star Bks.

Gidwitz, Adam. The Grimm Conclusion. 2014. (Grimm Ser.: 3). lib. bdg. 18.40 *(978-0-606-36187-3(1))* Turtleback Bks.

—In a Glass Grimmly. Santat, Dan, illus. 2013. (ENG.). 352p. (J). (gr. 5). pap. 7.99 *(978-0-14-242506-0(0),* Puffin Books) Penguin Young Readers Group.

—In a Glass Grimmly. D'Andrade, Hugh, illus. 2012. (ENG.). 336p. (J). (gr. 5). 16.99 *(978-0-525-42581-6(0),* Dutton Books for Young Readers) Penguin Young Readers Group.

—In a Glass Grimmly. 2013. (Grimm Ser.: 2). lib. bdg. 18.40 *(978-0-606-32135-8(7),* Turtleback) Turtleback Bks.

—The Inquisitor's Tale: Or, the Three Magical Children & Their Holy Dog. Aly, Hatem, illus. 2016. (ENG.). 384p. (J). (gr. 5). 17.99 *(978-0-525-42616-5(7),* Dutton Books for Young Readers) Penguin Young Readers Group.

—Star Wars - the Empire Strikes Back: So You Want to be a Jedi? McCaig, Iain, illus. 2015. (ENG.). 336p. (J). (gr. 3-7). 17.99 *(978-1-4847-0914-6(4),* 1392359, Disney Lucasfilm Press) Disney Publishing Worldwide.

A Gift to Share. 2005. (J). 17.00 *(978-0-9721457-1-8(0))* Silent Moon Bks.

Gil, Carmen. Que Fastidio Ser Princesa! 2012. (SPA & ENG., Illus.). 28p. (J). (gr. k-2). 14.95 *(978-84-15241-14-0(3))* Eastern National.

Gilbert, Heather. Skyler the Pirate, 1 vol. 2009. 25p. pap. 24.95 *(978-1-60813-820-3(8))* America Star Bks.

Gilbert, Julie. Dark Waters. 2017. (Dark Waters Ser.). (ENG.). 160p. (gr. 2-4). lib. bdg. 106.60 *(978-1-4965-4192-5(8))* Stone Arch Bks.

Gilbert, Marcie. Zee: Adventure One: Borrowing China. Krebs, Patricia, illus. l.t. ed. 2006. 48p. (J). per. 16.99 *(978-0-9771566-0-3(5))* Librujas.

Gilbert, Matthew. Friend or Foe? (Teenage Mutant Ninja Turtles) Random House, illus. 2014. (Junior Novel Ser.). (ENG.). 128p. (J). (gr. 3-7). 5.99 *(978-0-385-38505-3(6),* Random Hse. Bks. for Young Readers) Random Hse. Children's Bks.

—Night of the T-Machines (Teenage Mutant Ninja Turtles) Spaziante, Patrick, illus. 2016. (Pictureback(R) Ser.). (ENG.). 16p. (J). (gr. -1-2). 4.99 *(978-1-101-93866-9(8),* Random Hse. Bks. for Young Readers) Random Hse. Children's Bks.

Gilbert, Scott W. The Adventures of Willie the Worm: Willie's Big Adventure. 2012. 28p. pap. 19.99 *(978-1-4772-5407-3(2))* AuthorHouse.

Gilbert, William. The Last Lords of Gardonal. 2004. reprint ed. pap. 1.99 *(978-1-4192-6872-4(4))* Kessinger Publishing, LLC.

Gildea, Kathy. The Adventures of Baylee Beagle — Annabelle Beagle. Larson, Amanda, illus. 2005. 28p. (J). 7.95 *(978-0-9767096-1-9(9))* Maxim Pr.

—The Adventures of Baylee Beagle — Greenville. 2005. (Illus.). 20p. (J). 7.95 *(978-0-9767096-0-2(0))* Maxim Pr.

—The Adventures of Baylee Beagle — Hurricane Hound. Larson, Amanda, illus. 2005. 28p. (J). 7.95 *(978-0-9767096-2-6(7))* Maxim Pr.

Giles, Katharine. The Princess of Skye, an Archer Adventure. 2013. (ENG.). 280p. (YA). pap. 12.99 *(978-1-939927-79-8(X))* Telemachus Pr., LLC.

Giles, Lisa. The Adventures of Sunny the Bunny: The Easter Egg Hunt. 2010. 20p. 10.49 *(978-1-4520-1842-3(1))* AuthorHouse.

Giles, Mike, illus. Halloween Is Fun! 2009. (Yo Gabba Gabba! Ser.). (ENG.). 16p. (J). (gr. -1-1). pap. 6.99 *(978-1-4169-7824-4(0),* Simon Spotlight) Simon Spotlight.

Giles, S. A. A Home for All: How a Little Puppy Finds a Home. 2006. 20.00 *(978-0-8059-9076-8(3))* Dorrance Publishing Co., Inc.

Gill, David Macinnis. Invisible Sun. (Black Hole Sun Ser.: 2). (ENG.). (YA). (gr. 9). 2013. 400p. pap. 9.99 *(978-0-06-207333-4(8))* 2012. 384p. 16.99 *(978-0-06-207332-7(X))* HarperCollins Pubs. (Greenwillow Bks.).

—Shadow on the Sun. 2013. (Black Hole Sun Ser.: 3). (ENG.). 432p. (YA). (gr. 9). 17.99 *(978-0-06-207335-8(4),* Greenwillow Bks.) HarperCollins Pubs.

Gill, Heidi. Egypt. Carter, Kris, illus. 2012. (2 Kurious Kids Ser.: Vol. 5). (ENG.). 24p. (J). (gr. -1-5). 14.95 *(978-1-936319-93-0(4))* Mascot Bks., Inc.

—2 Kurious Kids: China. Carter, Kris, illus. 2012. 38p. (J). 14.95 *(978-1-936319-89-3(6))* Mascot Bks., Inc.

—2 Kurious Kids: France. Carter, Kris, illus. 2012. 38p. (J). 14.95 *(978-1-936319-90-9(X))* Mascot Bks., Inc.

—2 Kurious Kids: India. Carter, Kris, illus. 2012. 38p. (J). 14.95 *(978-1-936319-92-3(6))* Mascot Bks., Inc.

Gill, Heidi & Carter, Kris. 2 Kurious Kids: Mexico. 2012. (Illus.). 38p. (J). 14.95 *(978-1-936319-91-6(8))* Mascot Bks., Inc.

Gill, Margaret. Return of the Quetzal. 2003. (ENG.). 184p. 22.95 *(978-0-595-65609-7(9));* 182p. (YA). pap. 12.95 *(978-0-595-26531-2(6))* iUniverse, Inc. (Writers Club Pr.).

Gill, Paul. The Centaurs: An Adventure Fantasy. 2003. 54p. pap. 8.95 *(978-0-595-30260-4(2))* iUniverse, Inc.

Gill, Shelley. Prickly Rose. Cartwright, Shannon & Love, Judy, illus. 2014. (ENG.). 32p. (J). (gr. -1-3). pap. 7.95 *(978-1-57091-357-0(9));* lib. bdg. 17.95 *(978-1-57091-356-3(0))* Charlesbridge Publishing, Inc.

—Sitka Rose. Cartwright, Shannon, illus. 2005. (ENG.). 32p. (J). (gr. -1-3). per. 7.95 *(978-1-57091-364-8(1))* Charlesbridge Publishing, Inc.

Gillanders, Ann. Fairy Fleur & Doug the Dragonfly's Adventures in London: Ann Gillanders. 2012. (Illus.). 36p. pap. 22.88 *(978-1-4772-4358-9(5))* AuthorHouse.

Gilleland, Linda. I Love You, Baby Deer. Irish, Leigh Ann, illus. 2012. 56p. 19.99 *(978-1-61254-025-2(2))* Brown Books Publishing Group.

Gilley, Jane. The Adventures of Solly Polly & Georgie Porgy. 2008. 24p. pap. *(978-1-906210-70-0(5))* Grosvenor Hse. Publishing Ltd.

—Roodery's Birthday - Book One of the Troglodyte Trilogy. 2008. 16p. pap. *(978-1-906210-72-4(1))* Grosvenor Hse. Publishing Ltd.

Gilligan, Shannon. Cup of Death. Nugent, Suzanne, illus. 2006. (Choose Your Own Adventure Ser.). 144p. (J). (gr. 4-8). per. 6.99 *(978-1-933390-70-3(0))* Chooseco LLC.

—The Lake Monster Mystery. Newton, Keith, illus. 2009. (Dragonlarks Ser.). 80p. (J). (gr. k-3). pap. 7.99 *(978-1-933390-60-4(3))* Chooseco LLC.

—Struggle down Under. Burphon, S. et al, illus. 2007. (Choose Your Own Adventure Ser.: No. 21). 123p. (J). (gr. 4-7). pap. 6.99 *(978-1-933390-21-5(2))* Chooseco LLC.

Gillott, C. M. Nelson 'n' Deck & Friends: How the Adventures Began. 2010. (Illus.). 48p. pap. 17.49 *(978-1-4490-9593-2(3))* AuthorHouse.

Gillrie Fraser, Marg. The Dolphin Way. 2011. 156p. (gr. -1 — 1). 22.95 *(978-1-4502-8225-3(3));* pap. 12.95 *(978-1-4502-8224-6(5))* iUniverse, Inc.

Gillrie-Fraser, Margaret. The Dolphin Way. 2011. 120p. pap. 36.99 *(978-1-4634-3638-4(6))* AuthorHouse.

—The Dolphin Way: Learn about the amazing underwater sea world of Mattie the Dolphin as he soars through one exciting adventure after Another! 2011. 152p. pap. 42.21 *(978-1-4634-3635-3(1))* AuthorHouse.

Gilman, David. Blood Sun. 2012. (Danger Zone Ser.). (ENG.). 432p. (YA). (gr. 7). pap. 10.99 *(978-0-440-42241-9(8),* Ember) Random Hse. Children's Bks.

—The Devil's Breath Bk. 1. 2010. (Danger Zone Ser.). (ENG.). 416p. (YA). (gr. 7). pap. 9.99 *(978-0-440-42239-6(6),* Ember) Random Hse. Children's Bks.

Gilman, Phoebe. Pirate Pearl. 2004. (J). (gr. k-3). spiral bd. *(978-0-616-01657-2(3));* spiral bd. *(978-0-616-01658-9(1))* Canadian National Institute for the Blind/Institut National Canadien pour les Aveugles.

Gilmartin, Mary. Adventures with Easton: The Magical Journey. 2012. (ENG.). (J). pap. 16.95 *(978-1-4675-2418-6(2))* Independent Pub.

Gilmore, Dorina Lazo. A Stone in the Soup. Hires, Josh, illus. 2006. 39p. per. 15.00 *(978-0-938911-29-6(5))* Individualized Education Systems/Poppy Lane Publishing.

Gilroy, Henry. The Clone Wars: In Service of the Republic Vol. 1: the Battle of Khorm, 1 vol. Hepburn, Scott, illus. 2011. (Star Wars: the Clone Wars Ser.: No. 2). (ENG.). 24p. (J). (gr. 7-12). 24.21 *(978-1-59961-838-8(9))* Spotlight.

Gingras, Marie Claude. Let's Spend Summer with Fred. 2012. 198p. 24.95 *(978-1-4626-4413-1(9))* America Star Bks.

Giorgio, Marg. Maxi's Magical Dream. 2011. 24p. pap. 12.79 *(978-1-4634-4491-4(5))* AuthorHouse.

Gipson, Crash. Sheldon's Favorite Game. 2011. 36p. pap. 24.95 *(978-1-4626-4578-7(X))* America Star Bks.

Gipson, Morrell, ed. Stories of Mystery, Adventure & Fun from Calling All Girls. Dawson, Isabel, illus. 2011. 252p. 46.95 *(978-1-258-10497-9(0))* Literary Licensing, LLC.

Girard, Philippe. Gustave et le Capitaine Planète. Girard, Philippe, illus. 2004. (Mon Roman Ser.). (FRE., Illus.). 96p. (J). (gr. 2). pap. *(978-2-89021-649-5(7))* Diffusion du livre Mirabel (DLM).

Girard, Thomas. The Nameless Treasure. Girard, Thomas, illus. 2013. (Illus.). 58p. pap. *(978-0-9918736-0-9(2))* Bric-a-brac Bks.

Given, Cate. The Great Pogo Stick. Hill-Peterson, Jodi, illus. 2006. (J). *(978-0-9790057-0-1(1))* Paws In the Sand Publishing.

Gladiators. (Awesome Adventures Ser.). 16p. (J). *(978-2-7643-0169-2(3))* Phidal Publishing, Inc./Editions Phidal, Inc.

Glaser, P. H. Chrystallia & the Source of Light. 2011. (Illus.). 196p. (J). 18.99 *(978-1-60832-232-9(7))* Greenleaf Book Group.

Glass, Calliope. Tiana: The Stolen Jewel. 2013. (Disney Princess Early Chapter Bks.). (J). lib. bdg. 14.75 *(978-0-606-32291-1(4),* Turtleback) Turtleback Bks.

—World of Reading Star Wars at-At Attack! (Level 1) 2015. (World of Reading Ser.). (ENG.). 32p. (J). (gr. 1-3). pap. 3.99 *(978-1-4847-0549-0(1),* Disney Lucasfilm Press) Disney Publishing Worldwide.

Glass, Calliope & Kennedy, Caitlin. Star Wars ABC-3PO. Cook, Katie, illus. 2016. (ENG.). 48p. (J). (gr. -1-k). 12.99 *(978-1-4847-4142-9(0),* Disney Lucasfilm Press) Disney Publishing Worldwide.

Glass, Graeme. A Bee's Kiss. Trone, Jo, illus. 2012. 60p. pap. 21.50 *(978-1-61897-383-2(5),* Strategic Bk. Publishing) Strategic Book Publishing & Rights Agency (SBPRA).

Glaze, Dave. Danger in Dead Man's Mine, 1 vol. 2009. (1912: the Mackenzie Davis Files Ser.). (ENG., Illus.). 176p. (J). (gr. 4-7). pap. 8.95 *(978-1-55050-416-3(9))* Coteau Bks. CAN. Dist: Orca Bk. Pubs. USA.

Glazer, Maryann. The Adventures of Teddy Bark-Lee: Teddy Comes Home. 2009. 28p. pap. 13.99 *(978-1-4389-4569-9(8))* AuthorHouse.

Gleim, Jc. Leprechaun Kate. 2012. 56p. pap. 24.95 *(978-1-4626-7608-8(1))* America Star Bks.

Gleitzman, Morris. Toad Rage. 2005. (Toad Bks.). (ENG.). 176p. (J). (gr. 3-7). per. 6.99 *(978-0-375-82763-1(3),* Yearling) Random Hse. Children's Bks.

Glori, Debi. Muy Chiquitin. 2003.Tr. of Very Small. (SPA., Illus.). 32p. (J). (gr. k-2). *(978-84-480-1646-3(7),* TM30375) Timun Mas, Editorial S.A. ESP. Dist: Lectorum Pubns., Inc.

Glocke, Robin. Tiny Fish. 2006. 56p. pap. 16.95 *(978-1-4241-3777-0(2))* PublishAmerica, Inc.

Glover, Dennis W. The Cat in the Woods. 2010. 20p. pap. 10.49 *(978-1-4389-8492-6(8))* AuthorHouse.

Glynn, Eoin. Mischief at Se. 2009. 232p. pap. 14.49 *(978-1-4389-4919-2(7))* AuthorHouse.

Godby, Ron. The King of Imperial Hill. 2006. 76p. pap. 16.95 *(978-1-4241-1061-2(0))* PublishAmerica, Inc.

Goddard, D. L. Agondray: The Guardian of the Clouds. 2012. (Illus.). 100p. pap. 10.67 *(978-1-4678-8516-4(9))* AuthorHouse.

Godfrey, Jessica E. Night Hamster. 2012. 28p. pap. 15.99 *(978-1-4691-5083-3(2))* Xlibris Corp.

Godfrey, John. The Green Enamel Kid. 2008. 64p. per. 9.95 *(978-1-4357-0508-1(4))* Lulu Pr., Inc.

Godsey, J. P. "Gus". How Scooter Gets His Tail Back. Del Russo, John William, Sr., illus. 2014. (ENG.). 46p. (gr. 2-6). pap. 9.95 *(978-1-63047-003-6(1))* Morgan James Publishing.

Goebel, Jenny. Mission Hurricane. 2016. (39 Clues: Doublecross Ser.: 3). (ENG., Illus.). 192p. (J). (gr. 3-7). 12.99 *(978-0-545-76748-4(2))* Scholastic, Inc.

Goerzen, Christy. Farmed Out, 1 vol. 2011. (Orca Currents Ser.). (ENG.). 128p. (J). (gr. 5-9). pap. 9.95 *(978-1-55469-910-0(X));* lib. bdg. 16.95 *(978-1-55469-911-7(8))* Orca Bk. Pubs. USA.

Goetz, Bracha. Because of a Smile. 2012. (ENG.). (J). pap. *(978-1-4675-3550-2(8))* Independent Pub.

Goggins, Jean. The Adventures of Boo & Koty: Snow. 2009. 36p. pap. 21.99 *(978-1-4415-4670-8(7))* Xlibris Corp.

Gogolewski, Kathe, illus. Tato. 2008. (J). *(978-0-9800064-2-1(2))* Red Engine Pr.

Gogonya, Carol. The Adventure of Red Robin in the African Forest. 2012. 24p. pap. 28.03 *(978-1-4691-7922-3(9))* Xlibris Corp.

—The African Mermaid & Other Stories. 2011. 40p. pap. 32.70 *(978-1-4568-5416-4(X))* Xlibris Corp.

Goguen, Martha. Sissy Goes to Washington. Fowler, Faith, illus. 2013. 36p. pap. *(978-1-897435-59-5(2))* Agio Publishing Hse.

Gold, Gina. Monster High: Voltageous Adventure! 2017. (ENG., Illus.). 32p. (J). (gr. -1-3). pap. 3.99 ***(978-0-316-54793-2(X))*** Little, Brown Bks. for Young Readers.

Gold, Jeffrey. Brianna & the Search for the Cloudmaker. Date not set. (Illus.). (J). (gr. -1-8). *(978-0-615-11213-8(7))* Spoon Publishing Hse.

Gold, Rainbow. Dolphin Dreams. 2013. 72p. pap. 18.68 *(978-1-4797-6009-1(9))* Xlibris Corp.

Gold, Willa. Stella & Tulip: A Home for Us. 2010. (ENG.). 36p. (J). (gr. k-2). 17.99 *(978-0-930773-95-3(0))* Black Heron Pr.

Golden Books. ABC Animals (Dora the Explorer) McGee, Warner, illus. 2013. (Color Plus Card Stock Ser.). (ENG.). 48p. (J). (gr. -1-2). pap. 3.99 *(978-0-307-98218-6(1),* Golden Bks.) Random Hse. Children's Bks.

—The Art of the Ninja (Teenage Mutant Ninja Turtles) Golden Books, illus. 2014. (Doodle Book Ser.). (ENG., Illus.). 128p. (J). (gr. -1-2). pap. 5.99 (978-0-385-37851-2(3), Golden Bks.) Random Hse. Children's Bks.

—The Big Golden Book of Starships, Speeders, & Space Stations (Star Wars) Golden Books, illus. 2017. (Big Golden Book Ser.). (ENG., Illus.). 48p. (J). (gr. -1-2). 10.99 **(978-0-7364-3693-9(6)**, Golden Bks.) Random Hse. Children's Bks.

—Clash with the Kraang! (Teenage Mutant Ninja Turtles) Golden Books, illus. 2013. (Deluxe Reusable Sticker Book Ser.). (ENG., Illus.). 24p. (J). (gr. -1-2). pap. 6.99 (978-0-449-81883-1(7), Golden Bks.) Random Hse. Children's Bks.

—Class Pictures! (Bubble Guppies) Golden Books, illus. 2012. (Big Coloring Book Ser.). (ENG., Illus.). 48p. (J). (gr. -1-2). pap. 6.99 (978-0-307-93137-5(4), Golden Bks.) Random Hse. Children's Bks.

—Dinosaur Dig! (Bubble Guppies) Jackson, Mike, illus. 2013. (Paint Box Book Ser.). (ENG.). 48p. (J). (gr. -1-2). pap. 3.99 (978-0-307-98166-0(5), Golden Bks.) Random Hse. Children's Bks.

—Dora's Christmas Carol (Dora the Explorer) Goddard, Brenda & Haskett, Dan, illus. 2012. (Big Golden Book Ser.). (ENG.). 48p. (J). (gr. -1-2). 9.99 (978-0-307-97592-8(4), Golden Bks.) Random Hse. Children's Bks.

—Fearless Firemoose! (Rocky & Bullwinkle) Golden Books, illus. 2014. (Little Golden Book Ser.). (ENG., Illus.). 24p. (J). (-k). 3.99 (978-0-385-37152-0(7), Golden Bks.) Random Hse. Children's Bks.

—Fix It up! (Rusty Rivets) Lovett, Nate, illus. 2017. (Deluxe Paint Box Book Ser.). (ENG.). 128p. (J). (gr. -1-2). pap. 7.99 **(978-1-5247-1674-5(X)**, Golden Bks.) Random Hse. Children's Bks.

—Full Speed Ahead! (Blaze & the Monster Machines) Golden Books, illus. 2015. (Color Plus Crayons & Sticker Ser.). (ENG., Illus.). 48p. (J). (gr. -1-2). pap. 4.99 (978-0-553-52455-0(0), Golden Bks.) Random Hse. Children's Bks.

—Giant Adventures. Golden Books, illus. 2015. (Big Coloring Book Ser.). (ENG., Illus.). 48p. (J). (gr. -1-2). pap. 6.99 (978-0-553-52292-1(2), Golden Bks.) Random Hse. Children's Bks.

—Join the Team! (Team Umizoomi) Golden Books, illus. 2012. (Big Coloring Book Ser.). (ENG., Illus.). 48p. (J). (gr. -1-2). pap. 6.99 (978-0-307-93138-2(2), Golden Bks.) Random Hse. Children's Bks.

—Journey Beyond Sodor. Stubbs, Tommy, illus. 2017. (Little Golden Book Ser.). (ENG.). 24p. (J). (-k). 4.99 **(978-1-5247-1653-0(7)**, Golden Bks.) Random Hse. Children's Bks.

—Jumbo Coloring Adventures! (Nickelodeon) Golden Books, illus. 2015. (Super Jumbo Coloring Book Ser.). (ENG., Illus.). 416p. (J). (gr. -1-2). pap. 10.99 (978-0-553-52087-3(3), Golden Bks.) Random Hse. Children's Bks.

—Just Yelp for Help! (PAW Patrol) Golden Books, illus. 2015. (Giant Coloring Book Ser.). (ENG., Illus.). 40p. (J). (gr. -1-2). pap. 9.99 (978-0-553-53386-6(X), Golden Bks.) Random Hse. Children's Bks.

—Let's Get Epic! (Teenage Mutant Ninja Turtles) Golden Books, illus. 2014. (Big Coloring Book Ser.). (ENG., Illus.). 48p. (J). (gr. -1-2). pap. 6.99 (978-0-385-37849-9(1), Golden Bks.) Random Hse. Children's Bks.

—Love Is in the Hair! Golden Books, illus. 2016. (4 Color Plus Stkrs & Cards Ser.). (ENG., Illus.). 48p. (J). (gr. -1-2). pap. 7.99 (978-0-399-55892-4(6), Golden Bks.) Random Hse. Children's Bks.

—Night of the Ghost Pirate (Paw Patrol) Lovett, Nate, illus. 2015. (Hologramatic Sticker Book Ser.). (ENG.). 64p. (J). (gr. -1-2). pap. 4.99 (978-0-553-52390-4(2), Golden Bks.) Random Hse. Children's Bks.

—No Job Is Too Big! (Paw Patrol) Golden Books, illus. 2015. (Big Coloring Book Ser.). (ENG., Illus.). 48p. (J). (gr. -1-2). pap. 6.99 (978-0-553-52276-1(0), Golden Bks.) Random Hse. Children's Bks.

—PAW Patrol Awesome Sticker Collection (PAW Patrol) Golden Books, illus. 2017. (4 Color Plus 1,000 Stickers Ser.). (ENG., Illus.). 64p. (J). (gr. -1-2). pap. 12.99 **(978-1-5247-1682-0(0)**, Golden Bks.) Random Hse. Children's Bks.

—Race Across Gotham City. Golden Books, illus. 2016. (Big Golden Book Ser.). (ENG., Illus.). 48p. (J). (-k). 9.99 (978-0-399-55013-3(5), Golden Bks.) Random Hse. Children's Bks.

—Race Against Time (Mr. Peabody & Sherman) Fransisco, Tina, illus. 2014. (Super Color with Stickers Ser.). (ENG.). 96p. (J). (gr. -1-2). pap. 3.99 (978-0-385-37151-3(9), Golden Bks.) Random Hse. Children's Bks.

—Rainbow Rescue! (Dora the Explorer) Miller, Victoria, illus. 2014. (Color Plus Chunky Crayons Ser.). (ENG.). 48p. (J). (gr. -1-2). pap. 3.99 (978-0-385-37436-1(4), Golden Bks.) Random Hse. Children's Bks.

—Rusty's Robot Rescue (Rusty Rivets) Dynamo Limited, illus. 2017. (Color Plus Crayons & Sticker Ser.). (ENG.). 48p. (J). (gr. -1-2). pap. 4.99 **(978-1-5247-1675-2(8)**, Golden Bks.) Random Hse. Children's Bks.

—Start Your Engines! (Bubble Guppies) Golden Books, illus. 2015. (Color Plus Crayons & Sticker Ser.). (ENG., Illus.). 48p. (J). (gr. -1-2). pap. 4.99 (978-0-553-49764-9(2), Golden Bks.) Random Hse. Children's Bks.

—A Stroke of Magic (Shimmer & Shine) Garcia, Segundo, illus. 2016. (Deluxe Paint Box Book Ser.). (ENG.). 128p. (J). (gr. -1-2). pap. 7.99 (978-0-553-52363-8(5), Golden Bks.) Random Hse. Children's Bks.

—To the Limit! (Blaze & the Monster Machines) Hechtenkopf, Omar, illus. 2015. (Deluxe Paint Box Book Ser.). (ENG.). 128p. (J). (gr. -1-2). pap. 7.99 (978-0-553-52459-8(3), Golden Bks.) Random Hse. Children's Bks.

—Turtles to the Rescue! (Teenage Mutant Ninja Turtles) Johnson, Shane L., illus. 2012. (Color Plus Tattoos Ser.). (ENG.). 48p. (J). (gr. -1-2). pap. 3.99 (978-0-307-98069-4(3), Golden Bks.) Random Hse. Children's Bks.

—We Totally Rock! (Bubble Guppies) Jackson, Mike, illus. 2012. (Hologramatic Sticker Book Ser.). (ENG.). 48p. (J). (gr. -1-2). pap. 3.99 (978-0-307-93095-8(5), Golden Bks.) Random Hse. Children's Bks.

—Welcome to the City! (Dora & Friends) Sciarrone, Claudio, illus. 2014. (Color Plus Chunky Crayons Ser.). (ENG.). 48p. (J). (gr. -1-2). pap. 3.99 (978-0-385-38412-4(2), Golden Bks.) Random Hse. Children's Bks.

—Welcome to Wonderland! (Dora the Explorer) Miller, Victoria, illus. 2014. (Color Plus Chunky Crayons Ser.). (ENG.). 48p. (J). (gr. -1-2). pap. 3.99 (978-0-449-81760-5(1), Golden Bks.) Random Hse. Children's Bks.

Golden Books, illus. Little Golden Book Library, 5 vols. 2016. (ENG.). 24p. (J). (-k). 24.95 (978-0-449-81735-3(0), Golden Bks.) Random Hse. Children's Bks.

—The Star Wars Little Golden Book Library (Star Wars), 6 vols. 2015. (ENG.). 144p. (J). (-k). 29.94 (978-0-7364-3470-6(4), Golden Bks.) Random Hse. Children's Bks.

Golden Books Staff. All Fired up! (Paw Patrol) Lovett, Nate, illus. 2016. (Hologramatic Sticker Book Ser.). (ENG.). 64p. (J). (gr. -1-2). pap. 4.99 (978-1-101-93167-7(1), Golden Bks.) Random Hse. Children's Bks.

—All Paws on Deck! (Paw Patrol) Golden Books Staff & Lovett, Nate, illus. 2014. (Deluxe Paint Box Book Ser.). (ENG.). 128p. (J). (gr. -1-2). pap. 7.99 (978-0-385-38446-9(7), Golden Bks.) Random Hse. Children's Bks.

—Beyond the Clouds. Duarte, Pamela, illus. 2005. (Paint Box Book Ser.). (ENG.). 32p. (J). (gr. -1-2). pap. 3.99 (978-0-375-83362-5(5), Golden Bks.) Random Hse. Children's Bks.

—A Big Easter Adventure (Peter Cottontail) 2012. (Big Coloring Book Ser.). (ENG.). 48p. (J). (gr. -1-2). pap. 6.99 (978-0-375-86557-2(8), Golden Bks.) Random Hse. Children's Bks.

—Champions of the Sea! (SpongeBob SquarePants) Artifact Group Staff, illus. 2011. (Hologramatic Sticker Book Ser.). (ENG.). 48p. (J). (gr. -1-2). pap. 3.99 (978-0-375-87322-5(8), Golden Bks.) Random Hse. Children's Bks.

—Christmas Is Coming! (Dora the Explorer) McGee, Warner, illus. 2011. (Glitter Sticker Book Ser.). (ENG.). 64p. (J). (gr. -1-2). pap. 4.99 (978-0-375-87393-5(7), Golden Bks.) Random Hse. Children's Bks.

—Danger from the Deep. 2009. (Deluxe Coloring Book Ser.). (ENG., Illus.). 96p. (J). (gr. -1-2). pap. 3.99 (978-0-375-85328-9(6), Golden Bks.) Random Hse. Children's Bks.

—Dora the Explorer Fun Kit!, Kit. Golden Books Staff, illus. 2010. (Fun Kit Ser.). (ENG., Illus.). 64p. (J). (gr. -1-2). 9.99 (978-0-375-86527-5(6), Golden Bks.) Random Hse. Children's Bks.

—The Great Crayon Race. 2012. (Color Plus Chunky Crayons Ser.). (ENG.). 48p. (J). (gr. -1-2). pap. 3.99 (978-0-307-93027-9(0), Golden Bks.) Random Hse. Children's Bks.

—The Itty-Bitty Kitty Rescue (Paw Patrol) Golden Books Staff & Petrossi, Fabrizio, illus. 2014. (Little Golden Book Ser.). (ENG.). 24p. (J). (-k). 4.99 (978-0-553-50884-0(9), Golden Bks.) Random Hse. Children's Bks.

—Jumbo Coloring Party. Golden Books Staff, illus. 2010. (Jumbo Coloring Book Ser.). (ENG., Illus.). 224p. (J). (gr. -1-2). pap. 5.99 (978-0-375-86352-3(4), Golden Bks.) Random Hse. Children's Bks.

—May the Best Engine Win! Stubbs, Tommy, illus. Courtney, Richard, photos by. 2008. (Little Golden Book Ser.). (ENG.). 24p. (J). (gr. -1-2). 3.99 (978-0-375-84381-5(7), Golden Bks.) Random Hse. Children's Bks.

—Oh, the Things Spring Brings! Ruiz, Aristides, illus. 2013. (Color Plus Stencil Ser.). (ENG.). 64p. (J). (-k). pap. 5.99 (978-0-307-98123-3(1), Golden Bks.) Random Hse. Children's Bks.

—Rainbow Adventure. Miller, Victoria, illus. 2010. (Super Color with Stickers Ser.). (ENG.). 96p. (J). (gr. -1-2). pap. 3.99 (978-0-375-86350-9(8), Golden Bks.) Random Hse. Children's Bks.

—Rainbow Party! Golden Books Staff & Laguna, Fabio, illus. 2016. (Color Plus Rainbow Pencil Ser.). (ENG.). 128p. (J). (gr. -1-2). pap. 7.99 (978-0-399-55902-0(7), Golden Bks.) Random Hse. Children's Bks.

—Save the Unicorn King! Miller, Victoria, illus. 2011. (Paint Box Book Ser.). (ENG.). 48p. (J). (gr. -1-2). pap. 3.99 (978-0-375-87391-1(0), Golden Bks.) Random Hse. Children's Bks.

—Trainloads of Fun. Golden Books Staff, illus. 2010. (Jumbo Coloring Book Ser.). (ENG., Illus.). 224p. (J). (gr. -1-2). pap. 5.99 (978-0-375-86363-9(X), Golden Bks.) Random Hse. Children's Bks.

—Travel with Thomas. Santanach, Tino, illus. 2007. (Deluxe Coloring Book Ser.). (ENG.). 96p. (J). (gr. -1-2). pap. 3.99 (978-0-375-83953-5(4), Golden Bks.) Random Hse. Children's Bks.

—Trolls Little Golden Book (DreamWorks Trolls) Golden Books Staff, illus. 2016. (Little Golden Book Ser.). (ENG., Illus.). 24p. (J). (gr. -1-2). 4.99 (978-0-399-55893-1(4), Golden Bks.) Random Hse. Children's Bks.

Golden Books Staff & Smith, Geof. Green vs. Mean (Teenage Mutant Ninja Turtles) Golden Books Staff & Lambe, Steve, illus. 2015. (Little Golden Book Ser.). (ENG.). 24p. (J). (-k). 4.99 (978-1-101-93465-4(4), Golden Bks.) Random Hse. Children's Bks.

Golden, Christopher & Lebbon, Tim. The Sea Wolves Bk. 2, Bk. 2. Ruth, Greg, illus. 2012. (Secret Journeys of Jack London Ser.: 2). (ENG.). 400p. (YA). (gr. 8). 16.99 (978-0-06-186320-2(3), HarperTeen) HarperCollins Pubs.

—The Wild. Ruth, Greg, illus. (Secret Journeys of Jack London Ser.: 1). (ENG.). (YA). (gr. 5-18). 2011. 368p. 15.99 (978-0-06-186317-2(3))Bk. 1. 2012. 400p. pap. 7.99 (978-0-06-186319-6(X)) HarperCollins Pubs. (HarperTeen).

Golden, Christopher & Sniegoski, Thomas E. The Un-Magician. 2004. (OutCast Ser.: 1). (ENG., Illus.). 240p. (J). (gr. 5-9). pap. 12.95 (978-0-689-86661-6(5), Simon & Schuster/Paula Wiseman Bks.) Simon & Schuster/Paula Wiseman Bks.

Goldhawk, Emma. Little Lamb. Lambert, Jonathan, illus. 2014. (Snuggle Puppet Ser.). (ENG.). 10p. (J). (gr. -1). bds. 14.95 (978-1-62686-014-8(9), Silver Dolphin Bks.) Readerlink Distribution Services, LLC.

Golding, Julia. Mel Foster & the Demon Butler. 2016. (Mel Foster Ser.: 1). (ENG., Illus.). 288p. (J). (gr. 4-7). pap. 8.99 (978-1-4052-7734-1(3)) Egmont Bks., Ltd. GBR. Dist: Independent Pubs. Group.

—Mel Foster & the Time Machine. 2017. (Mel Foster Ser.: 2). (ENG., Illus.). 288p. (J). (gr. 4-7). pap. 8.99 (978-1-4052-7971-0(0)) Egmont Bks., Ltd. GBR. Dist: Independent Pubs. Group.

Goldrush, Jds. The Adventures of Chris & Tom's Grandp: Great Grand Pappy's Treasure Map & the Bat Gold Cave. 2011. 50p. pap. 15.99 (978-1-4628-9660-8(X)) Xlibris Corp.

Goldson, Ashea S. Jayden & the Magic Pants. 2012. 42p. pap. 12.99 (978-0-9767933-2-8(6)) Goldwrite Publishing.

Goldstein, Bobby. The Story of the Pink Gorilla Monster. 2012. 40p. pap. 17.99 (978-1-4490-6377-1(2)) AuthorHouse.

Gomi, Taro. The Great Day. 2014. (ENG., Illus.). 40p. (J). (gr. -1 — 1). 16.99 (978-1-4521-1125-4(1)) Chronicle Bks. LLC.

Gomolski, Mark F. Ginny's Adventures: Little Ginny. 2013. (ENG.). 72p. pap. 9.95 (978-1-4787-2490-2(0)) Outskirts Pr., Inc.

Goncalves, Regina. Mathematics - what beast Is This? 2008. 214p. pap. 15.95 (978-1-4092-2673-4(5)) Lulu Pr., Inc.

Gonder, Glen W. Poudre Canyon. Gonder, Sharon J., ed. Grove, Gladys, illus. Date not set. (Adventures of Willy Whacker Ser.: Vol. 9). 161p. (YA). (gr. 6-8). lib. bdg. 8.95 (978-1-58389-004-2(1)) Osage Bend Publishing Co.

Goniwicha, William. Spike a Relli: A Week at the Lake. 2009. 28p. pap. 13.99 (978-1-4389-2902-6(1)) AuthorHouse.

—Spike a Relli: The Mini Doberman. 2009. 28p. pap. 13.99 (978-1-4389-5678-7(9)) AuthorHouse.

Gonnard, Christel, et al. The Planet of Okidians. 2015. (Little Prince Ser.: 21). (ENG., Illus.). 48p. (J). (gr. 4-8). pap. 7.95 (978-1-4677-6024-9(2), Graphic Universe™) Lerner Publishing Group.

Gonzalez, Ada Acosta. Mayte & the Bogeyman/Mayte y el Cuco. Rodriguez, Christina, illus. 2006. (ENG & SPA.). 32p. (J). (gr. -1-2). 16.95 (978-1-55885-442-0(8), Piñata Books) Arte Publico Pr.

Gonzalez, Christina Diaz. Return Fire. (Moving Target Ser.: 2). (ENG.). (J). (gr. 3-7). 2017. 224p. pap. 6.99 **(978-0-545-77323-2(7))** 2016. 352p. 17.99 (978-0-545-77322-5(9)) Scholastic, Inc. (Scholastic Pr.).

Gonzalez, Owner Lucy. Puppy Trapped in Cyberspace! 2010. 57p. pap. 15.29 (978-0-557-44662-9(7)) Lulu Pr., Inc.

Gonzßlez Valdts, Alberto Domingo. Sueños de Obama/Obama's Dreams. 2008. (SPA.). 164p. pap. 15.00 (978-1-4389-3773-1(3)) AuthorHouse.

Goode, John. Eye of the Storm. 2016. (ENG., Illus.). (J). 24.99 **(978-1-63533-011-3(4)**, Harmony Ink Pr.) Dreamspinner Pr.

Goode, John & Morgan, J.G. The Unseen Tempest. (ENG., Illus.). (YA). 2016. (Lords of Arcadia Ser.: Vol. 3). (gr. 8-12). 24.99 **(978-1-63477-980-7(0))** 2014. 248p. pap. 14.99 (978-1-63216-189-5(3)) Dreamspinner Pr. (Harmony Ink Pr.).

Goodell, Mary. The Chicken Pox Puppy: Kate & Jen's Daily Adventures. Goodell, Mary, illus. 2007. (Illus.). 29p. (J). per. 11.99 (978-1-59879-382-6(9)) Lifevest Publishing, Inc.

Goodhart, Pippa. Little Monster & the Spooky Party. Sharratt, Nick, illus. 2016. (ENG.). 16p. (J). (gr. -1-k). 12.99 **(978-1-4052-7742-6(4))** Egmont Bks., Ltd. GBR. Dist: Independent Pubs. Group.

Goodier, Eleanor, et al. The Vermin Family Adventures (Book 1) 2010. 68p. pap. 9.50 (978-1-4457-5617-2(X)) Lulu Pr., Inc.

Gooding-Alber, Karry. Red Shoelace, 1 vol. 2010. 16p. pap. 24.95 (978-1-4489-6255-6(2)) America Star Bks.

Goodman, Joan Elizabeth. Paradise: Inspired by a True Story of Survival. 2006. (ENG., Illus.). 224p. (YA). (gr. 7). pap. 12.95 (978-0-618-49481-1(2)) Houghton Mifflin Harcourt Publishing Co.

Goodman, Larry. The Cowboy & Other Stories. 2008. 36p. pap. 24.95 (978-1-60813-546-2(2)) America Star Bks.

Goodman, Nancy. The Camping Kids Adventures. 2010. 74p. pap. 10.99 (978-1-60957-474-1(5)) Salem Author Services.

Goodrich, C. C. Barnabee: At the Picnic. 2009. (Illus.). 32p. pap. 13.99 (978-1-4389-8388-2(3)) AuthorHouse.

—Barnabee: Goes Shopping. 2009. (Illus.). 32p. pap. 13.99 (978-1-4389-9728-5(0)) AuthorHouse.

—Barnabee: Goes to Work. 2009. (Illus.). 32p. pap. 13.99 (978-1-4389-8461-2(8)) AuthorHouse.

—Barnabee: In the Beehive. 2009. (Illus.). 24p. pap. 12.99 (978-1-4389-7560-3(0)) AuthorHouse.

—Barnabee: In the Meadow. 2009. (Illus.). 24p. pap. 12.99 (978-1-4389-8389-9(1)) AuthorHouse.

—Barnabee: Meets New Friends. 2009. (Illus.). 24p. pap. 12.99 (978-1-4389-8390-5(5)) AuthorHouse.

Goodspeed, Jdy. Perky Turkey's 4th of July Adventure. 2008. (Illus.). 24p. (J). per. (978-0-9801376-1-3(6)) Dragonfly Publishing, Inc.

Goodspeed, Judy. Perky Turkey's 4th of July Adventure. 2008. (Illus.). 24p. (J). lib. bdg. (978-0-9801376-0-6(8)) Dragonfly Publishing, Inc.

Goodwin, Aimee. A Fish Named Luke. 2011. 24p. 11.32 (978-1-4567-3497-8(0)) AuthorHouse.

Goodwin, Anne. No Business Like Ghost Business. 2010. 60p. pap. 14.95 (978-1-4520-7593-8(X)) AuthorHouse.

Goodwin, Archie. Secret Agent Corrigan, 1977-1980, 5 vols., Vol. 5. Williamson, Al, illus. 2013. (X-9 Ser.). (ENG.). 288p. 49.99 (978-1-61377-542-4(3), 9781613775424) Idea & Design Works, LLC.

Goodwin, Carol. Does This Belong Here? A Twiggyleaf Adventure. McDaniel, Thomas, illus. I.t. ed. 2003. 32p. (J). 14.95 (978-0-9741072-1-9(2)) CornerWind Media, L.L.C.

—The Great Acorn: A Twiggyleaf Adventure. McDaniel, Thomas, illus. I.t. ed. 2004. 32p. (J). 14.95 (978-0-9741072-2-6(0)) CornerWind Media, L.L.C.

—Tippy Needs A Home: A Twiggyleaf Adventure. McDaniel, Thomas, illus. I.t. ed. 32p. (J). 2004. 14.95 (978-0-9741072-3-3(9)) 2003. per. 14.95 (978-0-09-741072-2(1)) CornerWind Media, L.L.C.

—What's the Hurry, Furry? A Twiggyleaf Adventure. McDaniel, Thomas, illus. I.t. ed. 2003. 32p. (J). 14.95 (978-0-9741072-0-2(4)) CornerWind Media, L.L.C.

Goody, C. A. Charlie Goes Camping: Charlie's Great Adventure #4. 2004. (Charlie's Great Adventures). (Illus.). 112p. (J). per. 5.95 (978-0-9702546-0-3(1)) GoodyGoody Bks.

Gorbachev, Valeri. Christopher Counting. Gorbachev, Valeri, illus. 2008. (ENG., Illus.). 32p. (J). (gr. -1-3). 16.99 (978-0-399-24629-6(0), Philomel Bks.) Penguin Young Readers Group.

—Me Too! Gorbachev, Valeri, illus. 2014. (I Like to Read(r) Ser.). (ENG., Illus.). 24p. (J). (gr. -1-3). 6.99 (978-0-8234-3179-3(7)) Holiday Hse., Inc.

Gordon, Glenn. The Bubble Heads. 2007. 36p. per. 24.95 (978-1-4241-8038-7(4)) America Star Bks.

Gordon, Mike, illus. Little Red Riding Hood. 2007. (Picture Book Classics Ser.). 24p. (J). (gr. 1-4). 9.99 (978-0-7945-1787-8(0), Usborne) EDC Publishing.

Gordon, Mike & Gordon, Carl, illus. The Magic Porridge Pot. 2008. (Usborne First Reading: Level 3 Ser.). 48p. (J). (gr. -1-3). 8.99 (978-0-7945-1883-7(4), Usborne) EDC Publishing.

Gordon, Pauline C. Animals in My Backyard! Joey, the Flying Squirrel. 2012. 28p. pap. 15.99 (978-1-4771-1961-7(2)) Xlibris Corp.

Gordon, Roderick. Closer, 12 vols. (Tunnels Ser.: 4). (J). 121.75 (978-1-4498-2159-3(6)); 296.75 (978-1-4498-2158-6(8)); 1.25 (978-1-4498-2165-4(0)); 2011. 132.75 (978-1-4498-2163-0(4)); 2011. 134.75 (978-1-4498-2161-6(8)) Recorded Bks., Inc.

—Deeper, 15 vols. 2009. (J). 128.75 (978-1-4361-3717-1(9)); 134.75 (978-1-4361-3721-8(7)); 301.75 (978-1-4361-3718-8(7)); 1.25 (978-1-4361-3714-0(4)); 126.75 (978-1-4361-3719-5(5)); 132.75 (978-1-4361-3723-2(3)) Recorded Bks., Inc.

—Spiral, 9 vols. 2012. (Tunnels Ser.: 5). (J). 296.75 (978-1-4618-4515-7(7)); 121.75 (978-1-4618-4516-4(5)); 132.75 (978-1-4618-4519-5(X)); 134.75 (978-1-4618-4517-1(3)) Recorded Bks., Inc.

Gordon, Roderick & Williams, Brian. The Tunnels. 2009. (Tunnels Ser.: 1). (ENG.). 496p. (J). (gr. 3-7). pap. 8.99 (978-0-545-07881-8(4), Scholastic Paperbacks) Scholastic, Inc.

Gordon, Roderick & Williams, Brian James. Terminal. 2013. (J). (978-0-545-47963-9(0)) Scholastic, Inc.

Gordon, Sylvia. Further Adventures of the Potty Wizard & His Cat, Muddles. 2009. (Illus.). 60p. pap. 10.49 (978-1-4389-6819-3(1)) AuthorHouse.

Gorman, Katie. Wondrous Adventures, 1 vol. 2009. 24p. pap. 24.95 (978-1-60749-878-0(2)) America Star Bks.

Gormley, Greg. Mummy's Big Day Out. 2007. (Fantastic Phones Ser.). (ENG., Illus.). 12p. (J). (gr. k-k). bds. 9.99 (978-0-7475-8380-6(3)) Bloomsbury Publishing Plc GBR. Dist: Independent Pubs. Group.

Goscinny, René. Asterix & the Class Act. Uderzo, Albert, illus. 2004. (ENG.). 56p. pap. 12.99 (978-0-7528-6640-6(0), Orion) Orion Publishing Group, Ltd. GBR. Dist: Hachette Bk. Group.

Goscinny, René & Bell, Anthea. Nicholas. Sempé, Jean-Jacques, illus. 2011. (ENG.). 136p. (gr. 7-17). pap. 9.95 (978-0-7148-6115-9(4)) Phaidon Pr., Inc.

Goscinny, René & Uderzo, Albert. Asterix & the Class Act. Bell, Anthea & Hockridge, Derek, trs. from FRE. Uderzo, Albert, illus. 2003. (ENG., Illus.). 56p. 17.99 (978-0-7528-6068-8(2), Orion) Orion Publishing Group, Ltd. GBR. Dist: Hachette Bk. Group.

Goscinny, René, et al. Lucky Luke: The Dashing White Cowboy. 2008. (ENG.). 48p. (J). (gr. 2-4). pap. (978-81-8386-014-7(1)) India Research Pr. IND. Dist: Independent Pubs. Group.

—Lucky Luke - Jesse James. 2008. (ENG.). 48p. (J). (gr. 2-4). pap. (978-81-8386-016-1(8)) India Research Pr. IND. Dist: Independent Pubs. Group.

—Lucky Luke - Ma Dalton. 2008. (ENG.). 48p. (J). (gr. 2-4). pap. (978-81-8386-015-4(X)) India Research Pr. IND. Dist: Independent Pubs. Group.

—Lucky Luke - the Tender Foot. 2008. (ENG.). 48p. (J). (gr. 2-4). pap. (978-81-8386-017-8(6)) India Research Pr. IND. Dist: Independent Pubs. Group.

Gosling, Sharon. The Ruby Airship. 2015. (Diamond Thief Ser.). (ENG.). 496p. (gr. 9-12). 16.95 (978-1-63079-004-2(4)) Switch Pr.

—The Sapphire Cutlass. 2016. (Diamond Thief Ser.). (ENG.). 336p. (gr. 9-12). 16.95 (978-1-63079-041-7(9)) Switch Pr.

Gosselin, Jake & Gosselin, Laura. The Pinkaboos: Bitterly & the Giant Problem. 2016. (Pinkaboos Ser.: 1). (ENG.). 96p. (J). pap. 7.99 (978-1-4494-7831-5(X)) Andrews McMeel Publishing.

Gosule, Bette & Longmire, Lynda. Sneakers Hangs Out. Dewitt, Kenny, illus. 2012. 26p. (J). 14.95 (978-1-60131-129-0(X), Castlebridge Bks.) Big Tent Bks.

Gott, Ricky. I Wish, I Wish... I Wish to Fish / IT. 2011. (Illus.). 80p. (J). pap. 24.95 (978-0-9837334-1-6(4)) Digi-Tall Media.

Gottesfeld, Jeff. Killer Flood, 1 vol. 2014. (Red Rhino Ser.). (ENG.). 64p. (J). (gr. 4-6). pap. 7.95 (978-1-62250-946-1(3)) Saddleback Educational Publishing, Inc.

—Standing by Emma. 2014. (Red Rhino Ser.). (J). lib. bdg. 18.40 (978-0-606-36246-7(0)) Turtleback Bks.

Gough, Bill. The Adventures of Stumpman. 2010. 36p. pap. 17.00 (978-0-557-40582-4(3)) Lulu Pr., Inc.

Gould, Cecily. Island of the White Toothed Shrew. 2003. (ENG.). 132p. 20.95 (978-0-595-65469-7(X)); 128p. pap. 10.95 (978-0-595-25963-2(4)) iUniverse, Inc. (Writers Club Pr.).

Gould, Robert & Duey, Kathleen. Time Soldiers - Rex. Epstein, Eugene, illus. Gould, Robert, photos by. 2005. (Time Soldiers Ser.: Bk. 1). (ENG.). 96p. (J). (gr. k-2). per. 5.95 (978-1-929945-53-5(1)); per. 5.95 (978-1-929945-54-2(X)) Big Guy Bks., Inc.

Gould, Susan Lynn. A Gift from Grandma. Verkruysse, Toni, illus. 2013. 56p. pap. 20.50 (978-1-61897-230-9(8), Strategic Bk. Publishing) Strategic Book Publishing & Rights Agency (SBPRA).

Gould, Terry. The Adventures of Sir Sniffsalot & His Friends. Proulx, Denis, illus. 2007. 48p. (gr. -1-3). pap. 15.99 (978-0-9789057-3-6(3)) Huntington Ludlow Media Group.

—The Adventures of Sir Sniffsalot & His Friends. 2009. (Illus.). 48p. pap. 15.99 (978-0-615-26181-2(7)) Write Away.

Goulis, Julie. Something Shiny, Something Round. Ferguson, John, illus. 2005. 32p. (J). (gr. 3-7). 14.99 (978-0-9754621-1-9(3)) Bubblegum Bks.

—The Things a String Can Be. Ferguson, John, illus. 2005. 32p. (J). (gr. -1-3). 14.99 (978-0-9754621-0-2(5)) Bubblegum Bks.

—The Topsy-Turvy Towel. Ferguson, John H., illus. 2006. 32p. (J). (gr. -1-2). 14.95 *(978-0-9754621-2-6(1))* Bubblegum Bks.
Gourley, Barbara. The True Adventures of Tip the Catahoula-Leopard Cowdog. 2011. 28p. pap. 17.95 *(978-1-4634-2316-2(0))* AuthorHouse.
Gout, Leopoldo. Genius: The Game. 2016. (Genius Ser.: 1). (ENG., Illus.). 304p. (YA). 17.99 *(978-1-250-04581-2(9)*, 9781250045812) Feiwel & Friends.
—Genius: The Game. 2017. (Genius Ser.: 1). (ENG., Illus.). 320p. (YA). pap. 10.99 *(978-1-250-11527-0(2)*, 9781250115270) Square Fish.
—Genius: the Con. 2017. (Genius Ser.: 2). (ENG.). 288p. (YA). 18.99 *(978-1-250-04582-9(7)*, 9781250045829) Feiwel & Friends.
Govan, Christine Noble. The Surprising Summer. Sari, illus. 2013. 178p. pap. 9.95 *(978-1-61427-449-0(5))* Martino Fine Bks.
—Tilly's Strange Secret. 2013. 194p. pap. 12.95 *(978-1-61427-452-0(5))* Martino Fine Bks.
Gownley, Jimmy. Superheroes. 2012. (Amelia Rules! Ser.: No. 3). (ENG., Illus.). 176p. (J). (gr. -1-12). pap. 14.95 *(978-1-59687-830-3(4))* ibooks, Inc.
Grace, Ann Marie. The Secret Gift. 2013. 18p. pap. 12.99 *(978-1-4808-0411-1(8))* Archway Publishing.
Grace, Hannah. The Popcorn MacHine. 2013. 56p. *(978-1-4602-3282-8(8))* FriesenPress.
Graeber, Mark. Collin Conway: The First Adventure with. 2005. 77p. pap. 16.95 *(978-1-4137-9542-4(0))* PublishAmerica, Inc.
Graham, Cheryl. Stephanie's Shoes. 2010. 28p. pap. 9.95 *(978-1-4327-5944-5(2))* Outskirts Pr., Inc.
Graham, David. The Adventures of Inky - Escape from London. 2011. (Illus.). 98p. pap. *(978-1-908105-76-9(3))* Grosvenor Hse. Publishing Ltd.
Graham, Deborah. The Magic Comes Back: A Max & Sam Adventure. 2012. 66p. (gr. 2-4). pap. 8.95 *(978-1-4759-4758-8(5))* iUniverse, Inc.
Graham, Frank. The Adventures of Lil' Bull. 2009. 40p. pap. 16.50 *(978-1-60693-582-8(8)*, Eloquent Bks.) Strategic Book Publishing & Rights Agency (SBPRA).
Graham, H. P. & De Bats, M. On the Heels of the Hunted. 2013. 346p. pap. *(978-1-78148-067-0(2))* Grosvenor Hse. Publishing Ltd.
Graham, J. Lee. In the Nick of Time. 2008. 108p. pap. 10.95 *(978-0-595-52621-5(7))* iUniverse, Inc.
Graham, Judith A. The Didley-Doo's Go on an Adventure, 1 vol. 2009. 33p. pap. 24.95 *(978-1-60749-897-1(9))* America Star Bks.
Graham, L. B. All My Holy Mountain. 2008. (YA). pap. *(978-0-87552-724-6(8))* P & R Publishing.
Graham, Oakley. Fun Adventures. Crisp, Dan, illus. 2016. (Sticker Fun Bks.). (ENG.). 144p. (J). (gr. k-5). pap. 16.99 *(978-1-78445-656-6(X))* Top That! Publishing PLC GBR. Dist: Independent Pubs. Group.
Grahame, Kenneth. Dream Days. Shepard, Ernest H., illus. 2004. reprint ed. pap. 21.95 *(978-1-4179-0979-7(X))* Kessinger Publishing, LLC.
—The Wind in the Willows. Roberts, David, illus. 2013. (ENG.). 256p. (J). (gr. 5). 24.99 *(978-0-7636-6526-5(6))* Candlewick Pr.
—The Wind in the Willows. Ingpen, Robert R., illus. 2012. (Sterling Illustrated Classics Ser.). (ENG.). 224p. (J). (gr. 2-8). 19.95 *(978-1-4027-8283-1(7))* Sterling Publishing Co., Inc.
—The Wind in the Willows. Leplar, Anna, illus. 256p. (J). *(978-1-4054-3774-5(X))* Parragon, Inc.
—The Wind in the Willows. l.t. ed. 2007. (ENG.). 174p. pap. 21.99 *(978-1-4264-6997-8(7))* Creative Media Partners, LLC.
Grammy Sunshine. The Adventures of Mouse: The Mouse Who Wanted to Be A Pig. 2009. 20p. pap. 12.49 *(978-1-4389-9268-6(8))* AuthorHouse.
Grandma. Harry's Adventure, 1 vol. 2009. 17p. pap. 24.95 *(978-1-60836-943-0(9))* America Star Bks.
Grandma Bette. The Excellent Adventures of Max & Madison: Bedtime Stories for Youngsters. 2013. 36p. pap. 16.95 *(978-1-4525-7270-3(4))*; 32p. pap. 16.95 *(978-1-4525-7268-0(2))*; 32p. pap. 16.95 *(978-1-4525-7264-2(X))*; 32p. pap. 16.95 *(978-1-4525-7266-6(6))* Author Solutions, Inc. (Balboa Pr.).
Grandma Geny Heywood, Geny Heywood & Grandma Geny Heywood. Proto: What do you do when a dinosaur Is born in your Garden? 2009. 48p. pap. 19.49 *(978-1-4490-0993-9(X))* AuthorHouse.
Grandmother Littlewolf. Littlestar, 1 vol. Macpherson, Carol, illus. 2010. (ENG.). 19p. pap. 24.95 *(978-1-4489-8619-4(2))* America Star Bks.
Grandpa Casey. Another Müsh-Mice Adventure. Brennan, Lisa, illus. 2012. 48p. 24.95 *(978-1-4626-9379-5(2))* America Star Bks.
—Another Müsh-Mice Adventure: Florida Vacation, 1 vol. Brennan, Lisa, illus. 2009. 45p. pap. 24.95 *(978-1-60813-329-1(X))* America Star Bks.
—Going Green: Another Müsh-Mice Adventure, 1 vol. Brennan, Lisa, illus. 2010. 34p. pap. 24.95 *(978-1-4489-7375-0(9))* America Star Bks.
—The Trilogy: Three Adventures of the Müsh-Mice. Brenn, Lisa, illus. 2012. 46p. 24.95 *(978-1-4626-9378-8(4))* America Star Bks.
Grandpa Peeps. The Squire & the White Dragon. 2011. 24p. 11.95 *(978-1-4567-1872-5(X))* AuthorHouse.
Grange, Emma. Empire Strikes Back. 2014. (DK Readers Ser.). (ENG.). 32p. (J). (gr. 1-3). 14.99 *(978-1-4654-2028-2(2)*, DK Children) Dorling Kindersley Publishing, Inc.
—A New Hope. 2014. (DK Readers Ser.). (ENG.). 32p. (J). (gr. k-4). 14.99 *(978-1-4654-2026-8(6)*, DK Children) Dorling Kindersley Publishing, Inc.
Granger, Barbara. Down to Earth with a Bump. 2009. (Illus.). 40p. pap. 16.99 *(978-1-4389-1211-0(0))* AuthorHouse.
Granny J. Pinky Makes a New Friend: Pinky Frink's Adventures. 2012. 36p. pap. 17.99 *(978-1-105-82663-4(5))* Lulu Pr., Inc.
—Pinky Visits Outer Space: Pinky Frink's Adventures. 2012. 38p. pap. 17.99 *(978-1-300-06064-2(6))* Lulu Pr., Inc.
Granny Vanishes. 2008. (Looney Tunes 8*8 Ser.). 24p. pap. *(978-1-4075-2641-6(3))*; pap. *(978-1-4075-2631-7(6))* Parragon, Inc.
Granny's Favorite Tales. 2006. (Illus.). 156p. (J). per. 39.95 *(978-1-60002-098-8(4)*, 3915) Mountain Valley Publishing, LLC.
Granstrom, Brita & Manning, Mick. Wild Adventures. 2017. (ENG., Illus.). 48p. (J). (gr. 1-4). pap. 11.99 *(978-1-84780-754-0(2)*, Frances Lincoln Children's Bks.) Quarto Publishing Group UK GBR. Dist: Hachette Bk. Group.
Grant, Carolyn E. Maggie's Neighborhood. 2009. 24p. pap. 11.99 *(978-1-4389-7230-5(X))* AuthorHouse.
Grant, Crystal. Warrior Boy. 2007. (ENG.). 92p. per. 16.95 *(978-1-4241-3978-1(3))* PublishAmerica, Inc.
Grant, Holly. The Witch's Glass. 2017. (League of Beastly Dreadfuls Ser.: Bk. 3). (ENG., Illus.). 320p. (J). (gr. 3-7). 16.99 ***(978-1-101-93366-4(6)***, Random Hse. Bks. for Young Readers) Random Hse. Children's Bks.
Grant, Katy. Fearless. 2010. (Summer Camp Secrets Ser.). (ENG.). 240p. (J). (gr. 3-7). pap. 7.99 *(978-1-4169-9162-5(X)*, Aladdin) Simon & Schuster Children's Publishing.
Grant, Michael. The Call. (Magnificent 12 Ser.: 1). (ENG.). (J). (gr. 3-7). 2011. 272p. pap. 6.99 *(978-0-06-183367-0(3))* 2010. (Illus.). 256p. 16.99 *(978-0-06-183366-3(5))* HarperCollins Pubs. (Tegen, Katherine Bks).
—The Key. (Magnificent 12 Ser.: 3). (ENG.). (J). (gr. 3-7). 2013. 304p. pap. 5.99 *(978-0-06-183371-7(1))* 2012. (Illus.). 288p. 16.99 *(978-0-06-183370-0(3))* HarperCollins Pubs. (Tegen, Katherine Bks).
—The Power. 2013. (Magnificent 12 Ser.: 4). (ENG.). 288p. (J). (gr. 3-7). 16.99 *(978-0-06-183372-4(X)*, Tegen, Katherine Bks) HarperCollins Pubs.
—The Trap. (Magnificent 12 Ser.: 2). (ENG.). (J). (gr. 3-7). 2012. 320p. pap. 5.99 *(978-0-06-183369-4(X))* 2011. 304p. 16.99 *(978-0-06-183368-7(1))* HarperCollins Pubs. (Tegen, Katherine Bks).
Grant, Myrna. Ivan & the American Journey. 2006. (Flamingo Fiction 9-13s Ser.). (ENG., Illus.). 144p. (J). (gr. 4-7). per. 6.99 *(978-1-84550-131-0(4)*, 219b73c2-7f68-49a8-b40f-d5dbfb745039) Christian Focus Pubns. GBR. Dist: Bookmasters Distribution.
—Ivan & the Daring Escape. 2006. (Flamingo Fiction 9-13s Ser.). (ENG., Illus.). 144p. (J). (gr. 4-7). per. 6.99 *(978-1-84550-132-7(2)*, 24be2b87-de69-4377-8a1b-bc7b2ad8cd87) Christian Focus Pubns. GBR. Dist: Bookmasters Distribution.
—Ivan & the Moscow Circus. 2006. (Flamingo Fiction 9-13s Ser.). (ENG., Illus.). 160p. (J). (gr. 4-7). per. 6.99 *(978-1-84550-135-8(7)*, 4a6719e2-1a18-4f7c-9b8f-fed8a960777e) Christian Focus Pubns. GBR. Dist: Bookmasters Distribution.
—Ivan & the Secret in the Suitcase. 2006. (Flamingo Fiction 9-13s Ser.). (ENG., Illus.). 144p. (J). (gr. 4-7). per. 6.99 *(978-1-84550-136-5(5)*, 90ba43f9-c4f3-4eac-aa9d-e552a2ffb74d) Christian Focus Pubns. GBR. Dist: Bookmasters Distribution.
Grant, Natalie. Light up New York, 1 vol. 2017. (Faithgirlz / Glimmer Girls Ser.). (ENG.). 208p. (J). pap. 8.99 *(978-0-310-75274-5(4))* Zonderkidz.
Grant, Tess. Flying in the Dark. 2013. 186p. pap. 10.99 *(978-1-62237-167-9(4))* Turquoise Morning Pr.
Grant, V. F. Stories from Grimley Forest. 2011. 48p. (gr. 1-2). pap. 19.50 *(978-1-4567-4709-1(6))* AuthorHouse.
Grantham, Jared James. Ashley & the Dollmaker. 2004. (J). 14.95 *(978-1-58597-270-8(3))* Leathers Publishing.
Graphman, W. M. . Matthew. Chel & Riley Adventures: The Great Mountain Adventure. 2011. 80p. (gr. 4-6). pap. 9.99 *(978-1-4567-5592-8(7))* AuthorHouse.
Graphman, Wm. Matthew. Chel & Riley Adventures: The K9 Kidnapping Adventure. 2011. 80p. (gr. 4-6). pap. 9.99 *(978-1-4567-9574-0(0))* AuthorHouse.
Gratz, Alan. The Dragon Lantern: A League of Seven Novel. 2015. (League of Seven Ser.: 2). (ENG., Illus.). 336p. (J). (gr. 5-9). 17.99 *(978-0-7653-3823-5(8)*, 9780765338235, Starscape) Doherty, Tom Assocs., LLC.
—The League of Seven. Helquist, Brett, illus. 2015. (League of Seven Ser.: 1). (ENG.). 352p. (J). (gr. 5-9). pap. 9.99 *(978-0-7653-3825-9(4)*, 9780765338259, Starscape) Doherty, Tom Assocs., LLC.
Graves, Brandon Beebe. In Beaner's Backyard. 2012. 24p. pap. 17.99 *(978-1-4685-9549-9(0))* AuthorHouse.
Graves, Mary. The Adventures of Peanut George. 2007. 72p. per. 19.95 *(978-1-4241-8274-9(3))* America Star Bks.
Graves, Peter, tr. from SWE. Nils Holgersson's Wonderful Journey Through Sweden, 2 vols. 2013. (ENG., Illus.). 382p. pap. 32.00 *(978-1-870041-97-3(6))*; 360p. pap. 32.00 *(978-1-870041-96-6(8))* Norvik Pr. GBR. Dist: Dufour Editions, Inc.
Graves, Rose M. The Mudwalker. 2009. 24p. pap. 11.49 *(978-1-4389-4394-7(6))* AuthorHouse.
Gravley, Debbie Bybee. Golden Lace & the Magical Mossy Woods. 2005. 25.00 *(978-0-9771793-0-5(3))* Gravley, Debbie Bybee.
Gray, Anne. Rites of the Healer, 1 vol. 2007. (ENG.). 288p. (YA). (gr. 7-12). per. *(978-1-894549-59-2(7)*, Sumach Pr.) Canadian Scholars.
Gray, Anthony. The Confederate Adventure of Jed Bodine & Ruefus: The Old Tulip Train Raid. 2012. (ENG.). (J). pap. 4.99 *(978-1-4675-2270-0(8))* Independent Pub.
Gray, Bianca. Back to School: Adventures of Alex & Joey. 2013. 20p. pap. 17.99 *(978-1-4817-0425-0(7))* AuthorHouse.
Gray, C. M. Zombiefied!: Apocalypse. 2017. (Zombiefied Ser.: 04). 192p. pap. 5.99 *(978-0-7333-3424-5(5))* ABC Bks. AUS. Dist: HarperCollins Pubs.
—Zombiefied!: Outbreak. 3rd ed. 2017. (Zombiefied Ser.: 03). 160p. pap. 5.99 *(978-0-7333-3423-8(7))* ABC Bks. AUS. Dist: HarperCollins Pubs.
Gray, Claudia. Ten Thousand Skies above You. (Firebird Ser.: 2). (YA). (gr. 9). 2016. 448p. pap. 9.99 *(978-0-06-227900-2(9)*, HarperTeen) 2015. (ENG.). 432p. 17.99 *(978-0-06-227899-9(1))* HarperCollins Pubs.
—Ten Thousand Skies above You. 2016. (Firebird Ser.: 2). (ENG.). 448p. (YA). (gr. 9). 20.85 *(978-0-606-39263-1(7))* Turtleback Bks.
Gray, Clio. Peder & the Skincatcher. 2013. 188p. (J). pap. *(978-1-78299-157-1(3))* FeedARead.com.
Gray, Grandpa. The Land of the Three Elves: Inside the Curve of the River. 2013. (ENG.). 268p. (YA). pap. 14.95 *(978-1-4787-0314-3(8))* Outskirts Pr., Inc.
—The Land of the Three Elves Vol. 1: Beginnings. 2012. (ENG.). 317p. pap. 14.95 *(978-1-4327-9551-1(1))* Outskirts Pr., Inc.
Gray, Jacky. Rory. 2010. 199p. pap. 16.95 *(978-1-4461-5021-4(6))* Lulu Pr., Inc.
Gray, Jennifer. Atticus Claw Settles a Score. Ecob, Mark, illus. 2016. (Atticus Claw Ser.). (ENG.). 240p. (gr. 1-4). 7.95 *(978-0-571-28681-2(X))* Faber & Faber, Inc.
Gray, Jennifer, et al. Guinea Pigs Online: Viking Victory. 2014. (Guinea Pigs Online Ser.: 3). (ENG., Illus.). 160p. (J). (gr. 1-4). 12.99 *(978-1-62365-347-7(9)*, Quercus) Quercus NA.
Gray, Kes. Daisy & the Trouble with Coconuts. Sharratt, Nick & Parsons, Garry, illus. 2013. (Daisy Ser.). (ENG.). 272p. (J). (gr. 2-4). pap. 11.99 *(978-1-84941-678-8(8)*, Red Fox) Random House Children's Books GBR. Dist: Independent Pubs. Group.
Gray, P. J. The Accident. 2015. (Trippin' Ser.: 2). (YA). lib. bdg. 19.60 *(978-0-606-36834-6(5))* Turtleback Bks.
—The Lab Book 3, 1 vol. 2015. (Trippin' Ser.). (ENG.). 64p. (YA). (gr. 9-12). pap. 8.95 *(978-1-62250-933-1(1))* Saddleback Educational Publishing, Inc.
Graydon, William Murray. Canoe Boys & Campfires: Adventures on Winding Waters. 2007. (ENG.). 204p. per. 20.99 *(978-1-4346-4409-1(X))*; 214p. per. 22.99 *(978-1-4346-4410-7(3))* Creative Media Partners, LLC.
—The Jungle Boy; or, Sexton Blake's Adventures in India. 2007. 120p. per. 14.99 *(978-1-4344-0189-2(8))* Wildside Pr., LLC.
Graziani, Maria. The Adventures of Valeria Veterinarian: Las Aventuras de Valeria Veterinaria. 1. Elejalde, Eliana, illus. l.t. ed. 2004. (SPA.). 23p. (J). 7.00 *(978-0-9762361-0-8(9))* Ed. Acespanish S.A.C.- Lima, Peru.
The Great Bird Adventure. 2003. (J). lib. bdg. *(978-0-9725485-1-9(3))* Waterfall Ridge.
Greathouse, Lisa. Johnny Appleseed, 1 vol. 2009. (Building Fluency Through Reader's Theater Ser.). (ENG.). 24p. (J). (gr. 2-4). pap. 6.99 *(978-1-4333-0990-8(4))* Teacher Created Materials, Inc.
Green, Amy. Escape from Riddler's Pass, Vol. 2. 2011. (ENG., Illus.). 176p. (J). pap. 7.99 *(978-1-59317-433-0(0))* Warner Pr., Inc.
Green, Andi. The Monster in the Bubble. 2009. (WorryWoo Monsters Ser.). 68p. (J). 14.99 *(978-0-9792860-2-5(6))* Monsters in My Head, LLC, The.
Green, Caroline. Fragments. 2014. (ENG.). 272p. (YA). (gr. 8). pap. 11.99 *(978-1-84812-364-9(7))* Bonnier Publishing GBR. Dist: Independent Pubs. Group.
Green, Corey. Brainstorm: Buckley School Books #2. 2011. 167p. (J). pap. 7.99 *(978-1-934437-05-6(0))* Abligio Bks.
—Managing Stan: Buckley School Books #1. 2007. (ENG.). 162p. (J). 16.95 *(978-1-934437-01-8(8))*; pap. 7.99 *(978-1-934437-02-5(6))* Abligio Bks.
Green, D. L. Zeke Meeks, 1 vol. Alves, Josh, illus. 2014. (Zeke Meeks Ser.). (ENG.). 128p. (gr. 2-2). 45.30 *(978-1-4795-2045-9(4)*, Zeke Meeks) Picture Window Bks.
Green, Elaine. The Adventures of Abigale Green in Spain. Alston, Brad, illus. 2012. 38p. (J). 14.95 *(978-1-937406-10-3(5))* Mascot Bks., Inc.
Green, Jack. Dusty the Dust Devil. 2011. 70p. pap. 19.95 *(978-1-4560-8507-0(7))* America Star Bks.
—The Microchip Kid. 2011. 52p. pap. 16.95 *(978-1-4560-8494-3(1))* America Star Bks.
Green, Jim. The Ghost Dancer. 2007. (YA). pap. 15.95 *(978-1-59705-923-7(4))* Wings ePress, Inc.
—Shadows of the Moon... Dancing. 2007. (YA). pap. 14.95 *(978-1-59705-872-8(6))* Wings ePress, Inc.
Green, Judy. The Little Blue Octopus. 2009. 28p. pap. 21.99 *(978-1-4415-3393-7(1))* Xlibris Corp.
Green, Kevin M. Livy Bug & Ally Gator in Best Friends. 2008. 16p. per. 24.95 *(978-1-4241-9385-1(0))* America Star Bks.
Green, Kim. Rinny Rhino Wants Pink Pearls & a Polka Dotted Penguin. 2013. 46p. pap. 14.99 *(978-1-61863-530-3(1))* Bookstand Publishing.
Green, Poppy. The Clover Curse. Bell, Jennifer A., illus. 2016. (Adventures of Sophie Mouse Ser.: 7). (ENG.). 128p. (J). (gr. k-4). 16.99 *(978-1-4814-5184-0(7)*, Little Simon) Little Simon.
—The Emerald Berries. Bell, Jennifer A., illus. 2015. (Adventures of Sophie Mouse Ser.: 2). (ENG.). 128p. (J). (gr. k-4). pap. 5.99 *(978-1-4814-2835-4(7)*, Little Simon) Little Simon.
—The Great Big Paw Print. Bell, Jennifer A., illus. 2016. (Adventures of Sophie Mouse Ser.: 9). (ENG.). 128p. (J). (gr. k-4). 16.99 *(978-1-4814-7149-7(X)*, Little Simon) Little Simon.
Green, Rich. Pearlsus. 2007. 140p. 20.95 *(978-0-595-91189-9(7))*; per. 10.95 *(978-0-595-45166-1(7))* iUniverse, Inc.
Green, Rico. Super Animals! 2016. (Illus.). 23p. (J). *(978-1-4806-9876-5(8))* Random Hse., Inc.
Green, Robert James. Hawk of the Nile. Miller, Shane, illus. 2012. 222p. 44.95 *(978-1-258-25119-2(1))*; pap. 29.95 *(978-1-258-25551-0(0))* Literary Licensing, LLC.
Green, Roger Lancelyn. The Adventures of Robin Hood. Hall, Arthur, illus. 2010. (Puffin Classics Ser.). (ENG.). 320p. (J). (gr. 5-7). pap. 5.99 *(978-0-14-132938-3(6)*, Puffin Books) Penguin Young Readers Group.
Green, Sally. Half Bad. 2015. (Half Bad Trilogy Ser.: 1). lib. bdg. 20.85 *(978-0-606-36606-9(7))* Turtleback Bks.
Green, Scooter. Ituke's First Hunt. 2012. 32p. 24.95 *(978-1-4626-9503-4(4))* America Star Bks.
Green, Terry. Moonstone. 2010. 188p. pap. 14.49 *(978-1-4520-4634-1(4))* AuthorHouse.
Greenberg, Penny. The Adventures of Toby the Turtle & Mighty Magoo. 2008. 16p. pap. 8.49 *(978-1-4389-1014-7(2))* AuthorHouse.
Greenburg, J. C. In the Garbage. Gerardi, Jan, illus. 2010. (Rise & Shine Ser.: Bk. 13). (ENG.). 96p. (C). (gr. 1-4). 6.95 *(978-0-375-83562-9(8))* National Geographic School Publishing, Inc.
—With the Bats. Gerardi, Jan, illus. 2006. (Andrew Lost Ser.: 14). (ENG.). 96p. (J). (gr. 1-4). 3.99 *(978-0-375-83563-6(6)*, Random Hse. Bks. for Young Readers) Random Hse. Children's Bks.
Greene, Brenda. Dog Gone: Boomer's Story. Cheryl H. Hahn, illus. 2005. 127p. (YA). per. 8.99 *(978-0-9770279-0-3(2))* Three Willows Pr.
Greene, Janice. The Dark Lady. 2005. (Quickreads Ser.). (Illus.). 32p. (J). pap. 2.95 *(978-1-56254-741-7(0)*, SP7410) Saddleback Educational Publishing, Inc.
Greene, Janice. Hamlet's Trap (Suspense), 1 vol. 2017. (Pagetumers Ser.). (ENG.). 76p. (YA). (gr. 9-12). 8.95 ***(978-1-68021-404-8(7))*** Saddleback Educational Publishing, Inc.
Greene, Janice & Thomas, Terri. Read My Lips, 1 vol. unabr. ed. 2010. (Q Reads Ser.). (ENG.). 32p. (YA). (gr. 9-12). pap. 6.95 *(978-1-61651-216-3(4))* Saddleback Educational Publishing, Inc.
Greene, John McBride. Encounter at Ogre Island. Julich, Jenniffer, illus. 2006. 96p. pap. 9.50 *(978-0-9772809-0-2(X))* Comprecom.
Greene, Karen. The Adventures of Jack. 2003. pap. 15.00 *(978-0-8059-6322-9(7))* Dorrance Publishing Co., Inc.
Greene, Kristy. How Penguins Lost Their Flight. 2012. 20p. pap. 24.95 *(978-1-4626-7697-2(9))* America Star Bks.
Greene, Reggie. The Adventures of Swami Somewhere- the Supermarket. Graham, Michael, illus. 2011. 32p. (J). 14.95 *(978-1-60131-095-8(1))* Big Tent Bks.
Greene, Richard. Lawrence the Locomotive. 2004. 49p. pap. 16.95 *(978-1-4137-5704-0(9))* America Star Bks.
Greene, Sefton. Space Painters. 2003. 18p. bds. *(978-1-904502-30-2(X))* MediaWorld/BestBooks.
Greenham, Caz. The Adventures of Eric Seagull. Homfray, Nick, illus. 2013. 40p. pap. *(978-1-78132-093-8(4))* SilverWood Bks.
—The Adventures of Eric Seagull 'Story-Teller' Book 2 a Fairy's Wish. Homfray, Nick, illus. 2013. 48p. pap. *(978-1-78132-110-2(8))* SilverWood Bks.
Greenhill, Ms Jane. Jolly Olde Teenage Alien. 2013. 258p. pap. *(978-0-9918766-2-4(8))* Greenhill, Jane.
Greenhut, Josh & Brown, Jeff. The Flying Chinese Wonders. Pamintuan, Macky, illus. 2011. (Flat Stanley's Worldwide Adventures Ser.: 7). (ENG.). 96p. (J). (gr. 1-5). 15.99 *(978-0-06-143003-9(X))*; pap. 4.99 *(978-0-06-143002-2(1))* HarperCollins Pubs.
Greenwald, Tom. My Dog Is Better Than Your Dog. Stower, Adam, illus. 2015. 198p. (J). pap. *(978-0-545-91669-1(0)*, Scholastic Pr.) Scholastic, Inc.
Greenwald, Tommy. It's a Doggy Dog World. Stower, Adam, illus. 2016. (Crimebiters Ser.: 2). (ENG.). 240p. (J). (gr. 3-7). 12.99 *(978-0-545-78397-2(6)*, Scholastic Pr.) Scholastic, Inc.
—My Dog Is Better Than Your Dog (Crimebiters! #1) Stower, Adam, illus. 2015. (Crimebiters Ser.: 1). (ENG.). 208p. (J). (gr. 3-7). 12.99 *(978-0-545-77332-4(6)*, Scholastic Pr.) Scholastic, Inc.
Greenwood, Grace. Stories from Famous Ballads for Children by Grace Greenwood [Pseud] with Illustrations by Billings. 2006. 160p. per. 18.99 *(978-1-4255-1221-7(6))* Michigan Publishing.
Greenwood, Mark. The Greatest Liar on Earth. Lessac, Frané, illus. 2012. (ENG.). 32p. (J). (gr. 2-5). 16.99 *(978-0-7636-6155-7(4))* Candlewick Pr.
Greenwood, R. L. A Visit to the Kingdom of Camelot. 2013. 62p. (gr. 2-2). pap. 8.95 *(978-1-4759-8097-4(3))* iUniverse, Inc.
Greer, Hannah. The Castle Ivengless: The Velvet Bag Memoirs, Bk. 3. 2009. 145p. pap. 24.95 *(978-1-60749-105-7(2))* America Star Bks.
—The Gift of Re, the Adventures of the Whiz Kids. 2009. 200p. 24.50 *(978-1-60860-466-1(7)*, Eloquent Bks.) Strategic Book Publishing & Rights Agency (SBPRA).
—The Lighthouse Summer Greer, Tica, illus. 2009. 156p. pap. 24.95 *(978-1-60813-493-9(8))* America Star Bks.
—The Pharos Legacy Book: The Whiz Kids Adventures. 2010. 122p. 21.95 *(978-1-60860-902-4(2)*, Strategic Bk. Publishing) Strategic Book Publishing & Rights Agency (SBPRA).
—The Velvet Bag Memoirs, Bk. 1. 2008. 132p. pap. 24.95 *(978-1-60672-190-2(9))* America Star Bks.
Greer, Tom C. Honey's Peanut Butter Adventure. Faust, Laurie A., illus. 2007. (Adventures of Honey Ser.). (J). per. 9.95 *(978-0-9789227-1-9(9))* Weeping Willow Publishing.
Gregar, Steve. Al the Alien. 2004. 23p. pap. 14.98 *(978-1-4116-1149-8(7))* Lulu Pr., Inc.
Gregg, Stacy. Comet & the Champion's Cup, 5. 2015. (Pony Club Secrets Ser.: 5). (ENG., Illus.). 256p. (J). pap. 6.99 *(978-0-00-727030-9(5)*, HarperCollins Children's Bks.) HarperCollins Pubs. Ltd. GBR. Dist: HarperCollins Pubs.
—Destiny & the Wild Horses, 3. 2015. (Pony Club Secrets Ser.: 3). (ENG., Illus.). 256p. (J). pap. 6.99 *(978-0-00-724518-5(1)*, HarperCollins Children's Bks.) HarperCollins Pubs. Ltd. GBR. Dist: HarperCollins Pubs.
—Mystic & the Midnight Ride, 1. 2014. (Pony Club Secrets Ser.: 1). (ENG., Illus.). 208p. (J). pap. 6.99 *(978-0-00-724519-2(X)*, HarperCollins Children's Bks.) HarperCollins Pubs. Ltd. GBR. Dist: HarperCollins Pubs.
—Stardust & the Daredevil Ponies, 4. 2015. (Pony Club Secrets Ser.: 4). (ENG., Illus.). 240p. (J). pap. 6.99 *(978-0-00-724516-1(5)*, HarperCollins Children's Bks.) HarperCollins Pubs. Ltd. GBR. Dist: HarperCollins Pubs.
Gregory, David. Visions of Reality. 2007. 236p. per. 15.95 *(978-0-595-44969-9(7))* iUniverse, Inc.
Gregory, Philippa. Changeling, 10 vols. 2012. (Order of Darkness Ser.). (YA). 92.75 *(978-1-4640-4583-7(6))*; 90.75 *(978-1-4640-4587-5(9))*; 265.75 *(978-1-4640-4584-4(4))*; 90.75 *(978-1-4640-4586-8(0))* Recorded Bks., Inc.
—Changeling. van Deelen, Fred & Taylor, Sally, illus. 2013. (Order of Darkness Ser.: 1). (ENG.). 352p. (YA). (gr. 9). pap. 9.99 *(978-1-4424-5345-6(1)*, Simon Pulse) Simon Pulse.
—Changeling. Taylor, Sally & van Deelen, Fred, illus. 2012. (Order of Darkness Ser.: 1). (ENG.). 272p. (YA). (gr. 9). 18.99 *(978-1-4424-5344-9(3)*, Simon Pulse) Simon Pulse.
—Fools' Gold. van Deelen, Fred, illus. 2014. (Order of Darkness Ser.: 3). (ENG.). 384p. (YA). (gr. 9). pap. 9.99 *(978-1-4424-7691-2(5))*; 19.99 *(978-1-4424-7690-5(7))* Simon Pulse. (Simon Pulse).
—Stormbringers. van Deelen, Fred, illus. 2013. (Order of Darkness Ser.: 2). (ENG.). 336p. (YA). (gr. 9). pap. 9.99 *(978-1-4424-7688-2(5))*; 17.99 *(978-1-4424-7687-5(7))* Simon Pulse. (Simon Pulse).

Greig, Allison. Stacey's Adventures. 2006. (Illus.). 64p. pap. (978-1-84401-035-6(X)) Athena Pr.

Grein, Josh. Petunia Bobbin & the Baby Robin: A Christmas Adventure. 2012. 48p. (-18). 28.95 (978-1-4582-0614-5(9)); pap. 20.95 (978-1-4582-0615-2(7)) Author Solutions, Inc. (Abbott Pr.).

Greiner, Gail. Patchwork Helps a Friend. Schmidt, Jacqueline, illus. 2013. (ENG.). 40p. (J). (gr. -1-2). 17.95 (978-1-57687-642-8(X), powerHouse Bks.) powerHouse Cultural Entertainment, Inc.

Grennan, Michael F. The Adventures of E-Lane: Maple Syrul Heaven. 2012. 36p. (-18). pap. 20.99 (978-1-4772-8794-1(9)) AuthorHouse.

Gresh, Dannah & Anderson, Chizuruoke. Yuzi's False Alarm. 2008. (Secret Keeper Girl Fiction Ser.). (ENG.). 96p. pap. 7.99 (978-0-8024-8704-9(1)) Moody Pubs.

Gresham, P. A. Anything Could Be Any Thing. 2005. 128p. pap. 12.95 (978-1-4116-4353-6(4)) Lulu Pr., Inc.

Gresham, Xanthe. Thumbelina. Gastaut, Charlotte, illus. 2016. 48p. (J). (gr. 1-5). pap. 9.99 (978-1-78285-276-6(X)) Barefoot Bks., Inc.

Greve, Meg. Painting Party. Anglicas, Louise, illus. 2013. (ENG.). 24p. (gr. -1-1). pap. 8.95 (978-1-62169-207-2(8)) Rourke Educational Media.

Grey, Allan. Alienology. Steer, Dugald A., ed. Carrell, Douglas, illus. 2010. (Ologies Ser.: 10). (ENG.). 32p. (J). (gr. 3-7). 21.99 (978-0-7636-4565-6(6)) Candlewick Pr.

Grey, C. R. Animas, Book Two Flight of the King. 2016. (Animas Ser.). (ENG.). 320p. (J). (gr. 3-7). pap. 7.99 (978-1-4231-8467-6(X)) Hyperion Bks. for Children.

Grey, Jacob. Ferals. 2015. (Ferals Ser.: 1). (ENG.). 288p. (J). (gr. 3-7). 16.99 (978-0-06-232103-9(X)) HarperCollins Pubs.

—The White Widow's Revenge. 2016. (Ferals Ser.: 3). 272p. (J). (gr. 3-7). 16.99 (978-0-06-232109-1(9)) HarperCollins Pubs.

Grey, Mini. Traction Man Is Here! 2012. lib. bdg. 18.40 (978-0-606-26385-6(3), Turtleback) Turtleback Bks.

Griffin, Adele. Steg-O-Normous. Wu, Mike, illus. 2016. (Oodlethunks Ser.: Bk. 2). (ENG.). 160p. (J). (gr. 3-7). 12.99 (978-0-545-73284-0(0), Scholastic Pr.) Scholastic, Inc.

Griffin, Bethany. The Dance of the Red Death. (Masque of the Red Death Ser.: 2). (ENG.). (YA). (gr. 9). 2015. 352p. pap. 9.99 (978-0-06-210783-1(6)) 2013. 336p. 17.99 (978-0-06-210782-4(8)) HarperCollins Pubs. (Greenwillow Bks.).

—Masque of the Red Death. 2013. (Masque of the Red Death Ser.: 1). (ENG.). 336p. (YA). (gr. 9). pap. 9.99 (978-0-06-210780-0(1), Greenwillow Bks.) HarperCollins Pubs.

Griffin, Daniel. The Adventures of Merlin the Mouse 2005. (Illus.). 44p. (J). (978-0-9768348-0-9(4)) DiGuiseppi, Joseph.

Griffin, Dawnell. Osenplots! 2003. pap. 9.00 (978-0-8059-6220-8(4)) Dorrance Publishing Co., Inc.

Griffin, Dorothy J. What Goes Around Comes Around. 2013. 20p. pap. 12.45 (978-1-4908-1053-9(6), WestBow Pr.) Author Solutions, Inc.

Griffin, Wiley Chase. Chase the Shark: Flies Like a Bird. 2010. 28p. pap. 12.50 (978-1-4520-5173-4(9)) AuthorHouse.

Griffith, Andrew, illus. Transformers: Movie Prequel: Foundation: Vol 1: Dark of the Moon, 1 vol. 2012. (Transformers: Dark of the Moon Movie Prequel Ser.). (ENG.). 24p. (J). 24.21 (978-1-59961-971-2(7), Graphic Novels) Spotlight.

—Transformers: Movie Prequel: Foundation: Vol 2, 1 vol. 2012. (Transformers: Dark of the Moon Movie Prequel Ser.). (ENG.). 24p. (J). 24.21 (978-1-59961-972-9(5), Graphic Novels) Spotlight.

—Transformers: Movie Prequel: Foundation: Vol 3, 1 vol. 2012. (Transformers: Dark of the Moon Movie Prequel Ser.). (ENG.). 24p. (J). 24.21 (978-1-59961-973-6(3), Graphic Novels) Spotlight.

—Transformers: Movie Prequel: Foundation: Vol 4, 1 vol. 2012. (Transformers: Dark of the Moon Movie Prequel Ser.). (ENG.). 24p. (J). 24.21 (978-1-59961-974-3(1), Graphic Novels) Spotlight.

Griffiths, Allen & Godinez, Mary. Rusty Finds a Home: A Christmas Miracle. Ulrich, Kelly, illus. 2012. 32p. pap. (978-1-4602-0937-0(0)) FriesenPress.

Griffiths, Andy. The Day My Butt Went Psycho! 2003. (Andy Griffiths' Butt Ser.). (ENG.). 240p. (J). (gr. 3-7). pap. 6.99 (978-0-439-42469-1(0)) Scholastic, Inc.

—The Day My Butt Went Psycho! 2003. (gr. 5-8). lib. bdg. 17.20 (978-0-613-62939-3(6), Turtleback) Turtleback Bks.

—The 39-Story Treehouse. Denton, Terry, illus. 2015. (Treehouse Bks.). (ENG.). 352p. (J). (gr. 1-5). 13.99 (978-1-250-02692-7(X), 9781250026927) Feiwel & Friends.

—The 39-Story Treehouse. Barcellona, Christine, ed. Denton, Terry, illus. 2016. (Treehouse Bks.: 3). (ENG.). 368p. (J). pap. 6.99 (978-1-250-07511-6(4), 9781250075116) Square Fish.

Griffiths, Robert. Adventures of Clive. 2005. 45p. (J). pap. 10.01 (978-1-4116-5332-0(7)); 89p. pap. 8.81 (978-1-4116-5191-3(X)) Lulu Pr., Inc.

Griggs, Joyce. Imanis Good Deed. 2006. pap. 9.95 (978-1-4327-0071-3(5)) Outskirts Pr., Inc.

Griggs, Rosemarie. The Adventures of Donkey Tom Volume 2: Crystal Forest. 2012. 40p. pap. 32.70 (978-1-4797-0553-5(5)) Xlibris Corp.

Griggs, Terry. The Silver Door Teacher Guide. 2004. 4p. pap. (978-1-55192-705-3(5)) Raincoast Bk. Distribution CAN. Dist: Publishers Group West (PGW).

Grimm, Jacob. Tom Thumb/Pulgarcito. 2004. (Illus.). (J). cd-rom (978-1-933530-38-3(3)) Bingo Bks., Inc.

Grimm, Jacob & Grimm, Wilhelm K. The Fisherman & His Wife/ El Pescador y Su Esposa. 2004. (Illus.). (J). (978-1-933530-20-8(0)) Bingo Bks., Inc.

—Hansel & Gretel/Hansel y Gretel. 2004. (Illus.). (J). (978-1-933530-14-7(6)) Bingo Bks., Inc.

—Little Red Riding Hood/Caperucita Roja. 2004. (Illus.). (J). (978-1-933530-15-4(4)) Bingo Bks., Inc.

—Rapunzel/Raponchigo. 2004. (Illus.). (J). (978-1-933530-16-1(2)) Bingo Bks., Inc.

—Rumpelstiltskin. 2004. (Illus.). (J). (978-1-933530-17-8(0)) Bingo Bks., Inc.

—Snow White/Blancanieves. 2004. (Illus.). (J). (978-1-933530-19-2(7)) Bingo Bks., Inc.

—Tom Thumb/Pulgarcito. 2004. (Illus.). (J). (978-1-933530-24-6(3)) Bingo Bks., Inc.

—The Water of Life/ El Aqua de Vida. 2004. (Illus.). (J). (978-1-933530-23-9(5)) Bingo Bks., Inc.

Grindley, Sally. Danger in the Dust. 2013. (ENG.). 128p. (YA). (gr. 3-6). pap. 10.99 (978-1-4088-1946-3(5), 9781408819463, Bloomsbury USA Childrens) Bloomsbury Publishing USA.

—Feathers in the Wind. 2012. (ENG.). 128p. (YA). (gr. 5-7). pap. 10.99 (978-1-4088-1947-0(3), 9781408819470) Bloomsbury Publishing USA.

Grine, Chris. Time Shifters. 2017. (ENG.). 272p. (J). (gr. 3-7). 24.99 **(978-0-545-92659-1(9))**; pap. 12.99 **(978-0-545-92657-7(2))** Scholastic, Inc. (Graphix).

Grinnell, George Bird. Jack in the Rockies or A Boys Adventures. 2006. (Illus.). pap. 28.95 (978-1-4286-2952-3(1)) Kessinger Publishing, LLC.

Grinnell, Suzanne. Where Is Beau? Peter, Joshua, illus. 2008. 24p. pap. 12.99 (978-1-59858-612-1(2)) Dog Ear Publishing, LLC.

Grisham, John. The Fugitive. 2015. (Theodore Boone Ser.: 5). (ENG.). 256p. (J). (gr. 3-7). 17.99 (978-0-525-42638-7(8), Dutton Books for Young Readers) Penguin Young Readers Group.

—The Fugitive. 2016. (Theodore Boone Ser.: 5). 272p. lib. bdg. 18.40 (978-0-606-38847-4(8)) Turtleback Bks.

—The Scandal. 2016. (Theodore Boone Ser.: 6). (ENG.). 224p. (J). (gr. 3-7). 17.99 (978-0-525-42639-4(6), Dutton Books for Young Readers) Penguin Young Readers Group.

—Theodore Boone Box Set, 5 vols. 2013. (Theodore Boone Ser.). (ENG.). 816p. (J). (gr. 3-7). 50.97 (978-0-525-42637-0(X), Dutton Books for Young Readers) Penguin Young Readers Group.

Griswold, Elaine. The Fairy Walk: A True Story of Imagination. 2013. 34p. pap. 14.95 (978-1-4575-2394-6(9)) Dog Ear Publishing, LLC.

Gritton, Steve. Plain Fish. 2007. (Illus.). (J). 17.95 (978-0-9795361-2-0(X)) Bad Frog Art/SMG Bks.

Grizzell, Larry. What Would You Like to Do Today? Fun in the Snow. 2006. (Illus.). 30p. (J). 16.95 (978-0-9759542-1-8(0)) Adventures Galore.

Groethe, Kd. The Virtual Adventures of Megan & Timmy. 2012. 230p. (gr. 4-6). 27.99 (978-1-4685-5050-4(0)); pap. 16.95 (978-1-4685-5049-8(7)) AuthorHouse.

Groffman, Simcha. Awesome Days. 164p. 19.99 (978-1-58330-713-7(3)) Feldheim Pubs.

Grogan, John. Marley: Firehouse Dog. Cowdrey, Richard & Halverson, Lydia, illus. 2012. (I Can Read Level 2 Ser.). (ENG.). 32p. (J). (gr. -1-3). 16.99 (978-0-06-207484-3(9)); pap. 3.99 (978-0-06-207483-6(0)) HarperCollins Pubs.

—Marley Storybook Treasury. Cowdrey, Richard, illus. 2012. (I Can Read Level 2 Ser.). (ENG.). 192p. (J). (gr. k-3). 11.99 (978-0-06-212331-2(9)) HarperCollins Pubs.

—Marley's Big Adventure. 2009. (Marley: I Can Read! Ser.). (J). lib. bdg. 13.55 (978-0-606-06942-7(9), Turtleback) Turtleback Bks.

Grogan, John & Hill, Susan. Marley's Big Adventure. Cowdrey, Richard & Halverson, Lydia, illus. 2009. (I Can Read Book 2 Ser.). 32p. (J). (gr. -1-3). 16.99 (978-0-06-185384-5(4)); (ENG.). (gr. k-3). pap. 3.99 (978-0-06-185383-8(6)) HarperCollins Pubs.

—Strike Three, Marley! Cowdrey, Richard & Beier, Ellen, illus. 2010. (I Can Read Level 2 Ser.). (ENG.). 32p. (J). (gr. k-3). pap. 3.99 (978-0-06-185386-9(0)) HarperCollins Pubs.

Groggins, Anita. The Adventures of Little Cappedo: Cobwebs in the Sky. 2011. 28p. pap. 15.99 (978-1-4568-7476-6(4)) Xlibris Corp.

Grosgebauer, Clare Ham. Snickerdoodle & the Roller-Skating Horse! Rissing, Karen, illus. 3rd ed. 2005. 36p. (J). (gr. -1-3). 12.99 (978-0-9741888-4-3(0)) Small Wonders Enterprises.

Gross, Roxanna. The Pit Monster. 2007. 93p. pap. 9.95 (978-0-615-16398-7(X)) Gross, Roxanna.

Grotholt, Yannick. Chi Quest! 2014. (LEGO Legends of Chima Graphic Novels Ser.: 3). (J). lib. bdg. 18.40 (978-0-606-36135-4(9)) Turtleback Bks.

—Playing with Fire. 2016. (LEGO Legends of Chima Graphic Novels Ser.: 6). (J). lib. bdg. 18.40 (978-0-606-38370-7(0)) Turtleback Bks.

Group/McGraw-Hill, Wright. Crazy Adventurers: Magazine Anthology: Level 6, 6 vols. (Comprehension Strand Ser.). (gr. 4-8). 54.00 (978-0-322-09860-2(2)) Wright Group/McGraw-Hill.

—Secrets & Strays, 6 vols. (D-Man Beans Ser.). 47p. (gr. 4-6). 42.50 (978-0-322-06258-0(6)) Wright Group/McGraw-Hill.

Grout, Claire. Emil & Ordi: Friends for All Time. 2012. 24p. pap. 15.99 (978-1-4691-6279-9(2)) Xlibris Corp.

Grove, Malachai. Malachai Grove Plunt Solinatry: The Song of Malachai. 2010. 24p. 14.99 (978-1-4520-6441-3(5)) AuthorHouse.

Grove, S. E. The Crimson Skew. 2017. (Mapmakers Ser.: 3). lib. bdg. 19.65 **(978-0-606-40081-7(8))** Turtleback Bks.

Grover, Neha Lamba. Shaurya's Adventures. 2010. 43p. pap. 17.40 (978-0-557-12636-1(3)) Lulu Pr., Inc.

Grubbs, Darlene. The Children of the Ember: World War III, 1 vol. 2009. 48p. pap. 16.95 (978-1-61546-573-6(1)) America Star Bks.

Gruber, Ben. The Next Generation, Vol. 4. 2009. (Illus.). 112p. pap. 7.99 (978-1-60010-388-9(X)) Diamond Bk. Distributors.

Gruber, Daveda. More Tales of a Tiny Dog. 2009. 71p. pap. 32.50 (978-1-4092-6657-0(5)) Lulu Pr., Inc.

—Tales of a Tiny Dog. 2010. 74p. pap. 29.50 (978-0-557-43600-2(1)) Lulu Pr., Inc.

Guarneri, Cristina. Wiley's Adventure. 2009. 64p. pap. 10.49 (978-1-4389-5244-4(9)) AuthorHouse.

Gubernatis, Loretto. Dimitrius & the Gladiolas. 2011. 356p. pap. 19.99 (978-1-4568-2907-0(6)) Xlibris Corp.

Guerin, F. A. The Witch at NO46: Verbrola. 2011. (Illus.). 140p. pap. 14.69 (978-1-4567-7118-8(3)) AuthorHouse.

Guerra, Elisa Puricelli. The City of Lizards. Zeni, Marco, tr. from ITA. Bernstein, Gabriel León, illus. 2015. (Minerva Mint Ser.). (ENG.). 160p. (gr. 2-4). lib. bdg. 25.32 (978-1-4342-9671-9(7)) Stone Arch Bks.

—The Forest of Talking Trees. Zeni, Marco, tr. from ITA. Bernstein, Gabriel León, illus. 2015. (Minerva Mint Ser.). (ENG.). 160p. (gr. 2-4). lib. bdg. 25.32 (978-1-4342-9673-3(3)) Stone Arch Bks.

Guerra, R. R. Gabirochi y la Isla de la Vid. 2010. 168p. pap. 31.90 (978-1-59754-554-9(6)) Editorial Libros en Red.

Guerras, Safia. Lou Lou. 2012. (Illus.). 40p. (978-1-78132-021-1(7)); pap. (978-1-78132-019-8(5)) SilverWood Bks.

Guerras Safia. Lou Lou. Kemble, Mai S., illus. 2013. (ENG.). 24p. (J). pap. 16.95 (978-1-4787-2359-2(9)) Outskirts Pr., Inc.

Guerrera, Debra. The Adventures of Baby Caterpillar & His Traveling Butterfly Family. 2011. 28p. pap. 15.99 (978-1-4628-9982-1(X)) Xlibris Corp.

Guerrera, Jeannette D. The Dumb-Dumb Angel. 2012. 20p. pap. 17.99 (978-1-4685-5426-7(3)) AuthorHouse.

—The Pot of Gold. 2012. 20p. pap. 17.99 (978-1-4685-5883-8(8)) AuthorHouse.

Guerrero, Rhonda. It's Me, Penny! The Hot Air Balloon Adventure. Leech, Jacob, illus. 2011. 28p. pap. 24.95 (978-1-4489-7070-4(9)) America Star Bks.

Guess Who, Elmo! Adivina Quién! 2014. (Guess Who Ser.). (ENG., Illus.). 10p. (J). (gr. -1-k). 10.99 (978-0-7944-3212-6(3)) Reader's Digest Assn., Inc., The.

Guest, Jacqueline. War Games, 1 vol. 2008. (Lorimer SideStreets Ser.). (ENG.). 184p. (YA). (gr. 9-12). 9.95 (978-1-55277-035-1(4), 9781552770351); 16.95 (978-1-55277-036-8(2), 9781552770368) Lorimer, James & Co., Ltd., Pubs. CAN. Dist: Casemate Pubs. & Bk. Distributors, LLC.

Guia Del Entrenador Pokemon. (SPA.). 102p. 9.95 (978-84-488-1003-0(1)) Beascoa, Ediciones S.A. ESP. Dist: Distribooks, Inc.

Guibert, Emmanuel. Sardine in Outer Space 5. Pezzali, Walter & Sfar, Joann, illus. 5th ed. 2008. (Sardine in Outer Space Ser.: 5). (ENG.). 112p. (J). (gr. 1-5). pap. 17.99 (978-1-59643-380-9(9), 9781596433809, First Second Bks.) Roaring Brook Pr.

Guibert, Susan Mullen & O'Shaughnessy, Brendan. Clashmore Mike Comes Home. Pynaert, Andrea, illus. 2012. 24p. (J). 19.95 (978-0-9859377-3-7(4)) Corby Books.

Guignard, Lars. The Yogi's Curse. 2013. 342p. pap. (978-0-9877753-9-9(1)) Guignard, Lars.

Guillain, Adam. Bella Balistica & the African Safari. 2007. (Bella Balistica Ser.). (ENG., Illus.). 250p. (J). (gr. 4-7). per. 9.95 (978-1-84059-482-9(9)) Milet Publishing.

—Bella Balistica & the Forgotten Kingdom. 2009. (Bella Balistica Ser.). (ENG., Illus.). 180p. (J). (gr. 4-7). pap. 9.95 (978-1-84059-526-0(4)) Milet Publishing.

—Bella Balistica & the Indian Summer. 2005. (Bella Balistica Ser.). (ENG., Illus.). 350p. (J). (gr. 4-7). pap. 9.95 (978-1-84059-407-2(1)) Milet Publishing.

—Bella Balistica & the Izta Warriors. 2012. (Bella Balistica Ser.). (ENG., Illus.). 170p. (J). (gr. 4-7). pap. 9.95 (978-1-84059-771-4(2)) Milet Publishing.

Guilloppé, Antoine. One Scary Night. 2007. (ENG., Illus.). 32p. (J). (gr. 4-7). 15.95 (978-1-59687-185-4(7)) IBks., Inc.

Guiza, Vic, illus. Bat in the Bunk: Summer Camp Stories Seires. 2015. (ENG.). 32p. (J). (gr. 1-18). 19.99 (978-0-9863743-0-2(X)) Summer Camp Stories LLC.

Gulliksen, Anne. A Boy from Nøtterøy. 2009. 108p. pap. 13.00 (978-1-59858-939-9(3)) Dog Ear Publishing, LLC.

Gunby, Stephanie. The Clever Clouds. 2010. 56p. pap. 24.20 (978-1-4269-3902-0(7)) Trafford Publishing.

Gunderson, J. The Last Rider: The Final Days of the Pony Express. Ruiz, Jose Alfonso Ocampo & Woodman, Ned, illus. 2007. (Historical Fiction Ser.). (ENG.). 56p. (gr. 2-3). pap. 6.25 (978-1-59889-407-3(2), Graphic Flash) Stone Arch Bks.

Gunderson, Jessica. Passage to Fortune: Searching for Saguenay. Kurtz, Rory, illus. 2016. (Discovering the New World Ser.). (ENG.). 96p. (gr. 3-4). lib. bdg. 26.65 (978-1-4965-3481-1(6), Connect) Stone Arch Bks.

—Passage to Fortune: Searching for Saguenay. Kurtz, Rory, illus. 2016. (Discovering the New World Ser.). (ENG.). 96p. (gr. 3-4). pap. 7.95 (978-1-4965-3482-8(4), Connect) Stone Arch Bks.

Gunlock, Sheila. Groovy Granny & the Character Bees. 2012. 24p. (-18). pap. 10.95 (978-1-4497-6910-9(1), WestBow Pr.) Author Solutions, Inc.

Gunning, P. M. The Adventures of Corrie & Trix. 2012. (Illus.). 36p. pap. 22.88 (978-1-4772-1950-8(1)) AuthorHouse.

Gunter, Jacob Ben, et al. The Daily Bugle Stories. 2004. (Spider-Man 2 Ser.). (Illus.). 144p. pap. (978-0-00-717815-5(8), HarperCollins Entertainment) HarperCollins Pubs. Ltd.

Guojing. The Only Child. 2015. (ENG., Illus.). 112p. (J). (gr. k-4). 22.99 (978-0-553-49705-2(7), Schwartz & Wade Bks.) Random Hse. Children's Bks.

Gurden, Gloria. The Adventures of Wersel Driftwood. 2011. 58p. (gr. 2-4). pap. 10.16 (978-1-4269-9254-4(8)) Trafford Publishing.

Gurney, James. Dinotopia: The World Beneath. 20th anniv. ed. 2012. (Calla Editions Ser.). (ENG., Illus.). 192p. (gr. 3). 30.00 (978-1-60660-033-7(8)) Dover Pubns., Inc.

—Dinotopia - First Flight. 20th anniv. ed. 2014. (ENG., Illus.). 112p. (gr. 5). 25.00 (978-1-60660-057-3(5)) Dover Pubns., Inc.

—Dinotopia, Journey to Chandara. 2017. (Calla Editions Ser.). (ENG., Illus.). 192p. 35.00 (978-1-60660-100-6(8)) Dover Pubns., Inc.

Guthrie, Janelle. Rachel & the Pink & Green Dragon. 2012. 50p. (-18). pap. 11.95 (978-1-4772-8198-7(3)) AuthorHouse.

Gutierrez-Haley, Lisa. The New Pet: Adventures of Hayden & Jace. 2011. 20p. pap. 24.95 (978-1-4626-1872-9(3)) America Star Bks.

Gutknecht, Allison. Don't Wear Polka-Dot Underwear with White Pants: And Other Lessons I've Learned. Lewis, Stevie, illus. 2013. (ENG.). 160p. (J). (gr. 2-5). pap. 6.99 (978-1-4424-8392-7(X), Aladdin) Simon & Schuster Children's Publishing.

—Don't Wear Polka-Dot Underwear with White Pants: And Other Lessons I've Learned. Lewis, Stevie, illus. 2013. (ENG.). 160p. (J). (gr. 2-5). 15.99 (978-1-4424-8393-4(8), Simon & Schuster/Paula Wiseman Bks.) Simon & Schuster/Paula Wiseman Bks.

Gutman, Colas. The Pointless Leopard: What Good Are Kids Anyway? Seegmuller, Stephanie, tr. from FRE. Perret, Delphine, illus. 2014. (ENG.). 48p. (J). (gr. 2-4). pap. 9.99 (978-1-78269-040-5(9), Pushkin Press) Steerforth Pr.

Gutman, Dan. Back to School, Weird Kids Rule! Paillot, Jim, illus. 2014. (My Weird School Special Ser.). 144p. (J). (gr. 1-5). lib. bdg. 16.89 (978-0-06-220686-2(9)) HarperCollins Pubs.

—From Texas with Love. 2014. (ENG.). (J). (gr. 3-7). (Genius Files Ser.: 4). 304p. pap. 6.99 (978-0-06-182775-4(4)); (Genius Files Ser.: Bk. 4). (Illus.). 288p. 16.99 (978-0-06-182773-0(8)) HarperCollins Pubs.

—From Texas with Love. 2014. (Genius Files Ser.: 4). (J). lib. bdg. 17.20 (978-0-606-36462-1(5)) Turtleback Bks.

—The Genius Files #5: License to Thrill. 2016. (Genius Files Ser.: 5). (Illus.). 272p. (J). (gr. 3-7). pap. 6.99 (978-0-06-223633-3(4)) HarperCollins Pubs.

—License to Thrill. 2015. (Genius Files Ser.: 5). (ENG.). 272p. (J). (gr. 3-7). 16.99 (978-0-06-223632-6(6)) HarperCollins Pubs.

—License to Thrill. 2016. (Genius Files Ser.: 5). (J). lib. bdg. 17.20 (978-0-606-38167-3(8)) Turtleback Bks.

—The Lincoln Project. 2016. (Flashback Four Ser.: 1). 240p. (J). (gr. 3-7). 16.99 (978-0-06-237441-7(9)) HarperCollins Pubs.

—The Lincoln Project. 2017. (Flashback Four Ser.). (J). lib. bdg. 17.20 **(978-0-606-39606-6(3))** Turtleback Bks.

—Mission Unstoppable. 2011. (Genius Files Ser.: 1). (ENG.). 304p. (J). (gr. 3-7). pap. 6.99 (978-0-06-182766-2(5)); (Illus.). 16.99 (978-0-06-182764-8(9)) HarperCollins Pubs.

—Mission Unstoppable. 2011. (Genius Files Ser.: 1). (J). lib. bdg. 17.20 (978-0-606-23559-4(0), Turtleback) Turtleback Bks.

—Mr. Tony Is Full of Baloney! Paillot, Jim, illus. 2010. (My Weird School Daze Ser.: 11). 112p. (J). (gr. 1-5). (ENG.). pap. 4.99 (978-0-06-170399-7(0)); lib. bdg. 15.89 (978-0-06-170400-0(8)) HarperCollins Pubs.

—Never Say Genius. 2012. (Genius Files Ser.: 2). (J). (gr. 3-7). (ENG.). 304p. pap. 6.99 (978-0-06-182769-3(X)); (ENG.). 288p. 16.99 (978-0-06-182767-9(3)); 288p. lib. bdg. 17.89 (978-0-06-182768-6(1)) HarperCollins Pubs.

—Never Say Genius. 2012. (Genius Files Ser.: 2). (J). lib. bdg. 17.20 (978-0-606-27128-8(7), Turtleback) Turtleback Bks.

—You Only Die Twice. 2013. (Genius Files Ser.: 3). (J). (gr. 3-7). (ENG.). 320p. pap. 6.99 (978-0-06-182772-3(X)); (ENG., Illus.). 304p. 16.99 (978-0-06-182770-9(3)); (Illus.). 304p. lib. bdg. 17.89 (978-0-06-182771-6(1)) HarperCollins Pubs.

—You Only Die Twice. 2013. (Genius Files Ser.: 3). (J). lib. bdg. 17.20 (978-0-606-35043-3(8), Turtleback) Turtleback Bks.

Guyot, Rebecca. Flyin' Ryan the Rescue Ranger: In: the Puzzleton Storm, 1 vol. 2009. 20p. pap. 24.95 (978-1-60836-856-3(4)) America Star Bks.

H. P. Lawrence. The Adventures of Wilfred & Henri: The Staff of Knowledge. 2009. 88p. pap. 10.49 (978-1-4389-6374-7(2)) AuthorHouse.

Haarsma, P. J. The Softwire: Betrayal on Orbis 2. 2009. (Softwire Ser.: 2). (ENG., Illus.). 320p. (YA). (gr. 7). 7.99 (978-0-7636-4269-3(X)) Candlewick Pr.

Haas, Jessie. Bramble & Maggie: Snow Day. Friend, Alison, illus. 2016. (ENG.). 56p. (J). (gr. k-3). 14.99 (978-0-7636-7364-2(1)) Candlewick Pr.

—Bramble & Maggie Spooky Season. Friend, Alison, illus. 2016. (Candlewick Sparks Ser.). (ENG.). 56p. (J). (gr. k-3). pap. 3.99 (978-0-7636-8743-4(X)) Candlewick Pr.

Habel, Lia. Dearly, Departed. 2012. (ENG.). 496p. (YA). (gr. 8-12). pap. 10.99 (978-0-345-52332-7(6), Del Rey) Random House Publishing Group.

Habro Transformers Staff. Transformers Rescue Bots Roll to the Rescue! A Lift-the-Flap Book. 2013. (Lift-The-Flap Ser.: 1). (ENG.). 10p. (J). (gr. -1-k). bds. 9.99 (978-0-7944-2849-5(5), Reader's Digest Children's Bks.) Studio Fun International.

Haddix, Margaret Peterson. Among the Brave. (Shadow Children Ser.: 5). (ENG., Illus.). (J). (gr. 3-7). 2005. 256p. pap. 7.99 (978-0-689-85795-9(0)) 2004. 240p. 17.99 (978-0-689-85794-2(2)) Simon & Schuster Bks. For Young Readers. (Simon & Schuster Bks. For Young Readers).

—Children of Refuge. 2017. (Children of Exile Ser.: 2). (ENG., Illus.). 272p. (J). (gr. 5). 17.99 **(978-1-4424-5006-6(1)**, Simon & Schuster Bks. For Young Readers) Simon & Schuster Bks. For Young Readers.

—Found. 2008. (Missing Ser.: 1). (ENG.). 320p. (J). (gr. 3-7). 17.99 (978-1-4169-5417-0(1), Simon & Schuster Bks. For Young Readers) Simon & Schuster Bks. For Young Readers.

—Running Out of Time. 184p. (YA). (gr. 5-18). pap. 4.99 (978-0-8072-1529-6(5), Listening Library) Random Hse. Audio Publishing Group.

Hadley, Sally C. Little Sally Girl's Greatest Adventure Series. 2013. (ENG.). 38p. (J). 27.95 (978-1-4787-2067-6(0)) Outskirts Pr., Inc.

Haesche, Richard, Sr. The Bull of Death. 2007. (ENG.). 218p. (YA). 10.50 (978-0-9798536-4-7(8)) Kreative X-Pressions Pubns.

—The Werewolf Syndrome. 3rd ed. 2007. (ENG.). 218p. (YA). pap. 9.95 (978-0-9798536-0-9(5)) Kreative X-Pressions Pubns.

Hafiz, Caroline Owen. The Return of the Fossil. 2007. 76p. per. (978-1-897312-26-1(1)) Adlibbed Ltd.

Hagen, George. Gabriel Finley & the Raven's Riddle. 2016. (ENG.). 384p. (J). (gr. 4-7). 7.99 (978-0-399-55222-9(7), Yearling) Random Hse. Children's Bks.

—Gabriel Finley & the Raven's Riddle. Bakal, Scott, illus. 2014. (ENG.). 384p. (J). (gr. 4-7). 16.99 (978-0-385-37103-2(9), Schwartz & Wade Bks.) Random Hse. Children's Bks.

Hager, Mickey. Clarence Duntz & the Monkey Spell. 2010. 62p. pap. 11.33 (978-0-557-14381-8(0)) Lulu Pr., Inc.

Haggard, H. Rider. Allan Quatermain #3: Allan+s Wife. 2007. 116p. per. 7.99 (978-1-934451-87-8(8)) Wilder Pubns., Corp.

—King Solomon's Mines. Marcos, Pablo, illus. 2005. (Great Illustrated Classics Ser.). 239p. (J). (gr. 3-8). 21.35 (978-1-59679-244-9(2), Abdo & Daughters) ABDO Publishing Co.

—Pearl-Maiden. Kou, Christopher D. & McHugh, Michael J., eds. 2003. 372p. (YA). pap. 9.95 (978-1-930367-89-0(9)) Christian Liberty Pr.

Haggarty, Holly. Summer Dragons. 2007. (ENG.). 176p. (J). (gr. 3-18). per. 9.95 (978-1-894917-52-0(9), Napoleon & Co.) Dundurn CAN. Dist: Ingram Publisher Services.

Haggarty, S. Little Muddy Bear. 2009. 52p. pap. 11.99 *(978-1-4389-4071-7(8))* AuthorHouse.
Haggerty, Robert. Bailey's Day. 2010. (Illus.). 45p. (J). pap. 17.95 *(978-1-4327-4550-9(6))* Outskirts Pr., Inc.
Hahn, Jan. Albert & the Milk Pail. 2012. 118p. (gr. -1). pap. 12.19 *(978-1-4669-7409-8(5))* Trafford Publishing.
Hahn, Molly. Under the Sneep Tree: The Wamboozling of a Village. 2009. pap. *(978-1-61623-907-7(7))* Independent Pub.
Hahnl, John. Pocket & Toast, 1 vol. Hahnl, Olivia, illus. 2010. 40p. 24.95 *(978-1-4489-8425-1(4))* PublishAmerica, Inc.
Haidar, Hanna. Earl's Big Adventure in Costa Rica. Hutcheson, Meredith, ed. Newton, Kimberly, illus. 2007. 22p. (J). per. 7.99 *(978-0-9800975-0-4(9))* Old Silver Pr.
—Earl's Big Adventure in Costa Rica. Newton, Kimberly, illus. 2nd ed. 2012. 22p. (J). *(978-0-9800975-2-8(5))* Old Silver Pr.
—Earl's Big Adventure in Japan. Newton, Kimberly, illus. 2012. 26p. (J). *(978-0-9800975-1-1(7))* Old Silver Pr.
Hajj, Sharon. Zula Blackburn & the Rising Sun Festival. 2012. 146p. 34.94 *(978-1-105-79464-3(4))* Lulu.com GBR. Dist: Lulu Pr., Inc.
Hale, Aaron. Addy Gets Made. 2008. 27p. pap. 24.95 *(978-1-60610-339-5(3))* America Star Bks.
Hale, Bruce. The Chameleon Wore Chartreuse. unabr. ed. 2004. (Chet Gecko Mystery Ser.: No. 1). 112p. (J). (gr. 3-6). pap. 17.00 incl. audio *(978-0-8072-0342-2(4)*, Listening Library) Random Hse. Audio Publishing Group.
—Fat Cat of Underwhere. Hillman, Shane, illus. 2009. (Underwhere Ser.). 176p. (J). pap. 5.99 *(978-0-06-085135-4(X))* HarperCollins Pubs.
—Pirates of Underwhere. Hillman, Shane, illus. (Underwhere Ser.: 2). (J). (gr. 3-7). 2009. (ENG.). 176p. pap. 6.99 *(978-0-06-085129-3(5))* 2008. 164p. lib. bdg. 16.89 *(978-0-06-085128-6(7))* HarperCollins Pubs.
—Prince of Underwhere. Hillman, Shane, illus. 2009. (Underwhere Ser.: 1). (ENG.). 176p. (J). (gr. 3-7). pap. 5.99 *(978-0-06-085126-2(0))* HarperCollins Pubs.
—Tooth Trouble. 2014. (Clark the Shark: I Can Read Level 1 Ser.). (J). lib. bdg. 13.55 *(978-0-606-36459-1(5))* Turtleback Bks.
Hale, Daniel J. & LaBrot, Matthew. Red Card. 2004. (Zeke Armstrong Mysteries Ser.: Vol. 1). 170p. (gr. 4-9). 8.95 *(978-1-929976-15-7(1))* Top Pubns., Ltd.
Hale, Lucretia Peabody. The Last of the Peterkins: With Others of Their Kin. 2007. (ENG.). 142p. pap. 18.99 *(978-1-4346-2126-9(X))*; 154p. pap. 21.99 *(978-1-4346-2145-0(6))* Creative Media Partners, LLC.
Hale, Mary. Karly & Sheila's Walk. 2012. (ENG.). 23p. (J). pap. 11.95 *(978-1-4327-8647-2(4))* Outskirts Pr., Inc.
Hale, Shannon. The Book of a Thousand Days. Smith, James Noel, illus. 2007. (ENG.). 320p. (YA). (gr. 7-12). 17.95 *(978-1-59990-051-3(3)*, 9781599900513, Bloomsbury USA Childrens) Bloomsbury Publishing USA.
—Dangerous. (ENG.). 416p. (YA). (gr. 7). 2015. pap. 9.99 *(978-1-61963-819-8(3)*, 9781619638198) 2014. 17.99 *(978-1-59990-168-8(4)*, 9781599901688) Bloomsbury Publishing USA. (Bloomsbury USA Childrens).
Hale, Shannon & Hale, Dean. Rapunzel's Revenge. Hale, Nathan, illus. 2008. (ENG.). 144p. (YA). (gr. 5-8). pap. 16.99 *(978-1-59990-288-3(5)*, 9781599902883, Bloomsbury USA Childrens) Bloomsbury Publishing USA.
Haley, Annie. Rumpus & Bumpus: If we could do Anything... ... 2008. 32p. pap. 13.95 *(978-1-59858-803-3(6))* Dog Ear Publishing, LLC.
Haley, Barbara. Boot Camp. 2006. (Flamingo Fiction 9-13s Ser.). (ENG., Illus.). 128p. (J). (gr. 4-7). per. 6.99 *(978-1-84550-128-0(4)*, b92d6d0e-c252-4095-839b-1c07c368f656) Christian Focus Pubns. GBR. Dist: Bookmasters Distribution.
Haley, Jeannette. The Adventures of Zack & Mira. 2013. 116p. pap. 12.95 *(978-0-9891683-0-4(1))* Hidden Manna Pubns.
Hall, Angela Marie. Priscilla Pennybrook: Hello World, I Have Arrived!, 1 vol. 2009. 55p. pap. 16.95 *(978-1-61582-899-9(0))* America Star Bks.
Hall, Annalisa. Tak & Lolly: Santa Clause at Church. 2009. 51p. pap. 6.99 *(978-0-557-04923-3(7))* Lulu Pr., Inc.
Hall, Caroline V. Rhett & Abby: Abby's New Home. 2011. 40p. pap. 15.95 *(978-1-4497-1887-9(6)*, WestBow Pr.) Author Solutions, Inc.
Hall, J. Darroll. The Lollipop Club. 2011. (ENG.). 290p. pap. 4.99 *(978-0-615-56231-5(0))* Fantasy Island Bk. Publishing.
Hall, Jennie. The Viking Tales. 2008. 88p. pap. 8.15 *(978-1-60459-529-1(9))* Wilder Pubns., Corp.
Hall, Jennifer. Reginald's Broken Arm. 2008. 28p. pap. 16.95 *(978-1-4343-7532-2(3))* AuthorHouse.
Hall, John. Jeffrey Takes on the World. 2005. 48p. pap. 16.95 *(978-1-4137-9832-6(2))* PublishAmerica, Inc.
Hall, John & Gilpin, Stephen. If the Earth Had a Zipper. 2006. (Illus.). 48p. 15.99 *(978-1-59379-069-1(4))* White Stone Bks.
Hall, Kathleen. Billy & Bobby's Adventures. 2008. pap. 10.00 *(978-0-8059-8589-4(1))* Dorrance Publishing Co., Inc.
Hall, Kirsten. Help! All about Telling Time. Luedecke, Bev, illus. 2004. (Beastieville Ser.). (ENG.). 32p. (J). (gr. k-1). pap. 3.95 *(978-0-516-24655-0(0)*, Children's Pr.) Scholastic Library Publishing.
Hall, Maggie. The Ends of the World. 2017. (Conspiracy of Us Ser.: 3). (ENG.). 320p. (YA). (gr. 7). 17.99 ***(978-0-399-16652-5(1)***, G.P. Putnam's Sons Books for Young Readers) Penguin Young Readers Group.
Hall, Maggie. Map of Fates. 2016. (Conspiracy of Us Ser.). (ENG.). 320p. (YA). (gr. 7). 17.99 *(978-0-399-16651-8(3)*, G.P. Putnam's Sons Books for Young Readers) Penguin Young Readers Group.
Hall, Marjorie. The Talismon Tales No. 1: Wiggleton's Courageous Adventure. 2003. 136p. 18.95 *(978-1-4140-3006-7(1))* AuthorHouse.
—The Talismon Tales No. 1: Wiggleton's Courageous Adventure. 2003. 146p. 21.95 *(978-0-595-65790-2(7))*; pap. 11.95 *(978-0-595-28414-6(0))* iUniverse, Inc.
Hall, Mary Kathleen. Marland's Mysterious Mazes: Past the Mailbox. 2010. 40p. pap. 16.99 *(978-1-4490-7824-9(9))* AuthorHouse.
Hall, Natalie Susan. Andy Anole's Adventure, 1 vol. 2009. 26p. pap. 24.95 *(978-1-60813-350-5(8))* America Star Bks.
Hall, S. M. & Quarto Generic Staff. Breaking the Circle. 2012. (ENG.). 352p. (J). (gr. 7-10). pap. 8.99 *(978-1-84780-122-7(6)*, Frances Lincoln) Quarto Publishing Group UK GBR. Dist: Hachette Bk. Group.
Hall, Shirley. The Adventure of Molly the Mouse. 2012. (ENG.). (J). pap. 14.95 *(978-1-4675-1717-1(8))* Independent Pub.
Hall, Susan, illus. Robot Repairman to the Rescue! 2009. (Backyardigans Ser.). (ENG.). 24p. (J). (gr. -1-2). pap. 3.99 *(978-1-4169-9012-3(7)*, Simon Spotlight/Nickelodeon) Simon Spotlight/Nickelodeon.
Hall, Susan & Hall, Susan, illus. Diego Saves the Tree Frogs. 2006. (Go, Diego, Go! Ser.). (ENG.). 24p. (J). (gr. -1-1). pap. 3.99 *(978-1-4169-1574-4(5)*, Simon Spotlight/Nickelodeon) Simon Spotlight/Nickelodeon.
Hall, Susan Liberty. Scented Adventures of the Bouquet Sisters in Fairyland. Josephine, Wall, illus. 2011. 85p. (YA). pap. 21.50 *(978-0-9833247-6-8(X))* Inkwell Books LLC.
Hall, Terri L. Denny & Denise: A Story of Two Ducks: Introducing Pretty Boy & Fella, 1 vol. Hall, Terri L. & Babeaux, Dennis, photos by. 2009. (Illus.). 42p. pap. 24.95 *(978-1-60749-609-0(7))* America Star Bks.
Hallagin, Janet. The Way of Courage. 2006. 30.99 *(978-1-4257-1249-5(5))*; pap. 20.99 *(978-1-4257-1248-8(7))* Xlibris Corp.
Hallam, Gwion. Disgwyl a Disgwyl. 2005. (WEL., Illus.). 16p. pap. *(978-1-85644-750-8(2))* CAA.
Haller, Reese. The Adventures Begin. Lynn, Galsterer, illus. 2005. (Fred the Mouse Ser.). 108p. (J). (gr. -1-3). per. 4.97 *(978-0-9616046-8-4(9))* Personal Power Pr.
—Giving & Receiving. Haller, Reese, illus. 2007. (Fred the Mouse Ser.). (Illus.). 104p. (J). (gr. 4-7). per. 4.97 *(978-0-9772321-5-4(8))* Personal Power Pr.
Halley, Jane E. The Unidentified Flight-Less Object. 2008. 52p. pap. 22.49 *(978-1-4343-6491-3(7))* AuthorHouse.
Halliday, Keith. Aurore of the Yukon: A Girl's Adventure in the Klondike Gold Rush. 2006. 134p. (J). (gr. 1-1). pap. 11.95 *(978-0-595-39546-0(5))* iUniverse, Inc.
Halloran, Craig. The Chronicles of Dragon: Dragon Bones & Tombstones (Book 2) 2013. 226p. pap. 9.99 *(978-0-9896216-0-1(X))* Two-Ten Bk. Pr.
—The Chronicles of Dragon: Terror at the Temple (Book 3) 2013. 276p. pap. 9.99 *(978-0-9896216-2-5(6))* Two-Ten Bk. Pr.
Hallstrand, John & Sarah & Hawley, Karen. Zoey Helps the Mystery Dog Find a Home. 2011. 24p. pap. 11.99 *(978-1-4634-1094-0(8))* AuthorHouse.
Halpern, Jake & Kujawinski, Peter. Dormia. 2010. (ENG.). 528p. (J). (gr. 5-7). pap. 7.99 *(978-0-547-32887-4(7))* Houghton Mifflin Harcourt Publishing Co.
—Edgeland. 2017. (ENG., Illus.). 272p. (J). (gr. 5). 17.99 *(978-0-399-17581-7(4)*, G.P. Putnam's Sons Books for Young Readers) Penguin Young Readers Group.
Halsey, Jacqueline. Bluenose Adventure. Orchard, Eric, illus. 2013. (ENG.). 32p. (J). (gr. -1-3). 16.95 *(978-1-4595-0280-2(9)*, 9781459502802) Formac Publishing Co., Ltd. CAN. Dist: Casemate Pubs. & Bk. Distributors, LLC.
Halstead, Stefanie Merie. The Night of the Festival. 2008. 36p. pap. 24.95 *(978-1-60703-697-5(5))* America Star Bks.
Halvorson, Marilyn. Blue Moon, 1 vol. 2004. (Orca Soundings Ser.). (ENG.). 128p. (YA). (gr. 8-12). pap. 9.95 *(978-1-55143-320-2(6)*, 1234488) Orca Bk. Pubs. USA.
Hama, Larry & Dixon, Chuck. G. I. JOE: the IDW Collection Volume 1: The IDW Collection Volume 1. Mutti, Andrea et al, illus. 2013. (G. I. Joe Ser.). (ENG.). 352p. 49.99 *(978-1-61377-549-3(0)*, 9781613775493) Idea & Design Works, LLC.
Hama, Larry, et al. G. I. Joe Vol. 6: A Real American Hero. Frenz, Ron & Buscema, Sal, illus. 2013. (G. I. Joe Ser.). (ENG.). 128p. pap. 19.99 *(978-1-61377-582-0(2)*, 9781613775820) Idea & Design Works, LLC.
Hamburger, Carole. The Zippity-Do-Dot: The Dot Who Dared to Pick Her Knows. Hamburger, Carole, illus. 2008. (Illus.). 40p. (J). 16.95 *(978-0-9764921-1-5(3))* Cherry Street Pr.
Hamilton, Alwyn. Rebel of the Sands. (Rebel of the Sands Ser.). (ENG.). (YA). (gr. 7). 2017. 336p. pap. 10.99 *(978-0-14-751797-5(4)*, Speak) 2016. 320p. 18.99 *(978-0-451-47753-8(7)*, Viking Books for Young Readers) Penguin Young Readers Group.
Hamilton, Annie. The Unforgettable Night. 2013. (Illus.). 70p. pap. *(978-1-78148-617-7(4))* Grosvenor Hse. Publishing Ltd.
Hamilton, Covette J. Begethie Wenferd Meets King Tut. 2012. 32p. pap. *(978-1-77097-189-9(0))* FriesenPress.
Hamilton, Eric E. Buddy the Bassett Hound Follows His Nose. 2013. 94p. pap. 17.95 *(978-1-4137-7764-2(3))* America Star Bks.
Hamilton, George. Seeing Red: Story Seeds Vol 1. Hazel, Andrew, illus. 2008. 20p. pap. 13.99 *(978-1-4343-8004-3(1))* AuthorHouse.
Hamilton, John. Dog Friday. 2010. (Illus.). 60p. pap. 21.99 *(978-1-4490-9468-3(6))* AuthorHouse.
Hamilton, Katharine E. Susie at Your Service. 2012. 24p. pap. 17.99 *(978-1-4772-2426-7(2))* AuthorHouse.
Hamilton, Kersten. The Ire of Iron Claw. Hamilton, James, illus. (Gadgets & Gears Ser.: 2). (ENG.). (J). (gr. 2-5). 2016. 192p. pap. 6.99 *(978-0-544-66854-6(5)*, HMH Books For Young Readers) 2015. 176p. 16.99 *(978-0-544-22502-2(3))* Houghton Mifflin Harcourt Publishing Co.
—The Tick-Tock Man. Hamilton, James, illus. 2016. (Gadgets & Gears Ser.: 3). (ENG.). 144p. (J). (gr. 2-5). 16.99 *(978-0-544-43300-7(9))* Houghton Mifflin Harcourt Publishing Co.
—When the Stars Threw down Their Spears. 2013. (ENG.). 400p. (YA). (gr. 7). 16.99 *(978-0-547-73964-9(8))* Houghton Mifflin Harcourt Publishing Co.
Hamilton, Leslie. The Story of Peter Little Bear: A Lamprey River Adventure. 2005. (J). per. 12.95 *(978-1-933002-02-6(6))* PublishingWorks.
Hamilton, Pat. Peaches the Private Eye Poodle: The Missing Muffin Caper. 2008. 32p. pap. 13.50 *(978-1-60693-277-3(2)*, Eloquent Bks.) Strategic Book Publishing & Rights Agency (SBPRA).
Hamilton, Patricia D. Peaches the Private Eye Poodle: Finding Dipsey Doodle. 2008. 32p. pap. 13.50 *(978-1-60693-276-6(4)*, Eloquent Bks.) Strategic Book Publishing & Rights Agency (SBPRA).
—Peaches the Private Eye Poodle: Finding Foster a Home. 2010. 36p. (gr. -1-3). pap. 13.50 *(978-1-60911-108-3(7)*, Eloquent Bks.) Strategic Book Publishing & Rights Agency (SBPRA).
—Peaches the Private Eye Poodle: Where Is Loosey Goosey? 2009. 32p. pap. 13.50 *(978-1-60860-063-2(7)*, Eloquent Bks.) Strategic Book Publishing & Rights Agency (SBPRA).
Hamilton, Seymour. The Laughing Princess. 2012. (ENG.). 146p. (J). pap. 7.99 *(978-1-937291-45-7(6))* Acedrex Publishing.
Hamilton-Sturdy, K. The Tree of Dreams. 2013. 138p. pap. *(978-1-78299-683-5(4))* FeedARead.com.
Hamilton, Tisha. Piratas del Caribe. el viaje al fin del Mundo: Pirates of the Caribbean: at the World's End. 2007. (Illus.). 38p. (J). *(978-970-718-532-6(5)*, Silver Dolphin en Español) Advanced Marketing, S. de R. L. de C. V.
Hamlett, Martha. Bats in the Air, Bats in My Hair. 2008. 32p. pap. 13.99 *(978-1-4389-2358-1(9))* AuthorHouse.
Hammock, Sarah Owens. You Can't Get into More Trouble Than Gator Pervis!! Cocciolone, Kathy Roberts, illus. 2007. 32p. (J). 12.95 *(978-1-934246-27-6(1))* Peppertree Pr., The.
Hammon, Darrel L. Christmas Beneath the Lake: From the Adventures of Bob the Bullfrog. 2012. (ENG.). 25p. (J). (-18). pap. 23.95 *(978-1-4327-7916-0(8))* Outskirts Pr., Inc.
Hammond, Barbara, illus. The Duffy Chronicles. Hammond, Barbara, . 2007. 60p. pap. 11.99 *(978-0-9800675-4-5(5))* Mirror Publishing.
Hammond, James F. Ski Challenge. 2008. 100p. pap. 16.95 *(978-1-60703-493-3(X))* PublishAmerica, Inc.
Hammond, John & Hutchison, Gary. The Bewildering Bond: A Novel for Teenagers. 2004. 182p. (YA). pap. 13.99 *(978-1-885631-86-2(3))* Hutchison, G.F. Pr.
Hammond, Ron J. The Dig: Journey of a Lost Tribe. unabr. ed. 2004. 186p. (YA). pap. 10.95 *(978-1-932280-47-0(2)*, 80472) Granite Publishing & Distribution.
Hampshire, Anthony. Fast Track. 2004. (Redline Racing Ser.: Bk. 1). (Illus.). 104p. (YA). pap. 3.99 *(978-1-55305-007-0(X))* Cygnet Publishing Group, Inc./Coolreading.com CAN. Dist: Orca Bk. Pubs. USA.
—Full Throttle. 2004. (Redline Racing Ser.: Bk. 2). (Illus.). 108p. (YA). pap. 3.99 *(978-1-55305-008-7(8))* Cygnet Publishing Group, Inc./Coolreading.com CAN. Dist: Orca Bk. Pubs. USA.
Hampton, Francesca. Children's Voyage the Long Journey Home. 2010. 222p. pap. 13.96 *(978-0-557-23497-4(2))* Lulu Pr., Inc.
Hampton, Patrick. Down by the Mulberry Tree, 1 vol. 2009. 15p. pap. 24.95 *(978-1-60703-672-2(X))* America Star Bks.
Hancock, H. Irving. The High School Boys' Training Hike. 2007. 176p. per. *(978-1-4065-1986-0(3))* Dodo Pr.
—The Young Engineers in Arizona. 2007. 180p. per. *(978-1-4065-1992-1(8))* Dodo Pr.
—The Young Engineers in Colorado. 2007. 180p. per. *(978-1-4065-1993-8(6))* Dodo Pr.
—The Young Engineers on the Gulf. 2007. 176p. per. *(978-1-4065-1996-9(0))* Dodo Pr.
Handford, Martin. Where's Waldo? the Great Picture Hunt. 2010. (Where's Waldo? Ser.). lib. bdg. 18.40 *(978-0-606-14541-1(9)*, Turtleback) Turtleback Bks.
Handy Manny Pop-up Tool Book. 2009. 6p. 12.99 *(978-1-4231-2114-5(7))* Disney Pr.
Hanes, Tracey. The Adventures of Kung Foo Poo. 2009. 84p. pap. 15.99 *(978-1-4415-4045-4(8))* Xlibris Corp.
Hanington, John G. The Adventures of Quick Fox. 2006. (ENG.). 92p. per. 9.95 *(978-0-7414-3223-0(4))* Infinity Publishing.
Hankins, Jim. Teddy Scares Volume 3. 2008. (Illus.). 52p. (YA). pap. 6.95 *(978-0-9791050-2-9(1))* Ape Entertainment.
Hankins, Larry. Stickboy at the Fair. 2011. 32p. pap. 24.95 *(978-1-4512-2206-7(8))* America Star Bks.
Hanley, Victoria. Seize the Story: A Handbook for Teens Who Like to Write. 2008. (ENG.). 208p. (J). (gr. 6). pap. 15.95 *(978-1-877673-81-8(1))* Cottonwood Pr., Inc.
Hannaford, Linda S. Petie the Parrot's Amazing Adventures: P. D. Q., 1 vol. Lee, George T., illus. 2010. 16p. pap. 24.95 *(978-1-61582-767-1(6))* PublishAmerica, Inc.
Hannam, John-Pierre M., Sr. Uncle Jake's Hat. 2009. 43p. pap. 20.00 *(978-0-557-02568-8(0))* Lulu Pr., Inc.
Hanny, Diane. Wispy Willy. Baskey, Kim, illus. 2011. 24p. pap. 12.00 *(978-1-4520-9975-0(8))* AuthorHouse.
Hano, Patricia. Tyler Meets the Moon. 2010. 28p. pap. 11.99 *(978-1-60911-189-2(3)*, Eloquent Bks.) Strategic Book Publishing & Rights Agency (SBPRA).
Hansel, Karen & Ham, Ken. Charlie & Trike Grand Canyon Adventure. 2010. (Illus.). 24p. (J). spiral bd. 15.99 *(978-0-89051-569-3(7))* Master Bks.
Hansell, Robin. Mason & Monkey's Big Adventure. 2013. 52p. pap. 23.99 *(978-1-4808-0254-4(9))* Archway Publishing.
Hansen, Ace. Julius Caesar Brown & the Green Gas Mystery. 2013. 114p. pap. *(978-1-77127-424-1(7))* MuseItUp Publishing.
Hansen, Alli. Huevos Rancheros. 2008. 32p. pap. 24.95 *(978-1-60672-993-9(4))* PublishAmerica, Inc.
Hansen, Dustin. Microsaurs: Adventure Awaits. Hansen, Dustin, illus. 2017. (Microsaurs Ser.: 1). (ENG., Illus.). 224p. (J). 13.99 *(978-1-250-09021-8(0)*, 9781250090218) Feiwel & Friends.
Hansen, Eric. The Isle of Nam. Meier, Paul, illus. 2004. (J). bds. 9.99 *(978-1-4183-0016-6(0))* Christ Inspired, Inc.
Hansen, Kate. Spike the Sewer Cat. Illustrations byVoigt, Karen S., illus. 2008. 27p. pap. 24.95 *(978-1-60474-094-3(9))* America Star Bks.
Hansen, Marc. Ralph Snart Adventures: Comic Collection #2. 2007. (Illus.). 128p. (YA). pap. 14.95 *(978-0-9794643-1-7(5))* Hansen, Marc Stuff!
Hansen, Marc. Ralph Snart Adventures: Comic Collection #1. Hansen, Marc, . 2007. (Illus.). (YA). per. 14.95 *(978-0-9794643-0-0(7))* Hansen, Marc Stuff!
Hansen, Paul. The Adventures of Gray Tail. 2011. 20p. 13.99 *(978-1-4567-2958-5(6))* AuthorHouse.
Hansen, Tevin. Hole in the Wall: (humorous Action & Adventure - Ages 8+) Cochran, Shaun, illus. l.t. ed. 2014. (ENG.). 300p. (J). (gr. 2-7). pap. 11.99 *(978-1-941429-00-6(9))* Handersen Publishing.
Hanson, Bonnie Compton. Lost on Monster Mountain. 2004. (Ponytail Girls Ser.). (Illus.). 208p. (J). pap. 7.99 *(978-1-58411-031-6(7)*, Legacy Pr.) Rainbow Pubs. & Legacy Pr.
Hanson, Ed. Amazon Adventure. 2003. (Barclay Family Adventure Ser.: Bk. 1). 64p. (J). (gr. k-6). per. 3.95 *(978-1-56254-550-5(7)*, SP 5507) Saddleback Educational Publishing, Inc.
—Danger at 20 Fathoms. 2003. (Barclay Family Adventure Ser.: Bk. 2). (Illus.). 64p. (J). (gr. k-6). per. 3.95 *(978-1-56254-551-2(5)*, SP 5515) Saddleback Educational Publishing, Inc.
—Falsely Accused. 2005. (Barclay Family Adventures 2 Ser.). 63p. (J). per. 3.95 *(978-1-56254-802-5(6)*, SP8026) Saddleback Educational Publishing, Inc.
—Free Fall. 2005. (Barclay Family Adventures 2 Ser.). 64p. (J). per. 3.95 *(978-1-56254-804-9(2)*, SP8042) Saddleback Educational Publishing, Inc.
—Iron Mountain. 2005. (Barclay Family Adventures 2 Ser.). 64p. (J). per. 3.95 *(978-1-56254-806-3(9)*, SP8069) Saddleback Educational Publishing, Inc.
—Lost at Sea. 2003. (Barclay Family Adventure Ser.: Bk. 6). (Illus.). 64p. (J). (gr. k-6). per. 3.95 *(978-1-56254-555-0(8)*, SP 5558) Saddleback Educational Publishing, Inc.
—The Pass. 2003. (Barclay Family Adventure Ser.: Bk. 9). (Illus.). 64p. (J). (gr. k-6). per. 3.95 *(978-1-56254-557-4(4)*, SP 5574) Saddleback Educational Publishing, Inc.
—The Swamp. 2003. (Barclay Family Adventure Ser.: Bk. 10). (Illus.). 64p. (J). (gr. k-6). per. 3.95 *(978-1-56254-558-1(2))* Saddleback Educational Publishing, Inc.
Hanson, Jonathan. Victor el Zopilote Renuente! Duffek, Kim Kanoa, illus. 2012. 36p. (J). pap. 16.95 *(978-1-886679-46-7(0))* Arizona Sonora Desert Museum Pr.
—Victor, the Reluctant Vulture. Duufek, Kim Kanoa, illus. 2012. 36p. (J). pap. 16.95 *(978-1-886679-45-0(2))* Arizona Sonora Desert Museum Pr.
Hanson, Robert Karl. Bluey & the Great Spirit Moon. 2012. 48p. pap. 17.45 *(978-1-4525-0730-9(9))* Balboa Pr.
Hanson, Ted & Hanson, Jackie. Dakota's First Roundup. 2012. 60p. (gr. 2-4). pap. 11.95 *(978-1-4772-9096-5(6))* AuthorHouse.
Hapka, Catherine, pseud. Blue Ribbon Day. Kennedy, Anne, illus. 2013. (I Can Read Level 2 Ser.). (ENG.). 32p. (J). (gr. -1-3). pap. 3.99 *(978-0-06-208676-1(6))* HarperCollins Pubs.
—Chasing Gold. 2014. (Ponies of Chincoteague Ser.: 3). lib. bdg. 17.20 *(978-0-606-36099-9(9))* Turtleback Bks.
—Meet the Buddies! Lyon, Tammie, illus. 2013. (World of Reading Ser.). (ENG.). 32p. (J). (gr. 1-3). pap. 3.99 *(978-1-4231-6946-8(8))* Disney Pr.
—One Big Blue Family. 2014. (I Can Read Level 2 Ser.). (ENG.). 32p. (J). (gr. -1-3). pap. 3.99 *(978-0-06-228498-3(3))* HarperCollins Pubs.
—Plants vs. Zombies: Save Your Brains! 2014. (I Can Read Level 2 Ser.). (ENG.). 32p. (J). (gr. -1-3). pap. 3.99 *(978-0-06-229496-8(2))* HarperCollins Pubs.
—Pony Scouts - The Camping Trip. Kennedy, Anne, illus. 2014. (I Can Read Level 2 Ser.). (ENG.). 32p. (J). (gr. -1-3). pap. 3.99 *(978-0-06-208663-1(4))* HarperCollins Pubs.
—Pony Scouts: the Camping Trip. Kennedy, Anne, illus. 2014. (I Can Read Level 2 Ser.). (ENG.). 32p. (J). (gr. -1-3). 16.99 *(978-0-06-208665-5(0))* HarperCollins Pubs.
—Rio - Learning to Fly. 2011. (I Can Read Level 2 Ser.). (ENG.). 32p. (J). (gr. k-3). pap. 3.99 *(978-0-06-201488-7(9)*, HarperFestival) HarperCollins Pubs.
—Rio 2: Vacation in the Wild. 2014. (I Can Read Level 2 Ser.). (ENG.). 32p. (J). (gr. -1-3). pap. 3.99 *(978-0-06-228499-0(1))* HarperCollins Pubs.
—Roaring In. 6th ed. 2009. 288p. pap. 7.99 *(978-1-4231-1669-1(0))* Disney Pr.
Hapka, Cathy, pseud. Jungle Adventure. 2014. (LEGO Friends Chapter Bks.: 6). lib. bdg. 14.75 *(978-0-606-36363-1(7))* Turtleback Bks.
—LEGO Friends: Mystery in the Whispering Woods (Chapter Book #3) 2013. (LEGO Friends Ser.). (ENG.). 64p. (J). (gr. 2-5). pap. 4.99 *(978-0-545-56669-8(X))* Scholastic, Inc.
Harbo, Gary. The Northern Woods Adventure: Advanced Reader, 6 vols. Harbo, Gary, illus. l.t. ed. 2004. (If You Want to Succeed, You Need to Read! Ser.: 6). (Illus.). 33p. (J). per. 10.95 *(978-1-884149-15-3(4))* Kutie Kari Bks., Inc.
—The Northern Woods Adventure: Early Reader. Harbo, Gary, illus. l.t. ed. 2004. (If You Want to Succeed, You Need to Read! Ser.: 6). (Illus.). 33p. (J). 10.95 *(978-1-884149-16-0(2))* Kutie Kari Bks., Inc.
Harbour, Kathi. The Adventures of Kat VanDrat. 2013. (ENG.). 111p. (YA). pap. 11.95 *(978-1-4787-1010-3(1))* Outskirts Pr., Inc.
Harbridge, Paul. Helena's Voyage: A Mystic Adventure. 2008. (HEB, ARA & ENG., Illus.). 48p. (J). (gr. -1-2). pap. 9.95 *(978-1-84694-114-6(8)*, Our Street Bks.) Hunt, John Publishing Ltd. GBR. Dist: National Bk. Network.
Hardcastle, Henry. Explorer: A Daring Guide for Young Adventurers. Steer, Dugald A., ed. 2007. (Genuine & Moste Authentic Guide Ser.). (ENG., Illus.). 32p. (J). (gr. 1-4). 15.99 *(978-0-7636-3648-7(7))* Candlewick Pr.
Harder, Linda Janet. Kittens in the Classroom. 2011. 40p. (gr. -1). pap. 16.59 *(978-1-4567-6414-2(4))* AuthorHouse.
Hardie, Richard. Leap of Faith. 2013. (Illus.). 272p. pap. *(978-1-909841-26-0(9))* Crooked Cat Publishing.
Hardin, Holly. Aurora of the Northern Lights. 2009. 31p. (J). pap. 18.95 *(978-1-4327-2439-9(8))* Outskirts Pr., Inc.
Hardinge, Frances. A Face Like Glass. 2017. (ENG.). 496p. (YA). (gr. 7-17). 19.95 *(978-1-4197-2484-8(3)*, Amulet Bks.) Abrams, Inc.
Hardman, John. Little Miss Daredevil, Vol. 1. Beach, Bryan, illus. 2012. (ENG.). 80p. (J). pap. 6.99 *(978-1-4215-4072-6(X))* Viz Media.
Hardy Boys Adventures: Secret of the Red Arrow; Mystery of the Phantom Heist; the Vanishing Game; into Thin Air. 2013. (Hardy Boys Adventures Ser.). (ENG., Illus.). 608p. (J). (gr. 3-7). pap. 27.99 *(978-1-4424-8897-7(2)*, Aladdin) Simon & Schuster Children's Publishing.
Hardy, Emelia J. The Adventures of Maureen & Maury: For Children of All Ages! 2003. 158p. (J). pap. 12.95 *(978-0-595-29536-4(3))* iUniverse, Inc.
Hardy, Emma-Rose. Vampuric Slayer Blood. 2010. 155p. pap. 7.94 *(978-1-4461-5652-0(4))* Lulu Pr., Inc.
Hardy, Zoey. Brockway High. 2006. 318p. per. 12.95 *(978-0-9765423-1-5(5))* Eudon Publishing.
Hargrave, Kiran Millwood. The Cartographer's Daughter. 2016. (ENG.). 224p. (J). (gr. 5). 16.99 *(978-0-553-53528-0(5)*,

Knopf Bks. for Young Readers) Random Hse. Children's Bks.

Haris, Martha & Haris, Kimberli. The Adventures of Fairyella the Tooth Fairy & Dragonfly Floyd. 2012. 24p. pap. 14.95 *(978-1-4575-1039-7(1))* Dog Ear Publishing, LLC.

harkins, charles. Naptime Adventures of Luksi the Turtle. 2010. 174p. pap. 20.96 *(978-0-557-28695-9(6))* Lulu Pr., Inc.

Harkness, Peter T. Andy the Acrobat. 2007. 184p. per. *(978-1-4065-2349-2(6))* Dodo Pr.

—Andy the Acrobat: Out with the Greatest Show on Earth. 2006. (ENG.). 162p. pap. 19.99 *(978-1-4264-4077-9(4))* 2007. 180p. pap. 21.99 *(978-1-4264-4136-3(3))* Creative Media Partners, LLC.

Harlan. My Best Friend. 2011. 28p. pap. 9.95 *(978-1-4327-7164-5(7))* Outskirts Pr., Inc.

Harley, Bill. The Amazing Flight of Darius Frobisher, 1 vol. 2009. (ENG.). 160p. (J). pap. 7.95 *(978-1-56145-494-5(X))* Peachtree Pubs.

Harley, Stephen. The Christmastime Dog Rescue. 2013. 24p. pap. 10.95 *(978-1-4624-0774-3(9)*, Inspiring Voices) Author Solutions, Inc.

Harlow, Honey. Honey's Shoes. 2013. 28p. pap. 9.95 *(978-1-4327-9921-2(5))* Outskirts Pr., Inc.

Harman, Ian. The Adventures of Terry Tool Bench: Book 1 Terry Is Born. 2009. 36p. pap. 16.99 *(978-1-4490-0048-6(7))* AuthorHouse.

Harmon, Alison L. The Adventures of Feeda Fox; Everybody's Different. 2010. 24p. 14.99 *(978-0-557-05931-7(3))* Lulu Pr., Inc.

Harmon, Douglas. Momma Whats a Stranger. 2011. 28p. pap. *(978-1-4269-7247-8(4))* Trafford Publishing (UK) Ltd.

Harms, Carol. What If? 2010. 20p. 10.49 *(978-1-4520-8463-3(7))* AuthorHouse.

Harper, Benjamin. Greetings from Rio! 2011. (Rio Ser.). (ENG.). 24p. (J). (gr. -1-2). pap. 3.99 *(978-0-06-202266-0(0)*, HarperFestival) HarperCollins Pubs.

—Star Wars: the Chewbacca Story. 2016. (ENG.). 32p. (J). (gr. k-3). 17.99 *(978-0-7944-3741-1(9)*, Reader's Digest Children's Bks.) Studio Fun International.

—Star Wars: the Force Awakens: Movie Theater Storybook & BB-8 Projector. 2016. (ENG.). 40p. (J). (gr. 1-3). 24.99 *(978-0-7944-3789-3(3))* Studio Fun International.

Harper, Jamie. Miles to Go. Harper, Jamie, illus. 2013. (ENG., Illus.). 32p. (J). (gr. -1-2). pap. 4.99 *(978-0-7636-6469-5(3))* Candlewick Pr.

Harper, Ken. Mystery in Mansfield. 2008. 60p. pap. 19.95 *(978-1-60441-055-6(8))* America Star Bks.

HarperCollins Publishers Ltd. Staff & Auerbach, Annie. Paddington: Paddington's Adventures. 2014. (I Can Read Level 1 Ser.). (ENG., Illus.). 32p. (J). (gr. -1-3). pap. 3.99 *(978-0-06-235001-5(3))* HarperCollins Pubs.

HarperCollins Publishers Ltd. Staff, et al. James Cameron's Avatar. movie tie-in ed. 2009. (James Cameron's Avatar Ser.). (ENG., Illus.). 48p. (J). (gr. -1-2). pap. 7.99 *(978-0-06-180124-2(0)*, HarperFestival) HarperCollins Pubs.

Harrar, Frank W. Wee Dragonslayers. Galan-Robles, Francisco, illus. 2008. 45p. pap. 24.95 *(978-1-60610-851-2(4))* America Star Bks.

Harrell, Rob. Life of Zarf: The Trouble with Weasels. 2016. (Life of Zarf Ser.: 3). (ENG., Illus.). 272p. (J). (gr. 3-7). 15.99 *(978-0-8037-4105-8(7)*, Dial Bks) Penguin Young Readers Group.

—The Trouble with Weasels. 2014. (Life of Zarf Ser.: 1). (ENG.). 288p. (J). (gr. 3-7). 14.99 *(978-0-8037-4103-4(0)*, Dial Bks) Penguin Young Readers Group.

Harrington, Linda. Holly's Backyard Adventures, 1 vol. 2010. 20p. pap. 24.95 *(978-1-4512-9277-0(5))* PublishAmerica, Inc.

Harrington, Sean. Jack-in-the-Box Madness. 2006. (Illus.). 32p. (YA). 4.99 *(978-0-9778042-0-7(8))* Harrington Artwerkes Booksellers.

Harris, Carrie. Sally Slick & the Steel Syndicate. Valentine, Amanda, ed. 2014. (Illus.). 200p. (YA). pap. 15.00 *(978-1-61317-063-2(7))* Evil Hat Productions LLC.

Harris, Charles Edward. Ice Angels. 2007. 60p. pap. 30.50 *(978-1-84799-750-0(3))* Lulu Pr., Inc.

Harris, Christine. Undercover Girl #5: Twisted. 2007. (ENG.). 136p. (J). per. 10.95 *(978-1-59594-151-0(7)*, Wingspan Pr.) WingSpan Publishing.

Harris, David. Pussy Footin' 2010. 190p. pap. 26.50 *(978-1-4457-8092-4(5))* Lulu Pr., Inc.

Harris-Davies, Dafydd, et al. Caleb a Tyg. 2005. (WEL., Illus.). 24p. pap. *(978-0-86381-854-7(4))* Gwasg Carreg Gwalch.

Harris, Dee. I Am Not a Hippopotamus, I Am a Little Girl , Book. Bohart, Lisa, illus. 2011. 24p. pap. 12.95 *(978-1-61493-005-1(8))* Peppertree Pr., The.

Harris, Donna. Dust Bunnies Do Love Donuts. 2009. 40p. pap. 16.99 *(978-1-4490-0628-0(0))* AuthorHouse.

—Lucie & the Garden Fairies. 2008. (Illus.). 40p. pap. 18.49 *(978-1-4389-1312-4(5))* AuthorHouse.

—Ruff Life. 2011. 240p. pap. 17.99 *(978-1-4567-5081-7(X))* AuthorHouse.

Harris, Jane Ellen. Room for One More. Cole, Al, illus. 2007. 24p. (J). (gr. -1-3). pap. 11.98 *(978-0-9800733-0-0(8)*, LSP) LSP Digital, LLC.

Harris, Janice. The Journey: Subtle Lessons in Spiritual Awakening. 2007. 180p. per. 19.95 *(978-1-4327-0795-8(7))* Outskirts Pr., Inc.

Harris, Joe. Narda. 2005. (J). *(978-0-9772259-0-3(9))* Character Arts.

Harris, Kimberly Anne. Only in a Dream Series: Caught in a Web ~ the Trees Are My Friends~What Is All the Buzz About? 2012. 60p. pap. 24.99 *(978-1-4772-7005-9(1))* AuthorHouse.

Harris, Mary Beth. Susie Sunflower. Pederson, Gunda, illus. 2010. 24p. 16.49 *(978-1-4520-5171-0(2))* AuthorHouse.

Harris, Nelson. Andrew of the Antimites. 2006. 83p. pap. 16.95 *(978-1-4241-3429-8(3))* PublishAmerica, Inc.

Harris, Nikki. Adventures in Friendship for Benji Butterfly & Tom Turkey. 2013. 24p. pap. 24.95 *(978-1-63004-741-2(4))* America Star Bks.

Harris, Patricia. The Car of Many Colors. 2017. (Colorful Cars Ser.). 24p. (gr. 4-6). pap. 8.25 ***(978-1-5383-2087-7(8)***, PowerKids Pr.) Rosen Publishing Group, Inc., The.

Harris, Philip. Trever & the Phoenix. 2009. 40p. pap. 16.99 *(978-1-4389-9537-3(7))* AuthorHouse.

Harris, Shelly Jones. Little Elephant Is a Lifesaver. 2012. 24p. pap. 10.99 *(978-1-4497-6092-2(9)*, WestBow Pr.) Author Solutions, Inc.

Harris, Stephanie C. The Wonders of Monkey Mac! 2009. 302p. pap. 15.95 *(978-1-60693-257-5(8)*, Eloquent Bks.) Strategic Book Publishing & Rights Agency (SBPRA).

Harris, Todd V. Heroes & Haters. 2008. 75p. pap. 19.95 *(978-1-60563-157-8(4))* America Star Bks.

Harris, Tumeka. The Broken Law. Sea Breeze Productions & Phelps, Janice, eds. Miller, Linzi, illus. 2006. 32p. (J). 14.95 *(978-0-9769366-0-2(7))* Dividion Group, LLC, The.

—The Goody Bag. Sea Breeze Productions, ed. Miller, Linzi, illus. 2006. 36p. (J). 14.95 *(978-0-9769366-2-6(3))* Dividion Group, LLC, The.

—Home Sweet Home. Sea Breeze Productions, ed. Miller, Linzi, illus. 2006. 36p. (J). 14.95 *(978-0-9769366-3-3(1))* Dividion Group, LLC, The.

—Trouble in Paradise. Sea Breeze Productions & Phelps, Janice, eds. Miller, Linzi, illus. 2006. 36p. (J). 14.95 *(978-0-9769366-1-9(5))* Dividion Group, LLC, The.

Harrison, Charles C. Dick Turpin. 2003. (Historias de Siempre Ser.). (SPA., Illus.). 92p. (J). (gr. 5-8). pap. 12.95 *(978-84-204-5701-7(9))* Santillana USA Publishing Co., Inc.

Harrison, Christy Gremore. Once upon A Monday. 2010. 40p. pap. 16.99 *(978-1-4490-5854-8(X))* AuthorHouse.

Harrison, F. Bayford. The Battlefield Treasure. 2004. reprint ed. pap. 15.95 *(978-1-4191-5373-0(0))*; pap. 1.99 *(978-1-4192-5373-7(5))* Kessinger Publishing, LLC.

Harrison, Lisi. Boys R Us. 2009. (Clique Ser.: 11). (ENG.). 320p. (YA). (gr. 7-17). pap. 9.99 *(978-0-316-00682-8(3)*, Tingley, Megan Bks.) Little, Brown Bks. for Young Readers.

Harrison, Megan Bernadette. The Adventures of Kitty Tom & Blossom: Book One. 2009. 36p. pap. 24.95 *(978-1-60749-257-3(1))* America Star Bks.

Harrison, Michelle. The Thirteen Secrets. 2014. (ENG.). 400p. (YA). pap. 8.99 *(978-1-4711-2169-2(0)*, Simon & Schuster Children's) Simon & Schuster, Ltd. GBR. Dist: Simon & Schuster, Inc.

Harrison, Paul. Undersea Adventure. Nascimbeni, Barbara, illus. 2011. 32p. pap. *(978-1-84089-638-1(8))* Zero to Ten, Ltd.

Harrison, Paula. The Moonlight Mystery. 2013. (Rescue Princesses Ser.: 3). (ENG., Illus.). 128p. (J). (gr. 2-5). pap. 4.99 *(978-0-545-50915-2(7)*, Scholastic Paperbacks) Scholastic, Inc.

—The Stolen Crystals. 2013. (Rescue Princesses Ser.: 4). (ENG.). 128p. (J). (gr. 2-5). pap. 4.99 *(978-0-545-50916-9(5)*, Scholastic Paperbacks) Scholastic, Inc.

Harriton, Maxine. A School Trip to the Fruit Planet, 1. l.t. ed. 2006. 34p. (J). (gr. -1-1). lib. bdg. 18.95 *(978-0-9787248-0-1(1)*, 00-01-851-447X) UpTree Publishing.

Harrold, A. F. Fizzlebert Stump: The Boy Who Cried Fish. Horne, Sarah, illus. 2014. (Fizzlebert Stump Ser.). (ENG.). 288p. (YA). (gr. 2-4). pap. 10.99 *(978-1-4088-4246-1(7)*, 9781408842461, Bloomsbury USA Childrens) Bloomsbury Publishing USA.

—Fizzlebert Stump: The Boy Who Did P. E. in His Pants. Horne, Sarah, illus. 2017. (ENG.). 320p. (J). pap. 10.99 *(978-1-4088-5339-9(6)*, 9781408853399, Bloomsbury USA Childrens) Bloomsbury Publishing USA.

—Fizzlebert Stump: The Boy Who Ran Away from the Circus (And Joined the Library) Horne, Sarah, illus. 2013. (Fizzlebert Stump Ser.). (ENG.). 256p. (YA). (gr. 3-6). pap. 10.99 *(978-1-4088-3003-1(5)*, 9781408830031, Bloomsbury USA Childrens) Bloomsbury Publishing USA.

—Fizzlebert Stump & the Bearded Boy. Horne, Sarah, illus. 2014. (Fizzlebert Stump Ser.). (ENG.). 272p. (YA). (gr. 3-6). pap. 10.99 *(978-1-4088-3521-0(5)*, 9781408835210, Bloomsbury USA Childrens) Bloomsbury Publishing USA.

—Fizzlebert Stump & the Girl Who Lifted Quite Heavy Things. Horne, Sarah, illus. 2015. (Fizzlebert Stump Ser.). (ENG.). 304p. (YA). (gr. 1-3). pap. 10.99 *(978-1-4088-5331-3(0)*, 9781408853313, Bloomsbury USA Childrens) Bloomsbury Publishing USA.

—Fizzlebert Stump & the Great Supermarket Showdown. Horne, Sarah, illus. 2017. (Fizzlebert Stump Ser.). (ENG.). 304p. (J). pap. 10.99 *(978-1-4088-6945-1(4)*, 9781408869451, Bloomsbury USA Childrens) Bloomsbury Publishing USA.

—The Imaginary. Gravett, Emily, illus. 2015. (ENG.). 240p. (YA). (gr. 3-6). 16.99 *(978-0-8027-3811-0(7)*, 9780802738110, Bloomsbury USA Childrens) Bloomsbury Publishing USA.

Harry How Books. Just Luke. l.t. ed. 2006. (ENG., Illus.). 28p. per. 9.95 *(978-1-4327-0178-9(9))* Outskirts Pr., Inc.

Harshbarger, D. The Treasures of Dawn. 2011. 44p. pap. 19.99 *(978-1-4634-1585-3(0))* AuthorHouse.

Hart, J. Tristan. The Adventures of Friendly & Barnackel: Book 1 Friendly & Barnackel. 2010. 36p. pap. 15.49 *(978-1-4490-9721-9(9))* AuthorHouse.

—The Adventures of Friendly & Barnackel: Book 2. 2011. 36p. pap. 15.14 *(978-1-4567-6284-1(2))* AuthorHouse.

—The Adventures of Friendly & Barnackel: Book 3 Ollie the Octopus. 2011. 32p. 12.77 *(978-1-4567-2602-7(1))* AuthorHouse.

—The Adventures of Friendly & Barnackel: Book 4 Jaybird the BlueJay. 2010. 32p. 12.99 *(978-1-4490-8919-1(4))* AuthorHouse.

Hart, Janice. Henry & the Oranges: Henry's Wild Adventures. McDonald, Suzi, illus. 2010. 32p. pap. 13.00 *(978-1-60860-911-6(1)*, Eloquent Bks.) Strategic Book Publishing & Rights Agency (SBPRA).

Hart, Teresa. The Ant & the Alligator. 2007. 84p. per. 19.95 *(978-1-4241-7182-8(2))* America Star Bks.

Harter, Debbie. De Paseo Por la Selva. Ugalde, Raquel, tr. Harter, Debbie, illus. 2003. (SPA., Illus.). 32p. (J). pap. 6.99 *(978-1-84148-995-7(6))* Barefoot Bks., Inc.

Hartley, A. J. Steeplejack. 2016. (Steeplejack Ser.: 1). (ENG.). 336p. (YA). 17.99 *(978-0-7653-8342-6(X)*, 9780765383426, Tor Teen) Doherty, Tom Assocs., LLC.

Hartley Bellows, Carol. Icabog Bear. 2009. 24p. pap. 15.50 *(978-1-4389-3856-1(X))* AuthorHouse.

Hartley, Grandpa. Further Jolly Bedtime Tales for Big & Little People. 2010. 88p. pap. 30.99 *(978-1-4490-8267-3(X))* AuthorHouse.

Hartley, Susan. Abby's Adventures: Abby the Pirate. Kane, Brenden, illus. 2005. 37p. pap. 24.95 *(978-1-4137-4491-0(5))* PublishAmerica, Inc.

Hartman, Brett. Cadillac Chronicles. 2012. (ENG.). 304p. (J). (gr. 10). 16.95 *(978-1-935955-41-2(1))* Cinco Puntos Pr.

Hartman, Ms. Joan. Mischiefs & Misadventures of the Hooligans. 2012. 40p. pap. 21.99 *(978-1-4691-9255-0(1))* Xlibris Corp.

Hartry, Nancy. Smokescreen. 2013. (ENG., Illus.). 204p. (YA). (gr. 7). 17.95 *(978-1-77049-405-3(7)*, Tundra Bks.) Tundra Bks. CAN. Dist: Penguin Random Hse. LLC.

Harvey, Autumn. Putty. 2009. 16p. pap. 8.99 *(978-1-4389-4421-0(7))* AuthorHouse.

Harvey, Charlene A. The Adventures of the Tiger Club. 2011. 14p. pap. 10.99 *(978-1-61215-027-7(6))* Salem Author Services.

Harvey, Damian & Remphry, Martin. Robin & the Friar. 2009. (Hopscotch Adventures Ser.). (Illus.). 31p. (J). (gr. 1). lib. bdg. 25.65 *(978-1-59771-177-7(2))* Sea-To-Sea Pubns.

—Robin & the Monk. 2009. (Hopscotch Adventures Ser.). (Illus.). 31p. (J). (gr. 1). lib. bdg. 25.65 *(978-1-59771-179-1(9))* Sea-To-Sea Pubns.

Harvey, Gwendolyn Fowlkes. The Backyard Plum Tree. 2009. (J). pap. *(978-1-61623-481-2(4))* Independent Pub.

Harvey, M. A. Attack of the Jaguar: Dare to Take the Test. 2004. (Illus.). 128p. (J). pap. *(978-1-84458-051-4(2)*, Pavilion Children's Books) Pavilion Bks.

—The Scorpion Secret: Dare to Take the Test. 2004. (Illus.). 128p. (J). pap. *(978-1-84458-050-7(4)*, Pavilion Children's Books) Pavilion Bks.

Harvey, Natalie. Peppermint Pixie. Winfield, Amy, illus. 2013. 44p. pap. *(978-1-909202-10-8(X))* Little Acorns Publishing.

Harvey, Pam & Panckridge, Michael. Taking the Chequered Flag. 2008. 208p. *(978-0-207-20062-5(9))* HarperCollins Pubs. Australia.

Harvey, Paul E., Jr. The Adventures of Shamus the Leprechaun. 2009. 48p. pap. 15.50 *(978-1-60693-924-6(6)*, Strategic Bk. Publishing) Strategic Book Publishing & Rights Agency (SBPRA).

Harvey, Sharon M. Legend of the Pumpkin Carver. 2010. 100p. pap. 22.95 *(978-1-4327-1214-3(4))* Outskirts Pr., Inc.

Harvey, Tom. Creature Teachers. 2013. 72p. pap. 24.27 *(978-1-4669-9417-1(7))* Trafford Publishing.

—Guido, the Swan with an Attitude. 2011. 44p. (gr. -1). pap. 17.99 *(978-1-4269-6855-6(8))* Trafford Publishing.

—Rat in the Red Truck. 2011. 44p. 17.99 *(978-1-4269-6236-3(3))* Trafford Publishing.

Harvie, Ronald Anthony. The Adventures of Peter Potato & Friends. 2005. (Illus.). 71p. (J). per. 15.95 *(978-0-9771939-0-5(X)*, 0002) New World Publishing.

Hasan, Jamal I. A Journey to Remember. 2007. 64p. per. 8.95 *(978-0-595-43375-9(8))* iUniverse, Inc.

Hasany, Syed M. Stop the Train, Monkey! 2013. 28p. pap. 16.09 *(978-1-4669-7792-1(2))* Trafford Publishing.

Hasbro. Roll Out & Read Adventures. 2014. (Transformers Passport to Reading Ser.). (J). lib. bdg. 18.40 *(978-0-606-35294-9(5))* Turtleback Bks.

—Transformers Rescuebots: Robots to the Rescue! 2016. (ENG.). 12p. (J). (gr. -1-1). bds. 10.99 *(978-0-7944-3685-8(4))* Studio Fun International.

Hasbro & King, Trey. Transformers Rescue Bots. 2015. (ENG., Illus.). 12p. (J). (gr. -1-1). pap. 6.99 *(978-0-316-40560-7(4))* Little, Brown Bks. for Young Readers.

Hasbro & Shea, Lisa. Transformers: Rescue Bots: Meet Chase the Police-Bot. 2013. (Passport to Reading Level 1 Ser.). (ENG.). 32p. (J). (gr. -1-1). 3.99 *(978-0-316-22829-9(X))* Little, Brown Bks. for Young Readers.

Hasbro Inc. Staff & King, Trey. Transformers Rescue Bots: Training Academy: Firefighters! 2016. (Passport to Reading Level 2 Ser.). (ENG., Illus.). 32p. (J). (gr. -1-1). pap. 3.99 *(978-0-316-38982-2(X))* Little, Brown Bks. for Young Readers.

Hasbro Industries Incorporated Staff. My Little Pony Winning Style: Stories, Activites, & Tattoos. 2014. (ENG.). 24p. (J). (gr. -1-1). pap. 7.99 *(978-0-7944-3030-6(9)*, Reader's Digest Children's Bks.) Studio Fun International.

Hasbro My Little Pony, Hasbro My. My Little Pony New Episode 2014. 2014. (Panorama Sticker Storybook Ser.: 12). (ENG.). 24p. (J). (gr. -1-2). pap. 7.99 *(978-0-7944-3117-4(8))* Reader's Digest Assn., Inc., The.

Haskamp, Steven, illus. Eight Silly Monkeys. 2007. (ENG.). 18p. (J). (gr. -1-3). bds. 15.95 *(978-1-58117-577-6(9)*, Intervisual/Piggy Toes) Bendon, Inc.

Haskell, Merrie. Handbook for Dragon Slayers. 2013. (ENG.). 336p. (J). (gr. 3-7). 16.99 *(978-0-06-200816-9(1))* HarperCollins Pubs.

Hastings, Brian. Song of the Deep. 2016. (ENG., Illus.). 176p. (J). (gr. 3-7). 12.95 *(978-1-4549-2096-0(3))* Sterling Publishing Co., Inc.

Hasty, Vicki Sterling. Eliza & the Analogies of Burnshire. 2009. 150p. pap. 24.95 *(978-1-60813-216-4(1))* America Star Bks.

Hatch, Thomas. Larry the Moose. 2009. 32p. pap. 15.99 *(978-1-4389-8533-6(9))* AuthorHouse.

Hatfield, Ruth. The Book of Shadows. 2017. (Book of Storms Trilogy Ser.: 3). (ENG., Illus.). 288p. (J). 16.99 *(978-1-62779-003-1(9)*, 9781627790031, Holt, Henry & Co. Bks. For Young Readers) Holt, Henry & Co.

—The Book of Storms. Call, Greg, illus. 2015. (Book of Storms Trilogy Ser.: 1). (ENG.). 368p. (J). (gr. 5-9). 16.99 *(978-0-8050-9998-0(0)*, 9780805099980, Holt, Henry & Co. Bks. For Young Readers) Holt, Henry & Co.

—The Color of Darkness. 2016. (Book of Storms Trilogy Ser.: 2). (ENG., Illus.). 336p. (J). 16.99 *(978-1-62779-001-7(2)*, 9781627790017, Holt, Henry & Co. Bks. For Young Readers) Holt, Henry & Co.

Hathaway, Lucinda Churchman. 'Round the World: Takashi Sails Home. 2008. (Illus.). 135p. (J). 12.95 *(978-1-59322-034-1(0))* Down The Shore Publishing Corp.

Hathorn, Libby. The River. Wong, Stanley, illus. 2003. 40p. 28.95 *(978-1-86366-516-2(1))* Education Services Australia Ltd. AUS. Dist: Cheng & Tsui Co.

Hathorn, Sarah Alexandra. Teenagents: World Challenge. 2012. 240p. pap. 12.99 *(978-2-9700738-2-6(X))* Simon & Schuster, Inc.

Hatke, Ben. Mighty Jack. (Mighty Jack Ser.: 2). (ENG., Illus.). 208p. (J). 2017. 22.99 ***(978-1-62672-267-5(6)***, 9781626722675) 2017. pap. 14.99 ***(978-1-62672-266-8(8)***, 9781626722668) 2016. pap. 14.99 *(978-1-62672-264-4(1)*, 9781626722644) Roaring Brook Pr. (First Second Bks.).

—Mighty Jack. 2017. (Mighty Jack Ser.). (J). lib. bdg. 26.95 ***(978-0-606-40540-9(2))*** Turtleback Bks.

Hatke, Ben. Nobody Likes a Goblin. 2016. (ENG., Illus.). 40p. (J). 17.99 *(978-1-62672-081-7(9)*, 9781626720817, First Second Bks.) Roaring Brook Pr.

Hattan, Ann. Jake & Bobby's Magical Christmas. 2012. (Illus.). 16p. pap. 18.30 *(978-1-4772-2748-0(2))* AuthorHouse.

Hattaway, Carol. Dinky Duck's Adventure. Cotton, Sue Lynn, illus. 2012. 16p. pap. 12.95 *(978-1-61493-128-7(3))* Peppertree Pr., The.

The Haunted House. 2007. (Choose Your Own Adventure Ser.). (Illus.). 80p. (J). (gr. 4-7). pap. 7.99 *(978-1-933390-51-2(4))* Chooseco LLC.

Hauser, Judy. The Legend of Punzel's Pond. 2005. (Illus.). 126p. (YA). per. 9.95 *(978-0-9713603-0-3(8))* Fen's Rim.

Hausman, Gerald. Timeswimmer. 2009. (Island Fiction Ser.). 187p. (J). (gr. 5-16). pap. *(978-1-4050-9898-4(8))* Macmillan Caribbean.

Hautman, Pete. All-In. 2008. (ENG., Illus.). 208p. (YA). (gr. 7). mass mkt. 5.99 *(978-1-4169-1326-9(2)*, Simon Pulse) Simon Pulse.

Hautzig, Deborah. Lewis Carroll's Alice in Wonderland. Rathke, Kathryn, illus. 2010. (Penguin Young Readers, Level 4 Ser.). (ENG.). 48p. (J). (gr. 3-4). mass mkt. 3.99 *(978-0-448-45269-2(3)*, Penguin Young Readers) Penguin Young Readers Group.

Havel, Geoff. Babies Bite. 2004. (Illus.). 146p. (J). pap. 13.50 *(978-1-920731-87-8(3))* Fremantle Pr. AUS. Dist: Independent Pubs. Group.

Havens, J. C. In My World: The Beginning. 2012. (ENG.). 117p. pap. 12.95 *(978-1-4327-9444-6(2))* Outskirts Pr., Inc.

Havran, Melissa. George Washington. 2013. 32p. pap. 19.99 *(978-1-4817-0157-0(6))* AuthorHouse.

Hawes, Alison. The Enormous Watermelon. Rodriguez, Elba, illus. 2016. (Cambridge Reading Adventures Ser.). (ENG.). 16p. pap. 6.56 *(978-1-107-54924-1(8))* Cambridge Univ. Pr.

—The Last Lemon Pink B Band. Anegón, Tamara, illus. 2016. (Cambridge Reading Adventures Ser.). (ENG.). 16p. pap. 6.56 *(978-1-107-54909-8(4))* Cambridge Univ. Pr.

Hawes, Charles Boardman. The Dark Frigate. unabr. ed. 2004. 246p. (J). (gr. 7-18). pap. 38.00 incl. audio *(978-0-8072-0448-1(X)*, Listening Library) Random Hse. Audio Publishing Group.

Hawking, Stephen W. & Hawking, Lucy. George's Secret Key to the Universe. Parsons, Garry, illus. (George's Secret Key Ser.). (ENG.). (J). (gr. 3-7). 2009. 336p. pap. 12.99 *(978-1-4169-8584-6(0))* 2007. 304p. 22.99 *(978-1-4169-5462-0(7))* Simon & Schuster Bks. For Young Readers. (Simon & Schuster Bks. For Young Readers).

Hawkins, Colin. Pirate Ship: A Pop-up Adventure. Hawkins, Colin et al, illus. 2006. 28p. (J). (gr. 4-8). reprint ed. 20.00 *(978-0-7567-9827-7(2))* DIANE Publishing Co.

Hawkins, Linda J. Who Gives a Hoot? Hunter Hoot,the Great Horned Owl. 2012. (ENG., Illus.). 40p. (J). pap. 9.99 *(978-1-937008-06-2(1))* Heart to Heart Publishing, Inc.

Hawkins, Mia K. The Broken Guild of Twelve Pirates, 1 vol. 2009. 201p. pap. 24.95 *(978-1-61546-333-6(X))* PublishAmerica, Inc.

Hawkins, Rachel. Rebel Belle. 2014. (Rebel Belle Ser.: 1). (ENG.). 352p. (YA). (gr. 7). 17.99 *(978-0-399-25693-6(8)*, G.P. Putnam's Sons Books for Young Readers) Penguin Young Readers Group.

Hawks, K. J. Lu-Don & the Kingdoms of Trent. 2012. 72p. pap. 27.49 *(978-1-4520-6359-1(1))* AuthorHouse.

Haws, Jacob. Telarthia: The Taln Crystal. 2013. 336p. pap. 29.95 *(978-1-63000-906-9(7))* PublishAmerica, Inc.

Hay, Louise L. & Olmos, Dan. The Adventures of Lulu. Smith-Moore, J. J., illus. 2005. (ENG.). 96p. per. 12.95 *(978-1-4019-0553-8(6))* Hay Hse., Inc.

Hayden, Gwendolen Lampshire. Mary Martha's Really Truly Stories: Book 3. 3rd ed. 2013. 130p. pap. 11.95 *(978-1-4796-0105-9(5))* TEACH Services, Inc.

Haydon, David J. The Spuds - the Circus Comes to Town. 2012. 20p. pap. *(978-1-78222-051-0(8))* Paragon Publishing, Rothersthorpe.

—The Spuds - the Fancy Dress Party. Ferns, Kevin, illus. 2011. 20p. pap. *(978-1-908341-08-2(4))* Paragon Publishing, Rothersthorpe.

Haydon, Elizabeth. The Tree of Water. Dorman, Brandon, illus. 2014. (Lost Journals of Ven Polypheme Ser.: 4). (ENG.). 400p. (J). (gr. 5-9). 17.99 *(978-0-7653-2059-9(2)*, 9780765320599, Starscape) Doherty, Tom Assocs., LLC.

Hayes, Angela. Just an Existence, 1 vol. 2010. 50p. pap. 16.95 *(978-1-60749-035-7(8))* PublishAmerica, Inc.

Hayes, Celeste. Cacao & the Jaded Orb: A Sphinx & Trevi Adventure. 2011. (Illus.). 62p. (J). pap. 22.95 *(978-0-9785695-2-5(0))* Adam's Creations Publishing, LLC.

—Enchanted Fairyland: A Sphinx & Trevi Adventure. 2011. (Illus.). 30p. (J). pap. 19.95 *(978-0-9785695-4-9(7))* Adam's Creations Publishing, LLC.

—The Puzzle Box of Nefertiti: A Sphinx & Trevi Adventure. Bishop, Christina, illus. 2011. 42p. (J). pap. 19.95 *(978-0-9785695-3-2(9))* Adam's Creations Publishing, LLC.

Hayes, Clair W. The Boy Allies in the Trenches: Midst Shot & Shell along the Aisne. 2007. (ENG.). 180p. pap. 19.99 *(978-1-4346-2323-2(8))*; 192p. pap. 21.99 *(978-1-4346-2381-2(5))* Creative Media Partners, LLC.

Hayes, Clyde & Jacobson, Pat. The Tunnels of Tecsuna. 2003. 122p. (J). pap. 9.95 *(978-1-55517-739-3(5)*, 1232038, Bonneville Bks.) Cedar Fort, Inc./CFI Distribution.

Hayes, Dale. Kc the Good Little Diggy Dog Who Does Naughty Things... Is Going Home. 2013. 32p. pap. *(978-1-4602-0428-3(X))* FriesenPress.

Hayes, John C. Splurge & the Theatre of Magic. 2008. 348p. pap. 22.00 *(978-1-84426-500-8(5))* Upfront Publishing Ltd. GBR. Dist: Printondemand-worldwide.com.

Hayes, Karel. The Christmas Visitors. 2013. (ENG., Illus.). 32p. (J). (gr. -1-3). 16.95 *(978-1-60893-248-1(6))* Down East Bks.

Hayes, Malcolm. The Dreamcatchers. 2006. 282p. pap. 20.14 *(978-1-4120-8320-1(6))* Trafford Publishing.

Hayes, Terri. The Day the Blue Puff Trees Bloomed. 2011. 36p. pap. 24.95 *(978-1-4560-6096-1(1))* America Star Bks.

Hayes, Tracey J. Bartina in Trouble Again. 2009. 64p. pap. 15.99 *(978-1-4415-2050-0(3))* Xlibris Corp.

Hayhurst, James L. The Adventures of Mercury Lane: Bad Commandments, Book No. 1. 2008. (Illus.). 212p. (YA). pap. 13.95 *(978-0-9729380-1-3(X)*, Parascension Pr.) Parascension, Inc.
Hayhurst/Parascension Press, James/Lyle. The Adventures of Mercury Lane: Bad Commandments, Book No.1. 2008. (Illus.). 212p. (YA). lib. bdg. 21.95 *(978-0-615-18212-4(7)*, Parascension Pr.) Parascension, Inc.
Haynes, Betsy. The Creepazoid's Nostrils. 2013. 118p. pap. 9.99 *(978-1-60820-858-6(3))* MLR Pr., LLC.
Haynes, Cate. Groovy Granny. Tholen, Shane, illus. 2003. 32p. (J). pap. 13.50 *(978-1-86368-332-6(1))* Fremantle Pr. AUS. Dist: Independent Pubs. Group.
Hays, Sharon. The Tumbleweed Family. 2011. 28p. pap. 15.99 *(978-1-4568-6825-3(X))* Xlibris Corp.
Hays, Steve. Beauty & the Boy: An Old Man's Story for a Dying Boy. 2006. (YA). 24.95 *(978-0-9759902-1-6(7))* Before Christmas Pr.
Hays, Tommy. What I Came to Tell You. 2013. (ENG.). 304p. (J). (gr. 5-7). 16.99 *(978-1-60684-433-5(4)*, Carolrhoda Bks.) Lerner Publishing Group.
Hazell, Carolyn. Pav the Plumber Saves the Day. 2011. 84p. (gr. 4-6). pap. 11.76 *(978-1-4567-8148-4(0))* AuthorHouse.
Hazell, Mark. Gift of the Wind Dancers. 2004. 140p. pap. *(978-1-84401-029-5(5))* Athena Pr.
—Miners of the Rainbow Stone (the Forest Children Series) 2006. 308p. pap. *(978-1-84401-625-9(0))* Athena Pr.
Head, Mat. Warduff & the Pelican Pirates. 2014. (ENG., Illus.). 32p. (J). (-k). pap. 9.99 *(978-1-84939-567-0(5))* Andersen Pr. GBR. Dist: Independent Pubs. Group.
Headford, Cheryl. The Face in the Window. 2013. 288p. pap. 14.99 *(978-1-60820-893-7(1))* MLR Pr., LLC.
Headley, Maria Dahvana. Aerie. 2016. (Magonia Ser.: 2). 320p. (YA). (gr. 8). 17.99 *(978-0-06-232055-1(6))* HarperCollins Pubs.
Healey, Bruce. The Delightfully Dreadful Tale of King Drod, 1 vol. 2009. 48p. pap. 16.95 *(978-1-61582-545-2(2))* America Star Bks.
Healy, Tim. The Birthday Chronicles: Volume I. 2013. 36p. pap. 15.99 *(978-1-4624-0628-9(9)*, Inspiring Voices) Author Solutions, Inc.
Heape, David. R. That's What Friends Do. l.t. ed. 2006. (ENG., Illus.). 28p. per. 9.95 *(978-1-4327-0177-2(0))* Outskirts Pr., Inc.
Heapy, Teresa. Very Little Red Riding Hood. Heap, Sue, illus. 2014. (Very Little Ser.). (ENG.). 32p. (J). (gr. -1-3). 16.99 *(978-0-544-28000-7(8)*, HMH Books For Young Readers) Houghton Mifflin Harcourt Publishing Co.
Hearn, Julie & Yankus, Marc. Sign of the Raven. 2005. (ENG., Illus.). 336p. (YA). 16.95 *(978-0-689-85734-8(9)*, Atheneum Bks. for Young Readers) Simon & Schuster Children's Publishing.
Hearn, Lian. Leyendas de los Otori I. 2004. (SPA.). 312p. (YA). (gr. 8-12). pap. 13.95 *(978-956-239-300-3(3))* Santillana USA Publishing Co., Inc.
Heath, Kathy. Camp Crazy Kids. 2006. 157p. pap. 24.95 *(978-1-4241-0260-0(X))* PublishAmerica, Inc.
Heaton, Layce D. The Many Tracks of Lap'n Tap, 1. Heaton, Layce D., illus. 2006. (Illus.). 32p. (J). lib. bdg. 18.95 *(978-0-9761128-3-9(3))* KB Bks. & More.
Hebert, Pamela. Elliot Finley's Jus' Plain Ole Daisy. 2005. pap. 14.95 *(978-0-9767696-0-6(3))* Oak Court Pr.
Heckler, Naomi & Kyelberg, Hope. The Adventures of Little Caesar ... Little Caesar's Christmas Adventure. 2008. 32p. pap. 14.98 *(978-0-557-00878-0(6))* Lulu Pr., Inc.
Heckman, Ashley. The Last Three Words. 2013. 104p. pap. *(978-1-77130-651-5(3))* Evernight Publishing.
Hedderwick, Mairi. Island Stories. Hedderwick, Mairi, illus. 2010. (Katie Morag Ser.: 12). (ENG., Illus.). 32p. (J). (gr. k-2). pap. 19.99 *(978-1-84941-088-5(7)*, Red Fox) Random House Children's Books GBR. Dist: Independent Pubs. Group.
—Katie Morag & the Grand Concert. Hedderwick, Mairi, illus. 2010. (Katie Morag Ser.: 6). (ENG., Illus.). 32p. (J). (gr. k-2). pap. 12.99 *(978-1-84941-087-8(9)*, Red Fox) Random House Children's Books GBR. Dist: Independent Pubs. Group.
—Katie Morag & the Riddles. Hedderwick, Mairi, illus. 2010. (Katie Morag Ser.: 10). (ENG., Illus.). 32p. (J). (gr. k-2). pap. 12.99 *(978-1-84941-092-2(5)*, Red Fox) Random House Children's Books GBR. Dist: Independent Pubs. Group.
—Katie Morag & the Two Grandmothers. Hedderwick, Mairi, illus. 2010. (Katie Morag Ser.: 2). (ENG., Illus.). 32p. (J). (gr. k-2). pap. 12.99 *(978-1-84941-086-1(0)*, Red Fox) Random House Children's Books GBR. Dist: Independent Pubs. Group.
—Katie Morag Delivers the Mail. Hedderwick, Mairi, illus. 2010. (Katie Morag Ser.: 1). (ENG., Illus.). 32p. (J). (gr. k-2). pap. 12.99 *(978-1-84941-091-5(7)*, Red Fox) Random House Children's Books GBR. Dist: Independent Pubs. Group.
Heddle, Rebecca. Puzzle Journey through Time. Spenceley, Annabel, illus. 2003. 32p. (J). pap. 6.95 *(978-0-7945-0440-3(X)*, Usborne) EDC Publishing.
Heder, Thyra. Fraidyzoo. 2013. (ENG., Illus.). 48p. (J). (gr. k-2). 16.95 *(978-1-4197-0776-6(0)*, Abrams Bks. for Young Readers) Abrams, Inc.
Heer, Dusty Rhoades. The Forest That Rains Frogs. 2012. (ENG.). 58p. pap. 19.95 *(978-1-4327-9303-6(9))* Outskirts Pr., Inc.
Hees, Miriam. The Adventures of Jilly & Brad: Noises in the Attic. Kinneman, D. Michael, illus. 2003. 128p. (J). pap. 5.95 *(978-0-9718348-4-2(9))* Blooming Tree Pr.
Heflick, LaMonte. The Story of Boney & Clyde. 2004. (Illus.). 64p. pap. 3.99 *(978-1-56175-911-8(2))* Remedia Pubns.
Heflin, Ronald. Caddo Lake. 2011. 156p. pap. 24.95 *(978-1-4626-0093-9(X))* America Star Bks.
Hegarty, Carol, ed. Teacher's Resource Guide. 2005. (Barclay Family Adventures 2 Ser.). (Illus.). 48p. (J). per. 9.95 *(978-1-56254-813-1(1)*, SP8131) Saddleback Educational Publishing, Inc.
Heger, Bryan. Valor & Virtues from the Mind of a Child, 1 vol. 2009. 124p. pap. 19.95 *(978-1-60749-625-0(9))* America Star Bks.
Heible, Beverly. A River Row: Andrew & Luke Fishing with Grandpa. 2012. 24p. 24.95 *(978-1-4626-6648-5(5))* America Star Bks.
Heide, Florence Parry. The Shrinking of Treehorn. 60p. (J). (gr. 1-3). pap. 6.95 *(978-0-8072-1327-8(6)*, Listening Library) Random Hse. Audio Publishing Group.
Heiden, Gina. Zippy, Lolly & Surfer Dude. 2009. 28p. pap. 16.50 *(978-1-60693-172-1(5)*, Eloquent Bks.) Strategic Book Publishing & Rights Agency (SBPRA).
Heil, Christopher. Wish Rings: A Second Beginning. 2003. 196p. pap. 14.95 *(978-0-595-29582-1(7)*, Writers Club Pr.) iUniverse, Inc.
Heilig, Heidi. The Ship Beyond Time. 2017. (Illus.). 464p. (YA). (gr. 8). 17.99 *(978-0-06-238078-4(8)*, Greenwillow Bks.) HarperCollins Pubs.
Heimbuch, Carol. Shadow Stallion. 2011. 170p. pap. 11.50 *(978-1-59330-693-9(8))* Aventine Pr.
Heimbuch, Carol Jo. Condor Caper. Martin, Fred, illus. 2008. 128p. pap. 11.50 *(978-1-59330-560-4(5))* Aventine Pr.
—Twilight Tracks. 2007. 112p. per. 10.95 *(978-1-59330-466-9(8))* Aventine Pr.
Heimerdinger, Chris. Escape from Zarahemla. 2011. 263p. (YA). pap. *(978-1-60861-539-1(1))* Covenant Communications.
Hein, Connie L. Toliver in Time; for a Journey West: History in a Nutshell. Theobald, Denise, illus. l.t. ed. 2005. 28p. (J). lib. bdg. 17.95 *(978-0-9740855-6-2(1))*; per. 9.95 *(978-0-9740855-7-9(X))* Still Water Publishing.
Heinlein, Robert A. Sixth Column. lib. bdg. 22.95 *(978-0-8488-1982-8(9))* Amereon Ltd.
The Heir of King Meldh: Book One of the Geometry of Power. 2004. (YA). per. 10.95 *(978-0-9747441-0-0(7))* Brainerd Enterprises.
Helakoski, Leslie. Woolbur. Harper, Lee, illus. 2008. 32p. (J). (gr. -1-3). 17.89 *(978-0-06-084727-2(1))* HarperCollins Pubs.
Hele, Bonita Jewel. Adventures That Lead to Home. Butler, Lisa, illus. 2012. (ENG.). 32p. (J). (gr. -1-3). 12.99 *(978-0-615-50182-6(6))* Hartlyn Kids Media, LLC.
Helemano, Butch. Sleeping Giant of Waimea. 2008. 25p. 9.95 *(978-0-9754567-1-2(7))* Kana'i Records.
Helget, Nicole. Wonder at the Edge of the World. 2017. (ENG., Illus.). 400p. (J). (gr. 3-7). pap. 7.99 *(978-0-316-24508-1(9))* Little, Brown Bks. for Young Readers.
Helixon, Tracy Schuldt. Little Isaac's Big Adventure. Foster, Jack, illus. 2012. 16p. pap. 9.95 *(978-1-61633-321-8(9))* Guardian Angel Publishing, Inc.
Hellberg, Joanne S. The Alv. Hellberg, Kristian & Hellberg, Madalyn, illus. 2010. 68p. pap. 23.49 *(978-1-4490-6868-4(5))* AuthorHouse.
Heller, Alyson. Raggedy Ann's Beach Bag. Thomas, Laura, illus. 2009. (Raggedy Ann & Me! Ser.). (ENG.). 10p. (J). (gr. -1-k). bds. 5.99 *(978-1-4169-5546-7(1)*, Little Simon) Little Simon.
Heller, Andrew. A Fine Mess. 2003. (J). 7.99 *(978-0-9722038-6-9(9))* Mr Do It All, Inc.
Hellman, Charles. Adventures in Sportsand - the Baseball Bully (with accompanying CD) The Baseball Bully. Tiritilli, Robert, illus. 2008. (Adventures in SportsLand: the Bully Ser.). 32p. pap. 19.95 *(978-0-935938-27-2(3))* Stogo, Malcolm Assocs.
—Adventures in SportsLand - the Basketball Bully (with accompanying CD) Tiritilli, Robert, illus. 2008. (Adventures in SportsLand: the Bully Ser.). 32p. (J). (gr. -1-3). 19.95 *(978-0-935938-28-9(1))* Stogo, Malcolm Assocs.
—Adventures in SportsLand - the Football Bully (with accompanying CD) Tiritilli, Robert, illus. 2008. (Adventures in SportsLand: the Bully Ser.). 32p. (J). (gr. -1-3). 19.95 *(978-0-935938-30-2(3))* Williams, Michael.
—Adventures in SportsLand - the Soccer Bully (with accompanying CD) Tiritilli, Robert, illus. 2008. (Adventures in SportsLand: the Bully Ser.). 32p. (gr. -1-3). pap. 19.95 *(978-0-935938-26-5(5))* Stogo, Malcolm Assocs.
Hellman, Charles S. The Baseball Bully. Tiritilli, Robert A., illus. 2013. 34p. pap. 9.25 *(978-0-935938-19-7(2))* LuckySports.
—The Football Bully. Tiritilli, Robert A., illus. 2013. 34p. pap. 9.25 *(978-0-935938-22-7(2))* LuckySports.
—The Hockey Bully. Tiritilli, Robert A., illus. 2013. 34p. pap. 9.25 *(978-0-935938-23-4(0))* LuckySports.
—The Volleyball Bully. Tiritilli, Robert A., illus. 2013. 34p. pap. 9.25 *(978-0-935938-53-1(2))* LuckySports.
Hellman, Charles S. & Tiritilli, Robert A. The Tennis Bully. 2013. 34p. pap. 9.25 *(978-0-935938-24-1(9))* LuckySports.
Hello Kitty: Fashion Music Wonderland. 2015. (ENG.). 48p. (J). pap. 6.99 *(978-1-4215-5903-2(X))* Viz Media.
Helm, Julie G. The Lost Monster Tales. Cary, Debbi, illus. 2010. 212p. pap. 14.49 *(978-1-4490-3823-6(9))* AuthorHouse.
Helmer, Marilyn. Pirate Island Treasure, 1 vol. Parkins, David, illus. 2013. (Orca Echoes Ser.). (ENG.). 64p. (J). (gr. 2-3). pap. 6.95 *(978-1-4598-0165-3(2))* Orca Bk. Pubs. USA.
Helmintoller, Matt & Baiz, Mark. One December Night. 2013. 30p. pap. 16.95 *(978-1-4908-1576-3(7)*, WestBow Pr.) Author Solutions, Inc.
Helvig, Kristi. Strange Skies. 2015. (ENG.). 272p. (YA). (gr. 9-12). 17.99 *(978-1-5124-0171-4(4)*, Carolrhoda Lab™) Lerner Publishing Group.
Hemmerle, Jamie. The Lost & Found Summer. 2010. (Illus.). 312p. pap. 15.95 *(978-1-4327-6268-1(0))* Outskirts Pr., Inc.
Hemphill, Rick, illus. The Adventures of Kirra & Rincon: Li'l Kids, Big Waves. 2005. 32p. (J). 17.99 *(978-0-9766408-0-6(5))* Kerr, Justin & Shelley.
Hemyng, Bracebridge. Jack Harkaway & His Son's Escape from the Brigands of Greece. 2004. reprint ed. pap. 37.95 *(978-1-4191-2705-2(5))* Kessinger Publishing, LLC.
Hen, Ms. Lucky Lottie. 2012. 58p. pap. 6.99 *(978-1-300-09653-5(5))* Lulu Pr., Inc.
Henderson, Dianne. The Frightening Old Mansion. 2006. 116p. pap. 19.95 *(978-1-4241-2486-2(7))* PublishAmerica, Inc.
Henderson, Hugh. VanDland. 2012. 112p. pap. 10.95 *(978-1-61204-859-8(5)*, Strategic Bk. Publishing) Strategic Book Publishing & Rights Agency (SBPRA).
Henderson, Mary Anne. The Adventures of Linda's Little Frog. 2004. 252p. 29.50 *(978-1-4184-1576-1(6))* AuthorHouse.
Henderson, Richard. One Christmas Night. Shackelford, David, illus. 2008. 32p. (J). 15.95 *(978-0-615-17629-1(1))* St. Clair Publishing.
Hendley, Jeff. Stump. Hendley, Tess, illus. 2007. (J). pap. *(978-0-9762014-7-2(X))* L'Edge Pr.
Hendrickson, Kevis. The Legend of Witch Bane. 2008. 348p. per. 11.95 *(978-1-4327-1298-3(5))* Outskirts Pr., Inc.
Hendrix, Jennifer & Schmitt, Laura. Oscar. 2012. 50p. pap. 20.95 *(978-1-4525-4938-5(9))* Balboa Pr.
Hendry, Frances. Quest for a Queen: The Lark. 2006. (Illus.). 251p. pap. *(978-1-905665-04-4(0))* Pollinger In Print.
Heneghan, James. Safe House, 1 vol. 2006. (ENG.). 160p. (J). (gr. 5-9). per. 8.95 *(978-1-55143-640-1(X))* Orca Bk. Pubs. USA.
Heneghan, James & McBay, Bruce. Nannycatch Chronicles, 1 vol. Valério, Geraldo, illus. 2005. (ENG.). 88p. (J). (gr. 3-5). 16.95 *(978-1-896580-56-2(4))* Tradewind Bks. CAN. Dist: Orca Bk. Pubs. USA.
Heneghan, Judith. The Magician's Apprentice. 2008. (Illus.). 168p. (J). (gr. 3-7). 16.95 *(978-0-8234-2150-3(3))* Holiday Hse., Inc.
Heneghan, Lou. The Turnarounders & the Arbuckle Rescue. Maguire, Jake, illus. 2013. 496p. pap. *(978-0-9573523-1-5(X))* Natus Publishing.
Henham, R. D. Bronze Dragon Codex. 2008. (Dragon Codices Ser.). (ENG., Illus.). 256p. (J). (gr. 4-7). 9.95 *(978-0-7869-4930-4(9)*, Mirrorstone) Wizards of the Coast.
Henkel, Pat. Jeffrey's Great Day. Elliott, Luke, illus. 2012. 16p. pap. 24.95 *(978-1-4626-7993-5(5))* America Star Bks.
Henkes, Kevin. Lilly's Big Day Standee. 2006. (J). *(978-0-06-087311-0(6))* HarperCollins Pubs.
Henley, Christian A. Adventures with Norky: Teamwork. 2005. (J). pap. 7.99 *(978-0-9744178-2-0(3))* Daughters Arise, LLC.
Hennessy, B. G. The Once upon a Time Map Book: Take a Tour of Six Enchanted Lands. Joyce, Peter, illus. 2010. (ENG.). 16p. (J). (gr. 1-4). pap. 8.99 *(978-0-7636-2682-2(1))* Candlewick Pr.
Hennesy, Carolyn. Pandora Gets Angry. (Mythic Misadventures Ser.). (ENG.). (YA). (gr. 3-7). 2011. 320p. 14.99 *(978-1-59990-440-5(3)*, 9781599904405) Vol. 5. 2012. 336p. pap. 7.99 *(978-1-59990-734-5(8)*, 9781599907345) Bloomsbury Publishing USA. (Bloomsbury USA Childrens).
—Pandora Gets Frightened. (Mythic Misadventures Ser.). (ENG.). 320p. (YA). (gr. 3-6). 2014. pap. 7.99 *(978-1-61963-251-6(9)*, 9781619632516) 2013. 16.99 *(978-1-59990-442-9(X)*, 9781599904429) Bloomsbury Publishing USA. (Bloomsbury USA Childrens).
—Pandora Gets Greedy. (Mythic Misadventures Ser.). (ENG., (YA). (gr. 3-6). 2013. Illus.). 320p. pap. 7.99 *(978-1-61963-010-9(9)*, 9781619630109) 2012. 304p. 15.99 *(978-1-59990-441-2(1)*, 9781599904412) Bloomsbury Publishing USA. (Bloomsbury USA Childrens).
—Pandora Gets Heart, No. 4. 2010. (Mythic Misadventures Ser.). (ENG.). 272p. (YA). (gr. 3-7). 14.99 *(978-1-59990-439-9(X)*, 9781599904399, Bloomsbury USA Childrens) Bloomsbury Publishing USA.
—Pandora Gets Jealous. 2009. (Mythic Misadventures Ser.). (ENG., Illus.). 288p. (YA). (gr. 3-6). pap. 7.99 *(978-1-59990-291-3(5)*, 9781599902913, Bloomsbury USA Childrens) Bloomsbury Publishing USA.
—Pandora Gets Lazy. (Mythic Misadventures Ser.). (ENG.). (YA). (gr. 3-6). 2010. 304p. pap. 7.99 *(978-1-59990-481-8(0)*, 9781599904818) 2009. 288p. 14.99 *(978-1-59990-198-5(6)*, 9781599901985) Bloomsbury Publishing USA. (Bloomsbury USA Childrens).
—Pandora Gets Vain. (Mythic Misadventures Ser.). (ENG., 288p. (YA). (gr. 3-6). 2008. Illus.). 14.99 *(978-1-59990-197-8(8)*, 9781599901978) Vol. 2. 2009. pap. 7.99 *(978-1-59990-329-3(6)*, 9781599903293) Bloomsbury Publishing USA. (Bloomsbury USA Childrens).
Henny, Rose. Teddy Finds His Way: A Teddy Tale. Henny, Rose, illus. l.t. ed. 2005. (Illus.). 22p. (J). per. 17.95 *(978-0-9705458-7-9(8))* Royalty Bks. International, Inc.
Henrikson, Jerilynn. Teddy, the Ghost Dog of Red Rocks. 2013. 72p. pap. 11.95 *(978-1-939054-23-4(0))* Rowe Publishing and Design.
Henry, Heather French. Claire's Magic Shoes. Henry, Heather French, illus. 2004. (Claire's Everyday Adventures Ser.). (ENG., Illus.). 32p. (J). (gr. k-4). 15.95 *(978-0-9706341-3-9(7)*, 1231609) Cubbie Blue Publishing.
Henry, Judy. Woodland Stories for Our Grandchildren. 2013. 40p. pap. 19.99 *(978-1-4669-7752-5(3))* Trafford Publishing.
Henry, Kristina. The Turtle Tank, 1 vol. Ambler, Laura & Brown, Amanda, illus. 2011. (ENG.). 32p. (J). 16.99 *(978-0-7643-3843-4(9)*, 9780764338434, Schiffer Publishing Ltd) Schiffer Publishing, Ltd.
Henry, LaTosha. Dino Treasure Hunt, 1 vol. Friesen, Wayne, illus. 2010. 16p. 24.95 *(978-1-4489-3966-4(6))* PublishAmerica, Inc.
Henry, Pam. Cold Call. 2011. 200p. *(978-1-84903-066-3(9))*; pap. *(978-1-84903-065-6(0))* Schiel & Denver Publishing Ltd.
Henry, T. K. Rickey & Rachel, the Cats without Tails & Their Awesome Adventure. 2007. 40p. (J). pap. 8.00 *(978-0-8059-7224-5(2))* Dorrance Publishing Co., Inc.
Henry, William. Tir na NOg: A New Adventure. Amault, Delphine, illus. 2009. (ENG.). 128p. (J). pap. 25.95 *(978-1-85635-597-1(7))* Mercier Pr., Ltd., The IRL. Dist: Dufour Editions, Inc.
Hensel, Gege. The a B C Animal Adventures. 2012. 68p. pap. 32.99 *(978-1-62419-788-8(4))* Salem Author Services.
Hensel, Rita. Whooo's the Chicken Thief, a Humble Stew Book, 1 vol. 2010. 50p. pap. 16.95 *(978-1-61546-640-5(1))* America Star Bks.
Hensel, Sylvia. The a B C Animal Adventures. 2012. 68p. 42.99 *(978-1-62419-789-5(2))* Salem Author Services.
Hensler, K. Why Worry? The Adventures of Bay/Bob/A/Loo/Bop Everything in Moderation. 2008. 48p. pap. 24.95 *(978-1-60610-813-0(1))* America Star Bks.
Henty, George Alfred. Bravest of the Brave. 2006. pap. *(978-1-4068-1274-9(9))* Echo Library.
—The Cat of Bubastes. 2006. (ENG.). pap. 33.95 *(978-1-4286-0382-0(4))* Kessinger Publishing, LLC.
—The Cat of Bubastes: A Tale of Ancient Egypt. 2011. 344p. pap. 19.95 *(978-1-61179-125-9(1))* Fireship Pr.
—In Freedom's Cause: A Story of Wallace & Bruce. 2004. reprint ed. pap. 1.99 *(978-1-4192-2572-7(3))* Kessinger Publishing, LLC.
—In Freedom's Cause: A Tale of Wallace & Bruce. 2011. 372p. pap. 19.95 *(978-1-61179-152-5(9))* Fireship Pr.
—In the Heart of the Rockies. l.t. ed. 2006. 322p. pap. 24.99 *(978-1-4264-3253-8(4))* Creative Media Partners, LLC.
—In the Heart of the Rockies. 2004. reprint ed. pap. 27.95 *(978-1-4191-2600-0(8))*; pap. 1.99 *(978-1-4192-2600-7(2))* Kessinger Publishing, LLC.
—In the Heart of the Rockies: An Adventure on the Colorado River. 2005. (Dover Children's Classics Ser.). (ENG.). 304p. (YA). (gr. 3-8). per. 8.95 *(978-0-486-44214-3(4))* Dover Pubns., Inc.
—A March on London: A Story of Wat Tyler's Insurrection. l.t. ed. 2005. 596p. pap. *(978-1-84637-209-4(7))* Echo Library.
—A March on London: A Story of Wat Tyler's Insurrection. 2004. reprint ed. pap. 27.95 *(978-1-4191-0224-0(9))*; pap. 1.99 *(978-1-4192-0224-7(3))* Kessinger Publishing, LLC.
—A March on London: Being a Story of Wat Tyler's Insurrection. l.t. ed. 2007. 316p. pap. 24.99 *(978-1-4264-3096-1(5))* Creative Media Partners, LLC.
—No Surrender! A Tale of the Rising in la Vendee. l.t. ed. 2007. 330p. pap. 24.99 *(978-1-4346-3575-4(9))* Creative Media Partners, LLC.
—The Stone Chest or the Secret of Cedar Island. 2004. reprint ed. pap. 1.99 *(978-1-4192-8354-3(5))*; pap. 15.95 *(978-1-4191-8354-6(0))* Kessinger Publishing, LLC.
—Through Three Campaigns: A Story of Chitral Tirah & Ashanti. 2007. (ENG.). 318p. pap. 23.99 *(978-1-4346-4617-0(3))*; 356p. pap. 26.99 *(978-1-4346-4618-7(1))* Creative Media Partners, LLC.
—The Treasure of the Incas: The Treasure of the Incas. 2007. (ENG.). 308p. pap. 23.99 *(978-1-4264-4045-8(6))* Creative Media Partners, LLC.
—True to the Old Flag. 2007. 286p. pap. 21.99 *(978-1-4264-4288-9(2))*; (ENG.). 318p. pap. 24.99 *(978-1-4264-4352-7(8))* Creative Media Partners, LLC.
—Under Drake's Flag: A Tale of the Spanish Main. 2007. (ENG.). 290p. pap. 21.99 *(978-1-4346-3056-8(0))*; 322p. pap. 24.99 *(978-1-4346-3070-4(6))* Creative Media Partners, LLC.
—Under Drake's Flag: A Tale of the Spanish Main. 2005. (Dover Children's Classics Ser.). (ENG., Illus.). 304p. (J). (gr. 3-8). per. 6.99 *(978-0-486-44215-0(2))* Dover Pubns., Inc.
—With Buller in Natal: Or a Born Leader. 2007. (ENG.). 290p. pap. 21.99 *(978-1-4264-9358-4(4))*; 324p. pap. 24.99 *(978-1-4264-9739-1(3))* Creative Media Partners, LLC.
—Wulf the Saxon. 2007. 322p. pap. 23.99 *(978-1-4264-2278-2(4))*; (ENG.). 360p. pap. 26.99 *(978-1-4264-2313-0(6))* Creative Media Partners, LLC.
Hepfler, Caroline Ann. Huckleberrys Hiccups. 2009. 20p. pap. 11.25 *(978-1-60693-917-8(3)*, Strategic Bk. Publishing) Strategic Book Publishing & Rights Agency (SBPRA).
Hepola, Catherine R. The Great Toadie. 2009. 60p. pap. 23.99 *(978-1-4389-3451-8(3))* AuthorHouse.
Herbach, Geoff. Nothing Special. 2012. (Felton Reinstein Trilogy Ser.: 2). (ENG., Illus.). 304p. (YA). (gr. 7-12). pap. 12.99 *(978-1-4022-6507-5(7))* Sourcebooks, Inc.
Herbert, Bethany Zohner. The Perfect Fool. 2015. 279p. (YA). pap. 17.99 *(978-1-4621-1620-1(5))* Cedar Fort, Inc./CFI Distribution.
Herbert, Frances. Fran's Van & the Arran Adventure. 2017. (ENG., Illus.). (J). (gr. k-2). pap. ***(978-1-78222-498-3(X))*** Paragon Publishing, Rothersthorpe.
—Fran's Van & the Magic Box. Herbert, Frances, illus. 2013. (Illus.). 24p. pap. *(978-1-78222-085-5(2))* Paragon Publishing, Rothersthorpe.
—Fran's Van & the Naughty Terrier. Herbert, Frances, illus. 2013. (Illus.). 32p. pap. *(978-1-78222-164-7(6))* Paragon Publishing, Rothersthorpe.
Herbert Hilligan & His Magical Adventure Curriculum Guide. 2004. ring bd. 24.95 *(978-0-9743335-4-0(9))* Imaginative Publishing, Ltd.
Herbert Hilligan's Lone Star Adventure Curriculum Guide. 2004. ring bd. 24.95 *(978-0-9743335-7-1(3))* Imaginative Publishing, Ltd.
Herbert Hilligan's Prehistoric Adventure Curriculum Guide. 2004. ring bd. 24.95 *(978-0-9743335-5-7(7))* Imaginative Publishing, Ltd.
Herbert Hilligan's Tropical Adventure Curriculum Guide. 2004. ring bd. 24.95 *(978-0-9743335-6-4(5))* Imaginative Publishing, Ltd.
Herda, Frank A. The Cup of Death: Cronicles of the Dragons of the Magi. 2007. 180p. 16.95 *(978-1-4327-0922-8(4))*; 212p. per. 9.95 *(978-1-4327-1412-3(0))* Outskirts Pr., Inc.
Hereford, L. F. Gerry the Grape. Skardarasy, Doreen L., illus. 2005. (J). pap. *(978-0-9728969-9-3(6))* Acorn Publishing.
Hergé. The Adventures of Tintin, 8. collector's gif. ed. Set. 2008. (ENG.). (gr. 3-17). 165.00 *(978-0-316-00668-2(8))* Vol. 1. 2009. 192p. 18.99 *(978-0-316-18979-8(0))* Vol. 2. 2009. 192p. 18.99 *(978-0-316-18983-5(9))* Vol. 3. 2009. 192p. 18.99 *(978-0-316-18986-6(3))* Vol. 4. 2009. 192p. 18.99 *(978-0-316-18987-3(1))* Little, Brown Bks. for Young Readers.
—America. Orig. Title: Tintin en Amerique. (Illus.). 62p. (J). 24.95 *(978-0-8288-5000-1(3))* French & European Pubns., Inc.
—Der Arumbaya-Fetisch. (GER., Illus.). 62p. (J). pap. 19.95 *(978-0-8288-5008-7(9))* French & European Pubns., Inc.
—El Asunto Tornasol. (SPA., Illus.). 62p. (J). 19.95 *(978-0-8288-5009-4(7))* French & European Pubns., Inc.
—Aterrizaje en la Luna. (SPA., Illus.). 62p. (J). 19.95 *(978-0-8288-5010-0(0))* French & European Pubns., Inc.
—The Black Island. (Illus.). 62p. (J). 19.95 *(978-0-8288-5012-4(7))* French & European Pubns., Inc.
—The Black Island. 2012. (Adventures of Tintin: Young Readers Edition Ser.). (ENG., Illus.). 96p. (J). (gr. 3-17). pap. 11.00 *(978-0-316-13387-6(6))* Little, Brown Bks. for Young Readers.
—Der Blaue Lotos. (GER., Illus.). 62p. (J). pap. 19.95 *(978-0-8288-5013-1(5))* French & European Pubns., Inc.
—The Blue Lotus. (Illus.). (J). 19.95 *(978-0-8288-5480-1(7))* French & European Pubns., Inc.
—The Blue Lotus. 2011. (Adventures of Tintin: Young Readers Edition Ser.). (ENG., Illus.). 96p. (J). (gr. 3-17). pap. 9.99 *(978-0-316-13382-1(5))* Little, Brown Bks. for Young Readers.
—The Broken Ear. (Illus.). 62p. (J). 24.95 *(978-0-8288-5086-5(0))* French & European Pubns., Inc.
—The Broken Ear. 2011. (Adventures of Tintin: Young Readers Edition Ser.). (ENG., Illus.). 96p. (J). (gr. 3-17). pap.

11.00 (978-0-316-13385-2(X)) Little, Brown Bks. for Young Readers.
—The Calculus Affair. (Illus.). 62p. (J). 19.95 (978-0-8288-5014-8(3)) French & European Pubns., Inc.
—El Cangrejo Pinzas Oro. (SPA., Illus.). 62p. (J). 19.95 (978-0-8288-5015-5(1)) French & European Pubns., Inc.
—The Castafiore Emerald. (Illus.). 62p. (J). 19.95 (978-0-8288-5016-2(X)) French & European Pubns., Inc.
—El Cetro de Ottokar. (SPA., Illus.). 62p. (J). 19.95 (978-0-8288-5017-9(8)) French & European Pubns., Inc.
—El Cetro de Ottokar. 2007. (Aventuras de Tintin Ser.). (SPA., Illus.). 62p. reprint ed. 22.95 (978-1-59497-345-1(8)) Public Square Bks.
—Les Cigares du Pharaon.Tr. of Cigars of the Pharaoh. (FRE., Illus.). 62p. (J). 19.95 (978-0-8288-5020-9(8)) French & European Pubns., Inc.
—Los Cigarros del Faraon. (SPA., Illus.). 62p. (J). 19.95 (978-0-8288-5019-3(4)) French & European Pubns., Inc.
—Cigars of the Pharaoh.Tr. of Cigares du Pharoan. (Illus.). 62p. (J). 19.95 (978-0-8288-5021-6(6)) French & European Pubns., Inc.
—Cigars of the Pharaoh. 2011. (Adventures of Tintin: Young Readers Edition Ser.).Tr. of Cigares du Pharoan. (ENG., Illus.). 96p. (J). (gr. 3-17). pap. 11.00 (978-0-316-13388-3(4)) Little, Brown Bks. for Young Readers.
—The Crab with the Golden Claws. (Illus.). 62p. (J). (gr. 3-8). 19.95 (978-0-8288-5023-0(2)) French & European Pubns., Inc.
—The Crab with the Golden Claws. 2012. (Adventures of Tintin: Young Readers Edition Ser.). (ENG., Illus.). 96p. (J). (gr. 3-17). pap. 8.99 (978-0-316-19876-9(5)) Little, Brown Bks. for Young Readers.
—Le Crabe aux Pinces d'Or.Tr. of Crab with the Golden Claws. (FRE., Illus.). (J). (gr. 7-9). ring bd. 19.95 (978-0-8288-5025-4(9)) French & European Pubns., Inc.
—Destination Moon.Tr. of Objectif Lune. (J). (gr. 3-8). ring bd. 19.95 (978-0-8288-5026-1(7)); (Illus.). 62p. 19.95 (978-0-8288-5027-8(5)) French & European Pubns., Inc.
—Il Drago Blu. (ITA., Illus.). 62p. (J). pap. 19.95 (978-0-8288-5028-5(3)) French & European Pubns., Inc.
—La Estrella Misteriosa. (SPA., Illus.). 62p. (J). 19.95 (978-0-8288-5029-2(1)) French & European Pubns., Inc.
—Explorers of the Moon. (Illus.). 62p. (J). 19.95 (978-0-8288-5031-5(3)) French & European Pubns., Inc.
—Der Fall Bienlein. (GER., Illus.). 62p. (J). pap. 19.95 (978-0-8288-5033-9(X)) French & European Pubns., Inc.
—Flight 714. (Illus.). 62p. (J). 19.95 (978-0-8288-5034-6(8)) French & European Pubns., Inc.
—Flug 714 nach Sydney. (GER., Illus.). 62p. (J). pap. 19.95 (978-0-8288-5035-3(6)) French & European Pubns., Inc.
—Das Geheimnis der "Einhorn" (GER., Illus.). 62p. (J). pap. 19.95 (978-0-8288-5036-0(4)) French & European Pubns., Inc.
—Der Geheimnisvolle Stern. (GER., Illus.). 62p. (J). pap. 19.95 (978-0-8288-5037-7(2)) French & European Pubns., Inc.
—Il Granchio d'Oro. (ITA., Illus.). 62p. (J). pap. 19.95 (978-0-8288-5038-4(0)) French & European Pubns., Inc.
—L' Ile Noire.Tr. of Black Island. (FRE., Illus.). (J). (gr. 7-9). ring bd. 19.95 (978-0-8288-5039-1(9)) French & European Pubns., Inc.
—Im Reiche des Schwarzen Goldes. (GER., Illus.). 62p. (J). pap. 19.95 (978-0-8288-5040-7(2)) French & European Pubns., Inc.
—La Isla Negra. (SPA., Illus.). 62p. (J). 19.95 (978-0-8288-5041-4(0)) French & European Pubns., Inc.
—La Isla Negra. 2007. (Aventuras de Tintin Ser.). (SPA., Illus.). 62p. reprint ed. 22.95 (978-1-59497-344-4(X)) Public Square Bks.
—Las Joyas de la Castafiore. (SPA., Illus.). 62p. (J). 19.95 (978-0-8288-5042-1(9)) French & European Pubns., Inc.
—Die Juwelen der Sangerin. (GER., Illus.). 62p. (J). pap. 19.95 (978-0-8288-5043-8(7)) French & European Pubns., Inc.
—King Ottokar's Sceptre. (Illus.). 62p. (J). 19.95 (978-0-8288-5044-5(5)) French & European Pubns., Inc.
—Kohle an Bord. (GER., Illus.). 62p. (J). pap. 19.95 (978-0-8288-5045-2(3)) French & European Pubns., Inc.
—Konig Ottokar's Zepter. (GER., Illus.). 62p. (J). pap. 19.95 (978-0-8288-5046-9(1)) French & European Pubns., Inc.
—Die Krabbe mit den Goldenen Scheren. (GER., Illus.). 62p. (J). pap. 19.95 (978-0-8288-5047-6(X)) French & European Pubns., Inc.
—Land of Black Gold. Orig. Title: Tintin au Pays de l'Or Noir. (Illus.). 62p. (J). 19.95 (978-0-8288-5048-3(8)) French & European Pubns., Inc.
—Lo Scettro di Ottokar. (ITA., Illus.). 62p. (J). pap. 19.95 (978-0-8288-5061-2(5)) French & European Pubns., Inc.
—El Loto Azul.Tr. of Blue Lotus. (SPA., Illus.). 62p. (J). 19.95 (978-0-8288-5049-0(6)) French & European Pubns., Inc.
—El Loto Azul. (Tintin Ser.).Tr. of Blue Lotus. (SPA.). 64p. (J). 14.95 (978-84-261-1418-1(0)) Juventud, Editorial ESP. Dist: Distribooks, Inc.
—Le Lotus Bleu.Tr. of Blue Lotus. (FRE.). (J). (gr. 2-9). 19.95 (978-0-8288-5050-6(X)) French & European Pubns., Inc.
—Objectif Lune.Tr. of Destination Moon. (FRE., Illus.). (J). (gr. 7-9). ring bd. 19.95 (978-0-8288-5051-3(8)) French & European Pubns., Inc.
—Objetivo la Luna. (SPA., Illus.). 62p. (J). 19.95 (978-0-8288-5052-0(6)) French & European Pubns., Inc.
—On a Marche sur la Lune. (Tintin Ser.).Tr. of Explorers on the Moon. (FRE.). (J). pap. 21.95 (978-2-203-00116-9(X)) Casterman, Editions FRA. Dist: Distribooks, Inc.
—On a Marche sur la Lune.Tr. of Explorers on the Moon. (FRE., Illus.). (J). (gr. 7-9). ring bd. 19.95 (978-0-8288-5053-7(4)) French & European Pubns., Inc.
—L' Oreille Cassee.Tr. of Broken Ear. (FRE., Illus.). 62p. (J). 19.95 (978-0-8288-5054-4(2)) French & European Pubns., Inc.
—La Oreja Rota. (SPA., Illus.). 62p. (J). 19.95 (978-0-8288-5055-1(0)) French & European Pubns., Inc.
—Prisoners of the Sun. (Illus.). 62p. (J). 24.95 (978-0-8288-5056-8(9)) French & European Pubns., Inc.
—Prisoners of the Sun. 2014. (Adventures of Tintin: Young Readers Edition Ser.). (ENG., Illus.). 96p. (J). (gr. 3-17). pap. 9.00 (978-0-316-40917-9(0)) Little, Brown Bks. for Young Readers.
—Red Rackham's Treasure. Orig. Title: Tresor de Rackham le Rouge. (Illus.). 62p. (J). 24.95 (978-0-8288-5057-5(7)) French & European Pubns., Inc.
—Red Rackham's Treasure. Orig. Title: Tresor de Rackham le Rouge. (ENG., Illus.). (J). (gr. 3-17). 2012. 64p. 60.00 (978-0-316-23054-4(5)) 2011. 96p. pap. 9.99 (978-0-316-13384-5(1)) Little, Brown Bks. for Young Readers.
—The Red Sea Sharks. (Illus.). (J). (gr. 3-8). 24.95 (978-0-8288-5058-2(5)) French & European Pubns., Inc.
—Reiseziel Mond. (GER., Illus.). 62p. (J). pap. 24.95 (978-0-8288-5059-9(3)) French & European Pubns., Inc.
—Le Sceptre d' Ottokar.Tr. of King Ottokar's Sceptre. (FRE., Illus.). (J). (gr. 7-9). ring bd. 24.95 (978-0-8288-5060-5(7)) French & European Pubns., Inc.
—Der Schatz Rackhams des Roten. (GER., Illus.). 62p. (J). pap. 24.95 (978-0-8288-5062-9(3)) French & European Pubns., Inc.
—Schritte auf dem Mond. (GER., Illus.). 62p. (J). pap. 24.95 (978-0-8288-5063-6(1)) French & European Pubns., Inc.
—Die Schwarze Insel. (GER., Illus.). 62p. (J). pap. 24.95 (978-0-8288-5064-3(X)) French & European Pubns., Inc.
—Secret de la Licorne.Tr. of Secret of the Unicorn. (FRE., Illus.). (J). (gr. 7-9). 24.95 (978-0-8288-5065-0(8)) French & European Pubns., Inc.
—The Secret of the Unicorn. Orig. Title: Secret de la Licorne. (Illus.). 62p. (J). 24.95 (978-0-8288-5066-7(6)) French & European Pubns., Inc.
—The Secret of the Unicorn. Orig. Title: Secret de la Licorne. (ENG., Illus.). (J). (gr. 3-17). 2012. 64p. 60.00 (978-0-316-23055-1(3)) 2011. 96p. pap. 9.99 (978-0-316-13386-9(8)) Little, Brown Bks. for Young Readers.
—El Secreto del Unicornio. (SPA., Illus.). 62p. (J). 24.95 (978-0-8288-5067-4(4)) French & European Pubns., Inc.
—Il Segreto del Liocorno. (ITA., Illus.). 62p. (J). pap. 24.95 (978-0-8288-5068-1(2)) French & European Pubns., Inc.
—Sept Boules de Cristal. (FRE., Illus.). (J). (gr. 7-9). 24.95 (978-0-8288-5069-8(0)) French & European Pubns., Inc.
—Le Sette Sfere di Cristallo. (ITA., Illus.). 62p. (J). pap. 24.95 (978-0-8288-5070-4(4)) French & European Pubns., Inc.
—The Seven Crystal Balls. (Illus.). 62p. (J). (gr. 3-8). 24.95 (978-0-8288-5071-1(2)) French & European Pubns., Inc.
—The Shooting Star. (Illus.). (J). (gr. 3-8). ring bd. 24.95 (978-0-8288-5073-5(9)) French & European Pubns., Inc.
—The Shooting Star. 2012. (Adventures of Tintin: Young Readers Edition Ser.). (ENG., Illus.). 96p. (J). (gr. 3-7). pap. 8.99 (978-0-316-19875-2(7)) Little, Brown Bks. for Young Readers.
—Die Sieben Kristallkugeln. (GER., Illus.). 62p. (J). pap. 24.95 (978-0-8288-5072-8(0)) French & European Pubns., Inc.
—Las Siete Bolas de Cristal. (SPA., Illus.). 62p. (J). 24.95 (978-0-8288-5074-2(7)) French & European Pubns., Inc.
—I Sigari del Faraone. (ITA., Illus.). 62p. (J). pap. 24.95 (978-0-8288-5075-9(5)) French & European Pubns., Inc.
—Der Sonnentempel. (GER., Illus.). 62p. (J). pap. 24.95 (978-0-8288-5076-6(3)) French & European Pubns., Inc.
—Stock de Coque. (FRE., Illus.). 62p. (J). 24.95 (978-0-8288-5077-3(1)) French & European Pubns., Inc.
—Temple du Soleil. (FRE., Illus.). (J). (gr. 7-9). 24.95 (978-0-8288-5078-0(X)) French & European Pubns., Inc.
—El Templo del Sol. (SPA., Illus.). 62p. (J). 24.95 (978-0-8288-5079-7(8)) French & European Pubns., Inc.
—Il Templo del Sol. (ITA., Illus.). 62p. (J). pap. 24.95 (978-0-8288-5080-3(1)) French & European Pubns., Inc.
—El Tesoro de Rackham el Rojo. (SPA., Illus.). 62p. (J). 24.95 (978-0-8288-5081-0(X)) French & European Pubns., Inc.
—Il Tesoro di Rakam. (ITA., Illus.). 62p. (J). pap. 24.95 (978-0-8288-5082-7(8)) French & European Pubns., Inc.
—Tim und der Haifschsee. (GER., Illus.). 62p. (J). pap. 24.95 (978-0-8288-5084-1(4)) French & European Pubns., Inc.
—Tim und die Picaros. (GER., Illus.). 62p. (J). pap. 24.95 (978-0-8288-5085-8(2)) French & European Pubns., Inc.
—Tim und Struppi 19. Tim in Tibet. (GER., Illus.). 62p. (J). pap. 24.95 (978-0-8288-5083-4(6)) French & European Pubns., Inc.
—Tintin: El cangrejo de las pinzas de Oro. 2007. (SPA., Illus.). 64p. reprint ed. 22.95 (978-1-59497-346-8(6)) Public Square Bks.
—Tintin & the Golden Fleece. (J). (gr. 3-8). 24.95 (978-0-8288-5087-2(9)) French & European Pubns., Inc.
—Tintin & the Lake of Sharks. (Illus.). 62p. (J). 24.95 (978-0-416-78950-8(1)) French & European Pubns., Inc.
—Tintin & the Picaros. Orig. Title: Tintin et les Picaros. (Illus.). 62p. (J). 24.95 (978-0-8288-5089-6(5)) French & European Pubns., Inc.
—Tintin au Congo. (FRE., Illus.). (J). (gr. 7-9). 24.95 (978-0-8288-5090-2(9)) French & European Pubns., Inc.
—Tintin au Pays de l'Or Noir.Tr. of Land of Black Gold. (FRE.). (J). (gr. 7-9). 24.95 (978-0-8288-5091-9(7)) French & European Pubns., Inc.
—Tintin au Tibet.Tr. of Tintin in Tibet. (J). (gr. 7-9). ring bd. 24.95 (978-0-8288-5092-6(5)) French & European Pubns., Inc.
—Tintin en Amerique. Orig. Title: Tintin in America. (Illus.). 62p. (J). (SPA.). 24.95 (978-0-8288-5094-0(1)); (FRE., 24.95 (978-0-8288-5093-3(3)) French & European Pubns., Inc.
—Tintin en el Congo. (SPA., Illus.). 62p. (J). 24.95 (978-0-8288-5095-7(X)) French & European Pubns., Inc.
—Tintin en el Pais del Oro Negro.Tr. of Land of Black Gold. (SPA., Illus.). 62p. (J). 24.95 (978-0-8288-4995-1(1)) French & European Pubns., Inc.
—Tintin en Tibet. (SPA., Illus.). 62p. (J). 24.95 (978-0-8288-4996-8(X)) French & European Pubns., Inc.
—Tintin et les Picaros.Tr. of Tintin & the Picaros. (FRE., Illus.). 62p. (J). 24.95 (978-0-8288-4997-5(8)) French & European Pubns., Inc.
—Tintin im Amerika.Tr. of Tintin in America. (GER., Illus.). 62p. (J). pap. 24.95 (978-0-8288-4999-9(4)) French & European Pubns., Inc.
—Tintin im Kongo. (GER., Illus.). 62p. (J). pap. 24.95 (978-0-8288-4998-2(6)) French & European Pubns., Inc.
—Tintin in America. 2011. (Adventures of Tintin: Young Readers Edition Ser.). Orig. Title: Tintin en Amerique. (ENG., Illus.). 96p. (J). (gr. 3-17). pap. 9.99 (978-0-316-13380-7(9)) Little, Brown Bks. for Young Readers.
—Tintin in Tibet. Orig. Title: Tintin au Tibet. (Illus.). 62p. (J). 24.95 (978-0-8288-5001-8(1)) French & European Pubns., Inc.
—Tintin y los Picaros. (SPA., Illus.). 62p. (J). 24.95 (978-0-8288-5002-5(X)) French & European Pubns., Inc.
—Tresor de Rackham le Rouge.Tr. of Red Rackham's Treasure. (FRE., Illus.). 62p. (J). (gr. 7-9). 24.95 (978-0-8288-5003-2(8)) French & European Pubns., Inc.
—Vol 714 Pour Sydney Vol. 714: Flight 714 for Sydney. (FRE., Illus.). 62p. 21.95 (978-2-203-00121-3(6)) Casterman, Editions FRA. Dist: Distribooks, Inc.
—Vuelo 714 para Sidney. (SPA., Illus.). 62p. (J). 24.95 (978-0-8288-5004-9(6)) French & European Pubns., Inc.
—Y las Naranjas Azules. (SPA., Illus.). 62p. (J). 24.95 (978-0-8288-5005-6(4)) French & European Pubns., Inc.
—Die Zigarren des Pharaos. (GER., Illus.). 62p. (J). pap. 24.95 (978-0-8288-5006-3(2)) French & European Pubns., Inc.
Hergé & Egmont Books Staff. Tintin & the Picaros. 2003. Orig. Title: Tintin et les Picaros. (ENG.). 64p. (978-1-4052-0823-9(6)) Egmont Bks., Ltd.
—Tintin in Tibet. 2003. Orig. Title: Tintin au Tibet. (ENG., Illus.). 64p. (978-1-4052-0819-2(8)) Egmont Bks., Ltd.
Hergé & I, Herge-tintin Rustica. Los Cigarros del Faraon. (Tintin Ser.). (SPA.). 46p. (J). 14.95 (978-84-261-1406-8(7)) Juventud, Editorial ESP. Dist: Distribooks, Inc.
—La Isla Negra. (Tintin Ser.). (SPA.). 64p. (J). 14.95 (978-84-261-1417-4(2)) Juventud, Editorial ESP. Dist: Distribooks, Inc.
—La Oreja Rota. (Tintin Ser.). (SPA.). 64p. (J). 14.95 (978-84-261-1424-2(5)) Juventud, Editorial ESP. Dist: Distribooks, Inc.
—Tintin en Amerique. (Tintin Ser.). Orig. Title: Tintin in America. (SPA.). 64p. (J). 14.95 (978-84-261-1400-6(8)) Juventud, Editorial ESP. Dist: Distribooks, Inc.
—Tintin en el Congo. (Tintin Ser.). (SPA.). 64p. (J). 14.95 (978-84-261-1401-3(6)) Juventud, Editorial ESP. Dist: Distribooks, Inc.
Hergé & Ii, Herge-tintin Cartone. El Tesoro de Rackham el Rojo. 19th ed. 2008. (SPA., Illus.). 64p. (J). (gr. 5-7). pap. 19.99 (978-84-261-1036-7(3)) Juventud, Editorial ESP. Dist: Lectorum Pubns., Inc.
Hergé & Ii, Herge-tintin Rustica. La Estrella Misteriosa. (Tintin Ser.). (SPA.). 64p. (J). 14.95 (978-84-261-1416-7(4)) Juventud, Editorial ESP. Dist: Distribooks, Inc.
—El Secreto del Unicornio. (Tintin Ser.). (SPA.). 64p. (J). 14.95 (978-84-261-1420-4(2)) Juventud, Editorial ESP. Dist: Distribooks, Inc.
Hergé & Iv, Herge-tintin Rustica. Tintin y los Picaros. (Tintin Ser.). (SPA.). 64p. (J). 14.95 (978-84-261-1389-4(3)) Juventud, Editorial ESP. Dist: Distribooks, Inc.
—Vuelo 714 para Sidney. (Tintin Ser.). (SPA.). 64p. (J). 14.95 (978-84-261-1404-4(0)) Juventud, Editorial ESP. Dist: Distribooks, Inc.
Hergé, et al. El Cetro de Ottokar. (Tintin Ser.). (SPA.). 64p. (J). 14.95 (978-84-261-1415-0(6)) Juventud, Editorial ESP. Dist: Distribooks, Inc.
—Objetivo la Luna. (Tintin Ser.). (SPA.). 64p. (J). 14.95 (978-84-261-1419-8(9)) Juventud, Editorial ESP. Dist: Distribooks, Inc.
—The Secret of the Unicorn. 2003. Orig. Title: Secret de la Licorne. (ENG.). 64p. (978-1-4052-0810-9(4)) Egmont Bks., Ltd.
—Las Siete Bolas de Cristal. (Tintin Ser.). (SPA.). 64p. (J). 14.95 (978-84-261-1423-5(7)) Juventud, Editorial ESP. Dist: Distribooks, Inc.
—Stock de Coque. (Tintin Ser.). (FRE & SPA.). (J). pap. 14.95 (978-84-261-1422-8(9)) Juventud, Editorial ESP. Dist: Distribooks, Inc.
—El Tesoro de Rackham el Rojo. (Tintin Ser.). (SPA.). 4p. (J). 14.95 (978-84-261-1399-3(0)) Juventud, Editorial ESP. Dist: Distribooks, Inc.
Hergenroeder, Ernie, illus. Little Drop of Water. 2007. 24p. (J). 15.00 (978-0-9724272-4-1(4)) Katydid Publishing LLC.
Hering, Marianne & Younger, Marshal. Escape to the Hiding Place. 2012. (AIO Imagination Station Bks.: 9). (ENG., Illus.). 128p. (J). pap. 4.99 (978-1-58997-693-1(2)) Tyndale Hse. Pubs.
Herman, Alison & Grossman, Lynne. Dolly Goes on Vacation. Eve, Lealand, illus. 2007. 22p. (J). 24.95 (978-0-9746153-2-5(3)) DMH Pr., Inc.
—Dolly Goes to the Beach. Eve, Lealand, illus. 2007. 24p. (J). 24.95 (978-0-9746153-1-8(5)) DMH Pr., Inc.
—Dolly Goes to the Supermarket. Eve, Lealand, illus. 2007. 22p. (J). 24.96 (978-0-9746153-0-1(7)) DMH Pr., Inc.
Herman, Eleanor. Empire of Dust. 2016. (Blood of Gods & Royals Ser.: 2). (ENG., Illus.). 384p. 19.99 (978-0-373-21192-0(9), Harlequin Teen) Harlequin Enterprises, Ltd. CAN. Dist: HarperCollins Pubs.
Herman, Gail. Scooby-Doo in the Lighthouse Mystery, 1 vol. 2016. (Scooby-Doo! Set 3 Ser.). (ENG., Illus.). 32p. (J). (gr. k-4). lib. bdg. 24.21 (978-1-61479-410-3(3)) Spotlight.
Herman-O'Neal, Jackie. Moctezuma's Zoo: A Tale from an Enchanted City. 2013. 28p. pap. 24.95 (978-1-62709-271-5(4)) America Star Bks.
Hernandez, David. Land of the Pharaohs, 1 vol. 2003. (Adventures of Toby Digz Ser.: 1). (ENG., Illus.). 96p. pap. 5.99 (978-1-4003-0195-9(5)) Nelson, Thomas Inc.
—The Mighty Armor, 1 vol., Vol. 2. 2003. (Adventures of Toby Digz Ser.: 2). (ENG., Illus.). 96p. pap. 5.99 (978-1-4003-0196-6(3)) Nelson, Thomas Inc.
Hernandez, Gilbert. The Adventures of Venus. 2012. (ENG., Illus.). 104p. (gr. 4-9). 9.99 (978-1-60699-540-2(5), 699540) Fantagraphics Bks.
Hernández, Miguel & Hernández, Miguel. Miguel Hernandez para Ninos. Alonso, Juan Ramon, illus. 2003. (SPA.). 178p. (978-84-305-9548-8(1), SU30133) Susaeta Ediciones, S.A. ESP. Dist: Lectorum Pubns., Inc.
Hernandez, Natalie. Stowaway to California: Adventures with Father Junipero Serra, 3. 2003. (Illus.). 138p. (J). per. 10.95 (978-1-885852-29-8(0)) James Stevenson Pub.
Hernandez, Natalie Nelson. Captain Sutter's Fort: Adventures with John A. Sutter. 2003. (Illus.). 108p. (J). per. 9.95 (978-1-885852-28-1(2)) James Stevenson Pub.
—Mapmakers of the Western Trails: Adventures with John Chrles Fremont, 3 bks. 2003. (Illus.). 130p. (J). per. 10.95 (978-1-885852-31-1(2)) James Stevenson Pub.
Hernandez, Peter. A New Day with Rhyming Robin. 2011. 32p. pap. (978-1-4269-5817-5(X)) Trafford Publishing (UK) Ltd.
Hernandez, Regina. Texas Roundup: Jake the Beagle's Crazy Adventures. Woods, Carol, ed. Fetherston, Catherine & Miller, Tom, illus. 2003. (Jake the Beagle Crazy Adventure Ser.: 2). 90p. (J). pap. 5.99 (978-0-9727771-2-4(1)) Regal Enterprises.
Herndon, Lee G. The Land of Always & Forever: The Trilogy, 1 vol. 2009. 77p. pap. 19.95 (978-1-60836-898-3(X)) America Star Bks.
Herodotus. The Wright Brothers Adventure. 2005. (Illus.). (J). (978-0-9762509-1-3(8)) Society For The Understanding Of Early Child Development.
Herr, Brandy. The Adventures of Freddie Spaghetti & Meat Ball. 2012. 24p. pap. 24.95 (978-1-4626-7834-1(3)) America Star Bks.
Herr, Margaret J. Fritz, the Donut-Tailed Dog. 2013. 62p. pap. 17.95 (978-1-63000-635-8(1)) America Star Bks.
Herrera, Joaquin. Horris, Little Eli & the Lens of Truth. 2007. (DreamFever Chronicles Ser.: Bk. 1). 208p. (978-1-59258-245-7(1)) Hylas Publishing.
Herrick, Amy. The Time Fetch. (ENG.). (J). (gr. 4-7). 2014. 336p. pap. 6.95 (978-1-61620-453-2(2), 73453) 2013. 320p. 16.95 (978-1-61620-220-0(3), 73220) Algonquin Bks. of Chapel Hill.
Herrick, Ann. Walk Softly & Watch Out for Bigfoot. 2006. (YA). pap. 9.95 (978-0-7599-4489-3(X)) Hard Shell Word Factory.
Herrick, Steven. Kissing Annabel: Love, Ghosts, & Facial Hair & a Place Like This. 2009. (ENG.). 272p. (YA). (gr. 9). pap. 7.99 (978-1-4169-8287-6(6), Simon Pulse) Simon Pulse.
Herring, Bruce D. The Wizard of Wonderland, 1 vol. 2010. 192p. pap. 24.95 (978-1-4489-5844-3(X)) America Star Bks.
Hersh, Kristin. Toby Snax. 2016. (ENG., Illus.). 40p. (J). 14.95 (978-1-4773-1127-1(0)) Univ. of Texas Pr.
Hervey, Cheston & Doane, Darren. Kill the Dragon, Get the Girl. 2017. (J). pap. **(978-1-59128-188-7(1))** Canon Pr.
Herwick Rice, Dona & Paris, Stephanie. Sal Fink, 1 vol. 2009. (Building Fluency Through Reader's Theater Ser.). (ENG.). 24p. (J). (gr. 2-4). pap. 6.99 (978-1-4333-0995-3(5)) Teacher Created Materials, Inc.
Herzog, Mary Ann. The Buddy Tails. 2008. 49p. pap. 16.95 (978-1-60441-760-9(9)) America Star Bks.
Hess, Brian F. Lynquest & the Search for Greatness. 2006. (ENG.). 116p. per. 19.95 (978-1-4241-4503-4(1)) PublishAmerica, Inc.
Hesse, George. Malcolm & the Magic Shoe... a Peek into Heaven. 2012. 30p. pap. 17.99 (978-1-62419-858-8(9)) Salem Author Services.
Hesselbein, Deborah A. Tail Talks. Claycomb, Norma L., illus. 2008. 48p. per. 15.95 (978-1-59858-560-5(6)) Dog Ear Publishing, LLC.
Hest, Amy. You Can Do It, Sam. Jeram, Anita, illus. 2007. (Sam Bks.). (ENG.). 32p. (J). (gr. -1-k). pap. 4.99 (978-0-7636-3688-3(6)) Candlewick Pr.
Hester, Beth Landis. Ninjago: Secret World of the Ninja. 2015. (ENG.). 96p. (J). (gr. 2-5). 16.99 (978-1-4654-2137-1(8), DK Children) Dorling Kindersley Publishing, Inc.
Hester, Beth Landis & Dorling Kindersley Publishing Staff. Secret World of the Ninja. 2015. (ENG., Illus.). 96p. (J). (gr. 2-5). 16.99 (978-1-4654-2078-7(9), DK Children) Dorling Kindersley Publishing, Inc.
Heston, L. L. The Story of Pan Doo: A Panda's Progress. 2012. 24p. pap. 15.99 (978-1-4771-2392-8(X)) Xlibris Corp.
Heuer, Christoph, illus. Lola & Fred & Tom. 2007. (Lola & Fred Ser.). (ENG.). 48p. (J). (gr. -1-3). 15.95 (978-0-9741319-9-3(7)) 4N Publishing LLC.
Hewett, Katherine. Magic Bubble Bath. 2012. 40p. pap. 25.10 (978-0-578-09202-7(6)) Hewett, Katherine J.E.
Hewitt-Barker, Marsha E. The Dachshund Who Sprouted Wings. 2012. 32p. pap. 19.99 (978-1-4772-8887-0(2)) AuthorHouse.
Hewitt, Christine. A Mystical Journey. 2009. 80p. pap. 12.45 (978-0-557-06314-7(0)) Lulu Pr., Inc.
Heyliger, William. Bill Darrow's Victory. Salg, Bert, illus. 2011. 202p. 44.95 (978-1-258-07262-9(9)) Literary Licensing, LLC.
Heywood, La Abuelita Geny. Proto: ¿Qué hacer cuando un dinosaurio nace en tu Jardín? 2010. 52p. pap. 22.49 (978-1-4490-5628-5(8)) AuthorHouse.
Hiatt, Fred. Nine Days. 2014. (ENG.). 252p. (YA). (gr. 7). pap. 8.99 (978-0-385-74281-8(9), Ember) Random Hse. Children's Bks.
Hibbs, Gillian. Tilly's at Home Holiday. Hibbs, Gillian, illus. 2014. (Child's Play Library). (ENG., Illus.). 32p. (J). (978-1-84643-601-7(X)) Child's Play International Ltd.
Hickery Dickery. 2004. (J). per. (978-1-57657-426-3(1)) Paradise Pr., Inc.
Hickey, David. A Very Small Something. Griggs-Burr, Alexander & Griggs-Burr, Alexander, illus. 2012. (ENG.). 32p. (J). (gr. -1). 15.95 (978-1-926845-37-1(4)) Biblioasis CAN. Dist: Consortium Bk. Sales & Distribution.
Hickey, Joshalyn M. Good Morning Lovey! Chaveevah, Banks Ferguson, illus. 2005. (ENG.). 28p. (J). 12.00 (978-0-9718939-3-1(4)) BaHar Publishing, L.C.
Hicks, Angie, illus. The Fairy Horse. 2012. (ENG.). 24p. (J). 9.95 (978-1-84135-834-5(7)) Award Pubns. Ltd. GBR. Dist: Parkwest Pubns., Inc.
Hicks, Deron R. Secrets of Shakespeare's Grave. Geyer, Mark Edward, illus. (Shakespeare Mysteries Ser.: 1). (ENG.). (J). (gr. 2-5). 2012. 304p. 16.99 (978-0-547-84034-5(9))Bk. 1. 2013. 320p. pap. 7.99 (978-0-544-10504-1(4)) Houghton Mifflin Harcourt Publishing Co.
—Tower of the Five Orders. Geyer, Mark Edward, illus. 2013. (Shakespeare Mysteries Ser.: 2). (ENG.). 320p. (J). (gr. 5-7). 16.99 (978-0-547-83953-0(7)) Houghton Mifflin Harcourt Publishing Co.
—Tower of the Five Orders: The Shakespeare Mysteries, Book 2. Geyer, Mark Edward, illus. 2014. (Shakespeare Mysteries Ser.). (ENG.). 320p. (J). (gr. 5-7). pap. 7.99 (978-0-544-33630-8(5), HMH Books For Young Readers) Houghton Mifflin Harcourt Publishing Co.
Hicks, Esther & Hicks, Jerry. Solomon's Fine Featherless Friends. 2nd ed. 2007. (ENG., Illus.). 256p. pap. 15.99 (978-1-4019-1159-1(5)) Hay Hse., Inc.
Hicks, Esther, et al. Sara Learns the Secret about the Law of Attraction. Garrett, Caroline S., illus. 2nd ed. 2007. (ENG.). 192p. per. 14.99 (978-1-4019-1158-4(7)) Hay Hse., Inc.

Hicks, Faith Erin. The Stone Heart. 2017. (Nameless City Ser.: 2). (ENG., Illus.). 256p. (J). pap. 14.99 *(978-1-62672-158-6(0)*, 9781626721586, First Second Bks.) Roaring Brook Pr.
—The Stone Heart. 2017. (Nameless City Ser.: 2). (J). lib. bdg. 26.95 ***(978-0-606-40349-8(3))*** Turtleback Bks.
Hicks, John. Divided World. 2003. 192p. (YA). per. 6.50 *(978-0-9742829-1-6(X))* Quiet Man Publishing.
—My Buddypack. ltd. ed. 2003. (Illus.). 160p. (J). per. 5.99 *(978-0-9742829-0-9(1))* Quiet Man Publishing.
Hicks, John Bryant. The Day Charlie Lost His Weirdiness. 2nd ed. 2007. (J). per. 5.99 *(978-0-9742829-4-7(4))* Quiet Man Publishing.
Hicks, Michael Christopher. Tales of Drake: The Tale of the Lost Dog. 2011. 40p. pap. 18.99 *(978-1-4634-1823-6(X))* AuthorHouse.
Hicks, Rebecca. Little Vampires. Hicks, Rebecca, illus. 2007. (Illus.). 56p. per. 8.95 *(978-0-9799290-0-7(8))* Lunasea Studios.
Hidalgo, Pablo. The Phantom Menace. 2012. (Star Wars Ser.). (ENG.). 64p. (J). (gr. -1-3). 9.99 *(978-0-545-38986-0(0))* Scholastic, Inc.
—Star Wars Rebels: Head to Head. 2014. lib. bdg. 19.65 *(978-0-606-36071-5(9))* Turtleback Bks.
—Star Wars Rebels: Head to Head. 2014. (ENG.). 64p. (J). (gr. 3-7). pap. 8.99 *(978-0-545-74642-7(6))* Scholastic, Inc.
Hierl, Christine Gormican. Wyatt Walker Turbo Talker. Thompson, Michelle Gormican & Thompson, Janet M., illus. 2004. 28p. *(978-0-9760680-0-6(1))* Cedar Shamrock Publishing.
Higesanbon. Mo Mo Mo Mo Monster: Mon Monster. 2011. 56p. pap. 34.95 *(978-1-4327-4149-5(7))* Outskirts Pr., Inc.
Higgins, F. E. A Game of Ghouls. unabr. ed. 2014. (Phenomenals Ser.: 2). (ENG.). 240p. (J). (gr. 4-6). pap. 8.99 *(978-0-330-50756-1(7))* Pan Macmillan GBR. Dist: Independent Pubs. Group.
Higgins, Jack & Richards, Justin. Death Run. 2009. (Rich & Jade Ser.: Bk. 2). (ENG.). 288p. (YA). (gr. 7-18). 8.99 *(978-0-14-241475-0(1)*, Speak) Penguin Young Readers Group.
—First Strike. 2011. (Rich & Jade Ser.: Bk. 4). (ENG.). 240p. (YA). (gr. 7-18). 8.99 *(978-0-14-241909-0(5)*, Speak) Penguin Young Readers Group.
—Sharp Shot. 2010. (Rich & Jade Ser.: Bk. 3). (ENG.). 240p. (YA). (gr. 7-18). 8.99 *(978-0-14-241730-0(0)*, Speak) Penguin Young Readers Group.
—Sure Fire. 2008. (Rich & Jade Ser.: Bk. 1). (ENG.). 272p. (YA). (gr. 7-18). 8.99 *(978-0-14-241213-8(9)*, Speak) Penguin Young Readers Group.
Higgins, Jim. The Enchanted Nursery: Heather & Hamish, Fun in Florida, Reggie Rabbit at the Seaside, Percy Penguin's Friends. 2009. (Illus.). 36p. pap. 15.49 *(978-1-4389-9904-3(6))* AuthorHouse.
—The Enchanted Nursery: Nessie's Friends. 2008. 24p. pap. 11.49 *(978-1-4343-8993-0(6))* AuthorHouse.
Higgins, Nadia. Sleeping Beauty & the Snapdragons, 1 vol. Johnson, Meredith, illus. 2009. (Fiona & Frieda's Fairy-Tale Adventures Ser.). (ENG.). 80p. (J). (gr. 2-5). 27.07 *(978-1-60270-576-0(3))* Magic Wagon.
—Snow White & the Candy Apple, 1 vol. Johnson, Meredith, illus. 2009. (Fiona & Frieda's Fairy-Tale Adventures Ser.). (ENG.). 80p. (J). (gr. 2-5). 27.07 *(978-1-60270-577-7(1))* Magic Wagon.
Higginson, Sheila Sweeny. Diego rescata al bebé manatí (Diego's Manatee Rescue) McGee, Warner, illus. 2009. (Go, Diego, Go! Ser.). (SPA.). 24p. (J). pap. 3.99 *(978-1-4169-7983-8(2)*, Libros Para Ninos) Libros Para Ninos.
Highlights for Children Editorial Staff, compiled by. Whoo & Coo's Barnyard Adventure. 2016. (Highlights(tm) Story Puzzle Fun Ser.). (ENG.). 24p. (J). (gr. -1-k). pap. 4.99 *(978-1-62979-549-2(6)*, Highlights) Boyds Mills Pr.
Higson, Charlie. The Hunted (an Enemy Novel) 2016. (Enemy Novel Ser.). (ENG.). 480p. (YA). (gr. 9-17). pap. 9.99 *(978-1-4231-6637-5(X))* Hyperion Bks. for Children.
Hildebrand, Jens. Team 002: The Abduction of the Queen. Garcia, Juan F., illus. 2013. 224p. pap. *(978-3-929892-46-8(4))* Hildebrand, Jutta Warped Tomato Publishing.
—Team 002 und das Utopia-Element. Garcia, Juan F., illus. 2013. 270p. pap. *(978-3-929892-39-0(1))* Hildebrand, Jutta Warped Tomato Publishing.
—Team 002 und Die Entführung der Queen. Garcia, Juan F., illus. 2013. 240p. pap. *(978-3-929892-37-6(5))* Hildebrand, Jutta Warped Tomato Publishing.
Hilderbrandt, Sandra June. Wilbur's Great Adventure. Whispering Pine Press International, Inc. Staff, ed. Merrell, Vernon R., illus. 2011. (ENG.). 32p. (J). per. 12.95 *(978-1-59434-312-4(8))* Whispering Pine Pr. International, Inc.
Hile, Doretta. A Place for All of Us. Barnes, William, illus. 2007. 36p. per. 14.94 *(978-1-59858-421-9(9))* Dog Ear Publishing, LLC.
Hili, Marvin. Playland. 2007. 96p. pap. 14.95 *(978-1-84799-888-0(7))* Lulu Pr., Inc.
Hill, C. J. Echo in Time. 2013. (Erasing Time Ser.: 2). (ENG.). 400p. (YA). (gr. 8). pap. 9.99 *(978-0-06-212396-1(3)*, Tegen, Katherine Bks) HarperCollins Pubs.
—Slayers: Friends & Traitors. 2013. (Slayers Ser.: 2). (ENG.). 400p. (YA). (gr. 7). 16.99 *(978-1-250-02461-9(7)*, 9781250024619) Feiwel & Friends.
Hill, Eveline. Hugo & Oscar Go Travelling: Continuing the Adventures of Hugo & Oscar. 2012. (Illus.). 52p. pap. 27.45 *(978-1-4772-2733-6(4))* AuthorHouse.
Hill, Janet Muirhead. The Many Adventures of Miranda & Starlight: Six Books in One Package. rev. ed. 2008. (Illus.). 790p. (J). pap. 60.00 *(978-0-9772525-8-9(2))* Raven Publishing Inc. of Montana.
—Miranda & Starlight. 2013. (J). cd-rom 19.00 *(978-1-937849-08-5(2))* Raven Publishing Inc. of Montana.
Hill, Kevin Kelvin. The Red Baron, the Knight of Many Talents. 2009. 40p. pap. 20.99 *(978-1-4490-0642-6(6))* AuthorHouse.
—The Supreme Sorcerer Ollie Tooth Pick & His Two Henchmen versus the Magical Dragons. 2011. 40p. 20.76 *(978-1-4567-3254-7(4))* AuthorHouse.
Hill, Leah. The Adventures of Prince Phillip & the Fairytale Creatures: The Giant Problem. 2013. (ENG.). 26p. (J). pap. 10.95 *(978-1-4787-0696-0(1))* Outskirts Pr., Inc.
Hill, Nick. Carlton Casey: Alien Incident. 2007. 100p. per. 9.95 *(978-1-59800-310-9(0))* Outskirts Pr., Inc.
Hill, Robert E. The Day of the Monarch. 2013. 250p. (gr. 10-12). 26.95 *(978-1-4759-7478-2(7))*; pap. 16.95 *(978-1-4759-7476-8(0))* iUniverse, Inc.
Hill, Sarah. Posie Pixie & the Copper Kettle. O'Gorman, Sarah, ed. Mauchline, Sarah, illus. 2013. 52p. pap. *(978-1-909302-20-4(1))* Abela Publishing.
Hill, Susanna Leonard. Airplane Flight! Larrañaga, Ana Martín, illus. 2009. (ENG.). 12p. (J). (gr. -1-k). bds. 7.99 *(978-1-4169-7832-9(1)*, Little Simon) Little Simon.
—Freight Train Trip! A Lift-the-Flap Adventure. Larrañaga, Ana Martín, illus. 2009. (ENG.). 12p. (J). (gr. -1-k). bds. 7.99 *(978-1-4169-7833-6(X)*, Little Simon) Little Simon.
Hill, Will. Battle Lines: A Department 19 Novel. 2013. (Department Nineteen Ser.: 3). (ENG.). 608p. (J). (gr. 9). 18.99 *(978-1-59514-408-9(0)*, Razorbill) Penguin Young Readers Group.
Hillan, Pam & Dyan, Penelope. Dem Bones, Dem Bones! 2013. 110p. pap. 8.95 *(978-1-61477-122-7(7))* Bellissima Publishing, LLC.
Hillan, Pamela & Dyan, Penelope. The Discovery in the Old Mine. Weigand, John, photos by. 2013. (Illus.). 116p. pap. 8.95 *(978-1-61477-095-4(6))* Bellissima Publishing, LLC.
—The Hidden Treasure at Dragon Lake. 2013. 112p. pap. 8.95 *(978-1-61477-101-2(4))* Bellissima Publishing, LLC.
—The Jewels of the Crown. Weigand, John, photos by. 2013. (Illus.). 128p. pap. 8.95 *(978-1-61477-111-1(1))* Bellissima Publishing, LLC.
—The Mummy's Secret. Weigand, John, photos by. 2013. (Illus.). 112p. pap. 8.95 *(978-1-61477-099-2(9))* Bellissima Publishing, LLC.
—The Mystery on Burgundy Street. 2013. 134p. pap. 8.95 *(978-1-61477-086-2(7))* Bellissima Publishing, LLC.
—The Ring of Evil. Weigand, John D., photos by. 2013. (Illus.). 124p. pap. 8.95 *(978-1-61477-114-2(6))* Bellissima Publishing, LLC.
—The Secret at Fort Huachuca. 2013. 130p. pap. 8.95 *(978-1-61477-093-0(X))* Bellissima Publishing, LLC.
Hillert, Margaret. Dear Dragon Goes to the Beach. Pullan, Jack, illus. 2015. (BeginningtoRead Ser.). (ENG.). 32p. (J). (gr. k-2). pap. 11.94 *(978-1-60357-789-2(0))* Norwood Hse. Pr.
Hills, Tad. Duck & Goose Go to the Beach. 2014. (Duck & Goose Ser.). (ENG., Illus.). 40p. (J). (gr. -1-2). 17.99 *(978-0-385-37235-0(3)*, Schwartz & Wade Bks.) Random Hse. Children's Bks.
Hilton, Charlotte. Adventure of the Pen Pot Pals. 2009. 36p. pap. 16.99 *(978-1-4389-4434-0(9))* AuthorHouse.
Hilton, Fern A. Jesse & Henry Save the Day. 2012. 24p. pap. 14.50 *(978-1-4772-9282-2(9))* AuthorHouse.
—Jesse & Wee. 2012. 20p. pap. 12.99 *(978-1-4685-7613-9(5))* AuthorHouse.
Hilton, N. E. The Spell. 2010. (Illus.). 216p. pap. 15.95 *(978-1-4452-7791-2(3))* Lulu Pr., Inc.
Himekawa, Akira. The Legend of Zelda Box Set, 10 vols. 2011. (ENG., Illus.). 2000p. (J). pap. 79.99 *(978-1-4215-4242-3(0))* Viz Media.
—The Legend of Zelda, Vol. 10. Himekawa, Akira, illus. 2010. (ENG., Illus.). 200p. (J). (gr. 2-5). pap. 9.99 *(978-1-4215-3724-5(9))* Viz Media.
—The Legend of Zelda, Vol. 5. Himekawa, Akira, illus. 2009. (ENG., Illus.). 200p. (J). pap. 9.99 *(978-1-4215-2331-6(0))* Viz Media.
—The Legend of Zelda, Vol. 6. Himekawa, Akira, illus. 2009. (ENG., Illus.). 200p. (J). pap. 9.99 *(978-1-4215-2332-3(9))* Viz Media.
—The Legend of Zelda, Vol. 9. Himekawa, Akira, illus. 2010. (ENG., Illus.). 192p. (YA). pap. 9.99 *(978-1-4215-2335-4(3))* Viz Media.
Himes, John. The Adventures of an Alligator Named Ally. 2012. 24p. pap. 17.99 *(978-1-4772-9676-9(X))* AuthorHouse.
Himmelman, John. Bunjitsu Bunny's Best Move. Himmelman, John, illus. 2016. (Bunjitsu Bunny Ser.: 2). (ENG., Illus.). 128p. (J). (gr. 1-3). 16.00 *(978-0-606-39298-3(X))* Turtleback Bks.
Hinckley, Betts. Mr Bumble. 2011. 24p. pap. 15.99 *(978-1-4568-9714-7(4))* Xlibris Corp.
Hinds, Gareth. The Odyssey. Hinds, Gareth, illus. 2010. (ENG., Illus.). 256p. (YA). (gr. 7-18). 24.99 *(978-0-7636-4266-2(5))*; pap. 14.99 *(978-0-7636-4268-6(1))* Candlewick Pr.
hines, j. Finding Raven. 2007. 101p. pap. 8.95 *(978-0-615-17723-6(9))* Hines, Jerry.
Hinkler Books, ed. Ghostly Glow in the Haunted House. 2012. (Glow & Learn Ser.). (Illus.). 16p. (J). bds. 12.99 *(978-1-74308-808-1(6))* Hinkler Bks. Pty, Ltd. AUS. Dist: Ideals Pubns.
Hinkler Books Staff, reader. Barney's Outer Space Adventure. 2004. (J). 9.99 incl. audio compact disk *(978-1-86515-996-6(4))* Hinkler Bks. Pty, Ltd. AUS. Dist: Penton Overseas, Inc.
Hinson, Paw Paw. Country Days: Duck Pond. 2010. 12p. 11.95 *(978-1-4490-7030-4(2))* AuthorHouse.
Hinton, Nigel. Collision Course. 2005. 156p. (J). (gr. 5-8). pap. 5.95 *(978-1-903015-42-1(1))* Barn Owl Bks, London GBR. Dist: Independent Pubs. Group.
Hinton, S. E. Rebeldes. 2003. (SPA., Illus.). 192p. (YA). (gr. 5-8). pap. 13.95 *(978-968-19-0831-7(7)*, AF4535) Aguilar Editorial MEX. Dist: Lectorum Pubns., Inc., Santillana USA Publishing Co., Inc.
—Rebeldes. 2nd ed. (SPA., Illus.). 200p. (YA). (gr. 5-8). 13.95 *(978-84-204-4797-1(8))* Ediciones Alfaguara ESP. Dist: Santillana USA Publishing Co., Inc.
Hipp, Helen C. A Different Kind of Safari. Diaco, Paula Tedford, ed. Glass, Hilary Ann Love, illus. 2013. 32p. 17.95 *(978-0-9890134-0-6(5))* A Different Kind of Safari LLC.
Hirsch, Alex, et al. Gravity Falls: Journal 3. Gonsalves, Andy & Ramirez, Stephanie, illus. 2017. (ENG.). 288p. (J). (gr. 3-7). 150.00 ***(978-1-368-00250-9(1))*** Disney Pr.
Hirsch, Andy. Varmints. 2016. (J). lib. bdg. 29.40 *(978-0-606-39563-2(6))* Turtleback Bks.
Hit Entertainment. Lost at Sea! Stubbs, Tommy, illus. 2010. (Pictureback(R) Ser.). (ENG.). 24p. (J). (gr. -1-2). pap. 3.99 *(978-0-375-84754-7(5)*, Random Hse. Bks. for Young Readers) Random Hse. Children's Bks.
Hitchcock, Alfred. Misterio de la Arana de Plata. (Alfred Hitchcock y los Tres Investigadores Ser.). (SPA.). (YA). 8.95 *(978-84-272-4908-0(X)*, MO60) Molino, Editorial ESP. Dist: Continental Bk. Co., Inc.
—Misterio de la Calavera Parlante. (Alfred Hitchcock y los Tres Investigadores Ser.). (SPA.). (YA). 8.95 *(978-84-272-4911-0(X)*, MO63) Molino, Editorial ESP. Dist: Continental Bk. Co., Inc.
—Misterio de la Cueva de los Lamentos. (Alfred Hitchcock y los Tres Investigadores Ser.). (SPA.). 160p. (YA). 8.95 *(978-84-272-4910-3(1)*, MO62) Molino, Editorial ESP. Dist: Continental Bk. Co., Inc.
—Misterio de la Montana del Monstruo. (Alfred Hitchcock y los Tres Investigadores Ser.). (SPA.). (YA). 8.95 *(978-84-272-4920-2(9)*, MO72) Molino, Editorial ESP. Dist: Continental Bk. Co., Inc.
—Misterio de Leon Mervioso. (Alfred Hitchcock y los Tres Investigadores Ser.). (SPA.). 192p. (YA). 8.95 *(978-84-272-4916-5(0)*, MO68) Molino, Editorial ESP. Dist: Continental Bk. Co., Inc.
—Misterio del Dragon. (Alfred Hitchcock y los Tres Investigadores Ser.). (SPA.). 176p. (YA). 8.95 *(978-84-272-4914-1(4)*, MO66) Molino, Editorial ESP. Dist: Continental Bk. Co., Inc.
—Misterio del Gato de Trapo. (Alfred Hitchcock y los Tres Investigadores Ser.). (SPA.). 152p. (YA). 8.95 *(978-84-272-4913-4(6)*, MO65) Molino, Editorial ESP. Dist: Continental Bk. Co., Inc.
Hitchcock, Fleur. Ghosts on Board. 2016. (Shrunk! Adventure Ser.: 3). (ENG., Illus.). 192p. (J). (gr. 3-7). pap. 9.99 *(978-1-84812-483-7(X))* Bonnier Publishing GBR. Dist: Independent Pubs. Group.
—Mayhem & Meteorites. 2016. (Shrunk! Adventure Ser.: 2). (ENG., Illus.). 256p. (J). (gr. 3-7). pap. 9.99 *(978-1-84812-481-3(3))* Bonnier Publishing GBR. Dist: Independent Pubs. Group.
Hiti, Samuel, creator. End Times - Tiempos Finales Vol. 1: English / Spanish. 2004. Orig. Title: Bloody Demon Guts. (Illus.). 128p. (YA). per. 9.95 net. *(978-0-9755193-0-1(1))* La Luz Comics.
Hoadley, Jo. Miss Creant: The Adventures of a little Red Hen. l.t. ed. 2004. (Illus.). 127p. (J). per. 15.99 *(978-0-9765088-0-9(X))* Billy Jo Bks.
Hobbs, Brice Edward. Beth's Woodpecker. 2004. 108p. 26.45 *(978-1-4208-0135-4(X))* AuthorHouse.
Hobbs, Constance. Dreamers. 436p. 2008. 50.50 *(978-0-9556783-6-3(6))* 2007. pap. 35.95 *(978-0-9556783-0-1(7))* Hobbs, Constance GBR. Dist: Lulu Pr., Inc.
Hobbs, Leigh. Mr Badger & the Missing Ape. l.t. ed. 2012. 120p. (J). pap. *(978-1-4596-3344-5(X))* ReadHowYouWant.com, Ltd.
Hobbs, Valerie. Sheep. 2009. (ENG.). 144p. (J). (gr. 3-7). pap. 7.99 *(978-0-312-56116-1(4)*, 9780312561161) Square Fish.
—Wolf. 2013. (ENG.). 128p. (J). (gr. 3-7). 15.99 *(978-0-374-31575-7(2)*, 9780374315757, Farrar, Straus & Giroux (BYR)) Farrar, Straus & Giroux.
Hobbs, Will. Beardance. 2004. (ENG., Illus.). 208p. (J). (gr. 5-9). pap. 7.99 *(978-0-689-87072-9(8)*, Simon & Schuster/Paula Wiseman Bks.) Simon & Schuster Children's Publishing.
—The Big Wander. 2004. (ENG., Illus.). 192p. (J). (gr. 5-9). pap. 6.99 *(978-0-689-87070-5(1)*, Simon & Schuster/Paula Wiseman Bks.) Simon & Schuster/Paula Wiseman Bks.
—Never Say Die. 224p. (J). (gr. 3-7). 2014. (ENG.). pap. 6.99 *(978-0-06-170880-0(1))* 2013. (ENG.). 16.99 *(978-0-06-170878-7(X))* 2013. lib. bdg. 17.89 *(978-0-06-170879-4(8))* HarperCollins Pubs.
Hobson, Joseph. The Snake River Adventures: Floating the Snake. 2012. 88p. pap. 10.95 *(978-1-938223-04-4(7))* Salem Author Services.
Hobson, Mark. Raindrop. 2013. 76p. pap. 12.95 *(978-1-937216-45-0(4))* Dog Ear Publishing, LLC.
Hochenauer, Mary & Hochenauer-Fox, Lois. Sunny & Wondrous, Cat Cousins. 2007. (ENG.). 32p. (J). 16.95 *(978-0-9778005-0-6(4))* Gnatcatcher Children'S Bks.
Hock, Dan. The Afternoon Auction: An Iggy & Igor Mystery. 2004. (Illus.). 48p. (J). per. 4.99 *(978-0-9754046-0-7(1))* Anticipation Pr.
Hocking, Amanda. Ice Kissed. 2015. (Kanin Chronicles Ser.: 2). (ENG., Illus.). 320p. (YA). (gr. 7-12). 22.99 *(978-1-250-07534-5(3)*, 9781250075345); pap. 10.99 *(978-1-250-04987-2(3)*, 9781250049872) St. Martin's Pr. (St. Martin's Griffin).
Hodes, Loren. Thirty-One Cakes: A Hashvas Aveida Adventure. Rosenfeld, Devorah Leah, ed. Klineman, Harvey, illus. 2003. (J). 10.95 *(978-1-929628-13-1(7))* Hachai Publishing.
Hodges, Jim. Electronic Lollipops. 2013. 52p. pap. 21.88 *(978-1-4669-8858-3(4))* Trafford Publishing.
Hodgson, Jesse. Pongo. 2013. (ENG., Illus.). 32p. (J). (gr. -1-2). 16.95 *(978-1-909263-09-3(5))* Flying Eye Bks. GBR. Dist: Consortium Bk. Sales & Distribution.
Hodgson, Julie. The Mothaich. 2008. 185p. 41.95 *(978-1-4092-3819-5(9))* Lulu Pr., Inc.
Hodgson, William Hope. The Sea Horses. 2004. reprint ed. pap. 1.99 *(978-1-4192-8166-2(6))* Kessinger Publishing, LLC.
Hodson, Ann & Mason, David. The Adventures of Kef, Dael & Emma. 2010. (Illus.). 84p. pap. 28.99 *(978-1-4520-2138-6(4))* AuthorHouse.
Hoena, B. A. & Barrie, J. M. Peter Pan. Cano, Fernando, illus. 2015. (Graphic Revolve: Common Core Editions Ser.). (ENG.). 72p. (gr. 2-3). lib. bdg. 27.99 *(978-1-4965-0372-5(4))* Stone Arch Bks.
Hoena, Blake A. Eek & Ack Early Chapter Books, 1 vol. 2014. (Eek & Ack Early Chapter Bks.). (ENG.). 32p. (gr. k-2). 90.60 *(978-1-4342-8457-0(3))* Stone Arch Bks.
Hoena, Blake A. & Terrell, Brandon. Tony Hawk's 900 Revolution. 2013. (Tony Hawk's 900 Revolution Ser.). (ENG.). 128p. (gr. 3-4). 106.60 *(978-1-4342-4109-2(2)*, Tony Hawk's 900 Revolution) Stone Arch Bks.
Hoena, Blake A. & Tortosa, Wilson. Amplified, Vol. 5. Ito, Leonardo, illus. 2012. (Tony Hawk's 900 Revolution Ser.). (ENG.). 128p. (gr. 3-4). pap. 7.19 *(978-1-4342-3887-0(3))*; lib. bdg. 26.65 *(978-1-4342-3311-0(1))* Stone Arch Bks. (Tony Hawk's 900 Revolution).
Hoes, Holly. When Aliens Took over the World. 2012. 44p. pap. 21.99 *(978-1-4797-4870-9(6))* Xlibris Corp.
Hoff, Syd. Danny & the Dinosaur: a Very Dino Christmas. Hoff, Syd & Cutting, David, illus. 2017. 24p. (J). (gr. -1-3). pap. 6.99 ***(978-0-06-241046-7(6)***, HarperFestival) HarperCollins Pubs.
—Danny & the Dinosaur: Big Reading Collection. Hoff, Syd, illus. 2017. (I Can Read Level 1 Ser.). (Illus.). 190p. (J). (gr. -1-3). pap. 16.99 ***(978-0-06-241047-4(4))*** HarperCollins Pubs.
Hoffman, Joey. The Greedy Courier. 2013. 280p. (gr. -1). pap. 17.48 *(978-1-4907-1362-5(X))* Trafford Publishing.
Hoffman, Mary. City of Secrets. (Stravaganza Ser.). (ENG.). (YA). 2010. 416p. (gr. 7). pap. 8.99 *(978-1-59990-451-1(9)*, 9781599904511) 2008. 400p. (gr. 5-18). 17.99 *(978-1-59990-202-9(8)*, 9781599902029) Bloomsbury Publishing USA. (Bloomsbury USA Childrens).
—City of Ships. 2010. (Stravaganza Ser.). (ENG.). 368p. (YA). (gr. 7-18). 17.99 *(978-1-59990-491-7(8)*, 9781599904917, Bloomsbury USA Childrens) Bloomsbury Publishing USA.
—Stravaganza: City of Ships. 2012. (Stravaganza Ser.). (ENG.). 384p. (YA). (gr. 7). pap. 9.99 *(978-1-59990-832-8(8)*, 9781599908328, Bloomsbury USA Childrens) Bloomsbury Publishing USA.
—Stravaganza: City of Swords. 2012. (Stravaganza Ser.). (ENG.). 368p. (YA). (gr. 7-12). 18.99 *(978-1-59990-842-7(5)*, 9781599908427, Bloomsbury USA Childrens) Bloomsbury Publishing USA.
Hoffman, Mary Ann. Elbert Takes a Trip. 2006. (Neighborhood Readers Ser.). (ENG., Illus.). 12p. (gr. 1-3). pap. 5.90 *(978-1-4042-6847-0(2)*, Rosen Classroom) Rosen Publishing Group, Inc., The.
Hoffman, Robert M. The Adventures of Mia & Squeaky: Tails of Imagination. 2011. 32p. pap. 14.99 *(978-1-257-37254-6(8))* Lulu Pr., Inc.
Hoffmann, Arthur W. The Blue King. 2003. (Illus.). 31p. (J). 21.95 incl. audio compact disk *(978-0-9742967-0-8(8))* ASK Publishing, L.L.C.
Hoffmann, Dana. The Golden Tale: A Goldentail Adventure Story Book. O'Leary Brown, Erin, illus. 2004. (ENG.). 44p. (J). 19.95 *(978-0-9753106-0-1(7))* Hoffmann Partnership, The.
Hoffmann, Dana Marie. El Cuento Dorado, un Libro de Aventura, la Historia de Goldentail. O'Leary Brown, Erin, illus. 2004. (SPA.). 42p. (J). 9.95 *(978-0-9753106-1-8(5))* Hoffmann Partnership, The.
—The Golden Tale, A Goldentail Adventure Story Book. O'Leary Brown, Erin, illus. 2004. 42p. (J). 9.95 *(978-0-9753106-3-2(1))* Hoffmann Partnership, The.
Hoffpauir, J. R. Wibeau Flies! 2013. 26p. pap. 14.95 *(978-1-62838-118-4(3))* Page Publishing Inc.
Hofkin, Sabrina. Magnolia, 1. 2005. 168p. (YA). per. 9.95 *(978-0-9763916-0-9(0))* Manzanita Falls Pubs.
Hofmeister, Alan, et al. The Mask. (Reading for All Learners Ser.). (Illus.). (J). pap. 5.00 *(978-1-56861-139-6(0))* Swift Learning Resources.
—Ruff. (Reading for All Learners Ser.). (Illus.). (J). pap. *(978-1-56861-137-2(4))* Swift Learning Resources.
—Run, Feet, Run. (Reading for All Learners Ser.). (Illus.). (J). pap. *(978-1-56861-095-5(5))* Swift Learning Resources.
—We Will Run. (Reading for All Learners Ser.). (Illus.). (J). pap. *(978-1-56861-099-3(8))* Swift Learning Resources.
Hofmeister, Nick. Adventures of Eli Deuce - SPECIAL EDITION - Fourth & Final Part Added. 2009. 360p. pap. 23.50 *(978-0-557-12192-2(2))* Lulu Pr., Inc.
Hofsess, William. My Very First Dinosaur. 2012. 28p. pap. 15.99 *(978-1-4691-6057-3(9))* Xlibris Corp.
Hogan, Barbora. How Ryan & Aiden Saved the Ocean. 2013. 36p. pap. 16.99 *(978-1-4525-7776-0(5)*, Balboa Pr.) Author Solutions, Inc.
Hohl, Valicity. When I Grow Up. 2012. 20p. pap. 17.99 *(978-1-4772-3685-7(6))* AuthorHouse.
Hohlbein, Wolfgang. Avalon Projekt. pap. 30.95 *(978-3-426-61866-0(4))* Droemersche Verlagsanstalt Th. Knaur Nachf. - GmbH & Co. DEU. Dist: Distribooks, Inc.
Holbrook, L. E. Victoria & the Door to Travarmis. 2007. 108p. per. 19.95 *(978-1-4241-6934-4(8))* America Star Bks.
Holdman, Shirley Terrill. The Adventures of Giggles & Owen: A True Story. Riecks Goss, Carol, illus. 2010. 26p. pap. 14.95 *(978-1-60844-490-8(2))* Dog Ear Publishing, LLC.
Holechek, Max. Edsel Mcfarlan's New Car. Toland, Darrell, illus. 2010. 52p. (J). *(978-1-935359-40-1(1))* Book Pubs. Network.
Holland, Amy L. The Adventures of Bubba & Sis: Book One. 2009. 16p. pap. 8.49 *(978-1-4389-5941-2(9))* AuthorHouse.
Holland, Dwayne K. Princess Laura & the Magic Waterfall. 2010. 42p. pap. 15.50 *(978-1-60860-744-0(5)*, Strategic Bk. Publishing) Strategic Book Publishing & Rights Agency (SBPRA).
Holland, Frances. Ryan's Praying Mantis, 1 vol. 2009. 19p. pap. 24.95 *(978-1-60749-432-4(9))* PublishAmerica, Inc.
Holland, Jesse J. Finn's Story. 2016. (Star Wars the Force Awakens Chapter Bks.). (J). lib. bdg. 16.00 ***(978-0-606-39920-3(8))*** Turtleback Bks.
Holland, Maryjo. The Broken Shadow. 2008. 157p. pap. 19.50 *(978-1-4357-3052-6(6))* Lulu Pr., Inc.
Hollaway, David. Quigley Mccormick: And the Curse of the Polka Dotted Pig, 3 vols. l.t. ed. 2005. (Illus.). 156p. (J). (gr. -1-3). per. 15.95 *(978-1-933211-54-1(7))* Quackenworth Publishing.
Holley, Kim. Rollie Pollie Review. Hawkins, Kristen, illus. 2013. 16p. pap. 10.00 *(978-1-939054-22-7(2))* Rowe Publishing and Design.
Holliday, D. L. Adventures of Tommy. 2013. (ENG.). 34p. (J). pap. 14.95 *(978-1-4787-0953-4(7))* Outskirts Pr., Inc.
Holliday, Susan. Dream Cave. l.t. ed. 2007. 216p. per. *(978-1-905665-23-5(7))* Pollinger In Print.
—The Time Street Gang & the Rag & Bone Boy. l.t. ed. 2007. 132p. pap. *(978-1-905665-64-8(4))* Pollinger In Print.
Hollingsworth, Suzi. Birding with Bobbie. 2011. 23p. (J). pap. 15.95 *(978-1-4327-6422-7(5))* Outskirts Pr., Inc.

A
B

Hollins, Jack. Charlie's Christmas Adventure. 2006. 16.95 *(978-0-9788725-0-2(9))* Alli Kat Publishing.
Holly, Julia. Mrs Winkler's Cure. Holly, Julia, illus. 2010. (Illus.). 214p. pap. 19.99 *(978-1-883376-45-1(9))* Stellium Pr.
Holm, Jennifer L. Turtle in Paradise. 2012. (CHI.). 187p. (J). (gr. 3-7). pap. *(978-7-221-10316-1(X))* Guizhou People's Publishing Hse.
—Turtle in Paradise. 2009. 9.14 *(978-0-7848-3781-8(3),* Everbind) Marco Bk. Co.
—Turtle in Paradise. 2011. (ENG.). 224p. (J). (gr. 3-7). pap. 7.99 *(978-0-375-83690-9(X),* Yearling) Random Hse. Children's Bks.
—Turtle in Paradise. 2011. lib. bdg. 18.40 *(978-0-606-23877-9(8),* Turtleback) Turtleback Bks.
Holmes, Anna. Emmet's Awesome Day. Scholastic, Inc. Staff, illus. 2014. (LEGO: the LEGO Movie Ser.). (ENG.). 32p. (J). (gr. 1-3). pap. 3.99 *(978-0-545-79539-5(7))* Scholastic, Inc.
—Emmet's Awesome Day. 2014. lib. bdg. 13.55 *(978-0-606-36364-8(5))* Turtleback Bks.
—Tickety Toc: Pirate Time. 2014. (ENG.). 24p. (J). (gr. -1-k). pap. 3.99 *(978-0-545-61475-7(9))* Scholastic, Inc.
—Wyldstyle: The Search for the Special. 2014. lib. bdg. 13.55 *(978-0-606-36366-2(1))* Turtleback Bks.
—Wyldstyle - The Search for the Special. 2014. (LEGO: the LEGO Movie Ser.). (ENG., Illus.). 24p. (J). (gr. -1-3). pap. 3.99 *(978-0-545-79540-1(0))* Scholastic, Inc.
Holmes, Kimberly. Digibots Classroom Adventures. Lawson, Devin, illus. 2004. (J). *(978-0-9755725-0-4(4),* 1238415) Digibots Corp.
Holmes, Quentin. Real Street Kidz: Art of Authenticity. 2011. 92p. (gr. 3-7). pap. 10.99 *(978-1-4575-0268-2(2))* Dog Ear Publishing, LLC.
—Real Street Kidz: Chasing Action. 2010. 88p. pap. 10.99 *(978-1-60844-521-9(6))* Dog Ear Publishing, LLC.
Holmes, S. D. The Adventures of Mister. 2009. 56p. pap. 23.99 *(978-1-4389-3786-1(5))* AuthorHouse.
Holsather, Kent /Wilson. Sara's Moon. 2007. (Illus.). 176p. (YA). per. 12.95 *(978-0-9729101-3-2(1))* Lonejack Mountain Pr.
Holsey, Alvin I. Dinosaur Haunt. 2008. 188p. pap. 13.95 *(978-1-60693-282-7(9),* Eloquent Bks.) Strategic Book Publishing & Rights Agency (SBPRA).
Holstein, Ima. A Dragons Daydream. 2011. 24p. pap. 12.99 *(978-1-4634-0430-7(1))* AuthorHouse.
Holt, Christopher. Dark Waters. 2013. (Last Dogs Ser.: 2). (J). lib. bdg. 18.40 *(978-0-606-35308-3(9))* Turtleback Bks.
—Journey's End. 2014. (Last Dogs Ser.: 4). (J). lib. bdg. 18.40 *(978-0-606-35944-3(3))* Turtleback Bks.
—The Last Dogs: The Vanishing. Call, Greg, illus. 2012. (Last Dogs Ser.: 1). (ENG.). 384p. (J). (gr. 3-7). 16.99 *(978-0-316-20005-9(0))* Little, Brown Bks. for Young Readers.
—The Last Dogs - The Vanishing. 2013. (Last Dogs Ser.: 1). (J). lib. bdg. 18.45 *(978-0-606-31744-3(9),* Turtleback) Turtleback Bks.
—The Last Dogs: Dark Waters. Douglas, Allen, illus. 2013. (Last Dogs Ser.: 2). (ENG.). 352p. (J). (gr. 3-7). pap. 7.99 *(978-0-316-20009-7(3))* Little, Brown Bks. for Young Readers.
—The Last Dogs: Journey's End. Douglas, Allen, illus. 2014. (Last Dogs Ser.: 4). (ENG.). 320p. (J). (gr. 3-7). 17.00 *(978-0-316-20007-3(7))* Little, Brown Bks. for Young Readers.
—The Last Dogs: the Long Road. Douglas, Allen, illus. 2014. (Last Dogs Ser.: 3). (ENG.). 352p. (J). (gr. 3-7). pap. 7.99 *(978-0-316-20016-5(6))* Little, Brown Bks. for Young Readers.
—The Long Road. 2014. (Last Dogs Ser.: 3). (J). lib. bdg. 18.40 *(978-0-606-35309-0(7))* Turtleback Bks.
—The Vanishing. Call, Greg, illus. 2013. (Last Dogs Ser.: 1). (ENG.). 400p. (J). (gr. 3-7). pap. 8.99 *(978-0-316-20004-2(2))* Little, Brown Bks. for Young Readers.
Holt, K. A. Gnome-A-geddon. Jack, Colin, illus. 2017. (ENG.). 304p. (J). (gr. 3-7). 16.99 ***(978-1-4814-7845-8(1),*** McElderry, Margaret K. Bks.) McElderry, Margaret K. Bks.
—Gnomeageddon. 2017. (Illus.). 285p. (J). pap. ***(978-1-4814-7846-5(X),*** McElderry, Margaret K. Bks.) McElderry, Margaret K. Bks.
Holt, Martha. The Adventures of Jillian & Sam: Tiger in Our Town. 2009. 28p. pap. 12.49 *(978-1-4389-6773-8(X))* AuthorHouse.
Holthaus, Abbey. The Treasures of Christmas. Downs, Braden, illus. 2008. 126p. pap. 19.95 *(978-1-60672-152-0(6))* America Star Bks.
Holtz-Bacha, Christina. Second Chance. 2007. 96p. 8.95 *(978-0-9773082-6-2(X))* LBF Bks., LLC.
Holub, Joan & Williams, Suzanne. Apollo & the Battle of the Birds. 2014. (Heroes in Training Ser.: 6). lib. bdg. 16.00 *(978-0-606-35442-4(5))* Turtleback Bks.
—Artemis the Loyal. 2011. (Goddess Girls Ser.: 7). (ENG.). 288p. (J). (gr. 3-7). pap. 7.99 *(978-1-4424-3377-9(9),* Aladdin) Simon & Schuster Children's Publishing.
—Athena the Proud. 2014. (Goddess Girls Ser.: 13). lib. bdg. 18.40 *(978-0-606-35441-7(7))* Turtleback Bks.
—Crius & the Fright of Night. Phillips, Craig, illus. 2015. (Heroes in Training Ser.: 9). (ENG.). 96p. (J). (gr. 1-4). pap. 5.99 *(978-1-4814-3506-2(X),* Aladdin) Simon & Schuster Children's Publishing.
—Cronus & the Threads of Dread. 2014. (Heroes in Training Ser.: 8). lib. bdg. 16.00 *(978-0-606-36092-0(1))* Turtleback Bks.
—Goddess Girls the Glittering Collection: Athena the Wise - Aphrodite the Diva - Artemis the Loyal - Medusa the Mean. 2013. (Goddess Girls Ser.). (ENG., Illus.). 1088p. (J). (gr. 3-7). pap. 23.99 *(978-1-4424-9925-6(7),* Aladdin) Simon & Schuster Children's Publishing.
—Goldilocks Breaks In. 2015. (Grimmtastic Girls Ser.: 6). (ENG.). 192p. (J). (gr. 3-7). pap. 5.99 *(978-0-545-78394-1(1),* Scholastic Paperbacks) Scholastic, Inc.
—Hephaestus & the Island of Terror. 2015. (Heroes in Training Ser.: 10). lib. bdg. 16.00 *(978-0-606-37130-8(3))* Turtleback Bks.
—Hyperion & the Great Balls of Fire. Phillips, Craig, illus. 2013. (Heroes in Training Ser.: 4). (ENG.). 144p. (J). (gr. 1-4). pap. 5.99 *(978-1-4424-5269-5(2),* Aladdin) Simon & Schuster Children's Publishing.
—Hyperion & the Great Balls of Fire. Phillips, Craig, illus. 2013. (Heroes in Training Ser.: 4). (ENG.). 144p. (J). (gr. 1-4). 16.99 *(978-1-4424-5803-1(8),* Simon & Schuster/Paula Wiseman Bks.) Simon & Schuster/Paula Wiseman Bks.
—Nyx the Mysterious. 2017. (Goddess Girls Ser.: 22). lib. bdg. 18.40 ***(978-0-606-39742-1(6))*** Turtleback Bks.
—Pallas the Pal. 2016. (Goddess Girls Ser.: 21). lib. bdg. 18.40 *(978-0-606-39495-6(8))* Turtleback Bks.
—Perseus & the Monstrous Medusa. Phillips, Craig, illus. 2016. (Heroes in Training Ser.: 12). (ENG.). 128p. (J). (gr. 1-4). 16.99 *(978-1-4814-3516-1(7));* pap. 5.99 *(978-1-4814-3515-4(9))* Simon & Schuster Children's Publishing. (Aladdin).
—Perseus & the Monstrous Medusa. 2016. (Heroes in Training Ser.: 12). lib. bdg. 16.00 *(978-0-606-38248-9(8))* Turtleback Bks.
—Red Riding Hood Gets Lost. 2014. (Grimmtastic Girls Ser.: 2). (ENG.). 192p. (J). (gr. 3-7). pap. 5.99 *(978-0-545-51984-7(5))* Scholastic, Inc.
—Typhon & the Winds of Destruction. Phillips, Craig, illus. 2013. (Heroes in Training Ser.: 5). (ENG.). 112p. (J). (gr. 1-4). 16.99 *(978-1-4424-8844-1(1));* pap. 5.99 *(978-1-4424-8842-7(5))* Simon & Schuster Children's Publishing. (Aladdin).
—Typhon & the Winds of Destruction. 2013. (Heroes in Training Ser.: 5). lib. bdg. 16.00 *(978-0-606-32330-7(9),* Turtleback) Turtleback Bks.
—Uranus & the Bubbles of Trouble. 2015. (Heroes in Training Ser.: 11). lib. bdg. 16.00 *(978-0-606-37842-0(1))* Turtleback Bks.
—Zeus & the Thunderbolt of Doom. Phillips, Craig, illus. 2012. (Heroes in Training Ser.: 1). (ENG.). 112p. (J). (gr. 1-4). 16.99 *(978-1-4424-5787-4(2));* pap. 5.99 *(978-1-4424-5263-3(3))* Simon & Schuster Children's Publishing. (Aladdin).
Holyoak, Kathleen & Summers, Sherry. Flowers in Heaven. 2009. 32p. pap. 14.49 *(978-1-4389-4607-8(4))* AuthorHouse.
Holyoke, Polly. The Neptune Project. 2014. (ENG.). 352p. (J). (gr. 3-7). pap. 7.99 *(978-1-4231-5979-7(9))* Hyperion Bks. for Children.
Homer. La Iliada. (SPA., Illus.). 192p. (YA). 11.95 *(978-84-7281-104-1(2),* AF1104) Auriga, Ediciones S.A. ESP. Dist: Continental Bk. Co., Inc.
—La Odisea. (SPA., Illus.). 192p. (YA). 11.95 *(978-84-7281-079-2(8),* AF1079) Auriga, Ediciones S.A. ESP. Dist: Continental Bk. Co., Inc.
Homer, Elizabeth. Peter Wolfe & the Scepter of Myleah. 2008. 212p. pap. 13.95 *(978-1-60693-197-4(0),* Eloquent Bks.) Strategic Book Publishing & Rights Agency (SBPRA).
Homfray, Jenny. The Adventures of Parker the Parrot. 2008. 36p. pap. 15.49 *(978-1-4389-1229-5(3))* AuthorHouse.
Hone, Sallie. Phoenix. 2011. (Illus.). 48p. 20.36 *(978-1-4567-0074-4(X))* AuthorHouse.
Hong, Catherine Thao. The Adventures of Miss Turtle. Pipe, Jasper, illus. 2012. 24p. (J). pap. *(978-0-9873790-0-9(3))* Icky Grass Books.
Hong, J. Gabriela Gil. Chaos & Mother Earth / Caos y Madre Tierr. 2012. 44p. pap. 17.44 *(978-1-4669-6969-8(5))* Trafford Publishing.
Hoobler, David. Zonk & the Secret Lagoon: The Further Adventures of Zonk the Dreaming Tortoise. Hoobler, David, illus. l.t. ed. 2005. (Illus.). 32p. (J). lib. bdg. 18.95 *(978-0-9706537-1-0(9))* Zonk Galleries and Pubns.
Hood, Ann. Alexander Graham Bell: Master of Sound. Zilber, Denis, illus. 2013. (Treasure Chest Ser.: 7). (ENG.). 192p. (J). (gr. 3-7). 6.99 *(978-0-448-45730-7(X),* Grosset & Dunlap) Penguin Young Readers Group.
—Amelia Earhart: Lady Lindy. Zilber, Denis, illus. 2014. (Treasure Chest Ser.: 8). (ENG.). 176p. (J). (gr. 3-7). 6.99 *(978-0-448-45731-4(8),* Grosset & Dunlap) Penguin Young Readers Group.
—Leonardo Da Vinci No. 9: Renaissance Master. Zilber, Denis, illus. 2014. (Treasure Chest Ser.: 9). (ENG.). 224p. (J). (gr. 3-7). 15.99 *(978-0-448-46768-9(2),* Grosset & Dunlap) Penguin Young Readers Group.
Hood, Karen Jean Matsko. Adventures of My Dentist & the Tooth Fairy Activity & Coloring Book Second Edition. 2nd rev. ed. 2010. (Educational Activity & Coloring Book Ser.). (Illus.). (J). 19.95 *(978-1-930948-59-4(X))* Whispering Pine Pr. International, Inc.
—Goodnight, I Wish You Goodnight, Vol. 1. Whispering Pine Press International, Inc. Staff, ed. Hatakeyama, Hiroshi, illus. 2014. (Hood Picture Book Ser.). (ENG.). 44p. (J). 24.95 *(978-1-930948-97-6(2))* Whispering Pine Pr. International, Inc.
—Goodnight, I Wish You Goodnight, Bilingual English & Icelandic, Vol. 1. Whispering Pine Press International, ed. Hatakeyama, Hiroshi, illus. 2015. (Hood Picture Book Ser.). (ENG & ICE.). 60p. (J). 94.99 *(978-1-930948-83-9(2))* Whispering Pine Pr. International, Inc.
—Jesus Loves the Little Children: Activity & Coloring Book, Vol. 8. Whispering Pine Press International, ed. Artistic Design Service Staff, illus. 2016. (Educational Activity & Coloring Book Ser.). (ENG & SPA.). (J). spiral bd. 21.95 *(978-1-59434-087-1(0))* Whispering Pine Pr. International, Inc.
—Spokane Falls. Whispering Pine Press International, ed. Artistic Design Service, illus. l.t. ed. 2015. (Banacek & Flannigan Mystery Ser.). 224p. pap. 22.95 *(978-1-59434-223-3(7));* Vol. 1. 29.95 *(978-1-59434-228-8(8));* Vol. 1. per. 19.95 *(978-1-59434-226-4(1))* Whispering Pine Pr. International, Inc.
—Tanka Thoughts: A Collection of Poetry, bk. 11. Whispering Pine Press International, ed. Artistic Design Service Staff, illus. l.t. ed. 2014. (Hood Poetry Ser.). 224p. pap. 22.95 *(978-1-59808-648-5(0))* Whispering Pine Pr. International, Inc.
Hoogstad, Alice. BOLDER & BOAT. 2008. (ENG.). 32p. (J). (gr. 1-7). 13.95 *(978-1-60136-015-1(0))* Audio Holdings, LLC.
Hook. Wrinkled Crinkled Grapes: A Purple Monster. 2007. 52p. per. 8.95 *(978-0-595-42310-1(8))* iUniverse, Inc.
Hook, Derek. He Walked & He Walked & He Walked. 2012. 110p. 23.95 *(978-1-937902-08-7(0))* Karina Library Pr.
Hook, Francis. Finding the Djinn. 2009. (Hodder African Readers Ser.). (Illus.). 112p. pap. 12.95 *(978-0-340-99029-2(5))* Hodder Education Group GBR. Dist: Trans-Atlantic Pubns., Inc.
Hook, J. E. Magic Square. 2010. 142p. pap. 16.95 *(978-0-557-30383-0(4))* Lulu Pr., Inc.
Hooke, R. Schuyler. Thomas & the Treasure. Palone, Terry & Permane, Terry, photos by. 2008. (Thomas & Friends Ser.). (ENG., Illus.). 24p. (J). (gr. -1-2). pap. 3.99 *(978-0-375-84287-0(X),* Random Hse. Bks. for Young Readers) Random Hse. Children's Bks.
Hooke, R. Schuyler & Awdry, W. Thomas & the Great Discovery. Stubbs, Tommy, illus. 2009. (Little Golden Book Ser.). (ENG.). 24p. (J). (gr. -1-2). 4.99 *(978-0-375-85153-7(4),* Golden Bks.) Random Hse. Children's Bks.
Hooley, Rachelle B. & Butler, Mackay M. The Halloween Chase. Jarman, Brandy S., illus. 2012. 36p. 24.95 *(978-1-4626-7160-1(8))* America Star Bks.
Hooper, R. M. J. The Secret of Crescent Grey. 2009. 340p. pap. 19.99 *(978-1-4363-3206-4(0))* Xlibris Corp.
Hooser, Betty. A Flying House for Entertainment. 2012. 28p. pap. 24.95 *(978-1-4626-7582-1(4))* America Star Bks.
Hoover, P. J. The Emerald Tablet. 2012. (ENG.). 296p. (J). (gr. 6-9). pap. 8.95 *(978-1-933767-19-2(7))* CBAY Bks.
—Tut. 2016. (J). lib. bdg. 20.85 *(978-0-606-38442-1(1))* Turtleback Bks.
—Tut: My Epic Battle to Save the World. 2017. (Tut: My Immortal Life Ser.: 2). (ENG.). 336p. (J). 16.99 *(978-0-7653-9082-0(5),* 9780765390820, Starscape) Doherty, Tom Assocs., LLC.
—Tut: The Story of My Immortal Life. 2014. (Tut: My Immortal Life Ser.: 1). (ENG.). 320p. (J). (gr. 4-7). 15.99 *(978-0-7653-3468-8(2),* 9780765334688, Starscape) Doherty, Tom Assocs., LLC.
Hope, Anthony. Prisoner of Zenda: Reader, Pack. 2nd ed. 2016. (ENG.). x, 86p. (C). pap. 10.99 incl. cd-rom ***(978-1-4082-7649-5(6))*** Pearson Education.
Hope, B. T. The Curse of the Bone Pirates: Nui Island Eco-Logical Adventures. 2008. 198p. (J). pap. 9.95 *(978-0-9817388-0-2(X))* Nui Media & Entertainment, LLC.
Hope, Laura Lee. The Bobbsey Twins in a Great City. 2007. (ENG.). 138p. pap. 18.99 *(978-1-4264-9426-0(2));* 152p. pap. 21.99 *(978-1-4264-9807-7(1))* Creative Media Partners, LLC.
—The Bobbsey Twins in Volcano Land. 2011. 190p. 42.95 *(978-1-258-04953-9(8))* Literary Licensing, LLC.
—The Bobbsey Twins in Washington. 2007. 256p. 29.95 *(978-1-4344-8591-5(9));* per. 17.95 *(978-1-4344-8590-8(0))* Wildside Pr., LLC.
—The Bobbsey Twins on Blueberry Island. 2007. (ENG.). 136p. pap. 18.99 *(978-1-4346-3610-2(0));* 154p. pap. 21.99 *(978-1-4346-3611-9(9))* Creative Media Partners, LLC.
—Bunny Brown & His Sister Sue in the Bi. 2006. 26.95 *(978-1-4218-2974-6(6));* pap. 11.95 *(978-1-4218-3074-2(4))* 1st World Publishing, Inc.
—The Moving Picture Girls at Oak Farm. 2007. 180p. (gr. -1-7). 25.96 *(978-1-4218-3890-8(7),* 1st World Library - Literary Society) 1st World Publishing, Inc.
—The Moving Picture Girls at Sea: Or A Pictured Shipwreck That Became Real. l.t. ed. 2007. (ENG.). 154p. pap. 21.99 *(978-1-4264-9792-6(X))* Creative Media Partners, LLC.
—The Moving Picture Girls under the Palms: Or Lost in the Wilds of Florida. 2007. 140p. pap. 18.99 *(978-1-4346-0717-1(8));* (ENG.). 158p. pap. 21.99 *(978-1-4346-0777-5(1))* Creative Media Partners, LLC.
—Outdoor Girls at Ocean View. 2006. 26.95 *(978-1-4218-2981-4(9));* pap. 11.95 *(978-1-4218-3081-0(7))* 1st World Publishing, Inc.
—The Outdoor Girls at Ocean View: Or the Box That Was Found in the Sand. 2007. 140p. pap. 18.99 *(978-1-4264-9639-4(7));* (ENG.). 150p. pap. 19.99 *(978-1-4264-2712-1(3))* Creative Media Partners, LLC.
—The Outdoor Girls at Rainbow Lake. 2005. 180p. pap. 11.95 *(978-1-4218-1163-5(4),* 1st World Library - Literary Society) 1st World Publishing, Inc.
—The Outdoor Girls at the Hostess House. 2005. 180p. pap. 11.95 *(978-1-4218-1162-8(6),* 1st World Library - Literary Society) 1st World Publishing, Inc.
—The Outdoor Girls at the Hostess House: Or, doing their best for the Soldiers. 2006. (ENG.). 138p. pap. 18.99 *(978-1-4264-7589-4(6))* Creative Media Partners, LLC.
—The Outdoor Girls at Wild Rose Lodge. 2005. 168p. pap. 11.95 *(978-1-4218-1160-4(X),* 1st World Library - Literary Society) 1st World Publishing, Inc.
—The Outdoor Girls at Wild Rose Lodge. l.t. ed. 2007. (ENG.). 144p. pap. 19.99 *(978-1-4264-4399-2(4))* Creative Media Partners, LLC.
—The Outdoor Girls at Wild Rose Lodge: The Outdoor Girls at Wild Rose Lodge. 2007. (ENG.). 134p. pap. 18.99 *(978-1-4264-4361-9(7))* Creative Media Partners, LLC.
—The Outdoor Girls in a Motor Car. 2007. 180p. 26.95 *(978-1-4218-3284-5(4));* per. 11.95 *(978-1-4218-3384-2(0))* 1st World Publishing, Inc. (1st World Library - Literary Society).
—The Outdoor Girls in Army Service. 2005. 26.95 *(978-1-4218-1061-4(1));* 176p. pap. 11.95 *(978-1-4218-1161-1(8))* 1st World Publishing, Inc. (1st World Library - Literary Society).
—The Outdoor Girls in Army Service: Or Doing Their Bit for the Soldier Boys. 2007. (ENG.). 134p. pap. 18.99 *(978-1-4264-9612-7(5));* 148p. pap. 19.99 *(978-1-4264-9993-7(0))* Creative Media Partners, LLC.
—The Outdoor Girls in Florida: Or Wintering in the Sunny South. 2007. 130p. pap. 18.99 *(978-1-4264-9645-5(1));* 144p. pap. 19.99 *(978-1-4264-4927-7(5))* Creative Media Partners, LLC.
—The Outdoor Girls in the Saddle: Or the Girl Miner of Gold Run. 2007. (ENG.). 138p. pap. 18.99 *(978-1-4264-9648-6(6));* 150p. pap. 19.99 *(978-1-4264-6870-4(9))* Creative Media Partners, LLC.
—The Outdoor Girls of Deepdale. 2005. 26.95 *(978-1-4218-1064-5(6));* 180p. pap. 11.95 *(978-1-4218-1164-2(2))* 1st World Publishing, Inc. (1st World Library - Literary Society).
—The Outdoor Girls on Pine Island: Or A Cave & What It Contained. 2007. (ENG.). 144p. pap. 18.99 *(978-1-4264-9638-7(9));* 162p. pap. 21.99 *(978-1-4264-1870-9(1))* Creative Media Partners, LLC.
—Six Little Bunkers at Cousin Tom's. rev. ed. 2006. 192p. 26.95 *(978-1-4218-1795-8(0));* pap. 11.95 *(978-1-4218-1895-5(7))* 1st World Publishing, Inc. (1st World Library - Literary Society).
—Six Little Bunkers at Cowboy Jack's. 2007. 180p. 25.96 *(978-1-4218-3888-5(5),* 1st World Library - Literary Society) 1st World Publishing, Inc.
—Six Little Bunkers at Grandma Bell's. 2005. 26.95 *(978-1-4218-1066-9(2));* 188p. pap. 11.95 *(978-1-4218-1166-6(9))* 1st World Publishing, Inc. (1st World Library - Literary Society).
—Six Little Bunkers at Grandpa Ford's. 2007. 188p. 25.96 *(978-1-4218-3889-2(3),* 1st World Library - Literary Society) 1st World Publishing, Inc.
Hope, Lee Laura. The Outdoor Girls in a Motor Car: The Haunted Mansion of Shadow Valley. 2007. (ENG.). 134p. pap. 18.99 *(978-1-4346-3200-5(8));* 150p. pap. 19.99 *(978-1-4346-3201-2(6))* Creative Media Partners, LLC.
—The Outdoor Girls in a Motor Car or the Haunted Mansion of Shadow Valley. 2007. 156p. 41.99 *(978-1-4280-7518-4(6));* per. 35.99 *(978-1-4280-7519-1(4))* IndyPublish.com.
—The Outdoor Girls in a Winter Camp: Glorious Days on Skates & Ice Boats. 2007. (ENG.). 138p. pap. 18.99 *(978-1-4346-3216-6(4));* 152p. pap. 21.99 *(978-1-4346-3217-3(2))* Creative Media Partners, LLC.
—The Outdoor Girls in a Winter Camp or Glorious Days on Skates & Ice Boats. 2007. 156p. 41.99 *(978-1-4280-7498-9(8));* per. 35.99 *(978-1-4280-7509-2(7))* IndyPublish.com.
—Six Little Bunkers at Aunt Jo's. 2007. 164p. 95.99 *(978-1-4280-7622-8(0));* per. 89.99 *(978-1-4280-7620-4(4))* IndyPublish.com.
—Six Little Bunkers at Cowboy Jack's. 2007. 156p. 95.99 *(978-1-4280-7668-6(9));* per. 89.99 *(978-1-4280-7677-8(8))* IndyPublish.com.
Hopkins, Nicolia. What was Grandma Doing? Wiggins, Margaret W., illus. 2007. (J). per. 9.99 *(978-0-9768579-8-3(7))* eVision, LLC.
Hopkinson, Deborah. The Long Trail. Farnsworth, Bill, illus. 2005. 2004p. (J). lib. bdg. 15.00 *(978-1-59054-904-9(X))* Fitzgerald Bks.
Hopper, Ada. A Case of the Clones. Ricks, Sam, illus. 2016. (DATA Set Ser.: 5). (ENG.). 128p. (J). (gr. k-4). pap. 5.99 *(978-1-4814-7113-8(9),* Little Simon) Little Simon.
—Don't Disturb the Dinosaurs. Ricks, Sam, illus. 2016. (DATA Set Ser.: 2). (ENG.). 128p. (J). (gr. k-4). pap. 5.99 *(978-1-4814-5731-6(4),* Little Simon) Little Simon.
—Invasion of the Insects. Ricks, Sam, illus. 2017. (DATA Set Ser.: 6). (ENG.). 128p. (J). (gr. -1-4). 16.99 *(978-1-4814-7117-6(1),* Little Simon) Little Simon.
—March of the Mini Beasts. Ricks, Sam, illus. 2016. (DATA Set Ser.: bk.1). (ENG.). 128p. (J). (gr. k-4). pap. 5.99 *(978-1-4814-5728-6(4),* Little Simon) Little Simon.
—The Sky Is Falling. Ricks, Sam, illus. 2016. (DATA Set Ser.: bk.3). (ENG.). 128p. (J). (gr. k-4). pap. 5.99 *(978-1-4814-6309-6(8),* Little Simon) Little Simon.
Hopper, Bobby E. Bleep the Purple Bear. Hopper, Andy Lee, illus. 2009. 36p. pap. 18.99 *(978-1-4389-1908-9(5))* AuthorHouse.
Hopper, Celia. The Merry Adventures of Blade & Friends. 2006. (J). lib. bdg. 26.95 *(978-0-9779662-8-8(3))* Creative Bk. Pubs.
Horan, Pamela. Newman the Gnome. 2012. 66p. pap. 17.95 *(978-1-4626-9461-7(6))* America Star Bks.
Horender, Philip M. A Brave New Mouse: Ellis Island Approved Immigrant, 1 vol. Wolek, Guy, illus. 2013. (Maximilian P. Mouse, Time Traveler Ser.). (ENG.). 112p. (J). (gr. 3-6). lib. bdg. 27.07 *(978-1-61641-961-5(X),* Calico Chapter Bks) Magic Wagon.
—Head West, Young Mouse: Transcontinental Railroad Traveler, 1 vol. Wolek, Guy, illus. 2013. (Maximilian P. Mouse, Time Traveler Ser.). (ENG.). 112p. (J). (gr. 3-6). lib. bdg. 27.07 *(978-1-61641-959-2(8),* Calico Chapter Bks) Magic Wagon.
—Homeward Bound: Civil Rights Mouse Leader, 1 vol. Wolek, Guy, illus. 2013. (Maximilian P. Mouse, Time Traveler Ser.). (ENG.). 112p. (J). (gr. 3-6). lib. bdg. 27.07 *(978-1-61641-962-2(8),* Calico Chapter Bks) Magic Wagon.
—The Mighty Maximilian: Samuel Clemens's Traveling Companion, 1 vol. Wolek, Guy, illus. 2013. (Maximilian P. Mouse, Time Traveler Ser.). (ENG.). 112p. (J). (gr. 3-6). lib. bdg. 27.07 *(978-1-61641-960-8(1),* Calico Chapter Bks) Magic Wagon.
—Patriotic Mouse: Boston Tea Party Participant, 1 vol. Wolek, Guy, illus. 2013. (Maximilian P. Mouse, Time Traveler Ser.). (ENG.). 112p. (J). (gr. 3-6). lib. bdg. 27.07 *(978-1-61641-957-8(1),* Calico Chapter Bks) Magic Wagon.
—Yankee Mouse: Gettysburg Address Observer, 1 vol. Wolek, Guy, illus. 2013. (Maximilian P. Mouse, Time Traveler Ser.). (ENG.). 112p. (J). (gr. 3-6). lib. bdg. 27.07 *(978-1-61641-958-5(X),* Calico Chapter Bks) Magic Wagon.
Horn, Shannon. Pirates of the Mississippian: The Adventures of Jerry & Draco. 2012. 24p. pap. 17.99 *(978-1-4772-6991-6(6))* AuthorHouse.
Horne, Jane & Page, Claire. I Really Like Puppies. 2010. (ENG., Illus.). 12p. (J). (gr. -1-k). bds. 9.99 *(978-1-84610-963-8(9))* Make Believe Ideas GBR. Dist: Nelson, Thomas Inc.
Hornung, E. W. The Return Match. 2004. reprint ed. pap. 1.99 *(978-1-4192-8039-9(2));* pap. 15.95 *(978-1-4191-8039-2(8))* Kessinger Publishing, LLC.
Horowitz, Anthony. Ark Angel. (Alex Rider Ser.: Bk. 6). (ENG.). (J). (gr. 5-18). 2007. 352p. 8.99 *(978-0-14-240738-7(0),* Puffin Books) 2006. 336p. 17.99 *(978-0-399-24152-9(3),* Philomel Bks.) Penguin Young Readers Group.
—Ark Angel. 2007. (Alex Rider Ser.: Bk. 6). 326p. (gr. 5-9). 19.00 *(978-0-7569-8134-1(4))* Perfection Learning Corp.
—Ark Angel. 2007. (Alex Rider Ser.: 6). 326p. lib. bdg. 19.65 *(978-1-4177-7664-1(1),* Turtleback) Turtleback Bks.
—Crocodile Tears. (Alex Rider Ser.: Bk. 8). (ENG.). (J). (gr. 5-18). 2010. 416p. 8.99 *(978-0-14-241719-5(X),* Puffin Books) 2009. 400p. 18.99 *(978-0-399-25056-9(5),* Philomel Bks.) Penguin Young Readers Group.
—Crocodile Tears, 9 vols. 2010. (Alex Rider Adventure Ser.: 8). (J). 81.75 *(978-1-4407-5451-7(9));* 79.75

(978-1-4407-5453-1(5)); 100.75 (978-1-4407-5458-6(6)); 102.75 (978-1-4407-5456-2(X)); 1.25 (978-1-4407-5459-3(4)) Recorded Bks., Inc.
—Crocodile Tears. 2010. (Alex Rider Ser.: 8). lib. bdg. 19.65 (978-0-606-23639-3(2), Turtleback) Turtleback Bks.
—The Devil & His Boy. 2007. (ENG.). 192p. (J). (gr. 3-7). 6.99 (978-0-14-240797-4(6), Puffin Books) Penguin Young Readers Group.
—Eagle Strike. (Alex Rider Ser.). (ENG.). (J). (gr. 5-18). 2006. 368p. 8.99 (978-0-14-240613-7(9), Puffin Books) 2004. (Illus.). 272p. 17.99 (978-0-399-23979-3(0), Philomel Bks.) Penguin Young Readers Group.
—The Falcon's Malteser. 2004. (Diamond Brothers Ser.: No. 1). (ENG.). 208p. (J). (gr. 3-7). 6.99 (978-0-14-240219-1(2), Puffin Books) Penguin Young Readers Group.
—Russian Roulette. 2014. (Alex Rider Ser.: 10). lib. bdg. 19.65 (978-0-606-36189-7(8)) Turtleback Bks.
—Russian Roulette: The Story of an Assassin. 2013. (Alex Rider Ser.). (ENG.). 384p. (J). (gr. 6-9). 17.99 (978-0-399-25441-3(2), Philomel Bks.) Penguin Publishing Group.
—Russian Roulette: The Story of an Assassin. 2014. (Alex Rider Ser.). (ENG.). 432p. (J). (gr. 5). pap. 8.99 (978-0-14-751231-4(X), Puffin Books) Penguin Young Readers Group.
—Snakehead. (Alex Rider Ser.: Bk. 7). (ENG.). (gr. 5-18). 2008. 432p. (J). pap. 8.99 (978-0-14-241212-1(0), Puffin Books) 2007. 400p. (YA). 17.99 (978-0-399-24161-1(2), Philomel Bks.) Penguin Young Readers Group.
Horowitz, Anthony & Johnston, Antony. Point Blank. Yuzuru & Kanako, illus. 2007. (Alex Rider Ser.). (ENG.). 176p. (J). (gr. 5-18). 14.99 (978-0-399-25026-2(3), Philomel Bks.) Penguin Young Readers Group.
Horowitz, Jeanine. Latch Key Kid. 2006. 75p. (YA). lib. bdg. 12.99 (978-1-934190-10-4(1)) Ocean Front Bk. Publishing, Inc.
Horse, Harry. The Last Castaways. Horse, Harry, illus. 2009. (ENG., Illus.). 128p. (J). (gr. 1-5). 12.95 (978-1-56145-439-6(7)) Peachtree Pubs.
—The Last Cowboys. Horse, Harry, illus. 2008. (ENG., Illus.). 128p. (J). (gr. 1-5). 12.95 (978-1-56145-451-8(6), Peachtree Junior) Peachtree Pubs.
—The Last Gold Diggers: Being as It Were, an Account of a Small Dog's Adventures, down Under. Horse, Harry, illus. 2008. (ENG., Illus.). 128p. (J). (gr. 1-5). 12.95 (978-1-56145-435-8(4)) Peachtree Pubs.
Horsfall, S. J. Jodie & Lilly... & the Fake Mansion. 2009. 58p. pap. 7.50 (978-0-557-12474-9(3)) Lulu Pr., Inc.
Horton, Jim. The Foot Log Incident. 2008. 30p. pap. 24.95 (978-1-60610-706-5(2)) America Star Bks.
Hosler, Jay. Last of the Sandwalkers. 2015. (ENG., Illus.). 320p. (YA). (gr. 5). pap. 17.99 (978-1-62672-024-4(X), 9781626720244, First Second Bks.) Roaring Brook Pr.
—The Sandwalk Adventures. 2nd ed. 2003. (ENG., Illus.). 152p. (YA). (gr. 6-9). pap. 20.00 (978-0-9677255-1-2(8)) Active Synapse.
Houck, Colleen. Reawakened. 2015. (Reawakened Ser.: Bk. 1). (ENG.). 400p. (YA). (gr. 9-12). 17.99 (978-0-385-37656-3(1), Delacorte Pr.) Random Hse. Children's Bks.
Houdek, Andi. Stop That Pudding! Collier, Kevin, illus. 2010. 16p. pap. 9.95 (978-1-61633-079-8(1)) Guardian Angel Publishing, Inc.
Houk, Amanda. Mommy's New Heart, 1 vol. 2010. 22p. 24.95 (978-1-4512-9377-7(1)) PublishAmerica, Inc.
House, David James. The Key to Space. 2006. (ENM.). 364p. (YA). 24.95 (978-0-9777086-0-4(8)) House, David.
Houseman, D. L. Harvey & His Friends Great Fishing Adventure. 2010. pap. 18.95 (978-0-578-05355-4(1)) Stuff on Paper.
Houston, Meradeth. Colors Like Memories. 2013. 178p. pap. (978-1-77127-371-8(2)) MuseItUp Publishing.
Hovaguimian, Vroni. Deep in the Woods. 2011. 32p. pap. 13.00 (978-0-557-70332-6(8)) Lulu Pr., Inc.
Hovanec, Deb. Lots & Lots of Friends! 2012. 28p. pap. 15.99 (978-1-4797-6208-8(3)) Xlibris Corp.
Howard, A. G. Untamed (Splintered Series Companion) A Splintered Companion. 2016. (Splintered Ser.). (ENG., Illus.). 304p. (J). (gr. 9-17). pap. 9.95 (978-1-4197-2203-5(4), Amulet Bks.) Abrams, Inc.
Howard, Ann. The Mystery of Dragon Bridge: A Peach Blossom Village Story. 2014. (ENG & CHI., Illus.). 40p. (J). (gr. 2-5). pap. 16.95 (978-1-58394-813-2(9)) North Atlantic Bks.
Howard, Assuanta. Doggie Bets. Sandoz, Matt, illus. 2013. 32p. pap. 7.99 (978-1-934947-76-0(8)) Asta Publications, LLC.
Howard, Becky L. Harrison Goes Camping. Pine, Margherita N., ed. Howard, Becky L., illus. 2nd ed. 2012. (Illus.). 26p. (-18). pap. 11.98 (978-0-9848782-1-5(1)) Palmetto Street Publishing.
Howard, Brenda Lynette. Cadi's Weekend Adventure. 2013. 60p. pap. 25.36 (978-1-4669-7057-1(X)) Trafford Publishing.
Howard, Cheryl L. Mikhael the Mighty: Be True to Who You Are & You Can Never Go Wrong. 2009. 52p. pap. 18.50 (978-1-60860-760-0(7), Strategic Bk. Publishing) Strategic Book Publishing & Rights Agency (SBPRA).
Howard, Cheryl Lynne. Captured by Love: A Wild Horse Story Based on Psalm 139. 2011. 48p. pap. 11.00 (978-1-4567-1822-0(3)) AuthorHouse.
Howard, Chris. Night Speed. 2016. 416p. (YA). (gr. 8). 17.99 (978-0-06-241534-9(4), Tegen, Katherine Bks) HarperCollins Pubs.
Howard, Eva. League of Archers. 2016. (League of Archers Ser.: 1). (ENG., Illus.). 288p. (J). (gr. 4-8). 16.99 (978-1-4814-6037-8(4), Aladdin) Simon & Schuster Children's Publishing.
Howard, Jennifer. Lucy & the Land of Lost Socks. 2009. 56p. pap. 10.49 (978-1-4389-5362-5(3)) AuthorHouse.
Howard, Jenny. Bittersweet Voyage. 2012. 172p. pap. 12.95 (978-1-4685-7573-6(2)) AuthorHouse.
Howard, Jonathan L. Katya's War. 2013. (ENG.). 320p. (YA). (gr. 9). pap. 9.99 (978-1-908844-19-4(1), Strange Chemistry) Watkins Media Limited GBR. Dist: Penguin Random Hse. LLC.
—Katya's World. 2012. (Strange Chemistry Ser.). (ENG.). 320p. (J). (gr. 9-12). pap. 9.99 (978-1-908844-13-2(2), Strange Chemistry) Watkins Media Limited GBR. Dist: Penguin Random Hse. LLC.
Howard, Kate. The Lego Movie. movie tie-in ed. 2013. (ENG.). 144p. (J). (gr. 2-5). pap. 5.99 (978-0-545-62464-0(9)) Scholastic, Inc.
—The Search for Zane. 2015. (Lego Ninjago Ser.: 7). (ENG.). 80p. (J). (gr. 2-5). pap. 4.99 (978-0-545-75054-7(7)) Scholastic, Inc.
Howard, Martin. Shaun the Sheep: Flock to the Seaside. Janes, Andy, illus. 2015. (Tales from Mossy Bottom Farm Ser.). (ENG.). 112p. (J). (gr. k-3). pap. 4.99 (978-0-7636-8058-9(3), Candlewick Entertainment) Candlewick Pr.
—Shaun the Sheep: on the Ball. Janes, Andy, illus. 2015. (Tales from Mossy Bottom Farm Ser.). (ENG.). 112p. (J). (gr. k-3). pap. 4.99 (978-0-7636-8059-6(1), Candlewick Entertainment) Candlewick Pr.
Howard, Monique. The Moon Creeper. 2010. (Illus.). 40p. (J). pap. 7.95 (978-1-935706-07-6(1)) Wiggles Pr.
—The Moon Creeper (Simplified Chinese & English) Li, Helen, tr. Howard, Monique, illus. 2010. (CHI & ENG., Illus.). 40p. (YA). pap. 7.95 (978-1-935706-24-3(1)) Wiggles Pr.
Howard, Peggy Ann. Zorees: Land of Dreams. 2007. (YA). per. 16.95 (978-0-9795519-0-1(0)) Dream Scape Publishing, LLC.
Howard, Pyle. A Modern Aladdin or the Wonderful Adventures of Oliver Munier: an Extravaganza in Four Acts. 2009. (ENG.). 278p. pap. 23.99 (978-1-110-32516-0(9)); pap. 21.99 (978-1-110-32512-2(6)) Creative Media Partners, LLC. (BiblioLife).
Howard, Roger. Safety First. 2008. 328p. pap. 12.95 (978-1-4327-0449-0(4)) Outskirts Pr., Inc.
Howard, Rushton. Sebastian Reckless. Howard, Rushton, illus. 2005. (Illus.). 263p. (J). per. 8.99 (978-0-9768088-0-0(3)) Abdiel Productions.
Howard, S. Paul. Hawehyo's Tale, 1 vol. 2008. (ENG.). 31p. pap. 24.95 (978-1-60441-577-3(0)) America Star Bks.
Howard, Victoria. The Adventures of Max: Max & His Friends Save the World. 2013. 68p. pap. 28.99 (978-1-4817-0732-9(9)) AuthorHouse.
—The Adventures of Max: The Bolognese Dog. 2012. 72p. pap. 28.99 (978-1-4772-6560-4(0)) AuthorHouse.
—The Adventures of Max & Molly: A Love Story about a Dog & a Horse. 2012. 52p. pap. 24.99 (978-1-4772-4866-9(8)) AuthorHouse.
Howat, Irene. Adoniram Judson: Danger on the Streets of Gold. 2007. (Trailblazers Ser.). (ENG.). 160p. (J). mass mkt. 8.99 (978-1-85792-660-6(9), aa09dd00-c28c-4172-8dee-7bb4c77f28dc) Christian Focus Pubns. GBR. Dist: Bookmasters Distribution.
Howe, James. Bunnicula in a Box: Bunnicula; Howliday Inn; the Celery Stalks at Midnight; Nighty-Nightmare; Return to Howliday Inn; Bunnicula Strikes Again; Bunnicula Meets Edgar Allan Crow. Payne, C. F., illus. 2013. (Bunnicula & Friends Ser.). (ENG.). 1136p. (J). (gr. 3-7). pap. 48.99 (978-1-4424-8521-1(3), Atheneum Bks. for Young Readers) Simon & Schuster Children's Publishing.
Howe, Peter. Waggit's Tale. Rayyan, Omar, illus. 2009. (Waggit Ser.: 1). (ENG.). 304p. (J). (gr. 5). pap. 6.99 (978-0-06-124263-2(2)) HarperCollins Pubs.
Howe, Tina Field. Alysa of the Fields: Book One in the Tellings of Xunar-kun. 2006. (Illus.). 320p. (YA). 30.95 (978-0-9768585-2-2(5)) Howe, Tina Field.
—Snailsworth, a slow little Story. Howe, Tina Field, illus. 2007. (Illus.). 24p. (J). per. 12.95 (978-0-9768585-3-9(3)) Howe, Tina Field.
Howell, David. Swan Songs-in Search of the Staffstone. 2005. per. 13.99 (978-1-59781-002-9(9)) Salem Author Services.
Howell, Gail L. Sarah & the Blue Sled: Sarah's World (Series) 2010. 32p. pap. 12.99 (978-1-4389-7597-9(X)) AuthorHouse.
Howell, Hayley L. Sammy's Two Left Feet: Groovin' with Mr. Smooth: Discovering How to Believe in Yourself. 2010. 32p. pap. 15.95 (978-1-4520-5733-0(8)) AuthorHouse.
Howell, Julie Ann. Mrs Owl's Nest of Rhymes. LaGrange, Tiffany, illus. 2008. 24p. pap. 12.95 (978-0-9818683-8-7(X)) Peppertree Pr., The.
Howells, Angela. The Tails of Victoria Way. 2009. (Illus.). 32p. pap. 12.99 (978-1-4490-4432-9(8)) AuthorHouse.
Howland, Ashley. The Homework Goblin. 2013. 24p. pap. 13.97 (978-1-62516-301-1(0), Strategic Bk. Publishing) Strategic Book Publishing & Rights Agency (SBPRA).
—Obi the Super Puppy & the Mystery of the Red Mist. 2011. 88p. pap. 12.97 (978-1-61204-276-7(3), Strategic Bk. Publishing) Strategic Book Publishing & Rights Agency (SBPRA).
Hoyle, K. B. The Six. 2016. (ENG., Illus.). (J). 29.99 **(978-1-61213-396-6(7))** 2012. 230p. pap. 22.50 (978-1-61213-052-1(6)) Writer's Coffee Shop, The.
Hoyle, Tom. Survivor. 2015. (ENG.). 272p. (YA). (gr. 7). 10.99 **(978-1-4472-8675-2(8))** Pan Macmillan GBR. Dist: Independent Pubs. Group.
Hoylie, Gerry. Byron Unleashed. 2005. 60p. pap. 14.95 (978-1-59113-670-5(9)) Booklocker.com, Inc.
Hoyt, Charlene. Where the Leprechauns Hide. Fischer, Sandi, illus. 2007. (ENG.). 40p. per. 12.99 (978-0-9792258-9-5(2)) Bezalel Bks.
Hozjan, Michael. The Adventures of Tibo & Friends. 2011. 44p. pap. 24.95 (978-1-4626-4486-5(4)) America Star Bks.
Hritzay, Tami. The Hole in the Wall: J. B. & the Pirates. 2013. pap. 11.45 (978-0-7414-8266-2(5)) Infinity Publishing.
Hsiao, Christie. Journey to Rainbow Island. 2013. (ENG., Illus.). 40p. (J). (gr. 2-7). 17.95 (978-1-939529-24-4(7)) BenBella Bks.
Hu, Jennifer. Dodo's Story: Journey in America. 2010. 40p. 16.99 (978-1-4520-6095-8(9)) AuthorHouse.
Huang, Yu-Hsuan. Alien Adventure. 2017. (ENG., Illus.). 10p. (J). (gr. -1-k). bds. 7.99 **(978-1-5098-3579-9(2))** Pan Macmillan GBR. Dist: Independent Pubs. Group.
Hubbard, Kirsten. Race the Night. 2016. (ENG.). 288p. (J). (gr. 3-7). 16.99 (978-1-4847-0834-7(2)) Hyperion Bks. for Children.
—Race the Night. 2017. (J). lib. bdg. 18.40 **(978-0-606-40711-3(1))** Turtleback Bks.
Hubbard, L. Ron, contrib. by. On Blazing Wings: Literature Guide for Teachers & Librarians Based on Common Core ELA Standards for Classrooms 6-9. 2013. (Stories from the Golden Age Ser.). (ENG.). 35p. (gr. 6-9). pap., tchr. ed. 14.95 (978-1-61986-253-1(0)) Galaxy Pr., LLC.
—Tomb of the Ten Thousand Dead: Literature Guide for Teachers & Librarians Based on Common Core ELA Standards for Classrooms 6-9. 2013. (Stories from the Golden Age Ser.). (ENG.). 35p. (gr. 6-9). pap., tchr. ed. 14.95 (978-1-61986-219-7(0)) Galaxy Pr., LLC.
—The Toughest Ranger: Literature Guide for Teachers & Librarians, Based on Common Core ELA Standards for Classrooms 6-9. 2013. (Stories from the Golden Age Ser.). (ENG.). 35p. (gr. 6-9). pap., tchr. ed. 14.95 (978-1-61986-220-3(4)) Galaxy Pr., LLC.
Hubbard, Sharron/Y. Link & Rosie Pick Berries. Schleihs, Krostin, illus. 2007. (J). bds. 7.95 (978-0-9762434-2-7(3)) Link & Rosie Pr.
Hubbell, Mary A. The Miracle of Annie's Ring. 2010. 138p. pap. 11.50 (978-1-60911-530-2(9), Eloquent Bks.) Strategic Book Publishing & Rights Agency (SBPRA).
Huber, Randy. Of Heroes & Heroines. 2008. 48p. pap. 16.95 (978-1-4241-5421-0(9)) America Star Bks.
Huchel, Gerald D. She-Devil & the Pup. 2012. 32p. (-18). pap. 16.95 (978-1-62709-156-5(4)) America Star Bks.
Huckleberry Finn. (ARA., Illus.). 48p. (J). 12.00 (978-0-86685-623-2(4)) International Bk. Ctr., Inc.
Hudgins, Larry. My Dog Spike, 1 vol. 2009. 55p. pap. 16.95 (978-1-60836-421-3(6)) America Star Bks.
Hudgins, Mary Jane. Quacker Jack the Duck, 1 vol. 2010. 20p. pap. 24.95 (978-1-4489-8188-5(3)) PublishAmerica, Inc.
Hudson, Wade. Puddin', Jeffrey & Leah. 2008. (Illus.). 16p. (gr. -1). 6.95 (978-1-60349-006-1(X), Marimba Bks.) Hudson Publishing Group, The.
Hudspith, Will. Stairgate - Gordon's Adventures on Everest. 2013. 64p. pap. (978-1-4602-1219-6(3)) FriesenPress.
Huelin, Jodi. Alvin & the Chipmunks: Alvin & the Big Art Show. Artful Doodlers Limited Staff, illus. 2013. (I Can Read Level 2 Ser.). (ENG.). 32p. (J). (gr. -1-3). pap. 3.99 (978-0-06-225225-8(9), HarperFestival) HarperCollins Pubs.
—Batman & the Toxic Terror. Gordon, Steven E., illus. 2011. (ENG.). 24p. (J). (gr. -1-3). pap. 3.99 (978-0-06-188530-3(4), HarperFestival) HarperCollins Pubs.
—Batman Versus Bane. Tong, Andie, illus. 2012. (I Can Read Book 2 Ser.). (ENG.). 32p. (J). (gr. -1-3). pap. 3.99 (978-0-06-213224-6(5)) HarperCollins Pubs.
—The Movie Storybook. 2011. (Rio Ser.). (ENG.). 48p. (J). (gr. -1-2). pap. 8.99 (978-0-06-202270-7(9), HarperFestival) HarperCollins Pubs.
—The Reason for the Season. Artful Doodlers Ltd Staff, illus. 2013. (Alvin & the Chipmunks Ser.). (ENG.). 24p. (J). (gr. -1-3). pap. 4.99 (978-0-06-225221-0(6), HarperFestival) HarperCollins Pubs.
Huffman, Nancy E. The Misadventures of Taylor R. Bailey. 2010. 112p. 23.99 (978-1-4490-5791-6(8)); pap. 13.99 (978-1-4490-5790-9(X)) AuthorHouse.
Huggett, Christopher. The Magic Man. 2011. 216p. pap. 24.95 (978-1-4560-6701-4(X)) America Star Bks.
Hughes, Carol. The Princess & the Unicorn. 2010. (ENG.). 288p. (J). (gr. 3-7). 7.99 (978-0-375-85563-4(7), Bluefire) Random Hse. Children's Bks.
Hughes, Diane. Wilbur Meets Aunt Lucy. 2009. 12p. pap. 8.49 (978-1-4490-1241-0(8)) AuthorHouse.
Hughes, Diane Marie. Meet Wilbur the Squirrel. 2004. 21p. pap. 24.95 (978-1-4137-2758-6(1)) PublishAmerica, Inc.
Hughes, Donna L. Charly's Adventure, 1 vol. Johnson, Kenny Ray, illus. 2009. 14p. pap. 24.95 (978-1-4489-1822-5(7)) America Star Bks.
Hughes, Jenny. Sea Horses. 2013. (ENG., Illus.). 224p. (J). (gr. 3-7). pap. 9.95 (978-1-62124-006-8(1)) Breakaway Bks.
Hughes, Julie. The Fantastic Christmas. Sharpley, Kate, illus. 2013. 34p. pap. (978-0-9868344-9-3(1)) Yodoki Inc.
Hughes, Shirley. Digby O'Day in the Fast Lane. Vulliamy, Clara, illus. 2014. (ENG.). 128p. (J). (gr. k-3). 12.99 (978-0-7636-7369-7(2)) Candlewick Pr.
—Digby O'Day up, up, & Away. Vulliamy, Clara, illus. 2016. (ENG.). 136p. (J). (gr. k-3). 12.99 (978-0-7636-7444-1(3)) Candlewick Pr.
—Hero on a Bicycle. 2013. (ENG., Illus.). 224p. (J). (gr. 5-9). 16.99 (978-0-7636-6037-6(X)) Candlewick Pr.
Hughes, Stephen B. The Adventures of Bruno a Dogg & Bowser T Houn' 2009. 80p. pap. 14.98 (978-1-4389-8677-7(7)) AuthorHouse.
Hughes, Thomas. Tom Brown's School Days by an Old Boy. 2004. reprint ed. pap. 1.99 (978-1-4192-9039-8(8)) Kessinger Publishing, LLC.
Hugo, Victor. Les Misérables. Flores, Catty, illus. adapted ed. 2014. (ENG.). 64p. pap. 6.95 (978-1-906230-79-1(X)) Real Reads Ltd. GBR. Dist: Casemate Pubs. & Bk. Distributors, LLC.
Huiner, Jacque. Anna Ate. 2009. 36p. pap. 21.99 (978-1-4389-1765-8(1)) AuthorHouse.
Hulet, Paul. Bruce the Moose Is on the Loose. 2009. (Illus.). 36p. (gr. -1-7). pap. 13.95 (978-1-60860-473-9(X), Strategic Bk. Publishing) Strategic Book Publishing & Rights Agency (SBPRA).
Hulk. 2003. (J). per. (978-1-57657-856-8(9)) Paradise Pr., Inc.
Hulk the Hero. 2003. (J). per. (978-1-57657-821-6(6)) Paradise Pr., Inc.
Hulk to the Rescue. 2003. (J). per. (978-1-57657-811-7(9)) Paradise Pr., Inc.
Hulk's Big Mess. 2003. (J). per. (978-1-57657-822-3(4)) Paradise Pr., Inc.
Hull, Claire. Frozen in Time. 2013. 60p. pap. 15.95 (978-0-9887836-7-6(3)) Taylor and Seale Publishing, LLC.
—Isn;T That Silly. 2012. 82p. pap. 15.95 (978-0-9846558-7-8(5)) Taylor and Seale Publishing, LLC.
Humm, Sharlene. Jack & Jill in the Special Wish. 2008. 40p. per. 24.95 (978-1-4241-9458-2(X)) America Star Bks.
Hummel, Jim. A Bubble C. 2009. 32p. pap. 14.95 (978-1-4269-0034-1(1)) Trafford Publishing.
—The Hunters. 2010. 36p. 15.49 (978-1-4269-4216-7(8)) Trafford Publishing.
—Imagination: On Planet Hic-Cup. 2013. 36p. pap. 15.49 (978-1-4669-8903-0(3)) Trafford Publishing.
Huneck, Stephen. Sally's Great Balloon Adventure. 2010. (ENG., Illus.). 32p. (J). (gr. 1-4). 16.95 (978-0-8109-8331-1(1), Abrams Bks. for Young Readers) Abrams, Inc.
—Sally's Snow Adventure. Huneck, Stephen, illus. 2006. (ENG., Illus.). 32p. (J). (gr. -1-3). 15.95 (978-0-8109-7061-8(9)) Abrams, Inc.
Hunsaker, Joan. A Dagger in Time. 2008. 116p. 18.99 (978-1-58930-218-1(4)); pap. 11.99 (978-1-58930-216-7(8)) Selah Publishing Group, LLC.
Hunt, Bonnie. Danger! Keep Out! The Grayson Twins Adventures. 2008. 96p. pap. 19.95 (978-1-60563-202-5(3)) America Star Bks.
—The Missing Chimp: A Grayson Twins Adventures, 1 vol. 2009. 100p. pap. 19.95 (978-1-60813-481-6(4)) America Star Bks.
Hunt, Debbie Colleen. Wollie the Wheelbarrow. Burket, Shelia, illus. 2012. 24p. 24.95 (978-1-4626-9969-8(3)) America Star Bks.
Hunt, Elizabeth Singer. The Escape of the Deadly Dinosaur - USA. Williamson, Brian, illus. 2007. (Secret Agent Jack Stalwart Ser.: 1). (ENG.). 128p. (J). (gr. 1-4). per. 5.99 (978-1-60286-004-9(1), Weinstein Bks.) Perseus Bks. Group.
—The Fight for the Frozen Land, Bk.12. Williamson, Brian, illus. 2009. (Secret Agent Jack Stalwart Ser.: 12). (ENG.). 128p. (J). (gr. 1-4). pap. 5.99 (978-1-60286-099-5(8), Weinstein Bks.) Perseus Bks. Group.
—The Mystery of the Mona Lisa, Bk. 3. Williamson, Brian, illus. 2007. (Secret Agent Jack Stalwart Ser.: 3). (ENG.). 128p. (J). (gr. 1-4). per. 5.99 (978-1-60286-001-8(7), Weinstein Bks.) Perseus Bks. Group.
—Peril at the Grand Prix - Italy, Bk. 8. 2009. (Secret Agent Jack Stalwart Ser.: 8). (ENG.). 144p. (J). (gr. 1-4). pap. 5.99 (978-1-60286-019-3(X), Weinstein Bks.) Perseus Bks. Group.
—The Pursuit of the Ivory Poachers: Kenya. Williams, Brian, illus. 2008. (Secret Agent Jack Stalwart Ser.: 6). (ENG.). 144p. (J). (gr. 1-4). pap. 5.99 (978-1-60286-021-6(1), Weinstein Bks.) Perseus Bks. Group.
—The Puzzle of the Missing Panda, Bk. 7. Williamson, Brian, illus. 2008. (Secret Agent Jack Stalwart Ser.: 7). (ENG.). 128p. (J). (gr. 1-4). pap. 5.99 (978-1-60286-020-9(3), Weinstein Bks.) Perseus Bks. Group.
—The Search for the Sunken Treasure. Williamson, Brian, illus. 2007. (Secret Agent Jack Stalwart Ser.: 2). (ENG.). 128p. (J). (gr. 1-4). per. 5.99 (978-1-60286-002-5(5), Weinstein Bks.) Perseus Bks. Group.
—The Search for the Sunken Treasure Bk. 2: Australia. 2007. (Illus.). 110p. (J). (978-1-4242-4190-3(1), Weinstein Bks.) Perseus Bks. Group.
—Secret Agents Jack & Max Stalwart: Book 1: the Battle for the Emerald Buddha: Thailand. Williamson, Brian, illus. 2017. (Secret Agents Jack & Max Stalwart Ser.: 1). (ENG.). 144p. (gr. 1-4). pap. 5.99 **(978-1-60286-359-0(8)**, Weinstein Bks.) Perseus Bks. Group.
—Secret Agents Jack & Max Stalwart: Book 2: the Adventure in the Amazon: Brazil. Williamson, Brian, illus. 2017. (Secret Agents Jack & Max Stalwart Ser.: 2). (ENG.). 128p. (gr. 1-4). pap. 5.99 **(978-1-60286-361-3(X)**, Weinstein Bks.) Perseus Bks. Group.
Hunt, Elizabeth Singer. Theft of the Samurai Sword: Japan #11. 2009. (ENG., Illus.). 128p. (J). lib. bdg. 15.38 (978-1-4242-4452-2(8)) Fitzgerald Bks.
Hunt, Elizabeth Singer & Weinstein Books Staff. The Theft of the Samurai Sword: Japan. Williamson, Brian, illus. 2009. (Secret Agent Jack Stalwart Ser.: 11). (ENG.). 128p. (J). (gr. 1-4). pap. 5.99 (978-1-60286-098-8(X), Weinstein Bks.) Perseus Bks. Group.
The Hunt for Pirate Gold, 6 vols., Vol. 2. (Woodland Mysteriestm Ser.). 133p. (gr. 3-7). 42.50 (978-0-7802-7934-6(4)) Wright Group/McGraw-Hill.
Hunt, Graham. Smillbow & the Land of Titch'wee. 2010. (Illus.). 92p. pap. (978-1-84748-673-8(8)) Athena Pr.
Hunt, Leo. Eight Rivers of Shadow. 2017. (ENG.). 368p. (YA). (gr. 9). pap. 9.99 **(978-0-7636-9457-9(6))** Candlewick Pr.
Hunt, Leo. Thirteen Days of Midnight. 2015. (ENG.). 336p. (YA). (gr. 9). 13.00 (978-0-7636-7865-4(1)) Candlewick Pr.
Hunter, A. J. Myth Raiders. De la Rue, James, illus. 2017. (Myth Raiders Ser.). (ENG.). 192p. (J). (gr. 4-6). pap. 6.99 **(978-0-349-12436-0(1))** Little, Brown Bks. for Young Readers.
Hunter, Derek. Brainwash Escape Victims, Vol. 2. 2006. (ENG., Illus.). 144p. (YA). pap. 12.95 (978-1-59362-051-6(9), 9781593620516) Slave Labor Bks.
Hunter, Elizabeth. Home Oasis. 2009. (Illus.). 36p. pap. 15.49 (978-1-4389-6284-9(3)) AuthorHouse.
Hunter, Erin. After the Flood. 2012. (Warriors — SkyClan & the Stranger Ser.: 3). (J). lib. bdg. 17.20 (978-0-606-23597-6(3), Turtleback) Turtleback Bks.
—Bluestar's Prophecy. McLoughlin, Wayne, illus. 2009. (Warriors Super Edition Ser.: 2). (ENG.). 544p. (J). (gr. 3-7). 17.99 (978-0-06-158247-9(6)) HarperCollins Pubs.
—Dark River. (Warriors: Power of Three Ser.: 2). (ENG.). (J). (gr. 3-7). 2015. 368p. pap. 7.99 (978-0-06-236709-9(9)) 2008. 368p. pap. 6.99 (978-0-06-089207-4(2)) 2007. (Illus.). 352p. 16.99 (978-0-06-089205-0(6)) HarperCollins Pubs.
—Darkness Falls. (Survivors Ser.: 3). (J). (gr. 3-7). 2014. (ENG.). 320p. pap. 7.99 (978-0-06-210266-9(4)) 2013. 304p. lib. bdg. 17.89 (978-0-06-210265-2(6)) 2013. (ENG.). 304p. 16.99 (978-0-06-210264-5(8)) HarperCollins Pubs.
—Darkness Falls. 2014. (Survivors Ser.: 3). (J). lib. bdg. 18.40 (978-0-606-35496-7(4)) Turtleback Bks.
—Dawn. 2015. (Warriors — the New Prophecy Ser.: 3). (J). lib. bdg. 18.40 (978-0-606-36502-4(8)) Turtleback Bks.
—Eclipse. (Warriors: Power of Three Ser.: 4). (ENG.). (J). (gr. 3-7). 2015. 368p. pap. 7.99 (978-0-06-236711-2(0)) 2009. 336p. pap. 7.99 (978-0-06-089213-5(7)) 2008. (Illus.). 336p. 16.99 (978-0-06-089211-1(0)) HarperCollins Pubs.
—The Empty City. (Survivors Ser.: 1). (J). (gr. 3-7). 2013. (ENG.). 304p. pap. 7.99 (978-0-06-210258-4(3)) 2012. (ENG.). 288p. 16.99 (978-0-06-210256-0(7)) 2012. 288p. lib. bdg. 17.89 (978-0-06-210257-7(5)) HarperCollins Pubs.
—The Empty City. 2013. (Survivors Ser.: 1). (J). lib. bdg. 18.40 (978-0-606-31803-7(8), Turtleback) Turtleback Bks.
—The Empty City & a Hidden Enemy. 2014. (Survivors Ser.). (ENG.). 592p. (J). (gr. 3-7). pap. 7.99 (978-0-06-232146-6(3)) HarperCollins Pubs.
—The Endless Lake. 2014. (Survivors Ser.: 5). 320p. (J). (gr. 3-7). (ENG.). 16.99 (978-0-06-210272-0(9)); lib. bdg. 17.89 (978-0-06-210273-7(7)) HarperCollins Pubs.

—Fading Echoes. Richardson, Owen & Douglas, Allen, illus. (Warriors: Omen of the Stars Ser.: 2). (ENG.). (J). (gr. 3-7). 2011. 368p. pap. 6.99 (978-0-06-155514-5(2)) 2010. 352p. 16.99 (978-0-06-155512-1(6)) HarperCollins Pubs.

—The First Battle. McLoughlin, Wayne & Douglas, Allen, illus. 2015. (Warriors: Dawn of the Clans Ser.: 3). (ENG.). 352p. (J). (gr. 3-7). pap. 6.99 (978-0-06-206356-4(1)) HarperCollins Pubs.

—Forest of Secrets. Stevenson, Dave, illus. 2004. (Warriors: the Prophecies Begin Ser.: 3). (ENG.). 336p. (J). (gr. 3-7). pap. 6.99 (978-0-06-052561-3(4)) HarperCollins Pubs.

—Forest of Secrets, In to the Wild, Fire & Ice. 2006. (Warriors Ser.: Bks. 1-3). (Illus.). 1056p. (J). (gr. 3-7). pap. 15.99 (978-0-06-089190-9(4)) HarperCollins Pubs.

—The Forgotten Warrior. Richardson, Owen & Douglas, Allen, illus. 2012. (Warriors: Omen of the Stars Ser.: 5). (ENG.). 384p. (J). (gr. 3-7). pap. 6.99 (978-0-06-155526-8(6)) HarperCollins Pubs.

—The Fourth Apprentice. Richardson, Owen & Douglas, Allen, illus. 2009. (Warriors: Omen of the Stars Ser.: 1). (ENG.). 352p. (J). (gr. 3-7). 16.99 (978-0-06-155509-1(6)) HarperCollins Pubs.

—A Hidden Enemy. (Survivors Ser.: 2). (J). (gr. 3-7). 2014. (ENG.). 304p. pap. 7.99 (978-0-06-210262-1(1)) 2013. 288p. lib. bdg. 17.89 (978-0-06-210261-4(3)) 2013. (ENG.). 288p. 16.99 (978-0-06-210260-7(5)) HarperCollins Pubs.

—A Hidden Enemy. 2014. (Survivors Ser.: 2). (J). lib. bdg. 18.40 (978-0-606-35056-3(X), Turtleback) Turtleback Bks.

—Into the Wild. Stevenson, Dave, illus. 2004. (Warriors: the Prophecies Begin Ser.: 1). (ENG.). 288p. (J). (gr. 3-7). pap. 6.99 (978-0-06-052550-7(9)) HarperCollins Pubs.

—Into the Wild. 2003. (Warriors Ser.: Bk. 1). (Illus.). 304p. (J). pap. (978-0-00-714002-2(9), HarperCollins Children's Bks.) HarperCollins Pubs. Ltd.

—The Last Hope. Richardson, Owen & Douglas, Allen, illus. (Warriors: Omen of the Stars Ser.: 6). (ENG.). (J). (gr. 3-7). 2013. 400p. pap. 7.99 (978-0-06-155529-9(0)) 2012. 384p. 16.99 (978-0-06-155527-5(4)) HarperCollins Pubs.

—Long Shadows. (Warriors: Power of Three Ser.: 5). (ENG.). (J). (gr. 3-7). 2015. 368p. pap. 7.99 (978-0-06-236712-9(9)) 2009. 352p. pap. 7.99 (978-0-06-089216-6(1)) 2008. 336p. 16.99 (978-0-06-089214-2(5)) HarperCollins Pubs.

—The Melting Sea. 2013. (Seekers: Return to the Wild Ser.: 2). (ENG.). 304p. (J). (gr. 3-7). pap. 6.99 (978-0-06-199639-9(4)) HarperCollins Pubs.

—The Melting Sea. 2013. (Seekers: Return to the Wild Ser.: 2). (J). lib. bdg. 17.20 (978-0-606-31816-7(X), Turtleback) Turtleback Bks.

—Midnight. 2015. (Warriors — the New Prophecy Ser.: 1). (J). lib. bdg. 18.40 (978-0-606-36500-0(1)) Turtleback Bks.

—Night Whispers. Richardson, Owen & Douglas, Allen, illus. (Warriors: Omen of the Stars Ser.: 3). (ENG.). (J). (gr. 3-7). 2011. 368p. pap. 6.99 (978-0-06-155517-6(7)) 2010. 352p. 16.99 (978-0-06-155515-2(0)) HarperCollins Pubs.

—Outcast. (Warriors: Power of Three Ser.: 3). (ENG.). (J). (gr. 3-7). 2015. 368p. pap. 7.99 (978-0-06-236710-5(2)) 2008. (Illus.). 352p. 16.99 (978-0-06-089208-1(0)) HarperCollins Pubs.

—River of Lost Bearsrs No. 3. 2013. (Seekers: Return to the Wild Ser.: 3). (ENG., Illus.). 320p. (J). (gr. 3-7). 16.99 (978-0-06-199640-5(8)) HarperCollins Pubs.

—Seekers: Return to the Wild #6: the Longest Day. 2016. (Seekers: Return to the Wild Ser.: 6). (Illus.). 336p. (J). (gr. 3-7). 16.99 (978-0-06-199649-8(1)) HarperCollins Pubs.

—Shadows of the Clans. 2016. (Warriors Ser.). (J). lib. bdg. 18.40 (978-0-606-38146-8(5)) Turtleback Bks.

—Shattered Peace. Barry, James L., illus. 2009. (Warriors Manga Ser.: 1). (ENG.). 112p. (J). (gr. 3-7). pap. 6.99 (978-0-06-168865-2(7)) HarperCollins Pubs.

—Sign of the Moon. Richardson, Owen & Douglas, Allen, illus. (Warriors: Omen of the Stars Ser.: 4). (J). (gr. 3-7). 2011. (ENG.). 352p. 16.99 (978-0-06-155518-3(5)) 2011. 352p. lib. bdg. 17.89 (978-0-06-155520-6(7))No. 4. 2012. (ENG.). 368p. pap. 6.99 (978-0-06-155521-3(5)) HarperCollins Pubs.

—Sign of the Moon. 2015. (Warriors — Omen of the Stars Ser.: 4). (J). lib. bdg. 17.20 (978-0-606-37725-6(5)) Turtleback Bks.

—Skyclan's Destiny. McLoughlin, Wayne, illus. 2011. (Warriors Super Edition Ser.: 3). (ENG.). 528p. (J). (gr. 3-7). pap. 7.99 (978-0-06-169996-2(9)) HarperCollins Pubs.

—Storm of Dogs. 2015. (Survivors Ser.: 6). (J). (gr. 3-7). (ENG.). 304p. pap. 7.99 (978-0-06-210278-2(8)); (ENG.). 288p. 16.99 (978-0-06-210276-8(1)); 288p. lib. bdg. 17.89 (978-0-06-210277-5(X)) HarperCollins Pubs.

—The Sun Trail. McLoughlin, Wayne & Douglas, Allen, illus. 2013. (Warriors: Dawn of the Clans Ser.: 1). (ENG.). 352p. (J). (gr. 3-7). 16.99 (978-0-06-206346-5(4)) HarperCollins Pubs.

—The Sun Trail. 2016. (Warriors — Dawn of the Clans Ser.: 1). (J). lib. bdg. 18.40 (978-0-606-38161-1(9)) Turtleback Bks.

—Sunrise. (Warriors: Power of Three Ser.: 6). (ENG.). (J). (gr. 3-7). 2010. 368p. pap. 7.99 (978-0-06-089219-7(6)) 6th ed. 2009. 352p. 16.99 (978-0-06-089217-3(X)) HarperCollins Pubs.

—Sunrise. 2015. (Warriors — Power of Three Ser.: 6). (J). lib. bdg. 18.40 (978-0-606-36975-6(9)) Turtleback Bks.

—Sunset. Stevenson, Dave, illus. 2006. (Warriors: the New Prophecy Ser.: 6). (ENG.). 320p. (J). (gr. 3-7). 16.99 (978-0-06-082769-4(6)) HarperCollins Pubs.

—Sunset. 2015. (Warriors — the New Prophecy Ser.: 6). (J). lib. bdg. 18.40 (978-0-606-36507-9(9)) Turtleback Bks.

—Survivors: the Gathering Darkness #3: into the Shadows. Kubinyi, Laszlo & Green, Julia, illus. 2017. (Survivors: the Gathering Darkness Ser.: 3). (J). (gr. 3-7). 336p. pap. 7.99 **(978-0-06-234343-7(2))**; 320p. 16.99 (978-0-06-234341-3(6)) HarperCollins Pubs.

—Survivors: the Gathering Darkness #4: Red Moon Rising. Kubinyi, Laszlo & Green, Julia, illus. 2017. (Survivors: the Gathering Darkness Ser.: 4). 304p. (J). (gr. 3-7). 16.99 **(978-0-06-234345-1(9))** HarperCollins Pubs.

—Tallstar's Revenge. Barry, James L., illus. (Warriors Super Edition Ser.: 6). (J). (gr. 3-7). 2014. (ENG.). 560p. pap. 7.99 (978-0-06-221806-3(9)) 2013. (ENG.). 544p. 18.99 (978-0-06-221804-9(2)) 2013. 544p. lib. bdg. 19.89 (978-0-06-221805-6(0)) HarperCollins Pubs.

—Warriors, Vols. 1 to 6. 2015. (Warriors: Power of Three Ser.). (ENG.). 2256p. (J). (gr. 3-7). pap. 44.99 (978-0-06-236716-7(1)) HarperCollins Pubs.

—Warriors - Sunrise. 2015. (Warriors: Power of Three Ser.: 6). (ENG.). 368p. (J). (gr. 3-7). pap. 7.99 (978-0-06-236713-6(7)) HarperCollins Pubs.

—Warriors: a Vision of Shadows #2: Thunder & Shadow. (Warriors: a Vision of Shadows Ser.: 2). (J). (gr. 3-7). 2017. 416p. pap. 7.99 **(978-0-06-238643-4(3))** 2016. (Illus.). 400p. 16.99 (978-0-06-238641-0(7)) 2016. (Illus.). 400p. lib. bdg. 17.89 (978-0-06-238642-7(5)) HarperCollins Pubs.

—Warriors: a Vision of Shadows #3: Shattered Sky. 2017. (Warriors: a Vision of Shadows Ser.: 3). 320p. (J). (gr. 3-7). 16.99 (978-0-06-238645-8(X)); lib. bdg. 17.89 (978-0-06-238646-5(8)) HarperCollins Pubs.

—Warriors: a Vision of Shadows #4: Darkest Night. 2017. (Warriors: a Vision of Shadows Ser.: 4). 336p. (J). (gr. 3-7). 16.99 **(978-0-06-238649-6(2))**; (ENG.). lib. bdg. 17.89 **(978-0-06-238650-2(6))** HarperCollins Pubs.

—Warriors: Dawn of the Clans #1: the Sun Trail. McLoughlin, Wayne & Douglas, Allen, illus. 2016. (Warriors: Dawn of the Clans Ser.: 1). 368p. (J). (gr. 3-7). pap. 7.99 (978-0-06-241000-9(8)) HarperCollins Pubs.

—Warriors: Legends of the Clans. 2017. (Warriors Novella Ser.). 336p. (J). (gr. 3-7). pap. 7.99 (978-0-06-256087-2(5)) HarperCollins Pubs.

—Warriors: Omen of the Stars Box Set: Volumes 1 To 6. 2013. (Warriors: Omen of the Stars Ser.). (ENG.). 2256p. (J). (gr. 3-7). pap. 36.99 (978-0-06-226887-7(2)) HarperCollins Pubs.

—Yellowfang's Secret. 2014. (Warriors Super Edition Ser.). (J). lib. bdg. 18.40 (978-0-606-35074-7(8), Turtleback) Turtleback Bks.

Hunter, Erin & Jolley, Dan. Bramblestar's Storm. 2016. (Warriors Super Edition Ser.). (J). lib. bdg. 18.40 (978-0-606-38180-2(5)) Turtleback Bks.

—Escape from the Forest. Hudson, Don, illus. 2008. (Warriors Manga Ser.: 2). (ENG.). 112p. (J). (gr. 3-7). pap. 7.99 (978-0-06-154793-5(X)) HarperCollins Pubs.

Hunter, R. C. Moon Kids. 2010. 64p. pap. 11.99 (978-1-4490-7846-1(X)) AuthorHouse.

Hunter, Skillman "Kim". El Becerrito en Valle Grande. Ritthaler, Sarah Pilcher, tr. Sundstrom, Mary, illus. 2006.Tr. of Little Cow in Valle Grande. (SPA & ENG.). 32p. (J). (gr. -1-k). 16.95 (978-0-8263-4044-3(X)) Univ. of New Mexico Pr.

Hunton, Robert L. Secrets of the Medicine Pouch. 2012. 260p. pap. (978-0-9852737-4-3(7)) Roxby Media Ltd.

Hurst, Joshua. One Day at the North Pole. Johnson, Jared, illus. 2008. 44p. pap. 24.95 (978-1-60703-327-1(5)) America Star Bks.

Hurwitz, Johanna. Magical Monty. McGrory, Anik, illus. 2013. (Monty Ser.). (ENG.). 112p. (J). (gr. k-4). pap. 5.99 (978-0-7636-6457-2(X)) Candlewick Pr.

Huser, Glen. The Runaway, 1 vol. 2012. (ENG., Illus.). 147p. (YA). (gr. 6-9). pap. 12.95 (978-1-896580-21-0(1)) Tradewind Bks. CAN. Dist: Orca Bk. Pubs. USA.

Hussey, Charmian. The Valley of Secrets. Crump, Christopher, illus. 2006. (ENG.). 400p. (J). (gr. 7-12). per. 17.99 (978-1-4169-0015-3(2), Simon Pulse) Simon Pulse.

Huston, Harriette "Ree". The Rescue of Buster Bus: A True Adventure Mystery with Sparkling Intrigue for All Ages. 2012. 36p. pap. 21.99 (978-1-4771-1658-6(3)) Xlibris Corp.

Hutchens, Calvin. The Adventures of Otis Possum. 2007. 52p. per. 16.95 (978-1-4241-7065-4(6)) America Star Bks.

Hutchins, Hazel. TJ & the Quiz Kids, 1 vol. 2007. (Orca Young Readers Ser.). (ENG.). 136p. (J). (gr. 3-6). pap. 5.95 (978-1-55143-731-6(7)) Orca Bk. Pubs. USA.

Hutchison, D. W. Storm Hags. 2010. 139p. pap. 20.50 (978-1-4461-7086-1(1)) Lulu Pr., Inc.

Hutton, Fiona. The Adventures of Henrietta - the Camden Girl. 2012. 24p. pap. (978-1-78222-056-5(9)) Paragon Publishing, Rothersthorpe.

Hutton, Gaila. Frank the Colorful Frog. Knox, Anna Mae, illus. 2011. 28p. pap. 24.95 (978-1-4560-5607-0(7)) America Star Bks.

Hutton, Laurie S. & Marsham, Liz. Wonder Woman Classic - A Hero for All. Hood, Josh et al, illus. 2017. 24p. (J). (gr. -1-3). pap. 3.99 (978-0-06-236081-6(7), HarperFestival) HarperCollins Pubs.

Huxley, Sheila M. One Lovely Summer: The Stories of One Little Butterfly & His Friends. 2009. (Illus.). 48p. pap. 19.49 (978-1-4389-2987-3(0)) AuthorHouse.

Hveem, Todd. The Adventures of Celtic. 2011. 36p. pap. 15.14 (978-1-4567-0076-8(6)) AuthorHouse.

—The Adventures of Celtic: Road Trip. 2011. 44p. pap. 18.46 (978-1-4634-4703-8(5)) AuthorHouse.

Hyde, E. A. Watson. Little Sisters to the Camp Fire Girls. 2004. reprint ed. pap. 15.95 (978-1-4179-9442-7(8)) Kessinger Publishing, LLC.

Hyde, Noreen. The Adventures of Miss Chief: Miss Chief Goes to School. Pushee, Marisa, illus. 2007. 28p. per. 9.95 (978-1-59858-368-7(9)) Dog Ear Publishing, LLC.

Hyman, Jack G. Breakfast with the Birds. 2013. 216p. pap. 15.99 (978-1-4525-8453-9(2), Balboa Pr.) Author Solutions, Inc.

I DOUBLE Dare You. 2008. (Illus.). 36p. (J). (978-0-9792686-5-6(6)) Lehman Publishing.

I Know My Colors the Adventures of Little Darlings Child Care. 2007. (978-0-9793490-1-0(X)) Dynasty Publishing, Inc.

Ian Pugh. Wolfstorm: The First Danny Piper Adventure. 2010. 388p. pap. 22.95 (978-1-4269-0238-3(7)) Trafford Publishing.

Ibarrola, Begonia. The Adventures of a Water Drop. Tejado, Irene, illus. 2013. (ENG.). 32p. (J). (978-84-95923-96-7(3)) Primera Persona.

Ibbotson, Eva. Journey to the River Sea. Hawkes, Kevin, illus. 2003. 298p. (gr. 3-7). 18.00 (978-0-7569-1552-0(X)) Perfection Learning Corp.

—Journey to the River Sea. Hawkes, Kevin, illus. 2003. (ENG.). 304p. (J). (gr. 3-7). pap. 8.99 (978-0-14-250184-9(0), Puffin Books) Penguin Young Readers Group.

—Journey to the River Sea. 5th unabr. ed. 2008. (ENG.). 304p. (J). (gr. 10-14). 14.95 (978-0-330-39715-5(X), Macmillan) Pan Macmillan GBR. Dist: Trans-Atlantic Pubns., Inc.

—The Ogre of Oglefort. 2012. (ENG.). 272p. (J). (gr. 3-7). pap. 6.99 (978-0-14-242135-2(9), Puffin Books) Penguin Young Readers Group.

Icanberry, Mark. A Pirate's Feast. 2011. (Illus.). 48p. 14.95 (978-1-893327-08-5(6)); pap. 7.95 (978-1-893327-09-2(4)) Ten Speed Pr. (Tricycle Pr.).

Ice Water Press Staff. Secrets of the Deep. 2010. (J). pap. (978-1-921639-95-1(4)) Ripley Entertainment, Inc.

Idowu, Cathy. Light for the Sacra Vellum: The Graceville Chronicles Book One. 2008. (Illus.). (J). (978-0-9801484-0-4(5)) Rite Quest.

If You're Gonna be a Monster do it Right. 2005. (YA). per. (978-1-59872-088-4(0)) Instant Pub.

Ignatow, Amy. Love & Other Fiascos with Lydia Goldblatt & Julie Graham-Chang, Bk. 6. 2013. (Popularity Papers). (ENG., Illus.). 208p. (J). (gr. 3-7). 16.95 (978-1-4197-0859-6(7), Amulet Bks.) Abrams, Inc.

—The Mighty Odds. 2016. (Odds Ser.). (ENG., Illus.). 240p. (J). (gr. 5-9). 15.95 (978-1-4197-1271-5(3), Amulet Bks.) Abrams, Inc.

—The Popularity Papers: Book Four: the Rocky Road Trip of Lydia Goldblatt & Julie Graham-Chang. 2013. (Popularity Papers). (ENG., Illus.). 208p. (J). (gr. 3-7). pap. 8.95 (978-1-4197-0972-2(0), Amulet Bks.) Abrams, Inc.

Igneri, David S. The Boy & Girl Who Hated History. Wigley, Audrey Watson, illus. 2009. 44p. pap. 24.95 (978-1-61546-828-7(5)) America Star Bks.

Ihara, Shigekatsu. Pokémon - Diamond & Pearl Adventure!, Vol. 4. Ihara, Shigekatsu, illus. 2009. (ENG., Illus.). 192p. (J). pap. 9.99 (978-1-4215-2674-4(3)) Viz Media.

—Pokémon: Diamond & Pearl Adventure!, Vol. 1. Ihara, Shigekatsu, illus. 2008. (ENG., Illus.). 208p. (J). (gr. k). pap. 9.99 (978-1-4215-2286-9(1)) Viz Media.

—Pokémon: Diamond & Pearl Adventure!, Vol. 2. Ihara, Shigekatsu, illus. 2008. (ENG., Illus.). 192p. (J). (gr. 1). pap. 9.99 (978-1-4215-2287-6(X)) Viz Media.

—Pokémon: Diamond & Pearl Adventure!, Vol. 3. Ihara, Shigekatsu, illus. 2009. (ENG., Illus.). 200p. (J). pap. 9.99 (978-1-4215-2574-7(7)) Viz Media.

—Pokémon: Diamond & Pearl Adventure!, Vol. 6. Ihara, Shigekatsu, illus. 2010. (ENG., Illus.). 192p. (J). pap. 9.99 (978-1-4215-3170-0(4)) Viz Media.

—Pokémon: Diamond & Pearl Adventure!, Vol. 7. Ihara, Shigekatsu, illus. 2010. (ENG., Illus.). 192p. (J). pap. 9.99 (978-1-4215-3491-6(6)) Viz Media.

Illich, Maria. The Morcant Twins & the Curse of the Griseum. 2013. 248p. pap. (978-1-927384-11-4(7)) Zeta Comics.

I'm Just the Right Size. 2004.Tr. of Soy del tamano correcto! (SPA.). 24p. 8.99 (978-1-59185-423-4(7), Casa Creacion) Charisma Media.

Imagine This, James Robert: Individual Title, 6 packs. (Action Packs Ser.). 120p. (gr. 3-5). 44.00 (978-0-7635-8418-4(5)) Rigby Education.

Imholtz, August & Tannenbaum, Alison. Alice Eats Wonderland. Carr, A. E. K., illus. 2009. (ENG.). 120p. pap. 14.95 (978-1-4290-9106-0(1)) Applewood Bks.

Imwalle, Candice, et al. Sir Morgan & the Kingdom of Horrible Food. 2012. 32p. 20.00 (978-1-4349-7356-6(5), RoseDog Bks.) Dorrance Publishing Co., Inc.

In Search of the Little People & the Normand Key, 1vol., 1vol. 3rd ed. 2005. (ENG., Illus.). 170p. (J). reprint ed. per. 11.99 (978-0-9760045-2-3(6), Reluctant Reader Bks.) Cronus College.

In the Clubhouse. 2003. (J). per. (978-1-57657-872-8(0)) Paradise Pr., Inc.

Inagaki, Riichiro. Eyeshield 21, Vol. 12. Murata, Yusuke, illus. 2007. (ENG.). 208p. pap. 9.99 (978-1-4215-1061-3(8)) Viz Media.

—Eyeshield 21, Vol. 13. Murata, Yusuke, illus. 2007. (ENG.). 216p. pap. 7.99 (978-1-4215-1062-0(6)) Viz Media.

Inches, Alison. The Adventures of a Plastic Bottle: A Story about Recycling. Whitehead, Pete, illus. 2009. (Little Green Bks.). (ENG.). 24p. (J). (gr. -1-1). pap. 3.99 (978-1-4169-6788-0(5), Little Simon) Little Simon.

—The Adventures of an Aluminum Can: A Story about Recycling. Whitehead, Pete & Chambers, Mark L., illus. 2009. (Little Green Bks.). (ENG.). 24p. (J). (gr. -1-1). pap. 3.99 (978-1-4169-7221-1(8), Little Simon) Little Simon.

—Diego's Buzzing Bee Adventure. Zalme, Ron, illus. 2008. (Go, Diego, Go! Ser.: 7). (ENG.). 24p. (J). (gr. -1-1). pap. 3.99 (978-1-4169-4776-9(0), Simon Spotlight/Nickelodeon) Simon Spotlight/Nickelodeon.

—Súper Bebés! Miller, Victoria, illus. 2006. (Dora la Exploradora Ser.). (SPA.). 24p. (J). (gr. -1-3). pap. 3.99 (978-1-4169-2461-6(2), Libros Para Ninos) Libros Para Ninos.

The Incredible Hulk Storm. 2003. (J). per. (978-1-57657-812-4(7)) Paradise Pr., Inc.

Indian Trail. 2007. (Choose Your Own Adventure - Dragonlarks Ser.). (Illus.). 64p. (J). (gr. 4-7). pap. 7.99 (978-1-933390-53-6(0)) Chooseco LLC.

Inez, Peggy. The Gully. 2007. 140p. per. 7.95 (978-1-59858-400-4(6)) Dog Ear Publishing, LLC.

The Infinite Adventures of Rodney Appleseed in Something Happens. 2007. (YA). per. (978-0-9727894-5-5(6)) Arizona Blueberry Studios.

Ing, Dean. It's up to Charlie Hardin. 2015. (Baen Ser.: 1). (ENG.). 256p. (YA). (gr. 5). 16.99 (978-1-4767-8030-6(7)) Baen Bks.

Ingelow, Jean. Mopsa the Fairy. 2006. pap. 19.95 (978-1-4304-4177-9(1)) Kessinger Publishing, LLC.

Ingham, Janis. Flip & Flop Celebrate Family. 2009. 32p. pap. 16.49 (978-1-4389-2152-5(7)) AuthorHouse.

Inglis, Lucy. City of Halves. 2015. (ENG.). 368p. (J). (gr. 7). 17.99 (978-0-545-82958-8(5), Chicken Hse., The) Scholastic, Inc.

Ingram, Catherine. Arnold's Extraordinary Art Museum. Stoten, Jim, illus. 2016. (ENG.). 64p. (J). (gr. 2-6). 19.95 (978-1-78067-863-4(0)) King, Laurence Publishing GBR. Dist: Hachette Bk. Group.

Ingram, Fiona. The Secret of the Sacred Scarab. 2008. 272p. (gr. -1 — 1). 27.95 (978-0-595-71977-8(5)); pap. 17.95 (978-0-595-45716-8(9)) iUniverse, Inc.

Inkpen, Mick. A to Z: An Alphabet Adventure. 2005. (Kipper Ser.). (ENG., Illus.). 64p. (J). (gr. -1-3). pap. 7.99 (978-0-15-205441-0(3)) Houghton Mifflin Harcourt Publishing Co.

—Beachmoles & Bellvine. 2005. (ENG., Illus.). 32p. (J). (gr. -1-k). pap. 9.99 (978-0-340-87866-8(5)) Hodder & Stoughton GBR. Dist: Hachette Bk. Group.

—Ploo & the Terrible Gnobbler. (ENG., Illus.). (J). (gr. -1). 2006. (Blue Nose Island Ser.: Bk. 1). 11.95 (978-1-84032-988-9(2)) 2003. 32p. 17.99 (978-0-340-85573-7(8)) Hodder & Stoughton GBR. Dist: Trafalgar Square Publishing, Hachette Bk. Group.

Inner Voice. 80p. (YA). (gr. 6-12). pap. 10.50 (978-0-8224-3927-1(1)) Globe Fearon Educational Publishing.

Innis, Amy. The Adventures of Princess Lilyan: The Shimmering Beauty Ball. 2009. 48p. pap. 16.95 (978-1-60749-318-1(7)) America Star Bks.

Inns, Chris & Woods, Dave. Florence Nightingirl. 2014. (ENG., Illus.). 64p. (J). (gr. k-2). pap. 5.99 (978-1-4083-1363-3(4)) Hodder & Stoughton GBR. Dist: Hachette Bk. Group.

Inoue, Momota. Pokémon the Movie: Genesect & the Legend Awakened. Inoue, Momota, illus. 2013. (ENG., Illus.). 192p. (J). pap. 9.99 (978-1-4215-6804-1(7)) Viz Media.

The Invisible Boat, 1 vol. 2013. (ENG.). 336p. pap. 18.00 (978-1-936367-44-3(0)) Waldorf Publications.

Ipcar, Dahlov. Stripes & Spots, 1 vol. 2012. (ENG.). 42p. (J). 17.95 (978-1-934031-70-4(4), 2e66d329-f317-4896-abd2-ae101e429c86) Islandport Pr., Inc.

Iribarren, Elena, ed. Mambru se fue a la Guerra. Calderon, Gloria, illus. 2005. (SPA.). 27p. (gr. -1-2). reprint ed. pap. 14.00 (978-0-7567-8948-0(6)) DIANE Publishing Co.

Irish, Rosario A. Lamy. 2012. 28p. pap. 13.54 (978-1-4669-6232-3(1)) Trafford Publishing.

Irvin, David. Rusty, the Rainbow Trout: Moving Day. Irvin, Sioux, illus. 2007. 24p. per. 24.95 (978-1-4241-8455-2(X)) America Star Bks.

Irvin-Marston, Hope. My Little Book of River Otters. Magdalena-Brown, Maria, illus. 2nd ed. 2004. 32p. (J). pap. 7.95 (978-0-89317-051-6(8), WW-0518, Windward Publishing) Finney Co., Inc.

Irvin, William. The Adventures of Winston & Hazel: Episode 1: the Silver Medallion. 2006. 11.00 (978-0-8059-8220-6(5)) Dorrance Publishing Co., Inc.

Irvine, Alex. Phase Three: Marvel's Captain America: Civil War. 2017. (ENG.). 208p. (J). (gr. 3-7). 12.99 (978-0-316-27150-9(0)) Little, Brown Bks. for Young Readers.

—Phase Two: Marvel's Captain America: the Winter Soldier. 2016. (Marvel Cinematic Universe Ser.). (ENG., Illus.). 208p. (J). (gr. 3-7). 10.99 (978-0-316-25678-0(1)) Little, Brown Bks. for Young Readers.

Irvine, Alex & Wyatt, Chris. Phase Two: Marvel's Guardians of the Galaxy. 2015. (Marvel Cinematic Universe Ser.). (ENG.). 192p. (J). (gr. 3-7). 10.99 (978-0-316-25675-9(7)) Little, Brown Bks. for Young Readers.

Irvine, Kitty. Mysterious Moorings with Mouse. 2017. (ENG.). 96p. (J). pap. 11.95 **(978-1-78693-220-4(2)**, 2bcedaac-1c94-4640-ab5f-7088dc6903a6) Austin, Stan AUS. Dist: Bookmasters Distribution.

Irwin, Bindi & Black, Jess. Roar! 2011. (Bindi's Wildlife Adventures Ser.: 6). (ENG.). 112p. (J). (gr. 3-6). pap. 4.99 (978-1-4022-5931-9(X), Sourcebooks Jabberwocky) Sourcebooks, Inc.

Irwin, Bindi & Kunz, Chris. Croc Capers: Bindi Wildlife Adventures. 2012. (Bindi's Wildlife Adventures Ser.: 7). (ENG.). 112p. (J). (gr. 3-6). pap. 4.99 (978-1-4022-7373-5(8), Sourcebooks Jabberwocky) Sourcebooks, Inc.

Irwin, Daniel. The Adventures of Tylor Bear & Mana. 2004. 144p. pap. 24.95 (978-1-4137-5580-0(1)) America Star Bks.

Irwin, Gerald. Harry the Spider & His Friend Charlie. 2012. 28p. pap. 19.99 (978-1-4772-6620-5(8)) AuthorHouse.

Irwin, John P. The Cubby Files; Tales of a Pennsylvania Black Bear Growing Up. 2009. 96p. pap. 15.99 (978-1-4415-0209-4(2)) Xlibris Corp.

Isbell, Shaun. The Mouse & the Witch, 1 vol. 2009. 56p. pap. 16.95 (978-1-61546-892-8(7)) PublishAmerica, Inc.

Isbell, Tessa J. Animal Adventures: Goosey & Beauty Take a Mystery Magic Carpet Ride to Jamaica. 2013. 48p. pap. 21.99 (978-1-4669-7217-9(3)) Trafford Publishing.

Isenhoff, Michelle. The Quill Pen. 2011. (ENG.). 168p. pap. 9.98 (978-1-4664-9691-0(6)) CreateSpace Independent Publishing Platform.

Island of the Blue Dolphins. 2011. 9.00 (978-0-7848-3655-2(8), Everbind) Marco Bk. Co.

Isom, Michelle. Human Dogs. 2012. 28p. (-18). pap. 16.09 (978-1-4669-5842-5(1)) Trafford Publishing.

Ito, Jerilyn. Double Rainbow Island: The Mauka Adventure. Wong, Melissa Oliaivar, illus. 2013. 36p. pap. 10.95 (978-1-937260-99-6(2)) Sleepytown Pr.

Itow, Rebecca Chiyoko & Anderson II, Norman E. A Boy, A Dog & Persnickety Log. 2007. 50p. pap. 24.50 (978-0-615-14376-7(8)) R&N Productions.

Ivanoff, George. Gamers' Quest. 2009. (Gamers Ser.: Bk. 1). (ENG.). 208p. (YA). pap. (978-1-876462-86-4(8), Ford Street Publishing) Hybrid Pubs.

Ivers, Steven A. The Family Menaces: Runaway Babies. 2012. 40p. pap. 24.95 (978-1-4626-7673-6(1)) America Star Bks.

Iverson-Noel, Gayle. Brown Beary's Adventures with Jon-Paul. 2011. 32p. pap. 21.99 (978-1-4628-9875-6(0)) Xlibris Corp.

Ives, Bob. The Three Ants & the Cat. Fairy, Meg, illus. 2003. 40p. (J). (978-1-920832-07-0(6)) Four Heads Publishing Group Pty, Ltd.

Ives, David. Scrib. 2005. 208p. (J). (gr. 5-18). lib. bdg. 17.89 (978-0-06-059842-6(5)) HarperCollins Pubs.

Ivo. Charles & Amand: The Adventuresome Frogs. 2012. 40p. pap. 14.95 (978-1-61897-129-6(8), Strategic Bk. Publishing) Strategic Book Publishing & Rights Agency (SBPRA).

Iwamura, Kazuo. Seven Little Mice Have Fun on the Ice. 2011. (ENG., Illus.). 32p. (J). (gr. -1-2). 16.95 (978-0-7358-4048-5(2)) North-South Bks., Inc.

Izzo, Donna. Frilly Lilly's Candyland Express. 2011. 24p. pap. 15.99 (978-1-4653-6159-2(6)) Xlibris Corp.

—Mischievous Michael's 1st Day of School. 2011. 28p. pap. 15.99 (978-1-4568-5531-4(X)) Xlibris Corp.

J, Granny. Pinky Gets a New Puppy: Pinky Frink's Adventures. 2012. 38p. pap. 17.99 (978-1-105-86479-7(0)) Lulu Pr., Inc.

J., Henry. The Big Gray House: The Adventures of Franklin Meyers. 2010. 96p. (gr. -1-2). pap. 12.00 (978-1-4269-4255-6(9)) Trafford Publishing.

Jablonski, Carla. The Travelers, Bk. 1. 2009. (Pendragon: Before the War Ser.: 1). (ENG.). 256p. (J). (gr. 5-9). pap. 7.99 *(978-1-4169-6522-0(X),* Aladdin) Simon & Schuster Children's Publishing.
Jachimczyk, Victoria. Max's Tale: Home Sweet Home. 2012. 24p. pap. 17.99 *(978-1-4772-2115-0(8))* AuthorHouse.
Jack R. Wilder. Devil with a Halo. 2009. 256p. pap. 24.95 *(978-1-4251-1283-7(8))* Trafford Publishing.
Jackowski, Rosemarie. Busy Ants under Red Bricks. 2011. 24p. pap. 11.69 *(978-1-4634-1716-1(0))* AuthorHouse.
—Super Duper Diaper-Poopin' Hero. 2011. 24p. pap. 12.99 *(978-1-4634-2211-0(3))* AuthorHouse.
Jacks, C. S. The Adventures of Pisten Billy: Pisten Billy Makes the Grade! 2010. 32p. pap. 12.99 *(978-1-4520-6624-0(8))* AuthorHouse.
Jackson, Anitha L. Gabby'may Digsby: When I grow up, I wanna Be.... . 2011. 68p. pap. 26.99 *(978-1-4628-5385-4(4))* Xlibris Corp.
Jackson, Bridgett. The Bobos Save the Day: Book One of Tales from the Creek. 2008. 36p. pap. 14.49 *(978-1-4389-2034-4(2))* AuthorHouse.
—The Monster on the Moon: Book Three of Tales from the Creek. 2009. 40p. pap. 18.49 *(978-1-4389-3540-9(4))* AuthorHouse.
Jackson, Ciandress. Chloe the Jumbo Jet: Fantastic Friends Around the World. 2013. 24p. pap. 9.99 *(978-1-61286-195-1(4))* Avid Readers Publishing Group.
—Chloe the Jumbo Jet: First Class to Seoul! Let's Rock & Roll. 2013. 26p. pap. 9.99 *(978-1-61286-196-8(2))* Avid Readers Publishing Group.
Jackson, Debra. Canines on Patrol: Special Lessons. 2009. (Illus.). 28p. pap. 12.49 *(978-1-4343-8806-3(9))* AuthorHouse.
Jackson, Gary. The Sunny Side of the Apple. 2005. 28p. (J). per. 14.99 net. *(978-1-59975-034-7(1))* Independent Pub.
Jackson, Glenda K. Friends of the Hills. 2012. 20p. pap. 17.99 *(978-1-4685-4082-6(3))* AuthorHouse.
Jackson, Jocelyn. Ariel's Adventures: the Series: Ariel's New Home. 2010. 32p. pap. 13.95 *(978-1-4497-0383-7(6),* WestBow Pr.) Author Solutions, Inc.
Jackson, Kimberly. Volcano Adventures of Keikilani. Spachner, Karen D., illus. 2009. 32p. pap. 8.95 *(978-0-9643512-1-9(8))* Mouse! Publishing.
Jackson, Lyn D. The Perilous Journey Home. 2009. 200p. pap. 14.49 *(978-1-4389-4651-1(1))* AuthorHouse.
Jackson, Marjorie. Beach Feet. Cohen, Lynda, illus. 2005. (ENG.). 8p. (J). pap. 5.75 *(978-1-57274-750-0(1),* 2123, Bks. for Young Learners) Owen, Richard C. Pubs., Inc.
Jackson, Paul B. Luke & Mcnashty's Treasure. 2006. 96p. pap. 16.95 *(978-1-4241-2909-6(5))* PublishAmerica, Inc.
Jackson, Stephen. Mundoespejo. 2005. (SPA., Illus.). 28p. (J). (gr. 2-4). 15.95 *(978-84-666-1495-5(8))* Ediciones B ESP. Dist: Independent Pubs. Group.
Jaco, Paul. The Leopards of Sh'ong. 2010. 260p. pap. *(978-0-7981-4930-3(2))* NB Pubs. Ltd.
Jacob, Annie. When I Was a Kid. 2013. 24p. pap. 14.93 *(978-1-4669-9740-0(0))* Trafford Publishing.
Jacobellis, Michelle. Dachshund Tales: Adventures on the Great South Bay. 2012. 60p. pap. 17.95 *(978-1-62709-104-6(1))* America Star Bks.
Jacobs Cfp, Sheila. Jake's Big Bang. 2012. 28p. pap. 11.99 *(978-1-4685-5736-7(X))* AuthorHouse.
Jacobs, Edgar P. Atlantis Mystery. 2012. (Blake & Mortimer Ser.: 12). (ENG., Illus.). 72p. (J). (gr. 5-12). pap. 15.95 *(978-1-84918-107-5(1))* CineBook GBR. Dist: National Bk. Network.
Jacobs, Jerry L. Koda. 2013. 80p. pap. 12.99 *(978-0-9855202-5-0(6))* Kids At Heart Publishing, LLC.
Jacobs, Jordan. Samantha Sutton & the Labyrinth of Lies. 2012. (Samantha Sutton Ser.: 0). (ENG., Illus.). 368p. (J). (gr. 4-7). pap. 6.99 *(978-1-4022-7560-9(9),* 1350497, Sourcebooks Jabberwocky) Sourcebooks, Inc.
—Samantha Sutton & the Winter of the Warrior Queen. 2014. (Samantha Sutton Ser.: 2). (ENG.). 368p. (J). (gr. 4-7). pap. 6.99 *(978-1-4022-7563-0(3),* 9781402275630, Sourcebooks Jabberwocky) Sourcebooks, Inc.
Jacobs, Leslie. The Adventure of the Tall giraffe & the Short Duck. 2009. (J). 14.99 *(978-1-61584-646-7(8))* Independent Pub.
Jacobs, Lily. The Littlest Bunny: An Easter Adventure. Dunn, Robert, illus. 2015. (ENG.). 32p. (J). (-3). 9.99 *(978-1-4926-1012-0(7),* Sourcebooks Jabberwocky) Sourcebooks, Inc.
—The Littlest Bunny in Alabama: An Easter Adventure. 2015. (ENG.). 32p. (J). (-3). 9.99 *(978-1-4926-1015-1(1),* Sourcebooks Jabberwocky) Sourcebooks, Inc.
—The Littlest Bunny in Alaska: An Easter Adventure. 2015. (ENG.). 32p. (J). (-3). 9.99 *(978-1-4926-1018-2(6),* Sourcebooks Jabberwocky) Sourcebooks, Inc.
—The Littlest Bunny in Albuquerque: An Easter Adventure. Dunn, Robert, illus. 2015. (ENG.). 32p. (J). (-3). 9.99 *(978-1-4926-1021-2(6),* Sourcebooks Jabberwocky) Sourcebooks, Inc.
—The Littlest Bunny in Arizona: An Easter Adventure. 2015. (ENG.). 32p. (J). (-3). 9.99 *(978-1-4926-1024-3(0),* Sourcebooks Jabberwocky) Sourcebooks, Inc.
—The Littlest Bunny in Arkansas: An Easter Adventure. 2015. (ENG.). 32p. (J). (-3). 9.99 *(978-1-4926-1027-4(5),* Sourcebooks Jabberwocky) Sourcebooks, Inc.
—The Littlest Bunny in Austin. Dunn, Robert, illus. 2016. (ENG.). 32p. (J). (-7). 9.99 *(978-1-4926-3347-1(X),* 9781492633471, Sourcebooks Jabberwocky) Sourcebooks, Inc.
—The Littlest Bunny in Bentonville: An Easter Adventure. 2015. (ENG.). 32p. (J). (-3). 9.99 *(978-1-4926-1030-4(5),* Sourcebooks Jabberwocky) Sourcebooks, Inc.
—The Littlest Bunny in Boise: An Easter Adventure. 2015. (ENG.). 32p. (J). (-3). 9.99 *(978-1-4926-1033-5(X),* Sourcebooks Jabberwocky) Sourcebooks, Inc.
—The Littlest Bunny in Boston: An Easter Adventure. 2015. (ENG.). 32p. (J). (-3). 9.99 *(978-1-4926-1036-6(4),* Sourcebooks Jabberwocky) Sourcebooks, Inc.
—The Littlest Bunny in Calgary: An Easter Adventure. Dunn, Robert, illus. 2015. (ENG.). 32p. (J). (-3). 11.99 *(978-1-4926-1039-7(9),* Sourcebooks Jabberwocky) Sourcebooks, Inc.
—The Littlest Bunny in Canada: An Easter Adventure. Dunn, Robert, illus. 2015. (ENG.). 32p. (J). (-3). 11.99 *(978-1-4926-1045-8(3),* Sourcebooks Jabberwocky) Sourcebooks, Inc.
—The Littlest Bunny in Charleston: An Easter Adventure. 2015. (ENG.). 32p. (J). (-3). 9.99 *(978-1-4926-1048-9(8),* Sourcebooks Jabberwocky) Sourcebooks, Inc.
—The Littlest Bunny in Cincinnati: An Easter Adventure. Dunn, Robert, illus. 2015. (ENG.). 32p. (J). (-3). 9.99 *(978-1-4926-1054-0(2),* Sourcebooks Jabberwocky) Sourcebooks, Inc.
—The Littlest Bunny in Colorado: An Easter Adventure. 2015. (ENG.). 32p. (J). (-3). 9.99 *(978-1-4926-1057-1(7),* Sourcebooks Jabberwocky) Sourcebooks, Inc.
—The Littlest Bunny in Connecticut: An Easter Adventure. 2015. (ENG.). 32p. (J). (-3). 9.99 *(978-1-4926-1060-1(7),* Sourcebooks Jabberwocky) Sourcebooks, Inc.
—The Littlest Bunny in Delaware: An Easter Adventure. Dunn, Robert, illus. 2015. (ENG.). 32p. (J). (-3). 9.99 *(978-1-4926-1063-2(1),* Sourcebooks Jabberwocky) Sourcebooks, Inc.
—The Littlest Bunny in Edmonton: An Easter Adventure. Dunn, Robert, illus. 2015. (ENG.). 32p. (J). (-3). 11.99 *(978-1-4926-1066-3(6),* Sourcebooks Jabberwocky) Sourcebooks, Inc.
—The Littlest Bunny in Florida: An Easter Adventure. Dunn, Robert, illus. 2015. (ENG.). 32p. (J). (-3). 9.99 *(978-1-4926-1069-4(0),* Sourcebooks Jabberwocky) Sourcebooks, Inc.
—The Littlest Bunny in Georgia: An Easter Adventure. 2015. (ENG.). 32p. (J). (-3). 9.99 *(978-1-4926-1072-4(0),* Sourcebooks Jabberwocky) Sourcebooks, Inc.
—The Littlest Bunny in Hawaii: An Easter Adventure. 2015. (ENG.). 32p. (J). (-3). 9.99 *(978-1-4926-1075-5(5),* Sourcebooks Jabberwocky) Sourcebooks, Inc.
—The Littlest Bunny in Idaho: An Easter Adventure. 2015. (ENG.). 32p. (J). (-3). 9.99 *(978-1-4926-1078-6(X),* Sourcebooks Jabberwocky) Sourcebooks, Inc.
—The Littlest Bunny in Illinois: An Easter Adventure. Dunn, Robert, illus. 2015. (ENG.). 32p. (J). (-3). 9.99 *(978-1-4926-1081-6(X),* Sourcebooks Jabberwocky) Sourcebooks, Inc.
—The Littlest Bunny in Indiana: An Easter Adventure. Dunn, Robert, illus. 2015. (ENG.). 32p. (J). (-3). 9.99 *(978-1-4926-1084-7(4),* Sourcebooks Jabberwocky) Sourcebooks, Inc.
—The Littlest Bunny in Iowa: An Easter Adventure. 2015. (ENG.). 32p. (J). (-3). 9.99 *(978-1-4926-1087-8(9),* Sourcebooks Jabberwocky) Sourcebooks, Inc.
—The Littlest Bunny in Kansas: An Easter Adventure. 2015. (ENG.). 32p. (J). (-3). 9.99 *(978-1-4926-1090-8(9),* Sourcebooks Jabberwocky) Sourcebooks, Inc.
—The Littlest Bunny in Kansas City: An Easter Adventure. Dunn, Robert, illus. 2015. (ENG.). 32p. (J). (-3). 9.99 *(978-1-4926-1093-9(3),* Sourcebooks Jabberwocky) Sourcebooks, Inc.
—The Littlest Bunny in Kentucky: An Easter Adventure. Dunn, Robert, illus. 2015. (ENG.). 32p. (J). (-3). 9.99 *(978-1-4926-1096-0(8),* Sourcebooks Jabberwocky) Sourcebooks, Inc.
—The Littlest Bunny in Las Vegas: An Easter Adventure. 2015. (ENG.). 32p. (J). (-3). 9.99 *(978-1-4926-1099-1(2),* Sourcebooks Jabberwocky) Sourcebooks, Inc.
—The Littlest Bunny in Los Angeles: An Easter Adventure. 2015. (ENG.). 32p. (J). (-3). 9.99 *(978-1-4926-1102-8(6),* Sourcebooks Jabberwocky) Sourcebooks, Inc.
—The Littlest Bunny in Louisiana: An Easter Adventure. Dunn, Robert, illus. 2015. (ENG.). 32p. (J). (-3). 9.99 *(978-1-4926-1105-9(0),* Sourcebooks Jabberwocky) Sourcebooks, Inc.
—The Littlest Bunny in Maine: An Easter Adventure. 2015. (ENG.). 32p. (J). (-3). 9.99 *(978-1-4926-1108-0(5),* Sourcebooks Jabberwocky) Sourcebooks, Inc.
—The Littlest Bunny in Maryland: An Easter Adventure. Dunn, Robert, illus. 2015. (ENG.). 32p. (J). (-3). 9.99 *(978-1-4926-1111-0(5),* Sourcebooks Jabberwocky) Sourcebooks, Inc.
—The Littlest Bunny in Massachusetts: An Easter Adventure. 2015. (ENG.). 32p. (J). (-3). 9.99 *(978-1-4926-1114-1(X),* Sourcebooks Jabberwocky) Sourcebooks, Inc.
—The Littlest Bunny in Minnesota: An Easter Adventure. Dunn, Robert, illus. 2015. (ENG.). 32p. (J). (-3). 9.99 *(978-1-4926-1120-2(4),* Sourcebooks Jabberwocky) Sourcebooks, Inc.
—The Littlest Bunny in Mississippi: An Easter Adventure. Dunn, Robert, illus. 2015. (ENG.). 32p. (J). (-3). 9.99 *(978-1-4926-1123-3(9),* Sourcebooks Jabberwocky) Sourcebooks, Inc.
—The Littlest Bunny in Missouri: An Easter Adventure. Dunn, Robert, illus. 2015. (ENG.). 32p. (J). (-3). 9.99 *(978-1-4926-1126-4(3),* Sourcebooks Jabberwocky) Sourcebooks, Inc.
—The Littlest Bunny in Montana: An Easter Adventure. Dunn, Robert, illus. 2015. (ENG.). 32p. (J). (-3). 9.99 *(978-1-4926-1129-5(8),* Sourcebooks Jabberwocky) Sourcebooks, Inc.
—The Littlest Bunny in Nebraska: An Easter Adventure. Dunn, Robert, illus. 2015. (ENG.). 32p. (J). (-3). 9.99 *(978-1-4926-1132-5(8),* Sourcebooks Jabberwocky) Sourcebooks, Inc.
—The Littlest Bunny in Nevada: An Easter Adventure. Dunn, Robert, illus. 2015. (ENG.). 32p. (J). (-3). 9.99 *(978-1-4926-1135-6(2),* Sourcebooks Jabberwocky) Sourcebooks, Inc.
—The Littlest Bunny in New England: An Easter Adventure. Dunn, Robert, illus. 2015. (ENG.). 32p. (J). (-3). 9.99 *(978-1-4926-1138-7(7),* Sourcebooks Jabberwocky) Sourcebooks, Inc.
—The Littlest Bunny in New Hampshire: An Easter Adventure. Dunn, Robert, illus. 2015. (ENG.). 32p. (J). (-3). 9.99 *(978-1-4926-1141-7(7),* Sourcebooks Jabberwocky) Sourcebooks, Inc.
—The Littlest Bunny in New Jersey: An Easter Adventure. Dunn, Robert, illus. 2015. (ENG.). 32p. (J). (-3). 9.99 *(978-1-4926-1144-8(1),* Sourcebooks Jabberwocky) Sourcebooks, Inc.
—The Littlest Bunny in New Mexico: An Easter Adventure. Dunn, Robert, illus. 2015. (ENG.). 32p. (J). (-3). 9.99 *(978-1-4926-1147-9(6),* Sourcebooks Jabberwocky) Sourcebooks, Inc.
—The Littlest Bunny in New York: An Easter Adventure. Dunn, Robert, illus. 2015. (ENG.). 32p. (J). (-3). 9.99 *(978-1-4926-1150-9(6),* Sourcebooks Jabberwocky) Sourcebooks, Inc.
—The Littlest Bunny in New York City: An Easter Adventure. Dunn, Robert, illus. 2015. (ENG.). 32p. (J). (-3). 9.99 *(978-1-4926-1153-0(0),* Sourcebooks Jabberwocky) Sourcebooks, Inc.
—The Littlest Bunny in North Carolina: An Easter Adventure. Dunn, Robert, illus. 2015. (ENG.). 32p. (J). (-3). 9.99 *(978-1-4926-1156-1(5),* Sourcebooks Jabberwocky) Sourcebooks, Inc.
—The Littlest Bunny in North Dakota: An Easter Adventure. Dunn, Robert, illus. 2015. (ENG.). 32p. (J). (-3). 9.99 *(978-1-4926-1159-2(X),* Sourcebooks Jabberwocky) Sourcebooks, Inc.
—The Littlest Bunny in Ohio: An Easter Adventure. Dunn, Robert, illus. 2015. (ENG.). 32p. (J). (-3). 9.99 *(978-1-4926-1162-2(X),* Sourcebooks Jabberwocky) Sourcebooks, Inc.
—The Littlest Bunny in Oklahoma: An Easter Adventure. Dunn, Robert, illus. 2015. (ENG.). 32p. (J). (-3). 9.99 *(978-1-4926-1165-3(4),* Sourcebooks Jabberwocky) Sourcebooks, Inc.
—The Littlest Bunny in Omaha: An Easter Adventure. Dunn, Robert, illus. 2015. (ENG.). 32p. (J). (-3). 9.99 *(978-1-4926-1168-4(9),* Sourcebooks Jabberwocky) Sourcebooks, Inc.
—The Littlest Bunny in Oregon: An Easter Adventure. Dunn, Robert, illus. 2015. (ENG.). 32p. (J). (-3). 9.99 *(978-1-4926-1171-4(9),* Sourcebooks Jabberwocky) Sourcebooks, Inc.
—The Littlest Bunny in Ottawa: An Easter Adventure. Dunn, Robert, illus. 2015. (ENG.). 32p. (J). (-3). 11.99 *(978-1-4926-1174-5(3),* Sourcebooks Jabberwocky) Sourcebooks, Inc.
—The Littlest Bunny in Pennsylvania: An Easter Adventure. Dunn, Robert, illus. 2015. (ENG.). 32p. (J). (-3). 9.99 *(978-1-4926-1177-6(8),* Sourcebooks Jabberwocky) Sourcebooks, Inc.
—The Littlest Bunny in Philadelphia: An Easter Adventure. Dunn, Robert, illus. 2015. (ENG.). 32p. (J). (-3). 9.99 *(978-1-4926-1180-6(8),* Sourcebooks Jabberwocky) Sourcebooks, Inc.
—The Littlest Bunny in Pittsburgh: An Easter Adventure. Dunn, Robert, illus. 2015. (ENG.). 32p. (J). (-3). 9.99 *(978-1-4926-1183-7(2),* Sourcebooks Jabberwocky) Sourcebooks, Inc.
—The Littlest Bunny in Portland: An Easter Adventure. Dunn, Robert, illus. 2015. (ENG.). 32p. (J). (-3). 9.99 *(978-1-4926-1186-8(7),* Sourcebooks Jabberwocky) Sourcebooks, Inc.
—The Littlest Bunny in San Francisco: An Easter Adventure. Dunn, Robert, illus. 2015. (ENG.). 32p. (J). (-3). 9.99 *(978-1-4926-1192-9(1),* Sourcebooks Jabberwocky) Sourcebooks, Inc.
—The Littlest Bunny in South Carolina: An Easter Adventure. Dunn, Robert, illus. 2015. (ENG.). 32p. (J). (-3). 9.99 *(978-1-4926-1195-0(6),* Sourcebooks Jabberwocky) Sourcebooks, Inc.
—The Littlest Bunny in South Dakota: An Easter Adventure. Dunn, Robert, illus. 2015. (ENG.). 32p. (J). (-3). 9.99 *(978-1-4926-1198-1(0),* Sourcebooks Jabberwocky) Sourcebooks, Inc.
—The Littlest Bunny in St. Louis: An Easter Adventure. Dunn, Robert, illus. 2015. (ENG.). 32p. (J). (-3). 9.99 *(978-1-4926-1201-8(4),* Sourcebooks Jabberwocky) Sourcebooks, Inc.
—The Littlest Bunny in Tampa Bay: An Easter Adventure. Dunn, Robert, illus. 2015. (ENG.). 32p. (J). (-3). 9.99 *(978-1-4926-1204-9(9),* Sourcebooks Jabberwocky) Sourcebooks, Inc.
—The Littlest Bunny in Tennessee: An Easter Adventure. Dunn, Robert, illus. 2015. (ENG.). 32p. (J). (-3). 9.99 *(978-1-4926-1207-0(3),* Sourcebooks Jabberwocky) Sourcebooks, Inc.
—The Littlest Bunny in Texas: An Easter Adventure. Dunn, Robert, illus. 2015. (ENG.). 32p. (J). (-3). 9.99 *(978-1-4926-1210-0(3),* Sourcebooks Jabberwocky) Sourcebooks, Inc.
—The Littlest Bunny in Toronto: An Easter Adventure. Dunn, Robert, illus. 2015. (ENG.). 32p. (J). (-3). 11.99 *(978-1-4926-1213-1(8),* Sourcebooks Jabberwocky) Sourcebooks, Inc.
—The Littlest Bunny in Tulsa: An Easter Adventure. Dunn, Robert, illus. 2015. (ENG.). 32p. (J). (-3). 9.99 *(978-1-4926-1216-2(2),* Sourcebooks Jabberwocky) Sourcebooks, Inc.
—The Littlest Bunny in Utah: An Easter Adventure. Dunn, Robert, illus. 2015. (ENG.). 32p. (J). (-3). 9.99 *(978-1-4926-1219-3(7),* Sourcebooks Jabberwocky) Sourcebooks, Inc.
—The Littlest Bunny in Vancouver: An Easter Adventure. Dunn, Robert, illus. 2015. (ENG.). 32p. (J). (-3). 11.99 *(978-1-4926-1222-3(7),* Sourcebooks Jabberwocky) Sourcebooks, Inc.
—The Littlest Bunny in Vermont: An Easter Adventure. Dunn, Robert, illus. 2015. (ENG.). 32p. (J). (-3). 9.99 *(978-1-4926-1225-4(1),* Sourcebooks Jabberwocky) Sourcebooks, Inc.
—The Littlest Bunny in Virginia: An Easter Adventure. Dunn, Robert, illus. 2015. (ENG.). 32p. (J). (-3). 9.99 *(978-1-4926-1228-5(6),* Sourcebooks Jabberwocky) Sourcebooks, Inc.
—The Littlest Bunny in Washington: An Easter Adventure. 2015. (ENG.). 32p. (J). (-3). 9.99 *(978-1-4926-1231-5(6),* Sourcebooks Jabberwocky) Sourcebooks, Inc.
—The Littlest Bunny in Washington, DC: An Easter Adventure. Dunn, Robert A., illus. 2015. (ENG.). 32p. (J). (-3). 9.99 *(978-1-4926-1234-6(0),* Sourcebooks Jabberwocky) Sourcebooks, Inc.
—The Littlest Bunny in West Virginia: An Easter Adventure. 2015. (ENG.). 32p. (J). (-3). 9.99 *(978-1-4926-1237-7(5),* Sourcebooks Jabberwocky) Sourcebooks, Inc.
—The Littlest Bunny in Wisconsin: An Easter Adventure. 2015. (ENG.). 32p. (J). (-3). 9.99 *(978-1-4926-1240-7(5),* Sourcebooks Jabberwocky) Sourcebooks, Inc.
—The Littlest Bunny in Wyoming: An Easter Adventure. 2015. (ENG.). 32p. (J). (-3). 9.99 *(978-1-4926-1243-8(X),* Sourcebooks Jabberwocky) Sourcebooks, Inc.
Jacobs, Sherry. Grampa's Teeth. 2012. (ENG.). 42p. (J). pap. 16.95 *(978-1-4327-8104-0(9))* Outskirts Pr., Inc.
Jacobs, Z. D. Ari & the Dybbuk. 2012. 144p. (gr. 4-6). pap. 14.95 *(978-1-4685-3671-3(0))* AuthorHouse.
Jacobsen, Annie. Ole Mackerel. Everson, Mya, illus. 2012. 32p. (J). 9.98 *(978-0-9778276-5-7(8))* Pickled Herring Pr.
Jacobson, Jennifer Richard. Small as an Elephant. 2011. (ENG., Illus.). 288p. (J). (gr. 4-7). 15.99 *(978-0-7636-4155-9(3))* Candlewick Pr.
Jacobson, John. The Quest: Adventure Story & Songs. Wilson, Roberta, illus. 2005. (ENG.). 48p. pap. 12.95 incl. audio compact disk *(978-1-4234-0019-6(4),* 1423400194) Leonard, Hal Corp.
Jacobson, Ryan. Jack London's Call of the Wild - A Choose Your Path Book. 2011. (Can You Survive? Ser.). (ENG.). 160p. (J). (gr. 3-8). pap. 8.95 *(978-0-9774122-3-5(7))* Lake 7 Creative, LLC.
Jacoby, Sue. The Sneakies in Las Vegas: A Coby Jay Adventure. 2012. 128p. (gr. 4-6). 22.60 *(978-1-4669-6672-7(6));* pap. 12.60 *(978-1-4669-6670-3(X))* Trafford Publishing.
Jacqueline Juin Snow. A Potato Tale. 2009. 16p. pap. 8.49 *(978-1-4389-6360-0(2))* AuthorHouse.
Jacques, Brian. The Bellmaker. Curless, Allan, illus. 2004. (Redwall Ser.). (ENG.). 352p. (J). (gr. 5-18). reprint ed. pap. 8.99 *(978-0-14-240030-2(0),* Firebird) Penguin Young Readers Group.
—Die Mauer. pap. 19.95 *(978-3-570-26021-0(6))* Bertelsman, Verlagsgruppe C. GmbH DEU. Dist: Distribooks, Inc.
—Outcast of Redwall: A Tale from Redwall. 2004. (Redwall Ser.). (ENG., Illus.). 368p. (J). (gr. 5-5). 8.99 *(978-0-14-240142-2(0),* Firebird) Penguin Young Readers Group.
—Pearls of Lutra. 2004. (Redwall Ser.). (ENG., Illus.). 416p. (J). (gr. 5-5). 8.99 *(978-0-14-240144-6(7),* Firebird) Penguin Young Readers Group.
—Redwall. Blevins, Bret, illus. 2007. (Redwall Ser.). (ENG.). 148p. (J). (gr. 5-18). 12.99 *(978-0-399-24481-0(6),* Philomel Bks.) Penguin Young Readers Group.
—Voyage of Slaves: A Tale from the Castaways of the Flying Dutchman. 2007. (ENG.). 320p. (gr. 12-18). 7.99 *(978-0-441-01528-3(X),* Ace Bks.) Penguin Publishing Group.
Jacques, Marcie. Booba-Lou. 2005. (Illus.). (J). bds. 9.95 *(978-0-9764114-0-6(7))* Little People Bks.
Jae-Jones, S. Wintersong. 2017. (ENG.). 448p. (YA). 18.99 *(978-1-250-07921-3(7),* 9781250079213) St. Martin's Pr.
Jafa, Manorama. Sadako of Hiroshima (English) 2013. (ENG.). 16p. pap. 4.95 *(978-93-5036-084-2(5))* Ratna, Sagar Pvt. Ltd. IND. Dist: Midpoint Trade Bks., Inc.
Jaggi, Harleen. Mystery at the Book Store. 2007. (J). per. *(978-0-9790896-0-2(3))* Booksmart Pubns.
Jaimet, Kate. Edge of Flight, 1 vol. 2012. (Orca Sports Ser.). (ENG.). 160p. (YA). (gr. 6-10). pap. 9.95 *(978-1-4598-0160-8(1))* Orca Bk. Pubs. USA.
Jake's Big Adventure. 2008. (Jake Flocked Board Ser.). 8p. bds. *(978-1-4075-1818-3(6))* Parragon, Inc.
Jakobs, D. Despicable Me 2: the Anti-Villain League Handbook. 2013. (Despicable Me 2 Ser.). (ENG., Illus.). 80p. (J). (gr. 3-7). pap. 4.99 *(978-0-316-24557-9(7))* Little, Brown Bks. for Young Readers.
—Meet Blades the Copter-Bot. 2014. (Transformers Passport to Reading Ser.). (J). lib. bdg. 14.75 *(978-0-606-35295-6(3))* Turtleback Bks.
Jakubowski, Michele. Perfectly Poppy, 1 vol. 2014. (Perfectly Poppy Ser.). (ENG.). 32p. (gr. k-2). 90.60 *(978-1-4795-4544-5(9))* Picture Window Bks.
—The Sleuths of Somerville, 4 vols. Pinelli, Amerigo, illus. 2016. (Sleuths of Somerville Ser.). (ENG.). 144p. (gr. 4-6). 103.96 *(978-1-4965-3207-7(4))* Stone Arch Bks.
Jalonen, Nicole. Magical Animal Army Adventures. 2012. 28p. pap. 15.99 *(978-1-4691-7544-7(4))* Xlibris Corp.
Jamal L. Q'Ettelle. Jayden & the Return of the Jalon Warriors. 2010. 120p. pap. 10.95 *(978-1-4502-0288-6(8))* iUniverse, Inc.
James, Arthur. Jason & the Kodikats. 2013. 118p. pap. *(978-0-9918166-2-0(5))* Flower Pr.
James, Brian. Attack on the High Seas!, No. 3. Zivoin, Jennifer, illus. 2007. (Pirate School Ser.: 3). (ENG.). 64p. (J). (gr. 1-3). pap. 3.99 *(978-0-448-44645-5(6),* Grosset & Dunlap) Penguin Young Readers Group.
—The Curse of Snake Island. Zivoin, Jennifer, illus. 2007. (Pirate School Ser.: 1). (ENG.). 64p. (J). (gr. 1-3). pap. 3.99 *(978-0-448-44574-8(3),* Grosset & Dunlap) Penguin Young Readers Group.
—Port of Spies. Zivoin, Jennifer, illus. 2007. (Pirate School Ser.: 4). (ENG.). 64p. (J). (gr. 1-3). pap. 3.99 *(978-0-448-44646-2(4),* Grosset & Dunlap) Penguin Young Readers Group.
—Treasure Trouble. Zivoin, Jennifer, illus. 2008. (Pirate School Ser.: 5). (ENG.). 64p. (J). (gr. 1-3). pap. 3.99 *(978-0-448-44782-7(7),* Grosset & Dunlap) Penguin Young Readers Group.
—Yo-Ho-Ho! Zivoin, Jennifer, illus. 2008. (Pirate School Ser.: 7). (ENG.). 64p. (J). (gr. 1-3). pap. 3.99 *(978-0-448-44887-9(4),* Grosset & Dunlap) Penguin Young Readers Group.
James, Brokenlily. Pine Needle Shoes. 2007. 108p. per. 10.99 *(978-1-60477-154-1(2))* Salem Author Services.
James, Dalton. The Heroes of Googley Woogley. 2009. 22p. (J). pap. 10.95 *(978-1-4327-2782-6(6))* Outskirts Pr., Inc.
—The Sneakiest Pirates. 2008. 20p. pap. 10.95 *(978-1-4327-2477-1(0))* Outskirts Pr., Inc.
James, Debra & James, Jessica. The Social Pyramid. 2010. 57p. pap. 7.50 *(978-0-557-40789-7(3))* Lulu Pr., Inc.
James, Eric. A Halloween Scare in Connecticut. Le Ray, Marina, illus. 2015. (ENG.). 32p. (J). (-5). 9.99

(978-1-4926-2370-0(9), 9781492623700, Sourcebooks Jabberwocky) Sourcebooks, Inc.
—A Halloween Scare in Idaho. Le Ray, Marina, illus. 2015. (ENG.). 32p. (J). (-5). 9.99 (978-1-4926-2374-8(1), 9781492623748, Sourcebooks Jabberwocky) Sourcebooks, Inc.
—A Halloween Scare in Missouri. Le Ray, Marina, illus. 2015. (ENG.). 32p. (J). (-5). 9.99 (978-1-4926-2383-0(0), 9781492623830, Sourcebooks Jabberwocky) Sourcebooks, Inc.
—A Halloween Scare in Nebraska. Le Ray, Marina, illus. 2015. (ENG.). 32p. (J). (-5). 9.99 (978-1-4926-2385-4(7), 9781492623854, Sourcebooks Jabberwocky) Sourcebooks, Inc.
—A Halloween Scare in Omaha. Le Ray, Marina, illus. 2015. (ENG.). 32p. (J). (-5). 9.99 (978-1-4926-2392-2(X), 9781492623922, Sourcebooks Jabberwocky) Sourcebooks, Inc.
—A Halloween Scare in Philadelphia. Le Ray, Marina, illus. 2015. (ENG.). 32p. (J). (-5). 9.99 (978-1-4926-2395-3(4), 9781492623953, Sourcebooks Jabberwocky) Sourcebooks, Inc.
—A Halloween Scare in Portland. Le Ray, Marina, illus. 2015. (ENG.). 32p. (J). (-5). 9.99 (978-1-4926-2397-7(0), 9781492623977, Sourcebooks Jabberwocky) Sourcebooks, Inc.
—A Halloween Scare in South Dakota. Le Ray, Marina, illus. 2015. (ENG.). 32p. (J). (-5). 9.99 (978-1-4926-2400-4(4), 9781492624004, Sourcebooks Jabberwocky) Sourcebooks, Inc.
—A Halloween Scare in the Carolinas. Le Ray, Marina, illus. 2014. (ENG.). 32p. (J). (-5). 9.99 (978-1-4926-0576-8(X), 9781492605768, Sourcebooks Jabberwocky) Sourcebooks, Inc.
—A Halloween Scare in Utah. Le Ray, Marina, illus. 2015. (ENG.). 32p. (J). (-5). 9.99 (978-1-4926-2405-9(5), 9781492624059, Sourcebooks Jabberwocky) Sourcebooks, Inc.
—A Halloween Scare in Virginia. Le Ray, Marina, illus. 2014. (ENG.). 32p. (J). (-5). 9.99 (978-1-4926-0636-9(7), 9781492606369, Sourcebooks Jabberwocky) Sourcebooks, Inc.
—A Halloween Scare in Washington. Le Ray, Marina, illus. 2014. (ENG.). 32p. (J). (-5). 9.99 (978-1-4926-0639-0(1), 9781492606390, Sourcebooks Jabberwocky) Sourcebooks, Inc.
—A Halloween Scare in West Virginia. Le Ray, Marina, illus. 2015. (ENG.). 32p. (J). (-5). 9.99 (978-1-4926-2409-7(8), 9781492624097, Sourcebooks Jabberwocky) Sourcebooks, Inc.
—A Halloween Scare in Wisconsin. Le Ray, Marina, illus. 2014. (ENG.). 32p. (J). (-5). 9.99 (978-1-4926-0642-0(1), 9781492606420, Sourcebooks Jabberwocky) Sourcebooks, Inc.
—Santa's Sleigh Is on Its Way to Alaska: A Christmas Adventure. Dunn, Robert, illus. 2016. (ENG.). 32p. (J). (-2). 12.99 (978-1-4926-4314-2(9), 9781492643142, Sourcebooks Jabberwocky) Sourcebooks, Inc.
—Santa's Sleigh Is on Its Way to Albuquerque: A Christmas Adventure. Dunn, Robert, illus. 2016. (ENG.). 32p. (J). (-2). 12.99 (978-1-4926-4315-9(7), 9781492643159, Sourcebooks Jabberwocky) Sourcebooks, Inc.
—Santa's Sleigh Is on Its Way to Arizona: A Christmas Adventure. Dunn, Robert, illus. 2016. (ENG.). 32p. (J). (-2). 12.99 (978-1-4926-4316-6(5), 9781492643166, Sourcebooks Jabberwocky) Sourcebooks, Inc.
—Santa's Sleigh Is on Its Way to Arkansas: A Christmas Adventure. Dunn, Robert, illus. 2016. (ENG.). 32p. (J). (-2). 12.99 (978-1-4926-4317-3(3), 9781492643173, Sourcebooks Jabberwocky) Sourcebooks, Inc.
—Santa's Sleigh Is on Its Way to Boise: A Christmas Adventure. Dunn, Robert, illus. 2016. (ENG.). 32p. (J). (-2). 12.99 (978-1-4926-4318-0(1), 9781492643180, Sourcebooks Jabberwocky) Sourcebooks, Inc.
—Santa's Sleigh Is on Its Way to Boston: A Christmas Adventure. Dunn, Robert, illus. 2016. (ENG.). 32p. (J). (-2). 12.99 (978-1-4926-4319-7(X), 9781492643197, Sourcebooks Jabberwocky) Sourcebooks, Inc.
—Santa's Sleigh Is on Its Way to Calgary: A Christmas Adventure. Dunn, Robert, illus. 2016. (ENG.). 32p. (J). (-2). 12.99 (978-1-4926-4320-3(3), 9781492643203, Sourcebooks Jabberwocky) Sourcebooks, Inc.
—Santa's Sleigh Is on Its Way to Canada: A Christmas Adventure. Dunn, Robert, illus. 2016. (ENG.). 32p. (J). (-2). 12.99 (978-1-4926-4321-0(1), 9781492643210, Sourcebooks Jabberwocky) Sourcebooks, Inc.
—Santa's Sleigh Is on Its Way to Charleston: A Christmas Adventure. Dunn, Robert, illus. 2016. (ENG.). 32p. (J). (-2). 12.99 (978-1-4926-4322-7(X), 9781492643227, Sourcebooks Jabberwocky) Sourcebooks, Inc.
—Santa's Sleigh Is on Its Way to Chicago: A Christmas Adventure. Dunn, Robert, illus. 2016. (ENG.). 32p. (J). (-2). 12.99 (978-1-4926-4323-4(8), 9781492643234, Sourcebooks Jabberwocky) Sourcebooks, Inc.
—Santa's Sleigh Is on Its Way to Cincinnati: A Christmas Adventure. Dunn, Robert, illus. 2016. (ENG.). 32p. (J). (-2). 12.99 (978-1-4926-4324-1(6), 9781492643241, Sourcebooks Jabberwocky) Sourcebooks, Inc.
—Santa's Sleigh Is on Its Way to Connecticut: A Christmas Adventure. Dunn, Robert, illus. 2016. (ENG.). 32p. (J). (-2). 12.99 (978-1-4926-4325-8(4), 9781492643258, Sourcebooks Jabberwocky) Sourcebooks, Inc.
—Santa's Sleigh Is on Its Way to Delaware: A Christmas Adventure. Dunn, Robert, illus. 2016. (ENG.). 32p. (J). (-2). 12.99 (978-1-4926-4326-5(2), 9781492643265, Sourcebooks Jabberwocky) Sourcebooks, Inc.
—Santa's Sleigh Is on Its Way to Edmonton: A Christmas Adventure. Dunn, Robert, illus. 2016. (ENG.). 32p. (J). (-2). 12.99 (978-1-4926-4327-2(0), 9781492643272, Sourcebooks Jabberwocky) Sourcebooks, Inc.
—Santa's Sleigh Is on Its Way to Hawaii: A Christmas Adventure. Dunn, Robert, illus. 2016. (ENG.). 32p. (J). (-2). 12.99 (978-1-4926-4328-9(9), 9781492643289, Sourcebooks Jabberwocky) Sourcebooks, Inc.
—Santa's Sleigh Is on Its Way to Idaho: A Christmas Adventure. Dunn, Robert, illus. 2016. (ENG.). 32p. (J). (-2). 12.99 (978-1-4926-4329-6(7), 9781492643296, Sourcebooks Jabberwocky) Sourcebooks, Inc.
—Santa's Sleigh Is on Its Way to Kansas: A Christmas Adventure. Dunn, Robert, illus. 2016. (ENG.). 32p. (J). (-2). 12.99 (978-1-4926-4330-2(0), 9781492643302, Sourcebooks Jabberwocky) Sourcebooks, Inc.
—Santa's Sleigh Is on Its Way to Kansas City: A Christmas Adventure. Dunn, Robert, illus. 2016. (ENG.). 32p. (J). (-2). 12.99 (978-1-4926-4331-9(9), 9781492643319, Sourcebooks Jabberwocky) Sourcebooks, Inc.
—Santa's Sleigh Is on Its Way to Las Vegas: A Christmas Adventure. Dunn, Robert, illus. 2016. (ENG.). 32p. (J). (-2). 12.99 (978-1-4926-4332-6(7), 9781492643326, Sourcebooks Jabberwocky) Sourcebooks, Inc.
—Santa's Sleigh Is on Its Way to Los Angeles: A Christmas Adventure. Dunn, Robert, illus. 2016. (ENG.). 32p. (J). (-2). 12.99 (978-1-4926-4333-3(5), 9781492643333, Sourcebooks Jabberwocky) Sourcebooks, Inc.
—Santa's Sleigh Is on Its Way to Maine: A Christmas Adventure. Dunn, Robert, illus. 2016. (ENG.). 32p. (J). (-2). 12.99 (978-1-4926-4334-0(3), 9781492643340, Sourcebooks Jabberwocky) Sourcebooks, Inc.
—Santa's Sleigh Is on Its Way to Maryland: A Christmas Adventure. Dunn, Robert, illus. 2016. (ENG.). 32p. (J). (-2). 12.99 (978-1-4926-4335-7(1), 9781492643357, Sourcebooks Jabberwocky) Sourcebooks, Inc.
—Santa's Sleigh Is on Its Way to Massachusetts: A Christmas Adventure. Dunn, Robert, illus. 2016. (ENG.). 32p. (J). (-2). 12.99 (978-1-4926-4336-4(X), 9781492643364, Sourcebooks Jabberwocky) Sourcebooks, Inc.
—Santa's Sleigh Is on Its Way to Mississippi: A Christmas Adventure. Dunn, Robert, illus. 2016. (ENG.). 32p. (J). (-2). 12.99 (978-1-4926-4337-1(8), 9781492643371, Sourcebooks Jabberwocky) Sourcebooks, Inc.
—Santa's Sleigh Is on Its Way to Montana: A Christmas Adventure. Dunn, Robert, illus. 2016. (ENG.). 32p. (J). (-2). 12.99 (978-1-4926-4338-8(6), 9781492643388, Sourcebooks Jabberwocky) Sourcebooks, Inc.
—Santa's Sleigh Is on Its Way to Nebraska: A Christmas Adventure. Dunn, Robert, illus. 2016. (ENG.). 32p. (J). (-2). 12.99 (978-1-4926-4339-5(4), 9781492643395, Sourcebooks Jabberwocky) Sourcebooks, Inc.
—Santa's Sleigh Is on Its Way to Nevada: A Christmas Adventure. Dunn, Robert, illus. 2016. (ENG.). 32p. (J). (-2). 12.99 (978-1-4926-4340-1(8), 9781492643401, Sourcebooks Jabberwocky) Sourcebooks, Inc.
—Santa's Sleigh Is on Its Way to New England: A Christmas Adventure. Dunn, Robert, illus. 2016. (ENG.). 32p. (J). (-2). 12.99 (978-1-4926-4341-8(6), 9781492643418, Sourcebooks Jabberwocky) Sourcebooks, Inc.
—Santa's Sleigh Is on Its Way to New Hampshire: A Christmas Adventure. Dunn, Robert, illus. 2016. (ENG.). 32p. (J). (-2). 12.99 (978-1-4926-4342-5(4), 9781492643425, Sourcebooks Jabberwocky) Sourcebooks, Inc.
—Santa's Sleigh Is on Its Way to New Mexico: A Christmas Adventure. Dunn, Robert, illus. 2016. (ENG.). 32p. (J). (-2). 12.99 (978-1-4926-4343-2(2), 9781492643432, Sourcebooks Jabberwocky) Sourcebooks, Inc.
—Santa's Sleigh Is on Its Way to New York City: A Christmas Adventure. Dunn, Robert, illus. 2016. (ENG.). 32p. (J). (-2). 12.99 (978-1-4926-4344-9(0), 9781492643449, Sourcebooks Jabberwocky) Sourcebooks, Inc.
—Santa's Sleigh Is on It's Way to Newfoundland: A Christmas Adventure. Dunn, Robert, illus. 2016. (ENG.). 32p. (J). (-2). 12.99 (978-1-4926-4505-4(2), 9781492645054, Sourcebooks Jabberwocky) Sourcebooks, Inc.
—Santa's Sleigh Is on Its Way to North Dakota: A Christmas Adventure. Dunn, Robert, illus. 2016. (ENG.). 32p. (J). (-2). 12.99 (978-1-4926-4345-6(9), 9781492643456, Sourcebooks Jabberwocky) Sourcebooks, Inc.
—Santa's Sleigh Is on It's Way to Nova Scotia: A Christmas Adventure. Dunn, Robert, illus. 2016. (ENG.). 32p. (J). (-2). 12.99 (978-1-4926-4508-5(7), 9781492645085, Sourcebooks Jabberwocky) Sourcebooks, Inc.
—Santa's Sleigh Is on Its Way to Oklahoma: A Christmas Adventure. Dunn, Robert, illus. 2016. (ENG.). 32p. (J). (-2). 12.99 (978-1-4926-4346-3(7), 9781492643463, Sourcebooks Jabberwocky) Sourcebooks, Inc.
—Santa's Sleigh Is on Its Way to Omaha: A Christmas Adventure. Dunn, Robert, illus. 2016. (ENG.). 32p. (J). (-2). 12.99 (978-1-4926-4347-0(5), 9781492643470, Sourcebooks Jabberwocky) Sourcebooks, Inc.
—Santa's Sleigh Is on Its Way to Oregon: A Christmas Adventure. Dunn, Robert, illus. 2016. (ENG.). 32p. (J). (-2). 12.99 (978-1-4926-4348-7(3), 9781492643487, Sourcebooks Jabberwocky) Sourcebooks, Inc.
—Santa's Sleigh Is on Its Way to Philadelphia: A Christmas Adventure. Dunn, Robert, illus. 2016. (ENG.). 32p. (J). (-2). 12.99 (978-1-4926-4350-0(5), 9781492643500, Sourcebooks Jabberwocky) Sourcebooks, Inc.
—Santa's Sleigh Is on Its Way to Pittsburgh: A Christmas Adventure. Dunn, Robert, illus. 2016. (ENG.). 32p. (J). (-2). 12.99 (978-1-4926-4351-7(3), 9781492643517, Sourcebooks Jabberwocky) Sourcebooks, Inc.
—Santa's Sleigh Is on Its Way to Portland: A Christmas Adventure. Dunn, Robert, illus. 2016. (ENG.). 32p. (J). (-2). 12.99 (978-1-4926-4352-4(1), 9781492643524, Sourcebooks Jabberwocky) Sourcebooks, Inc.
—Santa's Sleigh Is on Its Way to Rhode Island: A Christmas Adventure. Dunn, Robert, illus. 2016. (ENG.). 32p. (J). (-2). 12.99 (978-1-4926-4353-1(X), 9781492643531, Sourcebooks Jabberwocky) Sourcebooks, Inc.
—Santa's Sleigh Is on Its Way to San Francisco: A Christmas Adventure. Dunn, Robert, illus. 2016. (ENG.). 32p. (J). (-2). 12.99 (978-1-4926-4354-8(8), 9781492643548, Sourcebooks Jabberwocky) Sourcebooks, Inc.
—Santa's Sleigh Is on Its Way to South Dakota: A Christmas Adventure. Dunn, Robert, illus. 2016. (ENG.). 32p. (J). (-2). 12.99 (978-1-4926-4355-5(6), 9781492643555, Sourcebooks Jabberwocky) Sourcebooks, Inc.
—Santa's Sleigh Is on Its Way to St. Louis: A Christmas Adventure. Dunn, Robert, illus. 2016. (ENG.). 32p. (J). (-2). 12.99 (978-1-4926-4356-2(4), 9781492643562, Sourcebooks Jabberwocky) Sourcebooks, Inc.
—Santa's Sleigh Is on Its Way to Tampa Bay: A Christmas Adventure. Dunn, Robert, illus. 2016. (ENG.). 32p. (J). (-2). 12.99 (978-1-4926-4357-9(2), 9781492643579, Sourcebooks Jabberwocky) Sourcebooks, Inc.
—Santa's Sleigh Is on Its Way to Tulsa: A Christmas Adventure. Dunn, Robert, illus. 2016. (ENG.). 32p. (J). (-2). 12.99 (978-1-4926-4359-3(9), 9781492643593, Sourcebooks Jabberwocky) Sourcebooks, Inc.
—Santa's Sleigh Is on Its Way to Utah: A Christmas Adventure. Dunn, Robert, illus. 2016. (ENG.). 32p. (J). (-2). 12.99 (978-1-4926-4360-9(2), 9781492643609, Sourcebooks Jabberwocky) Sourcebooks, Inc.
—Santa's Sleigh Is on Its Way to Vermont: A Christmas Adventure. Dunn, Robert, illus. 2016. (ENG.). 32p. (J). (-2). 12.99 (978-1-4926-4362-3(9), 9781492643623, Sourcebooks Jabberwocky) Sourcebooks, Inc.
—Santa's Sleigh Is on Its Way to Washington, D. C. A Christmas Adventure. Dunn, Robert, illus. 2016. (ENG.). 32p. (J). (-2). 12.99 (978-1-4926-4363-0(7), 9781492643630, Sourcebooks Jabberwocky) Sourcebooks, Inc.
—Santa's Sleigh Is on Its Way to West Virginia: A Christmas Adventure. Dunn, Robert, illus. 2016. (ENG.). 32p. (J). (-2). 12.99 (978-1-4926-4364-7(5), 9781492643647, Sourcebooks Jabberwocky) Sourcebooks, Inc.
James, Henry. The Turn of the Screw. 2005. 96p. per. 4.95 (978-1-4209-2244-8(0)) Digireads.com Publishing.
—The Turn of the Screw. l.t. ed. 2006. 240p. pap. (978-1-84637-294-0(1)) Echo Library.
James, Kristopher. Lyrian. 2009. (Illus.). 171p. pap. 16.95 (978-1-4092-8986-9(9)) Lulu Pr., Inc.
James, Laura. Captain Pug: The Dog Who Sailed the Seas. 2017. (J). lib. bdg. 17.20 **(978-0-606-40346-7(9))** Turtleback Bks.
James, Martha. Jack Tenfield's Star: A Story of Yankee. 2005. pap. 30.95 (978-1-4179-9285-0(9)) Kessinger Publishing, LLC.
James, Richard E., III. Adventures of the Elements Vol. 3: Dangerous Games. Lyle, Maryann, ed. Welch, Chad, illus. 2004. 169p. (YA). (gr. 3-12). pap. 5.95 (978-0-9675901-2-7(4)) Alchemy Creative, Inc.
James, Shilah & James, Michael. Little Land Adventures - Little Bird. Castles, Heather, illus. 2010. 24p. pap. (978-1-926635-33-0(7)) Adlibbed, Ltd.
—Little Land Adventures - Little Iguan. Castles, Heather, illus. 2010. 24p. pap. (978-1-926635-34-7(5)) Adlibbed, Ltd.
—Little Land Adventures - Little Pig. Castles, Heather, illus. 2010. 24p. pap. (978-1-926635-35-4(3)) Adlibbed, Ltd.
—Little Land Adventures - Little Racoon. Castles, Heather, illus. 2010. 24p. pap. (978-1-926635-36-1(1)) Adlibbed, Ltd.
Jameson, Bernadette. The Boy Who Played His Way to Freedom. 2012. 80p. pap. 12.95 (978-1-4710-6968-0(0)) Lulu Pr., Inc.
Jameson, Pam. The Betty Book! The Life & Times of Betty. 2012. (ENG.). 33p. (J). pap. 12.95 (978-1-4327-8915-2(5)) Outskirts Pr., Inc.
Jameson, Rosemary. Mortimer & Teasdale's Adventures. 2009. 44p. pap. 14.50 (978-1-60693-441-8(4), Eloquent Bks.) Strategic Book Publishing & Rights Agency (SBPRA).
Jamieson, B. Goldstrike. (Illus.). xiii, 252p. (J). (gr. k-6). 39.95 (978-0-09-174260-7(9), Arrow Bks., Ltd.) Random Hse. GBR. Dist: Trafalgar Square Publishing.
Jamiol, Paul. Bikers Are Animals: A Children's Book on Motorcycling. Habib, Linda, ed. 2009. 38p. pap. 14.95 (978-1-60844-232-4(2)) Dog Ear Publishing, LLC.
Jane, Kelsey. The Autumn Adventure. 2011. 32p. 15.00 (978-1-4567-0153-6(3)) AuthorHouse.
Jane, Rebecca. Hamster Heroes to the Rescue: The Mystery of the Shadow in the Yard & Retirement. 2012. 84p. 19.95 (978-1-4626-6862-5(3)) America Star Bks.
Janeway, Paul. Dragon Eye Connection. 2011. 202p. pap. 14.95 (978-1-60976-854-6(X), Strategic Bk. Publishing) Strategic Book Publishing & Rights Agency (SBPRA).
Janicke, Gregory. The Shadow Beasts, 1 vol. Janicke, Gregory, illus. 2007. (Outcasts Ser.: Bk. 1). (ENG., Illus.). 276p. (YA). (gr. 8-12). pap. 6.99 (978-0-7614-5364-2(4)) Marshall Cavendish Corp.
Janisch, Heinz. The Fantastic Adventures of Baron Munchausen. Cooper, Belinda, tr. from GER. Blau, Aljoscha, illus. 2010. (ENG.). 32p. (J). (gr. -1-3). 17.95 (978-1-59270-091-2(8)) Enchanted Lion Bks., LLC.
Janjua, Sajid. Dusty the Kitten. 2012. (Illus.). 20p. pap. 19.82 (978-1-4772-2225-6(1)) AuthorHouse.
Jannazo, Michelle A. Isabella's Shoes. 2012. 28p. pap. 11.95 (978-1-4327-9019-6(6)) Outskirts Pr., Inc.
Janni, Rebecca. Nellie Sue, Happy Camper. Avril, Lynne, illus. 2013. (Every Cowgirl Ser.). (ENG.). 32p. (J). (gr. 1-2). 14.99 (978-0-448-46507-4(8)); mass mkt. 3.99 (978-0-448-46387-2(3)) Penguin Young Readers Group. (Penguin Young Readers).
Janow, Jody. Eddie's Great Escape. 2010. 44p. pap. 19.99 (978-1-4520-1764-8(6)) AuthorHouse.
Janowski, Alice. The Adventures of Inka the Feline. Smith, Jerry, illus. 2010. 36p. pap. 14.00 (978-1-60844-576-9(3)) Dog Ear Publishing, LLC.
Janson, Marilyn June. Tommy Jenkins: First Teleported Kid: A Fearless Series Book. 2007. 30p. (J). pap. 8.95 (978-0-7414-3912-3(3)) Infinity Publishing.
Janssen, Ian. The Perils of Pierre Book 2, Hunger Rules. 2013. 26p. pap. 13.95 (978-1-61160-823-6(6)) Whiskey Creek Restorations.
Jansson, Tove. Moominsummer Madness. Warburton, Thomas, tr. Jansson, Tove, illus. 2010. (Moomins Ser.: 4). (ENG., Illus.). 176p. (J). (gr. 4-7). pap. 7.99 (978-0-312-60891-0(8), 9780312608910) Square Fish.
Jaramillo, J.C. Best Buggies, 1 vol. 2010. 16p. 24.95 (978-1-4489-4928-1(9)) PublishAmerica, Inc.
Jardine, Alan. Sloop John B: A Pirate's Tale. Pickering, Jimmy, illus. 2005. 32p. 17.95 (978-0-689-03596-8(9), Milk & Cookies) ibooks, Inc.
Jardine, Alan. Sloop John B -A Pirate's Tale. Pickering, Jimmy, illus. 2016. (ENG.). (J). (gr. k-4). 32.00 **(978-1-59687-511-1(9)**, ipicturebooks) ibooks, Inc.
Jardine, Kathy & Jardine, Ashley. The Durples: Go to School. 2010. 28p. pap. 17.99 (978-1-4490-3405-4(5)) AuthorHouse.
Jarkins, Sheila. Marco Flamingo Under the Sea. 2009. (Rip Squeak Ser.). (ENG.). 32p. (J). (gr. -1-3). 16.95 (978-1-934960-68-4(3), Raven Tree Pr.,Csi) Continental Sales, Inc.
—Marco Flamingo under the Sea/Las Aventuras Submarinas de Marco Flamenco. 2009. (ENG & SPA.). 32p. (J). (gr. -1-3). 16.95 (978-1-934960-66-0(7), Raven Tree Pr.,Csi) Continental Sales, Inc.
Jarman, Julia. Harry the Clever Spider at School. Fowkes, Charlie, illus. 2007. (Collins Big Cat Ser.). (ENG.). 128p. (J). (gr. 1-2). pap. 6.99 (978-0-00-718670-9(3)) HarperCollins Pubs. Ltd. GBR. Dist: Independent Pubs. Group.
Jarmes, Jon Jeffery. Jason Post: Magic at the Downs. 2006. (YA). 19.95 (978-0-9770483-0-4(6)) Speech Publishing Hse.
Jarratt, Laura. By Any Other Name. 2014. (ENG.). 368p. (YA). (gr. 7). pap. 10.99 (978-1-4052-5673-5(7)) Egmont Bks., Ltd. GBR. Dist: Independent Pubs. Group.
Jarrell, Pamela R. The Tod Squad Can Pretend. 2006. (Tod Squad Ser.). (Illus.). 12p. (J). (gr. -1-k). bds. 7.99 (978-1-57332-413-7(2), HighReach Learning, Incorporated) Carson-Dellosa Publishing, LLC.
Jarvis, Cathy. Red Beard Santa's Biker Buddy. 2013. 36p. pap. 15.49 (978-1-4669-9587-1(4)) Trafford Publishing.
Jarvis, James & Waterman, Russell. Vortigern's Machine: And the Great Sage of Wisdom. Jarvis, James, illus. 2006. (Illus.). 48p. per. 24.00 (978-3-89955-098-6(6)) Die Gestalten Verlag DEU. Dist: Prestel Publishing.
Jarvis, Robin. Dark Waters of Hagwood. 2013. (Hagwood Trilogy Ser.: 2). (ENG.). 318p. (J). (gr. 4-6). pap. 14.99 (978-1-4532-9920-3(3), Open Road Media E-riginal) Open Road Integrated Media, Inc.
—War in Hagwood. 2016. (Hagwood Trilogy Ser.: 3). (ENG.). 310p. (J). (gr. 4-6). pap. 14.99 (978-1-4532-9922-7(X), Open Road Media E-riginal) Open Road Integrated Media, Inc.
Jarvis, Rowles Mary. Dick Lionheart. 2007. 68p. per. 87.99 (978-1-4280-7645-7(X)) IndyPublish.com.
Jasnoch, Dorothy. Adventure of Little Mouse Maggie. Kern, Kimberly, ed. Jasnoch, Dorothy, illus. 2012. (ENG., Illus.). 36p. pap. 14.99 (978-1-937752-06-4(2)) Owl About Bks. Pub., Inc.
—The Adventures of Oskar: Oskar's New School. Korzeniowski, Samson O., ed. Jasnoch, Dorothy, illus. 2013. (Illus.). 32p. 18.99 (978-1-937752-27-9(5)) Owl About Bks. Pub., Inc.
Javaherbin, Mina. Soccer Star. Alarcao, Renato, illus. 2014. (ENG.). 40p. (J). (gr. k-3). 16.99 (978-0-7636-6056-7(6)) Candlewick Pr.
Jay, Basil. The Adventures of Twig. 2011. (Illus.). 120p. pap. 32.90 (978-1-4567-8631-1(8)) AuthorHouse.
Jay, Eli. Poppy & the Stranger. 2012. (ENG.). 41p. (J). pap. 21.95 (978-1-4327-9752-2(2)) Outskirts Pr., Inc.
—Poppy, the Wandering Balloon. 2011. 33p. (J). pap. 19.95 (978-1-4327-6855-3(7)) Outskirts Pr., Inc.
Jay, Stacey. Princess of Thorns. 2016. (ENG.). 400p. (YA). (gr. 9). pap. 9.99 (978-0-385-74323-5(8), Ember) Random Hse. Children's Bks.
Jayne, Hannah. Truly, Madly, Deadly. 2013. (ENG.). 272p. (YA). (gr. 7-12). pap. 10.99 (978-1-4022-8121-1(8), 9781402281211) Sourcebooks, Inc.
Jaz. Lost Lake: An Adventure for Kids of All Ages. 2008. 172p. pap. 24.95 (978-1-60703-398-1(4)) America Star Bks.
Jazynka, Kitson. Boys Camp: Nate's Story. Orback, Craig, illus. 2015. (ENG.). 144p. (J). (gr. 1-5). pap. 9.95 (978-1-62914-806-9(7), Sky Pony Pr.) Skyhorse Publishing Co., Inc.
Jean, Heather. Secret of the Golden Pyramid. 2013. 44p. pap. 20.45 (978-1-4525-1042-2(3), Balboa Pr.) Author Solutions, Inc.
Jeanne Taylor Thomas Illustrator: Pr. Austin & Harlow's First Adventure. Hardy, Pris, illus. 2011. 28p. pap. 24.95 (978-1-4560-8383-0(X)) America Star Bks.
Jeb. Destinations in Time. 2008. 101p. pap. 19.95 (978-1-60672-653-2(6)) America Star Bks.
Jebiwool Art Museum Staff. Destination Blackbeard: Destinations in Time, Book 2, 1 vol. 2009. 101p. pap. 19.95 (978-1-60749-626-7(7)) America Star Bks.
Jee, Derek. The Time Travelling Clock. 2017. (ENG.). 94p. (J). pap. 11.95 **(978-1-78693-931-9(2)**, 99c4dc7f-1492-4cdf-beb7-43277fa0ca0b) Austin, Stan AUS. Dist: Bookmasters Distribution.
Jefferson, A. C. The Adventures of Lucy the Wiener Dog. 2012. 24p. pap. 17.99 (978-1-4772-7214-5(3)) AuthorHouse.
Jefferson, Barbara. The Luck of the Dragonfly. Jefferson, Daniel E., illus. 2008. 31p. pap. 24.95 (978-1-60672-283-1(2)) America Star Bks.
Jefferson Elementary Art Club, illus. Domino. 2007. 32p. (J). 15.00 (978-0-9767244-2-1(1)) SkyMacSyd Publishing.
Jeffrey, Mark. Max Quick: The Pocket & the Pendant. 2011. (ENG., Illus.). 304p. (J). (gr. 3-7). 15.99 (978-0-06-198892-9(8)) HarperCollins Pubs.
Jeffrey, Rosemary. Allio, Are you Free. 2010. 176p. pap. 12.00 (978-0-557-75342-0(2)) Lulu Pr., Inc.
Jelenic, Michael. Justice League vs. Bizarro League. 2015. (LEGO DC Super Heroes Chapter Book Ser.). lib. bdg. 14.75 (978-0-606-37794-2(8)) Turtleback Bks.
Jenkins, Amanda. Pecos Bill & Sluefoot Sue: An American Tall Tale. 2006. (J). pap. (978-1-4108-7158-9(4)) Benchmark Education Co.
—Wally Smithers Tames the River. Fagan, Martin, illus. 2017. (Text Connections Guided Close Reading Ser.). (J). (gr. 2). (978-1-4900-1842-3(5)) Benchmark Education Co.
Jenkins, Amanda & Benchmark Education Co., LLC. The Secret Life of Wally Smithers. Fagan, Martin, illus. 2014. (Text Connections Ser.). (J). (gr. 3). (978-1-4509-9656-3(6)) Benchmark Education Co.
Jenkins Bathe, Bettina. Violet the Pilot in Canada. 2004. (Illus.). 20p. (J). 14.35 (978-1-4120-3215-5(6)) Trafford Publishing.
Jenkins, Carla LaVern. The Disappearance of Mrs. Brown: A Jenkins Girl Mystery. 2010. 72p. 23.55 (978-1-4269-4537-3(X)); pap. 13.55 (978-1-4251-6659-5(8)) Trafford Publishing.
Jenkins, Emily. Toy Dance Party. Zelinsky, Paul O., illus. 2010. (Toys Go Out Ser.). (ENG.). 176p. (J). (gr. 1-4). 6.99 (978-0-375-85525-2(4), Yearling) Random Hse. Children's Bks.
—Toy Dance Party: Being the Further Adventures of a Bossyboots Stingray, a Courageous Buffalo, & a Hopeful Round Someone Called Plastic. Zelinsky, Paul O., illus.

2008. (Toys Go Out Ser.). (ENG.). 176p. (J). (gr. 1-4). 16.99 *(978-0-375-83935-1(6),* Schwartz & Wade Bks.) Random Hse. Children's Bks.

—Toys Come Home: Being the Early Experiences of an Intelligent Stingray, a Brave Buffalo, & a Brand-New Someone Called Plastic. Zelinsky, Paul O., illus. 2016. (Toys Go Out Ser.). (ENG.). 144p. (J). (gr. 1-4). 6.99 *(978-0-449-81592-2(7),* Yearling) Random Hse. Children's Bks.

—Toys Go Out: Being the Adventures of a Knowledgeable Stingray, a Toughy Little Buffalo, & Someone Called Plastic. Zelinsky, Paul O., illus. (Toys Go Out Ser.). (ENG.). (J). (gr. 1-4). 2008. 144p. 6.99 *(978-0-385-73661-9(4),* Yearling) 2006. 128p. 16.95 *(978-0-375-83604-6(7),* Schwartz & Wade Bks.) Random Hse. Children's Bks.

Jenkins, Henry A. The Adventures of Monkey Squirrel & Frogman: Sand Trap. 2009. 16p. pap. 8.49 *(978-1-4343-7827-9(6))* AuthorHouse.

Jenkins, Jerry B. Crash at Cannibal Valley, 1 vol. 2006. (AirQuest Adventures Ser.). (ENG.). 160p. (J). (gr. 3-7). pap. 6.99 *(978-0-310-71347-0(1))* Zonderkidz.

—Disaster in the Yukon, 1 vol. 2006. (AirQuest Adventures Ser.). (ENG., Illus.). 160p. (J). (gr. 3-7). pap. 6.99 *(978-0-310-71345-6(5))* Zonderkidz.

—Terror: In Branco Grande, 1 vol. 2006. (AirQuest Adventures Ser.). (ENG., Illus.). 160p. (J). (gr. 3-7). pap. 6.99 *(978-0-310-71346-3(3))* Zonderkidz.

Jenkins, Jerry B. & Fabry, Chris. The Author's Blood. 2008. (Wormling Ser.: 5). (ENG.). 368p. (J). (gr. 5-9). per. 7.99 *(978-1-4143-0159-4(6),* Tyndale Kids) Tyndale Hse. Pubs.

—The Book of the King. 2007. (Wormling Ser.: 1). (ENG.). 288p. (J). (gr. 5-9). per. 7.99 *(978-1-4143-0155-6(3))* Tyndale Hse. Pubs.

—The Changeling. 2007. (Wormling Ser.: 3). (ENG.). 336p. (J). (gr. 5-9). per. 7.99 *(978-1-4143-0157-0(X))* Tyndale Hse. Pubs.

—El Libro del Rey. 2008. (Lombricero Ser.: 1).Tr. of Book of the King. (SPA.). 304p. (J). pap. 7.99 *(978-1-4143-2216-2(X),* Tyndale Espanol) Tyndale Hse. Pubs.

—The Minions of Time. 2008. (Wormling Ser.: 4). (ENG.). 336p. (J). (gr. 5-9). per. 7.99 *(978-1-4143-0158-7(8))* Tyndale Hse. Pubs.

—Sword of the Wormling. 2007. (Wormling Ser.: 2). (ENG.). 336p. (J). (gr. 5-9). per. 7.99 *(978-1-4143-0156-3(1))* Tyndale Hse. Pubs.

Jenkins, Jerry B. & LaHaye, Tim. The Mark of the Beast: Witness Behind Bars. 2003. (Left Behind Ser.). 146p. (J). 13.65 *(978-0-7569-3532-0(6))* Perfection Learning Corp.

Jenkins, June M. All about Me: Tales for Tiny Tots. 2008. (Illus.). 52p. per. *(978-1-84748-222-8(8))* Athena Pr.

Jenkins, Steven. The Spider House: Battle for the Wall. 2007. 264p. 26.95 *(978-0-595-69910-0(3));* per. 16.95 *(978-0-595-44488-5(1))* iUniverse, Inc.

Jenner, Kendall Nicole, et al. Rebels, City of Indra: The Story of Lex & Livia. 2016. (Story of Lex & Livia Ser.: 1). (ENG.). 352p. pap. 11.99 *(978-1-4516-9455-0(5))* Simon & Schuster, Inc.

Jennette, Mairead. Ten Green Bottles. 2013. 98p. pap. *(978-3-7103-0181-0(5))* united p.c. Verlag.

Jennewein, James & Parker, Tom S. RuneWarriors. 2008. (RuneWarriors Ser.). 320p. (J). (gr. 3-7). lib. bdg. 17.89 *(978-0-06-144937-6(7),* Geringer, Laura Book) HarperCollins Pubs.

—Shield of Odin. 2009. (RuneWarriors Ser.: 1). (ENG.). 336p. (J). (gr. 3-7). pap. 6.99 *(978-0-06-144938-3(5))* HarperCollins Pubs.

—Ship of the Dead. 2010. (RuneWarriors Ser.: 3). (ENG.). 304p. (J). (gr. 3-7). 17.99 *(978-0-06-144942-0(3))* HarperCollins Pubs.

—Sword of Doom. 2009. (RuneWarriors Ser.: 2). (ENG.). 432p. (J). (gr. 3-7). 17.99 *(978-0-06-144939-0(3))* HarperCollins Pubs.

Jennicrai, Susanna. Button & Bow: Friends Forever. 2013. 28p. pap. 16.09 *(978-1-4669-8779-1(0))* Trafford Publishing.

Jennings, L. N. Seven Splinters. 2012. 426p. pap. 22.50 *(978-1-105-54636-5(5))* Lulu Pr., Inc.

Jennings, Regina & Kuhn, Suzanne Brooks. A Scary Little Christmas. 2017. (ENG., Illus.). 192p. (J). 14.99 *(978-1-943785-06-3(6),* 9781943785063) Rabbit Pubs.

Jennings, Sharon, et al, adapted by. Franklin & the Stopwatch. 2007. (Kids Can Read Ser.). (ENG., Illus.). 32p. (J). (gr. 1-2). 3.95 *(978-1-55337-891-4(1))* Kids Can Pr., Ltd. CAN. Dist: Hachette Bk. Group.

Jennings, Steven J. The Bodacious Adventures of Joe & Barb. 2006. 399p. 38.00 *(978-1-4116-7509-4(6))* Lulu Pr., Inc.

Jensen, Brandi Ann & Courtright, Jordan K. The Hilarious & Brave Adventures of Hog & Dog. 2011. 40p. pap. 16.95 *(978-1-4560-3955-4(5))* America Star Bks.

Jensen, Jeff. X-Factor. Ranson, Arthur, illus. 2003. (X-Men Ser.: Vol. 1). 96p. (YA). pap. 9.99 *(978-0-7851-1016-3(X))* Marvel Worldwide, Inc.

Jensen, Kathryn. Splash! 2012. 194p. 29.95 *(978-1-4489-6574-8(8))* America Star Bks.

Jensen, Lars, et al. Donald Duck Adventures, Vol. 18. Clark, John, ed. 2006. (ENG., Illus.). 128p. (YA). pap. 7.95 *(978-1-888472-30-1(8),* 9781888472301) Gemstone Publishing, Inc.

Jepson, Jeanette. The Adventures of Theodore Tortoise - Claude's Big Adventure: Claude's Big Adventure. 2011. 24p. pap. 15.99 *(978-1-4628-8646-3(9))* Xlibris Corp.

Jeremiatt, Omani. Paper Boy. Rollins, Bernic, illus. 2003. 40p. (J). (gr. 6-8). pap. 10.00 *(978-1-929188-09-3(9))* Morton Bks.

Jesperson, Per. Wonder & Magic: The David Tales. 2003. 50p. pap. *(978-1-84401-017-2(1))* Athena Pr.

Jess & Jaylen (Set), 8 vols. 2014. (Jess & Jaylen Ser.). (ENG.). (J). (gr. 1-4). 216.56 *(978-1-60973-168-7(9),* 208272) Child's World, Inc., The.

Jessi Swanson And Jessica Swanson & Swanson, Jessica. An Adventurous Day for Lucy. 2011. 28p. pap. 24.95 *(978-1-4626-2426-3(X))* America Star Bks.

Jessica Hoel. Adam B Brave. Samantha Nowak, illus. 2009. 20p. pap. 12.49 *(978-1-4389-3240-8(5))* AuthorHouse.

Jessup, VonDa. Wanda the Witch at the Happy Haunted House. 2008. (Illus.). 44p. pap. 18.50 *(978-1-60693-149-3(0),* Eloquent Bks.) Strategic Book Publishing & Rights Agency (SBPRA).

Jewel Robbery. 2008. (Looney Tunes 8*8 Ser.). 24p. pap. *(978-1-4075-2632-4(4));* pap. *(978-1-4075-2642-3(1))* Parragon, Inc.

Jewell, M. B. Tales of Amanda O' 2008. 80p. pap. 15.99 *(978-1-4363-2215-7(4))* Xlibris Corp.

Jewett, Sarah Orne. Betty Leicester: A Story for Girls. 2004. reprint ed. pap. 20.95 *(978-1-4191-0978-2(2));* pap. 1.99 *(978-1-4192-0978-9(7))* Kessinger Publishing, LLC.

Jiang, Mingyan. Stella Doggy: Book One of Stella's Awesome Adventures. 2011. 88p. (gr. 4-6). 19.95 *(978-1-4620-4610-2(X));* pap. 9.95 *(978-1-4620-4608-9(8))* iUniverse, Inc.

Jimmie the Crab: An Adventure in the Chesapeake Bay. 2013. (Illus.). 28p. pap. 13.97 *(978-1-62516-364-6(9),* Strategic Bk. Publishing) Strategic Book Publishing & Rights Agency (SBPRA).

Jimmy. My Kayak Lives in a Tree at the Beach, 1 vol. 2009. 18p. pap. 24.95 *(978-1-60749-210-8(5))* America Star Bks.

Jin, Nayoung. Shooting Star Rider. Cote, Genevieve, illus. 2017. (ENG.). 36p. (J). (gr. -1-3). 16.95 *(978-1-77229-020-2(3))* Simply Read Bks. CAN. Dist: Ingram Publisher Services.

Jinks, Catherine. The Last Bogler. 2016. (How to Catch a Bogle Ser.: 3). (ENG., Illus.). 336p. (J). (gr. 5-7). 16.99 *(978-0-544-08696-8(1),* HMH Books For Young Readers) Houghton Mifflin Harcourt Publishing Co.

—Pagan in Exile. 2005. (Pagan Chronicles Ser.: 2). (ENG., Illus.). 336p. (YA). (gr. 7-18). reprint ed. pap. 6.99 *(978-0-7636-2691-4(0))* Candlewick Pr.

Jiya, Tapiwa. The Epic of Goz. 2008. 144p. pap. 11.99 *(978-1-4343-5730-4(9))* AuthorHouse.

Jobes, Cecily. Playtime. 2016. (It's Time Ser.). 24p. (gr. 1-1). pap. 8.25 *(978-1-4994-2284-9(9),* PowerKids Pr.) Rosen Publishing Group, Inc., The.

Jobling, Curtis. The Beast of Bone Creek. 2016. (Max Helsing: Monster Hunter Ser.: 2). (ENG., Illus.). 304p. (J). (gr. 5). 16.99 *(978-0-451-47480-3(5),* Viking Books for Young Readers) Penguin Young Readers Group.

—Nest of Serpents. 2015. (Wereworld Ser.: 4). (ENG.). 512p. (J). (gr. 5). 8.99 *(978-0-14-242193-2(6),* Puffin Books) Penguin Young Readers Group.

—Rage of Lions. 2013. (Wereworld Ser.: 2). (ENG.). 432p. (J). (gr. 5). pap. 8.99 *(978-0-14-242202-1(9),* Puffin Books) Penguin Young Readers Group.

—Rage of Lions. 2013. (Wereworld Ser.: 2). lib. bdg. 19.65 *(978-0-606-30041-4(4),* Turtleback) Turtleback Bks.

—Rise of the Wolf. 2012. (Wereworld Ser.: 1). (ENG.). 432p. (J). (gr. 5-18). pap. 8.99 *(978-0-14-242108-6(1),* Puffin Books) Penguin Young Readers Group.

—Rise of the Wolf. 2012. (Wereworld Ser.: 1). lib. bdg. 19.65 *(978-0-606-26084-8(6),* Turtleback) Turtleback Bks.

—Shadow of the Hawk. 2013. (Wereworld Ser.: 3). (ENG.). 496p. (J). (gr. 5). pap. 8.99 *(978-0-14-242192-5(8),* Puffin Books) Penguin Young Readers Group.

—Shadow of the Hawk. 2013. (Wereworld Ser.: 3). lib. bdg. 19.65 *(978-0-606-30044-5(9),* Turtleback) Turtleback Bks.

—Storm of Sharks. (Wereworld Ser.: 5). (ENG.). 480p. (J). (gr. 5). 2015. 8.99 *(978-0-14-242577-0(X),* Puffin Books) 2013. 16.99 *(978-0-670-78558-2(X),* Viking Books for Young Readers) Penguin Young Readers Group.

—War of the Werelords. 2013. (Wereworld Ser.: 6). (ENG.). 528p. (J). (gr. 5). 16.99 *(978-0-670-78559-9(8),* Viking Books for Young Readers) Penguin Young Readers Group.

Joe & Trish. The Adventures of Sasha, the Six-Fingered Cat. 2010. 36p. pap. 16.99 *(978-1-4520-8406-0(8))* AuthorHouse.

Joe Thomson-Swift. The Magic Stone. 2011. 92p. pap. *(978-1-908105-83-7(6))* Grosvenor Hse. Publishing Ltd.

Jofre, Paola. Lilliput Blasts Off! 2010. 36p. 17.50 *(978-1-4490-7450-0(2))* AuthorHouse.

Johansen, Zdenka. When You Give of Yourself. 2006. 28p. pap. 9.95 *(978-1-4327-0059-1(6))* Outskirts Pr., Inc.

Johns, Geoff, et al. Teen Titans, Vol. 1. rev. ed. 2004. (Teen Titans Go! Ser.: Vol. 1). (ENG., Illus.). 192p. pap. 16.99 *(978-1-4012-0308-5(6))* DC Comics.

Johns, Linda. Postcard Clues. 2004. (Shared Connections Ser.). (J). pap. *(978-1-4108-1644-3(3));* instr.'s gde. ed. 27.00 *(978-1-4108-1620-7(6))* Benchmark Education Co.

Johns, W. E. Biggles' Secret Assignments. 2014. (ENG., Illus.). 512p. pap. 29.95 *(978-1-85375-911-6(2))* Carlton Bks., Ltd. GBR. Dist: Independent Pubs. Group.

Johnson, Allen, Jr. My Brother's Story. McMorris, Kelley, illus. 2014. (Blackwater Novels Ser.: Vol. 1). (ENG.). 191p. (J). (gr. 4-7). 14.99 *(978-1-933725-37-6(0))* Premium Pr. America.

Johnson, Bud. Chirpy: Chirpy's First Time Flying. 2013. 32p. pap. 13.99 *(978-1-4525-6763-1(8))* Balboa Pr.

Johnson, C. Homecoming. 2007. (Illus.). 64p. per. 10.00 *(978-1-4251-1358-2(3))* Trafford Publishing.

Johnson, Cara. The Dream Travelers, Book Two: The Butterfly Voyage. 2007. 176p. (J). per. 9.99 *(978-0-9768870-1-0(0))* Whirling Dirvish Publishing.

Johnson, Carol V. Somerset Dreams. 2011. (Illus.). 112p. pap. 32.12 *(978-1-4567-9012-7(9))* AuthorHouse.

Johnson, Carolyn W. Sano Comes to the Farm, 1 vol. 2009. 13p. pap. 24.95 *(978-1-61546-091-5(8))* America Star Bks.

Johnson, Deanna. Blarron Creek Chronicles. 2009. 108p. 23.49 *(978-1-4389-5580-3(4))* AuthorHouse.

Johnson, Doris M. The Cookie Crumb Trail. Taylor, Jennifer Louise, illus. 2008. (ENG.). 28p. pap. 15.99 *(978-1-4196-9127-0(9))* CreateSpace Independent Publishing Platform.

Johnson, Esther A. The Princess & the Garden. Taylor, Carolyn, illus. 2012. 34p. pap. 19.99 *(978-1-62419-614-0(4))* Salem Author Services.

Johnson, H. E. Sequoia Secret Place: Redeeming the Stolen Kingdom. 2011. 74p. (gr. -1). pap. 10.77 *(978-1-4567-5923-0(X))* AuthorHouse.

Johnson, James A. The Beast & the Backpack. 2009. 64p. pap. 8.95 *(978-1-4401-5390-7(6))* iUniverse, Inc.

—The Terror & the Talking Stick: Sundown Stories II. 2011. 56p. pap. 8.95 *(978-1-4502-8156-0(7))* iUniverse, Inc.

Johnson, James Ray. Timmy Wee Pee & Castle Friends. 2009. 28p. pap. 24.95 *(978-1-60836-886-0(6))* America Star Bks.

Johnson, Julia, ed. Arabian Star. Climent, Henry, illus. 2009. (ENG.). 52p. 11.99 *(978-1-905299-84-3(2),* Stacey International) Stacey Publishing GBR. Dist: Casemate Pubs. & Bk. Distributors, LLC.

Johnson, K. Ii. Pig Farm: Adventures of Sal & Snapper. 2011. 52p. pap. 31.99 *(978-1-4653-5058-9(6))* Xlibris Corp.

Johnson, Kevin D. Around Every Corner. 2011. 24p. (gr. 1-2). pap. 11.32 *(978-1-4567-4869-2(6))* AuthorHouse.

Johnson, Lucille M. Titus the Magnificent: The Adventures of Titus. 2013. 32p. pap. 13.99 *(978-1-4624-0755-2(2),* Inspiring Voices) Author Solutions, Inc.

Johnson, Mar. Jack the Mighty Steed. 2011. 88p. pap. 19.95 *(978-1-4560-4916-4(X))* America Star Bks.

Johnson, Margaret. Gone! Starter/Beginner. 2009. (ENG.). 48p. pap. 11.00 *(978-84-8323-509-6(9))* Cambridge Univ. Pr.

—Running Wild Level 3 Lower-Intermediate. 2009. (ENG.). 80p. pap. 12.75 *(978-84-8323-501-0(3))* Cambridge Univ. Pr.

Johnson, Mark. Little Fish Lou. 2008. 28p. pap. 17.95 *(978-1-4327-2934-9(9))* Outskirts Pr., Inc.

Johnson-McCue, Joyce. Gizmo's Great Adventure. 2008. (Illus.). 32p. (J). pap. 8.00 *(978-0-8059-7550-5(0))* Dorrance Publishing Co., Inc.

Johnson, Michael E. Barley & Betsy: Journey #1 A cat & dog's great adventure to the Mall. Atchley, Kendra, illus. 2011. 36p. pap. 24.95 *(978-1-4560-4077-2(4))* America Star Bks.

Johnson, Mimi Evelyn. A Day in the Life of Div. 2011. 24p. pap. 15.99 *(978-1-4628-9649-3(9))* Xlibris Corp.

Johnson, Myrna. Let's Take a Hike. 2013. (ENG., Illus.). 32p. (gr. -1-1). pap. 13.95 *(978-1-936205-79-0(3))* Austin, Stephen F. State Univ. Pr.

Johnson, S. K. Billy & Bob. 2012. 28p. pap. 16.09 *(978-1-4669-0995-3(1))* Trafford Publishing.

Johnson, Sandra, adapted by. Shoobie, 1 vol. 2009. 15p. pap. 24.95 *(978-1-60813-705-3(8))* America Star Bks.

Johnson, Shane L., illus. OLIVIA la Princesa. 2011. (Olivia TV Tie-In Ser.). (ENG & SPA.). 24p. (J). (gr. -1-2). pap. 3.99 *(978-1-4424-4640-3(4),* Libros Para Ninos) Libros Para Ninos.

Johnson-Shelton, Nils. The Dragon King. 2013. (Otherworld Chronicles Ser.: 3). (ENG.). 352p. (J). (gr. 3-7). 16.99 *(978-0-06-207097-5(5))* HarperCollins Pubs.

—The Invisible Tower. 2012. (J). (Otherworld Chronicles Ser.: 1). (ENG.). 368p. (gr. 5). pap. 6.99 *(978-0-06-207088-3(6));* 335p. 9.99 *(978-0-06-213192-8(3));* (Otherworld Chronicles Ser.: 1). (ENG.). 352p. (gr. 5). 16.99 *(978-0-06-207086-9(X))* HarperCollins Pubs.

—Otherworld Chronicles #2: the Seven Swords. 2013. (Otherworld Chronicles Ser.: 2). (ENG.). 384p. (J). (gr. 3-7). pap. 6.99 *(978-0-06-207095-1(9))* HarperCollins Pubs.

—The Seven Swords. 2013. (Otherworld Chronicles Ser.: 2). (ENG.). 368p. (J). (gr. 3-7). 16.99 *(978-0-06-207094-4(0))* HarperCollins Pubs.

Johnson, T. The Beach Club: Magic Beach, Vol. 1. 2012. (ENG.). 131p. pap. 11.95 *(978-1-4327-9316-6(0))* Outskirts Pr., Inc.

Johnson, Terry David. As I Sat on My Grandpa's Knee. 2009. 32p. pap. 16.50 *(978-1-60860-202-5(8),* Eloquent Bks.) Strategic Book Publishing & Rights Agency (SBPRA).

Johnston, Annie Fellows. The Story of the Red Cross As Told to the Little Colonel. Goss, John, illus. 2007. 48p. per. *(978-1-4065-3517-4(6))* Dodo Pr.

Johnston-Brown, A. M. Life at Pleasant Grove. 2005. (J). per. 15.95 *(978-0-9760718-1-5(9))* Retriever Pr.

Johnston, Cindy. Zip, Burp & Hula. 2006. (Illus.). 32p. (J). per. 10.95 *(978-0-9787930-5-0(6))* Virtual Word Publishing.

Johnston, E. K. Prairie Fire. 2015. (J). 18.99 *(978-1-4677-6181-9(8));* (ENG.). 304p. (gr. 6-12). 18.99 *(978-1-4677-3909-2(X))* Lerner Publishing Group.

—The Story of Owen: Dragon Slayer of Trondheim. 2014. 312p. (J). (gr. 6-12). 17.95 *(978-1-4677-1066-4(0),* Carolrhoda Lab™) Lerner Publishing Group.

Johnston, Gayle. Adventures of Jazzi G: Search for the Missing Peace. 2016. (Adventures of Jazzi G Ser.: 1). (ENG., Illus.). 202p. (J). pap. 14.95 *(978-1-63047-840-7(7))* Morgan James Publishing.

Johnston, James D. The Adventures of Lucas & Celi: Lucas Stows Away. 2009. 32p. pap. 12.99 *(978-1-4343-6372-5(4))* AuthorHouse.

Johnston, Jan. Amélie the Most Amazing Butterfly: I Do So Love Being a Butterfly ... 2013. (Illus.). 24p. pap. 17.99 *(978-1-4817-8018-6(2))* AuthorHouse.

—Lisa Finds a Playful Tree Elf: No! I Am Not a Fairy! 2013. (Illus.). 24p. pap. 17.99 *(978-1-4817-8020-9(4))* AuthorHouse.

—Ruby - the Naughty Little Black Kitten: Hello! My Name Is Ruby ... 2013. (Illus.). 24p. pap. 17.99 *(978-1-4817-8023-0(9))* AuthorHouse.

Johnston, Kathy. Get That Grasshopper! 2012. 24p. pap. 12.56 *(978-1-4669-3743-7(2))* Trafford Publishing.

Johnston, Mark & Spizman, Robyn Freedman. The Secret Agents Strike Back. 2008. (ENG., Illus.). 160p. (J). (gr. 4-7). 16.99 *(978-1-4169-0086-3(1),* Atheneum Bks. for Young Readers) Simon & Schuster Children's Publishing.

Johnston, Tamra L. Libby the Little Leprechaun. 2012. 42p. pap. 20.99 *(978-1-4772-0750-5(3))* AuthorHouse.

—Libby the Little Leprechaun: And the Majestic Roller Coaster. 2012. 50p. pap. 21.99 *(978-1-4772-0752-9(X))* AuthorHouse.

—Libby the Little Leprechaun: Exploring the Opposite Side of South Africa. 2012. 50p. pap. 21.99 *(978-1-4772-0782-6(1))* AuthorHouse.

Johnston-Thomas, Lee Ann. The Hidden Treasure of the Forgotten Pharaoh. 2008. 136p. 21.95 *(978-0-595-71157-4(X));* pap. 11.95 *(978-0-595-47552-0(3))* iUniverse, Inc.

Johnstone, Ian. The Bell Between Worlds. 2016. (Mirror Chronicles Ser.: 1). (J). lib. bdg. 20.85 *(978-0-606-38185-7(6))* Turtleback Bks.

Jokisch, Kimberly. I Have Two Homes. 2009. 24p. pap. 11.99 *(978-1-4389-2823-4(8))* AuthorHouse.

Jolley, Dan. Agent Mongoose & the Hypno-Beam Scheme. Wendt, Matt, illus. 2009. (Twisted Journeys (r) Ser.: 9). (ENG.). 112p. (J). (gr. 4-7). 27.93 *(978-0-8225-6203-0(0));* pap. 7.95 *(978-0-8225-6204-7(9))* Lerner Publishing Group.

—Attack of the Mutant Meteors. Witt, David, illus. 2010. (Twisted Journeys (r) Ser.: 14). (ENG.). 112p. (J). (gr. 4-7). pap. 7.95 *(978-0-8225-9255-6(X),* Graphic Universe™); lib. bdg. 27.93 *(978-0-8225-9249-5(5))* Lerner Publishing Group.

—The Emerald Tablet. 2016. (Five Elements Ser.: 1). 304p. (J). (gr. 3-7). 16.99 *(978-0-06-241165-5(9))* HarperCollins Pubs.

—The Emerald Tablet. 2017. (Five Elements Ser.: 1). (ENG.). (J). (gr. 3-7). lib. bdg. 17.20 ***(978-0-606-40054-1(0))*** Turtleback Bks.

—Five Elements #2: the Shadow City. (Five Elements Ser.: 2). (J). (gr. 3-7). 2018. 288p. pap. 6.99 ***(978-0-06-241168-6(3))*** 2017. 272p. 16.99 ***(978-0-06-241167-9(5))*** HarperCollins Pubs.

—Guan Yu: Blood Brothers to the End [A Chinese Legend]. Randall, Ron, illus. 2009. (Graphic Myths & Legends Ser.). (ENG.). 48p. (gr. 4-8). pap. 8.95 *(978-1-58013-890-1(X))* Lerner Publishing Group.

—The Hero Twins: Against the Lords of Death [A Mayan Myth]. Witt, David, illus. 2009. (Graphic Myths & Legends Ser.). (ENG.). 48p. (gr. 4-8). pap. 8.95 *(978-1-58013-892-5(6))* Lerner Publishing Group.

—Shipwrecked on Mad Island. Huddleston, Courtney, illus. 2009. (Twisted Journeys (r) Ser.: 11). (ENG.). 112p. (J). (gr. 4-7). pap. 7.95 *(978-0-8225-8875-7(7),* Carolrhoda Bks.) Lerner Publishing Group.

—The Time Travel Trap. Wendt, Matt, illus. 2008. (Twisted Journeys (r) Ser.: 6). (ENG.). 112p. (J). (gr. 4-7). per. 7.95 *(978-0-8225-8874-0(9))* Lerner Publishing Group.

Jonas, Gennevive. Mary Loves Butterflies. Barrett, Karlish, illus. 2012. 40p. pap. 24.95 *(978-1-62709-061-2(4))* America Star Bks.

Jonell, Bob. Katie the Cricket. Prince, Brian, illus. 2009. 12p. pap. 24.95 *(978-1-61546-280-3(5))* America Star Bks.

Jonell, Lynne. The Secret of Zoom. 2009. (ENG.). 304p. (J). (gr. 4-7). 16.99 *(978-0-8050-8856-4(3),* 9780805088564, Holt, Henry & Co. Bks. For Young Readers) Holt, Henry & Co.

—The Secret of Zoom. 2011. (ENG.). 320p. (J). (gr. 4-7). pap. 7.99 *(978-0-312-65933-2(4),* 9780312659332) Square Fish.

—The Sign of the Cat. 2015. (ENG., Illus.). 368p. (J). (gr. 3-7). 16.99 *(978-0-8050-9683-5(3),* 9780805096835, Holt, Henry & Co. Bks. For Young Readers) Holt, Henry & Co.

Jones, Allan. The Six Crowns: Fair Wind to Widdershins. Chalk, Gary, illus. 2011. (Six Crowns Ser.: 2). 176p. (J). (gr. 2-5). 15.99 *(978-0-06-200626-4(6),* Greenwillow Bks.) HarperCollins Pubs.

—The Six Crowns: Sargasso Skies. Chalk, Gary, illus. 2013. (Six Crowns Ser.: 5). 176p. (J). (gr. 3-7). 16.99 *(978-0-06-200636-3(3),* Greenwillow Bks.) HarperCollins Pubs.

—The Six Crowns: the Ice Gate of Spyre. Chalk, Gary, illus. 2012. (Six Crowns Ser.: 4). 160p. (J). (gr. 3-7). 15.99 *(978-0-06-200633-2(9),* Greenwillow Bks.) HarperCollins Pubs.

—The Six Crowns: Trundle's Quest. Chalk, Gary, illus. 2011. (Six Crowns Ser.: 1). 176p. (J). (gr. 2-5). pap. 5.99 *(978-0-06-200625-7(8),* Greenwillow Bks.) HarperCollins Pubs.

Jones, Allan & Frewin, Jones. In the Zone. 2012. (ENG.). 128p. (J). (gr. 4-6). pap. 6.99 *(978-1-4440-0545-5(6),* Orion Children's Bks.) Hachette Children's Group GBR. Dist: Hachette Bk. Group.

Jones, Allan Frewin. Burning Sky. 2012. (ENG.). 208p. (J). (gr. 4-6). pap. 6.99 *(978-1-4440-0547-9(2),* Orion Children's Bks.) Hachette Children's Group GBR. Dist: Hachette Bk. Group.

—Fire over Swallowhaven. Chalk, Gary, illus. 2012. (Six Crowns Ser.: 3). 160p. (J). (gr. 2-5). 15.99 *(978-0-06-200629-5(0),* Greenwillow Bks.) HarperCollins Pubs.

—Legends of the Golden Elephant. 2006. 188p. *(978-0-439-85671-3(X))* Scholastic, Inc.

—Trundle's Quest. Chalk, Gary, illus. 2011. (Six Crowns Ser.: 1). 160p. (J). (gr. 2-5). 15.99 *(978-0-06-200623-3(1),* Greenwillow Bks.) HarperCollins Pubs.

Jones, Bedo. The Adventures of Rodeo Duck. 2008. 37p. pap. 24.95 *(978-1-60610-554-2(X))* America Star Bks.

Jones, Brandy. Petunia: The Plump Princess, 1 vol. 2010. 32p. 24.95 *(978-1-4489-4874-1(6))* PublishAmerica, Inc.

Jones, Brenda. The Adventures of Murphy the Mouse. Moore, Dwain, illus. 2007. (J). per. 12.99 *(978-1-59712-069-2(3))* Catawba Publishing Co.

Jones, Bruce & Austen, Chuck. The Call of Duty Vol. 2: The Precinct, 2 vols. Mandrake, Tom & Zezelj, Danijel, illus. 2003. (Call Ser.). 128p. (YA). pap. 9.99 *(978-0-7851-0974-7(9))* Marvel Worldwide, Inc.

Jones, Bryan. Go Hokies Go: An Interactive Book Featuring Virginia Tech University. Bowman, Hootie, illus. 2012. 1. 12p. 19.95 *(978-0-9836211-0-2(1))* Collegiate Kids Bks., LLC.

Jones, C. Ashley. Draconic Destiny: Birth Rite. 2007. 140p. per. 24.95 *(978-1-4241-9218-2(8))* America Star Bks.

Jones, C. B. Bog Hollow Boys. Green, Chris, illus. 2017. (Bog Hollow Boys Ser.). (ENG.). 72p. (gr. 4-5). 101.28 *(978-1-4965-4063-8(8))* Stone Arch Bks.

Jones, Carol. Lake of the Lost. 2005. (Illus.). 160p. pap. *(978-0-7344-0646-0(0),* Lothian Children's Bks.) Hachette Australia.

Jones, Carrie. Time Stoppers. 2017. (Time Stoppers Ser.). (ENG.). 400p. (J). pap. 7.99 *(978-1-68119-437-0(6),* 9781681194370, Bloomsbury USA Childrens) Bloomsbury Publishing USA.

Jones, Cheri. The Adventures of a Mermaid Princess. 2013. 76p. (gr. -1). pap. 10.84 *(978-1-4907-0598-9(8))* Trafford Publishing.

Jones, Cheryl. Where Are My Shoes? 2011. 28p. pap. 9.95 *(978-1-4327-7157-7(4))* Outskirts Pr., Inc.

Jones, Cheryl & Joseph, Rahzheena. Jojo the Dappled Dachshund. Simmons, Ann, illus. 2013. 30p. pap. 15.95 *(978-1-4787-0560-4(4))* Outskirts Pr., Inc.

Jones, Chris. Cameron Jack & the Ghosts of World War 2. 2010. 120p. pap. 12.49 *(978-1-4520-2839-2(7))* AuthorHouse.

—Cameron Jack & the Key to the Universe. 2010. (Illus.). 136p. pap. 10.99 *(978-1-4490-6547-8(3))* AuthorHouse.

Jones, Connie. On the Farm with Kaden & Moxie. 2010. 20p. 12.49 *(978-1-4490-8047-1(2))* AuthorHouse.

Jones, Dennis. The Adventures of the Fruitiebears: Book 2 Fruitiecars. 2011. (Illus.). 48p. pap. 19.48 *(978-1-4567-9001-1(3))* AuthorHouse.

—Fruitiebears: Yorkies Birthday Today: Book 1. 2010. 36p. pap. 18.99 *(978-1-4520-7037-7(7))* AuthorHouse.
—The Life of Socks. 2004. 27p. pap. 24.95 *(978-1-4137-2774-6(3))* PublishAmerica, Inc.
Jones, Diana Wynne. Fire & Hemlock. 2012. (ENG.). 496p. (YA). (gr. 7-18). 9.99 *(978-0-14-242014-0(X)*, Firebird) Penguin Young Readers Group.
Jones, Erasmus W. The Young Captives: A Story of Judah & Babylon. Hayne, Mark, illus. 2007. 200p. per. *(978-1-4065-2718-6(1))* Dodo Pr.
Jones, Gareth P. The Clan of the Scorpion. Finlayson, Luke, illus. 2013. (Ninja Meerkats Ser.: 1). (ENG.). 128p. (J). (gr. 2-4). pap. 5.99 *(978-1-250-01664-5(9)*, 9781250016645) Square Fish.
—The Eye of the Monkey. Finlayson, Luke, illus. 2013. (Ninja Meerkats Ser.: 2). (ENG.). 128p. (J). (gr. 2-4). pap. 5.99 *(978-1-250-01665-2(7)*, 9781250016652) Square Fish.
Jones, Gwyneth. The Hidden Ones. (Livewire Ser.). 144p. (YA). (gr. 6-9). pap. 7.99 *(978-0-7043-4910-0(8))* Women's Pr., Ltd., The GBR. Dist: Trafalgar Square Publishing.
Jones, Jeannelle. Henry's Adventure. 2011. 36p. pap. 18.00 *(978-1-4634-1664-5(4))* AuthorHouse.
Jones, Jenny. Shadowsong. 128p. (J). pap. 8.99 *(978-1-85881-708-8(0)*, Orion) Orion Publishing Group, Ltd. GBR. Dist: Trafalgar Square Publishing.
Jones, Karen. Around the World from a to Z. 2011. 56p. pap. 21.95 *(978-1-4567-6145-5(5))* AuthorHouse.
Jones, Katherine. The Forbidden Tree. 2013. 44p. pap. 19.57 *(978-1-4669-7447-0(8))* Trafford Publishing.
Jones, Kia. The Adventures of Shamya & Friends: The Thanksgiving Day Wish. 2009. 28p. pap. 12.49 *(978-1-4389-5127-0(2))* AuthorHouse.
Jones, Lonetha. Big Brother's Missing Shoes. 2010. 28p. pap. 9.95 *(978-1-4327-5926-1(4))* Outskirts Pr., Inc.
Jones, Mary Noble. Itsy Rabbit & Friends: Itsy's First Adventure. Jones, Mary Noble, illus. 2007. (Illus.). 28p. (J). per. 15.00 *(978-0-9796209-8-0(8))* Righter Publishing Co., Inc.
Jones, Michael. Finding Imagine Nation. 2007. (YA). per. 10.95 *(978-0-9789386-4-2(X))* Lucy Rose Publishing LLC.
Jones, Nathan Smith. Dragonkyn. 2017. (YA). pap. 14.99 ***(978-1-4621-1978-3(6))*** Cedar Fort, Inc./CFI Distribution.
Jones, Nicky. Toby Fletcher's Fly-Away Tree. 2013. 182p. pap. *(978-1-78299-798-6(9))* FeedARead.com.
Jones, Rachel. The Adventures of AJ & Hunter: Lost in the Back Yard. sheltrown, karen, illus. 2011. (ENG.). 24p. pap. 6.99 *(978-1-4681-0130-0(7))* CreateSpace Independent Publishing Platform.
Jones, Ralph E. The Adventures of Kele: Boy of the Rock Shelter. 2012. 156p. pap. 41.99 *(978-1-4772-9405-5(8))*; 56p. pap. 24.99 *(978-1-4685-7696-2(8))* AuthorHouse.
Jones, Rob Lloyd. Wild Boy: The Real Life of the Savage of Aveyron. 2013. (ENG.). 304p. (J). (gr. 5). 16.99 *(978-0-7636-6252-3(6))* Candlewick Pr.
—Wild Boy & the Black Terror. 2015. (ENG.). 336p. (J). (gr. 5). 16.99 *(978-0-7636-6253-0(4))* Candlewick Pr.
Jones, Ruth Fosdick. Boy of the Pyramids: A Mystery of Ancient Egypt. Morse, Dorothy Bayley, illus. 2011. 150p. 40.95 *(978-1-258-06798-4(6))* Literary Licensing, LLC.
Jones, Steven E. Blue Eagle Meets Double Trouble. Jones, Steven E., Jr., illus. 2008. (Blue Eagle Ser.). (ENG.). 40p. (J). (gr. -1-2). 15.95 *(978-0-9794655-0-5(8))* Blue Eagle Bks., Inc.
Jones, T. W. Derth. 2006. 165p. pap. 24.95 *(978-1-4241-0806-0(3))* PublishAmerica, Inc.
Jones, Wendy Lou. Quest for Golden Downs. 2013. 246p. pap. 10.95 *(978-0-9777110-2-4(1))* Royal Knight Inc.
Jordan, Apple. Baboons! (Disney Junior: the Lion Guard) RH Disney, illus. 2017. (Little Golden Book Ser.). (ENG.). 24p. (J). (-k). 4.99 *(978-0-7364-3563-5(8)*, Golden/Disney) Random Hse. Children's Bks.
—Oh, Brother! Random House Disney Staff, illus. 2012. (Step into Reading Ser.). (ENG.). 32p. (J). (gr. -1-1). pap. 3.99 *(978-0-7364-2887-3(9)*, RH/Disney) Random Hse. Children's Bks.
—A Spooky Adventure (Disney/Pixar Toy Story) Random House Disney Staff, illus. 2011. (Step into Reading Ser.). (ENG.). 32p. (J). (gr. k-3). pap. 3.99 *(978-0-7364-2777-7(5)*, RH/Disney) Random Hse. Children's Bks.
Jordan, Claire. Fanakapan & the Fairies - a Children's Fairy Story. Skou, Nick, illus. 2013. 52p. pap. *(978-1-78148-648-1(4))* Grosvenor Hse. Publishing Ltd.
Jordan, Devin. The Dragon's Pearl. Di Bartolo, Jim, illus. 2010. (ENG.). 352p. (YA). (gr. 5-9). pap. 8.99 *(978-1-4169-6411-7(8)*, Simon & Schuster Bks. For Young Readers) Simon & Schuster Bks. For Young Readers.
Jordan, Lana. The Sleepytime Ponies Trick a Trickster. Allen, Kd & Giraud, Teresa, illus. 2004. 32p. (J). 12.95 *(978-0-9710696-1-9(1))* Jorlan Publishing, Inc.
Jordan, Sophie. Hidden. 2012. (Firelight Ser.: 3). (ENG.). 272p. (YA). (gr. 8). 17.99 *(978-0-06-193512-1(3))* HarperCollins Pubs.
—Unleashed. (Uninvited Ser.: 2). (YA). (gr. 8). 2016. 384p. pap. 9.99 *(978-0-06-223367-7(X))* 2015. (ENG.). 368p. 17.99 *(978-0-06-223371-4(8))* HarperCollins Pubs. (HarperTeen).
Jordison, P. B. Maggie to the Rescue. 2009. 45p. pap. 22.95 *(978-1-4327-1916-6(5))* Outskirts Pr., Inc.
Jorgensen, Norman. A Fine Mess. 2004. 192p. (J). pap. 13.50 *(978-1-920731-02-1(4))* Fremantle Pr. AUS. Dist: Independent Pubs. Group.
Joseph, Curtis M. Max Baxter. 2008. 57p. pap. 16.95 *(978-1-60610-206-0(0))* America Star Bks.
—Order of Godalming: Max Baxter, 1 vol. 2009. 64p. pap. 19.95 *(978-1-60836-525-8(5))* America Star Bks.
Joseph, Doug. The Last Bye: Book Three of the Millennial Teleport Trilogy. 2011. (ENG.). 194p. pap. 9.95 *(978-1-4680-1209-5(6))* CreateSpace Independent Publishing Platform.
Josephine Breglia. The Adventures of Poke Sa' Baar. 2012. 28p. pap. 24.95 *(978-1-4626-8820-3(9))* America Star Bks.
Josephs, Rudy & Barba, Rick. The Gemini Agent. 2011. (ENG.). 224p. (YA). (gr. 7). 14.99 *(978-1-4424-1961-2(X))*; pap. 7.99 *(978-1-4424-1342-9(5))* Simon Spotlight. (Simon Spotlight).
Journey to see the King. 2006. (J). *(978-0-9791168-0-3(5))* Lighthouse Bk. Publishing.
Joy, Judith Bourassa. A Doorway Through Space: Winner of Mayhaven Award for Children's Fiction. 2008. (ENG.). 224p. (YA). 14.95 *(978-1-932278-17-0(6))* Mayhaven Publishing, Inc.
Joy, Linda. Little Wave & the Mission of Laura Hawksbill. 2012. 24p. pap. 15.99 *(978-1-4691-9178-2(4))* Xlibris Corp.
Joyal, Lisa. Swahili for Beginners, 1 vol. 2008. (ENG., Illus.). 176p. (YA). (gr. 5-9). pap. *(978-1-894549-69-1(4)*, Sumach Pr.) Canadian Scholars.
Joyce, Carol. Just Friends. 2011. 228p. (gr. 10-12). 33.95 *(978-1-4497-2972-1(X))*; pap. 17.95 *(978-1-4497-2971-4(1))* Author Solutions, Inc. (WestBow Pr.).
Joyce, S. E. Silas Saves the Friendly Crab: A Low Country Tale. 2011. 28p. (gr. 1-2). pap. 14.99 *(978-1-4634-0285-3(6))* AuthorHouse.
Joyce, Sandie May. Little Miss Alice & the Bookworm. 2007. 65p. pap. 24.95 *(978-1-4357-0328-5(6))* Lulu Pr., Inc.
Joyce, William. E. Aster Bunnymund & the Warrior Eggs at the Earth's Core!, Bk. 2. Joyce, William, illus. 2012. (Guardians Ser.: 2). (ENG., Illus.). 272p. (J). (gr. 2-6). 15.99 *(978-1-4424-3050-1(8)*, Atheneum Bks. for Young Readers) Simon & Schuster Children's Publishing.
—Ollie's Odyssey. Joyce, William, illus. 2017. (ENG., Illus.). 304p. (J). (gr. 2-6). pap. 9.99 *(978-1-4424-7356-0(8))* Simon & Schuster, Inc.
—The Sandman & the War of Dreams. Joyce, William, illus. 2013. (Guardians Ser.: 4). (ENG., Illus.). 240p. (J). (gr. 2-6). 15.99 *(978-1-4424-3054-9(0)*, Atheneum Bks. for Young Readers) Simon & Schuster Children's Publishing.
—Toothiana Bk. 3: Queen of the Tooth Fairy Armies. Joyce, William, illus. 2012. (Guardians Ser.: 3). (ENG., Illus.). 240p. (J). (gr. 2-6). 15.99 *(978-1-4424-3052-5(4)*, Atheneum Bks. for Young Readers) Simon & Schuster Children's Publishing.
Joyce, William & Geringer, Laura. Nicholas St. North & the Battle of the Nightmare King, Bk. 1. Joyce, William, illus. 2011. (Guardians Ser.: 1). (ENG., Illus.). 240p. (J). (gr. 2-6). 15.99 *(978-1-4424-3048-8(6)*, Atheneum Bks. for Young Readers) Simon & Schuster Children's Publishing.
Joyner, Andrew. Boris on the Move. 2013. (Boris Ser.: 1). lib. bdg. 14.75 *(978-0-606-31974-4(3)*, Turtleback) Turtleback Bks.
Juarbe, Cynthia. Callie the Caterpillar Collects Coins. 2011. 24p. pap. 13.50 *(978-1-4520-5641-8(2))* AuthorHouse.
Judge, Chris. The Great Explorer. 2012. (ENG., Illus.). 32p. (J). (gr. -1-2). pap. 13.99 *(978-1-84939-401-7(6))* Andersen Pr. GBR. Dist: Independent Pubs. Group.
Judge, Chris & Wickham, Mark. Brian & the Giant. 2016. (ENG., Illus.). 32p. (J). pap. 11.00 *(978-1-84717-773-5(5))* O'Brien Pr., Ltd., The IRL. Dist: Dufour Editions, Inc.
Judith Anne Moody. Golden Eye & the Killer Cat. 2009. 248p. pap. 19.49 *(978-1-4251-7684-6(4))* Trafford Publishing.
Judith Brown Lamb. Gaudy Goosey Gander. 2009. 28p. pap. 13.99 *(978-1-4389-4812-6(3))* AuthorHouse.
Judson, Clara Ingram. Mary Jane: Her Book. 2007. 88p. per. *(978-1-4065-4677-4(1))* Dodo Pr.
—Mary Jane: Her Visit. White, Frances, illus. 2007. 108p. per. *(978-1-4065-4676-7(3))* Dodo Pr.
—Mary Jane - Her Visit. White, Frances, illus. 2008. 220p. 22.95 *(978-1-934671-15-3(0))*; per. 12.95 *(978-1-934671-16-0(9))* Salem Ridge Press LLC.
Judybee. Danny Strikes Out in Americ: A R. E. A. d Book. Kecskés, Anna, illus. 2013. 32p. pap. *(978-1-78092-335-2(X))* MX Publishing, Ltd.
Jules. Bubble's World: Book Five Frogs & Fairies. 2011. 40p. pap. 16.59 *(978-1-4567-6730-3(5))* AuthorHouse.
—Bubble's World: Isabella's Magic Dream. 2012. 58p. pap. 24.99 *(978-1-4772-6956-5(8))* AuthorHouse.
Jules, Jacqueline. The Princess & the Ziz. Kahn, Katherine Janus, illus. 2008. 32p. (J). (gr. -1-3). lib. bdg. 17.95 *(978-0-8225-7377-6(6))*; (ENG.). pap. 7.95 *(978-0-8225-7382-1(2))* Lerner Publishing Group. (Kar-Ben Publishing).
Julie, Aunt. Paddleduck! Julie, A Little Girl from Texas. 2011. 56p. (gr. 2-4). pap. 8.95 *(978-1-4269-2584-9(0))* Trafford Publishing.
Julie Marie. The Adventures of Fred the Five Pound Note. 2009. (Illus.). 52p. pap. 10.49 *(978-1-4389-4921-5(9))* AuthorHouse.
Julius, Nicholas. The Mythfitz: Unee the Unicorn. 2012. (ENG., Illus.). 62p. 28.95 *(978-1-4327-9868-0(5))*; pap. 23.95 *(978-1-4327-9365-4(9))* Outskirts Pr., Inc.
Jumbo & the Stranger. 2004. (J). per. 15.99 *(978-0-9744205-5-4(7))* Golden Eagle Publishing Hse., Inc.
Jumbo Fun. 2003. (J). per. *(978-1-884907-22-7(9))*; per. *(978-1-884907-23-4(7))* Paradise Pr., Inc.
Jumbo, the Kids & the Babysitter. 2004. (J). per. 15.99 *(978-0-9744205-8-5(1))* Golden Eagle Publishing Hse., Inc.
Juncar, Nicola. The Legend of Thornton Wood. 2012. 238p. pap. *(978-1-78176-184-7(1))* FeedARead.com.
Junge, Alexandra. A Night-Time Tale. Connolly, Kate, tr. from GER. 2006. (Picture books from around the World Seri Ser.). (ENG., Illus.). 36p. (J). (gr. k-2). 16.95 *(978-1-905341-06-1(7))* WingedChariot Pr. GBR. Dist: Independent Pubs. Group.
Jungle Fun. 2017. (Jungle Fun Ser.). 24p. (gr. 4-6). 70.80 ***(978-1-5081-6182-0(8)***, PowerKids Pr.) Rosen Publishing Group, Inc., The.
Juravel, Rabbi. A Journey with Rabbi Juravel: Adventure in the Sky & other Stories, Vol. 2. 2003. (Illus.). 254p. (J). 22.95 *(978-1-931681-50-6(3))* Israel Bookshop Pubns.
—A Journey with Rabbi Juravel: The Great Escape & Other Stories, Vol. 3. 2004. (Illus.). 252p. (J). 22.95 *(978-1-931681-63-6(5))* Israel Bookshop Pubns.
Jurgens, Dan, et al. Thor Vol. 3: Gods on Earth, 3 vols. Raney, Tom & Bennett, Davis, illus. 2003. (Thor Ser.). 248p. (YA). pap. 21.99 *(978-0-7851-1126-9(3))* Marvel Worldwide, Inc.
Jury, Walter & Fine, Sarah. Burn. 2015. (ENG.). 352p. (YA). (gr. 7). bds. 17.99 *(978-0-399-16068-4(X)*, G.P. Putnam's Sons Books for Young Readers) Penguin Young Readers Group.
Juslin, Lee. Nurse Frosty & the Wond'ear'ful Adventure. 2010. 32p. pap. 21.99 *(978-0-557-52512-6(8))* Lulu Pr., Inc.
—Nurse Frosty Saves the Day. 2009. 35p. pap. 22.00 *(978-0-557-09486-8(0))* Lulu Pr., Inc.
Justice, Tonya. Millie Mathison's Imagination: Cowboys, Indians, & no Red Cards. 2009. 24p. pap. 11.99 *(978-1-4389-9519-9(9))* AuthorHouse.
K. B. Kendricks. Travis Taylor & the Dragon Quest. 2010. 344p. pap. 29.95 *(978-1-4502-0261-9(6))* iUniverse, Inc.
K. Hall. The Adventures of Ranald the Rugby Player: The First Game. 2012. (Illus.). 28p. pap. 21.35 *(978-1-4685-8319-9(0))* AuthorHouse.
K, Miller Mace. Not Without Power: Lost in Africa. 2013. 302p. pap. 14.95 *(978-1-60920-071-8(3))* Ajoyin Publishing, Inc.
Kaaberbøl, Lene. The Shamer's Daughter. 2006. (Shamer Chronicles Ser.: 1).Tr. of Skammerens Datter. (ENG.). 240p. (J). (gr. 5-9). pap. 14.99 *(978-0-8050-8111-4(9)*, 9780805081114, Holt, Henry & Co. Bks. For Young Readers) Holt, Henry & Co.
Kabaji, Egara. When the Dead Met the Living, 1 vol. 2009. 48p. pap. 16.95 *(978-1-61546-505-7(7))* America Star Bks.
Kaczmarczyk, Kyle J. The Misadventures of Silent Boy - Volume II: the Stupid Strikes Back. 2005. 52p. (YA). pap. 17.99 *(978-1-4116-5231-6(2))* Lulu Pr., Inc.
Kaczynski, Heather. Dare Mighty Things. 2017. 384p. (YA). (gr. 8). 17.99 ***(978-0-06-247986-0(5)***, HarperTeen) HarperCollins Pubs.
Kadilak, Kathy. Tommy Finds His Forever Home. 2009. 28p. pap. 12.49 *(978-1-4490-0177-3(7))* AuthorHouse.
Kaesshaefer, Charles. The Lost Princess. 2004. (J). mass mkt. 10.00 *(978-0-9744407-0-5(1))* Shelbykay Publishing Co.
Kagawa, Julie. The Iron Daughter. 2010. (Iron Fey Ser.: 2). lib. bdg. 20.85 *(978-0-606-14917-4(1)*, Turtleback) Turtleback Bks.
—The Iron King. 2010. (Iron Fey Ser.: 1). lib. bdg. 20.85 *(978-0-606-14909-9(0)*, Turtleback) Turtleback Bks.
Kahanek, Kristine Elizabeth. Katie & the Magic Umbrella: A Stormy Adventure. 2008. (Katie & the Magic Umbrella Ser.). (Illus.). 44p. (J). (gr. -1-4). 14.95 *(978-0-9801423-0-3(X))* K.Co.Kids, LLC.
Kahaney, Amelia. The Brokenhearted. 2014. (Brokenhearted Ser.: 1). (ENG.). 368p. (YA). (gr. 8). pap. 9.99 *(978-0-06-223093-5(X)*, HarperTeen) HarperCollins Pubs.
—The Invisible. 2014. (Brokenhearted Ser.: 2). (ENG.). 304p. (YA). (gr. 8). 17.99 *(978-0-06-223192-5(8)*, HarperTeen) HarperCollins Pubs.
—The Invisible: A Brokenhearted Novel. 2015. (Brokenhearted Ser.: 2). (ENG.). 304p. (YA). (gr. 8). pap. 9.99 *(978-0-06-223193-2(6)*, HarperTeen) HarperCollins Pubs.
Kahler, Janet C. 1918 Covered Wagon Adventure. 2006. (Illus.). 94p. per. 10.95 *(978-1-57258-444-0(0)*, 945-6305) TEACH Services, Inc.
Kahn, Colleen Alyssa. The Peadoaks, 1 vol. 2010. 36p. 24.95 *(978-1-4489-4774-4(X))* America Star Bks.
Kail, Leanna. The Owl Who Couldn't Whoo. Rottinger, Amy, illus. 2013. 24p. pap. 11.95 *(978-1-61244-129-0(7))* Halo Publishing International.
Kain, Wallace M. The Red Column: A Young Woman's Capture, Imprisonment & Escape in the Amazon Jungle. 2006. (YA). per. 12.95 *(978-0-9742148-1-8(7))* Inkberry Pr.
Kakkar, Renu. Granny's Return from Heaven as an Incredible Car. 2011. (Illus.). 180p. (gr. 4-6). pap. 14.49 *(978-1-4490-9859-9(2))* AuthorHouse.
Kalb, Deborah. The President & Me: George Washington & the Magic Hat, 1 vol. Lunsford, Robert, illus. 2016. (ENG.). 144p. (J). pap. 12.99 *(978-0-7643-5110-5(9)*, 9780764351105) Schiffer Publishing, Ltd.
Kalkipsakis, Thalia. Catch Me If You Can. Oswald, Ash, illus. 2008. (Go Girl! Ser.: 12). (ENG.). 96p. (J). (gr. 2-4). pap. 5.99 *(978-0-312-34654-6(9)*, 9780312346546) Feiwel & Friends.
Kalkowski, John. Red Cell. 2010. 164p. 21.95 *(978-1-4502-1209-0(3))*; pap. 11.95 *(978-1-4502-1207-6(7))* iUniverse, Inc.
Kallus, Ryder. Ryder the Red-Nosed Engine. 2012. 44p. pap. 24.95 *(978-1-4626-9292-7(3))* America Star Bks.
Kaltovich, Edith Rusconi. The Adventures of Juan, the Fox: Argentine Tales & Fables. 2010. 64p. pap. 26.49 *(978-1-4490-8778-4(7))* AuthorHouse.
Kamat Tarkar, Poorwa Yeshwant. The Cornelius Sign: & the Season Queen Business, 1 vol. 2009. 234p. pap. 24.95 *(978-1-61582-408-3(1))* America Star Bks.
Kamateros, Litsa & Morfonios, Nia. Sarah's Socks: My World of Autism. 2010. 24p. pap. 10.95 *(978-1-61633-023-1(6))* Guardian Angel Publishing, Inc.
Kaminski, Tom. Miss Olivia, the Little Red Poodle: Her First Big Adventure. Fallon, Lisa, illus. 2006. (J). pap. 16.00 *(978-0-8059-7253-5(6))* Dorrance Publishing Co., Inc.
Kanata, Konami. Chi's Sweet Home 11. 2014. (Chi's Sweet Home Ser.: 11). lib. bdg. 25.70 *(978-0-606-35893-4(5))* Turtleback Bks.
Kane, James. Tom & Katie's Greatest Adventure. 2005. 73p. pap. 14.95 *(978-1-4241-0776-6(8))* PublishAmerica, Inc.
Kane, P. B. & Kane, Paul. The Rainbow Man. 2013. 162p. pap. 9.99 *(978-0-9823322-3-8(8))* Rocket Ride Bks.
Kann, Victoria. Pinkalicious - Eggstraordinary Easter. Kann, Victoria, illus. 2014. (Pinkalicious Ser.). (ENG., Illus.). 24p. (J). (gr. -1-3). pap. 4.99 *(978-0-06-218772-7(4)*, HarperFestival) HarperCollins Pubs.
—Pinkalicious & Aqua, the Mini-Mermaid. Kann, Victoria, illus. 2016. (Pinkalicious Ser.). (Illus.). 24p. (J). (gr. -1-3). pap. 4.99 *(978-0-06-241075-7(X)*, HarperFestival) HarperCollins Pubs.
—Pinkalicious & the Perfect Present. Kann, Victoria, illus. 2014. (I Can Read Level 1 Ser.). (ENG., Illus.). 32p. (J). (gr. -1-3). 16.99 *(978-0-06-218789-5(9))*; pap. 3.99 *(978-0-06-218788-8(0))* HarperCollins Pubs.
—Pinkalicious: Story Time. Kann, Victoria, illus. 2016. (I Can Read Level 1 Ser.). (Illus.). 32p. (J). (gr. -1-3). pap. 3.99 *(978-0-06-241072-6(5))* HarperCollins Pubs.
—The Royal Tea Party. 2014. (Pinkalicious I Can Read Ser.). (J). lib. bdg. 13.55 *(978-0-606-35473-8(5))* Turtleback Bks.
—Soccer Star. Kann, Victoria, illus. 2012. (I Can Read Level 1 Ser.). (ENG., Illus.). 32p. (J). (gr. -1-3). 16.99 *(978-0-06-198965-0(7))* HarperCollins Pubs.
Kaplan, Arie. Face Off. White, Dave, illus. 2016. (Lego Star Wars Ser.). (ENG.). 64p. (J). (gr. 2-5). pap. 8.99 *(978-0-545-92541-9(X))* Scholastic, Inc.
Kaputa, Christine C. Bad Kitty! 2007. 16p. per. 9.95 *(978-1-59858-478-3(2))* Dog Ear Publishing, LLC.
Karalius, Kimberly. Love Fortunes & Other Disasters. 2015. (Grimbaud Ser.). (ENG.). 368p. (YA). (gr. 7). pap. 9.99 *(978-1-250-04720-5(X)*, 9781250047205) Feiwel & Friends.
Karandeev, Oleg. Dmitri II: The Kind Storyteller Book Two of Five. Ciesinska, Izabela, illus. 2007. 76p. (YA). per. 15.95 *(978-0-9793944-3-0(0))* Digi-Tall Media.
Karl, Mary Eileen. A Buddy in Winter: Lost & Found. Karl, Therese, illus. 2010. 44p. pap. 15.50 *(978-1-60911-424-4(8)*, Eloquent Bks.) Strategic Book Publishing & Rights Agency (SBPRA).
Karol, Leslee. Sylvie the Littlest Guardian Angel: Cassie Makes a Friend. 2013. 48p. pap. 21.99 *(978-1-4817-0864-7(3))* AuthorHouse.
Karr, D. A. The Legend of Pendyne: The King, the Horse, the Boy, & the Legend. 2006. 153p. pap. 24.95 *(978-1-4241-5161-5(9))* America Star Bks.
Karr, Lily. Spooky Boo: A Halloween Adventure. Poling, Kyle, illus. 2011. (ENG.). 12p. (J). (gr. -1 — 1). bds. 6.99 *(978-0-545-29867-4(9)*, Cartwheel Bks.) Scholastic, Inc.
Karwoski, Gail Langer. Quake! Disaster in San Francisco 1906, 1 vol. Papp, Robert, illus. 2004. (ENG.). 192p. (J). (gr. 3-7). 15.95 *(978-1-56145-310-8(2))* Peachtree Pubs.
Kass, Daniele L., ed. The City Trail: A Skip-Counting Tale. 2010. 40p. pap. 18.49 *(978-1-4520-1219-3(9))* AuthorHouse.
Kassel, Roger de. Mr P & the Bully Birds. 2013. (Illus.). 12p. pap. 8.75 *(978-1-78035-677-8(3)*, Fastprint Publishing) Upfront Publishing Ltd. GBR. Dist: Printondemand-worldwide.com.
—Mr P & the Red Poppy. 2013. (Illus.). 22p. pap. 8.75 *(978-1-78035-707-2(9)*, Fastprint Publishing) Upfront Publishing Ltd. GBR. Dist: Printondemand-worldwide.com.
—Mr P & the Silver Red Bag. 2013. (Illus.). 12p. pap. 7.00 *(978-1-78035-536-8(X)*, Fastprint Publishing) Upfront Publishing Ltd. GBR. Dist: Printondemand-worldwide.com.
—Mr P & the Sticky Gum. 2013. (Illus.). 12p. pap. 7.00 *(978-1-78035-537-5(8)*, Fastprint Publishing) Upfront Publishing Ltd. GBR. Dist: Printondemand-worldwide.com.
Kasten, Victoria. Mighty Stallion. 2005. (Illus.). 70p. (J). per. 8.95 *(978-0-9788850-0-7(7))* Kasten, Victoria.
—Mighty Stallion 2 Fury's Journey. 2006. (Illus.). 72p. (J). per. 8.95 *(978-0-9788850-1-4(5))* Kasten, Victoria.
Kastigar, Jessica. The King of Hearts. 2006. 49p. pap. 16.95 *(978-1-4241-3875-3(2))* PublishAmerica, Inc.
Katar, Al. Captain Scratch: The Island of Sirmarj. 2008. 48p. pap. 21.99 *(978-1-4363-4188-2(4))* Xlibris Corp.
Katheryn, Shelly. Legends of the New Worlds: In the Beginning. 2012. 116p. (J). (gr. -1). 22.19 *(978-1-4669-2112-2(9))*; pap. 12.19 *(978-1-4669-2114-6(5))* Trafford Publishing.
Kathleen, Jo Ann. Buddy Can't Tie Shoes. I.t. ed. 2006. (ENG., Illus.). 28p. per. 9.95 *(978-1-4327-0238-0(6))* Outskirts Pr., Inc.
—NATALIA, O' MIA, WHITE LACES & SHOES. I.t. ed. 2006. (ENG., Illus.). 28p. per. 9.95 *(978-1-4327-0314-1(5))* Outskirts Pr., Inc.
Kato, Shakila Maria Inviolata & Kato, Sharifa Maria Inviolata. The Adventures by the Magic Bicycle. 2012. 134p. 24.95 *(978-1-4137-5716-3(2))* America Star Bks.
Kats, Jewel. Teddy Bear Princess: A Story about Sharing & Caring. Arts, Richa Kinra, illus. 2012. 24p. (-18). pap. 13.95 *(978-1-61599-163-1(8)*, Marvelous Spirit Pr.) Loving Healing Pr., Inc.
Katschke, Judy. Shrek the Third. 2007. (Illus.). (J). *(978-0-696-23947-2(7))* Meredith Bks.
—Teeny Genie. Jennings, C. S., illus. 2009. (ENG.). 24p. (J). (gr. 1-17). pap. 3.99 *(978-1-58476-813-5(4))* Innovative Kids.
Katula, Bob. Larry y el Increíble Ataque de los Tapa Oídos. 2003.Tr. of Larry Boy & the Awful Earwacks Attacks. (SPA.). pap. 5.49 *(978-0-8297-3747-9(2))* Vida Pubs.
Katz, Gwen C. Among the Red Stars. 2017. 384p. (YA). (gr. 8). 17.99 ***(978-0-06-264274-5(X)***, HarperTeen) HarperCollins Pubs.
Katz, Welwyn W. Sun God, Moon Witch. (J). pap. 7.95 *(978-0-88899-246-8(7))* Groundwood Bks. CAN. Dist: Publishers Group West (PGW).
Kaupp, Rosemarie. The Amberella Tales: Amberella & Double Double Trouble. 2013. 144p. (gr. 2-4). 20.77 *(978-1-4669-9233-7(6))*; pap. 10.77 *(978-1-4669-9234-4(4))* Trafford Publishing.
—The Amberella Tales: Amberella in the City. 2012. 120p. (gr. 4-6). 22.33 *(978-1-4669-0594-8(8))*; pap. 12.33 *(978-1-4669-0595-5(6))* Trafford Publishing.
Kaur, K. S. The Homcastles & the Magnopeus Medicine. Kaur, Bal, illus. 2012. 154p. pap. *(978-1-78148-023-6(0))* Grosvenor Hse. Publishing Ltd.
Kawane, Michelle. The Little Dragon Who Wasn't Small after All: Adventures with Mathius Mccloud. 2010. 24p. pap. 14.49 *(978-1-4520-5787-3(7))* AuthorHouse.
Kay, Elizabeth. Felix y el Mundo Al Reves. Batlles, Camila, tr. 2007. (Illus.). 345p. (J). (gr. 4-7). *(978-84-96544-91-8(5))* Roca Editorial.
Kay, Ross. The Go Ahead Boys & Simon's Mine. 2007. 148p. pap. 18.99 *(978-1-4264-8426-1(7))*; 168p. pap. 21.99 *(978-1-4264-8484-1(4))* Creative Media Partners, LLC.
—The Go Ahead Boys & Simon's Mine. Owen, R. Emmett, illus. 2007. 184p. per. *(978-1-4065-1857-3(3))* Dodo Pr.
—The Go Ahead Boys & Simon's Mine. 2007. 112p. per. *(978-1-4068-1924-3(7))* Echo Library.
—The Go Ahead Boys & the Racing Motor-Boat. 2007. 176p. per. *(978-1-4065-1858-0(1))* Dodo Pr.
—The Go Ahead Boys & the Racing Motor Boat. 2007. 104p. per. *(978-1-4068-1923-6(9))* Echo Library.
—Go Ahead Boys & the Racing Motorboat. 2007. (ENG.). 154p. pap. 19.99 *(978-1-4264-3551-5(7))*; 176p. pap. 21.99 *(978-1-4264-3606-2(8))* Creative Media Partners, LLC.
Kayaalp, Suzan. The Adventures of Lucky the Duck. 2010. 90p. pap. 9.95 *(978-1-60693-716-7(2)*, Eloquent Bks.) Strategic Book Publishing & Rights Agency (SBPRA).
Kaye, Shelley. Saving Private Woods. 2012. (Illus.). 76p. pap. 8.50 *(978-1-78035-510-8(6)*, Fastprint Publishing) Upfront Publishing Ltd. GBR. Dist: Printondemand-worldwide.com.
Kayser, Eric. Champion: Graphic Novel Series. 3rd ed. 2007. (YA). 2.95 *(978-0-9785605-2-2(3))* Oasis Studios Inc.
Kayser, Eric, creator. Champion: Graphic Novel Series, 8. 2007. (Illus.). 28p. (YA). abr. ed. 2.95 *(978-0-9785605-3-9(1))* 2nd abr. ed. 2.95 *(978-0-9785605-1-5(5))* Vol. 1. 5th ed. (ENG., 2.95 *(978-0-9785605-4-6(X))* Oasis Studios Inc.
Kazenbroot, Nelly. Down the Chimney with Googal & Googolplex. 2004. 63p. (J). lib. bdg. 20.00 *(978-1-4242-1257-6(X))* Fitzgerald Bks.

Kearney Cooper, Nicole. Time for Bed: Andrew & April's Adventures. Broadnax, Charles, illus. 2005. (J). 7.00 (978-0-9766086-7-7(7)) nVision Publishing.

Keaton, Skeet. The Adventures of Jd Losey. 2005. pap. 9.99 (978-1-59781-353-2(2)) Salem Author Services.

Keay, Ben. Perfect Solution. Hsu, Florence, illus. 2009. (YA). (978-1-933791-09-8(8)) Finial Publishing.

Keeley, Jenny Conner. The Hollow: A Kansas Fairytale. 2011. 154p. pap. 15.95 (978-1-4327-6670-2(8)) Outskirts Pr., Inc.

Keene, Carolyn. Action!, No. 6. 6th ed. 2004. (Nancy Drew (All New) Girl Detective Ser.: 6). (ENG.). 144p. (J). (gr. 3-7). pap. 6.99 (978-0-689-86571-8(6), Aladdin) Simon & Schuster Children's Publishing.

—Bad Times, Big Crimes. 14th ed. 2005. (Nancy Drew (All New) Girl Detective Ser.: 14). (ENG.). 160p. (J). (gr. 3-7). pap. 6.99 (978-0-689-87883-1(4), Aladdin) Simon & Schuster Children's Publishing.

—Cape Mermaid Mystery. Pamintuan, Macky, illus. 2012. (Nancy Drew & the Clue Crew Ser.: 32). (ENG.). 96p. (J). (gr. 1-4). pap. 5.99 (978-1-4424-4625-0(0), Aladdin) Simon & Schuster Children's Publishing.

—Cat Burglar Caper. Pamintuan, Macky, illus. 2010. (Nancy Drew & the Clue Crew Ser.: 27). (ENG.). 96p. (J). (gr. 1-4). pap. 5.99 (978-1-4169-9436-7(X), Aladdin) Simon & Schuster Children's Publishing.

—False Notes. 3rd ed. 2004. (Nancy Drew (All New) Girl Detective Ser.: 3). (ENG.). 160p. (J). (gr. 3-7). pap. 5.99 (978-0-689-86568-8(6), Aladdin) Simon & Schuster Children's Publishing.

—Mardi Gras Masquerade. 28th ed. 2008. (Nancy Drew (All New) Girl Detective Ser.: 28). (ENG.). 144p. (J). (gr. 3-7). pap. 5.99 (978-1-4169-5103-2(2), Aladdin) Simon & Schuster Children's Publishing.

—Model Menace: Book Two in the Model Mystery Trilogy. 2009. (Nancy Drew (All New) Girl Detective Ser.: 37). (ENG.). 176p. (J). (gr. 3-7). pap. 5.99 (978-1-4169-7843-5(7), Aladdin) Simon & Schuster Children's Publishing.

—The Perfect Escape, Bk. 3. 32nd ed. 2008. (Nancy Drew (All New) Girl Detective Ser.: 32). (ENG.). 160p. (J). (gr. 3-7). pap. 5.99 (978-1-4169-5531-3(3), Aladdin) Simon & Schuster Children's Publishing.

—A Race Against Time. 2nd ed. 2004. (Nancy Drew (All New) Girl Detective Ser.: 2). (ENG.). 160p. (J). (gr. 3-7). pap. 6.99 (978-0-689-86567-1(8), Aladdin) Simon & Schuster Children's Publishing.

—Riverboat Ruse, Vol. 11. 11th ed. 2005. (Nancy Drew (All New) Girl Detective Ser.: 11). (ENG.). 160p. (J). (gr. 3-7). pap. 5.99 (978-0-689-87335-5(2), Aladdin) Simon & Schuster Children's Publishing.

—The Secret of the Scarecrow. Pamintuan, Macky, illus. 2013. (Nancy Drew & the Clue Crew Ser.: 36). (ENG.). 96p. (J). (gr. 1-4). pap. 4.99 (978-1-4424-5353-1(2), Aladdin) Simon & Schuster Children's Publishing.

—A Taste of Danger. 174th ed. 2003. (Nancy Drew Ser.: 174). (ENG.). 176p. (J). (gr. 3-7). pap. 5.99 (978-0-689-86154-3(0), Aladdin) Simon & Schuster Children's Publishing.

—Trade Wind Danger. 13th ed. 2005. (Nancy Drew (All New) Girl Detective Ser.: 13). (ENG.). 160p. (J). (gr. 3-7). pap. 5.99 (978-0-689-87641-7(6), Aladdin) Simon & Schuster Children's Publishing.

—Uncivil Acts. 10th ed. 2005. (Nancy Drew (All New) Girl Detective Ser.: 10). (ENG.). 160p. (J). (gr. 3-7). pap. 5.99 (978-0-689-86937-2(1), Aladdin) Simon & Schuster Children's Publishing.

—Where's Nancy? 2005. (Nancy Drew: Girl Detective Super Mystery Ser.: 1). (ENG.). 176p. (J). (gr. 3-7). pap. 5.99 (978-1-4169-0034-4(9), Aladdin) Simon & Schuster Children's Publishing.

—Without a Trace. 2004. (Nancy Drew (All New) Girl Detective Ser.: 1). (ENG.). 160p. (J). (gr. 3-7). pap. 5.99 (978-0-689-86566-4(X), Aladdin) Simon & Schuster Children's Publishing.

—Without a Trace Set: A Race Against Time - False Notes - High Risk. 2004. (Nancy Drew (All New) Girl Detective Ser.). (ENG., Illus.). 640p. (J). (gr. 3-7). pap. 23.99 (978-0-689-03691-0(4), Aladdin) Simon & Schuster Children's Publishing.

Keene, Carolyn & Dixon, Franklin W. Danger Overseas. 2008. (Nancy Drew/Hardy Boys Ser.: 2). (ENG., Illus.). 224p. (J). (gr. 3-7). pap. 5.99 (978-1-4169-5777-5(4), Aladdin) Simon & Schuster Children's Publishing.

Keene, Carolyn & Drew, Nancy. Lights, Camera... 5th ed. 2004. (Nancy Drew (All New) Girl Detective Ser.: 5). (ENG., Illus.). 160p. (J). (gr. 3-7). pap. 5.99 (978-0-689-86570-1(8), Aladdin) Simon & Schuster Children's Publishing.

Keene, Carolyn & Frost, Michael. Stop the Clock, Vol. 12. 12th ed. 2005. (Nancy Drew (All New) Girl Detective Ser.: 12). (ENG.). 160p. (J). (gr. 3-7). pap. 5.99 (978-0-689-87336-2(0), Aladdin) Simon & Schuster Children's Publishing.

Keeney, Stephen S. Spencer the Adventurer & the Castle of Bran. 2009. (ENG.). 256p. (J). pap. 14.99 (978-1-934135-31-0(3), Zumaya Thresholds) Zumaya Pubns. LLC.

The Keeper of Names. 2005. (YA). per. (978-0-9744448-3-3(9)) McCourtie, Anne.

Keeper of the Island. 2007. (Who? What? When? Where? Ser.). (Illus.). 246p. (J). (gr. 5-9). per. 10.95 (978-1-929976-39-3(9), TOP) Top Pubns., Ltd.

Kehoe, Tim. Furious Jones & the Assassin's Secret. 2014. (ENG., Illus.). 336p. (J). (gr. 3-7). 16.99 (978-1-4424-7337-9(1), Simon & Schuster Bks. For Young Readers) Simon & Schuster Bks. For Young Readers.

Kehret, Peg. Race to Disaster. 2008. (ENG.). 128p. (J). (gr. 3-7). pap. 7.99 (978-1-4169-9108-3(5), Simon & Schuster/Paula Wiseman Bks.) Simon & Schuster/Paula Wiseman Bks.

Keil, James. Tiger & the Poachers. 2010. 54p. pap. 15.52 (978-0-557-34105-4(1)) Lulu Pr., Inc.

Keith, David. Hands Across Time. 2010. 129p. pap. 10.98 (978-0-557-27121-4(5)) Lulu Pr., Inc.

Kelborne, Wenna. The Stinkozimus. 2012. 356p. pap. 24.34 (978-1-4772-2282-9(0)) AuthorHouse.

Kellenbarger, Sandy Hurst. Magic Gnomes. 2012. 24p. (gr. 2-4). pap. 14.93 (978-1-4669-6526-3(6)) Trafford Publishing.

—Magic Gnomes Treasure Hunt. 2013. 28p. pap. 16.09 (978-1-4669-8892-7(4)) Trafford Publishing.

Keller, John E. The Emperor's Elephant. 2006. 127p. (YA). per. 12.95 (978-0-942566-45-1(9)) LinguaText, LLC.

Keller, Laurie. Arnie the Doughnut. 2016. (Adventures of Arnie the Doughnut Ser.: 1). (J). lib. bdg. 19.65 (978-0-606-38549-7(5)) Turtleback Bks.

Kelley, Jane. The Desperate Adventures of Zeno & Alya. 2013. (ENG.). 208p. (J). (gr. 3-7). 15.99 (978-1-250-02348-3(3), 9781250023483) Feiwel & Friends.

Kelley, Lisa. Nutty. 2010. 20p. 10.49 (978-1-4520-0303-0(3)) AuthorHouse.

Kelley Ludovici, Joanne Dzioba. Maggie Stone Becomes Morning Starr. 2013. 28p. pap. 16.09 (978-1-4669-9291-7(3)) Trafford Publishing.

Kellogg, Catherine Berry. The Moose Who Ate My Fort: Stories from Bella Sage. 2008. 36p. pap. 24.95 (978-1-60441-696-1(3)) America Star Bks.

Kellogg, Elijah. The Ark of Elm Island. 2005. reprint ed. pap. 28.95 (978-1-4191-1833-3(1)) Kessinger Publishing, LLC.

Kellogg, Steven. Johnny Appleseed. Cohn, Amy, ed. Kellogg, Steven, illus. 2008. (ENG., Illus.). 48p. (J). (gr. -1-3). reprint ed. pap. 6.99 (978-0-688-14025-0(4)) HarperCollins Pubs.

Kellum Enterprises, 1st. The ADVENTURES of Diggle, Boogie & Lolo: Diggle Loses Lolo. 2007. (Illus.). 30p. (J). 19.99 (978-0-9801322-0-5(7)); pap. 9.99 (978-0-9801322-1-2(5)) W3 Publishing.

Kelly, Cheryl. Adam the Adventurous Ant. 2011. 24p. pap. 15.99 (978-1-4568-6366-1(5)) Xlibris Corp.

Kelly, David A. The Capital Catch. 2017. (Ballpark Mysteries Ser.: Bk. 13). lib. bdg. 14.75 **(978-0-606-39869-5(4))** Turtleback Bks.

Kelly, Kathy & Feder, Debbie. Jelly Bean's Art Museum Adventure. 2012. 40p. pap. 20.99 (978-1-4772-4828-7(5)) AuthorHouse.

Kelly, Lisa. The Many Adventures of Elysse: Her Journey Begins. 2012. 36p. pap. 16.99 (978-1-4525-5760-1(8)) Balboa Pr.

Kelly, Mark. Project Rescue. 2017. (Astrotwins Ser.: 2). lib. bdg. 18.40 **(978-0-606-39745-2(0))** Turtleback Bks.

Kelly, Marylee A. Quest to Obsidia: The Second Peter Mcfall Adventure. 2003. 126p. pap. 10.95 (978-0-595-29402-2(2), Writers Club Pr.) iUniverse, Inc.

Kelly, Stephen M. Symbala's River. 2006. (YA). lib. bdg. 6.99 (978-1-4276-0237-4(9)) Aardvark Global Publishing.

Kelly, Tess. Buko's Journey. 2004. 262p. (YA). 26.95 (978-0-595-66864-9(X)) iUniverse, Inc.

Kelman, Jennifer. Mrs Pinkelmeyer & Moopus Mcglinden Prance into New York City. 2011. 44p. pap. 15.99 (978-1-4575-0497-6(9)) Dog Ear Publishing, LLC.

Kelman, Marcy & Disney Book Group Staff. Ahoy, Izzy! Disney Storybook Art Team, illus. 2013. (ENG.). 24p. (J). (gr. -1-k). pap. 3.99 (978-1-4231-6393-0(1)) Disney Pr.

Kelsey, Juliet Grey. Nettie by the Sea Stories: Set I. 2010. 56p. pap. 23.99 (978-1-4490-9452-2(X)) AuthorHouse.

Kelso, Mary Jean. The Adventures of Andy & Spirit: Book 1. Snider, K. C., illus. 2010. 64p. pap. 9.95 (978-1-61633-069-9(4)) Guardian Angel Publishing, Inc.

Kelton, G F. The Land of Cigam. 2007. 144p. per. 10.95 (978-0-595-46947-5(7)) iUniverse, Inc.

Keltz, Karen. Sally Jo Survives Sixth Grade: A Journal. Carrigg, Susan, illus. 2013. 180p. pap. 9.99 (978-0-9857281-1-3(6)) HAPPY HOUSE PR.

Kemler, Nancy. Dragon Box: The Key to Magic. 2005. 108p. pap. 19.95 (978-1-4137-8445-9(3)) America Star Bks.

Kemp, Anna. The Great Brain Robbery. Smith, Alex T., illus. 2013. (ENG.). 288p. (J). pap. 6.99 (978-0-85707-996-1(4), Simon & Schuster Children's) Simon & Schuster, Ltd. GBR. Dist: Simon & Schuster, Inc.

Kemp, Dina. Milo & Unico Adventures. 2012. 40p. pap. 20.99 (978-1-4772-8129-1(0)) AuthorHouse.

Kemp, Mary Kay. The Adventures of Jimmy Joe & Tippy Toe: Show & Tell. 2011. 20p. (gr. 1-2). pap. 14.00 (978-1-4567-6170-7(6)) AuthorHouse.

Kempton, Linda. Jessica Sweetapple & the Battle. (Illus.). 183p. (J). 8.99 (978-0-7497-3905-8(3)) Egmont Bks., Ltd. GBR. Dist: Trafalgar Square Publishing.

Kendall, Bridget. Bond & the Big Green Hill. 2009. 28p. pap. 13.99 (978-1-4490-1458-2(5)) AuthorHouse.

Kendall, Carolyn. Phibby & Ribby. 2013. 32p. pap. (978-1-4602-0387-3(9)) FriesenPress.

Kendall, Gillian Murray. The Garden of Darkness. 2014. (ENG.). 336p. (YA). (gr. 6-12). pap. 9.99 (978-1-78108-248-5(0), Ravenstone) Rebellion GBR. Dist: Simon & Schuster, Inc.

Kendall, Sarita H. Al Rescate de Omacha. (SPA.). (YA). (gr. 5-8). 8.95 (978-958-04-2930-2(8), NR2139) Norma S.A. COL. Dist: Distribuidora Norma, Inc., Lectorum Pubns., Inc.

Kendall, Stan P. Samson Gets a Family. 2005. 22p. (J). 13.50 (978-1-4116-5756-4(X)) Lulu Pr., Inc.

Kendrick, Robert. Treasure Quest: Journey to the Jungle. 2004. (ENG.). 46p. 24.95 (978-1-4137-1467-8(6)) PublishAmerica, Inc.

Kennaway, James. Tunes of Glory. 2010. (ENG.). 192p. pap. 14.00 (978-0-86241-223-4(4)) Canongate Bks. GBR. Dist: Publishers Group West (PGW).

Kennedy, Hugh J. The Flowers & the Fairies. 2009. 32p. pap. 18.97 (978-1-4490-0265-7(X)) AuthorHouse.

Kennedy, J. Aday. Juggerum. Morris, Alexander, illus. 2012. 16p. pap. 9.95 (978-1-61633-348-5(0)) Guardian Angel Publishing, Inc.

Kennedy, James. The Order of Odd-Fish. 2010. (ENG.). 416p. (YA). (gr. 7-18). mass mkt. 8.99 (978-0-440-24065-5(4), Laurel Leaf) Random Hse. Children's Bks.

Kennedy, Katie. Learning to Swear in America. 2017. (ENG.). 368p. (YA). pap. 9.99 (978-1-61963-911-9(4), 9781619639119, Bloomsbury USA Childrens) Bloomsbury Publishing USA.

—What Goes Up. 2017. (ENG.). 336p. (YA). 17.99 (978-1-61963-912-6(2), 9781619639126, Bloomsbury USA Childrens) Bloomsbury Publishing USA.

Kennedy Tosten, S. Troy's Amazing Universe: A for Aliens. 2005. 124p. pap. 13.95 (978-1-59113-672-9(5)) Booklocker.com, Inc.

Kennerson, Vern. Love Stories for Children. Falk, Cathy Kennerson, illus. 2013. (ENG.). 67p. (YA). pap. 17.95 (978-1-4787-1665-5(7)) Outskirts Pr., Inc.

Kenny, Michael Daedalus. Little Miss Sunshine in: Here Comes the Sun!, Vol. 2. 2012. (ENG.). 80p. (J). pap. 6.99 (978-1-4215-4071-9(1)) Viz Media.

Kent, Elizabeth. The Enchanted Adventures of the Caroline Kemps. 2007. 148p. pap. 24.95 (978-1-4241-9915-0(8)) America Star Bks.

Kent, Jaden. #1: the Cave of Aaaaah! Doom! Bodnaruk, Iryna, illus. 2017. (Ella & Owen Ser.: 1). (ENG.). 112p. (J). (gr. 1-3). pap. 5.99 (978-1-4998-0368-6(0)) Little Bee Books Inc.

—#2: Attack of the Stinky Fish Monster! Bodnaruk, Iryna, illus. 2017. (Ella & Owen Ser.: 2). (ENG.). 112p. (J). (gr. 1-3). pap. 5.99 (978-1-4998-0369-3(9)) Little Bee Books Inc.

Kent, Neville. The Secrets of the Forest - the Time Zone. 2013. 88p. pap. (978-1-78299-795-5(4)) FeedARead.com.

Kenyon, Sherrilyn. Invision. 2016. (Chronicles of Nick Ser.: 7). (ENG.). 400p. (YA). (gr. 7-12). 19.99 (978-1-250-06388-5(4), 9781250063885, St. Martin's Griffin) St. Martin's Pr.

Kermani, Arax. The Wyrm, Bk. 1. 2003. 134p. (YA). pap. 10.95 (978-0-595-26775-0(0), Writers Club Pr.) iUniverse, Inc.

Kerr, P. B., pseud. The Grave Robbers of Genghis Khan. 2011. (Children of the Lamp Ser.: Vol. 7). (ENG.). 448p. (J). (gr. 3-7). 18.99 (978-0-545-12660-1(6), Orchard Bks.) Scholastic, Inc.

Kerr, Pat. Down to Earth. (Illus.). xii, 180p. (J). (gr. k-6). 29.95 (978-0-09-175159-3(4)) Random Hse. GBR. Dist: Trafalgar Square Publishing.

Kerr, Valerie. The Adventures of Selwyn & Robert. 2012. 64p. pap. 10.43 (978-1-4669-5998-9(3)) Trafford Publishing.

—The Adventures of Selwyn & Robert: Saving Whako the White Lion. 2013. 40p. pap. 16.46 (978-1-4669-9252-8(2)) Trafford Publishing.

Kerrin, Jessica Scott. Blazing Ahead! Kelly, Joseph, illus. 2006. (Martin Bridge Ser.). (ENG.). 112p. (J). (gr. 2-5). 6.95 (978-1-55337-962-1(4)) Kids Can Pr., Ltd. CAN. Dist: Hachette Bk. Group.

Kerwin, Betsy. The Adventures of Floret the Woodland Fairy: The Adventures Begin. 2008. 44p. pap. 18.49 (978-1-4343-9426-2(3)) AuthorHouse.

Kesecker, Jennifer. The Adventures of Mr. Feeny & Cinnamon. Thomas, James, illus. 2012. 20p. pap. 24.95 (978-1-4626-8858-6(6)) America Star Bks.

Kesinger, Brian. Coloring with Your Octopus: A Coloring Book for Domesticated Cephalopods. 2014. (ENG., Illus.). 48p. pap. 12.00 (978-1-61404-010-1(9)) Baby Tattoo Bks.

Kessler, Leonard P. Mrs. Pine Takes a Trip. Kessler, Leonard P., illus. 2005. (Illus.). (J). 16.00 (978-1-930900-25-7(2)) Purple Hse. Pr.

Kessler, Liz. Emily Windsnap & the Ship of Lost Souls. Gibb, Sarah, illus. 2015. (Emily Windsnap Ser.). (ENG.). 288p. (J). (gr. 3-7). 15.99 (978-0-7636-7688-9(8)) Candlewick Pr.

—Emily Windsnap: Six Swishy Tails of Land & Sea. 2016. (Emily Windsnap Ser.). (ENG.). (J). (gr. 3-7). pap. 34.99 (978-0-7636-9223-0(9)) Candlewick Pr.

—Emily Windsnap: Two Magical Mermaid Tales. Gibb, Sarah, illus. 2014. (Emily Windsnap Ser.). (ENG.). 464p. (J). (gr. 3-7). pap. 9.99 (978-0-7636-7452-6(4)) Candlewick Pr.

—Four Sparkling Underwater Adventures. Gibb, Sarah & Ledwidge, Natacha, illus. 2012. (Emily Windsnap Ser.). (ENG.). (J). (gr. 3-7). pap. 23.96 (978-0-7636-6295-0(X)) Candlewick Pr.

—Philippa Fisher & the Dream-Maker's Daughter. 2009. (Philippa Fisher Ser.: 2). (ENG., Illus.). 288p. (J). (gr. 3-7). 15.99 (978-0-7636-4202-0(9)) Candlewick Pr.

—Poppy the Pirate Dog. Phillips, Mike, illus. 2013. (ENG.). 64p. (J). (gr. k-3). 14.99 (978-0-7636-6569-2(X)) Candlewick Pr.

Ketter-Brust , Sandra. Sir Guinness of Wildridge. 2006. 48p. pap. 16.95 (978-1-4241-4626-0(7)) PublishAmerica, Inc.

Keyes, Joseph W. The Sparrows of Saint Thomas. 2007. 92p. pap. 14.95 (978-1-4303-1410-3(9)) Lulu Pr., Inc.

Keyworth, R. L. Gregory Giraffe's New Friends Adventure: Gregory Giraffe Is about to find some altogether different but new friends at his watering Hole. 2009. 20p. pap. 10.99 (978-1-4389-3284-2(7)) AuthorHouse.

Khamis, Johnny. Costi & the Raindrop Adventure. Belanger, Damon, illus. 2007. 32p. (J). (gr. -1-3). 6.95 (978-1-60005-029-9(8)) Happy About.

Khan, Aliyah. The Adventures of Solomon Spider: Solomon Sees the City. 2011. 28p. (gr. -1 — 1). pap. 14.09 (978-1-4490-1546-6(8)) AuthorHouse.

Khan, Farheen. Ibrahim Khan & the Mystery of the Haunted Lake. 2011. (Ibrahim Khan Ser.). (ENG., Illus.). 64p. (J). (gr. k-5). pap. 7.50 (978-0-86037-423-7(8)) Kube Publishing Ltd. GBR. Dist: Consortium Bk. Sales & Distribution.

Khan, Joshua. Shadow Magic. Hibon, Ben, illus. 2017. (ENG.). 352p. (J). (gr. 3-7). pap. 6.99 (978-1-4847-3788-0(1)) Hyperion Bks. for Children.

Khoo, Rowena. Where Is My Sock? 2012. 76p. pap. 42.05 (978-1-4771-5459-5(0)) Xlibris Corp.

Kiani, Sabra. Billy Ben's Fantastic Pictures. 2012. 48p. pap. 17.45 (978-1-4669-5157-0(5)) Trafford Publishing.

Kibera, Ngumi. Shaza's Trials. 2005. (Phoenix Young Readers Library). (Illus.). 103p. (978-9966-47-023-2(9)) Phoenix Pubs., Ltd.

Kibuishi, Kazu. The Cloud Searchers. 2010. (Amulet Ser.: 3). (ENG.). 208p. (J). (gr. 3-7). pap. 12.99 (978-0-545-20885-7(8), Graphix) Scholastic, Inc.

—Copper. 2010. lib. bdg. 24.50 (978-0-606-14274-8(6), Turtleback) Turtleback Bks.

—The Last Council. 2011. (Amulet Ser.: 4). (ENG.). 224p. (J). (gr. 3-7). pap. 12.99 (978-0-545-20887-1(4), Graphix) Scholastic, Inc.

—Prince of the Elves. 2012. (Amulet Ser.: 5). (ENG., Illus.). 208p. (J). (gr. 3-7). pap. 12.99 (978-0-545-20889-5(0), Graphix) Scholastic, Inc.

—Prince of the Elves. 2012. (Amulet Ser.: 5). lib. bdg. 24.50 (978-0-606-26499-0(X), Turtleback) Turtleback Bks.

—The Stonekeeper. 2008. (Amulet Ser.: 1). (ENG., Illus.). 192p. (J). (gr. 3-7). 24.99 (978-0-439-84680-6(3), Graphix) Scholastic, Inc.

Kidd, Jessica A. Zachary Zoom. 2009. 28p. pap. 12.25 (978-1-60860-502-6(7), Eloquent Bks.) Strategic Book Publishing & Rights Agency (SBPRA).

Kidd, Rob. The Age of Bronze, 1 vol. Orpinas, Jean-Paul, illus. 2009. (Pirates of the Caribbean, Jack Sparrow Ser.: Bk. 5). (ENG.). 144p. (gr. 3-6). 24.21 (978-1-59961-527-1(4)) Spotlight.

—City of Gold, 1 vol. Orpinas, Jean-Paul, illus. 2009. (Pirates of the Caribbean, Jack Sparrow Ser.: Bk. 7). (ENG.). 128p. (gr. 3-6). 24.21 (978-1-59961-529-5(0)) Spotlight.

—The Coming Storm, 1 vol. Orpinas, Jean-Paul, illus. 2009. (Pirates of the Caribbean, Jack Sparrow Ser.: Bk. 1). (ENG.). 144p. (gr. 3-6). 24.21 (978-1-59961-523-3(1)) Spotlight.

—Day of the Shadow. 4th ed. 2009. (Pirates of the Caribbean Ser.: No. 5). 256p. (YA). (gr. 5-18). pap. 6.99 (978-1-4231-1041-5(2)) Disney Pr.

—The Pirate Chase, 1 vol. Orpinas, Jean-Paul, illus. 2009. (Pirates of the Caribbean, Jack Sparrow Ser.: Bk. 3). (ENG.). 128p. (gr. 3-6). 24.21 (978-1-59961-525-7(8)) Spotlight.

—Silver, 1 vol. Orpinas, Jean-Paul, illus. 2009. (Pirates of the Caribbean, Jack Sparrow Ser.: Bk. 6). (ENG.). 128p. (gr. 3-6). 24.21 (978-1-59961-528-8(2)) Spotlight.

—The Siren Song, 1 vol. Orpinas, Jean-Paul, illus. 2009. (Pirates of the Caribbean, Jack Sparrow Ser.: Bk. 2). (ENG.). 128p. (gr. 3-6). 24.21 (978-1-59961-524-0(X)) Spotlight.

—The Sword of Cortes, 1 vol. Orpinas, Jean-Paul, illus. 2009. (Pirates of the Caribbean, Jack Sparrow Ser.: Bk. 4). (ENG.). 128p. (gr. 3-6). 24.21 (978-1-59961-526-4(6)) Spotlight.

—The Timekeeper, 1 vol. Orpinas, Jean-Paul, illus. 2009. (Pirates of the Caribbean, Jack Sparrow Ser.: Bk. 8). (ENG.). 128p. (gr. 3-6). 24.21 (978-1-59961-530-1(4)) Spotlight.

Kidd, Ronald, et al. Chasing George Washington. Hoyt, Ard, illus. 2009. (ENG.). 80p. (J). (gr. 2-5). 12.99 (978-1-4169-4858-2(9), Simon & Schuster Bks. For Young Readers) Simon & Schuster Bks. For Young Readers.

Kidwell, Justina. The Enchanted Garden & the Curse of the Evil Witch: The Kent Boys' Adventures. 2009. 68p. pap. 19.95 (978-1-60749-163-7(X)) America Star Bks.

—The Haunted Tree House, the Ghost Town, & the Dark Reaper: The Kent Boys' Adventures, 1 vol. 2009. 48p. pap. 16.95 (978-1-60813-234-8(X)) America Star Bks.

Kiely, Kevin. SOS Lusitania. 2013. (ENG.). 208p. (J). pap. 12.95 (978-1-84717-230-3(X)) O'Brien Pr., Ltd., The IRL. Dist: Dufour Editions, Inc.

Kienzle, Ed. The Last Buffalo. 2013. (ENG.). 214p. (YA). 29.95 (978-1-4787-0802-5(6)); pap. 13.95 (978-1-4787-0944-2(8)) Outskirts Pr., Inc.

Kieper, Rienhold Richard. Blue Thunder One. 2004. 30p. (J). pap. (978-0-9719284-0-4(1)) Blue Thunder One, Inc.

Kiernan, Kenny, illus. Save the Day! 2013. (J). (978-1-4844-0146-0(8)) Scholastic, Inc.

Kiesling, Ralph W. The Exploration, 1 vol. 2009. 253p. pap. 27.95 (978-1-61546-668-9(1)) America Star Bks.

Kiley, Christian Kennedy. Little Trixie's Big Adventure. 2004. (J). per. 10.99 (978-0-9758888-0-3(3)) IFLY Bks.

Kilgore, Lee. The Mr. Munch Adventures: Six Short Stories, 1 vol. 2010. 73p. pap. 19.95 (978-1-4489-2876-7(1)) America Star Bks.

Kilgus, Walter C. Bess Takes a Ride. 2008. 36p. pap. 17.49 (978-1-4257-8807-0(6)) Xlibris Corp.

Killaire, B. M. The Adventures of Betty & Bo-Bob: A Tale of One & a Half Frogs. Kwik, Penny Shannon, ed. Killaire, B. M., illus. 2012. (Illus.). 32p. pap. 24.95 (978-1-4626-6621-8(3)) America Star Bks.

Killen, Nicola. The Little Reindeer. Killen, Nicola, illus. 2017. (ENG., Illus.). 32p. (J). (gr. -1-3). 15.99 (978-1-4814-8686-6(1), Simon & Schuster/Paula Wiseman Bks.) Simon & Schuster/Paula Wiseman Bks.

Kilpatrick, Irene. Let's Use Our Imaginations! Giles, Mike, illus. 2009. (Yo Gabba Gabba! Ser.). (ENG.). 24p. (J). (gr. -1-2). pap. 3.99 (978-1-4169-7854-1(2), Simon Spotlight) Simon Spotlight.

—Meet the Gabba Gang. 2009. (Yo Gabba Gabba! Ser.: 1). (ENG.). 24p. (J). (gr. -1-2). pap. 3.99 (978-1-4169-7097-2(5), Simon Spotlight) Simon Spotlight.

—Welcome to Gabba Land! 2009. (Yo Gabba Gabba! Ser.). (ENG.). 14p. (J). (gr. -1-k). 8.99 (978-1-4169-7096-5(7), Simon Spotlight) Simon Spotlight.

Kilpatrick, Leanne. One Night on Earth: The Story of Christmas. 2013. 28p. pap. (978-0-906672-82-2(1)) Oleander Pr., The.

—Two by Two: Noah's Story in Rhyme. McCullough, Marilyn, illus. 2013. 28p. pap. (978-0-906672-67-9(8)) Oleander Pr., The.

Kim, F. S. Blueberry Muffin's Book: An Adventure in Blue. 2005. 39p. lib. bdg. (978-0-439-70468-7(5)) Scholastic, Inc.

Kim, Susan & Klavan, Laurence. Guardians. 2015. (Wasteland Ser.: 3). (ENG.). 432p. (YA). (gr. 9). 17.99 (978-0-06-211857-8(9), HarperTeen) HarperCollins Pubs.

—Wanderers. 2014. (Wasteland Ser.: 2). (ENG.). 368p. (YA). (gr. 9). 17.99 (978-0-06-211854-7(4), HarperTeen) HarperCollins Pubs.

Kimball, Angela. Of All the Silly Things. 2011. 52p. (gr. -1 — 1). pap. 25.49 (978-1-4567-2259-3(X)) AuthorHouse.

Kimball, Michael D. Alligator Bay: A Beary Tale. 2009. 132p. pap. 11.95 (978-1-4401-1804-3(3)) iUniverse, Inc.

Kimberly, Anne. Dark Well of Decision. 2007. 136p. per. 7.99 (978-0-9800356-5-0(1)) Highland Pr. Publishing.

Kimble-Ellis, Sonya. The Sancastle Kids: A Maya Adventure. 2010. pap. (978-1-61623-664-9(7)) Independent Pub.

Kimmel, Elizabeth Cody. Secret of the Mountain Dog. 2014. (ENG.). 208p. (J). (gr. 3-7). 16.99 (978-0-545-60369-0(2), Scholastic Pr.) Scholastic, Inc.

Kimmel, Jordan L. The Magic Gown. 2007. (Illus.). 144p. (J). (gr. 3-6). pap. (978-0-9785007-0-2(9)) Spring Tree Pr.

Kimmons, Janet M. The Jewel in the Attic & the Adventures of Tiger. Farmer, Zoe, illus. 2007. 108p. (J). (gr. 1-3). pap. (978-1-58690-028-1(5)) Mould, Paul Publishing.

Kimpton, Paul & Kimpton, Ann Kaczkowski. Summer of Firsts: WWII Is Ending, but the Music Adventures Are Just Beginning. 2013. (Adventures with Music Ser.: 3). (ENG., Illus.). 288p. (J). (gr. 4-7). pap. 8.95 (978-1-57999-972-8(7)) G I A Pubns., Inc.

Kincaid, S. J. Vortex. 2014. (Insignia Ser.: 2). (ENG.). 416p. (YA). (gr. 8). pap. 9.99 (978-0-06-209303-5(7), Tegen, Katherine Bks) HarperCollins Pubs.

Kincaid, Tracy. The Adventures of Casey the Lost Suitcase. 2007. (Illus.). 32p. (J). (gr. -1-3). 16.95 (978-0-929915-67-8(4)) Headline Bks., Inc.

Kinder, Connie & Virden, Carole. Dash's Pause: An Adventure in Being Found. 2012. (Illus.). 40p. pap. 20.95 (978-1-4497-6981-9(0), WestBow Pr.) Author Solutions, Inc.

Kinderman, Robert W. & Moore, Trudy E. Kelly Kapers: Adventures of Kelly & Her Family. Moore, Trudy E., illus.

2011. (Illus.). 42p. pap. 23.00 (978-1-4349-1035-6(0)) Dorrance Publishing Co., Inc.
Kindler, Jennifer. Rita's Fairytale. 2011. 68p. pap. 10.95 (978-1-4575-0277-4(1)) Dog Ear Publishing, LLC.
Kindt, Matt. Poppy! & the Lost Lagoon. 2016. (ENG., Illus.). 144p. (J). (gr. 3-7). 14.99 (978-1-61655-943-4(8)) Dark Horse Comics.
King-cargile, Gillian. Toy & the Test Drive. Krull, Kevin, illus. 2017. (Stuffed Bunny Science Adventure Ser.). (ENG.). 36p. (J). (gr. k-3). 18.99 **(978-0-87580-760-7(7))** Northern Illinois Univ. Pr.
King, Caro. Seven Sorcerers. 2011. (ENG.). 352p. (J). (gr. 3-7). 15.99 (978-1-4424-2042-7(1), Aladdin) Simon & Schuster Children's Publishing.
—Shadow Spell. 2012. (ENG.). 320p. (J). (gr. 3-7). pap. 6.99 (978-1-4423-3908-8(X), Aladdin) Simon & Schuster Children's Publishing.
—Shadow Spell. 2012. (ENG.). 320p. (J). (gr. 3-7). 15.99 (978-1-4424-2045-8(6), Simon & Schuster/Paula Wiseman Bks.) Simon & Schuster/Paula Wiseman Bks.
King, Caro & Bowater, Charlie. Seven Sorcerers. 2012. (ENG.). 352p. (J). (gr. 3-7). pap. 6.99 (978-1-4424-2043-4(X), Aladdin) Simon & Schuster Children's Publishing.
King, Carrie. Joni-Pip. Boddy, James & Moon, Paul, illus. 2010. 476p. pap. (978-0-9555246-9-1(5)) Bothy Bks., Corwall, A Div. of Grace & Patrick Pubs., Ltd.
—The Life in the Wood with Joni-Pip. 2007. (Illus.). 463p. (978-0-9555246-8-4(7)) Bothy Bks., Corwall, A Div. of Grace & Patrick Pubs., Ltd.
King-Chai, Sharon. Snail Mail. 2017. (ENG., Illus.). 32p. (J). (gr. -1-k). 17.99 (978-1-4449-2254-7(8)) Hachette Children's Group GBR. Dist: Hachette Bk. Group.
King, Diane. Elijah & the Talking Tree. 2012. (Illus.). 32p. pap. 21.99 (978-1-4691-4862-5(5)) Xlibris Corp.
King, Frank. Nina & Skeezix: The Problem of the Lost Ring. 2005. pap. 26.95 (978-1-4179-9654-4(4)) Kessinger Publishing, LLC.
King George the Thirty Third. Come Go with Me. 2017. (ENG.). 185p. pap. 13.95 **(978-1-78612-438-8(6),** 9781786124388) Austin, Stan AUS. Dist: Bookmasters Distribution.
King-Hanna, Shirley. The Ghost Child of Camay Lane, 1 vol. 2009. 143p. pap. 24.95 (978-1-60836-399-5(6)) America Star Bks.
King Iii, Dudley Allen. Skye's Big Fly'n Adventures: How Skye Gets His Name. 2012. 28p. pap. 10.95 (978-1-4626-7445-9(3)) America Star Bks.
King, J. R. Arianna Kelt & the Renegades of Time: Deluxe Edition, Wizards of Skyhall Book 2. 2008. (ENG.). 252p. (YA). per. 15.95 (978-1-57545-120-6(4)) RP Media.
—Arianna Kelt & the Renegades of Time: Signature Edition, Wizards of Skyhall Book 2. 2008. (ENG.). 256p. (J). 18.95 (978-1-57545-165-7(4), Reagent Pr. Echo) RP Media.
—Arianna Kelt & the Wizards of Skyhall: Deluxe Edition, Wizards of Skyhall Book 1. 2008. (ENG.). 200p. (YA). per. 14.95 (978-1-57545-170-1(0)) RP Media.
King, Jo. A Flight of Fancy. 2011. 58p. 24.99 (978-1-4691-3665-3(1)); pap. 15.99 (978-1-4653-9298-5(X)) Xlibris Corp.
King, Judy. When Summer Comes Again. King, Judy, illus. 2013. (Illus.). 160p. (J). pap. (978-1-884377-20-4(3)) Green Pastures Pr.
King, Julia. Bingo Explores the Farm. (ENG., Illus.). 46p. (J). 2012. pap. 8.99 (978-0-9839827-1-5(6)) 2011. lib. bdg. 15.99 (978-0-9839827-0-8(8)) King, Julia.
—Bingo's Big Adventure: A Cat's Tale. 2010. (ENG., Illus.). 36p. (J). pap. 8.99 (978-0-615-37032-3(2)) King, Julia.
King, Karen. Unicorn Magic. Hicks, Angie, illus. 2012. (ENG.). 24p. 9.95 (978-1-84135-832-1(0)) Award Pubns. Ltd. GBR. Dist: Parkwest Pubns., Inc.
King, Paulk, Sr. The Hero. 2005. per. 5.95 (978-0-9771476-1-8(4)) LJK Publishing LLC.
King, Sarah. The Great Adventures of Piggy the Peruvian Guinea Pig. 2016. (ENG., Illus.). 36p. (J). pap. 10.95 (978-1-63047-568-0(8)) Morgan James Publishing.
King-smith, Dick. The Stray. 139p. (J). (gr. 3-5). pap. 4.99 (978-0-8072-1507-4(4), Listening Library) Random Hse. Audio Publishing Group.
King Sr., Billy. The Story. 2010. 73p. pap. 11.95 (978-0-557-25606-8(2)) Lulu Pr., Inc.
King, Steve. The Stone Dragon. 2005. 80p. pap. 16.95 (978-1-4137-9628-5(1)) PublishAmerica, Inc.
King, Terrie. The Six-Toed Dog & the Big-Headed Puppy. 2008. 104p. pap. 19.95 (978-1-60672-765-2(6)) America Star Bks.
King, Trey. Friends & Foes! Wang, Sean, illus. 2015. (LEGO DC Super Heroes Ser.: 1). (ENG.). 24p. (J). (gr. -1-3). pap. 3.99 (978-0-545-78504-4(9)) Scholastic, Inc.
—Mystery on the Lego Express. Wang, Sean, illus. 2014. (Lego City Ser.). (ENG.). 24p. (J). (gr. -1-3). 3.99 (978-0-545-60366-9(8)) Scholastic, Inc.
—Sidekick Showdown! Wang, Sean, illus. 2016. (LEGO DC Super Heroes 8X8 Ser.). (ENG.). 24p. (J). (gr. -1-3). 13.55 (978-0-606-39149-8(5)) Turtleback Bks.
—Transformers Rescue Bots - Training Academy: Sharks & Other Sea Life! 2017. (Passport to Reading Level 2 Ser.). (ENG., Illus.). 32p. (J). (gr. -1-3). pap. 4.99 (978-0-316-36187-3(9)) Little, Brown Bks. for Young Readers.
—Transformers Rescue Bots: Training Academy: Construction! 2016. (Passport to Reading Level 2 Ser.). (ENG., Illus.). 32p. (J). (gr. -1-1). pap. 3.99 (978-0-316-38973-0(0)) Little, Brown Bks. for Young Readers.
—Treasure Time! 2014. (Tickety Toc Ser.). (ENG.). 16p. (J). (gr. -1-k). 6.99 (978-0-545-61474-0(0)) Scholastic, Inc.
King, Wesley. The Incredible Space Raiders from Space! 2015. (ENG., Illus.). 304p. (J). (gr. 3-7). 16.99 (978-1-4814-2319-9(3), Simon & Schuster Bks. For Young Readers) Simon & Schuster Bks. For Young Readers.
—The Incredible Space Raiders from Space! 2016. lib. bdg. 18.40 (978-0-606-38276-2(3)) Turtleback Bks.
—OCDaniel. (ENG., Illus.). 304p. (J). (gr. 3-7). 2017. pap. 8.99 (978-1-4814-5532-9(X)) 2016. 17.99 (978-1-4814-5531-2(1)) Simon & Schuster/Paula Wiseman Bks. (Simon & Schuster/Paula Wiseman Bks.).
—OCDaniel. 2017. lib. bdg. 18.40 **(978-0-606-39743-8(4))** Turtleback Bks.
King, Zola. Whatever Became of Charlie Caterpillar? 2011. 44p. pap. 16.59 (978-1-4634-7441-6(5)) AuthorHouse.
Kinger, Rachit. Zapp: The Squirrel Who Wanted to Fly. 2015. (ENG.). 100p. pap. 7.95 (978-81-8328-137-9(0)) Wisdom Tree IND. Dist: SCB Distributors.
Kingsley, Kaza. Erec Rex: The Dragon's Eye. Payne, John, ed. Grant, Melvyn, illus. 2006. 360p. (J). 17.99 (978-0-9786555-6-3(7)) Firelight Press, Inc.
Kingsley, Mike. The Haunted House. (Ace Adventures Ser.). (Illus.). 64p. (J). (gr. 4-6). (978-1-876367-21-3(0)) Wizard Bks.
—The Treasure of King Midas. (Ace Adventures Ser.). (Illus.). 64p. (J). (gr. 4-6). pap. (978-1-876367-12-1(1)) Wizard Bks.
Kingston, W. Aventuras en la Selva. (SPA., Illus.). 160p. (YA). 14.95 (978-84-7281-182-9(4), AF1182) Auriga, Ediciones S.A. ESP. Dist: Continental Bk. Co., Inc.
Kingston, W. H. G. In the Rocky Mountains. 2007. (Illus.). 228p. per. (978-1-4065-2892-3(7)) Dodo Pr.
Kinney, Sarah & Petrucha, Stefan. Secret Sand Sleuths. 2013. (Nancy Drew & the Clue Crew Ser.). (ENG., Illus.). 64p. (J). (gr. k-3). pap. 7.99 (978-1-59707-376-9(8), 9781597073769) Papercutz.
Kintz, Elizabeth. The Magic Hose. 2012. 30p. 16.95 (978-1-4575-1087-8(1)); pap. 14.00 (978-1-4575-0948-3(2)) Dog Ear Publishing, LLC.
Kipling, Rudyard. The Jungle Book. Detmold, Edward J. & Detmold, Maurice, illus. 2010. (Calla Editions Ser.). (ENG.). 192p. 30.00 (978-1-60660-009-2(5)) Dover Pubns., Inc.
—The Jungle Books. 2013. (ENG.). 384p. (gr. 12). mass mkt. 5.95 (978-0-451-41918-7(9), Signet) Penguin Publishing Group.
—Jungle Books. Nagai, Kaori, ed. 2013. (ENG.). 448p. (gr. 12). 11.00 (978-0-14-119665-7(3), Penguin Classics) Penguin Publishing Group.
—Kim. Trivedi, Harish & Montefiore, Jan, eds. 2011. (ENG., Illus.). 432p. (gr. 12). 10.00 (978-0-14-144237-2(9), Penguin Classics) Penguin Publishing Group.
—Kim. 2011. (Puffin Classics Ser.). (ENG.). 400p. (J). (gr. 5-7). 5.99 (978-0-14-133250-5(6), Puffin Books) Penguin Young Readers Group.
—Mowgli of the Jungle Book: The Complete Stories. 2016. (ENG.). 224p. (gr. 1). pap. 6.99 (978-1-944686-32-1(0), Racehorse Publishing) Skyhorse Publishing Co., Inc.
—Puck of Pook's Hill. 2010. 260p. pap. 20.95 (978-0-557-36212-7(1)) Lulu Pr., Inc.
Kirby, Matthew J. The Arctic Code. (Dark Gravity Sequence Ser.: 1). (J). (gr. 3-7). 2016. 352p. pap. 6.99 (978-0-06-222488-0(3)) 2015. (ENG.). 336p. 16.99 (978-0-06-222487-3(5)) HarperCollins Pubs.
—Cave of Wonders. 2013. (Infinity Ring Ser.: 5). (ENG.). 192p. (J). (gr. 3-7). 12.99 (978-0-545-38700-2(0)) Scholastic, Inc.
—Island of the Sun. 2016. (Dark Gravity Sequence Ser.: 2). 384p. (J). (gr. 3-7). 16.99 (978-0-06-222490-3(5)) HarperCollins Pubs.
—Last Descendants. 2016. (Last Descendants Ser.: 1). (ENG.). 320p. (J). (gr. 7). pap. 9.99 (978-0-545-85551-8(9)) Scholastic, Inc.
—The Lost Kingdom. 2013. (ENG.). 352p. (J). (gr. 3-7). 18.99 (978-0-545-27426-5(5), Scholastic Pr.) Scholastic, Inc.
—The Rogue World. 2017. (Dark Gravity Sequence Ser.: 3). 400p. (J). (gr. 3-7). 16.99 (978-0-06-222493-4(X)) HarperCollins Pubs.
—Spell Robbers. 2014. (Quantum League Ser.: No. 1). (ENG.). 272p. (J). (gr. 3-7). 16.99 (978-0-545-50226-9(8), Scholastic Pr.) Scholastic, Inc.
Kirby, Ruth M. Claudius Saves the Pumpkin Patch. Larson, Lisa K., illus. 2008. 20p. pap. 24.95 (978-1-60703-827-6(7)) America Star Bks.
Kirby, Stan. Captain Awesome & the Missing Elephants. 2014. (Captain Awesome Ser.: 10). lib. bdg. 16.00 (978-0-606-35440-0(9)) Turtleback Bks.
—The Captain Awesome Collection: A MI-TEE Boxed Set: Captain Awesome to the Rescue!; Captain Awesome vs. Nacho Cheese Man; Captain Awesome & the New Kid; Captain Awesome Takes a Dive. O'Connor, George, illus. 2013. (Captain Awesome Ser.). (ENG.). 512p. (J). (gr. k-2). pap. 23.99 (978-1-4424-8977-6(4), Little Simon) Little Simon.
—Captain Awesome Meets Super Dude! 2016. (Captain Awesome Ser.: 17). lib. bdg. 16.00 (978-0-606-38963-1(6)) Turtleback Bks.
—Captain Awesome Takes Flight. 2017. (Captain Awesome Ser.: 19). lib. bdg. 16.00 **(978-0-606-40202-6(0))** Turtleback Bks.
Kirby, Stan. Captain Awesome vs. the Sinister Substitute Teacher. 2016. (Captain Awesome Ser.: 16). lib. bdg. 16.00 (978-0-606-38247-2(X)) Turtleback Bks.
Kirker, Solveig. The Florida Pod. 2009. 32p. pap. 12.99 (978-1-4389-3137-1(9)) AuthorHouse.
Kirkland, Justin B. Jb Pumpernikel vs the Sock Monster. 2013. 74p. pap. 5.50 (978-0-615-81456-8(5)) KIRKLAND, JUSTIN B.
Kirkpatrick, Teresa. The Adventures of Four Friends on Vacation, 1 vol. 2009. 119p. pap. 19.95 (978-1-60836-927-0(7)) America Star Bks.
—Roscoe's Forest Adventures. 2008. 177p. pap. 24.95 (978-1-60672-328-9(6)) America Star Bks.
Kirkup, Mary. The Tales of Granny Grunt. 2008. 32p. pap. 12.99 (978-1-4389-1040-6(1)) AuthorHouse.
Kirkwood, Jeff. The Adventures of Little Mouse. 2008. (ENG.). 24p. pap. 12.99 (978-1-4389-2874-6(2)) AuthorHouse.
Kirsch, R. A. The Big One: (A Bicycle Tale), 1 vol. 2009. 191p. pap. 24.95 (978-1-60703-341-7(0)) PublishAmerica, Inc.
Kishimoto, Seishi. O-Parts Hunter, Vol. 3. Kishimoto, Seishi, illus. 2007. (O-Parts Hunter Ser.: 3). (ENG., Illus.). 200p. pap. 9.99 (978-1-4215-0857-3(5)) Viz Media.
—O-Parts Hunter, Vol. 2. Kishimoto, Seishi, illus. 2007. (ENG., Illus.). 200p. pap. 9.99 (978-1-4215-0856-6(7)) Viz Media.
Kitamura, Satoshi. Comic Adventures of Boots. Kitamura, Satoshi, illus. 2012. (ENG., Illus.). 32p. (J). (gr. k-4). pap. 10.99 (978-1-84270-908-5(9)) Andersen Pr. GBR. Dist: Independent Pubs. Group.
Kitchen, David. The Adventures of Chesed & Cadence. 2012. 28p. pap. 9.95 (978-1-4787-1712-6(2)) Outskirts Pr., Inc.
—The Adventures of David & Freddie Boo. 2012. 28p. pap. 9.95 (978-1-4327-6610-8(4)) Outskirts Pr., Inc.
Kithinji, Gerald, et al. Of Friends, Money & Gossip: 3 Stories & a Play. 2009. (Hodder African Readers Ser.). (Illus.). 96p. pap. 12.95 (978-0-340-99027-8(9)) Hodder Education Group GBR. Dist: Trans-Atlantic Pubns., Inc.
Kittredge, James M. The Three Little Explorers, 1 vol. Reyes, Glendalys, illus. 2010. 16p. pap. 24.95 (978-1-4489-8973-7(6)) PublishAmerica, Inc.
Kizer, Linda M. Plug, the Lonely Little Fire Hydrant. 2009. 60p. pap. 26.99 (978-1-4490-2873-2(X)) AuthorHouse.
Klass, David. Whirlwind. 2009. (Caretaker Trilogy Ser.: 2). (ENG.). 320p. (YA). (gr. 9-12). pap. 18.99 (978-0-312-38429-6(7), 9780312384296) Square Fish.
Klause, Annette Curtis. Freaks: Alive, on the Inside! (ENG.). 336p. (YA). 2007. (gr. 9). pap. 9.99 (978-0-689-87038-5(8)) 2006. (Illus.). (gr. 8-18). 16.95 (978-0-689-87037-8(X)) McElderry, Margaret K. Bks. (McElderry, Margaret K. Bks.).
Klavan, Andrew. The Last Thing I Remember, 1 vol. 2010. (Homelanders Ser.: 1). (ENG.). 352p. (YA). pap. 9.99 (978-1-59554-586-2(7)) Nelson, Thomas Inc.
Kleczka, John A. Flick the Butterfly: Flick & Mom Go to Grandma's. 2008. 48p. per. 24.95 (978-1-60441-290-1(9)) America Star Bks.
Klehr, Dawn. If You Wrong Us. 2015. (ENG.). 240p. (YA). pap. 11.99 (978-0-7387-4599-2(5), Flux) North Star Editions.
Klein, Abby. Camping Catastrophe! McKinley, John, illus. 2008. (Ready, Freddy! Ser.: Bk. 14). 95p. (J). (gr. -1-3). 11.65 (978-0-7569-8837-1(3)) Perfection Learning Corp.
—Homework Hassles. McKinley, John, illus. 2004. (Ready, Freddy! Ser.: 3). (ENG.). 96p. (J). (gr. -1-3). 5.99 (978-0-439-55600-2(7), Blue Sky Pr., The) Scholastic, Inc.
Klein, Joel & Klein, Abby. The Night I Saved the Universe: From the Files of the Galactic Police Department. 2009. 126p. (J). (978-0-545-12933-6(8)) Scholastic, Inc.
Klein, Judith Anne. Tuxedo Flyer. 2009. 28p. pap. 14.65 (978-1-4490-0635-8(3)) AuthorHouse.
Klepeis, Alicia. Mountains, Monsoons, & Mules. 2015. (ENG.). 96p. (gr. 3-6). 31.36 (978-1-63430-398-9(9)) Rourke Educational Media.
Klett, David. The Adventures of Willy & Billy Bk. 1: The Lake Lure Chronicles - Book 1. Lang, Carole, illus. l.t. ed. 2006. 32p. (J). lib. bdg. 17.95 (978-0-9779325-0-4(8)) Five Oaks Pr.
Kliever, S. I. A Slave's Quest. 2011. 284p. pap. (978-1-77069-178-0(2)) Word Alive Pr.
Klim, Christopher. Firecracker Jones Is on the Case. 2006. (Illus.). 116p. (J). lib. bdg. 19.95 (978-1-933435-11-4(9)) Hopewell Pubns., LLC.
Klimo, Kate. Rolf. 2017. (Dog Diaries: 10). lib. bdg. 18.40 **(978-0-606-40240-8(3))** Turtleback Bks.
Kline, Joel. Cookie's Colorful World. Borsch, Kim, illus. 2011. 32p. pap. 24.95 (978-1-4560-7578-1(0)) America Star Bks.
Kline, Spencer. The Adventures of Fujimori-San. Brown, E. Jackie, illus. 2010. 20p. 12.99 (978-1-4520-6275-4(7)) AuthorHouse.
Kline, Suzy. Horrible Harry & the Mud Gremlins. Remkiewicz, Frank, illus. 2004. (Horrible Harry Ser.). (ENG.). 64p. (J). (gr. 2-4). 4.99 (978-0-14-240123-1(4), Puffin Books) Penguin Young Readers Group.
Klingele, Lindsey. The Broken World. 2017. 432p. (YA). (gr. 8). 17.99 **(978-0-06-238036-4(2),** HarperTeen) HarperCollins Pubs.
Klinkerman, Anthonette. Battle of the Grandmas. 2012. (ENG.). 34p. (J). pap. 13.95 (978-1-4787-1930-4(3)) Outskirts Pr., Inc.
Klise, Kate. Pop Goes the Circus! Klise, M. Sarah, illus. 2015. (Three-Ring Rascals Ser.: 4). (ENG.). 144p. (J). (gr. 2-5). 15.95 (978-1-61620-464-8(8)) Algonquin Bks. of Chapel Hill.
Klitzner, Irene. Sean Michael K. Whistles the Wrong Way! Who, Carrie Lou, illus. 2011. 48p. (J). 18.95 (978-0-692-01275-8(3)) Attitude Pie Publishing.
Klitzner, Irene & Adams, Peggy. Today Is My Birthday & I Have Nothing to Wear! Lou Who, Carrie, illus. 2011. (ENG.). 48p. (J). 18.95 (978-0-9846496-0-0(3)) Attitude Pie Publishing.
Kloepfer, John. Empire State of Slime. DeGrand, Ned & DeGrand, David, illus. 2013. (Zombie Chasers Ser.: 4). (ENG.). 208p. (J). (gr. 3-7). 16.99 (978-0-06-223095-9(6)) HarperCollins Pubs.
—Nothing Left to Ooze. DeGrand, David, illus. 2014. (Zombie Chasers Ser.: 5). (ENG.). 224p. (J). (gr. 3-7). 16.99 (978-0-06-223098-0(0)) HarperCollins Pubs.
—The Zombie Chasers. Wolfhard, Steve, illus. 2011. (Zombie Chasers Ser.: 1). (ENG.). 224p. (J). (gr. 3-7). pap. 6.99 (978-0-06-185306-7(2)) HarperCollins Pubs.
—Zombies of the Caribbean. DeGrand, David, illus. 2015. (Zombie Chasers Ser.: 6). (ENG.). 240p. (J). (gr. 3-7). pap. 6.99 (978-0-06-229025-0(8)) HarperCollins Pubs.
The Klondike Kid. 2005. (J). pap. (978-1-60015-070-8(5)) Steps To Literacy, LLC.
Knapp, Jodi. The Adventures of Kelly & Lucky: The Beginning. 2010. 76p. pap. 20.99 (978-1-60976-090-8(5), Eloquent Bks.) Strategic Book Publishing & Rights Agency (SBPRA).
Kneblik, Debi. The Shipwreck of Knottingburg. 2009. (J). pap. 12.00 (978-1-61623-985-5(9)) Independent Pub.
Knechtel, Mark & Knechtel, Crystal. Pollywog Pickle's Great Big Plan. 2013. 40p. pap. (978-1-4602-0255-5(4)) FriesenPress.
Knee-Knock Rise. 133p. (J). (gr. 4-6). pap. 4.95 (978-0-8072-1488-6(4), Listening Library) Random Hse. Audio Publishing Group.
Kneisley, Amy. The Gentle Elephant. Tina, Dunnier, illus. 2013. 24p. pap. 8.99 (978-1-938768-21-7(3)) Gypsy Pubns.
Knesek, Marian. Sage & the Peacock. Buehrle, Jackie, illus. 2011. 28p. pap. 24.95 (978-1-4512-2211-1(4)) America Star Bks.
Knevels, Gertrude. The Wonderful Bed. Chamberlin, Emily Hall, illus. 2007. 124p. per. (978-1-4065-2920-3(6)) Dodo Pr.
Knight, Chris. Skaggy the Scarecrow: A Halloween Story. 2010. (Illus.). 40p. pap. 18.49 (978-1-4520-2473-8(1)) AuthorHouse.
Knight, Christopher. World Is Black & White. 2008. 459p. (YA). pap. 14.95 (978-1-893699-97-7(8)) AudioCraft Publishing, Inc.
Knight, Deidre Denise. The Wash Cloth & the Turtle. Milosevic, Tamara, illus. 2013. 36p. 17.95 (978-0-9893091-2-7(6)) Cube Marketing.
Knight, Diedre. Beanie's Backyard. 2012. 28p. pap. 12.95 (978-1-62141-812-2(X)) Booklocker.com, Inc.
Knight, J. A. Ben & Ken: The Odd Job Men. 2008. 56p. pap. 23.99 (978-1-4389-1144-1(0)) AuthorHouse.
Knight, P. B. The Secret Passage, 1 vol. 2009. 73p. pap. 14.95 (978-1-61546-421-0(2)) PublishAmerica, Inc.
Knight, Paul. Abbabuwas Mountain. 2006. 252p. per. (978-1-905529-65-0(1)) Grosvenor Hse. Publishing Ltd.
Knights, Nancy. Gracie's Hill. Norie, Rooney, illus. 2007. 28p. per. 7.95 (978-1-58275-192-4(7)) Black Forest Pr.
Knisley, Eric. The Adventures of Furlington Mackelthwaite. 2005. 40p. pap. 19.95 (978-1-4116-4792-3(0)) Lulu Pr., Inc.
Knoten, Erinn. Nickelas the Lost Nickel. 2012. 24p. pap. 16.99 (978-1-4772-9041-5(9)) AuthorHouse.
Knotoff, Karenann. The Island of Rouge. 2007. 96p. per. 19.95 (978-1-4241-7575-8(5)) America Star Bks.
Knowlen, Maralee Burdick. Ian's Christmas Tree. 2012. 48p. pap. 24.95 (978-1-4626-8932-3(9)) America Star Bks.
Knox-Henry, Kheri. The Invisible Car. 2010. 46p. pap. 9.95 (978-1-58275-219-8(2)) Black Forest Pr.
Knox, Thomas W. The Young Nimrods Around the World. 2005. reprint ed. pap. 28.95 (978-1-4179-6340-9(9)) Kessinger Publishing, LLC.
Kobert, Michael Gilead & Donato, Dona. Who Goes with That Nose? The Wild Adventures of Juicy Coppertoes. Fuller, Laurie, illus. 2005. 40p. (J). per. 9.95 (978-0-9770700-0-8(X)) Giggling Gorilla Productions, LLC.
Koch, Joann. Annie's World. 2009. 20p. (J). pap. 9.95 (978-1-4327-4063-4(6)) Outskirts Pr., Inc.
Kochalka, James. The Best Little Ghost in the World! 2008. (Johnny Boo Ser.: 1). (ENG., Illus.). 40p. (J). (gr. 2-5). 9.95 (978-1-60309-013-1(4), 9781603090131) Top Shelf Productions.
Kocsis, Konrád Hayward. The Adventures of the Krusaders & the Legend of Wilde Island. 2012. 238p. pap. 16.97 (978-1-61897-106-7(9), Strategic Bk. Publishing) Strategic Book Publishing & Rights Agency (SBPRA).
Koehler, Hanne Lore & Laraya-Coutts, Corie. A Tale of a Malipayon Warrior. 2010. 128p. 21.95 (978-1-4502-1344-8(8)); pap. 11.95 (978-1-4502-1346-2(4)) iUniverse, Inc.
Koeppel, Ruth. Nick Jr. Wonder Pets Adventures: Book & Magnetic Playset. 2009. 16p. (J). bds. 14.99 (978-0-7944-1769-7(8)) Reader's Digest Assn., Inc., The.
Koger, Danny K. The Misadventures of Carson & C J Crenshaw: In Search of the Book of Life. 2007. 184p. per. 13.95 (978-0-595-42365-1(5)) iUniverse, Inc.
Kogge, Michael. The Force Awakens. deluxe ed. 2016. (ENG.). 192p. (J). (gr. 3-7). 10.99 (978-1-4847-7584-4(8), Disney Lucasfilm Press) Disney Publishing Worldwide.
—Star Wars: The Force Awakens Junior Novel. 2016. (J). lib. bdg. 17.20 (978-0-606-38303-5(4)) Turtleback Bks.
—Star Wars Rebels: Battle to the End. 2015. (Star Wars Saga Chapter Book Ser.). (ENG.). 144p. (J). (gr. 1-3). pap. 5.99 (978-1-4847-0487-5(8), Disney Lucasfilm Press) Disney Publishing Worldwide.
Kogge, Michael & Disney Book Group Staff. The Force Awakens. 2016. (ENG.). 192p. (J). (gr. 3-7). pap. 6.99 (978-1-4847-0488-2(6), Disney Lucasfilm Press) Disney Publishing Worldwide.
Kohl, T. Michelle. The Magical Adventures of Bailey Boo the Cockatoo: When the Family's Away, the Parrots Will Play! 2012. 24p. pap. 24.95 (978-1-4626-6215-9(3)) America Star Bks.
Kohlhepp, Michael G. Within the Hearthstone Book 2: The Fountain of Balance. 2007. (ENG.). 184p. per. 24.95 (978-1-4241-4446-4(9)) PublishAmerica, Inc.
Kohlmann, Krista. Mapsume: Unscramble the Hero. 2003. 118p. (YA). pap. 10.95 (978-0-595-27182-5(0), Writers Club Pr.) iUniverse, Inc.
Kok, Gemma. Explore. 2008. 44p. pap. 18.50 (978-1-4092-2058-9(3)) Lulu Pr., Inc.
—Explore (Printed in black & White) 2008. 44p. pap. 8.00 (978-1-4092-2530-0(5)) Lulu Pr., Inc.
Kolar, Marsha. Little Brave Bear. Di Marco, Audrey, illus. 2005. 17p. (J). per. (978-0-9766804-0-6(8)) CottonWood Publishing Co.
Kolb, Andrew. Edmund Unravels. Kolb, Andrew, illus. 2015. (ENG., Illus.). 34p. (J). (gr. k-3). 16.99 (978-0-399-16914-4(8), Nancy Paulsen Books) Penguin Young Readers Group.
Koller, Jackie French. A Wizard Named Nell. Guay, Rebecca, illus. 2003. (ENG.). 208p. (J). (gr. 3-7). pap. 11.95 (978-0-689-85591-7(5), Aladdin) Simon & Schuster Children's Publishing.
—The Wizard's Apprentice. Guay, Rebecca, illus. 2003. (ENG.). 192p. (J). (gr. 3-7). pap. 9.99 (978-0-689-85592-4(3), Aladdin) Simon & Schuster Children's Publishing.
Komalasari, Arie. Kiki the Orangutan: The Big Banana Festival. 2017. (ENG., Illus.). 32p. (J). (gr. -1-3). 8.95 (978-0-8048-4811-4(4)) Tuttle Publishing.
Komarnitsky, Kara. The Grimalkin's Secret. 2013. 242p. pap. 16.99 (978-0-9825528-1-0(5)) Stone Arrow Bks.
Koncerak, Veronica. The Bubble That Never Popped. 2010. 24p. 11.49 (978-1-4520-3935-0(6)) AuthorHouse.
Kong, Anja & Sunkara, Naveena. The Battle Of: Secret of the Taj. 2010. 172p. 23.95 (978-1-4502-0954-0(8)); pap. 13.95 (978-1-4502-0952-6(1)) iUniverse, Inc.
Konigsburg, E. L. The E. L. Konigsburg Newbery Collection: From the Mixed-Up Files of Mrs. Basil E. Frankweiler; Jennifer, Hecate, Macbeth, William Mckinley, & Me, Elizabeth; the View from Saturday. 2013. (ENG., Illus.). 472p. (J). (gr. 3-7). pap. 23.99 (978-1-4424-9743-6(2), Atheneum Bks. for Young Readers) Simon & Schuster Children's Publishing.
—From the Mixed-up Files of Mrs. Basil E. Frankweiler. 159p. (J). (gr. 4-6). pap. 4.99 (978-0-8072-1386-5(1), Listening Library) Random Hse. Audio Publishing Group.
—From the Mixed-up Files of Mrs. Basil E. Frankweiler. 2007. (Illus.). 74p. (J). pap. (978-0-545-04173-7(2)) Scholastic, Inc.
—From the Mixed-up Files of Mrs. Basil E. Frankweiler. l.t. ed. 2005. 186p. pap. 10.95 (978-0-7862-7358-4(5), Large Print Pr.) Thorndike Pr.
Koniver, Laura. Jake, A Guinea Pig Finds Adventure. 2010. 40p. pap. 17.99 (978-0-557-64364-6(3)) Lulu Pr., Inc.

Kooser, Ted. The Bell in the Bridge. Root, Barry, illus. 2016. (ENG.). 32p. (J). (gr. 1-4). 16.99 (978-0-7636-6481-7(2)) Candlewick Pr.

Koraido, Beth S. Summers with Grampa Gus. 2008. 63p. pap. 19.95 (978-1-60703-384-4(4)) America Star Bks.

Korman, Gordon. The Climb. 2012. (Everest Ser.: 2). lib. bdg. 17.20 (978-0-606-23934-9(0), Turtleback) Turtleback Bks.

—Collision Course, Bk. 2. 2011. (Titanic Ser.: 2). (ENG.). 160p. (J). (gr. 3-7). pap. 6.99 (978-0-545-12332-7(1), Scholastic Paperbacks) Scholastic, Inc.

—The Contest. 2012. (Everest Ser.: 1). lib. bdg. 17.20 (978-0-606-23933-2(2), Turtleback) Turtleback Bks.

—Criminal Destiny. 2016. (Masterminds Ser.: 2). 320p. (J). (gr. 3-7). 16.99 (978-0-06-230002-7(4)) HarperCollins Pubs.

—Criminal Destiny. 2017. (Masterminds Ser.: 2). (J). lib. bdg. 18.40 **(978-0-606-39612-7(8))** Turtleback Bks.

—Escape. 2008. (Island (Playaway Audio) Ser.). (J). 34.99 (978-1-60514-854-0(7)) Findaway World, LLC.

—Framed. (J). 2011. (ENG.). 240p. (gr. 3-7). pap. 6.99 (978-0-545-19763-2(5), Scholastic Paperbacks) 2010. (978-0-545-27081-6(2), Scholastic Pr.) 2010. (Swindle Ser.: 3). (ENG.). 240p. (gr. 4-7). 16.99 (978-0-545-17849-5(5), Scholastic Pr.) Scholastic, Inc.

—Masterminds. (Masterminds Ser.: 2). (J). (gr. 3-7). 2017. 336p. 7.99 (978-0-06-230003-4(2)) 2016. 352p. pap. 7.99 (978-0-06-229999-4(9)) 2015. 336p. 16.99 (978-0-06-229996-3(4)) HarperCollins Pubs.

—Masterminds. 2016. (Masterminds Ser.: 1). (J). lib. bdg. 18.40 (978-0-606-38138-3(4)) Turtleback Bks.

—One False Note. 2009. (39 Clues Ser.: 2). (ENG.). 160p. (J). (gr. 3-7). 12.99 (978-0-545-06042-4(7)); (Illus.). 12.99 (978-0-545-09060-5(1)) Scholastic, Inc.

—Payback. 2017. (Masterminds Ser.: 3). 320p. (J). (gr. 3-7). 16.99 (978-0-06-230005-8(9)) HarperCollins Pubs.

—Showoff. 2012. (ENG.). 256p. (J). (gr. 3-7). pap. 6.99 (978-0-545-32060-3(7), Scholastic Paperbacks); (Swindle Ser.: 4). 16.99 (978-0-545-32059-7(3), Scholastic Pr.) Scholastic, Inc.

—Slacker. 2017. lib. bdg. 17.20 **(978-0-606-40143-2(1))** Turtleback Bks.

—The Summit. 2012. (Everest Ser.: 3). lib. bdg. 17.20 (978-0-606-23935-6(9), Turtleback) Turtleback Bks.

—Swindle. 2009. (ENG.). 256p. (J). (gr. 3-7). 6.99 (978-0-439-90345-5(9), Scholastic Paperbacks) Scholastic, Inc.

—Unsinkable, Bk. 1. 2011. (Titanic Ser.: 1). (ENG.). 160p. (J). (gr. 3-7). pap. 6.99 (978-0-545-12331-0(3), Scholastic Paperbacks) Scholastic, Inc.

—Unstoppable - Flashpoint. 2014. (39 Clues: Unstoppable Ser.: 4). (ENG.). 224p. (J). (gr. 3-7). 12.99 (978-0-545-52147-5(5)) Scholastic, Inc.

—Zoobreak. (J). 2010. (ENG.). 240p. (gr. 3-7). pap. 6.99 (978-0-545-12500-0(6), Scholastic Paperbacks) 2009. 230p. (978-0-545-20027-1(X), Scholastic Pr.) Scholastic, Inc.

Korman, Justine. Spring Is Here, Grumpy Bunny! McQueen, Lucinda, illus. 2008. (Clifford's Bedtime Ser.). (ENG.). 64p. (J). (gr. -1-3). pap. 4.99 (978-0-545-03402-9(7), Cartwheel Bks.) Scholastic, Inc.

Korman, Susan. Birds of a Feather. 2011. (Rio Ser.). (ENG.). 24p. (J). (gr. -1-2). pap. 3.99 (978-0-06-202267-7(9), HarperFestival) HarperCollins Pubs.

—Continental Drift. 2012. (Ice Age Ser.). (ENG.). 144p. (J). (gr. 3-7). pap. 5.99 (978-0-06-210485-4(3), HarperFestival) HarperCollins Pubs.

Korr, Mary. Winston the water Dog: Portuguese water dog tales book One. 2009. 40p. pap. 17.49 (978-1-4415-8406-9(4)) Xlibris Corp.

Korte, Steve. Beast Boy Bro-Down. 2016. (Teen Titans Go! Chapter Bks.). (J). lib. bdg. 16.00 (978-0-606-38327-1(1)) Turtleback Bks.

—Curse of the Stage Fright. Neely, Scott, illus. 2016. (Scooby-Doo Comic Chapter Bks.). (ENG.). 88p. (gr. 3-7). lib. bdg. 27.32 (978-1-4965-3583-2(9)) Capstone Press of Coughlan Cos.

—Wonder Woman - I Am an Amazon Warrior. Ferguson, Lee, illus. 2017. (I Can Read Level 2 Ser.). 32p. (J). (gr. -1-3). pap. 3.99 **(978-0-06-268184-3(2))** HarperCollins Pubs.

—Wonder Woman Movie Deluxe Junior Novel. 2017. 144p. (J). (gr. 1-5). 9.99 **(978-0-06-268190-4(7)**, HarperFestival) HarperCollins Pubs.

—Wonder Woman Movie Junior Novel. 2017. 144p. (J). (gr. 1-5). pap. 6.99 **(978-0-06-268188-1(5)**, HarperFestival) HarperCollins Pubs.

Kositsky, Lynne. Minerva's Voyage. 2009. (ENG., Illus.). 240p. (YA). (gr. 6-18). pap. 10.99 (978-1-55488-439-1(X), Dundurn Pr.) Dundurn CAN. Dist: Ingram Publisher Services.

Kotzwinkle, William, et al. Walter the Farting Dog Goes on a Cruise. Coleman, Audrey, illus. 2008. (ENG.). 32p. (J). (gr. k-3). pap. 6.99 (978-0-14-241142-1(6), Puffin Books) Penguin Young Readers Group.

Koumjian, Gay Melanie. Mojo's Mojo. 2013. (ENG.). 23p. (J). pap. 12.95 (978-1-4787-1623-5(1)) Outskirts Pr., Inc.

Kountz, Charity. Jason, Lizzy & the Snowman Village. Klock, Kimberly, illus. 2013. 132p. 24.99 (978-0-9859601-1-7(6)) Texas Pride Publishing.

Kovac, Tommy. Wonderland #1. 2006. (Illus.). 24p. (YA). pap. 3.50 (978-1-59362-039-4(X), Slave Labor Graphics) Slave Labor Bks.

—Wonderland #2: The Tulgey Wood & the Treacle Well. 2006. (Illus.). 3.50 (978-1-59362-050-9(0)) Slave Labor Bks.

Kovalski, Maryann. Jenny & Joanna Album. 2005. (978-1-55041-941-2(2)) Fitzhenry & Whiteside, Ltd.

Kraai, David. Gesta De Salomon. 2008. 120p. pap. 19.95 (978-1-933916-25-5(7)) Nelson Publishing & Marketing.

Krackow, Eric T. Have an Abominably Good Day, 1 vol. 2010. (ENG., Illus.). 64p. (J). 16.99 (978-0-7643-3496-2(4), 9780764334962) Schiffer Publishing, Ltd.

Kraegel, Kenneth. King Arthur's Very Great Grandson. Kraegel, Kenneth, illus. 2012. (ENG., Illus.). 40p. (J). (gr. k-3). 16.99 (978-0-7636-5311-8(X)) Candlewick Pr.

Krakower, Harold. The Adventures of Jacob & Mr Ludicus. 2010. 28p. pap. 12.49 (978-1-4520-1187-5(7)) AuthorHouse.

Kramer, Adam. Monkey of the Month, 1 vol. Kramer, David, illus. 2012. (ENG.). 40p. (J). 16.99 (978-0-7643-4156-4(1), 9780764341564) Schiffer Publishing, Ltd.

Kramer, Andrew. Pajama Pirates. Lammle, Leslie, illus. 2010. (ENG.). 40p. (J). (gr. k-3). 16.99 (978-0-06-125194-8(1)) HarperCollins Pubs.

Krapp, JoAnn Vergona. Missing Treasure Means Trouble. Rivera, Roberta, illus. 2012. 66p. (J). (gr. 3-5). pap. 12.95 (978-0-9722576-3-3(2)) JoAnn Vergona Krapp & Gene Zaner.

Krasnesky, Thad. I Always, Always Get My Way. Parkins, David, illus. 2009. (ENG.). 32p. (J). (gr. k-2). 16.95 (978-0-9799746-4-9(X)) Flashlight Pr.

Kraszewski. Surf Angel. 2009. 40p. (978-0-9821989-0-2(6)) Kraszewski, Terry.

Kratt, Chris & Kratt, Martin. Wild Kratts Step into Reading Bind-Up. Random House, illus. 2017. (Step into Reading Ser.). (ENG.). 160p. (J). (gr. -1-1). 7.99 (978-1-101-93900-0(1), Random Hse. Bks. for Young Readers) Random Hse. Children's Bks.

Krebs, Laurie. We All Went on Safari: A Counting Journey Through Tanzania. Cairns, Julia, illus. 2010. (J). 18.10 (978-0-7569-9319-1(9)) Perfection Learning Corp.

Kreder Sr., Edward G. & Kreder, Mary Ellen DeLuca. Sparkle's Journey. Vanden Berg, Myra, illus. 2013. 32p. pap. 5.99 (978-0-9913232-0-3(3)) Kreder, Mary Ellen DeLuca.

Kreidler, Shannon. The Adventures of Sally the Squirrel: Interactive... Educational & Earn Gold Stars. 2013. 28p. pap. 15.99 (978-1-4797-7674-0(2)) Xlibris Corp.

Kreilein, Debra. The Tombstone Treasure Mystery. 2013. 142p. pap. 12.99 (978-1-62509-458-2(2)) Salem Author Services.

Kreitzer, Dora. Summer in Connecticut. 2012. 18p. pap. 16.95 (978-1-4626-8665-0(6)) America Star Bks.

Krejewski, Sandra. Kitty Kitty. 2009. 16p. (J). 12.50 (978-1-60695-038-8(X)) Callanish Pr.

Krensky, Stephen. What Do You See? A Lift-the-Flap Book about Endangered Animals. Schimler, Amy, illus. 2009. (Little Green Bks.). (ENG.). 16p. (J). (gr. -1-k). 6.99 (978-1-4169-7123-8(8), Little Simon) Little Simon.

Kress, Adrienne. The Explorers: The Door in the Alley. 2017. (Explorers Ser.: 1). (ENG.). 320p. (J). (gr. 3-7). 16.99 (978-1-101-94005-1(0), Delacorte Bks. for Young Readers) Random Hse. Children's Bks.

Kretzer, Kimberly. The Mystic Valley Adventures of Kody & Kory: The Journey Begins. 2008. 25p. pap. 24.95 (978-1-60610-692-1(9)) America Star Bks.

Kretzmer, Alissa. Brandy's Day at the Beach. 2013. 16p. pap. 12.97 (978-1-61897-357-3(6), Strategic Bk. Publishing) Strategic Book Publishing & Rights Agency (SBPRA).

Kreuger, Jim & Averdonz, N. R. My Double-Edged Life, 1 vol. Padilla, Ariel, illus. 2007. (Z Graphic Novels / Tomo Ser.). (ENG.). 160p. (J). (gr. 3-7). pap. 6.99 (978-0-310-71301-2(3)) Zondervan.

Krings, Antoon. Gilberto Mariposa. 2005. (Bichitos Curiosos Ser.). (SPA & ENG., Illus.). 32p. (J). (gr. -1-k). 5.95 (978-84-932442-9-3(5)) Blume ESP. Dist: Independent Pubs. Group.

Krisp, Caleb. Anyone but Ivy Pocket. Cantini, Barbara, illus. 2015. (Ivy Pocket Ser.: 1). 400p. (J). (gr. 3-7). 17.99 (978-0-06-236434-0(0), Greenwillow Bks.) HarperCollins Pubs.

—Somebody Stop Ivy Pocket. 2016. (Ivy Pocket Ser.: 2). (Illus.). 416p. (J). (gr. 3-7). 17.99 (978-0-06-236437-1(5), Greenwillow Bks.) HarperCollins Pubs.

Kristie Smith-Armand M.Ed Ctvi. Adventures of Abby Diamond: Out of Sight. 2009. 300p. pap. 18.95 (978-1-4401-7013-3(4)) iUniverse, Inc.

Kristie Smith-Armand M.Ed Tvi. Adventures of Abby Diamond: Abby Diamond in Teenage Wizard & Secrets in the Attic. 2009. 276p. pap. 17.95 (978-1-4401-6626-6(9)) iUniverse, Inc.

Kropp, Joseph. Bowlegs' Bounty. 2005. 192p. (J). pap. 9.95 (978-1-890905-24-8(0)) Day to Day Enterprises.

Kropp, Joseph P. Nathan Meets His Monsters. Johnston, Phillip, illus. 2012. 34p. 16.95 (978-1-890905-59-0(3)); pap. 9.95 (978-1-890905-58-3(5)) Day to Day Enterprises.

Kropp, Paul. Avalanche. (Illus.). 91p. (978-1-897039-07-6(7)) High Interest Publishing (HIP).

Krosoczka, Jarrett J. The Frog Who Croaked. Krosoczka, Jarrett J., illus. 2013. (Platypus Police Squad Ser.: 1). (ENG., Illus.). 240p. (J). (gr. 3-7). 12.99 (978-0-06-207164-4(5), Waldon Pond Pr.) HarperCollins Pubs.

—Platypus Police Squad: Never Say Narwhal. Krosoczka, Jarrett J., illus. 2016. (Platypus Police Squad Ser.: 4). (Illus.). 256p. (J). (gr. 3-7). 12.99 (978-0-06-207170-5(X), Waldon Pond Pr.) HarperCollins Pubs.

Krpata, Mitch. The Lost Expedition. Merritt, Kory, illus. 2016. (Poptropica Ser.). (ENG.). 112p. (J). (gr. 1-4). 9.95 (978-1-4197-2129-8(1), Amulet Bks.) Abrams, Inc.

—The Lost Expedition. Merritt, Kory, illus. 2016. (Poptropica Graphic Novels Ser.: 2). (J). lib. bdg. 20.80 (978-0-606-39019-4(7)) Turtleback Bks.

Krueger, Jim & Rogers, Bud. The Argon Deception, 1 vol. Padilla, Ariel, illus. 2008. (Z Graphic Novels / Tomo Ser.). (ENG.). 160p. (J). (gr. 4-7). pap. 6.99 (978-0-310-71303-6(X)) Zondervan.

Krueger, K. S. Traegonia: The Ember Rune. 2011. 295p. 24.95 (978-1-4327-7718-0(1)); 304p. pap. 17.95 (978-1-4327-7604-6(5)) Outskirts Pr., Inc.

Krug, R. Lyding. The Treasure of Ferson Creek. 2006. 133p. (YA). pap. 9.95 (978-1-4116-3683-5(X)) Lulu Pr., Inc.

Kruger, Kat. The Night Has Claws. 2013. 280p. pap. (978-0-9917937-5-4(7)) Fierce ink Pr. Co-Op, Ltd.

Kruger, Malia. Naughty Elepaio. Furchgott, Eve, illus. 2008. 32p. 14.95 (978-0-87336-158-3(X)) Kamehameha Publishing.

Krulik, Nancy. Keep on Burpin' Blecha, Aaron, illus. 2012. (George Brown, Class Clown Ser.: No. 2). (ENG.). 384p. (J). (gr. 2-4). pap. 8.99 (978-0-448-46285-1(0), Grosset & Dunlap) Penguin Young Readers Group.

—Three Burps & You're Out! 2013. (George Brown, Class Clown Ser.: 10). lib. bdg. 14.75 (978-0-606-31682-8(5), Turtleback) Turtleback Bks.

Krum, Atticus. The Taming. Donaera, Patrizia, illus. 2014. (ENG.). 227p. (J). pap. 12.99 (978-0-9885349-1-9(6)) Huntly Hse.

Krumm, Brian & Kortenkamp, Steve. Exploring Space & Beyond. 2015. (Exploring Space & Beyond Ser.). (ENG.). (gr. 3-4). 114.61 (978-1-4914-6659-9(6), Connect) Stone Arch Bks.

Krumwiede, Lana. Archon. (Psi Chronicles Ser.). (ENG.). 320p. (J). (gr. 5). 2015. pap. 7.99 (978-0-7636-7659-9(4)) 2013. (Illus.). 16.99 (978-0-7636-6402-2(2)) Candlewick Pr.

—Freakling. 2014. (Psi Chronicles Ser.). (ENG.). 320p. (J). (gr. 5). pap. 7.99 (978-0-7636-6938-6(5)) Candlewick Pr.

Kruse, Donald W. Gorilla Soup! 2012. 48p. pap. 12.95 (978-1-59663-862-4(1), Castle Keep Pr.) Rock, James A. & Co. Pubs.

—There's a Goof on My Roof. Crank, Donny, illus. 2012. 48p. pap. 12.95 (978-1-59663-855-6(9), Castle Keep Pr.) Rock, James A. & Co. Pubs.

—Where's the Gold. Shipman, Josie, illus. 2012. 50p. pap. 12.95 (978-1-59663-857-0(5), Castle Keep Pr.) Rock, James A. & Co. Pubs.

Kruusval, Catarina. Franny's Friends. Sandin, Joan, tr. from SWE. 2008. (Illus.). 32p. (J). (gr. -1-1). 16.00 (978-91-29-66836-0(0)) R & S Bks. SWE. Dist: Macmillan.

Krymski, Walter A. The Adventures of Peter Pangler Puncker: Discovering the Pumping Heart. 2005. (Illus.). 16p. (J). 17.00 (978-0-8059-9940-2(X), RoseDog Bks.) Dorrance Publishing Co., Inc.

Krystosek, Richard. Chicken Scratch. 2013. 36p. pap. 24.95 (978-1-63000-536-8(3)) America Star Bks.

Kshir, Donna M. & Potter, Sandra Dawn. The Three Little Golden Retrievers. 2010. 32p. pap. 14.50 (978-0-557-30026-6(6)) Lulu Pr., Inc.

Kubert, Adam, et al, illus. Hellfire & Brimstone, 4 vols. 2006. (ENG.). 144p. (J). (gr. -1-17). pap. 12.99 (978-0-7851-1089-7(5)) Marvel Worldwide, Inc.

Kubert, Joe. The Adventures of Yaakov & Isaac. 64p. 9.99 (978-1-58330-741-0(9)) Feldheim Pubs.

Kubik, Dorothy. The Adventures of Elbert & Leopoldina. James, Annie, illus. 2006. 104p. (J). per. 15.00 (978-0-9790775-1-7(6)) Touchstone Communications.

Kubuitsile, Lauri. Oh Bella! Yellow Band. Brown, Steve, illus. 2016. (Cambridge Reading Adventures Ser.). (ENG.). 15p. pap. 6.56 (978-1-107-55070-4(X)) Cambridge Univ. Pr.

Kuc, Jessica. Mawby the Christmas Pony. 2011. 36p. pap. 15.14 (978-1-4634-2521-0(X)) AuthorHouse.

Kuchman, D. S. Krystal Steps: The Journey Begins. 2006. 57p. pap. 16.95 (978-1-4241-5135-6(X)) America Star Bks.

Kuhl, Debra. Black Bert the Pirate, 1 vol. 2009. 83p. pap. 19.95 (978-1-60749-968-8(1)) America Star Bks.

—Sammy's Magic Carpet Ride, 1 vol. 2009. 73p. pap. 14.95 (978-1-4489-9204-1(4)) PublishAmerica, Inc.

Kuhlman, Evan. Brother from a Box. Bruno, Iacopo, illus. (ENG.). 288p. (J). (gr. 4-7). 2013. pap. 6.99 (978-1-4424-2659-7(4)) 2012. 16.99 (978-1-4424-2658-0(6)) Simon & Schuster Children's Publishing. (Atheneum Bks. for Young Readers).

Kuhlmann, Torben. Armstrong: The Adventurous Journey of a Mouse to the Moon. 2016. (ENG., Illus.). 128p. (J). 19.95 (978-0-7358-4262-5(0)) North-South Bks., Inc.

Kuhn, Krystyna & Pessah, Jon. The Game. 2012. (ENG.). 320p. (YA). (gr. 7-17). 9.99 (978-1-907411-65-6(8)) Little, Brown Book Group Ltd. GBR. Dist: Hachette Bk. Group.

Kuhn, Suzanne Brooks. Mountain Mayhem. 2017. (ENG., Illus.). 208p. (J). pap. 14.99 (978-1-943785-18-6(X), 9781943785186) Rabbit Pubs.

Kuijpers, Justin. The Dragon Myth & the Mysterious Eyeball. 2010. 58p. pap. 7.90 (978-3-8391-5033-7(7)) Bks. on Demand.

Kuipers, Jennifer L. Lynn's Magic Trunk: An Adventure in King Arthur's Court. 2007. 76p. per. 19.95 (978-1-4241-9860-3(7)) America Star Bks.

Kulikovsky-Romanoff, Grand Duchess Olga Alexandrovna, illus. The Adventures of Three White Bears. 2011. 26p. (J). pap. (978-0-9716365-2-1(4), St. Nicholas Pr.) CrossBearers Publishing.

Kuno, Dorothy. Micah. 2012. 124p. (-18). 29.99 (978-1-4797-0546-7(2)); pap. 19.99 (978-1-4797-0545-0(4)) Xlibris Corp.

Kuperman, Marina. Turtle Feet, Surfer's Beat. 2007. 164p. (J). pap. 9.99 (978-0-9801109-0-6(4)) Kuperman, Marina.

Kurd, Tariq. Gordon the Goblin in Oh My! Is That a Pork Pie? Robertson, Laura, illus. 2012. 36p. pap. (978-1-907762-10-9(8)) Malt Publishing.

Kurtz, Chris. The Adventures of a South Pole Pig: A Novel of Snow & Courage. (ENG., Illus.). 288p. (J). (gr. 5-7). 2015. pap. 7.99 (978-0-544-54070-5(0), HMH Books For Young Readers) 2013. 16.99 (978-0-547-63455-5(2)) Houghton Mifflin Harcourt Publishing Co.

Kurtz, Scott. Rides Again, Vol. 3. 2005. (ENG., Illus.). 144p. pap. 11.99 (978-1-58240-553-7(0), 9781582405537) Toonhound Studios, LLC.

Kurup, Sindhu. Baby Bear's Favorite Food Pyramid. 2011. 28p. pap. 11.99 (978-1-935268-91-8(0)) Halo Publishing International.

Kusaka, Hidenori. Pokemon Adventures. 2015. (Pokemon Adventures Ser.: 29). lib. bdg. 20.85 (978-0-606-37897-0(9)) Turtleback Bks.

—Pokémon Adventures Vol. 1: Diamond & Pearl/Platinum. 2011. (ENG., Illus.). 208p. (J). pap. 9.99 (978-1-4215-3816-7(4)) Viz Media.

—Pokémon Adventures Vol. 2: Diamond & Pearl/Platinum. 2011. (ENG., Illus.). 208p. (J). pap. 9.99 (978-1-4215-3817-4(2)) Viz Media.

—Pokémon Adventures Vol. 3: Black & White. Yamamoto, Satoshi, illus. 2014. (ENG.). 208p. (J). pap. 9.99 (978-1-4215-6178-3(6)) Viz Media.

—Pokémon Adventures Vol. 3: Diamond & Pearl/Platinum. Satoshi, Yamamoto, illus. 2011. (ENG.). 200p. (J). pap. 9.99 (978-1-4215-3818-1(0)) Viz Media.

—Pokémon Adventures Vol. 5: Diamond & Pearl/Platinum. Yamamoto, Satoshi, illus. 2012. (ENG.). 208p. (J). pap. 9.99 (978-1-4215-3913-3(6)) Viz Media.

—Pokémon Adventures Vol. 9: Diamond & Pearl/Platinum. Yamamoto, Satoshi, illus. 2013. (Pokemon Ser.: 9). (ENG.). 192p. (J). pap. 9.99 (978-1-4215-5405-1(4)) Viz Media.

—Pokémon Adventures Vol. 11: Diamond & Pearl/Platinum. Yamamoto, Satoshi, illus. 2014. (ENG.). 192p. (J). pap. 9.99 (978-1-4215-6179-0(4)) Viz Media.

—Pokémon Adventures - Diamond & Pearl/Platinum. Yamamoto, Satoshi, illus. (ENG.). (J). Vol. 6. 2012. 208p. pap. 9.99 (978-1-4215-3914-0(4)) Vol. 7. 2013. 192p. pap. 9.99 (978-1-4215-4247-8(1)) Viz Media.

—Pokémon Adventures: Black 2 & White 2, Vol. 1. Yamamoto, Satoshi, illus. 2017. (Pokemon Ser.: 1). (ENG.). 200p. (J). pap. 9.99 (978-1-4215-8437-9(9)) Viz Media.

—Pokémon Adventures: Black & White, Vol. 2. Yamamoto, Satoshi, illus. 2013. (ENG.). 192p. (J). pap. 9.99 (978-1-4215-5899-8(8)) Viz Media.

—Pokémon Adventures: Black & White, Vol. 6. Yamamoto, Satoshi, illus. 2015. (ENG.). 224p. (J). pap. 9.99 (978-1-4215-7181-2(1)) Viz Media.

—Pokémon Adventures: Diamond & Pearl/Platinum, Vol. 4. 2012. (ENG., Illus.). 216p. (J). pap. 9.99 (978-1-4215-3912-6(8)) Viz Media.

—Pokémon Adventures: Diamond & Pearl/Platinum, Vol. 8. Yamamoto, Satoshi, illus. 2013. (ENG.). 192p. (J). pap. 9.99 (978-1-4215-5404-4(6)) Viz Media.

—Pokémon Adventures Gold & Silver Box Set (set includes Vol. 8-14) 2012. (ENG.). 1552p. (J). pap. 54.99 (978-1-4215-5007-7(5)) Viz Media.

—Pokémon Adventures: Heart Gold Soul Silver, Vol. 2. 2013. (ENG., Illus.). 272p. (J). pap. 9.99 (978-1-4215-5901-8(3)) Viz Media.

—Pokémon Adventures, Vol. 1 (2nd Edition) Kusaka, Hidenori, illus. 2nd ed. 2009. (ENG., Illus.). 200p. (J). pap. 9.99 (978-1-4215-3054-3(6)) Viz Media.

—Pokémon Adventures, Vol. 11. Mato, illus. 2011. (ENG.). 208p. (J). pap. 9.99 (978-1-4215-3545-6(9)) Viz Media.

—Pokémon Adventures, Vol. 12. Mato, illus. 2011. (ENG.). 208p. (J). pap. 9.99 (978-1-4215-3546-3(7)) Viz Media.

—Pokémon Adventures, Vol. 13. 2011. (ENG., Illus.). 208p. (J). pap. 9.99 (978-1-4215-3547-0(5)) Viz Media.

—Pokémon Adventures, Vol. 14. 2011. (ENG., Illus.). 208p. (J). pap. 9.99 (978-1-4215-3548-7(3)) Viz Media.

—Pokémon Adventures, Vol. 18. Mato, illus. 2013. (ENG.). 192p. (J). pap. 9.99 (978-1-4215-3552-4(1)) Viz Media.

—Pokémon Adventures, Vol. 19. Mato, illus. 2013. (ENG.). 192p. (J). pap. 9.99 (978-1-4215-3553-1(X)) Viz Media.

—Pokémon Adventures, Vol. 2 (2nd Edition) Kusaka, Hidenori, illus. 2nd ed. 2009. (ENG., Illus.). 200p. (J). pap. 9.99 (978-1-4215-3055-0(4)) Viz Media.

—Pokémon Adventures, Vol. 22. Yamamoto, Satoshi, illus. 2014. (ENG.). 184p. (J). pap. 9.99 (978-1-4215-3556-2(4)) Viz Media.

—Pokémon Adventures, Vol. 26. Mato, illus. 2015. (ENG.). 144p. (J). pap. 9.99 (978-1-4215-3560-9(2)) Viz Media.

—Pokémon Adventures, Vol. 27. Mato, illus. 2015. (ENG.). 208p. (J). pap. 9.99 (978-1-4215-3561-6(0)) Viz Media.

—Pokémon Adventures, Vol. 6 (2nd Edition) Kusaka, Hidenori, illus. 2nd ed. 2010. (ENG., Illus.). 208p. (J). pap. 9.99 (978-1-4215-3059-8(7)) Viz Media.

—Pokémon Adventures, Vol. 7 (2nd Edition) Kusaka, Hidenori, illus. 2nd ed. 2010. (ENG., Illus.). 200p. (J). pap. 9.99 (978-1-4215-3060-4(0)) Viz Media.

—Pokémon Adventures, Vol. 8. Kusaka, Hidenori, illus. 2010. (ENG., Illus.). 200p. (J). pap. 9.99 (978-1-4215-3061-1(9)) Viz Media.

—Pokémon Black & White, Vol. 10. Yamamoto, Satoshi, illus. 2013. (ENG.). 96p. (J). pap. 4.99 (978-1-4215-5894-3(7)) Viz Media.

—Pokémon Black & White, Vol. 11. Yamamoto, Satoshi, illus. 2013. (ENG.). 96p. (J). pap. 4.99 (978-1-4215-5895-0(5)) Viz Media.

—Pokémon Black & White, Vol. 13. Yamamoto, Satoshi, illus. 2013. (ENG.). 96p. (J). pap. 4.99 (978-1-4215-5897-4(1)) Viz Media.

—Pokémon Black & White, Vol. 15. Yamamoto, Satoshi, illus. 2014. (ENG.). 80p. (J). pap. 4.99 (978-1-4215-6767-9(9)) Viz Media.

—Pokémon Black & White, Vol. 17. Yamamoto, Satoshi, illus. 2014. (ENG.). 88p. (J). pap. 4.99 (978-1-4215-6769-3(5)) Viz Media.

—Pokémon Black & White, Vol. 4. 2011. (ENG.). 80p. (J). pap. 4.99 (978-1-4215-4114-3(9)) Viz Media.

—Pokémon Black & White, Vol. 5. Yamamoto, Satoshi, illus. 2012. (ENG.). 96p. (J). pap. 4.99 (978-1-4215-4280-5(3)) Viz Media.

—Pokémon Black & White, Vol. 7. Yamamoto, Satoshi, illus. 2012. (ENG.). 96p. (J). pap. 4.99 (978-1-4215-4282-9(X)) Viz Media.

—Pokémon Black & White, Vol. 8. Yamamoto, Satoshi, illus. 2012. (ENG.). 96p. (J). pap. 4.99 (978-1-4215-4283-6(8)) Viz Media.

—Pokémon Black & White, Vol. 9. Yamamoto, Satoshi, illus. 2013. (ENG.). 96p. (J). pap. 4.99 (978-1-4215-5893-6(9)) Viz Media.

Kutner, Richard, tr. from FRE. The Suspended Castle: a Philemon Adventure: A TOON Graphic. Fred, illus. 2015. (Philemon Adventures Ser.). (ENG.). 56p. (J). (gr. 2). 16.95 (978-1-935179-86-3(1)) TOON Books / RAW Junior, LLC.

—The Wild Piano. Fred, illus. 2015. (Philemon Adventures Ser.). (ENG.). 48p. (J). (gr. 2-7). 16.95 (978-1-935179-83-2(7)) TOON Books / RAW Junior, LLC.

Kuykendoll, Kim. The Adventures of the Coral Way Gang. 2008. 160p. pap. 13.99 (978-1-60477-840-3(7)) Salem Author Services.

Kvamstrom, Todd M. The King of Pete's Pond. 2011. 84p. pap. 28.68 (978-1-4634-3523-3(1)) AuthorHouse.

Kwarta, Darlene. Walking with King Tut. 2008. 48p. pap. 9.95 (978-1-60693-040-3(0), Eloquent Bks.) Strategic Book Publishing & Rights Agency (SBPRA).

Kwaymullina, Ambelin. The Interrogation of Ashala Wolf. 2016. (ENG.). 384p. (YA). (gr. 7). pap. 8.99 (978-0-7636-8020-6(6)) Candlewick Pr.

Kyi, Tanya Lloyd. The Crystal Connection, 1 vol. 2nd ed. 2003. (Science Squad Adventure Ser.). (ENG., Illus.). 160p. (J). pap. (978-1-55285-511-9(2)) Whitecap Bks., Ltd.

Kyne, Peter B. The Three Godfathers. 2005. reprint ed. pap. 15.95 (978-1-4179-0351-1(1)) Kessinger Publishing, LLC.

Kyriakou, Marie. Mike the Little Bean: Christmas with Mike. 2012. (Illus.). 32p. pap. 22.88 (978-1-4772-4646-7(0)) AuthorHouse.

—Mike the Little Bean: Flying to the Beach! 2012. (Illus.). 40p. pap. 22.88 (978-1-4772-3041-1(6)) AuthorHouse.

—Mike the Little Bean: I'm Gonna Tickle You! 2012. (Illus.). 40p. pap. 22.88 (978-1-4772-2310-9(X)) AuthorHouse.

La Flamme Beighey, Carole. The Waddodles of Hollow Lake: The Mighty Oak. 2009. 344p. 28.49 (978-1-4389-4037-3(8))

2008. 340p. pap. 17.99 *(978-1-4343-8201-6(X))* AuthorHouse.

La-Marr, Chiquita. Sally's Adventures. 2012. 12p. pap. 10.67 *(978-1-4669-4294-3(0))* Trafford Publishing.

Laaker, Terry, illus. Charlie the Spy: Charlie's Great Adventure #6. 2008. 104p. (J). pap. 5.95 *(978-0-9702546-7-2(9))* GoodyGoody Bks.

Laar-Yond C.T. Six Fingers & the Blue Warrior. Playcrib, illus. 2013. 36p. pap. 14.00 *(978-1-62212-177-9(5)*, Strategic Bk. Publishing) Strategic Book Publishing & Rights Agency (SBPRA).

Labadie, Sally. Tanner's Turtle. Jeremiah, illus. 2012. 32p. pap. 12.95 *(978-1-61244-085-9(1))* Halo Publishing International.

Labadie, Sally Zolkosky. The Schoolhouse Mouse. 2013. 32p. pap. *(978-1-4602-3128-9(7))* FriesenPress.

Labenne, Jonathan A. Annual Bear Dance. 2013. (Illus.). 64p. pap. 23.95 *(978-1-4525-6633-7(X))* Balboa Pr.

Laberje, Reji. Max Explores Chicago. Fenech, Liza, illus. 2014. (Max Explores Ser.). (ENG.). 20p. (J). (— 1). bds. 9.95 *(978-1-62937-003-3(7))* Triumph Bks.

—Max Explores New York. Fenech, Liza, illus. 2014. (Max Explores Ser.). (ENG.). 20p. (J). (— 1). bds. 9.95 *(978-1-62937-004-0(5))* Triumph Bks.

—Max Explores San Francisco. Fenech, Liza, illus. 2014. (Max Explores Ser.). (ENG.). 20p. (J). (— 1). bds. 9.95 *(978-1-62937-005-7(3))* Triumph Bks.

LaBrant, Kenneth R. Uncle Kenny's Crazy Bedtime Stories. 2008. 73p. pap. 19.95 *(978-1-60563-602-3(9))* America Star Bks.

LaBrot, Matthew & Daniel, Hale. Green Streak. 2004. (Zeke Armstrong Mysteries Ser.: 2). 236p. (J). per. 8.95 *(978-1-929976-28-7(3))* Top Pubns., Ltd.

Lacaille, Link. Roots, Rock, Rap & Reggae, 1 vol. 2009. 25p. pap. 24.95 *(978-1-60836-930-0(7))* America Star Bks.

Lacey, Josh. Island of Thieves. 2013. (ENG.). 240p. (J). (gr. 5-7). pap. 7.99 *(978-0-544-10485-3(4))* Houghton Mifflin Harcourt Publishing Co.

—The Sultan's Tigers. 2014. (ENG.). 304p. (J). (gr. 5-7). pap. 6.99 *(978-0-544-33629-2(1)*, HMH Books For Young Readers) Houghton Mifflin Harcourt Publishing Co.

Lacey, Josh & Pakenham, Sarah. Island of Thieves. 2012. (ENG.). 240p. (J). (gr. 5-7). 15.99 *(978-0-547-76327-9(1))* Houghton Mifflin Harcourt Publishing Co.

Lackey, Mercedes. Apex. 2017. (Hunter Ser.: 3). (ENG.). 304p. (YA). (gr. 7-17). 18.99 ***(978-1-4847-0786-9(9))*** Hyperion Bks. for Children.

—Elite: A Hunter Novel. (Hunter Ser.). (ENG.). (YA). (gr. 7-17). 2017. 384p. pap. 9.99 ***(978-1-4847-4784-1(4))*** 2016. (Illus.). 368p. 17.99 *(978-1-4847-0785-2(0))* Hyperion Bks. for Children.

—Elite: A Hunter Novel. 2017. (Hunter Ser.: 2). (YA). lib. bdg. 20.85 ***(978-0-606-40645-1(X))*** Turtleback Bks.

Lackey, Mercedes. Hunter. 2016. (Hunter Ser.). (ENG., Illus.). 400p. (YA). (gr. 7-12). pap. 9.99 *(978-1-4847-2543-6(3))* Hyperion Bks. for Children.

—Hunter. 2016. (Hunter Ser.: 1). (YA). lib. bdg. 20.85 *(978-0-606-38309-7(3))* Turtleback Bks.

Lackey, Mercedes, ed. Hunter. 2015. (Hunter Ser.). (ENG., Illus.). 380p. (YA). (gr. 7-12). 17.99 *(978-1-4847-0784-5(2))* Hyperion Bks. for Children.

Lacie, Tony. A Man Called Avalon. 2006. 156p. per. 15.63 *(978-1-4120-5609-0(8))* Trafford Publishing.

Lade, Linda. Peter Bunny: Adventures in the Kudzu Pat. 2006. 82p. pap. 16.95 *(978-1-4241-3818-0(3))* PublishAmerica, Inc.

Ladew, Donald. Troop 402: A Novel. 2003. 178p. (YA). pap. 13.95 *(978-0-595-27317-1(3)*, Writers Club Pr.) iUniverse, Inc.

Ladig, Kim. Ellie's Lake House. 2010. 48p. pap. 19.49 *(978-1-4490-5641-4(5))* AuthorHouse.

Ladybird, Ladybird & Swift, Jonathan. Gulliver's Travels. Duffy, Ciaran, illus. 2015. (Ladybird Classics Ser.). (ENG.). 72p. (J). (gr. 1-3). 8.99 *(978-1-4093-1127-0(9))* Penguin Bks., Ltd. GBR. Dist: Independent Pubs. Group.

LaFevers, R. L. The Basilisk's Lair. Murphy, Kelly, illus. (Nathaniel Fludd, Beastologist Ser.: 2). (ENG.). 160p. (J). (gr. 1-4). 2011. pap. 6.99 *(978-0-547-54957-6(1))* 2nd ed. 2010. 15.00 *(978-0-547-23867-8(3))* Houghton Mifflin Harcourt Publishing Co.

—Flight of the Phoenix Bk. 1. Murphy, Kelly, illus. 2010. (Nathaniel Fludd, Beastologist Ser.: 1). (ENG.). 144p. (J). (gr. 1-4). pap. 5.99 *(978-0-547-40845-3(5))* Houghton Mifflin Harcourt Publishing Co.

—Theodosia & the Serpents of Chaos. Tanaka, Yoko, illus. 2008. (ENG.). 352p. (J). (gr. 2-5). pap. 7.99 *(978-0-618-99976-7(0))* Houghton Mifflin Harcourt Publishing Co.

—The Wyverns' Treasure. 2012. (Nathaniel Fludd, Beastologist Ser.: 3). lib. bdg. 16.00 *(978-0-606-24516-6(2)*, Turtleback) Turtleback Bks.

LaFleur, James & Massie, Gordon. Order Of 5ive: The Complete First Season. Dalglish, Rich, ed. 2012. (ENG.). 308p. (YA). pap. 8.99 *(978-1-935702-09-2(2))* Middleton Publishing.

LaFleur, John & Dubin, Shawn. The Misadventures of Dreary & Naughty, 1 vol. 2013. (ENG., Illus.). 64p. (J). 14.99 *(978-0-7643-4494-7(3)*, 9780764344947) Schiffer Publishing, Ltd.

Lagasse, Paul. Seeing Through Clouds: The Story of an Airship Apprentice. 2006. 180p. per. 11.95 *(978-1-59858-115-7(5))* Dog Ear Publishing, LLC.

Lagerlöf, Selma. The Further Adventures of Nils. 2005. pap. 31.95 *(978-1-4179-9042-9(2))* Kessinger Publishing, LLC.

—The Further Adventures of Nils. Howard, Velma Swanston, tr. 2003. 284p. pap. 14.95 *(978-1-59224-320-4(7))*; 32.95 *(978-1-59224-541-3(2))* Wildside Pr., LLC.

—The Wonderful Adventures of Nils. l.t. ed. 2007. pap. 28.99 *(978-1-4346-2240-2(1))* Creative Media Partners, LLC.

—The Wonderful Adventures of Nils. Howard, Velma Swanston, tr. 2007. 440p. per. *(978-1-4065-2572-4(3))* Dodo Pr.

—The Wonderful Adventures of Nils. 2009. 360p. (gr. 4-7). pap. 10.99 *(978-1-60459-624-3(4))* Wilder Pubns., Corp.

Lagonegro, Melissa. A Tale of Two Sisters. Random House Disney Staff, illus. 2013. (Step into Reading Ser.). (ENG.). 32p. (J). (gr. -1-1). 3.99 *(978-0-7364-3120-0(9)*, RH/Disney) Random Hse. Children's Bks.

Lagonegro, Melissa & Redbank, Tennant. Five Toy Tales. 2012. (Step into Reading Level 1 Ser.). lib. bdg. 18.40 *(978-0-606-23853-3(0)*, Turtleback) Turtleback Bks.

Lagrow, Victoria. The Adventures of the Magical Hubcap Kid. 2005. pap. 33.49 *(978-1-4208-7981-0(2))* AuthorHouse.

Laguatan, Alwen & Buada, Joselito. Kobi. 2013. 40p. pap. 24.95 *(978-1-63000-853-6(2))* America Star Bks.

Lahan, Tim. Nosyhood. 2016. (ENG., Illus.). 60p. (gr. -1). 16.95 *(978-1-938073-93-9(2))* McSweeney's Publishing.

LaHaye, Tim & Jenkins, Jerry B. Dejados Atrás. 2003. (Left Behind Ser.).Tr. of Left Behind. (SPA., Illus.). 48p. 4.99 *(978-0-8054-2843-8(7))*; Vol. 2. pap. 4.99 *(978-0-8054-2847-6(X))*; Vol. 3. 4.99 *(978-0-8054-2844-5(5))* B&H Publishing Group.

Lahey, Thomas A. King of the Pygmies. 2005. pap. 28.95 *(978-1-4179-9360-4(X))* Kessinger Publishing, LLC.

Lai, Trevor. Tomo Explores the World. Lai, Trevor, illus. 2016. (Tomo's Adventure Journal Ser.). (ENG., Illus.). 40p. (J). 17.99 *(978-1-250-08545-0(4)*, 9781250085450) Imprint IND. Dist: Macmillan.

Laible, Steve William, ed. Dandylion. Berry, VacieAnna, illus. 2012. (ENG.). 38p. (J). pap. 9.95 *(978-0-9844784-6-0(9)*, Empire Holdins - Literary Division for Young Readers) Kodel Group, LLC, The.

Laidlaw, S. J. An Infidel in Paradise. 2013. (ENG., Illus.). 314p. (YA). (gr. 7). 19.95 *(978-1-77049-304-9(2)*, Tundra Bks.) Tundra Bks. CAN. Dist: Penguin Random Hse. LLC.

—The Voice Inside My Head. 2014. (ENG., Illus.). 252p. (YA). (gr. 9). 17.99 *(978-1-77049-565-4(7)*, Tundra Bks.) Tundra Bks. CAN. Dist: Penguin Random Hse. LLC.

LAIKA. The Boxtrolls: Make Your Own Boxtroll Punch-Out Activity Book. 2014. (ENG., Illus.). 12p. (J). (gr. 3-7). pap. 7.99 *(978-0-316-33268-2(2))* Little, Brown Bks. for Young Readers.

LAIKA & Fox, Jennifer. The Boxtrolls: Meet the Boxtrolls. 2014. (Passport to Reading Level 2 Ser.). (ENG., Illus.). 32p. (J). (gr. -1-3). pap. 3.99 *(978-0-316-33266-8(6))* Little, Brown Bks. for Young Readers.

Lairamore, Dawn. Ivy's Ever After. 2013. (ENG.). 192p. (J). (gr. 2-7). pap. 7.99 *(978-0-8234-2937-0(7))* Holiday Hse., Inc.

Lake, A. J. The Circle of Stone. 2008. (Darkest Age Ser.). (ENG.). 304p. (YA). (gr. 4-7). 16.95 *(978-1-59990-079-7(3)*, 9781599900797, Bloomsbury USA Childrens) Bloomsbury Publishing USA.

Lake, Autumn. The Terrible Day. 2011. 32p. pap. 24.95 *(978-1-4560-0949-6(4))* America Star Bks.

Lake, Nick. Blood Ninja. 2009. (ENG., Illus.). 384p. (YA). (gr. 7-18). 16.99 *(978-1-4169-8627-0(8)*, Simon & Schuster Bks. For Young Readers) Simon & Schuster Bks. For Young Readers.

—Hostage Three. 2014. (ENG.). 400p. (YA). (gr. 7). pap. 9.99 *(978-1-61963-438-1(4)*, 9781619634381, Bloomsbury USA Childrens) 2013. (ENG.). 384p. (YA). (gr. 7). 17.99 *(978-1-61963-123-6(7)*, 9781619631236, Bloomsbury USA Childrens) 2013. 368p. 17.99 *(978-1-61963-149-6(0))* Bloomsbury Publishing USA.

Lamar, Lloyd. The Pond. 2007. 92p. per. 9.99 *(978-1-60477-286-9(7))* Salem Author Services.

Lamb, Enelle. Christopher Collin & the True Okemus - the Adventure Begins. 2009. 123p. pap. 13.00 *(978-0-557-05783-2(3))* Lulu Pr., Inc.

Lamb, Jowana. Makhi & the Run Away Elephant. 2012. 28p. pap. 15.99 *(978-1-4771-3820-5(X))* Xlibris Corp.

Lamb, Lenny. Moving Blues: Greener Grass. 2011. 32p. pap. 24.95 *(978-1-4626-4398-1(1))* America Star Bks.

Lamb, Phillip C. Ace Canary & Dud Clutch. Lamb, Michael, illus. 2011. 40p. pap. 24.95 *(978-1-4626-0401-2(3))* America Star Bks.

Lamb, Tanya. Kyle's One Day Adventures. 2005. (J). pap. 16.00 *(978-0-8059-6683-1(8))* Dorrance Publishing Co., Inc.

Lambert, Nancy & Lamb, Anne. Help! 2017. (Beat Bugs Ser.). 24p. (J). (gr. -1-3). pap. 3.99 *(978-0-06-264060-4(7)*, HarperFestival) HarperCollins Pubs.

Lambert, Nancy R. Falcon Fear of Flying. 2016. (Marvel World of Reading Level 2 Ser.). (J). lib. bdg. 13.55 *(978-0-606-37537-5(6))* Turtleback Bks.

Lambert, Patricia. The Blue Ribbon Chicken. 2005. 36p. (J). pap. 14.93 *(978-1-4116-6163-9(X))* Lulu Pr., Inc.

Lammers, Elizabeth A. & McKinney, Dan. Pierre's Stupendous Birthday Bash. Epstein, Gabriela, illus. 2011. 48p. pap. 24.95 *(978-1-4560-4294-3(7))* America Star Bks.

—The Tale of the Black Igloo: Another Adventure of Pepe & Pierre, 1 vol. Epstein, Gabriela, illus. 2010. 26p. pap. 24.95 *(978-1-60610-433-0(0))* PublishAmerica, Inc.

Lamonica, Lisa. You & Me As Big As the Se. 2008. 20p. pap. 24.95 *(978-1-60563-390-9(9))* America Star Bks.

Lamont, Tracey. The Adventures of Speedy & Creedy: Mrs. Smith's Kitchen. 2008. (ENG.). 32p. 14.49 *(978-1-4389-3043-5(7))* AuthorHouse.

—The Adventures of Speedy & Creedy: The Surprise. 2009. 36p. pap. 16.50 *(978-1-4389-7541-2(4))* AuthorHouse.

La'more, Sheila. Runt: The Omega Wolf. 2007. 48p. per. 16.95 *(978-1-4241-8222-0(0))* PublishAmerica, Inc.

Lamphere-Slaughter, Sharyn. Droopy Drawers & the Peg Leg Pirate. 2009. 24p. pap. 12.99 *(978-1-4490-6055-8(2))* AuthorHouse.

Lampman, Evelyn Sibley. The Shy Stegosaurus of Cricket Creek. Buel, Hubert, illus. 2007. 218p. (J). (gr. 4-7). per. 12.00 *(978-1-930900-37-0(6))* Purple Hse. Pr.

Lancaster, Janie. Julie & the Lost Fairy Tale. 2006. (Illus.). 116p. (J). per. 10.95 *(978-1-932993-60-8(6))* Star Publish LLC.

Lancaster, Mike A. The Future We Left Behind. 2012. (ENG.). 384p. (J). (gr. 7). 16.99 *(978-1-60684-410-6(5)*, Carolrhoda Lab™) Lerner Publishing Group.

Lancaster, Susan. The Caves & the Skull. 2004. 160p. pap. *(978-0-9730350-1-8(3))* Snosrap Publishing.

Lancett, Peter. The Bridge of Dark Tears, 1 vol. unabr. ed. 2011. (Dark Man Ser.). (ENG.). 47p. (YA). (gr. 9-12). 7.95 *(978-1-61651-294-1(6))* Saddleback Educational Publishing, Inc.

—Dark Machine. 2007. (Dark Man Ser.). (ENG.). 36p. pap. *(978-1-84167-601-2(2))* Ransom Publishing Ltd.

—Day Is Dark. 2007. (Dark Man Ser.). (ENG.). 36p. pap. *(978-1-84167-606-7(3))* Ransom Publishing Ltd.

—Dying for the Dark. 2007. (Dark Man Ser.). (ENG.). 36p. pap. *(978-1-84167-604-3(7))* Ransom Publishing Ltd.

—Fear in the Dark (Blue Series), 1 vol. 2015. (Dark Man Ser.). (ENG.). 36p. (YA). (gr. 9-12). pap. 7.95 *(978-1-68021-128-3(5))* Saddleback Educational Publishing, Inc.

The Land Beyond Forever. 2006. 25.00 *(978-0-9785570-0-3(X))* Three Sisters Publishing Hse., Ltd.

Landers, Ace. Anakin to the Rescue! White, David A., illus. 2012. (Lego Star Wars Ser.). (ENG.). 24p. (J). (gr. -1-3). pap. 3.99 *(978-0-545-47066-7(8))* Scholastic, Inc.

—Emmet's Guide to Being Awesome. Scholastic, Inc. Staff, illus. 2014. (LEGO: the LEGO Movie Ser.). (ENG.). 128p. (J). (gr. 2-5). 9.99 *(978-0-545-79532-6(X))* Scholastic, Inc.

—The Padawan Menace. 2012. (Lego Star Wars Ser.). (ENG.). 32p. (J). (gr. 2-5). pap. 3.99 *(978-0-545-40450-1(9)*, Scholastic Paperbacks) Scholastic, Inc.

—Yoda's Secret Missions, Bk. 1. Ameet Studio Staff, illus. 2014. (Lego Star Wars Ser.). (ENG.). 64p. (J). (gr. 2-5). pap. 4.99 *(978-0-545-65700-6(8))* Scholastic, Inc.

Landers, Melissa. Starfall. 2017. (Starflight Ser.). (ENG.). 368p. (YA). (gr. 9-17). 17.99 *(978-1-4847-5025-4(X))* Hyperion Bks. for Children.

—Starflight. 2017. (ENG.). 384p. (YA). (gr. 9-17). pap. 9.99 *(978-1-4847-4786-5(0))* Hyperion Bks. for Children.

—Starflight. 2016. (ENG., Illus.). 364p. (YA). (gr. 7-12). 17.99 *(978-1-4847-2324-1(4))* Hyperion Pr.

Landis, David. Papercuttables. 2017. (ENG.). 80p. (J). (gr. 1-3). pap. 8.99 *(978-0-545-83488-9(0)*, Cartwheel Bks.) Scholastic, Inc.

Landy, Derek. The Faceless Ones: A California Gothic. 2007. (Skulduggery Pleasant Ser.: Bk. 3). (SPA.). 335p. *(978-84-675-1984-6(3))* SM Ediciones.

Lane, Amy. Triane's Son Reigning. 2nd ed. 2016. (ENG., Illus.). (J). 29.99 ***(978-1-63477-984-5(3))*** 2014. (Bitter Moon Ser.: Bk. 4). 320p. pap. 17.99 *(978-1-62798-343-3(0))* Dreamspinner Pr. (Harmony Ink Pr.).

Lane, Andrew. Snake Bite. 2014. (Sherlock Holmes: the Legend Begins Ser.: 5). (ENG.). 304p. (YA). (gr. 7-12). 17.99 *(978-0-374-37090-9(7)*, 9780374370909, Farrar, Straus & Giroux (BYR)) Farrar, Straus & Giroux.

Lane, Jean E. Lill & Mewe Journey to the Ocean of Runa. 2013. 122p. pap. 11.95 *(978-1-62212-538-8(X)*, Strategic Bk. Publishing) Strategic Book Publishing & Rights Agency (SBPRA).

Lane, Jessica E. The Secret of the Swans. 2009. 52p. pap. 31.99 *(978-1-4415-5517-5(X))* Xlibris Corp.

Lane, Leonie. Fork Tongue Freimon. 2006. 164p. per. *(978-1-84667-009-1(8))* Derwent Pr., The.

—The Retford Witch Catchers. 2005. 144p. per. *(978-1-84667-002-2(0))* Derwent Pr., The.

Lane, M. J. & Lane, M. J. Where in the World Is Snickers? 2011. 42p. pap. 19.99 *(978-0-557-81843-3(5))* Lulu Pr., Inc.

Lang, Valerie E. Jet's Day: A Whisker Team Story. 2011. 32p. pap. 13.00 *(978-1-61204-178-0(7)*, Strategic Bk. Publishing) Strategic Book Publishing & Rights Agency (SBPRA).

Langan, Paul. Summer of Secrets. Langan, Paul, ed. 2004. (Bluford Ser.: 10). 142p. (YA). mass mkt. 4.95 *(978-1-59194-018-0(4))* Townsend Pr.

Langan, Paul & Blackwell, D. M. Blood Is Thicker. Langan, Paul, ed. 2004. (Bluford Ser.: 8). 156p. (YA). mass mkt. 4.95 *(978-1-59194-016-6(8))* Townsend Pr.

Langen, Annette. Felix Explores Planet Earth. Droop, Constanza, illus. 2004. (Perfect for Earth Day Promotions! Ser.). 47p. (J). 14.99 *(978-1-59384-030-3(6))* Parklane Publishing.

Langley, C. Kevin. Brer Rabbit Comic. 2009. 16p. pap. 9.80 *(978-0-557-11631-7(7))* Lulu Pr., Inc.

Langner, Mark Eugene. The One Window. 2012. 264p. pap. 13.95 *(978-0-9840120-2-2(8))* Aliso Street Productions.

Langridge, Roger. Snarked, Vol. 3. 2013. (Snarked Ser.). (ENG., Illus.). 112p. (J). (gr. 4). pap. 14.99 *(978-1-60886-295-5(X))* Boom! Studios.

Langridge, Roger & Cox, Alex. Adventure Time Vol. 2: Sugary Shorts Mathematical Edition. 2016. lib. bdg. 33.05 *(978-0-606-38730-9(7))* Turtleback Bks.

Langrish, Katherine. Troll Blood. Stevens, Tim & Wyatt, David, illus. 2008. 352p. (gr. 5-8). (ENG.). (J). 16.99 *(978-0-06-111674-2(2))*; (YA). lib. bdg. 17.89 *(978-0-06-111675-9(0)*, Eos) HarperCollins Pubs.

Langworthy, John Luther. The Aeroplane Boys Flight. 2004. reprint ed. pap. 1.99 *(978-1-4192-5169-6(4))* Kessinger Publishing, LLC.

Lanier, Renee Comeaux. Ruby's Reading Tree. 2012. 24p. pap. 17.99 *(978-1-4772-0716-1(3))* AuthorHouse.

Lansdowne, Marcella. The Adventures of Patty & Annabel: Apache Lake & the Chakras. 2009. 28p. pap. 15.95 *(978-1-4389-1643-9(4))* AuthorHouse.

—The Adventures of Patty & Annabel: The Javelinas & Releasing the Cords. 2009. 28p. pap. 15.95 *(978-1-4389-1645-3(0))* AuthorHouse.

—The Adventures of Patty & Annabel: The Monsoon & the Auric Field. 2009. 28p. pap. 15.95 *(978-1-4389-4786-0(0))* AuthorHouse.

Lansky, Bruce. Polar BRRR Delivers. Wummer, Amy, illus. 2010. 10p. (J). bds. 6.99 *(978-1-4169-9318-6(5))* Meadowbrook Pr.

Lansky, Bruce & Johnson, Martha. Girls to the Rescue, Bk. 5. 108p. (J). pap. *(978-0-88166-315-0(8))* Meadowbrook Pr.

Lansley, Oliver. Holly & Ivan's Christmas Adventure. 2012. (ENG., Illus.). 96p. (J). (gr. k-5). pap. 16.95 *(978-1-84943-136-1(1))* Oberon Bks., Ltd. GBR. Dist: Consortium Bk. Sales & Distribution.

Lapid, Koty. The Wild Virtual Enchanted Garden. 2005. 41p. (J). per. 16.18 *(978-1-4116-2068-1(2))* Lulu Pr., Inc.

Lapin Feeblebunny. The Gang That Couldn't Think Straight. 2005. 83p. pap. 10.00 *(978-1-4134-9979-7(1))* Xlibris Corp.

LaPorte, Tom. Hembree Heiroglyphs. 2008. 98p. pap. 9.42 *(978-1-4357-5970-1(2))* Lulu Pr., Inc.

Lapytski, Serge & Lapytski, Kristina. The Heart of a Lion! E-Hare. 2011. 84p. pap. 12.84 *(978-1-4567-4281-2(7))* AuthorHouse.

LaReau, Kara. Unintentional Adventures of the Bland Sisters. Hill, Jen, illus. 2017. (ENG.). 176p. (J). (gr. 3-7). 14.95 *(978-1-4197-2136-6(4)*, Amulet Bks.) Abrams, Inc.

Larner, Eric. The Adventure of Paperman - Journey into Night. Schmolze, Ian, illus. 2013. 194p. pap. 16.99 *(978-1-883651-68-8(9))* Winters Publishing.

LaRochelle, David. Arlo's ARTrageous Adventure! Includes 50 Flaps to Flip. 2013. (ENG., Illus.). 28p. (J). (gr. -1-3). 14.95 *(978-1-4027-9226-7(3))* Sterling Publishing Co., Inc.

LaRocque, Greg. Crybaby: Extinction. Castillo, Cesar & Burruss, Melissa, illus. 2005. (YA). per. 9.99 *(978-1-933570-86-0(5))* Aardvark Global Publishing.

Larosa, Marjanita. Mosquit: The Very Disobedient Mosquito. 2012. 36p. pap. 16.95 *(978-1-4497-3283-7(6)*, WestBow Pr.) Author Solutions, Inc.

Larose, Melinda. Surfin' Turf. 2014. (World of Reading Ser.). (J). lib. bdg. 13.55 *(978-0-606-34108-0(0)*, Turtleback) Turtleback Bks.

LaRose, Melinda & Disney Book Group Staff. Bucky Makes a Splash! Disney Storybook Artists Staff, illus. 2013. (ENG.). 16p. (J). (gr. -1-k). pap. 4.99 *(978-1-4231-6389-3(3))* Disney Pr.

—The Croc Takes the Cake. Disney Storybook Artists Staff, illus. 2012. (World of Reading Ser.). (ENG.). 32p. (J). (gr. -1-k). pap. 3.99 *(978-1-4231-5543-0(2))* Disney Pr.

—Jake & the Never Land Pirates Treasure of the Tides. Disney Storybook Artists Staff, illus. 2014. (ENG.). 32p. (J). (gr. -1-k). pap. 3.99 *(978-1-4231-9422-4(5))* Disney Pr.

—Jake Hatches a Plan, Pre-Level 1. Disney Storybook Art Team, illus. 2012. (World of Reading Ser.). (ENG.). 32p. (J). (gr. -1-k). pap. 3.99 *(978-1-4231-5542-3(4))* Disney Pr.

Larry, H. I. Frozen Fear. Oswald, Ash, illus. 2008. (Zac Power Ser.: 4). (ENG.). 96p. (J). (gr. 3-6). pap. 4.99 *(978-0-312-34656-0(5)*, 9780312346560) Square Fish.

—Mind Games. Oswald, Ash, illus. 2008. (Zac Power Ser.: 3). (ENG.). 96p. (J). (gr. 3-6). pap. 4.99 *(978-0-312-34657-7(3)*, 9780312346577) Square Fish.

—Zac's Bank Bust. 2014. (Zac Power Test Drive Ser.: 7). (ENG.). 56p. (J). (gr. k-2). 7.99 *(978-1-921502-09-5(6))* Hardie Grant Egmont Pty, Ltd. AUS. Dist: Independent Pubs. Group.

—Zac's Shark Attack. 2014. (Zac Power Test Drive Ser.: 8). (ENG.). 56p. (J). (gr. k-2). 7.99 *(978-1-921502-10-1(X))* Hardie Grant Egmont Pty, Ltd. AUS. Dist: Independent Pubs. Group.

Larsa, Angela. Norman PhartEphant. 2009. (J). pap. *(978-1-61623-643-4(4))* Independent Pub.

Larsen, Alison. Thomas the Turtle's Adventures. 2006. (Illus.). 23p. (J). per. 14.95 *(978-1-60002-096-4(8)*, 3962) Mountain Valley Publishing, LLC.

Larsen, Elizabeth. Buster Hardings: Buster Makes New Friends. 2008. 104p. pap. 19.95 *(978-1-60563-951-2(6))* America Star Bks.

—Open House at Buster's New School: Season 1, Book 2: Buster Hardings, 1 vol. 2010. 85p. pap. 19.95 *(978-1-60749-559-8(7))* America Star Bks.

Larsen, Erik, et al. Image Comics. ltd. ed. 2005. (ENG., Illus.). 128p. (YA). 75.00 *(978-1-58240-257-4(4)*, 9781582402574) Image Comics.

Larsen, Kirsten. Dora & the Baby Crab. Roper, Robert, illus. 2008. (Dora the Explorer Ser.: 17). (ENG.). 24p. (J). (gr. -1-1). pap. 3.99 *(978-1-4169-5451-4(1)*, Simon Spotlight/Nickelodeon) Simon Spotlight/Nickelodeon.

Larson, Abigail. Alice's Wonderfilled Adventures: Coloring Pages for Adults up for a Wonderfilled Exploration of Wonderland. 2016. (ENG.). 144p. pap. 14.99 *(978-1-4403-4668-2(2)*, Impact) F&W Media, Inc.

Larson, Hope. Compass South. Mock, Rebecca, illus. 2016. (Four Points Ser.: 1). (ENG.). 224p. (J). 17.99 *(978-0-374-30043-2(7)*, 9780374300432, Farrar, Straus & Giroux (BYR)) Farrar, Straus & Giroux.

—Knife's Edge: A Graphic Novel. Mock, Rebecca, illus. 2017. (Four Points Ser.: 2). (ENG.). 224p. (J). 19.99 *(978-0-374-30044-9(5)*, 9780374300449, Farrar, Straus & Giroux (BYR)) Farrar, Straus & Giroux.

Larson, Kirby. Audacity Jones Steals the Show (Audacity Jones #2) 2017. (Audacity Jones Ser.: 2). (ENG.). 192p. (J). (gr. 3-7). 16.99 *(978-0-545-84065-1(1)*, Scholastic Pr.) Scholastic, Inc.

—Audacity Jones to the Rescue. 2016. (Audacity Jones Ser.: 1). (ENG.). 224p. (J). (gr. 3-7). pap. 6.99 *(978-0-545-84060-6(0))*; 16.99 *(978-0-545-84056-9(2))* Scholastic, Inc. (Scholastic Pr.).

—Audacity Jones to the Rescue. 2016. (Audacity Jones Ser.: 1). lib. bdg. 17.20 ***(978-0-606-39708-7(6))*** Turtleback Bks.

Larson, M. A. Pennyroyal Academy. 2014. (Pennyroyal Academy Ser.: 1). (ENG.). 320p. (J). (gr. 5). 16.99 *(978-0-399-16324-1(7)*, G.P. Putnam's Sons Books for Young Readers) Penguin Young Readers Group.

Larson, Mark. The Adventures of Pinky, the Pink Flamingo. 2008. 24p. pap. 24.95 *(978-1-60610-046-2(7))* America Star Bks.

Larson, Rachel. Jesse Strong & Courageous Runaway: There Comes A Time When the Roads of Destiny Will No Longer Wait... 2011. 192p. (J). (gr. -1). pap. 14.03 *(978-1-4520-0421-1(8))* AuthorHouse.

Larson, Sara B. Defy. 2014. (Defy Trilogy: Bk. 1). (ENG.). 336p. (J). (gr. 7). 17.99 *(978-0-545-59758-6(7)*, Scholastic Pr.) Scholastic, Inc.

—Endure. 2015. (Defy Trilogy: Bk. 3). (ENG.). 320p. (J). (gr. 7). 17.99 *(978-0-545-64490-7(9)*, Scholastic Pr.) Scholastic, Inc.

—Ignite. 2014. (Defy Trilogy: Bk. 2). (ENG.). 304p. (J). (gr. 7). 17.99 *(978-0-545-64474-7(7)*, Scholastic Pr.) Scholastic, Inc.

L.A.S., Alex. Magnificent Sir Johnny & Santa Claus. 2011. 36p. pap. 24.95 *(978-1-4626-3401-9(X))* America Star Bks.

Lashawn Graves, M. Ed. Listen & Embrace When Children Care. 2012. 28p. pap. 9.95 *(978-1-4327-8895-7(7))* Outskirts Pr., Inc.

Lasher, Kathy. Heinrich Streudleman Climbs Mt. Baker. 2010. 32p. pap. 14.49 *(978-1-4520-2090-7(6))* AuthorHouse.

Lasky, Kathryn. Blood Secret. 2004. (Illus.). 256p. (J). (gr. 7-18). lib. bdg. 16.89 *(978-0-06-000065-3(1))* HarperCollins Pubs.

—The Burning. 2004. (Guardians of Ga'hoole Ser.: 6). (ENG., Illus.). 224p. (J). (gr. 3-7). 6.99 *(978-0-439-40562-1(9)*, Scholastic Paperbacks) Scholastic, Inc.

—The Capture. 2003. (Guardians of Ga'hoole Ser.: 1). (ENG.). 240p. (J). (gr. 3-7). mass mkt. 6.99 *(978-0-439-40557-7(2)*, Scholastic Paperbacks) Scholastic, Inc.

—The First Collier. 2006. (Guardians of Ga'hoole Ser.: 9). (ENG.). 208p. (J). (gr. 3-7). 6.99 *(978-0-439-79568-5(0)*, Scholastic Paperbacks) Scholastic, Inc.

—Night Witches: A Novel of World War II. 2017. (ENG.). 224p. (J). (gr. 7). 17.99 (978-0-545-68298-5(3), Scholastic Pr.) Scholastic, Inc.

—Wild Blood. 2016. (Horses of the Dawn Ser.: 3). (ENG., Illus.). 208p. (J). (gr. 3-7). 16.99 (978-0-545-68300-5(9), Scholastic Pr.) Scholastic, Inc.

Lasky, Ricki & Siqueiros, Paula. The Brave Adventures of Captain Courage: The Bully. 2012. (Illus.). (J). 14.95 (978-1-62086-095-3(3)) Mascot Bks., Inc.

Lassiter, Erin & Garcia, Jolanda. EarTwiggle's Adventure 1: The Treasure Hunt. 2004. (Illus.). (J). 12.99 (978-0-9762573-0-1(0)) Ear Twiggles Productions, Inc.

Lassiter, Rhiannon. Shadows. 2011. (Hex Ser.: 2). (ENG.). 272p. (YA). (gr. 7). pap. 12.99 (978-1-4424-3103-4(2), Simon Pulse) Simon Pulse.

Last, Mary. The Ghost of Dark Swamp Road. 2011. 108p. pap. 7.95 (978-1-257-13238-6(5)) Lulu Pr., Inc.

Lathrop, Brandy. Jalen Goes to Mars. 2008. 22p. pap. 24.95 (978-1-4241-9010-2(X)) America Star Bks.

Latimer, Miriam. Little Red Riding Hood. 2013. (Classic Fairy Tale Pop-Ups Ser.). (ENG.). 12p. (J). (gr. -1-1). 12.99 (978-0-7641-6598-6(4)) Barron's Educational Series, Inc.

The Laughing Snowman. 2003. (J). per. (978-1-57657-924-4(7)) Paradise Pr., Inc.

Laura Beth. Two Girls 2 Cats: A Magical Mystery, 1 vol. 2010. 130p. pap. 24.95 (978-1-4489-4235-0(7)) PublishAmerica, Inc.

Laura Lee Hope. The Moving Picture Girls at Oak Farm. 2007. 180p. per. 11.95 (978-1-4218-3990-5(3), 1st World Library - Literary Society) 1st World Publishing, Inc.

—Six Little Bunkers at Cowboy Jack's. 2007. 180p. per. 11.95 (978-1-4218-3988-2(1), 1st World Library - Literary Society) 1st World Publishing, Inc.

—Six Little Bunkers at Grandpa Ford's. 2007. 188p. per. 11.95 (978-1-4218-3989-9(X), 1st World Library - Literary Society) 1st World Publishing, Inc.

Laurel Associates. Kidnapped Study Guide: The Complete Adventures of David Balfour. 2006. (Classics Ser.). (Illus.). 48p. (YA). per. 17.95 (978-1-56254-874-2(3)) Saddleback Educational Publishing, Inc.

Laurentine, Florianne Daphne. The Mystery Chronicles: The Unknown Masterpiece & the Case of the Practical Joker. 2012. 98p. pap. 7.99 (978-1-61667-427-4(X)) Raider Publishing International.

Laurie, Victoria. When. 2016. (YA). lib. bdg. 20.85 **(978-0-606-39883-1(X))** Turtleback Bks.

Lauterbach, B. L. Home-Grown Experiences. 2008. 68p. pap. 7.95 (978-1-4327-2620-1(X)) Outskirts Pr., Inc.

Lauzon, Christi. Where's Owen Goin'? 2009. 40p. pap. 14.75 (978-1-60860-543-9(4), Eloquent Bks.) Strategic Book Publishing & Rights Agency (SBPRA).

Lavigne, Mark Hunter. Les Aventures de Matilda la Fée des Dents: Premier Épisode. 2013. 28p. pap. 19.99 (978-1-4817-0124-2(X)) AuthorHouse.

Lavohn, Jodi. Sam's Adventure. 2011. 54p. pap. 16.95 (978-1-4560-7758-7(9)) America Star Bks.

Law, Jerel. Spirit Fighter, 1 vol. 2012. (Son of Angels, Jonah Stone Ser.). (ENG.). 256p. (J). pap. 9.99 (978-1-4003-1843-8(2)) Nelson, Thomas Inc.

—Truth Runner, 1 vol. 2013. (Son of Angels, Jonah Stone Ser.). (ENG.). 272p. (J). pap. 9.99 (978-1-4003-2287-9(1)) Nelson, Thomas Inc.

Lawati, A. The Jungle Adventure of Chimpoo. 2011. 40p. pap. 21.99 (978-1-4634-2921-8(5)) AuthorHouse.

Lawes, Alexander. Peter & the Enchanted Cavern. 2012. 140p. pap. (978-1-909395-25-1(0)) Legend Pr.

Lawhorn, Mary Joyce. When Annie Dreams. 2012. 74p. pap. 8.95 (978-1-4697-8819-7(5)) iUniverse, Inc.

Lawrence, Caroline. The Colossus of Rhodes. 2005. (ENG., Illus.). 224p. (gr. 7-9). pap. 10.99 (978-1-84255-138-7(8), Orion Children's Bks.) Hachette Children's Group GBR. Dist: Hachette Bk. Group.

—The Secrets of Vesuvius. 2004. (Roman Mysteries Ser.). (Illus.). 173p. (J). (gr. 3-7). 13.65 (978-0-7569-5947-0(0)) Perfection Learning Corp.

Lawrence, David L. The New Adventure of Geoffrey & Chongo: Book 2. 2011. 40p. pap. 16.75 (978-1-4634-4607-9(1)) AuthorHouse.

Lawrence, Hilary R. The Adventures of Little Ted. 2009. (ENG., Illus.). 154p. pap. (978-1-84748-587-8(1)) Athena Pr.

Lawrence, Iain. The Buccaneers. 2003. (High Seas Trilogy). (Illus.). 244p. (gr. 5-9). 16.50 (978-0-7569-1454-7(X)) Perfection Learning Corp.

—The Buccaneers. 2003. (ENG., Illus.). 256p. (J). (gr. 3-7). 7.99 (978-0-440-41671-5(X), Yearling) Random Hse. Children's Bks.

Lawrence, L. S. Escape by Sea. 2009. 208p. (J). (gr. 3-7). 16.95 (978-0-8234-2217-3(8)) Holiday Hse., Inc.

Lawrence, Michael. Ryan's Brain. 2006. (Jiggy Mccue Ser.). (ENG., Illus.). 336p. (J). (gr. 4-6). pap. 8.99 (978-1-84616-227-5(0)) Hodder & Stoughton GBR. Dist: Hachette Bk. Group.

Lawrence, Mike. The Macaroni Disaster! 2006. 44p. pap. 12.00 (978-1-4116-8613-7(6)) Lulu Pr., Inc.

—Star Scouts. 2017. (Star Scouts Ser.: 1). (ENG., Illus.). 192p. (J). pap. 14.99 (978-1-62672-280-4(3), 9781626722804, First Second Bks.) Roaring Brook Pr.

Lawrie, Robin. First among Losers. 2003. (Chain Gang Ser.). (Illus.). 32p. (YA). pap. (978-0-237-52562-0(3)) Evans Brothers, Ltd.

—Gone Green. 2003. (Chain Gang Ser.). (Illus.). 32p. (YA). pap. (978-0-237-52563-7(1)) Evans Brothers, Ltd.

—Paintball Panic. 2003. (Chain Gang Ser.). (Illus.). 32p. (YA). pap. (978-0-237-52559-0(3)) Evans Brothers, Ltd.

—Radar Riders. 2003. (Chain Gang Ser.). (Illus.). 32p. (YA). pap. (978-0-237-52560-6(7)) Evans Brothers, Ltd.

—Treetop Trauma. 2003. (Chain Gang Ser.). (Illus.). 32p. (YA). pap. (978-0-237-52564-4(X)) Evans Brothers, Ltd.

Lawrie, Robin & Lawrie, Chris, illus. Chain Reaction. 32p. pap. (978-0-237-52110-3(5)) Evans Brothers, Ltd.

—Fear 3.1. 32p. (J). pap. (978-0-237-52107-3(5)) Evans Brothers, Ltd.

—Muddy Mayhem. 32p. (J). pap. (978-0-237-52105-9(9)) Evans Brothers, Ltd.

—Winged Avenger. 32p. pap. (978-0-237-52106-6(7)) Evans Brothers, Ltd.

Laws, Jamie Lynn. Cameron & the Mysterious Shack. 2008. pap. 16.95 (978-1-60563-434-0(4)) America Star Bks.

Lawson, Barbara. An Ugly Black Bird, 1 vol. Lafarge, Kelly, illus. 2009. 35p. pap. 24.95 (978-1-61546-656-6(8)) America Star Bks.

Lawson, Jessica. The Actual & Truthful Adventures of Becky Thatcher. Bruno, Iacopo, illus. 2014. (ENG.). 224p. (J). (gr. 3-7). 16.99 (978-1-4814-0150-0(5), Simon & Schuster Bks. For Young Readers) Simon & Schuster Bks. For Young Readers.

Lawson, Jessica & Twain, Mark. The Tom Sawyer Collection: The Adventures of Tom Sawyer; the Adventures of Huckleberry Finn; the Actual & Truthful Adventures of Becky Thatcher. Bruno, Iacopo, illus. 2014. (ENG.). 944p. (J). (gr. 3-7). 50.99 (978-1-4814-0536-2(5), Simon & Schuster Bks. For Young Readers) Simon & Schuster Bks. For Young Readers.

Lawson, Peter & Smith, Kathryn. Animal Ambulance. 2009. (Turn the Wheel Ser.). (ENG., Illus.). 10p. (J). (gr. -1-k). bds. 5.95 (978-0-7892-1026-5(6), Abbeville Kids) Abbeville Pr., Inc.

Lawson, Shandy. The Loop. 2014. (ENG.). 208p. (YA). (gr. 7-12). pap. 8.99 (978-1-4231-6948-2(4)) Hyperion Bks. for Children.

Lawson-Williams, BerNadette. Blossom Bee's Golf Adventures. 2008. 76p. pap. 24.95 (978-1-4327-0874-0(0)) Outskirts Pr., Inc.

Lawton, Wilbur. The Boy Aviators' Polar Dash or Facing Death in the Antarctic. 2004. reprint ed. pap. 1.99 (978-1-4192-5497-0(9)) Kessinger Publishing, LLC.

Laybourne, Emmy. Sweet. 2016. (YA). lib. bdg. 20.85 (978-0-606-38561-9(4)) Turtleback Bks.

Layburn, Joe. Runaways. Williams, John, illus. 2014. (ENG.). 144p. (J). (gr. 4-7). pap. 8.95 (978-1-84780-080-0(7), Frances Lincoln) Quarto Publishing Group UK GBR. Dist: Hachette Bk. Group.

Layne, Steven L. Mergers, 1 vol. (ENG., Illus.). 208p. (YA). (gr. 6-10). 2007. per. 8.95 (978-1-58980-538-5(0)) 2006. 15.99 (978-1-58980-183-7(0)) Pelican Publishing Co., Inc.

Layton, Dan. Adventures in the Kingdom, the Dreamer. 2004. 64p. pap. 5.99 (978-0-9707919-4-8(1)) Mercy Place, Inc.

Layton, Dian. Seeker's Great Adventure. 2005. (Illus.). 64p. (J). (gr. 2-5). pap. 4.99 (978-0-9677402-1-8(5)) Destiny Image Pubs.

Layton, Roxanne A. Eddie Saves Cats. 2012. 26p. 24.95 (978-1-4626-6193-0(9)) America Star Bks.

Lazewnik, Libby. Three Cheers for Shira! 611p. 11.99 (978-1-58330-628-4(5)) Feldheim Pubs.

Le Gallienne, Richard. The Book Bills of Narcissus. 2004. reprint ed. pap. 15.95 (978-1-4191-5479-9(6)); pap. 1.99 (978-1-4192-5479-6(0)) Kessinger Publishing, LLC.

Le Gras, Gilbert. Joaquin & Olivier en Haute Mer! On the High Seas. 2009. 24p. pap. 8.20 (978-1-4251-1980-5(8)) Trafford Publishing.

Le Guin, Ursula K. Catwings Return. Schindler, S. D., illus. 2003. (Catwings Ser.: No. 2). (ENG.). 56p. (J). (gr. -1-3). 5.99 (978-0-439-55190-8(0)) Scholastic, Inc.

—Wonderful Alexander & the Catwings. Schindler, S. D., illus. 2003. (Catwings Ser.: No. 3). (ENG.). 48p. (J). (gr. -1-3). 5.99 (978-0-439-55191-5(9)) Scholastic, Inc.

Leach, Sara. Count Me In, 1 vol. 2011. (ENG.). 176p. (J). (gr. 4-7). pap. 9.95 (978-1-55469-404-4(3)) Orca Bk. Pubs. USA.

Leaf, Autumn. Coto, Child of the Ocean. 2008. 122p. pap. 19.95 (978-1-60703-843-6(9)) America Star Bks.

Leamon, Kevin. Oh No. Not Again! 2010. 27p. 14.95 (978-0-557-63078-3(9)) Lulu Pr., Inc.

Leatham, Marc Vincent. The Race. 2007. (Illus.). (J). (gr. -1-3). per. 15.99 (978-1-59879-274-4(1)) Lifevest Publishing, Inc.

—The Story of the Five Squirrels. Leatham, Marc Vincent, illus. 2007. (Illus.). (J). (gr. -1-3). per. 15.99 (978-1-59879-275-1(X)) Lifevest Publishing, Inc.

Leathers, Rain. Purple Mountain. 2008. 36p. pap. 20.95 (978-1-4327-2685-0(4)) Outskirts Pr., Inc.

Leavey, Peggy Dymond. Treasure at Turtle Lake. 2007. (ENG.). 152p. (J). (gr. 4-18). per. 9.95 (978-1-894917-49-0(9), Napoleon & Co.) Dundurn CAN. Dist: Ingram Publisher Services.

LeBaron, Cecilia. The Map. 2007. (Illus.). 16p. (J). 5.95 (978-0-9798869-1-1(0)) Crush Publishing.

—Nat & Tab. 2007. (Illus.). 16p. (J). 5.95 (978-0-9798869-0-4(2)) Crush Publishing.

—Sam & Val. 2007. (Illus.). 16p. (J). 5.95 (978-0-9798869-3-5(7)) Crush Publishing.

Leberer, Sigrid. The Adventures of the Three Best Friends. 2004. (Charming Collection of Five Short Stories Ser.). (Illus.). 22p. (J). bds. 6.99 (978-1-59384-056-3(X)) Parklane Publishing.

Leblanc, Avis Lyons. To Ride a Dragonfly. 2012. 94p. pap. 15.99 (978-1-4771-2222-8(2)) Xlibris Corp.

Leblanc, Margaret. Ms. Maddy Comes to Town. 2006. 76p. pap. 19.95 (978-1-4241-4103-6(6)) America Star Bks.

LeBlanc, Margaret Ann. The Mexico Adventure: Book Three of Ms. Maddy Series, 1 vol. 2010. 72p. pap. 19.95 (978-1-4489-8090-1(9)) America Star Bks.

Leblanc, Margaret Ann. Ms Maddy & the Lake Adventure. 2008. 89p. pap. 19.95 (978-1-60474-003-5(5)) America Star Bks.

LeBow, Michael. Sally Salli & the Case of the Tic Monster: A Book for Kids Who Tic. Barnett, Thora, illus. 2013. 75p. (J). pap. 18.95 (978-1-59630-060-6(4)) Science & Humanities Pr.

LeBreton, Heather. Rhyming with the Little Ones, 1 vol. LeBreton, Zachary, illus. 2009. 31p. pap. 24.95 (978-1-60749-114-9(1)) America Star Bks.

Lebscky, Ibi. Amadeus. Cardoni, Paolo, illus. (Coleccion Seran Famosos). (SPA.). 32p. (J). (gr. 2-4). 14.95 (978-84-233-1262-7(3)) Ediciones Destino ESP. Dist: AIMS International Bks., Inc.

Ledbetter, Penny S. Mushroom's Day Away. Garrett, Caroline S., illus. 2005. 32p. (J). 9.95 (978-1-933251-19-6(0)) Parkway Pubs., Inc.

Ledeaux, Lola. If A Dog Could Blog. 2010. 28p. 12.49 (978-1-4520-7575-4(1)) AuthorHouse.

Lederer, Ryan. The Adventures of Captain Candy. 2007. (Illus.). 48p. (J). (gr. 4-7). 15.95 (978-0-9795852-1-0(X)) Seven Locks Pr.

Lederhos, Lynn. Return to Her Roots: Revelations from a Young Girl's Journey Home. 2010. 40p. 20.99 (978-1-4520-3812-4(0)) AuthorHouse.

Ledray, Michael. Fifi Loves You! 2010. 40p. pap. 21.00 (978-0-557-27099-6(5)) Lulu Pr., Inc.

Lee, Anita Lynn. Kenny's Amazing Adventures. 2009. 36p. pap. 16.99 (978-1-4490-1588-6(3)) AuthorHouse.

Lee Badtke, Danica. Day Care. 2013. 26p. pap. 9.99 (978-1-937165-36-9(1)) Orange Hat Publishing.

Lee, Bonnie. Go Go Sadie. Taylor, Erin, illus. 2011. 46p. 24.00 (978-1-4349-8679-5(9), RoseDog Bks.) Dorrance Publishing Co., Inc.

Lee Coy, Amy. Duke Devlin the Daring Dogie. 2007. 48p. pap. 19.00 (978-0-615-14380-4(6)) Z Pr.

Lee Follen, Eliza. The Pedler of Dust Sticks. 2004. reprint ed. pap. 1.99 (978-1-4192-7694-1(8)) Kessinger Publishing, LLC.

—The Talkative Wig. 2004. reprint ed. pap. 1.99 (978-1-4192-8483-0(5)) Kessinger Publishing, LLC.

Lee, Ginger. Tessa T's Treasures, 1 vol. 2010. 22p. 29.95 (978-1-4489-4526-9(7)) America Star Bks.

Lee, Ingrid. George, the Best of All!, 1 vol. Denis, Stephane, illus. 2006. (Orca Echoes Ser.). (ENG.). 64p. (J). (gr. 2-3). per. 4.99 (978-1-55143-623-4(X)) Orca Bk. Pubs. USA.

—The True Story of George, 1 vol. Denis, Stephane, illus. 2004. (Orca Echoes Ser.). (ENG.). 64p. (J). (gr. 2-3). pap. 6.95 (978-1-55143-293-9(5)) Orca Bk. Pubs. USA.

Lee, Johnie. Courtney. 2012. 108p. pap. 11.99 (978-1-61996-498-3(8)) Salem Author Services.

Lee, Joshua. The Mysterious Quest of Johnathan Davis. 2012. 24p. pap. 16.95 (978-1-4626-9672-7(4)) America Star Bks.

Lee, Justus. YO-KAI WATCH: the MEOWny Faces of Jibanyan! 2017. (ENG., Illus.). 12p. (J). (gr. -1-3). pap. 6.99 (978-0-316-46468-0(6)) Little, Brown Bks. for Young Readers.

Lee, Karin. Zangadoo Kangaroo & the Mysterious Boomerang. Porterfield, Scott, illus. 2012. 94p. pap. 6.99 (978-0-9847428-2-0(4)) Zangadoo Entertainment.

Lee, Kathy. Captive in Rome. 2005. pap. (978-1-84427-088-0(2)) Scripture Union.

—A Captive in Rome. 2016. (ENG., Illus.). 146p. (J). pap. (978-0-281-07633-8(2)) SPCK Publishing.

—Hall of Mirrors. 2011. 144p. pap. (978-1-84427-506-9(X)) Scripture Union.

—The Runaway Train. 2011. 144p. pap. (978-1-84427-505-2(1)) Scripture Union.

Lee, Katie Bertoch. Ma Ma's Hair Is Everywhere. 2008. 28p. pap. 24.95 (978-1-60563-435-7(2)) America Star Bks.

Lee, Mackenzi. The Gentleman's Guide to Vice & Virtue. 2017. 528p. (YA). (gr. 8). 18.99 (978-0-06-238280-1(2), Tegen, Katherine Bks) HarperCollins Pubs.

—This Monstrous Thing. 2017. 400p. (YA). (gr. 8). pap. 9.99 (978-0-06-238278-8(0), Tegen, Katherine Bks) HarperCollins Pubs.

Lee, Margaret. The Adventures of Sebastian the Helpful Seagull. 2012. (Illus.). 72p. pap. 41.99 (978-1-4771-0672-3(3)) Xlibris Corp.

Lee, Mary Ellen. Danny & Life on Bluff Point: Blizzard of '95 revised Edition. 2009. 160p. (gr. 4-7). pap. 12.95 (978-0-595-53308-4(6)) iUniverse, Inc.

—Danny & Life on Bluff Point: Lost in the Dark. 2009. 160p. (gr. 4-7). 22.95 (978-1-4401-4607-7(1)); pap. 12.95 (978-1-4401-4608-4(X)) iUniverse, Inc.

Lee, Nancy. Baby Chipmunks & Backyard Friends. 2005. (J). 9.95 (978-0-9772078-2-4(X)) Journey Pubns., LLC.

Lee, Penny. Schoolio: Pets, Projects & Pandemonium. 2013. 72p. pap. (978-1-4602-0568-6(5)) FriesenPress.

Lee, Rex. Rann Braden Circus Showman A Circus Adve. 2006. (Illus.). pap. 27.95 (978-1-4286-5861-5(0)) Kessinger Publishing, LLC.

Lee, Shell. Teenie's Treehouse Adventures: The Magic Begins. 2004. 37p. pap. 24.95 (978-1-4137-2879-8(0)) PublishAmerica, Inc.

Lee, Stacey. Under a Painted Sky. 2015. (ENG.). 384p. (YA). (gr. 7). 16.99 (978-0-399-16803-1(6), G.P. Putnam's Sons Books for Young Readers) Penguin Young Readers Group.

—Under a Painted Sky. 2016. lib. bdg. 22.10 (978-0-606-38391-2(3)) Turtleback Bks.

Lee, Stan. Stan Lee's Superhero Christmas. Jessell, Tim, illus. 2nd ed. 2016. (ENG.). (gr. k-2). 27.95 **(978-1-59687-526-5(7)**, ipicturebooks) ibooks, Inc.

Lee, Stan. Thor, Vol. 2. 2005. (Thor Ser.). (Illus.). 584p. pap. 16.99 (978-0-7851-1591-5(9)) Marvel Worldwide, Inc.

Lee, Stan & Moore, Stuart. Convergence. Tong, Andie, illus. 2015. (Zodiac Ser.). (ENG.). 488p. (J). (gr. 3-7). 16.99 (978-1-4231-8085-2(2)) Disney Pr.

Lee, Steven. TruthQuest: In the Beginning. 2009. 72p. (J). pap. 6.95 (978-1-4327-3473-2(3)) Outskirts Pr., Inc.

Lee, Suzy. Shadow. 2010. (ENG., Illus.). 44p. (J). (gr. -1-3). 15.99 (978-0-8118-7280-5(7)) Chronicle Bks. LLC.

Lee, Tanith. Piratica: Being a Daring Tale of a Singular Girl's Adventure upon the High Seas. 2006. (ENG.). 304p. (YA). (gr. 7-18). per. 8.99 (978-0-14-240644-1(9), Firebird) Penguin Young Readers Group.

Lee, Wan, et al. A Fish Wish - Lunch for Patch - Squid Twins: BuildUp Unit 4 Lap Book. Moor, Beka et al, illus. 2015. (Build up Core Phonics Ser.). (J). (gr. 1). (978-1-4900-2603-9(7)) Benchmark Education Co.

Lees, Patricia. The Kingdom of Youu. 2012. 36p. pap. 16.99 (978-1-4670-7308-0(3)) AuthorHouse.

Leflore, Henry. The Aftermath: The Curse of the Blue Flamed Meteor. 2009. 112p. pap. 10.99 (978-1-4389-9588-5(1)) AuthorHouse.

The Legend of the Great Salt Mountain. 2005. (J). pap. (978-0-9771804-1-7(7)) Terra Tales.

LeGette, M. L. The Unicorn Girl. 2008. (ENG.). 416p. pap. 10.00 (978-1-4196-8696-2(8)) CreateSpace Independent Publishing Platform.

Leggat, Gillian. The Golden Highway. 2016. (ENG.). 189p. (YA). pap. 11.95 (978-1-78554-524-5(8), ef7fca95-1360-41bb-afab-3ab0fce00aba) Austin, Stan AUS. Dist: Bookmasters Distribution.

Legrand, Claire. Foxheart. Zollars, Jaime, illus. 2016. 480p. (J). (gr. 3-7). 16.99 (978-0-06-242773-1(3), Greenwillow Bks.) HarperCollins Pubs.

Legrand, Claire. Some Kind of Happiness. 2017. lib. bdg. 18.40 **(978-0-606-40127-2(X))** Turtleback Bks.

Legrand, H J, III. Paddle Tail's First Winter Adventure. Fair, Patricia Anne, illus. 2006. 64p. (J). per. 7.95 (978-1-59466-082-5(4), Growing Years) Port Town Publishing.

Lehane, Pearse. The Train That Never Came. 2008. 328p. pap. (978-1-84923-249-4(0)) YouWriteOn.

Lehman, Barbara. Rainstorm. 2007. (ENG., Illus.). 32p. (J). (gr. -1-3). 17.99 (978-0-618-75639-1(6)) Houghton Mifflin Harcourt Publishing Co.

Lehman, Jacques. The Adventures of Pepe Pandejo. 2007. 64p. per. 16.95 (978-1-4241-4980-3(0)) PublishAmerica, Inc.

Lehnert, R. B. The Adventures of Billy Butterfly. Garcia, Marc Khayam, illus. 2003. (J). per. (978-0-9747628-2-1(2)) BKB Group, Inc., The.

Leibold, Jay. Secret of the Ninja. Nugent, Suzanne & Marron, Jose, illus. 2007. (Choose Your Own Adventure Ser.: Vol. 16). 124p. (J). (gr. 4-7). per. 6.99 (978-1-933390-16-1(6)) Chooseco LLC.

Leigh, Anita L. Willow's Gift, 1 vol. 2009. 48p. pap. 16.95 (978-1-4489-9202-7(8)) America Star Bks.

Leigh-Anna Tehan. Beyond All Imagination: The First Souvenir. Paul Reising, illus. 2009. 44p. pap. 18.49 (978-1-4389-6452-2(8)) AuthorHouse.

Leigh, S. Runaway Pony. 2004. (Sandy Lane Stables Ser.). (J). (ENG.). 118p. pap. 4.95 (978-0-7945-0507-3(4)); 100p. lib. bdg. 12.95 (978-1-58086-575-3(5)) EDC Publishing.

—Uncle Pete's Pirate Adventure. rev. ed. 2004. (Young Puzzle Adventures Ser.). 32p. (J). (gr. 2-18). pap. 4.95 (978-0-7945-0401-4(9)); lib. bdg. 12.95 (978-1-58086-545-6(3)) EDC Publishing.

Leigh, Susan K. Luther: Echoes of the Hammer. 2011. 144p. pap. 12.99 (978-0-7586-2382-9(8)) Concordia Publishing Hse.

Leigh, Susannah. Puzzle Mountain. Waters, Gaby, ed. Haw, Brenda, illus. 2005. (Usborne Young Puzzles Ser.). 32p. (J). (gr. 1). lib. bdg. 14.95 (978-1-58086-694-1(8), Usborne) EDC Publishing.

—Puzzle Mountain. Haw, Brenda, illus. 2003. 32p. (J). pap. 6.95 (978-0-7945-0713-8(1), Usborne) EDC Publishing.

—Uncle Pete's Pirate Adventure. Stowell, Louie, ed. Haw, Brenda & Dawes, Will, illus. rev. ed. 2007. (Young Puzzle Adventures Ser.). 32p. (J). (gr. -1-3). pap. 4.99 (978-0-7945-1848-6(6), Usborne) EDC Publishing.

Leigh, Susannah, et al. Young Puzzle Adventures: Combined Volume. 2004. (Young Puzzle Adventures Ser.). (Illus.). 128p. (J). (gr. 2-18). pap. 12.95 (978-0-7945-0698-8(4), Usborne) EDC Publishing.

Leighfield, D. K. Abel's Song. 2013. 132p. (gr. 2-4). pap. 11.95 (978-1-4908-1327-1(6), WestBow Pr.) Author Solutions, Inc.

Leighton-Porter, Wendy. The Shadow of Camelot. 2013. 262p. pap. (978-1-909411-06-7(X)) Mauve Square Publishing.

—The Shadow of the Norman Arrow. 2013. 270p. pap. (978-1-909411-07-4(8)) Mauve Square Publishing.

Leighton, Robert. Bravest Boy in the Camp A Story of Adven. 2006. pap. 28.95 (978-1-4286-5937-7(4)) Kessinger Publishing, LLC.

Leija-Sysak, Viviana. My House Is Full of Light. 2008. 20p. 11.50 (978-1-4357-1606-3(X)) Lulu Pr., Inc.

Leiterman, Robert S. Operation Redwood Quest: Search for Answers. 2003. 351p. (YA). pap. 20.95 (978-0-595-30513-1(X)) iUniverse, Inc.

—Yeti or Not, Here We Come! Bigfoot in the Redwoods. 2003. 275p. (YA). pap. 16.95 (978-0-595-26561-9(8), Writers Club Pr.) iUniverse, Inc.

Lejeune, Leah. Sam & Jo: In the Adventure in the Woods. 2011. 58p. pap. 15.99 (978-1-4415-6027-8(0)) Xlibris Corp.

Leloup, Roger. On the Edge of Life. 2007. (Yoko Tsuno Ser.: 1). (ENG., Illus.). 48p. (J). (gr. 4-7). pap. 11.95 (978-1-905460-32-8(5)) CineBook GBR. Dist: National Bk. Network.

Lemay, Didi. A Winter Solstice Celebration. Campbell, Jacquie, illus. 2008. 56p. pap. 23.99 (978-1-4389-0998-1(5)) AuthorHouse.

Lemke, Donald. Batman - Who Is Clayface? Gordon, Steven E. & Gordon, Eric A., illus. 2013. (I Can Read Level 2 Ser.). (ENG.). 32p. (J). (gr. -1-3). pap. 3.99 (978-0-06-188525-9(8)) HarperCollins Pubs.

—Batman Classic: Battle in the Batcave. 2014. (ENG.). 24p. (J). (gr. -1-3). pap. 3.99 (978-0-06-220998-6(1), HarperFestival) HarperCollins Pubs.

—Batman Classic: Poison Ivy's Scare Fair. Tong, Andie, illus. 2017. 24p. (J). (gr. -1-3). pap. 3.99 (978-0-06-236077-9(9), HarperFestival) HarperCollins Pubs.

—Justice League Classic: Storm Surge. Spaziante, Patrick, illus. 2017. 24p. (J). (gr. -1-3). pap. 3.99 (978-0-06-236079-3(5), HarperFestival) HarperCollins Pubs.

—Nightmare in Gotham City. 2015. (Batman 8X8 Storybooks Ser.). (J). lib. bdg. 13.55 (978-0-606-36952-7(X)) Turtleback Bks.

—The Penguin's Arctic Adventure. Roberts, Jeremy, illus. 2014. (ENG.). 24p. (J). (gr. -1-3). pap. 3.99 (978-0-06-221000-5(9), HarperFestival) HarperCollins Pubs.

—Superman: A Giant Attack. 2015. (Justice League Classic: I Can Read! Ser.). (J). lib. bdg. 13.55 (978-0-606-36955-8(4)) Turtleback Bks.

—Superman Classic: Bizarro's Last Laugh. Spaziante, Patrick, illus. 2017. (I Can Read Level 2 Ser.). 32p. (J). (gr. -1-3). pap. 3.99 (978-0-06-236089-2(2)) HarperCollins Pubs.

—Who Is Clayface? 2013. (Justice League Classic: I Can Read! Ser.). (J). lib. bdg. 13.55 (978-0-606-31790-0(2), Turtleback) Turtleback Bks.

—Winter Wasteland. 2014. (Batman Classic I Can Read Level 2 Ser.). (J). lib. bdg. 13.55 (978-0-606-36458-4(7)) Turtleback Bks.

Lemke, Donald B. Drop In, 1 vol., Vol. 1. Majado, Caio et al, illus. 2011. (Tony Hawk's 900 Revolution Ser.). (ENG.). 128p. (gr. 3-4). pap. 7.19 (978-1-4342-3451-3(7)); lib. bdg. 26.65 (978-1-4342-3214-4(X)) Stone Arch Bks. (Tony Hawk's 900 Revolution).

Lemonade Zoo Monkeys. 2006. (Illus.). 33p. (YA). 10.95 (978-0-9765321-2-5(3)) Taven Hill Studio.

LeMonde', Stephanie. The Misty Forest. 2007. (Illus.). 154p. (J). (gr. -1-3). 14.95 (978-1-934138-13-7(4)) Bouncing Ball Bks., Inc.

L'Engle, Madeleine. A Wrinkle in Time Trilogy. 2012. (Wrinkle in Time Quintet Ser.). (ENG.). 800p. (J). (gr. 6-9). pap. 20.99 (978-1-250-00343-0(1), 9781250003430) Square Fish.

—The Young Unicorns. 2008. (Austin Family Ser.: 3). (ENG.). 304p. (J). (gr. 7-12). pap. 11.99 *(978-0-312-37933-9(1),* 9780312379339) Square Fish.

Lentini, Joe. Mickey the Monster's New Adventure: The Mysterious Fence. 2012. 28p. pap. 19.99 *(978-1-4685-8510-0(X))* AuthorHouse.

Lenzi, Danielle E. My Search for Prince Charming's Normal Brother. 2011. 136p. pap. 25.70 *(978-1-4634-0446-8(8))*; (gr. 10-12). 33.70 *(978-1-4634-0445-1(X))* AuthorHouse.

Leonard, Elise. Killer Lunch Lady. 2007. (Al's World Ser.: 2). (ENG.). 144p. (J). (gr. 5-9). pap. 8.99 *(978-1-4169-3465-3(0),* Simon & Schuster/Paula Wiseman Bks.) Simon & Schuster/Paula Wiseman Bks.

—Monday Morning Blitz. 2007. (Al's World Ser.: 1). (ENG.). 144p. (J). (gr. 5-9). pap. 8.99 *(978-1-4169-3464-6(2),* Simon & Schuster/Paula Wiseman Bks.) Simon & Schuster/Paula Wiseman Bks.

Leonard, M. G. Beetle Boy. 2017. lib. bdg. 17.20 ***(978-0-606-40151-7(2))*** Turtleback Bks.

Leonard, Niall. Shredder. 2015. (ENG.). 384p. (YA). (gr. 9). 17.99 *(978-0-385-74365-5(3),* Delacorte Pr.) Random Hse. Children's Bks.

Leone, Jason, illus. the Enchantress of Caratunk. Manna, Elizabeth, photos by. 2003. 30p. (J). (gr. 1-5). pap. 9.95 *(978-0-9729807-0-8(9))* Murray, David M.

Leoni, Nancy. Toby Goes to Camp, 1 vol. Leoni, Nancy, illus. 2009. (Illus.). 21p. pap. 24.95 *(978-1-61546-417-3(4))* America Star Bks.

Leopold, Astara Ladyvienna. The Stardream Chronicles, Vol. 2. Date not set. 128p. (J). (gr. 1-8). pap. 12.95 *(978-1-885226-45-7(4))* StarLineage Pubns.

Lepere, J. Mindseed. 2013. 120p. 28.99 *(978-1-4808-0016-8(3))*; pap. 11.99 *(978-1-4808-0014-4(7))* Archway Publishing.

Lepp, Kristin. Libby Louanne & the Amazing Hospital Mystery. 2010. 79p. pap. 10.95 *(978-0-557-61519-3(4))* Lulu Pr., Inc.

Lerangis, Peter. The Colossus Rises, Bk. 1. Norstrand, Torstein & Reagan, Mike, illus. 2013. (Seven Wonders Ser.: 1). (ENG.). 384p. (J). (gr. 3-7). pap. 6.99 *(978-0-06-207041-8(X))* HarperCollins Pubs.

—The Colossus Rises, Bk. 1. Reagan, Mike & Norstrand, Torstein, illus. 2013. (Seven Wonders Ser.: 1). (ENG.). 368p. (J). (gr. 3-7). 17.99 *(978-0-06-207040-1(1))* HarperCollins Pubs.

—The Colossus Rises, No. 1. Lerangis, Peter, illus. 2012. (Seven Wonders Ser.). (ENG., Illus.). 112p. (J). (gr. 3-7). 2.99 *(978-0-06-223889-4(2))* HarperCollins Pubs.

—The Colossus Rises. 2013. (Seven Wonders Ser.: 1). (J). lib. bdg. 17.20 *(978-0-606-32166-2(7),* Turtleback) Turtleback Bks.

—The Key. 2015. (Seven Wonders Journals: 3). (J). lib. bdg. 12.35 *(978-0-606-36487-4(0))* Turtleback Bks.

—The Legend of the Rift. 2016. (Seven Wonders Ser.: 5). (J). lib. bdg. 17.20 *(978-0-606-38738-5(2))* Turtleback Bks.

—Lost in Babylon. Norstrand, Torstein, illus. 2014. (Seven Wonders Ser.: 2). (ENG.). 400p. (J). (gr. 3-7). pap. 6.99 *(978-0-06-207044-9(4))* HarperCollins Pubs.

—Lost in Babylon. 2013. (Seven Wonders Ser.). (ENG., Illus.). 384p. (J). (gr. 3-7). 17.99 *(978-0-06-207043-2(6))* HarperCollins Pubs.

—Lost in Babylon. 2014. (Seven Wonders Ser.: 2). (J). lib. bdg. 17.20 *(978-0-606-35483-7(2))* Turtleback Bks.

—Max Tilt: Fire the Depths. 2017. (Max Tilt Ser.: 1). 368p. (J). (gr. 3-7). 17.99 ***(978-0-06-244100-3(0))*** HarperCollins Pubs.

—The Promise. 2016. (Seven Wonders Journals: 4). (J). lib. bdg. 12.35 *(978-0-606-38133-8(3))* Turtleback Bks.

—The Select & the Orphan. 2014. (Seven Wonders Journals). (ENG.). 144p. (J). (gr. 3-7). pap. 2.99 *(978-0-06-223891-7(4))* HarperCollins Pubs.

—The Select & the Orphans. 2014. (Seven Wonders Journals). (J). lib. bdg. 12.35 *(978-0-606-35484-4(0))* Turtleback Bks.

—Seven Wonders Book 4: the Curse of the King. Norstrand, Torstein, illus. 2016. (Seven Wonders Ser.: 4). 320p. (J). (gr. 3-7). pap. 6.99 *(978-0-06-207050-0(9))* HarperCollins Pubs.

—Seven Wonders Book 5: the Legend of the Rift. Norstrand, Torstein, illus. 2016. (Seven Wonders Ser.: 5). 448p. (J). (gr. 3-7). 17.99 *(978-0-06-207052-4(5))* HarperCollins Pubs.

—The Sword Thief. 2009. (39 Clues Ser.: 3). (ENG.). 160p. (J). (gr. 3-7). 12.99 *(978-0-545-06043-1(5),* Scholastic Pr.); (Illus.). 12.99 *(978-0-545-09059-9(8))* Scholastic, Inc.

—The Tomb of Shadows. Norstrand, Torstein, illus. (Seven Wonders Ser.: 3). (ENG.). (J). (gr. 3-7). 2015. 368p. pap. 6.99 *(978-0-06-207047-0(9))* 2014. 304p. 17.99 *(978-0-06-207046-3(0))* HarperCollins Pubs.

—The Tomb of Shadows. 2015. (Seven Wonders Ser.: 3). (J). lib. bdg. 17.20 *(978-0-606-36484-3(6))* Turtleback Bks.

Les, Papa. Gio the Friendly T-Rex & Friends: Hide-and-Seek. 2009. 24p. pap. 24.95 *(978-1-60749-731-8(X))* America Star Bks.

Lesler, Rebecca. The Magic Stone: Return of Two Kings. 2008. 73p. pap. 19.95 *(978-1-60610-101-8(3))* America Star Bks.

Lesley, Sharon. The Red Scarf & Other Stories. 2010. 165p. pap. 14.95 *(978-1-4457-6720-8(1))* Lulu Pr., Inc.

Leslie, Dawn Marie. Orthify. 2007. 33p. pap. 24.95 *(978-1-4241-8468-2(1))* America Star Bks.

Leslie, Lawrence J. With Trapper Jim in the North Woods. 2004. reprint ed. pap. 19.95 *(978-1-4191-9451-1(8))*; pap. 1.99 *(978-1-4192-9451-8(2))* Kessinger Publishing, LLC.

Leslie, Robyn. Rinny & the Trail of Clues. 2003. Orig. Title: Miss President & the Trail of Clues. (Illus.). 192p. (J). pap. 7.95 *(978-0-9727388-8-0(6))* Sugar Ducky Bks., Inc.

Leslie, Sherrie L. An Apple A Day: The Adventures of Grannie Annie & Pickles #1. 2011. 52p. (gr. 2-4). pap. 8.95 *(978-1-4620-4606-5(1))* iUniverse, Inc.

Lester, Sharon. The Boy Who Wouldn't Sit Still!, Vol. 2. Smith, Jeff, illus. 2nd ed. 2011. 40p. (J). 15.95 *(978-0-9802302-2-2(5))* Privileged Communications, LLC.

Leth, Kate. Adventure Time Vol. 4. 2014. lib. bdg. 24.50 *(978-0-606-36119-4(7))* Turtleback Bks.

Lethcoe, Jason. Amazing Adventures from Zoom's Academy. Lethcoe, Jason, illus. 2005. (ENG., Illus.). 160p. (J). (gr. 4-7). pap. 12.95 *(978-0-345-48355-3(3),* Ballantine Bks.) Random House Publishing Group.

Letourneau, Cameron. Skyriders. 2012. 288p. pap. *(978-1-77097-949-9(2))* FriesenPress.

Lettrick, Robert. The Murk. Disney Storybook Art Team, illus. 2015. (ENG.). 320p. (J). (gr. 5-9). 16.99 *(978-1-4231-8695-3(8))* Hyperion Bks. for Children.

Leung, Erika. The Dinosaur Hunt. 2010. 28p. pap. 12.99 *(978-1-4490-9584-0(4))* AuthorHouse.

Levandowski, Barbara. The Adventures of Muffin & Alexander: A New Home, a New Beginning. 2011. (SPA.). 28p. pap. 16.95 *(978-1-4269-5917-2(6))* Trafford Publishing.

—The Adventures of Muffin & Alexander: Let the Explorations Begin. 2011. 36p. pap. *(978-1-4269-8746-5(3))* Trafford Publishing (UK) Ltd.

Leveen, Tom. Hellworld. 2017. (ENG., Illus.). 304p. (YA). (gr. 9). 17.99 *(978-1-4814-6633-2(X),* Simon Pulse) Simon Pulse.

Levering-Duff, Judy. The Medallion of Tiben: Book Two of the Adventures of Princess Isabella. 2004. (YA). 265p. 23.95 *(978-0-9725874-9-5(7))*; pap. 9.50 *(978-1-932672-00-8(1))* Outskirts Pr., Inc.

Levey, Emma, illus. Hattie Peck. 2016. (ENG.). 32p. (J). (gr. -1-k). 16.99 *(978-1-63450-170-5(5),* Sky Pony Pr.) Skyhorse Publishing Co., Inc.

Levine, Gail Carson. Stolen Magic. 2015. (ENG., Illus.). 336p. (J). (gr. 3-7). 16.99 *(978-0-06-170637-0(X))* HarperCollins Pubs.

Levine, Susan Sachs. Harriett's Homecoming: A High-Flying Tour of Cincinnati. Burchwell, Erin, illus. 2012. (ENG.). 32p. (J). (gr. -1-3). 19.95 *(978-1-933197-97-5(8))* Orange Frazer Pr.

Levitt, Steve. Journey to the MountainA Roots Tale. 2007. 144p. pap. 19.95 *(978-1-84728-086-2(2))* Lulu Pr., Inc.

Levy, Janey. Edwin Visits Earth. 2006. (Neighborhood Readers Ser.). (ENG.). 16p. (gr. 1-3). pap. 6.50 *(978-1-4042-7160-9(0),* Rosen Classroom) Rosen Publishing Group, Inc., The.

Levy, Michael. The Inspiring Story of Little Goody Two Shoes. 2007. 139p. (YA). per. 12.95 *(978-0-9668069-9-1(9))* Point of Life, Inc.

Lewis. Tomboy Terror in Bunk 109. 2008. (ENG.). 128p. (YA). (gr. 7). pap. 7.95 *(978-1-4169-7539-7(X),* Simon Pulse) Simon Pulse.

Lewis, Anne G. A Perfect Tree for Christmas. Stahlberg, Carina, illus. 2013. (ENG.). (J). pap. 7.99 *(978-1-935666-55-4(X))* Nodin Pr.

Lewis, Anne Margaret. Fly Blanky Fly. Chavarri, Elisa, illus. 2012. (ENG.). 40p. (J). (gr. -1-2). 16.99 *(978-0-06-199996-3(2))* HarperCollins Pubs.

—The Runaway Mitten. Zenz, Aaron, illus. 2015. (ENG.). 40p. (J). (gr. -1-k). 15.99 *(978-1-63450-213-9(2),* Sky Pony Pr.) Skyhorse Publishing Co., Inc.

—The Runaway Pumpkin. Zenz, Aaron, illus. 2015. (ENG.). 40p. (J). (gr. -1-k). 15.99 *(978-1-63450-214-6(0),* Sky Pony Pr.) Skyhorse Publishing Co., Inc.

—The Runaway Santa. Zenz, Aaron, illus. 2015. (ENG.). 40p. (J). (gr. -1-k). 15.99 *(978-1-63450-589-5(1),* Sky Pony Pr.) Skyhorse Publishing Co., Inc.

Lewis, Axel. Arctic Adventure, 1 vol. 2014. (Robot Racers Ser.). (ENG., Illus.). 160p. (gr. 2-4). pap. 6.95 *(978-1-4342-7938-5(3))* Stone Arch Bks.

—Desert Disaster, 1 vol. 2014. (Robot Racers Ser.). (ENG., Illus.). 160p. (gr. 2-4). pap. 6.95 *(978-1-4342-7939-2(1))* Stone Arch Bks.

Lewis, C. A. Harold the Sparrow & His Bellybutton. 2013. 48p. pap. *(978-1-4602-1117-5(0))* FriesenPress.

Lewis, C. Robbie. Rapunzel. 2004. 228p. 23.95 *(978-1-4184-8779-9(1))* AuthorHouse.

Lewis, C. S. The Horse & His Boy. Baynes, Pauline, illus. (Chronicles of Narnia Ser.: 3). (ENG.). 240p. (J). (gr. 3-18). 2008. pap. 8.99 *(978-0-06-440501-0(X))* 2007. 17.99 *(978-0-06-023488-1(1))* HarperCollins Pubs.

—El Leon, la Bruja y el Ropero, 1 vol. 2005. (Cronicas de Narnia Ser.). (ESP, SPA & ENG.). 208p. pap. 9.99 *(978-0-06-084253-6(9))* HarperCollins Pubs.

Lewis, Calvin, Jr. & Wilhite, Susan L. It Comes in the Night: Speaking Eagle, Book One. 2006. pap. 9.95 *(978-1-934130-03-2(6),* 3002) Flood Crest Pr.

Lewis, Carolyn. Hairy Beary Book Two Bk. 2,Vol. 2: The Great Waterfall, 3 bks. DeVince, James, ed. Porcheron, Tammy, illus. 2003. (Hairy Beary Ser.: 2). 42p. (J). pap. 9.95 *(978-0-9712641-1-3(2))* J M D's Business Services.

Lewis, Carolyn & DeVince, James. The Hairy Beary Adventure Series, 3 bks. DeVince, James, ed. Porcheron, Tammy, illus. 2005. 122p. (J). pap. 24.95 *(978-0-9712641-3-7(9))* J M D's Business Services.

—Hairy Beary Book Three: The Blue Ribbon Hero, 3 bks., Vol. 3. DeVince, James, ed. Porcheron, Tammy, illus. 2003. (Hairy Beary Ser.: 3). 46p. (J). pap. 9.95 *(978-0-9712641-2-0(0))* J M D's Business Services.

Lewis, Cindy (Didas). Time to Head South with Cindy the Canadian Goose, 1 vol. 2010. 56p. pap. 16.95 *(978-1-4489-3879-7(1))* America Star Bks.

Lewis, Clarajane. The House on the Hill. 2012. (Illus.). 26p. pap. 12.00 *(978-1-78035-399-9(5),* Fastprint Publishing) Upfront Publishing Ltd. GBR. Dist: Printondemand-worldwide.com.

Lewis, David & Dugas, Lisa, eds. Hill House Speaks. 2006. 156p. (YA). pap. 18.00 *(978-0-9769114-7-0(7))* Leonard Pr.

Lewis, K. s. & Lewis, K. S. Happiness: A Charlie Travel Adventure Story. 2009. 28p. pap. 21.20 *(978-0-557-12094-9(2))* Lulu Pr., Inc.

Lewis, Kevin. Kj's Adventures. 2011. 28p. pap. 15.99 *(978-1-4653-3573-9(0))* Xlibris Corp.

Lewis, Kurt. The Improbable Barnsy & the Pocket Full of Teeth. 2009. 152p. pap. 12.96 *(978-0-557-11956-1(1))* Lulu Pr., Inc.

Lewis, Lisa. Tsunaxen's Journey. 2013. (ENG.). 23p. (J). pap. 14.95 *(978-1-4787-1979-3(6))* Outskirts Pr., Inc.

Lewis, Lorinne. Junior & Callie's Awesome Adventure. 2012. 36p. pap. 16.95 *(978-1-62709-269-2(2))* America Star Bks.

Lewis, Megan. The Girl Who Could Fly. l.t. ed. 2005. (Illus.). 30p. (J). per. 9.99 *(978-1-59879-029-0(3))* Lifevest Publishing, Inc.

Lewis, Phyllis. Legend of the Aneeka. 2003. 173p. pap. 24.95 *(978-1-59286-519-2(4))* PublishAmerica, Inc.

Lewis, Terence. Bani a Butterfly Adventure. 2012. 30p. pap. 8.99 *(978-1-62230-329-8(6))* Salem Author Services.

Lewman, David. Monster Mayhem! (Teenage Mutant Ninja Turtles) Golden Books, illus. 2017. (Big Golden Book Ser.). (ENG.). 48p. (J). (gr. -1-2). 9.99 ***(978-1-5247-1670-7(7),*** Golden Bks.) Random Hse. Children's Bks.

—The Rise of Tiger Claw. 2016. lib. bdg. 16.00 *(978-0-606-38489-6(8))* Turtleback Bks.

—SpongeBob, Soccer Star! Reed, Stephen, illus. 2010. (SpongeBob SquarePants Ser.). (ENG.). 24p. (J). (gr. -1-3). pap. 3.99 *(978-1-4169-9445-9(9),* Simon Spotlight/Nickelodeon) Simon Spotlight/Nickelodeon.

Leyendas Nordicas. (SPA., Illus.). 160p. (YA). 11.95 *(978-84-7281-056-3(9),* AF1056) Auriga, Ediciones S.A. ESP. Dist: Continental Bk. Co., Inc.

Lhomme, Sandrine & Piu, Amandine. Sammy the Snail's Amazing Day, 1 vol. Lhomme, Sandrine, illus. 2012. (My Baby Stories Ser.). (ENG., Illus.). 24p. (J). (gr. -1). bds. 9.95 *(978-2-7338-1981-4(X))* Auzou, Philippe Editions FRA. Dist: Consortium Bk. Sales & Distribution.

Libby, Lori Ann. The Adventures of Henry Hamper & the Flying Fish. Lee, Tricia Ting, illus. 2010. 34p. pap. 13.95 *(978-1-60911-493-0(0),* Eloquent Bks.) Strategic Book Publishing & Rights Agency (SBPRA).

Liberts, Jennifer. What Is a Princess? (Disney Princess) Harchy, Atelier Philippe, illus. 2016. (Step into Reading Ser.). (ENG.). 24p. (J). (gr. -1-1). pap. 4.99 *(978-0-7364-3666-3(9),* RH/Disney) Random Hse. Children's Bks.

Libra, Michael W. Dragons of Draegoni: Dragon Black's Revenge Book 2. 2012. (Illus.). 262p. pap. *(978-1-78148-505-7(4))* Grosvenor Hse. Publishing Ltd.

Liess, Claudia. A Stranger on Planet Earth. 2006. 76p. pap. 16.95 *(978-1-4241-0987-6(6))* PublishAmerica, Inc.

Liess, Claudia Schmidt. But Where Is Dad? 2007. 96p. per. 19.95 *(978-1-4241-6912-2(7))* America Star Bks.

—Harry the Hamster: Learns a Lesson. 2010. 32p. 14.49 *(978-1-4490-8864-4(3))* AuthorHouse.

—Henry the Magical, Mythical Dragon. 2008. 74p. pap. 19.95 *(978-1-60672-956-4(X))* America Star Bks.

Lift & Listen. pap. 15.98 *(978-0-7853-4251-9(6))* Publications International, Ltd.

Lifton, Betty Jean. Taka-Chan & I: A Dog's Journey to Japan by Runcible. Hosoe, Eikoh, photos by. 2012. (ENG., Illus.). 64p. (J). (gr. k-4). 16.95 *(978-1-59017-502-6(6),* NYR Children's Collection) New York Review of Bks., Inc., The.

Light, John & Light, Marilyn. TT Triangle. 2005. (Illus.). 26p. *(978-1-897968-27-7(2))* Photon Pr.

Light, Steve. Swap! Light, Steve, illus. 2016. (ENG., Illus.). 40p. (J). (gr. -1-2). 16.99 *(978-0-7636-7990-3(9))* Candlewick Pr.

—Zephyr Takes Flight. Light, Steve, illus. 2012. (ENG., Illus.). 40p. (J). (gr. -1-3). 16.99 *(978-0-7636-5695-9(X))* Candlewick Pr.

Light's Adventures: Light's Adventures with Doom & Gloom. 2003. (J). spiral bd. 7.00 *(978-0-9743223-0-8(X))* Jones, Augustine R.

Light's Adventures on the Playground. 2004. (J). spiral bd. 7.00 net. *(978-0-9743223-1-5(8))* Jones, Augustine R.

Light's Adventure's with Friends. 2005. (J). spiral bd. 7.00 *(978-0-9743223-2-2(6))* Jones, Augustine R.

Lihou, Gavin. Revenge of the Cannibal Chickens. Ross Kennedy, illus. 2013. 74p. pap. 10.50 *(978-1-62212-484-8(7),* Strategic Bk. Publishing) Strategic Book Publishing & Rights Agency (SBPRA).

Lillehaug-Collins, Yvonne. Little Dragon. 2009. 70p. pap. 21.00 *(978-1-60693-344-2(2),* Eloquent Bks.) Strategic Book Publishing & Rights Agency (SBPRA).

Lillis, Sonya. Fuzzy Bacon. 2008. 43p. pap. 24.95 *(978-1-60610-952-6(9))* America Star Bks.

Lilly, Stephanie. The Amazing Adventures of Ethan-Tyrannosaurus-Rex: The Escape from Raptor Forest. 2009. 28p. pap. 15.30 *(978-1-4490-1105-5(5))* AuthorHouse.

Lilly, Suzanne. Untellable. 2013. 158p. pap. 9.99 *(978-1-62237-218-8(2))* Turquoise Morning Pr.

Lim, Ronald & Rosenberg, Rachelle, illus. This Is Ant-Man. 2015. 31p. (J). ***(978-1-4844-5652-1(1))*** Disney Pr.

Limke, Jeff. Jason: Quest for the Golden Fleece, a Greek Myth. Seeley, Tim & Schulz, Barbara, illus. 2008. (Graphic Myths & Legends Ser.). (ENG.). 48p. (gr. 4-8). per. 8.95 *(978-0-8225-6571-0(4))* Lerner Publishing Group.

Lin, Alex. The Little Detective. 2012. 24p. (-18). pap. 15.99 *(978-1-4797-0286-2(2))* Xlibris Corp.

Lin, Grace. When the Sea Turned to Silver. (ENG.). (J). (gr. 3-7). 2017. 400p. pap. 9.99 ***(978-0-316-12594-9(6))*** 2016. (Illus.). 384p. 18.99 *(978-0-316-12592-5(X))* Little, Brown Bks. for Young Readers.

—When the Sea Turned to Silver. 2017. (J). lib. bdg. 20.85 ***(978-0-606-40629-1(8))*** Turtleback Bks.

Lin, Grace. The Year of the Rat. 2009. (Pacy Lin Novel Ser.). (ENG.). 208p. (J). (gr. 3-7). pap. 7.00 *(978-0-316-03361-9(8))* Little, Brown Bks. for Young Readers.

Linares, Jairo, illus. Pinocho. 2004. (Literatura Juvenil (Panamericana Editorial) Ser.).Tr. of Pinocchio. (SPA.). 283p. (J). (gr. 4-7). pap. *(978-958-30-0803-0(6),* PV30464) Centro de Informacion y Desarrollo de la Comunicacion y la Literatura MEX. Dist: Lectorum Pubns., Inc.

Lincoln, Jacqueline Michelle. The Adventures of Sheila the Awesome (Aussie) Dog. 2005. (J). 7.95 *(978-0-9748426-3-9(X),* Accent Pubns.) Ajoyin Publishing, Inc.

Lindgren, Astrid. Mio, My Son. Morgan, Jill, tr. from SWE. Wikland, Ilon, illus. 2015.Tr. of Mio, Min Mio. (ENG.). 184p. (J). (gr. 3-7). 16.95 *(978-1-59017-870-6(X),* NYR Children's Collection) New York Review of Bks., Inc., The.

—Mio, My Son. Wikland, Ilon, illus. 2003.Tr. of Mio, Min Mio. 179p. (J). 17.95 *(978-1-930900-23-3(6))* Purple Hse. Pr.

—Pippi Goes on Board. (Pippi Longstocking Ser.). 140p. (J). (gr. 3-5). pap. 3.99 *(978-0-8072-1401-5(9),* Listening Library) Random Hse. Audio Publishing Group.

—Pippi in the South Seas. Turner, Marianne, tr. from SWE. Ross, Tony, illus. 2006. 128p. pap. *(978-0-19-275481-3(5))* Oxford Univ. Pr.

—Pippi in the South Seas. (Pippi Longstocking Ser.). 125p. (J). (gr. 3-5). pap. 3.99 *(978-0-8072-1392-6(6),* Listening Library) Random Hse. Audio Publishing Group.

—Pippi Longstocking. (Pippi Longstocking Ser.). 160p. (J). (gr. 3-5). pap. 4.99 *(978-0-8072-1431-2(0),* Listening Library) Random Hse. Audio Publishing Group.

—The Tomten, 1 vol. Wiberg, Harald, illus. 2nd rev. ed. (ENG.). 32p. (J). 17.95 *(978-0-86315-153-8(1))* Floris Bks. GBR. Dist: SteinerBooks, Inc.

Lindgren, Astrid & Vang Nyman, Ingrid. Pippi Fixes Everything. Nunnally, Tiina, tr. from SWE. 2013. (ENG., Illus.). 56p. (J). 14.95 *(978-1-77046-131-4(0),* 9781770461314) Drawn & Quarterly Pubns. CAN. Dist: Macmillan.

Lindner, Brooke. Diego's Halloween Party. Mawhinney, Art, illus. 2008. (Go, Diego, Go! Ser.). (ENG.). 16p. (J). (gr. -1-k). bds. 5.99 *(978-1-4169-5497-2(X),* Simon Spotlight/Nickelodeon) Simon Spotlight/Nickelodeon.

Lindquist, Kaeti. Tyler Poncho's Amalgamated Menagerie. 2011. 56p. pap. 25.00 *(978-0-557-99490-8(X))* Lulu Pr., Inc.

Lindquist, N. J. In Time of Trouble: A Novel about Second Chances. 2016. (ENG., Illus.). (YA). pap. ***(978-1-927692-40-0(7))***; 282p. (J). pap. *(978-1-927692-24-0(5))* That's Life! Communications.

Lindsey, Audrey. Against the Dawn, 1 vol. 2010. 74p. pap. 19.95 *(978-1-60749-097-5(8))* America Star Bks.

Lindsey, Stephanie. Crabs in a Bucket. 2013. 28p. pap. 24.95 *(978-1-63000-538-2(X))* America Star Bks.

Lininger, Dianne. The Kingdom of Cydinah. 2006. (J). *(978-0-9790337-0-4(5))* Crosam Pr.

Linklater, Eric. The Pirates in the Deep Green Sea. 2013. (ENG.). 314p. (YA). pap. 16.99 *(978-1-4482-0582-0(4),* 9781448205820, Bloomsbury Reader) Bloomsbury Publishing Plc GBR. Dist: Macmillan.

Linkowski, Tami Leli. Lynn Can Fly, 1 vol. Selover, Lisa & Selover, Arthur, illus. 2009. 15p. pap. 24.95 *(978-1-60749-611-3(9))* America Star Bks.

Linney, Graham F. The Seaside Adventure of Carrot, Pea, & Friends. 2011. 32p. pap. 13.00 *(978-1-61204-435-4(2),* Strategic Bk. Publishing) Strategic Book Publishing & Rights Agency (SBPRA).

Linsner, Joseph Michael. Three Tiers, Vol. 3. 2006. (ENG., Illus.). 176p. (YA). 39.99 *(978-1-58240-573-5(5),* 9781582405735) Image Comics.

Linton, Chandra S. Colors, Colors, Colors, A World Filled with Colors, Who Made Them? 2011. 20p. (gr. 2-4). pap. 15.49 *(978-1-4567-6355-8(5))* AuthorHouse.

Linz, Kathryn. Jim Brandon's Adventures. 2006. (ENG.). 100p. per. 19.95 *(978-1-4241-3160-0(X))* America Star Bks.

Liora, Iimma. Flick. 2012. 24p. pap. 12.45 *(978-1-4525-0660-9(4))* Balboa Pr.

—Flick Goes Bush. 2013. 32p. pap. 16.95 *(978-1-4525-0819-1(4),* Balboa Pr.) Author Solutions, Inc.

—Flick Goes under the Sea! 2012. 32p. (-18). pap. 16.95 *(978-1-4525-0663-0(9))* Balboa Pr.

Lipkowitz, Daniel & Dorling Kindersley Publishing Staff. Batman, Visual Dictionary. 2012. (ENG.). 96p. (J). (gr. 2-5). 21.99 *(978-0-7566-9787-7(5),* DK Children) Dorling Kindersley Publishing, Inc.

Lippert-Martin, Kristen. Incognita. 2016. (Tabula Rasa Saga Ser.: 2). (ENG.). (YA). (gr. 7-12). 340p. 17.99 *(978-1-5124-0577-4(9),* Carolrhoda Bks.); 272p. 35.99 *(978-1-5124-0896-6(4),* Carolrhoda Lab™) Lerner Publishing Group.

—Tabula Rasa. (ENG.). 337p. (YA). (gr. 7-12). 2016. (Tabula Rasa Saga Ser.: 1). pap. 9.99 *(978-1-5124-2629-8(6))* 2014. 17.99 *(978-1-60684-518-9(7))* Lerner Publishing Group. (Carolrhoda Lab™).

Lisle, Janet Taylor. Black Duck. 2007. (ENG.). 256p. (J). (gr. 5-18). 7.99 *(978-0-14-240902-2(2),* Puffin Books) Penguin Young Readers Group.

Lisle, Rebecca. Amethyst. Hess, Paul, illus. 2007. (ENG.). 176p. (J). (gr. 4-7). per. 8.99 *(978-1-84270-541-4(5))* Andersen Pr. GBR. Dist: Independent Pubs. Group.

Lister, Tresina. Itty Bitty Birdie. Greengaard, Alex, illus. 2006. 20p. (J). per. 12.95 *(978-0-9791171-0-7(0))* Lister, Tresina.

Litchfield, Jo. Bit-Bot & the Blob. 2013. (ENG., Illus.). 40p. (J). (gr. -1-k). pap. 10.99 *(978-1-4052-5513-4(7))* Egmont Bks., Ltd. GBR. Dist: Independent Pubs. Group.

Litchmore, Michael. The MB Force: Heroes at the Best! 2007. 56p. pap. 9.00 *(978-0-8059-7399-0(0))* Dorrance Publishing Co., Inc.

Litrel, Suzanne. Jackie Tempo & the House of Wisdom. 2012. 150p. (gr. 10-12). 21.95 *(978-1-4620-5887-7(6))*; pap. 11.95 *(978-1-4620-5886-0(8))* iUniverse, Inc.

Littell, William Adams. Guillaume. 2008. 74p. pap. 10.00 *(978-0-8059-7757-8(0))* Dorrance Publishing Co., Inc.

Little Airplane Productions & Scanlon, Michael, illus. Off to School! 2009. (Wonder Pets! Ser.). (ENG.). 24p. (J). pap. 3.99 *(978-1-4169-7197-9(1),* Simon Spotlight/Nickelodeon) Simon Spotlight/Nickelodeon.

Little Reader Digital Storybook: Beauty & the Beast. 2005. (J). cd-rom 9.99 *(978-0-9767657-2-1(1),* oatb-ctvol1) Mullings Media.

Little Reader Digital Storybook: Rumplestiltskin. 2005. (J). cd-rom 7.99 *(978-0-9767657-6-9(4),* rum-cfvol1) Mullings Media.

Litwin, Mike. The Big Cowhuna. Litwin, Mike, illus. 2015. (Welcome to Bermooda! Ser.: 3). (ENG., Illus.). 160p. (J). (gr. 1-5). 14.99 *(978-0-8075-8720-1(6))* Whitman, Albert & Co.

—Crown of the Cowibbean. Litwin, Mike, illus. 2014. (Welcome to Bermooda! Ser.: 2). (ENG., Illus.). 144p. (J). (gr. 1-5). 14.99 *(978-0-8075-8719-5(2))* Whitman, Albert & Co.

—Lost in Bermooda. Litwin, Mike, illus. 2014. (Welcome to Bermooda! Ser.: Book 1). (ENG., Illus.). 144p. (J). (gr. 1-5). 14.99 *(978-0-8075-8718-8(4))* Whitman, Albert & Co.

Liv‡n, Paco. WHAT A SNOUT! 2007. (ENG., Illus.). 48p. (J). 18.95 *(978-84-96788-87-9(3))* OQO, Editora ESP. Dist: Baker & Taylor Bks.

Lively, Deborah Dreher. Hateya Sam. 2009. 32p. pap. 13.75 *(978-1-60860-029-8(7),* Eloquent Bks.) Strategic Book Publishing & Rights Agency (SBPRA).

Lively, Judy. Hanny Bonz. 2008. 24p. pap. 10.95 *(978-1-4327-2122-0(4))* Outskirts Pr., Inc.

Livingston, Eric. Brandon Marlowe & the Spirit Snatcher. 2011. 216p. 25.95 *(978-1-4502-9221-4(6))*; pap. 15.95 *(978-1-4502-9220-7(8))* iUniverse, Inc.

Livingston, Lesley. Transcendent. 2014. (Starling Trilogy Ser.: 3). (ENG.). 352p. (YA). (gr. 8). 17.99 *(978-0-06-206313-7(8),* HarperTeen) HarperCollins Pubs.

Livingston, R. E. Super Scamper & Jayden's Big Adventure. 2012. (Illus.). 16p. pap. 18.30 *(978-1-4772-1775-7(4))* AuthorHouse.

Lizzy Anne's Adventures Staff & Zarrella, Sharon. Lizzy Anne's Adventures, Vol. 1. Vasudevan, Vidya, illus. 2011. 52p. (J). (gr. k-4). pap. 5.99 *(978-0-9845887-2-5(8))* Lizzy Anne's Adventures.

Llewellyn, Claire. On the Track Blue Band. Ruffle, Mark, illus. 2016. (Cambridge Reading Adventures Ser.). (ENG.). 16p. pap. 6.56 *(978-1-316-50322-5(4))* Cambridge Univ. Pr.

Llewellyn, Sam. The Well Between the Worlds. 2010. (Lyonesse Ser.: 1). (ENG.). 368p. (J). (gr. 3-7). 7.99 *(978-0-439-93470-1(2)*, Scholastic Paperbacks) Scholastic, Inc.

Llongueras, Joan & Masnou, Merce. Kadingir: El Cetro de Zink. 2007. (SPA.). 365p. (J). 18.95 *(978-84-96544-64-2(8))* Roca Editorial ESP. Dist: Spanish Pubs., LLC.

Lloyd, Alison. Year of the Tiger. 2010. (ENG.). 228p. (YA). (gr. 5-18). pap. 16.95 *(978-0-8234-2277-7(1))* Holiday Hse., Inc.

Lloyd-Jones, Emily. Deceptive: An Illusive Novel. 2015. (Illusive Ser.: 2). (ENG.). 432p. (YA). (gr. 7-17). 18.00 *(978-0-316-25464-9(9))* Little Brown & Co.

Lloyd, Sylvia. A Little Turtle's Tale. 2005. pap. *(978-1-932077-96-4(0))* Athena Pr.

Lluch, Alex A. Alexander, It's Time for Bed! Defenbaugh, David, illus. 2006. (ENG.). 30p. (J). (gr. -1-3). 14.95 *(978-1-887169-59-2(8))* WS Publishing.

Lobdell, Scott. The Opposite Numbers. Rendon, Daniel et al, illus. 2006. 111p. (J). *(978-1-4156-9815-0(5))* Papercutz.

Lobel, Arnold. Frog & Toad Storybook Treasury. Lobel, Arnold, illus. 2013. (I Can Read Level 2 Ser.). (ENG., Illus.). 256p. (J). (gr. -1-3). 11.99 *(978-0-06-229258-2(7))* HarperCollins Pubs.

Lobiondo, Christine. Red Rock Capers. 2007. 56p. per. 19.95 *(978-1-4327-1039-2(7))* Outskirts Pr., Inc.

Lochhead, Joyce N. The Adventures of Mr Figaro Tailhead. 2008. 172p. pap. 11.99 *(978-1-4389-0790-1(7))* AuthorHouse.

Lochmandy, Sandy. Kids & Critters on an Adventure. 2009. 36p. pap. 14.95 *(978-1-60860-387-9(3)*, Eloquent Bks.) Strategic Book Publishing & Rights Agency (SBPRA).

Lockaby, Angie. Tad the Turtle It's Okay to Be Different. 2012. 28p. pap. 19.99 *(978-1-4772-7295-4(X))* AuthorHouse.

Lockard, Donna Lee. Sasha the Tortoise's Summer Vacation. 2013. (ENG.). 36p. (J). pap. 19.95 *(978-1-4787-0938-1(3))* Outskirts Pr., Inc.

Lockard, Lynn. Gone Batty!!! 2009. 40p. pap. 16.99 *(978-1-4389-8516-9(9))* AuthorHouse.

Locke, Terry. Spencer Hurley & the Aliens: Book One: the Abduction. Hucks, Robin, ed. 2008. (Spencer Hurley & the Aliens Ser.: 1). (ENG., Illus.). 256p. (J). 12.95 *(978-0-9786940-0-5(7)*, SHAB1V1E1CB) Dream Workshop Publishing Co., LLC, The.

—Spencer Hurley & the Aliens: Book One: the Abduction, Vol. 1. Hucks, Robin, ed. Locke, Terry, illus. 2008. (Spencer Hurley & the Aliens Ser.: 1). (Illus.). 256p. (J). per. 8.99 *(978-0-9786940-1-2(5))* Dream Workshop Publishing Co., LLC, The.

Locker, Thomas. Water Dance. 2010. (Rise & Shine Ser.). (ENG., Illus.). 32p. (C). pap. 11.95 *(978-0-15-216396-9(4))* National Geographic School Publishing, Inc.

Lockwood, Cara. Moby Clique. 2008. (Bard Academy Ser.: No. 3). (ENG.). 304p. (gr. 7-12). pap. 19.99 *(978-1-4165-5050-1(X)*, MTV Bks.) MTV Books.

—The Scarlet Letterman. 2007. (Bard Academy Ser.: 2). (ENG.). 272p. (gr. 7-12). pap. 17.99 *(978-1-4165-2490-8(8))* Pocket Books.

Lockwood, Penny. Boo's Bad Day. Johnson, Deborah C., illus. 2013. 32p. pap. 11.99 *(978-0-9852661-5-8(5))* 4RV Publishing, LLC.

LoDestro, Christine. The Littlest Cloud. 2005. 15p. (J). 12.01 *(978-1-4116-6377-0(2))* Lulu Pr., Inc.

LoDolce, Jodi. Johnny's Adventure at Sea. 2013. 18p. pap. 8.99 *(978-1-62839-102-2(2))* Salem Author Services.

Loeb, Jeph. Blue. Sale, Tim, illus. 2003. (Spider-Man Ser.). 160p. (YA). 21.99 *(978-0-7851-1062-0(3))* Marvel Worldwide, Inc.

Lofting, Hugh. La Historia del Doctor Dolittle. (SPA.). 136p. 12.95 *(978-84-239-9048-1(6))*; (Illus.). 184p. (YA). (gr. 5-8). 11.95 *(978-84-239-2733-3(4)*, EC2743) Espasa Calpe, S.A. ESP. Dist: Planeta Publishing Corp., Continental Bk. Co., Inc., Lectorum Pubns., Inc.

—The Voyages of Doctor Dolittle. 2004. (Dover Children's Classics Ser.). (ENG., Illus.). 224p. (J). (gr. 3-7). pap. 4.95 *(978-0-486-43491-9(5))* Dover Pubns., Inc.

—The Voyages of Doctor Dolittle. McKowen, Scott, illus. 2012. (Sterling Unabridged Classics Ser.). (ENG.). 256p. (J). (gr. 5). 9.95 *(978-1-4027-9721-7(4))* Sterling Publishing Co., Inc.

Loftus, Tracy. Lucky Pup & Miss Millie Go Home. 2012. 28p. pap. 19.99 *(978-1-4772-6922-0(3))* AuthorHouse.

Logan, Erika. The Tick Tribe. 2012. 188p. pap. 13.99 *(978-1-4525-0712-5(0)*, Balboa Pr.) Author Solutions, Inc.

Logan, June. Billy & His Underwater Adventures. 2005. (J). 9.00 *(978-1-59971-046-4(3))* Aardvark Global Publishing.

Lois, Lowry. Anastasia Vive Aqui. Alonso, Juan Ramon, illus. 2003. (Anastasia Krupnik Ser.). (SPA.). 160p. (J). 9.95 *(978-84-670-0073-3(2))* Espasa Calpe, S.A. ESP. Dist: Planeta Publishing Corp.

Loisillier, Maud & Morel, Diane. The Planet of Jade. Smith, Owen & Collins Smith, Anne, trs. ÉLyum Studio, illus. 2012. (Little Prince Ser.: 4). (ENG.). 56p. (J). (gr. 4-8). pap. 7.95 *(978-1-4677-0263-8(3)*, Graphic Universe™) Lerner Publishing Group.

Loiske, Jennifer. Black Diamond. 2013. 246p. (J). pap. 13.61 *(978-1-291-30145-8(3))* Lulu Pr., Inc.

Lokaisingh, Jasmine. The Tales of Mme. Bovarie Vache & Mr. P. Huggins: In Huggsie's Birthday. 2011. 16p. 8.32 *(978-1-4520-4071-4(0))* AuthorHouse.

Lomba, Ana. Le Petit Chaperon Rouge. Wenzel, Dominique, tr. Cornejo, Santiago, illus. 2006.Tr. of Little Red Riding Hood/The Fun Way to Learn 50 New French Words! (ENG & FRE.). 48p. (gr. -1-3). 17.00 incl. audio compact disk *(978-0-07-146167-2(1)*, 0071461671) McGraw-Hill Cos., The.

Lombardo, G. Where the Trees Grow Gumballs. 2006. 57p. pap. 16.95 *(978-1-4241-2978-2(8))* PublishAmerica, Inc.

London, Alex. Guardian. 2015. (ENG.). 368p. (YA). (gr. 7). pap. 9.99 *(978-0-14-750981-9(5)*, Speak) Penguin Young Readers Group.

London, C. Alexander. Moonlight Brigade. 2016. (Wild Ones Ser.: 2). (ENG.). 240p. (J). (gr. 3-7). 17.99 *(978-0-399-17100-0(2)*, Philomel Bks.) Penguin Young Readers Group.

—Outbreak. 2016. (39 Clues: Super Special Ser.: 1). (ENG.). 272p. (J). (gr. 3-7). 13.99 *(978-1-338-03705-0(6))* Scholastic, Inc.

—We Are Not Eaten by Yaks. (Accidental Adventure Ser.: 1). (ENG.). (J). (gr. 3-7). 2013. 384p. pap. 7.99 *(978-0-14-242056-0(5)*, Puffin Books) 2011. 224p. 12.99 *(978-0-399-25487-1(0)*, Philomel Bks.) Penguin Young Readers Group.

—We Dine with Cannibals. 2013. (Accidental Adventure Ser.: 2). (ENG.). 384p. (J). (gr. 3-7). pap. 7.99 *(978-0-14-242474-2(9)*, Puffin Books) Penguin Young Readers Group.

London, Jack. Brown Wolf & Other Stories. 2005. 156p. per. 13.95 *(978-1-59818-706-9(6))* Aegypan.

—The Call of the Wild. (Illus.). 184p. (J). 9.95 *(978-1-56156-370-8(6))* Kidsbooks, LLC.

—The Call of the Wild. Moser, Barry, illus. 2011. (ENG.). 144p. (J). (gr. 4-9). pap. 8.99 *(978-1-4424-3411-0(2)*, Simon & Schuster Bks. For Young Readers) Simon & Schuster Bks. For Young Readers.

—The Call of the Wild: Prestwick House Literary Touchstone Edition. 2005. 100p. (YA). per. 3.99 *(978-1-58049-584-4(2)*, PWH5842) Prestwick Hse., Inc.

—The Call of the Wild - Spotlight Edition. Grudzina, Douglas, ed. 2005. 100p. (YA). per. 5.95 *(978-1-58049-552-3(4)*, PWH5524) Prestwick Hse., Inc.

—Faith of Men. 2006. 116p. per. 9.95 *(978-1-59818-074-9(6))* Aegypan.

—Graphic Classics - Jack London, Vol. 5. Pomplun, Tom, ed. Emerson, Hunt, illus. 2003. (ENG.). 144p. (gr. 7-18). pap. 9.95 *(978-0-9712464-5-4(9)*, 9780971246454) Eureka Productions.

—Jack London. 2003. cd-rom 19.00 *(978-0-931968-52-5(6))* Samizdat Express.

—La Llamada de la Naturaleza. 2003. (Historias de Siempre Ser.).Tr. of Call of the Wild. (SPA., Illus.). 92p. (J). (gr. 5-8). pap. 10.95 *(978-84-204-5731-4(0))* Santillana USA Publishing Co., Inc.

—La Llamada de la Selva.Tr. of Call of the Wild. (SPA.). (YA). 8.00 *(978-958-04-6747-2(1))* Norma S.A. COL. Dist: Distribuidora Norma, Inc.

—Michael Brother of Jerry. 2006. 228p. per. 15.95 *(978-1-59818-075-6(4))* Aegypan.

—The Mutiny of the 'ElsinoreApos. 2006. 264p. per. 15.95 *(978-1-59818-834-9(8))* Aegypan.

—La Quimera del Oro.Tr. of Gold Rush. (SPA.). 256p. (YA). *(978-84-7525-004-5(1))* Ediciones Generales Anaya SA.

London, Jonathan. Bella, Bella. London, Sean, illus. 2016. (Aaron's Wilderness Ser.: 2). (ENG.). 180p. (J). pap. 12.99 *(978-0-88240-923-8(9)*, West Winds Pr.) Graphic Arts Ctr. Publishing Co.

—Bella Bella. London, Sean, illus. 2016. (Aaron's Wilderness Ser.: 2). (ENG.). 180p. (YA). 23.99 *(978-1-943328-33-8(1)*, West Winds Pr.) Graphic Arts Ctr. Publishing Co.

—Desolation Canyon. London, Sean, illus. 2015. (Aaron's Wilderness Ser.: 1). (ENG.). 168p. (YA). pap. 12.99 *(978-1-941821-29-9(4)*, West Winds Pr.) Graphic Arts Ctr. Publishing Co.

—Grizzly Peak. London, Sean, illus. 2017. (Aaron's Wilderness Ser.). (ENG.). 174p. (YA). pap. 12.99 *(978-1-943328-77-2(3)*, West Winds Pr.) Graphic Arts Ctr. Publishing Co.

—Here Comes Doctor Hippo: A Little Hippo Story. Eduar, Gilles, illus. (Little Hippo Ser.). (ENG.). 32p. (J). (gr. -1-k). 2013. pap. 6.95 *(978-1-62091-595-0(2))* 2012. 15.95 *(978-1-59078-851-6(6))* Boyds Mills Pr.

London, Matt. We Built This City. 2016. (8th Continent Ser.: 4). (ENG.). 208p. (J). (gr. 3-7). 12.99 *(978-1-59514-840-7(X)*, Razorbill) Penguin Young Readers Group.

—The 8th Continent. 2014. (8th Continent Ser.: 1). (ENG.). 224p. (J). (gr. 3-7). 12.99 *(978-1-59514-754-7(3)*, Razorbill) Penguin Young Readers Group.

London, Matt & Loftin, Nikki. Born to Be Wild. 2015. (8th Continent Ser.: 3). (ENG., Illus.). 192p. (J). (gr. 3-7). 12.99 *(978-1-59514-756-1(X)*, Razorbill) Penguin Young Readers Group.

—Welcome to the Jungle. 2015. (8th Continent Ser.: 2). (ENG.). 224p. (J). (gr. 3-7). 12.99 *(978-1-59514-755-4(1)*, Razorbill) Penguin Young Readers Group.

Long, Chad Michael, illus. The Lycan Journal. Long, Chad Michael, . 2nd ed. 2007. 141p. (YA). per. 12.95 *(978-0-615-18961-1(X))* Long Stories LLC.

Long, Cliff. Broadside Ben & the Big Brass Cannon. 2004. (Illus.). 46p. (J). per. 8.95 *(978-0-9754400-0-1(4))* Watermark Cruises.

Long, Ethan. Clara & Clem Take a Ride. Long, Ethan, illus. 2012. (Penguin Young Readers, Level 1 Ser.). (ENG., Illus.). 32p. (J). (gr. k-1). mass mkt. 3.99 *(978-0-448-46264-6(8)*, Penguin Young Readers) Penguin Young Readers Group.

Long, Loren. The Drummer Boy. Long, Loren, illus. 2008. (ENG., Illus.). 40p. (J). (gr. -1-k). 18.99 *(978-0-399-25174-0(X)*, Philomel Bks.) Penguin Young Readers Group.

—Drummer Boy. Long, Loren, illus. 2012. (ENG., Illus.). 40p. (J). (gr. -1-k). mass mkt. 7.99 *(978-0-14-242341-7(6)*, Puffin Books) Penguin Young Readers Group.

Long, Loren & Bildner, Phil. Great Balls of Fire. Long, Loren, illus. 2009. (Sluggers Ser.: 3). (ENG., Illus.). 224p. (J). (gr. 3-7). pap. 7.99 *(978-1-4169-1889-9(2)*, Simon & Schuster Bks. For Young Readers) Simon & Schuster Bks. For Young Readers.

Long, Matty. Super Happy Magic Forest. Long, Matty, illus. 2016. (ENG., Illus.). 32p. (J). (gr. -1-3). 17.99 *(978-0-545-86059-8(8)*, Scholastic Pr.) Scholastic, Inc.

—Super Slug of Doom: A Super Happy Magic Forest Story. Long, Matty, illus. 2017. (ENG., Illus.). 32p. (J). (gr. -1-3). 17.99 *(978-1-338-05435-4(X)*, Scholastic Pr.) Scholastic, Inc.

Long, Melinda. How I Became a Pirate. Shannon, David, illus. 2003. (ENG.). 44p. (J). (gr. -1-3). 16.99 *(978-0-15-201848-1(4))* Houghton Mifflin Harcourt Publishing Co.

Long, Susan Hill. The Magic Mirror: Concerning a Lonely Princess, a Foundling Girl, a Scheming King & a Pickpocket Squirrel. 2016. (ENG., Illus.). 320p. (J). (gr. 3-7). 16.99 *(978-0-553-51134-5(3)*, Knopf Bks. for Young Readers) Random Hse. Children's Bks.

Long, Trishia. How I Met Bigfoot. 2012. 40p. pap. 20.99 *(978-1-4685-9425-6(7))* AuthorHouse.

Longley, Joshua. Barnaby's Buccaneers. 2011. 240p. (gr. 4-6). 25.95 *(978-1-4620-6112-9(5))*; pap. 15.95 *(978-1-4620-6110-5(9))* iUniverse, Inc.

Longo, Kaitlin. The Secret in Olivia's Garden. 2012. 36p. pap. 20.99 *(978-1-4685-5222-5(8))* AuthorHouse.

Longus. The ADVENTURES of SILVANA & the MAGIC UNICORN. 2008. 48p. 18.95 *(978-1-4357-1877-7(1))* Lulu Pr., Inc.

Loos, Jody C. Alex the Alien: Bubble Magic. 2013. 24p. pap. 14.95 *(978-1-4787-0322-8(9))* Outskirts Pr., Inc.

Lopez, Bolivar. Z Finds a Kite. 2010. 32p. pap. 13.49 *(978-1-4490-8650-3(0))* AuthorHouse.

Lopez, Cece. Mini Munchkin Mania Mini Series Presents: Mini Munchkin in the Mirror. 2013. (ENG.). 25p. (J). pap. 18.95 *(978-1-4787-1572-6(3))* Outskirts Pr., Inc.

Lopez, Cheyene Montana. Blue Sky Rainbows: A Series of Children's Stories of the World of Dreams & Imaginations, 1 vol. 2009. 82p. pap. 16.95 *(978-1-61582-290-4(9))* PublishAmerica, Inc.

Lopez, David Mark. Maddie's Magic Markers: Ride Like an Indian. 2006. (J). (gr. 3-7). *(978-0-9744097-1-9(5))* Lopez, David.

—Walk Like an Egyptian. 2006. (J). (gr. 3-7). *(978-0-9744097-0-2(7))* Lopez, David.

Lopez Dekker, Anna. Everwhere. 2008. 137p. 31.95 *(978-1-4092-0318-6(2))* Lulu Pr., Inc.

Lopez, Joe. Solemates. 2013. 28p. pap. 9.95 *(978-1-4787-2494-0(3))* Outskirts Pr., Inc.

Lopez, Maria Lorena. The Bird's Party, Birds in the Tropical Dry Forest. 2009. 28p. pap. 13.00 *(978-1-60860-156-1(0)*, Eloquent Bks.) Strategic Book Publishing & Rights Agency (SBPRA).

Lopez, Sixto. Snarloff Duwaki's Adventures. 2011. 24p. pap. 24.95 *(978-1-4626-2557-4(6))* America Star Bks.

Loranger, Marc J. Diamond in the Rough. 2004. (J). *(978-1-59196-741-5(4))* Instant Pub.

—Down There. 2012. (ENG.). 277p. pap. 19.95 *(978-1-4327-9142-1(7))* Outskirts Pr., Inc.

Lord, Cynthia. Touch Blue. 2010. (ENG.). 192p. (J). (gr. 3-7). 16.99 *(978-0-545-03531-6(7)*, Scholastic Pr.) Scholastic, Inc.

Lord, Pia. The Adventures of M M , Music Mouse. 2011. 50p. pap. 16.95 *(978-1-4626-3755-3(8))* America Star Bks.

Lore, Pittacus. The Fall of Five. 2013. (I Am Number Four Ser.: Bk. 4). (ENG.). 416p. (YA). (gr. 9). 17.99 *(978-0-06-197461-8(7))* HarperCollins Pubs.

—I Am Number Four. 2012. (Lorien Legacies: the Lost Files Ser.). (ENG.). 416p. (YA). (gr. 9). pap. 9.99 *(978-0-06-221110-1(2))* HarperCollins Pubs.

—I Am Number Four: The Lost Files: Hidden Enemy, Vol. 3. 2014. (Lorien Legacies: the Lost Files Ser.). (ENG.). 416p. (YA). (gr. 9). pap. 9.99 *(978-0-06-228768-7(0))* HarperCollins Pubs.

Lorentz, Dayna. No Dawn Without Darkness, Bk. 3. 3rd ed. 2015. (No Safety in Numbers Ser.: 3). (ENG.). 256p. (YA). (gr. 7). pap. 9.99 *(978-0-14-242622-7(9)*, Speak) Penguin Young Readers Group.

—No Easy Way Out, Bk. 2. 2nd ed. 2014. (No Safety in Numbers Ser.: 2). (ENG.). 480p. (YA). (gr. 7). pap. 9.99 *(978-0-14-242524-4(9)*, Speak) Penguin Young Readers Group.

—The Pack. 2011. (Dogs of the Drowned City Ser.: No. 2). (ENG.). 240p. (J). (gr. 3-7). 16.99 *(978-0-545-27644-3(6)*, Scholastic Pr.) Scholastic, Inc.

Lorenz Guest, Donna. The Enchanted Ride. 2009. 32p. pap. 14.99 *(978-1-4389-8116-1(3))* AuthorHouse.

Lorenzo, Amanda. Clovis Escapes! Bks. 3: Runt Farm. Walker, Mark Evan, illus. 2009. 136p. 12.95 *(978-0-9800952-2-7(0))* BooktiMookti Pr.

Lorenzo, Mike. Allison's Summer Of '53. 2005. 53p. pap. 16.95 *(978-1-4241-1074-2(2))* PublishAmerica, Inc.

Lorimer, Janet. Boneyard (Suspense), 1 vol. 2017. (Pageturners Ser.). (ENG.). 84p. (YA). (gr. 9-12). 8.95 ***(978-1-68021-403-1(9))*** Saddleback Educational Publishing, Inc.

Lorimer, Janet. Ring of Fear, 1 vol. unabr. ed. 2010. (Q Reads Ser.). (ENG.). 32p. (YA). (gr. 9-12). pap. 6.95 *(978-1-61651-194-4(X))* Saddleback Educational Publishing, Inc.

Lorraine. The Adventures of Ruthy: Ruthy Gets Lost. 2012. 32p. pap. 19.99 *(978-1-4772-6000-5(5))* AuthorHouse.

Lorraine, Nancy. The Butterfly Adventure. Herron, Dorothy, illus. 2nd ed. 2013. 50p. 22.50 *(978-0-9886194-9-4(0))* ProsePress.

The Lost Treasure of Skull Island. 2012. (Illus.). (J). *(978-1-4351-4328-9(0))* Barnes & Noble, Inc.

Lotz, Dana. What It's Like to Still Be a Kid. 2005. 61p. pap. 16.95 *(978-1-4137-9257-7(X))* PublishAmerica, Inc.

Louchard, Anto. Plume dans le Whisky. pap. 12.95 *(978-2-84146-723-5(6))* Editions Milan FRA. Dist: Distribooks, Inc.

Lough, Whitney. Smoke Hole Adventure. Cosner, Jeff, illus. 2013. 36p. (J). 12.00 *(978-0-87012-833-2(7))* McClain Printing Co.

Loughead, Deb. Caught in the Act, 1 vol. 2013. (Orca Currents Ser.). (ENG.). 128p. (J). (gr. 5-9). pap. 9.95 *(978-1-4598-0496-8(1))*; lib. bdg. 16.95 *(978-1-4598-0510-1(0))* Orca Bk. Pubs. USA.

Louis, Robb. Monster in the Moat. 2011. (Illus.). 44p. (gr. -1). pap. 18.46 *(978-1-4567-4053-5(9))* AuthorHouse.

Love, Angela. 'Gwyngallion' Guardian of Little Children Lost in the Woods. 2009. (Illus.). 40p. pap. 16.99 *(978-1-4389-2017-7(2))* AuthorHouse.

Love, D. Anne. The Secret Prince. 2012. (ENG.). 240p. (J). (gr. 3-7). pap. 11.99 *(978-1-4424-5931-1(X)*, McElderry, Margaret K. Bks.) McElderry, Margaret K. Bks.

Love, Emily. The Beginning of Freedom. 2010. 81p. pap. 9.00 *(978-0-557-56598-6(7))* Lulu Pr., Inc.

Love, Judy. Praise Be & Rainbows. 2006. 51p. pap. 16.95 *(978-1-4241-0333-1(9))* PublishAmerica, Inc.

Love, Makada H. Harold's Adventures. Holt, Lindsey, illus. 2008. 92p. pap. 10.99 *(978-1-4343-6875-1(0))* AuthorHouse.

Lovelady, W. f. The Adventures of Johnny Saturday: Back to the Drawing Board. 2012. 76p. pap. 12.95 *(978-1-4685-5286-7(4))* AuthorHouse.

Lovell, H. N. Wootie's Great Adventure: Escape to Freedom. 2006. (J). pap. 12.95 *(978-0-9761182-1-3(1))* Alpha Run Pr., LLC.

Loveridge, Pamela. The Knife of Blood. 2012. 28p. pap. 32.70 *(978-1-4797-4804-4(8))* Xlibris Corp.

Lovett, Darrell. Hi, I'm Alex. l.t. ed. 2006. (ENG., Illus.). 28p. per. 9.95 *(978-1-4327-0195-6(9))* Outskirts Pr., Inc.

—My Dog Tony. l.t. ed. 2006. (ENG., Illus.). 28p. per. 9.95 *(978-1-4327-0187-1(8))* Outskirts Pr., Inc.

Lovett, Tracy M. Buck's Rodeo. Lovett, Tracy M., illus. 2012. (Illus.). 470p. pap. 16.50 *(978-0-9819736-6-1(3))* Inclement Pr.

Lovhaug, Lewis J. Angel Armor: Just a Boy. 2003. 224p. (YA). pap. 15.95 *(978-0-595-28475-7(2))* iUniverse, Inc.

Low, Chen-Chen-Chen. Lizzie May & Oshin. 2009. 46p. pap. 29.99 *(978-1-4092-5740-0(1))* Lulu Pr., Inc.

—Lizzie May & the Shoelaces. 2009. 44p. pap. 29.99 *(978-1-4092-5739-4(8))* Lulu Pr., Inc.

Lowe, Lana. The Three Little Girls & the Giant Sea Turtle. Beaumont, Peter, illus. 2006. (J). *(978-0-9777274-0-7(8))* Lone Star Publishing Co.

Lowe, Tom. Louie the Loon & the Moon. Leadlove, Ben, illus. 2011. 28p. pap. 11.00 *(978-1-61170-030-5(2))* Robertson Publishing.

Lowery, Linda & Keep, Richard. The Tale of la Llorona: A Mexican Folktale. Porter, Janice Lee, illus. 2007. (On My Own Folklore Ser.). (ENG.). 48p. (gr. 2-4). lib. bdg. 25.26 *(978-0-8225-6378-5(9)*, Millbrook Pr.) Lerner Publishing Group.

Lowery, Mike. Doodle Adventures: the Search for the Slimy Space Slugs! 2016. (Doodle Adventures Ser.). (ENG., Illus.). 112p. (J). (gr. 2-5). 12.95 *(978-0-7611-8719-6(7))* Workman Publishing Co., Inc.

—The Pursuit of the Pesky Pizza Pirate! 2016. (Doodle Adventures Ser.). (ENG., Illus.). 112p. (J). (gr. 2-5). 12.95 *(978-0-7611-8720-2(0))* Workman Publishing Co., Inc.

Lowery, Rae. Charlie & the Case of the Big Bully: The Adventures of Charlie #4, 1 vol. 2010. 108p. pap. 19.95 *(978-1-4489-5558-9(0))* America Star Bks.

Lowitz, Leza & Oketani, Shogo. Jet Black & the Ninja Wind. 2013. (ENG.). 320p. (J). (gr. 7-12). pap. 15.95 *(978-0-8048-4402-4(X))*; (Illus.). 17.99 *(978-4-8053-1284-1(X))* Tuttle Publishing.

Lowrey, Chris. Wonec Adventures: The Gift of Giving. 2008. 26p. pap. 24.95 *(978-1-60563-622-1(3))* America Star Bks.

Lowry, Mark & Bolton, Martha. Piper's Great Adventures. Myers, Kristen, illus. 2005. (ENG.). 124p. pap. 15.99 *(978-1-58229-474-2(7)*, Howard Bks.) Howard Books.

Loyd, Mark. Big Ben: A Little Known Story. Loyd, Mark, illus. 2005. (Illus.). (J). *(978-0-9773317-1-0(7))* Too Fun Publshing.

Loyd, Todd. Dark Ride. 2012. (ENG.). 320p. (YA). (gr. 7-9). pap. 15.00 *(978-1-936487-22-6(5)*, 1936487225) Franklin Green Publishing.

Loyie, Larry & Brissenden, Constance. As Long As the Rivers Flow, 1 vol. Holmlund, Heather D., illus. 2005. (ENG.). 40p. (J). (gr. 4-7). pap. 9.95 *(978-0-88899-696-1(9))* Groundwood Bks. CAN. Dist: Publishers Group West (PGW).

Lu, Marie. The Midnight Star. 2016. (Young Elites Novel Ser.: 3). (ENG., Illus.). 336p. (YA). (gr. 7). 18.99 *(978-0-399-16785-0(4)*, G.P. Putnam's Sons Books for Young Readers) Penguin Young Readers Group.

—The Rose Society. 2015. (Young Elites Ser.: 2). (ENG., Illus.). 416p. (YA). (gr. 7). 18.99 *(978-0-399-16784-3(6)*, G.P. Putnam's Sons Books for Young Readers) Penguin Publishing Group.

—The Rose Society. 2016. (Young Elites Novel Ser.). (ENG.). 432p. (YA). (gr. 7). pap. 10.99 *(978-0-14-751169-0(0)*, Speak) Penguin Young Readers Group.

—The Rose Society. l.t. ed. 2015. (Young Elites Ser.). (ENG.). 24.99 *(978-1-4104-8465-9(3))* Thorndike Pr.

—The Rose Society. 2016. (Young Elites Ser.: 2). (ENG.). 432p. (YA). (gr. 7). 22.10 *(978-0-606-39314-0(5))* Turtleback Bks.

Lu, Marie. The Young Elites. 2014. (ENG., Illus.). 368p. (YA). (gr. 7). 18.99 *(978-0-399-16783-6(8)*, G.P. Putnam's Sons Books for Young Readers) Penguin Publishing Group.

—The Young Elites. 2015. (Young Elites Novel Ser.). (ENG.). 384p. (YA). (gr. 7). pap. 10.99 *(978-0-14-751168-3(2)*, Speak) Penguin Young Readers Group.

—The Young Elites. 2015. (ENG.). (YA). (gr. 7). lib. bdg. 21.60 ***(978-1-68065-052-5(1))*** Perfection Learning Corp.

—The Young Elites. 2015. (Young Elites Ser.: 1). lib. bdg. 22.10 *(978-0-606-37575-7(9))* Turtleback Bks.

Lubar, David. Ghost Attack (Monster Itch #1) 2017. (Monster Itch Ser.: 1). (ENG.). 128p. (J). (gr. 2-5). pap. 4.99 ***(978-0-545-87348-2(7)***, Scholastic Paperbacks) Scholastic, Inc.

Lucan, Dawn. Daily Adventure Memories. 2010. 48p. pap. 16.95 *(978-0-557-53422-7(4))* Lulu Pr., Inc.

—My Challenge Memories. 2011. 108p. pap. 8.95 *(978-1-4583-4714-5(1))* Lulu Pr., Inc.

Lucas & His Long Loopy Laces. 2013. (Illus.). 48p. 16.99 *(978-0-9823519-4-9(1))* Tall Tails Publishing Hse.

Lucas Film Book Group. Luke Skywalker. 2016. (Star Wars: Force Awakens 8X8 Ser.). (J). lib. bdg. 14.75 ***(978-0-606-39175-7(4))*** Turtleback Bks.

—Star Wars Poe Dameron 8x8. 2017. (ENG.). 24p. (J). (gr. 1-3). pap. 4.99 *(978-1-4847-0506-3(8)*, Disney Lucasfilm Press) Disney Publishing Worldwide.

—Star Wars: Revenge of the Sith Read-Along Storybook & CD. 2017. (Read-Along Storybook & CD Ser.). (ENG.). 32p. (J). (gr. 1-3). pap. 6.99 *(978-1-4847-8181-4(3)*, Disney Lucasfilm Press) Disney Publishing Worldwide.

—Star Wars Star Wars: Attack of the Clones Read-Along Storybook & CD. 2017. (Read-Along Storybook & CD Ser.). (ENG.). 32p. (J). (gr. 1-3). pap. 6.99 *(978-1-4847-8180-7(5)*, Disney Lucasfilm Press) Disney Publishing Worldwide.

—Trouble on Tatooine. 2017. (Star Wars: World of Reading Ser.). (J). lib. bdg. 14.75 ***(978-0-606-39963-0(1))*** Turtleback Bks.

—World of Reading Star Wars Boxed Set: Level 2. 2017. (ENG.). 192p. (J). (gr. 1-3). pap. 12.99 ***(978-1-368-00587-6(X)***, Disney Lucasfilm Press) Disney Publishing Worldwide.

Lucas Film Book Group. World of Reading Star Wars Trouble on Tatooine (Level 2) 2017. (World of Reading Ser.). (ENG.).

32p. (J). (gr. 1-3). pap. 4.99 *(978-1-4847-9934-5(8),* Disney Lucasfilm Press) Disney Publishing Worldwide.

Lucas Film Book Group & Forbeck, Matt. Star Wars Rogue One Junior Novel. 2017. (ENG.). 192p. (J). (gr. 3-7). 10.99 *(978-1-4847-0509-4(2),* Disney Lucasfilm Press) Disney Publishing Worldwide.

Lucas Film Book Group & Fry, Jason. Luke & the Lost Jedi Temple. 2016. (ENG.). 24p. (J). (gr. 1-3). pap. 4.99 *(978-1-4847-0505-6(X),* Disney Lucasfilm Press) Disney Publishing Worldwide.

Lucas Film Book Group, et al. Join the Resistance, Bk. 1. Wu, Annie, illus. 2017. (Join the Resistance Ser.). (ENG.). 224p. (J). (gr. 5-7). 12.99 *(978-1-4847-0484-4(3),* Disney Lucasfilm Press) Disney Publishing Worldwide.

Lucas Film Book Group Editors. Poe Dameron. 2017. (Star Wars: Force Awakens 8X8 Ser.). (J). lib. bdg. 14.75 *(978-0-606-39506-9(7))* Turtleback Bks.

Lucas Film Book Group Staff & Holland, Jesse J. Star Wars Finn's Story. Rood, Brian, illus. 2016. (ENG.). 128p. (J). (gr. 1-3). pap. 5.99 *(978-1-4847-9022-9(7),* Disney Lucasfilm Press) Disney Publishing Worldwide.

Lucas, Gareth, illus. Dig, Dig, Digger! 2017. (Gareth Lucas Noisy Bks.). (ENG.). 12p. (J). (gr. -1). bds. 14.99 *(978-1-62686-936-3(7),* Silver Dolphin Bks.) Readerlink Distribution Services, LLC.

Lucas, Lexie. The Adventures of Little Boy Brown. 2011. (Illus.). 40p. pap. 16.59 *(978-1-4567-4035-1(0))* AuthorHouse.

Lucas, Nicole A. Sammy Bo Bo Hammy. 2012. 24p. pap. 17.99 *(978-1-4685-7251-3(2))* AuthorHouse.

Lucasfilm Book Group. The Heist. 2017. (Star Wars Adventures in Wild Space Ser.: 3). (J). lib. bdg. 16.00 ***(978-0-606-39961-6(5))*** Turtleback Bks.

—The Nest. 2017. (Star Wars Adventures in Wild Space Ser.: 2). (J). lib. bdg. 16.00 *(978-0-606-39562-5(8))* Turtleback Bks.

—The Snare. 2017. (Star Wars Adventures in Wild Space Ser.: 1). (J). lib. bdg. 16.00 *(978-0-606-39561-8(X))* Turtleback Bks.

LucasFilm Book Group. Star Wars Adventures in Wild Space the Heist: Book 3. 2017. (Adventures in Wild Space Ser.). (ENG.). 144p. (J). (gr. 1-3). pap. 5.99 *(978-1-368-00314-8(1),* Disney Lucasfilm Press) Disney Publishing Worldwide.

—Star Wars Galactic Maps: An Illustrated Atlas of the Star Wars Universe. 2016. (ENG.). 80p. (J). (gr. 3-7). 24.99 *(978-1-368-00306-3(0),* Disney Lucasfilm Press) Disney Publishing Worldwide.

—World of Reading Star Wars Finn & Poe Team Up! 2016. (ENG., Illus.). 32p. (J). (gr. 1-3). pap. 3.99 *(978-1-4847-4143-6(9),* Disney Lucasfilm Press) Disney Publishing Worldwide.

LucasFilm Book Group & Huddleston, Tom. The Nest. 2017. (Adventures in Wild Space Ser.). (ENG.). 144p. (J). (gr. 1-3). pap. 5.99 *(978-1-368-00316-2(8),* Disney Lucasfilm Press) Disney Publishing Worldwide.

LucasFilm Book Group & Scott, Cavan. The Snare. 2017. (Adventures in Wild Space Ser.). (ENG.). 144p. (J). (gr. 1-3). pap. 5.99 *(978-1-368-00275-2(7),* Disney Lucasfilm Press) Disney Publishing Worldwide.

LucasFilm Book Group Staff. World of Reading: Star Wars Listen along: Star Wars: 3 World of Reading Level 2 Readers with CD! 2016. (World of Reading Ser.). (ENG.). 96p. (J). (gr. -1-k). pap. 7.99 *(978-1-4847-9024-3(3),* Disney Lucasfilm Press) Disney Publishing Worldwide.

Lucasfilm Press. Han & the Rebel Rescue. 2017. (J). lib. bdg. 14.75 ***(978-0-606-39966-1(6))*** Turtleback Bks.

LucasFilm Press. Star Wars: 5-Minute Star Wars Stories. 2015. (ENG.). 176p. (J). (gr. 1-3). 12.99 *(978-1-4847-2820-8(3),* Disney Lucasfilm Press) Disney Publishing Worldwide.

LucasFilm Press Staff. The Force Awakens. Rood, Brian, illus. 2015. (World of Reading Ser.). (ENG.). 32p. (J). (gr. 1-3). pap. 3.99 *(978-1-4847-0481-3(9))* Disney Pr.

Lucci, Cindy. Bob the Builder: Big Book of Words. 2017. (ENG., Illus.). 12p. (J). (gr. -1 — 1). bds. 8.99 *(978-0-316-27299-5(X))* Little, Brown Bks. for Young Readers.

Lucero, Erik Kristofer. Ki-Ky the Cat. 2011. 24p. pap. 24.95 *(978-1-4560-3761-1(7))* America Star Bks.

Luciani, Brigitte & Tharlet, Eve. How Will We Get to the Beach?/Cómo Iremos a la Playa? An English-Spanish Guessing-Game Story. 2006. (Michael Neugebauer Books Ser.). (SPA., Illus.). 32p. (J). (gr. -1). pap. 7.95 *(978-0-7358-2038-8(4))* North-South Bks., Inc.

Luck, Gail. Bumduggle Davis Joins the Dots: Or It's All There in Black & White. 2012. 166p. pap. 13.50 *(978-1-62212-379-7(4),* Strategic Bk. Publishing) Strategic Book Publishing & Rights Agency (SBPRA).

Lucky, A. E. Kyle the Detective, 1 vol. 2010. 70p. pap. 19.95 *(978-1-4512-2042-1(1))* America Star Bks.

Lucky Foot Stable & Lady's Big Surprise. 2003. (J). *(978-0-9746561-7-5(8))* FT Richards Publishing.

LuckySports, illus. Adventures in SportsLand - the Golf Bully (with accompanying CD) The Golf Bully. LuckySports, . 2008. 32p. (J). pap. 19.95 *(978-0-935938-29-6(X))* Stogo, Malcolm Assocs.

Ludwig, Elisa. Pretty Crooked. 2014. (Pretty Crooked Trilogy Ser.: 1). (ENG.). 384p. (YA). (gr. 8). pap. 9.99 *(978-0-06-206607-7(2),* Tegen, Katherine Bks) HarperCollins Pubs.

Ludy, Mark. Jujo: The Youngest Tribesman. Ludy, Mark, illus. 2007. (ENG., Illus.). 32p. (J). (gr. k-2). 16.95 *(978-0-9664276-5-3(3))* Scribble & Sons.

Luedtke, Courtney. Baby Boo: The Happy Beginning. 2009. (Illus.). 72p. pap. 27.49 *(978-1-4389-2696-4(0))* AuthorHouse.

Luiken, Nichole & Luiken, Nicole. Amid Wind & Stone. 2016. (ENG., Illus.). 410p. (J). pap. 14.99 *(978-1-68281-126-9(3))* Entangled Publishing, LLC.

Luján, Jorge. Palabras Manzana. 2003. (Sopa de Libros Ser.). (SPA., Illus.). 94p. (gr. 2-4). pap. 13.99 *(978-84-667-2474-6(5))* Grupo Anaya, S.A. ESP. Dist: Lectorum Pubns., Inc.

Luke, Jacqueline. Yellow Pea in the Pod. 2009. 92p. pap. 30.49 *(978-1-4343-3716-0(2))* AuthorHouse.

Luke's Adventures: Individual Title Six-Packs. (gr. -1-2). 27.00 *(978-0-7635-9460-2(1))* Rigby Education.

Lumry, Amanda & Hurwitz, Laura. Amazon River Rescue. McIntyre, Sarah, illus. 2004. (Adventures of Riley Ser.). 36p. 15.95 *(978-0-9662257-9-2(1))* Eaglemont Pr.

—Polar Bear Puzzle. 2007. (Adventures of Riley Ser.). (Illus.). (J). (gr. -1-3). 33p. 15.95 *(978-1-60040-004-9(3));* 36p. 18.95 *(978-1-60040-005-6(1))* Eaglemont Pr.

Lund, Celia. Square Sails & Dragons. 2006. 284p. per. 19.95 *(978-1-4120-5758-5(2))* Trafford Publishing.

Lund, Wendy E. The Fly Away Balloon. 2010. 50p. pap. 16.50 *(978-1-60911-660-6(7),* Eloquent Bks.) Strategic Book Publishing & Rights Agency (SBPRA).

Lunetta, Demitria. In the End. 2014. (In the After Ser.: 2). (ENG.). 448p. (YA). (gr. 8). 17.99 *(978-0-06-210548-6(5),* HarperTeen) HarperCollins Pubs.

Lunn, John. The Mariner's Curse. 2004. (ENG.). 216p. (J). (gr. 4-7). pap. 8.95 *(978-0-88776-672-5(2),* Tundra Bks.) Tundra Bks. CAN. Dist: Penguin Random Hse. LLC.

Lunsford, Russell. Benjamin Nathan Tuggle: Adventurer: Daniel Boone & the Settlement of Boonesborough, Kentucky. 2010. 112p. (gr. 4-6). 20.95 *(978-1-4502-3361-3(9));* pap. 10.95 *(978-1-4502-3360-6(0))* iUniverse, Inc.

Lunsk, Robert. Kippy Berryfoote. 2012. (ENG.). (J). pap. *(978-1-4675-4313-2(6))* Independent Pub.

Luper, Eric. The Haunted Howl. 2016. (Key Hunters Ser.: 3). (ENG., Illus.). 128p. (J). (gr. 2-5). pap. 4.99 *(978-0-545-82211-4(4),* Scholastic Paperbacks) Scholastic, Inc.

—The Mysterious Moonstone. 2016. (Key Hunters Ser.: 1). (ENG., Illus.). 128p. (J). (gr. 2-5). pap. 4.99 *(978-0-545-82204-6(1))* Scholastic, Inc.

—The Spy's Secret. 2016. (Key Hunters Ser.: 2). (ENG.). 128p. (J). (gr. 2-5). pap. 4.99 *(978-0-545-82206-0(8))* Scholastic, Inc.

—The Titanic Treasure. 2017. (Key Hunters Ser.: 5). (ENG.). 128p. (J). (gr. 2-5). pap. 4.99 ***(978-1-338-14926-5(1),*** Scholastic Paperbacks) Scholastic, Inc.

—The Titanic Treasure (Key Hunters #5) 2017. (Key Hunters Ser.: 5). (ENG.). 128p. (J). (gr. 2-5). lib. bdg. 16.99 ***(978-1-338-14927-2(X),*** Scholastic Paperbacks) Scholastic, Inc.

Luper, Eric. The Wizard's War (Key Hunters #4) 2017. (Key Hunters Ser.: 4). (ENG.). 128p. (J). (gr. 2-5). pap. 4.99 *(978-0-545-82213-8(0),* Scholastic Paperbacks) Scholastic, Inc.

Lupica, Mike. Heavy Hitters. 2014. (Game Changers Ser.: 3). (ENG.). 240p. (J). (gr. 3-7). 16.99 *(978-0-545-38184-0(3))* Scholastic, Inc.

Lurie, Craig. Butterflies, Ladybugs, & Bumble Bees & the wonderful world this could Be .... 2011. 36p. (gr. -1). pap. 14.95 *(978-1-4567-6300-8(8))* AuthorHouse.

Lush, Nella. Gracie & Belle Never Again! 2007. 20p. per. 24.95 *(978-1-4241-8373-9(1))* America Star Bks.

Luster, Bonnie. The Adventures of Mrs. Tibbles & Her Toys: Spots. 2012. 28p. pap. 16.95 *(978-1-4497-6929-1(2),* WestBow Pr.) Author Solutions, Inc.

Lutz II, William. Quest of Brothers. 2007. 346p. pap. 18.99 *(978-0-615-15622-4(3))* Lutz, William G.

—Seeking Mason. 2009. 212p. pap. 14.00 *(978-0-557-03737-7(9))* Lulu Pr., Inc.

Luxa, Sue. A Cabin in Cripple Creek. 2004. (Illus.). 99p. (J). pap. 8.95 *(978-1-932738-04-9(5),* 1234249) Western Reflections Publishing Co.

Lyall, Casey. Howard Wallace, P. I. (Howard Wallace, P. I. Ser.). (ENG.). (J). (gr. 3-7). 2017. 288p. pap. 6.95 ***(978-1-4549-2604-7(X))*** 2016. 272p. 14.95 *(978-1-4549-1949-0(3))* Sterling Publishing Co., Inc.

Lyen, Taylor Samuel. Pembroke: The Adventures of Arthur Bacterium & Patty Virus. 2012. 180p. (-18). pap. 13.95 *(978-1-4759-5855-3(2))* iUniverse, Inc.

Lyford, Joan. Daisybelle & Dash, a Bedtime Story. 2012. 24p. pap. 14.93 *(978-1-4669-1154-3(9))* Trafford Publishing.

Lyga, Barry. The Secret Sea. 2016. (ENG.). 448p. (J). 16.99 *(978-1-250-07283-2(2),* 9781250072832) Feiwel & Friends.

Lyle, Cindy. The Creation Chronicles - the Dragon Within. 2013. 320p. *(978-1-4602-2618-6(6))* FriesenPress.

Lyle-Soffe, Shari. The Misadventures of Rooter & Snuffle. Collier, Kevin Scott, illus. 2008. 20p. pap. 9.95 *(978-1-933090-88-7(X))* 2006. 28p. (J). E-Book 5.00 incl. cd-rom *(978-1-933090-43-6(X))* Guardian Angel Publishing, Inc.

Lynch, Brendan Denis. The Document. 2012. 218p. pap. 8.99 *(978-0-9825243-2-9(3))* 1776 Pr.

Lynch, Chris. I Pledge Allegiance. 2011. (Vietnam Ser.: 1). (ENG.). 192p. (J). (gr. 3-7). 16.99 *(978-0-545-27029-8(4),* Scholastic Pr.) Scholastic, Inc.

Lynch, Keven R. What's a Buffalo Soldier? The Historical Adventures of Amber & Trevor. 2005. (J). pap. 12.00 *(978-0-8059-6750-0(8))* Dorrance Publishing Co., Inc.

Lynch, Lauren Boehm. The Yellow Butterfly. DeBroeck, Sarah, illus. 2011. 28p. pap. 24.95 *(978-1-4560-0982-3(6))* America Star Bks.

Lynes, William. Pirates, Scoundrels, & Kings. 2013. 450p. (gr. 10-12). 33.95 *(978-1-4759-6562-9(1));* pap. 23.95 *(978-1-4759-6561-2(3))* iUniverse, Inc.

Lynn, Catherine. The Great Sock Adventure. 2011. 32p. (gr. -1). pap. 16.49 *(978-1-4490-8062-4(6))* AuthorHouse.

Lynn, Deidre. Treasure Delight: A Sweet Story about the Joy in Sharing. Morris, Jessica, illus. 2013. 36p. pap. 12.95 *(978-0-9893181-0-5(9))* LoveLight Media.

Lynn, Jeffrey. The Adventures of Pablo. . the Ecuadorian Panda. 2004. (YA). per. *(978-0-9763025-0-6(0))* Penner/Lynn Publishing.

Lyon, Nathan W. & Ellis, Kevin L. Sam the Clam. 2010. 28p. pap. 14.95 *(978-1-4520-7784-0(3))* AuthorHouse.

Lyons, Jayne. 100% Wolf. Rivas, Victor, illus. 2010. (ENG.). 256p. (J). (gr. 2-7). pap. 7.99 *(978-1-4424-0252-2(0),* Atheneum Bks. for Young Readers) Simon & Schuster Children's Publishing.

Lyons, Maggie. Dewi & the Seeds of Doom. 2012. 70p. pap. 9.99 *(978-1-61244-094-1(0))* Halo Publishing International.

Lyons Stroud, Patricia. The Seven Keys to Adventure. 2007. 148p. 23.00 *(978-1-59048-252-0(2))* Long Riders' Guild Pr., The.

Lyttleton, Kay. Jean Craig in New York. 2005. pap. 24.95 *(978-1-4179-9293-5(X))* Kessinger Publishing, LLC.

Lyzenga, Antonia Babauta. Happy Island. 2012. 32p. pap. 21.99 *(978-1-4797-2037-8(2))* Xlibris Corp.

M. Eugenia Coeymans. The Universe of the Aurus. 2013. 60p. pap. 20.99 *(978-1-4808-0366-4(9))* Archway Publishing.

Ma, Wenhai, illus. Tang Monk Disciples Monkey King. 2005. (Adventures of Monkey King Ser.: No. 3). 32p. (J). 16.95 *(978-1-57227-084-8(5))* Pan Asia Pubns. (USA), Inc.

—Tang Monk Disciples Monkey King: English/Chinese. 2005. (Adventures of Monkey King Ser.: No. 3). (ENG & CHI.). 32p. (J). 16.95 *(978-1-57227-086-2(1))* Pan Asia Pubns. (USA), Inc.

Ma, Wing Shing. A Tale of No Name, Vol. 1. 2005. (Storm Riders Ser.). (Illus.). 300p. (YA). pap. 7.95 *(978-1-58899-375-5(2))* ComicsOne Corp./Dr. Masters.

Maartman, Ben. The Lost Treasures of Yucatan: A Belizean Saga. 2004. (Illus.). 106p. (YA). pap. 14.50 *(978-1-4120-1487-8(5))* Trafford Publishing.

Maas, Sarah J. A Court of Thorns & Roses. 2017. (ENG.). 96p. (YA). pap. 15.99 *(978-1-68119-576-6(3),* 9781681195766, Bloomsbury USA Childrens) Bloomsbury Publishing USA.

Mabbitt, Will. Mabel Jones & the Doomsday Book. 2016. (Mabel Jones Ser.). (ENG., Illus.). 336p. (J). (gr. 3-7). 16.99 *(978-1-101-99962-2(4),* Viking Books for Young Readers) Penguin Young Readers Group.

—Mabel Jones & the Forbidden City. Collins, Ross, illus. 2016. (Mabel Jones Ser.). (ENG.). 304p. (J). (gr. 3-7). 16.99 *(978-0-451-47197-0(0),* Viking Books for Young Readers) Penguin Young Readers Group.

—The Unlikely Adventures of Mabel Jones. Collins, Ross, illus. 2015. (Mabel Jones Ser.). (ENG.). 304p. (J). (gr. 3-7). 16.99 *(978-0-451-47196-3(2),* Viking Books for Young Readers) Penguin Young Readers Group.

Maberry, Jonathan. The Rot & Ruin Collection: Rot & Ruin; Dust & Decay; Flesh & Bone, Fire & Ash. 2013. (Rot & Ruin Ser.). (ENG., Illus.). 2016p. (YA). (gr. 7). 72.99 *(978-1-4424-9770-2(X),* Simon & Schuster Bks. For Young Readers) Simon & Schuster Bks. For Young Readers.

Mabille, Christine. Potato-Kid & the Adventure: Treasures Within, 1 vol. 2009. 76p. pap. 19.95 *(978-1-61582-981-1(4))* America Star Bks.

Mac Uistin, Liam. The Táin: Ireland's Epic Adventure. Teskey, Donald, illus. 2012. (ENG.). 112p. (J). pap. 10.95 *(978-1-84717-288-4(1))* O'Brien Pr., Ltd., The IRL. Dist: Dufour Editions, Inc.

Macaluso, Jennifer. Where Do the Bubbles Go? O'Shaughnessy, Nancy, illus. 2006. (ENG.). 40p. (J). (gr. -1-3). pap. 21.99 *(978-1-4259-3929-8(5))* AuthorHouse.

Macan, Darko. Soldier X. Kordey, Igor, illus. 2003. 144p. (YA). pap. 12.99 *(978-0-7851-1013-2(5))* Marvel Worldwide, Inc.

Macauley, Jo. Secrets & Spies, 1 vol. 2014. (Secrets & Spies Ser.). (ENG.). 224p. (gr. 4-7). 53.30 *(978-1-4342-8770-0(X))* Stone Arch Bks.

Macdangereuse, T. T. The Lonesome Outlaw. 2015. (Epic Tales from Adventure Time Ser.). lib. bdg. 17.20 *(978-0-606-37579-5(1))* Turtleback Bks.

—The Untamed Scoundrel. 2014. (Epic Tales from Adventure Time Ser.). lib. bdg. 17.20 *(978-0-606-35718-0(1))* Turtleback Bks.

MacDonald, George. The Carasoyn. 2008. 108p. 22.95 *(978-1-60664-921-3(3));* pap. 9.95 *(978-1-60664-041-8(0))* Aegypan.

—A Double Story. 2008. 108p. 22.95 *(978-1-60664-983-1(3))* Aegypan.

—The Golden Key: Classic fairy Tales. McCabe, Steve, illus. 2008. 104p. (J). pap. *(978-0-88835-045-9(7))* Meany, P. D. Pubs.

—History of GuttaPercha Willie. 2006. 116p. 22.95 *(978-1-59818-157-9(2))* Aegypan.

—Phantastes, a Faerie Romance. 2007. 164p. per. 12.95 *(978-1-60312-241-2(9));* 24.95 *(978-1-60312-819-3(0))* Aegypan.

—The Princess & the Goblin. 2010. 222p. pap. 13.95 *(978-0-557-47296-3(2))* Lulu Pr., Inc.

—Stephen Archer & Other Tales. 2008. 212p. 26.95 *(978-1-60664-985-5(X))* Aegypan.

MacDonald, Hugh. Morgan's Boat Ride, 1 vol. Bald, Anna, illus. 2014. (ENG.). 24p. (J). (gr. -1-3). pap. 12.95 *(978-1-894838-96-2(3))* Acorn Pr., The CAN. Dist: Orca Bk. Pubs. USA.

MacDonald, James. Levi, Adventures of a Police Dog. 2005. (Illus.). 96p. (J). 16.95 *(978-0-9716923-1-2(9))* Regency Hse., Ltd.

MacDonald, Jerry. Red Eyes & Crazy Jake. 2009. 24p. pap. 15.95 *(978-1-4389-2706-0(1))* AuthorHouse.

MacDonald, Suse. Alphabet Animals: A Slide-and-Peek Adventure. MacDonald, Suse, illus. 2008. (ENG., Illus.). 28p. (J). (gr. -1-k). 12.99 *(978-1-4169-5045-5(1),* Little Simon) Little Simon.

MacDonald, Tom. Secret of the Tree: Marcus Speer's Ecosentinel. Stieber, Joel, illus. 2009. 300p. 28.95 *(978-0-595-51985-9(7));* pap. 18.95 *(978-0-595-52402-0(8))* iUniverse, Inc.

Macenski, Geraldine. Healthy, Happy Gigi! 2009. 28p. pap. 15.99 *(978-1-4415-3644-0(2))* Xlibris Corp.

MacFarlane, John. Stormstruck! 2015. (ENG.). 160p. (J). (gr. 3-7). 16.95 *(978-0-8234-3394-0(3))* Holiday Hse., Inc.

MacFarlane, Stuart & MacFarlane, Linda. The Secret Diary of Adrian Cat. 2006. (ENG.). 286p. (J). (gr. 4-8). *(978-1-933255-23-1(4))* DNA Pr.

Macgoye, Marjorie Oludhe. The Black Hand Gang. 2003. (Illus.). 64p. (gr. 4-7). pap. *(978-9966-46-016-5(0))* Heinemann Kenya, Limited (East African Educational Publishers Ltd E.A.E.P.) KEN. Dist: Michigan State Univ. Pr.

MacGregor, Roy. Attack on the Tower of London, Vol. 19. 2004. (ENG., Illus.). 128p. (YA). mass mkt. 4.95 *(978-0-7710-5648-2(6),* Screech Owls) McClelland & Stewart CAN. Dist: Penguin Random Hse. LLC.

—The Screech Owls' Reunion, Vol. 20. 2004. (ENG., Illus.). 144p. (YA). mass mkt. 4.95 *(978-0-7710-5649-9(4),* Screech Owls) McClelland & Stewart CAN. Dist: Penguin Random Hse. LLC.

MacGregor, Roy & MacGregor, Roy. The Complete Screech Owls, Vol. 4. 2006. (Complete Screech Owls Ser.). (ENG.). 488p. (J). (gr. 3-7). per. 15.95 *(978-0-7710-5491-4(2),* Screech Owls) McClelland & Stewart CAN. Dist: Penguin Random Hse. LLC.

Machado, Ana María. Aunque Parezca Mentira. (SPA., Illus.). 64p. (J). 16.95 *(978-84-207-4412-4(3))* Grupo Anaya, S.A. ESP. Dist: Lectorum Pubns., Inc., Distribooks, Inc.

Machado, Antonio. ANTONIO MACHADO PARA NIÑOS. 2003. (SPA., Illus.). 248p. *(978-84-305-9532-7(5),* SU30132) Susaeta Ediciones, S.A. ESP. Dist: Lectorum Pubns., Inc.

MacHale, D. J. Black Water. (Pendragon Ser.: 5). (ENG., 448p. (J). (gr. 5-9). 2007. Illus.). 18.99 *(978-1-4169-5779-9(0))* 2004. pap. 10.99 *(978-0-689-86911-2(8))* Simon & Schuster Children's Publishing. (Aladdin).

—The Guide to the Territories of Halla. Ferguson, Peter, illus. 2005. (Pendragon Ser.). (ENG.). 48p. (J). (gr. 5-9). pap. 12.99 *(978-1-4169-0014-6(4),* Aladdin) Simon & Schuster Children's Publishing.

—The Lost City of Faar. 2007. (Pendragon Ser.: 2). (ENG.). 400p. (J). (gr. 5-9). 19.99 *(978-1-4169-3626-8(2),* Aladdin) Simon & Schuster Children's Publishing.

—The Merchant of Death. 2007. (Pendragon Ser.: 1). (ENG.). 384p. (J). (gr. 5-9). 19.99 *(978-1-4169-3625-1(4),* Aladdin) Simon & Schuster Children's Publishing.

—The Merchant of Death; The Lost City of Faar. 2005. (Pendragon Ser.: Bks. 1-2). 758p. (YA). 9.99 *(978-0-681-05434-9(4))* Borders Pr.

—The Never War. 2003. (Pendragon Ser.: 3). (ENG., Illus.). 352p. (J). (gr. 5-9). pap. 9.99 *(978-0-7434-3733-2(0),* Aladdin) Simon & Schuster Children's Publishing.

—Pendragon: The Merchant of Death; The Lost City of Fear; The Never War; The Reality Bug; Black Water. 2013. (Pendragon Ser.). (ENG., Illus.). 1968p. (J). (gr. 5-9). pap. 49.99 *(978-1-4424-9926-3(5),* Simon & Schuster/Paula Wiseman Bks.) Simon & Schuster/Paula Wiseman Bks.

—The Pilgrims of Rayne. (Pendragon Ser.: 8). (ENG.). (J). (gr. 5-9). 2008. 576p. pap. 9.99 *(978-1-4169-1417-4(X))* 2007. 560p. 19.99 *(978-1-4169-1416-7(1))* Simon & Schuster Children's Publishing. (Aladdin).

—The Quillan Games. (Pendragon Ser.: 7). (ENG.). (J). (gr. 5-9). 2007. 512p. pap. 9.99 *(978-0-689-86913-6(4))* 2006. 496p. 16.99 *(978-1-4169-1423-5(4))* Simon & Schuster Children's Publishing. (Aladdin).

—Raven Rise. 2009. (Pendragon Ser.: 9). (ENG.). 560p. (J). (gr. 5-9). pap. 10.99 *(978-1-4169-1419-8(6),* Aladdin) Simon & Schuster Children's Publishing.

—The Reality Bug. 2003. (Pendragon Ser.: 4). (ENG., Illus.). 384p. (J). (gr. 5-9). pap. 9.99 *(978-0-7434-3734-9(9),* Aladdin) Simon & Schuster Children's Publishing.

—The Rivers of Zadaa. 2006. (Pendragon Ser.: Bk. 6). 405p. (gr. 5-9). 19.00 *(978-0-7569-7040-6(7))* Perfection Learning Corp.

—The Rivers of Zadaa. (Pendragon Ser.: 6). (ENG.). 416p. (J). (gr. 5-9). 2006. pap. 9.99 *(978-0-689-86912-9(6))* 2005. 19.99 *(978-1-4169-0710-7(6))* Simon & Schuster Children's Publishing. (Aladdin).

—The Soldiers of Halla. (Pendragon Ser.: 10). (ENG.). 608p. (J). (gr. 5-9). 2010. pap. 9.99 *(978-1-4169-1421-1(8))* 2009. 17.99 *(978-1-4169-1420-4(X))* Simon & Schuster Children's Publishing. (Aladdin).

—Storm. 2014. (SYLO Chronicles Ser.: 2). (ENG.). (J). (gr. 3-7). 512p. pap. 9.99 *(978-1-59514-668-7(7));* 2nd ed. 496p. 17.99 *(978-1-59514-667-0(9))* Penguin Young Readers Group. (Razorbill).

MacHale, D.J. Pendragon Complete Collection: The Merchant of Death; the Lost City of Faar; the Never War; the Reality Bug; Black Water; the Rivers of Zadaa; the Quillan Games; the Pilgrims of Rayne; Raven Rise; the Soldiers of Halla. 2016. (Pendragon Ser.). (ENG., Illus.). 4720p. (J). (gr. 5-9). pap. 99.99 *(978-1-4814-9689-6(1),* Aladdin) Simon & Schuster Children's Publishing.

MacHalek, Bj. The Adventures of a Noble Duchess: Duchess on Yard Patrol. 2012. 32p. pap. 17.37 *(978-1-4389-6886-5(8))* AuthorHouse.

MacHoka, Rebecca. The Dog Sisters: One Missing Sister. 2010. 36p. pap. 15.49 *(978-1-4490-8306-9(4))* AuthorHouse.

Macieiski, Ellen. Little Raccoon's Adventures. 2012. 56p. pap. 24.99 *(978-1-4685-3854-0(3))* AuthorHouse.

Macinnis, Katherine. Kelsar. 2006. pap. 12.95 *(978-1-58939-876-4(9))* Virtualbookworm.com Publishing, Inc.

MacInnis, Katherine Grace. Kelsar. 2006. 140p. 19.95 *(978-1-58939-877-1(7))* Virtualbookworm.com Publishing, Inc.

Mack, Harry. The Treasure Mystery Clues. 2011. 70p. pap. 19.95 *(978-1-4626-2487-4(1))* America Star Bks.

Mack, Jeff. Hush Little Polar Bear. Mack, Jeff, illus. (ENG., Illus.). (J). (gr. -1-1). 2013. 36p. bds. 7.99 *(978-1-59643-945-0(9),* 9781596439450) 2008. 40p. 17.99 *(978-1-59643-368-7(X),* 9781596433687) Roaring Brook Pr.

Mack, Karen. The Magical Adventures of Sun Beams. 2009. 42p. 31.99 *(978-1-4415-3636-5(1))* Xlibris Corp.

Mack, Lorrie. DK Adventures: Ballet Academy: Ballet Academy. 2014. (DK Adventures Ser.). (ENG., Illus.). 128p. (J). (gr. 3-7). 16.99 *(978-1-4654-1970-5(5),* DK Children) Dorling Kindersley Publishing, Inc.

Mack, Lorrie & Dorling Kindersley Publishing Staff. Ballet Academy. 2014. (DK Adventures Ser.). (ENG., Illus.). 128p. (J). (gr. 3-7). pap. 5.99 *(978-1-4654-1969-9(1),* DK Children) Dorling Kindersley Publishing, Inc.

Mack, Paulette. Cookout at Grandma's House: The Adventures of Mielle & Cheeky. 2006. (ENG., Illus.). 24p. per. 10.95 *(978-1-59800-998-9(2))* Outskirts Pr., Inc.

MacKenzie, Buckley. PAW Patrol: Movie Theater Storybook & Movie Projector. 2016. (ENG.). 32p. (J). (gr. -1-1). 19.99 *(978-0-7944-3325-3(1),* Reader's Digest Children's Bks.) Studio Fun International.

MacKenzie, C. A. The Search for a Golden Eagle. 2013. (Illus.). 48p. pap. 10.95 *(978-0-7552-0712-1(2))* Authors OnLine, Ltd. GBR. Dist: Printondemand-worldwide.com.

MacKenzie, Catherine. The Lonely Grey Dog at No. 6: Tammy & Jake Learn about Love & Loyalty. 2005. (Tales from Canterbury Place Ser.). (ENG., Illus.). 160p. (J). per. 6.99 *(978-1-84550-103-7(9),* bb65d1c0-1fc5-4a1a-8cb0-8c01c9ccdb70) Christian Focus Pubns. GBR. Dist: Bookmasters Distribution.

MacKenzie-Krysko, Claudia & Krysko, Kenneth L. The Adventures of Granville, Coming to America. Cotton, Sue

Lynn, illus. 2013. 24p. pap. 12.95 *(978-1-61493-227-7(1))* Peppertree Pr., The.

MacKenzie, Maryellen. Sneekie & Snookie: And the Honey Tree. 2012. 24p. (-18). pap. 17.99 *(978-1-4772-7651-8(3))* AuthorHouse.

Mackey, Heather. Dreamwood. 2014. (ENG.). 352p. (J). (gr. 5). 16.99 *(978-0-399-25067-5(0),* G.P. Putnam's Sons Books for Young Readers) Penguin Young Readers Group.

Mackey, Stephen. Miki, Set. Mackey, Stephen, illus. 2012. (ENG., Illus.). 48p. (J). (gr. -1-k). 16.99 *(978-1-4449-0651-6(8))* Hodder & Stoughton GBR. Dist: Hachette Bk. Group.

MacKie, Ian. The Adventures of Hamish the Sea Eagle. Mackie, Marie-Anne, illus. 2013. 24p. *(978-1-78148-614-6(X))* Grosvenor Hse. Publishing Ltd.

MacKinnon, Art. Chloe's Great Blue Adventure. 2011. 36p. pap. 16.86 *(978-1-4634-1704-8(7))* AuthorHouse.

Mackinnon, Bernard. The Boy Who Turned Green. 2005. 119p. pap. 19.95 *(978-1-4137-7262-3(5))* America Star Bks.

Mackowiak Elson, Maya. Transformers: Rescue Bots: the Mystery of the Pirate Bell. 2013. (Transformers Rescue Bots Ser.). (ENG., Illus.). 24p. (J). (gr. -1-3). 3.99 *(978-0-316-22833-6(8))* Little, Brown Bks. for Young Readers.

MacLean, Alistair. Circus. (J). 24.95 *(978-0-89190-672-8(X))* Amereon Ltd.

—Circus. 2009. (ENG., Illus.). 288p. mass mkt. 9.99 *(978-0-00-616735-8(7))* HarperCollins Pubs.

MacLean, Betty. Jiali's Traveling Heart. Kinra, Richa, illus. 2013. 34p. (J). 17.95 *(978-1-60131-157-3(5),* Castlebridge Bks.) Big Tent Bks.

MacLean, Heather. The Moonicorn Fairies. 2011. 40p. pap. *(978-1-77067-687-9(2))* FriesenPress.

MacLean, Sarah. The Season. (J). 2010. (ENG.). 352p. (gr. 7). 8.99 *(978-0-545-04887-3(7),* Orchard Bks.) 2009. (ENG.). 352p. (gr. 7-18). 17.99 *(978-0-545-04886-6(9),* Orchard Bks.) 2009. 345p. *(978-0-545-24214-1(2))* Scholastic, Inc.

MacNeil, Stephen. Woolies & Worms. Sandford, John, illus. 2007. (ENG.). 192p. (J). (gr. 1-5). 16.95 *(978-0-8126-2751-0(2))* Cricket Bks.

MacPhee, Bill. Stella, Nothing Has Changed. 2008. 312p. 28.50 *(978-1-60693-230-8(6),* Strategic Bk. Publishing) Strategic Book Publishing & Rights Agency (SBPRA).

MacPherson, D. R. The First Wave. 2009. 68p. pap. 21.00 *(978-1-60860-456-2(X),* Eloquent Bks.) Strategic Book Publishing & Rights Agency (SBPRA).

MacPherson, Lorry. The Adventures of Super Keith! Alexander, Yvonne Rabdau, illus. 2010. 56p. pap. 19.50 *(978-1-60976-268-1(1),* Eloquent Bks.) Strategic Book Publishing & Rights Agency (SBPRA).

Macri, Thomas. Avengers: Happy Holidays! 2016. (Marvel 8x8s Ser.). (J). lib. bdg. 16.00 ***(978-0-606-39176-4(2))*** Turtleback Bks.

MacVicar, Andrea. Tales of Zoftic. Morse, Patti, illus. 2007. 58p. (J). per. 16.95 *(978-0-9798395-0-4(5))* Inspiration Pr. Inc.

Mad Dash. 2005. (J). 4.95 *(978-1-59792-011-7(8))* F.A.S.T. Learning LLC.

Madama, Khadi. The Adventures of Jade Charme: A Follow-Along Book with Nine Exciting Adventures to Solve. 2012. 178p. pap. 24.95 *(978-1-4626-6898-4(4))* America Star Bks.

Madden, Kerry. Jessie's Mountain. 2008. (ENG.). 320p. (J). (gr. 3-7). 16.99 *(978-0-670-06154-9(9),* Viking Books for Young Readers) Penguin Young Readers Group.

Maddock-Cowart, Donna. The Anhinga Tree. Mann, William A., illus. 2012. 74p. pap. 9.95 *(978-0-9836484-3-7(3))* Miglior Pr.

Maddock, Lisa. The Bridezilla Who Stole Christmas: A Teddy & Pip Story. 2009. 108p. pap. 9.95 *(978-1-60844-258-4(6))* Dog Ear Publishing, LLC.

—A Tale of Two Guinea Pigs. 2009. 184p. pap. 11.95 *(978-1-59858-960-3(1))* Dog Ear Publishing, LLC.

Maddox, Jake. Free Climb. Tiffany, Sean, illus. 2008. (Jake Maddox Sports Stories Ser.). (ENG.). 72p. (gr. 2-3). 25.32 *(978-1-4342-0784-5(6));* pap. 5.95 *(978-1-4342-0880-4(X))* Stone Arch Bks.

—Wild Hike. Tiffany, Sean, illus. 2008. (Jake Maddox Sports Stories Ser.). (ENG.). 72p. (gr. 2-3). 25.32 *(978-1-4342-0785-2(4));* pap. 5.95 *(978-1-4342-0881-1(8))* Stone Arch Bks.

Madge, Amy. The Adventures of Kwun-Gee & Uba Dooba Boy. 2012. 24p. 29.95 *(978-1-4626-9270-5(2))* America Star Bks.

Madrid, Bo. The Lunar Express. 2010. (Illus.). 32p. 12.99 *(978-1-4490-6949-0(5))* AuthorHouse.

The Madrona Heroes Register: Echoes of the Past. 2013. (Illus.). 344p. pap. 12.43 *(978-0-9899905-4-7(0))* Atelier Mythologie.

Madrzak, Carole. The Arronna Crystal. 2012. 234p. pap. 24.95 *(978-1-4137-9968-2(X))* America Star Bks.

Madsen, Shane. The Stevenson Chronicles: Deltom. 2013. 170p. (gr. 10-12). 23.96 *(978-1-4669-7614-6(4));* pap. 13.96 *(978-1-4669-7612-2(8))* Trafford Publishing.

Madsen, W. J. Arkeepers: Episode One. 2012. 142p. pap. 7.95 *(978-0-9830487-0-1(3))* little m Bks.

—Arkeepers: Episode Two. 2012. 206p. pap. 9.30 *(978-0-9830487-1-8(1))* little m Bks.

Mae, Darcie. Sammy & Robert's Animal Adventures. 2008. 32p. pap. 24.95 *(978-1-60703-987-7(7))* America Star Bks.

Maes, Nicholas. Fortuna: A Felix Taylor Adventure. 2013. (Felix Taylor Adventure Ser.: 2). (ENG., Illus.). 252p. (YA). pap. 10.99 *(978-1-4597-0561-6(0))* Dundurn CAN. Dist: Ingram Publisher Services.

—Laughing Wolf. 2009. (Felix Taylor Adventure Ser.: 1). (ENG.). 248p. (J). (gr. 7-18). pap. 10.99 *(978-1-55488-385-1(7),* Dundurn Pr.) Dundurn CAN. Dist: Ingram Publisher Services.

Maestas, Phillip. The Adventures of Little Big-Foot. 2009. 28p. pap. 13.99 *(978-1-4389-5753-1(X))* AuthorHouse.

Mafera, Sandra. Cloud of Dauphin Island. 2009. 28p. pap. 12.49 *(978-1-4389-5159-1(0))* AuthorHouse.

Mafi, Tahereh. Furthermore. 2016. (ENG.). 416p. (J). (gr. 4-7). 17.99 *(978-1-101-99476-4(2),* Dutton Books for Young Readers) Penguin Young Readers Group.

—Furthermore. 2017. lib. bdg. 19.65 ***(978-0-606-40493-8(7))*** Turtleback Bks.

Magaro, Dan. The Adventures of Fred & Daisymae. 2010. 48p. pap. 10.99 *(978-1-60957-407-9(9))* Salem Author Services.

Magee, Dolunay. Perrey's Adventures. 2012. (Illus.). 20p. pap. 19.82 *(978-1-4772-3501-0(9))* AuthorHouse.

Magellan, Mauro. Max the Apartment Cat. Magellan, Mauro, illus. 2013. (Illus.). 36p. pap. 12.95 *(978-0-89334-887-8(2))* Green Dragon Bks.

Magic Wagon Staff. A Flip-Flop Adventure, 1 vol. 2011. (Flip-Flop Adventure Ser.). (ENG., Illus.). 32p. 114.00 *(978-1-61641-650-8(5),* Looking Glass Library) Magic Wagon.

—Ghost Detectors Set 2, 1 vol. 2012. (Ghost Detectors Ser.: 6). (ENG., Illus.). 80p. 162.42 *(978-1-61641-622-5(X),* Calico Chapter Bks) Magic Wagon.

Magic Wagon Staff & ABDO Publishing Company Staff. Calico Illustrated Classics Set 4, 1 vol. 2012. (Calico Illustrated Classics Ser.: 12). (ENG., Illus.). 112p. 324.84 *(978-1-61641-609-6(2),* Calico Chapter Bks) Magic Wagon.

The Magical Adventures of Samuel the Squirrel & Oscar the Owl Journey to Mars. 2005. (J). per. 12.95 *(978-0-9762929-0-6(4))* Morning Glory Pubns.

Magill, Sharon L. Chloe Madison & the Beach Heists. 2009. 60p. pap. 10.49 *(978-1-4389-4191-2(9))* AuthorHouse.

Magnason, Andri Snaer. The Story of the Blue Planet. D'Arcy, Julian Meldon, tr. Jonsdottir, Aslaug, illus. 2013. (ENG.). 136p. (J). (gr. 2-5). pap. 9.95 *(978-1-60980-506-7(2),* Triangle Square) Seven Stories Pr.

Magness, Lee. Silver Dasher. 2003. 164p. pap. 12.95 *(978-0-595-29043-7(4))* iUniverse, Inc.

Magness, Robert. Silent Knife, Holy Knife. Glon, Nancy, illus. 2003. 345p. 10.00 *(978-0-9774577-0-0(2))* Magness, Robert Pubns., LLC.

Magness, Vicki. Victor the Victorious: And the Tale of Two Cities. 2012. 40p. pap. 21.99 *(978-1-4797-1955-6(2))* Xlibris Corp.

Magnet, Julien. The Planet of the Firebird. Klio Burrell, Carol, tr. ELyum Studio, illus. 2012. (Little Prince Ser.: 2). (ENG.). 56p. (J). (gr. 4-8). pap. 7.95 *(978-0-8225-9423-9(4),* Graphic Universe™) Lerner Publishing Group.

Magno, Carlos, illus. Transformers: Movie Prequel: Rising Storm: Vol 1, 1 vol. 2012. (Transformers: Dark of the Moon Movie Prequel Ser.). (ENG.). 24p. (J). 24.21 *(978-1-59961-975-0(X),* Graphic Novels) Spotlight.

—Transformers: Movie Prequel: Rising Storm: Vol 2, 1 vol. 2012. (Transformers: Dark of the Moon Movie Prequel Ser.). (ENG.). 24p. (J). 24.21 *(978-1-59961-976-7(8),* Graphic Novels) Spotlight.

—Transformers: Movie Prequel: Rising Storm: Vol 3, 1 vol. 2012. (Transformers: Dark of the Moon Movie Prequel Ser.). (ENG.). 24p. (J). 24.21 *(978-1-59961-977-4(6),* Graphic Novels) Spotlight.

—Transformers: Movie Prequel: Rising Storm: Vol 4, 1 vol. 2012. (Transformers: Dark of the Moon Movie Prequel Ser.). (ENG.). 24p. (J). 24.21 *(978-1-59961-978-1(4),* Graphic Novels) Spotlight.

Magnuson, James. Emma's First Agate, 1 vol. LeMay, Meagan, illus. 2014. (ENG.). 32p. (J). (gr. 1-2). pap. 7.95 *(978-1-59193-443-1(5))* Adventure Pubns.

Magoon, Kekla. Infinity Riders. 2016. (Voyager Ser.). (ENG.). 208p. (J). (gr. 3-7). 12.99 *(978-0-385-38667-8(2),* Random Hse. Bks. for Young Readers) Random Hse. Children's Bks.

—Rebellion of Thieves. 2016. (Robyn Hoodlum Adventure Ser.). (ENG.). 256p. (J). 16.99 *(978-1-61963-655-2(7),* 9781619636552, Bloomsbury USA Childrens) Bloomsbury Publishing USA.

—Rebellion of Thieves. 2017. (Robyn Hoodlum Ser.: 2). (J). lib. bdg. 18.40 ***(978-0-606-40596-6(8))*** Turtleback Bks.

Magoon, Kekla. Shadows of Sherwood. (Robyn Hoodlum Adventure Ser.). (ENG.). 368p. 2016. (J). pap. 7.99 *(978-1-68119-023-5(0),* 9781681190235) 2015. (YA). (gr. 3-6). 16.99 *(978-1-61963-634-7(4),* 9781619636347) Bloomsbury Publishing USA. (Bloomsbury USA Childrens).

Magsamen, Sandra. I Love California (an ABC Adventure) 2015. (ENG.). 40p. (J). (-5). 12.99 *(978-1-4926-2837-8(9),* Sourcebooks Jabberwocky) Sourcebooks, Inc.

—I Love Michigan (an ABC Adventure) 2015. (ENG.). 40p. (J). (-5). 12.99 *(978-1-4926-2844-6(1),* Sourcebooks Jabberwocky) Sourcebooks, Inc.

—I Love Ohio (an ABC Adventure) 2015. (ENG.). 40p. (J). (-5). 12.99 *(978-1-4926-2836-1(0),* Sourcebooks Jabberwocky) Sourcebooks, Inc.

—I Love Texas (an ABC Adventure) 2015. (ENG.). 40p. (J). (-5). 12.99 *(978-1-4926-2835-4(2),* Sourcebooks Jabberwocky) Sourcebooks, Inc.

—You! 2015. (ENG.). 24p. (J). (-3). 16.99 *(978-1-4926-1934-5(5),* 9781492619345, Sourcebooks Jabberwocky) Sourcebooks, Inc.

Maguire, Thomas Aquinas. A Growling Place. 2007. (ENG., Illus.). 32p. (J). (gr. -1-3). 16.95 *(978-1-894965-74-3(4))* Simply Read Bks. CAN. Dist: Ingram Publisher Services.

Mahabeer, Rishen. Anna & Timothy. 2012. 20p. pap. 13.77 *(978-1-4669-5509-7(0))* Trafford Publishing.

Maher, Liam. Blue Paint. Everett-Hawkes, Bonnie, illus. 2012. 20p. pap. 9.95 *(978-1-61633-290-7(5))* Guardian Angel Publishing, Inc.

—Golden Daffodils. Movshina, Marina, illus. 2010. 20p. pap. 10.95 *(978-1-61633-073-6(2))* Guardian Angel Publishing, Inc.

Maher, Mickle Brandt. Master Stitchum & the Moon. Dousias, Spiro, illus. 2003. (J). 19.99 *(978-1-932188-01-1(0))* Bollix Bks.

Mahon, Matthew. The Defenders of All Thats Fall. 2008. 56p. pap. 24.95 *(978-1-4327-3169-4(6))* Outskirts Pr., Inc.

Mahoney, Jan. Moose Tales. 2010. 12p. 9.99 *(978-1-4520-6950-0(6))* AuthorHouse.

Mahy, Margaret. The Green Bath. Kellogg, Steven, illus. 2013. (J). pap. *(978-0-545-20668-6(5));* (ENG.). 40p. (gr. -1-3). 16.99 *(978-0-545-20667-9(7))* Scholastic, Inc. (Levine, Arthur A. Bks.).

Mai, Lily. Bertie Boom's Trip to the Moon. 2010. (Illus.). 20p. 12.49 *(978-1-4520-1379-4(9))* AuthorHouse.

Maier, Gary B. Key Masters: The Tyrannosaur Rebellion. 2013. 124p. pap. 11.50 *(978-1-62516-403-2(3),* Strategic Bk. Publishing) Strategic Book Publishing & Rights Agency (SBPRA).

Maihack, Mike. Target Practice. 2014. (Cleopatra in Space Ser.: 1). (ENG.). 176p. (J). (gr. 3-7). 22.99 *(978-0-545-52842-9(9),* Graphix) Scholastic, Inc.

Mair, J. Samia. The Great Race to Sycamore Street. 2013. (ENG., Illus.). 196p. (J). (gr. 3-6). pap. 12.99 *(978-1-84774-057-1(X))* Kube Publishing Ltd. GBR. Dist: Consortium Bk. Sales & Distribution.

Major, Kevin. Far from Shore, 1 vol. 2004. (ENG.). 250p. (YA). pap. 9.95 *(978-0-88899-568-1(7))* Groundwood Bks. CAN. Dist: Publishers Group West (PGW).

Majors, J. Natty's Adventures. 2011. 28p. pap. 15.99 *(978-1-4568-5949-7(8))* Xlibris Corp.

Majumdar, Debu. Viku & the Elephant: A Story from the Forests of India. Wolfe, Lynn, illus. 2011. (ENG.). 54p. (J). pap. 12.99 *(978-0-9832227-0-5(3))* Bo-Tree Hse.

Mäkinen, Kirsti. The Kalevala: Tales of Magic & Adventure. Brooks, Kaarina, tr. from FIN. Surojegin, Pirkko-Liisa, illus. 2009. (ENG.). 214p. (YA). (gr. 4-18). 24.95 *(978-1-897476-00-0(0))* Simply Read Bks. CAN. Dist: Ingram Publisher Services.

MAKOTO, Mizobuchi. Pokémon: Arceus & the Jewel of Life. MAKOTO, Mizobuchi, illus. 2011. (ENG., Illus.). 200p. (J). pap. 9.99 *(978-1-4215-3802-0(4))* Viz Media.

Makumi, Joel. The Return of Njaga. 2005. (Phoenix Young Readers Library). (Illus.). 179p. *(978-9966-47-113-0(8))* Phoenix Pubs., Ltd.

Malaghan, Michael. The Lost Prophecies. 2014. (ENG.). 256p. (J). (gr. 4-6). pap. 9.99 *(978-1-84939-574-8(8))* Andersen Pr. GBR. Dist: Independent Pubs. Group.

Malaika: Safari Adventure to Kenya. 2006. (J). 4.99 *(978-0-9765982-0-6(5))* Simba Publishing Co.

Malatesta, Resa. Jewel & Chin Chin's Adventure. 2013. 20p. pap. 10.95 *(978-1-4525-7610-7(6),* Balboa Pr.) Author Solutions, Inc.

Malea. Princess Melia. 2007. 145p. (J). pap. 15.95 *(978-1-58909-367-6(4))* Bookstand Publishing.

Malik, Katherine. Giselle's Magical World, 1 vol. 2009. 150p. pap. 24.95 *(978-1-4489-1902-4(9))* America Star Bks.

Malinowski, Carrie. The Hand-Me-Down Bear. 2012. (ENG., Illus.). 28p. (J). pap. 12.99 *(978-1-937008-15-4(0))* Heart to Heart Publishing, Inc.

Malison, Anna. Through Thick & Thin. 2006. (ENG.). 136p. per. *(978-1-897117-14-9(0))* Gospel Folio Pr.

Malkin, Arlene Swinson. Adventures with Grandma & Grandpa: The Secret of the Old Trunk. 2006. 48p. pap. 16.95 *(978-1-4241-1621-8(X))* PublishAmerica, Inc.

Mallory, Nicole. I Wish I Was an Alligator. 2013. (ENG.). 29p. (J). pap. 15.95 *(978-1-4787-1066-0(7))* Outskirts Pr., Inc.

Malloy, Chris. Wizard Academies - A Special Kind of Talent. 2008. 142p. pap. 19.95 *(978-0-615-18505-7(3))* Wizard Academies, LLC.

Malokas, Ann. The Tag-a-long Trio: Zak, Lizze & Ben Too! Nicholas, Corasue, illus. 2007. (J). 15.95 *(978-0-9708415-8-2(2))* Guilty Mom Pr.

Malone, D. L. 52 Purple Monkeys. 2009. 24p. pap. 24.95 *(978-1-60749-085-2(4))* America Star Bks.

Malone, David P. The Adventures of Benny the Bunnyduck: Escape from Chindia. 2012. (ENG.). 45p. (J). pap. 23.95 *(978-1-4327-9352-4(7))* Outskirts Pr., Inc.

Maloney, Andrew. The Master Song. 2014. (Illus.). 352p. (YA). *(978-1-62911-176-6(7))* Whitaker Hse.

—Verse of Valor. 2015. 285p. (YA). *(978-1-62911-357-9(3))* Whitaker Hse.

Malot, Hector & Crewe-Jones, Florence. Nobody's Boy: Companion Story to Nobody's Girl. Gooch, Thelma & Gruelle, Johnny, illus. 2006. 237p. (J). pap. *(978-1-894666-75-6(5))* Inheritance Pubns.

—Nobody's Girl: Companion Story to Nobody's Boy. Gooch, Thelma, illus. 2006. 220p. (J). pap. *(978-1-894666-76-3(3))* Inheritance Pubns.

Mama Doo. Trevor's Adventure in Button Land, 1 vol. 2008. (ENG.). 47p. pap. 24.95 *(978-1-60672-349-4(9))* America Star Bks.

Mamah, Michael. Imp. 2013. 76p. pap. 10.85 *(978-1-61933-865-4(3))* FastPrncil, Inc.

Mammina, David. The Circle Stone Group: Book 1: the Beginning. 2009. 112p. pap. 13.35 *(978-1-4269-1478-2(4))* Trafford Publishing.

Man-Kong, Mary. Bubble Power! (Bubble Guppies) Jackson, Mike, illus. 2016. (Step into Reading Ser.). (ENG.). 24p. (J). (gr. -1-1). 4.99 *(978-0-553-52091-0(1),* Random Hse. Bks. for Young Readers) Random Hse. Children's Bks.

—It's Sparkle Time! 2015. (Color Plus Crayons & Sticker Ser.). (ENG., Illus.). 48p. (J). (gr. -1-2). pap. 4.99 *(978-0-553-50744-7(3),* Golden Bks.) Random Hse. Children's Bks.

The Man of Steel. 2013. (Man of Steel Ser.). (ENG.). 88p. (gr. 2-3). 213.20 *(978-1-4342-4811-4(9));* 106.60 *(978-1-4342-4812-1(7));* pap. 23.80 *(978-1-4342-4864-0(X));* pap. 47.60 *(978-1-4342-4863-3(1))* Stone Arch Bks. (DC Super Heroes).

Mancusi, Mari. Scorched. (Scorched Ser.: 1). (ENG.). (YA). (gr. 6-12). 2014. 368p. pap. 9.99 *(978-1-4022-9227-9(9))* 2013. 352p. 16.99 *(978-1-4022-8458-8(6),* 9781402284588) Sourcebooks, Inc.

—Shattered. (Scorched Ser.: 2). (ENG.). (YA). 2015. 416p. (gr. 8-12). pap. 9.99 *(978-1-4926-0869-1(6))* 2014. 400p. (gr. 7-12). 16.99 *(978-1-4022-8461-8(6),* 9781402284618) Sourcebooks, Inc.

Mandla. Garden Green Hills: And Finally Ants Run the Village. 2013. 102p. pap. 15.99 *(978-1-4797-1482-7(8))* Xlibris Corp.

Maness, Branda Edwards. Animal Tales of Hawaii. 2011. 28p. pap. 12.15 *(978-1-4634-3484-7(7))* AuthorHouse.

Maness, Patricia. Adventures of Ben & Golden. 2007. 192p. per. 24.95 *(978-1-4241-7721-9(9))* America Star Bks.

Manga University Staff. My First PC: The Comic Book That Teaches You about the Internet. 2012. 128p. (J). pap. 9.99 *(978-4-921205-28-7(0))* Japanime Co., Ltd. JPN. Dist: Diamond Bk. Distributors.

Mangano, Tom, illus. Dora's World Adventure! 2006. (Dora the Explorer Ser.). (ENG.). 24p. (J). (gr. -1-2). pap. 3.99 *(978-1-4169-2447-0(7),* Simon Spotlight/Nickelodeon) Simon Spotlight/Nickelodeon.

Mangual, Cynthia Ines. 3 Super Hero Tales (DC Super Friends) Random House & Doescher, Erik, illus. 2017. (Padded Board Book Ser.). (ENG.). 30p. (J). (— 1). bds. 11.99 ***(978-1-5247-1714-8(2),*** Random Hse. Bks. for Young Readers) Random Hse. Children's Bks.

Mankamyer, Laura. The Adventures of the Stonycreek Gang. Mankamyer, Laura, illus. l.t. ed. 2003. (Illus.). 84p. (J). 12.99 *(978-0-9728431-4-0(0))* Mankamyer, Laura.

Manley, Brenda Randazzo. The Misfits of Millville. 2010. (ENG.). 220p. pap. 14.99 *(978-1-4392-6496-6(1))* CreateSpace Independent Publishing Platform.

Manley, Candace. Skeeter's Dream. 2010. (ENG.). 192p. (J). (gr. 7-18). pap. 14.95 *(978-0-9785634-8-6(4))* La Frontera Publishing.

Manley, Francis G. Tellin Twins: The Great Art Scam. 2004. (Illus.). 132p. pap. *(978-1-84401-292-3(1))* Athena Pr.

Mann, Greyson. Lost in the Jungle: Secrets of a Minecraft Survivor. Sandford, Grace, illus. 2017. (Secrets of an Overworld Survivor Ser.). (ENG.). 112p. (J). (gr. 1-4). 13.99 *(978-1-5107-1325-3(5),* Sky Pony Pr.) Skyhorse Publishing Co., Inc.

—When Lava Strikes: Secrets of a Minecraft Survivor. Sandford, Grace, illus. 2017. (Secrets of an Overworld Survivor Ser.). (ENG.). 112p. (J). (gr. 1-4). 13.99 *(978-1-5107-1328-4(X),* Sky Pony Pr.) Skyhorse Publishing Co., Inc.

Mann, Jennifer Ann. Sunny Sweet Can So Get Lost. 2015. (Sunny Sweet Ser.). (ENG., Illus.). 208p. (YA). (gr. 3-6). 15.99 *(978-1-61963-505-0(4),* 9781619635050, Bloomsbury USA Childrens) Bloomsbury Publishing USA.

—Sunny Sweet Is So Dead Meat. 2014. (Sunny Sweet Ser.). (ENG., Illus.). 208p. (YA). (gr. 3-6). 15.99 *(978-1-59990-978-3(2),* 9781599909783, Bloomsbury USA Childrens) Bloomsbury Publishing USA.

—Sunny Sweet Is So Not Sorry. 2013. (Sunny Sweet Ser.). (ENG., Illus.). 208p. (YA). (gr. 3-6). 15.99 *(978-1-59990-977-6(4),* 9781599909776, Bloomsbury USA Childrens) Bloomsbury Publishing USA.

Mann, Seymour. The Purple Automobile & the Newspaper Girl. 2003. 112p. 20.95 *(978-0-595-66076-6(2));* pap. 10.95 *(978-0-595-29907-2(5))* iUniverse, Inc.

Mann, T. L. The Adventures of Magellan. 2009. 23p. (J). pap. 13.95 *(978-1-4327-3490-9(3))* Outskirts Pr., Inc.

Manning, Dennis & Crisalli, Joseph. The Turnip War. 2011. 120p. pap. 7.76 *(978-1-4357-1566-0(7))* Lulu Pr., Inc.

Manning, L. L. At the Roller Rink. 2011. 28p. pap. 15.99 *(978-1-4628-8449-0(0))* Xlibris Corp.

Manning, Matthew. Batgirl: New Hero of the Night (Backstories) 2017. (Backstories Ser.). lib. bdg. 16.00 ***(978-0-606-39731-5(0))*** Turtleback Bks.

Manning, Matthew. Batgirl: New Hero of the Night (Backstories) Spaziante, Patrick, illus. 2017. (Backstories Ser.). (ENG.). 128p. (J). (gr. 3-7). pap. 5.99 *(978-1-338-11741-7(6))* Scholastic, Inc.

Manning, Matthew K. U.S. Special Forces: Ghosts of the Night. Enecio, Jeremy, illus. 2016. (U. S. Special Ops Ser.). (ENG.). 96p. (gr. 3-4). E-Book 26.65 *(978-1-4965-3477-4(8),* Connect) Stone Arch Bks.

Manning, Matthew K. & Majado, Caio. Lockdown, Vol. 8. Ito, Leonardo, illus. 2012. (Tony Hawk's 900 Revolution Ser.). (ENG.). 128p. (gr. 3-4). pap. 7.19 *(978-1-4342-3890-0(3));* lib. bdg. 26.65 *(978-1-4342-3314-1(6))* Stone Arch Bks. (Tony Hawk's 900 Revolution).

Manning, Matthew K. & Sutton, Laurie S. You Choose Stories: Scooby-Doo. Neely, Scott, illus. 2017. (You Choose Stories: Scooby-Doo Ser.). (ENG.). 112p. (gr. 2-3). 457.10 *(978-1-4965-4341-7(6),* You Choose Bks.) Capstone Press of Coughlan Cos.

Manning, Sara. Wally the Whale: A Tale about a Whale with Seizures. 2011. 40p. pap. 18.46 *(978-1-4634-4160-9(6))* AuthorHouse.

Manny's Aventura de Motorcyle. 2009. (ENG.). 24p. pap. 4.99 *(978-1-4231-2266-1(6))* Disney Pr.

Manson, Beverlie, illus. The Mermaid's Secret Diaries. 2013. (ENG.). 96p. (J). (gr. -1-2). 9.95 *(978-1-907967-59-7(1))* Boxer Bks., Ltd. GBR. Dist: Sterling Publishing Co., Inc.

Manus, Willard. A Dog Called Leka. 2007. (ENG.). 122p. pap. 7.99 *(978-0-9740551-3-8(1))* Smith, Viveca Publishing.

Manushkin, Fran. Katie Woo, 1 vol. Lyon, Tammie, illus. 2014. (Katie Woo Ser.). (ENG.). 32p. (gr. k-2). lib. bdg. 639.60 *(978-1-4795-4813-2(8))* Picture Window Bks.

—Katie Woo, Set. Lyon, Tammie, illus. Incl. Big Lie. 21.32 *(978-1-4048-5497-0(5));* Boss of the World. 21.32 *(978-1-4048-5493-2(2));* Goodbye to Goldie. 21.32 *(978-1-4048-5495-6(9));* Happy Day. 21.32 *(978-1-4048-5496-3(7));* No More Teasing. 21.32 *(978-1-4048-5492-5(4));* Too Much Rain. 21.32 *(978-1-4048-5494-9(0));* (gr. k-2). (Katie Woo Ser.). (ENG., Illus.). 32p. 2009. 127.92 *(978-1-4048-5679-0(X))* Picture Window Bks.

—Katie Woo Book Club Kit. Lyon, Tammie, illus. 2013. (Katie Woo Ser.). (ENG.). 576p. (gr. k-2). pap. 29.70 *(978-1-4795-5120-0(1))* Picture Window Bks.

Manwiller, S. A. The Adventures of Jack & Max: What Jack & Max Love. Manwiller, S. A., illus. 2013. (Illus.). 30p. 19.99 *(978-0-9838427-4-3(4))* SevenHorns Publishing.

The Many Tracks of Lap'n Tap. 2007. (J). per. 10.95 *(978-0-9761128-4-6(1))* KB Bks. & More.

Many Ways to Be a Soldier. 2009. (On My Own History Ser.). (gr. 2-4). pap. 6.95 *(978-0-8225-9021-7(2),* First Avenue Editions) Lerner Publishing Group.

Mara, Cate. The Great Kieranski & the Bardbuy. 2012. 114p. pap. *(978-0-9873204-2-1(4))* Breedles Publishing.

Mara, Sarah Robinson. A Snug Little Island Hammond, Nancy Robinson, illus. 2005. 60p. (J). 18.50 *(978-0-9766737-0-5(3))* Pink Granite Pr.

Marbury, Stephon & Dean, Marshall. The Adventures of Young Starbury: Practice Makes Perfect. Nakai, Ryan, illus. 2007. 36p. (J). 12.99 *(978-0-9798250-0-2(8))* Godspeed Pr.

Marchesi, Stephen, illus. The Flights of Marceau: Week One. 2007. (ENG.). 56p. (J). 16.95 *(978-0-9797495-0-6(6))* Majestic Eagle Publishing.

Marchetti, Dave. Nestle's Big Adventure. 2012. 28p. pap. 21.99 *(978-1-4691-4672-0(X))* Xlibris Corp.

Marcolina, P. J. My Friend Grows Feathers - the True Story of Jackie the Crow. 2009. 52p. pap. 24.60 *(978-0-557-02706-4(3))* Lulu Pr., Inc.

Marcus, Mary J. The Digger. 2013. 180p. pap. 12.99 *(978-1-60820-872-2(9))* MLR Pr., LLC.

Marcus, Ms. Elena N. Devon: The Wild Adventures of Devon & Friends. 2012. (ENG., Illus.). 74p. (gr. 1-6). pap. 18.00 *(978-0-615-57545-2(5))* Elena Marcus Negoita.

Marcus, Richard. What Will Happen in Eragon IV: Who Lives, Who Dies, Who Becomes the Third Dragon Rider & How Will the Inheritance Cycle Finally End? 2009. (ENG.). 180p. (J). (gr. 3). pap. 12.95 *(978-1-56975-728-4(3))* Ulysses Pr.

Maresca, Wendi S. Alphabet Silly Time. 2005. (J). pap. *(978-0-9772897-0-7(2))* Maresca, Wendi.

Margie BluePockets. 2004. (J). *(978-0-9744448-1-9(2))* McCourtie, Anne.

Margolis, Leslie. One Tough Chick. 2014. (Annabelle Unleashed Ser.). (ENG.). 192p. (YA). (gr. 3-6). pap. 6.99 *(978-1-61963-161-8(X)*, 9781619631618, Bloomsbury USA Childrens) Bloomsbury Publishing USA.

Margo's Magic Trunk. 2006. (Illus.). 32p. (J). pap. 6.95 *(978-0-9789016-0-8(6))* Jodaviste Publishing.

Mariconda, Barbara. The Voyage of Lucy P. Simmons. 2012. (Voyage of Lucy P. Simmons Ser.: 1). (ENG.). 256p. (J). (gr. 3-7). 16.99 *(978-0-06-211979-7(6)*, Tegen, Katherine Bks) HarperCollins Pubs.

Marie, Anna. Hexon. 2012. (ENG.). 66p. pap. 9.95 *(978-1-4327-9112-4(5))* Outskirts Pr., Inc.

Marie, Barbara. Snowy & Felix Find Christmas. 2009. 24p. pap. 11.49 *(978-1-4389-7392-0(6))* AuthorHouse.

Marie, Christina. Where Would I Live?, 1 vol. 2010. 18p. 24.95 *(978-1-4489-7584-6(0))* PublishAmerica, Inc.

Marie, Jill Jana. Elsa Magda Val My Imaginary Pal. 2008. 24p. pap. 12.95 *(978-1-4389-3411-2(4))* AuthorHouse.

Marie, Tamara. The Adventures of Madison. 2010. 32p. pap. 17.99 *(978-1-60957-972-2(0))* Salem Author Services.

Marinaro, Stacy. Treasure Monkey. 2008. 32p. pap. 15.95 *(978-1-4357-2840-0(8))* Lulu Pr., Inc.

—The Walrus King. 2008. 32p. 29.95 *(978-1-4357-2885-1(8))* Lulu Pr., Inc.

Marino, Michael. Magi Adventure. 2012. 80p. 24.99 *(978-1-4691-3712-4(7))*; pap. 15.99 *(978-1-4691-3711-7(9))* Xlibris Corp.

Mario. Arriving to Planet Noah. 2011. 68p. 24.99 *(978-1-4628-5905-4(4))*; pap. 15.99 *(978-1-4628-5904-7(6))* Xlibris Corp.

Marion, L. K. Summer Holiday with Funny Bunny. 2012. 32p. pap. 17.25 *(978-1-4669-6475-4(8))* Trafford Publishing.

Markette, Paul Scott. I'm with Poppy!! Lee, Joe, illus. 2010. 24p. pap. 12.99 *(978-1-4520-6276-1(5))* AuthorHouse.

Markey, Andrew C. The Afterlife Phenomenon. 2009. 107p. pap. 9.98 *(978-0-615-19036-5(7))* Bug Boy Bks.

Marko, Cyndi. Bok! Bok! Boom! 2014. (Kung Pow Chicken Ser.: 2). lib. bdg. 14.75 *(978-0-606-35357-1(7))* Turtleback Bks.

Marks, Melanie. Phonics Comics: Super Sam - Level 3: Issue 1. Collins, Daryll, illus. 2006. (ENG.). 24p. (J). (gr. 1-17). per. 3.99 *(978-1-58476-420-5(1)*, IKIDS) Innovative Kids.

Markun, Alan F. New Revolution. (J). 8.95 *(978-0-8022-1062-3(7))* Philosophical Library, Inc.

Marlow, Susan K. Andrea Carter & the Long Ride Home: A Novel, 1 vol. 2016. (Circle C Adventures Ser.: 1). 144p. (J). pap. 8.99 ***(978-0-8254-4500-2(0))*** Kregel Pubns.

—Courageous Love: An Andrea Carter Book, 1 vol. 2017. (Circle C Milestones Ser.: 4). 192p. (YA). pap. 9.99 *(978-0-8254-4370-1(9))* Kregel Pubns.

—River of Peril, 1 vol. 2014. (Goldtown Adventures Ser.: 4). 144p. (J). pap. 7.99 *(978-0-8254-4297-1(4))* Kregel Pubns.

Marlowe, Amy Bell. When Oriole Came to Harbor Light. 2011. 318p. 50.95 *(978-1-258-10144-2(0))* Literary Licensing, LLC.

—When Oriole Traveled Westward. 2011. 310p. 50.95 *(978-1-258-10214-2(5))* Literary Licensing, LLC.

Marlowe, Paul. Sporeville. 2007. (Wellborn Conspiracy Ser.: Bk. 1). 250p. (YA). (gr. 8-12). pap. 10.95 *(978-0-9739505-4-0(4))* Sybertooth, Inc. CAN. Dist: Lightning Source, Inc.

Maroudas, N. G. The Adventures of Athena & Odysseus. 2011. (ENG.). 276p. pap. *(978-1-84876-593-1(2))* Troubador Publishing Ltd.

Maroulis, Danielle. Monk in the Trunk. 2011. 24p. (gr. 1-2). pap. 13.99 *(978-1-4634-0598-4(7))* AuthorHouse.

Marquess, Dana. Night of the Lighted Freedom - A Firefly Fantasy. 2006. (ENG., Illus.). 32p. (J). 19.95 *(978-1-932278-06-4(0))* Mayhaven Publishing, Inc.

Marquez, Sofia. Pepe Perez Mexican Mouse: Pepe Perez Comes to the United States: Book 1, 1 vol. Marquez, Sofia, illus. 2009. (Illus.). 20p. pap. 24.95 *(978-1-61546-496-8(4))* America Star Bks.

—Pepe Perez Mexican Mouse: Pepe Perez Comes to the United States: Book 1, 1 vol. 2010. 20p. 24.95 *(978-1-4489-6600-4(0))* PublishAmerica, Inc.

Marr, Ella J. The Adventures of Curtis & Grammy. 2006. 57p. pap. 16.95 *(978-1-4241-4743-4(3))* PublishAmerica, Inc.

Marrero, Rosa M. Nickolas Loves Toby. 2011. 28p. pap. 9.95 *(978-1-4327-7452-3(2))* Outskirts Pr., Inc.

Marriott, Zoë. Swan Kingdom. 2009. (ENG., Illus.). 272p. (YA). (gr. 7). pap. 8.99 *(978-0-7636-4293-8(2))* Candlewick Pr.

Marro, Barbara. Smitty's Cave Adventures. 2010. 147p. pap. 12.95 *(978-1-4327-4340-6(6))* Outskirts Pr., Inc.

Marroquin, Melissa. Tide Day, 1000 vols. 2016. (ENG., Illus.). (J). (gr. -1-3). 16.95 *(978-1-59298-684-2(6))* Beaver's Pond Pr., Inc.

Marrs, Christie, creator. The Promise Keeper: I B Hoofinit's Horse Tales. l.t. ed. 2003. (Illus.). 53p. (J). mass mkt. 5.99 *(978-1-928890-16-4(4))* I. B. Hoofinit Co.

Marryat, Frederick. Masterman Ready. l.t. ed. 2006. 276p. pap. 23.99 *(978-1-4264-0573-0(1))* Creative Media Partners, LLC.

Marsh, Carole. Adventure to the Eight Wonders of the World. 2007. (Field Trips (Gallopade International) Ser.). (Illus.). 118p. (J). (gr. 2-9). 14.95 *(978-0-635-06391-5(3))*; per. 5.99 *(978-0-635-06335-9(2))* Gallopade International.

—Adventure to the Pioneer Prairie! 2007. (Field Trips (Gallopade International) Ser.). (Illus.). 114p. (J). (gr. 2-9). pap. 14.95 *(978-0-635-06393-9(X))*; per. 5.99 *(978-0-635-06337-3(9))* Gallopade International.

—Adventure to the Planet Mars! 2007. (Field Trips (Gallopade International) Ser.). (Illus.). 114p. (J). (gr. 4-9). per. 5.99 *(978-0-635-06336-6(0))*; (gr. 2-9). 14.95 *(978-0-635-06392-2(1))* Gallopade International.

—The Behemoth Blizzard Mystery. (Masters of Disasters Ser.). (Illus.). 118p. (J). (gr. 3-5). 2008. per. 5.99 *(978-0-635-06464-6(2))* 2007. 14.95 *(978-0-635-06467-7(7))* Gallopade International.

—The Colonial Caper Mystery at Williamsburg. 2009. (Real Kids, Real Places Ser.). (J). (gr. 2-9). lib. bdg. 18.99 *(978-0-635-06832-3(X))*; (Illus.). 143p. (gr. 4-7). pap. 7.99 *(978-0-635-06826-2(5)*, Marsh, Carole Bks.) Gallopade International.

—The Curse of the Ancient Acropolis: Athens, Greece. 2008. (Carole Marsh Mysteries Ser.). 133p. (J). (gr. 3-5). per. 7.99 *(978-0-635-06470-7(7)*, Marsh, Carole Bks.) Gallopade International.

—The Earthshaking Earthquake Mystery. 2007. (Masters of Disasters Ser.). (Illus.). 118p. (J). (gr. 2-9). 14.95 *(978-0-635-06395-3(6))* Gallopade International.

—The Ferocious Forest Fire Mystery. 2008. (Masters of Disasters Ser.). (Illus.). 118p. (J). (gr. 3-5). 14.95 *(978-0-635-06468-4(5))*; per. 5.99 *(978-0-635-06465-3(0))* Gallopade International.

—The Giggling Ghost Girl Scout Mystery. 2012. (ENG., Illus.). 158p. (J). pap. 7.99 *(978-0-635-10230-0(7)*, Marsh, Carole Mysteries) Gallopade International.

—The Gosh Awful! Gold Rush Mystery. 2007. (Real Kids, Real Places Ser.). (Illus.). 146p. (J). (gr. 2-8). per. 5.95 *(978-0-635-06334-2(4))* Gallopade International.

—The Horrendous Hurricane Mystery. 2007. (Masters of Disasters Ser.). (Illus.). 118p. (J). (gr. 2-9). 14.95 *(978-0-635-06396-0(4))* Gallopade International.

—The Treacherous Tornado Mystery. 2007. (Masters of Disasters Ser.). (Illus.). 118p. (J). (gr. 2-9). 14.95 *(978-0-635-06394-6(8))*; per. 5.99 *(978-0-635-06338-0(7))* Gallopade International.

—The Voracious Volcano Mystery. 2008. (Masters of Disasters Ser.). (Illus.). 118p. (J). (gr. 3-5). 14.95 *(978-0-635-06466-0(9))*; per. 5.99 *(978-0-635-06463-9(4))* Gallopade International.

Marsh, David. Into the Abyss. 2004. (YA). 23.95 *(978-0-9742909-0-4(4))* Sea Chest Bks.

Marsh, Laura. Take a Leap! 2009. (Toot & Puddle Ser.). (ENG., Illus.). 24p. (J). (gr. -1-2). pap. 3.99 *(978-1-4263-0416-3(1))*; lib. bdg. 11.90 *(978-1-4263-0417-0(X))* National Geographic Society. (National Geographic Children's Bks.).

—Toot's Tour of India. 2009. (Toot & Puddle Ser.). (ENG., Illus.). 24p. (J). (gr. -1-2). pap. 3.99 *(978-1-4263-0418-7(8))*; lib. bdg. 11.90 *(978-1-4263-0419-4(6))* National Geographic Society. (National Geographic Children's Bks.).

Marsh, Mike. The Efelant Hunters Part One: Shipwreck! Jain, Priti, illus. 2013. 28p. pap. *(978-1-927506-21-9(2))* Yellow Toadstool Pr.

—The Skyrats Capture the Grumblies! Jain, Priti, illus. 2012. 28p. pap. *(978-1-927506-01-1(8))* Yellow Toadstool Pr.

Marsh, Richard Phillip. Mattress People Go to Bear Park. 2009. 44p. pap. 10.95 *(978-1-935125-39-6(7))* Robertson Publishing.

Marshall, Amelia. Big Truck's Road Adventure. 2016. (Big Machines Ser.). 32p. (gr. 2-1). pap. 10.00 *(978-1-4994-8099-3(7)*, Windmill Bks.) Rosen Publishing Group, Inc., The.

Marshall, Carly. The Babysitter & the Critter Hunt. 2012. 38p. 24.95 *(978-1-4626-9407-5(1))*; 40p. pap. 24.95 *(978-1-4626-7516-6(6))* America Star Bks.

—The Babysitter & the Hot Rainy Days. 2012. 48p. 24.95 *(978-1-4626-7515-9(8))*; pap. 24.95 *(978-1-4626-9644-4(9))* America Star Bks.

Marshall, Denise. The Adventures of Hip Hop: Hip Hop & the Blueberry Pancakes. Champagne, Heather, illus. 2012. 36p. pap. 14.75 *(978-1-62212-331-5(X)*, Strategic Bk. Publishing) Strategic Book Publishing & Rights Agency (SBPRA).

—The Adventures of Hip Hop: Hip Hop & the Yellow Hat. Schley, Cheri & Champagne, Heather, illus. 2011. 36p. pap. 14.75 *(978-1-60976-342-8(4)*, Eloquent Bks.) Strategic Book Publishing & Rights Agency (SBPRA).

Marshall, Kate. Mokes, Mines & Mayhem. 2008. 120p. pap. 10.95 *(978-1-60693-357-2(4)*, Eloquent Bks.) Strategic Book Publishing & Rights Agency (SBPRA).

Marshall, Ken. The Adventures of Maya & Grampa. 2005. 64p. pap. 9.95 *(978-0-7414-2472-3(X))* Infinity Publishing.

Marshall, Kenneth L. The Adventures of Maya & Grandpa, Bk. II. 2005. 65p. pap. 9.95 *(978-0-7414-2238-5(7))* Infinity Publishing.

Marshall, Melanie. Ladybug. 2006. 25.00 *(978-1-4122-0219-0(1))* Trafford Publishing.

Marshall, Sandra K. Tom's Space Adventure. 2007. 60p. per. 16.95 *(978-1-4241-7840-7(1))* America Star Bks.

Marsham, Liz. A Hero for All. 2017. (Justice League Classic 8X8 Ser.). lib. bdg. 13.55 ***(978-0-606-40076-3(1))*** Turtleback Bks.

Martell, Ray. Brox the Bungling Badger. 2012. (Illus.). 88p. pap. 15.50 *(978-1-78035-345-6(6)*, Fastprint Publishing) Upfront Publishing Ltd. GBR. Dist: Printondemand-worldwide.com.

Martens, Kara. The Two Missing Kids. 2008. 80p. pap. 11.49 *(978-1-4343-8696-0(1))* AuthorHouse.

Martha, Morales. Ariana Leaves San Francisco. Chiu, Bessie, illus. 2011. 28p. pap. 8.50 *(978-1-61170-017-6(5))* Robertson Publishing.

Martin, Amy. As You Wake. 2013. 294p. pap. 10.93 *(978-0-9882051-2-3(2))* Martin, Amy.

Martin, Ann M. Kristy's Great Idea. 2010. (Baby-Sitters Club Ser.: 1). (ENG.). 176p. (J). (gr. 3-7). 6.99 *(978-0-545-17475-6(9)*, Scholastic Paperbacks) Scholastic, Inc.

—Upon a Midnight Clear. Date not set. (J). 15.95 *(978-0-8050-6898-6(8)*, Holt, Henry & Co. Bks. For Young Readers) Holt, Henry & Co.

Martin, Bob. James' Night of Terror. Salinas, Alex, illus. 2010. 120p. (gr. 4-6). 20.95 *(978-1-4502-6500-3(6))*; pap. 10.95 *(978-1-4502-6498-3(0))* iUniverse, Inc.

Martin, Brenda Damley. Freddie, Hector & Tish: The Treasure-Hunt Fish. 2008. 36p. per. 24.95 *(978-1-60441-109-6(0))* America Star Bks.

Martin, Brian. The Gold of Angel Island. McDonald, Kim, illus. 2007. 46p. (J). *(978-0-9798059-0-5(2))* Lunchbox Stories Inc.

Martin, Carrie Waddington. Ham the Astrochimp: Anything Is Possible. 2012. 52p. (-18). pap. 24.99 *(978-1-4797-1059-1(8))* Xlibris Corp.

Martin, Chandra. Sintacs. 2012. 100p. 19.95 *(978-1-4626-7833-4(5))* America Star Bks.

Martin, Cynthia Bloom. Tryloc: The Quest. 2006. (J). per. 22.95 *(978-0-9787015-0-5(X))* T.C. McSears Publishing.

Martin, Gary & Pennebaker, H. I. Professor Tyme's Timeless Tales: Revenge of the Sargasso Sea Ogre. 2006. (ENG.). 160p. per. 24.95 *(978-1-4241-5701-3(3))* America Star Bks.

Martin, Gary & Rogers, Bud. The Raiders of Joppa, 1 vol. Cariello, Sergio, illus. 2008. (Z Graphic Novels / Son of Samson Ser.). (ENG.). 160p. (J). (gr. 4-7). pap. 6.99 *(978-0-310-71282-4(3))* Zonderkidz.

Martin, Herbert. Catch A Falling Leaf. 2006. (J). lib. bdg. 20.00 *(978-0-9761765-1-0(3))* Smartinbooks, Inc.

Martin, J. Marshall. The Bird. 2008. 88p. pap. 12.50 *(978-0-9801224-1-1(4))* Boys Read Bks.

Martin, JoElle. Moonlight in the Forest. 2009. (ENG.). 280p. (YA). pap. 14.99 *(978-1-59092-563-8(7))* Blue Forge Pr.

Martin, Justin McCory. The Planet Without Pronouns. Lee, Jared, illus. 2004. (Grammar Tales Ser.). (ENG.). 16p. (J). (gr. 3-7). pap. 3.25 *(978-0-439-45820-7(X))* Scholastic, Inc.

Martin, Kevin. Chomper the Stomper. 2012. 28p. pap. 11.00 *(978-0-578-10705-9(8))* Martin, Kevin.

Martin, L. & Beckett, G. The Adventures of Timothy in Early New South Wales. 2012. 32p. pap. 21.10 *(978-1-4669-3144-2(2))* Trafford Publishing.

Martin, Lance. The Little Hermit. 2008. 56p. pap. 14.95 *(978-0-9815573-1-1(7))* Highland Pr.

Martin, Laura. The Ark Plan. Deschamps, Eric, illus. (Edge of Extinction Ser.: 1). (J). (gr. 3-7). 2017. 384p. pap. 6.99 *(978-0-06-241623-0(5))* 2016. 368p. 16.99 *(978-0-06-241622-3(7))* HarperCollins Pubs.

—The Ark Plan. DesChamps, Eric, illus. 2017. (Edge of Extinction Ser.: 1). (ENG.). (J). (gr. 3-7). lib. bdg. 17.20 ***(978-0-606-40046-6(X))*** Turtleback Bks.

Martin, Lisa & Martin, Valerie. Anton & Cecil, Book 2: Cats on Track. Murphy, Kelly, illus. (Anton & Cecil Ser.: 2). (ENG.). 272p. (J). (gr. 3-7). 2016. pap. 6.95 *(978-1-61620-638-3(1))* 2015. 16.95 *(978-1-61620-419-8(2))* Algonquin Bks. of Chapel Hill.

—Anton & Cecil, Book 3: Cats Aloft. Murphy, Kelly, illus. 2016. (Anton & Cecil Ser.: 3). (ENG.). 272p. (J). (gr. 3-7). 16.95 *(978-1-61620-459-4(1))* Algonquin Bks. of Chapel Hill.

—Cats at Sea. (Anton & Cecil Ser.: 1). (ENG., Illus.). (J). 2015. 272p. pap. 6.95 *(978-1-61620-456-3(7)*, 73456) 2013. 256p. (gr. 3-7). 16.95 *(978-1-61620-246-0(7)*, 73246) Algonquin Bks. of Chapel Hill.

Martin, Michelle Nicole. Princess & Missy's Magical Adventures: The Crystal Heart. 2010. 55p. pap. 10.95 *(978-1-4327-4954-5(4))* Outskirts Pr., Inc.

Martin, Rachael Lynn. McKenzie Drew: Adventures with David. 2008. 56p. pap. 16.95 *(978-1-60610-389-0(X))* America Star Bks.

Martin, Rebecca. Joanna's Journey. Yoder, Laura & Weaver, Lisa, illus. 2006. 168p. (YA). pap. 9.99 *(978-1-933753-01-0(3))* Carlisle Pr.- Walnut Creek.

Martin, Sheila. Muddy Water. 2005. pap. 16.95 *(978-1-4137-8551-7(4))* PublishAmerica, Inc.

Martin, W. D. Dragonfly Valley: When Best Plans Go Awry. 2012. (ENG.). 176p. (J). pap. 11.95 *(978-1-4787-1832-1(3))* Outskirts Pr., Inc.

—Quest for the Cure: When Quitting Is Not an Option - Dragonfly Valley Series Book 2. 2013. 270p. pap. 15.95 *(978-1-4787-2098-0(0))* Outskirts Pr., Inc.

Martinez, Maureen Cerminaro. Just Be Yourself! the Adventures of Ted the Pom-Poo. 2013. 36p. pap. 15.95 *(978-1-4787-2005-8(0))* Outskirts Pr., Inc.

Martins, Sharon. Murray. 2007. 76p. per. 19.95 *(978-1-4241-7276-4(4))* America Star Bks.

Martone, Ginny. The White Stallion. 2006. (ENG.). 60p. per. 16.95 *(978-1-4241-4332-0(2))* PublishAmerica, Inc.

Maruno, Jennifer. Warbird. 2010. (ENG., Illus.). 120p. (J). (gr. 4-7). pap. 9.95 *(978-1-926607-11-5(2)*, Napoleon & Co.) Dundurn CAN. Dist: Ingram Publisher Services.

Marvel. Captain America - Civil War Reusable Sticker Book. 2016. (ENG., Illus.). 12p. (J). (gr. -1-1). pap. 6.99 *(978-0-316-27145-5(4))* Little, Brown Bks. for Young Readers.

—Captain America: Civil War Junior Novel. 2016. (ENG.). 144p. (J). (gr. 3-7). pap. 6.99 *(978-0-316-27142-4(X))* Little, Brown Bks. for Young Readers.

—Marvel Movie Theater Storybook & Movie Projector. 2016. (ENG.). 32p. (J). (gr. k-3). 19.99 *(978-0-7944-3728-2(1))* Studio Fun International.

—Marvel Super Heroes Assemble! Tattoos, Fantastic Facts, & Amazing Activites. 2014. (ENG.). 24p. (J). (gr. -1-1). pap. 7.99 *(978-0-7944-3008-5(2)*, Reader's Digest Children's Bks.) Studio Fun International.

—Marvel's Guardians of the Galaxy, Vol. 2. 2017. (ENG., Illus.). 12p. (J). (gr. -1-1). pap. 6.99 *(978-0-316-27170-7(5))* Little, Brown Bks. for Young Readers.

—Marvel's the Avengers Storybook Collection. 2015. (ENG., Illus.). 192p. (J). (gr. -1-3). 11.99 *(978-0-316-25631-5(5))* Little, Brown Bks. for Young Readers.

Marvel & Busse, R. R. Meet the Team! 2017. (Passport to Reading Level 2 Ser.). (ENG., Illus.). 32p. (J). (gr. -1-3). pap. 4.99 *(978-0-316-27167-7(5))* Little, Brown Bks. for Young Readers.

Marvel & Cho, Charles. The Return of Rocket & Groot. 2017. (ENG., Illus.). 24p. (J). (gr. -1-3). pap. 4.99 *(978-0-316-27162-2(4))* Little, Brown Bks. for Young Readers.

Marvel & Davis, Adam. Hulk to the Rescue. 2015. (Passport to Reading Level 2 Ser.). (ENG., Illus.). 32p. (J). (gr. -1-3). pap. 3.99 *(978-0-316-25640-7(4))* Little, Brown Bks. for Young Readers.

Marvel & McCann, Jim. Guardians of the Galaxy, Vol. 2. 2017. (ENG.). 176p. (J). (gr. 3-7). 9.99 *(978-0-316-27163-9(2))*; pap. 6.99 *(978-0-316-27165-3(9))* Little, Brown Bks. for Young Readers.

Marvel & Palacios, Tomas. Friends & Foes. 2015. (Passport to Reading Level 2 Ser.). (ENG., Illus.). 32p. (J). (gr. -1-3). pap. 3.99 *(978-0-316-25641-4(2))* Little, Brown Bks. for Young Readers.

Marvel & Strathearn, Chris. Captain America: Civil War 8x8. 2016. (ENG., Illus.). 24p. (J). (gr. -1-3). pap. 3.99 *(978-0-316-27139-4(X))* Little, Brown Bks. for Young Readers.

Marvel & Wyatt, Chris. Marvel's Ant-Man: the Junior Novel. 2015. (ENG.). 144p. (J). (gr. 3-7). pap. 6.99 *(978-0-316-25674-2(9))* Little, Brown Bks. for Young Readers.

—Marvel's Avengers: Age of Ultron: the Deluxe Junior Novel. 2015. (ENG., Illus.). 144p. (J). (gr. 3-7). 9.99 *(978-0-316-30105-3(1))* Little, Brown Bks. for Young Readers.

Marvel Book Group. The Avengers Storybook Collection. 2015. (Storybook Collection). (ENG.). 304p. (J). (gr. 1-3). 16.99 *(978-1-4847-0242-0(5)*, Marvel Pr.) Disney Publishing Worldwide.

—Captain America: the First Avenger Read-Along Storybook & CD. 2016. (Read-Along Storybook & CD Ser.). (ENG.). 32p. (J). (gr. -1-k). pap. 6.99 *(978-1-4847-5131-2(0)*, Marvel Pr.) Disney Publishing Worldwide.

—Iron-Man 2. 2016. (Read-Along Storybook & CD Ser.). (ENG.). 32p. (J). (gr. -1-k). pap. 6.99 *(978-1-4847-8630-7(0)*, Marvel Pr.) Disney Publishing Worldwide.

—Iron Man Read-Along Storybook & CD. 2016. (Read-Along Storybook & CD Ser.). (ENG.). 32p. (J). (gr. -1-k). pap. 6.99 *(978-1-4847-5182-4(5)*, Marvel Pr.) Disney Publishing Worldwide.

—A Mighty Marvel Chapter Book Amazing Adventures! 2016. (Mighty Marvel Chapter Book Ser.: 2). (ENG.). 384p. (J). (gr. 3-7). pap. 11.99 *(978-1-4847-6732-0(2)*, Marvel Pr.) Disney Publishing Worldwide.

—Thor Read-Along Storybook & CD. 2016. (Read-Along Storybook & CD Ser.). (ENG.). 32p. (J). (gr. -1-k). pap. 6.99 *(978-1-4847-8173-9(2)*, Marvel Pr.) Disney Publishing Worldwide.

—World of Reading: Avengers the New Team: Level 1. 2015. (World of Reading Ser.). (ENG.). 32p. (J). (gr. -1-1). pap. 3.99 *(978-1-4847-1454-6(7)*, Marvel Pr.) Disney Publishing Worldwide.

Marvel Book Group. World of Reading Listen Along. 2017. (World of Reading Ser.). (ENG.). 96p. (J). (gr. -1-k). pap. 7.99 ***(978-1-4847-9948-2(8)***, Marvel Pr.) Disney Publishing Worldwide.

Marvel Book Group & West, Alexandra. World of Reading Super Hero Adventures: Thwip! You Are It! Level Pre-1. 2017. (World of Reading Ser.). (ENG.). 32p. (J). (gr. -1-k). pap. 3.99 *(978-1-4847-8643-7(2)*, Marvel Pr.) Disney Publishing Worldwide.

—World of Reading Super Hero Adventures: Tricky Trouble! Level Pre-1. 2017. (World of Reading Ser.). (ENG.). 32p. (J). (gr. -1-k). pap. 3.99 *(978-1-4847-8644-4(0)*, Marvel Pr.) Disney Publishing Worldwide.

Marvel Book Group & Wong, Clarissa S. World of Reading Falcon: This Is Falcon: Level 1. Lim, Ron & Rosenberg, Rachelle, illus. 2015. (World of Reading Ser.). (ENG.). 32p. (J). (gr. 1-3). pap. 3.99 *(978-1-4847-2259-6(0)*, Marvel Pr.) Disney Publishing Worldwide.

Marvel Book Group & Wyatt, Chris. World of Reading: Hulk This Is Hulk. 2015. (World of Reading Ser.). (ENG.). 32p. (J). (gr. 1-3). pap. 3.99 *(978-1-4847-1658-8(2)*, Marvel Pr.) Disney Publishing Worldwide.

Marvel Books Group & Macri, Thomas. This Is Wolverine. 2013. (Marvel World of Reading Level 1 Ser.). (J). lib. bdg. 13.55 *(978-0-606-31751-1(1)*, Turtleback) Turtleback Bks.

Marvel Books Staff & Wyatt, Chris. Guardians of the Galaxy. 2014. (ENG.). 144p. (J). (gr. 3-7). pap. 6.99 *(978-0-316-29324-2(5))* Little, Brown Bks. for Young Readers.

Marvel Comics Staff & Mayer, Kirsten. Age of Ultron: Avengers Save the Day. 2015. (ENG., Illus.). 24p. (J). (gr. -1-3). pap. 4.99 *(978-0-316-25639-1(0))* Little, Brown Bks. for Young Readers.

Marvel Press Book Group. Astonishing Adventures!, 3 Bks In 1. 2016. (Mighty Marvel Chapter Book Ser.: 1). (ENG.). 400p. (J). (gr. 3-7). pap. 11.99 *(978-1-4847-6731-3(4)*, Marvel Pr.) Disney Publishing Worldwide.

—Spider-Man: an Amazing Book & Magnetic Play Set: Book & Magnetic Play Set. Marvel Press Book Group, illus. 2016. (Magnetic Dress-Up Book Ser.). (ENG., Illus.). 32p. (J). (gr. -1-k). 15.99 *(978-1-4847-6168-7(5)*, Marvel Pr.) Disney Publishing Worldwide.

—5-Minute Avengers Stories. 2015. (5-Minute Stories Ser.). (ENG.). 192p. (J). (gr. 1-3). 12.99 *(978-1-4847-4331-7(8)*, Marvel Pr.) Disney Publishing Worldwide.

Marvel Press Staff, et al. Thor: the Dark World Junior Novel. Disney Book Group Staff, illus. 2013. (ENG.). 128p. (J). (gr. 3-7). pap. 5.99 *(978-1-4231-7245-1(0))* Marvel Worldwide, Inc.

Marvel Staff & Busse, R. R. Captain America: Civil War Reader #2. 2016. (Passport to Reading Level 2 Ser.). (ENG., Illus.). 32p. (J). (gr. -1-3). pap. 3.99 *(978-0-316-27144-8(6))* Little, Brown Bks. for Young Readers.

Marvel Staff & Smith, A. Harrison. Captain America: Civil War Reader #1. 2016. (Passport to Reading Level 1 Ser.). (ENG., Illus.). 32p. (J). (gr. -1-3). pap. 3.99 *(978-0-316-27143-1(8))* Little, Brown Bks. for Young Readers.

Marvel Staff & Wyatt, Chris. Captain America: Civil War Deluxe Junior Novel. 2016. (ENG.). 144p. (J). (gr. 3-7). 9.99 *(978-0-316-27141-7(1))* Little, Brown Bks. for Young Readers.

Marvel Staff, et al. Captain America: Civil War 8x8 W/Add-On. 2016. (ENG.). 24p. (J). (gr. -1-3). pap. 4.99 *(978-0-316-27140-0(3))* Little, Brown Bks. for Young Readers.

Marvin, Susan. Birthday Dreamz. 2011. 36p. (gr. -1). pap. 15.99 *(978-1-4567-4173-0(X))* AuthorHouse.

Mary Barr. The Ditch Dog the Hedge Cat. 2009. 108p. 20.95 *(978-1-4401-5560-4(7))*; pap. 10.95 *(978-1-4401-5558-1(5))* iUniverse, Inc.

Mary John Lewis. Pookie in Paris. 2009. 24p. pap. 12.49 *(978-1-4389-6514-7(1))* AuthorHouse.

Mashima, Hiro. Rave. 2006. (Rave Ser.). (SPA., Illus.). reprint ed. Vol. 1. 185p. pap. 10.95 *(978-1-59497-175-4(7))* Vol. 3. 184p. pap. 10.95 *(978-1-59497-177-8(3))* Vol. 4. 188p. per. 10.95 *(978-1-59497-178-5(1))* Vol. 5. 192p. pap. 10.95 *(978-1-59497-179-2(X))* Vol. 6. 200p. pap. 10.95 *(978-1-59497-180-8(3))* Public Square Bks.

—Rave: Volume 2, Vol. 2. 2006. (Rave Ser.). (SPA., Illus.). 180p. reprint ed. pap. 10.95 *(978-1-59497-176-1(5))* Public Square Bks.

—Rave: Volume 7, Vol. 7. 2006. (Rave Ser.). (SPA., Illus.). 189p. reprint ed. pap. 10.95 *(978-1-59497-199-0(4))* Public Square Bks.

—Rave: Volume 9, Vol. 9. 2006. (Rave Ser.). (SPA., Illus.). 189p. reprint ed. pap. 10.95 *(978-1-59497-201-0(X))* Public Square Bks.
—Rave, Volume 8, Vol. 8. 2006. (Rave Ser.). (SPA., Illus.). 171p. reprint ed. pap. 10.95 *(978-1-59497-200-3(1))* Public Square Bks.
Mason, Charlene. Landon's Backyard Adventures. 2012. 24p. pap. 24.95 *(978-1-4626-7470-1(4))* America Star Bks.
Mason, Christine. The Mystery of Nan Madol a Pacific Island Adventure. 2011. 166p. pap. 11.95 *(978-1-61170-025-1(6))* Robertson Publishing.
Mason, Conrad. The Watchmen of Port Fayt. 2015. (ENG.). 400p. (J). (gr. 3-7). 17.99 *(978-0-545-83308-0(6))* Scholastic, Inc.
Mason, Dianne. Danny's Ghost. 2007. 156p. pap. 9.39 *(978-1-4116-4937-8(0))* Lulu Pr., Inc.
Mason, Tom & Danko, Dan. The Lost Scrolls: Fire. Spaziante, Patrick, illus. 2006. (Avatar Ser.). (ENG.). 64p. (J). pap. 4.99 *(978-1-4169-1880-6(9),* Simon Spotlight/Nickelodeon) Simon Spotlight/Nickelodeon.
Mason, Tom, et al. Honk That Horn! Shannon, David et al, illus. 2011. (Jon Scieszka's Trucktown Ser.). (ENG.). 24p. (J). (gr. -1-k). pap. 3.99 *(978-1-4169-4184-2(3),* Simon & Schuster Bks. For Young Readers) Simon & Schuster Bks. For Young Readers.
—Who's That Truck? Shannon, David et al, illus. 2008. (Jon Scieszka's Trucktown Ser.). (ENG.). 14p. (J). (gr. -1-1). bds. 7.99 *(978-1-4169-4175-0(4),* Little Simon) Little Simon.
Mass, Wendy. The Candymakers & the Great Chocolate Chase. (ENG.). (J). (gr. 3-7). 2017. 560p. pap. 8.99 ***(978-0-316-08918-0(4))*** 2016. 544p. 18.99 *(978-0-316-08919-7(2))* Little, Brown Bks. for Young Readers.
Mass, Wendy & Brawer, Michael. Archie Takes Flight. 2014. (Space Taxi Ser.: 1). (J). lib. bdg. 16.00 *(978-0-606-35305-2(4))* Turtleback Bks.
—B. U. R. P. Strikes Back. 2017. (Space Taxi Ser.: 5). (ENG., Illus.). 144p. (J). (gr. 1-5). pap. 5.99 *(978-0-316-30840-3(4))* Little, Brown Bks. for Young Readers.
—B. U. R. P. Strikes Back. 2017. (Space Taxi Ser.: 5). (J). lib. bdg. 16.00 ***(978-0-606-40226-2(8))*** Turtleback Bks.
—The Galactic B. U. R. P. 2016. (Space Taxi Ser.: 4). (ENG., Illus.). 128p. (J). (gr. 1-5). 14.99 *(978-0-316-24331-5(0));* pap. 5.99 *(978-0-316-24330-8(2))* Little, Brown Bks. for Young Readers.
—Space Taxi: Aliens on Earth. 2017. (Space Taxi Ser.: 6). (ENG., Illus.). 128p. (J). (gr. 1-5). 15.99 *(978-0-316-30842-7(0))* Little, Brown Bks. for Young Readers.
—Water Planet Rescue. 2014. (Space Taxi Ser.: 2). (ENG., Illus.). 128p. (J). (gr. 1-5). 15.00 *(978-0-316-24323-0(X))* Little, Brown Bks. for Young Readers.
Mass, Wendy & Michael Brawer. Aliens on Earth. 2017. (Space Taxi Ser.: 6). (J). lib. bdg. 16.00 ***(978-0-606-40227-9(6))*** Turtleback Bks.
Massaro, Michael. Tony Towne & the Fearful Summer. 2011. (ENG.). 192p. pap. 8.99 *(978-1-4564-7961-9(X))* CreateSpace Independent Publishing Platform.
Massey, Eithne. Where the Stones Sing: Who Are the Mysterious Voices in Christ Church? 2012. (ENG., Illus.). 208p. (J). pap. 12.95 *(978-1-84717-277-8(6))* O'Brien Pr., Ltd., The IRL. Dist: Dufour Editions, Inc.
Massey, K. J. Everyday Things with Morgan. Bowser, Katya, illus. 2013. 24p. 19.99 *(978-0-9910489-4-6(6))* NyreePr. Literary Group.
Masters, H. Pink Feathers,Murky Pools & a Witch: A Lellaland Adventure. Lie, Vivian, illus. 2003. 52p. pap. *(978-1-84401-098-1(8))* Athena Pr.
Masters, Jane E. Indy. 2013. 40p. pap. 9.99 *(978-1-62839-260-9(6))* Salem Author Services.
Mastro, M. L. Return to Baladah. 2011. 88p. (gr. 10-12). pap. 9.99 *(978-1-4520-7377-4(5))* AuthorHouse.
Matas, Carol. Tales of a Reluctant Psychic: The Freak, Visions, & Far. 2009. (ENG.). 424p. (YA). (gr. 7-18). pap. *(978-1-55470-203-9(8))* Me to We.
Matas, Carol & Nodelman, Perry. The Curse of the Evening Eye. 2009. (Ghosthunters Ser.). (ENG.). 216p. (J). (gr. 3-7). pap. *(978-1-55470-145-2(7))* Me to We.
Matchett, Gillian. The Adventures of Weston Super Cat with Activities. 2009. (Illus.). 92p. pap. 30.49 *(978-1-4389-2241-6(8))* AuthorHouse.
Mateboer, Hans. Peter the Cruise Ship. 2007. (Illus.). 32p. (J). 16.95 *(978-0-9759487-1-2(7))* Mateboer, Johannes Aart.
Matheis, Mickie. Balloon Blast! (Rusty Rivets) Flowers, Luke, illus. 2017. (Little Golden Book Ser.). (ENG.). 24p. (J). (-k). 4.99 ***(978-1-5247-1672-1(3),*** Golden Bks.) Random Hse. Children's Bks.
—Save the School Bus! (PAW Patrol) Petrossi, Fabrizio, illus. 2017. (Little Golden Book Ser.). (ENG.). 24p. (J). (-k). 4.99 ***(978-1-5247-1665-3(0),*** Golden Bks.) Random Hse. Children's Bks.
Matheos, George P. Pure Magic. 2011. 156p. (gr. 2-4). 22.95 *(978-1-4620-1619-8(7));* pap. 12.95 *(978-1-4620-1617-4(0))* iUniverse, Inc.
Matherly, Ashley Page. Wonderful White Wintery Day: The Marvelous Misadventure of Katy Bear, 1 vol. Fennewald, Joseph Grant, illus. 2009. 43p. pap. 24.95 *(978-1-61546-323-7(2))* PublishAmerica, Inc.
Matheron, Annaliese. Ninja Nan & Sidekick Grandad. 2013. 124p. pap. *(978-1-909411-20-3(5))* Mauve Square Publishing.
—Ninja Nan Strikes Again. 2013. 132p. pap. *(978-1-909411-21-0(3))* Mauve Square Publishing.
Matheson, Richard. Abu & the 7 Marvels. Stout, William, illus. 2003. 128p. (YA). pap. 21.95 *(978-1-887368-49-0(3))* Gauntlet, Inc.
Mathews, David George. We Can Do Anything! 2009. (Illus.). 28p. pap. 12.49 *(978-1-4490-5014-6(X))* AuthorHouse.
Mathews, Temple. The Sword of Armageddon. 2012. (ENG.). 274p. (J). (gr. 6-11). pap. 9.99 *(978-1-937856-19-9(4))* BenBella Bks.
Mathis, Tabitha. The Princess & the Tyger. 2012. 28p. pap. 24.95 *(978-1-4626-8265-2(0))* America Star Bks.
Mathisen, Michael. Abby & the Helping Mommy. Estill, Amy, illus. 2009. 28p. pap. 13.99 *(978-1-4389-5327-4(5))* AuthorHouse.
Matson, Lynne. Nil on Fire. 2016. (Nil Ser.: 3). (ENG.). 416p. (YA). 17.99 *(978-1-62779-295-0(3),* 9781627792950, Holt, Henry & Co. Bks. For Young Readers) Holt, Henry & Co.
Matsumoto, Lisa. The Adventures of Gary & Harry: A Tale of Two Turtles. Furuya, Michael, illus. 2006. (J). 16.95 *(978-0-9647491-4-6(9))* Lehua, Inc.
Matsumoto, Reiko Odate. The Princess with the Magic Bowl: As retold from the Japanese folk tale By. 2008. 48p. pap. 22.49 *(978-1-4389-1225-7(0))* AuthorHouse.
Matsumoto, Tomo. Beauty is the Beast, Vol. 4. Matsumoto, Tomo, illus. 2006. (ENG., Illus.). 208p. pap. 8.99 *(978-1-4215-0354-7(9))* Viz Media.
Matsuoka, Kyoko. Where Is Little Toko. 2005. (Illus.). 27p. (J). 11.95 *(978-4-902216-11-0(6))* R.I.C. Publications Asia Co, Inc. JPN. Dist: Continental Enterprises Group, Inc. (CEG).
Matte, Johane, et al. Flight Explorer, Vol. 1. Kibuishi, Kazu, ed. Armstrong, Matthew S., illus. 2008. (ENG.). 112p. (YA). pap. 16.00 *(978-0-345-50313-8(9),* Villard Bks.) Random House Publishing Group.
Mattei, Francesca. Caraselle. 2010. 36p. pap. *(978-1-4269-3219-9(7))* Trafford Publishing (UK) Ltd.
Matthew, Patricia D. THG-Mystery... Treehouse Gargoyle. 2006. 150p. pap. 24.95 *(978-1-4241-2587-6(1))* PublishAmerica, Inc.
Matthews, Curtis. Boots Meets the Grizzly Bears. 2007. 164p. per. 13.95 *(978-1-4343-3372-8(8))* AuthorHouse.
Matthews, Jackie. The Grand Adventure: Journey from the Castle of Safe. 2013. 28p. pap. 16.95 *(978-1-4908-0842-0(6),* WestBow Pr.) Author Solutions, Inc.
Matthews, John. The Barefoot Book of Giants, Ghosts, & Goblins. Manna, Giovanni, illus. 2008. (ENG.). 80p. (J). 21.99 *(978-1-84686-235-9(3))* Barefoot Bks., Inc.
—The Chronicles of Arthur: Sword of Fire & Ice. Collins, Mike, illus. 2009. (ENG.). 128p. (J). (gr. 3-7). pap. 14.99 *(978-1-4169-5908-3(4),* Aladdin) Simon & Schuster Children's Publishing.
—The Chronicles of Arthur: Sword of Fire & Ice. Collins, Mike, illus. 2009. (ENG.). 128p. (J). (gr. 3-7). 21.99 *(978-1-4169-8683-6(9),* Simon & Schuster/Paula Wiseman Bks.) Simon & Schuster/Paula Wiseman Bks.
—StoryWorld: Quests & Adventures: Create-A-Story. Matthews, Caitlín, illus. 2013. (Storyworld Ser.). (ENG.). (J). (gr. 4-7). 9.99 *(978-0-7636-5317-0(9),* Templar) Candlewick Pr.
Matthews, T. J. The Canoeing Safari. Rheburg, Judy, illus. 2004. (J). *(978-0-938978-35-0(7))* Wycliffe Bible Translators.
—The Village Safari. Rheburg, Judy, illus. 2005. (J). *(978-0-938978-36-7(5))* Wycliffe Bible Translators.
Matthies, Don-Oliver. Detective Mazes. 2004. (ENG., Illus.). 40p. (J). pap. 3.95 *(978-1-4027-1293-7(6))* Sterling Publishing Co., Inc.
Mattingly Jr., Joseph C. Logan's Big Surprise. 2013. 28p. pap. 24.95 *(978-1-62709-717-8(1))* America Star Bks.
Mattix, Tracy. Begging for Marshmallows. 2013. 44p. pap. 16.95 *(978-1-63000-542-9(8))* America Star Bks.
Matulewicz, Elisabeth Ann. Benny & Marshmallow. Sponaugle, Kim, illus. 2008. 31p. (J). pap. 15.00 *(978-0-9786211-7-9(4),* Ithaca Pr.) Authors & Artists Publishers of New York, Inc.
Matuszak, Pat. Simone's Secret, 2, Bk 2. 2009. (Angel Light Ser.: 2). (ENG.). 192p. (gr. 11). pap. 12.99 *(978-0-89957-876-7(4))* AMG Pubs.
Mauldin, Mary. What a Carrot-Astrophy! 2011. 32p. pap. 14.99 *(978-1-4634-3366-6(2))* AuthorHouse.
Maurer, Jayne. Grandpa Goes to Horse Camp. 2012. 40p. 16.95 *(978-1-62709-874-8(7));* pap. 16.95 *(978-1-62709-141-1(6))* America Star Bks.
Mawhinney, Art, illus. Diego's Arctic Rescue. 2009. (Go, Diego, Go! Ser.). (ENG.). 24p. (J). (gr. -1-2). pap. 3.99 *(978-1-4169-8504-4(2),* Simon Spotlight/Nickelodeon) Simon Spotlight/Nickelodeon.
—Diego's Wolf Pup Rescue. 2006. (Go, Diego, Go! Ser.: 1). (ENG.). 24p. (J). (gr. -1-2). pap. 3.99 *(978-1-4169-1559-1(1),* Simon Spotlight/Nickelodeon) Simon Spotlight/Nickelodeon.
—Dora & Diego Help the Dinosaur. 2011. (Dora & Diego Ser.). (ENG.). 24p. (J). pap. 3.99 *(978-1-4424-1400-6(6),* Simon Spotlight/Nickelodeon) Simon Spotlight/Nickelodeon.
—Look & Find Disney Princess Worlds of Wonder. 2006. (Look & Find Books). (J). pap. 24.98 *(978-1-4127-6490-2(4))* Publications International, Ltd.
Max & Mintie, 6 Pks. (gr. k-1). 23.00 *(978-0-7635-9054-3(1))* Rigby Education.
Maxwell, Andre L. & Maxwell, Amanda L. The Great Chicken Caper. Carter, Jill, illus. 2012. 34p. (-18). 18.00 *(978-0-9881811-1-3(8))* Maxwell, Andre.
May, Marcie & Zerhusen, Margaret. The Adventures of Penny & Tubs: The City on the Sea. Chamberlin, Maggie, illus. 2012. (ENG.). 32p. (J). 16.95 *(978-0-938467-61-8(1))* Headline Bks., Inc.
May, Sophie. Dotty Dimple Out West. 2005. reprint ed. pap. 22.95 *(978-1-4179-8845-7(2))* Kessinger Publishing, LLC.
May, Stephan. Leo the Entrepreneurial Hippo. 2008. (Illus.). 56p. pap. 10.95 *(978-1-4401-0480-0(8))* iUniverse, Inc.
Maya, Valorie & Sharma, Neal. Ivan Idea Has a Big Ide. 2012. 24p. pap. 17.99 *(978-1-4772-6673-1(9))* AuthorHouse.
Maya Z And Nadajia R. Hall. The New-Fangled Adventures of Alexia & Z: The Case of Grams' Missing Teeth. 2009. 36p. pap. 15.95 *(978-1-4389-4508-8(6))* AuthorHouse.
Mayberry, Becky. Always Listen to Your Mom, Even If She Is a Duck: Even If She Is A Duck. 2011. 28p. pap. 21.99 *(978-1-4628-7175-9(5))* Xlibris Corp.
Mayer, Kirsten. Despicable Me 2 - Undercover Super Spies. 2013. (ENG.). 24p. (J). (gr. -1-3). 4.99 *(978-0-316-23446-7(X))* Little, Brown Bks. for Young Readers.
—Disney Fairies: the Pirate Fairy: Adventure at Skull Rock. 2014. (ENG., Illus.). 24p. (J). (gr. -1-3). 3.99 *(978-0-316-28331-1(2))* Little, Brown Bks. for Young Readers.
—Dude-It-Yourself Adventure Journal. Spaziante, Patrick, illus. 2012. (Adventure Time Ser.). (ENG.). 112p. (J). (gr. 2-5). 7.99 *(978-0-8431-7244-7(4),* Price Stern Sloan) Penguin Young Readers Group.
—I Am Aquaman. 2013. (Justice League Classic: I Can Read! Ser.). (J). lib. bdg. 13.55 *(978-0-606-31794-8(5),* Turtleback) Turtleback Bks.
—Meet Team Prime. 2012. (Transformers Passport to Reading Ser.). (J). lib. bdg. 13.55 *(978-0-606-26148-7(6),* Turtleback) Turtleback Bks.
Mayer, Kirsten, text. The World's Greatest Villain. 2010. (Despicable Me Ser.). (ENG., Illus.). 24p. (J). (gr. 1-4). pap. 3.99 *(978-0-316-08377-5(1),* L,B Kids) Hachette Bk. Group.
Mayer, Linda & Mayer, Jason. Frankie: The World's Greatest Hot Dog. 2009. 24p. pap. 12.99 *(978-1-4389-4307-7(5))* AuthorHouse.
Mayer, Marianna. The Adventures of Tom Thumb. Craft, Kinuko Y., illus. 2005. 28p. (J). (gr. k-4). reprint ed. 16.00 *(978-0-7567-9642-6(3))* DIANE Publishing Co.
Mayer, Mercer. Going to the Sea Park. 2009. (Little Critter: I Can Read! Ser.). (J). lib. bdg. 13.55 *(978-0-606-06964-9(X),* Turtleback) Turtleback Bks.
—Just an Adventure at Sea. 2017. (Little Critter: I Can Read! Ser.). lib. bdg. 13.55 ***(978-0-606-40062-6(1))*** Turtleback Bks.
Mayer, Mercer. Just Critters Who Care. Mayer, Mercer, illus. 2010. (My First I Can Read Ser.). (ENG., Illus.). 32p. (J). (gr. -1-3). 16.99 *(978-0-06-083560-6(5));* pap. 3.99 *(978-0-06-083559-0(1))* HarperCollins Pubs.
Mayes, Rosey. Introducing... Max, 1 vol. Mayes, Steven, illus. 2010. 16p. 24.95 *(978-1-4489-3895-7(3))* PublishAmerica, Inc.
Mayfield, Jamie. Destiny. 2016. (ENG., Illus.). (J). 29.99 ***(978-1-63533-000-7(9))*** 2013. 310p. pap. 17.99 *(978-1-62380-864-8(2))* Dreamspinner Pr. (Harmony Ink Pr.).
Mayhew, James. Starlight Sailor. Morris, Jackie, illus. (ENG.). 24p. (J). 2012. pap. 6.99 *(978-1-84686-750-7(9))* 2009. (gr. -1-3). 16.99 *(978-1-84686-185-7(3))* Barefoot Bks., Inc.
Mayhew, James & MAYHEW, JAMES. Miranda Da la Vuelta Al Mundo. 2004. (SPA., Illus.). (J). 17.99 *(978-84-8488-094-3(X))* Serres, Ediciones, S. L. ESP. Dist: Lectorum Pubns., Inc.
Mayle, Peter. The Amazing Adventures of Chilly Billy. Robins, Arthur, illus. 2013. 72p. pap. *(978-1-908191-69-4(4))* Escargot Bks. Online, Ltd.
Maynard, Adam G. The Adventures of Dynamo Dog & the Case of the Missing Jewelery. 2010. 24p. 15.49 *(978-1-4490-9186-6(5))* AuthorHouse.
Mayo, Simon. Itch: The Explosive Adventures of an Element Hunter. 2014. (ENG.). 432p. (J). (gr. 6). pap. 9.95 *(978-1-4549-1427-3(0))* Sterling Publishing Co., Inc.
Mayowa-Harrison, Lady Paula Merry. The Buckaroos. 2006. (J). pap. 8.00 *(978-0-8059-6978-8(0))* Dorrance Publishing Co., Inc.
Mays, Stan. Wicked Little Camp Story. 2005. 248p. pap. 14.95 *(978-1-59113-674-3(1))* Booklocker.com, Inc.
Mazula, Derek. A Drifen's Tale. 2009. 48p. pap. 24.99 *(978-1-4490-2782-7(2))* AuthorHouse.
Mazur, Kathy. My Story... I'd like to Tell. 2005. (J). bds. 8.95 *(978-0-9761076-1-3(9))* Spring Ducks Bks., LLC.
Mazurke, Rachel. Mr. & Mrs. Duck: Busy Day, The Accident, New Home or the Brook, Dirty Water Again. 2008. (Illus.). 62p. (J). pap. 9.00 *(978-0-8059-7762-2(7))* Dorrance Publishing Co., Inc.
Mazzola, Lori. Tales of the Tree People to Tree... or. 2006. 48p. pap. 16.95 *(978-1-4241-5065-6(5))* PublishAmerica, Inc.
Mazzola, Lori E. The Forbidden Forest: Tales of the Tree People, 1 vol. 2009. 151p. pap. 24.95 *(978-1-4489-2656-5(4))* America Star Bks.
Mba, Ogochukwu. The Roaches, 1 vol. 2010. 20p. 24.95 *(978-1-4489-3951-0(8))* PublishAmerica, Inc.
Mbuyazi, Phiwayinkosi G. The Wiby Kids - How It All Began. 2011. 204p. pap. 12.99 *(978-1-61667-337-6(0))* Raider Publishing International.
Mc Shane, Mary. Karena the Fairy. 2011. 112p. pap. 10.95 *(978-1-4502-9297-9(6))* iUniverse, Inc.
Mcadams, Kate. Flynn the Post Office Mouse. 2010. 28p. pap. 12.49 *(978-1-4520-0816-5(7))* AuthorHouse.
McAdams Moore, Carol. Phonics Comics: Cave Dave - Level 1. Dammer, Mike, illus. 2007. (ENG.). 24p. (J). (gr. 1-17). per. 3.99 *(978-1-58476-552-3(6))* Innovative Kids.
McArthur, Cathy E. The Adventures of Elvis the Groundhog: The Golden Glow. 2005. 9.00 *(978-0-8059-8154-4(3))* Dorrance Publishing Co., Inc.
McArthur, Shallee. The Unhappening of Genesis Lee. 2014. (ENG.). 352p. (J). (gr. 6). 16.95 *(978-1-62914-647-8(1),* Sky Pony Pr.) Skyhorse Publishing Co., Inc.
McBee, Travis. A Little Holiday Thrill. 2008. 66p. pap. 10.99 *(978-0-557-03276-1(8))* Lulu Pr., Inc.
McBratney, Sam. Guess How Much I Love You Lap-Size Board Book. Jeram, Anita, illus. 2013. (Guess How Much I Love You Ser.). (ENG.). 24p. (J). (— 1). bds. 12.99 *(978-0-7636-7006-1(5))* Candlewick Pr.
McBride, Earvin, Jr. The Adventurous Cyborg. McBride, Earvin, Jr., illus. 2nd unabr. ed. 2003. (Amazing Sci-Fi & Adventure Heroes Ser.). (Illus.). 43p. (YA). (gr. 7-12). 4.95 *(978-1-892511-06-5(1))* MacBride, E. J. Pubn., Inc.
—The Eerie Adventures of Detective Omar Mendez. McBride, Earvin, Jr., illus. 2nd unabr. ed. 2003. (Earvin MacBride's Amazing Sci-Fi & Adventure Heroes Ser.). (Illus.). 329p. (J). (gr. 7-12). pap. 5.95 *(978-1-892511-08-9(8))* MacBride, E. J. Pubn., Inc.
McBride, Lish. Pyromantic. 2017. (Firebug Ser.). (ENG.). 336p. (YA). (gr. 9-17). 18.99 *(978-0-8050-9863-1(1),* 9780805098631, Holt, Henry & Co. Bks. For Young Readers) Holt, Henry & Co.
McBride M. D., Mark A., et al. The Chickens & the Ice Cream. 2010. 28p. pap. 12.99 *(978-1-4490-9172-9(5))* AuthorHouse.
McBride, Peter & McBride, Judith. Bug & Budgie Fly Away. 2013. 48p. *(978-1-4602-3312-2(3))* FriesenPress.
McBrier, Page. Beatrice's Goast. unabr. ed. 2005. (J). (gr. -1-3). 27.95 incl. audio *(978-0-8045-6938-5(X))* Spoken Arts, Inc.
McCaffrey, Laura Williams. Marked. 2016. (ENG.). 368p. (YA). (gr. 7-9). 17.99 *(978-0-547-23556-1(9),* Clarion Bks.) Houghton Mifflin Harcourt Trade & Reference Pubs.
Mccain-Buzzelli, Vic. The Adventures of Milly & Mikey: Womb Mates Book #1. 2010. 20p. pap. 10.49 *(978-1-4520-4654-9(9))* AuthorHouse.
McCall, Guadalupe Garcia. Summer of the Mariposas. 2012. (ENG.). 352p. (YA). 19.95 *(978-1-60060-900-8(7),* Tu Bks.) Lee & Low Bks., Inc.
McCall Smith, Alexander. Precious & the Puggies: Precious Ramotswe's Very First Case. Robertson, James, tr. from ENG. 2011. (ENG., Illus.). 96p. pap. 10.95 *(978-1-84502-332-4(3))* Black and White Publishing Ltd. GBR. Dist: Interlink Publishing Group, Inc.
McCall Smith, Alexander. The Sands of Shark Island. 2017. (School Ship Tobermory Ser.: 2). (ENG.). 256p. (J). (gr. 3-7). 15.99 ***(978-0-399-55401-8(7),*** Delacorte Bks. for Young Readers) Random Hse. Children's Bks.
McCallister, Colleen. Boaz the Ginger Cat & the Mysterious Mishap of the Kitchen Sponge. 2013. 36p. pap. 12.59 *(978-0-9787336-9-8(X))* CMC Publishing.
Mccants, Bruce C. Legend of the White Cockroach. 2012. 120p. 20.95 *(978-1-4759-4791-5(7));* pap. 10.95 *(978-1-4759-4792-2(5))* iUniverse, Inc.
McCarthy, Jon-Paul. Eddie the Egg. 2010. (Illus.). 32p. pap. 12.99 *(978-1-4490-4125-0(6))* AuthorHouse.
McCarthy, Sally J. & McCarthy, Arica G. Hope & Wishie. 2013. (Illus.). 42p. pap. 12.95 *(978-0-9898968-1-8(1))* McCarthy, Sally Studios.
McCarty, Bryan. Devyn's Gold. 2008. pap. 17.00 *(978-0-8059-8640-2(5))* Dorrance Publishing Co., Inc.
McCarty, Jerry. A Dog to Treasure. 2003. 130p. per. 14.95 *(978-1-59196-228-1(5))* Instant Pub.
McCarty, Peter. Fabian Escapes. McCarty, Peter, illus. rev. ed. 2007. (ENG., Illus.). 40p. (J). (gr. -1-1). 21.99 *(978-0-8050-7713-1(8),* 9780805077131, Holt, Henry & Co. Bks. For Young Readers) Holt, Henry & Co.
McCaughrean, Geraldine. Las Aventuras de Ulises. Barroso, Paz, tr. Ross, Tony, illus. 2005. (Mythology Series Collection Mitos Ser.). Tr. of Odysseus. (SPA.). 48p. (J). (gr. 2-3). 9.95 *(978-84-348-6426-9(6))* SM Ediciones ESP. Dist: Iaconi, Mariuccia Bk. Imports.
—The Death-Defying Pepper Roux. 2010. 336p. (J). (gr. 5-18). 16.99 *(978-0-06-183665-7(6))* HarperCollins Pubs.
—The Glorious Adventures of the Sunshine Queen. 2011. 336p. (J). (gr. 5). 16.99 *(978-0-06-200806-0(4))* HarperCollins Pubs.
—Peter Pan in Scarlet. Fischer, Scott M., illus. 2006. (ENG.). 320p. (J). (gr. 4-9). 19.99 *(978-1-4169-1808-0(6),* McElderry, Margaret K. Bks.) McElderry, Margaret K. Bks.
McCaughren, Tom. Legend of the Golden Key. (Illus.). 96p. 3.95 *(978-0-900068-73-7(6))* Penguin Publishing Group.
McClafferty, Lisa. Matilda Private Eye: The Case of the Missing Socks, 1 vol. Aines, Diane, illus. 2007. (ENG.). 31p. 24.95 *(978-1-4241-8637-2(4))* America Star Bks.
McClain, Charles. Big Jake Plants a Garden: Big Jake Adventures. Southern Lion Books, ed. McClain, Tania, illus. 2013. 26p. (J). *(978-1-935272-21-2(7))* Southern Lion Bks.
McClanahan, Teel, 3rd. Dragons' Truth. 2007. 208p. (YA). per. 12.99 *(978-1-934516-02-7(3))* Modern Evil Pr.
McClatchy, Lisa. Eloise's Pirate Adventure. Lyon, Tammie Speer & Lyon, Tammie, illus. 2007. (Eloise Ser.). (ENG.). 32p. (J). (gr. -1-1). pap. 3.99 *(978-1-4169-4979-4(8),* Simon Spotlight) Simon Spotlight.
McClellan, Rachel. Escape to Eden. 2016. (ENG.). 295p. (YA). pap. 17.99 *(978-1-4621-1777-2(5),* Sweetwater Bks.) Cedar Fort, Inc./CFI Distribution.
McClintock, Norah. Close to the Heel, 1 vol. 2012. (Seven (the Series) Ser.). (ENG., Illus.). 272p. (J). (gr. 5-10). pap. 9.95 *(978-1-55469-950-6(9))* Orca Bk. Pubs. USA.
—From the Dead, 1 vol. 2014. (Seven Sequels Ser.). (ENG., Illus.). 288p. (J). (gr. 5-10). pap. 10.95 *(978-1-4598-0537-8(2))* Orca Bk. Pubs. USA.
McCloskey, John J. Warrior Ching. 2006. 179p. pap. 24.95 *(978-1-4241-2389-6(5))* PublishAmerica, Inc.
McCLOUD, Scott. Superman Adventures. 2013. (Superman Adventures Ser.). (ENG.). 32p. (gr. 1-2). 90.40 *(978-1-4342-4859-6(3))* Stone Arch Bks.
McClure, Brian D. The Raindrop. 2006. (Illus.). 36p. (J). 14.95 *(978-1-933426-01-3(2))* Universal Flag Publishing.
McClure, Kim. Edgar the Seagull who was Afraid to Fly. 2009. 34p. pap. 16.70 *(978-0-557-05920-1(8))* Lulu Pr., Inc.
McClure, Wendy. Wanderville. 2014. (Wanderville Ser.: 1). (ENG.). (J). (gr. 3-7). 240p. pap. 7.99 *(978-1-59514-701-1(2));* 224p. 16.99 *(978-1-59514-700-4(4))* Penguin Young Readers Group. (Razorbill).
McCluskey, J. E. The Adventures of Peter the Pleasant Platypus & Friends: First Adventure, Tidy Time. 2004. 48p. pap. 24.95 *(978-1-4137-2546-9(5))* PublishAmerica, Inc.
—Platypus Tales. 2009. 120p. pap. 14.95 *(978-1-4357-2635-2(9))* Lulu Pr., Inc.
McCollum, Lynn Tragesser. The Green School Caper: The Adventures of the Five Amigos. 2008. 164p. pap. 9.95 *(978-1-4327-2564-8(5))* Outskirts Pr., Inc.
McConnell, Edith J. Their Times. 2004. 44p. (J). per. 11.66 *(978-1-4116-1370-6(8))* Lulu Pr., Inc.
McConville, Alexandra. The Adventures of Sass-O-Frask: A Tale of Kindness. 2012. 32p. pap. 19.99 *(978-1-4772-6006-7(4))* AuthorHouse.
McCooke, Valerie J. Grandfather's Chest. 2012. 40p. pap. 32.70 *(978-1-4771-0543-6(3))* Xlibris Corp.
McCorkle, Barbara. Bandit Raccoon. Taylor, David A., illus. I.t. ed. 2006. 39p. (J). 19.95 *(978-1-59879-170-9(2));* per. 13.99 *(978-1-59879-123-5(0))* Lifevest Publishing, Inc.
McCorkle, Mark & Schooley, Bob. Grudge Match. 2005. (Illus.). 80p. (J). *(978-1-4155-9100-0(8))* Disney Pr.
McCoy, Angie. Starchild's Adventures on Earth. McCoy, Derrick, illus. 2011. 24p. pap. 24.95 *(978-1-4560-5053-5(2))* America Star Bks.
McCranie, Stephen. Mal & Chad - The Biggest, Bestest Time Ever! McCranie, Stephen, illus. 2011. (Mal & Chad Ser.: 1). (ENG., Illus.). 224p. (J). (gr. 3-7). 9.99 *(978-0-399-25221-1(5),* Philomel Bks.) Penguin Young Readers Group.
McCredie, Elise. Nowhere Boys. 2016. (ENG.). 314p. (YA). (gr. 7). pap. 12.99 *(978-1-76012-016-0(2))* Hardie Grant Egmont Pty, Ltd. AUS. Dist: Independent Pubs. Group.
McCreedy, J. L. The Orphan of Torundi. 2014. (ENG.). 300p. (YA). pap. 10.99 *(978-0-9882369-2-9(3))* Penelope Pipp Publishing.
McCulley, Johnston. Zorro! (FRE.). pap. 19.95 incl. audio compact disk *(978-88-7754-819-1(3))* Cideb ITA. Dist: Distribooks, Inc.
—Zorro. (SPA.). pap. 20.95 incl. audio compact disk *(978-88-7754-895-5(9))* Cideb ITA. Dist: Distribooks, Inc.
McCullough, Dicy. Tired of School. 2011. 28p. pap. 15.99 *(978-1-4628-9229-7(9))* Xlibris Corp.

Mccullough, Kelly. School for Sidekicks. 2016. (J). lib. bdg. 18.40 *(978-0-606-38559-6(2))* Turtleback Bks.
McCullough, Myrina D. Feet. Schafrath, Ty, illus. 2013. 28p. pap. 15.00 *(978-0-9847740-1-2(7))* Systems Group, Inc., The.
McCune, Joshua. Talker 25. 2014. (Talker 25 Ser.: 1). (ENG.). 432p. (YA). (gr. 9). 17.99 *(978-0-06-212191-2(X),* Greenwillow Bks.) HarperCollins Pubs.
—Talker 25 #2: Invisible Monsters. 2016. (Talker 25 Ser.: 2). 448p. (YA). (gr. 8). pap. 9.99 *(978-0-06-212195-0(2),* Greenwillow Bks.) HarperCollins Pubs.
Mccutcheon, George B. The Purple Parasol. 2004. reprint ed. pap. 15.95 *(978-1-4191-7949-5(7))* Kessinger Publishing, LLC.
McCutcheon, George Barr. The Purple Parasol. 2004. reprint ed. pap. 1.99 *(978-1-4192-7949-2(1))* Kessinger Publishing, LLC.
McDaid, Mark. Billy the Bus. 2006. (Illus.). 48p. pap. *(978-1-84401-714-0(1))* Athena Pr.
Mcdaniel, Chris M. The Adventures of Dusty Popsallot. 2010. 52p. pap. 24.99 *(978-1-4520-0871-4(X))* AuthorHouse.
McDaniels, Preston, illus. The Prince of Ireland & the Three Magic Stallions. 2003. (ENG.). 32p. (J). (gr. k-3). tchr. ed. 16.95 *(978-0-8234-1573-1(2))* Holiday Hse., Inc.
—The Squire & the Scroll: A Tale of the Rewards of a Pure Heart. 2004. (ENG.). 32p. (J). 12.99 *(978-1-59317-079-0(3))* Warner Pr., Inc.
McDermott, John Francis. The Adventures of Izzy & Bitty Bee. 2007. (J). 0.01 net. *(978-1-60402-094-6(6))* Independent Pub.
McDiarmid, Gail S. & McGee, Marilyn S. Running for Home. Coffey, Durwood, illus. 2013. 76p. pap. 15.95 *(978-0-9854677-0-8(3))* SunDog Enterprises.
McDonagh, Christelle, et al. Mission Magic Bubble. 2009. (Illus.). 56p. pap. 23.99 *(978-1-4389-0640-9(4))* AuthorHouse.
McDonald, Ann-Eve. MaGook. 2005. (J). *(978-0-9770158-6-3(6))* BeachWalk Bks. Inc.
—The Tale of the Black Square. 2004. (J). *(978-0-9770158-2-5(3))* BeachWalk Bks. Inc.
McDonald, Diane O. The Adventures of Tweed. 2011. 52p. 24.99 *(978-1-4535-1701-7(4))*; pap. 15.99 *(978-1-4535-1700-0(6))* Xlibris Corp.
McDonald, Fiona. Ghost Doll & Jasper. 2012. (ENG., Illus.). 112p. (J). (gr. 2-7). 12.95 *(978-1-62087-174-4(2),* 620174, Sky Pony Pr.) Skyhorse Publishing Co., Inc.
McDonald, Janet. Chill Wind. 2006. (ENG.). 144p. (YA). (gr. 7-12). reprint ed. per. 12.99 *(978-0-374-41183-1(2),* 9780374411831, Farrar, Straus & Giroux (BYR)) Farrar, Straus & Giroux.
McDonald, Lisa. The Adventures of Penelope the Tea Cup Pig. 2012. 36p. pap. 32.70 *(978-1-4771-3182-4(5))* Xlibris Corp.
McDonald, Megan. Mad Rad. Reynolds, Peter H., illus. 2012. (Judy Moody Ser.: Bks. 7-9). (ENG.). (J). (gr. 1-4). pap. 17.97 *(978-0-7636-5410-8(8))* Candlewick Pr.
—Twice as Moody. Reynolds, Peter H., illus. 2011. (Judy Moody Ser.). (ENG.). 304p. (J). (gr. 1-4). pap. 8.99 *(978-0-7636-5740-6(9))* Candlewick Pr.
—When the Library Lights Go Out. Tillotson, Katherine, illus. 2009. (ENG.). 40p. (J). (gr. -1-1). 8.99 *(978-1-4169-8028-5(8),* Atheneum Bks. for Young Readers) Simon & Schuster Children's Publishing.
—When the Library Lights Go Out. Tillotson, Katherine, tr. Tillotson, Katherine, illus. 2005. (ENG.). 40p. (J). (gr. -1-3). 19.99 *(978-0-689-86170-3(2),* Atheneum/Richard Jackson Bks.) Simon & Schuster Children's Publishing.
McDonnell, Kathleen. The Songweavers, 1 vol. 2008. (Notherland Journeys Ser.: 3). (ENG.). 232p. (YA). (gr. 4-8). pap. 9.95 *(978-1-897187-42-5(4))* Second Story Pr. CAN. Dist: Orca Bk. Pubs. USA.
McDonnell, Patrick. Year of Yesh. 2016. lib. bdg. 33.05 *(978-0-606-39185-6(1))* Turtleback Bks.
McDonnell, Vincent. Can Timmy Save Toyland? 2006. (ENG., Illus.). 185p. (J). pap. 13.95 *(978-1-903464-86-1(2))* Collins Pr., The IRL. Dist: Dufour Editions, Inc.
—The Catalpa Adventure: Escape to Freedom. 2010. (ENG.). 128p. (J). pap. 12.95 *(978-1-84889-038-1(9))* Collins Pr., The IRL. Dist: Dufour Editions, Inc.
—Children of Stone. 2006. (ENG.). 206p. (J). pap. 11.95 *(978-1-903464-88-5(9))* Collins Pr., The IRL. Dist: Dufour Editions, Inc.
—The Knock Airport Mystery. 2006. (ENG., Illus.). 203p. (J). pap. 11.95 *(978-1-903464-87-8(0))* Collins Pr., The IRL. Dist: Dufour Editions, Inc.
McDoogle, Farrah. A Mystery in Gabba Land. Scanlon, Michael, illus. 2010. (Yo Gabba Gabba! Ser.). (ENG.). 24p. (J). (gr. -1-k). pap. 3.99 *(978-1-4424-0652-0(6),* Simon Spotlight) Simon Spotlight.
McDougall, Jill. Jinxed! 2008. (Lightning Strikes Ser.). 96p. (J). pap. *(978-1-921150-59-3(9))* Walker Bks. Australia Pty, Ltd.
McDowell, Andrew. Beyond the Forest. 2007. 286p. pap. 16.95 *(978-0-7414-4238-3(8))* Infinity Publishing.
McDunn, Rosemary. When Kids Dream & Trucks Fly. 2007. (ENG.). 52p. per. 12.99 *(978-0-9792258-6-4(8))* Bezalel Bks.
McElligott, Matthew. Mad Scientist Academy: the Space Disaster. 2017. (Mad Scientist Academy Ser.: 3). (ENG.). 40p. (J). (gr. k-3). lib. bdg. 20.99 ***(978-0-553-52383-6(X))***; (Illus.). 17.99 ***(978-0-553-52382-9(1))*** Random Hse. Children's Bks. (Crown Books For Young Readers).
McFall, Jessica & McFall, Ernest. Unselfish Love. l.t. ed. 2006. (ENG., Illus.). 28p. per. 9.95 *(978-1-4327-0076-8(6))* Outskirts Pr., Inc.
McFarland, John S. Annette a Big, Hairy Mom. 2013. 100p. pap. 9.95 *(978-1-59713-135-3(0))* Goose River Pr.
McFarland, Kim. A Refugee in Oz. 2010. 164p. pap. 11.95 *(978-0-557-48706-6(4))* Lulu Pr., Inc.
McFarlane, Brian. Fire in the North. 2007. (ENG.). 220p. (J). (gr. 2-7). pap. *(978-1-55168-243-3(5))* Magma.
—On the Hockey Highway, Vol. 2. 2nd ed. 2007. (Mitchell Brothers Ser.). (ENG.). 220p. (J). (gr. 2-7). pap. *(978-1-55168-245-7(1))* Magma.
—Trouble at Tumbling Waters. 3rd ed. 2007. (Mitchell Brothers Ser.). (ENG., Illus.). 200p. (J). (gr. 3-7). per. 6.99 *(978-1-55168-251-8(6))* Leaf Storm Pr.
McFarlane, Brian & McFarlene, Brain. Wizard the Wonder Horse. 2007. (Mitchell Brothers Ser.). (ENG.). 162p. (J). (gr. 3-7). pap. 6.99 *(978-1-55168-253-2(2))* Leaf Storm Pr.
McFarlane, Leslie. McGonigle Scores! 2006. (ENG.). 256p. (J). pap. 9.95 *(978-1-55263-834-7(0))* Leaf Storm Pr.
McGee. Logger's Return: The Continuing Adventures of our White-Tailed Deer Friend. 2011. 24p. pap. 24.95 *(978-1-4560-4230-1(0))* PublishAmerica, Inc.
Mcgee, Cotton. Bookman's Adventures: The Valley of the Frogs. 2011. 52p. pap. 22.28 *(978-1-4389-4771-6(2))* AuthorHouse.
McGee, Helen. Ikky Dikky Dak: Magical Adventures with Googler! Book Two. Kaltenborn, Karl, illus. 2011. pap. 21.95 *(978-1-60494-573-7(7))* Wheatmark, Inc.
McGee, Ron. Ryan Quinn & the Lion's Claw. Samnee, Chris, illus. 2017. (Ryan Quinn Ser.: 2). 352p. (J). (gr. 3-7). 16.99 ***(978-0-06-242169-2(7))*** HarperCollins Pubs.
McGee, Warner, illus. Diego's Egyptian Expedition. 2009. (Go, Diego, Go! Ser.). (ENG.). 24p. (J). pap. 3.99 *(978-1-4169-6870-2(9),* Simon Spotlight/Nickelodeon) Simon Spotlight/Nickelodeon.
Mcghee, Alison. Firefly Hollow. Denise, Christopher, illus. 2015. (ENG.). 304p. (J). (gr. 3-7). 16.99 *(978-1-4424-2336-7(6),* Atheneum Bks. for Young Readers) Simon & Schuster Children's Publishing.
—Song of Middle C. Menchin, Scott, illus. 2009. (ENG.). 32p. (J). (gr. k-3). 16.99 *(978-0-7636-3013-3(6))* Candlewick Pr.
McGhee, Heather. The Wild Adventures of a Curious Princess. Myers, Shari, illus. 2008. (J). per. 9.99 *(978-0-9788985-9-5(1))* Better Be Write Pub., A.
McGhee, Katie Mariah. The Case of the Missing Chimpanzee from Classroom C2. McGhee, Katie Mariah & Herrera, Aaron Jeremiah, illus. 2012. 28p. 24.95 *(978-1-4560-0039-4(X))* America Star Bks.
McGillicuddy, Barbara. Adventures in the Kingdom of Mim: Buddie Saves the Day. 2006. (J). per. 13.95 *(978-0-9774513-7-1(2))* Changing Lives Publishing.
McGinnis, Chelsea. Mk Frogg & the Lily Pad Adventures, 1 vol. 2009. 48p. pap. 24.95 *(978-1-60813-548-6(9))* America Star Bks.
McGirr, Randel W. Bible Camp. 2007. 176p. per. 13.95 *(978-0-595-44663-6(9))* iUniverse, Inc.
McGovern, Ann. Who Has a Secret? 2011. 52p. (gr. 1-2). pap. 9.95 *(978-1-4620-1273-2(6))* iUniverse, Inc.
McGovern, DeeDee. Zachary, the Adventure Boy!, 1 vol. 2009. 88p. pap. 19.95 *(978-1-4489-8249-3(9))* America Star Bks.
McGovern, DeeDee Jean. The Heartland of Home: Tight Quarters in the City. 2008. 58p. pap. 16.95 *(978-1-60610-058-5(0))* America Star Bks.
McGowan, Anthony. The Bare Bum Gang & the Holy Grail. 2009. (ENG., Illus.). 160p. (J). (gr. 2-4). pap. 11.99 *(978-1-86230-389-8(4),* Red Fox) Random House Children's Books GBR. Dist: Independent Pubs. Group.
McGowan, Keith. The Witch's Curse. Tanaka, Yoko, illus. 2014. (ENG.). 320p. (J). (gr. 4-7). pap. 7.99 *(978-1-250-04426-6(X),* 9781250044266) Square Fish.
McGowan, Michael. Newton Time Machine. 2008. (ENG., Illus.). 216p. (J). pap. 11.99 *(978-0-00-639550-8(3),* Harper Trophy) HarperCollins Pubs.
McGowan, Steve. The Adventures of Keke & the Golden Coconut. 2012. 48p. pap. 21.92 *(978-1-4251-4407-4(1))* Trafford Publishing.
Mcgranahan, Patrick D. Imaginary Jerry: And the Tale of His Daring Escape from Imaginaria. 2011. 292p. (gr. -1). 27.99 *(978-1-4389-4728-0(3))*; pap. 17.99 *(978-1-4389-4727-3(5))* AuthorHouse.
McGrath, Sheelagh. Magick It Up: A Children's Story for Grown Ups Too. 2012. (Illus.). 60p. pap. 23.95 *(978-1-4525-0498-8(9))* Balboa Pr.
McGraw, Eloise Jarvis. The Golden Goblet. l.t. ed. 2003. (LRS Large Print Cornerstone Ser.). 318p. (J). lib. bdg. 35.95 *(978-1-58118-113-5(2))* LRS.
McGraw, Penny Underwood. Jay's Vacation, 1 vol. 2009. 37p. pap. 24.95 *(978-1-61582-313-0(1))* America Star Bks.
McGreal, Sue. Jimmy Fox's Great Pet Adventure. 2013. 68p. pap. *(978-1-78299-607-1(9))* FeedARead.com.
McGregor, Don. Flights. Lima, Sidney, illus. 4th rev. ed. 2006. (Zorro Ser.). (ENG.). 96p. (J). pap. 7.95 *(978-1-59707-026-3(2))* Papercutz.
McGregor, Don & Lima, Sidney. Flights. 4th rev. ed. 2006. (Zorro Ser.). (ENG., Illus.). 96p. (J). 12.95 *(978-1-59707-027-0(0))* Papercutz.
McGregor, John. Daisy & Her Autumn & Winter Adventures. 2012. (Illus.). 77p. pap. 13.50 *(978-1-78035-482-8(7),* Fastprint Publishing) Upfront Publishing Ltd. GBR. Dist: Printondemand-worldwide.com.
McGregor, Melissa Lee. Ainsley & Owen: An Unexpected Friendship. 2013. 40p. pap. *(978-1-4602-0111-4(6))* FriesenPress.
McGregor, Suzy. The Garden Fairy & Mrs. Mouse. 2013. 58p. pap. 14.95 *(978-0-9824926-6-6(9))* Lollipop Media Productions, LP.
—Moon Leopard. 2013. 40p. pap. 11.95 *(978-0-9824926-5-9(0))* Lollipop Media Productions, LP.
McGuinness, Jeff. Paddy the Penguin's Adventure. Starr, Lisa, illus. l.t. ed. 2006. 33p. (J). 27.95 *(978-1-59879-231-7(8))*; (gr. -1-3). per. 15.95 *(978-1-59879-229-4(6))* Lifevest Publishing, Inc.
McGuire, Jeremy. O'shaughnessey: Boy & His Leprechaun. 2007. 140p. per. 14.95 *(978-1-4327-0892-4(9))* Outskirts Pr., Inc.
McGuire, Roberta Libby. The Adventures of the Cape Cod Bear. 2012. 24p. pap. 15.99 *(978-1-4771-5266-9(0))* Xlibris Corp.
McGuirk, Leslie. Tucker's Spooky Halloween. 2009. 32p. 14.99 *(978-0-7636-4468-0(4))* Candlewick Pr.
—Tucker's Spooky Halloween. McGuirk, Leslie, illus. 2009. (Candlewick Storybook Animations Ser.). (ENG., Illus.). 32p. (J). (gr. k-k). 14.99 *(978-0-7636-4469-7(2))* Candlewick Pr.
Mchale, Pat. Over the Garden Wall. 2016. lib. bdg. 33.05 *(978-0-606-39002-6(2))* Turtleback Bks.
McHaney, Eric & McHaney, Mandy. Rich the Itch. Smith, Jordyn, illus. l.t. ed. 2005. 20p. (J). *(978-0-9769086-0-9(3))* RTI Publishing, LLC.
McHugh, Rosetta. Poodiky Oglethorpe. 2009. 20p. pap. 24.95 *(978-1-60749-086-9(2))* America Star Bks.
—Poodiky Oglethorpe's First Christmas, 1 vol. 2010. 30p. 24.95 *(978-1-4512-0119-2(2))* PublishAmerica, Inc.
McIntosh, Kenneth. A Stranger's Voice: Forensic Speech. 2007. (Crime Scene Club: Fact & Fiction Ser.). (Illus.). 144p. (YA). (gr. 8-12). pap. 9.95 *(978-1-4222-0879-3(6))* Mason Crest.
Mcintosh Williams, Samantha. The Last Bear on Brandywine Crick. 2013. 276p. pap. 11.99 *(978-1-4575-1960-4(7))* Dog Ear Publishing, LLC.
McIntyre, Gary P. Jake Fall & Winter. 2011. 198p. pap. 24.95 *(978-1-4560-4085-7(5))* America Star Bks.
McIntyre, Sheila Adam. The Cave in the Forest. 2012. pap. 9.95 *(978-0-7414-7480-3(8))* Infinity Publishing.
McIntyre, Sterlynett. The Closing Argument. 2005. 97p. pap. 16.95 *(978-1-4137-9216-4(2))* PublishAmerica, Inc.
McIntyre, Will. Burning Midnight. 2016. (ENG.). 320p. (YA). (gr. 7). 17.99 *(978-0-553-53410-8(6),* Delacorte Pr.) Random Hse. Children's Bks.
McIsaac, Meaghan. The Boys of Fire & Ash. 2015. (ENG.). 336p. (J). (gr. 5). 19.99 *(978-0-375-99167-7(0),* Delacorte Bks. for Young Readers) Random Hse. Children's Bks.
McJarrow, Shandy. The Adventures of Papilio the Butterfly. 2009. 112p. 20.95 *(978-1-4401-3850-8(8))*; pap. 10.95 *(978-1-4401-3840-9(0))* iUniverse, Inc.
McKain, W. J. Morris Hollett - & St Vernon's Ward for Strange & Unusual Diseases. 2013. 140p. pap. *(978-1-78148-193-6(8))* Grosvenor Hse. Publishing Ltd.
McKay, Malcolm. Thistown. 2006. (ENG., Illus.). 200p. per. 18.95 *(978-0-9546912-5-7(3))* Aurora Metro Pubns. Ltd. GBR. Dist: Consortium Bk. Sales & Distribution.
McKay, Sindy. We Both Read-My Day Big Book. Johnson, Meredith, illus. 2006. (We Both Read Ser.). 40p. (J). (gr. -1-4). pap. 29.95 *(978-1-891327-93-3(3))* Treasure Bay, Inc.
McKee, David. The Adventures of King Rollo. 2016. (ENG., Illus.). 32p. (J). (-k). 19.99 *(978-1-78344-468-7(1))* Andersen Pr. GBR. Dist: Independent Pubs. Group.
—Elmer & the Whales. McKee, David, illus. 2014. (ENG., Illus.). 32p. (J). (gr. -1-3). 16.95 *(978-1-4677-3453-0(5))* Lerner Publishing Group.
—The Extraordinary Adventures of Mr Benn Diver. 2015. (Mr. Benn Ser.). (ENG., Illus.). 32p. (J). (gr. -1-k). pap. 9.99 *(978-1-4449-2204-2(1))* Hodder & Stoughton GBR. Dist: Hachette Bk. Group.
—Melric & the Sorcerer. 2014. (Melric Ser.). (ENG., Illus.). 32p. (J). (gr. -1-k). pap. 9.99 *(978-1-78344-036-8(8))* Andersen Pr. GBR. Dist: Independent Pubs. Group.
McKee, David & L'Ecole des loisirs/LeapFrog. Elmer. 2008. (J). 20.79 *(978-1-59319-950-0(3))* LeapFrog Enterprises, Inc.
McKee, Rosie. Captain of the Ship: What's the Problem? 2017. (Computer Science for the Real World Ser.). 16p. (gr. 7-8). pap. 7.95 ***(978-1-5383-5200-7(1),*** Rosen Classroom) Rosen Publishing Group, Inc., The.
McKelvey, Lonnie. Benny the Brave. Wooten, Neal, illus. 2008. 28p. (J). pap. 7.99 *(978-0-9817521-3-6(6))* Mirror Publishing.
McKelvie, Melissa, told to. Serena & the Turtle Eggs. 2007. (ENG.). 28p. pap. 15.99 *(978-1-4196-7780-9(2))* CreateSpace Independent Publishing Platform.
McKenna, James. The Mind Traveller. 2013. 212p. pap. *(978-0-9569723-8-5(1))* Lone Cloud Publishing.
McKenzie, C. Lee. Alligators Overhead. 2012. (ENG.). 216p. pap. 12.95 *(978-1-4327-8473-7(0))* Outskirts Pr., Inc.
McKenzie, Precious. Isle of Enchantment. 2015. (ENG.). 96p. (gr. 3-6). 31.36 *(978-1-63430-390-3(3))* Rourke Educational Media.
—A Vacation in Ruins. 2015. (ENG.). 96p. (gr. 3-6). 31.36 *(978-1-63430-393-4(8))* Rourke Educational Media.
McKenzie, Tiffany M. The Adventures of Alan & the Man-Eating Rabbits. 2013. 24p. pap. 24.95 *(978-1-63000-143-8(0))* America Star Bks.
McKernan, Victoria. Shackleton's Stowaway. 2006. (ENG.). 336p. (YA). (gr. 7-11). per. 7.99 *(978-0-440-41984-6(0),* Laurel Leaf) Random Hse. Children's Bks.
McKinlay, Meg. Bella & the Wandering House. 2016. (ENG.). 80p. (J). (gr. k-2). 11.99 *(978-1-925162-30-1(3))* Fremantle Pr. AUS. Dist: Independent Pubs. Group.
McKinley, Ryan. The Lost Crew. 2012. (ENG.). 144p. pap. 14.95 *(978-1-4327-9659-4(3))*; pap. 9.95 *(978-1-4327-9658-7(5))* Outskirts Pr., Inc.
McKissack, Fredrick L., et al. Cyborg. 2011. (Clone Codes Ser.: 2). (ENG.). 144p. (J). (gr. 3-7). 16.99 *(978-0-439-92985-1(7),* Scholastic Pr.) Scholastic, Inc.
McKissack, Patricia C., et al. The Visitors. 2012. (Clone Codes Ser.). (ENG.). 160p. (J). (gr. 3-7). 16.99 *(978-0-439-92987-5(3),* Scholastic Pr.) Scholastic, Inc.
McKown, Hunter. Meet Jack Truck! Shannon, David et al, illus. 2008. (Jon Scieszka's Trucktown Ser.). (ENG.). 14p. (J). (gr. -1-1). bds. 5.99 *(978-1-4169-4173-6(8),* Little Simon) Little Simon.
—Sand Castle Bash: Counting from 1 To 10. Shannon, David et al, illus. 2009. (Jon Scieszka's Trucktown Ser.). (ENG.). 26p. (J). (gr. -1-k). bds. 5.99 *(978-1-4169-4179-8(7),* Little Simon) Little Simon.
McKown, Martha. The Adventures of Zingway, the Monster. 2011. 28p. 12.03 *(978-1-4567-1087-3(7))* AuthorHouse.
McLaren-Tishler, Sylvia. Finn the Fireman. 2008. 33p. pap. 16.95 *(978-0-557-02552-7(4))* Lulu Pr., Inc.
McLaughlin, Julie. Mr. Gator's up the Creek. McKay, Ann Marie, illus. 2005. (J). 16.99 *(978-0-933101-23-4(6))* Legacy Pubns.
McLaughlin, Vicki. The Dancer of Her Dreams. 2006. 48p. pap. 16.95 *(978-1-4241-2723-8(8))* PublishAmerica, Inc.
McLaurin, Corey F. Larry, Lisa & the Missing Kite, 1 vol. Dixon, Corey, illus. 2009. 20p. pap. 24.95 *(978-1-61546-590-3(1))* America Star Bks.
McLean, Claire. Bo & the Ghosts of the White House Pets. 2012. 88p. pap. 17.95 *(978-1-4626-7416-9(X))* America Star Bks.
McLean, Matthew. A Bewitching Summer, 1 vol. 2009. 100p. pap. 19.95 *(978-1-60836-686-6(3))* America Star Bks.
—The Invisible War: Book One of the Disciple Trilogy. 2007. 236p. 25.95 *(978-0-595-69953-7(7))*; per. 15.95 *(978-0-595-46152-3(2))* iUniverse, Inc.
McLeese, Peggy Anne. The Magic. 2011. 64p. pap. 31.99 *(978-1-4568-9558-7(3))* Xlibris Corp.
McLeod, Kimberly. Little Mitchell Tried to Be Good, but Most of the Time He Was Misunderstood. 2012. 42p. 25.00 *(978-0-9829825-5-6(0))* Creative Energy, LLC.
Mcloughlin, Jane. At Yellow Lake. 2012. 368p. (J). pap. 8.99 *(978-1-84780-360-3(1),* Frances Lincoln) Quarto Publishing Group UK GBR. Dist: Littlehampton Bk Services, Ltd.
McLoughlin, Wayne, illus. Warriors - Tales from the Clans. 2014. (Warriors Novella Ser.). (ENG.). 320p. (J). (gr. 3-7). pap. 6.99 *(978-0-06-229085-4(1))* HarperCollins Pubs.
McMahan, Stephanie K. The Mystery of the Golden Rings. 2007. 140p. 21.95 *(978-0-595-68451-9(3))*; per. 11.95 *(978-0-595-43998-0(5))* iUniverse, Inc.
McMahen, Chris. Klutzhood, 1 vol. 2007. (ENG.). 168p. (J). (gr. 4-7). per. 7.95 *(978-1-55143-710-1(4))* Orca Bk. Pubs. USA.
McMahon, Kara. Dress up Dora! Aikins, Dave, illus. 2009. (Dora the Explorer Ser.). (ENG.). 12p. (J). 8.99 *(978-1-4169-6067-6(8),* Simon Spotlight/Nickelodeon) Simon Spotlight/Nickelodeon.
McMahon, Kim. The Curious Prince. 2011. 32p. pap. 24.95 *(978-1-4560-5089-4(3))* America Star Bks.
McMann, Lisa. Dragon Captives. 2017. (Unwanteds Quests Ser.: 1). (ENG., Illus.). 432p. (J). (gr. 3-7). 17.99 *(978-1-4814-5681-4(4),* Simon & Schuster/Paula Wiseman Bks.) Simon & Schuster/Paula Wiseman Bks.
—Dragon Captives. 2018. (Unwanteds Quests Ser.: 1). lib. bdg. 18.40 ***(978-0-606-40846-2(0))*** Turtleback Bks.
—Going Wild. (Going Wild Ser.: 1). (J). (gr. 3-7). 2017. 400p. pap. 6.99 ***(978-0-06-233715-3(7))*** 2016. 384p. 16.99 *(978-0-06-233714-6(9))* HarperCollins Pubs.
—Predator vs. Prey. 2017. (Going Wild Ser.: 2). 400p. (J). (gr. 3-7). 16.99 ***(978-0-06-233717-7(3))*** HarperCollins Pubs.
McMann, Lisa. The Trap Door. 2013. (Infinity Ring Ser.: Bk. 3). (ENG.). 192p. (J). (gr. 3-7). 16.99 *(978-0-545-48456-5(1))*; (Illus.). 12.99 *(978-0-545-38698-2(5))* Scholastic, Inc.
McMasters, Anne. Anne's Stories for Children of All Ages. 2008. 24p. pap. 12.50 *(978-1-4343-9204-6(X))* AuthorHouse.
McMillan, Angelo. The Adventures of W D: The Dreamers Series Vol. 1. 2012. 24p. 24.95 *(978-1-4626-5270-9(0))* America Star Bks.
McMillen, Charlotte Palmer. The Little Sea Rock & His Friend Arena. 2005. (Illus.). 32p. (J). per. 14.95 *(978-0-9771939-4-3(2),* 003) New World Publishing.
Mcmillen, Michelle. Brothers in the Storm. 2011. 120p. pap. 14.95 *(978-1-4670-2518-6(6))* AuthorHouse.
McMullan, Kate. Double Dragon Trouble. Basso, Bill, illus. 2005. (Dragon Slayers' Academy Ser.: 15). (ENG.). 112p. (J). (gr. 2-5). pap. 5.99 *(978-0-448-43821-4(6),* Grosset & Dunlap) Penguin Young Readers Group.
—Dragon Slayers' Academy Set 2. Basso, Bill, illus. 2007. (Dragon Slayers' Academy Ser.). (ENG.). 112p. 145.26 *(978-1-59961-375-8(1))* Spotlight.
—The Ghost of Sir Herbert Dungeonstone. Basso, Bill, illus. 2004. (Dragon Slayers' Academy Ser.: 12). (ENG.). 112p. (J). (gr. 2-5). pap. 4.99 *(978-0-448-43530-5(6),* Grosset & Dunlap) Penguin Young Readers Group.
—Hail! Hail! Camp Dragononka! Basso, Bill, illus. 2006. (Dragon Slayers' Academy Ser.: 17). (ENG.). 224p. (J). (gr. 2-5). pap. 6.99 *(978-0-448-44124-5(1),* Grosset & Dunlap) Penguin Young Readers Group.
—Never Trust a Troll! Basso, Bill, illus. 2006. (Dragon Slayers' Academy Ser.: 18). (ENG.). 112p. (J). (gr. 2-5). pap. 4.99 *(978-0-448-44393-5(7),* Grosset & Dunlap) Penguin Young Readers Group.
—Revenge of the Dragon Lady, 2 vols. Basso, Bill, illus. 2003. (Dragon Slayers' Academy Ser.: 2). (ENG.). 112p. (J). (gr. 2-5). mass mkt. 5.99 *(978-0-448-43109-3(2),* Grosset & Dunlap) Penguin Young Readers Group.
—Revenge of the Dragon Lady, 1 vol. Basso, Bill, illus. 2007. (Dragon Slayers' Academy Ser.: No. 2). (ENG.). 109p. (gr. -1-3). 24.21 *(978-1-59961-378-9(6))* Spotlight.
—School's Out... Forever! Basso, Bill & Gilpin, Stephen, illus. 2012. (Dragon Slayers' Academy Ser.: 20). (ENG.). 112p. (J). (gr. 2-5). pap. 4.99 *(978-0-448-44571-7(9),* Grosset & Dunlap) Penguin Young Readers Group.
McMullen, Beth. Mrs. Smith's Spy School for Girls. 2017. (Mrs. Smith's Spy School for Girls Ser.: 1). (ENG., Illus.). 304p. (J). (gr. 4-8). 16.99 ***(978-1-4814-9020-7(6),*** Aladdin) Simon & Schuster Children's Publishing.
—Mrs. Smith's Spy School for Girls. 2017. (J). pap. ***(978-1-4814-9021-4(4),*** Simon & Schuster/Paula Wiseman Bks.) Simon & Schuster/Paula Wiseman Bks.
McMullen, Brian & Jägel, Jason. Hang Glider & Mud Mask. 2012. (ENG., Illus.). 32p. (J). (gr. -1-3). 14.95 *(978-1-936365-83-8(9))* McSweeney's Publishing.
McMullen, Sean. Before the Storm. 2009. 262p. (Orig.). pap. 13.95 *(978-1-879462-50-2(8),* Ford Street Publishing) Hybrid Pubs. AUS. Dist: International Publishers Marketing.
McMurchy-Barber, Gina. A Bone to Pick: A Peggy Henderson Adventure. 2015. (Peggy Henderson Adventure Ser.: 4). (ENG.). 152p. (J). pap. 12.99 *(978-1-4597-3072-4(0))* Dundurn CAN. Dist: Ingram Publisher Services.
McNair, Barbara. Tea Parties with Grandm. Hogan, Eric, illus. 2009. 48p. pap. 24.95 *(978-1-60749-617-5(8))* America Star Bks.
McNamee, Graham. Acelercion. (SPA.). (YA). 9.95 *(978-958-04-7608-5(X))* Norma S.A. COL. Dist: Distribuidora Norma, Inc.
McNaney, Jeanne. Miracle in Sumatra: The Story of Gutsy Gus. Cochard, David, illus. 2009. (ENG.). 32p. (J). (gr. -1-3). 16.95 *(978-0-9814534-6-0(5))* Ovation Bks.
McNee, Ian, illus. Treasure Island. 2006. 158p. (J). (gr. 5-9). per. 4.99 *(978-0-7945-1230-9(5),* Usborne) EDC Publishing.
McNeece, Alexander. Sam Iver: Imminent Threat. 2009. 138p. pap. 10.95 *(978-1-935278-02-3(9),* iUniverse Star) iUniverse, Inc.
McNeil, Natalie. Wylli Nilly's Amazing Adventures. 2011. (Illus.). 56p. pap. 20.38 *(978-1-4567-7672-5(X))* AuthorHouse.
McNish, Cliff. Silver City. (ENG.). 256p. (J). (gr. 4-7). 2015. 9.99 *(978-1-4677-9454-1(6),* Carolrhoda Bks.) 2007. (Exceptional Reading & Language Arts Titles for Intermediate Grades Ser.). per. 6.95 *(978-0-8225-6780-6(6),* First Avenue Editions) 2006. (Silver Sequence Ser.: Bk. 2). 15.95 *(978-1-57505-926-6(6),* Carolrhoda Bks.) Lerner Publishing Group.
—Silver World. 2015. (ENG.). 248p. (J). (gr. 4-7). 9.99 *(978-1-4677-9457-2(0),* Carolrhoda Bks.) Lerner Publishing Group.

McPhate, Paul. The Puggles: The Adventures of Carly & Vinigin. 2006. (ENG.). 48p. per. 16.95 *(978-1-4241-4481-5(7))* PublishAmerica, Inc.
McPhate, Paul J. The Puggle King. 2008. 52p. pap. 16.95 *(978-1-60703-709-5(2))* America Star Bks.
McPhee, Peter. Out of Time, 1 vol. 2003. (Lorimer SideStreets Ser.). (ENG.). 168p. (YA). (gr. 9-12). 9.95 *(978-1-55028-796-7(6)*, 9781550287967); 16.95 *(978-1-55028-797-4(4)*, 9781550287974) Lorimer, James & Co., Ltd., Pubs. CAN. Dist: Casemate Pubs. & Bk. Distributors, LLC.
McPherson, Missie & O'Neill, Elizabeth. Alfred Visits Indiana. 2003. (ENG.). 24p. (J). pap. 12.00 *(978-0-9771836-0-9(2))* Lipp, G. Douglas & Assocs.
—Alfred Visits Washington, D. C. 2005. (ENG., Illus.). 24p. (J). (gr. -1-3). pap. 12.00 *(978-0-9771836-1-6(0))* Lipp, G. Douglas & Assocs.
McQueen, Amelia. A Penny for Your Thoughts. 2010. 56p. pap. 23.99 *(978-1-4490-8046-4(4))* AuthorHouse.
McQuerry, Maureen Doyle. The Peculiars. (ENG.). (YA). (gr. 7-17). 2014. 384p. pap. 8.95 *(978-1-4197-1206-7(3))* 2012. 368p. 17.95 *(978-1-4197-0178-8(9))* Abrams, Inc. (Amulet Bks.).
—Time Out of Time. 2015. (Time Out of Time Ser.). (ENG., Illus.). 368p. (J). (gr. 5-9). 16.95 *(978-1-4197-1494-8(5)*, Amulet Bks.) Abrams, Inc.
—Time Out of Time: Book One: Beyond the Door. 2015. (Time Out of Time Ser.). (ENG., Illus.). 400p. (J). (gr. 5-9). pap. 7.95 *(978-1-4197-1493-1(7)*, Amulet Bks.) Abrams, Inc.
—Time Out of Time: Book Two: the Telling Stone. 2016. (ENG., Illus.). 376p. (J). (gr. 3-7). pap. 8.95 *(978-1-4197-1916-5(5)*, Amulet Bks.) Abrams, Inc.
—Time Out of Time Bk. 1: Beyond the Door. 2014. (Time Out of Time Ser.). (ENG., Illus.). 384p. (J). (gr. 3-7). 16.95 *(978-1-4197-1016-2(8)*, Amulet Bks.) Abrams, Inc.
McShane, Pol. The Button That Should Never, Ever, Ever Be Pushed! 2008. 140p. pap. 11.95 *(978-0-595-53194-3(6)*, iUniverse, Inc.) iUniverse, Inc.
Mcshane, Pol. The Magic Elevator: The Adventures of Johnny & Joey. 2005. 129p. pap. 19.95 *(978-1-4241-0014-9(3))* PublishAmerica, Inc.
McShane, Pol. Return to Animal Land: The Adventures of Johnny & Joey. 2007. 132p. (J). per. 10.95 *(978-0-595-45804-2(1))* iUniverse, Inc.
McSorley, Paul J. & Bearss, Patricia. The Adventures of Forealdo: Finding Millie. 2012. 34p. 24.95 *(978-1-4626-6721-5(X))* America Star Bks.
McSpadden, Judy. Heart for Thunder. 2010. 148p. 22.95 *(978-1-4401-9487-0(4))* iUniverse, Inc.
McTague, Charles. Bernard Overall: The Russian Tom Sawyer. 2004. (J). pap. 7.00 *(978-0-8059-6404-2(5))* Dorrance Publishing Co., Inc.
McVay, Chrissy. Souls of the North Wind. 2005. 184p. (J). 23.95 *(978-0-595-67229-5(9))*; pap. 13.95 *(978-0-595-35527-3(7))* iUniverse, Inc.
McVeigh, Mark W. The Lizard's Legacy. Sazaklis, John, illus. 2009. (Spider-Man Ser.). 64p. (J). (gr. 2-5). pap. 4.99 *(978-0-06-162627-2(9)*, HarperFestival) HarperCollins Pubs.
Mcwherter, Barbara. The Wren & the Groundhog. Brandon, Vicky, illus. 2011. 40p. pap. 24.95 *(978-1-4560-5512-7(7))* America Star Bks.
Mcwilliams, Ronnie. The Leaf People: Philip & the Wolf. 2011. 16p. (gr. 1-2). pap. 9.36 *(978-1-4567-6583-5(3))* AuthorHouse.
Me Lees un Cuento, Por Favor?Tr. of Read Me a Story, Please? (SPA., Illus.). (gr. k-3). Vol. 1. (J). *(978-84-480-1622-7(X)*, TM7339) Vol. 2. 96p. (J). *(978-84-480-1624-1(6)*, TM0700) Vol. 3. 2003. 96p. *(978-84-480-1626-5(2)*, TM3568) Timun Mas, Editorial S.A. ESP. Dist: Lectorum Pubns., Inc.
Mead, Purnima & Kerber, Kathy. Bibia, the Butterfly. 2009. 24p. pap. 18.50 *(978-1-4389-6644-1(X))* AuthorHouse.
Mead, Richelle. Shadow Kiss. Vieceli, Emma, illus. 2013. (Vampire Academy Ser.: 3). (ENG.). 160p. (YA). (gr. 7). pap. 12.99 *(978-1-59514-431-7(5)*, Razorbill) Penguin Young Readers Group.
Meade, L. T. A Little Mother to the Others. 2007. (ENG.). 216p. pap. 20.99 *(978-1-4346-1019-5(5))*; 244p. pap. 22.99 *(978-1-4346-1223-6(6))* Creative Media Partners, LLC.
—Red Rose & Tiger Lily or in a Wider Wo. 2004. reprint ed. pap. 28.95 *(978-0-7661-8345-2(9))* Kessinger Publishing, LLC.
Meadowbrook Press. Meadowbrook Kids Three Book Back to School Set. 2005. 250p. pap. 26.85 *(978-0-689-05307-8(X))* Meadowbrook Pr.
Meadows, Daisy. Alicia the Snow Queen Fairy. 2016. (Rainbow Magic — Special Edition Ser.). lib. bdg. 17.20 ***(978-0-606-39728-5(0))*** Turtleback Bks.
—Amber the Orange Fairy. Ripper, Georgie, illus. 2005. (Rainbow Magic Ser.: 2). (ENG.). 80p. (J). (gr. -1-3). pap. 4.99 *(978-0-439-74465-2(2))* Scholastic, Inc.
—Carmen the Cheerleading Fairy. 2017. (Rainbow Magic: Special Edition Ser.). (ENG.). 176p. (J). (gr. 2-5). pap. 6.99 ***(978-1-338-05484-2(8)***, Scholastic Paperbacks) Scholastic, Inc.
—Grace Woollyhop's Musical Mystery (Magic Animal Friends #12) 2016. (Magic Animal Friends Ser.: 12). (ENG., Illus.). 112p. (J). (gr. 2-5). pap. 4.99 *(978-0-545-94079-5(6)*, Scholastic Paperbacks) Scholastic, Inc.
—Kylie the Carnival Fairy. Ripper, Georgie, illus. 2008. (Rainbow Magic Ser.). (ENG.). 192p. (J). (gr. -1-3). pap. 6.99 *(978-0-545-05475-1(3)*, Scholastic Paperbacks) Scholastic, Inc.
Meadows, Jodi. The Orphan Queen. 2015. (Orphan Queen Ser.: 1). (ENG., Illus.). 400p. (YA). (gr. 8). 17.99 *(978-0-06-231738-4(5)*, Tegen, Katherine Bks) HarperCollins Pubs.
Meadows, Melissa. What's the Word, Thunderbird? Book A: the Alamo. 2007. (Wishing Well Ser.). (Illus.). 81p. (J). (gr. k-3). per. 4.99 *(978-1-934517-00-0(3))* Firelight Press, Inc.
Means, J. D. Millie & Honey: The Incredible, Instantaneous, Interplanetary Adventure - Volume Ii - Appleopolis. 2012. 112p. pap. 12.95 *(978-1-4575-1394-7(3))* Dog Ear Publishing, LLC.
Mebus, Scott. Gods of Manhattan, 1 vol. 2009. (ENG.). 368p. (J). (gr. 3-7). 8.99 *(978-0-14-241307-4(0)*, Puffin Books) Penguin Young Readers Group.
—The Sorcerer's Secret, Bk. 3. 2011. (ENG.). 384p. (J). (gr. 5-18). 8.99 *(978-0-14-241878-9(1)*, Puffin Books) Penguin Young Readers Group.
—Spirits in the Park. 2009. (Gods of Manhattan Ser.: No. 2). (J). *(978-0-525-47963-5(5)*, Dutton Juvenile) Penguin Publishing Group.
—Spirits in the Park, Vol. 2. 2010. (ENG.). 400p. (J). (gr. 3-7). 8.99 *(978-0-14-241645-7(2)*, Puffin Books) Penguin Young Readers Group.
Meckler, Linda. Ghost Kids Trilogy. 2004. 139p. (YA). pap. 11.95 *(978-0-7414-2273-6(5))* Infinity Publishing.
Meddaugh, Susan. Campfire Stories. 2013. (Martha Speaks Ser.). (ENG., Illus.). 96p. (J). (gr. 1-4). pap. 5.99 *(978-0-547-97021-9(8))* Houghton Mifflin Harcourt Publishing Co.
—Haunted House. 2010. (Martha Speaks Ser.). (ENG., Illus.). 24p. (J). (gr. -1-3). pap. 3.99 *(978-0-547-21073-5(6))* Houghton Mifflin Harcourt Publishing Co.
—Martha Speaks: Campfire Stories (Chapter Book) 2013. (Martha Speaks Ser.). (ENG., Illus.). 96p. (J). (gr. 1-4). 14.99 *(978-0-547-97024-0(2))* Houghton Mifflin Harcourt Publishing Co.
—Martha Speaks: Haunted House (Reader) 2010. (Martha Speaks Ser.). (ENG., Illus.). 24p. (J). (gr. -1-3). 12.99 *(978-0-547-39353-7(9))* Houghton Mifflin Harcourt Publishing Co.
Meddour, Wendy. The Black Cat Detectives. 2012. (Cinnamon Grove Ser.). (Illus.). 176p. (J). pap. *(978-1-84780-226-2(5)*, Frances Lincoln) Quarto Publishing Group UK.
Medina, Jamie B. Juan Carlos & the Hairy-Chested Chili Pepper. 2008. 28p. pap. 24.95 *(978-1-4241-9869-6(0))* America Star Bks.
Medina, Kathleen. Born into Greyworld. 2008. 220p. 29.99 *(978-1-4363-2619-3(2))*; pap. 19.99 *(978-1-4363-2618-6(4))* Xlibris Corp.
Medina, Larry. The Adventures of Peek a Boo the Sea Lion. 2010. 40p. 21.00 *(978-1-4520-1499-9(X))* AuthorHouse.
Medina, Sylvia M. & B alloxk-Dixon, Saige J. Gorilla's Roar. Eagle, Joy, illus. 2012. 36p. pap. 11.49 *(978-0-9836602-5-5(5))* Green Kids Club, Inc.
Medina, Sylvia M. & Ballock-Dixon, Saige J. Jade Elephant. Eagle, Joy, illus. 2012. 36p. pap. 11.49 *(978-0-9836602-4-8(7))* Green Kids Club, Inc.
Medley, Shari. The Adventure of a Lifetime! LaGrange, Tiffany, illus. 2009. 24p. pap. 10.95 *(978-1-936051-20-5(6))* Peppertree Pr., The.
Meehan, William. Fife. 2006. (ENG.). 180p. (YA). (gr. 4-6). per. 12.95 *(978-0-595-39223-0(7))* iUniverse, Inc.
Meek, S. P. Surfman: The Adventures of A Coast Guard Dog. 2011. 284p. 48.95 *(978-1-258-08361-8(2))* Literary Licensing, LLC.
Meg. The Adventures of Meg: Wiggles Learns about Making Good Choices. 2010. 24p. pap. 9.99 *(978-1-60911-892-1(8)*, Eloquent Bks.) Strategic Book Publishing & Rights Agency (SBPRA).
Megerdichian, Janet. Pine Needle Pedro. Adams, Allysa, illus. 2010. 36p. pap. 16.99 *(978-1-4520-4422-4(8))* AuthorHouse.
Mehr, Bethany. Adventures of Reggie Elder & the Sourc. 2007. 126p. pap. 19.95 *(978-1-4241-5599-6(1))* America Star Bks.
Meister, Cari. Airplane Adventure, 1 vol. Janovitz, Marilyn, illus. 2010. (My First Graphic Novel Ser.). (ENG.). 32p. (gr. k-2). pap. 6.25 *(978-1-4342-2286-2(1)*, My First Graphic Novel) Stone Arch Bks.
—Rio 2 - Off & Flying. 2014. (Rio Ser.). (ENG.). 24p. (J). (gr. -1-3). pap. 3.99 *(978-0-06-228497-6(5)*, HarperFestival) HarperCollins Pubs.
—Tiny the Birthday Dog. 2013. (Penguin Young Readers Level 1 Ser.). lib. bdg. 13.55 *(978-0-606-31706-1(6)*, Turtleback) Turtleback Bks.
—Untamed Talent. 2014. (Rio Ser.). (ENG.). 24p. (J). (gr. -1-3). pap. 3.99 *(978-0-06-228496-9(7)*, HarperFestival) HarperCollins Pubs.
Meldrum, Margaret. Peter Panda & His Friends. 2009. (Illus.). 24p. pap. 11.49 *(978-1-4343-7826-2(8))* AuthorHouse.
Melean, Mary & Lascaris, Alexia. The Adventures of Don Quixote of la Mancha. 2011. 44p. pap. 18.46 *(978-1-4567-6131-8(5))* AuthorHouse.
Melendez-Shafe, Yvette. The Adventures of Mudpie. 2009. 100p. pap. 28.99 *(978-1-4389-6616-8(4))* AuthorHouse.
Melissa Strangway. Abigail's Mirror. 2010. 316p. pap. 18.95 *(978-1-4401-6176-6(3))* iUniverse, Inc.
Mellanby, Alex. Tregarthur's Promise. 2013. 220p. pap. *(978-0-9573155-4-9(6))* Cillian Pr. Ltd.
Mellon, David. Silent. 2017. (ENG.). 320p. (YA). (gr. 9-12). 17.99 *(978-1-5072-0168-8(0)*, Simon Pulse) Simon Pulse.
Mellor, Corinne & Ericksson, Ashe. Snowlies Find a Letter. 2007. 22p. (J). *(978-1-84666-410-6(1)*, Tide Mill Pr.) Top That! Publishing PLC.
Melodies. 2005. (J). 6.50 *(978-0-9776472-1-7(8))* MythSeries.
Meloy, Colin. Under Wildwood. Ellis, Carson, illus. (Wildwood Chronicles Ser.: 2). (ENG.). (J). (gr. 3). 2013. 592p. pap. 9.99 *(978-0-06-202473-2(6))* 2012. 576p. 17.99 *(978-0-06-202471-8(X))* HarperCollins Pubs.
—The Whiz Mob & the Grenadine Kid. Ellis, Carson, illus. 2017. 432p. (J). (gr. 3-7). 17.99 ***(978-0-06-234245-4(2))*** HarperCollins Pubs.
Meloy, Colin. Wildwood Imperium. Ellis, Carson, illus. 2014. (Wildwood Chronicles: Bk. 3). (ENG.). 592p. (J). (gr. 3). 17.99 *(978-0-06-202474-9(4))* HarperCollins Pubs.
Meloy, Maile. The After-Room. Schoenherr, Ian, illus. 2015. (Apothecary Ser.: 3). (ENG.). 432p. (J). (gr. 5). 17.99 *(978-0-399-17544-2(X)*, G.P. Putnam's Sons Books for Young Readers) Penguin Young Readers Group.
—The Apothecary. l.t. ed. 2012. (ENG.). 435p. (J). (gr. 4-7). 23.99 *(978-1-4104-4504-9(6))* Thorndike Pr.
—The Apprentices. Schoenherr, Ian, illus. 2013. (Apothecary Ser.: 2). (ENG.). 416p. (J). (gr. 5). 16.99 *(978-0-399-16245-9(3)*, G.P. Putnam's Sons Books for Young Readers) Penguin Young Readers Group.
Melrose, Laurie. Willow Wood. 2013. 238p. pap. 15.95 *(978-1-62646-375-2(1))* Booklocker.com, Inc.
Melton, David. The Wonder Years of Oscar the Raccoon. 2013. (ENG.). 32p. (J). 15.95 *(978-1-4327-9964-9(9))* Outskirts Pr., Inc.
Melton, Lexi. Buck Toothed Charlie & Other Stories. 2010. 72p. pap. 34.99 *(978-1-4490-6183-8(4))* AuthorHouse.
Melville, Herman. Moby Dick, or the Whale. 2005. (J). Pt. 1. cd-rom *(978-1-4105-0265-0(1))*Pt. 2. pap. 9.95 *(978-1-4105-0267-4(8))* Vol. 1. pap. 9.95 *(978-1-4105-0263-6(5))* Vol. 2. cd-rom *(978-1-4105-0269-8(4))* Johnston, Don Inc.
Melville, Herman & Huth, Michael. Moby Dick. 2004. (Veröffentlichung der Maximilian-Gesellschaft für die Jahre 2004/2005 Ser.). (GER., Illus.). 92p. (J). *(978-3-921743-52-2(4))* Maximilian-Gesellschaft e. V.
Melville, V. H. Livia the Scientist. 2007. 20p. per. 24.95 *(978-1-4241-8547-4(5))* America Star Bks.
Memories of John & Sonny's Childhood Adventures. 2006. (J). per. 7.95 *(978-0-9787540-0-6(X))* McNatmar Ventures LLC.
Menard, Lucille & Menard, Michele R. Inky's Missing Bow. 2013. 40p. pap. 13.75 *(978-0-9887969-8-0(8))* Four Menards, The.
Menard, Lucille R. & Menard, Michele R. Inky the Talent Scout. 2013. 38p. pap. 12.75 *(978-0-9891734-2-1(9))* Four Menards, The.
Menard, Michele R. The Canopy House - Lost among the Stars. 2013. 38p. pap. 13.95 *(978-0-9887969-4-2(5))* Four Menards, The.
—The Moon Means Business. 2013. 48p. pap. 14.50 *(978-0-9887969-2-8(9))* Four Menards, The.
Menchin, Scott. Goodnight Selfie. Collet-Derby, Pierre, illus. 2015. (ENG.). 32p. (J). (gr. -1-3). 14.99 *(978-0-7636-3182-6(5))* Candlewick Pr.
Mendenhall, Gaylee. My Teacher Is Bald! 2011. 28p. pap. 14.99 *(978-1-4634-5032-8(X))* AuthorHouse.
Mendoza, Madeleine. Simply & the Shiny Quarter. Abasta, Mary, illus. 2011. 24p. pap. 24.95 *(978-1-4560-3792-5(7))* America Star Bks.
Menefee, Angelo K. Billy's First Summer Vacation. 2007. (Illus.). (J). per. 16.95 *(978-1-60002-249-4(9))* Mountain Valley Publishing, LLC.
Menge, Dawn. Queen Vernita Visits the Islands of Enchantment. 2011. (ENG.). 32p. (J). pap. 16.95 *(978-1-4327-7312-0(7))* Outskirts Pr., Inc.
—Queen Vernita's Visitors. Switzer, Bobbi, illus. 2008. 36p. pap. 19.95 *(978-1-59800-714-5(9))* Outskirts Pr., Inc.
Menix, Cinda. Tenbrook Farms. Menix, Cinda & McGuire, Bryan, illus. 2007. 67p. (J). (gr. 4-7). per. 23.99 *(978-1-59879-338-3(1))* Lifevest Publishing, Inc.
Mentyka, Sharon. Chasing at the Surface: A Novel. 2016. (ENG., Illus.). 228p. (J). 23.99 *(978-1-943328-62-8(5)*, West Winds Pr.) Graphic Arts Ctr. Publishing Co.
Mercaldo, David. Little Boy Boo: The Adventures of A Yorkshire Terrier Who Thought He Was a Boy. 2009. 112p. pap. 11.99 *(978-1-61579-099-9(3))* Salem Author Services.
mercedes cecilia. Kusikiy A Child from Taquile, Peru. mercedes cecilia & mercedes cecilia, illus. 2011. (Illus.). (J). pap. 24.99 *(978-0-9844079-9-6(5))* Keepers of Wisdom and Peace Bks.
Mercer, Graham. The Secret Cave. 2009. 52p. pap. 10.50 *(978-1-4092-9055-1(7))* Lulu Pr., Inc.
Meredith Books Staff, creator. Kung Fu Panda. 2008. (Illus.). 22p. (J). 15.95 *(978-0-696-23482-8(3))* Meredith Bks.
Meredith-Markowitz, Susan. Charlie's Museum Adventure: Set Of 6. 2010. (Early Connections Ser.). (J). pap. 37.00 net. *(978-1-4108-1367-1(3))* Benchmark Education Co.
Meredith, Randy. Marvel Puzzle Peril! 2008. (Marvel Heroes Ser.). (Illus.). 10p. (J). (gr. 1-5). 9.95 *(978-1-57791-377-1(9))* Brighter Minds Children's Publishing.
Meriatt, James & Frainier, Tamara. Miles Grand Adventures: The Denver Broncos Mascot's A-to-Z Journey Around Colorado. Malone, Kyle, illus. 2004. 32p. (J). 19.95 *(978-0-9759579-2-9(9))* Denver Broncos.
Merkel, Jenna. The Troubles of a Snowball Kid. 2008. 42p. pap. 14.96 *(978-1-4357-4896-5(4))* Lulu Pr., Inc.
Meroto, Tina. The Tooth Gnashing Witch. 2007. (ENG., Illus.). 48p. (J). 18.95 *(978-84-96788-82-4(2))* OQO, Editora ESP. Dist: Baker & Taylor Bks.
Merry, Margaret. The Adventures of Princess the Pony. 2009. 64p. pap. 19.50 *(978-1-60860-936-9(7)*, Eloquent Bks.) Strategic Book Publishing & Rights Agency (SBPRA).
Mescall, Ron. The Adventures of Goo Goo Malou: A Parent's Guide for Teaching Values. 2009. 24p. pap. 10.96 *(978-1-4269-0836-1(9))* Trafford Publishing.
Messenger, Shannon. Neverseen. (Keeper of the Lost Cities Ser.: 4). (ENG., Illus.). 688p. (J). (gr. 3-7). 2016. pap. 9.99 *(978-1-4814-3230-6(3))* 2015. 19.99 *(978-1-4814-3229-0(X))* Simon & Schuster Children's Publishing. (Aladdin).
Messervy-Norman, J. Philos. 2007. 156p. pap. 16.50 *(978-1-84753-927-4(0))* Lulu Pr., Inc.
Messick, Maxine. Use Your Noodle! The Adventures of a Hollywood Poodle Named Doodle. Hodsdon-Carr, Sandra, ed. Urrwin-Camara, Nancy, tr. Carrillo, J. Raul, illus. 2004. (SPA.). 90p. 15.00 *(978-0-9753508-0-5(3))* Aurora Bks.
Messina, Leslie-Ann. The Adventures of Dolly the Dollar Bill: Dolly Meets Matilda. 2012. 32p. pap. 19.95 *(978-1-4772-9235-8(7))* AuthorHouse.
Messner, Kate. Capture the Flag. (ENG.). 240p. (J). (gr. 3-7). 2013. pap. 6.99 *(978-0-545-41974-1(3)*, Scholastic Paperbacks) 2012. 16.99 *(978-0-545-39539-7(9)*, Scholastic Pr.) Scholastic, Inc.
—Danger in Ancient Rome. McMorris, Kelley, illus. 2015. (Ranger in Time Ser.: 2). (ENG.). 160p. (J). (gr. 2-5). pap. 5.99 *(978-0-545-63917-0(4)*, Scholastic Pr.) Scholastic, Inc.
—Escape from the Great Earthquake. McMorris, Kelley, illus. 2017. (Ranger in Time Ser.: 6). (ENG.). 160p. (J). (gr. 2-5). pap. 5.99 ***(978-0-545-90983-9(X))*** Scholastic, Inc.
—Hide & Seek. (ENG.). 256p. (J). (gr. 3-7). 2015. pap. 7.99 *(978-0-545-79910-2(4)*, Scholastic Paperbacks) 2013. (Illus.). 16.99 *(978-0-545-41975-8(1)*, Scholastic Pr.) Scholastic, Inc.
—Journey Through Ash & Smoke. 2017. (Ranger in Time Ser.: 5). lib. bdg. 16.00 ***(978-0-606-39723-0(X))*** Turtleback Bks.
—Land of Fire & Ice. McMorris, Kelley, illus. 2017. (Ranger in Time Ser.: 5). (ENG.). 160p. (J). (gr. 2-5). pap. 5.99 *(978-0-545-90978-5(3))* Scholastic, Inc.
—Long Road to Freedom. McMorris, Kelley, illus. 2015. (Ranger in Time Ser.: 3). (ENG.). 160p. (J). (gr. 2-5). pap. 5.99 *(978-0-545-63920-0(4))* Scholastic, Inc.
—Race to the South Pole. McMorris, Kelley, illus. 2016. (Ranger in Time Ser.: 4). (ENG.). 160p. (J). (gr. 2-5). pap. 5.99 *(978-0-545-63925-5(5))* Scholastic, Inc.
—Rescue on the Oregon Trail. McMorris, Kelley, illus. 2015. (Ranger in Time Ser.: 1). (ENG.). 144p. (J). (gr. 2-5). pap. 5.99 *(978-0-545-63914-9(X)*, Scholastic Pr.) Scholastic, Inc.
—Wake up Missing. 2014. (ENG.). 288p. (YA). (gr. 5-8). pap. 7.99 *(978-0-8027-3748-9(X)*, 9780802737489, Bloomsbury USA Childrens) Bloomsbury Publishing USA.
Mestas. Nolan & the Magic Bridge. 2009. 28p. pap. 13.99 *(978-1-4490-0812-3(7))* AuthorHouse.
Metzger, Steve. Little Snowflake's Big Adventure. 2005. (Illus.). *(978-0-439-67619-9(3))* Scholastic, Inc.
—We're Going on a Leaf Hunt. Sakamoto, Miki, illus. 2008. (ENG.). 32p. (J). (gr. -1-3). pap. 6.99 *(978-0-439-87377-2(0)*, Cartwheel Bks.) Scholastic, Inc.
Meunier, Sylvain. Raffi's Island Adventure, 1 vol. Cummins, Sarah, tr. from FRE. Eudes-Pascal, Elisabeth, illus. 2008. (Formac First Novels Ser.). (ENG.). 64p. (J). (gr. 2-5). 5.95 *(978-0-88780-755-8(0)*, 9780887807558) Formac Publishing Co., Ltd. CAN. Dist: Casemate Pubs. & Bk. Distributors, LLC.
Meyer, C. The Very First Unicorn. 2013. 24p. pap. 24.95 *(978-1-63004-317-9(6))* America Star Bks.
Meyer, Dana. A Gift for Prince Eli. 2012. 24p. pap. 24.95 *(978-1-4626-5575-5(0))* America Star Bks.
Meyer, Diana. Samson's Great Adventure. 2009. 32p. pap. 10.50 *(978-1-60693-029-8(X)*, Eloquent Bks.) Strategic Book Publishing & Rights Agency (SBPRA).
Meyer, L. A. Bloody Jack: Being an Account of the Curious Adventures of Mary "Jacky" Faber, Ship's Boy. 2010. (Bloody Jack Adventures Ser.: 1). (Illus.). 301p. (gr. 8-12). lib. bdg. 20.85 *(978-0-613-71640-6(X)*, Turtleback) Turtleback Bks.
—Boston Jacky: Being an Account of the Further Adventures of Jacky Faber, Taking Care of Business. 2015. (Bloody Jack Adventures Ser.: 11). (ENG.). 384p. (YA). (gr. 9). pap. 9.99 *(978-0-544-43914-6(7)*, HMH Books For Young Readers) Houghton Mifflin Harcourt Publishing Co.
—Curse of the Blue Tattoo: Being an Account of the Misadventures of Jacky Faber, Midshipman & Fine Lady. 2nd ed. 2011. (Bloody Jack Adventures Ser.: 2). (ENG., Illus.). 496p. (YA). (gr. 7-12). reprint ed. pap. 9.99 *(978-0-15-205459-5(6))* Houghton Mifflin Harcourt Publishing Co.
—Rapture of the Deep: Being an Account of the Further Adventures of Jacky Faber, Soldier, Sailor, Mermaid, Spy. 2009. (Bloody Jack Adventures Ser.: 7). (ENG., Illus.). 464p. (YA). (gr. 9-18). 17.00 *(978-0-15-206501-0(6))* Houghton Mifflin Harcourt Publishing Co.
—Viva Jacquelina! Being an Account of the Further Adventures of Jacky Faber, over the Hills & Far Away. (Bloody Jack Adventures Ser.: 10). (ENG.). (YA). (gr. 9). 2014. 384p. pap. 9.99 *(978-0-544-23439-0(1)*, HMH Books For Young Readers) 2012. 368p. 16.99 *(978-0-547-76350-7(6))* Houghton Mifflin Harcourt Publishing Co.
—Wild Rover No More: Being the Last Recorded Account of the Life & Times of Jacky Faber. (Bloody Jack Adventures Ser.). (ENG.). 368p. (YA). (gr. 9). 2016. pap. 9.99 *(978-0-544-66842-3(1))* 2014. 17.99 *(978-0-544-21777-5(2))* Houghton Mifflin Harcourt Publishing Co. (HMH Books For Young Readers).
Meyer, Maggie. Big Foot Adventures down Under: Book One in the Series 'Spirits Alive' 2013. 244p. (gr. 1-1). 46.72 *(978-1-4797-4547-0(2))*; pap. 28.03 *(978-1-4797-4546-3(4))* Xlibris Corp.
Meyer, Ronald. Casey Cougar. 2007. (Illus.). 32p. (J). 19.95 *(978-0-9754701-2-1(4))* Natures Beauty Publishing.
Meyer, Shawna Rae. When the Baby-Sitter Comes. 2011. 28p. pap. 14.95 *(978-1-4567-3808-2(9))* AuthorHouse.
Meyer, Zachary. The Book Buddies' Adventures the Dragon Story. 2011. 76p. pap. 10.99 *(978-0-557-82961-3(5))* Lulu Pr., Inc.
Meyers, Susan. Bear in the Air. Bates, Amy, illus. 2010. (ENG.). 32p. (J). (gr. k-2). 15.95 *(978-0-8109-8398-4(2)*, Abrams Bks. for Young Readers) Abrams, Inc.
M.H.Pruitt. The Adventures of Rexie the Bear. 2009. 16p. pap. 8.99 *(978-1-4490-4211-0(2))* AuthorHouse.
Mi Primera Biblioteca Coleccion, 12 vols., Set. (SPA.). 288p. (J). (gr. k-3). *(978-84-392-8300-3(8)*, EV31247) Gaviota Ediciones ESP. Dist: Lectorum Pubns., Inc.
Micchelli, Lauren. I Love My Pet Elephant. 2015. (ENG., Illus.). 28p. (J). pap. 14.95 *(978-1-62287-880-2(9))* First Edition Design eBook Publishing.
—The Snootzytime Adventures of Maddie & Murphy - to the Moon & Back. 2015. (ENG., Illus.). 40p. (J). pap. 14.95 *(978-1-62287-843-7(4))* First Edition Design eBook Publishing.
Miceli, Robert L. The Adventures of Twilight. 2008. 80p. pap. 22.50 *(978-1-60693-241-4(1)*, Strategic Bk. Publishing) Strategic Book Publishing & Rights Agency (SBPRA).
Michael-Angelo Goes to School. 2012. (Illus.). 34p. pap. 9.99 *(978-1-937107-10-9(8))* Morning Joy Media.
Michael Batdorf. Pair of Jacks: A Novel. 2009. 332p. 29.95 *(978-1-4401-4482-0(6))*; pap. 19.95 *(978-1-4401-4479-0(6))* iUniverse, Inc.
Michael R. Zomber. Sweet Betsy That's Me: A child of the Civil War. 2009. 116p. pap. 10.95 *(978-1-4401-6323-4(5))* iUniverse, Inc.
Michael Ray Knauff. Roubidoux: A Story for 12-Year Olds & Those Who Wish They Still Were. 2009. 128p. pap. 10.99 *(978-1-4389-5391-5(7))* AuthorHouse.
Michaelides, M. Rainbow Angel. 2012. 120p. (gr. 4-6). 20.95 *(978-1-4759-6249-9(5))*; pap. 10.95 *(978-1-4759-6248-2(7))* iUniverse, Inc.
Michaelis, Antonia. The Secret of the Twelfth Continent. Hosmer-Dillard, Mollie, tr. from GER. Nievelstein, Ralf, illus. 2013. (ENG.). 288p. (J). (gr. 2-7). 14.95 *(978-1-62087-539-1(X)*, 620539, Sky Pony Pr.) Skyhorse Publishing Co., Inc.
Michaels, Doad. Tennyshoe Adventures: the Doghead Whistle. 2010. 92p. pap. 12.95 *(978-0-557-44028-3(9))* Lulu Pr., Inc.
—Tennyshoe Adventures: Treasure Hunters. 2010. 101p. pap. 12.95 *(978-0-557-70285-5(2))* Lulu Pr., Inc.
Michaels, Mishon. The Big Adventures of Little Again Sam. 2012. 28p. pap. 24.95 *(978-1-4626-8827-2(6))* America Star Bks.
Michel, Gay. CRONIÑON. 2003. (SPA.). 40p. *(978-84-8470-001-2(1))* Corimbo, Editorial S.L.

Michelle, Jean. Naba II: A Journey. Michelle, Jean & D'Ariggo, Jay, illus. 2011. 20p. pap. 24.95 *(978-1-4626-4381-3(7))* America Star Bks.

Michiko Florence, Debbi. Dorothy & Toto. Roe, Monika, illus. 2016. (Dorothy & Toto Ser.). (ENG.). 40p. (gr. k-2). 85.28 *(978-1-4795-8714-8(1))* Capstone Press of Coughlan Cos.

Middle, Myra. Rabi's Halloween Adventure. 2012. 28p. pap. 21.99 *(978-1-4691-5380-3(7))* Xlibris Corp.

Middleditch, Susan. Monty the Mountain Duck. 2013. (Illus.). 145p. pap. 9.50 *(978-1-78035-394-4(4),* Fastprint Publishing) Upfront Publishing Ltd. GBR. Dist: Printondemand-worldwide.com.

Middleton, Casey Olsson. Flying the Imaginarium: Book One, Coconut. 2007. 136p. per. 11.50 *(978-1-59330-507-9(9))* Aventine Pr.

Middleton Gray, Family Np. Maddie Goes to the Nurse Practitioner. 2008. 32p. pap. 13.50 *(978-1-4389-0220-3(4))* AuthorHouse.

Middleton, Julian. Joanna Beyond the Veil. 2012. 116p. pap. *(978-1-78176-977-5(X))* FeedARead.com.

Midnight at the August Tree House. 2004. (Illus.). 100p. (J). per. 15.95 *(978-0-9754823-1-5(9))* Pumpkin Patch Publishing.

Miguel, Angela. Harold the Duck. 2009. 52p. pap. 19.50 *(978-1-60693-658-0(1),* Eloquent Bks.) Strategic Book Publishing & Rights Agency (SBPRA).

Mihalek, Alex, et al. The Adventures of Captain Fishhook Waterflea: the Invasion of Lake Champlain. 2009. 34p. pap. 13.98 *(978-0-557-12868-6(4))* Lulu Pr., Inc.

Mika, Sharon Ann. Penny's Big Day. Wilson, Kay, illus. 2003. (J). 8.95 *(978-0-9747836-0-4(9))* Button Flower Pr.

Mikaelsen, Ben. Jungle of Bones. 2014. (ENG.). 224p. (J). (gr. 3-7). 16.99 *(978-0-545-44287-9(7))* Scholastic, Inc.

—Sparrow Hawk Red. 2010. (ENG.). 192p. (J). (gr. 3-7). pap. 5.99 *(978-1-4231-3361-2(7))* Hyperion Pr.

Miko-Ray, Yours Truly. June's Scrapbook. 2009. 54p. pap. 16.95 *(978-1-61546-926-0(5))* America Star Bks.

Miles, Colin. Naughty Nicky & the Good Ship Oggy. Miles, Gail, illus. 2013. 24p. pap. *(978-1-909202-16-0(9))* Little Acorns Publishing.

Miles, Lisa. Let's Be Friends! Follow the Reader Level 2. 2008. (Littlest Pet Shop Ser.). (ENG., Illus.). 24p. (J). (gr. -1-2). 24.99 *(978-1-4169-4994-7(1),* Simon Scribbles) Simon Scribbles.

Miles, Lisa & Chown, Xanna Eve. The Backyardigans Gang: Follow the Reader Level 1. 2008. (Backyardigans Ser.). (ENG.). 24p. (J). 24.99 *(978-1-4169-5844-4(4),* Simon Scribbles) Simon Scribbles.

Miles, Victoria. Magnifico, 1 vol. l.t. ed. 2006. (ENG.). 32p. (J). (gr. 4-7). *(978-1-55041-960-3(9))* Fitzhenry & Whiteside, Ltd.

Mill, Lynda. Let's Meet Harry, Ted & Mike. 2013. 40p. pap. 19.57 *(978-1-4669-9321-1(9))* Trafford Publishing.

Millar, Mark. Ultimate X-Men, 3 vols., Vol. 3. 2003. (Ultimate X-Men Ser.). (Illus.). 312p. 29.99 *(978-0-7851-1131-3(X))* Marvel Worldwide, Inc.

Millar, Mark & Austen, Chuck. Ultimate X-Men, 2 vols., Vol. 2. Kubert, Adam et al, illus. 2003. (Ultimate X-Men Ser.). 336p. (YA). 29.99 *(978-0-7851-1130-6(1))* Marvel Worldwide, Inc.

Millard, Mary Weeks. Live Wires & Lobster Pots. 2014. (Syding Adventures Ser.: Vol. 5). (ENG., Illus.). 112p. (J). (gr. 4-7). pap. *(978-1-84625-368-3(3))* DayOne Pubns.

Miller, Al. Patricia the Duck. 2013. 20p. pap. 14.95 *(978-1-4669-7798-3(1))* Trafford Publishing.

Miller, Amanda. The Library's Secret: A Hidden Adventure. 2010. 88p. pap. 10.49 *(978-1-4520-7012-4(1))* AuthorHouse.

—Pat the Enormous Brat! 2011. 80p. (gr. 4-6). pap. 11.24 *(978-1-4567-9391-3(8))* AuthorHouse.

Miller, Amanda K. Lily's Grand Adventures. 2011. 36p. pap. 24.95 *(978-1-4626-2493-5(6))* America Star Bks.

Miller, Barbara Anne. The Adventures of Emily-Faith. 2012. (ENG.). pap. 10.95 *(978-1-4675-1181-0(1))* Independent Pub.

Miller, Bobbi. Big River's Daughter. 2013. (ENG.). 224p. (J). (gr. 2-7). 16.95 *(978-0-8234-2752-9(8))* Holiday Hse., Inc.

Miller, Carol. Maurice the Mole: Can You Guess Series. 2007. (ENG., Illus.). 24p. (J). lib. bdg. 18.95 *(978-0-9771641-3-4(6))* Defiance In Print.

Miller, Chris & Miller, Allan. Hunter Brown & the Consuming Fire, 3 bks., Bk.2. 2009. (ENG., Illus.). 352p. (J). pap. 13.99 *(978-1-59317-357-9(1))* Warner Pr., Inc.

Miller, Christopher & Miller, Allan. Hunter Brown & the Eye of Ends, 3 bks., Bk.3. 2011. (J). pap. 13.99 *(978-1-59317-400-2(4))* Warner Pr., Inc.

—Hunter Brown & the Secret of the Shadow, 3 bks., Bk.1. 2008. (ENG., Illus.). 384p. (J). (gr. 9-18). pap. 13.99 *(978-1-59317-328-9(8))* Warner Pr., Inc.

Miller, Cindy M. The Little Green Truck: The Adventures of a 1998 Ford Ranger & Its Owner. 2012. 20p. pap. 15.00 *(978-1-4772-0319-4(2))* AuthorHouse.

Miller, Daniel, et al. A Miller Cousin Mystery. 2010. 120p. pap. 17.80 *(978-0-557-57118-5(9));* pap. 49.00 *(978-0-557-57235-9(5))* Lulu Pr., Inc.

Miller, Denise. Annie's Shoes. 2012. 28p. pap. 9.95 *(978-1-4787-2020-1(4))* Outskirts Pr., Inc.

Miller, Gary & Miller, Lynda. The Adventures of Bob & Betty. 2006. (J). spiral bd. *(978-1-933594-92-7(6))* FBC Pubns. & Printing.

Miller, Jeff. Close Encounters of the Nerd Kind. 2015. (Nerdy Dozen Ser.: 2). (ENG.). 272p. (J). (gr. 3-7). 16.99 *(978-0-06-227265-2(9))* HarperCollins Pubs.

—The Nerdy Dozen. (Nerdy Dozen Ser.: 1). (ENG.). (J). (gr. 3-7). 2015. 320p. pap. 6.99 *(978-0-06-227263-8(2))* 2014. 304p. 16.99 *(978-0-06-227262-1(4))* HarperCollins Pubs.

—The Nerdy Dozen #2: Close Encounters of the Nerd Kind. 2015. (Nerdy Dozen Ser.: 2). (ENG.). 288p. (J). (gr. 3-7). pap. 6.99 *(978-0-06-227266-9(7))* HarperCollins Pubs.

—The Nerdy Dozen #3 - 20,000 Nerds under the Sea. 2015. (Nerdy Dozen Ser.: 3). (ENG.). 208p. (J). (gr. 3-7). 16.99 *(978-0-06-227268-3(3))* HarperCollins Pubs.

—The Nerdy Dozen #3: 20,000 Nerds under the Sea. 2016. (Nerdy Dozen Ser.: 3). 208p. (J). (gr. 3-7). pap. 6.99 *(978-0-06-227269-0(1))* HarperCollins Pubs.

Miller-Johnston, Renee. Double Trouble for Courtney Logan Kennedy, 1 vol. 2009. 88p. pap. 19.95 *(978-1-60836-384-1(8))* America Star Bks.

Miller, Kathryn L. Abc's with Sadie: Sadie Goes to the Zoo. 2011. 32p. pap. 17.25 *(978-1-4269-5940-0(0))* Trafford Publishing.

Miller, Kristine Elizabeth. Albert's Lunch Box. 2008. 24p. pap. 24.95 *(978-1-60672-096-7(1))* America Star Bks.

Miller, Kyle Linda. Dillo - A Baby Armadillo's Adventure on Sanibel Island. Eddy, Randon T., illus. l.t. ed. 2005. (ENG.). 64p. (J). 16.95 *(978-0-9769332-0-5(9))* Jungle Hse. Pubns.

Miller, Larry, Jr. Long Live the Queen. 2003. 162p. (YA). pap. 12.95 *(978-0-595-27449-9(8))* iUniverse, Inc.

Miller, Larry W., Jr. Droptroopers: Gauntlet of Fear. 2007. 208p. per. 14.95 *(978-0-595-47591-9(4))* iUniverse, Inc.

Miller, Michael & Strickland, AdriAnne. Shadow Run. 2017. (ENG.). 400p. (YA). (gr. 7). 17.99 *(978-0-399-55253-3(7),* Delacorte Pr.) Random Hse. Children's Bks.

Miller, Michael John. Harry Hamster Adventures. 2012. 24p. pap. 15.99 *(978-1-4691-6861-6(8))* Xlibris Corp.

Miller, Mike S. Confession, 1 vol. Ninaltowski, Eric, illus. 2008. (Z Graphic Novels / Hand of the Morning Star Ser.). (ENG.). 160p. (YA). (gr. 8-11). pap. 6.99 *(978-0-310-71371-5(4))* Zondervan.

Miller, Mona. Hey, Buddy! Fruchter, Jason, illus. 2010. (Super Coloring Book Ser.). (ENG.). 96p. (J). (gr. -1-2). pap. 3.99 *(978-0-375-86155-0(6),* Golden Bks.) Random Hse. Children's Bks.

Miller, Mona. Poppy & Branch's Big Adventure. 2017. (Step into Reading Level 3 Ser.). lib. bdg. 14.75 ***(978-0-606-39851-0(1))*** Turtleback Bks.

Miller, Penelope. Farbedrook. 2008. 96p. pap. *(978-1-84748-104-7(3))* Athena Pr.

Miller, Ron Jay. The Medallion. 2003. 210p. 14.95 *(978-1-55517-737-9(9),* 77379) Cedar Fort, Inc./CFI Distribution.

Miller, Sara F. A Gift for Pooh. 2012. (ENG.). 24p. (J). (gr. -1-1). pap. 4.99 *(978-1-4231-3592-0(X))* Disney Pr.

Miller, Sibley & Lenhard, Elizabeth. Horses' Night Out. Chang, Tara Larsen & Gershman, Jo, illus. 2008. (Wind Dancers Ser.: 4). (ENG.). 80p. (J). (gr. 1-4). pap. 16.99 *(978-0-312-38283-4(9),* 9780312382834) Feiwel & Friends.

Miller, Suzanne. Pirates! That Is Who We Be! 2010. 28p. pap. 13.50 *(978-1-4490-6362-7(4))* AuthorHouse.

Miller, Tim. Moo Moo in a Tutu. Miller, Tim, illus. 2017. (Moo Moo & Mr. Quackers Book Ser.). (Illus.). 32p. (J). (gr. -1-3). 17.99 *(978-0-06-241440-3(2))* HarperCollins Pubs.

Millet, Jason, et al, illus. Beyond Escape! 2007. (Choose Your Own Adventure Ser.: No. 15). 118p. (J). (gr. 4-7). per. 6.99 *(978-1-933390-15-4(8),* CHCL15) Chooseco LLC.

Millet, Lydia. The Fires Beneath the Sea. 2012. (Dissenters Ser.). (ENG.). 256p. (J). (gr. 3-7). pap. 12.00 *(978-1-931520-47-8(X),* Big Mouth Hse.) Small Beer Pr.

—The Shimmers in the Night. 2012. (Dissenters Ser.). (ENG.). 256p. (J). (gr. 3-7). 16.95 *(978-1-931520-78-2(X),* Big Mouth Hse.) Small Beer Pr.

Millett, Peter. Take Zayan with You! Green Band. Daff, Russ, illus. 2016. (Cambridge Reading Adventures Ser.). (ENG.). 16p. pap. 6.56 *(978-1-107-57587-5(7))* Cambridge Univ. Pr.

Milligan, Chris & Smith, David. Check Mate! Two Boys Experience the Life & Death Fight for Control of the Hudson Bay Fur Trade. 2013. 192p. *(978-1-4602-1041-3(7));* pap. *(978-1-4602-1039-0(5))* FriesenPress.

Milligan, Peter. Good Omens, Vol. 1. Allred, Mike, illus. 2003. (X-Statix Ser.). 128p. (YA). pap. 11.99 *(978-0-7851-1059-0(3))* Marvel Worldwide, Inc.

—X-Force: Famous, Mutant & Mortal. Allred, Mike, illus. 2003. (X-Statix Ser.). 352p. (YA). 29.99 *(978-0-7851-1023-1(2))* Marvel Worldwide, Inc.

Millin, Christopher. The King of Arugula. 2007. (ENG.). 208p. (J). (gr. 1-7). per. 12.95 *(978-1-897235-21-8(6))* Thistledown Pr., Ltd. CAN. Dist: Univ. of Toronto Pr.

Millman, Calanitte. The Adventures of the Gimmel Gang IV: Triple Trouble, Vol. 4. 2007. (J). pap. 10.95 *(978-1-60091-005-0(X))* Israel Bookshop Pubns.

Millman, Dan. El Secreto Del Guerrero Pacifico. 2004. (SPA.). 32p. *(978-84-7720-903-4(0))* Ediciones Obelisco.

Millman, M. C. Always Something Else: The whimsical adventures of Elisheva Raskin. 2005. (Illus.). 160p. (J). 14.95 *(978-1-932443-23-3(1),* ASEH) Judaica Pr., Inc., The.

Millner, Robert W. The Chicken Coop Gang. 2011. 130p. 29.99 *(978-1-4568-5517-8(4));* pap. 19.99 *(978-1-4568-5516-1(6))* Xlibris Corp.

Mills, Claudia. 7 X 9 = Trouble! Karas, G. Brian, illus. 2004. (ENG.). 112p. (J). (gr. 2-5). pap. 6.99 *(978-0-374-46452-3(9),* 9780374464523) Square Fish.

Mills, G. Riley. Son of the Sea. 2012. 22.95 *(978-0-7414-7515-2(4));* pap. 11.95 *(978-0-7414-7514-5(6))* Infinity Publishing.

Mills, Linda Sue. Meet Toado & Friends. Mills, Lori, illus. l.t. ed. 2008. (ENG.). 30p. (J). 20.99 *(978-1-59879-246-1(6),* Lifevest) Lifevest Publishing, Inc.

Mills, Patricia Anne. Stevie's First Christmas. 2009. 28p. pap. 12.49 *(978-1-4490-3452-8(7))* AuthorHouse.

Mills, Paul A. Chipper & Fluffy's Big Adventure. 2003. per. *(978-1-59196-255-7(2))* Instant Pub.

Mills, Tessa L. The Adventures of Avery & Cali. 2007. 60p. per. 16.95 *(978-1-4241-7982-4(3))* America Star Bks.

Milne, A. A. A Gallery of Children. Le Mair, Henriette Willebeek, illus. 2006. 79p. (J). (gr. k-4). reprint ed. 20.00 *(978-1-4223-5106-2(8))* DIANE Publishing Co.

—Giant. Shepard, Ernest H., illus. 2009. (Winnie-The-Pooh Ser.). (ENG.). 12p. (J). (gr. -1-k). bds. 9.99 *(978-0-525-42088-0(6),* Dutton Books for Young Readers) Penguin Young Readers Group.

Milne, J. E. The Adventures of Haole the Penguin: The Inner Game of Surfing. 2011. 264p. 25.95 *(978-1-4327-7160-7(4));* pap. 13.95 *(978-1-4327-7142-3(6))* Outskirts Pr., Inc.

Milne, Rg. Quibble Tales: The Adventures of Bobin Hood of Sherworm Forest. 2012. 28p. 24.95 *(978-1-4626-6755-0(4))* America Star Bks.

Milo, Margaret D. Matthew Pet Adventure. 2012. 24p. 24.95 *(978-1-4626-6850-2(X))* America Star Bks.

Milroy, Jill & Milroy, Gladys. Eagle, Crow & Emu: Bird Stories. 2017. (ENG.). 88p. (J). (gr. 2-4). 9.95 ***(978-1-925163-71-1(7))*** Fremantle Pr. AUS. Dist: Independent Pubs. Group.

Milway, Alex. Alien Moon. Milway, Alex, illus. 2014. (ENG., Illus.). 240p. (J). pap. 5.99 *(978-1-61067-164-4(3))* Kane Miller.

—The Curse of Mousebeard. 2011. (ENG.). 368p. (J). (gr. 3-7). pap. 6.99 *(978-0-316-07745-3(3))* Little, Brown Bks. for Young Readers.

—The Magma Conspiracy: Armed, Dangerous & Covered in Fur! Milway, Alex, illus. 2013. (ENG., Illus.). 224p. (J). pap. 5.99 *(978-1-61067-159-0(7))* Kane Miller.

—Operation Robot Storm: The Mythical 9th Division. Milway, Alex, illus. 2013. (ENG., Illus.). 224p. (J). pap. 5.99 *(978-1-61067-074-6(4))* Kane Miller.

—Pigsticks & Harold & the Tuptown Thief. Milway, Alex, illus. 2017. (Candlewick Sparks Ser.). (ENG., Illus.). 80p. (J). (gr. k-4). pap. 3.99 *(978-0-7636-9400-5(2))* Candlewick Pr.

—Pigsticks & Harold & the Tuptown Thief. Milway, Alex, illus. 2017. (Candlewick Sparks Ser.). (ENG., Illus.). (J). (gr. k-4). lib. bdg. 13.55 ***(978-0-606-39840-4(6))*** Turtleback Bks.

Mims-Word, Marsha. The Great Vacation. 2011. 36p. pap. 21.99 *(978-1-4568-9675-1(X))* Xlibris Corp.

Minarik, Else Holmelund. Little Bear. 2003. (Little Bear: I Can Read! Ser.). (J). (gr. k-3). lib. bdg. 13.55 *(978-0-8085-2618-6(9),* Turtleback) Turtleback Bks.

—Little Bear & the Marco Polo. Doubleday, Dorothy, illus. 2010. (I Can Read Level 1 Ser.). (ENG.). 32p. (J). (gr. k-3). 16.99 *(978-0-06-085485-0(5));* pap. 3.99 *(978-0-06-085487-4(1))* HarperCollins Pubs.

Mindel, Nissan. Eight Chanukah Tales. Toron, Eli & Graybar, Shmuel, illus. 2007. 78p. (J). 10.95 *(978-0-8266-0039-4(5))* Kehot Pubn. Society.

Mindes, Erin. Missy Moo, Where Are You off to? Surfing Adventure. Harston, David, illus. 2011. (J). 14.95 *(978-0-9841558-8-0(0))* Tasty Minstrel Games.

Miner, Sharon. Octavia's Quest. 2005. 113p. pap. 11.95 *(978-0-7414-2647-5(1))* Infinity Publishing.

Ming, Markay. Bear's Great Adventure, 1 vol. 2010. 32p. 24.95 *(978-1-4489-5792-7(3))* PublishAmerica, Inc.

Minhós Martins, Isabel. At Our House. Matoso, Madalena, illus. 2013. (ENG.). 28p. 12.95 *(978-1-84976-049-2(7))* Tate Publishing, Ltd. GBR. Dist: Abrams, Inc.

Minich, Eric. Digger & the Search for Home. 2006. 48p. pap. 16.95 *(978-1-4241-0321-8(5))* PublishAmerica, Inc.

Minix, Holly. What Does Mommy Do at Night? 2009. 68p. pap. 25.00 *(978-1-60693-705-1(7),* Strategic Bk. Publishing) Strategic Book Publishing & Rights Agency (SBPRA).

Minks, Joshua. Humania & the Legend of Commander Pancreator. 2010. 44p. pap. 20.00 *(978-1-4490-3333-0(4))* AuthorHouse.

Minshall, Caleigh. Blue: Voyage to the Sky. 2005. 54p. (J). pap. 19.95 net. *(978-1-59975-284-6(0))* Independent Pub.

Minz-Kammer, Koda. Pinpot Tiger & the Lost Monkey. 2008. 54p. pap. 20.00 *(978-0-557-01646-4(0))* Lulu Pr., Inc.

Miot, Ray. Alexis the Wizard Rabbit: Pascale & Alain Adventures. 2009. 36p. pap. 17.99 *(978-1-4389-3440-2(8))* AuthorHouse.

Miracle, Joan. Tia's Shoes. 2013. 28p. pap. 9.95 *(978-1-4787-2603-6(2))* Outskirts Pr., Inc.

Miranda, Twyla. Longfeather Ponds: A Chipmunk's Tale. 2006. 82p. pap. 16.95 *(978-1-4241-1785-7(2))* PublishAmerica, Inc.

Miranda, Twyla T. The Beagles' Tale: A Longfeather Ponds Adventure, 1 vol. 2010. 82p. pap. 19.95 *(978-1-4512-1547-2(9))* America Star Bks.

Mirarchi, Anthony J. The King's Challenge. 2007. (Cristo's Chronicles Ser.). (ENG., Illus.). 224p. (YA). (gr. 4-7). pap. *(978-1-933255-32-3(3))* DNA Pr.

Mireles, Debbie. The Map & the Pirate Ship. 2009. 74p. pap. 19.95 *(978-1-61582-417-5(0))* America Star Bks.

Miro. The Watermelon Story. Brown, Nick, illus. 2003. 103p. (J). pap. *(978-1-84426-258-8(8))* Upfront Publishing Ltd.

The Misadventures of Wags & Freckles. (J). 4.00 *(978-1-56230-043-2(1))* Syndistar, Inc.

The Missing Earrings. 2005. (Georgie Giraffe Set 1 Ser.). (J). 7.33 *(978-1-932570-39-7(X))* Pioneer Valley Bks.

Mistretta, T. P. C. Jay Francis. The Parkour Code. 2010. 114p. pap. 13.95 *(978-0-557-38476-1(1))* Lulu Pr., Inc.

Mitcham Davis, Zipporah. The Fox & Emily's Long Migration. 2008. 28p. pap. 13.99 *(978-1-4389-0326-2(X))* AuthorHouse.

Mitchell, Andrew B. Bubbles, Bubbles & More Bubbles. 2013. 24p. pap. 15.99 *(978-1-4797-3916-5(2))* Xlibris Corp.

Mitchell, Carolyn. The Tale of the Pumpkin Seed Squad. 2006. (ENG.). 40p. per. 16.99 *(978-1-4259-7004-8(4))* AuthorHouse.

Mitchell, Charlie. The Great M & M Caper. 2009. 82p. pap. 15.99 *(978-1-4415-2242-9(5))* Xlibris Corp.

Mitchell, Denise K. Starbyte the Computer Fairy Collection. 2009. 67p. pap. 10.68 *(978-1-4452-2435-0(6))* Lulu Pr., Inc.

Mitchell, Jack. The Ancient Ocean Blues. 2008. (ENG.). 200p. (YA). (gr. 5-8). pap. 9.95 *(978-0-88776-832-3(6),* Tundra Bks.) Tundra Bks. CAN. Dist: Penguin Random Hse. LLC.

Mitchell, Lakeya Geneene. Devon Iscariot. 2010. 48p. pap. 7.83 *(978-0-557-19062-1(2))* Lulu Pr., Inc.

Mitchell, Lance B. The Penguin Adventures of Ping & Pong. 2008. 32p. pap. 24.95 *(978-1-60474-124-7(4))* America Star Bks.

Mitchell, Mary Esther. The Adventures of Timmy Gills. 2005. (J). pap. 20.00 *(978-0-8059-9660-9(5),* RoseDog Bks.) Dorrance Publishing Co., Inc.

Mitchell, N. J. W. The Search. 2003. 110p. pap. 9.95 *(978-0-595-27251-8(7),* Writers Club Pr.) iUniverse, Inc.

Mitchell, Stan R. Oskar & Myer at the Lake. 2013. 24p. pap. 24.95 *(978-1-63000-414-9(6))* America Star Bks.

—Oskar Wins the Race. 2013. 28p. pap. 24.95 *(978-1-63000-407-1(3))* America Star Bks.

Mitchell, Trish. Noah Pals: Noah & Friends Awesome Adventure. 2011. 56p. pap. 23.88 *(978-1-4520-0459-4(5))* AuthorHouse.

Mitchen, Scott. Will of the Pirates. 2008. 180p. 22.95 *(978-0-595-70652-5(5))* iUniverse, Inc.

Mitchum, Lynn Tyner. Happy Being Me. Mitchum, Lynn Tyner, illus. 2006. (Illus.). (J). bds. 21.95 *(978-0-9745191-0-4(3))* Lynn Tyner Mitchum & James Rogers.

Mittal, Amitabh. The Heir Apparent. 2009. 32p. pap. 14.99 *(978-1-4389-7845-1(6))* AuthorHouse.

Mittal, Anjali. The Convent Rules. 2009. (Illus.). 80p. pap. 10.49 *(978-1-4389-8575-6(4))* AuthorHouse.

Mitton, Tony. African Adventure. 2015. (Amazing Animals Ser.). (ENG., Illus.). 24p. (J). (gr. -1-1). pap. 4.99 *(978-0-7534-7230-9(9),* 9780753472309, Kingfisher) Roaring Brook Pr.

—Forest Adventure. Parker, Ant, illus. 2015. (Amazing Animals Ser.). (ENG.). 24p. (J). (gr. -1-1). pap. 4.99 *(978-0-7534-7229-3(5),* 9780753472293, Kingfisher) Roaring Brook Pr.

Miyazaki, Hayao. Castle In The Sky, Vol. 1. Miyazaki, Hayao, illus. 2003. (ENG., Illus.). 164p. pap. 9.95 *(978-1-59116-170-7(3))* Viz Media.

—Castle In The Sky, Vol. 2. Miyazaki, Hayao, illus. 2003. (ENG., Illus.). 164p. pap. 9.95 *(978-1-59116-171-4(1))* Viz Media.

—Castle In The Sky, Vol. 3. Miyazaki, Hayao, illus. 2003. (ENG., Illus.). 164p. pap. 9.95 *(978-1-59116-172-1(X))* Viz Media.

—Castle In The Sky, Vol. 4. Miyazaki, Hayao, illus. novel ed. 2003. (ENG., Illus.). 164p. pap. 9.95 *(978-1-59116-173-8(8))* Viz Media.

—My Neighbor Totoro Picture Book (New Edition) 2013. (ENG., Illus.). 112p. (J). 19.99 *(978-1-4215-6122-6(0))* Viz Media.

—Ponyo Film Comic, Vol. 3. Miyazaki, Hayao, illus. movie tie-in ed. 2009. (ENG., Illus.). 172p. (J). pap. 9.99 *(978-1-4215-3079-6(1))* Viz Media.

—Ponyo Film Comic, Vol. 4. Miyazaki, Hayao, illus. movie tie-in ed. 2009. (ENG., Illus.). 172p. (J). pap. 9.99 *(978-1-4215-3080-2(5))* Viz Media.

—Ponyo Picture Book, Vol. 1. Miyazaki, Hayao, illus. 2009. (ENG., Illus.). 152p. (J). (gr. 2-7). 19.99 *(978-1-4215-3065-9(1))* Viz Media.

Mizielinska, Aleksandra & Mizielinski, Daniel. Welcome to Mamoko. 2013. (ENG., Illus.). 16p. (J). (gr. k-3). 17.99 *(978-0-7636-6891-4(5),* Big Picture Press) Candlewick Pr.

Mlynowski, Sarah. Abby in Wonderland. 2017. (Whatever After Ser.). (ENG.). 256p. (J). (gr. 3-7). 16.99 ***(978-0-545-74664-9(7),*** Scholastic Pr.) Scholastic, Inc.

Mlynowski, Sarah. Sink or Swim. 2014. (Whatever After Ser.: 3). (ENG.). 176p. (J). (gr. 3-7). pap. 5.99 *(978-0-545-41570-5(5),* Scholastic Pr.) Scholastic, Inc.

Mock, Katelyn Marie. The Lost Herd: Callie's Adventure. 2012. 46p. 19.95 *(978-1-4626-5393-5(6))* America Star Bks.

Moeling, Nell. The Secret Adventures of Prince Justin & the Dragon. 2010. 40p. 17.99 *(978-1-4520-4996-0(3))* AuthorHouse.

Moesta, Rebecca & Anderson, Kevin J. Space Station Crisis. 2011. (Star Challengers Ser.). 184p. (J). (gr. 4-7). 11.99 *(978-1-934857-66-3(1),* Catalyst Game Labs) InMediaRes Productions.

Moesta, Rebecca, et al. Star Challengers Trilogy. 2013. (J). pap. 18.99 *(978-1-61475-124-3(2),* WordFire Pr.) WordFire Pr.

Moffat, Nichola. High Voltage Smile. 2009. 256p. pap. 21.50 *(978-1-4092-7480-3(2))* Lulu Pr., Inc.

Moffett, Slyvia. The Missionary Kids Adventure Series: Bo. 2006. 48p. pap. 16.95 *(978-1-4241-2854-9(4))* PublishAmerica, Inc.

Moger, Susan. Of Better Blood. 2016. (ENG.). 304p. (YA). (gr. 8-12). 16.99 *(978-0-8075-4774-8(3))* Whitman, Albert & Co.

Moghimi, Salmeh. The Adventures of Anoo & Pashmack. 2013. (ENG.). 44p. (J). 19.95 *(978-1-4525-5857-8(4),* Balboa Pr.) Author Solutions, Inc.

Molesworth. Cuckoo Clock. 2006. 216p. per. *(978-1-4067-1668-9(5),* Hesperides Pr.) Read Bks.

—The Cuckoo Clock. 2007. 172p. per. 12.99 *(978-1-59986-835-6(0))* Filiquarian Publishing, LLC.

Molla, Jean. Sobibor. McLean, Polly, tr. from FRE. 2006. (ENG.). 200p. per. 16.95 *(978-0-9546912-4-0(5))* Aurora Metro Pubns. Ltd. GBR. Dist: Consortium Bk. Sales & Distribution.

—Sobibor. rev. ed. 2006. (ENG., Illus.). 200p. (YA). (gr. 10). pap. 8.95 *(978-970-20-0857-6(3))* Castillo, Ediciones, S. A. de C. V. MEX. Dist: Macmillan.

Molloy, Sheila. Jack - King of the Dogs. Steed, Tobias, ed. Molloy, Michael, illus. 2004. (Jack Ser.: 1). (ENG.). 100p. (J). (gr. 4-7). pap. 9.99 *(978-1-904872-30-6(1),* Can of Worms Kids Pr.) Can of Worms Pr. GBR. Dist: Independent Pubs. Group.

Molock, Anthony. The Adventures of Cocoa Pelou: Cocoa Pelou Meets Alabama Black. 2011. 24p. pap. 14.00 *(978-1-4634-4118-0(5))* AuthorHouse.

Monaghan, Annabel. Double Digit. (ENG.). 192p. (YA). (gr. 7). 2015. pap. 7.99 *(978-0-544-33620-9(8),* HMH Books For Young Readers) 2014. 16.99 *(978-0-544-10577-5(X))* Houghton Mifflin Harcourt Publishing Co.

—A Girl Named Digit: Under Cover, under Pressure, under Estimated. 2013. (ENG.). 192p. (YA). (gr. 7). pap. 8.99 *(978-0-544-02248-5(3))* Houghton Mifflin Harcourt Publishing Co.

—A Girl Named Digit: Undercover, under Pressure, & Underestimated. 2012. (ENG., Illus.). 192p. (YA). (gr. 7). 16.99 *(978-0-547-66852-9(X))* Houghton Mifflin Harcourt Publishing Co.

Monahan, Holly. Flip Wanders Off, 1 vol. 2010. 18p. pap. 24.95 *(978-1-4489-5609-8(9))* PublishAmerica, Inc.

Monge, Nieves. The Adventures of Three Raccoons Raised by a Human Mother. 2004. (J). pap. 8.00 *(978-0-8059-6472-1(X))* Dorrance Publishing Co., Inc.

Mongillo, Michael. The Philistine: Anthology/Chronology, 1 book. Zittel, Michael, illus. 2003. 216p. (YA). pap. 24.95 *(978-0-9743086-0-9(9))* United Comics.

Monica, Monica L. Freckles Goes to Grand Cayman Island. 2010. 24p. pap. 12.99 *(978-1-4520-5082-9(1))* AuthorHouse.

Moniz, Michael. Tristan: The Changeling Prince (Book 2) 2013. 252p. (J). pap. 11.95 *(978-1-938083-25-9(3))* Silver Knight Publishing, LLC.

—The Whalemaster. 2016. (ENG., Illus.). 235p. (J). (gr. 4-7). pap. 9.95 *(978-1-927018-79-8(X))* Simply Read Bks. CAN. Dist: Ingram Publisher Services.

Monk, Carol & O'Connor, Ruth. The Walking Adventures of Ruthie & Coco. 2005. (Illus.). 29p. (J). pap. 12.95 *(978-1-56167-881-5(3))* American Literary Pr.

Monkey Business. 2005. (J). 4.95 *(978-1-59792-015-5(0))* F.A.S.T. Learning LLC.

Monkey Girl Staff. Jay Travels to the U S A. 2012. 20p. pap. 17.99 *(978-1-4685-4778-8(X))* AuthorHouse.

Monks, Barbara. Thank You Weasel Abbs! 2011. (Illus.). 72p. pap. 24.83 *(978-1-4567-7816-3(1))* AuthorHouse.
Monlongo, Jorge & Chabot, Jacob. Hello Kitty: Just Imagine. Monlongo, Jorge, illus. 2014. (ENG., Illus.). 64p. (J). pap. 7.99 *(978-1-4215-7362-5(8))* Viz Media.
Montague, Chester. Timmy's Vacation. 2008. 40p. pap. 24.95 *(978-1-60441-225-3(9))* America Star Bks.
Montana, Brenda. Jamie & Lacy & the Adventures of the White Chihuahuas Book. 2011. 48p. pap. 15.99 *(978-1-4653-6752-5(7))* Xlibris Corp.
Montelongo, Monica. The Adventures of Roxy & Mozart. 2009. 28p. pap. 14.50 *(978-1-60860-458-6(6)*, Eloquent Bks.) Strategic Book Publishing & Rights Agency (SBPRA).
Montes, Graciela. Habia una Vez una Nube. Legnazzi, Claudia, illus. 2006. 23p. (J). (gr. -1-3). 8.95 *(978-1-59820-214-4(6)*, Alfaguara) Santillana USA Publishing Co., Inc.
—Habia una Vez una Princesa. Torres, Elena, illus. 2006. (Alfaguara Infantil Ser.). 26p. (J). 8.95 *(978-1-59820-215-1(4)*, Alfaguara) Santillana USA Publishing Co., Inc.
Montgomery, Anson. Dragon Day. 2011. (Illus.). 80p. (J). (gr. k-3). 7.99 *(978-1-933390-61-1(1))* Chooseco LLC.
—Escape from the Haunted Warehouse. 2015. (ENG.). 144p. (J). pap. 6.99 *(978-1-937133-47-4(8))* Chooseco LLC.
—Moon Quest. Semionov, Vladimir, illus. 2008. (Choose Your Own Adventure Ser.: No. 26). 144p. (J). (gr. 2-7). pap. 6.99 *(978-1-933390-26-0(3))* Chooseco LLC.
—Your Grandparents Are Spies. 2016. (Illus.). (J). pap. 7.99 *(978-1-937133-51-1(6))* Chooseco LLC.
Montgomery, E. j. Hailey Walker & the Mystery of the Absent Professor. 2013. 180p. pap. 13.95 *(978-1-4575-2068-6(0))* Dog Ear Publishing, LLC.
Montgomery, L. M. The Blue Castle. Date not set. (J). 22.95 *(978-0-8488-2370-2(2))* Amereon Ltd.
—Rainbow Valley. 2007. (ENG.). 234p. pap. 20.99 *(978-1-4346-5245-4(9))*; 258p. pap. 23.99 *(978-1-4346-5246-1(7))* Creative Media Partners, LLC.
Montgomery, R. A. The Abominable Snowman Peguy, Laurence, illus. 2006. (Choose Your Own Adventure Ser.). 144p. (J). (gr. 4-8). per. 6.99 *(978-1-933390-01-7(8)*, CHCL01) Chooseco LLC.
—Always Picked Last. 2009. 64p. (J). pap. 7.99 *(978-1-933390-38-3(7))* Chooseco LLC.
—Behind the Wheel. 2010. 144p. pap. 6.99 *(978-1-933390-35-2(2))* Chooseco LLC.
—Beyond Escape. 2005. (Choose Your Own Adventure Ser.). (Illus.). 118p. (gr. 4-8). pap. 5.50 *(978-0-7608-9703-4(4))* Sundance/Newbridge Educational Publishing.
—Blood on the Handle. 2010. (Illus.). 144p. (J). pap. 6.99 *(978-1-933390-33-8(6))* Chooseco LLC.
—The Brilliant Dr. Wogan. 2005. (Choose Your Own Adventure Ser.). (Illus.). 112p. (gr. 4-8). pap. 5.50 *(978-0-7608-9705-8(0))* Sundance/Newbridge Educational Publishing.
—Choose Your Own Adventure 4 Book Boxed Set #3: Lost on the Amazon; Prisoner of the Ant People; Trouble on Planet Earth; War with the Evil Power Master. 2006. (Illus.). 144p. (J). pap. 22.99 *(978-1-933390-96-3(4))* Chooseco LLC.
—Dragonlark Bind Up-#02. 2009. 0192p. pap. 6.99 *(978-1-933390-89-5(1))* Chooseco LLC.
—Escape. 2005. (Illus.). 127p. (J). pap. *(978-0-7608-9696-9(8))* Sundance/Newbridge Educational Publishing.
—Escape. Millet, Jason, illus. 2006. (Choose Your Own Adventure Ser.: No. 8). 144p. (J). (gr. 4-8). per. 6.99 *(978-1-933390-08-6(5)*, CHCL08) Chooseco LLC.
—House of Danger. 2005. (Choose Your Own Adventure Ser.). (Illus.). 108p. (gr. 4-8). pap. 5.50 *(978-0-7608-9694-5(1))* Sundance/Newbridge Educational Publishing.
—House of Danger. Sundaravej, Sittisan, illus. 2006. (Choose Your Own Adventure Ser.: No. 6). 144p. (J). (gr. 4-8). per. 6.99 *(978-1-933390-06-2(9)*, CHCL06) Chooseco LLC.
—Island of Time. Louie, Wes & Cannella, Marco, illus. 2008. 144p. (J). (gr. 2-7). pap. 6.99 *(978-1-933390-28-4(X))* Chooseco LLC.
—Lost Dog! 2011. (Dragonlarks Ser.). (Illus.). 80p. (J). (gr. k-3). pap. 7.99 *(978-1-933390-00-0(X))* Chooseco LLC.
—The Lost Jewels of Nabooti. Kommaneeroj, T. et al, illus. 2006. (Choose Your Own Adventure Ser.: No. 4). 144p. (J). (gr. 4-8). per. 6.99 *(978-1-933390-04-8(2)*, CHCL04) Chooseco LLC.
—Lost on the Amazon. 2007. 144p. (J). pap. *(978-1-86504-931-1(X))* Chooseco LLC.
—Lost on the Amazon. 2005. (Choose Your Own Adventure Ser.). (Illus.). 114p. (gr. 4-8). pap. 5.50 *(978-0-7608-9697-6(6))* Sundance/Newbridge Educational Publishing.
—Monsters of the Deep. 2010. 64p. pap. 7.99 *(978-1-933390-37-6(9))* Chooseco LLC.
—Prisoner of the Ant People. 2007. 144p. (J). pap. *(978-1-86504-932-8(8))* Chooseco LLC.
—Prisoner of the Ant People. Millet, Jason, illus. 2006. (Choose Your Own Adventure Ser.: No. 10). 144p. (J). (gr. 4-8). per. 6.99 *(978-1-933390-10-9(7)*, CHCL10) Chooseco LLC.
—Prisoner of the Ant People. 2005. (Illus.). 115p. (J). pap. *(978-0-7608-9698-3(4))* Sundance/Newbridge Educational Publishing.
—Project UFO. Semionov, Vladimir & Cannella, Marco, illus. 2008. 144p. (J). (gr. 4-7). pap. 6.99 *(978-1-933390-27-7(1))* Chooseco LLC.
—Punishment: Earth. 2010. 144p. pap. 6.99 *(978-1-933390-36-9(0))* Chooseco LLC.
—Return to Atlantis. 2005. (Choose Your Own Adventure Ser.). (Illus.). 119p. (gr. 4-8). pap. 5.50 *(978-0-7608-9706-5(9))* Sundance/Newbridge Educational Publishing.
—Sand Castle. Newton, Keith, illus. 2008. 80p. (J). (gr. k-3). pap. 7.99 *(978-1-933390-59-8(X))* Chooseco LLC.
—Smoke Jumpers. Peguy, Laurence, illus. 2009. (Choose Your Own Adventure Ser.: No. 29). 144p. (J). (gr. 2-7). pap. 6.99 *(978-1-933390-29-1(8))* Chooseco LLC.
—The Trail of Lost Time. 2011. (Illus.). 144p. (J). mass mkt. 6.99 *(978-1-937133-03-0(6))* Chooseco LLC.
—Your Grandparents Are Zombies! 2010. (Illus.). 64p. (J). pap. 7.99 *(978-1-933390-90-1(5))* Chooseco LLC.
—Your Very Own Robot Goes Cuckoo Bananas. 2009. (Illus.). 80p. (J). pap. 7.99 *(978-1-933390-39-0(5))* Chooseco LLC.
Montgomery, Ramsey. U. N. Adventure: Mission to Molowa. 2009. 144p. (J). pap. 6.99 *(978-1-933390-32-1(8))* Chooseco LLC.
Montgomery, Ross. Perijee & Me. 2016. (ENG.). 224p. (J). (gr. 3-7). 16.99 *(978-0-399-55397-4(5)*, Lamb, Wendy Bks.) Random Hse. Children's Bks.
Montijo, Rhode. Chews Your Destiny. 2017. (Gum Girl Ser.: 1). (J). lib. bdg. 16.00 ***(978-0-606-39969-2(0))*** Turtleback Bks.
Moon, Catherine R. & Everette, Maureen C. The Adventures of NanaCat & Her Children: Someone New. Richardson, Kara, illus. 2004. 32p. (J). per. 6.95 *(978-0-930507-02-2(9))* GRAND Media, LLC.
Moon, Cliff, ed. Slumbery Stumble in the Jungle. 2015. (Collins Big Cat Ser.). (ENG.). 24p. (J). (gr. 2-2). pap. 6.95 *(978-0-00-759105-3(5))* HarperCollins Pubs. Ltd. GBR. Dist: Independent Pubs. Group.
Moone, Colin. Wonderful Adventures of the Margicans: The One Bad Apple. 2003. 164p. pap. *(978-1-84426-189-5(1))* Upfront Publishing Ltd.
Mooney, Stephen. Half Past Danger. 2014. (ENG., Illus.). 200p. 29.99 *(978-1-61377-849-4(X)*, 9781613778494) Idea & Design Works, LLC.
Moore, Alan, et al. Promethea, Bk. 2. 2nd rev. ed. 2003. (ENG., Illus.). 176p. pap. 17.99 *(978-1-56389-957-7(4)*, Wildstorm) DC Comics.
Moore, Angela. Rebecca's Ducks, 1 vol. Keating, Nancy, illus. 2007. (ENG.). 32p. (J). (gr. -1-2). pap. 8.95 *(978-1-897174-00-5(4)*, Tuckamore Bks) Creative Bk. Publishing CAN. Dist: Orca Bk. Pubs. USA.
Moore, Ann C. Looking for a Place to Take a Long Winter Nap. 2009. 32p. pap. 14.49 *(978-1-4490-0852-9(6))* AuthorHouse.
Moore, Ashley L. The Story of Princess K. 2012. 20p. pap. 24.95 *(978-1-4626-6800-7(3))* America Star Bks.
Moore, Brenna L. Out of Place in Outer Space. 2013. 28p. pap. 11.95 *(978-1-4787-0706-6(2))* Outskirts Pr., Inc.
Moore, Daniel. Abdallah Jones & the DisappearingDust. 2006. 168p. pap. 17.00 *(978-0-615-13570-0(6))* Ecstatic Exchange, The.
Moore, Graeme. Ruin. 2009. 240p. pap. 21.50 *(978-1-4092-8737-7(8))* Lulu Pr., Inc.
Moore, Inga. Captain Cat. Moore, Inga, illus. 2013. (ENG., Illus.). 48p. (J). (gr. -1-2). 15.99 *(978-0-7636-6151-9(1))* Candlewick Pr.
Moore, Jordan. Sinbad the Sailor, 1 vol. rev. ed. 2013. (Fiction Readers Ser.). (ENG., Illus.). 32p. (J). (gr. 3-3). pap. 8.99 *(978-1-4333-5647-6(3))* Shell Educational Publishing.
Moore, Ken A. Ghost Island & the Mystery of Charmander: An Unofficial Adventure for Pokémon GO Fans. 2016. (ENG.). 236p. (J). (gr. 2-7). pap. 9.99 *(978-1-5107-2296-5(3)*, Sky Pony Pr.) Skyhorse Publishing Co., Inc.
Moore, Kevin. The Road Maker. 2008. 52p. pap. 31.99 *(978-1-4363-7007-3(8))* Xlibris Corp.
Moore, Mykela. Meet the Super Sisters. Garrett, Myers, illus. 2013. (J). 9.99 *(978-0-9852746-9-6(7))* Hope of Vision Publishing.
Moore, Natascha. Little Bear Kleiner Bär. 2012. 28p. pap. 19.99 *(978-1-4772-6055-5(2))* AuthorHouse.
Moore, Perry. Hero. 2009. (ENG.). 432p. (J). (gr. 5-9). pap. 9.99 *(978-1-4231-0196-3(0))* Hyperion Pr.
Moore, Roland D. Bugging in the City. 2011. 80p. pap. 32.26 *(978-1-4567-4130-3(6))* AuthorHouse.
Moore, Rosey. Dreams. 2010. 228p. pap. 14.49 *(978-1-4520-7485-6(2))* AuthorHouse.
Moore, S. D. The Adventures of Pj & Split Pea. Switzer, Bobbi, illus. 2008. 36p. per. 12.95 *(978-1-4327-1288-4(8))* Outskirts Pr., Inc.
—The Adventures of PJ & Split Pea Vol. II: Nothing but the Tooth. 2010. 37p. (J). pap. 12.95 *(978-1-4327-1289-1(6))* Outskirts Pr., Inc.
Moore, Sherry. The Crab Is Back in Town. 2007. (ENG.). 100p. (J). per. *(978-1-894936-78-1(7))* Saga Bks.
Moore, Stephanie Perry & Moore, Derrick. Real Diva/Man Up, 2014. (Grovehill Giants Ser.). (YA). lib. bdg. 26.90 *(978-0-606-31879-2(8)*, Turtleback) Turtleback Bks.
Moore, Suse. Ella Power & the Sun Puppies: A Power Families Adventure. Elkerton, Andy, illus. 2011. (ENG.). 40p. (J). 17.99 *(978-0-9837863-2-0(1))* Jack Hook Publishing.
Moore, Ted. Eagle Eye & the Fall of Creek Canyon. 2007. 112p. per. 10.95 *(978-0-595-43133-5(X))* iUniverse, Inc.
Moore, Thomas. Zoe & the Back Yard Boys: The Magic Garden Haunted House Adventure. 2012. 24p. pap. 17.99 *(978-1-4772-9086-6(9))* AuthorHouse.
Moore, Yvonne. The Listening Gift. 2012. 24p. pap. 17.99 *(978-1-4772-9313-3(2))* AuthorHouse.
Morah, Chizoba. The Anderson Twins. 2007. 76p. per. 19.95 *(978-1-60441-015-0(9))* America Star Bks.
Moraja, Melissa Perry. Jake's Adventures - the Secret of the Shark Tooth Crab Claw. Moraja, Melissa Perry, illus. 2012. (Illus.). 118p. pap. *(978-0-9834751-8-7(0))* Roxby Media Ltd.
—Madison & Ga: Tale of the Messed up Talent Show. 2013. 156p. pap. *(978-0-9898293-1-1(6))* Roxby Media Ltd.
Moran, Katy. Bloodline. 2009. (ENG., Illus.). 320p. (YA). (gr. 7). 16.99 *(978-0-7636-4083-5(2))* Candlewick Pr.
Moran, Mary C. Digby's Rescue. 2012. 28p. pap. 15.95 *(978-1-105-96859-4(6))* Lulu Pr., Inc.
Mörchen, Roland. Wir Gehen in Die Bibliothek - A Visit to the Library: Deutsch-Englische Ausgabe. Kiefer, Katja, illus. 2010. (ENG.). 40p. (J). (gr. 3-7). 19.99 *(978-3-487-08843-3(6))* Olms, Georg Verlag AG DEU. Dist: Independent Pubs. Group.
—Wir Gehen Ins Fernsehstudio. Kiefer, Katja, illus. 2010. (ENG.). 40p. (J). (gr. 3-7). 19.99 *(978-3-487-08836-5(3))* Olms, Georg Verlag AG DEU. Dist: Independent Pubs. Group.
Morden, Daniel & Lupt, Hugh. Adventures of Odysseus. 2017. (ENG., Illus.). 96p. (J). (gr. 1-4). 16.99 ***(978-1-78285-356-5(1))*** Barefoot Bks., Inc.
Moreau, Chris. The Professor's Telescope. Marek, Jane, illus. 2006. (YA). 10.95 *(978-0-9785399-0-0(7))*; cd-rom 7.95 *(978-0-9785399-2-4(3))* Windows of Discovery.
Moree, Katie. Jesse's Peekaboo Safari. 2008. 20p. pap. 24.95 *(978-1-60672-473-6(8))* America Star Bks.
Morgan, Allen. Matthew & the Midnight Firefighters. 2004. (Illus.). (J). (gr. k-3). spiral bd. *(978-0-616-07242-4(2))* Canadian National Institute for the Blind/Institut National Canadien pour les Aveugles.
Morgan, Beverly. Gregory & the Stars: A Little Story about Independence. Joyful Noise, ed. 2005. (Illus.). 26p. (J). 4.95 *(978-0-9772109-0-9(1))* Joyful Noise.
Morgan, C. M. Silver Doorway #3: An Elf's Adventure. 2004. 104p. (J). pap. 6.99 *(978-0-9702189-4-0(X))* Sabledrake Enterprises.
MOrgan, C. M. Silver Doorway #4: Dragon on the Loose. 2004. 104p. (J). pap. 6.99 *(978-0-9702189-7-1(4))* Sabledrake Enterprises.
Morgan, C. M. Silver Doorway #6: The Alchemist's Girl. 2008. 108p. pap. 6.99 *(978-0-9771005-2-1(9))* Sabledrake Enterprises.
Morgan, Charles. Flight of the Solar Ducks. 2009. 219p. pap. 15.01 *(978-0-557-07503-4(3))* Lulu Pr., Inc.
Morgan, Clay. The Boy Who Returned from the Sea. 2009. (ENG.). 256p. (J). (gr. 3-7). pap. 7.99 *(978-0-14-241395-1(X)*, Puffin Books) Penguin Young Readers Group.
Morgan, Derek T. Cats Tails. 2011. 378p. pap. 20.95 *(978-1-60976-729-7(2)*, Eloquent Bks.) Strategic Book Publishing & Rights Agency (SBPRA).
Morgan, G. A. Chantarelle, 1 vol. 2015. (Five Stones Trilogy Ser.: 2). (ENG.). 316p. (J). pap. 18.95 *(978-1-939017-63-5(7)*, a178678b-3da7-4c5c-96c5-09386c28787e) Islandport Pr., Inc.
—The Kinfolk, 1 vol. 2016. (Five Stones Trilogy Ser.: 3). (ENG.). 300p. (J). 18.95 *(978-1-934031-82-7(8)*, 8d77caad-23f8-4ae6-8704-a88c1b35f25d) Islandport Pr., Inc.
Morgan, Gloria. Dream Me Home. 2012. 294p. pap. 13.50 *(978-1-84426-661-6(3)*, Fastprint Publishing) Upfront Publishing Ltd. GBR. Dist: Printondemand-worldwide.com.
Morgan, Jack. The True Story of How Lacy Gasper Solved the Crime Spree. 2007. 220p. per. 24.95 *(978-1-4241-7120-0(2))* America Star Bks.
Morgan, Kristy. The Adventures of Rocky & Skeeter: Rocky Goes to Jail. 2011. 52p. pap. 8.95 *(978-1-4620-2219-9(7))* iUniverse, Inc.
Morgan, Marlee. Soujon's Journey. 2010. 380p. (J). pap. 10.00 *(978-0-9789247-6-8(2)*, INDI Best) INDI, LLC.
Morgan-McCray, Sheila. Untied Shoes. 2008. 28p. pap. 9.95 *(978-1-4327-1093-4(1))* Outskirts Pr., Inc.
Morgan, Melissa J. Camp Confidential - Complete First Summer. 2009. (Camp Confidential Ser.: Nos. 1-4). (ENG.). 624p. (J). (gr. 3-7). pap. 14.99 *(978-0-448-45188-6(3)*, Grosset & Dunlap) Penguin Young Readers Group.
—Second Time's the Charm. 7th ed. 2006. (Camp Confidential Ser.: 7). (ENG.). 160p. (J). (gr. 3-7). pap. 4.99 *(978-0-448-44265-5(5)*, Grosset & Dunlap) Penguin Young Readers Group.
Morgan, Nicola. The Highwayman's Curse. 2009. (J). *(978-0-7636-4066-8(2))* Candlewick Pr.
—The Highwayman's Curse. 2007. 368p. (YA). pap. *(978-1-4063-0312-4(7))* Walker Bks., Ltd.
Morgan, Ruth. Jess & the Bean Root. Vagnozzi, Barbara, illus. 2005. (ENG.). 24p. (J). lib. bdg. 23.65 *(978-1-59646-732-3(0))* Dingles & Co.
Morgan, Vicky S. Jim & Me & Theo T. 2011. 28p. pap. 21.99 *(978-1-4568-8124-5(8))* Xlibris Corp.
Morgan, Winter. Attack of the Ender Dragon: An Unofficial Minetrapped Adventure, #6. 2016. (Unofficial Minetrapped Adventure Ser.: 6). (ENG.). 112p. (J). (gr. 1-7). pap. 7.99 *(978-1-5107-0602-6(X)*, Sky Pony Pr.) Skyhorse Publishing Co., Inc.
—Attack of the Goblin Army: Tales of a Terrarian Warrior, Book One. 2016. (ENG.). 112p. (J). (gr. 1-7). pap. 7.99 *(978-1-5107-1682-7(3)*, Sky Pony Pr.) Skyhorse Publishing Co., Inc.
—Battle in the Overworld: The Unofficial Minecrafters Academy Series, Book Three. 2016. (Unofficial Minecrafters Academy Ser.). (ENG.). 112p. (J). (gr. 1-7). pap. 7.99 *(978-1-5107-0596-8(1)*, Sky Pony Pr.) Skyhorse Publishing Co., Inc.
—Creeper Invasion: An Unofficial Minetrapped Adventure, #5. 2016. (Unofficial Minetrapped Adventure Ser.: 5). (ENG., Illus.). 112p. (J). (gr. 1-7). pap. 7.99 *(978-1-5107-0601-9(1)*, Sky Pony Pr.) Skyhorse Publishing Co., Inc.
—Ghastly Battle: An Unofficial Minetrapped Adventure, #4. 2016. (Unofficial Minetrapped Adventure Ser.: 4). (ENG.). 112p. (J). (gr. 1-7). pap. 7.99 *(978-1-5107-0600-2(3)*, Sky Pony Pr.) Skyhorse Publishing Co., Inc.
—Hidden in the Overworld: League of Griefers Series, Book Two. 2015. (League of Griefers Ser.: 2). (ENG.). 112p. (J). (gr. 1-7). pap. 7.99 *(978-1-63450-595-6(6)*, Sky Pony Pr.) Skyhorse Publishing Co., Inc.
—Lost in the End: Lost Minecraft Journals, Book Three. 2016. (Lost Minecraft Journals Ser.). (ENG.). 112p. (J). (gr. 1-7). pap. 7.99 *(978-1-5107-0352-0(7)*, Sky Pony Pr.) Skyhorse Publishing Co., Inc.
—Mobs in the Mine: An Unofficial Minetrapped Adventure, #2. 2016. (Unofficial Minetrapped Adventure Ser.: 2). (ENG.). 112p. (J). (gr. 1-7). pap. 7.99 *(978-1-5107-0598-2(8)*, Sky Pony Pr.) Skyhorse Publishing Co., Inc.
—Terror on a Treasure Hunt: An Unofficial Minetrapped Adventure, #3. 2016. (Unofficial Minetrapped Adventure Ser.: 3). (ENG.). 112p. (J). (gr. 1-7). pap. 7.99 *(978-1-5107-0599-9(6)*, Sky Pony Pr.) Skyhorse Publishing Co., Inc.
—Trapped in the Overworld: An Unofficial Minetrapped Adventure, #1. 2016. (Unofficial Minetrapped Adventure Ser.: 1). (ENG.). 112p. (J). (gr. 1-7). pap. 7.99 *(978-1-5107-0597-5(X)*, Sky Pony Pr.) Skyhorse Publishing Co., Inc.
—Treasure Hunters in Trouble: A Minecraft Gamer's Adventure, Bk 4. 2015. (Unofficial Gamer's Adventure Ser.). (ENG.). 112p. (J). (gr. 1-7). pap. 7.99 *(978-1-63450-090-6(3)*, Sky Pony Pr.) Skyhorse Publishing Co., Inc.
—Wicked Warrior: Tales of a Terrarian Warrior, Book Three. 2017. (ENG.). 112p. (J). (gr. 1-7). pap. 7.99 *(978-1-5107-2195-1(9)*, Sky Pony Pr.) Skyhorse Publishing Co., Inc.
—Zombie Invasion: The Unofficial Minecrafters Academy Series, Book One. 2016. (Unofficial Minecrafters Academy Ser.). (ENG.). 112p. (J). (gr. 1-7). pap. 7.99 *(978-1-5107-0594-4(5)*, Sky Pony Pr.) Skyhorse Publishing Co., Inc.
Morganti, Jerre. The World of Priscilla Gingold. 2008. 135p. pap. 24.95 *(978-1-60474-122-3(8))* America Star Bks.
Morimoto, Sango. Taro & the Terror of Eats Street. Morimoto, Sango, illus. 2011. (Adventures of Taro Ser.). (ENG., Illus.). 96p. (J). (gr. 1-4). pap. 7.99 *(978-1-4215-3525-8(4))* Viz Media.
Morin, Al. Brandon Abroad: The Mystery of the Ruins. 2017. (ENG., Illus.). (J). pap. 7.99 ***(978-1-911079-61-3(1)***, Acorn) Heinemann-Raintree.
Morino, Sakana. Becoming a Dragon. Morino, Sakana, illus. 2014. (Illus.). (J). 8.95 *(978-1-935523-67-3(8))* World Tribune Pr.
Morley, Elizabeth. Let Sleeping Hedgehogs Spy. 2013. (Illus.). 154p. pap. *(978-1-78299-107-6(7))* FeedARead.com.
Morningforest, Chris & Raymond, Rebecca. Princess Underdrawers & the Dragon. 2006. 37p. (J). pap. 15.58 *(978-1-4116-8837-7(6))* Lulu Pr., Inc.
Moroney, Trace. Bathtime: Baxter Bear Chubby. Moroney, Trace, illus. 2008. (Baxter Bear Collection). (Illus.). 10p. (J). (gr. -1-1). bds. *(978-1-86463-175-3(9))* Brimax Books Ltd.
Morphew, Chris. Blood in the Ashes. 2017. (Phoenix Files Ser.: 2). (ENG.). 512p. (YA). (gr. 6). pap. 12.99 ***(978-1-76012-426-7(5))*** Hardie Grant Egmont Pty, Ltd. AUS. Dist: Independent Pubs. Group.
Morpurgo, Michael. Kaspar the Titanic Cat. Foreman, Michael, illus. 2012. 208p. (J). (gr. 3-7). 16.99 *(978-0-06-200618-9(5))* HarperCollins Pubs.
—Kensuke's Kingdom. 2004. (ENG.). 176p. (J). (gr. 4-7). mass mkt. 6.99 *(978-0-439-59181-2(3)*, Scholastic Paperbacks) Scholastic, Inc.
—The Nine Lives of Montezuma. 2004. (Illus.). 120p. (J). pap. 8.99 *(978-1-4052-0189-6(4))* Egmont Bks., Ltd. GBR. Dist: Trafalgar Square Publishing.
—Not Bad for a Bad Lad. Foreman, Michael, illus. 2016. (ENG.). 128p. (J). (gr. 2-4). pap. 9.99 *(978-1-84812-471-4(6))* Bonnier Publishing GBR. Dist: Independent Pubs. Group.
—El Reino de Kensuke. Aguilar, Carmen, tr. Foreman, Michael, illus. 2006.Tr. of Kensuke's Kingdom. (SPA.). 155p. (J). (gr. 5-8). 16.99 *(978-84-7901-420-9(2))* RBA Libros, S.A. ESP. Dist: Santillana USA Publishing Co., Inc.
Morris, April. Eldon the Elephant. 2004. (J). lib. bdg. 25.95 *(978-1-893595-49-1(8))* Four Seasons Bks., Inc.
Morris, Ashara. Let's Find Lucy! 2008. (Illus.). 32p. pap. 17.95 *(978-1-4327-3221-9(8))* Outskirts Pr., Inc.
Morris, Bob. Tommy Tott's Raft Adventure. 2013. 36p. pap. 16.99 *(978-1-4624-0724-8(2)*, Inspiring Voices) Author Solutions, Inc.
Morris, Chad. Cragbridge Hall, Book 3: The Impossible Race. 2015. (Cragbridge Hall Ser.: 3). (ENG., Illus.). 432p. (J). (gr. 3-9). 18.99 *(978-1-60907-979-6(5)*, Shadow Mountain) Shadow Mountain Publishing.
Morris, Dawn. Concorde the Beautiful Flying Collie. 2012. 32p. pap. 21.99 *(978-1-4691-8098-4(7))* Xlibris Corp.
Morris, Gerald. The Lioness & Her Knight. 2008. (Squire's Tales Ser.: 7). (ENG.). 352p. (J). (gr. 5-7). pap. 7.99 *(978-0-547-01485-2(6))* Houghton Mifflin Harcourt Publishing Co.
—The Quest of the Fair Unknown. 2008. (Squire's Tales Ser.: 8). (ENG.). 272p. (J). (gr. 5-7). pap. 7.99 *(978-0-547-01484-5(8))* Houghton Mifflin Harcourt Publishing Co.
Morris, J. S. The Jewel. 2007. 204p. pap. 22.95 *(978-1-4357-0140-3(2))* Lulu Pr., Inc.
Morris, Kerry Nicole. The Baby Who Just... WON't Sleep! Parker's Story. 2004. 35p. pap. 24.95 *(978-1-4137-3724-0(2))* PublishAmerica, Inc.
Morris, Kim. Tinker Bell & the Great Fairy Rescue. 2010. (ENG.). 32p. 12.99 *(978-1-4231-2925-7(3))* Disney Pr.
Morris, Kirkland. The Alley that Wanted to be a Street: Kirkland Morris. Kinra, Richa, illus. 2012. (ENG.). 27p. (J). pap. 11.95 *(978-1-4327-7844-6(7))* Outskirts Pr., Inc.
Morris, Lynn. Belinda the Butterfly's Beautiful Colors. 2011. 48p. (gr. -1). pap. 19.26 *(978-1-4567-3521-0(7))* AuthorHouse.
—Don't eat your Broccoli! Mettler, Joe, illus. 2007. 32p. (J). per. 6.95 *(978-0-9755548-2-1(4))* Log Cabin Bks.
Morrison, Anna C. & Movshina, Marina. Silly Moments. 2010. 16p. pap. 9.95 *(978-1-61633-039-2(2))* Guardian Angel Publishing, Inc.
Morrison, D. F. The Lapis Key Adventures of Ernie & Daisy. 2012. 104p. pap. *(978-1-77097-515-6(2))* FriesenPress.
Morrison, David. The Mind Map Level 3 Lower-Intermediate. 2009. (ENG.). 80p. pap. 12.75 *(978-84-8323-537-9(4))* Cambridge Univ. Pr.
Morrison, Kenny. Sevenlives & the Woof Pack. 2011. (Illus.). 104p. pap. 13.32 *(978-1-4567-8595-6(8))* AuthorHouse.
Morrison, Megan. Grounded: The Tale of Rapunzel. 2015. (Illus.). 374p. (J). *(978-0-545-75468-2(2))* Scholastic, Inc.
Morrissette, Cora. Adventures in the Land of Make Believe. 2011. 88p. pap. 17.95 *(978-1-4327-6766-2(6))* Outskirts Pr., Inc.
Morse, Scott. Magic Pickle. Morse, Scott, illus. 2008. (Magic Pickle Ser.). (ENG., Illus.). 112p. (J). (gr. 2-5). pap. 9.99 *(978-0-439-87995-8(7)*, Graphix) Scholastic, Inc.
Morse, William A. Kurkle Kids: Pirate Lostman's Great Adventure. 2010. 44p. pap. 16.99 *(978-1-4490-6187-6(7))* AuthorHouse.
Moseley, Marlon Paul. Still Skylarkin. 2015. (ENG., Illus.). 40p. pap. 11.95 *(978-1-84963-820-3(9)*, 943995e4-1535-4f77-ae53-975feaf5201a) Austin, Stan AUS. Dist: Bookmasters Distribution.
Moseley, Sophia. The Adventures of Charlie. Delderfield, Angela, illus. 2012. 106p. pap. *(978-1-78148-757-0(X))* Grosvenor Hse. Publishing Ltd.
Moseley, Steven. The Trailer Park King. 2013. (ENG.). 48p. (J). pap. 8.95 *(978-1-4787-1765-2(3))* Outskirts Pr., Inc.
Mosier, Pamela. Elizabeth, the Eastern Gray Squirrel. 2008. 44p. pap. 18.95 *(978-1-4357-5407-2(7))* Lulu Pr., Inc.
Moss, Anne H. The Amazing, True-To-Life Tale of Me Do It. 2012. 28p. pap. 19.99 *(978-1-4772-2072-6(0))* AuthorHouse.

Moss, Christopher Hawthorne. Beloved Pilgrim. 2nd ed. 2016. (ENG., Illus.). (J). 29.99 **(978-1-63477-939-5(8))** 2014. 304p. pap. 17.99 (978-1-62798-538-3(7)) Dreamspinner Pr. (Harmony Ink Pr.).

Moss, Helen. The Serpent King. 2017. (Secrets of the Tombs Ser.). (ENG., Illus.). 272p. (J). (gr. 4-6). 10.99 (978-1-4440-1043-5(3), Orion Children's Bks.) Hachette Children's Group GBR. Dist: Hachette Bk. Group.

Moss, J. P. The Kind Fairy Adventures: 3 Loving Fairy Tales from the Land of the Faye. 2010. (Illus.). 52p. pap. 22.99 (978-1-4520-3868-1(6)) AuthorHouse.

Moss, Marissa. Alien Eraser Reveals the Secret of Evolution. Moss, Marissa, illus. 2009. (ENG., Illus.). 56p. (J). (gr. 3-7). pap. 6.99 (978-0-7636-4419-2(6)) Candlewick Pr.

Moss, Yvonne. Seasons Through the Eyes of A Child: The Snow, the Spring, the Summer, the Fall. 2010. 12p. pap. 9.49 (978-1-4520-3757-8(4)) AuthorHouse.

Mother Goose Staff & Studio Mouse Staff. Sugar & Spice, 6 Bks. 2005. (ENG., Illus.). 10p. (J). 12.95 (978-1-59249-471-2(4), 1D100) Soundprints.

Mothershead, Martha Fulford. Petoskey Stone Soup. Clarkson, Janet M., illus. 2006. 32p. (J). 18.95 (978-0-9785465-0-2(4)) Leelanau Pr.

Motto, Bernadine. The Adventures of Fluff the Bunny. 2007. 32p. per. 11.95 (978-1-59800-908-8(7)) Outskirts Pr., Inc.

Moulton, Bob. Rosey & Josey Meet Big Feet. 2010. 20p. 10.49 (978-1-4490-9151-4(2)) AuthorHouse.

Moulton, Erin E. Flutter: The Story of Four Sisters & an Incredible Journey. 2012. (ENG.). 224p. (J). (gr. 3-7). pap. 6.99 (978-0-14-242133-8(2), Puffin Books) Penguin Young Readers Group.

Moulton, Eugena. The Age of Merrik: The Anointing. 2007. 200p. 24.95 (978-0-595-67899-0(8)); per. 14.95 (978-0-595-41367-6(6)) iUniverse, Inc.

Moulton, Mike. Tina Talinka's Travels Vol. 1: Tina Talinka & the Knights of Sacrifice & Tina Talinka & the Echo of the Allohom. 2004. 260p. (YA). 27.99 (978-1-59507-044-9(3), ArcheBooks) ArcheBooks Publishing, Inc.

Moundlic, Charlotte. The Bathing Costume. Tallec, Olivier & Sorman, Joy, illus. 2013. (ENG.). 40p. (J). (gr. k-3). 15.95 (978-1-59270-141-4(8)) Enchanted Lion Bks., LLC.

Mount, Jill. The Mystery of the Dirty Bike. 2005. 9.00 (978-0-8059-9778-1(4)) Dorrance Publishing Co., Inc.

Mounteer, J. B. I Think My Brother Is a Werewolf. 2012. 50p. pap. 8.22 (978-1-4669-4868-6(X)) Trafford Publishing.

Mourlevat, Jean-Claude. Winter's End. Bell, Anthea, tr. from FRE. 2009. (ENG., Illus.). 432p. (YA). (gr. 9-18). 17.99 (978-0-7636-4450-5(1)) Candlewick Pr.

Mouser, Mary. Chigger: A Prairie Dog Tale. 2007. 152p. per. 24.95 (978-1-4241-9791-0(0)) America Star Bks.

Mowll, Joshua. Operation Storm City, Bk. 3. 2009. (Guild of Specialists Ser.). (ENG., Illus.). 288p. (J). (gr. 5). 16.99 (978-0-7636-4224-2(X)) Candlewick Pr.

Mowry, Chris. Revenge of the Fallen: Alliance, 1 vol. Milne, Alex, illus. 2010. (Transformers: Revenge of the Fallen Movie Prequel Ser.). (ENG.). 24p. (J). (gr. 3-6). Vol. 1. 24.21 (978-1-59961-717-6(X)) Vol. 2. 24.21 (978-1-59961-718-3(8)) Vol. 3. 24.21 (978-1-59961-719-0(6)) Vol. 4. 24.21 (978-1-59961-720-6(X)) Spotlight.

—Revenge of the Fallen: Defiance, 1 vol., Vol. 1. Khanna, Dan, illus. 2010. (Transformers: Revenge of the Fallen Movie Prequel Ser.). (ENG.). 24p. (J). (gr. 3-6). 24.21 (978-1-59961-721-3(8)) Spotlight.

—Revenge of the Fallen: Defiance, 1 vol., Vol. 2. Khanna, Dan & Griffith, Andrew, illus. 2010. (Transformers: Revenge of the Fallen Movie Prequel Ser.). (ENG.). 24p. (J). (gr. 3-6). 24.21 (978-1-59961-722-0(6)) Spotlight.

—Revenge of the Fallen: Defiance, 1 vol., Vol. 4. Duendes del Sur, illus. 2010. (Transformers: Revenge of the Fallen Movie Prequel Ser.). (ENG.). 24p. (J). (gr. 3-6). 24.21 (978-1-59961-724-4(2)) Spotlight.

Mowry, Jess. Tyger Tales. 2007. 227p. per. 14.99 (978-1-59092-358-0(8)) Blue Forge Pr.

Moyer, Bess. Gypsies of the Air. 2004. reprint ed. pap. 19.95 (978-1-4179-9112-9(7)) Kessinger Publishing, LLC.

Moynahan, Jamie. Ben at the Seaside. 2009. (Illus.). 20p. pap. 15.49 (978-1-4389-6999-2(6)) AuthorHouse.

—Fly with Ben. 2009. (Illus.). 24p. pap. 14.99 (978-1-4389-7001-1(3)) AuthorHouse.

—Tiger Bunnies. 2009. (Illus.). 16p. pap. 9.49 (978-1-4389-7000-4(5)) AuthorHouse.

Moyston, Connaelia. God's Faith Is Real. 2013. 44p. pap. 21.99 (978-1-4817-0155-6(X)) AuthorHouse.

Mr. Cheesehead Goes for a Ride... 2nd rev. ed. 2005. (Illus.). 32p. (J). 12.99 (978-0-9764463-1-6(6)) Vertigo Publishing.

Ms. T. A Chincoteague Pony Finds a Friend. 2009. 28p. pap. 12.49 (978-1-4389-7981-6(9)) AuthorHouse.

Mucha, Mark. Adventures with Edison & His Friends Vol. 1: "Crab in a Bucket" 2008. 58p. pap. 11.95 (978-1-934449-29-5(6)) Legacy Publishing Services, Inc.

Muchamore, Robert. Brigands M. C. 2016. (Cherub Ser.: 11). (ENG., Illus.). 416p. (YA). (gr. 9). 17.99 (978-1-4814-5671-5(7), Simon Pulse) Simon Pulse.

—The Dealer. (Cherub Ser.: 2). (ENG.). (YA). (gr. 7). 2011. 336p. pap. 11.99 (978-1-4424-1361-0(1)) 2010. 320p. 18.99 (978-1-4169-9941-6(8)) Simon Pulse. (Simon Pulse).

—The General. 2016. (Cherub Ser.: 10). (ENG., Illus.). 352p. (YA). (gr. 9). 17.99 (978-1-4814-5666-1(0), Simon Pulse) Simon Pulse.

—Maximum Security. (Cherub Ser.: 3). (ENG.). 320p. (YA). (gr. 7). 2012. pap. 9.99 (978-1-4424-1362-7(X)) 2011. lib. bdg. 17.99 (978-1-4169-9942-3(6)) Simon Pulse. (Simon Pulse).

—The Sleepwalker. 2015. (Cherub Ser.: 9). (ENG., Illus.). 336p. (YA). (gr. 7). 17.99 (978-1-4814-5663-0(6), Simon Pulse) Simon Pulse.

Mudaly, Jessica. And That's Just the Trouble with Cats! 2011. 116p. pap. 10.95 (978-1-61204-186-5(8), Eloquent Bks.) Strategic Book Publishing & Rights Agency (SBPRA).

—Cats Can Be So Cattish! 2013. 116p. pap. 10.95 (978-1-62212-084-0(1), Strategic Bk. Publishing) Strategic Book Publishing & Rights Agency (SBPRA).

Mueller, Paul G. Abigail & Blueboy. 2010. 152p. 22.95 (978-1-60860-881-2(6), Eloquent Bks.) Strategic Book Publishing & Rights Agency (SBPRA).

Muench-Williams, Heather & Jarrell, Pamela R. Caillou's Hiking Adventure. Storch, Ellen N., illus. l.t. ed. 2005. (HRL Board Book Ser.). (J). (gr. k-18). pap. 10.95 (978-1-57332-329-1(2), HighReach Learning, Incorporated) Carson-Dellosa Publishing, LLC.

Muha, Christina. Porchville. 2009. 16p. pap. 8.52 (978-1-4389-8139-0(2)) AuthorHouse.

Muhammad, Shahid. The Adventures of the Math Doctor: Book One: King Jafiz & the Evil Farmer Nimra. 2007. (J). per. 7.95 (978-1-59872-778-4(8)) Instant Pub.

Muir, Sabine. Meeting Wolfie: A Story about Mozart. 2006. 129p. pap. 19.95 (978-1-4241-3968-2(6)) PublishAmerica, Inc.

Muir, Suzanne. The Magic Tile. 2007. (Illus.). 48p. (J). lib. bdg. 15.00 (978-1-4242-1619-2(2)) Dingles & Co.

mulholland, robin. Bolivia & the sunshine King. 2008. 147p. pap. 14.98 (978-0-557-01401-9(8)) Lulu Pr., Inc.

Mull, Brandon. Arcade Catastrophe. 2012. (Candy Shop War Ser.: 2). (ENG.). 448p. (J). (gr. 5). 18.99 (978-1-60907-179-0(4), Shadow Mountain) Shadow Mountain Publishing.

—Arcade Catastrophe. 2014. (Candy Shop War Ser.: 2). lib. bdg. 18.40 (978-0-606-35795-1(5)) Turtleback Bks.

—The Candy Shop War. 2011. E-Book 6.64 (978-1-60641-649-5(9)) Deseret Bk. Co.

—The Candy Shop War. (Candy Shop War Ser.: Bk. 1). 2008. 368p. pap. 6.99 (978-1-59038-970-6(0)) 2007. (Illus.). 409p. (J). (gr. 3-7). 19.99 (978-1-59038-783-2(X)) Shadow Mountain Publishing. (Shadow Mountain).

—The Candy Shop War. 2014. (Candy Shop War Ser.: 1). lib. bdg. 18.40 (978-0-606-35794-4(7)) Turtleback Bks.

—The Caretaker's Guide to Fablehaven. Dorman, Brandon, illus. 2015. (ENG.). 128p. (J). (gr. 4). 24.99 (978-1-62972-091-3(7), Shadow Mountain) Shadow Mountain Publishing.

—Chasing the Prophecy. 2014. (Beyonders Ser.: 3). lib. bdg. 19.65 (978-0-606-35435-6(2)) Turtleback Bks.

—Crystal Keepers. (Five Kingdoms Ser.: 3). (ENG., Illus.). (J). (gr. 3-7). 2016. 512p. pap. 8.99 (978-1-4424-9707-8(6), Aladdin) 2015. 496p. 17.99 (978-1-4424-9706-1(8), Aladdin Library) Simon & Schuster Children's Publishing.

—Death Weavers. 2016. (Five Kingdoms Ser.: 4). (ENG., Illus.). 512p. (J). (gr. 3-7). 17.99 (978-1-4424-9709-2(2), Aladdin) Simon & Schuster Children's Publishing.

—Death Weavers. 2017. (Five Kingdoms Ser.: 4). lib. bdg. 19.65 **(978-0-606-39758-2(2))** Turtleback Bks.

—Grip of the Shadow Plague. Dorman, Brandon, illus. 2009. (Fablehaven Ser.: 3). (ENG.). 512p. (J). (gr. 3-8). pap. 8.99 (978-1-4169-8603-4(0), Aladdin) Simon & Schuster Children's Publishing.

—Rogue Knight. (Five Kingdoms Ser.: 2). (ENG., Illus.). (J). (gr. 3-7). 2015. 496p. pap. 8.99 (978-1-4424-9704-7(1)) 2014. 480p. 17.99 (978-1-4424-9703-0(3)) Simon & Schuster Children's Publishing. (Aladdin).

—Rogue Knight. 2015. (Five Kingdoms Ser.: 2). lib. bdg. 19.65 (978-0-606-38254-0(2)) Turtleback Bks.

—Sky Raiders. (Five Kingdoms Ser.: 1). (ENG., Illus.). (J). (gr. 3-7). 2015. 448p. pap. 7.99 (978-1-4424-9701-6(7)) 2014. 432p. 17.99 (978-1-4424-9700-9(9)) Simon & Schuster Children's Publishing. (Aladdin).

—Sky Raiders. 2015. (Five Kingdoms Ser.: 1). lib. bdg. 18.40 (978-0-606-36303-7(3)) Turtleback Bks.

Mullaney, Polly. Three Kids Gripped by Evil. 2013. 158p. pap. 10.62 (978-1-291-38027-9(2)) Lulu Pr., Inc.

Mullendore, Bryan L. Scott's Many Adventures. 2010. 54p. pap. 22.95 (978-0-557-63648-8(5)) Lulu Pr., Inc.

Muller, Seth. Keepers of the WindClaw Chronicles: The Day of Storms, 3 vols., Vol. 2. Dubay, Tayloe, ed. Whitethorne, Bahe, Jr., illus. 2nd ed. 2010. 224p. (J). pap. 12.95 (978-1-893354-10-4(5)) Salina Bookshelf Inc.

—Keepers of the WindClaw Chronicles: The Mockingbird's Manual. Tayloe, McConnell Dubay, ed. Whitethorne, Bahe, Jr., illus. 2009. (ENG.). 128p. (J). (gr. 4-7). pap. 12.95 (978-1-893354-04-3(0)) Salina Bookshelf Inc.

Mulligan, Andy. Return to Ribblestrop. 2016. (Ribblestrop Ser.). (ENG., Illus.). 352p. (J). (gr. 3-7). 17.99 (978-1-4424-9907-2(9), Beach Lane Bks.) Beach Lane Bks.

—Ribblestrop. (Ribblestrop Ser.). (ENG., Illus.). (J). (gr. 3-7). 2016. 400p. pap. 7.99 (978-1-4424-9905-8(2)) 2014. 384p. 16.99 (978-1-4424-9904-1(4)) Beach Lane Bks. (Beach Lane Bks.).

—Ribblestrop Forever! 2016. (Ribblestrop Ser.). (ENG., Illus.). 320p. (J). (gr. 3-7). 16.99 (978-1-4424-9910-2(9), Beach Lane Bks.) Beach Lane Bks.

Mullin, Michael & Skewes, John. Larry Gets Lost in the Twin Cities. Skewes, John, illus. 2012. (Larry Gets Lost Ser.). (ENG., Illus.). 32p. (J). (gr. -1-2). 17.99 (978-1-57061-754-6(6), Little Bigfoot) Sasquatch Bks.

Mullins, Norman D. Mountain Boy: The Adventures of Orion Saddler. 2004. 104p. (YA). per. 9.95 (978-0-9724867-4-3(7)) Woodland Pr., LLC.

Mullins, Rebecca. Tristan, 1 vol. 2009. 23p. pap. 24.95 (978-1-60672-257-2(3)) America Star Bks.

Mulrain, Sabrina. A Prince's Happy Ever After. 2011. 40p. pap. 24.95 (978-1-4560-3251-7(8)) America Star Bks.

—Ultimate Dreamer. 2011. 44p. pap. 24.95 (978-1-4560-3670-6(X)) America Star Bks.

Mulvihill, Tina. Ollie's Geometry Adventure. 2008. 24p. pap. 24.95 (978-1-60441-299-4(2)) America Star Bks.

Mumford, Carole. Caribbean Cruise Summer Vacation: A Magnificent Six Adventure, 1 vol. 2009. 96p. pap. 16.95 (978-1-61546-760-0(2)) PublishAmerica, Inc.

—Christmas Vacation in Colorado: A Magnificent Six Adventure, 1 vol. 2009. 75p. pap. 19.95 (978-1-60749-231-3(8)) America Star Bks.

—The Magnificent: Their Yellowstone Adventure, 1 vol. 2009. 73p. pap. 19.95 (978-1-60813-595-0(0)) America Star Bks.

Mun-Ensor, Michelle. The Angel's Garden. 2011. 48p. pap. 24.95 (978-1-4560-5596-7(8)) America Star Bks.

Munch, Donna. Dark Tales of the Tower. 2005. (J). pap. 9.95 (978-1-932196-71-9(4)) WordWright.biz, Inc.

Munday, Dj. The Secret Dummy of Joshua Bean. 2008. 84p. pap. (978-1-84923-029-2(3)) YouWriteOn.

Mundy, Charlene & Chapline, Jo. David's Donkey Tales. 2007. 73p. pap. 12.50 (978-0-615-16825-8(6)) Knee-High Adventures.

Mundy, Talbot. For the Salt He Had Eaten. 2004. reprint ed. pap. 1.99 (978-1-4192-2024-1(1)); pap. 15.95 (978-1-4191-2024-4(7)) Kessinger Publishing, LLC.

Munro, Ken. Fireball. 2003. (Sammy & Brian Mystery Ser.: No. 15). (J). pap. 6.95 (978-1-930353-84-8(7)) Masthof Pr.

Munro, Rosemary. The Adventures of Fidget the Monkey. 2017. (ENG., Illus.). (J). (gr. 1-2). pap. **(978-1-78222-509-6(9))** Paragon Publishing, Rothersthorpe.

Munroe, Kirk. Flamingo Feather. 2006. 120p. 22.95 (978-1-59818-510-2(1)) Aegypan.

Munsch, Robert. Murmel, Murmel, Murmel. Martchenko, Michael, illus. 2014. (ENG.). 26p. (J). (gr. -1 — 1). bds. 7.99 (978-1-55451-656-8(0), 9781554516568) Annick Pr., Ltd. CAN. Dist: Publishers Group West (PGW).

Munsell, Jill. What a Day for a Parade. 2010. 48p. pap. 19.95 (978-1-4389-9080-4(4)) AuthorHouse.

Munves, James. We Were There with Lewis & Clark. 2006. 128p. (J). pap. 13.95 (978-0-9779000-0-8(2)) American Home-School Publishing, LLC.

Munzel, Alexander. Where the Holy Thistle Blooms. 2003. (Illus.). 98p. (J). per. (978-0-9672566-1-0(5)) Technical Software, Inc.

Murdock, Catherine Gilbert. Wisdom's Kiss. 2013. (ENG.). 320p. (YA). (gr. 7). pap. 8.99 (978-0-547-85540-0(0)) Houghton Mifflin Harcourt Publishing Co.

—Wisdom's Kiss: A Thrilling & Romantic Adventure, Incorporating Magic, Villany, & a Cat. 2011. (ENG.). 304p. (YA). (gr. 7). 16.99 (978-0-547-56687-0(5)) Houghton Mifflin Harcourt Publishing Co.

Murguia, Bethanie Deeney. I Feel Five! Murguia, Bethanie Deeney, illus. 2014. (ENG., Illus.). 32p. (J). (gr. -1-3). 14.99 (978-0-7636-6291-2(7)) Candlewick Pr.

Murphy, Bonnie S. The Puzzle Piece Thief. 2010. 28p. pap. 15.99 (978-1-4500-2649-9(4)) Xlibris Corp.

Murphy, Breena. The Fairy Seekers - the Sand Fairy. Waid, Sara Joyce & Waid, Antoinette M., illus. l.t. ed. 2006. 284p. (J). 24.95 (978-0-9788010-1-4(5)) Edes Publishing Co.

—The Fairy Seekers - the Sand Fairy, 1. Waid, Sara J. & Waid, Antoinette M., illus. l.t. ed. 2006. 284p. (J). per. 14.95 (978-0-9788010-0-7(8)) Edes Publishing Co.

Murphy, Harriet. Diego in Action! Follow the Reader Level 2. 2007. (Go, Diego, Go! Ser.). (ENG., Illus.). 24p. (J). (gr. -1-2). 24.99 (978-1-4169-4993-0(3), Simon Scribbles) Simon Scribbles.

Murphy, Jill. Lista para Salir.Tr. of All in One Piece. (SPA., Illus.). (J). (gr. k-2). (978-84-350-9192-3(9), EH0377) Edhasa ESP. Dist: Lectorum Pubns., Inc.

Murphy, Peg. I Can Do Anything. l.t. ed. 2006. (ENG., Illus.). 28p. per. 9.95 (978-1-4327-0175-8(4)) Outskirts Pr., Inc.

Murphy, Stuart J. & Murphy. Treasure Map. Tusa, Tricia, illus. 2004. (MathStart 3 Ser.). (ENG.). 40p. (J). (gr. 2-18). pap. 5.99 (978-0-06-446738-4(3)) HarperCollins Pubs.

Murphy, T. M. Saving Santa's Seals. Taylor, Adam, illus. 2009. (LeapKids Ser.). (ENG.). 170p. (J). (gr. 1-5). pap. 10.95 (978-0-9815148-8-8(X)) Leapfrog Pr.

Murphy, Thomas. Island Boy. 2007. 124p. per. 19.95 (978-1-4241-7940-4(8)) America Star Bks.

Murphy, Timothy. Sugarbowl. 2013. 140p. pap. 11.95 (978-1-62857-019-9(9), Strategic Bk. Publishing) Strategic Book Publishing & Rights Agency (SBPRA).

Murphy, Tracy. Everyday Adventures with Mickey & Seed. 2011. (Illus.). 68p. (gr. -1). pap. 25.80 (978-1-4567-7351-9(8)) AuthorHouse.

Murray, C. J. Shayna Gladstone: In Search of the Scientist. 2011. 148p. 22.95 (978-1-4502-8992-4(4)); pap. 12.95 (978-1-4502-8990-0(8)) iUniverse, Inc.

Murray, Caryn Eve. Philomena's Homecoming: The (mostly) true story of a New York prairie dog's search for a Family. 2010. 48p. pap. 8.95 (978-1-4502-2769-8(4)) iUniverse, Inc.

Murray, George. The Tales of Molly Brand & MacNessie. 2008. 70p. pap. 14.95 (978-1-4092-3724-2(9)) Lulu Pr., Inc.

Murray, Helen. Awesome Adventures. 2013. (DK Readers Ser.). (ENG.). 32p. (J). (gr. 1-3). 14.99 (978-1-4654-1696-4(X), DK Children) Dorling Kindersley Publishing, Inc.

—Calling All Master Builders!, Level 1. 2013. (DK Readers Ser.). (ENG.). 32p. (J). (gr. 2-4). pap. 3.99 (978-1-4654-1697-1(8), DK Children) Dorling Kindersley Publishing, Inc.

Murray, Regina Waldron. The Very Exciting Train Ride: An Adventure. 2006. (J). per. 15.95 (978-0-9664042-1-0(1)) Murray, Regina Waldron.

Murray, Rosalie. Bobby & Bun Bun's Afternoon Adventure. Swope, Brenda, illus. 2012. 32p. pap. 24.95 (978-1-4560-5090-0(7)) America Star Bks.

Murray, Scott. Granny's Christmas Blunder. 2012. 28p. pap. 18.00 (978-1-4772-0990-5(5)) AuthorHouse.

Murrell, Belinda. The Locket of Dreams. (ENG.). 288p. (J). (gr. 4-7). 2015. pap. 12.99 (978-0-85798-695-5(3)) 2nd ed. 2013. 17.99 (978-0-85798-021-2(1)) Random Hse. Australia AUS. Dist: Independent Pubs. Group.

Murrow, Vita. The Whale. Murrow, Ethan, illus. 2016. (ENG.). 32p. (J). (gr. -1-3). 17.99 (978-0-7636-7965-1(8), Templar) Candlewick Pr.

Murtagh, Ciaran. Blackbeard & the Monster of the Deep. Aardvark, Nathan, illus. 2014. (Collins Big Cat Progress Ser.). (ENG.). 32p. (J). (gr. 2-3). pap. 7.99 (978-0-00-751931-6(1)) HarperCollins Pubs. Ltd. GBR. Dist: Independent Pubs. Group.

Muschinske, Victoria. Honey Pie Pony's Book: A Fun with Fillies Adventure. 2005. (Illus.). 39p. (978-0-439-70471-7(5)) Scholastic, Inc.

Muschla, Gary Robert. Crusader. 2006. (YA). pap. (978-0-88092-491-7(8)) Royal Fireworks Publishing Co.

—The Sword & the Cross. 2009. (YA). lib. bdg. (978-0-88092-471-9(3)) Royal Fireworks Publishing Co.

Muscia, Marilena Carrubba. Misses Cowy to the Rescue. 2011. 24p. (gr. -1). 12.99 (978-1-4567-3582-1(9)) AuthorHouse.

Musco, Rance. The Hunt: Adventures of Austin & Rance. 2010. 28p. pap. 14.95 (978-1-4490-5838-8(8)) AuthorHouse.

Muse, Ludi. My Day at the Park. 2007. 32p. per. 13.95 (978-1-4259-6563-1(6)) AuthorHouse.

Musgrove, Marianne. Forget-Me-Not Fairy Treasury. MacCarthy, Patricia, illus. 2013. (ENG.). 192p. (J). (gr. -1-3). (978-1-74308-536-3(2)) Hinkler Bks. Pty, Ltd.

Mussi, Sarah. The Door of No Return. (ENG.). 400p. (YA). (gr. 7). 2009. pap. 10.99 (978-1-4169-6825-2(3)) 2008. 17.99 (978-1-4169-1550-8(8)) McElderry, Margaret K. Bks. (McElderry, Margaret K. Bks.).

The Mutant Race. 2003. (J). per. (978-1-57657-865-0(8)) Paradise Pr., Inc.

Mutcherson, Toni. The Adventures of Jett Antoinette: Where Does Time Go? 2013. 24p. pap. 15.99 (978-1-4797-8161-4(4)) Xlibris Corp.

Mutchnick, Brenda & Casden, Ron. A Noteworthy Tale. Penney, Ian, illus. 2004. 30p. (J). (gr. k-4). reprint ed. 19.00 (978-0-7567-7654-1(6)) DIANE Publishing Co.

Mutrie, Matthew. Brady O'Brian Saves the Day. Morales, Andrew, illus. 2007. 37p. pap. 24.95 (978-1-4241-9009-6(6)) America Star Bks.

Mwangi, Meja. The Mzungu Boy, 1 vol. 2006. (ENG.). 152p. (J). (gr. 4-7). pap. 8.95 (978-0-88899-664-0(0)) Groundwood Bks. CAN. Dist: Publishers Group West (PGW).

My Day- Pillow Fight. 2003. (J). per. (978-1-57657-159-0(9)) Paradise Pr., Inc.

Mydin, Liza. The Three Village Boys of Al Haidar: The First Adventure. 2012. 20p. pap. 16.00 (978-1-4669-2792-6(5)) Trafford Publishing.

Myers, Benjamin J. Blood Alchemy. 2010. (ENG.). 384p. (978-1-84255-641-2(X)) Orion Publishing Group, Ltd. GBR. Dist: Hachette Bk. Group.

Myers, Bill. The Chamber of Lies, 1 vol. 2009. (Elijah Project Ser.). (ENG.). 128p. (J). (gr. 4-7). pap. 6.99 (978-0-310-71196-4(7)) Zonderkidz.

—The Enemy Closes In, 1 vol. 2009. (Elijah Project Ser.). (ENG.). 128p. (J). (gr. 4-7). pap. 6.99 (978-0-310-71194-0(0)) Zonderkidz.

—My Life As a Prickly Porcupine from the Planet Pluto, 1 vol. 2004. (Incredible Worlds of Wally Mcdoogle Ser.: 23). (ENG.). 128p. pap. 6.99 (978-0-8499-5994-3(2)) Nelson, Thomas Inc.

Myers, Bill & Riordan, James. On the Run, 1 vol. 2009. (Elijah Project Ser.). (ENG.). 128p. (J). (gr. 4-7). pap. 4.99 (978-0-310-71193-3(2)) Zonderkidz.

Myers, Janice Limb. Carolee Sings in the Christmas Choir: A Christmas Story for Children of All Ages. Velica, Teodora, illus. 2013. 48p. pap. 13.77 (978-0-9897175-1-9(8)) LJM Publishing.

Myers, Marion P. Never That! Whatever... Duh, get with the program & follow the Rules! 2011. 40p. pap. 21.99 (978-1-4568-8561-8(8)) Xlibris Corp.

Myers, Robin. Pinky Rabbit Learns to Share. 2008. 20p. pap. 24.95 (978-1-60703-937-2(0)) America Star Bks.

Myers, Roger. Oh, What a Joy It Is! An Adventure. 2011. (ENG.). 36p. pap. 7.00 (978-1-4679-0636-4(0)) CreateSpace Independent Publishing Platform.

Myhre, J. A. A Bird, a Girl, & a Rescue. 2016. (Illus.). ix, 133p. (J). pap. 15.99 (978-1-942572-69-5(7)) New Growth Pr.

Myhre, Jennifer. A Chameleon, a Boy, & a Quest. 2015. (ENG., Illus.). 160p. (J). pap. 15.99 (978-1-942572-08-4(5)) New Growth Pr.

Myklusch, Matt. The End of Infinity. 2013. (Jack Blank Adventure Ser.: 3). (ENG., Illus.). 416p. (J). (gr. 3-7). pap. 8.99 (978-1-4169-9568-5(4), Aladdin) Simon & Schuster Children's Publishing.

—The End of Infinity. 2012. (Jack Blank Adventure Ser.: 3). (ENG., Illus.). 416p. (J). (gr. 3-7). 16.99 (978-1-4169-9567-8(6), Simon & Schuster/Paula Wiseman Bks.) Simon & Schuster/Paula Wiseman Bks.

—The Jack Blank Collection: The Accidental Hero; The Secret War; The End of Infinity. 2013. (Jack Blank Adventure Ser.: Bks. 1-3). (ENG., Illus.). 1472p. (J). (gr. 3-7). pap. 23.99 (978-1-4424-8718-5(6), Aladdin) Simon & Schuster Children's Publishing.

Myracle, Lauren. Rodney's SsssSolution - Big Book. Renooy, "Cosmic" Ray, illus. 2003. (J). spiral bd. (978-1-884272-88-2(6)) Premier Schl. Agendas.

Mysterious Chills & Thrills: 10 creepy, strange, adventurous short stories for kids to tickle the imagination. 2004. (J). per. 6.95 (978-0-9749013-0-5(X)) LH Pubns. & Productions.

Mystery of the Maya: Choose Your Own Adventure. 2004. per. 5.95 (978-0-9745356-3-0(X)) Chooseco LLC.

Mystery on Church Hill. 2013. 196p. (J). pap. 8.99 (978-0-9893414-3-1(7)) MyBoys3 Pr.

Mystic. Talon Hawke: A Journey Through Darkness. 2007. 228p. per. 15.95 (978-0-595-46386-2(X)) iUniverse, Inc.

Mystical World of Nebe: Sky of Dreams. 2006. (YA). 14.95 (978-0-9779369-0-8(2)) Adamson, Mac.

Nabors, V. L. Mad Craze Middle School; the Case of the Crumpled Balls. 2010. 215p. pap. 16.95 (978-0-557-44140-2(4)) Lulu Pr., Inc.

Naderi, Babak. The Adventures of Captain Zero. 2009. 16p. pap. 9.00 (978-1-4251-8693-7(9)) Trafford Publishing.

Nadja. Cinco Deditos. 2004. (SPA.). 12p. (gr. -1-k). bds. 16.99 (978-84-8470-019-7(4)) Corimbo, Editorial S.L. ESP. Dist: Lectorum Pubns., Inc.

Nagaraj, Josephine. Bubble Power! 2016. (Step into Reading Level 2 Ser.). lib. bdg. 14.75 (978-0-606-38478-0(2)) Turtleback Bks.

Nagy, Jennifer. Goats in Coats. Broughton, Ilona & Szigyarto, Cynthia, illus. 2009. 20p. pap. 12.99 (978-1-4389-6586-4(9)) AuthorHouse.

Nagy, Jim. Daniel the Spaniel- Let's Go Home! 2010. 36p. (J). pap. 15.95 (978-1-4327-5310-8(X)) Outskirts Pr., Inc.

Nahorniak, Mike. Kalico Jack. 2016. (ENG., Illus.). (J). 16.95 **(978-1-5069-0333-0(9))**; pap. 14.95 **(978-1-5069-0290-6(1))** First Edition Design eBook Publishing.

Naidoo, V. J. The Castle on Daisy Drive. 2017. (ENG.). 106p. pap. 13.95 **(978-1-78629-989-5(5)**, 77820b98-3ccd-4538-b45b-503435f53d78) Austin, Stan AUS. Dist: Bookmasters Distribution.

Naliboff, Jane. The Only One Club. Hopkins, Jeff, illus. 2013. (ENG.). 32p. (J). (gr. k-2). 6.95 (978-1-936261-30-7(8)) Flashlight Pr.

Nambiar, Vinesh. Adventures in Human Values - Series 1: Courage, Kindness, Forgiveness, Teamwork, Compassion, Listening, Caring, Self-Confidence, Sharing. 2007. (Illus.). (J). pap. 9.99 (978-0-9798986-0-0(9)) Human Values 4 Kids Foundation, The.

—Adventures in Human Values - Series 4: Strength, Bravery, Gratitude, Acceptance, Discipline, Happiness, Cooperation, Hope, Self-Control. Raite, Albert Lalmuanpuia, illus. 2012. (J). pap. 9.99 (978-0-9798986-3-1(3)) Human Values 4 Kids Foundation, The.

Nanavati, Daniel. Midrak Earthshaker. Pryor, John-Thomas, illus. 2013. 132p. pap. (978-1-908867-06-3(X)) FootSteps Pr.

Nancy St. Paul-Martin. Go to the Nurse: Peanut Puffs & Snicker-Doodles. 2009. 28p. pap. 15.49 (978-1-4389-7653-2(4)) AuthorHouse.

Napoli, Linda. Sailing Away on a Windy Day. 2012. 24p. pap. 17.32 (978-1-4797-2962-3(0)) Xlibris Corp.

Naranjo, K. L. The Adventures of Ariel & Eden & the Lost Treasures of Zion. 2013. 50p. pap. 10.95 (978-1-62516-835-1(7), Strategic Bk. Publishing) Strategic Book Publishing & Rights Agency (SBPRA).

Narayan, Natasha. The Shaman's Secret. 2011. (Kit Salter Adventures Ser.). (ENG., Illus.). 272p. (J). (gr. 4-6). pap. 8.99 (978-1-84916-555-6(6)) Quercus GBR. Dist: Hachette Bk. Group.

Narine, Vidya D. Kari. 2011. 66p. 24.99 (978-1-4568-5348-8(1)); pap. 15.99 (978-1-4568-5347-1(3)) Xlibris Corp.

Narsimhan, Mahtab. The Deadly Conch: Tara Trilogy. 2011. (Tara Trilogy Ser.: 3). (ENG.). 288p. (YA). (gr. 9). pap. 12.99 (978-1-55488-794-1(1)) Dundurn CAN. Dist: Ingram Publisher Services.

—The Silver Anklet. 2009. (Tara Trilogy Ser.: 2). (ENG.). 272p. (YA). (gr. 5-18). pap. 10.99 (978-1-55488-445-2(4), Dundurn Pr.) Dundurn CAN. Dist: Ingram Publisher Services.

Narvick, the Whark (or a Shwale) 2003. (J). 8.95 (978-0-9729703-1-0(2)) Kidderature Publishing.

Nash, David. A Pete & Charley Adventure: The Sheri. 2005. 131p. pap. 24.95 (978-1-4137-9449-6(1)) PublishAmerica, Inc.

Nash, Ronza R. The Chocolate Wonders: The Adventures of Lila & Lester. 2011. 36p. pap. 16.86 (978-1-4634-1619-5(9)) AuthorHouse.

Nash, Susan Smith. The Good Deeds Society: Family Plot. 2008. (Illus.). 220p. (YA). pap. 18.00 (978-0-9797573-2-7(0)) Texture Pr.

Nash, Tim. The Club. 2009. 112p. pap. 12.49 (978-1-4490-2087-3(9)) AuthorHouse.

Nathoo, Aalaynah. The World above Us!!! 2012. 16p. pap. 15.99 (978-1-4772-3222-4(2)) AuthorHouse.

Natl Children's Book & Literacy Alliance. The Exquisite Corpse Adventure. 2011. (ENG., Illus.). 288p. (J). (gr. 4-7). pap. 7.99 (978-0-7636-5773-4(5)) Candlewick Pr.

Naughton, Colin Charles. Not So Spooky Book Series: Book One. 2012. 28p. pap. 24.95 (978-1-4626-7856-3(4)) America Star Bks.

Naylor, Phyllis Reynolds. Emily & Jackson Hiding Out. (ENG.). 176p. (J). (gr. 2-5). 2013. 6.99 (978-0-375-87185-6(3), Yearling) 2012. (Illus.). 14.99 (978-0-385-74097-5(2), Delacorte Bks. for Young Readers) Random Hse. Children's Bks.

—Going Where It's Dark. 2017. lib. bdg. 18.40 **(978-0-606-39872-5(4))** Turtleback Bks.

—The Grand Escape. Daniel, Alan, illus. 2005. (ENG.). 160p. (J). (gr. 3-7). pap. 7.99 (978-0-689-87407-9(3), Atheneum Bks. for Young Readers) Simon & Schuster Children's Publishing.

—The Healing of Texas Jake. Daniel, Alan, illus. 2005. (ENG.). 128p. (J). (gr. 3-7). pap. 6.99 (978-0-689-87406-2(5), Atheneum Bks. for Young Readers) Simon & Schuster Children's Publishing.

—It's Not Like I Planned It This Way: Including Alice; Alice on Her Way; Alice in the Know. 2010. (Alice Ser.). (ENG.). 816p. (YA). (gr. 7). pap. 12.99 (978-1-4424-1720-5(X), Atheneum Bks. for Young Readers) Simon & Schuster Children's Publishing.

—Polo's Mother. Daniel, Alan, illus. 2006. (ENG.). 176p. (J). (gr. 3-7). pap. 6.99 (978-0-689-87404-8(9), Atheneum Bks. for Young Readers) Simon & Schuster Children's Publishing.

—Roxie & the Hooligans. Boiger, Alexandra, illus. 2007. 115p. (gr. 2-5). 16.00 (978-0-7569-8284-3(7)) Perfection Learning Corp.

—Roxie & the Hooligans. Boiger, Alexandra, illus. (ENG.). 128p. (J). 2007. (gr. 3-5). pap. 6.99 (978-1-4169-0244-7(9), Simon & Schuster/Paula Wiseman Bks.) 2006. (gr. 2-5). 17.99 (978-1-4169-0243-0(0), Atheneum Bks. for Young Readers) Simon & Schuster Children's Publishing.

Nazarian, Leslie. Orelda & Corelda's Ocean Voyage. 2007. 52p. (J). 15.94 (978-1-4116-2373-6(8)) Lulu Pr., Inc.

Neal-Bailey, Ashley L. I Don't Want To. 2007. 20p. per. 24.95 (978-1-4241-8928-1(4)) America Star Bks.

Neal, Terry L. The Find It Club. 2007. 80p. per. 19.95 (978-1-4241-7490-4(2)) America Star Bks.

Neale, J. B. In the Shadow of the Guillotine. 2008. 180p. pap. 13.95 (978-1-4092-0391-9(3)) Lulu Pr., Inc.

Neale, Jonathan. Himalaya. 2004. 160p. (J). (gr. 5-9). 16.00 (978-0-618-55203-0(0)) Houghton Mifflin Harcourt Trade & Reference Pubs.

Neeck, Alessa. Bella Bunhead. 2013. 34p. pap. 9.99 (978-0-9894402-0-2(6)) Bella & Bruno Bks.

Neff, Ethel Maxine. Packy: The Runaway Elephant. 2004. (Illus.). 39p. (J). 5.99 (978-0-8163-2061-5(6)) Pacific Pr. Publishing Assn.

Neighbors, Jolene. Nobody's Dog. 2010. 107p. pap. 14.95 (978-1-4327-5957-5(4)) Outskirts Pr., Inc.

Neil, Deanna. The Land of Curiosities (Book 2)) Lost in Yellowstone, 1872-1873. 2009. 320p. (J). pap. 12.95 (978-0-9798800-2-5(5)) EcoSeekers, The.

Neilson, G. E. F. Cosmic Aviators - Book 1 - Flight Edition. 2013. 288p. pap. (978-0-9576132-5-6(3)) Buzzword Pr.

—Cosmic Aviators - Nathaniel's 1st Adventure. 2013. 248p. (978-0-9576132-4-9(5)); 332p. pap. (978-0-9576132-0-1(2)) Buzzword Pr.

Neiman, Jahcolyn Russell. Kekula. 2011. 32p. pap. 13.99 (978-1-4520-8086-4(0)) AuthorHouse.

Neimark, Susie. The Adventures of Sunny & the Chocolate Dog: Sunny & the Chocolate Dog Go to the Beach. Hammerstrom, Kent, illus. 2003. per. (978-0-9725945-1-6(5)) Sunny & The Chocolate Dog, LLC.

—The Adventures of Sunny & the Chocolate Dog: Sunny & the Chocolate Dog Go to the Doctor. Hammerstrom, Kent, illus. 2003. per. (978-0-9725945-2-3(3)) Sunny & The Chocolate Dog, LLC.

—The Adventures of Sunny & the Chocolate Dog: Sunny Meets Her Baby Sister. Hammerstrom, Kent, illus. 2003. per. (978-0-9725945-0-9(7)) Sunny & The Chocolate Dog, LLC.

Nekrasov, Andrei. The Adventures of Captain Vrungel. Kay, Nicole, tr. from ENG. 2006. (RUS.). (J). (978-0-9754433-1-6(3), Language Transformer Bks.) Velichko, Vera.

Nelson, Carmen R. Jacob & Katie in Japan: The Adventures of Tcks in a New Home. 2013. 26p. pap. 13.95 (978-1-935986-38-6(4)) Liberty University Press.

Nelson, Gail M. & Nelson, Katie M. Go Eat, Pete. Nelson, Gail M., illus. 2013. (Illus.). 32p. pap. 9.99 (978-1-936499-05-2(3)) Jewel Publishing LLC.

Nelson, James Gary. Dientecito y la Placa Peligros. Bumstead, Debbie, illus. 2011. 16p. pap. 9.95 (978-1-61633-132-0(1)) Guardian Angel Publishing, Inc.

—Smileytooth & Bushwack Plaque. Bumstead, Debbie, illus. 2009. 16p. pap. 9.95 (978-1-61633-009-5(0)) Guardian Angel Publishing, Inc.

—Smileytooth & the Plaque Attack. Bumstead, Debbie, illus. 2008. 20p. pap. 10.95 (978-1-935137-48-1(4)) Guardian Angel Publishing, Inc.

Nelson, Jim. Crosstown Crush. 2005. 82p. Vol. 1, Bk. 1. (YA). pap. 9.00 (978-1-4116-5266-8(5)) Vol. 1,Bk. 2. pap. 9.00 (978-1-4116-6654-2(2)) Lulu Pr., Inc.

Nelson, Lori. Hillary's BIG Business Adventure. 2008. (Illus.). 32p. (J). (gr. -1-3). 16.95 (978-0-9794171-0-8(4), Adventures of Hillary, The) Nelson Publishing, LLC.

Nelson, Peter. Creature Keepers & the Burgled Blizzard-Bristles. Rao, Rohitash, illus. 2016. (Creature Keepers Ser.: 3). 336p. (J). (gr. 3-7). 12.99 (978-0-06-223647-0(4)) HarperCollins Pubs.

—Herbert's Wormhole: AeroStar & the 3 1/2-Point Plan of Vengeance. Rao, Rohitash, illus. 2014. (Herbert's Wormhole Ser.: 3). (ENG.). 368p. (J). (gr. 3-7). pap. 6.99 (978-0-06-201221-0(5)) HarperCollins Pubs.

Nelson, Sean. Bungles Does the Bunny Op. 2012. 36p. pap. 16.95 (978-1-4575-1106-6(1)) Dog Ear Publishing, LLC.

—Bungles Loses His Marbles. 2008. 36p. pap. 16.95 (978-1-59858-605-3(X)) Dog Ear Publishing, LLC.

Nelson, Sheila K. The Backpack Bears' Adventure: Friendship. 2009. 24p. pap. 16.50 (978-1-4490-0554-2(3)) AuthorHouse.

Nelson, Sybil. Priscilla the Great: The Kiss of Life. 2013. 218p. 17.99 (978-1-939947-01-7(4)) Little Prince Publishing.

Nelson, Theresa. Devil Storm. 2016. (ENG.). 228p. (J). (gr. 6-11). pap. 12.99 **(978-1-5040-4071-6(6))** Open Road Integrated Media, Inc.

Nelson, Valerie. I Can Do It Myself! 2008. (Illus.). 20p. (J). pap. (978-0-9794171-1-5(2)) Nelson Publishing, LLC.

Nemec, Thomas F., creator. Owenopolis: A New Childrens Book, Created by Thomas Nemec-N. Y. C. 2007. (J). lib. bdg. 15.00 (978-0-9791612-0-9(7)) Goon Dog Publishing.

Neno, Michael. The Children's Magical Adventure: 1 the Rescue. 2011. (Illus.). 48p. (gr. -1). pap. 19.59 (978-1-4567-7887-3(0)) AuthorHouse.

Nesbit, E. Harding's Luck. 2006. 164p. (gr. 4-7). per. 13.95 (978-1-59818-878-3(X)); 25.95 (978-1-59818-170-8(X)) Aegypan.

—In Homespun. 2007. 136p. 25.95 (978-1-4218-3841-0(9)); per. 10.95 (978-1-4218-3941-7(5)) 1st World Publishing, Inc. (1st World Library - Literary Society).

—New Treasure Seekers. 2009. 172p. (gr. 4-7). 25.95 (978-1-60664-665-6(6)); pap. 13.95 (978-1-60664-293-1(6)) Rodgers, Alan Bks.

—The Phoenix & the Carpet. 2009. 156p. pap. 4.95 (978-1-60459-693-9(7)) Wilder Pubns., Corp.

—The Story of the Amulet. 2009. 176p. (gr. -1-7). pap. 4.95 (978-1-60459-694-6(5)) Wilder Pubns., Corp.

—The Story of the Treasure Seekers. 2009. 128p. (gr. 4-7). pap. 5.50 (978-1-60459-695-3(3)) Wilder Pubns., Corp.

—These Little Ones. 2006. 132p. per. 10.95 (978-1-59818-961-2(1)); 24.95 (978-1-59818-175-3(0)) Aegypan.

—Wet Magic. 2006. 188p. (gr. -1-7). per. 13.95 (978-1-59818-932-2(8)); 26.95 (978-1-59818-174-6(2)) Aegypan.

—Wet Magic. 2006. 200p. (gr. -1-7). per. (978-1-84350-095-7(7)) Soft Editions Ltd.

—The Wouldbegoods. 2007. 272p. per. 13.95 (978-1-4218-3947-9(4), 1st World Library - Literary Society) 1st World Publishing, Inc.

—The Wouldbegoods. 2007. (ENG.). 216p. pap. 20.99 (978-1-4346-5229-4(7)); 240p. pap. 22.99 (978-1-4346-5230-0(0)) Creative Media Partners, LLC.

—The Wouldbegoods. l.t. ed. 2005. 428p. pap. (978-1-84637-208-7(9)) Echo Library.

—7 Books in 1 - "The Railway Children", "Five Children & It", "The Phoenix & the Carpet", "The Story of the Amulet", "The Story of the Treasure-Seekers", "The Would-Be-Goods" & "The Enchanted Castle" 2004. 472p. pap. (978-0-9548401-0-5(0)) Shoes & Ships & Sealing Wax Ltd.

Nesbø, Jo. Bubble in the Bathtub. Chace, Tara F., tr. Lowery, Mike, illus. 2011. (Doctor Proctor's Fart Powder Ser.). (ENG.). 448p. (J). (gr. 3-7). pap. 7.99 (978-1-4169-7975-3(1), Aladdin) Simon & Schuster Children's Publishing.

—Bubble in the Bathtub. Chace, Tara, tr. from NOR. Lowery, Mike, illus. 2011. (Doctor Proctor's Fart Powder Ser.). (ENG.). 432p. (J). (gr. 3-7). 17.99 (978-1-4169-7974-6(3), Aladdin) Simon & Schuster Children's Publishing.

—The Magical Fruit. 2014. (Doctor Proctor's Fart Powder Ser.). (ENG., Illus.). 320p. (J). (gr. 3-7). pap. 7.99 (978-1-4424-9343-8(7), Aladdin) Simon & Schuster Children's Publishing.

—The Magical Fruit. Chace, Tara F., tr. from NOR. Lowery, Mike, illus. 2013. (Doctor Proctor's Fart Powder Ser.). (ENG.). 320p. (J). (gr. 3-7). 17.99 (978-1-4424-9342-1(9), Aladdin) Simon & Schuster Children's Publishing.

—Silent (but Deadly) Night. Lowery, Mike, illus. 2017. (J). pap. **(978-1-5344-1000-8(7)**, Simon & Schuster/Paula Wiseman Bks.) Simon & Schuster/Paula Wiseman Bks.

Nesbø, Jo. Who Cut the Cheese? Chace, Tara F., tr. Lowery, Mike, illus. 2012. (Doctor Proctor's Fart Powder Ser.). (ENG.). 464p. (J). (gr. 3-7). pap. 7.99 (978-1-4424-3308-3(6), Aladdin) Simon & Schuster Children's Publishing.

—Who Cut the Cheese? Chace, Tara, tr. from NOR. Lowery, Mike, illus. 2012. (Doctor Proctor's Fart Powder Ser.). (ENG.). 464p. (J). (gr. 3-7). 17.99 (978-1-4424-3307-6(8), Aladdin) Simon & Schuster Children's Publishing.

Nestell, Mark. Gordon & the Magic Fishbowl, 1 vol. Daley-Prado, M. J., illus. 2010. 26p. pap. 24.95 (978-1-4489-8495-4(5)) America Star Bks.

Nettles, Sarah A. Benjamin, the Bully & the Butterfly. 2012. 24p. pap. 17.99 (978-1-4772-7195-7(3)) AuthorHouse.

Nettrour, Nelani. Banshees Bk. 2: Dragon Lands. Nettrour, Heather, illus. l.t. ed. 2003. 114p. (J). pap. 11.95 (978-1-932657-03-6(7)) Third Millennium Pubns.

—Nunkey's Adventures, Bk. 1. Nettrour, Autumn, illus. 2003. 70p. (J). pap. 11.95 (978-1-929381-17-3(4), Third Millennium Publishing) Sci Fi-Arizona, Inc.

—Sun Griffins: Dragonlands, Book 4. 2007. (Illus.). 190p. (J). pap. 16.95 (978-1-932657-90-6(8)) Third Millennium Pubns.

Neubert, Oliver. Chantel's Quest for the Enchanted Medallion. 2009. (Cozy Classics Ser.). (ENG., Illus.). 224p. (J). (gr. 3-6). 16.95 (978-1-897476-15-4(9)) Simply Read Bks. CAN. Dist: Ingram Publisher Services.

Neuenschwander, B. L. That's Not a Unicorn. 2013. 48p. pap. 16.00 (978-0-9827753-2-5(6)) Interdimensional Pr.

Neuman, Carolyn. Adventures with the Winglets. 2012. 134p. (-18). pap. 10.33 (978-1-4669-6753-3(6)) Trafford Publishing.

Neumann, Jeff. How Do You Do? 2005. 39p. 8.00 (978-1-4116-6201-8(6)) Lulu Pr., Inc.

Neuschwander, Angel & Johnston, Becky. Gretchen Asks, How Do Cars Work? 2009. 24p. pap. 12.99 (978-1-4389-2886-9(6)) AuthorHouse.

Nevins, Paul. Dante's War. 2003. 168p. (YA). pap. 12.95 (978-0-595-26743-9(2), Writers Club Pr.) iUniverse, Inc.

Newberry, Gabriel S. Elli & Gabe's Big Christmas Adventure. 2012. 20p. pap. 13.77 (978-1-4669-6941-4(5)) Trafford Publishing.

Newbigging, Robert Delford. Robert Rat Has A Problem: A Tale of Broccoli. 2010. 44p. pap. 16.99 (978-1-4520-2134-8(1)) AuthorHouse.

Newcomb, Ambrose. Flying the Coast Skyways or Jack Ralston. 2005. pap. 26.95 (978-1-4179-8975-1(0)) Kessinger Publishing, LLC.

Newcomb, Kristene. Molly Q's Trash Travels Through the Water Cycle. Paschall, Patricia, ed. Newcomb, Kristene, illus. 2007. (Illus.). 32p. (J). per. 8.00 (978-0-9760790-9-5(7)) Folsom Fallies Pr.

Newcomer, Carolyn. Barf's First Flight. Raschke, Andrea, illus. 2009. 40p. (J). 14.95 (978-0-9792583-8-1(3)) White Stag Pr.

Newland, James P. A Smile Says It All. 2009. 48p. pap. 17.49 (978-1-4490-3438-2(1)) AuthorHouse.

Newland, Trevor. The Scallywag Solution, 1 vol. 2014. (ENG., Illus.). 64p. (J). (gr. k-7). 15.95 (978-0-88962-990-5(0), 9780889629905) Mosaic Pr. CAN. Dist: Independent Pubs. Group.

Newman, C. Edward. The Little Leaguer Wore #7. 2008. 76p. pap. 19.95 (978-1-60563-347-3(X)) America Star Bks.

Newman, Samantha. Sammy Skizzors & the Rainbow Knight. 2010. 32p. 14.99 (978-1-4520-9976-7(6)) AuthorHouse.

Newsome, Eric. The Adventures of Eric: Starry Beginnings. 2009. 51p. pap. 14.95 (978-1-4327-4075-7(X)) Outskirts Pr., Inc.

Newsome, Richard. The Emerald Casket. Duddle, Jonny, illus. (Archer Legacy Ser.). (J). (gr. 3-7). 2012. 384p. pap. 6.99 (978-0-06-194493-2(9)) 2011. 368p. 16.99 (978-0-06-194492-5(0)) HarperCollins Pubs. (Waldon Pond Pr.).

—The Mask of Destiny. Duddle, Jonny, illus. 2013. 384p. (J). (gr. 3-7). pap. 6.99 (978-0-06-194495-6(5), Waldon Pond Pr.) HarperCollins Pubs.

Newton, Renae. Having Fun with Granny. 2010. 16p. 9.00 (978-1-4520-0000-8(X)) AuthorHouse.

Ngo, Lap. The Teaser Monster. Ngo, illus. 2012. 24p. (J). 11.99 (978-0-9838321-9-5(6)) Higher Ground Pr.

Nguy, Hoa X. The Bamboo Girl. 2007. 84p. (J). pap. 20.00 (978-0-8059-7562-8(4)) Dorrance Publishing Co., Inc.

Nguyen, Taohuu. Mighty Mite 2: Zoo Gone Wild. Nguyen, Taohuu, illus. 2007. (Illus.). (J). 14.95 (978-0-9788469-2-3(3)) Amazing Factory, The.

Nicholai, Rachel, et al. Bird Adventures. Nicholai, Rachel et al, illus. 2006. (Adventure Story Collection Ser.). 28p. (J). (gr. 2-6). pap. 10.00 (978-1-58084-246-4(1)) Lower Kuskokwim Schl. District.

Nicholas, Nicki. Peter & Lil's Summer Day Adventure. 2011. 24p. pap. 15.50 (978-1-4269-5358-3(5)) Trafford Publishing.

Nichols, C. D. Kids Courageous. 2010. 66p. pap. 9.99 (978-1-60911-809-9(X), Eloquent Bks.) Strategic Book Publishing & Rights Agency (SBPRA).

Nichols, Earline. Through the Eyes of Casey. 2012. 32p. pap. 21.99 (978-1-4797-1403-2(8)) Xlibris Corp.

Nichols, Niki. Your Karma, DeeDee. 2005. 141p. pap. 24.95 (978-1-4137-9690-2(7)) PublishAmerica, Inc.

Nichols, Willie Charles. The Adventures of Bo & His Pal Boboy. 2004. pap. 8.00 (978-0-8059-6175-1(5)) Dorrance Publishing Co., Inc.

Nicholson, Devon, et al. Fundi the Snail. 2008. 48p. pap. 26.50 (978-1-4357-1551-6(9)) Lulu Pr., Inc.

Nicholson, Melissa. Prissy & Pop - Big Day Out. Nicholson, Melissa, illus. 2016. (Illus.). 32p. (J). (gr. -1-3). 17.99 (978-0-06-243995-6(2)) HarperCollins Pubs.

Nicholson, Simon. The Demon Curse. 2015. (Young Houdini Ser.: 2). (ENG.). 240p. (J). (gr. 5-8). 15.99 (978-1-4926-0335-1(X), 9781492603351, Sourcebooks Jabberwocky) Sourcebooks, Inc.

—The Magician's Fire. (Young Houdini Ser.: 1). (ENG.). (J). 2015. 272p. (gr. 4-7). pap. 7.99 (978-1-4926-0949-0(8)) 2014. (Illus.). 240p. (gr. 5-8). 15.99 (978-1-4926-0332-0(5), 9781492603320, Sourcebooks Jabberwocky) Sourcebooks, Inc.

Nicholson, William. Noman: Book Three of the Noble Warriors. 2009. (Noble Warriors Ser.: 3). (ENG., Illus.). 368p. (J). (gr. 7). pap. 15.95 (978-0-15-206656-7(X)) Houghton Mifflin Harcourt Publishing Co.

—Noman: La Orden de los Guerreros Misticos. 2009. (SPA.). 352p. (YA). 18.95 (978-84-666-4051-0(7)) Ediciones B ESP. Dist: Spanish Pubs., LLC.

—El Silbador del Viento. Manero, Laura, tr. 3rd ed. 2005. (Escritura desatada Ser.). (SPA.). 336p. (J). (gr. 4-8). 17.95 (978-84-666-0279-2(8)) Ediciones B ESP. Dist: Independent Pubs. Group.

—Viento en Llamas: Son del Fuego. Manero Jiménez, Laura, tr. 2008. (Escritura desatada Ser.). (SPA.). 368p. 17.95 (978-84-666-1232-6(7)) Ediciones B ESP. Dist: Spanish Pubs., LLC.

Nick Barry. Revenge of Poseidon's Trident: An Ethan Sparks Adventure. 2010. 176p. 23.95 (978-1-4502-1090-4(2)); pap. 13.95 (978-1-4502-1088-1(0)) iUniverse, Inc.

Nick, Papa. Never Ending Stories. 2011. 44p. pap. 24.95 (978-1-4626-3792-8(2)) America Star Bks.

Nickel, Scott. Curse of the Red Scorpion, 1 vol. Harpster, Steve, illus. 2006. (Graphic Sparks Ser.). (ENG.). 40p. (gr. 1-3). per. 5.95 (978-1-59889-169-0(3), Graphic Sparks) Stone Arch Bks.

—Double Trouble, 1 vol. Harpster, Steve, illus. 2007. (Jimmy Sniffles Ser.). (ENG.). 40p. (gr. 1-3). lib. bdg. 23.99 (978-1-59889-314-4(9)); per. 5.95 (978-1-59889-411-0(0)) Stone Arch Bks. (Graphic Sparks).

—The Super-Powered Sneeze. Harpster, Steve, illus. 2007. (Graphic Sparks Ser.). (ENG.). 40p. (gr. 1-3). per. 5.95 (978-1-59889-409-7(9), Graphic Sparks) Stone Arch Bks.

Nickelodeon. PAW Patrol: the Night Before Christmas. 2016. (ENG.). 10p. (J). (gr. -1-k). bds. 8.99 (978-0-7944-3800-5(8), Reader's Digest Children's Bks.) Studio Fun International.

—Surf's Up, SpongeBob! 2013. (SpongeBob Squarepants 8X8 Ser.). lib. bdg. 14.75 (978-0-606-31934-8(4), Turtleback) Turtleback Bks.

Nickerson, Jane. Strands of Bronze & Gold. 2014. (ENG.). 368p. (YA). (gr. 9). pap. 9.99 (978-0-307-97599-7(1), Ember) Random Hse. Children's Bks.

Nickles, Clay & Ayres, Ella. Ali's Treasure. l.t. ed. 2005. (Illus.). 38p. (J). per. 16.95 (978-1-59879-006-1(4)) Lifevest Publishing, Inc.

Nicolas, Ron. Northern Lights: A Wilderness Adventure. 2005. 228p. (YA). per. 15.85 (978-0-9770043-2-4(5)) New Global Publishing.

Nicoll, David. Bean at the Beach. 2012. 24p. pap. 15.99 (978-1-4691-7042-8(6)) Xlibris Corp.

—Bean at the Fair. 2012. 24p. pap. 15.99 (978-1-4691-4706-2(8)) Xlibris Corp.

—Bean on the Farm. 2012. 24p. pap. 15.99 (978-1-4691-7837-0(0)) Xlibris Corp.

Nicolle, Ethan. Kill the Devil. 2008. (ENG., Illus.). 120p. (YA). pap. 10.95 (978-1-59362-099-8(3), 9781593620998) Slave Labor Bks.

Niedda, Jeshica. A Bird Name Baby Blue. 2012. 28p. pap. 19.99 (978-1-4772-7067-7(1)) AuthorHouse.

Nielsen, Jennifer A. Behind Enemy Lines. 2013. (Infinity Ring Ser.: 6). (ENG.). 192p. (J). (gr. 3-7). 12.99 (978-0-545-38701-9(9)) Scholastic, Inc.

—The Scourge. 2016. (ENG.). 368p. (J). (gr. 4-7). 16.99 (978-0-545-68245-9(2), Scholastic Pr.) Scholastic, Inc.

—The Shadow Throne. (ENG.). 336p. (J). 2015. (Ascendance Trilogy Ser.: 3). (gr. 3-7). pap. 7.99 (978-0-545-28418-9(X), Scholastic Paperbacks) 2014. (Ascendance Trilogy: Bk. 3). (gr. 5-9). 17.99 (978-0-545-28417-2(1), Scholastic Pr.) Scholastic, Inc.

—Wrath of the Storm. 2017. (Mark of the Thief Ser.: 3). (ENG.). 352p. (J). (gr. 4-7). 16.99 (978-0-545-56207-2(4), Scholastic Pr.) Scholastic, Inc.

Nielsen, Jon. Laney Gets Her Ridge. 2011. 32p. pap. 17.99 (978-1-4567-3618-7(3)) AuthorHouse.

Niemann, Christoph. The Pet Dragon: A Story about Adventure, Friendship, & Chinese Characters. Niemann, Christoph, illus. 2008. (ENG., Illus.). 40p. (J). (gr. -1-3). 16.99 (978-0-06-157776-5(6), Greenwillow Bks.) HarperCollins Pubs.

Nieting, Sherry. Adventures in Hope Forest: Isabelle's Search for God. 2011. 24p. pap. 10.95 (978-1-4497-2518-1(X), WestBow Pr.) Author Solutions, Inc.

Night & Day Studios. Peekaboo Barn Farm Day. Night & Day Studios, illus. 2017. (Peekaboo Ser.). (ENG., Illus.). 20p. (J). (— 1). bds. 7.99 (978-0-7636-7566-0(0), Candlewick Entertainment) Candlewick Pr.

Night Beast. 2005. (J). 4.95 (978-1-59792-018-6(5)) F.A.S.T. Learning LLC.

Night of the Cougar. 2005. (J). 4.95 (978-1-59792-014-8(2)) F.A.S.T. Learning LLC.

Night Visitor. 2005. (J). 4.95 (978-1-59792-019-3(3)) F.A.S.T. Learning LLC.

Nightingale, Clare Theresa. The Adventures of Fishkins & Pepperjacket. 2011. (Illus.). 220p. pap. 56.49 (978-1-4520-8803-7(9)) AuthorHouse.

Nightmare: Individual Title Six-Packs. (Action Packs Ser.). 120p. (gr. 3-5). 44.00 (978-0-7635-8392-7(8)) Rigby Education.

Nihart, Gene. The Fox Island Cup. 2004. (YA). pap. (978-1-59404-023-8(0)) Peanut Butter Publishing.

Nimmo, Jenny. The Box Boys & the Magic Shell. (Box Boys Ser.). (Illus.). 64p. (J). pap. (978-0-340-73290-8(3)) Hodder & Stoughton.

Nino, Jairo Aníbal. Zoro. 2003. (SPA., Illus.). 97p. (YA). (gr. -1-7). pap. (978-958-30-0291-5(7), PV4489) Panamericana Editorial COL. Dist: Lectorum Pubns., Inc.

The Ninth Life. 2005. (J). 4.95 (978-1-59792-017-9(7)) F.A.S.T. Learning LLC.

Nix, Garth. Across the Wall: A Tale of the Abhorsen & Other Stories. 2006. (ENG.). 432p. (YA). (gr. 8-12). pap. 8.99 (978-0-06-074715-2(3), HarperTeen) HarperCollins Pubs.

—A Confusion of Princes. 2012. 352p. (YA). (gr. 8). (ENG.). 17.99 (978-0-06-009694-6(2)); lib. bdg. 18.89 (978-0-06-009695-3(0)) HarperCollins Pubs.

—The Fall. 2004. (Seventh Tower Ser.). 195p. (gr. 4-7). 18.00 (978-0-7569-3516-0(4)) Perfection Learning Corp.

—Frogkisser! 2017. (ENG.). 384p. (J). (gr. 7). 18.99 (978-1-338-05208-4(X), Scholastic Pr.) Scholastic, Inc.

—Into Battle. 2004. (Seventh Tower Ser.). 201p. (gr. 3-7). 17.00 (978-0-7569-3515-3(6)) Perfection Learning Corp.

—Newt's Emerald. 2015. (ENG.). 304p. (YA). (gr. 8-12). 18.99 (978-0-06-236004-5(3)) HarperCollins Pubs.

Nix, Garth & Williams, Sean. The Missing. 2014. (Troubletwisters Ser.: 4). (ENG.). 320p. (J). (gr. 3-7). 17.99 (978-0-545-25900-2(2), Scholastic Pr.) Scholastic, Inc.

Nix, Pamela. Tummel the Tumbleweed. Barnes, Trisha, ed. Paulson, Arlie & Nix, Pamela, illus. 2011. 26p. (J). pap. 7.99 (978-0-9815914-9-0(3)) River Canyon Pr.

Nixon, Joan Lowery & Harwood, John. The Séance. 2004. (ENG.). 224p. (YA). (gr. 7-12). pap. 14.95

(978-0-15-205029-0(9)) Houghton Mifflin Harcourt Publishing Co.

Noble, Sarah. Hannah & Horatio Pea. 2006. (Illus.). 336p. pap. (978-1-84401-673-0(0)) Athena Pr.

Nocenti, Ann. Typhoid Mary, 4 vols. Romita, John, Jr., illus. 2003. (Daredevil Legends Ser.: Vol. 4). 224p. (YA). pap. 19.99 (978-0-7851-1041-5(0)) Marvel Worldwide, Inc.

Noel Paul, Chrisana B. The Crescent Street Crew: A novel teens & young adults can identify With. 2008. 69p. pap. 8.95 (978-1-4327-2466-5(5)) Outskirts Pr., Inc.

Nolan, Alan. Destination: Homicide! 2012. (ENG., Illus.). 80p. (J). pap. 12.95 (978-1-84717-256-3(3)) O'Brien Pr., Ltd., The IRL. Dist: Dufour Editions, Inc.

Noland, Charles. The Adventures of Drew & Ellie: The Daring Rescue. Moyer, Tom, illus. 2nd ed. 2006. 92p. (J). per. 7.95 (978-0-9789297-2-5(1)) TMD Enterprises.

—The Adventures of Drew & Ellie: The Magical Dress. Baker, Sherri, illus. 2006. (J). (978-0-9789297-1-8(3)); 2nd rev. ed. 84p. per. 7.95 (978-0-9789297-0-1(5)) TMD Enterprises.

Noland, Monica. Slide. 2006. 116p. pap. 19.95 (978-1-4241-4966-7(5)) PublishAmerica, Inc.

Nolen, Gale. Johnny, My Favorite Mouse. Cain, Doreyl Ammons, illus. 2007. 32p. (J). per. 18.95 (978-0-9753023-7-8(X)) Ammons Communications, Ltd.

Nolen, T. K. The Magical Fantastical Big Red Balloon. 2009. 20p. pap. 11.49 (978-1-4389-5183-6(3)) AuthorHouse.

Nooks, Nanny. Nina in the Forest of Faces. 2011. 46p. pap. 16.00 (978-1-61204-606-8(1), Strategic Bk. Publishing) Strategic Book Publishing & Rights Agency (SBPRA).

Noonan, Loretta. My Gramma Doesn't Knit. 2010. 24p. 12.99 (978-1-4520-5661-6(7)) AuthorHouse.

Nordqvist, Sven. The Camping Trip: The Adventures of Pettson & Findus. Nordqvist, Sven, illus. 2017. (ENG., Illus.). 32p. (J). (gr. -1-3). 17.95 (978-0-7358-4277-9(9)) North-South Bks., Inc.

—The Fox Chase: The Adventures of Findus & Pettson. Nordqvist, Sven, illus. 2015. (Adventures of Pettson & Findus Ser.). (ENG., Illus.). 32p. (J). 17.95 (978-0-7358-4215-1(9)) North-South Bks., Inc.

—Pancakes for Findus. Nordqvist, Sven, illus. 2008. (Findus & Pettson Ser.). (ENG., Illus.). 28p. (J). (978-1-903458-79-2(X)) Hawthorn Pr.

Norman, Claire. At the End of the Lane. 2012. (Illus.). 48p. (gr. 1-2). pap. 13.66 (978-1-4685-8237-6(2)) AuthorHouse.

Norman, Dayle. Tre's Surprise the Move. I.t. ed. 2005. 35p. (J). per. 8.00 (978-1-59196-896-2(8)) Instant Pub.

Norrie, Louise Rosalyn. The Adventures of Flat Cat. 2011. 144p. 29.99 (978-1-4628-9397-3(X)); pap. 19.99 (978-1-4628-9396-6(1)) Xlibris Corp.

Norris, Christine. Talisman of Zandria, 1. Nagy, Robert, illus. 2005. 187p. (YA). pap. 14.95 (978-1-885093-44-8(6), LBF/Hadrosaur) Hadrosaur Pr.

—The Talisman of Zandria. 2013. 240p. pap. 14.99 (978-1-61271-220-8(7)) Zumaya Pubns. LLC.

Norris, David A. The CBARCs of Cannon Bay: Storm Clouds over Cannon Bay, 5 bks, Bk.3. Norris, Judy-Jo Harris, illus. 2012. 128p. (YA). pap. 16.95 (978-1-937493-30-1(X)) Dancing Moon Pr.

Norris, Elizabeth. Unbreakable. 2014. (Unraveling Ser.: 2). (ENG.). 496p. (YA). (gr. 9). pap. 9.99 (978-0-06-210377-2(6)) HarperCollins Pubs.

Norris, L. Wayne. The Adventures of Ricky Raccoon & Jodi the Cat with Boomer. I.t. ed. 2003. (Illus.). 36p. (J). pap. (978-0-9709408-1-0(5)) Pinetree Pubns.

Norris, Siân. Greta & Boris: A Daring Rescue. 2013. (ENG., Illus.). 98p. (J). (gr. -1-12). pap. 9.95 (978-1-78099-623-3(3), Our Street Bks.) Hunt, John Publishing Ltd. GBR. Dist: National Bk. Network.

Norris, Zack. Danger on Shadow Mountain. 2012. (Double Detectives Ser.). (ENG.). 144p. (J). (gr. 3-7). pap. 4.95 (978-1-4027-9146-8(1)) Sterling Publishing Co., Inc.

North, Ryan. Adventure Time, Vol. 4. 2014. (Adventure Time Graphic Novels Ser.: 4). lib. bdg. 26.95 (978-0-606-35463-9(8)) Turtleback Bks.

North, Ryan & Paroline, Shelli. Adventure Time Vol.4 - Mathematical Edition. 2014. (Illus.). 144p. (978-1-78276-171-6(3), Titan Bks.) Titan Bks. Ltd.

Northfield, Gary. Derek the Sheep. Northfield, Gary, illus. 2009. (ENG., Illus.). 64p. (J). (gr. k-2). 16.95 (978-0-7475-9424-6(4)) Bloomsbury Publishing Plc GBR. Dist: Independent Pubs. Group.

Northrop, Michael. Book of the Dead. 2015. (TombQuest Ser.: Bk. 1). (J). 197p. (978-1-76015-315-1(X)); 208p. pap. (978-1-74362-924-6(9)) Scholastic, Inc.

—The Final Kingdom. 2016. (TombQuest Ser.: 5). (ENG.). 192p. (J). (gr. 3-7). 12.99 (978-0-545-72342-8(6)); 16.99 (978-0-545-87111-2(5)) Scholastic, Inc. (Scholastic Pr.).

—The Stone Warriors. 2015. (TombQuest Ser.: 4). (ENG.). 192p. (J). (gr. 3-7). 12.99 (978-0-545-72341-1(8), Scholastic Pr.) Scholastic, Inc.

—Valley of Kings. 2015. (TombQuest Ser.: 3). (ENG.). 192p. (J). (gr. 3-7). 16.99 (978-0-545-87104-4(2)); 12.99 (978-0-545-72340-4(X), Scholastic Pr.) Scholastic, Inc.

Norton, Andre. The Time Traders. 2007. 236p. per. 12.95 (978-1-4218-2734-6(4)); 27.95 (978-1-4218-2634-9(8)) 1st World Publishing, Inc. (1st World Library - Literary Society).

Norton, Charles. The Perfect Plan & the Four Brother's Pact. 2012. 24p. pap. 15.99 (978-1-4691-6503-5(1)) Xlibris Corp.

Norton, George. Papa Golley's Journey Home. Hutcherson, Darren, illus. Date not set. 14.95 (978-1-889506-06-7(0)) Kendar Publishing, Inc.

Norton, Jack, Jr., as told by. Brave from Thunders. 2003. pap. 15.00 (978-0-9740071-3-7(7)) Ctr. for the Affirmation of Responsible Education.

Norton, Mary. The Borrowers. Krush, Beth & Krush, Joe, illus. 2003. (Borrowers Ser.: 1). (ENG.). 192p. (J). (gr. 2-5). pap. 7.99 (978-0-15-204737-5(9)) Houghton Mifflin Harcourt Publishing Co.

—Borrowers. 50th anniv. ed. 2003. (Illus.). (YA). (978-0-15-204768-9(9), Harcourt Children's Bks) Harcourt Children's Bks.

—The Borrowers Afield. Krush, Beth & Krush, Joe, illus. 50th anniv. ed. 2003. (Borrowers Ser.: 2). (ENG.). 224p. (J). (gr. 2-5). pap. 7.99 (978-0-15-204732-0(8)) Houghton Mifflin Harcourt Publishing Co.

—The Borrowers Afloat. Krush, Beth & Krush, Joe, illus. 2003. (Borrowers Ser.: 3). (ENG.). 192p. (J). (gr. 2-5). pap. 7.99 (978-0-15-204733-7(6)) Houghton Mifflin Harcourt Publishing Co.

—The Borrowers Avenged. Krush, Joe et al, illus. 50th anniv. ed. 2003. (Borrowers Ser.: 5). (ENG.). 304p. (J). (gr. 2-5). pap. 7.99 (978-0-15-204731-3(X)) Houghton Mifflin Harcourt Publishing Co.

—Borrowers Collection. 2016. (Borrowers Ser.). (ENG., Illus.). 1104p. (J). (gr. 2-5). 24.99 (978-0-544-84213-7(8), HMH Books For Young Readers) Houghton Mifflin Harcourt Publishing Co.

Norville, Rod. Moonshine Express: Revised Edition with a History of Moonshine Today & Yesterday. 2003. 178p. (YA). per. 13.95 (978-1-891929-99-1(2)) Four Seasons Pubs.

Nosov, Nikolai. The Adventures of Dunno & His Friends. Kay, Nicole, tr. from ENG. 2006. (RUS.). (J). (978-0-9754433-2-3(1), Language Transformer Bks.) Velichko, Vera.

Nosy Crow Staff. Bizzy Bear: Space Rocket. Davies, Benji, illus. 2015. (Bizzy Bear Ser.). (ENG.). 8p. (J). (— 1). bds. 6.99 (978-0-7636-8003-9(6), Nosy Crow) Candlewick Pr.

—Bizzy Bear: Spooky House. Davies, Benji, illus. 2017. (Bizzy Bear Ser.). (ENG.). 8p. (J). (— 1). bds. 6.99 **(978-0-7636-9327-5(8)**, Nosy Crow) Candlewick Pr.

Nosy Crow Staff. Jack & the Beanstalk: a Nosy Crow Fairy Tale. Bryan, Ed, illus. 2017. (ENG.). 32p. (J). (gr. -1-2). 9.99 (978-0-7636-9332-9(4), Nosy Crow) Candlewick Pr.

Noto, Nick & Noto, Larissa. The Adventures of Pyrgos: Volume 1. 2011. 36p. pap. 16.39 (978-1-4634-5250-6(0)) AuthorHouse.

Noufer, M. M. The Adventures of Millie & May: Millie & Maya Discover the New World. 2009. 32p. pap. 13.99 (978-1-4490-0711-9(2)) AuthorHouse.

Novara, Joe. Road Wrangler: Cowboys on Wheels. Lawson, Robert & Spatrisano, Kimberly, illus. 2007. 112p. (J). pap. 8.95 (978-1-58980-507-1(0)) Pelican Publishing Co., Inc.

November, Deborah, et al. Let's Visit Sesame Street. Mathieu, Joe, illus. 2010. (ENG.). 24p. (J). bds. 14.99 (978-0-7944-2101-4(6)) Reader's Digest Assn., Inc., The.

Novis, Jovita. The Tiny Ballerina in the Garden. 2013. 40p. pap. 15.95 (978-1-4497-9104-9(2), WestBow Pr.) Author Solutions, Inc.

Noyes, Alfred. The Highwayman. Kimber, Murray, illus. 2005. (Visions in Poetry Ser.). (ENG.). 48p. (J). (gr. 5-9). 17.95 (978-1-55337-425-1(8)) Kids Can Pr., Ltd. CAN. Dist: Hachette Bk. Group.

Numeroff, Laura Joffe. Time for School, Mouse! Lap Edition. Bond, Felicia, illus. 2016. (If You Give... Ser.). 24p. (J). (gr. -1-3). bds. 12.99 (978-0-06-242741-0(5)) HarperCollins Pubs.

Nunes, Bill. 301 Things a Bright St Louis Southern Illinois Girl Can Do. 2011. 344p. pap. 29.95 (978-0-9787994-6-5(1)) Nunes, H. William.

Nunez, Kent Hamilton. Mish: The Desert. 2007. 152p. per. 11.95 (978-0-595-47808-8(5)) iUniverse, Inc.

Nuri, Alya & Nuri, Alya. Amr's Adventure in Europe. 2013. 68p. pap. (978-1-935948-29-2(6)) Roxby Media Ltd.

Nurse, Holly. Meridian Brown Goes to School. 2009. (Illus.). 60p. pap. (978-1-84748-535-9(9)) Athena Pr.

Nurston, Nicholas. The Adventures of Smoky: (It's a Cat's Life) 2012. (Illus.). 44p. pap. 21.99 (978-1-4797-3585-3(X)) Xlibris Corp.

Nusz, Janean. The Littlest Cowboy. 2005. 26p. 12.30 (978-1-4116-4019-1(5)) Lulu Pr., Inc.

Nwapa-Ibuaka, Njideka. Tales from Animal Kingdom. I.t. unabr. ed. 2003. (Illus.). 30p. (gr. 2-5). pap. 7.95 (978-0-9661598-5-1(3)) Ekwike Bks. & Publishing.

Nybo, B. J. Elmo Jackson Great Yellow Ball. 2005. (978-0-9742322-0-1(3)) New Art & Vision, LLC.

Nye, Barry. Hannah & the Magic Blanket - Land of the Dinosaurs. 2009. 40p. pap. 18.50 (978-0-557-03682-0(8)) Lulu Pr., Inc.

—Hannah & the Magic Blanket - Land of the Robots. 2009. 40p. pap. 18.50 (978-0-557-06602-5(6)) Lulu Pr., Inc.

Nye, Bill & Mone, Gregory. Jack & the Geniuses: At the Bottom of the World. Iluzada, Nicholas, illus. 2017. (ENG.). 256p. (J). (gr. 3-7). 13.95 (978-1-4197-2303-2(0), Amulet Bks.) Abrams, Inc.

Nyikos, Stacy. Dizzy. Lee, Kary, illus. I.t. ed. 2006. 32p. (J). (gr. -1-3). 15.95 (978-0-9764199-2-1(0), 888-867-1927) Stonehorse Publishing, LLC.

Nykko. The Master of Shadows, 3 vols. Bannister, illus. 2009. (Elsewhere Chronicles Ser.: Bk. 3). (ENG.). 48p. (J). (gr. 4-8). lib. bdg. 27.93 (978-0-7613-4461-2(6)) Lerner Publishing Group.

—The Shadow Door. Bannister, illus. 2009. (Elsewhere Chronicles Ser.: Bk. 1). (ENG.). 48p. (J). (gr. 4-8). pap. 8.99 (978-0-7613-3963-2(9)) Lerner Publishing Group.

—The Shadow Spies, 2 vols. Bannister, illus. 2009. (Elsewhere Chronicles Ser.: Bk. 2). (ENG.). 48p. (J). (gr. 4-8). lib. bdg. 27.93 (978-0-7613-4460-5(8)) Lerner Publishing Group.

O' Byrne, Lorraine. The Hippity Dippity Witch. Martin, Laura & Kennedy, Seamus, illus. 2012. 138p. pap. (978-1-78176-391-9(7)) FeedARead.com.

Oberne, Sharon. Kelsey. 2006. 88p. (YA). pap. 13.95 (978-1-58909-340-9(2)) Bookstand Publishing.

O'Berry, Jan. The Journey Home. 2003. 198p. pap. 13.95 (978-0-595-27195-5(2), Writer's Showcase Pr.) iUniverse, Inc.

Obiols, Anna. Triceratops: the Strongest Dinosaur. Subi, illus. 2012. (Dinosaur Bks.). (ENG.). 36p. (J). (gr. -1-1). pap. 6.99 (978-1-4380-0108-1(8)) Barron's Educational Series, Inc.

O'Brien, Carola. Bobby Dazzler & the Three Rubies of Ishmalan. 2010. 236p. 28.99 (978-1-60911-285-1(7), Eloquent Bks.) Strategic Book Publishing & Rights Agency (SBPRA).

Obrien, Elaime F. Anita of Rancho del Mar. 2005. 171p. (Orig.). (J). (gr. 5-6). reprint ed. pap. 995.00 (978-1-885375-14-8(X), Shore Line Pr.) Pacific Bks.

O'Brien, Johnny. Day of Deliverance. Hardcastle, Nick, illus. 2010. (Jack Christie Adventure Ser.: 2). (ENG.). 192p. (J). (gr. 4-7). 15.99 (978-0-7636-5075-9(7), Templar) Candlewick Pr.

—Day of the Assassins. Hardcastle, Nick, illus. 2010. (Jack Christie Adventure Ser.: 1). (ENG.). 224p. (J). (gr. 4-7). pap. 6.99 (978-0-7636-4995-1(3), Templar) Candlewick Pr.

—Day of the Assassins: A Jack Christie Novel. Hardcastle, Nick, illus. 2009. (Jack Christie Adventure Ser.: 1). (ENG.). 224p. (J). (gr. 4-7). 15.99 (978-0-7636-4595-3(8), Templar) Candlewick Pr.

O'Brien, Thomas E. The Magic of Finbar. 2011. 68p. pap. 19.95 (978-1-4560-4235-6(1)) America Star Bks.

O'Callaghan, G. The Eternals. 2007. 376p. per. (978-1-84693-055-3(3)) Best Global Publishing Ltd.

O'Campo, Allicia. Tinky Goes to North Americ. 2009. 28p. pap. 15.50 (978-1-60860-412-8(8), Eloquent Bks.) Strategic Book Publishing & Rights Agency (SBPRA).

Ocean Front Books. Coloring Book. I.t. ed. 2006. (Illus.). (J). lib. bdg. (978-1-934190-02-9(0)) Ocean Front Bk. Publishing, Inc.

Ochse, Bobbie Collinton. Nana's Magic Closet. 2010. 40p. pap. 16.99 (978-1-4520-7663-8(4)) AuthorHouse.

O'Connor, Barbara. The Fantastic Secret of Owen Jester. 2010. (ENG.). 176p. (J). (gr. 3-7). 15.99 (978-0-374-36850-0(3), 9780374368500, Farrar, Straus & Giroux (BYR)) Farrar, Straus & Giroux.

—The Fantastic Secret of Owen Jester. 2011. (ENG.). 192p. (J). (gr. 3-7). pap. 7.99 (978-0-312-67430-4(9), 9780312674304) Square Fish.

—The Small Adventure of Popeye & Elvis. 2011. (ENG.). 176p. (J). (gr. 3-7). pap. 7.99 (978-0-312-65932-5(6), 9780312659325) Square Fish.

O'Connor, Jane. Fancy Nancy & the Fall Foliage. Glasser, Robin Preiss, illus. 2014. (Fancy Nancy Ser.). (ENG.). 24p. (J). (gr. -1-3). pap. 4.99 (978-0-06-208630-3(8), HarperFestival) HarperCollins Pubs.

—Girl on the Go: A Doodle & Draw Book. Glasser, Robin Preiss et al, illus. 2012. (Fancy Nancy Ser.). (ENG.). 64p. (J). (gr. -1-3). pap. 6.99 (978-0-06-188282-1(8), HarperFestival) HarperCollins Pubs.

—Nancy Clancy: My Secret Diary. Glasser, Robin Preiss, illus. 2015. (Fancy Nancy Ser.). (ENG.). 144p. (J). (gr. 1-5). pap. 11.99 (978-0-06-234983-5(X)) HarperCollins Pubs.

—Nancy Clancy - Secret of the Silver Key. Glasser, Robin Preiss, illus. 2015. (Nancy Clancy Ser.: 4). (ENG.). 144p. (J). (gr. 1-5). pap. 4.99 (978-0-06-208422-4(4)) HarperCollins Pubs.

—Nancy Clancy Sees the Future. Glasser, Robin Preiss, illus. 2015. (Fancy Nancy Ser.). (ENG.). 256p. (J). (gr. 1-5). 12.99 (978-0-06-240365-0(6)) HarperCollins Pubs.

—Nancy Clancy, Star of Stage & Screen. Glasser, Robin Preiss, illus. 2015. (Nancy Clancy Ser.: Bk. 5). (ENG.). 128p. (J). (gr. 1-5). 9.99 (978-0-06-226964-5(X)) HarperCollins Pubs.

Oddo, Jennifer M. Asim the Awesome Possum: Asim Gets His Awesome. Lamb, T. S., illus. 2012. 36p. 16.95 (978-0-9855906-2-8(9)) Pie Plate Publishing Co.

Ode, Eric. The Boy & the Dragon, 1 vol. Harris, Jim, illus. 2013. (ENG.). 32p. (J). (gr. k-3). 16.99 (978-1-4556-1813-2(6)) Pelican Publishing Co., Inc.

O'Dea, Rory & Benchmark Education Co. Staff. Books That Changed My Life. 2014. (Text Connections Ser.). (J). (gr. 5). (978-1-4900-1366-4(0)) Benchmark Education Co.

O'Dell, Scott. Black Star, Bright Dawn. 2008. (ENG., Illus.). 144p. (J). (gr. 5-7). pap. 6.99 (978-0-547-05319-6(3)) Houghton Mifflin Harcourt Publishing Co.

—The Seven Serpents Trilogy. 2009. (ENG.). 560p. (J). (gr. 4-6). pap. 19.99 (978-1-4022-1836-1(2), Sourcebooks Jabberwocky) Sourcebooks, Inc.

Odems, Carlee. A Thin Line. 2008. 88p. pap. 9.95 (978-0-595-50829-7(4)) iUniverse, Inc.

Odhiambo, Tori. Close to Home: The African Savannah. 2012. 32p. pap. 21.99 (978-1-4691-9510-0(0)) Xlibris Corp.

Odom, Mel. A Conspiracy Revealed. 2013. (Hunter's League Ser.: 1). (ENG.). 256p. (YA). (gr. 7). pap. 16.99 (978-1-4814-0152-4(1), Simon Pulse) Simon Pulse.

—His Legacy Avenged. 2013. (Hunter's League Ser.: 4). (ENG.). 256p. (YA). (gr. 7). pap. 16.99 (978-1-4814-0157-9(2), Simon Pulse) Simon Pulse.

—The Mystery Unravels. 2013. (Hunter's League Ser.: 2). (ENG.). 256p. (YA). (gr. 7). pap. 16.99 (978-1-4814-0154-8(8), Simon Pulse) Simon Pulse.

—The Secret Explodes. 2013. (Hunter's League Ser.: 3). (ENG.). 240p. (J). (gr. 7). pap. 15.99 (978-1-4814-0156-2(4), Simon Pulse) Simon Pulse.

O'Donnell, E. E. Father Browne's Galway. Browne, Frank, photos by. 2007. (ENG., Illus.). 112p. 45.95 (978-1-85607-938-9(4)) Currach Pr. IRL. Dist: Dufour Editions, Inc.

O'Donnell, Liam. Ganked: Geeked Out Mysteries #1. 2013. 214p. pap. (978-0-9919281-3-2(X)) Feeding Change Media.

—Ramp Rats: A Graphic Guide Adventure, 1 vol. Deas, Mike, illus. 2008. (Graphic Guides). (ENG.). 64p. (J). (gr. 3-7). pap. 9.95 (978-1-55143-880-1(1)) Orca Bk. Pubs. USA.

—Soccer Sabotage: A Graphic Guide Adventure, 1 vol. Deas, Mike, illus. 2009. (Graphic Guides). (ENG.). 64p. (J). (gr. 3-7). pap. 9.95 (978-1-55143-884-9(4)) Orca Bk. Pubs. USA.

—United Force. Rooth, Mike, illus. 2007. 44p. (J). lib. bdg. 23.08 (978-1-4242-1633-8(8)) Fitzgerald Bks.

Odu, Nkemakolam. My Horrible Trip to New York. 2012. (Illus.). 74p. (gr. 4-6). pap. 13.66 (978-1-4685-8217-8(8)) AuthorHouse.

Oechsle, Michael. The Lost Cipher. 2016. (ENG.). 272p. (J). (gr. 3-7). 14.99 (978-0-8075-8063-9(5)) Whitman, Albert & Co.

Oehmichen, Ariel. Chosen Last. Du Pont, Brittany, illus. 2012. 28p. pap. 9.99 (978-1-937165-26-0(4)) Orange Hat Publishing.

Oelrich, Ryan. The Grand Adventures of Carson the Balloonatic! A Peculiar Hero Story for Children & Adults Who Are Brave Enough to Believe in the Unbelievable. 2011. 36p. 16.99 (978-1-4567-0030-0(8)) AuthorHouse.

Ogden, Charles. Rare Beasts. Carton, Rick, illus. 2006. (Edgar & Ellen Ser.: 1). (ENG.). 144p. (J). (gr. 3-7). 22.99 (978-1-4169-1409-6(9), Aladdin) Simon & Schuster Children's Publishing.

—Tourist Trap. Carton, Rick, illus. 2006. (Edgar & Ellen Ser.: 2). (ENG.). 176p. (J). (gr. 3-7). 23.99 (978-1-4169-1411-2(0), Simon & Schuster/Paula Wiseman Bks.) Simon & Schuster/Paula Wiseman Bks.

—Under Town. Carton, Rick, illus. 2006. (Edgar & Ellen Ser.: 3). (ENG.). 160p. (J). (gr. 3-7). 22.99 (978-1-4169-1412-9(9), Simon & Schuster/Paula Wiseman Bks.) Simon & Schuster/Paula Wiseman Bks.

O'Grady, Standish Hayes. The Pursuit of the Gilla Decair & His Horse. 2004. reprint ed. pap. 1.99 (978-1-4192-7950-8(5)) Kessinger Publishing, LLC.

Oguneye, Kunle. Sikulu & Harambe by the Zambezi River: An African Vversion of the Good Samaritan Story. McCorkindale, Bruce & Youtsey, Scott, illus. 2008. 32p. (J). (gr. -1-5). 14.99 (978-0-9777382-4-3(8)) Blue Brush Media.

Oh, Ellen. Prophecy. 2013. (Prophecy Ser.: 1). (ENG.). (YA). (gr. 8). 352p. pap. 9.99 (978-0-06-209110-9(7)); (Illus.). 320p. 17.99 (978-0-06-209109-3(3)) HarperCollins Pubs. (HarperTeen).

—Warrior. (Prophecy Ser.: 2). (ENG.). (YA). (gr. 8). 2015. 352p. pap. 9.99 (978-0-06-209113-0(1)) 2013. 336p. 17.99 (978-0-06-209112-3(3)) HarperCollins Pubs. (HarperTeen).

O'Hagan, William. Anything Else but Me. 2008. 36p. pap. 24.95 (978-1-60563-701-3(7)) America Star Bks.

O'Hara, Susan. Christie Plays Softball. Barrett, Rebecca, illus. 2013. 48p. pap. 15.97 (978-1-62516-519-0(6), Strategic Bk. Publishing) Strategic Book Publishing & Rights Agency (SBPRA).

—Tim's First Soccer Game. Barrett, Rebecca, illus. 2012. 38p. pap. 14.97 (978-1-61897-199-9(9), Strategic Bk. Publishing) Strategic Book Publishing & Rights Agency (SBPRA).

O'Hart, Sinead. Eye of the North. 2017. (ENG.). 352p. (J). (gr. 3-7). 16.99 (978-1-101-93503-3(0), Knopf Bks. for Young Readers) Random Hse. Children's Bks.

O'Hearn, Kate. Valkyrie. 2016. (Valkyrie Ser.: 1). (ENG., Illus.). 352p. (J). (gr. 4-8). 17.99 (978-1-4814-4737-9(8), Simon & Schuster/Paula Wiseman Bks.) Simon & Schuster/Paula Wiseman Bks.

O'Hely, Eileen. Penny in Space. Phelan, Nicky, illus. 2009. (ENG.). 225p. (J). pap. 14.95 (978-1-85635-571-1(3)) Mercier Pr., Ltd., The IRL. Dist: Dufour Editions, Inc.

Oja, L. G. Little Miss Izzy's Adventures - Miss Izzy & the Monsters. 2013. 24p. pap. (978-1-4602-1421-3(8)) FriesenPress.

Okamoto, Rod. Kingdom of Nu - TJ's Tale: TJ's Tale. Okamoto, Alan, illus. 2006. (J). per. 19.95 (978-0-9764116-0-4(1)) Nutrishare Publishing.

Okaty, Nicole. Custard & Pupcake's Book: A Pet Pals Adventure. 2005. 39p. (978-0-439-70470-0(7)) Scholastic, Inc.

Oklahoma Energy Resoures Board, creator. The Road to Petroville: Petro Pete's Adventure. 2008. 15.00 (978-0-615-19844-6(9)) Oklahoma Energy Resources Board.

Okorafor-Mbachu, Nnedi. Zahrah the Windseeker. 2008. (ENG., Illus.). 320p. (J). (gr. 5-7). pap. 8.99 (978-0-547-02028-0(7)) Houghton Mifflin Harcourt Publishing Co.

Okugas, Juanaiga. The tales of Mew the Cat. 2011. 92p. pap. 35.30 (978-1-4567-3480-0(6)) AuthorHouse.

Okwu, Bernadette. Unbeatable Brothers: The Adventures of Three Brothers. 2013. (ENG.). 38p. 14.95 (978-1-4787-1397-5(6)) Outskirts Pr., Inc.

O'Laughlin, Ann. The Amazing Bi-Ski Rescue. Foster-Fell, Jeremy, ed. 2013. 34p. (J). pap. (978-0-9843477-1-1(2)) Roxby Media Ltd.

Old Man Winter: The New Season. 2005. (Illus.). 32p. (J). bds. 15.99 (978-1-933079-03-5(7)) Core Publishing & Consulting, Inc.

Old Mcdonald. 2004. (J). per. (978-1-57657-425-6(3)) Paradise Pr., Inc.

Oldenburg, Richard. The Three Little Green Pigs, Llc: A Recycling Pig Tale. Samantha May Cerney, illus. 2013. 28p. 23.50 (978-1-62516-753-8(9), Strategic Bk. Publishing) Strategic Book Publishing & Rights Agency (SBPRA).

—The Three Little Green Pigs, Llc: A Recycling Pig Tale. Cerney, Samantha May, illus. 2013. 28p. pap. 12.50 (978-1-62516-649-4(4), Strategic Bk. Publishing) Strategic Book Publishing & Rights Agency (SBPRA).

O'Leary, John. ¡En Busca del Tesoro del Pirata! 2005. (SPA & ENG., Illus.). 14p. (J). (gr. -1-k). 15.95 (978-84-7864-794-1(5)) Combel Editorial, S.A. ESP. Dist: Independent Pubs. Group.

Olena Rudge. The Adventures of Sophie & Katia in the Enchanted Forest. 2013. 220p. pap. (978-3-85438-685-8(0)) united p.c. Verlag.

Olesha, Yuri. The Three Fat Men. Kay, Nicole, tr. from RUS. 2006. (J). (978-0-9754433-0-9(5), Language Transformer Bks.) Velichko, Vera.

Oleson, Susan. Sammy Tails: Finding a Home, 1. 2006. (Illus.). 28p. (J). pap. (978-0-9779251-0-0(2)) Oleson, Susan.

Olien, Jessica. Adrift: An Odd Couple of Polar Bears. Olien, Jessica, illus. 2017. (Illus.). 40p. (J). (gr. -1-3). 17.99 (978-0-06-245177-4(4)) HarperCollins Pubs.

Olin, Rita & Olin, Spencer. Trouble in Soccertown: A Lazer Mcnulty Adventure. 2009. 108p. 20.95 (978-1-4401-5374-7(4)); pap. 10.95 (978-1-4401-5376-1(0)) iUniverse, Inc.

Olive Branch Publishing, ed. Boogaloboo Meets Ranger Bob. 2007. (Adventures of Boogaloboo Ser.). (Illus.). 32p. (J). (978-0-9793147-0-4(4)) OlivesAngels Publishing, LLC.

Oliveira, Luis. The Children of Hope 3. 2009. 56p. pap. 15.49 (978-0-578-00420-4(8)) Desktop Prepress Services.

Oliver, Andrew. Haunted Hill. 2006. (Sam & Stephanie Mystery Ser.). 268p. (J). (gr. 5-9). per. 12.95 (978-0-9661009-7-6(2)) Adams-Pomeroy Pr.

—If Photos Could Talk. 2005. (Sam & Stephanie Mystery Ser.). 264p. (J). per. 12.95 (978-0-9661009-6-9(4)) Adams-Pomeroy Pr.

Oliver, Helen. Ellen's First Swim. 2009. 32p. pap. 16.49 (978-1-4389-9828-2(7)) AuthorHouse.

Oliver, Lin. Beware! Shadows in the Night. Kallis, Samantha, illus. 2016. (Fantastic Frame Ser.: 3). (ENG.). 128p. (J). (gr. 2-4). 11.99 (978-0-448-48091-6(3), Grosset & Dunlap) Penguin Young Readers Group.

—Danger! Tiger Crossing. 2016. (Illus.). 115p. (J). pap. (978-0-448-48086-2(7), Grosset & Dunlap) Penguin Young Readers Group.

—Splat! Another Messy Sunday 2. 2016. (Fantastic Frame Ser.: 2). (ENG., Illus.). 128p. (J). (gr. 2-4). 11.99 (978-0-448-48089-3(1), Grosset & Dunlap) Penguin Young Readers Group.

Ollie. 2006. (J). 6.99 (978-0-9778922-0-4(4)) Hudson, Jessie.

Olsen, J. J. The Mystic Kingdom: A Jenny Dewberry Series. 2008. 400p. pap. 17.99 *(978-1-4389-2598-1(0))* AuthorHouse.

Olsen, Mary-Kate & Olsen, Ashley. New Adventures, 20 Copies, Vol. 36. 2003. pap. 90.00 *(978-0-06-057176-4(4),* Harper Entertainment) HarperCollins Pubs.

—Twist & Shout. 2005. (ENG., Illus.). 112p. *(978-0-00-718092-9(6))* HarperCollins Pubs. Australia.

Olshan, Matthew. A Voyage in the Clouds: The (Mostly) True Story of the First International Flight by Balloon in 1785. Blackall, Sophie, illus. 2016. (ENG.). 40p. (J). 17.99 *(978-0-374-32954-9(0),* 9780374329549, Farrar, Straus & Giroux (BYR)) Farrar, Straus & Giroux.

Olson, D. A. The Treasure Map. 2011. 36p. pap. 24.95 *(978-1-4626-3655-6(1))* America Star Bks.

Olson, Jennifer Lynn. Chef Charlie & the Great Escape, 1 vol. 2010. 18p. 24.95 *(978-1-4489-5638-8(2))* PublishAmerica, Inc.

Olson, John J. Wild Child & Annie. 2010. 44p. pap. 26.49 *(978-0-557-32534-4(X))* Lulu Pr., Inc.

Olson, Kevin Noel. Eerey Tocsin in the Cryptoid Zoo. Hammack, Debi, illus. 2006. (ENG.). 176p. (YA). per. 15.95 *(978-1-887560-17-7(3),* Cornerstone Bk. Publishers) Poll, Michael Publishing.

Olson, Tod. How to Get Rich on the Oregon Trail. Allred, Scott & Proch, Gregory, illus. 2009. (How to Get Rich Ser.). (ENG.). 48p. (J). (gr. 5-9). 18.95 *(978-1-4263-0412-5(9),* National Geographic Children's Bks.) National Geographic Society.

—How to Get Rich on the Oregon Trail. Proch, Gregory & Allred, Scott, illus. 2009. (How to Get Rich Ser.). (ENG.). 48p. (J). (gr. 5-9). lib. bdg. 27.90 *(978-1-4263-0413-2(7),* National Geographic Children's Bks.) National Geographic Society.

Olswanger, Anna. Shlemiel Crooks. Koz, Paula Goodman, illus. 2005. 36p. (J). (gr. 2-4). 15.95 *(978-1-58838-165-1(X))* NewSouth, Inc.

Onajin, Alaba. The Adventures of Atioro: the Rainmaker of Aramada (Colour Edition) 2010. 78p. pap. 37.95 *(978-0-557-34753-7(X))* Lulu Pr., Inc.

O'Nan, Lawrence W. & O'Nan, Gerald D. The Adventures of Andy Ant: The Swimming Hole Disaster. McGary, Norman, illus. 2014. (ENG.). 34p. (gr. -1-4). pap. 9.95 *(978-1-61448-799-9(5))* Morgan James Publishing.

Once upon a Time Spanish Version-Little Red Riding Hood. 2005. (J). *(978-1-57022-562-8(1))* ECS Learning Systems, Inc.

Once upon a Time Spanish Version-the Three Little Pigs. 2005. (J). *(978-1-57022-565-9(6))* ECS Learning Systems, Inc.

Once upon My Summer Camp Dream. 2003. spiral bd. 14.95 *(978-0-9744437-1-3(9))* Imagination Workshop, The.

O'Neal-Thorpe, Rochelle. The Adventures of Captain Remarkable: Companion chapter book to Captain Remarkable. Tamang, Mayan, illus. 2nd ed. 2010. 124p. (J). pap. 10.95 *(978-0-9823906-0-3(2))* Wiggles Pr.

O'Neill, Elizabeth. Alfred Visits Georgia. 2007. (Illus.). 24p. (gr. -1-3). pap. 12.00 *(978-0-9799121-0-8(5))* Global Business Information Strategies, Inc.

Oneill, Elizabeth. Alfred Visits Maryland. 2008. 24p. (J). pap. 12.00 *(978-0-9799121-7-7(2))* Global Business Information Strategies, Inc.

O'Neill, Elizabeth. Alfred Visits New Jersey. 2007. 24p. (J). pap. 12.00 *(978-0-9790240-7-8(2))* Global Business Information Strategies, Inc.

O'Neill, Elizabeth. Alfred Visits Oregon. 2008. 24p. pap. 12.00 *(978-0-9799121-8-4(0))* Global Business Information Strategies, Inc.

O'Neill, Elizabeth. Alfred Visits Rhode Island. 2007. (Illus.). 24p. (J). pap. 12.00 *(978-0-9790240-6-1(4))* Global Business Information Strategies, Inc.

—Alfred Visits Texas. 2007. 24p. (J). pap. 12.00 *(978-0-9790240-9-2(9))* Global Business Information Strategies, Inc.

Oneill, Elizabeth. Alfred Visits Vermont. 2008. 24p. pap. 12.00 *(978-0-9799121-9-1(9))* Global Business Information Strategies, Inc.

O'Neill, Joe. Legends of the Rif, bk. 3. Addicott, Sara & Walton, Bedelia C., eds. 2015. (Red Hand Adventures Ser.: 3). (ENG., Illus.). 311p. (gr. 3-7). pap. 9.95 *(978-0-9851969-8-1(X))* Blacklock Nature Photography.

O'Neill, Sean. Rocket Robinson & the Secret of the Saint. 2016. (Rocket Robinson Ser.). (ENG.). 240p. (J). (gr. 4-7). pap. 19.95 *(978-0-9893655-2-9(2))* Independent Pubs. Group.

O'Neill, Tom. Old Friends. 2010. (ENG.). 436p. (J). (gr. 3-7). pap. 12.99 *(978-1-84840-941-5(9))* Little Island IRL. Dist: Independent Pubs. Group.

Onyumbe, Jacob. Kevin the Wild Boy: The Diaries of a Survivor, 1 vol. 2010. 166p. pap. 24.95 *(978-1-4489-4673-0(5))* America Star Bks.

Oppel, Kenneth. The Boundless. Tierney, Jim, illus. 2014. (ENG.). 336p. (J). (gr. 3-7). 17.99 *(978-1-4424-7288-4(X),* Simon & Schuster Bks. For Young Readers) Simon & Schuster Bks. For Young Readers.

—Firewing. 2008. (Silverwing Trilogy Ser.). (ENG.). 336p. (J). (gr. 3-7). pap. 7.99 *(978-1-4169-4999-2(2),* Simon & Schuster Bks. For Young Readers) Simon & Schuster Bks. For Young Readers.

—The Silverwing Collection: Silverwing; Sunwing; Firewing. 2014. (Silverwing Trilogy Ser.). (ENG., Illus.). 896p. (J). (gr. 3-7). pap. 23.99 *(978-1-4814-2725-8(3),* Simon & Schuster Bks. For Young Readers) Simon & Schuster Bks. For Young Readers.

—Starclimber. 400p. (YA). (gr. 8). 2010. pap. 9.99 *(978-0-06-085059-3(0))* 2009. (Illus.). 17.99 *(978-0-06-085057-9(4))* HarperCollins Pubs.

Optic, Oliver, pseud. Haste & Waste; or, the Young Pilot of Lake Champlain. 2007. 112p. (gr. 4-7). per. *(978-1-4068-3636-3(2))* Echo Library.

—Haste & Waste or the Young Pilot of Lake Champlain A Story for Young People. 2004. reprint ed. pap. 1.99 *(978-1-4192-2291-7(0))* Kessinger Publishing, LLC.

—Northern Lands: Or, Young America in Russia & Prussia; A Story of Travel & Adventure / by William T. Adams (Oliver Optic). 2006. 384p. per. 26.99 *(978-1-4255-4074-6(0))* Michigan Publishing.

—Northern Lands; or, Young America in Russia & Prussia a Story of Travel & Adventure. 2006. 376p. per. 26.99 *(978-1-4255-3923-8(8))* Michigan Publishing.

—Now or Never: The Adventures of Bobby Bright. 2007. (ENG.). 144p. pap. 18.99 *(978-1-4346-3166-4(4));* 164p. pap. 21.99 *(978-1-4346-3167-1(2))* Creative Media Partners, LLC.

—Now or Never; or, the Adventures of Bobby Bright. 2007. 108p. per. *(978-1-4068-3637-0(0))* Echo Library.

—Outward Bound. 2007. 180p. (gr. 4-7). per. *(978-1-4068-4343-9(1))* Echo Library.

—Sunny Shores; or, Young America in Italy & Austria a Story of Travel & Adventure by William T Adams. 2006. 428p. per. 26.99 *(978-1-4255-4627-4(7))* Michigan Publishing.

—[the Boat Club; or, the Bunkers of Rippleton a Tale for Boys by Oliver Optic, Pseud. 2006. 252p. per. 23.99 *(978-1-4255-2253-7(X))* Michigan Publishing.

Orci, Roberto, et al. Transformers Official Movie Adaptation Issue #2, 1 vol. Milne, Alex, illus. 2008. (Transformers: Official Movie Adaptation Ser.). (ENG.). 24p. (J). (gr. 2-7). 24.21 *(978-1-59961-482-3(0))* Spotlight.

—Transformers Official Movie Adaptation Issue #3, 1 vol. Milne, Alex, illus. 2008. (Transformers: Official Movie Adaptation Ser.). (ENG.). 24p. (J). (gr. 2-7). 24.21 *(978-1-59961-483-0(9))* Spotlight.

—Transformers Official Movie Adaptation Issue #4, 1 vol. Milne, Alex, illus. 2008. (Transformers: Official Movie Adaptation Ser.). (ENG.). 24p. (J). (gr. 2-7). 24.21 *(978-1-59961-484-7(7))* Spotlight.

Orczy, Emmuska. Castles in the Air. 2008. 160p. 25.95 *(978-1-60664-927-5(2));* pap. 14.95 *(978-1-60664-047-0(X))* Aegypan.

—The Gallant Pimpernel - Unabridged - Lord Tony's Wife, the Way of the Scarlet Pimpernel, Sir Percy Leads the Band, the Triumph of the Scarlet Pimperne. 2012. 804p. *(978-1-78139-227-0(7))* Benediction Classics.

—The Scarlet Pimpernel. 2008. 208p. 27.95 *(978-1-60664-862-9(4));* pap. 14.95 *(978-1-60664-109-5(3))* Aegypan.

—The Scarlet Pimpernell. 2016. (J). pap. *(978-1-5124-2624-3(5))* Lerner Publishing Group.

—Unto Caesar. 2008. 260p. 29.95 *(978-1-60664-863-6(2));* pap. 15.95 *(978-1-60664-110-1(7))* Aegypan.

O'Reilly, Sean. Ezra: Egyptian Exchange. 2005. (YA). 9.95 *(978-0-9763095-4-3(8))* Arcana Studio, Inc.

Organ, Beryl E. Tiggy's World. 2010. 26p. pap. 15.99 *(978-1-4500-7915-0(6))* Xlibris Corp.

Origlio, Peter, illus. Charlie & Albert. 2007. 22p. (J). pap. 12.95 *(978-0-9801329-0-8(8))* Charlie & Albert.

Orlando, Kristen, et al. You Don't Know My Name. 2017. (Black Angel Chronicles Ser.). (ENG.). 304p. (YA). 16.99 *(978-1-250-08411-8(3),* 9781250084118) Feiwel & Friends.

Orlando, Mardi. The Wishall. 2009. 156p. pap. 15.34 *(978-1-4269-1704-2(X))* Trafford Publishing.

Orlean, Susan & Bradford, Chris. Young Samurai the Way of the Warrior. l.t. ed. 2011. (Young Samurai Ser.). (ENG.). 628p. (J). 23.99 *(978-1-4104-4329-8(9))* Thorndike Pr.

Orliac, Catherine. Te Tumu o Rapa Nui: El Arbolito de Rapa Nui. the Little Tree of Rapa Nui. le Petit Arbre de Rapa Nui. Haoa Cardinali, Viki et al, trs. Willemin, Veronique, illus. 2005. (FRE, SPA & ENG.). 40p. (J). spiral bd. 12.00 *(978-1-880636-02-2(6))* Easter Island Foundation.

Orman, Roscoe. Ricky & Mobo. 2013. 34p. pap. 9.95 *(978-1-62901-048-9(0))* Inkwater Pr.

Ormand, Kate & Louise, Kate. Dark Days. 2014. (ENG.). 256p. (J). (gr. 6). 16.95 *(978-1-62873-594-9(5),* Sky Pony Pr.) Skyhorse Publishing Co., Inc.

Orme, Helen. Wet! 2008. (Siti's Sisters Ser.). (ENG., Illus.). 36p. pap. *(978-1-84167-688-3(8))* Ransom Publishing Ltd.

Ormondroyd, Edward. Castaways on Long Ago. 2003. (Illus.). 188p. (gr. 5-18). 12.95 *(978-0-9714612-8-4(7))* Green Mansion Pr. LLC.

—David & the Phoenix. Raysor, Joan, illus. 2012. (ENG.). 191p. (J). (gr. 3-6). pap. 2.99 *(978-1-930900-58-5(9))* Purple Hse. Pr.

—David & the Phoenix. 2009. 76p. (gr. 4-7). pap. 4.75 *(978-1-60459-691-5(0))* Wilder Pubns., Corp.

Ormsbee, K. E. The Doorway & the Deep. 2016. (ENG., Illus.). 480p. (J). (gr. 3-7). 16.99 *(978-1-4521-3636-3(X))* Chronicle Bks. LLC.

—The Water & the Wild. Mora, Elsa, illus. 2015. (ENG.). 448p. (J). (gr. 3-7). 16.99 *(978-1-4521-1386-9(6))* Chronicle Bks. LLC.

Oroge, Sabinah. Oluwatofarati & Friends. 2013. 28p. pap. 9.95 *(978-1-4787-0520-8(5))* Outskirts Pr., Inc.

O'Rourke, Molly. The Adventures of Gleeson & Cormac: Why Do People Cry? 2013. 28p. pap. 12.50 *(978-1-62212-880-8(X),* Strategic Bk. Publishing) Strategic Book Publishing & Rights Agency (SBPRA).

O'Rourke, Ryan. Bella Lost & Found. O'Rourke, Ryan, illus. 2014. (ENG., Illus.). 40p. (J). (gr. -1-3). 17.99 *(978-0-06-221861-2(1))* HarperCollins Pubs.

—Bella, Up, Up & Away. O'Rourke, Ryan, illus. 2016. (Illus.). 40p. (J). (gr. -1-3). 17.99 *(978-0-06-221863-6(8))* HarperCollins Pubs.

Orr, Ryan. Jeremy Ruhl Africa. 2004. 420p. (YA). per. 25.95 *(978-0-9641861-9-4(5),* RWP Bks.) Redhawk Publishing.

—Jeremy Ruhl Savannah Wars, 1. 2005. 400p. (YA). per. 25.95 net. *(978-0-9641861-3-2(6),* JRSW, RWP Bks.) Redhawk Publishing.

Orris, Cornelius F. The Curious Adventures of Nigel & Viol. 2010. 94p. 19.99 *(978-1-4500-4463-9(8))* Xlibris Corp.

Orsi, Tea. Tinker Bell & the Pirate Fairy. 2015. (Disney Fairies Graphic Novels Ser.: 16). (J). lib. bdg. 18.40 *(978-0-606-37294-7(6))* Turtleback Bks.

Ortega, Ingrid. Cuentos Golosos. Welin, Raquel, illus. 2006. (SPA.). 64p. (J). mass mkt. 12.50 *(978-1-59835-012-8(9))* Cambridge BrickHouse, Inc.

Ortegon, Sharon A. Cookie Planet. 2013. 16p. pap. 12.70 *(978-1-4669-8283-3(7))* Trafford Publishing.

—Return to Cookie Planet. 2013. 16p. pap. 12.68 *(978-1-4669-9792-9(3))* Trafford Publishing.

Ortiz, Andrea. Snowflakes in June. Ortega, James, illus. 2013. 36p. 14.00 *(978-0-9884237-9-4(0))* CLF Publishing.

Ortiz, Tracy. As Dreamtime Unfolds. 2009. 20p. pap. 24.95 *(978-1-60749-359-4(4))* America Star Bks.

Ortiz, Zirzeria. The Queen in Me & My Bumblebee. 2008. 48p. pap. 24.95 *(978-1-60441-045-7(0))* America Star Bks.

O'Ryan, Ray. Ready, Set, Blast Off! 2017. (Galaxy Zack Ser.: 15). lib. bdg. 16.00 ***(978-0-606-39737-7(X))*** Turtleback Bks.

Osa, Nancy. The Battle of Zombie Hill: Defenders of the Overworld #1. 2015. (Defenders of the Overworld Ser.). (ENG.). 272p. (J). (gr. 6). pap. 9.99 *(978-1-63450-996-1(X),* Sky Pony Pr.) Skyhorse Publishing Co., Inc.

Osborn, D. W. Why Can't I Ribbit?, 1 vol. 2009. 48p. pap. 16.95 *(978-1-61582-641-4(6))* America Star Bks.

Osborne, Jill. Riley Mae & the Sole Fire Safari, 1 vol. 2014. (Faithgirlz / the Good News Shoes Ser.). (ENG.). 256p. (J). pap. 7.99 *(978-0-310-74283-8(8))* Zonderkidz.

Osborne, Kent. Adventure Time: Banana Guard Academy. 2015. lib. bdg. 33.05 *(978-0-606-37099-8(4))* Turtleback Bks.

Osborne, Mary Pope. Abe Lincoln at Last! Murdocca, Sal, illus. 2011. (Magic Tree House Merlin Mission Ser.: No. 19). (ENG.). 128p. (J). (gr. 2-5). 12.99 *(978-0-375-86825-2(9),* Random Hse. Bks. for Young Readers) Random Hse. Children's Bks.

—Afternoon on the Amazon. unabr. ed. 2004. (Magic Tree House Ser.: No. 6). 67p. (J). (gr. k-3). pap. 17.00 incl. audio *(978-0-8072-0339-2(4),* S FTR 217 SP, Listening Library) Random Hse. Audio Publishing Group.

—Balto of the Blue Dawn. Murdocca, Sal, illus. 2016. (Magic Tree House Merlin Missions Ser.: No. 26). (ENG.). 128p. (J). (gr. 2-5). 13.99 *(978-0-553-51085-0(1),* Random Hse. Bks. for Young Readers) Random Hse. Children's Bks.

—Dolphins at Daybreak; Ghost Town at Sundown; Lions at Lunchtime; Polar Bears Past Bedtime, 4 vols. Murdocca, Sal, illus. 2003. (Magic Tree House Ser.: Nos. 9-12). (ENG.). 96p. (J). (gr. 1-4). 23.96 *(978-0-375-82553-8(3),* Random Hse. Bks. for Young Readers) Random Hse. Children's Bks.

—Eve of the Emperor Penguin. Murdocca, Sal, illus. 2008. (Magic Tree House Merlin Mission Ser.: No. 12). (ENG.). 128p. (J). (gr. 2-5). 11.99 *(978-0-375-83733-3(7),* Random Hse. Bks. for Young Readers) Random Hse. Children's Bks.

—Hurry up, Houdini! Murdocca, Sal, illus. 2015. (Magic Tree House Merlin Mission Ser.: No. 22). (ENG.). 144p. (J). (gr. 2-5). 5.99 *(978-0-307-98048-9(0),* Random Hse. Bks. for Young Readers) Random Hse. Children's Bks.

—Magic Tree House: Vacation under the Volcano; Day of the Dragon King; Viking Ships at Sunrise; Hour of the Olympics, 4 vols. Murdocca, Sal, illus. 2008. (Magic Tree House Ser.: Nos. 13-16). (ENG.). 96p. (J). (gr. k-3). 23.96 *(978-0-375-84661-8(1),* Random Hse. Bks. for Young Readers) Random Hse. Children's Bks.

—Magic Tree House Volumes 21-24 Boxed Set: American History Quartet, 4 vols. Murdocca, Sal, illus. 2014. (ENG.). 96p. (J). (gr. 1-4). 23.96 *(978-0-385-38957-0(4),* Random Hse. Bks. for Young Readers) Random Hse. Children's Bks.

—The Mysteries of Spider Kane. 2006. (ENG.). 240p. (J). (gr. 3-7). 6.99 *(978-0-440-42097-2(0),* Yearling) Random Hse. Children's Bks.

—Night of the Ninjas. unabr. ed. 2004. (Magic Tree House Ser.: No. 5). 69p. (J). (gr. k-3). pap. 17.00 incl. audio *(978-0-8072-0338-5(6),* Listening Library) Random Hse. Audio Publishing Group.

—Shadow of the Shark. 2017. (Magic Tree House Merlin Mission Ser.: 25). (ENG., Illus.). 144p. (J). (gr. 2-5). 5.99 ***(978-0-553-51084-3(3),*** Random Hse. Bks. for Young Readers) Random Hse. Children's Bks.

—Shadow of the Shark. Murdocca, Sal, illus. 2015. (Magic Tree House Merlin Mission Ser.: No. 25). (ENG.). 144p. (J). (gr. 2-5). lib. bdg. 15.99 *(978-0-553-51082-9(7),* Random Hse. Bks. for Young Readers) Random Hse. Children's Bks.

—Sunset of the Sabertooth. unabr. ed. 2004. (Magic Tree House Ser.: No. 7). 67p. (J). (gr. k-3). pap. 17.00 incl. audio *(978-0-8072-0340-8(8),* Listening Library) Random Hse. Audio Publishing Group.

—Winter of the Ice Wizard. Murdocca, Sal, illus. 2011. (Magic Tree House Merlin Mission Ser.: 4). (ENG.). 144p. (J). (gr. 2-5). 5.99 *(978-0-375-87395-9(3),* Random Hse. Bks. for Young Readers) Random Hse. Children's Bks.

Oshida, Tim, illus. The Society's Traitor. 2nd ed. 2015. (The Discoveries of Arthur Grey ser.: 1). (ENG.). 304p. (J). (gr. 4-8). 27.99 *(978-1-943317-00-4(3))* Panama Hat Publishing, Ltd.

Osmer, Janice. Timmy & the Captain. 2009. 20p. pap. 10.49 *(978-1-4389-4683-2(X))* AuthorHouse.

Osmond, Joanne H. A Fishy Adventure. Osmond, Jack, illus. 2013. 152p. pap. 12.99 *(978-1-933334-26-4(6))* Vision Tree, Ltd., The.

Osorio, Rick. The Great Adventure of Sally Rock & el Lobo. 2007. (ENG.). 96p. per. 19.95 *(978-1-4241-5869-0(9))* America Star Bks.

—The Great Adventure of Sally Rock & the Cretaceous Chicken. 2006. 65p. pap. 16.95 *(978-1-4241-0971-5(X))* PublishAmerica, Inc.

—The Great Adventure of Sally Rock & the Secret of Man, 1 vol. 2009. 164p. pap. 24.95 *(978-1-60813-596-7(9))* America Star Bks.

Osteen, Victoria. Unexpected Treasures. Palmisciano, Diane, illus. 2009. (ENG.). 32p. (J). (gr. -1-3). 17.99 *(978-1-4169-5550-4(X),* Little Simon Inspirations) Little Simon Inspirations.

Ostermeyer Photography. Frosty & Snowy's Arctic Adventures. 2011. (Illus.). 18.95 *(978-0-9794228-5-0(X))* Ostermeyer Photography.

Ostow, Micol. House of Shards. 2006. (Charmed Ser.). (ENG.). 192p. (YA). (gr. 8-12). mass mkt. 6.99 *(978-1-4169-2531-6(7))* Pocket Books.

Ostrander, P. Martin. P Martin Ostrander's Dangerous Four Series: Book #1. 2007. 112p. 20.95 *(978-0-595-68250-8(2));* per. 10.95 *(978-0-595-43582-1(3))* iUniverse, Inc.

Ostrom, Gladys. Leggys in Number-land. Suits, Rosella, illus. 2011. 40p. (J). pap. 12.95 *(978-0-9841721-6-0(5))* Open Door Publishers, Inc.

O'Sullivan, Darren. The Sleep Taker. 2013. 158p. pap. *(978-1-78333-233-5(6),* AUK Authors) Andrews UK Ltd.

O'Sullivan, Helen. The Magic Piano. Busuttil, Conor, illus. 2013. 34p. pap. *(978-1-908773-36-4(7))* Iponymous Publishing, Ltd.

Ota, Yuko & Panagariya, Ananth. Adventure Time: Candy Capers. 2014. lib. bdg. 33.05 *(978-0-606-35468-4(9))* Turtleback Bks.

Others, et al. Avatar - The Last Airbender - The Lost Adventures. Gurihiru, illus. 2011. (ENG.). 240p. pap. 14.99 *(978-1-59582-748-7(X))* Dark Horse Comics.

Otis, James. Calvert of Maryland: A Story of Lord Baltimore's Colony. 2007. 140p. per. 9.95 *(978-0-9790876-6-0(X))* Living Bks. Pr.

—A District Messenger Boy & a Necktie Party. 2007. 60p. per. *(978-1-4068-4366-8(0))* Echo Library.

—Peter of New Amsterdam: A story of Old New York. 2007. 136p. per. 9.95 *(978-0-9790876-2-2(7))* Living Bks. Pr.

—Ruth of Boston: A story of the Massachusetts Bay Colony. 2007. 140p. per. 9.95 *(978-0-9790876-3-9(5))* Living Bks. Pr.

—Stephen of Philadelphi: A Story of Penn's Colony. 2007. 144p. per. 9.95 *(978-0-9790876-5-3(1))* Living Bks. Pr.

Ottaviani, Jim. T-Minus: The Race to the Moon. Cannon, Kevin & Cannon, Zander, illus. 2009. (ENG.). 128p. (J). (gr. 3-7). 21.99 *(978-1-4169-8682-9(0),* Simon & Schuster/Paula Wiseman Bks.) Simon & Schuster/Paula Wiseman Bks.

Otten, Charlotte. The Flying Mouse. Crawford, Greg, illus. 2014. (ENG.). 32p. (J). 17.95 *(978-1-59373-152-6(3))* Bunker Hill Publishing, Inc.

Our Story... for All to See. 2005. (J). bds. 8.95 *(978-0-9761076-2-0(7))* Spring Ducks Bks., LLC.

Outram, Evelyn. Sav & Josh O Lucky's Christmas Adventure & Magic Street. 2010. 56p. pap. 17.95 *(978-1-60911-876-1(6),* Eloquent Bks.) Strategic Book Publishing & Rights Agency (SBPRA).

Outram, Richard. The Adventures of Exokid: Growing Financial Wings. 2013. 40p. pap. 13.95 *(978-1-4575-2130-0(X))* Dog Ear Publishing, LLC.

Overstreet, Tommy & Vest, Dale G. The Graham Cracker Kid & the Calico Girl. Anderson, Jesse, illus. 2012. 46p. 12.95 *(978-1-62016-014-5(5))* AWOC.COM.

Owen, Chris. Hairy Mole & the Precious Islands. 2008. (ENG., Illus.). 132p. pap. *(978-1-84167-564-0(4))* Ransom Publishing Ltd.

Owen, Dan. Ellen. 2006. 32p. (J). pap. 11.99 *(978-1-4116-9069-1(9))* Lulu Pr., Inc.

Owen, Sarah. The Adventures of Molly & Polly. 2009. 43p. pap. 26.95 *(978-1-4452-5925-3(7))* Lulu Pr., Inc.

Owens, C. Denise. Help! I Can't Find My Shoes. 2013. 28p. pap. 9.95 *(978-1-4787-2550-3(8))* Outskirts Pr., Inc.

Owens, Donna. NIBBLES: Volume 2, Nibbles Adventures. 2008. 38p. pap. 14.95 *(978-1-4357-4621-3(X))* Lulu Pr., Inc.

—NIBBLES:Volume one, Nibbles finds a Home. 2008. 39p. pap. 14.96 *(978-1-4357-4410-3(1))* Lulu Pr., Inc.

Owens, Jeanette. The Adventures of Raj: The Snow Tiger. 2012. (Illus.). 28p. pap. 19.99 *(978-1-4678-8937-7(7))* AuthorHouse.

Owings, Jeff. Tiny Todd: Swooped Away. 2009. 20p. pap. 10.49 *(978-1-4490-1214-4(0))* AuthorHouse.

—Tiny Todd: Tiny Todd's First Pet. 2009. 20p. pap. 10.49 *(978-1-4490-1216-8(7))* AuthorHouse.

Owl, Grey. The Adventures of Sajo & Her Beaver People - with Original Bw Illustrations & a Glossary of Ojibway Indian Words. 2011. 164p. pap. *(978-1-84902-422-8(7))* Benediction Classics.

Oxley, J. Mcdonald. The Young Woodsman: Life in the Forests of Canada. 2007. 90p. pap. 16.99 *(978-1-4346-4267-7(4));* 100p. pap. 18.99 *(978-1-4346-4268-4(2))* Creative Media Partners, LLC.

Oxley, Jennifer & Aronson, Billy. Peg + Cat: the Lemonade Problem. 2017. (Peg + Cat Ser.). (ENG.). 32p. (J). (gr. -1-2). 12.99 *(978-0-7636-9436-4(3),* Candlewick Entertainment) Candlewick Pr.

Ozgur, Lynne Emily. Darryl & the Mountain. Abay, Ismail, illus. 2009. (ENG.). 32p. (J). (gr. 2-4). 9.95 *(978-1-59784-138-2(2))* Tughra Bks.

Pabbaraju, S. Adventures of Andreux: Book One - Aranya. 2008. 176p. 23.95 *(978-1-4401-0075-8(6));* pap. 13.95 *(978-0-595-40964-8(4))* iUniverse, Inc.

Pace, Anne Marie. Pigloo. Hussey, Lorna, illus. 2016. (ENG.). 32p. (J). 16.99 *(978-1-62779-202-8(3),* 9781627792028, Holt, Henry & Co. Bks. For Young Readers) Holt, Henry & Co.

Pace, Renee. The Forsaken. 2013. 204p. pap. 10.99 *(978-1-939194-79-4(2))* Etopia Pr.

Pace, Terri L. The Christmas Dream, 1 vol. 2009. 116p. pap. 19.95 *(978-1-60813-532-5(2))* America Star Bks.

Pacileo, Janis. A Shrimp Called Pee Wee. 2012. 24p. pap. 12.45 *(978-1-4624-0135-2(X),* Inspiring Voices) Author Solutions, Inc.

Packard, Debbie. Smokey's Silly Christmas Adventures, 1 vol. 2010. 26p. 24.95 *(978-1-4512-0080-5(3))* PublishAmerica, Inc.

Packard, Edward. The Forbidden Castle. Willis, Drew, illus. 2013. (U-Ventures Ser.). (ENG.). 192p. (J). (gr. 3-7). pap. 5.99 *(978-1-4424-3428-8(7),* Simon & Schuster Bks. For Young Readers) Simon & Schuster Bks. For Young Readers.

—Return to the Cave of Time. Willis, Drew, illus. 2012. (U-Ventures Ser.). (ENG.). 160p. (Orig.). (J). (gr. 3-7). pap. 5.99 *(978-1-4424-3427-1(9),* Simon & Schuster Bks. For Young Readers) Simon & Schuster Bks. For Young Readers.

—Through the Black Hole. Willis, Drew, illus. 2012. (U-Ventures Ser.). (ENG.). 160p. (J). (gr. 3-7). pap. 5.99 *(978-1-4424-3426-4(0),* Simon & Schuster Bks. For Young Readers) Simon & Schuster Bks. For Young Readers.

& Packer, Knife & McCoshan, Duncan. Captain Fact's Creepy Crawly Adventure. 2004. (Illus.). 96p. (J). pap. *(978-1-4052-0834-5(1))* Egmont Bks., Ltd.

Padilla, Claudia. Las Aventuras de Ceci y Azul. 2003. 96p. (J). per. *(978-1-931456-45-6(3))* Athena Pr.

Page, Cecelia Frances. Adventures on Ancient Continents. 2007. 172p. per. 13.95 *(978-0-595-46358-9(4))* iUniverse, Inc.

—Phenomenal Experiences. 2007. 144p. per. 11.95 *(978-0-595-46360-2(6))* iUniverse, Inc.

Page, J. & Rainier, S. T. Ben & Elvis: The Miracle of a Stormy Christmas. Moyer, J., illus. 2012. 28p. pap. 8.99 *(978-0-9829669-4-5(6))* Elv Enterprises.

Page, Louise. Furballs' Fables. 2008. 100p. pap. 17.50 *(978-1-4092-1068-9(5))* Lulu Pr., Inc.

Page, P. K. Uirapurú: Based on a Brazilian Legend. Bridgeman, Kristi, illus. 2010. (ENG.). 32p. (J). 19.95

(978-0-88982-264-1(6)) Oolichan Bks. CAN. Dist: Univ. of Toronto Pr.

Pagel, Stace. Fletcher the Fly. 2008. (Illus.). 32p. pap. 14.95 *(978-1-4389-2196-9(9))* AuthorHouse.

Paine, Walter. Cousin John: The Story of a Boy & a Small Smart Pig. Dodson, Bert, illus. 2006. (ENG.). 96p. (J). (gr. 3-4). 17.95 *(978-1-59373-057-4(8))* Bunker Hill Publishing, Inc.

Painter, Grace. The Harry Bear Story. Kacer, Stephen, illus. 2011. 28p. pap. 24.95 *(978-1-4626-3327-2(7))* America Star Bks.

Pajarofior. 2003. (SPA.). pap. *(978-956-13-1080-3(5),* AB8005) Bello, Andres CHL. Dist: Lectorum Pubns., Inc.

Pakkala, Christine. Last-But-Not-Least Lola & a Knot the Size of Texas. Hoppe, Paul, illus. 2016. (Last-But-Not-Least Lola Ser.). (ENG.). 169p. (J). (gr. 1-5). 16.95 *(978-1-62979-324-5(8))* Boyds Mills Pr.

—Last-But-Not-Least Lola & the Wild Chicken. Hoppe, Paul, illus. 2014. (Last-But-Not-Least Lola Ser.). (ENG.). 216p. (J). (gr. 2-5). 15.95 *(978-1-59078-983-4(0))* Boyds Mills Pr.

Palacios, Tomas. Guardians of the Galaxy: The Story of the Guardians. 2014. (World of Reading Ser.). (ENG.). 32p. (J). (gr. 1-3). pap. 3.99 *(978-1-4847-0065-5(1),* Marvel Pr.) Disney Publishing Worldwide.

—Guardians of the Galaxy Hallo-Scream Spook-Tacular!!! 2016. (J). lib. bdg. 16.00 *(978-0-606-38338-7(7))* Turtleback Bks.

—These Are the Guardians of the Galaxy. 2014. (Marvel World of Reading Level 1 Ser.). (J). lib. bdg. 13.55 *(978-0-606-35280-2(5))* Turtleback Bks.

Palacios, Tomas & Hosten, Colin. Guardians of the Galaxy Hallo-Scream Spook-tacular!!! 2016. (ENG.). 24p. (J). (gr. 1-3). pap. 5.99 *(978-1-4847-3214-4(6),* Marvel Pr.) Disney Publishing Worldwide.

Palacios, Tomas & Wright, Edgar. Ant-Man: I Am Ant-Man. 2015. (Passport to Reading Level 2 Ser.). (J). lib. bdg. 13.55 *(978-0-606-37219-0(9))* Turtleback Bks.

PaleoJoe & Caszatt-Allen, Wendy. Raptor's Revenge. 2007. (ENG.). 184p. (J). (gr. 2-5). pap. 8.95 *(978-1-934133-37-8(X),* Mackinac Island Press, Inc.) Charlesbridge Publishing, Inc.

Paley, Allison. The Sky Is Burning. 2010. 32p. pap. 15.60 *(978-0-557-46402-9(1))* Lulu Pr., Inc.

Paling, Chris. The Adventures of Rumble, Tumble, & Titch: Uncertain Times. 2010. 62p. pap. 9.99 *(978-1-60911-263-9(6),* Eloquent Bks.) Strategic Book Publishing & Rights Agency (SBPRA).

Pallas-Luke, Barbara. Cryptic Society. 2005. (YA). 5.00 *(978-0-9765637-0-9(3))* Iris Pallas-Luke E-Writings/E-Literature.

Pallock, Ruth. The Planet Mazol: Book 2 of World Adventures of Jayden. 2011. 82p. pap. 19.95 *(978-1-4560-9004-3(6))* America Star Bks.

Pallone, Robert. The Adventures of Main Man: A Child's View of the World. 2010. 28p. pap. 12.95 *(978-1-4490-5598-1(2))* AuthorHouse.

Palma, B. El Dorado: A Palo Alto Adventure. 2012. 136p. (gr. -1). 23.99 *(978-1-4634-3110-5(4));* pap. 13.99 *(978-1-4634-3111-2(2))* AuthorHouse.

Palmer, Deokie Savie. My Little Baby Sister & I, on a Cold Winter Day. 2007. 38p. 17.95 *(978-1-4303-2061-6(3))* Lulu Pr., Inc.

Palmer, Nigel. The Heart Family Adventures. 2010. (Illus.). 28p. pap. 13.99 *(978-1-4520-0969-8(4))* AuthorHouse.

Palmerlee, B. P. Legend of Darious: The First Part of the Chronicles of Arattoss. 2006. 69p. pap. 16.95 *(978-1-4241-1464-1(0))* PublishAmerica, Inc.

Palmieri, Kathryn & Palmieri, Patricia. GYPSY McPHEE: The New Kid in Town. 2011. (Illus.). 40p. (J). pap. 12.95 *(978-1-58909-750-6(5))* Bookstand Publishing.

Pampalone, Donna. The Adventures of Koco Koala & Friends: Book One: Cuisin' with Cameron. 2007. 60p. per. 16.95 *(978-1-4241-8095-0(3))* America Star Bks.

PAN Macmillan, P. A. N. Pirates. Van De Leijgraaf, Deborah, illus. 2015. (First Sticker Story Fun Ser.). (ENG.). 30p. (J). (gr. -1-k). pap. 9.99 ***(978-1-4472-8674-5(X))*** Pan Macmillan GBR. Dist: Independent Pubs. Group.

Panagopoulos, Janie Lynn. Mark of the Bear Claw. 2007. 224p. (J). pap. 8.95 *(978-0-938682-83-7(0))* River Road Pubns., Inc.

Panamkat, Matthew. Karan Quma & the Meluha Tree. 2007. 348p. per. 19.95 *(978-0-595-41816-9(3))* iUniverse, Inc.

Panckridge, Michael & Lee, Brett. Toby Jones & the Clash with Father Time. 5th ed. 2007. 208p. *(978-0-207-20047-2(5))* HarperCollins Pubs. Australia.

Pandya, Mamata. The Hare Scare: Based on the Original Gujarati Story by Gijubhai Badheka. 2004. (Illus.). 24p. (J). *(978-81-291-0441-0(5))* Rupa & Co.

Panes, Kerry. Knowledge of Good & Evil. 2012. 406p. pap. 22.95 *(978-1-4759-4035-0(1))* iUniverse, Inc.

Panik, Alison Saeger. Berry Best Friends Book: A Fun with Friends Adventure. 2005. 39p. lib. bdg. *(978-0-439-70469-4(3))* Scholastic, Inc.

Panitch, Amanda. Damage Done. 2015. (ENG.). 304p. (YA). (gr. 9). 17.99 *(978-0-553-50749-2(4),* Random Hse. Bks. for Young Readers) Random Hse. Children's Bks.

Pantelo, Amber. The Totally Meaningless Summer. 2004. 75p. (YA). pap. 12.95 *(978-0-7414-1914-9(9))* Infinity Publishing.

Pantoja, Stephen. The Amalaganimals: Eracism Sc. 2010. 33p. pap. 23.90 *(978-0-557-31722-6(3))* Lulu Pr., Inc.

Paoline, Dyann. Cecilia's Fitness Adventure. 2011. 24p. pap. 15.75 *(978-1-4634-0797-1(1))* AuthorHouse.

Paolini, Christopher. Eragon. 2003. (Inheritance Cycle Ser.: Bk. 1). (ENG., Illus.). 528p. (YA). (gr. 7-18). 18.95 *(978-0-375-82668-9(8),* Knopf Bks. for Young Readers) Random Hse. Children's Bks.

—Eragon; Eldest. (Inheritance Cycle Ser.: Bks. 1-2). (ENG.). (YA). (gr. 7). 2008. 1216p. pap. 19.99 *(978-0-375-85704-1(4))*Set. 2005. 1232p. 39.95 *(978-0-375-83658-9(6))* Random Hse. Children's Bks. (Knopf Bks. for Young Readers).

Papa Rolly. Sam the Semi Goes to Chicago. 2012. (Illus.). 36p. pap. 18.40 *(978-1-4669-1137-6(9))* Trafford Publishing.

Papaj, Dana. Blackjack's Hare Raising Adventure. Dixon, Gary, illus. 2005. (J). *(978-1-932583-20-5(3))* digital@batesjackson llc.

Papa's Gold. 2013. 196p. pap. 11.97 *(978-0-9851274-4-2(9))* Pen-L Publishing.

Papineau, Lucie. Gontrand et le Croissant des Cavernes. 2004. (FRE., Illus.). (J). (gr. k-3). spiral bd. *(978-0-616-11145-1(2))* Canadian National Institute for the Blind/Institut National Canadien pour les Aveugles.

Papp, Robert, illus. The Game Store Mystery. 2005. (Boxcar Children Mysteries Ser.: 104). (ENG.). (J). (gr. 1-5). 128p. 14.99 *(978-0-8075-2738-2(6));* 144p. per. 6.99 *(978-0-8075-2739-9(4))* Whitman, Albert & Co.

—The Pumpkin Head Mystery, No. 124. 2010. (Boxcar Children Mysteries Ser.: 124). (ENG.). 128p. (J). (gr. 1-5). pap. 5.99 *(978-0-8075-6669-5(1))* Whitman, Albert & Co.

Papp, Robert & Papp, Kathy, illus. The Pumpkin Head Mystery. 2010. (Boxcar Children Mysteries Ser.: 124). (ENG.). 128p. (J). (gr. 1-5). 14.99 *(978-0-8075-6668-8(3))* Whitman, Albert & Co.

Paquette, Ammi-Joan. Princess Juniper of the Anju. 2016. (Princess Juniper Ser.). (ENG., Illus.). 272p. (J). (gr. 3-7). 16.99 *(978-0-399-17152-9(5),* Philomel Bks.) Penguin Young Readers Group.

Paquette, Ammi-Joan. Princess Juniper of Torr. 2017. (Princess Juniper Ser.). (ENG.). 256p. (J). (gr. 3-7). 16.99 ***(978-0-399-17153-6(3),*** Philomel Bks.) Penguin Young Readers Group.

Paradis, Anne. Caillou - The Best Day Ever! Sévigny, Eric, illus. 2013. (Caillou (Board Books) Ser.). (ENG.). 24p. (J). (gr. -1-1). bds. 9.99 *(978-2-89718-097-3(8))* Caillouet, Gerry.

Pardoe, David. Jasper Tippett's Amazing Journey to Page 42. 2006. (Illus.). 132p. pap. *(978-1-84401-785-0(0))* Athena Pr.

Parent, David D. Drummers Forward! Marching with Angels: The Exciting Tale of a Drummer Boy Serving with the First Vermont Brigade & His Adventures During the Americ. 2013. 188p. pap. 13.50 *(978-1-62516-582-4(X),* Strategic Bk. Publishing) Strategic Book Publishing & Rights Agency (SBPRA).

Parille, Anna. Teddy & His Magical Paw: A New Home for the Honeypies. 2010. 52p. pap. 22.99 *(978-1-4520-5711-8(7))* AuthorHouse.

Parish, Alex. Peter & the Flying Sergeant. 2009. 30p. 21.50 *(978-0-9561613-0-7(8))* Parish, Alex GBR. Dist: Lulu Pr., Inc.

Parish, Herman. Amelia Bedelia. Avril, Lynne, illus. 2017. (I Can Read Level 1 Ser.). 160p. (J). (gr. -1-3). pap. 16.99 *(978-0-06-244357-1(7),* Greenwillow Bks.) HarperCollins Pubs.

—Amelia Bedelia Goes Wild! 2014. (Amelia Bedelia Chapter Book Ser.: 4). (J). lib. bdg. 14.75 *(978-0-606-35077-8(2),* Turtleback) Turtleback Bks.

—Amelia Bedelia Joins the Club. 2014. (Amelia Bedelia: I Can Read! Ser.). (J). lib. bdg. 13.55 *(978-0-606-35051-8(9),* Turtleback) Turtleback Bks.

—Amelia Bedelia Road Trip! Avril, Lynne, illus. 2013. (Amelia Bedelia Ser.: No. 3). (ENG.). 160p. (J). (gr. 1-5). 15.99 *(978-0-06-209503-9(X));* pap. 5.99 *(978-0-06-209502-2(1))* HarperCollins Pubs. (Greenwillow Bks.).

—Amelia Bedelia Talks Turkey. 2009. (Amelia Bedelia: I Can Read! Ser.). (J). lib. bdg. 13.55 *(978-0-606-06937-3(2),* Turtleback) Turtleback Bks.

—Amelia Bedelia Tries Her Luck. Avril, Lynne, illus. 2013. (I Can Read Level 1 Ser.). (ENG.). 32p. (J). (gr. -1-3). 16.99 *(978-0-06-222128-5(0));* pap. 3.99 *(978-0-06-222127-8(2))* HarperCollins Pubs. (Greenwillow Bks.).

—Amelia Bedelia's First Field Trip. Avril, Lynne, illus. 2013. (Amelia Bedelia Ser.). (ENG.). 32p. (J). (gr. -1-3). pap. 6.99 *(978-0-06-196415-2(8),* Greenwillow Bks.) HarperCollins Pubs.

Parish, Peggy. Amelia Bedelia. Siebel, Fritz, illus. 2017. (I Can Read Level 2 Ser.). 72p. (J). (gr. -1-3). 9.99 ***(978-0-06-257279-0(2),*** Greenwillow Bks.) HarperCollins Pubs.

Parisi, Anthony. Baby Harp Seal's Snowy Day. 2010. (ENG.). 16p. (J). (gr. -1). 6.95 *(978-1-60727-136-9(2))* Soundprints.

Park, Barbara. Jingle Bells, Batman Smells! (P. S. So Does May.) Brunkus, Denise, illus. 2005. (Junie B. Jones Ser.: No. 8). (ENG.). 128p. (J). (gr. 1-4). 11.95 *(978-0-375-82808-9(7),* Random Hse. Bks. for Young Readers) Random Hse. Children's Bks.

—Junie B., First Grader (At Last!) unabr. ed. 2004. (Junie B., First Grader Ser.: No. 1). 70p. (J). (gr. k-3). pap. 17.00 incl. audio *(978-0-8072-1020-8(X),* S FTR 258 SP, Listening Library) Random Hse. Audio Publishing Group.

—Junie B. Jones Complete Kindergarten Collection, 17 vols. Brunkus, Denise, illus. 2014. (ENG.). 96p. (J). (gr. 1-4). 84.83 *(978-0-385-37694-5(4),* Random Hse. Bks. for Young Readers) Random Hse. Children's Bks.

—Junie B. Jones Is a Graduation Girl. unabr. ed. 2004. (Junie B. Jones Ser.: No. 17). 69p. (J). (gr. k-3). pap. 17.00 incl. audio *(978-0-8072-1019-2(6),* S FTR 257 SP, Listening Library) Random Hse. Audio Publishing Group.

—Junie B. Jones Is Captain Field Day. unabr. ed. 2004. (Junie B. Jones Ser.: No. 16). 80p. (J). (gr. k-3). pap. 17.00 incl. audio *(978-0-8072-0337-8(8),* Listening Library) Random Hse. Audio Publishing Group.

Park, Barbara & Wotherspoon, John. The Adventures of Lily Leaf. 2011. (Illus.). 28p. pap. 11.36 *(978-1-4567-8648-9(2))* AuthorHouse.

Park, Devin & Lee, Claudia. Howl Michigan. 2011. 138p. pap. 24.95 *(978-1-4560-8895-8(5))* America Star Bks.

Park, Linda Sue. Trust No One. 2012. (39 Clues: Cahills vs. Vespers Ser.: Bk. 5). (ENG.). 192p. (J). (gr. 3-7). 12.99 *(978-0-545-32415-1(7))* Scholastic, Inc.

Park, Louise. New Girl. May, Kyla & Matthews, Melanie, illus. 2015. (Star Girl Ser.). (ENG.). 80p. (gr. 1-4). lib. bdg. 22.65 *(978-1-4795-8275-4(1))* Picture Window Bks.

—Odd One Out. May, Kyla & Matthews, Melanie, illus. 2015. (Star Girl Ser.). (ENG.). 80p. (gr. 1-4). lib. bdg. 22.65 *(978-1-4795-8276-1(X))* Picture Window Bks.

—Three's a Crowd. May, Kyla & Matthews, Melanie, illus. 2015. (Star Girl Ser.). (ENG.). 80p. (gr. 1-4). lib. bdg. 22.65 *(978-1-4795-8278-5(6))* Picture Window Bks.

—Winning Moves. May, Kyla & Matthews, Melanie, illus. 2015. (Star Girl Ser.). (ENG.). 80p. (gr. 1-4). lib. bdg. 22.65 *(978-1-4795-8277-8(8))* Picture Window Bks.

Parker, A. J. The Table of Shadows. 2007. 273p. pap. 16.95 *(978-1-84753-762-1(6))* Lulu Pr., Inc.

Parker, Andy. Ciberbichos: Cyber Bugs, Spanish-Language Edition. 2005. (Mekanimals Ser.). (SPA., Illus.). 8p. (J). bds. *(978-970-718-323-0(3),* Silver Dolphin en Español) Advanced Marketing, S. de R. L. de C. V.

Parker, Beth. Tom Turtle's Fishing Tail, 1 vol. 2010. 26p. 24.95 *(978-1-4489-4134-6(2))* America Star Bks.

Parker, Emma. Safari Adventure. 2010. (Illus.). pap. *(978-1-877561-29-0(0))* First Edition Ltd.

Parker, Gilbert. Carnac's Folly. 2009. 168p. pap. 13.95 *(978-1-60664-417-1(3))* Rodgers, Alan Bks.

—Michel & Angele. 2009. 124p. pap. 10.95 *(978-1-60664-418-8(1))* Rodgers, Alan Bks.

Parker, Jake. Rescue on Tankium, No. 3. 2011. (Missile Mouse Ser.: 2). (ENG.). 160p. (J). (gr. 3-7). pap. 10.99 *(978-0-545-11717-3(8),* Graphix) Scholastic, Inc.

—Rescue on Tankium3. 2011. (Missile Mouse Ser.: 2). (ENG.). 160p. (J). (gr. 3-7). 21.99 *(978-0-545-11716-6(X),* Graphix) Scholastic, Inc.

Parker, Meeta. Cookie the Clown. 2007. 56p. per. 16.95 *(978-1-4241-7917-6(3))* America Star Bks.

Parker, Mike. Break-In. 2008. 208p. pap. 6.95 *(978-0-86327-898-3(1))* Wolfhound Pr. IRL. Dist: Interlink Publishing Group, Inc.

Parker, Patti. Book of Ominook: The Journey Begins. 2012. 28p. pap. 9.95 *(978-1-936587-98-8(X))* Brighton Publishing LLC.

Parker, Patty J. Little Puppy Saves the Day. 2012. 24p. (-18). pap. 17.32 *(978-1-4797-4186-1(8))* Xlibris Corp.

Parker, Ron. Teen Wars. 2010. 170p. pap. 9.42 *(978-1-4452-5000-7(4))* Lulu Pr., Inc.

Parker, Sydney. Scoop That Snow! Shannon, David et al, illus. 2009. (Jon Scieszka's Trucktown Ser.). (ENG.). 12p. (J). (gr. -1-k). 7.99 *(978-1-4169-4182-8(7),* Little Simon) Little Simon.

Parkins, Joanne. The Adventures of Little Bear: Little Bear & the Potty. 2012. (Illus.). 12p. pap. 18.30 *(978-1-4772-2673-5(7))* AuthorHouse.

Parkins, Rebecca Katherine. Lilly the Little Lava Mouse. 2009. 180p. pap. 43.49 *(978-1-4389-4330-5(X))* AuthorHouse.

Parkinson, Curtis. Sea Chase. 2004. (ENG.). 192p. (J). (gr. 5). pap. 8.95 *(978-0-88776-682-4(X),* Tundra Bks.) Tundra Bks. CAN. Dist: Penguin Random Hse. LLC.

—Storm-Blast. 2003. (ENG., Illus.). 160p. (J). (gr. 5-9). pap. 7.95 *(978-0-88776-630-5(7),* Tundra Bks.) Tundra Bks. CAN. Dist: Penguin Random Hse. LLC.

Parnell, Paul. Talking Rocks. 2009. 52p. pap. 16.95 *(978-1-61546-651-1(7))* America Star Bks.

Parr, Maria. Adventures with Waffles. Forrester, Kate, illus. 2015. (ENG.). 240p. (J). (gr. 2-4). 15.99 *(978-0-7636-7281-2(5))* Candlewick Pr.

Parr, Susan Sherwood. Christopher's Adventures: Chris Visits the Hospital, Vol. 2. Paraschiv, Doina, illus. 2nd alt. ed. 2013. (ENG.). 24p. (J). pap. 8.95 *(978-0-9827998-8-8(8),* KID-E Bks.) Word Prodns.

Parra, Jen. Crazy Old Lou. Meier, Paul, illus. 2005. (J). bds. 9.99 *(978-1-4183-0063-0(2))* Christ Inspired, Inc.

Parragon Staff. Mickey Mouse: Adventure Tales & Stories. 2010. (Disney Diecut Classics). 72p. (J). (gr. -1-1). *(978-1-4075-8937-4(7))* Parragon, Inc.

—Tigger's Adventure. 2010. (Disney Diecut Classics). 72p. (J). (gr. -1-1). *(978-1-4075-8903-9(2))* Parragon, Inc.

Parrish, Amanda. Greyhound Travels: Puma Travels to Italy. 2010. 28p. pap. 12.49 *(978-1-4490-9453-9(8))* AuthorHouse.

Parrish, Edith. Sarah the Purple Goose Gets Lost. Odom, Kelly, illus. 2011. 34p. 23.95 *(978-1-60844-930-9(0))* Dog Ear Publishing, LLC.

Parrish, Edith E. Sara the Purple Goose & Susan the Black Swan. 2010. 24p. pap. 17.99 *(978-1-4490-8879-8(1))* AuthorHouse.

Parrish, Emma. Lou. 2010. 106p. pap. 15.95 *(978-1-4452-6573-5(7))* Lulu Pr., Inc.

Parrish, Fayrene. Pancho Saves the Day: Shipmates Learning Adventures Venture. Parrish, Fayrene, illus. 2010. (Illus.). 42p. (J). 15.95 *(978-0-9826717-8-8(4))* Parrish, Fayrene.

Parrish, Harry. Kate & Alice. 2009. 28p. pap. 13.40 *(978-1-4389-3120-3(4))* AuthorHouse.

Parsons, Bruce. Siah Carter & the Ship Monitor. 2009. 36p. pap. 16.99 *(978-1-4490-3435-1(7))* AuthorHouse.

Parsons, Caroline Renee. The Coffins in the Basement. 2008. 134p. pap. 24.95 *(978-1-60563-140-0(X))* America Star Bks.

Parsons, Julie. Julianne & the Jinn, the Evil Genie. 2008. 56p. pap. 16.95 *(978-1-60703-984-6(2))* America Star Bks.

Partee, Andrea. Jed, the Boy, the Snake & the Window. 2007. 160p. 30.99 *(978-1-4257-6401-2(0));* per. 20.99 *(978-1-4257-6399-2(5))* Xlibris Corp.

Particular, Nowen N. Boomtown, 1 vol. 2010. (ENG.). 320p. pap. 9.99 *(978-1-4003-1553-6(0))* Nelson, Thomas Inc.

Parton, Paula. Room 17 - Where History Comes Alive - Missions. Parton, Paula, illus. 2010. (Illus.). 126p. pap. 8.95 *(978-1-935630-19-7(9))* Bellissima Publishing, LLC.

—Room 17 'Where History Comes Alive!' Book Ii, Explorers. 2008. 120p. pap. 8.95 *(978-0-9794815-3-6(8))* Bellissima Publishing, LLC.

Parus, M. V. The Adventures of Mamma Simone, Jodie & Zed: The Mystery of the Pirate's Lost Treasure. 2006. 115p. (YA). per. 12.95 *(978-1-58374-148-1(8))* Chicago Spectrum Pr.

Parvensky Barwell, Catherine A. Tommi Goes Camping, 4 vols. Barwell, Matthew W. et al, eds. Parvensky Barwell, Catherine A., illus. 2006. (Illus.). 40p. (J). 14.95 *(978-0-9774409-3-1(1),* TL004) ILT Publishing.

—Tommi Goes to the Beach, 4 vols. Barwell, Matthew W. & Parvensky, Mary T., eds. 2006. (Illus.). 40p. (J). *(978-0-9774409-2-4(3),* TL003) ILT Publishing.

—Tommi Lance Grows Up, 4 vols. 2006. (Illus.). 30p. (J). *(978-0-9774409-0-0(7),* TL001) ILT Publishing.

—Tommi's First Snowfall, 4 vols. 2006. (Illus.). 32p. (J). *(978-0-9774409-1-7(5),* TL002) ILT Publishing.

Pascal, Francine. Fearless 3: Rebel; Heat; Blood. 2014. (Fearless Ser.: 3). (ENG., Illus.). 656p. (YA). (gr. 9). pap. 10.99 *(978-1-4814-0270-5(6),* Simon Pulse) Simon Pulse.

—Kill Game. 2005. (Fearless FBI Ser.: 1). (ENG.). 272p. (YA). (gr. 11). pap. 11.99 *(978-0-689-87821-3(4),* Simon Pulse) Simon Pulse.

—Lucha por la Fama. Orig. Title: Claim to Fame. (SPA.). 128p. (J). 6.95 *(978-84-272-3793-3(6))* Molino, Editorial ESP. Dist: AIMS International Bks., Inc.

—Mocosos. Orig. Title: Jessica & the Brat Attack. (SPA.). 112p. (J). 6.95 *(978-84-272-3590-8(9))* Molino, Editorial ESP. Dist: AIMS International Bks., Inc.

Pascal, Francine & Frost, Michael. Live Bait. 2005. (Fearless FBI Ser.: 2). (ENG.). 208p. (YA). (gr. 11). pap. 10.99 *(978-0-689-87822-0(2),* Simon Pulse) Simon Pulse.

Pascoe, Bruce. Sea Horse. 2016. (ENG.). 110p. (J). (gr. 4-7). pap. 12.99 *(978-1-921248-93-1(9))* Magabala Bks. AUS. Dist: Independent Pubs. Group.

Pascual, Dennis Mark. The Adventures of Dj the Butterfly & Friends Series Presents Dj's Birthday Party. 2012. 20p. pap. 10.15 *(978-1-105-35838-8(0))* Lulu Pr., Inc.

Pasha, Georgia. Jelly Bean & Key Mystery. 2005. 17.00 *(978-0-8059-9909-9(4),* RoseDog Bks.) Dorrance Publishing Co., Inc.

Passaniti, Connie. The Fairy Garden Zodiac Adventure. 2012. 38p. pap. 25.49 *(978-1-4478-7060-9(3))* Lulu Pr., Inc.

Passen, Lisa. Monkey Mountain. 2013. 234p. pap. 14.99 *(978-1-60820-880-7(X))* MLR Pr., LLC.

Pastor, N. Allie Mckay: And the Keepers of the Golden Cross. 2008. 280p. 25.99 *(978-1-60647-248-4(8));* pap. 15.99 *(978-1-60647-247-7(X))* Salem Author Services.

Pastor, Norma. The Young Alchemists & the Vatican's Legion of Evil. 2013. 472p. pap. 30.95 *(978-1-4633-6179-2(3))* Palibrio.

Pastor Wil. It's Good, Okay, & Alright, 1 vol. 2010. 28p. pap. 24.95 *(978-1-4489-7065-0(2))* PublishAmerica, Inc.

A Pat on the Back. 2003. (J). per. *(978-1-57657-879-7(8))* Paradise Pr., Inc.

Patchett, Mary Elwyn. Ajax: Golden Dog of the Australian Bush. Tansley, Eric, illus. 2011. 172p. 42.95 *(978-1-258-01103-1(4))* Literary Licensing, LLC.

—The Great Barrier Reef. Monroe, Joan Kiddell, illus. 2011. 210p. 44.95 *(978-1-258-08492-9(9))* Literary Licensing, LLC.

Patchett, Terry. Nation. 2011. 10.36 *(978-0-7848-3498-5(9),* Everbind) Marco Bk. Co.

Patey, Nicola. Aspireland & the story of George. 2010. 101p. pap. 16.95 *(978-1-4457-2458-4(8))* Lulu Pr., Inc.

Pati, Geeta. Finny's Voyage Through the Universe: Nebula, Supernova, Open Star Cluster. 2007. 100p. per. 11.95 *(978-1-59526-422-0(1),* Llumina Pr.) Aeon Publishing Inc.

Paticoff, Melanie. Sophie's Tales: Overcoming Obstacles. Vales, Chrissie, illus. 2012. 42p. 25.95 *(978-0-9851575-6-2(9))* Sophie's Tales, LLC.

Patrick, David. Nero Demare & the Legend of the Vampires. 2007. 284p. (YA). per. 17.95 *(978-0-595-42014-8(1))* iUniverse, Inc.

Patrick, Jim. The Adventures of Artemous Bk. 1: Mouse in the Museum. 2015. (ENG., Illus.). 52p. (J). pap. 12.95 *(978-1-62287-915-1(5))* First Edition Design eBook Publishing.

Patrick.J.Jardine. S r b U: Sir. Robert, Belmont, Uberdon the Third. 2011. 16p. pap. 13.99 *(978-1-4490-4336-0(4))* AuthorHouse.

Patten, E. J. The Legend Thief. Rocco, John, illus. 2014. (Hunter Chronicles Ser.: 2). (ENG.). 384p. (J). (gr. 3-7). pap. 7.99 *(978-1-4424-2036-6(7),* Simon & Schuster Bks. For Young Readers) Simon & Schuster Bks. For Young Readers.

Patten, Laurien. The Left Hand of Aneryn. Date not set. (Illus.). 352p. (YA). *(978-1-885173-95-9(4))* Write Way Publishing.

Patterson, Eric. Carl Nose the Truth. Wright, Christopher, illus. 2007. 104p. (J). pap. 6.95 *(978-0-9797106-6-7(9))* Avid Readers Publishing Group.

—Fluffy, a Puppy with a Purpose. Mathis, Leslie, illus. 2013. 146p. pap. 6.99 *(978-1-61286-150-0(4))* Avid Readers Publishing Group.

—Nature Boy. Wright, Christopher, illus. 2007. 112p. (J). pap. 6.95 *(978-0-9797106-0-5(X))* Avid Readers Publishing Group.

—Nature Boy Nature Strikes Back. Wright, Chris, illus. 2008. 108p. pap. 6.95 *(978-1-935105-15-2(9))* Avid Readers Publishing Group.

—Something Lurking in the Bell Tower. Christopher, Wright, illus. 2007. 99p. (J). pap. 6.95 *(978-0-9797106-1-2(8))* Avid Readers Publishing Group.

Patterson, James. Angel. 2011. (Maximum Ride Ser.). (YA). 54.99 *(978-1-60941-970-7(7))* Findaway World, LLC.

—Angel. (Maximum Ride Ser.: 7). (ENG.). (gr. 5-17). 2012. 352p. pap. 10.00 *(978-0-316-03832-4(6))* 2011. 384p. pap. 22.99 *(978-0-316-12201-6(7))* Little Brown & Co. (Jimmy Patterson).

—Angel. 2012. (Maximum Ride Ser.: 7). lib. bdg. 20.85 *(978-0-606-23452-8(7),* Turtleback) Turtleback Bks.

—The Angel Experiment. 2nd rev. ed. 2007. (Maximum Ride Ser.: 1). (ENG., Illus.). 464p. (YA). (gr. 5-17). per. 10.00 *(978-0-316-06795-9(4),* Jimmy Patterson) Little Brown & Co.

—Fang. (ENG.). 2014. (Best of Maximum Ride Ser.: 3). 352p. mass mkt. 8.00 *(978-1-4555-3070-0(0))* 2011. (Maximum Ride Ser.: 6). 368p. (YA). (gr. 5-17). pap. 10.00 *(978-0-316-03831-7(8))* 2010. (Maximum Ride Ser.: 6). 416p. (gr. 5-17). pap. 23.99 *(978-0-316-07106-2(4))* Little Brown & Co. (Jimmy Patterson).

—The Final Warning. 2008. (Maximum Ride Ser.: 4). (ENG.). 304p. (YA). (gr. 5-17). pap. 10.00 *(978-0-316-00287-5(9),* Jimmy Patterson) Little Brown & Co.

—The Final Warning. l.t. ed. 2009. (Maximum Ride Ser.: No. 4). 420p. (YA). 23.95 *(978-1-4104-1626-1(7))* Thorndike Pr.

—Max. 2009. (Maximum Ride Ser.: 5). (ENG.). (YA). (gr. 5-17). 352p. pap. 9.99 *(978-0-316-00290-5(9),* Jimmy Patterson); 416p. 23.99 *(978-0-316-03759-4(1))* Little Brown & Co.

—Maximum Ride. 2015. (Maximum Ride: the Manga Ser.: 9). lib. bdg. 24.50 *(978-0-606-38045-4(0))* Turtleback Bks.

—Maximum Ride Forever. 2015. (Maximum Ride Ser.: 9). (ENG.). 400p. (YA). (gr. 7-17). 19.00 *(978-0-316-20750-8(0),* Jimmy Patterson) Little Brown & Co.

—Nevermore: The Final Maximum Ride Adventure. 2012. (Maximum Ride Ser.: 8). (ENG.). 384p. (YA). (gr. 5-17). 17.99 *(978-0-316-10184-4(2),* Jimmy Patterson) Little Brown & Co.

—Saving the World: And Other Extreme Sports. 3rd rev. ed. 2008. (Maximum Ride Ser.: 3). (ENG.). 432p. (YA). (gr. 5-17). pap. 10.00 *(978-0-316-15427-7(X),* Jimmy Patterson) Little Brown & Co.

—Saving the World & Other Extreme Sports. 2008. (Maximum Ride Ser.: Bk. 5). 429p. (gr. 4-7). 18.00 *(978-0-7569-8353-6(3))* Perfection Learning Corp.

—Saving the World & Other Extreme Sports. l.t. ed. 2007. (Maximum Ride Ser.: No. 3). 489p. (J). (gr. 3-7). 23.95 *(978-0-7862-9887-7(1))* Thorndike Pr.

—School's Out - Forever. rev. ed. 2007. (Maximum Ride Ser.: 2). (ENG., Illus.). 448p. (YA). (gr. 5-17). per. 10.00 *(978-0-316-06796-6(2),* Jimmy Patterson) Little Brown & Co.
—School's Out - Forever. 2008. (Maximum Ride Ser.: Bk. 2). 418p. (gr. 4-7). 18.00 *(978-0-7569-8349-9(5))* Perfection Learning Corp.
—School's Out - Forever. 2007. (Maximum Ride Ser.: 2). (YA). lib. bdg. 20.85 *(978-1-4177-7493-7(2),* Turtleback) Turtleback Bks.
Patterson, James & Dembowski, Jill. The Kiss. 2013. (Witch & Wizard Ser.: 4). (ENG.). 384p. (YA). (gr. 7-17). pap. 10.00 *(978-0-316-10176-9(1),* Jimmy Patterson) Little Brown & Co.
Patterson, James & Grabenstein, Chris. Danger down the Nile. Neufeld, Juliana, illus. 2014. (Treasure Hunters Ser.). (ENG.). 480p. (J). (gr. 3-7). 14.99 *(978-0-316-37086-8(X),* Jimmy Patterson) Little Brown & Co.
—Secret of the Forbidden City. Neufeld, Juliana, illus. 2015. (Treasure Hunters Ser.: 3). (ENG.). 448p. (J). (gr. 3-7). 14.99 *(978-0-316-28480-6(7),* Jimmy Patterson) Little Brown & Co.
—Treasure Hunters. Neufeld, Juliana, illus. (Treasure Hunters Ser.: 1). (ENG.). 480p. (J). (gr. 3-7). 2015. pap. 8.00 *(978-0-316-20757-7(8))* 2013. 14.99 *(978-0-316-20756-0(X))* Little Brown & Co. (Jimmy Patterson).
—Treasure Hunters. 2015. (Treasure Hunters Ser.: 1). (J). lib. bdg. 18.45 *(978-0-606-37305-0(5))* Turtleback Bks.
—Word of Mouse. Sutphin, Joe, illus. 2016. (ENG.). 304p. (J). (gr. 3-7). 13.99 *(978-0-316-34956-7(9),* Jimmy Patterson) Little Brown & Co.
Patterson, James, et al. Treasure Hunters. Neufeld, Juliana, illus. 2013. 451p. (J). *(978-0-316-24262-2(4))* Little Brown & Co.
Patterson, Michael. The Adventures of Spot: Cody, Boozer & Aaliyah, 1 vol. 2010. 68p. pap. 19.95 *(978-1-4489-5517-6(3))* America Star Bks.
Patterson, Nancy Ruth. A Simple Gift. 2009. 128p. (gr. 3-7). pap. 10.95 *(978-1-4401-1206-5(1))* iUniverse, Inc.
Patterson, Sandra Jean. Crabby Crab. 2006. bds. 12.95 *(978-1-59700-246-2(1))* Island Heritage Publishing.
Patton, Jack. The Chameleon Attack (Battle Bugs #4) 2015. (Battle Bugs Ser.: 4). (ENG., Illus.). 128p. (J). (gr. 2-5). pap. 4.99 *(978-0-545-70784-8(6),* Scholastic Paperbacks) Scholastic, Inc.
—The Dragonfly Defense. 2016. (Battle Bugs Ser.: 7). (ENG.). 128p. (J). (gr. 2-5). pap. 4.99 *(978-0-545-94509-7(7),* Scholastic Paperbacks) Scholastic, Inc.
—The Poison Frog Assault (Battle Bugs #3) 2015. (Battle Bugs Ser.: 3). (ENG.). 128p. (J). (gr. 2-5). pap. 4.99 *(978-0-545-70744-2(7),* Scholastic Paperbacks) Scholastic, Inc.
—The Spider Siege. 2015. (Battle Bugs Ser.: 2). (ENG.). 128p. (J). (gr. 2-5). pap. 4.99 *(978-0-545-70742-8(0),* Scholastic Paperbacks) Scholastic, Inc.
Pattou, Edith. Fire Arrow: The Second Song of Eirren. 2005. (ENG., Illus.). 348p. (YA). (gr. 7-12). pap. 7.95 *(978-0-15-205530-1(4))* Houghton Mifflin Harcourt Publishing Co.
Pau Pau. The Princess' Adventure. 2007. 52p. pap. 16.95 *(978-1-60441-069-3(8))* America Star Bks.
Paul, Donita K. Two Renegade Realms, 1 vol. 2014. (Realm Walkers Ser.). (ENG.). 416p. (YA). pap. 13.99 *(978-0-310-73581-6(5))* Zondervan.
Paul J McSorley; Illustrated By Patricia. The Adventures of Forealdo. Bearss, Patricia, illus. 2011. 36p. pap. 24.95 *(978-1-4560-8429-5(1))* America Star Bks.
Paul, John. Copters. Young, Bill, illus. 2012. 36p. 24.95 *(978-1-4626-9458-7(6))* America Star Bks.
Paula, Cristina De. Sweet Pomchu. 2011. 28p. pap. 15.99 *(978-1-4568-5816-2(5))* Xlibris Corp.
Paulding, James Kirke. Westward Ho! 2004. reprint ed. pap. 26.95 *(978-1-4191-9343-9(0));* pap. 1.99 *(978-1-4192-9343-6(5))* Kessinger Publishing, LLC.
Paulding, Steve. The Wonderful Adventures of Bradley the Bat. Schmidt, Caleb & Schmidt, Carter, illus. 2013. 70p. pap. 18.95 *(978-0-615-74591-6(1))* Slow on the Draw Productions.
Pauley, Christa. Manda Panda & the Loons. 2013. 32p. pap. 19.99 *(978-1-62697-016-8(5))* Salem Author Services.
Pauline, Christi. Hullabaloo at the Zoo. 2008. 28p. pap. 14.95 *(978-1-4389-1204-2(8))* AuthorHouse.
Paull, John W. The Great Stampede: A Jimmy James Story. 2010. 28p. 16.09 *(978-1-4269-4698-1(8))* Trafford Publishing.
Paulsen, Gary. Brian's Hunt. (Hatchet Adventure Ser.). (ENG.). (YA). 2012. 144p. (gr. 5). pap. 9.99 *(978-0-307-92959-4(0),* Ember) 2003. 112p. (gr. 7). 14.95 *(978-0-385-74647-2(4),* Lamb, Wendy Bks.) Random Hse. Children's Bks.
—The Legend of Bass Reeves: Being the True & Fictional Account of the Most Valiant Marshal in the West. 2008. (ENG., Illus.). 160p. (YA). (gr. 7-9). mass mkt. 6.99 *(978-0-553-49429-7(5),* Laurel Leaf) Random Hse. Children's Bks.
—Masters of Disaster. 2011. (ENG.). 112p. (J). (gr. 3-7). 5.99 *(978-0-375-86610-4(8),* Yearling) Random Hse. Children's Bks.
—The River. unabr. ed. 2004. (Middle Grade Cassette Librariestm Ser.). 132p. (J). (gr. 5-9). pap. 29.00 incl. audio *(978-0-8072-8704-0(0),* S YA 241 SP, Listening Library) Random Hse. Audio Publishing Group.
—Tucket's Travels: Francis Tucket's Adventures in the West, 1847-1849. 2003. (Francis Tucket Bks.: Bks. 1-5). (ENG.). 560p. (J). (gr. 3-7). pap. 8.99 *(978-0-440-41967-9(0),* Yearling) Random Hse. Children's Bks.
Paulsen, Gary & Roberts, Esyllt Nest. Craig y Diafol. 2005.Tr. of Devil's Wall. (WEL.). 64p. pap. *(978-0-86381-684-0(3))* Gwasg Carreg Gwalch.
—Plygu Amser. 2005. (WEL.). 80p. pap. *(978-0-86381-683-3(5))* Gwasg Carreg Gwalch.
Paulsen, Gary, et al. Paraswt! 2005.Tr. of Skydive! (WEL.). 66p. pap. *(978-0-86381-685-7(1))* Gwasg Carreg Gwalch.
Paulson, Elizabeth. Dead upon a Time. 2015. (ENG.). 224p. (J). (gr. 7). 17.99 *(978-0-545-64046-6(6),* Scholastic Pr.) Scholastic, Inc.
Paulson, Michael William. The Baker Street Bunch & the Missing Bracelet Mystery. 2005. (Illus.). (J). per. *(978-0-9754241-2-4(2))* MiMar Publishing.
Pavanello, Roberto. The Chilly Mammoth, 1 vol. Zeni, Marco, tr. from ITA. Pisapia, Biasco & Brughera, Pamela, illus. 2013. (Echo & the Bat Pack Ser.). (ENG.). 128p. (gr. 2-3). 9.95 *(978-1-4342-4889-3(5))* Stone Arch Bks.
Pavelka, Patricia. The Adventures of Victor. 2003. (ENG., Illus.). 32p. (J). per. 7.99 *(978-0-9722918-1-1(4))* Husky Trail Pr. LLC.
Pavelka, Pavelka. Foodle. 2004. (ENG., Illus.). 32p. (J). per. 7.99 *(978-0-9722918-2-8(2))* Husky Trail Pr. LLC.
Pavese, Candace. Caught in the Net. Holroyd, Geraldine, illus. 2013. 84p. pap. 9.95 *(978-1-937449-19-3(X))* YAV.
Pavlova, Elena. Adventures at Tall Oaks: New Friends. 2004. (Illus.). 80p. (J). 19.95 *(978-0-9755839-0-6(5))* Read 2 Children.
P.A.W. My Summer Road Trip. 2012. 28p. pap. 15.99 *(978-1-4691-5077-2(8))* Xlibris Corp.
PAW Patrol, P. A. W. PAW Patrol: Chase to the Rescue. 2016. (ENG.). 24p. (J). (gr. -1 — 1). 18.99 *(978-0-7944-3801-2(6),* Reader's Digest Children's Bks.) Studio Fun International.
Payjack, Amy J. The Valorean. 2012. 426p. 34.99 *(978-1-4771-5239-3(3));* pap. 23.99 *(978-1-4771-5238-6(5))* Xlibris Corp.
Payne, Gaynell. I Go Exploring. Buffinet, Jacqueline, illus. 2012. 34p. 21.99 *(978-0-9884657-0-1(1))* DreamLand Mediaworks LLC.
Payne, Gregory. Chase to the Brazen Head. 2010. (ENG.). 228p. (YA). (gr. 4-7). pap. 11.95 *(978-988-18094-6-9(0))* Haven Bks.
Payne, Rachel. Autumn Secrets of the Equinox. 2004. (Iggy Colvin Adventure Ser.: Bk. 2). 286p. 27.95 *(978-0-595-66647-8(7))* iUniverse, Inc.
Payne, Raymond. Shelter from the Storm. rev. ed. 2004. 144p. (YA). pap. 9.95 *(978-0-9740552-1-3(2))* Harbourside Pr.
Payson, Howard. The Boy Scouts at the Panama Canal. 2005. reprint ed. pap. 30.95 *(978-1-4179-2457-8(8))* Kessinger Publishing, LLC.
Pea, M. J. The adventures of Benje & Sammy: Probably the naughtiest dogs in the World. 2011. (Illus.). 72p. (gr. -1). pap. 24.83 *(978-1-4567-7812-5(9))* AuthorHouse.
Peace, Bob. The Wicked Witch Pop Quiz. Rasheed, M., illus. 2013. 132p. pap. 12.95 *(978-0-9824741-4-3(8))* Sojourner Publishing, Inc.
Peachey, Ann. The Adventures of a Greek Cat Called Mani. 2012. (Illus.). 44p. pap. 24.40 *(978-1-4685-8206-2(2))* AuthorHouse.
Peachey, Ted. The Adventures of Ryan & His Magic Carrot. 2010. 90p. pap. 9.99 *(978-1-60911-222-6(9),* Eloquent Bks.) Strategic Book Publishing & Rights Agency (SBPRA).
PeachMoon Publishing. The Adventures of Lucky the Lizard Las aventuras del lagarto Lucky. 2008. (ENG & SPA., Illus.). 100p. (J). pap. 19.95 *(978-0-9795831-4-8(4))* PeachMoon Publishing.
Peacock, Shane. Double You, 1 vol. 2014. (Seven Sequels Ser.). (ENG., Illus.). 272p. (J). (gr. 5-10). pap. 10.95 *(978-1-4598-0534-7(8))* Orca Bk. Pubs. USA.
—Last Message, 1 vol. 2012. (Seven (the Series) Ser.). (ENG., Illus.). 256p. (J). (gr. 5-10). pap. 9.95 *(978-1-55469-935-3(5))* Orca Bk. Pubs. USA.
Peacock-Williams, Carol A. & Williams, Christy Jo. Benny the Beetle, 1 vol. Peacock, Bessie Merle, illus. 2010. 28p. 24.95 *(978-1-4489-8373-5(8))* PublishAmerica, Inc.
Peagler, Melissa. Lost Creek Rising Volume 2 of the Lost Creek Saga Series. 2012. 198p. pap. 12.95 *(978-1-939289-04-9(1),* Little Creek Bks.) Jan-Carol Publishing, INC.
Pearce, Bryony. Phoenix Rising. 2017. (ENG.). 336p. (J). (gr. 4). 15.99 *(978-1-5107-0734-4(4),* Sky Pony Pr.) Skyhorse Publishing Co., Inc.
Pearce, Jackson. The Inside Job: (and Other Skills I Learned As a Superspy) 2016. (ENG.). 272p. (J). 16.99 *(978-1-61963-420-6(1),* 9781619634206, Bloomsbury USA Childrens) Bloomsbury Publishing USA.
Pearce, Jacqueline. Emily's Dream, 1 vol. 2005. (Orca Young Readers Ser.: Sequel to Discovering Emily). (ENG., Illus.). 128p. (J). (gr. 3-6). per. 5.95 *(978-1-55143-368-4(0))* Orca Bk. Pubs. USA.
Pearce, Jonathan. Nobody's Fault: Surprises from the Earth & the Heart. 2006. 234p. (J). per. *(978-0-9765479-3-8(7))* Balona Bks.
Pearce, Margaret. Jumping into Trouble Book 3: Missing! a Horse. 2013. 66p. pap. *(978-1-922066-61-9(3))* Writers Exchange E-Publishing.
—Jumping into Trouble Series Book 1: Wanted! a Horse. 2013. 108p. pap. *(978-1-922066-59-6(1))* Writers Exchange E-Publishing.
Pearl, B. B. Poerava's Heaven. 2011. (Illus.). 88p. pap. 12.85 *(978-1-4567-8985-5(6))* AuthorHouse.
Pearson Education Staff. Pirates of the Caribbean the Curse of the Black Pearl. 2nd ed. 2008. (ENG.). 48p. pap. 11.99 *(978-1-4058-8170-8(4))* Pearson Education.
Pearson, J. J. Anita & Ing: Garden Adventure. 2012. 24p. pap. 12.95 *(978-1-4525-4248-5(1))* Balboa Pr.
Pearson, Jean W. & Dutto, Lisa M. Gravity Rocks. 2012. (Illus.). 60p. pap. 35.99 *(978-1-4685-2813-8(0))* AuthorHouse.
Pearson, Kathleen. We Love You a Lot, Little Polka Dot. 2011. 28p. (gr. -1). pap. 12.49 *(978-1-4567-4449-6(6))* AuthorHouse.
Pearson, Kimberly Ann. Mystling Glen Book I: The Tale of A Prince. 2009. 207p. pap. 14.95 *(978-1-4327-4169-3(1))* Outskirts Pr., Inc.
Pearson, Ridley. The Initiation. 2016. (Lock & Key Ser.: 1). 384p. (J). (gr. 3-7). 17.99 *(978-0-06-239901-4(2))* HarperCollins Pubs.
Pearson, Ridley. Lock & Key: the Downward Spiral. 2017. (Lock & Key Ser.: 2). 432p. (J). (gr. 3-7). 17.99 ***(978-0-06-239904-5(7))*** HarperCollins Pubs.
Pearson, Ridley & Barry, Dave. Peter & the Secret of Rundoon. Call, Greg, illus. rev. ed. 2009. (Peter & the Starcatchers Ser.: Bk. 3). (ENG.). 496p. (J). (gr. 5-9). pap. 9.99 *(978-1-4231-2326-2(3))* Hyperion Pr.
Pearson, Susan. We're Going on a Ghost Hunt, 0 vols. Schindler, S. D., illus. 2012. (ENG.). 32p. (J). (gr. -1-3). 16.99 *(978-0-7614-6307-8(0),* 9780761463078, Amazon Children's Publishing) Amazon Publishing.
Pease, D. Robert. Noah Zarc: Declaration. l.t. ed. 2013. 3. (ENG.). 226p. (gr. 3-8). pap. 11.95 *(978-1-62253-408-1(5))* Evolved Publishing.
—Noah Zarc: Mammoth Trouble. 2nd l.t. ed. 2013. 1. (ENG.). 214p. (gr. 3-8). pap. 11.95 *(978-1-62253-404-3(2))* Evolved Publishing.
—Noah Zarc: Omnibus. l.t. ed. 2013. 4. (ENG.). 630p. (gr. 3-8). 36.95 *(978-1-62253-410-4(7))* Evolved Publishing.
Peaty, Mary Alice. The Girl Who Lived on the Moon. 2008. 44p. pap. 26.95 *(978-0-557-02225-0(8))* Lulu Pr., Inc.
Peck, Lisa J. CTR Club Adventure Series: (Four-book Set), 4 bks. 2005. (J). pap. 24.95 *(978-0-9749241-9-9(9))* Golden Wings Enterprises.
Peck, Richard. The Mouse with the Question Mark Tail. 2014. (ENG.). 256p. (J). (gr. 3-7). pap. 7.99 *(978-0-14-242530-5(3),* Puffin Books) Penguin Young Readers Group.
—The Mouse with the Question Mark Tail. Murphy, Kelly, illus. 2013. (ENG.). 240p. (J). (gr. 3-7). 16.99 *(978-0-8037-3838-6(2),* Dial Bks) Penguin Young Readers Group.
—Secrets at Sea. 2012. (ENG.). 272p. (J). (gr. 3-7). pap. 7.99 *(978-0-14-242183-3(9),* Puffin Books) Penguin Young Readers Group.
—Secrets at Sea. Murphy, Kelly, illus. 2011. (ENG.). 256p. (J). (gr. 3-7). 16.99 *(978-0-8037-3455-5(7),* Dial Bks) Penguin Young Readers Group.
Peckover, Lyn. Sparkling Gold Dust. 2010. 86p. pap. 6.99 *(978-1-61667-074-0(6))* Raider Publishing International.
Pederson, Katie. The Point of No Return. 2006. 304p. pap. 29.95 *(978-1-4137-9945-3(0))* PublishAmerica, Inc.
Pedley, Linda J. A Journey of Brothers. 2013. 96p. pap. *(978-0-9878319-7-2(6))* Dream Write Publishing, Ltd.
Peebles, Joseph. The Stickman & the Crow. 2004. (ENG.). (YA). pap. 10.95 *(978-0-9644758-4-7(7))* Peebco Publishing Hse., The.
Peek-a-Boo, Hulk. 2003. (J). per. *(978-1-57657-816-2(X))* Paradise Pr., Inc.
Peek, Megan. Friendly Furries: The Annual Animal County Hop-a-Thon , the un-Surprise Birthday , the New Soccer Friend , the School Play , the Cook-off Contest. 2007. 76p. per. 19.95 *(978-1-4241-6193-5(2))* America Star Bks.
Peekhaus, Jennifer. The Little Red House. 2009. 16p. pap. 19.50 *(978-1-4389-1857-0(7))* AuthorHouse.
Peeler, Gail. Jackson's Magic Wishing Well. 2008. 25p. 35.50 *(978-1-4357-2950-6(1))* Lulu Pr., Inc.
Peeler, Penny. The Adventures of Spike & Sally. 2011. 52p. pap. 15.99 *(978-1-4568-9981-3(3))* Xlibris Corp.
Peep for Keeps. 2005. 43p. (J). 3.99 *(978-0-9763213-4-7(3))* OHC Group LLC.
Peet, Rosie. Amazing Battles! 2015. (DK Reader Level 2 Ser.). lib. bdg. 13.55 *(978-0-606-36686-1(5))* Turtleback Bks.
Pefferly, Lawrence. Larry Tyler & the Planet Buksdahud. 2007. 312p. pap. 16.95 *(978-0-9789969-2-5(5));* 24.95 *(978-0-9789969-1-8(7))* Tradition Publishing.
Peirce, Lincoln. Big Nate on a Roll. Peirce, Lincoln, illus. 2015. (Big Nate Ser.: 3). (ENG., Illus.). 224p. (J). (gr. 3-7). pap. 6.99 *(978-0-06-228357-3(X))* HarperCollins Pubs.
—Big Nate Triple Play Box Set. Peirce, Lincoln, illus. 2013. (Big Nate Ser.: 3). (ENG., Illus.). (J). (gr. 3-7). pap. 16.99 *(978-0-06-228360-3(X))* HarperCollins Pubs.
—Great Minds Think Alike. 2014. (Big Nate Ser.: 8). (ENG.). 224p. (J). 9.99 *(978-1-4494-3635-3(8))* Andrews McMeel Publishing.
Pekkalainen, Leena. Mummies, Monsters, & the Ship of Millions. 2017. (ENG., Illus.). 128p. pap. 18.95 ***(978-977-416-851-2(8))*** American Univ. in Cairo Pr.
Pelelo-Ray, Sam. Athenrei. 2006. 56p. pap. 16.95 *(978-1-4137-9946-0(9))* PublishAmerica, Inc.
Pellegata, Donna, illus. The Harp Mouse Chooses Her Home: The Adventure Begins. 2008. 24p. (J). pap. 6.95 *(978-0-9742174-1-3(7))* Heart & Harp LLC.
Pelton, Lisa. Logos & Adoption: Remi's Journey. 2012. 40p. pap. 14.95 *(978-1-4497-5378-8(7),* WestBow Pr.) Author Solutions, Inc.
Pemberton, Bernadette. Marshall's Marvelous Shoes. 2012. 24p. pap. 15.99 *(978-1-4771-4309-4(2))* Xlibris Corp.
Pemberton, Bert. Three for Adventure. 2013. 70p. pap. *(978-1-910053-03-4(1))* Legend Pr.
Peña-Solis, Marcia. Minna Vu & Her Super Special One of a Kind Fabulous Sparkly New Shoes. 2009. 40p. pap. 21.99 *(978-1-4363-8578-7(4))* Xlibris Corp.
Penberthy, Stephen. The Adventures of Bird Dog & Friends. 2009. 24p. pap. 10.99 *(978-1-4269-0977-1(2))* Trafford Publishing.
Pendergrass, D. Louis, a Blue Dragon. 2009. 32p. pap. 15.00 *(978-1-4389-9036-1(7))* AuthorHouse.
Pendergrass, Daphne. Riders of Berk: A Fiery Discovery. 2015. lib. bdg. 13.55 *(978-0-606-36311-2(4))* Turtleback Bks.
Penecale Jr., Richard P. The Luckiest Frog. 2009. 33p. (J). pap. 24.95 *(978-1-4327-3023-9(1))* Outskirts Pr., Inc.
Penlington, Nathan. The Boy in the Book: One Man's Adventure in Search of a Lost Childhood. 2015. (ENG., Illus.). 272p. 14.99 *(978-0-7553-6570-8(4))* Headline Publishing Group GBR. Dist: Hachette Bk. Group.
Penn, Audrey. Mystery at Blackbeard's Cove. Howard, Philip & Miller, Joshua, illus. 2004. (ENG.). 263p. (J). (gr. 2-7). per. 7.95 *(978-1-933718-09-5(9))* Tanglewood Pr.
—Mystery at Blackbeard's Cove. Howard, Philip & Miller, Josh, illus. 2004. (ENG.). 200p. (J). (gr. 3-7). 14.95 *(978-0-9749303-1-2(8))* Tanglewood Pr.
Penn, Linda M. Clayton's Birding Adventure: A Young Boy Learns the Secret Ways of Birds. 2013. 46p. pap. 10.95 *(978-0-9852488-5-7(8))* Racing to Joy Pr. LLC.
Penner, Stephen. Professor Barrister's Dinosaur Mysteries #1: The Case of the Truncated Troodon. Penner, Stephen, illus. 2010. (Illus.). 44p. pap. 19.25 *(978-1-60888-005-8(2))* Nimble Bks. LLC.
—Professor Barrister's Dinosaur Mysteries #2: The Case of the Armored Allosaurus. 2010. 54p. pap. 19.60 *(978-1-60888-018-8(4))* Nimble Bks. LLC.
Penny Z. The Adventures of Little Brother. 2012. 36p. pap. 16.95 *(978-1-4497-4480-9(X),* WestBow Pr.) Author Solutions, Inc.
Penovi, Celina. Alboroto a la Hora Del Desayuno / Scrambled Breakfast. 2009. 20p. pap. 14.99 *(978-1-4490-2743-8(1))* AuthorHouse.
—The Clumsy Stork - la Cigüeña Despistad. 2009. 32p. pap. 17.50 *(978-1-4490-2746-9(6))* AuthorHouse.
Penrose, Margaret. Dorothy Dale: A Girl of To-day. 2006. 152p. pap. 19.99 *(978-1-4264-1944-7(9))* Creative Media Partners, LLC.
—Dorothy Dale s Camping Days. 2007. (ENG.). 148p. pap. 18.99 *(978-1-4264-9201-3(4))* Creative Media Partners, LLC.
—Dorothy Dale's Camping Days. l.t. ed. 2007. (ENG.). 166p. pap. 21.99 *(978-1-4264-9258-7(8))* Creative Media Partners, LLC.
—The Motor Girls. 2007. (ENG.). 152p. pap. 19.99 *(978-1-4264-1903-4(1))* Creative Media Partners, LLC.
—The Motor Girls. 2004. reprint ed. pap. 1.99 *(978-1-4192-7466-4(X))* Kessinger Publishing, LLC.
—The Motor Girls on a Tour. 2007. 152p. pap. 19.99 *(978-1-4346-5779-4(5));* 172p. pap. 21.99 *(978-1-4346-5780-0(9))* Creative Media Partners, LLC.
—The Motor Girls on Cedar Lake: Or the Hermit of Fern Island. 2007. (ENG.). 156p. pap. 19.99 *(978-1-4346-5783-1(3));* 178p. pap. 21.99 *(978-1-4346-5784-8(1))* Creative Media Partners, LLC.
—The Motor Girls on the Coast or the Waif from the Se. 2011. 140p. pap. 9.99 *(978-1-61203-219-1(2))* Bottom of the Hill Publishing.
—The Motor Girls on Waters Blue. rev. ed. 2006. 228p. 27.95 *(978-1-4218-1802-3(7));* pap. 12.95 *(978-1-4218-1902-0(3))* 1st World Publishing, Inc. (1st World Library - Literary Society).
—The Motor Girls on Waters Blue. 2007. (ENG.). 164p. pap. 19.99 *(978-1-4264-2184-6(2))* Creative Media Partners, LLC.
—The Motor Girls on Waters Blue. 2004. reprint ed. pap. 1.99 *(978-1-4192-7467-1(8));* pap. 22.95 *(978-1-4191-7467-4(3))* Kessinger Publishing, LLC.
—The Motor Girls Through New England: Or Held by the Gypsies. 2007. (ENG.). 154p. pap. 19.99 *(978-1-4346-5805-0(8));* 172p. pap. 21.99 *(978-1-4346-5806-7(6))* Creative Media Partners, LLC.
Pepper, Sly. Dugan Peckles Through the Manhole. 2004. 190p. (gr. 4-6). pap. 5.99 *(978-0-9747668-0-5(1))* MindMaze Publishing Co.
Peralta, Joaquin. An Almost Private Eye: Mystery of the Starfighter. 2008. 260p. (YA). (gr. 8-18). per. 17.00 *(978-1-934376-17-1(5))* Balona Bks.
—Emma Snow: At the Edge of the World. 2009. 206p. (J). pap. 17.00 *(978-1-934376-19-5(1))* Balona Bks.
Percy, Richard & Baudet. The Silver Arrow. (Illus.). 128p. (J). pap. 7.95 *(978-0-233-99516-8(1))* Andre Deutsch GBR. Dist: Trafalgar Square Publishing.
Pereira, William. The Adventures of LC, the Lucky Calf. Bowlsby, Tina Marie, illus. 2005. (J). 18.95 *(978-0-9773133-0-3(1))* Little Tule Bks.
Perelman, Helen. A Candy Fairies Sweet Collection: Chocolate Dreams; Rainbow Swirl; Caramel Moon; Cool Mint. Waters, Erica-Jane, illus. 2013. (Candy Fairies Ser.). (ENG.). 512p. (J). (gr. 2-5). pap. 23.99 *(978-1-4424-9390-2(9),* Aladdin) Simon & Schuster Children's Publishing.
—Double Dip. Waters, Erica-Jane, illus. 2012. (Candy Fairies Ser.: 9). (ENG.). 128p. (J). (gr. 2-5). pap. 5.99 *(978-1-4424-2219-3(X),* Aladdin) Simon & Schuster Children's Publishing.
—Double Dip. Waters, Erica-Jane, illus. 2012. (Candy Fairies Ser.: 9). (ENG.). 128p. (J). (gr. 2-5). 15.99 *(978-1-4424-5972-4(7),* Simon & Schuster/Paula Wiseman Bks.) Simon & Schuster/Paula Wiseman Bks.
—A Royal Wedding: Super Special. Waters, Erica-Jane, illus. 2013. (Candy Fairies Ser.). (ENG.). 208p. (J). (gr. 2-5). pap. 5.99 *(978-1-4424-8898-4(0),* Aladdin) Simon & Schuster Children's Publishing.
—A Royal Wedding: Super Special. Waters, Erica-Jane, illus. 2013. (Candy Fairies Ser.). (ENG.). 208p. (J). (gr. 2-5). 15.99 *(978-1-4424-8899-1(9),* Simon & Schuster/Paula Wiseman Bks.) Simon & Schuster/Paula Wiseman Bks.
—A Valentine's Surprise. Waters, Erica-Jane, illus. 2011. (Candy Fairies Ser.: 7). (ENG.). 128p. (J). (gr. 2-5). pap. 5.99 *(978-1-4424-2215-5(7),* Aladdin) Simon & Schuster Children's Publishing.
Perera, Hilda. Mumu. (SPA.). (YA). (gr. 5-8). 100p. *(978-84-216-2557-6(8),* BU1696); 128p. 8.95 *(978-84-216-1207-1(7),* BU3780); 64p. 8.76 *(978-84-216-1611-6(0),* BU4757) Bruño, Editorial ESP. Dist: Lectorum Pubns., Inc.
Peretti, Frank E. The Cooper Kids, 4 vols. 2004. (Cooper Kids Adventure Ser.). 576p. pap., pap., pap. 27.96 *(978-1-58134-691-6(3))* Crossway.
—The Cooper Kids Adventure Series. 2004. (Cooper Kids Adventure Ser.). (gr. 5-7). 23.96 *(978-0-89107-901-9(7))* Crossway.
—The Deadly Curse of Toco-Rey. Life Publishers International Staff, tr. from ENG. 2005. (RUS., Illus.). 156p. (J). *(978-0-7361-0347-3(3))* Life Pubs. International.
—The Door in the Dragon's Throat. 2004. (Cooper Kids Adventure Ser.: 1). 128p. (J). (gr. 3-6). pap. 6.99 *(978-1-58134-618-3(2))* Crossway.
—Escape from the Island of Aquarius, Vol. 2. 2004. (Cooper Kids Adventure Ser.: 2). 160p. (J). pap. 6.99 *(978-1-58134-619-0(0))* Crossway.
—The Tombs of Anak. 2004. (Cooper Kids Adventure Ser.: No. 3). 144p. (gr. 4-7). 5.99 *(978-0-89107-593-6(3))* Crossway.
—Trapped at the Bottom of the Sea. 2004. (Cooper Kids Adventure Ser.: No. 4). 144p. (gr. 4-7). 5.99 *(978-0-89107-594-3(1));* Vol. 4. (J). (gr. 3-6). pap. 6.99 *(978-1-58134-621-3(2))* Crossway.
Pérez-Foncea, Juan Antonio & Caro, Stephen. Ivan of Aldenuri: The Forest of the Tauros. 2007. (J). *(978-1-59835-058-6(7))* Cambridge BrickHouse, Inc.
Perez-Martinez, Irella. Suyensita & Her Adventures. 2011. 48p. pap. 21.99 *(978-1-4568-5767-7(3))* Xlibris Corp.
Perez, Melissa E. Adventures of Camron, Tiffany & Lydi. 2011. 24p. pap. 24.95 *(978-1-4626-3724-9(8))* America Star Bks.
Perisic, Zoran. An Alien Called Freddy. 2012. 152p. pap. 9.95 *(978-1-60594-907-9(8),* Llumina Pr.) Aeon Publishing Inc.
Perkins, Kevin John. The Circlet. 2010. 316p. pap. *(978-1-907211-33-1(0))* Grosvenor Hse. Publishing Ltd.
Perkins, Lucy Fitch. The Irish Twins. 2008. 164p. pap. 9.95 *(978-1-59915-122-9(7))* Yesterday's Classics.

Perkins, Lynne Rae. As Easy As Falling off the Face of the Earth. (YA). (gr. 8). 2012. (ENG., Illus.). 384p. pap. 9.99 *(978-0-06-187092-7(7))* 2010. (ENG.). 368p. 16.99 *(978-0-06-187090-3(0))* 2010. 368p. lib. bdg. 17.89 *(978-0-06-187091-0(9))* HarperCollins Pubs. (Greenwillow Bks.).

—Nuts to You. Perkins, Lynne Rae, illus. 2014. (ENG., Illus.). 272p. (J). (gr. 3-7). 16.99 *(978-0-06-009275-7(0),* Greenwillow Bks.) HarperCollins Pubs.

Perrigo, Brad. Tuffy Mcnasty: The Rogue Elf Who Terrorized Christmas! 2012. 48p. pap. 21.88 *(978-1-4669-6147-0(3))* Trafford Publishing.

Perritano, John. Madness of Captain Cyclops, 1 vol. 2014. (Kid Squad Saves the World Ser.). (ENG.). 112p. (J). (gr. 8-12). lib. bdg. 27.07 *(978-1-62402-040-7(2),* Calico Chapter Bks) Magic Wagon.

Perry, Adam. Mister Ray. 2011. 230p. pap. 9.95 *(978-1-61646-084-6(9))* Coachwhip Pubns.

Perry, Brad Lee. Clumsy Claudia & the Gentle Forest Friends, 1 vol. Perry, Diana Torri, illus. 2010. 56p. pap. 16.95 *(978-1-4489-4633-4(6))* America Star Bks.

Perry, Dennis. Yakabou Must Choose: An African Adventure for Boys & Girls. 2004. 108p. (YA). pap. 10.95 *(978-0-7414-1766-4(9))* Infinity Publishing.

Perry, Douglas M. Boomer Likes to Point. 2013. 32p. pap. 24.95 *(978-1-62709-377-4(X))* America Star Bks.

Perry, Fred. Gold Digger, Vol. 6. 2011. (ENG.). 660p. (YA). pap., pap. 59.95 *(978-0-9831823-2-0(9),* 9780983182320) Antarctic Pr., Inc.

—Time Lincoln, Vol. 1. 2011. (ENG.). 122p. (YA). pap., pap. 19.95 *(978-0-9831823-7-5(X),* 9780983182375) Antarctic Pr., Inc.

Perry, Holly Lynn. Spinner's Mystic Travels: Lost in the Black Forest. 2003. pap. 9.00 *(978-0-8059-6291-8(3))* Dorrance Publishing Co., Inc.

Perry, M. LaVora. Taneesha's Treasures of the Heart. 2006. 56p. pap. 5.65 *(978-0-9759251-9-5(9))* Forest Hill Publishing, LLC.

Perry, Melanie Denise. Johnathan & Geneva the Adventures of Zeallionaire Kid's. Neal, Albert, ed. Ovakimyan, Liza, illus. 2013. 34p. pap. 11.99 *(978-0-9911077-1-1(3))* Sankofa Pr.

—Jonathan y Geneva Las Aventuras de Los Zeallionaire Kids. Neal, Albert, ed. Ovakimyan, Liza, illus. 2013. 34p. pap. 11.99 *(978-0-9911077-0-4(5))* Sankofa Pr.

Perry, Pete. The Saints in Paradise: Another Crazy Story for Crazy Kids. 2009. (Illus.). 76p. pap. 24.99 *(978-1-4490-1311-0(2))* AuthorHouse.

Perry, Shelly. Duckling's First Adventure. Loebel, Bonnie, illus. 2006. (ENG.). 56p. (J). per. 9.95 *(978-0-9787740-3-5(5))* Peppertree Pr., The.

Perry, Tally. Saving Sunny Stream, a Wormie Wormald Adventure. 2009. 60p. pap. 22.00 *(978-1-60860-296-4(6),* Eloquent Bks.) Strategic Book Publishing & Rights Agency (SBPRA).

Persaud, Sandhya S. One Day. Ahmad, Maryam & Ramotar, Alexandra, illus. 2009. 12p. pap. 12.99 *(978-1-4389-4437-1(3))* AuthorHouse.

Pertzborn, Cindy. How Do We Get to Heaven? 2012. 36p. pap. 16.95 *(978-1-4497-4585-1(7),* WestBow Pr.) Author Solutions, Inc.

Perugini, Donna. The Adventures of Amelia Airheart Butterfly. 2010. 36p. pap. 9.99 *(978-0-88144-537-4(1))* Yorkshire Publishing Group.

Peruzzo, Nicolas. Safari Dreams. Peruzzo, Nicolas, illus. 2012. (Illus.). 26p. pap. 9.99 *(978-1-61225-162-2(5))* Mirror Publishing.

Peschke, Marci. Kylie Jean, 1 vol. Mourning, Tuesday, illus. 2014. (Kylie Jean Ser.). (ENG.). 112p. (gr. 2-3). 317.10 *(978-1-4795-4545-2(7),* Kylie Jean) Picture Window Bks.

Peter & the Wolf. 2004. (Illus.). (J). *(978-1-84458-040-8(7),* Pavilion Children's Books) Pavilion Bks.

Peter & the Wolf. 2016. (Ladybird Tales Ser.). (ENG., Illus.). 48p. (J). (gr. k-2). 9.99 *(978-0-7232-9448-1(8))* Penguin Bks., Ltd. GBR. Dist: Independent Pubs. Group.

Peter L. Ward. Freya & the Fenris-Wolf. 2010. 184p. 24.50 *(978-1-4269-2511-5(5))*; pap. 14.50 *(978-1-4269-2510-8(7))* Trafford Publishing.

Peter Piper: 6 Small Books. (gr. k-2). 23.00 *(978-0-7635-8495-5(9))* Rigby Education.

Peterfreund, Diana. The Forbidden Fortress. 2017. (Omega City Ser.: 2). 304p. (J). (gr. 3-7). 16.99 *(978-0-06-231088-0(7))* HarperCollins Pubs.

—Omega City. 2015. (Omega City Ser.: 1). (ENG.). 336p. (J). (gr. 3-7). 16.99 *(978-0-06-231085-9(2))* HarperCollins Pubs.

Peterka, Edward S. Zoe Isabella Goes to the Zoo. 2011. 32p. pap. 12.77 *(978-1-4520-0305-4(X))* AuthorHouse.

Peters, Andrew. Ravenwood. 2011. (ENG.). 368p. (J). (gr. 5-9). 16.99 *(978-0-545-30550-1(0),* Chicken Hse., The) Scholastic, Inc.

Peters, Andrew Fusek. Dragon & Mousie. Wade, Gini, illus. 2006. (ENG.). 32p. (J). pap. 7.95 *(978-0-86243-650-6(8))* Y Lolfa GBR. Dist: Dufour Editions, Inc.

Peters, Andrew J. Banished Sons of Poseidon. 2015. (ENG.). 240p. (J). (gr. 7). pap. 11.95 *(978-1-62639-441-4(5))* Bold Strokes Bks.

Peters, E. G. The Voyage of Noah's Ark. 2011. 166p. 29.99 *(978-1-4653-4080-1(7))*; pap. 19.99 *(978-1-4653-4079-5(3))* Xlibris Corp.

Peters, Kara L. The Adventures of the Peters Family: A Dolphin of a Time. 2013. 12p. pap. 15.99 *(978-1-4685-4404-6(7))* AuthorHouse.

Peters, Stephanie True. Sleeping Beauty, Magic Master: A Graphic Novel. Lopez, Alex, illus. 2016. (Far Out Fairy Tales Ser.). (ENG.). 40p. (gr. 3-4). lib. bdg. 25.32 *(978-1-4965-3784-3(X),* Far Out Fairy Tales) Stone Arch Bks.

Petersen, Jean. Moose Shoes. Morrow, E., illus. 2007. 52p. per. 24.95 *(978-1-4241-8399-9(5))* America Star Bks.

Peterson, Brian. The Popcornmaker. 2007. 232p. 25.95 *(978-0-595-70458-3(1))*; per. 15.95 *(978-0-595-46727-3(X))* iUniverse, Inc.

Peterson, Jim. Kittens in the Mall. 2006. 76p. pap. 16.95 *(978-1-4241-2604-0(5))* PublishAmerica, Inc.

Peterson, Ruth. Its Time for Bed Stephanie... , but First. 2005. (J). per. *(978-1-932721-64-5(9))* My Heart Yours Publishing.

Peterson, Sara Budinger. The Journey of Perm. Kaufman, Mary Bee, illus. 2004. 96p. pap. 11.95 *(978-0-9665282-3-7(9))* Saranjon Publishing.

Peterson, Shelley. Stagestruck: The Saddle Creek Series. 2017. (Saddle Creek Ser.: 1). (ENG.). 344p. (YA). pap. 12.99 ***(978-1-4597-3945-1(0))*** Dundurn CAN. Dist: Ingram Publisher Services.

Petit, Karen. The Mystery of the Stolen Stallion. 2007. (Illus.). 246p. (J). per. 14.95 *(978-0-9794420-4-9(4))* Red Letter Pr.

Petkovich, David. The Story of Pete the Pig: A Truly Twisted Tail. 2012. 52p. pap. 24.99 *(978-1-4817-0043-6(X))* AuthorHouse.

Petri, Michelle. The Fvantom: Omegapocalypse. 2007. 212p. per. 14.95 *(978-0-595-45723-6(1))* iUniverse, Inc.

Petrucha, Stefan & Kinney, Sarah. Vampire Slayer, No. 2. 2010. (Nancy Drew the New Case Files Ser.). (ENG., Illus.). 64p. (J). (gr. 3-7). pap. 6.99 *(978-1-59707-233-5(8),* 9781597072335) Papercutz.

Petrucha, Stefan, et al. Papercutz Slices Boxed Set: Vol #1-3. 2012. (ENG., Illus.). 192p. (J). (gr. 5-12). 19.99 *(978-1-59707-274-8(5),* 9781597072748) Papercutz.

Petty, Kate. The Nightspinners. Smith, Mary Claire, illus. 2004. 32p. (J). pap. 8.99 *(978-1-84255-105-9(1),* Dolphin Paperbacks) Orion Publishing Group, Ltd. GBR. Dist: Trafalgar Square Publishing.

Pevear, Ted F. & Pevear, Linda W. The Date in the Junk Yard. 2012. 28p. 24.95 *(978-1-62709-781-9(3))* America Star Bks.

Peyo. Benny Breakiron #2: Madame Adolphine. 2013. (Benny Breakiron Ser.). (ENG., Illus.). 64p. (J). (gr. 2-12). 11.99 *(978-1-59707-436-0(5),* 9781597074360) Papercutz.

—Smurfiness to Go! A Smurfin' Big Adventure, Meet Smurfette!, Lazy Smurf Takes a Nap, the Thankful Smurf, Rain, Rain Smurf Away, the 100th Smurf. Peyo, illus. 2012. (Smurfs Classic Ser.). (ENG., Illus.). 144p. (J). (gr. -1-2). pap. 15.99 *(978-1-4424-6520-6(4),* Simon Spotlight) Simon Spotlight.

Peyton, K. M. Minna's Quest IR. 2013. (Roman Pony Trilogy Ser.). 186p. (J). pap. 5.99 *(978-0-7945-3143-0(1),* Usborne) EDC Publishing.

—No Turning Back IR. 2013. pap. 5.99 *(978-0-7945-3148-5(2),* Usborne) EDC Publishing.

Peyton, Km. Far from Home. 2014. (ENG., Illus.). 183p. (J). (gr. 4-7). pap. 5.99 *(978-0-7945-3292-5(6),* Usborne) EDC Publishing.

Pez, Christine & Duggins, Shirley. Casey & the Junkyard Cats: Pudgy's New Hero. 2010. 16p. 10.99 *(978-1-4520-8518-0(8))* AuthorHouse.

Pfeffer, Wendy. Life in a Coral Reef. Jenkins, Steve, illus. 2009. (Let's-Read-And-Find-Out Science 2 Ser.). (ENG.). 40p. (J). (gr. 1-4). pap. 5.99 *(978-0-06-445222-9(0))* HarperCollins Pubs.

—Light So Bright. Date not set. 40p. (J). (gr. -1-1). lib. bdg. 16.89 *(978-0-06-029122-8(2))* HarperCollins Pubs.

Pfister, Marcus. The Adventures of Rainbow Fish. 2014. (Rainbow Fish Ser.). (ENG., Illus.). 144p. (J). 19.95 *(978-0-7358-4185-7(3))* North-South Bks., Inc.

—Rainbow Fish Deep Sea Adventure Sticker & Coloring Storybook. 2010. (Rainbow Fish Ser.). (ENG.). 24p. (gr. -1-2). 5.95 *(978-0-7358-2318-1(9))* North-South Bks., Inc.

—Rainbow Fish Finds His Way. James, J. Alison, tr. from GER. Pfister, Marcus, illus. 2006. (Rainbow Fish Ser.). (ENG., Illus.). 32p. (J). (gr. k-3). 18.95 *(978-0-7358-2084-5(8))* North-South Bks., Inc.

Pfitsch, Patricia Curtis. Riding the Flume. 2004. (ENG., Illus.). 240p. (J). (gr. 5-9). pap. 11.99 *(978-0-689-86692-0(5),* Simon & Schuster/Paula Wiseman Bks.) Simon & Schuster/Paula Wiseman Bks.

Phanton, Rick. Boston & the Bean. 2012. 112p. pap. 19.95 *(978-1-4626-4809-2(6))* America Star Bks.

Pharaohs. (Awesome Adventures Ser.). 16p. (J). *(978-2-7643-0166-1(9))* Phidal Publishing, Inc./Editions Phidal, Inc.

Phelan, Matt. Around the World. Phelan, Matt, illus. (ENG., Illus.). 240p. (J). (gr. 4-7). 2014. pap. 12.99 *(978-0-7636-6925-6(3))* 2011. 24.99 *(978-0-7636-3619-7(3))* Candlewick Pr.

—Druthers. Phelan, Matt, illus. 2014. (ENG., Illus.). 32p. (J). (-k). 15.99 *(978-0-7636-5955-4(X))* Candlewick Pr.

Phelps, Ethel Johnston. The Hunter Maiden: Feminist Folktales from Around the World. Boynton, Suki, illus. 2017. (Feminist Folktales Ser.: 4). (ENG.). 200p. (J). (gr. 2-7). 14.95 ***(978-1-55861-434-5(6))*** Feminist Pr. at The City Univ. of New York.

Philbrick, Rodman. The Big Dark. (ENG.). 192p. (J). (gr. 3-7). 2017. pap. 6.99 ***(978-0-545-78976-9(1))*** 2016. 17.99 *(978-0-545-78975-2(3))* Scholastic, Inc. (Blue Sky Pr., The).

—Freak the Mighty. 169p. (J). pap. 4.99 *(978-0-8072-1521-0(X),* Listening Library) Random Hse. Audio Publishing Group.

—The Mostly True Adventures of Homer P. Figg. (ENG.). (J). (gr. 3-7). 2011. 240p. pap. 7.99 *(978-0-439-66821-7(2),* Scholastic Paperbacks) 2009. 224p. 16.99 *(978-0-439-66818-7(2),* Blue Sky Pr., The) Scholastic, Inc.

Phillips, Barry. Cave Express. 2010. 84p. pap. 12.61 *(978-0-557-25038-7(2))* Lulu Pr., Inc.

Phillips, Beth Ann. Crystal Kingdom, 1 vol. 2009. 63p. pap. 19.95 *(978-1-60813-003-0(7))* America Star Bks.

Phillips, Dee. Resistance Fighter, 1 vol., Bk. 10. 2015. (Yesterday's Voices Ser.). (ENG.). 48p. (YA). (gr. 9-12). pap. 8.95 *(978-1-62250-912-6(9))* Saddleback Educational Publishing, Inc.

Phillips, Dee & Ticktock Media, Ltd. Staff. What Do Kangaroos Do? 2009. (What Do Animals Do? Ser.). (ENG.). 5p. (J). (gr. k — 1). bds. 4.95 *(978-1-84696-959-1(X),* TickTock Books) Octopus Publishing Group GBR. Dist: Independent Pubs. Group.

Phillips, Dixie. Angel Eyes. Sponaugle, Kim, illus. 2008. 24p. pap. 10.95 *(978-1-933090-74-0(X))* Guardian Angel Publishing, Inc.

Phillips, Dixie & Snider, K. C. Stilts the Stork. 2011. 20p. pap. 10.95 *(978-1-61633-143-6(7))* Guardian Angel Publishing, Inc.

Phillips, Kent. The Red Eyed Black Dragon. 2011. 28p. pap. 15.99 *(978-1-4568-3795-2(8))* Xlibris Corp.

Phillips, Liam & Plumm, Gabi. Mumble & Jumble & the Great Corpsicle Conundrum. 2009. 278p. pap. 24.50 *(978-1-4092-5577-2(8))* Lulu Pr., Inc.

Phillips, Lorri. Ragamuffin Friends. 2010. 71p. pap. 14.00 *(978-0-557-73860-1(1))* Lulu Pr., Inc.

Phillips, Terrie. The Ski Trip. 2006. (Illus.). 38p. (J). lib. bdg. 12.95 *(978-0-9789449-0-2(9))* Tbooks Publishing Co.

Phillips, Valerie A. A Wish upon a Star. 2010. 28p. pap. 14.99 *(978-1-4520-7712-3(6))* AuthorHouse.

Philpot, Graham, illus. The Fish That Talked. 2008. (Usborne First Reading: Level 3 Ser.). 48p. (J). 8.99 *(978-0-7945-1945-2(8),* Usborne) EDC Publishing.

—Hansel & Gretel. 2007. (First Fairy Tales Ser.). 32p. (J). (gr. -1-3). lib. bdg. 28.50 *(978-1-59771-075-6(X))* Sea-To-Sea Pubns.

Phineas and Ferb. Phineas & Ferb Batter Up! 2010. pap. 5.99 *(978-1-4231-2408-5(1))* Disney Pr.

Phleger, Marjorie. Pilot Down, Presumed Dead. 206p. (J). (gr. 5-6). pap. 5.95 *(978-0-8072-1426-8(4))* Random Hse. Audio Publishing Group.

Picano, Jaime Gianna. The Mood Ring Adventure. 2008. 128p. pap. 11.95 *(978-0-595-47958-0(8))* iUniverse, Inc.

Pichon, Liz. Tom Gates That's Me! (Books One, Two, Three) Pichon, Liz, illus. 2016. (Tom Gates Ser.). (ENG., Illus.). (J). (gr. 3-7). pap. 23.97 *(978-0-7636-9216-2(6))* Candlewick Pr.

Pickering, Amanda. Alfred the Alien: Number Adventure. 2011. 18p. pap. 15.95 *(978-1-4327-7522-3(7))* Outskirts Pr., Inc.

Pickering, Lynne. James & the Naughty Seagull. Pickering, Lynne, illus. 2013. (Illus.). 32p. pap. 13.50 *(978-1-62857-333-6(3),* Strategic Bk. Publishing) Strategic Book Publishing & Rights Agency (SBPRA).

Pickering, Sean & Morrill, Scott. The Adventures of Danny & Spike: Underground. 2007. 92p. per. 9.95 *(978-0-595-44365-9(6))* iUniverse, Inc.

Pickford, Sue. Bob & Rob. 2014. (ENG., Illus.). 32p. (J). (gr. -1-2). 17.99 *(978-1-84780-343-6(1),* Frances Lincoln) Quarto Publishing Group UK GBR. Dist: Hachette Bk. Group.

Picou, Lin. Best Boat Race Ever! Reasoner, John, illus. 2012. (ENG.). 24p. (gr. 1-2). pap. 8.95 *(978-1-61810-317-8(2))* Rourke Educational Media.

Pier, Stanwood. The Jester of St. Timothy's. 2007. (ENG.). 116p. pap. 18.99 *(978-1-4346-1157-4(4))*; 128p. pap. 19.99 *(978-1-4346-1228-1(7))* Creative Media Partners, LLC.

Pierce, Ricky. Bouncing Billy. 2008. 24p. per. 10.95 *(978-1-4327-1696-7(4))* Outskirts Pr., Inc.

Pierce, Tamora. First Test. 2004. (Protector of the Small Ser.: No. 1). (ENG.). 240p. (YA). (gr. 7). pap. 9.99 *(978-0-375-82905-5(9),* Ember) Random Hse. Children's Bks.

—Lady Knight. 2004. (Protector of the Small Ser.: 4). (ENG.). 464p. (YA). (gr. 7-12). pap. 9.99 *(978-0-375-82908-6(3),* Ember) Random Hse. Children's Bks.

—Page. 2004. (Protector of the Small Ser.: 2). (ENG.). 288p. (YA). (gr. 7). pap. 9.99 *(978-0-375-82907-9(5),* Ember) Random Hse. Children's Bks.

—Squire. 2004. (Protector of the Small Ser.: 3). (ENG.). 432p. (YA). (gr. 7). pap. 9.99 *(978-0-375-82906-2(7),* Ember) Random Hse. Children's Bks.

—Wolf-Speaker. 2005. (Immortals Ser.: 2). (ENG.). 368p. (YA). (gr. 7). pap. 7.99 *(978-1-4169-0344-4(5),* Simon Pulse) Simon Pulse.

Pierpoint, Eric. The Last Ride of Caleb O'Toole. 2013. (ENG.). 304p. (J). (gr. 4-7). pap. 7.99 *(978-1-4022-8171-6(4),* 9781402281716, Sourcebooks Jabberwocky) Sourcebooks, Inc.

Pierre, Dana. Mousey, Mousey Finds Cheese? Illustrated by Wellon Pierre. 2006. 17.00 *(978-0-8059-9867-2(5))* Dorrance Publishing Co., Inc.

Pierson, Jan. The Haunted Horse of Gold Hill. 2005. (Ghostowners Ser.: Vol. 4). (Illus.). 109p. (J). per. 9.95 *(978-0-9721800-3-0(6))* WildWest Publishing.

Pighin, Marcel. Tickles the Bear Goes on a Cruise, 1 bk. Mitchell, Hazel, illus. 2006. 48p. (J). per. 10.49 *(978-0-9776679-7-0(9))* MP2ME Enterprise.

Pigott, Kat. Green Dinosaur Pancakes, 1 vol. Sibley, Mason, illus. 2016. (ENG.). 32p. (J). (gr. k-3). 16.99 *(978-1-4556-2177-4(3))* Pelican Publishing Co., Inc.

Pigott, Louise. Squirrel Me Timbers. 2016. (Fiction Picture Bks.). (ENG., Illus.). 24p. (gr. k-1). lib. bdg. 24.65 *(978-1-4795-9177-0(7),* Fiction Picture Bks.) Picture Window Bks.

Pikachu Press, . Catch Oshawott! Set: A Pokémon Look & Listen. 2012. (Pokemon Pikachu Press Ser.). (ENG.). 32p. (J). (gr. 3-6). 12.99 *(978-1-60438-158-0(2))* Pokemon, USA, Inc.

—Catch Snivy! A Pokémon Look & Listen Set. 2012. (Pokemon Pikachu Press Ser.). (ENG.). 32p. (J). (gr. 3-6). 12.99 *(978-1-60438-157-3(4))* Pokemon, USA, Inc.

—Catch Tepig! Set: A Pokémon Look & Listen. 2012. (Pokemon Pikachu Press Ser.). (ENG.). 32p. (J). (gr. 3-6). 12.99 *(978-1-60438-159-7(0))* Pokemon, USA, Inc.

—Pokémon Find 'Em All! Welcome to Unova! 2012. (Pokemon Pikachu Press Ser.). (ENG.). 42p. (J). (gr. 3-6). 9.99 *(978-1-60438-161-0(2))* Pokemon, USA, Inc.

Pike, Aprilynne. Glitter. 2016. (ENG., Illus.). 384p. (YA). (gr. 9). 17.99 *(978-1-101-93370-1(4),* Random Hse. Bks. for Young Readers) Random Hse. Children's Bks.

Pilcher, Steve. Pixar Animation Studio Artist Showcase over There. Pilcher, Steve, illus. 2014. (Pixar Animation Studios Artist Showcase Ser.). (ENG., Illus.). 40p. (J). (gr. -1-k). 17.99 *(978-1-4231-4793-0(6))* Hyperion Bks. for Children.

Pileggi, Joe. No Greater Love. 2009. 24p. pap. 10.49 *(978-1-4389-9377-5(3))* AuthorHouse.

Pilger, Seamus. Blast from the Past. Gilpin, Stephen, illus. 2017. (Fart Squad Ser.: 6). 128p. (J). (gr. 1-5). pap. 4.99 *(978-0-06-229055-7(X))* HarperCollins Pubs.

—The Toilet Vortex. Gilpin, Stephen, illus. 2016. (Fart Squad Ser.: 4). 112p. (J). (gr. 1-5). pap. 4.99 *(978-0-06-229051-9(7))* HarperCollins Pubs.

Pilkey, Dav. The Adventures of Super Diaper Baby. 2003. (Captain Underpants Ser.). (SPA & ENG., Illus.). 128p. (J). mass mkt. 5.99 *(978-0-439-55120-5(X),* Scholastic en Espanol) Scholastic, Inc.

—El Capitan Calzoncillos y la Feroz Batalla Contra el Nino Mocobionico Pt. 2: La Venganza de los Ridiculos Mocorobots. Azaola, Miguel, tr. Pilkey, Dav, illus. 2005. (Captain Underpants Ser.: Bk. 7). Orig. Title: Captain Underpants & the Big, Bad Battle of the Bionic Booger Boy, Part 2: The Revenge of the Ridiculous Robo-Boogers. (SPA & ENG., Illus.). 176p. (J). (gr. 2-5). pap. 5.99 *(978-0-439-66205-5(2),* Scholastic en Espanol) Scholastic, Inc.

—Captain Underpants & the Terrifying Return of Tippy Tinkletrousers. Pilkey, Dav, illus. 2012. (Captain Underpants Ser.: 9). (ENG., Illus.). 304p. (J). (gr. 2-5). 9.99 *(978-0-545-17534-0(8))* Scholastic, Inc.

—Captain Underpants & the Terrifying Return of Tippy Tinkletrousers. 2012. (Captain Underpants Ser.: 9). lib. bdg. 20.85 *(978-0-606-26523-2(6),* Turtleback) Turtleback Bks.

—Dog Man. Pilkey, Dav, illus. 2016. (Dog Man Ser.: 1). (ENG., Illus.). 240p. (J). (gr. 2). 9.99 *(978-0-545-58160-8(5),* Graphix) Scholastic, Inc.

—Dog Man Unleashed. 2016. (Dog Man Ser.: 2). (ENG., Illus.). 224p. (J). (gr. 2-7). 9.99 *(978-0-545-93520-3(2),* Graphix) Scholastic, Inc.

—Dog Man Unleashed. 2016. (Dog Man Ser.: 2). (ENG.). (J). (gr. 2). lib. bdg. 20.85 ***(978-0-606-39709-4(4))***; 240p. 20.85 *(978-0-606-39115-3(0))* Turtleback Bks.

—Ricky Ricotta's Mighty Robot. 2014. (Ricky Ricotta's Mighty Robot Ser.: 1). lib. bdg. 16.00 *(978-0-606-35799-9(8))* Turtleback Bks.

Pilkey, Dav. A Tale of Two Kitties. 2017. (Dog Man Ser.: bk.3). (ENG., Illus.). 256p. (J). (gr. 2-5). 9.99 ***(978-0-545-93521-0(0)***, Graphix) Scholastic, Inc.

—A Tale of Two Kitties. 2017. (Dog Man Ser.: 3). lib. bdg. 20.85 ***(978-0-606-40547-8(X))*** Turtleback Bks.

Pilling, Ann. The Year of the Worm. 172p. (J). (gr. 4-7). pap. 7.50 *(978-0-7459-4294-0(6),* Lion Books) Lion Hudson PLC GBR. Dist: Trafalgar Square Publishing.

Pillsbury, Samuel H. Mission to California. Kantrowitz, David, illus. 2003. (Planet Wampetter Adventure Ser.). 140p. (J). pap. 8.95 *(978-1-930085-03-9(6))* Perspective Publishing, Inc.

Pillsworth, Anne M. Fathomless. 2015. (Redemption's Heir Ser.: 2). (ENG.). 320p. (YA). 18.99 *(978-0-7653-3590-6(5),* 9780765335906, Tor Teen) Doherty, Tom Assocs., LLC.

Pilney, Dovie. Charlie the Cocky Rooster. 2010. 44p. pap. 18.49 *(978-1-4490-9806-3(1))* AuthorHouse.

—Charlie the Cocky Rooster: Another Adventure. 2008. 52p. pap. 20.95 *(978-1-4389-3517-1(X))* AuthorHouse.

—Charlie the Cocky Rooster: Leader of the Pack. 2011. 44p. (gr. -1). pap. 20.46 *(978-1-4567-4197-6(7))* AuthorHouse.

Pilot Point Pranksters. 2008. 56p. pap. 6.99 *(978-0-8341-2343-4(6),* 083-412-3436) Beacon Hill Pr. of Kansas City.

Pinkwater, Daniel M. Mrs. Noodlekugel. Stower, Adam, illus. 2013. (Mrs. Noodlekugel Ser.). (ENG.). 80p. (J). (gr. k-4). pap. 5.99 *(978-0-7636-6452-7(9))* Candlewick Pr.

—The Yggyssey: How Iggy Wondered What Happened to All the Ghosts, Found Out Where They Went, & Went There. 2010. (ENG., Illus.). 256p. (J). (gr. 5-7). pap. 6.99 *(978-0-547-32865-2(6))* Houghton Mifflin Harcourt Publishing Co.

Pinnington, Andrea. The Pirate Creativity Book. 2011. (Creativity Bks.). (ENG.). 80p. (J). (gr. 1-4). pap. 12.99 *(978-0-7641-4778-4(1))* Barron's Educational Series, Inc.

Pinson, Joseph. Joey & Big Wooley's Adventures. 2010. 88p. pap. 30.49 *(978-1-4520-4718-8(9))* AuthorHouse.

Pinter, Karin. Niki Owl: Leap of Faith. 2012. 172p. (gr. 4-6). 27.99 *(978-1-4772-8023-2(5))*; pap. 16.95 *(978-1-4772-8024-9(3))* AuthorHouse.

Pinto, Ferando. Little Heroes. 2012. (ENG.). (J). pap. 14.99 *(978-1-4507-8573-0(5))* Independent Pub.

Pirates of the Caribbean Dead Mans Chest. 2006. incl. audio compact disk *(978-1-4054-7260-9(X))* Parragon Bk. Service Ltd.

Pirnot, Karen Hutchins. Night Traveler. Pirnot, Karen Hutchins, illus. 2007. (Illus.). 24p. per. 12.95 *(978-1-934246-97-9(2))* Peppertree Pr., The.

—Sam's Perfect Plan. Ross, Julie, illus. 2008. 32p. pap. 12.95 *(978-0-9814894-8-3(6))* Peppertree Pr., The.

Pisarik, Michael E. Loonhaunt. 2006. (J). per. 19.95 *(978-1-59872-600-8(5))* Instant Pub.

Pitman, Colin. The House That Talked. 2012. (Illus.). 78p. pap. 13.66 *(978-1-4772-2639-1(7))* AuthorHouse.

Pitman, Sandra. 10 Busy Bumble Bees, 1 vol. Sizemore, Carmen, illus. 2009. 20p. pap. 24.95 *(978-1-60749-683-0(6))* America Star Bks.

Pitt, Darrell. Lost Sword. 2016. (Jack Mason Adventure Ser.). (ENG., Illus.). 256p. (J). (gr. 2-7). 7.99 *(978-1-925240-18-4(5))* Text Publishing Co. AUS. Dist: Consortium Bk. Sales & Distribution.

—The Monster Within. 2015. (Jack Mason Adventure Ser.). (ENG., Illus.). 264p. (J). (gr. 2-7). 7.99 *(978-1-922182-87-6(7))* Text Publishing Co. AUS. Dist: Consortium Bk. Sales & Distribution.

Pittar, Gill. Milly & Molly Go Camping (book W/dolls) 2006. 28p. pap. *(978-1-86972-097-1(0))* Milly Molly Bks.

—Milly, Molly & Beefy. 2004. (Illus.). 28p. *(978-1-86972-006-3(7))* Milly Molly Bks.

—Milly, Molly & Betelgeuse. 2004. (Illus.). 28p. *(978-1-86972-005-6(9))* Milly Molly Bks.

—Milly, Molly & Taffy Bogle. 2004. (Illus.). 28p. *(978-1-86972-001-8(6))* Milly Molly Bks.

—Milly, Molly & the Tree Hut. 2004. 28p. *(978-1-86972-028-5(8))* Milly Molly Bks.

—Milly, Molly & What Was That? 2004. 28p. *(978-1-86972-031-5(8))* Milly Molly Bks.

Pittman, Eddie. Red's Planet. 2016. (Red's Planet Ser.). (ENG., Illus.). 192p. (J). (gr. 3-7). 19.95 *(978-1-4197-1907-3(6),* Amulet Bks.) Abrams, Inc.

Pittman, Michael. Mackey's first Adventure. 2011. 24p. pap. 14.93 *(978-1-4269-5175-6(2))* Trafford Publishing.

Pittman, Seth. Raggy's Island. 2010. 124p. pap. 9.95 *(978-0-557-59557-0(6))* Lulu Pr., Inc.

Pitzorno, Blanca. La Casa del Arbol. 4th ed.Tr. of Casa sull'albero. (SPA., Illus.). 128p. (J). *(978-84-207-7771-9(4))* Grupo Anaya, S.A. ESP. Dist: Lectorum Pubns., Inc.

Pixar, told to. Monsters University Look & Find. 2013. 24p. (J). (gr. 1-3). 7.99 *(978-1-4127-9649-1(0),* ce47602a-38de-4bb7-82b3-69fb3502ef5d) Phoenix International Publications, Inc.

—Monsters University Play a Sound. 2013. (Illus.). 24p. (J). (gr. 1-3). 12.98 *(978-1-4508-1607-6(X),* 0e9ec920-3cca-43ee-9d08-a87cc2047168) Phoenix International Publications, Inc.

Pixie, B. R. Just a Little Human. 2011. 98p. pap. 19.95 *(978-1-4512-3551-7(8))* America Star Bks.
Plant, Marilyn. Trinka's Magic Bracelet. 2012. 40p. pap. *(978-1-77067-956-6(1))* FriesenPress.
—Trinka's Music Lessons. 2013. 48p. pap. *(978-1-4602-1273-8(8))* FriesenPress.
Platt, Kin. The Blue Man. 3rd collector's ed. 2005. (YA). 125.00 *(978-1-59885-000-0(8))*; 192p. 24.95 *(978-1-59885-001-7(6))* Two Lakes Pr., Inc.
Platt, Richard. Pirate Diary: The Journal of Jake Carpenter. Riddell, Chris, illus. 2014. (ENG.). 128p. (J). (gr. 4-7). pap. 6.99 *(978-0-7636-7361-1(7))* Candlewick Pr.
Platt, Richard & Dorling Kindersley Publishing Staff. Galactic Mission. 2014. (DK Adventures Ser.). (ENG.). 128p. (J). (gr. 3-7). pap. 5.99 *(978-1-4654-1977-4(2)*, DK Children) Dorling Kindersley Publishing, Inc.
Platt, Richard & Gifford, Clive. Spies Revealed. 2008. (ENG., Illus.). 32p. (J). (gr. 1-7). 21.99 *(978-1-4169-7113-9(0)*, Atheneum Bks. for Young Readers) Simon & Schuster Children's Publishing.
Pledger, Maurice. Billy Bunny & the Butterflies. 2013. (ENG., Illus.). 16p. (J). bds. 10.95 *(978-1-60710-808-5(9)*, Silver Dolphin Bks.) Readerlink Distribution Services, LLC.
—Dinosaur World. 2013. (Pledger Sticker Book Ser.). (ENG., Illus.). 80p. (J). (gr. -1). pap. 10.95 *(978-1-60710-819-1(4)*, Silver Dolphin Bks.) Readerlink Distribution Services, LLC.
Plez, Josey. My Adventures with Granny Roo - Riding Jessy. 2011. 24p. pap. 19.95 *(978-1-4626-3139-1(8))* America Star Bks.
Pliszka, Jodi. Bella & Gizmo's Adventures — Bella Gets A New Sweater. 2005. 32p. (J). per. 18.95 *(978-1-933449-26-5(8))* Nightengale Pr.
—Bella & Gizmo's Adventures — the Hairless Sphynx Cats. 2005. (Illus.). 30p. (J). per. 18.95 *(978-1-933449-27-2(6))* Nightengale Pr.
Plitt, Kay. Why Isn't Bobby Like Me, Mom? 2010. 32p. 14.75 *(978-1-4269-4038-5(6))* Trafford Publishing.
Plotkin, Andy. The Black Block Legend. 2007. 64p. per. 19.95 *(978-1-4241-9190-1(4))* America Star Bks.
Plotz, John. Time & the Tapestry. Saroff, Phyllis, illus. 2014. (ENG.). 192p. (YA). (gr. 4-6). 18.50 *(978-1-59373-145-8(0))* Bunker Hill Publishing, Inc.
Plourde, Josee & Barrette, Doris. Une Ombre au Tableau. 2003. (Roman Jeunesse Ser.). (FRE., Illus.). 96p. (J). (gr. 4-7). pap. *(978-2-89021-616-7(0))* Diffusion du livre Mirabel (DLM).
Plumberg, William. The Legend of Peggy Postue: The Girl with the Upturned Nose. 2011. 28p. pap. 15.99 *(978-1-4568-9635-5(0))* Xlibris Corp.
Plumides, Damon & Boerke, Arthur Mark. The Adventures of Caterwaul the Cat: Feline Pie. 2011. (ENG., Illus.). 226p. (J). (gr. 4-7). pap. 17.95 *(978-1-937084-19-6(1))* Boutique of Quality Books Publishing Co., Inc.
Plumier, Lea. The Story of Rhu the Fairy. Rambo, Angela, illus. 2012. 208p. pap. 11.95 *(978-1-61477-039-8(5))* Bellissima Publishing, LLC.
Pocha, Michael J. Thomas James & the Ringmaster. 2011. 180p. pap. 24.95 *(978-1-4560-6904-9(7))* America Star Bks.
Pociask, Stephen. Black Hole of Sacred Mountain. 2005. 109p. 18.95 *(978-0-9763811-0-5(9))* Loquacious Publishing Co.
Pockat, Alison A. Adam's Bubble. 2010. 76p. pap. 10.49 *(978-1-4490-9287-0(X))* AuthorHouse.
Poe, Mark Allen & Poe, Mark Andrew. Haunted Pizza. 2017. (ENG., Illus.). 184p. (J). 14.99 *(978-1-943785-38-4(4)*, 9781943785384) Rabbit Pubs.
Poe, Mark Andrew. Ending Easter. 2017. (ENG., Illus.). 216p. (J). 14.99 ***(978-1-943785-21-6(X)***, 9781943785216) Rabbit Pubs.
—Harry & His Time Machine. 2017. (ENG., Illus.). 180p. (YA). (gr. 6-8). 14.99 *(978-1-943785-04-9(X)*, 9781943785049) Rabbit Pubs.
—Harry's Christmas Carol. 2017. (ENG., Illus.). 213p. (J). 14.99 ***(978-1-943785-24-7(4)***, 9781943785247) Rabbit Pubs.
—Inkadink. 2017. (ENG., Illus.). 180p. (YA). 24.95 *(978-1-943785-10-0(4)*, 9781943785100) Rabbit Pubs.
—The Scary Smart House. 2017. (ENG., Illus.). 208p. (J). 14.99 *(978-1-943785-30-8(9)*, 9781943785308) Rabbit Pubs.
—Spooky Socks. 2017. (ENG., Illus.). 216p. (J). 14.99 ***(978-1-943785-34-6(1)***, 9781943785346) Rabbit Pubs.
Poe, Mark Andrew. Wand-Paper-Scissors. 2017. (ENG., Illus.). (J). 216p. 16.99 ***(978-1-943785-59-9(7)***, 9781943785599); 236p. 14.99 *(978-1-943785-00-1(7)*, 9781943785001) Rabbit Pubs.
Poe, Mark Andrew & Kuhn, Suzanne Brooks. Shades & Shenanigans. 2017. (ENG., Illus.). 224p. (YA). 14.99 *(978-1-943785-16-2(3)*, 9781943785162) Rabbit Pubs.
Pogo the Clown. Along Little Dogie: Harley's Great Adventures. Miller, Richard, illus. 2005. (J). 12.95 *(978-0-9755253-3-3(6))* Chiliric Pubns.
—A Brave Little Lion: Harley's Great Adventures. Miller, Richard D., illus. 2005. (J). 12.95 *(978-0-9755253-5-7(2))* Chiliric Pubns.
—The Great Blue Sky: Harley's Great Adventures. Miller, Richard D., illus. 2005. (J). 12.95 *(978-0-9755253-6-4(0))* Chiliric Pubns.
—A Little Gray Mouse: Harley's Great Adventures. Miller, Richard D., illus. 2005. (J). 12.95 *(978-0-9755253-7-1(9))* Chiliric Pubns.
—A Taste of Shrimp: Harley's Great Adventures. Miller, Richard D., illus. 2005. (J). 12.95 *(978-0-9755253-4-0(4))* Chiliric Pubns.
Poh, Jennie. Herbie's Big Adventure. Poh, Jennie, illus. 2016. (Fiction Picture Bks.). (ENG., Illus.). 40p. (gr. 1-2). lib. bdg. 23.32 *(978-1-5158-0234-1(5)*, Fiction Picture Bks.) Picture Window Bks.
Pohl, William L. The Amazing Flight of Daisy: A Runaway Kite Circles the World on the Back of the Wind. 2006. 72p. 20.00 *(978-1-4257-0666-1(5))* Xlibris Corp.
Poison Patrol: Coloring/Activity Book (English) 2005. (Illus.). (J). 2.99 *(978-1-933934-01-3(8))* Mighty Kids Media.
Poison Patrol: Coloring/Activity (English) Incl. Posters, Stickers. 2007. (J). 2.99 *(978-1-933934-53-2(0))* Mighty Kids Media.
Poison Patrol: Picture Book 8x8. 2007. (J). 5.99 *(978-1-933934-40-2(9))* Mighty Kids Media.
Poison Patrol: Picture Book (English) 9x9 with Snipe. 2007. (J). 5.99 *(978-1-933934-50-1(6))* Mighty Kids Media.
Pokémon Adventures: Black & White, Vol. 5. 2014. (ENG., Illus.). 208p. (J). pap. 9.99 *(978-1-4215-6181-3(6))* Viz Media.
Pokémon Adventures, Vol. 24. 2014. (ENG., Illus.). 216p. (J). pap. 9.99 *(978-1-4215-3558-6(0))* Viz Media.
Pokémon Adventures, Vol. 25. 2014. (ENG., Illus.). 208p. (J). pap. 9.99 *(978-1-4215-3559-3(9))* Viz Media.
Polan, Alex. Catching the Jigglypuff Thief. 2016. (Unofficial Adventures for Pokemon GO Players Ser.: 1). lib. bdg. 18.40 ***(978-0-606-39657-8(8))*** Turtleback Bks.
—Catching the Jigglypuff Thief: PokéStop Stories, Book One. 2016. (ENG.). 112p. (J). (gr. 1-7). pap. 7.99 *(978-1-5107-2157-9(6)*, Sky Pony Pr.) Skyhorse Publishing Co., Inc.
—Chasing Butterfree. 2016. (Unofficial Adventures for Pokemon GO Players Ser.: 3). lib. bdg. 18.40 ***(978-0-606-39655-4(1))*** Turtleback Bks.
—Chasing Butterfree: Unofficial Adventures for Pokémon GO Players, Book Three. 2016. (Unofficial Adventures for Pokémon GO Players Ser.). (ENG.). 112p. (J). (gr. 1-7). pap. 7.99 *(978-1-5107-2204-0(1)*, Sky Pony Pr.) Skyhorse Publishing Co., Inc.
—Cracking the Magikarp Code: Unofficial Adventures for Pokémon GO Players, Book Four. 2016. (Unofficial Adventures for Pokémon GO Players Ser.). (ENG.). 112p. (J). (gr. 1-7). pap. 7.99 *(978-1-5107-2205-7(X)*, Sky Pony Pr.) Skyhorse Publishing Co., Inc.
—Following Meowth's Footprints. 2016. (Unofficial Adventures for Pokemon GO Players Ser.: 2). lib. bdg. 18.40 ***(978-0-606-39658-5(6))*** Turtleback Bks.
Polan, Alex. Following Meowth's Footprints: PokéStop Stories, Book Two. 2016. (ENG.). 112p. (J). (gr. 1-7). pap. 7.99 *(978-1-5107-2158-6(4)*, Sky Pony Pr.) Skyhorse Publishing Co., Inc.
Polanco, Amparo. The Magical Forest. 2016. (ENG., Illus.). (J). 16.95 ***(978-1-5069-0268-5(5))***; pap. 12.95 ***(978-1-5069-0269-2(3))*** First Edition Design eBook Publishing.
Poland, Pitch & Poland, Inglan. Lost & Found. Rose, Drew, illus. 2013. 30p. (J). *(978-0-9853430-0-2(1))* Little P Pr. Co.
Polden, Kelly Carper. Puppy Tales: The Adventures of Adam the Australian Sheppard. 2007. (ENG.). 72p. pap. 11.99 *(978-1-4196-7458-7(7))* CreateSpace Independent Publishing Platform.
Polette, Keith. Paco & the Giant Chile Plant/Paco y la Planta de Chile Gigante. de la Vega, Eida, tr. Dulemba, Elizabeth, illus. 2008. (SPA & ENG.). 32p. (J). (gr. -1-3). lib. bdg. 16.95 *(978-0-9770906-2-4(0)*, Raven Tree Pr.,Csi) Continental Sales, Inc.
Police, Gerard. Herbert the Frog Goes to the Store. 2008. 20p. pap. 13.50 *(978-1-60693-066-3(4)*, Eloquent Bks.) Strategic Book Publishing & Rights Agency (SBPRA).
Poling Kilough, Melissa. Titus the Turtle & the Hard Shell Story. 2009. 28p. pap. 13.99 *(978-1-4490-0962-5(X))* AuthorHouse.
Politi, Leo. Emmet. 2009. (ENG., Illus.). 32p. 16.95 *(978-0-89236-992-8(2))* Oxford Univ. Pr., Inc.
Polk, Douglas. The Legend of Garle Pond. 2008. 60p. pap. 16.95 *(978-1-60703-985-3(0))* America Star Bks.
Pollock, J. A. Titus & Otis & the Arctic Adventure. 2009. 151p. pap. 12.00 *(978-0-557-03427-7(2))* Lulu Pr., Inc.
Poltera, Anne. Castle Magic & the Sinister Encroaching Fir Wood. 2012. (Illus.). 256p. (-18). pap. 19.76 *(978-1-4772-3943-8(X))* AuthorHouse.
Ponti, James. Blue Moon. 2013. (Dead City Ser.: 2). (ENG., Illus.). 336p. (J). (gr. 4-8). 17.99 *(978-1-4424-4131-6(3)*, Aladdin) Simon & Schuster Children's Publishing.
Pooker, J. D. The Ifs. 2013. (ENG.). 148p. (J). pap. 7.95 *(978-0-9858280-3-5(X))* Little Devil Bks.
Pool, Catherine. Catrina's Journey to Her Musical Friends, 1 vol. 2010. 18p. pap. 24.95 *(978-1-4489-7237-1(X))* PublishAmerica, Inc.
Poole, Richard. The Iron Angel. 2007. (Book of Lowmoor Ser.: 3). (ENG., Illus.). 384p. (J). (gr. 7). 19.95 *(978-0-689-87550-2(9))* Simon & Schuster, Ltd. GBR. Dist: Simon & Schuster, Inc.
Poole, Vera. The Adventures of Natsoodatie: The Stolen Blankets. 2013. 24p. pap. 14.93 *(978-1-4669-8719-7(7))* Trafford Publishing.
Pope, Brennan & Pope, Janet. The Adventures of William Walkingstick. 2007. 132p. (gr. 2-2). per. 11.95 *(978-0-595-45786-1(X))*; Vol. 1. 21.95 *(978-0-595-69866-0(2))* iUniverse, Inc.
Pope, Cheryl Lynn. The Adventures of Princess Zari. Nyamor, Eric, illus. 2009. 34p. pap. 12.99 *(978-0-9840660-1-8(2))* Second Time Media & Communications.
Pope, Cody/Louis Ray. Andy & the Dragons. 2008. (Illus.). 48p. (J). per. *(978-0-9798792-1-0(3))* Scavenger's Pubns.
Pope, P. R. Queens of Antares: Volume 1 of the Bloodline Trilogy: Bloodline Returned: Bloodline Returned. 2012. (ENG., Illus.). 224p. pap. *(978-1-908168-01-6(3)*, Elsewhen Pr.) Alnpete Ltd.
Pope, Paul. Sugary Shorts. 2013. (Adventure Time Ser.: 1). (ENG.). 144p. (J). (gr. 4). 34.99 *(978-1-60886-333-4(6))* Boom! Studios.
Pope, Paul & Petty, J. T. The Rise of Aurora West. Rubín, David, illus. 2014. (Battling Boy Ser.). (ENG.). 160p. (J). (gr. 5-12). pap. 9.99 *(978-1-62672-009-1(6)*, 9781626720091, First Second Bks.) Roaring Brook Pr.
Pope, Paul & Renier, Aaron. Adventure Time Vol. 1: Sugary Shorts. 2014. lib. bdg. 33.05 *(978-0-606-35466-0(2))* Turtleback Bks.
Popke, Suzanne L. The Adventures of Tolei Mergen. 2013. 36p. pap. 24.95 *(978-1-4626-8863-0(2))* America Star Bks.
Popper, Garry. High Noon in Didley Pidley. Forshaw, John, illus. 2004. (Bret the Vet Ser.). 40p. 7.00 *(978-1-84161-013-9(5))* Ravette Publishing, Ltd. GBR. Dist: Parkwest Pubns., Inc.
Porfirio, Guy. Jump! 2012. (J). *(978-1-933855-81-3(9))* Rio Nuevo Pubs.
Porteous, Barbara. Little Cloud's Christmas Adventure. 2011. (Illus.). 32p. pap. 15.66 *(978-1-4520-0176-0(6))* AuthorHouse.
Porter, Alan J. Cars: Route 66 Dash! Gladfelter, Allen, illus. 2010. (Cars Ser.). (ENG.). 112p. (J). (gr. 3-6). pap. 9.99 *(978-1-60886-585-7(1))* Boom! Studios.
Porter, Amber Leann. To Be a Champion. 2008. 31p. pap. 24.95 *(978-1-60610-222-0(2))* PublishAmerica, Inc.
Porter, Kevin Don. Missing. 2013. 166p. pap. 11.99 *(978-0-9857014-7-5(1))* Artists' Orchard, LLC, The.
Portman, Michelle Eva. Compost, by Gosh! An Adventure with Vermicomposting. Portman, Michelle Eva, illus. l.t. ed. 2003. (ENG., Illus.). 42p. (J). 16.95 *(978-0-942256-16-1(6)*, Falcon Guides) Globe Pequot Pr., The.
Posner-Sanchez, Andrea & Hitchcock, Laura. Moana Little Golden Book (Disney Moana) RH Disney & Sastrawinata-Lemay, Griselda, illus. 2016. (Little Golden Book Ser.). (ENG.). 24p. (J). (-k). 4.99 *(978-0-7364-3603-8(0)*, Golden/Disney) Random Hse. Children's Bks.
Posner-Sanchez, Andrea & Julius, Jessica. Oaken's Invention (Disney Frozen) Random House Disney Staff, illus. 2016. (Pictureback(R) Ser.). (ENG.). 24p. (J). (gr. -1-2). 4.99 *(978-0-7364-3632-8(4)*, RH/Disney) Random Hse. Children's Bks.
Posnock, Michael A. The Adventures of Wilbur the Wave. 2013. 44p. pap. 17.99 *(978-1-4808-0132-5(1))* Archway Publishing.
Post, Bobby. The Adventures of Jimmy. 2007. 48p. per. 16.95 *(978-1-4137-8704-7(5))* America Star Bks.
Post, Grace. Three Dogs Go Walking. Mogyorosi, Nicole, illus. 2009. 32p. pap. 24.95 *(978-1-61546-147-9(7))* America Star Bks.
Poth, Karen, et al. The Pirates Who Don't Do Anything & Me! 2004. (Big Idea Books / VeggieTales Ser.). (ENG., Illus.). 32p. (J). 7.99 *(978-0-310-70725-7(0))* Zonderkidz.
Potter, Alan Mitchell & Williams, Virginia. Hoo-Hoo Hooty-Hoo-Who. 2005. 9.00 *(978-0-8059-9807-8(1))* Dorrance Publishing Co., Inc.
Potter, Beatrix. The Classic Tale of Peter Rabbit: And Other Cherished Stories. Santore, Charles, illus. 2013. (ENG.). 68p. (J). 19.95 *(978-1-60433-376-3(6)*, Applesauce Pr.) Cider Mill Pr. Bk. Pubs., LLC.
—El Conejo Pedro. 2003. (Coleccion el Mundo de Peter Rabbit). (SPA., Illus.). (J). (gr. k-2). pap. *(978-950-07-1718-2(2)*, SA30684) Editorial Sudamericana S.A. ARG. Dist: Lectorum Pubns., Inc.
—Mystery Thief! 2013. (Peter Rabbit Animation Ser.). (ENG.). 32p. (J). (gr. -1-k). 3.99 *(978-0-7232-8041-5(X)*, Warne) Penguin Young Readers Group.
—Peter & Friends Sticker Activity Book. 2013. (Peter Rabbit Animation Ser.). (ENG., Illus.). 16p. (J). (gr. -1-2). pap. 6.99 *(978-0-7232-8042-2(8)*, Warne) Penguin Young Readers Group.
—The Peter Rabbit & Friends Treasury. Potter, Beatrix, illus. 2006. (Illus.). 240p. (J). (gr. k-4). reprint ed. 20.00 *(978-1-4223-5452-0(0))* DIANE Publishing Co.
—The Tale of Peter Rabbit. 2010. (ENG.). 30p. pap. 9.49 *(978-1-4538-2670-6(X))* CreateSpace Independent Publishing Platform.
Potter, David. The Left Behinds: Abe Lincoln & the Selfie That Saved the Union. 2016. (Left Behinds Ser.). (ENG.). 304p. (J). (gr. 3-7). 16.99 *(978-0-385-39060-6(2)*, Crown Books For Young Readers) Random Hse. Children's Bks.
—The Left Behinds: the iPhone That Saved George Washington. 2016. (Left Behinds Ser.). (ENG.). 368p. (J). (gr. 3-7). 7.99 *(978-0-385-39059-0(9)*, Yearling) Random Hse. Children's Bks.
Potter, Ellen. The Kneebone Boy. 2011. (ENG.). 304p. (J). (gr. 4-7). pap. 8.99 *(978-0-312-67432-8(5)*, 9780312674328) Square Fish.
Potter, George. The Wisemen of Bountiful. Harmon, Glenn, illus. 2005. per. 11.99 *(978-1-55517-814-7(6))* Cedar Fort, Inc./CFI Distribution.
Potter, Kay. I Hate Fairies! the Adventures of Katie James. 2013. 140p. pap. 13.97 *(978-1-62212-127-4(9)*, Strategic Bk. Publishing) Strategic Book Publishing & Rights Agency (SBPRA).
Pottorf, Patricia D. Hebee, the Quibber. 2012. 64p. pap. 19.50 *(978-1-61897-350-4(9)*, Strategic Bk. Publishing) Strategic Book Publishing & Rights Agency (SBPRA).
Potts, Christiane Elenes. Lola & the Caterpillar. 2011. 28p. pap. 13.99 *(978-1-4520-2563-6(0))* AuthorHouse.
Potvin, James E. The Adventures of Forest the Ferret: Forest's First Snowfall & Forest's Cottage. 2007. 32p. per. 13.95 *(978-1-4327-0556-5(3))* Outskirts Pr., Inc.
Poulsen, David A. No Time Like the Past. 3rd rev. ed. 2007. (Salt & Pepper Chronicles). (ENG., Illus.). 160p. (J). (gr. 4-7). 6.95 *(978-1-55263-807-1(3))* Leaf Storm Pr.
—The Prisoners & the Paintings. 5th ed. 2008. (Salt & Pepper Chronicles: No. 5). (ENG.). 176p. (J). (gr. 2-7). *(978-1-55470-015-8(9))* Me to We.
—Shivers & Shakes. 2009. (Salt & Pepper Chronicles Ser.). (ENG.). 176p. (J). (gr. 3-7). pap. *(978-1-55470-144-5(9))* Me to We.
Poulter, David. Morris & Mini Minor & Friends: A Day at the Seaside. 2010. (ENG., Illus.). 50p. pap. *(978-1-84748-774-2(2))* Athena Pr.
Powell, Christine. Bootsie's Underground Adventure. 2012. 28p. pap. 24.95 *(978-1-4626-7449-7(6))* America Star Bks.
Powell, Gail. The Adventures of Harold J. Kat. 2008. 40p. pap. 16.99 *(978-1-4259-6334-7(X))* AuthorHouse.
Powell, Gary Allison. In That Land There Are Giants. Johnston, Jillian S., illus. 2011. 38p. pap. 14.50 *(978-1-60860-891-1(3)*, Eloquent Bks.) Strategic Book Publishing & Rights Agency (SBPRA).
Powell, Gregg E. Goobadabers. Lea, Corinne, illus. 2011. 24p. pap. 24.95 *(978-1-4626-0734-1(9))* America Star Bks.
Powell, Huw. Spacejackers. 2015. (Spacejackers Ser.). (ENG.). 336p. (YA). (gr. 3-6). 16.99 *(978-1-61963-515-9(1)*, 9781619635159, Bloomsbury USA Childrens) Bloomsbury Publishing USA.
Powell, Jim S. The Mystery of the Totem Trees: A Plumroy Pack Adventure. 2009. 124p. pap. 10.95 *(978-1-4401-3921-5(0))* iUniverse, Inc.
Powell, Lenora Y. Ardo: The Mysterious New House. 2008. 105p. pap. 19.95 *(978-1-60672-133-9(X))* America Star Bks.
Powell, Richard. Bear. Gardner, Louise, illus. 2014. (Bathing Beauties Ser.). (ENG.). 8p. (J). (gr. -1 — 1). 7.99 *(978-1-4380-7441-2(7))* Barron's Educational Series, Inc.
—Duck. Gardner, Louise, illus. 2014. (Bathing Beauties Ser.). (ENG.). 8p. (J). (gr. -1 — 1). 7.99 *(978-1-4380-7442-9(5))* Barron's Educational Series, Inc.
—Frog. Gardner, Louise, illus. 2014. (Bathing Beauties Ser.). (ENG.). 8p. (J). (gr. -1 — 1). 7.99 *(978-1-4380-7443-6(3))* Barron's Educational Series, Inc.
Power, Barry. The First Ice Pigeon of London. 2009. 80p. pap. 10.49 *(978-1-4490-3070-4(X))* AuthorHouse.
Power, Laura. Air-Born. 2013. 322p. pap. 16.99 *(978-0-9894792-4-0(2))* Winter Goose Publishing.
Power, Molly. Up & down with Lena Larocha. Carter, Barbara, illus. 2013. 169p. pap. 15.00 *(978-1-60571-176-8(4)*, Shires Press) Northshire Pr.
Power, Nicholas D. Paudie's Magical Adventures. 2009. 236p. 24.75 *(978-1-60693-534-7(8)*, Strategic Bk. Publishing) Strategic Book Publishing & Rights Agency (SBPRA).
The Power of Chocolate. 2005. (YA). *(978-0-9771020-0-6(9))* Savas, Bachtsoglou.
Powers, J. L. & Powers, M. A. Broken Circle. 2017. (ENG.). 320p. (J). (gr. 6). pap. 14.95 ***(978-1-61775-580-4(X)***, Black Sheep) Akashic Bks.
Powers, Nelda Means & Terrell, Caitlyn. Puddle Puppy Goes to the Farm. 2012. 32p. pap. *(978-1-77067-628-2(7))* FriesenPress.
Pranali. The Secret Storybook. 2013. 64p. pap. 23.95 *(978-1-4828-0147-7(7))* Partridge Pub.
Prasad, Sunayna. Alyssa's African Adventures. 2011. pap. 11.95 *(978-0-7414-6619-8(8))* Infinity Publishing.
Pratcher, Roger & Pratcher, Birgit. June Bear Adventures: The Missing Pies. 2007. 236p. per. 11.95 *(978-1-4327-0352-3(8))* Outskirts Pr., Inc.
Pratchett, Terry. Dodger. 368p. (YA). (gr. 8). 2013. pap. 9.99 *(978-0-06-200951-7(6))* 2012. 17.99 *(978-0-06-200949-4(4))* 2012. lib. bdg. 18.89 *(978-0-06-200950-0(8))* HarperCollins Pubs.
Pratt, Pierre. Marcel et Andre. 2003. (Picture Bks.). (FRE., Illus.). 32p. (J). (gr. -1). *(978-2-89021-633-4(0))* Diffusion du livre Mirabel (DLM).
Pratt, Sally. The Adventures of Bernie the Bee in Sally's Garden. 2013. 46p. pap. 21.99 *(978-1-4772-9759-9(6))* AuthorHouse.
Praveeta. Imagine Travelling to the Most Mysterious & Unusual Places! Ash, illus. 2011. (ENG.). 146p. (J). pap. *(978-0-9872096-0-3(4)*, Travel Tales of Elves) Praveeta Kumar.
Pray, Linda. Characters in the Wild. 2011. 44p. pap. 16.95 *(978-1-4560-7904-8(2))* America Star Bks.
—Characters of Adventure. 2011. 54p. pap. 16.95 *(978-1-4560-5787-9(1))* America Star Bks.
Prehistoria. 2005. (Coleccion Las Grandes Aventuras Ser.). (SPA.). (J). 21.95 *(978-968-7381-52-7(3))*; pap. 17.95 *(978-968-7381-48-0(5))* Tecolote, Ediciones, S.A. de C.V. MEX. Dist: Iaconi, Mariuccia Bk. Imports.
Preik, Christel D. Growing up Joyfully. 2012. 36p. pap. 15.49 *(978-1-4669-0869-7(6))* Trafford Publishing.
—Sharing the Love. 2013. 36p. pap. 15.49 *(978-1-4669-9975-6(6))* Trafford Publishing.
Preller, James. The Courage Test. 2016. (ENG.). 224p. (J). 16.99 *(978-1-250-09391-2(0)*, 9781250093912) Feiwel & Friends.
Prentice, Amy. Mouser Cats' Story. 2004. reprint ed. pap. 1.99 *(978-1-4192-3542-9(7))*; pap. 15.95 *(978-1-4191-3542-2(2))* Kessinger Publishing, LLC.
Prenzlau & Suttom. The by Times' Kid Sisters: Three-in-One 1-3, 4-6, 7-9, 10-12, 12 vols. 355p. 15.99 *(978-1-56871-239-0(1))* Targum Pr., Inc.
Preston, Helen M. Gra Gra's Stories. 2012. 72p. pap. 28.99 *(978-1-4772-9783-4(9))* AuthorHouse.
Pretty Little Lilly & the Dragon's Slumber. 2008. (Illus.). 38p. (J). pap. *(978-0-9777241-4-7(X))* Cepia LLC.
Preus, Margi. The Bamboo Sword. (ENG., Illus.). (YA). (gr. 5-9). 2016. 368p. pap. 8.95 *(978-1-4197-0824-4(4))* 2015. 352p. 16.95 *(978-1-4197-0807-7(4))* Abrams, Inc. (Amulet Bks.).
—Shadow on the Mountain. 2012. (ENG., Illus.). 304p. (YA). (gr. 3-7). 17.95 *(978-1-4197-0424-6(9)*, Amulet Bks.) Abrams, Inc.
Previn, Stacey. Aberdeen. 2016. (ENG., Illus.). 40p. (J). (-k). 16.99 *(978-0-451-47148-2(2)*, Viking Books for Young Readers) Penguin Young Readers Group.
Prevost, Pamela Ms Ed. The Adventures of Charlie: The Curious Cat & Me. 2012. 32p. (-18). pap. 21.99 *(978-1-4797-4280-6(5))* Xlibris Corp.
Price & Wilkinson. The Saga of Aslak. 2004. (ENG., Illus.). 96p. 8.95 *(978-0-7136-4076-2(6)*, A&C Black) Bloomsbury Publishing Plc GBR. Dist: Consortium Bk. Sales & Distribution.
Price, David J. Tom & Emily's Incredible Adventure to the World of the Gossamerians. 2013. 130p. pap. *(978-1-909740-41-9(1))* Legend Pr.
Price, Kevin, ed. The Mystery of Love: A Born Storyteller Collection of Mystery Adventure & Science Fiction Stories. 2013. (Illus.). 308p. pap. *(978-0-9872559-6-9(7)*, Crotchet Quaver) Logorythm.
Price, Roger & Stern, Leonard, creators. Ninjas Mad Libs. 2011. (Mad Libs Ser.). (ENG.). 48p. (J). (gr. 3-7). 4.99 *(978-0-8431-9897-3(4)*, Mad Libs) Penguin Young Readers Group.
Price, Roger, et al. Fionna & Cake Mad Libs. 2013. (Adventure Time Ser.). (ENG.). 48p. (J). (gr. 3-7). 3.99 *(978-0-8431-7528-8(1)*, Mad Libs) Penguin Young Readers Group.
Price, Roy. The Gnome Guardian: Polly's Adventure. 2012. 64p. pap. 13.66 *(978-1-4678-9701-3(9))* AuthorHouse.
Priddy, Roger. Follow Me. 2016. (Finger Mazes Ser.). (ENG.). 16p. (J). bds. 9.99 *(978-0-312-52058-8(1)*, 9780312520588, Priddy Bks.) St. Martin's Pr.
Priebe, Trisha & Jenkins, Jerry B. The Ruby Moon. 2016. (Thirteen Ser.). (ENG.). 240p. 14.99 *(978-1-63409-903-5(6))* Barbour Publishing, Inc.
Primavera, Elise. Making Mistakes on Purpose. 2016. (Ms. Rapscott's Girls Ser.). (ENG., Illus.). 160p. (J). (gr. 3-7). 16.99 *(978-0-8037-3824-9(2)*, Dial Bks) Penguin Young Readers Group.
—Secret Order Gumm Street Girl, No. 2. 2006. *(978-0-06-056950-1(6))*; *(978-0-06-056949-5(2))* HarperCollins Canada, Ltd.

Prime, Derek. Sarah & Paul Go on Holiday Again: Discover about Being a Christian. 2006. (Sarah & Paul Ser.). (ENG., Illus.). 128p. (J). per. 6.99 *(978-1-84550-162-4(4),* 94175d0d-6922-46f5-bc95-9e8edf2f526c) Christian Focus Pubns. GBR. Dist: Bookmasters Distribution.

—Sarah & Paul Go to the Seaside. 2006. (Sarah & Paul Ser.). (ENG., Illus.). 128p. (J). (gr. 2-5). per. 6.99 *(978-1-84550-159-4(4),* e21a5ea6-3d41-4387-977e-93990141367d) Christian Focus Pubns. GBR. Dist: Bookmasters Distribution.

Prince, Cheryl. Belle's Wild Journey. 2012. 24p. pap. 24.95 *(978-1-4626-9794-6(1))* America Star Bks.

Prince, Ricky. What Made That Noise? 2008. 35p. pap. 24.95 *(978-1-60474-601-3(7))* America Star Bks.

Princess Protection Program Staff. The Palace of Mystery, No. 4. 2010. (Princess Protection Program Ser.). 144p. pap. 4.99 *(978-1-4231-2727-7(7))* Disney Pr.

Prineas, Sarah. Ash & Bramble. 2016. 480p. (YA). (gr. 8). pap. 9.99 *(978-0-06-233795-5(5),* HarperTeen) HarperCollins Pubs.

—Found. Caparo, Antonio Javier, illus. 2011. (Magic Thief Ser.: 3). (ENG.). 384p. (J). (gr. 5). pap. 7.99 *(978-0-06-137595-8(0))* HarperCollins Pubs.

Prins, Piet. The Search for Sheltie. Kramer, Jaap, illus. 2006. 137p. (J). pap. *(978-1-894666-43-5(7))* Inheritance Pubns.

Prioleau, J. N. Clyde. 2008. 24p. 13.95 *(978-0-615-25200-1(1))* Prioleau, Jivonne.

Prior, Natalie Jane. Lily Quench & the Lighthouse of Skellig Mor, Vol. 4. 2004. (ENG., Illus.). 160p. (J). (gr. 3-7). 6.99 *(978-0-14-240059-3(9),* Puffin Books) Penguin Young Readers Group.

Prior, Natalie Jane & Dawson, Kathy. Lily Quench & the Magician's Pyramid, Vol. 5. 2004. (ENG., Illus.). 176p. (Orig.). (J). (gr. 3-7). 6.99 *(978-0-14-240163-7(3),* Puffin Books) Penguin Young Readers Group.

Pritchard, Gabby. Turtle Is a Hero Green Band. Di Baldo, Fabrizio, illus. 2016. (Cambridge Reading Adventures Ser.). (ENG.). 16p. pap. 6.56 *(978-1-107-55046-9(7))* Cambridge Univ. Pr.

Pritchard, Jean. Bobcat Bootcamp in Orange City. Dakins, Todd, illus. 2007. (J). *(978-0-9652491-6-4(6))* Cook, Ken Co.

Probst, Jeff & Tebbetts, Christopher. Forbidden Passage. 2014. (Stranded Ser.: 4). (ENG.). 176p. (J). (gr. 3-7). 6.99 *(978-0-14-751388-5(X),* Puffin Books) Penguin Young Readers Group.

—Survivors. 2013. (Stranded Ser.: 3). (ENG.). 224p. (J). (gr. 3). pap. 6.99 *(978-0-14-242426-1(9),* Puffin Books) Penguin Publishing Group.

Prochaska, Dan J. Courage, 1 vol. 2009. 48p. pap. 16.95 *(978-1-61582-995-8(4))* PublishAmerica, Inc.

Project-00. 2003. (J). 15.95 *(978-0-9743843-0-6(5))* Endeavor Publishing.

Prokash, Marie. Madison's Adventure. 2012. 28p. pap. 17.99 *(978-1-4772-3334-4(2))* AuthorHouse.

The Promise. 2012. 218p. pap. *(978-1-78176-337-7(2))* FeedARead.com.

Protasov, Alexander. Fairy-Tales & Fantasies. 2010. (Illus.). 52p. pap. 22.49 *(978-1-4490-7847-8(8))* AuthorHouse.

Proulx, Roxanna Darling. The Princes of Pleasant Valley: A Day in the Life of Zyler & Xavier, 1 vol. Sandon, Gina, illus. 2010. 46p. 24.95 *(978-1-4489-7641-6(3))* PublishAmerica, Inc.

Prouty, Krista. George Monkeys Around, 1 vol. 2010. 42p. 24.95 *(978-1-4489-4936-6(X))* PublishAmerica, Inc.

La Prueba Continua. (SPA.). 62p. 4.95 *(978-84-488-1002-3(3))* Beascoa, Ediciones S.A. ESP. Dist: Distribooks, Inc.

Pruitt, Patti B. Meeting Paddy O'Rourke: Book One. 2007. 68p. (J). pap. 9.00 *(978-0-8059-7656-4(6))* Dorrance Publishing Co., Inc.

Pruitt, Vasta Z. Buttons & Babs Run Life's Race: Heavenly Pals Series. 2011. 168p. (gr. 4-6). 22.99 *(978-1-4567-6792-1(5));* pap. 13.99 *(978-1-4567-6793-8(3))* AuthorHouse.

Pryce, Denise. Alexander & the Ring of Destiny. 2009. 72p. pap. 24.99 *(978-1-4251-8887-0(7))* Trafford Publishing.

Pryce, Sasha. Labby's Adventures. 2009. 52p. pap. 14.95 *(978-1-4092-8020-0(9))* Lulu Pr., Inc.

Pryce, Trevor & Naftali, Joel. The Rainbow Serpent. Greene, Sanford, illus. 2015. (Kulipari Ser.). (ENG.). 320p. (J). (gr. 3-7). pap. 8.95 *(978-1-4197-1657-7(3),* Amulet Bks.) Abrams, Inc.

Pryke, Gary. The Adventures of Spike & Johnny: Somewhere Close to Forty. 2011. 120p. (gr. -1). pap. 13.88 *(978-1-4269-2705-8(3))* Trafford Publishing.

Pryor, Bonnie. Captain Hannah Pritchard: The Hunt for Pirate Gold. 2011. (Historical Fiction Adventures (HFA) Ser.). (Illus.). 160p. (J). (gr. 3-18). pap. 10.95 *(978-1-59845-283-9(5));* (gr. 4-7). lib. bdg. 29.27 *(978-0-7660-3817-2(3))* Enslow Pubs., Inc.

Pryor, Michael. Leo Da Vinci vs the Furniture Overlord. Faber, Jules, illus. 2016. (Leo Da Vinci Ser.: 2). (ENG.). 192p. (J). (gr. 4-6). pap. 8.99 *(978-0-85798-839-3(5))* Random Hse. Australia AUS. Dist: Independent Pubs. Group.

—Leo Da Vinci vs the Ice-Cream Domination League. Faber, Jules, illus. 2015. (Leo Da Vinci Ser.). (ENG.). 144p. (J). (gr. 4-7). 8.99 *(978-0-85798-837-9(9))* Random Hse. Australia AUS. Dist: Independent Pubs. Group.

PSSC Staff. Secrets of the Power Ring. 2011. (Green Lantern Ser.). (ENG.). 20p. (J). (gr. -1-k). pap., act. bk. ed. 6.99 *(978-0-8431-9844-7(3),* Price Stern Sloan) Penguin Publishing Group.

Publications International Ltd. Staff. Elmo PNO BK. 2008. 10p. (J). 16.98 *(978-1-4127-8995-0(8))* Phoenix International Publications, Inc.

—Interactive Sound Pirates of the Caribbean 3. 2007. 24p. (J). 16.98 *(978-1-4127-8111-4(6))* Publications International, Ltd.

—Phineas & Ferb (Looks & Find) 2011. 24p. (J). 7.98 *(978-1-4508-1103-3(5))* Phoenix International Publications, Inc.

—Rio Large Play As Ound. 2011. 24p. (J). 17.98 *(978-1-4508-0735-7(6))* Phoenix International Publications, Inc.

—Teenage Mutant Ninja Turtles - Ninja Heroes: Flashlight Adventure Sound Book. 2013. 14p. (J). (gr. 1-3). bds. 17.98 *(978-1-4127-5339-5(2),* 0c51eeb7-c20f-4b72-a87f-c492bcc6f86f) Phoenix International Publications, Inc.

—Wall E Large Sound BK. 2008. 24p. (J). 17.98 *(978-1-4127-8991-2(5),* PIL Kids) Publications International, Ltd.

Publications International Ltd. Staff, creator. Fairy Tales: Keepsake Collection. 2007. (Illus.). 96p. 12.98 *(978-1-4127-7453-6(5))* Publications International, Ltd.

—Let's Dance!/Vamos a Bailar! 2007. (Play-A-Sound Ser.). (J). 17.98 *(978-1-4127-9276-9(2))* Publications International, Ltd.

—We've Got a Mission! 2007. (Disney's Little Einsteins Ser.). (Illus.). 12p. (J). (gr. -1-3). bds. 9.98 *(978-1-4127-7415-4(2))* Publications International, Ltd.

Publications International Ltd. Staff, ed. Baby Einstein. 2007. 18p. (J). bds. *(978-1-4127-8436-8(0),* 1412784360) Phoenix International Publications, Inc.

—Dance Mat Sound Book Dora Lets Dance. 2007. (J). 17.98 *(978-1-4127-8305-7(4))* Publications International, Ltd.

—Diego What a Team. 2007. (J). 10.98 *(978-1-4127-6744-6(X))* Publications International, Ltd.

—Discover the Day. 2010. 12p. (J). bds. 9.98 *(978-1-4127-6747-7(4))* Phoenix International Publications, Inc.

—Disney(r) Frozen: Giant Look & Find(tm) 2014. 24p. (J). *(978-1-4508-9769-3(X),* 145089769X) Publications International, Ltd.

—Disney(r) Frozen Little Look & Find(tm) 2014. 24p. (J). *(978-1-4508-9259-9(0),* 1450892590) Publications International, Ltd.

—Disney(r) Junior Little Look & Find(tm) Fun with Friends. 2014. 24p. (J). *(978-1-4508-9479-1(8),* 1450894798) Publications International, Ltd.

—Disney Pixar. 2007. (J). 15.98 *(978-1-4127-8326-2(7))* Publications International, Ltd.

—Disney(r) Pixar Inside Out: Play-A-Sound(r). 2015. 24p. (J). 12.98 *(978-1-4508-9117-2(9),* 1450891179) Publications International, Ltd.

—Disney Princess: Follow Your Dreams. 2010. 24p. (J). 19.98 *(978-1-4127-5357-9(0),* PIL Kids) Publications International, Ltd.

—Doc to the Rescue. 2013. 14p. (J). (gr. k-4). bds. 12.99 *(978-1-4508-6567-8(4),* 1d5bc35b-26cc-4030-a099-b7fac495ca53) Phoenix International Publications, Inc.

—Dora Little Stars, Big Adventure. 2013. 14p. (J). bds. 16.98 *(978-1-4127-8950-9(8),* 1412789508) Phoenix International Publications, Inc.

—Dora the Explorer: Little Star's Big Adventure. 2010. (J). 10.98 *(978-1-4508-0391-5(1))* Phoenix International Publications, Inc.

—Dora the Explorer: Little Star's Big Adventure (Flashlight Adventure Book & Dora Plush) 2010. (J). 24.98 *(978-1-4508-0129-4(3))* Publications International, Ltd.

—Dora the Explorer, Ding Dong! It's Dora! 2009. 12p. (J). bds. 11.98 *(978-1-4127-7598-4(1))* Phoenix International Publications, Inc.

—Dragon Boat Festival. 2009. 9p. (J). bds. 10.98 *(978-1-4127-7782-7(8),* PIL Kids) Publications International, Ltd.

—Finding Nemo - Let's Go to School. 2011. 12p. (J). bds. *(978-1-4508-0510-0(8))* Publications International, Ltd.

—Flashlight Book Disney Pixar Cars. 2008. (J). 17.10 *(978-1-4127-8958-5(3))* Phoenix International Publications, Inc.

—Go Diego Go. 2007. (J). 5.98 *(978-1-4127-6725-5(3))* Publications International, Ltd.

—Head to Toe! Go! Go! Go! 2009. 24p. (J). 17.98 *(978-0-7853-1321-2(4),* PIL Kids) Publications International, Ltd.

—Look & Find - Captain America: The First Avenger. 2011. 24p. (J). 3.75 net. *(978-1-4508-1877-3(3))* Phoenix International Publications, Inc.

—Look & Find Activity Pad Mickey Mouse. 2011. 64p. (J). 10.98 *(978-1-4508-0733-3(X))* Publications International, Ltd.

—Look & Find Green Lantern. 2011. 24p. (J). 7.98 *(978-1-4508-1179-8(5))* Publications International, Ltd.

—Look & Find: Nickelodeon: Teenage Mutant Ninja Turtles. 2013. 24p. (J). (gr. 1-3). 7.98 *(978-1-4508-1972-5(9),* ceaa0b59-853d-401a-91e5-5d3db3d7adab) Phoenix International Publications, Inc.

—Look & Find Pirates of the Caribbean 3. 2007. 24p. (J). 7.10 *(978-1-4127-8019-3(5))* Publications International, Ltd.

—Look & Find: Snoopy. 2013. 24p. (J). (gr. 1-3). 7.99 *(978-1-4127-1722-9(1),* 6273d751-5dbd-41ad-a19f-1ef74baf570f) Phoenix International Publications, Inc.

—Mickey Mouse Clubhouse: Mickey's Silly Shadow Book. 2011. 14p. (J). bds. 8.45 net. *(978-1-4508-0564-3(7))* Phoenix International Publications, Inc.

—Mickey Mouse Clubhouse (book Block) 2010. (J). 10.98 *(978-1-4508-0673-2(2))* Publications International, Ltd.

—Mickey Mouse Clubhouse Super Look & Find Activity Pad with Stickers. 2010. 64p. (J). *(978-1-4508-0732-6(1),* 1450807321) Phoenix International Publications, Inc.

—Mickey Mouse Clubhouse Super Look & Find Activity Pad with Stickers. 2011. 64p. (J). 10.98 *(978-1-4508-1887-2(0))* Publications International, Ltd.

—Mickey's Adventure. 2010. 24p. (J). bds. 16.98 *(978-1-4127-4599-4(3))* Phoenix International Publications, Inc.

—My First Look & Find - Chuggington. 2011. 18p. (J). bds. 9.98 *(978-1-4508-0036-5(X))* Phoenix International Publications, Inc.

—Nickelodeon Dora the Explorer: Choo, Choo, Let's Go! 2014. 12p. (J). bds. 12.98 *(978-1-4508-7591-2(2),* 9eb3d955-9235-4e60-b5f1-58f6e60ec19b) Publications International, Ltd.

—Rudolph the Red-Nosed Reindeer(r): A Flashlight Adventure Sound Book. 2014. 14p. (J). *(978-1-4508-9047-2(4),* 1450890474) Publications International, Ltd.

—Sesame Street, Ding Dong, Elmo's Here! 2009. 12p. (J). bds. 11.98 *(978-1-4127-9613-2(X))* Phoenix International Publications, Inc.

—Sesame Street Happy Birthday to You. 2013. 12p. (J). bds. 9.98 *(978-1-4508-6159-5(8),* 0fc64c9f-9454-4eb3-b56f-9c42ccb72c61) Phoenix International Publications, Inc.

—Soft! Furry! Bumpy! A Touch, Hear, & Learn with Elmo Book. 2010. 10p. (J). bds. 11.98 *(978-1-4127-5805-5(X),* PIL Kids) Publications International, Ltd.

—Teenage Mutant Ninja Turtles(tm) Dojo: A Flashlight Adventure Sound Book. 2013. 12p. (J). bds. *(978-1-4508-7438-0(X),* 145087438X) Publications International, Ltd.

—Toy Story 3: New Friends. 2010. 12p. (J). bds. 10.98 *(978-1-4127-4584-0(5),* PIL Kids) Publications International, Ltd.

—Treasure Hunt. 2010. 12p. (J). bds. 9.98 *(978-1-4127-9885-3(X))* Phoenix International Publications, Inc.

—Up & down! Play-a-Sound Book & Huggable Kai-lan. 2010. (J). 14.98 *(978-1-4127-5591-7(3))* Publications International, Ltd.

—What Do You See? 2012. (Illus.). 14p. (J). (gr. 2-4). 17.98 *(978-1-4508-4545-8(2),* 23956fd6-2821-435f-aef0-d47191d0621e) Phoenix International Publications, Inc.

—What's Different. 2009. 24p. (J). 7.98 *(978-1-4127-1725-0(6),* PIL Kids) Publications International, Ltd.

—Wonder Pets: Save the Baby Kitten. 2008. (J). bds. 10.98 *(978-1-4127-9198-4(7))* Publications International, Ltd.

—9 Button Record Song Dora Superstar. 2011. 18p. 19.98 *(978-1-4508-1913-8(3))* Phoenix International Publications, Inc.

Puckett, Annie Marie. Pedro Learns about Salvation. 2006. 56p. per. 9.95 *(978-1-57258-453-2(X),* 945-6314) TEACH Services, Inc.

Puffy. 2006. (J). *(978-0-9779521-0-6(X))* City on a Hill, Inc.

Puffy: The Cloud That Couldn't Rain. 2005. (J). 8.95 *(978-0-9755348-0-9(7))* Kids Life Pr.

Pugh, Ian. Wolfstorm: The First Danny Piper Adventure. 2010. 388p. 32.95 *(978-1-4269-0239-0(5))* Trafford Publishing.

Pugh, Tracey D. A Show & Tell Lesson. McCracken, Jaime, photos by. l.t. ed. 2006. (Illus.). 32p. (J). 12.95 *(978-1-59879-105-1(2))* Lifevest Publishing, Inc.

Pugin-Rodas, M. C. The Eight Ball Club: Ocean of Fire. 2007. (ENG., Illus.). 144p. pap. 15.95 *(978-0-9793761-2-2(2))* ESOL Publishing.

Pullein-Thompson, Christine. Phantom Horse. 2012. (ENG., Illus.). 176p. (J). pap. 9.95 *(978-1-84135-820-8(7))* Award Pubns. Ltd. GBR. Dist: Parkwest Pubns., Inc.

—Phantom Horse Comes Home. 2012. (ENG., Illus.). 176p. (J). pap. 9.95 *(978-1-84135-822-2(3))* Award Pubns. Ltd. GBR. Dist: Parkwest Pubns., Inc.

—Phantom Horse Disappears. 2012. (ENG., Illus.). 176p. (J). pap. 9.95 *(978-1-84135-821-5(5))* Award Pubns. Ltd. GBR. Dist: Parkwest Pubns., Inc.

—Phantom Horse Island Mystery. 2012. (ENG., Illus.). 176p. (J). pap. 9.95 *(978-1-84135-825-3(8))* Award Pubns. Ltd. GBR. Dist: Parkwest Pubns., Inc.

—Wait for Me. 2012. (ENG., Illus.). 176p. (J). pap. 9.95 *(978-1-84135-823-9(1))* Award Pubns. Ltd. GBR. Dist: Parkwest Pubns., Inc.

Pullen, Zachary. Friday My Radio Flyer Flew. Pullen, Zachary, illus. 2008. (ENG., Illus.). 32p. (J). (gr. -1-2). 18.99 *(978-1-4169-3983-2(0),* Simon & Schuster Bks. For Young Readers) Simon & Schuster Bks. For Young Readers.

Pullman, Philip. The Adventures of John Blake: Mystery of the Ghost Ship. Fordham, Fred, illus. 2017. (ENG.). 160p. (J). (gr. 3-7). 19.99 ***(978-1-338-14912-8(1),*** Graphix) Scholastic, Inc.

—The Adventures of John Blake: Mystery of the Ghost Ship. Fordham, Fred, illus. 2017. lib. bdg. 33.05 ***(978-0-606-40195-1(4))*** Turtleback Bks.

—The Golden Compass Graphic Novel, Complete Edition. 2017. (His Dark Materials Ser.). (ENG.). 224p. (J). (gr. 5). 21.99 ***(978-0-553-53516-7(1));*** pap. 12.99 ***(978-0-553-53517-4(X));*** lib. bdg. 24.99 ***(978-0-553-53518-1(8))*** Random Hse. Children's Bks. (Knopf Bks. for Young Readers).

—Once upon a Time in the North. 2008. (His Dark Materials Ser.). (ENG., Illus.). 112p. *(978-0-385-61432-0(2))* Fickling, David Bks.

—Once upon a Time in the North. Lawrence, John, illus. 2008. (His Dark Materials Ser.). (ENG.). 112p. (J). (gr. 5-12). 12.99 *(978-0-375-84510-9(0),* Knopf Bks. for Young Readers) Random Hse. Children's Bks.

—Les Royaumes du Nord. (FRE.). pap. 19.95 *(978-2-07-054188-1(6))* Gallimard, Editions FRA. Dist: Distribooks, Inc.

—The Scarecrow & His Servant. Bailey, Peter, illus. (ENG.). 240p. (J). (gr. 3-7). 2007. 7.99 *(978-0-440-42130-6(6),* Yearling) 2005. 15.95 *(978-0-375-81531-7(7),* Knopf Bks. for Young Readers) Random Hse. Children's Bks.

—The Tin Princess. 2008. (Sally Lockhart Ser.). (ENG.). 304p. (YA). (gr. 7). pap. 7.99 *(978-0-375-84514-7(3),* Knopf Bks. for Young Readers) Random Hse. Children's Bks.

—La Tour des Anges. (FRE.). pap. 19.95 *(978-2-07-054189-8(4))* Gallimard, Editions FRA. Dist: Distribooks, Inc.

—Two Crafty Criminals! And How They Were Captured by the Daring Detectives of the New Cut Gang. (ENG.). 288p. (J). (gr. 3-7). 2013. 7.99 *(978-0-307-93035-4(1),* Yearling) 2012. (Illus.). 16.99 *(978-0-375-87029-3(6),* Knopf Bks. for Young Readers) Random Hse. Children's Bks.

Pundir, Annie. Gauri & the Crocodile: Smiley Crocodiley. 2009. 28p. pap. 12.50 *(978-1-4389-8611-1(4))* AuthorHouse.

Punnett, Dick. Count the Possums: A Talk-along Book. Punnett, Yvonne, ed. 2nd ed. 2005. (Talk-Along Bks.). (Illus.). 32p. (J). pap. 6.99 *(978-0-9657211-4-1(0))* Tomoka Pr.

—Help Jumbo Escape: A Talk-along Book. Dunnington, Tom, illus. 2nd ed. 2005. (Talk-Along Bks.). 32p. (J). pap. 6.99 *(978-0-9657211-2-7(4))* Tomoka Pr.

Punter, R. Pirate Adventures. 2009. (Kid Kits Ser.). 48p. (J). 16.99 *(978-1-60130-155-0(3));* 16.99 *(978-1-60130-154-3(5))* EDC Publishing. (Usborne).

Punter, Russell. Pirate Adventures. Fox, Christyan, illus. 2007. (Usborne Young Reading: Series One Ser.). 48p. (J). (gr. 4-7). pap. 5.99 *(978-0-7945-1447-1(2),* Usborne) EDC Publishing.

—Stories of Cowboys. Fiorin, Fabiano, illus. 2008. (Usborne Young Reading: Series One Ser.). 48p. (J). 8.99 *(978-0-7945-1822-6(2),* Usborne) EDC Publishing.

Puppel, Douglas. A Hero Named Mark. Verrill, William, illus. 2012. (J). lib. bdg. 25.00 *(978-0-9788980-6-9(0))* Public Education Foundation, The.

Puzzi, Jessica. Rosy & Simon's Front Yard Adventure, 1 vol. 2010. 18p. pap. 24.95 *(978-1-4489-2601-5(7))* PublishAmerica, Inc.

Pybus, Judith. The Ladder. 2009. 136p. pap. 10.99 *(978-1-4490-0298-5(6))* AuthorHouse.

Pyle, Ernie Howard. Men of Iron. 2005. 272p. 28.95 *(978-1-4218-0617-4(7),* 1st World Library - Literary Society) 1st World Publishing, Inc.

Pyle, Howard. The Adventures of Robin Hood. 2014. (ENG.). 416p. 17.50 *(978-1-78270-045-6(5))* Award Pubns. Ltd. GBR. Dist: Parkwest Pubns., Inc.

—A Modern Aladdin: Or, the Wonderful Adventures of Oliver Munier. 2011. 276p. pap. 27.75 *(978-1-179-68213-6(0))* Creative Media Partners, LLC.

—A Modern Aladdin: Or the Wonderful Adventures of Oliver Munier, an Extravaganza in Four Acts (1892) 2009. 100p. pap. 14.14 *(978-1-151-72659-9(1))* General Bks. LLC.

—A Modern Aladdin: Or the Wonderful Adventures of Oliver Munier, an Extravaganza in Four Acts (1892) 2010. 282p. 34.36 *(978-1-164-31521-6(8))* 2010. 282p. pap. 22.36 *(978-1-163-97479-7(X))* 2008. 280p. 42.95 *(978-0-548-98196-2(5))* 2007. (ENG.). 284p. per. 27.95 *(978-0-548-66551-0(6))* Kessinger Publishing, LLC.

—A Modern Aladdin - or, the Wondferful Adventures of Oliver Munier. 2009. 276p. pap. *(978-1-4446-0435-1(X))* Read Bks.

—A Modern Aladdin, or, the Wonderful Adventures of Oliver Munier, an Extravaganza in Four Acts. 2010. (ENG.). 284p. pap. 28.75 *(978-1-176-84578-7(0))* 2009. 280p. 30.99 *(978-1-110-32521-4(5))* 2009. 280p. pap. 26.75 *(978-1-110-32518-4(5))* Creative Media Partners, LLC.

—A Modern Aladdin, or, the Wonderful Adventures of Oliver Munier, an Extravaganza in Four Acts. 2010. 82p. pap. 14.31 *(978-1-151-74489-0(1))* General Bks. LLC.

—A Modern Aladdin, or, the Wonderful Adventures of Oliver Munier, an Extravaganza in Four Acts. 2012. 290p. pap. *(978-1-290-29400-3(3))* HardPr.

—The Story of Jack Ballister's Fortunes: Being the Narrative of the Adventures of a Young Gentleman of Good Family, Who Was Kidnapped in the Year 1719 & Carried to the Plantations of the Continent of Virginia, Where He Fell in with That Famous Pirate Captain Edward Teach, or Blackbeard: of His Escape from the Pirates & the Rescue of a Young Lady from Out Their Hands. unabr. ed. 2012. (Illus.). 436p. 49.99 *(978-1-4622-8858-8(8))* Repressed Publishing LLC.

—Twilight Land. 2006. (ENG.). pap. *(978-1-4068-3431-4(9))* Echo Library.

—Within the Capes. 2004. reprint ed. pap. 27.95 *(978-1-4179-3855-1(2))* Kessinger Publishing, LLC.

Pyne, Jane. Tommy's Secret. 2009. 86p. pap. 10.49 *(978-1-4389-9102-3(9))* AuthorHouse.

Quackenbush, Robert. Detective Mole. 2010. 68p. (J). (gr. k-4). pap. 8.95 *(978-1-4502-1529-9(7))* iUniverse, Inc.

—Piet Potter Returns: A Piet Potter Mystery. 2010. 52p. (J). (gr. k-4). pap. 8.95 *(978-1-4502-1352-3(9))* iUniverse, Inc.

—Piet Potter Strikes Again: A Piet Potter Mystery. 2010. 52p. (J). (gr. k-4). pap. 8.95 *(978-1-4502-1530-5(0))* iUniverse, Inc.

Qualls, Millie Marie. Miss Cooney & Her New Home. 2012. 24p. 24.95 *(978-1-4626-7426-8(7))* America Star Bks.

Qualls, Shirley. Marigold Duck Comes to Our School. 2009. 28p. pap. 12.49 *(978-1-4389-8386-8(7))* AuthorHouse.

Quarles, Bernadict. Chronicles of Maya & Quincy: When I Grow Up. 2013. 28p. pap. 24.95 *(978-1-4626-7832-7(7))* America Star Bks.

The Quest for Courage. 2006. (Amazing Travels of Wannabeb Ser.). (Illus.). 32p. (J). (gr. -1-3). 8.99 *(978-0-7847-1801-8(6),* 04127) Standard Publishing.

Quest for God's Hidden Creatures: The Legacy of the Doors. 2006. (J). per. 9.95 *(978-0-9777725-0-6(0))* bazow, thomas.

Quest for Gold. 2003. (J). per. *(978-1-57657-976-3(X))* Paradise Pr., Inc.

The Quest for Seven Castles. 2006. (J). per. 7.99 *(978-0-9785523-1-2(8))* Cross & Crown Publishing.

Quetel, Julie. The Adventures of Shayne & His Flying Grandma. 2011. 60p. (gr. -1). pap. 10.49 *(978-1-4490-5553-0(2))* AuthorHouse.

Quigley, Michael. A Monkey's Riddle. 2013. 24p. pap. 24.95 *(978-1-63000-506-1(1))* America Star Bks.

Quihuis, Albert. The Search for the Lost Art of Making Tortillas. 2012. 38p. pap. 16.95 *(978-0-9884576-0-7(1))* Perfect Bound Marketing.

Quiller-Couch, Arthur Thomas. Naughts & Crosses. 2009. 188p. 26.95 *(978-1-60664-671-7(0))* Rodgers, Alan Bks.

—True Tilda. 2006. 224p. per. 15.95 *(978-1-59818-052-7(5))* Aegypan.

Quiller-Couch, Arthur Thomas & Q. Naughts & Crosses. 2009. 188p. pap. 13.95 *(978-1-60664-299-3(5))* Rodgers, Alan Bks.

Quinn, Jordan. The Lost Stone. McPhillips, Robert, illus. 2014. (Kingdom of Wrenly Ser.: 1). (ENG.). 128p. (J). (gr. k-4). pap. 5.99 *(978-1-4424-9690-3(8),* Little Simon) Little Simon.

—The Lost Stone. 2014. (Kingdom of Wrenly Ser.: 1). lib. bdg. 16.00 *(978-0-606-35443-1(3))* Turtleback Bks.

—The Scarlet Dragon. McPhillips, Robert, illus. 2014. (Kingdom of Wrenly Ser.: 2). (ENG.). 128p. (J). (gr. k-4). pap. 5.99 *(978-1-4424-9693-4(2),* Little Simon) Little Simon.

—The Scarlet Dragon. 2014. (Kingdom of Wrenly Ser.: 2). lib. bdg. 16.00 *(978-0-606-35444-8(1))* Turtleback Bks.

—Sea Monster! McPhillips, Robert, illus. 2014. (Kingdom of Wrenly Ser.: 3). (ENG.). 128p. (J). (gr. k-4). pap. 5.99 *(978-1-4814-0072-5(X),* Little Simon) Little Simon.

Quinn, Timothy. Marvelous Miriam's Magnificent Hawaiian Adventure. 2011. 56p. pap. 16.95 *(978-1-4560-9630-4(3))* America Star Bks.

Quinones, Juan Carlos. The Gang & the Biggest Book in the World. Ortiz Montanez, Nivea, illus. 2004. (Purple Ser.). 48p. (J). *(978-1-57581-438-4(2))* Ediciones Santillana, Inc.

—La Pandilla Bajo el Arbol. Ortiz Montanez, Nivea, illus. 2004. (Purple Ser.). (SPA.). 44p. (J). (gr. 3-5). pap. 5.95 *(978-1-57581-439-1(0))* Santillana USA Publishing Co., Inc.

Quint, M. The Defiant. Padula, Lily, illus. 2015. (ENG.). 256p. (gr. 2-7). 18.99 (978-1-936365-54-8(5)) McSweeney's Publishing.

Quintanilla, Efren. Aventuras de Bartolillo. (SPA.). (J). 7.95 (978-84-241-5634-3(X)) Torres, Eliseo & Sons.

Quiroga, Horacio. The Lazy Bee. Leal, Mireya Fonseca, ed. Porras, Javier Fernando, illus. 2003. (Library of Tale Ser.). (SPA.). 12p. (J). (gr. -1-7). pap. (978-958-30-0988-4(1)) Panamericana Editorial.

Quisenberry, Stacey. Dinosaur George Pre-hysterical Adventures: What Color Were Dinosaurs? Browning, Suzan, illus. 2007. (J). 3.95 (978-0-9797304-3-6(0)) Raining Popcorn Media.

Quixley, Barbara. Island Adventures of Jacki-Jacki. 2012. 116p. pap. 61.99 (978-1-4771-4616-3(4)) Xlibris Corp.

R. M. Ballantyne. The Coral Island. 2007. 316p. per. 14.95 (978-1-4218-4004-8(9), 1st World Library - Literary Society) 1st World Publishing, Inc.

Raab, Ralph. The Dewey Deception: The First Adventure from the Biblio Files. 2009. (ENG.). 248p. 26.95 (978-1-4401-4687-9(X)); pap. 16.95 (978-1-4401-4685-5(3)) iUniverse, Inc.

Raabe, Emily. Lost Children of the Far Islands. 2014. (ENG.). 288p. (J). (gr. 3-7). 16.99 (978-0-375-87091-0(1), Knopf Bks. for Young Readers) Random Hse. Children's Bks.

Rabe, Tish. Big Snowman, Little Snowman. Random House Disney Staff, illus. 2013. (Step into Reading Ser.). (ENG.). 32p. (J). (gr. -1-1). 3.99 (978-0-7364-3119-4(5), RH/Disney) Random Hse. Children's Bks.

—The Thinga-Ma-Jigger Is Coming Today! Moroney, Christopher, illus. 2010. (Little Golden Book Ser.). (ENG.). 24p. (J). (gr. -1-2). 4.99 (978-0-375-85927-4(6), Golden Bks.) Random Hse. Children's Bks.

Rabelo-Beacroft, Katia. The Grumpy Monkey Who Only Eats Bananas. 2012. 28p. pap. 16.10 (978-1-4669-3957-8(5)) Trafford Publishing.

Rabideau, Dianna. A Den for Ben. 2009. 24p. pap. 12.99 (978-1-4490-0886-4(0)) AuthorHouse.

Racine, Patrice. The Quest of the Last Dodo Bird. 2011. (Adventures of Cosmo the Dodo Bird Ser.). (ENG., Illus.). 112p. (J). (gr. 4-7). pap. 10.95 (978-1-77049-241-7(0), Tundra Bks.) Tundra Bks. CAN. Dist: Penguin Random Hse. LLC.

Rack, Charlene. The Adventures of Delaware Bear & Young Abraham Lincoln. 2011. 24p. (gr. -1). pap. 12.79 (978-1-4567-5619-2(2)) AuthorHouse.

Rackham, Katelyn. The Storyteller. 2007. (ENG.). 284p. per. 15.95 (978-0-7414-3845-4(3)) Infinity Publishing.

Rad, Charles J. The Boy they called a Snowball. 2007. 140p. pap. 20.95 (978-1-84753-461-3(9)) Lulu Pr., Inc.

Radlauer. Molly Goes Hiking. 2007. (ENG.). 32p. (J). (gr. -1-2). 8.99 (978-1-4169-6834-4(2), Simon & Schuster/Paula Wiseman Bks.) Simon & Schuster/Paula Wiseman Bks.

Rady, Michael. The Quest for Neveragain. 2011. 138p. pap. 24.95 (978-1-4560-7019-9(3)) America Star Bks.

Rae, Jaci. Collista's Search for the True Meaning of Christmas. 2007. (Illus.). 59p. per. 14.95 (978-0-9746229-1-0(5)) North Shore Records, Inc.

Rae Strawn, Evelyn. Moncho the Mule. 2010. 24p. 12.99 (978-1-4389-8751-4(X)) AuthorHouse.

Rafferty, Michael. The TAB Boys Meet the Blue Boy. 2008. 66p. pap. 7.95 (978-1-4357-3465-4(3)) Lulu Pr., Inc.

Raffle, Diana. Moondragon. 2006. 161p. pap. 24.95 (978-1-4241-0626-4(5)) PublishAmerica, Inc.

Ragan, Lyn. Berc's Inner Voice. 2013. 24p. 21.95 (978-0-9860205-4-4(0)) HourGlass Publishing.

—Berc's Inner Voice. Meyer, Alison, illus. 2013. 24p. pap. 14.95 (978-0-9860205-3-7(2)) HourGlass Publishing.

Ragin, M. K. Mildred Row & Improper Bounds. 2006. 185p. pap. 24.95 (978-1-4137-9724-4(5)) America Star Bks.

Raheb, Donna. The Adventures of Henrietta Ham. 2007. 32p. per. 14.95 (978-1-4327-0142-0(8)) Outskirts Pr., Inc.

—The Adventures of Henrietta Ham: Gone Fishing. 2008. 36p. pap. 14.95 (978-1-4327-2565-5(3)) Outskirts Pr., Inc.

Rainbolt, Jo Ann Sayman. The Mountain Journey, 1 vol. 2010. 52p. pap. 16.95 (978-1-61582-599-8(1)) America Star Bks.

The Rainbow's End. 2003. 14.95 (978-1-929489-75-6(7)) Platinum Medallion Children's Bks.

Raine, Ame. A Ray of Light: Key Keepers Book #3. 2008. 180p. pap. 13.95 (978-0-595-53464-7(3)) iUniverse, Inc.

Raine, Amelie. The Misadventures of Mallomar the Horse. 2009. 32p. pap. 12.99 (978-1-4389-8371-4(9)) AuthorHouse.

Rains, Michael. The House on the Corner. 2010. 112p. 28.95 (978-1-4497-0200-7(7)); pap. 11.95 (978-1-4497-0198-7(1)) Author Solutions, Inc. (WestBow Pr.).

Ralles, H. J. Keeper of the Realm, Vol. 2. 2003. (Illus.). 248p. (J). pap. 9.95 (978-1-929976-21-8(6)) Top Pubns., Ltd.

Ralph, Brian. Cave In. 2013. (ENG., Illus.). 96p. (J). (gr. 7-12). pap. 14.95 (978-1-77046-094-2(2), 9781770460942) Drawn & Quarterly Pubns. CAN. Dist: Macmillan.

Ralphson, G. Harvey. Boy Scouts in a Submarine. 2007. 104p. per. (978-1-4068-3726-1(1)) Echo Library.

—Boy Scouts in an Airship. 2007. 104p. per. (978-1-4068-3727-8(X)) Echo Library.

—Boy Scouts in Mexico. 2007. 112p. (gr. 4-7). per. (978-1-4068-3728-5(8)) Echo Library.

—Boy Scouts in Mexico,Or on Guard with Uncle Sam. 2003. 136p. pap. 14.99 (978-1-59224-085-2(2)) Wildside Pr., LLC.

—Boy Scouts in Southern Waters. 2007. 128p. (gr. -1-7). per. (978-1-4068-3730-8(X)) Echo Library.

—Boy Scouts in the Philippines. 2007. 112p. per. (978-1-4068-3729-2(6)) Echo Library.

—Boy Scouts on Motorcycles. 2007. 100p. per. (978-1-4068-3731-5(8)) Echo Library.

Ramage, Rosalyn Rikel. The Graveyard: N/a. 2012. 184p. (gr. 4-6). pap. 11.88 (978-1-4669-5033-7(1)) Trafford Publishing.

Ramani, Madhvi. Nina & the Kung-Fu Adventure. 2013. (Nina Ser.: 2). (ENG., Illus.). 96p. (J). (gr. 2-4). 8.99 (978-1-84853-091-1(9)) Transworld Publishers Ltd. GBR. Dist: Independent Pubs. Group.

—Nina & the Travelling Spice Shed. 2012. (Nina Ser.: 1). (ENG., Illus.). 96p. (J). (gr. 2-4). pap. 7.99 (978-1-84853-089-8(7)) Transworld Publishers Ltd. GBR. Dist: Independent Pubs. Group.

The Rambunctious Tommy Turnpike. 2nd ed. 2005. (J). (978-0-9773760-0-1(1)) Johnson, Anthony.

Rameaka, T. Where's Dorothy? 2005. 73p. pap. 16.95 (978-1-4137-9117-4(4)) PublishAmerica, Inc.

Ramirez, Martha. The Fabulous Adventures of Fred the Frog. 2008. 48p. pap. 24.95 (978-1-60474-799-7(4)) America Star Bks.

Ramsey, Byra L. Little Stick. 2009. 28p. pap. 13.99 (978-1-4490-3371-2(7)) AuthorHouse.

Ramsey, Dave. Dave Ramsey's 6 Kids Books Boxed Set. 2005. (J). 39.95 (978-0-9774895-8-9(2)) Ramsey Pr.

Ramsey, Jo. Jet Black. 2012. 220p. pap. 12.99 (978-1-60820-630-8(0)) MLR Pr., LLC.

Ramsey, R. M. The Browser Bunch: The Browser Files Presents... the Big Lie. 2006. (J). pap. 8.00 (978-0-8059-7172-9(6)) Dorrance Publishing Co., Inc.

Rand, Jason. Helios. 2007. (Illus.). 152p. (YA). pap. 15.99 (978-0-9738966-3-3(9)) Speakeasy Comics CAN. Dist: Diamond Bk. Distributors.

Rand, Johnathan. Freddie Fernortner #8: Chippers Crazy Carnival. 2008. 96p. (J). pap. 4.99 (978-1-893699-77-9(3)) AudioCraft Publishing, Inc.

—Freddie Fernortner #9: Attack of the Dust Bunnies from Outer Space. 2008. 96p. (J). pap. 4.99 (978-1-893699-95-3(1)) AudioCraft Publishing, Inc.

—Michigan Chillers #11 Great Lakes Ghost Ship. 2005. (Michigan Chillers: No. 11). 208p. (J). pap. 5.99 (978-1-893699-84-7(6)) AudioCraft Publishing, Inc.

Rand, Jonathan. Freddie Fernortner #7 Bk 7: Fearless First Grader: the Magical Wading Pool. 2007. pap. 4.99 (978-1-893699-91-5(9)) AudioCraft Publishing, Inc.

Randall, Bob & McInerney, Kunyi June-Anne. Tracker Tjugingji. 2003. (ENG.). 36p. (J). pap. 22.95 incl. audio compact disk (978-1-86465-030-3(3)) IAD Pr. AUS. Dist: Independent Pubs. Group.

Randolph, Robert. Ben Goes to the Farmer's Market, 1 vol. 2009. 37p. pap. 24.95 (978-1-4489-1934-5(7)) PublishAmerica, Inc.

Random House. The Adventure Bay Treasury (PAW Patrol) Random House, illus. 2017. (Padded Board Book Ser.). (ENG., Illus.). 30p. (J). (— 1). bds. 11.99 (978-0-399-55881-8(0), Random Hse. Bks. for Young Readers) Random Hse. Children's Bks.

—Adventure Story Collection (Nickelodeon) Random House, illus. 2016. (ENG., Illus.). 320p. (J). (gr. -1-2). 15.99 (978-1-101-93417-3(4), Random Hse. Bks. for Young Readers) Random Hse. Children's Bks.

—All about the Troll. Random House, illus. 2016. (Step into Reading Ser.). (ENG., Illus.). 32p. (J). (gr. -1-2). pap. 4.99 (978-0-399-55903-7(5), Random Hse. Bks. for Young Readers) Random Hse. Children's Bks.

—Barbie Star Light Adventure. 2016. (Barbie Chapters Ser.). (ENG., Illus.). 64p. (J). (gr. 1-4). 5.99 (978-1-101-94020-4(4), Random Hse. Bks. for Young Readers) Random Hse. Children's Bks.

—Everything That Glitters Is Guy! Laguna, Fabio, illus. 2017. (Pictureback(R) Ser.). (ENG.). 16p. (J). (gr. -1-2). pap. 5.99 (978-1-5247-1732-2(0), Random Hse. Bks. for Young Readers) Random Hse. Children's Bks.

—Feel the Power (Blaze & the Monster Machines) Hechtenkopf, Omar, illus. 2016. (Touch-And-Feel Ser.). (ENG.). 10p. (J). (— 1). bds. 12.99 (978-0-399-55372-1(X), Random Hse. Bks. for Young Readers) Random Hse. Children's Bks.

—Follow That Egg! (Team Umizoomi) Aikins, David, illus. 2014. (Glitter Board Book Ser.). (ENG.). 12p. (J). (-k). bds. 6.99 (978-0-385-37518-4(2), Random Hse. Bks. for Young Readers) Random Hse. Children's Bks.

—Gold Rush Pups! (PAW Patrol) MJ Illustrations, illus. 2017. (Pictureback(R) Ser.). (ENG.). 16p. (J). (gr. -1-2). pap. 5.99 (978-1-5247-1684-4(7), Random Hse. Bks. for Young Readers) Random Hse. Children's Bks.

—GoldieBlox Chapter Book #2 (GoldieBlox) Random House et al, illus. 2017. (Stepping Stone Book(TM) Ser.). (ENG.). 128p. (J). (gr. 1-4). 6.99 (978-0-399-55636-4(2), Random Hse. Bks. for Young Readers) Random Hse. Children's Bks.

—Let's Find Adventure! (Paw Patrol) Jackson, Mike, illus. 2015. (Nifty Lift-And-Look Ser.). (ENG.). 12p. (J). (-k). bds. 5.99 (978-0-553-51027-0(4), Random Hse. Bks. for Young Readers) Random Hse. Children's Bks.

—Pawsome Puppy Adventures! Random House, illus. 2016. (Pictureback Favorites Ser.). (ENG., Illus.). 96p. (J). (gr. -1-2). 9.99 (978-1-5247-1438-3(0), Random Hse. Bks. for Young Readers) Random Hse. Children's Bks.

—Pizza Party! (Teenage Mutant Ninja Turtles) Random House, illus. 2017. (Step into Reading Ser.). (ENG., Illus.). 24p. (J). (gr. -1-1). pap. 4.99 (978-1-5247-6982-6(7)); lib. bdg. 12.99 (978-1-5247-6983-3(5)) Random Hse. Children's Bks. (Random Hse. Bks. for Young Readers).

—Poppy Follows Her Nose! Random House, illus. 2017. (Scratch-And-Sniff Book Ser.). (ENG., Illus.). 24p. (J). (gr. -1-2). 9.99 (978-1-5247-6642-9(9), Random Hse. Bks. for Young Readers) Random Hse. Children's Bks.

—Rough-And-Tumble Turtles! (Teenage Mutant Ninja Turtles: Half-Shell Heroes) Spaziante, Patrick, illus. 2016. (Touch-And-Feel Ser.). (ENG.). 10p. (J). (— 1). bds. 12.99 (978-1-101-94029-7(8), Random Hse. Bks. for Young Readers) Random Hse. Children's Bks.

—Saved by the Shell! (Teenage Mutant Ninja Turtles) Random House, illus. 2017. (Pictureback(R) Ser.). (ENG., Illus.). 24p. (J). (gr. -1-2). pap. 5.99 (978-1-5247-6984-0(3), Random Hse. Bks. for Young Readers) Random Hse. Children's Bks.

—Small Pups, Big Adventures! (PAW Patrol) Random House, illus. 2017. (ENG., Illus.). 24p. (J). (— 1). bds. 6.99 (978-0-399-55879-5(9), Random Hse. Bks. for Young Readers) Random Hse. Children's Bks.

—The Spooky Cabin (PAW Patrol) Fruchter, Jason, illus. 2017. (Step into Reading Ser.). (ENG.). 24p. (J). (gr. -1-1). pap. 4.99 (978-1-5247-1694-3(4)); lib. bdg. 12.99 (978-1-5247-1695-0(2)) Random Hse. Children's Bks. (Random Hse. Bks. for Young Readers).

—Thomas & Friends: the Adventure Begins (Thomas & Friends) 2015. (Pictureback(R) Ser.). (ENG., Illus.). 24p. (J). (gr. -1-2). 3.99 (978-0-553-53553-2(6), Random Hse. Bks. for Young Readers) Random Hse. Children's Bks.

—Trolls: the Deluxe Junior Novelization (DreamWorks Trolls) Random House, illus. 2016. (Junior Novel Ser.). (ENG., Illus.). 144p. (J). (gr. 2-5). 9.99 (978-0-399-55909-9(4), Random Hse. Bks. for Young Readers) Random Hse. Children's Bks.

—Trolls: the Junior Novelization (DreamWorks Trolls) Random House, illus. 2016. (Junior Novel Ser.). (ENG., Illus.). 144p. (J). (gr. 2-5). 6.99 (978-0-399-55910-5(8), Random Hse. Bks. for Young Readers) Random Hse. Children's Bks.

Random House. 1, 2, 3, Tea! (Shimmer & Shine) Cespedes-Alicea, Marcela, illus. 2017. (ENG.). 24p. (J). (— 1). bds. 6.99 (978-1-5247-1719-3(3), Random Hse. Bks. for Young Readers) Random Hse. Children's Bks.

Random House & Miller, Mona. Poppy & Branch's Big Adventure. Random House, illus. 2017. (Step into Reading Ser.). (ENG., Illus.). 32p. (J). (gr. -1-2). pap. 4.99 (978-0-399-55870-2(5), Random Hse. Bks. for Young Readers) Random Hse. Children's Bks.

Random House Australia Staff & Malone, Jen. Follow Your Art. Random House Australia Staff, illus. 2016. (Stepping Stone Book(TM) Ser.). (ENG., Illus.). 208p. (J). (gr. 3-7). 12.99 (978-0-399-55747-7(4), Random Hse. Bks. for Young Readers) Random Hse. Children's Bks.

Random House Disney. Moana Junior Novelization. Random House Disney, illus. 2016. (Junior Novel Ser.). (ENG., Illus.). 144p. (J). (gr. 2-5). 17.20 (978-0-606-39357-7(9)) Turtleback Bks.

Random House Disney Staff. Anna's Act of Love - Elsa's Icy Magic, 2 bks. in 1. Random House Disney Staff, illus. 2013. (Pictureback(R) Ser.). (ENG., Illus.). 24p. (J). (gr. -1-2). 4.99 (978-0-7364-3061-6(X), RH/Disney) Random Hse. Children's Bks.

—Big Bear, Little Bear. Random House Disney Staff, illus. 2012. (Step into Reading Ser.). (ENG., Illus.). 32p. (J). (gr. -1-1). pap. 3.99 (978-0-7364-2915-3(8), RH/Disney) Random Hse. Children's Bks.

—Big Hero 6. Random House Disney Staff, illus. 2014. (Little Golden Book Ser.). (ENG., Illus.). 24p. (J). (-k). 4.99 (978-0-7364-3168-2(3), Golden Bks.) Random Hse. Children's Bks.

—Big Hero 6 Big Golden Book (Disney Big Hero 6) Random House Disney Staff, illus. 2014. (Big Golden Book Ser.). (ENG., Illus.). 48p. (J). (gr. k-4). 9.99 (978-0-7364-3186-6(1), Golden Bks.) Random Hse. Children's Bks.

—Brave Big Golden Book (Disney/Pixar Brave) Random House Disney Staff, illus. 2012. (Big Golden Book Ser.). (ENG., Illus.). 64p. (J). (gr. -1-2). 9.99 (978-0-7364-2918-4(2), Golden/Disney) Random Hse. Children's Bks.

—Disney Frozen: Special Edition Junior Novelization (Disney Frozen) Random House Disney Staff, illus. 2014. (Junior Novel Ser.). (ENG., Illus.). 128p. (J). (gr. 3-7). 12.99 (978-0-7364-3296-2(5), RH/Disney) Random Hse. Children's Bks.

—Disney/Pixar Story Collection. Random House Disney Staff, illus. 2008. (Step into Reading Ser.). (ENG., Illus.). 160p. (J). (gr. k-3). pap. 7.99 (978-0-7364-2554-4(3), RH/Disney) Random Hse. Children's Bks.

—Dusty to the Rescue (Disney Planes: Fire & Rescue) Random House Disney Staff, illus. 2014. (Pictureback Ser.). (ENG., Illus.). 24p. (J). (gr. -1-2). 4.99 (978-0-7364-3255-9(8), RH/Disney) Random Hse. Children's Bks.

—Finding Nemo. 2004. (Read-Aloud Board Book Ser.). (ENG., Illus.). 24p. (J). (gr. k — 1). bds. 4.99 (978-0-7364-2249-9(8), RH/Disney) Random Hse. Children's Bks.

—Frozen Junior Novelization (Disney Frozen) Random House Disney Staff, illus. 2013. (Junior Novel Ser.). (ENG., Illus.). 128p. (J). (gr. 3-7). 4.99 (978-0-7364-3118-7(7), RH/Disney) Random Hse. Children's Bks.

—Frozen Little Golden Book (Disney Frozen) Random House Disney Staff, illus. 2013. (Little Golden Book Ser.). (ENG., Illus.). 24p. (J). (-k). 3.99 (978-0-7364-3051-7(2), Golden/Disney) Random Hse. Children's Bks.

—Little Man of Disneyland (Disney Classic) Walt Disney Studios Staff, illus. 2015. (Little Golden Book Ser.). (ENG.). 24p. (J). (-k). 4.99 (978-0-7364-3485-0(2), Golden/Disney) Random Hse. Children's Bks.

—Look Out for Mater! Random House Disney Staff, illus. 2009. (Little Golden Book Ser.). (ENG., Illus.). 24p. (J). (gr. -1-2). 4.99 (978-0-7364-2582-7(9), Golden/Disney) Random Hse. Children's Bks.

—Poppy's Party. Random House Disney Staff & Matta, Gabriella, illus. 2016. (Step into Reading Ser.). (ENG.). 32p. (J). (gr. -1-2). pap. 4.99 (978-0-399-55906-8(X), Random Hse. Bks. for Young Readers) Random Hse. Children's Bks.

—Race Team. Random House Disney Staff, illus. 2008. (Step into Reading Ser.). (ENG., Illus.). 32p. (J). (gr. k-3). pap. 3.99 (978-0-7364-2571-1(3), RH/Disney) Random Hse. Children's Bks.

—Super Spies. Random House Disney Staff, illus. 2011. (Step into Reading Ser.). (ENG., Illus.). 32p. (J). (gr. k-3). pap. 3.99 (978-0-7364-2807-1(0), RH/Disney) Random Hse. Children's Bks.

—Up. Random House Disney Staff, illus. 2009. (Little Golden Book Ser.). (ENG., Illus.). 24p. (J). (gr. -1-2). 4.99 (978-0-7364-2581-0(0), Golden/Disney) Random Hse. Children's Bks.

—Zootopia Big Golden Book (Disney Zootopia) Random House Disney Staff, illus. 2016. (Big Golden Book Ser.). (ENG., Illus.). 64p. (J). (gr. -1-2). 9.99 (978-0-7364-3384-6(8), Golden/Disney) Random Hse. Children's Bks.

Random House Disney Staff & Green, Rico. Super Animals! Random House Disney Staff & Disney Storybook Art Team, illus. 2016. (Step into Reading Ser.). (ENG.). 24p. (J). (gr. -1-1). 4.99 (978-0-7364-3454-6(2), RH/Disney) Random Hse. Children's Bks.

Random House Disney Staff & Scollon, Bill. The Big Case. Random House Disney Staff & Disney Storybook Art Team, illus. 2016. (Step into Reading Ser.). (ENG.). 32p. (J). (gr. -1-1). 4.99 (978-0-7364-3456-0(9), RH/Disney) Random Hse. Children's Bks.

Random House Editors. Nickelodeon Story Time Collection (Nickelodeon) Random House Editors & Golden Books Staff, illus. 2014. (ENG.). 320p. (J). (gr. -1-2). 15.99 (978-0-385-38777-4(6), Random Hse. Bks. for Young Readers) Random Hse. Children's Bks.

—Too Much Ooze! (Teenage Mutant Ninja Turtles) Random House Editors & Spaziante, Patrick, illus. 2015. (Step into Reading Ser.). (ENG.). 24p. (J). (gr. -1-1). 4.99 (978-0-553-50866-6(0), Random Hse. Bks. for Young Readers) Random Hse. Children's Bks.

—Wishes & Surprises! (Shimmer & Shine) Random House Editors & Cho, Mu Young, illus. 2017. (Nifty Lift-And-Look Ser.). (ENG.). 12p. (J). (-k). bds. 9.99 (978-1-101-93983-3(4), Random Hse. Bks. for Young Readers) Random Hse. Children's Bks.

Random House Staff. Chase Is on the Case! (Paw Patrol) Random House Staff & Petrossi, Fabrizio, illus. 2014. (Step into Reading Ser.). (ENG.). 24p. (J). (gr. -1-1). 3.99 (978-0-385-38447-6(5), Random Hse. Bks. for Young Readers) Random Hse. Children's Bks.

—I Am Baymax. 2015. (Step into Reading Level 2 Ser.). lib. bdg. 14.75 (978-0-606-36383-9(1)) Turtleback Bks.

—Legend of the Blue Mermaid (Team Umizoomi) Fruchter, Jason, illus. 2013. (Pictureback(R) Ser.). (ENG.). 24p. (J). (gr. -1-2). 3.99 (978-0-449-81758-2(X), Random Hse. Bks. for Young Readers) Random Hse. Children's Bks.

—Railway Adventures. Random House Staff, illus. 2010. (Step into Reading Ser.). (ENG., Illus.). 160p. (J). (gr. -1-1). pap. 7.99 (978-0-375-86653-1(1), Random Hse. Bks. for Young Readers) Random Hse. Children's Bks.

Random House Staff, illus. Barbie Fairytale Collection. 2011. (Step into Reading Ser.). (ENG.). 160p. (J). (gr. -1-1). pap. 7.99 (978-0-375-87255-6(8), Random Hse. Bks. for Young Readers) Random Hse. Children's Bks.

—Hero Story Collection (DC Super Friends) 2012. (Step into Reading Ser.). (ENG.). 160p. (J). (gr. -1-1). pap. 7.99 (978-0-375-87298-3(1), Random Hse. Bks. for Young Readers) Random Hse. Children's Bks.

Randy. The Adventures of Rico. 2010. 28p. pap. 13.79 (978-1-4490-8353-3(6)) AuthorHouse.

Rangel, Graciela. Anthony's Journey to God's Ark. 2007. 84p. pap. 8.95 (978-1-59526-907-2(X), Llumina Christian Bks.) Aeon Publishing Inc.

Ranjalkar, Shreyans. My Sunny British Days - Stories for Children by a Child. 2013. (Illus.). 70p. pap. (978-1-78148-596-5(8)) Grosvenor Hse. Publishing Ltd.

Rankin, Debbie. Butch the Blue Jay. 2010. 36p. pap. 20.00 (978-1-4490-7809-6(5)) AuthorHouse.

Rankine-Van Wassenhoven, Jacqueline. Three Pumpkin Pies for Three Good Neighbors. 2009. 20p. pap. 11.00 (978-1-4389-3242-2(1)) AuthorHouse.

Ransom, Candice. The Life-Saving Adventure of Sam Deal, Shipwreck Rescuer. Trover, Zachary, illus. 2010. (History's Kid Heroes Ser.). (ENG.). 32p. (gr. 3-5). lib. bdg. 26.60 (978-0-7613-6177-0(4)) Lerner Publishing Group.

Ransome, Arthur. Great Northern? 2003. (Swallows & Amazons Ser.). (ENG., Illus.). 352p. (J). pap. 14.95 (978-1-56792-259-2(7)) Godine, David R. Pub.

—Old Peter's Russian Tales. 2005. 35.00 (978-1-55742-465-5(9)); pap. 15.95 (978-1-55742-456-3(X)) Wildside Pr., LLC.

—Swallows & Amazons. Ransome, Arthur, illus. 2010. (Swallows & Amazons Ser.). (Illus.). 351p. (J). pap. 14.95 (978-1-56792-420-6(4)) Godine, David R. Pub.

—Swallows & Amazons. 2013. (ENG.). 384p. (gr. 4-13). 22.95 (978-1-4683-0661-3(8), 460661) Overlook Pr., The.

Rao, Chatura. Amie & the Chawl of Colour. Pathak, Ashutosh, illus. 2004. 100p. pap. (978-0-14-333592-4(8), Puffin) Penguin Publishing Group.

Rao, Lisa. Diego & the Baby Sea Turtles. McGee, Warner, illus. 2008. (Go, Diego, Go! Ser.: 8). (ENG.). 24p. (J). pap. 3.99 (978-1-4169-5450-7(3), Simon Spotlight/Nickelodeon) Simon Spotlight/Nickelodeon.

—Dora's Magic Watering Can. Miller, Victoria, illus. 2008. (Dora the Explorer Ser.). (ENG.). 16p. (J). (gr. -1-1). pap. 4.99 (978-1-4169-4772-1(8), Simon Spotlight/Nickelodeon) Simon Spotlight/Nickelodeon.

—Iron Man: I Am Iron Man! Guidi, Guido, illus. 2008. (I Can Read Bks.). 32p. (J). (gr. -1-2). pap. 3.99 (978-0-06-082193-7(0), Harper Trophy) HarperCollins Pubs.

Rapoport, Cindy. The Adventures of Poca & Flea Bert. 2008. 64p. pap. 19.95 (978-1-60672-901-4(2)) America Star Bks.

Rapson, Helen. One Lucky Goose, 1 vol. 2005. (ENG.). 32p. 24.95 (978-1-4137-2852-1(9)) PublishAmerica, Inc.

—Reggie Did It!, 1 vol. 2009. 49p. pap. 16.95 (978-1-60813-161-7(0)) America Star Bks.

Rasheed, M. Monsters 101, Book One. 2007. 152p. pap. 15.00 (978-1-4303-2946-6(7)) Lulu Pr., Inc.

Raskin, Ellen. The Mysterious Disappearence of Leon. Raskin, Ellen, illus. 2011. (ENG., Illus.). 176p. (J). (gr. 3-7). 6.99 (978-0-14-241700-3(9), Puffin Books) Penguin Young Readers Group.

Raspe, Rudolph. Surprising Adventures of Baron Munchause. 2006. 62.99 (978-1-4219-8906-8(9)) IndyPublish.com.

Ratcliff, Carol J. Grannie's Secret Garden: (Somewhere in England) 2009. (Illus.). 48p. pap. 19.49 (978-1-4490-4355-1(0)) AuthorHouse.

Ratcliff, Charline. The Princess, the Toad & the Whale. 2012. (ENG.). 36p. (J). (-18). pap. 12.95 (978-1-4787-1672-3(X)) Outskirts Pr., Inc.

Rath, Tom H. Donkey Oatie's Impossible Dream. MacAdam, Reegory, illus. 2012. 24p. pap. (978-0-9866065-5-7(3)) Wood Islands Prints.

Rathborne, St. George. Canoe Mates in Canada; or, Three Boys Afloat on the Saskatchewan. 2007. 100p. per. (978-1-4068-3746-9(6)) Echo Library.

—The House Boat Boys. 2007. 160p. per. (978-1-4065-4243-1(1)) Dodo Pr.

Raun, Robert L. Tales of the Clam Club: Turtle Soup. 2012. (ENG.). pap. (978-1-4675-1923-6(5)) Independent Pub.

Rautenberg, Karen Rita. Lady Lucy's Gallant Knight. 2007. (ENG.). 156p. (J). (gr. 4-7). per. (978-1-933255-22-4(6)) DNA Pr.

Rawls, Wilson. Where the Red Fern Grows. l.t. ed. 2017. (ENG.). 378p. 22.99 (978-1-4328-3845-4(8)) Cengage Gale.

Ray, Ann. Just Imagine What You Can Do! 2008. 20p. pap. 12.99 (978-1-4343-8874-2(3)) AuthorHouse.

Ray, Baltazar, creator. The Adventures of the FancyCrazyHydrants: The Mission 2004. (Illus.). 162p. (J). per. 17.95 (978-0-9745386-9-3(8)) FancyCrazy Publishing.

Ray, Christie Jones & Ray, Christie Jones. Eliza & a Cottage Door. 2012. (Illus.). 40p. pap. 15.00 (978-0-9853223-0-4(6)) Rose Water Cottage Pr.

—Eliza Has a Cousin. 2012. (Illus.). 32p. pap. 15.00 *(978-0-9853223-5-9(7))* Rose Water Cottage Pr.

Ray, Joanna Z. 'elaran! Isithan!' 2007. (ENG.). 92p. (YA). per. 15.95 *(978-1-4116-9393-7(0))* Lulu Pr., Inc.

Ray, Keri. The Saving Journey. 2009. 48p. pap. 10.49 *(978-1-4389-5008-2(X))* AuthorHouse.

Raye, Marianna & Raye, Daniel. Olis & the Big Outside. 2011. (Illus.). 32p. pap. 14.09 *(978-1-4567-7157-7(4))* AuthorHouse.

Raynor, Michelle. A Magical World. 2011. 20p. pap. 11.99 *(978-1-257-65025-5(4))* Lulu Pr., Inc.

RAZ. 'Cuz That's Just My Way. Kerchner, Janet Hall, illus. 2005. 32p. (J). bds. 15.95 *(978-0-9712070-4-2(6))* B2Z Publishing, Inc.

Razilov, Evelyn. The Little Ant & the Apple Tree. 2013. 24p. pap. 12.56 *(978-1-4669-7729-7(9))* Trafford Publishing.

Razzell, Mary. Runaway at Sea. unabr. ed. 2005. (ENG., Illus.). 150p. (YA). (gr. 7-9). 9.95 *(978-1-55017-327-7(8))* Harbour Publishing Co., Ltd. CAN. Dist: Midpoint Trade Bks., Inc.

R.D.Haire & Francis, Richard E. When Good Got Better: The Adventures of Fred the Friendly Shark. 2012. 24p. pap. 15.99 *(978-1-4797-3797-0(6))* Xlibris Corp.

Rea, Monique. Toulouse the Moose & the Mystery Guests. 2012. 34p. pap. 13.99 *(978-0-9788926-4-7(X))* Trails of Discovery.

Read, Kit. Alexis Ant Marooned in Afric. 2012. 152p. *(978-1-4602-0314-9(3))*; pap. *(978-1-4602-0313-2(5))* FriesenPress.

Read, Laurie. Blacky Longlegs Meets Freddy the Fly. 2008. 20p. pap. 14.00 *(978-1-4389-1231-8(5))* AuthorHouse.

Reader's Digest Staff. Mickey Mouse Clubhouse Gift Set. 2012. (ENG.). 64p. (J). 39.98 *(978-0-7944-2669-9(7))* Reader's Digest Assn., Inc., The.

—Rise of the Guardians: Worlds of Wonder. Primeau, Chuck, illus. deluxe ed. 2012. (ENG.). 24p. (J). (gr. k-2). 19.99 *(978-0-7944-2803-7(7))* Reader's Digest Assn., Inc., The.

Readler, Blaine C. Under the Radar: The Spy Drone Adventure. 2006. (ENG.). 248p. (J). (gr. 7-12). per. *(978-1-933255-18-7(8))* DNA Pr.

RealBuzz Studios Staff. Out of the Soup. 2007. (Goofyfoot Gurl Ser.: No. 4). 96p. (YA). pap. 4.97 *(978-1-59789-576-7(8))* Barbour Publishing, Inc.

Reardon, A. C. Galish: The adventure of Isabelle & Eva. 2011. 168p. pap. 14.69 *(978-1-4567-7818-7(8))* AuthorHouse.

Reason, Diane. Travis the Traveling Turtle & the Beautiful Butterfly. 2011. 32p. pap. 14.98 *(978-1-4634-0206-8(6))* AuthorHouse.

Reasoner, Charles. Charles Reasoner's Little Cuddles. Llewhellin, Gareth, illus. 2015. (Charles Reasoner's Little Cuddles Ser.). (ENG.). 10p. (gr. -1 — 1). bds. 17.97 *(978-1-4795-8061-3(9),* Charles Reasoners Little Cuddles) Picture Window Bks.

Rebal, Tara. Sarah Sue Smith: A Crooked Wharf Adventure. 2010. 52p. pap. 22.49 *(978-1-4520-7165-7(9))* AuthorHouse.

The Rebel Princess. 2014. pap. 12.99 *(978-1-4621-1430-6(X))* Cedar Fort, Inc./CFI Distribution.

Rebello, Kevin. Julia & Mckinley's Day at the Beach. 2009. 32p. pap. 12.99 *(978-1-4389-7330-2(6))* AuthorHouse.

Reberg, Evelyne. Tom Tom et la impossible Na. pap. 21.95 *(978-2-227-73101-1(X))* Bayard Editions FRA. Dist: Distribooks, Inc.

—Tom Tom et les idees Explosi. pap. 21.95 *(978-2-227-73106-6(0))* Bayard Editions FRA. Dist: Distribooks, Inc.

Rebert, Brenda. Rooster Went A' Walkin' 2009. 28p. pap. 13.99 *(978-1-4389-3414-3(9))* AuthorHouse.

Rechlin, Ted. ComicQuest TIME TRAVEL TROUBLE. 2013. (Dover Children's Activity Bks.). (ENG.). 48p. (J). (gr. 3-8). pap. 4.99 *(978-0-486-49949-9(9))* Dover Pubns., Inc.

Rector, Lori. Adventures of A. 2013. (ENG.). 21p. (J). pap. 12.95 *(978-1-4787-1005-9(5))* Outskirts Pr., Inc.

Redbank, Tennant. The Great Mountain Adventure. RH Disney et al, illus. 2016. (Disney Chapters Ser.). (ENG.). 64p. (J). (gr. 1-4). 5.99 *(978-0-7364-3636-6(7),* RH/Disney) Random Hse. Children's Bks.

Reddy's Golden Adventure. 2004. (J). 15.95 *(978-0-9639670-0-8(2))* twhiteart.

Redenius, John. Escaping the Yard, the Little Adventure of a Puppy Named Splinter. 2009. 88p. pap. 12.50 *(978-1-60693-985-7(8),* Eloquent Bks.) Strategic Book Publishing & Rights Agency (SBPRA).

Redepenning, George. The Adventures of Webster. 2008. pap. 9.00 *(978-0-8059-8629-7(4))* Dorrance Publishing Co., Inc.

Redfern, Holly. The Adventures of Remmington the Dog: An Unexpected Friend. Burton, Claudia, illus. 2007. 28p. (gr. -1-3). per. 14.95 *(978-1-59858-317-5(4))* Dog Ear Publishing, LLC.

Redmond, Mark L. Arty's Long Day. Ury, Laura, illus. 2003. 102p. pap. *(978-0-87398-042-5(5))* Sword of the Lord Pubs.

Redmond, Zelie. The Adventures of Sister Regina Marie: Sister Finds a Friend. Redmond, Zelie, . 2005. (J). per. 6.95 *(978-0-9774345-0-3(8))* Joy of my Youth Pubns., The.

Rednose, Skiddles. Tale of the Land of Umble. 2013. 126p. pap. 18.99 *(978-1-938487-14-9(1))* Big Country Publishing, LLC.

Redondo, Kurt. Treasure Map. 2006. (Neighborhood Readers Ser.). (ENG.). 12p. (gr. -1-3). pap. 5.90 *(978-1-4042-6463-2(9),* Rosen Classroom) Rosen Publishing Group, Inc., The.

Redwine, C. J. The Wish Granter. 2017. (Ravenspire Ser.: 2). (Illus.). 432p. (YA). (gr. 8). 17.99 *(978-0-06-236027-4(2))* HarperCollins Pubs.

Reed, Bliss & Reed, Sinclair. This Summer I Plan to Rule the World. rev. ed. 2009. (ENG., Illus.). 100p. (J). (gr. k-7). pap. *(978-0-9822200-2-3(2))* Temmen, Edition, Horst Temmen.

Reed-Guldin, Emily. Sarah & Sammi's Playhouse: Mermaid Adventure. 2009. 36p. pap. 16.99 *(978-1-4389-9342-3(0))* AuthorHouse.

Reed, Jennifer. Hadi's Journey. 2003. 110p. pap. 10.95 *(978-0-595-29375-9(1))* iUniverse, Inc.

Reed, Joel B. Grandpa's New Kitty. Reed, Joel B., illus. 2008. (Illus.). 28p. pap. 12.95 *(978-1-933482-65-1(6))* White Turtle Bks.

Reed, Master Amy. The Adventures of A Dragon Named Ryung: Journey to Black Belt. 2010. 56p. pap. 30.99 *(978-1-4520-0145-6(6))* AuthorHouse.

Reed, T. K. Quasar & the Eye of the Serpent. 2009. 136p. 21.95 *(978-1-4401-2753-3(0))*; pap. 11.95 *(978-1-4401-2751-9(4))* iUniverse, Inc.

Reedy, Trent. The Last Full Measure. 2017. (Divided We Fall Ser.: 3). (ENG.). 464p. (J). (gr. 9-9). pap. 9.99 ***(978-0-545-54878-6(0))*** Scholastic, Inc.

Reel FX Inc. Staff, et al, illus. A Tale of Two Friends. 2014. (Book of Life Ser.). (ENG.). 32p. (J). (gr. k-2). pap. 3.99 *(978-1-4814-2573-5(0),* Simon Spotlight) Simon Spotlight.

Rees, Celia. The Fool's Girl. 2010. (ENG.). 304p. (YA). (gr. 7-18). 16.99 *(978-1-59990-486-3(1),* 9781599904863, Bloomsbury USA Childrens) Bloomsbury Publishing USA.

—Pirates! 2003. (ENG.). 384p. (YA). (gr. 7). 16.95 *(978-1-58234-816-2(2),* 9781582348162, Bloomsbury USA Childrens) Bloomsbury Publishing USA.

—Pirates! The True & Remarkable Adventures of Minerva Sharpe & Nancy Kington, Female Pirates. 2005. (Illus.). 379p. (YA). (gr. 9-12). 16.60 *(978-0-7569-6304-0(4))* Perfection Learning Corp.

—The Wish House. 2006. (ENG.). 272p. (YA). (gr. 9-12). 15.99 *(978-0-7636-2951-9(0))* Candlewick Pr.

Rees, Margaret. Primrose & the Mystery of Frangipani Bay. 2015. (ENG., Illus.). 45p. (J). (gr. 3-4). pap. 11.95 *(978-1-78455-832-1(X),* 18de55dc-6e2c-45a7-b765-ce2b58e00c12) Austin, Stan AUS. Dist: Bookmasters Distribution.

Rees, Susan. The First Adventure of Baby Bee. 2011. 36p. pap. 16.86 *(978-1-4567-9434-7(5))* AuthorHouse.

Reese, Jenn. Horizon. (Above World Ser.). (ENG.). 400p. (J). (gr. 5). 2015. pap. 7.99 *(978-0-7636-7667-4(5))* 2014. 16.99 *(978-0-7636-6417-6(0))* Candlewick Pr.

—Mirage. 2013. (Above World Ser.). (ENG.). 368p. (J). (gr. 5). 16.99 *(978-0-7636-5418-4(3))* Candlewick Pr.

Reeve, Penny. The Back Leg of a Goat: A Tania Abbey Adventure. Apps, Fred, illus. 2008. (Tania Abbey Adventure Ser.). (ENG.). 96p. (J). pap. 6.99 *(978-1-84550-340-6(6),* c8e23bb3-9904-4201-971e-e57faa66b8f3) Christian Focus Pubns. GBR. Dist: Bookmasters Distribution.

—Water or Goo? Apps, Fred, illus. 2008. (Tania Abbey Adventure Ser.). (ENG.). 96p. (J). pap. 6.99 *(978-1-84550-341-3(4),* 748295d7-9d18-4862-90d7-b454340bafc1) Christian Focus Pubns. GBR. Dist: Bookmasters Distribution.

Reeve, Philip. Black Light Express. 2017. (ENG.). 352p. (gr. 9-12). 17.95 ***(978-1-63079-096-7(6))*** Switch Pr.

—Goblins. 2013. (ENG.). 352p. (J). (gr. 3-7). 17.99 *(978-0-545-22220-4(6),* Scholastic Pr.) Scholastic, Inc.

—Oliver & the Sea Monkeys. McIntyre, Sarah, illus. 2016. (Not-So-Impossible Tale Ser.). (ENG.). 224p. (J). (gr. 2-5). pap. 6.99 *(978-0-385-38789-7(X),* Yearling) Random Hse. Children's Bks.

—Oliver & the Seawigs. McIntyre, Sarah, illus. 2014. (Not-So-Impossible Tale Ser.). (ENG.). 208p. (J). (gr. 2-5). 12.99 *(978-0-385-38788-0(1),* Random Hse. Bks. for Young Readers) Random Hse. Children's Bks.

—Pugs of the Frozen North. McIntyre, Sarah, illus. 2016. (Not-So-Impossible Tale Ser.). (ENG.). 224p. (J). (gr. 2-5). 12.99 *(978-0-385-38796-5(2),* Random Hse. Bks. for Young Readers) Random Hse. Children's Bks.

—Railhead. 2016. (ENG.). 352p. (gr. 9-12). 16.95 *(978-1-63079-048-6(6))* Switch Pr.

Reeves, Amy Carol. Resurrection. 2014. (Ripper Novel Ser.: 3). (ENG.). 336p. (YA). pap. 9.99 *(978-0-7387-3877-2(8),* Flux) North Star Editions.

Reeves, Claire. Adventures of Boots the One Eyed Cat 2003. (Illus.). 32p. (J). 15.95 *(978-0-9743048-1-6(6))* LTI Publishing.

Reeves, Janet. The Acorn Treasure. 2010. 32p. pap. 14.49 *(978-1-4520-5024-9(4))* AuthorHouse.

Reeves, Jeni, illus. Anansi & the Box of Stories: A West African Folktale. 2007. (On My Own Folklore Ser.). 48p. (J). (gr. 2-5). lib. bdg. 25.26 *(978-0-8225-6741-7(5),* Millbrook Pr.) Lerner Publishing Group.

Regan, Marti. Lazy Daisy, the Love Dog. 2013. (Illus.). 40p. pap. 16.46 *(978-1-4669-7789-1(2))* Trafford Publishing.

Regan, Peter. A Fresh Start. Myler, Terry, illus. 2004. (Shannon Harps Ser.: 03). (ENG.). 112p. (J). per. 10.95 *(978-1-901737-49-3(7))* Anvil Bks., Ltd. IRL. Dist: Dufour Editions, Inc.

—Something New, Vol. 2. Myler, Terry, illus. 2004. (Shannon Harps Ser.: 02). (ENG.). 112p. (J). pap. 10.95 *(978-1-901737-52-3(7))* Anvil Bks., Ltd. IRL. Dist: Dufour Editions, Inc.

Reger, Rob & Gruner, Jessica. Dark Times. Reger, Rob & Parker, Buzz, illus. 2011. (Emily the Strange Ser.: 3). (ENG.). 248p. (YA). (gr. 8). pap. 8.99 *(978-0-06-145237-6(8))* HarperCollins Pubs.

Reh, Rusalka. The Secret of the Water Knight, 0 vols. Derbyshire, Katy, tr. unabr. ed. 2011. (ENG.). 100p. (J). (gr. 4-7). pap. 9.95 *(978-1-61109-006-2(7),* 9781611090062) Amazon Publishing.

Reibold, Mary. Ninya's Great Adventure: A Cat's Tale. 2007. 96p. per. 19.95 *(978-1-4241-7135-4(0))* America Star Bks.

Reich, J. J. Deer Dad: Kampp Tales Outdoor Adventures. Johnathan, Kuehl, illus. 2006. (BAT.). 32p. (J). *(978-0-9762971-0-9(8))* Outdoor Originals LLC.

Reich, Robert E. Harry MacFly's the Old Mill Adventure. Reich, Robert E., illus. 2013. (ENG., Illus.). 28p. (J). pap. 9.95 *(978-0-9895323-1-0(3))* Black Creek Publishing Group.

Reichs, Kathy. Code. 2013. (Virals Ser.: 3). (ENG.). 432p. (J). (gr. 5). pap. 8.99 *(978-1-59514-572-7(9),* Puffin Books) Penguin Young Readers Group.

Reichs, Kathy & Reichs, Brendan. Code. 2013. (Virals Ser.: 3). lib. bdg. 19.65 *(978-0-606-32140-2(3),* Turtleback) Turtleback Bks.

Reid, Alastair. A Balloon for a Blunderbuss. Gill, Bob, illus. 2008. (ENG.). 36p. (gr. -1-3). 14.95 *(978-0-7148-4873-0(5))* Phaidon Pr., Inc.

Reid Banks, Lynne & Stephenson, Omri. Polly & Jake. 2010. 36p. pap. 25.50 *(978-1-4457-5277-8(8))* Lulu Pr., Inc.

Reid, Barbara. The Subway Mouse. Reid, Barbara, illus. 2005. (Illus.). (J). *(978-0-439-77430-7(6))* Scholastic, Inc.

Reid, James. Ready, Set, Go!, 1 vol. rev. ed. 2013. (Fiction Readers Ser.). (ENG., Illus.). 20p. (J). (gr. 1-1). 4.99 *(978-1-4333-5488-5(8))*; pap. 15.96 *(978-1-4807-1144-0(6))* Shell Educational Publishing.

—This Is My Story by Frederick G. Frog, 1 vol. rev. ed. 2013. (Fiction Readers Ser.). (ENG., Illus.). 20p. (J). (gr. 1-1). pap. 4.99 *(978-1-4333-5484-7(5))*; pap. 15.96 *(978-1-4807-1140-2(3))* Shell Educational Publishing.

Reid, Mayne. The Boy Hunters or Adventures in Search of a White Buffalo. 2005. reprint ed. pap. 30.95 *(978-1-4179-0412-9(7))* Kessinger Publishing, LLC.

—Young Yagers or A Narrative of Hunting A. 2006. (Illus.). pap. 31.95 *(978-1-4286-2205-0(5))* Kessinger Publishing, LLC.

Reid, Nakeil W. & Reid, Neil W. The Adventure of Avery the Ant: Experience the Next Children?ÇÖS Classic. 2011. 49p. pap. 14.95 *(978-1-4327-6597-2(3))* Outskirts Pr., Inc.

Reid, P. D. The Adventures of Sam the Suitcase. 2014. (ENG.). 63p. (gr. 1-2). pap. 8.95 *(978-1-84963-439-7(4),* 4bbcce1e-4a8d-4be3-bb14-7c66fec25522) Austin, Stan AUS. Dist: Bookmasters Distribution.

Reid, Roger. Longleaf. 2007. 133p. (J). (gr. 3-7). 19.95 *(978-1-58838-194-1(3),* Junebug Bks.) NewSouth, Inc.

Reid, Thomas M. Forged. 2003. 320p. (YA). per. 7.99 *(978-1-59263-010-3(3))* Bastion Pr., Inc.

Reide, MacKenzie. The Adventurers the Mask of the Troll. 2013. 326p. pap. *(978-0-9869647-2-5(7))* MR Bks.

Reidy, Hannah. Crazy Creature Capers. Mackie, Clare, illus. 2003. (Crazy Creatures Ser.). 26p. (J). pap. *(978-1-84089-222-2(6))* Zero to Ten, Ltd.

Reilly, Carmel & Miesen, Christina. The Call of the Wolf. 2008. (Rigby Focus Forward: Level H Ser.). (Illus.). 24p. (J). (gr. 4-7). pap. *(978-1-4190-3722-1(6),* Rigby) Pearson Education Australia.

Reilly, Carmel & Young, Karen. Buzz Takes Over. 2008. (Rigby Focus Forward: Level I Ser.). (Illus.). 24p. (J). (gr. 4-7). pap. *(978-1-4190-3743-6(9),* Rigby) Pearson Education Australia.

Reimiller, Diane L. Ike & Jamie. Jastrzebski, Brandy, illus. 2008. 32p. pap. 24.95 *(978-1-60610-227-5(3))* America Star Bks.

Reinhart, Matthew. The Jungle Book: A Pop-Up Adventure. Reinhart, Matthew, illus. 2006. (ENG., Illus.). 12p. (J). 34.99 *(978-1-4169-1824-0(8),* Little Simon) Little Simon.

—Marvel's the Avengers - Age of Ultron: A Pop-Up Book. Reinhart, Matthew, illus. 2015. (ENG., Illus.). 10p. (J). (gr. 1-17). 14.99 *(978-0-316-34086-1(3))* Little, Brown Bks. for Young Readers.

Reinhart, Matthew & Lucasfilm. A Galactic Pop-Up Adventure. ltd. ed. 2012. (Star Wars Ser.). (ENG.). 10p. (J). (gr. 2-5). 300.00 *(978-0-545-44246-6(X),* Orchard Bks.) Scholastic, Inc.

Reinheimer, Melinda T. Little Blue Kite Makes A Friend: Another Adventure of the Little Blue Kite. 2005. 24p. (J). per. 9.95 *(978-1-59196-908-2(5))* Instant Pub.

Reinlein, Ann. The Adventures of Mister Squirrel Acorn. 2008. 32p. pap. 15.00 *(978-1-4389-1879-2(8))* AuthorHouse.

Reis, Jason & Hurley, Meagan. The Adventures of Burt: Burt & the Big Race. 2012. 28p. pap. 19.99 *(978-1-4634-4126-5(6))* AuthorHouse.

Reisinger, John. The Duckworth Chronicles. 2005. pap. 11.95 *(978-1-59330-269-6(X))* Aventine Pr.

Reisner, Molly. Dora's Birthday Surprise! Aikins, David, illus. 2010. (Little Golden Book Ser.). (ENG.). 24p. (J). (gr. -1-2). 3.99 *(978-0-375-86163-5(7),* Golden Bks.) Random Hse. Children's Bks.

—Halloween Hoedown! 2013. (Dora the Explorer 8X8 Ser.). lib. bdg. 13.55 *(978-0-606-32217-1(5),* Turtleback) Turtleback Bks.

—Halloween Hoedown! (Dora the Explorer) Aikins, David, illus. 2013. (Pictureback(R) Ser.). (ENG.). 24p. (J). (gr. -1-2). 3.99 *(978-0-449-81762-9(8),* Random Hse. Bks. for Young Readers) Random Hse. Children's Bks.

Reiss, Johanna. La Habitacion de Arriba. (SPA., Illus.). 213p. (YA). (gr. 5-8). pap. *(978-84-239-8852-5(X),* EC0945) Espasa Calpe, S.A. ESP. Dist: Lectorum Pubns., Inc.

Reiss, Kathryn. Pale Phoenix. 2003. (ENG., Illus.). 336p. (J). (gr. 5-7). pap. 15.95 *(978-0-15-204927-0(4))* Houghton Mifflin Harcourt Publishing Co.

Reisz, Kristopher. Unleashed. 2008. (ENG.). 352p. (YA). (gr. 9). pap. 7.99 *(978-1-4169-4001-2(4),* Simon Pulse) Simon Pulse.

Remender, Rick & Comtois, Joelle. Girl Afraid, 4 vols., Vol. 1. 2006. (ENG., Illus.). 104p. (YA). per. 12.99 *(978-1-58240-543-8(3),* 9781582405438) Image Comics.

Remole, Arnulf. The Island of Alphebia. 2007. 34p. 24.55 *(978-1-4303-2720-2(0))* Lulu Pr., Inc.

Renier Nash, Oliver. The Primate Puzzle: A tale of two friends & the missing long-nosed Monkeys. 2009. 272p. pap. 15.49 *(978-1-4490-3099-5(8))* AuthorHouse.

Renninson, Lou. Frontalknutschen. pap. 17.95 *(978-3-570-30008-4(0))* Bertelsman, Verlagsgruppe C. GmbH DEU. Dist: Distribooks, Inc.

Renshaw, Douglas. Around Our Feeder with George the Groundhog & Friends. Lamb, Janie, illus. 2008. 48p. pap. 24.95 *(978-1-60610-657-0(0))* America Star Bks.

Rentala, Sita Kanaka Valli. Ocean Flows: In Prose: Zcumby's Judo (on Global Warming) 2010. 44p. (J). pap. 19.99 *(978-1-4490-8780-7(9))* AuthorHouse.

Renzetti, Rob & Hirsch, Alex. Gravity Falls Journal 3. Disney Storybook Art Team, illus. 2016. (ENG.). 288p. (J). (gr. 3-7). 19.99 *(978-1-4847-4669-1(4))* Disney Pr.

Rescue Flight! 2003. 150p. (J). (gr. 4-6). per. 12.95 *(978-0-9740202-0-4(6))* Skyword Pr.

Ressy-Nieves, Cynthia Ann. Keek-A-Poo's Adventures. 2010. 48p. pap. 24.99 *(978-1-4535-1479-5(1))* Xlibris Corp.

Reva Jean Rohe. Adventures of Tomtom the Duck. 2009. 52p. pap. 22.49 *(978-1-4343-7811-8(X))* AuthorHouse.

Revenson, Jody. Candy Bonanza. 2015. (Fancy Nancy Picture Bks.). (J). lib. bdg. 14.75 *(978-0-606-36965-7(1))* Turtleback Bks.

ReWalt, Nancy E. Rental: A Trip to Remember. Cranford, Darren, illus. 2010. 32p. (J). 16.95 *(978-0-9821110-1-7(0))* Ronan Enterprises, Inc.

Rex, Adam. Champions of Breakfast. 2014. (Cold Cereal Saga Ser.: 3). (ENG., Illus.). 368p. (J). (gr. 3-7). 16.99 *(978-0-06-206008-2(2))* HarperCollins Pubs.

—Cold Cereal. (Cold Cereal Saga Ser.: 1). (ENG.). (J). (gr. 3-7). 2013. 448p. pap. 7.99 *(978-0-06-206003-7(1))* 2012. 432p. 16.99 *(978-0-06-206002-0(3))* HarperCollins Pubs.

—Smek for President! Rex, Adam, illus. (Smek Smeries Ser.). (ENG., Illus.). 272p. (J). (gr. 3-7). 2016. pap. 7.99 *(978-1-4847-0969-6(1))* 2015. 16.99 *(978-1-4847-0951-1(9))* Hyperion Bks. for Children.

—Unlucky Charms. 2013. (Cold Cereal Saga Ser.: 2). (ENG., Illus.). 400p. (J). (gr. 3-7). 16.99 *(978-0-06-206005-1(8))* HarperCollins Pubs.

Rex, Annmarie. Black's Adventure in the Big, Scary, Hairy World. 2007. (Illus.). 46p. (J). 19.99 *(978-1-59879-365-9(9),* Lifevest) Lifevest Publishing, Inc.

—Black's Adventure in the Big, Scary, Hairy World. Rex, Annmarie, illus. 2007. (Illus.). 46p. (J). (gr. -1-3). per. 15.99 *(978-1-59879-364-2(0),* Lifevest) Lifevest Publishing, Inc.

Rey, H. A. Curious George Curious about Learning Boxed Set. 2012. (Curious George Ser.). (ENG., Illus.). 144p. (J). (gr. -1-3). 16.99 *(978-0-547-58209-2(9))* Houghton Mifflin Harcourt Publishing Co.

—Curious George Discovers Recycling (science Storybook) 2017. (Curious George Ser.). (ENG., Illus.). 32p. (J). (gr. -1-3). 14.99 *(978-0-544-88035-1(8),* HMH Books For Young Readers) Houghton Mifflin Harcourt Publishing Co.

—Curious George Farm to Table. 2016. (Curious George TV Tie-In 8x8 Ser.). lib. bdg. 14.75 *(978-0-606-37991-5(6))* Turtleback Bks.

—Curious George Subway Train Adventure. 2016. (Curious George Ser.). (ENG., Illus.). 24p. (J). (gr. 1-4). 12.99 *(978-0-544-78585-4(1),* HMH Books For Young Readers) Houghton Mifflin Harcourt Publishing Co.

—Jorge el Curioso y la Pinata. 2009. (Curious George Ser.).Tr. of Curious George Pinata Party. (SPA & ENG., Illus.). 24p. (J). (gr. -1-3). pap. 3.99 *(978-0-547-23830-2(4))* Houghton Mifflin Harcourt Publishing Co.

—My Curious Dreamer, Set. gif. ed. 2010. (Curious Baby Curious George Ser.). (ENG., Illus.). 10p. (J). (gr. k — 1). 14.99 *(978-0-547-24308-5(1))* Houghton Mifflin Harcourt Publishing Co.

—Pinata Party. 2009. (Curious George Ser.). (ENG., Illus.). 24p. (J). (gr. -1-3). pap. 3.99 *(978-0-547-11962-5(3))* Houghton Mifflin Harcourt Publishing Co.

Rey, H. A. & Rey, Margret. Big Book of Adventures: 12 Beginning Readers in One. 2013. (Curious George Ser.). (ENG., Illus.). 296p. (J). (gr. -1-3). 15.99 *(978-0-544-08463-6(2))* Houghton Mifflin Harcourt Publishing Co.

—The Complete Adventures of Curious George: 75th Anniversary Edition. 75th ed. 2016. (Curious George Ser.). (ENG., Illus.). 432p. (J). (gr. -1-3). 34.99 *(978-0-544-64448-9(4),* HMH Books For Young Readers) Houghton Mifflin Harcourt Publishing Co.

—Curious George Flies a Kite, 1 vol. 2008. (Curious George Ser.). (ENG., Illus.). 80p. (J). (gr. -1-3). audio compact disk 10.99 *(978-0-618-99884-5(5))* Houghton Mifflin Harcourt Publishing Co.

—Curious George to the Rescue. 2007. (Curious George Ser.). (ENG., Illus.). 12p. (J). (gr. -1-3). 8.99 *(978-0-618-72401-7(X))* Houghton Mifflin Harcourt Publishing Co.

—Jorge el Curioso. Català, Josep Maria & Tusquets, Eugenia, trs. 2008. (Curious George Ser.).Tr. of Curious George. (SPA & ENG., Illus.). 64p. (J). (gr. -1-3). pap. 7.99 *(978-0-618-88411-7(4))* Houghton Mifflin Harcourt Publishing Co.

—Shapes. 2008. (Curious George Ser.). (ENG., Illus.). 10p. (J). (gr. k — 1). bds. 6.99 *(978-0-618-89198-6(X))* Houghton Mifflin Harcourt Publishing Co.

—Where Is Curious George? A Look & Find Book. 2013. (Curious George Ser.). (ENG., Illus.). 32p. (J). (gr. -1-3). 9.99 *(978-0-547-91416-9(4))* Houghton Mifflin Harcourt Publishing Co.

Rey, H. A. & Rey, Margret, creators. Curious George Loves to Ride. 2016. (Curious George Ser.). (ENG., Illus.). 20p. (J). (gr. -1-3). bds. 6.99 *(978-0-544-61102-3(0),* HMH Books For Young Readers) Houghton Mifflin Harcourt Publishing Co.

Rey, Margret & Rey, H. A. The New Adventures of Curious George. Vipah Interactive Staff, illus. 2006. (Curious George Ser.). (ENG.). 208p. (J). (gr. -1-3). 10.99 *(978-0-618-66373-6(8))* Houghton Mifflin Harcourt Publishing Co.

Reyes, Laurisa White. The Rock of Ivanore. (Celestine Chronicles Ser.). (ENG.). (J). (gr. 2-7). 2013. 349p. pap. 9.95 *(978-1-933718-92-7(7))* 2012. (Illus.). 356p. 16.95 *(978-1-933718-60-6(9))* Tanglewood Pr.

Reyes, Sharon D. Frank, 1 vol. 2010. 48p. pap. 24.95 *(978-1-4489-6114-6(9))* PublishAmerica, Inc.

Reyes, Yazmin. Fairies vs. Wizards: The Last Battle, 1 vol. 2009. 48p. pap. 16.95 *(978-1-4489-9527-1(2))* America Star Bks.

Reynolds, Aaron. Tiger Moth: Adventures of an Insect Ninja, 1 vol. Lervold, Erik, illus. 2011. (Tiger Moth Ser.). (ENG.). 128p. (gr. 2-5). pap. 7.95 *(978-1-4342-3032-4(5),* Graphic Sparks) Stone Arch Bks.

Reynolds, Carl. The Turkey Mountain Gang's.... Christmas Adventure! 2010. 44p. pap. 18.49 *(978-1-4520-6514-4(4))* AuthorHouse.

Reynolds, Carl Stanley. The Turkey Mountain Gang: The Adventures Begin. 2009. 52p. pap. 22.50 *(978-1-4389-7496-5(5))* AuthorHouse.

Reynolds, E. E. Behind the Ranges: Tales of Explorers, Pioneers & Travellers. Tresilian, S., illus. 2011. (ENG.). 128p. pap. 15.99 *(978-0-521-13526-9(5))* Cambridge Univ. Pr.

Reynolds, Grahame. The Grafs of Arran Towers. 2013. 180p. pap. 15.28 *(978-1-291-38827-5(3))* Lulu Pr., Inc.

Reynolds, Jason. Miles Morales. Nelson, Kadir, illus. 2017. (Marvel YA Novel Ser.). (ENG.). 272p. (YA). (gr. 7-12). 17.99 ***(978-1-4847-8748-9(X),*** Marvel Pr.) Disney Publishing Worldwide.

Reynolds, Mariem. The World in Between. 2008. 87p. pap. 16.95 *(978-1-60672-144-5(5))* PublishAmerica, Inc.

Reynolds, Mignon C. Life as Bonkers. 2006. 137p. pap. 12.95 *(978-1-4116-7357-1(3))* Lulu Pr., Inc.

Reynolds, Peter H. The Dot. Reynolds, Peter H., illus. 2005. (Illus.). 34p. (J). bds. 19.95 *(978-0-9769313-0-0(3))* BrailleInk.

Reznik, Anastasia, ed. The Little Horse Gornok: Russian Fairy Tale. 2009. 40p. pap. 18.95 *(978-1-4343-9830-7(7))* AuthorHouse.

Rešcek, Sanja, illus. One Elephant Went Out to Play. 2009. (Classic Books with Holes US Soft Cover with CD Ser.). (ENG.). 16p. (J). (gr. -1-1). pap. incl. audio compact disk *(978-1-84643-258-3(8))* Child's Play International Ltd.
—One Elephant Went Out to Play. 2009. (Classic Books with Holes Big Book Ser.). (ENG.). 16p. (J). (gr. -1-1). *(978-1-84643-209-5(X))* Child's Play International Ltd.
RH Disney. Beware the Kakamora! RH Disney, illus. 2016. (Pictureback(R) Ser.). (ENG., Illus.). 24p. (J). (gr. -1-2). 4.99 *(978-0-7364-3601-4(4),* RH/Disney) Random Hse. Children's Bks.
—Disney Princess Beginnings: Ariel Makes Waves (Disney Princess) RH Disney, illus. 2017. (Stepping Stone Book(TM) Ser.). (ENG., Illus.). 128p. (J). (gr. 1-4). 6.99 ***(978-0-7364-3733-2(9))***; lib. bdg. 12.99 ***(978-0-7364-8196-0(6))*** Random Hse. Children's Bks. (RH/Disney).
—Dory's Story. RH Disney, illus. 2016. (Step into Reading Ser.). (ENG., Illus.). 24p. (J). (gr. -1-1). 4.99 *(978-0-7364-3498-0(4),* RH/Disney) Random Hse. Children's Bks.
—Finding Dory Big Golden Book (Disney/Pixar Finding Dory) RH Disney, illus. 2016. (Big Golden Book Ser.). (ENG., Illus.). 48p. (J). (gr. -1-2). 9.99 *(978-0-7364-3506-2(9),* Golden/Disney) Random Hse. Children's Bks.
—Finding Dory Little Golden Book (Disney/Pixar Finding Dory) RH Disney, illus. 2016. (Little Golden Book Ser.). (ENG., Illus.). 24p. (J). (-k). 4.99 *(978-0-7364-3511-6(5),* Golden/Disney) Random Hse. Children's Bks.
—Finding Dory: the Deluxe Junior Novelization (Disney/Pixar Finding Dory) RH Disney, illus. 2016. (Deluxe Junior Novel Ser.). (ENG., Illus.). 144p. (J). (gr. 2-5). 9.99 *(978-0-7364-3573-4(5),* RH/Disney) Random Hse. Children's Bks.
—Hello, Dory! RH Disney, illus. 2016. (Tabbed Board Book Ser.). (ENG., Illus.). 16p. (J). (— 1). bds. 7.99 *(978-0-7364-3625-0(1),* RH/Disney) Random Hse. Children's Bks.
—Moana Big Golden Book (Disney Moana) RH Disney, illus. 2016. (Big Golden Book Ser.). (ENG., Illus.). 48p. (J). (gr. -1-2). 9.99 *(978-0-7364-3602-1(2),* Golden/Disney) Random Hse. Children's Bks.
—Moana Deluxe Step into Reading #1 (Disney Moana) RH Disney, illus. 2016. (Step into Reading Ser.). (ENG., Illus.). 24p. (J). (gr. -1-1). pap. 4.99 *(978-0-7364-3644-1(8),* RH/Disney) Random Hse. Children's Bks.
—Moana Junior Novelization. RH Disney, illus. 2016. (Junior Novel Ser.). (ENG., Illus.). 144p. (J). (gr. 2-5). 6.99 *(978-0-7364-3600-7(6),* RH/Disney) Random Hse. Children's Bks.
—Moana: the Deluxe Junior Novelization (Disney Moana) RH Disney, illus. 2016. (Deluxe Junior Novel Ser.). (ENG., Illus.). 144p. (J). (gr. 2-5). 9.99 *(978-0-7364-3574-1(3),* RH/Disney) Random Hse. Children's Bks.
—An Ocean Adventure. RH Disney, illus. 2016. (Magnetic Play Book Ser.). (ENG., Illus.). 8p. (J). (-k). bds. 9.99 *(978-0-7364-3626-7(X),* Random Hse. Bks. for Young Readers) Random Hse. Children's Bks.
—Quest for the Heart. RH Disney, illus. 2016. (Step into Reading Ser.). (ENG., Illus.). 32p. (J). (gr. -1-1). pap. 4.99 *(978-0-7364-3646-5(4),* RH/Disney) Random Hse. Children's Bks.
—Where Monsters Live. RH Disney, illus. 2016. (Pictureback(R) Ser.). (ENG., Illus.). 24p. (J). (gr. -1-2). 4.99 *(978-0-7364-3649-6(9),* RH/Disney) Random Hse. Children's Bks.
RH Disney Staff. Anna's Icy Adventure. RH Disney Staff, illus. 2013. (Golden First Chapters Ser.). (ENG., Illus.). 80p. (J). (gr. 1-4). 4.99 *(978-0-7364-8132-8(X),* Golden/Disney) Random Hse. Children's Bks.
—The Big Battle. RH Disney Staff, illus. 2014. (Step into Reading Ser.). (ENG., Illus.). 32p. (J). (gr. k-3). 4.99 *(978-0-7364-3245-0(0),* RH/Disney) Random Hse. Children's Bks.
—Brave Little Golden Book (Disney/Pixar Brave) RH Disney Staff, illus. 2012. (Little Golden Book Ser.). (ENG., Illus.). 24p. (J). (gr. k-k). 4.99 *(978-0-7364-2901-6(8),* Golden/Disney) Random Hse. Children's Bks.
—Cars 2 Little Golden Book (Disney/Pixar Cars 2) RH Disney Staff, illus. 2011. (Little Golden Book Ser.). (ENG., Illus.). 24p. (J). (gr. -1-2). 3.99 *(978-0-7364-2781-4(3),* Golden/Disney) Random Hse. Children's Bks.
—Frozen Big Golden Book (Disney Frozen) RH Disney Staff, illus. 2013. (Big Golden Book Ser.). (ENG., Illus.). 64p. (J). (gr. -1-2). 9.99 *(978-0-7364-3065-4(2),* Golden/Disney) Random Hse. Children's Bks.
—Olaf's 1-2-3. RH Disney Staff, illus. 2013. (Glitter Board Book Ser.). (ENG., Illus.). 12p. (J). (— 1). bds. 6.99 *(978-0-7364-3064-7(4),* Golden/Disney) Random Hse. Children's Bks.
—Welcome to Whisker Haven (Disney Palace Pets: Whisker Haven Tales) RH Disney Staff, illus. 2016. (Big Golden Book Ser.). (ENG., Illus.). 32p. (J). (gr. -1-2). 9.99 *(978-0-7364-3474-4(7),* Golden/Disney) Random Hse. Children's Bks.
RH Disney Staff & Rabe, Tish. Frozen - Big Snowman, Little Snowman. RH Disney Staff, illus. 2013. (Step into Reading Ser.). (ENG., Illus.). 32p. (J). (gr. -1-1). lib. bdg. 12.99 *(978-0-7364-8130-4(3),* RH/Disney) Random Hse. Children's Bks.
RH Disney Staff & Scollon, Bill. Fight to the Finish! RH Disney Staff & Disney Storybook Art Team, illus. 2014. (Step into Reading Ser.). (ENG.). 48p. (J). (gr. k-3). 3.99 *(978-0-7364-3189-7(6),* RH/Disney) Random Hse. Children's Bks.
Rhae, Sympne. My Name Is Johnson? l.t. ed. 2006. (Illus.). 53p. (J). per. 13.75 *(978-0-977043-9-3(2))* New Global Publishing.
Rhoden, Chris J. B. How Niseag Became a Legend in Scot. 2008. 48p. pap. 23.99 *(978-1-4343-5461-7(X))* AuthorHouse.
Rhodes, Carol. Gene the Pumpkin Man. 2008. 32p. pap. 16.95 *(978-1-4327-1416-1(3))* Outskirts Pr., Inc.
Rhodes, Genee M. & Travers, Jasmine. Gloria Gets Glasses. 2013. 32p. pap. 11.00 *(978-2-01-300710-8(8))* Rhodes, EL. Bks., LLC.
Rhodes, Jennifer. The Adventures of Kirby. Balogh, Jared, illus. 2012. 46p. 24.95 *(978-1-4626-9473-0(X))* America Star Bks.
Rhodes, Morgan. Rebel Spring. 2013. (Falling Kingdoms Ser.: 2). (ENG.). 416p. (YA). (gr. 7). 18.99 *(978-1-59514-593-2(1),* Razorbill) Penguin Young Readers Group.
Rhue, Morton. Die Welle: Bericht über einen Unterrichtsversuch, der zu weit ging. (GER.). pap. 14.95 *(978-3-473-58008-8(2))* Ravensburger Buchverlag Otto Maier GmbH DEU. Dist: Distribooks, Inc.
Rhyne, Nancy. The Crab Boys. 2007. (J). pap. 6.95 *(978-0-87844-183-9(2))* Sandlapper Publishing Co., Inc.
Riad, Hala. Haunted Backyard. 2012. 24p. 24.95 *(978-1-4626-2530-7(4))* America Star Bks.
Ricchi, Brenda. The Grandchildren's Bible Journey-the Big Fall. 2010. 32p. pap. 15.51 *(978-0-557-38645-1(4))* Lulu Pr., Inc.
—The Grandchildren's Bible Journeys - the Creation Story. 2010. 35p. pap. 17.00 *(978-0-557-14903-2(7))* Lulu Pr., Inc.
Ricchiazzi, Lisa Gail. The Adventures of Fella & Dawn: Help One Another. 2012. 20p. pap. 13.77 *(978-1-4669-7170-7(3))* Trafford Publishing.
Ricci, Christine. Dora in the Deep Sea. Roper, Robert, illus. 2003. (Dora the Explorer Ser.: Vol. 3). (ENG.). 24p. (J). pap. 3.99 *(978-0-689-85845-1(0),* Simon Spotlight/Nickelodeon) Simon Spotlight/Nickelodeon.
—Dora's Valentine Adventure. A and J Studios Staff, illus. 2006. (Dora the Explorer Ser.). (ENG.). 14p. (J). (gr. -1-k). bds. 6.99 *(978-1-4169-1754-0(3),* Simon Spotlight/Nickelodeon) Simon Spotlight/Nickelodeon.
—Legend Hunters! McGee, Warner, illus. 2007. (Backyardigans Ser.: 9). (ENG.). 24p. (J). (gr. -1-2). pap. 3.99 *(978-1-4169-4058-6(8),* Simon Spotlight/Nickelodeon) Simon Spotlight/Nickelodeon.
Ricci, Laura. Dr. Mike's Adventures. 2006. 63p. pap. 16.95 *(978-1-4241-2653-8(3))* PublishAmerica, Inc.
Rice, Dona Herwick. Paul Bunyan, 1 vol. 2009. (Building Fluency Through Reader's Theater Ser.). (ENG.). 24p. (J). (gr. 2-4). pap. 6.99 *(978-1-4333-0994-6(7))* Teacher Created Materials, Inc.
Rice, June K. The Little Blue Tree. 2009. 20p. pap. 10.99 *(978-1-4389-4806-5(9))* AuthorHouse.
Rich, Carol Bak. The Running Nose Book. Rich, Bobbie, illus. 2013. (ENG.). 41p. (J). pap. 9.95 *(978-1-4787-0062-3(9))* Outskirts Pr., Inc.
Richard, Lolita Louise. Walking with a B C Big Book Adventure. 2009. 60p. pap. 31.99 *(978-1-4415-3719-5(8))* Xlibris Corp.
Richard Richtmyer. A Bit of Magic: A Novel. 2009. 116p. pap. 10.95 *(978-1-4401-5565-9(8))* iUniverse, Inc.
Richards, C. J. The Junkyard Bot. 2016. (Robots Rule Ser.: 1). lib. bdg. 17.20 *(978-0-606-37980-9(0))* Turtleback Bks.
Richards, Jane. Tombs, Temples, & Thrones. 2005. 125p. pap. 19.95 *(978-1-4137-9084-9(4))* PublishAmerica, Inc.
Richards, Jasmine. The Book of Wonders. 2012. (ENG.). 416p. (J). (gr. 3-7). 16.99 *(978-0-06-201007-0(7))* HarperCollins Pubs.
—Keeper of Myths. 2017. (Secrets of Valhalla Ser.: 2). 256p. (J). (gr. 3-7). 16.99 *(978-0-06-201011-7(5))* HarperCollins Pubs.
—Secrets of Valhalla. 2016. (Secrets of Valhalla Ser.: 1). 320p. (J). (gr. 3-7). 16.99 *(978-0-06-201009-4(3))* HarperCollins Pubs.
Richards, Justin. The Chaos Code. 2007. (ENG.). 400p. (YA). (gr. 7-12). 17.95 *(978-1-59990-124-4(2),* 9781599901244, Bloomsbury USA Childrens) Bloomsbury Publishing USA.
—Thunder Raker, 1. 2008. (Agent Alfie Ser.: 1). (ENG., Illus.). 144p. (J). (gr. 2-4). pap. 6.99 *(978-0-00-727357-7(6),* HarperCollins Children's Bks.) HarperCollins Pubs. Ltd. GBR. Dist: HarperCollins Pubs.
Richards, Laura E. Captain January. 2004. reprint ed. pap. 15.95 *(978-1-4191-1199-0(X))* Kessinger Publishing, LLC.
Richards, Lynne. The Fearless Four: Braced for Battle. Semple, Dave, illus. 2009. (ENG.). 24p. (J). (gr. 1-17). pap. 3.99 *(978-1-58476-814-2(2))* Innovative Kids.
Richards, Stephen J. The Twins First Snow. 2010. 28p. pap. 13.99 *(978-1-4490-8853-8(8))* AuthorHouse.
Richardson, Bernard. Freddy Weller's Holiday. 2011. 50p. 24.99 *(978-1-4628-9548-9(4))*; pap. 15.99 *(978-1-4628-9547-2(6))* Xlibris Corp.
Richardson, Deborra. Treasures at the Museum. 2011. (Illus.). 64p. (J). pap. 5.99 *(978-0-9824945-1-6(3))* Elevator Group, The.
Richardson, Duncan. Revenge. Edwards, Rebecca, illus. 2005. 30p. (J). pap. *(978-1-876682-69-9(8))* Post Pressed.
Richardson, J. J. It's about Time. 2008. (ENG.). 92p. pap. 12.99 *(978-1-4196-5707-8(0))* CreateSpace Independent Publishing Platform.
Richardson, Jeffery. Wormwood Adventures New Friends. 2010. 49p. pap. 8.50 *(978-1-4452-5758-7(0))* Lulu Pr., Inc.
Richardson, Levae. Skip & Marty. Richardson, Kayla, illus. 2007. 20p. per. 24.95 *(978-1-4241-8469-9(X))* America Star Bks.
Richardson, S. Lee. The Backyard Series Volume Two: The Baby Bear Scare Story. 2012. 28p. pap. 24.95 *(978-1-4626-9615-4(5))* America Star Bks.
Richardson, Steve. Alexander Trout's Amazing Adventure. Lowe, Wesley, illus. 2008. 75p. 16.95 *(978-0-9786422-2-8(8))* Impossible Dreams Publishing Co.
Richburg, Sheila. The Story of Panhandle Pete Part One. 2010. 19p. 16.95 *(978-0-557-15382-4(4))* Lulu Pr., Inc.
Richmond, Caroline Tung. Darkest Hour. 2016. (ENG.). 320p. (J). (gr. 7). 17.99 *(978-0-545-80127-0(3),* Scholastic Pr.) Scholastic, Inc.
Richter, Conrad. The Light in the Forest. (YA). (gr. 7-18). 21.95 *(978-0-89190-333-8(X))* Amereon Ltd.
Richter, Debra A. Hamster on the Run, Let's Play in the Snow. LiveLearn, Robert, illus. 2012. 28p. pap. 24.95 *(978-1-4626-5064-4(3))* America Star Bks.
—Two Frogs & the Lost Wedding Band. 2012. 32p. 24.95 *(978-1-4626-4343-1(4))* America Star Bks.
Rickards, Lynne. Hide & Seek Green Band. Pérez, Moni, illus. 2016. (Cambridge Reading Adventures Ser.). (ENG.). 16p. pap. 6.56 *(978-1-107-57599-8(0))* Cambridge Univ. Pr.
—Playgrounds Yellow Band. 2016. (Cambridge Reading Adventures Ser.). (ENG.). 16p. pap. 6.56 *(978-1-316-50318-8(6))* Cambridge Univ. Pr.
Rickards, Lynne & Roberts, Ley Honor. Diego Fandango Yellow Band. Rogers, Alan, illus. 2016. (Cambridge Reading Adventures Ser.). (ENG.). 16p. pap. 6.56 *(978-1-107-55021-6(1))* Cambridge Univ. Pr.
Riddell, Andrew G. The Curse of Blackbeard's Ghost. 2010. 122p. (gr. 4-6). pap. 10.95 *(978-1-4502-6952-0(4))* iUniverse, Inc.
Riddell, Chris & Stewart, Paul. The Curse of the Gloamglozer. 2009. (Edge Chronicles Ser.). (ENG.). 384p. (J). (gr. 3-7). 8.99 *(978-0-440-42099-6(7),* Yearling) Random Hse. Children's Bks.
Riddell, J. H. The Open Door. 2004. reprint ed. pap. 1.99 *(978-1-4192-7623-1(9))* Kessinger Publishing, LLC.
Riddle, A. Yogi & Me. 2006. 48p. pap. 16.95 *(978-1-4241-0565-6(X))* PublishAmerica, Inc.
Rideout, Henry. Dragons Blood. 2006. 144p. per. 11.95 *(978-1-59818-051-0(7))*; 24.95 *(978-1-59818-548-5(9))* Aegypan.
Rider, Jason. Dawn of Hope. 2008. 180p. pap. 11.95 *(978-1-935118-10-7(2))* Bellissima Publishing, LLC.
Rider, John Russell. The Adventures of Acorn & Pinecone. 2010. 64p. pap. 25.95 *(978-1-4520-8354-4(1))* AuthorHouse.
Ridgers, Denise J. Elspeth's Great Adventure. 2007. (Illus.). 60p. (J). pap. 9.00 *(978-0-8059-7471-3(7))* Dorrance Publishing Co., Inc.
Riding, Will. Ebenezer's Tale. 2008. (Illus.). 188p. pap. 14.49 *(978-1-4343-9694-5(0))* AuthorHouse.
Rieback, Milton. The Adventures of Webb Ellis, a Tale from the Heart of Africa: The Return of the Protectors. Crowley, Cheryl, illus. 2006. (J). lib. bdg. 19.95 *(978-0-9777440-0-8(0))* Inyati Press.
Riebe, C. V. Jonathan Jameson in the Crossroad Chronicles: Adventures in Heaven, Vol. 1. 2008. 64p. pap. 10.95 *(978-1-4327-3709-2(0))* Outskirts Pr., Inc.
Riedl, Sheila. Elijah & the Elephant. 2011. 24p. pap. 15.99 *(978-1-4653-5796-0(3))* Xlibris Corp.
Riegelman, Rianna. Red Roger to the Rescue. Schorr, Bill, illus. 2012. (ENG.). 28p. (J). (gr. -1-3). 16.99 *(978-1-4494-2189-2(X))* Andrews McMeel Publishing.
Riegelman, Rianna & Accord Publishing Staff. Safari: A Build & Play Story. Chandler, Shannon, illus. 2012. (ENG.). 10p. (J). (gr. -1-1). bds. 15.99 *(978-1-4494-2191-5(1))* Andrews McMeel Publishing.
Rifkin, L. The Nine Lives of Romeo Crumb: Life 6. Hartman, Kurt, illus. 2010. 246p. (YA). pap. 8.95 *(978-0-9743221-8-6(0))* Sunrise Publishing Co.
Rift. The Wise Little Butterfly, 1 vol. Rift, illus. 2009. (Illus.). 39p. pap. 19.95 *(978-1-61546-493-7(X))* PublishAmerica, Inc.
Rigby & Gem: A Guberif Adventure. 2005. (J). *(978-0-9773775-0-3(4))* Don Rand's Classy Collectibles.
Rigby Education Staff. Peter Piper. (gr. k-2). 21.00 *(978-0-7635-2407-4(7))* Rigby Education.
Riggs, Darla L. Hooney Bacooney: Caught Red Handed. 2004. (Illus.). 12p. (J). 4.98 *(978-0-9747883-0-2(9))* Little League Pr.
Riley, Clifford. Operation Trinity. 2012. (39 Clues: the Cahill Files Ser.). (ENG.). 144p. (J). (gr. 3-7). 9.99 *(978-0-545-43143-9(3))* Scholastic, Inc.
Riley, J. D. Axel the Truck: Rocky Road. Dorman, Brandon, illus. 2013. (My First I Can Read Ser.). (ENG.). 32p. (J). (gr. -1-3). pap. 3.99 *(978-0-06-222231-2(7),* Greenwillow Bks.) HarperCollins Pubs.
—Rocky Road. Dorman, Brandon, illus. 2013. (My First I Can Read Ser.). (ENG.). 32p. (J). (gr. -1-3). 16.99 *(978-0-06-222232-9(5),* Greenwillow Bks.) HarperCollins Pubs.
Riley, James. Half upon a Time. (Half upon a Time Ser.: 1). (ENG.). (J). (gr. 3-7). 2011. 432p. pap. 7.99 *(978-1-4169-9594-4(3))* 2010. 400p. 17.99 *(978-1-4169-9593-7(5))* Simon & Schuster Children's Publishing. (Aladdin).
—The Half upon a Time Trilogy: Half upon a Time; Twice upon a Time; Once upon the End. 2014. (Half upon a Time Ser.). (ENG., Illus.). 1168p. (J). (gr. 3-7). pap. 23.99 *(978-1-4424-9966-9(4),* Aladdin) Simon & Schuster Children's Publishing.
—Once upon the End. 2014. (Half upon a Time Ser.: 3). (ENG., Illus.). 400p. (J). (gr. 3-7). pap. 7.99 *(978-1-4424-7421-5(1),* Aladdin) Simon & Schuster Children's Publishing.
—Once upon the End. 2013. (Half upon a Time Ser.: 3). (ENG.). 384p. (J). (gr. 3-7). 17.99 *(978-1-4424-7422-2(X),* Simon & Schuster/Paula Wiseman Bks.) Simon & Schuster/Paula Wiseman Bks.
—Once upon the End. 2014. (Half upon a Time Ser.: 3). lib. bdg. 18.40 *(978-0-606-35427-1(1))* Turtleback Bks.
—Secret Origins. 2017. (Story Thieves Ser.: 3). (ENG., Illus.). 384p. (J). (gr. 3-7). 17.99 *(978-1-4814-6125-2(7),* Simon & Schuster/Paula Wiseman Bks.) Simon & Schuster/Paula Wiseman Bks.
—The Stolen Chapters. 2016. (Story Thieves Ser.: 2). (ENG., Illus.). 368p. (J). (gr. 3-7). 17.99 *(978-1-4814-0922-3(0),* Aladdin) Simon & Schuster Children's Publishing.
—Story Thieves. 2015. (Story Thieves Ser.: 1). (ENG., Illus.). (J). (gr. 3-7). 416p. pap. 7.99 *(978-1-4814-0920-9(4))*; 400p. 17.99 *(978-1-4814-0919-3(0))* Simon & Schuster Children's Publishing. (Aladdin).
—Story Thieves. 2015. (Story Thieves Ser.: Vol. 1). (ENG.). (J). (gr. 3-7). lib. bdg. 18.40 ***(978-0-606-39444-4(3))*** Turtleback Bks.
Riley, James. Twice upon a Time. (Half upon a Time Ser.: 2). (ENG.). (J). (gr. 3-7). 2013. 384p. pap. 8.99 *(978-1-4169-9597-5(8))* 2012. 352p. 17.99 *(978-1-4169-9596-8(X))* Simon & Schuster Children's Publishing. (Aladdin).
—Twice upon a Time. 2013. (Half upon a Time Ser.: 2). lib. bdg. 18.40 *(978-0-606-35426-4(3))* Turtleback Bks.
Riley, Lehman, et al. The Adventures of Papa Lemon's Little Wanderers Bk. 2: The Dangerous Escape from Slavery. 2005. 52p. pap. 5.99 *(978-0-9760523-1-9(8))* Matter of Africa America Time.
Riley, Penelope A. Christmas Away! A Duckie Dan Adventure Book. 2012. 48p. pap. 21.99 *(978-1-4772-7554-2(1))* AuthorHouse.
Riley, Vicki. Squirt's Adventures: Episode 1. 2010. 48p. pap. 16.50 *(978-1-60911-627-9(5),* Eloquent Bks.) Strategic Book Publishing & Rights Agency (SBPRA).
Rinaldo, Jim. Wally the Worm's Adventures on the Farm. 2011. 28p. pap. 15.99 *(978-1-4568-9102-2(2))* Xlibris Corp.
Rinehart, J. D. A Kingdom Rises. 2017. (Crown of Three Ser.: 3). (ENG., Illus.). 432p. (J). (gr. 4-8). 18.99 ***(978-1-4814-2449-3(1),*** Aladdin) Simon & Schuster Children's Publishing.
Riner, Kendall F. The Rescue Adventures of Fireman Frank. 2006. (Illus.). 52p. (J). pap. 12.00 *(978-0-9786369-1-3(0))* Warwick Hse. Publishing.
Ringley, Patrick & Brown, Anne Corbett. The Adventures of the Nutters, the Tree Highway. Cotton, Sue Lynn, illus. 2013. 48p. pap. 19.95 *(978-1-61493-207-9(7))* Peppertree Pr., The.
Ringwald, Whitaker. The Secret Box. 2015. (Secret Box Ser.: 1). (ENG.). 320p. (J). (gr. 3-7). pap. 6.99 *(978-0-06-221615-1(5),* Tegen, Katherine Bks) HarperCollins Pubs.
—The Secret Fire. 2016. (Secret Box Ser.: 3). 208p. (J). (gr. 3-7). 16.99 *(978-0-06-221620-5(1),* Tegen, Katherine Bks) HarperCollins Pubs.
Riordan, Rick. The Dark Prophecy. 2017. (Trials of Apollo Ser.: bk.2). (ENG.). 432p. (J). (gr. 5-9). 19.99 *(978-1-4847-4642-4(2))* Hyperion Bks. for Children.
—The Hammer of Thor. 2016. (Magnus Chase & the Gods of Asgard Ser.: Bk. 2). (ENG.). 480p. (J). (gr. 5-9). 19.99 *(978-1-4231-6092-2(4))* Hyperion Bks. for Children.
—The Heroes of Olympus, Book Five the Blood of Olympus. 2016. (Heroes of Olympus Ser.). (ENG.). 544p. (J). (gr. 5-9). pap. 9.99 *(978-1-4231-4678-0(6))* Hyperion Bks. for Children.
—The Hidden Oracle. l.t. ed. 2016. (Trials of Apollo Ser.: 1). (ENG.). 488p. (J). 25.99 *(978-1-4104-8945-6(0))* Cengage Gale.
—The Hidden Oracle. 2016. (Trials of Apollo Ser.: Bk. 1). (ENG.). 384p. (J). (gr. 5-9). 19.99 *(978-1-4847-3274-8(X))* Hyperion Bks. for Children.
—The Hidden Oracle. 2017. (Trials of Apollo Ser.: 1). (J). lib. bdg. 20.85 ***(978-0-606-40605-5(0))*** Turtleback Bks.
—The House of Hades. 2013. (Heroes of Olympus Ser.). (ENG.). 608p. (J). (gr. 5-17). 19.99 *(978-1-4231-4672-8(7))* Hyperion Pr.
—The Kane Chronicles Box Set. Rocco, John, illus. 2013. (Kane Chronicles Ser.). (ENG.). 1472p. (J). (gr. 3-7). pap. 26.99 *(978-1-4231-9962-5(6))* Hyperion Bks. for Children.
—The Last Olympian, Bk. 5. (Percy Jackson & the Olympians Ser.). (ENG.). (J). (gr. 5-9). 2011. 432p. pap. 7.99 *(978-1-4231-0150-5(2))* 5th ed. 2009. 400p. 17.99 *(978-1-4231-0147-5(2))* Hyperion Pr.
—The Maze of Bones. 2008. (39 Clues Ser.: 1). (ENG.). 224p. (J). (gr. 3-7). 12.99 *(978-0-545-06039-4(7),* Scholastic Pr.); (Illus.). 12.99 *(978-0-545-09054-4(7))* Scholastic, Inc.
—Percy Jackson & the Olympians, Set. 2010. (ENG.). 1744p. (J). (gr. 5-17). 89.99 *(978-1-4231-4189-1(X))* Hyperion Pr.
—Percy Jackson & the Olympians. l.t. ed. 2009. (Percy Jackson & the Olympians Ser.). (ENG.). 485p. (YA). 23.95 *(978-1-4104-1678-0(X))* Thorndike Pr.
—Percy Jackson & the Olympians. 2011. (Percy Jackson & the Olympians Ser.: 5). (J). lib. bdg. 18.40 *(978-0-606-10567-5(0,* Turtleback) Turtleback Bks.
—The Red Pyramid. 2011. (ENG.). 544p. (J). (gr. 5-17). pap. 9.99 *(978-1-4231-1345-4(4))* Disney Publishing Worldwide.
—The Red Pyramid. 2010. (Kane Chronicles Ser.). (ENG.). 528p. (J). (gr. 5-9). 17.99 *(978-1-4231-1338-6(1))* Hyperion Pr.
—The Red Pyramid, Bk. 1. Collar, Orpheus, illus. 2012. (Kane Chronicles Ser.). (ENG.). 192p. (J). (gr. 5-9). pap. 12.99 *(978-1-4231-5069-5(4))* Hyperion Pr.
—The Red Pyramid. 2009. (Kane Chronicles: Bk. 1). 11.04 *(978-0-7848-3733-7(3),* Everbind) Marco Bk. Co.
—The Red Pyramid. 2012. 20.00 *(978-1-61383-660-6(0))* Perfection Learning Corp.
—The Red Pyramid. 2010. pap. *(978-0-545-40016-9(3))* Scholastic, Inc.
—The Red Pyramid. l.t. ed. 2010. (Kane Chronicles: Bk. 1). (ENG.). 671p. 23.95 *(978-1-4104-2536-2(3))* Thorndike Pr.
—The Red Pyramid. (Kane Chronicles Graphic Novels Ser.: 1). (J). 2012. lib. bdg. 24.50 *(978-0-606-37510-8(4))* 2011. lib. bdg. 20.85 *(978-0-606-39216-7(5))* Turtleback Bks.
—The Serpent's Shadow. (Kane Chronicles Ser.). (ENG.). (gr. 5-17). 2013. 464p. (J). pap. 9.99 *(978-1-4231-4202-7(0))*Bk. 3. 2012. 416p. (YA). 19.99 *(978-1-4231-4057-3(5))* Hyperion Pr.
—The Serpent's Shadow. 2012. 416p. *(978-0-14-133568-1(8),* Puffin) Penguin Bks., Ltd.
—The Serpent's Shadow. l.t. ed. 2012. (Kane Chronicles: Bk. 3). (ENG.). 521p. (gr. 5-12). 23.99 *(978-1-4104-4789-0(8))* Thorndike Pr.
—The Throne of Fire. 2011. (Kane Chronicles: Bk. 2). 452p. (J). pap. *(978-1-4231-5059-6(7))* Disney Pr.
—The Throne of Fire. 2nd ed. 2012. (ENG.). 464p. (YA). (gr. 5-9). pap. 9.99 *(978-1-4231-6703-7(1))* Hyperion Bks. for Children.
—The Throne of Fire, Bk. 2. (ENG.). 464p. (gr. 5-17). 2012. (YA). pap. 9.99 *(978-1-4231-4201-0(2))* 2011. (J). 18.99 *(978-1-4231-4056-6(7))* Hyperion Pr.
—The Throne of Fire. 2011. (Kane Chronicles: Bk. 2). (ENG., Illus.). 451p. 28.25 *(978-0-85757-231-8(8))*; 2nd ed. 554p. pap. *(978-0-14-133566-7(1))* Penguin Publishing Group. (Puffin).
—The Throne of Fire. l.t. ed. 2011. (Kane Chronicles: Bk. 2). (ENG.). 591p. 23.99 *(978-1-4104-3607-8(1))* Thorndike Pr.
—The Throne of Fire. (Kane Chronicles Graphic Novels Ser.: 2). 2015. lib. bdg. 24.50 *(9770-0-606-37509-2(0))* 2012. (YA). lib. bdg. 20.85 *(978-0-606-39217-4(3))* Turtleback Bks.
Riordan, Rick & Venditti, Robert. Heroes of Olympus, Book One the Lost Hero: the Graphic Novel. Powell, Nathan, illus. 2014. (Heroes of Olympus Ser.). (ENG.). 192p. (J). (gr. 5-9). pap. 12.99 *(978-1-4231-6325-1(7))* Hyperion Bks. for Children.
—The Titan's Curse. Futaki, Attila & Guilhaumond, Gregory, illus. 2013. (Percy Jackson & the Olympians Ser.). (ENG.). 128p. (J). (gr. 5-9). pap. 14.99 *(978-1-4231-4551-6(8))* Hyperion Pr.

—The Titan's Curse. 2013. (Percy Jackson & the Olympians Graphic Novels Ser.: 3). (J). lib. bdg. 26.95 *(978-0-606-32286-7(8),* Turtleback) Turtleback Bks.

Ripley, T. P. Lily Lovebug & the Unconquered Planet. 2013. 170p. pap. 9.99 *(978-1-908910-43-1(7))* Crooked Cat Publishing.

Ripley's Believe It or Not Editors & Ripley's Believe It Or Not! Staff. Sub-Zero Survival. 2010. (Rbi Ser.: 6). (ENG.). 128p. (J). pap. 4.99 *(978-1-893951-57-0(X))* Ripley Entertainment, Inc.

—Wings of Fear. 2010. (Rbi Ser.: 5). (ENG.). 128p. (J). pap. 4.99 *(978-1-893951-56-3(1))* Ripley Entertainment, Inc.

Ripley's Believe It Or Not! Staff. The Lost Island. 2010. (Rbi Ser.: 8). (ENG.). 128p. (J). pap. 4.99 *(978-1-893951-59-4(6))* Ripley Entertainment, Inc.

—Secrets of the Deep. 2010. (Rbi Ser.: 4). (ENG.). 128p. (J). pap. 4.99 *(978-1-893951-54-9(5))* Ripley Entertainment, Inc.

—Shock Horror. 2010. (Rbi Ser.: 7). (ENG.). 128p. (J). pap. 4.99 *(978-1-893951-58-7(8))* Ripley Entertainment, Inc.

Rippin, Sally. The Bad Butterfly: Billie B. Brown. Fukuoka, Aki, illus. 2013. (ENG.). 48p. (J). pap. 4.99 *(978-1-61067-095-1(7))* Kane Miller.

—The Midnight Feast. Fukuoka, Aki, illus. 2013. (ENG.). 48p. (J). pap. 4.99 *(978-1-61067-097-5(3))* Kane Miller.

—The Soccer Star. Fukuoka, Aki, illus. 2013. (ENG.). 48p. (J). pap. 4.99 *(978-1-61067-096-8(5))* Kane Miller.

Risselada, Melissa. Seven Cats & the Big Gray Fence. Kalpart, illus. 2013. 28p. pap. 12.50 *(978-1-62516-777-4(6),* Strategic Bk. Publishing) Strategic Book Publishing & Rights Agency (SBPRA).

Rissman, Angelica. Julius & the Lost Letter to Santa. 2003. (J). 7.99 *(978-1-59384-019-8(5))* Parklane Publishing.

Ritchey, Carmil White. The Adventures of Pine Cone the Cat. 2012. 24p. pap. 17.99 *(978-1-4685-9470-6(2))* AuthorHouse.

Ritchie, Joseph R. Knock, Knock, Who's There? Rose, Drew, illus. 2005. (ENG.). 12p. (J). bds. 7.95 *(978-0-8249-6613-3(9),* Ideal Pubns.) Worthy Publishing.

Rive, Myrtle. Sam's Adventures. 2009. (Illus.). 154p. pap. 38.99 *(978-1-4490-0821-5(6))* AuthorHouse.

Rivera, Raquel. Orphan Ahwak, 1 vol. 2007. (ENG.). 144p. (J). (gr. 4-8). per. 7.95 *(978-1-55143-653-1(1))* Orca Bk. Pubs. USA.

Rivers, Katie. A Winter's Dream. 2005. 31p. (J). per. 2.95 *(978-0-9721640-1-6(4))* Whispering Wind Publishing Inc.

Rivers, Phoebe. Mischief Night. 2012. (Saranormal Ser.: 3). (ENG.). 160p. (J). (gr. 3-7). 15.99 *(978-1-4424-5380-7(X));* pap. 5.99 *(978-1-4424-5221-3(8))* Simon Spotlight. (Simon Spotlight).

Rivot, Jean Mahassel. The Secret of Pet Heaven. 2013. 46p. pap. 12.00 *(978-0-9888901-0-7(0))* Night Sky, LLC.

Rix, Jamie. Panda Panic: Running Wild. 2013. (Awesome Animals Ser.). (ENG., Illus.). 192p. (J). (gr. 2-6). pap. 6.99 *(978-1-4380-0308-5(0))* Barron's Educational Series, Inc.

Rixon, Denise. The Owl That Barked: Tammy, 1 vol. 2009. 203p. pap. 24.95 *(978-1-4489-8472-5(6))* America Star Bks.

Rizy, Brock, illus. Emily Edison: Volume 1. 2006. 139p. (gr. 8-18). pap. 12.95 *(978-0-9777883-2-3(6))* Viper Comics.

Road Trip. 2003. (J). per. *(978-1-57657-958-9(1))* Paradise Pr., Inc.

Roane, E. M. Quincy's First Year. 2013. 56p. pap. 15.99 *(978-1-4797-8075-4(8))* Xlibris Corp.

Robaard, Jedda. Milo & Millie. Robaard, Jedda, illus. 2014. (ENG., Illus.). 32p. (J). (-k). 14.99 *(978-0-7636-6783-2(8))* Candlewick Pr.

Robberecht, Thierry. Superhero School. Goossens, Philippe, illus. 2012. (ENG.). 30p. (J). (gr. -1-k). 16.95 *(978-1-60537-140-5(8))* Cobblestone Publishing Co.

Robbins, Karen. Care for Our World Play Set. 2012. (ENG.). (J). 34.95 *(978-1-935414-63-6(1))* Casemate Pubs. & Bk. Distributors, LLC.

Robbins, Neal. The Island of the Three Sapphires. Mayfield, Helen, illus. 98p. (J). (gr. 6-18). pap. 4.00 *(978-1-884993-04-6(4))* Koldarana Pubns.

Roberge, Tracy. Jacob & Alec Explore Shenzhen's Windows of the World. 2011. 40p. pap. 17.99 *(978-1-257-76087-9(4))* Lulu Pr., Inc.

—Jacob & Alec Move to Hong Kong. 2011. 32p. pap. 17.99 *(978-1-257-01739-3(X))* Lulu Pr., Inc.

Roberson, Margaret. Maggie Poo the Kangaroo Adventures. 2008. 36p. pap. 14.95 *(978-1-4327-0674-6(8))* Outskirts Pr., Inc.

Roberson, T. S. Riley's Race. 2012. 24p. pap. 15.99 *(978-1-4691-6428-1(0))* Xlibris Corp.

Robert, Lytle. Mr. Blair's Labyrinth. Gayle, Vandercook, illus. 2011. (J). 10.95 *(978-0-9798088-4-5(7))* EDCO Publishing, Inc.

Robert, Nadine. Toshi's Little Treasures. Aki, illus. 2016. (ENG.). 32p. (J). (gr. -1-2). 17.95 *(978-1-77138-573-2(1))* Kids Can Pr., Ltd. CAN. Dist: Hachette Bk. Group.

Roberts, Barbara. The Adventures of Phoebe Flower: Stories of a Girl with ADHD. 2010. (ENG.). 176p. (J). (gr. 2-6). pap. 14.95 *(978-0-9714609-6-6(5))* Advantage Bks., LLC.

Roberts, Carmen. Inseparable: The Tale of the Amulet. 2009. 120p. 21.49 *(978-1-4490-3394-1(6));* pap. 10.99 *(978-1-4490-3396-5(2))* AuthorHouse.

Roberts, Charles G. D. Children of the Wild. 2007. 112p. per. *(978-1-4068-3939-5(6))* Echo Library.

Roberts, Christa. Rio 2. 2014. (Ramona Ser.). (ENG.). 144p. (J). (gr. 3-7). pap. 5.99 *(978-0-06-228504-1(1),* HarperFestival) HarperCollins Pubs.

Roberts, Constance. Sigil in Shadow. 2016. (ENG.). (J). pap. 15.99 *(978-1-4621-1873-1(9),* Sweetwater Bks.) Cedar Fort, Inc./CFI Distribution.

Roberts, Curt. The Story of Scruffy of Smithfield, Virginia. Traylor, Waverley, ed. Roberts, Curt & Traylor, Waverley, illus. Lt. ed. 2005. 14p. (J). (gr. k-6). pap. 3.95 *(978-0-9715068-4-8(1))* Traylor, Waverley Publishing.

Roberts, D. W. Pep Squad Mysteries Book 1: Cavern in the Hills. 2009. 71p. pap. 8.99 *(978-0-557-05513-5(X))* Lulu Pr., Inc.

—Pep Squad Mysteries Book 2:the Haunting of Townsand Hall. 2009. 77p. pap. 8.95 *(978-0-557-05289-9(0))* Lulu Pr., Inc.

—Pep Squad Mysteries Book 4: Prediction of Danger. 2010. 90p. pap. 8.99 *(978-0-557-46495-1(1))* Lulu Pr., Inc.

Roberts, Daniel. The Adventures of Tumbleweed Smith. 2012. 220p. pap. 12.99 *(978-1-105-84675-5(X))* Lulu Pr., Inc.

Roberts, Dw. Pep Squad Mysteries Book: Cavern in the Hills. 2008. (Illus.). 68p. pap. 9.96 *(978-0-557-02446-9(3))* Lulu Pr., Inc.

—Pep Squad Mysteries Book: Mystery in the Lions' Maze. 2012. 102p. pap. 9.95 *(978-1-257-92360-1(9))* Lulu Pr., Inc.

—Pep Squad Mysteries Book: Trouble on Avalance Mountain. 2010. (Illus.). 86p. pap. 8.99 *(978-0-557-16575-9(X))* Lulu Pr., Inc.

—Pep Squad Mysteries Book 7: The Deadly Doll. 2012. 120p. pap. 9.95 *(978-1-105-49215-0(X))* Lulu Pr., Inc.

—Pep Squad Mysteries Book 8: Shock of the Scarecrow. 2012. (Illus.). 124p. pap. 9.95 *(978-1-105-83468-4(9))* Lulu Pr., Inc.

Roberts, Heather H. Raven & the Forest Angels. 2012. 66p. pap. 27.95 *(978-1-4525-5739-7(X))* Balboa Pr.

Roberts, Kelly Hughes. The Road to Chianti. 2012. 214p. (gr. 4-6). 33.99 *(978-1-4525-5963-6(5));* pap. 15.99 *(978-1-4525-5961-2(9))* Balboa Pr.

Roberts, Nick H. Tyler the Tumbleweed & His Family Adventure. 2013. 28p. pap. 13.55 *(978-1-4669-7782-2(5))* Trafford Publishing.

Roberts, Phyllis. Teeny Tiny Star. 2007. (Illus.). 30p. (J). lib. bdg. 19.95 *(978-1-933732-40-4(7))* Big Ransom Studio.

Roberts, Rachel. Circles in the Stream. 2007. (Avalon Ser.: Bk. 1). 175p. (J). 9.99 *(978-1-933164-64-9(6))* Seven Seas Entertainment, LLC.

Roberts, Scott A. The Rollicking Adventures of Tam O'Hare. Roberts, Scott A., illus. 2007. (ENG., Illus.). 228p. (J). (gr. 4-7). per. 16.95 *(978-1-60037-289-6(9))* Morgan James Publishing.

Roberts, Tim. The Portal to Chalicu. 2005. 218p. pap. 24.95 *(978-1-4137-9680-3(X))* PublishAmerica, Inc.

Roberts, Tina. Dream Watchman: Quest for the Missing Talisman Book I. 2011. 244p. pap. 15.95 *(978-1-60976-636-8(9),* Eloquent Bks.) Strategic Book Publishing & Rights Agency (SBPRA).

Robertson, Dan. Zoe Pencarrow & the River of Life. 2013. 84p. pap. 10.99 *(978-1-62697-108-0(0))* Salem Author Services.

Robertson, Elysia Hill. Dottie Goes to School. Robertson, Elysia Hill, illus. 2005. (Illus.). 30p. (J). per. 6.95 *(978-0-9764444-8-0(8))* E. J. Publishing.

Robertson, Neil. The Captain & the Infinite Watch Dog. 2015. (ENG., Illus.). 136p. (J). pap. *(978-1-78222-437-2(8))* Paragon Publishing, Rothersthorpe.

Robins, Eleanor. It Does Matter. 2005. (Carter High Chronicles Senior Year Ser.). (Illus.). 48p. (J). per. 3.95 *(978-1-56254-770-7(4),* SP7704) Saddleback Educational Publishing, Inc.

Robinson, Aquila. Septic Zombie - a Short Story. 2012. 28p. pap. 4.99 *(978-0-9840423-6-4(9))* Breakneck Media.

Robinson, Arlene. The Adventures of Wheelie Weenie & His Friends: A Brave & Wonderful Little Friend. 2011. (Illus.). 43p. pap. 12.95 *(978-1-4327-6861-4(1))* Outskirts Pr., Inc.

Robinson, Bonita. The Little Seed That Could. 2011. 24p. pap. 24.95 *(978-1-4626-4234-2(9))* America Star Bks.

Robinson Ed. D., Shannon R. The Adventures of Katie Koala: Oops! My Momma Is Lost!, 1 vol. Swope, Brenda, illus. 2009. 23p. pap. 24.95 *(978-1-60749-733-2(6))* America Star Bks.

Robinson, Gary. Danny Blackgoat, Rugged Road to Freedom. 2014. (ENG.). (YA). pap. 9.95 *(978-1-939053-05-3(6),* 7th Generation) Book Publishing Co.

Robinson, George. Elmer the Elf & the Magical Jingle Bells, 1 vol. Foster, Janet, illus. 2008. (ENG.). 33p. 24.95 *(978-1-60610-606-8(6))* America Star Bks.

Robinson, Gwen. The Renshaw Diversion. 2007. (Illus.). 204p. per. *(978-0-7552-0275-1(9))* Authors OnLine, Ltd.

Robinson, Hilary & Catling, Andy. Aladdin & the Lamp. 2009. (Hopscotch Adventures Ser.). (Illus.). 31p. (J). (gr. 1). lib. bdg. 25.65 *(978-1-59771-181-4(0))* Sea-To-Sea Pubns.

Robinson, Jennifer. Isabella's Shoes. 2009. 20p. pap. 10.95 *(978-1-60860-553-8(1),* Strategic Bk. Publishing) Strategic Book Publishing & Rights Agency (SBPRA).

Robinson, Keith. Valley of Monsters. 2013. 212p. pap. *(978-0-9843906-6-3(9))* Roxby Media Ltd.

Robinson, Kelley. The Magic of Lo: Book 1, lo Trilogy. Lt. ed. 2004. (Illus.). 160p. (YA). per. 9.95 *(978-0-9745865-0-2(1),* SarahRose Children's Bks.) SarahRose Publishing.

Robinson, Margaret Richardson. Wally's Wish. 2010. 28p. 16.99 *(978-1-4490-2168-9(9))* AuthorHouse.

Robinson, Mary. Days of Terriers. 2008. 32p. pap. 13.50 *(978-1-60693-481-4(3),* Eloquent Bks.) Strategic Book Publishing & Rights Agency (SBPRA).

Robinson, Michael. Bloodline. 2009. 144p. pap. 19.99 *(978-1-4415-1070-9(2))* Xlibris Corp.

Robinson, Sabra A. Micky, Ticky, Boo! Says Hello. 2003. (J). per. 9.99 *(978-1-59196-230-4(7))* Instant Pub.

Robinson, T. J. The Academy Defenders. 2012. 326p. pap. 14.99 *(978-1-936850-46-4(X))* Rhemalda Publishing.

Robinson, W. Heath. The Adventures of Uncle Lubin. 2013. (Dover Children's Classics Ser.). (ENG., Illus.). 128p. (J). (gr. 6-8). pap. 9.95 *(978-0-486-49821-8(2))* Dover Pubns., Inc.

Robledo, Ronald J. Sasquatch for Dinner. Robledo, Victoria, ed. Magno, Ryan, illus. 2013. 32p. 18.99 *(978-0-578-12711-8(3))* One Little Spark.

Roby, Ian. Surface Diver Tommy & the Sea Critters, 1 vol. 2010. 40p. 24.95 *(978-1-4489-6161-0(0))* PublishAmerica, Inc.

Roche, Art. The Knights of Boo'Gar. 2017. (ENG.). 176p. (J). pap. 9.99 *(978-1-4494-7987-9(1))* Andrews McMeel Publishing.

Roche, Louise. The Amazing Adventures of Libby Lightfoot: Book 1: Book 1. 2011. 40p. 17.50 *(978-1-4567-3443-5(1))* AuthorHouse.

Rochfort, Barry. The Adventures of Mortimer the Marmot. 2015. (ENG.). 107p. (J). (gr. 2-3). mass mkt. 11.95 *(978-1-78554-739-3(9),* dd7dabfb-8041-475e-8062-7133d7abcf1d) Austin, Stan AUS. Dist: Bookmasters Distribution.

Rock, Jonathan. Out of Bounds Bk. 1, Bk. 1. 2013. (Survival Squad Ser.: 1). (ENG., Illus.). 272p. (J). (gr. 4-7). pap. 8.99 *(978-1-86230-965-4(5),* Red Fox) Random House Children's Books GBR. Dist: Independent Pubs. Group.

—Search & Rescue Bk. 2, Bk. 2. 2013. (Survival Squad Ser.: 2). (ENG., Illus.). 256p. (J). (gr. 4-7). pap. 12.99 *(978-1-86230-966-1(3),* Red Fox) Random House Children's Books GBR. Dist: Independent Pubs. Group.

—White Water, Bk. 4. 2013. (Survival Squad Ser.: 4). (ENG., Illus.). 256p. (J). (gr. 4-7). pap. 8.99 *(978-1-86230-968-5(X),* Red Fox) Random House Children's Books GBR. Dist: Independent Pubs. Group.

Rock, Zack. Homer Henry Hudson's Curio Museum. 2014. (ENG., Illus.). 32p. (J). (gr. 1-3). 18.99 *(978-1-56846-260-8(3),* Creative Editions) Creative Co., The.

Rockliff, Mara. Pieces of Another World, 1 vol. Alikhan, Salima, illus. 2005. (ENG.). 32p. (J). (gr. k-4). 15.95 *(978-0-9764943-2-4(9))* Arbordale Publishing.

Rocklin, Joanne. The Five Lives of Our Cat Zook. 2013. (ENG.). 240p. (J). (gr. 3-7). pap. 7.95 *(978-1-4197-0525-0(3),* Amulet Bks.) Abrams, Inc.

The Rocks. 2005. (J). 4.95 *(978-1-59792-013-1(4))* F.A.S.T. Learning LLC.

Rockwell, Carey. On the Trail of Space Pirates. Ley, Willy, ed. 2007. 140p. per. 11.95 *(978-1-60312-283-2(4))* Aegypan.

—On the Trail of Space Pirates. 2007. 140p. 24.95 *(978-1-60312-781-3(X))* Aegypan.

—The Revolt on Venus. 2007. 120p. per. *(978-1-4068-3961-6(2))* Echo Library.

—The Revolt on Venus: The TOM CORBETT Space Cadet Adventure. 2007. (ENG.). 180p. pap. 19.99 *(978-1-4264-9548-9(X));* 202p. pap. 22.99 *(978-1-4264-9929-6(9))* Creative Media Partners, LLC.

—The Space Pioneers. 2007. 120p. per. *(978-1-4068-3962-3(0))* Echo Library.

Rockwell, Carey & Ley, Willy. The Space Pioneers: A Tom Corbett Space Cadet Adventure. Glanzman, Louis, illus. 2011. 220p. 44.95 *(978-1-258-10097-1(5))* Literary Licensing, LLC.

Rockwell, D. R. The Jessicas: The Adventures of Five City Girls. 2005. (J). pap. 9.95 *(978-0-9767711-0-4(1))* CLOJ Publishing.

Rockwood, Roy. Dave Dashaway & His Hydroplane. 2009. 128p. 23.95 *(978-1-60664-625-0(7));* pap. 10.95 *(978-1-60664-364-8(9))* Rodgers, Alan Bks.

—Jack North's Treasure Hunt: Or, Daring Adventures in South America. 2007. (ENG.). 142p. pap. 18.99 *(978-1-4264-2654-4(2));* 146p. pap. 19.99 *(978-1-4264-2711-4(5))* Creative Media Partners, LLC.

—On a Torn-Away World. 2008. 136p. pap. 12.95 *(978-1-60664-174-3(3))* Aegypan.

—On a Torn-Away World: Or, the Captives of the Great Earthquake. 2007. 252p. 32.95 *(978-1-4344-9622-5(8));* per. 22.95 *(978-1-4344-9621-8(X))* Wildside Pr., LLC.

—Through Space to Mars. 2008. 128p. (gr. 4-7). pap. 11.95 *(978-1-60664-173-6(5))* Aegypan.

—The Wizard of the Se. 2008. 124p. 23.95 *(978-1-60664-931-2(0));* pap. 10.95 *(978-1-60664-051-7(8))* Aegypan.

—The Wizard of the Sea. 2007. 84p. per. *(978-1-4068-3969-2(8))* Echo Library.

Rodda, Emily. Deltora Quest 2. Niwano, Makoto, illus. 2011. (Deltora Quest Ser.). (ENG.). 206p. (gr. 8-12). pap. 10.99 *(978-1-935429-29-6(9))* Kodansha America, Inc.

—Deltora Quest 3. Niwano, Makoto, illus. 2011. (Deltora Quest Ser.). (ENG.). 208p. (gr. 8-12). pap. 10.99 *(978-1-935429-30-2(2))* Kodansha America, Inc.

—The Golden Door. 2012. (ENG.). 272p. (J). (gr. 3-7). 16.99 *(978-0-545-42990-0(0),* Scholastic Pr.) Scholastic, Inc.

—The Silver Door. 2013. (Illus.). (J). 278p. pap. *(978-0-545-42993-1(5));* (ENG., 288p. (gr. 3-7). 16.99 *(978-0-545-42992-4(7))* Scholastic, Inc. (Scholastic Pr.).

—The Third Door. 2013. (J). pap. *(978-0-545-42995-5(1),* Scholastic Pr.) Scholastic, Inc.

—The Wizard of Rondo. 2009. (ENG.). 400p. (J). (gr. 3-7). 16.99 *(978-0-545-11516-2(7),* Scholastic Pr.) Scholastic, Inc.

Roddy, Lee. Dooger, the Grasshopper Hound. 2008. (D. J. Dillon Adventure Ser.: No. 3). (J). 7.99 *(978-0-88062-267-7(9))* Mott Media.

—Escape down the Raging Rapids. 2008. (D. J. Dillon Adventure Ser.: No. 10). (J). 7.99 *(978-0-88062-274-5(1))* Mott Media.

—The Ghost Dog of Stoney Ridge. 2008. (D. J. Dillon Adventure Ser.: No. 4). (J). 7.99 *(978-0-88062-268-4(7))* Mott Media.

—Ghost of the Moaning Mansion. 2008. (D. J. Dillon Adventure Ser.: No. 8). (J). 7.99 *(978-0-88062-272-1(5))* Mott Media.

—The Hermit of Mad River. 2008. (D. J. Dillon Adventure Ser.: No. 9). (J). 8.99 *(978-0-88062-273-8(3))* Mott Media.

—Hunted in the Alaskan Wilderness. 2008. (Ladd Family Adventure Ser.: Vol. 13). (Illus.). 149p. (Orig.). (J). (gr. 3-7). per. 7.99 *(978-0-88062-262-2(8))* Mott Media.

—The Legend of the White Raccoon. 2008. (D. J. Dillon Adventure Ser.: No. 6). (J). 7.99 *(978-0-88062-270-7(9))* Mott Media.

—Mad Dog of Lobo Mountain. 2008. (D. J. Dillon Adventure Ser.: No. 5). (J). 7.99 *(978-0-88062-269-1(5))* Mott Media.

—The Mystery of the Black Hole Mine. 2008. (D. J. Dillon Adventure Ser.: No. 7). (J). 8.99 *(978-0-88062-271-4(7))* Mott Media.

—Peril at Pirate's Point. 2006. (Ladd Family Adventure Ser.: Vol. 7). (Illus.). 153p. (J). (gr. 4-7). per. 7.99 *(978-0-88062-256-1(3))* Mott Media.

Rodenbur, Susan. The Boy Who Captured the Sun. Kirkpatrick, Karen, illus. 2007. 32p. per. 12.95 *(978-1-59858-515-5(0))* Dog Ear Publishing, LLC.

Rodkey, Geoff. Blue Sea Burning. 2015. (Chronicles of Egg Ser.: 3). (ENG.). 400p. (J). (gr. 5). 7.99 *(978-0-14-751443-1(6),* Puffin Books) Penguin Young Readers Group.

—Deadweather & Sunrise. 2013. (Chronicles of Egg Ser.: 1). (ENG.). 320p. (J). (gr. 5). pap. 7.99 *(978-0-14-242662-3(8),* Puffin Books) Penguin Young Readers Group.

Rodman, Sean. Infiltration, 1 vol. 2011. (Orca Soundings Ser.). (ENG.). (gr. 8-12). 128p. (J). 16.95 *(978-1-55469-986-5(X));* 144p. (YA). pap. 9.95 *(978-1-55469-985-8(1))* Orca Bk. Pubs. USA.

Rodrigue, Nancy Temple. Hidden Mickey Adventures 1: Peter & the Wolf. 2nd ed. 2017. (Hidden Mickey Adventures Ser.: 1). (ENG.). 194p. (gr. 4-17). pap. 14.99 **(978-1-938319-30-3(3),** DOUBLE R Bks.) Rodrigue & Sons Co./Double R Books Publishing.

—Hidden Mickey Adventures 2: Peter & the Missing Mansion, vol. 2. (Hidden Mickey Adventures Ser.: 2). (ENG.). 2015. 182p. (YA). (gr. 4-17). lib. bdg. 29.99 *(978-1-938319-19-8(2),* DOUBLE-R BKS.) 2nd ed. 2017. 198p. (gr. 5-17). pap. 14.99 **(978-1-938319-31-0(1),** DOUBLE R Bks.) Rodrigue & Sons Co./Double R Books Publishing.

—Hidden Mickey Adventures 3: The Mermaid's Tale, vol. 3. 2014. (Hidden Mickey Adventures Ser.: 3). (ENG.). 272p. (YA). (gr. 4-17). pap. 14.99 *(978-1-938319-05-1(2),* DOUBLE-R BKS.) Rodrigue & Sons Co./Double R Books Publishing.

Rodriguez, AJ. A Cajun Crawfish Tale. 2009. 20p. pap. 12.49 *(978-1-4389-5529-2(4))* AuthorHouse.

—Cycle of Life. 2009. 20p. pap. 12.49 *(978-1-4389-5528-5(6))* AuthorHouse.

Rodriguez, Angelica. Mia y Primos/Mia & Cousins: Yo grito,corro y grito / I scream, run & Scream. 2009. 24p. pap. 12.49 *(978-1-4389-7095-0(1))* AuthorHouse.

Rodriguez, Elaine M. Nerposito & Planet Earth. 2012. 36p. pap. 15.49 *(978-1-4669-5972-9(X))* Trafford Publishing.

Rodriguez, Marisela. Violet's Shoes. 2012. 28p. pap. 9.95 *(978-1-4327-9616-7(X))* Outskirts Pr., Inc.

Rodriguez, Odette B. Lezama. The Last Golden Egg. 2011. 32p. pap. 19.95 *(978-1-4327-5931-5(0))* Outskirts Pr., Inc.

Rodriguez, Raul. Runaway Baby / el Bebe' Travieso. 2005. (SPA., Illus.). 13p. (J). per. 9.99 *(978-1-932338-63-8(2))* Lifevest Publishing, Inc.

Rodriguez, Robert & Rodriguez, Racer. The Adventures of Shark Boy & Lava Girl: The Movie Storybook. 2005. (Illus.). 65p. (J). *(978-1-933104-02-7(3))* Troublemaker Publishing, LP.

Rodriguez, Robert, et al. The Day Dreamer. Toader, Alex, illus. 2005. (Shark Boy & Lava Girl Adventures Ser.: Bk. 1). 162p. (J). (gr. -1-7). per. *(978-1-933104-04-1(X))* Troublemaker Publishing, LP.

Rodriguez, Sergio R. Little Santa & Snowboy: The Childhood Adventures of Santa Claus. 2007. (Illus.). 32p. (J). pap. 8.95 *(978-0-615-17411-2(6))* Little Santa Bks., Inc.

Roemermann, Jennifer. The Long Grass Tunnel. 2012. 50p. pap. 18.68 *(978-1-4797-0300-5(1))* Xlibris Corp.

Roeser, Matt. Oh No, Astro! Woodard, Brad, illus. 2016. (ENG.). 40p. (J). (gr. -1-3). 17.99 *(978-1-4814-3976-3(6),* Simon & Schuster Bks. For Young Readers) Simon & Schuster Bks. For Young Readers.

Rogers, Andy. The Puppy Brothers Adventures with Forest Friends - Children's Picture Book for Ages 3 To 8. 2013. 38p. pap. 10.00 *(978-1-63022-036-5(1))* Speedy Publishing LLC.

Rogers, Anne. The magic rainbow large Print. 2008. 332p. pap. 30.95 *(978-1-4092-3059-5(7))* Lulu Pr., Inc.

—The magic rainbow very large Print. 2008. 502p. pap. 39.50 *(978-1-4092-3065-6(1))* Lulu Pr., Inc.

Rogers, Bud & Martin, Gary. The Witch of Endor, 1 vol. Cariello, Sergio, illus. 2008. (Z Graphic Novels / Son of Samson Ser.). (ENG.). 160p. (J). pap. 6.99 *(978-0-310-71283-1(1))* Zonderkidz.

Rogers, Carol J. The Adventures of Buttonballs' Trails. 2012. 28p. pap. 19.99 *(978-1-4772-4481-4(6))* AuthorHouse.

Rogers, Christopher M., illus. Homer the Helicopter Grand Canyon Adventures. 2007. 72p. (J). 18.95 *(978-0-9786352-3-7(X))* Buscher, Julie W.

Rogers, Don. The Adventures of Shawn & Jeremy. 2011. 20p. pap. 24.95 *(978-1-4626-3674-7(8))* America Star Bks.

—The Adventures of Shawn & Jeremy with Sister Nicole & the Hot Air Balloon: Volume Two. 2012. 24p. pap. 24.95 *(978-1-4626-7649-1(9))* America Star Bks.

Rogers, Jacqueline. Jack Jones off to the Post Office. 2012. 20p. pap. 13.77 *(978-1-4669-0808-6(4))* Trafford Publishing.

Rogers, Martha. Bernie Finds a Friend. 2013. 36p. pap. 15.99 *(978-1-4497-8288-7(4),* WestBow Pr.) Author Solutions, Inc.

—Bernie Goes to the Beach: Bernie's Journey. 2012. 32p. pap. 13.99 *(978-1-4497-5187-6(3),* WestBow Pr.) Author Solutions, Inc.

Rogers, Meghan. Enemy Exposure. 2017. (Raven Files Ser.: 2). (ENG.). 320p. (YA). (gr. 7). 17.99 *(978-0-399-17618-0(7),* Philomel Bks.) Penguin Young Readers Group.

Rogers, Michelle Elizabeth. The Adventures of Brutus & Baby: A Haunted Halloween. Collier, Kevin Scott, illus. 2010. 50p. pap. 16.50 *(978-1-60860-592-7(2),* Eloquent Bks.) Strategic Book Publishing & Rights Agency (SBPRA).

Rogers, Terry, illus. Androcles & the Lion: A Roman Legend. 2003. (Dominie Collection of Myths & Legends). (SPA.). 20p. (J). lib. bdg. *(978-0-7685-2419-2(9))* Dominie Pr., Inc.

—Androcles & the Lion: A Roman Legend. 2004. (SPA & ENG.). 20p. (J). (gr. 3-3). pap. 6.47 net. *(978-0-7685-2122-1(X),* Dominie Elementary) Pearson Schl.

Rogers, Wanda Gayle. Miss Bean & the Great Tricycle Rescue: The Great Tricycle Rescue. 2007. (J). 7.95 *(978-1-59872-735-7(4))* Instant Pub.

Rogger. The Fifty-Fifth Bear & the Awkward Rabbits: An Amazing Thick Blue Wood Bear Adventure. 2009. (Illus.). 60p. pap. 21.99 *(978-1-4389-1672-9(8))* AuthorHouse.

Roginsky, Renata. The Simulacrum & the Book of Spells. 2005. 173p. pap. 9.25 *(978-1-4116-2451-1(3))* Lulu Pr., Inc.

Roh, Grace S. Booyoung & Sea Turtle's Adventure: God's Creatures' Adventures Series 1. Park, Mi-Ok, illus. 2013. 52p. pap. 17.50 *(978-1-62212-718-4(8),* Strategic Bk. Publishing) Strategic Book Publishing & Rights Agency (SBPRA).

Rohan, Julia K. Weaverworld: Grimsnipe's Revenge. 2012. 382p. 31.95 *(978-1-4697-0031-1(X));* pap. 21.95 *(978-1-4697-0032-8(8))* iUniverse, Inc.

Rohan, Margaret de. Celia & Granny Meg go to Paris: A survival Guide. 2011. (ENG., Illus.). 184p. pap. *(978-1-84876-650-1(5))* Troubador Publishing Ltd.

—Celia & Granny Meg Return to Paris: The man with no Face. 2012. (ENG., Illus.). 176p. pap. *(978-1-78088-243-7(2))* Troubador Publishing Ltd.

Rohen, Sean. Unprincess Nermine. 2009. 84p. pap. 26.99 *(978-1-4490-3592-1(2))* AuthorHouse.

Rohmer, Sax, pseud. The Quest of the Sacred Slipper. 2007. 136p. per. 11.95 *(978-1-60312-363-1(6));* 24.95 *(978-1-60312-701-1(1))* Aegypan.

Rohmer, Sax, pseud, et al. Adventure Classics, Vol. 12. Pomplun, Tom, ed. 2005. (ENG., Illus.). 144p. pap. 11.95 *(978-0-9746648-4-2(7),* 9780974664842) Eureka Productions.

Rohr, Rebecca. Flocks: A Buster Bird Adventure. 2011. pap. 8.95 *(978-0-7414-6735-5(6))* Infinity Publishing.

Rohrer, Kim. The Adventures of Little Dooey: The Doctor. 2012. 24p. pap. 9.95 *(978-0-9848050-7-5(9),* Little Creek Bks.) Jan-Carol Publishing, INC.

Rokker, H. M. The Adventures of Ralph in the Search for Blackbeard's Gold, 1 vol. 2009. 41p. pap. 24.95 *(978-1-60474-259-6(3))* America Star Bks.

Roland-James, Patricia & James, Robert L. Something Wicked in the Land of Picatrix. Chidgey, Scarlett, ed. Verhoef, Sharon & Pinkham, Pamela, illus. 2007. 281p. (J). pap. 12.95 *(978-0-9760789-9-9(6))* Aquila Ink Publishing.

Rollason, Jane. Freddie's War Level 6 Advanced. 2010. (ENG.). 128p. pap. 14.50 *(978-84-8323-909-4(4))* Cambridge Univ. Pr.

—Freddie's War Level 6 Advanced Book with CD-ROM & Audio CDs (3), 1 vol. 2010. (ENG.). 128p. cd-rom, audio compact disk 18.25 *(978-84-8323-662-8(1))* Cambridge Univ. Pr.

Roller, Pat Kellogg. Pink Hat's Adventure with Kites. Salazar, Riana, illus. Roller, John, photos by. 2009. 36p. pap. 10.95 *(978-1-59858-957-3(1))* Dog Ear Publishing, LLC.

Rollins, Danielle. Burning. 2017. (ENG.). 368p. (YA). pap. 9.99 *(978-1-68119-205-5(5),* 9781681192055, Bloomsbury USA Childrens) Bloomsbury Publishing USA.

Rollins, James. Jake Ransom & the Howling Sphinx. 2012. (Jake Ransom Ser.: 2). (ENG.). 384p. (J). (gr. 5). pap. 7.99 *(978-0-06-147384-5(7))* HarperCollins Pubs.

—Jake Ransom & the Skull King's Shadow. 2009. (Jake Ransom Ser.: 1). (ENG.). 416p. (J). (gr. 5-18). 16.99 *(978-0-06-147379-1(0))* HarperCollins Pubs.

Rolón, Rebecca Alisa. Rebecca's Tales. 2007. 48p. pap. 16.95 *(978-1-4241-9198-7(X))* America Star Bks.

Roman, Javier. Adventures of Tinturu & Kumachan the M. 2007. (Illus.). 48p. pap. 16.95 *(978-1-4241-1626-3(0))* PublishAmerica, Inc.

Roman, Stacey. Some of Us Want Wrinkles. Wurster, Laurie, illus. 2005. (J). per. 16.95 *(978-1-59858-033-4(7))* Dog Ear Publishing, LLC.

Romay, Alexis. Diego Saves the Sloth! Mawhinney, Art, illus. 2007. (Go, Diego, Go! Ser.: 4). (ENG.). 24p. (J). (gr. -1-2). pap. 3.99 *(978-1-4169-3470-7(7),* Simon Spotlight/Nickelodeon) Simon Spotlight/Nickelodeon.

Romero, Vivian. On the Lam with Lambert. 2009. 24p. pap. 12.99 *(978-1-4490-2773-5(3))* AuthorHouse.

Romeu, Emma. Naufragio en las Filipinas. 2003.Tr. of Shipwrecked in the Philippines. (SPA., Illus.). 162p. (J). (gr. 5-8). pap. 9.95 *(978-968-19-0555-2(5))* Santillana USA Publishing Co., Inc.

Romolino, Kimberly. A Day at Sea. 2009. 15p. pap. 24.95 *(978-1-60813-803-6(8))* America Star Bks.

Romoulous. Katalambano: Invasion of the Terror Dome. 2005. *(978-0-9773064-5-9(3))* MIROGLYPHICS.

Root, Phyllis. Lilly & the Pirates. Shepperson, Rob, illus. (ENG.). (J). 2013. 180p. (gr. 3-7). pap. 8.95 *(978-1-62091-027-6(6))* 2010. 116p. (gr. 4-6). 16.95 *(978-1-59078-583-6(5),* Front Street) Boyds Mills Pr.

Rosano, John. Molly Monkey. 2008. (Illus.). (J). 14.95 *(978-1-60131-013-2(7))* Big Tent Bks.

Rosciti, Donna. The Birthday Train: Book 1. 2013. (ENG.). 48p. (J). 24.95 *(978-1-4787-2236-6(3))* Outskirts Pr., Inc.

Rose, C. T. Don't Play with the Craft, 1 vol. 2009. 82p. pap. 19.95 *(978-1-61582-871-5(0))* America Star Bks.

Rose, Caroline Starr. Jasper & the Riddle of Riley's Mine. 2017. (ENG.). 288p. (J). (gr. 5). 16.99 *(978-0-399-16811-6(7),* G.P. Putnam's Sons Books for Young Readers) Penguin Young Readers Group.

Rose, Chloe Gayle & Rose, Tammy Marie. The Snake That Eats Cake. 2012. 28p. pap. 24.95 *(978-1-4626-9882-0(4))* America Star Bks.

Rose, John. Wikker. 2007. 248p. pap. 17.95 *(978-1-4303-1523-0(7))* Lulu Pr., Inc.

Rose, Robin. Reaching for the Stars. 2008. 24p. pap. 11.95 *(978-1-4389-2299-7(X))* AuthorHouse.

Rose, S. J. Plant Agriculture Education: 2012 Edition. collector's ed. 2011. (ENG., Illus.). 176p. per. 5.00 *(978-0-9729057-2-5(3))* Training Grounds.

Rose, Simon. The Clone Conspiracy, 1 vol. 2005. (ENG., Illus.). 96p. (J). (gr. 4-6). per. 7.95 *(978-1-896580-80-7(7))* Tradewind Bks. CAN. Dist: Orca Bk. Pubs. USA.

Rosen, Lucy. I Am Bane. Cohn, Scott, illus. 2012. (Dark Knight Rises Ser.). (ENG.). 24p. (J). (gr. -1-2). pap. 3.99 *(978-0-06-213222-2(9),* HarperFestival) HarperCollins Pubs.

—Planet 51. 2009. (Planet 51 Ser.). 12p. (J). pap. 6.99 *(978-0-06-184418-8(7),* HarperFestival) HarperCollins Pubs.

—Teen Titans Go! - Meet the Teen Titans! 2014. (Passport to Reading Level 2 Ser.). (ENG., Illus.). 32p. (J). (gr. -1-3). pap. 4.99 *(978-0-316-33330-6(1))* Little, Brown Bks. for Young Readers.

Rosen, Michael. Send for a Superhero! McEwen, Katharine, illus. 2014. (ENG.). 40p. (J). (gr. -1-2). 16.99 *(978-0-7636-6438-1(3))* Candlewick Pr.

—Uncle Gobb & the Green Heads. Layton, Neal, illus. 2017. (ENG.). 272p. (J). 17.99 *(978-1-4088-5133-3(4),* 9781408851333, Bloomsbury USA Childrens) Bloomsbury Publishing USA.

Rosenberg, Michael. Chilly Goes to Hong Kong & China: Another Chilly the Toy Polar Bear Adventure. 2013. 36p. pap. 13.95 *(978-1-62212-841-9(9),* Strategic Bk. Publishing) Strategic Book Publishing & Rights Agency (SBPRA).

—The Little Lost Tune: More Adventures from Bendalot. 2010. 30p. pap. 13.00 *(978-1-60911-881-5(2),* Eloquent Bks.) Strategic Book Publishing & Rights Agency (SBPRA).

—The Story of Bendalot. 2008. 40p. pap. 16.99 *(978-1-4343-9932-8(X))* AuthorHouse.

—The Story of Bendalot Part: The Return Home. 2009. (Illus.). 36p. pap. 15.49 *(978-1-4389-8294-6(1))* AuthorHouse.

Rosenblum, Gregg. Revolution 19. 2013. (Revolution 19 Ser.: 1). (ENG.). 272p. (YA). (gr. 8). 17.99 *(978-0-06-212595-8(8),* HarperTeen) HarperCollins Pubs.

Rosenow, Ty. The Historical Adventures of Thomas Balfour. 2012. 186p. pap. 17.95 *(978-1-105-94011-8(X))* Lulu Pr., Inc.

Rosenthal, Adam. Adventures of Snizznsnozz. 2011. 24p. pap. 11.32 *(978-1-4634-0736-0(X))* AuthorHouse.

Rosenthal, Eileen. Bobo the Sailor Man! Rosenthal, Marc, illus. 2013. (ENG.). 40p. (J). (gr. -1-1). 15.99 *(978-1-4424-4443-0(6))* Simon & Schuster Children's Publishing.

Rosenthal, Michele Marie. The Frog & the Tadpole's Great Swamp Adventure, 1 vol. 2009. 22p. pap. 24.95 *(978-1-61546-178-3(7))* America Star Bks.

Rosoff, Meg. Picture Me Gone. 2014. (ENG.). 256p. (YA). (gr. 7). pap. 9.99 *(978-0-14-751226-0(3),* Speak) Penguin Young Readers Group.

Ross, Daisy T. Ty & the Moon. 2012. 80p. pap. 25.25 *(978-1-4772-6950-3(9))* AuthorHouse.

Ross, Dev. We Both Read-Frank & the Giant. 2005. (We Both Read Ser.). (Illus.). 44p. (J). (gr. -1-2). 7.99 *(978-1-891327-59-9(3));* per. 4.99 *(978-1-891327-60-5(7))* Treasure Bay, Inc.

—We Both Read-Frank & the Tiger. Reinhart, Larry, illus. 2012. 44p. (J). pap. 4.99 *(978-1-60115-260-2(4))* Treasure Bay, Inc.

Ross, Emily. Half in Love with Death. 2015. (ENG.). 224p. (YA). 17.99 *(978-1-4405-8903-4(8),* Simon Pulse) Simon Pulse.

Ross, Gary. Bartholomew Biddle & the Very Big Wind. Myers, Matthew, illus. 2012. (ENG.). 96p. (J). (gr. 1-4). 17.99 *(978-0-7636-4920-3(1))* Candlewick Pr.

Ross, Joel. Beast & Crown. 2017. 384p. (J). (gr. 3-7). 16.99 ***(978-0-06-248459-8(1))*** HarperCollins Pubs.

—The Fog Diver. (Fog Diver Ser.: 1). (J). (gr. 3-7). 2016. 352p. pap. 6.99 *(978-0-06-235294-1(6))* 2015. (ENG.). 336p. 16.99 *(978-0-06-235293-4(8))* HarperCollins Pubs.

—The Fog Diver. 2016. (J). lib. bdg. 17.20 *(978-0-606-38745-3(5))* Turtleback Bks.

—The Lost Compass. (Fog Diver Ser.: 2). (J). (gr. 3-7). 2017. 368p. pap. 6.99 ***(978-0-06-235309-2(8))*** 2016. 352p. 16.99 *(978-0-06-235297-2(0))* HarperCollins Pubs.

—The Lost Compass. 2017. (Fog Diver Ser.: Vol. 2). (ENG.). (J). (gr. 3-7). lib. bdg. 17.20 ***(978-0-606-40052-7(4))*** Turtleback Bks.

Ross, Marlene. The Adventures of Donny the Doorknob. Hallam, Colleen and Peggy, illus. 2009. 32p. pap. 24.95 *(978-1-61546-539-2(1))* America Star Bks.

Ross, Melissa. Today I Am a Penguin. Ross, Melissa, illus. 2012. (Illus.). 24p. pap. 10.95 *(978-1-61633-306-5(5))* Guardian Angel Publishing, Inc.

Ross, Sherry Lazarus. The Light of Lucinda. Date not set. (Illus.). 253p. (J). (gr. 2-6). pap. *(978-0-615-11146-9(7))* Well Fire Pubns.

Rossell, Judith. Withering-By-Sea. Rossell, Judith, illus. 2017. (ENG., Illus.). 288p. (J). (gr. 3-7). pap. 7.99 *(978-1-4814-4368-5(2))* Simon & Schuster Children's Publishing.

Rossi, Veronica. Riders. 2016. (ENG.). 368p. (YA). 17.99 *(978-0-7653-8254-2(7),* 9780765382542, Tor Teen) Doherty, Tom Assocs., LLC.

—Seeker. 2017. (Riders Ser.: 2). (ENG.). 352p. (YA). 17.99 *(978-0-7653-8256-6(3),* 9780765382566, Tor Teen) Doherty, Tom Assocs., LLC.

Roth, David. The Adventures of the Magnificent Seven. 2009. 347p. pap. 26.88 *(978-0-557-09999-3(4))* Lulu Pr., Inc.

Roth-Fisch, Marla. Sensitive Sam: Sam's Sensory Adventure Has a Happy Ending! 2009. (ENG., Illus.). 29p. (J). pap. 9.95 *(978-1-932565-86-7(8))* Future Horizons, Inc.

Roth, Matthue. Candy in Action. 2007. (ENG.). 224p. (gr. 9-18). *(978-1-933368-63-4(2))* CSA Telltapes, Ltd.

—Candy in Action: A Novel. 2009. (ENG., Illus.). 208p. (gr. 8). pap. *(978-1-59376-228-5(3))* Ebury Publishing.

Roth, Silke. Creak, Thump, Bonk! 2007. (ENG.). 40p. (J). (gr. -1-3). 11.99 *(978-1-4169-6159-8(3),* Simon & Schuster/Paula Wiseman Bks.) Simon & Schuster/Paula Wiseman Bks.

Rothfuss, Patrick. The Adventures of the Princess & Mr. Whiffle: The Thing Beneath the Bed. Taylor, Nate, illus. 2010. 68p. 25.00 *(978-1-59606-313-6(0))* Subterranean Pr.

Rothstein, Arminio & Brixler, Andreas. TOBY & TOBIAS: Die Abenteuer aus dem ZiRKUS HABAKUK. 2010. 134p. pap. 14.90 *(978-3-8391-0292-3(8))* Bks. on Demand.

Rothwell, David. The Voyage of the Pilchard. 2009. 162p. pap. 13.95 *(978-1-4092-1071-9(5))* Lulu Pr., Inc.

Rothwell, Tammy. The Adventures of Lewis the Dragon: The journey Begins... 2008. (Illus.). 89p. (J). per. *(978-0-615-18912-3(1))* Rothwell Digital Imagery.

Rotman, Stuart. Welcome to Trashtown. 2007. 192p. 34.95 *(978-1-4303-2662-5(X))* Lulu Pr., Inc.

Rotstein, Adira. Little Jane & the Nameless Isle: A Little Jane Silver Adventure. 2012. (Little Jane Silver Adventure Ser.: 2). (ENG.). 264p. (YA). pap. 12.99 *(978-1-4597-0420-6(7))* Dundurn CAN. Dist: Ingram Publisher Services.

—Little Jane Silver. 2011. (Little Jane Silver Adventure Ser.: 1). (ENG., Illus.). 288p. (YA). (gr. 7). pap. 12.99 *(978-1-55488-878-8(6),* Dundurn Pr.) Dundurn CAN. Dist: Ingram Publisher Services.

Roudon Jr., James. The Adventures of Ratsy & Kitten: Which Way Is Home? 2007. 56p. per. 16.95 *(978-1-4241-8549-8(1))* America Star Bks.

Rough Riders. 2005. (J). 4.95 *(978-1-59792-020-9(7))* F.A.S.T. Learning LLC.

Rouncville, Bibi. Bog Nymphs & Tiger Stones. 2008. 52p. pap. 15.50 *(978-1-4357-3966-6(3))* Lulu Pr., Inc.

—Castle at Trail's End. 2008. 52p. pap. 9.50 *(978-1-4357-3967-3(1))* Lulu Pr., Inc.

—Gimbels & Gooseberries. 2010. 52p. pap. 9.50 *(978-0-557-21585-0(4))* Lulu Pr., Inc.

—Sea Bugs & Moose Eggs. 2009. 52p. pap. 9.50 *(978-1-4357-4004-4(1))* Lulu Pr., Inc.

—Trouble at Binka Bridge. 2010. 52p. pap. 9.50 *(978-0-557-16051-8(0))* Lulu Pr., Inc.

Rousay II, Richard A. Choose the Right & Walk with Noah. 2008. 82p. pap. 17.50 *(978-0-615-19773-9(6))* P.F.P. Pubs.

—Choose the Right 'Walk with Alma' 2010. 94p. pap. 17.50 *(978-0-557-13491-5(9))* Lulu Pr., Inc.

Rouse, Betty Munn. The Adventures of the Phillyfab Family. 2011. 68p. pap. 12.95 *(978-1-4567-3005-5(3))* AuthorHouse.

Rouse, Walt. The Adventures of Clever Kitty. Bowker, Margie, illus. 2013. 56p. pap. *(978-1-4602-1254-7(1))* FriesenPress.

Rousseau, Leon. Fritz Deelman en die Woestynrowers. 2004. 160p. pap. *(978-0-7981-4425-4(4))* Human & Rousseau.

Roux, Madeleine. Escape from Asylum. 2016. (Asylum Ser.: 4). (Illus.). 352p. (YA). (gr. 9). 17.99 *(978-0-06-242442-6(4))* HarperCollins Pubs.

Rouzer, Walter. Rebel Stone & the Ghost Whisperers. 2009. 304p. 28.95 *(978-0-595-51192-1(9));* pap. 18.95 *(978-0-595-52313-9(7))* iUniverse, Inc.

Rovetch, L. Bob. And the Surprisingly Slobbery Attack of the Dog-Wash Doggies. Whamond, Dave, illus. 2007. (Hot Dog & Bob Ser.: HOTD). (ENG.). 96p. (J). (gr. 1-5). per. 4.95 *(978-0-8118-5746-8(8))* Chronicle Bks. LLC.

—Hot Dog & Bob: And the Particularly Pesky Attack of the Pencil People. Whamond, Dave, illus. 2006. (Hot Dog & Bob Ser.: HOTD). (ENG.). 96p. (J). (gr. 1-5). pap. 4.95 *(978-0-8118-5322-4(5))* Chronicle Bks. LLC.

Rowland, Dawn. The Adventures of Little Sprout. Oliver, Angel, illus. 2010. 32p. 12.99 *(978-1-4490-7725-9(0))* AuthorHouse.

Rowling, J. K. Harry Potter y el Caliz de Fuego. 2004. (Harry Potter Ser.: Year 4).Tr. of Harry Potter & the Goblet of Fire. (SPA., Illus.). 240p. (YA). 19.95 *(978-84-7888-645-6(1),* SAL30169) Emece Editores ESP. Dist: Lectorum Pubns., Inc.

Rowntree, G. M. Wizards Spell Magic in the Legends of Mere Leander. 2010. 291p. pap. 32.50 *(978-1-4452-6812-5(4))* Lulu Pr., Inc.

—Wizards Spell Magic in the Legends of Mere Leander - US Trade Size. 2010. 291p. pap. 24.95 *(978-1-4452-9266-3(1))* Lulu Pr., Inc.

Rowohlt, Harry & Trier, Walter. The Jolly Steamship. Trier, Walter, illus. 2013. (ENG., Illus.). 32p. (J). (gr. -1-3). 17.95 *(978-0-7358-4127-7(6))* North-South Bks., Inc.

Roxy. The Adventure of Benny Franklin: A Boy Tale. 2012. 26p. 19.95 *(978-1-4626-7972-0(2))* America Star Bks.

Roy, Lillian Elizabeth. Polly in New York. Barbour, H. S., illus. 2004. reprint ed. pap. 28.95 *(978-1-4179-0068-8(7))* Kessinger Publishing, LLC.

Roy, Oscar. I Was Captured by Pirates. 2013. 110p. pap. 11.00 *(978-1-62212-790-0(0),* Strategic Bk. Publishing) Strategic Book Publishing & Rights Agency (SBPRA).

Roy, Pat & Roy, Sandy. Jonathan Park: a New Beginning. 2013. (Jonathan Park Adventure Fiction Ser.: Vol. 2). (ENG.). 145p. (J). (gr. 4-7). pap. 10.00 *(978-1-937460-60-0(6))* Vision Forum, Inc., The.

—Jonathan Park: a Startling Discovery. 2013. (Jonathan Park Adventure Fiction Ser.: Vol. 1). (ENG.). 136p. (J). (gr. 4-7). pap. 10.00 *(978-1-937460-59-4(2))* Vision Forum, Inc., The.

Roy, Philip. Seas of South Africa. 2013. (ENG.). 250p. pap. 11.95 *(978-1-55380-247-1(0))* Ronsdale Pr. CAN. Dist: SPD-Small Pr. Distribution.

—Submarine Outlaw. 2008. (ENG., Illus.). 254p. pap. 10.95 *(978-1-55380-058-3(3))* Ronsdale Pr. CAN. Dist: SPD-Small Pr. Distribution.

Roy Rockwood. Through the Air to the North Pole: Or the Wonderful Cruise of the Electric Monarch. l.t. ed. 2007. 78p. pap. 21.99 *(978-1-4264-8207-6(8))* Creative Media Partners, LLC.

Roy, Ron. The Missing Mummy. (A to Z Mystery Ser.: Vol. 13). (J). 11.32 *(978-0-7383-3465-3(0))* Booksource, The.

Roy, Ronald. The Castle Crime. Gurney, John Steven, illus. 2014. (to Z Mysteries Ser.: No. 6). (ENG.). 144p. (J). (gr. 1-4). 5.99 *(978-0-385-37159-9(4),* Random Hse. Bks. for Young Readers) Random Hse. Children's Bks.

Royce, Richard. Hard Day for Harry. 2006. (Illus.). (J). spiral bd. *(978-0-9777735-1-0(5))* Everwas Publishing.

Roys, Julie. Outside the Window. 2012. 24p. pap. 21.00 *(978-1-4669-3092-6(6))* Trafford Publishing.

Roytman, Arkady. The Adventures of King Arthur Coloring Book. 2013. (ENG., Illus.). 32p. (J). (gr. 3-12). pap. 3.99 *(978-0-486-49829-4(8))* Dover Pubns., Inc.

Rozevskis, Diana. Crystal Waters & on to North America. 2013. 280p. pap. *(978-1-78299-851-8(9))* FeedARead.com.

Rubalcaba, Jill. The Wadjet Eye. 2006. (ENG.). 160p. (J). (gr. 5-7). pap. 7.99 *(978-0-618-68927-9(3))* Houghton Mifflin Harcourt Publishing Co.

Rubens, Michael. Emily & the Spellstone. 2017. (ENG.). 288p. (J). (gr. 5-7). 16.99 *(978-0-544-79086-5(3))* Houghton Mifflin Harcourt Publishing Co.

Rubin, Diana. King Choco the Great. 2009. 45p. (J). pap. 10.95 *(978-1-4327-2972-1(1))* Outskirts Pr., Inc.

Rubinacci, Mary Ellen. Srepsihw: The Land of Quiet? 2012. 36p. 19.95 *(978-1-4626-5872-5(5))* America Star Bks.

Rubino, Tony. Animal Farm. 2013. 24p. pap. 24.95 *(978-1-62709-615-7(9))* America Star Bks.

Ruby, Anne. Children of the Sea. Meier, Ty, illus. 2007. (YA). per. *(978-0-9787881-0-0(9))* Seachild.

Ruby, Laura. York: The Shadow Cipher. 2017. (York Ser.: 1). (ENG.). 496p. (J). (gr. 3-7). E-Book *(978-0-06-230695-1(2),* Waldon Pond Pr.) HarperCollins Pubs.

—York: The Shadow Cipher. Stevenson, Dave, illus. 2017. (York Ser.: 1). 496p. (J). (gr. 3-7). 17.99 *(978-0-06-230693-7(6),* Waldon Pond Pr.) HarperCollins Pubs.

Ruck-Pauquet, Gina. Los Ninos Mas Encantadores del Mundo. 2003. (SPA.). 192p. (J). (gr. 3-5). 8.95 *(978-84-204-4772-8(2))* Ediciones Alfaguara ESP. Dist: Santillana USA Publishing Co., Inc.

Rucker, Noah. Mystery of the Shadows. 2005. 27p. (J). 5.00 *(978-1-882695-21-8(6))* Patagonia Pr.

Ruckman, Ivy. Night of the Twisters. 2003. (Trophy Bk.). (ENG.). 160p. (J). (gr. 3-6). reprint ed. pap. 7.99 *(978-0-06-440176-0(6))* HarperCollins Pubs.

Rudnick, Elizabeth. Hulk Versus the World, 1 vol. Marvel Illustrators, illus. 2012. (Avengers: Earth's Mightiest Heroes! Ser.). (ENG.). 24p. (J). (gr. -1-4). lib. bdg. 24.21 *(978-1-61479-002-0(7))* Spotlight.

—Iron Man Is Born, 1 vol. Marvel Illustrators, illus. 2012. (Avengers: Earth's Mightiest Heroes! Ser.). (ENG.). 24p. (J). (gr. -1-4). lib. bdg. 24.21 *(978-1-61479-003-7(5))* Spotlight.

Ruebush, McKenna. Enter a Glossy Web. Zollars, Jaime, illus. 2016. (ENG.). 400p. (YA). 16.99 *(978-1-62779-370-4(4),* 9781627793704, Holt, Henry & Co. Bks. For Young Readers) Holt, Henry & Co.

Ruellan, Susan. The Lost Treasure of Finistere. 2008. (ENG & FRE., Illus.). 83p. (J). (gr. 4-7). pap. 9.95 *(978-1-933916-24-8(9))* Nelson Publishing & Marketing.

Ruggiero, Wilma. The Orange Barnge. 2011. 40p. 24.00 *(978-1-4520-9778-7(X))* AuthorHouse.

Ruiz, Jackson. It's Cool in the Furnace: The first graphic novel by Jackson Ruiz. 2010. 32p. pap. 16.99 *(978-1-4520-2634-3(3))* AuthorHouse.

Rule, Rebecca. The Iciest, Diciest, Scariest Sled Ride Ever!, 1 vol. Thermes, Jennifer, illus. 2012. (ENG.). 36p. (J). 17.95 *(978-1-934031-88-9(7),* 7e0b5554-6142-497e-ae8f-c0cb24d9743a) Islandport Pr., Inc.

Ruley, Garrett. Hollin. 2011. 226p. pap. 15.00 *(978-0-557-55873-5(5))* Lulu Pr., Inc.

Rumble, Chris. My Dad Is Coming to Career Day but Hopefully the Earth Will Be Destroyed. 2013. 218p. pap. 8.95 *(978-0-9832491-2-2(1))* Thunder Enlightening.

Rundell, Katherine. The Explorer. 2017. (ENG., Illus.). 336p. (J). (gr. 3-7). 16.99 ***(978-1-4814-1945-1(5),*** Simon & Schuster Bks. For Young Readers) Simon & Schuster Bks. For Young Readers.

Rundstrom, Teressa. The Adventures of Tommy Toad. Marshall, Setsu, illus. 2004. 40p. (J). per. *(978-1-932062-41-0(6))* Hability Solution Services, Inc.

—I Love to Leap! Miller, Bryan, illus. 2004. 35p. (J). per. *(978-1-932062-42-7(4))* Hability Solution Services, Inc.

Rupp, Rebecca. The Dragon of Lonely Island. 2006. (Dragon of Lonely Island Ser.). (ENG.). 192p. (J). (gr. 4-7). 6.99 *(978-0-7636-2805-5(0))* Candlewick Pr.

Ruppelius, Jeffrey & Ruppelius, Conrad. Conrad's Hiking Adventure. Ruppelius, Conrad, illus. 2006. (Illus.). (J). per. 12.95 *(978-0-9774143-3-8(7))* Little Dog Pubns.

Rusch, Elizabeth. Muddy Max: The Mystery of Marsh Creek. Lawrence, Mike, illus. 2014. (ENG.). 224p. (J). pap. 9.99 *(978-1-4494-3561-5(0))* Andrews McMeel Publishing.

Rusch, Elizabeth & Lawrence, Mike. Muddy Max: The Mystery of Marsh Creek. 2016. (ENG., Illus.). (J). (gr. 2-6). 37.99 ***(978-1-4494-7388-4(1))*** Andrews McMeel Publishing.

Rushdie, Salman. Luka & the Fire of Life. 2009. 14.75 *(978-0-7848-3731-3(7),* Everbind) Marco Bk. Co.

—Luka & the Fire of Life. 2011. (ENG.). 240p. (J). (gr. 7). pap. 17.00 *(978-0-679-78347-3(4),* Random Hse. Trade Paperbacks) Random House Publishing Group.

Russell, Allyson. The Lizard Who Wanted to Be a Mouse. Bubp, Jennifer, illus. 2009. 28p. pap. 12.95 *(978-1-59858-938-2(5))* Dog Ear Publishing, LLC.

Russell, B. M. My Friend Bianca. 2010. 32p. 13.95 *(978-1-4497-0168-0(X),* WestBow Pr.) Author Solutions, Inc.

Russell Brown, Eleanor. The Ring of Rats: An Other World Dimension. 2009. 28p. pap. 12.99 *(978-1-4490-0393-7(1))* AuthorHouse.

Russell, Christopher & Russell, Christine. Warrior Sheep Go Jurassic. 2014. (Warrior Sheep Ser.). (ENG.). 256p. (J). (gr. 2-4). pap. 7.99 *(978-1-4052-6718-2(6))* Egmont Bks., Ltd. GBR. Dist: Independent Pubs. Group.

Russell, Elaine. Martin Mcmillan & the Lost Inca City. Cornell du Houx, Emily M. D., illus. 2005. 128p. (gr. 5-18). pap. 10.00 *(978-1-882190-86-7(6))* Polar Bear & Co.

Russell, J. L. Sugabear Goes to Bed. 2010. 24p. pap. 15.99 *(978-1-4535-2940-9(3))* Xlibris Corp.

Russell, James. The Dragon Riders. Choi, Link, illus. 2017. (Dragon Brothers Ser.: 3). (ENG.). 32p. (J). (-4). 16.99 ***(978-1-4926-4867-3(1),*** Sourcebooks Jabberwocky) Sourcebooks, Inc.

Russell, John. Sam & Socrates. 2012. 60p. (gr. 4-6). pap. 8.95 *(978-1-4620-6830-2(8))* iUniverse, Inc.

Russell, Maureen Annette. MR & Mrs Universe & Their Four Best Friends. Caiafa, Laura, illus. 2017. (ENG.). (J). (gr. k-2). ***(978-1-84327-934-1(7))*** Electric Bk. Co.

Russell, P. M. The Wormhole Adventures: Travel Is Relative. 2007. 57p. pap. 16.95 *(978-1-60441-426-4(X))* America Star Bks.

Russell, Peggy. Patsy Goes to a New Home: The Patsy Adventures Volume 1. Scott, Larry, illus. 2008. 16p. pap. 24.95 *(978-1-60703-799-6(8))* America Star Bks.

Russell-Peter, Jasmine. Biddle in the Middle. 2013. 28p. pap. 17.99 *(978-1-4817-0295-9(5))* AuthorHouse.

Russell, Rachel Renée. Middle School Mayhem. Russell, Rachel Renée, illus. 2017. (Misadventures of Max Crumbly Ser.: 2). (ENG., Illus.). 240p. (J). (gr. 4-8). 13.99 ***(978-1-4814-6003-3(X),*** Aladdin) Simon & Schuster Children's Publishing.

Russell, Sharman Apt. Teresa of the New World. 2015. (ENG.). 192p. (gr. 6). 14.99 *(978-1-63158-042-0(6),* Yucca Publishing) Skyhorse Publishing Co., Inc.

Russo, Anthony. Abby. Sampson, Jody, illus. 2003. 18p. (J). 7.95 *(978-1-59466-006-1(9),* Little Ones) Port Town Publishing.

Russo, Bud. The Magic Picture. 2007. 156p. pap. 10.95 *(978-1-4357-0110-6(0))* Lulu Pr., Inc.

Russo, Mary. The Adventures of Wizahickon. 2010. 28p. pap. 13.99 *(978-1-4520-1831-7(6))* AuthorHouse.

Rust, Ned. Patrick Griffin's First Birthday on Ith. 2017. (Patrick Griffin & the Three Worlds Ser.: 2). (ENG.). 304p. (J). 16.99 *(978-1-62672-344-3(3),* 9781626723443) Roaring Brook Pr.

Rustrian, Edvin E. The Adventures of Timmy & Jay. 2010. 24p. pap. 15.99 *(978-1-4535-3792-3(9))* Xlibris Corp.

Rusu, Meredith. Charmer Girls Rock! 2016. (Scholastic Reader, Level 1 Ser.). (ENG.). 32p. (J). (gr. -1-1). pap. 5.99 *(978-1-338-03730-2(7))* Scholastic, Inc.

—Legend of the Brown Ninja. 2016. (LEGO Ninjago Ser.). (ENG.). 80p. (J). (gr. 2-5). pap. 4.99 *(978-1-338-04466-9(4))* Scholastic, Inc.

—Legend of the Brown Ninja. 2016. (LEGO Ninjago Chapter Bks.: 10). (ENG.). 80p. (J). (gr. 2-5). 14.75 *(978-0-606-39151-1(7))* Turtleback Bks.

—A Merry Shopkins Christmas. 2016. (Shopkins Ser.). (ENG.). 24p. (J). (gr. -1-3). pap. 4.99 *(978-1-338-03800-2(1))* Scholastic, Inc.

—The New Ninja. 2016. (Illus.). 78p. (J). ***(978-1-5182-0305-3(1))*** Scholastic, Inc.

—Police Pursuit! 2017. (LEGO City 8X8 Ser.). lib. bdg. 13.55 ***(978-0-606-39732-2(9))*** Turtleback Bks.

—Python's Revenge. 2017. (LEGO Ninjago Chapter Bks.: 11). lib. bdg. 14.75 ***(978-0-606-39733-9(7))*** Turtleback Bks.

Ruth, Greg. The Lost Boy. 2013. (ENG.). 192p. (J). (gr. 3-7). pap. 12.99 *(978-0-439-82332-6(3),* Graphix) Scholastic, Inc.

Ruth-Kilgore, Chanacee. Alphabet Soup. 2012. 108p. pap. 9.99 *(978-1-936453-13-9(4))* Bezalel Bks.

Rutledge, Eddie. Amani's World: Amani & Friends Go to New York City. 2012. 24p. pap. 17.99 *(978-1-4772-9554-0(2))* AuthorHouse.

—Amani's World: Amani Goes to Washington D. C. Anderson, Susan, illus. 2009. 16p. pap. 8.75 *(978-1-4490-2095-8(X))* AuthorHouse.

Rutley, Erika L. Adventures in Pup-A-Dupping. 2012. 36p. pap. 24.95 *(978-1-62709-710-9(4))* America Star Bks.

Ruzima, Keza. Girl Power: The Adventures of a Teenage Circle. 2009. 112p. pap. 23.75 (978-1-60860-647-4(3), Eloquent Bks.) Strategic Book Publishing & Rights Agency (SBPRA).

Ruzycki, Dan Dan. The Adventures of Pillow Head: The Fallen Star. Hunter, Robbie Chase, illus. 2012. 26p. (J). 13.95 (978-0-9834315-5-8(8)) Dan Dan Fantasy.

Ruzzier, Sergio. Two Mice. 2015. (ENG., Illus.). 32p. (J). (gr. -1-3). 12.99 (978-0-544-30209-9(5)) Houghton Mifflin Harcourt Publishing Co.

Ryals, Marie M. Mama, Tell about It: The Helen Stories. 2010. 38p. (J). pap. 16.95 (978-1-4327-4664-3(2)) Outskirts Pr., Inc.

Ryan, Carol. A Bridge Through Time, 1 vol. 2010. 276p. pap. 27.95 (978-1-4489-4254-1(3)) PublishAmerica, Inc.

Ryan, Carrie. Divide & Conquer. 2012. (Infinity Ring Ser.: 2). (ENG.). 192p. (J). (gr. 3-7). 16.99 (978-0-545-48455-8(3)); 12.99 (978-0-545-38697-5(7)) Scholastic, Inc.

Ryan, Carrie & Davis, John Parke. City of Thirst. (Map to Everywhere Ser.: 2). (ENG., Illus.). (J). (gr. 3-7). 2016. 416p. pap. 7.99 (978-0-316-24082-6(6)) 2015. 400p. 17.00 (978-0-316-24084-0(2)) Little, Brown Bks. for Young Readers.

—The Map to Everywhere. 2014. (Map to Everywhere Ser.: Bk. 1). (ENG., Illus.). 448p. (J). (gr. 3-7). 17.00 (978-0-316-24077-2(X)) Little Brown & Co.

—The Map to Everywhere. 2015. (Map to Everywhere Ser.: 1). (ENG., Illus.). 464p. (J). (gr. 3-7). pap. 8.99 (978-0-316-24078-9(8)) Little, Brown Bks. for Young Readers.

—Shadows of the Lost Sun. 2017. (Map to Everywhere Ser.: 3). (ENG., Illus.). 368p. (J). (gr. 3-7). 17.99 (978-0-316-24088-8(5)) Little, Brown Bks. for Young Readers.

Ryan, Frank P. The Snowmelt River. 2013. (Three Powers Ser.: 1). (ENG.). 720p. (J). (gr. 7-17). 15.95 (978-1-62365-048-3(8), Jo Fletcher Books) Quercus NA.

Ryan, Jeanne. Nerve. (ENG.). (YA). (gr. 9). 2012. 304p. 17.99 (978-0-8037-3832-4(3), Dial Bks) 2016. 320p. pap. 10.99 (978-0-14-242283-0(5), Speak) Penguin Young Readers Group.

Ryan, John. Pugwash Aloft. Ryan, John, illus. 2008. (ENG., Illus.). 32p. (J). (gr. -1-2). 16.95 (978-1-84507-822-5(5), Frances Lincoln) Quarto Publishing Group UK GBR. Dist: Hachette Bk. Group.

Ryan, Tom. Tag Along, 1 vol. 2013. (ENG.). 208p. (YA). (gr. 8-12). pap. 12.95 (978-1-4598-0297-1(7)) Orca Bk. Pubs. USA.

Rycroft, Frederick. Young World: Book Two - Friends 'Til the End. 2012. 568p. pap. 23.99 (978-1-4797-1311-0(2)) Xlibris Corp.

Ryherd, Saundra. The Adventures of Sparky, 1 vol. 2009. 48p. pap. 16.95 (978-1-60813-516-5(0)) America Star Bks.

Ryland, John B., told to. Wisdom for the Little People. 2005. (Illus.). (J). pap. (978-0-9743985-2-5(7)) DJ Blues Publishing.

Rylander, Chris. Codename Zero. (Codename Conspiracy Ser.: 1). (ENG.). (J). (gr. 3-7). 2015. 384p. pap. 6.99 (978-0-06-212009-0(3)) 2014. 368p. 16.99 (978-0-06-212008-3(5)) HarperCollins Pubs. (Walden Pond Pr.).

—Countdown Zero. (Codename Conspiracy Ser.: 2). (J). (gr. 3-7). 2016. 384p. pap. 6.99 (978-0-06-212012-0(3)) 2015. (ENG.). 368p. 16.99 (978-0-06-212011-3(5)) HarperCollins Pubs. (Waldon Pond Pr.).

—The Fourth Stall, Pt. 3. 2014. (Fourth Stall Ser.: 3). (ENG.). 320p. (J). (gr. 3-7). pap. 6.99 (978-0-06-212006-9(9), Waldon Pond Pr.) HarperCollins Pubs.

Rylant, Cynthia. Henry & Mudge Ready-To-Read Value Pack #2: Henry & Mudge & the Long Weekend; Henry & Mudge & the Bedtime Thumps; Henry & Mudge & the Big Sleepover; Henry & Mudge & the Funny Lunch; Henry & Mudge & the Great Grandpas; Henry & Mudge & the Tall Tree House. Stevenson, Suçie, illus. 2013. (Henry & Mudge Ser.). (ENG.). 240p. (J). (gr. k-2). pap. 15.96 (978-1-4424-9441-1(7), Simon Spotlight) Simon Spotlight.

—The High-Rise Private Eyes Series. Karas, G. Brian, illus. 2003. pap. 61.95 incl. audio (978-1-59112-430-6(1)); pap. 68.95 incl. audio compact disk (978-1-59112-858-8(7)) Live Oak Media.

—La Tormenta. 2012.Tr. of Storm. (SPA.). 104p. (gr. 3-5). pap. 10.99 (978-958-04-7077-9(4)) Norma S.A. COL. Dist: Lectorum Pubns., Inc.

—The Whale. McDaniels, Preston, illus. (Lighthouse Family Ser.: 2). (ENG.). 64p. (J). (gr. 1-5). 2004. pap. 5.99 (978-0-689-84883-4(8)) 2003. 15.99 (978-0-689-84881-0(1)) Simon & Schuster Bks. For Young Readers. (Simon & Schuster Bks. For Young Readers).

Rymas-Loomis, Cathy. Calamity Clancey: The Calamity Cat from Kalvesta Kansas. 2007. 40p. per. 12.97 (978-1-932344-85-1(3)) Thornton Publishing, Inc.

Ryshpan-Harris, Joanne. The Great Adventures of Bottom the Bassett Hound. Bouganim, Revital, illus. 2008. 60p. (J). pap. 5.95 (978-1-4259-8558-5(0)) AuthorHouse.

S. P. Glynn, Annie S. P. Glynn. Jodie's Adventures with Aunty Ann. 2016. (ENG.). 26p. (J). (gr. 3-4). mass mkt. 10.95 (978-1-78612-838-6(1), 66ce91c5-aae4-4fb3-864f-1d2ff1cbc8b5) Austin, Stan AUS. Dist: Bookmasters Distribution.

Sabo-Western, Deborah. Peter Penny: Discovers the Gift. 2007. (ENG.). 46p. pap. 15.99 (978-1-4196-8115-8(X)) CreateSpace Independent Publishing Platform.

Sackanay, Kathleen. Adventures in the Forest. Wood, Morgan, illus. 2007. 24p. (J). pap. 8.45 (978-0-9791276-2-5(9)) Athanatos Publishing Group.

Sackett, Frances. The Misadventures of the Magician's Dog. 2013. (ENG.). 192p. (J). (gr. 2-7). 16.95 (978-0-8234-2869-4(9)) Holiday Hse., Inc.

Saddleback Educational Publishing Staff, creator. Barclay Family Adventures Resource Guide. 2003. (Barclay Family Adventure Ser.). 48p. tchr. ed., per. 9.95 (978-1-56254-560-4(4), SP 5604) Saddleback Educational Publishing, Inc.

Saddleback Educational Publishing Staff, ed. Camp, 1 vol. unabr. ed. 2011. (Heights Ser.). (ENG.). 50p. (gr. 5-8). pap. 7.95 (978-1-61651-284-2(9)) Saddleback Educational Publishing, Inc.

—Sail, 1 vol. unabr. ed. 2011. (Heights Ser.). (ENG.). 50p. (gr. 5-8). 7.95 (978-1-61651-622-2(4)) Saddleback Educational Publishing, Inc.

—Twister, 1 vol. unabr. ed. 2011. (Heights Ser.). (ENG.). 49p. (gr. 5-8). 7.95 (978-1-61651-626-0(7)) Saddleback Educational Publishing, Inc.

Sage, Angie. Araminta Spookie: The Sword in the Grotto. Pickering, Jimmy, illus. 2006. (Araminta Spookie Ser.: Bk. 2). 160p. (J). (gr. 2-5). 8.99 (978-0-06-077484-4(3), Tegen, Katherine Bks) HarperCollins Pubs.

—Frognapped. Pickering, Jimmy, illus. 2007. (Araminta Spookie Ser.: Bk. 3). (J). (gr. 2-5). 128p. 8.99 (978-0-06-077487-5(8)); 208p. lib. bdg. 14.89 (978-0-06-077488-2(6)) HarperCollins Pubs. (Tegen, Katherine Bks).

—Pathfinder. 2015. (Septimus Heap: TodHunter Moon Ser.: 1). (J). lib. bdg. 18.40 (978-0-606-37612-9(7)) Turtleback Bks.

—The Sword in the Grotto. Pickering, Jimmy, illus. 2008. (Araminta Spookie Ser.: 2). (ENG.). 176p. (J). (gr. 2-5). pap. 5.99 (978-0-06-077486-8(X), Tegen, Katherine Bks) HarperCollins Pubs.

—Todhunter Moon. Zug, Mark, illus. 2015. (World of Septimus Heap Ser.: 1). (ENG.). 496p. (J). (gr. 3-7). pap. 7.99 (978-0-06-227246-1(2), Tegen, Katherine Bks) HarperCollins Pubs.

—Vampire Brat. Pickering, Jimmy, illus. (Araminta Spookie Ser.: 4). (J). (gr. 2-5). 2009. (ENG.). 224p. pap. 6.99 (978-0-06-077492-9(4), Tegen, Katherine Bks) 2007. 128p. 8.99 (978-0-06-077490-5(8)) HarperCollins Pubs.

Sage, Cathryn. Destiny's Secret. 2012. 44p. (-18). pap. 21.99 (978-1-4389-1530-2(6)) AuthorHouse.

Sage, David. Adzul, the Heirs of the Medallion Book 1. 2013. 168p. pap. 7.99 (978-0-9894210-0-3(7)) Sage, David.

Sagner, Sibel, et al. A Day at the Museum Blue Band. Pérez, Moni, illus. 2016. (Cambridge Reading Adventures Ser.). (ENG.). 16p. pap. 6.56 (978-1-316-50320-1(8)) Cambridge Univ. Pr.

Saha, Tulika. 'Kosho & Sid on the Rainbow' 2014. 22p. pap. 13.99 (978-1-4828-1762-1(4)) Partridge Pub.

Sainlouis, Kercise. Danielle's Amazing Day. 2008. 24p. pap. 12.00 (978-1-4343-9990-8(7)) AuthorHouse.

Sainsbury, Kylee. Anna Banana Goes to Se. 2009. 32p. pap. 12.99 (978-1-4490-0222-0(6)) AuthorHouse.

Sakade, Florence & Hayashi, Yoshio. Urashima Taro & Other Japanese Children's Favorite Stories. Kurosaki, Yoshisuke, illus. 2008. (ENG.). 48p. (J). (gr. -1-3). 12.95 (978-4-8053-0997-1(0)) Tuttle Publishing.

Sakai, Stan. The Adventures of Nilson Groundthumper & Hermy. Wright, Brendan, ed. Sakai, Stan, illus. 2014. (ENG., Illus.). 112p. 14.99 (978-1-61655-341-8(3)) Dark Horse Comics.

—Usagi Yojimbo Vol. 4: Estaciones. 2007. (SPA., Illus.). 200p. reprint ed. pap. 15.95 (978-1-59497-320-8(2)) Public Square Bks.

—Usagi Yojimbo Vol. 5: Segadora. 2007. (SPA., Illus.). 256p. reprint ed. pap. 17.95 (978-1-59497-321-5(0)) Public Square Bks.

—Usagi Yojimbo Vol. 6: Primeras Andanzas. 2007. (SPA., Illus.). 128p. reprint ed. pap. 12.95 (978-1-59497-322-2(9)) Public Square Bks.

—Usagi Yojimbo Vol. 7: Samurai (en Español) 2007. (SPA., Illus.). 144p. reprint ed. pap. 14.95 (978-1-59497-323-9(7)) Public Square Bks.

Sakowski, Nadeen. The Adventures of Bailey Wiggins. 2009. 70p. pap. 26.50 (978-0-557-06610-0(7)) Lulu Pr., Inc.

Sala, George Augustus. Captain Dangerous. 2011. 130p. 24.95 (978-1-4638-9899-1(1)); 126p. pap. 10.95 (978-1-4638-0141-0(6)); 130p. pap. 10.95 (978-1-4638-0140-3(8)); 124p. pap. 10.95 (978-1-4638-0142-7(4)) Rodgers, Alan Bks.

Salane, Jeffrey. Justice. 2015. (ENG.). 288p. (J). (gr. 3-7). 16.99 (978-0-545-45031-7(4), Scholastic Pr.) Scholastic, Inc.

—The Lego Movie. Kiernan, Kenny, illus. 2013. (ENG.). 64p. (J). (gr. 2-5). pap. 5.99 (978-0-545-62462-6(2)) Scholastic, Inc.

—Mayhem. 2016. (Lawless Ser.: 3). (ENG.). 304p. (J). (gr. 3-7). 17.99 (978-0-545-45033-1(0), Scholastic Pr.) Scholastic, Inc.

Salas-Tristan, M. U. Rocky's ABC Book with His Friends: Photographic Bilingual. 2012. (ENG.). 32p. (J). pap. 29.95 (978-1-4327-9381-4(0)) Outskirts Pr., Inc.

Salazar, L. J. Chin & the Magic Stones: Book One - Becoming Guardians. 2009. 108p. 20.95 (978-0-595-63627-3(6)); pap. 10.95 (978-0-595-53157-8(1)) iUniverse, Inc.

Saldaña, René. The Lemon Tree Caper: A Mickey Rangel Mystery / la Intriga del limonero: Colección Mickey Rangel, detective Privado. Rosales-Yeomans, Natalia, tr. from ENG. 2011. (SPA & ENG.). (J). pap. 9.95 (978-1-55885-709-4(5), Piñata Books) Arte Publico Pr.

Saldivar, Jose A. The Adventures of Oskar: Oskar's New School. Nilsson, Janet Busbey, ed. Jasnoch, Dorothy, illus. 2013. 32p. pap. 13.99 (978-1-937752-14-9(3)) Owl About Bks. Pub., Inc.

Salerno, Tony. Dog Tired: A Learning Adventure in Perseverance, 4 vols. 2005. 56p. (J). 14.99 (978-0-89221-605-5(0)) New Leaf Pub. Group.

—A Sticky Situation: A Learning Adventure in Honesty. 2005. 56p. (J). 14.99 (978-0-89221-606-2(9)) New Leaf Pub. Group.

—Wise Quacks: A Learning Adventure in Self-Control, 4 vols. 2005. 56p. (J). 14.99 (978-0-89221-604-8(2)) New Leaf Pub. Group.

Salisbury, Linda. Earthquake Surprise: A Bailey Fish Adventure. Tornatore, Carol, illus. 2012. 192p. (J). pap. 8.95 (978-1-881539-65-0(2)) Tabby Hse. Bks.

Salmassian, Jennifer. Sally Saves the Mice. 2007. (J). per. 0.01 net. (978-1-60402-115-8(2)) Independent Pub.

—Sally the Firefighter. 2007. (J). per. 0.01 net. (978-1-60402-164-6(0)) Independent Pub.

Salmon, Casey. The Adventures of Mabel & Stinky: Mabel, Stinky, & the Terrified Toad. 2009. 44p. pap. 19.99 (978-1-4389-7454-5(X)) AuthorHouse.

Salmon, Nina. Nola & the Sprickle. 2012. 232p. pap. (978-1-78148-137-0(7)) Grosvenor Hse. Publishing Ltd.

Salmon, Sheryl. The Adventures of Kaptain Kristian. 2010. 68p. pap. 9.99 (978-1-60911-829-7(4), Eloquent Bks.) Strategic Book Publishing & Rights Agency (SBPRA).

Salote, Ana. Oy Yew. 2013. 276p. pap. (978-1-78299-659-0(1)) FeedARead.com.

Salsi, Lynn. Jack & the Giants. Young, James, illus. 2012. (ENG.). 32p. (J). 16.95 (978-0-938467-52-6(2)) Headline Bks., Inc.

Salten, Felix. A Forest World. Greenburger, Sanford Jerome & Milton, Paul R., trs. 2013. (Bambi's Classic Animal Tales Ser.). (ENG., Illus.). 288p. (J). (gr. 3-7). pap. 6.99 (978-1-4424-8637-9(6), Aladdin) Simon & Schuster Children's Publishing.

—A Forest World. Greenburger, Sanford Jerome & Milton, Paul R., trs. 2013. (Bambi's Classic Animal Tales Ser.). (ENG., Illus.). 288p. (J). (gr. 3-7). 16.99 (978-1-4424-8638-6(4), Simon & Schuster/Paula Wiseman Bks.) Simon & Schuster/Paula Wiseman Bks.

Salti, Kim. Riley's Imagination Super Highway - Adventures in Dreamworld. 2012. 56p. pap. 12.00 (978-1-105-81460-0(2)) Lulu Pr., Inc.

Salzman, Jeremiah. The Day of the Sandwich. Smith, Stephan, illus. 2010. (Very Small Adventures of Daisie Pup! Ser.). 48p. (J). pap. 8.99 (978-0-9842632-8-8(4)) Scandora.

—Mike's Adventure Packs: England. Smith, Stephan, illus. 2010. (Mike's Adventure Packs Ser.). 144p. (J). pap. 16.95 (978-0-9842632-5-7(X)) Scandora.

Sambar, Syma. This Is Olivia. Spaziante, Patrick, illus. 2009. (Olivia TV Tie-In Ser.). (ENG.). 12p. (J). (gr. -1-2). 7.99 (978-1-4169-8709-3(6), Simon Spotlight) Simon Spotlight.

Sammartino, Joseph & Ozimkowski, Edward. The Legend of Kringle. 2009. 48p. pap. 19.95 (978-1-4490-5241-6(X)) AuthorHouse.

Sammel, Rocheile. Tales of Two Mouse Brothers. 2008. 45p. pap. 24.95 (978-1-4241-9798-6(8)) America Star Bks.

Samphire, Patrick. The Emperor of Mars. Holmes, Jeremy, illus. 2017. (Secrets of the Dragon Tomb Ser.). (ENG.). 368p. (J). 16.99 (978-0-8050-9908-9(5), 9780805099089, Holt, Henry & Co. Bks. For Young Readers) Holt, Henry & Co.

Sample, Matthew C. What a Day! 2010. 20p. pap. 12.49 (978-1-4389-9853-4(8)) AuthorHouse.

Sampson, Brent. Aidan's Shoes. Switzer, Bobbi, illus. 2006. (ENG.). 28p. per. 12.95 (978-1-59800-684-1(3)) Outskirts Pr., Inc.

—One Wacky Wasp: The Perfect Children's Book for Kids Ages 3-6 Who Are Learning to Read. 2010. 24p. (J). 14.95 (978-1-4327-6217-9(6)); pap. 9.95 (978-1-4327-0465-0(6)) Outskirts Pr., Inc.

Sams, Carl R., II & Stoick, Jean. Lost in the Woods: A Photographic Fantasy. Herrick, Mark J., illus. 2005. (Connect-It Ser.). 68p. (J). (gr. -1-3). pap. 24.95 (978-0-9749412-2-6(0)) EDCO Publishing, Inc.

Sams, Laura & Sams, Robert. A Pirate's Quest: For His Family Heirloom Peg Leg. Hertling, Heiner, illus. 2008. 48p. (J). 19.95 (978-0-9770108-7-5(2)) Sams, II, Carl R. Photography, Inc.

Samuel, Josiah C. Mr. Tortoise Funny Life, Bk. 1. 2013. 132p. pap. 45.07 (978-1-4669-9904-6(7)) Trafford Publishing.

Samuel, R. Skull & Bones: A Pirate's Odyssey. 2011. 192p. (gr. 1-2). 27.99 (978-1-4634-0319-5(4)); (gr. 10-12). pap. 18.49 (978-1-4634-0320-1(8)) AuthorHouse.

Samuels, Vallerie. The Village of Time. 2005. 9.00 (978-0-8059-9709-5(1)) Dorrance Publishing Co., Inc.

Sanchez, Anita. The Invasion of Sandy Bay. 2008. (ENG.). 148p. (J). (gr. 5-7). 16.95 (978-1-59078-560-7(6), Calkins Creek) Boyds Mills Pr.

Sanchez, Kevin & Sanchez, Laura. Nikki's Hurricane Adventure. 2011. 24p. pap. 11.32 (978-1-4567-1452-9(X)) AuthorHouse.

Sanchez, Priscilla. Champ the Boxing Boxer. 2011. 12p. pap. 8.32 (978-1-4634-7423-2(7)) AuthorHouse.

Sandemose, Iben. Gracie & Grandma. Sandemose, Iben, illus. 2008. (Gracie & Grandma Ser.). (Illus.). 36p. (J). (gr. -1-1). 14.95 (978-0-9790347-3-2(6)) Mackenzie Smiles, LLC.

Sander, Sonia. Calling All Cars! 2010. (Lego City Ser.). (ENG.). 32p. (J). (gr. -1-k). pap. 3.99 (978-0-545-15523-6(1)) Scholastic, Inc.

—Help Is on the Way! 2009. (Lego City Ser.). (ENG.). 32p. (J). (gr. -1-k). pap. 3.99 (978-0-545-15068-2(X)) Scholastic, Inc.

—Scooby-Doo in Shiver Me Timbers, 1 vol. 2016. (Scooby-Doo! Set 3 Ser.). (ENG., Illus.). 32p. (J). (gr. k-4). lib. bdg. 24.21 (978-1-61479-408-0(1), 1401184) Spotlight.

Sander, Sonia & Scieszka, Jon. Smash That Trash! Shannon, David et al, illus. 2009. (Jon Scieszka's Trucktown Ser.). (ENG.). 14p. (J). (gr. -1-k). 7.99 (978-1-4169-4180-4(0), Little Simon) Little Simon.

Sanders, Alex. Un Lobo! (SPA.). 36p. (978-84-95150-34-9(4)) Corimbo, Editorial S.L.

—Un Lobo! (SPA.). 36p. 16.95 (978-84-95150-24-0(7)) Corimbo, Editorial S.L. ESP. Dist: Distribooks, Inc.

Sanders, E. T. Ninja Grandm. 2012. 24p. pap. 28.03 (978-1-4691-9063-1(X)) Xlibris Corp.

Sanders, Gaye Lynn. Chameleon Girl Again. 2012. 86p. 19.95 (978-1-4626-7378-0(3)) America Star Bks.

Sanders, Jeane F. Ramón. 2008. 100p. pap. 19.95 (978-1-60610-768-3(2)) America Star Bks.

Sanders, Stephanie & Pauling, Galen T. Q. T. Pie's Rescue Adventure. 2003. (Illus.). 36p. (J). (gr. -1-6). mass mkt. 4.99 (978-0-9670875-3-5(8), 313-533-7383) SanPaul Group, LLC, The.

Sanders, Stephanie S. Villain School: Good Curses Evil. 2011. (ENG.). 240p. (YA). (gr. 3-12). pap. 6.99 (978-1-59990-848-9(4), 9781599908489, Bloomsbury USA Childrens) Bloomsbury Publishing USA.

Sanders, Ted. The Keepers #2: the Harp & the Ravenvine. Bruno, Iacopo, illus. 2017. (Keepers Ser.: 2). 688p. (J). (gr. 3-7). pap. 7.99 (978-0-06-227586-8(0)) HarperCollins Pubs.

Sanders, Ted. The Keepers #3: the Portal & the Veil. 2017. (Keepers Ser.: 3). 592p. (J). (gr. 3-7). 16.99 **(978-0-06-227588-2(7))** HarperCollins Pubs.

Sanderson, Brandon. Calamity. (Reckoners Ser.). (ENG.). (YA). (gr. 7). 2017. 448p. pap. 10.99 (978-0-385-74361-7(0), Ember) 2016. 432p. lib. bdg. 21.99 (978-0-375-99123-3(9), Delacorte Pr.) 2016. 432p. 18.99 (978-0-385-74360-0(2), Delacorte Pr.) Random Hse. Children's Bks.

—Firefight. 2016. (SPA.). 432p. pap. 28.95 (978-84-666-5836-2(X)) Ediciones B ESP. Dist: Spanish Pubs., LLC.

—Firefight. (Reckoners Ser.: Bk. 2). (ENG.). (YA). (gr. 7). 2016. 448p. pap. 10.99 (978-0-385-74359-4(9), Ember) 2015. 432p. 18.99 (978-0-385-74358-7(0), Delacorte Pr.) Random Hse. Children's Bks.

—Firefight. 2016. (Reckoners Ser.: 2). lib. bdg. 22.10 (978-0-606-38447-6(2)) Turtleback Bks.

—The Reckoners, 3 vols. 2016. (ENG.). (YA). (gr. 7). 56.97 (978-0-399-55168-0(9), Delacorte Pr.) Random Hse. Children's Bks.

—Steelheart. (SPA.). 416p. pap. 27.95 (978-84-666-5296-4(5)); 2015. pap. 14.95 (978-84-9070-095-2(8)) Ediciones B ESP. Dist: Spanish Pubs., LLC.

—Steelheart. 2013. 386p. (YA). (978-0-385-38371-4(1), Delacorte Pr) Random House Publishing Group.

—Steelheart. (Reckoners Ser.: 1). (ENG.). (YA). (gr. 7). 2014. 416p. pap. 9.99 (978-0-385-74357-0(2), Ember) 2013. 400p. 18.99 (978-0-385-74356-3(4), Delacorte Pr.) Random Hse. Children's Bks.

—Steelheart. 2014. (Reckoners Ser.: 1). lib. bdg. 20.85 (978-0-606-36027-2(1)) Turtleback Bks.

Sanderson, Nancy. Summer of the Painted Horse. 2009. 188p. pap. 14.49 (978-1-4490-2312-6(6)) AuthorHouse.

Sandford, John, pseud & Cook, Michele. Outrage. 2015. (Singular Menace Ser.: Bk. 2). (ENG.). 336p. (YA). (gr. 9). 18.99 (978-0-385-75309-8(8), Knopf Bks. for Young Readers) Random Hse. Children's Bks.

—Rampage. (Singular Menace Ser.: 3). (ENG.). 336p. (YA). (gr. 9). 2017. pap. 10.99 (978-0-385-75315-9(2), Ember) 2016. 18.99 (978-0-385-75313-5(6), Knopf Bks. for Young Readers) Random Hse. Children's Bks.

—Uncaged. (Singular Menace Ser.: Bk. 1). (ENG.). 416p. (gr. 9). 2015. (YA). pap. 10.99 (978-0-385-75305-0(5), Ember) 2014. (J). 18.99 (978-0-385-75306-7(3), Knopf Bks. for Young Readers) 2014. (YA). lib. bdg. 21.99 (978-0-385-75307-4(1), Knopf Bks. for Young Readers) Random Hse. Children's Bks.

Sandifer, Audie Cavett. The Exciting Adventures of Eekie & Squeeky. 2011. 52p. (gr. -1). pap. 12.95 (978-1-4567-4289-8(2)) AuthorHouse.

Sandra De Mos. Cleo's Playground Adventure. 2009. 40p. pap. 16.99 (978-1-4389-2049-8(0)) AuthorHouse.

Sands, Kathryn N. Billy's Big Adventure. 2012. 32p. pap. 24.95 (978-1-4626-2327-3(1)) America Star Bks.

Sands, Kevin. The Blackthorn Key. 2016. lib. bdg. 18.40 (978-0-606-38966-2(0)) Turtleback Bks.

Sanford, Barry. The Shoes. 2007. 84p. per. 19.95 (978-1-4241-8700-3(1)) America Star Bks.

Sanford, Joyce. Goldenlocks & Her 3 Homes. 2013. (ENG.). 34p. (J). 24.95 (978-1-4787-0151-4(X)) Outskirts Pr., Inc.

Sanjo, Riku. Beet the Vandel Buster, Vol. 4. Inada, Koji, illus. 2005. (ENG.). 208p. pap. 7.99 (978-1-59116-750-1(7)) Viz Media.

Sankey, Alice. Roy Rogers & the Desert Treasure. Souza, Paul, illus. 2011. 26p. 35.95 (978-1-258-03927-1(3)) Literary Licensing, LLC.

Sansone, V. K. A Daunting Quest for Quincy & Quigley. 2009. 32p. pap. 8.98 (978-0-557-03594-6(5)) Lulu Pr., Inc.

—Katie Bear: Fun Days at School. WillowRaven, Aidana, illus. 2007. 84p. pap. 16.95 (978-0-9798154-7-8(9)) Living Waters Publishing Co.

Santacroce, John P. Running Across the Moon. 2013. 146p. pap. 14.98 (978-0-615-76887-8(3)) Santacroce, John.

Santaniello, Shelly W. Tommy's Needham Rocket. 2011. 53p. pap. 10.95 (978-1-4327-7000-6(4)) Outskirts Pr., Inc.

Sante, Andrew R. The Silver Heart Chronicles: The Voyage. 2012. 50p. 24.99 (978-1-4771-4700-9(4)); pap. 15.99 (978-1-4771-4699-6(7)) Xlibris Corp.

Santiago, Brianna A. Why Is the Moon Following Us? 2008. 16p. pap. 24.95 (978-1-60474-944-1(X)) America Star Bks.

Santiago, Chiori. Home to Medicine Mountain. Lowry, Judith, illus. 2013. (ENG.). 32p. (J). (gr. 1-18). pap. 12.95 (978-0-89239-176-9(6)) Lee & Low Bks., Inc.

Santiago, Shelly. The Fairies of Tythian. 2010. 40p. pap. 14.95 (978-1-60976-143-1(X), Eloquent Bks.) Strategic Book Publishing & Rights Agency (SBPRA).

Santini, Philip. Harvey's Adventures. Chambers, Z., illus. 2011. 44p. pap. 24.95 (978-1-4626-2078-4(7)) America Star Bks.

Santos, Ray. I Am Green Lantern. 2013. (Justice League Classic: I Can Read! Ser.). (J). lib. bdg. 13.55 (978-0-606-32152-5(7), Turtleback) Turtleback Bks.

Saper, Lee & Lee, Brian. The Tales of Tranquility. 2004. 178p. 23.95 (978-0-595-66392-7(3)) iUniverse, Inc.

Sapp, Brent. Teknon & the Champion Warriors. Cariello, Sergio, illus. 2003. 7.99 (978-1-57229-219-2(9)) FamilyLife.

Sapre, Reshma. Patnaxi's Crazy Long Journey Home. 2012. (ENG.). 40p. 16.95 (978-0-9829362-1-4(4)) Hathi Chiti Bks. for Kids.

Sargeant, Glen. Ghost Ship: A y-Files Mystery. 2012. 128p. pap. 19.95 (978-1-4626-8020-7(8)) America Star Bks.

Sargeant, Theresa. The Drainpipe Gang - the Adventures of Chris & Andy Smy. 2011. 112p. pap. (978-1-907256-80-6(6)) Abela Publishing.

Sargent, Alan E. Fortitude: The Adventures of the Esteem Team. Wade, Jerry, illus. 2013. 84p. pap. 10.95 (978-1-62516-984-6(1), Strategic Bk. Publishing) Strategic Book Publishing & Rights Agency (SBPRA).

Sargent-Barker, Erika. Casey Moore, the Littlest Leprechaun, 1 vol. 2010. 16p. pap. 24.95 (978-1-4489-5419-3(3)) PublishAmerica, Inc.

Sargent, Dave. Hiding Place #4, 10 vols. 2007. (Little Stinker Ser.: 4). (J). lib. bdg. 23.60 (978-1-59381-282-9(5)) Ozark Publishing.

—Hiding Place #4 (PB), 10 vols. 2007. (Little Stinker Ser.: 4). (J). pap. 10.95 (978-1-59381-283-6(3)) Ozark Publishing.

—Sammy's Hiding Place #9, 10 vols. 2007. (Little Stinker Ser.: 9). (J). lib. bdg. 23.60 (978-1-59381-297-3(3)) Ozark Publishing.

—Sammy's Hiding Place #9 (PB), 10 vols. 2007. (Little Stinker Ser.: 9). (J). pap. 10.95 (978-1-59381-298-0(1)) Ozark Publishing.

—Tornado & Sweep, Bk. II. Bowen, Debbie, ed. Zapata, Miguel, tr. from ENG. Lenoir, Jane, illus. (SPA.). (Orig.). (J). (gr. k-6). pap. 6.95 (978-1-56763-126-5(6)); pap. 6.95 (978-1-56763-123-4(1)) Ozark Publishing.

Sargent, Dave & Sargent, Pat. Big Jake: I'm Very Curious, 56 vols., Vol. 12. Huff, Jeane, illus. 2nd rev. ed. 2003. (Animal Pride Ser.: 12). 42p. (J). lib. bdg. 20.95 (978-1-56763-781-6(7)) Ozark Publishing.

—The Chuck Wagon: Don't Be Stubborn, 10 vols., Vol. 7. Lenoir, Jane, illus. 2005. (Colorado Cowboys Ser.: 10). 32p. (J). pap. 10.95 *(978-1-59381-099-3(7))*; lib. bdg. 23.60 *(978-1-59381-098-6(9))* Ozark Publishing.

—The Colorado Blizzard: Be Determined, 10 vols., Vol. 8. Lenoir, Jane, illus. 2005. (Colorado Cowboys Ser.: 10). 32p. (J). pap. 10.95 *(978-1-59381-027-6(X))* Ozark Publishing.

—The Drought: Have Faith, 10 vols., Vol. 9. Lenoir, Jane, illus. 2005. (Colorado Cowboys Ser.: 10). 32p. (J). pap. 10.95 *(978-1-59381-103-7(9))*; lib. bdg. 23.60 *(978-1-59381-102-0(0))* Ozark Publishing.

—The Fire: A Second Chance, 10 vols., Vol. 10. Lenoir, Jane, illus. 2005. (Colorado Cowboys Ser.: 10). 32p. (J). pap. 10.95 *(978-1-59381-105-1(5))* Ozark Publishing.

—Valley Oak Acorns: (Maidu) Be Helpful, 20 vols., Vol. 20. Lenoir, Jane, illus. l.t. ed. 2005. (Story Keeper Ser.: 20). 42p. (J). (gr. -1 — 1). lib. bdg. 23.60 *(978-1-56763-941-4(0))* Ozark Publishing.

Sargent, Dave, et al. Fierce Warriors Vol. 7: (Comanche) Learn Skills, 20 vols. Lenoir, Jane, illus. l.t. ed. 2004. (Story Keeper Ser.: 7). 48p. (J). pap. 10.95 *(978-1-56763-916-2(X))* Ozark Publishing.

—Summer Milky Way: (Blackfeet) Be Compassionate, 20 vols., Vol. 16. Lenoir, Jane, illus. l.t. ed. 2004. (Story Keeper Ser.). 48p. (J). lib. bdg. 23.60 *(978-1-56763-933-9(X))*; pap. 10.95 *(978-1-56763-934-6(8))* Ozark Publishing.

—Truth, Power & Freedom Vol. 19: (Sioux) Show Respect, 20 vols., Vol. 19. Lenoir, Jane, illus. l.t. ed. 2004. (Story Keeper Ser.: 19). 42p. (J). pap. 10.95 *(978-1-56763-940-7(2))* Ozark Publishing.

—Valley Oaks Acorns Vol. 20: (Maidu) Be Helpful, 20 vols. Lenoir, Jane, illus. l.t. ed. 2004. (Story Keeper Ser.: 20). 48p. (J). pap. 10.95 *(978-1-56763-942-1(9))* Ozark Publishing.

Sarmiento-Waring, D. We Are the One Race Kids. 2010. 30p. pap. 17.99 *(978-1-60957-900-5(3))* Salem Author Services.

Sarnella, Jeanette. Santini's Magic Castle. 2010. 28p. 15.49 *(978-1-4520-4908-3(4))* AuthorHouse.

Sarno, J. P. Little Paddle the Platypus & His First Day Outing Adventure. 2012. 136p. pap. 71.99 *(978-1-4691-8746-4(9))* Xlibris Corp.

Satterlee, Chuck. Smoke & Mirror Vol. 1: Time & Again. 2006. (Illus.). 152p. (YA). pap. 15.99 *(978-0-9738966-2-6(0))* Speakeasy Comics CAN. Dist: Diamond Bk. Distributors.

Satterly, Denise B. The Adventures of Icky & Weezy: Fall Has Arrived. 2011. 20p. (gr. -1 — 1). pap. 10.03 *(978-1-4520-2046-4(9))* AuthorHouse.

Satterwhite, William. Stealth, Vol. 1. 2005. 44p. (YA). pap. 5.75 *(978-1-4116-2395-8(9))* Lulu Pr., Inc.

Sattler, Jennifer. Chick 'n' Pug. 2013. (ENG., Illus.). 30p. (J). (gr. -1-1). bds. 7.99 *(978-1-61963-078-9(8))*, 9781619630789, Bloomsbury USA Childrens) Bloomsbury Publishing USA.

—Chick 'n' Pug Meet the Dude. (ENG., Illus.). (J). (gr. -1-1). 2014. 30p. bds. 7.99 *(978-1-61963-402-2(3))*, 9781619634022) 2013. 32p. 17.89 *(978-1-59990-760-4(7))*, 9781599907604) 2013. 32p. 16.99 *(978-1-59990-600-3(7))*, 9781599906003) Bloomsbury Publishing USA. (Bloomsbury USA Childrens).

Sattler, Jennifer Gordon. Chick 'n' Pug. 2010. (ENG., Illus.). 32p. (J). (gr. -1-1). 14.99 *(978-1-59990-534-1(5))*, 9781599905341, Bloomsbury USA Childrens) Bloomsbury Publishing USA.

Saugstad, Edward. Oakee Doakee & the Ego Bomb. 2008. 108p. pap. 19.95 *(978-0-9551503-9-5(6))* Checkpoint Pr. IRL. Dist: Printondemand-worldwide.com.

—Oakee Doakee & the Hate Wave. 2008. 88p. pap. 18.95 *(978-0-9551503-6-4(1))* Checkpoint Pr. IRL. Dist: Printondemand-worldwide.com.

Saunders, Catherine. DK Readers L4: LEGO NINJAGO: Team Ninja. 2016. (ENG., Illus.). 96p. (J). (gr. 3-7). pap. 3.99 *(978-1-4654-5191-0(9))*, DK Children) Dorling Kindersley Publishing, Inc.

Saunders, George P. The Last Elf. 2007. 180p. per. 13.95 *(978-0-595-40843-6(5))* iUniverse, Inc.

Saunders, Harry M. Teenagers on an Adventure: Journey of Two Boys & a Girl. 2013. 168p. pap. 19.95 *(978-1-62709-466-5(0))* America Star Bks.

Saunders, Kate. The Curse of the Chocolate Phoenix. 2016. (ENG.). 272p. (J). (gr. 5). 6.99 *(978-0-385-39105-4(6))*, Yearling) Random Hse. Children's Bks.

—The Curse of the Chocolate Phoenix: A Companion to the Whizz Pop Chocolate Shop. 2015. (ENG.). 272p. (J). (gr. 5). 19.99 *(978-0-375-99183-7(2))*, Delacorte Bks. for Young Readers) Random Hse. Children's Bks.

—The Whizz Pop Chocolate Shop. (ENG.). 304p. (J). (gr. 5). 2014. 7.99 *(978-0-385-74302-0(5))*, Yearling) 2013. 16.99 *(978-0-385-74301-3(7))*, Delacorte Bks. for Young Readers) Random Hse. Children's Bks.

Saunders, Len. Joey the Kangaroo: An Adventure in Exercise. 2010. 32p. pap. 14.95 *(978-1-4389-3992-6(2))* AuthorHouse.

—Spunky the Monkey: An Adventure in Exercise. 2010. 32p. pap. 14.95 *(978-1-4389-3991-9(4))* AuthorHouse.

Saunders, Maggie. The Adventures of Morgan & Malyk: The Lost Dog Mystery. 2012. 48p. (gr. 1-2). pap. 8.99 *(978-1-4582-0338-0(7))*, Abbott Pr.) Author Solutions, Inc.

Saunders, Margaret Marshall. Tilda Jane: A Rambunctious Orphan's Misadventures Finding a Home in the Early 1900s. 2008. (Fiction Treasures Ser.). (ENG.). 318p. pap. 16.95 *(978-0-88780-780-0(1))*, 9780887807800) Formac Publishing Co., Ltd. CAN. Dist: Casemate Pubs. & Bk. Distributors, LLC.

Saunders, Vivien. The Adventures of Annika. Muckle, Christine, illus. 2013. 42p. pap. *(978-1-909730-02-1(5))* Abbotsley Publishing.

Saupé, Rick. Moses P Rose Has Broken His Nose. DeBroeck, Sarah, illus. 2012. 28p. pap. 24.95 *(978-1-4626-0547-7(8))* America Star Bks.

Sava, Scott Christian. Animal Crackers. 2011. (Illus.). 152p. pap. 11.99 *(978-1-60010-619-4(6))* Idea & Design Works, LLC.

—Ed's Terrestrials. 2006. 84p. 19.95 *(978-0-9789168-1-7(6))* Blue Dream Studios.

—Gary the Pirate. 2008. (Illus.). 112p. 12.95 *(978-0-9789168-5-5(9))* Blue Dream Studios.

Savage, Bridgette Z. Fly Like the Wind. Savage, Charles J., ed. Savage, Bridgette Z., illus. Savage, Charles J., photos by. 2005. (ENG., Illus.). 112p. (YA). (gr. 5). per. 16.99 *(978-0-9771494-0-7(4))* Buckbeech Studios.

Savage, J. Scott. Gears of Revolution. 2016. (Mysteries of Cove Ser.: 2). 342p. (J). 17.99 *(978-1-62972-223-8(5))*, Shadow Mountain) Deseret Bk. Co.

—Making the Team. Holgate, Doug, illus. 2015. (Case File 13 Ser.: 2). (ENG.). 288p. (J). (gr. 3-7). pap. 6.99 *(978-0-06-213335-9(7))* HarperCollins Pubs.

Savage, Tawanna. Anna Mischievous: The Early Years. 2005. Orig. Title: ANNA MISCHIEVOUS: the Early Years. (J). spiral bd. *(978-0-9754147-9-8(8))* ASP Corp. Entertainment Group, Inc.

Savageau, Tony. The Mud House Mystery: A Wild Bunch Adventure. Raditz, JoAnne, illus. 2004. (J). pap. 9.95 *(978-0-9759737-0-7(3))* Blue Mustang Pr.

Saveley, Barb. Curse of Moonstone Island. 2009. (Illus.). 36p. pap. 16.99 *(978-1-4389-4938-3(3))* AuthorHouse.

Savitsky, Steve, illus. Dora's Pirate Treasure Hunt. 2010. (Dora the Explorer Ser.). (ENG.). 12p. (J). (gr. -1-1). 6.99 *(978-1-4169-9927-0(2))*, Simon Spotlight/Nickelodeon) Simon Spotlight/Nickelodeon.

Sawaski, James H. The Next Chess Team: A Novel. 2012. 120p. (gr. 10-12). pap. 10.95 *(978-1-4759-2425-1(9))* iUniverse, Inc.

Sawler, Kimberly. Rocket & the Magical Cosmic Candies. Walls, Ty, illus. 2006. 32p. (J). (gr. 4-7). 18.95 *(978-1-933285-51-1(6))* Brown Books Publishing Group.

Sawyer, Jacqueline. Little Racer Big Heart. 2012. 28p. pap. 16.95 *(978-1-62709-783-3(X))* America Star Bks.

Saxon, Lucy. The Almost King. 2016. (ENG., Illus.). 400p. (YA). (gr. 7-12). 17.99 *(978-1-61963-627-9(1))*, 9781619636279, Bloomsbury USA Childrens) Bloomsbury Publishing USA.

—Take Back the Skies. 2014. (ENG.). 384p. (YA). (gr. 7). 17.99 *(978-1-61963-367-4(1))*, 9781619633674, Bloomsbury USA Childrens) Bloomsbury Publishing USA.

Saxon, Victoria. Ready to Play! (Disney Infinity) RH Disney Staff & Doescher, Erik, illus. 2015. (Step into Reading Ser.). (ENG.). 32p. (J). (gr. k-3). 4.99 *(978-0-7364-3427-0(5))*, RH/Disney) Random Hse. Children's Bks.

Say Please, Says Squeeze. 2009. (ENG.). 32p. pap. 3.99 *(978-1-4231-1755-1(7))* Disney Pr.

Sazaklis, John. Batman Classic: Dawn of the Dynamic Duo. Gordon, Eric A. & Gordon, Steven E., illus. 2011. (I Can Read Level 2 Ser.). (ENG.). 32p. (J). (gr. -1-3). pap. 3.99 *(978-0-06-188520-4(7))* HarperCollins Pubs.

—Batman Classic - Eternal Enemies. Tong, Andie, illus. 2013. (ENG.). 24p. (J). (gr. -1-3). pap. 3.99 *(978-0-06-220997-9(3))*, HarperFestival) HarperCollins Pubs.

—Battle - Battle in Metropolis. Smith, Andy & Vancata, Brad, illus. 2013. (ENG.). 24p. (J). (gr. -1-3). pap. 3.99 *(978-0-06-188537-2(1))*, HarperFestival) HarperCollins Pubs.

—Fowl Play. Gordon, Steven E. & Gordon, Eric A., illus. 2012. (ENG.). 24p. (J). (gr. -1-3). pap. 3.99 *(978-0-06-188536-5(3))*, HarperFestival) HarperCollins Pubs.

—I Am the Flash. 2014. (Justice League Classic: I Can Read! Ser.). (J). lib. bdg. 13.55 *(978-0-606-35073-0(X))*, Turtleback) Turtleback Bks.

—Land Before Prime. 2015. (Transformers 8x8 Ser.). (J). lib. bdg. 13.55 *(978-0-606-35937-5(0))* Turtleback Bks.

—Man of Steel. 2013. (Man of Steel Ser.). (ENG.). 12p. (J). (gr. -1-3). pap. 6.99 *(978-0-06-223605-0(9))*, HarperFestival) HarperCollins Pubs.

—The Mystery of the Maze Monster, 1 vol. Neely, Scott, illus. 2014. (You Choose Stories: Scooby-Doo Ser.). (ENG.). 112p. (gr. 2-3). pap. 6.95 *(978-1-4342-7928-6(6))*, You Choose Bks.) Capstone Press of Coughlan Cos.

—Superman: Escape from the Phantom Zone. Gordon, Steven E., illus. 2011. (I Can Read Level 2 Ser.). (ENG.). 32p. (J). (gr. -1-3). pap. 3.99 *(978-0-06-188519-8(3))* HarperCollins Pubs.

—Thunder Strike! (Marvel: Thor) Spaziante, Patrick, illus. 2017. (Little Golden Book Ser.). (ENG.). 24p. (J). (-k). 4.99 **(978-1-5247-1730-8(4)**, Golden Bks.) Random Hse. Children's Bks.

Sazaklis, John. You Choose Stories: Batman. Beavers, Ethen, illus. 2016. (You Choose Stories: Batman Ser.). (ENG.). 112p. (gr. 2-3). 261.20 *(978-1-4965-3100-1(0))*, DC Super Heroes) Stone Arch Bks.

Sazaklis, John & Merkel, Joe F. Day of the Undead. Tong, Andie, illus. 2013. (ENG.). 24p. (J). (gr. -1-3). pap. 3.99 *(978-0-06-220999-3(X))*, HarperFestival) HarperCollins Pubs.

Sazaklis, John & Phillips, Ruby Ann. Krystal Ball, 1 vol. 2014. (Krystal Ball Ser.). (ENG.). 112p. (gr. 2-3). 50.64 *(978-1-4795-4547-6(3))* Picture Window Bks.

Scafuro, Lisa. Adventures at Cedar Hollow: Tigre Encounters the Great Horned Owl. 2005. (J). 18.00 *(978-0-8059-6635-0(8))* Dorrance Publishing Co., Inc.

Scala, Vincent. Beep Beep Goes the Bus Driver, 1 vol. 2013. (ENG., Illus.). 32p. (J). 16.99 *(978-0-7643-4493-0(5))*, 9780764344930) Schiffer Publishing, Ltd.

Scanes, Amy. The Chosen: Book Two of the Abon Trilogy. 2007. 304p. per. 18.95 *(978-0-595-45990-2(0))* iUniverse, Inc.

Scarlett Giblin, Alison. Children of Conygre & the Time Capsule. 2006. 220p. per. *(978-1-905529-41-4(4))* Grosvenor Hse. Publishing Ltd.

Scarry, Richard. Richard Scarry's Lowly Worm's Applecar. 2014. (Richard Scarry's Lift the Flaps Bks.). (ENG.). 10p. (J). (gr. -1 — 1). 7.99 *(978-0-7641-6673-0(5))* Barron's Educational Series, Inc.

Schaaf, Ron. Tiger's Quest: Rounding Cape Horn. 2007. (J). *(978-0-9787555-0-8(2))* Hickory Tales Publishing.

Schachner, Judy. A Surprise for Mama. 2008. (Skippyjon Jones Ser.). (ENG., Illus.). 16p. (J). (gr. -1-k). pap. 5.99 *(978-0-448-44816-9(5))*, Grosset & Dunlap) Penguin Young Readers Group.

Schade, Susan. Simon's Dream. Buller, Jon, illus. 2009. (Fog Mound Ser.: 3). (ENG.). 208p. (J). (gr. 3-7). pap. 12.99 *(978-0-689-87689-9(0))*, Aladdin) Simon & Schuster Children's Publishing.

—Travels of Thelonious. Buller, Jon, illus. 2007. (Fog Mound Ser.: 1). (ENG.). 224p. (J). (gr. 3-7). pap. 11.99 *(978-0-689-87685-1(8))*, Aladdin) Simon & Schuster Children's Publishing.

Schade, Susan & Buller, Jon. Faradawn. 2008. (Fog Mound Ser.: 2). (ENG., Illus.). 208p. (J). (gr. 3-7). pap. 12.99 *(978-0-689-87687-5(4))*, Aladdin) Simon & Schuster Children's Publishing.

Schaefer, Elizabeth. Star Wars: the Phantom Menace Read-Along Storybook & CD. Rood, Brian, illus. 2017. (Read-Along Storybook & CD Ser.). (ENG.). 32p. (J). (gr. 1-3). pap. 6.99 *(978-1-4847-8182-1(1))*, Disney Lucasfilm Press) Disney Publishing Worldwide.

Schaefer, Lola M. Mittens at School. Hartung, Susan Kathleen, illus. 2012. (My First I Can Read Ser.). (ENG.). 32p. (J). (gr. -1-3). 16.99 *(978-0-06-170224-2(2))*; pap. 3.99 *(978-0-06-170223-5(4))* HarperCollins Pubs.

Schaffer, Jacqueline. Porsha & the Great Snowmen Adventure. 2009. 36p. pap. 15.99 *(978-1-4490-5421-2(8))* AuthorHouse.

Schalow, Al. The Adventure down Crunchy Road. 2004. (Illus.). vii, 69p. (J). 19.95 *(978-0-9654963-4-6(1))* Medwag Publishing.

Schandle, Julie. Little Wishes Big Dreams: Around the World. 2005. (Illus.). 22p. (J). 11.95 *(978-0-9771868-0-8(6))*, 303-503-3289) Big Dreams Publishing.

Scheber, George. Earl Joins the Circus. Spicer, Bridgett, illus. l.t. ed. 2005. (Adventures of Earl the Squirrel Ser.). 32p. (J). (gr. -1-3). 12.95 *(978-1-878847-01-0(5))* Make Me A Story Pr.

Scherer, Catherine W. Simon & Barklee in China, Book 2 - the Mountains. 2008. (Another Country Calling Ser.). (J). per. 15.00 *(978-0-9714502-7-1(7))*, Explorer Media) Simon & Barklee, Inc./ExplorerMedia.

—Simon & Barklee in China, Book 3 - the North. 2008. (Another Country Calling Ser.). (J). per. 15.00 *(978-0-9714502-8-8(5))*, Explorer Media) Simon & Barklee, Inc./ExplorerMedia.

Schermbrucker, Reviva. An African Christmas Cloth. 2007. (ENG.). 36p. 27.95 *(978-1-77009-081-1(9))* Jacana Media ZAF. Dist: Independent Pubs. Group.

Schettler, Amanda. The Adventures of Mike & Fanny: A Story about A Dog & A Goat. 2011. 50p. 35.95 *(978-1-258-08538-4(0))* Literary Licensing, LLC.

Schexnayder, Paul, illus. The Kajun Kween. 2003. (ENG.). 100p. (J). per. 22.00 *(978-0-9650977-1-0(4))* Border Pr.

Schifferli, Paul Phillip. Darryl's Daring Deed. Schifferli, Paul Phillip, illus. 2006. (Illus.). (J). 9.95 *(978-0-9765304-7-3(3))* Windsor Media Enterprises, Inc.

Schiller, Friedrich. Guillermo Tell.Tr. of William Tell. (SPA., Illus.). 160p. (YA). 11.95 *(978-84-7281-088-4(7))*, AF1088) Auriga, Ediciones S.A. ESP. Dist: Continental Bk. Co., Inc.

Schirmer, Jodi L. Dear Deer Friend. 2008. 24p. pap. 11.95 *(978-1-4327-2540-2(8))* Outskirts Pr., Inc.

Schlegl, Stacey Lynn. Little Frog. 2008. (J). per. 8.95 *(978-0-9801504-0-7(X))* Jan-Carol Publishing, INC.

Schlegl, Stacey Lynn & Schlegl, Abigail. MerMountain. 2012. 84p. (J). pap. 11.95 *(978-0-9850272-2-3(3))* Jan-Carol Publishing, INC.

Schlesinger, Gretchen. Send Me the Soap #2: The Amazon Adventure. Pietila, David, illus. 2007. (J). 11.95 *(978-0-9778536-2-5(4))* Eco-thumb Publishing Co.

Schliewen, Richard. Paulina's Teddy Bear Journey. Visaya, Artemio, illus. 2012. 104p. 24.95 *(978-1-62709-055-1(X))*; pap. 19.95 *(978-1-4626-9597-3(3))* America Star Bks.

Schlimm, John, ed. Stand Up! 75 Young Activists Who Rock the World & How You Can, Too! 2013. (ENG.). 284p. (J). (gr. 7-7). pap. 16.95 *(978-0-9850602-9-9(8))* Publishing Syndicate LLC.

Schlitt, Jayme & Schlitt, Ron. Rags, Riches & the Robe. 2010. 32p. 17.25 *(978-1-4269-4666-0(X))* Trafford Publishing.

Schlitz, Laura Amy. The Night Fairy. Barrett, Angela, illus. (ENG.). 128p. (J). (gr. 2-5). 2011. pap. 6.99 *(978-0-7636-5295-1(4))* 2010. 16.99 *(978-0-7636-3674-6(6))* Candlewick Pr.

Schlosser, Jeffrey A. Little Jacky Yooper: Kid Fisherman. 2011. (Illus.). 20p. pap. 8.50 *(978-1-4567-5163-0(8))* AuthorHouse.

Schmatjen, Marc. My Giraffe Makes Me Laugh. 2010. 24p. 12.95 *(978-1-4520-0941-4(4))* AuthorHouse.

Schmidt, Tiffany. Break Me Like a Promise: Once upon a Crime Family. 2017. (ENG.). 416p. (YA). pap. 9.99 *(978-1-68119-404-2(X))*, 9781681194042, Bloomsbury USA Childrens) Bloomsbury Publishing USA.

Schmidt, Werner. The Forests of Adventure. 2005. 137p. pap. 12.50 *(978-1-4116-4721-3(1))* Lulu Pr., Inc.

—Prisoners of the Witchaliks. 2005. 173p. pap. 12.50 *(978-1-4116-4728-2(9))* Lulu Pr., Inc.

Schnell, Selynn. The Backpack Jungle. 2011. 48p. pap. 16.95 *(978-1-4560-3332-3(8))* America Star Bks.

Schnitzler, Arthur. Meistererzählungen. Weigel, Hans, ed. (GER.). pap. 25.95 *(978-3-257-21016-3(7))* Diogenes Verlag AG CHE. Dist: Distribooks, Inc.

Schnur, Dawn. Bailey's Tree House Adventures. 2013. 138p. pap. 12.99 *(978-1-62697-613-9(9))* Salem Author Services.

Schnur, Steven. Mrs. Popham's Library. 2003. 48p. (J). pap. 8.95 *(978-0-595-30163-8(0))* iUniverse, Inc.

Schoen, Sarah. Omar the Smiling Labrador, 1 vol. 2010. 26p. pap. 24.95 *(978-1-4489-6231-0(5))* PublishAmerica, Inc.

Schoening, Dan, illus. Green Lantern, 12 vols., Set. Incl. Battle of the Blue Lanterns. Acampora, Michael V. lib. bdg. 26.65 *(978-1-4342-2608-2(5))*; Beware Our Power! Sonneborn, Scott. 26.65 *(978-1-4342-2607-5(7))*; Escape from the Orange Lanterns. Acampora, Michael Vincent. lib. bdg. 26.65 *(978-1-4342-2622-8(0))*; Fear the Shark. Sutton, Laurie S. lib. bdg. 26.65 *(978-1-4342-2620-4(4))*; Guardian of Earth. Dahl, Michael. lib. bdg. 26.65 *(978-1-4342-2611-2(5))*; High-Tech Terror. Steele, Michael A. lib. bdg. 26.65 *(978-1-4342-2609-9(3))*; Last Super Hero. Dahl, Michael. lib. bdg. 26.65 *(978-1-4342-2612-9(3))*; Light King Strikes! Sutton, Laurie S. lib. bdg. 26.65 *(978-1-4342-2610-5(7))*; Prisoner of the Ring. Sonneborn, Scott. lib. bdg. 26.65 *(978-1-4342-2624-2(7))*; Red Lanterns' Revenge. Acampora, Michael Vincent. lib. bdg. 26.65 *(978-1-4342-2623-5(9))*; Savage Sands. Bright, J. E. lib. bdg. 26.65 *(978-1-4342-2619-8(0))*; Web of Doom. Steele, Michael A. lib. bdg. 26.65 *(978-1-4342-2621-1(2))*; (Illus.). (gr. 2-3)., DC Super Heroes (Green Lantern Ser.). (ENG.). 56p. 2011. Set lib. bdg. 319.80 *(978-1-4342-3240-3(9))* Stone Arch Bks.

Schofield Sr., Derrick. A Frog's Tale. 2012. 20p. pap. 13.77 *(978-1-4669-2009-5(2))* Trafford Publishing.

Scholastic. Day of the Departed (LEGO Ninjago: Reader) 2016. (Lego Ninjago Ser.). (ENG.). 32p. (J). (gr. -1-3). pap. 3.99 *(978-1-338-11369-3(0))* Scholastic, Inc.

—Fun at the Fair: a Sticker Storybook (Peppa Pig) Eone, illus. 2016. (Peppa Pig Ser.). (ENG.). 24p. (J). (gr. -1-k). pap. 7.99 *(978-1-338-03281-9(X))* Scholastic, Inc.

—The Legend of Shogunyan. 2016. (Yo-Kai Watch Ser.). (ENG.). 32p. (J). (gr. 2-5). pap. 3.99 *(978-1-338-05825-3(8))* Scholastic, Inc.

—Macy & the King's Tournament. 2017. (LEGO NEXO Knights Ser.). (ENG.). 32p. (J). (gr. 1-3). pap. 3.99 *(978-1-338-05558-0(5))* Scholastic, Inc.

Scholastic, et al. Forbidden Power. 2017. (LEGO NEXO Knights Ser.: 1). (ENG.). 192p. (J). (gr. 2-5). 12.99 *(978-1-338-04183-5(5))* Scholastic, Inc.

Scholastic Editors. Classic Collector's Handbook: An Official Guide to the First 151 Pokemon. 2016. lib. bdg. 19.65 *(978-0-606-39550-2(4))* Turtleback Bks.

—The Quest for the Crystal. 2015. (Ninjago Readers Ser.: 14). lib. bdg. 13.55 *(978-0-606-38109-3(0))* Turtleback Bks.

Scholastic Editors & Howard, Kate. Return of the Djinn. 2016. (Lego Ninjago Ser.). (ENG.). 32p. (J). (gr. 1-3). pap. 3.99 *(978-0-545-92553-2(3))* Scholastic, Inc.

Scholastic, Inc. Staff. Cahills vs Vespers, Pack. 2011. (39 Clues: Cahills vs. Vespers Ser.). (ENG.). 16p. (J). (gr. 3-7). 6.99 *(978-0-545-31640-8(5))* Scholastic, Inc.

—A Construir la Ciudad! 2011. (Lego City Ser.). (SPA.). 24p. (J). (gr. -1-3). pap. 3.99 *(978-0-545-34464-7(6))*, Scholastic en Espanol) Scholastic, Inc.

—Pokemon: Kalos Region Handbook. 2014. (ENG.). 272p. (J). (gr. 2-5). pap. 8.99 *(978-0-545-64602-4(2))* Scholastic, Inc.

—The Quest for the Crystal. 2015. (Lego Ninjago Ser.). (ENG., Illus.). 32p. (J). (gr. 1-3). pap. 3.99 *(978-0-545-90589-3(3))* Scholastic, Inc.

—Spy vs. Spy. 2015. (Ninjago Readers Ser.: 13). lib. bdg. 13.55 *(978-0-606-37080-6(3))* Turtleback Bks.

Scholastic, Inc. Staff, contrib. by. Adventures in LEGO City, Set. 2nd ed. 2015. (Lego City Ser.). (ENG.). (J). (gr. -1-3). pap. 24.99 *(978-0-545-80861-3(8))* Scholastic, Inc.

—The Story of Peppa Pig. 2013. (Peppa Pig Ser.). (ENG.). 32p. (J). (gr. -1-k). 8.99 *(978-0-545-46805-3(1))* Scholastic, Inc.

Scholastic, Inc. Staff & Farshtey, Greg. Lego Ninjago. 2011. (Lego Ninjago Ser.). (ENG., Illus.). 112p. (J). (gr. 2-5). pap. 7.99 *(978-0-545-36258-0(X))* Scholastic, Inc.

Scholastic, Inc. Staff & Fry, Jason. Darth Maul - Shadow Conspiracy. 2013. (Star Wars Ser.). (ENG.). 160p. (J). (gr. 3-7). pap. 5.99 *(978-0-545-47063-6(3))* Scholastic, Inc.

Scholastic, Inc. Staff & Marsham, Liz. Movie Flip Book. 2016. (Batman vs. Superman: Dawn of Justice Ser.). (ENG.). 112p. (J). (gr. 3-7). pap. 9.99 *(978-0-545-91627-1(5))* Scholastic, Inc.

Scholastic, Inc. Staff & Sander, Sonia. Ready for Takeoff! 2010. (Lego City Ser.). (ENG.). 32p. (J). (gr. -1-k). pap. 3.99 *(978-0-545-21986-0(8))* Scholastic, Inc.

Scholastic, Inc. Staff & Steele, Michael Anthony. Fix That Truck! Dynamo Limited Staff, illus. 2012. (Lego City Ser.). (ENG.). 24p. (J). (gr. -1-3). pap. 3.99 *(978-0-545-47061-2(7))* Scholastic, Inc.

Scholastic, Inc. Staff & Watson, Jude. Doublecross - Mission Titanic, Bk. 1. 2015. (39 Clues: Doublecross Ser.: 1). (ENG.). 224p. (J). (gr. 3-7). 12.99 *(978-0-545-76719-4(9))* Scholastic, Inc.

Scholastic, Inc. Staff & Weisman, Greg. Traveler. Didier, Samwise, illus. 2016. (World of Warcraft Ser.). (ENG.). 384p. (J). (gr. 3-7). 14.99 *(978-0-545-90667-8(9))* Scholastic, Inc.

Scholastic, Inc. Staff & Wheeler, Alex. Hostage. 2009. (Star Wars: Rebel Force Ser.: 2). (ENG.). 176p. (J). (gr. 3-7). 6.99 *(978-0-545-11218-5(4))* Scholastic, Inc.

Scholastic, Inc. Staff & Windham, Ryder. Return of the Jedi. novel ed. 2004. (Star Wars Ser.). (ENG., Illus.). 160p. (J). (gr. 3-7). pap. 6.99 *(978-0-439-68126-1(X))* Scholastic, Inc.

Scholistic Editors & Rusu, Meredith. Official Guide. 2016. (Yo-Kai Watch Ser.). (ENG.). 128p. (J). (gr. 2-5). pap. 7.99 *(978-1-338-05442-2(2))* Scholastic, Inc.

Schomberger, Mary. The Adventures of Goldy the Mouse. 2013. 36p. pap. 16.95 *(978-1-4908-0375-3(0))*, WestBow Pr.) Author Solutions, Inc.

Schooley, Bob & McCorkle, Mark. Liar of Kudzu. 2008. (ENG.). 192p. (J). (gr. 5-9). pap. 9.99 *(978-1-4169-1489-1(7))*, Simon & Schuster Bks. For Young Readers) Simon & Schuster Bks. For Young Readers.

Schoombee, Cherese. Frilly Lilly. 2009. 28p. 16.95 *(978-1-84799-435-6(0))* Lulu Pr., Inc.

Schopp, Bernice Frances. The Legend of Moon-Goblin Town. 2012. 32p. pap. 21.99 *(978-1-4771-4475-6(7))* Xlibris Corp.

Schorr, Titus. A Playground Adventure, 01 vols., 1. 2016. (Rosen REAL Readers: STEM & STEAM Collection). (ENG.). 8p. (J). pap. 5.46 *(978-1-5081-1469-7(2))*, Rosen Classroom) Rosen Publishing Group, Inc., The.

Schrader, Racheal. Doodlebugs: Trouble On Moss Farm. Schrader, Racheal, illus. 2008. (Illus.). 156p. (YA). per. 7.99 *(978-0-9815274-0-6(X))* Schrader, Racheal.

Schraff, Anne. The Darkest Secret. 2008. (Passages Ser.). 114p. (YA). (gr. 7-9). lib. bdg. 13.95 *(978-0-7569-8376-5(2))* Perfection Learning Corp.

—A Horse Called Courage (Adventure), 1 vol. 2017. (Pageturners Ser.). (ENG.). 76p. (YA). (gr. 9-12). 8.95 **(978-1-68021-378-2(4))** Saddleback Educational Publishing, Inc.

—Planet Doom (Adventure), 1 vol. 2017. (Pageturners Ser.). (ENG.). 76p. (YA). (gr. 9-12). 8.95 **(978-1-68021-379-9(2))** Saddleback Educational Publishing, Inc.

—The Quality of Mercy. 2011. (Urban Underground — Harriet Tubman High School Ser.). (YA). lib. bdg. 20.80 *(978-0-606-14800-9(0))*, Turtleback) Turtleback Bks.

—The Terrible Orchid Sky (Adventure), 1 vol. 2017. (Pageturners Ser.). (ENG.). 76p. (YA). (gr. 9-12). 8.95 **(978-1-68021-380-5(6))** Saddleback Educational Publishing, Inc.

—Up Rattler Mountain (Adventure), 1 vol. 2017. (Pageturners Ser.). (ENG.). 76p. (YA). (gr. 9-12). 8.95 **(978-1-68021-381-2(4))** Saddleback Educational Publishing, Inc.

—Who Has Seen the Beast? (Adventure), 1 vol. 2017. (Pageturners Ser.). (ENG.). 76p. (YA). (gr. 9-12). 8.95

(978-1-68021-382-9(2)) Saddleback Educational Publishing, Inc.

Schraff, Anne E. Second Chances. 2013. (Urban Underground — Harriet Tubman High School Ser.). (YA). lib. bdg. 20.80 *(978-0-606-31584-5(5)*, Turtleback) Turtleback Bks.

Schram, Kristina. The Chronicles of Anaedor: The Lost Ones. 2013. 442p. pap. 15.99 *(978-0-9884774-5-2(9))* Hive Collective.

—The Chronicles of Anaedor: The Uprising. 2013. 462p. pap. 15.99 *(978-0-9884774-6-9(7))* Hive Collective.

Schreck, Tabatha M. Welcome to God's Big Backyard: Little Mouse's Adventure. 2012. 28p. pap. 14.95 *(978-1-4520-5524-4(6))* AuthorHouse.

Schrefer, Eliot. Threatened. 2014. (ENG., Illus.). 288p. (J). (gr. 7). 17.99 *(978-0-545-55143-4(9)*, Scholastic Pr.) Scholastic, Inc.

Schreiber, Joe. Perry's Killer Playlist. (ENG.). 224p. (YA). (gr. 9). 2013. pap. 8.99 *(978-0-544-10489-1(7))* 2012. 16.99 *(978-0-547-60117-5(4))* Houghton Mifflin Harcourt Publishing Co.

Schroeder, Erin, illus. Oh no! it's the helpful hound... & the days of the Week. Schroeder, Erin, . 2006. (FRE, JPN, SPA & GER.). 27p. (J). per. 7.95 *(978-0-9779155-0-7(6))* Erinsillart.

Schrowang, Irene. Sam & Joey's Pirate Ship Adventure. 2013. 16p. pap. 15.99 *(978-1-4817-0333-8(1))* AuthorHouse.

Schueler, M. A. Penny the Beach Westie Big Trouble for a Little Dog. 2009. 24p. pap. 16.50 *(978-1-60860-424-1(1)*, Eloquent Bks.) Strategic Book Publishing & Rights Agency (SBPRA).

Schuette, Leslie Elaine. The Adventures of Little Autumn. Walker, Bradley, illus. 2013. 24p. 24.95 *(978-1-63004-507-4(1))* America Star Bks.

—The Adventures of Little Autumn. Walker, Bradley, illus. 2013. 24p. pap. 24.95 *(978-1-4626-9778-6(X))* America Star Bks.

—Little Autumn's Adventure in the Smoky Mountains. 2013. 30p. 24.95 *(978-1-63004-952-2(2))*; 32p. pap. 24.95 *(978-1-4626-9924-7(3))* America Star Bks.

Schuh, Eileen. The Traz. 2012. 202p. pap. *(978-0-9869388-2-5(3))* Kastle Harbour Publishing.

Schulkers, Robert. The Gray Ghost: A Seckatary Hawkins Mystery. 2016. (ENG., Illus.). 352p. 24.95 *(978-0-8131-6794-7(9))* Univ. Pr. of Kentucky.

—Stoner's Boy: A Seckatary Hawkins Mystery. 2016. (ENG., Illus.). 380p. 24.95 *(978-0-8131-6791-6(4))* Univ. Pr. of Kentucky.

Schult, Sherry. There's a Horse in My Closet..., 1 vol. 2010. 48p. pap. 16.95 *(978-1-4489-5412-4(6))* PublishAmerica, Inc.

Schultz, Aronka. A Dinosaur on the Loose. 2010. 32p. pap. 12.99 *(978-1-4520-4400-2(7))* AuthorHouse.

Schultz, Brenda. Wanda & Willie. Albano, Jennifer, illus. 2008. 25p. pap. 24.95 *(978-1-60703-446-9(8))* America Star Bks.

Schultz, Edward L. Pix, 1 vol. 2009. 48p. pap. 16.95 *(978-1-60749-393-8(4))* PublishAmerica, Inc.

Schultz, Heidi. The Twelve Dreams of Christmas. 2012. pap. 11.95 *(978-0-7414-7532-9(4))* Infinity Publishing.

Schultz, Leslie & Braulick, J. J. M. And Sometimes Y. Newman, Heather, illus. 2013. 302p. pap. 12.99 *(978-1-937848-07-1(8))* Do Life Right, Inc.

Schulz, Hal. Dak's Country Visit: The Painter & His Cat. 2011. 32p. pap. *(978-1-4269-6743-6(8))* Trafford Publishing (UK) Ltd.

Schulz, Heidi. Hook's Revenge. 2015. (Hook's Revenge Ser.: 1). (J). lib. bdg. 18.40 *(978-0-606-37398-2(5))* Turtleback Bks.

Schulz, Heidi. Hook's Revenge, Book 2: the Pirate Code. Hendrix, John, illus. 2016. (Hook's Revenge Ser.: 2). (ENG.). (J). (gr. 3-7). lib. bdg. 18.40 ***(978-0-606-39169-6(X))*** Turtleback Bks.

Schulz, Lori. Papa's Plan for Buddy Bee. 2012. 40p. pap. 13.95 *(978-1-4497-3652-1(1)*, WestBow Pr.) Author Solutions, Inc.

Schurch, Maylan. The Sword of Denis Anwyck. 2009. (J). pap. 10.99 *(978-0-8280-2425-9(1))* Review & Herald Publishing Assn.

Schurch, Vicky. A Little Songbird Named Annie. 2009. 32p. pap. 14.49 *(978-1-4490-2134-4(4))* AuthorHouse.

Schuster, Judith A. No Place to Call Home: Book Two-the Eddie Brewster Adventures. 2008. 196p. pap. 24.95 *(978-1-60563-559-0(6))* PublishAmerica, Inc.

Schwartz, Anna L. Okie the Wonder Dog. Dumm, Brian Caleb, illus. 2016. 62p. (J). pap. *(978-1-63293-111-5(7))* Sunstone Pr.

Schwartz, B. J. The Adventures of Max & I. 2011. 54p. pap. 24.99 *(978-1-4670-2434-1(1))* AuthorHouse.

—The Adventures of Max & I: Dream Pirates. 2011. 32p. pap. 15.99 *(978-1-4670-2435-8(X))* AuthorHouse.

Schwartz, Bennett L. Khadim & the Wanderers. 2010. 227p. 39.08 *(978-0-557-22262-9(1))* Lulu Pr., Inc.

Schwartz, Ellen. The Case of the Missing Deed. 2011. (Teaspoon Detectives Ser.). (ENG., Illus.). 154p. (J). (gr. 4-7). 15.95 *(978-0-88776-959-7(4)*, Tundra Bks.) Tundra Bks. CAN. Dist: Penguin Random Hse. LLC.

Schwartz, Roslyn. The Complete Adventures of the Mole Sisters. Schwartz, Roslyn, illus. 2004. (ENG., Illus.). 168p. (J). (gr. -1-k). 19.95 *(978-1-55037-883-2(X)*, 9781550378832) Annick Pr., Ltd. CAN. Dist: Publishers Group West (PGW).

Schwartz, Suzanne & Schwartz, Robert. My Friend Hibby: A Tropical Adventure. Schwartz, Suzanne & Schwartz, Robert, illus. 2005. (Illus.). 20p. (J). spiral bd. 6.00 *(978-0-9764152-0-6(8))* Seascay Productions.

Schwarz, S. L. Treasure at Lure Lake. 2016. (Illus.). 185p. (J). pap. 12.99 *(978-1-4621-1790-1(2))*; ***(978-1-4621-2600-2(6))*** Cedar Fort, Inc./CFI Distribution.

Schwarz, Viviane. How to Find Gold. Schwarz, Viviane, illus. 2016. (ENG., Illus.). 32p. (J). (-k). 16.99 *(978-0-7636-8104-3(0))* Candlewick Pr.

Schwarzkopf, Tom. The Ghost at Mahone Bay, 1 vol. 2007. (ENG., Illus.). 128p. (J). (gr. 4-7). pap. 10.95 *(978-1-55109-526-4(2))* Nimbus Publishing, Ltd. CAN. Dist: Orca Bk. Pubs. USA.

—Trouble Twins Save Christmas, 1 vol. 2007. (ENG.). 96p. (J). (gr. 3-7). pap. 10.95 *(978-1-55109-619-3(6))* Nimbus Publishing, Ltd. CAN. Dist: Orca Bk. Pubs. USA.

Schwind, Beverly Lahote. Patches & Her Backpack Adventures. 2013. (Illus.). 142p. 14.00 *(978-0-9745810-8-8(9))* Potters Publishing LLC.

Scieszka, Jon. Ay, Samuray!Tr. of Sam Samurai. (SPA.). (J). 7.95 *(978-958-04-6867-7(2))* Norma S.A. COL. Dist: Distribuidora Norma, Inc.

—Domingo, el Dia del Vikingo. (SPA.). (J). 7.95 *(978-958-04-7448-7(6))* Norma S.A. COL. Dist: Distribuidora Norma, Inc.

—Tu Mama Era Neanderthal. Smith, Lane, illus. (SPA.). (J). (gr. 5-8). 7.95 *(978-958-04-5045-0(5)*, NR3076) Norma S.A. COL. Dist: Distribuidora Norma, Inc., Lectorum Pubns., Inc.

—Tut, Tut, No. 6. Smith, Lane, illus. 2004. (Time Warp Trio Ser.: 6). (ENG.). 80p. (J). (gr. 2-4). pap. 5.99 *(978-0-14-240047-0(5)*, Puffin Books) Penguin Young Readers Group.

—Tut, Tut. Smith, Lane, illus. 2004. (Time Warp Trio Ser.: No. 6). 74p. (gr. 4-7). 15.00 *(978-0-7569-4050-8(8))* Perfection Learning Corp.

—Walt Disney's Alice in Wonderland (Reissue) Blair, Mary, illus. 2016. (ENG.). 64p. (J). (gr. -1-k). 16.99 *(978-1-4847-3041-6(0))* Disney Pr.

Scieszka, Jon & Christopher Healy. Heroes & Villains. 2017. (Guys Read Ser.). (J). lib. bdg. 17.20 ***(978-0-606-39637-0(3))*** Turtleback Bks.

Sclafani, Terry. The Thompson Twins Cruise Adventure. 2007. 84p. per. 10.95 *(978-1-4327-1542-7(9))* Outskirts Pr., Inc.

—The Thompson Twins Western Adventure. 2009. 114p. pap. 11.95 *(978-1-4327-3783-2(X))* Outskirts Pr., Inc.

Scollon, Bill. The Big Case. 2016. (Step into Reading Level 3 Ser.). lib. bdg. 14.75 *(978-0-606-38488-9(X))* Turtleback Bks.

—Disney*Pixar Finding Dory Movie Theater Storybook & Movie Projector. 2016. (Movie Theater Ser.: 1). (ENG.). 32p. (J). (gr. -1-2). 19.99 *(978-0-7944-3668-1(4)*, Reader's Digest Children's Bks.) Studio Fun International.

—Moana Guide Book (Disney Moana) Random House Disney Staff, illus. 2016. (Essential Guide Ser.). (ENG.). 64p. (J). (gr. 4-7). pap. 7.99 *(978-0-7364-3673-1(1)*, RH/Disney) Random Hse. Children's Bks.

—Super Adventure. Disney Book Group Staff & Disney Storybook Artists Staff, illus. 2013. (ENG.). 24p. (J). (gr. -1-k). pap. 4.99 *(978-1-4231-8657-1(5))* Disney Pr.

Scollon, William & Disney Book Group Staff. The Great Treasure Hunt. Disney Storybook Art Team, illus. 2013. (ENG.). 10p. (J). (gr. -1-k). bds. 8.99 *(978-1-4231-6396-1(6))* Disney Pr.

—Mickey & Donald Have a Farm. Disney Storybook Art Team, illus. 2012. (ENG.). 32p. (J). (gr. -1-k). pap. 5.99 *(978-1-4231-4946-0(7))* Disney Pr.

Sconyers, Jennifer. John Bunny Goes on Vacation. 2010. 20p. pap. 12.99 *(978-1-4490-7774-7(9))* AuthorHouse.

—The Map. 2010. 24p. pap. 12.99 *(978-1-4490-5731-2(4))* AuthorHouse.

Scotford, Groenewald & Scotford, Tina. A Bush Buffet in the Land of Kachoo. 2014. (Land of Kachoo Ser.). (ENG.). 32p. (J). (gr. k-2). pap. 10.95 *(978-1-4314-0761-3(5))* Jacana Media ZAF. Dist: Independent Pubs. Group.

Scotford, Tina. Saving the Rhino in the Land of Kachoo: The Land of Kachoo Series. Groenewald, Frans, illus. 2014. (Land of Kachoo Ser.). (ENG.). 32p. (J). (gr. k-2). pap. 10.95 *(978-1-4314-0760-6(7))* Jacana Media ZAF. Dist: Independent Pubs. Group.

Scott, B. L. The Adventures of Babadoodle Kit Kit. 2008. 52p. pap. 22.99 *(978-1-4389-1812-9(7))* AuthorHouse.

Scott, Brandon James, illus. The Big Pet Story. 2013. (Justin Time Ser.). (ENG.). 36p. (J). (gr. -1-3). 15.95 *(978-1-59702-041-1(9))* Immedium.

Scott, Cathy. Lily Mouse. 2011. (Illus.). 32p. pap. 12.95 *(978-1-4575-0305-4(0))* Dog Ear Publishing, LLC.

Scott, Chay L. Henry the Hippo. 2012. 32p. pap. 32.70 *(978-1-4797-1168-0(3))* Xlibris Corp.

Scott, Dee Mary. The Adventures of Charles & Camilla Chinchilla. 2012. (Illus.). 46p. pap. 6.99 *(978-1-78035-389-0(8)*, Fastprint Publishing) Upfront Publishing Ltd. GBR. Dist: Printondemand-worldwide.com.

Scott, Elizabeth M. Adventures with Mama Scottie & the Kids. Jackson, Kay Whytock, illus. 2008. 60p. pap. 8.95 *(978-0-595-51760-2(9))* iUniverse, Inc.

Scott, Gwen. Blackberry Junction. Baker, David, illus. 2011. 28p. pap. 24.95 *(978-1-4560-0951-9(6))* America Star Bks.

—In Between the Cracks: The Search for Zar. 2013. 20p. pap. 16.95 *(978-1-63000-080-6(9))* America Star Bks.

Scott, Jeff. The Discovery of Monkey Island. 2008. 64p. pap. 19.95 *(978-1-60610-921-2(9))* America Star Bks.

Scott, Lisa Ann. Dreams That Sparkle (Enchanted Pony Academy #4) 2017. (Enchanted Pony Academy Ser.: 4). (ENG.). 128p. (J). (gr. 2-5). pap. 4.99 *(978-0-545-90897-9(3)*, Scholastic Paperbacks) Scholastic, Inc.

Scott, Luke. Through a Crystal Doorknob. 2012. 88p. 24.95 *(978-1-4626-9420-4(9))*; pap. 19.95 *(978-1-4626-7361-2(9))* America Star Bks.

Scott, Martin J. A Boy Knight. 2011. 132p. pap. 12.99 *(978-1-61203-307-5(5))* Bottom of the Hill Publishing.

Scott, Shirley A. The Adventures of Jack & Dobbie: Happy Tails. 2010. 32p. pap. 13.95 *(978-1-4490-9865-0(7))* AuthorHouse.

—The Adventures of Jack & Dobbie: The Beginning. 2009. 32p. pap. 13.95 *(978-1-4389-4840-9(9))* AuthorHouse.

—The Adventures of Jack & Dobbie: Traveling Buddies. 2012. 30p. pap. 18.99 *(978-1-4772-7851-2(6))* AuthorHouse.

Scott, Terrence. Bryce Coris Blessing. 2006. 28p. pap. 9.95 *(978-1-4327-0000-3(6))* Outskirts Pr., Inc.

Scott, Victoria. Hear the Wolves. 2017. (ENG.). 240p. (J). (gr. 3-7). 16.99 *(978-1-338-04358-7(7)*, Scholastic Pr.) Scholastic, Inc.

—Titans. 2017. (ENG.). 320p. (J). (gr. 7). pap. 9.99 *(978-1-338-09555-5(2)*, Scholastic Pr.) Scholastic, Inc.

Scotton, Rob. Back to School, Splat! Scotton, Rob, illus. 2011. (Splat the Cat Ser.). (ENG., Illus.). 24p. (J). (gr. -1-3). pap. 3.99 *(978-0-06-197851-7(5)*, HarperFestival) HarperCollins Pubs.

—On with the Show. Scotton, Rob, illus. 2013. (Splat the Cat Ser.). (ENG., Illus.). 24p. (J). (gr. -1-3). pap. 3.99 *(978-0-06-209010-2(0)*, HarperFestival) HarperCollins Pubs.

—Oopsie-Daisy. Scotton, Rob, illus. 2014. (Splat the Cat Ser.). (ENG., Illus.). 24p. (J). (gr. -1-3). pap. 4.99 *(978-0-06-211585-0(5)*, HarperFestival) HarperCollins Pubs.

—Splat the Cat: What Was That? Scotton, Rob, illus. deluxe ed. 2013. (Splat the Cat Ser.). (ENG., Illus.). 16p. (J). (gr. k-3). pap. 6.99 *(978-0-06-197863-0(9)*, HarperFestival) HarperCollins Pubs.

—Up in the Air at the Fair. Scotton, Rob, illus. 2014. (I Can Read Level 1 Ser.). (ENG., Illus.). 32p. (J). (gr. -1-3). 16.99 *(978-0-06-211596-6(0))*; pap. 3.99 *(978-0-06-211595-9(2))* HarperCollins Pubs.

—A Whale of a Tale. Scotton, Rob, illus. 2013. (I Can Read Level 1 Ser.). (ENG., Illus.). 32p. (J). (gr. -1-3). pap. 3.99 *(978-0-06-209022-5(4))* HarperCollins Pubs.

Scriber, Christian. The Adventures of Almighty Mouse: And Tales of His Friends. 2009. 112p. pap. 10.99 *(978-1-4389-4313-8(X))* AuthorHouse.

Scribner, Don. Bennie & Thomas & the Battle at Worldsend, 1 vol. 2009. 84p. pap. 19.95 *(978-1-60836-630-9(8))* America Star Bks.

—Bennie & Thomas & the Rescue at Razor's Edge: Volume I. Scribner, Peter, illus. 2012. 44p. pap. 24.95 *(978-1-4626-8957-6(4))* America Star Bks.

—Bennie & Thomas & the Rescue at Razor's Edge: Volume II. Scribner, Peter, illus. 2012. 48p. pap. 24.95 *(978-1-4626-9472-3(1))* America Star Bks.

Scrimger, Richard. Into the Ravine. 2007. (ENG.). 264p. (YA). (gr. 5-12). per. 9.95 *(978-0-88776-822-4(9)*, Tundra Bks.) Tundra Bks. CAN. Dist: Penguin Random Hse. LLC.

—The Wolf & Me, 1 vol. 2014. (Seven Sequels Ser.). (ENG., Illus.). 256p. (J). (gr. 5-10). pap. 10.95 *(978-1-4598-0531-6(3))* Orca Bk. Pubs. USA.

Scrivanich, Kerry Ann. My Gifted & Talented Adventure. 2010. 28p. pap. 14.99 *(978-1-4490-8502-5(4))* AuthorHouse.

Scudamore, Beverly. Ice Dreams, 1 vol. 2003. (Lorimer Sports Stories Ser.). (ENG.). 112p. (J). (gr. 4-8). 16.95 *(978-1-55028-813-1(X)*, 9781550288131) Lorimer, James & Co., Ltd., Pubs. CAN. Dist: Casemate Pubs. & Bk. Distributors, LLC.

Seabrooke, Brenda. The Boy Who Saved the Town, 1 vol. Burns, Howard M., illus. 2009. (ENG.). 30p. (J). (gr. 2-5). 8.95 *(978-0-87033-405-4(0)*, 9780870334054, Cornell Maritime Pr./Tidewater Pubs.) Schiffer Publishing, Ltd.

Seagull, Robert. The Adventure to Septumus Sevusere & the Magic Glowing Rings. 2013. 60p. pap. 7.00 *(978-1-927558-43-0(3))* Birch Tree Publishing.

—Mindbender's Revenge Book One. 2013. 90p. pap. 8.00 *(978-1-927558-44-7(1))* Birch Tree Publishing.

Seals, Arthur. The Three Little Heroes: Book One of Kirk, Chelsea, & Samantha's Adventures. 2007. 84p. per. 8.95 *(978-0-595-44083-2(5))* iUniverse, Inc.

Seaman, John E. The Captain's Secret: A Lost Boy's Odyssey in Old New York. 2008. 220p. pap. 15.95 *(978-0-595-51753-4(6))* iUniverse, Inc.

—On the Road with Ruben Doyle. 2010. 170p. 29.99 *(978-1-4500-3196-7(X))*; pap. 19.99 *(978-1-4500-3195-0(1))* Xlibris Corp.

Searles, Rachel. The Lost Planet. 2014. (Lost Planet Ser.: 1). (ENG.). 384p. (YA). (gr. 4-8). 16.99 *(978-1-250-03879-1(0)*, 9781250038791) Feiwel & Friends.

Sebastian, Teresa L. & Harrell, Angel R. The Kootie Kids & the Attack of the Poot Troop. 2012. 28p. 24.95 *(978-1-4626-6019-3(3))* America Star Bks.

Sebring, Ruthie. Charlie, Itty's Guinea Pig, 1 vol. 2010. 30p. 24.95 *(978-1-4489-4391-3(4))* PublishAmerica, Inc.

Seddon, Jane. Tales of Bermy Wood, 1 vol. 2010. 64p. pap. 19.95 *(978-1-4489-2195-9(3))* America Star Bks.

Sedgwick, Julian. The Black Dragon. Moffett, Patricia, illus. 2016. (Mysterium Ser.: 1). (ENG.). 352p. (gr. 4-8). 18.99 *(978-1-4677-7567-0(3))*; 38.65 *(978-1-4677-9555-5(0))* Lerner Publishing Group. (Carolrhoda Bks.).

—The Palace of Memory. Moffett, Patricia, illus. 2017. (Mysterium Ser.: 2). (ENG.). 352p. (J). (gr. 4-8). 18.99 *(978-1-4677-7568-7(1)*, Carolrhoda Bks.) Lerner Publishing Group.

Sedgwick, Marcus. Floodland. unabr. ed. 2004. (Middle Grade Cassette Librariestm Ser.). 154p. (J). (gr. 4-7). pap. 29.00 incl. audio *(978-0-8072-0979-0(1)*, S YA 282 SP, Listening Library) Random Hse. Audio Publishing Group.

Sedwick, Helen. Coyote Winds. 2013. 268p. (gr. 7-10). pap. 10.99 *(978-0-9883021-2-9(8))* Ten Gallon Pr.

See, Ee Lin. My Kiasu Teenage Life in Singapore. 2005. (ENG., Illus.). 1p. per. 12.95 *(978-981-05-3016-7(1))* Monsoon Bks. Pte. Ltd. SGP. Dist: Tuttle Publishing.

Seeger, K R. Asa-Birdie Com. 2007. 244p. 26.95 *(978-0-595-69522-5(1))*; per. 16.95 *(978-0-595-45553-9(0))* iUniverse, Inc.

Segal, John. Alistair & Kip's Great Adventure! Segal, John, illus. 2008. (ENG., Illus.). 32p. (J). (gr. -1-3). 17.99 *(978-1-4169-0280-5(5)*, McElderry, Margaret K. Bks.) McElderry, Margaret K. Bks.

Segvic-Boudreaux, Ivana. Desperately Seeking Talent: A Puppy's Journey. 2010. 108p. pap. 13.95 *(978-1-4327-6112-7(9))* Outskirts Pr., Inc.

Seibers, Elexis. Jasmine & the Mystery of the Disappearing Shoes. 2011. 28p. pap. 9.95 *(978-1-4327-7626-8(6))* Outskirts Pr., Inc.

Seider, Sharon J. The Door in the Garden Wall. 2003. 139p. (J). pap. 13.95 *(978-0-7414-1712-1(X))* Infinity Publishing.

Seidman, Amy. The Adventures of Bebop Bunny. 2009. (Illus.). 20p. pap. 14.95 *(978-0-9824530-1-8(9)*, Epigraph Bks.) Monkfish Bk. Publishing Co.

Seidon, Bonnie Bale. The Adventures of Trevor & the Tiger. 2012. 104p. 21.79 *(978-1-4669-4389-6(0))*; pap. 11.79 *(978-1-4669-4391-9(2))* Trafford Publishing.

Seifert, Brandon. Disney Kingdoms: Seekers of the Weird. 2014. (ENG., Illus.). 120p. (J). (gr. -1-17). 24.99 *(978-0-7851-5452-5(3))* Marvel Worldwide, Inc.

Seitz, Melissa. Stewie Meets New Friends. Accrocco, Anthony, illus. 2012. 26p. pap. 12.95 *(978-1-61244-079-8(7))* Halo Publishing International.

Selby, Vicki L. Sleepy Sierra & the Great Blanket Adventure. 2011. 20p. (gr. 1-2). pap. 11.32 *(978-1-4567-3099-4(1))* AuthorHouse.

Seleccion de Oro: Libro Morado.Tr. of Golden Selection: Purple Book. (SPA.). (J). 13.48 *(978-84-8426-240-4(5))* Susaeta Ediciones, S.A. ESP. Dist: AIMS International Bks., Inc.

Selfors, Suzanne. Smells Like Dog. 2011. (Smells Like Dog Ser.: 1). (ENG.). 384p. (J). (gr. 3-7). pap. 7.99 *(978-0-316-04397-7(4))* Little, Brown Bks. for Young Readers.

—Smells Like Pirates. 2013. (Smells Like Dog Ser.: 3). (ENG.). 384p. (J). (gr. 3-7). pap. 8.99 *(978-0-316-20595-5(8))* Little, Brown Bks. for Young Readers.

Selig, Josh. Go, Wonder Pets! Little Airplane Productions, illus. 2008. (Wonder Pets! Ser.). (ENG.). 26p. (J). bds. 5.99 *(978-1-4169-4723-3(X)*, Simon Spotlight/Nickelodeon) Simon Spotlight/Nickelodeon.

Sell, Jeff. The Quarry Cave. 2006. 51p. pap. 16.95 *(978-1-4241-1188-6(9))* PublishAmerica, Inc.

Selznick, Brian. The Marvels. 2016. (CHI.). (J). ***(978-986-479-039-5(0))*** Commonwealth Publishing Co., Ltd.

—The Marvels. Selznick, Brian, illus. 2015. (ENG., Illus.). 672p. (J). (gr. 5-7). 32.99 *(978-0-545-44868-0(9)*, Scholastic Pr.) Scholastic, Inc.

Semerad, Emma & Semerad, Johnnie. Josh W. Time Out. Semerad, Johnnie, illus. 2003. (Illus.). 32p. (J). 15.00 *(978-0-9744251-0-8(9))* Quiet Man.

Sempebwa, Christina. Tales of Zindan. 2012. 154p. pap. *(978-1-908895-48-6(9))* FeedARead.com.

Send Me the Soap #2: The Amazon Adventure (lib. Binding) 2007. (J). lib. bdg. 11.95 *(978-0-9778536-3-2(2))* Eco-thumb Publishing Co.

Send-up, Maurice. Where the Mild Things Are: A Very Meek Parody. Leick, Bonnie, illus. 2009. (ENG.). 40p. (J). (gr. -1-3). 16.99 *(978-1-4169-9551-7(X)*, Simon & Schuster Bks. For Young Readers) Simon & Schuster Bks. For Young Readers.

Senior, Patricia. Mischief on Mumpit Mountain. 2009. 36p. pap. 14.75 *(978-1-60693-661-0(1)*, Eloquent Bks.) Strategic Book Publishing & Rights Agency (SBPRA).

Sensel, Joni. The Farwalker's Quest. (ENG.). 384p. (YA). (gr. 3-6). 2010. pap. 7.99 *(978-1-59990-450-4(0)*, 9781599904504) 2009. 16.99 *(978-1-59990-272-2(9)*, 9781599902722) Bloomsbury Publishing USA. (Bloomsbury USA Childrens).

Sente, Yves & Juillard, Andre. The Gondwana Shrine. 2012. (Blake & Mortimer Ser.: 11). (ENG., Illus.). 64p. pap. 15.95 *(978-1-84918-094-8(6))* CineBook GBR. Dist: National Bk. Network.

—The Sarcophagi of the Sixth Continent, Pt. 2. 2011. (Blake & Mortimer Ser.: 10). (ENG., Illus.). 64p. pap. 15.95 *(978-1-84918-077-1(6))* CineBook GBR. Dist: National Bk. Network.

Senzai, N. H. Ticket to India. 2015. (ENG., Illus.). 288p. (J). (gr. 3-7). 16.99 *(978-1-4814-2258-1(8)*, Simon & Schuster/Paula Wiseman Bks.) Simon & Schuster/Paula Wiseman Bks.

Sepulveda, Sandra. The Adventures of Halo & Manny: Lost in the City. 2008. 176p. pap. 14.99 *(978-1-4389-0156-5(9))* AuthorHouse.

Serafin, Michael. 4 Seasons of Baghdad. 2007. (ENG.). 60p. per. 16.95 *(978-1-4241-2303-2(8))* PublishAmerica, Inc.

Serban, Milica. Little Bag with Two Gold Coins. 2012. 20p. pap. 17.99 *(978-1-4772-1132-8(2))* AuthorHouse.

Sergeant, Kate. It's a Very Good Night. 2005. (J). *(978-0-9770158-5-6(8))* BeachWalk Bks. Inc.

Serino, Robert. The Adventures of Pea-Shooter: Into the Forbidden Forest. Lally, Cory, illus. 2012. 32p. pap. 24.95 *(978-1-4626-8019-1(4))* America Star Bks.

Serpa, Dylon J. Moosey's Adventures: The Way Home. 2013. 28p. pap. 24.95 *(978-1-62709-256-2(0))* America Star Bks.

Serrano, Pet. Best Friends No Matter What. 2007. (Illus.). 32p. (J). pap. *(978-0-9770497-9-0(5)*, Itty Bitty Kitty) Singing Moon Pr.

Serrano, Tomas. Salfon el Limpiador de Tejados. (SPA.). 48p. (J). (gr. 1-3). pap. *(978-84-264-3746-4(X))* Editorial Lumen ESP. Dist: Lectorum Pubns., Inc.

Serwacki, Kevin & Pallace, Chris. Joey & Johnny, the Ninjas: Epic Fail. Serwacki, Kevin & Pallace, Chris, illus. 2016. (Joey & Johnny, the Ninjas Ser.: 2). (Illus.). 384p. (J). (gr. 3-7). 12.99 *(978-0-06-229935-2(2))* HarperCollins Pubs.

Sesame Street Staff. Fairly Furry 2 bk Big Red Riding Hood 3 Little Grouches. 2007. 15.99 *(978-1-59069-625-5(5))* Studio Mouse LLC.

Session, Garry. Odessa Bluegill & The Star Ship: Odessa Bluegill & The Space Ship. 2008.Tr. of Odessa Bluegill Y Lanave espacial. (SPA., Illus.). 45p. (J). per. 9.95 *(978-0-9658006-3-1(6))* Session Family.

Sesso, Karen A. Off They Swam, 1 vol. 2009. 37p. pap. 19.95 *(978-1-61546-453-1(0))* PublishAmerica, Inc.

Seton, Ernest Thompson. Rolf in the Woods: The Adventures of a Boy Scout with Indian Quonab & Little Dog Skookum. 2013. (ENG., Illus.). 400p. (J). (gr. 6-17). pap. 14.95 *(978-1-62087-386-1(9)*, 620386) Skyhorse Publishing Co., Inc.

—Two Little Savages: The Adventures of Two Boys Who Lived As American Indians. Seton, Ernest Thompson, illus. 2010. (ENG., Illus.). 313p. (J). (gr. 4-7). pap. 18.00 *(978-1-60419-033-5(7))* Axios Pr.

—Wild Animals I Have Known. 2009. 116p. pap. 9.50 *(978-1-60459-623-6(6))* Wilder Pubns., Corp.

Seuss, Dr. Gatola da Cartola. pap. 23.95 *(978-85-7406-085-9(2))* Schwarcz, Editora Ltda, Companhia das Letrinhas BRA. Dist: Distribooks, Inc.

Seven, John. The Alchemist War, 1 vol. Phillips, Craig, illus. 2013. (Time-Tripping Faradays Ser.). (ENG.). 160p. (gr. 4-5). 9.95 *(978-1-62370-011-9(6))*; (YA). pap. 5.95 *(978-1-4342-6438-1(6))*; (gr. 4-5). lib. bdg. 26.65 *(978-1-4342-6028-4(3))* Stone Arch Bks.

—The Dragon of Rome, 1 vol. Phillips, Craig, illus. 2013. (Time-Tripping Faradays Ser.). (ENG.). 160p. (gr. 4-5). 9.95 *(978-1-62370-012-6(4))*; lib. bdg. 26.65 *(978-1-4342-6029-1(1))* Stone Arch Bks.

—The Outlaw of Sherwood Forest, 1 vol. Hans, Stephanie, illus. 2014. (Time-Tripping Faradays Ser.). (ENG.). 192p. (gr. 4-5). lib. bdg. 26.65 *(978-1-4342-9174-5(X))* Stone Arch Bks.

—The Terror of the Tengu, 1 vol. Hans, Stephanie, illus. 2014. (Time-Tripping Faradays Ser.). (ENG.). 192p. (gr. 4-5). 26.65 *(978-1-4342-9173-8(1))* Stone Arch Bks.

—The Time-Tripping Faradays, 1 vol. Phillips, Craig, illus. (Time-Tripping Faradays Ser.). (ENG.). 160p. (gr. 4-5). 2014.

53.30 *(978-1-4342-9473-9(0))* 2013. 53.30 *(978-1-4342-8994-0(X))* Stone Arch Bks.

Seven, John & Phillips, Craig. The Dragon of Rome, 1 vol. 2013. (ENG.). 160p. (YA). pap. *(978-1-4342-6439-8(4))* Stone Arch Bks.

The Seven Little Kids. 2005. (Folk Tales Set 2 Ser.). (J). 5.33 *(978-1-58453-305-4(6))* Pioneer Valley Bks.

Severine Rugumamu. Further Adventures of the Black Hand Gang. 2005. 64p. pap. *(978-9966-25-422-1(6))* Heinemann Kenya, Limited (East African Educational Publishers Ltd E.A.E.P.) KEN. Dist: Michigan State Univ. Pr.

Sévigny, Eric, illus. Caillou, Search & Count: Fun Adventures! 2013. (Coloring & Activity Book Ser.). (ENG.). 16p. (J). (gr. -1-1). bds. 9.99 *(978-2-89718-034-8(X))* Caillouet, Gerry.

Sewell, Kele. Beewee & Meager to the Rescue! the Underbed Entertainment Network. 2008. 28p. pap. 12.50 *(978-1-60693-326-8(4),* Eloquent Bks.) Strategic Book Publishing & Rights Agency (SBPRA).

Seybold, Celisa. The Keys to Adventure Take Flight. 2011. 48p. pap. 9.95 *(978-1-257-06278-2(6))* Lulu Pr., Inc.

Seykora, Teresa. The Case of the Missing Peanut Butter: The Adventures of Peanut Butter Bob. Drewes, Dan, illus. 2010. 32p. 12.99 *(978-1-4520-2678-7(5))* AuthorHouse.

Seykora, Teresa M. Peanut Butter Bob's Alphabet Book: The Adventures of Peanut Butter Bob. 2010. 36p. pap. 15.49 *(978-1-4520-4184-1(9))* AuthorHouse.

Sezgin, Orhan. The Adventures of Little Selim. 2011. (ENG., Illus.). 48p. pap. 4.95 *(978-1-59784-237-2(0))* Tughra Bks.

Shaboo, Joseph R. Shalamazoo. Churchill, Jessica, photos by. Date not set. (Illus.). 56p. (J). (gr. 2-5). *(978-0-9700380-0-5(3))* Purple Pig Publishing.

Shackleford, Maudie. An Upside-Down Tale. 2013. 114p. pap. 12.50 *(978-1-62212-156-4(2),* Strategic Bk. Publishing) Strategic Book Publishing & Rights Agency (SBPRA).

Shacter, Sara F. Heading to the Wedding: You're Invited to Join Patrick & Evie on the Great Adventure of Becoming (Almost) Perfect Guests. Thornton, Christine, illus. 2006. (ENG.). 32p. (J). (gr. -1-3). 18.95 *(978-1-933176-05-5(9))* Red Rock Pr., Inc.

Shade, Jeff. An Unusual Education. 2010. (J). pap. *(978-0-88092-317-0(2))* Royal Fireworks Publishing Co.

Shadow, Jak. Space Plague. 2005. (F. E. A. R. Adventures S. Ser.). (ENG., Illus.). 126p. (J). 8.00 *(978-1-84046-694-2(4),* Wizard Books) Icon Bks., Ltd. GBR. Dist: Publishers Group Canada.

Shaffer, J. E. Mrs. Mugsy & Nolan Grant's Island Adventure, 1 vol. 2010. 30p. 24.95 *(978-1-4489-4770-6(7))* PublishAmerica, Inc.

Shaffer, Jason. The Quick Brown Fox Jumps over the Lazy Dog. 2012. 36p. pap. 21.99 *(978-1-4771-3824-3(2))* Xlibris Corp.

Shaffert, Charles F. Googus to the Rescue. Stringer, Margaret, illus. l.t. ed. 2005. 31p. (J). per. 10.00 *(978-1-59879-043-6(9))* Lifevest Publishing, Inc.

Shah, Yasmin. Abby & the Feather Quest. 2010. (Illus.). 48p. pap. 10.49 *(978-1-4343-9839-0(0))* AuthorHouse.

Shakespeare, Strawberry. Hope's Horse: The Mystery of Shadow Ridge. 2013. 94p. pap. 11.97 *(978-0-9774335-6-8(0))* Diamond Star Pr.

Shalant, Phyllis. Beware of Kissing Lizard Lips. 2010. 196p. pap. 13.95 *(978-1-4401-8339-3(2))* iUniverse, Inc.

—When Pirates Came to Brooklyn. 2010. 224p. pap. 14.95 *(978-1-4401-8338-6(4))* iUniverse, Inc.

Shaler, Robert. The Boy Scouts As Country Fair Guides. 2005. pap. 21.95 *(978-1-4191-2256-9(8))* Kessinger Publishing, LLC.

—The Boy Scouts in the Great Flood. 2005. pap. 21.95 *(978-1-4191-2257-6(6))* Kessinger Publishing, LLC.

Shan, Darren, pseud. Bec. 2008. (ENG.). 256p. (YA). (gr. 10-17). pap. 10.00 *(978-0-316-01390-1(0))* Little, Brown Bks. for Young Readers.

—Vampire Mountain, Vol. 4. 2010. (Cirque du Freak, the Manga Ser.: 4). lib. bdg. 24.55 *(978-0-606-14433-9(1),* Turtleback) Turtleback Bks.

—Zom-B. Pleece, Warren, illus. 2016. (ENG.). 208p. (YA). (gr. 7-17). 15.00 *(978-0-316-33845-5(1))* Little Brown & Co.

—Zom-B. 2015. (Zom-B Ser.: 11). (ENG., Illus.). 192p. (gr. 7-17). 15.99 *(978-0-316-21409-4(4))* Little Brown & Co.

Shand, Patrick. Marvel Guardians of the Galaxy: Space Riot. 2017. lib. bdg. 24.50 ***(978-0-606-40199-9(7))*** Turtleback Bks.

Shanghai Animation Studio Staff & Tang, Sanmu. Monkey Makes Havoc in Heaven. Xiaozhen, Wu, tr. from CHI. 2010. (Favorite Children's Ser.). (ENG., Illus.). 32p. (J). (gr. -1-3). pap. 5.95 *(978-1-60220-974-9(X))* BetterLink Pr., Inc.

Shank, Diane S. Minnow Kisses. Bailey, Terri L., illus. 2011. 34p. pap. 12.95 *(978-1-936343-60-7(6))* Peppertree Pr., The.

Shanker, Tarun & Zekas, Kelly. These Ruthless Deeds. 2017. (These Vicious Masks Ser.). (ENG.). 320p. (YA). pap. 10.99 *(978-1-250-12795-2(5),* 9781250127952) Feiwel & Friends.

Shankman, Ed. I Went to the Party in Kalamazoo. Frank, Dave, illus. 2013. (ENG.). 40p. pap. 12.95 *(978-1-938700-22-4(8),* Commonwealth Editions) Applewood Bks.

Shanks, Cindy. Emilia Camina la Vereda de Borregos. 2009. 48p. pap. 19.95 *(978-1-4490-2388-1(6))* AuthorHouse.

—Emily Walks the Sheep Trail. 2009. 48p. pap. 19.95 *(978-1-4490-2208-2(1))* AuthorHouse.

Shannon, David. Uh-Oh, David! A David Sticker Book. Shannon, David, illus. 2013. (ENG., Illus.). 16p. (J). (gr. -1-k). 6.99 *(978-0-545-43768-4(7),* Cartwheel Bks.) Scholastic, Inc.

Shannon, Ronnie Jay. Samurai Force: the Final Hope: The Junior Novel. 2007. (ENG.). 76p. per. 19.95 *(978-1-4241-6528-5(8))* America Star Bks.

Shaposhnik, Alina. A Warm Yellow Pancake, 1 vol. 2010. 22p. 24.95 *(978-1-4489-7067-4(9))* PublishAmerica, Inc.

Sharkey, Niamh. Santasaurus. Sharkey, Niamh, illus. 2005. (ENG., Illus.). 32p. (J). (gr. -1-2). 15.99 *(978-0-7636-2671-6(6))* Candlewick Pr.

Sharma, Shivan. The Castle, Dragons & a Cricket Ball. 2009. 76p. pap. *(978-1-84549-415-5(6),* Swirl) arima publishing.

Sharmat, Andrew & Sharmat, Marjorie Weinman. Nate the Great & the Missing Birthday Snake. Wheeler, Jody, illus. 2017. (Nate the Great Ser.). (ENG.). 64p. (J). (gr. 1-4). 12.99 ***(978-1-101-93467-8(0))***; lib. bdg. 15.99 ***(978-1-101-93469-2(7))*** Random Hse. Children's Bks. (Delacorte Bks. for Young Readers).

Sharmat, Marjorie Weinman. Nate the Great Goes Undercover. Simont, Marc, illus. unabr. ed. 2004. (Nate the Great Ser.: No. 2). 48p. (J). (gr. 1-3). pap. 17.00 incl. audio *(978-0-8072-0201-2(0),* FTR172SP, Listening Library) Random Hse. Audio Publishing Group.

Sharp, Kevin. The Amazing Adventures of Ted Shuttle: Book One. 2012. (Illus.). 24p. pap. 19.82 *(978-1-4772-4286-5(4))* AuthorHouse.

Sharp, Margery. The Rescuers. Williams, Garth, illus. 2016. (ENG.). 160p. (J). (gr. 4-7). pap. 9.99 *(978-1-68137-007-1(7),* NYRB Kids) New York Review of Bks., Inc., The.

Sharpe, Gerald. Parade of Lights. Moya, Patricia, illus. 2007. (What Lies Beneath the Bed Ser.). 487p. (J). per. 11.00 *(978-1-933894-01-0(6))* IJN Publishing, Inc.

—Tommy's Tales. Moya, Patricia, illus. 2006. (Tommy's Tales Ser.). 300p. (J). per. 7.00 *(978-1-933894-00-3(8))* IJN Publishing, Inc.

Sharpless, Sheila M. Mystery on Bear's Island: A Short Adventure Novel for Girls Aged 8-11. 2012. 74p. 24.99 *(978-1-4691-3576-2(0))*; pap. 15.99 *(978-1-4691-3575-5(2))* Xlibris Corp.

Shasek, Judy & Schulz, Wendy Anderson. E-Wally & the Renegades. 2003. per. *(978-0-9729599-0-2(4))* invenTEAM, LLC.

Shaughnessy, Adam. The Trickster's Tale, Bk. 1. 2016. (Unbelievable FIB Ser.: 1). (ENG.). 288p. (J). (gr. 3-7). pap. 6.95 *(978-1-61620-637-6(3))* Algonquin Bks. of Chapel Hill.

Shava, Ryder. Undersea Adventure, 01 vols., 1. 2016. (Rosen REAL Readers: STEM & STEAM Collection). (ENG.). 12p. (J). pap. 6.33 *(978-1-5081-1599-1(0),* Rosen Classroom) Rosen Publishing Group, Inc., The.

Shaw, Alexander William. The Adventures of A Teenage Time Traveller. 2009. 84p. pap., pap. 12.95 *(978-0-9561592-2-9(2))* Hetman Publishing GBR. Dist: Lulu Pr., Inc.

Shaw-Burns, Carol. Grandma's House: Jacob's Adventure. 2012. 24p. pap. 17.99 *(978-1-4685-5318-5(6))* AuthorHouse.

Shaw, Daniel, illus. Journey to Pansophigus. 2005. (J). per. 9.95 *(978-0-9772168-0-2(2))* Water Lily Pr., Inc.

Shaw, Dawn. Anthony's First Ant March. 2008. 36p. pap. 24.95 *(978-1-60672-992-2(6))* America Star Bks.

Shaw, Debra. Riley & Ginger's Big Adventure. 2013. 24p. pap. 10.95 *(978-1-4808-0099-1(6))* Archway Publishing.

Shaw, Murray & Cosson, M. J. Sherlock Holmes & the Adventure at the Abbey Grange. Rohrbach, Sophie, illus. 2010. (On the Case with Holmes & Watson Ser.: 2). (ENG.). 48p. (J). (gr. 4-6). pap. 6.95 *(978-0-7613-6200-5(2),* Graphic Universe™) Lerner Publishing Group.

—Sherlock Holmes & the Adventure of the Blue Gem. Rohrbach, Sophie, illus. 2010. (On the Case with Holmes & Watson Ser.: 3). (ENG.). 48p. (J). (gr. 4-6). pap. 6.95 *(978-0-7613-6202-9(9),* Graphic Universe™) Lerner Publishing Group.

—Sherlock Holmes & the Adventure of the Dancing Men. Rohrbach, Sophie, illus. 2010. (On the Case with Holmes & Watson Ser.: 4). (ENG.). 48p. (J). (gr. 4-6). pap. 6.95 *(978-0-7613-6199-2(5),* Graphic Universe™) Lerner Publishing Group.

—Sherlock Holmes & the Adventure of the Speckled Band. Rohrbach, Sophie, illus. 2010. (On the Case with Holmes & Watson Ser.: 5). (ENG.). 48p. (J). (gr. 4-6). 27.93 *(978-0-7613-6186-2(3))*; pap. 6.95 *(978-0-7613-6198-5(7),* Graphic Universe™) Lerner Publishing Group.

—Sherlock Holmes & the Adventure of the Sussex Vampire. Rohrbach, Sophie, illus. 2010. (On the Case with Holmes & Watson Ser.: 6). (ENG.). 48p. (J). (gr. 4-6). pap. 6.95 *(978-0-7613-6201-2(0),* Graphic Universe™) Lerner Publishing Group.

Shaw, Patricia. Gilly the Duck Meets the Magical Lady. 2013. 36p. pap. 20.99 *(978-1-4817-0288-1(2))* AuthorHouse.

Shaw, Sandy. The Adventures of Dilly Dog: Dilly at the Lakes. 2017. (ENG., Illus.). 16p. (J). pap. 13.95 ***(978-1-78693-586-1(4),*** 5d695943-b94e-4707-ab27-a18a86393def) Austin, Stan AUS. Dist: Bookmasters Distribution.

Shaw, Sandy. Do You Know Where the Bus Driver Will Go? 2012. 24p. pap. 15.99 *(978-1-4771-2107-8(2))* Xlibris Corp.

Shaw, Scott. Shrek - Living Green, Vol. 2. 2012. (ENG.). 52p. pap. 6.95 *(978-1-936340-19-4(4),* 9781936340194) Ape Entertainment.

Shaw, Susan. Star. 2003. 112p. pap. 11.45 *(978-1-4107-2451-9(4))* AuthorHouse.

Shea, Christine. Las Aventuras de Max, el Camión Volteador: El Mejor Día de Nieve! = the Adventures of Max the Dump Truck: The Greatest Snow Day Ever! Chase, Michelle B. & Chase, Tanor R., illus. 2007. (ENG & SPA.). (J). *(978-1-933002-01-9(8))* PublishingWorks.

Shea, Lisa. Meet Chase the Police-Bot. 2013. (Transformers Passport to Reading Ser.). (J). lib. bdg. 13.55 *(978-0-606-31736-8(8),* Turtleback) Turtleback Bks.

—Transformers: Rescue Bots: Meet Heatwave the Fire-Bot. 2013. (Passport to Reading Level 1 Ser.). (ENG., Illus.). 32p. (J). (gr. -1-1). 4.99 *(978-0-316-22830-5(3))* Little, Brown Bks. for Young Readers.

Sheard, Jean. A Chinese Fantasy - Cave in a Casket. 2007. 128p. 34.95 *(978-1-84753-349-4(3))*; (Illus.). pap. 10.50 *(978-1-84753-249-7(7))* Lulu Pr., Inc.

Shearer, Alex. The Cloud Hunters. 2013. (ENG.). 288p. (J). (gr. 6-8). 14.95 *(978-1-62636-216-1(5),* 263216, Sky Pony Pr.) Skyhorse Publishing Co., Inc.

—Sea Legs. 2006. (ENG.). 320p. (J). (gr. 5-9). per. 17.99 *(978-0-689-87144-3(9),* Simon & Schuster/Paula Wiseman Bks.) Simon & Schuster/Paula Wiseman Bks.

—Sky Run. 2014. (Cloud Hunters Ser.). (ENG.). 288p. (J). (gr. 2-7). 14.95 *(978-1-62873-593-2(7),* Sky Pony Pr.) Skyhorse Publishing Co., Inc.

Sheehan, Jennifer E. Chicky Dickey's Animal Pancakes. 2003. (Illus.). 32p. (J). 15.95 *(978-0-9700952-9-5(5))* Bumples.

Sheehan, Peter. Willy Wagtail grows Up. 2010. 32p. pap. 19.99 *(978-1-4461-3281-4(1))* Lulu Pr., Inc.

Sheen, C. D. McKnight. Morphani: And the Valley of the Coloured Doorway's. 2012. 76p. 37.37 *(978-1-4691-7680-2(7))*; pap. 18.68 *(978-1-4691-7679-6(3))* Xlibris Corp.

Sheets, Katherine. Captured by Henrey, 1 vol. 2010. 48p. pap. 16.95 *(978-1-4489-4538-2(0))* America Star Bks.

Shein, Erik. The Pillow Princess: Mystoryland Friends Brand. 2014. (ENG., Illus.). 32p. (J). 8.95 *(978-0-9765358-0-5(7))* Ark Watch Holdings LLC.

Shelby, Anne. The Adventures of Molly Whuppie & Other Appalachian Folktales. McArdle, Paula, illus. 2007. (ENG.). 96p. (J). (gr. 3-7). 20.00 *(978-0-8078-3163-2(8))* Univ. of North Carolina Pr.

Sheley, Kristen. Partners in Time #5: A Change of Course. 2010. 236p. 25.95 *(978-1-4502-6658-1(4))*; pap. 15.95 *(978-1-4502-6657-4(6))* iUniverse, Inc.

Shelley Ann Boutcher-Caldwell. The Naughty Little Birdie & the Surprise Cake. 2009. 40p. pap. 16.99 *(978-1-4389-4896-6(4))* AuthorHouse.

Shelton, Dave. A Boy & a Bear in a Boat. 2013. (ENG.). 304p. (J). (gr. 2-5). 6.99 *(978-0-449-81060-6(7),* Yearling) Random Hse. Children's Bks.

Shelton, Rick. Hoggle's Christmas. Gates, Donald, illus. 2007. 80p. (J). pap. 11.95 *(978-1-60306-026-4(X))* NewSouth, Inc.

Shepard, Aaron. The Adventures of Mouse Deer. Gamble, Kim, illus. 2005. 48p. (J). (gr. -1-4). pap. 10.00 *(978-0-938497-32-5(4),* Skyhook Pr.) Shepard Pubns.

—The Legend of Lightning Larry. Goffe, Toni, illus. 2005. 48p. (J). pap. 10.00 *(978-0-938497-28-8(6),* Skyhook Pr.) Shepard Pubns.

Shepard, Sara. Burned. 2012. (Pretty Little Liars Ser.: 12). (ENG.). 336p. (YA). (gr. 9). 17.99 *(978-0-06-208192-6(6),* HarperTeen) HarperCollins Pubs.

Shepherd, Deborah. A Thread Through Time. 2013. 102p. pap. *(978-0-9571756-5-5(5))* Shepline Words.

Shepherd, JaiLeen. Lea's Song: The Life of a Special Little Horse. 2006. (J). per. 13.95 *(978-1-889743-54-7(2))* Robbie Dean Pr.

Shepherd, Megan. The Gauntlet. 2017. (Cage Ser.: 3). 400p. (YA). (gr. 8). 17.99 *(978-0-06-224312-6(8))* HarperCollins Pubs.

—The Hunt. 2016. (Cage Ser.: 2). 368p. (YA). (gr. 8). 17.99 *(978-0-06-224308-9(X))* HarperCollins Pubs.

Shepherd, Wilf. Behind the Whiskers: Tales for the Young at Heart. 2012. 282p. pap. 28.03 *(978-1-4797-0473-6(3))* Xlibris Corp.

Shepperson, Jacqueline Ruth. The Blue Jay Tales. 2005. 89p. pap. 19.95 *(978-1-4137-3884-1(2))* America Star Bks.

Shepple, Sue Ann. Christopher & Grammy Join the Circus. 2011. 28p. pap. 15.99 *(978-1-4628-6245-0(4))* Xlibris Corp.

Sheridan, Celi. Tolly & Maisie's Ghastly Adventure. 2011. (Illus.). 48p. (gr. -1). pap. 11.95 *(978-1-4670-0397-1(2))* AuthorHouse.

Sheriff, Jeanne. Walkabout Kid. 2013. 172p. pap. 12.95 *(978-1-4787-2130-7(8))* Outskirts Pr., Inc.

Sherman, Brandi. The Sweetest Dreams. 2013. (ENG.). 26p. (J). pap. 15.95 *(978-1-4327-9976-2(2))* Outskirts Pr., Inc.

Sherman, Harold Morrow. Fight 'Em Big Three. 2011. 272p. 47.95 *(978-1-258-07552-1(0))* Literary Licensing, LLC.

Sherman, Josepha. Land of Endless Night. 2007. 124p. pap. 4.99 *(978-1-931567-68-8(9))* Margaret Weis Productions, Ltd.

Sherman, M. Zachary. Bloodlines, 4 vols., Set. Casas, Fritz, illus. Incl. Blood Brotherhood. 26.65 *(978-1-4342-2559-7(3))*; Control under Fire. lib. bdg. 26.65 *(978-1-4342-2561-0(5))*; Fighting Phantoms. lib. bdg. 26.65 *(978-1-4342-2560-3(7))*; Time for War. 26.65 *(978-1-4342-2558-0(5))*; (gr. 4-8). (Bloodlines Ser.). (ENG., Illus.). 88p. 2011. Set lib. bdg. 106.60 *(978-1-4342-3140-6(2))* Stone Arch Bks.

—Impulse, Vol. 2. Majado, Caio et al, illus. 2011. (Tony Hawk's 900 Revolution Ser.). (ENG.). 128p. (gr. 3-4). pap. 7.19 *(978-1-4342-3452-0(5))*; lib. bdg. 26.65 *(978-1-4342-3203-8(4))* Stone Arch Bks. (Tony Hawk's 900 Revolution).

Sherrill, Rusty & Miers, Doug. Kid Nitro & the Sinister Slorp. Sherrill, Cathy, ed. Sherrill, Rusty, illus. 2007. (Illus.). 273p. (YA). per. 14.95 *(978-0-9787729-0-1(3))* RS Art Studio.

Sherwood-Sitts, Herm. The Secret of Cypress Swamp. 2011. 20p. pap. 24.95 *(978-1-4560-6166-1(6))* America Star Bks.

Shickman, Allan Richard. Zan-Gah: A Prehistoric Adventure. 2007. 160p. (J). (gr. 4-7). per. 9.95 *(978-0-9790357-0-8(8))* Earthshaker Bks.

Shields, Christine. The Tiny Little Scary Mouse. 2012. 20p. pap. 12.68 *(978-1-4669-2147-4(1))* Trafford Publishing.

Shields, Gillian. Holly Takes a Risk. Turner, Helen, illus. 2008. (Mermaid S. O. S. Ser.: 4). (ENG.). 96p. (J). (gr. 1-4). pap. 4.50 *(978-1-59990-214-2(1),* 9781599902142, Bloomsbury USA Childrens) Bloomsbury Publishing USA.

—Sophie Makes a Splash. Turner, Helen, illus. 2008. (Mermaid S. O. S. Ser.: 3). (ENG.). 96p. (J). (gr. 1-4). pap. 4.50 *(978-1-59990-212-8(5),* 9781599902128, Bloomsbury USA Childrens) Bloomsbury Publishing USA.

Shields, Lew. Legend of Pleasant Island. 2004. 203p. (YA). pap. 18.95 *(978-1-930002-55-5(6))* I & L Publishing.

Shine, Joe. I Become Shadow. 2015. (ENG.). 304p. (YA). (gr. 9). pap. 10.99 *(978-1-61695-537-3(6),* Soho Teen) Soho Pr., Inc.

Shirer, Priscilla. The Prince Warriors & the Swords of Rhema. 2017. (Prince Warriors Ser.). (ENG.). 312p. (J). (gr. 3-7). 12.99 *(978-1-4336-9021-1(7),* B&H Kids) B&H Publishing Group.

Shirer, Priscilla & Detwiler, Gina. The Prince Warriors. 2016. (Prince Warriors Ser.). (ENG.). 288p. (J). (gr. 3-7). 12.99 *(978-1-4336-9019-8(5),* B&H Kids) B&H Publishing Group.

Shirley Russak Wachtel. Howie Rocket — World Traveler-Detective: The Search for the Lovely Precious. 2010. 100p. pap. 9.95 *(978-1-4401-9993-6(0))* iUniverse, Inc.

Shiro, S. P. Postcards from the Beyond. 2012. 194p. pap. *(978-1-78176-408-4(5))* FeedARead.com.

Shirt, Virginia. Angels of Clover Farm. Lane, Rob, ed. 2012. 132p. pap. *(978-1-78176-546-3(4))* FeedARead.com.

Shoals, Cinda. Ashley Says. 2008. 16p. pap. 24.95 *(978-1-60672-600-6(5))* America Star Bks.

Shock, Tanya & Thomson, Roger. Walking in Courage: Stories of Virtue's Forest. 2012. 24p. pap. 12.95 *(978-1-4497-3443-5(X),* WestBow Pr.) Author Solutions, Inc.

Shoesmith-Bateman, Amanda. The Magic Tree House, 1 vol. Beitz-Grant, Heather, illus. 2010. 22p. 24.95 *(978-1-4489-3866-7(X))* PublishAmerica, Inc.

Shon. Henry Boothill: The Return of Nidagall, 1 vol. 2010. 52p. pap. 16.95 *(978-1-4512-8700-4(3))* America Star Bks.

Shondalae. The Great Giver of Life, No. 8. 2008. 49p. pap. 16.95 *(978-1-60672-071-4(6))* America Star Bks.

Shooter, Darlene D. The Adventures of the Tree Frog Family: My Favorite Little Critters. 2009. 19p. (J). pap. 16.95 *(978-1-4327-3483-1(0))* Outskirts Pr., Inc.

Shores, Lloyd. The Adventures of Mr. Ant. 2013. 28p. pap. 13.95 *(978-1-4497-9747-8(4),* WestBow Pr.) Author Solutions, Inc.

Shorrock, Anne. The Secret Adventures of Amelia & Rainbow. 2008. 36p. pap. 15.95 *(978-1-60693-011-3(7),* Eloquent Bks.) Strategic Book Publishing & Rights Agency (SBPRA).

Shotz, Jennifer Li. Hero: Hurricane Rescue. 2017. (Hero Ser.: 2). 192p. (J). (gr. 3-7). 12.99 ***(978-0-06-279139-9(7))***; pap. 7.99 *(978-0-06-256043-8(3))* HarperCollins Pubs.

Shoup, Andrew J. Andy & Elmer's Apple Dumpling Adventure. 2nd ed. 2007. (J). 16.95 *(978-0-9720436-3-2(2))* TokoBooks, LLC.

—Andy & Elmer's Apple Dumpling Adventure Coloring & Activity Book. Shoup, Andrew J., illus. 2007. (Illus.). 36p. (J). 3.95 *(978-0-9720436-2-5(4))* TokoBooks, LLC.

Shreeve, Elizabeth. Hector Afloat. Levy, Pamela R., illus. 2004. (Ready-For-Chapters Ser.: 3). (ENG.). 64p. (J). (gr. 1-4). pap. 6.99 *(978-0-689-86416-2(7),* Simon & Schuster/Paula Wiseman Bks.) Simon & Schuster/Paula Wiseman Bks.

Shreve, Steve. The Adventures of Benny, 0 vols. 2013. (ENG.). 160p. (J). (gr. 3-6). pap. 9.99 *(978-1-4778-1607-3(0),* 9781477816073, Amazon Children's Publishing) Amazon Publishing.

—The Adventures of Charlie: Bigfoot or the Value of a Smelly Friend. Shreve, Steve, illus. 2010. (Adventures of Charlie Ser.). (Illus.). 32p. pap. *(978-0-237-54284-9(6))* Evans Brothers, Ltd.

—The Bogey Man: Or a Good Argument for Not Picking Your Nose. Shreve, Steve, illus. 2010. (Adventures of Charlie Ser.). (Illus.). 32p. pap. *(978-0-237-54287-0(0))* Evans Brothers, Ltd.

—Monkey Island: Or the Advantage of Opposable Thumbs. Shreve, Steve, illus. 2010. (Adventures of Charlie Ser.). (Illus.). 32p. pap. *(978-0-237-54288-7(9))* Evans Brothers, Ltd.

—The Mummy: Or Another Great Use for Toilet Paper. 2010. (Adventures of Charlie Ser.). (Illus.). 32p. pap. *(978-0-237-54285-6(4))* Evans Brothers, Ltd.

—Pirates: Or the Truth about Life on the High Seas. Shreve, Steve, illus. 2010. (Adventures of Charlie Ser.). (Illus.). 32p. pap. *(978-0-237-54286-3(2))* Evans Brothers, Ltd.

Shubin, Masha. The Camp Caper: A Shubin Cousins Adventure. Hayes, Kathy & Hayes, David, illus. 2013. 88p. pap. 6.95 *(978-0-9792145-1-6(3))* Anno Domini.

—The Fairytale Fracas: A Shubin Cousins Adventure. Shubin, Jon, illus. 2012. 200p. pap. 7.95 *(978-0-9792145-8-5(0))* Anno Domini.

Shuff, Chrissi. The Dancing Tree & other Stories. 2010. (Illus.). 80p. pap. 28.99 *(978-1-4520-0054-1(9))* AuthorHouse.

Shuff, Lana Tanaka. Kira Helps A Friend. l.t. ed. 2007. (ENG., Illus.). 28p. (J). per. 9.95 *(978-1-4327-0810-8(4))* Outskirts Pr., Inc.

Shukla, Subir. The Boy Who Loved Colour. Sabnani, Nina, illus. 2004. (ENG & HIN.). (J). *(978-81-8146-042-4(1))* Tulika Pubs.

Shulda, Daron M. Dragon Boots. 2009. 40p. pap. 18.49 *(978-1-4389-7022-6(6))* AuthorHouse.

Shulman, Polly. The Grimm Legacy. (ENG.). (J). (gr. 5-18). 2011. 352p. 8.99 *(978-0-14-241904-5(4),* Puffin Books) 2010. (Illus.). 336p. 16.99 *(978-0-399-25096-5(4),* G.P. Putnam's Sons Books for Young Readers) Penguin Young Readers Group.

Shultz, D. B. The World Adventures of Sahara the Mummy: The Magical Exploration of Ancient Egypt. 2012. 28p. pap. 17.99 *(978-1-4772-3310-8(5))* AuthorHouse.

Shurtliff, Liesl. Jack: The True Story of Jack & the Beanstalk. 2015. (ENG.). 304p. (J). (gr. 3-7). 16.99 *(978-0-385-75579-5(1),* Knopf Bks. for Young Readers) Random Hse. Children's Bks.

—Red: the True Story of Red Riding Hood. (ENG.). 256p. (J). (gr. 3-7). 2017. 7.99 *(978-0-385-75586-3(4),* Yearling) 2016. 16.99 *(978-0-385-75583-2(X),* Knopf Bks. for Young Readers) Random Hse. Children's Bks.

Shusterman, Neal. Hawking's Hallway. 2017. (Accelerati Ser.: 3). (J). lib. bdg. 19.65 *(978-0-606-39502-1(4))* Turtleback Bks.

—Ship Out of Luck. 2014. (ENG.). 320p. (YA). (gr. 7). pap. 7.99 *(978-0-14-242624-1(5),* Puffin Books) Penguin Young Readers Group.

—Speeding Bullet. 2004. (ENG.). 208p. (YA). (gr. 7). pap. 11.95 *(978-0-689-87348-5(4),* Simon Pulse) Simon Pulse.

Shusterman, Neal. UnBound: Stories from the Unwind World. 2016. (Unwind Dystology Ser.). lib. bdg. 23.30 ***(978-0-606-39748-3(5))*** Turtleback Bks.

Shvarts, Andrew. Royal Bastards. 2017. (Royal Bastards Ser.). (ENG.). 352p. (YA). (gr. 9-17). 18.99 ***(978-1-4847-6765-8(9))*** Hyperion Bks. for Children.

Sibille, Lucinda. Dragon Swirl: Book II. 2009. 28p. pap. 14.95 *(978-1-4490-1057-7(1))* AuthorHouse.

—Dragon Swirl: Book III. 2009. 32p. pap. 14.95 *(978-1-4490-1072-0(5))* AuthorHouse.

—Dragon Swirl: Book IV. 2009. 32p. pap. 14.95 *(978-1-4490-1075-1(X))* AuthorHouse.

—Dragon Swirl: In the Beginning. 2009. 32p. pap. 14.95 *(978-1-4490-0965-6(4))* AuthorHouse.

Sica, Diane. The Adventures of Sammy & Vinney. 2012. 48p. pap. 11.95 *(978-1-4685-6883-7(3))* AuthorHouse.

Siclari, Theresa. The Pond Behind Grandmother's House. 2007. 32p. per. 24.95 *(978-1-4137-8597-5(2))* America Star Bks.

Sid, Fleischman. The Whipping Boy. 2014. (HarperClassics Ser.). (ENG.). 96p. (J). (gr. 3-8). 10.24 *(978-1-63245-335-8(5))* Lectorum Pubns., Inc.

Sidney, Maragret. Five Little Peppers Abroad. 2007. (ENG.). 236p. pap. 20.99 *(978-1-4264-5079-2(6))*; 262p. pap. 23.99 *(978-1-4264-5380-9(9))* Creative Media Partners, LLC.

Sidney, Margaret. The Adventures of Joel Pepper. 2007. (ENG.). 234p. pap. 20.99 *(978-1-4264-2360-4(8))*; 250p. pap. 22.99 *(978-1-4264-2408-3(6))* Creative Media Partners, LLC.

—The Adventures of Joel Pepper. 2008. 192p. 26.95 (978-1-60664-740-0(7)) Rodgers, Alan Bks.
—Margaret Sidney: Little Peppers. 2003. (J). cd-rom 19.00 (978-0-931968-61-7(5)) Samizdat Express.
Siegel, Jan. The Devil's Apprentice. 2013. (ENG.). 384p. (YA). (gr. 6). pap. 9.99 (978-1-78108-147-1(6), Ravenstone) Rebellion GBR. Dist: Simon & Schuster, Inc.
Siegel, Mark & Siegel, Alexis. The Sand Warrior. Bouma, Xanthe et al, illus. 2017. (5 Worlds Ser.: 1). (ENG.). 256p. (J). (gr. 3-7). 18.99 **(978-1-101-93586-6(3))**; pap. 12.99 **(978-1-101-93588-0(X))**; lib. bdg. 21.99 **(978-1-101-93587-3(1))** Random Hse. Children's Bks. (Random Hse. Bks. for Young Readers).
—The Sand Warrior. Bouma, Xanthe et al, illus. 2017. (5 Worlds Ser.: 1). lib. bdg. 24.50 **(978-0-606-40243-9(8))** Turtleback Bks.
Siegel, Rv. A Bee Called Kangaroo. 2005. 81p. pap. 9.16 (978-1-4116-2890-8(X)) Lulu Pr., Inc.
Siemens, Cindy Louetta. The Adventures of Mr Grizz. 2011. 24p. pap. 15.99 (978-1-4568-4816-3(X)) Xlibris Corp.
Sierra i Fabra, Jordi. La Asombrosa Historia del Viajero de las Estrellas. (SPA.). (YA). 8.95 (978-958-04-6872-1(9)) Norma S.A. COL. Dist: Distribuidora Norma, Inc.
Siglain, Michael. Finn & Rey Escape! 2015. (Star Wars: Force Awakens 8X8 Ser.). (J). lib. bdg. 14.75 (978-0-606-38311-0(5)) Turtleback Bks.
—Han & Chewie Return! 2015. (Star Wars: Force Awakens 8X8 Ser.). (J). lib. bdg. 13.55 (978-0-606-38310-3(7)) Turtleback Bks.
Siglain, Michael, adapted by. Zeb to the Rescue. 2014. (Illus.). 32p. (J). (978-1-4844-3445-1(5)) Disney Publishing Worldwide.
Signor, Priscilla M. The Adventures of Hooch & Mile-A-Minute-Freebee. Buehrle, Jacquelyn, illus. 2011. 28p. pap. 24.95 (978-1-4560-0936-6(2)) America Star Bks.
Silbaugh, Michael John. Crosseyed Puzzle. 2009. 28p. pap. 15.99 (978-1-4415-8779-4(9)) Xlibris Corp.
Silcox, Beth Douglass. Little Rumely Man. Peters, Darcy, illus. 2012. 36p. pap. 12.99 (978-0-9832514-2-2(8)) Gypsy Heart Pr.
Silk, Max V. Whiskers. Hirsch, Kerry, illus. 2004. (J). pap. 12.00 (978-0-9748524-6-1(5)) Biblio Bks. International.
Silva, Paula M. The Ice Cream Dream. 2012. 24p. pap. 15.95 (978-1-4567-9401-9(9)) AuthorHouse.
Silver Dolphin en Español Editors. Magical Magnets: Pixar. 2006. (SPA., Illus.). 8p. (J). bds. 12.95 (978-970-718-319-3(5)) Readerlink Distribution Services, LLC.
Silver Dolphin en Español Staff, creator. Musica en Casa Libro de Cuentos. 2007. (Illus.). 38p. (J). (gr. -1-3). incl. audio compact disk (978-970-718-494-7(9), Silver Dolphin en Español) Advanced Marketing, S. de R. L. de C. V.
Silver Dolphin en Español Staff, ed. Cine en casa: Cars: Movie Theater: Cars. 2007. (Cine en casa Disney Ser.). (Illus.). 46p. (J). (978-970-718-508-1(2), Silver Dolphin en Español) Advanced Marketing, S. de R. L. de C. V.
Silver Dragon Books Staff, et al. Jump Start. 2012. (ENG., Illus.). 80p. pap., act. bk. ed. 5.99 (978-0-9830404-7-7(8), 9780983040477) Zenescope Entertainment.
Silver, Ruth. Aberrant. 2013. 250p. pap. 14.99 (978-0-9917897-8-8(4)) Patchwork Pr.
Silvera, Adam. They Both Die at the End. 2017. 384p. (YA). (gr. 9). 17.99 **(978-0-06-245779-0(9))** HarperCollins Pubs.
Silverberg, Beth. The Adventures of Mattie Mae: Life Lessons Through the Eyes of A Puppy. 2009. 76p. pap. 12.99 (978-1-4389-4587-3(6)) AuthorHouse.
Silverthorne, Jill. SOS Titanic. 2012. (Faith Finders Ser.). (ENG.). 126p. (YA). pap. (978-1-84625-308-9(X)) DayOne Pubns.
Silverthorne, Judith & Coteau Books Staff. Dinosaur Hideout. 1 vol. 2006. (Dinosaur Adventure Ser.). (ENG.). 220p. (J). (gr. 4-7). pap. 6.95 (978-1-55050-226-8(3)) Coteau Bks. CAN. Dist: Orca Bk. Pubs. USA.
Silvestre, R. Un Secreto en la Tormenta. (Raton de Biblioteca Coleccion). (SPA., Illus.). 128p. (J). (gr. 3). 7.95 (978-84-88061-69-0(2)) Serres, Ediciones, S. L. ESP. Dist: Lectorum Pubns., Inc.
Silvestri, Enzo & Silvestri, Karen Hamilton. War in the Heavens: Episode 6. 2013. 84p. pap. 6.59 (978-0-9899318-1-6(1)) Karenzo Media.
Silvey, Diane. Spirit Quest. 2009. (ENG., Illus.). 64p. (J). (gr. 6). pap. 11.99 (978-1-55002-831-7(6), Sandcastle Bks.) Dundurn CAN. Dist: Ingram Publisher Services.
—Time of the Thunderbird. Mantha, John, illus. 2008. (ENG.). 88p. (J). (gr. 6-5). pap. 11.99 (978-1-55002-792-1(1), Sandcastle Bks.) Dundurn CAN. Dist: Ingram Publisher Services.
Siminovich, Lorena. Alex & Lulu: Two of a Kind. Siminovich, Lorena, illus. 2009. (ENG., Illus.). 32p. (J). (gr. -1-3). 14.99 (978-0-7636-4423-9(4), Templar) Candlewick Pr.
Simko, Joe. The Sweet Rot, Book 2: Raiders of the Lost Art, 1 vol. 2011. (ENG., Illus.). 80p. (J). 19.99 (978-0-7643-3828-1(5), 9780764338281, Schiffer Publishing Ltd) Schiffer Publishing, Ltd.
Simmions, Glenn. My Father's Work. 2008. 19p. pap. 24.95 (978-1-60672-196-4(8)) America Star Bks.
Simmons, Celeste. The Adventures of Booger Malone: Busted in the Backseat. 2007. (J). per. 10.95 (978-0-9777041-2-5(2)) Third Dimension Publishing.
Simmons, J. A. Hannah's First Airplane Ride. 2013. 32p. pap. 24.95 (978-1-63004-197-7(1)) America Star Bks.
Simmons, Kristen. Metaltown. 2016. (ENG.). 384p. (YA). 17.99 (978-0-7653-3662-0(6), 9780765336620, Tor Teen) Doherty, Tom Assocs., LLC.
Simon, Coco. Katie Sprinkled Secrets. 2015. (Cupcake Diaries: 25). lib. bdg. 17.20 (978-0-606-37133-9(8)) Turtleback Bks.
Simon, Elizabeth. Tyler Adams & the Adventures of Bravura: the First Quest. 2009. 49p. pap. 19.95 (978-0-557-06290-4(X)) Lulu Pr., Inc.
Simon, Francesca. Jogger's Big Adventure. Bolam, Emily, illus. 2012. (ENG.). 64p. (J). (gr. -1-k). 7.99 (978-1-4440-0202-7(3), Orion Children's Bks.) Hachette Children's Group GBR. Dist: Hachette Bk. Group.
Simon, Jay. Deep Freeze. 2004. 255p. (YA). per. 7.99 (978-0-931764-17-2(3)) Roberts Publishing Co.
Simon, Nadine. The Treasured Dream. 2009. 52p. pap. 9.95 (978-1-60693-274-2(8), Eloquent Bks.) Strategic Book Publishing & Rights Agency (SBPRA).
Simon, Romain, illus. Forest Animals. 2011. 90p. 38.95 (978-1-258-10284-5(6)) Literary Licensing, LLC.
Simon Spotlight, creator. Adventures to Go! 2006. (Nick Jr. Carry-Along Boxed Set Ser.). (ENG., Illus.). 144p. (J). (gr. -1-2). pap. 9.99 (978-1-4169-1558-4(3), Simon Spotlight/Nickelodeon) Simon Spotlight/Nickelodeon.
Simoneau, Shelly. The Cows Came Running & the Horses Did Too! 2011. 28p. pap. 14.99 (978-1-4567-3107-6(6)) AuthorHouse.
Simons, Alan L. The Incredible Adventures of Captain Cameron MacDuddyfunk in Cuggermuggerland. Boggelen-Heutink, Ellen van, illus. 2013. 98p. pap. (978-0-9877503-8-9(0)) Baronel Bks.
Simons, D. M. Keep Her Safe. 2011. (ENG.). 232p. pap. (978-1-84876-697-6(1)) Troubador Publishing Ltd.
Simonson, Louise. Battling Bigfoot. Elston, James W., illus. 2007. (Extreme Monsters Ser.). 94p. (J). (gr. 2-5). per. 3.99 (978-1-57791-275-0(6), Penny Candy Pr.) Brighter Minds Children's Publishing.
—Meet Mr. Hydeous, Vol. 3. Elston, James W., illus. gif. ed. 2006. (Extreme Monsters Ser.). 96p. (J). per. 3.99 (978-1-57791-255-2(1)) Brighter Minds Children's Publishing.
Simonson, Walter. Meltdown, 3 vols. Simonson, Louise et al, illus. 2003. (Wolverine Legends Ser.: Vol. 2). 200p. (YA). pap. 19.99 (978-0-7851-1048-4(8)) Marvel Worldwide, Inc.
Simpson, Albert. The Adventures of Billy, Ras, & Al. 2012. 24p. pap. 17.99 (978-1-4772-1641-5(3)) AuthorHouse.
Simpson, Craig. Resistance. 2007. (ENG., Illus.). 368p. (YA). (gr. 7). pap. 15.99 (978-0-552-55571-5(1)) Transworld Publishers Ltd. GBR. Dist: Independent Pubs. Group.
Simpson, D. C. Closer to the Void: Ozy & Millie 2006-2007. 2008. 127p. pap. 12.45 (978-1-4357-0504-3(1)) Lulu Pr., Inc.
Simpson, Dana. A Heavenly Nostrils Chronicle. 2014. (Phoebe & Her Unicorn Ser.: 1). (ENG., Illus.). 224p. (J). 9.99 (978-1-4494-4620-8(5)) Andrews McMeel Publishing.
—Razzle Dazzle Unicorn: Another Phoebe & Her Unicorn Adventure. 2016. (Phoebe & Her Unicorn Ser.: 4). (ENG., Illus.). 184p. (J). pap. 9.99 (978-1-4494-7791-2(7)) Andrews McMeel Publishing.
—Unicorn Crossing: Another Phoebe & Her Unicorn Adventure. 2017. (Phoebe & Her Unicorn Ser.: 5). (ENG., Illus.). 176p. (J). pap. 9.99 (978-1-4494-8357-9(7)) Andrews McMeel Publishing.
Simpson-Tweedie, Karen. Treasure on Chincoteague Island. 2003. (Illus.). 153p. (J). per. 12.95 (978-0-9742205-0-5(7)) Sheepdog Pr.
Sims, Anthony. Princess Zoe. 2012. (Illus.). 44p. pap. 24.40 (978-1-4772-2365-9(7)) AuthorHouse.
Sims, Lesley. Agent Arthur's Island Adventures. Mounter, Paddy, illus. 2003. (Puzzle Adventures Ser.). 48p. (J). (gr. 3). lib. bdg. 12.95 (978-1-58086-463-3(5)) EDC Publishing.
—Illustrated Classics Action & Adventure Stories for Young Readers. 2015. (Illustrated Stories Ser.). (ENG.). 384p. (J). (gr. k-5). 19.99 (978-0-7945-3565-0(8), Usborne) EDC Publishing.
—Island Adventures. 2004. (Puzzle Adventures Ser.). (Illus.). 48p. (J). pap. 4.95 (978-0-7945-0091-7(9), Usborne) EDC Publishing.
Sims, Lesley, ed. Illustrated Adventure Stories. 2014. (Usborne Illustrated Stories Ser.). (ENG., Illus.). 324p. (J). (gr. 4-7). 19.99 (978-0-7945-2649-2(X), Usborne) EDC Publishing.
Sims, Lori. Starvin' Marvin & Skinny Minnie Melt Minnesota. 2010. 115p. pap. 11.95 (978-1-4327-5628-4(1)) Outskirts Pr., Inc.
—Starvin' Marvin & Skinny Minnie Shake up San Francisco. 2009. 78p. (YA). pap. 9.95 (978-1-4327-3651-4(5)) Outskirts Pr., Inc.
Sina-Atanda, Moyin. The Phenomenal Four: Four on a Mission to Save the Animals. 2013. 52p. (gr. 4-6). pap. 10.03 (978-1-4669-7291-9(2)) Trafford Publishing.
Sinclair, Howard. Ego: And the Chocolate-Covered Worms. 2013. (ENG.). 28p. (J). pap. 9.95 (978-1-4787-0089-0(0)) Outskirts Pr., Inc.
Sinden, David, et al. Bang Goes a Troll, Bk. 3. Duddle, Jonny, illus. 2009. (Awfully Beastly Business Ser.: 3). (ENG.). 208p. (J). (gr. 3-7). 9.99 (978-1-4169-8651-5(0), Aladdin) Simon & Schuster Children's Publishing.
—Sea Monsters & Other Delicacies. Duddle, Jonny, illus. 2009. (Awfully Beastly Business Ser.: 2). (ENG.). 208p. (J). (gr. 3-7). 9.99 (978-1-4169-8650-8(2), Aladdin) Simon & Schuster Children's Publishing.
—Werewolf Versus Dragon. Duddle, Jonny, illus. 2009. (Awfully Beastly Business Ser.: 1). (ENG.). 192p. (J). (gr. 3-7). 9.99 (978-1-4169-8649-2(9), Aladdin) Simon & Schuster Children's Publishing.
Singer, Isaac Bashevis. Mazel y Schlimazel. (SPA.). 30p. (YA). (gr. 5-18). 17.75 (978-84-264-3574-3(2), LM3116) Editorial Lumen ESP. Dist: Lectorum Pubns., Inc.
Singh, Navneet. The Key to Light & Darkness: Everything Can Feel Like a Dream... 2013. 344p. pap. 19.92 (978-1-4907-0948-2(7)) Trafford Publishing.
Singhose, Rose. Granny's GIGGLES BOOK EIGHT. 2010. 32p. pap. 16.95 (978-0-557-61005-1(2)) Lulu Pr., Inc.
Singhose, Rose & StGermain, Annetta. Gramma's Sure Fire Cure for Insomnia in the Very Young. 2010. 67p. pap. 27.50 (978-0-557-08697-9(3)) Lulu Pr., Inc.
Singleton, Linda Joy. Dead Girl Dancing. 2009. (Dead Girl Ser.: 2). (ENG.). 264p. (YA). pap. 9.95 (978-0-7387-1406-6(2), Flux) Llewellyn Pubns.
Singley, George. Mutation. 2007. (Illus.). 144p. (YA). pap. 14.99 (978-0-9738388-6-2(8)) Speakeasy Comics CAN. Dist: Diamond Bk. Distributors.
Singley, George T. Silent Ghost. 2006. (Illus.). 136p. (YA). pap. 14.99 (978-0-9738388-8-6(4)) Speakeasy Comics CAN. Dist: Diamond Bk. Distributors.
Sipperley, Keli. Gingerbread with Abigail Adams. 2016. (Time Hop Sweets Shop Ser.). (ENG.). 32p. (gr. k-3). 25.65 (978-1-68191-378-0(X)) Rourke Educational Media.
—Ice Cream with Albert Einstein. 2016. (Time Hop Sweets Shop Ser.). (ENG.). 32p. (gr. k-3). 25.65 (978-1-68191-376-6(3)) Rourke Educational Media.
Sirod, G. p. & Sirod, G. P. Scabs. 2010. 190p. pap. (978-1-84923-457-3(4)) YouWriteOn.
Sisler, Celeste. Disney Fairies: Meet the Fairies: A Collection of Reading Adventures. 2015. (Passport to Reading Level 1 Ser.). (ENG., Illus.). 160p. (J). (gr. -1-3). 9.99 (978-0-316-33739-7(0)) Little, Brown Bks. for Young Readers.
Sister Flowers. When Boo Boo Wakes Up!, 1 vol. Smith, Brenda, illus. 2009. 36p. pap. 24.95 (978-1-61546-250-6(3)) America Star Bks.
Sitomer, Alan Lawrence. Noble Warrior. 2016. (Caged Warrior Ser.). (ENG., Illus.). 400p. (YA). (gr. 7-12). pap. 9.99 (978-1-4847-3416-2(5)) Hyperion Bks. for Children.
Siwinski, Deborah. The Adventures of Teddy & Freddy Summer Safari. Siwinski, Deborah, illus. Lt. ed. 2006. (Illus.). 41p. (J). per. 8.95 (978-1-59879-097-9(8)) Lifevest Publishing, Inc.
Skae, Hilda T. The Adventure League. 2013. 138p. pap. 9.00 (978-1-927558-40-9(9)) Birch Tree Publishing.
Skandle, D. L. Little Duckie's Day. 2010. 28p. pap. 15.49 (978-1-4490-9705-9(7)) AuthorHouse.
Skelton, K. Magic from the Wishing Well. 2009. 28p. pap. 12.49 (978-1-4389-8747-7(1)) AuthorHouse.
Skewes, John & Mullin, Michael. Larry Gets Lost in Philadelphia. Skewes, John, illus. 2013. (Larry Gets Lost Ser.). (ENG., Illus.). 32p. (J). (gr. -1-2). 17.99 (978-1-57061-792-8(9), Little Bigfoot) Sasquatch Bks.
Skidmore, Lauren. What Is Lost. 2015. 217p. (YA). pap. 16.99 (978-1-4621-1621-8(3)) Cedar Fort, Inc./CFI Distribution.
Skidmore, Marlene. Wesley's Swoo-Foo. 2008. 28p. pap. 9.99 (978-0-9821408-5-7(1)) Faithful Life Pubs.
Skilbeck, Carol. Adventures of Melonhead. 2011. 56p. 24.99 (978-1-4568-7464-3(0)); pap. 15.99 (978-1-4568-7463-6(2)) Xlibris Corp.
Skinner, Tina. Christopher Wren Avian Architect, 1 vol. LouLou, illus. 2008. (ENG.). 32p. (J). 15.99 (978-0-7643-3169-5(8), 9780764331695) Schiffer Publishing, Ltd.
Skorlinski, Cynthia. My Little Erica. 2013. 28p. pap. 13.99 (978-1-4808-0181-3(X)) Archway Publishing.
Skotnicki, Jill. Ham & Beans: Have You Seen the Color Green? 2010. 28p. pap. 12.49 (978-1-4520-6452-9(0)) AuthorHouse.
Skrbina, Daniel William. A Knight to Remember: Gulliver's Journey Continues, 1 vol. 2009. 74p. pap. 19.95 (978-1-60836-737-5(1)) America Star Bks.
Sky Rock. 2005. (J). 4.95 (978-1-59792-012-4(6)) F.A.S.T. Learning LLC.
Skye, Lucy. The Adventure of Maisie Voyager. 2012. (ENG.). 240p. (J). pap. 15.95 (978-1-84905-287-0(5), 4927) Kingsley, Jessica Pubs. GBR. Dist: Macmillan Distribution Ltd.
Skye, obert. The Eyes of the Want. Sowards, Ben, illus. 2008. (Leven Thumps Ser.: 3). (ENG.). 464p. (J). (gr. 3-7). pap. 9.99 (978-1-4169-4719-6(1), Aladdin) Simon & Schuster Children's Publishing.
—Leven Thumps & the Eyes of the Want. 2007. (Leven Thumps Ser.: Bk. 3). (Illus.). 406p. (J). (gr. 4-7). 18.95 (978-1-59038-800-6(3), Shadow Mountain) Shadow Mountain Publishing.
—The Whispered Secret. 2006. (Leven Thumps Ser.: Bk. 2). (ENG., Illus.). 432p. (J). (gr. 4-7). 18.95 (978-1-59038-490-9(3), Shadow Mountain) Shadow Mountain Publishing.
Slack, Michael. Shorty & Clem. Slack, Michael, illus. 2017. (Illus.). 40p. (J). (gr. -1-3). 17.99 (978-0-06-242158-6(1)) HarperCollins Pubs.
Slade, Mark. A Week of Mushrooming Book One. 2013. 88p. pap. 8.00 (978-1-927558-14-0(X)) Birch Tree Publishing.
Slagle, Clark. Axel Cecil & the Rising Sun Adventures: the Janwah. 2009. 105p. pap. 9.95 (978-0-615-24135-7(2)) Wold Creative Group.
Slanina, Anne M. Baby Brother Goes to the Hospital. Agnew, Alicia, illus. 2007. (Adventures of Annie Mouse Ser.: Bk. 2). 28p. (J). 18.99 (978-0-9793379-1-8(7)); per. 9.99 (978-0-9793379-0-1(9)) Annie Mouse Bks.
Slanina, Anne Maro. Annie Mouse's Route 66 Adventure: A Photo Journal, vols. 6, vol. 5. Collins, Kelsey, illus. 2011. (ENG.). 48p. (J). pap. 14.99 (978-0-9793379-6-3(8)) Annie Mouse Bks.
Slate, Kelly. The Adventures of Santa Claws: At Amelia Island. 2012. 28p. pap. 16.99 (978-1-4772-2093-1(3)) AuthorHouse.
Slater, David Michael. David Michael Slater: Missy Swiss & More - 6 Titles, 6 vols., Set. Incl. Comin' Through. Rooney, Ronnie, illus. 28.50 (978-1-60270-008-6(7)); Flour Girl: A Recipe for Disaster. Brooks, S. G., illus. 28.50 (978-1-60270-009-3(5)); Missy Swiss. Reibeling, Brandon, illus. 28.50 (978-1-60270-010-9(9)); Ned Loses His Head. 28.50 (978-1-60270-011-6(7)); Seven Ate Nine. Trover, Zachary, illus. 28.50 (978-1-60270-012-3(5)); Sharpest Tool in the Shed. Reibeling, Brandon, illus. 28.50 (978-1-60270-013-0(3)); (gr. -1-4). (Missy Swiss & More Ser.). (ENG.). 32p. 2007. 171.00 (978-1-60270-007-9(9), Looking Glass Library) ABDO Publishing Co.
Slater, Jean M. The Adventures of Hopper. Slater, Jean M., illus. 2003. (Illus.). 8p. (J). bds. 16.00 (978-0-9743149-3-8(5)) Slater Software, Inc.
Sled, Robert A. The Adventures of Daisy Snowball: The Journey Begins. 2012. 56p. (gr. 4-6). pap. 10.16 (978-1-4269-7424-3(8)) Trafford Publishing.
Sleigh, Barbara. The Kingdom of Carbonel. Kennedy, Richard, illus. 2009. (ENG.). 240p. (J). (gr. 4-7). 17.95 (978-1-59017-315-2(5), NYR Children's Collection) New York Review of Bks., Inc., The.
Sleiman, Dina L. Dauntless. 2015. (Valiant Hearts Ser.: 1). (ENG.). 368p. (YA). pap. 13.99 (978-0-7642-1312-0(1)) Bethany Hse. Pubs.
Slezak, Roy E. Marsha the Manatee. 2012. 32p. (-18). pap. 24.95 (978-1-4626-9465-5(9)) America Star Bks.
Slider-Baker, Belinda. Lost Stripes, Please Return. 2008. 32p. pap. 24.95 (978-1-60813-075-7(4)) America Star Bks.
Slim, Lillian, et al. Subsistence Adventures. Slim, Lillian et al, illus. 2006. (Adventure Story Collection Ser.). 28p. (J). (gr. 2-6). pap. 10.00 (978-1-58084-252-5(6)) Lower Kuskokwim Schl. District.
Sloan, William. Of Bees & Bats of Crocodiles & Cats. 2009. 73p. pap. 14.95 (978-1-4092-9470-2(6)) Lulu Pr., Inc.
Sloane, Richard. Back to the Dark Ages! 2013. 138p. (gr. 4-6). 22.95 (978-1-4669-7401-2(X)); pap. 12.95 (978-1-4669-7399-2(4)) Trafford Publishing.
Slote, Alfred. Jake. 2013. 160p. pap. 11.99 (978-0-9886988-2-6(X)) Arborville Bks.
Sloyer, Elliot. The Safety Pin: Summer Camp Stories. Guiza, Victor, illus. 2014. (ENG.). 32p. (J). 16.95 (978-1-60131-182-5(6), Castlebridge Bks.) Big Tent Bks.
Slutsky, Adam & Croce, Pat. Plunder ARC. 2015. (ENG., Illus.). 336p. (J). pap. 16.95 (978-1-63026-894-7(1)) Turner Publishing Co.
Small, Charlie. The Daredevil Desperados of Destiny. 2009. (Charlie Small Ser.: Bk. 4). (ENG.). 208p. (J). (gr. 1-4). 6.99 (978-0-385-75141-4(9)) Fickling, David Bks. GBR. Dist: Penguin Random Hse. LLC.
—The Hawk's Nest. 2014. (Charlie Small Journals). (ENG., Illus.). 176p. (J). (gr. 2-4). 12.99 (978-1-78295-330-2(2), Red Fox) Random House Children's Books GBR. Dist: Independent Pubs. Group.
small world creations ltd. Blubb, Blubb! 2017. (Magic Bath Bks.). (ENG.). 8p. (J). (gr. -1 — 1). 5.99 **(978-1-4380-7843-4(9))** Barron's Educational Series, Inc.
Small, Wylie J. The Great Prune Caper. 2009. 94p. pap. 9.98 (978-1-84728-350-4(0)) Lulu Pr., Inc.
Smalley, Roger. Big Cat Trouble. Shaw, Charles, illus. 2005. (J). (978-1-933248-13-4(0)) World Quest Learning.
—Rick's Dream Adventure. 2005. (J). (978-1-933248-10-3(6)) World Quest Learning.
Smallwood, Edward. J. Frankles: Space Adventures. 2003. (Illus.). 24p. (J). 9.95 (978-0-9741282-0-7(1), 00001) Smallwood, Edward.
Smart, Andy. Bob'n Joe Book One: Lunch Time. Smart, Andy, illus. 2013. (Illus.). 42p. (J). pap. (978-0-9919196-1-1(0)) Beckon Creative.
Smedes, Marty. Goldie Bear & the Three Lockes. 2009. 24p. pap. 12.99 (978-1-4389-7216-9(4)) AuthorHouse.
Smedley, Garrett. The Adventures of Chi Chi. 2008. 50p. pap. 16.95 (978-1-60672-356-2(1)) America Star Bks.
Smedley, Mike. Emily & the Mysterious Potato. 2013. (Illus.). 30p. pap. 7.95 (978-1-78035-652-5(8), Fastprint Publishing) Upfront Publishing Ltd. GBR. Dist: Printondemand-worldwide.com.
Smelcer, John. Edge of Nowhere. 2014. (ENG.). 194p. (J). (gr. 6). pap. 9.99 (978-1-935248-57-6(X)) Leapfrog Pr.
—Savage Mountain. 2015. (ENG., Illus.). 160p. (J). (gr. 6). pap. 12.00 (978-1-935248-65-1(0)) Leapfrog Pr.
The Smile of A Golden Child. 2004. (J). per. 16.99 (978-0-9753533-6-3(5)) Golden Eagle Publishing Hse., Inc.
Smiley, Jeremy. Chester: Little Turtle, Big Adventure, 1 vol. 2009. 36p. pap. 24.95 (978-1-60703-489-6(1)) America Star Bks.
Smiley, Sophie. Man of the Match. Foreman, Michael, illus. 2005. (ENG.). 80p. (J). (gr. 2-4). per. 9.99 (978-1-84270-420-2(6)) Andersen Pr. GBR. Dist: Independent Pubs. Group.
Smileytooth & the Plaque Attack: The Adventures of Smileytooth. 2006. (J). 6.95 (978-0-9778456-0-6(5)) Pontrelli, Jeany.
Smirl, Mike. Crysta Lun. 2012. 48p. pap. 14.95 (978-0-615-43657-9(9)) crysta luna studios.
Smith, Adelene Keeler. Sophie Gets Curtains! 2010. 28p. (J). pap. 12.99 (978-1-4520-8943-0(4)) AuthorHouse.
Smith, Alex. Home. Smith, Alex, illus. 2011. (ENG., Illus.). 32p. pap. 7.95 (978-1-58925-433-6(3)) Tiger Tales.
Smith, Alexander Gordon. Hellraisers. 2015. (Devil's Engine Ser.: 1). (ENG.). 352p. (YA). (gr. 7). 17.99 (978-0-374-30169-9(7), 9780374301699, Farrar, Straus & Giroux (BYR)) Farrar, Straus & Giroux.
Smith, Andrew Christopher John. Soi. 2009. (Illus.). 40p. pap. 16.99 (978-1-4490-3591-4(4)) AuthorHouse.
Smith, Anne & Smith, Owen. Safari Survivor. Rayas, Rubén, illus. 2012. (Twisted Journeys (r) Ser.: 21). (ENG.). 112p. (J). (gr. 4-7). pap. 7.95 (978-1-57505-943-3(6), Graphic Universe™) Lerner Publishing Group.
Smith-Armand, Kristie. Diamond in the Rough: More Fun Adventures with Abby Diamond. 2010. 256p. pap. 16.95 (978-1-4502-4618-7(4)) iUniverse, Inc.
Smith, B. M. Evan & Cassie Go on a Train Meet, 1 vol. Smith, Mandy M., illus. 2009. 35p. pap. 24.95 (978-1-60836-552-4(2)) America Star Bks.
—My Very Own Picnic Basket: An Evan & Cassie Adventure. 2012. 28p. pap. 24.95 (978-1-4626-7551-7(4)) America Star Bks.
Smith, Barbara. Lost Diary Secrets. 2011. 78p. pap. 19.95 (978-1-4560-6056-5(2)) America Star Bks.
Smith, C. E. Draupner's Curse. 2009. 208p. 24.95 (978-1-4401-6797-3(4)); pap. 14.95 (978-1-4401-6799-7(0)) iUniverse, Inc.
Smith, Carrie. Going to the Beach: Small Book. 2004. (Shared Connections Ser.). (J). pap. (978-1-4108-1639-9(7)) Benchmark Education Co.
Smith, Clara Batton. Elliott & Anastaci. Smith, Clara Batton, illus. 2012. (Illus.). 16p. pap. 9.95 (978-1-61633-233-4(6)) Guardian Angel Publishing, Inc.
Smith, Cleveland W. Billabongo. 2008. 172p. pap. (978-1-84923-100-8(1)) YouWriteOn.
Smith, David R. The Door to Andara. 2005. 180p. pap. 8.14 (978-1-4116-1894-7(7)) Lulu Pr., Inc.
Smith, David Thomas. Frenchie the Grass Seed's Journey Around the World to Learn How to Sow a Lawn. 2012. 28p. pap. 24.95 (978-1-4626-8112-9(3)) America Star Bks.
Smith, Debora Ann Baker. The Magnificent Fairy Party. 2010. (Illus.). 30p. pap. 13.00 (978-1-60911-404-6(3), Eloquent Bks.) Strategic Book Publishing & Rights Agency (SBPRA).
Smith, Dee. The Pigs of Pineapple Beach Anthology. 2009. (Illus.). 80p. pap. 15.00 (978-1-59858-961-0(X)) Dog Ear Publishing, LLC.
Smith, Dianne M. Stuck! 2004. 20p. (J). per. (978-1-59196-580-0(2)) Instant Pub.
Smith, Duane. Heritage Revealed Series, 3. (J). (gr. 2-9). pap. 13.95 (978-1-886218-00-0(5)) Azimuth Pr.
Smith, E. The Adventures of Sir Ambrose Elephant: A Visit to the City. Apa, Ivy Marie, illus. 2012. 19p. pap. 9.95 (978-1-4691-8378-7(1)) Xlibris Corp.
Smith, Frederick D. The Black Premiere, 1 vol. 2009. 196p. pap. 24.95 (978-1-60813-605-6(1)) PublishAmerica, Inc.

Smith, Grahame Baker. George's Magic Day. 2005. (ENG., Illus.). 32p. (J). (gr. -1-k). pap. 6.99 *(978-0-340-87550-6(X))* Hodder & Stoughton GBR. Dist: Hachette Bk. Group.

Smith-Henderson, Susie. The Adventures of Snorro & the Keepers from Sleep. 2009. 32p. pap. 14.18 *(978-0-557-08682-5(5))* Lulu Pr., Inc.

Smith, Holly C. Tyler the Monkey & Andy the Mouse. 2012. 28p. (-18). pap. 24.95 *(978-1-4626-9501-0(9))* America Star Bks.

Smith, I. J. The Legend of Scary Mary: The Journey to Leadership Collection Adventure 2. Pollard, Deborah Hanna, illus. 2004. 96p. (J). 16.95 *(978-0-9727273-1-0(0))* Green Owl, Inc.

—The Musical Fort. Pollard, Deborah Hanna, illus. 2003. 53p. (J). 14.95 *(978-0-9727273-0-3(2))* Green Owl, Inc.

Smith, J. Albert. The Adventures of the Molly Dollys. 2011. 28p. (J). pap. 16.95 *(978-1-4327-4313-0(9))* Outskirts Pr., Inc.

Smith, J. E. Complex City: All in a Day's Work. 2003. 120p. per. 12.95 *(978-0-9728070-0-5(4))* Better Comics.

Smith, James J. Mikey's Monster. 2013. (Step into Reading Level 4 Ser.). lib. bdg. 13.55 *(978-0-606-32223-2(X),* Turtleback) Turtleback Bks.

Smith, Jane. Adventure on White High Island. 2006. (YA). per. *(978-0-9777074-0-9(7))* Beverly Hills Publishing.

Smith, Jeff. Eyes of the Storm. Smith, Jeff & Hamaker, Steve, illus. 2006. (Bone Ser.: 3). (ENG.). 192p. (J). (gr. 3-7). 26.99 *(978-0-439-70625-4(4));* pap. 12.99 *(978-0-439-70638-4(6))* Scholastic, Inc. (Graphix).

—The Great Cow Race. Smith, Jeff & Hamaker, Steve, illus. 2005. (Bone Ser.: 2). (ENG.). 144p. (J). (gr. 4-7). 26.99 *(978-0-439-70624-7(6),* Graphix) Scholastic, Inc.

—Rock Jaw: Master of the Eastern Border. Smith, Jeff & Hamaker, Steve, illus. 2007. (Bone Ser.: 5). (ENG.). 128p. (J). (gr. 4-7). pap. 12.99 *(978-0-439-70636-0(X),* Graphix) Scholastic, Inc.

—Rock Jaw: Master of the Eastern Border. Hamaker, Steve & Smith, Jeff, illus. 2007. (Bone Ser.: 5). (ENG.). 128p. (J). (gr. 4-7). 24.99 *(978-0-439-70627-8(0),* Graphix) Scholastic, Inc.

Smith, Jeff & Sniegoski, Tom. Tall Tales. Smith, Jeff, illus. 2010. (Bone Ser.). (ENG., Illus.). 128p. (J). (gr. 4-7). pap. 12.99 *(978-0-545-14096-6(X),* Graphix) Scholastic, Inc.

Smith, Josephine A. It's Okay on a Winters Day! Hickle Pickle Books Presents Adventures of Hickle the Pickle. 2005. (J). per. *(978-1-881958-10-9(8))* Hickle Pickle Publishing.

Smith, Kathy. New Shoes for Chili Bean: Adventures of a Little Red Mule. 2011. 28p. (J). pap. 19.95 *(978-1-4327-6524-8(8));* pap. 30.95 *(978-1-4327-6965-9(0))* Outskirts Pr., Inc.

Smith, Keeley. First Soul. 2013. 204p. pap. *(978-1-78299-452-7(1))* FeedARead.com.

Smith, Kourtney. The Adventures of Stanley the Staple. 2013. 28p. pap. 24.95 *(978-1-63004-276-9(5))* America Star Bks.

Smith, Kristie Lyn. Dottie & Dots See Animal Spots: Learning Braille with Dots & Dottie. 2007. 52p. per. 8.95 *(978-0-595-47130-0(7))* iUniverse, Inc.

Smith, Latisha. Mama Always Knows Best. 2009. 28p. pap. 12.49 *(978-1-4389-9951-7(8))* AuthorHouse.

Smith, Lauren E. Ashley Enright Investigations. 2006. 48p. pap. 16.95 *(978-1-4241-2963-8(X))* America Star Bks.

Smith, Lesley & Award Publications Staff. Brer Rabbit & the Honey Pot. 2014. (ENG., Illus.). 24p. (J). pap. 6.95 *(978-1-84135-961-8(0))* Award Pubns. Ltd. GBR. Dist: Parkwest Pubns., Inc.

—Brer Rabbit & the Tar Baby. 2014. (ENG., Illus.). 24p. (J). pap. 6.95 *(978-1-84135-964-9(5))* Award Pubns. Ltd. GBR. Dist: Parkwest Pubns., Inc.

Smith, Lesley, et al. Brer Rabbit & the Great Race. 2014. (ENG., Illus.). 24p. (J). pap. 6.95 *(978-1-84135-963-2(7))* Award Pubns. Ltd. GBR. Dist: Parkwest Pubns., Inc.

Smith, Linda. The Piper of Shadonia, 1 vol. 2012. (ENG.). 352p. (YA). (gr. 7-12). pap. 14.95 *(978-1-55050-516-0(5))* Coteau Bks. CAN. Dist: Orca Bk. Pubs. USA.

Smith, Lindsay. Skandal. 2015. (Sekret Ser.: Vol. 2). (ENG.). 336p. (YA). (gr. 7-12). 17.99 *(978-1-62672-005-3(3),* 9781626720053) Roaring Brook Pr.

—Skandal. 2016. (Sekret Ser.: 2). (ENG.). 352p. (YA). pap. 9.99 *(978-1-250-07369-3(3),* 9781250073693) Square Fish.

Smith, Maudie. The Out of This World Adventure. 2016. (Opal Moonbaby Ser.). (ENG.). 304p. (J). (gr. 2-4). 7.99 *(978-1-4440-1582-9(6),* Orion Children's Bks.) Hachette Children's Group GBR. Dist: Hachette Bk. Group.

Smith, Nerissia. Prince de'Mario's Adventure, 1 vol. Dartes, Staci, illus. 2009. 29p. pap. 24.95 *(978-1-61582-972-9(5))* America Star Bks.

Smith, Owen & Smith, Anne. Safari Survivor. Rubine, illus. 2012. (Twisted Journeys (r) Ser.: 21). (ENG.). 112p. (J). (gr. 4-7). lib. bdg. 27.93 *(978-0-7613-6727-7(6),* Graphic Universe™) Lerner Publishing Group.

Smith, Peggy. The Champ: The Adventures of a Boy & His New Puppy. Told in One-syllable Words for the Barton Reading & Spelling System. 2003. (J). pap. 7.95 *(978-0-9744343-3-9(7),* SA-304) Bright Solutions for Dyslexia, LLC.

Smith, Roger. The Adventures of Xavier Winfield & His Pal Oggie, the Great Camping Adventure. 2013. 184p. pap. 7.99 *(978-0-9854439-0-0(1))* Backpack Pubs.

Smith, Roland. Chupacabra. (J). 2015. (ENG.). 304p. (gr. 3-7). pap. 7.99 *(978-0-545-17818-1(5),* Scholastic Paperbacks) 2013. (Illus.). xv, 285p. pap. *(978-0-545-62984-3(5),* Scholastic Pr.) Scholastic, Inc.

—The Edge. 2016. (Peak Marcello Adventure Ser.). (ENG.). 240p. (YA). (gr. 7). pap. 7.99 *(978-0-544-81354-0(5),* HMH Books For Young Readers) Houghton Mifflin Harcourt Publishing Co.

—Kitty Hawk. 2012. (I, Q Ser.: Bk. 3). (ENG., Illus.). 240p. (J). (gr. 5). pap. 8.95 *(978-1-58536-604-0(8));* lib. bdg. 15.95 *(978-1-58536-605-7(6))* Sleeping Bear Pr.

—Mutation. (ENG.). 352p. (J). (gr. 3-7). 2016. (Cryptid Hunters Ser.: 4). pap. 6.99 *(978-0-545-08181-8(5))* 2014. 16.99 *(978-0-545-08180-1(7))* Scholastic, Inc. (Scholastic Pr.).

—Shatterproof. 2012. (39 Clues: Cahills vs. Vespers Ser.: 4). (ENG.). 192p. (J). (gr. 3-7). 12.99 *(978-0-545-29842-1(3));* Bk. 4. (Illus.). lib. bdg. 12.99 *(978-0-545-32413-7(0))* Scholastic, Inc.

—Tentacles. (ENG.). 336p. (J). (gr. 3-7). 2011. pap. 7.99 *(978-0-545-17816-7(9),* Scholastic Paperbacks) 2009. 16.99 *(978-0-545-16688-1(8),* Scholastic Pr.) Scholastic, Inc.

—Walkabout. 2003. 224p. (J). 15.99 *(978-0-7868-0588-4(9))* Hyperion Bks. for Children.

Smith, Ruth. Buddy Bear: Visits Michigan Lighthouses. 2010. 28p. pap. 13.99 *(978-1-4490-8363-2(3))* AuthorHouse.

Smith, Sherri L. The Toymaker's Apprentice. 2015. (ENG., Illus.). 400p. (J). (gr. 5). 16.99 *(978-0-399-25295-2(9),* G.P. Putnam's Sons Books for Young Readers) Penguin Young Readers Group.

—The Toymaker's Apprentice. 2016. (ENG.). 400p. (J). (gr. 5). 19.65 *(978-0-606-39322-5(6))* Turtleback Bks.

Smith, Sherrie. Not Another Dog. 2007. 61p. pap. 19.95 *(978-1-60441-434-9(0))* America Star Bks.

Smith, Sindy. Ervin & Alma's Little Mouse House. 2013. 38p. 24.95 *(978-1-63004-209-7(9));* 40p. pap. 24.95 *(978-1-62709-189-3(0))* America Star Bks.

Smith, Steven K. Summer of the Woods. 2013. 158p. pap. 7.99 *(978-0-9893414-1-7(0))* MyBoys3 Pr.

Smith, Timothy R. The Salmon Stop Running. 2008. (ENG., Illus.). 80p. (J). pap. 5.95 *(978-1-934133-34-7(5),* Mackinac Island Press, Inc.) Charlesbridge Publishing, Inc.

Smith, Vicki. Jamaican Adventure with Tori & Paul. 2012. (ENG., Illus.). 24p. (J). pap. 13.95 *(978-1-4327-8578-9(8))* Outskirts Pr., Inc.

Smithem, Beth. Cocoa Bean & Squirt. 2010. 68p. pap. 10.49 *(978-1-4520-1929-1(0))* AuthorHouse.

—Dust Bunny's Mission. 2010. 84p. pap. 10.49 *(978-1-4520-1934-5(7))* AuthorHouse.

—The Misadventures of Dust Bunny. 2009. 84p. pap. 10.49 *(978-1-4389-4093-9(9))* AuthorHouse.

Smithey, Donna. Nichisan & the Ancient Ones. 2012. 36p. pap. 24.99 *(978-1-62419-240-1(8))* Salem Author Services.

Smyth, Jimmy. Causeway Coast. 2013. 34p. pap. *(978-0-9569314-6-7(4))* Smith, Jimmy.

—The Leprechaun. Ozzy, illus. 2013. 32p. pap. *(978-0-9569314-1-2(3))* Smith, Jimmy.

—The Lost Fairy. 2013. 34p. pap. *(978-0-9569314-3-6(X))* Smith, Jimmy.

—The Magic Garden. 2013. 36p. pap. *(978-0-9569314-7-4(2))* Smith, Jimmy.

—Titanic the Untold Story. 2013. 34p. pap. *(978-0-9569314-4-3(8))* Smith, Jimmy.

Snead, D. J. E. D. Nasty Nathan (the No-good Gnat who Never Listened to Nobody) 2005. (Illus.). 34p. (J). per. 11.95 *(978-0-9769033-0-7(X))* Moonwater Products.

Snedeker, Erin. The Littlest Elf: Marvin Mcgee & the Candle of Fate. Drotleff, David J., illus. 2010. 44p. pap. 15.50 *(978-1-60911-194-6(X),* Eloquent Bks.) Strategic Book Publishing & Rights Agency (SBPRA).

Sneed, Elouise M. Who Is Mr Buzz? 2008. 24p. pap. 13.95 *(978-1-4327-2774-1(5))* Outskirts Pr., Inc.

Snell, Roy J. The Blue Envelope. 2009. 112p. 22.95 *(978-1-60664-675-5(3));* pap. 9.95 *(978-1-60664-304-4(5))* Rodgers, Alan Bks.

—Little White Fox & His Arctic Friends. 2008. 108p. 22.95 *(978-1-60664-935-0(3))* Aegypan.

—Triple Spies. 2008. 112p. (gr. -1-7). 22.95 *(978-1-60664-743-1(1));* pap. 9.95 *(978-1-60664-242-9(1))* Rodgers, Alan Bks.

Snell, Roy Judson. Curlie Carson Listens In. 2007. (ENG.). 120p. pap. 18.99 *(978-1-4264-9605-9(2));* 132p. pap. 19.99 *(978-1-4264-9678-3(8))* Creative Media Partners, LLC.

Snicket, Lemony, pseud. Una Academia Muy Austera. 2004. (Coleccion Una Serie de Catastroficas Desdichas A Series of Unfortunate Events Ser.). (SPA., Illus.). 189p. (YA). 12.95 *(978-84-8441-214-4(8))* Grijalbo Mondadori, S.A.-Montena ESP. Dist: Lectorum Pubns., Inc.

—The Complete Wreck, Bks. 1-13. Helquist, Brett, illus. 2006. (Series of Unfortunate Events Ser.: Bks. 1-13). (J). (gr. 5). 180.00 *(978-0-06-111906-4(7))* HarperCollins Pubs.

—The Grim Grotto. Helquist, Brett & Kupperman, Michael, illus. 2004. (Series of Unfortunate Events Ser.: 11). (ENG.). 352p. (J). (gr. 5-6). 13.99 *(978-0-06-441014-4(5))* HarperCollins Pubs.

—Piege au College. pap. 24.95 *(978-2-09-282599-0(2))* Nathan, Fernand FRA. Dist: Distribooks, Inc.

—Tout Commence Mal. (FRE.). pap. *(978-2-09-282353-8(1))* Editions Rouge et Or.

—29 Myths on the Swinster Pharmacy. Brown, Lisa, illus. 2014. (ENG.). 32p. (gr. 1). 14.95 *(978-1-938073-78-6(9))* McSweeney's Publishing.

Snider, Brandon T. Guardians of the Galaxy Doodles. Montalvo-Lagos, Tomás, illus. 2017. (Doodle Book Ser.). (ENG.). 128p. (J). (gr. 1-3). pap. 12.99 *(978-1-4847-8767-0(6),* Marvel Pr.) Disney Publishing Worldwide.

—Slice of Life with Pizza Steve. 2015. (Uncle Grandpa Ser.). (ENG., Illus.). 80p. (J). (gr. 3-7). pap. 8.99 *(978-0-8431-8314-6(4),* Cartoon Network Books) Penguin Young Readers Group.

—Transformers Rescue Bots: Dangerous Rescue. 2016. (ENG., Illus.). 24p. (J). (gr. -1-3). pap. 3.99 *(978-0-316-26546-1(2))* Little, Brown Bks. for Young Readers.

Sniegoski, Thomas E. The Brimstone Network. 2008. (Brimstone Network Ser.: 1). (ENG.). 304p. (J). (gr. 4-8). pap. 14.99 *(978-1-4169-5104-9(0),* Simon & Schuster/Paula Wiseman Bks.) Simon & Schuster/Paula Wiseman Bks.

—The Shroud of A'Ranka. Howard, Zachariah, illus. 2008. (Brimstone Network Ser.: 2). (ENG.). 288p. (J). (gr. 4-8). pap. 5.99 *(978-1-4169-5105-6(9),* Simon & Schuster/Paula Wiseman Bks.) Simon & Schuster/Paula Wiseman Bks.

—Specter Rising. 2009. (Brimstone Network Ser.: 3). (ENG.). 288p. (J). pap. 5.99 *(978-1-4169-5106-3(7),* Simon & Schuster/Paula Wiseman Bks.) Simon & Schuster/Paula Wiseman Bks.

Sniegoski, Thomas E. & Golden, Christopher. Battle for Arcanum. 2013. (Magic Zero Ser.: 4). (ENG., Illus.). 240p. (J). (gr. 3-7). pap. 6.99 *(978-1-4424-7315-7(0),* Aladdin) Simon & Schuster Children's Publishing.

—Battle for Arcanum. 2013. (Magic Zero Ser.: 4). (ENG., Illus.). 240p. (J). (gr. 3-7). 17.99 *(978-1-4424-7316-4(9),* Simon & Schuster/Paula Wiseman Bks.) Simon & Schuster/Paula Wiseman Bks.

—Dragon Secrets. 2013. (Magic Zero Ser.: 2). (ENG.). 320p. (J). (gr. 3-7). pap. 6.99 *(978-1-4424-7309-6(6),* Aladdin) Simon & Schuster Children's Publishing.

—Dragon Secrets. 2013. (Magic Zero Ser.: 2). (ENG.). 320p. (J). (gr. 3-7). 17.99 *(978-1-4424-7310-2(X),* Simon & Schuster/Paula Wiseman Bks.) Simon & Schuster/Paula Wiseman Bks.

Sniegoski, Tom. Quest for the Spark. Smith, Jeff, illus. (Bone Ser.). (ENG.). (J). (gr. 3-7). 2012. 240p. pap. 10.99 *(978-0-545-14104-8(4))*Bk. 2. 2012. 240p. 26.99 *(978-0-545-14103-1(6))*Bk. 3. 2013. 288p. pap. 10.99 *(978-0-545-14106-2(0))*No. 3. 2013. 288p. 22.99 *(978-0-545-14105-5(2))* Scholastic, Inc. (Graphix).

—Quest for the Spark. (Bone: Quest for the Spark Ser.: 3). 2013. lib. bdg. 22.10 *(978-0-606-31497-8(0))* 2012. lib. bdg. 22.10 *(978-0-606-23947-9(2))* Turtleback Bks. (Turtleback).

Sniegoski, Tom & Smith, Jeff. Quest for the Spark, Bk. 1. Smith, Jeff, illus. 2011. (BONE: Quest for the Spark Ser.: 1). (ENG., Illus.). 224p. (J). (gr. 3-7). 26.99 *(978-0-545-14101-7(X),* Graphix) Scholastic, Inc.

—Tall Tales. Smith, Jeff, illus. 2010. (Bone Ser.). (ENG., Illus.). 128p. (J). (gr. 4-7). 26.99 *(978-0-545-14095-9(1),* Graphix) Scholastic, Inc.

Snow, Alan. Worse Things Happen at Sea! A Tale of Pirates, Poison, & Monsters. Snow, Alan, illus. 2014. (Ratbridge Chronicles Ser.: 2). (ENG., Illus.). 352p. (J). (gr. 3-9). pap. 9.99 *(978-0-689-87050-7(7),* Atheneum Bks. for Young Readers) Simon & Schuster Children's Publishing.

Snowden, Gary. The Lost Treasure of Hawkins Cave. Pierce Clark, Donna, illus. 2013. 112p. pap. 7.99 *(978-1-938768-10-1(8))* Gypsy Pubns.

The Snowman. 2007. (Magical Magnetic Play Scene Ser.). 10p. (J). (gr. -1). *(978-1-84666-214-0(1))* Top That! Publishing PLC.

Snyder, Deanna Sytek. Lee the Pe. 2009. 24p. pap. 12.99 *(978-1-4389-2405-2(4))* AuthorHouse.

Snyder, Karen. Camp Charlie, the Adventures of Grandma Lipstick. LaGrange, Tiffany, illus. 2013. 20p. pap. 12.95 *(978-1-61493-218-5(2))* Peppertree Pr., The.

Snyder, Lavinia Branca. Mission in Space: Softi's Adventures. 2003. (Illus.). (J). mass mkt. *(978-1-932233-35-3(0))* Aurora Libris Corp.

Sobol, Donald J. Encyclopedia Brown, Boy Detective. Shortall, Leonard W., illus. 2009. (Encyclopedia Brown Ser.). 88p. lib. bdg. 15.00 *(978-1-60686-386-2(X))* Perfection Learning Corp.

—Encyclopedia Brown Gets His Man. Shortall, Leonard W., illus. 2009. (Encyclopedia Brown Ser.). 96p. lib. bdg. 15.00 *(978-1-60686-464-7(5))* Perfection Learning Corp.

Soda, Cynthia. Lolly's Basement Crawlies. 2011. 28p. (gr. 1-2). pap. 13.59 *(978-1-4567-4562-2(X))* AuthorHouse.

Soderberg, Erin. Catnapped! 2016. (Puppy Pirates Ser.). (ENG., Illus.). 96p. (J). (gr. 1-4). lib. bdg. 12.99 *(978-0-553-51174-1(2),* Random Hse. Bks. for Young Readers) Random Hse. Children's Bks.

—Ghost Ship. 2016. (Puppy Pirates Ser.: 1). (ENG., Illus.). 128p. (J). (gr. 1-4). 5.99 *(978-1-101-93773-0(4),* Random Hse. Bks. for Young Readers) Random Hse. Children's Bks.

—Puppy Pirates #5: Search for the Sea Monster. 2016. (Puppy Pirates Ser.). (ENG., Illus.). 96p. (J). (gr. 1-4). 4.99 *(978-1-101-93776-1(9),* Random Hse. Bks. for Young Readers) Random Hse. Children's Bks.

Soderberg, Erin. Puppy Pirates Super Special #2: Best in Class. 2017. (Puppy Pirates Ser.: 2). (ENG.). 128p. (J). (gr. 1-4). lib. bdg. 12.99 ***(978-1-5247-1329-4(5))***; (Illus.). 5.99 ***(978-1-5247-1328-7(7))*** Random Hse. Children's Bks. (Random Hse. Bks. for Young Readers).

Soderberg, Erin & Wasserman, Robin. Stowaway! 2015. (Puppy Pirates Ser.: 1). (ENG., Illus.). 96p. (J). (gr. 1-4). pap. 4.99 *(978-0-553-51167-3(X));* lib. bdg. 12.99 *(978-0-553-51168-0(8))* Random Hse. Children's Bks. (Random Hse. Bks. for Young Readers).

Soffe, Caroline Dawn. The Burrows of Trother. 2011. 60p. pap. 19.95 *(978-1-4560-5202-7(0))* America Star Bks.

Sohn, Emily & Timmons, Anne. Adventures in Sound with Max Axiom, Super Scientist. Martin, Cynthia & Timmons, Anne, illus. 2007. (Graphic Science Ser.). (ENG.). 32p. (gr. 3-4). 30.65 *(978-0-7368-6836-5(4),* Graphic Library) Capstone Press of Coughlan Cos.

Soisson, Chelsea. Tate's Wayward Voyage. 2012. (ENG.). (J). pap. 17.99 *(978-1-4675-2651-7(7));* pap. 17.99 *(978-1-4675-2650-0(9))* Independent Pub.

Sola, Lawrence H. Jeremy's Adventures: Miracle on Main Street. 2012. 88p. *(978-1-77097-843-0(7));* pap. *(978-1-77097-598-9(5))* FriesenPress.

Soli, Doris. Jango the Little Dragon: The Wondrous Adventures of Little Dragon. 2011. (Illus.). 36p. pap. 17.07 *(978-1-4567-8487-4(0))* AuthorHouse.

Solice, Deborah. The Eye of the Undead: The Hidden Channel: an Adventure Series in Time. l.t. ed. 2005. (ENG., Illus.). 100p. (J). per. 7.59 *(978-1-933300-01-6(9))* Wandering Sage Pubns., LLC.

Solis, Javier Rene. The Adventures of Tony the Turtle: La Familia the Family. 2008. 24p. pap. 14.99 *(978-1-4389-1421-3(0))* AuthorHouse.

Sollinger, Emily. Diego's Ocean Adventure: A Book of Facts about Ocean Animals. Mawhinney, Art, illus. 2008. (Go, Diego, Go! Ser.). (ENG.). 16p. (J). (gr. -1-2). pap. 6.99 *(978-1-4169-4781-3(7),* Simon Spotlight/Nickelodeon) Simon Spotlight/Nickelodeon.

Soloman, Debra. Don't Look under the Bridge. 2006. 25p. 21.00 *(978-1-4116-7114-0(7))* Lulu Pr., Inc.

Solomon, Barbara. The Girl Who Wanted to Become a Princess. 2013. 50p. pap. 12.99 *(978-1-62839-354-5(8))* Salem Author Services.

Solomon, Chad. Adventures of Rabbit & Bear Paws: The Voyageurs. 2008. (ENG.). 32p. pap. *(978-0-9739906-2-1(7))* Little Spirit Bear Productions CAN. Dist: Lone Pine Publishing.

Soman, David. Three Bears in a Boat. Soman, David, illus. 2014. (ENG., Illus.). 40p. (J). (gr. -1-k). 17.99 *(978-0-8037-3993-2(1),* Dial Bks) Penguin Publishing Group.

Sommer, Isabell & Reinhardt, Swen. CHIP CHIPS JAM - 4: Der Schatz in der Elbe. 2010. 86p. pap. *(978-3-8391-0219-0(7))* Books on Demand GmbH.

Sommer, Sharon. The Adventures of Summer Hills: Rowdy Red's Lesson. 2008. 28p. per. 24.95 *(978-1-4241-9374-5(5))* America Star Bks.

Somper, Justin. Black Heart. 2010. (Vampirates Ser.: 4). (ENG.). 512p. (J). (gr. 3-7). pap. 8.99 *(978-0-316-02088-6(5))* Little, Brown Bks. for Young Readers.

Sones, Sonya. To Be Perfectly Honest: A Novel Based on an Untrue Story. 2013. (ENG., Illus.). 496p. (YA). (gr. 7). 17.99 *(978-0-689-87604-2(1),* Simon & Schuster Bks. For Young Readers) Simon & Schuster Bks. For Young Readers.

Song, Amira. Horse Lovers Forever. 2012. 64p. pap. *(978-1-4602-0144-2(2))* FriesenPress.

Song Hà. Indebted As Lord Chom/No Nhu Chua Chom: The Legend of the Forbidden Street. Smith, William, tr. from VIE. Ly, Thu Hà, illus. 2006. (ENG & VIE.). 32p. (J). (gr. 1-4). 16.95 *(978-0-9701654-6-6(3))* East West Discovery Pr.

Sonja Johannesen & Alice Johannesen. Ola & Jens' Christmas Adventure. 2011. 32p. pap. 21.99 *(978-1-4628-6498-0(8))* Xlibris Corp.

Sonnebom, Scott. Feet First. Banks, Timothy, illus. 2014. (Frankenstein Journals). (ENG.). 80p. (gr. 2-3). 22.65 *(978-1-4342-8999-5(0))* Stone Arch Bks.

—The Frankenstein Journals, 1 vol. Banks, Timothy, illus. 2014. (Frankenstein Journals). (ENG.). 160p. (gr. 2-3). 9.95 *(978-1-4342-9130-1(8))* Stone Arch Bks.

—The Frankenstein Journals: Guts or Bust. Banks, Timothy, illus. 2015. (Frankenstein Journals). (ENG.). 160p. (gr. 2-3). 9.95 *(978-1-4965-0223-0(X))* Stone Arch Bks.

—I for an Eye. Banks, Timothy, illus. 2014. (Frankenstein Journals). (ENG.). 80p. (gr. 2-3). 22.65 *(978-1-4342-9000-7(X))* Stone Arch Bks.

—No Guts, No Gloria. Banks, Timothy, illus. 2015. (Frankenstein Journals). (ENG.). 80p. (gr. 2-3). 22.65 *(978-1-4965-0221-6(3))* Stone Arch Bks.

—A Pain in the Butt. Banks, Timothy, illus. 2015. (Frankenstein Journals). (ENG.). 80p. (gr. 2-3). 22.65 *(978-1-4965-0222-3(1))* Stone Arch Bks.

Sontag, Mary G. Bruno's Adventures. 2009. 128p. pap. 38.49 *(978-1-4490-1769-9(X))* AuthorHouse.

Soper, Stuart A. Milky Saves Christmas. 2011. (Illus.). 290p. pap. 16.00 *(978-1-60976-193-6(6),* Strategic Bk. Publishing) Strategic Book Publishing & Rights Agency (SBPRA).

Sorensen, Launa. The King's First Journey, Bk. 1. 2007. 280p. (YA). pap. 15.99 *(978-1-59092-572-0(6))* Blue Forge Pr.

Sorenson, E. Randy. The First Reindeer Couldn't Fly. 2007. (Illus.). 32p. (J). 17.99 *(978-0-615-16939-2(2))* Sorenson, E. Randy.

Sorenson, Jack R. Eibhlin & Her Dragon, 1 vol. 2009. 131p. pap. 24.95 *(978-1-60749-634-2(8))* America Star Bks.

Sorrells, Walter. The Travelers, Bk. 2. 2009. (Pendragon: 2). (ENG.). 240p. (J). (gr. 5-9). pap. 6.99 *(978-1-4169-6523-7(8),* Aladdin) Simon & Schuster Children's Publishing.

Sosna, Marvin. Brandon's Trail. 2006. 220p. per. 13.95 *(978-1-58939-875-7(0))* Virtualbookworm.com Publishing, Inc.

Soto, Gary. Chato Goes Cruisin' Guevara, Susan, illus. 2008. (Chato Ser.). (J). pap. 16.95 *(978-1-59519-905-8(5))* Live Oak Media.

—Crazy Weekend. 2003. (ENG.). 160p. (gr. 4-7). pap. 10.95 *(978-0-89255-286-3(7),* 255286) Persea Bks., Inc.

Southall, Donna. The Bubble Trailer. 2004. (J). 15.00 *(978-0-8059-6585-8(8))* Dorrance Publishing Co., Inc.

Southard, Patricia. Captain Andre's Adventure in the Sky. 2008. 27p. pap. 24.95 *(978-1-4241-8613-6(7))* America Star Bks.

Sovago-Royal, Sandra. Magimus. 2009. 33p. (J). pap. 19.95 *(978-1-4327-4375-8(9))* Outskirts Pr., Inc.

Sowder, G. Wesley & Sowder, Joseph, told to. Hunter-Lee & the Toy Monster: Book One. 2008. 48p. pap. 16.95 *(978-1-60703-137-6(X))* America Star Bks.

Sowerby, Dale. The Adventures of Baggy & Paxton: Trouble in Dawlish Warren. 2010. (ENG., Illus.). 48p. pap. *(978-1-84748-704-9(1))* Athena Pr.

Space Jam Audio Action Adventure. (Illus.). 28p. (J). (gr. 1-7). pap. 9.89 incl. audio *(978-1-56826-707-4(X),* KR1) Rhino Entertainment Co, A Warner Music Group Co.

Spalding, Andrea. Behind the Sorcerer's Cloak, 1 vol. 2006. (Summer of Magic Quartet Ser.: 4). (ENG., Illus.). 240p. (J). (gr. 4-7). per. 8.95 *(978-1-55143-627-2(2))* Orca Bk. Pubs. USA.

Spalding, Andrea & Spalding, David. The Silver Boulder. (Adventure Net Ser.). 8p. tchr. ed. 3.95 *(978-1-55285-160-9(5),* Walrus Bks.) Whitecap Bks., Ltd. CAN. Dist: Graphic Arts Ctr. Publishing Co.

Spalding, Esta. Look Out for the Fitzgerald-Trouts. Smith, Sydney, illus. 2017. (ENG.). 272p. (J). (gr. 3-7). pap. 6.99 *(978-0-316-29857-5(3))* Little, Brown Bks. for Young Readers.

Spanabel, H. A. Skyler & the Skunks. 2009. 48p. pap. *(978-1-84923-954-7(1))* YouWriteOn.

Spangenberg, Greg. A Christmas Eve Victory. Lodwick, Sarah, illus. l.t. ed. 2006. 32p. (J). 16.99 *(978-1-59879-140-2(0))* Lifevest Publishing, Inc.

Spann, Bill. The Agents of Little Woods. 2005. 116p. pap. 19.95 *(978-1-4137-6574-8(2))* America Star Bks.

Spanton, Elizabeth & Bright, Laren. Golden Voyages. 2013. 84p. pap. 27.99 *(978-1-4525-7213-0(5),* Balboa Pr.) Author Solutions, Inc.

The Sparkling Beauty. 2006. Orig. Title: Televisual Book. (J). 18.99 *(978-0-9779672-0-9(4))* Karsonkina, Tatiana.

Sparks, Matthew Landon. The Little Hoss Adventures. 2010. 54p. pap. 22.20 *(978-0-557-55200-9(1))* Lulu Pr., Inc.

Sparrow, Steve. The Wooden Tiger. 2009. 52p. pap. *(978-1-84923-773-4(5))* YouWriteOn.

Spaziano, Layna. Shane & Molly's Magical Journey, 1 vol. 2010. 28p. pap. 24.95 *(978-1-4489-6261-7(7))* PublishAmerica, Inc.

Spaziante, Patrick. Too Much Ooze! 2015. (Step into Reading Level 2 Ser.). lib. bdg. 14.75 *(978-0-606-36399-0(8))* Turtleback Bks.

Spaziante, Patrick, illus. Creatures of Crime: A Guide to the Bad Guys. 2016. (Batman Ser.). (ENG.). 24p. (J). (gr. -1-2). pap. 3.99 *(978-1-4814-7837-3(0),* Simon Spotlight) Simon Spotlight.

—Heroes of Gotham City. 2016. (Batman Ser.). (ENG.). 32p. (J). (gr. k-2). pap. 3.99 *(978-1-4814-7721-5(8)*, Simon Spotlight) Simon Spotlight.

—Sokka, the Sword Master. 2008. (Avatar Ser.: 1). (ENG.). 32p. (J). (gr. 1-3). pap. 3.99 *(978-1-4169-5491-0(0)*, Simon Spotlight/Nickelodeon) Simon Spotlight/Nickelodeon.

Speakman, David. The Adventures of Sierra Rae: The Forgotten Map, 1 vol. 2009. 59p. pap. 16.95 *(978-1-4489-2657-2(2))* PublishAmerica, Inc.

Spector, Baron. Approaching the Undead, 1 vol. Kneupper, Setch, illus. 2012. (Graveyard Diaries Ser.). (ENG.). 128p. (J). (gr. 3-8). lib. bdg. 27.07 *(978-1-61641-899-1(0)*, Calico Chapter Bks) Magic Wagon.

Spedding, Steven. Boriscat & the Quest for the Golden Carp. 2010. 136p. pap. 10.99 *(978-1-4520-5759-0(1))* AuthorHouse.

Speer, Scott. Battle Angel. 2014. (Immortal City Ser.: 3). (ENG.). 320p. (YA). (gr. 7). pap. 9.99 *(978-1-59514-598-7(2)*, Razorbill) Penguin Young Readers Group.

Spellman, Frankie. Pinky & Bubs' Stinky Night Out. Spellman, Susan, illus. 2005. (ENG.). 32p. (J). (gr. -1-3). per. 12.95 *(978-1-933002-16-3(6))* PublishingWorks.

Spellmeyer, William. Ick-N-Pog: The Encounter Book 2. 2012. 104p. (gr. 2-4). pap. 12.81 *(978-1-4251-9237-2(8))* Trafford Publishing.

Spelvin, Justin. Deep-Sea Countdown. McGee, Warner, illus. 2006. (Backyardigans Ser.). (ENG.). 26p. (J). (gr. -1). bds. 5.99 *(978-1-4169-1484-6(6)*, Simon Spotlight/Nickelodeon) Simon Spotlight/Nickelodeon.

—Riding the Range. 2006. (Illus.). 24p. (J). lib. bdg. 9.00 *(978-1-4242-0248-5(5))* Fitzgerald Bks.

Spence, Cliff. Noah C. 2011. 28p. pap. 13.59 *(978-1-4634-2167-0(2))* AuthorHouse.

Spence, Stephen Mark. African Knights. 2005. 340p. (J). pap. 14.95 *(978-0-9705324-4-2(X))* Spence, Stephen Mark.

Spencer, Debbie. Monty & His Amazing Adventures at Christmas. 2015. (ENG.). 25p. (J). (gr. 2-3). mass mkt. 13.95 *(978-1-78554-708-9(9)*, c404417d-e519-44a9-b243-445d307c70e4) Austin, Stan AUS. Dist: Bookmasters Distribution.

Spencer, Nick. Morning Glories, Vol. 4. 2013. (ENG., Illus.). 216p. pap. 14.99 *(978-1-60706-727-6(7)*, 9781607067276) Image Comics.

Spencer, Pamela. Timeless Treasures. 2005. (J). per. 13.95 *(978-0-9748426-5-3(6)*, Accent Pubns.) Ajoyin Publishing, Inc.

Spendlove, Joanna. The Adventures of Gooky & Spinnet: The Universe, Our Wonderland. 2011. 24p. 14.99 *(978-1-4567-1066-8(4))* AuthorHouse.

Spendlove, Owen. Stanley Brambles & the Pirate's Treasure. 2007. 320p. per. 18.95 *(978-0-595-43792-4(3))* iUniverse, Inc.

Sperry, Brendan. Captain Dino & the Revenge of Roberto. 2012. 20p. pap. 24.95 *(978-1-4626-8260-7(X))* America Star Bks.

Spickett, D. M. The Adventures of Sarah the Seahorse, 1 vol. 2009. 21p. pap. 24.95 *(978-1-61546-205-6(8))* America Star Bks.

Spies, Ben. Weirdo. Spies, Robert, illus. 2015. (ENG.). 54p. (J). pap. *(978-0-473-33563-2(8))* Spies Publishing.

Spiewak, Chet. An Ornament's Tale. 2006. (Illus.). 32p. (J). spiral bd. 16.95 *(978-0-9785827-0-8(5))* CWS Studios, Inc.

—Vinney the Bug Man: The Journey Begins. 2007. (Illus.). 80p. (J). per. 9.95 *(978-0-9785827-1-5(3))* CWS Studios, Inc.

Spikes, James L. The Adventures of LemonHead & Mudd Duck: What to do if Someone Tries to Grab You. 2005. 36p. (J). lib. bdg. 19.95 net. *(978-0-9749202-7-6(4))* Excel Digital Pr.

Spinale, Wendy. Everland. (ENG.). (J). (gr. 7). 2017. (Everland Ser.: 1). 336p. pap. 9.99 *(978-1-338-09553-1(6)*, Scholastic Paperbacks) 2016. 320p. 17.99 *(978-0-545-83694-4(8)*, Scholastic Pr.) Scholastic, Inc.

Spires, Ashley. Binky: License to Scratch. Spires, Ashley, illus. 2013. (Binky Adventure Ser.). (ENG., Illus.). 64p. (J). (gr. 2-5). pap. 7.95 *(978-1-55453-964-2(1))* Kids Can Pr., Ltd. CAN. Dist: Hachette Bk. Group.

The Spirited Little Fisherman: A Pip Adventure. 2005. lib. bdg. 11.95 *(978-1-932341-00-3(5))* Lotti, Marc.

Spiritworks. Sleep, 1 vol. Foster, Jonathan, illus. 2010. 18p. 24.95 *(978-1-4489-4930-4(0))* PublishAmerica, Inc.

Spoonmore, Scott. Seymour the Semi- Space Truckin' Sponaugle, Kim, illus. 2012. 24p. 19.95 *(978-1-61633-282-2(4))*; pap. 11.95 *(978-1-61633-283-9(2))* Guardian Angel Publishing, Inc.

Spotswood, Jessica. A Tyranny of Petticoats. 2016. (ENG.). 368p. (YA). (gr. 9). 17.99 *(978-0-7636-7848-7(1))* Candlewick Pr.

Spradlin, Michael P. Killer Species #4: Ultimate Attack. 2014. (Killer Species Ser.: 4). (ENG.). 192p. (J). (gr. 3-7). pap. 5.99 *(978-0-545-50678-6(6)*, Scholastic Paperbacks) Scholastic, Inc.

Sprague, Howard Lee. Snowflake's Vacation. Borrajero, Judy, illus. 2011. 40p. pap. 9.95 *(978-1-881276-16-6(3))* Serey/Jones Pubs.

Spreng, Robert C. The Tahoe Tiger & the Lahontan Lion. 2008. 38p. pap. 14.50 *(978-0-557-02370-7(X))* Lulu Pr., Inc.

Springer, Michael. The Bootlegger's Secret. 2010. (Illus.). 164p. pap. 15.95 *(978-1-4327-5792-2(X))* Outskirts Pr., Inc.

Springer, Nancy. The Case of the Gypsy Goodbye. 2011. (Enola Holmes Mystery Ser.: 6). (ENG.). 192p. (J). (gr. 3-7). 6.99 *(978-0-14-241888-8(9)*, Puffin Books) Penguin Young Readers Group.

—Lionclaw: A Tale of Rowan Hood. 2004. (ENG.). 128p. (J). (gr. 3-7). 7.99 *(978-0-14-240053-1(X)*, Puffin Books) Penguin Young Readers Group.

—Wild Boy: A Tale of Rowan Hood. 2005. (ENG.). 128p. (J). (gr. 3-7). 6.99 *(978-0-14-240395-2(4)*, Puffin Books) Penguin Young Readers Group.

Springer, Paul. Ink Thief. 2003. (ENG., Illus.). 176p. mass mkt. 6.99 *(978-0-330-33714-4(9)*, Pan) Pan Macmillan GBR. Dist: Trafalgar Square Publishing.

Springer, Susan Woodward. Seldovia Sam & the Blueberry Bear, Vol. 4. Meissner, Amy, illus. 2005. (Misadventures of Seldovia Sam Ser.). (ENG.). 64p. (J). (gr. -1-4). per. 6.95 *(978-0-88240-603-9(5)*, Alaska Northwest Bks.) Graphic Arts Ctr. Publishing Co.

—Seldovia Sam & Wildfire Escape. Meissner, Amy, illus. 2005. (Misadventures of Seldovia Sam Ser.: Bk. 3). (ENG.). 64p. (J). (gr. -1-4). per. 6.95 *(978-0-88240-601-5(9))* Graphic Arts Ctr. Publishing Co.

Spudich, Giulietta. The Amber Giant. 2017. 142p. (J). pap. 7.99 ***(978-1-941429-49-5(1))*** Handersen Publishing.

Spurgeon, S. The Great Kitten Mystery. 2008. 73p. pap. 19.95 *(978-1-60610-798-0(4))* America Star Bks.

Spurlock, Necole. Rocky & Rudy's Wild Adventure, 1 vol. 2009. 48p. pap. 16.95 *(978-1-61582-600-1(9))* America Star Bks.

Spyri, Johanna. Erick & Sally. 2006. pap. *(978-1-4068-0692-2(7))* Echo Library.

—Otra Vez Heidi. (SPA., Illus.). 160p. (YA). 11.95 *(978-84-7281-091-4(7)*, AF1091) Auriga, Ediciones S.A. ESP. Dist: Continental Bk. Co., Inc.

—Veronica. 2006. 120p. (gr. 4-7). per. 10.95 *(978-1-59818-863-9(1))* Aegypan.

Squatrito, J. Michael, Jr. The Talisman of Unification: The Overlords. 2007. (ENG., Illus.). 424p. (YA). per. 22.95 *(978-0-595-47343-4(1))* iUniverse, Inc.

Sretaw. Homonym Hunt. 2010. 24p. pap. 28.03 *(978-1-4500-5228-3(2))* Xlibris Corp.

St. George, Victoria. Barnyard Bandits. 2011. 28p. pap. 12.99 *(978-1-4567-3040-6(1))* AuthorHouse.

St. John, Laurence. Metatron: The Angel Has Risen. 2012. 102p. pap. *(978-1-926997-64-3(6))* Imajin Bks.

St. Pierre, Joe, creator. Bold Blood. 2005. (YA). per. 5.95 *(978-0-9772727-0-9(2))* Astronaut Ink.

Stack, Edward. Food, Spirits, Lodging. 2003. (YA). per. 19.95 *(978-1-929374-18-2(6))* Fire Mountain Pr.

Stacy, Dorothy. Erie Canal Cousins. Stacy, Dorothy, illus. 2007. (Illus.). 110p. (J). per. 9.95 *(978-0-9792947-0-9(3))* Blackberry Hill Pr.

—Three Weeks in Utica. Stacy, Dorothy, illus. 2008. (Illus.). 120p. (J). pap. 9.95 *(978-0-9792947-1-6(1))* Blackberry Hill Pr.

Stadler, Terrie. Who's Knocking at My Door? A Country Pond Tale. 2013. (ENG., Illus.). 26p. (J). pap. 10.95 *(978-1-4787-0453-9(5))* Outskirts Pr., Inc.

Staffen, Julie. Krista Kay MacKinac Island Adventures. 2011. (ENG.). 148p. (YA). pap. 10.95 *(978-1-60920-024-4(1))* Ajoyin Publishing, Inc.

—Krista Kay Summer Adventures. 2010. 156p. pap. 10.95 *(978-1-60920-005-3(5))* Ajoyin Publishing, Inc.

Stafford, Mary. Lincoln & the Lilac Lilies. Dennis, Nadine, illus. 2005. (Fantastic World of Lincoln Llama Ser.). 24p. 6.95 *(978-0-9735663-0-7(2))* Amethyst Hse Publishing, Inc. CAN. Dist: Hushion Hse. Publishing, Ltd.

—Lincoln's Day of Discovery, Vol. 2. Dennis, Nadine, illus. 2005. (Fantastic World of Lincoln Llama Ser.). 24p. 6.95 *(978-0-9735663-1-4(0))* Amethyst Hse Publishing, Inc. CAN. Dist: Hushion Hse. Publishing, Ltd.

—Lincoln's Journey of Journeys, Vol. 3. Dennis, Nadine, illus. 2005. (Fantastic World of Lincoln Llama Ser.). 24p. 6.95 *(978-0-9735663-2-1(9))* Amethyst Hse Publishing, Inc. CAN. Dist: Hushion Hse. Publishing, Ltd.

Stagliano, Michael F. Wesley's Stories: Afterschool Adventures. 2008. 208p. 24.95 *(978-0-595-50215-8(6))*; pap. 14.95 *(978-0-595-50637-8(2))* iUniverse, Inc.

Stahlberg, L. R. The Three Musketeers. Cabrera, Eva, illus. 2016. (Graphic Revolve: Common Core Editions Ser.). (ENG.). 72p. (gr. 2-3). pap. 6.95 *(978-1-4965-3565-8(0)*, Graphic Revolve) Stone Arch Bks.

—The Three Musketeers. Cabrera, Eva, illus. 2016. (Graphic Revolve: Common Core Editions Ser.). (ENG.). 72p. (gr. 2-3). lib. bdg. 27.99 *(978-1-4965-3563-4(4)*, Graphic Revolve) Stone Arch Bks.

Stahnke, Rich. Furious Fist of the Drunken Monkey: Origin of the Species #3. 2007. (Illus.). 2.95 *(978-0-9791192-4-8(3))* Silent Devil Productions.

Staley, Samuel. The Pirate of Panther Bay Classroom Guide. 2007. 75p. spiral bd. 15.00 *(978-0-9764684-2-4(5))* IZS, Inc.

Staller, Mary J. Meet Sandy Gull. 2013. 20p. pap. 10.00 *(978-1-4251-3171-5(9))* Trafford Publishing.

Stamps, Sarah. Our Gang & the Shrinking Machine. Workman, Paula J., illus. 2008. 33p. pap. 24.95 *(978-1-60610-953-3(7))* PublishAmerica, Inc.

Standish, Burt L. Dick Merriwell Abroad. Rudman, Jack, ed. 2003. (Frank Merriwell Ser.). pap. 9.95 *(978-0-8373-9118-2(0))* Merriwell, Frank Inc.

—Dick Merriwell Adrift. Rudman, Jack, ed. 2003. (Frank Merriwell Ser.). pap. 9.95 *(978-0-8373-9154-0(7))* Merriwell, Frank Inc.

—Dick Merriwell at Fardale. Rudman, Jack, ed. 2003. (Frank Merriwell Ser.). 29.95 *(978-0-8373-9376-6(0))*; pap. 9.95 *(978-0-8373-9076-5(1))* Merriwell, Frank Inc.

—Dick Merriwell Doubted. Rudman, Jack, ed. 2003. (Frank Merriwell Ser.). pap. 9.95 *(978-0-8373-9164-9(4))* Merriwell, Frank Inc.

—Dick Merriwell, Freshman. Rudman, Jack, ed. 2003. (Frank Merriwell Ser.). pap. 9.95 *(978-0-8373-9142-7(3))* Merriwell, Frank Inc.

—Dick Merriwell in the Wilds. Rudman, Jack, ed. 2003. (Frank Merriwell Ser.). pap. 9.95 *(978-0-8373-9167-0(9))* Merriwell, Frank Inc.

—Dick Merriwell on the Gridiron. Rudman, Jack, ed. 2003. (Frank Merriwell Ser.). pap. 9.95 *(978-0-8373-9102-1(4))* Merriwell, Frank Inc.

—Dick Merriwell, the Wizard. Rudman, Jack, ed. 2003. (Frank Merriwell Ser.). pap. 9.95 *(978-0-8373-9126-7(1))* Merriwell, Frank Inc.

—Dick Merriwell's Ability. Rudman, Jack, ed. 2003. (Frank Merriwell Ser.). 29.95 *(978-0-8373-9390-2(6))*; pap. 9.95 *(978-0-8373-9090-1(7))* Merriwell, Frank Inc.

—Dick Merriwell's Assurance. Rudman, Jack, ed. 2003. (Frank Merriwell Ser.). pap. 9.95 *(978-0-8373-9109-0(1))* Merriwell, Frank Inc.

—Dick Merriwell's Backers. Rudman, Jack, ed. 2003. (Frank Merriwell Ser.). pap. 9.95 *(978-0-8373-9149-6(0))* Merriwell, Frank Inc.

—Dick Merriwell's Backstop. Rudman, Jack, ed. 2003. (Frank Merriwell Ser.). 29.95 *(978-0-8373-9396-4(5))*; pap. 9.95 *(978-0-8373-9096-3(6))* Merriwell, Frank Inc.

—Dick Merriwell's Best Work. Rudman, Jack, ed. 2003. (Frank Merriwell Ser.). pap. 9.95 *(978-0-8373-9150-2(4))* Merriwell, Frank Inc.

—Dick Merriwell's Black Star. Rudman, Jack, ed. 2003. (Frank Merriwell Ser.). pap. 9.95 *(978-0-8373-9158-8(X))* Merriwell, Frank Inc.

—Dick Merriwell's Cleverness. Rudman, Jack, ed. 2003. (Frank Merriwell Ser.). pap. 9.95 *(978-0-8373-9124-3(5))* Merriwell, Frank Inc.

—Dick Merriwell's Close Call. Rudman, Jack, ed. 2003. (Frank Merriwell Ser.). pap. 9.95 *(978-0-8373-9156-4(3))* Merriwell, Frank Inc.

—Dick Merriwell's Dare. Rudman, Jack, ed. 2003. (Frank Merriwell Ser.). pap. 9.95 *(978-0-8373-9136-6(9))* Merriwell, Frank Inc.

—Dick Merriwell's Dash. Rudman, Jack, ed. 2003. (Frank Merriwell Ser.). 29.95 *(978-0-8373-9389-6(2))*; pap. 9.95 *(978-0-8373-9089-5(3))* Merriwell, Frank Inc.

—Dick Merriwell's Day. Rudman, Jack, ed. 2003. (Frank Merriwell Ser.). pap. 9.95 *(978-0-8373-9114-4(8))* Merriwell, Frank Inc.

—Dick Merriwell's Debt. Rudman, Jack, ed. 2003. (Frank Merriwell Ser.). pap. 9.95 *(978-0-8373-9152-6(0))* Merriwell, Frank Inc.

—Dick Merriwell's Defense. Rudman, Jack, ed. 2003. (Frank Merriwell Ser.). 29.95 *(978-0-8373-9392-6(2))*; pap. 9.95 *(978-0-8373-9092-5(3))* Merriwell, Frank Inc.

—Dick Merriwell's Delivery. Rudman, Jack, ed. 2003. (Frank Merriwell Ser.). 29.95 *(978-0-8373-9384-1(1))*; pap. 9.95 *(978-0-8373-9084-0(2))* Merriwell, Frank Inc.

—Dick Merriwell's Diamond. Rudman, Jack, ed. 2003. (Frank Merriwell Ser.). 29.95 *(978-0-8373-9387-2(6))*; pap. 9.95 *(978-0-8373-9087-1(7))* Merriwell, Frank Inc.

—Dick Merriwell's Disguise. Rudman, Jack, ed. 2003. (Frank Merriwell Ser.). pap. 9.95 *(978-0-8373-9103-8(2))* Merriwell, Frank Inc.

—Dick Merriwell's Distrust. Rudman, Jack, ed. 2003. (Frank Merriwell Ser.). pap. 9.95 *(978-0-8373-9151-9(2))* Merriwell, Frank Inc.

—Dick Merriwell's Downfall. Rudman, Jack, ed. 2003. (Frank Merriwell Ser.). pap. 9.95 *(978-0-8373-9116-8(4))* Merriwell, Frank Inc.

—Dick Merriwell's Example. Rudman, Jack, ed. 2003. (Frank Merriwell Ser.). pap. 9.95 *(978-0-8373-9166-3(0))* Merriwell, Frank Inc.

—Dick Merriwell's Five. Rudman, Jack, ed. 2003. (Frank Merriwell Ser.). pap. 9.95 *(978-0-8373-9130-4(X))* Merriwell, Frank Inc.

—Dick Merriwell's Glory. Rudman, Jack, ed. 2003. (Frank Merriwell Ser.). 29.95 *(978-0-8373-9377-3(9))*; pap. 9.95 *(978-0-8373-9077-2(X))* Merriwell, Frank Inc.

—Dick Merriwell's Grit. Rudman, Jack, ed. 2003. (Frank Merriwell Ser.). pap. 9.95 *(978-0-8373-9108-3(3))* Merriwell, Frank Inc.

—Dick Merriwell's Home Run. Rudman, Jack, ed. 2003. (Frank Merriwell Ser.). pap. 9.95 *(978-0-8373-9135-9(0))* Merriwell, Frank Inc.

—Dick Merriwell's Honors. Rudman, Jack, ed. 2003. (Frank Merriwell Ser.). pap. 9.95 *(978-0-8373-9173-1(3))* Merriwell, Frank Inc.

—Dick Merriwell's Influence. Rudman, Jack, ed. 2003. (Frank Merriwell Ser.). pap. 9.95 *(978-0-8373-9141-0(5))* Merriwell, Frank Inc.

—Dick Merriwell's Joke. Rudman, Jack, ed. 2003. (Frank Merriwell Ser.). pap. 9.95 *(978-0-8373-9144-1(X))* Merriwell, Frank Inc.

—Dick Merriwell's Long Slide. Rudman, Jack, ed. 2003. (Frank Merriwell Ser.). pap. 9.95 *(978-0-8373-9110-6(5))* Merriwell, Frank Inc.

—Dick Merriwell's Magnetism. Rudman, Jack, ed. 2003. (Frank Merriwell Ser.). pap. 9.95 *(978-0-8373-9148-9(2))* Merriwell, Frank Inc.

—Dick Merriwell's Marked Money. Rudman, Jack, ed. 2003. (Frank Merriwell Ser.). pap. 9.95 *(978-0-8373-9100-7(8))* Merriwell, Frank Inc.

—Dick Merriwell's Mastery. Rudman, Jack, ed. 2003. (Frank Merriwell Ser.). pap. 9.95 *(978-0-8373-9153-3(9))* Merriwell, Frank Inc.

—Dick Merriwell's Model. Rudman, Jack, ed. 2003. (Frank Merriwell Ser.). 29.95 *(978-0-8373-9393-3(0))*; pap. 9.95 *(978-0-8373-9093-2(1))* Merriwell, Frank Inc.

—Dick Merriwell's Mystery. Rudman, Jack, ed. 2003. (Frank Merriwell Ser.). 29.95 *(978-0-8373-9394-0(9))*; pap. 9.95 *(978-0-8373-9094-9(X))* Merriwell, Frank Inc.

—Dick Merriwell's Narrow Escape. Rudman, Jack, ed. 2003. (Frank Merriwell Ser.). 29.95 *(978-0-8373-9380-3(9))*; pap. 9.95 *(978-0-8373-9080-2(X))* Merriwell, Frank Inc.

—Dick Merriwell's Persistence. Rudman, Jack, ed. 2003. (Frank Merriwell Ser.). pap. 9.95 *(978-0-8373-9113-7(X))* Merriwell, Frank Inc.

—Dick Merriwell's Polo Team. Rudman, Jack, ed. 2003. (Frank Merriwell Ser.). pap. 9.95 *(978-0-8373-9132-8(6))* Merriwell, Frank Inc.

—Dick Merriwell's Pranks. Rudman, Jack, ed. 2003. (Frank Merriwell Ser.). pap. 9.95 *(978-0-8373-9120-5(2))* Merriwell, Frank Inc.

—Dick Merriwell's Promise. Rudman, Jack, ed. 2003. (Frank Merriwell Ser.). 29.95 *(978-0-8373-9378-0(7))*; pap. 9.95 *(978-0-8373-9078-9(8))* Merriwell, Frank Inc.

—Dick Merriwell's Racket. Rudman, Jack, ed. 2003. (Frank Merriwell Ser.). 29.95 *(978-0-8373-9381-0(7))*; pap. 9.95 *(978-0-8373-9081-9(8))* Merriwell, Frank Inc.

—Dick Merriwell's Regret. Rudman, Jack, ed. 2003. (Frank Merriwell Ser.). pap. 9.95 *(978-0-8373-9147-2(4))* Merriwell, Frank Inc.

—Dick Merriwell's Reputation. Rudman, Jack, ed. 2003. (Frank Merriwell Ser.). pap. 9.95 *(978-0-8373-9171-7(7))* Merriwell, Frank Inc.

—Dick Merriwell's Rescue. Rudman, Jack, ed. 2003. (Frank Merriwell Ser.). 29.95 *(978-0-8373-9379-7(5))*; pap. 9.95 *(978-0-8373-9079-6(6))* Merriwell, Frank Inc.

—Dick Merriwell's Resource. Rudman, Jack, ed. 2003. (Frank Merriwell Ser.). pap. 9.95 *(978-0-8373-9129-8(6))* Merriwell, Frank Inc.

—Dick Merriwell's Return. Rudman, Jack, ed. 2003. (Frank Merriwell Ser.). pap. 9.95 *(978-0-8373-9128-1(8))* Merriwell, Frank Inc.

—Dick Merriwell's Ruse. Rudman, Jack, ed. 2003. (Frank Merriwell Ser.). 29.95 *(978-0-8373-9383-4(3))*; pap. 9.95 *(978-0-8373-9083-3(4))* Merriwell, Frank Inc.

—Dick Merriwell's Stanchness. Rudman, Jack, ed. 2003. (Frank Merriwell Ser.). pap. 9.95 *(978-0-8373-9161-8(X))* Merriwell, Frank Inc.

—Dick Merriwell's Threat. Rudman, Jack, ed. 2003. (Frank Merriwell Ser.). pap. 9.95 *(978-0-8373-9112-0(1))* Merriwell, Frank Inc.

—Dick Merriwell's Trap. Rudman, Jack, ed. 2003. (Frank Merriwell Ser.). 29.95 *(978-0-8373-9391-9(4))*; pap. 9.95 *(978-0-8373-9091-8(5))* Merriwell, Frank Inc.

—Dick Merriwell's Way. Rudman, Jack, ed. 2003. (Frank Merriwell Ser.). pap. 9.95 *(978-0-8373-9169-4(5))* Merriwell, Frank Inc.

—Dick Merriwell's Western Mission. Rudman, Jack, ed. 2003. (Frank Merriwell Ser.). 29.95 *(978-0-8373-9397-1(3))*; pap. 9.95 *(978-0-8373-9097-0(4))* Merriwell, Frank Inc.

—Dick Merriwell's Wonders. Rudman, Jack, ed. 2003. (Frank Merriwell Ser.). 29.95 *(978-0-8373-9385-8(X))*; pap. 9.95 *(978-0-8373-9085-7(0))* Merriwell, Frank Inc.

—Frank Merriwell in Maine. Rudman, Jack, ed. 2003. (Frank Merriwell Ser.). (YA). (gr. 9-18). 29.95 *(978-0-8373-9328-5(0))*; pap. 9.95 *(978-0-8373-9028-4(1)*, FM-028) Merriwell, Frank Inc.

—Frank Merriwell in the Rockies. Rudman, Jack, ed. 2003. (Frank Merriwell Ser.). pap. 9.95 *(978-0-8373-9119-9(9))* Merriwell, Frank Inc.

—Frank Merriwell on the Boulevards. Rudman, Jack, ed. 2003. (Frank Merriwell Ser.). pap. 9.95 *(978-0-8373-9045-1(1))* Merriwell, Frank Inc.

—Frank Merriwell on the Road. Rudman, Jack, ed. 2003. (Frank Merriwell Ser.). 29.95 *(978-0-8373-9334-6(5))*; pap. 9.95 *(978-0-8373-9034-5(6))* Merriwell, Frank Inc.

—Frank Merriwell on Top. Rudman, Jack, ed. 2003. (Frank Merriwell Ser.). 29.95 *(978-0-8373-9355-1(8))*; pap. 9.95 *(978-0-8373-9055-0(9))* Merriwell, Frank Inc.

—Frank Merriwell's Air Voyage. Rudman, Jack, ed. 2003. (Frank Merriwell Ser.). pap. 9.95 *(978-0-8373-9157-1(1))* Merriwell, Frank Inc.

—Frank Merriwell's Alarm. Rudman, Jack, ed. 2003. (Frank Merriwell Ser.). (YA). (gr. 9-18). 29.95 *(978-0-8373-9316-2(7))*; pap. 9.95 *(978-0-8373-9016-1(8)*, FM-016) Merriwell, Frank Inc.

—Frank Merriwell's Athletes. Rudman, Jack, ed. 2003. (Frank Merriwell Ser.). (YA). (gr. 9-18). 29.95 *(978-0-8373-9317-9(5))*; pap. 9.95 *(978-0-8373-9017-8(6)*, FM-017) Merriwell, Frank Inc.

—Frank Merriwell's Backers. Rudman, Jack, ed. 2003. (Frank Merriwell Ser.). 296.95 *(978-0-8373-9395-7(7))*; pap. 9.95 *(978-0-8373-9095-6(8))* Merriwell, Frank Inc.

—Frank Merriwell's Bicycle Tour. Rudman, Jack, ed. 2003. (Frank Merriwell Ser.). (YA). (gr. 9-18). 29.95 *(978-0-8373-9313-1(2))*; pap. 9.95 *(978-0-8373-9013-0(3)*, FM-013) Merriwell, Frank Inc.

—Frank Merriwell's Bravery. 2007. 232p. per. 19.95 *(978-1-4344-0153-3(7))* Wildside Pr., LLC.

—Frank Merriwell's Brother. Rudman, Jack, ed. 2003. (Frank Merriwell Ser.). 29.95 *(978-0-8373-9373-5(6))*; pap. 9.95 *(978-0-8373-9073-4(7))* Merriwell, Frank Inc.

—Frank Merriwell's Challengers. Rudman, Jack, ed. 2003. (Frank Merriwell Ser.). pap. 9.95 *(978-0-8373-9122-9(9))* Merriwell, Frank Inc.

—Frank Merriwell's Champions. Rudman, Jack, ed. 2003. (Frank Merriwell Ser.). (YA). (gr. 9-18). 29.95 *(978-0-8373-9319-3(1))*; pap. 9.95 *(978-0-8373-9019-2(2)*, FM-019) Merriwell, Frank Inc.

—Frank Merriwell's Chase. Rudman, Jack, ed. 2003. (Frank Merriwell Ser.). (YA). (gr. 9-18). 29.95 *(978-0-8373-9327-8(2))*; pap. 9.95 *(978-0-8373-9027-7(3)*, FM-027) Merriwell, Frank Inc.

—Frank Merriwell's Chums. 2007. (ENG.). 228p. pap. 20.99 *(978-1-4346-3282-1(2))*; 264p. pap. 23.99 *(978-1-4346-3283-8(0))* Creative Media Partners, LLC.

—Frank Merriwell's Club. Rudman, Jack, ed. 2003. (Frank Merriwell Ser.). 29.95 *(978-0-8373-9368-1(X))*; pap. 9.95 *(978-0-8373-9068-0(0))* Merriwell, Frank Inc.

—Frank Merriwell's Courage. Rudman, Jack, ed. 2003. (Frank Merriwell Ser.). (YA). (gr. 9-18). 29.95 *(978-0-8373-9314-8(0))*; pap. 9.95 *(978-0-8373-9014-7(1)*, FM-014) Merriwell, Frank Inc.

—Frank Merriwell's Cruise. Rudman, Jack, ed. 2003. (Frank Merriwell Ser.). (YA). (gr. 9-18). 29.95 *(978-0-8373-9326-1(4))*; pap. 9.95 *(978-0-8373-9026-0(5)*, FM-026) Merriwell, Frank Inc.

—Frank Merriwell's Danger. Rudman, Jack, ed. 2003. (Frank Merriwell Ser.). (YA). (gr. 9-18). 29.95 *(978-0-8373-9322-3(1))*; pap. 9.95 *(978-0-8373-9022-2(2)*, FM-022) Merriwell, Frank Inc.

—Frank Merriwell's Daring. Rudman, Jack, ed. 2003. (Frank Merriwell Ser.). (YA). (gr. 9-18). 29.95 *(978-0-8373-9315-5(9))*; pap. 9.95 *(978-0-8373-9015-4(X)*, FM-015) Merriwell, Frank Inc.

—Frank Merriwell's Duel. Rudman, Jack, ed. 2003. (Frank Merriwell Ser.). 29.95 *(978-0-8373-9346-9(9))*; pap. 9.95 *(978-0-8373-9046-8(X))* Merriwell, Frank Inc.

—Frank Merriwell's Encounter. Rudman, Jack, ed. 2003. (Frank Merriwell Ser.). 29.95 *(978-0-8373-9399-5(X))*; pap. 9.95 *(978-0-8373-9099-4(0))* Merriwell, Frank Inc.

—Frank Merriwell's Encouragement. Rudman, Jack, ed. 2003. (Frank Merriwell Ser.). pap. 9.95 *(978-0-8373-9172-4(5))* Merriwell, Frank Inc.

—Frank Merriwell's Endurance. Rudman, Jack, ed. 2003. (Frank Merriwell Ser.). pap. 9.95 *(978-0-8373-9123-6(7))* Merriwell, Frank Inc.

—Frank Merriwell's Fortune. Rudman, Jack, ed. 2003. (Frank Merriwell Ser.). 29.95 *(978-0-8373-9339-1(6))*; pap. 9.95 *(978-0-8373-9039-0(7))* Merriwell, Frank Inc.

—Frank Merriwell's Fun. Rudman, Jack, ed. 2003. (Frank Merriwell Ser.). 29.95 *(978-0-8373-9351-3(5))*; pap. 9.95 *(978-0-8373-9051-2(6))* Merriwell, Frank Inc.

—Frank Merriwell's Great Scheme. Rudman, Jack, ed. 2003. (Frank Merriwell Ser.). 29.95 *(978-0-8373-9343-8(4))*; pap. 9.95 *(978-0-8373-9043-7(5))* Merriwell, Frank Inc.

—Frank Merriwell's Hard Case. Rudman, Jack, ed. 2003. (Frank Merriwell Ser.). pap. 9.95 *(978-0-8373-9162-5(8))* Merriwell, Frank Inc.

—Frank Merriwell's Iron Nerve. Rudman, Jack, ed. 2003. (Frank Merriwell Ser.). 29.95 *(978-0-8373-9362-9(0))*; pap. 9.95 *(978-0-8373-9062-8(1))* Merriwell, Frank Inc.

—Frank Merriwell's Loyalty. Rudman, Jack, ed. 2003. (Frank Merriwell Ser.). (YA). (gr. 9-18). 29.95 (978-0-8373-9323-0(X)); pap. 9.95 (978-0-8373-9023-9(0), FM-023) Merriwell, Frank Inc.

—Frank Merriwell's Marvel. Rudman, Jack, ed. 2003. (Frank Merriwell Ser.). 29.95 (978-0-8373-9374-2(4)); pap. 9.95 (978-0-8373-9074-1(5)) Merriwell, Frank Inc.

—Frank Merriwell's Mascot. Rudman, Jack, ed. 2003. (Frank Merriwell Ser.). 29.95 (978-0-8373-9357-5(4)); pap. 9.95 (978-0-8373-9057-4(5)) Merriwell, Frank Inc.

—Frank Merriwell's New Comedian. Rudman, Jack, ed. 2003. (Frank Merriwell Ser.). 29.95 (978-0-8373-9340-7(X)); pap. 29.95 (978-0-8373-9040-6(0)) Merriwell, Frank Inc.

—Frank Merriwell's Nomads. Rudman, Jack, ed. 2003. (Frank Merriwell Ser.). pap. 9.95 (978-0-8373-9101-4(6)) Merriwell, Frank Inc.

—Frank Merriwell's Opportunity. Rudman, Jack, ed. 2003. (Frank Merriwell Ser.). 29.95 (978-0-8373-9331-5(0)); pap. 9.95 (978-0-8373-9031-4(1)) Merriwell, Frank Inc.

—Frank Merriwell's Own Company. Rudman, Jack, ed. 2003. (Frank Merriwell Ser.). 29.95 (978-0-8373-9335-3(3)); pap. 9.95 (978-0-8373-9035-2(4)) Merriwell, Frank Inc.

—Frank Merriwell's Party. Rudman, Jack, ed. 2003. (Frank Merriwell Ser.). (YA). (gr. 9-18). 29.95 (978-0-8373-9312-4(4)); pap. 29.95 (978-0-8373-9012-3(5), FM-012) Merriwell, Frank Inc.

—Frank Merriwell's Peril. Rudman, Jack, ed. 2003. (Frank Merriwell Ser.). pap. 9.95 (978-0-8373-9115-1(6)) Merriwell, Frank Inc.

—Frank Merriwell's Phantom. Rudman, Jack, ed. 2003. (Frank Merriwell Ser.). 29.95 (978-0-8373-9359-9(0)); pap. 9.95 (978-0-8373-9059-8(1)) Merriwell, Frank Inc.

—Frank Merriwell's Power. Rudman, Jack, ed. 2003. (Frank Merriwell Ser.). 29.95 (978-0-8373-9364-3(7)); pap. 9.95 (978-0-8373-9064-2(8)) Merriwell, Frank Inc.

—Frank Merriwell's Pride. Rudman, Jack, ed. 2003. (Frank Merriwell Ser.). pap. 9.95 (978-0-8373-9121-2(0)) Merriwell, Frank Inc.

—Frank Merriwell's Problem. Rudman, Jack, ed. 2003. (Frank Merriwell Ser.). 29.95 (978-0-8373-9338-4(8)); pap. 9.95 (978-0-8373-9038-3(9)) Merriwell, Frank Inc.

—Frank Merriwell's Prosperity. Rudman, Jack, ed. 2003. (Frank Merriwell Ser.). 29.95 (978-0-8373-9341-4(8)); pap. 9.95 (978-0-8373-9041-3(9)) Merriwell, Frank Inc.

—Frank Merriwell's Protege. Rudman, Jack, ed. 2003. (Frank Merriwell Ser.). 29.95 (978-0-8373-9333-9(7)); pap. 9.95 (978-0-8373-9033-8(8)) Merriwell, Frank Inc.

—Frank Merriwell's Pursuit. Rudman, Jack, ed. 2003. (Frank Merriwell Ser.). pap. 9.95 (978-0-8373-9117-5(2)) Merriwell, Frank Inc.

—Frank Merriwell's Races. Rudman, Jack, ed. 2003. (Frank Merriwell Ser.). (YA). (gr. 9-18). 29.95 (978-0-8373-9311-7(6)); pap. 9.95 (978-0-8373-9011-6(7), FM-011) Merriwell, Frank Inc.

—Frank Merriwell's Rescue. Rudman, Jack, ed. 2003. (Frank Merriwell Ser.). 29.95 (978-0-8373-9398-8(1)); pap. 9.95 (978-0-8373-9098-7(2)) Merriwell, Frank Inc.

—Frank Merriwell's Return to Yale. Rudman, Jack, ed. 2003. (Frank Merriwell Ser.). (YA). (gr. 9-18). 29.95 (978-0-8373-9320-9(5)); pap. 9.95 (978-0-8373-9020-8(6), FM-020) Merriwell, Frank Inc.

—Frank Merriwell's Reward. Rudman, Jack, ed. 2003. (Frank Merriwell Ser.). 29.95 (978-0-8373-9358-2(2)); pap. 9.95 (978-0-8373-9058-1(3)) Merriwell, Frank Inc.

—Frank Merriwell's Rough Deal. Rudman, Jack, ed. 2003. (Frank Merriwell Ser.). pap. 9.95 (978-0-8373-9111-3(3)) Merriwell, Frank Inc.

—Frank Merriwell's Search. Rudman, Jack, ed. 2003. (Frank Merriwell Ser.). 29.95 (978-0-8373-9367-4(1)); pap. 9.95 (978-0-8373-9067-3(2)) Merriwell, Frank Inc.

—Frank Merriwell's Secret. Rudman, Jack, ed. 2003. (Frank Merriwell Ser.). (YA). (gr. 9). 29.95 (978-0-8373-9321-6(3)); pap. 9.95 (978-0-8373-9021-5(4), FM-021) Merriwell, Frank Inc.

—Frank Merriwell's Setback. Rudman, Jack, ed. 2003. (Frank Merriwell Ser.). 29.95 (978-0-8373-9366-7(3)); pap. 9.95 (978-0-8373-9066-6(4)) Merriwell, Frank Inc.

—Frank Merriwell's Shrewdness. Rudman, Jack, ed. 2003. (Frank Merriwell Ser.). 29.95 (978-0-8373-9365-0(5)); pap. 9.95 (978-0-8373-9065-9(6)) Merriwell, Frank Inc.

—Frank Merriwell's Skill. Rudman, Jack, ed. 2003. (Frank Merriwell Ser.). (YA). (gr. 9-18). 29.95 (978-0-8373-9318-6(3)); pap. 9.95 (978-0-8373-9018-5(4), FM-018) Merriwell, Frank Inc.

—Frank Merriwell's Stage Hit. Rudman, Jack, ed. 2003. (Frank Merriwell Ser.). 29.95 (978-0-8373-9342-1(6)); pap. 9.95 (978-0-8373-9042-0(7)) Merriwell, Frank Inc.

—Frank Merriwell's Steadying Hand. Rudman, Jack, ed. 2003. (Frank Merriwell Ser.). pap. 9.95 (978-0-8373-9165-6(2)) Merriwell, Frank Inc.

—Frank Merriwell's Strategy. Rudman, Jack, ed. 2003. (Frank Merriwell Ser.). pap. 9.95 (978-0-8373-9106-9(7)) Merriwell, Frank Inc.

—Frank Merriwell's Strong Arm. Rudman, Jack, ed. 2003. (Frank Merriwell Ser.). 29.95 (978-0-8373-9371-1(X)); pap. 9.95 (978-0-8373-9071-0(0)) Merriwell, Frank Inc.

—Frank Merriwell's Struggle. Rudman, Jack, ed. 2003. (Frank Merriwell Ser.). (YA). (gr. 9-18). pap. 9.95 (978-0-8373-9029-1(X)) Merriwell, Frank Inc.

—Frank Merriwell's Support. Rudman, Jack, ed. 2003. (Frank Merriwell Ser.). 29.95 (978-0-8373-9375-9(2)); pap. 9.95 (978-0-8373-9075-8(3)) Merriwell, Frank Inc.

—Frank Merriwell's Talisman. Rudman, Jack, ed. 2003. (Frank Merriwell Ser.). pap. 9.95 (978-0-8373-9145-8(8)) Merriwell, Frank Inc.

—Frank Merriwell's Temptation. Rudman, Jack, ed. 2003. (Frank Merriwell Ser.). 29.95 (978-0-8373-9354-4(X)); pap. 9.95 (978-0-8373-9054-3(0)) Merriwell, Frank Inc.

—Frank Merriwell's Tigers. Rudman, Jack, ed. 2003. (Frank Merriwell Ser.). pap. 9.95 (978-0-8373-9131-1(8)) Merriwell, Frank Inc.

—Frank Merriwell's Tricks. Rudman, Jack, ed. 2003. (Frank Merriwell Ser.). 29.95 (978-0-8373-9353-7(1)); pap. 9.95 (978-0-8373-9053-6(2)) Merriwell, Frank Inc.

—Frank Merriwell's Trip West. Rudman, Jack, ed. (Frank Merriwell Ser.). (YA). (gr. 9-18). 29.95 (978-0-8373-9304-9(3)); pap. 9.95 (978-0-8373-9004-8(4), FM-004) Merriwell, Frank Inc.

—Frank Merriwell's Triumph. Rudman, Jack, ed. 2003. (Frank Merriwell Ser.). pap. 9.95 (978-0-8373-9107-6(5)) Merriwell, Frank Inc.

—Frank Merriwell's Trump Card. Rudman, Jack, ed. 2003. (Frank Merriwell Ser.). pap. 9.95 (978-0-8373-9105-2(9)) Merriwell, Frank Inc.

—Frank Merriwell's Trust. Rudman, Jack, ed. 2003. (Frank Merriwell Ser.). 29.95 (978-0-8373-9369-8(8)); pap. 9.95 (978-0-8373-9069-7(9)) Merriwell, Frank Inc.

—Frank Merriwell's Vacation. Rudman, Jack, ed. 2003. (Frank Merriwell Ser.). (YA). (gr. 9-18). 29.95 (978-0-8373-9325-4(6)); pap. 9.95 (978-0-8373-9025-3(7), FM-025) Merriwell, Frank Inc.

—Frank Merriwell's Victories. Rudman, Jack, ed. 2003. (Frank Merriwell Ser.). 29.95 (978-0-8373-9361-2(2)); pap. 9.95 (978-0-8373-9061-1(3)) Merriwell, Frank Inc.

—Frank Merriwell's Winners. Rudman, Jack, ed. 2003. (Frank Merriwell Ser.). 29.95 (978-0-8373-9388-9(4)); pap. 9.95 (978-0-8373-9088-8(5)) Merriwell, Frank Inc.

—Frank Merriwell's Wizard. Rudman, Jack, ed. 2003. (Frank Merriwell Ser.). pap. 9.95 (978-0-8373-9174-8(1)) Merriwell, Frank Inc.

—Frank Merriwell's Worst Boy. Rudman, Jack, ed. 2003. (Frank Merriwell Ser.). pap. 9.95 (978-0-8373-9155-7(5)) Merriwell, Frank Inc.

Standish, Burt L. & Rudman, Jack. Frank Merriwell on the Boulevards. 2003. (Frank Merriwell Ser.). 29.95 (978-0-8373-9345-2(0)) Merriwell, Frank Inc.

Standish, Joyce, ed. The Adventures of Ryan Lincoln. Cooper, Nicole, illus. 2012. 46p. (J). pap. 10.00 (978-0-9716244-5-0(3)) TLS Publishing.

Stanek, Mary Beth. The Fire Keepers: Mystery at Manitou Beach. Stanek, Mary Beth, illus. Stanek, Linda, photos by. 2003. (Illus.). (J). pap. 20.00 (978-0-9747556-0-1(5)) Stanek, Mary Beth.

Stanek, Robert, pseud. Adventures with Letters & Words (Buster Bee's Learning Series #1, the Bugville Critters) 2009. (Illus.). 28p. 7.25 (978-1-57545-194-7(8)) RP Media.

—The Art of Ruin Mist: Heroes & Villains. 2007. (ENG.). 60p. (YA). per. 16.00 (978-1-57545-163-3(8)) RP Media.

—Break Their Bad Habits. deluxe ed. 2009. (Bugville Critters Ser.: No. 9). (Illus.). 24p. 9.99 (978-1-57545-213-5(8), Reagent Pr. Bks. for Young Readers) RP Media.

—Break Their Bad Habits: (the Bugville Critters, Lass's Adventures Series #2) 2009. (Bugville Critters Ser.: No. 9). (Illus.). 52p. (J). pap. 14.95 (978-1-57545-205-0(7), Reagent Pr. Bks. for Young Readers) RP Media.

—The Bugville Critters Go on Vacation. 2008. (ENG., Illus.). (J). 32p. per. 9.95 (978-1-57545-148-0(4)); 52p. per. 19.95 (978-1-57545-125-1(5)) RP Media.

—The Bugville Critters Go to School. 2007. (ENG.). 28p. (J). per. 9.99 (978-1-57545-145-9(X)) RP Media.

—The Bugville Critters Make New Friends: Buster Bee's School Days #2. 2008. (ENG., Illus.). 60p. (J). per. 18.95 (978-1-57545-168-8(9)) RP Media.

—The Bugville Critters Play Their First Big Game. 2008. (ENG., Illus.). (J). 32p. per. 9.95 (978-1-57545-149-7(2)); 52p. per. 16.95 (978-1-57545-127-5(1)) RP Media.

—The Bugville Critters Rush to the Hospital. 2008. (ENG., Illus.). (J). 32p. per. 9.95 (978-1-57545-150-3(6)); 52p. per. 19.95 (978-1-57545-126-8(3)) RP Media.

—The Bugville Critters Vacation Surprise: Buster Bee's School Days #3. 2008. (ENG., Illus.). 68p. (J). per. 18.95 (978-1-57545-172-5(7)) RP Media.

—The Bugville Critters Visit Dad & Mom at Work. 2007. (ENG.). (J). 28p. per. 9.99 (978-1-57545-144-2(1)); (Illus.). 52p. per. 19.95 (978-1-57545-121-3(2), Reagent Pr. Bks. for Young Readers) RP Media.

—The Bugville Critters Visit Garden Box Farms. (ENG.). (J). 2008. 28p. per. 10.99 (978-1-57545-147-3(6)) 2007. (Illus.). 52p. per. 19.95 (978-1-57545-124-4(7)) RP Media.

—Buster Bee's Adventures with Letters & Words. (ENG., Illus.). (J). 2008. 52p. per. 19.95 (978-1-57545-169-5(7)) 2007. 28p. pap. 9.99 (978-1-57545-156-5(5)) RP Media.

—Catching a Cup of Sunshine. 2010. (Illus.). 36p. pap. 9.99 (978-1-57545-195-4(6), Reagent Pr. Bks. for Young Readers) RP Media.

—The Elf Queen & the King III. 2007. 232p. (YA). pap. 15.00 (978-1-57545-086-5(0)) RP Media.

—The Elf Queen & the King IV. 2008. 238p. (YA). pap. 15.00 (978-1-57545-087-2(9)) RP Media.

—Every Day Is Different. 2010. 32p. pap. 8.99 (978-1-57545-180-0(8), Reagent Pr. Bks. for Young Readers) RP Media.

—Go on Vacation. 2008. (ENG., Illus.). 32p. (J). pap. 5.59 (978-1-57545-191-6(3)) RP Media.

—Go to School. 2008. (ENG., Illus.). 28p. (J). pap. 5.29 (978-1-57545-188-6(3)) RP Media.

—Have a Backyard Picnic. 2009. (Bugville Critters Ser.: No. 14). (ENG., Illus.). 52p. (J). 14.95 (978-1-57545-210-4(3), Reagent Pr. Bks. for Young Readers) RP Media.

—Have a Bad Day. 2009. (Bugville Critters Ser.: No. 11). (ENG., Illus.). 52p. (J). 14.95 (978-1-57545-207-4(3), Reagent Pr. Bks. for Young Readers) RP Media.

—Have a Sleepover. 2008. (ENG., Illus.). 28p. (J). pap. 5.29 (978-1-57545-189-3(1)) RP Media.

—Have a Surprise Party. 2009. (Bugville Critters Ser.: No. 13). (ENG., Illus.). 52p. (J). 14.95 (978-1-57545-209-8(X), Reagent Pr. Bks. for Young Readers) RP Media.

—Have Trouble at School. 2009. (Illus.). 24p. pap. 9.99 (978-1-57545-212-8(X)); 52p. (J). pap. 14.95 (978-1-57545-204-3(9)) RP Media. (Reagent Pr. Bks. for Young Readers).

—In the Service of Dragons. 2007. (ENG., Illus.). 280p. (YA). 19.99 (978-1-57545-134-3(4)) RP Media.

—In the Service of Dragons II. 2007. (ENG., Illus.). 284p. (YA). 19.99 (978-1-57545-135-0(2)) RP Media.

—In the Service of Dragons III. 2007. (ENG., Illus.). 268p. (YA). 19.99 (978-1-57545-136-7(0)) RP Media.

—In the Service of Dragons IV. 2007. 264p. (YA). 19.99 (978-1-57545-137-4(9)) RP Media.

—In the Service of Dragons IV: Keeper Martin's Tales, Book 8. 2006. (ENG.). 180p. (YA). (gr. 8-12). per. 11.25 (978-1-57545-119-0(0), Reagent Pr. Echo) RP Media.

—Into the Stone Land. 2011. (Best Fantasy Ser.: Bk. 2). 242p. (J). pap. 11.00 (978-1-57545-092-6(5)) RP Media.

—Journey Beyond the Beyond. (J). 2007. (ENG.). 156p. per. 14.00 (978-1-57545-132-9(8)) 2007. (ENG., Illus.). 156p. 18.95 (978-1-57545-133-6(6)) 2006. (Illus.). 112p. pap. 14.95 (978-1-57545-108-4(5)) RP Media.

—The Kingdoms & the Elves of the Reaches: Signature, Keeper Martin's Tales, Bk. 1. 2007. (Illus.). 240p. (YA). 35.00 (978-1-57545-128-2(X)) RP Media.

—The Kingdoms & the Elves of the Reaches II: Signature, Keeper Martin's Tales, Bk. 2. 2007. (Illus.). 244p. (J). (gr. 4-7). 35.00 (978-1-57545-129-9(8)) RP Media.

—The Kingdoms & the Elves of the Reaches Ii (Reader's Choice Edition, Keeper Martin's Tales Book 2) 2008. (Illus.). 244p. pap. 15.95 (978-1-57545-197-8(2)) RP Media.

—The Kingdoms & the Elves of the Reaches Iv. 2008. (Illus.). 244p. 35.00 (978-1-57545-131-2(X)) RP Media.

—The Kingdoms & the Elves of the Reaches Iv (Reader's Choice Edition, Keeper Martin's Tales Book 4) 2008. (Illus.). 244p. pap. 15.95 (978-1-57545-199-2(9)) RP Media.

—Play Their First Big Game. 2008. (ENG., Illus.). 32p. (J). pap. 5.59 (978-1-57545-193-0(X)) RP Media.

—Robert Stanek's Bugville Critters Storybook Treasury. 2008. (ENG., Illus.). 132p. (J). per. 24.95 (978-1-57545-171-8(9)) RP Media.

—Robert Stanek's Bugville Critters Storybook Treasury Volume 2 (the Bugville Critters Storybook Collection, Volume 2), 4 vols., Vol. 2. 2008. (ENG., Illus.). 124p. (J). per. 24.95 (978-1-57545-173-2(5)) RP Media.

—Rush to the Hospital. 2008. (ENG., Illus.). 32p. (J). pap. 5.59 (978-1-57545-192-3(1)) RP Media.

—The Secrets, Mysteries & Magic of Robert Stanek's Ruin Mist. 2008. 200p. (YA). pap. 15.00 (978-1-57545-037-7(2), Ruin Mist Pubns.) RP Media.

—Stay after School. 2009. (Bugville Critters Ser.: No. 10). (ENG., Illus.). 52p. (J). 14.95 (978-1-57545-206-7(5), Reagent Pr. Bks. for Young Readers) RP Media.

—Student's Classroom Handbook for the Kingdoms & the Elves of the Reaches II. 2nd ed. 2007. (ENG.). 128p. pap. 15.00 (978-1-57545-036-0(4), Ruin Mist Pubns.) RP Media.

—Visit City Hall. 2009. (Bugville Critters Ser.: No. 12). (ENG., Illus.). 52p. (J). 14.95 (978-1-57545-208-1(1), Reagent Pr. Bks. for Young Readers) RP Media.

—Visit Dad & Mom at Work. 2008. (ENG., Illus.). 28p. (J). pap. 5.29 (978-1-57545-187-9(5)) RP Media.

—Visit Garden Box Farms. 2008. (ENG., Illus.). 28p. (J). pap. 5.29 (978-1-57545-190-9(5)) RP Media.

Stanfield, Michael. Bucky & Becky - the Magic of Wigglepoo Mountain. 2009. 144p. pap. 14.96 (978-0-557-02614-2(8)) Lulu Pr., Inc.

Stanford, K. B. Sixteen Wishes (paperback) 2008. 188p. pap. 15.47 (978-1-4357-1773-2(2)) Lulu Pr., Inc.

Stangherlin, Tonia. T-Bird & the Island of Lost Cats. 2006. 116p. pap. 14.99 (978-1-4116-6697-9(6)) Lulu Pr., Inc.

Stanislaus, Justin. The Purple Elephant in the Room. 2008. 44p. pap. 24.95 (978-1-60474-707-2(2)) America Star Bks.

Staniszewski, Anna. My Epic Fairy Tale Fail. 2013. (My Very Unfairy Tale Life Ser.: 2). (ENG.). 224p. (J). (gr. 4-7). pap. 6.99 (978-1-4022-7930-0(2), 9781402279300, Sourcebooks Jabberwocky) Sourcebooks, Inc.

—My Sort of Fairy Tale Ending. 2013. (My Very Unfairy Tale Life Ser.: 3). (ENG.). 224p. (J). (gr. 4-7). pap. 6.99 (978-1-4022-7933-1(7), Sourcebooks Jabberwocky) Sourcebooks, Inc.

Stanley, Andy. Go Fish: Because of What's on the Line. 2005. (North Point Resources Ser.). (ENG.). 96p. stu. ed., per., pupil's gde. ed. 9.99 (978-1-59052-548-7(5), Multnomah Bks.) Crown Publishing Group.

Stanmore, Tony. Tide of Chance: A Holiday Adventure. 2010. (Illus.). 60p. pap. 10.49 (978-1-4520-0650-5(4)) AuthorHouse.

Stansberry, Don. Inky & the Missing Gold. 2007. (Illus.). 128p. (YA). per. 15.95 (978-0-929915-10-4(0), Publisher Page) Headline Bks., Inc.

Stanton, Nicholas Sheridan. KK Undercover Mystery: The Cookie Caper. 2011. 80p. (gr. 4-6). pap. 26.01 (978-1-4567-6597-2(3)) AuthorHouse.

Stanwood Pier, Arthu. The Jester of St. Timothy's. 2006. pap. 14.95 (978-1-55742-546-1(9)) Wildside Pr., LLC.

Stapley, Giles. Plinktus, the Little Pink Dinosaur. 2010. 84p. pap. 23.50 (978-1-60911-796-2(4), Eloquent Bks.) Strategic Book Publishing & Rights Agency (SBPRA).

star, celina. Paw Prints on the Road. 2008. 79p. pap. 9.96 (978-0-557-02420-9(X)) Lulu Pr., Inc.

Star, Nancy. The Case of the Sneaky Strangers. 2006. 77p. pap. (978-0-439-67267-2(8)) Scholastic, Inc.

Star Wars Staff & Valois, Rob. Sticker Storyteller. 2008. (Star Wars). (ENG.). 48p. (J). (gr. 1-3). pap. 12.99 (978-0-448-45058-2(5)) Penguin Publishing Group.

Star Wars Staff, et al. Renegade. 2009. (Star Wars: Rebel For Ser.: 3). (ENG.). 176p. (J). (gr. 3-7). pap. 6.99 (978-0-545-11211-6(7)) Scholastic, Inc.

Star Wars, Star. Star Wars - The Force Awakens Mask Book: Which Side Are You On? 2016. (ENG.). 24p. (J). (gr. -1-1). pap. 9.99 (978-0-7944-3740-4(0), Reader's Digest Children's Bks.) Studio Fun International.

Stark, Henry. Heart Lessons. 2008. (ENG.). 502p. pap. 19.99 (978-1-4196-4881-6(0)) CreateSpace Independent Publishing Platform.

Starkey, R. Hawk. Mysterious Magical Circus Family Kids: The Chocolate Cake Turkey Lip Crumb Trail Mystery Adventure. 2008. 192p. pap. 13.95 (978-1-4327-3096-3(7)) Outskirts Pr., Inc.

Starks, Nicole. Childrens Story Book Rainbow. 2013. 16p. pap. 12.68 (978-1-4669-7189-9(4)) Trafford Publishing.

Starr, Fredro. Lil Freddy: The Red Sock. 2011. 24p. pap. 12.74 (978-1-4634-1118-3(9)) AuthorHouse.

Starwolf. Tiny Dancer. 2012. 36p. pap. 15.49 (978-1-4669-5247-8(4)) Trafford Publishing.

Stasco, Raymond. The Adventures of Mr Mccroak. 2009. 48p. pap. 21.99 (978-1-4363-4244-5(9)) Xlibris Corp.

Staton, Debbie. Twiggle. Patzelt, Kasie, illus. 2007. (J). (gr. -1-3). 17.99 (978-1-59879-362-8(4)); 26p. per. 12.99 (978-1-59879-199-0(0)) Lifevest Publishing, Inc.

Staunton, Ted. Coda, 1 vol. 2014. (Seven Sequels Ser.). (ENG., Illus.). 224p. (J). (gr. 5-10). pap. 10.95 (978-1-4598-0549-1(6)) Orca Bk. Pubs. USA.

—Jump Cut, 1 vol. 2012. (Seven (the Series) Ser.). (ENG., Illus.). 232p. (J). (gr. 5-10). pap. 9.95 (978-1-55469-947-6(9)) Orca Bk. Pubs. USA.

Stead, Rebecca. First Light. 2008. (ENG.). 336p. (J). (gr. 3-7). 7.99 (978-0-440-42222-8(1), Yearling) Random Hse. Children's Bks.

Steadman, Ralph. Little. com. 2014. (Illus.). 32p. (J). 16.95 (978-1-56792-520-3(0)) Godine, David R. Pub.

Steck-Vaughn Staff. Three Cheers for May. 2005. (gr. -1-k). pap. 12.99 (978-0-7398-9825-3(6)) Harcourt Schl. Pubs.

Steedman, Judith & Mitchell-Cranfield, Robin. Foggy. 2008. (Windy Ser.). (ENG., Illus.). 32p. (J). (gr. -1-3). 15.95 (978-1-894965-96-5(5)) Simply Read Bks. CAN. Dist: Ingram Publisher Services.

Steel, Flora. The Adventures of Akbar. 2007. 116p. per. 9.95 (978-1-60312-207-8(9)) Aegypan.

Steele, Andrew. The Galaxy Boys & the Sphere. 2008. (ENG.). 285p. (J). (gr. 4-7). pap. (978-1-85756-687-1(4)) Janus Publishing Co.

Steele, Giselle. The off-Limits Watermelon Patch. 2006. (Illus.). 35p. (J). per. 12.95 (978-0-9769949-0-9(9)) Stuart & Weitz Publishing Group.

Steele, Giselle V. Nicholas & the Magical Wind. 2005. 32p. 23.95 (978-1-58275-093-4(9)) Stuart & Weitz Publishing Group.

Steele, Michael Anthony. Night at the Museum: Secret of the Tomb. 3rd ed. 2014. (ENG.). 176p. (J). (gr. 3-7). pap. 5.99 (978-1-4380-0524-9(5)) Barron's Educational Series, Inc.

Steele, William O. The Buffalo Knife. 2004. (ENG., Illus.). 144p. (J). (gr. 2-5). pap. 11.95 (978-0-15-205215-7(1)) Houghton Mifflin Harcourt Publishing Co.

Steffen, Tim & Thornton, Susan. The Adventures of Baby Cat in Cherry Grove: Home Sweet Home. 2006. (Illus.). (J). per. 15.00 (978-0-9779518-0-2(4)) Cardinal Pr.

Steffen, Tim & Thornton, Susan Ann. The Adventures of Baby Cat in Cherry Grove: Finding Faith. Thornton, Susan Ann, illus. 2007. (Illus.). 50p. (J). per. 12.00 (978-0-9779518-1-9(2)) Cardinal Pr.

—The Golden Dragonfly: The Adventures of Baby Cat in Cherry Grove. Thornton, Susan Ann, illus. 2009. (Illus.). 76p. pap. 8.95 (978-1-4401-4804-0(X)) iUniverse, Inc.

Steig, William. Abel's Island. 2007. (Illus.). 117p. (J). (gr. 4-7). 17.20 (978-1-4177-9383-9(X), Turtleback) Turtleback Bks.

—Dominic. Steig, William, illus. 2007. (ENG., Illus.). 160p. (J). (gr. 3-7). per. 6.99 (978-0-312-37144-9(6), 9780312371449) Square Fish.

—The Zabajaba Jungle. 2nd ed. 2016. (ENG., Illus.). 32p. (J). (gr. -1-3). pap. 8.99 (978-1-250-05761-7(2), 9781250057617) Square Fish.

Stein, A. K. EZEKIEL MAYHILL & the Crystal of God. 2007. 196p. pap. 16.96 (978-1-4303-2540-6(2)) Lulu Pr., Inc.

Stein, Evaleen. Our Little Crusader Cousin of Long Ago. Meister, Charles E., illus. 2007. 136p. per. 8.95 (978-1-59915-243-1(6)) Yesterday's Classics.

—Our Little Frankish Cousin of Long Ago. Landau, Helena Von & Meister, Charles, illus. 2007. 92p. per. 8.95 (978-1-59915-244-8(4)) Yesterday's Classics.

—Our Little Norman Cousin of Long Ago. Goss, John, illus. 2007. 112p. per. 8.95 (978-1-59915-245-5(2)) Yesterday's Classics.

Stein, Mathilde. The Child Cruncher. Van Hout, Mies, illus. 2008. (ENG.). 32p. (J). (gr. -1-3). 16.95 (978-1-59078-635-2(1)) Lemniscaat USA.

Stein, Uriel Von. Gretta's & Graci's Bright, Bright, Moonlit Night. 2011. 24p. pap. 12.79 (978-1-4634-0225-9(2)) AuthorHouse.

Steinberg, D. J. Mac Attack! Smith, Brian, illus. 2008. (Daniel Boom Aka Loud Boy Ser.: 2). (ENG.). 96p. (J). (gr. 1-4). pap. 6.99 (978-0-448-44699-8(5), Grosset & Dunlap) Penguin Young Readers Group.

Steiner, Dawn. The Silver Squirrel & Friends: The Original Book. 2009. 16p. pap. 8.99 (978-1-4389-2944-6(7)) AuthorHouse.

Steiner, Matt. Mission Possible. 2011. 108p. (gr. 4-6). 20.95 (978-1-4620-0028-9(2)); pap. 10.95 (978-1-4620-0027-2(4)) iUniverse, Inc.

Steinke, Misty. Who Hung the Moon. 2013. 20p. pap. 6.99 (978-1-938768-17-0(5)) Gypsy Pubns.

Steinlage, Ben. Bird Boy. 2011. 290p. pap. 17.95 (978-1-4327-6667-2(8)) Outskirts Pr., Inc.

Stellinga, Mark. Buster Boogernose & the Bank Robbers. l.t. ed. 2007. (ENG.). 65p. (J). per. 9.95 (978-0-9796421-0-4(8)) Stellinga, Mark.

—Buster Boogernose & the Boxcar. 2007. (ENG.). 46p. (J). per. 9.95 (978-0-9796421-1-1(6)) Stellinga, Mark.

—Buster Boogernose & the Bully. 2007. (ENG.). 49p. (J). per. 9.95 (978-0-9796421-2-8(4)) Stellinga, Mark.

—Buster Boogernose & the Copper Mine. 2007. (ENG.). 53p. (J). per. 9.95 (978-0-9796421-3-5(2)) Stellinga, Mark.

—Buster Boogernose & the Grizzly Bear. 2007. (ENG.). 57p. (J). per. 9.95 (978-0-9796421-4-2(0)) Stellinga, Mark.

—Buster Boogernose & the Junkyard. 2007. (ENG.). 56p. (J). per. 9.95 (978-0-9796421-6-6(7)) Stellinga, Mark.

—Buster Boogernose & the Liar. 2007. (ENG.). 41p. (J). per. 9.95 (978-0-9796421-7-3(5)) Stellinga, Mark.

—Buster Boogernose & the Old Mansion. 2007. (ENG.). 53p. (J). per. 9.95 (978-0-9796421-5-9(9)) Stellinga, Mark.

—Buster Boogernose & the Secret Cave. 2007. (ENG.). 55p. (J). per. 9.95 (978-0-9796421-8-0(3)) Stellinga, Mark.

—Buster Boogernose & the Tramp. 2007. (ENG.). 68p. (J). per. 9.95 (978-0-9796421-9-7(1)) Stellinga, Mark.

—Satellite Detectives. 2008. (ENG.). 120p. per. 9.95 (978-0-9762011-8-2(6)) Stellinga, Mark.

Stellings, Caroline. Skippers at Cape Spear. 2012. (ENG., Illus.). 32p. pap. (978-1-55081-174-2(6)) Breakwater Bks., Ltd.

Stem, Jacqueline C. The Secret of the Dragonfly Pin. 2006. (Hollow Tree Mystery Ser.: 7). 115p. (J). (gr. 3-7). per. 12.95 (978-1-57168-264-2(3), Eakin Pr.) Eakin Pr.

Stephanie K. McMahan. Sylvan Tales: The Secret of Elfenore. 2009. 152p. 22.95 (978-1-4401-5507-9(0)); pap. 12.95 (978-1-4401-5505-5(4)) iUniverse, Inc.

Stephanie Wheeler Maier. Vincent VanDersnoot Finds His Purpose! Why God Made the Earth, Why He Made People, & the Meaning of Everything. 2009. (Illus.). 128p. pap. 39.95 (978-1-4343-9547-4(2)) AuthorHouse.

Stephens, Berin L. Time Gangsters. 2012. pap. 14.99 (978-1-59955-966-7(8)) Cedar Fort, Inc./CFI Distribution.

Stephens, Helen. The Big Adventure of the Smalls. Stephens, Helen, illus. 2012. (ENG., Illus.). 32p. (J). (gr. -1-3). 15.99 (978-1-4424-5058-5(4), Aladdin) Simon & Schuster Children's Publishing.

Stephens, Jay. Doc Phantom, Vol. 2. 2003. (ENG., Illus.). 80p. (gr. 12-18). pap. 12.95 (978-1-929998-27-2(9), 9781929998272) Oni Pr., Inc.

Stephenson, Alan. The Adventures of Roy & Rosie Rabbit. 2011. (Illus.). 48p. pap. 19.51 (978-1-4567-9728-7(X)) AuthorHouse.

Stephenson, Kristina. Sir Charlie Stinky Socks & the Really Big Adventure. 2015. (Sir Charlie Stinky Socks Ser.). (ENG., Illus.). 32p. (J). (gr. -1-k). pap. 12.99 (978-1-4052-7768-6(8)) Egmont Bks., Ltd. GBR. Dist: Independent Pubs. Group.

—Sir Charlie Stinky Socks & the Really Dreadful Spell. 2015. (Sir Charlie Stinky Socks Ser.). (ENG., Illus.). 32p. (J). (gr. -1-k). pap. 12.99 (978-1-4052-7770-9(X)) Egmont Bks., Ltd. GBR. Dist: Independent Pubs. Group.

—Sir Charlie Stinky Socks & the Really Frightful Night. 2015. (Sir Charlie Stinky Socks Ser.). (ENG., Illus.). 32p. (J). (gr. -1-k). pap. 12.99 (978-1-4052-7769-3(6)) Egmont Bks., Ltd. GBR. Dist: Independent Pubs. Group.

—Sir Charlie Stinky Socks & the Tale of the Terrible Secret. 2016. (Sir Charlie Stinky Socks Ser.). (ENG., Illus.). 32p. (J). (gr. -1-k). pap. 12.99 (978-1-4052-7771-6(8)) Egmont Bks., Ltd. GBR. Dist: Independent Pubs. Group.

—Sir Charlie Stinky Socks & the Tale of the Two Treasures. 2016. (Sir Charlie Stinky Socks Ser.). (ENG., Illus.). 32p. (J). (gr. -1-k). pap. 12.99 (978-1-4052-7772-3(6)) Egmont Bks., Ltd. GBR. Dist: Independent Pubs. Group.

—Sir Charlie Stinky Socks & the Wizard's Whisper. 2016. (Sir Charlie Stinky Socks Ser.). (ENG., Illus.). 32p. (J). (gr. -1-k). pap. 12.99 (978-1-4052-7773-0(4)) Egmont Bks., Ltd. GBR. Dist: Independent Pubs. Group.

—Sir Charlie Stinkysocks - The Pirate's Curse. 2015. (Sir Charlie Stinky Socks Ser.). (ENG., Illus.). 32p. (J). 17.99 (978-1-4052-6809-7(3)) Egmont Bks., Ltd. GBR. Dist: Independent Pubs. Group.

Stephenson, Norman E. God's Blood: The Fate of the Lost Templar Treasure. 2007. 176p. per. 13.95 (978-0-595-47539-1(6)) iUniverse, Inc.

Stephenson, Omri. Freddie Finds Out. 2010. 34p. pap. 21.50 (978-1-4457-5726-1(5)) Lulu Pr., Inc.

Steps To Literacy Staff, compiled by. Beast Quest Collection Grades 2-5: Class Pack (6 Titles, 6 Each) 2010. (ENG.). (J). pap. 170.75 (978-1-60923-616-8(5)) Steps To Literacy, LLC.

—Beast Quest Collection Grades 2-5: Variety Pack (6 Titles, 1 Each) 2010. (ENG.). (J). pap. 29.90 (978-1-60923-615-1(7)) Steps To Literacy, LLC.

—Capitol Mysteries: Gen014. 2005. (ENG., Illus.). (J). (978-1-59564-732-0(5)) Steps To Literacy, LLC.

—Eragon/Eldest Box Set: Variety Pack (2 Titles, 1 Each) 2010. (ENG.). (J). pap. 23.85 (978-1-61267-194-9(2)) Steps To Literacy, LLC.

—The Mysterious Benedict Society Collection: Class Pack (3 titles, 6 Each) 2010. (ENG.). (J). pap. 125.82 (978-1-61267-335-6(X)) Steps To Literacy, LLC.

—The Mysterious Benedict Society Collection: Variety Pack (3 titles, 1 Each) 2010. (ENG.). (J). pap. 20.97 (978-1-61267-334-9(1)) Steps To Literacy, LLC.

—Percy Jackson & the Olympians Series: Variety Pack (5 Titles, 1 Each) 2010. (J). pap. 39.95 (978-1-60923-745-5(5)) Steps To Literacy, LLC.

Stern, D. G. Disappearing Diamonds: An Upton Charles Adventure. Bartlett, Rebecca, illus. 2008. (ENG.). 126p. (J). pap. 9.99 (978-0-9754676-9-5(7)) Yeoman Hse.

Sternfeld, Nathan. All about Motti & His Adventures with Rebbe Mendel. Bichman, David, illus. 2004. 220p. (J). 20.99 (978-1-58330-669-7(2)) Feldheim Pubs.

Steve Chering. There's Something in Granny's Garden! 2013. 48p. pap. (978-3-85040-854-7(X)) Chytra-Verlag Vindobona.

Stevens, A. P. The Volcano: The Adventures of Antboy & Mr Cricket. Finn, N. K., ed. Deskcube, illus. 2008. (ENG.). 29p. pap. 9.95 (978-0-9798886-0-1(3)) Mugsy and Sugar Pressed.

Stevens, Cara. Let's Save Pirate Day! (Dora & Friends) Aikins, David, illus. 2014. (Pictureback(R) Ser.). (ENG.). 24p. (J). (gr. -1-2). 4.99 (978-0-385-37440-8(2), Random Hse. Bks. for Young Readers) Random Hse. Children's Bks.

Stevens, Dan. The Magic of the Brass Ring. 2009. 84p. pap. 19.95 (978-1-4489-7759-8(2)) America Star Bks.

Stevens-Egerton, Drema. Three Wishes for Christmas: A Stevens Children Adventure. 2007. 35p. pap. 24.95 (978-1-60441-780-7(3)) America Star Bks.

Stevens, Lynda. The Lawn Monster: A Book to Help Kids Learn to Be Brave. 2012. 44p. pap. 21.99 (978-1-4771-0291-6(4)) Xlibris Corp.

Stevens, Michael J. Silver Spitfire. 2010. 164p. pap. (978-1-907652-13-4(2)) Grosvenor Hse. Publishing Ltd.

Stevens, Roger & Quarto Generic Staff. The Comic Café. 2012. (ENG.). 288p. (J). (gr. 4-7). pap. 8.99 (978-1-84780-270-5(2), Frances Lincoln) Quarto Publishing Group UK GBR. Dist: Hachette Bk. Group.

Stevens, Serita. The Adventure Begins. 2004. (Illus.). 182p. (978-0-9753548-1-0(7)) Palm Publishing LLC.

Stevenson, Chris. The Drum of Destiny. 2016. (Middle-Grade Novels Ser.). (ENG., Illus.). 224p. (gr. 4-7). lib. bdg. 26.65 (978-1-4965-2673-1(2)) Stone Arch Bks.

Stevenson-Ringo, Angela. Keith's Shoes. 2009. 28p. pap. 9.95 (978-1-4327-2344-6(8)) Outskirts Pr., Inc.

—Where Are My Shoes? 2009. 28p. pap. 9.95 (978-1-4327-2343-9(X)) Outskirts Pr., Inc.

Stevenson, Robert Louis. The Black Arrow. l.t. ed. 2005. 448p. pap. (978-1-84637-164-6(3)) Echo Library.

—La Flecha Negra.Tr. of Black Arrow. (SPA., Illus.). 160p. (YA). 11.95 (978-84-7281-142-3(5), AF1142) Auriga, Ediciones S.A. ESP. Dist: Continental Bk. Co., Inc.

—La Flecha Negra. (Coleccion Clasicos de la Juventud).Tr. of Black Arrow. (SPA., Illus.). (J). 12.95 (978-84-7189-100-6(X), ORT304) Ortells, Alfredo Editorial S.L. ESP. Dist: Continental Bk. Co., Inc.

—La Isla del Tesoro. (Coleccion Clasicos de la Juventud).Tr. of Treasure Island. (SPA., Illus.). 188p. (J). 12.95 (978-84-7189-017-7(8), ORT301) Ortells, Alfredo Editorial S.L. ESP. Dist: Continental Bk. Co., Inc.

—La Isla del Tesoro. (Coleccion Estrella).Tr. of Treasure Island. (SPA., Illus.). 64p. (J). 14.95 (978-950-11-0009-9(X), SGM009) Sigmar ARG. Dist: Continental Bk. Co., Inc.

—Kidnapped. 2004. (Fast Track Classics Ser.). (ENG., Illus.). 48p. (J). pap. 8.99 (978-0-237-52403-6(1)) Evans Brothers, Ltd. GBR. Dist: Independent Pubs. Group.

—Kidnapped. Kennedy, Cam, illus. 2007. (ENG.). 64p. (YA). (gr. 5). pap. 11.95 (978-0-88776-843-9(1), Tundra Bks.) Tundra Bks. CAN. Dist: Penguin Random Hse. LLC.

—Kidnapped. 2009. (Puffin Classics Ser.). (ENG.). 352p. (J). (gr. 5-7). 5.99 (978-0-14-132602-3(6), Puffin Books) Penguin Young Readers Group.

—Kidnapped. 2006. per. 8.95 (978-1-57646-970-5(0)) Quiet Vision Publishing.

—Kidnapped. 2006. (Classics Ser.). (Illus.). 80p. (YA). (gr. 4-7). per. 8.95 (978-1-56254-873-5(5)) Saddleback Educational Publishing, Inc.

—Kidnapped. Kumar, Naresh, illus. 2011. (Campfire Graphic Novels Ser.). (ENG.). 72p. (YA). (gr. 3-7). pap. 9.99 (978-93-80028-52-1(0), Campfire) Steerforth Pr.

—Kidnapped, 1 vol. Fisher, Eric Scott, illus. 2011. (Calico Illustrated Classics Ser.: No. 3). (ENG.). 112p. (YA). (gr. 3-6). 27.07 (978-1-61641-105-3(8)) Magic Wagon.

—Kidnapped: Adapted for Young Readers. Kliros, Thea, illus. abr. ed. 2011. (Dover Children's Thrift Classics Ser.). (ENG.). 96p. (J). (gr. 3-8). reprint ed. pap. 4.00 (978-0-486-29354-7(8)) Dover Pubns., Inc.

—Kidnapped: Bring the Classics to Life. 2008. (Bring the Classics to Life Ser.). (ENG., Illus.). 72p. (gr. 3-12). pap., act. bk. ed. 10.95 (978-0-931334-65-8(9), EDCTR-303B) EDCON Publishing Group.

—Kidnapped & Catriona. 2007. (ENG.). 496p. per. (978-1-84697-033-7(4)) Birlinn, Ltd.

—Secuestrado. 3rd ed. (Coleccion Clasicos en Accion).Tr. of Kidnapped. (SPA., Illus.). 80p. (YA). (gr. 5-8). 15.95 (978-84-241-5781-4(8), EV1487) Everest Editora ESP. Dist: Lectorum Pubns., Inc.

—Treasure Island. Corvino, Lucy, illus. 2005. (Classic Starts(tm) Ser.). (ENG.). 160p. (J). (gr. 2-4). 6.95 (978-1-4027-1318-7(5)) Sterling Publishing Co., Inc.

—Treasure Island. Lawrence, John, illus. 2009. (Candlewick Illustrated Classics Ser.). (ENG.). 272p. (J). (gr. 4-7). 24.99 (978-0-7636-4445-1(5)) Candlewick Pr.

—Treasure Island. 2014. (Graphic Classics Ser.). 48p. (gr. 3-6). 37.10 (978-1-908973-91-7(9)) Book Hse. GBR. Dist: Black Rabbit Bks.

—Treasure Island. Date not set. (Nelson Readers Ser.). (J). pap. (978-0-17-556699-0(2)) Addison-Wesley Longman, Inc.

—Treasure Island. 2016. (ENG., Illus.). (J). pap. **(978-3-7433-2049-9(5))** Creation Pubs.

—Treasure Island. 2016. (ENG., Illus.). (J). 26.95 **(978-1-358-35578-3(9))** Creative Media Partners, LLC.

—Treasure Island. 2005. 116p. per. 5.95 (978-1-4209-2258-5(0)) Digireads.com Publishing.

—Treasure Island. 2004. reprint ed. pap. 1.99 (978-1-4192-9097-8(5)) Kessinger Publishing, LLC.

—Treasure Island. (Young Collector's Illustrated Classics Ser.). (Illus.). 192p. (J). (gr. 3-7). 9.95 (978-1-56156-456-9(7)) Kidsbooks, LLC.

—Treasure Island. Rhead, Louis, illus. 2015. (J). pap. (978-1-4677-7821-3(4), First Avenue Editions) Lerner Publishing Group.

—Treasure Island. Chapman, Neil, illus. 2004. 320p. (J). (978-1-4054-3773-8(1)) Parragon, Inc.

—Treasure Island. 2014. (Word Cloud Classics Ser.). (ENG., Illus.). 208p. pap. 14.99 (978-1-62686-256-2(7), Thunder Bay Pr.) Readerlink Distribution Services, LLC.

—Treasure Island. 2005. (Enriched Classics Ser.). (ENG.). 304p. mass mkt. 4.95 (978-1-4165-0029-2(4)) Simon & Schuster.

—Treasure Island, 1 vol. Gully, Mario & Davidson, Pat, illus. 2009. (Treasure Island Ser.). (ENG.). 24p. (gr. 5-8). 24.21 (978-1-59961-601-8(7));Pt. 2. 24.21 (978-1-59961-602-5(5)) Spotlight.

—Treasure Island. Corvino, Lucy, illus. abr. ed. 2010. (Classic Starts(tm) Ser.). (ENG.). 160p. (J). (gr. 2-4). cd-rom 9.95 (978-1-4027-7358-7(1)) Sterling Publishing Co., Inc.

—Treasure Island: The Treasure Map. Comport, Sally Wern, illus. 2008. (Easy Reader Classics Ser.). (ENG.). 32p. (gr. -1-3). lib. bdg. 24.21 (978-1-59961-342-0(5)) Spotlight.

—Treasure Island: With a Discussion of Courage. 2003. (Values in Action Illustrated Classics Ser.). (J). (978-1-59203-054-5(8)) Learning Challenge, Inc.

—Treasure Island: With Story of the Treasure of Norman Island. Date not set. (J). (gr. 5-6). reprint ed. lib. bdg. 22.95 (978-0-89190-236-2(8), American Reprint Co.) Amereon Ltd.

—Treasure Island (Quality Library Classics) 2005. (YA). pap. 14.95 (978-1-57545-701-7(6)) RP Media.

Stevenson, Robert Louis & Ballaz, Jesus. Treasure Island. 2007. (Illustrated Classics Ser.). (Illus.). 40p. (gr. 3-6). lib. bdg. 26.00 (978-0-8368-7665-9(2), Gareth Stevens Learning Library) Stevens, Gareth Publishing LLLP.

Stevenson, Robert Louis & Gaston, Charles Robert. Treasure Island. 2016. (ENG., Illus.). (J). 25.95 **(978-1-358-93415-5(0))** Creative Media Partners, LLC.

Stevenson, Robert Louis & Vance, Hiram Albert. Treasure Island. 2016. (ENG., Illus.). (J). 25.95 **(978-1-359-06744-9(2))**; 25.95 **(978-1-358-73513-4(1))** Creative Media Partners, LLC.

Stevenson, Robert Louis & Wyeth, N. C. Kidnapped. Wyeth, N. C., illus. 2004. (Scribner Storybook Classics Ser.). (ENG., Illus.). 64p. (J). (gr. 3-7). 19.99 (978-0-689-86542-8(2), Atheneum Bks. for Young Readers) Simon & Schuster Children's Publishing.

Stevenson, Robert Louis, et al. Treasure Island. 2016. (ENG., Illus.). (J). 26.95 **(978-1-357-83050-2(5))** Creative Media Partners, LLC.

Stevenson, Robin. Desolación, 1 vol. 2012. (Spanish Soundings Ser.). (SPA.). 160p. (YA). (gr. 8-12). pap. 9.95 (978-1-4598-0305-3(1)) Orca Bk. Pubs. USA.

Stevenson, Steve. The Crown of Venice, No. 7. Turconi, Stefano, illus. 2014. (Agatha: Girl of Mystery Ser.: 7). (ENG.). 144p. (J). (gr. 2-5). 5.99 (978-0-448-46225-7(7), Grosset & Dunlap) Penguin Young Readers Group.

—The Crown of Venice. 2014. (Agatha Girl of Mystery Ser.: 7). lib. bdg. 16.00 (978-0-606-36164-4(2)) Turtleback Bks.

—The Curse of the Pharaoh. Turconi, Stefano, illus. 2013. (Agatha: Girl of Mystery Ser.: 1). (ENG.). 144p. (J). (gr. 2-5). pap. 6.99 (978-0-448-46217-2(6), Grosset & Dunlap) Penguin Young Readers Group.

—The Curse of the Pharaoh. 2013. (Agatha Girl of Mystery Ser.: 1). lib. bdg. 17.20 (978-0-606-29986-2(6), Turtleback) Turtleback Bks.

—The Eiffel Tower Incident. 2014. (Agatha Girl of Mystery Ser.: 5). lib. bdg. 16.00 (978-0-606-34153-0(6), Turtleback) Turtleback Bks.

—The Heist at Niagara Falls. 2013. (Agatha Girl of Mystery Ser.: 4). lib. bdg. 16.00 (978-0-606-32128-0(4), Turtleback) Turtleback Bks.

—The Kenyan Expedition #8. Turconi, Stefano, illus. 2015. (Agatha: Girl of Mystery Ser.: 8). (ENG.). 144p. (J). (gr. 3-7). 5.99 (978-0-448-48679-6(2), Grosset & Dunlap) Penguin Young Readers Group.

—The King of Scotland's Sword. Turconi, Stefano, illus. 2013. (Agatha: Girl of Mystery Ser.: 3). (ENG.). 144p. (J). (gr. 2-5). pap. 5.99 (978-0-448-46220-2(6), Grosset & Dunlap) Penguin Young Readers Group.

—The Pearl of Bengal. Turconi, Stefano, illus. 2013. (Agatha: Girl of Mystery Ser.: 2). (ENG.). 144p. (J). (gr. 2-5). pap. 6.99 (978-0-448-46219-6(2), Grosset & Dunlap) Penguin Young Readers Group.

—The Pearl of Bengal. 2013. (Agatha Girl of Mystery Ser.: 2). lib. bdg. 17.20 (978-0-606-30016-2(3), Turtleback) Turtleback Bks.

—The Treasure of the Bermuda Triangle, No. 6. Turconi, Stefano, illus. 2014. (Agatha: Girl of Mystery Ser.: 6). (ENG.). 144p. (J). (gr. 2-5). 6.99 (978-0-448-46224-0(9), Grosset & Dunlap) Penguin Young Readers Group.

—The Treasure of the Bermuda Triangle. 2014. (Agatha Girl of Mystery Ser.: 6). lib. bdg. 17.20 (978-0-606-35700-5(9)) Turtleback Bks.

Stevenson, William. Ricky's Dream Trip to Ancient Egypt. 2012. 30p. (J). pap. 12.99 (978-1-936517-71-8(X), Pop Pop Pr.) Micro Publishing Media, Inc.

—Ricky's Dream Trip to Ancient Greece. 2012. 36p. pap. 14.00 (978-1-936517-77-0(9)) Micro Publishing Media, Inc.

—Ricky's Dream Trip under the Sea. 2013. 38p. pap. 13.50 (978-1-936517-85-5(X)) Micro Publishing Media, Inc.

Stever, Karen Malloy. Jabin, the Talking Donkey: In Jerusalem. 2012. 24p. pap. 24.95 (978-1-4626-8285-0(5)) America Star Bks.

Stewart, Angela. The Curious Adventures of India Sophia. Stuart, Mitchell, illus. 2004. (Juvenile Novel Ser.). 176p. (J). (gr. 4-6). pap. 9.95 (978-1-895836-78-3(6)) River Bks. CAN. Dist: Fitzhenry & Whiteside, Ltd.

Stewart, Bob. Baily Bumble Bee. 2009. 32p. pap. 14.49 (978-1-4389-7254-1(7)) AuthorHouse.

Stewart, Chuck. Angels at Rickwood. 2009. (J). pap. 10.00 (978-1-61584-842-3(8)) Independent Pub.

Stewart, Dianne C. Quimbaya. 2008. (ENG.). 200p. (gr. 1-18). pap. 8.95 (978-0-9667359-8-7(6), BeanPole Bks.) Harren Communications, LLC.

—Season of the Cold Moon. 2011. (ENG.). 108p. (J). (gr. 2). pap. 8.95 (978-0-9831032-0-2(8), BeanPole Bks.) Harren Communications, LLC.

Stewart, E. J. The Wayfaring Dolphin. 2010. 298p. pap. 16.95 (978-0-557-33701-9(1)) Lulu Pr., Inc.

Stewart, Emma. The Adventures of Fillmore the Gerbil. 2008. 24p. pap. 13.50 (978-1-60693-033-5(8), Eloquent Bks.) Strategic Book Publishing & Rights Agency (SBPRA).

Stewart-Goodair, Madonna. Key to the Golden Gates: The Mystic Soldier, Book 1, 1 vol. 2009. 48p. pap. 16.95 (978-1-61582-625-4(4)) PublishAmerica, Inc.

Stewart III, Freddie Leonard. Night Night Birmingham. 2009. 24p. 12.00 (978-0-557-08775-4(9)) Lulu Pr., Inc.

Stewart, Jane L. The Camp Fire Girls at Long Lake: Bessie King in Summer Camp. l.t. ed. 2007. (ENG.). 126p. pap. 19.99 (978-1-4346-2353-9(X)) Creative Media Partners, LLC.

—A Campfire Girl's Test of Friendship. 2004. reprint ed. pap. 26.95 (978-1-4179-3874-2(9)) Kessinger Publishing, LLC.

Stewart, Justus. Kyle Oaks: A Traitor on Nighta. 2007. 144p. per. 11.95 (978-0-595-47708-1(9)) iUniverse, Inc.

Stewart, Martin. Riverkeep. 2017. lib. bdg. 22.10 **(978-0-606-40100-5(8))** Turtleback Bks.

Stewart, Nancy. One Pelican at a Time: A Story of the Gulf Oil Spill. Bell, Samantha, illus. 2011. 26p. (J). 19.95 (978-1-61633-138-2(0)); pap. 11.95 (978-1-61633-139-9(9)) Guardian Angel Publishing, Inc.

Stewart, Paul. The Curse of Magoria. 2008. (Thrillers Ser.). 125p. (YA). (gr. 5-18). per. 4.99 (978-0-7945-1816-5(8), Usborne) EDC Publishing.

—Far-Flung Adventures: Hugo Pepper. 2012. (Far-Flung Adventures Ser.). (ENG.). 272p. (J). (gr. 3-7). 7.99 (978-0-385-75223-7(7), Yearling) Random Hse. Children's Bks.

Stewart, Paul & Riddell, Chris. Bloodhoney. 2013. (Wyrmeweald Trilogy Ser.: 2). (ENG.). 368p. (YA). (gr. 9-12). pap. 14.99 (978-1-4804-1598-0(7), Open Road Media E-riginal) Open Road Integrated Media, Inc.

—The Bone Trail. 2013. (Wyrmeweald Trilogy Ser.: 3). (ENG.). 384p. (YA). (gr. 9-12). pap. 16.99 (978-1-4804-1611-6(8), Open Road Media E-riginal) Open Road Integrated Media, Inc.

—Dragon's Hoard. Riddell, Chris, illus. 2014. (Knight's Story Ser.: 3). (ENG., Illus.). 144p. (J). (gr. 2-6). pap. 13.99 (978-1-4814-2890-3(X), Atheneum Bks. for Young Readers) Simon & Schuster Children's Publishing.

—Far-Flung Adventures: Fergus Crane. 2011. (Far-Flung Adventures Ser.). (ENG.). 240p. (J). (gr. 3-7). 7.99 (978-0-385-75112-4(5), Yearling) Random Hse. Children's Bks.

—Joust of Honor. Riddell, Chris, illus. 2014. (Knight's Story Ser.: 2). (ENG., Illus.). 144p. (J). (gr. 2-6). pap. 13.99 (978-1-4814-2889-7(6), Atheneum Bks. for Young Readers) Simon & Schuster Children's Publishing.

—Lake of Skulls. Riddell, Chris, illus. 2014. (Knight's Story Ser.: 1). (ENG., Illus.). 144p. (J). (gr. 2-6). pap. 13.99 (978-1-4814-2888-0(8), Atheneum Bks. for Young Readers) Simon & Schuster Children's Publishing.

—Returner's Wealth. 2013. (Wyrmeweald Trilogy Ser.: 1). (ENG.). 374p. (YA). (gr. 9-12). pap. 14.99 (978-1-4804-1610-9(X), Open Road Media E-riginal) Open Road Integrated Media, Inc.

Stewart, Shawn. Donny & the Doorman's Nightmare. 2004. 54p. pap. 8.11 (978-1-4116-2188-6(3)) Lulu Pr., Inc.

Stewart, Shawna. Amazing Tails of Zomber Doodles & Buttons, 1 vol. 2010. 30p. pap. 24.95 (978-1-4489-7913-4(7)) PublishAmerica, Inc.

Stewart, Trenton Lee. The Extraordinary Education of Nicholas Benedict. Sudyka, Diana, illus. (Mysterious Benedict Society Ser.). (ENG.). (J). (gr. 3-7). 2013. 496p. pap. 9.99 (978-0-316-17620-0(6)) 2012. 480p. 18.99 (978-0-316-17619-4(2)) Little, Brown Bks. for Young Readers.

—The Extraordinary Education of Nicholas Benedict. 2013. (Mysterious Benedict Society Ser.: 0). (J). lib. bdg. 19.65 (978-0-606-31743-6(0), Turtleback) Turtleback Bks.

—The Mysterious Benedict Society. Tingley, Megan, ed. Sudyka, Diana, illus. 2010. (Mysterious Benedict Society Ser.: 3). (ENG.). 400p. (J). (gr. 3-7). pap. 8.99 (978-0-316-04550-6(0)) Little, Brown Bks. for Young Readers.

—The Mysterious Benedict Society. Ellis, Carson, illus. (Mysterious Benedict Society Ser.: 1). (ENG.). (J). (gr. 3-7). 2008. 512p. pap. 9.99 (978-0-316-00395-7(6)) 2007. 496p. 19.00 (978-0-316-05777-6(0), Tingley, Megan Bks.) 2015. 512p. 12.99 (978-0-316-26501-0(2)) Little, Brown Bks. for Young Readers.

—The Mysterious Benedict Society. unabr. ed. 2007. (Mysterious Benedict Society Ser.: Bk. 1). (ENG.). (J). (gr. 3-7). 25.50 (978-0-307-28440-2(9), Listening Library (Audio)) Penguin Random House Audio Publishing Group.

—The Mysterious Benedict Society. 2009. 17.45 (978-1-60686-527-9(7)) Perfection Learning Corp.

—The Mysterious Benedict Society. 2010. (Mysterious Benedict Society Ser.: 3). (J). lib. bdg. 19.65 (978-0-606-15117-7(6), Turtleback) Turtleback Bks.

—The Mysterious Benedict Society. Ellis, Carson, illus. 2008. (Mysterious Benedict Society Ser.: 1). 485p. (J). (gr. 3-7). lib. bdg. 19.65 (978-1-4178-1817-4(4), Turtleback) Turtleback Bks.

—The Mysterious Benedict Society: 10th Anniversary Edition. Ellis, Carson, illus. 2017. (ENG.). 528p. (J). (gr. 3-7). 18.99 (978-0-316-46491-8(0)) Little, Brown Bks. for Young Readers.

—The Mysterious Benedict Society & the Perilous Journey. Sudyka, Diana, illus. 2009. (Mysterious Benedict Society Ser.: 2). (ENG.). 464p. (J). (gr. 3-7). pap. 8.99 (978-0-316-03673-3(0)) Little Brown & Co.

—The Mysterious Benedict Society & the Perilous Journey. Sudyka, Diana, illus. 2008. (Mysterious Benedict Society Ser.: 2). (ENG.). 448p. (J). (gr. 3-7). 18.99 (978-0-316-05780-6(0)) Little, Brown Bks. for Young Readers.

—The Mysterious Benedict Society & the Perilous Journey. 2009. (Mysterious Benedict Society Ser.: 2). (J). lib. bdg. 19.65 (978-0-606-07462-9(7), Turtleback) Turtleback Bks.

—The Mysterious Benedict Society & the Prisoner's Dilemma. Sudyka, Diana, illus. 2009. (Mysterious Benedict Society Ser.: 3). (ENG.). 400p. (J). (gr. 3-7). 18.99 (978-0-316-04552-0(7)) Little, Brown Bks. for Young Readers.

—The Secret Keepers. Sudyka, Diana, illus. 2017. (ENG.). 512p. (J). (gr. 3-7). pap. 8.99 **(978-0-316-38954-9(4))** Little, Brown Bks. for Young Readers.

—The Secret Keepers. 2016. (ENG., Illus.). 512p. (J). (gr. 3-7). 18.99 (978-0-316-38955-6(2)) Little, Brown Bks. for Young Readers.

—The Secret Keepers. 2017. (J). lib. bdg. 19.65 **(978-0-606-40551-5(8))** Turtleback Bks.

Stewart, Yale. The Amazing Adventures of Superman! Stewart, Yale, illus. 2014. (Amazing Adventures of Superman! Ser.). (ENG., Illus.). 32p. (gr. k-2). 101.28 (978-1-4795-5816-2(8), DC Super Heroes) Stone Arch Bks.

Stiefvater, Maggie. Forever. 2014. (Shiver Ser.: 3). (ENG.). 416p. (J). (gr. 9). pap. 9.99 (978-0-545-68280-0(0)) Scholastic, Inc.

—Forever. 2014. (Wolves of Mercy Falls Ser.: 3). lib. bdg. 20.85 (978-0-606-36649-6(0)) Turtleback Bks.

Stiefvater, Maggie & Pearce, Jackson. Pip Bartlett's Guide to Unicorn Training. 2017. (Pip Bartlett Ser.: 2). (ENG.). 192p. (J). (gr. 3-7). 9.99 (978-0-545-70929-3(6), Scholastic Pr.) Scholastic, Inc.

Stier, Roy E. Son of Bunyan & the Sacred Moonstone. 2003. (Illus.). 158p. (J). per. 15.95 (978-1-892264-10-7(2)) Timeless Voyager Pr.

Stierle, Cynthia. Cars 2 CarryAlong(r) Play Book. Disney Artists Staff, illus. 2011. (Carry along Play Book Ser.). (ENG.). 14p. (J). (gr. -1-k). bds. 14.99 (978-0-7944-2323-0(X)) Reader's Digest Assn., Inc., The.

—Grand Prix Garage: Storybook & Garage. 2011. (Storybook & Playset Ser.). (ENG., Illus.). 24p. (J). (gr. -1-1). 19.99 (978-0-7944-2311-7(6)) Reader's Digest Assn., Inc., The.

Stig Gjerlaug & Dallas Stebanuk, Gjerla & Stig Gjerlaug & Dallas Stebanuk. Good Morning Mr Frubus. 2010. 20p. pap. 9.14 (978-1-4269-1538-3(1)) Trafford Publishing.

Stillman, Norma. Forest Adventures: Book # 1 - Digger the Gopher & Hoppity the Frog. 2010. 20p. 12.77 (978-1-4520-1693-1(3)) AuthorHouse.

Stilton, Geronimo. The Amazing Voyage. Barozzi, Danilo, illus. 2011. (Geronimo Stilton & the Kingdom of Fantasy Ser.: 3). (ENG.). 320p. (J). (gr. 2-5). 14.99 (978-0-545-30771-0(6)) Scholastic, Inc.

—Attack of the Bandit Cats. Wolf, Matt, illus. 2004. (Geronimo Stilton Ser.: 8). (ENG.). 128p. (J). (gr. 2-5). pap. 7.99 (978-0-439-55970-6(7), Scholastic Paperbacks) Scholastic, Inc.

—Cat & Mouse in a Haunted House. 2004. (Geronimo Stilton Ser.: 3). (gr. 3-6). lib. bdg. 18.40 (978-0-613-72224-7(8), Turtleback) Turtleback Bks.

—The Curse of the Cheese Pyramid. 2004. (Geronimo Stilton Ser.: 2). (gr. 3-6). lib. bdg. 18.40 (978-0-613-72223-0(X), Turtleback) Turtleback Bks.

—Don't Wake the Dinosaur! 2014. (Geronimo Stilton Cavemice Ser.: 6). (ENG.). 128p. (J). (gr. 2-5). pap. 7.99 (978-0-545-65603-0(6), Scholastic Paperbacks) Scholastic, Inc.

—Don't Wake the Dinosaur! 2014. (Geronimo Stilton Cavemice Ser.: 6). lib. bdg. 18.40 *(978-0-606-36057-9(3))* Turtleback Bks.

—Down & Out down Under. 2007. (Geronimo Stilton Ser.: 29). (ENG., Illus.). 128p. (J). (gr. 2-5). pap. 7.99 *(978-0-439-84120-7(8)*, Scholastic Paperbacks) Scholastic, Inc.

—Down & Out down Under. 2007. (Geronimo Stilton Ser.: 29). lib. bdg. 18.40 *(978-1-4177-7837-9(7)*, Turtleback) Turtleback Bks.

—The Dragon of Fortune: An Epic Kingdom of Fantasy Adventure. 2017. (Geronimo Stilton & the Kingdom of Fantasy Ser.: 2). (ENG.). 592p. (J). (gr. 2-5). 19.99 ***(978-1-338-15939-4(9)***, Scholastic Paperbacks) Scholastic, Inc.

—The Dragon Prophecy. 2012. (Geronimo Stilton & the Kingdom of Fantasy Ser.: Bk. 4). (ENG.). 320p. (J). (gr. 2-5). 14.99 *(978-0-545-39351-5(5)*, Scholastic Paperbacks) Scholastic, Inc.

—A Fabumouse School Adventure. 2009. (Geronimo Stilton Ser.: 38). (ENG.). 128p. (J). (gr. 2-5). pap. 7.99 *(978-0-545-02138-8(3)*, Scholastic Paperbacks) Scholastic, Inc.

—A Fabumouse School Adventure. 2009. (Geronimo Stilton Ser.: 38). lib. bdg. 18.40 *(978-0-606-00229-5(4)*, Turtleback) Turtleback Bks.

—The Fast & the Frozen. 2014. (Geronimo Stilton Cavemice Ser.: 4). (ENG., Illus.). 128p. (J). (gr. 2-5). pap. 7.99 *(978-0-545-64291-0(4)*, Scholastic Paperbacks) Scholastic, Inc.

—Flight of the Red Bandit. 2014. (ENG., Illus.). 128p. (J). (gr. 2-5). pap. 7.99 *(978-0-545-55630-9(9)*, Scholastic Paperbacks) Scholastic, Inc.

—Flight of the Red Bandit. 2014. (Geronimo Stilton Ser.: 56). lib. bdg. 18.40 *(978-0-606-35195-9(7))* Turtleback Bks.

—Four Mice Deep in the Jungle. Wolf, Matt & Keys, Larry, illus. 2004. (Geronimo Stilton Ser.: 5). (ENG.). 128p. (J). (gr. 2-5). pap. 7.99 *(978-0-439-55967-6(7)*, Scholastic Paperbacks) Scholastic, Inc.

—Fright Night. 2013. (Creepella Von Cacklefur Ser.: 5). (ENG.). 128p. (J). (gr. 2-5). pap. 7.99 *(978-0-545-39349-2(3)*, Scholastic Paperbacks) Scholastic, Inc.

—The Galactic Goal. 2015. (Geronimo Stilton Spacemice Ser.: 4). (ENG., Illus.). 128p. (J). (gr. 2-5). pap. 7.99 *(978-0-545-74620-5(5)*, Scholastic Paperbacks) Scholastic, Inc.

—Un granizado de moscas para el Conde. Wolf, Matt, illus. (SPA.). 128p. (J). (gr. 3-5). pap. 7.95 *(978-1-59437-452-4(X))* Santillana USA Publishing Co., Inc.

—The Haunted Castle. 2011. (ENG.). 128p. (J). (gr. 2-5). pap. 7.99 *(978-0-545-10374-9(6)*, Scholastic Paperbacks) Scholastic, Inc.

—Help, I'm in Hot Lava! 2013. (Geronimo Stilton Cavemice Ser.: 3). (ENG., Illus.). 128p. (J). (gr. 2-5). pap. 7.99 *(978-0-545-64290-3(6)*, Scholastic Paperbacks) Scholastic, Inc.

—Help, I'm in Hot Lava! 2013. (Geronimo Stilton Cavemice Ser.: 3). lib. bdg. 17.20 *(978-0-606-32407-6(0)*, Turtleback) Turtleback Bks.

—Ice Planet Adventure. 2015. (Geronimo Stilton Spacemice Ser.: 3). (ENG., Illus.). 128p. (J). (gr. 2-5). pap. 7.99 *(978-0-545-74619-9(1)*, Scholastic Paperbacks) Scholastic, Inc.

—Ice Planet Adventure. 2015. (Geronimo Stilton Spacemice Ser.: 3). lib. bdg. 18.40 *(978-0-606-36353-2(X))* Turtleback Bks.

—I'm Too Fond of My Fur! Wolf, Matt, illus. 2004. (Geronimo Stilton Ser.: No. 4). 116p. (J). lib. bdg. 10.00 *(978-1-4242-0698-8(7))* Fitzgerald Bks.

—I'm Too Fond of My Fur! Wolf, Matt & Keys, Larry, illus. 2004. (Geronimo Stilton Ser.: 4). (ENG.). 128p. (J). (gr. 2-5). pap. 7.99 *(978-0-439-55966-9(9)*, Scholastic Paperbacks) Scholastic, Inc.

—I'm Too Fond of My Fur! 2004. (Geronimo Stilton Ser.: 4). (gr. 3-6). lib. bdg. 18.40 *(978-0-613-72225-4(6)*, Turtleback) Turtleback Bks.

—Journey Through Time. 2014. (Geronimo Stilton Special Edition Ser.). (ENG.). 320p. (J). (gr. 2-5). 14.99 *(978-0-545-55623-1(6)*, Scholastic Paperbacks) Scholastic, Inc.

—Lost Treasure of the Emerald Eye. Wolf, Matt, illus. 2004. (Geronimo Stilton Ser.: No. 1). 116p. (J). lib. bdg. 10.00 *(978-1-4242-0695-7(2))* Fitzgerald Bks.

—Lost Treasure of the Emerald Eye. Wolf, Matt & Keys, Larry, illus. 2004. (Geronimo Stilton Ser.: 1). (ENG.). 128p. (J). (gr. 2-5). pap. 7.99 *(978-0-439-55963-8(4)*, Scholastic Paperbacks) Scholastic, Inc.

—Mighty Mount Kilimanjaro. 2010. (Geronimo Stilton Ser.: 41). (ENG.). 128p. (J). (gr. 2-5). 7.99 *(978-0-545-10371-8(1)*, Scholastic Paperbacks) Scholastic, Inc.

—El Misterio Del Ojo Esmeralda. (SPA., Illus.). 128p. (J). (gr. 3-5). pap. 7.95 *(978-1-59437-453-1(8))* Santillana USA Publishing Co., Inc.

—Mouse House Hunter. 2015. (Geronimo Stilton Ser.: 61). lib. bdg. 18.40 *(978-0-606-37780-5(8))* Turtleback Bks.

—The Mummy with No Name. 2006. (Geronimo Stilton Ser.: 26). (ENG., Illus.). 128p. (J). (gr. 2-5). pap. 7.99 *(978-0-439-84117-7(8)*, Scholastic Paperbacks) Scholastic, Inc.

—The Mysterious Cheese Thief. 2007. (Geronimo Stilton Ser.: 31). (ENG., Illus.). 128p. (J). (gr. 2-5). pap. 7.99 *(978-0-439-02312-2(2))* Scholastic, Inc.

—The Quest for Paradise. 2010. (Geronimo Stilton & the Kingdom of Fantasy Ser.: 2). (ENG.). 320p. (J). (gr. 2-5). 14.99 *(978-0-545-25307-9(1))* Scholastic, Inc.

—The Race Across America. 2009. (Geronimo Stilton Ser.: 37). (ENG.). 128p. (J). (gr. 2-5). pap. 7.99 *(978-0-545-02137-1(5)*, Scholastic Paperbacks) Scholastic, Inc.

—The Race Against Time: The Third Journey Through Time. 2016. (Geronimo Stilton Journey Through Time Ser.: 3). (ENG.). 320p. (J). (gr. 2-5). 14.99 *(978-0-545-87241-6(3)*, Scholastic Paperbacks) Scholastic, Inc.

—Rescue Rebellion. 2015. (Geronimo Stilton Spacemice Ser.: 5). lib. bdg. 17.20 *(978-0-606-37775-1(1))* Turtleback Bks.

—Return of the Vampire. 2012. (Creepella Von Cacklefur Ser.: 4). (ENG.). 128p. (J). (gr. 2-5). pap. 7.99 *(978-0-545-39348-5(5)*, Scholastic Paperbacks) Scholastic, Inc.

—Ride for Your Life! 2014. (Creepella Von Cacklefur Ser.: 6). (ENG., Illus.). 128p. (J). (gr. 2-5). pap. 7.99 *(978-0-545-64659-8(6)*, Scholastic Paperbacks) Scholastic, Inc.

—The Search for Treasure. 2014. (ENG.). 320p. (J). (gr. 2-5). 14.99 *(978-0-545-65604-7(4)*, Scholastic Paperbacks) Scholastic, Inc.

—Secret Agent. 2008. (Geronimo Stilton Ser.: 34). (ENG., Illus.). 128p. (J). (gr. 2-5). pap. 7.99 *(978-0-545-02134-0(0)*, Scholastic Paperbacks) Scholastic, Inc.

—The Secret of Cacklefur Castle. 2005. (Geronimo Stilton Ser.: 22). (ENG., Illus.). 128p. (J). (gr. 2-5). pap. 7.99 *(978-0-439-69145-1(1)*, Scholastic Paperbacks) Scholastic, Inc.

—The Ship of Secrets (Geronimo Stilton & the Kingdom of Fantasy #10) 2017. (Geronimo Stilton & the Kingdom of Fantasy Ser.: 10). (ENG.). 320p. (J). (gr. 2-5). 14.99 ***(978-1-338-08880-9(7)***, Scholastic Paperbacks) Scholastic, Inc.

—The Stinky Cheese Vacation. 2014. (Geronimo Stilton Ser.: 57). lib. bdg. 18.40 *(978-0-606-35843-9(9))* Turtleback Bks.

—The Stone of Fire. 2013. (Geronimo Stilton Cavemice Ser.: 1). lib. bdg. 18.40 *(978-0-606-31526-5(8)*, Turtleback) Turtleback Bks.

—The Temple of the Ruby of Fire. Wolf, Matt, illus. 2004. (Geronimo Stilton Ser.: No. 14). 109p. (J). lib. bdg. 10.00 *(978-1-4242-0283-6(3))* Fitzgerald Bks.

—The Temple of the Ruby of Fire. 2004. (Geronimo Stilton Ser.: 14). (ENG., Illus.). 128p. (J). (gr. 2-5). pap. 7.99 *(978-0-439-66163-8(3)*, Scholastic Paperbacks) Scholastic, Inc.

—The Volcano of Fire. 2013. (Geronimo Stilton & the Kingdom of Fantasy Ser.: Bk. 5). (ENG., Illus.). 320p. (J). (gr. 2-5). 14.99 *(978-0-545-55625-5(2)*, Scholastic Paperbacks) Scholastic, Inc.

—Watch Your Tail! 2013. (Geronimo Stilton Cavemice Ser.: 2). lib. bdg. 18.40 *(978-0-606-31998-0(0)*, Turtleback) Turtleback Bks.

—The Way of the Samurai. 2012. (Geronimo Stilton Ser.: No. 49). (ENG.). 128p. (J). (gr. 2-5). pap. 7.99 *(978-0-545-34101-1(9)*, Scholastic Paperbacks) Scholastic, Inc.

—The Way of the Samurai. 2012. (Geronimo Stilton Ser.: 49). lib. bdg. 18.40 *(978-0-606-26094-7(3)*, Turtleback) Turtleback Bks.

—The Wild, Wild West. 2005. (Geronimo Stilton Ser.: 21). (ENG., Illus.). 128p. (J). (gr. 2-5). pap. 7.99 *(978-0-439-69144-4(3)*, Scholastic Paperbacks) Scholastic, Inc.

—You're Mine, Captain! 2014. (Geronimo Stilton Spacemice Ser.: 2). lib. bdg. 18.40 *(978-0-606-35845-3(5))* Turtleback Bks.

Stilton, Geronimo & Dami, Elisabetta. The Enchanted Charms: The Seventh Adventure in the Kingdom of Fantasy. Barozzi, Danilo, illus. 2015. (ENG.). 320p. (J). (gr. 2-5). 14.99 *(978-0-545-74615-1(9))* Scholastic, Inc.

—The Phoenix of Destiny. 2015. (Geronimo Stilton & the Kingdom of Fantasy: Special Edition Ser.). (ENG.). 592p. (J). (gr. 2-5). 19.99 *(978-0-545-82907-6(0))* Scholastic, Inc.

Stilton, Geronimo & Stilton, Thea. Thea Stilton & the Blue Scarab Hunt. 2012. (Thea Stilton Ser.: 11). (ENG.). 176p. (J). (gr. 2-5). pap. 8.99 *(978-0-545-34104-2(3)*, Scholastic Paperbacks) Scholastic, Inc.

—Thea Stilton & the Ghost of the Shipwreck. 2010. (Thea Stilton Ser.: 3). (ENG., Illus.). 176p. (J). (gr. 2-5). mass mkt. 8.99 *(978-0-545-15059-0(0)*, Scholastic Paperbacks) Scholastic, Inc.

—Thea Stilton & the Ghost of the Shipwreck. 2010. (Thea Stilton Ser.: 3). lib. bdg. 19.65 *(978-0-606-06843-7(0)*, Turtleback) Turtleback Bks.

—Thea Stilton & the Ice Treasure. 2011. (Thea Stilton Ser.: 9). (ENG., Illus.). 176p. (J). (gr. 2-5). pap. 8.99 *(978-0-545-33134-0(X)*, Scholastic Paperbacks) Scholastic, Inc.

—Thea Stilton & the Mountain of Fire. 2009. (Thea Stilton Ser.: 2). (ENG.). 176p. (J). (gr. 2-5). pap. 8.99 *(978-0-545-15060-6(4)*, Scholastic Paperbacks) Scholastic, Inc.

—Thea Stilton & the Mystery on the Orient Express. 2012. (Thea Stilton Ser.: 13). (ENG.). 176p. (J). (gr. 2-5). pap. 8.99 *(978-0-545-34105-9(1)*, Scholastic Paperbacks) Scholastic, Inc.

—Thea Stilton & the Prince's Emerald. 2012. (Thea Stilton Ser.: 12). (ENG.). 176p. (J). (gr. 2-5). pap. 8.99 *(978-0-545-34108-0(6)*, Scholastic Paperbacks) Scholastic, Inc.

Stilton, Geronimo & Wolf, Matt. All Because of a Cup of Coffee. 2004. (Geronimo Stilton Ser.: No. 10). (Illus.). 112p. (J). lib. bdg. 10.00 *(978-1-4242-0279-9(5))* Fitzgerald Bks.

Stilton, Geronimo, et al. The Journey Through Time. 2014. (Illus.). 94p. (J). *(978-0-545-61129-9(6))* Scholastic, Inc.

Stilton, Thea. Big Trouble in the Big Apple. 2011. (Thea Stilton Ser.: 8). (ENG., Illus.). 176p. (J). (gr. 2-5). pap. 8.99 *(978-0-545-22775-9(5)*, Scholastic Paperbacks) Scholastic, Inc.

—The Secret of the Fairies. 2013. (Thea Stilton Ser.). (ENG., Illus.). 320p. (J). (gr. 2-5). 14.99 *(978-0-545-55624-8(4)*, Scholastic Paperbacks) Scholastic, Inc.

—The Spanish Dance Mission. 2013. (Thea Stilton Ser.: 16). (ENG., Illus.). 176p. (J). (gr. 2-5). pap. 8.99 *(978-0-545-55626-2(0)*, Scholastic Paperbacks) Scholastic, Inc.

—Thea Stilton & the Frozen Fiasco: a Geronimo Stilton Adventure (Thea Stilton #25) 2017. (Thea Stilton Ser.: 25). (ENG.). 176p. (J). (gr. 2-5). pap. 8.99 ***(978-1-338-08786-4(X)***, Scholastic Paperbacks) Scholastic, Inc.

—Thea Stilton & the Hollywood Hoax. 2016. (Thea Stilton Ser.: 23). (ENG., Illus.). 176p. (J). (gr. 2-5). pap. 7.99 *(978-0-545-87242-3(1)*, Scholastic Paperbacks) Scholastic, Inc.

—Thea Stilton & the Journey to the Lion's Den. 2013. (Thea Stilton Ser.: 17). (ENG.). 176p. (J). (gr. 2-5). pap. 8.99 *(978-0-545-55627-9(9)*, Scholastic Paperbacks) Scholastic, Inc.

—Thea Stilton & the Legend of the Fire Flowers. 2013. (Thea Stilton Ser.: 15). lib. bdg. 19.65 *(978-0-606-32000-9(8)*, Turtleback) Turtleback Bks.

—Thea Stilton & the Madagascar Madness: A Geronimo Stilton Adventure. 2016. (Thea Stilton Ser.: 24). (ENG.). 176p. (J). (gr. 2-5). pap. 8.99 *(978-1-338-03289-5(5)*, Scholastic Paperbacks) Scholastic, Inc.

—Thea Stilton & the Madagascar Madness: A Geronimo Stilton Adventure. 2016. (Thea Stilton Ser.: 24). (ENG.). 176p. (J). (gr. 2-5). 19.65 *(978-0-606-39136-8(3))* Turtleback Bks.

—Thea Stilton & the Missing Myth. 2014. (Thea Stilton Ser.: 20). (ENG.). 176p. (J). (gr. 2-5). pap. 8.99 *(978-0-545-65601-6(X)*, Scholastic Paperbacks) Scholastic, Inc.

—Thea Stilton & the Mystery on the Orient Express. 2012. (Thea Stilton Ser.: 13). lib. bdg. 19.65 *(978-0-606-26757-1(3)*, Turtleback) Turtleback Bks.

—Thea Stilton & the Prince's Emerald. 2012. (Thea Stilton Ser.: 12). lib. bdg. 19.65 *(978-0-606-26534-8(1)*, Turtleback) Turtleback Bks.

—Thea Stilton & the Secret City. 2010. (Thea Stilton Ser.: 4). (ENG.). 176p. (J). (gr. 2-5). 8.99 *(978-0-545-15061-3(2)*, Scholastic Paperbacks) Scholastic, Inc.

—Thea Stilton & the Spanish Dance Mission. 2013. (Thea Stilton Ser.: 16). lib. bdg. 19.65 *(978-0-606-32381-9(3)*, Turtleback) Turtleback Bks.

—The Treasure of the Sea. 5th ed. 2016. (Thea Stilton Special Edition Ser.: 5). (ENG.). 320p. (J). (gr. 2-5). 14.99 *(978-1-338-03290-1(9)*, Scholastic Paperbacks) Scholastic, Inc.

Stilton, Thea & Stilton, Geronimo. Secret of the Snow: A Geronimo Stilton Adventure. 2014. (Thea Stilton Special Edition Ser.). (ENG.). 320p. (J). (gr. 2-5). 14.99 *(978-0-545-65605-4(2)*, Scholastic Paperbacks) Scholastic, Inc.

Stine, Fay. Star Ship Fantasy: The New Frontier of Space. 2008. 52p. pap. 10.95 *(978-1-4327-2703-1(6))* Outskirts Pr., Inc.

Stine, Faye. The Magic Forest: The Magic of Childhood. 2009. 117p. (J). pap. 10.95 *(978-1-4327-3617-0(5))* Outskirts Pr., Inc.

—Wolf: A Story of the Wild. 2012. (ENG.). 64p. pap. 10.95 *(978-1-4787-2054-6(9))* Outskirts Pr., Inc.

Stine, R. L. The Adventures of Shrinkman, 0 vols. unabr. ed. 2012. (ENG.). 140p. (J). (gr. 3-7). pap. 4.99 *(978-1-61218-328-2(X)*, 9781612183282, Amazon Children's Publishing) Amazon Publishing.

—Broken Hearts. 2011. (Fear Street Superchillers Ser.: Bk. 3). (ENG.). 224p. (YA). (gr. 7). pap. 10.99 *(978-1-4424-4273-3(5)*, Simon Pulse) Simon Pulse.

—Escape from HorrorLand. 2009. (Goosebumps Horrorland Ser.: 11). (ENG.). 160p. (J). (gr. 3-7). 6.99 *(978-0-439-91879-4(0)*, Scholastic Paperbacks) Scholastic, Inc.

—Party Games: A Fear Street Novel. 2014. (Fear Street Ser.). (ENG.). 288p. (YA). (gr. 7-12). 17.99 *(978-1-250-05161-5(4)*, 9781250051615, St. Martin's Griffin) St. Martin's Pr.

—Slappy New Year! 2010. (Goosebumps Horrorland Ser.: 18). (ENG.). 160p. (J). (gr. 3-7). pap. 6.99 *(978-0-545-16199-2(1)*, Scholastic Paperbacks) Scholastic, Inc.

—Weirdo Halloween. 2010. (Goosebumps Horrorland Ser.: 16). (ENG.). 240p. (J). (gr. 3-7). 7.99 *(978-0-545-16197-8(5)*, Scholastic Paperbacks) Scholastic, Inc.

—Who's Your Mummy? 2009. (Goosebumps Horrorland Ser.: 6). (ENG.). 160p. (J). (gr. 3-7). 6.99 *(978-0-439-91874-9(X)*, Scholastic Paperbacks) Scholastic, Inc.

—Why I Quit Zombie School. 2011. (Goosebumps Hall of Horrors Ser.: 4). (ENG.). 160p. (J). (gr. 3-7). pap. 6.99 *(978-0-545-28932-0(7)*, Scholastic Paperbacks) Scholastic, Inc.

Stingley, Quinton. My Little Adventure. 2013. 60p. pap. 21.34 *(978-1-4669-6231-6(3))* Trafford Publishing.

Stinson, Aimee & Somson, Kathy. The Bearless City, 1 vol. 2009. 22p. pap. 24.95 *(978-1-60749-406-5(X))* America Star Bks.

Stinson, June. A Basset Named Fred. 2012. 28p. pap. 24.95 *(978-1-4626-8190-7(5))* America Star Bks.

—Yellow Kitty Rags. 2013. 24p. pap. 24.95 *(978-1-4626-8191-4(3))* America Star Bks.

Stitch Up. 2016. (ENG.). 368p. (YA). (gr. 8). pap. 11.99 *(978-1-84877-423-0(0))* Bonnier Publishing GBR. Dist: Independent Pubs. Group.

Stockdale, Stephanie. Sidney Visits Australi. 2009. 44p. pap. 18.99 *(978-1-4389-8698-2(X))* AuthorHouse.

Stockham, Jessica, illus. Little Red Riding Hood. 2005. (Flip-Up Fairy Tales Ser.). (ENG.). 24p. (J). pap. *(978-1-904550-22-8(3))* Child's Play International Ltd.

Stocks, David. Moon Rabbit. 2008. 276p. pap. *(978-1-84747-838-2(7))* Chipmunkapublishing.

Stockton, Frank Richard. The Associate Hermits. 2005. pap. 27.95 *(978-1-4179-2511-7(6))* Kessinger Publishing, LLC.

—The Captain's Toll-Gate. 2005. pap. 31.95 *(978-1-4179-2498-1(5))* Kessinger Publishing, LLC.

—A Jolly Fellowship. 2008. 168p. 26.95 *(978-1-60664-873-5(X))*; pap. 13.95 *(978-1-60664-120-0(4))* Aegypan.

—Kate Bonnet: The Romance of a Pirate's Daughter. reprint ed. pap. 28.00 *(978-1-4047-8937-1(5))* Classic Textbooks.

—Kate Bonnet: The Romance of a Pirate's Daughter. 2007. 364p. (J). (gr. -1-7). 46.95 *(978-0-548-02295-5(X))* Kessinger Publishing, LLC.

—Kate Bonnet: The Romance of a Pirate's Daughter. 2005. 29.95 *(978-1-59818-254-5(4))* Wildside Pr., LLC.

Stockton, Lucille. Hallo, Mallo & Pallo: The Ostracized Ostrich Family. Sampson, April, illus. 2005. 31p. (J). 19.95 *(978-1-59408-511-6(0))* Cork Hill Pr.

Stockwell, Jeff. Fandango: The Key to the Wind. Stockwell, Pel, illus. 2007. 58p. (YA). per. 22.50 *(978-0-9785594-0-3(1))* Stockwell Publishing.

Stohl, Margaret. Black Widow: Forever Red. (Black Widow Novel Ser.). (ENG.). (YA). (gr. 7-12). 2016. 432p. pap. 9.99 *(978-1-4847-7645-2(3))* 2015. 416p. 17.99 *(978-1-4847-2643-3(X))* Disney Publishing Worldwide. (Marvel Pr.).

Stokes, Jonathan W. Addison Cooke & the Treasure of the Incas. 2016. (Addison Cooke Ser.). (ENG., Illus.). 336p. (J). (gr. 3-7). 16.99 *(978-0-399-17377-6(3)*, Philomel Bks.) Penguin Young Readers Group.

Stokes, Katherine. Motor Maids in Fair Japan. 2006. pap. *(978-1-4068-3090-3(9))* Echo Library.

Stokes, Roy Eliot. Andy at Yale: Or the Great Quadrangle Mystery. 2007. (ENG.). 202p. pap. 20.99 *(978-1-4264-9506-9(4))*; 222p. pap. 22.99 *(978-1-4264-9887-9(X))* Creative Media Partners, LLC.

Stoklasa, JoAnne. Oliver & I: The Long Way Home. 2012. 20p. pap. 11.59 *(978-1-4669-5287-4(3))* Trafford Publishing.

Stompin' Boots. 2013. (Illus.). 24p. pap. *(978-1-4602-2767-1(0))* FriesenPress.

Stone Arch Books (Firm: Afton, Minn.) Staff. Hansel & Gretel: The Graphic Novel, 1 vol. Dietrich, Sean, illus. 2008. (Graphic Spin Ser.). (ENG.). 40p. (gr. 1-3). pap. 5.95 *(978-1-4342-0863-7(X)*, Graphic Revolve) Stone Arch Bks.

Stone, Charlene. The Greatest Fishing Adventure of a Lifetime: American Kids Greatest Adventures. 2004. 47p. pap. 24.95 *(978-1-4137-2862-0(6))* PublishAmerica, Inc.

Stone, Emma. Loholt Scrimminge & the Moor-Land Quest. 2007. 140p. per. *(978-1-906210-19-9(5))* Grosvenor Hse. Publishing Ltd.

Stone, Jeff. Five Ancestors Out of the Ashes: Phoenix. 2013. (Five Ancestors Out of the Ashes Ser.: 1). (ENG.). 304p. (J). (gr. 4-7). 6.99 *(978-0-375-87097-2(0)*, Yearling) Random Hse. Children's Bks.

—Five Ancestors Out of the Ashes #1: Phoenix. 2012. (Five Ancestors Out of the Ashes Ser.). (ENG.). 288p. (J). (gr. 4-7). 16.99 *(978-0-375-87018-7(0)*, Random Hse. Bks. for Young Readers) Random Hse. Children's Bks.

—Five Ancestors Out of the Ashes #2: Lion. 2014. (Five Ancestors Out of the Ashes Ser.). (ENG.). 256p. (J). (gr. 4-7). 6.99 *(978-0-375-87099-6(7)*, Yearling) Random Hse. Children's Bks.

—Five Ancestors Out of the Ashes #3: Jackal. 2014. (Five Ancestors Out of the Ashes Ser.). (ENG.). 192p. (J). (gr. 4-7). 16.99 *(978-0-375-87020-0(2)*, Random Hse. Bks. for Young Readers) Random Hse. Children's Bks.

—Lion. 2013. (Five Ancestors Out of the Ashes Ser.). (ENG.). 240p. (J). (gr. 4-7). 16.99 *(978-0-375-87019-4(9)*, Random Hse. Bks. for Young Readers) Random Hse. Children's Bks.

Stone, Judith. Billie the Buffalo Goes to Great Sand Dunes National Park. 2009. 24p. pap. 15.95 *(978-1-4490-1495-7(X))* AuthorHouse.

—Billie the Buffalo Goes to Town. 2008. 20p. pap. 12.95 *(978-1-4389-2877-7(7))* AuthorHouse.

Stone, Pam. Oscar's Adventures in the Woods: True story about a turtle that comes back every year to find his Friend. 2011. 15p. (J). pap. 14.95 *(978-1-4327-6382-4(2))* Outskirts Pr., Inc.

Stone, Reuben. Guardians of the Cambrian Lode: An Ancient People - A Timeless Quest. 2005. 254p. (YA). (gr. 8-12). per. 7.99 *(978-0-9550034-0-0(7))* Bethania Bks. GBR. Dist: Send The Light Distribution LLC.

Storck, Patrick & Rik Hoskin. Dreamworks Madagascar Comics Collection. 2017. (J). lib. bdg. 20.85 *(978-0-606-39426-0(5))* Turtleback Bks.

Storer, Megan. Cowbelle - Snow Day. 2005. (Illus.). 54p. (J). per. 6.99 *(978-0-9769856-0-0(8)*, 0-9769856-0-8) Little River Bookshelf.

Storm Is Coming. 2003. (J). per. *(978-1-57657-866-7(6))* Paradise Pr., Inc.

Storm, Jeff. No Return Land: You Are the Hero of This Book! Chan, Harvey, illus. 2015. (Determine Your Destiny Ser.: Vol. 2). (ENG.). 176p. (J). (gr. 4-7). pap. *(978-1-77143-247-4(0))* CCB Publishing.

—Petrified World, Determine Your Destiny No. 1: You Are the Hero of This Book! Chan, Harvey, illus. 2nd ed. 2014. 160p. pap. *(978-1-77143-159-0(8)*, CCB Publishing) CCB Publishing.

Storm, Michael. Pulp7: A Sweet Deal, a Killer Calling, & a Man Inside. 2nd enl. ed. 2005. (YA). 23.95 *(978-0-9744929-6-4(5))* Leeway Pubs.

—The Roboshop. 2005. (J). 12.95 *(978-0-9744929-5-7(7))* Leeway Pubs.

Storm, Zed. Will Solvit & the Cannibal Cavemen. 2010. (Will Solvit Ser.: Bk. 5). (Illus.). 128p. (J). (gr. 1-7). pap. *(978-1-4075-8983-1(0))* Parragon, Inc.

—Will Solvit & the Deadly Gladiator. 2010. (Will Solvit Ser.: Bk. 6). (Illus.). 128p. (J). (gr. 1-7). pap. *(978-1-4075-8984-8(9))* Parragon, Inc.

—Will Solvit & the Dreaded Droids. 2010. (Will Solvit Ser.: Bk. 4). (Illus.). 128p. (J). (gr. 1-7). pap. *(978-1-4075-8980-0(6))* Parragon, Inc.

—Will Solvit & the Mission of Menace. 2010. (Will Solvit Ser.: Bk. 2). (Illus.). 128p. (J). (gr. 1-7). pap. *(978-1-4075-8981-7(4))* Parragon, Inc.

—Will Solvit & the Mummy's Curse. 2010. (Will Solvit Ser.: Bk. 3). (Illus.). 128p. (J). (gr. 1-7). pap. *(978-1-4075-8979-4(2))* Parragon, Inc.

—Will Solvit & the T-Rex Terror. 2010. (Will Solvit Ser.: Bk. 1). (Illus.). 128p. (J). (gr. 1-7). pap. *(978-1-4075-8982-4(2))* Parragon, Inc.

Stormer, Kate. Casey's Unexpected Friend. Lowes, Tom, illus. l.t. ed. 2003. 38p. (J). 16.95 *(978-0-9722099-7-7(2)*, CUF) Caseys World Bks.

A Stormy Adventure: Facing the Fear of Storms. 2004. (J). 6.99 *(978-0-9753870-3-0(0))* Write On!

Storr, Catherine. The Chinese Egg. 2012. (ENG.). 266p. (J). pap. *(978-1-4482-0816-6(5)*, 157982, Bloomsbury Reader) Bloomsbury Publishing Plc.

Storrie, Paul. Perseus: The Hunt for Medusa's Head [A Greek Myth]. Yeates, Thomas, illus. 2009. (Graphic Myths & Legends Ser.). (ENG.). 48p. (gr. 4-8). pap. 8.95 *(978-1-58013-888-8(8))* Lerner Publishing Group.

Storrie, Paul D. Nightmare on Zombie Island. Witt, David, illus. 2008. (Twisted Journeys (r) Ser.: 5). (ENG.). 112p. (J). (gr. 4-7). per. 7.95 *(978-0-8225-6200-9(6))* Lerner Publishing Group.

Storrie, Paul D., et al. Twisted Journeys(r): Spring 2012 New Releases. 2012. (Twisted Journeys Ser.). (Illus.). 112p. (J). (gr. 4-7). lib. bdg. 55.86 *(978-0-7613-8910-1(5)*, Graphic Universe™) Lerner Publishing Group.

Story Time Book: Rhyme Time & Story Time. 2004. reprint ed. pap. 15.95 *(978-1-4191-1380-2(1))* Kessinger Publishing, LLC.

Storytime with Dora & Diego. 2009. (Dora & Diego Ser.). (ENG.). 192p. (J). (gr. -1-2). 12.99 *(978-1-4169-7093-4(2),* Simon Spotlight/Nickelodeon) Simon Spotlight/Nickelodeon.

Stoudemire, Amar'e. Schooled. 2013. (STAT: Standing Tall & Talented Ser.: 4). lib. bdg. 16.00 *(978-0-606-32378-9(3),* Turtleback) Turtleback Bks.

Strachan, Linda. Hamish Mchaggis & the Edinburgh Adventure. Collins, Sally J., illus. 2005. (Hamish Mchaggis Ser.). 26p. (J). per. 9.00 *(978-0-9546701-7-7(5))* GW Publishing GBR. Dist: Wilson & Assocs.

—Hamish Mchaggis & the Ghost of Glamis. Collins, Sally J., illus. 2005. (Hamish Mchaggis Ser.). 26p. (J). per. 9.00 *(978-0-9546701-9-1(1))* GW Publishing GBR. Dist: Wilson & Assocs.

—Hamish Mchaggis & the Search for the Loch Ness Monster. Collins, Sally J., illus. 2005. 32p. (J). pap. 9.00 *(978-0-9546701-5-3(9))* GW Publishing GBR. Dist: Wilson & Assocs.

—Hamish Mchaggis & the Skye Surprise. Collins, Sally J., illus. 2005. (Hamish Mchaggis Ser.). 26p. (J). pap. 9.00 *(978-0-9546701-8-4(3))* GW Publishing GBR. Dist: Wilson & Assocs.

Strachen, Iona. Adventures in a Red Tartan Duffle Coat. 2003. 62p. pap. *(978-1-84401-090-5(2))* Athena Pr.

Stracher, Cameron. The Water Wars. 2011. (ENG.). 256p. (YA). (gr. 7-12). pap. 10.99 *(978-1-4022-6759-8(2),* 9781402267598) Sourcebooks, Inc.

Strack, Beth. Sammy the Snail's Bright Ideas. 2013. 32p. pap. 9.99 *(978-0-9898991-0-9(1))* Strack, Beth.

Straczynski, J. Michael. Best of Spider-Man, Vol. 3. Youngquist, Jeff, ed. 2004. (Spider-Man Ser.). (Illus.). 368p. (YA). 29.99 *(978-0-7851-1339-3(8))* Marvel Worldwide, Inc.

—The Book of Ezekiel, Vol. 7. Romita, John, Jr., illus. 2004. (Spider-Man Ser.). 144p. (YA). pap. 12.99 *(978-0-7851-1525-0(0))* Marvel Worldwide, Inc.

Straker, Bethany, illus. The Funny Bunny Fly. 2014. (ENG.). 32p. (J). (gr. -1-k). 14.95 *(978-1-62914-610-2(2),* Sky Pony Pr.) Skyhorse Publishing Co., Inc.

Stranaghan, Crystal. The 13th Floor: Colouring Outside the Lines. Bzymek, Izabela, illus. 2012. 34p. (-18). *(978-1-926691-25-1(3))* Gumboot Bks.

Strand, Jeff. I Have a Bad Feeling about This. 2014. (ENG.). 256p. (YA). (gr. 7-12). pap. 8.99 *(978-1-4022-8455-7(1),* 9781402284557) Sourcebooks, Inc.

Strand, Kai. The Wishing Well. 2012. 104p. 19.95 *(978-1-61633-301-0(4));* pap. 9.95 *(978-1-61633-302-7(2))* Guardian Angel Publishing, Inc.

Strang, Herbert. Round the World in Seven Days. 2006. pap. *(978-1-4068-2304-2(X))* Echo Library.

Strasser, Todd. Battle Drift. Phillips, Craig, illus. 2006. (DriftX Ser.: 2). (ENG.). 224p. (YA). (gr. 9-12). pap. 10.99 *(978-1-4169-0582-0(0),* Simon Pulse) Simon Pulse.

—Cut Back. 2004. (ENG.). 320p. (YA). (gr. 9). mass mkt. 5.99 *(978-0-689-87030-9(2),* Simon Pulse) Simon Pulse.

—Sideways Glory. Phillips, Craig, illus. 2006. (DriftX Ser.: 3). (ENG.). 208p. (YA). (gr. 9-12). pap. 10.99 *(978-1-4169-0583-7(9),* Simon Pulse) Simon Pulse.

—Slide or Die. Phillips, Craig, illus. 2006. (DriftX Ser.: 1). (ENG.). 224p. (YA). (gr. 9-18). pap. 10.99 *(978-1-4169-0581-3(2),* Aladdin) Simon & Schuster Children's Publishing.

—Take Off. 2004. (ENG.). 320p. (YA). (gr. 9). mass mkt. 5.99 *(978-0-689-87029-3(9),* Simon Pulse) Simon Pulse.

Stratemeyer, Edward. Richard Dare's Venture. 2007. 232p. 26.95 *(978-1-4218-4146-5(0));* per. 11.95 *(978-1-4218-4244-8(0))* 1st World Publishing, Inc. (1st World Library - Literary Society).

—Richard Dare's Venture. 2004. reprint ed. pap. 21.95 *(978-1-4191-4479-0(0));* pap. 1.99 *(978-1-4192-4479-7(5))* Kessinger Publishing, LLC.

—The Rover Boys at Colby Hall: Or the Struggles of the Young Cadets. 2007. (ENG.). 190p. pap. 19.99 *(978-1-4346-4319-3(0));* 218p. pap. 22.99 *(978-1-4346-4320-9(4))* Creative Media Partners, LLC.

—The Rover Boys at College or the Right R. 2004. reprint ed. pap. 22.95 *(978-1-4191-8114-6(9))* Kessinger Publishing, LLC.

—The Rover Boys at College or the Right Road & the Wrong. 2004. reprint ed. pap. 1.99 *(978-1-4192-8114-3(3))* Kessinger Publishing, LLC.

—The Rover Boys at School: Or the Cadets of Putnam Hall. 2007. (ENG.). 164p. pap. 19.99 *(978-1-4264-2004-7(8))* Creative Media Partners, LLC.

—The Rover Boys in Business or the Search. 2004. reprint ed. pap. 22.95 *(978-1-4191-8116-0(5))* Kessinger Publishing, LLC.

—The Rover Boys in Business or the Search for the Missing Bonds. 2004. reprint ed. pap. 1.99 *(978-1-4192-8116-7(X))* Kessinger Publishing, LLC.

—The Rover Boys on the Ocean: Or, a Chase for a Fortune. 2007. (ENG.). 158p. pap. 19.99 *(978-1-4264-2766-4(2));* 170p. pap. 21.99 *(978-1-4264-2804-3(9))* Creative Media Partners, LLC.

Strathearn, Chris. Ant-Man: The Incredible Shrinking Suit. 2015. (Marvel 8x8s Ser.). (J). lib. bdg. 13.55 *(978-0-606-37217-6(2))* Turtleback Bks.

Stratton, Allan. Borderline. 2012. (ENG.). 320p. (YA). (gr. 8). pap. 9.99 *(978-0-06-145113-3(4),* HarperTeen) HarperCollins Pubs.

—The Grave Robber's Apprentice. 2012. 288p. (J). (gr. 5). 16.99 *(978-0-06-197608-7(3))* HarperCollins Pubs.

Stratton, Bart. Arctic Mail Adventure. Riddle, Scott, illus. 2010. 28p. pap. 15.95 *(978-1-60844-558-5(5))* Dog Ear Publishing, LLC.

Straub-Martin, Susan M. Legends, Loves & Great Lakes. 2013. 28p. pap. 15.00 *(978-0-9830321-6-8(5))* Strauberry Studios.

Strauch, Brenda. Tragic Endings: The Unwritten Series. 2011. 292p. (gr. -1). 24.99 *(978-1-4567-4176-1(4));* pap. 14.99 *(978-1-4567-4177-8(2))* AuthorHouse.

Stravinskas, Janice. Pam the Dog: A Hawaiian Adventure. 2009. 32p. pap. 13.00 *(978-1-60860-692-4(9),* Eloquent Bks.) Strategic Book Publishing & Rights Agency (SBPRA).

Streit, Jakob. Puck The Gnome. Mitchell, David S., ed. Kuettel, Nina, tr. from GER. 2004. Orig. Title: Puck der Zwerg. (ENG., Illus.). 100p. (J). per. 15.00 *(978-1-888365-54-2(4))* Waldorf Publications.

Strickland, A. W. The Adventures of Ralph & Elmer This Potato Is for You. 2012. 38p. pap. 14.95 *(978-0-9820649-9-3(3))* Andromeda Pr., Inc.

Strickland, Brad & Fuller, Thomas E. The Guns of Tortuga. Saponaro, Dominick, illus. 2003. (ENG.). 208p. (J). (gr. 3-7). pap. 10.99 *(978-0-689-85297-8(5),* Simon & Schuster/Paula Wiseman Bks.) Simon & Schuster/Paula Wiseman Bks.

—Marooned! 2004. (Mars Year One Ser.: 1). (ENG., Illus.). 192p. (J). (gr. 3-7). pap. 9.99 *(978-0-689-86400-1(0),* Aladdin) Simon & Schuster Children's Publishing.

Strickland, Deborah. Mary Reeder, Prairie Girl. 2007. 68p. per. 8.95 *(978-0-595-44514-1(4))* iUniverse, Inc.

Strickland, James R. Lincoln's Lost Papers. 2008. 131p. (J). pap. 11.95 *(978-0-7414-4601-5(4))* Infinity Publishing.

Strobel-Cort, Joanne. Emillee Kart & the Seven Saving Signs: The Tale of Beasley's Bonnet. 2007. 204p. per. 24.95 *(978-1-4241-8597-9(1))* America Star Bks.

Strong, Louise. The Island Adventures of Frodo Mcadoo. 2005. (Illus.). 196p. (J). per. 12.95 *(978-0-9770950-0-1(2))* Strong, Louise dev.

The Strongest of Them All. 2003. (J). per. *(978-1-57657-862-9(3))* Paradise Pr., Inc.

Stroschin, Jane H. Atsa & Ga: A Story from the High Desert. Stich, Carolyn R., illus. 2005. 32p. (J). (gr. k-6). *(978-1-883960-29-2(0))* Henry Quill Pr.

Stroud, Jonathan. The Amulet of Samarkand. 2004. (Bartimaeus Novel Ser.). (ENG.). 480p. (J). (gr. 5-9). reprint ed. pap. 9.99 *(978-0-7868-5255-0(0))* Hyperion Pr.

—Heroes of the Valley. 2009. (JPN., Illus.). 587p. (YA). *(978-4-652-07954-6(0))* Fukuinkan Shoten.

—Heroes of the Valley. 2010. (ENG.). 496p. (J). (gr. 5-9). pap. 8.99 *(978-1-4231-0967-9(8))* Hyperion Pr.

—Lockwood & Co. 2017. (Lockwood & Co Ser.). (ENG.). 480p. (J). (gr. 3-7). pap. 7.99 ***(978-1-4847-1190-3(4))*** Hyperion Bks. for Children.

—Lockwood & Co. Book Three the Hollow Boy. 2016. (Lockwood & Co Ser.). (ENG.). 416p. (J). (gr. 3-7). pap. 7.99 *(978-1-4847-1189-7(0))* Hyperion Bks. for Children.

—Ptolemy's Gate, Bk. 3. 3rd rev. ed. 2007. (Bartimaeus Novel Ser.). (ENG.). 512p. (J). (gr. 5-9). per. 9.99 *(978-0-7868-3868-4(X))* Hyperion Pr.

Strouss, Jessica & Strouss, Stephen. There's a Dog at My Feet when I Eat. 2010. 36p. 15.49 *(978-1-4269-4342-3(3))* Trafford Publishing.

Strout, Morgan. Petri's Adventures. 2013. 18p. pap. 8.95 *(978-1-4575-2094-5(X))* Dog Ear Publishing, LLC.

Strunk, Peter, illus. & creator. Two Inch Hero: The Adventures of Lorenzo Lizard. Strunk, Peter, creator. 2006. (J). 17.95 *(978-0-9785961-0-1(2))* Smile Time Publishing.

Stuart, Lisa Marie. The Little Cat, the Wonderful Witch, & the Clever Mouse. Potter, Lori, illus. 2008. 60p. pap. 21.95 *(978-1-59858-691-6(2))* Dog Ear Publishing, LLC.

Stuart, Raff. A Roman Odyssey: Book One of the chronicles of Adam Black the Teenage Time Traveller. 2009. 228p. pap. 14.49 *(978-1-4389-7407-1(8))* AuthorHouse.

Stuart-Russell, C. Playtime with the Animals. 2007. 61p. pap. 19.95 *(978-1-4241-5473-9(1))* America Star Bks.

Stubben, Michael. Clark vs. the Rainforest. 2012. 110p. pap. 9.99 *(978-1-105-54615-0(2))* Lulu Pr., Inc.

Studio Mouse, ed. Jojo's Circus Get up & Move! Flat Learn & Carry 4 Board Books & CD. rev. ed. 2007. (ENG.). 12.99 *(978-1-59069-548-7(8))* Studio Mouse LLC.

Studio Mouse Editorial. Belle: The Power of Love. 2008. (ENG., Illus.). 36p. (gr. -1-k). 7.99 *(978-1-59069-435-0(X))* Studio Mouse LLC.

Studio Mouse Staff. Pooh & Friends ABCs & 123s: First Concepts. rev. ed. 2007. (ENG., Illus.). 24p. (J). (gr. -1-3). 4.99 *(978-1-59069-606-4(9))* Studio Mouse LLC.

—Pooh & Tigger. 2008. (ENG., Illus.). 36p. (J). (gr. -1). 7.99 *(978-1-59069-417-6(1))* Studio Mouse LLC.

—Space Adventure. rev. ed. 2008. (ENG., Illus.). (J). 12.99 *(978-1-59069-609-5(3))* Studio Mouse LLC.

—Tinkerbell's Magic Story Writer. rev. ed. 2008. (ENG.). 30p. (J). 14.99 *(978-1-59069-616-3(6))* Studio Mouse LLC.

Stull, Judy. From Darkness to Color: A Trilogy. 2005. (J). per. *(978-0-9765738-3-8(0))* Stull, Judy.

—The Gray World. 2005. (Illus.). (J). per. *(978-0-9765738-0-7(6))* Stull, Judy.

—The Great Connection. 2005. (J). per. *(978-0-9765738-2-1(2))* Stull, Judy.

—The Secret Mission. 2005. (J). per. *(978-0-9765738-1-4(4))* Stull, Judy.

Stumpe, Jennifer. Aunt Jo Jo's Magical Gifts: Amazing Underwater Adventure. 2011. 32p. (gr. 1-2). pap. 14.95 *(978-1-4567-3160-1(2))* AuthorHouse.

—Aunt Jo Jo's Magical Gifts: Ethan's Great African Journey. 2012. 32p. pap. 17.95 *(978-1-4772-9097-2(4))* AuthorHouse.

Stupp, Robert Dock. The Fable of Freddy & the Frockett. 2011. 194p. pap. 16.95 *(978-1-4327-4327-7(9))* Outskirts Pr., Inc.

Sturm, James. Fantastic Four: Unstable Molecules. Davis, Guy & Sikoryak, Bob, illus. 2003. (Fantastic Four Legends Ser.: Vol. 1). 128p. (YA). pap. 13.99 *(978-0-7851-1112-2(3))* Marvel Worldwide, Inc.

Sturm, James, et al. Characters in Action! Sturm, James, illus. 2013. (Adventures in Cartooning Ser.). (ENG., Illus.). 64p. (J). (gr. 1-5). pap. 10.99 *(978-1-59643-732-6(4),* 9781596437326, First Second Bks.) Roaring Brook Pr.

—Hocus Focus. 2017. (Adventures in Cartooning Ser.). (ENG., Illus.). 40p. (J). 14.99 *(978-1-59643-654-1(9),* 9781596436541, First Second Bks.) Roaring Brook Pr.

Sturtevant, Karen. The Adventures of Gert & Stu & Zippy Too. 2012. 36p. pap. 18.99 *(978-1-4772-9360-7(4))* AuthorHouse.

Stute, Lela LaBree. When Pugs Fly! 2011. 36p. pap. 24.95 *(978-1-4489-5484-1(3))* America Star Bks.

Stute, Lela Labree & Stute, Lela LaBree. Three Pugs & a Canadian Spy. 2011. 74p. pap. 26.90 *(978-1-257-82229-4(2))* Lulu Pr., Inc.

Styles, Showell. The Flying Ensign: Greencoats Against Napoleon. 2003. (Budget Bks.). Orig. Title: Greencoat Against Napoleon. 297p. (YA). pap. 14.95 *(978-1-883937-70-6(1))* Bethlehem Bks.

Subrina. Jacko the Monkey. 2013. 16p. pap. 24.95 *(978-1-63000-145-2(7))* America Star Bks.

Suchowacki, William. The Adventures of Maggie & Mikey. 2013. 20p. pap. 10.99 *(978-1-4582-1113-2(4),* Abbott Pr.) Author Solutions, Inc.

Suderman, Colleen C. Norgee Does the Laundry, 1 vol. 2010. 34p. pap. 24.95 *(978-1-4489-2453-0(7))* PublishAmerica, Inc.

Sue-A-Quan, Goomatie. A Seal Fascination at Sea: A Fascinating Seal. 2008. (Illus.). 38p. (J). pap. 19.00 *(978-0-8059-7517-8(9))* Dorrance Publishing Co., Inc.

Suggs, Dona. The Adventures of Ms Dee & Misti the Kitten. 2010. 19p. pap. 13.95 *(978-1-4327-6514-9(0))* Outskirts Pr., Inc.

Sullivan, told to. The Adventures of the Pink Shovel & the Red Pail. 2004. (J). pap. 9.00 *(978-0-8059-6263-5(8))* Dorrance Publishing Co., Inc.

Sullivan, Ayn Cates. Sparkle & the Light. duCray, Belle Crow, illus. 2013. (ENG.). (J). (gr. 1-4). 19.99 *(978-0-9884537-0-8(3))* Infinite Light Publishing.

Sullivan, Candida. Zippy y Las Rayas de Valor. Foster, Jack, illus. 2013. 40p. pap. 13.99 *(978-1-937331-51-1(2))* ShadeTree Publishing, LLC.

Sullivan, Michael. Escapade Johnson & Mayhem at Mount Moosilauke. Kolitsky, Joy, illus. 2007. (Escapade Johnson Ser.). (ENG.). 96p. (J). (gr. 2-4). per. 3.95 *(978-1-929945-70-2(1))* Big Guy Bks., Inc.

—Escapade Johnson & the Witches of Belknap County. Kolitsky, Joy, illus. 2008. (Escapade Johnson Ser.). (ENG.). 99p. (J). (gr. 2-4). pap. 3.95 *(978-1-929945-90-0(6))* Big Guy Bks., Inc.

Sullivan, Sarah. All That's Missing. 2013. (ENG.). 368p. (J). (gr. 3-7). 16.99 *(978-0-7636-6102-1(3))* Candlewick Pr.

Sullivan, Stephen D. Fantastic Four: The Junior Novel. 2005. (Fantastic Four Ser.). (ENG., Illus.). 144p. (gr. 3-7). pap. 4.99 *(978-0-06-078619-9(1),* HarperFestival) HarperCollins Pubs.

Summers, Darien. The Mischievous Hare. 2009. (Illus.). 48p. pap. 9.95 *(978-1-4327-4602-5(2))* Outskirts Pr., Inc.

Summers, Everette. Grandaddy's Short Stories. 2006. 48p. pap. 16.95 *(978-1-4241-2468-8(9))* PublishAmerica, Inc.

Summers, Gillian. The Secret of the Dread Forest: The Faire Folk Trilogy. 2009. (Faire Folk Saga Ser.: 3). (ENG.). 288p. (YA). pap. 9.95 *(978-0-7387-1411-0(9),* Flux) North Star Editions.

Sumner, M. C. Common Enemy. 2013. (Extreme Zone Ser.: 5). (ENG., Illus.). 192p. (YA). (gr. 11). pap. 13.99 *(978-1-4814-2115-7(8),* Simon Pulse) Simon Pulse.

—Deadly Secrets. 2013. (Extreme Zone Ser.: 4). (ENG., Illus.). 192p. (YA). (gr. 11). pap. 13.99 *(978-1-4814-2125-6(5),* Simon Pulse) Simon Pulse.

—Night Terrors. 2013. (Extreme Zone Ser.: 1). (ENG., Illus.). 208p. (YA). (gr. 11). pap. 14.99 *(978-1-4814-2126-3(3),* Simon Pulse) Simon Pulse.

Sundance/Newbridge LLC Staff. Mystery of the Maya. 2005. (Choose Your Own Adventure Ser.). (gr. 4-8). pap. 5.50 *(978-0-7608-9692-1(5))* Sundance/Newbridge Educational Publishing.

Sundaravej, Sittisan & Thongmoon, Kriangsak, illus. Return to Atlantis. 2007. (Choose Your Own Adventure Ser.: No. 18). 119p. (J). (gr. 4-7). per. 6.99 *(978-1-933190-18-5(2),* CHCL18) Chooseco LLC.

Sunday, Bonnie. Sparkles, Dragons, & Dragonfly Land. 2012. 32p. pap. 19.99 *(978-1-4772-2914-9(0))* AuthorHouse.

Sundberg, Peggy. Jazmine's Incredible Story. Wiles, Pat, illus. 2006. 32p. (J). 16.95 *(978-0-9721057-5-0(1),* Cowgirl Peg Bks.) Cowgirl Peg Enterprises.

Sundell, Joanne. Arctic Shadow. 2015. (Watch Eyes Trilogy Ser.: 2). (ENG.). 278p. (YA). 25.95 *(978-1-4328-3008-3(2),* Five Star Trade) Cengage Gale.

—Arctic Will. 2016. (ENG.). 326p. (YA). 25.95 *(978-1-4328-3175-2(5),* Five Star) Cengage Gale.

Sundstrom, Dainel H. The Return of Oz. 2007. pap. 10.00 *(978-0-8059-8944-1(7))* Dorrance Publishing Co., Inc.

Super Kids Nutrition, creator. Super Baby Abigail's Lunch Time Advenutre. 2008. (Illus.). 30p. (J). *(978-0-9801148-0-5(2))* SuperKids Nutrition Inc.

Superman Adventures. 2013. (Superman Adventures Ser.). (ENG.). 32p. (gr. 1-2). 180.80 *(978-1-4342-4860-2(7))* Stone Arch Bks.

Surget, Alain. The Ghost Ship. 2015. (Jolly Roger Ser.). (Illus.). 96p. (gr. 3-6). 28.50 *(978-1-909645-41-7(9))* Book Hse. GBR. Dist: Black Rabbit Bks.

Surget, Alain & Yeardley, Glynne. Caesar, Who's He? Parme, Fabrice, illus. 2014. 95p. (J). *(978-1-4351-5328-8(6))* Barnes & Noble, Inc.

—Danger at the Circus! Parme, Fabrice, illus. 2014. 95p. (J). *(978-1-4351-5334-9(0))* Barnes & Noble, Inc.

—Prisoners in the Pyramid. Parme, Fabrice, illus. 2014. 94p. (J). *(978-1-4351-5326-4(X))* Barnes & Noble, Inc.

Suritsch, Gina. Magical Tales from India: The Secret of the White Elephant & Mukti the Lion Finds Himself. 2013. 44p. pap. 22.99 *(978-1-4828-1435-4(8))* Partridge Pub.

Sutcliff, Rosemary. The Eagle of the Ninth. 2010. (Roman Britain Trilogy Ser.: 1). (ENG.). 240p. (YA). (gr. 7). pap. 9.99 *(978-0-312-64429-1(9),* 9780312644291) Square Fish.

Sutcliffe, William. Circus of Thieves & the Raffle of Doom. Tazzyman, David, illus. 2016. (ENG.). 224p. (J). pap. 7.99 *(978-1-4711-2023-7(6),* Simon & Schuster Children's) Simon & Schuster, Ltd. GBR. Dist: Simon & Schuster, Inc.

Sutherland, David. Samantha Cardigan & the Genie's Revenge. Roberts, David, illus. 2005. (Red Bananas Ser.). (ENG.). 48p. (J). lib. bdg. *(978-0-7787-1070-7(X))* Crabtree Publishing Co.

—Samantha Cardigan & the Ghastly Twirling Sickness. Roberts, David, illus. 2005. (Red Bananas Ser.). (ENG.). 48p. (J). lib. bdg. *(978-0-7787-1069-1(6))* Crabtree Publishing Co.

Sutherland, David & Roberts, David. Samantha Cardigan & the Genie's Revenge. 2005. (Red Bananas Ser.). (ENG., Illus.). 48p. (J). (gr. 1-3). *(978-0-7787-1086-8(6))* Crabtree Publishing Co.

—Samantha Cardigan & the Ghastly Twirling Sickness. 2005. (Red Bananas Ser.). (ENG., Illus.). 48p. (J). (gr. 1-3). *(978-0-7787-1085-1(8))* Crabtree Publishing Co.

Sutherland, David, et al. Siriol Llywelyn a Dial y Bwgan. 2005. (WEL., Illus.). 48p. pap. *(978-1-85596-678-9(6))* Dref Wen.

—Siriol Llywelyn A'r Salwch Chwyrlio Erchyll. Roberts, David, illus. 2005. (WEL.). 48p. pap. *(978-1-85596-679-6(4))* Dref Wen.

Sutherland, E. B. Tallie's in a Sea of Trouble. 2013. 44p. pap. 21.99 *(978-1-4797-3988-2(X))* Xlibris Corp.

Sutherland, Keith. Two Tubby Teddies Have a Very Busy Week. 2013. 40p. pap. *(978-0-9545288-7-4(5))* D S Press.

Sutherland, Tui T. The Brightest Night. 2014. (Wings of Fire Ser.: Bk. 5). (ENG., Illus.). 336p. (J). (gr. 3-7). 16.99 *(978-0-545-34922-2(2),* Scholastic Pr.) Scholastic, Inc.

—The Dark Secret. (Wings of Fire Ser.: 4). (ENG.). 336p. (J). (gr. 3-7). 2014. pap. 6.99 *(978-0-545-34926-0(5))* 2013. (Illus.). 16.99 *(978-0-545-34921-5(4))* Scholastic, Inc. (Scholastic Pr.).

—The Dark Secret. 2014. (Wings of Fire Ser.: 4). lib. bdg. 17.20 *(978-0-606-36033-3(6))* Turtleback Bks.

—Darkstalker. 2016. (Wings of Fire Ser.). (ENG., Illus.). 400p. (J). (gr. 3-7). 17.99 *(978-1-338-05361-6(2),* Scholastic Pr.) Scholastic, Inc.

—The Dragonet Prophecy. (Wings of Fire Ser.: 1). 2013. (ENG.). 336p. (J). (gr. 3-7). pap. 6.99 *(978-0-545-34923-9(0))* 2012. (ENG.). 336p. (J). (gr. 3-7). 16.99 *(978-0-545-34918-5(4))* 2012. (Illus.). 304p. pap. *(978-0-545-48603-3(3))* Scholastic, Inc. (Scholastic Pr.).

—The Dragonet Prophecy. 2013. (Wings of Fire Ser.: 1). lib. bdg. 17.20 *(978-0-606-31952-2(2),* Turtleback) Turtleback Bks.

—Escaping Peril. (Wings of Fire Ser.: 8). (ENG.). 336p. (J). (gr. 3-7). 2017. pap. 6.99 ***(978-0-545-68545-0(1))*** 2015. (Illus.). 16.99 *(978-0-545-68544-3(3))* Scholastic, Inc. (Scholastic Pr.).

—The Hidden Kingdom. (Wings of Fire Ser.: 3). (ENG.). 336p. (J). (gr. 3-7). 2014. pap. 6.99 *(978-0-545-34925-3(7))* 2013. (Illus.). 16.99 *(978-0-545-34920-8(6),* Scholastic Pr.) Scholastic, Inc.

—The Lost Heir. 2013. (Wings of Fire Ser.: 2). (ENG.). 336p. (J). (gr. 3-7). pap. 6.99 *(978-0-545-34924-6(9));* 16.99 *(978-0-545-34919-2(2))* Scholastic, Inc. (Scholastic Pr.).

—The Lost Heir. 2013. (Wings of Fire Ser.: 2). lib. bdg. 17.20 *(978-0-606-32341-3(4),* Turtleback) Turtleback Bks.

—Winter Turning. 2015. (Wings of Fire Ser.: Bk. 7). (ENG., Illus.). 336p. (J). (gr. 3-7). 16.99 *(978-0-545-68537-5(0),* Scholastic Pr.) Scholastic, Inc.

—Winter Turning. 2016. (Wings of Fire Ser.: 7). lib. bdg. 17.20 ***(978-0-606-39706-3(X))*** Turtleback Bks.

Sutherland, Tui T. & Sutherland, Kari. Dragon on Trial. 2014. (Menagerie Ser.: 2). (ENG.). 304p. (J). (gr. 3-7). 16.99 *(978-0-06-085143-9(0))* HarperCollins Pubs.

Sutiff, Jamie. The Elves of Owl's Head Mountain. Blumberg, Christine A., ed. Evens, Kevin C., illus. 2007. 276p. pap. 10.95 *(978-0-9712867-8-8(7))* Cold River Pubns.

—The Elves of Owl's Head Mountain. Blumberg, Christine A., ed. Evans, Kevin, illus. 2007. 280p. (gr. 8-12). 26.95 *(978-0-9712867-7-1(9))* Cold River Pubns.

Sutton, Kelsey. Gardenia. 2017. (ENG.). 260p. pap. 13.99 *(978-1-62681-841-5(X))* Diversion Publishing Corp.

Sutton, Laurie S. The Case of the Clown Carnival. Neely, Scott, illus. 2017. (You Choose Stories: Scooby-Doo Ser.). (ENG.). 112p. (gr. 2-3). lib. bdg. 32.65 *(978-1-4965-4333-2(5),* You Choose Bks.) Capstone Press of Coughlan Cos.

—Goldilocks & the Three Vampires: A Graphic Novel. Jennings, C. S., illus. 2016. (Far Out Fairy Tales Ser.). (ENG.). 40p. (gr. 3-4). lib. bdg. 25.32 *(978-1-4965-3783-6(1),* Far Out Fairy Tales) Stone Arch Bks.

—The Secret of the Sea Creature, 1 vol. Neely, Scott, illus. 2014. (You Choose Stories: Scooby-Doo Ser.). (ENG.). 112p. (gr. 2-3). pap. 6.95 *(978-1-4342-7925-5(1),* You Choose Bks.) Capstone Press of Coughlan Cos.

—The Terror of the Bigfoot Beast, 1 vol. Neely, Scott, illus. 2014. (You Choose Stories: Scooby-Doo Ser.). (ENG.). 112p. (gr. 2-3). pap. 6.95 *(978-1-4342-7926-2(X),* You Choose Bks.) Capstone Press of Coughlan Cos.

Sutton, Laurie S. & Bright, J. E. Batman & Robin Adventures. Vecchio, Luciano, illus. 2016. (Batman & Robin Adventures Ser.). (ENG.). 88p. (gr. 2-3). 106.60 *(978-1-4965-2551-2(5),* DC Super Heroes) Stone Arch Bks.

Sutton, Margaret. The Discovery at Dragon's Mouth, No. 31. Doane, Pelagie, illus. 2008. (Judy Bolton Mysteries Ser.). (ENG.). 196p. (J). (gr. 4-7). pap. 14.95 *(978-1-4290-9051-3(0))* Applewood Bks.

Sutton, Nicky C. Blake's Oddity. 2010. 169p. pap. 14.95 *(978-1-4461-9729-5(8))* Lulu Pr., Inc.

Swan, Bill. Off Track, 1 vol. 2003. (Lorimer Sports Stories Ser.: 62). (ENG.). 112p. (J). (gr. 4-8). 16.95 *(978-1-55028-807-0(5),* 9781550288070); 8.95 *(978-1-55028-806-3(7),* 9781550288063) Lorimer, James & Co., Ltd., Pubs. CAN. Dist: Casemate Pubs. & Bk. Distributors, LLC.

Swanepoel, Sharon. The Adventures of Seek & Save Volume 3: The Village. Locsinto, Lucas, illus. 2011. (J). *(978-0-9772647-6-6(9))* God's Glory Media.

Swann, Stephen. The Magical TV. 2009. 43p. pap. 21.50 *(978-1-4452-3001-6(1))* Lulu Pr., Inc.

—Where's Our Submarine. 2009. 58p. pap. 21.50 *(978-1-4452-3146-4(8))* Lulu Pr., Inc.

Swanson Sateren, Shelley. Adventures at Hound Hotel. Melmon, Deborah, illus. 2016. (Adventures at Hound Hotel Ser.). (ENG.). 72p. (gr. 2-3). 202.56 *(978-1-5158-0078-1(4),* Adventures at Hound Hotel) Picture Window Bks.

Swecker, Susan J. Who's Looking for Cheese! 2012. 16p. pap. 15.99 *(978-1-4685-4637-8(6))* AuthorHouse.

Sweet, George M. The Old Alligator & the Young Bird. 2011. 52p. pap. 19.39 *(978-1-4269-5357-6(7))* Trafford Publishing.

Sweet, J. H. Foo & Friends Storybook. 2013. 290p. 26.94 *(978-1-936660-04-9(0))* Sweet, Joanne.

Sweren-Becker, Daniel. The Ones, Bk. 1. 2016. (Ones Ser.: 1). (ENG.). 304p. (YA). 17.99 *(978-1-250-08314-2(1),* 9781250083142) Imprint IND. Dist: Macmillan.

Swick, Carmen D. Patch Land Adventures Book 2 Camping at Mimi's Ranch. Lambert, Page, ed. Manfre, Joey, illus. 2012. 40p. pap. 12.99 *(978-0-9831380-1-3(X))* Presbeau Publishing, Inc.

Swift, Carolyn. Robbers in the House. (Illus.). 96p. 2.95 *(978-0-900068-59-1(0))* Penguin Publishing Group.

Swift, Jonathan, et al. The Adventure Collection: Treasure Island, the Jungle Book, Gulliver's Travels, White Fang, the

Merry Adventures of Robin Hood, 0 vols. Macdonald, Ross, illus. unabr. ed. 2012. (Heirloom Collection: 0). (ENG.). 1588p. 99.99 *(978-1-61218-416-6(2)*, 9781612184166) Amazon Publishing.

Swift, K. Marie. The Adventures of Jake & George: Jake Gets a New Brother. Paul, Kate, illus. 2010. 26p. pap. 11.75 *(978-1-60693-863-8(0)*, Eloquent Bks.) Strategic Book Publishing & Rights Agency (SBPRA).

Swift, Melanie. Rioc & Elber's Arctic Adventure. 2011. 120p. pap. *(978-1-84549-511-4(X)*, Swirl) arima publishing.

Swindells, Robert. Blackout. 2011. (ENG.). 224p. (J). (gr. 3-6). pap. 9.99 *(978-0-552-56154-9(1))* Transworld Publishers Ltd. GBR. Dist: Independent Pubs. Group.

—The Ghosts of Givenham Keep. 2015. (ENG., Illus.). 108p. (J). pap. 9.99 *(978-1-78270-056-2(0))* Award Pubns. Ltd. GBR. Dist: Parkwest Pubns., Inc.

—Kidnap at Denton Farm. 2015. (ENG., Illus.). 106p. (J). pap. 9.99 *(978-1-78270-055-5(2))* Award Pubns. Ltd. GBR. Dist: Parkwest Pubns., Inc.

—Ruby Tanya. 2005. (ENG.). 256p. (J). (gr. 7). per. 15.99 *(978-0-440-86398-4(8))* Transworld Publishers Ltd. GBR. Dist: Independent Pubs. Group.

—Shrapnel. 2009. (ENG., Illus.). 224p. (YA). (gr. 7-18). pap. 14.99 *(978-0-552-55930-0(X))* Transworld Publishers Ltd. GBR. Dist: Independent Pubs. Group.

—A Skull in Shadows Lane. 2012. (ENG.). 240p. (J). (gr. 4-7). pap. 12.99 *(978-0-552-56409-0(5))* Transworld Publishers Ltd. GBR. Dist: Independent Pubs. Group.

—The Strange Tale of Ragger Bill. 2015. (ENG., Illus.). 103p. (J). pap. 9.99 *(978-1-78270-058-6(7))* Award Pubns. Ltd. GBR. Dist: Parkwest Pubns., Inc.

—We Didn't Mean to, Honest! 2015. (ENG., Illus.). 107p. (J). pap. 9.99 *(978-1-78270-054-8(4))* Award Pubns. Ltd. GBR. Dist: Parkwest Pubns., Inc.

Swinger-Ellbogen, Sue. Campfire Kids, 1 vol. 2010. 54p. pap. 16.95 *(978-1-4489-5493-3(2))* America Star Bks.

Swinney, Kay. Marty Moose & the Mystical Reunion, 1 vol. 2009. 73p. pap. 19.95 *(978-1-61546-867-6(6))* America Star Bks.

Syed, Jaweria T. Enchantment Realm's First Adventure. 2012. 94p. 24.99 *(978-1-4771-1695-1(8))*; pap. 15.99 *(978-1-4771-1694-4(X))* Xlibris Corp.

Sykes, Harold S. The Beacon of Airport Seven. 2004. reprint ed. pap. 1.99 *(978-1-4192-5375-1(1))* Kessinger Publishing, LLC.

Sylvester, Kevin. Neil Flambé & the Marco Polo Murders. Sylvester, Kevin, illus. 2014. (Neil Flambe Capers Ser.: 1). (ENG., Illus.). 320p. (J). (gr. 3-7). pap. 7.99 *(978-1-4424-4605-2(6)*, Simon & Schuster Bks. For Young Readers) Simon & Schuster Bks. For Young Readers.

—The Neil Flambé Capers Collection: Neil Flambé & the Marco Polo Murders; Neil Flambé & the Aztec Abduction; Neil Flambé & the Crusader's Curse; Neil Flambé & the Tokyo Treasure. Sylvester, Kevin, illus. 2014. (Neil Flambe Capers Ser.). (ENG., Illus.). 1344p. (J). (gr. 3-7). pap. 31.99 *(978-1-4814-3238-2(9)*, Simon & Schuster Bks. For Young Readers) Simon & Schuster Bks. For Young Readers.

Sylvester, Sr. Land of the Angels, 1 vol. Morrison, Nancy, illus. 2009. 32p. pap. 24.95 *(978-1-60836-888-4(2))* America Star Bks.

Sylvester Sr, John S. Our Day on the Farm, 1 vol. 2010. 44p. pap. 24.95 *(978-1-4489-7139-8(X))* PublishAmerica, Inc.

Symons, Brandy. Peek A Boo, I See You. 2010. 32p. pap. 12.99 *(978-1-4490-1841-2(6))* AuthorHouse.

Szkop, Catherine. The Adventures of Arathmatar. 2009. 48p. pap. 12.99 *(978-1-4389-4318-3(0))* AuthorHouse.

Szpirglas, Jeff & Saint-Onge, Danielle. Messy Miranda, 1 vol. Whamond, Dave, illus. 2013. (Orca Echoes Ser.). (ENG.). 64p. (J). (gr. 2-3). pap. 6.95 *(978-1-4598-0117-2(2))* Orca Bk. Pubs. USA.

T. The Adventures of Sugar the Pup. Baker, David, illus. 2011. 36p. pap. 24.95 *(978-1-4560-5724-4(3))* America Star Bks.

Taaffe, Gary. Bullies: Billy's Gotta Survive the City. 2013. 130p. (YA). pap. *(978-0-9874937-1-2(X))* Bunya Publishing.

Tabares, Veronica. Monkeys on an Island. Tabares, Bridgitt, illus. 2012. 32p. (J). pap. 14.50 *(978-1-60916-005-0(3))* Sun Break Publishing.

Taber, Kristen. Ærenden - the Child Returns. 2012. 382p. (YA). pap. 13.99 *(978-0-9851200-0-9(2))* Sean Tigh Pr.

Tabibi, Alexis Deeba. An Unusual World. 2011. 16p. pap. 8.32 *(978-1-4670-3798-3(2))* AuthorHouse.

Tabor, Corey R. Fox & the Bike Ride. Tabor, Corey R., illus. 2017. (Illus.). 32p. (J). (gr. -1-3). 17.99 ***(978-0-06-239875-8(X))*** HarperCollins Pubs.

Taborn, Deborah V. Donia & Her Marvelous Bag of Cents. 2011. 36p. pap. 16.99 *(978-1-4567-6934-5(0))* AuthorHouse.

Taeryn, M. S. Chosen Four: The Faelan Prophecies, Book One. 2010. 444p. (gr. 10-12). pap. 23.95 *(978-1-4502-4797-9(0))*; (J). 33.95 *(978-1-4502-5634-6(1))* iUniverse, Inc.

Tafoya, Jody. Sammy: A Day in the Life of a Snail. 2012. 24p. pap. 24.95 *(978-1-62709-389-7(3))* America Star Bks.

Tait, Elena. The Twisted Fairy Tale. 2009. 36p. pap. 16.99 *(978-1-4389-2774-9(6))* AuthorHouse.

Taitano, Janice G. The Legend of Lutung. 2006. 260p. pap. 29.00 *(978-1-59752-482-7(4)*, Resource Pubns.(OR)) Wipf & Stock Pubs.

Talbot, Ethel. The Natural History Story Book. Noble, Edwin & Grieve, Walter G., illus. 2008. 336p. pap. 13.95 *(978-1-59915-295-0(9))* Yesterday's Classics.

Talbot Healy, John Adrian. The Flea & the Cauliflower. 2009. (Illus.). 92p. pap. 30.49 *(978-1-4490-1360-8(0))* AuthorHouse.

Talbot, Kathy. Camille's Rainy Day Adventure. 2011. 24p. pap. 8.32 *(978-1-4634-5998-7(X))* AuthorHouse.

—My Magic Swing. 2010. 28p. pap. 12.50 *(978-1-4567-1027-9(3))* AuthorHouse.

Talbot, Rose. The Adventures of Peanut, the Sugar Glider. 2007. 80p. per. 15.99 *(978-1-4257-9629-7(X))* Xlibris Corp.

—The Adventures of Peanut, the Sugar Glider: Holiday Celebrations & Outings. 2012. 88p. (gr. 1-2). pap. 13.95 *(978-1-4772-5439-4(0))* AuthorHouse.

Talbot, Sophie. Chloe. 2011. (Fabulous Terrible Ser.). 280p. (YA). (gr. 7-18). pap. 12.99 *(978-1-933390-77-2(8))* Chooseco LLC.

Talburt, Tony. The History on the Page: Adventures in Black British History. 2012. 182p. pap. *(978-1-909039-23-0(3))* Legend Pr.

The Tale of Jackie Berry. 2005. (J). per. 12.95 *(978-0-9677047-5-3(8))* Marble Hse. Editions.

Talhah, Abu & Books, Greenbird. My Sister Saarah. Fowler, Claire, illus. 2013. 30p. pap. *(978-0-9576379-6-2(9))* Greenbird Bks.

Tamang, Mayan, illus. Captain Remarkable; Girls can be Superheroes Too! 2009. 28p. (J). pap. 10.95 *(978-0-9823906-1-0(0))* Wiggles Pr.

Tamayo, Alex. Horizons Set 1, 5 books. Shea, Steve, ed. 2013. (Illus.). 48p. (YA). pap. 24.00 *(978-1-57128-809-7(0))* High Noon Bks.

Tamura, Mitsuhisa. BakéGyamon, Vol. 4. Tamura, Mitsuhisa, illus. 2009. (Bakégyamon Ser.: 4). (ENG., Illus.). 216p. (J). pap. 7.99 *(978-1-4215-1882-4(1))* Viz Media.

Tamura, Yumi. Book of Justice. Tamura, Yumi, illus. 2003. (Chicago Ser.: Vol. 2). (ENG., Illus.). 200p. pap. 15.95 *(978-1-56931-829-4(8))* Viz Media.

Tan, Valerie Genevivie. Hello! I'm Sha Sha: Join Sha Sha in Her New School. 2009. (Illus.). 50p. (J). pap. 14.95 *(978-1-4327-4195-2(0))* Outskirts Pr., Inc.

Tanaka, Rika. Kilala Princess, Vol. 2. 2016. (ENG.). 208p. (J). pap. 10.99 *(978-1-4278-5663-0(X)*, 9781427856630) TOKYOPOP, Inc.

Tanner, Lian. Battlesong. Szabla, Liz, ed. 2017. (Icebreaker Trilogy Ser.: 3). (ENG.). 304p. (J). 16.99 *(978-1-250-05218-6(1)*, 9781250052186) Feiwel & Friends.

—City of Lies. 2012. (Keepers Trilogy: Bk. 2). (ENG.). 288p. (J). (gr. 4-7). 6.99 *(978-0-375-85979-3(9)*, Yearling) Random Hse. Children's Bks.

—Museum of Thieves. (Keepers Ser.: Bk. 1). (ENG.). 320p. (J). (gr. 3-7). 2011. 8.99 *(978-0-375-85978-6(0)*, Yearling) 2010. 16.99 *(978-0-385-73905-4(2)*, Delacorte Bks. for Young Readers) Random Hse. Children's Bks.

—Path of Beasts. 2013. (Keepers Trilogy: Bk. 3). (ENG.). 352p. (J). (gr. 4-7). 8.99 *(978-0-375-85980-9(2)*, Yearling) Random Hse. Children's Bks.

Tanner, Suzan. The Most Unusual Adventures of Black Shadow Smokey & the Blue Streak. 2003. 108p. 21.95 *(978-1-4140-0911-7(9))* AuthorHouse.

Tanos, Elaine. Anadarko & Pugwash: The Delbert Adventures. 2006. (J). spiral bd. 6.79 *(978-0-9764666-6-6(X))* TanosBooks Publishing.

Tapia, Rayner. The Adventures of Tom Mcguire: Morkann's Revenge. 2010. (Illus.). 156p. pap. 11.99 *(978-1-4490-8183-6(5))* AuthorHouse.

—The Adventures of Tom Mcguire: The Bard of Typheousina. 2009. (Illus.). 112p. 21.49 *(978-1-4389-3905-6(1))*; pap. 12.49 *(978-1-4389-3906-3(X))* AuthorHouse.

Tapley-Milton, Katherine. The Adventures of Sir Lancelot the Cat. 2013. 16p. pap. 7.99 *(978-1-4497-8838-4(6)*, WestBow Pr.) Author Solutions, Inc.

Tarasova, Julia. Daniel's Travels. 2008. 48p. 21.50 *(978-1-4357-1249-2(8))* Lulu Pr., Inc.

Tarbett, Debbie. Ten Wriggly Wiggly Caterpillars. (Illus.). 24p. (J). bds. 19.95 *(978-1-84506-027-5(X))* Little Tiger Pr.

Tarore, Martha. The Runaway Bubble. 2011. (ENG.). 35p. (J). pap. 16.95 *(978-1-4327-5898-1(5))* Outskirts Pr., Inc.

Tarshis, Lauren. I Survived the Destruction of Pompeii, AD 79. Dawson, Scott, illus. 2014. 95p. (J). ***(978-0-545-77568-7(X)***, Scholastic Pr.) Scholastic, Inc.

Tarshis, Lauren. I Survived the Japanese Tsunami 2011. Dawson, Scott, illus. 2013. (I Survived Ser.: No. 8). 83p. (J). *(978-0-545-62981-2(0))* Scholastic, Inc.

Tarter, Mildred. Alexis Uses the Elements of Nature. 2011. 24p. pap. 16.49 *(978-1-4389-6879-7(5))* AuthorHouse.

Tashlikowich, Natasha. The Secret of the Seven Stones. 2009. 117p. pap. 18.97 *(978-0-557-03747-6(6))* Lulu Pr., Inc.

Tate, Cynthia Wagoner. Gordy's Grimy but Groovy Adventure. 2006. 24p. 12.98 *(978-1-4116-6297-1(0))* Lulu Pr., Inc.

Tate, J. The Pops. 2012. (Illus.). 36p. pap. 19.99 *(978-1-4678-8958-2(X))* AuthorHouse.

Tate, Micheal R. The Adventures of Sugarcube. 2012. 52p. pap. 24.99 *(978-1-4772-4823-2(4))* AuthorHouse.

Tate, Nancy. Grandmother Ellie's Attic. 2010. 232p. pap. 32.50 *(978-1-60976-033-5(6)*, Eloquent Bks.) Strategic Book Publishing & Rights Agency (SBPRA).

Tate, Nikki. The Battle for Camillo, 1 vol. Williams, E. Colin, illus. 2003. (Estorian Chronicles Ser.: 2). (ENG.). 322p. (J). (gr. 4-8). pap. 8.95 *(978-1-55039-127-5(5))* Sono Nis Pr. CAN. Dist: Orca Bk. Pubs. USA.

Tate, Nikki. Deadpoint. 2017. (Orca Sports Ser.). lib. bdg. 20.80 ***(978-0-606-40454-9(6))*** Turtleback Bks.

Tavener, Carys. The Adventures of T. C & Friends. 2011. (Illus.). 132p. pap. 38.72 *(978-1-4567-7096-9(9))* AuthorHouse.

Taylor, Angela. Izzy's Quest for Gold. 2015. (ENG., Illus.). 92p. (J). pap. *(978-1-78222-415-0(7))* Paragon Publishing, Rothersthorpe.

Taylor, Carol K. Behind the Fence. 2009. 24p. pap. 12.99 *(978-1-4389-4352-7(0))* AuthorHouse.

Taylor, Centrella P. Little Miss Sunshine, 1 vol. 2009. 48p. pap. 16.95 *(978-1-61546-936-9(2))* America Star Bks.

Taylor, Christine. Red Riding Hood & the Toad. 2009. (Illus.). 44p. (gr. -1 — 1). 18.49 *(978-1-4389-3483-9(1))* AuthorHouse.

Taylor, Clifford. Taylor's Tales. 2004. 108p. 20.95 *(978-0-595-66558-7(6))* iUniverse, Inc.

Taylor, Cora. Champlain & Cartier, 1 vol. 2004. (Ghost Voyages Ser.: No. 4). (ENG., Illus.). 128p. (J). (gr. 3-6). pap. 7.95 *(978-1-55050-374-6(X))* Coteau Bks. CAN. Dist: Orca Bk. Pubs. USA.

—The Matthew, 1 vol. 2008. (Ghost Voyages Ser.). (ENG.). 128p. (J). (gr. 3-6). pap. 5.95 *(978-1-55050-198-8(4))* Coteau Bks. CAN. Dist: Orca Bk. Pubs. USA.

Taylor, Edward C. Ted Strong's Motor Car or Fast & Furio. 2006. pap. *(978-1-4068-0774-5(5))* Echo Library.

Taylor, Emma. Adventures of Bunting, the Turtle. 2011. 24p. pap. 15.99 *(978-1-4568-5911-4(0))* Xlibris Corp.

Taylor, G. P. The Tizzle Sisters & Erik. 2007. 188p. *(978-1-905692-22-4(6))* Markosia Enterprises, Ltd.

—Wormwood. 2004. (Illus.). 272p. (J). (gr. 3-6). 17.99 *(978-1-59185-626-9(4))* Charisma Media.

Taylor, Greg. Killer Pizza. 2011. (ENG.). 368p. (YA). (gr. 5-9). pap. 10.99 *(978-0-312-67485-4(6)*, 9780312674854) Square Fish.

—Killer Pizza: the Slice. 2012. (ENG.). 368p. (YA). (gr. 5-9). pap. 10.99 *(978-1-250-00478-9(0)*, 9781250004789) Square Fish.

Taylor, Jennifer. Dragon Sitter. 2005. 36p. (J). 14.99 *(978-1-4116-6449-4(3))* Lulu Pr., Inc.

Taylor, Jo-Ann. The Alchemist's Secret. 2011. 268p. pap. *(978-1-907652-87-5(6))* Grosvenor Hse. Publishing Ltd.

Taylor, K. C. Easier Without. 2005. 177p. (YA). lib. bdg. 12.95 *(978-0-9728549-2-4(4))* Y-IREAD Publishing.

Taylor, Kay Lovelace. Princess Aisha & the Cave of Judgment. Rhine, Karen C., illus. 2007. 32p. (J). 19.95 *(978-0-9799119-0-3(7))* KLT & Assocs.

Taylor, Kim. Accion. (SPA., Illus.). (J). (gr. 5-8). pap. *(978-84-216-1812-7(1)*, BU4732) Bruño, Editorial ESP. Dist: Lectorum Pubns., Inc.

Taylor, Laini. Strange the Dreamer. 2017. 536p. (YA). ***(978-0-316-43120-0(6))*** Little Brown & Co.

—Strange the Dreamer. 2017. (ENG.). (J). 544p. (gr. 10-17). 18.99 *(978-0-316-34168-4(1))*; 704p. (gr. 9-17). 20.99 *(978-0-316-46427-7(9))* Little, Brown Bks. for Young Readers.

Taylor, Mari Jo. Not One of the Robot Children. 2005. 11.00 *(978-0-8059-9791-0(1))* Dorrance Publishing Co., Inc.

Taylor, Mark. Henry Explores the Jungle. Booth, Graham, illus. 2012. (ENG.). 48p. (J). (gr. -1-3). 18.95 *(978-1-930900-56-1(2))* Purple Hse. Pr.

—Henry the Castaway. Booth, Graham, illus. 2010. 48p. (J). (gr. -1-3). 18.95 *(978-1-930900-47-9(3))* Purple Hse. Pr.

Taylor, Mildred D. Roll of Thunder, Hear My Cry. 25th anniv. ed. 2004. (Puffin Modern Classics Ser.). (ENG., Illus.). 288p. (J). (gr. 5-7). 7.99 *(978-0-14-240112-5(9)*, Puffin Books) Penguin Young Readers Group.

Taylor, Pearl Fleming. Snowbird Weenie, 1 vol. 2009. 59p. pap. 16.95 *(978-1-60836-745-0(2))* America Star Bks.

Taylor, Richard B. Chispita Service Dog Extraordinaire: Volume 2. the Pack Trip. 2010. 52p. pap. 20.49 *(978-1-4490-5326-0(2))* AuthorHouse.

—Chispita Service Dog Extraordinaire: Volume 3. Alaskan Cruise. 2010. 52p. pap. 20.49 *(978-1-4490-5563-9(X))* AuthorHouse.

—Chispita Service Dog Extraordinaire: Volume 4. Alaskan Land Cruise. 2010. 68p. pap. 23.49 *(978-1-4490-5613-1(X))* AuthorHouse.

—Chispita Service Dog Extraordinaire: Volume 5. Indian Country. 2010. 60p. pap. 21.99 *(978-1-4490-5617-9(2))* AuthorHouse.

—Chispita Service Dog Extraordinaire Volume 1: Introduction. 2010. 44p. pap. 16.99 *(978-1-4490-5540-0(0))* AuthorHouse.

Taylor, Rose. Johnny's Great Adventure, 1 vol. 2009. 40p. pap. 24.95 *(978-1-60813-662-9(0))* America Star Bks.

Taylor, Rosemary. Eddie's Rocket Adventure. 2011. 28p. pap. 13.54 *(978-1-4670-2537-9(2))* AuthorHouse.

Taylor, Roy. Matilda's Magic Wand: Dreamland Adventure. 2008. 36p. (J). pap. 9.00 *(978-0-8059-7716-5(3))* Dorrance Publishing Co., Inc.

Taylor, S. S. The Expeditioners & the Secret of King Triton's Lair. Roy, Katherine, illus. 2014. (ENG.). 320p. (gr. 4-9). 22.00 *(978-1-940450-20-9(9))* McSweeney's Publishing.

—The Expeditioners & the Treasure of Drowned Man's Canyon. Roy, Katherine, illus. 2013. (ENG.). 384p. pap. 12.95 *(978-1-938073-71-7(1))* McSweeney's Publishing.

Taylor, Theodore & Taylor, Theodore. Billy the Kid: A Novel. 2006. (ENG., Illus.). 224p. (YA). (gr. 7-12). reprint ed. pap. 14.95 *(978-0-15-205651-3(3))* Houghton Mifflin Harcourt Publishing Co.

Taylor, Thomas. Haunters. 2013. (J). 327p. *(978-0-545-50253-5(5))*; (ENG.). 336p. (gr. 5-9). 17.99 *(978-0-545-49644-5(6))* Scholastic, Inc.

Taylor, Tijuana. The Adventures of Buddy Blue Bug & the Critters of the Gospel. 2012. 34p. pap. 19.99 *(978-1-61996-655-0(7))* Salem Author Services.

Taylor, Tom. The Deep: The Vanishing Island, Vol. 2. Edwards, Gary, ed. 2013. (ENG., Illus.). 80p. (J). pap. 11.95 *(978-1-922023-05-6(1))* Gestalt Publishing Pty, Ltd. AUS. Dist: Diamond Comic Distributors, Inc.

Taylor, Travis S. & Nye, Jody Lynn. Moon Beam. 2017. (ENG.). 320p. (J). (gr. 5). 18.99 ***(978-1-4814-8252-3(1))*** Baen Bks.

Taylor, Vacen. Starchild: The City of Souls. 2013. (ENG.). 176p. (J). pap. 13.95 *(978-1-922200-12-9(3))* Odyssey Bks. AUS. Dist: Lightning Source, Inc.

TBD. DreamWorks Trolls: Storybook with Poppy Collectible. 2016. (ENG.). 24p. (J). (gr. -1-2). 14.99 *(978-0-7944-3845-6(8)*, Reader's Digest Children's Bks.) Studio Fun International.

tbd. Paw Patrol - Here to Help! 2016. (ENG.). 10p. (J). (gr. -1 — 1). bds. 8.99 *(978-0-7944-3585-1(8)*, Reader's Digest Children's Bks.) Studio Fun International.

Teacher Created Resources Staff & Collins, Susan. A Guide for Using Time Soldiers in the Classroom. 2009. (ENG.). 48p. pap. 9.99 *(978-1-4206-2003-0(7))* Teacher Created Resources, Inc.

Teague, David. Henry Cicada's Extraordinary Elktonium Escapade. 2016. 320p. (J). (gr. 3-7). 16.99 *(978-0-06-237745-6(0))* HarperCollins Pubs.

Teague, Mark. The Secret Shortcut. 2004. (J). (gr. k-3). spiral bd. *(978-0-616-04563-3(8))*; spiral bd. *(978-0-616-03059-2(2))* Canadian National Institute for the Blind/Institut National Canadien pour les Aveugles.

Tegan-Olsen, Sandra, illus. Joey's adventures by the Sea: Jellyfish Everywhere! 2008. 20p. (J). per. 9.95 *(978-0-9801527-0-8(4))* Freefox Publishing.

Teitelbaum, Michael. Cine en casa: Heroes de Cine: Movie Theater: Marvel Heroes. 2007. (Cine en casa Disney Ser.). (Illus.). 46p. (J). *(978-970-718-535-7(X)*, Silver Dolphin en Español) Advanced Marketing, S. de R. L. de C. V.

—I Am Superman. 2009. (Justice League Classic: I Can Read! Ser.). (J). lib. bdg. 13.55 *(978-0-606-06951-9(8)*, Turtleback) Turtleback Bks.

—Meet the Super Heroes. 2009. (Justice League Classic: I Can Read! Ser.). (J). lib. bdg. 13.55 *(978-0-606-06941-0(0)*, Turtleback) Turtleback Bks.

—Mutant Origin: Michelangelo/Raphael (Teenage Mutant Ninja Turtles) Random House Staff, illus. 2012. (Junior Novel Ser.). (ENG.). 128p. (J). (gr. 3-7). 4.99 *(978-0-449-80994-5(3)*, Random Hse. Bks. for Young Readers) Random Hse. Children's Bks.

—The Secret Life of Black Cat. Sazaklis, John, illus. 2009. (Spider-Man Ser.). 64p. (J). (gr. 2-5). pap. 4.99 *(978-0-06-162626-5(0)*, HarperFestival) HarperCollins Pubs.

—Tale of Zuko. Spaziante, Patrick, illus. 2008. (Avatar Ser.). (ENG.). 96p. (J). (gr. 2-6). pap. 5.99 *(978-1-4169-4984-8(4)*, Simon Spotlight/Nickelodeon) Simon Spotlight/Nickelodeon.

—Teenage Mutant Ninja Turtles Wheel Power Book & Skateboard. 2013. (ENG.). 48p. (J). 12.99 *(978-0-7944-2796-2(0))* Reader's Digest Assn., Inc., The.

Teitelbaum, Michael & Scieszka, Jon. On the Move! Shannon, David et al, illus. 2009. (Jon Scieszka's Trucktown Ser.). (ENG.). 10p. (J). (gr. -1-k). bds. 6.99 *(978-1-4169-4178-1(9)*, Little Simon) Little Simon.

Tela, Carl M. Squnky's Big Awakening. Tela, Donna L., illus. 2009. 140p. pap. 14.99 *(978-1-4251-8145-1(7))* Trafford Publishing.

Telmosse, Gerard. The Curse of the Sourlands. 2008. 132p. pap. 14.51 *(978-1-4357-0169-4(0))* Lulu Pr., Inc.

Temple, Bob. Protecting the Prairie, 1 vol. Horrocks, Savannah, illus. 2008. (Read-It! Chapter Books: Science Tales: Biome Battles Ser.). (ENG.). 64p. (gr. 2-4). lib. bdg. 22.65 *(978-1-4048-3651-8(9)*, Chapter Readers) Picture Window Bks.

Temple, Valerie. Mud Witch Boy of Ghost Canyon. 2009. 113p. pap. 21.95 *(978-1-4327-1133-7(4))* Outskirts Pr., Inc.

Ten Hagen, Evelyn. Malcolm Dooswaddles Good Day. Hutchinson, Michelle, illus. 2013. 82p. pap. 12.95 *(978-1-59930-415-1(5))* TAG Publishing, LLC.

Tennant, Linda. Polly & Meril & the Wicked Spell. 2009. (Illus.). 20p. pap. 15.49 *(978-1-4389-7471-2(X))* AuthorHouse.

TenNapel, Doug. Battle for Amphibopolis. 2017. (Nnewts Ser.: 3). (ENG.). 224p. (J). (gr. 3-7). 19.99 ***(978-0-545-67664-9(9))***; pap. 10.99 ***(978-0-545-67670-0(3))*** Scholastic, Inc. (Graphix).

Tennapel, Doug. The Battle for Amphibopolis. 2017. (Nnewts Ser.: 3). lib. bdg. 22.10 ***(978-0-606-40194-4(6))*** Turtleback Bks.

Tennapel, Doug. Cardboard. 2012. (ENG., Illus.). 288p. (J). (gr. 4-7). 24.99 *(978-0-545-41872-0(0))*; pap. 12.99 *(978-0-545-41873-7(9))* Scholastic, Inc. (Graphix).

TenNapel, Doug. Escape from the Lizzarks. 2015. (Nnewts Ser.: 1). (ENG., Illus.). 192p. (J). (gr. 3-7). pap. 10.99 *(978-0-545-67646-5(0)*, Graphix) Scholastic, Inc.

Tennapel, Doug. Ghostopolis. 2010. (ENG.). 272p. (J). (gr. 4-7). pap. 12.99 *(978-0-545-21028-7(3)*, Graphix) Scholastic, Inc.

TenNapel, Doug. The Rise of Herk. 2016. (Nnewts Ser.: 2). (ENG.). 208p. (J). (gr. 3-7). 19.99 *(978-0-545-67652-6(5)*, Graphix) Scholastic, Inc.

Tennyson, Patrick & Bickford, Nicole. Tarantula Tracks: Rosie's Wild Adventure. l.t. ed. 2004. (Illus.). 32p. (J). 2.95 *(978-0-9729000-1-0(2))* Butterfly Pavilion.

Terango, Christine. Teddy's Surprise Adventure. 2011. 24p. 12.95 *(978-1-4567-4069-6(5))* AuthorHouse.

Terman, Douglas. By Balloon to the Sahara. 2015. (ENG.). 144p. (J). pap. 6.99 *(978-1-937133-48-1(6))* Chooseco LLC.

Terpening, Lori. Hey! You Bug Me. 2012. 28p. pap. 21.99 *(978-1-4691-9529-2(1))* Xlibris Corp.

Terrell, Andrea M. The Adventures of Sammy the Squirrel: Buying Shoes. Mitchell, Anthony W., illus. 2008. (ENG.). 28p. pap. 13.99 *(978-1-4343-5608-6(6))* AuthorHouse.

Terrell, Brandon. Horizon, 1 vol. Dal Bello, Thiago & Tortosa, Wilson, illus. 2013. (Tony Hawk's 900 Revolution Ser.). (ENG.). 128p. (gr. 3-4). pap. 7.19 *(978-1-4342-6218-9(9))*; lib. bdg. 26.65 *(978-1-4342-6032-1(1))* Stone Arch Bks.

Terrell, Brandon & Majado, Caio. Tunnel Vision, Vol. 6. Ito, Leonardo, illus. 2012. (Tony Hawk's 900 Revolution Ser.). (ENG.). 128p. (gr. 3-4). pap. 7.19 *(978-1-4342-3888-7(1))*; lib. bdg. 26.65 *(978-1-4342-3312-7(X))* Stone Arch Bks. (Tony Hawk's 900 Revolution).

Terrell, Brandon & Tortosa, Wilson. Exiled, Vol. 7. Ito, Leonardo, illus. 2012. (Tony Hawk's 900 Revolution Ser.). (ENG.). 128p. (gr. 3-4). pap. 7.19 *(978-1-4342-3889-4(X))*; lib. bdg. 26.65 *(978-1-4342-3313-4(8))* Stone Arch Bks. (Tony Hawk's 900 Revolution).

Terrill Holdman, Shirley. The Adventures of Giggles & Owen: Adventure Three - Unlimited Pawsibilities. Leeds, Marjorie M., illus. 2013. 50p. pap. 17.95 *(978-1-4575-2175-1(X))* Dog Ear Publishing, LLC.

—The Adventures of Giggles & Owen: Adventure Two - Pawsistance Pays Off. Wright, Wendy L., illus. 2011. 46p. pap. 17.95 *(978-1-4575-0568-3(1))* Dog Ear Publishing, LLC.

Terry, Alana. What Hurricane? My Solar-Powered History on a Supply Ship to the Jamestown Colony. Steffen, Jeremy, illus. 2013. 136p. pap. 12.99 *(978-1-937848-05-7(1))* Do Life Right, Inc.

Tesler, Monica. The Tundra Trials. 2016. (Bounders Ser.: 2). (ENG., Illus.). 384p. (J). (gr. 5-9). 16.99 *(978-1-4814-4596-2(0)*, Simon & Schuster/Paula Wiseman Bks.) Simon & Schuster/Paula Wiseman Bks.

Testa, Dom. Galahad 1: The Comet's Curse. 2005. 224p. (YA). per. 8.95 *(978-0-9760564-0-9(2))* Profound Impact Group, Inc.

—Galahad 2: The Web of Titan. 2006. (YA). per. 8.95 *(978-0-9760564-1-6(0))* Profound Impact Group, Inc.

—Galahad 3: The Cassini Code. 2008. 272p. (YA). pap. 9.95 *(978-0-9760564-4-7(5))* Profound Impact Group, Inc.

—The Galahad Archives Book Three: A New Life. 2016. (Galahad Ser.: 3). (ENG.). 512p. (YA). pap. 16.99 *(978-0-7653-8341-9(1)*, 9780765383419, Tor Teen) Doherty, Tom Assocs., LLC.

Testa, Maggie. Max's Big Show. Shannon, David et al, illus. 2010. (Jon Scieszka's Trucktown Ser.). (ENG.). 32p. (J). (gr. -1-1). 4.99 *(978-1-4169-4191-0(6)*, Simon Scribbles) Simon Scribbles.

Tetirick, Jack E. Joey the Motor Home Mouse. 2012. 110p. 20.95 *(978-1-4759-3702-2(4))*; pap. 10.95 *(978-1-4759-3703-9(2))* iUniverse, Inc.

Tetzlaff, Wendy Jo. A Girl Named Frannie. 2008. 28p. pap. 24.95 *(978-1-60703-055-3(1))* America Star Bks.

—Summertime: A Girl Named Frannie, 1 vol. 2010. 38p. pap. 24.95 *(978-1-4489-2598-8(3))* PublishAmerica, Inc.

Tewee, Laqaixit. Winterbloom & the Magical Swan: Book 1 Discovery of the Moon Treasure. 2012. 68p. pap. 31.99 *(978-1-4653-9933-5(X))* Xlibris Corp.

Thakkar, Ravina. Adventure of a Lifetime. 2013. (ENG.). 128p. (J). (gr. 3-6). pap. 6.99 *(978-1-4022-6914-1(5),* Sourcebooks Jabberwocky) Sourcebooks, Inc.

Thaler, Mike. The Class Trip from the Black Lagoon. Lee, Jared, illus. 2004. (Black Lagoon Adventures Ser.: 1). (ENG.). 64p. (J). (gr. 2-5). pap. 3.99 *(978-0-439-42927-6(7),* Scholastic Paperbacks) Scholastic, Inc.

—The New Kid from the Black Lagoon. 2004. (Black Lagoon Ser.). (Illus.). 32p. *(978-0-439-55719-1(4))* Scholastic, Inc.

—The Principal from the Black Lagoon. Lee, Jared, illus. 2008. (Black Lagoon Adventures Ser.). (ENG.). 32p. (J). (gr. -1-3). pap. 3.99 *(978-0-545-06932-8(7),* Cartwheel Bks.) Scholastic, Inc.

Thames, Bob, illus. Hermy the Hermit Crab Goes Shrimping. 2007. 44p. (J). 16.99 *(978-0-933101-05-0(8))* Legacy Pubns.

Thank You, Thank You, Thank You. 2003. (J). 10.95 *(978-0-9745798-0-1(7))* Pen & Sword Publishing Co., The.

Thanos, Jerald. A Princess Christmas. 2009. 32p. pap. 14.49 *(978-1-4389-6752-3(7))* AuthorHouse.

Tharp, Barbara, et al. Tillena Lou's Day in the Sun. Denk, James, ed. Lewis, T., illus. 2nd ed. 2013. (My World & Me Ser.). (ENG.). 32p. (J). (gr. k-2). pap. *(978-1-888997-44-6(3),* BioEd) Baylor College of Medicine.

Tharp, Shari. Gertrude & Toby's Friday Adventure, bks. 3. Heath, Jim, illus. l.t. ed. 2016. 1. (ENG.). (J). (gr. -1-3). bk. 3. 48p. 16.99 *(978-0-9969679-0-7(7))*Bk.1. 46p. pap. 7.99 *(978-0-9969679-1-4(5))* Atlas Publishing LLC. (Atlas Publishing).

The Calaiacovo Family. The Amazing Adventures of Ruby & Rubette: San Francisco. 2010. 32p. pap. 14.49 *(978-1-4490-6948-3(7))* AuthorHouse.

The Duda Family. The Adventures of Newo: Newo & Emma Visit Their Furry Friends. 2008. 28p. pap. 12.49 *(978-1-4343-9766-9(1))* AuthorHouse.

The Guide Dog, Thelma. For the Love of My Pet. Hartley, Joshua, illus. 2012. (ENG.). 26p. (gr. k-5). pap. 14.95 *(978-1-61448-338-0(8))* Morgan James Publishing.

The Series, Superdaddies. Superdaddies; the Series, Presents: Daddy, I Broke My Snowball! 2009. 32p. pap. 14.49 *(978-1-4490-2632-5(X))* AuthorHouse.

The Strode Family. The Magical Land of Far, Far Away. 2011. 16p. pap. *(978-1-4269-5570-9(7))* Trafford Publishing (UK) Ltd.

The 2nd & 7 Foundation. The Hog Mollies & the Camp Carmen Campfire. rev. ed. 2012. (ENG.). 32p. pap. 16.95 *(978-1-4652-0604-6(3))* Kendall Hunt Publishing Co.

Thea Stilton Staff. The Cloud Castle. 2015. (Thea Stilton Special Edition Ser.: 4). (ENG.). 320p. (J). (gr. 2-5). 14.99 *(978-0-545-83536-7(4),* Scholastic Paperbacks) Scholastic, Inc.

Theiss, Lewis E. The Secret Wireless: Or the Spy Hunt of the Camp Brady Patrol. 2007. (ENG.). 160p. pap. 19.99 *(978-1-4346-4429-9(4))* Creative Media Partners, LLC.

Themerson, Franciszka & Themerson, Franciszka. My First Nursery Book. 2009. (ENG., Illus.). 72p. (J). (gr. k-2). 16.95 *(978-0-8109-7978-9(0),* Abrams Bks. for Young Readers) Abrams, Inc.

Therriault - Bruder, Dovie G. Life on the Farm: Story One Adventure with the Chickens. 2011. 36p. pap. 15.14 *(978-1-4670-3797-6(4))* AuthorHouse.

—Life on the Farm - Adventure with the Dogs: Story Ten. 2012. 36p. pap. 20.99 *(978-1-4685-6347-4(5))* AuthorHouse.

Theval, Lio. Angela's Lost Turtle. 2007. 20p. 23.70 *(978-1-4357-0020-8(1))* Lulu Pr., Inc.

Thewes Nicolai, Susan. The Thirteenth Butterfly: A Lizzie's Life Novel. 2009. 192p. pap. 14.49 *(978-1-4389-9975-3(5))* AuthorHouse.

Thiele, Colin. River Murray Mary. (Illus.). 160p. pap. *(978-0-7344-0414-5(X),* Lothian Children's Bks.) Hachette Australia.

Thierry, Raphael. Green Butterfly. 2007. (Superdog Adventure Ser.). (ENG., Illus.). 24p. (J). (gr. -1-k). pap. 6.99 *(978-1-84270-449-3(4))* Transworld Publishers Ltd. GBR. Dist: Independent Pubs. Group.

Thomas, Amy A. The Abominog. Williams, Gail, illus. 2013. 120p. pap. 6.99 *(978-0-9898579-0-1(5))* Passionate Purpose.

Thomas, Amy T. The Story of Rocco on Satterwhite Ridge: Spring Surprises. Lester, Roseanna, illus. 2009. 16p. pap. 8.49 *(978-1-4389-3142-5(5))* AuthorHouse.

Thomas, Bette. Herman's Adventures: Book 1. 2009. 24p. pap. 14.49 *(978-1-4389-8018-8(3))* AuthorHouse.

Thomas, C. Gordon. The Adventures of Jack & Jim. 2008. 132p. 26.54 *(978-1-4251-5909-2(5))* Trafford Publishing.

Thomas, Christina L. Lizzie Thompson: My Dog Knows Kung Fu! 2013. 60p. (gr. 2-4). pap. 10.30 *(978-1-4669-9997-8(7))* Trafford Publishing.

Thomas, Dale. Soot & Frogskin. 2008. 118p. pap. 12.50 *(978-0-9559798-0-4(3))* Inane Blabbering Bks. GBR. Dist: Lulu Pr., Inc.

Thomas, Debbie. Jungle Tangle. MacDonald, Stella, illus. 2013. (ENG.). 320p. (J). pap. 14.95 *(978-1-78117-116-5(5))* Mercier Pr., Ltd., The IRL. Dist: Dufour Editions, Inc.

—Monkie Business. 2014. (ENG., Illus.). 320p. (J). pap. 14.95 *(978-1-78117-170-7(X))* Mercier Pr., Ltd., The IRL. Dist: Dufour Editions, Inc.

Thomas, Gene. Tales from the Tree House. 2011. 112p. (gr. 10-12). 20.95 *(978-1-4620-1864-2(5));* pap. 10.95 *(978-1-4620-1863-5(7))* iUniverse, Inc.

Thomas, Geraint. Agent Mouse: Snowdon Adventure. 2013. 172p. pap. *(978-1-908773-54-8(5))* Iponymous Publishing, Ltd.

Thomas, Gerry. The Umbrella Race. 2010. 25p. (J). pap. 25.95 *(978-1-4327-6006-9(8))* Outskirts Pr., Inc.

Thomas, Gwyn. King Arthur. Jones, Margaret, illus. 2006. (ENG.). 144p. (J). pap. 21.95 *(978-0-86243-798-5(9))* Y Lolfa GBR. Dist: Dufour Editions, Inc.

Thomas, Jane. Zioc Saves His Planet. 2009. (Illus.). 208p. pap. 14.49 *(978-1-4389-4930-7(8))* AuthorHouse.

Thomas, Janet. Can I Play? Bartlett, Alison, illus. 2005. 32p. (J). 8.99 *(978-1-4052-0597-9(0))* Egmont Bks., Ltd. GBR. Dist: Trafalgar Square Publishing.

Thomas, Jason. The Adventures of Bird & Gator: Best Friends. 2012. 24p. pap. 12.56 *(978-1-4669-4973-7(2))* Trafford Publishing.

Thomas, Jeanne Taylor. Kerry Mcdaniels & the Cave. 2012. (ENG.). 276p. pap. 18.95 *(978-1-4327-7296-3(1))* Outskirts Pr., Inc.

Thomas, Jim. Super Slam Turtles! Spaziante, Patrick, illus. 2005. 22p. (J). lib. bdg. 15.00 *(978-1-4242-0971-2(4))* Fitzgerald Bks.

Thomas, Kerrie Annette. Jinja of the Munjyburr. Jacobs, D. K., illus. 2011. 34p. pap. 13.50 *(978-1-61204-421-7(2),* Eloquent Bks.) Strategic Book Publishing & Rights Agency (SBPRA).

Thomas, Michelle. Bubble World & the Enchanted Garden. 2010. (Illus.). 28p. pap. 12.49 *(978-1-4490-9088-3(5))* AuthorHouse.

—Bubble World & the Olympics. 2010. 28p. 12.49 *(978-1-4520-1682-5(8))* AuthorHouse.

Thomas, Mike. The Mysterious Treasure of Jerry Lee Thorton. 2013. 154p. pap. 12.95 *(978-0-578-12603-6(6))* Moss Press Publishing.

Thomas Nelson. Touch & Feel Robbie Reindeer's Snowy Adventure. 2016. (ENG.). 12p. (gr. -1). bds. *(978-1-78598-437-2(3))* Make Believe Ideas.

Thomas Nelson Publishing Staff. Light Rangers: Mending the Maniac Madness: Protect the Children of Angeltown. 2008. cd-rom 19.95 *(978-0-9754280-5-4(5))* Nelson, Thomas Inc.

—The Pirates Who Don't Do Anything: A VeggieTales Movie: Discovery Bay. 2008. 64p. (J). pap. 12.99 *(978-1-4003-1234-4(5))* Nelson, Thomas Inc.

Thomas, Nigel. Tom Travis: The Lost People of Orion. 2006. 193p. pap. 24.95 *(978-1-4241-0382-9(7))* PublishAmerica, Inc.

Thomas, Rich. Thor: An Origin Story. Olliffe, Pat, illus. 2013. (Origin Story Ser.). (ENG.). 48p. (J). (gr. 1-3). 8.99 *(978-1-4231-7215-4(9))* Marvel Worldwide, Inc.

Thomas, Rich, Jr. & Siglain, Michael. Captain America: The Tomorrow Army. Disney Book Group Staff et al, illus. 2014. (Mighty Marvel Chapter Book Ser.: 2). (ENG.). 144p. (J). (gr. 1-3). pap. 5.99 *(978-1-4231-4303-1(5),* Marvel Pr.) Disney Publishing Worldwide.

Thomas, Roy & Stevenson, Robert Louis. Death in the Forest, 1 vol., Vol. 4. Gully, Mario, illus. 2011. (Kidnapped! Ser.). (ENG.). 24p. (J). (gr. 5-9). 24.21 *(978-1-59961-784-8(6))* Spotlight.

—The End of the Quest, 1 vol., Vol. 5. Gully, Mario, illus. 2011. (Kidnapped! Ser.). (ENG.). 24p. (YA). (gr. 5-9). 24.21 *(978-1-59961-785-5(4))* Spotlight.

—I Go to Sea, 1 vol., Vol. 2. Gully, Mario, illus. 2011. (Kidnapped! Ser.). (ENG.). 24p. (J). (gr. 5-9). 24.21 *(978-1-59961-782-4(X))* Spotlight.

—The Loss of the Brig, 1 vol., Vol. 3. Gully, Mario, illus. 2011. (Kidnapped! Ser.). (ENG.). 24p. (YA). (gr. 5-9). 24.21 *(978-1-59961-783-1(8))* Spotlight.

Thomas, Sara. McCoy & the Pond. 2013. 24p. pap. 24.95 *(978-1-62709-793-2(7))* America Star Bks.

Thomas, Susan. Beyond the Mist: Sequel to Mist on the Window. 2012. 352p. pap. 24.34 *(978-1-4772-4627-6(4))* AuthorHouse.

Thomas, Terri. The Barge Ghost, 1 vol. unabr. ed. 2010. (Q Reads Ser.). (ENG.). 32p. (YA). (gr. 9-12). pap. 6.95 *(978-1-61651-211-8(3))* Saddleback Educational Publishing, Inc.

Thomas the Tank Engine. 2012. *(978-0-7948-3764-8(6))* Egmont Bks., Ltd.

Thomas, Warren. The Adventures of Mu-Mu Lost in the Outback. 2012. 44p. pap. 8.99 *(978-1-60746-566-9(3))* FastPrncil, Inc.

Thomasian, Sara. Charlie's Magical Night. Harrington, David, illus. 2007. (J). per. 11.99 *(978-1-59879-381-9(0))* Lifevest Publishing, Inc.

Thomes, William Henry. The Bushrangers a Yankee's Adventures During His Second Visit to Australia by William H Thomes. 2006. 420p. per. 26.99 *(978-1-4255-4567-3(X))* Michigan Publishing.

Thompson, Berine. Tedi the Bear & His Pals Adventure at the Zoo! 2005. 44p. per. 21.99 *(978-1-4208-1007-3(3))* AuthorHouse.

Thompson, Bill. The Legend of Gunners Cove. 2012. (ENG.). 132p. pap. 14.95 *(978-1-4327-9817-8(0))* Outskirts Pr., Inc.

Thompson, C. Michael. Twinsational. 2009. 120p. (YA). pap. 14.95 *(978-1-4327-3033-8(9))* Outskirts Pr., Inc.

Thompson, Carolyn. BJ S Bean Patch. 2013. 18p. pap. 9.99 *(978-1-62419-724-6(8))* Salem Author Services.

Thompson, Craig. Space Dumplins. 2015. lib. bdg. 26.95 *(978-0-606-37760-7(3))* Turtleback Bks.

Thompson, Deirdre. Nana, Dey, & Peanut's Adventures. 2011. 48p. pap. 15.99 *(978-1-4568-8388-1(7))* Xlibris Corp.

Thompson Ii, Roger E. A Sister's Love: A Novel. 2007. 80p. per. 8.95 *(978-0-595-44549-3(7))* iUniverse, Inc.

Thompson, Jan & Sharpe, Jaime. Amara's Magical Playhouse: The Adventure Begins. 2010. 108p. pap. 37.99 *(978-1-4520-8284-4(7))* AuthorHouse.

Thompson, Jenean. All in a Day's Play. Thompson, Jenean, illus. l.t. ed. 2005. (Illus.). 40p. (J). 14.95 *(978-1-59879-066-5(8))* Lifevest Publishing, Inc.

Thompson, Joan R. Terrible Turnoff & Me. 2006. pap. 11.95 *(978-0-595-39902-4(8),* Backinprint.com) iUniverse, Inc.

Thompson, Kate. Highway Robbery. Dress, Robert & Duddle, Johnny, illus. 2009. (ENG.). 128p. (J). (gr. 5-18). 15.99 *(978-0-06-173034-4(3),* Greenwillow Bks.) HarperCollins Pubs.

—La Musica del Tiempo. Delgado, Diana, tr. 2nd ed. 2007. (SPA., Illus.). 317p. (J). (gr. 4-7). 18.95 *(978-84-96544-97-0(4))* Roca Editorial ESP. Dist: Spanish Pubs., LLC.

Thompson, Kim. Eldritch Manor. 2013. 212p. pap. *(978-1-4596-6312-1(8))* ReadHowYouWant.com, Ltd.

Thompson, Kim Mitzo. The Wheels on the Bus. Holm, Sharon Lane, illus. 2010. (Padded Board Book W/CD Ser.). 8p. (J). (gr. k-2). bds. 10.99 incl. audio compact disk *(978-1-59922-580-7(8))* Twin Sisters IP, LLC.

Thompson, Kimberly. Toulouse Tangled up in Lights. Easey, Chris, illus. 2011. 64p. (J). 19.95 *(978-0-9818976-1-5(4))* Little Pigeon Bks.

Thompson, Lauren. Little Quack Counts. Anderson, Derek, illus. 2009. (Super Chubbies Ser.). (ENG.). 26p. (J). (gr. -1 — 1). bds. 5.99 *(978-1-4169-6093-5(7),* Little Simon) Little Simon.

—Little Quack's ABC's. Anderson, Derek, illus. 2010. (Super Chubbies Ser.). (ENG.). 26p. (J). (gr. -1 — 1). bds. 5.99 *(978-1-4169-6091-1(0),* Little Simon) Little Simon.

Thompson, Mary G. Wuftoom. 2013. (ENG.). 256p. (YA). (gr. 7). pap. 8.99 *(978-0-544-02247-8(5))* Houghton Mifflin Harcourt Publishing Co.

Thompson, Paul B. The Battle for the Brightstone: Book III of the Brightstone Saga. 2013. (Brightstone Saga Ser.). 176p. (J). 18.95 *(978-0-7660-3984-1(6))* Enslow Pubs., Inc.

Thompson-Swift, Joseph. The Adventures of Primrose Perfect. 2011. 248p. pap. *(978-1-907652-88-2(4))* Grosvenor Hse. Publishing Ltd.

Thompson, Teresa. The Adventures of Shasta & Nikki: A True Friendship. 2004. 34p. pap. 24.95 *(978-1-4137-1967-3(8))* PublishAmerica, Inc.

Thompson, Vinny. Vinny & Bud. 2009. 64p. pap. 11.99 *(978-1-4490-2551-9(X))* AuthorHouse.

Thoms, Gigi. Noble Pocket. 2016. (YA). pap. 18.99 *(978-1-4621-1773-4(2),* Horizon Pubs.) Cedar Fort, Inc./CFI Distribution.

Thomson, Carly. Truth Seekers. 2013. 60p. pap. 9.99 *(978-1-62839-189-3(8))* Salem Author Services.

Thomson, Elizabeth & Albert, Sarah. Andros: the Last Villager. 2008. 226p. pap. 17.04 *(978-1-4357-3557-6(9))* Lulu Pr., Inc.

Thomson, Rachel Starr. Theodore Pharris Saves the Universe. 2013. 176p. pap. *(978-1-927658-18-5(7))* Little Dozen Press.

Thomson, Sarah L. Deadly Flowers: A Ninja's Tale. 2016. (Ninja's Journey Ser.). (ENG., Illus.). 272p. (J). (gr. 4-9). 17.95 *(978-1-62979-214-9(4),* 1402729) Boyds Mills Pr.

—The Eureka Key. (Secrets of the Seven Ser.). (ENG.). (J). 2017. 256p. pap. 7.99 *(978-1-68119-061-7(3),* 9781681190617) 2016. 240p. 16.99 *(978-1-61963-731-3(6),* 9781619637313) Bloomsbury Publishing USA. (Bloomsbury USA Childrens).

Thomson-Swift, Joe. The Monkeyboy & the Gruffits. 2011. (Illus.). 44p. pap. *(978-1-908105-63-9(1))* Grosvenor Hse. Publishing Ltd.

—The Twig People of Mossdown Woods. 2011. (Illus.). 36p. pap. *(978-1-908105-35-6(6))* Grosvenor Hse. Publishing Ltd.

Thore, Maria Nilsson. Stay-At-Home Sammy & the Runaway Spot. 2017. (ENG.). 36p. (J). (gr. -1-3). 15.95 *(978-0-8234-3677-4(2))* Holiday Hse., Inc.

Thornburg, Michael. The Monster Kids' Adventures: The Retur. 2005. pap. 19.95 *(978-1-4137-8556-2(5))* PublishAmerica, Inc.

Thorne, K. C. The Troll of MacKinac. Johnson, Vickie, illus. 2010. 32p. pap. 13.00 *(978-1-60911-178-6(8),* Eloquent Bks.) Strategic Book Publishing & Rights Agency (SBPRA).

Thornton, Vera E. The Useless Donkey. 2007. 36p. per. 24.95 *(978-1-4241-8736-2(2))* America Star Bks.

Thorp, Gloria J. & Ruotsala, Charity Aili. Anna's Hats: Anna has a hat for every Adventure. 2009. 40p. pap. 19.49 *(978-1-4389-8967-9(9))* AuthorHouse.

Thorpe, Kiki. Disney's Kim Possible: Chapter Book, 4 vols. 2004. (ENG.). 320p. (J). (gr. 2-5). pap. 9.99 *(978-0-7868-3585-0(0))* Disney Pr.

—Far from Shore. RH Disney Staff & Christy, Jana, illus. 2015. (Never Girls Ser.: 8). (ENG.). 128p. (J). (gr. 1-4). lib. bdg. 12.99 *(978-0-7364-8166-3(4),* RH/Disney) Random Hse. Children's Bks.

Thorpe, Roslyn C. Rayray's Amazing Dream: An Adventurous Week. 2012. 24p. pap. 15.99 *(978-1-4771-5366-6(7))* Xlibris Corp.

Thoughts Staff. PNUT BUDDY & JUDDY (the adventures Of) #1. 2005. 38p. (J). pap. 16.99 *(978-1-4116-2574-7(9))* Lulu Pr., Inc.

A Thousand Pieces of You. 2014. (Firebird Ser.: 1). (ENG.). 368p. (YA). (gr. 9). 17.99 *(978-0-06-227896-8(7))* HarperCollins Pubs.

Thrasher, Amanda M. A Fairy Match in the Mushroom Patch. 2013. (ENG., Illus.). 162p. (J). (gr. 2-4). pap. 7.99 *(978-0-9888568-1-3(6))* Rising Phoenix Pr.

—The Ghost of Whispering Willow. Dunigan, Anne, ed. 2013. (ENG., Illus.). 258p. (J). (gr. 4-7). pap. 10.95 *(978-0-615-74990-7(9))* Rising Phoenix Pr.

—The Ghost of Whispering Willow. 2012. 222p. 26.50 *(978-1-61897-881-3(0));* pap. 13.95 *(978-1-61897-630-7(3))* Strategic Book Publishing & Rights Agency (SBPRA). (Strategic Bk. Publishing).

—Mischief in the Mushroom Patch. 2013. (ENG., Illus.). 146p. (J). (gr. 2-4). pap. 7.99 *(978-0-9888568-0-6(8))* Rising Phoenix Pr.

Threatt, Cedric, Sr. A Boy Called Short Rock: The Early Years. 2007. (ENG.). 115p. (J). pap. 9.95 *(978-0-9720543-4-8(0))* Threatt, Cedric L.

Thwin, Soe Soe. The Story of Inle in the Galapagos. 2009. 44p. pap. 15.95 *(978-1-60860-361-9(X),* Strategic Bk. Publishing) Strategic Book Publishing & Rights Agency (SBPRA).

Thyroff, Brad. Albert & Freddie. Gillen, Rosemarie, illus. 2013. 24p. pap. 9.99 *(978-1-61286-190-6(3))* Avid Readers Publishing Group.

Tibke, Terry. Upgrader: Re-Engineered. 2011. 137p. (YA). pap. 6.99 *(978-1-933925-32-5(9),* Actionopolis) Komikwerks, LLC.

Tibo, Gilles. Le Grand Voyage de Monsieur. 2004. (FRE., Illus.). (J). (gr. k-3). spiral bd. *(978-0-616-14600-2(0))* Canadian National Institute for the Blind/Institut National Canadien pour les Aveugles.

Tidball, Lee. Windfork Secrets. 2013. 256p. pap. *(978-1-927384-12-1(5))* Zeta Comics.

Tidwell, Mae B. & Hancock, Vicki. Kyle Wants to Be a Monkey, 1 vol. 2009. 24p. pap. 24.95 *(978-1-60749-751-6(4))* America Star Bks.

Tieri, Frank. Weapon X: The Underground, Vol. 2. Youngquist, Jeff, ed. Jeanty, Georges, illus. 2004. (X-Men Ser.). 184p. pap. 19.99 *(978-0-7851-1253-2(7))* Marvel Worldwide, Inc.

Tiernan, Cate. Darkness Falls. 2012. (Immortal Beloved Ser.: 2). (ENG.). 416p. (YA). (gr. 7-17). pap. 8.99 *(978-0-316-03594-1(7),* Poppy) Little, Brown Bks. for Young Readers.

Tierney, John. Jack, Tommy & the Phoenix Street Firefighters. Algar, James, illus. 2012. 70p. pap. 11.99 *(978-1-78035-416-3(9),* Fastprint Publishing) Upfront Publishing Ltd. GBR. Dist: Printondemand-worldwide.com.

Tierney, Melissa. Elly's True Colors. 2009. 32p. pap. 14.99 *(978-1-4389-3901-8(9))* AuthorHouse.

Till, Danelle. Max's Moving Adventure: A Coloring Book for Kids on the Move. Spooner, Joe, illus. 2006. 52p. (J). 8.95 *(978-0-912301-64-8(3))* First Bks.

Till, Nan. Solomon Finds His Spots. 2009. 24p. (J). pap. 15.95 *(978-1-4327-5134-0(4))* Outskirts Pr., Inc.

Tiller, Steve. La Colonia de Arco Iris. Cremeans, Robert, illus. Date not set. (SPA.). (J). 15.95 *(978-1-932317-02-2(3))* Right Stuff Kids Bks.

Tilley. Damaged. 2011. (ENG.). 260p. (gr. 9-13). pap. 11.95 *(978-988-18967-0-4(3))* Haven Bks.

Tilley, Adrian. The Spider's Web. 2010. (ENG.). 232p. (YA). (gr. 4-7). pap. 11.95 *(978-988-18094-5-2(2))* Haven Bks.

Tilley, Steve, et al. Airlock: Arrival. 2004. 80p. pap. *(978-1-84427-047-7(5))* Scripture Union.

Tillson, M. C. Secret of Bete Grise Bay: A Michigan Lighthouse Adventure. Bailey, Lisa, illus. 2008. (ENG.). (J). (gr. 1-5). pap. 9.95 *(978-0-9764824-2-0(8))* A & M Writing and Publishing.

Tillworth, Mary. All Bottled up! (Shimmer & Shine) Laviosa, Mattia Francesco, illus. 2017. (Pictureback(R) Ser.). (ENG.). 16p. (J). (gr. -1-2). pap. 5.99 ***(978-1-5247-1718-6(5),*** Random Hse. Bks. for Young Readers) Random Hse. Children's Bks.

—Boots & Dora Forever! (Dora & Friends) Aikins, David, illus. 2016. (Pictureback(R) Ser.). (ENG.). 16p. (J). (gr. -1-2). 4.99 *(978-0-553-53836-6(5),* Random Hse. Bks. for Young Readers) Random Hse. Children's Bks.

—Busy as a Bee! Moroney, Christopher, illus. 2012. (Write-On/Wipe-off Activity Book Ser.). (ENG.). 12p. (J). (gr. k — 1). bds. 9.99 *(978-0-307-93011-8(4),* Golden Bks.) Random Hse. Children's Bks.

—Dora in Wonderland. 2014. (Dora the Explorer 8X8 Ser.). lib. bdg. 13.55 *(978-0-606-35557-5(X))* Turtleback Bks.

—A Fairytale Adventure. 2014. (Dora the Explorer 8X8 Ser.). lib. bdg. 13.55 *(978-0-606-36010-4(7))* Turtleback Bks.

—A Fairytale Adventure (Dora the Explorer) Jackson, Mike, illus. 2014. (Pictureback(R) Ser.). (ENG.). 24p. (J). (gr. -1-2). 3.99 *(978-0-385-37443-9(7),* Random Hse. Bks. for Young Readers) Random Hse. Children's Bks.

—Meet My Friends! (Dora & Friends) Aikins, David, illus. 2014. (Step into Reading Ser.). (ENG.). 24p. (J). (gr. -1-1). 3.99 *(978-0-385-38462-9(9),* Random Hse. Bks. for Young Readers) Random Hse. Children's Bks.

Tillworth, Mary. Rusty Rocks! (Rusty Rivets) Aikins, Dave, illus. 2017. (Pictureback(R) Ser.). (ENG.). 24p. (J). (gr. -1-2). pap. 5.99 ***(978-1-5247-1721-6(5),*** Random Hse. Bks. for Young Readers) Random Hse. Children's Bks.

Tilson, Gina L. Patches: Adventures of a Country Cavalier. 2011. 48p. pap. 9.99 *(978-1-4567-6386-2(5))* AuthorHouse.

Tim, Tornado. Tornado Chaser: Life on the Edge. 2003. 92p. (YA). pap. 8.95 *(978-0-595-27381-2(5),* Writers Club Pr.) iUniverse, Inc.

Timberlake, Amy. One Came Home. 2014. (ENG., Illus.). 272p. (J). (gr. 5-7). 7.99 *(978-0-375-87345-4(7),* Yearling) Random Hse. Children's Bks.

Timberlake, Gail. The Rescue of the Lady's Slipper. 2010. 52p. pap. 22.49 *(978-1-4490-8503-2(2))* AuthorHouse.

Time Soldiers Book: Rex. 2003. tchr. ed. *(978-1-929945-30-6(2))* Big Guy Bks., Inc.

Time Soldiers Book Vol. 2: Rex 2. 2003. tchr. ed. *(978-1-929945-31-3(0))* Big Guy Bks., Inc.

Tingwald, Jady Ann. The Adventures of Rady Red Comb. Powell, James, illus. 2005. 33p. (J). (gr. 1-6). 9.00 *(978-0-9706728-1-0(0))* New Millenium Pr., The.

Tintera, Amy. Avenged. (Ruined Ser.: 2). (YA). (gr. 8). 2018. (ENG.). 432p. pap. 9.99 ***(978-0-06-239664-8(1))*** 2017. 416p. 17.99 *(978-0-06-239663-1(3))* HarperCollins Pubs. (HarperTeen).

—Rebel. (Reboot Ser.: 2). 352p. (YA). (gr. 8). 2015. (ENG.). pap. 9.99 *(978-0-06-221711-0(9))* 2014. pap. 12.00 *(978-0-06-233790-0(4))* HarperCollins Pubs. (HarperTeen).

—Reboot. 2013. (Reboot Ser.: 1). (ENG.). 384p. (YA). (gr. 8). 17.99 *(978-0-06-221707-3(0),* HarperTeen) HarperCollins Pubs.

Tinti, Natalie. Magic in Us. the Healing Circle, bks. 2, vol. 2. Tinti, Natalie, illus. 2013. (Sewing a Friendship Ser.). (ENG., Illus.). 96p. (J). 25.95 *(978-0-9830884-4-8(6))* Tintinatie Publishing Hse.

—Magic in Us. the Healing Circle: The Healing Circle, bks. 2, vol. 2. Tinti, Natalie, illus. 2013. (Sewing a Friendship Ser.: 3). (ENG., Illus.). 96p. (J). pap. 12.95 *(978-0-9830884-0-0(3))* Tintinatie Publishing Hse.

—Magic in Us. the Power of Imagination: The Power of Imagination, bks. 1, vol. 2. T, N., illus. ed. 2013. (Sewing a Friendship Ser.). (ENG.). 116p. (J). pap. 12.95 *(978-0-9842625-3-3(9))* Tintinatie Publishing Hse.

Tipton, Annie. Diary of a Real Payne Book 3: Oh Baby! 2014. (ENG.). 192p. (J). pap. 5.99 *(978-1-62836-864-2(0),* Barbour Bks.) Barbour Publishing, Inc.

Tipton, Scott. Teenage Mutant Ninja Turtles: New Animated Adventures: Volume 3, 1 vol. 2016. (Teenage Mutant Ninja Turtles: New Animated Adventures Ser.). (ENG.). 24p. (J). lib. bdg. 24.21 *(978-1-61479-461-5(8),* Graphic Planet) Magic Wagon.

Tirado, Raquel. That Sticky Cat. 2012. 20p. pap. 17.99 *(978-1-4685-8857-6(5))* AuthorHouse.

Tisha Admire Duncan. My Dirty Cat Mutt. 2009. 28p. pap. 17.99 *(978-1-4389-5684-8(3))* AuthorHouse.

Titelman, Becky. The Wonky Witch & the Witching Well. 2009. 364p. pap. 19.99 *(978-1-4490-2673-8(7))* AuthorHouse.

Tobin, Paul. The Genius Factor - How to Capture an Invisible Cat. Lafontaine, Thierry, illus. 2016. (ENG.). 272p. (J). 16.99 *(978-1-61963-840-2(1),* 9781619638402, Bloomsbury USA Childrens) Bloomsbury Publishing USA.

—The Genius Factor: How to Capture an Invisible Cat. Lafontaine, Thierry, illus. 2017. (ENG.). 288p. (J). pap. 7.99 *(978-1-68119-278-9(0),* 9781681192789, Bloomsbury USA Childrens) Bloomsbury Publishing USA.

—How to Outsmart a Billion Robot Bees. Lafontaine, Thierry & Abey, Katie, illus. 2017. (ENG.). 320p. (J). 16.99 *(978-1-61963-897-6(5),* 9781619638976, Bloomsbury USA Childrens) Bloomsbury Publishing USA.

Todd, Anne. Teddy Powers: The Stone Keepers. 2012. 394p. pap. 13.99 *(978-1-938993-00-8(4))* Keogh, Anne.

Todd-Stanton, Joe, illus. The Secret of Black Rock. 2017. (ENG.). 40p. (J). (gr. -1-2). 16.95 *(978-1-911171-25-6(9))*

Flying Eye Bks. GBR. Dist: Consortium Bk. Sales & Distribution.

Todorov, Boriana & Todorov, Vladimir. The Moon Rock. 2007. (ENG., Illus.). 110p. (J). (gr. 2-6). 19.95 *(978-1-894965-77-4(9))* Simply Read Bks. CAN. Dist: Ingram Publisher Services.

Toft, Julie. Blot on the Landscape. 2010. (Illus.). 48p. pap. 10.49 *(978-1-4490-6453-2(1))* AuthorHouse.

Tofte, Mavis. Doogie Dork & Marta. 2005. (Illus.). 64p. (J). per. 5.75 *(978-0-9709906-4-8(2))* Creative Quill Publishing, Inc.

—Doogie Dork & the Storm. Tofte, Mavis, illus. 2006. (Illus.). 64p. (J). per. 6.75 *(978-0-9709906-5-5(0))* Creative Quill Publishing, Inc.

—Doogie Dork's Wish. Tofte, Mavis, illus. 2003. (Illus.). (J). per. 5.75 *(978-0-9709906-2-4(6))* Creative Quill Publishing, Inc.

—Franny Frumpel's Secret. 2007. (Illus.). 64p. (J). per. 6.00 *(978-0-9709906-7-9(7))* Creative Quill Publishing, Inc.

Tolkien, J. R. R. Las Aventuras de Tom Bombadil/the Adventures of Tom Bombadil: Y Otros Poemas de el Libro Rojo/and Other Verses from the Red Book. 2006. (SPA., Illus.). 157p. 22.95 *(978-84-450-7194-6(7))* Minotauro Ediciones ESP. Dist: Planeta Publishing Corp.

—Senhor dos Aneis, Vol. 3. pap. 34.95 *(978-85-336-1339-3(3))* Livraria Martins Editora BRA. Dist: Distribooks, Inc.

Tolkien, Michael. Woodsy. 2014. 78p. pap. *(978-1-910162-44-6(2))* Legend Pr.

Tolson, Aaron J. Washington Putter. 2005. 248p. (YA). per. 22.00 *(978-1-58982-243-6(9)*, Bedside Bks.) American Bk. Publishing Group.

Tomasi-Dubois, Mary. Danger in the Jeweled City: A Matt & Heather Thriller. 2007. 188p. (YA). per. 15.95 *(978-0-9798633-5-6(X))* Robertson Publishing.

Tomasso, Phillip. King Gauthier & the Little Dragon Slayer. l.t. ed. 2003. (Illus.). 61p. (J). per. *(978-0-9740833-5-3(6))* Port Town Publishing.

Tombo. The Magic Nickel: A Fable about an Unhappy Salesman, a Sad Retired Person, & an Invisible Monster. 2012. 26p. pap. 16.99 *(978-1-4624-0280-9(1)*, Inspiring Voices) Author Solutions, Inc.

Tomlin, James C. The Adventures of I Am, I Can & I Feel: A Journey into Positive. 2008. 126p. (J). pap. 11.95 *(978-0-7414-4840-8(8))* Infinity Publishing.

Tomlin, S. E. Children of Baimbough Forest. 2012. (ENG.). 79p. pap. 17.95 *(978-1-4787-1735-5(1))*; pap. 9.95 *(978-1-4327-9857-4(X))* Outskirts Pr., Inc.

Tomlinson, Jill. The Otter Who Wanted to Know. Howard, Paul, illus. 2014. (ENG., Illus.). 96p. (J). (gr. -1-2). pap. 8.99 *(978-1-4052-7194-3(9))* Egmont Bks., Ltd. GBR. Dist: Independent Pubs. Group.

tomlinson, rick. The Adventures of Bob & Mr. Ant the MAZE. 2010. 84p. pap. 17.00 *(978-0-557-58728-5(X))* Lulu Pr., Inc.

Tompkins, Robyn Lee. Miss Molly's Adventure in the Park: Another Great Adventure Brought to You by Miss Molly & Her Dog Reyburn. 10 vols. Carson, Shawn K., illus. l.t. ed. 2005. (ENG.). 60p. (J). per. *(978-0-9741647-6-2(3))* NRG Pubns.

—Miss Molly's Adventure on the Farm: Another great adventure brought to you by Miss Molly & her dog Reyburn. Carson, Shawn, illus. 2006. (J). per. *(978-0-9741647-7-9(1))* NRG Pubns.

Tony Hawk's 900 Revolution. 2013. (Tony Hawk's 900 Revolution Ser.). (ENG.). 128p. (gr. 3-4). 319.80 *(978-1-4342-4110-8(6)*, Tony Hawk's 900 Revolution) Stone Arch Bks.

Toombs, Tom. The Big Camping Adventure: Little Tommy Learns Lessons from the Great Outdoors. Wells-Smith, Abby, illus. 2013. 32p. pap. 12.95 *(978-1-61314-035-2(5))* Innovo Publishing, LLC.

Tooth, Lucy. Star the Tooth Fairy Wants to Know If You Need Braces? 2009. 36p. 16.95 *(978-0-557-07542-3(4))* Lulu Pr., Inc.

Tooty. Patches in Winter. 2012. 32p. pap. 9.00 *(978-1-4349-7288-0(7)*, RoseDog Bks.) Dorrance Publishing Co., Inc.

Top That, ed. Sammy the Snake. 2008. (Story Book Ser.). 18p. (J). (gr. -1). *(978-1-84666-541-7(8)*, Tide Mill Pr.) Top That! Publishing PLC.

Toral, Miguel A. Babu Goes Back to the Zoo. 2009. 32p. pap. 15.70 *(978-1-4389-6330-3(0))* AuthorHouse.

Torbert, Wayne E. Twelve for Thebes, a Tale of Ancient Greece. Torbert, Wayne E., illus. 2009. (Illus.). 82p. pap. 8.95 *(978-1-936051-73-1(7))* Peppertree Pr., The.

Torday, Piers. The Last Wild. 2014. (Last Wild Ser.: 1). (ENG., Illus.). 336p. (J). (gr. 3-7). 16.99 *(978-0-670-01554-2(7)*, Viking Books for Young Readers) Penguin Young Readers Group.

Toreeva, Natalia G. Greg & the Sea Monster. 2011. 34p. pap. 14.50 *(978-1-61204-332-6(1)*, Eloquent Bks.) Strategic Book Publishing & Rights Agency (SBPRA).

Toriyama, Akira. Dragon Ball: Chapter Book, Vol. 9. Toriyama, Akira, illus. 2010. (ENG., Illus.). 80p. (J). pap. 4.99 *(978-1-4215-3125-0(9))* Viz Media.

—Dragon Ball Full Color Freeza Arc, Volume 4. 2016. (Dragon Ball Freeza Ser.: 4). lib. bdg. 33.05 *(978-0-606-39489-5(3))* Turtleback Bks.

—Dragon Ball Z, Vol. 26. Toriyama, Akira, illus. 2006. (ENG., Illus.). 208p. pap. 9.99 *(978-1-4215-0636-4(X))* Viz Media.

—Fight to the Finish! Toriyama, Akira, illus. 2010. (Dragon Ball Ser.: 8). (ENG., Illus.). 80p. (J). pap. 4.99 *(978-1-4215-3124-3(0))* Viz Media.

—Strongest under the Heavens. Toriyama, Akira, illus. 2010. (Dragon Ball Ser.: 10). (ENG., Illus.). 80p. (J). pap. 4.99 *(978-1-4215-3126-7(7))* Viz Media.

Torphy, William & Gowack, Paul. Snakebite. 2005. (Illus.). 115p. (J). per. 12.95 *(978-0-9749502-4-2(6))* Ithuriel's Spear.

Torres, J. The Collected Alison Dare Little Miss Adventures. Bone, J., illus. 2005. (J). *(978-1-4156-1359-7(1))* Oni Pr., Inc.

Torres, J., et al. Teen Titans GO!, 1 vol. 2014. (Teen Titans GO! Ser.). (ENG., Illus.). 32p. (gr. 2-3). 67.80 *(978-1-4342-9516-3(8))*; 90.40 *(978-1-4342-8765-6(3))* Stone Arch Bks.

Torres, Mario J. The Incredible Adventures of Kaplan & Dylan: Book One: Present, 1 vol. 2009. 159p. pap. 24.95 *(978-1-4489-9513-4(2))* PublishAmerica, Inc.

Tossell, David H. Charlie & Chippo Meet a Ghost. Pritchard, Louise, illus. 2012. 24p. pap. *(978-1-908773-25-8(1))* Iponymous Publishing, Ltd.

Tosten, Sharon. Troy's Amazing Universe: K for Karate. 2006. 144p. per. 13.95 *(978-0-9743185-2-3(3))* Booklocker.com, Inc.

Tóth-Jones, Dee S. The Street Cats of Marrakech. Stevenson, Seline, illus. 2013. 34p. pap. *(978-1-908794-08-6(9))* Chiaroscuro Bks.

Toufexis, George. MONSTER MASH-Up — Rise of the Predators. 2014. (ENG., Illus.). 48p. (J). (gr. 4). pap. 4.99 *(978-0-486-49224-7(9))* Dover Pubns., Inc.

Tougas, Shelley. Finders Keepers. 2015. (ENG.). 288p. (J). (gr. 3-7). 16.99 *(978-1-59643-990-0(4)*, 9781596439900) Roaring Brook Pr.

Touma, Patricia. Happy Times, Book: Ish & Mish Go to the Carnival. 2007. 56p. per. 9.95 *(978-1-59899-093-5(4))* Long Dash Publishing.

—Happy Times, the Adventures of Ish & Mish Vol. 1: Ish & Mish Go to the Circus. 2005. per. 7.00 *(978-1-58396-873-4(3))* Blue Unicorn Edition, LLC.

Toussaint, Simone. Sharing My Shoes. 2010. 28p. pap. 9.95 *(978-1-4327-5701-4(6))* Outskirts Pr., Inc.

Tower, Cory L. The Adventures of Courtney, Morgan & the Magic Toy Bears Book 2: In the Beginning. 2012. 24p. pap. 24.95 *(978-1-4626-8395-6(9))* America Star Bks.

Townsan, Judy. The Wishing Flower, 1 vol. Rosado, Michael, illus. 2009. 13p. pap. 24.95 *(978-1-61546-179-0(5))* America Star Bks.

Townsend, Amber C. The Hungry Chickens. 2007. (Illus.). (J). per. 7.95 *(978-0-9801297-4-8(5))* G Publishing LLC.

Townsend, Charlene. The Trap & the Trip. 2013. 90p. pap. 8.99 *(978-1-4808-0219-3(0))* Archway Publishing.

Townsend, Kari. Fused. 2010. (ENG.). 208p. (J). (gr. 5-7). pap. 7.99 *(978-1-4022-4042-3(2)*, Sourcebooks Jabberwocky) Sourcebooks, Inc.

Townsend, Marjorie. Wee's Moving Day. 2008. 24p. pap. 14.95 *(978-1-4327-2828-1(8))* Outskirts Pr., Inc.

Townsend, Vanessa. What's in Molly's.... Bedroom? 2012. (Illus.). 24p. pap. 15.99 *(978-1-4797-3248-7(6))* Xlibris Corp.

Townson, Hazel. Dark Deeds at Deathwood. 2006. (Deathwood Letters Ser.). (ENG., Illus.). 92p. (J). (gr. 4-7). per. 8.99 *(978-1-84270-486-8(9))* Andersen Pr. GBR. Dist: Independent Pubs. Group.

Towson, Robert. The Wrong Bus, 1 vol. 2010. 34p. 24.95 *(978-1-4489-4345-6(0))* PublishAmerica, Inc.

ToyBox Innovations, creator. The Curse of the Black Pearl. 2006. (Pirates of the Caribbean Ser.). (ENG., Illus.). 24p. (J). (gr. -1-3). pap. *(978-0-7634-2176-2(6))* Walt Disney Records.

—Disney Pixar's Toy Story: Read-along. 2006. (Disney's Read Along Ser.). (ENG., Illus.). 24p. (J). (gr. -1-3). pap. *(978-0-7634-2179-3(0))* Walt Disney Records.

—Disney Princess: Cinderella/Snow White/Sleeping Beauty. unabr. abr. ed. 2005. (Disney Princess Ser.). (J). pap. *(978-0-7634-1150-3(7))* Walt Disney Records.

Toybox Innovations, creator. Pirates of the Caribbean: the Complete Collection: The Curse of the Black Pearl/Dead Man's Chest/at World's End. 2007. (Disney's Read along Collection). (ENG., Illus.). (J). (gr. -1-3). pap. *(978-0-7634-2194-6(4))* Walt Disney Records.

Toybox Innovations & Toybox Innovations, creators. At Worlds End. 2007. (Pirates of the Caribbean Ser.). (ENG., Illus.). (J). (gr. -1-3). pap. *(978-0-7634-2186-1(3))* Walt Disney Records.

Toybox Innovations Staff & Toybox Innovations, creators. Disney Read along Little Mermaid Collection, 3 vols. 2009. (ENG., Illus.). (J). (gr. -1-1). *(978-0-7634-1202-9(3))* Walt Disney Records.

Tozer, S. J. MI29: Mouseweb International to the Rescue! Salaman, Rosy, illus. 2014. (ENG.). 80p. (J). pap. 12.95 *(978-1-84905-496-6(7)*, 7004) Kingsley, Jessica Pubs. GBR. Dist: Macmillan Distribution Ltd.

Tozier, Christopher. Olivia Brophie & the Pearl of Tagelus. 2012. (ENG.). 208p. (J). pap. 12.95 *(978-1-56164-519-0(2))* Pineapple Pr., Inc.

—Olivia Brophie & the Sky Island. 2014. (ENG.). 304p. (J). pap. 12.95 *(978-1-56164-680-7(6))* Pineapple Pr., Inc.

Trafton, Jennifer. The Rise & Fall of Mount Majestic. Helquist, Brett, illus. 2011. (ENG.). 352p. (J). (gr. 3-7). 6.99 *(978-0-14-241934-2(6)*, Puffin Books) Penguin Young Readers Group.

The Trail of the Wooden Horse. 2007. 32p. pap. 4.50 *(978-0-8341-2284-0(7)*, 083-412-2847) Beacon Hill Pr. of Kansas City.

The TrailFolk of Xunar-kun: Book Two in the Tellings of Xunar-kun. 2008. (YA). 30.95 *(978-0-9768585-5-3(X))*; pap. 16.95 *(978-0-9768585-4-6(1))* Howe, Tina Field.

Tran, Hensley. Agatha's Stolen Curve. 2013. 80p. (gr. 4-6). 18.95 *(978-1-4759-7312-9(8))*; pap. 8.95 *(978-1-4759-7310-5(1))* iUniverse, Inc.

The Transformation. 2003. (J). per. *(978-1-57657-863-6(1))* Paradise Pr., Inc.

Travers, James A. Kitten & the Barn. 2008. 44p. pap. 24.95 *(978-1-4241-8771-3(0))* America Star Bks.

Travis, Alva. Secret of the Hidden Chamber. 2006. pap. 16.95 *(978-1-4241-2071-0(3))* PublishAmerica, Inc.

Trayer, Edward. The Struggles of Felicity Brady. 2004. (YA). per. 14.95 *(978-1-59571-043-7(4))* Word Association Pubs.

Trayer, Edward H. Struggles of Felicity Brady: Articulus Quest. 2005. (YA). per. 14.95 *(978-1-59571-091-8(4))* Word Association Pubs.

Treadway, Clifton. Benny & Bugsy. 2013. 36p. pap. 15.95 *(978-1-4624-0492-6(8)*, Inspiring Voices) Author Solutions, Inc.

Treasure Found. 2005. 32p. (J). 12.99 *(978-0-9758709-2-1(0)*, A.W.A. Gang) Journey Stone Creations, LLC.

Treasures. 2005. (J). 6.50 *(978-0-9776472-0-0(X))* MythSeries.

Trechsel, Kelli. A Whale Set Sail. Renfroe, Leisa, illus. 2011. 28p. (J). pap. 14.95 *(978-1-936085-42-2(9))* DSA Publishing & Design, Inc.

Trees, Annie Mae. The Last Days of Summer: A Mystery of Two Children & Their Grandma Set Out on an Adventure. 2012. 40p. pap. 24.95 *(978-1-4626-6103-9(3))* America Star Bks.

Trelogan, Stephanie. Mask Parade: Forest Animals. Armstrong, Katharine, illus. 2008. (ENG.). 14p. (J). (gr. -1). 12.95 *(978-1-58117-790-9(9)*, Intervisual/Piggy Toes) Bendon, Inc.

Tremblay, Alain Ulysse. Le Don de Jonathan. Malepart, Celine, tr. 2003. (Roman Jeunesse Ser.). (FRE., Illus.). 96p. (J). (gr. 4-7). pap. *(978-2-89021-635-8(7))* Diffusion du livre Mirabel (DLM).

Tremblay, Amanda. The Tornado Trial. 2010. 65p. pap. 12.00 *(978-0-557-14051-0(X))* Lulu Pr., Inc.

Trenchard, Robert. The Famous Frog Fiasco. 2008. 265p. (J). pap. 13.99 *(978-0-615-20974-6(2))* Soxwings Publishing.

Trent, Rodney. Sadie Mae's Big Adventure. 2012. 28p. pap. 19.99 *(978-1-4772-6536-9(8))* AuthorHouse.

Trent, Sandy Chase. Tommy's Amazing Journey: The Cat that Could Fly. 2011. 16p. pap. 24.95 *(978-1-4626-2363-1(8))* America Star Bks.

Trest, Candace D. Zack & Tripp & the Indian Village. 2007. 64p. per. 9.99 *(978-1-60477-526-6(2))* Salem Author Services.

Trevayne, Emma. Gamescape - Overworld. 2016. (Gamescape Ser.: 1). 416p. (YA). (gr. 9). 17.99 *(978-0-06-240876-1(3)*, Greenwillow Bks.) HarperCollins Pubs.

—The House of Months & Years. 2017. (ENG., Illus.). 288p. (J). (gr. 3-7). 16.99 *(978-1-4814-6255-6(5)*, Simon & Schuster Bks. For Young Readers) Simon & Schuster Bks. For Young Readers.

Trevethan, Glenn A. The Adventures of Sammi Snake: Sammi's Coat. 2012. 24p. pap. 13.97 *(978-1-61897-926-1(4)*, Strategic Bk. Publishing) Strategic Book Publishing & Rights Agency (SBPRA).

Trevino, David. A Colorful Carnival of Kids in the Kingdom of Marbles: Mission #1 the Cemetery Ghost. 2011. 126p. pap. 19.95 *(978-1-4626-1087-7(0))* America Star Bks.

Tribolet, Leslie L. Danny's Tale: Adventures of an Arabian Horse in his Own Words. 2010. (Illus.). 112p. 24.95 *(978-1-4490-6065-7(X))* AuthorHouse.

Triffo, Kahini H. Relentless Tears. 2011. 108p. (gr. 10-12). pap. 11.92 *(978-1-4269-6288-2(6))* Trafford Publishing.

Trilling, Richard J. More Stories of Stephanie & Friends: Volume 2 in the Stephanie Stories. 2011. 64p. pap. 19.50 *(978-1-61204-034-9(9)*, Eloquent Bks.) Strategic Book Publishing & Rights Agency (SBPRA).

Trimble, Tonya. Curiosity, with a Capital S. Enik, Ted, illus. 2011. 144p. (J). pap. 9.95 *(978-0-9816453-9-1(9))*; 16.95 *(978-0-9829421-5-4(X))* Tell Me Pr., LLC.

Trine, Greg. The Brotherhood of the Traveling Underpants. Montijo, Rhode, illus. 7th ed. 2009. (Melvin Beederman, Superhero Ser.: 7). (ENG.). 144p. (J). (gr. 2-5). pap. 8.99 *(978-0-8050-8163-3(1)*, 9780805081633) Square Fish.

—Wyatt Burp Rides Again. Dormer, Frank W., illus. 2012. (Adventures of Jo Schmo Ser.: 2). (ENG.). 112p. (J). (gr. 1-4). 12.99 *(978-0-547-80795-9(3))* Houghton Mifflin Harcourt Publishing Co.

Tripp, Ben. The Accidental Highwayman: Being the Tale of Kit Bristol, His Horse Midnight, a Mysterious Princess, & Sundry Magical Persons Besides. 2014. (ENG., Illus.). 304p. (YA). (gr. 6). 17.99 *(978-0-7653-3549-4(2)*, Tor Teen) Doherty, Tom Assocs., LLC.

Trivette, Donna K. One Special Christmas. 2012. 44p. pap. 24.95 *(978-1-4626-9363-4(6))* America Star Bks.

Trod, Mariano, et al, illus. The Brilliant Dr. Wogan. 2007. (Choose Your Own Adventure Ser.: No. 17). 112p. (J). (gr. 4-7). per. 6.99 *(978-1-933390-17-8(4)*, CHC:17) Chooseco LLC.

Trooboff, Rhoda. Punkinhead's Veggie Adventure: And the Strange Contraption in the Kitchen. Easton, Susan, illus. Rosenbaum, Elizabeth, photos by. 2013. (ENG.). 56p. (J). (gr. -1). pap. 15.00 *(978-0-9773536-7-5(2))* Transigar Co. LLC.

The Troubles of Johnny Cannon. 2014. (ENG., Illus.). 304p. (J). (gr. 3-7). 16.99 *(978-1-4814-0003-9(7)*, Simon & Schuster Bks. For Young Readers) Simon & Schuster Bks. For Young Readers.

Trout, Holly Christian. The Firefly Who Lost Her Way. 2013. 24p. pap. 24.95 *(978-1-62709-594-5(2))* America Star Bks.

Trout, Richard. Czar of Alaska: The Cross of Charlemagne, 1 vol. 2005. (MacGregor Family Adventure Ser.: 4). (ENG.). 256p. (YA). (gr. k-3). 16.99 *(978-1-58980-328-2(0))* Pelican Publishing Co., Inc.

—Devil's Breath Volcano, 1 vol. 2008. (MacGregor Family Adventure Ser.: 6). (ENG., Illus.). 208p. (YA). (gr. 6-10). 16.99 *(978-1-58980-558-3(5))* Pelican Publishing Co., Inc.

—Eclipse of the Jaguar, 1 vol. 2011. (ENG., Illus.). 224p. (YA). (gr. 8-12). 16.99 *(978-1-58980-872-0(X))* Pelican Publishing Co., Inc.

—Sign of the Dragon, 1 vol. 2007. (MacGregor Family Adventure Ser.: 5). (ENG.). 272p. (YA). (gr. 5-12). 16.99 *(978-1-58980-476-0(7))* Pelican Publishing Co., Inc.

Trout, Richard E. Cayman Gold: Lost Treasure of Devils Grotto, 1 vol. 2005. (MacGregor Family Adventure Ser.: 1). (ENG., Illus.). 224p. (YA). (gr. 5-12). 15.95 *(978-1-58980-323-7(X))* Pelican Publishing Co., Inc.

Trowell, Michelle. Pilot Your Own Deep-Sea Submarine. Dronsfield, Paul, illus. 2007. 22p. (J). (gr. -1-3). *(978-1-84666-352-9(0)*, Tide Mill Pr.) Top That! Publishing PLC.

Truax, Lois. Grandmothers Are Magic. 2010. 28p. pap. 5.95 *(978-1-935355-01-4(5))* New Shelves Bks.

Truckey, Don. The Adventures of Caraway Kim... Southpaw. Macintyre, R P, ed. 2006. (ENG.). 192p. pap. 10.95 *(978-1-894345-90-3(8))* Thistledown Pr., Ltd. CAN. Dist: Univ. of Toronto Pr.

True, J. J. Billy Brite: Africa & Beyond. 2011. (Illus.). 112p. pap. 14.03 *(978-1-4567-7281-9(3))* AuthorHouse.

True, John Preston. The Iron Star. 2007. 88p. per. *(978-1-4068-1787-4(2))* Echo Library.

—The Iron Star. 2004. reprint ed. pap. 15.95 *(978-1-4191-6767-6(7))*; pap. 1.99 *(978-1-4192-6767-3(1))* Kessinger Publishing, LLC.

Trussell-Cullen, Alan. The Lonely Penguin's Blog, 1 vol. 2013. (Fiction Readers Ser.). (ENG., Illus.). 28p. (J). (gr. 2-2). pap. 6.99 *(978-1-4333-5559-2(0))* Shell Educational Publishing.

Tsang, Evonne. Kung Fu Masters, No. 12. Martinez, Alitha E., illus. 2009. (Twisted Journeys (r) Ser.: 12). (ENG.). 112p. (J). (gr. 4-7). 27.93 *(978-0-8225-8878-8(1)*, Graphic Universe™) Lerner Publishing Group.

Tsavalas, Helena Macree. The Dazzling Beast. 2007. 56p. per. 10.00 *(978-1-4257-4295-9(5))* Xlibris Corp.

Tsong, Jing Jing. Sam Surfs. 2010. 20p. (J). pap. 7.95 *(978-1-933067-33-9(0))* Beachhouse Publishing, LLC.

Tubb, Kristin O'Donnell. The 13th Sign. 2013. (ENG.). 272p. (J). (gr. 5-9). 16.99 *(978-0-312-58352-1(4)*, 9780312583521) Feiwel & Friends.

—The 13th Sign. 2014. (ENG.). 288p. (J). (gr. 5-9). pap. 9.99 *(978-1-250-05059-5(6)*, 9781250050595) Square Fish.

Tuchman, Lauryn & Silverhardt, Lauryn. A Visit to the Firehouse. Craig, Karen, illus. 2009. (Blue's Clues Ser.). (ENG.). 24p. (J). (gr. -1-2). pap. 3.99 *(978-1-4169-7193-1(9)*, Simon Spotlight/Nickelodeon) Simon Spotlight/Nickelodeon.

Tuck Everlasting. 8.97 *(978-0-13-437487-1(8))* Prentice Hall PTR.

Tuck, Helen. The House at the Bend of Contently Creek. Melton, Eric, illus. 2003. 107p. (J). pap. 11.95 *(978-0-7414-1682-7(4))* Infinity Publishing.

Tucker, Mark. Super Phil. Petete, Christine, illus. 2003. (J). 4.50 *(978-1-882440-00-9(5))* God's World Pubns. Inc.

—Super Phil & the Missing Mom. Petete, Christine, illus. 2003. 24p. (J). 4.50 *(978-1-882440-01-6(3))* God's World Pubns. Inc.

—Super Phil & the Sphiddle of the Rinks. Patete, Christine, illus. 2003. (J). 4.50 *(978-1-882440-02-3(1))* God's World Pubns. Inc.

Tucker, Sally A. Leo & Apollo: The Forbidden Land. 2012. 28p. pap. 15.00 *(978-1-105-60121-7(8))* Lulu Pr., Inc.

Tucker, Susan K. Ridiculously Ridiculous. Foster, Jack, illus. 2012. 16p. pap. 9.95 *(978-1-61633-346-1(4))* Guardian Angel Publishing, Inc.

Tugman, Etta. Smokey Mountain Bears. 2006. 9.00 *(978-0-8059-8189-6(6))* Dorrance Publishing Co., Inc.

Tuitel, Johnnie & Lamson, Sharon. The Light in Bradford Manor. 2004. (Gun Lake Adventures Ser.). (Illus.). 130p. (J). (gr. -1-7). per. 5.99 *(978-0-9658075-5-5(X))* Cedar Tree Publishing.

Tulik, Alice, et al. Fishing Adventures. Tulik, Alice et al, illus. 2006. (Adventure Story Collection Ser.). 36p. (J). (gr. 2-6). pap. 12.00 *(978-1-58084-248-8(8))* Lower Kuskokwim Schl. District.

Tullson, Diane. The Darwin Expedition, 1 vol. 2007. (Orca Soundings Ser.). (ENG.). 128p. (YA). (gr. 8-12). per. 9.95 *(978-1-55143-676-0(0))* Orca Bk. Pubs. USA.

—Red Sea, 1 vol. 2005. (ENG.). 176p. (YA). (gr. 8-12). per. 13.00 *(978-1-55143-331-8(1))* Orca Bk. Pubs. USA.

—Sea Change, 1 vol. 2010. (Orca Soundings Ser.). (ENG.). 128p. (YA). (gr. 8-12). pap. 9.95 *(978-1-55469-332-0(2))* Orca Bk. Pubs. USA.

Tully, Justin. Lost from the Christmas Mansion. 2008. 141p. pap. 16.95 *(978-1-4092-5106-4(3))* Lulu Pr., Inc.

Tunbridge, J. L. The Jellybean Tree. 2012. 40p. pap. 15.95 *(978-1-4525-0813-9(5))* Balboa Pr.

Tunstall, Tiki. Will You Be My Friend? 2009. 36p. pap. 15.49 *(978-1-4490-2230-3(8))* AuthorHouse.

Turchan, Monique. Mydoit. Turchan, Monique, illus. 2013. (Illus.). 24p. pap. 11.95 *(978-1-61244-144-3(0))* Halo Publishing International.

Turcios, Omar. David, Peces, Pinguinos ... 2012. (SPA & ENG.). 36p. (J). (gr. -1-k). 14.95 *(978-84-15241-95-9(X))* Eastern National.

Turnbull, Ann. Deep Water. 3rd ed. 2013. 102p. pap. *(978-1-78132-160-7(4))* SilverWood Bks.

Turnbull, Elizabeth. Janjak & Freda Go to the Iron Market. Turnbull, Wally, tr. Jones, Mark, illus. 2013. 36p. 18.95 *(978-1-61153-072-8(5))* Light Messages Publishing.

Turnbull, Elizabeth J. Janjak & Freda Go to the Iron Market. Turnbull, Wally R., tr. Jones, Mark, illus. 2013. 36p. pap. 12.95 *(978-1-61153-062-9(8))* Light Messages Publishing.

Turner, Corey W. Little Benjamin & the Red Fire Ants. 2009. 24p. pap. 14.99 *(978-1-4389-1747-4(3))* AuthorHouse.

Turner, Daniel. Cinnamon the Adventurous Guinea Pig Goes to Devil's Island. Skinner, Gayle, illus. 2013. (ENG.). 48p. (J). pap. 10.95 *(978-1-4787-1753-9(X))* Outskirts Pr., Inc.

Turner, Dannie E. You Don't Know Beans: the Great Frog Adventure. 2008. 28p. pap. 24.95 *(978-1-60474-711-9(0))* America Star Bks.

Turner, Darlene. Tommy Gets Lost! Rottinger, Amy, illus. 2012. 24p. pap. 12.95 *(978-1-61244-064-4(9))* Halo Publishing International.

Turner, Ethel. Seven Little Australians. 2005. 27.95 *(978-1-4218-0333-3(X))*; 204p. pap. 12.95 *(978-1-4218-0433-0(6))* 1st World Publishing, Inc. (1st World Library - Literary Society).

—Seven Little Australians. 2007. (ENG.). 142p. pap. 18.99 *(978-1-4264-1638-5(5))* Creative Media Partners, LLC.

—Seven Little Australians. 2004. reprint ed. pap. 1.99 *(978-1-4192-4679-1(8))*; pap. 20.95 *(978-1-4191-4679-4(3))* Kessinger Publishing, LLC.

Turner, Julie Anne. A Tale of Summerland. 2007. (Illus.). 72p. pap. *(978-1-84401-902-1(0))* Athena Pr.

Turner, Megan Whalen. A Conspiracy of Kings. (Queen's Thief Ser.: 4). (ENG.). (YA). (gr. 8). 2017. 368p. pap. 9.99 *(978-0-06-264299-8(5))* 2011. 352p. pap. 7.99 *(978-0-06-187095-8(1))* 2010. 336p. 16.99 *(978-0-06-187093-4(5))* HarperCollins Pubs. (Greenwillow Bks.).

—A Conspiracy of Kings, 6 vols. 2010. (Queen's Thief Ser.: BK.4). (YA). (ENG.). 73.75 *(978-1-4498-4570-4(3))*; (ENG.). 230.75 *(978-1-4498-4569-8(X))*; 1.25 *(978-1-4498-4574-2(6))*; 88.75 *(978-1-4498-4573-5(8))*; No. 4. (ENG.). 90.75 *(978-1-4498-4571-1(1))* Recorded Bks., Inc.

—The King of Attolia. (Queen's Thief Ser.: 3). (ENG.). (YA). (gr. 8). 2017. 432p. pap. 9.99 *(978-0-06-264298-1(7))* 2007. 432p. pap. 7.99 *(978-0-06-083579-8(6))* 2006. 400p. 17.99 *(978-0-06-083577-4(X))* HarperCollins Pubs. (Greenwillow Bks.).

—The King of Attolia. 2007. (Queen's Thief Ser.: BK.3). 387p. (YA). 18.00 *(978-0-7569-8106-8(9))* Perfection Learning Corp.

—The King of Attolia. (YA). 2008. (Queen's Thief Ser.: BK.3). (ENG.). 84.49 *(978-1-4281-8027-7(3))* 2007. (Attolia Ser.: 3). 119.75 *(978-1-4281-1722-8(9))* 2007. (Queen's Thief Ser.: BK.3). (ENG.). 92.75 *(978-1-4281-1716-7(4))* 2006. (Queen's Thief Ser.: BK.3). (ENG.). 90.75 *(978-1-4281-1718-1(0))* 2006. (Queen's Thief Ser.: BK.3). (ENG.). 122.75 *(978-1-4281-1720-4(2))* 2006. (Queen's Thief Ser.: BK.3). (ENG.). 1.25 *(978-1-4281-1713-6(X))*

2006. (Queen's Thief Ser.: BK.3). (ENG.). 251.75 (978-1-4281-1717-4(2)) 2006. (Queen's Thief Ser.: BK.3). 281.75 (978-1-4281-1721-1(0)) Recorded Bks., Inc.
—The Queen of Attolia. (Queen's Thief Ser.: 2). (ENG.). (YA). (gr. 8). 2017. 416p. pap. 9.99 (978-0-06-264297-4(9)) 2006. 368p. pap. 6.99 (978-0-06-084182-9(6)) HarperCollins Pubs. (Greenwillow Bks.).
—The Queen of Attolia, 8 vols. (Attolia Ser.: 2). (J). 2013. 188.75 (978-1-4281-5237-3(7)) 2009. 73.75 (978-1-4361-6574-7(1)) 2008. 104.75 (978-1-4281-5236-6(9)) 2008. 75.75 (978-1-4281-5234-2(2)) 2007. 78.75 (978-1-4281-5232-8(6)) 2007. 1.25 (978-1-4281-5229-8(6)) 2007. 101.75 (978-1-4281-5238-0(5)) 2007. 162.75 (978-1-4281-5233-5(4)) Recorded Bks., Inc.
—The Queen of Attolia. 2017. (Queen's Thief Ser.: BK.2). (ENG.). (YA). lib. bdg. 20.85 **(978-0-606-40331-3(0))** Turtleback Bks.
—Thick As Thieves. 2017. (Queen's Thief Ser.: 5). (ENG.). 352p. (YA). (gr. 8). 17.99 (978-0-06-256824-3(8), Greenwillow Bks.) HarperCollins Pubs.
—The Thief. (Queen's Thief Ser.: 1). (ENG.). (YA). 2017. 320p. (gr. 8). pap. 9.99 (978-0-06-264296-7(0)) 2005. 304p. (gr. 5). reprint ed. pap. 8.99 (978-0-06-082497-6(2)) HarperCollins Pubs. (Greenwillow Bks.).
—The Thief. 2009. (Queen's Thief Ser.: BK.1). (ENG.). (YA). 9.00 (978-0-7848-3718-4(X)); 8.32 (978-0-7848-3065-9(7)) Marco Bk. Co. (Everbind).
—The Thief, 7 vols. (Queen's Thief Ser.: BK.1). (ENG.). (YA). 2005. 169.75 (978-1-4025-5458-2(3)) 2004. 92.75 (978-1-4025-5457-5(5)) Recorded Bks., Inc.
—The Thief. (Queen's Thief Ser.: BK.1). (ENG.). 2017. (YA). lib. bdg. 20.85 **(978-0-606-40328-3(0))** 2005. (J). lib. bdg. 17.20 (978-1-4177-4836-5(2), Turtleback) Turtleback Bks.
Turner, Tracie & Dyson, Kyree. The Adventures of Kyree the Chocolate Moose. 2013. 20p. pap. 24.95 (978-1-62709-178-7(5)) America Star Bks.
Turquoise Class. George's Dragon Adventure. 2012. (Illus.). 24p. pap. 19.82 (978-1-4772-1427-5(5)) AuthorHouse.
Tutor, Margaret. A Make-Do Christmas, 1 vol. 2009. 74p. pap. 19.95 (978-1-4489-0849-3(3)) America Star Bks.
Twain, Mark, pseud. Adventures of Huckleberry Finn. Powell, Eric, illus. 2012. (ENG.). 276p. 19.99 (978-1-61377-086-3(3), 9781613770863) Idea & Design Works, LLC.
—The Adventures of Huckleberry Finn. 96p. (J). pap. 4.95 (978-0-7910-4108-6(5), Chelsea Hse.) Facts On File, Inc.
—The Adventures of Huckleberry Finn. (Coleccion Clasicos de la Juventud). (SPA., Illus.). 192p. (J). 12.95 (978-84-7189-027-6(5), ORT313) Ortells, Alfredo Editorial S.L. ESP. Dist: Continental Bk. Co., Inc.
—The Adventures of Huckleberry Finn. McKowen, Scott, illus. 2006. (Sterling Unabridged Classics Ser.). (ENG.). 320p. (J). (gr. 5-7). 14.95 (978-1-4027-2600-2(7)) Sterling Publishing Co., Inc.
—The Adventures of Huckleberry Finn. 2008. (Puffin Classics Ser.). 386p. (gr. 3-7). lib. bdg. 16.00 (978-0-613-63913-2(8), Turtleback) Turtleback Bks.
—The Adventures of Tom Sawyer. Ingpen, Robert R., illus. 2010. (Sterling Illustrated Classics Ser.). (ENG.). 240p. (J). (gr. 5-18). 19.95 (978-1-4027-6762-3(5)) Sterling Publishing Co., Inc.
—The Adventures of Tom Sawyer. Corvino, Lucy, illus. 2005. (Classic Starts(tm) Ser.). (ENG.). 160p. (J). (gr. 2-4). 6.95 (978-1-4027-1216-6(2)) Sterling Publishing Co., Inc.
—The Adventures of Tom Sawyer - Literary Touchstone Edition. 2005. 216p. (YA). per. 4.99 (978-1-58049-596-7(6), PWH5966) Prestwick Hse., Inc.
—The Adventures of Tom Sawyer, Complete. l.t. ed. 2006. 408p. pap. (978-1-84637-320-6(4)) Echo Library.
—Las Aventuras de Tom Sawyer. 2003. (Advanced Reading Ser.).Tr. of Adventures of Tom Sawyer. (SPA.). 124p. (J). 11.95 (978-84-239-9045-0(1)) Espasa Calpe, S.A. ESP. Dist: Planeta Publishing Corp.
—Avventure di Tom Sawyer. pap. 15.95 (978-88-451-2151-7(8)) Fabbri Editori - RCS Libri ITA. Dist: Distribooks, Inc.
—No. 44, the Mysterious Stranger. 2004. 160p. pap. 11.95 (978-1-59540-326-1(4), 1st World Library - Literary Society) 1st World Publishing, Inc.
—The Prince & the Pauper. (J). 19.95 (978-0-8488-0849-5(5)) Amereon Ltd.
—The Prince & the Pauper. 2008. (Bring the Classics to Life Ser.). (Illus.). 72p. (gr. 2-12). pap., act. bk. ed. 10.95 (978-1-55576-096-0(1), EDCTR-206B) EDCON Publishing Group.
—The Prince & the Pauper. 2003. (Modern Library Classics Ser.). (ENG., Illus.). 240p. pap. 11.00 (978-0-375-76112-6(8), Modern Library) Random House Publishing Group.
—The Prince & the Pauper. Akib, Jamel, illus. 2007. (Classic Starts(tm) Ser.). (ENG.). 160p. (J). (gr. 2-4). 6.95 (978-1-4027-3687-2(8)) Sterling Publishing Co., Inc.
—The Prince & the Pauper: With a Discussion of Respect. 2003. (Values in Action Illustrated Classics Ser.). (J). (978-1-59203-052-1(1)) Learning Challenge, Inc.
—El Principe y el Mendigo.Tr. of Prince & the Pauper. (SPA., Illus.). 144p. (YA). 11.95 (978-84-7281-073-0(9), AF1073) Auriga, Ediciones S.A. ESP. Dist: Continental Bk. Co., Inc.
—El Principe y el Mendigo. Castro, Patricia & Avila, Jorge, illus. 2003. (Literatura Juvenil (Panamericana Editorial) Ser.).Tr. of Prince & the Pauper. (SPA.). 314p. (YA). (gr. 4-7). pap. (978-958-30-0146-8(5)) Panamericana Editorial.
—Tom Sawyer. 2004. 264p. pap. 13.95 (978-1-59540-318-6(3), 1st World Library - Literary Society) 1st World Publishing, Inc.
—Tom Sawyer. 2006. (Classic Retelling Ser.). (Illus.). 224p. (YA). (gr. 8-12). (978-0-618-12053-6(X), 2-00218) Holt McDougal.
—Tom Sawyer, 1 vol. Mullarkey, Lisa, illus. 2010. (Calico Illustrated Classics Ser.: No. 1). (ENG.). 112p. (J). (gr. 3-6). 27.07 (978-1-60270-704-7(9)) Magic Wagon.
—Tom Sawyer. (Coleccion Clasicos de la Juventud). (SPA., Illus.). 220p. (J). 12.95 (978-84-7189-029-0(1), ORT310) Ortells, Alfredo Editorial S.L. ESP. Dist: Continental Bk. Co., Inc.
—Tom Sawyer. 2009. 196p. (gr. 4-7). pap. 12.99 (978-1-934941-63-8(8)) Red & Black Pubs.
—Tom Sawyer. 2003. (Timeless Classics Ser.). (SPA., Illus.). 95p. (J). (gr. 5-8). pap. 12.95 (978-84-372-2235-6(4)) Santillana USA Publishing Co., Inc.
—Tom Sawyer. l.t. ed. 2006. (Classics Ser.). (ENG.). 363p. (J). (gr. 4-7). 22.95 (978-0-7862-8640-9(7)) Thorndike Pr.
—Tom Sawyer, Detective. (SPA., Illus.). 160p. (YA). 11.95 (978-84-7281-062-4(3), AF0623) Auriga, Ediciones S.A. ESP. Dist: Continental Bk. Co., Inc.
Twain, Mark, pseud & Clemens, Samuel L. The Prince & the Pauper. 2013. (Works of Mark Twain). 425p. reprint ed. lthr. 79.00 (978-0-7812-1120-8(4)) Reprint Services Corp.
Twain, Mark, pseud, et al. The Prince & the Pauper. Kliros, Thea, illus. abr. ed. 2011. (Dover Children's Thrift Classics Ser.). (ENG.). 112p. (J). (gr. 3-8). reprint ed. pap. 4.00 (978-0-486-29383-7(1)) Dover Pubns., Inc.
Tweed, Susan Larned. A Sailor's Adventure: Sailing Stormy Seas. 2012. 24p. pap. 11.50 (978-1-61897-522-5(6), Strategic Bk. Publishing) Strategic Book Publishing & Rights Agency (SBPRA).
Twiford, Jerod. Kisho. 2005. pap. 16.95 (978-1-4241-0525-0(0)) PublishAmerica, Inc.
Twigger, J. Nicci & Her Amazing Adventure. 2008. (Illus.). 40p. pap. 18.49 (978-1-4389-1295-0(1)) AuthorHouse.
Twinkle Books. Terrible Tommy. 2006. (J). 14.98 (978-0-9792992-6-1(8)) Twinkle Bks.
Twitty, Mary F. Ashley Visits Urchin Village. 2008. 92p. pap. 51.99 (978-1-4363-5578-0(8)) Xlibris Corp.
Two Sisters Circle. The Lady of the Lane. 2013. 116p. pap. 19.95 (978-1-63004-330-8(3)) America Star Bks.
Tye, Peter. Crocodile Tours. Howe, Norma, illus. 2012. 80p. pap. (978-1-78176-536-4(7)) FeedARead.com.
Tyle, Shirley. Where Is Time, 1 vol. 2010. 30p. 24.95 (978-1-4489-5976-1(4)) PublishAmerica, Inc.
Tyler, Tanith. Aegis Rising. 2007. (Illus.). 179p. (978-0-9800860-0-3(0)) TNT Publishing Co.
Typaldos, Melanie. Celeste & the Adorable Kitten. Tayts, Alexandra, illus. 2013. 244p. 14.99 (978-0-9899847-0-6(2)) Capybara Madness.
Tyson, Delilah Cottingham. Color Us Rainbow. 2012. 24p. pap. 15.99 (978-1-4797-5711-4(X)) Xlibris Corp.
Tzingoker, Lilach. Sonny's Adventure in Mystery Park. 2010. 44p. pap. 19.95 (978-1-60911-927-0(4), Eloquent Bks.) Strategic Book Publishing & Rights Agency (SBPRA).
Tzvi, G. J. The Great Adventure of la Gang du Sept. 2008. 177p. pap. 14.95 (978-1-4116-8291-7(2)) Lulu Pr., Inc.
Tzvieli, Neta. The Private Eyes & the Mysterious Submarine. 2009. 149p. 17.99 (978-1-59826-286-5(6)) Feldheim Pubs.
U. S. National Geographic Society Staff. Get with the Beat! 2009. (Toot & Puddle Ser.). (ENG., Illus.). 24p. (J). (gr. -1-2). lib. bdg. 11.90 (978-1-4263-0485-9(4), National Geographic Children's Bks.) National Geographic Society.
—Get with the Beat. 2009. (Toot & Puddle Ser.). (ENG., Illus.). 24p. (J). (gr. -1-2). pap. 3.99 (978-1-4263-0484-2(6), National Geographic Children's Bks.) National Geographic Society.
—The Great Cheese Chase. 2008. (Toot & Puddle Ser.). (ENG., Illus.). 24p. (J). (gr. -1-2). lib. bdg. 11.90 (978-1-4263-0371-5(8), National Geographic Children's Bks.) National Geographic Society.
—The Mystery of the Disappearing Swing. 2008. (Toot & Puddle Ser.). (ENG., Illus.). 24p. (J). (gr. -1-2). pap. 3.99 (978-1-4263-0224-4(X)); lib. bdg. 11.90 (978-1-4263-0372-2(6)) National Geographic Society. (National Geographic Children's Bks.).
Uahc, Ecarg. Adventures of I. Firebrace: The Battle in the Underground. 2011. 124p. pap. 10.95 (978-1-4502-9785-1(4)); (gr. 4-6). 20.95 (978-1-4502-9786-8(2)) iUniverse, Inc.
Udvari, Joseph G. Courage. 2012. 132p. pap. (978-1-84961-169-5(6)) RealTime Publishing.
Ueno, Haruki. Big Hero 6, Vol. 2. 2015. (Big Hero 6 Graphic Novel Ser.: 2). lib. bdg. 23.30 (978-0-606-37926-7(6)) Turtleback Bks.
Ueyama, Michiro. Chaotic Century. Ueyama, Michiro, illus. (Zoids Ser.). (ENG., Illus.). Vol. 11. 2004. 82p. pap. 5.95 (978-1-56931-858-4(1)) Vol. 12. 2003. 72p. pap. 5.95 (978-1-56931-867-6(0)) Viz Media.
Uglow, Lorna. The Fairy in the Potting Shed. 2008. (Illus.). 100p. pap. 28.99 (978-1-4389-0858-8(X)) AuthorHouse.
Ugon, Gabriela Armand. El Secreto de la Casa Gris. (SPA.). (J). 8.95 (978-958-04-7349-7(8)) Norma S.A. COL. Dist: Distribuidora Norma, Inc.
Uihlein, Mary. Hello Little Owl, I Am Hermit Crab! Uihlein, Mary, illus. 2013. (Illus.). 28p. 24.95 (978-1-61493-159-1(3)); pap. 12.95 (978-1-61493-158-4(5)) Peppertree Pr., The.
Ullrich, Hortense. La Aventura de Lorenzo. (SPA.). (J). 7.95 (978-958-04-7447-0(8)) Norma S.A. COL. Dist: Distribuidora Norma, Inc.
Ullrich, Nai D. Octo-Annie: Home-Help Super Star. 2012. 24p. pap. 15.99 (978-1-4797-0928-1(X)) Xlibris Corp.
Umansky, Kaye. Belinda & the Bears & the New Chair. Jevons, Chris, illus. 2016. (Early Reader Ser.). (ENG.). 80p. (J). (gr. k-2). 6.99 (978-1-4440-1351-1(3), Orion Children's Bks.) Hachette Children's Group GBR. Dist: Hachette Bk. Group.
Uncle Bernie. Michaels Adventures in the Land of Nod Book: Michaels Trip to Orange County. 2008. 32p. pap. 12.99 (978-1-4389-1097-0(5)) AuthorHouse.
Uncle Chuck. The Monkey Puzzle Tree. 2011. 32p. pap. 24.95 (978-1-4560-6992-6(6)) America Star Bks.
Uncle E. The ADVENTURES of Diggle, Boogie & Lolo: Boogie & the Bubbles, 1 volume. 2008. (Illus.). 36p. (J). Vol. 1, Bk. 2. 17.99 (978-0-9801322-2-9(3))vol. 1, Bk. 2. pap. 9.99 (978-0-9801322-3-6(1)) W3 Publishing.
Uncle Markie. Piglетté & Bobo Christmas in Palm Springs. 2003. (YA). ring bd. 9.95 (978-1-933129-10-5(7)) Studio 403.
—Piglеtté & Bobo in Estonia. 2003. (YA). ring bd. 9.95 (978-1-933129-13-6(1)) Studio 403.
—Piglеtté & Bobo in Kansas City. 2003. (YA). ring bd. 9.95 (978-1-933129-08-2(5)) Studio 403.
—Piglеtté & Bobo in Sud Africa. 2003. (YA). ring bd. 9.95 (978-1-933129-15-0(8)) Studio 403.
—Piglеtté & Bobo in the New Territories. 2003. (YA). ring bd. 9.95 (978-1-933129-06-8(9)) Studio 403.
—Piglеtté & Bobo in the United Kingdom. 2003. (YA). ring bd. 9.95 (978-1-933129-14-3(X)) Studio 403.
—Piglеtté & Bobo on Safari. 2003. (YA). ring bd. 9.95 (978-1-933129-16-7(6)) Studio 403.
Unger-Pengilly, Elaine. Rat. Trockstad, Marcy, illus. 2013. 120p. (978-1-4602-2262-1(8)) FriesenPress.
Ungerer, Tomi. Fog Island. 2013. (ENG., Illus.). 48p. 16.95 (978-0-7148-6535-5(4)) Phaidon Pr., Inc.
—The Mellops Go Diving for Treasure. 2011. (ENG., Illus.). 32p. (gr. -1-2). 12.95 (978-0-7148-6248-4(7)) Phaidon Pr., Inc.
Ungermann Marshall, Yana. Gilda Gets Wise. Ungermann Marshall, Yana, illus. 2008. (Illus.). 34p. (J). pap. (978-0-9670982-6-5(2)) Yana's Kitchen.
Universal & Chesterfield, Sadie. Despicable Me 3: the Deluxe Junior Novel. 2017. (ENG.). 144p. (J). (gr. 3-7). 9.99 **(978-0-316-50756-1(3))** Little, Brown Bks. for Young Readers.
Universal & King, Trey. Minions: The Road to Villain-Con - Reusable Sticker Book. 2015. (ENG., Illus.). 12p. (J). (gr. -1-1). pap. 6.99 (978-0-316-29996-1(0)) Little, Brown Bks. for Young Readers.
Ünlükoç, Müge. Real Race. 2013. 32p. pap. 17.99 (978-1-105-98879-0(1)) Lulu Pr., Inc.
Upham, Linda. Divided Loyalties. Littlejohn, Anna, illus. 2007. 188p. per. (978-0-7552-0302-4(X)) Authors OnLine, Ltd.
Urbach, Jourdan. Leaving Jeremiah. 2003. (Illus.). 108p. (J). 19.95 (978-1-930648-57-9(X), 207-832-6665); per. 10.95 (978-1-930648-50-0(2), 207-832-6665) Goose River Pr.
Urban, Linda. Milo Speck, Accidental Agent. (ENG., Illus.). 272p. (J). (gr. 2-5). 2017. pap. 7.99 (978-0-544-93523-5(3)) 2015. 16.99 (978-0-544-41951-3(0)) Houghton Mifflin Harcourt Publishing Co. (HMH Books For Young Readers).
Ure, Jean. Born to Dance, 1. 2017. (Dance Trilogy Ser.: 1). (ENG.). 256p. (J). 6.99 (978-0-00-816452-2(5), HarperCollins Children's Bks.) HarperCollins Pubs. Ltd. GBR. Dist: HarperCollins Pubs.
Urey, Gary. Pursued. 2017. (Secrets of the X-Point Ser.: 1). (ENG.). 288p. (J). (gr. 3-7). 16.99 (978-0-8075-6684-8(5)); pap. 9.99 **(978-0-8075-6686-2(1))** Whitman, Albert & Co.
—Super Schnoz Boxed Set #1-3. Long, Ethan & Frawley, Keith, illus. 2017. (Super Schnoz Ser.). (ENG.). 480p. (J). (gr. 3-7). pap., pap., pap. 19.99 (978-0-8075-9989-1(1)) Whitman, Albert & Co.
Urish, J. D. The Adventures of Rex Bolton Volume 1. 2010. 60p. pap. 9.98 (978-0-578-03676-2(2)) Jentmedia.
Ursu, Anne. The Immortal Fire. Swaab, Neil, illus. 2010. (Cronus Chronicles Ser.: 3). (ENG.). 528p. (J). (gr. 3-7). pap. 7.99 (978-1-4169-0592-9(8), Atheneum Bks. for Young Readers) Simon & Schuster Children's Publishing.
—The Siren Song. Fortune, Eric, illus. (Cronus Chronicles Ser.: 2). (ENG.). (J). (gr. 3-7). 2008. 464p. pap. 7.99 (978-1-4169-0590-5(1)) 2007. 448p. 19.99 (978-1-4169-0589-9(8)) Simon & Schuster Children's Publishing. (Atheneum Bks. for Young Readers).
Usher, Carolyn. Chip Takes Off. 2013. (ENG.). 167p. (YA). pap. 8.95 (978-1-4787-1637-2(1)) Outskirts Pr., Inc.
Uwuigiaren, Omoruyi. The Adventures of Nihu. Ayalomeh, Shedrach, illus. 2007. 158p. (J). (gr. 2-8). 16.95 (978-1-934138-15-1(0)) Bouncing Ball Bks., Inc.
Uy, Katherine Nepomuceno. The Adventures of Tess: Tessa & the Secret Tunnel. 2012. 70p. pap. 15.99 (978-1-4771-1367-7(3)) Xlibris Corp.
V. Isabelle's Star. 2010. 16p. 8.49 (978-1-4490-8584-1(9)) AuthorHouse.
Vachon, Mary Beth. Mac s Mackinac Island Adventure. Rusky, Ann G., illus. 2005. 216p. (J). pap. 17.95 (978-0-9766104-1-0(8)) Arbutus Pr.
Vagabond One. Date not set. (J). pap. 140.40 (978-0-590-39614-1(5)) Scholastic, Inc.
Vail, Rochelle Kelly. Critters: A Dog's Tale. 2007. 140p. per. 11.95 (978-1-4327-0826-9(0)) Outskirts Pr., Inc.
Vakker, Hans Alric. The Riddle of the Jade Collar: A Twelve Cousins Book. 2013. 292p. 26.95 (978-1-4759-7522-2(8)); pap. 16.95 (978-1-4759-7521-5(X)) iUniverse, Inc.
Valencia, O. R. Savior in the Blue Mermaid. 2008. 180p. pap. 14.35 (978-1-4251-2824-1(6)) Trafford Publishing.
Valent, Fred. The Tiniest Raindrop, 1 vol. 2008. (ENG.). 31p. 24.95 (978-1-60441-393-9(X)) America Star Bks.
Valente, Catherynne M. The Girl Who Soared over Fairyland & Cut the Moon in Two. Juan, Ana, illus. 2013. (Fairyland Ser.: 3). (ENG.). 256p. (YA). (gr. 5-9). 16.99 (978-1-250-02350-6(5), 9781250023506) Feiwel & Friends.
Valentine, Sophie. Zoo Hullabaloo, 1 vol. rev. ed. 2013. (Fiction Readers Ser.). (ENG., Illus.). 12p. (J). (gr. 1-1). pap. 12.96 (978-1-4807-1137-2(3)); pap. 4.99 (978-1-4333-5458-8(6)) Shell Educational Publishing.
Valeska, John & Fripp, Jean. The Secret of the Sand. Fripp, Jean, ed. Moussa, Karen M., illus. 2003. (Dolphin Watch Ser.). 32p. (J). (gr. k-5). pap. 5.99 (978-0-9701008-2-5(5)) Bicast, Inc.
Valois, Rob & Caravan Studios Staff. Spyro & the Giants. 2013. (Penguin Young Readers Level 3 Ser.). lib. bdg. 13.55 (978-0-606-31693-4(0), Turtleback) Turtleback Bks.
Valor, De. Pirate Adventures of Sea Worthy: Featuring: the Treasure of Captain Blue Beard & the Return of Captain Blue Beard. 2013. 150p. (gr. 2-2). 20.35 (978-1-4669-7483-8(4)); pap. 10.35 (978-1-4269-9551-4(2)) Trafford Publishing.
Van Allsburg, Chris. Jumanji. 30th anniv. ed. 2011. (ENG., Illus.). 32p. (J). (gr. 1-4). 18.99 (978-0-547-60838-9(1)) Houghton Mifflin Harcourt Publishing Co.
—The Wreck of the Zephyr. 2014. 32p. pap. 9.00 (978-1-61003-222-3(5)) Center for the Collaborative Classroom.
—The Wreck of the Zephyr. 30th anniv. ed. 2013. (ENG., Illus.). 32p. (J). (gr. -1-3). 18.99 (978-0-544-05005-1(3)) Houghton Mifflin Harcourt Publishing Co.
Van Camp, Katie. Cookiebot! A Harry & Horsie Adventure. Agnew, Lincoln, illus. 2011. (Harry & Horsie Adventures Ser.: 2). (ENG.). 32p. (J). (gr. -1-1). 16.99 (978-0-06-197445-8(5)) HarperCollins Pubs.
—Harry & Horsie. Agnew, Lincoln, illus. 2009. (Harry & Horsie Adventures Ser.: 1). (ENG.). 32p. (J). (gr. -1-1). 16.99 (978-0-06-175598-9(2)) HarperCollins Pubs.
Van Der Watt, Tony. Balthazar, the Wolf Who Reformed. 2010. 48p. pap. 12.50 (978-1-60911-125-0(7), Eloquent Bks.) Strategic Book Publishing & Rights Agency (SBPRA).
Van Draanen, Wendelin. The Gecko & Sticky: the Power Potion. Gilpin, Stephen, illus. 2011. (Gecko & Sticky Ser.). (ENG.). 240p. (J). (gr. 3-7). 6.99 (978-0-440-42245-7(0), Yearling) Random Hse. Children's Bks.
—The Greatest Power. Gilpin, Stephen, illus. 2011. (Gecko & Sticky Ser.: Bk. 1). (ENG.). 208p. (J). (gr. 3-7). 7.99 (978-0-440-42243-3(4), Yearling) Random Hse. Children's Bks.
—Sinister Substitute. Gilpin, Stephen, illus. (Gecko & Sticky Ser.: Bk. 3). (ENG.). 224p. (J). (gr. 3-7). 2011. 7.99 (978-0-440-42244-0(2), Yearling) 2010. 12.99 (978-0-375-84378-5(7), Knopf Bks. for Young Readers) Random Hse. Children's Bks.
—Swear to Howdy. 2005. (ENG.). 144p. (J). (gr. 3-7). reprint ed. 6.99 (978-0-440-41943-3(3), Yearling) Random Hse. Children's Bks.
Van Dyne, Edith. Aunt Jane's Nieces out West. 2005. 27.95 (978-1-4218-1425-4(0)); 212p. pap. 12.95 (978-1-4218-1525-1(7)) 1st World Publishing, Inc. (1st World Library - Literary Society).
van Genechten, Guido. Floppy. 2004. (ENG & CHI., Illus.). 28p. (J). pap. (978-1-85269-550-7(1)) Mantra Lingua.
Van Gessel, Chad. Demons: The Titan Clash. 2007. 216p. per. (978-1-84549-252-6(8)) arima publishing.
Van Hamme, Jean. The Curse of the 30 Pieces of Silver, Pt. 1. Sterne, René & De Spiegeleer, Chantal, illus. 2012. (Blake & Mortimer Ser.: 13). (ENG.). 62p. (J). (gr. 5-12). pap. 15.95 (978-1-84918-125-9(X)) CineBook GBR. Dist: National Bk. Network.
—The Curse of the 30 Pieces of Silver, Vol. 14, Pt. 2. Shreder, Etienne & Aubin, Antoine, illus. 2012. (Blake & Mortimer Ser.: 14). (ENG.). 64p. (J). (gr. 5-12). pap. 15.95 (978-1-84918-130-3(6)) CineBook GBR. Dist: National Bk. Network.
Van Hauten, Jacques. Llega el Zorro. 2003. (SPA., Illus.). 144p. (J). (gr. 5-8). 9.95 (978-84-372-2192-2(7), SAN1927) Altea, Ediciones, S.A. - Grupo Santillana ESP. Dist: Santillana USA Publishing Co., Inc.
Van Sise, George W. Wonderfultales from the Land of the Seven Kingdoms. 2010. 437p. pap. 22.95 (978-1-4327-6200-1(1)) Outskirts Pr., Inc.
Van Slyke, Lucille. Little Miss by-the-Day. 2007. 136p. per. (978-1-4068-1625-9(6)) Echo Library.
Van Stockum, Hilda. King Oberon's Forest. 2012. 164p. pap. 11.95 (978-0-7414-6693-8(7)) Infinity Publishing.
Van Straaten, Harmen. Tough guy Tim. 2008. (ENG.). 24p. (J). (gr. 1-7). 12.95 (978-1-60136-002-1(9)) Audio Holdings, LLC.
Van Tassel, Mary. Beach Ball's Journey, 1 vol. 2010. 18p. pap. 24.95 (978-1-4489-9618-6(X)) America Star Bks.
Van Tassel, Mary A. Beach Ball's Discovery. 2013. 24p. pap. 24.95 (978-1-4626-9698-7(8)) America Star Bks.
VanArsdale, Anthony, illus. The Clue in the Papyrus Scroll. 2017. (Boxcar Children Great Adventure Ser.: 2). (ENG.). 160p. (J). (gr. 1-5). 12.99 **(978-0-8075-0698-1(2))**; 6.99 **(978-0-8075-0699-8(0))** Whitman, Albert & Co.
—The Detour of the Elephants. 2017. (Boxcar Children Great Adventure Ser.: 3). (ENG.). 144p. (J). (gr. 1-5). 6.99 **(978-0-8075-0685-1(0))**; 12.99 **(978-0-8075-0684-4(2))** Whitman, Albert & Co.
—Journey on a Runaway Train. 2017. (Boxcar Children Great Adventure Ser.: 1). (ENG.). 160p. (J). (gr. 1-5). 12.99 **(978-0-8075-0695-0(8))**; 6.99 **(978-0-8075-0696-7(6))** Whitman, Albert & Co.
Vanasse, Deb. Cold Spell. 2014. (Alaska Literary Ser.). 224p. pap. 15.95 (978-1-60223-242-6(3)) Univ. of Alaska Pr.
Vance, Alexander. Behind the Canvas. 2016. (ENG.). 336p. (J). 16.99 (978-1-250-02970-6(8), 9781250029706) Feiwel & Friends.
Vance Barnum. Frank & Andy Afloat. 2007. 212p. per. 12.95 (978-1-4218-4011-6(1), 1st World Library - Literary Society) 1st World Publishing, Inc.
—Joe Strong the Boy Fire-Eater. 2007. 180p. per. 11.95 (978-1-4218-4012-3(X), 1st World Library - Literary Society) 1st World Publishing, Inc.
Vancil, Marybelle. Adventures with Macy & the Sneezy, Sneezy Dog: First Adventure: We Visit Indians. 2010. (Illus.). 43p. (J). pap. 23.95 (978-1-4327-5038-1(0)) Outskirts Pr., Inc.
Vande Velde, Vivian. Frogged. 2014. (ENG.). 208p. (J). (gr. 5-7). pap. 7.99 (978-0-544-22546-6(5), HMH Books For Young Readers) Houghton Mifflin Harcourt Publishing Co.
VanDenberg, Saidat. Tadias & the Pitbully Tree. 2012. 36p. pap. 21.99 (978-1-4797-0172-8(6)) Xlibris Corp.
Vandercook, Margaret. Camp Fire Girls at Sunrise Hill, the (Fi. 2006. pap. 55.99 (978-1-4219-9140-5(3)) IndyPublish.com.
—The Red Cross Girls with the Russian Army. 2007. 156p. per. (978-1-4065-4738-2(7)) Dodo Pr.
Vanderpool, Clare. Navigating Early. (ENG.). (J). (gr. 5). 2014. 336p. pap. 7.99 (978-0-307-93065-1(3), Yearling) 2013. 320p. 16.99 (978-0-385-74209-2(6), Delacorte Bks. for Young Readers) 2013. 320p. lib. bdg. 19.99 (978-0-375-99040-3(2), Delacorte Bks. for Young Readers) Random Hse. Children's Bks.
—Navigating Early. 2014. lib. bdg. 18.40 (978-0-606-36420-1(X)) Turtleback Bks.
VanDerpool, Jessie. Little Rose Becomes a Hunter. 2013. 24p. pap. 24.95 (978-1-4626-9554-6(X)) America Star Bks.
Vanier, Jolie. Puwaii Adventures with Joliea & Friends. 2006. 16.95 (978-0-9787949-1-0(5)) Puwaii International, LLC.
Vann, Donna. Corin's Quest. 2003. (Tales Out of Time Ser.). (ENG.). 192p. (J). (gr. 4-8). reprint ed. mass mkt. 6.99 (978-1-85792-218-9(2), 9781857922189) Christian Focus Pubns. GBR. Dist: Bookmasters Distribution.
VanNuys, Elroy. The Mysterious Cave. 2010. 108p. 24.49 (978-1-4490-9224-5(1)); pap. 13.99 (978-1-4490-9223-8(3)) AuthorHouse.
VanRiper, Justin & VanRiper, Gary. The Lost Lighthouse. Gary, Glenn, illus. 2003. (Adirondack Kids Ser.: Vol. 3). 82p. (J). (gr. 2-7). pap. 9.95 (978-0-9707044-2-9(9), ADK3) Adirondack Kids Pr.
Varacchi, Barbara. Desiree & Daisy Mae & All That Love. 2012. 24p. pap. 17.99 (978-1-4685-6146-3(4)) AuthorHouse.
—Desiree's Adventures with Her Friends. 2009. 36p. pap. 16.99 (978-1-4389-1603-3(5)) AuthorHouse.
Various. DC Super Hero Girls. 2017. (ENG.). 64p. (gr. 3-7). pap. 7.99 **(978-1-4012-7458-0(7))** DC Comics.

Various. Donald Duck Adventures, Vol. 2. 2003. (ENG., Illus.). 128p. pap. 7.95 (978-0-911903-11-9(9), 9780911903119) Gemstone Publishing, Inc.
Various, illus. Dora's 10 Best Adventures. 2010. (Dora the Explorer Ser.). (ENG.). 248p. (J). 15.99 (978-1-4424-0967-5(3), Simon Spotlight/Nickelodeon) Simon Spotlight/Nickelodeon.
—OLIVIA Loves to Read: Olivia Trains Her Cat; Olivia & Her Ducklings; Olivia Takes a Trip; Olivia & the Snow Day; Olivia Plants a Garden; Olivia Goes Camping. 2012. (Olivia TV Tie-In Ser.). (ENG.). 144p. (J). (gr. -1-1). pap. 15.99 (978-1-4424-5879-6(8), Simon Spotlight) Simon Spotlight.
Varsell, Linda. A Journey for Rainbows. Curtis, E., illus. 2003. 166p. (YA). per. 6.00 (978-0-9725479-1-8(6)) Rainbow Communications.
Varveris, Ariana Eleni. The Adventures of Magic Island: Book I- Welcome to Magic Island. 2012. 122p. (gr. 2-2). pap. 9.95 (978-1-4620-5751-1(9)) iUniverse, Inc.
Vasquez, Elisa Irene. My Little Piggy: A Bilingual English-Spanish Children's Book. 2010. 28p. 14.95 (978-1-4490-8716-6(7)) AuthorHouse.
Vaughn, Deborah. Sneaky Secret Steff & Her Problem Solving Adventure. 2004. (J). per. 7.95 (978-1-932560-25-1(4)) Aeon Publishing Inc.
Vaughn, Richard. Rowena & the Magic Hawk, the First Adventure. 2009. 224p. pap. 14.95 (978-1-60860-157-8(9), Eloquent Bks.) Strategic Book Publishing & Rights Agency (SBPRA).
Vazov, George D. The Other Side of the Mushroom. 2006. 12.00 (978-0-8059-9018-8(6)) Dorrance Publishing Co., Inc.
Vega, Diego. The Iron Brand. 2007. (Young Zorro Ser.). 240p. (YA). (gr. 3-7). pap. 6.99 (978-0-06-083947-5(3), Rayo) HarperCollins Pubs.
Vegas, Peter. The Iron Tomb. 2016. (Pyramid Hunters Ser.: 1). (ENG., Illus.). 304p. (J). (gr. 5-9). 16.99 (978-1-4814-4578-8(2), Aladdin) Simon & Schuster Children's Publishing.
Velástegui, Cecilia. Olinguito Speaks Up. 2013. (ENG., Illus.). 36p. (J). 19.99 (978-0-9851769-7-6(0)) Libros Publishing.
Velazquez, Anna. Stewart's Airplane Adventure. 2008. 40p. pap. 24.95 (978-1-60441-486-8(3)) America Star Bks.
Velez, Walter, illus. Little Red Riding Hood: A Tale about Staying Safe. 2006. (J). 6.99 (978-1-59939-021-5(3)) Cornerstone Pr.
Velvet, Black. The Adventures of Sam in Space: Planet of the Sweets. 2007. 32p. (J). pap. 8.00 (978-0-8059-7367-9(2)) Dorrance Publishing Co., Inc.
Venable Jr, Al B. Captain Tom, the Sea Adventurer. 2013. 40p. pap. 16.95 (978-1-63004-037-6(1)) America Star Bks.
Venditti, Robert & Riordan, Rick. The Titan's Curse. Futaki, Attila & Guilhaumond, Gregory, illus. 2013. (Percy Jackson & the Olympians Ser.). (ENG.). 128p. (J). (gr. 5-9). 19.99 (978-1-4231-4530-1(5)) Disney Pr.
Vendrell, Maria Martinez & Capdevila, Roser. La Noche. 2003.Tr. of Night. (SPA.). 24p. (J). 7.95 (978-84-233-1455-3(3)) Ediciones Destino ESP. Dist: Planeta Publishing Corp.
Veneziano, Chuckie. My Time on Nantucket. 2005. (Illus.). 56p. (J). lib. bdg. 17.95 (978-0-9755078-0-3(X)) Sweet Punkin Pr.
Ventrillo, James & Ventrillo, Nick. Rick & Bobo: Two Brothers. One a Genius. One Not, 4 vols. Kunardi, Marco, illus. 2009. 332p. (YA). pap. 13.95 (978-0-615-28865-9(0)) Vanir Bks.
Venturini, Claudia, illus. Ali Baba & the Forty Thieves. 2009. (Flip-Up Fairy Tales Ser.). (ENG.). 24p. (J). (gr. -1-2). audio compact disk (978-1-84643-294-1(4)) Child's Play International Ltd.
Veranda, Molly. Molly & Tucker get Shanghaied. 2009. 41p. pap. 9.96 (978-0-557-04210-4(0)) Lulu Pr., Inc.
Verano, Vladimir, illus. The Prince, the Demon King, & the Monkey Warrior. 2011. (ENG.). 96p. (J). (gr. 3-6). pap. 9.95 (978-1-934159-30-9(1)) ThingsAsian Pr.
Verhoeff, Carolyn. All about Johnnie Jones. 2007. 80p. per. (978-1-4068-1628-0(0)) Echo Library.
Verne, Jules. The Adventures of a Special Correspondent. 2009. 180p. 25.95 (978-1-60664-635-9(4)) Rodgers, Alan Bks.
—Around the World in 80 Days. 2004. (Young Reading Series Two Ser.). 64p. (J). (gr. 2-18). pap. 5.95 (978-0-7945-0741-1(7), Usborne) EDC Publishing.
—Around the World in 80 Days. Soleilhac, Aude, illus. 2011. (Classics Illustrated Deluxe Graphic Nove Ser.). (ENG.). 144p. (J). (gr. 3-9). 17.99 (978-1-59707-284-7(2), 9781597072847) Papercutz.
—Around the World in 80 Days. 2006. (Classics Ser.). (Illus.). 48p. per. (978-1-56254-864-3(6)); 80p. (J). (gr. 4-7). per. (978-1-56254-863-6(8)) Saddleback Educational Publishing, Inc.
—Around the World in 80 Days. Akib, Jamel, illus. 2007. (Classic Starts(tm) Ser.). (ENG.). 160p. (J). (gr. 2-4). 6.95 (978-1-4027-3689-6(4)) Sterling Publishing Co., Inc.
—Around the World in 80 Days. 2007. (Illustrated Classics Ser.). (Illus.). 40p. (gr. 3-6). lib. bdg. 26.00 (978-0-8368-7662-8(8), Gareth Stevens Learning Library) Stevens, Gareth Publishing LLLP.
—Around the World in Eighty Days. Ingpen, Robert R., illus. 2012.Tr. of Tour du Monde en Quatre-Vingts Jours. (ENG.). 224p. (J). (gr. 4-7). 24.99 (978-0-9564942-5-2(0)) Palazzo Editions, Ltd. GBR. Dist: Independent Pubs. Group.
—Un Capitan de Quince Anos.Tr. of Fifteen Year Old Captain. (SPA., Illus.). (YA). 14.95 (978-84-7281-049-5(6), AF1049) Auriga, Ediciones S.A. ESP. Dist: Continental Bk. Co., Inc.
—Dick Sand. Munro, George, tr. 2008. 296p. 29.95 (978-1-60664-752-3(0)); pap. 15.95 (978-1-60664-253-5(7)) Rodgers, Alan Bks.
—Dick Sands: The Boy Captain. ELLEN E. FREWER, tr. 2007. (ENG.). 298p. pap. 21.99 (978-1-4264-3403-7(0)) Creative Media Partners, LLC.
—Dick Sands: The Boy Captain. Frewer, Ellen E., tr. l.t. ed. 2007. (ENG.). 328p. pap. 24.99 (978-1-4264-3453-2(7)) Creative Media Partners, LLC.
—The English at the North Pole. 2009. 160p. 24.95 (978-1-60664-684-7(2)); pap. 13.95 (978-1-60664-313-6(4)) Rodgers, Alan Bks.
—The Field of Ice: Part II of the Adventures of Captain Hatteras. 2007. (ENG.). 154p. pap. 19.99 (978-1-4264-3591-1(6)); 170p. pap. 21.99 (978-1-4264-3642-0(4)) Creative Media Partners, LLC.
—La Isla Misteriosa. (SPA., Illus.). 192p. (YA). 11.95 (978-84-7281-105-8(0), AF1105) Auriga, Ediciones S.A. ESP. Dist: Continental Bk. Co., Inc.
—A Journey to the Center of the Earth. Kumar, Vinod, illus. 2011. (Campfire Graphic Novels Ser.). (ENG.). 72p. (YA). (gr. 5-12). pap. 9.99 (978-93-80028-40-8(7), Campfire) Steerforth Pr.
—Miguel Strogoff. (SPA., Illus.). 176p. (YA). 11.95 (978-84-7281-109-6(3), AF1109) Auriga, Ediciones S.A. ESP. Dist: Continental Bk. Co., Inc.
—Topsy-Turvy. Ogilvie, J. G., tr. 2009. 108p. 22.95 (978-1-60664-685-4(0)); pap. 9.95 (978-1-60664-314-3(2)) Rodgers, Alan Bks.
—20,000 Leagues under the Sea. (Illus.). (J). 9.95 (978-1-56156-307-4(2)) Kidsbooks, LLC.
Verne, Jules, illus. Viaje al Centro de la Tierra. Orig. Title: Journey to the Center of the Earth. (SPA.). 160p. (YA). 11.95 (978-84-7281-084-6(4), AF1084) Auriga, Ediciones S.A. ESP. Dist: Continental Bk. Co., Inc.
Verne, Jules & Lokus, Rex. Around the World in 80 Days. Smith, Tod G., illus. 2015. (Graphic Revolve: Common Core Editions Ser.). (ENG.). 72p. (gr. 2-3). pap. 6.95 (978-1-4965-0381-7(3)) Stone Arch Bks.
Verne, Jules & Verne, Julio. Los Hijos del Capitan Grant. (Coleccion Clasicos de la Juventud). (SPA., Illus.). 324p. (J). 12.95 (978-84-7189-098-6(4), ORT314) Ortells, Alfredo Editorial S.L. ESP. Dist: Continental Bk. Co., Inc.
—Miguel Strogoff. (Coleccion Clasicos de la Juventud). (SPA., Illus.). 236p. (J). 12.95 (978-84-7189-106-8(9), ORT305) Ortells, Alfredo Editorial S.L. ESP. Dist: Continental Bk. Co., Inc.
—20,000 Leguas de Viaje Submarino. (Coleccion Clasicos de la Juventud). (SPA., Illus.). 232p. (J). 12.95 (978-84-7189-019-1(4), ORT309) Ortells, Alfredo Editorial S.L. ESP. Dist: Continental Bk. Co., Inc.
Vernon, Ursula. Dani Bocafuego. la Salchicha Maldita. 2012. (SPA.). 204p. (J). (gr. 4-6). pap. 20.99 (978-84-246-3597-8(3)) La Galera, S.A. Editorial ESP. Dist: Lectorum Pubns., Inc.
—The Frozen Menace. 2016. (Dragonbreath Ser.: 11). (ENG., Illus.). 208p. (J). (gr. 3-7). 12.99 (978-0-8037-3986-4(9), Dial Bks) Penguin Young Readers Group.
—Harriet the Invincible. 2015. (Hamster Princess Ser.: 1). (ENG., Illus.). 208p. (J). (gr. 3-7). 12.99 (978-0-8037-3983-3(4), Dial Bks) Penguin Young Readers Group.
—Knight-Napped! 2015. (Dragonbreath Ser.: 10). (ENG.). 208p. (J). (gr. 3-7). 12.99 (978-0-8037-3849-2(8), Dial Bks) Penguin Young Readers Group.
—Lair of the Bat Monster. 4th ed. (Dragonbreath Ser.: 4). (ENG.). 208p. (J). (gr. 3-7). 2014. pap. 6.99 (978-0-14-751320-5(0), Puffin Books) 2011. 12.99 (978-0-8037-3525-5(1), Dial Bks) Penguin Young Readers Group.
—Lair of the Bat Monster. 2014. (Dragonbreath Ser.: 4). lib. bdg. 17.20 (978-0-606-35711-1(4)) Turtleback Bks.
—Nightmare of the Iguana. 2013. (Dragonbreath Ser.: 8). (ENG., Illus.). 208p. (J). (gr. 3-7). 12.99 (978-0-8037-3846-1(3), Dial Bks) Penguin Publishing Group.
—Nurk: The Strange, Surprising Adventures of a (Somewhat) Brave Shrew. 2008. (ENG., Illus.). 144p. (J). (gr. 3-7). 16.00 (978-0-15-206375-7(7)) Houghton Mifflin Harcourt Publishing Co.
—Ratpunzel. 2016. (Hamster Princess Ser.: 3). (ENG., Illus.). 240p. (J). (gr. 3-7). 12.99 (978-0-8037-3985-7(0), Dial Bks) Penguin Young Readers Group.
—When Fairies Go Bad, No. 7. 7th ed. 2012. (Dragonbreath Ser.: 7). (ENG.). 208p. (J). (gr. 3-7). 12.99 (978-0-8037-3678-8(9), Dial Bks) Penguin Young Readers Group.
Veronica Dauber. Mudslide. 2009. 176p. 23.95 (978-1-4401-6228-2(X)) iUniverse, Inc.
Verrett, Michael. It Followed Me Home Can I Keep It? 2010. 35p. pap. 10.00 (978-0-557-28827-4(4)) Lulu Pr., Inc.
—It Followed Me Home Can I Keep It? (full Color) 2010. 35p. pap. 19.00 (978-0-557-29796-2(6)) Lulu Pr., Inc.
—The White Alligator Crown Quatro. 2010. 147p. pap. 13.95 (978-0-557-58121-4(4)) Lulu Pr., Inc.
—The White Alligator (paper Back) 2010. 116p. pap. 17.30 (978-0-557-28042-1(7)) Lulu Pr., Inc.
—The White Alligator (paperback full Color) 2010. 116p. pap. 42.00 (978-0-557-36924-9(X)) Lulu Pr., Inc.
Verrico, Susan. The Privateer's Apprentice, 1 vol. 2012. (ENG.). 224p. (J). 15.95 (978-1-56145-633-8(0)) Peachtree Pubs.
Verrone, Patric C. W. Sharktooth. 2009. 229p. pap. 14.76 (978-0-557-09535-3(2)) Lulu Pr., Inc.
Verstraete, Majanka. The Doll Maker: Weirdville. l.t. ed. 2013. 1. (ENG.). 86p. (gr. 2-6). pap. 9.95 (978-1-62253-065-6(9)) Evolved Publishing.
—Fright Train: Weirdville. l.t. ed. 2013. 3. (ENG.). 88p. (gr. 2-6). pap. 9.95 (978-1-62253-069-4(1)) Evolved Publishing.
—House of Horrors: Weirdville. l.t. ed. 2013. 2. (ENG.). 90p. (gr. 2-6). pap. 9.95 (978-1-62253-067-0(5)) Evolved Publishing.
—Valentina & the Whackadoodle Witch: Valentina's Spooky Adventures. Giffin, Noelle, illus. l.t. ed. 2013. 2. (ENG.). 46p. (gr. k-4). pap. 10.95 (978-1-62253-059-5(4)) Evolved Publishing.
Vescio & LohnRiver, Jenna. Rainbow Journey Screen Play (with Pictures) 2005. 65p. pap. 20.00 (978-1-4116-3288-2(5)) Lulu Pr., Inc.
Vetsch, Rita Kaye. The Many Colors of Friendship. 2009. 40p. pap. 16.50 (978-1-60693-756-3(1), Eloquent Bks.) Strategic Book Publishing & Rights Agency (SBPRA).
Vevers, Rachel. Quest for the Unicorn. 2012. 222p. pap. (978-1-78176-316-2(X)) FeedARead.com.
Viagem de Babar. pap. 19.95 (978-85-85466-78-7(2)) Companhia das Letras BRA. Dist: Distribooks, Inc.
El Viaje de Ash. (SPA.). 62p. 4.95 (978-84-488-1001-6(5)) Beascoa, Ediciones S.A. ESP. Dist: Distribooks, Inc.
Vickery-Bharadwaj, Janice. Valentino & His Friends: It's Magic! 2012. 28p. pap. 12.99 (978-1-4691-7709-0(9)) Xlibris Corp.
Victor, Appleton. Tom Swift among the Fire Fighters: Or Battling with Flames from the Air. 2007. (ENG.). 136p. pap. 18.99 (978-1-4346-1489-6(1)) Creative Media Partners, LLC.
—Tom Swift & His Aerial Warship: Or the Naval Terror of the Seas. 2007. (ENG.). 144p. pap. 18.99 (978-1-4346-1484-1(0)) Creative Media Partners, LLC.
—Tom Swift & His Air Scout: Or Uncle Sam's Mastery of the Sky. 2007. (ENG.). 144p. pap. 18.99 (978-1-4346-1486-5(7)) Creative Media Partners, LLC.
—Tom Swift & His Wizard Camera: Or Thrilling Adventures While Taking Moving Pictu. 2007. (ENG.). 132p. pap. 18.99 (978-1-4346-1485-8(9)) Creative Media Partners, LLC.
Victoria's Tooth Fairy Adventure. 2007. (Illus.). 40p. (J). 19.95 (978-0-615-17773-1(5)) Created For You.
Vicuna, Claudio Orrego. The Surprising Adventures of Balthazar. 2011. (Peace, Justice, Human Rights, & Freedom in Latin America Ser.). (SPA & ENG.). 160p. 15.00 (978-1-58966-218-6(0)) Univ. of Scranton Pr.
Vil, Steve. Arvid & Hornschwatz Go Skunk Scoffing. Witt, Eddie, illus. 2011. 32p. pap. 24.95 (978-1-4560-6043-5(0)) America Star Bks.
Vili, Fane. Mano: The Awakening. Frakes, Clint, ed. 2006. (Illus.). (YA). per. 19.95 (978-0-9774074-0-8(3)) Plankton Pr.
Villalobos, Serenity. Yasso's Adventure: Written by Serenity M. Villalobos Illustrated & Designed by Alisha & Kristen Villalobos & Yes Even Dad AKA Jody Villalobos Helped! 2007. pap. 17.00 (978-0-8059-8749-2(5)) Dorrance Publishing Co., Inc.
Villar Liébana, Luisa. El Ladron Sin Huellas. 2005. (Investigator Big Ears Ser.). (SPA., Illus.). 78p. (J). (gr. 2-3). 8.95 (978-84-348-9434-1(3)) SM Ediciones ESP. Dist: Iaconi, Mariuccia Bk. Imports.
Villareal, Ray. Don't Call Me Hero. 2011. (J). pap. 10.95 (978-1-55885-711-7(7), Piñata Books) Arte Publico Pr.
Villeneuve, Kevin J. The Adventures of Nick the Ecologist & His Robot O-Zone: The Mystery of the Missing Trees. 2007. 96p. per. 9.95 (978-0-595-42362-0(0)) iUniverse, Inc.
Vincent, Patti. The Village Heroes Meet the Dragon. 2008. 44p. pap. 19.95 (978-1-4389-1764-1(3)) AuthorHouse.
Vincolisi, Marnie. The House Who Found Its Home. Clarke, Benjamin S., illus. 2013. 32p. pap. 10.95 (978-0-9823732-3-1(6)) Light Internal Publishing.
Vine, Joshua M. Gnomey & Froggie. 2012. 46p. pap. 21.99 (978-1-4772-7529-0(0)) AuthorHouse.
Vines, Connie. Un Murmullo Sobre el Agua. Perez, Laura C., tr. 2005. (SPA & ENG.). 144p. (YA). per. 9.95 (978-0-7599-3932-5(2)) Hard Shell Word Factory.
Vinsh, Aara J. Playtime Adventures. Leijs, Tommie, illus. 2011. 48p. pap. 24.95 (978-1-4560-9982-4(5)) America Star Bks.
Vinson, Haley. Horizons Set 2, 5 books. Shea, Steve, ed. 2013. (Illus.). 48p. (YA). pap. 24.00 (978-1-57128-815-8(5)) High Noon Bks.
Virginia H. Lasher. The Secret of Crooked Creek. 2006. 58p. 20.00 (978-1-59926-625-1(3)); pap. 10.00 (978-1-4134-9728-1(4)) Xlibris Corp.
Virjan, Emma J. What This Story Needs Is a Bang & a Clang. Virjan, Emma J., illus. 2017. (Pig in a Wig Book Ser.). (Illus.). 40p. (J). (gr. -1-3). 9.99 (978-0-06-241530-1(1)) HarperCollins Pubs.
Vischer, Frans. A Very Fuddles Christmas. Vischer, Frans, illus. 2013. (ENG., Illus.). 32p. (J). (gr. -1-2). 15.99 (978-1-4169-9156-4(5), Aladdin) Simon & Schuster Children's Publishing.
Vischer, Lisa. Three Pirates & You! 2004. (Big Idea Books / VeggieTales Ser.). (ENG., Illus.). 32p. (J). 7.99 (978-0-310-70724-0(2)) Zonderkidz.
Vivat, Booki. Frazzled #2: Ordinary Mishaps & Inevitable Catastrophes. Vivat, Booki, illus. 2017. (Illus.). 224p. (J). (gr. 3-7). 12.99 **(978-0-06-239881-9(4))** HarperCollins Pubs.
Vivès, Bastien, et al. The Chase. 2015. (Last Man Ser.: 3). (ENG., Illus.). 208p. (gr. 9). pap. 9.99 (978-1-62672-048-0(7), 9781626720480, First Second Bks.) Roaring Brook Pr.
—The Royal Cup. 2015. (Last Man Ser.: 2). (ENG., Illus.). 208p. (gr. 9). pap. 9.99 (978-1-62672-047-3(9), 9781626720473, First Second Bks.) Roaring Brook Pr.
Vivinetto, Gina. With Superman & Wonder Woman. Farley, Rick & Tripp, Kanila, illus. 2011. (ENG.). 24p. (J). (gr. -1-3). pap. 3.99 (978-0-06-188531-0(2), HarperFestival) HarperCollins Pubs.
Viz Media Staff & Mizobuchi, Makoto. Pokémon: Ranger & the Temple of the Sea. Mizobuchi, Makoto, illus. 2008. (ENG., Illus.). 192p. (J). (gr. 1). pap. 9.99 (978-1-4215-2288-3(8)) Viz Media.
Viz Media Staff & Takamisaki, Ryo. Pokémon: The Rise of Darkrai. Takamisaki, Ryo, illus. 2008. (ENG., Illus.). 192p. (J). (gr. 1). pap. 9.99 (978-1-4215-2289-0(6)) Viz Media.
Vizoso Veiga, Xoán Antón. The READING LESSON: Adventures of Huckleberry Finn. 2008. 72p. pap. 13.50 (978-1-4092-0361-2(1)) Lulu Pr., Inc.
Voake, Steve. Hooey Higgins & the Shark. Dodson, Emma, illus. 2012. (ENG.). 112p. (J). (gr. 2-5). 14.99 (978-0-7636-5782-6(4)) Candlewick Pr.
Voelkel, J. P. The Lost City. 2015. (Jaguar Stones Ser.: 4). (ENG., Illus.). 368p. (J). (gr. 5-12). 16.99 (978-1-5124-0184-4(6), Darby Creek) Lerner Publishing Group.
Voelkel, J&P. The Lost City. 2017. (Jaguar Stones Ser.: 4). (ENG., Illus.). 368p. (gr. 5-12). 9.99 (978-1-5124-4148-2(1), Darby Creek) Lerner Publishing Group.
Voelkel, Jon & Voelkel, Pamela. The End of the World Club, Bk. 2. 2010. (Jaguar Stones Ser.: Bk. 2). (ENG.). 384p. (gr. 5-6). 16.99 (978-1-60684-072-6(X), Darby Creek) Lerner Publishing Group.
—Middleworld. 2007. (Jaguar Stones Ser.: Bk. 1). (Illus.). 397p. (gr. 6-9). (978-1-57525-561-3(8)) Smith & Kraus Pubs., Inc.
—The River of No Return, Bk. 3. 2012. (Jaguar Stones Ser.: Bk. 3). (ENG.). 352p. (J). (gr. 5). 16.99 (978-1-60684-073-3(8), Darby Creek) Lerner Publishing Group.
Vogel, Peter C. Mike Duffy & His Adventure Witht the World's Smallest Person. 2008. 112p. pap. 9.95 (978-1-59526-796-2(4), Llumina Pr.) Aeon Publishing Inc.
Vogel-Placides, Joan Katherine. The Safe Place. Placides, Del S., illus. 2013. 58p. 13.99 (978-0-9888718-3-0(1)) DOMINIONHOUSE Publishing & Design.
Vogel, Sean. Celtic Run. 2012. 159p. (978-0-9850814-0-9(6)) MB Publishing, LLC.
Voght, Victor A. Fun with Huff & Puff, 1 vol. 2009. 15p. pap. 24.95 (978-1-60749-853-7(7)) America Star Bks.
Voigt, Cynthia. The Book of Secrets. 2015. (Mister Max Ser.: 2). lib. bdg. 17.20 (978-0-606-37702-7(6)) Turtleback Bks.
—Mister Max: the Book of Kings: Mister Max 3. Bruno, Iacopo, illus. 2016. (Mister Max Ser.). (ENG.). 352p. (J). (gr. 3-7). 7.99 (978-0-307-97688-8(2), Yearling) Random Hse. Children's Bks.
—The Tale of Birle. 2015. (Tales of the Kingdom Ser.: 2). (ENG., Illus.). 416p. (YA). (gr. 7). 19.99 (978-1-4424-8356-9(3), Atheneum Bks. for Young Readers) Simon & Schuster Children's Publishing.
—The Tale of Oriel. 2015. (Tales of the Kingdom Ser.: 3). (ENG., Illus.). 544p. (YA). (gr. 7). 19.99 (978-1-4814-0323-8(0), Atheneum Bks. for Young Readers) Simon & Schuster Children's Publishing.
—The Book of Kings. Bruno, Iacopo, illus. 2015. (Mister Max Ser.). (ENG.). 352p. (J). (gr. 3-7). 16.99 (978-0-307-97687-1(4), Knopf Bks. for Young Readers) Random Hse. Children's Bks.
—Young Fredle. Yates, Louise, illus. 2011. (ENG.). 240p. (J). (gr. 3-7). 16.99 (978-0-375-86457-5(1), Knopf Bks. for Young Readers) Random Hse. Children's Bks.
Volk, Gretchen. The Amazing Adventures of Tristy Ruth, Raisin Girl. 2012. 258p. pap. (978-1-105-51531-6(1)) Lulu.com.
Vollmer, Howard R. Adventures of the Chipmunks Three. 2011. 60p. pap. 24.95 (978-1-4567-3240-0(4)) AuthorHouse.
Volpi, Sophia. White Fawn. 2004. 160p. 22.95 (978-0-595-66708-6(2)) iUniverse, Inc.
von Bissing, Ronimund. La Tierra del Oro Ardiente. (SPA.). 184p. (YA). (gr. 5-8). (978-84-216-1045-9(7), BU4764) Bruño, Editorial ESP. Dist: Lectorum Pubns., Inc.
Von Kanel, Liz. The Search for Cuddles & Jonathan's Dream. 2012. 40p. pap. (978-1-77097-158-5(0)) FriesenPress.
von Rosenberg, Byron. Dale the Uniclyde: An adventure in Friendship. Parrott, Heather, illus. 2007. 22p. (J). 11.95 (978-0-9759858-6-1(8)) Red Mountain Creations.
Von Schlichten, David. H-E-Double Hockey Stick. 2011. 124p. pap. 19.95 (978-1-4560-9019-7(4)) America Star Bks.
Voorhees, Coert. In Too Deep. 2014. (ENG.). 336p. (YA). (gr. 7-12). pap. 8.99 (978-1-4231-4473-1(2)) Hyperion Bks. for Children.
Vorster, Nicola. A Monkeys' Wedding. 2012. (Illus.). 24p. pap. 21.35 (978-1-4772-3126-5(9)) AuthorHouse.
Voudrie, Krista. Sisters of Destiny. 2011. 96p. pap. 19.95 (978-1-4560-5636-0(0)) America Star Bks.
Voyager, Beatrice Nambouy. Mama Minko: A Survival Quest. 2010. (Illus.). 28p. pap. 15.49 (978-1-4490-5797-8(7)) AuthorHouse.
Vyff, Shannon. 21st Century Kids. 2007. 280p. pap. 14.95 (978-1-886057-00-5(1)) Warren Publishing, Inc.
Vyvyan, Taylor. Beyond the Waterfall. 2009. 92p. pap. (978-1-84748-551-9(0)) Athena Pr.
—A Dragon's Odyssey. 2012. 120p. pap. (978-1-78281-021-6(8)) Athena Pr.
Wach, Martin. The Great West Virginia Snow Adventure: Teddy Bear Guardians of the Rain Forest. 2006. (Illus.). 32p. (J). 16.95 (978-0-929915-42-5(9)) Headline Bks., Inc.
Wacker, Eileen. Black Tortoise & the Dynasty Dragon. Low, Alan M., illus. 2012. (Fujimini Adventure Ser.: Vol. 5). (ENG.). 40p. (J). (gr. -1-3). 10.99 (978-1-4675-1741-6(0)) Oncekids.
—The Fujimini Adventure Series Box Set. 2013. (Fujimini Adventure Ser.). (ENG.). 128p. (J). (gr. 1-3). 29.99 (978-1-4675-1747-8(X)) Oncekids.
—Rainbow Panda & the Firecracker Fiasco. 2013. (Fujimini Adventure Ser.). (ENG.). 40p. (J). 10.99 (978-1-4675-1749-2(6)) Oncekids.
Waddell, Barbara. Hooray, Hooray, Today's the Day. 2010. 36p. 15.49 (978-1-4269-4477-2(2)) Trafford Publishing.
Wade, Joan. Zoey Finds a New Home. Swope, Brenda, illus. 2011. 28p. pap. 24.95 (978-1-4560-0899-4(4)) PublishAmerica, Inc.
Wade, Judith. Faelen, the Horse from the Sea. 2007. 107p. (J). mass mkt. 5.99 (978-0-9728958-5-9(X)) Riley Pr.
Wade, Taylor. The Magical Well. 2008. 33p. pap. 12.95 (978-1-4357-5175-0(2)) Lulu Pr., Inc.
Wafer, C. K. The Adventures of Brady Bean: Operation: Canine Caper. Myers, Alishea, illus. 2008. (J). pap. 5.95 (978-0-9797580-1-0(7)) CK Bks.
Wafer, C. K. & Wafer, C. K. The Adventures of Brady Bean: Operation: Georgie Porgie. Myers, Alishea, illus. 2007. (J). pap. 5.95 (978-0-9797580-0-3(9)) CK Bks.
Waggaman, Mary T. Con of Misty Mountain. 2013. 190p. pap. 8.95 (978-0-9719230-4-1(3)) St. Aidan Pr., Inc.
Wagner, Lloyd S. Ghosts at Gettysburg: An Oliver Family Adventure. 2007. 144p. 21.95 (978-0-595-70995-3(8)); per. 11.95 (978-0-595-46877-5(2)) iUniverse, Inc.
Wagner, Lori. Gateway of the Sun. 2007. 120p. pap. 9.95 (978-0-9798627-2-4(8)) Affirming Faith.
Wagner, Rachel A. Bogie the Boxer: Gardens. 2012. 24p. pap. 9.99 (978-0-9885180-4-9(X)) Mindstir Media.
Wagner-Robertson, Garry. The Evil Mailbox & the Super Burrito, 1 vol. Wagner, Connie, illus. 2011. (ENG.). 96p. (J). 16.99 (978-0-7643-3856-4(0), 9780764338564, Schiffer Publishing Ltd) Schiffer Publishing, Ltd.
Wagner, Yulia. The Flying-Fur Bus. 2011. 16p. pap. (978-1-4269-8835-6(4)) Trafford Publishing (UK) Ltd.
Wagoner, Timothy Allen. The Adventures of Jacque & Wanderwan Bk. 1: Naoo. 2005. (J). pap. 14.99 (978-0-9761739-2-2(1)) Grandoc Publishing.
Wagstaff, Janiel. Stella Tells Her Story. 2015. (ENG.). pap. 7.95 (978-1-63133-023-0(3)) Staff Development for Educators.
Waguespack, Michael. The Deer Hunting Book. 2013. 104p. pap. 7.95 (978-0-9754624-6-1(6)) Country Kid Publishing LLC.
Wahl, Jan. Cobweb Castle. 2014. (ENG., Illus.). 32p. (J). 14.95 (978-0-7649-6801-3(7)) Pomegranate Communications, Inc.
Waid, Mark. Imaginauts. Wieringo, Mike, illus. 2003. (Fantastic Four Ser.: Vol. 1). 144p. (YA). pap. 12.99 (978-0-7851-1063-7(1)) Marvel Worldwide, Inc.
Waid, Mark & Haspiel, Dean. The Fox - Freak Magnet. Haspiel, Dean, illus. 2014. (Fox Ser.). (ENG., Illus.). 144p. pap. 14.99 (978-1-936975-93-8(9), Dark Circle Comics) Archie Comic Pubns., Inc.
Wainwright, Joann M. Winston, the Polite St Bernard. Ross, Adam, illus. 2009. 28p. pap. 14.99 (978-1-4389-2704-6(5)) AuthorHouse.

Wakefield, Beth. The Cleaner. 2010. 151p. pap. 14.50 *(978-1-4457-6809-0(7))* Lulu Pr., Inc.

Wakem, Samantha. Milly's Magic Play House: The Hospital, 1 vol. Herridge, Debbie, illus. 2010. 20p. 24.95 *(978-1-4489-5114-7(3))* PublishAmerica, Inc.

Walden, Mark. Rogue. (H. I. V. E. Ser.: 5). (ENG.). (J). (gr. 3-7). 2012. 320p. pap. 8.99 *(978-1-4424-1369-6(7))* 2011. 304p. 16.99 *(978-1-4424-2187-5(8))* Simon & Schuster Bks. For Young Readers. (Simon & Schuster Bks. For Young Readers).

Waldman, Alan/A. Erica from America & the Start of the Gang of Four. Scobie, Andrea, illus. 2013. 44p. pap. *(978-0-9840514-2-7(2))* Roxby Media Ltd.

Waldrep, Susan. Papa Ant's Picnic. 2008. 24p. 15.00 *(978-1-4357-1129-7(7))* Lulu Pr., Inc.

Waldron, Douglas E. Cody Sackett of Montana: Tales of Adventure. 2008. 188p. per. 24.95 *(978-1-4241-9781-1(3))* America Star Bks.

Waldron, Douglas Edward. Pathway to Montan: The Settlers Rest, 1 vol. 2009. 104p. pap. 19.95 *(978-1-60836-313-1(9))* America Star Bks.

Wales, Sid. Freddie & Mee. Bryant, Kerry, illus. 2013. 28p. pap. *(978-1-78222-097-8(6))* Paragon Publishing, Rothersthorpe.

Walker, Anna. Peggy: A Brave Chicken on a Big Adventure. (ENG., Illus.). 32p. (J). (gr. -1-3). 2017. pap. 6.99 *(978-0-544-92819-0(9),* HMH Books For Young Readers) 2014. 16.99 *(978-0-544-25900-3(9))* Houghton Mifflin Harcourt Publishing Co.

—Peggy: A Brave Chicken on a Big Adventure. 2017. (ENG.). (J). (gr. -1-3). lib. bdg. 17.20 ***(978-0-606-39828-2(7))*** Turtleback Bks.

Walker, Dan. Summer of Trespass. 2016. (ENG.). 182p. (YA). pap. 12.99 *(978-1-943328-42-0(0),* Alaska Northwest Bks.) Graphic Arts Ctr. Publishing Co.

Walker, Johnny. The Planet Blue: The Adventures of Harry Lee & Bingo. 2011. 24p. pap. 11.32 *(978-1-4567-4879-1(3))* AuthorHouse.

Walker-Jones, Alexandra & Herrera, Hanna. The Adventures of Hobnob & Raisin - Paris Airport. 2013. 32p. 9.99 *(978-0-9830470-0-1(6))* O.L.D. Inc.

Walker, Jorge. Little Winston's Desire. 2011. 20p. pap. 9.49 *(978-1-4567-2396-5(0))* AuthorHouse.

Walker, Landry. Secrets & Lies. Takara, Marcio, illus. 2010. (Incredibles Ser.). 112p. (J). (gr. 3-8). pap. 9.99 *(978-1-60886-583-3(5))* Boom! Studios.

—Teenage Mutant Ninja Turtles Amazing Adventures, Vol. 1. 2016. (Teenage Mutant Ninja Turtles Amazing Adventures Ser.: 1). lib. bdg. 30.60 *(978-0-606-37809-3(X))* Turtleback Bks.

Walker, Melissa & Walker, Richard. A Place for Delta. 2010. (Illus.). 266p. (J). 16.95 *(978-0-9824784-0-0(2))* Whale Tale Pr.

Walker, Melzina. Little Melvin's Blue Coat. 2007. (Illus.). 32p. (J). pap. 8.00 *(978-0-8059-7389-1(3))* Dorrance Publishing Co., Inc.

Walker, Nicole. Gingersnap. 2005. (YA). per. 15.99 *(978-0-9677379-2-8(3))* North Gap Publishing.

Walker, Peter. The Magic Airplane. 2006. (ENG.). 160p. per. 12.95 *(978-1-59526-416-9(7))* Aeon Publishing Inc.

Walker, Peter Lancaster. Space Travelers Land at Buckingham Palace. Dixit, Rama, illus. 2007. 275p. (J). 19.95 *(978-1-934138-12-0(6))* Bouncing Ball Bks., Inc.

Walker, Rhonda. Willie Out West. 2013. 24p. pap. 12.95 *(978-1-4497-9848-2(9),* WestBow Pr.) Author Solutions, Inc.

Walker, Richard. The Barefoot Book of Pirates. Whelan, Olwyn, illus. 2008. (Barefoot Bks.). (ENG.). 64p. (J). 19.99 *(978-1-84686-237-3(X))* Barefoot Bks., Inc.

—Jack & the Beanstalk. 2009. (ENG., Illus.). (J). 16.99 *(978-1-84686-297-7(3))* Barefoot Bks., Inc.

—Juan y los Frijoles Magicos. 2008. (ENG & SPA., Illus.). 40p. (J). (gr. -1-1). 10.99 *(978-1-84686-216-8(7))* Barefoot Bks., Inc.

Walker, Russell D. Michelle & the Magic Timepiece. 2006. 108p. pap. 19.95 *(978-1-4241-3143-3(X))* PublishAmerica, Inc.

Walker, Rysa. Time's Edge, 0 vols. 2014. (Chronos Files Ser.: 2). (ENG.). 450p. (J). (gr. 7-12). pap. 9.99 *(978-1-4778-2582-2(7),* 9781477825822, Skyscape) Amazon Publishing.

Walkup, Jennifer. Second Verse. unabr. ed. 2013. (ENG.). 200p. (YA). (gr. 7-12). 15.95 *(978-1-935462-86-6(5))* Luminis Bks., Inc.

Wall, Anne. The Librarius Quest. 2012. (Illus.). 216p. (gr. 2-2). pap. 16.95 *(978-1-4678-8466-2(9))* AuthorHouse.

Wallace, Barbara Brooks. The Interesting Thing That Happened at Perfect Acres, Inc. 2007. 148p. per. 11.95 *(978-0-595-45763-2(0),* Backinprint.com) iUniverse, Inc.

Wallace, Bill. The Legend of Thunderfoot. 2006. (ENG.). 160p. (J). (gr. 3-7). 15.95 *(978-1-4169-0691-9(6),* Simon & Schuster/Paula Wiseman Bks.) Simon & Schuster/Paula Wiseman Bks.

Wallace, Bonny. The Raymond Wikins' Adventures, Children of Straw. 2009. 70p. pap. 9.95 *(978-1-60860-699-3(6),* Eloquent Bks.) Strategic Book Publishing & Rights Agency (SBPRA).

Wallace, Carol & Wallace, Bill. Bub, Snow, & the Burly Bear Scare. Gurney, John Steven, illus. 2003. (ENG.). 128p. (J). (gr. 3-7). pap. 7.99 *(978-0-7434-0640-6(0),* Aladdin) Simon & Schuster Children's Publishing.

Wallace, Clinton. H. The Adventures of Roger Eldemire. 2013. 28p. pap. 9.95 *(978-1-4787-2493-3(5))* Outskirts Pr., Inc.

Wallace, Daniel. Star Wars: Ship Factory. 2016. (ENG.). 24p. (J). (gr. 3-8). 19.99 *(978-0-7944-3739-8(7),* Reader's Digest Children's Bks.) Studio Fun International.

Wallace, Dillon. Troop One of the Labrador. 2007. (ENG.). 158p. pap. 19.99 *(978-1-4264-9191-7(3));* 178p. pap. 21.99 *(978-1-4264-9248-8(0))* Creative Media Partners, LLC.

—Ungava Bob. 2007. (ENG.). 196p. pap. 19.99 *(978-1-4346-0196-4(X));* 216p. pap. 22.99 *(978-1-4346-0270-1(2))* Creative Media Partners, LLC.

Wallace, James. Tsunami: Ghost Eagle 1. 2003. 149p. (YA). pap. 11.95 *(978-0-595-27372-0(6))* iUniverse, Inc.

Wallace, Jim. Terror on the Titanic. Sundaravej, Sittisan & Barchus, Nathan, illus. 2007. (Choose Your Own Adventure Ser.: No. 24). (ENG.). 122p. (J). (gr. 4-7). pap. 6.99 *(978-1-933390-24-6(7))* Chooseco LLC.

Wallace, Karen & Chapman, Neil. Arthur the King. 2009. (Hopscotch Adventures Ser.). (Illus.). 31p. (J). (gr. 1). lib. bdg. 25.65 *(978-1-59771-173-9(X))* Sea-To-Sea Pubns.

—The Round Table. 2009. (Hopscotch Adventures Ser.). (Illus.). 31p. (J). (gr. 1). lib. bdg. 25.65 *(978-1-59771-175-3(6))* Sea-To-Sea Pubns.

—Sir Lancelot & the Ice Castle. 2009. (Hopscotch Adventures Ser.). (Illus.). 31p. (J). (gr. 1). lib. bdg. 25.65 *(978-1-59771-174-6(8))* Sea-To-Sea Pubns.

Wallace, Rich. Double-Crossed at Cactus Flats: An Up2 U Western Adventure, 1 vol. Mitchell, Hazel, illus. 2013. (Up2U Adventures Ser.). (ENG.). 80p. (J). (gr. 2-5). lib. bdg. 27.07 *(978-1-61641-966-0(0),* Calico Chapter Bks) Magic Wagon.

Wallace, Sharolyn. The Adventures of Bruce, Ben & Gerry: Bruce's Dream. 2012. 28p. pap. 17.99 *(978-1-4772-0249-4(8))* AuthorHouse.

—The Adventures of Bruce, Ben & Gerry: Training Day. 2012. 24p. pap. 17.99 *(978-1-4772-5397-7(1))* AuthorHouse.

Wallace, Sheila Ryan. Miss Abigail's Antique Treasures. 2007. (ENG.). 152p. per. 15.95 *(978-0-7414-3942-0(5))* Infinity Publishing.

Wallace, Wade. Escape from Lego City! 2011. (Lego City Ser.). (ENG.). 16p. (J). (gr. -1-k). pap. 6.99 *(978-0-545-28095-2(8))* Scholastic, Inc.

Waller, Sharon Biggs. The Forbidden Orchid. 2016. (ENG., Illus.). 416p. (YA). (gr. 7). 18.99 *(978-0-451-47411-7(2),* Viking Books for Young Readers) Penguin Young Readers Group.

Waller, Stephen & Pearson Education Staff. Run for Your Life, Level 1. 2nd ed. 2009. (ENG., Illus.). 32p. pap. 11.99 *(978-1-4058-6970-6(4))* Pearson Education.

Walls, Pamela June. Sp Abby Lost at Sea. 2003. (Abby Ser.). pap. 6.99 *(978-0-7899-0967-1(7))* Editorial Unilit.

—Sp Abby Secret at Cutter Grove. 2003. (Abby Ser.). pap. 6.99 *(978-0-7899-0970-1(7))* Editorial Unilit.

Wally the Walleye. 2004. (J). lib. bdg. *(978-0-9725485-3-3(X))* Waterfall Ridge.

Walser, Jo. Chasing the Rising Moon. 2012. 452p. pap. 14.95 *(978-1-935807-04-9(8))* Stansbury Publishing.

Walsh, Ann. The Doctor's Apprentice: A Barkerville Mystery. 2007. (Barkerville Mystery Ser.: 2). (ENG.). 160p. (J). pap. 9.99 *(978-1-55002-633-7(X),* Sandcastle Bks.) Dundurn CAN. Dist: Ingram Publisher Services.

—Moses, Me, & Murder: A Barkerville Mystery. 2nd ed. 2013. (Barkerville Mystery Ser.: 1). (ENG., Illus.). 112p. (J). pap. 10.99 *(978-1-4597-0967-6(5))* Dundurn CAN. Dist: Ingram Publisher Services.

Walsh, Bill. The Dog Show. 2010. 32p. pap. 19.95 *(978-0-557-24059-3(X))* Lulu Pr., Inc.

Walsh, Franny. Who Cat: A Louisiana Tale. 2013. (ENG.). 32p. (J). pap. 16.95 *(978-1-4787-0280-1(X))* Outskirts Pr., Inc.

Walsh, Kim Carmen. Safari Finn. 2009. 28p. pap. 12.49 *(978-1-4389-0361-3(8))* AuthorHouse.

Walsh, Meg. Mama, Won't You Play with Me? 2009. 28p. pap. 13.99 *(978-1-4490-1424-7(0))* AuthorHouse.

Walsh, Patrick M., Jr. The Derby: A Timmy Wallings Story. McGriff, Aaron C., ed. WFM Services, illus. 2012. 188p. (J). *(978-0-9842929-4-3(2))* Daddy Bean Bks.

Walsh, Sara. The Dark Light. (ENG., (YA). (gr. 9). 2013. Illus.). 512p. pap. 9.99 *(978-1-4424-3458-5(9))* 2012. 496p. 16.99 *(978-1-4424-3455-4(4))* Simon Pulse. (Simon Pulse).

Walsh, Sheila. Will, God's Mighty Warrior, 1 vol. Johnson, Meredith, illus. 2006. (Will, God's Mighty Warrior Ser.: 1). (ENG.). 32p. (gr. -1-3). 14.99 *(978-1-4003-0805-7(4))* Nelson, Thomas Inc.

Walsleben, Edda Brigitte. Scotty the Little Westie Dog & His Diary. 2013. 268p. 25.00 *(978-1-937911-49-2(7));* pap. 15.00 *(978-1-937911-48-5(9))* Heavenly Realm Publishing.

Walter-Sereg, D. Bonnie Catches Lights in the Night Sky. 28p. 2013. 24.95 *(978-1-4137-9977-4(9))* 2012. pap. 24.95 *(978-1-4626-5856-5(3))* America Star Bks.

—Bonnie, the Trapeze Artist. 2013. 30p. 24.95 *(978-1-4137-6032-3(5))* 2012. 32p. pap. 24.95 *(978-1-4626-5858-9(X))* America Star Bks.

—Bonnie Tracks a Jungle Animal. 2012. 24p. 24.95 *(978-1-4626-5857-2(1))* America Star Bks.

Walters, Eric. Alexandria of Africa. 2008. (ENG.). 208p. (J). (gr. 7). pap. 12.95 *(978-0-385-66639-8(X),* Doubleday Canada) Penguin Random House Canada Young Readers CAN. Dist: Penguin Random Hse. LLC.

—Between Heaven & Earth, 1 vol. 2012. (Seven (the Series) Ser.). (ENG., Illus.). 264p. (J). (gr. 5-10). pap. 9.95 *(978-1-55469-941-4(X))* Orca Bk. Pubs. USA.

—Hunter, 1 vol. 2012. (ENG.). 208p. (J). (gr. 4-7). pap. 9.95 *(978-1-4598-0157-8(1))* Orca Bk. Pubs. USA.

—I've Got an Idea. 2004. 166p. (J). pap. *(978-0-00-639196-8(6),* HarperTrophy) HarperCollins Canada, Ltd.

—Overdrive, 1 vol. 2004. (Orca Soundings Ser.). (ENG.). 112p. (YA). (gr. 8-12). pap. 9.95 *(978-1-55143-318-9(4))* Orca Bk. Pubs. USA.

—The Rule of Three. 2014. (Rule of Three Ser.: 1). (ENG.). 416p. (YA). (gr. 7). 18.99 *(978-0-374-35502-9(9),* 9780374355029, Farrar, Straus & Giroux (BYR)) Farrar, Straus & Giroux.

—Visions. 2011. (ENG.). 208p. (J). pap. *(978-1-55455-122-4(6))* Fitzhenry & Whiteside, Ltd.

Walters, Janis. Adventures of Libby & Sophie: Sometimes Our Friends Can Get Us into Trouble. 2012. 24p. pap. 15.99 *(978-1-4771-2628-8(7))* Xlibris Corp.

Walthers, Joanie. The Fish Smuggler. Walthers, Don, illus. 2013. (ENG.). 24p. (J). 19.95 *(978-1-4787-1167-4(1))* Outskirts Pr., Inc.

Waltz, Dan. Dragon Fly: A Gnome's Great Adventure. Waltz, Dan, illus. 2007. (Illus.). 360p. (YA). per. 12.49 *(978-0-9741774-7-2(4))* D. W. Publishing.

Wand, Dana. Shanie June Jumped over the Moon. Tinling, Molly, illus. 2013. 32p. pap. *(978-1-4602-0466-5(2))* FriesenPress.

Wandless, David. Natural Magic. 2010. 344p. pap. 27.50 *(978-1-4461-4163-2(2))* Lulu Pr., Inc.

—Natural Magic Book 3 - the Milk Stone & the Tauren. 2010. 134p. pap. 20.95 *(978-1-4461-5162-4(X))* Lulu Pr., Inc.

Wang, Jen. Fionna & Cake Card Wars. 2016. (Adventure Time Graphic Novels Ser.). lib. bdg. 33.05 *(978-0-606-39000-2(6))* Turtleback Bks.

Wang, Kateri. Wang Ming: The Greatest of the Great Pandas. 2012. 32p. pap. 19.99 *(978-1-4772-9042-2(7))* AuthorHouse.

Ward, James M. The Time Curse. 2007. (Paths of Doom Ser.). (Illus.). 128p. (J). per. 4.99 *(978-1-931567-72-5(7))* Margaret Weis Productions, Ltd.

Ward, Jean Elizabeth. A Barbara Anne Bushy Tale: Book #2 in a Series. 2007. 188p. per. 16.95 *(978-0-595-45726-7(6))* iUniverse, Inc.

Ward, Kari. Marley & Maverick & the Haunted Maze. 2012. 34p. (-18). pap. *(978-1-897512-61-6(9))* Saga Bks.

—Marley & Maverick Go Fishing. 2012. 26p. pap. *(978-1-897512-54-8(6))* Saga Bks.

Ward, Lindsay. Please Bring Balloons. 2013. (ENG., Illus.). 32p. (J). (gr. -1-k). 16.99 *(978-0-8037-3878-2(1),* Dial Bks) Penguin Young Readers Group.

Ward, M. The Evergreens Get Wet: The Evergreens. 2009. (Illus.). 28p. pap. 12.49 *(978-1-4389-8960-0(1))* AuthorHouse.

Ward, M. P. Sam & the Sea Witch. 2013. 158p. pap. *(978-1-77127-397-8(6))* MuseItUp Publishing.

Ward, Marcia. The Girl Who Found Her Voice. 2013. (ENG.). 276p. pap. 14.99 *(978-1-939927-28-6(5))* Telemachus Pr., LLC.

Ward, Ruth. The Adventures of Bloor Bone. 2005. (J). lib. bdg. 18.00 *(978-1-59094-105-8(5))* Jawbone Publishing Corp.

Ward, Teresa. Blackie's Day Out. Ward, Juliana, illus. 2011. 32p. pap. *(978-1-77067-933-7(2))* FriesenPress.

Wardale, David. Psico. 2013. 302p. (J). pap. *(978-1-78299-172-4(7))* FeedARead.com.

Wardlow, Lynn. Friends with My Brother. 2012. 28p. pap. 9.95 *(978-1-4787-1384-5(4))* Outskirts Pr., Inc.

Wareh, Denny T. Nee Nee the Woodpecker. 2011. 36p. pap. 24.95 *(978-1-4560-5680-3(8))* America Star Bks.

—School Bound Nee Nee the Woodpecker. 2011. 36p. pap. 24.95 *(978-1-4560-8900-9(5))* America Star Bks.

Wargin, Kathy-jo. Mitt & Minn at the Wisconsin Cheese Jamboree. Holman, Karen Busch, illus. 2007. (Mitt Midwest Ser.: 3). (ENG.). 144p. (J). (gr. k-7). 14.95 *(978-1-58726-305-7(X),* Mitten Pr.) Ann Arbor Editions LLC.

—Mitt & Minn's Illinois Adventure. Holman, Karen Busch, illus. 2007. (Mitt Midwest Ser.: 4). (ENG.). 144p. (J). (gr. k-7). 14.95 *(978-1-58726-306-4(8),* Mitten Pr.) Ann Arbor Editions LLC.

—Mitt, the Michigan Mouse. Holman, Karen Busch, illus. 2015. (Mitt Midwest Ser.: 1). (ENG.). 160p. (J). (gr. k-7). pap. 8.95 *(978-1-938170-65-2(2),* Mitten Pr.) Ann Arbor Editions LLC.

Warnack, Rhonda. Kelsey's Candy World Adventure. 2009. 48p. pap. 17.49 *(978-1-4490-4438-1(7))* AuthorHouse.

Warnasuriya, Chandrani. Children's Stories of Wit & Humor: Stories from Sri Lanka (The Grand-Old-Man & The Big Five) 2008. 50p. pap. 16.95 *(978-1-60672-624-2(2))* America Star Bks.

Warne. Peter's Favorite Places (Sticker Stories) 2014. (Peter Rabbit Animation Ser.). (ENG., Illus.). 16p. (J). (gr. -1-2). pap. 6.99 *(978-0-14-135005-9(9),* Warne) Penguin Young Readers Group.

Warner, Deborah. Phineas Willerbee - in the Code of the Realm: The Chosen One Revealed. 2013. (ENG.). 36p. (J). pap. 9.95 *(978-1-4787-0955-8(3))* Outskirts Pr., Inc.

Warner, Gertrude Chandler. The Boxcar Children Guide to Adventure: A How-To for Mystery Solving, Make-It-Yourself Projects, & More. 2014. (Boxcar Children Mysteries Ser.). (ENG.). 144p. (J). (gr. 1-5). 12.99 *(978-0-8075-0905-0(1))* Whitman, Albert & Co.

—The Clue in the Papyrus Scroll. 2017. (Boxcar Children Great Adventure Ser.: 2). (J). lib. bdg. 17.20 ***(978-0-606-40316-0(7))*** Turtleback Bks.

—Journey on a Runaway Train. 2017. (Boxcar Children Great Adventure Ser.: 1). (J). lib. bdg. 17.20 ***(978-0-606-40315-3(9))*** Turtleback Bks.

Warner, Gertrude Chandler, creator. The Boxcar Children, 12 bks. 2010. (Boxcar Children Mysteries Ser.: 1). (ENG.). 1p. (J). (gr. 1-5). pap. 59.99 *(978-0-8075-0855-8(1))* Whitman, Albert & Co.

Warner, Jeremy. Hidden Mickeys: A Mouse in the Land. Warner, Danielle, illus. 2012. 68p. pap. 5.95 *(978-0-9853555-2-4(2))* Portrait Health Publishing.

Warner, Larry. Chocolate Island, 1 vol. 2010. 42p. pap. 24.95 *(978-1-4489-7372-9(4))* PublishAmerica, Inc.

Warnock, Chris. Toys Overboard!, 1 vol. 2009. (ENG.). 48p. 24.95 *(978-1-60672-197-1(6))* America Star Bks.

Warren, Tania Catherine. All about Charlie Horse: Charlie Horse & His Adventures. Warren, Steven Mathew, illus. 2012. 26p. 24.95 *(978-1-4626-5442-0(8))* America Star Bks.

Warren, Vince H. The Adventures of Meka & Her Two Cubs. 2013. (ENG.). 28p. (J). pap. 7.95 *(978-1-4787-0308-2(3))* Outskirts Pr., Inc.

Warren, Wendy Ann. Potato Chip, an Irish Tale. 2008. 28p. pap. 15.99 *(978-1-4363-0551-8(9))* Xlibris Corp.

The Wars. Date not set. (J). *(978-0-679-40067-7(2),* Random Hse. Bks. for Young Readers) Random Hse. Children's Bks.

Washer, Mark Gregory. Blue Bonnie Butterfly: Tale of Two Tails. 2013. 36p. pap. 18.41 *(978-1-4669-8434-9(1))* Trafford Publishing.

Washer, S. N. The Wingate Adventures: Our New Friends. 2006. 164p. pap. 11.95 *(978-1-59800-510-3(3))* Outskirts Pr., Inc.

Washington, Sharalee Marie Shepherd. Little Bear Rabbit Goes to London. 2012. 80p. 24.99 *(978-1-4797-2677-6(X));* pap. 15.99 *(978-1-4797-2676-9(1))* Xlibris Corp.

Washington Sr., Terence B. Terry, Bear & Duck, 1 vol. 2009. 20p. pap. 24.95 *(978-1-60836-291-2(4))* America Star Bks.

Wasserman, Robin. Crashed. 2009. (ENG.). 448p. (YA). (gr. 9-18). 16.99 *(978-1-4169-7453-6(9),* Simon Pulse) Simon Pulse.

Wasserman, Robin & Soderberg, Erin. X Marks the Spot. 2015. (Puppy Pirates Ser.: No. 2). (ENG., Illus.). 96p. (J). (gr. 1-4). 4.99 *(978-0-553-51170-3(X),* Random Hse. Bks. for Young Readers) Random Hse. Children's Bks.

Wassillie, Eliza, et al. Four Legged Adventures. Wassillie, Eliza et al, illus. 2006. (Adventure Story Collection Ser.). 28p. (J). (gr. 2-6). pap. 10.00 *(978-1-58084-250-1(X))* Lower Kuskokwim Schl. District.

Watase, Yuu & Caselman, Lance. Alice 19th, Vol. 2, 7 vols. JN Productions Staff, tr. from JPN. Watase, Yuu, illus. 2003. (ENG., Illus.). 200p. pap. 9.95 *(978-1-59116-229-2(7))* Viz Media.

Waterhouse, Raymond & Lawrie, Gabrielle. Yoppi A Bear Story. 2007. 158p. pap. 19.50 *(978-1-84753-876-5(2))* Lulu Pr., Inc.

Waters, Michael. Tommy & his Flying Saucer of Milk. 2009. 32p. 18.95 *(978-1-4092-8450-5(6));* pap. 16.95 *(978-1-4357-4802-6(6))* Lulu Pr., Inc.

Watkins, Fred L. Sue, Mary & Charles, 1 vol. 2009. 127p. pap. 19.95 *(978-1-60749-110-1(9))* America Star Bks.

Watkins, T. a. Joey & the Ancient Horn: A Mystery Revealed. Davis, Marcus, illus. 2007. 333p. (J). (gr. -1). per. 12.95 *(978-0-9762788-0-1(4))* Great I-AM Publishing Co., The.

Watlington, Elizabeth. Binky's Big Adventure. 2004. (YA). pap. 7.95 *(978-0-9723102-3-9(1))* Bush Publishing Inc.

Watson, Casey. Dirty Heart Clean Heart. 2013. 30p. pap. 9.99 *(978-1-62509-564-0(3))* Salem Author Services.

Watson, Don. The Legend of Red Leaf. Robbins, Ashley, illus. l.t. ed. 2005. 125p. (J). pap. 9.95 *(978-0-9714358-6-5(3))* Longhorn Creek Pr.

Watson, Gayle. Catie Corn & the Corn Cops. Fautsch, Jackie, illus. l.t. ed. 22p. (J). 2006. 15.99 *(978-1-59879-098-6(6))* 2005. per. 9.99 *(978-1-59879-079-5(X))* Lifevest Publishing, Inc.

Watson, H. B. Marriott. The Stone Chamber. 2004. reprint ed. pap. 1.99 *(978-1-4192-8353-6(7))* Kessinger Publishing, LLC.

Watson, J. R. Wizard down Under. 2009. 160p. 23.50 *(978-1-60860-138-7(2),* Eloquent Bks.) Strategic Book Publishing & Rights Agency (SBPRA).

Watson, Jude. Beyond the Grave. 2009. (39 Clues Ser.: 4). (ENG.). 192p. (J). (gr. 3-7). 12.99 *(978-0-545-06044-8(3))* Scholastic, Inc.

—In Too Deep. 2009. (39 Clues Ser.: 6). (ENG.). 208p. (J). (gr. 3-7). 12.99 *(978-0-545-09064-3(4));* 12.99 *(978-0-545-06046-2(X))* Scholastic, Inc.

—A King's Ransom. 2011. (39 Clues: Cahills vs. Vespers Ser.: 2). (ENG.). 192p. (J). (gr. 3-7). 12.99 *(978-0-545-29840-7(7),* Scholastic Pr.);Bk. 2. 12.99 *(978-0-545-32410-6(6))* Scholastic, Inc.

—Loot. 2014. (ENG.). 272p. (J). (gr. 3-7). 17.99 *(978-0-545-46802-2(7),* Scholastic Pr.) Scholastic, Inc.

—Nowhere to Run. 2013. (39 Clues Ser.: Bk. 1). (ENG., Illus.). 272p. (J). (gr. 3-7). 12.99 *(978-0-545-52137-6(8))* Scholastic, Inc.

—The 39 Clues # 6: En Las Profundidades. 2012. (SPA.). 208p. (J). (gr. 5-8). pap. 14.99 *(978-84-08-10768-2(2))* Noguer y Caralt Editores, S. A. ESP. Dist: Lectorum Pubns., Inc.

Watson, M. Desmond & the Challenge on Mudwig Mountain. 2005. 109p. pap. *(978-1-84401-010-3(4))* Athena Pr.

—Veg Patch Gang. 2005. (Illus.). 40p. pap. *(978-1-84401-005-9(8))* Athena Pr.

Watson, M. C. V. Fairy Tales & Pixie Trails: From the Series. 2012. 48p. pap. 21.99 *(978-1-4771-5249-2(0))* Xlibris Corp.

Watson, Michael. Search, Secrets, & Spies. 2011. 32p. pap. 13.00 *(978-1-61204-357-9(7),* Strategic Bk. Publishing) Strategic Book Publishing & Rights Agency (SBPRA).

—Treasure, Trash, & Turtles. 2010. 24p. pap. 11.50 *(978-1-60911-500-5(7),* Eloquent Bks.) Strategic Book Publishing & Rights Agency (SBPRA).

Watson, Philip & Ofiesh, Nicole. The Treasure Chest. 2011. 52p. 20.50 *(978-1-4269-5350-7(X));* pap. 10.50 *(978-1-4269-5269-2(4))* Trafford Publishing.

Watson, Tom. Stick Dog & Stick Dog Wants a Hot Dog. 2017. (Stick Dog Ser.). 416p. (J). (gr. 3-7). 25.98 ***(978-0-06-274810-2(6))*** HarperCollins Pubs.

Watt, J. S. The Hall of Sorrows. 2006. 67p. pap. 16.95 *(978-1-4241-2984-3(2))* PublishAmerica, Inc.

Watters, Shannon, ed. Adventure Time - Cover Gallery, Vol. 1. 2013. (ENG., Illus.). 128p. (J). (gr. 4). 24.99 *(978-1-60886-343-3(9))* Boom! Studios.

Watts, Jan. CAKE! A comedy script for young People. 2010. 55p. pap. 21.95 *(978-1-4452-4587-4(6))* Lulu Pr., Inc.

Watts, Jane & Nobel, DeAnna. The Adventures of Alligator Tater. 2007. 64p. per. 10.95 *(978-1-4327-0228-1(9))* Outskirts Pr., Inc.

Watts, Katherine. Tiger Tails. 2008. 76p. pap. 35.95 *(978-0-9556878-0-8(2))* Watts, Katherine GBR. Dist: Lulu Pr., Inc.

Watts, Robin Queen. The Adventures of Beauty & Sam. 2009. 20p. pap. 10.50 *(978-1-4269-1286-3(2))* Trafford Publishing.

Wax, Wendy. Diego y Papi al Rescate. Ziegler, Argentina Palacios, tr. Hom, John, illus. 2008. (Go, Diego, Go! Ser.).Tr. of Diego & Papi to the Rescue. (SPA.). 24p. (J). (gr. -1-2). pap. 3.99 *(978-1-4169-5044-8(3),* Libros Para Ninos) Libros Para Ninos.

Weakley, David. Rowley to the Rescue. 2009. 72p. pap. 24.00 *(978-1-60860-295-7(8),* Eloquent Bks.) Strategic Book Publishing & Rights Agency (SBPRA).

Wealth, Viktoria. Aadom Kingdom of the Dragons' Light: Book-I. 2003. 214p. (YA). pap. 14.95 *(978-0-595-28175-6(3))* iUniverse, Inc.

Weatherbee, Tabatha. Dream Sharers: Love/Hate. 2013. 336p. (J). pap. 19.00 *(978-1-62212-978-2(4),* Strategic Bk. Publishing) Strategic Book Publishing & Rights Agency (SBPRA).

Weathers, Andrea. Hermy the Hermit Crab: The Adventure Begins. 2004. (J). pap. 15.99 *(978-0-933101-22-7(8))* Legacy Pubns.

Weaver, Jack W. Cat & Dog Breath Meet the Last Pirates: How to Fly a Basset Hound. 2012. 164p. 24.95 *(978-1-4626-6652-2(3))* America Star Bks.

Weaver, Jo. Paul Bunyan: A Very Tall Tale, 1 vol. rev. ed. 2013. (Fiction Readers Ser.). (ENG., Illus.). 20p. (J). (gr. 1-1). pap. 15.96 *(978-1-4807-1153-2(5));* pap. 4.99 *(978-1-4333-5497-7(7))* Shell Educational Publishing.

Weaver, Joyce A. Mckissick. The Adventures of Mopey Bear & His Two Brothers, 1 vol. 2009. 48p. pap. 16.95 *(978-1-60813-775-6(9))* America Star Bks.

Webb, Catherine. The Extraordinary & Unusual Adventures of Horatio Lyle. 2006. (ENG.). 320p. (gr. 8). 9.95 *(978-1-904233-61-9(9))* Little, Brown Book Group Ltd. GBR. Dist: Hachette Bk. Group.

—The Obsidian Dagger: Being the Further Extraordinary Adventures of Horatio Lyle. 2007. (ENG.). 336p. (gr. 7). pap.

11.95 *(978-1-904233-79-4(1))* Little, Brown Book Group Ltd. GBR. Dist: Hachette Bk. Group.

Webb, Heather. The Frog & the Fly. Sanderson, Constance, illus. 2008. 29p. pap. 24.95 *(978-1-60441-380-9(8))* America Star Bks.

Webb, Holly. The Brave Kitten. Williams, Sophy, illus. 2016. (Pet Rescue Adventures Ser.). (ENG.). 128p. (J). (gr. 2-6). 4.99 *(978-1-58925-480-0(5))* Tiger Tales.

—The Rescued Puppy. Williams, Sophy, illus. 2017. (Pet Rescue Adventures Ser.). (ENG.). 128p. (J). (gr. 2-6). 19.99 ***(978-1-68010-051-8(3))*** Tiger Tales.

—Sammy the Shy Kitten. Williams, Sophy, illus. 2017. (Pet Rescue Adventures Ser.). (ENG.). 128p. (J). (gr. 2-6). 19.99 ***(978-1-68010-050-1(5))*** Tiger Tales.

—The Secret Kitten. Williams, Sophy, illus. 2017. (Pet Rescue Adventures Ser.). (ENG.). 128p. (J). (gr. 2-6). 19.99 ***(978-1-68010-049-5(1))*** Tiger Tales.

Webb, Jane K. My Super Stupendous Day at the Beach. Cupolo, Eileen, illus. 2012. 24p. pap. 12.95 *(978-1-61493-044-0(9))* Peppertree Pr., The.

Webb, Mack H., Jr. Webb's Wondrous Tales Book 2. Webb, Celia, illus. 2007. 156p. (J). per. 14.95 *(978-0-9779576-3-7(2))* Plinut Pr., Inc.

Webb, Ryan. Buddy: Dog of the Smoky Mountains. 2013. (Illus.). 34p. (J). pap. 12.00 *(978-0-9847836-3-2(6))* Celtic Cat Publishing.

Webber, Barbara. Feeling Loved: A Ted E. Bear Story. 2013. 40p. pap. 15.95 *(978-1-4525-7162-1(7),* Balboa Pr.) Author Solutions, Inc.

Webber, Gail. Time of the Cats. 2013. 132p. 28.95 *(978-1-4582-1233-7(5),* Abbott Pr.) Author Solutions, Inc.

Weber, Erec-Michael Ollier. Bryce & the Blood Ninjas. Harvey II, Alvin, illus. 2013. 38p. pap. 20.00 *(978-0-9716481-9-7(0))* Kila Springs Pr.

Webster, Andrea K. Pigeon in the Park. 2012. 28p. pap. 19.99 *(978-1-4772-2530-1(7))* AuthorHouse.

Webster, Christy. Big Fish, Little Fish. 2016. (Illus.). 24p. (J). E-Book ***(978-0-7364-3705-9(3))*** Random Hse., Inc.

—Double-Team! (Teenage Mutant Ninja Turtles) Spaziante, Patrick, illus. 2014. (Step into Reading Ser.). (ENG.). 48p. (J). (gr. 2-4). 3.99 *(978-0-385-37434-7(8),* Random Hse. Bks. for Young Readers) Random Hse. Children's Bks.

—Green Team! 2012. (Step into Reading Level 4 Ser.). lib. bdg. 13.55 *(978-0-606-26801-1(4),* Turtleback) Turtleback Bks.

—Green Team! (Teenage Mutant Ninja Turtles) Spaziante, Patrick, illus. 2012. (Step into Reading Ser.). (ENG.). 48p. (J). (gr. k-3). pap. 3.99 *(978-0-307-98070-0(7),* Random Hse. Bks. for Young Readers) Random Hse. Children's Bks.

Webster, Christy. Thomas & the Buzzy Bees. 2017. (Thomas & Friends Step into Reading Ser.). lib. bdg. 14.75 ***(978-0-606-39861-9(9))*** Turtleback Bks.

Webster, Clare L., retold by. The Elf, 1 vol. 2009. 27p. pap. 24.95 *(978-1-60836-775-7(4))* America Star Bks.

Webster, David. Book Two of the Naxos Island Mages: The War of the Dark Mages. 2004. 190p. pap. 13.95 *(978-0-595-31302-0(7))* iUniverse, Inc.

Webster, David Scott. Book One of the Naxos Island Mages: The Grand Adventure. 2003. 200p. 24.95 *(978-0-595-75137-2(7));* pap. 14.95 *(978-0-595-29933-1(4))* iUniverse, Inc.

Webster, Frank V. The Boy from the Ranch: Or, Roy Bradner's City Experiences. 2007. (ENG.). 132p. pap. 18.99 *(978-1-4346-4347-6(6));* 148p. pap. 19.99 *(978-1-4346-4348-3(4))* Creative Media Partners, LLC.

—The Boy Scouts of Lenox: Or the Hike over Big Bear Mountain. 2007. 146p. pap. 18.99 *(978-1-4346-4443-5(X))* Creative Media Partners, LLC.

—Dick the Bank Boy. 2007. 184p. 26.95 *(978-1-4218-3231-9(3),* 1st World Library - Literary Society) 1st World Publishing, Inc.

Webster, Jean. Papaito-Piernas-Largas. (SPA.). (YA). (gr. 5-8). pap. *(978-950-08-1515-4(X),* AA7255) Atlantida ARG. Dist: Lectorum Pubns., Inc.

Webster, Wendy. Magicus Perfecticum. 2009. (Illus.). 60p. pap. 11.49 *(978-1-4490-0765-2(1))* AuthorHouse.

Wechsler, Nathalie. Once upon A Fly: The Adventures of Lamouche. Wechsler, Nathalie, illus. 2005. (Illus.). 24p. (J). per. 7.99 *(978-0-9766998-1-1(8))* Finlay Prints, Inc.

—Once upon A Fly - Hardcover: The Adventures of Lamouche. Wechsler, Nathalie, illus. 2005. (Illus.). 24p. (J). 10.95 *(978-0-9766998-0-4(X))* Finlay Prints, Inc.

Wedgeworth, Anthony G. Nums of Shoreview: Baka's Curse. 2010. 68p. pap. 9.97 *(978-0-578-04710-2(1))* Wedgeworth, Anthony G.

Weeks Millard, Mary. A Bilingual Parrot. 2017. (From Disgrace to Honour Ser.: Vol. 4). (ENG.). pap. ***(978-1-84625-519-9(8))*** DayOne Pubns.

Weeks, Sarah. Woof. Berry, Holly, illus. 2009. (ENG.). 32p. (J). (gr. -1-3). 16.99 *(978-0-06-025007-2(0))* HarperCollins Pubs.

Weeks, Timothy A. The Wise Mullet of Cook Bayou I.t. ed. 2004. (Illus.). 48p. (J). per. *(978-0-9713573-8-9(2))* Thomas Expressions, LLC.

Wegelius, Jakob. The Murderer's Ape. 2017. (ENG.). 624p. (YA). (gr. 7). 17.99 *(978-1-101-93175-2(2),* Delacorte Pr.) Random Hse. Children's Bks.

Wegelius, Jakob & Graves, Peter. The Murderer's Ape. 2017. (YA). lib. bdg. *(978-1-101-93176-9(0),* Delacorte Pr) Random House Publishing Group.

Wehrman, Tom. Grandpa's a Martian. Dunnier, Tina, illus. 2013. 28p. pap. 8.99 *(978-1-938768-27-9(2))* Gypsy Pubns.

Wehrmeijer, Annelien. Noah & Dexter. van de Liejgraaf, Deborah, illus. 2014. (My Best Friend & Me Ser.). (ENG.). 10p. (J). (gr. -1 — 1). bds. 6.99 *(978-0-7641-6662-4(X))* Barron's Educational Series, Inc.

Weilerstein, Sadie Rose. K'tonton's Sukkot Adventure. 2016. (ENG., Illus.). 32p. pap. 11.95 *(978-0-8276-1268-6(0))* Jewish Pubn. Society.

Wein, Elizabeth. Black Dove, White Raven. 2015. (ENG.). 368p. (YA). (gr. 7-12). 17.99 *(978-1-4231-8310-5(X))* Hyperion Bks. for Children.

—Rose under Fire. 2013. (ENG.). 368p. (YA). (gr. 9-17). 17.99 *(978-1-4231-8309-9(6))* Hyperion Pr.

Weinberg, Moshe. The Unforgettable Journey. 2004. 142p. (J). 12.95 *(978-1-56871-306-9(1))* Targum Pr., Inc.

Weing, Drew. The Creepy case files of Margo Maloo. 2016. (Creepy Case Files of Margo Maloo Ser.). (ENG., Illus.). 128p. (J). 15.99 *(978-1-62672-339-9(7),* 9781626723399, First Second Bks.) Roaring Brook Pr.

Weinman, Logan & Bennett, Jeffrey. Max's Ice Age Adventure. 2007. (Science Adventures with Max the Dog Ser.). (ENG., Illus.). 32p. (J). (gr. k-2). 12.00 *(978-0-9721819-2-1(X))* Big Kid Science.

Weis, Claudia Brigitte. A B R A H A M: Bist du neugierig? 2010. 88p. pap. 17.90 *(978-3-8391-0698-3(2))* Bks. on Demand.

Weisenfluh, Craig. ABC's in the Trees, a LittleWeeds Adventure: A book for Little Ones. 2007. (Illus.). (J). 11.95 *(978-0-9746782-1-4(X))* B'Squeak Productions.

Weishampel, W. A. The Mystery of the Green Stone, 1 vol. 2010. 122p. pap. 19.95 *(978-1-60749-761-5(1))* America Star Bks.

Weisman, Greg. Gargoyles #1. 2006. (Illus.). 24p. (YA). pap. 3.50 *(978-1-59362-040-0(3),* Slave Labor Graphics) Slave Labor Bks.

—Rain of the Ghosts. 2013. (Rain of the Ghosts Ser.: 1). (ENG., Illus.). 240p. (YA). (gr. 6-13). pap. 9.99 *(978-1-250-02979-9(1),* 9781250029799, St. Martin's Griffin) St. Martin's Pr.

Weiss, Ellen. Lucky Duck. Lies, Brian, illus. 2004. (Ready-to-Read Ser.). 31p. (J). (gr. -1-1). 11.65 *(978-0-7569-5618-9(8))* Perfection Learning Corp.

—The Mystery of Microsneezia: A ClueFinders Mystery Adventure. 2004. (Illus.). 96p. (J). pap. *(978-0-7630-7619-1(8))* Magma.

Weiss, Rebecca J. Grandpa & Me Love Hotdogs! 2012. 36p. pap. 20.99 *(978-1-4772-8714-9(0))* AuthorHouse.

Weissmann, Joe, illus. The Gingerbread Man. 2005. (J). 7.95 *(978-0-9770473-0-7(X))* Heersink, Roland.

Welch, Eric. Jimmy the Gnome Won't Leave His Home, 1 vol. Natelli, Kenny, illus. 2009. 17p. pap. 24.95 *(978-1-60836-679-8(0))* America Star Bks.

Welch, J. D. The Darwin Code. 2017. (ENG.). 320p. pap. 14.95 ***(978-1-78693-389-8(6),*** cdc8fcca-0f1f-4aed-9fb5-864761d67852) Austin, Stan AUS. Dist: Bookmasters Distribution.

Welch, Sheila Kelly. The Shadowed Unicorn. 2011. 192p. (gr. -1). pap. 12.95 *(978-1-4502-6991-9(5))* iUniverse, Inc.

Welling, Martin. Eston Discovers Home: A Dog Discovers Freedom, Fear and, Finally, Family. 2011. (Illus.). 42p. (J). 29.95 *(978-1-4327-7038-9(1))* Outskirts Pr., Inc.

Wellings, Chris. Sparkles Visits the Farm. Paluseka, Julia, illus. 2011. 36p. pap. 24.95 *(978-1-4560-4102-1(9))* America Star Bks.

Wellings, Chris R. How Sparkles Came About: The Adventures of Sparkles. Nunnally, Carson, illus. 2011. 32p. pap. 24.95 *(978-1-4560-4119-9(3))* America Star Bks.

—Sparkles Meets the Easter Bunny: The Adventures of Sparkles. Hammersley, Karen, illus. 2011. 48p. pap. 24.95 *(978-1-4560-7063-2(0))* America Star Bks.

Wells, Carolyn. Patty's Butterfly Days. 2011. 166p. 25.95 *(978-1-4638-9970-7(X));* pap. 13.95 *(978-1-4638-0167-0(X))* Rodgers, Alan Bks.

Wells, Craig. Fangs for God: A Vampire Satire. 2011. 252p. pap. 16.95 *(978-1-4620-2136-9(0))* iUniverse, Inc.

Wells, Dan. Ruins. 2014. (Partials Sequence Ser.: 3). (ENG.). 464p. (YA). (gr. 9). 17.99 *(978-0-06-207110-1(6))* HarperCollins Pubs.

Wells, Helen. Cherry Ames Boxed Set: Volumes 17-20. 2007. 896p. (J). 39.95 *(978-0-8261-0439-7(8))* Springer Publishing Co., Inc.

—The Silver Ring Mystery: The Vicki Barr Flight Stewardess Series. 2011. 190p. 42.95 *(978-1-258-10005-6(3))* Literary Licensing, LLC.

Wells, Jane. Bird on Fire. 2013. 84p. pap. 14.95 *(978-1-939880-10-9(6))* Crumm, David Media, LLC.

Wells, Janet F. For Petey's Sake! 2013. 24p. pap. 10.99 *(978-1-4525-8297-9(1),* Balboa Pr.) Author Solutions, Inc.

Wells, R. W. Black Mountain Express: A Smoky Mountain Bedtime Tale. 2007. 53p. pap. 16.95 *(978-1-60441-396-0(4))* America Star Bks.

Wells, Rita. Janie Plants a Tree. 2013. 26p. pap. 16.95 *(978-1-4497-8903-9(X),* WestBow Pr.) Author Solutions, Inc.

Wells, Rosemary. On the Blue Comet. Ibatoulline, Bagram, illus. (ENG.). 336p. (J). (gr. 5). 2012. pap. 8.99 *(978-0-7636-5815-1(4))* 2010. 16.99 *(978-0-7636-3722-4(X))* Candlewick Pr.

—Yoko Finds Her Way. 2014. (Yoko Book Ser.). (ENG.). 32p. (J). (gr. -1-k). 16.99 *(978-1-4231-6512-5(8))* Hyperion Pr.

Wells, Shannon Nicole. Gold! A Tall Tale. 2009. (J). pap. 7.00 *(978-1-61623-111-8(4))* Independent Pub.

Wells, Zachariah, et al. Anything but Hank! Orchard, Eric, illus. 2008. (ENG.). 50p. (J). (gr. k-3). 19.95 *(978-1-897231-36-4(9))* Biblioasis CAN. Dist: Consortium Bk. Sales & Distribution.

Welsh Books Staff. Llyfr Liwio Sali Mali. 2nd ed. 2005. (WEL., Illus.). 24p. pap. *(978-1-902416-88-5(0))* Cymdeithas Lyfrau Ceredigion.

Welsh, C. E. L. Space Race. Jones, K. L., illus. 2011. (Campfire Graphic Novels Ser.). (ENG.). 68p. (YA). (gr. 5-12). pap. 9.99 *(978-93-80028-62-0(8),* Campfire) Steerforth Pr.

Welsh, Lisa. Sammy Swan: The Big Storm. 2010. 24p. pap. 14.49 *(978-1-4490-7234-6(8))* AuthorHouse.

Welty, Carolyn. Look at Little Lucy, 1 vol. Pratt, Susan, illus. 2009. 16p. pap. 24.95 *(978-1-60813-444-1(X))* America Star Bks.

Welvaert, Scott R. & Jungman, Ann. The Curse of the Wendigo: An Agate & Buck Adventure, 1 vol. Garvey, Brann, illus. 2006. (Vortex Bks.). (ENG.). 112p. (gr. 2-3). pap. 7.19 *(978-1-59889-282-6(7),* Vortex Bks.) Stone Arch Bks.

Wenger, Brahm. Dewey's Magical Sleigh. 2005. (ENG.). 32p. (J). (gr. -1-2). 15.95 *(978-0-9745143-5-2(7))* RandallFraser Publishing.

Wentz, Tim. Dark Secret at Twenty-Five Feet. 2012. 220p. 24.95 *(978-1-62709-663-8(9))* America Star Bks.

Werlin, Nancy. And Then There Were Four. 2017. (ENG.). 416p. (YA). (gr. 9). 18.99 *(978-0-8037-4072-3(7),* Dial Bks) Penguin Young Readers Group.

Werner, Michael. Aspey's Adventures with Asperger's. 2012. 32p. pap. 21.99 *(978-1-4771-0800-0(9))* Xlibris Corp.

West, Alma Brown. Princess Logan & the Shy Spell. 2010. 54p. pap. 15.99 *(978-1-4535-3513-4(6))* Xlibris Corp.

West, C. The Adventures of Ice Cream & Honey Buns: A Day in the Park. 2012. 28p. pap. 16.09 *(978-1-4669-4700-9(4))* Trafford Publishing.

—The Adventures of Ice Cream & Honey Buns: Ready to Learn. 2012. 28p. pap. 16.09 *(978-1-4669-4739-9(X))* Trafford Publishing.

—The Adventures of Ice Cream & Honey Buns: What Time Is It? 2013. 28p. pap. 16.09 *(978-1-4669-5671-1(2))* Trafford Publishing.

West, Denis. Sam of the Forest Railway. 2012. 66p. pap. 13.50 *(978-1-78035-361-6(8),* Fastprint Publishing) Upfront Publishing Ltd. GBR. Dist: Printondemand-worldwide.com.

West, Joyce. The Drovers Road Collection: Three New Zealand Adventures, 3 vols. West, Joyce, illus. 2003. (Bethlehem Budget Bks.). (Illus.). 416p. (YA). pap. 16.95 *(978-1-883937-69-0(8))* Bethlehem Bks.

West, Kathryn E. Garden of Roses. 2007. 328p. 29.95 *(978-0-595-70333-3(X));* per. 19.95 *(978-0-595-45295-8(7))* iUniverse, Inc.

West, Nancy. Chips - the War Dog: Based on the True-Life Adventures of the World War II K-9 Hero. 2nd ed. 2004. 183p. (J). per. 8.95 *(978-0-9743659-1-6(2))* Hero Dog Pubns.

West, Paul & Denslow, W. W. The Pearl & the Pumpkin: A Classic Halloween Tale. Denslow, W. W., illus. 2009. (Dover Children's Classics Ser.). (ENG., Illus.). 264p. (J). (gr. 2-5). pap. 12.99 *(978-0-486-47031-3(8))* Dover Pubns., Inc.

West, Robert. Attack of the Spider Bots, 1 vol. 2008. (Star-Fighters of Murphy Street Ser.). (ENG., Illus.). 160p. (J). (gr. 4-7). pap. 6.99 *(978-0-310-71426-2(5))* Zonderkidz.

—Escape from the Drooling Octopod!, 1 vol. 2008. (Star-Fighters of Murphy Street Ser.). (ENG., Illus.). 144p. (J). (gr. 4-7). pap. 6.99 *(978-0-310-71427-9(3))* Zonderkidz.

—There's a Spaceship in My Tree!, 1 vol. 2008. (Star-Fighters of Murphy Street Ser.). (ENG., Illus.). 144p. (J). (gr. 4-7). pap. 6.99 *(978-0-310-71425-5(7))* Zonderkidz.

West, Stephen Earl. My Grandfather's Farm. Eller, Jerod R., illus. 2011. 20p. pap. 24.95 *(978-1-4560-6628-4(5))* America Star Bks.

West, Tracey. Attack of the Nindroids. 2014. (Ninjago Readers Ser.: 8). lib. bdg. 13.55 *(978-0-606-35413-4(1))* Turtleback Bks.

—Chronicles of Ninjago. 2014. (Lego Ninjago Ser.). (ENG.). 64p. (J). (gr. 2-5). pap. 5.99 *(978-0-545-74638-0(8))* Scholastic, Inc.

—Enemy Rising. Phillips, Craig, illus. 2010. (Hiro's Quest Ser.: 1). (ENG.). 96p. (J). (gr. 2-5). 4.99 *(978-0-545-16288-3(2),* Scholastic Paperbacks) Scholastic, Inc.

—Flight of the Moon Dragon. Jones, Damien, illus. 2016. (Dragon Masters Ser.: 6). (ENG.). 96p. (J). (gr. 1-3). pap. 4.99 *(978-0-545-91392-8(6))* Scholastic, Inc.

—The Haunted Gym. 2003. (Pokemon Readers Ser.: No. 3). (ENG.). 32p. (J). pap. 3.99 *(978-0-439-42988-7(9))* Scholastic, Inc.

—Mario & the Incredible Rescue. 2006. 76p. (J). pap. *(978-0-439-84366-9(9))* Scholastic, Inc.

—Power of the Fire Dragon. Howells, Graham, illus. 2015. (Dragon Masters Ser.: No. 4). (ENG.). 96p. (J). (gr. 1-3). pap. 4.99 *(978-0-545-64631-4(6))* Scholastic, Inc.

—Rabbit Hood: Stealing Laughs in Sherwood Forest. 2004. (Illus.). 57p. *(978-0-439-56600-1(2))* Scholastic, Inc.

—Rise of the Snakes. 2012. (Lego Ninjago Ser.). (ENG.). 32p. (J). (gr. -1-3). pap. 3.99 *(978-0-545-43592-5(7))* Scholastic, Inc.

—Roar of the Thunder Dragon: a Branches Book. Jones, Damien, illus. 2017. (Dragon Masters Ser.: 8). (ENG.). 96p. (J). (gr. 1-3). lib. bdg. 15.99 ***(978-1-338-04293-1(9))***; pap. 4.99 ***(978-1-338-04292-4(0))*** Scholastic, Inc.

—Rogue City. 2017. (LEGO Batman Movie Ser.: 1). (ENG.). 176p. (J). (gr. 2-5). pap. 6.99 ***(978-1-338-13442-1(6))*** Scholastic, Inc.

—Sadness Saves the Day! 2016. lib. bdg. 16.00 *(978-0-606-38485-8(5))* Turtleback Bks.

—Search for the Lightning Dragon: a Branches Book (Dragon Masters #7) Jones, Damien, illus. 2017. (Dragon Masters Ser.: 7). (ENG.). 96p. (J). (gr. 1-3). pap. 4.99 *(978-1-338-04288-7(2))* Scholastic, Inc.

West, Tracey & Howard, Kate. Attack of the Nindroids. 2014. (Lego Ninjago Ser.). (ENG.). 32p. (J). (gr. -1-3). pap. 3.99 *(978-0-545-64390-0(2))* Scholastic, Inc.

—Techno Strike! 2014. (Lego Ninjago Ser.). (ENG.). 32p. (J). (gr. -1-3). pap. 3.99 *(978-0-545-66384-7(9))* Scholastic, Inc.

—The Titanium Ninja. 2014. (Lego Ninjago Ser.: Reader #10). (ENG.). 32p. (J). (gr. -1-3). pap. 3.99 *(978-0-545-66386-1(5))* Scholastic, Inc.

Westerfeld, Scott. Horizon. 2017. (Horizon Ser.: 1). (ENG.). 256p. (J). (gr. 4-7). 16.99 ***(978-1-338-19658-0(8))*** Scholastic, Inc.

Westerfeld, Scott. So Yesterday. (ENG.). (YA). (gr. 7-12). 2004. 240p. 16.99 *(978-1-59514-000-5(X))* 2005. 256p. reprint ed. 8.99 *(978-1-59514-032-6(8))* Penguin Young Readers Group. (Razorbill).

Westerfeld, Scott & Lanagan, Margo. Swarm. 2018. (Zeroes Ser.: 2). lib. bdg. 24.50 ***(978-0-606-40832-5(0))*** Turtleback Bks.

Westerfeld, Scott, et al. Swarm. 2016. (Zeroes Ser.: 2). (ENG., Illus.). 464p. (YA). (gr. 9). 19.99 *(978-1-4814-4339-5(9),* Simon Pulse) Simon Pulse.

—Zeroes. (Zeroes Ser.: 1). (ENG.). (YA). (gr. 9). 2016. 576p. pap. 12.99 *(978-1-4814-4337-1(2))* 2015. (Illus.). 560p. 19.99 *(978-1-4814-4336-4(4))* Simon Pulse. (Simon Pulse).

Weston, Avalon. All the Sky. 2013. 138p. pap. *(978-1-78407-151-6(X))* FeedARead.com.

Weston, Greg. The Man Upstairs. 2007. 212p. pap. 14.95 *(978-1-84799-957-3(3))* Lulu Pr., Inc.

—Ocean View Terrace & the Blue Pirate Eater. 2008. 232p. pap. 14.95 *(978-1-4092-0278-3(X))* Lulu Pr., Inc.

Weston, Robert Paul. Zorgamazoo. 2010. (ENG.). 288p. (J). (gr. 3-7). 8.99 *(978-1-59514-295-5(9),* Razorbill) Penguin Young Readers Group.

Weston Woods Staff, creator. Harold & the Purple Crayon. 2011. 18.95 *(978-0-439-72691-7(3));* 38.75 *(978-0-439-72693-1(X));* 29.95 *(978-0-439-73474-5(6))* Weston Woods Studios, Inc.

—The Island of the Skog. 2011. 38.75 *(978-0-545-23367-5(4));* 29.95 *(978-0-545-23365-1(8));* 18.95 *(978-0-545-23366-8(6))* Weston Woods Studios, Inc.

Westover, Steve. Crater Lake: Battle for Wizard Island. 2012. pap. 14.99 *(978-1-59955-960-5(9))* Cedar Fort, Inc./CFI Distribution.

—Return of the Mystic Gray. 2013. 15.99 *(978-1-4621-1187-9(4))* Cedar Fort, Inc./CFI Distribution.

Westra, Elizabeth. Alexander & the Stallion. Ampel, Kenneth Robert, illus. 2003. (Books for Young Learners). 16p. (J). per. 5.75 net. *(978-1-57274-534-6(7),* 2721, Bks. for Young Learners) Owen, Richard C. Pubs., Inc.

Wetherby, Mark. The Tales of Mossy Dell. 2009. (Illus.). 88p. pap. 10.49 *(978-1-4389-7726-3(3))* AuthorHouse.

Wethington, Constance. The Adventures of One-Eyed Jack. 2012. 28p. pap. 24.95 *(978-1-4626-8286-7(3))* America Star Bks.

Wetterer, Margaret K. The Midnight Adventure of Kate Shelley, Train Rescuer. Trover, Zachary, illus. 2010. (History's Kid Heroes Ser.). (ENG.). 32p. (gr. 3-5). pap. 8.95 *(978-0-7613-6192-3(8),* Graphic Universe™) Lerner Publishing Group.

Wetterer, Margaret K. & Wetterer, Charles M. The Snowshoeing Adventure of Milton Daub, Blizzard Trekker. 2010. pap. 51.02 *(978-0-7613-6921-9(X))* Lerner Publishing Group.

—The Snowshoeing Adventure of Milton Daub, Blizzard Trekker. Trover, Zachary, illus. 2010. (History's Kid Heroes Ser.). (ENG.). 32p. (gr. 3-5). pap. 8.95 *(978-0-7613-6194-7(4),* Graphic Universe™); lib. bdg. 26.60 *(978-0-7613-6175-6(8))* Lerner Publishing Group.

Wewers, Jason. The Candy Bar Adventures: March of the Evil Mard. 2007. 156p. pap. 12.99 *(978-1-4357-0438-1(X))* Lulu Pr., Inc.

Weyn, Suzanne. The Titanic Locket. 2014. (Haunted Museum Ser.: 1). (ENG.). 208p. (J). (gr. 3-7). pap. 6.99 *(978-0-545-58842-3(1),* Scholastic Paperbacks) Scholastic, Inc.

Whalen, Erin T. Charlie Gets Spooked, 3 vols. 2004. (Illus.). 32p. (J). (gr. k-3). 16.95 *(978-1-929265-04-6(2));* pap. 8.95 *(978-1-929265-05-3(0))* Lily & Co. Publishing.

Whamond, O. T. Wiffin & Wussell Go Digging. 2009. (Illus.). 16p. pap. 8.49 *(978-1-4389-4236-0(2))* AuthorHouse.

What's in the Suitcase, Grandma? My Solar-Powered History, Book 3. 2013. (Illus.). 116p. pap. 12.99 *(978-1-937848-08-8(6))* Do Life Right, Inc.

Wheatley, Sandra. Marmaduke the Mighty. 2010. (Illus.). 28p. (gr. -1). 13.99 *(978-1-4490-4290-5(2))* AuthorHouse.

Wheeler-Cribb, Peggy. Madeline Becomes a Star. Bensch, April, illus. 2013. 50p. 29.95 *(978-0-9886194-1-8(5))* ProsePress.

Wheeler, J. D. Gummery & Lubber. 2008. 56p. pap. 16.95 *(978-1-60563-432-6(8))* America Star Bks.

Wheeler, Jordan. Just a Walk. 2009. (ENG., Illus.). 32p. (J). (gr. -1-k). pap. 8.95 *(978-1-894778-82-4(0))* Theytus Bks., Ltd. CAN. Dist: Univ. of Toronto Pr.

Wheeler, Kim. The Adventures of Jonny Plumb. 2013. 174p. pap. *(978-0-7552-1568-3(0),* Bright Pen) Authors OnLine, Ltd.

—Even More Adventures of Jonny Plumb. 2013. 186p. pap. *(978-0-7552-1570-6(2),* Bright Pen) Authors OnLine, Ltd.

—Jonny Plumb's New Adventures... 2013. 172p. pap. *(978-0-7552-1569-0(9),* Bright Pen) Authors OnLine, Ltd.

Wheeler, Ron. Stinky Stevens: The Missing Soggy Soccer Shoe (Book 3) 2012. 114p. pap. 6.95 *(978-0-9829377-6-1(8))* Written World Communications.

Wheelie, P. The Fishing Trip: The tales of Tommy the tortoise & Friends. 2009. (Illus.). 32p. pap. 12.99 *(978-1-4389-6414-0(5))* AuthorHouse.

Wheiler, Robert. Herphus & the importance of Aroooo. 2010. 68p. pap. 10.00 *(978-0-557-29769-6(9))* Lulu Pr., Inc.

—Snowflake a Christmas Gift. 2010. 39p. pap. 11.50 *(978-0-557-47524-7(4))* Lulu Pr., Inc.

When all the locusts had Eaten. 2006. (YA). per. 12.99 *(978-1-59872-460-8(6))* Instant Pub.

When All the Locusts Had Eaten. 2006. (YA). per. 13.99 *(978-1-59872-534-6(3))* Instant Pub.

Wheres Lily? 2006. (Illus.). (J). per. 8.95 *(978-0-9786404-0-8(3))* Damiano Sara, Janeen.

Wherry, Alwyn. The Hungry Little Mouse. 2006. 17p. (J). 12.08 *(978-1-4116-8056-2(1))* Lulu Pr., Inc.

Whilldin, Sunny. Alex P. Maxwell's Rainy Day Adventure. 2009. 38p. pap. 25.40 *(978-0-557-13284-3(3))* Lulu Pr., Inc.

Whipple, Wayne. Radio Boys Cronies. 2004. reprint ed. pap. 1.99 *(978-1-4192-4378-3(0))* Kessinger Publishing, LLC.

Whirlwhim. The Baffelgagging Blundernagging Brothers: In Curse of the Bog Frog. 2008. (Illus.). 192p. (YA). 29.95 *(978-0-9800274-0-2(3))* Whirlwhim.

Whistler, Charles W. A Sea-Queen's Sailing. Groome, W. H. C., illus. 2011. 346p. 24.95 *(978-1-934671-42-9(8))* Salem Ridge Press LLC.

Whitaker, Sue. And Jake Makes Three. Ludlam, Jamie, illus. 2013. 108p. pap. *(978-1-907978-16-6(X))* ETA Publishing Hse.

—And Jake Makes Three & the Secret of Badlands. Ludlam, Jamie, illus. 2013. 92p. pap. *(978-1-907978-26-5(7))* ETA Publishing Hse.

—And Jake Makes Three in the Snow. Ludlam, Jamie, illus. 2013. 104p. pap. *(978-1-907978-21-0(6))* ETA Publishing Hse.

—And Jake Makes Three in the Vampires Den. Thomas-Brown, Cauline, ed. Ludlam, Jamie, illus. 2013. 86p. pap. *(978-1-907978-31-9(3))* ETA Publishing Hse.

White. Naja Plays Hide-Go-Seek, 1 vol. Hyatt, Sean, illus. 2010. 28p. pap. 24.95 *(978-1-4489-8842-6(X))* America Star Bks.

White-Adams, Beverly. The Adventures of Rusty: Rusty Goes to Maine Vol. 3. 2012. 40p. pap. 19.57 *(978-1-4669-5442-7(6))* Trafford Publishing.

—The Adventures of Rusty: Rusty Goes to Tennessee the Adventures Continue Vol. 4. 2013. 32p. pap. 17.25 *(978-1-4669-8583-4(6))* Trafford Publishing.

White, Alexis. Three Peas in a Pod. 2008. 56p. pap. 11.95 *(978-1-4327-1869-5(X))* Outskirts Pr., Inc.

White, Cecily. Conspiracy Boy. 2016. (ENG., Illus.). 280p. (YA). (gr. 7). pap. 14.99 *(978-1-68281-125-2(5))* Entangled Publishing, LLC.

White, Chris. The Great Jammy Adventures: The Flying Cowboy. 2010. (J). pap. 14.99 *(978-0-9827705-6-6(1))* StoneHouse Ink.

White, David. The Bad Luck Gang & the Ghost That Wasn't. 2007. 76p. per. 19.95 *(978-1-4241-7504-8(6))* America Star Bks.

White, E. B. Le Avventure di Stuart Little.Tr. of Stuart Little. (ITA.). pap. 17.95 *(978-88-451-2736-6(2))* Fabbri Editori - RCS Libri ITA. Dist: Distribooks, Inc.

White, Ellen Emerson. Webster: Tale of an Outlaw. 2016. (ENG., Illus.). 256p. (J). (gr. 3-7). pap. 7.99 *(978-1-4814-2202-4(2),* Aladdin) Simon & Schuster Children's Publishing.

White, J. A. Well of Witches. Offermann, Andrea, illus. 2017. (Thickety Ser.: 3). 528p. (J). (gr. 5). pap. 7.99 *(978-0-06-225731-4(5),* Tegen, Katherine Bks) HarperCollins Pubs.

White, Janet. Tales of Leafy Lane. White, Lee et al, illus. 2007. 88p. per. *(978-1-84748-196-2(5))* Athena Pr.

White, June. The Amazing Adventure of Tiptoe & the Yellow Balloon. Starkey, Fiona, illus. 2011. 32p. pap. *(978-0-7552-1345-0(9))* Authors OnLine, Ltd.

White, K. B. Adrianna Angelica Andrea Mystery Stories: The Case of the Missing Bath Towel. 2012. 24p. pap. 17.99 *(978-1-4772-7058-5(2))* AuthorHouse.

—Adrianna*Angelica*Andrea Mystery Stories: The Case of the Missing Dog. 2012. 20p. pap. 17.99 *(978-1-4772-4549-1(9))* AuthorHouse.

White, Kittie. The Magic Butterfly: And Other Tales. 2008. (ENG.). 52p. pap. 11.99 *(978-1-4196-9096-9(5))* CreateSpace Independent Publishing Platform.

White, Marcia. The Adventures of Ragpatch: Love Lost & Found. 2012. 28p. pap. 13.99 *(978-1-4624-0150-5(3),* Inspiring Voices) Author Solutions, Inc.

White, Margaret (Kintner). 18 Lives: The Adventures of Sam & Emil. 2008. 84p. pap. 8.95 *(978-0-595-46521-7(8))* iUniverse, Inc.

White, Pamela. Poppa Full of Pictures. 2012. 16p. pap. 15.99 *(978-1-4772-9223-5(3))* AuthorHouse.

White, Paul. Jungle Doctor in Slippery Places. 2011. (Flamingo Fiction 9-13s Ser.). (ENG., Illus.). 160p. (J). (gr. 4-7). pap. 8.99 *(978-1-84550-298-0(1),* ad8bbad9-6595-4aeb-8c4f-f089b189b088) Christian Focus Pubns. GBR. Dist: Bookmasters Distribution.

—Jungle Doctor on the Hop. 2015. (Flamingo Fiction 9-13s Ser.). (ENG., Illus.). 160p. (J). (gr. 4-7). per. 8.99 *(978-1-84550-297-3(3),* 941c8ee3-121e-4dda-84ae-b6809a4d4b39) Christian Focus Pubns. GBR. Dist: Bookmasters Distribution.

—Jungle Doctor Spots a Leopard. 2008. (Flamingo Fiction 9-13s Ser.). (ENG., Illus.). 176p. (J). (gr. 5-7). per. 8.99 *(978-1-84550-301-7(5),* 6c36bf51-d79e-4a21-bb4f-54dc3b30085b) Christian Focus Pubns. GBR. Dist: Bookmasters Distribution.

—Jungle Doctor's Enemies. 2011. (Flamingo Fiction 9-13s Ser.). (ENG., Illus.). 160p. (J). (gr. 5-7). pap. 8.99 *(978-1-84550-300-0(7),* c2552503-49be-450c-84cc-9ec522751da8) Christian Focus Pubns. GBR. Dist: Bookmasters Distribution.

White, Ramy Allison. Sunny Boy & His Playmates. 2007. 104p. pap. 18.99 *(978-1-4346-1569-5(3));* (ENG.). 112p. pap. 19.99 *(978-1-4346-1782-8(3))* Creative Media Partners, LLC.

White, Robb. The Lion's Paw. Ray, Ralph, illus. 2008. 243p. (J). (gr. 4-7). 29.95 *(978-0-9820932-0-7(9))* A. W. Ink, Inc.

White, Sandi. Playing with Rain. 2010. 36p. pap. 21.99 *(978-1-4500-1534-9(4))* Xlibris Corp.

White, Steve. Cleo the Curious Cat. 2009. 32p. pap. 19.98 *(978-1-4092-5464-5(X))* Lulu Pr., Inc.

White, T. Diogenes in a Barrel of Fun. 2004. (J). 15.95 *(978-0-9639670-2-2(9))* twhiteart.

White, Tom. Lost in the Texas Desert. 2004. (Illus.). 132p. per. 7.95 *(978-0-9753611-0-8(4))* Arlington Pubns.

White, Wade Albert. The Adventurer's Guide to Dragons (and Why They Keep Biting Me) 2017. (Adventurer's Guide Ser.: 2). (ENG.). 384p. (J). (gr. 3-7). 16.99 ***(978-0-316-30531-0(6))*** Little, Brown Bks. for Young Readers.

—The Adventurer's Guide to Successful Escapes. 2017. (Adventurer's Guide Ser.: 1). (ENG.). 400p. (J). (gr. 3-7). pap. 6.99 ***(978-0-316-30526-6(X))*** Little, Brown Bks. for Young Readers.

Whited, Melissa F. The Bear Brothers' Big Adventure, 1 vol. 2009. 23p. pap. 24.95 *(978-1-60749-258-0(X))* America Star Bks.

Whited, Wayne & Burns, Robert David. The Adventures of Orie Alexander - the Story Thief (Paperback Edition) 2010. 70p. pap. 7.95 *(978-0-557-63433-0(4))* Lulu Pr., Inc.

Whitehill, Simcha. First Partner. 2017. (Pokémon Ser.). (ENG.). 96p. (J). (gr. 2-5). pap., instr.'s hndbk. ed. 7.99 ***(978-1-338-18533-1(0))*** Scholastic, Inc.

Whitehill, Simcha. World of Sinnoh. 2009. (Pokemon Ser.). (ENG.). 96p. (J). (gr. 2-5). instr.'s gde. ed. 7.99 *(978-0-545-09936-7(2))* Scholastic, Inc.

Whitehouse, Anna. The Last Sant. 2012. 118p. pap. *(978-1-78176-289-9(9))* FeedARead.com.

Whitehouse, Howard. The Strictest School in the World: Being the Tale of a Clever Girl, a Rubber Boy & a Collection of Flying Machines, Mostly Broken. Slavin, Bill, illus. 2006. (Mad Misadventures of Emmaline & Rubberbones Ser.). (ENG.). 256p. (J). (gr. 4-7). 16.95 *(978-1-55337-882-2(2))* Kids Can Pr., Ltd. CAN. Dist: Hachette Bk. Group.

Whitlock, Bonnie. Momma Yeti & the Terribly Tiresome Goodnight. 2009. 40p. pap. 18.49 *(978-1-4389-5147-8(7))* AuthorHouse.

Whitman Guszcza, Helen Suzanne. Little Lilli & Willy Live Here. 2012. (Illus.). 80p. pap. 19.95 *(978-1-4575-1026-7(X))* Dog Ear Publishing, LLC.

Whitmore, Hugh. The Three Madelines. Wilson, Raylene Jenee & Gibbons, Deanna, illus. 2012. 124p. pap. 15.95 *(978-0-9848314-4-9(4))* Sincerity Publishing.

Whittaker, Liz. Manawl's Treasure. 2005. (ENG.). 190p. (J). pap. 11.95 *(978-0-86243-785-5(7))* Y Lolfa GBR. Dist: Dufour Editions, Inc.

Whittingham, Stephen. The Best Summer Holiday. 2012. 100p. pap. 8.99 *(978-1-4525-0425-4(3))* Balboa Pr.

Who's My Opposite? (Peek A Boo Pockets Ser.). 12p. (J). bds. *(978-2-89393-973-5(2))* Phidal Publishing, Inc./Editions Phidal, Inc.

Whybrow, Ian. Boy Racer. 2017. (ENG., Illus.). 64p. (J). (gr. 1-6). pap. 7.99 ***(978-1-4449-3576-9(3))*** Hachette Children's Group GBR. Dist: Hachette Bk. Group.

—Ella the Superstar. McCullen, Sam, illus. 2007. (Collins Big Cat Ser.). (ENG.). 32p. (J). (gr. 1-2). pap. 6.99 *(978-0-00-718681-5(9))* HarperCollins Pubs. Ltd. GBR. Dist: Independent Pubs. Group.

—It's Much Too Early! Watson, Laura, illus. 2016. (Cambridge Reading Adventures Ser.). (ENG.). 16p. pap. 6.56 *(978-1-107-56032-1(2))* Cambridge Univ. Pr.

—Little Wolf's Haunted Hall for Small Horrors. Ross, Tony, illus. 2004. (Middle Grade Fiction Ser.). 125p. (J). (gr. 4-7). per. 6.95 *(978-1-57505-794-1(8))* Lerner Publishing Group.

—Malicia para Principiantes: Una Aventura de Lobito y Apestosito. Quintana, Joela, tr. Ross, Tony, illus. 2005. (Libros Ilustrados (Picture Bks.)). (SPA.). 32p. (J). (gr. k-2). 16.95 *(978-0-8225-3211-8(5),* Ediciones Lerner) Lerner Publishing Group.

—Sinbad & the Roc Purple Band. Schon, Nick, illus. 2016. (Cambridge Reading Adventures Ser.). (ENG.). 24p. pap. 7.19 *(978-1-316-50340-9(2))* Cambridge Univ. Pr.

—That Naughty Meerkat! Parsons, Garry, illus. 2016. (ENG.). 32p. (J). 17.99 *(978-0-00-813945-2(8),* HarperCollins Children's Bks.) HarperCollins Pubs. Ltd. GBR. Dist: HarperCollins Pubs.

Wick. Elfish Fantasy: The Great Chocolate Caper. 2003. 128p. (YA). pap. 11.95 *(978-0-595-29038-3(8))* iUniverse, Inc.

Wick, Kimberly. Reaching for Heaven. 2009. 36p. pap. 16.99 *(978-1-4389-2268-3(X))* AuthorHouse.

Wicke, Ed. Akayzia Adams & the Masterdragon's Secret. 2003. 280p. (J). per. 9.99 *(978-0-9677652-3-5(4),* BlackenBlue Pr. UK) Blacknblue Pr.

—Mattie & the Highwaymen. 2012. 216p. (J). per. 9.99 *(978-0-9677652-1-1(8),* BlacknBlue Pr. UK) Blacknblue Pr.

Wicks, Valerie. Seven Spectral: The Orange World Outlaw. Lang, Leslie, ed. Ingram, Charles, illus. 2013. 342p. pap. 12.99 *(978-0-9912594-0-3(8))* Wicks, Valerie.

Wielkiewicz, Richard M. Okay, Riders, Set 'Em Up: A Nate Walker BMX Adventure. Dwyer, Corinne et al, illus. 2005. 140p. (J). pap. 12.95 *(978-0-9774129-0-7(3))* Main Event Pr.

Wiesner, David. Flotsam. 2006. (ENG., Illus.). 40p. (J). (gr. -1-3). 18.99 *(978-0-618-19457-5(6))* Houghton Mifflin Harcourt Publishing Co.

—Los Tres Cerditos. 2003.Tr. of Three Little Pigs. (SPA.). 40p. (J). (gr. k-2). 21.99 *(978-84-261-3291-8(X))* Juventud, Editorial ESP. Dist: Lectorum Pubns., Inc.

Wiesner, Karen Sue. Cody Knows. Hardy, Candace J., illus. 2012. 16p. pap. 9.95 *(978-1-61633-260-0(3))* Guardian Angel Publishing, Inc.

Wiesner, Leona Shew. Lundy: Adventures of A Little Boy in Early America. 2007. 72p. per. 8.95 *(978-0-595-47200-0(1))* iUniverse, Inc.

Wiggin, Kate Douglas. New Chronicles of Rebecca. 2006. (ENG.). 300p. per. 21.45 *(978-1-59462-367-7(8),* 403, Book Jungle) Standard Pubns., Inc.

—Penelope's Postscripts. 2008. 96p. (gr. 4-7). pap. 8.95 *(978-1-60664-193-4(X))* Aegypan.

Wiggins, D. L. Where Dreams Are Born. Carter, Kelly, illus. 2012. 26p. (J). 16.95 *(978-1-60131-128-3(1),* Castlebridge Bks.) Big Tent Bks.

Wiggins, Rosie. Adventures at a Ray of Hope Preschool. 2007. 32p. per. 12.95 *(978-1-4327-1657-8(3))* Outskirts Pr., Inc.

Wightman, Jillian C. The Adventures of Erin Mctavitt. 2008. 68p. pap. 19.95 *(978-1-4327-3164-9(5))* Outskirts Pr., Inc.

Wilce, Ysabeau S. Flora's Fury: How a Girl of Spirit & a Red Dog Confound Their Friends, Astound Their Enemies, & Learn the Importance of Packing Light. 2013. (ENG.). 528p. (YA). (gr. 7). pap. 7.99 *(978-0-15-205415-1(4))* Houghton Mifflin Harcourt Publishing Co.

Wilde, Oscar. The Selfish Giant & Other Classic Tales. Thorne, Jenny, illus. 2014. (ENG.). 96p. (J). (gr. k-5). pap. 9.99 *(978-1-86147-403-2(2),* Armadillo) Anness Publishing GBR. Dist: National Bk. Network.

Wilder, Chase. Jungle Trek. 2016. (Temple Run Ser.: 1). (ENG., Illus.). 160p. (J). (gr. 2-4). pap. 9.99 *(978-1-4052-7167-7(1))* Egmont Bks., Ltd. GBR. Dist: Independent Pubs. Group.

Wilder, Laura Ingalls. Animal Adventures. 2017. (Little House Chapter Book Ser.: 3). (Illus.). 112p. (J). (gr. 1-5). pap. 4.99 *(978-0-06-237712-8(4))* HarperCollins Pubs.

Wildes, Emma. Mr. Poot's Christmas [a Scary Baby Adventure]. 2013. 30p. 16.95 *(978-1-61160-926-4(7))* Whiskey Creek Restorations.

The Wildlife Adventures of Mugwa & Washtucna. 2008. (Illus.). 54p. (J). 19.95 *(978-0-9799493-0-2(0))* Carol Kalhagen-Tamanaha.

Wiles, Faith R. The Pumpkin who couldn't say BOO!, 1 vol. 2010. 20p. 24.95 *(978-1-4489-4242-8(X))* PublishAmerica, Inc.

Wiley. The Extraordinary Adventures of Ordinary Basil: Island of the Volcano Monkeys. 2007. (Ordinary Basil Ser.). (J). pap. *(978-0-439-86133-5(0))* Blue Sky Pr.

Wiley, Jean. Sweet Dreams for Sydney: A Book to Help Dissipate Nightmares, 1 vol. Green, Burt, illus. 2009. 25p. pap. 24.95 *(978-1-60703-002-7(0))* America Star Bks.

Wilhelm, Doug. Curse of the Pirate Mist. 2011. (Illus.). 144p. (J). pap. 6.99 *(978-1-937133-02-3(8))* Chooseco LLC.

Wilkerson, Alison. The Adventures of Tabby Cat. 2009. (Illus.). 104p. pap. 12.49 *(978-1-4389-6695-3(4))* AuthorHouse.

Wilkerson, Dawn. Katie & Katoa Travel down the River. 2009. 48p. pap. 16.95 *(978-1-61582-862-3(1))* America Star Bks.

Wilkey, David. Through the Black Hole: The Incredible Adventures of Justin Hart. 2003. 154p. pap. 12.95 *(978-0-595-29497-8(9))* iUniverse, Inc.

Wilkie, E. m. The Garden of Eden Adventure. Wilkie, E. m., illus. 2012. (Illus.). 42p. (J). pap. 9.99 *(978-0-9846685-7-1(8),* Indie Christian Book Group) IndieGo Publishing LLC.

—The Noah's Ark Adventure. 2013. 38p. pap. 9.99 *(978-0-9887048-3-1(8))* IndieGo Publishing LLC.

Wilkins, LaTanya. The Adventures of Dedan & Dylan Jackson: The Second Day of School. 2010. 48p. pap. 13.99 *(978-1-4520-5963-1(2))* AuthorHouse.

Wilkins, Lisa. The Key Seekers. 2005. 68p. pap. 16.95 *(978-1-4137-8681-1(2))* PublishAmerica, Inc.

Wilkins, Phil Cole. Dragog & the Seven Weeks of Summer. 2012. 164p. (gr. -1). pap. 15.60 *(978-1-4567-8998-5(8))* AuthorHouse.

Wilkinson, Richard Fergus. Wilkinson Tales: A Collection of Adventure Short Stories for Young People. Murphy, Andrea, illus. 2010. 88p. pap. 27.49 *(978-1-4490-5489-2(7))* AuthorHouse.

Wilks, Peter. The Foragers. 2006. (ENG., Illus.). 166p. *(978-1-905886-07-4(1))* Troubador Publishing Ltd.

Will I Ever. 2003. per. *(978-0-9740182-0-1(1))* HuntForMo Creations.

Willard, Claudette. Chloe & Banana Island. 2008. 40p. pap. 16.99 *(978-1-4343-8756-1(9))* AuthorHouse.

Willard F. Baker. The Boy Ranchers among the Indians. 2007. 180p. per. 11.95 *(978-1-4218-4020-8(0),* 1st World Library - Literary Society) 1st World Publishing, Inc.

Willems, Mo. I Love My New Toy! Willems, Mo, illus. 2008. (Elephant & Piggie Book Ser.). (ENG., Illus.). 64p. (J). (gr. -1-k). 9.99 *(978-1-4231-0961-7(9))* Hyperion Pr.

—I Will Surprise My Friend! Willems, Mo, illus. 2008. (Elephant & Piggie Book Ser.). (ENG., Illus.). 64p. (J). (gr. -1-k). 9.99 *(978-1-4231-0962-4(7))* Hyperion Pr.

Willever, Lisa & Funari-Willever, Lisa. Nicky Fifth's Garden State Adventure. 2004. 160p. pap. 5.95 *(978-0-9760469-2-9(X),* 329-005) Franklin Mason Pr.

Williams, Alan. Archy the Flying Dolphin & the Vampire's Curse. 2007. pap. 15.38 *(978-1-4251-3151-7(4))* Trafford Publishing.

Williams, Allen. Claude the Backward-Jumping Bullfrog: Space Shuttle Commander. 2009. 32p. pap. 17.99 *(978-1-4490-0479-8(2))* AuthorHouse.

—Claude the Backward Jumping Bullfrog - Firefighter: Buster's Great Adventure. 2009. 36p. pap. 16.99 *(978-1-4389-7817-8(0))* AuthorHouse.

Williams, Alix Elise. The Adventures of Prince Thaddeus: The Glamorous Guest. 2010. 56p. pap. 11.49 *(978-1-4520-5437-7(1))* AuthorHouse.

Williams, Ann. The Multifarious Adventures of Fred the Raindrop. 2005. 22p. (J). 8.00 *(978-1-4116-4175-4(2))* Lulu Pr., Inc.

Williams, Billie. Angela's Bedtime Adventures, 1 vol. 2009. 31p. pap. 24.95 *(978-1-60749-112-5(5))* America Star Bks.

Williams, Billie A. Fourteen Is Too Many: The Survivors. 2013. 24p. pap. 24.95 *(978-1-63004-179-3(3))* America Star Bks.

Williams, Brenda Gail. Little Mo Weep. 2004. (J). per. 7.95 *(978-1-59427-027-7(9))* Aglob Publishing.

Williams, Brenda May. The Shop of Magical Things. 2013. (Illus.). 44p. pap. 13.50 *(978-1-78035-526-9(2),* Fastprint Publishing) Upfront Publishing Ltd. GBR. Dist: Printondemand-worldwide.com.

Williams, C. B. Walkers. 2012. 118p. pap. 6.95 *(978-0-9881814-0-3(1))* BRYN WILLIAMS LLC.

Williams, C. G., illus. The Incredibly Helpful Helper. 2008. (ENG.). 40p. (J). (gr. -1-k). 14.95 *(978-0-7892-1001-2(0),* Abbeville Kids) Abbeville Pr., Inc.

Williams, Carol Lynch & Earl, Cheri Pray. Sweet Secrets in Pennsylvania. Oliphant, Manelle, illus. 2013. (Just in Time Ser.: 2). (ENG.). 152p. (J). (gr. 3-7). pap. 9.95 *(978-1-938301-76-6(5))* Familius LLC.

—Wizard of Menlo Park, New Jersey. Oliphant, Manelle, illus. 2014. (Just in Time Ser.). (ENG.). 140p. (J). pap. 9.95 *(978-1-938301-77-3(3))* Familius LLC.

Williams, David Morgan. Ebony & Ivory. 2007. (ENG.). 136p. (J). pap. 11.95 *(978-0-86243-972-9(8))* Y Lolfa GBR. Dist: Dufour Editions, Inc.

Williams, Donald & Williams, Ronald. The Adventures of Wacko Rabbit. 2012. (Illus.). (J). 14.95 *(978-1-62086-058-8(9))* Mascot Bks., Inc.

Williams, Emma. The Adventures of Emma & Scruffy. 2010. 50p. 24.99 *(978-1-4500-3908-6(1));* pap. 15.99 *(978-1-4500-3907-9(3))* Xlibris Corp.

Williams, Fawn. The Adventures of Jj the Amazon Parrot. 2011. 32p. pap. 24.95 *(978-1-4626-4251-9(9))* America Star Bks.

Williams-Garcia, Rita. Bottle Cap Boys on Royal Street. 2009. (Illus.). 32p. (J). 16.95 *(978-1-60349-030-6(2),* Marimba Bks.) Hudson Publishing Group, The.

Williams, Geoffrey T. The Devil Fish. Artful Doodlers, illus. Campbell, Tom, photos by. 2008. (Save Our Seas Adventure Bks.). (ENG.). 64p. (J). (gr. 4-7). 8.95 *(978-0-9800444-1-6(3))* Save Our Seas, Ltd.

—The Great White Red Alert. Artful Doodlers, illus. Campbell, Tom, photos by. 2008. (Save Our Seas Adventure Bks.). (ENG.). 64p. (J). (gr. 4-7). 8.95 *(978-0-9800444-0-9(5))* Save Our Seas, Ltd.

—The Hammerheads of Treasure Island. 2010. (ENG., Illus.). 64p. (J). (gr. 3-7). 8.95 *(978-0-9800444-2-3(1))* Save Our Seas, Ltd.

Williams, Hal G. Qudola's Quest. 2011. 48p. pap. 16.95 *(978-1-4560-5167-9(9))* America Star Bks.

Williams, Hap. Henry the Elf. Graves, Michelle, illus. 2012. 28p. pap. 24.95 *(978-1-4626-8999-6(X))* America Star Bks.

Williams-Hines, Jacqueline. Joshua, That's Sooo Slimming! 2009. 28p. pap. 13.99 *(978-1-4389-0342-2(1))* AuthorHouse.

Williams, Jason & Felt, Jeremy. The Adventures of Sam & Rowdy: Two Best Friends. 2013. 16p. pap. 15.99 *(978-1-4817-1268-2(3))* AuthorHouse.

Williams, Katie. The Space Between Trees. 2013. (ENG., Illus.). 280p. (J). (gr. 8-17). pap. 9.99 *(978-1-4521-1959-5(7))* Chronicle Bks. LLC.

Williams, Larry. The League of Clique. Williams, Larry, illus. 2007. (ENG., Illus.). 80p. per. 19.95 *(978-1-4241-5976-5(8))* America Star Bks.

Williams, Levester. The Adventures od Crunchy & Munchy Squirrel: Field Nuts. 2005. pap. *(978-0-9774418-0-8(6))* L.Patrick Publishing.

Williams, Mandi Tillotson. The Many Adventures of Mortimer Crump: Mortimer's Sweet Retreat. 2011. 28p. pap. 13.83 *(978-1-4634-2637-8(2))* AuthorHouse.

Williams, Mark. Hooty & Pig: The Missing Christmas Pudding. Garrett, Keith, illus. 2013. 24p. pap. *(978-1-78132-133-1(7))* SilverWood Bks.

Williams, Noele. The Little Red Frog. Kern, Debb, illus. 2012. 54p. pap. 14.99 *(978-1-61807-066-1(5),* Little Blue Flower Pr.) Grey Gate Media, LLC.

Williams, Renee Pierce. Buck the Good Doog. 2012. 28p. pap. 15.99 *(978-1-4691-5325-4(4))* Xlibris Corp.

Williams, Rufus. The Frog & the Butterfly. 2012. 88p. pap. 10.00 *(978-1-61897-380-1(0),* Strategic Bk. Publishing) Strategic Book Publishing & Rights Agency (SBPRA).

Williams, Sandra. Look with Me. 2012. (Illus.). 40p. pap. 20.99 *(978-1-4772-1318-6(X))* AuthorHouse.

Williams, Sherri. The Adventures of Little Mouse: (Life Outside the Mouse Hole) 2012. 48p. pap. 21.99 *(978-1-4772-2937-8(X))* AuthorHouse.

Williams, Suzanna. Ninety-Five Percent Human. 2013. 270p. pap. *(978-0-9574662-2-7(6))* Beresford Publishing Hse.

Williams, Suzanne. The Gigantic, Genuine Genie. Gonzales, Chuck, illus. 2007. (Princess Power Ser.: No. 6). 128p. (J). 15.99 *(978-0-06-078309-9(5))* HarperCollins Pubs.

—The Mysterious, Mournful Maiden. Gonzales, Chuck, illus. 2007. 112p. (J). 15.99 *(978-0-06-078305-1(2))* HarperCollins Pubs.

Williams, Tracy. The Mini Adventures of Lally Lola. 2012. (SPA.). (J). pap. 10.95 *(978-1-4675-4739-0(5))* Independent Pub.

Williams, Ursula Moray. Adventures of the Little Wooden Horse. Brisley, Joyce Lankester, illus. 2013. (ENG.). 256p. (J). (gr. -1-2). 15.99 *(978-0-230-75495-9(3))* Pan Macmillan GBR. Dist: Independent Pubs. Group.

Williams, Vanessa A. The Missing Penny. 2013. 28p. pap. 9.95 *(978-1-4787-2429-2(3))* Outskirts Pr., Inc.

Williamson, Greg. How Do I Cure This Cold? Popko, Wendy, illus. 2005. (J). 7.99 *(978-0-9666076-4-2(3))* Peerless Publishing, L.L.C.

Williamson, Liza. Emily to the Rescue. Keddy, Brian, illus. 2011. 28p. pap. 24.95 *(978-1-4626-3342-5(0))* America Star Bks.

Willis, Jeanne. Penguin Pandemonium: the Rescue. 2013. (Awesome Animals Ser.). (ENG., Illus.). 176p. (J). (gr. 2-6). pap. 6.99 *(978-1-4380-0306-1(4))* Barron's Educational Series, Inc.

Willis Jr., Joseph H. Silly the Scarecrow. 2010. 65p. pap. 26.00 *(978-0-557-27167-2(3))* Lulu Pr., Inc.

Willis, Tacey Lynn. Ellie, Tellie & Mellie: Best Jungle Friends Forever. 2010. 28p. pap. 12.49 *(978-1-4520-1903-1(7))* AuthorHouse.

Willis, Wren. Why Is My Name September? 2005. 155p. pap. 11.39 *(978-1-4116-6534-7(1))* Lulu Pr., Inc.

Willocks, Tim. Doglands. 2012. (ENG.). 324p. (YA). (gr. 7). pap. 9.99 *(978-0-375-85818-5(0),* Ember) Random Hse. Children's Bks.

Willoughby, Bebe. Saving Emma. Dacus, Bobbie, illus. 2005. (J). pap. 12.95 *(978-0-9763945-0-1(2))* King St Bks./Stabler-Leadbeater Apothecary Museum.

Willowbough, W. K. A Day at the Old Man's Garden. 2005. (J). 19.95 *(978-0-9761138-0-5(5))* Kaseberg, W. G. Publishing.

Wills, Julia. Fleeced! an Aries Adventure. 2016. (Aries Adventure Ser.). (ENG.). 400p. (J). (gr. 4-7). pap. 10.99 *(978-1-84812-476-9(7))* Bonnier Publishing GBR. Dist: Independent Pubs. Group.

—Rampage! an Aries Adventure. 2016. (Aries Adventure Ser.). (ENG.). 416p. (J). (gr. 4-7). pap. 10.99 *(978-1-84812-477-6(5))* Bonnier Publishing GBR. Dist: Independent Pubs. Group.

Willsea, Hedley. The Heath of the Graves. 2009. 371p. pap. 31.50 *(978-1-4092-2226-2(8))* Lulu Pr., Inc.

Wilson, Sarah. Dora's Halloween Adventure. Savitsky, Steven, illus. 2003. (Dora the Explorer Ser.). (ENG.). 14p. (J). bds. 5.99 *(978-0-689-85844-4(2),* Simon Spotlight/Nickelodeon) Simon Spotlight/Nickelodeon.

Wilson, Barbara Rogers. Deva & the Soul Snatcher an Environmental Fantasy. 2nd ed. 2013. 216p. pap. 11.95 *(978-0-9834956-9-7(6),* SpiritBooks) Portal Ctr. Pr.

Wilson, Bob. Stanley Bagshaw & the Fourteen-Foot Wheel. 2005. (Stanley Bagshaw Ser.). (Illus.). 32p. (J). (gr. -1-k). pap. 5.95 *(978-1-903015-40-7(5))* Barn Owl Bks, London GBR. Dist: Independent Pubs. Group.

Wilson, David. The Adventures of Jack Bennett James Bay or Bust. 2013. 190p. pap. *(978-0-9919509-1-1(7))* Wilson, David.

—The Adventures of Jack Bennett Winter Rescue. 2013. 116p. pap. *(978-0-9919509-0-4(9))* Wilson, David.

Wilson, Db. Teale Tales: Wyv Land of Magik. 2012. 266p. pap. *(978-1-78176-345-2(3))* FeedARead.com.

Wilson, Douglas. Blackthorn Winter. Bently, Peter, illus. 2003. 141p. (J). per. 12.00 *(978-1-932168-10-5(9))* Veritas Pr., Inc.

Wilson, Essdale. Horses, Tigers & Neighbors. 2007. 160p. per. 24.95 *(978-1-4241-5811-9(7))* America Star Bks.

Wilson, Gerrard. Alice on Top of the World. 2009. 159p. pap. 17.50 *(978-0-9561553-0-6(8))* Wilson, Gerrard IRL. Dist: Lulu Pr., Inc.

Wilson, J. M. & Zolkowski, Cathy A. Blue: Adventures of a Gymnast. 2004. 150p. (YA). per. 11.95 *(978-0-9667037-5-7(8))* Verona (Bk.) Publishing, Inc.

Wilson, Jacqui. Little Johnny's Faith Adventures: Creation Curiosity! 2012. 30p. pap. 15.95 *(978-1-4497-5994-0(7),* WestBow Pr.) Author Solutions, Inc.

Wilson, Jessica. Stary's Secret. Tintjer, Birgit, illus. 2007. 28p. pap. 24.95 *(978-1-4241-9089-8(4))* America Star Bks.

Wilson, John. Broken Arrow, 1 vol. 2014. (Seven Sequels Ser.). (ENG., Illus.). 240p. (J). (gr. 5-10). pap. 10.95 *(978-1-4598-0540-8(2))* Orca Bk. Pubs. USA.

—Ghost Moon, 1 vol. 2011. (Desert Legend Trilogy Ser.: 2). (ENG.). 192p. (YA). (gr. 8-12). pap. 12.95 *(978-1-55469-879-0(0))* Orca Bk. Pubs. USA.

Wilson, Laurie Harman. The Treasures of Destiny. 2012. 72p. pap. 7.95 *(978-0-9848050-3-7(6),* Little Creek Bks.) Jan-Carol Publishing, INC.

Wilson, Leonard W. Realms of Flimenia Jeremyaes Journey. 2008. 136p. pap. 11.95 *(978-0-595-51523-3(1))* iUniverse, Inc.

Wilson, Mark A. The Amazing Gift from the Woods. 2008. 48p. pap. 16.95 *(978-1-60563-056-4(X))* America Star Bks.

—The Legend of Crawley Creek. 2008. 104p. pap. 9.95 *(978-1-60693-423-4(6),* Eloquent Bks.) Strategic Book Publishing & Rights Agency (SBPRA).

Wilson, N. D. Empire of Bones. (Ashtown Burials Ser.: Bk. 3). (ENG.). (J). (gr. 3-7). 2014. 464p. 7.99 *(978-0-375-86398-1(2),* Yearling) 2013. 352p. 16.99 *(978-0-375-86441-4(5),* Random Hse. Bks. for Young Readers) Random Hse. Children's Bks.

—Leepike Ridge. 2008. (ENG., Illus.). 256p. (J). (gr. 3-7). 6.99 (978-0-375-83874-3(0), Yearling) Random Hse. Children's Bks.
—Outlaws of Time: The Legend of Sam Miracle. 2016. (Outlaws of Time Ser.: 1). 336p. (J). (gr. 3-7). 16.99 (978-0-06-232726-0(7), Tegen, Katherine Bks) HarperCollins Pubs.
Wilson, Robert. Pippy: The Miracle of A Dream. 2011. 136p. 21.95 (978-1-4620-6634-6(8)); pap. 11.95 (978-1-4620-6633-9(X)) iUniverse, Inc.
Wilson, Rosalee. A Mushy Mouse Tale. 2009. 69p. pap. 24.58 (978-0-557-10084-2(4)) Lulu Pr., Inc.
Wilson, Sheba. Down & Out in Halfville. 2013. 36p. pap. 11.99 (978-1-62697-904-8(9)) Salem Author Services.
Wilson, Veronica B. Aswald's ABC Adventure. 2008. 28p. pap. 24.95 (978-1-60441-691-6(2)) America Star Bks.
Wilson, W. Shane. The sprite Adventure. 2010. 97p. pap. 12.99 (978-0-557-42603-4(0)) Lulu Pr., Inc.
—The world of Ice. 2009. 134p. pap. 13.24 (978-0-578-03299-3(6)) Wilson, W. Shane.
Wiltbank, Ryan. The Land of Bland: Illustrations by Dan Cooper on the Title Page. 2012. 28p. pap. 17.99 (978-1-4772-7376-0(X)) AuthorHouse.
Winbolt-Lewis, Martin. The Soggy Saga of Samuel Sprat. Mason, Abi, illus. 2013. 24p. pap. (978-1-78222-152-4(2)) Paragon Publishing, Rothersthorpe.
Wind, Chuck T. The Test of Love. 2011. 24p. pap. 24.95 (978-1-4626-2398-3(0)) America Star Bks.
Windham, Ryder. Ezra's Gamble. 2014. (Star Wars Rebels Chapter Bks.). 154p. (J). lib. bdg. 17.20 (978-0-606-35283-3(X)) Turtleback Bks.
—Island of Lost Masks. Scholastic, Inc. Staff, illus. 2015. (LEGO Bionicle Ser.: 1). (ENG.). 128p. (J). (gr. 2-5). pap. 5.99 (978-0-545-87325-3(8)) Scholastic, Inc.
—A New Hope: The Life of Luke Skywalker. 2009. 208p. (J). (978-0-545-16177-0(0)) Scholastic, Inc.
—Revenge of the Skull Spiders. 2015. (LEGO Bionicle Ser.: 2). (ENG.). 128p. (J). (gr. 2-5). pap. 5.99 (978-0-545-90590-9(7)) Scholastic, Inc.
Windham, Ryder & Weyn, Suzanne. Indiana Jones Collector's Edition. 2008. (Illus.). 657p. (J). (978-0-545-09183-1(7)) Scholastic, Inc.
The Windsor Caper. 2013. (Illus.). 258p. pap. (978-0-9576554-0-9(1)) Good, Martin.
Wines, Michael P. Stupid Alabama: A Laugh-So-Hard-You-Will-Snot about Growing up to Discover Not All Things Are Stupid but a Lot of Them Are. Gierhart, Steve, ed. Floyd, Claire, illus. 2013. (ENG.). 244p. (YA). pap. 17.95 (978-1-938667-13-8(1)) Ardent Writer Pr., LLC, The.
Winfield, A. C. The Star Pirate. 2013. (Illus.). 184p. pap. (978-1-909202-11-5(8)) Little Acorns Publishing.
Winfield, Arthur M. The Mystery at Putnam Hall. 2007. 272p. 26.95 (978-1-4218-4130-4(4)); per. 11.95 (978-1-4218-4228-8(9)) 1st World Publishing, Inc. (1st World Library - Literary Society).
—Putnam Hall Champions or Bound to Win Ou. 2006. pap. 28.95 (978-1-4286-2346-0(9)) Kessinger Publishing, LLC.
—The Rover Boys at College. 2007. 264p. 27.95 (978-1-4218-4131-1(2)); per. 12.95 (978-1-4218-4229-5(7)) 1st World Publishing, Inc. (1st World Library - Literary Society).
—The Rover Boys in the Air. 2007. 264p. 29.95 (978-1-4218-4134-2(7)); per. 14.95 (978-1-4218-4232-5(7)) 1st World Publishing, Inc. (1st World Library - Literary Society).
—The Rover Boys in the Jungle. 2007. 212p. 27.95 (978-1-4218-4135-9(5)); per. 12.95 (978-1-4218-4233-2(5)) 1st World Publishing, Inc. (1st World Library - Literary Society).
Winfield, Arthur M. The Rover Boys in the Jungle. 2004. reprint ed. pap. 21.95 (978-1-4191-8118-4(1)); pap. 1.99 (978-1-4192-8118-1(6)) Kessinger Publishing, LLC.
Winfield, Arthur M. The Rover Boys in the Mountains. 2005. 27.95 (978-1-4218-1009-6(3), 1st World Library - Literary Society) 1st World Publishing, Inc.
—The Rover Boys in the Mountains or a Hunt for Fun & Fortune. 2006. (ENG.). 268p. per. 27.95 (978-1-4286-4100-6(9)) Kessinger Publishing, LLC.
—The Rover Boys on Land & Sea. 2007. 252p. 26.95 (978-1-4218-4136-6(3)); per. 11.95 (978-1-4218-4234-9(3)) 1st World Publishing, Inc. (1st World Library - Literary Society).
—The Rover Boys on the Great Lakes. 2007. 244p. 26.95 (978-1-4218-4137-3(1)); per. 11.95 (978-1-4218-4235-6(1)) 1st World Publishing, Inc. (1st World Library - Literary Society).
—The Rover Boys on the Ocean. 2007. 232p. 26.95 (978-1-4218-4138-0(X)); per. 11.95 (978-1-4218-4236-3(X)) 1st World Publishing, Inc. (1st World Library - Literary Society).
—The Rover Boys on the Plains or the Mystery of Red Rock Ranch. 2004. reprint ed. pap. 27.95 (978-1-4179-2626-8(0)) Kessinger Publishing, LLC.
—The Rover Boys Out West. 2007. 228p. 26.95 (978-1-4218-4140-3(1)); per. 11.95 (978-1-4218-4238-7(6)) 1st World Publishing, Inc. (1st World Library - Literary Society).
—The Rover Boys Out West. 2004. reprint ed. pap. 21.95 (978-1-4191-8120-7(3)) Kessinger Publishing, LLC.
Winfield, Arthur M. The Rover Boys Out West. 2004. reprint ed. pap. 1.99 (978-1-4192-8120-4(8)) Kessinger Publishing, LLC.
Wingate, Frank. Herman the Hedgehog: Bedtime Tales from the Woodland. 2009. (Illus.). 84p. pap. 10.49 (978-1-4389-9134-4(7)) AuthorHouse.
Winick, Judd. The Great Big Boom. 2017. (Hilo Ser.: 3). (ENG., Illus.). 208p. (J). (gr. 3-7). 13.99 (978-0-385-38620-3(6)); lib. bdg. 16.99 (978-0-385-38621-0(4)) Random Hse. Children's Bks. (Random Hse. Bks. for Young Readers).
Wininger, Stephen T. The Adventure of Pirate Pete Moss. 2004. (J). pap. (978-1-59196-466-7(0)) Instant Pub.
Winkel, Andrew. Raceboy & Super Qwok Adventures. Brault, Christopher, illus. 2012. (ENG.). 356p. (J). pap. 16.00 (978-0-9837905-1-8(5)) Hierophantasm.
Winkler, Ashley & Winkler, Michael. One Good Quest Deserves Another: A Crown of Amaranth Story. 2009. 292p. 28.95 (978-0-595-71039-3(5)); pap. 18.95 (978-0-595-47365-6(2)) iUniverse, Inc.
Winkler, Henry & Oliver, Lin. Always Dance with a Hairy Buffalo. 2013. (Ghost Buddy Ser.: 4). (ENG.). 192p. (J). (gr. 3-7). pap. 5.99 (978-0-545-29885-8(7), Scholastic Paperbacks) Scholastic, Inc.
—Ghost Buddy: Always Dance with a Hairy Buffalo. 2013. (Ghost Buddy Ser.: 4). (ENG.). 192p. (J). (gr. 3-7). 17.99 (978-0-545-29890-2(3), Scholastic Pr.) Scholastic, Inc.
—Life of Me: Enter at Your Own Risk. Watson, Jesse Joshua, illus. 2008. (Hank Zipzer Ser.: 14). (ENG.). 256p. (J). (gr. 3-7). pap. 6.99 (978-0-448-44376-8(7), Grosset & Dunlap) Penguin Young Readers Group.
Winn, Don M. The Tortoise & the Hairpiece. Hefflin, Toby, illus. 2009. 20p. pap. 7.99 (978-0-88144-452-0(9)) Yorkshire Publishing Group.
Winn, L. B. Butterpod Jerome & the Planet of Gabool. Winn, L. B., illus. 2007. (Illus.). (J). pap. 18.95 (978-0-9791884-0-4(7)) Winn, Lynnette.
Winn, Sheridan. The Sprite Sisters: Magic at Drysdale's School (Vol 7) Winn, Christopher, illus. 2013. 256p. pap. (978-0-9574231-2-1(8)) Winn, Sheridan.
Winnard, Rebecca Victoria & Winnard, Linda. Giraffe Liberation: An Act of Freedom. 2006. 53p. pap. 16.95 (978-1-4241-0552-6(8)) PublishAmerica, Inc.
Winnette, Sandy. A Snow Angel Story Book: Little Beth & the Snow Angel. 2008. 108p. pap. 11.99 (978-1-4343-8133-0(1)) AuthorHouse.
Winnie the Pooh. Goodbye, Honeypot! 2010. 12p. 6.99 (978-1-4231-3098-7(7)) Disney Pr.
Winslow, Theresa. Katie the Bear & Her Adventure for Honey, 1 vol. 2009. 20p. pap. 24.95 (978-1-60836-893-8(9)) America Star Bks.
Winstanley, Liz. The Adventures of Abra & His Magic Carpet. 2012. 32p. pap. 14.97 (978-1-62212-406-0(5), Strategic Bk. Publishing) Strategic Book Publishing & Rights Agency (SBPRA).
Winter, Barbara. Trapped in Gallipoli. 2007. (Illus.). 48p. (YA). lib. bdg. 15.00 (978-1-4242-1643-7(5)) Dingles & Co.
Winter, Christopher. Henrietta the Farmer & the Long, Long, Long, Long Vacation! O'Shea, Bonnie, illus. 2012. 32p. pap. 13.95 (978-1-60594-856-0(X)) Aeon Publishing Inc.
Winter, P. K. Back at Eagle Lake: More Eagle Lake Giant Stories. Winter, P. K., illus. 2009. (Illus.). 182p. pap. 18.50 (978-1-4251-8831-3(1)) Trafford Publishing.
Wirt, Mildred A. Guilt of the Brass Thieves. 2011. 178p. pap. 9.99 (978-1-935774-80-8(8), Resurrected Pr.) Intrepid Ink, LLC.
—Saboteurs on the River. 2011. 174p. pap. 12.99 (978-1-935774-86-0(7), Resurrected Pr.) Intrepid Ink, LLC.
—Signal in the Dark. 2011. 170p. pap. 9.99 (978-1-935774-82-2(4), Resurrected Pr.) Intrepid Ink, LLC.
—Swamp Island. 2011. 176p. pap. 12.99 (978-1-935774-85-3(9), Resurrected Pr.) Intrepid Ink, LLC.
—Voice from the Cave. 2011. 168p. pap. 9.99 (978-1-935774-81-5(6), Resurrected Pr.) Intrepid Ink, LLC.
Wisham Fenstermacher, Mary. Pablo Visits the Desert. 2010. 52p. pap. 22.49 (978-1-4490-5180-8(4)) AuthorHouse.
Wishinsky, Frieda. Flying High! Griffiths, Dean & Owlkids Books Inc. Staff, illus. 2007. (Canadian Flyer Adventures Ser.: 5). (ENG.). 96p. (J). (gr. 1-4). per. 7.95 (978-1-897066-99-7(6), Owlkids) Owlkids Bks. Inc. CAN. Dist: Publishers Group West (PGW).
—Halifax Explodes! Lewis-MacDougall, Patricia Ann & Owlkids Books Inc. Staff, illus. 2011. (Canadian Flyer Adventures Ser.: 17). (ENG.). 96p. (J). (gr. 1-4). pap. 7.95 (978-1-926818-98-6(9), Maple Tree Pr.) Owlkids Bks. Inc. CAN. Dist: Publishers Group West (PGW).
—Hurry, Freedom. Griffiths, Dean & Owlkids Books Inc. Staff, illus. 2008. (Canadian Flyer Adventures Ser.: 7). (ENG.). 96p. (J). (gr. 1-4). per. 9.95 (978-1-897349-15-1(7), Maple Tree Pr.) Owlkids Bks. Inc. CAN. Dist: Publishers Group West (PGW).
—Make It Fair!, No. 15. Lewis-MacDougall, Patricia Ann & Owlkids Books Inc. Staff, illus. 2010. (Canadian Flyer Adventures Ser.: 15). (ENG.). 96p. (J). (gr. 1-4). pap. 7.95 (978-1-897349-99-1(8), Maple Tree Pr.) Owlkids Bks. Inc. CAN. Dist: Publishers Group West (PGW).
—On the Case. Franson, Leanne et al, illus. 2009. (Canadian Flyer Adventures Ser.: 12). (ENG.). 96p. (J). (gr. 1-4). pap. 7.95 (978-1-897349-55-7(6), Owlkids) Owlkids Bks. Inc. CAN. Dist: Publishers Group West (PGW).
Wishinsky, Frieda & Griffiths, Dean. Lost in the Snow. Franson, Leanne & Owlkids Books Inc. Staff, illus. 2008. (Canadian Flyer Adventures Ser.: 10). (ENG.). 96p. (J). (gr. 1-4). pap. 7.95 (978-1-897349-41-0(6), Owlkids) Owlkids Bks. Inc. CAN. Dist: Publishers Group West (PGW).
Withers, Pam. Andreo's Race. 2015. (ENG., Illus.). 216p. (J). (gr. 7). pap. 12.99 (978-1-77049-766-5(8), Tundra Bks.) Tundra Bks. CAN. Dist: Penguin Random Hse. LLC.
—Daredevil Club, 1 vol. 2006. (Orca Currents Ser.). (ENG.). 112p. (J). (gr. 5-9). per. 9.95 (978-1-55143-614-2(0)) Orca Bk. Pubs. USA.
—First Descent. (ENG., Illus.). (YA). (gr. 7). 2014. 266p. pap. 9.99 (978-1-77049-412-1(X)) 2011. 268p. 17.95 (978-1-77049-257-8(7)) Tundra Bks. CAN. (Tundra Bks.). Dist: Penguin Random Hse. LLC.
Withers, Pam. Tracker's Canyon. 2017. (ENG.). 184p. (YA). pap. 12.99 **(978-1-4597-3963-5(9))** Dundurn CAN. Dist: Ingram Publisher Services.
Witschen, Kay. Clinker's Dragon. 2006. (J). 6.95 (978-0-9741352-2-9(4)) Dwitt Publishing.
Wittner, Shirley. Kemira & the Ancient Book of Spells. 2006. 51p. pap. 16.95 (978-1-4241-4840-0(5)) PublishAmerica, Inc.
Woebkenberg, Valerie & Ingels, Diane. The Story the Little Christmas Tree Told. 2012. pap. 11.95 (978-0-7414-8095-8(6)) Infinity Publishing.
Wofford, Delaney. For Courage. 2010. 229p. pap. 17.98 (978-0-557-17045-6(1)) Lulu Pr., Inc.
Wofford, Sherry Lynn. Introducing the Adventures of Jerry Giraffe & Feather Bird. 2011. 36p. pap. 16.95 (978-1-4560-3238-8(0)) America Star Bks.
Wohl, David, et al. Top Cow's Best of Michael Turner. 2006. (ENG., Illus.). 240p. (YA). pap. 24.99 (978-1-58240-544-5(1), 9781582405445) Image Comics.
Wojciechowska, Maia. Shadow of the Bull. 141p. (YA). (gr. 5-18). pap. 3.95 (978-0-8072-1506-7(6), Listening Library) Random Hse. Audio Publishing Group.
Wolf, Clarissa. Orange Fizz. Wolf, Myron, photos by. 2009. (Illus.). 32p. pap. 9.99 (978-1-935105-39-8(6)) Avid Readers Publishing Group.
Wolf, Fred Alan. Dr. Quantum in the Grandfather Paradox. 2007. (Dr. Quantum Ser.). (Illus.). 176p. (J). (gr. 4-7). per. 12.95 (978-0-9786813-3-3(9)) Elora Media, LLC.
Wolf, Justin. The Adventures of Silly Monkey & Jack. 2011. 20p. (gr. 1-2). pap. 12.99 (978-1-4567-6452-4(7)) AuthorHouse.
Wolf, Mária. Maggy Cans. 2012. 52p. (gr. 4-6). pap. 11.95 (978-1-4772-6093-5(6)) AuthorHouse.
Wolfe, D. K. Flap Doodle & the Incredible Kibbil Caper 2005. (Illus.). 247p. (J). (gr. 4-6). 16.95 (978-1-59810-031-0(9)) Jeriger Pr.
Wolfe, Jack & Wolfe, Jennifer. The Tales of Spy Dogs Archie & Hazel. 2011. 44p. pap. 16.59 (978-1-4567-6244-5(3)) AuthorHouse.
Wolfel, Ursula. Fliegender Stern. pap. 14.95 (978-3-570-26064-7(X)) Bertelsman, Verlagsgruppe C. GmbH DEU. Dist: Distribooks, Inc.
Wolff, D. O. Precious Little. 2012. 132p. (gr. 4-6). pap. 14.95 (978-1-4772-7224-4(0)) AuthorHouse.
Wolff, Susan. Quackers Wants to Fly. Currie, Justin, illus. 2013. 32p. pap. 8.95 (978-1-60653-074-0(7)) High Hill Pr.
Wolff, Tracy. Book 1: Crisis. 2016. (Mars Bound Ser.). (ENG.). (J). (gr. 2-8). lib. bdg. 28.50 **(978-1-62402-197-8(2))** ABDO Publishing Co.
—Book 4: Arrival. 2016. (Mars Bound Ser.). (ENG.). (J). (gr. 2-8). lib. bdg. 28.50 **(978-1-62402-200-5(6))** ABDO Publishing Co.
Wolfinger, Sheri. Has Anyone Seen Puff? A Billy & Jake Adventure. 2012. 20p. pap. 11.59 (978-1-4669-1377-6(0)) Trafford Publishing.
Wolfson, Steve. Monster Cheese. Johnson, Bill, illus. 2013. 34p. pap. 10.95 (978-0-9798324-3-7(8)) Argami Productions, LLC.
Wolverton, Barry. The Dragon's Gate. Stevenson, Dave, illus. 2016. (Chronicles of the Black Tulip Ser.: 2). 336p. (J). (gr. 3-7). 16.99 (978-0-06-222193-3(0), Waldon Pond Pr.) HarperCollins Pubs.
Womack, Rowena. Popcorn. Archer, Angela, illus. 2013. 26p. (J). 16.99 (978-1-61160-595-2(4)) Whiskey Creek Restorations.
Wonder Forge Staff, creator. Horton Hears a Who! - You to the Rescue! Game. 2007. (J). (978-0-9797123-1-9(9)) Wonder Forge, Inc.
The Wonderful Wizard of OZ: Twiggle Book. 2004. (Illus.). 26p. (J). 1.99 (978-0-9762573-2-5(7)) Ear Twiggles Productions, Inc.
Wong, Clarissa S. The Story of the Guardians of the Galaxy. 2014. (Marvel World of Reading Level 2 Ser.). (J). lib. bdg. 13.55 (978-0-606-35279-6(1)) Turtleback Bks.
—World of Reading: Black Widow This Is Black Widow. Di Vito, Andrea, illus. 2015. (World of Reading Ser.). (ENG.). 32p. (J). (gr. 1-3). pap. 3.99 (978-1-4847-2517-7(4), Marvel Pr.) Disney Publishing Worldwide.
Wood, Amanda. Amazing Baby Look & Play! 2005. (Illus.). 12p. (J). 15.95 (978-1-59223-528-5(X), Silver Dolphin Bks.) Readerlink Distribution Services, LLC.
—Amazing Baby Touch & Play! 2005. (Illus.). 12p. (J). 15.95 (978-1-59223-529-2(8), Silver Dolphin Bks.) Readerlink Distribution Services, LLC.
Wood, Barbie. The Adventure of Mookin Munchkin. Klick, Gloria, illus. 2013. 32p. pap. 24.95 (978-1-63004-041-3(X)) America Star Bks.
Wood, Cary D. Davis & Pop Go Hiking. Turner, Cecilia, illus. 2014. (ENG.). (gr. -1-4). 30p. 34.95 (978-1-63047-217-7(4)); 32p. pap. 14.95 (978-1-63047-068-5(6)) Morgan James Publishing.
Wood, Francis Eugene. Return to Winterville. Pickett, Elizabeth & Dean, Tina, eds. Larsen, Dan, illus. 2004. 96p. (YA). per. 14.95 net. (978-0-9746372-1-1(1)) Tip-Of-The-Moon Publishing Co.
Wood, Franklin. Teddy the Cat That Barks. 2011. 24p. pap. 15.99 (978-1-4628-7908-3(X)) Xlibris Corp.
Wood, Gary. Bertrand - The Story of a Cat. 2008. 80p. pap. 16.95 (978-1-60703-744-6(0)) PublishAmerica, Inc.
Wood, Kate. Twinkle. 2013. (Illus.). 60p. (J). pap. 20.00 (978-0-9837334-9-2(X)) Digi-Tall Media.
Wood, Kristen. Find Masked Rider. 2008. 19.95 (978-1-935159-06-3(2)) My Campus Adventure, Inc.
Wood, Lisa. The Human Hotel. 2010. 36p. pap. 15.49 (978-1-4389-7466-8(3)) AuthorHouse.
Wood, T. L. Eldohr Adventures: Quest for Windsoar (Book 2) 2013. 280p. pap. 11.99 (978-0-9859110-4-1(2)) Hobbes End Publishing, LLC.
Woodard, Amy. The Day the Teacher Rode a Horse to School. 2008. 24p. pap. 24.95 (978-1-60441-736-4(6)) America Star Bks.
Woodard, April & White-Petaway, Davida. The Adventures of Frankie & Lucy. 2009. 32p. 6.95 (978-0-60349-028-3(0), Marimba Bks.) Hudson Publishing Group, The.
Woodberry, Gareth. Gakeva Gluntok's New School. 2005. 65p. pap. 16.95 (978-1-4137-9894-4(2)) PublishAmerica, Inc.
Woodell, Rejoice. Kohara, the White Veiled City. 2011. 138p. pap. 19.99 (978-1-4568-7969-3(3)) Xlibris Corp.
Wooden, John. Fiesta. Cornelison, Susan F., illus. 2007. (Coach John Wooden for Kids Ser.). 63p. (J). (gr. k-3). lib. bdg. 11.65 (978-0-7569-7791-7(6)); pap., per. 4.99 (978-0-7891-7187-0(2)) Perfection Learning Corp.
Wooden, Walter. Little Bear's Journey. 2011. 32p. pap. 21.99 (978-1-4628-4440-1(5)) Xlibris Corp.
Wooderson, Philip. Arf & the Tarantula. 2005. (978-0-7136-7640-2(X), A&C Black) Bloomsbury Publishing Plc.
Woodfield, Gary. The Time Thief. 2004. (J). per. 19.95 (978-0-9761289-2-2(6)); (Illus.). (YA). 26.95 (978-0-9743348-9-9(8)) Nightengale Pr.
Woodford, Pamela. King Giggle. 2013. (Brighter Little Minds Ser.). (ENG., Illus.). 24p. (J). pap. 10.95 (978-1-871305-80-7(2)) Orpen Pr. IRL. Dist: Dufour Editions, Inc.
—Lilly & Harry. 2013. (Brighter Little Minds Ser.). (ENG., Illus.). 24p. (J). pap. 10.95 (978-1-871305-79-1(9)) Orpen Pr. IRL. Dist: Dufour Editions, Inc.
—Sid, Spark & the Signal Man. 2013. (Brighter Little Minds Ser.). (ENG., Illus.). 24p. (J). pap. 9.99 (978-1-871305-82-1(9)) Orpen Pr. IRL. Dist: M.H. Gill & Co. U. C.
—Sortof the Snail. 2013. (Brighter Little Minds Ser.). (ENG., Illus.). 24p. (J). pap. 9.99 (978-1-871305-83-8(7)) Orpen Pr. IRL. Dist: M.H. Gill & Co. U. C.
Wooding, Chris. Havoc. 2010. (Malice Ser.: 2). (ENG., Illus.). 400p. (J). (gr. 3-7). 16.99 (978-0-545-16045-2(6), Scholastic Pr.) Scholastic, Inc.
—Malice, Bk. 1. Chernett, Dan, illus. 2009. (Malice Ser.: 1). (ENG.). 384p. (J). (gr. 7-12). 14.99 (978-0-545-16043-8(X)) Scholastic, Inc.
—Malice #2: Havoc. 2012. (Malice Ser.: 2). (ENG.). 400p. (J). (gr. 3-7). pap. 9.99 (978-0-545-16046-9(4), Scholastic Pr.) Scholastic, Inc.
—Pale. 2012. (Stoke Books Titles Ser.). (ENG.). 72p. (YA). (gr. 8-12). pap. 6.95 (978-1-78112-091-0(9)); lib. bdg. 22.60 (978-1-78112-092-7(7)) Lerner Publishing Group.
Woodruff, Elvira. Fearless. 2011. (ENG.). 240p. (J). (gr. 3-7). pap. 6.99 (978-0-439-67704-2(1), Scholastic Pr.) Scholastic, Inc.
Woodruff, M. C. The Woods of Arreth. 2012. 248p. pap. 24.95 (978-1-4626-8817-3(9)) America Star Bks.
Woods, Dave & Inns, Chris. Junior Caesar. 2014. (ENG., Illus.). 64p. (J). (gr. k-2). pap. 5.99 (978-1-4083-1362-6(6)) Hodder & Stoughton GBR. Dist: Hachette Bk. Group.
Woods, Rebecca. Rising Winds of Silver Falls. 2012. (Silver Falls Ser.: Vol. 3). (ENG.). 191p. (J). pap. 15.99 (978-1-59955-998-8(6), Sweetwater Bks.) Cedar Fort, Inc./CFI Distribution.
Woods, Valerie. Princess Portia's Enchanted Journey, 1 vol. 2010. 36p. pap. 24.95 (978-1-4489-9673-5(2)) America Star Bks.
Woods, Wendy. Welcome Home, Indigeaux: A Louisiana Adventure. Martin, Sherry, illus. 2013. (ENG.). (J). (gr. -1-3). 14.95 (978-1-62086-246-9(8)) Mascot Bks., Inc.
Woods-Whitaker, Kim. Elijah's Big Imagination: A Ball of an Adventure. 2010. 20p. 11.49 (978-1-4490-1518-3(2)) AuthorHouse.
Woodward, J. Howland. A Moment in Time. 2006. 55p. pap. 16.95 (978-1-4241-1334-7(2)) America Star Bks.
Woody, John. Ernie Tales. Byars, Bob M., illus. 2012. pap. 13.95 (978-0-9848019-9-2(5)) Inkwell Books LLC.
Woolf, Julia, illus. Snowman Surprise. 2008. (ENG.). 10p. (J). bds. 4.95 (978-1-58117-812-8(3), Intervisual/Piggy Toes) Bendon, Inc.
Worcester, Daryl D. The Story of the Famous Traves Travlslot. 2006. 48p. pap. 16.95 (978-1-4241-2417-6(4)) America Star Bks.
—Traves Travlslot: The North American Adventure, 1 vol. 2010. 54p. pap. 16.95 (978-1-60474-853-6(2)) America Star Bks.
Word, Brian H. Jenks Jupiter. 2011. 48p. pap. 17.50 (978-1-4634-2051-2(X)) AuthorHouse.
World Almanac Editors, et al. Historical Adventure: A Connecticut Yankee in King Arthur's Court/ Around the World in 80 Days/the Prisoner of Zenda. 2007. (Bank Street Graphic Novels Ser.). (Illus.). 56p. (gr. 5-8). lib. bdg. 31.00 (978-0-8368-7927-8(9)) Stevens, Gareth Publishing LLLP.
Worley, Michelle. Buster Goes to the White House, 1 vol. 2009. 48p. pap. 16.95 (978-1-61546-352-7(6)) PublishAmerica, Inc.
Worley, Roger A. 14 Wishes, 1 vol. 2009. 164p. pap. 24.95 (978-1-61582-419-9(7)) America Star Bks.
Wormell, Chris. The Sea Monster. Wormell, Chris, illus. 2005. (ENG., Illus.). 32p. (J). (gr. k-2). pap. 12.99 (978-0-09-945147-1(6), Red Fox) Random House Children's Books GBR. Dist: Independent Pubs. Group.
Worrell, Maryellen. The Accidental Hero. 2008. 101p. pap. 19.95 (978-1-60672-145-2(3)) America Star Bks.
Worthen, Diane. Oliver's Wish: A Tale from the Garden. 2012. 36p. pap. 20.99 (978-1-4685-4005-5(X)) AuthorHouse.
Worthington, Michelle. Noah Chases the Wind. Cowman, Joseph, illus. 2015. (ENG.). 32p. (J). (gr. -1-3). 16.95 (978-1-60554-356-7(X)) Redleaf Pr.
Worthington, Sandi. An Adventure with Rainy Twostep. 2012. (ENG.). pap. 8.95 (978-1-4675-1305-0(9)) Independent Pub.
Woszczylo, Noushka. Escape. 2012. 36p. pap. 21.99 (978-1-4771-5035-1(8)) Xlibris Corp.
Wozniak, Paul. Stranded in a Snowstorm! Webber, Mike, illus. 2014. (ENG.). 82p. pap. 11.95 (978-1-63047-173-6(9)) Morgan James Publishing.
Wrate, Richard. Din-o-mite in Aarons Closet. 2009. 28p. (J). 14.99 (978-0-615-19210-9(6)) Show n' Tell Publishing.
Wrecks, Billy. Batman: Adventures of the Dark Knight. 2016. (DK Adventures Ser.). lib. bdg. 16.00 (978-0-606-38229-8(1)) Turtleback Bks.
—Bizarro Day! 2013. (Step into Reading Level 2 Ser.). lib. bdg. 13.55 (978-0-606-26971-1(1), Turtleback) Turtleback Bks.
—Bizarro Day! (DC Super Friends) Legramandi, Francesco, illus. 2013. (Step into Reading Ser.). (ENG.). 32p. (J). (gr. k-3). pap. 3.99 (978-0-307-98119-6(3), Random Hse. Bks. for Young Readers) Random Hse. Children's Bks.
—Catch Catwoman! DeCarlo, Mike & Tanguay, David D., illus. 2013. (Step into Reading Ser.). (ENG.). 32p. (J). (gr. -1-1). 3.99 (978-0-449-81616-5(8), Random Hse. Bks. for Young Readers) Random Hse. Children's Bks.
—The Courageous Captain America. Golden Books Staff, illus. 2016. (Little Golden Book Ser.). (ENG.). 24p. (J). (gr. -1-k). 4.99 (978-0-307-93050-7(5), Golden Bks.) Random Hse. Children's Bks.
—Crime Wave! 2012. (Step into Reading Level 2 Ser.). lib. bdg. 13.55 (978-0-606-23739-0(9), Turtleback) Turtleback Bks.
—Crime Wave! (DC Super Friends) Schoening, Dan, illus. 2012. (Step into Reading Ser.). (ENG.). 32p. (J). (gr. -1-1). pap. 3.99 (978-0-375-86898-6(4), Random Hse. Bks. for Young Readers) Random Hse. Children's Bks.
—Green Lantern vs. the Meteor Monster! Random House Staff, illus. 2011. (Pictureback Ser.). (ENG.). 24p. (J). (gr. -1-2). pap. 3.99 (978-0-375-87297-6(3), Random Hse. Bks. for Young Readers) Random Hse. Children's Bks.

A
B

—Heroes! Golden Books Staff, illus. 2011. (Hologramatic Sticker Book Ser.). (ENG.). 48p. (J). (gr. -1-2). pap. 3.99 (978-0-375-85331-9(6), Golden Bks.) Random Hse. Children's Bks.

—Heroes vs. Villains/Space Chase! (DC Super Friends) Doescher, Erik et al, illus. 2013. (Pictureback(R) Ser.). (ENG.). 32p. (J). (gr. -1-2). pap. 4.99 (978-0-307-97616-1(5), Random Hse. Bks. for Young Readers) Random Hse. Children's Bks.

—The Mighty Thor. Golden Books Staff, illus. 2016. (Little Golden Book Ser.). (ENG.). 24p. (J). (gr. -1-k). 4.99 (978-0-307-93051-4(3), Golden Bks.) Random Hse. Children's Bks.

—Nemo's Big Adventure (Disney/Pixar Finding Nemo) RH Disney Staff, illus. 2012. (Pictureback(R) Ser.). (ENG.). 16p. (J). (gr. -1-2). pap. 4.99 (978-0-7364-2968-9(9), RH/Disney) Random Hse. Children's Bks.

—Reptile Rumble! Doescher, Erik, illus. 2014. (Step into Reading Ser.). (ENG.). 32p. (J). (gr. -1-1). 3.99 (978-0-385-37403-3(8), Random Hse. Bks. for Young Readers) Random Hse. Children's Bks.

—Reptile Rumble! 2014. (Step into Reading Level 2 Ser.). lib. bdg. 13.55 (978-0-606-35541-4(3)) Turtleback Bks.

—Shark Attack! Doescher, Erik, illus. 2017. 24p. (J). **(978-1-5182-2649-6(3))** Random Hse., Inc.

Wrecks, Billy. Time-Travel Trouble! 2014. (Step into Reading Level 2 Ser.). lib. bdg. 13.55 (978-0-606-36281-8(9)) Turtleback Bks.

Wrecks, Billy & Shealy, Dennis. T. Rex Trouble! Random House Staff et al, illus. 2011. (Step into Reading Ser.). (ENG.). 32p. (J). (gr. -1-1). pap. 3.99 (978-0-375-86777-4(5), Random Hse. Bks. for Young Readers) Random Hse. Children's Bks.

Wrede, Patricia C. The Far West. 2012. (ENG.). 384p. (J). (gr. 7-7). 17.99 (978-0-545-03344-2(6), Scholastic Pr.) Scholastic, Inc.

Wrench, Peter. The Web She Wove. 2013. 186p. pap. (978-1-78299-872-3(1)) FeedARead.com.

Wright, Deana. The Playground. 2009. 48p. pap. 9.95 (978-1-60693-680-1(8), Eloquent Bks.) Strategic Book Publishing & Rights Agency (SBPRA).

Wright, Dee. The Peanut Butter Finger Mystery. 2013. (Little Ruth Ser.). (ENG., Illus.). 38p. (J). pap. (978-1-59684-606-7(2)) Penman Publishers.

Wright, Gail. The Adventures of Alfred in Mom, I'm Growing up Now: Decision Making. 2012. 108p. (gr. 4-6). 28.95 (978-1-4497-6639-9(0)); pap. 11.95 (978-1-4497-6637-5(4)) Author Solutions, Inc. (WestBow Pr.).

Wright Johnson, Shelli. Falcon in the Nest: A Story of Bes Adventure. 2004. 273p. pap. 27.95 (978-1-4137-5263-2(2)) America Star Bks.

Wright, Kiyah. Vacation Fun. 2011. 24p. pap. 14.95 (978-1-4634-4055-8(3)) AuthorHouse.

Wright, Marcus. Raincloud. 2007. 172p. pap. 9.88 (978-0-615-15579-1(0)) Digitex-U Pubns.

Wright, Mary. Co-Man & Poppa Meet Kanka. Dewitt, Levi, illus. 2013. 24p. pap. 24.95 (978-1-62709-328-6(1)) America Star Bks.

Wright, Mary H. & Frontiera, Deborah K. Simon & Company: Flea Market Mice. Scott, Korey, illus. l.t. ed. 2016. (ENG.). 110p. (J). (gr. 2). pap. 11.99 (978-1-940591-04-9(X)) By Grace Enterprises.

Wright, Neville. Cop Car: And the Phantom Street Gang. 2010. 16p. 8.49 (978-1-4520-2881-1(8)) AuthorHouse.

Wright, S. B. Lissa Discovers the Secrets of the Castle, 1 vol. 2010. 62p. pap. 19.95 (978-1-4489-9692-6(9)) America Star Bks.

Wright, Shamekia. Mr. Fatty Mcfatterton. 2013. 20p. pap. 24.95 (978-1-63000-401-9(4)) America Star Bks.

Wright, Sky'asia. The Big, Blue Raspberry. 2012. 30p. pap. 5.99 (978-0-9857095-1-8(0)) RRJ Publishing, Inc.

Wright, Terry. The One-Eyed Monster. 2006. 48p. pap. 16.95 (978-1-4241-3696-4(2)) PublishAmerica, Inc.

Wright, Tish. The Boy & the Blue Painted Pony. 2012. 94p. (gr. -1). pap. 13.95 (978-1-4685-6606-2(7)) AuthorHouse.

Wright, Unasue Sellers. Dr. Chubby. 2013. 32p. pap. 13.95 (978-1-4497-8931-2(5), WestBow Pr.) Author Solutions, Inc.

Wronski, Gareth. Holly Farb & the Princess of the Galaxy. 2017. (ENG., Illus.). 320p. (J). (gr. 3-7). 16.99 **(978-1-4814-7177-0(5)**, Aladdin) Simon & Schuster Children's Publishing.

Wu, Nicholas. The Princess & the Pea, 1 vol. rev. ed. 2013. (Fiction Readers Ser.). (ENG., Illus.). 20p. (J). (gr. 1-1). pap. 4.99 (978-1-4333-5489-2(6)) Shell Educational Publishing.

—The Princess & the Pea: A Retelling of Hans Christian Andersen's Story, 1 vol. rev. ed. 2013. (Fiction Readers Ser.). (ENG., Illus.). 20p. (J). (gr. 1-1). pap. 15.96 (978-1-4807-1145-7(4)) Shell Educational Publishing.

Wyant, J. Anamnesis: The Further Adventures of Struth Digger. 2013. (ENG.). 107p. (YA). 23.95 (978-1-4787-1512-2(X)) Outskirts Pr., Inc.

Wyant, Sharon Kay. The Adventures of Brody. 2011. 56p. pap. 31.99 (978-1-4568-7560-2(4)) Xlibris Corp.

Wyatt, Cherokee. The Adventures of Margaret Mouse: Harvest Carnival. l.t. ed. 2006. (Illus.). 32p. (J). 6.95 (978-0-9761326-5-3(6)) www.margaretmouse.com publishing co.

—The Adventures of Margaret Mouse: School Days. Redmon, Angela M., illus. l.t. ed. 2004. 32p. (J). 6.95 (978-0-9761326-0-8(5)) www.margaretmouse.com publishing co.

—The Adventures of Margaret Mouse: The Magic Star. l.t. ed. 2006. (Illus.). 32p. (J). 6.95 (978-0-9761326-6-0(4)) www.margaretmouse.com publishing co.

—The Adventures of Margaret Mouse: The Picnic. Redmon, Angela M., illus. 2004. 32p. (J). 6.95 (978-0-9761326-1-5(3)) www.margaretmouse.com publishing co.

Wyatt, Chris. Falcon: Fight or Flight. 2015. (Mighty Marvel Chapter Bks.). (J). lib. bdg. 16.00 (978-0-606-36905-3(8)) Turtleback Bks.

—Star-Lord: Knowhere to Run. 2014. (Mighty Marvel Chapter Bks.). (J). lib. bdg. 16.00 (978-0-606-35920-7(6)) Turtleback Bks.

—World of Reading: Ant-Man This Is Ant-Man: Level 1. Lim, Ron & Rosenberg, Rachelle, illus. 2015. (World of Reading Ser.). (ENG.). 32p. (J). (gr. -1-k). pap. 3.99 (978-1-4847-1455-3(5), Marvel Pr.) Disney Publishing Worldwide.

Wyche, Wofford, Jane. Adventures at Hi-Lonesome Ranch: The Magic Cabin, Book Two. 2014. 194p. pap. 17.95 (978-1-4908-1824-5(3), WestBow Pr.) Author Solutions, Inc.

Wyke-Smith, E. A. The Marvellous Land of Snergs. Morrow, George, illus. 2006. (Dover Children's Classics Ser.). (ENG.). 224p. (gr. 3-12). per. 11.95 (978-0-486-45255-5(7)) Dover Pubns., Inc.

Wyler, Melissa. The Adventures of Henry the Sports Bug: Book 1. 2012. 36p. pap. 19.99 (978-1-105-64532-7(0)) Lulu Pr., Inc.

Wyllie, Ruth G. The Adventures of George the Turtle. 2012. 16p. pap. 15.99 (978-1-4772-5284-0(3)) AuthorHouse.

Wyman, Dorothy. Kaysell the Dragon Pup. 2011. 28p. pap. 13.54 (978-1-4269-4802-2(6)) Trafford Publishing.

Wynne-Jones, Tim. Secret Agent Man Goes Shopping for Shoes. Won, Brian, illus. 2016. (ENG.). 32p. (J). (gr. -1-3). 16.99 (978-0-7636-7119-8(3)) Candlewick Pr.

Wynne, Nick. Florida Tales. 2007. 128p. pap. 12.95 (978-0-9771079-6-4(5), Chapin Hse. Bks.) Florida Historical Society.

Wynne, Rhys. The Magic Pencil, 1 vol. 2009. 13p. pap. 24.95 (978-1-60749-089-0(7)) America Star Bks.

Wyre, Yvonne. The Further Adventures of Cuthbert the Coal Lorry & all His Friends. 2007. (Illus.). 204p. pap. (978-1-84401-801-7(6)) Athena Pr.

Wyss, Johann. The Swiss Family Robinson. 2005. pap. 16.95 (978-1-59818-422-8(9)) Rodgers, Alan Bks.

Wyss, Johann David. The Swiss Family Robinson. 2006. (Charming Classics). 208p. (J). pap. 6.99 (978-0-06-087587-9(9), HarperFestival) HarperCollins Pubs.

—The Swiss Family Robinson: Or Adventures in a Desert Island. l.t. ed. 2007. (ENG.). 354p. pap. 26.99 (978-1-4264-5633-6(6)) Creative Media Partners, LLC.

Wyss, Tyan. Night Flyer. Immelman, Sarita, illus. 2006. 40p. (J). per. 14.95 (978-1-58939-916-7(1)) Virtualbookworm.com Publishing, Inc.

The X-Factor. 2009. (Hardy Boys (All New) Undercover Brothers Ser.: 30). (ENG.). 176p. (J). (gr. 3-7). pap. 5.99 (978-1-4169-7802-2(X), Aladdin) Simon & Schuster Children's Publishing.

X-Plosion. 2009. (Hardy Boys (All New) Undercover Brothers Ser.: 29). (ENG.). 160p. (J). (gr. 3-7). pap. 6.99 (978-1-4169-7870-1(4), Aladdin) Simon & Schuster Children's Publishing.

Xavier V, Sajjad. Baboonia. 2010. 191p. pap. 14.99 (978-0-557-04174-9(0)) Lulu Pr., Inc.

Xu, Lei. Graveyard of a Queen. Mok, Kathy, tr. Verano, Vladimir, illus. 2014. (Grave Robbers' Chronicles Ser.: 6). (ENG.). pap. 9.95 (978-1-934159-36-1(0)) ThingsAsian Pr.

Yaccarino, Dan. Class Pet Squad: Journey to the Center of Town. 2016. (ENG., Illus.). 144p. (J). 13.99 (978-1-250-02462-6(5), 9781250024626) Feiwel & Friends.

—Journey to the Center of Town. 2017. (Class Pet Squad Ser.: 1). (J). lib. bdg. 17.20 **(978-0-606-39943-2(7))** Turtleback Bks.

Yaccarino, Dan. Lawn to Lawn. 2010. (ENG.). 40p. (J). (gr. -1-2). 17.99 (978-0-375-85574-0(2), Knopf Bks. for Young Readers) Random Hse. Children's Bks.

Yager, Karen & Williams, Kiersten. Krickle Forest Adventures, Wizbet's Notebook. Walsh, Jennifer, illus. 2012. 60p. pap. 7.95 (978-0-9855997-0-6(7)) Krickle Forest Adventures.

Yalmeh, Jacklin. Scruffy & the Blue Hazelnut Tree. 2013. 38p. pap. 10.95 (978-0-9885898-1-0(8)) i ZGOOL Media.

—Scruffy & the Walnuts. 2013. 38p. pap. 10.95 (978-0-9885898-2-7(6)) i ZGOOL Media.

Yan, Wing & Tung, King. King of Fighters 2003, Vol. 4. 2008. (ENG., Illus.). 140p. (YA). pap. 13.95 (978-1-59796-010-6(1)) DrMaster Pubns. Inc.

Yan, Wing Tung, et al. King of Fighters 2003, Vol. 5. 2008. (ENG., Illus.). 140p. (YA). pap. 13.95 (978-1-59796-011-3(X)) DrMaster Pubns. Inc.

Yancey, Rick. Alfred Kropp: the Thirteenth Skull. 2015. (Alfred Kropp Ser.). (ENG.). 304p. (YA). (gr. 7). pap. 9.99 (978-1-61963-918-8(1), 9781619639188, Bloomsbury USA Childrens) Bloomsbury Publishing USA.

—The Monstrumologist Collection: Monstrumologist; Curse of the Wendigo; Isle of Blood; Final Descent. 2014. (Monstrumologist Ser.). (ENG., Illus.). 1808p. (YA). (gr. 9). pap. 46.99 (978-1-4814-3012-8(2), Simon & Schuster Bks. For Young Readers) Simon & Schuster Bks. For Young Readers.

—The Thirteenth Skull. (Alfred Kropp Ser.). (ENG.). 304p. (YA). (gr. 7). 2009. mass mkt. 6.99 (978-1-59990-363-7(6), 9781599903637) 2008. 16.99 (978-1-59990-114-5(5), 9781599901145) Bloomsbury Publishing USA. (Bloomsbury USA Childrens).

Yang, Angela. Within the Mist. 2013. 198p. pap. 12.99 (978-0-578-12358-5(4)) Yang, Jennifer.

Yang, Gene Luen. Secrets & Sequences. Holmes, Mike, illus. 2017. (Secret Coders Ser.: 3). (ENG.). 112p. (J). pap. 10.99 (978-1-62672-077-0(0), 9781626720770, First Second Bks.) Roaring Brook Pr.

—Secrets & Sequences. 2017. (Secret Coders Ser.: 3). (J). lib. bdg. 22.10 **(978-0-606-40345-0(0))** Turtleback Bks.

Yang, Gene Luen. The Shadow Hero. Liew, Sonny, illus. 2014. (ENG.). 176p. (YA). (gr. 7-12). pap. 17.99 (978-1-59643-697-8(2), 9781596436978, First Second Bks.) Roaring Brook Pr.

—The Shadow Hero. Liew, Sonny, illus. 2014. (YA). lib. bdg. 30.60 (978-0-606-35521-6(9)) Turtleback Bks.

Yang, Gladys. The Frog Rider & Other Folktales from Chin. 2008. 116p. 19.95 (978-1-59654-569-4(0)) Disruptive Publishing.

Yarbray Brucke, Candice & Moore, Dawnyelle. Wrappers Wanted: A Mathematical Adventure in Surface Area. 2009. 32p. pap. 15.00 (978-1-4389-7468-2(X)) AuthorHouse.

Yardley Hastings Primary School. Tim & Holly's Olympic Adventure. 2012. 74p. pap. (978-1-909039-52-0(7)) Legend Pr.

Yardley, Liz. The Firefly Legacy - Book Vi. Yardley, Liz, illus. 2013. (Illus.). 336p. pap. (978-0-9872013-1-7(X)) BlueFlower Bks.

Yarrow, Peter & Lipton, Lenny. Puff, the Magic Dragon. Puybaret, Eric, illus. 2007. (ENG.). 24p. (J). 16.95 (978-1-4027-5219-3(9)); 16.95 (978-1-4027-5279-7(2)) Sterling Publishing Co., Inc.

Yasko, Carmen R. Buddy & His Buddies. 2012. 40p. pap. 22.65 (978-1-4797-4710-8(6)) Xlibris Corp.

Yasso, C. D. The Adventures of Penn & Penelope in Washington, Dc. 2012. 32p. pap. 15.75 (978-1-105-64108-4(2)) Lulu Pr., Inc.

Yayo. The Tales of Pop & Grace: Pop's Lucky Token. 2013. 94p. (gr. 2-4). pap. 10.67 (978-1-4817-8033-9(6)) AuthorHouse.

Yazdani, Aliza. Protection: How far Would you go to Save a Brother? 2012. 84p. pap. 11.11 (978-1-4669-0895-6(5)) Trafford Publishing.

Yearling, A. K. My Little Pony Set: The Daring Do Adventure Collection. 2014. (ENG.). 624p. (J). (gr. 5-7). 75.00 (978-0-316-40612-3(0)) Little, Brown Bks. for Young Readers.

Yee, Linda L. Big Red Things. 2005. 20.00 (978-0-8059-9855-9(1)) Dorrance Publishing Co., Inc.

Yeh, Julie. Poppie's Adventures: Serpents in Paradise. Hsu, Jack, illus. 2003. 48p. (J). per. (978-0-9742386-0-9(0)) Way Out Comics.

Yellowknife, Jessica. Spring Break Adventure. 2011. 84p. pap. 11.11 (978-1-4269-6952-2(X)) Trafford Publishing.

Yerges, Karen. The Adventures of Scooper the Beagle Dog: Las aventuras de Scooper el perrito Beagle. 2004. (SPA., Illus.). 60p. (J). per. 19.95 (978-0-9764384-0-3(2)) Mitre's Touch Gallery, The.

Ylvisaker, Anne. The Curse of the Buttons. 2014. (ENG.). 240p. (J). (gr. 3-7). 15.99 (978-0-7636-6138-0(4)) Candlewick Pr.

—Little Klein. 2009. (ENG.). 192p. (J). (gr. 3-7). pap. 6.99 (978-0-7636-4338-6(6)) Candlewick Pr.

Yoder, Greg, illus. The Swing: A Storybook to Color. 2003. (J). 4.00 (978-1-930353-88-6(X)) Masthof Pr.

Yolen, Jane. Dragon's Blood. 2004. (Pit Dragon Chronicles Ser.: 1). (ENG., Illus.). 320p. (YA). (gr. 7-12). pap. 7.99 (978-0-15-205126-6(0)) Houghton Mifflin Harcourt Publishing Co.

—Foiled. 2010. (J). lib. bdg. 30.60 (978-0-606-14452-0(8), Turtleback) Turtleback Bks.

—Heart's Blood, Vol. 2. 2004. (Pit Dragon Chronicles Ser.: 2). (ENG., Illus.). 368p. (YA). (gr. 7-12). pap. 7.99 (978-0-15-205118-1(X)) Houghton Mifflin Harcourt Publishing Co.

—The Last Dragon. Guay, Rebecca, illus. 2011. (ENG.). 144p. (J). (gr. 7-7). pap. 29.99 (978-1-59582-798-2(6)) Dark Horse Comics.

—A Sending of Dragons Vol. 3. 2004. (Pit Dragon Chronicles Ser.: 3). (ENG., Illus.). 320p. (YA). (gr. 7-12). pap. 8.99 (978-0-15-205128-0(7)) Houghton Mifflin Harcourt Publishing Co.

Yolen, Jane & Harris, Robert J. Atalanta & the Arcadian Beast. 2003. (Young Heroes Ser.: Bk. 3). 256p. (J). 15.99 (978-0-06-029454-0(X)) HarperCollins Pubs.

Yolen, Jane & Stemple, Adam. The Hostage Prince. 2014. (Seelie Wars Ser.). (ENG.). 256p. (J). (gr. 3-7). pap. 7.99 (978-0-14-242234-2(7), Puffin Books) Penguin Young Readers Group.

Yomtov, Nel. Adventures in Science. O'Neill, Sean et al, illus. 2012. (Adventures in Science Ser.). (ENG.). 32p. (gr. 3-4). pap. 190.80 (978-1-4296-8470-5(4)); pap. 31.80 (978-1-4296-8469-9(0)) Capstone Press of Coughlan Cos. (Graphic Library).

Yomtov, Nel, et al. Adventures in Science. O'Neill, Sean et al, illus. 2012. (Adventures in Science Ser.). (ENG.). 32p. (gr. 3-4). lib. bdg. 91.95 (978-1-4296-8172-8(1), Graphic Library) Capstone Press of Coughlan Cos.

Yonge, Charlotte M. Little Lucy's Wonderful Globe. 2007. 52p. per. (978-1-4065-5529-5(0)) Dodo Pr.

—Little Lucy's Wonderful Globe. 2008. 152p. 36.95 (978-0-548-97272-4(9)) 2007. 156p. per. 21.95 (978-0-548-67542-7(2)) Kessinger Publishing, LLC.

Yontz, Barbara J. The Adventures of Baby Z & the Rabbit of Oz. 2012. 24p. pap. 15.99 (978-1-4797-3514-3(0)) Xlibris Corp.

Yoon, Salina. Penguin's Big Adventure. 2015. (Penguin Ser.). (ENG., Illus.). 40p. (J). (gr. -1-1). 14.99 (978-0-8027-3828-8(1), 9780802738288, Bloomsbury USA Childrens) Bloomsbury Publishing USA.

Yoon, Salina. Pingüino Enamorado. 2017. 36p. (J). (gr. k). 20.99 **(978-84-8470-545-1(5))** Corimbo, Editorial S.L. ESP. Dist: Lectorum Pubns., Inc.

York, John Randall. King Bronty in the Days of the Dinosaurs. 2012. 48p. pap. 9.95 (978-1-60076-332-8(4)) StoneGarden.net Publishing.

York, M. J. The Boy at the Dike: A Dutch Folktale. Freeman, Laura, illus. 2012. (Folktales from Around the World Ser.). (ENG.). 24p. (J). (gr. k-3). 28.50 (978-1-61473-219-8(1), 204914) Child's World, Inc., The.

Yost-Filgate, Susan. Rip Squeak & Friends: the Adventure. Filgate, Leonard, illus. 2005. (Rip Squeak Ser.). (ENG.). 32p. (J). (gr. -1-3). 16.95 (978-0-9672422-9-3(0), Raven Tree Pr.,Csi) Continental Sales, Inc.

—Rip Squeak & His Friends. Filgate, Leonard, illus. 2009. (ENG.). 32p. (J). (gr. -1-3). 16.95 (978-1-934960-40-0(3), Raven Tree Pr.,Csi) Continental Sales, Inc.

—The Treasure. 2009. (ENG.). 32p. (J). (gr. -1-3). 16.95 (978-1-934960-41-7(1), Raven Tree Pr.,Csi) Continental Sales, Inc.

—The Treasure: A Rip Squeak Book. Filgate, Leonard, illus. 2005. (Rip Squeak Ser.). (ENG.). 32p. (J). (gr. -1-3). 16.95 (978-0-9747825-1-5(3), Raven Tree Pr.,Csi) Continental Sales, Inc.

You Can Make a Difference, Maddie Morrison. 2008. 123p. (J). pap. 7.99 (978-0-9786117-1-2(3)) Neal Morgan Publishing.

You Choose Stories: Batman. 2016. (You Choose Stories: Batman Ser.). (ENG.). 112p. (gr. 2-3). pap. 13.90 (978-1-4965-3103-2(5)); pap. 55.60 (978-1-4965-3104-9(3)) Stone Arch Bks. (DC Super Heroes).

Young, Andrea. Finny & the Boy from Horse Mountain. 2016. (ENG.). 320p. (J). (gr. 6). pap. 9.99 (978-1-63450-166-8(7), Sky Pony Pr.) Skyhorse Publishing Co., Inc.

Young, Brett. The Twontle. 2005. (ENG., Illus.). 48p. (J). pap. 12.99 (978-0-9725230-7-3(3)) Wandering Sage Pubns., LLC.

Young, Caroline. Grubby Finn Robinson. 2009. 52p. pap. 10.55 (978-1-4251-3002-2(X)) Trafford Publishing.

Young, Chris. Boko & the Big Red Bag. 2012. 36p. pap. 18.41 (978-1-4669-6497-6(9)) Trafford Publishing.

Young, Craig. Arrr Marks the Spot. 2011. 32p. pap. (978-1-926959-06-1(X)) 1889 Labs Ltd.

Young, Elizabeth L. Dozens & Dozens of Cousins & Cousins. Perkins, Ruth, illus. 2012. 30p. 20.95 (978-1-61633-353-9(7)); pap. 12.95 (978-1-61633-352-2(9)) Guardian Angel Publishing, Inc.

Young, Franklin. S P o T S. 2012. 198p. pap. (978-0-9869350-0-8(X)) Awesome Bks.

Young, Heather. Norman. 2012. 36p. pap. 21.99 (978-1-4797-1356-1(2)) Xlibris Corp.

Young, Helen Ann. Hellie & the Sensational Magic Carpet. Young, Tim, illus. 2013. 106p. pap. (978-1-908353-02-3(3)) Young Editions.

Young, J. E. Horror in Space. Huddleston, Courtney, illus. 2011. (Twisted Journeys (r) Ser.: 18). (ENG.). 112p. (J). (gr. 4-7). pap. 7.95 (978-0-8225-9273-0(8), Graphic Universe™) Lerner Publishing Group.

Young, Kristi. The Secret Club - the Powder Puff Club Book 1. 2007. (ENG.). 140p. (J). per. 12.95 (978-1-59594-070-4(7), Wingspan Pr.) WingSpan Publishing.

Young, Lauren. Ally M. & Ally G. Rooney, Sandra, illus. 2006. 20p. (J). 9.95 (978-1-4120-8518-2(7)) Trafford Publishing.

Young, Linda P. The Adventures of Anna & Andy Hummingbird: Anna & Andy Meet the Grandchildren, Book 3 Stories 11, 12 And 13. 2012. 32p. pap. 21.99 (978-1-4797-1637-1(5)) Xlibris Corp.

Young, Lynn. Adventures with Looka, 1 vol. 2009. 48p. pap. 16.95 (978-1-60813-959-0(X)) America Star Bks.

Young, Marlene Lauster. Before Summer's End. 2012. 36p. (-18). pap. 20.99 (978-1-4772-6810-0(3)) AuthorHouse.

Young, Steve. Winchell Mink: The Misadventure Begins. 2004. 144p. (J). 16.89 (978-0-06-053500-1(8)) HarperCollins Pubs.

Young, Suzanne Marie. A Dedication to Free Spirit. 2011. 62p. pap. 19.95 (978-1-4626-3425-5(7)) America Star Bks.

Young, Valerie. The Adventures of Todd & Friends. 2009. 20p. pap. 12.49 (978-1-4389-3196-8(4)) AuthorHouse.

Youngberg, Yvette M. The Tooting Squirrel. 2009. (Illus.). 20p. pap. 10.95 (978-1-4389-1967-6(0)) AuthorHouse.

Younge, Cathy. The Tale of Sidney Elderberry - an Ordinary Boy with Extraordinary Bowels. Taylor, Mark, illus. 2013. 32p. pap. (978-1-78148-838-6(X)) Grosvenor Hse. Publishing Ltd.

Younger, David. The Mysterious Moat Maiden: A Wandering Firefly Fairy Adventure, 1 vol. 2009. 15p. pap. 24.95 (978-1-61546-213-1(9)) America Star Bks.

Your Purrr-Fect Birthday. 2007. (Dragonlarks Ser.). (Illus.). 64p. (J). (gr. k-3). per. 7.99 (978-1-933390-55-0(7)) Chooseco LLC.

Your Very Own Robot. 2007. (Choose Your Own Adventure Ser.). (Illus.). 80p. (J). (gr. 4-7). pap. 7.99 (978-1-933390-52-9(2)) Chooseco LLC.

Yourgrau, Barry. Another Nastybook: The Curse of the Tweeties. DeJesus, Robert, illus. 2006. 171p. (J). (gr. 5-9). lib. bdg. 13.89 (978-0-06-057982-1(X), Cotler, Joanna Books) HarperCollins Pubs.

—Nasty Book. 2005. (ENG.). 192p. (J). (gr. 5-9). 11.99 (978-0-06-057978-4(1)) HarperCollins Pubs.

—Nastybook. 2007. (ENG.). 192p. (J). (gr. 5-9). pap. 5.99 (978-0-06-057980-7(3), Harper Trophy) HarperCollins Pubs.

YoYo. Vermonia 7: Battle for the Turtle Realm, 1. 2014. (Vermonia Ser.). (ENG.). 208p. (J). (gr. 3-6). pap. 11.75 (978-1-61533-651-7(6), Windmill Bks.) Rosen Publishing Group, Inc., The.

Yoyo Books Staff. Princess Charlotte's Journey Through History. 2005. 32p. (978-90-5843-458-6(3)) YoYo Bks.

Yu, Li, et al. The Holy Spark: Rogel & the Goddess of Liberty. 2006. (J). (978-1-931907-42-2(0)) Homa & Sekey Bks.

Yukkie the Yorkie, A. K. A. Marilyn J. Sanders. The Adventures of Yukkie the Yorkie: The Beginning. 2008. (Illus.). 32p. (J). 16.00 (978-0-8059-7606-9(X)) Dorrance Publishing Co., Inc.

Yusuf. Butterfly & Bumble Bee: Adventure in Yellow Stone National Park. 2010. 16p. 8.49 (978-1-4520-4022-6(2)) AuthorHouse.

Yusuf, Hanna S. & Day, Cansarra. Katie Mcchoir. 2010. 80p. pap. 10.49 (978-1-4490-7378-7(6)) AuthorHouse.

Zabel, Randy & Broesch, Valerie, illus. Al-the-Gator & Freddy Frog. 2007. 48p. (J). per. 18.99 (978-0-9797513-0-1(6)) 4RV Publishing, LLC.

Zabriskie, Cindy. The Daily Adventures of Ruckus & Otis. Benger, Chelsi L., illus. 2008. 24p. pap. 24.95 (978-1-60672-829-1(6)) America Star Bks.

Zabrosky, Joseph. Herbie Hanson, 1 vol., 4 bks. l.t. ed. 2005. (Illus.). 32p. (J). per. (978-0-9768831-0-4(4)) Elohim Bks.

Zadrozny, Alicia & Church, Caroline Jayne. The Wild Little Jungle: A Mix-and-Match Flap Book. 2008. (ENG.). 10p. (J). bds. 12.99 (978-0-7944-1605-8(5)) Reader's Digest Assn., Inc., The.

Zafrilla, Marta. Little Chick & Mommy Cat. 2012. (ENG., Illus.). 32p. (J). (gr. k-2). (978-84-15241-96-6(8)) D P & G Military Pubs.

Zagorski, Steve. The River of Wisdom. 2010. pap. 17.95 (978-0-578-05364-6(0)) Zagorski, Steve.

Zaionz, Ruth. Morris the Friendly Dinosaur. 2010. 24p. pap. 12.99 (978-1-4490-6981-0(9)) AuthorHouse.

Zak, Faith. Naptime Adventures: Christmas Tree. 2012. 24p. pap. 24.95 (978-1-4626-5279-2(4)) America Star Bks.

—Naptime Adventures: Train. 2012. 24p. 24.95 (978-1-4626-5000-2(7)) America Star Bks.

Zakon, Miriam, creator. Baker's Dozen: Three-in-One 1-3, 4-6, 7-9, 10-12, 13-15, 16-17, 3 vols. Vols. 1-3. 16.95 (978-1-56871-200-0(6))Vols. 10-12. 16.99 (978-1-56871-297-0(9))Vols. 13-15. 16.99 (978-1-56871-266-6(9)) Targum Pr., Inc.

Zales, S. R. Jenny & the Hummingbird Faeries. 2012. 152p. pap. 14.95 (978-1-4575-1330-5(7)) Dog Ear Publishing, LLC.

Zamenhof, Robert. The Adventures of Armadillo Baby & Annabelli. Baker, Sara, illus. 2013. 56p. pap. 9.29 (978-0-615-80196-4(X)) RGZ Consulting.

Zamor, Nehemie Djose. The Adventures of Naoomi. 2011. 34p. pap. 14.99 (978-1-61379-327-5(8)) Salem Author Services.

Zappa, Ahmet & Muldoon Zappa, Shana. Star Darlings Libby & the Class Election. Bonatakis, Shannon & Disney

Storybook Art Team, illus. 2015. (Star Darlings Ser.: 2). (ENG.). 176p. (J). (gr. 3-7). pap. 6.99 *(978-1-4231-7766-1(5))* Disney Pr.

Zappa, Shana Muldoon & Zappa, Ahmet. Star Darlings: Scarlet Discovers True Strength. Disney Storybook Art Team, illus. 2016. (Star Darlings Ser.: 5). (ENG.). 176p. (J). (gr. 3-7). pap. 6.99 *(978-1-4847-1424-9(5))* Disney Pr.

Zarcinas, Scott. The Golden Chalice: A Pilgrim's Chronicle. 2013. 200p. pap. *(978-0-9875975-9-5(0))* DoctorZed Publishing.

—The Golden Chalice: A Pilgrim's Chronicle (Large Print 16pt) l.t. ed. 2013. 284p. (YA). pap. *(978-1-4596-7063-1(9))* ReadHowYouWant.com, Ltd.

Zaugg, Sandra L. A Prayer for Mother. 2005. (Illus.). 95p. (J). *(978-0-8163-2056-1(X))* Pacific Pr. Pubns.

Zaugg, Sandy. Murdock Mystery #1: A House Called Fernley Manor. 2009. 103p. (J). pap. 10.95 *(978-1-4327-2914-1(4))* Outskirts Pr., Inc.

Zdenek, Joseph. Heart of Courage: The Narscix War. 2007. 372p. (gr. -1-7). per. 20.95 *(978-0-595-43187-8(9))* iUniverse, Inc.

Zehring Fischer, Nancy. Children of the Mission. 2013. 52p. pap. 7.95 *(978-1-61170-129-6(5))* Robertson Publishing.

Zeidman, Bob. The Amazing Adventure of Edward & Dr. Sprechtmachen. 2012. 76p. (J). (gr. k-10). pap. 5.95 *(978-0-9702276-1-4(2))* Swiss Creek Pubns.

Zellers, Michelle. Maya's Magic Carpet. 2006. (J). per. 11.95 *(978-1-889743-48-6(8))* Robbie Dean Pr.

Zeman, Ludmila, retold by. Sindbad's Secret. 2003. (ENG., Illus.). 32p. (J). (gr. 1-4). 17.95 *(978-0-88776-462-2(2),* Tundra Bks.) Tundra Bks. CAN. Dist: Penguin Random Hse. LLC.

Zemeckis, Robert, et al. The Polar Express Movie Shadowbook: An Interactive Shadow-Casting Bedtime Story. Van Allsburg, Chris, illus. 2006. 12p. (J). (gr. 4-18). reprint ed. 13.00 *(978-1-4223-5172-7(6))* DIANE Publishing Co.

Zenescope Entertainment Staff, et al. Never Underestimate a Hermit Crab. 2014. (ENG., Illus.). 48p. (J). pap. 9.99 *(978-1-939683-25-0(4),* 9781939683250) Zenescope Entertainment.

Zera, Beata. Little Puppy Swifty & Elle. 2008. 64p. pap. 21.99 *(978-1-4257-6703-7(6))* Xlibris Corp.

Zerbe, Tim. The King of Pumpkin Ridge. 2012. 28p. pap. 9.95 *(978-1-937600-80-8(7))* Salem Author Services.

Zhang, Kat. Echoes of US. 2014. (Hybrid Chronicles Ser.: 3). (ENG.). 368p. (YA). (gr. 8). 17.99 *(978-0-06-211493-8(X))* HarperCollins Pubs.

—The Emperor's Riddle. 2017. (ENG., Illus.). 256p. (J). (gr. 3-7). 16.99 ***(978-1-4814-7862-5(1),*** Aladdin) Simon & Schuster Children's Publishing.

Zhang, Kat. Once We Were: The Hybrid Chronicles, Book 2. 2013. (Hybrid Chronicles Ser.: 2). (ENG.). 352p. (YA). (gr. 8). 17.99 *(978-0-06-211490-7(5))* HarperCollins Pubs.

Ziegesar, Cecily von. Love the One You're With. 2009. (Gossip Girl: the Carlyles Ser.: 4). (ENG.). 240p. (YA). (gr. 10-17). pap. 10.99 *(978-0-316-02067-1(2),* Poppy) Little, Brown Bks. for Young Readers.

Ziegler, Jennifer. Revenge of the Happy Campers. 2017. (Brewster Triplets Ser.). (ENG.). 272p. (J). (gr. 3-7). 16.99 ***(978-1-338-09119-9(0),*** Scholastic Pr.) Scholastic, Inc.

Zielinski, Valerie & Skaletski, Roslyn. The Adventures of Bella. 2011. 48p. pap. 14.00 *(978-1-4634-2018-5(8))* AuthorHouse.

Zimelman, Nathan. The Great Adventure of Wo Ti. 2013. (ENG., Illus.). 32p. (J). (gr. -1-3). 16.99 *(978-1-4814-2142-3(5),* Simon & Schuster Bks. For Young Readers) Simon & Schuster Bks. For Young Readers.

Zimmerman, Andrea & Clemesha, David. Train Man. Zimmerman, Andrea & Clemesha, David, illus. 2017. (ENG., Illus.). 32p. (J). bds. 8.99 *(978-1-62779-504-3(9),* 9781627795043, Holt, Henry & Co. Bks. For Young Readers) Holt, Henry & Co.

Zimmerman, Carol. Charlie the Spider. 2011. 32p. pap. 13.95 *(978-1-4567-9523-8(6))* AuthorHouse.

Zimmerman, Ron. Ultimate Adventures Vol. 1: One Tin Soldier. 2005. (Hank Kipple Ser.). (Illus.). 144p. (YA). pap. 12.99 *(978-0-7851-1043-9(7))* Marvel Worldwide, Inc.

Zimmerman, Virginia. The Rosemary Spell. (ENG.). (J). (gr. 5-7). 2017. 288p. pap. 7.99 *(978-0-544-93699-7(X),* HMH Books For Young Readers) 2015. 280p. 16.99 *(978-0-544-44537-6(6))* Houghton Mifflin Harcourt Publishing Co.

Zimmerman, W. Frederick. Unauthorized Harry Potter & the Alchemist's Cell News: Half-Blood Prince Analysis & Speculation. 2006. 160p. per. 14.94 *(978-0-9777424-7-9(4))* Nimble Bks. LLC.

—Unauthorized Harry Potter & the Chariots of Light News: Half-Blood Prince Analysis & Speculation. 2006. 160p. per. 14.94 *(978-0-9777424-8-6(2))* Nimble Bks. LLC.

Zimmermann, Andreas. Shard. 2012. 302p. 28.95 *(978-1-4620-8351-0(X));* pap. 18.95 *(978-1-4620-8350-3(1))* iUniverse, Inc.

Zimmerschied, P. Grampa Paul's Adventure Stories for Children. 2011. 112p. (gr. -1). 23.99 *(978-1-4634-2885-3(5));* pap. 13.99 *(978-1-4634-2883-9(9))* AuthorHouse.

Zindel, Paul. The Pigman's Legacy. 2005. 168p. (YA). (gr. 7-12). 13.65 *(978-0-7569-4962-4(9))* Perfection Learning Corp.

Zoboi, Ibi. American Street. 2017. 336p. (YA). (gr. 9). 17.99 *(978-0-06-247304-2(2))* HarperCollins Pubs.

Zomerdyke, Joy. Polar & Grizzly Find Christmas. 2013. 24p. pap. 17.99 *(978-1-4817-1155-5(5))* AuthorHouse.

Zorro: Crypts. 2006. (J). pap. 7.95 *(978-1-59707-032-4(7))* NBM Publishing Co.

Zschock, Martha Day. Hello, San Francisco! 2012. (Hello! Ser.). (ENG., Illus.). 16p. (J). (gr. -1-k). bds. 9.95 *(978-1-933212-65-4(9),* Commonwealth Editions) Applewood Bks.

Zub, Jim. Figment: Journey into Imagination. 2016. (Figment: Journey into Imagination Ser.: 5). (ENG.). 24p. (J). (gr. k-5). lib. bdg. 121.05 *(978-1-61479-444-8(8),* Graphic Planet) Magic Wagon.

—Figment: Journey into Imagination: Volume 1, 1 vol. 2016. (Figment: Journey into Imagination Ser.). (ENG., Illus.). 24p. (J). (gr. k-5). lib. bdg. 24.21 *(978-1-61479-445-5(6),* Graphic Planet) Magic Wagon.

—Figment: Journey into Imagination: Volume 2, 1 vol. 2016. (Figment: Journey into Imagination Ser.). (ENG., Illus.). 24p. (J). (gr. k-5). lib. bdg. 24.21 *(978-1-61479-446-2(4),* Graphic Planet) Magic Wagon.

—Figment: Journey into Imagination: Volume 3, 1 vol. 2016. (Figment: Journey into Imagination Ser.). (ENG., Illus.). 24p. (J). (gr. k-5). lib. bdg. 24.21 *(978-1-61479-447-9(2),* Graphic Planet) Magic Wagon.

—Figment: Journey into Imagination: Volume 4, 1 vol. 2016. (Figment: Journey into Imagination Ser.). (ENG., Illus.). 24p. (J). (gr. k-5). lib. bdg. 24.21 *(978-1-61479-448-6(0),* Graphic Planet) Magic Wagon.

—Figment: Journey into Imagination: Volume 5, 1 vol. 2016. (Figment: Journey into Imagination Ser.). (ENG., Illus.). 24p. (J). (gr. k-5). lib. bdg. 24.21 *(978-1-61479-449-3(9),* Graphic Planet) Magic Wagon.

Zucker, Jonny. Mission 1: Game On. Woodman, Ned, illus. 2013. (Max Flash Ser.: 1). (ENG.). 144p. (gr. 2-5). pap. 7.95 *(978-1-4677-1465-5(8));* lib. bdg. 27.93 *(978-1-4677-1207-1(8))* Lerner Publishing Group. (Darby Creek).

—Mission 2: Supersonic. Woodman, Ned, illus. 2013. (Max Flash Ser.: 2). (ENG.). 144p. (gr. 2-5). pap. 7.95 *(978-1-4677-1482-2(8));* lib. bdg. 27.93 *(978-1-4677-1208-8(6))* Lerner Publishing Group. (Darby Creek).

—Mission 3: In Deep. Woodman, Ned, illus. 2013. (Max Flash Ser.: 3). (ENG.). 144p. (gr. 2-5). pap. 7.95 *(978-1-4677-1473-0(9));* lib. bdg. 27.93 *(978-1-4677-1209-5(4))* Lerner Publishing Group. (Darby Creek).

—Mission 4: Grave Danger. Woodman, Ned, illus. 2013. (Max Flash Ser.: 4). (ENG.). 144p. (gr. 2-5). pap. 7.95 *(978-1-4677-1466-2(6));* lib. bdg. 27.93 *(978-1-4677-1210-1(8))* Lerner Publishing Group. (Darby Creek).

—Mission 5: Subzero. Woodman, Ned, illus. 2013. (Max Flash Ser.: 5). (ENG.). 144p. (gr. 2-5). pap. 7.95 *(978-1-4677-1481-5(X));* lib. bdg. 27.93 *(978-1-4677-1212-5(4))* Lerner Publishing Group. (Darby Creek).

Zuckerberg, Randi. Dot. Berger, Joe, illus. 2013. (ENG.). 32p. (J). (gr. -1-3). 17.99 *(978-0-06-228751-9(6))* HarperCollins Pubs.

Zuckerman, Lilla & Zuckerman, Nora. Beauty Queen Blowout. 2003. (ENG.). 240p. pap. 15.99 *(978-0-7432-3846-5(X),* Touchstone) Touchstone.

Zuggo, Violeta & Zuggo, Jutka. Story Time for Kids with Nlp by the English Sisters: The Little Grasshopper & the Big Ball of Dung. Kecskés, Anna, illus. 2013. 24p. pap. *(978-1-78092-493-9(3))* MX Publishing, Ltd.

Zuhdi, Darla. A South Sea Adventure, Vol. 4. 2005. (Cat Detectives Present Ser.: 4). (Illus.). 104p. (J). per. 6.99 *(978-0-9706062-6-6(5))* catBOX Entertainment, Inc.

Zupsic, Kelly. Mrs. Sneeze & the Three Legged Goat. 2013. 28p. pap. 24.95 *(978-1-62709-791-8(0))* America Star Bks.

Zwingelberg, Wc. The Adventures of Will W. Wilson. 2006. (Illus.). 80p. per. 12.00 *(978-1-4251-0579-2(3))* Trafford Publishing.

123 Sesame Street, ed. Abby in Wonderland. 2009. (ENG.). 20p. 16.99 *(978-1-59069-834-1(7))* Studio Mouse LLC.

—A Year Starts Here. 2009. (ENG.). 24p. 7.99 *(978-1-59069-829-7(0))* Studio Mouse LLC.

2nd and 7 Foundation. The Hog Mollies & the Amazing Aquatic Adventure (Soft Cover) rev. ed. 2011. (ENG.). 32p. pap. 6.95 *(978-0-7575-9147-1(7))* Kendall Hunt Publishing Co.

2nd and 7 Foundation Staff. The Hog Mollies & the Amazing Aquatic Adventure. rev. ed. 2011. 32p. pap. 12.95 *(978-0-7575-9148-8(5))* Kendall Hunt Publishing Co.

ADVENTURE STORIES

see Adventure And Adventurers—Fiction

ADVERTISING

see also Commercial Art; Marketing; Posters; Propaganda; Sales Personnel; Signs and Signboards

Bodden, Valerie. Identify & Evaluate Advertising. 2015. (Info Wise Ser.). (ENG., Illus.). 40p. (J). (gr. 4-6). pap. 8.99 *(978-1-4677-7580-9(0));* lib. bdg. 30.65 *(978-1-4677-5226-8(6))* Lerner Publishing Group. (Lerner Pubns.).

Donovan, Sandy. Media: From News Coverage to Political Advertising. 2015. (ENG.). 64p. (J). (gr. 6-8). 26.65 *(978-1-4677-7909-8(1))* Lerner Publishing Group.

Espejo, Roman. How Does Advertising Impact Teen Behavior? 2011. (At Issue Ser.). (ENG.). 128p. (gr. 10-12). 39.40 *(978-0-7377-5578-7(4))* Cengage Gale.

Espejo, Roman, ed. How Does Advertising Impact Teen Behavior. 2011. (At Issue Ser.). 128p. pap. 24.45 *(978-0-7377-5579-4(2),* Greenhaven Pr., Inc.) Cengage Gale.

Freese, Susan M. Craigslist: The Company & Its Founder, 1 vol. 2011. (Technology Pioneers Set 1 Ser.). (ENG., Illus.). 112p. (J). (gr. 6-12). lib. bdg. 35.64 *(978-1-61714-806-4(7))* ABDO Publishing Co.

Fromm, Megan. Understanding Advertising & Monetization, 1 vol. 2015. (ENG.). 48p. (YA). 30.25 *(978-1-4777-8064-0(5),* Rosen Reference) Rosen Publishing Group, Inc., The.

Goodbody, Slim & Burstein, John. Big Fat Lies: Advertising Tricks. 2008. (Slim Goodbody's Lighten Up! Ser.). (ENG., Illus.). 32p. (J). (gr. 3-7). pap. *(978-0-7787-3931-9(7));* lib. bdg. *(978-0-7787-3913-5(9))* Crabtree Publishing Co.

Graydon, Shari. Made You Look: How Advertising Works & Why You Should Know. Lamoreaux, Michelle, illus. 2nd rev. ed. 2013. (ENG.). 160p. (J). (gr. 6-12). 26.95 *(978-1-55451-561-5(0),* 9781554515615); pap. 16.95 *(978-1-55451-560-8(2),* 9781554515608) Annick Pr., Ltd. CAN. Dist: Publishers Group West (PGW).

Green, Jen. Advertising. 2017. (Ethical Debates Ser.). (ENG., Illus.). 48p. (J). (gr. 6-11). pap. 12.99 ***(978-0-7502-9745-5(X),*** Wayland) Hachette Children's Group GBR. Dist: Hachette Bk. Group.

—Advertising. 2011. (Ethical Debates Ser.). (ENG.). 48p. (YA). (gr. 5-8). pap. 11.75 *(978-1-4488-7007-3(0));* lib. bdg. 29.25 *(978-1-4488-6018-0(0))* Rosen Publishing Group, Inc., The. (Rosen Reference).

Hicks, Aubrey. Advertising: Does Advertising Tell the Truth? 2014. (J). lib. bdg. *(978-1-62712-404-1(7))* Cavendish Square Publishing.

Lusted, Marcia Amidon. Advertising to Children, 1 vol. 2008. (Essential Viewpoints Set 3 Ser.). (ENG.). 112p. (J). (gr. 6-12). lib. bdg. 35.64 *(978-1-60453-107-7(X))* ABDO Publishing Co.

Mierau, Christina B. Accept No Substitutes! The History of American Advertising. 2005. (People's History Ser.). (Illus.). 96p. (gr. 6-12). lib. bdg. 26.60 *(978-0-8225-1742-9(6))* Lerner Publishing Group.

Minden, Cecilia & Roth, Kate. How to Write an Ad. 2011. (Explorer Junior Library: Language Arts Explorer Junior Ser.). (ENG.). 24p. (gr. 1-4). lib. bdg. 25.64 *(978-1-61080-107-2(5),* 201116) Cherry Lake Publishing.

Nagle, Jeanne. Careers in Internet Advertising & Marketing. 2013. 80p. (YA). (gr. 9-12). 33.25 *(978-1-4488-9596-0(0))* Rosen Publishing Group, Inc., The.

Newman, Heather. Creating Digital Brochures. Petelinsek, Kathleen, illus. 2013. (Explorer Library: Information Explorer Ser.). (ENG.). 32p. (J). (gr. 4-8). 28.50 *(978-1-62431-128-4(8),* 202832); pap. 14.21 *(978-1-62431-260-1(8),* 202834) Cherry Lake Publishing.

Perdew, Laura. Asking Questions about Food Advertising. 2015. (21st Century Skills Library: Asking Questions about Media Ser.). (ENG., Illus.). 32p. (J). (gr. 4-8). 29.93 *(978-1-63362-487-0(0),* 206856) Cherry Lake Publishing.

Raum, Elizabeth. Let's Think about the Power of Advertising, 1 vol. 2014. (Let's Think About Ser.). (ENG., Illus.). 48p. (gr. 3-6). 33.32 *(978-1-4846-0290-4(0));* pap. 8.99 *(978-1-4846-0295-9(1))* Heinemann-Raintree. (Heinemann InfoSearch).

Rissman, Rebecca. Asking Questions about Body Image in Advertising. 2015. (21st Century Skills Library: Asking Questions about Media Ser.). (ENG., Illus.). 32p. (J). (gr. 4-8). 29.93 *(978-1-63362-486-3(2),* 206852) Cherry Lake Publishing.

Rustad, Martha E. H. Learning about Ads. 2015. (Media Literacy for Kids Ser.). (ENG.). 24p. (gr. k-1). lib. bdg. 26.65 *(978-1-4914-1830-7(3),* Pebble Plus) Capstone Press of Coughlan Cos.

Schuh, Mari C. Let's Find Ads in Magazines. 2016. (First Step Nonfiction — Learn about Advertising Ser.). (ENG., Illus.). 24p. (J). (gr. k-2). pap. 6.99 *(978-1-4677-9653-8(0))* Lerner Publishing Group.

—Let's Find Ads on Clothing. 2016. (First Step Nonfiction — Learn about Advertising Ser.). (ENG., Illus.). 24p. (J). (gr. k-2). pap. 6.99 *(978-1-4677-9655-2(7))* Lerner Publishing Group.

—Let's Find Ads on Food Packages. 2016. (First Step Nonfiction — Learn about Advertising Ser.). (ENG., Illus.). 24p. (J). (gr. k-2). 23.99 *(978-1-4677-9468-8(6))* Lerner Publishing Group.

—Let's Find Ads on Signs. 2016. (First Step Nonfiction — Learn about Advertising Ser.). (ENG.). 24p. (J). (gr. k-2). 23.99 *(978-1-4677-9465-7(1))* Lerner Publishing Group.

—Let's Find Ads on the Internet. 2016. (First Step Nonfiction — Learn about Advertising Ser.). (ENG., Illus.). 24p. (J). (gr. k-2). 23.99 *(978-1-4677-9464-0(3))* Lerner Publishing Group.

—Let's Find Ads on TV. 2016. (First Step Nonfiction — Learn about Advertising Ser.). (ENG., Illus.). 24p. (J). (gr. k-2). 23.99 *(978-1-4677-9466-4(X))* Lerner Publishing Group.

Staley, Erin. Vloggers & Vlogging. 2016. (Digital & Information Literacy Ser.). 00048p. (J). (gr. 6-6). pap. 11.75 *(978-1-5081-7333-5(8))* Rosen Publishing Group, Inc., The.

ADVERTISING, ART IN

see Commercial Art

ADVERTISING—FICTION

Apted, Violet. Jasmin & the Nature Fairies. Hollinrake, Chriss, illus. 2012. 16p. pap. 10.00 *(978-1-61897-806-6(3),* Strategic Bk. Publishing) Strategic Book Publishing & Rights Agency (SBPRA).

Carroll, Lewis, pseud & Sweeney, Kevin. Exeunt Alice. 2009. 87p. pap. *(978-0-9556938-1-6(0))* Black Rainbow Pr.

DeVillers, Julia & Roy, Jennifer. Double Feature. 2012. (Mix Ser.). (ENG.). 288p. (J). (gr. 4-8). pap. 7.99 *(978-1-4424-3403-5(1),* Aladdin) Simon & Schuster Children's Publishing.

Edwards, Leo. Andy Blake's Comet Coaster. Salg, Bert, illus. 2011. 274p. 47.95 *(978-1-258-06587-4(8))* Literary Licensing, LLC.

Hanson, Ed. Hostages. 2003. (Barclay Family Adventure Ser.: Bk. 5). (Illus.). 64p. (J). (gr. k-6). per. 3.95 *(978-1-56254-554-3(X),* SP 554X) Saddleback Educational Publishing, Inc.

Kain, P. G. Famous for Thirty Seconds. 2012. (Commercial Breaks Ser.: 1). (ENG.). 320p. (J). (gr. 4-8). pap. 6.99 *(978-1-4169-9786-3(5),* Aladdin) Simon & Schuster Children's Publishing.

Kelman, Marcy & Disney Book Group Staff. Trick or Treasure? Disney Storybook Artists Staff, illus. 2013. (ENG.). 24p. (J). (gr. -1-k). pap. 5.99 *(978-1-4231-7140-9(3))* Disney Pr.

Mehnert, Robert. Spelunkers. 2012. 108p. pap. 19.95 *(978-1-62709-036-0(3))* America Star Bks.

Naylor, Phyllis Reynolds. Anyone Can Eat Squid!, 0 vols. Ramsey, Marcy, illus. 2009. (Simply Sarah Ser.: 0). (ENG.). 80p. (J). (gr. 2-5). pap. 9.99 *(978-0-7614-5540-0(X),* 9780761455400, Amazon Children's Publishing) Amazon Publishing.

Paul, J. D. The Little Lost Dog, 1 vol. 2010. 12p. pap. 24.95 *(978-1-4489-9251-5(6))* PublishAmerica, Inc.

Standish, Burt L. Dick Merriwell's Revenge. Rudman, Jack, ed. 2003. (Frank Merriwell Ser.). 29.95 *(978-0-8373-9382-7(5));* pap. 9.95 *(978-0-8373-9082-6(6))* Merriwell, Frank Inc.

Warner Bros. Entertainment Staff. Harry Potter Poster Collection: The Quintessential Images. 2012. (Insights Poster Collections). (ENG., Illus.). 40p. (gr. 2). pap. 24.99 *(978-1-60887-142-1(8))* Insight Editions.

Warner Bros. Entertainment Staff & Warner Bros. Consumer Products Inc. Staff. Harry Potter Poster Collection: The Definitive Movie Posters. 2012. (Insights Poster Collections). (ENG., Illus.). 40p. (gr. 2). pap. 24.99 *(978-1-60887-113-1(4))* Insight Editions.

ADVERTISING, PICTORIAL

see Commercial Art; Posters

ADVERTISING—VOCATIONAL GUIDANCE

Ferguson. Advertising & Marketing. 2nd rev. ed. 2009. (Careers in Focus Ser.). 202p. (gr. 6-12). 32.95 *(978-0-8160-7295-8(7),* Ferguson Publishing Co.) Facts On File, Inc.

Haegele, Katie. E-Advertising & E-Marketing: Online Opportunities. 2005. (Library of e-Commerce & Internet Careers Ser.). (Illus.). 64p. (YA). (gr. 7-12). lib. bdg. 31.95 *(978-0-8239-3426-3(8))* Rosen Publishing Group, Inc., The.

—E-Advertising & E-Marketing Online Opportunities. 2009. (Library of E-Commerce & Internet Careers Ser.). 64p. (gr. 5-5). 58.50 *(978-1-60853-585-9(1))* Rosen Publishing Group, Inc., The.

Petley, Julian. Advertising. 2003. (Media Wise Ser.). 64p. (J). lib. bdg. 28.50 *(978-1-58340-255-9(1))* Black Rabbit Bks.

AENEAS (LEGENDARY CHARACTER)

Williams, Rose. The Labors of Aeneas: What a Pain It Was to Found the Roman Race. 2003. (Illus.). (YA). 18.00 *(978-0-86516-556-4(4))* Bolchazy-Carducci Pubs.

AERIAL PHOTOGRAPHY

Giraudon, David, illus. Our Living Earth: A Story of People, Ecology, & Preservation. Arthus-Bertrand, Yann, photos by. 2008. (ENG.). 160p. (J). (gr. 3-7). 24.95 *(978-0-8109-7132-5(1),* Abrams Bks. for Young Readers) Abrams, Inc.

AERIAL ROCKETS

see Rockets (Aeronautics)

AERODYNAMICS

see also Aeronautics

Enz, Tammy. Building Vehicles That Fly. 2017. (Young Engineers Ser.). (ENG., Illus.). 32p. (gr. 1-2). lib. bdg. 27.32 *(978-1-4846-3747-0(X),* Heinemann First Library) Heinemann-Raintree.

—The Science Behind Superman's Flight. 2017. (Science Behind Superman Ser.). (ENG., Illus.). 24p. (gr. 1-2). lib. bdg. 25.32 *(978-1-5157-5097-0(3),* DC Super Heroes) Stone Arch Bks.

—Soaring the Skies: Superman & the Science of Flight. 2016. (Superman Science Ser.). (ENG., Illus.). 32p. (gr. 3-4). lib. bdg. 27.32 *(978-1-5157-0913-8(2),* DC Super Heroes) Stone Arch Bks.

Meredith, Susan Markowitz, et al. How Do Aircraft Fly? 2009. (Science in the Real World Ser.). (Illus.). 32p. (gr. 4-6). 28.00 *(978-1-60413-464-3(X),* Chelsea Clubhouse) Facts On File, Inc.

Moore, Rob. Why Do Airplanes Fly? 2010. (Solving Science Mysteries Ser.). (Illus.). 24p. (J). pap. 8.25 *(978-1-61531-912-1(3),* PowerKids Pr.); (YA). (gr. 3-6). lib. bdg. 22.60 *(978-1-61531-890-2(9))* Rosen Publishing Group, Inc., The.

Parker, Steve. Tabletop Scientist — the Science of Air: Projects & Experiments with Air & Flight. 2013. (ENG., Illus.). 32p. (J). (gr. 3-8). pap. 6.99 *(978-0-486-49265-0(6))* Dover Pubns., Inc.

Richards, Jon. Air & Flight. 2009. (Science Factory Ser.). 32p. (gr. 4-5). 50.50 *(978-1-60853-018-2(3),* PowerKids Pr.) Rosen Publishing Group, Inc., The.

Schwartz, Heather E. The Science of a Race Car: Reactions in Action. 2010. (Action Science Ser.). (ENG.). 32p. (gr. 3-4). pap. 47.70 *(978-1-4296-5074-8(5),* Fact Finders) Capstone Press of Coughlan Cos.

Spiro, Ruth & Chan, Irene. Baby Loves Aerospace Engineering! 2016. (Baby Loves Science Ser.). (ENG., Illus.). 20p. (J). (— 1). bds. 8.95 *(978-1-58089-541-5(7))* Charlesbridge Publishing, Inc.

VanVoorst, Jenny Fretland. Paper Airplanes. 2016. (Early Physics Fun). 24p. (J). (gr. 2-5). lib. bdg. 25.65 *(978-1-62031-317-6(0),* Pogo) Jump! Inc.

AERODYNAMICS, SUPERSONIC

Alvarez, Carlos & Finn, Denny Von. Supersonic Jets. 2009. (World's Fastest Ser.). (ENG., Illus.). 24p. (J). (gr. 3-7). lib. bdg. 25.95 *(978-1-60014-287-1(7))* Bellwether Media.

Herold, Vickey. Discover the Sound Barrier. 2006. (J). pap. *(978-1-4108-6490-1(1))* Benchmark Education Co.

Niver, Heather Moore. Breaking the Sound Barrier. 2015. (Incredible True Adventures Ser.). (ENG.). 32p. (J). (gr. 3-4). pap. 10.50 *(978-1-4824-2030-2(9))* Stevens, Gareth Publishing LLLP.

Pierce, Alan. Breaking the Sound Barrier, 1 vol. 2005. (American Moments Ser.). (ENG.). 48p. (gr. 4-8). 27.07 *(978-1-59197-730-8(4),* Abdo & Daughters) ABDO Publishing Co.

Suen, Anastasia. Aviones supersónicos (Supersonic Jets) 2009. (Vehículos de alta tecnología (High-Tech Vehicles) Ser.). (SPA.). 24p. (gr. 2-3). 42.50 *(978-1-60854-717-3(5),* Editorial Buenas Letras) Rosen Publishing Group, Inc., The.

AERONAUTICAL SPORTS

see also names of specific sports, e.g. Airplane Racing; Skydiving; etc.

Bach, Rachel. The Hot Air Balloon Race. 2016. (Let's Race Ser.). (ENG.). 16p. (J). (gr. k-3). 17.95 *(978-1-60753-914-8(4))* Amicus Publishing.

Butler, Erin K. Extreme Air Sports. 2017. (Sports to the Extreme Ser.). (ENG.). 32p. (gr. 3-4). lib. bdg. 27.99 ***(978-1-5157-7861-5(4),*** Edge Bks.) Capstone Press of Coughlan Cos.

Hansen, Ole Steen. Flying for Fun. 2003. (Story of Flight Ser.). (ENG., Illus.). 32p. (J). (gr. 4). pap. *(978-0-7787-1227-5(3));* lib. bdg. *(978-0-7787-1211-4(7))* Crabtree Publishing Co.

Kalman, Bobbie & Crossingham, John. Extreme Skydiving. 2006. (Extreme Sports No Limits! Ser.). (ENG., Illus.). 32p. (J). (gr. 3-7). pap. *(978-0-7787-1730-0(5));* lib. bdg. *(978-0-7787-1684-6(8))* Crabtree Publishing Co.

Kelley, K. C. Bungee Jumping. 2011. (Extreme Sports Ser.). (ENG., Illus.). 32p. (J). (gr. 2-5). lib. bdg. 28.50 *(978-1-60973-206-6(5),* 201122) Child's World, Inc., The.

Luke, Andrew. Air Sports. 2017. (Illus.). 48p. (J). ***(978-1-4222-3705-2(2))*** Mason Crest.

McFee, Shane. Bungee Jumping. (Living on the Edge Ser.). 24p. (gr. 2-3). 2009. 42.50 *(978-1-61514-296-5(7),* PowerKids Pr.) 2008. (Illus.). (J). lib. bdg. 22.60 *(978-1-4042-4216-6(3))* Rosen Publishing Group, Inc., The.

AERONAUTICS

see also Aerodynamics; Aeronautical Sports; Airplanes; Airships; Astronautics; Balloons; Flight; Gliders (Aeronautics); Helicopters; High-Speed Aeronautics; Kites; Parachutes; Rocketry; Rockets (Aeronautics); Unidentified Flying Objects

Amato, William. Aviones Supersonicos. 2004. (Vehículos de Alta Tecnología (High-Tech Vehicles) Ser.). (SPA & ENG., Illus.). 24p. (J). (gr. 2-4). lib. bdg. 22.60 (978-0-8239-6880-0(4)) Rosen Publishing Group, Inc., The.

Arnold, Quinn M. Antonov An-225 Mriya. 2016. (Illus.). 24p. (J). (978-1-60818-711-9(X), Creative Education) Creative Co., The.

Bailey, Gerry. Flight. 2009. (Simply Science Ser.). (Illus.). 32p. (YA). (gr. 3-6). lib. bdg. 26.00 (978-1-4339-0032-7(7)) Stevens, Gareth Publishing LLLP.

Bingham, Jane. The Wright Brothers: First Flight. 2017. (Fact Cat: History Ser.). (ENG., Illus.). 24p. (J). (gr. k-2). pap. 9.99 **(978-0-7502-9039-5(0)**, Wayland) Hachette Children's Group GBR. Dist: Hachette Bk. Group.

Blair, Margaret Whitman. The Roaring 20: The First Cross-Country Air Race for Women. 2006. (ENG., Illus.). 112p. (gr. 5-9). lib. bdg. 32.90 (978-0-7922-5390-7(6), National Geographic Children's Bks.) National Geographic Society.

—The Roaring Twenty: The First Cross-Country Air Race for Women. 2006. (National Geographic Ser.). (ENG., Illus.). 112p. (gr. 5-9). 21.95 (978-0-7922-5389-1(2), National Geographic Children's Bks.) National Geographic Society.

Boothroyd, Jennifer. How Do Hang Gliders Work? 2013. (Lightning Bolt Books (tm) — How Flight Works). (ENG., Illus.). 32p. (gr. k-2). lib. bdg. 26.60 (978-0-7613-8970-5(9)) Lerner Publishing Group.

Brooks, Felicity & Durber, Matt. Airport Magnet Book. 2009. (Magnet Bks). 10p. (J). bds. 19.99 (978-0-7945-2363-3(3), Usborne) EDC Publishing.

Buckley, James. Who Were the Wright Brothers? Foley, Tim, illus. 2014. 106p. (J). (978-1-101-99527-3(0)) Penguin Publishing Group.

Burke, Michelle Prater. The Story of the Wright Brothers. Johnson, Meredith, illus. 2016. (J). (978-0-8249-1986-3(6), Ideal Pubns.) Worthy Publishing.

Calhoun, Marmaduke Randolph. The Story of an Aviator. Twist, Clint, ed. Wallis, Diz & Hardcastle, Nick, illus. 2008. (Amazing Wonders Collection: 2). (ENG.). 16p. (J). (gr. 1-4). 19.99 (978-0-7636-3906-8(0)) Candlewick Pr.

Candlewick Press, Candlewick. The Story of Flight: Panorama Pops. Holcroft, John, illus. 2015. (ENG.). 30p. (J). (gr. k-4). 8.99 (978-0-7636-7700-8(0)) Candlewick Pr.

Candlewick Press Staff & Arnold, Nick. Flying Machines. Kearney, Brendan, illus. 2014. (ENG.). (J). (gr. 3-7). 19.99 (978-0-7636-7107-5(X)) Candlewick Pr.

Civardi, Anna. Going on a Plane Sticker Book. 2009. (First Experiences Sticker Book Ser.). 16p. (J). pap. 6.99 (978-0-7945-2180-6(0), Usborne) EDC Publishing.

Clark, Willow. Planes on the Move. 2010. (Transportation Station Ser.). 24p. (J). (ENG.). pap. 8.25 (978-1-4358-9752-6(8)); (Illus.). (gr. 2-5). lib. bdg. 22.60 (978-1-4358-9332-0(8)) Rosen Publishing Group, Inc., The. (PowerKids Pr.).

Clemson, Wendy & Clemson, David. Rocket to the Moon. 2007. (Math Adventures Ser.). (Illus.). 32p. (gr. 1-4). (SPA.). pap. 10.50 (978-0-8368-8140-0(0)); lib. bdg. 26.00 (978-0-8368-7841-7(8)) Stevens, Gareth Publishing LLLP. (Gareth Stevens Learning Library).

Close, Edward. Wheels, Wings, & Motors, 1 vol., 1. 2014. (Discovery Education: How It Works). (ENG.). 32p. (gr. 3-6). 26.25 (978-1-4777-6313-1(9), PowerKids Pr.) Rosen Publishing Group, Inc., The.

Collins, Francis. The Boys' Book of Model Aeroplanes: How to Build & Fly Them: with the Story of the Evolution of the Flying Machine. 2004. (Illus.). 308p. (YA). per. 16.95 (978-0-9758914-3-8(X)) Gustav's Library.

Community Connections: How Does It Fly?, 8 vols., Set. Incl. How Does It Fly? Blimp. Nittinger, Sharon. lib. bdg. 25.64 (978-1-61080-071-6(0), 201068); How Does It Fly? Bomber Plane. Mullins, Matt. lib. bdg. 25.64 (978-1-61080-067-9(2), 201060); How Does It Fly? Fighter Plane. Mullins, Matt. lib. bdg. 25.64 (978-1-61080-066-2(4), 201058); How Does It Fly? Glider. Masters, Nancy Robinson. lib. bdg. 25.64 (978-1-61080-072-3(9), 201070); How Does It Fly? Helicopter. Mullins, Matt. lib. bdg. 25.64 (978-1-61080-065-5(6), 201056); How Does It Fly? Hot Air Balloon. Masters, Nancy Robinson. lib. bdg. 25.64 (978-1-61080-068-6(0), 201062); How Does It Fly? Jet Plane. Mullins, Matt. lib. bdg. 25.64 (978-1-61080-069-3(9), 201064); How Does It Fly? Propeller Plane. Masters, Nancy Robinson. lib. bdg. 25.64 (978-1-61080-070-9(2), 201066); 24p. (gr. 2-5). 2011. Set lib. bdg. 205.12 (978-1-61080-146-1(6)) Cherry Lake Publishing.

The Complete History of Aviation: From Ballooning to Supersonic Flight. 2011. (Transportation & Society Ser.). (ENG.). 184p. (YA). (gr. 10-12). 77.50 (978-1-61530-768-5(0)) Rosen Publishing Group, Inc., The.

Crompton, Samuel Willard. The Wright Brothers: First in Flight. 2007. (Milestones in American History Ser.). (Illus.). 128p. (YA). (gr. 7-12). lib. bdg. 35.00 (978-0-7910-9356-6(5)) Facts On File, Inc.

Curley, Robert, ed. The Complete History of Aviation: From Ballooning to Supersonic Flight. 2011. (Transportation & Society Ser.). (ENG., Illus.). 184p. (J). (gr. 10-12). lib. bdg. 38.75 (978-1-61530-667-1(6), 1337129) Rosen Publishing Group, Inc., The.

Dailey, Franklyn E., Jr. The Triumph of Instrument Flight: A Retrospective in the Century of U. S. Aviation. 2004. (Illus.). 335p. per. 18.95 (978-0-9666251-3-4(7)) Dailey International Pubs.

Dakers, Diane. Orville & Wilbur Wright: Pioneers of the Age of Flight. 2016. (Crabtree Groundbreaker Biographies Ser.). (ENG.). 112p. (J). (gr. 5-8). (978-0-7787-2609-8(6)) Crabtree Publishing Co.

deMarin, Layne. To Fly in the Sky, 1 vol. 2011. (Wonder Readers Fluent Level Ser.). (ENG.). (gr. -1-2). 32p. pap. 5.99 (978-1-4296-7943-5(3)); 16p. pap. 35.94 (978-1-4296-8189-6(6)) Capstone Press of Coughlan Cos. (Wonder Readers).

Dibben, Colin. Flight. 2006. (Illus.). 48p. (J). lib. bdg. 29.95 (978-1-60044-259-9(5)) Rourke Educational Media.

Dorling Kindersley Publishing Staff. Ultimate Sticker Book: Airplanes & Other Flying Machines. 2017. (Ultimate Sticker Bks.). (ENG.). 32p. (J). (gr. k-4). pap. 6.99 (978-1-4654-5695-3(3), DK Children) Dorling Kindersley Publishing, Inc.

Editors of Kingfisher. Fantastic Fliers. 2016. (It's All About... Ser.). (ENG.). 32p. pap. 5.99 (978-0-7534-7286-6(4), 9780753472866, Kingfisher) Roaring Brook Pr.

Enz, Tammy. The Science Behind Batman's Flying Machines. Vecchio, Luciano, illus. 2016. (Science Behind Batman Ser.). (ENG.). 24p. (gr. 1-2). lib. bdg. 25.32 (978-1-5157-2036-2(5), DC Super Heroes) Stone Arch Bks.

Eppard, Jon. Aircraft. 2012. (ENG., Illus.). 24p. (J). pap. (978-1-60014-853-8(0)); (gr. 3-8). 25.95 (978-1-60014-808-8(5), Express Bks.) Bellwether Media.

Faust, Daniel R. Flying Robots. 2016. (Robots & Robotics Ser.). (Illus.). 32p. (J). (gr. 5-5). pap. 11.75 (978-1-4994-2167-5(2), PowerKids Pr.) Rosen Publishing Group, Inc., The.

Flying Machines. (First Facts about Ser.). 24p. (J). (gr. 3-7). pap. (978-1-882210-17-6(4)) Action Publishing, Inc.

Flying Machines. Date not set. (I Can Draw Ser.). 32p. (J). 4.98 (978-1-4054-0019-0(6)) Parragon, Inc.

Gerdes, Louise I. Drones. Greenhaven Press Editors & Gale Editors, eds. 2014. (At Issue Ser.). (ENG.). 128p. (gr. 10-12). pap. 27.80 (978-0-7377-6833-6(9), Greenhaven Pr., Inc.) Cengage Gale.

—Drones. Greenhaven Press Editors & Gale, Anthony, eds. 2014. (At Issue Ser.). (ENG.). 128p. (gr. 10-12). lib. bdg. 39.40 (978-0-7377-6832-9(0), Greenhaven Pr., Inc.) Cengage Gale.

Gilpin, Daniel & Pang, Alex. Record Breakers. 2010. (Machines Close-Up Ser.). 32p. (J). (gr. 4-7). 28.50 (978-1-60870-113-1(1)) Marshall Cavendish Corp.

Graham, Ian. In the Air. 2008. (QEB Machines at Work Ser.). (Illus.). 36p. (YA). (gr. 4-7). 19.95 (978-1-59566-315-3(0)) QEB Publishing Inc.

Graham, Ian & Salariya, David. Planes, Rockets — And Other — Flying Machines. Hewetson, N. J., illus. 2014. (Time Shift Speed Ser.). 32p. (gr. 3-6). 31.35 **(978-1-908973-95-5(1))** Book Hse. GBR. Dist: Black Rabbit Bks.

Gregory, Josh. From Birds to... Aircraft. 2012. (21st Century Skills Innovation Library: Innovations from Nature Ser.). (ENG.). 32p. (gr. 4-8). 28.50 (978-1-61080-497-4(X), 202107); pap. 14.21 (978-1-61080-671-8(9), 202281) Cherry Lake Publishing.

Grist, Julie. Flying: Just Plane Fun. Grist, Julie, illus. 2006. (ENG., Illus.). 24p. (J). (gr. k-7). pap. 8.95 (978-0-9725750-2-7(2)) Spoonbender Bks.

Group/McGraw-Hill, Wright. Great Aviators Take Flight, 6 vols. (Book2WebTM Ser.). (gr. 4-8). 36.50 (978-0-322-04467-8(7)) Wright Group/McGraw-Hill.

Grove, Tim & National Air and Space Museum, National Air. Milestones of Flight: From Hot-Air Balloons to SpaceShipOne. 2016. (ENG., Illus.). 112p. (J). (gr. 5-9). 21.95 (978-1-4197-2003-1(1), Abrams Bks. for Young Readers) Abrams, Inc.

Gunston, Bill, et al. The World of Flight. 2012. (ENG., Illus.). 48p. 15.00 (978-1-899762-89-7(2)) Award Pubns. Ltd. GBR. Dist: Parkwest Pubns., Inc.

Hansen, Ole Steen. Air Combat. 2003. (Story of Flight Ser.). (ENG., Illus.). 32p. (J). (gr. 4). pap. (978-0-7787-1222-0(2)) Crabtree Publishing Co.

—Flying for Fun. 2003. (Story of Flight Ser.). (ENG., Illus.). 32p. (J). (gr. 4). pap. (978-0-7787-1227-5(3)); lib. bdg. (978-0-7787-1211-4(7)) Crabtree Publishing Co.

—Seaplanes & Naval Aviation. 2003. (Story of Flight Ser.). (ENG., Illus.). 32p. (J). (gr. 4). pap. (978-0-7787-1225-1(7)) Crabtree Publishing Co.

Hayes, Amy. How a Plane Is Made. 2016. (Engineering Our World Ser.). (ENG., Illus.). 24p. (J). (gr. 2-3). pap. 8.15 (978-1-4824-3931-1(X)) Stevens, Gareth Publishing LLLP.

High Flying: Level P, 6 vols., Vol. 3. (Explorers Ser.). 32p. (gr. 3-6). 44.95 (978-0-7699-0619-5(2)) Shortland Pubns. (U. S. A.) Inc.

Hill, Lee Sullivan. The Flyer Flew! The Invention of the Airplane. Orback, Craig, illus. 2006. (On My Own Science Ser.). 48p. (J). (gr. 3-7). per. 6.95 (978-1-57505-855-9(3)); (gr. k-3). lib. bdg. 25.26 (978-1-57505-758-3(1), Millbrook Pr.) Lerner Publishing Group.

Holzweiss, Kristina. Amazing MakerSpace DIY Fliers. 2017. (True Book — MakerSpace Projects Ser.). (ENG.). 48p. (J). lib. bdg. 31.00 **(978-0-531-23846-2(6)**, Children's Pr.) Scholastic Library Publishing.

Holzweiss, Kristina A. Fliers. 2017. (True Book — MakerSpace Projects Ser.). (ENG.). 48p. (J). pap. 7.95 **(978-0-531-24097-7(5)**, Children's Pr.) Scholastic Library Publishing.

Houran, Lori Haskins. The $25,000 Flight. Lowe, Wesley, illus. 2014. (Totally True Adventures Ser.). (ENG.). 112p. (J). (gr. 2-5). 4.99 (978-0-385-38284-7(7), Random Hse. Bks. for Young Readers) Random Hse. Children's Bks.

Humphreys, Pauline A. Romance of the Airman. 2005. pap. 43.95 (978-1-4191-0278-3(8)) Kessinger Publishing, LLC.

Hunter, Ryan Ann, et al. Into the Air: An Illustrated Timeline of Flight. Nascimbene, Yan, illus. 2003. (ENG.). 48p. (J). (gr. -1-3). 16.95 (978-0-7922-5120-0(2), National Geographic Children's Bks.) National Geographic Society.

Hustad, Douglas. Discover Drones. 2016. (Searchlight Books (tm) — What's Cool about Science? Ser.). (ENG., Illus.). 40p. (J). (gr. 3-5). 30.65 (978-1-5124-0810-2(7)) Lerner Publishing Group.

Ikids Staff. Junior Groovies: Things That Fly (Storybook, Fun Facts & Toys) Randazzo, Tony, illus. 2011. (ENG.). 10p. (J). (gr. -1-1). 15.99 (978-1-60169-148-4(3)) Innovative Kids.

Inside the World of Drones. 2016. (Inside the World of Drones Ser.). 00064p. (J). (gr. 7-7). 206.70 (978-1-5081-7369-4(9), Rosen Young Adult) Rosen Publishing Group, Inc., The.

Istakhorov, *Selma*. Solving Real World Problems with Aerospace Engineering, 01 vols., 1. 2016. (Let's Find Out! Ser.). (ENG., Illus.). 32p. (J). pap. 12.90 (978-1-5081-0073-7(X), Britannica Educational Publishing) Rosen Publishing Group, Inc., The.

Jepson, Edgar. The Admirable Tinker: Child of the World. 2007. (ENG.). 174p. pap. 19.99 (978-1-4264-9536-6(6)); 194p. pap. 21.99 (978-1-4264-9917-3(5)) Creative Media Partners, LLC.

—The Admirable Tinker: Child of the World. Eckerson, Margaret, illus. 2007. 204p. per. (978-1-4065-2736-0(X)) Dodo Pr.

Karst, Ken. Area 51: Enduring Mysteries. 2014. (Illus.). 48p. (J). pap. (978-1-60818-399-9(8)) Creative Co., The.

Kawa, Katie. My First Trip on an Airplane: Mi Primer Viaje en Avión. 2012. (My First Adventures / Mis primeras aventuras Ser.). (SPA & ENG., Illus.). 24p. (J). (gr. k-2). lib. bdg. 22.60 (978-1-4339-7370-3(7)) Stevens, Gareth Publishing LLLP.

Kids Can Press Staff. This Is Daniel Cook on a Plane. 2006. (This Is Daniel Cook Ser.). (ENG., Illus.). 24p. (J). (gr. -1-1). 4.95 (978-1-55453-082-3(2)) Kids Can Pr., Ltd. CAN. Dist: Hachette Bk. Group.

Kinmont, Ritchie. Every Kid Needs Things That Fly, 1 vol. Casey, Robert, photos by. 2005. (ENG., Illus.). 136p. (J). pap. 14.95 (978-1-58685-509-3(3), 1241179) Gibbs Smith, Publisher.

Kuskowski, Alex & Craig, Diane. Super Simple Aircraft Projects: Inspiring & Educational Science Activities, 1 vol. 2016. (ENG., Illus.). 32p. (J). (978-1-62403-728-3(3)) ABDO Publishing Co.

Lewis, Simon. Adventures in the Air. 2009. (Difficult & Dangerous Ser.). (J). 28.50 (978-1-59920-161-0(5)) Black Rabbit Bks.

Lindeen, Mary. Drones & Flying Robots. 2017. (Cutting-Edge Robotics Ser.). (ENG.). 32p. (J). (gr. 3-6). 27.99 (978-1-5124-4009-6(4)) Lerner Publishing Group.

Loves, June. Flight Series, 6 bks. Incl. Balloons, Kites, Airships & Gliders. (Illus.). (J). (gr. 5-18). 2001. 27.00 (978-0-7910-6563-1(4), 010302, Chelsea Hse.); (Illus.). 101.70 (978-0-7910-6557-0(X), 101300S, Chelsea Hse.) Facts On File, Inc.

Lynch, Christopher. Albert Bond Lambert: Aviation Pioneer. 2015. (ENG., Illus.). 48p. (J). pap. 24.00 (978-1-61248-155-5(8)) Truman State Univ. Pr.

MacLeod, Elizabeth. The Wright Brothers. Krystoforski, Andrej, illus. 2008. (Kids Can Read Ser.). (ENG.). 32p. (J). (gr. 1-3). 14.95 (978-1-55453-053-3(9)); pap. 3.95 (978-1-55453-054-0(7)) Kids Can Pr., Ltd. CAN. Dist: Hachette Bk. Group.

Marsico, Katie. Drones. 2016. (True Book(tm) — Engineering Wonders Ser.). (ENG., Illus.). 48p. (J). pap. 6.95 (978-0-531-22270-6(5), Children's Pr.) Scholastic Library Publishing.

Maynard, Christopher. I Wonder Why Planes Have Wings: And Other Questions about Transportation. 2012. (I Wonder Why Ser.). (ENG., Illus.). 32p. (J). (gr. k-3). pap. 6.99 (978-0-7534-6703-9(8), 9780753467039, Kingfisher) Roaring Brook Pr.

Mayo, Gretchen Will, et al. The Wright Brothers. 2006. (Graphic Biographies Ser.). (Illus.). 32p. (gr. 5-8). pap. 10.50 (978-0-8368-6251-5(1)) Stevens, Gareth Publishing LLLP.

McHaffie, Natalie. C-Growl: The Daring Little Airplane. McHaffie, Natalie, illus. 2004. (Illus.). 32p. 14.95 (978-1-55125-015-1(2)) Vanwell Publishing, Ltd. CAN. Dist: Casemate Pubs. & Bk. Distributors, LLC.

Meet NASA Inventor Kendra Short & Her Printable Probes & Cosmic Confetti. 2017. (J). **(978-0-7166-6158-0(6))** World Bk., Inc.

Mellett, Peter. Find Out about Flight: With 18 Projects & More Than 240 Pictures. 2013. (ENG., Illus.). 64p. (J). (gr. 3-7). 9.99 (978-1-84322-869-1(6)) Anness Publishing GBR. Dist: National Bk. Network.

Mellett, Peter, et al. What Is Flight? Birds; Planes; Kites; Balloons. 2015. (ENG., Illus.). 64p. (J). (gr. k-6). 12.99 (978-1-86147-401-8(6), Armadillo) Anness Publishing GBR. Dist: National Bk. Network.

Milbourne, Anna. Viaje a la Luna. 2005. (SPA.). 24p. (J). 9.99 (978-0-7460-6632-4(5), Usborne) EDC Publishing.

Mills, Nathan & Weir, William. The Wright Brothers: The First to Fly. 2012. (Rosen Readers Ser.). (ENG., Illus.). 24p. (J). (gr. 1-2). pap. 8.25 (978-1-4488-8863-4(8), Rosen Classroom) Rosen Publishing Group, Inc., The.

Molzahn, Arlene Bourgeois. Airplanes. 2003. (Transportation & Communication Ser.). (Illus.). 48p. (J). (gr. 1-4). lib. bdg. 25.27 (978-0-7660-2026-9(6)) Enslow Pubs., Inc.

Montgomery, Christine. Marie Meyer Fower: Barnstormer. 2015. (ENG., Illus.). 48p. (J). 24.00 (978-1-61248-149-4(3)) Truman State Univ. Pr.

Moore, Rob. Why Do Airplanes Fly? All about Flight. 2010. 24p. (J). 49.50 (978-1-61531-923-7(9), PowerKids Pr.) Rosen Publishing Group, Inc., The.

Murphy, Pat. Air Power: Rocket Science Made Simple. 2014. (ENG.). 48p. (J). (gr. 3). 16.99 (978-0-545-64778-6(9)) Klutz.

Murray, Jennifer. Flight & Fancy: The Airline Industry. 2007. (Shockwave: Economics & Geography Ser.). (ENG., Illus.). 36p. (J). (gr. 4-6). lib. bdg. 25.00 (978-0-531-17796-9(3), Children's Pr.) Scholastic Library Publishing.

Nolan, Carla. Someone I Love Is in the Air Force. 2009. 24p. pap. 15.99 (978-1-4415-3738-6(4)) Xlibris Corp.

O'Brien, Patrick. Fantastic Flights: One Hundred Years of Flying on the Edge. 2003. (Illus.). 40p. (J). 18.85 (978-0-8027-8881-8(5)) Walker & Co.

Olivera, Ramon. ABCs on Wings. Olivera, Ramon, illus. 2015. (ENG., Illus.). 40p. (J). (gr. -1-2). 17.99 (978-1-4814-3242-9(7), Little Simon) Little Simon.

Otfinoski, Steven. Drones: Science, Technology, & Engineering. 2016. (Calling All Innovators: a Career for You Ser.). (ENG., Illus.). 64p. (J). lib. bdg. 32.00 (978-0-531-21866-2(X), Children's Pr.) Scholastic Library Publishing.

Parker, Steve. In the Air. 2010. (J). 28.50 (978-1-59920-284-6(0)) Black Rabbit Bks.

Parker, Steven. By Air. 2011. (Future Transport Ser.). (Illus.). 32p. (J). (gr. 4). 28.50 (978-1-60870-777-5(6)) Marshall Cavendish Corp.

Penguin Books Staff, ed. Things That Fly. (Information Activity Ser.). 24p. (J). 3.50 (978-0-7214-3443-8(6), Dutton Juvenile) Penguin Publishing Group.

Perish, Patrick. Wilderness Rescue Pilot. 2015. (Dangerous Jobs Ser.). (ENG., Illus.). 24p. (J). (gr. 3-7). lib. bdg. 25.95 (978-1-62617-199-2(8), Torque Bks.) Bellwether Media.

Perkis, Andrea. The Wright Brothers Make History! 2012. (InfoMax Readers Ser.). (ENG., Illus.). 24p. (J). (gr. 1-2). pap. 8.25 (978-1-4488-9076-7(4), Rosen Classroom) Rosen Publishing Group, Inc., The.

Reed, Jennifer. Daring American Heroes of Flight: Nine Brave Fliers. 2009. (Great Scientists & Famous Inventors Ser.). (Illus.). 128p. (J). (gr. 5-9). lib. bdg. 34.60 (978-1-59845-081-1(6)) Enslow Pubs., Inc.

—Wilbur & Orville Wright: Trailblazers of the Sky. 2007. (Inventors Who Changed the World Ser.). (Illus.). 128p. (J). (gr. 5). lib. bdg. 34.60 (978-1-59845-054-5(9), MyReportLinks.com Bks.) Enslow Pubs., Inc.

Rees, Peter. How Does It Fly? The Science of Flight. 2007. (Shockwave: Technology & Manufacturing Ser.). (ENG., Illus.). 36p. (J). (gr. 4-6). lib. bdg. 25.00 (978-0-531-17587-3(1), Children's Pr.) Scholastic Library Publishing.

Reynolds, Toby & Calver, Paul. Aviation. 2017. (Visual Explorers Ser.). (ENG.). 32p. (J). (gr. 3-7). pap. 6.99 **(978-1-4380-1080-9(X))** Barron's Educational Series, Inc.

Riehle, Mary Ann McCabe. A Is for Airplane: An Aviation Alphabet. Craig, David, illus. 2009. (Science Alphabet Ser.). (ENG.). 40p. (J). (gr. 1-4). 16.95 (978-1-58536-358-2(8), 202143) Sleeping Bear Pr.

Roby, Cynthia A. Building Aircraft & Spacecraft: Aerospace Engineers, 01 vols., 1. 2016. (Engineers Rule Ser.). (ENG., Illus.). 32p. (J). pap. 11.75 (978-1-5081-4528-8(8), PowerKids Pr.) Rosen Publishing Group, Inc., The.

Rooney, Anne. Aerospace Engineering & the Principles of Flight. 2012. (ENG.). 32p. (J). (978-0-7787-7495-2(3)) Crabtree Publishing Co.

Rose, Simon. Agricultural Drones. 2017. (Drones Ser.). (ENG., Illus.). 32p. (gr. 3-4). pap. 7.95 (978-1-5157-3775-9(6), Edge Bks.) Capstone Press of Coughlan Cos.

Rose, Simon, et al. Drones. 2017. (Drones Ser.). (ENG.). 32p. (gr. 3-4). pap. 31.80 (978-1-5157-3799-5(3), Edge Bks.) Capstone Press of Coughlan Cos.

Rustad, Martha E. H. NASA, 1 vol. 2012. (Exploring Space Ser.). (ENG.). 24p. (gr. k-1). pap. 7.29 (978-1-4296-7894-0(1)); pap. 41.70 (978-1-4296-8329-6(5)) Capstone Press of Coughlan Cos. (Pebble Plus).

Schulz, Walter A. Johnny Moore & the Wright Brothers' Flying Machine. Bowles, Doug, illus. 2011. (History Speaks: Picture Books Plus Reader's Theater Ser.). 48p. pap. 56.72 (978-0-7613-7633-0(X)); (ENG.). (gr. 2-4). lib. bdg. 27.93 (978-0-7613-5876-3(5), Millbrook Pr.) Lerner Publishing Group.

Schulz, Walter A. & Schultz, Walter A. Johnny Moore & the Wright Brothers' Flying Machine. Bowles, Doug, illus. 2011. (History Speaks: Picture Books Plus Reader's Theater Ser.). (ENG.). 48p. (gr. 2-4). pap. 9.95 (978-0-7613-7117-5(6)) Lerner Publishing Group.

The Science of a Plane Crash. 2014. (21st Century Skills Library: Disaster Science Ser.). (ENG., Illus.). 32p. (J). (gr. 4-8). 28.50 (978-1-63137-626-9(8), 205287) Cherry Lake Publishing.

Sibila, Tom. SpaceShipOne: Making Dreams Come True. 2005. (High Five Reading - Blue Ser.). (ENG., Illus.). 48p. (gr. 3-4). per. 9.00 (978-0-7368-5744-4(3), High Five Reading (RBL)) Capstone Press of Coughlan Cos.

Silverman, Buffy. How Do Hot Air Balloons Work? 2013. (Lightning Bolt Books (tm) — How Flight Works). (ENG., Illus.). 32p. (gr. k-2). pap. 7.95 (978-1-4677-0785-5(6)) Lerner Publishing Group.

Silverstein, Janna. Close Encounters with Aliens. 2009. (Unsolved Mysteries: the Secret Files Ser.). 48p. (gr. 5-8). 53.00 (978-1-60854-693-0(4), Rosen Reference) Rosen Publishing Group, Inc., The.

Solar-Wind-Riding Electric Sail: Meet NASA Inventor Bruce Wiegmann & His Team's. 2017. (J). **(978-0-7166-6162-7(4))** World Bk., Inc.

Solway, Andrew. Secrets of Flight. 2010. (Science Secrets Ser.). 32p. (gr. 4). 28.50 (978-1-60870-136-0(0)) Marshall Cavendish Corp.

Spilsbury, Louise. Flight, 1 vol. 2012. (Science Behind Ser.). (ENG.). 32p. (gr. 3-3). pap. 8.29 (978-1-4109-4502-0(2)); lib. bdg. 30.65 (978-1-4109-4491-7(3)) Heinemann-Raintree. (Raintree Perspectives).

Spizzirri, Peter M. Aircraft. Spizzirri, Linda, ed. unabr. ed. (Educational Coloring Book & Cassette Ser.). (J). (gr. 1-8). pap. 6.95 incl. audio (978-0-86545-109-4(5)) Spizzirri Pr., Inc.

Sproule, Anna. The Wright Brothers. 2005. (Giants of Science Bilingual Ser.). (J). 9.95 (978-1-4103-0507-7(4), Blackbirch Pr., Inc.) Cengage Gale.

Taking to the Air: Individual Title Six-Packs. (Action Packs Ser.). 120p. (gr. 3-5). 44.00 (978-0-7635-8396-5(0)) Rigby Education.

Tiner, John Hudson. Airplanes. (Illus.). 32p. 2004. pap. 8.95 (978-0-89812-387-6(9), Creative Paperbacks) 2003. (J). lib. bdg. 18.95 (978-1-58341-258-9(1), Creative Education) Creative Co., The.

Van Vleet, Carmella. Aviation: Cool Women Who Fly. Chandhok, Lena, illus. 2016. (Girls in Science Ser.). (ENG.). 112p. (gr. 3-7). 19.95 (978-1-61930-436-9(8)) Open City Bks.

Weir, William. The Wright Brothers: The First to Fly. 2012. (Beginning Biographies Ser.). (ENG., Illus.). 24p. (J). (gr. 1-3). 22.60 (978-1-4488-8597-8(3), PowerKids Pr.) Rosen Publishing Group, Inc., The.

Wilgus, Alison. Science Comics: Flying Machines: How the Wright Brothers Soared. Brooks, Molly, illus. 2017. (Science Comics Ser.). (ENG.). 128p. (J). pap. 12.99 (978-1-62672-139-5(4), 9781626721395, First Second Bks.) Roaring Brook Pr.

Williams, Zachary. How Do Airplanes Fly? 2009. (Reading Room Collection 2 Ser.). 24p. (gr. 3-4). 42.50 (978-1-60851-969-9(4), PowerKids Pr.) Rosen Publishing Group, Inc., The.

Winchester, Jim. Record Breakers. 2006. (Aircraft of the World Ser.). (Illus.). 32p. (gr. 2-6). lib. bdg. 26.00 (978-0-8368-6905-7(2), Gareth Stevens Learning Library) Stevens, Gareth Publishing LLLP.

Wright, Craig, ed. Things That Fly. 2010. (ENG., Illus.). 14p. act. bk. ed. 4.06 (978-0-19-440166-1(9)) Oxford Univ. Pr., Inc.

Wyckoff, Edwin Brit. Helicopter Man: Igor Sikorsky & His Amazing Invention. 2010. (Genius at Work! Great Inventor Biographies Ser.). (Illus.). 32p. (J). 23.94 (978-0-7660-3445-7(3)) Enslow Pubs., Inc.

Yasuda, Anita. Explore Flight! With 25 Great Projects. Stone, Bryan, illus. 2013. (Explore Your World Ser.). (ENG.). 96p. (J). (gr. k-4). pap. 13.95 (978-1-61930-176-4(8)) Open City Bks.

3,2,1 Liftoff! Level M, 6 vols. 128p. (gr. 2-3). 41.95 (978-0-7699-1024-6(6)) Shortland Pubns. (U. S. A.) Inc.

AERONAUTICS—ACCIDENTS

see Aircraft Accidents

AERONAUTICS—BIOGRAPHY

see also Air Pilots; Women in Aeronautics

Benge, Janet & Benge, Geoff. Heroes of History - Orville Wright: The Flyer. 2006. (ENG.). (YA). pap. 9.99 (978-1-932096-34-7(5)) Emerald Bks.

Brown, Jonatha A. Los Hermanos Wright. 2004. (People We Should Know Ser.).Tr. of Wright Brothers. (SPA.). 24p. (gr. 1-4). pap. 8.15 (978-0-8368-4363-7(0), GHS33824, Weekly Reader Leveled Readers) Stevens, Gareth Publishing LLLP.

—The Wright Brothers. 2004. (People We Should Know Ser.). (Illus.). 24p. (gr. 1-4). lib. bdg. 22.00 (978-0-8368-4314-9(2), Weekly Reader Leveled Readers) Stevens, Gareth Publishing LLLP.

Buckley, James, Jr. Who Were the Wright Brothers? Foley, Tim & Harrison, Nancy, illus. 2014. (Who Was? Ser.). (ENG.). 112p. (J). (gr. 3-7). 5.99 (978-0-448-47951-4(6), Grosset & Dunlap) Penguin Young Readers Group.

Burke, Michelle Prater. The Story of the Wright Brothers. Johnson, Meredith, illus. 2008. (ENG.). 26p. (J). (gr. -1-3). bds. 6.99 (978-0-8249-6729-1(1), Ideal Pubns.) Worthy Publishing.

Collins, Mary. Airborne: A Photobiography of Wilbur & Orville Wright. (Photobiographies Ser.). (ENG., Illus.). 64p. (J). (gr. 5). 2015. pap. 7.99 (978-1-4263-2221-1(6)) 2003. 18.95 (978-0-7922-6957-1(8), 53238483) National Geographic Society. (National Geographic Children's Bks.).

Dorfman, Janet. The Wright Brothers. 2011. (Early Connections Ser.). (J). (978-1-61672-564-8(8)) Benchmark Education Co.

Dunn, Joe. The Wright Brothers, 1 vol. Dunn, Ben, illus. 2007. (Bio-Graphics Ser.). (ENG.). 32p. (gr. 3-6). 28.50 (978-1-60270-071-0(0), Graphic Planet- Nonfiction) ABDO Publishing Co.

Helfand, Lewis. The Wright Brothers. Banerjee, Sankha, illus. 2011. (Campfire Graphic Novels Ser.). (ENG.). 72p. (YA). (gr. 5-9). pap. 9.99 (978-93-80028-46-0(6), Campfire) Steerforth Pr.

James, Emily. The Wright Brothers. 2017. (Great Scientists & Inventors Ser.). (ENG.). 24p. (gr. k-1). lib. bdg. 26.65 (978-1-5157-3885-5(X)) Capstone Press of Coughlan Cos.

Jenner, Caryn. First Flight Vol. 4: The Story of the Wright Brothers. 2004. (DK Readers Ser.). (Illus.). 48p. (gr. -1-3). 14.00 (978-0-7569-3361-6(7)) Perfection Learning Corp.

Jenner, Caryn & Garrett, Leslie. First Flight, Level 4: The Story of the Wright Brothers. 2003. (DK Readers Ser.). (ENG., Illus.). 48p. (J). (gr. 3-7). pap. 3.99 (978-0-7894-9291-3(1), DK Children) Dorling Kindersley Publishing, Inc.

Knoke, Paul. The Storm on Godfather Mountain: A True Story. 2010. 24p. pap. 14.99 (978-1-4490-5773-2(X)) AuthorHouse.

Mayo, Gretchen Will & O'Hern, Kerri. Los Hermanos Wright. Isaacs, Rebekah & Timmons, Jonathan, illus. 2007. (Biografías Gráficas (Graphic Biographies) Ser.). (SPA.). 32p. (gr. 5-8). lib. bdg. 27.00 (978-0-8368-7883-7(3)) Stevens, Gareth Publishing LLLP.

—The Wright Brothers. Isaacs, Rebekah & Timmons, Jonathan, illus. 2006. (Graphic Biographies Ser.). 32p. (gr. 5-8). lib. bdg. 27.00 (978-0-8368-6199-0(X)) Stevens, Gareth Publishing LLLP.

McCormick, Lisa Wade. Wright Brothers. 2005. (Scholastic News Nonfiction Readers Ser.). (Illus.). 24p. (J). pap. (978-0-516-24786-1(7)) Children's Pr., Ltd.

McPherson, Stephanie Sammartino & Gardner, Joseph Sammartino. Wilbur & Orville Wright: Taking Flight. 2004. (Trailblazer Biography Ser.). (Illus.). 120p. (J). 30.60 (978-1-57505-443-8(4), Carolrhoda Bks.) Lerner Publishing Group.

Niz, Xavier, et al. The Wright Brothers & the Airplane, 1 vol. Erwin, Steve et al, illus. 2007. (Inventions & Discovery Ser.). (ENG.). 32p. (gr. 3-4). 30.65 (978-0-7368-6845-7(3), Graphic Library) Capstone Press of Coughlan Cos.

Niz, Xavier W., et al. The Wright Brothers & the Airplane, 1 vol. Erwin, Steve, illus. 2007. (Inventions & Discovery Ser.). (ENG.). 32p. (gr. 3-4). per. 8.10 (978-0-7368-7897-5(1), Graphic Library) Capstone Press of Coughlan Cos.

O'Hern, Kerri & Will Mayo, Gretchen. Los Hermanos Wright. 2007. (Biografías Gráficas (Graphic Biographies) Ser.). (SPA.). 32p. (gr. 5-8). pap. 10.50 (978-0-8368-7890-5(6)) Stevens, Gareth Publishing LLLP.

Old, Wendie C. The Wright Brothers: Aviation Pioneers & Inventors. 2015. (Legendary American Biographies Ser.). 96p. (J). (gr. 6-12). 27.94 (978-0-7660-6505-5(7)); pap. 10.95 (978-0-7660-6506-2(5)) Enslow Pubs., Inc.

Orr, Tamra B. The Dawn of Aviation: The Story of the Wright Brothers. 2005. (Monumental Milestones Ser.). (Illus.). 48p. (YA). (gr. 4-7). lib. bdg. 29.95 (978-1-58415-396-2(2), 1244922) Mitchell Lane Pubs., Inc.

Rausch, Monica L. Los Hermanos Wright y el Avion. 2007. (Inventores y sus descubrimientos (Inventors & Their Discoveries) Ser.). (SPA., Illus.). 24p. (gr. 1-4). pap. 8.15 (978-0-8368-8001-4(3)); lib. bdg. 22.00 (978-0-8368-7996-4(1)) Stevens, Gareth Publishing LLLP. (Weekly Reader Leveled Readers).

—The Wright Brothers & the Airplane. 2007. (Inventors & Their Discoveries Ser.). (Illus.). 24p. (gr. 1-4). pap. 8.15 (978-0-8368-7733-5(0)); lib. bdg. 22.00 (978-0-8368-7502-7(8)) Stevens, Gareth Publishing LLLP. (Weekly Reader Leveled Readers).

Spilsbury, Louise. The Wright Brothers & the Airplane, 01 vols., 1. 2016. (Inventions That Changed the World Ser.). (ENG.). 32p. (J). pap. 10.00 (978-1-5081-4643-8(8), PowerKids Pr.) Rosen Publishing Group, Inc., The.

Stoltz, Paul. The Wright Brothers. 2009. (Real Life Readers Ser.). 12p. (gr. 2-3). pap. 5.90 (978-1-4042-7955-1(5), Rosen Classroom) Rosen Publishing Group, Inc., The.

Tieck, Sarah. Wright Brothers, 1 vol. 2006. (First Biographies Ser.). (ENG., Illus.). 32p. (gr. -1-3). 27.07 (978-1-59679-790-1(8), Buddy Bks.) ABDO Publishing Co.

Troupe, Thomas Kingsley. The Wright Brothers' First Flight: a Fly on the Wall History. Tejido, Jomike, illus. 2017. (Fly on the Wall History Ser.). (ENG.). 32p. (gr. 1-3). pap. 7.95 (978-1-4795-9791-8(0)); lib. bdg. 27.32 (978-1-4795-9787-1(2)) Picture Window Bks.

Van Steenwyk, Elizabeth. One Fine Day: A Radio Play. Farnsworth, Bill, illus. 2004. 32p. (J). (gr. 3-5). 16.00 (978-0-8028-5234-2(3)) Eerdmans, William B. Publishing Co.

Venezia, Mike. The Wright Brothers: Inventors Whose Ideas Really Took Flight. 2010. (Getting to Know the World's Greatest Inventors & Scientists Ser.). 32p. (J). (gr. 3-4). pap. 6.95 (978-0-531-22353-6(1), Children's Pr.) Scholastic Library Publishing.

—The Wright Brothers: Inventors Whose Ideas Really Took Flight. Venezia, Mike, illus. 2010. (Getting to Know the World's Greatest Inventors & Scientists Ser.). (ENG., Illus.). 32p. (J). (gr. 3-4). 28.00 (978-0-531-23732-8(X)) Scholastic Library Publishing.

Wadsworth, Ginger. The Wright Brothers. 2004. (History Maker Bios Ser.). (Illus.). 47p. (J). 26.60 (978-0-8225-0199-2(6), Lerner Pubns.) Lerner Publishing Group.

AERONAUTICS, COMMERCIAL

see also Airlines

Canavan, Andrea. The Federal Aviation Administration: Your Government: How it Works. 2006. (Illus.). 64p. (J). (gr. 4-8). reprint ed. 20.00 (978-1-4223-5544-2(6)) DIANE Publishing Co.

Eden, Paul. The World's Most Powerful Civilian Aircraft. 2016. (World's Most Powerful Machines Ser.). 00224p. (J). (gr. 9-9). 45.10 (978-1-4994-6588-4(2), Rosen Young Adult) Rosen Publishing Group, Inc., The.

Faust, Daniel R. Commercial Drones, 01 vols., 1. 2016. (Drones: Eyes in the Skies Ser.). (ENG.). 32p. (J). pap. 11.75 (978-1-5081-4490-8(7), PowerKids Pr.) Rosen Publishing Group, Inc., The.

Finn, Denny Von. V-22 Ospreys. 2014. (Military Vehicles Ser.). (ENG., Illus.). 24p. (J). (gr. 3-7). lib. bdg. 25.95 (978-1-62617-083-4(5), Epic Bks.) Bellwether Media.

Gilbert, Sara. The Story of FedEx. 2012. (Built for Success Ser.). (Illus.). 48p. (J). (gr. 5-12). 23.95 (978-1-60818-177-3(4), Creative Education) Creative Co., The.

Kallen, Stuart A. What Is the Future of Drones? 2016. (ENG.). (J). (gr. 5-12). lib. bdg. (978-1-68282-062-9(9)) ReferencePoint Pr., Inc.

Kamberg, Mary-Lane. Drones & Commerce. 2016. (Inside the World of Drones Ser.). 00064p. (J). (gr. 7-7). 34.45 (978-1-5081-7341-0(9)) Rosen Publishing Group, Inc., The.

Kawa, Katie. My First Trip on an Airplane. 2012. (My First Adventures Ser.). (Illus.). 24p. (gr. k-2). 69.20 (978-1-4339-8046-6(0)) Stevens, Gareth Publishing LLLP.

La Bella, Laura. Drones & Entertainment. 2016. (Inside the World of Drones Ser.). 00064p. (J). (gr. 7-7). 34.45 (978-1-5081-7339-7(7)) Rosen Publishing Group, Inc., The.

Parker, Steve & Parker, Vic. My First Trip on an Airplane, 1 vol. 2011. (Growing Up Ser.). (ENG.). 24p. (gr. k-2). 23.32 (978-1-4329-4801-6(6)); pap. 6.79 (978-1-4329-4811-5(3)) Heinemann-Raintree. (Heinemann Read & Learn).

Rober, Harold. Going on an Airplane. 2017. (Bumba Books (tm) — Fun Firsts Ser.). (ENG.). 24p. (J). (gr. -1-1). 12.99 **(978-1-5124-3681-5(X))**; 38.65 **(978-1-5124-2750-9(0))**; 38.65 **(978-1-5124-3680-8(1))** Lerner Publishing Group. (Lerner Pubns.).

Rober, Harold T. Going on an Airplane. 2017. (Bumba Books (tm) — Fun Firsts Ser.). (ENG., Illus.). 24p. (J). (gr. -1-1). 25.32 (978-1-5124-2554-3(0)) Lerner Publishing Group.

Wright, John. The U. S. Transportation Security Administration. 2004. (Rescue & Prevention Ser.). (Illus.). 96p. (YA). (gr. 7-18). lib. bdg. 22.95 (978-1-59084-412-0(2)) Mason Crest.

AERONAUTICS—FICTION

Appleton, Victor. Tom Swift among the Diamond Makers. 2005. 26.95 (978-1-4218-1086-7(7)); 196p. pap. 11.95 (978-1-4218-1186-4(3)) 1st World Publishing, Inc. (1st World Library - Literary Society).

—Tom Swift among the Diamond Makers. 2007. 224p. 29.95 (978-1-4344-9458-0(6)); per. 19.95 (978-1-4344-9457-3(8)) Wildside Pr., LLC.

—Tom Swift among the Diamond Makers or Th. 2006. pap. (978-1-4065-0892-5(6)) Dodo Pr.

—Tom Swift & His Air Scout: Or Uncle Sam's Mastery of the Sky. l.t. ed. 2007. (ENG.). 158p. pap. 21.99 (978-1-4346-1580-0(4)) Creative Media Partners, LLC.

—Tom Swift & His Air Scout or Uncle Sam. 2006. pap. (978-1-4065-0896-3(9)) Dodo Pr.

—Tom Swift & his Sky Racer. 2005. 26.95 (978-1-4218-1504-6(4)); 192p. pap. 11.95 (978-1-4218-1604-3(0)) 1st World Publishing, Inc. (1st World Library - Literary Society).

—Tom Swift & His Sky Racer or the Quick. 2006. pap. (978-1-4065-0907-6(8)) Dodo Pr.

Bailey, Gerry & Foster, Karen. The Wright Brothers' Glider. Radford, Karen & Noyes, Leighton, illus. 2008. (Stories of Great People Ser.). (ENG.). 40p. (J). (gr. 3-8). pap. (978-0-7787-3715-5(2)); lib. bdg. (978-0-7787-3693-6(8)) Crabtree Publishing Co.

Beasley, Ava. Akeem's Airplane: Breaking down the Problem. 2017. (Computer Science for the Real World Ser.). 16p. (gr. 7-8). pap. 7.95 **(978-1-5383-5204-5(4)**, Rosen Classroom) Rosen Publishing Group, Inc., The.

Brier, Howard M. Skycruiser. 2005. pap. 26.95 (978-1-4191-1033-7(0)) Kessinger Publishing, LLC.

Brooks, Walter R. Freddy & the Perilous Adventure. Wiese, Kurt, illus. 2012. (ENG.). 256p. 10.99 (978-1-59020-742-0(4), 902742) Overlook Pr., The.

Burtis, Thomson. Flying Blackbirds. Gretta, J. Clemens, illus. 2011. 256p. 47.95 (978-1-258-07554-5(7)) Literary Licensing, LLC.

Carlson, Glenn E. Angie the Aviator. Robinson, Helen, ed. Storey, Linda & Nielson, Doug, illus. l.t. ed. 2004. 55p. (J). (gr. 2-9). 21.95 (978-0-9611954-4-1(4)) Watosh Publishing.

Clark, Ruth E. Airport Mouse Activity Fun Book 1. Jones, Phil, illus. 2010. 16p. (J). pap. 5.99 (978-0-9792963-6-9(6)) Huntington Ludlow Media Group.

—Airport Mouse Becomes a VIP/VIM World Traveler Activity Fun Book 4. Jones, Phil, illus. 2010. 16p. (J). pap. 5.99 (978-0-9792963-9-0(0)) Huntington Ludlow Media Group.

—Airport Mouse Explores on Opening Day Activity Fun Book 3. Jones, Phil, illus. 2010. 16p. (J). pap. 5.99 (978-0-9792963-8-3(2)) Kimball, Jane A.

—Airport Mouse Works the Night Shift Activity Fun Book 2. Jones, Phil, illus. 2010. 16p. (J). pap. 5.99 (978-0-9792963-7-6(4)) Huntington Ludlow Media Group.

Fitzhugh, Percy K. Tom Slade with the Flying Corps. 2005. (Illus.). pap. 27.95 (978-1-885529-87-9(2)) Stevens Publishing.

Frederick, Rachel. I'm Going to Be a Pilot! 2011. 24p. pap. 15.99 (978-1-4628-4891-1(5)) Xlibris Corp.

Garis, Howard Roger. Dick Hamilton's Airship or, A Young Millionaire in the Clouds. 2007. 220p. per. (978-1-4065-2767-4(X)) Dodo Pr.

Gosling, Sharon. The Ruby Airship. 2015. (Diamond Thief Ser.). (ENG.). 496p. (gr. 9-12). 16.95 (978-1-63079-004-2(4)) Switch Pr.

Kelly, Mark. Astrotwins — Project Rescue. 2016. (Astrotwins Ser.). (ENG., Illus.). 256p. (J). (gr. 3-7). 16.99 (978-1-4814-2458-5(0), Simon & Schuster/Paula Wiseman Bks.) Simon & Schuster/Paula Wiseman Bks.

Langworthy, John Luther. The Aeroplane Boys on the Wing: Aeroplane Chums in the Tropics. 2007. (ENG.). 138p. pap. 18.99 (978-1-4346-2165-8(0)); 158p. pap. 21.99 (978-1-4346-2225-9(8)) Creative Media Partners, LLC.

—The Airplane Boys among the Clouds: Or, Young Aviators in a Wreck. 2007. (ENG.). 140p. pap. 18.99 (978-1-4346-4339-1(5)); 160p. pap. 21.99 (978-1-4346-4340-7(9)) Creative Media Partners, LLC.

Lefevre-Garros. The Wright Brothers. 2009. (ENG., Illus.). 48p. pap. 11.95 (978-1-905460-73-1(2)) CineBook GBR. Dist: National Bk. Network.

Mathiews, Franklin K. Skyward Ho! 2005. pap. 26.95 (978-1-4191-1034-4(9)) Kessinger Publishing, LLC.

McGeachy, Andrew. The Flight of Louis Blaireau. 2010. 36p. pap. 13.95 (978-1-60911-206-6(7), Eloquent Bks.) Strategic Book Publishing & Rights Agency (SBPRA).

Meadows, Michelle. Pilot Pups. Andreasen, Dan, illus. 2008. (ENG.). 32p. (J). (gr. -1-3). 17.99 (978-1-4169-2484-5(1), Simon & Schuster Bks. For Young Readers) Simon & Schuster Bks. For Young Readers.

Messner, Kate. Capture the Flag. 2013. (ENG.). 240p. (J). (gr. 3-7). pap. 6.99 (978-0-545-41974-1(3), Scholastic Paperbacks) Scholastic, Inc.

Montes, Hugo & Montes, Michelle. Young Eagles Armor Academy: Caught in the Storm, V02. 2010. 76p. (J). pap. 5.99 (978-1-60683-022-2(8)) Harrison House Pubs.

—Young Eagles Armor Academy: Fear of Flying, V01. 2010. 76p. (J). pap. 5.99 (978-1-60683-021-5(X)) Harrison House Pubs.

—Young Eagles Armor Academy: The Whispering Cave, V03. 2010. 76p. (J). pap. 5.99 (978-1-60683-023-9(6)) Harrison House Pubs.

—Young Eagles Armor Academy Box Set: Volumes 1 - 3. 2010. (J). pap. 17.97 (978-1-60683-024-6(4)) Harrison House Pubs.

Oechsli, Helen. Fly Away. 2013. (ENG., Illus.). 32p. (J). (gr. -1-3). 16.99 (978-1-4814-2168-3(9), Simon & Schuster Bks. For Young Readers) Simon & Schuster Bks. For Young Readers.

Olivas, John D. Endeavour's Long Journey: Celebrating 19 Years of Space Exploration. Roski, Gayle Garner, illus. 2013. (J). pap. (978-0-9856237-3-9(X)) East West Discovery Pr.

Oliver, Lin. Revenge of the Itty-Bitty Brothers. Gilpin, Stephen, illus. 2010. (Who Shrunk Daniel Funk? Ser.: 3). (ENG.). 176p. (J). (gr. 3-7). pap. 6.99 (978-1-4169-0962-0(1), Simon & Schuster Bks. For Young Readers) Simon & Schuster Bks. For Young Readers.

Reid, Charles. Hurricanes over London. 2005. (ENG., Illus.). 152p. (J). (gr. 3-9). pap., tchr. ed. 8.95 (978-0-921870-82-1(5)) Ronsdale Pr. CAN. Dist: Literary Pr. Group of Canada.

Roberts, Willo Davis. What Could Go Wrong? 2016. (ENG., Illus.). 240p. (J). (gr. 3-7). pap. 7.99 (978-1-4814-7489-4(8), Aladdin) Simon & Schuster Children's Publishing.

Rockwood, Roy. Dave Dashaway & His Hydroplane. 2009. 128p. 23.95 (978-1-60664-625-0(7)); pap. 10.95 (978-1-60664-364-8(9)) Rodgers, Alan Bks.

Semionov, Vladimir, illus. Silver Wings. 2007. (Choose Your Own Adventure Ser.: No. 23). 107p. (J). (gr. 4-7). pap. 6.99 (978-1-933390-23-9(9)) Chooseco LLC.

Service, Pamela F. Alien Envoy. Gorman, Mike, illus. 2011. (Alien Agent Ser.: 6). (ENG.). 176p. (J). (gr. 4-6). 16.95 (978-0-7613-5364-5(X)) Lerner Publishing Group.

Seybold, Celisa. The Keys to Adventure Take Flight. 2011. 48p. pap. 9.95 (978-1-257-06278-2(6)) Lulu Pr., Inc.

Snape, Emily. Motor Mix, Flight: Invent Your Own Mix-And-Match Vehicles! Alexander, Rilla, illus. 2017. (ENG.). 16p. (J). (gr. -1 — 1). bds. 9.99 (978-1-4521-4839-7(2)) Chronicle Bks. LLC.

Snell, Roy Judson. Sparky Ames of the Ferry Command. Darwin, Erwin L., illus. 2012. 246p. 46.95 (978-1-258-25306-6(2)); pap. 31.95 (978-1-258-25572-5(3)) Literary Licensing, LLC.

Terman, Douglas. By Balloon to the Sahara. 2015. (ENG.). 144p. (J). pap. 6.99 (978-1-937133-48-1(6)) Chooseco LLC.

Victor, Appleton. Tom Swift & His Air Scout: Or Uncle Sam's Mastery of the Sky. 2007. (ENG.). 144p. pap. 18.99 (978-1-4346-1486-5(7)) Creative Media Partners, LLC.

Winfield, Arthur M. The Rover Boys in the Air or from College Campus to the Clouds. 2006. (ENG.). 316p. per. 30.95 (978-1-4286-4103-7(3)) Kessinger Publishing, LLC.

Wright, Philip Lee & Foster, John. The Mail Pilot's Hunch: Or A Crash in Death Valley. 2011. 218p. 44.95 (978-1-258-10021-6(5)) Literary Licensing, LLC.

AERONAUTICS—FLIGHTS

see also Space Flight

Benchmark Education Co., LLC. Up in the Sky Big Book. 2014. (Shared Reading Foundations Ser.). (J). (gr. -1). (978-1-4509-9446-0(6)) Benchmark Education Co.

Borden, Louise, et al. Touching the Sky: The Flying Adventures of Wilbur & Orville Wright. Fiore, Peter M., illus. 2003. (ENG.). 64p. (J). (gr. k-3). 19.99 (978-0-689-84876-6(5), McElderry, Margaret K. Bks.) McElderry, Margaret K. Bks.

Finkelstein, Norman H. Three Across: The Great Transatlantic Air Race Of 1927. 2008. (ENG., Illus.). 136p. (J). (gr. 4-18). 17.95 (978-1-59078-462-4(6), Calkins Creek) Boyds Mills Pr.

Grove, Tim. First Flight Around the World: The Adventures of the American Fliers Who Won the Race. 2015. (ENG., Illus.). 96p. (J). (gr. 5-9). 21.95 (978-1-4197-1482-5(1)) Abrams, Inc.

Koestler-Grack, Rachel A. Spirit of St. Louis, 1 vol. 2005. (American Moments Ser.). (ENG., Illus.). 48p. (gr. 4-8). 27.07 (978-1-59197-940-1(4), Abdo & Daughters) ABDO Publishing Co.

McAneney, Caitlin. The First Flight Across the Atlantic. 2015. (Incredible True Adventures Ser.). (ENG., Illus.). 32p. (J). (gr. 3-4). pap. 10.50 (978-1-4824-2034-0(1)) Stevens, Gareth Publishing LLLP.

Pimm, Nancy Roe. The Jerrie Mock Story: The First Woman to Fly Solo Around the World. 2016. (Biographies for Young Readers Ser.). (ENG., Illus.). 168p. (J). (gr. 1-6). 28.95 (978-0-8214-2215-1(4)) Ohio Univ. Pr.

AERONAUTICS, HIGH SPEED

see High-Speed Aeronautics

AERONAUTICS—HISTORY

Berger, Melvin & Berger, Gilda. Can You Fly High, Wright Brothers? Dorman, Brandon, illus. 2007. (Scholastic Science Supergiants Ser.: Vol. 1). (ENG.). 48p. (J). (gr. 2-5). pap. 4.99 (978-0-439-83378-3(7)) Scholastic, Inc.

Bledsoe, Karen E. Daredevils of the Air: Thrilling Tales of Pioneer Aviators. 2003. (Avisson Young Adult Ser.). (Illus.). 155p. (J). pap. 19.95 (978-1-888105-58-2(5)) Avisson Pr., Inc.

Brasch, Nicholas. Conquering the Sky. 2013. (Discovery Education: Discoveries & Inventions Ser.). 32p. (J). (gr. 3-6). pap. 60.00 (978-1-4777-1505-5(3), PowerKids Pr.) Rosen Publishing Group, Inc., The.

Brasch, Nicolas. Conquering the Sky. 2013. (Discovery Education: Discoveries & Inventions Ser.). (ENG., Illus.). 32p. (J). (gr. 3-6). pap. 10.00 (978-1-4777-1504-8(5)); lib. bdg. 25.25 (978-1-4777-1331-0(X)) Rosen Publishing Group, Inc., The. (PowerKids Pr.).

Brown, Jonatha A. The Wright Brothers. 2004. (People We Should Know Ser.). (Illus.). 24p. (gr. 1-4). lib. bdg. 22.00 (978-0-8368-4314-9(2), Weekly Reader Leveled Readers) Stevens, Gareth Publishing LLLP.

Burkett, Molly. Pioneers of the Air. 2010. (History of Exploration Ser.). 48p. 32.80 (978-1-84898-306-9(9)) Black Rabbit Bks.

Davis, Lynn. The Wright Brothers, 1 vol. 2016. (ENG., Illus.). 24p. (J). (978-1-62403-726-9(7)) ABDO Publishing Co.

Dorling Kindersley Publishing Staff & Nahum, Andrew. Flight. 2011. (DK Eyewitness Bks.). (ENG.). 72p. (J). (gr. 3-7). 16.99 (978-0-7566-7317-8(8), DK Children) Dorling Kindersley Publishing, Inc.

Dougherty, Martin J. Aircraft. 2012. (Modern Weapons: Compared & Contrasted Ser.). (ENG., Illus.). 48p. (YA). (gr. 9-12). 29.25 (978-1-4488-9246-4(5), Rosen Reference) Rosen Publishing Group, Inc., The.

Finkelstein, Norman H. Three Across: The Great Transatlantic Air Race Of 1927. 2008. (ENG., Illus.). 136p. (J). (gr. 4-18). 17.95 (978-1-59078-462-4(6), Calkins Creek) Boyds Mills Pr.

Ford, Carin T. The Wright Brothers: Heroes of Flight. 2003. (Famous Inventors Ser.). (Illus.). 32p. (J). (gr. 1-4). lib. bdg. 23.94 (978-0-7660-2002-3(9)) Enslow Pubs., Inc.

The Future Takes Wing: San Diego International Airport - 75 Years of Flight. 2nd ed. 2003. per. (978-0-9745294-0-0(0)) San Diego County Regional Airport Authority.

Golden Cosmos Staff, contrib. by. High Times: A History of Aviation. 2012. (Leporello Ser.). (ENG., Illus.). 20p. (gr. k). 16.00 (978-1-907704-35-2(3)) Nobrow Ltd. GBR. Dist: Consortium Bk. Sales & Distribution.

Goldstone, Lawrence. Higher, Steeper, Faster: The Daredevils Who Conquered the Skies. 2017. (ENG., Illus.). 256p. (J). (gr. 3-7). 18.99 (978-0-316-35023-5(0)) Little Brown & Co.

Hamen, Susan E. The Wright Brothers, 1 vol. 2007. (Essential Lives Set 1 Ser.). (ENG., Illus.). 112p. (J). (gr. 6-12). lib. bdg. 35.64 (978-1-59928-846-8(X)) ABDO Publishing Co.

Hansen, Ole Steen. The Story of Flight. 2003. (Illus.). 190p. (J). (978-0-7787-1212-1(5)) Crabtree Publishing Co.

—The Story of Flight, 12 bks. Incl. Amazing Flights: The Golden Age. (gr. 4). 2002. lib. bdg. (978-0-7787-1202-2(8)); Commercial Aviation. (gr. 4). 2002. lib. bdg. (978-0-7787-1205-3(2)); Flying for Fun. (gr. 4). 2003. lib. bdg. (978-0-7787-1211-4(7)); Military Aircraft of WWI. (gr. 4). 2002. lib. bdg. (978-0-7787-1201-5(X)); Modern Military Aircraft. (gr. 4). 2002. lib. bdg. (978-0-7787-1204-6(4)); Seaplanes & Naval Aviation. (gr. 4). 2003. lib. bdg. (978-0-7787-1209-1(5)); Space Flight. (gr. 2-9). 2003. lib. bdg. (978-0-7787-1207-7(9)); Weird & Wonderful Aircraft. (gr. 4). 2003. lib. bdg. (978-0-7787-1210-7(9)); Wright Brothers & Other Pioneers of Flight. (gr. 4). 2002. lib. bdg. (978-0-7787-1200-8(1)); 32p. (J). (Illus.). 2003. (978-0-7787-1198-8(6)); Set pap. (978-0-7787-1214-5(1)) Crabtree Publishing Co.

Hardesty, Von. Flight. 2011. (Insiders Ser.). (ENG., Illus.). 64p. (J). (gr. 3-7). 17.99 (978-1-4424-3277-2(2), Simon & Schuster Bks. For Young Readers) Simon & Schuster Bks. For Young Readers.

Harding, Les. McCurdy & the Silver Dart, 1 vol. 2nd ed. 2014. (ENG., Illus.). 96p. pap. (978-1-927492-77-2(7)) Cape Breton Univ. Pr.

Hofer, Charles. Airplanes. (World's Fastest Machines Ser.). 24p. 2009. (gr. 2-3). 42.50 (978-1-60854-851-4(1)) 2008. (Illus.). (J). (gr. 3-7). lib. bdg. 22.60 (978-1-4042-4173-2(6)) Rosen Publishing Group, Inc., The. (PowerKids Pr.).

Jeffrey, Gary. The History of Flight. (Graphic Discoveries Ser.). (ENG.). 48p. 2009. (YA). (gr. 5-5). 58.50 (978-1-61512-938-6(3), Rosen Reference) 2008. (gr. 3-8). pap. 14.05 (978-1-4042-9589-6(5)) 2008. (Illus.). (J). (gr. 5-9). lib. bdg. 31.95 (978-1-4042-1087-5(3)) Rosen Publishing Group, Inc., The.

Jenner, Caryn. First Flight Vol. 4: The Story of the Wright Brothers. 2004. (DK Readers Ser.). (Illus.). 48p. (gr. -1-3). 14.00 (978-0-7569-3361-6(7)) Perfection Learning Corp.

LaFontaine, Bruce. BOOST the Story of the Wright Brothers Coloring Book. 2013. (BOOST Educational Ser.). (ENG.). 32p. (J). (gr. 3-5). pap. 4.99 (978-0-486-49440-1(3)) Dover Pubns., Inc.

Lefèvre-Garros, J. P. The Wright Brothers, Vol. 3: Uderzo, M., illus. 2012. (Cinebook Recounts Ser.: 3). (ENG.). 48p. (YA).

(gr. 6-17). pap. 11.95 *(978-1-84918-100-6(4))* CineBook GBR. Dist: National Bk. Network.

Lowery, Lawrence F. Up, Up in a Balloon. 2013. (I Wonder Why Ser.). (ENG., Illus.). 36p. (J). (gr. k-3). pap. 11.95 *(978-1-938946-14-1(6))* National Science Teachers Assn.

Masters, Nancy Robinson. The Airplane. 2006. (Inventions That Shaped the World Ser.). (Illus.). 80p. (gr. 4-7). 19.95 *(978-0-7569-6852-6(6))* Perfection Learning Corp.

—Airplanes. 2008. (21st Century Skills Library: Global Products Ser.). (ENG.). 32p. (gr. 4-8). lib. bdg. 28.50 *(978-1-60279-119-0(8)*, 200091) Cherry Lake Publishing.

Morris, Neil. Air Pioneers. (Illus.). 48p. (YA). (gr. 5-18). lib. bdg. 29.95 *(978-1-932333-81-7(9))* Chrysalis Education.

Nagelhout, Ryan. The Problem with Early Flying Machines. 2015. (Bloopers of Invention Ser.). (ENG., Illus.). 24p. (J). (gr. 2-3). 22.60 *(978-1-4824-2766-0(4))* Stevens, Gareth Publishing LLLP.

O'Brien, Patrick. Fantastic Flights: One Hundred Years of Flying on the Edge. 2003. (Illus.). 40p. (J). 18.85 *(978-0-8027-8881-8(5))* Walker & Co.

Otfinoski, Steven. Air Travel: Science Technology Engineering. 2015. (ENG., Illus.). 64p. (J). pap. 8.95 *(978-0-531-21174-8(6)*, Orchard Bks.) Scholastic Library Publishing.

Salzmann, Mary Elizabeth. Biggest, Baddest Book of Flight, 1 vol. 2014. (Biggest, Baddest Books Set 2 Ser.). (ENG., Illus.). 24p. (J). (gr. k-4). 25.65 *(978-1-62403-515-9(9))* ABDO Publishing Co.

Sandler, Martin W. Flying over the USA: Airplanes in American Life. 2006. (Illus.). 61p. (J). (gr. 4-8). reprint ed. 20.00 *(978-1-4223-5623-4(X))* DIANE Publishing Co.

Shetterly, Margot Lee. Hidden Figures. Freeman, Laura, illus. 2018. (ENG.). 40p. (J). (gr. -1-3). 17.99 ***(978-0-06-274246-9(9))*** HarperCollins Pubs.

—Hidden Figures. 2016. 240p. (J). (gr. 3-7). 16.99 *(978-0-06-266238-5(4))*; (Illus.). pap. 7.99 *(978-0-06-266237-8(6))* HarperCollins Pubs.

—Hidden Figures. 2016. (Illus.). 231p. (J). lib. bdg. 18.40 ***(978-0-606-39623-3(3))*** Turtleback Bks.

Smithsonian Institution Staff, creator. Extreme Aircraft! Q&A. 2007. (Illus.). 48p. (J). (gr. 3-5). 16.99 *(978-0-06-089943-1(3))* HarperCollins Pubs.

Spilsbury, Louise & Spilsbury, Richard. The Airplane, 1 vol. 2010. (Tales of Invention Ser.). (ENG.). 32p. (gr. 3-5). 30.65 *(978-1-4329-3830-7(4))*; pap. 8.95 *(978-1-4329-3837-6(1))* Heinemann-Raintree. (NA-h).

Tieck, Sarah. Wright Brothers, 1 vol. 2006. (First Biographies Ser.). (ENG., Illus.). 32p. (gr. -1-3). 27.07 *(978-1-59679-790-1(8)*, Buddy Bks.) ABDO Publishing Co.

Weitzman, David. Jenny: The Airplane That Taught America to Fly. Weitzman, David, illus. 2006. (Illus.). 27p. (J). (gr. k-4). reprint ed. 19.00 *(978-1-4223-5582-4(9))* DIANE Publishing Co.

West, David. Ten of the Best Adventures in the Sky. 2015. (Ten of the Best: Stories of Exploration & Adventure Ser.). (ENG., Illus.). 24p. (J). (gr. 3-6). lib. bdg. *(978-0-7787-1838-3(7))* Crabtree Publishing Co.

White, Rowland. Cleared for Takeoff! The Ultimate Book of Flight. 2016. (ENG., Illus.). 320p. (J). (gr. 3-7). 21.99 *(978-1-4521-3550-2(9))* Chronicle Bks. LLC.

World Book, Inc Staff, contrib. by. A Dream Takes Flight: A Supplement to Childcraft, the How & Why Library. 2013. (Illus.). 26p. (J). *(978-0-7166-0629-1(1))* World Bk., Inc.

AERONAUTICS, MILITARY

see also Air Bases; Aircraft Carriers; Airplanes, Military; Parachute Troops

also names of wars with the subdivision Aerial Operations

Abell, Tracy. All about Drones. 2017. (Cutting-Edge Technology (hardcover) Ser.). (ENG., Illus.). 32p. (J). (gr. 4-7). lib. bdg. 28.50 ***(978-1-63517-012-2(5)***, Focus Readers) North Star Editions.

Abramovitz, Melissa. Unbelievable Military Aircraft, 1 vol. 2014. (Ready for Military Action Ser.). (ENG.). 48p. (gr. 3-6). lib. bdg. 32.79 *(978-1-62403-656-9(2))* ABDO Publishing Co.

Alvarez, Carlos. V-22 Ospreys. 2010. (Military Machines Ser.). (ENG., Illus.). 24p. (J). (gr. 3-7). lib. bdg. 25.95 *(978-1-60014-333-5(4))* Bellwether Media.

Bolitho, Mark. Fold Your Own Origami Air Force. 2013. 32p. (J). (gr. 3-6). 26.50 *(978-1-4777-1319-8(0))*; pap. 11.75 *(978-1-4777-1469-0(3))* Rosen Publishing Group, Inc., The. (PowerKids Pr.).

Broyles, Janell. Chemical & Biological Weapons in a Post-9/11 World. 2009. (Library of Weapons of Mass Destruction Ser.). 64p. (gr. 5-5). 58.50 *(978-1-60853-951-2(2))* Rosen Publishing Group, Inc., The.

—Chemical Biological Incident Response Force. 2009. (Inside Special Operations Ser.). 64p. (gr. 6-6). 58.50 *(978-1-61513-551-6(0)*, Rosen Reference) Rosen Publishing Group, Inc., The.

David, Jack. HH-60 Pavehawk Helicopters. 2008. (Military Machines Ser.). (ENG., Illus.). 24p. (YA). (gr. 3-7). lib. bdg. 25.95 *(978-1-60014-223-9(0))* Bellwether Media.

Dougherty, Martin J. Air Warfare. 2010. (Modern Warfare Ser.). 32p. (YA). (gr. 2-5). lib. bdg. 26.00 *(978-1-4339-2720-1(9))* Stevens, Gareth Publishing LLLP.

Fold Your Own Origami Air Force. 2013. (Origami Army Ser.). 32p. (J). (gr. 3-6). pap. 70.50 *(978-1-4777-1470-6(7)*, PowerKids Pr.) Rosen Publishing Group, Inc., The.

Gordon, Nick. Army Night Stalkers. 2013. (U. S. Military Ser.). (ENG., Illus.). 24p. (J). (gr. 3-7). lib. bdg. 25.95 *(978-1-60014-874-3(3)*, Epic Bks.) Bellwether Media.

Gray, Judy Silverstein & Kiland, Taylor Baldwin. The Military GPS: Cutting-Edge Global Positioning System. 2016. (Military Engineering in Action Ser.). 48p. (J). (gr. 6-5). pap. 11.70 *(978-0-7660-7515-3(X))* Enslow Pubs., Inc.

Hamilton, John. Uh-60 Black Hawk. 2013. (Xtreme Military Aircraft Set 2 Ser.). 32p. (J). (gr. 3-9). lib. bdg. 27.07 *(978-1-61783-689-3(3)*, Abdo & Daughters) ABDO Publishing Co.

Hansen, Ole Steen. Air Combat. 2003. (Story of Flight Ser.). (ENG., Illus.). 32p. (J). (gr. 4). pap. *(978-0-7787-1222-0(2))* Crabtree Publishing Co.

—Seaplanes & Naval Aviation. 2003. (Story of Flight Ser.). (ENG., Illus.). 32p. (J). (gr. 4). pap. *(978-0-7787-1225-1(7))*; lib. bdg. *(978-0-7787-1209-1(5))* Crabtree Publishing Co.

Harmon, Daniel E. Chemical & Biological Weapons: Agents of War & Terror. 2009. (Science & Society Ser.). 64p. (gr. 5-6). 58.50 *(978-1-60853-007-6(8))* Rosen Publishing Group, Inc., The.

Larson, Kirsten W. Drones. 2017. (Robotics in Our World Ser.). (ENG.). 32p. (gr. 1-4). 20.95 *(978-1-68151-140-5(1))* Amicus Publishing.

Loveless, Antony. Fighter Pilots. 2009. (World's Most Dangerous Jobs Ser.). (ENG., Illus.). 32p. (J). (gr. 3-6). pap. *(978-0-7787-5110-6(4))*; lib. bdg. *(978-0-7787-5096-3(5))* Crabtree Publishing Co.

Marcovitz, Hal. Biological & Chemical Warfare, 1 vol. 2010. (Essential Issues Set 1 Ser.). (ENG.). 112p. (J). (gr. 6-12). lib. bdg. 35.64 *(978-1-60453-951-6(8)*, Essential Library) ABDO Publishing Co.

Masters, Nancy Robinson. Drone Pilot. 2012. (21st Century Skills Library: Cool Military Careers Ser.). (ENG.). 32p. (gr. 4-8). 28.50 *(978-1-61080-448-6(1)*, 202058); pap. 14.21 *(978-1-61080-622-0(0)*, 202232) Cherry Lake Publishing.

Miller, Roger G. Billy Mitchell: Evangelist of Airpower. 2007. (Illus.). 152p. (J). (gr. 10-18). lib. bdg. 25.95 *(978-1-59556-025-4(4))* OTTN Publishing.

Noll, Elizabeth. Flying Robots. 2017. (World of Robots Ser.). (ENG., Illus.). 32p. (J). (gr. 3-8). lib. bdg. 26.95 ***(978-1-62617-688-1(4)***, Blastoff! Discovery) Bellwether Media.

Parks, Peggy J. Fighter Pilot. 2005. (Exploring Careers Ser.). (ENG., Illus.). 48p. (J). (gr. 4-8). lib. bdg. 29.15 *(978-0-7377-3079-1(X)*, Kidhaven) Cengage Gale.

Person, Stephen. Army Night Stalkers in Action. 2013. (Special Ops II Ser.). 32p. (J). (gr. 2-7). lib. bdg. 26.60 *(978-1-61772-889-1(6))* Bearport Publishing Co., Inc.

Turner, Tracy. Weapons of War. 2015. (Head-To-Head Ser.). (ENG., Illus.). 24p. (gr. 3-8). 28.50 *(978-1-62588-151-9(7))* Black Rabbit Bks.

WWII Airplanes. (Color & Learn Ser.). 36p. (J). (gr. 1-5). pap. *(978-1-882210-01-5(8))* Action Publishing, Inc.

AERONAUTICS, NAVAL

see Aeronautics, Military

AERONAUTICS—PILOTING

see Airplanes—Piloting

AERONAUTICS—SAFETY MEASURES

Leavitt, Amie Jane. Anatomy of a Plane Crash. (Disasters Ser.). (ENG.). 48p. (gr. 3-4). 2011. pap. 59.70 *(978-1-4296-7362-4(1))* 2010. lib. bdg. 31.99 *(978-1-4296-4796-0(5))* Capstone Press of Coughlan Cos.

AERONAUTICS—VOCATIONAL GUIDANCE

Aviation. 2nd rev. ed. 2010. (Careers in Focus Ser.). (Illus.). 192p. (gr. 6-12). 32.95 *(978-0-8160-8023-6(2)*, Ferguson Publishing Co.) Facts On File, Inc.

Casil, Amy Sterling. Choosing a Career in Aircraft Maintenance. 2009. (World of Work Ser.). 64p. (gr. 5-5). 58.50 *(978-1-60854-328-1(5))* Rosen Publishing Group, Inc., The.

—Choosing a Career in Aircraft Mechanic. 2005. (World of Work Ser.). (Illus.). 64p. (YA). (gr. 7-12). lib. bdg. 31.95 *(978-0-8239-3567-3(1))* Rosen Publishing Group, Inc., The.

Hutchings, Amy. What Happens at an Airport? 2009. (Where People Work Ser.). 24p. (J). (gr. -1-3). lib. bdg. 22.00 *(978-1-4339-0072-3(6)*, Weekly Reader Leveled Readers) Stevens, Gareth Publishing LLLP.

—What Happens at an Airport? (¿Qué pasa en un Aeropuerto?) 2009. (Where People Work Ser.). 24p. (gr. -1-3). pap. 8.15 *(978-1-4339-0136-2(6)*, Weekly Reader Leveled Readers) Stevens, Gareth Publishing LLLP.

Hutchings, Amy & Nations, Susan. What Happens at an Airport? (?;¿Qué pasa en un Aeropuerto?) 2009. (Where People Work/Dónde Trabaja la Gente? Ser.). (SPA & ENG.). 24p. (gr. -1-3). pap. 8.15 *(978-1-4339-0144-7(7)*, Weekly Reader Leveled Readers) Stevens, Gareth Publishing LLLP.

—What Happens at an Airport?/¿Qué Pasa en un Aeropuerto? 2009. (Where People Work/Dónde Trabaja la Gente? Ser.). (SPA & ENG.). 24p. (J). (gr. -1-3). lib. bdg. 22.00 *(978-1-4339-0080-8(7)*, Weekly Reader Leveled Readers) Stevens, Gareth Publishing LLLP.

Otfinoski, Steven. Air Travel: Science Technology Engineering. 2015. (ENG., Illus.). 64p. (J). pap. 8.95 *(978-0-531-21174-8(6)*, Orchard Bks.) Scholastic Library Publishing.

Tetrick, Byron. Choosing a Career as a Pilot. (World of Work Ser.). 64p. 2009. (gr. 5-5). 58.50 *(978-1-60854-325-0(0))* 2005. (Illus.). (YA). (gr. 7-12). lib. bdg. 31.95 *(978-0-8239-3571-0(X))* Rosen Publishing Group, Inc., The.

Thomas, William. Wilderness Rescue Pilot. 2010. (Benchmark Rockets: Dirty & Dangerous Jobs Ser.). 32p. (J). (gr. 3-6). 28.50 *(978-1-60870-180-3(8))* Marshall Cavendish Corp.

AERONAUTICS—VOYAGES

see Aeronautics—Flights

AERONAUTICS IN METEOROLOGY

Jeffrey, Gary. Hurricane Hunters & Tornado Chasers. 2009. (Graphic Careers Ser.). (ENG.). 48p. (YA). (gr. 5-5). 58.50 *(978-1-61512-885-3(9)*, Rosen Reference) Rosen Publishing Group, Inc., The.

—Hurricane Hunters & Tornado Chasers. Garofalo, Gianluca, illus. 2008. (Graphic Careers Ser.). (ENG.). 48p. (gr. 5-8). per. 14.05 *(978-1-4042-1459-0(3))*; (YA). lib. bdg. 31.95 *(978-1-4042-1458-3(5))* Rosen Publishing Group, Inc., The.

AEROSPACE MEDICINE

see Space Medicine

AFFECTION

see Friendship; Love

AFGHANISTAN

Ali, Sharifah Enayat. Afghanistan. 2013. (Cultures of the World 4 Ser.). 144p. (J). (gr. 6-9). pap. 23.51 *(978-1-62712-157-6(9))* Cavendish Square Publishing.

—Afghanistan. 2nd rev. ed. 2006. (Cultures of the World Ser.). (Illus.). 144p. (gr. 6-7). lib. bdg. 42.79 *(978-0-7614-2064-4(9)*, Benchmark Bks.) Marshall Cavendish Corp.

Behnke, Alison. Afghanistan in Pictures. 2nd ed. 2003. (Visual Geography Series, Second Ser.). (ENG., Illus.). 80p. (gr. 5-12). 31.93 *(978-0-8225-4683-2(3))* Lerner Publishing Group.

Berlatsky, Noah. The Taliban. 2011. (Opposing Viewpoints Ser.). (ENG.). 224p. (gr. 12-12). pap. 33.80 *(978-0-7377-5240-3(8))*; lib. bdg. 48.80 *(978-0-7377-5239-7(4))* Cengage Gale. (Greenhaven Pr., Inc.).

Bjorklund, Ruth. Afghanistan. 2011. (Enchantment of the World Ser.). (ENG., Illus.). 144p. (J). (gr. 5-9). lib. bdg. 40.00 *(978-0-531-25350-2(3))* Scholastic Library Publishing.

Brownell, Richard. War in Afghanistan. 2011. (Hot Topics Ser.). (ENG., Illus.). 128p. (J). (gr. 7-10). lib. bdg. 39.40 *(978-1-4205-0554-2(8))* Cengage Gale.

Carlisle, Rodney P. Afghanistan War. 2010. (America at War Ser.). 958p. (gr. 6-12). 45.00 *(978-0-8160-8119-6(0)*, Chelsea Hse.) Facts On File, Inc.

Doeden, Matt & Hoena, Blake. War in Afghanistan: An Interactive Modern History Adventure, 1 vol. 2014. (You Choose: Modern History Ser.). (ENG.). 112p. (gr. 3-4). pap. 6.95 *(978-1-4765-5221-7(5))*; 31.99 *(978-1-4765-4190-7(6))* Capstone Press of Coughlan Cos. (You Choose Bks.).

Downing, David & Cavendish, Marshall. Afghanistan. 2008. (Global Hotspots Ser.). 32p. (gr. 5-18). lib. bdg. 18.56 *(978-0-7614-3177-0(2)*, Benchmark Bks.) Marshall Cavendish Corp.

Ellis, Deborah. Kids of Kabul: Living Bravely Through a Never-Ending War, 1 vol. 2012. (ENG., Illus.). 128p. (J). (gr. 6). 15.95 *(978-1-55498-181-6(6))* Groundwood Bks. CAN. Dist: Publishers Group West (PGW).

Fordyce, Deborah. Afghanistan. 2010. (Welcome to My Country Ser.). 48p. (gr. 3). 28.50 *(978-1-60870-149-0(2))* Marshall Cavendish Corp.

Fordyce, Deborah & Kazem, Halima. Welcome to Afghanistan. 2004. (Welcome to My Country Ser.). (Illus.). 48p. (gr. 2-5). lib. bdg. 27.00 *(978-0-8368-2557-2(8))* Stevens, Gareth Publishing LLLP.

Gaag, Nikki Van Der. Focus on Afghanistan. 2007. (World in Focus Ser.). (Illus.). 64p. (gr. 5-12). lib. bdg. 34.00 *(978-0-8368-6748-0(3)*, Gareth Stevens Secondary Library) Stevens, Gareth Publishing LLLP.

Gerber, Larry. The Taliban in Afghanistan. 2010. (In the News Ser.). (ENG.). 64p. (YA). pap. 12.95 *(978-1-4488-1677-4(7))*; (gr. 7-12). lib. bdg. 31.95 *(978-1-4358-9445-7(6))* Rosen Publishing Group, Inc., The.

Gerszak, Rafal. Beyond Bullets: A Photo Journal of Afganistan. 3rd ed. 2011. (ENG., Illus.). 128p. (J). (gr. 7-18). 19.95 *(978-1-55451-293-5(X)*, 9781554512935) Annick Pr., Ltd. CAN. Dist: Publishers Group West (PGW).

Glynne, Andy. Ali's Story: A Real-Life Account of His Journey from Afghanistan. 2017. (Seeking Refuge Ser.). (ENG.). 32p. (gr. 3-4). 27.32 ***(978-1-5158-1412-2(2))*** Picture Window Bks.

Greenhaven Press Editors & Gillard, Arthur, eds. The War in Afghanistan. 2013. (Issues That Concern You Ser.). (ENG., Illus.). 144p. (gr. 7-10). lib. bdg. 36.95 *(978-0-7377-6301-0(9))* Cengage Gale.

Gunderson, Cory Gideon. Afghanistan's Struggles. 2003. (World in Conflict (Edina, Minn.) Ser.). 32p. (gr. 4-8). 27.07 *(978-1-59197-410-9(0)*, Abdo & Daughters) ABDO Publishing Co.

Haskins, James & Benson, Kathleen. Count Your Way Through Afghanistan. Moore, Megan, illus. 2006. (Count Your Way Ser.). 40p. (J). (gr. -1-3). lib. bdg. 19.93 *(978-1-57505-880-1(4)*, Millbrook Pr.) Lerner Publishing Group.

Hatton, Thomas & George, Enzo. The Afghanistan & Iraq Wars: War Against Extremism. 2014. (Voices of War Ser.). 48p. (J). (gr. 4-6). lib. bdg. 31.36 *(978-1-62712-879-7(4))* Cavendish Square Publishing.

Hunter, Nick. Hoping for Peace in Afghanistan. 2012. (Peace Pen Pals Ser.). (Illus.). 48p. (J). (gr. 6-8). pap. 14.05 *(978-1-4339-7724-9(4))*; lib. bdg. 31.95 *(978-1-4339-7723-7(0))* Stevens, Gareth Publishing LLLP.

Jeffrey, Gary. The Soviet War in Afghanistan. Spender, Nik, illus. 2013. (ENG.). 48p. (J). *(978-0-7787-1235-0(4))*; pap. *(978-0-7787-1239-8(7))* Crabtree Publishing Co.

Juarez, Christine. Afghanistan, 1 vol. 2013. (Countries Ser.). (ENG.). 24p. (gr. k-1). 26.65 *(978-1-4765-3078-9(5)*, Pebble Plus); pap. 6.95 *(978-1-4765-3518-0(3)*, Pebble Bks.) Capstone Press of Coughlan Cos.

Kavanaugh, Dorothy. War in Afghanistan: Overthrow of the Taliban & Aftermath, Vol. 11. Musteen, Jason R., ed. 2015. (Major U. S. Historical Wars Ser.). (Illus.). 64p. (J). (gr. 7). lib. bdg. 23.95 *(978-1-4222-3360-3(X))* Mason Crest.

Kiesbye, Stefan. How Should the U. S. Proceed in Afghanistan? 2009. (At Issue Ser.). (ENG., Illus.). 128p. (gr. 10-12). 24.45 *(978-0-7377-4425-5(1))*; 39.40 *(978-0-7377-4424-8(3))* Cengage Gale. (Greenhaven Pr., Inc.).

Levete, Sarah. The Afghanistan War: Frontline Soldiers & Their Families. 2015. (Frontline Families Ser.). (ENG., Illus.). 48p. (J). (gr. 5-6). pap. 14.05 *(978-1-4824-3049-3(5))* Stevens, Gareth Publishing LLLP.

MacCarald, Clara. The War in Afghanistan: 12 Things to Know. 2017. (America at War Ser.). (ENG., Illus.). 32p. (J). (gr. 3-6). 21.95 *(978-1-63235-268-2(0))* Pr. Room Editions LLC.

Mason, Helen. A Refugee's Journey from Afghanistan. 2017. (Leaving My Homeland Ser.). (ENG., Illus.). 32p. (J). pap. ***(978-0-7787-3129-0(4))*** Crabtree Publishing Co.

Mattern, Joanne. Afghanistan. 2016. (Exploring World Cultures Ser.). 32p. (J). pap. 10.58 *(978-1-5026-2150-4(9))*; lib. bdg. 28.50 *(978-1-5026-2152-8(5))* Cavendish Square Publishing.

Milivojevic, Jovanka J. Afghanistan, 1 vol. 2011. (Countries Around the World Ser.). (ENG.). 48p. (gr. 3-6). pap. 9.95 *(978-1-4329-5220-4(X)*, NA-h) Heinemann-Raintree.

Miller, Raymond H. The War in Afghanistan. 2003. (American War Library). (ENG., Illus.). 112p. (J). 30.85 *(978-1-59018-331-1(2)*, Lucent Bks.) Cengage Gale.

Mortenson, Greg. Stones into Schools: Promoting Peace, One School at a Time. 2011. (ENG.). 240p. (J). (gr. 3-18). 16.99 *(978-0-8037-3687-0(8)*, Dial) Penguin Publishing Group.

Mortenson, Greg & Relin, David Oliver. Three Cups of Tea: One Man's Journey to Change the World... One Child at a Time. 2009. (ENG.). 240p. (J). (gr. 3-7). 8.99 *(978-0-14-241412-5(3)*, Puffin Books) Penguin Young Readers Group.

—Three Cups of Tea: One Man's Journey to Change the World... One Child at a Time. ed. 2009. lib. bdg. 19.65 *(978-0-606-07164-2(4)*, Turtleback) Turtleback Bks.

Mortenson, Greg, et al. Three Cups of Tea: One Man's Journey to Change the World... One Child at a Time. adapted ed. 2009. 10.36 *(978-0-7848-3360-5(5)*, Everbind) Marco Bk. Co.

Murray, Julie. Afghanistan, 1 vol. 2016. (Explore the Countries Set 3 Ser.). (ENG., Illus.). 40p. (J). (gr. 2-5). 29.93 *(978-1-68078-065-9(4))* ABDO Publishing Co.

Orr, Tamra. We Visit Afghanistan. 2011. (Your Land & My Land Ser.). (Illus.). 64p. (J). (gr. 4-7). lib. bdg. 33.95 *(978-1-58415-959-9(6))* Mitchell Lane Pubs., Inc.

Owings, Lisa. Afghanistan. 2011. (Exploring Countries Ser.). (ENG., Illus.). 32p. (J). (gr. 3-7). lib. bdg. 26.95 *(978-1-60014-590-2(6)*, Blastoff! Readers) Bellwether Media.

Piddock, Charles. Afghanistan. 2006. (Nations in the News Ser.). (Illus.). 48p. (gr. 5-12). pap. 14.05 *(978-0-8368-6713-8(0))*; lib. bdg. 31.00 *(978-0-8368-6706-0(8))* Stevens, Gareth Publishing LLLP. (Gareth Stevens Secondary Library).

Pohl, Kathleen. Looking at Afghanistan. 2008. (Looking at Countries Ser.). 32p. (gr. 1-5). (J). lib. bdg. 26.00 *(978-0-8368-9054-9(X))*; pap. 10.50 *(978-0-8368-9055-6(8))* Stevens, Gareth Publishing LLLP. (Gareth Stevens Learning Library).

Pohl, Kathleen & Nations, Susan. Descubramos Afganistán. 2008. (Descubramos países del mundo (Looking at Countries) Ser.). (SPA., Illus.). 32p. (J). (gr. 1-5). lib. bdg. 26.00 *(978-0-8368-9056-3(6)*, Gareth Stevens Learning Library) Stevens, Gareth Publishing LLLP.

Romano, Amy. A Historical Atlas of Afghanistan. 2009. (Historical Atlases of South Asia, Central Asia, & the Middle East Ser.). 64p. (gr. 6-6). 61.20 *(978-1-61513-315-4(1))* Rosen Publishing Group, Inc., The.

Roraback, Amanda. Afghanistan in a Nutshell. 2004. (Nutshell Notes). (Illus.). 60p. (YA). pap. 7.95 *(978-0-9702908-7-8(X))* Enisen Publishing.

Scherer, Lauri S. The Taliban. 2013. (Introducing Issues with Opposing Viewpoints Ser.). (ENG., Illus.). 144p. (gr. 7-10). lib. bdg. 42.00 *(978-0-7377-6283-9(7)*, Greenhaven Pr., Inc.) Cengage Gale.

Sheen, Barbara. Foods of Afghanistan. 2011. (Taste of Culture Ser.). 64p. (J). lib. bdg. 30.45 *(978-0-7377-5420-9(6)*, Kidhaven) Cengage Gale.

Shroder, John F., et al. Afghanistan. 3rd rev. ed. 2011. (Modern World Nations Ser.). (Illus.). 136p. (J). (gr. 6-12). 35.00 *(978-1-60413-941-9(2)*, Chelsea Hse.) Facts On File, Inc.

Spilsbury, Richard. Discover Afghanistan. 2012. (Discover Countries Ser.). (ENG., Illus.). 32p. (J). (gr. 3-5). pap. 10.60 *(978-1-4488-7044-8(5))*; lib. bdg. 26.50 *(978-1-4488-6619-9(7))* Rosen Publishing Group, Inc., The. (PowerKids Pr.).

Steele, Philip. Afghanistan: From War to Peace? 2012. (Our World Divided Ser.). (ENG., Illus.). 48p. (J). (gr. 5-8). 27.95 *(978-1-4488-6030-2(X)*, Rosen Reference) Rosen Publishing Group, Inc., The.

Taylor, Trace. Afghanistan. (1G Our World Ser.). 2016. (ENG., Illus.). 16p. (J). pap. 5.99 *(978-1-63437-474-3(6))* 2010. pap. 39.62 *(978-1-61541-135-1(6))* American Reading Co.

Taylor, Trace & Sánchez, Lucía M. Afghanistan. 2010. (1Y Nuestro Mundo Ser.). (SPA.). 16p. (J). (gr. k-1). pap. 6.99 *(978-1-61541-157-3(7))* American Reading Co.

Taylor, Trace & SáNchez, LucíA M. Afghanistan. 2010. pap. 39.62 *(978-1-61541-158-0(5))* American Reading Co.

Understanding Afghanistan Today. 2014. (Illus.). 64p. (gr. 3-6). 33.95 *(978-1-61228-652-5(6))* Mitchell Lane Pubs., Inc.

Wahab, Shaista & Youngerman, Barry. Afghanistan. 2nd ed. 2010. (Brief History Ser.). (Illus.). 368p. (C). (gr. 9). pap. 19.95 *(978-0-8160-8219-3(7)*, Checkmark Bks.); 49.50 *(978-0-8160-8218-6(9))* Facts On File, Inc.

Weber, Valerie J. I Come from Afghanistan. 2006. (This Is My Story Ser.). (Illus.). 24p. (gr. 1-4). pap. 8.15 *(978-0-8368-7240-8(1))*; lib. bdg. 22.00 *(978-0-8368-7233-0(9))* Stevens, Gareth Publishing LLLP. (Weekly Reader Leveled Readers).

Whitehead, Kim. Afghanistan. (Major Muslim Nations Ser.). 2010. 136p. (YA). (gr. 5-18). lib. bdg. 25.95 *(978-1-4222-1403-9(6))* 2008. (YA). pap. 14.95 *(978-1-4222-1433-6(8))* 2006. (Illus.). 128p. (YA). lib. bdg. 25.95 *(978-1-59084-833-3(0))* Vol. 13. 2015. (Illus.). 136p. (J). (gr. 7). lib. bdg. 25.95 *(978-1-4222-3439-6(8))* Mason Crest.

Whitfield, Susan & National Geographic Kids Staff. Afghanistan. 2008. (Countries of the World Ser.). (ENG., Illus.). 64p. (J). (gr. 5). lib. bdg. 27.90 *(978-1-4263-0256-5(8)*, National Geographic Children's Bks.) National Geographic Society.

Willis, Terri. Afghanistan. 2008. (Enchantment of the World Ser.). (ENG., Illus.). 144p. (J). (gr. 5-9). 39.00 *(978-0-531-18483-7(8))* Scholastic Library Publishing.

Winter, Jeanette. Nasreen's Secret School: A True Story from Afghanistan. Winter, Jeanette, illus. 2009. (ENG., Illus.). 40p. (J). (gr. 1-4). 17.99 *(978-1-4169-9437-4(8)*, Beach Lane Bks.) Beach Lane Bks.

Winter, Max. The Afghanistan War. 2015. (Wars in U. S. History Ser.). (ENG.). 32p. (J). (gr. 2-5). 28.50 *(978-1-63143-712-0(7)*, 208535) Child's World, Inc., The.

Wittekind, Erika. Afghanistan, 1 vol. 2013. (Countries of the World Set 2 Ser.). (ENG.). 144p. (J). (gr. 6-12). lib. bdg. 37.07 *(978-1-61783-625-1(7)*, Essential Library) ABDO Publishing Co.

Wolny, Philip. American Troops in Afghanistan: Building a New Nation. (Frontline Coverage of Current Events Ser.). 48p. 2009. (gr. 5-5). 53.00 *(978-1-61512-653-8(8))* 2004. (Illus.). (J). lib. bdg. 29.25 *(978-1-4042-0343-3(5))* Rosen Publishing Group, Inc., The.

—Hamid Karzai: President of Afghanistan. 2007. (Newsmakers Ser.). (Illus.). 112p. (YA). (gr. 7-12). lib. bdg. 34.60 *(978-1-4042-1902-1(1))* Rosen Publishing Group, Inc., The.

Zeiger, Jennifer. The War in Afghanistan. 2011. (Cornerstones of Freedom, Third Ser.). (Illus.). 64p. (J). (ENG.). pap. 8.95 *(978-0-531-26569-7(2))*; lib. bdg. 30.00 *(978-0-531-25044-0(X))* Scholastic Library Publishing. (Children's Pr.).

Zimmerman, W. Frederick. Cool Maps for Curious Kids #2: Afghanistan, an Unauthorized Tour of the Land of A THOUSAND SPLENDID SUNS & the KITE RUNNER. 2007. 36p. per. 17.81 *(978-1-934840-00-9(9))* Nimble Bks. LLC.

Zullo, Allan. Battle Heroes. 2014. (10 True Tales Ser.). (ENG.). 160p. (J). (gr. 3-7). pap. 5.99 *(978-0-545-81810-0(9)*, Scholastic Nonfiction) Scholastic, Inc.

AFGHANISTAN—FICTION

Abawi, Atia. The Secret Sky. 2015. (ENG.). 304p. (YA). (gr. 9). pap. 9.99 *(978-0-14-242406-3(4)*, Speak) Penguin Young Readers Group.

Avalon-Pai, Phyllis. Children's Stories from Around the World. Arrott, Nancy, illus. 2008. 70p. pap. 9.95 *(978-0-9788283-8-7(0))* Acacia Publishing, Inc.

Bowen, Carl & Fuentes, Benny. Long Shadow. Tortosa, Wilson, illus. 2015. (Shadow Squadron Ser.). (ENG.). 112p. (gr. 4-8). pap. 5.95 *(978-1-4965-0388-6(0))* Stone Arch Bks.

Brereton, Libby. The King & the Cobbler: A Tale from Afghanistan. Ginerva, Dante, illus. 2016. 24p. (J). pap. *(978-1-927244-63-0(3))* Flying Start Bks.

—The King & the Cobbler (Big Book Edition) A Tale from Afghanistan. Ginerva, Dante, illus. 2016. 24p. (J). pap. *(978-1-927244-73-9(0))* Flying Start Bks.

Clements, Andrew. Extra Credit. Elliott, Mark, illus. (ENG.). (J). (gr. 3-7). 2011. 224p. pap. 7.99 *(978-1-4169-4931-2(3))* 2009. 192p. 16.99 *(978-1-4169-4929-9(1))* Simon & Schuster Children's Publishing. (Atheneum Bks. for Young Readers).

Dando-Collins, Stephen. Caesar the War Dog - Operation Black Shark. 2016. (Caesar the War Dog Ser.: 5). (ENG.). 288p. (J). (gr. 4-6). pap. 11.99 *(978-0-85798-863-8(8))* Random Hse. Australia AUS. Dist: Independent Pubs. Group.

Deborah, Ellis. The Breadwinner. 2014. (ENG.). 176p. (J). 13.20 *(978-1-63245-145-3(X))* Lectorum Pubns., Inc.

Doller, Trish. Something Like Normal. (ENG.). (YA). (gr. 9). 2013. 240p. pap. 9.99 *(978-1-61963-146-5(6)*, 9781619631465) 2012. 224p. 16.99 *(978-1-59990-844-1(1)*, 9781599908441) Bloomsbury Publishing USA. (Bloomsbury USA Childrens).

Edison-Clark, Gina. I Just Want My Daddy! Newkirk, Errol Q., illus. 2008. 13p. pap. 24.95 *(978-1-60672-026-4(0))* America Star Bks.

Ellis, Deborah. The Breadwinner. unabr. ed. 2004. 170p. (J). (gr. 5-7). pap. 29.00 incl. audio *(978-0-8072-0982-0(1)*, S YA 411 SP, Listening Library) Random Hse. Audio Publishing Group.

—The Breadwinner. 2013. 164p. pap. *(978-1-4596-6483-8(3))* ReadHowYouWant.com, Ltd.

—Mud City, 1 vol. 2015. (Breadwinner Ser.). (ENG., Illus.). 168p. (J). (gr. 4-9). pap. 9.95 *(978-1-55498-773-3(3))* Groundwood Bks. CAN. Dist: Publishers Group West (PGW).

—Mud City. 2013. 156p. pap. *(978-1-4596-6445-6(0))* ReadHowYouWant.com, Ltd.

—Parvana's Journey, 1 vol. 2015. (Breadwinner Ser.). (ENG., Illus.). 200p. (J). (gr. 4-9). pap. 9.95 *(978-1-55498-770-2(9))* Groundwood Bks. CAN. Dist: Publishers Group West (PGW).

—Parvana's Journey. 2013. 184p. pap. *(978-1-4596-6476-0(0))* ReadHowYouWant.com, Ltd.

Eulate, Ana. The Sky of Afghanistan. 2012. (ENG., Illus.). 24p. (J). (gr. k-2). *(978-84-15503-04-0(0))* D P & G Military Pubs.

Hashimi, Nadia. One Half from the East. 2016. 272p. (J). (gr. 3-7). 16.99 *(978-0-06-242190-6(5))* HarperCollins Pubs.

Henty, George Alfred. For Name & Fame: Or Through Afghan Passes. 2007. (ENG.). 240p. per. 20.99 *(978-1-4346-4487-9(1))*; 264p. per. 23.99 *(978-1-4346-4488-6(X))* Creative Media Partners, LLC.

Khan, Rukhsana. Wanting Mor, 1 vol. 2010. (ENG.). 192p. (J). (gr. 4-9). pap. 9.95 *(978-0-88899-862-0(7))* Groundwood Bks. CAN. Dist: Publishers Group West (PGW).

King, Dedie. I See the Sun in Afghanistan. Vahidi, Mohd, tr. Inglese, Judith, illus. 2011. (I See the Sun In ... Ser.: 0). (PER & ENG.). 40p. (J). (gr. k). pap. 12.95 *(978-0-9818720-8-7(5))* Satya Hse. Pubns.

Liddiment, Carol, illus. The Wooden Sword: A Jewish Folktale from Afghanistan. 2012. (ENG.). 32p. (J). (gr. k-3). 16.99 *(978-0-8075-9201-4(3))* Whitman, Albert & Co.

London, C. Alexander. Semper Fido. 2013. (Dog Tags Ser.: 1). (ENG.). 224p. (J). (gr. 5-9). pap. 5.99 *(978-0-545-47704-8(2))* Scholastic, Inc.

Maddox, Jake. Snowboard Hero. 2015. (Jake Maddox JV Ser.). (ENG.). 96p. (gr. 3-4). lib. bdg. 25.99 *(978-1-4342-9636-8(9))* Stone Arch Bks.

Manning, Matthew K. U. S. Special Forces: Ghosts of the Night. Enecio, Jeremy, illus. 2016. (U. S. Special Ops Ser.). (ENG.). 96p. (gr. 3-4). lib. bdg. 26.65 *(978-1-4965-3475-0(1)*, Connect) Stone Arch Bks.

Massey, David. Torn. 2013. (ENG.). 288p. (J). (gr. 9). 17.99 *(978-0-545-49645-2(4))* Scholastic, Inc.

McKay, Sharon E. Thunder over Kandahar. Gerszak, Rafal, photos by. 2010. (ENG., Illus.). 264p. (YA). (gr. 7-12). 19.95 *(978-1-55451-267-6(0)*, 9781554512676); 3rd ed. pap. 12.95 *(978-1-55451-266-9(2)*, 9781554512669) Annick Pr., Ltd. CAN. Dist: Publishers Group West (PGW).

Morpurgo, Michael. Shadow. 2012. (ENG.). 192p. (J). (gr. 5-9). 16.99 *(978-0-312-60659-6(1)*, 9780312606596) Feiwel & Friends.

—Shadow. 2014. (ENG.). 208p. (J). (gr. 5-9). pap. 6.99 *(978-1-250-03996-5(7)*, 9781250039965) Square Fish.

Phillips, Dee. Eject, 1 vol. 2014. (Right Now! Ser.). (ENG.). 48p. (YA). (gr. 9-12). pap. 8.95 *(978-1-62250-881-5(5))* Saddleback Educational Publishing, Inc.

Reedy, Trent. Words in the Dust. (ENG.). 272p. (J). 2013. (gr. 5-9). pap. 6.99 *(978-0-545-26126-5(0))* 2011. (gr. 4-7). 17.99 *(978-0-545-26125-8(2))* Scholastic, Inc. (Levine, Arthur A. Bks.).

Sherman, M. Zachary. Control under Fire, 1 vol. Casas, Fritz, illus. 2011. (Bloodlines Ser.). (ENG.). 88p. (gr. 4-8). pap. 6.95 *(978-1-4342-3100-0(3))*; lib. bdg. 26.65 *(978-1-4342-2561-0(5))* Stone Arch Bks.

Smith, Roland. The Edge. 2015. (Peak Marcello Adventure Ser.). (ENG.). 240p. (YA). (gr. 7). 17.99 *(978-0-544-34122-7(8)*, HMH Books For Young Readers) Houghton Mifflin Harcourt Publishing Co.

—The Edge. 2016. (Peak Marcello Adventure Ser.). (ENG.). 240p. (YA). (gr. 7). pap. 7.99 *(978-0-544-81354-0(5)*, HMH Books For Young Readers) Houghton Mifflin Harcourt Publishing Co.

Staples, Suzanne Fisher. Under the Persimmon Tree. 2008. (Illus.). 281p. (gr. 7-12). 20.00 *(978-0-7569-9004-6(1))* Perfection Learning Corp.

—Under the Persimmon Tree. 2008. (ENG., Illus.). 304p. (YA). (gr. 7-12). pap. 9.99 *(978-0-312-37776-2(2)*, 9780312377762) Square Fish.

Suneby, Elizabeth. Razia's Ray of Hope: One Girl's Dream of an Education. Verelst, Suana, illus. 2013. (CitizenKid Ser.). (ENG.). 32p. (J). (gr. 3-7). 18.95 *(978-1-55453-816-4(5))* Kids Can Pr., Ltd. CAN. Dist: Hachette Bk. Group.

AFRICA

Africa: Progress & Problems, 13 vols., Set. Incl. AIDS & Health Issues. Gelletly, LeeAnne. 126p. (YA). (gr. -1-3). 2008. lib. bdg. 24.95 *(978-1-59084-954-5(X))*; Governance & Leadership in Africa. Rotberg, Robert I. 112p. (J). (gr. 7-18). 2006. lib. bdg. 24.95 *(978-1-59084-957-6(4))*; Helping Africa Help Itself: A Global Effort. Shah, Anup. 124p. (YA). (gr. 7-18). 2008. lib. bdg. 24.95 *(978-1-59084-923-1(X))*; Population & Overcrowding. Obadina, Tunde. 110p. (YA). (gr. 7-18). 2008. lib. bdg. 24.95 *(978-1-59084-997-2(3))*; (Illus.). 2006. Set lib. bdg. 324.35 *(978-1-59084-952-1(3))* Mason Crest.

Altman, Linda Jacobs. African Mythology Rocks! Bock, William Sauts, illus. 2011. (Mythology Rocks! Ser.). 112p. (J). (gr. 6-18). pap. 10.95 *(978-1-59845-328-7(9))* Enslow Pubs., Inc.

Aspen-Baxter, Linda. Africa. 2006. (Continents Ser.). (Illus.). 32p. (J). (gr. 4-6). lib. bdg. 26.00 *(978-1-59036-316-4(7))* Weigl Pubs., Inc.

AZ Books Staff. Visiting Africa. Zuk, Valentina, ed. 2012. (Lively Pictures Ser.). (ENG.). 10p. (J). (gr. -1-k). bds. 9.95 *(978-1-61889-179-2(0))* AZ Bks. LLC.

Barker, Geoff & Marshall Cavendish Corporation Staff. Sudan. 2008. (Global Hotspots Ser.). 32p. (gr. 5-18). lib. bdg. 18.56 *(978-0-7614-3182-4(9)*, Benchmark Bks.) Marshall Cavendish Corp.

Baughan, Brian. Human Rights in Africa. Ojakorotu, Victor & Rotberg, Robert I., eds. 2013. (Africa: Progress & Problems Ser.: 13). (Illus.). 112p. (J). (gr. 7-18). 24.95 *(978-1-4222-2942-2(4))* Mason Crest.

Benchmark Education Co., LLC. The Geography of Africa. 2014. (PRIME Ser.). (J). (gr. 6-8). pap. *(978-1-4509-9503-0(9))* Benchmark Education Co.

Borgert-Spaniol, Megan. Cape Buffalo. 2014. (Animal Safari Ser.). (ENG.). 24p. (J). (gr. k-3). lib. bdg. 25.95 *(978-1-60014-965-8(0)*, Blastoff! Readers) Bellwether Media.

Bowden, Rob. Africa. 2005. (Continents of the World Ser.). (Illus.). 64p. (gr. 5-12). lib. bdg. 34.00 *(978-0-8368-5910-2(3)*, Gareth Stevens Secondary Library) Stevens, Gareth Publishing LLLP.

Brennan, Kristine. Burundi. Rotberg, Robert I., ed. 2012. (Evolution of Africa's Major Nations Ser.). (Illus.). 80p. (J). (gr. 7). 22.95 *(978-1-4222-2177-8(6))* Mason Crest.

—Burundi. 2011. (J). pap. *(978-1-4222-2205-8(5))* Mason Crest.

Brown, Don. Uncommon Traveler: Mary Kingsley in Africa. 2003. (ENG., Illus.). 32p. (J). (gr. -1-3). 7.99 *(978-0-618-36916-4(3))* Houghton Mifflin Harcourt Publishing Co.

Chanek, Sherilin & National Geographic Learning Staff. Africa - Geography & Environments. 2007. (Reading Expeditions Ser.). (ENG., Illus.). 64p. (J). pap. 25.95 *(978-0-7922-4364-9(1))* CENGAGE Learning.

Chapman, Simon. On Safari. Chapman, Simon, illus. 2005. (Illus.). 111p. (J). lib. bdg. 20.00 *(978-1-4242-0633-9(2))* Fitzgerald Bks.

Croze, Harvey. Africa for Kids: Exploring a Vibrant Continent - 19 Activities. 2006. (For Kids Ser.). (ENG., Illus.). 144p. (J). (gr. 4-7). 19.99 *(978-1-55652-598-8(2))* Chicago Review Pr., Inc.

Darmani, L. Stories from Africa, Vol. 3. 2003. (Illus.). 48p. pap. *(978-9964-87-854-2(0))* African Christian Pr. GHA. Dist: Michigan State Univ. Pr.

De Villiers, Les. Africa 2004. 4th ed. 2004. (Illus.). 400p. pap. 28.95 *(978-0-916673-13-0(8))* Business Bks. International.

Diaw, Boris. Hoops to Hippos! True Stories of a Basketball Star on Safari! 2015. (NGK Chapters Ser.). (ENG., Illus.). 112p. (J). (gr. 2-5). pap. 5.99 *(978-1-4263-2052-1(3)*, National Geographic Children's Bks.) National Geographic Society.

Diaz, Joanne Ruelos. Animals on the African Savanna, 1 vol. Mendez, Simon, illus. 2014. (Animals All Day! Ser.). (ENG.). 32p. (gr. k-2). 27.27 *(978-1-4795-5701-1(3))* Picture Window Bks.

DiPiazza, Francesca Davis. Sudan in Pictures. 2006. (Visual Geography Ser.). (Illus.). 80p. (YA). (gr. 7-12). lib. bdg. 27.93 *(978-0-8225-2678-0(6))* Lerner Publishing Group.

Donaldson, Madeline. Africa. 2005. (Pull Ahead Bks.). (Illus.). 32p. (gr. k-3). (J). lib. bdg. 22.60 *(978-0-8225-4720-4(1))*; (ENG., pap. 7.95 *(978-0-8225-2489-2(9))* Lerner Publishing Group.

Ellis, Gerry & Novesky, Amy. Natumi Takes the Lead: The True Story of an Orphan Elephant Who Finds Family. 2016. (ENG., Illus.). 32p. (J). (gr. -1-3). 16.99 *(978-1-4263-2561-8(4))*; lib. bdg. 26.90 *(978-1-4263-2562-5(2))* National Geographic Society. (National Geographic Children's Bks.).

Encyclopaedia Britannica, Inc. Staff, compiled by. My First Britannica: Africa. 2008. (gr. 7-12). *(978-1-59339-408-0(X))* Encyclopaedia Britannica, Inc.

—Views of Africa. 2003. (Illus.). 64p. 14.95 *(978-1-59339-042-6(4))* Encyclopaedia Britannica, Inc.

Encyclopaedia Britannica Publishers, Inc. Staff. Views of Africa. 2003. (Britannica Learning Library). (Illus.). 14.95 *(978-1-59339-011-2(4))* Encyclopaedia Britannica, Inc.

Friedenthal, Lora & Kavanaugh, Dorothy. Religions of Africa. Ojakorotu, Victor & Rotberg, Robert I., eds. 2013. (Africa: Progress & Problems Ser.: 13). (Illus.). 112p. (J). (gr. 7-18). 24.95 *(978-1-4222-2947-7(5))* Mason Crest.

Friedman, Mel. Africa. 2009. (True Bks.). (ENG.). 48p. (J). pap. 6.95 *(978-0-531-21825-9(2)*, Children's Pr.) Scholastic Library Publishing.

Gelletly, LeeAnne. Ecological Issues. Ojakorotu, Victor & Rotberg, Robert I., eds. 2013. (Africa: Progress & Problems Ser.: 13). (Illus.). 112p. (J). (gr. 7-18). 24.95 *(978-1-4222-2937-8(8))* Mason Crest.

—Somalia. 2010. (Major Muslim Nations Ser.). (Illus.). 112p. (YA). (gr. 5-18). lib. bdg. 25.95 *(978-1-4222-1395-7(1))* Mason Crest.

Gibbs, Maddie. African Buffalo. 2011. (Safari Animals Ser.). (Illus.). 24p. (J). 22.60 *(978-1-4488-2508-0(3))*; pap. 8.25 *(978-1-4488-2604-9(7))* Rosen Publishing Group, Inc., The. (PowerKids Pr.).

—Antelope / Antílopes. 2011. (Safari Animals / Animales de Safari Ser.). (ENG & SPA., Illus.). 24p. (J). (gr. -1-2). 22.60 *(978-1-4488-3122-7(9))* Rosen Publishing Group, Inc., The.

—Flamingos. 2011. (Safari Animals Ser.). (Illus.). 24p. (J). 22.60 *(978-1-4488-3184-5(9))*; pap. 8.25 *(978-1-4488-3185-2(7))* Rosen Publishing Group, Inc., The. (PowerKids Pr.).

Glencoe McGraw-Hill Staff, creator. Exploring Our World - Eastern Hemisphere: People, Places, & Cultures. 2nd ed. 2007. (WORLD & ITS PEOPLE EASTERN Ser.). (ENG., Illus.). 766p. (gr. 6-8). lib. bdg., stu. ed. 98.00 *(978-0-07-874578-2(0*, 0078745780) McGraw-Hill Education.

Haas, Robert B. African Critters. 2008. (ENG., Illus.). 96p. (J). (gr. 1-4). lib. bdg. 26.90 *(978-1-4263-0318-0(1)*, National Geographic Children's Bks.) National Geographic Society.

Haas, Robert B. & National Geographic Kids Staff. African Critters. 2008. (ENG., Illus.). 96p. (J). (gr. 1-4). 17.95 *(978-1-4263-0317-3(3)*, National Geographic Children's Bks.) National Geographic Society.

Hall, Derek. Africa. 2008. (Facts at Your Fingertips Ser.). (Illus.). 64p. (YA). (gr. 7-12). lib. bdg. 34.25 *(978-1-933834-08-5(0))* Brown Bear Bks.

Harmon, Daniel E. Algeria. 2012. (J). pap. *(978-1-4222-2219-5(5))* Mason Crest.

—Algeria. Rotberg, Robert I., ed. 2012. (Evolution of Africa's Major Nations Ser.). (Illus.). 80p. (J). (gr. 7). 22.95 *(978-1-4222-2191-4(1))* Mason Crest.

Hassig, Susan M. & Latif, Zawiah Abdul. Somalia. 2nd rev. ed. 2007. (Cultures of the World Ser.). 144p. (gr. 6). lib. bdg. 42.79 *(978-0-7614-2082-8(7)*, Benchmark Bks.) Marshall Cavendish Corp.

Hovanec, Erin M. An Online Visit to Africa. 2009. (Internet Field Trips Ser.). 24p. (gr. 3-3). 45.00 *(978-1-61513-601-8(0)*, PowerKids Pr.) Rosen Publishing Group, Inc., The.

Hunkins, Boehm Armstrong & McGraw-Hill Education Editors. Exploring Our World: People, Places, & Cultures. 2007. (WORLD & ITS PEOPLE EASTERN Ser.). (ENG., Illus.). 95p. (gr. 6-9). pap. 6.48 *(978-0-07-877743-1(7)*, 0078777437) McGraw-Hill Higher Education.

Joubert, Beverly & Joubert, Dereck. African Animal Alphabet. 2011. (ENG., Illus.). 48p. (J). (gr. -1-k). 26.90 *(978-1-4263-0782-9(9)*, National Geographic Children's Bks.) National Geographic Society.

Kalman, Bobbie & Sjonger, Rebecca. Explore Africa. 2007. (Explore the Continents Ser.). (ENG., Illus.). 32p. (J). (gr. 3-7). lib. bdg. *(978-0-7787-3070-5(0))*; (gr. 1-5). pap. *(978-0-7787-3084-2(0))* Crabtree Publishing Co.

Kneib, Martha. Benin. 2007. (Cultures of the World Ser.). (Illus.). 144p. (J). (gr. 3-7). lib. bdg. 39.93 *(978-0-7614-2328-7(1)*, Benchmark Bks.) Marshall Cavendish Corp.

Koopmans, Andy. Rwanda. Rotberg, Robert I., ed. 2012. (Evolution of Africa's Major Nations Ser.). (Illus.). 88p. (J). (gr. 7). 22.95 *(978-1-4222-2183-9(0))* Mason Crest.

—Rwanda. 2011. (J). pap. *(978-1-4222-2211-9(X))* Mason Crest.

Kushner, Jill Menkes. Who on Earth Is Dian Fossey? Defender of the Mountain Gorillas. 2009. (Scientists Saving the Earth Ser.). (Illus.). 112p. (J). (gr. 5-9). lib. bdg. 33.27 *(978-1-59845-117-7(0))* Enslow Pubs., Inc.

Lawrence, Ellen. Time to Play. 2015. (My World Your World Ser.). (ENG.). 24p. (J). (gr. -1-3). lib. bdg. 23.93 *(978-1-910549-06-3(1))* Bearport Publishing Co., Inc.

Lee, Justin. How to Draw African Animals. 2009. (Kid's Guide to Drawing Ser.). 24p. (gr. 3-3). 47.90 *(978-1-61511-008-7(9)*, PowerKids Pr.) Rosen Publishing Group, Inc., The.

Levy, Patricia & Latif, Zawiah Abdul. Sudan. 2nd rev. ed. 2007. (Cultures of the World Ser.). 144p. (gr. 6). lib. bdg. 42.79 *(978-0-7614-2083-5(5)*, Benchmark Bks.) Marshall Cavendish Corp.

Marsh, Carole. Africa: A Safari Through Its Amazing Nations! 2009. (It's Your World Ser.). 48p. (J). (gr. 2-9). pap. 7.99 *(978-0-635-06814-9(1))* Gallopade International.

McGraw-Hill Education Editors. Exploring Our World: People, Places, & Cultures - Eastern Hemisphere. 2007. (WORLD & ITS PEOPLE EASTERN Ser.). (ENG., Illus.). 192p. (gr. 6-8). per. 23.20 *(978-0-07-878166-7(3)*, 0078781663) McGraw-Hill Education.

McGraw-Hill Staff. Exploring Our World, Eastern Hemisphere, Interactive Tutor Self Assessment. 2007. (WORLD & ITS PEOPLE EASTERN Ser.). (ENG.). (gr. 6-8). cd-rom 104.00 *(978-0-07-879098-0(0)*, 0078790980) McGraw-Hill Education.

McNeil, Niki, et al. Africa. 2007. (In the Hands of a Child: Project Pack Continent Study Ser.). (Illus.). 116p. spiral bd. 24.00 *(978-1-60308-052-1(X))* In the Hands of a Child.

Montgomery, Sy. Chasing Cheetahs: The Race to Save Africa's Fastest Cats. Bishop, Nic, illus. Bishop, Nic, photos by. 2014. (Scientists in the Field Ser.). (ENG.). 80p. (J). (gr. 5-7). 18.99 *(978-0-547-81549-7(2)*, HMH Books For Young Readers) Houghton Mifflin Harcourt Publishing Co.

NgCheong-Lum, Roseline. Eritrea. 2nd rev. ed. 2010. (Cultures of the World 22 Ser.). 144p. (gr. 6). 42.79 *(978-1-60870-454-5(8))* Marshall Cavendish Corp.

Obadina, Elizabeth. Ethnic Groups in Africa. Ojakorotu, Victor & Rotberg, Robert I., eds. 2013. (Africa: Progress & Problems Ser.: 13). (Illus.). 112p. (J). (gr. 7-18). 24.95 *(978-1-4222-2939-2(4))* Mason Crest.

Oelschlager, Vanita. Bonyo Bonyo. Blackwood, Kristin & Blanc, Mike, illus. 2010. (ENG.). 42p. (J). (gr. -1-3). pap. 8.95 *(978-0-9819714-5-X))*; 15.95 *(978-0-9819714-3-8(1))* VanitaBooks.

Oppong, Joseph R. Rwanda. 2008. (Modern World Nations Ser.). 120p. (gr. 6-12). 35.00 *(978-0-7910-9669-7(6)*, Chelsea Hse.) Facts On File, Inc.

Oxlade, Chris. Introducing Africa, 1 vol. 2013. (Introducing Continents Ser.). (ENG.). 32p. (gr. 1-3). 27.32 *(978-1-4329-8038-2(6))*; pap. 8.95 *(978-1-4329-8046-7(7))* Heinemann-Raintree. (Heinemann First Library).

Prebeg, Rick. Into the Jungle. Prebeg, Rick, photos by. 2005. (Illus.). (J). *(978-1-933248-05-9(X))* World Quest Learning.

Putumayo Kids Staff, creator. African Sticker Collection. 2010. (J). 11.95 *(978-1-58759-273-7(8))* Putumayo World Music & Crafts.

Rappoport, Bernice. Habitats of Africa: Set Of 6. 2011. (Navigators Ser.). (J). pap. 44.00 net. *(978-1-4108-5074-4(9))* Benchmark Education Co.

Rice, William B. African Grasslands, 1 vol. 2nd rev. ed. 2012. (Nonfiction Readers Ser.). (ENG.). 32p. (J). (gr. 3-3). pap. 8.99 *(978-1-4333-3670-6(7))* Teacher Created Materials, Inc.

Rotberg, Robert I., ed. Africa: Continent in the Balance 2, 13 vols., Set. Incl. African Union. Roberts, Russell. 80p. lib. bdg. 21.95 *(978-1-4222-0093-3(0))*; Botswana. Wittman, Kelly. 79p. lib. bdg. 21.95 *(978-1-4222-0087-2(6))*; Liberia. Baughan, Brian. 87p. lib. bdg. 21.95 *(978-1-4222-0088-9(4))*; Libya. Hasday, Judy L. 79p. lib. bdg. 21.95 *(978-1-4222-0083-4(3))*; Sierra Leone. Hasday, Judy L. 79p. lib. bdg. 21.95 *(978-1-4222-0092-6(2))*; (Illus.). (YA). (gr. 3-7). 2009. 2007. Set lib. bdg. 285.35 *(978-1-4222-0080-3(9))* Mason Crest.

Rustad, Martha E. H. On a Safari 5, 10, 15: A Counting by Fives Book. 2016. (1, 2, 3 Count with Me Ser.). (ENG., Illus.). 24p. (J). (gr. k-3). 20.95 *(978-1-60753-922-3(5))* Amicus Publishing.

Sayre, April Pulley. Good Morning, Africa! 2003. 32p. (J). (gr. 2-5). pap. 7.95 *(978-0-7613-1993-1(X))*; (Celebrate the Continents Ser.: 4). (Illus.). lib. bdg. 21.90 *(978-0-7613-2121-7(7))* Lerner Publishing Group. (Millbrook Pr.).

Schaefer, A. R. Spotlight on Africa, 1 vol. 2010. (Spotlight on the Continents Ser.). (ENG.). 24p. (gr. 1-2). lib. bdg. 25.32 *(978-1-4296-6624-4(2)*, First Facts) Capstone Press of Coughlan Cos.

Snyder, Gail. Sudan. rev. ed. 2010. (Major Muslim Nations Ser.). 112p. (YA). (gr. 4-8). 25.95 *(978-1-4222-1394-0(3))* Mason Crest.

Sol & K'naan. When I Get Older: The Story Behind Wavin' Flag. Gutierrez, Rudy, illus. 2012. (ENG.). 1p. (J). (gr. 1-4). 17.95 *(978-1-77049-302-5(6)*, Tundra Bks.) Tundra Bks. CAN. Dist: Penguin Random Hse. LLC.

Somervill, Barbara A. Niger. 2016. (Enchantment of the World(tm) Ser.). (ENG., Illus.). 144p. (J). lib. bdg. 40.00 *(978-0-531-21883-9(X)*, Children's Pr.) Scholastic Library Publishing.

Spilsbury, Richard & Spilsbury, Louise. Animals in Danger in Africa, 1 vol. 2013. (Animals in Danger Ser.). (ENG.). 32p. (gr. 1-3). 27.32 *(978-1-4329-7672-9(9))*; pap. 8.95 *(978-1-4329-7679-8(6))* Heinemann-Raintree. (Heinemann First Library).

St. John, Warren. Outcasts United: The Story of a Refugee Soccer Team That Changed a Town. 2013. (ENG.). 240p. (YA). (gr. 7). pap. 9.99 *(978-0-385-74195-8(2)*, Ember) Random Hse. Children's Bks.

Staeger, Rob. Angola. 2012. (J). pap. *(978-1-4222-2220-1(9))* Mason Crest.

—Angola. Rotberg, Robert I., ed. 2012. (Evolution of Africa's Major Nations Ser.). (Illus.). 88p. (J). (gr. 7). 22.95 *(978-1-4222-2192-1(X))* Mason Crest.

Steele, Philip. Sudan, Darfur & the Nomadic Conflicts. 2012. (Our World Divided Ser.). (ENG., Illus.). 48p. (J). (gr. 5-8). 27.95 *(978-1-4488-6028-9(8)*, Rosen Reference) Rosen Publishing Group, Inc., The.

Taylor, Jacqui. African ABC. 2005. (ENG., Illus.). 96p. 14.95 *(978-1-86872-703-2(3))* Penguin Random House Grupo Editorial ESP. Dist: Casemate Pubs. & Bk. Distributors, LLC.

Thomas, Isabel. City Safari, 1 vol. 2014. (City Safari Ser.). (ENG.). 24p. (gr. 1-1). lib. bdg. 139.92 *(978-1-4329-8812-8(3)*, Heinemann Read & Learn) Heinemann-Raintree.

Tuchman, Gail. Safari. 2015. (National Geographic Readers: Pre-Reader Ser.). (ENG.). (gr. -1-k). 19.95 *(978-1-4301-1889-3(X))* Live Oak Media.

Vierow, Wendy. Africa. (Atlas of the Seven Continents Ser.). 24p. (gr. 3-3). 2009. 42.50 *(978-1-61511-476-4(9)*, PowerKids Pr.) 2004. (Illus.). (YA). lib. bdg. 22.60 *(978-0-8239-6687-5(9))* Rosen Publishing Group, Inc., The.

Walden, Katherine. Leopards of the African Plains. 2009. (Safari Animals Ser.). (Illus.). 24p. (J). (gr. k-3). pap. 8.25 *(978-1-4358-3064-6(4))*; 24p. (gr. 1-1). 42.50 *(978-1-60852-953-7(3))*; (J). lib. bdg. 22.60 *(978-1-4358-2690-8(6))* Rosen Publishing Group, Inc., The. (PowerKids Pr.).

Walters, Eric. An African Alphabet, 1 vol. Todd, Sue, illus. 2017. (ENG.). 28p. (J). (gr. -1-k). bds. 9.95 *(978-1-4598-1070-9(8))* Orca Bk. Pubs. USA.

Watson, Galadriel Findlay. The Bushmen of South Africa. 2005. (Indigenous Peoples Ser.). 32p. pap. 9.95 *(978-1-59036-254-9(3))* Weigl Pubs., Inc.

Weintraub, Aileen. Discovering Africa's Land, People, & Wildlife: A MyReportLinks. com Book. 2004. (Continents of the World Ser.). (Illus.). 48p. (J). lib. bdg. 25.26 *(978-0-7660-5204-8(4)*, MyReportLinks.com Bks.) Enslow Pubs., Inc.

World Book, Inc Staff, contrib. by. Wild Animals. 2007. (J). *(978-0-7166-7733-8(4))* World Bk., Inc.

AFRICA—ANTIQUITIES

Howell, Izzi. Benin. 2017. (Explore! Ser.). (ENG., Illus.). 32p. (J). (gr. 4-6). 16.99 *(978-1-5263-0084-3(2)*, Wayland) Hachette Children's Group GBR. Dist: Hachette Bk. Group.

Pacchini, Fiorenzo. A Day with Homo Habilis: Life 2,000,000 Years Ago. 2003. (Early Humans Ser.). (Illus.). 48p. (gr. 6-18). lib. bdg. 23.90 *(978-0-7613-2765-3(7)*, Twenty-First Century Bks.) Lerner Publishing Group.

AFRICA—BIOGRAPHY

Abella, Tomas. E de Escuela. 2005. (SPA.). 26p. (J). (gr. 2-7). 18.95 *(978-84-89970-69-4(6))* Fundacion Intermon ESP. Dist: Iaconi, Mariuccia Bk. Imports.

Anumbor, Justina U. The African Girl: African Folklores. 2013. 138p. (gr. 10-12). 28.95 *(978-1-4497-8807-0(6)*, WestBow Pr.) Author Solutions, Inc.

Briscoe, Diana. Jane Goodall Set: Finding Hope in the Wilds of Africa, 6 vols. 2004. (High Five Reading - Purple Ser.). (ENG.). 64p. (gr. 3-4). pap. 54.00 *(978-0-7368-3869-6(4)*, High Five Reading (RBL)) Capstone Press of Coughlan Cos.

Collin, Grace. Man of Destiny: The Life of Leopold Sedar Senghor. Bostic, Alex, illus. 2006. 32p. (J). lib. bdg. 16.95 *(978-1-886366-15-2(2))* Sights Productions.

A
B

Cooke, Tim. The Exploration of Africa. 2013. (Explorers Discovering the World Ser.). (Illus.). 48p. (J). (gr. 4-6). pap. 14.05 *(978-1-4339-8612-3(4))*; lib. bdg. 31.95 *(978-1-4339-8611-6(6))* Stevens, Gareth Publishing LLLP.

Dau, John Bul. Lost Boy Lost Girl: Escaping Civil War in Sudan. 2010. (ENG., Illus.). 160p. (YA). (gr. 7-18). 23.90 *(978-1-4263-0709-6(8))*, National Geographic Children's Bks.) National Geographic Society.

Dau, John Bul & Akech, Martha Arual. Lost Boy, Lost Girl: Escaping Civil War in Sudan. 2010. (ENG., Illus.). 160p. (YA). (gr. 7-18). 15.95 *(978-1-4263-0708-9(X))*, National Geographic Children's Bks.) National Geographic Society.

Doeden, Matt. SpaceX & Tesla Motors Engineer Elon Musk. 2015. (STEM Trailblazer Bios Ser.). (ENG., Illus.). 32p. (J). (gr. 2-5). lib. bdg. 26.60 *(978-1-4677-5791-1(8))*, Lerner Pubns.) Lerner Publishing Group.

Dougherty, Steve. Idi Amin. 2010. (Wicked History Ser.). 128p. (J). (gr. 6-12). pap. 5.95 *(978-0-531-22354-3(X))*, Watts, Franklin) Scholastic Library Publishing.

Dougherty, Steven. Idi Amin. 2010. (Wicked History Ser.). (ENG., Illus.). 128p. (J). (gr. 5-8). 31.00 *(978-0-531-20754-3(4))* Scholastic Library Publishing.

Green, Richard L. A Salute to Historic African Kings & Queens. 2011. (Empak "Black History" Publication Ser.: Vol. 6). (J). *(978-0-9616156-5-9(6))* Empak Publishing Co.

Greenhaven Press Staff, ed. Muammar El-Qaddafi. 2012. (People in the News Ser.). (ENG., Illus.). 128p. (J). (gr. 7-10). lib. bdg. 33.95 *(978-1-4205-0759-1(1))*, Lucent Bks.) Cengage Gale.

Havemeyer, Janie. Njinga the Warrior Queen. Malone, Peter, illus. 2011. (Thinking Girl's Treasury of Dastardly Dames Ser.). (ENG.). 32p. (J). (gr. 3-8). 18.95 *(978-0-9834256-6-3(3))* Goosebottom Bks. LLC.

Jal, David. David's Journey: The Story of David Jal, One of the Lost Boys of Sudan. Bezesky, Tracy, illus. 2012. 32p. 20.00 *(978-1-934478-30-1(X))* Sunray Publishing.

Kamkwamba, William. The Boy Who Harnessed the Wind: Creating Currents of Electricity & Hope. 2009. 14.44 *(978-0-7848-3872-3(0))*, Everbind) Marco Bk. Co.

—The Boy Who Harnessed the Wind: Creating Currents of Electricity & Hope. Hymas, Anna, illus. 2015. (ENG.). 304p. (J). (gr. 5). 18.99 *(978-0-8037-4080-8(8))*, Dial Bks) Penguin Young Readers Group.

Kamkwamba, William & Mealer, Bryan. The Boy Who Harnessed the Wind: Young Readers Edition. Zunon, Elizabeth, illus. (ENG.). (J). 2016. 304p. (gr. 5). 8.99 *(978-0-14-751042-6(2))*, Puffin Books) 2012. 32p. (gr. 1-3). 17.99 *(978-0-8037-3511-8(1))*, Dial Bks) Penguin Young Readers Group.

Lee, George L. Worldwide Interesting People: 162 History Makers of African Descent. 1 vol. alt. ed. 2012. (ENG., Illus.). 144p. pap. 19.99 *(978-0-7864-6768-6(1))*, 5efb588e-8e35-4188-81bd-86ff635cdb1d) McFarland & Co., Inc. Pubs.

Leidenfrost, Lisa. At the Edge of the Village: Musings of a Missionary Wife. 2004. Orig. Title: African Sketches. (ENG., Illus.). 212p. (YA). pap. 17.00 *(978-1-59128-017-0(6))* Canon Pr.

Moses: The True Story of an Elephant Baby. 2014. (ENG., Illus.). 48p. (J). (gr. -1-3). 17.99 *(978-1-4424-9603-3(7))*, Atheneum Bks. for Young Readers) Simon & Schuster Children's Publishing.

O'Connell, Caitlin & Jackson, Donna M. The Elephant Scientist. Rodwell, Timothy, illus. 2016. (Scientists in the Field Ser.). (ENG.). 80p. (J). (gr. 5-7). 9.99 *(978-0-544-66830-0(8))*, HMH Books For Young Readers) Houghton Mifflin Harcourt Publishing Co.

—The Elephant Scientist. Rodwell, Timothy, illus. O'Connell, Caitlin & Rodwell, Timothy, photos by. 2011. (Scientists in the Field Ser.). (ENG.). 80p. (J). (gr. 5-7). 18.99 *(978-0-547-05344-8(4))* Houghton Mifflin Harcourt Publishing Co.

Otfinoski, Steven. David Livingstone: Deep in the Heart of Africa. 2006. (Great Explorations Ser.). (Illus.). 79p. (J). (gr. 3-7). lib. bdg. 32.79 *(978-0-7614-2226-6(9))*, Benchmark Bks.) Marshall Cavendish Corp.

Stefoff, Rebecca. Redbeard. 2015. (True-Life Pirates Ser.). (ENG.). 48p. (J). (gr. 3-3). 31.36 *(978-1-5026-0199-5(0))* Cavendish Square Publishing.

Sutherland, Adam. Political Leaders. 2012. (Black History Makers Ser.). (ENG., Illus.). 24p. (J). (gr. 3-8). pap. 8.25 *(978-1-4488-7056-1(9))*; lib. bdg. 22.60 *(978-1-4488-6639-7(1))* Rosen Publishing Group, Inc., The. (PowerKids Pr.).

Weintraub, Aileen. The Barbarossa Brothers: 16th-Century Pirates of the Barbary Coast. 2009. (Library of Pirates Ser.). 24p. (gr. 3-3). 42.50 *(978-1-60853-814-0(1))*, PowerKids Pr.) Rosen Publishing Group, Inc., The.

Winter, Jeanette. Wangari's Trees of Peace: A True Story from Africa. Winter, Jeanette, illus. 2008. (ENG., Illus.). 32p. (J). (gr. -1-3). 17.99 *(978-0-15-206545-4(8))* Houghton Mifflin Harcourt Publishing Co.

AFRICA, CENTRAL

Hassig, Susan M., et al. Somalia. 3rd ed. 2017. (J). ***(978-1-5026-2607-3(1))*** Cavendish Square Publishing.

Hughes, Christopher. Rwanda. 2003. (Nations in Conflict Ser.). 48p. (J). 26.19 *(978-1-56711-542-0(X))*, Blackbirch Pr., Inc.) Cengage Gale.

Kneib, Martha. Chad. 2006. (Cultures of the World Ser.). (Illus.). 144p. (gr. 6-7). lib. bdg. 42.79 *(978-0-7614-2327-0(3))*, Benchmark Bks.) Marshall Cavendish Corp.

Koopmans, Andy. Rwanda. 2006. (Africa Ser.). (Illus.). 87p. (YA). lib. bdg. 21.95 *(978-1-59084-812-8(8))* Mason Crest.

Zuchora-Walske, Christine. Chad in Pictures. 2009. (Visual Geography Series, Second Ser.). (ENG.). 80p. (gr. 5-12). 31.93 *(978-1-57505-956-3(8))*, Twenty-First Century Bks.) Lerner Publishing Group.

AFRICA, CENTRAL—FICTION

Bowen, Carl & Fuentes, Benny. Guardian Angel. Tortosa, Wilson, illus. 2015. (Shadow Squadron Ser.). (ENG.). 112p. (gr. 4-8). lib. bdg. 26.65 *(978-1-4965-0382-4(1))* Stone Arch Bks.

—Rogue Agent. Tortosa, Wilson, illus. 2015. (Shadow Squadron Ser.). (ENG.). 224p. (gr. 4-8). pap. 8.95 *(978-1-62370-296-0(8))* Capstone Young Readers of Coughlan Cos.

AFRICA, EAST

Feelings, Muriel L. Moja Means One: A Swahili Counting Book. Feelings, Tom, illus. 2004. 20p. (J). (gr. k-4). reprint ed. pap. 5.00 *(978-0-7567-7108-9(0))* DIANE Publishing Co.

Gelletly, LeeAnne. Somalia. 2008. (Illus.). 112p. (YA). pap. 14.95 *(978-1-4222-1425-1(7))* Mason Crest.

Hamilton, Janice. Somalia in Pictures. 2007. (Visual Geography Series, Second Ser.). (ENG., Illus.). 80p. (gr. 5-12). lib. bdg. 31.93 *(978-0-8225-6586-4(2))* Lerner Publishing Group.

Heale, Jay & Wong, Winnie. Tanzania. 2nd rev. ed. 2008. (Cultures of the World Ser.). 144p. (gr. 6-18). lib. bdg. 42.79 *(978-0-7614-3417-7(8))*, Benchmark Bks.) Marshall Cavendish Corp.

Morrow, James. Djibouti. 2003. (Modern Middle East Nations & Their Strategic Place in the World Ser.). (Illus.). 112,128p. (YA). (gr. 7-18). lib. bdg. *(978-1-59084-525-7(0))* Mason Crest.

Nardo, Don. The Rwanda Genocide. 2011. (World History Ser.). 128p. (J). lib. bdg. 34.95 *(978-1-4205-0567-2(X))*, Lucent Bks.) Cengage Gale.

Pacchini, Fiorenzo. A Day with Homo Habilis: Life 2,000,000 Years Ago. 2003. (Early Humans Ser.). (Illus.). 48p. (gr. 6-18). lib. bdg. 23.90 *(978-0-7613-2765-3(7))*, Twenty-First Century Bks.) Lerner Publishing Group.

Patterson, John Henry. The Man-Eaters of Tsavo. 2011. 148p. pap. 7.49 *(978-1-61382-001-8(1))* Simon & Brown.

AFRICA, EAST—FICTION

Bull, Schuyler. Through Tsavo: A Story of an East African Savanna. 2005. (Soundprints' Wild Habitats Ser.). (ENG., Illus.). 32p. (J). (gr. 1-4). 8.95 *(978-1-59249-096-7(4))*, SC7008) Soundprints.

Castleton, Chaffee. Runty's Adventure: A Story of Love. Queen, Dana, illus. 2010. 97p. (J). pap. 17.95 *(978-0-578-06109-2(0))* Castleton, Julia J.

Dukes, Martin. Worm Winds of Zanzibar. 2013. 420p. pap. *(978-0-9575679-0-0(1))* Dukes, Martin.

Jomo & Mata: Evaluation Guide. 2006. (J). *(978-1-55942-411-0(7))* Witcher Productions.

Kola, Pamela, ed. East African How Stories. 2003. (Illus.). 48p. pap. *(978-9966-46-472-9(7))* Heinemann Kenya, Limited (East African Educational Publishers Ltd E.A.E.P.) KEN. Dist: Michigan State Univ. Pr.

Lively, Deborah Dreher. Vanishing Treasure of the Virungas. 2008. 88p. pap. 11.50 *(978-1-934925-54-6(3))*, Strategic Bk. Publishing) Strategic Book Publishing & Rights Agency (SBPRA).

Massey, David. Taken. 2014. 311p. (YA). *(978-0-545-66129-4(3))*; (ENG.). 320p. (J). (gr. 9). 18.99 *(978-0-545-66128-7(5))*, Chicken Hse., The) Scholastic, Inc.

Nanji, Shenaaz. Child of Dandelions. 2008. (ENG., Illus.). 208p. (J). (gr. 6-9). 17.95 *(978-1-932425-93-2(4))*, Front Street) Boyds Mills Pr.

Park, Linda Sue. A Long Walk to Water: Based on a True Story. (ENG., 128p. (J). (gr. 5-7). 2011. Illus.). pap. 7.99 *(978-0-547-57731-9(1))* 2010. 17.99 *(978-0-547-25127-1(0))* Houghton Mifflin Harcourt Publishing Co.

—A Long Walk to Water: Based on a True Story. 2009. 8.32 *(978-0-7848-3885-3(2))*, Everbind) Marco Bk. Co.

—A Long Walk to Water: Based on a True Story. 2011. 18.00 *(978-1-61383-124-3(2))* Perfection Learning Corp.

—A Long Walk to Water: Based on a True Story. 2011. lib. bdg. 18.40 *(978-0-606-23406-1(3))*, Turtleback) Turtleback Bks.

Whelan, Gloria. Listening for Lions. 2006. (ENG.). 208p. (J). (gr. 5-9). pap. 6.99 *(978-0-06-058176-3(X))* HarperCollins Pubs.

—Listening for Lions. 2007. 194p. (gr. 5-9). 16.00 *(978-0-7569-7800-6(9))* Perfection Learning Corp.

Wilton, Briar. The Strongest Mouse: A Tale from East Africa. Corke, Estelle, illus. 2016. 24p. (J). pap. *(978-1-927244-59-3(5))* Flying Start Bks.

—The Strongest Mouse (Big Book Edition) A Tale from East Africa. Corke, Estelle, illus. 2016. 24p. (J). pap. *(978-1-927244-69-2(2))* Flying Start Bks.

AFRICA—FICTION

Alakija, Polly, et al. Catch That Goat! 2004. (Avenues Ser.). (ENG., Illus.). 32p. (C). pap. 11.95 *(978-1-84148-161-5(0))* National Geographic School Publishing, Inc.

Alfred Sole. Pandi's Adventures in Afric. Patradol Kitcharoen, illus. 2012. 86p. pap. 23.97 *(978-1-61897-493-8(9))*, Strategic Bk. Publishing) Strategic Book Publishing & Rights Agency (SBPRA).

Allen, Christina G. Hippos in the Night: Autobiographical Adventures in Africa. 2003. (Illus.). 144p. (J). 17.89 *(978-0-688-17827-7(8))* HarperCollins Pubs.

Allen, Harry. Ibarajo Road. 2012. 352p. (YA). pap. *(978-1-84780-320-7(2))*, Frances Lincoln) Quarto Publishing Group UK.

Amenii, Nehprii. Memories of the Little Elephant. 2008. (Illus.). 60p. (J). 24.95 *(978-0-9797010-0-9(7))* Khunum Productions, Inc.

Anderson, Jane. Anansi the Spider & the Sky King: A Tale from Africa. 2006. (J). pap. *(978-1-4108-6175-7(9))* Benchmark Education Co.

Asare, Meshack. L' Appel de Sosu (Sosu's Call) Keita, Fatou, tr. 2003. (FRE., Illus.). 37p. pap. *(978-9988-550-48-6(0))* Sub-Saharan Pubs. & Traders GHA. Dist: Michigan State Univ. Pr.

—Sosu's Call. Asare, Meshack, illus. 2006. (ENG., Illus.). 40p. (J). (gr. k-4). 11.99 *(978-1-929132-21-8(2))* Kane Miller.

Atinuke. No 1 Car Spotter & the Firebird. Johnson Cadwell, Warwick, illus. 2012. (Fiction Ser.). (ENG.). 112p. (J). pap. 4.99 *(978-1-61067-052-4(3))* Kane Miller.

Auntie Annie. Knute: Dreams of Africa. 2013. 32p. pap. 17.25 *(978-1-4669-7519-4(9))* Trafford Publishing.

Ausbeth-Ajagu, Anuli C. The King's Verdict. 2003. (Illus.). 31p. pap. *(978-978-2951-65-6(X))* CSS Bookshops, Ltd., Agency & Publishing Div.

Axtell, David. We're Going on a Lion Hunt. Axtell, David, illus. 2007. (ENG., Illus.). 32p. (J). (gr. -1-1). 8.99 *(978-0-8050-8219-7(0))*, 9780805082197) Square Fish.

AZ Books. In Hot Africa. 2013. (Talking Flaps Ser.). (ENG.). 10p. (J). (gr. -1-k). bds. 9.95 *(978-1-61889-087-0(5))* AZ Bks. LLC.

Bailey, Carla R. A. Inner Beauty. 2013. 24p. pap. *(978-1-4602-1535-7(4))* FriesenPress.

Ballantyne, R. M. Gorilla Hunters A Tale of the Wilds of A. 2006. pap. 36.95 *(978-1-4286-5952-0(8))* Kessinger Publishing, LLC.

Base, Graeme. Jungle Drums. 2004. (ENG., Illus.). 40p. (J). (gr. -1-3). 19.95 *(978-0-8109-5044-3(8))* Abrams, Inc.

Bassoff, Leah & DeLuca, Laura. Lost Girl Found, 1 vol. 2014. (ENG., Illus.). 192p. (J). (gr. 7). 16.95 *(978-1-55498-416-9(5))* Groundwood Bks. CAN. Dist: Publishers Group West (PGW).

Baxter, Nicola. Josie the Giraffe & the Starry Night. Fox, Lisa, illus. 2016. (ENG.). 16p. (J). (gr. -1-12). 7.99 *(978-0-85723-526-8(5))*, Armadillo) Anness Publishing GBR. Dist: National Bk. Network.

Beake, Lesley. Home Now. Littlewood, Karin, illus. 2007. 32p. (J). (ENG.). (gr. -1-3). pap. 6.95 *(978-1-58089-163-9(2))*; (gr. k-3). 16.95 *(978-1-58089-162-2(4))* Charlesbridge Publishing, Inc.

—Rough Luck: Diamonds in the Kalahari. 2009. (Hodder African Readers Ser.). (Illus.). 112p. pap. 12.95 *(978-0-340-99028-5(7))* Hodder Education Group GBR. Dist: Trans-Atlantic Pubns., Inc.

Beard, Alex. The Jungle Grapevine. 2009. (ENG., Illus.). 48p. (J). (gr. k-2). 17.95 *(978-0-8109-8001-3(0))*, Abrams Bks. for Young Readers) Abrams, Inc.

—Monkey See, Monkey Draw. 2011. (ENG., Illus.). 48p. (J). (gr. k-2). 17.95 *(978-0-8109-8970-2(0))*, Abrams Bks. for Young Readers) Abrams, Inc.

Bergin, Jennifer J. Jungle Jim & Jungle Jen in the African Savannahs. 2012. 68p. pap. 8.99 *(978-1-4525-5314-6(9))* Balboa Pr.

Berkes, Marianne. Over in the Grasslands: On an African Savanna, 1 vol. Dubin, Jill, illus. 2016. (ENG.). 32p. (J). (gr. -1-2). 16.95 *(978-1-58469-567-7(6))* Dawn Pubns.

Berry, Nessa. Protectors of Little Africa. 2005. 108p. per. 9.99 *(978-1-58832-132-9(0))* Unlimited Publishing LLC.

Bess, Clayton, et al. Story for a Black Night. 2004. (ENG.). 112p. (YA). (gr. 7). pap. 8.95 *(978-0-618-49483-5(9))* Houghton Mifflin Harcourt Publishing Co.

Bester, Maryanne. The Missing Ball. Bester, Shayle, illus. 2010. (Cool Nguni Ser.: 4). (ENG.). 32p. (J). (gr. k-2). 12.00 *(978-1-77009-704-9(X))* Jacana Media ZAF. Dist: Independent Pubs. Group.

Birch, Beverley. Rift. 2008. (ENG., Illus.). 224p. (YA). (gr. 7-18). pap. 9.95 *(978-1-4052-1589-3(5))* Egmont Bks., Ltd. GBR. Dist: Independent Pubs. Group.

Birch, Beverley. Two Animal Tales from Africa: Band 15/Emerald. 2017. (Collins Big Cat Tales Ser.). (ENG., Illus.). 48p. (J). (gr. 3-4). pap. 8.99 ***(978-0-00-817942-7(5))*** HarperCollins Pubs. Ltd. GBR. Dist: Independent Pubs. Group.

Blessing, Charlotte. New Old Shoes. Phillips, Gary R., illus. 2009. (ENG.). 32p. (J). (gr. k-3). 16.95 *(978-0-9792035-6-5(2))* Pleasant St. Pr.

Bloch, Joanne. A Few Little Lies. 2009. (Hodder African Readers Ser.). (Illus.). 96p. pap. 12.95 *(978-0-340-98415-4(5))* Hodder Education Group GBR. Dist: Trans-Atlantic Pubns., Inc.

Boor, Annarie. Bapsie in the Bushveld. 2007. 148p. 26.50 *(978-1-4251-2717-6(7))* Trafford Publishing.

Borgeson, Grace. Douwlina: A Rhino's Story. 2012. (ENG., Illus.). 32p. 19.95 *(978-1-936474-53-9(8))*, 87298107-73d6-41ce-8918-67bd7c8ae307) Bright Sky Pr.

Bowen, Betsy, illus. Dhegdheer: A Scary Somali Folktale. 2007. (SOM & ENG.). *(978-1-931016-19-3(4))*; *(978-1-931016-18-6(6))* Minnesota Humanities Ctr.

Brailsford, David. Confessions of Anansi. 2004. (ENG., Illus.). 136p. pap. 6.99 *(978-976-8184-51-1(5))* Penguin Publishing Group.

Brain, Helen. No More Secrets. 2009. (Hodder African Readers Ser.). (Illus.). 144p. pap. 12.95 *(978-0-340-98419-2(8))* Hodder Education Group GBR. Dist: Trans-Atlantic Pubns., Inc.

Brenda, Jones. No, I Don't Want to Play Today: An African Tale about Bullying. 2010. 40p. pap. 14.95 *(978-1-60911-387-2(X))*, Eloquent Bks.) Strategic Book Publishing & Rights Agency (SBPRA).

Brett, Jan. Honey... Honey... Lion! A Story from Africa. Brett, Jan, illus. 2014. (ENG., Illus.). 40p. (J). (gr. -1-3). 7.99 *(978-0-14-751352-6(9))*, Puffin Books) Penguin Young Readers Group.

Broach, Elise. Gumption! Egielski, Richard, illus. 2010. (ENG.). 40p. (J). (gr. k-3). 18.99 *(978-1-4169-1628-4(8))*, Atheneum Bks. for Young Readers) Simon & Schuster Children's Publishing.

Brown, Jeff. The African Safari Discovery. Pamintuan, Macky, illus. 2010. (Flat Stanley's Worldwide Adventures Ser.: 6). (ENG.). 112p. (J). (gr. 2-5). pap. 4.99 *(978-0-06-143000-8(5))*; No. 6. 15.99 *(978-0-06-143001-5(3))* HarperCollins Pubs.

Brown, Paul Henry. Grandpa Still Remembers: Life Changing Stories for Kids of All Ages from a Missionary Kid in Africa. Deborah, Brown Armes, illus. 2013. 162p. pap. 14.95 *(978-1-61153-027-8(X))* Light Messages Publishing.

Brown-Wood, Janay. Imani's Moon. Mitchell, Hazell, illus. 2014. (ENG.). 32p. (J). (gr. 1-4). pap. 7.95 *(978-1-934133-58-3(2))*, Mackinac Island Press, Inc.) Charlesbridge Publishing, Inc.

Bryan, Ashley. Can't Scare Me! Bryan, Ashley, illus. 2013. (ENG., Illus.). 40p. (J). (gr. -1-3). 16.99 *(978-1-4424-7657-8(5))*, Atheneum Bks. for Young Readers) Simon & Schuster Children's Publishing.

—Who Built the Stable? A Nativity Poem. Bryan, Ashley, illus. 2012. (ENG., Illus.). 40p. (J). (gr. -1-3). 16.99 *(978-1-4424-0934-7(7))*, Atheneum Bks. for Young Readers) Simon & Schuster Children's Publishing.

Burchett, Jan & Vogler, Sara. Desert Danger, 1 vol. Le Feyer, Diane, illus. 2013. (Wild Rescue Ser.). (ENG.). 152p. (gr. 3-6). 9.95 *(978-1-4342-4892-3(5))* Stone Arch Bks.

—Desert Danger, 1 vol. Le Feyer, Diane & Kennedy, Sam, illus. 2012. (Wild Rescue Ser.). (ENG.). 152p. (gr. 3-6). lib. bdg. 25.32 *(978-1-4342-3773-6(7))* Stone Arch Bks.

The Captain, His Daughter, & Their Discovery. 2007. 48p. pap. 6.50 *(978-0-8341-2296-3(0))*, 083-412-2960) Beacon Hill Pr. of Kansas City.

Carlson, Bert H. The Perilous African Adventures of Sir Bert & Sir Gilbert. 2013. 106p. pap. 32.10 *(978-1-4669-8744-9(8))* Trafford Publishing.

Carrasco, Jose Manuel, illus. El viaje de las semillas. 2008. 48p. *(978-84-95225-83-2(2))* Saure, Jean-Francois Editor.

Carter, Jani R. Long Ago in the African Jungle. 2008. 108p. pap. 10.99 *(978-1-4389-1233-2(1))* AuthorHouse.

Casey, Mark. An African Princess: Deasha's Wild Adventure. 2010. (Illus.). 54p. pap. 11.95 *(978-1-4327-3864-8(X))* Outskirts Pr., Inc.

Chanani, Gloria. Fearful Frannie's African Safari. 2006. 95p. pap. 16.95 *(978-1-4241-2617-0(7))* PublishAmerica, Inc.

Cherubini. Pinocchio in Africa. 2004. reprint ed. pap. 1.99 *(978-1-4192-4166-6(4))*; pap. 15.95 *(978-1-4191-4166-9(X))* Kessinger Publishing, LLC.

Cherubini, E. Pinocchio in Africa. 2007. pap. *(978-1-4065-1442-1(X))* Dodo Pr.

Chichester Clark, Emma, illus. No More Kissing! 2015. (J). ***(978-1-4351-5751-4(6))*** Barnes & Noble, Inc.

Chidebelu-Eze/Dove Publishing, Chibueze / Obi. The Tales of Tortoise: Inspirational Stories of Wisdom. Newborne, David / F., illus. 2005. (ENG.). 76p. (J). 16.00 *(978-0-9766578-0-4(5))* Dove Publishing, Inc.

Chisiya. Afrikan Lullaby: Folk Tales from Zimbabwe. 2012. (Illus.). 56p. pap. 31.99 *(978-1-4691-7174-6(0))* Xlibris Corp.

Chukovsky, Kornei. Doctor Ouch. Seabaugh, Jan, tr. from RUS. Seabaugh, Jan, illus. 2004. (Children's International Ser.: 1). Orig. Title: Aibolit. 43p. (J). pap. 6.99 *(978-0-9740551-0-7(7))* Smith, Viveca Publishing.

Constans, Gabriel. Skin of Lions. 2009. 63p. pap. 13.75 *(978-1-60695-014-2(2))* Callanish Pr.

Cooney, Caroline B. Diamonds in the Shadow. 2009. (ENG.). 240p. (YA). 9.99 *(978-1-4000-7424-2(X))*, WaterBrook Pr.) Crown Publishing Group.

Courlander, Harold & Herzog, George. The Cow-Tail Switch: And Other West African Stories. Chastain, Madye Lee, illus. 2008. (ENG.). 160p. (J). (gr. 3-7). pap. 8.99 *(978-0-312-38006-9(2))*, 9780312380069) Square Fish.

Cox, Dorothy Ayling. Children's Stories. 2013. 108p. pap. 11.95 *(978-1-4787-0220-7(6))* Outskirts Pr., Inc.

Croall, Marie P. Marwe: Into the Land of the Dead - An East African Folktale. Lago, Ray & Hamilton, Craig, illus. 2008. (Graphic Myths & Legends Ser.). (ENG.). 48p. (gr. 4-8). 27.93 *(978-0-8225-7134-6(X))*, Graphic Universe™) Lerner Publishing Group.

Crowder, Melanie. Parched. (ENG.). 160p. (J). (gr. 5-7). 2014. pap. 7.99 *(978-0-544-33631-5(3))*, HMH Books For Young Readers) 2013. 15.99 *(978-0-547-97651-8(8))* Houghton Mifflin Harcourt Publishing Co.

Daly, Jude. Sivu's Six Wishes: A Taoist Tale. 2010. (ENG., Illus.). 36p. (J). (gr. 1-5). 17.00 *(978-0-8028-5369-1(2))*, Eerdmans Bks For Young Readers) Eerdmans, William B. Publishing Co.

Daly, Niki. Pretty Salma: A Little Red Riding Hood Story from Africa. Daly, Niki, illus. 2007. (ENG., Illus.). 32p. (J). (gr. -1-3). 17.99 *(978-0-618-72345-4(5))* Houghton Mifflin Harcourt Publishing Co.

Daniels, Katie C. Danny's Adventure in Afric. 2009. 24p. pap. 12.99 *(978-1-4389-3404-4(1))* AuthorHouse.

Davey, Keith Peter. Squeaks Narrow Squeaks. Frost, Justine, illus. 2009. 32p. pap. 14.62 *(978-1-4120-4402-8(2))* Trafford Publishing.

Davies, Stephen. Don't Spill the Milk! Corr, Christopher, illus. 2013. 32p. 16.95 *(978-1-4677-2028-1(3))* Anderson Pr.

Davis, Cynthia. Drink the Rain. 2007. (Illus.). 256p. (YA). per. 12.95 *(978-0-9712163-1-0(2))* Greenroom Bks.

De Matos, Isabel Freire. Una Carta de Delke. Saez, Sofia, illus. 2004. (SPA.). 32p. (gr. k-3). pap. 8.95 *(978-1-57581-573-2(7))* Santillana USA Publishing Co., Inc.

Del Riego, Erica. The Heart of Life. 2010. 36p. pap. 17.75 *(978-1-4389-7572-6(4))* AuthorHouse.

Dell'orco, Antonio. The Wolf Lion & Whistle: Two Children's Stories. 2013. 68p. 22.95 *(978-0-9755471-8-2(6))* Divine Mercy Pr.

DeNucci, Sharon. Ava Goes to Africa. DeNucci, Corinne, illus. 2010. 32p. pap. 16.99 *(978-1-4520-4091-2(5))* AuthorHouse.

Doan, Lisa. Jack & the Wild Life. Stevanovic, Ivica, illus. 2014. (Berenson Schemes Ser.: 2). (ENG.). 144p. (J). (gr. 4-6). 17.95 *(978-1-4677-1077-0(6))* Lerner Publishing Group.

Doder, Joshua. Grk: Operation Tortoise. 2009. 219p. (J). pap. *(978-0-440-42152-8(7))*, Delacorte Pr) Random House Publishing Group.

Don, Lari. The Tortoise's Gift: A Story from Zambia. Williamson, Melanie, illus. 2012. (Animal Stories Ser.). (ENG.). 48p. (J). (gr. 1-4). pap. 8.99 *(978-1-84686-774-3(6))* Barefoot Bks., Inc.

Donald, David R. I Am Thabek. 2012. 78p. pap. 15.99 *(978-1-4797-5138-9(3))* Xlibris Corp.

Duey, Kathleen. Ella the Baby Elephant: A Baby Elephant's Story. Gurin, Lara, illus. 2008. (My Animal Family Ser.). (ENG.). 32p. (J). (gr. -1-3). 12.99 *(978-0-8249-5584-7(6))*, Ideal Pubns.) Worthy Publishing.

Dyer, Hadley. Les Savanes. 2012. (FRE.). 32p. (J). pap. 9.95 *(978-2-89579-443-1(X))* Bayard Canada CAN. Dist: Crabtree Publishing Co.

Earhart, Kristin. Savanna Showdown. 2016. (Illus.). 138p. (J). ***(978-1-5182-0302-2(7))*** Scholastic, Inc.

—Savanna Showdown. 2015. (Race the Wild Ser.: 4). (ENG., Illus.). 144p. (J). (gr. 2-5). lib. bdg. 14.75 *(978-0-606-38080-5(9))* Turtleback Bks.

Ebbers, Susan M. Jamie's Journey: The Savannah. Godbey, Cory, illus. 2012. 38p. 17.99 *(978-0-9833971-8-2(X))*; pap. 9.99 *(978-0-9833971-9-9(8))* Rowe Publishing and Design.

Eke, Vincent. The Turtle's Shell. 2013. (Illus.). 46p. pap. *(978-1-909688-00-1(2))* Lionpen Publishing.

An Elephant's Tail. 2010. 47p. pap. 6.00 *(978-81-7806-190-0(2))* Unicorn Bks. Pvt Ltd. IND. Dist: Mahal, Pustak Pubs., Booksellers & Order Suppliers.

Ewing, Deborah. Secret Celebrity. 2009. (Hodder African Readers Ser.). (Illus.). 112p. pap. 12.95 *(978-0-340-98420-8(1))* Hodder Education Group GBR. Dist: Trans-Atlantic Pubns., Inc.

Farish, Terry. The Good Braider. 0 vols. 2014. (ENG.). 224p. (YA). (gr. 9-12). pap. 9.99 *(978-1-4778-1628-8(3))*, 9781477816288, Amazon Children's Publishing) Amazon Publishing.

Faundez, Anne. The Day the Rains Fell. Littlewood, Karin, illus. 2010. (ENG.). 32p. (J). (gr. k-2). pap. 9.99

(978-1-84853-015-7(3), Tamarind) Transworld Publishers Ltd. GBR. Dist: Independent Pubs. Group.

Ferrone, John M. Margo Goes on Safari. Ferrone, John M., illus. Date not set. (Illus.). 36p. (J). (gr. -1-5). pap. 16.95 *(978-1-928811-04-6(3))* Story Stuff, Inc.

Finch, Donna. The Big Dig: The Continuing Adventures of Brandy the Golden Retriever, 1 vol. 2010. 46p. 24.95 *(978-1-4489-8797-9(0))* PublishAmerica, Inc.

Foster, Jesse, et al. The Night Before Christmas in Africa, 1 vol. Christodoulou, Jean, illus. 2010. (Night Before Christmas Ser.). (ENG.). 32p. (J). (gr. k-3). 16.99 *(978-1-58980-847-8(9))* Pelican Publishing Co., Inc.

Friend, Amanda. Lisa & Laura: African Safari Park Adventure. 2012. (Illus.). 40p. pap. 17.00 *(978-1-84426-856-6(X)*, Fastprint Publishing) Upfront Publishing Ltd. GBR. Dist: Printondemand-worldwide.com.

Gabriel, Elizabeth P. & Gabriel, Pamela P. Ziccah Blows Her Horn. 2008. 24p. pap. 12.99 *(978-1-4389-2447-2(X))* AuthorHouse.

Garstang, Michael. Ntombazana: A Story of an African Elephant Family. 2008. (ZUL., Illus.). 208p. pap. 17.50 *(978-0-615-18904-8(0))* Angel Applications.

Gillies, Mark. Imvula, Child of the Rain. 2007. (Illus.). 80p. per. *(978-1-84401-965-6(9))* Athena Pr.

Gilligan, Alison. Search for the Black Rhino. 2011. (Illus.). 144p. (J). pap. 6.99 *(978-1-937133-01-6(X))* Chooseco LLC.

Gleeson, Brian. Koi & the Kola Nuts, 1 vol. Ruffins, Reynold, illus. 2007. (Rabbit Ears: A Classic Tale Ser.). (ENG.). 36p. (gr. k-3). 25.65 *(978-1-59961-310-9(7))* Spotlight.

Godley, Christina. Lion at the Gateway. 2010. 36p. pap. 16.99 *(978-1-4520-4508-5(9))* AuthorHouse.

Gomez, Luis Marcelino. Memorias de Angola: Cuentos Africanos. Vallejo, Esperanza, illus. 2004. (Letras Latinoamericanas Ser.). (SPA.). 131p. (YA). (gr. -1-7). per. *(978-958-30-1257-0(2))* Panamericana Editorial.

Gorg, Gwyn. I Am the Blues. Alfandolo, Koffi, illus. 2012. 26p. pap. 19.95 *(978-0-9840204-2-3(X))* Pacific Raven Pr.

Gravett, Emily. Meerkat Mail. Gravett, Emily, illus. 2007. (ENG., Illus.). 32p. (J). (gr. -1-3). 17.99 *(978-1-4169-3473-8(1)*, Simon & Schuster Bks. For Young Readers) Simon & Schuster Bks. For Young Readers.

Grifalconi, Ann. The Village That Vanished. Nelson, Kadir, illus. 2004. (ENG.). 40p. (J). (gr. k-3). reprint ed. pap. 7.99 *(978-0-14-240190-3(0)*, Puffin Books) Penguin Young Readers Group.

Groenewald, Catherine. I Could Be Anywhere. 2011. (ENG.). 16p. (J). (gr. 2-4). pap. 6.99 *(978-1-77009-833-6(X))* Jacana Media ZAF. Dist: Independent Pubs. Group.

—Jingle-Jingle in My Pocket. 2011. (ENG.). 16p. (J). (gr. 2-4). pap. 7.95 *(978-1-77009-832-9(1))* Jacana Media ZAF. Dist: Independent Pubs. Group.

—The Little Girl Who Didn't Want to Grow Up. 2011. (Best Loved Tales for Africa Ser.). (ENG., Illus.). 32p. (J). (gr. k-2). pap. 10.95 *(978-1-77009-819-0(4))* Jacana Media ZAF. Dist: Independent Pubs. Group.

Hadithi, Mwenye & Kennaway, Adrienne. Handsome Hog. 2010. (ENG., Illus.). 32p. (J). (gr. k-2). pap. 10.99 *(978-0-340-97035-5(9))* Hodder & Stoughton GBR. Dist: Hachette Bk. Group.

Haggard, H. Rider. Allan Quatermain #3: Allan+s Wife. 2007. 116p. per. 7.99 *(978-1-934451-87-8(8))* Wilder Pubns., Corp.

Hahn, Nancy. One Lost Boy. Ayoub, Hamid, illus. 2012. pap. 19.95 *(978-1-4276-5351-2(8))* Aardvark Global Publishing.

Hanson, Ed. African Safari. 2005. (Barclay Family Adventures 2 Ser.). 64p. (J). per. 3.95 *(978-1-56254-800-1(X)*, SP800X) Saddleback Educational Publishing, Inc.

Hassan, Marian A. Bright Star, Blue Sky. 2005.Tr. of Xidig Bidhaanta, Cir Buluug Ah. (SOM.). 7.00 *(978-0-9766616-0-3(8))* Hassan, Marian.

Hawksley, Gerald. See Through Safari. Spengler, Margaret, illus. 2005. (J). bds. *(978-1-890647-15-5(2))* TOMY International, Inc.

Hazlewood, Leyland. Chester Goes to Afric. 2011. 32p. pap. 21.99 *(978-1-4568-6466-8(1))* Xlibris Corp.

Heer, Andrew De. Three African Short Stories for Young Readers: For Young Readers. 2011. 32p. pap. 21.99 *(978-1-4568-7973-0(1))* Xlibris Corp.

Hill, Ros. Unexpected Tails: Africa Like You've Never Seen It Before. 2nd ed. 2017. (ENG., Illus.). (J). (gr. k-3). 19.95 ***(978-1-59687-541-8(0)**, ipicturebooks) ibooks, Inc.

Hipp, Helen C. A Different Kind of Safari. Diaco, Paula Tedford, ed. Glass, Hilary Ann Love, illus. 2013. 32p. 17.95 *(978-0-9890134-0-6(5))* A Different Kind of Safari LLC.

Holmqvist, Carin. African Tales. 2010. 64p. pap. 28.70 *(978-0-557-18184-1(4))* Lulu Pr., Inc.

Hook, Francis. Finding the Djinn. 2009. (Hodder African Readers Ser.). (Illus.). 112p. pap. 12.95 *(978-0-340-99029-2(5))* Hodder Education Group GBR. Dist: Trans-Atlantic Pubns., Inc.

Hutton, Keely. Soldier Boy. 2017. (ENG.). 336p. (YA). 17.99 *(978-0-374-30563-5(3)*, 9780374305635, Farrar, Straus & Giroux (BYR)) Farrar, Straus & Giroux.

Isadora, Rachel. I Just Want to Say Good Night. Isadora, Rachel, illus. 2017. (ENG., Illus.). 32p. (J). (-k). 17.99 *(978-0-399-17384-4(6)*, Nancy Paulsen Books) Penguin Young Readers Group.

—Old Mikamba Had a Farm. Isadora, Rachel, illus. 2013. (ENG., Illus.). 40p. (J). (gr. -1-k). 17.99 *(978-0-399-25740-7(3)*, Nancy Paulsen Books) Penguin Young Readers Group.

—The Twelve Dancing Princesses. Isadora, Rachel, illus. 2009. (ENG., Illus.). 32p. (J). (gr. k-3). pap. 6.99 *(978-0-14-241450-7(6)*, Puffin Books) Penguin Young Readers Group.

Jackson, Maureen. You Count Too. 2012. 20p. pap. 17.99 *(978-1-4772-1241-7(8))* AuthorHouse.

Jameson, Bernadette. The Boy Who Played His Way to Freedom. 2012. 80p. pap. 12.95 *(978-1-4710-6968-0(0))* Lulu Pr., Inc.

Jansen, Hanna. Over a Thousand Hills I Walk with You. Crawford, Elizabeth D., tr. from GER. 2006. (ENG.). 344p. (YA). (gr. 7-12). lib. bdg. 16.95 *(978-1-57505-927-3(4)*, Carolrhoda Bks.) Lerner Publishing Group.

Janski, Beverly. A Little Birdie Told Me. 2012. 48p. pap. 14.95 *(978-1-4497-5263-7(2)*, WestBow Pr.) Author Solutions, Inc.

Johnson, Julia. Cheetah's Tale. Stacey International Staff, ed. Keeble, Susan, illus. 2004. (ENG.). 56p. 16.95 *(978-1-900988-87-2(9)*, Stacey International) Stacey Publishing GBR. Dist: Casemate Pubs. & Bk. Distributors, LLC.

Johnson, Sandi. The Peaceful Lion. Johnson, Britt, ed. Kraft, Lauri, illus. l.t. ed. 2014. (ENG.). 28p. (J). (gr. k-5). pap. 12.99 *(978-1-929063-95-6(4)*, 325) Moons & Stars Publishing For Children.

Jones, Vanessa. I Dreamed It Snowed in Afric. 2007. 40p. per. 14.95 *(978-1-4327-1535-9(6))* Outskirts Pr., Inc.

Joosse, Barbara M. & Lavallee, Barbara. Papa, Do You Love Me? Lavallee, Barbara, illus. 2005. (Mama Ser.: MAMA). (ENG., Illus.). 36p. (J). (gr. -1-7). 15.99 *(978-0-8118-4265-5(7))* Chronicle Bks. LLC.

Judybee. Queen Amina of Zari: Queens of Africa Book 1. LittlePinkPebble, illus. 2011. 28p. pap. *(978-1-908218-43-8(6))* MX Publishing, Ltd.

—Queen Esther: Queens of Africa Book 4. LittlePinkPebble, illus. 2011. 28p. pap. *(978-1-908218-52-0(5))* MX Publishing, Ltd.

—Queen Idi: Queens of Africa Book 5. LittlePinkPebble, illus. 2011. 24p. pap. *(978-1-908218-55-1(X))* MX Publishing, Ltd.

—Queen Maked: Queens of Africa Book 2. LittlePinkPebble, illus. 2011. 28p. pap. *(978-1-908218-46-9(0))* MX Publishing, Ltd.

—Queen Moremi: Queens of Africa Book 3. LittlePinkPebble, illus. 2011. 28p. pap. *(978-1-908218-49-0(5))* MX Publishing, Ltd.

K, Miller Mace. Not Without Power: Lost in Africa. 2013. 302p. pap. 14.95 *(978-1-60920-071-8(3))* Ajoyin Publishing, Inc.

Kabaji, Egara. When the Dead Met the Living, 1 vol. 2009. 48p. pap. 16.95 *(978-1-61546-505-7(7))* America Star Bks.

Karr, Kathleen. Born for Adventure, 0 vols. unabr. ed. 2013. (ENG.). 208p. (YA). (gr. 7-10). pap. 9.99 *(978-1-4778-1701-8(8)*, 9781477817018, Amazon Children's Publishing) Amazon Publishing.

Katschke, Judy. The Imaginary Okapi (Disney Junior: the Lion Guard) Matta, Gabriella & Legramandi, Francesco, illus. 2017. (Little Golden Book Ser.). (ENG.). 24p. (J). (-k). 4.99 ***(978-0-7364-3719-6(3)**, Golden/Disney) Random Hse. Children's Bks.

Khulekani, Magubane. Angels Salvation. 2007. 96p. pap. *(978-1-86900-865-9(0))* UmSinsi Pr. ZAF. Dist: Michigan State Univ. Pr.

Kim, JiYu. The Wise Boy. Hwang, YoSeob, illus. 2014. (MySELF Bookshelf Ser.). (ENG.). 32p. (J). (gr. k-2). pap. 11.94 *(978-1-60357-690-1(8))*; lib. bdg. 25.27 *(978-1-59953-655-2(2))* Norwood Hse. Pr.

Kimani, Kamande. Why the Hyena Has Short Hind Legs. Therrian, John, illus. 2011. 40p. pap. 24.95 *(978-1-4560-5468-7(6))* America Star Bks.

Kinch, Michael. The Blending Time. 2010. (Blending Time Ser.: 1). (ENG.). 264p. (YA). (gr. 9-18). pap. 9.95 *(978-0-7387-2067-8(4)*, Flux) North Star Editions.

—The Fires of New Sun. 2012. (Blending Time Ser.: 2). (ENG.). 288p. (YA). pap. 9.95 *(978-0-7387-3076-9(9)*, Flux) North Star Editions.

—The Rebels of New SUN. 2013. (Blending Time Ser.: 3). (ENG.). 288p. (YA). pap. 9.99 *(978-0-7387-3151-3(X)*, Flux) North Star Editions.

Kithinji, Gerald, et al. Of Friends, Money & Gossip: 3 Stories & a Play. 2009. (Hodder African Readers Ser.). (Illus.). 96p. pap. 12.95 *(978-0-340-99027-8(9))* Hodder Education Group GBR. Dist: Trans-Atlantic Pubns., Inc.

Koh, Jennifer Pretious. Zindi's Journey: Finding Gem. 2013. 54p. pap. 23.99 *(978-1-4525-7057-0(4)*, Balboa Pr.) Author Solutions, Inc.

Kok, Gemma. Explore. 2008. 44p. pap. 18.50 *(978-1-4092-2058-9(3))* Lulu Pr., Inc.

—Explore (Printed in black & White) 2008. 44p. pap. 8.00 *(978-1-4092-2530-0(5))* Lulu Pr., Inc.

—Scribble. 2008. 42p. pap. 17.94 *(978-1-4092-2060-2(5))* Lulu Pr., Inc.

—Scribble (Printed in black & White) 2008. 42p. pap. 7.96 *(978-1-4092-2531-7(3))* Lulu Pr., Inc.

Kosgei, William. The Talented & Gifted: African Writers Series. 2013. 106p. pap. 10.95 *(978-1-62516-165-9(4)*, Strategic Bk. Publishing) Strategic Book Publishing & Rights Agency (SBPRA).

¿Lâdo¿Ù, F¿Lák¿'. Ajàyí Gb' Ìtum' Ìlù. Lowe, Wesley, illus. 2013. 34p. *(978-0-9866435-1-4(3))* Adubi Publishing.

Laird, Elizabeth & Quarto Generic Staff. The Ogress & the Snake: And Other Stories from Somalia. Fowles, Shelley, illus. 2009. (ENG.). 96p. (J). (gr. 3-6). pap. 7.95 *(978-1-84507-870-6(5)*, Frances Lincoln) Quarto Publishing Group UK GBR. Dist: Hachette Bk. Group.

Landstrom, Lena. A Hippo's Tale. Sandin, Joan, tr. from SWE. 2007. (Illus.). 32p. (J). (gr. -1-1). 15.00 *(978-91-29-66603-8(1))* R & S Bks. SWE. Dist: Macmillan.

Langley, C. Kevin. Brer Rabbit Comic. 2009. 16p. pap. 9.80 *(978-0-557-11631-7(7))* Lulu Pr., Inc.

The Legend of the Great Salt Mountain. 2005. (J). pap. *(978-0-9771804-1-7(7))* Terra Tales.

Lester, Julius. The Girl Who Saved Yesterday. Angel, Carl, illus. 2016. (ENG.). 32p. (J). (gr. -1-4). 16.99 *(978-1-939547-24-8(5))* Creston Bks.

Lewis, Gill. Gorilla Dawn. Meyer, Susan, illus. 2017. (ENG.). 432p. (J). (gr. 4-9). 16.99 *(978-1-4814-8657-6(8)*, Atheneum/Caitlyn Dlouhy Books) Simon & Schuster Children's Publishing.

London, C. Alexander. Honor Bound. 2014. (Tides of War Ser.: 2). (ENG.). 224p. (J). (gr. 5-9). pap. 5.99 *(978-0-545-66301-4(6)*, Scholastic Paperbacks) Scholastic, Inc.

Louise, Verna & McKinney, Doris. Tales & Rhymes for Children: Cute Little Stories for Kids. 2012. 64p. pap. 20.95 *(978-1-4497-3339-1(5)*, WestBow Pr.) Author Solutions, Inc.

Lumry, Amanda, et al. Safari in South Africa. 2003. (Adventures of Riley Ser.: Bk. 2). (Illus.). 36p. (gr. k-3). 15.95 *(978-0-9662257-8-5(3))* Eaglemont Pr.

Lynch, Stephen D. The Travels of Kui, the African Spurred Tortoise. Richard, Keisha Luana, illus. 2007. 36p. per. 24.95 *(978-1-4137-1802-7(7))* America Star Bks.

MacLachlan, Patricia. Your Moon, My Moon: A Grandmother's Words to a Faraway Child. Collier, Bryan, illus. 2011. (ENG.). 32p. (J). (gr. -1-3). 16.99 *(978-1-4169-7950-0(6)*, Simon & Schuster Bks. For Young Readers) Simon & Schuster Bks. For Young Readers.

Magona, Sindiwe. The Ugly Duckling. Hinrichsen, Natalie, illus. 2011. (Best Loved Tales for Africa Ser.). (ENG.). 32p. (J). (gr. k-2). pap. 10.95 *(978-1-77009-823-7(2))* Jacana Media ZAF. Dist: Independent Pubs. Group.

Mama Jamie. I Will Call Myself Future. 2012. 34p. pap. 15.95 *(978-1-4497-5500-3(3)*, WestBow Pr.) Author Solutions, Inc.

Mamburay, Yankuba & Mamburay, Khadijah. A Day at Grandma's Farm. 2011. 20p. pap. 24.95 *(978-1-4560-6707-6(9))* America Star Bks.

Marino, Gianna. Meet Me at the Moon. 2012. (ENG.). 32p. (J). (gr. -1-k). 16.99 *(978-0-670-01313-5(7)*, Viking Books for Young Readers) Penguin Young Readers Group.

Marsh, Laura F. Big Enough. 2009. (Mama Mirabelle Ser.). (ENG., Illus.). 24p. (J). (gr. -1-2). pap. 3.99 *(978-1-4263-0432-3(3)*, National Geographic Children's Bks.) National Geographic Society.

—What's in a Tail? 2009. (Mama Mirabelle Ser.). (ENG., Illus.). 24p. (J). (gr. -1-2). pap. 3.99 *(978-1-4263-0430-9(7))*; lib. bdg. 11.90 *(978-1-4263-0431-6(5))* National Geographic Society. (National Geographic Children's Bks.).

Marshall, Melanie. Ladybug. 2006. 25.00 *(978-1-4122-0219-0(1))* Trafford Publishing.

Mary, Nanette. Ashby, the Happy Little Elephant. 2007. (Illus.). 40p. (J). per. 12.95 *(978-0-9787112-7-6(0)*, 01002) New World Publishing.

Masilela, Johnny. We Shall Not Weep. 2010. (ENG.). 132p. pap. *(978-0-7957-0147-4(0))* NB Pubs. Ltd.

Mason, Charlene. Landon's Backyard Adventures. 2012. 24p. pap. 24.95 *(978-1-4626-7470-1(4))* America Star Bks.

Mazzola, Lori E. The Forbidden Forest: Tales of the Tree People, 1 vol. 2009. 151p. pap. 24.95 *(978-1-4489-2656-5(4))* America Star Bks.

Mbairamadji, Koffi. African Savannah Stories: Volume 2 Of 2. 2009. (Illus.). 48p. pap. 19.49 *(978-1-4389-2375-8(9))* AuthorHouse.

—African Savannah Stories, Volume 1. Mbairamadji, Koffi, illus. 2006. (Illus.). 40p. (J). per. 17.49 *(978-1-59879-277-5(6))* Lifevest Publishing, Inc.

McGee, Ron. Ryan Quinn & the Lion's Claw. Samnee, Chris, illus. 2017. (Ryan Quinn Ser.: 2). 352p. (J). (gr. 3-7). 16.99 ***(978-0-06-242169-2(7))*** HarperCollins Pubs.

McIntosh, Gavin. Hausaland Tales from the Nigerian Market Place. 2005. (Illus.). 98p. (J). (gr. 5-9). reprint ed. 22.00 *(978-0-7567-9714-0(4))* DIANE Publishing Co.

McKay, Sharon E. & Lafrance, Daniel. War Brothers: The Graphic Novel. Lafrance, Daniel, illus. 2013. (ENG., Illus.). 176p. (YA). (gr. 9-12). 2nd ed. 27.95 *(978-1-55451-489-2(4)*, 9781554514892) 3rd ed. pap. 18.95 *(978-1-55451-488-5(6)*, 9781554514885) Annick Pr., Ltd. CAN. Dist: Publishers Group West (PGW).

McKenzie, Lyn. Lavinia's Shoes. 2007. (J). pap. 12.95 *(978-0-9788628-5-5(6))* Just Write Bks.

McMahan, Virginia, told to. Mushgnome Legend of the African Spear. 2003. 38p. pap. 15.56 *(978-1-4116-0222-9(6))* Lulu Pr., Inc.

McMullan, Kate. A Wedding for Wiglaf?, 1 vol. Basso, Bill, illus. 2007. (Dragon Slayers' Academy Ser.: No. 4). (ENG.). 109p. (gr. 4-7). 24.21 *(978-1-59961-380-2(8))* Spotlight.

Meachen Rau, Dana. The Lion in the Grass. 2006. (Nature Ser.). (SPA., Illus.). 24p. (gr. k-1). lib. bdg. 15.95 *(978-0-7614-2305-8(2)*, Benchmark Bks.) Marshall Cavendish Corp.

Mead, Alice. Year of No Rain. 2005. (Illus.). 129p. (gr. 4-7). 15.50 *(978-0-7569-5158-0(5))* Perfection Learning Corp.

Medina, Sylvia M. & B alloxk-Dixon, Saige J. Gorilla's Roar. Eagle, Joy, illus. 2012. 36p. pap. 11.49 *(978-0-9836602-5-5(5))* Green Kids Club, Inc.

Meintjes, Chris. Angel's Flight. 2009. 156p. 25.99 *(978-1-4269-0843-9(1))*; pap. 15.99 *(978-1-4269-0842-2(3))* Trafford Publishing.

Mello, Craig. Difference: the Rainbow Zebra: An African Tale of Diversity. 2007. 40p. per. 24.95 *(978-1-4241-8269-5(7))* PublishAmerica, Inc.

Messimer, Wanda Fay. Tiny Teacup & Pot Belly Pig Go to Africa to Meet the 'Great Lion' 2013. 24p. pap. 24.95 *(978-1-4626-8736-7(9))* America Star Bks.

Meyrick, Rich. Jaspa's Journey: The Great Migration. 2015. (ENG., Illus.). 276p. (J). (gr. 4-6). pap. *(978-1-62815-313-2(X))* Speaking Volumes, LLC.

Miles, Robin, reader. Mufaro's Beautiful Daughters: An African Tale. 2003. (Illus.). (J). (gr. -1-2). pap. 35.95 incl. audio compact disk *(978-1-59112-541-9(3))* Live Oak Media.

Milway, Katie Smith. One Hen: How One Small Loan Made a Big Difference. Fernandes, Eugenie, illus. 2008. (CitizenKid Ser.). (ENG.). 32p. (J). (gr. 3-7). 18.95 *(978-1-55453-028-1(8))* Kids Can Pr., Ltd. CAN. Dist: Hachette Bk. Group.

Min, SooHyeon. The Drummer Boy. Nille, Peggy, illus. 2014. (MySELF Bookshelf Ser.). (ENG.). 32p. (J). (gr. k-2). pap. 11.94 *(978-1-60357-696-3(7))*; lib. bdg. 25.27 *(978-1-59953-661-3(7))* Norwood Hse. Pr.

Montgomery, R. A. The Lost Jewels of Nabooti. Kornmaneeroj, T. et al, illus. 2006. (Choose Your Own Adventure Ser.: No. 4). 144p. (J). (gr. 4-8). per. 6.99 *(978-1-933390-04-8(2)*, CHCL04) Chooseco LLC.

—Race Forever. 2005. (Illus.). 122p. (J). *(978-0-7608-9695-2(X))* Sundance/Newbridge Educational Publishing.

—Race Forever. Sundaravej, Sittisan, illus. 2006. (Choose Your Own Adventure Ser.: No. 7). 144p. (J). (gr. 4-8). per. 6.99 *(978-1-933390-07-9(7)*, CHCL07) Chooseco LLC.

Morpurgo, Michael. Dear Olly. Birmingham, Christian, illus. 2007. (ENG.). 128p. (J). (gr. 4-7). mass mkt. 7.99 *(978-0-00-675333-9(7)*, HarperCollins Children's Bks.) HarperCollins Pubs. Ltd. GBR. Dist: HarperCollins Pubs.

Morris, Neil. African Myths. Sansom, Fiona & Kennedy, Graham, illus. 2009. (Myths from Many Lands Ser.). 48p. (YA). (gr. 4-7). 29.25 *(978-1-60754-215-5(3))* Windmill Bks.

Musariri, Blessing. Going Home: A Tree's Story. 2005. (Illus.). 29p. pap. *(978-1-77922-042-4(1))* Weaver Pr. ZWE. Dist: Michigan State Univ. Pr.

Muszynski, Julie. Henley on Safari. 2012. (ENG., Illus.). 48p. (J). (gr. -1-12). 20.00 *(978-0-9832702-3-2(6))* Glitterati, Inc.

My African Safari. 2004. (J). ring bd. 3.25 *(978-0-9762740-4-9(3)*, Flat Kids) Smart Smiles Co., The.

Myhre, J. A. A Bird, a Girl, & a Rescue. 2016. (Illus.). ix, 133p. (J). pap. 15.99 *(978-1-942572-69-5(7))* New Growth Pr.

Myhre, Jennifer. A Chameleon, a Boy, & a Quest. 2015. (ENG., Illus.). 160p. (J). pap. 15.99 *(978-1-942572-08-4(5))* New Growth Pr.

Nagda, Ann Whitehead. Kevin Keeps Up. 2012. (ENG.). 96p. (J). 15.95 *(978-0-8234-2657-7(2))* Holiday Hse., Inc.

Naidoo, Beverley. Who Is King? Grobler, Piet, illus. 2015. (ENG.). 72p. (J). (gr. k-4). 22.99 *(978-1-84780-514-0(0)*, Frances Lincoln) Quarto Publishing Group UK GBR. Dist: Hachette Bk. Group.

Namukasa, Glaydah. Voice of a Dream. 2006. (Illus.). 97p. *(978-1-4050-9592-1(X))* Macmillan/McGraw-Hill Schl. Div.

Neiman, Jahcolyn Russell. Kekula. 2011. 32p. pap. 13.99 *(978-1-4520-8086-4(0))* AuthorHouse.

Neru, Enna. An African Tale. 2009. 159p. (YA). pap. 13.95 *(978-1-4327-2348-4(0))* Outskirts Pr., Inc.

Newman, Gwill York. Bingo Bear Was Here: A Toy Bear's Climb to the Top of Africa's Highest Mountain. Babcock, Jeff, illus. 2003. 48p. (J). pap. 8.95 *(978-0-86534-395-5(0))* Sunstone Pr.

Nielsen, Jon. Laney Gets Her Ridge. 2011. 32p. pap. 17.99 *(978-1-4567-3618-7(3))* AuthorHouse.

Nnabuchi, Afam. Emeka Transforms in the Pit. 2013. 78p. (J). pap. 12.95 *(978-1-4772-9679-0(4))* AuthorHouse.

Nuckolls, Les. Chester the Chimpanzee. 2012. 14.99 *(978-1-4621-1131-2(9))* Cedar Fort, Inc./CFI Distribution.

Ocelot, Michel. Kirikou et la Sorciere. pap. 14.95 *(978-2-01-321877-1(X))* Hachette Groupe Livre FRA. Dist: Distribooks, Inc.

Oduwole, Ben. The Flying Tortoise. 2009. 182p. pap. 43.50 *(978-1-60693-611-5(5)*, Eloquent Bks.) Strategic Book Publishing & Rights Agency (SBPRA).

Oguneye, Kunle. Sikulu & Harambe by the Zambezi River: An African Vversion of the Good Samaritan Story. McCorkindale, Bruce & Youtsey, Scott, illus. 2008. 32p. (J). (gr. -1-5). 14.99 *(978-0-9777382-4-3(8))* Blue Brush Media.

O'Neill, Gemma. Oh Dear, Geoffrey! O'Neill, Gemma, illus. 2014. (ENG., Illus.). 32p. (J). (gr. -1-2). 15.99 *(978-0-7636-6659-0(9)*, Templar) Candlewick Pr.

Opal, Paola. Saffy Looks for Rain. 2009. (Simply Small Ser.). (ENG., Illus.). 24p. (J). (gr. k — 1). bds. 7.95 *(978-1-897476-03-1(5))* Simply Read Bks. CAN. Dist: Ingram Publisher Services.

Oram, Hiawyn. Counting Leopard's Spots & other Stories. Warnes, Tim, illus. 2005. 96p. (J). (gr. k-4). reprint ed. 17.00 *(978-0-7567-9252-7(5))* DIANE Publishing Co.

Orford, Margie. The Little Red Hen. Lilje, Karen, illus. 2011. (Best Loved Tales for Africa Ser.). (ENG.). 32p. (J). (gr. k-2). pap. 10.95 *(978-1-77009-821-3(6))* Jacana Media ZAF. Dist: Independent Pubs. Group.

Ormsby, Nathaniel Hosea. Timeless Tales of Anansi: Ancestral Realm of Africa. 2006. 108p. pap. 19.95 *(978-1-4241-3396-3(3))* PublishAmerica, Inc.

Parker, Emma. Safari Adventure. 2010. (Illus.). pap. *(978-1-877561-29-0(0))* First Edition Ltd.

Parnell, Fran. The Mother of Monsters: A Story from South Africa. Fatus, Sophie, illus. 2011. (Monster Stories Ser.). (ENG.). 48p. (J). (gr. 1-5). pap. 8.99 *(978-1-84686-560-2(3))* Barefoot Bks., Inc.

Parragon Staff. Lion King. 2010. (Disney Diecut Classics). 72p. (J). (gr. -1-1). *(978-1-4075-8936-7(9))* Parragon, Inc.

Patterson, James & Grabenstein, Chris. Danger down the Nile. Neufeld, Juliana, illus. 2014. (Treasure Hunters Ser.). (ENG.). 480p. (J). (gr. 3-7). 14.99 *(978-0-316-37086-8(X)*, Jimmy Patterson) Little Brown & Co.

Paulsen, Aimee. Mambo & the Runaway Gorill. 2011. (Illus.). 40p. pap. 21.99 *(978-1-4628-5878-1(3))* Xlibris Corp.

Peet, Mal & Graham, Elspeth. Mysterious Traveler. Lynch, P. J., illus. 2013. (ENG.). 48p. (J). (gr. k-3). 15.99 *(978-0-7636-6232-5(1))* Candlewick Pr.

Peretti, Frank E. & Thomas Nelson & Sons Staff. The Secret of the Desert Stone, 1 vol. 2005. (Cooper Kids Adventure Ser.: 5). (ENG.). 160p. pap. 6.99 *(978-1-4003-0574-2(8))* Nelson, Thomas Inc.

Peruzzo, Nicolas. Safari Dreams. Peruzzo, Nicolas, illus. 2012. (Illus.). 26p. pap. 9.99 *(978-1-61225-162-2(5))* Mirror Publishing.

Pinguilly, Yves. Contes et legendes d Afrique. (FRE., Illus.). 230p. pap. 19.95 *(978-2-09-282309-5(4))* Nathan, Fernand FRA. Dist: Distribooks, Inc.

Pinkney, Andrea Davis. The Red Pencil. Evans, Shane W., illus. 2015. (ENG.). 368p. (J). (gr. 4-17). pap. 8.99 *(978-0-316-24782-5(0))* Little, Brown Bks. for Young Readers.

Pixton, Amy. Mary Had a Little Lamb. 2010. (Indestructibles Ser.). (ENG., Illus.). 12p. (J). (gr. k — 1). pap. 5.95 *(978-0-7611-5860-8(X)*, 15860) Workman Publishing Co., Inc.

Prasad, Sunayna. Alyssa's African Adventures. 2011. pap. 11.95 *(978-0-7414-6619-8(8))* Infinity Publishing.

Price, Matt. Out on a Limb. 2006. 32p. 4.50 *(978-0-8341-2229-1(4))* Beacon Hill Pr. of Kansas City.

Publications International Ltd. Staff, ed. Disney Lion King - We Can Share. 2011. 12p. (J). bds. *(978-1-4508-1383-9(6))* Publications International, Ltd.

Read, Kit. Alexis Ant Marooned in Afric. 2012. 152p. *(978-1-4602-0314-9(3))*; pap. *(978-1-4602-0313-2(5))* FriesenPress.

Redmond, Valerie. Emma & the African Wishing Bead. Victoria, Kirton, illus. 2013. 28p. pap. 13.95 *(978-1-61244-115-3(7))* Halo Publishing International.

Reece, William James. The Great Hippo Migration. 2007. 92p. per. 19.95 *(978-1-4241-9770-5(8))* America Star Bks.

Reid Banks, Lynne & Stephenson, Omri. Polly & Jake. 2010. 36p. pap. 25.50 *(978-1-4457-5277-8(8))* Lulu Pr., Inc.

Richardson, Dick. The Oglin: A Hero's Journey Across Africa... Towards the Tomorrows. Feek, Cathy, illus. 2004. 417p. (J). 24.95 *(978-0-9759440-3-5(7))* Savanna Pr.

Rodanas, Kristina. The Blind Hunter, 1 vol. Rodanas, Kristina, illus. 2003. (ENG., Illus.). 32p. (J). (gr. 1-4). 16.95 *(978-0-7614-5132-7(3))* Marshall Cavendish Corp.

Rolle, Joan & Thompson, Tracey. I Am Special. 2012. 36p. pap. 21.99 *(978-1-4653-6951-2(1))* Xlibris Corp.

Roy, Pat & Roy, Sandy. Jonathan Park: a New Beginning. 2013. (Jonathan Park Adventure Fiction Ser.: Vol. 2). (ENG.). 145p. (J). (gr. 4-7). pap. 10.00 *(978-1-937460-60-0(6))* Vision Forum, Inc., The.

—Jonathan Park: a Startling Discovery. 2013. (Jonathan Park Adventure Fiction Ser.: Vol. 1). (ENG.). 136p. (J). (gr. 4-7). pap. 10.00 (978-1-937460-59-4(2)) Vision Forum, Inc., The.
Roy, Philip. Seas of South Africa. 2013. (ENG.). 250p. pap. 11.95 (978-1-55380-247-1(0)) Ronsdale Pr. CAN. Dist: SPD-Small Pr. Distribution.
San Souci, Robert D. & Burroughs, Edgar Rice. Tarzan. McCurdy, Michael, illus. 2004. 31p. (J). (gr. k-4). reprint ed. 16.00 (978-0-7567-7576-6(0)) DIANE Publishing Co.
Sareva, Ibrahim. West of Kilimanjaro 1: Book 1. 2010. 44p. pap. 16.99 (978-1-4520-3006-7(5)) AuthorHouse.
Savory, Phyllis. The Best of African Folklore. 2015. (ENG., Illus.). 128p. pap. 12.00 (978-1-4323-0342-6(2)) Penguin Random House Grupo Editorial ESP. Dist: Casemate Pubs. & Bk. Distributors, LLC.
Schrefer, Eliot. Threatened. 2014. (ENG., Illus.). 288p. (J). (gr. 7). 17.99 (978-0-545-55143-4(9), Scholastic Pr.) Scholastic, Inc.
Schweizer, Chris. The Crogan Adventures. 2015. (ENG., Illus.). 224p. (J). pap. 17.99 (978-1-62010-243-5(9), 9781620102435) Oni Pr., Inc.
Severine Rugumamu. Further Adventures of the Black Hand Gang. 2005. 64p. pap. (978-9966-25-422-1(6)) Heinemann Kenya, Limited (East African Educational Publishers Ltd E.A.E.P.) KEN. Dist: Michigan State Univ. Pr.
Shea-Gass, Lucille. How Animals Sleep Vol. 1: In Africa. 2004. 48p. pap. 24.95 (978-1-4137-2039-6(0)) PublishAmerica, Inc.
Smart, Kimberly. A New Home for Gabril. 2008. 32p. 15.95 (978-1-4357-0762-7(1)) Lulu Pr., Inc.
The Smartest Thing. 2004. (YA). (978-0-9762904-8-3(0)) Layne Morgan Media, Inc.
Smith, Roland. Cryptid Hunters. 2006. (ENG.). 352p. (J). (gr. 5-17). pap. 6.99 (978-0-7868-5162-1(7)) Hyperion Pr.
Smithem, Beth. Dust Bunny's Mission. 2010. 84p. pap. 10.49 (978-1-4520-1934-5(7)) AuthorHouse.
Soli, Doris. Jango the Little Dragon: The Wondrous Adventures of Little Dragon. 2011. (Illus.). 36p. pap. 17.07 (978-1-4567-8487-4(0)) AuthorHouse.
Spalding, Andrea. An Island of My Own. 2008. (ENG., Illus.). 112p. (YA). (gr. 8-12). pap. 11.99 (978-1-55002-635-1(6), Sandcastle Bks.) Dundurn CAN. Dist: Ingram Publisher Services.
Spence, Stephen Mark. African Knights. 2005. 340p. (J). pap. 14.95 (978-0-9705324-4-2(X)) Spence, Stephen Mark.
St. John, Patricia. I Needed a Neighbour. 2003. 128p. 6.49 (978-0-86201-454-4(9)) Scripture Union GBR. Dist: Gabriel Resources.
Stassen, Jean-Philippe. Deogratias. 2006. (Illus.). 96p. (J). pap. (978-0-330-44467-5(0), First Second Bks.) Roaring Brook Pr.
Stephenson, Omri. Freddie Finds Out. 2010. 34p. pap. 21.50 (978-1-4457-5726-1(5)) Lulu Pr., Inc.
Stevenson, Steve. The Kenyan Expedition #8. Turconi, Stefano, illus. 2015. (Agatha: Girl of Mystery Ser.: 8). (ENG.). 144p. (J). (gr. 3-7). 5.99 (978-0-448-48679-6(2), Grosset & Dunlap) Penguin Young Readers Group.
Stewart, Dianne & Heale, Jay. African Myths & Legends. 2004. (Illus.). 96p. (978-1-86872-705-6(X)) Penguin Random House South Africa.
Stiegemeyer, Julie. Under the Baobab Tree, 1 vol. Lewis, E. B., illus. 2012. (ENG.). 32p. (J). 16.99 (978-0-310-72561-9(5)) Zonderkidz.
Stilton, Geronimo. Mighty Mount Kilimanjaro. 2010. (Geronimo Stilton Ser.: 41). (ENG.). 128p. (J). (gr. 2-5). 7.99 (978-0-545-10371-8(1), Scholastic Paperbacks) Scholastic, Inc.
Stockland, Patricia M. Anthill Home Repair, 1 vol. Haugen, Ryan, illus. 2008. (Safari Friends Ser.). (ENG.). 32p. (gr. -1-3). 28.50 (978-1-60270-082-6(6), Looking Glass Library) ABDO Publishing Co.
—The Big Banana Hunt, 1 vol. Haugen, Ryan, illus. 2008. (Safari Friends Ser.). (ENG.). 32p. (gr. -1-3). 28.50 (978-1-60270-083-3(4), Looking Glass Library) ABDO Publishing Co.
—Clean up the Watering Hole!, 1 vol. Haugen, Ryan, illus. 2008. (Safari Friends Ser.). (ENG.). 32p. (gr. -1-3). 28.50 (978-1-60270-084-0(2), Looking Glass Library) ABDO Publishing Co.
—Peanut Picking, 1 vol. Haugen, Ryan, illus. 2008. (Safari Friends Ser.). (ENG.). 32p. (gr. -1-3). 28.50 (978-1-60270-085-7(0), Looking Glass Library) ABDO Publishing Co.
—Stop the Grassfires!, 1 vol. Haugen, Ryan, illus. 2008. (Safari Friends Ser.). (ENG.). 32p. (gr. -1-3). 28.50 (978-1-60270-086-4(9), Looking Glass Library) ABDO Publishing Co.
—Tiger Toothache, 1 vol. Haugen, Ryan, illus. 2008. (Safari Friends Ser.). (ENG.). 32p. (gr. -1-3). 28.50 (978-1-60270-087-1(7), Looking Glass Library) ABDO Publishing Co.
Stojic, Manya. Rain. Stojic, Manya, illus. 2009. (Rise & Shine Ser.). (ENG., Illus.). 32p. (J). (gr. -1-2). pap. 7.99 (978-0-385-73729-6(7), Dragonfly Bks.) Random Hse. Children's Bks.
Stratton, Allan. Chanda's Secrets. 2004. (ENG., Illus.). 200p. (YA). (gr. 9-18). 3rd ed. pap. 11.95 (978-1-55037-834-4(1), 9781550378344) 4th ed. 19.95 (978-1-55037-835-1(X), 9781550378351) Annick Pr., Ltd. CAN. Dist: Publishers Group West (PGW).
—Chanda's Wars. 2009. (ENG.). 416p. (J). mass mkt. 7.99 (978-1-55468-566-0(4), Harper Trophy); (YA). (gr. 8). pap. 8.99 (978-0-06-087265-6(9), HarperTeen) HarperCollins Pubs.
—Chanda's Wars. 2011. 10.36 (978-0-7848-3486-2(5), Everbind) Marco Bk. Co.
Stumpe, Jennifer. Aunt Jo Jo's Magical Gifts: Ethan's Great African Journey. 2012. 32p. pap. 17.95 (978-1-4772-9097-2(4)) AuthorHouse.
Swarabi, Fatma Abdulla & El Amin, Khalid Hamid. Marim & Her Grandmother. 2010. 28p. pap. 13.99 (978-1-4490-8156-0(8)) AuthorHouse.
Taylor, Kay Lovelace. Princess Aisha & the Cave of Judgment. Rhine, Karen C., illus. 2007. 32p. (J). 19.95 (978-0-9799119-0-3(7)) KLT & Assocs.
Trammell, Menlia Moss. Rob & Rex Prevent a Poaching. 2012. 36p. pap. 16.95 (978-1-4626-7811-2(4)) America Star Bks.
Trodd, Mark. Hippo in the Stable. 2012. 36p. pap. 32.70 (978-1-4797-1561-9(1)) Xlibris Corp.
U. S. National Geographic Society Staff. Get with the Beat! 2009. (Toot & Puddle Ser.). (ENG., Illus.). 24p. (J). (gr. -1-2). lib. bdg. 11.90 (978-1-4263-0485-9(4), National Geographic Children's Bks.) National Geographic Society.
—Get with the Beat. 2009. (Toot & Puddle Ser.). (ENG., Illus.). 24p. (J). (gr. -1-2). pap. 3.99 (978-1-4263-0484-2(6), National Geographic Children's Bks.) National Geographic Society.
Udo, Victoria. The Children & the Yard Animals: Children of an African Village Volume 1. 2004. 31p. pap. 24.95 (978-1-4137-3215-3(1)) PublishAmerica, Inc.
Van Gorder, Vivian Ezeife. Master Kofi & Friskey the Dog. 2012. 20p. pap. 17.99 (978-1-4772-6817-9(0)) AuthorHouse.
Verde, Susan & Badiel, Georgie. The Water Princess. Reynolds, Peter H., illus. 2016. (ENG.). 40p. (J). (gr. k-3). 17.99 (978-0-399-17258-8(0), G.P. Putnam's Sons Books for Young Readers) Penguin Young Readers Group.
Voyager, Beatrice Nambouy. Mama Minko: A Survival Quest. 2010. (Illus.). 28p. pap. 15.49 (978-1-4490-5797-8(7)) AuthorHouse.
Wachtel, Shirley Russak. Brad Sureshot — Coach-Detective: The Baffling Case of the Disappearing Dribbler. 2007. 76p. per. 8.95 (978-0-595-47266-6(4)) iUniverse, Inc.
Wagler, Elizabeth. Sojourn in Africa. 2003. (Travels with Aunt Laura Ser.: Vol. 1). (Illus.). v, 256p. (J). (978-0-87813-607-0(X)) Christian Light Pubns., Inc.
Walker, Lisa & Coyne, Adrian. The Boy Who Brought Thunder. 2012. (Illus.). 40p. pap. 12.95 (978-9987-08-222-3(X)) Mkuki na Nyoka Pubs. TZA. Dist: African Bks. Collective, Ltd.
Wallace, Jim. Search for the Mountain Gorillas. Nugent, Suzanne & Donploypetch, Jintanan, illus. 2008. (Choose Your Own Adventure Ser.: No. 25). 125p. (J). (gr. 4-7). pap. 6.99 (978-1-933390-25-3(5)) Chooseco LLC.
Walters, Eric. Alexandria of Africa. 2008. (ENG.). 208p. (J). (gr. 7). pap. 12.95 (978-0-385-66639-8(X), Doubleday Canada) Penguin Random House Canada Young Readers CAN. Dist: Penguin Random Hse. LLC.
Watkins, Steve. Awol in North Africa. 2016. (Ghosts of War Ser.: 3). (ENG.). 208p. (J). (gr. 3-7). pap. 5.99 (978-0-545-83706-4(5)) Scholastic, Inc.
Watson-Doost, Valeria. Issa. 2009. 55p. pap. 9.95 (978-0-557-03625-7(9)) Lulu Pr., Inc.
Watts, Tammy E. From Libya to Namibi. 2012. 24p. 24.95 (978-1-4626-5928-9(4)) America Star Bks.
Weeks Millard, Mary. A Bilingual Parrot. 2017. (From Disgrace to Honour Ser.: Vol. 4). (ENG.). pap. **(978-1-84625-519-9(8))** DayOne Pubns.
Weston Woods Staff, creator. Mufaro's Beautiful Daughters. 2011. 29.95 (978-0-439-73504-9(1)) Weston Woods Studios, Inc.
—A Story-A Story. 2011. 18.95 (978-0-439-72891-1(6)); 29.95 (978-0-439-73521-6(1)) Weston Woods Studios, Inc.
—A Story-Astory. 2011. 38.75 (978-0-439-72892-8(4)) Weston Woods Studios, Inc.
Whelan, Gloria. Yatandou. Sylvada, Peter, illus. rev. ed. 2007. (Tales of the World Ser.). (ENG.). 32p. (J). (gr. -1-3). 17.95 (978-1-58536-211-0(5)) Sleeping Bear Pr.
White, Paul. Jungle Doctor's Africa. 2011. (Flamingo Fiction 9-13s Ser.). (ENG., Illus.). 144p. (J). 8.99 (978-1-84550-388-6(0), 97eef3f6-1cd9-4ca5-866c-66b47f498800) Christian Focus Pubns. GBR. Dist: Bookmasters Distribution.
Whitman, Sylvia. The Milk of Birds. (ENG., Illus.). 384p. (YA). (gr. 9). 2014. pap. 10.99 (978-1-4424-4683-0(8)) 2013. 16.99 (978-1-4424-4682-3(X), Atheneum Bks. for Young Readers) Simon & Schuster Children's Publishing.
Wilhelm, Hans. A Hole in the Wall. Wilhelm, Hans, illus. 2016. (ENG., Illus.). 32p. (J). 16.95 (978-0-8234-3535-7(0)) Holiday Hse., Inc.
Williams, Karen Lynn. Galimoto. Stock, Catherine, illus. 2015. 32p. pap. 7.00 (978-1-61003-604-7(2)) Center for the Collaborative Classroom.
—Lubuto Means Light. Grifalconi, Ann, illus. 2010. (ENG.). 32p. 16.95 (978-1-59078-716-8(1)) Boyds Mills Pr.
Wilson, Anna. Monkey Madness: The Only Way Is Africa! unabr. ed. 2014. (ENG., Illus.). 224p. (J). (gr. 2-4). pap. 9.99 (978-1-4472-3664-1(5)) Pan Macmillan GBR. Dist: Independent Pubs. Group.
Winfield, Arthur M. The Rover Boys in the Jungle. 2007. 212p. 27.95 (978-1-4218-4135-9(5)); per. 12.95 (978-1-4218-4233-2(5)) 1st World Publishing, Inc. (1st World Library - Literary Society).
Winmilawe. Shango's Son. Melchishua, Tewodross, illus. 2012. 20p. pap. 9.95 (978-0-9839318-0-5(1)) Gazing In Publishing.
Wooden, Itanza L. The Chill Street Gang Spring Break Vacation. 2006. (J). pap. 6.99 (978-0-9664506-3-7(9)) Dukes World, Inc.
Wright, Sabrina L. & Griffin, Dexter. Kallah: the Whispered Promise. 2005. 159p. (J). (gr. 4-7). per. 12.95 (978-0-9770363-0-1(8)) First-Sight Publishing.
Writing Club, Dancing Pencils, compiled by. Budding Words: An Anthology. 2007. 60p. pap. (978-1-86900-871-0(5)) UmSinsi Pr. ZAF. Dist: Michigan State Univ. Pr.
Wyneken, Cherise. Spaceship Lands in Africa, 1 vol. 2010. 50p. pap. 16.95 (978-1-4489-5417-9(7)) America Star Bks.
Wyss, Tyan. African Dream. Immelman, Sarita, illus. 2006. 48p. (J). pap. 15.95 (978-1-58939-915-0(3)) Virtualbookworm.com Publishing, Inc.
Young, Caroline. Grubby Finn Robinson. 2009. 52p. pap. 10.55 (978-1-4251-3002-2(X)) Trafford Publishing.
Young, Karen. A Chimpanzee Tale. 2009. (Illus.). 36p. pap. 16.99 (978-1-4389-2448-9(8)) AuthorHouse.
Youree, Barbara. Senegal Sleuths. 2006. 56p. 7.75 (978-0-8341-2226-0(X)) Beacon Hill Pr. of Kansas City.

AFRICA—HISTORY

Alexander, Richard. The Transatlantic Slave Trade: The Forced Migration of Africans to America (1607-1830), 01 vols., 1. 2016. (Spotlight on Immigration & Migration Ser.). (ENG.). 24p. (J). pap. 10.00 (978-1-5081-4100-6(2), PowerKids Pr.) Rosen Publishing Group, Inc., The.
Allen, John. Idi Amin. 2003. (History's Villains Ser.). (Illus.). 112p. (J). 28.70 (978-1-56711-759-2(7), Blackbirch Pr., Inc.) Cengage Gale.
Altman, Linda Jacobs. African Mythology Rocks! Bock, William Sauts, illus. 2011. (Mythology Rocks! Ser.). 112p. (J). (gr. 6-18). lib. bdg. 33.27 (978-0-7660-3896-7(3)) Enslow Pubs., Inc.
Amstutz, Lisa J., et al. Awesome African Animals. 2015. (Awesome African Animals! Ser.). (ENG.). 32p. (gr. 1-2). lib. bdg. 163.92 (978-1-4914-1783-6(8), Aplus Bks.) Capstone Press of Coughlan Cos.
Apseloff, Stanford S. African Animals Alphabet Book. 2010. (Illus.). (J). (978-0-9647934-8-4(2)) Ohio Distinctive Publishing, Inc.
Aretha, David. The Middle Passage. 2014. xvi, 585p. (J). (978-1-59935-408-8(X)) Reynolds, Morgan Inc.
Aspen-Baxter, Linda. Africa. (J). 2016. **(978-1-4896-5737-4(1))** 2012. 28.55 (978-1-61913-443-0(8)) 2012. pap. 13.95 (978-1-61913-444-7(6)) Weigl Pubs., Inc.
Badcott, Nicholas. Pocket Explorer: African Civilizations. 2010. (ENG.). 32p. 13.95 (978-1-56656-804-3(8), Interlink Bks.) Interlink Publishing Group, Inc.
Bankston, John. We Visit Rwanda. 2012. (J). lib. bdg. 33.95 (978-1-61228-307-4(1)) Mitchell Lane Pubs., Inc.
Banting, Erinn. Great Barrier Reef. 2012. (J). (978-1-61913-525-3(6)); pap. (978-1-61913-438-6(1)) Weigl Pubs., Inc.
Bauer, Susan Wise & Weiss, Jim. Early Modern Times Vol. 3: From Elizabeth the First to the Forty-Niners. 2nd unabr. ed. 2008. (Story of the World Ser.: 0). (ENG.). 1p. cd-rom 49.95 (978-1-933339-17-7(9), 333917) Well-Trained Mind Pr.
Cairns, Conrad. The African Knights: The Armies of Sokotu, Bornu & Bagirmi in the Nineteenth Century. 2006. (Illus.). 62p. pap. 24.95 (978-1-901543-08-7(0)) Foundry Bks. GBR. Dist: Casemate Pubs. & Bk. Distributors, LLC.
Campbell, Rusty & Porter, Malcolm. Atlas of Africa. 2009. (Atlases of the World Ser.). (Illus.). 48p. (YA). (gr. 5-8). 29.25 (978-1-4358-8454-0(X), Rosen Reference) Rosen Publishing Group, Inc., The.
Clifford, Barry. Real Pirates: The Untold Story of the Whydah from Slave Ship to Pirate Ship. Manchess, Gregory, illus. Garrett, Kenneth, photos by. 2008. (ENG.). 32p. (J). (gr. 5). 16.95 (978-1-4263-0279-4(7)); lib. bdg. 25.90 (978-1-4263-0280-0(0)) National Geographic Society. (National Geographic Children's Bks.).
Cohen, Robert Z. Discovering the Asante Kingdom. 2013. (Exploring African Civilizations Ser.). (Illus.). 64p. (J). (gr. 5-8). 31.95 (978-1-4777-1880-3(X), Rosen Reference) Rosen Publishing Group, Inc., The.
Coletti, Sharon. Everything You Need to Teach Africa. 2005. (YA). ring bd. 149.95 (978-1-933558-00-4(8)) InspirEd Educators.
Conklin, Wendy. Ancient Civilizations - China - India - Africa - Mesopotamia: All-in-One Resource with Background Information, Map Activities, Simulations & Games, & a Read-Aloud Play to Support Comprehension & Critical Thinking in Social Studies, Grades 5 & Up. 2006. (Ancient Civilizations Ser.). (ENG., Illus.). 96p. (gr. 5). per. 14.99 (978-0-439-53993-7(5), Teaching Resources) Scholastic, Inc.
Conrad, David C. Empires of Medieval West Africa, Revised Edition. 2nd rev. ed. 2009. (Great Empires of the Past Ser.). (Illus.). 152p. (gr. 6-12). 35.00 (978-1-60413-164-2(0), Chelsea Hse.) Facts On File, Inc.
Cook, Diane. Cameroon. 2012. (J). pap. (978-1-4222-2222-5(5)) Mason Crest.
—Cameroon. Rotberg, Robert I., ed. 2012. (Evolution of Africa's Major Nations Ser.). (Illus.). 80p. (J). (gr. 7). 22.95 (978-1-4222-2194-5(6)) Mason Crest.
Cooper, Ross Gordon. Common Antelope in Africa, 1 vol. 2010. 22p. pap. 24.95 (978-1-4489-5552-7(1)) PublishAmerica, Inc.
Craats, Rennay. Maasai. 2012. (J). (978-1-61913-171-2(4)) Weigl Pubs., Inc.
Cuthbert, Megan. Africa. 2014. (J). (978-1-4896-0934-2(2)) Weigl Pubs., Inc.
Dau, John Bul. Lost Boy Lost Girl: Escaping Civil War in Sudan. 2010. (ENG., Illus.). 160p. (YA). (gr. 7-18). 23.90 (978-1-4263-0709-6(8), National Geographic Children's Bks.) National Geographic Society.
Dau, John Bul & Akech, Martha Arual. Lost Boy, Lost Girl: Escaping Civil War in Sudan. 2010. (ENG., Illus.). 160p. (YA). (gr. 7-18). 15.95 (978-1-4263-0708-9(X), National Geographic Children's Bks.) National Geographic Society.
Davenport, John. A Brief Political & Geographic History of Africa: Where Are... Belgian Congo, Rhodesia, & Kush. 2007. (Places in Time Ser.). (Illus.). 112p. (YA). (gr. 5-9). lib. bdg. 37.10 (978-1-58415-624-6(4)) Mitchell Lane Pubs., Inc.
Doeden, Matt. Central African Republic in Pictures. 2009. (Visual Geography Series, Second Ser.). (ENG., Illus.). 80p. (J). (gr. 5-12). 31.93 (978-1-57505-952-5(5)) Lerner Publishing Group.
Donn, Lin & Donn, Don. Ancient & Medieval Africa. 2012. (World History: Mr. Donn & Maxie's Always Something You Can Use Ser.). (ENG., Illus.). 115p. pap. 24.95 (978-1-59647-411-6(4)) Good Year Bks.
Eszterhas, Suzi. Eye on the Wild: Lion. 2012. (Eye on the Wild Ser.: 3). (Illus.). 32p. (J). (978-1-84780-310-8(5), Frances Lincoln) Quarto Publishing Group UK.
Exploration of Africa: The Emerging Nations. 2005. (Exploration of Africa Ser.). 144p. (gr. 6-12). 245.00 (978-0-7910-6267-8(6), Chelsea Hse.) Facts On File, Inc.
Exploring African Civilizations. 2013. (Exploring African Civilizations Ser.). 64p. (J). (gr. 5-8). 191.70 (978-1-4777-1892-6(3), Rosen Reference) Rosen Publishing Group, Inc., The.
Focus on Africa. 2016. (Focus on Africa Ser.). 128p. (YA). lib. bdg. 273.84 (978-1-5026-2385-0(4)) Cavendish Square Publishing.
Friedman, Mel. Africa. 2008. (True Book(tm), A — Continents Ser.). (ENG., Illus.). 48p. (J). (gr. 2-5). 31.00 (978-0-531-16863-9(8)) Scholastic Library Publishing.
Gibbs, Maddie. Flamingos: Flamencos. 2011. (Safari Animals / Animales de Safari Ser.). (SPA & ENG., Illus.). 24p. (J). (gr. -1-2). lib. bdg. 22.60 (978-1-4488-3213-2(6)) Rosen Publishing Group, Inc., The.
Giles, Bridget. West African Myths. 2010. (Myths from Around the World Ser.). 48p. (gr. 6-8). (YA). lib. bdg. 31.00 (978-1-4339-3536-7(8)); (Illus.). (J). pap. 14.05 (978-1-4339-3537-4(6)) Stevens, Gareth Publishing LLLP. (Gareth Stevens Secondary Library).
Glynne, Andy. Hamid's Story: A Real-Life Account of His Journey from Eritrea. 2017. (Seeking Refuge Ser.). (ENG.). 32p. (gr. 3-4). 27.32 **(978-1-5158-1413-9(0))** Picture Window Bks.
Green, Nehanda. The Adventures of Jaja & Jamila Going to Africa: Going to Africa, no. 2009. (ENG., Illus.). 47p. (J). pap. 7.95 (978-0-9824506-0-4(5)) Keira Pr.
Group/McGraw-Hill, Wright. Africa: Rich in Land & History, 6 vols. (Book2WebTM Ser.). (gr. 4-8). 36.50 (978-0-322-04439-5(1)) Wright Group/McGraw-Hill.
Gumede, William. A Kite's Flight. Sereda, Maja, illus. 2011. (ENG.). 32p. (J). (gr. k-2). pap. 11.00 (978-1-77009-804-6(6)) Jacana Media ZAF. Dist: Independent Pubs. Group.
Hay, Jeff. The Crisis in Darfur. Gale Editors, ed. 2011. (Perspectives on Modern World History Ser.). 224p. (YA). (gr. 10-12). lib. bdg. 42.45 (978-0-7377-5257-1(2), Greenhaven Pr., Inc.) Cengage Gale.
Hirsch, Rebecca E. Africa. 2012. (ENG., Illus.). 32p. (J). lib. bdg. 23.00 (978-0-531-28975-4(3)); (gr. -1-1). pap. 5.95 (978-0-531-29275-4(4)) Scholastic Library Publishing.
Hynson, Colin. Exploration of Africa. 2010. (History of Exploration Ser.). 48p. 32.80 (978-1-84898-300-7(X)) Black Rabbit Bks.
Jal, David. David's Journey: The Story of David Jal, One of the Lost Boys of Sudan. Bezesky, Tracy, illus. 2012. 32p. 20.00 (978-1-934478-30-1(X)) Sunray Publishing.
Kalman, Bobbie & Sjonger, Rebecca. Explora África. 2007. (Explora Los Continentes Ser.). (SPA., Illus.). 32p. (J). (gr. 3-7). pap. (978-0-7787-8295-7(6)) Crabtree Publishing Co.
Katis, Alex. Africa: People, Places, & Cultures. 2005. (ENG., Illus.). 50p. (gr. 4-12). 9.95 (978-0-7611-3978-2(8), 13978) Workman Publishing Co., Inc.
Kavanaugh, Dorothy. Sudan. 2012. (J). pap. (978-1-4222-2213-3(6)) Mason Crest.
—Sudan & Southern Sudan. Rotberg, Robert I., ed. 2012. (Evolution of Africa's Major Nations Ser.). (Illus.). 80p. (J). (gr. 7). 22.95 (978-1-4222-2185-3(7)) Mason Crest.
Keedle, Jayne. West African Americans. 2009. (New Americans Ser.). (Illus.). 80p. (J). (gr. 5-8). 35.64 (978-0-7614-4313-1(4)) Marshall Cavendish Corp.
Kennedy, Mike & Stewart, Mark. Soccer in Africa. 2011. (Smart about Soccer Ser.). 24p. (J). (gr. k-3). lib. bdg. 22.60 (978-1-59953-441-1(X)) Norwood Hse. Pr.
King, David C. Mozambique. 2006. (Cultures of the World Ser.). (Illus.). 144p. (gr. 6-7). lib. bdg. 42.79 (978-0-7614-2331-7(1), Benchmark Bks.) Marshall Cavendish Corp.
—Rwanda. 2006. (Cultures of the World Ser.). (Illus.). 144p. (gr. 6-7). lib. bdg. 42.79 (978-0-7614-2333-1(8), Benchmark Bks.) Marshall Cavendish Corp.
Klepeis, Alicia. Africa, 1 vol. 2013. (Continents Ser.). (ENG.). 48p. (J). (gr. 3-6). lib. bdg. 32.79 (978-1-61783-928-3(0)) ABDO Publishing Co.
Koontz, Robin Michal. Learning about Africa. 2015. (ENG., Illus.). 40p. (J). (gr. 3-5). 29.32 (978-1-4677-8013-1(8), Lerner Pubns.) Lerner Publishing Group.
Kummer, Patricia K. Africa. 2013. (J). (978-0-7614-8088-4(9)) Marshall Cavendish Corp.
Lekuton, Joseph Lemasolai & Viola, Herman. Facing the Lion: Growing up Maasai on the African Savanna. 2005. (ENG.). 128p. (YA). (gr. 7-12). pap. 6.95 (978-0-7922-7297-7(8), National Geographic Children's Bks.) National Geographic Society.
Levy, Janey. Genocide in Darfur. 2009. (Genocide in Modern Times Ser.). 64p. (gr. 6-6). 58.50 (978-1-61512-673-6(2)) Rosen Publishing Group, Inc., The.
Lewin, Ted. Look! Lewin, Ted, illus. (I Like to Read(r) Ser.). (ENG., Illus.). 24p. (J). (gr. -1-3). 2014. 6.99 (978-0-8234-3059-8(6)) 2013. 14.95 (978-0-8234-2607-2(6)) Holiday Hse., Inc.
Lewis, Susan Grant. Education in Africa. Rotberg, Robert I. & Ojakorotu, Victor, eds. 2013. (Africa: Progress & Problems Ser.: 13). (Illus.). 112p. (J). (gr. 7-18). 24.95 (978-1-4222-2938-5(6)) Mason Crest.
Lewis, Wendy. Sabrina, the Girl with a Hole in Her Heart. 2011. 16.95 (978-0-615-47819-7(0)) Two Dolphins Publishing Group.
Linde, Barbara M. Mapping Africa. 2013. (Mapping the World Ser.). 24p. (J). (gr. 2-5). pap. 48.90 (978-1-4339-9091-5(1)); (Illus.). 22.60 (978-1-4339-9089-2(X)); (Illus.). pap. 8.15 (978-1-4339-9090-8(3)) Stevens, Gareth Publishing LLLP.
Lonely Planet Publications Staff. Africa: Everything You Ever Wanted to Know, 1 vol. 2013. (Lonely Planet Kids Ser.). (ENG., Illus.). 96p. (J). pap. 12.99 (978-1-74321-911-9(3), 4625) Lonely Planet Pubns.
Lonely Planet Publications Staff, et al. Let's Explore... Safari, 1 vol. 2016. (Lonely Planet Kids Ser.). (ENG.). 48p. (J). pap. 9.99 (978-1-76034-039-1(1), 5145) Lonely Planet Pubns.
Lowery, Zoe & Spalding, Frank. The Rwandan Genocide. 2016. (Bearing Witness: Genocide & Ethnic Cleansing in the Modern World Ser.). 64p. (J). (gr. 6-6). 34.45 (978-1-4777-8570-6(1)) Rosen Publishing Group, Inc., The.
Madison, Amelia. Predators of Europe & Africa. 2015. (J). lib. bdg. (978-1-62713-553-5(7)) Cavendish Square Publishing.
Manning, Paul. Nile River. 2014. (River Adventures Ser.). (J). lib. bdg. 31.35 (978-1-59920-917-3(9)) Black Rabbit Bks.
Marsh, Laura. Great Migrations - Elephants. 2010. (Readers Ser.). (ENG., Illus.). 48p. (J). (gr. 2-4). 13.90 (978-1-4263-0744-7(6)); pap. 3.99 (978-1-4263-0743-0(8)) National Geographic Society. (National Geographic Children's Bks.).
Marshall Cavendish. The Lost Boys of Sudan. 2011. (Great Escapes Ser.). 80p. (gr. 6). 34.21 (978-1-60870-475-0(0)) Marshall Cavendish Corp.
Mason, Paul. Daily Life in Ancient Benin. 2015. (Daily Life in Ancient Civilizations Ser.). (ENG., Illus.). 48p. (gr. 3-6). pap. 8.99 (978-1-4846-2580-4(3)) Heinemann-Raintree.
Matthews, Caitlin & Williams, Sophy. Secret Bride, Runaway Princess: Two Stories from Rwanda. 2006. (J). (978-1-905236-90-9(5)) Barefoot Bks., Inc.
Medieval Africa DBA. 2003. spiral bd. 16.95 (978-1-56004-170-2(6)) Social Studies Schl. Service.
Michele, Tracey. African Art. 2011. (Learn-Abouts Ser.). (Illus.). 16p. (J). pap. 7.95 (978-1-59920-637-0(4)) Black Rabbit Bks.

Miller, Danny & National Geographic Learning Staff. African Journeys, 1850-1900. 2007. (Reading Expeditions Ser.). (ENG., Illus.). 32p. (J). pap. 17.95 *(978-0-7922-4545-2(8))* CENGAGE Learning.

Miller, Derek L. The Economy in Contemporary Africa. 2016. (Focus on Africa Ser.). 128p. (YA). 45.64 *(978-1-5026-2374-4(9))* Cavendish Square Publishing.

Mulroy, Tanya. Mozambique. 2012. (J). pap. *(978-1-4222-2210-2(1))* Mason Crest.

Murray, Jocelyn. Africa. 3rd rev. ed. 2007. (Cultural Atlas for Young People Ser.). (Illus.). 96p. (YA). (gr. 5-9). 35.00 *(978-0-8160-6826-5(7))* Facts On File, Inc.

Napoli, Tony. Vasco Da Gama: Discovering the Sea Route to India. 2010. (Great Explorers of the World Ser.). (Illus.). 112p. (J). (gr. 7-12). 33.27 *(978-1-59845-127-6(8))* Enslow Pubs., Inc.

Nardo, Don. The European Colonization of Africa. 2011. (World History Ser.). (Illus.). 112p. 28.95 *(978-1-59935-142-1(0))* Reynolds, Morgan Inc.

Oachs, Emily Rose. Africa. (Africa Ser.). 24p. (J). (gr. k-3). 2017. pap. 6.99 ***(978-1-61891-254-1(2))*** 2016. (ENG., Illus.). lib. bdg. 25.95 *(978-1-62617-323-1(0))* Bellwether Media. (Blastoff! Readers).

Obadina, Tunde. The Making of Modern Africa. Ojakorotu, Victor & Rotberg, Robert I., eds. 2013. (Africa: Progress & Problems Ser.: 13). (Illus.). 128p. (J). (gr. 7-18). 24.95 *(978-1-4222-2944-6(0))* Mason Crest.

O'Brien, Cynthia. Explore with Stanley & Livingstone. 2016. (Travel with the Great Explorers Ser.). (ENG., Illus.). 32p. (J). (gr. 3-6). *(978-0-7787-2848-1(X))* Crabtree Publishing Co.

O'Connell, Caitlin. A Baby Elephant in the Wild. O'Connell, Caitlin & Rodwell, Timothy, illus. 2014. (ENG.). 40p. (J). (gr. -1-3). 17.99 *(978-0-544-14944-1(0),* HMH Books For Young Readers) Houghton Mifflin Harcourt Publishing Co.

Onyefulu, Ifeoma. Home. 2013. (ENG., Illus.). 32p. (J). (gr. -1-k). 17.99 *(978-1-84780-266-8(4),* Frances Lincoln) Quarto Publishing Group UK GBR. Dist: Hachette Bk. Group.

—Look at This! - Play. 2013. (ENG., Illus.). 32p. (J). (gr. -1-k). 17.99 *(978-1-84780-267-5(2),* Frances Lincoln) Quarto Publishing Group UK GBR. Dist: Hachette Bk. Group.

Otfinoski, Steven. World War II Infantrymen: An Interactive History Adventure. 2013. (You Choose: World War II Ser.). (ENG., 112p. (gr. 3-4). Illus.). pap. 6.95 *(978-1-62065-716-4(3));* lib. bdg. 31.99 *(978-1-4296-9964-8(7))* Capstone Press of Coughlan Cos. (You Choose Bks.).

Owings, Lisa. Somalia. 2015. (Exploring Countries Ser.). (ENG., Illus.). 32p. (J). (gr. 3-7). lib. bdg. 26.95 *(978-1-62617-177-0(7),* Blastoff! Readers) Bellwether Media.

—South Sudan. 2012. (Exploring Countries Ser.). (ENG., Illus.). 32p. (J). (gr. 3-7). lib. bdg. 26.95 *(978-1-60014-765-4(8),* Blastoff! Readers) Bellwether Media.

Paquet, Laura Byrne. The Environment in Contemporary Africa. 2016. (Focus on Africa Ser.). 128p. (YA). 45.64 *(978-1-5026-2393-5(5))* Cavendish Square Publishing.

Peppas, Lynn. Piracy. 2013. (ENG.). 48p. (J). *(978-0-7787-1103-2(X));* pap. *(978-0-7787-1123-0(4))* Crabtree Publishing Co.

Peterson, Megan Cooley & Rustad, Martha E. H. Zebras Are Awesome! 2015. (Awesome African Animals! Ser.). (ENG.). 32p. (gr. 1-2). lib. bdg. 27.32 *(978-1-4914-1764-5(1))* Capstone Press of Coughlan Cos.

Peyton, Katherine & George, Enzo. World War II in Europe & North Africa: Preserving Democracy. 2014. (Voices of War Ser.). 48p. (J). (gr. 4-6). lib. bdg. 31.36 *(978-1-62712-864-3(6))* Cavendish Square Publishing.

Pipe, Jim. Hoping for Peace in Sudan. 2012. (Peace Pen Pals Ser.). (Illus.). 48p. (J). (gr. 6-8). pap. 14.05 *(978-1-4339-7740-4(0));* lib. bdg. 31.95 *(978-1-4339-7739-8(7))* Stevens, Gareth Publishing LLLP.

Randolph, Joanne. Number Crunch Your Way Around Africa. 2015. (Math Exploration: Using Math to Learn about the Continents Ser.). (ENG., Illus.). 32p. (J). (gr. 3-4). pap. 10.00 *(978-1-4994-1234-5(7),* PowerKids Pr.) Rosen Publishing Group, Inc., The.

Rebus, Anna. Victoria Falls: One of the World's Most Spectacular Waterfalls. 2006. (Natural Wonders Ser.). (Illus.). 32p. (gr. 3-7). 17.95 *(978-0-7569-6998-1(0))* Perfection Learning Corp.

Rice, William B. African Grasslands, 1 vol. 2nd rev. ed. 2014. (TIME for KIDS(r) Nonfiction Readers Ser.). (ENG., Illus.). 32p. (J). (gr. 3-3). pap. 25.96 *(978-1-4807-1079-5(2))* Shell Educational Publishing.

Richardson, Hazel. Life in Ancient Africa. 2005. (Peoples of the Ancient World Ser.). (ENG., Illus.). 32p. (J). (gr. -1-9). pap. *(978-0-7787-2073-7(X))* Crabtree Publishing Co.

Roberts, Russell. The African Union. Rotberg, Robert I., ed. 2012. (Evolution of Africa's Major Nations Ser.). (Illus.). 80p. (J). (gr. 7). 22.95 *(978-1-4222-2190-7(3))* Mason Crest.

—The African Union. 2011. (J). pap. *(978-1-4222-2218-8(7))* Mason Crest.

—The African Union. Rotberg, Robert I., ed. 2009. (Africa Ser.). (Illus.). 80p. (YA). (gr. 3-7). lib. bdg. 21.95 *(978-1-4222-0093-3(0))* Mason Crest.

Rockett, Paul. Mapping Africa. 2016. (Illus.). 32p. (J). *(978-0-7787-2612-8(6))* Crabtree Publishing Co.

Rotberg, Robert I., ed. Africa: Continent in the Balance, 13 vols., Set. 2005. (Illus.). 88p. (YA). lib. bdg. *(978-1-59084-807-4(1))* Mason Crest.

Roth, Susan L. & Trumbore, Cindy. The Mangrove Tree: Planting Trees to Feed Families. Roth, Susan L., illus. 2011. (ENG., Illus.). 40p. (J). (gr. 1-6). 19.95 *(978-1-60060-459-1(5))* Lee & Low Bks., Inc.

Roumanis, Alexis. Africa. 2014. (Illus.). 24p. (J). *(978-1-4896-3022-3(8))* Weigl Pubs., Inc.

Sánchez, Lucía M. & Taylor, Trace. Guinea (Spanish) 2011. (2Y Nuestro Mundo Ser.). (SPA.). 16p. (J). pap. 6.99 *(978-1-61406-060-4(6))* American Reading Co.

Schomp, Virginia. The Ancient Africans. 2008. (Myths of the World Ser.). 96p. (gr. 6-18). lib. bdg. 34.21 *(978-0-7614-3099-5(7),* Benchmark Bks.) Marshall Cavendish Corp.

Sheehan, Sean. Ancient African Kingdoms. 2010. (Exploring the Ancient World Ser.). (Illus.). 64p. (YA). (gr. 6-8). lib. bdg. 34.60 *(978-1-4339-4157-3(0),* Gareth Stevens Secondary Library) Stevens, Gareth Publishing LLLP.

Sheehan, Sean & Elias, Josie. Cameroon. 2nd rev. ed. 2010. (Cultures of the World 21 Ser.). 144p. (gr. 6). lib. bdg. 42.79 *(978-1-60870-214-5(6))* Marshall Cavendish Corp.

Sherrow, Victoria. Ancient Africa: Archaeology Unlocks the Secrets of Africa's Past. 2007. (National Geographic Investigates Ser.). (ENG., Illus.). 64p. (J). (gr. 5). 17.95 *(978-0-7922-5384-6(1));* lib. bdg. 27.90 *(978-0-7922-5399-0(X))* National Geographic Society. (National Geographic Children's Bks.).

Shuter, Jane. Ancient West African Kingdoms, 1 vol. 2003. (History Opens Windows Ser.). (ENG., Illus.). 32p. (J). (gr. 2-4). pap. 7.50 *(978-1-4034-0083-3(0))* Heinemann-Raintree.

Sjonger, Rebecca. L'Afrique. 2012. (FRE.). 32p. (J). pap. 9.95 *(978-2-89579-455-4(3))* Bayard Canada CAN. Dist: Crabtree Publishing Co.

Spalding, Frank. Genocide in Rwanda. (Genocide in Modern Times Ser.). 64p. 2009. (gr. 6-6). 58.50 *(978-1-61512-674-3(0))* 2008. (Illus.). (YA). (gr. 9-12). lib. bdg. 31.95 *(978-1-4042-1823-9(8))* Rosen Publishing Group, Inc., The.

Spears-Johnson, Dedra. Remember Who You Are. 2006. 28p. per. 15.95 *(978-1-59858-230-7(5))* Dog Ear Publishing, LLC.

Steele, Philip. Benin. 2015. (Collins Big Cat Ser.). (ENG., Illus.). 56p. (J). (gr. 5-6). pap. 9.95 *(978-0-00-812794-7(8))* HarperCollins Pubs. Ltd. GBR. Dist: Independent Pubs. Group.

Sudan. 2010. (Modern World Nations Ser.). (Illus.). 136p. (gr. 6-12). 35.00 *(978-1-60413-620-3(0),* Chelsea Hse.) Facts On File, Inc.

Toler, Pamela D. Transatlantic Slave Networks. 2017. (J). ***(978-1-5026-2696-7(9))*** Cavendish Square Publishing.

UNESCO. Njinga Mbandi: Queen of Ndonga & Matamba. 2016. (ENG., Illus.). 112p. (J). (gr. 3-7). 13.95 *(978-0-00-814937-6(2))* HarperCollins Pubs. Ltd. GBR. Dist: Independent Pubs. Group.

—Women Soldiers of Dahomey. 2016. (ENG., Illus.). 112p. (J). (gr. 3-7). 13.95 *(978-0-00-814936-9(4))* HarperCollins Pubs. Ltd. GBR. Dist: Independent Pubs. Group.

White, Bender Richardson, et al. African Traditional Religion. 3rd rev. ed. 2009. (World Religions Ser.). (Illus.). 144p. (gr. 6-12). 40.00 *(978-1-60413-103-1(9),* Chelsea Hse.) Facts On File, Inc.

Wiedemer & Steel, Abigail. Africa. 2013. (Collins Big Cat Phonics Progress Ser.). (ENG., Illus.). 16p. (J). (gr. 1-2). pap. 6.95 *(978-0-00-751634-6(7))* HarperCollins Pubs. Ltd. GBR. Dist: Independent Pubs. Group.

Wildlife Safari Africa, Swahili & English: Who's Who in the African Jungle & Savanna, a Swahili/English Multicultural Book. 2004. (J). per. 9.95 *(978-0-9742688-2-8(8))* Ndegwa, Catherine W.

Wilson, Ray. Kelsey's Lessons on Africa Vol 2. 2013. 42p. pap. 12.00 *(978-0-9857741-1-0(8))* Village Publishing.

Wolny, Philip. Discovering the Empire of Mali. 2013. (Exploring African Civilizations Ser.). 64p. (J). (gr. 5-8). 31.95 *(978-1-4777-1883-4(4),* Rosen Reference) Rosen Publishing Group, Inc., The.

Woods, Michael & Woods, Mary B. Seven Natural Wonders of Africa. 2009. (Seven Wonders Ser.). (ENG., Illus.). 80p. (gr. 5-8). lib. bdg. 33.26 *(978-0-8225-9071-2(9))* Lerner Publishing Group.

World Book, Inc Staff, contrib. by. Endangered & Threatened Species of Africa. 2014. (J). *(978-0-7166-5621-0(3))* World Bk., Inc.

Zamosky, Lisa. Mansa Musa: Leader of Mali, 1 vol. 2007. (Primary Source Readers Ser.). (ENG.). 32p. (J). (gr. 4-4). pap. 8.99 *(978-0-7439-0439-1(7))* Shell Educational Publishing.

AFRICA, NORTH

Benchmark Education Company. Kingdom of Kush (Teacher Guide) 2005. *(978-1-4108-4654-9(7))* Benchmark Education Co.

Bowden, Rob. The Middle East & North Africa. 2016. (Regions of the World Ser.). (ENG.). 64p. pap. 9.99 *(978-1-4846-4021-0(7),* NA-h) Heinemann-Raintree.

Brannon, Barbara. Discover the Kingdom of Kush. 2005. (J). pap. *(978-1-4108-5160-4(5))* Benchmark Education Co.

Levy, Patricia, et al. Sudan. 2017. (J). ***(978-1-5026-2611-0(X))*** Cavendish Square Publishing.

Piddock, Charles. Sudan. 2006. (Nations in the News Ser.). 48p. (gr. 5-12). pap. 14.05 *(978-0-8368-6718-3(1));* (Illus.). lib. bdg. 31.00 *(978-0-8368-6711-4(4))* Stevens, Gareth Publishing LLLP. (Gareth Stevens Secondary Library).

Ryall, Michael. The Kingdom of Kush. 2005. (J). pap. *(978-1-4108-4606-8(7))* Benchmark Education Co.

Stefoff, Rebecca. Redbeard. 2015. (J). lib. bdg. *(978-1-62713-533-7(2))* Cavendish Square Publishing.

Weintraub, Aileen. The Barbarossa Brothers: 16th-Century Pirates of the Barbary Coast. 2009. (Library of Pirates Ser.). 24p. (gr. 3-3). 42.50 *(978-1-60853-814-0(1),* PowerKids Pr.) Rosen Publishing Group, Inc., The.

AFRICA, NORTH—FICTION

Grant, Karima. Sofie & the City. Montecalvo, Janet, illus. 2006. (ENG.). 32p. (J). (gr. 1-3). 15.95 *(978-1-59078-273-6(9))* Boyds Mills Pr.

Lynch, Chris. The Right Fight. 2014. 189p. (YA). *(978-0-545-63728-2(7),* Scholastic Pr.) Scholastic, Inc.

—World War II Book 1: the Right Fight. 2014. (World War II Ser.). (ENG.). 192p. (J). (gr. 5-9). 18.99 *(978-0-545-52294-6(3),* Scholastic Pr.) Scholastic, Inc.

Pinkney, Andrea Davis. The Red Pencil. Evans, Shane W., illus. 2014. (ENG.). 336p. (J). (gr. 4-17). 17.99 *(978-0-316-24780-1(4))* Little, Brown Bks. for Young Readers.

St. John, Patricia. Secret of the Fourth Candle. rev. ed. 2003. (Illus.). 94p. 6.49 *(978-1-85999-511-2(X))* Scripture Union GBR. Dist: Gabriel Resources.

AFRICA—POLITICS AND GOVERNMENT

Childress, Diana. Omar Al-Bashir's Sudan. 2009. (Dictatorships Ser.). (ENG., Illus.). 160p. (J). (gr. 9-12). 38.60 *(978-0-8225-9096-5(4),* 1299570) Lerner Publishing Group.

Habeeb, William Mark. Civil Wars in Africa. Ojakorotu, Victor & Rotberg, Robert I., eds. 2013. (Africa: Progress & Problems Ser.: 13). (Illus.). 112p. (J). (gr. 7-18). 24.95 *(978-1-4222-2936-1(X))* Mason Crest.

Marcovitz, Hal. Islam in Africa. Ojakorotu, Victor & Rotberg, Robert I., eds. 2013. (Africa: Progress & Problems Ser.: 13). (Illus.). 112p. (J). (gr. 7-18). 24.95 *(978-1-4222-2943-9(2))* Mason Crest.

Obadina, Tunde. Population & Overcrowding. Ojakorotu, Victor & Rotberg, Robert I., eds. 2013. (Africa: Progress & Problems Ser.: 13). (Illus.). 112p. (J). (gr. 7-18). 24.95 *(978-1-4222-2945-3(9))* Mason Crest.

Roberts, Russell. The African Union. Rotberg, Robert I., ed. 2012. (Evolution of Africa's Major Nations Ser.). (Illus.). 80p. (J). (gr. 7). 22.95 *(978-1-4222-2190-7(3))* Mason Crest.

—The African Union. 2011. (J). pap. *(978-1-4222-2218-8(7))* Mason Crest.

Rotberg, Robert I. Governance & Leadership in Africa. Rotberg, Robert I. & Ojakorotu, Victor, eds. 2013. (Africa: Progress & Problems Ser.: 13). (Illus.). 112p. (J). (gr. 7-18). 24.95 *(978-1-4222-2940-8(8))* Mason Crest.

Shah, Anup. Helping Africa Help Itself: A Global Effort. Ojakorotu, Victor & Rotberg, Robert I., eds. 2013. (Africa: Progress & Problems Ser.: 13). (Illus.). 112p. (J). (gr. 7-18). 24.95 *(978-1-4222-2941-5(6))* Mason Crest.

Trussell-Cullen, Alan. Nelson Mandela. 2009. pap. 13.25 *(978-1-60559-067-7(3))* Hameray Publishing Group, Inc.

AFRICA—SOCIAL LIFE AND CUSTOMS

African Dance. 2nd rev. ed. 2010. (World of Dance Ser.). (Illus.). 136p. (C). (gr. 9-18). 35.00 *(978-1-60413-477-3(1),* Chelsea Hse.) Facts On File, Inc.

Alexanyan, Karina. An African Odyssey. 2004. 96p. pap. *(978-0-9688648-6-9(4))* Parkhurst Publishing, Ltd.

Badcott, Nicholas. Pocket Explorer: African Civilizations. 2010. (ENG.). 32p. 13.95 *(978-1-56656-804-3(8),* Interlink Bks.) Interlink Publishing Group, Inc.

Centore, Michael & Lebeko, Tshwarelo. My Teenage Life in South Africa. 2017. (Illus.). 128p. (J). ***(978-1-4222-3911-7(X))*** Mason Crest.

Cohen, Robert Z. Discovering the Asante Kingdom. 2013. (Exploring African Civilizations Ser.). (Illus.). 64p. (J). (gr. 5-8). 31.95 *(978-1-4777-1880-3(X),* Rosen Reference) Rosen Publishing Group, Inc., The.

CultureGrams 2006 World Edition - the Americas. 2005. (YA). per. 129.99 *(978-1-931694-93-3(1),* CultureGrams World Edition) ProQuest LLC.

Diakite, Baba Wague. A Gift from Childhood: Memories of an African Boyhood, 1 vol. 2013. (ENG., Illus.). 136p. (J). (gr. 4). pap. 12.95 *(978-1-55498-421-3(1))* Groundwood Bks. CAN. Dist: Publishers Group West (PGW).

Gadri, Stephen Awudi. The Revealed Myths about Trokosi Slavery: Human Rights Violations. 2010. 96p. pap. 28.99 *(978-1-4490-3702-4(X))* AuthorHouse.

Habeeb, William Mark. Civil Wars in Africa. Ojakorotu, Victor & Rotberg, Robert I., eds. 2013. (Africa: Progress & Problems Ser.: 13). (Illus.). 112p. (J). (gr. 7-18). 24.95 *(978-1-4222-2936-1(X))* Mason Crest.

Harvey, Miles. Look What Came from Africa. 2003. (Look What Came from... Ser.). (ENG., Illus.). 32p. (J). (gr. 2-4). pap. 6.95 *(978-0-531-16626-0(0))* Scholastic Library Publishing.

Hinds, Kathryn. The Pharaoh's Court. 2006. (Life in Ancient Egypt Ser.). (Illus.). 80p. (gr. 6-7). lib. bdg. 34.21 *(978-0-7614-2183-2(1),* Benchmark Bks.) Marshall Cavendish Corp.

Howell, Izzi. Benin. 2017. (Explore! Ser.). (ENG., Illus.). 32p. (J). (gr. 4-6). 16.99 *(978-1-5263-0084-3(2),* Wayland) Hachette Children's Group GBR. Dist: Hachette Bk. Group.

Klepeis, Alicia. Kenya. 2017. (J). pap. 19.95 ***(978-1-5026-2504-5(0))*** Cavendish Square Publishing.

Kuskowski, Alex. Super Simple African Art: Fun & Easy Art from Around the World, 1 vol. 2012. (ENG.). 32p. 27.07 *(978-1-61783-210-9(3),* Super SandCastle) ABDO Publishing Co.

Lekuton, Joseph Lemasolai. Facing the Lion: Growing up Maasai on the African Savanna. 2003. (ENG., Illus.). 144p. (YA). (gr. 7-18). 15.95 *(978-0-7922-5125-5(3),* National Geographic Children's Bks.) National Geographic Society.

Macdonald, Fiona. The Egyptians. 2011. (Children in History Ser.). (Illus.). 32p. (YA). (gr. 4-7). lib. bdg. 28.50 *(978-1-59771-269-9(8),* 1324614) Sea-To-Sea Pubns.

Meade, Deborah & National Geographic Learning Staff. Africa. 2007. (Reading Expeditions Ser.). (ENG., Illus.). 64p. (J). pap. 25.95 *(978-0-7922-4365-6(X))* CENGAGE Learning.

Musgrove, Margaret. Ashanti to Zulu: African Traditions. Dillon, Leo & Dillon, Diane, illus. 2004. 28p. (YA). (gr. 4-8). reprint ed. pap. 14.00 *(978-0-7567-7106-5(4))* DIANE Publishing Co.

NASA Astronauts of Color: African American, Hispanic, Chinese, Japanese & Indian 2nd Edition 2009. 2009. (My Ancestors — My Heroes Ser.: Vol. 3). (ENG., Illus.). 190p. (J). (gr. 3-4). cd-rom 18.95 *(978-1-893091-02-3(3),* My Ancestors, My Heroes) Parker-Wallace Publishing Co., LLC.

Onyefulu, Ifeoma. A de Africa. 2005. (SPA.). 28p. (J). (gr. 2-7). 18.95 *(978-84-89970-67-0(X))* Fundacion Intermon ESP. Dist: Iaconi, Mariuccia Bk. Imports.

—My Grandfather Is a Magician: Work & Wisdom in an African Village. 2006. (ENG., Illus.). 32p. (J). (gr. -1-3). pap. 8.95 *(978-1-84507-510-1(2),* Frances Lincoln) Quarto Publishing Group UK GBR. Dist: Hachette Bk. Group.

—Your Name Is Dede: An African Baby's Naming Ceremony. 2003. (Illus.). 32p. (J). *(978-0-7112-1938-0(9))* ReiseArt Buchhandlung GmbH.

Schomp, Virginia. The Ancient Africans. 2008. (Myths of the World Ser.). 96p. (gr. 6-18). lib. bdg. 34.21 *(978-0-7614-3099-5(7),* Benchmark Bks.) Marshall Cavendish Corp.

Shoveller, Herb. Ryan & Jimmy: And the Well in Africa That Brought Them Together. 2006. (CitizenKid Ser.). (ENG., Illus.). 56p. (J). (gr. 3-7). 16.95 *(978-1-55337-967-6(5))* Kids Can Pr., Ltd. CAN. Dist: Hachette Bk. Group.

Taylor, Dereen. The World of Food - Nigeria. 2010. (World of Food Ser.). 32p. (YA). (gr. 4-7). lib. bdg. 24.95 *(978-1-934545-14-0(7))* Oliver Pr., Inc.

Ward, Chris. Discover Kenya. 2010. (Discover Countries Ser.). (Illus.). 32p. (J). (gr. 3-5). 26.50 *(978-1-61532-296-1(5))* Rosen Publishing Group, Inc., The.

Welcome to Africa, Swahili & English: Fun & Adventure, a Swahili/English Multicultural Book. 2004. (J). per. 9.95 *(978-0-9742688-1-1(X))* Ndegwa, Catherine W.

White, Bender Richardson, et al. African Traditional Religion. 3rd rev. ed. 2009. (World Religions Ser.). (Illus.). 144p. (gr. 6-12). 40.00 *(978-1-60413-103-1(9),* Chelsea Hse.) Facts On File, Inc.

Winget, Mary. Cooking the North African Way. 2nd rev. ed. 2003. (Easy Menu Ethnic Cookbooks 2nd Edition Ser.). (ENG., Illus.). 72p. (gr. 5-12). 25.26 *(978-0-8225-4169-1(6),* Lerner Pubns.) Lerner Publishing Group.

AFRICA, SOUTHERN

Here are entered works on the area south of Congo (Democratic Republic) and Tanzania. Works on the Republic of South Africa are entered under South Africa.

Bodden, Valerie. To the Heart of Africa. 2011. (Illus.). 48p. (J). 35.65 *(978-1-60818-066-0(2),* Creative Education) Creative Co., The.

Cornell, Kari & Thomas, Peter. Cooking the Southern African Way. 2nd rev. ed. 2005. (Easy Menu Ethnic Cookbooks 2nd Edition Ser.). (ENG., Illus.). 72p. (gr. 5-12). 25.26 *(978-0-8225-1239-4(4),* Lerner Pubns.) Lerner Publishing Group.

Hamilton, Janice. South Africa in Pictures. 2nd ed. 2003. (Visual Geography Series, Second Ser.). (ENG., Illus.). 80p. (gr. 5-12). 31.93 *(978-0-8225-0938-7(5))* Lerner Publishing Group.

AFRICA, SOUTHERN—FICTION

Brett, Jan. The 3 Little Dassies. Brett, Jan, illus. 2010. (ENG., Illus.). 32p. (J). (gr. -1-k). 17.99 *(978-0-399-25499-4(4),* G.P. Putnam's Sons Books for Young Readers) Penguin Young Readers Group.

Haggard, H. Rider. King Solomon's Mines. Marcos, Pablo, illus. 2005. (Great Illustrated Classics Ser.). 239p. (J). (gr. 3-8). 21.35 *(978-1-59679-244-9(2),* Abdo & Daughters) ABDO Publishing Co.

Pow, Tom. When the Rains Come. Favre, Malika, illus. 2012. (ENG.). 48p. (J). (gr. k-2). pap. *(978-1-84697-206-5(X))* Birlinn, Ltd.

Sithole, Thelma. The Little Monkey & the Crocodile. Montague, Christine, illus. 2007. 32p. per. 12.00 *(978-1-59858-204-8(6))* Dog Ear Publishing, LLC.

St. John, Lauren. Dolphin Song. 2009. (ENG.). 272p. (J). (gr. 3-7). 7.99 *(978-0-14-241375-3(5),* Puffin Books) Penguin Young Readers Group.

AFRICA, SOUTHERN—HISTORY

see also South African War, 1899-1902

Bodden, Valerie. Victoria Falls. 2010. (Big Outdoors Ser.). 24p. (J). (gr. k-3). 16.95 *(978-1-58341-819-2(9))* Creative Co., The.

Klepeis, Alicia. Zimbabwe. 2017. (J). pap. 19.95 ***(978-1-5026-2496-3(6))*** Cavendish Square Publishing.

Leigh, Nila K. Learning to Swim in Swaziland - A Child's-Eye View of a Southern African Country (PDF Download) 2008. (Illus.). 48p. (J). (gr. k-4). stu. ed. 9.95 *(978-1-60855-067-8(2))* Real World Productions.

—Learning to Swim in Swaziland: A child's-eye view of a southern African Country. 2008. (Illus.). 48p. (J). (gr. k-4). pap., stu. ed. 9.95 *(978-1-60855-010-4(9))* Real World Productions.

Oluonye, Mary N. Madagascar. 2010. (Country Explorers Ser.). (ENG., Illus.). 48p. (J). (gr. 2-4). lib. bdg. 29.27 *(978-1-58013-601-3(X),* 1306314) Lerner Publishing Group.

AFRICA, SUB-SAHARAN

Ellis, Deborah. Our Stories, Our Songs: African Children Talk about AIDS, 1 vol. 2005. (ENG., Illus.). 104p. (J). (gr. 4-7). *(978-1-55041-913-9(7))* Fitzhenry & Whiteside, Ltd.

Zamosky, Lisa. Sub-Saharan Africa, 1 vol. 2007. (Primary Source Readers Ser.). (ENG.). 32p. (J). (gr. 5-5). pap. 8.99 *(978-0-7439-0438-4(9))* Shell Educational Publishing.

AFRICA, SUB-SAHARAN—HISTORY

Bodden, Valerie. To the Heart of Africa. 2012. (Great Expeditions Ser.). (ENG.). 48p. (J). (gr. 4-7). pap. 12.00 *(978-0-89812-664-8(9),* Creative Paperbacks) Creative Co., The.

Humphreys, Jessica Dee & Chikwanine, Michel. Child Soldier: When Boys & Girls Are Used in War. Dávila, Claudia, illus. 2015. (CitizenKid Ser.). (ENG.). 48p. (J). (gr. 5-9). 17.95 *(978-1-77138-126-0(4))* Kids Can Pr., Ltd. CAN. Dist: Hachette Bk. Group.

Sub-Saharan Africa: Regions of the World. 2003. spiral bd. 16.95 *(978-1-56004-161-0(7))* Social Studies Schl. Service.

Throp, Claire. The Nile River, 1 vol. 2012. (Explorer Tales Ser.). (ENG.). 32p. (gr. 1-3). 29.99 *(978-1-4109-4784-0(X),* Read Me!) Heinemann-Raintree.

AFRICA, WEST

Conrad, David C. Empires of Medieval West Africa, Revised Edition. 2nd rev. ed. 2009. (Great Empires of the Past Ser.). (Illus.). 152p. (gr. 6-12). 35.00 *(978-1-60413-164-2(0),* Chelsea Hse.) Facts On File, Inc.

Klobuchar, Lisa. Africans of the Ghana, Mali, & Songhai Empires. 2009. (J). *(978-0-7166-2134-8(7))* World Bk., Inc.

La Bella, Laura. Discovering the Songhay Empire. 2013. (Exploring African Civilizations Ser.). (Illus.). 64p. (J). (gr. 5-8). 31.95 *(978-1-4777-1885-8(0),* Rosen Reference) Rosen Publishing Group, Inc., The.

Sheehan, Sean & Yong, Jui Lin. Angola. 2nd rev. ed. 2009. (Cultures of the World 18 Ser.). 144p. (gr. 6). 42.79 *(978-0-7614-4845-7(4))* Marshall Cavendish Corp.

Shuter, Jane. Ancient West African Kingdoms, 1 vol. 2003. (History Opens Windows Ser.). (ENG., Illus.). 32p. (J). (gr. 2-4). pap. 7.50 *(978-1-4034-0083-3(0))* Heinemann-Raintree.

AFRICA, WEST—BIOGRAPHY

Diakite, Baba Wague. A Gift from Childhood: Memories of an African Boyhood, 1 vol. 2013. (ENG., Illus.). 136p. (J). (gr. 4). pap. 12.95 *(978-1-55498-421-3(1))* Groundwood Bks. CAN. Dist: Publishers Group West (PGW).

Hicks, Kyra E. Martha Ann's Quilt for Queen Victoria. Fodi, Lee Edward, illus. 2006. 28p. (J). (gr. -1-3). 16.95 *(978-1-933285-59-7(1))* Brown Books Publishing Group.

Obregón, José María. Didier Drogba. 2009. (World Soccer Stars / Estrellas Del Fútbol Mundial Ser.). (SPA & ENG.). 24p. (J). lib. bdg. 22.60 *(978-1-4358-2967-1(0),* Editorial Buenas Letras) Rosen Publishing Group, Inc., The.

AFRICA, WEST—FICTION

Aardema, Verna. Why Mosquitoes Buzz in People's Ears. 2004. 29.95 *(978-1-55592-491-1(3))* Weston Woods Studios, Inc.

A B

Cleveland, Rob. The Clever Monkey: A Folktale from West Africa. Hoffmire, Baird, illus. 2006. (Story Cove Ser.). (ENG.). 32p. (J). (gr. -1-3). pap. 4.95 *(978-0-87483-801-5(0))* August Hse. Pubs., Inc.

Cunnane, Kelly. Deep in the Sahara. Hadadi, Hoda, illus. 2013. (ENG.). 40p. (J). (gr. -1-3). 17.99 *(978-0-375-87034-7(2),* Schwartz & Wade Bks.) Random Hse. Children's Bks.

Davies, Stephen. All Aboard for the Bobo Road. Corr, Christopher, illus. 2016. (ENG.). 32p. (J). (gr. -1-3). 17.99 *(978-1-5124-1598-8(7))* Andersen Pr. GBR. Dist: Lerner Publishing Group.

Davis, Anthony C. I Ain't Lying. 2008. 112p. pap. 19.95 *(978-1-60474-087-5(6))* America Star Bks.

Fontes, Justine & Fontes, Ron. Sunjata: Warrior King of Mali [A West African Legend]. Carruthers, Sandy, illus. 2009. (Graphic Myths & Legends Ser.). (ENG.). 48p. (gr. 4-8). pap. 8.95 *(978-1-58013-891-8(8))* Lerner Publishing Group.

Hergé. Tintin im Kongo. (GER., Illus.). 62p. (J). pap. 24.95 *(978-0-8288-4998-2(6))* French & European Pubns., Inc.

Isabella, Jude. The Red Bicycle: The Extraordinary Story of One Ordinary Bicycle. Shin, Simone, illus. 2015. (CitizenKid Ser.). (ENG.). 32p. (J). (gr. 3-7). 18.95 *(978-1-77138-023-2(3))* Kids Can Pr., Ltd. CAN. Dist: Hachette Bk. Group.

Kimmel, Eric A. Anansi's Party Time. Stevens, Janet, illus. 2008. (ENG.). 32p. (J). (gr. -1-3). 17.95 *(978-0-8234-1922-7(3))* Holiday Hse., Inc.

LaFevers, R. L. The Basilisk's Lair. Murphy, Kelly, illus. 2011. (Nathanial Fludd, Beastologist Ser.: 2). (ENG.). 160p. (J). (gr. 1-4). pap. 6.99 *(978-0-547-54957-6(1))* Houghton Mifflin Harcourt Publishing Co.

Lewis, Gill. Wild Wings. Onoda, Yuta, illus. (ENG.). 304p. (J). (gr. 3-7). 2012. pap. 7.99 *(978-1-4424-1446-4(4))* 2011. 18.99 *(978-1-4424-1445-7(6))* Simon & Schuster Children's Publishing. (Atheneum Bks. for Young Readers).

Malaspina, Ann. Guinea Fowl & Rabbit Get Justice: An African Folktale. Wendland, Paula, illus. 2013. (Folktales from Around the World Ser.). (ENG.). 24p. (J). (gr. k-3). 28.50 *(978-1-62323-614-4(2),* 206381) Child's World, Inc., The.

A Monkey Ate My Homework. 2007. 32p. pap. 4.50 *(978-0-8341-2287-1(1),* 083-412-2871) Beacon Hill Pr. of Kansas City.

Nnodim, Paul. The Tortoise & the Birds. Pierotti, Yvonne, illus. 32p. (J). 2012. 24.95 *(978-1-937622-09-1(6))* 2010. 14.95 *(978-0-9825842-9-3(6))* Africana Homestead Legacy Pubs., Inc. (Nefu Bks.).

Norfolk, Bobby & Norfolk, Sherry. Anansi & the Sky Kingdom. Hoffmire, Baird, illus. 2008. (Story Cove Ser.). (ENG.). 32p. (J). (gr. -1-3). pap. 4.95 *(978-0-87483-881-7(9))* August Hse. Pubs., Inc.

—Anansi Goes to Lunch. Hoffmire, Baird, illus. 2007. (Story Cove Ser.). (ENG.). 32p. (J). (gr. -1-3). pap. 4.95 *(978-0-87483-852-7(5))* August Hse. Pubs., Inc.

Nwokolo, Nwanneka. Zara: The Girl Traveller. 2004. (ENG.). 80p. *(978-1-904744-58-0(3))* Troubador Publishing Ltd.

Nyamnjoh, Francis B. Stories from Abakwa. 2007. *(978-9956-558-00-1(1))* Langaa Research & Publishing Common Initiative Group CMR. Dist: Michigan State Univ. Pr.

Polisar, Barry Louis. Stolen Man: The Story of the Amistad Rebellion. 2007. (ENG.). 32p. (J). (gr. 4-7). per. 7.95 *(978-0-938663-50-8(X))* Rainbow Morning Music Alternatives.

Saikia, Mayur, illus. Anansi & His Children. 2010. (J). *(978-1-60617-139-4(9))* Teaching Strategies, LLC.

Scherer, Catherine W. Simon & Barklee in West Africa. Richardson, Kara, illus. 2006. (Another Country Calling Ser.). 80p. (J). per. 15.00 *(978-0-9714502-4-0(2),* Explorer Media) Simon & Barklee, Inc./ExplorerMedia.

USCCB Department of Justice, Peace, and Human Development. Drop by Drop. 2015. (ENG., Illus.). 40p. (J). (gr. 1-5). pap. 7.95 *(978-0-8294-4100-0(X))* Loyola Pr.

Watson, Peter. The Heart of the Lion. Watson, Mary, illus. 2005. (ENG.). 32p. (J). (gr. 4-7). 15.95 *(978-0-9726614-1-6(7))* Shenanigan Bks.

Wingard, Lucinda. The Turn-Around Bird. 2012. 296p. pap. 16.00 *(978-0-9848400-1-4(X))* Plicata Pr. LLC.

AFRICAN AMERICAN ACTORS

Armand, Glenda & Cooper, Floyd. Ira's Shakespeare Dream. 1 vol. 2015. (ENG., Illus.). 40p. (J). 18.95 *(978-1-62014-155-7(8),* 9781620000000) Lee & Low Bks., Inc.

Bill Cosby: Entertainer & Activist. 2nd rev. ed. 2010. (Black Americans of Achievement Legacy Edition Ser.). (Illus.). 104p. (gr. 6-12). 35.00 *(978-1-60413-711-8(8))* Facts On File, Inc.

Doeden, Matt. Will Smith. 2007. (Illus.). 112p. (J). pap. 9.95 *(978-0-8225-7064-6(5))* Lerner Publishing Group.

Dougherty, Terri. Raven-Symoné. 2007. (Role Model Entertainers Ser.). (Illus.). 64p. (YA). pap. 9.95 *(978-1-4222-0795-6(1))* Mason Crest.

Feinstein, Stephen. Oprah Winfrey. 2007. (African-American Heroes Ser.). (Illus.). 24p. (J). (gr. 1-3). lib. bdg. 22.60 *(978-0-7660-2764-0(3),* Enslow Elementary) Enslow Pubs., Inc.

—Will Smith. 2007. (African-American Heroes Ser.). (Illus.). 24p. (J). (gr. 1-3). lib. bdg. 22.60 *(978-0-7660-2765-7(1),* Enslow Elementary) Enslow Pubs., Inc.

Hinds, Maurene J. Halle Berry. (Sharing the American Dream Ser.). 64p. (YA). (gr. 7-12). 2009. 22.95 *(978-1-4222-0596-9(7))* 2007. pap. 9.95 *(978-1-4222-0738-3(2))* Mason Crest.

Leavitt, Amie. Raven-Symone. 2007. (Robbie Reader Ser.). (Illus.). 32p. (YA). (gr. 2-5). lib. bdg. 25.70 *(978-1-58415-593-5(0))* Mitchell Lane Pubs., Inc.

Paprocki, Sherry. Oprah Winfrey. 2008. (Black Americans of Achievement: Legacy Edition Ser.). 112p. (gr. 6-12). pap. 11.95 *(978-1-60413-326-4(0,* Checkmark Bks.) Facts On File, Inc.

Paprocki, Sherry Beck. Oprah Winfrey: Talk Show Host & Media Magnate. 2006. (Black Americans of Achievement Legacy Edition Ser.). (Illus.). 100p. (YA). (gr. 7-12). lib. bdg. 35.00 *(978-0-7910-9226-2(7))* Facts On File, Inc.

Sapet, Kerrily. Halle Berry. (Transcending Race in America Ser.). (Illus.). 64p. (J). 2010. (gr. 4-8). 22.95 *(978-1-4222-1612-5(8))* 2009. (gr. 5-18). pap. 9.95 *(978-1-4222-1626-2(8))* Mason Crest.

Schuman, Michael. Halle Berry: A Biography of an Oscar-Winning Actress. 2013. (African-American Icons Ser.). 104p. (J). (gr. 6-12). lib. bdg. 27.94 *(978-0-7660-3993-3(5))* Enslow Pubs., Inc.

Schuman, Michael A. Will Smith: A Biography of a Rapper Turned Movie Star. 2013. (African-American Icons Ser.). 104p. (J). (gr. 6-12). pap. 10.95 *(978-1-59845-397-3(1))* Enslow Pubs., Inc.

Westen, Robin. Oprah Winfrey: A Biography of a Billionaire Talk Show Host. 2013. (African-American Icons Ser.). 104p. (J). (gr. 6-12). lib. bdg. 27.94 *(978-0-7660-3991-9(9))* Enslow Pubs., Inc.

—Oprah Winfrey: I Don't Believe in Failure. 2005. (African-American Biography Library). (Illus.). 128p. (J). (gr. 6-12). lib. bdg. 33.27 *(978-0-7660-2462-5(8))* Enslow Pubs., Inc.

Wooten, Sara McIntosh. Denzel Washington: Academy Award-Winning Actor. 2003. (African-American Biographies Ser.). (Illus.). 128p. (J). lib. bdg. 26.60 *(978-0-7660-2131-0(9))* Enslow Pubs., Inc.

Young, Jeff C. Amazing African-American Actors. 2012. (African-American Collective Biographies Ser.). (Illus.). 112p. (J). (gr. 5-18). 33.27 *(978-1-59845-135-1(9))* Enslow Pubs., Inc.

AFRICAN AMERICAN ART

Arora, Sabina G. The Great Migration & the Harlem Renaissance. 2015. (African American Experience: from Slavery to the Presidency Ser.). (ENG., Illus.). 80p. (J). (gr. 7-8). 32.90 *(978-1-68048-045-0(6),* Britannica Educational Publishing) Rosen Publishing Group, Inc., The.

Britton, Crystal A. African American Art. 2017. (Art Collections: Vol. 7). (ENG., Illus.). (YA). (gr. 9-12). 26.95 ***(978-1-4222-3931-5(4))*** Mason Crest.

Haskins, James. The Harlem Renaissance. 2004. (J). pap. 10.95 *(978-0-940975-95-8(5),* Sankofa Bks.) Just Us Bks., Inc.

Kallen, Stuart A. A Travel Guide to Harlem Renaissance. 2003. (Travel Guide To Ser.). (ENG.). (J). 30.85 *(978-1-59018-358-8(4),* Lucent Bks.) Cengage Gale.

Lassieur, Allison. Harlem Renaissance: An Interactive History Adventure. 2013. (You Choose: History Ser.). (ENG.). 112p. (gr. 3-4). pap. 6.95 *(978-1-4765-3609-5(0));* 31.99 *(978-1-4765-0256-4(0))* Capstone Press of Coughlan Cos. (You Choose Bks.).

Robson, David. The Black Arts Movement. 2008. (Lucent Library of Black History Ser.). (ENG., Illus.). 104p. (YA). (gr. 7-10). 34.80 *(978-1-4205-0053-0(8),* Lucent Bks.) Cengage Gale.

Worth, Richard. The Harlem Renaissance: An Explosion of African-American Culture. 2008. (America's Living History Ser.). (Illus.). 128p. (J). (gr. 5-9). lib. bdg. 33.27 *(978-0-7660-2907-1(7))* Enslow Pubs., Inc.

Yasuda, Anita & Goldsworthy, Kaite. Art. 2011. (Great African Americans Ser.). (Illus.). 48p. (J). (gr. 1-4). 29.99 *(978-1-61690-659-7(6))* Weigl Pubs., Inc.

Yasuda, Anita & Goldsworthy, Katie. Art. 2011. (J). (gr. 5-8). pap. 14.95 *(978-1-61690-663-4(4),* AV2 by Weigl) Weigl Pubs., Inc.

AFRICAN AMERICAN ARTISTS

Benson, Kathleen. Draw What You See: The Life & Art of Benny Andrews. Andrews, Benny, illus. 2015. (ENG.). 32p. (J). (gr. -1-3). 17.99 *(978-0-544-10487-7(0),* Clarion Bks.) Houghton Mifflin Harcourt Trade & Reference Pubs.

Bryan, Ashley. Ashley Bryan: Words to My Life's Song. Bryan, Ashley, illus. McGuinness, Bill, photos by. 2009. (ENG., Illus.). 64p. (J). (gr. -1-18). 19.99 *(978-1-4169-0541-7(3),* Atheneum Bks. for Young Readers) Simon & Schuster Children's Publishing.

Chandler, Alton. A Salute to African American Architects: Learning Activities. Chapman, Loring F., ed. Still, Wayne A., illus. 24p. (Orig.). (J). (gr. 3-8). pap. 1.75 *(978-1-877804-16-8(9))* Chandler/White Publishing Co.

Ellis, Carol. African American Artists. 2012. (Illus.). 64p. (J). pap. *(978-1-4222-2385-7(X))* Mason Crest.

—African American Artists. Hill, Marc Lamont, ed. 2012. (Major Black Contributions from Emancipation to Civil Rights Ser.). (Illus.). 64p. (J). (gr. 5). 22.95 *(978-1-4222-2372-7(8))* Mason Crest.

Goldsworthy, Kaite. Entertainers. 2016. *(978-1-5105-1158-3(X))* SmartBook Media, Inc.

Igus, Toyomi. Going Back Home: An Artist Returns to the South. Wood, Michele, illus. 2013. (ENG.). 32p. (J). (gr. 1-18). pap. 9.95 *(978-0-89239-197-4(9),* Children's Book Press) Lee & Low Bks., Inc.

Oprah Winfrey. 2004. (Illus.). 112p. pap. 9.95 *(978-0-8225-5320-5(1))* Lerner Publishing Group.

Randolph, Joanne. African American Artists & Writers. 2017. (J). ***(978-0-7660-9251-8(8))*** Enslow Pubs., Inc.

Rembert, Winfred. Don't Hold Me Back: My Life & Art. Rembert, Winfred, illus. 2003. (ENG., Illus.). 48p. (J). 19.95 *(978-0-8126-2703-9(2))* Cricket Bks.

Ringgold, Faith. Henry Ossawa Tanner: His Boyhood Dream Comes True. Ringgold, Faith, illus. 2011. (ENG., Illus.). 32p. (J). (gr. 1-2). 17.50 *(978-1-59373-092-5(6))* Bunker Hill Publishing, Inc.

Todd, Anne M. Chris Rock: Comedian & Actor. 2006. (Black Americans of Achievement Legacy Edition Ser.). (Illus.). 100p. (YA). (gr. 7-12). lib. bdg. 35.00 *(978-0-7910-9225-5(9))* Facts On File, Inc.

Venezia, Mike. Faith Ringgold. Venezia, Mike, illus. 2008. (Getting to Know the World's Greatest Artists Ser.). (ENG., Illus.). 32p. (J). (gr. 3-4). pap. 6.95 *(978-0-531-14757-3(6),* Children's Pr.) Scholastic Library Publishing.

—Horace Pippin. Venezia, Mike, illus. 2008. (Getting to Know the World's Greatest Artists Ser.). (ENG., Illus.). 32p. (J). (gr. 3-4). pap. 6.95 *(978-0-531-14758-0(4),* Children's Pr.) Scholastic Library Publishing.

AFRICAN AMERICAN ATHLETES

Anderson, Richard. A Home Run for Bunny. Purnell, Gerald, illus. 2013. (ENG.). (J). (gr. -1-3). 16.95 *(978-0-9855417-2-9(5))* Inspire Every Child dba Illumination Arts.

Anniss, Matt. Kevin Durant in the Community. 1 vol., 1. 2014. (Making a Difference: Athletes Who Are Changing the World Ser.). (ENG.). 48p. (J). (gr. 5-8). 25.85 *(978-1-62275-180-8(9))* Rosen Publishing Group, Inc., The.

Buckley, James. Who Is Muhammad Ali? 2014. (Who Was... ? Ser.). lib. bdg. 16.00 *(978-0-606-35696-1(7))* Turtleback Bks.

Burlingame, Jeff. Jesse Owens: I Always Loved Running. 2011. (African-American Biography Library). (Illus.). 128p. (J). (gr. 7-12). lib. bdg. 33.27 *(978-0-7660-3497-6(6))* Enslow Pubs., Inc.

Danakas, John. Choice of Colours: The Pioneering African-American Quarterbacks Who Changed the Face of Football. 2007. (Lorimer Recordbooks Ser.). (ENG., Illus.). (YA). 120p. (gr. 4-9). 16.95 *(978-1-55028-993-0(4),* 9781550289930); 128p. (gr. 7-12). 9.95 *(978-1-55028-991-6(8),* 9781550289916) Lorimer, James & Co., Ltd., Pubs. CAN. Dist: Casemate Pubs. & Bk. Distributors, LLC.

Frisaro, Joe. Reggie Miller: From Downtown. 2003. (Superstar Ser.: Vol. 6). (Illus.). 96p. (gr. 4-7). pap. 4.95 *(978-1-58261-180-8(7))* Sports Publishing, LLC.

Gitlin, Marty. Kevin Durant: Basketball Star. 2017. (Biggest Names in Sports (paperback) Ser.). (ENG., Illus.). 32p. (J). (gr. 4-7). pap. 9.95 ***(978-1-63517-096-2(6),*** Focus Readers) North Star Editions.

Graves, Will. Robert Griffin III: NFL Sensation: RGIII, 1 vol. 2013. (Playmakers Set 4 Ser.). (ENG.). 32p. (gr. 2-6). lib. bdg. 27.07 *(978-1-61783-700-5(8),* SportsZone) ABDO Publishing Co.

Howse, Jennifer. Sports: African American History. 2011. (J). (gr. 5-8). pap. 14.95 *(978-1-61690-664-1(2),* AV2 by Weigl); (Illus.). 48p. (YA). (gr. 1-4). 29.99 *(978-1-61690-660-3(X))* Weigl Pubs., Inc.

James, Lebron, et al. Lebron James. 2015. (Quotes from the Greatest Athletes Ser.). (ENG., Illus.). 24p. (J). lib. bdg. 12.95 *(978-1-4896-3361-3(8),* AV2 by Weigl) Weigl Pubs., Inc.

Jesse Owens. 2004. (Illus.). 112p. pap. 9.95 *(978-0-8225-5318-2(X))* Lerner Publishing Group.

Kirkpatrick, Rob. Florence Griffith Joyner: Olympic Runner. 2009. (Great Record Breakers in Sports Ser.). 24p. (gr. 3-3). 42.50 *(978-1-61513-187-7(6),* PowerKids Pr.) Rosen Publishing Group, Inc., The.

Lang, Heather. Queen of the Track: Alice Coachman, Olympic High-Jump Champion. Cooper, Floyd, illus. 2012. (ENG.). 40p. (J). (gr. k). 16.95 *(978-1-59078-850-9(8))* Boyds Mills Pr.

Mattern, Joanne. LeBron James: Basketball Superstar. 1 vol. 2011. (Superstar Athletes Ser.). (ENG.). 24p. (gr. 1-2). pap. 7.29 *(978-1-4296-7309-5(9));* pap. 41.70 *(978-1-4296-7310-5(9))* Capstone Press of Coughlan Cos.

McKissack, Patricia C. & McKissack, Fredrick L. Jesse Owens: Legendary Track Star. 2013. (Famous African Americans Ser.). 24p. (J). (gr. k-3). pap. 7.95 *(978-1-4644-0199-2(3),* Enslow Elementary) Enslow Pubs., Inc.

Meltzer, Brad. I Am Jackie Robinson. Eliopoulos, Christopher, illus. 2015. (Ordinary People Change the World Ser.). (ENG.). 40p. (J). (gr. k-3). 14.99 *(978-0-8037-4086-0(7),* Dial Bks) Penguin Young Readers Group.

Mooney, Carla, ed. African Americans in Sports. 2012. (Lucent Library of Black History Ser.). (ENG., Illus.). 128p. (gr. 7-10). lib. bdg. 34.80 *(978-1-4205-0675-4(7),* Lucent Bks.) Cengage Gale.

Nasium, James. African Americans in Sports. 2012. (J). pap. *(978-1-4222-2394-9(9))* Mason Crest.

—African Americans in Sports. Hill, Marc Lamont, ed. 2012. (Major Black Contributions from Emancipation to Civil Rights Ser.). 64p. (J). (gr. 5). 22.95 *(978-1-4222-2381-9(7))* Mason Crest.

Raatma, Lucia & O'Hern, Kerri. Jackie Robinson. Campbell, Alex & Spay, Anthony, illus. 2007. (Biografias Graficas (Graphic Biographies) Ser.). (SPA.). 32p. (gr. 5-8). pap. 10.50 *(978-0-8368-7889-9(2))* Stevens, Gareth Publishing LLLP.

Savage, Jeff. Lebron James. 2nd rev. ed. 2014. (Amazing Athletes Ser.). (ENG., Illus.). 32p. (gr. 2-5). pap. 7.95 *(978-1-4677-3853-8(0))* Lerner Publishing Group.

Shuster, Rachel. LeBron James: King of the Court. 2017. (J). ***(978-1-5026-2836-7(8))*** Cavendish Square Publishing.

Smith-Llera, Danielle. Black Power Salute: How a Photograph Captured a Political Protest. 2017. (Captured History Sports Ser.). (ENG.). 64p. (gr. 5-7). lib. bdg. 34.65 *(978-0-7565-5526-9(4),* CPB Grades 4-8) Compass Point Bks.

Stauffacher, Sue. Nothing but Trouble: The Story of Althea Gibson. Couch, Greg, illus. 2011. (ENG.). 40p. (J). (gr. -1-2). pap. 7.99 *(978-0-375-86544-2(6),* Dragonfly Bks.) Random Hse. Children's Bks.

Time for Kids Editors. Jesse Owens: Running into History. 2007. (Time for Kids Ser.). (ENG., Illus.). 48p. (J). (gr. 2-4). pap. 3.99 *(978-0-06-057620-2(0),* Collins) HarperCollins Pubs.

Twemlow, Nick. Josh Gibson. 2009. (Baseball Hall of Famers of the Negro Leagues Ser.). 112p. (gr. 5-8). 63.90 *(978-1-61511-523-5(4),* Rosen Reference) Rosen Publishing Group, Inc., The.

Weatherford, Carole Boston. A Negro League Scrapbook. 2005. (ENG., Illus.). 48p. (J). (gr. 2-7). 19.95 *(978-1-59078-091-6(4))* Boyds Mills Pr.

AFRICAN AMERICAN AUTHORS

African-American Writers. 2010. (Multicultural Voices Ser.). (Illus.). 142p. (gr. 6-12). 35.00 *(978-1-60413-311-0(2),* Chelsea Hse.) Facts On File, Inc.

Angelou, Maya & Kirkpatrick, Patricia. Maya Angelou. 2003. (Voices of Poetry Ser.). (Illus.). 48p. 19.95 *(978-1-58341-281-7(6),* Creative Education) Creative Co., The.

Anthony, David H. Langston Hughes: Harlem Renaissance Writer. 1 vol. 2011. (Primary Source Readers Ser.). (ENG., Illus.). 32p. (J). (gr. 4-4). pap. 8.99 *(978-1-4333-1520-6(3))* Teacher Created Materials, Inc.

Bloom, Harold, ed. Maya Angelou's I Know Why the Caged Bird Sings. 2nd rev. ed. 2009. (Bloom's Modern Critical Interpretations Ser.). 141p. (C). (gr. 9-18). 45.00 *(978-1-60413-187-1(X),* Chelsea Hse.) Facts On File, Inc.

Bloom, Harold, intro. Alice Walker. 2nd ed. 2007. (Modern Critical Views Ser.). 223p. (C). (gr. 9). lib. bdg. 45.00 *(978-0-7910-9611-6(4),* Chelsea Hse.) Facts On File, Inc.

Bowman, Chris. Christopher Paul Curtis. 2017. (Children's Storytellers Ser.). (ENG., Illus.). 24p. (J). (gr. 2-5). lib. bdg. 25.95 *(978-1-62617-550-1(0),* Blastoff! Readers) Bellwether Media.

Bryan, Ashley. Ashley Bryan: Words to My Life's Song. Bryan, Ashley, illus. McGuinness, Bill, photos by. 2009. (ENG., Illus.). 64p. (J). (gr. -1-18). 19.99 *(978-1-4169-0541-7(3),* Atheneum Bks. for Young Readers) Simon & Schuster Children's Publishing.

Crayton, Lisa A. Reading & Interpreting the Works of Toni Morrison. 2016. (Lit Crit Guides). (ENG., Illus.). 152p. (J). (gr. 8-8). lib. bdg. 39.93 *(978-0-7660-7352-4(1))* Enslow Pubs., Inc.

Early, Gerald Lyn. Ralph Ellison: Invisible Man. 2009. (Writers & Their Works 4 Ser.). 144p. (gr. 7). 42.79 *(978-0-7614-4275-2(8))* Marshall Cavendish Corp.

Ernest J. Gaines. 2010. (Who Wrote That? Ser.). (Illus.). 120p. (gr. 6-12). 35.00 *(978-1-60413-683-8(9),* Chelsea Hse.) Facts On File, Inc.

Fradin, Dennis Brindell & Fradin, Judith Bloom. Zora! The Life of Zora Neale Hurston. 2012. (ENG., Illus.). 192p. (J). (gr. 5-7). 17.99 *(978-0-547-00695-6(0))* Houghton Mifflin Harcourt Publishing Co.

Gaines, Ann. Christopher Paul Curtis. 2004. (Blue Banner Biography Ser.). (Illus.). 32p. (J). lib. bdg. 25.70 *(978-1-58415-330-6(X))* Mitchell Lane Pubs., Inc.

Graham, Amy. Celebrated African-American Novelists. 2012. (African-American Collective Biographies Ser.). 112p. (J). pap. 10.95 *(978-1-4644-0037-7(7));* (Illus.). (gr. 5-18). 33.27 *(978-1-59845-138-2(3))* Enslow Pubs., Inc.

Harkins, Susan and William. Walter Dean Myers. 2007. (YA). lib. bdg. *(978-1-58415-534-8(5))* Mitchell Lane Pubs., Inc.

Hart, Joyce. Native Son: The Story of Richard Wright. 2004. (World Writers Ser.). (Illus.). 128p. (YA). (gr. 6-12). 23.95 *(978-1-931798-06-8(0))* Reynolds, Morgan Inc.

Herron, Carolivia. Always an Olivia: A Remarkable Family History. Tugeau, Jeremy, illus. 2012. (Jewish Identity Ser.). (ENG.). 32p. (J). (gr. 2-4). pap. 9.95 *(978-0-7613-9100-5(2),* Kar-Ben Publishing) Lerner Publishing Group.

Herron, Carolivia. Always an Olivia: A Remarkable Family History. Tugeau, Jeremy, illus. 2007. (Jewish Identity Ser.). 32p. (J). (gr. -1-3). 17.95 *(978-0-8225-7049-3(1),* Kar-Ben Publishing) Lerner Publishing Group.

Hoover, Elizabeth. Walter Dean Myers. Greenhaven Press Staff, ed. 2014. (People in the News Ser.). (ENG., Illus.). 128p. (gr. 7-10). lib. bdg. 39.40 *(978-1-4205-0859-8(8),* Lucent Bks.) Cengage Gale.

Houghton, Gillian. Mildred Taylor. (Library of Author Biographies Ser.). 112p. 2009. (gr. 5-8). 63.90 *(978-1-60853-548-4(7),* Rosen Reference) 2005. (Illus.). (YA). 34.60 *(978-1-4042-0330-3(3))* Rosen Publishing Group, Inc., The.

Jordan, Denise M. Walter Dean Myers: A Biography of an Award-Winning Urban Fiction Author. 2013. (African-American Icons Ser.). 104p. (J). (gr. 6-12). pap. 10.95 *(978-1-59845-393-5(9))* Enslow Pubs., Inc.

Kite, L. Patricia. Maya Angelou. 2006. (Just the Facts Biographies Ser.). (Illus.). 112p. (J). (gr. 3-7). pap. 9.95 *(978-0-8225-5997-9(8));* (ENG., (gr. 5-12). lib. bdg. 27.93 *(978-0-8225-3426-6(6))* Lerner Publishing Group. (Lerner Pubns.).

Kramer, Barbara. Toni Morrison: A Biography of a Nobel Prize-Winning Writer. 2013. (African-American Icons Ser.). 104p. (J). (gr. 6-12). pap. 10.95 *(978-1-59845-392-8(0))* Enslow Pubs., Inc.

Lasky, Kathryn. A Voice of Her Own: A Story of Phillis Wheatley, Slave Poet. 2012. lib. bdg. 14.75 *(978-0-606-26940-7(1),* Turtleback) Turtleback Bks.

Levin, Judy & Draper, Allison Stark. Christopher Paul Curtis. annot. ed. 2005. (Library of Author Biographies Ser.). (Illus.). 112p. (J). (gr. k-3). lib. bdg. 34.60 *(978-1-4042-0458-4(X))* Rosen Publishing Group, Inc., The.

Levy, Debbie. Richard Wright: A Biography. 2007. (Literary Greats Ser.). (ENG., Illus.). 160p. (gr. 7-12). lib. bdg. 33.26 *(978-0-8225-6793-6(8),* Twenty-First Century Bks.) Lerner Publishing Group.

Litwin, Laura Baskes. Zora Neale Hurston: I Have Been in Sorrow's Kitchen. 2007. (African-American Biography Library). (Illus.). 128p. (J). (gr. 6-12). lib. bdg. 33.27 *(978-0-7660-2536-3(5))* Enslow Pubs., Inc.

Loos, Pamela. A Reader's Guide to Lorraine Hansberry's a Raisin in the Sun. 2008. (Multicultural Literature Ser.). (Illus.). 128p. (YA). (gr. 9-12). lib. bdg. 33.27 *(978-0-7660-2830-2(5))* Enslow Pubs., Inc.

Mangal, Melina. Mildred Taylor. 2004. (Classic Storytellers Ser.). (Illus.). 48p. (J). (gr. 4-8). lib. bdg. 29.95 *(978-1-58415-311-5(3))* Mitchell Lane Pubs., Inc.

Mangrum, Allison. African American Writers Who Inspired Change. 2005. (Illus.). 79p. 17.00 *(978-1-55501-650-0(2))* Ballard & Tighe Pubs.

Marsico, Katie. Zora Neale Hurston. 1 vol. 2008. (Essential Lives Set 2 Ser.). (ENG., Illus.). 112p. (J). (gr. 6-12). lib. bdg. 35.64 *(978-1-60453-036-0(7))* ABDO Publishing Co.

Mattern, Joanne. Tyler Perry. 2012. (J). lib. bdg. 25.70 *(978-1-61228-334-0(9))* Mitchell Lane Pubs., Inc.

Miller, William. Zora Hurston & the Chinaberry Tree. 2004. (Illus.). (J). (gr. k-3). spiral bd. *(978-0-616-03099-8(1))* Canadian National Institute for the Blind/Institut National Canadien pour les Aveugles.

Parker-Rock, Michelle. Patricia & Fredrick Mckissack: Authors Kids Love. 2008. (Authors Kids Love Ser.). (Illus.). 48p. (J). (gr. 3-4). lib. bdg. 25.27 *(978-0-7660-2759-6(7),* Enslow Elementary) Enslow Pubs., Inc.

Randolph, Joanne. African American Artists & Writers. 2017. (J). ***(978-0-7660-9251-8(8))*** Enslow Pubs., Inc.

Roza, Greg. Guide My Pen: The Poems of Phillis Wheatley. 2009. (Great Moments in American History Ser.). 32p. (gr. 3-3). 47.90 *(978-1-61513-133-4(7))* Rosen Publishing Group, Inc., The.

Rubini, Julie K. Virginia Hamilton: America's Children's Book Author. 2017. (Biographies for Young Readers Ser.). (ENG., Illus.). 152p. (J). (gr. 1-6). pap. 14.95 *(978-0-8214-2269-4(3))* Ohio Univ. Pr.

Rubini, Julie K. Virginia Hamilton: Her Story. 2017. (Biographies for Young Readers Ser.). (ENG., Illus.). 152p. (J). (gr. 1-6). 28.95 ***(978-0-8214-2268-7(5))*** Ohio Univ. Pr.

Sammons, Sandra Wallus. Zora Neale Hurston. 2014. (ENG.). 80p. (J). (gr. 4-6). pap. 9.95 *(978-1-56164-682-1(2))* Pineapple Pr., Inc.

Scarbrough, Mary Hertz. African American Writers & Journalists. 2012. pap. *(978-1-4222-2389-5(2))* Mason Crest.

—African American Writers & Journalists. Hill, Marc Lamont, ed. 2012. (Major Black Contributions from Emancipation to Civil Rights Ser.). 64p. (J). (gr. 5). 22.95 *(978-1-4222-2376-5(0))* Mason Crest.

Sickels, Amy. Walter Dean Myers. 2008. (Who Wrote That? Ser.). 128p. (gr. 6-12). 35.00 *(978-0-7910-9524-9(X),* Chelsea Hse.) Facts On File, Inc.

Simons, Lisa M. Bolt. Kadir Nelson. Byers, Michael, illus. 2017. (Your Favorite Authors Ser.). (ENG.). 24p. (gr. 1-2). lib. bdg. 25.32 *(978-1-5157-3556-4(7),* First Facts) Capstone Press of Coughlan Cos.

Smith, Emily R. Phillis Wheatley, 1 vol. 2004. (Primary Source Readers Ser.). (ENG.). 24p. (J). (gr. 4-4). pap. 8.99 *(978-0-7439-8743-1(8))* Shell Educational Publishing.

Tahir, Rana. Countee Cullen. 2016. (Artists of the Harlem Renaissance Ser.). (ENG.). 128p. (J). (gr. 9-9). lib. bdg. 45.64 *(978-1-5026-1068-3(X))* Cavendish Square Publishing.

Taylor, Charlotte. Phillis Wheatley: Colonial African-American Poet. 2016. (Exceptional African Americans Ser.). (ENG., Illus.). 24p. (J). (gr. 3-3). 22.60 *(978-0-7660-7326-5(2))* Enslow Pubs., Inc.

Uschan, Michael V., ed. Tyler Perry. 2010. (People in the News Ser.). (ENG.). 96p. (YA). (gr. 7-12). 33.95 *(978-1-4205-0309-8(X))* Cengage Gale.

Watson, Galadriel Findlay. Toni Morrison. 2005. (Great African American Women for Kids Ser.). (Illus.). 24p. (J). (gr. 2-3). lib. bdg. 24.45 *(978-1-59036-334-8(5))* Weigl Pubs., Inc.

AFRICAN AMERICAN COOKING

Raabe, Emily. A Kwanzaa Holiday Cookbook. 2009. (Festive Foods for the Holidays Ser.). 24p. (gr. 3-3). 42.50 *(978-1-61512-596-8(5),* PowerKids Pr.) Rosen Publishing Group, Inc., The.

AFRICAN AMERICAN FOLKLORE

see African Americans—Folklore

AFRICAN AMERICAN LITERATURE (ENGLISH)

see American Literature—African American Authors

AFRICAN AMERICAN MUSIC

see African Americans—Music

AFRICAN AMERICAN MUSICIANS

Aretha, David. Awesome African-American Rock & Soul Musicians. 2012. (African-American Collective Biographies Ser.). 112p. (J). (gr. 5-18). 33.27 *(978-1-59845-140-5(5))* Enslow Pubs., Inc.

Collins, Terry. King of Pop: The Story of Michael Jackson. Byers, Michael, illus. 2012. (American Graphic Ser.). (ENG.). 32p. (gr. 3-4). pap. 47.70 *(978-1-4296-8476-7(3),* Graphic Library) Capstone Press of Coughlan Cos.

—Louis Armstrong: Jazz Legend. Pope, Richie, illus. 2012. (American Graphic Ser.). (ENG.). 32p. (gr. 3-4). pap. 47.70 *(978-1-4296-9337-0(1),* Graphic Library) Capstone Press of Coughlan Cos.

Donatelli, Jen Jones. Sean Diddy Combs: A Biography of a Music Mogul. 2014. (African-American Icons Ser.). 104p. (J). pap. 10.95 *(978-1-4644-0537-2(9))* Enslow Pubs., Inc.

Embacher, Eric. Will Smith: The Funny, Funky, & Confident Fresh Prince. 2003. (High Five Reading - Red Ser.). (ENG., Illus.). 48p. (gr. 3-4). per. 9.00 *(978-0-7368-2829-1(X),* High Five Reading (RBL)) Capstone Press of Coughlan Cos.

Feinstein, Stephen. Incredible African-American Jazz Musicians. 2012. (African-American Collective Biographies Ser.). (Illus.). 112p. (J). (gr. 5-18). 33.27 *(978-1-59845-137-5(5))* Enslow Pubs., Inc.

Ford, Carin T. Duke Ellington: I Live with Music. 2007. (African-American Biography Library). (Illus.). 128p. (J). (gr. 6-12). lib. bdg. 33.27 *(978-0-7660-2702-2(3))* Enslow Pubs., Inc.

Foy, Debbie. Musicians. 2012. (Black History Makers Ser.). (ENG., Illus.). 24p. (J). (gr. 3-8). pap. 8.25 *(978-1-4488-7052-3(6));* lib. bdg. 22.60 *(978-1-4488-6637-3(5))* Rosen Publishing Group, Inc., The. (PowerKids Pr.).

Gelfand, Dale Evva. Jimi Hendrix: Musician. 2006. (Black Americans of Achievement Ser.). (Illus.). 120p. (YA). (gr. 7-12). lib. bdg. 35.00 *(978-0-7910-9214-9(3))* Facts On File, Inc.

Gigliotti, Jim. Who Is Stevie Wonder? Marchesi, Stephen, illus. 2016. (Who Was? Ser.). (ENG.). 112p. (J). (gr. 3-7). lib. bdg. 15.99 *(978-0-399-54243-5(4),* Grosset & Dunlap) Penguin Young Readers Group.

Goldsworthy, Kaite. Entertainers. 2016. *(978-1-5105-1158-3(X))* SmartBook Media, Inc.

Greenhaven Press Staff, ed. Wyclef Jean. 2012. (People in the News Ser.). (ENG., Illus.). 128p. (J). (gr. 7-10). lib. bdg. 33.95 *(978-1-4205-0763-8(X),* Lucent Bks.) Cengage Gale.

Harrah, Madge. Blind Boone: Piano Prodigy. 2004. (Trailblazers Biographies Ser.). (Illus.). 112p. (J). (gr. 5-9). lib. bdg. 30.60 *(978-1-57505-057-7(9))* Lerner Publishing Group.

Hegel, Claudette. African-American Musicians. 2012. (J). pap. *(978-1-4222-2387-1(6))* Mason Crest.

—African-American Musicians. Hill, Marc Lamont, ed. 2012. (Major Black Contributions from Emancipation to Civil Rights Ser.). 64p. (J). (gr. 5). 22.95 *(978-1-4222-2374-1(4))* Mason Crest.

Holland, Gini & O'Hern, Kerri. Louis Armstrong. Spay, Anthony & Campbell, Alex, illus. 2007. (Biografías Gráficas (Graphic Biographies) Ser.). (SPA.). 32p. (gr. 5-8). lib. bdg. 27.00 *(978-0-8368-7878-3(7))* Stevens, Gareth Publishing LLLP.

Josephson, Judith Pinkerton. Louis Armstrong. 2008. (History Maker Biographies Ser.). (Illus.). 47p. (J). (gr. 3-7). lib. bdg. 26.60 *(978-0-8225-7169-8(2),* Lerner Pubns.) Lerner Publishing Group.

Mattern, Joanne. Count Basie. 2012. (J). lib. bdg. 29.95 *(978-1-61228-270-1(9))* Mitchell Lane Pubs., Inc.

Mitchell, Barbara. Raggin' A Story about Scott Joplin. Mitchell, Hetty, illus. 2003. (Creative Minds Biographies Ser.). (ENG.). 56p. (gr. 4-8). pap. 8.95 *(978-0-87614-589-0(6),* Carolrhoda Bks.) Lerner Publishing Group.

O'Hern, Kerri & Holland, Gini. Louis Armstrong. Spay, Anthony & Campbell, Alex, illus. 2007. (Biografías Gráficas (Graphic Biographies) Ser.). (SPA.). 32p. (gr. 5-8). pap. 10.50 *(978-0-8368-7885-1(X))* Stevens, Gareth Publishing LLLP.

Orgill, Roxane. Skit-Scat Raggedy Cat: Ella Fitzgerald. Qualls, Sean, illus. 2012. (Candlewick Biographies Ser.). (ENG.). 48p. (J). (gr. 3-7). 14.99 *(978-0-7636-6459-6(6));* pap. 4.99 *(978-0-7636-6458-9(8))* Candlewick Pr.

Overbey, Theresa. Michael Jackson. Lt. ed. 2003. (Blue Banner Biography Ser.). (Illus.). 32p. (J). (gr. 3-8). lib. bdg. 25.70 *(978-1-58415-216-3(8))* Mitchell Lane Pubs., Inc.

Partridge, Kenneth. Louis Armstrong. 2nd rev. ed. 2011. (Black Americans of Achievement Legacy Edition Ser.). 120p. (YA). (gr. 6-12). 35.00 *(978-1-60413-833-7(5))* Facts On File, Inc.

Pizer, Carol. Michael Jackson, 1 vol. Saddleback Educational Publishing Staff, ed. unabr. ed. 2011. (Graphic Biographies Ser.). (ENG.). 25p. (YA). (gr. 9-12). pap. 7.95 *(978-1-61651-265-1(2))* Saddleback Educational Publishing, Inc.

Rice, Earle. Charlie Parker. 2012. (J). lib. bdg. 29.95 *(978-1-61228-266-4(0))* Mitchell Lane Pubs., Inc.

Rockwell, Anne F. Hey, Charleston! The True Story of the Jenkins Orphanage Band. Bootman, Colin, illus. 2013. 32p. pap. 16.95 *(978-0-7613-8843-2(5));* (ENG.). (J). (gr. 2-5). lib. bdg. 16.95 *(978-0-7613-5565-6(0),* Carolrhoda Bks.) Lerner Publishing Group.

Shabazz, Ilyasah. Malcolm Little: The Boy Who Grew up to Become Malcolm X. Ford, A. G., illus. 2014. (ENG.). 48p. (J). (gr. 1-5). 17.99 *(978-1-4424-1216-3(X))* Simon & Schuster Children's Publishing.

Sheafer, Silvia Anne. The Life of Aretha Franklin: Queen of Soul. 2015. (Legendary African Americans Ser.). 96p. (J). (gr. 6-12). pap. 10.95 *(978-0-7660-6226-9(0))* Enslow Pubs., Inc.

Stevie Wonder: Musician. 2010. (Black Americans of Achievement Legacy Edition Ser.). (Illus.). 112p. (gr. 6-12). 35.00 *(978-1-60413-685-2(5))* Facts On File, Inc.

Weinstein, Muriel Harris. Play, Louis, Play! The True Story of a Boy & His Horn. Morrison, Frank, illus. (ENG.). 112p. (J). (gr. 2-4). 2013. pap. 5.99 *(978-1-59990-994-3(4),* 9781599909943) 2010. 15.99 *(978-1-59990-375-0(X),* 9781599903750) Bloomsbury Publishing USA. (Bloomsbury USA Childrens).

Weston Woods Staff, creator. Duke Ellington. 2011. 38.75 *(978-0-545-02759-5(4));* 18.95 *(978-0-545-02757-1(8))* Weston Woods Studios, Inc.

—Ella Fitzgerald. 2011. 18.95 *(978-0-545-02761-8(6));* 38.75 *(978-0-545-02763-2(2))* Weston Woods Studios, Inc.

Wilder, Stephanie. Legends of the Blues. 2005. (ENG., Illus.). 24p. (J). (gr. 5-5). pap. 5.97 net. *(978-0-328-13542-4(9),* Scott Foresman) Pearson Schl.

AFRICAN AMERICAN POETRY (ENGLISH)

see American Poetry—African American Authors

AFRICAN AMERICAN SCIENTISTS

Abrams, Dennis. George Washington Carver: Scientist & Educator. 2008. (Black Americans of Achievement Ser.). (Illus.). 119p. (gr. 6-12). lib. bdg. 35.00 *(978-0-7910-9717-5(X),* Chelsea Hse.) Facts On File, Inc.

Currie, Stephen. African-American Inventors. 2010. (Lucent Library of Black History Ser.). (Illus.). 128p. (gr. 7-10). 34.80 *(978-1-4205-0121-6(6),* Lucent Bks.) Cengage Gale.

Davidson, Tish. African American Scientists & Inventors. 2012. (J). pap. *(978-1-4222-2388-8(4))* Mason Crest.

—African American Scientists & Inventors. Hill, Marc Lamont, ed. 2012. (Major Black Contributions from Emancipation to Civil Rights Ser.). 64p. (J). (gr. 5). 22.95 *(978-1-4222-2375-8(2))* Mason Crest.

Jones, Natalya. George Washington Carver: Peanut Scientist. 2009. (Real Life Readers Ser.). 16p. (gr. 2-3). pap. 7.05 *(978-1-4358-0085-4(0),* Rosen Classroom) Rosen Publishing Group, Inc., The.

Keller, Shana. Ticktock Banneker's Clock. Gardner, David C., illus. 2016. (ENG.). 32p. (J). (gr. 1-4). 16.99 *(978-1-58536-956-0(X),* 204114) Sleeping Bear Pr.

Litwin, Laura Baskes. The Life of Benjamin Banneker: Astronomer & Mathematician. 2014. (Legendary African Americans Ser.). (Illus.). 96p. (J). (gr. 6-12). 27.94 *(978-0-7660-6112-5(4))* Enslow Pubs., Inc.

Martin, Isabel. Benjamin Banneker, 1 vol. 2014. (Great African-Americans Ser.). (ENG.). 24p. (gr. k-1). pap. 5.95 *(978-1-4914-0506-2(6),* Pebble Bks.) Capstone Press of Coughlan Cos.

National Geographic Kids Staff & Jazynka, Kitson. George Washington Carver. 2016. (Readers Bios Ser.). (ENG., Illus.). 32p. (J). (gr. -1-1). pap. 3.99 *(978-1-4263-2285-3(2),* National Geographic Children's Bks.) National Geographic Society.

Randolph, Joanne. African American Inventors & Scientists. 2017. (J). ***(978-0-7660-9248-8(8))*** Enslow Pubs., Inc.

Shaffer, Jody Jensen. Benjamin Banneker: Self-Made Man. 2016. (Primary Source Readers Ser.). (Illus.). 32p. (J). (gr. 4-5). pap. 8.99 *(978-1-4938-3082-4(1))* Teacher Created Materials, Inc.

Spangenburg, Ray, et al. African Americans in Science, Math, & Invention. 2nd rev. ed. 2011. (to Z of African Americans Ser.). 270p. (C). (gr. 9). 49.50 *(978-0-8160-8331-2(2))* Facts On File, Inc.

Wadsworth, Ginger. Benjamin Banneker: Pioneering Scientist. Orback, Craig, illus. 2003. (On My Own Biography Ser.). (ENG.). 48p. (gr. 2-4). 25.26 *(978-0-87614-916-4(6))* Lerner Publishing Group.

—Benjamin Banneker: Pioneering Scientist. Orback, Craig, illus. 2006. (On My Own Biographies Ser.). 47p. (gr. 2-5). 17.00 *(978-0-7569-6705-5(8))* Perfection Learning Corp.

Wagner, Heather Lehr. Benjamin Banneker. 2010. (Leaders of the Colonial Era Ser.). 104p. (gr. 5-8). 35.00 *(978-1-60413-744-6(4),* Chelsea Hse.) Facts On File, Inc.

Welch, Catherine A. Benjamin Banneker. 2008. (History Maker Biographies Ser.). (Illus.). 48p. (J). (gr. 3-7). lib. bdg. 26.60 *(978-0-8225-7167-4(6),* Lerner Pubns.); pap. 52.95 *(978-0-8225-9386-7(6))* Lerner Publishing Group.

Young, Jeff C. Brilliant African-American Scientists: Nine Exceptional Lives. 2009. (Great Scientists & Famous Inventors Ser.). (Illus.). 128p. (J). (gr. 5-9). lib. bdg. 34.60 *(978-1-59845-083-5(2))* Enslow Pubs., Inc.

AFRICAN AMERICAN SOLDIERS

Baumann, Susan K. Black Civil War Soldiers: The 54th Massachusetts Regiment. 2013. (Jr. Graphic African American History Ser.). (ENG., Illus.). 24p. (J). (gr. 3-6). pap. 10.60 *(978-1-4777-1457-7(X));* lib. bdg. 25.25 *(978-1-4777-1316-7(6))* Rosen Publishing Group, Inc., The. (PowerKids Pr.).

Black Civil War Soldiers: The 54th Massachusetts Regiment. 2013. (Jr. Graphic African American History Ser.). 24p. (J). (gr. 3-6). pap. 63.60 *(978-1-4777-1458-4(8),* PowerKids Pr.) Rosen Publishing Group, Inc., The.

Burgan, Michael. The Untold Story of the Black Regiment: Fighting in the Revolutionary War. 2015. (What You Didn't Know about the American Revolution Ser.). (ENG.). 64p. (gr. 4-8). 34.65 *(978-0-7565-4975-6(2))* Compass Point Bks.

Drama of African-American History, 5 bks., Set. Incl. Africa: A Look Back. Haskins, James & Benson, Kathleen. 80p. (J). (gr. 6-7). lib. bdg. 35.64 *(978-0-7614-2148-1(3));* Civil War. Jordan, Anne Devereaux. 72p. (J). (gr. 3-7). lib. bdg. 35.64 *(978-0-7614-2179-5(3));* Reconstruction Era. Stroud, Bettye. 80p. (gr. 6-7). lib. bdg. 35.64 *(978-0-7614-2181-8(5));* Slave Trade & the Middle Passage. Sharp, S. Pearl. 80p. (gr. 6-7). lib. bdg. 35.64 *(978-0-7614-2176-4(9));* Slavery & Resistance. Jordan, Anne Devereaux. 80p. (gr. 6-7). lib. bdg. 35.64 *(978-0-7614-2178-8(5));* (Illus.). 2006. 2007. Set lib. bdg. 178.21 *(978-0-7614-2174-0(2),* Benchmark Bks.) Marshall Cavendish Corp.

Dreyer, Ellen. A Band of Brave Men: The Story of the 54th Massachusetts Regiment. 2004. (ENG., Illus.). 31p. (J). (gr. 5-5). pap. 11.47 net. *(978-0-7652-5247-0(3),* Celebration Pr.) Pearson Schl.

Figley, Marty Rhodes. Prisoner for Liberty. Orback, Craig, illus. 2009. (On My Own History Ser.). (ENG.). 48p. (gr. 2-4). pap. 6.95 *(978-0-8225-9022-4(0),* First Avenue Editions) Lerner Publishing Group.

Figley, Mary Rhodes. Prisoner for Liberty. 2009. pap. 40.95 *(978-0-7613-4796-5(8))* Lerner Publishing Group.

Ford, Carin T. African-American Soldiers in the Civil War: Fighting for Freedom. 2004. (Civil War Library). (Illus.). 48p. (J). (gr. 3-4). lib. bdg. 25.27 *(978-0-7660-2254-6(4))* Enslow Pubs., Inc.

—The Civil War's African-American Soldiers Through Primary Sources. 2013. (Civil War Through Primary Sources Ser.). 48p. (J). (gr. 4-10). pap. 8.95 *(978-1-4644-0183-1(7));* 25.27 *(978-0-7660-4125-7(5))* Enslow Pubs., Inc.

Garstecki, Julia. Buffalo Soldiers. 2017. (All-American Fighting Forces Ser.). (ENG., Illus.). 32p. (J). (gr. 3-7). 31.35 ***(978-1-68072-000-6(7))*** Black Rabbit Bks.

Gastel, Tiffany & Benchmark Education Co. Staff. The Red-Tail Angels. 2014. (Text Connections Ser.). (J). (gr. 6). *(978-1-4900-1537-8(X))* Benchmark Education Co.

Honders, Christine. Buffalo Soldiers. 2015. (Heroes of Black History Ser.). (ENG., Illus.). 32p. (J). (gr. 3-4). pap. 10.50 *(978-1-4824-2900-8(4))* Stevens, Gareth Publishing LLLP.

Howse, Jennifer. The Civil War. 2008. (African American History Ser.). (Illus.). 48p. (YA). (gr. 5-8). pap. 10.95 *(978-1-59036-877-0(0));* lib. bdg. 29.05 *(978-1-59036-876-3(2))* Weigl Pubs., Inc.

Lewis, J. Patrick. Harlem Hellfighters. Kelley, Gary, illus. 2014. (ENG.). 32p. (J). (gr. 4-7). 19.99 *(978-1-56846-246-2(8),* Creative Editions) Creative Co., The.

Morrison, Jessica. Military. 2016. (Illus.). 48p. (J). *(978-1-5105-1160-6(1))* SmartBook Media, Inc.

—Military. 2011. (J). (gr. 5-8). pap. 14.95 *(978-1-61690-665-8(0),* AV2 by Weigl); (Illus.). 48p. (YA). (gr. 1-4). 29.99 *(978-1-61690-661-0(8))* Weigl Pubs., Inc.

Nell, William C. Black Patriots of the American Revolution, with Sketches of Several Distinguished Black Persons to Which Is Added a Brief Survey of the Condition & Prospects of Black Americans. 2017. (ENG., Illus.). 396p. (J). (gr. 4-12). act. bk. ed. incl. cd-rom *(978-1-892824-87-5(6))* AFCHRON.

Orr, Tamra. What's So Great About the Buffalo Soldiers. 2009. (What's So Great About...? Ser.). 32p. (J). (gr. 2-4). lib. bdg. 25.70 *(978-1-58415-831-8(X))* Mitchell Lane Pubs., Inc.

Raabe, Emily. Buffalo Soldiers & the Western Frontier. (Westward Ho! Ser.). 24p. 2009. (gr. 2-3). 42.50 *(978-1-60854-759-3(0))* 2003. (Illus.). (J). lib. bdg. 22.60 *(978-0-8239-6495-6(7))* Rosen Publishing Group, Inc., The. (PowerKids Pr.).

Stone, Tanya Lee. Courage Has No Color - The True Story of the Triple Nickles: America's First Black Paratroopers. 2013. (ENG., Illus.). 160p. (J). (gr. 5). pap. 17.99 *(978-0-7636-6548-7(7));* 24.99 *(978-0-7636-5117-6(6))* Candlewick Pr.

AFRICAN AMERICAN SOLDIERS—FICTION

Ballard, Allen. Where Im Bound. 2006. pap. 18.95 *(978-0-595-39856-0(1),* Backinprint.com) iUniverse, Inc.

Garland, Sherry. The Buffalo Soldier, 1 vol. Himler, Ronald, illus. 2006. (ENG.). 32p. (J). (gr. k-3). 16.99 *(978-1-58980-391-6(4))* Pelican Publishing Co., Inc.

Moore, Stephanie Perry & Moody Publishing Staff. Finding Your Faith 2009. (Yasmin Peace Ser.: 1). (ENG.). 176p. (gr. 7-10). pap. 7.99 *(978-0-8024-8602-8(9),* Lift Every Voice) Moody Pubs.

Myers, Walter Dean. Invasion. 2013. (YA). *(978-0-545-57659-8(8));* (ENG.). 224p. (J). (gr. 7). 17.99 *(978-0-545-38428-5(1))* Scholastic, Inc. (Scholastic Pr.).

AFRICAN AMERICAN SONGS

see African Americans—Music

AFRICAN AMERICAN SPIRITUALS

see Spirituals (Songs)

AFRICAN AMERICANS

Here are entered works on citizens of the United States of black African descent. Works on blacks outside the United States are entered under Blacks. A to Z of African Americans, 8 vols., Set. 2011. (A to Z of African Americans Ser.). (C). (gr. 9). 396.00 (978-0-8160-8312-1(6)) Facts On File, Inc.

African-American Achievers. (Illus.). (gr. 6-12). lib. bdg. 69.65 *(978-0-7910-8444-1(2));* 2005. 144p. 90.00 *(978-0-7910-7720-7(9))* Facts On File, Inc. (Chelsea Hse.).

African-American Contributions. 2005. (American Mosaic:African-American Contributions Ser.). (Illus.). 112p. (gr. 6-12). 120.00 *(978-0-7910-7271-4(1),* Chelsea Hse.) Facts On File, Inc.

Allen, Thomas B. Harriet Tubman, Secret Agent: How Daring Slaves & Free Blacks Spied for the Union During the Civil War. Bauer, Carla, illus. 2006. (National Geographic Ser.). (ENG.). 192p. (gr. 5-8). 16.95 *(978-0-7922-7889-4(5));* lib. bdg. 25.90 *(978-0-7922-7890-0(9))* National Geographic Society. (National Geographic Children's Bks.).

Amazing African-Americans. 2007. (Illus.). 28p. (J). pap. 6.00 *(978-0-9815308-2-6(6))* Amazement Square.

Ashley, Michele. Who Is This? 2014. (Little Books of Answers: Level a Ser.). (Illus.). 16p. (gr. k-2). pap. 7.95 *(978-1-927136-00-3(8))* Three Crows Media NZL. Dist: RiverStream Publishing.

Banting, Erinn. Halle Berry. 2005. (Great African American Women for Kids Ser.). (Illus.). 24p. (J). (gr. 2-3). lib. bdg. 24.45 *(978-1-59036-333-1(7));* (gr. 3-7). per. 9.95 *(978-1-59036-339-3(6))* Weigl Pubs., Inc.

Bloom, Harold, ed. Bloom's Literary Criticism 20th Anniversary Collection. (Illus.). (gr. 9-13). pap. *(978-0-7910-8394-9(2),* Chelsea Hse.) Facts On File, Inc.

Bloom's Literary Criticism. 20th anniv. ed. Incl. Dramatists & Drama. Bloom, Harold, ed. 45.00 *(978-0-7910-8226-3(1),* Checkmark Bks.); Epic. Bloom, Harold. 45.00 *(978-0-7910-8229-4(6),* Chelsea Hse.); Essayists & Prophets. Bloom, Harold, ed. 45.00 *(978-0-7910-8523-3(6),* Chelsea Hse.); Novelists & Novels. Bloom, Harold, ed. 45.00 *(978-0-7910-8227-0(X),* Checkmark Bks.); Poets & Poems. Bloom, Harold. 45.00 *(978-0-7910-8225-6(3),* Chelsea Hse.); Short Story Writers & Short Stories. Bloom, Harold. 45.00 *(978-0-7910-8228-7(8),* Chelsea Hse.); 200p. (C). (gr. 9-14). 2004. (Bloom's 20th Anniversary Collection Ser.). (Illus.). 300p. 2005. 270.00 *(978-0-7910-8480-9(9),* Chelsea Hse.) Facts On File, Inc.

Braun, Eric. Booker T. Washington: Great American Educator. Martin, Cynthia, illus. 2005. (Graphic Biographies Ser.). (ENG.). 32p. (gr. 3-4). 30.65 *(978-0-7368-4630-1(1),* Graphic Library) Capstone Press of Coughlan Cos.

Bridges, Ruby. Ruby Bridges Goes to School: My True Story. 2009. (Scholastic Reader Level 2 Ser.). (ENG.). 32p. (J). (gr. -1-3). pap. 3.99 *(978-0-545-10855-3(1))* Scholastic, Inc.

Brill, Marlene Targ. Michelle Obama: From Chicago's South Side to the White House. 2009. (Gateway Biographies Ser.). (ENG., Illus.). 48p. (gr. 4-8). 26.60 *(978-0-7613-5033-0(0))* Lerner Publishing Group.

Brown, Margery W. Afro-Bets Book of Shapes. Blair, Culverson & Simpson, Howard, illus. 2nd ed. 2004. (Afro-Bets Ser.). 24p. (J). (gr. -1-1). pap. 3.95 *(978-0-940975-58-3(0),* Sankofa Bks.) Just Us Bks., Inc.

—Book of Colors: Meet the Color Family. Blair, Culverson & Simpson, Howard, illus. 2nd ed. 2004. (Afro-Bets Ser.). 24p. (J). (gr. -1-1). pap. 3.95 *(978-0-940975-57-6(2),* Sankofa Bks.) Just Us Bks., Inc.

Chandler, Alton. A Salute to African American in Medicine: Learning. Chapman, L., ed. Still, Wayne A., illus. 24p. (Orig.). (J). (gr. 3-8). pap. 1.75 *(978-1-877804-17-5(7))* Chandler/White Publishing Co.

Colbert, David. Michelle Obama: An American Story. 2008. (ENG., Illus.). 160p. (J). (gr. 2-5). pap. 6.99 *(978-0-547-24770-0(2))* Houghton Mifflin Harcourt Publishing Co.

Crowe, Chris. Getting Away with Murder: The True Story of the Emmett till Case. 2003. (ENG., Illus.). 144p. (J). (gr. 7-18). 18.99 *(978-0-8037-2804-2(2),* Dial Bks) Penguin Young Readers Group.

Currie, Stephen. African-American Inventors. 2010. (Lucent Library of Black History Ser.). (Illus.). 128p. (gr. 7-10). 34.80 *(978-1-4205-0121-6(6),* Lucent Bks.) Cengage Gale.

Drew, Mary E. C. One Common Country for One Common People. 2011. 120p. 29.99 *(978-1-4628-8720-0(1));* pap. 19.99 *(978-1-4628-8719-4(8))* Xlibris Corp.

Ganeri, Anita. Harriet Tubman: The Life of an African-American Abolitionist. Shone, Rob, illus. 2005. (Graphic Biographies Ser.). (ENG.). 48p. (gr. 5-8). pap. 14.05 *(978-1-4042-5172-4(3))* Rosen Publishing Group, Inc., The.

George, Charles. Black Nationalism. 2009. (Lucent Library of Black History Ser.). (ENG., Illus.). 128p. (gr. 7-10). 39.40 *(978-1-4205-0083-7(X),* Lucent Bks.) Cengage Gale.

Green, Jen. The Africans: We Came to North America. 2006. (Illus.). 32p. (J). (gr. 4-8). reprint ed. pap. 19.00 *(978-0-7567-9901-4(5))* DIANE Publishing Co.

Greenfield, Eloise. How They Got Over: African Americans & the Call of the Sea. Date not set. 80p. (J). pap. 6.99 *(978-0-06-443693-9(4))* HarperCollins Pubs.

Gunderson, Jessica. A Biography of Malcolm X. Hayden, Seitu, illus. 2010. (American Graphic Ser.). (ENG.). 32p. (gr. 3-4). lib. bdg. 30.65 *(978-1-4296-5471-5(6),* Graphic Library) Capstone Press of Coughlan Cos.

Hansen-Krening, Nancy, et al, eds. Kaleidoscope: A Multicultural Booklist for Grades K-8. 4th ed. 2003. (NCTE Bibliography Ser.). (Illus.). 118p. (J). pap. 30.95 *(978-0-8141-2539-7(5),* 25395) National Council of Teachers of English.

Herkert, Barbara. Sewing Stories: Harriet Powers' Journey from Slave to Artist. Brantley-Newton, Vanessa, illus. 2015. (ENG.). 40p. (J). (gr. -1-3). 17.99 *(978-0-385-75462-0(0),* Knopf Bks. for Young Readers) Random Hse. Children's Bks.

Hill, Laban Carrick. Harlem Stomp! A Cultural History of the Harlem Renaissance. 2009. (ENG., Illus.). 160p. (J). (gr. 7-17). pap. 20.00 *(978-0-316-03424-1(X))* Little, Brown Bks. for Young Readers.

Hoblin, Paul. Great Hitters of the Negro Leagues, 1 vol. 2012. (Negro Baseball Leagues Ser.). (ENG.). 64p. (J). (gr. 5-8). lib. bdg. 32.79 *(978-1-61783-507-0(2),* SportsZone) ABDO Publishing Co.

—Great Pitchers of the Negro Leagues, 1 vol. 2012. (Negro Baseball Leagues Ser.). (ENG.). 64p. (J). (gr. 5-8). lib. bdg. 32.79 *(978-1-61783-508-7(0),* SportsZone) ABDO Publishing Co.

Hudak, Heather C. Oprah Winfrey. 2005. (Great African American Women for Kids Ser.). (Illus.). 24p. (J). (gr. 2-3). lib. bdg. 24.45 *(978-1-59036-335-5(3));* (gr. 3-7). per. 8.95 *(978-1-59036-341-6(8))* Weigl Pubs., Inc.

Huey, Lois Miner. Forgotten Bones: Uncovering a Slave Cemetery. 2015. (ENG., Illus.). 56p. (J). (gr. 4-8). lib. bdg. 30.65 *(978-1-4677-3393-9(8),* Millbrook Pr.) Lerner Publishing Group.

Igus, Toyomi. I See the Rhythm of Gospel, 1 vol. Wood, Michele, illus. 2010. (ENG.). 40p. (J). (gr. 4-7). 16.99 *(978-0-310-71819-2(8))* Zonderkidz.

Jeffrey, Gary. The Little Rock Nine & the Fight for Equal Education. 2012. (Graphic History of the Civil Rights Movement Ser.). (Illus.). 24p. (J). (gr. 3-8). lib. bdg. 23.95 *(978-1-4339-7483-0(5))* Stevens, Gareth Publishing LLLP.

Johnson, Angela. In Daddy's Arms, I Am Tall. 2004. (Illus.). (J). (gr. k-3). spiral bd. (978-0-616-03094-3(0)) Canadian National Institute for the Blind/Institut National Canadien pour les Aveugles.

Johnson, Claudia. Women's Issues in Alice Walker's the Color Purple. 2011. (Social Issues in Literature Ser.). (Illus.). 224p. (ENG.). (gr. 12-12). lib. bdg. 46.40 (978-0-7377-5270-0(X)); (J). pap. 28.45 (978-0-7377-5271-7(8)) Cengage Gale. (Greenhaven Pr., Inc.).

Kallen, Stuart A. The Harlem Renaissance. 2009. (American History Ser.). (ENG.). 128p. (J). (gr. 7-10). 34.80 (978-1-4205-0104-9(6), Lucent Bks.) Cengage Gale.

—A Travel Guide to Harlem Renaissance. 2003. (Travel Guide To Ser.). (ENG.). (J). 30.85 (978-1-59018-358-8(4), Lucent Bks.) Cengage Gale.

Keedle, Jayne. West African Americans. 2009. (New Americans Ser.). (Illus.). 80p. (J). (gr. 5-8). 35.64 (978-0-7614-4313-1(4)) Marshall Cavendish Corp.

King, Wilma. Children of the Emancipation. 2005. (Picture the American Past Ser.). (Illus.). 48p. (gr. 2-5). 22.60 (978-1-57505-396-7(9)) Lerner Publishing Group.

Kirkpatrick, Rob. Evander Holyfield: Campeón de los Pesos Pesados (Heavyweight Champion) 2009. (Grandes Idolos (Hot Shots) Ser.). (SPA.). 24p. (gr. 1-1). 42.50 (978-1-61512-736-8(4), Editorial Buenas Letras) Rosen Publishing Group, Inc., The.

Koopmans, Andy. The Harlem Renaissance. 2005. (Lucent Library of Black History). (ENG., Illus.). 112p. (YA). (gr. 7-10). lib. bdg. 33.45 (978-1-59018-702-9(4), Lucent Bks.) Cengage Gale.

Lane, Mitchell. Contemporary African-American Collection, 14 vols., Set. 2003. (Illus.). (J). (gr. 3-8). lib. bdg. 223.30 (978-1-58415-189-0(7)) Mitchell Lane Pubs., Inc.

Lucas, Eileen. The Little Rock Nine Stand up for Their Rights. Gustavson, Adam, illus. 2011. 48p. pap. 9.95 (978-0-7613-7118-2(4)); pap. 56.72 (978-0-7613-7634-7(8)); (ENG.). (gr. 2-4). lib. bdg. 27.93 (978-0-7613-5874-9(9), Millbrook Pr.) Lerner Publishing Group.

Lüsted, Marcia Amidon. Lyndon B. Johnson & the Civil Rights ACT. 2017. (J). **(978-1-5383-8048-2(X))** Rosen Publishing Group, Inc., The.

Magee, Kanika A. M. Today I Got Saved, 1 book. Thomas, Sonya, illus. 2003. 20p. (J). 10.00 net. (978-0-9748834-0-3(9)) Ebenezer A.M.E. Church.

Maloof, Torrey. Abolitionists: What We Need Is Action (America in The 1800s) 2017. (Primary Source Readers Ser.). (Illus.). 32p. (J). (gr. 4-5). pap. 8.99 **(978-1-4938-3801-1(6))** Teacher Created Materials, Inc.

Marbury, Ja'Nitta. All Mixed Up. Marbury, Ja'Nitta, illus. 2003. (Illus.). 22p. (J). pap. 22.50 (978-0-9718307-3-8(8)) Shades of Me Publishing.

Marsh, Carole. Barack Obama - America's 44th President. 2009. (Here & Now Ser.). 40p. (J). (gr. 2-9). 29.99 (978-0-635-06983-2(0)) Gallopade International.

McKissack, Patricia C. & McKissack, Fredrick L. Carter G. Woodson: Black History Pioneer. 2013. (Famous African Americans Ser.). (Illus.). 24p. (J). (gr. k-18). lib. bdg. 22.60 (978-0-7660-4109-7(3), Enslow Elementary) Enslow Pubs., Inc.

—Ida B. Wells-Barnett: Fighter for Justice. 2013. (Famous African Americans Ser.). 24p. (J). (gr. k-3). pap. 7.95 (978-1-4644-0198-5(5), Enslow Elementary) Enslow Pubs., Inc.

McLendon, Jacquelyn Y. Phillis Wheatley: A Revolutionary Poet. 2005. (Library of American Lives & Times). (Illus.). 112p. (YA). (gr. 4-8). lib. bdg. 34.60 (978-0-8239-5750-7(0)) Rosen Publishing Group, Inc., The.

Michelson, Richard. Twice as Good: The story of William Powell & Clearview, the only golf course designed, built, & owned by an African-American. 2012. (ENG., Illus.). 32p. (J). (gr. 1-4). 16.95 (978-1-58536-466-4(5), 202308) Sleeping Bear Pr.

Moore-Chambers, Robin. Dark Skin, Light Skin, Straight or Nappy... It's All Good! An Educational Coloring Book about the Beauty & Diversity of African-American Features. 2011. 47p. pap. 12.95 (978-1-4327-3545-6(4)) Outskirts Pr., Inc.

Nell, William C. Black Patriots of the American Revolution, with Sketches of Several Distinguished Black Persons to Which Is Added a Brief Survey of the Condition & Prospects of Black Americans. 2017. (ENG., Illus.). 396p. (J). (gr. 4-12). act. bk. ed. incl. cd-rom (978-1-892824-87-5(6)) AFCHRON.

Nelson, Kadir. We Are the Ship: The Story of Negro League Baseball. 2009. 88p. (J). 19.00 (978-1-4379-6953-5(4)) DIANE Publishing Co.

—We Are the Ship: The Story of Negro League Baseball. Nelson, Kadir, illus. 2008. (ENG., Illus.). 96p. (J). (gr. 3-7). 19.99 (978-0-7868-0832-8(2), Jump at the Sun) Hyperion Bks. for Children.

No Easy Answers: Bayard Rustin & the Civil Rights Movement. 2005. (Civil Rights Leaders Ser.). (Illus.). 160p. (J). (gr. 6-12). 26.95 (978-1-931798-43-3(5)) Reynolds, Morgan Inc.

Novesky, Amy. Mister & Lady Day: Billie Holiday & the Dog Who Loved Her. Brantley Newton, Vanessa, illus. 2017. (ENG.). 32p. (J). (gr. -1-3). 6.99 (978-0-544-80905-5(X), HMH Books For Young Readers) Houghton Mifflin Harcourt Publishing Co.

Oliver, Patrick M., ed. Turn the Page & You Don't Stop: Sharing Successful Chapters in Our Lives with Youth. 2006. (Illus.). 156p. pap. 12.00 (978-0-9779499-0-8(7)) Say It Loud! Readers & Writers Series.

Ovations. Incl. Barry Bonds. Goodman, Michael E. lib. bdg. 21.30 (978-0-88682-694-9(2)); Grant Hill. Goodman, Michael E. lib. bdg. (978-0-88682-831-8(7)); Hillary Rodham Clinton. Loewen, Nancy. lib. bdg. (978-0-88682-636-9(5)); Jeff Gordon. Bach, Julie S. pap. (978-0-88682-939-1(9)); Monica Seles. Goodman, Michael E. lib. bdg. 21.30 (978-0-88682-699-4(3)); Shaquille O'Neal. Goodman, Michael E. lib. bdg. (978-0-88682-633-8(0)); Spike Lee. Chapman, Ferguson. lib. bdg. (978-0-88682-697-0(7)); Whoopi Goldberg. DeBoer, Andy. 21.30 (978-0-88682-696-3(9)); (Illus.). 32p. (YA). (gr. 4-7). 1998. 59.80 (978-0-88682-693-2(4), Creative Education) Creative Co., The.

Peete, Holly Robinson, et al. Same but Different: Teen Life on the Autism Express. 2016. (ENG.). 224p. (J). (gr. 7). 17.99 (978-0-545-09468-9(2), Scholastic Pr.) Scholastic, Inc.

Ponto, Joanna & Leeper, Angela. Juneteenth. 2016. (Story of Our Holidays Ser.). (Illus.). 32p. (J). pap. 10.52 (978-0-7660-8336-3(5)) Enslow Pubs., Inc.

Porterfield, Jason. Frederick Douglass: Abolitionist & Fighter for Equality. 2017. (J). **(978-1-5383-0019-0(2)**, Britannica Educational Publishing) Rosen Publishing Group, Inc., The.

Powell, Patricia Hruby. Josephine: The Dazzling Life of Josephine Baker. Robinson, Christian, illus. 2014. (ENG.). 104p. (J). (gr. 2-5). 17.99 (978-1-4521-0314-3(3)) Chronicle Bks. LLC.

The River Is My Life: Six-Pack. (Greetings Ser.: Vol. 3). (gr. 3-5). 31.00 (978-0-7635-1823-3(9)) Rigby Education.

Rossi, Ann. Freedom Struggle: The Anti-Slavery Movement 1830-1865. 2005. (Crossroads America Ser.). (ENG., Illus.). 40p. (J). (gr. 5-9). 12.95 (978-0-7922-7828-3(3)); 21.90 (978-0-7922-8061-3(X)) National Geographic Society. (National Geographic Children's Bks.).

Sanders, Nancy I. D Is for Drinking Gourd: An African American Alphabet. Lewis, E. B., illus. 2007. (ENG.). 40p. (J). (gr. k-6). 17.95 (978-1-58536-293-6(X)) Sleeping Bear Pr.

Seba, Jaime. Gallup Guides for Youth Facing Persistent Prejudice: Blacks. 2012. (Gallup Guides for Youth Facing Persistent Prejudice Ser.). 64p. (J). (gr. 7-8). 22.95 (978-1-4222-2464-9(3)) Mason Crest.

Shabazz, Ilyasah & Magoon, Kekla. X. 2016. (ENG.). 384p. (YA). (gr. 9). 19.65 (978-0-606-39098-9(7)) Turtleback Bks.

Shone, Rob & Ganeri, Anita. Harriet Tubman: The Life of an African-American Abolitionist. 2005. (Graphic Nonfiction Biographies Ser.). (ENG., Illus.). 48p. (J). (gr. 4-7). lib. bdg. 31.95 (978-1-4042-0245-0(5)) Rosen Publishing Group, Inc., The.

Smith, Charles R., Jr. Brick by Brick. Cooper, Floyd, illus. 2012. (ENG.). 32p. (J). (gr. -1-3). 17.99 (978-0-06-192082-0(7), Amistad) HarperCollins Pubs.

Smolka, Bo. The Negro Leagues' Integration Era, 1 vol. 2012. (Negro Baseball Leagues Ser.). (ENG.). 64p. (J). (gr. 5-8). lib. bdg. 32.79 (978-1-61783-509-4(9), SportsZone) ABDO Publishing Co.

—The Story of the Negro Leagues, 1 vol. 2012. (Negro Baseball Leagues Ser.). (ENG.). 64p. (J). (gr. 5-8). lib. bdg. 32.79 (978-1-61783-510-0(2), SportsZone) ABDO Publishing Co.

Sorey, Barbara J. Florida Girl: Short Stories of Family, Community & History. 2007. 72p. per. 9.95 (978-0-595-47438-7(1)) iUniverse, Inc.

Taylor-Butler, Christine. Thurgood Marshall. 2006. (Rookie Biographies Ser.). (ENG., Illus.). 32p. (J). (gr. 1-2). pap. 4.95 (978-0-516-27099-9(0), Children's Pr.) Scholastic Library Publishing.

Thompson, Craig. ABC's of Black Inventors: A Children's Guide. 2009. (ENG.). 32p. (J). 14.95 (978-0-9823876-2-7(8)) Beckham Pubns. Group, Inc.

Tisdale, Rachel. The Little Rock Nine, 1 vol., 1. 2014. (We Shall Overcome Ser.). (ENG.). 32p. (J). (gr. 3-6). 26.25 (978-1-4777-6057-4(1), PowerKids Pr.) Rosen Publishing Group, Inc., The.

Toth, Henrietta. The Murder of Emmett Till. 2017. pap. **(978-1-5383-8054-3(4))** Rosen Publishing Group, Inc., The.

Tougas, Shelley. Little Rock Girl 1957: How a Photograph Changed the Fight for Integration, 1 vol. 2011. (Captured History Ser.). (ENG.). 64p. (gr. 5-7). pap. 9.10 (978-0-7565-4512-3(9)); lib. bdg. 34.65 (978-0-7565-4440-9(8)) Compass Point Bks. (CPB Grades 4-8).

Troupe, Thomas Kingsley. Harriet Tubman's Escape: a Fly on the Wall History. Tejido, Jomike, illus. 2017. (Fly on the Wall History Ser.). (ENG.). 32p. (gr. 1-3). lib. bdg. 27.32 (978-1-4795-9788-8(0)) Picture Window Bks.

Turner, Glennette Tilley. An Apple for Harriet Tubman. Keeter, Susan, illus. 2016. (ENG.). 24p. (J). (gr. -1-3). pap. 6.99 (978-0-8075-0396-6(7)) Whitman, Albert & Co.

Wheeler, Jill C. Mae Jemison: Awesome Astronaut, 1 vol. 2012. (Women in Science Ser.). (ENG., Illus.). 32p. (J). (gr. 3-6). lib. bdg. 27.07 (978-1-61783-447-9(5), Checkerboard Library) ABDO Publishing Co.

—Thurgood Marshall. 2003. (Breaking Barriers Ser.). 64p. (gr. 3-8). 27.07 (978-1-57765-907-5(4), Abdo & Daughters) ABDO Publishing Co.

AFRICAN AMERICANS—ALABAMA

Haldy, Emma E. Rosa Parks. Bane, Jeff, illus. 2016. (My Early Library: My Itty-Bitty Bio Ser.). (ENG.). 24p. (J). (gr. k-1). 28.50 (978-1-63470-481-6(9), 207655) Cherry Lake Publishing.

Kemp, Kristin. Amazing Americans: Rosa Parks, 1 vol. rev. ed. 2014. (Primary Source Readers Content & Literacy Ser.). (ENG., Illus.). 32p. (gr. 3-3). pap. 8.99 (978-1-4333-7375-6(0)) Teacher Created Materials, Inc.

Miller, Jake. The March from Selma to Montgomery: African Americans Demand the Vote. 2004. (Library of the Civil Rights Movement Ser.). (Illus.). 24p. (J). lib. bdg. 22.60 (978-0-8239-6254-9(7), PowerKids Pr.) Rosen Publishing Group, Inc., The.

Pingry, Patricia A. The Story of Rosa Parks. Walker, Steven, illus. 2008. (ENG.). 24p. (J). (gr. 3-7). bds. 7.69 (978-0-8249-6687-4(2), Ideal Pubns.) Worthy Publishing.

Rubin, Susan Goldman. The Quilts of Gee's Bend. 2017. (ENG., Illus.). 56p. (J). (gr. 3-7). 21.95 (978-1-4197-2131-1(3), Abrams Bks. for Young Readers) Abrams, Inc.

Tougas, Shelley. Birmingham 1963: How a Photograph Rallied Civil Rights Support, 1 vol. 2011. (Captured History Ser.). (ENG.). 64p. (gr. 5-7). lib. bdg. 34.65 (978-0-7565-4398-3(3), CPB Grades 4-8) Compass Point Bks.

Whiting, Jim. Rosa Parks. 2007. (What's So Great About... ? Ser.). (Illus.). 32p. (YA). (gr. 2-4). lib. bdg. 25.70 (978-1-58415-573-7(6)) Mitchell Lane Pubs., Inc.

AFRICAN AMERICANS—ALABAMA—MONTGOMERY

Aretha, David. The Story of Rosa Parks & the Montgomery Bus Boycott in Photographs. 2014. (Story of the Civil Rights Movement in Photographs Ser.). 48p. (J). 25.27 (978-0-7660-4234-6(0)) Enslow Pubs., Inc.

Banting, Erinn. Rosa Parks. 2005. (Great African American Women for Kids Ser.). (Illus.). 24p. (J). (gr. 2-3). lib. bdg. 26.00 (978-1-59036-336-2(1)); (gr. 3-7). per. 8.95 (978-1-59036-342-3(6)) Weigl Pubs., Inc.

Daly, Ruth. Rosa Parks. 2014. (J). (978-1-4896-2452-9(X)) Weigl Pubs., Inc.

Dubowski, Cathy East. Rosa Parks: Don't Give In! 2005. (Defining Moments Ser.). (Illus.). 32p. (J). (gr. 2-5). lib. bdg. 25.27 (978-1-59716-078-0(4)) Bearport Publishing Co., Inc.

Edison, Erin. Rosa Parks, 1 vol. 2013. (Great Women in History Ser.). (ENG.). 24p. (gr. k-1). pap. 6.29 (978-1-62065-863-5(1)); pap. 35.70 (978-1-62065-864-2(X)); (Illus.). lib. bdg. 21.99 (978-1-62065-071-4(1)) Capstone Press of Coughlan Cos. (Pebble Bks.).

Fine, Edith Hope. Rosa Parks: Meet a Civil Rights Hero. 2004. (Meeting Famous People Ser.). (Illus.). 32p. (J). lib. bdg. 23.94 (978-0-7660-2099-3(1)) Enslow Pubs., Inc.

Giovanni, Nikki. Rosa. Collier, Bryan, illus. rev. ed. 2005. (ENG.). 40p. (J). (gr. -1-3). 17.99 (978-0-8050-7106-1(7), 9780805071061, Holt, Henry & Co. Bks. For Young Readers) Holt, Henry & Co.

Gitlin, Martin. The Montgomery Bus Boycott: A History Perspectives Book. 2013. (Perspectives Library). (ENG., Illus.). 32p. (J). (gr. 4-8). 28.50 (978-1-62431-418-6(X), 202792); pap. 14.21 (978-1-62431-494-0(5), 202794) Cherry Lake Publishing.

Hurt, Avery Elizabeth. Rosa Parks: Civil Rights Activist. 2017. (J). pap. **(978-1-5383-8102-1(8))** Rosen Publishing Group, Inc., The.

Kishel, Ann-Marie. Rosa Parks: A Life of Courage. 2006. (Pull Ahead Books-Biographies Ser.). (ENG., Illus.). 32p. (gr. k-3). lib. bdg. 22.60 (978-0-8225-3478-5(9), Lerner Pubns.) Lerner Publishing Group.

—Rosa Parks: Una Vida de Valentia. Translations.com Staff, tr. 2006. (Libros para Avanzar-Biografías (Pull Ahead Books-Biographies) Ser.). (ENG & SPA., Illus.). 32p. (gr. k-3). lib. bdg. 22.60 (978-0-8225-6239-9(1)) Lerner Publishing Group.

Mara, Wil. Rosa Parks. 2004. (Rookie Biographies Ser.). (ENG., Illus.). 32p. (J). (gr. 1-2). pap. 4.95 (978-0-516-27916-9(5), Children's Pr.) Scholastic Library Publishing.

—Rosa Parks: Mother of the Civil Rights Movement. 2014. (Rookie Biographies(r) Ser.). (ENG.). 32p. (J). pap. 5.95 (978-0-531-21204-2(1)) Scholastic Library Publishing.

McDonough, Yona Zeldis. Who Was Rosa Parks? Harrison, Nancy & Marchesi, Stephen, illus. 2010. (Who Was? Ser.). (ENG.). 112p. (J). (gr. 3-7). pap. 5.99 (978-0-448-45442-9(4), Grosset & Dunlap) Penguin Young Readers Group.

Mis, Melody S. Meet Rosa Parks. 2009. (Civil Rights Leaders Ser.). 24p. (gr. 2-3). 42.50 (978-1-61511-855-7(1), PowerKids Pr.) Rosen Publishing Group, Inc., The.

Morris, Roz. Rosa Parks: Mother of the Civil Rights Movement. 2003. (Alabama Roots Biography Ser.). (Illus.). 109p. (J). (978-1-878561-57-2(X)) Seacoast Publishing, Inc.

Pingry, Patricia A. Meet Rosa Parks. Walker, Steven, illus. 2008. (ENG.). 32p. (J). (gr. k-3). per. 7.99 (978-0-8249-5578-6(1), Ideal Pubns.) Worthy Publishing.

Rinaldo, Denise. Rosa Parks: With a Discussion of Courage. 2003. (Values in Action Ser.). (J). (978-1-59203-061-3(0)) Learning Challenge, Inc.

Ringgold, Faith. If a Bus Could Talk: The Story of Rosa Parks. Ringgold, Faith, illus. 2003. (ENG., Illus.). 32p. (J). (gr. k-4). pap. 7.99 (978-0-689-85676-1(8), Aladdin) Simon & Schuster Children's Publishing.

Schraff, Anne E. Rosa Parks: Tired of Giving In. 2005. (African-American Biography Library). (Illus.). 128p. (J). (gr. 6-12). lib. bdg. 33.27 (978-0-7660-2463-2(6)) Enslow Pubs., Inc.

Summer, L. S. Rosa Parks. 2009. (Journey to Freedom Ser.). (ENG., Illus.). 32p. (J). (gr. 4-7). 29.93 (978-1-60253-133-8(1), 200399) Child's World, Inc., The.

Tracy, Kathleen. The Life & Times of Rosa Parks. 2008. (Illus.). 48p. (J). (gr. 4-8). lib. bdg. 29.95 (978-1-58415-666-6(X)) Mitchell Lane Pubs., Inc.

Weidt, Maryann N. Rosa Parks. (History Maker Bios Ser.). (Illus.). (J). 2004. 48p. pap. 8.95 (978-0-8225-4805-8(4)) 2003. 47p. 26.60 (978-0-8225-4673-3(6)) Lerner Publishing Group. (Lerner Pubns.).

Weston Woods Staff, creator. Rosa. 2011. 18.95 (978-0-545-14962-4(2)); 38.75 (978-0-545-14963-1(0)) Weston Woods Studios, Inc.

Wheeler, Jill C. Rosa Parks, Set II. 2003. (Breaking Barriers Ser.). 64p. (gr. 3-8). 27.07 (978-1-57765-640-1(7), Abdo & Daughters) ABDO Publishing Co.

AFRICAN AMERICANS—BIOGRAPHY

Abdul-Jabbar, Kareem & Obstfeld, Raymond. What Color Is My World? The Lost History of African-American Inventors. Boos, Ben & Ford, A. G., illus. (ENG.). (J). (gr. 3-7). 2013. 96p. pap. 6.99 (978-0-7636-6442-8(1)) 2012. 44p. 17.99 (978-0-7636-4564-9(8)) Candlewick Pr.

Abnett, Dan. Harriet Tubman & the Underground Railroad. (Jr. Graphic Biographies Ser.). (ENG.). 24p. 2009. (J). (gr. 2-3). 47.90 (978-1-61513-816-6(1), PowerKids Pr.) 2007. (Illus.). (J). (gr. 2-5). lib. bdg. 25.25 (978-1-4042-3393-5(8)) 2007. (Illus.). (gr. 3-8). pap. 10.60 (978-1-4042-2146-8(8), PowerKids Pr.) Rosen Publishing Group, Inc., The.

Abrams, Dennis. George Washington Carver: Scientist & Educator. 2008. (Black Americans of Achievement Ser.). (Illus.). 119p. (gr. 6-12). lib. bdg. 35.00 (978-0-7910-9717-5(X), Chelsea Hse.) Facts On File, Inc.

—Gregory Hines. 2008. (Black Americans of Achievement Ser.). (Illus.). 98p. (gr. 6-12). lib. bdg. 35.00 (978-0-7910-9718-2(8), Chelsea Hse.) Facts On File, Inc.

—Jay-Z. 2007. (Hip-Hop Stars Ser.). (Illus.). 112p. (YA). (gr. 7-12). lib. bdg. 30.00 (978-0-7910-9551-5(7)) Facts On File, Inc.

Acker, Kerry. Nina Simone. 2003. (Women in the Arts Ser.). (Illus.). 112p. (gr. 6-12). 30.00 (978-0-7910-7456-5(0), Chelsea Hse.) Facts On File, Inc.

Adler, David A. Frederick Douglass: A Noble Life. 2010. (ENG., Illus.). 144p. (J). (gr. 5-18). 21.95 (978-0-8234-2056-8(6)) Holiday Hse., Inc.

—Harriet Tubman & the Underground Railroad. 2012. (ENG.). 144p. (J). 18.95 (978-0-8234-2365-1(4)) Holiday Hse., Inc.

—Heroes for Civil Rights. Farnsworth, Bill, illus. 2007. (ENG.). 32p. (J). (gr. -1-3). 17.95 (978-0-8234-2008-7(6)) Holiday Hse., Inc.

—A Picture Book of Frederick Douglass. Byrd, Samuel, illus. unabr. ed. 2005. (Picture Book Readalongs Ser.). (J). (gr. k-4). 25.95 incl. audio (978-1-59519-373-5(1)); pap. 28.95 incl. audio compact disk (978-1-59519-377-3(4));Set. pap. 37.95 incl. audio (978-1-59519-374-2(X));Set. pap. 39.95 incl. audio compact disk (978-1-59519-378-0(2)) Live Oak Media.

—A Picture Book of Martin Luther King, Jr. Casilla, Robert, illus. 2004. (Picture Book Biography Ser.). (J). (gr. -1-3). pap. 18.95 incl. audio compact disk (978-1-59112-773-4(4)) Live Oak Media.

—A Picture Book of Rosa Parks. Casilla, Robert, illus. 2015. 32p. pap. 8.00 (978-1-61003-405-0(8)) Center for the Collaborative Classroom.

—A Picture Book of Rosa Parks. Casilla, Robert, illus. 2004. (J). (gr. -1-2). 28.95 incl. audio compact disk (978-1-59112-762-8(9)) Live Oak Media.

African-American Biographies, 43 bks., Set. (Illus.). (YA). (gr. 6-12). lib. bdg. 900.85 (978-0-89490-775-3(1)) Enslow Pubs., Inc.

African-American Environmentalists. Date not set. (My Ancestors — My Heroes Ser.: Vol. 32). (J). (gr. 3-4). (978-1-893091-31-3(7)) Parker-Wallace Publishing Co., LLC.

African American Eras. 2010. (978-1-4144-3600-5(9)); (978-1-4144-3599-2(1)); (978-1-4144-3597-8(5)); (978-1-4144-3598-5(3)) Cengage Gale. (UXL).

African-American Writers. 2010. (Multicultural Voices Ser.). (Illus.). 142p. (gr. 6-12). 35.00 (978-1-60413-311-0(2), Chelsea Hse.) Facts On File, Inc.

Agins, Donna Brown. Maya Angelou: A Biography of an Award-Winning Poet & Civil Rights Activist. 2013. (African-American Icons Ser.). 104p. (J). (gr. 6-12). pap. 10.95 (978-1-59845-395-9(5)); lib. bdg. 27.94 (978-0-7660-3992-6(7)) Enslow Pubs., Inc.

Alagna, Magdalena. Mae Jemison: The First African American Woman in Space. (Women Hall of Famers in Mathematics & Science Ser.). 112p. (gr. 5-8). 2009. 63.90 (978-1-60854-813-2(9)) 2004. (Illus.). lib. bdg. 34.60 (978-0-8239-3878-0(6)) Rosen Publishing Group, Inc., The. (Rosen Reference).

Alexander, Carol. Bessie Coleman. 2016. (Rookie Biographies(tm) Ser.). (ENG.). 32p. (J). lib. bdg. 25.00 (978-0-531-22545-5(3), Children's Pr.) Scholastic Library Publishing.

Allen, Richard, contrib. by. Charlie Parker Played Be Bop. 2003. (Illus.). (J). (gr. -1-2). pap. 35.95 incl. audio compact disk (978-1-59112-602-7(9)) Live Oak Media.

—Mysterious Thelonious. abr. ed. 2003. (Illus.). (J). (gr. -1-2). audio compact disk 28.95 (978-1-59112-422-1(0)) Live Oak Media.

Allen, Thomas B. Harriet Tubman, Secret Agent: How Daring Slaves & Free Blacks Spied for the Union During the Civil War. 2008. (ENG., Illus.). 192p. (J). (gr. 5). 5.95 (978-1-4263-0401-9(3), National Geographic Children's Bks.) National Geographic Society.

Aller, Susan Bivin. Madam C. J. Walker. 2007. (History Maker Biographies Ser.). (ENG., Illus.). 48p. (gr. 3-6). lib. bdg. 27.93 (978-0-8225-6582-6(X), Lerner Pubns.) Lerner Publishing Group.

Andersen, Richard. Walter Dean Myers. 2014. (J). lib. bdg. (978-1-62712-262-7(1)) Cavendish Square Publishing.

Anderson, Jameson. Kevin Durant, 1 vol. 2014. (Awesome Athletes Ser.). (ENG.). 32p. (gr. 8-12). lib. bdg. 27.07 (978-1-62403-329-2(6), Checkerboard Library) ABDO Publishing Co.

Anderson, Jennifer Joline. Langston Hughes, 1 vol. 2013. (Great American Authors Ser.). (ENG.). 48p. (J). (gr. 3-6). lib. bdg. 32.79 (978-1-61783-718-0(0)) ABDO Publishing Co.

Anniss, Matt. Venus & Serena Williams in the Community, 1 vol., 1. 2014. (Making a Difference: Athletes Who Are Changing the World Ser.). (ENG.). 48p. (J). (gr. 5-8). 25.85 (978-1-62275-170-9(1)) Rosen Publishing Group, Inc., The.

Aretha, David. Awesome African-American Rock & Soul Musicians. 2012. (African-American Collective Biographies Ser.). 112p. (J). (gr. 5-18). 33.27 (978-1-59845-140-5(5)) Enslow Pubs., Inc.

—A Time for Martyrs: The Life of Malcolm X. 2012. (YA). 28.95 (978-1-59935-328-9(8)) Reynolds, Morgan Inc.

Aretha Franklin: Singer. 2nd rev. ed. 2010. (Black Americans of Achievement Legacy Edition Ser.). (Illus.). 104p. (gr. 6-12). 35.00 (978-1-60413-712-5(6)) Facts On File, Inc.

Armand, Glenda & Cooper, Floyd. Ira's Shakespeare Dream, 1 vol. 2015. (ENG., Illus.). 40p. (J). 18.95 (978-1-62014-155-7(8), 9781620000000) Lee & Low Bks., Inc.

Armstrong, Linda J. African-American Stage, Radio, Film, & TV Entertainers. 2012. (978-1-4222-2393-2(0)) Mason Crest.

—African-American Stage, Radio, Film, & TV Entertainers. Hill, Marc Lamont, ed. 2012. (Major Black Contributions from Emancipation to Civil Rights Ser.). 64p. (J). (gr. 5). 22.95 (978-1-4222-2380-2(9)) Mason Crest.

Arora, Sabina G. The Great Migration & the Harlem Renaissance. 2015. (African American Experience: from Slavery to the Presidency Ser.). (ENG., Illus.). 80p. (J). (gr. 7-8). 32.90 (978-1-68048-045-0(6), Britannica Educational Publishing) Rosen Publishing Group, Inc., The.

Ashby, Ruth. Rosa Parks: Freedom Rider. 2008. (Sterling Biographies(r) Ser.). (ENG., Illus.). 128p. (J). (gr. 5). pap. 5.95 (978-1-4027-4865-3(5)) Sterling Publishing Co., Inc.

Asim, Jabari. Fifty Cents & a Dream: Young Booker T. Washington. 2012. (ENG., Illus.). 48p. (J). (gr. -1-3). 16.99 (978-0-316-08657-8(6)) Little Brown & Co.

—Preaching to the Chickens: The Story of Young John Lewis. Lewis, E. B., illus. 2016. (ENG.). 32p. (J). (gr. k-3). 17.99 (978-0-399-16856-7(7), Nancy Paulsen Books) Penguin Young Readers Group.

Asselin, Kristine Carlson. Martin Luther King Jr: Civil Rights Leader, 1 vol. 2013. (Essential Lives Set 8 Ser.). (ENG.). 112p. (J). (gr. 6-12). lib. bdg. 35.64 (978-1-61783-891-0(8), Essential Library) ABDO Publishing Co.

B. Yes I Can for Kids. 2009. 36p. pap. 17.95 (978-1-4490-1585-5(9)) AuthorHouse.

Bader, Bonnie. Who Was Martin Luther King, Jr. ? Wolf, Elizabeth & Harrison, Nancy, illus. 2007. (Who Was? Ser.). (ENG.). 112p. (J). (gr. 3-7). pap. 5.99 (978-0-448-44723-0(1), Grosset & Dunlap) Penguin Young Readers Group.

—Who Was Martin Luther King, Jr. ? Wolf, Elizabeth, illus. 2008. (Who Was... ? Ser.). 105p. (J). (gr. 2-5). 12.65 (978-0-7569-8935-4(3)) Perfection Learning Corp.

Baer, Peter. Wilma Rudolph: Gold-Medal Winner. 2013. (InfoMax Readers Ser.). (ENG.). 24p. (J). (gr. 2-3). pap. 49.50 (978-1-4777-2383-8(8)); pap. 8.25 (978-1-4777-2381-4(1)) Rosen Publishing Group, Inc., The. (Rosen Classroom).

Baer, Peter & Castle, Grace. Olympic Champion: Wilma Rudolph. 2013. (Rosen Readers Ser.). (ENG.). 24p. (J). (gr. 2-3). pap. 8.25 (978-1-4777-2385-2(4)); pap. 49.50 (978-1-4777-2386-9(2)) Rosen Publishing Group, Inc., The. (Rosen Classroom).

Bailey, Diane. Physics. 2017. (Illus.). 64p. (J). (978-1-4222-3554-6(8)) Mason Crest.

—Venus & Serena Williams: Tennis Champions. 2010. (Sports Families Ser.). 48p. (YA). (gr. 5-8). lib. bdg., E-Book 53.00 (978-1-4488-0124-4(9)) Rosen Publishing Group, Inc., The.

Bailey, Gerry & Foster, Karen. Martin Luther King Jr.'s Microphone. Radford, Karen & Noyes, Leighton, illus. 2008. (Stories of Great People Ser.). (ENG.). 40p. (J). (gr. 3-8). pap. (978-0-7787-3711-7(X)); lib. bdg. (978-0-7787-3689-9(X)) Crabtree Publishing Co.

Bailey, Tom. A.G. Gaston: Visionary Businessman. 2003. (Alabama Roots Biography Ser.). (Illus.). 111p. (J). pap. (978-1-878561-99-2(5)) Seacoast Publishing, Inc.

Baker, Brynn. Tuskegee Airmen: Freedom Flyers of World War II. 2015. (Military Heroes Ser.). (ENG., Illus.). 32p. (gr. 3-4). lib. bdg. 27.32 (978-1-4914-4839-7(3)) Capstone Press of Coughlan Cos.

Bankston, John. Bow Wow. l.t. ed. 2004. (Blue Banner Biography Ser.). (Illus.). 32p. (J). (gr. 3-8). lib. bdg. 25.70 (978-1-58415-220-0(6)) Mitchell Lane Pubs., Inc.

—Ja Rule. l.t. ed. 2004. (Blue Banner Biography Ser.). (Illus.). 32p. (J). (gr. 3-8). lib. bdg. 25.70 (978-1-58415-221-7(4)) Mitchell Lane Pubs., Inc.

—Jay-Z. l.t. ed. 2004. (Blue Banner Biography Ser.). (Illus.). 32p. (J). (gr. 3-8). lib. bdg. 25.70 (978-1-58415-223-1(0)) Mitchell Lane Pubs., Inc.

—The Life & Times of Duke Ellington. 2004. (Masters of Music Ser.). (Illus.). 48p. (gr. 4-8). lib. bdg. 20.95 (978-1-58415-248-4(6)) Mitchell Lane Pubs., Inc.

—The Life & Times of Scott Joplin. 2004. (Masters of Music Ser.). (Illus.). 48p. (gr. 4-8). lib. bdg. 20.95 (978-1-58415-270-5(2)) Mitchell Lane Pubs., Inc.

—Missy Elliott: Hip-Hop Superstar. l.t. ed. 2004. (Blue Banner Biography Ser.). (Illus.). 32p. (J). (gr. 3-8). lib. bdg. 25.70 (978-1-58415-219-4(2)) Mitchell Lane Pubs., Inc.

Banting, Erinn. Condoleeza Rice. 2007. (Remarkable People Ser.). (Illus.). 24p. (J). (gr. 3-7). lib. bdg. 24.45 (978-1-59036-639-4(5)) Weigl Pubs., Inc.

—Condoleezza Rice. 2007. (Remarkable People Ser.). (Illus.). 24p. (J). (gr. 3-7). pap. 8.95 (978-1-59036-640-0(9)) Weigl Pubs., Inc.

—Rosa Parks. 2005. (Great African American Women for Kids Ser.). (Illus.). 24p. (J). (gr. 2-3). lib. bdg. 26.00 (978-1-59036-336-2(1)); (gr. 3-7). per. 8.95 (978-1-59036-342-3(6)) Weigl Pubs., Inc.

Barack Obama. 2007. (Political Profiles Ser.). (Illus.). 128p. (YA). (gr. 5-9). lib. bdg. 27.95 (978-1-59935-045-5(9)) Reynolds, Morgan Inc.

Barasch, Lynne. Knockin' on Wood: Starring Peg Leg Bates. 2004. (ENG., Illus.). 32p. (J). 16.95 (978-1-58430-170-7(8)) Lee & Low Bks., Inc.

Barbara Jordan. 2004. 12p. (gr. k-4). 2.95 (978-0-635-02616-3(3)) Gallopade International.

Barber, Tiki & Barber, Ronde. By My Brother's Side. Root, Barry, illus. 2004. (ENG.). 32p. (J). (gr. 1-5). 17.99 (978-0-689-86559-6(7), Simon & Schuster/Paula Wiseman Bks.) Simon & Schuster/Paula Wiseman Bks.

Barbour, Karen. Mr. Williams. Barbour, Karen, illus. rev. ed. 2005. (ENG., Illus.). 32p. (J). (gr. 1-5). 18.99 (978-0-8050-6773-6(6), 9780805067736, Holt, Henry & Co. Bks. For Young Readers) Holt, Henry & Co.

Barron, Patricia. Meet Judge Patricia Barron. Barron, Robert, photos by. 2006. (Illus.). 40p. per. 14.95 (978-1-59858-301-4(8)) Dog Ear Publishing, LLC.

Barton, Chris. The Amazing Age of John Roy Lynch. Tate, Don, illus. 2015. (ENG.). 50p. (J). 17.00 (978-0-8028-5379-0(X), Eerdmans Bks For Young Readers) Eerdmans, William B. Publishing Co.

—Whoosh! Lonnie Johnson's Super-Soaking Stream of Inventions. Tate, Don, illus. 2016. (ENG.). 32p. (J). (gr. 2-5). lib. bdg. 16.95 (978-1-58089-297-1(3)) Charlesbridge Publishing, Inc.

Barton, Jen. What's Your Story, Harriet Tubman? 2015. (Cub Reporter Meets Famous Americans Ser.). (ENG., Illus.). 32p. (J). (gr. k-3). pap. 8.99 (978-1-4677-8533-4(4), Lerner Pubns.) Lerner Publishing Group.

Basen, Ryan. Dwight Howard: Gifted & Giving Basketball Star. 2010. (Sports Stars Who Give Back Ser.). (Illus.). 128p. (YA). (gr. 5-9). 33.27 (978-0-7660-3586-7(7)) Enslow Pubs., Inc.

Baumann, Susan K. Harriet Tubman. 2013. (Jr. Graphic African American History Ser.). 24p. (J). (gr. 3-6). 25.25 (978-1-4777-1312-9(3)); pap. 10.60 (978-1-4777-1449-2(9)) Rosen Publishing Group, Inc., The. (PowerKids Pr.).

—Harriet Tubman: Conductor of the Underground Railroad. 2013. (Jr. Graphic African American History Ser.). 24p. (J). (gr. 3-6). pap. 63.60 (978-1-4777-1450-8(2), PowerKids Pr.) Rosen Publishing Group, Inc., The.

Beckman, Wendy Hart. Harlem Renaissance Artists & Writers. 2013. (Inspiring Collective Biographies Ser.). 112p. (J). (gr. 5-12). pap. 10.95 (978-1-4644-0269-2(8)) Enslow Pubs., Inc.

Bedesky, Baron. Peary & Henson: The Race to the North Pole. 2006. (In the Footsteps of Explorers Ser.). (ENG., Illus.). 32p. (J). (gr. 4-7). lib. bdg. (978-0-7787-2426-1(3)) Crabtree Publishing Co.

Bednar, Chuck. Rosa Parks. 2010. (Transcending Race in America Ser.). (Illus.). 64p. (YA). (gr. 5-18). lib. bdg. 22.95 (978-1-4222-1615-6(2)) Mason Crest.

Beier, Anne. Crispus Attucks: Hero of the Boston Massacre. 2004. (Famous People in American History Ser.). (Illus.). 32p. (gr. 4-8). (ENG.). pap. 10.00 (978-0-8239-4178-0(7)); (SPA & ENG., (J). lib. bdg. 22.50 (978-0-8239-4154-4(X)) Rosen Publishing Group, Inc., The.

—Crispus Attucks: Hero of the Boston Massacre / Héroe de la masacre de Boston. 2009. (Famous People in American History/Grandes personajes en la historia de los Estados Unidos Ser.). (ENG & SPA.). 32p. (gr. 2-3). 47.90 (978-1-61512-541-8(8), Editorial Buenas Letras) Rosen Publishing Group, Inc., The.

—Crispus Attucks: Heroe de la masacre de Boston. 2004. (Grandes personajes en la historia de los Estados Unidos Ser.). (SPA.). 32p. (gr. 3-6). pap. 10.00 (978-0-8239-4224-4(4), Rosen Classroom) Rosen Publishing Group, Inc., The.

—Crispus Attucks: Héroe de la masacre de Boston (Crispus Attucks: Hero of the Boston Massacre) 2009. (Grandes personajes en la historia de los Estados Unidos (Famous People in American History) Ser.). (SPA.). 32p. (gr. 2-3). 47.90 (978-1-61512-793-1(3), Editorial Buenas Letras) Rosen Publishing Group, Inc., The.

Belinda, Rochelle. Witnesses to Freedom: Young People Who Fought for Civil Rights. 2014. (ENG.). 116p. (J). 12.24 (978-1-63245-230-6(8)) Lectorum Pubns., Inc.

Benge, Janet & Benge, Geoff. Ben Carson: A Chance at Life. 2014. (ENG., Illus.). 192p. (YA). pap. 9.99 (978-1-62486-034-8(6)) Emerald Bks.

Benjamin, Lisa. Jackie Robinson: Changing the Game. 2005. (Voices Reading Ser.). (Illus.). 32p. (J). (978-0-7367-2937-6(2)) Zaner-Bloser, Inc.

Bennett, Doraine. Jackie Robinson. 2008. (J). pap. (978-1-935077-11-4(2)); (ENG., Illus.). 24p. lib. bdg. 19.93 (978-1-935077-04-6(X)) State Standards Publishing, LLC.

Benson, Kathleen. Draw What You See: The Life & Art of Benny Andrews. Andrews, Benny, illus. 2015. (ENG.). 32p. (J). (gr. -1-3). 17.99 (978-0-544-10487-7(0), Clarion Bks.) Houghton Mifflin Harcourt Trade & Reference Pubs.

Benson, Kathleen & Haskins, Jim. John Lewis in the Lead: A Story of the Civil Rights Movement, 1 vol. Andrews, Benny, illus. 2006. (ENG.). 40p. (gr. 2-7). 17.95 (978-1-58430-250-6(X)) Lee & Low Bks., Inc.

Bernard, Catherine. Sojourner Truth: Women's Rights Activist & Abolitionist. 2016. (Heroes of the Women's Suffrage Movement Ser.). 128p. (gr. 6-6). 37.27 (978-0-7660-7887-1(6)) Enslow Pubs., Inc.

Berne, Emma Carlson. Face of Freedom: How the Photos of Frederick Douglass Celebrated Racial Equality. 2017. (Captured History Ser.). (ENG.). 64p. (gr. 5-7). lib. bdg. 34.65 **(978-0-7565-5617-4(1)**, CPB Grades 4-8) Compass Point Bks.

Berne, Emma Carlson. What's Your Story, Jackie Robinson? 2015. (ENG., Illus.). 32p. (J). (gr. k-3). 26.65 (978-1-4677-7964-7(4)) Lerner Publishing Group.

Bernstein, Ross. Barry Bonds. 2004. (Sports Heroes & Legends Ser.). (ENG., Illus.). 112p. (gr. 5-12). lib. bdg. 30.60 (978-0-8225-1791-7(4)) Lerner Publishing Group.

—Shaquille O'Neal. (Amazing Athletes Ser.). 32p. 2005. (Illus.). (gr. 3-4). lib. bdg. 22.60 (978-0-8225-3689-5(7)) 2004. (Illus.). (J). (gr. 2-5). pap. 5.95 (978-0-8225-2042-9(7)) 2004. (Illus.). (J). (gr. 2-5). pap. 5.95 (978-0-8225-2042-9(7)) 2009. (ENG.). (gr. 2-5). pap. 7.95 (978-0-7613-4489-6(6), First Avenue Editions) Lerner Publishing Group.

—Sports Great Daunte Culpepper. 2003. (Sports Great Bks.). (Illus.). 64p. (J). lib. bdg. 23.94 (978-0-7660-2037-5(1)) Enslow Pubs., Inc.

Berry, S. L. Langston Hughes. 2014. lib. bdg. 35.65 (978-1-60818-327-2(0)) Creative Co., The.

Beyer, Mark. Stevie Wonder. (Rock & Roll Hall of Famers Ser.). 112p. (gr. 5-8). 2009. 63.90 (978-1-60852-475-4(2), Rosen Reference) 2006. (Illus.). (YA). lib. bdg. 34.60 (978-0-8239-3525-3(6)) Rosen Publishing Group, Inc., The.

Bill Cosby: Entertainer & Activist. 2nd rev. ed. 2010. (Black Americans of Achievement Legacy Edition Ser.). (Illus.). 104p. (gr. 6-12). 35.00 (978-1-60413-711-8(8)) Facts On File, Inc.

Billus, Kathleen. Judy Johnson. 2009. (Baseball Hall of Famers of the Negro Leagues Ser.). 112p. (gr. 5-8). 63.90 (978-1-61511-524-2(2), Rosen Reference) Rosen Publishing Group, Inc., The.

Bjornlund, Lydia D. Women of the Suffrage Movement. 2003. (Women in History Ser.). (ENG., Illus.). 112p. (J). 33.45 (978-1-59018-173-7(5), Lucent Bks.) Cengage Gale.

Black Americans of Achievement. (Illus.). 104-144p. (J). (gr. 5). 219.45 (978-0-7910-5216-7(8)); 40p. (J). (gr. 5). pap. 109.45 (978-0-7910-5217-4(6)); (gr. 6-12). pap. 119.40 (978-0-7910-8396-3(9)); (gr. 6-12). lib. bdg. 275.40 (978-0-7910-8419-9(1)) Facts On File, Inc. (Chelsea Hse.).

Blakely, Gloria. Condoleezza Rice. 2003. (African American Leaders Ser.). (Illus.). 112p. (gr. 6-12). 30.00 (978-0-7910-7683-5(0), Chelsea Hse.) Facts On File, Inc.

Blashfield, Jean F. Oprah Winfrey. 2003. (Trailblazers of the Modern World Ser.). (ENG & SPA., Illus.). 48p. (gr. 5-12). pap. 14.05 (978-0-8368-5247-9(8), Gareth Stevens Secondary Library) Stevens, Gareth Publishing LLLP.

Bloom, Harold, ed. Bloom's BioCritiques. (Illus.). (gr. 9-13). pap. (978-0-7910-8483-0(3)); lib. bdg. 1115.85 (978-0-7910-8482-3(5)) Facts On File, Inc. (Chelsea Hse.).

—Bloom's Guides. (Illus.). (gr. 9-13). pap. (978-0-7910-8068-9(4)); lib. bdg. 527.85 (978-0-7910-8481-6(7)) Facts On File, Inc. (Chelsea Hse.).

—Bloom's Major Literary Characters. (Illus.). 180p. (gr. 9-13). lib. bdg. 111.60 (978-0-7910-8070-2(6)); lib. bdg. 383.40 (978-0-7910-7881-5(7)) Facts On File, Inc. (Chelsea Hse.).

—Maya Angelou, New Edition. 2nd rev. ed. 2009. (Bloom's Modern Critical Views Ser.). 200p. (C). (gr. 9-18). 45.00 (978-1-60413-177-2(2), Chelsea Hse.) Facts On File, Inc.

—Maya Angelou's I Know Why the Caged Bird Sings. 2nd rev. ed. 2009. (Bloom's Modern Critical Interpretations Ser.). 141p. (C). (gr. 9-18). 45.00 (978-1-60413-187-1(X), Chelsea Hse.) Facts On File, Inc.

Bloom, Harold, intro. Alice Walker. 2nd ed. 2007. (Modern Critical Views Ser.). 223p. (C). (gr. 9). lib. bdg. 45.00 (978-0-7910-9611-6(4), Chelsea Hse.) Facts On File, Inc.

Blumenthal, Deborah. Fancy Party Gowns: The Story of Ann Cole Lowe. Freeman, Laura, illus. 2017. (ENG.). 40p. (J). (gr. -1-3). 17.99 (978-1-4998-0239-9(0)) Little Bee Books Inc.

Bodden, Valerie. Michelle Obama: First Lady & Role Model, 1 vol. 2009. (Essential Lives Set 4 Ser.). (ENG., Illus.). 112p. (J). (gr. 6-12). lib. bdg. 35.64 (978-1-60453-703-1(5)) ABDO Publishing Co.

Boehme, Gerry. John Lewis & Desegregation. 2016. (Primary Sources of the Civil Rights Movement Ser.). (Illus.). 64p. (J). (gr. 6-6). 34.21 (978-1-5026-1868-9(0)) Cavendish Square Publishing.

Boehme, Gerry. Serena Williams: Setting New Standards. 2017. (J). **(978-1-5026-2762-9(0))** Cavendish Square Publishing.

Bohannon, Lisa Frederiksen. Freedom Cannot Rest: Ella Baker & the Civil Rights Movement. 2005. (Civil Rights Leaders Ser.). (Illus.). 176p. (YA). (gr. 6-12). lib. bdg. 26.95 (978-1-931798-71-6(0)) Reynolds, Morgan Inc.

Bolden, Tonya. Capital Days: Michael Shiner's Journal & the Growth of Our Nation's Capital. 2015. (ENG., Illus.). 96p. (J). (gr. 3-7). 21.95 (978-1-4197-0733-9(7), Abrams Bks. for Young Readers) Abrams, Inc.

—M. L. K. The Journey of a King. Adelman, Bob, ed. 2007. (ENG., Illus.). 128p. (J). (gr. 5-9). 27.95 (978-0-8109-5476-2(1), Abrams Bks. for Young Readers) Abrams, Inc.

—Maritcha: A Nineteenth-Century American Girl. (ENG., Illus.). (J). (gr. k-4). 2015. 56p. 9.95 (978-1-4197-1626-3(3), Abrams Bks. for Young Readers) 2005. 48p. 19.95 (978-0-8109-5045-0(6)) Abrams, Inc.

—Pathfinders: The Journeys of 16 Extraordinary Black Souls. 2017. (ENG., Illus.). 128p. (J). (gr. 5-9). 24.95 (978-1-4197-1455-9(4), Abrams Bks. for Young Readers) Abrams, Inc.

—Portraits of African-American Heroes. Pitcairn, Ansel, illus. 2005. (ENG.). 96p. (J). (gr. 3-7). pap. 12.99 (978-0-14-240473-7(X), Puffin Books) Penguin Young Readers Group.

—Searching for Sarah Rector: The Richest Black Girl in America. 2014. (ENG., Illus.). 80p. (J). (gr. 3-7). 21.95 (978-1-4197-0846-6(5), Abrams Bks. for Young Readers) Abrams, Inc.

—W. E. B. du Bois: A Twentieth-Century Life. 2008. (Up Close Ser.). (ENG.). 224p. (YA). (gr. 7-18). 16.99 (978-0-670-06302-4(9), Viking Books for Young Readers) Penguin Young Readers Group.

Boone, Mary. 50 Cent. 2006. (Blue Banner Biography Ser.). (Illus.). 32p. (YA). (gr. 4-7). lib. bdg. 25.70 (978-1-58415-523-2(X), 1259604) Mitchell Lane Pubs., Inc.

Bourcier, Cammy S. Barack Obama. 2009. (Sharing the American Dream Ser.). (Illus.). 64p. (YA). (gr. 7-12). 22.95 (978-1-4222-0574-7(6)) Mason Crest.

—Carlos Mencia. 2007. (Sharing the American Dream Ser.). 64p. (YA). (gr. 7-18). pap. 9.95 (978-1-4222-0756-7(0)) Mason Crest.

—Malcolm X. 2009. (Sharing the American Dream Ser.). (Illus.). 64p. (YA). (gr. 7-12). 22.95 (978-1-4222-0577-8(0)) Mason Crest.

Bowman, Chris. Nikki Grimes. 2017. (Children's Storytellers Ser.). (ENG., Illus.). 24p. (J). (gr. k-3). lib. bdg. 25.95 **(978-1-62617-650-8(7)**, Blastoff! Readers) Bellwether Media.

Boyd, Herb. Martin Luther King, Jr. Marcos, Pablo, illus. 2005. (Heroes of America Ser.). 239p. (gr. 3-8). 27.07 (978-1-59679-258-6(2), Abdo & Daughters) ABDO Publishing Co.

Boyd, Herb. Martin Luther King Jr. 2006. (Heinle Reading Library: Biography Collection). (ENG.). 240p. pap. 16.95 **(978-1-4240-0546-8(9))** Cengage Heinle.

Bozzuti-Jones, Mark Francisco. The Miter Fits Just Fine: A Story about the Rt. Rev. Barbara Clementine Harris, Suffragan Bishop, Diocese of Massachusetts. 2003. (ENG.). 86p. pap. 10.95 (978-1-56101-220-6(3)) Cowley Pubns.

Bradley, Michael. Donovan McNabb. 2004. (Benchmark All-Stars 2 Ser.). (Illus.). 48p. (gr. 4). 21.95 (978-0-7614-1756-9(7), Benchmark Bks.) Marshall Cavendish Corp.

Brandt, Keith & Mattern, Joanne. Rosa Parks: Freedom Rider. Griffith, Gershom, illus. 2006. 54p. (J). pap. (978-0-439-66045-7(9)) Scholastic, Inc.

Braun, Eric. Booker T. Washington: Great American Educator, 1 vol. Martin, Cynthia, illus. 2006. (Graphic Biographies Ser.). (ENG.). 32p. (gr. 3-4). per. 8.10 (978-0-7368-6190-8(4), Graphic Library) Capstone Press of Coughlan Cos.

—Loretta Lynch: First African American Woman Attorney General. 2016. (Gateway Biographies Ser.). (ENG., Illus.). 48p. (J). (gr. 4-8). 26.65 (978-1-5124-0586-6(8)); 39.99 (978-1-5124-0587-3(6)) Lerner Publishing Group. (Lerner Pubns.).

Bridges, Ruby. Ruby Bridges Goes to School: My True Story. 2009. (Scholastic Reader Level 2 Ser.). lib. bdg. 13.55 (978-0-606-06808-6(2), Turtleback) Turtleback Bks.

Bridges, Ruby & Maccarone, Grace. Let's Read About — Ruby Bridges. Van Wright, Cornelius & Hu, Ying-Hwa, illus. 2003. (Scholastic First Biographies Ser.). (J). (978-0-439-51362-3(6)) Scholastic, Inc.

Brill, Marlene Targ. Barack Obama: Working to Make a Difference. 2006. (J). pap. 6.95 (978-0-8225-6056-2(9), First Avenue Editions); (Illus.). 48p. 23.93 (978-0-8225-3417-4(7)) Lerner Publishing Group.

—Barack Obama (Revised Edition) 2009. pap. 52.95 (978-0-7613-5031-6(4)) Lerner Publishing Group.

—Marshall Major Taylor: World Champion Bicyclist, 1899-1901. 2007. (Trailblazer Biographies Ser.). (ENG., Illus.). 112p. (gr. 5-9). lib. bdg. 31.93 (978-0-8225-6610-6(9), Twenty-First Century Bks.) Lerner Publishing Group.

Brimner, Larry Dane. Booker T. Washington: Getting into the Schoolhouse. 2008. (American Heroes Ser.). 48p. (YA). (gr. 3-18). lib. bdg. 29.93 (978-0-7614-3063-6(6), Benchmark Bks.) Marshall Cavendish Corp.

—We Are One: The Story of Bayard Rustin. 2007. (ENG., Illus.). 48p. (J). (gr. 4-6). 18.95 (978-1-59078-498-3(7)) Boyds Mills Pr.

Broadwater, Andrea. The Life of Marian Anderson: Diva & Humanitarian. 2015. (Legendary African Americans Ser.). 96p. (J). (gr. 6-12). 27.94 (978-0-7660-6285-6(6)); pap. 10.95 (978-0-7660-6286-3(4)) Enslow Pubs., Inc.

Brophy, David B. Michelle Obama: Meet the First Lady. 2008. 128p. (J). pap. 6.99 (978-0-06-177990-9(3)) HarperCollins Pubs.

Brophy, David Bergen. Michelle Obama: Meet the First Lady. 2009. (ENG.). 128p. (J). (gr. 3-7). 16.99 (978-0-06-177991-6(1), Collins) HarperCollins Pubs.

Brown, Jonatha A. Martin Luther King, Jr. 2005. (People We Should Know Ser.). (Illus.). 24p. (gr. 1-4). pap. 8.15 (978-0-8368-4474-0(2)); lib. bdg. 22.00 (978-0-8368-4467-2(X)); (ENG & SPA., lib. bdg. 22.00 (978-0-8368-4583-9(8)) Stevens, Gareth Publishing LLLP. (Weekly Reader Leveled Readers).

—Muhammad Ali. 2005. (People We Should Know Ser.). (Illus.). 24p. (J). (gr. 1-4). lib. bdg. 22.00 (978-0-8368-4743-7(1), Weekly Reader Leveled Readers) Stevens, Gareth Publishing LLLP.

—Rosa Parks. 2005. (People We Should Know Ser.). (Illus.). 24p. (gr. 1-4). pap. 8.15 (978-0-8368-4755-0(5)); (ENG & SPA., pap. 8.15 (978-0-8368-4769-7(5)); (ENG & SPA., lib. bdg. 22.00 (978-0-8368-4762-8(8)); lib. bdg. 22.00 (978-0-8368-4748-2(2)) Stevens, Gareth Publishing LLLP. (Weekly Reader Leveled Readers).

Brown, Jonatha A. & Raatma, Lucia. Jackie Robinson. 2004. (People We Should Know Ser.). (Illus.). 24p. (gr. 1-4). pap. 8.15 (978-0-8368-4318-7(5)); lib. bdg. 22.00 (978-0-8368-4311-8(8)) Stevens, Gareth Publishing LLLP. (Weekly Reader Leveled Readers).

Brown, Susan Taylor. Robert Smalls Sails to Freedom. Marshall, Felicia, illus. 2006. (On My Own History Ser.). 48p. (J). (gr. 3-7). pap. 6.95 (978-0-8225-6051-7(8), First Avenue Editions); (ENG.). (gr. 2-4). lib. bdg. 25.26 (978-1-57505-872-6(3)) Lerner Publishing Group.

Bruchac, Joseph. Jim Thorpe's Bright Path, 1 vol. Nelson, S. D., tr. Nelson, S. D., illus. 2004. (ENG.). 40p. (J). (gr. 1-4). 17.95 (978-1-58430-166-0(X)) Lee & Low Bks., Inc.

Bryant, Jennifer. A Splash of Red: The Life & Art of Horace Pippin. Sweet, Melissa, illus. 2013. (ENG.). 40p. (J). (gr. k-3). 17.99 (978-0-375-86712-5(0)); lib. bdg. 20.99 (978-0-375-96712-2(5)) Random Hse. Children's Bks. (Knopf Bks. for Young Readers).

Buckley, Annie. Robert L. Johnson. 2007. (21st Century Skills Library: Life Skills Biographies Ser.). (ENG., Illus.). 48p. (gr. 4-8). lib. bdg. 31.36 (978-1-60279-072-8(8), 200046) Cherry Lake Publishing.

Buckley, James. Kevin Durant. 2017. (Amazing Americans: Olympians Ser.). (ENG.). 24p. (J). (gr. -1-3). 17.95 **(978-1-68402-242-7(8))** Bearport Publishing Co., Inc.

Buckley, James, Jr. Muhammad Ali. 2004. (Trailblazers of the Modern World Ser.). (Illus.). 48p. (J). (gr. 5-12). pap. 14.05 (978-0-8368-5256-1(7)); lib. bdg. 31.00 (978-0-8368-5096-3(3)) Stevens, Gareth Publishing LLLP. (Gareth Stevens Secondary Library).

Buckley, James. Who Was Jesse Owens? 2015. (Who Was... ? Ser.). lib. bdg. 16.00 (978-0-606-36754-7(3)) Turtleback Bks.

Bull, Angela. The Story of Martin Luther King, Level 4. 2009. (DK Readers Ser.). (ENG.). 48p. (J). (gr. 3-7). 3.99 (978-0-7566-5615-7(X), DK Children) Dorling Kindersley Publishing, Inc.

Burchard, Peter. Frederick Douglass: For the Great Family of Man. 2007. (ENG., Illus.). 240p. (YA). (gr. 7). pap. 13.95 (978-1-4169-6752-1(4), Atheneum Bks. for Young Readers) Simon & Schuster Children's Publishing.

Burgan, Michael. Daring Play: How a Courageous Jackie Robinson Transformed Baseball. 2016. (Captured History Sports Ser.). (ENG.). 64p. (gr. 5-7). lib. bdg. 34.65 (978-0-7565-5291-6(5), CPB Grades 4-8) Compass Point Bks.

Burlingame, Jeff. Jesse Owens: I Always Loved Running. 2011. (African-American Biography Library). (Illus.). 128p. (J). (gr. 7-12). lib. bdg. 33.27 (978-0-7660-3497-6(6)) Enslow Pubs., Inc.

—Malcolm X: "I Believe in the Brotherhood of Man, All Men" 2010. (American Rebels Ser.). 160p. (YA). (gr. 7-12). 35.94 (978-0-7660-3384-9(8)) Enslow Pubs., Inc.

Butler, Mary. Sojourner Truth: From Slave to Activist for Freedom. 2009. (Library of American Lives & Times Ser.). 112p. (gr. 5-5). 69.20 (978-1-60853-505-7(3)) Rosen Publishing Group, Inc., The.

Butler, Mary G. Sojourner Truth: From Slave to Activist for Freedom. 2005. (Library of American Lives & Times). (Illus.). 112p. (YA). (gr. 4-8). lib. bdg. 34.60 (978-0-8239-5736-1(5)) Rosen Publishing Group, Inc., The.

Calkhoven, Laurie. Jesse Owens. Vukovic, Elizabet, illus. 2017. (You Should Meet Ser.). (ENG.). 48p. (J). (gr. 1-3). pap. 3.99 (978-1-4814-8095-6(2), Simon Spotlight) Simon Spotlight.

—Mae Jemison. Dong, Monique, illus. 2016. (You Should Meet Ser.). (ENG.). 48p. (J). (gr. 1-3). pap. 3.99 (978-1-4814-7649-2(1), Simon Spotlight) Simon Spotlight.

—Misty Copeland. Dong, Monique, illus. 2016. (You Should Meet Ser.). (ENG.). 48p. (J). (gr. 1-3). pap. 3.99 (978-1-4814-7043-8(4), Simon Spotlight) Simon Spotlight.

Caravantes, Peggy. Marcus Garvey: Black Nationalist. 2004. (Twentieth Century Leaders Ser.). (Illus.). 128p. (YA). (gr. 6-12). 23.95 (978-1-931798-14-3(1)) Reynolds, Morgan Inc.

Carlisle, Brady. Tony Dungy. (Sharing the American Dream Ser.). 64p. (YA). (gr. 7-12). 2009. (Illus.). 22.95 (978-1-4222-0588-4(6)) 2007. pap. 9.95 (978-1-4222-0743-7(9)) Mason Crest.

Carson, Mary Kay. What Was Your Dream, Dr. King? And Other Questions About... Martin Luther King, Jr. Madsen, Jim, illus. 2013. (Good Question! Ser.). (ENG.). 32p. (J). (gr. 2). pap. 5.95 (978-1-4027-9045-4(7)) Sterling Publishing Co., Inc.

—Who Was the Hair-Care Millionaire? Madam C. J. Walker. 2012. (I Like Inventors! Ser.). (Illus.). 24p. (J). (gr. k-3). pap. 7.95 (978-1-4644-0133-6(0)); 22.60 (978-0-7660-3973-5(0)) Enslow Pubs., Inc. (Enslow Elementary).

Cefrey, Holly. From Slave to Cowboy: The Nat Love Story. 2009. (Great Moments in American History Ser.). 32p. (gr. 3-3). 47.90 (978-1-61513-142-6(6)) Rosen Publishing Group, Inc., The.

—The Inventions of Granville Woods: The Railroad Telegraph System & the "Third Rail" 2003. (19th Century American Inventors Ser.). (Illus.). 24p. (J). lib. bdg. 22.60 (978-0-8239-6442-0(6), PowerKids Pr.) Rosen Publishing Group, Inc., The.

—The Inventions of Granville Woods: The Railroad Telegraph System & the Third Rail. 2009. (19th Century American Inventors Ser.). 24p. (gr. 2-3). 42.50 (978-1-60854-952-8(6), PowerKids Pr.) Rosen Publishing Group, Inc., The.

Chavez, Emilio. Thurgood Marshall: Supreme Court Justice. 2013. (InfoMax Readers Ser.). (ENG.). 24p. (J). (gr. 3-4). pap. 8.25 (978-1-4777-2599-3(7)); pap. 49.50 (978-1-4777-2600-6(4)) Rosen Publishing Group, Inc., The. (Rosen Classroom).

Cheng, Andrea. Etched in Clay: The Life of Dave, Enslaved Potter & Poet. Cheng, Andrea, illus. 2013. (ENG., Illus.).

146p. (J). 17.95 *(978-1-60060-451-5(X))* Lee & Low Bks., Inc.

Christie, R. Gregory. It Jes' Happened: When Bill Traylor Started to Draw, 1 vol. Tate, Don, illus. 2012. (ENG.). 1p. (J). 17.95 *(978-1-60060-260-3(6))* Lee & Low Bks., Inc.

Christopher, Matt. Michael Jordan: Legends in Sports. rev. ed. 2008. (ENG., Illus.). 176p. (gr. 3-7). pap. 6.99 *(978-0-316-02380-1(9))* Little, Brown Bks. for Young Readers.

—On the Court With... Shaquille O'Neil. 2003. (ENG., Illus.). 112p. (J). (gr. 3-7). pap. 16.99 *(978-0-316-16473-3(9))* Little, Brown Bks. for Young Readers.

Ciovacco, Justine. LeBron James: NBA Champion. 2015. (Living Legends of Sports Ser.). (ENG., Illus.). 48p. (J). (gr. 5-6). 25.85 *(978-1-68048-104-4(5)*, Britannica Educational Publishing) Rosen Publishing Group, Inc., The.

Civil Rights Leaders, bks. 13, vol. 13. Incl. A. Philip Randolph & the African American Labor Movement. Miller, Calvin Craig. (Illus.). 160p. (YA). (gr. 6-12). 2005. 26.95 *(978-1-931798-50-1(8))*; Eternal Vigilance: The Story of Ida B. Wells-Barnett. Hinman, Bonnie. 128p. (gr. 6-10). 2011. lib. bdg. 28.95 *(978-1-59935-111-7(0))*; Freedom Cannot Rest: Ella Baker & the Civil Rights Movement. Bohannon, Lisa Frederiksen. (Illus.). 176p. (YA). (gr. 6-12). 2005. lib. bdg. 26.95 *(978-1-931798-71-6(0))*; Liberator: The Story of William Lloyd Garrison. Esty, Amos. 144p. 2011. 28.95 *(978-1-59935-137-7(4))*; No Compromise: The Story of Harvey Milk. Aretha, David. 100p. (YA). (gr. 5-9). 2009. lib. bdg. 28.95 *(978-1-59935-129-2(3))*; No Easy Answers: Bayard Rustin & the Civil Rights Movement. (Illus.). 160p. (J). (gr. 6-12). 2005. 26.95 *(978-1-931798-43-3(5))*; Roy Wilkins: Leader of the NAACP. Miller, Calvin Craig. (Illus.). 176p. (YA). (gr. 6-12). 2005. 26.95 *(978-1-931798-49-5(4))*; Stranger in My Own House: The Story of W. E. B. du Bois. Hinman, Bonnie. (Illus.). 176p. (gr. 6-12). 2005. 28.95 *(978-1-931798-45-7(1))*; Unbound & Unbroken: The Story of Frederick Douglass. Esty, Amos. 144p. (gr. 8-10). 2011. 28.95 *(978-1-59935-136-0(6))*; 2008. Set lib. bdg. 376.35 *(978-1-931798-99-0(0))* Reynolds, Morgan Inc.

Cline-Ransome, Lesa. Major Taylor, Champion Cyclist. Ransome, James E., illus. 2004. (ENG.). 40p. (J). (gr. 1-5). 18.99 *(978-0-689-83159-1(5)*, Atheneum Bks. for Young Readers) Simon & Schuster Children's Publishing.

—Satchel Paige. Ransome, James E., illus. 2004. 31p. (J). (gr. k-4). reprint ed. pap. 7.00 *(978-0-7567-7799-9(2))* DIANE Publishing Co.

—Satchel Paige. Ransome, James E., illus. 2003. (ENG.). 40p. (J). (gr. 1-5). 8.99 *(978-0-689-85681-5(4)*, Simon & Schuster/Paula Wiseman Bks.) Simon & Schuster/Paula Wiseman Bks.

—Words Set Me Free: The Story of Young Frederick Douglass. Ransome, James E., illus. 2012. (ENG.). 32p. (J). (gr. k-4). 17.99 *(978-1-4169-5903-8(3)*, Simon & Schuster/Paula Wiseman Bks.) Simon & Schuster/Paula Wiseman Bks.

Clinton, Catherine. When Harriet Met Sojourner. Evans, Shane W., illus. 2007. (ENG.). 32p. (J). (gr. k-2). 16.99 *(978-0-06-050425-0(0)*, Tegen, Katherine Bks) HarperCollins Pubs.

Cohen, Joel H. Oscar Robertson. 2009. (Basketball Hall of Famers Ser.). 112p. (gr. 5-8). 63.90 *(978-1-61511-535-8(8)*, Rosen Reference) Rosen Publishing Group, Inc., The.

Colbert, David. Martin Luther King Jr. 2008. (10 Days Ser.). (ENG.). 160p. (J). (gr. 3-8). pap. 7.99 *(978-1-4169-6805-4(9)*, Aladdin) Simon & Schuster Children's Publishing.

Coles, Robert. The Story of Ruby Bridges. 2009. 8.44 *(978-0-7848-3016-1(9)*, Everbind) Marco Bk. Co.

—The Story of Ruby Bridges. 2011. 17.00 *(978-1-61383-173-1(0))* Perfection Learning Corp.

—The Story of Ruby Bridges. Ford, George, illus. 50th anniv. ed. 2010. (ENG.). 32p. (J). (gr. -1-3). pap. 6.99 *(978-0-439-47226-5(1)*, Scholastic Paperbacks) Scholastic, Inc.

—The Story of Ruby Bridges. 2010. lib. bdg. 17.20 *(978-0-606-23189-3(7)*, Turtleback) Turtleback Bks.

Colins, Luke. George Washington Carver, 1 vol. 2014. (Great African-Americans Ser.). (ENG.). 24p. (gr. k-1). lib. bdg. 21.99 *(978-1-4765-3957-7(X)*, Pebble Bks.) Capstone Press of Coughlan Cos.

—Mae Jemison, 1 vol. 2014. (Great African-Americans Ser.). (ENG.). 24p. (gr. k-1). lib. bdg. 21.99 *(978-1-4765-3954-6(5)*, Pebble Bks.) Capstone Press of Coughlan Cos.

—Thurgood Marshall, 1 vol. 2014. (Great African-Americans Ser.). (ENG.). 24p. (gr. k-1). lib. bdg. 21.99 *(978-1-4765-3956-0(1)*, Pebble Bks.) Capstone Press of Coughlan Cos.

Collard, Sneed B., III. Jacob Lawrence: A Painter's Story. 2009. (American Heroes Ser.). 48p. (gr. 3-18). 29.93 *(978-0-7614-4058-1(5))* Marshall Cavendish Corp.

—Phillis Wheatley: She Loved Words. 2009. (American Heroes Ser.). 48p. (gr. 3-18). 29.93 *(978-0-7614-4057-4(7))* Marshall Cavendish Corp.

—Rosa Parks: The Courage to Make a Difference. 2006. (American Heroes Ser.). (Illus.). 48p. (gr. 3-5). lib. bdg. 29.93 *(978-0-7614-2163-4(7)*, Benchmark Bks.) Marshall Cavendish Corp.

Collins, Kathleen. Sojourner Truth: Defensora de los derechos Civiles. 2004. (Grandes personajes en la historia de los Estados Unidos Ser.). (SPA.). 32p. (gr. 3-6). pap. 10.00 *(978-0-8239-4239-8(2)*, Rosen Classroom) Rosen Publishing Group, Inc., The.

—Sojourner Truth: Defensora de los derechos civiles (Sojourner Truth: Equal Rights Advocate) 2009. (Grandes personajes en la historia de los Estados Unidos (Famous People in American History) Ser.). (SPA.). 32p. (gr. 2-3). 47.90 *(978-1-61512-808-2(5)*, Editorial Buenas Letras) Rosen Publishing Group, Inc., The.

—Sojourner Truth: Equal Rights Advocate. (Primary Sources of Famous People in American History Ser.). 32p. 2009. (gr. 2-3). 47.90 *(978-1-60851-727-5(6))* 2004. (ENG., Illus.). (gr. 4-8). pap. 10.00 *(978-0-8239-4193-3(0))* Rosen Publishing Group, Inc., The.

—Sojourner Truth: Equal Rights Advocate / Defensora de los derechos Civiles. 2009. (Famous People in American History/Grandes personajes en la historia de los Estados Unidos Ser.). (ENG & SPA.). 32p. (gr. 2-3). 47.90 *(978-1-61512-556-2(6)*, Editorial Buenas Letras) Rosen Publishing Group, Inc., The.

Connors, Kathleen. The Life of Harriet Tubman, Vol. 1. 2014. (Famous Lives Ser.). (ENG.). 24p. (J). (gr. 1-2). 22.60 *(978-1-4824-0412-8(5))* Stevens, Gareth Publishing LLLP.

—The Life of Rosa Parks, Vol. 1. 2014. (Famous Lives Ser.). (ENG.). 24p. (J). (gr. 1-2). 22.60 *(978-1-4824-0419-7(2))* Stevens, Gareth Publishing LLLP.

Cook, Michelle. Our Children Can Soar: A Celebration of Rosa, Barack, & the Pioneers of Change. Ford, A. G. et al, illus. 2009. (ENG.). 32p. (J). (gr. -1-3). 16.99 *(978-1-59990-418-4(7)*, 9781599904184, Bloomsbury USA Childrens) Bloomsbury Publishing USA.

Cooper, Floyd. Jump! From the Life of Michael Jordan. Cooper, Floyd, illus. 2004. (ENG., Illus.). 40p. (J). (gr. 1-4). 17.99 *(978-0-399-24230-4(9)*, Philomel Bks.) Penguin Young Readers Group.

Cornell, Karl. Urban Biologist Danielle Lee. 2016. (STEM Trailblazer Bios Ser.). (ENG., Illus.). 32p. (J). (gr. 2-5). 26.65 *(978-1-4677-9529-6(1)*, Lerner Pubns.) Lerner Publishing Group.

Cosson, M. J. Harriet Tubman, 1 vol. 2007. (Essential Lives Set 1 Ser.). (ENG., Illus.). 112p. (J). (gr. 6-12). lib. bdg. 35.64 *(978-1-59928-842-0(7))* ABDO Publishing Co.

Cox, Vicki. Clarence Thomas. 2008. (Black Americans of Achievement Ser.). (Illus.). 120p. (YA). (gr. 7-12). 35.00 *(978-1-60413-048-5(2))* Facts On File, Inc.

Coy, John. Game Changer: John McLendon & the Secret Game. DuBurke, Randy, illus. 2015. (ENG.). 32p. (J). (gr. 2-5). 17.99 *(978-1-4677-9055-0(9)*, Carolrhoda Bks.); 17.99 *(978-1-4677-8810-6(4)*, Carolrhoda Bks.); 9.99 *(978-1-4677-9056-7(7)*, Carolrhoda Bks.); 17.99 *(978-1-4677-2604-7(4))* Lerner Publishing Group.

Crawford, Ann Fears. Barbara Jordan: Breaking the Barriers. 2003. (Illus.). 90p. (J). (gr. 7-9). lib. bdg. 19.95 *(978-1-931823-11-1(1))* Halcyon Pr., Ltd.

Crow, Joseph Medicine & Viola, Herman. Counting Coup: Becoming a Crow Chief on the Reservation & Beyond. 2006. (ENG., Illus.). 128p. (J). (gr. k-4). 15.95 *(978-0-7922-5391-4(4))*; lib. bdg. 23.90 *(978-0-7922-5392-1(2))* National Geographic Society. (National Geographic Children's Bks.).

Cruz, Barbara C. Alvin Ailey: Celebrating African-American Culture in Dance. 2004. (African-American Biographies Ser.). (Illus.). 112p. (J). lib. bdg. 26.60 *(978-0-7660-2293-5(5))* Enslow Pubs., Inc.

Cunningham, Kevin. Condoleezza Rice. 2009. (Journey to Freedom Ser.). (ENG., Illus.). 32p. (J). (gr. 4-7). 29.93 *(978-1-60253-120-8(X)*, 200386) Child's World, Inc., The.

Cunningham, Meghan Engsberg. Bill Bojangles Robinson. 2016. (Artists of the Harlem Renaissance Ser.). (ENG.). 128p. (YA). (gr. 9-9). lib. bdg. 45.64 *(978-1-5026-1073-7(6))* Cavendish Square Publishing.

Dakers, Diane. Magic Johnson: Basketball Legend, Entrepreneur, & HIV/AIDS Activist. 2016. (Crabtree Groundbreaker Biographies Ser.). (ENG.). 112p. (J). (gr. 5-8). *(978-0-7787-2608-1(8))* Crabtree Publishing Co.

—Oprah Winfrey: Media Legend & Inspiration to Millions. 2015. (Crabtree Groundbreaker Biographies Ser.). (ENG., Illus.). 112p. (J). (gr. 5-8). *(978-0-7787-2559-6(6))* Crabtree Publishing Co.

Daly, Ruth. Rosa Parks. 2014. (J). *(978-1-4896-2452-9(X))* Weigl Pubs., Inc.

Davidson, Tish. African American Scientists & Inventors. 2012. (J). pap. *(978-1-4222-2388-8(4))* Mason Crest.

—African American Scientists & Inventors. Hill, Marc Lamont, ed. 2012. (Major Black Contributions from Emancipation to Civil Rights Ser.). 64p. (J). (gr. 5). 22.95 *(978-1-4222-2375-8(2))* Mason Crest.

Davies, Ross. Bobo Brazil. 2009. (Wrestling Greats Ser.). 112p. (gr. 5-5). 63.90 *(978-1-60854-863-7(5))* Rosen Publishing Group, Inc., The.

Davis, Kenneth C. In the Shadow of Liberty: The Hidden History of Slavery, Four Presidents, & Five Black Lives. 2016. (ENG., Illus.). 304p. (J). 17.99 *(978-1-62779-311-7(9)*, 9781627793117, Holt, Henry & Co. Bks. For Young Readers) Holt, Henry & Co.

Davis, Mo'ne & TBD Staff. Mo'Ne - Remember My Name: My Story from First Pitch to Game Changer. 2015. (ENG., Illus.). 208p. (J). (gr. 3-7). 16.99 *(978-0-06-239752-2(4))* HarperCollins Pubs.

De la Peña, Matt. A Nation's Hope: The Story of Boxing Legend Joe Louis. Nelson, Kadir, illus. 2011. (ENG.). 40p. (J). (gr. 1-3). 17.99 *(978-0-8037-3167-7(1)*, Dial Bks) Penguin Young Readers Group.

—A Nation's Hope: The Story of Boxing Legend Joe Louis. 2013. lib. bdg. 19.65 *(978-0-606-34169-1(2)*, Turtleback) Turtleback Bks.

De Marco, Tony. Jackie Robinson. 2009. (Journey to Freedom Ser.). (ENG., Illus.). 32p. (J). (gr. 4-7). 29.93 *(978-1-60253-125-3(0)*, 200391) Child's World, Inc., The.

De Medeiros, Michael. Barack Obama. 2008. (Remarkable People Ser.). (Illus.). 24p. (J). (gr. 4-6). pap. 8.95 *(978-1-59036-989-0(0))*; lib. bdg. 24.45 *(978-1-59036-988-3(2))* Weigl Pubs., Inc.

Dean, Myers Walter. Bad Boy: A Memoir. 2014. (Amistad Ser.). (ENG.). 224p. (J). 14.24 *(978-1-63245-084-5(4))* Lectorum Pubns., Inc.

Deans, Karen. Playing to Win: The Story of Althea Gibson. Brown, Elbrite, illus. 2007. (ENG.). 32p. (J). (gr. -1-3). 16.95 *(978-0-8234-1926-5(6))* Holiday Hse., Inc.

DeFord, Diane. Harriet Tubman. 2009. pap. 13.25 *(978-1-60559-061-5(4))* Hameray Publishing Group, Inc.

Dell, Pamela. Memoir of Susie King Taylor: A Civil War Nurse. 2017. (First-Person Histories Ser.). (ENG.). 32p. (gr. 3-4). pap. 8.95 *(978-1-5157-3356-0(4))*; (Illus.). lib. bdg. 27.32 *(978-1-5157-3354-6(8))* Capstone Press of Coughlan Cos. (Fact Finders).

Derby, Sally. Jump Back, Paul: The Life & Poems of Paul Laurence Dunbar. Qualls, Sean, illus. 2015. (ENG.). 128p. (J). (gr. 4-7). 16.99 *(978-0-7636-6070-3(1))* Candlewick Pr.

deRubertis, Barbara. Let's Celebrate Martin Luther King, Jr. Day. 2013. 32p. pap. 16.95 *(978-1-57565-639-7(6))* Kane Press, Inc.

Devaney, Sherri, et al. Barack Obama. 2009. (People in the News Ser.). (ENG.). 104p. (YA). (gr. 7-12). lib. bdg. 33.45 *(978-1-4205-0206-0(9)*, LML02109-248525) Cengage Gale.

Dickinson, Stephanie. Jacob Lawrence. 2016. (Artists of the Harlem Renaissance Ser.). (ENG.). 128p. (YA). (gr. 9-9). 45.64 *(978-1-5026-1070-6(1))* Cavendish Square Publishing.

Ditchfield, Christin. Condoleezza Rice: America's Leading Stateswoman. 2006. (Great Life Stories Ser.). (ENG., Illus.). 112p. (J). (gr. 6-8). lib. bdg. 30.50 *(978-0-531-13874-8(7)*, Watts, Franklin) Scholastic Library Publishing.

Doak, Robin S. Harriet Tubman. 2015. (ENG., Illus.). 48p. (J). pap. 6.95 *(978-0-531-21757-3(4))*; lib. bdg. *(978-0-531-21595-1(4))* Scholastic, Inc. (Orchard Bks.).

—Michelle Obama, 1 vol. 2014. (Extraordinary Women Ser.). (ENG., Illus.). 48p. (gr. 6-6). lib. bdg. 32.65 *(978-1-4109-5940-9(6))* Heinemann-Raintree.

—Phillis Wheatley: The Inspiring Life Story of the American Poet. 2016. (Inspiring Stories Ser.). (ENG., Illus.). 112p. (J). (gr. 5-7). lib. bdg. 35.99 *(978-0-7565-5166-7(8)*, CPB Grades 4-8) Compass Point Bks.

Doeden, Matt. Dwyane Wade: Basketball Superstar, 1 vol. 2014. (Superstar Athletes Ser.). (ENG.). 24p. (gr. 1-2). pap. 7.29 *(978-1-4765-9429-3(5))*; lib. bdg. 25.32 *(978-1-4765-8599-4(7))* Capstone Press of Coughlan Cos.

—George Washington Carver. 2008. pap. 52.95 *(978-0-8225-9390-4(4))* Lerner Publishing Group.

—George Washington Carver. Butler, Tad, illus. 2007. (History Maker Biographies Ser.). 48p. (J). (gr. 3-7). lib. bdg. 26.60 *(978-0-8225-7605-1(8)*, Lerner Pubns.) Lerner Publishing Group.

—A Marked Man: The Assassination of Malcolm X. 2013. (ENG., Illus.). 88p. (J). (gr. 6-12). lib. bdg. 33.27 *(978-0-7613-5484-0(0)*, Twenty-First Century Bks.) Lerner Publishing Group.

—Tony Dungy. 2009. (Sports Heroes & Legends Ser.). (ENG.). 120p. (gr. 5-12). 30.60 *(978-0-7613-4225-0(7))* Lerner Publishing Group.

—Will Smith. 2007. (Illus.). 112p. (J). pap. 9.95 *(978-0-8225-7064-6(5))* Lerner Publishing Group.

—Wilt Chamberlain. 2010. (Sports Heroes & Legends Ser.). (ENG.). 120p. (gr. 5-12). lib. bdg. 30.60 *(978-0-7613-5369-0(0))* Lerner Publishing Group.

Donaldson, Madeline. Ruby Bridges. 2009. (History Maker Biographies Ser.). (ENG., Illus.). 48p. (gr. 3-6). 27.93 *(978-0-7613-4220-5(6)*, Lerner Pubns.) Lerner Publishing Group.

—Venus & Serena Williams. (Amazing Athletes Ser.). 32p. 2005. (Illus.). (gr. 3-4). lib. bdg. 22.60 *(978-0-8225-3316-0(2))* 2nd rev. ed. 2011. (J). pap. 45.32 *(978-0-7613-7654-5(2))* Lerner Publishing Group.

Donnelly, Karen. Deacon Jones. 2009. (Football Hall of Famers Ser.). 112p. (gr. 5-8). 2009. 63.90 *(978-1-61512-624-8(4))* 2003. (Illus.). (YA). lib. bdg. 34.60 *(978-0-8239-3606-9(6))* Rosen Publishing Group, Inc., The. (Rosen Reference).

Donohue, Moira Rose. L. Douglas Wilder. 2012. (Illus.). 32p. (J). *(978-1-935884-63-7(8))*; pap. *(978-1-935884-69-9(7))* State Standards Publishing, LLC.

—Maggie L. Walker. 2012. (Illus.). 32p. (J). *(978-1-935884-62-0(X))*; pap. *(978-1-935884-68-2(9))* State Standards Publishing, LLC.

Donohue, Moira Rose & Scott, Clarke C. Arthur R. Ashe, Jr. 2012. (Illus.). 32p. (J). *(978-1-935884-58-3(1))*; pap. *(978-1-935884-64-4(6))* State Standards Publishing, LLC.

D'Orio, Wayne. Al Sharpton. 2nd rev. ed. 2011. (Black Americans of Achievement Legacy Edition Ser.). 128p. (gr. 6-12). 35.00 *(978-1-60413-834-4(3))* Facts On File, Inc.

Dorrie, Roxanne. Venus & Serena Williams: The Smashing Sisters. 2003. (High Five Reading - Red Ser.). (ENG., Illus.). 48p. (gr. 3-4). per. 9.00 *(978-0-7368-2827-7(3)*, High Five Reading (RBL)) Capstone Press of Coughlan Cos.

Dougherty, Terri. Raven-Symoné. (Role Model Entertainers Ser.). (Illus.). 64p. (YA). 2010. (gr. 7-12). 22.95 *(978-1-4222-0508-2(8))* 2007. pap. 9.95 *(978-1-4222-0795-6(1))* Mason Crest.

—Tyra Banks. 2009. (People in the News Ser.). (Illus.). 128p. (YA). (gr. 7-12). 33.95 *(978-1-4205-0161-2(5))* Cengage Gale.

Draper, Allison Stark. The Assassination of Malcolm X. 2009. (Library of Political Assassinations Ser.). 64p. (gr. 5-5). 58.50 *(978-1-60853-827-0(3))* Rosen Publishing Group, Inc., The.

Dray, Philip. Yours for Justice, Ida B. Wells: The Daring Life of a Crusading Journalist, 1 vol. Alcorn, Stephen, illus. 2008. (ENG.). 48p. (J). (gr. 5-9). 18.95 *(978-1-56145-417-4(6))* Peachtree Pubs.

Driggs, Lorin. Biddy Mason: Becoming a Leader. 2017. (Primary Source Readers Ser.). (Illus.). 32p. (gr. 4-4). 9.99 ***(978-1-4258-3239-1(3))*** Teacher Created Materials, Inc.

Dubowski, Cathy East. Rosa Parks: Don't Give In! 2005. (Defining Moments Ser.). (Illus.). 32p. (J). (gr. 2-5). lib. bdg. 25.27 *(978-1-59716-078-0(4))* Bearport Publishing Co., Inc.

Dunn, Joe. Jackie Robinson, 1 vol. Espinosa, Rod, illus. 2007. (Bio-Graphics Ser.). (ENG.). 32p. (gr. 3-6). 28.50 *(978-1-60270-068-0(0)*, Graphic Planet- Nonfiction) ABDO Publishing Co.

Dunn, Joeming W. Booker T. Washington, 1 vol. Allen, Chris, illus. 2008. (Bio-Graphics Ser.). (ENG.). 32p. 28.50 *(978-1-60270-177-9(6)*, Graphic Planet- Nonfiction) ABDO Publishing Co.

—George Washington Carver, 1 vol. Allen, Chris, illus. 2008. (Bio-Graphics Ser.). (ENG.). 32p. 28.50 *(978-1-60270-171-7(7)*, Graphic Planet- Nonfiction) ABDO Publishing Co.

—Martin Luther King, Jr, 1 vol. Allen, Chris, illus. 2008. (Bio-Graphics Ser.). (ENG.). 32p. 28.50 *(978-1-60270-175-5(X)*, Graphic Planet- Nonfiction) ABDO Publishing Co.

Durden, Robert F. The Life of Carter G. Woodson: Father of African-American History. 2014. (Legendary African Americans Ser.). (ENG.). 96p. (J). (gr. 6-12). pap. 10.95 *(978-0-7660-6123-1(X))* Enslow Pubs., Inc.

Durden, Robert Franklin. The Life of Carter G.Woodson: Father of African-American History. 2014. (Legendary African Americans Ser.). 96p. (J). (gr. 6-12). 27.94 *(978-0-7660-6122-4(1))* Enslow Pubs., Inc.

Earl, Sari. Benjamin O. Davis, Jr: Air Force General & Tuskegee Airmen Leader, 1 vol. 2010. (Military Heroes Ser.). (ENG.). 112p. (J). (gr. 6-12). lib. bdg. 35.64 *(978-1-60453-961-5(5))* ABDO Publishing Co.

Early, Gerald Lyn. Ralph Ellison: Invisible Man. 2009. (Writers & Their Works 4 Ser.). 144p. (gr. 7). 42.79 *(978-0-7614-4275-2(8))* Marshall Cavendish Corp.

Edison, Erin. Harriet Tubman, 1 vol. 2013. (Great Women in History Ser.). (ENG.). 24p. (gr. k-1). pap. 6.29 *(978-1-62065-859-8(3))*; pap. 35.70 *(978-1-62065-860-4(7))* Capstone Press of Coughlan Cos. (Pebble Bks.).

—Rosa Parks, 1 vol. 2013. (Great Women in History Ser.). (ENG.). 24p. (gr. k-1). pap. 6.29 *(978-1-62065-863-5(1))*; pap. 35.70 *(978-1-62065-864-2(X))*; (Illus.). lib. bdg. 21.99 *(978-1-62065-071-4(1))* Capstone Press of Coughlan Cos. (Pebble Bks.).

Edwards, Linda McMurry. George Washington Carver: The Life of the Great American Agriculturist. 2009. (Library of American Lives & Times Ser.). 112p. (gr. 5-5). 69.20 *(978-1-60853-485-2(5))* Rosen Publishing Group, Inc., The.

Edwards, Pamela Duncan. The Bus Ride That Changed History: The Story of Rosa Parks. Shanahan, Danny, illus. 2009. (ENG.). 32p. (J). (gr. -1-3). pap. 6.99 *(978-0-547-07674-4(6))* Houghton Mifflin Harcourt Publishing Co.

Edwards, Roberta. Barack Obama: Presidente de Estados Unidos. Call, Ken, illus. 2009.Tr. of Barack Obama: United States President. (SPA.). 64p. (J). (gr. 2-5). pap. 9.99 ***(978-1-63113-956-7(8)**, Loqueleo)* Santillana USA Publishing Co., Inc.

—Barack Obama: United States President. Call, Ken, illus. rev. exp. ed. 2009. (ENG.). 64p. (J). (gr. 1-3). mass mkt. 5.99 *(978-0-448-45234-0(0)*, Grosset & Dunlap) Penguin Young Readers Group.

—Michelle Obama: Primera Dama y Primera Mama. Call, Ken, illus. 2010. (SPA.). 48p. (gr. 3-5). pap. 9.99 *(978-1-60396-946-8(2))* Santillana USA Publishing Co., Inc.

Ellis, Carol. African American Activists. 2012. (J). pap. *(978-1-4222-2384-0(1))* Mason Crest.

—African American Activists. Hill, Marc Lamont, ed. 2012. (Major Black Contributions from Emancipation to Civil Rights Ser.). 64p. (J). (gr. 5). 22.95 *(978-1-4222-2371-0(X))* Mason Crest.

Embacher, Eric. Will Smith: The Funny, Funky, & Confident Fresh Prince. 2003. (High Five Reading - Red Ser.). (ENG., Illus.). 48p. (gr. 3-4). per. 9.00 *(978-0-7368-2829-1(X)*, High Five Reading (RBL)) Capstone Press of Coughlan Cos.

Endsley, Kezia. Michelle Obama: 44th First Lady & Health & Education Advocate. 2014. (Leading Women Ser.). 112p. (YA). (gr. 7-11). lib. bdg. 39.93 *(978-1-62712-975-6(8))* Cavendish Square Publishing.

Epstein, Brad M. Barack Obama 101. I.t. ed. 2009. (My First Presidential Board Book Ser.). (Illus.). 28p. (J). (gr. -1-1). bds. *(978-1-60730-044-1(3)*, 101 Bk.) Michaelson Entertainment.

Epstein, Dwayne. Denzel Washington. 2009. (People in the News Ser.). (ENG.). (YA). (gr. 7-12). 33.95 *(978-1-4205-0157-5(7))* Cengage Gale.

Ernest J. Gaines. 2010. (Who Wrote That? Ser.). (Illus.). 120p. (gr. 6-12). 35.00 *(978-1-60413-683-8(9)*, Chelsea Hse.) Facts On File, Inc.

Eskridge, Ann E. Slave Uprisings & Runaways: Fighting for Freedom & the Underground Railroad. 2004. (Slavery in American History Ser.). (Illus.). 128p. (J). lib. bdg. 27.94 *(978-0-7660-2154-9(8))* Enslow Pubs., Inc.

Exceptional African Americans. 2015. (Exceptional African Americans Ser.). (ENG.). 24p. (J). (gr. 3-4). 135.60 *(978-0-7660-6670-0(3))* Enslow Pubs., Inc.

Falk, Laine. Meet President Barack Obama. 2009. (Scholastic News Nonfiction Readers Ser.). (ENG.). 24p. (J). (gr. 1-2). 20.00 *(978-0-531-23403-7(7)*, Children's Pr.) Scholastic Library Publishing.

Fandel, Jennifer. Martin Luther King, Jr. 2005. (Genius Ser.). (Illus.). 48p. (J). (gr. 5-9). lib. bdg. 21.95 *(978-1-58341-329-6(4)*, Creative Education) Creative Co., The.

—Martin Luther King, Jr: Great Civil Rights Leader, 1 vol. Bascle, Brian, illus. 2006. (Graphic Biographies Ser.). (ENG.). 32p. (gr. 3-4). 30.65 *(978-0-7368-6498-5(9)*, Graphic Library) Capstone Press of Coughlan Cos.

Farris, Christine King. My Brother Martin: A Sister Remembers Growing up with the Rev. Dr. Martin Luther King Jr. Soentpiet, Chris K., illus. 2003. (ENG.). 32p. (J). (gr. 1-6). 19.99 *(978-0-689-84387-7(9)*, Simon & Schuster Bks. For Young Readers) Simon & Schuster Bks. For Young Readers.

Fay, Gail. Malcolm X, 1 vol. 2012. (American Biographies Ser.). (ENG.). 48p. (gr. 4-6). pap. 9.95 *(978-1-4329-6467-2(4)*, NA-h) Heinemann-Raintree.

—Malcolm X, 1 vol. Oxford Bible Staff, illus. 2012. (American Biographies Ser.). (ENG.). 48p. (gr. 4-6). lib. bdg. 32.65 *(978-1-4329-6456-6(9)*, NA-h) Heinemann-Raintree.

Feinstein, Stephen. Barack Obama. 2008. (African-American Heroes Ser.). (Illus.). 24p. (J). (gr. 1-3). lib. bdg. 22.60 *(978-0-7660-2893-7(3)*, Enslow Elementary) Enslow Pubs., Inc.

—Chris Rock. 2008. (African-American Heroes Ser.). (Illus.). 24p. (J). (gr. 3-7). lib. bdg. 22.60 *(978-0-7660-2894-4(1)*, Enslow Elementary) Enslow Pubs., Inc.

—Colin Powell. 2007. (African-American Heroes Ser.). (Illus.). 24p. (J). (gr. 1-3). lib. bdg. 22.60 *(978-0-7660-2761-9(9)*, Enslow Elementary) Enslow Pubs., Inc.

—Denzel Washington. 2008. (African-American Heroes Ser.). (Illus.). 24p. (J). (gr. 1-3). lib. bdg. 22.60 *(978-0-7660-2895-1(X)*, Enslow Elementary) Enslow Pubs., Inc.

—Incredible African-American Jazz Musicians. 2012. (African-American Collective Biographies Ser.). (Illus.). 112p. (J). (gr. 5-18). 33.27 *(978-1-59845-137-5(5))* Enslow Pubs., Inc.

—Inspiring African-American Civil Rights Leaders. 2012. (African-American Collective Biographies Ser.). (Illus.). 112p. (J). (gr. 5-18). 33.27 *(978-1-59845-136-8(7))* Enslow Pubs., Inc.

—Lee sobre Martin Luther King, Jr. 2006. (I Like Biographies! Bilingual Ser.).Tr. of Read about Martin Luther King, Jr. (ENG & SPA., Illus.). 24p. (J). (gr. 1-3). lib. bdg. 22.60 *(978-0-7660-2745-9(7)*, Enslow Elementary) Enslow Pubs., Inc.

—Mae Jemison. 2007. (African-American Heroes Ser.). (Illus.). 24p. (J). (gr. 1-3). lib. bdg. 22.60 *(978-0-7660-2762-6(7)*, Enslow Elementary) Enslow Pubs., Inc.

—Oprah Winfrey. 2007. (African-American Heroes Ser.). (Illus.). 24p. (J). (gr. 1-3). lib. bdg. 22.60 (978-0-7660-2764-0(3), Enslow Elementary) Enslow Pubs., Inc.

—Read about Harriet Tubman. 2005. (I Like Biographies! Ser.). (Illus.). 24p. (J). lib. bdg. 22.60 (978-0-7660-2591-2(8), Enslow Elementary) Enslow Pubs., Inc.

—Read about Martin Luther King, Jr. 2004. (I Like Biographies! Ser.). (Illus.). 24p. (J). lib. bdg. 24.95 (978-0-7660-2300-0(1)) Enslow Pubs., Inc.

—Savion Glover. 2008. (African-American Heroes Ser.). (Illus.). 24p. (J). (gr. 1-3). lib. bdg. 22.60 (978-0-7660-2897-5(6), Enslow Elementary) Enslow Pubs., Inc.

—Wynton Marsalis. 2007. (African-American Heroes Ser.). (Illus.). 24p. (J). (gr. 1-3). lib. bdg. 22.60 (978-0-7660-2766-4(X), Enslow Elementary) Enslow Pubs., Inc.

Feldman, Heather. Marion Jones: Atleta de Categoría Internacional (World-Class Runner) 2009. (Superestrellas del Deporte (Superstars of Sports) Ser.). (SPA.). 24p. (gr. 1-2). 42.50 (978-1-60853-227-8(5), Editorial Buenas Letras) Rosen Publishing Group, Inc., The.

—Marion Jones: World Class Runner. 2009. (Sports Superstars Ser.). 24p. (gr. 1-1). 42.50 (978-1-60853-179-0(1), PowerKids Pr.) Rosen Publishing Group, Inc., The.

—Venus Williams: Campeona de Tenis (Tennis Champion) 2009. (Superestrellas del Deporte (Superstars of Sports) Ser.). (SPA.). 24p. (gr. 1-2). 42.50 (978-1-60853-229-2(1), Editorial Buenas Letras) Rosen Publishing Group, Inc., The.

—Venus Williams: Tennis Champion. 2009. (Sports Superstars Ser.). 24p. (gr. 1-1). 42.50 (978-1-60853-183-7(X), PowerKids Pr.) Rosen Publishing Group, Inc., The.

—Venus Williams: Tennis Champion / Campeona de Tenis. 2009. (Superstars of Sports/Superestrellas del deporte Ser.). (ENG & SPA.). 24p. (gr. 1-2). 42.50 (978-1-60853-241-4(0), Editorial Buenas Letras) Rosen Publishing Group, Inc., The.

—Venus Williams, Tennis Champion/Campeona del Tenis. De Leon, Mauricio Velzaquez, tr. 2008. (Reading Power Ser.). (ENG., Illus.). 24p. (gr. 1-6). per. 8.85 (978-0-8239-6212-9(1)) Rosen Publishing Group, Inc., The.

Ferris, Jeri Chase. Demanding Justice: A Story about Mary Ann Shadd Cary. Smith, Kimanne, illus. 2003. (Creative Minds Biographies Ser.). (ENG.). 64p. (gr. 4-8). 22.60 (978-1-57505-177-2(X)); pap. 8.95 (978-0-87614-928-7(X), Carolrhoda Bks.) Lerner Publishing Group.

Figley, Marty Rhodes. Prisoner for Liberty. Orback, Craig, illus. (On My Own History Ser.). (ENG.). 48p. (gr. 2-4). 2009. pap. 6.95 (978-0-8225-9022-4(0), First Avenue Editions) 2008. lib. bdg. 25.26 (978-0-8225-7280-0(X), Millbrook Pr.) Lerner Publishing Group.

—Washington Is Burning. Orback, Craig, illus. (On My Own History Ser.). 48p. (gr. 2-4). 2007. (ENG.). per. 6.95 (978-0-8225-6050-0(X), First Avenue Editions) 2006. (J). lib. bdg. 25.26 (978-1-57505-875-7(8)) Lerner Publishing Group.

Figley, Mary Rhodes. Prisoner for Liberty. 2009. pap. 40.95 (978-0-7613-4796-5(8)) Lerner Publishing Group.

Findley, Violet. Easy Reader Biographies: Harriet Tubman: Follow the North Star. 2007. (ENG.). 16p. pap. 2.99 (978-0-439-92330-9(1), Teaching Resources) Scholastic, Inc.

Fine, Edith Hope. Martin Luther King, Jr: Champion of Civil Rights. 2006. (Heroes of American History Ser.). (Illus.). 32p. (J). (gr. 3-7). lib. bdg. 23.94 (978-0-7660-2466-3(0), Enslow Elementary) Enslow Pubs., Inc.

—Rosa Parks: Meet a Civil Rights Hero. 2004. (Meeting Famous People Ser.). (Illus.). 32p. (J). lib. bdg. 23.94 (978-0-7660-2099-3(1)) Enslow Pubs., Inc.

Finlayson, Reggie. Colin Powell. 2005. (Biography Ser.). (Illus.). 112p. (gr. 6-12). lib. bdg. 27.93 (978-0-8225-4966-6(2)) Lerner Publishing Group.

Fisher-Shumpert, Sharon Y. Sadie's Hero. 2007. 42p. (J). pap. 10.00 (978-0-9794871-0-1(2)) SYS Publishing.

Fishman, Jon M. Kevin Durant. 2017. (Sports All-Stars Ser.). (ENG.). 32p. (J). (gr. 2-5). 26.65 **(978-1-5124-3453-8(1))** Lerner Publishing Group.

—LeBron James. 2017. (Sports All-Stars Ser.). (ENG.). 32p. (J). (gr. 2-5). pap. 8.99 **(978-1-5124-5617-2(9))**; (Illus.). 26.65 **(978-1-5124-3452-1(3)**, Lerner Pubns.) Lerner Publishing Group.

Fishman, Jon M. Serena Williams. 2016. (Amazing Athletes Ser.). (ENG., Illus.). 32p. (J). (gr. 2-5). 26.65 (978-1-5124-1334-2(8)) Lerner Publishing Group.

Fleischman, John. Black & White Airmen: Their True History. 2007. (ENG., Illus.). 160p. (gr. 5-12). 28.80 (978-1-4287-3953-6(X), Follettbound) Follett School Solutions.

Fleming, Alice. Frederick Douglass: From Slave to Statesman. 2009. (Library of American Lives & Times Ser.). 112p. (gr. 5-5). 69.20 (978-1-60853-482-1(0)) Rosen Publishing Group, Inc., The.

—Martin Luther King, Jr. A Dream of Hope. 2008. (Sterling Biographies(r) Ser.). (ENG., Illus.). 128p. (J). (gr. 5). pap. 5.95 (978-1-4027-4439-6(0)) Sterling Publishing Co., Inc.

Flowers, Arthur. I See the Promised Land: A Life of Martin Luther King, Jr., 1 vol. Chitrakar, Manu, illus. rev. ed. 2013. (ENG.). 156p. (J). (gr. 6). 16.95 (978-1-55498-328-5(2)) Groundwood Bks. CAN. Dist: Publishers Group West (PGW).

Flynn, Riley. Bessie Coleman, 1 vol. 2014. (Great African-Americans Ser.). (ENG., Illus.). 24p. (gr. k-1). lib. bdg. 21.99 (978-1-4765-3955-3(3), Pebble Bks.) Capstone Press of Coughlan Cos.

—Booker T. Washington, 1 vol. 2014. (Great African-Americans Ser.). (ENG.). 24p. (gr. k-1). lib. bdg. 21.99 (978-1-4765-3952-2(9), Pebble Bks.) Capstone Press of Coughlan Cos.

—Martin Luther King Jr, 1 vol. 2014. (Great African-Americans Ser.). (ENG.). 24p. (gr. k-1). lib. bdg. 21.99 (978-1-4765-3953-9(7), Pebble Bks.) Capstone Press of Coughlan Cos.

Ford, Carin T. Muhammad Ali: I Am the Greatest. 2006. (African-American Biography Library). (Illus.). 128p. (J). (gr. 6-12). lib. bdg. 33.27 (978-0-7660-2460-1(1)) Enslow Pubs., Inc.

—Paul Robeson: I Want to Make Freedom Ring. 2007. (African-American Biography Library). (Illus.). 128p. (J). (gr. 3-7). lib. bdg. 33.27 (978-0-7660-2703-9(1)) Enslow Pubs., Inc.

—Ray Charles: I Was Born with Music Inside Me. 2007. (African-American Biography Library). (Illus.). 128p. (J). (gr. 6-12). lib. bdg. 33.27 (978-0-7660-2701-5(5)) Enslow Pubs., Inc.

Franzen, Lenore. Venus Williams. 2003. (Ovations Ser.). (Illus.). 32p. (J). (978-1-58341-249-7(2), Creative Education) Creative Co., The.

Freedman, Russell. Abraham Lincoln & Frederick Douglass: The Story Behind an American Friendship. 2012. (ENG., Illus.). 128p. (J). (gr. 5-7). 18.99 (978-0-547-38562-4(5)) Houghton Mifflin Harcourt Publishing Co.

—Freedom Walkers: The Story of the Montgomery Bus Boycott. (ENG., Illus.). 112p. (J). 2009. (gr. 3-7). pap. 14.95 (978-0-8234-2195-4(3)) 2006. (gr. 5-10). 18.95 (978-0-8234-2031-5(0)) Holiday Hse., Inc.

—The Voice That Challenged a Nation: Marian Anderson & the Struggle for Equal Rights. (ENG., Illus.). 128p. (J). (gr. 5-7). 2011. pap. 10.99 (978-0-547-48034-3(2)) 2004. tchr. ed. 18.00 (978-0-618-15976-5(2)) Houghton Mifflin Harcourt Publishing Co.

—The Voice That Challenged a Nation: Marian Anderson & the Struggle for Equal Rights, 2 vols. 2005. (J). 45.75 (978-1-4193-3970-7(2)) Recorded Bks., Inc.

Frey, Wendy. Citizen Heroes. 2007. (Illus.). 68p. (J). (978-1-4105-0888-1(9)); (978-1-4105-0887-4(0)) Johnston, Don Inc.

Frisch, Aaron. Lebron James. 2013. (Illus.). 24p. (J). 25.65 (978-1-60818-337-1(8), Creative Education) Creative Co., The.

Gallagher, Brigid. Langston Hughes, 1 vol. 2012. (American Biographies Ser.). (ENG.). 48p. (gr. 4-6). pap. 9.95 (978-1-4329-6466-5(6), NA-h) Heinemann-Raintree.

Ganeri, Anita. I Have a Dream: Martin Luther King, Jr. & the Fight for Equal Rights. 2013. (Turning Points in History Ser.). (Illus.). 48p. (gr. 5-12). 37.10 (978-1-59920-972-2(1)) Black Rabbit Bks.

Garstecki, Julia. Tuskegee Airmen. 2017. (All-American Fighting Forces Ser.). (ENG.). 32p. (gr. 3-7). 31.35 **(978-1-68072-004-4(X)**, Bolt) Black Rabbit Bks.

Gastel, Tiffany & Benchmark Education Co. Staff. The Red-Tail Angels. 2014. (Text Connections Ser.). (J). (gr. 6). (978-1-4900-1537-8(X)) Benchmark Education Co.

Gatto, Kimberly. LeBron James: A Basketball Star Who Cares. 2011. (Sports Stars Who Care Ser.). (Illus.). 48p. (J). (gr. 3-18). pap. 8.95 (978-1-59845-231-0(2), Enslow Elementary); (gr. 2-5). lib. bdg. 25.27 (978-0-7660-3776-2(2)) Enslow Pubs., Inc.

Gayle, Sharon. Harriet Tubman & the Freedom Train. Marshall, Felicia, illus. 2003. (Ready-To-read SOFA Ser.). (ENG.). 32p. (J). (gr. 1-3). pap. 3.99 (978-0-689-85480-4(3), Simon Spotlight) Simon Spotlight.

Gelfand, Dale Evva. Coretta Scott King: Civil Rights Activist. 2nd rev. ed. 2006. (Black Americans of Achievement Legacy Edition Ser.). (Illus.). 137p. (YA). (gr. 7-12). lib. bdg. 35.00 (978-0-7910-9522-5(3)) Facts On File, Inc.

Gentry, Tony. Jesse Owens: Champion Athlete. 2005. (Black Americans of Achievement Ser.). (Illus.). 112p. (gr. 6-12). 35.00 (978-0-7910-8252-2(0), Chelsea Hse.) Facts On File, Inc.

Gibson, Karen Bush. The Historic Fight for the 2008 Democratic Presidential Nomination: The Obama View. 2009. (Monumental Milestones Ser.). (Illus.). 48p. (YA). (gr. 4-7). lib. bdg. 29.95 (978-1-58415-732-8(1)) Mitchell Lane Pubs., Inc.

Gill, Joel Christian. Strange Fruit Vol. 1: Uncelebrated Narratives from Black History. 2014. (ENG., Illus.). 176p. (YA). (gr. 7). pap. 23.95 (978-1-938486-29-6(3)) Fulcrum Publishing.

Giovanni, Nikki. Lincoln & Douglass: An American Friendship. Collier, Bryan, illus. 2008. (ENG.). 40p. (J). (gr. 2-6). 16.95 (978-0-8050-8264-7(6), 9780805082647, Holt, Henry & Co. Bks. For Young Readers) Holt, Henry & Co.

—Rosa. Collier, Bryan, illus. rev. ed. 2005. (ENG.). 40p. (J). (gr. -1-3). 17.99 (978-0-8050-7106-1(7), 9780805071061, Holt, Henry & Co. Bks. For Young Readers) Holt, Henry & Co.

—Rosa. Collier, Bryan, illus. 2007. (ENG.). 40p. (J). (gr. -1-3). per. 8.99 (978-0-312-37602-4(2), 9780312376024) Square Fish.

—Rosa. Collier, Bryan, illus. 2011. (J). (gr. 2-5). 29.95 (978-0-545-04261-1(5)) Weston Woods Studios, Inc.

Gitenstein, Judy. Alvin Ailey. 2009. (Library of American Choreographers Ser.). 48p. (gr. 5-8). 53.00 (978-1-60853-455-5(3), Rosen Reference) Rosen Publishing Group, Inc., The.

Gitlin, Martin. Chris Rock: A Biography of a Comic Genius. 2014. (African-American Icons Ser.). 104p. (J). lib. bdg. 27.94 (978-0-7660-4229-2(4)) Enslow Pubs., Inc.

—Kevin Durant: NBA Superstar, 1 vol. 2012. (Playmakers Set 3 Ser.). (ENG.). 32p. (J). (gr. 2-6). lib. bdg. 27.07 (978-1-61783-547-6(1), SportsZone) ABDO Publishing Co.

—Tyler Perry: A Biography of a Movie Mogul. 2014. (African-American Icons Ser.). 104p. (J). lib. bdg. 27.94 (978-0-7660-4241-4(3)) Enslow Pubs., Inc.

Glover, Maria Robinson. Who Do I Want to Be? Contemporary Black Women from A to Z. Glover, Maria Robinson, illus. 2006. (Illus.). (J). 16.95 (978-0-9787940-0-2(1)) HotComb Pr.

Gold, Susan Dudley. Harriet Tubman & the Underground Railroad. 2015. (Primary Sources of the Abolitionist Movement Ser.). (ENG., Illus.). 64p. (J). (gr. 6-6). 34.21 (978-1-5026-0522-1(8)) Cavendish Square Publishing.

Goldsworthy, Steve. Politicians. 2016. (Illus.). 48p. (J). (978-1-5105-1162-0(8)) SmartBook Media, Inc.

Golenbock, Peter. Hank Aaron: Brave in Every Way. Lee, Paul, illus. 2005. (ENG.). 32p. (J). (gr. -1-3). reprint ed. pap. 6.99 (978-0-15-205250-8(X)) Houghton Mifflin Harcourt Publishing Co.

Golus, Carrie. Josh Gibson. 2010. (Sports Heroes & Legends Ser.). (ENG.). 120p. (gr. 5-12). lib. bdg. 30.60 (978-0-7613-5367-6(4)) Lerner Publishing Group.

Gomez, Rebecca. Jackie Robinson, 1 vol. 2003. (First Biographies Ser.). (ENG., Illus.). 32p. (gr. k-4). 27.07 (978-1-57765-949-5(X), Buddy Bks.) ABDO Publishing Co.

Gordon, Katherine. Michael Jackson: Ultimate Music Legend. 2010. (Illus.). 48p. (J). pap. 8.95 (978-0-7613-6002-5(6), Lerner Pubns.) Lerner Publishing Group.

Gosman, Gillian. Harriet Tubman. 2011. (Life Stories Ser.). (Illus.). 24p. (J). pap. 8.25 (978-1-4488-2761-9(2), PowerKids Pr.); (gr. 1-4). lib. bdg. 22.60 (978-1-4488-2586-8(5), PowerKids Pr.); (ENG & SPA., (gr. 1-4). lib. bdg. 22.60 (978-1-4488-3220-0(9)) Rosen Publishing Group, Inc., The.

—Martin Luther King, Jr. 2011. (Life Stories Ser.). (Illus.). 24p. (J). pap. 8.25 (978-1-4488-2755-8(8), PowerKids Pr.); (gr. 1-4). lib. bdg. 22.60 (978-1-4488-2583-7(0), PowerKids Pr.); (ENG & SPA., (gr. 1-4). lib. bdg. 22.60 (978-1-4488-3217-0(9)) Rosen Publishing Group, Inc., The.

—Rosa Parks. 2011. (Life Stories Ser.). (Illus.). 24p. (J). pap. 8.25 (978-1-4488-2757-2(4), PowerKids Pr.); (gr. 1-4). lib. bdg. 22.60 (978-1-4488-2584-4(9), PowerKids Pr.); (ENG & SPA., (gr. 1-4). lib. bdg. 22.60 (978-1-4488-3218-7(7)) Rosen Publishing Group, Inc., The.

Gotsch, Patrice. Martin Luther King, Jr: Changing Lives. Arreola, Gil, illus. 2006. 19p. pap. 6.30 (978-1-55501-779-8(7)) Ballard & Tighe Pubs.

Gould, Jane H. George Washington Carver. 2013. (Jr. Graphic American Inventors Ser.). (ENG., Illus.). 24p. (J). (gr. 3-6). pap. 10.60 (978-1-4777-0141-6(9)); lib. bdg. 25.25 (978-1-4777-0078-5(1)) Rosen Publishing Group, Inc., The. (PowerKids Pr.).

Graham, Amy. Celebrated African-American Novelists. 2012. (African-American Collective Biographies Ser.). (Illus.). 112p. (J). (gr. 5-18). 33.27 (978-1-59845-138-2(3)) Enslow Pubs., Inc.

Graves, Jeseca, illus. Bessie Coleman: The Story of an Aviation Pioneer. 2007. 24p. (J). (978-0-9745294-1-7(9)) San Diego County Regional Airport Authority.

Graves, Will. Robert Griffin III: NFL Sensation: RGIII, 1 vol. 2013. (Playmakers Set 4 Ser.). (ENG.). 32p. (gr. 2-6). lib. bdg. 27.07 (978-1-61783-700-5(8), SportsZone) ABDO Publishing Co.

Green, Michelle Y. A Strong Right Arm: The Story of Mamie Peanut Johnson. Nelson, Kadir, illus. 2004. (ENG.). 128p. (J). (gr. 3-7). 5.99 (978-0-14-240072-2(6), Puffin Books) Penguin Young Readers Group.

Green, Richard L., et al, eds. A Salute to Black Civil Rights Leaders. Dobson, S. Gaston, illus. (Empak "Black History" Publication). (J). pap. 1.00 (978-0-9616156-3-5(X)) Empak Publishing Co.

Greenberger, Robert. Wilt Chamberlain. 2009. (Basketball Hall of Famers Ser.). 112p. (gr. 5-8). 63.90 (978-1-61511-536-5(6), Rosen Reference) Rosen Publishing Group, Inc., The.

Greenfield, Eloise. Paul Robeson. Ford, George, illus. 2009. (ENG.). 40p. (J). (gr. 1-6). pap. 10.95 (978-1-60060-262-7(2)) Lee & Low Bks., Inc.

Greenfield, Eloise & Ford, George. Paul Robeson. 2009. (ENG., Illus.). 40p. (J). (gr. 1-6). 10.95 (978-1-60060-256-6(8)) Lee & Low Bks., Inc.

Gregory, Josh. Frederick Douglass. 2015. (ENG., Illus.). 48p. (J). lib. bdg. (978-0-531-21597-5(0), Orchard Bks.) Scholastic, Inc.

—Jackie Robinson. 2015. (ENG., Illus.). 48p. (J). lib. bdg. (978-0-531-21598-2(9)) Children's Pr., Ltd.

—Jackie Robinson. 2015. (True Book(tm) — Biographies Ser.). (ENG.). 48p. (J). pap. 6.95 (978-0-531-21760-3(4), Children's Pr.) Scholastic Library Publishing.

—Lebron James. 2014. (Basketball Heroes Making a Difference Ser.). 24p. (J). (gr. 1-6). lib. bdg. 23.93 (978-1-62724-082-6(9)) Bearport Publishing Co., Inc.

—Martin Luther King Jr. 2015. (ENG., Illus.). 48p. (J). pap. 6.95 (978-0-531-21208-0(4), Orchard Bks.) Scholastic Library Publishing.

Grimes, Nikki. Barack Obama: Son of Promise, Child of Hope. Collier, Bryan, illus. 2012. (ENG.). 48p. (J). (gr. k-3). pap. 9.99 (978-1-4424-5077-6(0), Little Simon) Little Simon.

—Barack Obama: Son of Promise, Child of Hope. Collier, Bryan, illus. 2012. (ENG.). 48p. (J). (gr. k-3). 9.99 (978-1-4424-4092-0(9), Simon & Schuster Bks. For Young Readers) Simon & Schuster Bks. For Young Readers.

Gunderson, Jessica. Jay-Z: Hip-Hop Icon. Kinsella, Pat, illus. 2012. (American Graphic Ser.). (ENG.). 32p. (gr. 3-4). pap. 47.70 (978-1-4296-8475-0(5), Graphic Library) Capstone Press of Coughlan Cos.

—X: A Biography of Malcolm X. Hayden, Seitu, illus. 2011. (American Graphic Ser.). (ENG.). 32p. (gr. 3-4). pap. 8.10 (978-1-4296-6267-3(0)); pap. 47.70 (978-1-4296-6438-7(X)) Capstone Press of Coughlan Cos. (Graphic Library).

Gutman, Dan. Jackie Robinson & the Big Game. Garvin, Elaine, illus. 2006. 32p. (J). lib. bdg. 15.00 (978-1-4242-0957-6(9)) Fitzgerald Bks.

—Jackie Robinson & the Big Game. Garvin, Elaine, illus. 2006. (Ready-To-read COFA Ser.). (ENG.). 32p. (J). (gr. k-2). pap. 3.99 (978-0-689-86239-7(3), Simon & Schuster/Paula Wiseman Bks.) Simon & Schuster/Paula Wiseman Bks.

Haegele, Katie. Monte Irvin. 2009. (Baseball Hall of Famers of the Negro Leagues Ser.). 112p. (gr. 5-8). 63.90 (978-1-61511-525-9(0), Rosen Reference) Rosen Publishing Group, Inc., The.

Haldy, Emma E. Booker T. Washington. Bane, Jeff, illus. 2016. (My Early Library: My Itty-Bitty Bio Ser.). (ENG.). 24p. (J). (gr. k-1). 28.50 (978-1-63471-018-3(5), 208152) Cherry Lake Publishing.

—Frederick Douglass. Bane, Jeff, illus. 2016. (My Early Library: My Itty-Bitty Bio Ser.). (ENG.). 24p. (J). (gr. k-1). 28.50 (978-1-63470-479-3(7), 207647) Cherry Lake Publishing.

—Jackie Robinson. Bane, Jeff, illus. 2016. (My Early Library: My Itty-Bitty Bio Ser.). (ENG.). 24p. (J). (gr. k-1). 28.50 (978-1-63471-021-3(5), 208164) Cherry Lake Publishing.

—Marian Anderson. Bane, Jeff, illus. 2016. (My Early Library: My Itty-Bitty Bio Ser.). (ENG.). 24p. (J). (gr. k-1). 28.50 (978-1-63471-023-7(1), 208172) Cherry Lake Publishing.

—Martin Luther King, Jr. Bane, Jeff, illus. 2016. (My Early Library: My Itty-Bitty Bio Ser.). (ENG.). 24p. (J). (gr. k-1). 28.50 (978-1-63470-477-9(0), 207639) Cherry Lake Publishing.

—Maya Angelou. Bane, Jeff, illus. 2017. (My Early Library: My Itty-Bitty Bio Ser.). (ENG.). 24p. (J). (gr. k-1). lib. bdg. 28.50 (978-1-63472-153-0(5), 209184) Cherry Lake Publishing.

—Rosa Parks. Bane, Jeff, illus. 2016. (My Early Library: My Itty-Bitty Bio Ser.). (ENG.). 24p. (J). (gr. k-1). 28.50 (978-1-63470-481-6(9), 207655) Cherry Lake Publishing.

Haley, Alex. The Autobiography of Malcolm X. Bloom, Harold, ed. annot. ed. 2008. (Bloom's Guides). 168p. (C). (gr. 9). 30.00 (978-0-7910-9832-5(X), Chelsea Hse.) Facts On File, Inc.

Halfmann, Janet. Seven Miles to Freedom: The Robert Smalls Story. Smith, Duane, illus. 2008. 40p. (J). (gr. 1-6). 17.95 (978-1-60060-232-0(0)) Lee & Low Bks., Inc.

Halfmann, Janet & Smith, Duane. Seven Miles to Freedom: The Robert Smalls Story, 1 vol. 2008. (ENG., Illus.). 40p. (J). pap. 10.95 (978-1-60060-986-2(4)) Lee & Low Bks., Inc.

Hall, M. C. Martin Luther King, Jr. Civil Rights Leader, 1 vol. Soud, illus. 2008. (Beginner Biographies Ser.). (ENG.). 32p. (gr. -1-3). 28.50 (978-1-60270-251-6(9), Looking Glass Library- Nonfiction) Magic Wagon.

Hall, Ron & Moore, Denver. Same Kind of Different As Me for Kids, 1 vol. 2017. (ENG., Illus.). 32p. (J). 14.99 (978-0-7180-9179-8(5)) Nelson, Thomas Inc.

Hally, Ashleigh. Coretta Scott King. 2012. (Illus.). 24p. (J). (978-1-935884-78-1(6)); pap. (978-1-935884-84-2(0)) State Standards Publishing, LLC.

—Lugenia Burns Hope. 2012. (Illus.). 24p. (J). lib. bdg. (978-1-935884-76-7(X)) State Standards Publishing, LLC.

Hammer, Maxwell. LeBron James: NBA MVP & Champion. 2015. (Today's MVPs & Champions Ser.). (ENG.). 24p. (J). (gr. 2-5). 27.07 (978-1-63143-737-3(2), 208571) Child's World, Inc., The.

Hanft, Joshua E. Jackie Robinson. Marcos, Pablo, illus. 2005. (Heroes of America Ser.). 238p. (gr. 3-8). 27.07 (978-1-59679-259-3(0), Abdo & Daughters) ABDO Publishing Co.

Hansen, Grace. Martin Luther King, Jr. Civil Rights Leader, 1 vol. 2014. (History Maker Biographies Ser.). (ENG., Illus.). 24p. (J). (gr. 2-4). lib. bdg. 28.50 (978-1-62970-704-4(X)) ABDO Publishing Co.

Hanson, Joyce A. Mary McLeod Bethune & Black Women's Political Activism. 2003. (ENG., Illus.). 264p. (C). (gr. 13-17). 45.00 (978-0-8262-1451-5(7)) Univ. of Missouri Pr.

Harris, Laurie Lanzen. Biography for Beginners: African-American Leaders. 2007. (J). lib. bdg. 30.00 (978-1-931360-35-7(9)) Favorable Impressions.

Harris, Laurie Lanzen, ed. Biography for Beginners Vol. 2: African-American Leaders. 2008. 316p. (YA). (gr. 5-10). lib. bdg. 30.00 (978-1-931360-36-4(7)) Favorable Impressions.

Hart, Joyce. Native Son: The Story of Richard Wright. 2004. (World Writers Ser.). (Illus.). 128p. (YA). (gr. 6-12). 23.95 (978-1-931798-06-8(0)) Reynolds, Morgan Inc.

Hasday, Judy L. & Crompton, Samuel Willard. Barry Sanders. 2008. (Football Superstars Ser.). (Illus.). 120p. (J). (gr. 7-12). 30.00 (978-0-7910-9667-3(X)) Facts On File, Inc.

Haskins, Jim. African American Entrepreneurs. 2012. (Black Stars Ser.). (ENG.). 192p. (J). (gr. 5-9). pap. 27.00 (978-1-118-43613-4(X), Wiley) Wiley, John & Sons, Inc.

Haskins, Jim, et al. John Lewis in the Lead: A Story of the Civil Rights Movement, 1 vol. 2006. (ENG., Illus.). 40p. (J). pap. 11.95 (978-1-60060-849-0(3)) Lee & Low Bks., Inc.

Hayhurst, Chris. Bill Russell. 2009. (Basketball Hall of Famers Ser.). 112p. (gr. 5-8). 63.90 (978-1-61511-530-3(7), Rosen Reference) Rosen Publishing Group, Inc., The.

Head, David L. Granville T. Woods: African American Communication & Transportation Pioneer. 2013. 140p. pap. 30.00 (978-1-4349-7841-7(9), RoseDog Bks.) Dorrance Publishing Co., Inc.

Healy, Nick. Muhammad Ali. 2005. (Genius Ser.). (Illus.). 48p. (J). (gr. 5-9). lib. bdg. 21.95 (978-1-58341-333-3(2), Creative Education) Creative Co., The.

Helfand, Lewis & Teitelbaum, Michael. Martin Luther King. Banerjee, Sankha, illus. 2013. (Campfire Graphic Novels Ser.). (ENG.). 88p. (YA). (gr. 5). pap. 11.99 (978-93-80028-69-9(5), Campfire) Steerforth Pr.

Henneberg, Susan. James Baldwin, 1 vol. 2015. (ENG.). 112p. (YA). 35.60 (978-1-4777-7897-5(7), Rosen Young Adult) Rosen Publishing Group, Inc., The.

Herweck, Dona. Martin Luther King Jr., 1 vol. 2nd rev. ed. 2011. (TIME for KIDS(r) Nonfiction Readers Ser.). (ENG.). 28p. (J). (gr. 2-2). pap. 6.99 (978-1-4333-3641-6(3)) Teacher Created Materials, Inc.

Hicks, Kyra E. Martha Ann's Quilt for Queen Victoria. Födi, Lee Edward, illus. 2012. 32p. (J). pap. 12.95 (978-0-9824796-8-1(9)) Black Threads Pr.

—Martha Ann's Quilt for Queen Victoria. Fodi, Lee Edward, illus. 2006. 28p. (J). (gr. -1-3). 16.95 (978-1-933285-59-7(1)) Brown Books Publishing Group.

Hill, Anne E. Lebron James: King of Shots. 2012. (USA TODAY Lifeline Biographies Ser.). (ENG., Illus.). 112p. (gr. 6-12). lib. bdg. 34.60 (978-0-7613-8641-4(6)) Lerner Publishing Group.

Hill, Christine M. Gwendolyn Brooks: Poetry Is Life Distilled. 2005. (African-American Biography Library). (Illus.). 128p. (J). (gr. 6-12). lib. bdg. 33.27 (978-0-7660-2292-8(7)) Enslow Pubs., Inc.

Hill, Laban Carrick. Dave the Potter: Artist, Poet, Slave. Collier, Bryan, illus. 2010. (ENG.). 40p. (J). (gr. -1-3). 18.99 (978-0-316-10731-0(X)) Little, Brown Bks. for Young Readers.

Hill, Laban Carrik. Dave the Potter: Artist, Poet, Slave. 2011. (J). (978-1-4618-1706-2(4)) Recorded Bks., Inc.

Hind, Devon & Bergstresser, Kate, trs. Jesse Owens: World's Fastest Human. 2003. (Alabama Roots Biography Ser.). (Illus.). 120p. (J). (978-1-878561-38-1(3)) Seacoast Publishing, Inc.

Hinman, Bonnie. Eternal Vigilance: The Story of Ida B. Wells-Barnett. 2011. (Civil Rights Leaders Ser.). 128p. (gr. 6-10). lib. bdg. 28.95 (978-1-59935-111-7(0)) Reynolds, Morgan Inc.

—A Stranger in My Own House: The Story of W. E. B. du Bois. 2005. (Civil Rights Leaders Ser.). (Illus.). 176p. (gr. 6-12). 28.95 (978-1-931798-45-7(1)) Reynolds, Morgan Inc.

Hinton, Kaa Vonia. Jacqueline Woodson. 2007. (Classic Storytellers Ser.). (Illus.). 48p. (J). (gr. 4-8). lib. bdg. 29.95 (978-1-58415-533-1(7)) Mitchell Lane Pubs., Inc.

Hinton, KaaVonia. Martin Luther King, Jr. 2008. (What's So Great About... ? Ser.). (Illus.). 32p. (YA). (gr. 2-4). lib. bdg. 25.70 (978-1-58415-724-3(0)) Mitchell Lane Pubs., Inc.

Hobkirk, Lori. Madam C. J. Walker. 2009. (Journey to Freedom Ser.). (ENG., Illus.). 32p. (J). (gr. 4-7). 29.93 *(978-1-60253-127-7(7)*, 200393) Child's World, Inc., The.

Hoe, Susan. Rosa Parks. 2007. (Sharing the American Dream Ser.). 64p. (YA). (gr. 7-18). pap. 9.95 *(978-1-4222-0760-4(9))* Mason Crest.

Hoe, Susan C. Rosa Parks. 2009. (Sharing the American Dream Ser.). 64p. (YA). (gr. 7-12). 22.95 *(978-1-4222-0597-6(5))* Mason Crest.

Hoffman, Mary Ann. Dwayne Wade: Basketball Star. 2009. (Sports Superstars Ser.). 24p. (gr. 1-1). 42.50 *(978-1-60853-176-9(7)*, PowerKids Pr.) Rosen Publishing Group, Inc., The.

—Dwayne Wade: Basketball Star/Estrella del Baloncesto. 2009. (Amazing Athletes/Atletas increíbles Ser.). (ENG & SPA.). 24p. (gr. 1-2). 42.50 *(978-1-61511-305-7(3)*, Editorial Buenas Letras) Rosen Publishing Group, Inc., The.

—LeBron James: Basketball Star. 2009. (Sports Superstars Ser.). 24p. (gr. 1-1). 42.50 *(978-1-60853-178-3(3)*, PowerKids Pr.) Rosen Publishing Group, Inc., The.

—LeBron James: Basketball Star/Estrella del Baloncesto. 2009. (Amazing Athletes/Atletas increíbles Ser.). (ENG & SPA.). 24p. (gr. 1-2). 42.50 *(978-1-61511-306-4(1)*, Editorial Buenas Letras) Rosen Publishing Group, Inc., The.

Holliday, Laurel. Dreaming in Color Living in Black & White: Our Own Stories of Growing up Black in America. 2012. (ENG.). 208p. (YA). (gr. 7). pap. 10.99 *(978-1-4424-7177-1(8)*, Simon Pulse) Simon Pulse.

Homemaker, Nellie. Journey with a Woman of the Gullah Cultu. 2006. pap. 10.00 *(978-1-4257-1916-6(3))* Xlibris Corp.

Hoose, Phillip. Claudette Colvin: Twice Toward Justice. 2010. (ENG., Illus.). 160p. (YA). (gr. 8-12). pap. 9.99 *(978-0-312-66105-2(3)*, 9780312661052) Square Fish.

Hopkinson, Deborah. Keep On! The Story of Matthew Henson, Co-Discoverer of the North Pole. 1 vol. Alcorn, Stephen, illus. 2009. (ENG.). 36p. (J). (gr. 1-5). 17.95 *(978-1-56145-473-0(7))* Peachtree Pubs.

—Michelle. Ford, A. G., illus. 2009. 32p. (J). (gr. -1-2). 17.99 *(978-0-06-182739-6(8))* HarperCollins Pubs.

—Sweet Land of Liberty. 1 vol. Jenkins, Leonard, illus. 2007. (ENG.). 32p. (J). (gr. 1-5). 16.95 *(978-1-56145-395-5(1))* Peachtree Pubs.

Hord, Colleen. Muhammad Ali. 2013. (ENG., Illus.). 24p. (J). (gr. k-3). pap. 8.95 *(978-1-61810-285-0(0))* Rourke Educational Media.

Horn, Geoffrey M. Thurgood Marshall. 2004. (Trailblazers of the Modern World Ser.). (Illus.). 48p. (gr. 5-12). pap. 14.05 *(978-0-8368-5258-5(3))*; lib. bdg. 31.00 *(978-0-8368-5098-7(X))* Stevens, Gareth Publishing LLLP. (Gareth Stevens Secondary Library).

Hubbard-Brown, Janet. Ray Charles. 2008. (Black Americans of Achievement Ser.). (Illus.). 112p. (gr. 6-12). 35.00 *(978-1-60413-001-0(6)*, Chelsea Hse.) Facts On File, Inc.

Hubbard, Crystal. The Last Black King of the Kentucky Derby: The Story of Jimmy Winkfield. McGuire, Robert, illus. 2008. (ENG.). 40p. (J). (gr. 1-6). 17.95 *(978-1-58430-274-2(7))* Lee & Low Bks., Inc.

Hubbard, Crystal & McGuire, Robert. The Last Black King of the Kentucky Derby. 2005. (ENG., Illus.). 40p. (J). pap. 11.95 *(978-1-60060-891-9(4))* Lee & Low Bks., Inc.

Hudson, Wade. Scientists Healers & Inventors, Vol. 3. 2004. (Book of Black Heroes Ser.: Vol. 3). (Illus.). 72p. (J). (gr. 4-7). pap. 9.95 *(978-0-940975-97-2(1)*, Sankofa Bks.) Just Us Bks., Inc.

Hugh Granville Tilley North Carolina House of Representatives 1887 And 1889. 1 book. l.t. ed. 2007. (ENG., Illus.). 50p. lib. bdg. 36.99 *(978-0-9722724-3-8(7))* Blackfoot Burkino Cherokee Publishing.

Hulick, Kathryn. Kimberly Bryant: Founder of Black Girls Code. 2017. (J). ***(978-1-5026-2703-2(5))*** Cavendish Square Publishing.

Hull, Mary. Rosa Parks: Civil Rights Leader. 2nd rev. ed. 2006. (Black Americans of Achievement Ser.). (Illus.). 122p. (YA). (gr. 7-12). lib. bdg. 35.00 *(978-0-7910-9523-2(1))* Facts On File, Inc.

Hull, Mary & Gelfand, Dale Evva. Rosa Parks. 2nd rev. ed. 2008. (Black Americans of Achievement: Legacy Edition Ser.). 128p. (gr. 6-12). pap. 11.95 *(978-1-60413-325-7(2)*, Checkmark Bks.) Facts On File, Inc.

Hunt, Rameck, et al. We Beat the Street: How a Friendship Pact Led to Success. 2006. (ENG., Illus.). 208p. (J). (gr. 5-18). 7.99 *(978-0-14-240627-4(9)*, Puffin Books) Penguin Young Readers Group.

Hunter-Gault, Charlayne. To the Mountaintop: My Journey Through the Civil Rights Movement. 2014. (New York Times Ser.). (ENG., Illus.). 224p. (YA). (gr. 7). pap. 12.99 *(978-1-250-04062-6(0)*, 9781250040626) Square Fish.

Hurt, Avery Elizabeth. Rosa Parks: Civil Rights Activist. 2017. (J). ***(978-1-5383-8105-2(2))*** Rosen Publishing Group, Inc., The.

Irving, Barrington & Peppe, Holly. Touch the Sky. 2012. (J). *(978-0-531-22525-7(9))* Scholastic, Inc.

Isbell, Hannah. Misty Copeland: Ballerina. 2016. (Junior Biographies Ser.). 24p. (J). pap. 9.35 *(978-0-7660-8177-2(X))* Enslow Pubs., Inc.

Jackson, Garnet N. Shirley Chisholm, Congresswoman. 2012. (ENG., Illus.). (J). (gr. 1-4). pap. 7.47 net. *(978-0-8136-5247-4(2)*, Modern Curriculum Pr.) Pearson Schl.

Jakoubek, Robert. Martin Luther King Jr. 2008. (Black Americans of Achievement: Legacy Edition Ser.). 112p. (gr. 6-12). pap. 11.95 *(978-1-60413-328-8(7)*, Checkmark Bks.) Facts On File, Inc.

Jakoubek, Robert E. Martin Luther King, Jr. Civil Rights Leader. 2004. (Black Americans of Achievement Ser.). (Illus.). 112p. (gr. 6-12). 35.00 *(978-0-7910-8161-7(3)*, Chelsea Hse.) Facts On File, Inc.

James, Betty R. Against All Odds: Artist Dean Mitchell's Story. 2007. (Illus.). 64p. (J). 13.95 *(978-0-942407-83-9(0))* Father & Son Publishing.

Jarnow, Jesse. Phillis Wheatley. 2004. (Primary Sources of Famous People in American History Ser.). (ENG., Illus.). 32p. (gr. 4-8). pap. 10.00 *(978-0-8239-4191-9(4))* Rosen Publishing Group, Inc., The.

—Phillis Wheatley: African American Poet / Poeta Afroamericana. 2009. (Famous People in American History/Grandes personajes en la historia de los Estados Unidos Ser.). (ENG & SPA.). 32p. (gr. 2-3). 47.90 *(978-1-61512-554-8(X)*, Editorial Buenas Letras) Rosen Publishing Group, Inc., The.

—Phillis Wheatley: Poeta afroamericana (Phillis Wheatley: African American Poet) 2009. (Grandes personajes en la historia de los Estados Unidos (Famous People in American History) Ser.). (SPA.). 32p. (gr. 2-3). 47.90 *(978-1-61512-807-5(7)*, Editorial Buenas Letras) Rosen Publishing Group, Inc., The.

Jazynka, Kitson. National Geographic Readers: Martin Luther King, Jr. 2012. (Readers Bios Ser.). (ENG.). 48p. (J). (gr. k-3). pap. 3.99 *(978-1-4263-1087-4(0))*; lib. bdg. 13.90 *(978-1-4263-1088-1(9))* National Geographic Society. (National Geographic Children's Bks.).

—National Geographic Readers: Rosa Parks. 2015. (Readers Bios Ser.). (ENG., Illus.). 32p. (J). (gr. k-3). pap. 3.99 *(978-1-4263-2141-2(4)*, National Geographic Children's Bks.) National Geographic Society.

Jeffrey, Gary. Martin Luther King Jr: The Life of a Civil Rights Leader. 2009. (Graphic Nonfiction Biographies Ser.). (ENG.). 48p. (YA). (gr. 4-5). 58.50 *(978-1-61513-021-4(7)*, Rosen Reference) Rosen Publishing Group, Inc., The.

—Martin Luther King Jr: The Life of a Civil Rights Leader. Forsey, Chris, illus. 2007. (Graphic Nonfiction Biographies Ser.). (ENG.). 48p. (YA). (gr. 4-7). lib. bdg. 31.95 *(978-1-4042-0858-2(5))* Rosen Publishing Group, Inc., The.

—Martin Luther King Jr: The Life of a Civil Rights Leader. Forsey, Christopher, illus. 2007. (Graphic Biographies Ser.). (ENG.). 48p. (gr. 5-8). pap. 14.05 *(978-1-4042-0921-3(2))* Rosen Publishing Group, Inc., The.

—Rosa Parks & the Montgomery Bus Boycott. 2012. (Graphic History of the Civil Rights Movement Ser.). (Illus.). 24p. (J). (gr. 3-8). pap. 8.15 *(978-1-4339-7500-4(9))*; lib. bdg. 23.95 *(978-1-4339-7499-1(1))* Stevens, Gareth Publishing LLLP.

Johnson, Claudia Durst. Slavery & Racism in the Narrative Life of Freddrick Douglass. 2014. (Social Issues in Literature Ser.). (ENG., Illus.). 224p. (gr. 7-12). lib. bdg. 46.40 *(978-0-7377-6986-9(6)*, Greenhaven Pr., Inc.) Cengage Gale.

Johnson, Dolores. Onward: A Photobiography of African-American Polar Explorer Matthew Henson. 2005. (Photobiographies Ser.). (ENG., Illus.). 64p. (gr. k-3). 17.95 *(978-0-7922-7914-3(X))*; 27.90 *(978-0-7922-7915-0(8))* National Geographic Society. (National Geographic Children's Bks.).

Jones, Amy Robin. Mary McLeod Bethune. 2009. (Journey to Freedom Ser.). (ENG., Illus.). 32p. (J). (gr. 4-7). 29.93 *(978-1-60253-129-1(3)*, 200395) Child's World, Inc., The.

Jones, Lynda. Mrs. Lincoln's Dressmaker: The Unlikely Friendship of Elizabeth Keckley & Mary Todd Lincoln. 2009. (ENG., Illus.). 80p. (J). (gr. 5). lib. bdg. 27.90 *(978-1-4263-0378-4(5))*; 18.95 *(978-1-4263-0377-7(7))* National Geographic Society. (National Geographic Children's Bks.).

Jones, Natalya. George Washington Carver: Peanut Scientist. 2009. (Real Life Readers Ser.). 16p. (gr. 2-3). pap. 7.05 *(978-1-4358-0085-4(0)*, Rosen Classroom) Rosen Publishing Group, Inc., The.

Jones, Rob Lloyd. Martin Luther King, Jr. 2006. (Illus.). 62p. (J). pap. *(978-0-439-02299-6(1))* Scholastic, Inc.

Jones, Veda Boyd. Jazz Age Poet: A Story about Langston Hughes. Kiwak, Barbara, illus. 2005. (Creative Minds Biographies Ser.). (ENG.). 64p. (gr. 4-8). lib. bdg. 22.60 *(978-1-57505-757-6(3)*, Carolrhoda Bks.) Lerner Publishing Group.

Jordan, Denise. Walter Dean Myers: A Biography of an Award-Winning Urban Fiction Author. 2013. (African-American Icons Ser.). 104p. (J). (gr. 6-12). lib. bdg. 27.94 *(978-0-7660-3990-2(0))* Enslow Pubs., Inc.

Jordan, Denise M. Muhammad Ali: Meet the Champion. 2003. (Meeting Famous People Ser.). (Illus.). 32p. (J). lib. bdg. 22.60 *(978-0-7660-2272-0(2))* Enslow Pubs., Inc.

—Walter Dean Myers: A Biography of an Award-Winning Urban Fiction Author. 2013. (African-American Icons Ser.). 104p. (J). (gr. 6-12). pap. 10.95 *(978-1-59845-393-5(9))* Enslow Pubs., Inc.

Jordin Sparks. 2013. (Rising Stars Ser.). 32p. (J). (gr. 3-6). pap. 63.00 *(978-1-4339-8983-4(2))* Stevens, Gareth Publishing LLLP.

Josephson, Judith Pinkerton. Louis Armstrong. 2008. pap. 52.95 *(978-0-8225-9392-8(0))* Lerner Publishing Group.

Kaiser, Lisbeth. Maya Angelou. Salaberria, Leire, illus. 2016. (Little People, Big Dreams Ser.). (ENG.). 32p. (J). (gr. k-3). 14.99 *(978-1-84780-889-9(1)*, Frances Lincoln Children's Bks.) Quarto Publishing Group UK GBR. Dist: Hachette Bk. Group.

Kallen, Stuart A. Marcus Garvey & the Back to Africa Movement. 2006. (Lucent Library of Black History). (ENG., Illus.). 112p. (YA). (gr. 7-10). lib. bdg. 34.80 *(978-1-59018-838-5(1)*, Lucent Bks.) Cengage Gale.

Keiser, Cody. Thurgood Marshall: Civil Rights Leader. 2013. (Rosen Readers Ser.). (ENG.). 24p. (J). (gr. 3-4). pap. 49.50 *(978-1-4777-2546-7(6))*; pap. 8.25 *(978-1-4777-2545-0(8))* Rosen Publishing Group, Inc., The. (Rosen Classroom).

Kemp, Kristin. Amazing Americans: Thurgood Marshall, 1 vol. rev. ed. 2014. (Primary Source Readers Content & Literacy Ser.). (ENG., Illus.). 32p. (gr. 3-3). pap. 8.99 *(978-1-4333-7374-9(2))* Teacher Created Materials, Inc.

Kennedy, Mike. Lebron James. 2009. (People We Should Know Ser.). 32p. (gr. 3-5). (J). lib. bdg. 31.00 *(978-1-4339-0016-7(5))*; pap. 10.50 *(978-1-4339-0161-4(7))* Stevens, Gareth Publishing LLLP. (Gareth Stevens Learning Library).

Kent, Daniel T. Muhammad Ali & Laila Ali. 2004. (Famous Families Ser.). (Illus.). 48p. (J). lib. bdg. 29.25 *(978-1-4042-0261-0(7))* Rosen Publishing Group, Inc., The.

Kent, Deborah. Phillis Wheatley: First Published African-American Poet. 2003. (Our People Ser.). (ENG., Illus.). 32p. (J). (gr. 3-6). 29.93 *(978-1-59296-009-5(X)*, 200649) Child's World, Inc., The.

Kent, Jacqueline C. Phillis Wheatley. 2003. (Women of the Revolution Ser.). (J). pap. *(978-1-58417-089-1(1))*; lib. bdg. *(978-1-58417-026-6(3))* Lake Street Pubs.

Kernan, Elizabeth. Harriet Tubman: A Lesson in Bravery. 2009. (Reading Room Collection 2 Ser.). 24p. (gr. 3-4). 42.50 *(978-1-60851-966-8(X)*, PowerKids Pr.) Rosen Publishing Group, Inc., The.

King Farris, Christine. My Brother Martin: A Sister Remembers Growing up with the Rev. Dr. Martin Luther King Jr. Soentpiet, Chris K., illus. 2005. 35p. (J). (gr. 4-7). 15.65 *(978-0-7569-6552-5(7))* Perfection Learning Corp.

King, Meet Martin Luther, Jr. Meet Martin Luther King Jr. 2004. (ENG., Illus.). 32p. (J). 8.75 *(978-0-8249-5486-4(6)*, Ideal Pubns.) Worthy Publishing.

Kirkpatrick, Rob. Evander Holyfield: Heavyweight Champion / Campeón de los Pesos Pesados. 2009. (Hot Shots/Grandes ídolos Ser.). (ENG & SPA.). 24p. (gr. 1-1). 42.50 *(978-1-61513-414-4(X)*, Editorial Buenas Letras) Rosen Publishing Group, Inc., The.

—Grant Hill: Basketball All-Star. 2003. (Reading Power Ser.). (Illus.). 24p. (J). (gr. 1). lib. bdg. 17.25 *(978-0-8239-5538-1(9)*, PowerKids Pr.) Rosen Publishing Group, Inc., The.

—Kobe Bryant: Campeón de Slam Dunk (Slam Dunk Champion) 2009. (Deportistas de Poder (Power Players) Ser.). (SPA.). 24p. (gr. 1-1). 42.50 *(978-1-61512-158-8(7)*, Editorial Buenas Letras) Rosen Publishing Group, Inc., The.

—Kobe Bryant: Slam Dunk Champion / Campeón de Slam Dunk. 2009. (Power Players / Deportistas de Poder Ser.). (ENG & SPA.). 24p. (gr. 1-2). 42.50 *(978-1-60851-331-4(9)*, Editorial Buenas Letras) Rosen Publishing Group, Inc., The.

—Kobe Bryant, Slam Dunk Champion/Campeon del Slam Dunk. De Leon, Mauricio Velzaquez, tr. 2008. (Reading Power Ser.). (ENG., Illus.). 24p. (gr. 1-6). pap. 8.85 *(978-1-4042-7544-7(4))* Rosen Publishing Group, Inc., The.

—Michael Jordan: Basketball Superstar. 2009. (Great Record Breakers in Sports Ser.). 24p. (gr. 3-3). 42.50 *(978-1-61513-190-7(6)*, PowerKids Pr.) Rosen Publishing Group, Inc., The.

—Terrell Davis: Corredor de Superbowl (Super Bowl Running Back) 2009. (Deportistas de Poder (Power Players) Ser.). 24p. (gr. 1-1). 42.50 *(978-1-61512-161-8(7)*, Editorial Buenas Letras) Rosen Publishing Group, Inc., The.

Kishel, Ann-Marie. Rosa Parks: A Life of Courage. 2006. (Pull Ahead Books-Biographies Ser.). (ENG., Illus.). 32p. (gr. k-3). lib. bdg. 22.60 *(978-0-8225-3478-5(9)*, Lerner Pubns.) Lerner Publishing Group.

Kite, L. Patricia. Maya Angelou. 2006. (Just the Facts Biographies Ser.). (Illus.). 112p. (J). (gr. 3-7). pap. 9.95 *(978-0-8225-5997-9(8)*, Lerner Pubns.) Lerner Publishing Group.

Klein, Adria F. Barack Obama. 2009. pap. 13.25 *(978-1-60559-055-4(X))* Hameray Publishing Group, Inc.

Kneib, Martha. Kareem Abdul-Jabbar. 2009. (Basketball Hall of Famers Ser.). 112p. (gr. 5-8). 63.90 *(978-1-61511-533-4(1)*, Rosen Reference) Rosen Publishing Group, Inc., The.

Korb, Rena B. Pulling down the Walls: The Struggle of African American Performers. 2005. (ENG., Illus.). 24p. (J). (gr. 6-6). pap. 5.97 net. *(978-0-328-13625-4(5)*, Scott Foresman) Pearson Schl.

Kovatch, Sarah & Crumpler, Rebecca Lee. Rebecca Lee Crumpler. 2005. (Illus.). 16p. (J). *(978-0-7367-2891-1(0))* Zaner-Bloser, Inc.

Kramer, Barbara. The Life of George Washington Carver: Inventor & Scientist. 2015. (Legendary African Americans Ser.). 96p. (J). (gr. 6-12). 27.94 *(978-0-7660-6270-2(8))*; pap. 10.95 *(978-0-7660-6271-9(6))* Enslow Pubs., Inc.

—Mahalia Jackson: The Voice of Gospel & Civil Rights. 2003. (African-American Biographies Ser.). (Illus.). 128p. (J). lib. bdg. 26.60 *(978-0-7660-2115-0(7))* Enslow Pubs., Inc.

—Toni Morrison: A Biography of a Nobel Prize-Winning Writer. 2013. (African-American Icons Ser.). 104p. (J). (gr. 6-12). pap. 10.95 *(978-1-59845-392-8(0))* Enslow Pubs., Inc.

—Toni Morrison: A Biography of a Noble Prize-Winning Writer. 2013. (African-American Icons Ser.). 104p. (J). (gr. 6-12). lib. bdg. 27.94 *(978-0-7660-3989-6(7))* Enslow Pubs., Inc.

Krasner, Barbara. Harriet Tubman: Abolitionist & Conductor of the Underground Railroad. 2017. (Women Who Changed History Ser.). 48p. (gr. 10-12). lib. bdg. 26.85 ***(978-1-68048-659-9(4)***, Britannica Educational Publishing) Rosen Publishing Group, Inc., The.

Krass. Sojourner Truth. 2004. (Black Americans of Achievement Ser.). (Illus.). 112p. (gr. 6-12). 35.00 *(978-0-7910-8165-5(6)*, Chelsea Hse.) Facts On File, Inc.

Krohn, Katherine E. Madam C. J. Walker & New Cosmetics, 1 vol. Dominguez, Richard et al, illus. 2006. (Inventions & Discovery Ser.). (ENG.). 32p. (gr. 3-4). 8.10 *(978-0-7368-9647-4(3)*, Graphic Library) Capstone Press of Coughlan Cos.

—Madam C. J. Walker & New Cosmetics, 1 vol. Dominquez, Richard et al, illus. 2006. (Inventions & Discovery Ser.). (ENG.). 32p. (gr. 3-4). 30.65 *(978-0-7368-6485-5(7)*, Graphic Library) Capstone Press of Coughlan Cos.

—Oprah Winfrey. 2003. (Biography Ser.). (Illus.). 112p. (J). (gr. 6-18). pap. 7.95 *(978-0-8225-5000-6(8))* Lerner Publishing Group.

Krull, Kathleen. Wilma Unlimited. Diaz, David, illus. 2015. 44p. pap. 7.00 *(978-1-61003-502-6(X))* Center for the Collaborative Classroom.

Krull, Kathleen & Freeman, Laura. Coretta Scott King: I Kept on Marching. 2015. (Women Who Broke the Rules Ser.). (ENG., Illus.). 48p. (J). (gr. 1-4). pap. 6.99 *(978-0-8027-3827-1(3)*, 9780802738271, Bloomsbury USA Childrens) Bloomsbury Publishing USA.

Kudlinski, Kathleen. Sojourner Truth: Voice for Freedom. Wooden, Lenny, illus. 2003. (Childhood of Famous Americans Ser.). (ENG.). 160p. (Orig.). (J). (gr. 3-7). mass mkt. 7.99 *(978-0-689-85274-9(6)*, Simon & Schuster/Paula Wiseman Bks.) Simon & Schuster/Paula Wiseman Bks.

Kulling, Monica. All Aboard! Elijah McCoy's Steam Engine. Slavin, Bill, illus. 2013. (ENG.). 32p. (C). (gr. k-3). pap. 12.95 *(978-1-77049-514-2(2))* National Geographic School Publishing, Inc.

—To the Rescue! Garrett Morgan Underground. Parkins, David, illus. (Great Idea Ser.). (ENG.). 32p. (J). (gr. k-3). 2017. pap. 6.99 *(978-1-101-91882-1(9))* 2016. 17.99 *(978-1-77049-520-3(7))* Tundra Bks. CAN. (Tundra Bks.). Dist: Penguin Random Hse. LLC.

Labrecque, Ellen. George Washington Carver, 1 vol. 2014. (Science Biographies Ser.). (ENG.). 32p. (gr. 2-4). lib. bdg. 30.65 *(978-1-4109-6240-9(7)*, Raintree Perspectives) Heinemann-Raintree.

Labrecque, Ellen. Who Was Maya Angelou? Putra, Dede, illus. 2016. 105p. (J). ***(978-1-4844-6937-8(2)***, Grosset & Dunlap) Penguin Publishing Group.

Lantier, Patricia. Harriet Tubman: Conductor on the Underground Railroad. 2009. (Voices for Freedom Ser.). (ENG., Illus.). 64p. (J). (gr. 5-8). pap. *(978-0-7787-4838-0(3))*; lib. bdg. *(978-0-7787-4822-9(7))* Crabtree Publishing Co.

Lantier, Patricia & Michael Horn, Geoffrey. Sojourner Truth: Speaking up for Freedom. 2009. (Voices for Freedom Ser.). (ENG.). 64p. (J). (gr. 5-8). pap. *(978-0-7787-4840-3(5))*; lib. bdg. *(978-0-7787-4824-3(3))* Crabtree Publishing Co.

Lapham, Steven Sellers & Walton, Eugene. Philip Reid Saves the Statue of Freedom. 2014. (ENG.). (J). *(978-1-58536-819-8(9))* Sleeping Bear Pr.

Lasky, Kathryn. Vision of Beauty: The Story of Sarah Breedlove Walker. Bennett, Nneka, illus. 2012. (Candlewick Biographies Ser.). (ENG.). 56p. (J). (gr. 3-7). 14.99 *(978-0-7636-6428-2(6))*; pap. 4.99 *(978-0-7636-6092-5(2))* Candlewick Pr.

—A Voice of Her Own: The Story of Phillis Wheatley, Slave Poet. Lee, Paul, illus. 2012. (Candlewick Biographies Ser.). (ENG.). 48p. (J). (gr. 3-7). 14.99 *(978-0-7636-6427-5(8))*; pap. 4.99 *(978-0-7636-6091-8(4))* Candlewick Pr.

Lazo, Caroline Evensen. Alice Walker: Freedom Writer. 2005. (Lerner Biographies Ser.). (Illus.). 128p. (gr. 6-12). 27.93 *(978-0-8225-4960-4(3))* Lerner Publishing Group.

Leavitt, Amie Jane. George Washington Carver. 2007. (What's So Great About... ? Ser.). (Illus.). 32p. (YA). (gr. 2-4). lib. bdg. 25.70 *(978-1-58415-580-5(9))* Mitchell Lane Pubs., Inc.

—Harriet Tubman. 2007. (What's So Great About... ? Ser.). (Illus.). 32p. (J). (gr. 2-4). lib. bdg. 25.70 *(978-1-58415-577-5(9))* Mitchell Lane Pubs., Inc.

LeBron James. 2014. (ENG., Illus.). 48p. (J). lib. bdg. 29.00 *(978-0-531-21198-4(3))* Scholastic Library Publishing.

Lee, George L. Worldwide Interesting People: 162 History Makers of African Descent, 1 vol. alt. ed. 2012. (ENG., Illus.). 144p. pap. 19.99 *(978-0-7864-6768-6(1)*, 5efb588e-8e35-4188-81bd-86ff635cdb1d) McFarland & Co., Inc. Pubs.

The Legend of Jocko: Hero of the American Revolution. 2003. (YA). pap. 9.95 *(978-0-9761778-0-7(3))* Lefall & Co., Inc.

Levinson, Cynthia. The Youngest Marcher: The Story of a Young Civil Rights Activist. Brantley-Newton, Vanessa, illus. 2017. (ENG.). 40p. (J). (gr. k-5). 17.99 *(978-1-4814-0070-1(3))* Simon & Schuster, Inc.

Levy, Debbie. Richard Wright: A Biography. 2007. (Literary Greats Ser.). (ENG., Illus.). 160p. (gr. 7-12). lib. bdg. 33.26 *(978-0-8225-6793-6(8)*, Twenty-First Century Bks.) Lerner Publishing Group.

Lewis, Gregg & Lewis, Deborah Shaw. Gifted Hands: The Ben Carson Story. 1 vol. rev. ed. 2014. (ZonderKidz Biography Ser.). (ENG., Illus.). 176p. (J). pap. 7.99 *(978-0-310-73830-5(X))* Zonderkidz.

Linde, Barbara M. Jesse Jackson. 2011. (Civil Rights Crusaders Ser.). 24p. (gr. 2-5). (J). pap. 8.15 *(978-1-4339-5684-3(5)*, Gareth Stevens Learning Library); (YA). lib. bdg. 22.60 *(978-1-4339-5682-9(9))* Stevens, Gareth Publishing LLLP.

—Malcolm X. 2011. (Civil Rights Crusaders Ser.). 24p. (J). (gr. 2-5). pap. 8.15 *(978-1-4339-5688-1(8)*, Gareth Stevens Learning Library); lib. bdg. 22.60 *(978-1-4339-5686-7(1))* Stevens, Gareth Publishing LLLP.

—Martin Luther King Jr. 2011. (Civil Rights Crusaders Ser.). (Illus.). 24p. (gr. 2-5). (J). pap. 8.15 *(978-1-4339-5692-8(6)*, Gareth Stevens Learning Library); (YA). lib. bdg. 22.60 *(978-1-4339-5690-4(X))* Stevens, Gareth Publishing LLLP.

—Rosa Parks. 2011. (Civil Rights Crusaders Ser.). (Illus.). 24p. (gr. 2-5). (J). pap. 8.15 *(978-1-4339-5696-6(9)*, Gareth Stevens Learning Library); (YA). lib. bdg. 22.60 *(978-1-4339-5694-2(2))* Stevens, Gareth Publishing LLLP.

Linney, Susan. Martin Luther King, Jr: With a Discussion of Responsibility. 2004. (Values in Action Ser.). (J). *(978-1-59203-069-9(6))* Learning Challenge, Inc.

Littleton, Baron J. Your Little Black Book on African American Inventions & Inventors. 2006. vi, 153p. (J). per. 9.95 *(978-0-9791883-0-5(X))* Disciple One Publishing.

Litwin, Laura Baskes. A Reader's Guide to Zora Neale Hurston's Their Eyes Were Watching God. 2010. (Multicultural Literature Ser.). (Illus.). 128p. (YA). (gr. 8-18). 33.27 *(978-0-7660-3164-7(0))* Enslow Pubs., Inc.

Lochte, Hilary. W. E. B. du Bois. 2015. (Heroes of Black History Ser.). (ENG., Illus.). 32p. (J). (gr. 3-4). 26.60 *(978-1-4824-2922-0(5))* Stevens, Gareth Publishing LLLP.

Lohse, Joyce B. Justina Ford, Medical Pioneer. 2005. (Now You Know Bio Ser.). (Illus.). 56p. (J). pap. *(978-0-86541-074-9(7))* Filter Pr., LLC.

Looye, Juliette. Ruby Bridges. (Voices Reading Ser.). (Illus.). 16p. (J). pap. *(978-0-7367-2913-0(5))* Zaner-Bloser, Inc.

Lowery, Linda. Aunt Clara Brown: Official Pioneer. Porter, Janice Lee, illus. 2006. (On My Own Biographies Ser.). 48p. 16.95 *(978-0-7569-6699-7(X))* Perfection Learning Corp.

Machajewski, Sarah. Malcolm X in His Own Words. 2014. (Eyewitness to History Ser.). 32p. (J). (gr. 4-6). pap. 63.00 *(978-1-4824-1220-8(9))* Stevens, Gareth Publishing LLLP.

—Michelle Obama. 2016. (Superwomen Role Models Ser.). (Illus.). 32p. (J). (gr. 4-3). 26.25 *(978-1-5081-4812-8(0)*, PowerKids Pr.) Rosen Publishing Group, Inc., The.

MacLeod, Elizabeth. George Washington Carver: An Innovative Life. 2007. (Snapshots: Images of People & Places in History Ser.). (ENG., Illus.). 32p. (J). (gr. 3-7). 6.95 *(978-1-55337-907-2(1))*; 14.95 *(978-1-55337-906-5(3))* Kids Can Pr., Ltd. CAN. Dist: Hachette Bk. Group.

MacMillan, Dianne M. Martin Luther King, Jr. Day. rev. ed. 2008. (Best Holiday Bks.). (Illus.). 48p. (J). (gr. 3-7). lib. bdg. 25.27 *(978-0-7660-3043-5(1))* Enslow Pubs., Inc.

Macnow, Glen. Sports Great Allen Iverson. 2003. (Sports Great Bks.). (Illus.). 64p. (J). (gr. 4-10). lib. bdg. 22.60 *(978-0-7660-2063-4(0))* Enslow Pubs., Inc.

Malaspina, Ann. Harriet Tubman. 2009. (Leaders of the Civil War Era Ser.). (Illus.). 120p. (gr. 6-12). 35.00 *(978-1-60413-303-5(1)*, Chelsea Hse.) Facts On File, Inc.

Malcolm X & the Black Pride Movement. 2009. (Lucent Library of Black History Ser.). 128p. (gr. 7-10). 34.80 *(978-1-4205-0123-0(2)*, Lucent Bks.) Cengage Gale.

Mallin, Jay. Al Sharpton: Community Activist. 2007. (Great Life Stories Ser.). (Illus.). 111p. (J). *(978-0-531-13672-0(8)*, Franklin Watts) Hachette Children's Group.

Maloof, Torrey. Harriet Tubman: Leading Others to Liberty. 2017. (Primary Source Readers Ser.). (Illus.). 32p. (J). (gr. 4-5). pap. 8.99 *(978-1-4938-3802-8(4))* Teacher Created Materials, Inc.

—Martin Luther King Jr: Destined to Lead. 2016. (Primary Source Readers Ser.). (Illus.). 32p. (gr. 2-2). 8.99 *(978-1-4938-2559-2(3))* Teacher Created Materials, Inc.

Maloof, Torrey. True Life: Frederick Douglass. 2017. (J). pap. 9.97 ***(978-1-4938-3634-5(X))*** Teacher Created Materials, Inc.

—True Life: Frederick Douglass. 2017. (Time for Kids Nonfiction Readers Ser.). lib. bdg. 20.85 ***(978-0-606-40287-3(X))*** Turtleback Bks.

Mancini, Candice. Racism in the Autobiography of Malcolm X. 2008. (Social Issues in Literature Ser.). (ENG., Illus.). 175p. (YA). (gr. 10-12). 28.45 *(978-0-7377-4261-9(5)*, LML02109-243175); pap. 40.95 *(978-0-7377-4260-2(7)*, LML02109-243171) Cengage Gale. (Greenhaven Pr., Inc.).

Mandel, Peter. Say Hey! A Song of Willie Mays. Tate, Don, illus. 2004. 30p. (J). (gr. k-2). reprint ed. 16.00 *(978-0-7567-8162-0(0))* DIANE Publishing Co.

Mangal, Melina. Mildred Taylor. 2004. (Classic Storytellers Ser.). (Illus.). 48p. (J). (gr. 4-8). lib. bdg. 29.95 *(978-1-58415-311-5(3))* Mitchell Lane Pubs., Inc.

Manheimer, Ann S. James Beckwourth: Legendary Mountain Man. 2005. (Trailblazer Biographies Ser.). (ENG., Illus.). 112p. (gr. 5-9). lib. bdg. 31.93 *(978-1-57505-892-4(8)*, Twenty-First Century Bks.) Lerner Publishing Group.

—Martin Luther King Jr: Dreaming of Equality. 2004. (Trailblazer Biographies Ser.). (ENG., Illus.). 112p. (gr. 5-9). 31.93 *(978-1-57505-627-2(5)*, Carolrhoda Bks.) Lerner Publishing Group.

Manolis, Kay & Leslie, Tonya. Rosa Parks: A Life of Courage. 2007. (People of Character Ser.). (ENG., Illus.). 24p. (J). (gr. 2-5). lib. bdg. 25.95 *(978-1-60014-088-4(2))* Bellwether Media.

Mantell, Paul. Arthur Ashe: Young Tennis Champion. Henderson, Meryl, illus. 2006. (Childhood of Famous Americans Ser.). (ENG.). 224p. (J). (gr. 3-7). pap. 10.99 *(978-0-689-87346-1(8)*, Simon & Schuster/Paula Wiseman Bks.) Simon & Schuster/Paula Wiseman Bks.

Mara, Wil. Rosa Parks. (Rookie Biographies Ser.). (ENG., Illus.). 32p. (J). (gr. 1-2). 2004. pap. 4.95 *(978-0-516-27916-9(5))* 2007. pap. 4.95 *(978-0-531-12592-2(0))* Scholastic Library Publishing. (Children's Pr.).

—Rosa Parks: Mother of the Civil Rights Movement. 2014. (Rookie Biographies(tm) Ser.). (ENG.). 32p. (J). lib. bdg. 25.00 *(978-0-531-20561-7(4))*; pap. 5.95 *(978-0-531-21204-2(1))* Scholastic Library Publishing.

—Thurgood Marshall: Champion for Civil Rights. 2004. (Great Life Stories Ser.). (ENG., Illus.). 125p. (J). 30.50 *(978-0-531-12058-3(9)*, Watts, Franklin) Scholastic Library Publishing.

Marcovitz, Hal. Barack. 2007. (Obamas Ser.). (Illus.). 64p. (YA). (gr. 3-6). pap. 9.95 *(978-1-4222-1484-8(2))*; (gr. 4-7). lib. bdg. 19.95 *(978-1-4222-1477-0(X))* Mason Crest.

—Eddie Murphy. 2nd rev. ed. 2011. (Black Americans of Achievement Legacy Edition Ser.). 112p. (gr. 6-12). 35.00 *(978-1-60413-844-3(0))* Facts On File, Inc.

—Michelle. 2007. (Obamas Ser.). 64p. (YA). (gr. 3-6). pap. 9.95 *(978-1-4222-1485-5(0))*; (gr. 4-7). lib. bdg. 19.95 *(978-1-4222-1478-7(8))* Mason Crest.

Markel, Rita J. Jimi Hendrix. 2005. (Biography Ser.). (Illus.). 112p. (J). (gr. 6-12). lib. bdg. 27.93 *(978-0-8225-4990-1(5))* Lerner Publishing Group.

Marlowe, Sam. Learning about Dedication from the Life of Frederick Douglass. 2009. (Character Building Book Ser.). 24p. (gr. 2-3). 42.50 *(978-1-60854-970-2(4)*, PowerKids Pr.) Rosen Publishing Group, Inc., The.

Marsh, Carole. Barack Obama: Biography FunBook. 2009. (J). (gr. 2-9). pap. 3.99 *(978-0-635-07053-1(7))* Gallopade International.

—Benjamin Banneker. 2003. 12p. (gr. k-4). 2.95 *(978-0-635-02129-8(3))* Gallopade International.

—Carol Moseley Braun. 2003. 12p. (gr. k-4). 2.95 *(978-0-635-02384-1(9))* Gallopade International.

—Charles Drew: Dedicated Doctor. 2004. (1000 Readers Ser.). (Illus.). 12p. (J). (gr. k-4). per. 2.95 *(978-0-635-02528-9(0))* Gallopade International.

—Condoleezza Rice. 2003. 12p. (gr. k-4). 2.95 *(978-0-635-02385-8(7))* Gallopade International.

—Frederick Douglass. 2003. 12p. (gr. k-4). 2.95 *(978-0-635-02125-0(0))* Gallopade International.

—Garrett Morgan, Innovative Inventor. 2004. 12p. (gr. k-4). 2.95 *(978-0-635-02526-5(4))* Gallopade International.

—General Colin Powell. 2003. 12p. (gr. k-4). 2.95 *(978-0-635-02359-9(8))* Gallopade International.

—Granville Woods: Excellent Inventor. 2004. (1000 Readers Ser.). (Illus.). 14p. (J). (gr. k-4). pap. 2.95 *(978-0-635-02527-2(2))* Gallopade International.

—Meet Shirley Franklin, Mayor of Atlanta! 2003. 32p. (gr. 3-8). 21.95 *(978-0-635-01141-1(7))* Gallopade International.

—Michelle Obama: Biography FunBook. 2009. (J). (gr. 2-9). pap. 3.99 *(978-0-635-07054-8(5))* Gallopade International.

—Phillis Wheatley. 2003. 12p. (gr. k-4). 2.95 *(978-0-635-02371-1(7))* Gallopade International.

—Roberto Clemente: Baseball Hero & Humanitarian: Baseball Hero & Humanitarian. 2003. 12p. (gr. k-4). 2.95 *(978-0-635-02140-3(4))* Gallopade International.

—Sojourner Truth. 2003. 12p. (gr. k-4). 2.95 *(978-0-635-02355-1(5))* Gallopade International.

Marsico, Katie. Madame C. J. Walker. 2007. (21st Century Skills Library: Life Skills Biographies Ser.). (ENG.). 48p. (gr. 4-8). lib. bdg. 32.79 *(978-1-60279-074-2(4)*, 200043) Cherry Lake Publishing.

Martin, Isabel. Frederick Douglass, 1 vol. 2014. (Great African-Americans Ser.). (ENG., Illus.). 24p. (gr. k-1). pap. 5.95 *(978-1-4914-0507-9(4)*, Pebble Bks.) Capstone Press of Coughlan Cos.

—Jackie Robinson, 1 vol. 2014. (Great African-Americans Ser.). (ENG., Illus.). 24p. (gr. k-1). pap. 5.95 *(978-1-4914-0508-6(2)*, Pebble Bks.) Capstone Press of Coughlan Cos.

Martin, Michael & Martin, Michael J. Harriet Tubman & the Underground Railroad, 1 vol. Hoover, Dave & Anderson, Bill, illus. 2005. (Graphic History Ser.). (ENG.). 32p. (gr. 3-4). 30.65 *(978-0-7368-3829-0(5)*, Graphic Library) Capstone Press of Coughlan Cos.

Martin, Michael J. Harriet Tubman & the Underground Railroad, 1 vol. Hoover, Dave & Anderson, Bill, illus. 2005. (Graphic History Ser.). (ENG.). 32p. (gr. 3-4). per. 8.10 *(978-0-7368-5245-6(X)*, Graphic Library) Capstone Press of Coughlan Cos.

Martin, Oscar, Jr., creator. Doctors l.t. ed. 2003. (Illus.). 25p. (J). E-Book 19.95 incl. cd-rom *(978-0-9748416-5-6(X))* Build Your Story.

—Famous Women l.t. ed. 2003. (Illus.). 25p. (J). E-Book 19.95 incl. cd-rom *(978-0-9748416-8-7(4))* Build Your Story.

Marvis, Barbara. Day by Day with Lebron James. 2010. (Randy's Corner Ser.). (Illus.). 32p. (YA). (gr. -1-2). lib. bdg. 25.70 *(978-1-58415-858-5(1))* Mitchell Lane Pubs., Inc.

Marzollo, Jean. The Little Plant Doctor: The Story of George Washington Carver. Wilson-Max, Ken, illus. 2011. (ENG.). 32p. (J). (gr. -1-3). 16.95 *(978-0-8234-2325-5(5))* Holiday Hse., Inc.

Massie, Elizabeth. African American Educators. 2012. (J). pap. *(978-1-4222-2386-4(8))* Mason Crest.

—African American Educators. Hill, Marc Lamont, ed. 2012. (Major Black Contributions from Emancipation to Civil Rights Ser.). 64p. (J). (gr. 5). 22.95 *(978-1-4222-2373-4(6))* Mason Crest.

Mattern, Joanne. Coretta Scott King: Civil Rights Activist. (Women Who Shaped History Ser.). 24p. 2009. (gr. 2-3). 42.50 *(978-1-60854-816-3(3))* 2003. (Illus.). (J). lib. bdg. 19.95 *(978-0-8239-6504-5(X))* Rosen Publishing Group, Inc., The. (PowerKids Pr.).

—The Cost of Freedom: Crispus Attucks & the Boston Massacre. (Great Moments in American History Ser.). 32p. 2009. (gr. 3-3). 47.90 *(978-1-61513-153-2(1))* 2004. (Illus.). (J). (gr. 4-7). lib. bdg. 22.50 *(978-0-8239-4341-8(0))* Rosen Publishing Group, Inc., The.

—Count Basie. 2012. (J). lib. bdg. 29.95 *(978-1-61228-270-1(9))* Mitchell Lane Pubs., Inc.

—Donovan Mcnabb. 2004. (Robbie Reader Ser.). (Illus.). 32p. (J). (gr. 1-4). lib. bdg. 25.70 *(978-1-58415-294-1(X))* Mitchell Lane Pubs., Inc.

—LeBron James: Basketball Superstar, 1 vol. 2011. (Superstar Athletes Ser.). (ENG.). 24p. (gr. 1-2). pap. 7.29 *(978-1-4296-7309-9(5))*; pap. 41.70 *(978-1-4296-7310-5(9))*; lib. bdg. 25.32 *(978-1-4296-6562-9(9))* Capstone Press of Coughlan Cos.

—Simone Biles: Superstar Gymnast. 2017. (Rookie Biographies Ser.). (ENG.). 32p. (J). lib. bdg. 25.00 ***(978-0-531-23228-6(X)***, Children's Pr.) Scholastic Library Publishing.

Mattern, Joanne. Sojourner Truth: Early Abolitionist. (Women Who Shaped History Ser.). 24p. 2009. (gr. 2-3). 42.50 *(978-1-60854-821-7(X))* 2003. (Illus.). (J). lib. bdg. 22.60 *(978-0-8239-6502-1(3))* Rosen Publishing Group, Inc., The. (PowerKids Pr.).

Maurer, Tracy Nelson. LeBron James. 2015. (Famous Athletes Ser.). (ENG., Illus.). 24p. (gr. k-1). lib. bdg. 26.65 *(978-1-4914-6236-2(1))* Capstone Press of Coughlan Cos.

Maya Angelou. 2006. (Black Americans of Achievement Legacy Edition Ser.). (Illus.). 128p. (YA). (gr. 7-12). lib. bdg. 35.00 *(978-0-7910-9224-8(0))* Facts On File, Inc.

McCaffrey, Paul. Michelle Obama. 2010. (Women of Achievement Ser.). 144p. (gr. 6-12). 35.00 *(978-1-60413-911-2(0)*, Chelsea Hse.) Facts On File, Inc.

McClaurin, Irma & Schomp, Virginia. Facing the Future. 2007. (Drama of African-American History Ser.). 80p. (gr. 6). lib. bdg. 35.64 *(978-0-7614-2644-8(2)*, Benchmark Bks.) Marshall Cavendish Corp.

McDonnell, Julia. Harriet Tubman in Her Own Words. 2016. (Eyewitness to History Ser.). (ENG., Illus.). 32p. (J). (gr. 4-5). pap. 10.50 *(978-1-4824-4066-9(0))* Stevens, Gareth Publishing LLLP.

McDonough, Yona Zeldis. Who Was Harriet Tubman? Harrison, Nancy, illus. 2003. (Who Was... ? Ser.). 106p. (gr. 4-7). 15.00 *(978-0-7569-1590-2(2))* Perfection Learning Corp.

—Who Was Louis Armstrong? O'Brien, John A. & Harrison, Nancy, illus. 2004. (Who Was? Ser.). (ENG.). 112p. (J). (gr. 3-7). pap. 5.99 *(978-0-448-43368-4(0)*, Grosset & Dunlap) Penguin Young Readers Group.

—Who Was Rosa Parks? Harrison, Nancy & Marchesi, Stephen, illus. 2010. (Who Was? Ser.). (ENG.). 112p. (J). (gr. 3-7). pap. 5.99 *(978-0-448-45442-9(4)*, Grosset & Dunlap) Penguin Young Readers Group.

Mcdonough, Yona Zeldis. Who Was Sojourner Truth? 2015. (Who Was... ? Ser.). lib. bdg. 16.00 *(978-0-606-37560-3(0))* Turtleback Bks.

McDonough, Yona Zeldis & dePaola, Tomie. Who Was Sojourner Truth? Eldridge, Jim, illus. 2015. (Who Was? Ser.). (ENG.). 112p. (J). (gr. 3-7). 5.99 *(978-0-448-48678-9(4)*, Grosset & Dunlap) Penguin Young Readers Group.

McKissack, Patricia C. & McKissack, Fredrick, Jr. Sojourner Truth: Ain't I a Woman? 2003. (Illus.). 186p. (gr. 4-7). 17.20 *(978-0-7857-2515-2(6)*, Turtleback) Turtleback Bks.

McKissack, Patricia C. & McKissack, Fredrick L. Booker T. Washington: African-American Leader. 2013. (Famous African Americans Ser.). 24p. (J). (gr. k-3). pap. 7.95 *(978-1-4644-0194-7(2))*; (Illus.). lib. bdg. 22.60 *(978-0-7660-4100-4(X))* Enslow Pubs., Inc. (Enslow Elementary).

—Carter G. Woodson: Black History Pioneer. 2013. (Famous African Americans Ser.). 24p. (J). (gr. k-3). pap. 7.95 *(978-1-4644-0195-4(0)*, Enslow Elementary) Enslow Pubs., Inc.

—Frederick Douglass: Fighter Against Slavery. 2013. (Famous African Americans Ser.). 24p. (J). (gr. k-3). pap. 7.95 *(978-1-4644-0196-1(9)*, Enslow Elementary) Enslow Pubs., Inc.

—George Washington Carver: Scientist & Inventor. 2013. (Famous African Americans Ser.). 24p. (J). (gr. k-3). pap. 7.95 *(978-1-4644-0197-8(7))*; (Illus.). lib. bdg. 22.60 *(978-0-7660-4102-8(6))* Enslow Pubs., Inc. (Enslow Elementary).

—Madam C. J. Walker: Inventor & Millionaire. 2013. (Famous African Americans Ser.). 24p. (J). (gr. k-3). pap. 7.95 *(978-1-4644-0201-2(9)*, Enslow Elementary); (Illus.). 22.60 *(978-0-7660-4105-9(0))* Enslow Pubs., Inc.

—Paul Robeson: A Voice for Change. 2013. (Famous African Americans Ser.). 24p. (J). (gr. k-3). pap. 7.95 *(978-1-4644-0205-0(1))*; (Illus.). 22.60 *(978-0-7660-4107-3(7))* Enslow Pubs., Inc. (Enslow Elementary).

McLeese, Don. Crispus Attucks. 2005. (Heroes of the American Revolution Ser.). (Illus.). 32p. (gr. 2-5). 19.95 *(978-1-59515-218-3(0))* Rourke Educational Media.

McLendon, Jacquelyn. Phillis Wheatley: A Revolutionary Poet. 2009. (Library of American Lives & Times Ser.). 112p. (gr. 5-5). 69.20 *(978-1-60853-499-9(5))* Rosen Publishing Group, Inc., The.

McMickle, Marvin Andrew. Profiles in Black: Phat Facts for Teens. Elster, Jean Alicia, ed. 2008. (Illus.). 176p. (J). pap. 22.00 *(978-0-8170-1508-4(6))* Judson Pr.

McPherson, Stephanie Sammartino. Biography Coretta Scott King. 2007. (Biography Ser.). (Illus.). 112p. (YA). (gr. 7-12). lib. bdg. 29.27 *(978-0-8225-7156-8(0))* Twenty First Century Bks.

Meltzer, Brad. I Am Jackie Robinson. Eliopoulos, Christopher, illus. 2015. (Ordinary People Change the World Ser.). (ENG.). 40p. (J). (gr. k-3). 14.99 *(978-0-8037-4086-0(7)*, Dial Bks) Penguin Young Readers Group.

—I Am Martin Luther King, Jr. Eliopoulos, Christopher, illus. 2016. (Ordinary People Change the World Ser.). (ENG.). 40p. (J). (gr. k-3). 14.99 *(978-0-525-42852-7(6)*, Dial Bks) Penguin Young Readers Group.

—I Am Rosa Parks. Eliopoulos, Christopher, illus. 2014. (Ordinary People Change World Ser.). (ENG.). 40p. (J). (gr. -1-k). 14.99 *(978-0-8037-4085-3(9)*, Dial Bks) Penguin Publishing Group.

Melvin, Leland & Caulkhoven, Laurie. Chasing Space Young Readers' Edition. 2017. (Illus.). 240p. (J). (gr. 3-7). 17.99 *(978-0-06-266592-8(8)*, Amistad) HarperCollins Pubs.

Mendell, David & Thomson, Sarah L. Obama: A Promise of Change. 2008. (ENG., Illus.). 192p. (J). (gr. 3-7). pap. 6.99 *(978-0-06-169700-5(1)*, Amistad) HarperCollins Pubs.

Michelle Obama. 2009. (Political Profiles Ser.). 112p. (YA). (gr. 5-9). lib. bdg. 28.95 *(978-1-59935-090-5(4))* Reynolds, Morgan Inc.

Michelson, Richard. As Good As Anybody. Colón, Raúl, illus. 2013. (ENG.). 40p. (J). (gr. 1-4). 7.99 *(978-0-385-75387-6(X)*, Dragonfly Bks.) Random Hse. Children's Bks.

Miller, Barbara Kiely. Frederick Douglass. 2007. (Great Americans Ser.). 24p. (gr. 1-4). pap. 8.15 *(978-0-8368-8322-0(5))*; (SPA.). pap. 8.15 *(978-0-8368-8335-0(7))*; lib. bdg. 22.00 *(978-0-8368-8315-2(2))*; (SPA., Illus.). lib. bdg. 22.00 *(978-0-8368-8328-2(4))* Stevens, Gareth Publishing LLLP. (Weekly Reader Leveled Readers).

—George Washington Carver. 2007. (Great Americans Ser.). 24p. (gr. 1-4). pap. 8.15 *(978-0-8368-8320-6(9))*; lib. bdg. 22.00 *(978-0-8368-8313-8(6))*; (SPA., Illus.). pap. 8.15 *(978-0-8368-8334-3(9))*; (SPA., Illus.). lib. bdg. 22.00 *(978-0-8368-8327-5(6))* Stevens, Gareth Publishing LLLP. (Weekly Reader Leveled Readers).

Miller, Calvin Craig. A. Philip Randolph & the African American Labor Movement. 2005. (Civil Rights Leaders Ser.). (Illus.). 160p. (YA). (gr. 6-12). 26.95 *(978-1-931798-50-1(8))* Reynolds, Morgan Inc.

—Roy Wilkins: Leader of the NAACP. 2005. (Civil Rights Leaders Ser.). (Illus.). 176p. (YA). (gr. 6-12). 26.95 *(978-1-931798-49-5(4))* Reynolds, Morgan Inc.

Miller, Connie Colwell. Rosa Parks & the Montgomery Bus Boycott, 1 vol. Kalal, Dan, illus. 2006. (Graphic History Ser.). (ENG.). 32p. (gr. 3-4). 30.65 *(978-0-7368-6495-4(4)*, Graphic Library) Capstone Press of Coughlan Cos.

—Rosa Parks & the Montgomery Bus Boycott, 1 vol. Kalal, Dan, illus. 2006. (Graphic History Ser.). (ENG.). 32p. (gr. 3-4). per. 8.10 *(978-0-7368-9658-0(9)*, Graphic Library) Capstone Press of Coughlan Cos.

Miller, Moses. The Barack in Me: An Inspirational Novel for Young African American Males. 2009. 116p. pap. 10.99 *(978-0-9786929-2-6(6))* Mind Candy, LLC.

Miller, Ray. Shaquille O'Neal. 2003. (Stars of Sports Ser.). (ENG., Illus.). 48p. (J). 27.50 *(978-0-7377-1422-7(0)*, Kidhaven) Cengage Gale.

Miller, Raymond H. Kobe Bryant. 2003. (Stars of Sports Ser.). (ENG., Illus.). 48p. (J). 27.50 *(978-0-7377-1538-5(3)*, Greenhaven Pr., Inc.) Cengage Gale.

Miller, Robert H. Reflections of a Black Cowboy: Buffalo Soldiers. 2004. (J). pap. 9.95 *(978-0-940975-69-9(6)*, Sankofa Bks.) Just Us Bks., Inc.

—Reflections of a Black Cowboy: Cowboys. 2004. (J). pap. 9.95 *(978-0-940975-70-5(X)*, Sankofa Bks.) Just Us Bks., Inc.

Miller, William. Zora Hurston & the Chinaberry Tree. 2004. (Illus.). (J). (gr. k-3). spiral bd. *(978-0-616-03099-8(1))* Canadian National Institute for the Blind/Institut National Canadien pour les Aveugles.

Mills, Clifford W. Tupac Shakur. 2007. (Hip-Hop Stars Ser.). (Illus.). 104p. (YA). (gr. 7-12). lib. bdg. 30.00 *(978-0-7910-9495-2(2))* Facts On File, Inc.

Mis, Melody S. Meet Al Sharpton. (Civil Rights Leaders Ser.). 24p. (gr. 2-3). 2009. 42.50 *(978-1-61511-850-2(0)*, PowerKids Pr.) 2008. (Illus.). (YA). lib. bdg. 22.60 *(978-1-4042-4213-5(9))* Rosen Publishing Group, Inc., The.

—Meet Coretta Scott King. (Civil Rights Leaders Ser.). 24p. (gr. 2-3). 2009. 42.50 *(978-1-61511-851-9(9)*, PowerKids Pr.) 2008. (Illus.). (YA). lib. bdg. 22.60 *(978-1-4042-4211-1(2))* Rosen Publishing Group, Inc., The.

—Meet Jesse Jackson. (Civil Rights Leaders Ser.). 24p. (gr. 2-3). 2009. 42.50 *(978-1-61511-852-6(7)*, PowerKids Pr.) 2008. (Illus.). (YA). lib. bdg. 22.60 *(978-1-4042-4212-8(0))* Rosen Publishing Group, Inc., The.

—Meet Malcolm X. (Civil Rights Leaders Ser.). 24p. (gr. 2-3). 2009. 42.50 *(978-1-61511-853-3(5)*, PowerKids Pr.) 2008. (Illus.). (YA). lib. bdg. 22.60 *(978-1-4042-4214-2(7))* Rosen Publishing Group, Inc., The.

—Meet Martin Luther King Jr. 2009. (Civil Rights Leaders Ser.). 24p. (gr. 2-3). 42.50 *(978-1-61511-854-0(3)*, PowerKids Pr.) Rosen Publishing Group, Inc., The.

—Meet Martin Luther King Jr. 2008. (Civil Rights Leaders Ser.). (Illus.). 24p. (YA). (gr. 2-5). lib. bdg. 22.60 *(978-1-4042-4209-8(0))* Rosen Publishing Group, Inc., The.

—Meet Rosa Parks. (Civil Rights Leaders Ser.). 24p. (gr. 2-3). 2009. 42.50 *(978-1-61511-855-7(1)*, PowerKids Pr.) 2008. (Illus.). (YA). lib. bdg. 22.60 *(978-1-4042-4210-4(4))* Rosen Publishing Group, Inc., The.

Mohamed, Paloma. A Man Called Garvey: The Life & Times of the Great Leader Marcus Garvey. Braithwaithe, Barrington, illus. l.t. ed. 2004. (Majority Press Inc., Wisdom for Children Ser.: No. 1). (ENG.). 36p. (J). 12.95 *(978-0-912469-40-9(4))* Majority Pr., The.

Monceaux, Morgan & Katcher, Ruth. My Heroes, My People: African Americans & Native Americans in Thewest. Monceaux, Morgan, illus. 2004. (Illus.). 63p. (J). (gr. k-4). reprint ed. 18.00 *(978-0-7567-7868-2(9))* DIANE Publishing Co.

Moore, Barbara R. Sojourner Truth. 2005. (Illus.). 16p. (J). *(978-0-618-56039-4(4))* Houghton Mifflin Harcourt Publishing Co.

Moore, Cathy. Ellen Craft's Escape from Slavery. Braught, Mark, illus. 2010. (History Speaks: Picture Books Plus Reader's Theater Ser.). (ENG.). 48p. (gr. 2-4). pap. 9.95 *(978-0-7613-6672-0(5))*; lib. bdg. 27.93 *(978-0-7613-5875-6(7)*, Millbrook Pr.) Lerner Publishing Group.

Moore, Johnny Ray. The Story of Martin Luther King Jr. Wummer, Amy, illus. 2016. (J). *(978-0-8249-1974-0(2)*, Ideal Pubns.) Worthy Publishing.

Moore, Mary. Blacks in Ohio II, Vol. 1. Caesor, Ebraska, ed. Clay, Cliff, illus. (YA). (gr. 6-18). pap. 12.95 *(978-0-913678-31-2(7))* New Day Pr.

Morgan, Terri. Venus & Serena Williams: Grand Slam Sisters. (Sports Achievers Biographies Ser.). (Illus.). 2005. 80p. (gr. 7-12). lib. bdg. 22.60 *(978-0-8225-3684-0(6))* 2003. 64p. (J). (gr. 4-9). pap. 5.95 *(978-0-8225-9866-4(3)*, Carolrhoda Bks.) Lerner Publishing Group.

Moriarty, J. T. Phillis Wheatley: African American Poet. 2009. (Primary Sources of Famous People in American History Ser.). 32p. (gr. 2-3). 47.90 *(978-1-60851-717-6(9))* Rosen Publishing Group, Inc., The.

Morretta, Alison. Ida B. Wells-Barnett & the Crusade Against Lynching. 2016. (Primary Sources of the Civil Rights Movement Ser.). (Illus.). 64p. (J). (gr. 6-6). 34.21 *(978-1-5026-1874-0(5))* Cavendish Square Publishing.

—Rosa Parks & Civil Disobedience. 2016. (Primary Sources of the Civil Rights Movement Ser.). (Illus.). 64p. (J). (gr. 6-6). 34.21 *(978-1-5026-1870-2(2))* Cavendish Square Publishing.

Morris, Roz. Rosa Parks: Mother of the Civil Rights Movement. 2003. (Alabama Roots Biography Ser.). (Illus.). 109p. (J). *(978-1-878561-57-2(X))* Seacoast Publishing, Inc.

Morrison, Jessica. Hank Aaron: Home Run Hero. 2010. (Crabtree Groundbreaker Biographies Ser.). (ENG., Illus.). 112p. (J). pap. *(978-0-7787-2547-3(2))*; (gr. 5-8). lib. bdg. *(978-0-7787-2538-1(3))* Crabtree Publishing Co.

Murcia, Rebecca Thatcher. The Civil Rights Movement. 2005. (Monumental Milestones Ser.). (Illus.). 48p. (YA). (gr. 4-7). lib. bdg. 29.95 *(978-1-58415-401-3(2))* Mitchell Lane Pubs., Inc.

Murphy, Patricia J. Garrett Morgan: Inventor of the Traffic Light & Gas Mask. 2004. (Famous Inventors Ser.). (Illus.). 32p. (J). lib. bdg. 23.94 *(978-0-7660-2274-4(9))* Enslow Pubs., Inc.

Myers, Walter Dean. Frederick Douglass: The Lion Who Wrote History. Cooper, Floyd, illus. 2017. 40p. (J). (gr. -1-3). 17.99 *(978-0-06-027709-3(2))* HarperCollins Pubs.

—Ida B. Wells: Let the Truth Be Told. Christensen, Bonnie, illus. (ENG.). 40p. (J). (gr. -1-3). 2015. pap. 6.99 *(978-0-06-054468-3(6))* 2008. 16.99 *(978-0-06-027705-5(X))* HarperCollins Pubs. (Amistad).

—I've Seen the Promised Land: The Life of Dr. Martin Luther King, Jr. Jenkins, Leonard, illus. 2012. (ENG.). 40p. (J). (gr. -1-3). pap. 6.99 *(978-0-06-225002-5(7)*, Amistad) HarperCollins Pubs.

—Muhammad Ali: The People's Champion. Delinois, Alix, illus. 40p. (J). (gr. -1-3). 2016. pap. 6.99 *(978-0-06-443718-9(3)*, Amistad) 2009. (ENG.). 16.99 *(978-0-06-029131-0(1)*, Collins) HarperCollins Pubs.

Naden, Corinne J. & Blue, Rose. Mae Jeminson: Out of This World. 2003. (Gateway Biography Ser.: 4). (Illus.). 48p. lib. bdg. 23.90 *(978-0-7613-2570-3(0)*, Millbrook Pr.) Lerner Publishing Group.

Nagelhout, Ryan. Kevin Durant: Champion Basketball Star. 2017. (Sports Star Champions Ser.). 48p. (J). (gr. 5-6). lib. bdg. 27.93 ***(978-0-7660-8692-0(5))*** Enslow Pubs., Inc.

—Martin Luther King Jr. 2015. (Heroes of Black History Ser.). (ENG.). 32p. (J). (gr. 3-4). 26.60 *(978-1-4824-2906-0(3))* Stevens, Gareth Publishing LLLP.

—Serena Williams. 2016. (Sports MVPs Ser.). (Illus.). 24p. (J). (gr. 2-1). 22.60 *(978-1-4824-4642-5(1))* Stevens, Gareth Publishing LLLP.

Nagle, Jeanne. Chris Rock, 01 vols., 1. 2016. (Giants of Comedy Ser.). (ENG., Illus.). 112p. (J). 35.60 *(978-1-4994-6262-3(X)*, Rosen Young Adult) Rosen Publishing Group, Inc., The.

Nat Love. 2010. (Legends of the Wild West Ser.). (Illus.). 104p. (gr. 6-12). 35.00 *(978-1-60413-599-2(9)*, Chelsea Hse.) Facts On File, Inc.

Neis, Therese. Extraordinary African-American Poets. 2012. (African-American Collective Biographies Ser.). 112p. (J). (gr. 5-18). 33.27 *(978-1-59845-139-9(1))* Enslow Pubs., Inc.

Nelson, Maria. Coretta Scott King. 2011. (Civil Rights Crusaders Ser.). 24p. (gr. 2-5). (J). pap. 8.15 *(978-1-4339-5680-5(2)*, Gareth Stevens Learning Library); (YA). lib. bdg. 22.60 *(978-1-4339-5678-2(0))* Stevens, Gareth Publishing LLLP.

Nelson, Robin. George Washington Carver: A Life of Devotion. (Pull Ahead Books-Biographies Ser.). 32p. 2007. (ENG.). (gr. k-3). pap. 7.95 *(978-0-8225-6455-3(6))* 2006. (Illus.). (J). (gr. 3-7). lib. bdg. 22.60 *(978-0-8225-6461-4(0)*, Lerner Pubns.) Lerner Publishing Group.

Nelson, Vaunda Micheaux. Bad News for Outlaws: The Remarkable Life of Bass Reeves, Deputy U. S. Marshall. Christie, R. Gregory, illus. 2009. (Exceptional Social Studies Titles for Intermediate Grades). (ENG.). 40p. (J). (gr. 3-6). lib. bdg. 17.95 *(978-0-8225-6764-6(4))* Lerner Publishing Group.

Nichols, Catherine. Madam C.J. Walker. 2005. (Scholastic News Nonfiction Readers Ser.). (Illus.). 24p. (J). pap. 6.95

(978-0-516-24784-7(0), Children's Pr.) Scholastic Library Publishing.

Nichols, Kaitlyn. Martin Luther King. 2009. pap. 13.25 (978-1-60559-065-3(7)) Hameray Publishing Group, Inc.

Niver, Heather Moore. Sojourner Truth. 2015. (Heroes of Black History Ser.). (ENG., Illus.). 32p. (J). (gr. 3-4). pap. 10.50 (978-1-4824-2912-1(8)) Stevens, Gareth Publishing LLLP.

Norwich, Grace. I Am Lebron James. Simon, Ute, illus. 2014. 127p. (J). (978-0-545-79428-2(5)) Scholastic, Inc.

—Martin Luther King, Jr. Alba, Elisabeth, illus. 2012. (I Am Ser.: 4). (ENG.). 128p. (J). (gr. 2-5). pap. 5.99 (978-0-545-44780-5(1), Scholastic Paperbacks) Scholastic, Inc.

Ochiltree, Dianne. Molly, by Golly! The Legend of Molly Williams, America's First Female Firefighter. Kemly, Kathleen, illus. 2012. (ENG.). 32p. (J). (gr. 2-4). 16.95 (978-1-59078-721-2(8), Calkins Creek) Boyds Mills Pr.

O'Hern, Kerri & Raatma, Lucia. Jackie Robinson. 2006. (Graphic Biographies Ser.). (Illus.). 32p. (gr. 5-8). pap. 10.50 (978-0-8368-6250-8(3)) Stevens, Gareth Publishing LLLP.

Ollhoff, Jim. Pioneers of Equality, 1 vol. 2011. (African American History Ser.). (ENG., Illus.). 32p. (YA). (gr. 5-9). lib. bdg. 27.07 (978-1-61714-712-8(5)) ABDO Publishing Co.

Olson, Nathan. George Washington Carver: Ingenious Inventor, 1 vol. Tucker, Keith, illus. 2006. (Graphic Biographies Ser.). (ENG.). 32p. (gr. 3-4). 30.65 (978-0-7368-5484-9(3), Graphic Library) Capstone Press of Coughlan Cos.

Oprah Winfrey. 2004. (Illus.). 112p. pap. 9.95 (978-0-8225-5320-5(1)) Lerner Publishing Group.

Overbey, Theresa. Michael Jackson. I.t. ed. 2003. (Blue Banner Biography Ser.). (Illus.). 32p. (J). (gr. 3-8). lib. bdg. 25.70 (978-1-58415-216-3(8)) Mitchell Lane Pubs., Inc.

Paley, Caitlyn. Slave Narratives & the Writings of Freedmen. 2015. (Primary Sources of the Abolitionist Movement Ser.). (ENG., Illus.). 64p. (J). (gr. 6-6). 34.21 (978-1-5026-0524-5(4)) Cavendish Square Publishing.

Paprocki, Sherry. Oprah Winfrey. 2008. (Black Americans of Achievement: Legacy Edition Ser.). 112p. (gr. 6-12). pap. 11.95 (978-1-60413-326-4(0), Checkmark Bks.) Facts On File, Inc.

Paris, Stephanie Herweck. Jonathan Clarkson Gibbs: Reconstruction Revolutionary. 2016. (Primary Source Readers Ser.). 32p. (J). (gr. 4-4). pap. 8.99 (978-1-4938-3540-9(8)) Teacher Created Materials, Inc.

Passaro, John. Frederick Douglass. 2009. (Journey to Freedom Ser.). (ENG., Illus.). 32p. (J). (gr. 4-7). 29.93 (978-1-60253-122-2(6), 200388) Child's World, Inc., The.

Patrick, Denise Lewis. Jackie Robinson Strong Inside & Out. 2005. 44p. (J). lib. bdg. 15.00 (978-1-4242-0850-0(5)) Fitzgerald Bks.

—A Lesson for Martin Luther King, Jr. Pate, Rodney S., illus. 2003. (Ready-To-read COFA Ser.). (ENG.). 32p. (J). (gr. k-2). pap. 3.99 (978-0-689-85397-5(1), Simon Spotlight) Simon Spotlight.

Patrick, Denise Lewis & Time for Kids Editors. Jackie Robinson - Strong Inside & Out. 2005. (Time for Kids Ser.). (ENG., Illus.). 48p. (J). (gr. 2-4). pap. 3.99 (978-0-06-057600-4(6)) HarperCollins Pubs.

Payment, Simone. Buck Leonard. 2009. (Baseball Hall of Famers of the Negro Leagues Ser.). 112p. (gr. 5-8). 63.90 (978-1-61511-521-1(8), Rosen Reference) Rosen Publishing Group, Inc., The.

Penn, Sarah. Nat Love: African American Cowboy. 2009. (Primary Sources of Famous People in American History Ser.). 32p. (gr. 2-3). 47.90 (978-1-60851-706-0(3)) Rosen Publishing Group, Inc., The.

—Nat Love: African American Cowboy / Vaquero Afroamericano. 2009. (Famous People in American History/Grandes personajes en la historia de los Estados Unidos Ser.). (ENG & SPA.). 32p. (gr. 2-3). 47.90 (978-1-61512-551-7(5), Editorial Buenas Letras) Rosen Publishing Group, Inc., The.

—Nat Love: Vaquero Afroamericano. 2004. (Grandes personajes en la historia de los Estados Unidos Ser.). (SPA.). 32p. (gr. 4-8). pap. 10.00 (978-0-8239-4234-3(1), Rosen Classroom) Rosen Publishing Group, Inc., The.

—Nat Love: Vaquero afroamericano (Nat Love: African American Cowboy) 2009. (Grandes personajes en la historia de los Estados Unidos (Famous People in American History) Ser.). (SPA.). 32p. (gr. 2-3). 47.90 (978-1-61512-804-4(2), Editorial Buenas Letras) Rosen Publishing Group, Inc., The.

Perry, Clayton. Black Profiles: The North American Experience, Vol. 1. 2004. (Illus.). 50p. (YA). 12.99 (978-0-9762837-0-6(0)) Nubiano Project, Inc., The.

Peters, Gregory N. Serena & Venus Williams Tennis Stars, 1 vol. 2014. (Sports & Recreation Ser.). (ENG.). 48p. (gr. 4-12). 31.99 (978-1-4765-8075-3(8)) Capstone Press of Coughlan Cos.

Petry, Ann & Reynolds, Jason. Harriet Tubman: Conductor on the Underground Railroad. 2007. (ENG.). 256p. (J). (gr. 3-7). pap. 7.99 (978-0-06-446181-8(5), Amistad) HarperCollins Pubs.

Pferdehirt, Julia. Blue Jenkins: Working for Workers. 2011. (Badger Biographies Ser.). (ENG., Illus.). 160p. (J). pap. 12.95 (978-0-87020-427-2(0)) Wisconsin Historical Society.

Pingry, Patricia A. Meet Rosa Parks. Walker, Steven, illus. 2008. (ENG.). 32p. (J). (gr. k-3). per. 7.99 (978-0-8249-5578-6(1), Ideal Pubns.) Worthy Publishing.

—The Story of Coretta Scott King. Walker, Steven, illus. 2007. (ENG.). 26p. (J). (gr. 3-7). bds. 7.69 (978-0-8249-6717-8(8), Ideal Pubns.) Worthy Publishing.

—The Story of Rosa Parks. Walker, Steven, illus. (J). 2016. (978-0-8249-1987-0(4)) 2008. (ENG.). 24p. (gr. 3-7). bds. 7.69 (978-0-8249-6687-4(2)) Worthy Publishing. (Ideal Pubns.).

Pinkard, Alquan. Barcelona Brownsville: Life in the Hood. 2013. 136p. pap. 20.00 (978-0-9840204-7-8(0)) Pacific Raven Pr.

Pinkney, Andrea Davis. Duke Ellington. Pinkney, Brian, illus. 2006. (ENG.). 32p. (J). (gr. k-4). pap. 6.99 (978-0-7868-1420-6(9), Jump at the Sun) Hyperion Bks. for Children.

—Ella Fitzgerald: The Tale of a Vocal Virtuosa. Pinkney, Brian, illus. 2007. (ENG.). 32p. (J). (gr. k-4). pap. 6.99 (978-0-7868-1416-9(0), Jump at the Sun) Hyperion Bks. for Children.

—Hand in Hand: Ten Black Men Who Changed America. Pinkney, Brian, illus. 2012. (ENG.). 243p. (YA). (gr. 4-7). 19.99 (978-1-4231-4257-7(8)) Hyperion Pr.

Pittman, Rickey. Jim Limber Davis: A Black Orphan in the Confederate White House, 1 vol. Hierstein, Judith, illus. 2007. (ENG.). 32p. (J). (gr. k-3). 16.99 (978-1-58980-435-7(X)) Pelican Publishing Co., Inc.

Pizer, Carol. Michael Jackson, 1 vol. Saddleback Educational Publishing Staff, ed. unabr. ed. 2011. (Graphic Biographies Ser.). (ENG.). 25p. (YA). (gr. 9-12). pap. 7.95 (978-1-61651-265-1(2)) Saddleback Educational Publishing, Inc.

Plantz, Connie. The Life of Bessie Coleman: First African-American Woman Pilot. 2014. (Legendary African Americans Ser.). (Illus.). 96p. (J). (gr. 6-12). 27.94 (978-0-7660-6117-0(5)) Enslow Pubs., Inc.

Ponto, Joanna & Gnojewski, Carol. Martin Luther King Jr. Day. 2016. (Story of Our Holidays Ser.). (Illus.). 32p. (J). pap. 10.52 (978-0-7660-8340-0(3)) Enslow Pubs., Inc.

Poolos, Jamie & Poolos, J. Hank Aaron. 2007. (Baseball Superstars Ser.). (Illus.). 122p. (YA). (gr. 7-12). lib. bdg. 30.00 (978-0-7910-9536-2(3)) Facts On File, Inc.

Porter, Esther. Serena Williams. 2016. (Women in Sports Ser.). (ENG., Illus.). 24p. (gr. k-1). pap. 6.95 (978-1-4914-8569-9(8), Pebble Plus) Capstone Press of Coughlan Cos.

Porterfield, Jason. Frederick Douglass: Abolitionist & Fighter for Equality. 2017. (J). pap. **(978-1-68048-802-9(3)**, Britannica Educational Publishing) Rosen Publishing Group, Inc., The.

Prince, April Jones. Jackie Robinson - He Led the Way. Casilla, Robert, illus. 2007. (Penguin Young Readers, Level 3 Ser.). (ENG.). 48p. (J). (gr. 1-3). mass mkt. 3.99 (978-0-448-44721-6(5), Penguin Young Readers) Penguin Young Readers Group.

—Who Was Frederick Douglass? Squier, Robert & Harrison, Nancy, illus. 2014. (Who Was? Ser.). (ENG.). 112p. (J). (gr. 3-7). 5.99 (978-0-448-47911-8(7), Grosset & Dunlap) Penguin Young Readers Group.

Project Boy: Too Blessed to be Stressed, 1 bk. 2004. 117p. pap. 10.00 (978-0-9760441-0-9(2)) In The Hse. Publishing Co.

Raatma, Lucia. Barbara Jordan. 2013. 96p. (YA). (gr. 7-12). 39.93 (978-0-7614-4956-0(6)); pap. 19.99 (978-1-62712-114-9(5)) Cavendish Square Publishing.

—Michelle Obama, 1 vol. 2010. (First Ladies Ser.). (ENG.). 24p. (gr. k-1). lib. bdg. 26.65 (978-1-4296-5008-3(7), Pebble Plus) Capstone Press of Coughlan Cos.

—Shirley Chisholm. 2010. (Leading Women Ser.). 96p. (YA). (gr. 7-12). 39.93 (978-0-7614-4953-9(1)) Marshall Cavendish Corp.

Raber, Thomas R. Michael Jordan: Returning Champion. 4th rev. ed. 2005. (Sports Achievers Biographies Ser.). (Illus.). 80p. (gr. 7-12). pap. 5.95 (978-0-8225-0473-3(1)) Lerner Publishing Group.

Rajczak Nelson, Kristen. China Anne McClain: Actress, Singer, & Songwriter. 2016. (Junior Biographies Ser.). 24p. (J). pap. 9.35 (978-0-7660-8184-0(2)) Enslow Pubs., Inc.

—Serena Williams: Tennis Star. 2016. (Junior Biographies Ser.). (Illus.). 24p. (J). pap. 9.35 (978-0-7660-8181-9(8)) Enslow Pubs., Inc.

Rameck, Hunt, et al. We Beat the Street: How a Friendship Pact Led to Success. 2014. (ENG.). 208p. (J). 12.24 (978-1-63245-093-7(3)) Lectorum Pubns., Inc.

Randolph, Joanne. African American Explorers. 2017. (J). **(978-0-7660-9249-5(6))** Enslow Pubs., Inc.

—African American Inventors & Scientists. 2017. (J). **(978-0-7660-9248-8(8))** Enslow Pubs., Inc.

—African American Musicians & Entertainers. 2017. **(978-0-7660-9250-1(X))** Enslow Pubs., Inc.

—African American Politicians & Civil Rights Activists. 2017. (J). **(978-0-7660-9252-5(6))** Enslow Pubs., Inc.

Randolph, Ryan P. Black Cowboys. 2009. (Library of the Westward Expansion Ser.). 24p. (gr. 3-4). 42.50 (978-1-60853-933-8(4), PowerKids Pr.) Rosen Publishing Group, Inc., The.

Ransom, Candice. Maggie L. Walker: Pioneering Banker & Community Leader. 2008. (Trailblazer Biographies Ser.). (ENG.). 112p. (gr. 5-9). lib. bdg. 31.93 (978-0-8225-6611-3(7)) Lerner Publishing Group.

Rappaport, Doreen. Frederick's Journey: The Life of Frederick Douglass. Ladd, London, illus. 2015. (Big Words Ser.). (ENG.). 48p. (J). (gr. 1-3). 17.99 (978-1-4231-1438-3(8)) Disney Pr.

Raschka, Chris. Mysterious Thelonious. Raschka, Chris, illus. (Illus.). pap. 18.95 incl. audio compact disk (978-1-59112-421-4(2)) Live Oak Media.

Raum, Elizabeth. Lebron James. 2017. (Pro Sports Biographies Ser.). (ENG.). 24p. (gr. 1-4). 20.95 **(978-1-68151-138-2(X))** Amicus Publishing.

—Pro Sports Biographies: Lebron James. 2017. (Pro Sports Biographies Ser.). (ENG.). 24p. (J). (gr. 1-3). pap. 8.99 **(978-1-68152-169-5(5))** Amicus.

—Pro Sports Biographies: Serena Williams. 2017. (Pro Sports Biographies Ser.). (ENG.). 24p. (J). (gr. 1-3). pap. 8.99 **(978-1-68152-170-1(9))** Amicus.

—Serena Williams. 2017. (Pro Sports Biographies Ser.). (ENG.). 24p. (gr. 1-4). 20.95 **(978-1-68151-139-9(8))** Amicus Publishing.

Rausch, Monica. Crispus Attucks. 2007. (Grandes personajes (Spanish- Great Americans) Ser.). 24p. (gr. 1-4). (SPA.). pap. 8.15 (978-0-8368-7987-2(2)); (Illus.). lib. bdg. 22.00 (978-0-8368-7681-9(4)) Stevens, Gareth Publishing LLLP. (Weekly Reader Leveled Readers).

—Harriet Tubman. 2007. (Great Americans Ser.). (Illus.). 24p. (gr. 1-4). lib. bdg. 22.00 (978-0-8368-7686-4(5), Weekly Reader Leveled Readers) Stevens, Gareth Publishing LLLP.

Rausch, Monica L. Crispus Attucks. 2007. (Grandes personajes (Great Americans) Ser.). (SPA., Illus.). 24p. (gr. 1-4). lib. bdg. 22.00 (978-0-8368-7980-3(5), Weekly Reader Leveled Readers) Stevens, Gareth Publishing LLLP.

—Harriet Tubman. 2007. (Grandes personajes (Great Americans) Ser.). (ENG & SPA., Illus.). 24p. (gr. 1-4). lib. bdg. 22.00 (978-0-8368-7985-8(6), Weekly Reader Leveled Readers) Stevens, Gareth Publishing LLLP.

Redgrave, Naida. Shonda Rhimes: TV Producer, Screenwriter, & Showrunner. 2017. (Influential Lives Ser.). 128p. (J). (gr. 7-8). lib. bdg. 37.27 **(978-0-7660-8503-9(1))** Enslow Pubs., Inc.

Reef, Catherine. The Life of Paul Laurence Dunbar: Portrait of a Poet. 2014. (Legendary African Americans Ser.). (Illus.). 96p. (J). (gr. 6-12). 27.94 (978-0-7660-6152-1(3)); pap. 10.95 (978-0-7660-6153-8(1)) Enslow Pubs., Inc.

—William Grant Still: African-American Composer. 2004. (Modern Music Masters Ser.). (Illus.). 112p. (YA). (gr. 6-12). 23.95 (978-1-931798-11-2(7)) Reynolds, Morgan Inc.

Regis, Frankye. A Voice from the Civil Rights Era, 1 vol. 2004. (Voices of Twentieth-Century Conflict Ser.). (Illus.). 184p. (C). 43.00 (978-0-313-32998-2(2), GR2998, Greenwood) ABC-CLIO, LLC.

Rhynes, Martha E. Gwendolyn Brooks: Poet from Chicago. 2004. (World Writers Ser.). (Illus.). 112p. (YA). (gr. 6-12). 23.95 (978-1-931798-05-1(2)) Reynolds, Morgan Inc.

Ribke, Simone T. Ruby Bridges. 2015. (Rookie Biographies(r) Ser.). (ENG., Illus.). 32p. (J). pap. 5.95 (978-0-531-20993-6(8)) Scholastic Library Publishing.

Rice, Condoleezza. Condoleezza Rice: A Memoir of My Extraordinary, Ordinary Family & Me. 2012. (ENG.). 336p. (J). (gr. 5). pap. 8.99 (978-0-385-73880-4(3), Ember) Random Hse. Children's Bks.

Rice, Dona. Jackie Robinson: Hometown Hero. 2016. (Primary Source Readers Ser.). (Illus.). 32p. (J). (gr. 2-2). 8.99 (978-1-4938-2560-8(7)) Teacher Created Materials, Inc.

Rice, Earle. Charlie Parker. 2012. (J). lib. bdg. 29.95 (978-1-61228-266-4(0)) Mitchell Lane Pubs., Inc.

Rich, Mari. Computer Science, Vol. 10. Gilmore, Malinda & Pouson, Mel, eds. 2016. (Black Achievement in Science Ser.). (Illus.). 64p. (J). (gr. 7). 23.95 (978-1-4222-3557-7(2)) Mason Crest.

—Engineering, Vol. 10. Gilmore, Malinda & Pouson, Mel, eds. 2016. (Black Achievement in Science Ser.). 64p. (J). (gr. 7). 23.95 (978-1-4222-3558-4(0)) Mason Crest.

—Inventors, Vol. 10. Gilmore, Malinda & Pouson, Mel, eds. 2016. (Black Achievement in Science Ser.). 64p. (J). (gr. 7). 23.95 (978-1-4222-3560-7(2)) Mason Crest.

—Medicine, Vol. 10. Gilmore, Malinda & Pouson, Mel, eds. 2016. (Black Achievement in Science Ser.). (Illus.). 64p. (J). (gr. 7). 23.95 (978-1-4222-3561-4(0)) Mason Crest.

—Space, Vol. 10. Gilmore, Malinda & Pouson, Mel, eds. 2016. (Black Achievement in Science Ser.). (Illus.). 64p. (J). (gr. 7). 23.95 (978-1-4222-3563-8(7)) Mason Crest.

—Technology, Vol. 10. Gilmore, Malinda & Pouson, Mel, eds. 2016. (Black Achievement in Science Ser.). (Illus.). 64p. (J). (gr. 7). 23.95 (978-1-4222-3564-5(5)) Mason Crest.

Ridley, Sarah. Martin Luther King: ...And the Fight for Equality. 2013. (History Makers Ser.). (Illus.). 24p. (J). (gr. 2-4). 25.65 (978-1-59771-389-4(9)) Sea-To-Sea Pubns.

Rigby Education Staff. John Henry. (Illus.). 16p. (J). pap. 30.00 (978-0-7635-6490-2(7), 764907C99) Rigby Education.

Riley, John B. George Washington Carver: A Photo Biography. l.t. ed. 2004. (First Biographies Ser.). (Illus.). 24p. (YA). (gr. 5-18). 16.95 (978-1-883846-62-6(5), First Biographies) Reynolds, Morgan Inc.

Rinaldo, Denise. Rosa Parks: With a Discussion of Courage. 2003. (Values in Action Ser.). (J). (978-1-59203-061-3(0)) Learning Challenge, Inc.

Ringgold, Faith. Henry Ossawa Tanner: His Boyhood Dream Comes True. Ringgold, Faith, illus. 2011. (ENG., Illus.). 32p. (J). (gr. 1-2). 17.50 (978-1-59373-092-5(6)) Bunker Hill Publishing, Inc.

—If a Bus Could Talk: The Story of Rosa Parks. Ringgold, Faith, illus. 2003. (ENG., Illus.). 32p. (J). (gr. k-4). pap. 7.99 (978-0-689-85676-1(8), Aladdin) Simon & Schuster Children's Publishing.

Rivera, Sheila. Martin Luther King Jr: A Life of Determination. 2006. (Pull Ahead Bks.). (Illus.). 32p. (J). (gr. 3-7). lib. bdg. 22.60 (978-0-8225-3477-8(0), Lerner Pubns.) Lerner Publishing Group.

Rivera, Ursula. Aretha Franklin. (Rock & Roll Hall of Famers Ser.). 112p. (gr. 5-8). 2009. 63.90 (978-1-60852-467-9(1), Rosen Reference) 2006. (Illus.). (YA). lib. bdg. 34.60 (978-0-8239-3639-7(2)) Rosen Publishing Group, Inc., The.

—The Supremes. (Rock & Roll Hall of Famers Ser.). 112p. (gr. 5-8). 2009. 63.90 (978-1-60852-479-2(5), Rosen Reference) 2006. (Illus.). (YA). lib. bdg. 34.60 (978-0-8239-3527-7(2)) Rosen Publishing Group, Inc., The.

Robbins, Trina. Bessie Coleman: Daring Stunt Pilot, 1 vol. Steacy, Ken, illus. 2007. (Graphic Biographies Ser.). (ENG.). 32p. (gr. 3-4). per. 8.10 (978-0-7368-7903-3(X), Graphic Library) Capstone Press of Coughlan Cos.

Roberts, Russell. C. C. Sabathia. 2011. (Blue Banner Biography Ser.). (Illus.). 32p. (YA). (gr. 4-7). lib. bdg. 25.70 (978-1-61228-053-0(6)) Mitchell Lane Pubs., Inc.

Robertson, Theda Robinson. Journey to a Free Land: The Story of Nicodemus, the First All Black Town West of the Mississippi. 2006. (Illus.). (J). (978-0-9705721-6-5(6)) Written Images, Inc.

Robinson, Sharon. Promises to Keep: How Jackie Robinson Changed America. 2004. (ENG., Illus.). 64p. (J). (gr. 3-7). 17.99 (978-0-439-42592-6(1)) Scholastic, Inc.

Robson, David. Soledad O'Brien. 2010. (Transcending Race in America: Biographies of Biracial Achievers Ser.). (Illus.). 64p. (J). (gr. 5-18). lib. bdg. 22.95 (978-1-4222-1617-0(9)) Mason Crest.

Roby, Cynthia A. & Rohan, Rebecca. Langston Hughes. 2016. (Artists of the Harlem Renaissance Ser.). (ENG.). 128p. (J). (gr. 9-9). lib. bdg. 45.64 (978-1-5026-1064-5(7)) Cavendish Square Publishing.

Rohan, Rebecca Carey. Thurgood Marshall: The First African-American Supreme Court Justice. 2016. (Great American Thinkers Ser.). 128p. (J). (gr. 9-9). 45.64 (978-1-5026-1932-7(6)) Cavendish Square Publishing.

Rolfe, John. Ken Griffey, Jr. Superstar Centerfielder. 2009. (Sports Illustrated for Kids Bks). 176p. (gr. 7-12). 63.90 (978-1-60853-149-3(X)) Rosen Publishing Group, Inc., The.

Rolfe, John, et al. Ken Griffey, Jr. Superstar Centerfielder. 2005. (Sports Illustrated for Kids Books Ser.). (Illus.). 176p. (YA). (gr. 7-12). lib. bdg. 33.25 (978-0-8239-3687-8(2)) Rosen Publishing Group, Inc., The.

Roome, Hugh. Martin Luther King Jr. 2017. (Rookie Biographies Ser.). (ENG.). 32p. (J). pap. 5.95 **(978-0-531-23861-5(X)**, Children's Pr.) Scholastic Library Publishing.

Roop, Peter & Roop, Connie. Let's Dream, Martin Luther King, Jr.! 2004. (Scholastic Chapter Book Biography Ser.). (Illus.). 59p. (J). pap. (978-0-439-55443-5(8)) Scholastic, Inc.

Rowh, Mark. The Life of W. E. B. du Bois: Civil Rights Champion. 2015. (Legendary African Americans Ser.). 96p. (J). (gr. 6-12). 27.94 (978-0-7660-6280-1(5)); pap. 10.95 (978-0-7660-6281-8(3)) Enslow Pubs., Inc.

Roza, Greg. Venus & Serena Williams: The Sisters of Tennis. 2006. (Tony Stead Nonfiction Independent Reading Collection). (ENG.). 24p. (gr. 3-6). pap. 8.85 (978-1-4042-5537-1(0)) Rosen Publishing Group, Inc., The.

Ruffin, Frances E. Her Story, Her Words: The Narrative of Sojourner Truth. (Great Moments in American History Ser.). 32p. 2009. (gr. 3-3). 47.90 (978-1-61513-144-0(2)) 2004. (Illus.). (gr. 4-8). lib. bdg. 22.50 (978-0-8239-4387-6(9), Rosen Reference) Rosen Publishing Group, Inc., The.

—Sally Hemings. 2009. (American Legends Ser.). 24p. (gr. 3-3). 42.50 (978-1-61511-386-6(X), PowerKids Pr.) Rosen Publishing Group, Inc., The.

—Sojourner Truth: Early Abolitionist. 2009. (American Legends Ser.). 24p. (gr. 3-3). 42.50 (978-1-61511-387-3(8), PowerKids Pr.) Rosen Publishing Group, Inc., The.

Ruiz, Rachel. When Rosa Parks Went Fishing. Fedele, Chiara, illus. 2017. (Leaders Doing Headstands Ser.). (ENG.). 32p. (gr. 2-3). lib. bdg. 27.99 **(978-1-5158-1574-7(9))** Picture Window Bks.

Russell-Brown, Katheryn. Little Melba & Her Big Trombone. Morrison, Frank, illus. 2014. (ENG.). 40p. (J). 18.95 (978-1-60060-898-8(1)) Lee & Low Bks., Inc.

Ryan, Pam Muñoz. When Marian Sang: The True Recital of Marian Anderson. Selznick, Brian, illus. pap. incl. audio compact disk (978-1-59112-949-3(4)); pap. 18.95 incl. audio compact disk (978-1-59112-947-9(8)); pap. incl. audio (978-1-59112-945-5(1)); pap. 16.95 incl. audio (978-1-59112-943-1(5)) Live Oak Media.

Saddleback Educational Publishing Staff. Beyonce, 1 vol. 2015. (Hip-Hop Biographies Ser.). (ENG.). 48p. (YA). (gr. 9-12). 11.95 (978-1-62250-927-0(7)) Saddleback Educational Publishing, Inc.

—Sean Combs, 1 vol. 2015. (Hip-Hop Biographies Ser.). (ENG.). 48p. (YA). (gr. 9-12). 11.95 (978-1-62250-929-4(3)) Saddleback Educational Publishing, Inc.

Saddleback Educational Publishing Staff, ed. Jackie Robinson, 1 vol. unabr. ed. 2008. (Graphic Biographies Ser.). (ENG., Illus.). 25p. (YA). (gr. 9-12). pap. 7.95 (978-1-59905-225-0(3)) Saddleback Educational Publishing, Inc.

—Martin Luther King Jr., 1 vol. unabr. ed. 2008. (Graphic Biographies Ser.). (ENG., Illus.). 25p. (YA). (gr. 9-12). pap. 7.95 (978-1-59905-227-4(X)) Saddleback Educational Publishing, Inc.

Salazar, Sam. Jordin Sparks. 2013. (Rising Stars Ser.). 32p. (J). (gr. 3-6). pap. 10.50 (978-1-4339-8982-7(4)) Stevens, Gareth Publishing LLLP.

Salazar, Sam & Kennon, Michou. Jordin Sparks. 2013. 32p. (J). (gr. 3-6). 25.25 (978-1-4339-8981-0(6)) Stevens, Gareth Publishing LLLP.

Sammons, Sandra Wallus. Zora Neale Hurston: Wrapped in Rainbows. 2014. (Illus.). 67p. (J). pap. (978-1-56164-611-1(3)) Pineapple Pr., Inc.

Sanders, Nancy I. Frederick Douglass for Kids: His Life & Times, with 21 Activities. 2012. (For Kids Ser.). (ENG., Illus.). 144p. (J). (gr. 4). pap. 16.95 (978-1-56976-717-7(3)) Chicago Review Pr., Inc.

Sandler, Michael & Zegers, Charlie. Amar'E Stoudemire. 2012. (Basketball Heroes Making a Difference Ser.). 24p. (J). (gr. 1-6). lib. bdg. 23.93 (978-1-61772-442-8(4)) Bearport Publishing Co., Inc.

—Derrick Rose. 2012. (Basketball Heroes Making a Difference Ser.). 24p. (J). (gr. 1-6). lib. bdg. 23.93 (978-1-61772-439-8(4)) Bearport Publishing Co., Inc.

—Dwyane Wade. 2012. (Basketball Heroes Making a Difference Ser.). 24p. (J). (gr. 1-6). lib. bdg. 23.93 (978-1-61772-441-1(6)) Bearport Publishing Co., Inc.

—Kevin Durant. 2012. (Basketball Heroes Making a Difference Ser.). 24p. (J). (gr. 1-6). lib. bdg. 23.93 (978-1-61772-440-4(8)) Bearport Publishing Co., Inc.

Sapet, Kerrily. Halle Berry. (Transcending Race in America Ser.). (Illus.). 64p. (J). 2010. (gr. 4-8). 22.95 (978-1-4222-1612-5(8)) 2009. (gr. 5-18). pap. 9.95 (978-1-4222-1626-2(8)) Mason Crest.

—Halle Berry: Academy Award/Winning Actress. 2012. (Transcending Race Ser.). 64p. (J). (gr. 5). 22.95 (978-1-4222-2729-9(4)) Mason Crest.

—John Lewis. 2009. (Political Profiles Ser.). 100p. (YA). (gr. 5-9). 28.95 (978-1-59935-130-8(7)) Reynolds, Morgan Inc.

Savage, Jeff. Barry Bonds. 2008. pap. 40.95 (978-1-58013-717-1(2)) 2004. (ENG., Illus.). 32p. (gr. 2-5). lib. bdg. 25.26 (978-0-8225-3688-8(9)) 2008. (Illus.). 32p. (J). (gr. 3-7). lib. bdg. 23.93 (978-1-58013-611-2(7), Lerner Pubns.) Lerner Publishing Group.

—Barry Bonds: Record Breaker. 2nd rev. ed. 2003. (Sports Achievers Biographies Ser.). (Illus.). 64p. (J). (gr. 4-9). 5.95 (978-0-8225-0472-6(3), Carolrhoda Bks.) Lerner Publishing Group.

—Kobe Bryant. (Amazing Athletes Ser.). (Illus.). 32p. (gr. 2-5). 2005. (YA). lib. bdg. 22.60 (978-0-8225-1300-1(5)) 2003. (J). pap. 6.95 (978-0-8225-9849-7(3)) Lerner Publishing Group.

—LeBron James (3rd Revised Edition) 2016. (Amazing Athletes Ser.). (ENG., Illus.). 32p. (J). (gr. 2-5). pap. 7.95 (978-1-5124-0416-6(0)) Lerner Publishing Group.

—Prince Fielder. 2013. (Amazing Athletes Ser.). (ENG., Illus.). 32p. (gr. 2-5). lib. bdg. 25.26 (978-0-7613-8668-1(8)) Lerner Publishing Group.

Sawyer, Kem Knapp. Harriet Tubman - A Photographic Story of a Life. 2010. (DK Biography Ser.). (ENG.). 128p. (J). (gr. 5-12). 6.99 (978-0-7566-5806-9(3), DK Children) Dorling Kindersley Publishing, Inc.

Scarbrough, Mary Hertz. African American Writers & Journalists. 2012. pap. (978-1-4222-2389-5(2)) Mason Crest.

—African American Writers & Journalists. Hill, Marc Lamont, ed. 2012. (Major Black Contributions from Emancipation to Civil Rights Ser.). 64p. (J). (gr. 5). 22.95 (978-1-4222-2376-5(0)) Mason Crest.

Schier, Helga. George Washington Carver: Agricultural Innovator, 1 vol. 2008. (Essential Lives Set 2 Ser.). (ENG.,

Illus.). 112p. (J). (gr. 6-12). lib. bdg. 35.64 *(978-1-60453-035-3(9))* ABDO Publishing Co.

Schoell, William. "I Can Do Anything" The Sammy Davis, Jr. Story. 2004. (Avisson Young Adult Ser.). (Illus.). 116p. (J). pap. 19.95 *(978-1-888105-61-2(5))* Avisson Pr., Inc.

Scholastic Library Publishing Staff, contrib. by. African American Biographies, 10 vols. 2006. (Illus.). (YA). (gr. 6-12). 529.00 *(978-0-7172-6090-4(9)*, Grolier Online) Scholastic Library Publishing.

Schraff, Anne. Charles Drew: Pioneer in Medicine. 2003. (Famous Inventors Ser.). (Illus.). 32p. (J). (gr. 1-4). lib. bdg. 22.60 *(978-0-7660-2008-5(8))* Enslow Pubs., Inc.

—Dr. Charles Drew: Blood Bank Innovator. 2003. (African-American Biographies Ser.). (Illus.). 112p. (J). (gr. 6-12). lib. bdg. 27.94 *(978-0-7660-2117-4(3))* Enslow Pubs., Inc.

—The Life of Dr. Charles Drew: Blood Bank Innovator. 2015. (Legendary African Americans Ser.). 96p. (J). (gr. 6-12). pap. 10.95 *(978-0-7660-6266-5(X))* Enslow Pubs., Inc.

—The Life of Frederick Douglass: Speaking Out Against Slavery. 2014. (Legendary African Americans Ser.). (Illus.). 96p. (J). (gr. 6-12). pap. 10.95 *(978-0-7660-6133-0(7))* Enslow Pubs., Inc.

—The Life of Harriet Tubman: Moses of the Underground Railroad. 2014. (Legendary African Americans Ser.). (Illus.). 96p. (J). (gr. 6-12). 27.94 *(978-0-7660-6137-8(X))* Enslow Pubs., Inc.

—Marcus Garvey: Controversial Champion of Black Pride. 2004. (African-American Biographies Ser.). (Illus.). 128p. (J). lib. bdg. 26.60 *(978-0-7660-2168-6(8))* Enslow Pubs., Inc.

—Wilma Rudolph: The Greatest Woman Sprinter in History. 2004. (African-American Biographies Ser.). (Illus.). 112p. (J). lib. bdg. 26.60 *(978-0-7660-2291-1(9))* Enslow Pubs., Inc.

Schraff, Anne E. Booker T. Washington: Character Is Power. 2006. (African-American Biography Library). (Illus.). 128p. (J). (gr. 3-7). lib. bdg. 33.27 *(978-0-7660-2535-6(7))* Enslow Pubs., Inc.

—Ida B. Wells-Barnett: Strike a Blow Against Glaring Evil. 2008. (African-American Biography Library). (Illus.). 128p. (J). (gr. 6-18). lib. bdg. 33.27 *(978-0-7660-2704-6(X))* Enslow Pubs., Inc.

—Martin Luther King, Jr: We Shall Overcome. 2005. (African-American Biography Library). (Illus.). 128p. (J). (gr. 6-13). lib. bdg. 33.27 *(978-0-7660-1774-0(5))* Enslow Pubs., Inc.

—Rosa Parks: Tired of Giving In. 2005. (African-American Biography Library). (Illus.). 128p. (J). (gr. 6-12). lib. bdg. 33.27 *(978-0-7660-2463-2(6))* Enslow Pubs., Inc.

Schroeder, Alan. Baby Flo: Florence Mills Lights up the Stage. Van Wright, Cornelius & Hu, Ying-Hwa, illus. 2012. (ENG.). 40p. (J). 18.95 *(978-1-60060-410-2(2))* Lee & Low Bks., Inc.

—Booker T. Washington: Educator & Racial Spokesman. 2004. (Black Americans of Achievement Ser.). (Illus.). 112p. (gr. 6-12). 35.00 *(978-0-7910-8253-9(9)*, Chelsea Hse.) Facts On File, Inc.

Schroeder, Alan & National Geographic Learning Staff. In Her Hands: The Story of Sculptor Augusta Savage. Bereal, JaeMe, illus. 2009. (ENG.). 48p. (C). pap. 16.95 *(978-1-60060-989-3(9))* National Geographic School Publishing, Inc.

Schroeder, Alan & Wagner, Heather Lehr. Josephine Baker: Entertainer. 2006. (Black Americans of Achievement Ser.). (Illus.). 119p. (YA). (gr. 7-12). lib. bdg. 35.00 *(978-0-7910-9212-5(7))* Facts On File, Inc.

Schroff, Laura & Tresniowski, Alex. An Invisible Thread Christmas Story. Root, Barry, illus. 2015. (ENG.). 32p. (J). (gr. -1-3). 17.99 *(978-1-4814-1930-7(7)*, Little Simon) Little Simon.

Schuette, Sarah L. Garrett Morgan, 1 vol. 2014. (Great African-Americans Ser.). (ENG.). 24p. (gr. k-1). lib. bdg. 21.99 *(978-1-4914-0504-8(X)*, Pebble Bks.) Capstone Press of Coughlan Cos.

Schuette, Sarah L., et al. Great African-Americans, 1 vol. 2014. (Great African-Americans Ser.). (ENG.). 24p. (gr. k-1). 131.94 *(978-1-4914-0524-6(4)*, Pebble Bks.) Capstone Press of Coughlan Cos.

Schuldt, Lori Meek. Martin Luther King, Jr: With Profiles of Mohandas K. Gandhi & Nelson Mandela. 2006. (Biographical Connections Ser.). (Illus.). 112p. (J). *(978-0-7166-1822-5(2))* World Bk., Inc.

Schulman, Arlene. Muhammad Ali. (Just the Facts Biographies Ser.). (Illus.). (J). (gr. 6-12). 2005. 112p. 27.93 *(978-0-8225-2448-9(1))* 2003. 128p. pap. 7.95 *(978-0-8225-9693-6(8)*, Lerner Pubns.) Lerner Publishing Group.

Schuman, Michael. Will Smith: A Biography of Rapper Turned Movie Star. 2013. (African-American Icons Ser.). 104p. (J). (gr. 6-12). 27.94 *(978-0-7660-3994-0(3))* Enslow Pubs., Inc.

Schuman, Michael A. Barack Obama: We Are One People. 2008. (African-American Biography Library). (Illus.). 128p. (J). (gr. 3-7). lib. bdg. 33.27 *(978-0-7660-2891-3(7))* Enslow Pubs., Inc.

—Barack Obama: We Are One People, Revised & Expanded. rev. ed. 2009. (African-American Biography Library). (Illus.). 160p. (J). (gr. 6). lib. bdg. 33.27 *(978-0-7660-3649-9(9))* Enslow Pubs., Inc.

—Frederick Douglass: Truth Is of No Color. 2009. (Americans—the Spirit of a Nation Ser.). (Illus.). 128p. (J). (gr. 5-12). lib. bdg. 33.27 *(978-0-7660-3025-1(3))* Enslow Pubs., Inc.

—Halle Berry: Beauty Is Not Just Physical. 2006. (African-American Biography Library). (Illus.). 112p. (J). (gr. 6-12). lib. bdg. 33.27 *(978-0-7660-2467-0(9))* Enslow Pubs., Inc.

—The Life of Martin Luther King, Jr: Leader for Civil Rights. 2014. (Legendary African Americans Ser.). (Illus.). 96p. (J). (gr. 6-12). 27.94 *(978-0-7660-6147-7(7))* Enslow Pubs., Inc.

—Will Smith: A Biography of a Rapper Turned Movie Star. 2013. (African-American Icons Ser.). 104p. (J). (gr. 6-12). pap. 10.95 *(978-1-59845-397-3(1))* Enslow Pubs., Inc.

—Will Smith: I Like Blending a Message with Comedy. 2006. (African-American Biography Library). (Illus.). 128p. (J). (gr. 6). lib. bdg. 33.27 *(978-0-7660-2465-6(2)*, 1250489) Enslow Pubs., Inc.

Schuman, Michael A. & Schraff, Anne E. Martin Luther King Jr: Fighting for Civil Rights. 2017. (Rebels with a Cause Ser.). 128p. (gr. 8-8). lib. bdg. 37.27 ***(978-0-7660-8511-4(2))*** Enslow Pubs., Inc.

Schwartz, Heather E. Mary McLeod Bethune: Education & Equality. 2016. (Primary Source Readers Ser.). 32p. (J). (gr. 4-4). pap. 8.99 *(978-1-4938-3545-4(9))* Teacher Created Materials, Inc.

—NASA Mathematician Katherine Johnson. 2017. (STEM Trailblazer Bios Ser.). (ENG.). 32p. (J). (gr. 2-5). 26.65 ***(978-1-5124-5703-2(5))*** Lerner Publishing Group.

—Super Soaker Inventor Lonnie Johnson. 2017. (STEM Trailblazer Bios Ser.). (ENG.). 32p. (J). (gr. 2-5). 26.65 ***(978-1-5124-3447-7(7))*** Lerner Publishing Group.

Schwartz, Simon. First Man: Reimagining Matthew Henson. Watkinson, Laura, tr. 2015. (ENG., Illus.). 160p. (YA). (gr. 8-12). 31.99 *(978-1-4677-8856-4(2)*, Graphic Universe™) Lerner Publishing Group.

—First Man: The Voyages of Matthew Henson. Watkinson, Laura, tr. from GER. 2015. (ENG., Illus.). 160p. (J). (gr. 8-12). 31.99 *(978-1-4677-5842-0(6)*, Graphic Universe™) Lerner Publishing Group.

Scraper, Katherine. George Washington Carver. 2011. (Early Connections Ser.). (J). *(978-1-61672-551-8(6))* Benchmark Education Co.

Sexton, Colleen. Jackie Robinson: A Life of Determination. 2007. (People of Character Ser.). (ENG., Illus.). 24p. (J). (gr. 2-5). lib. bdg. 25.95 *(978-1-60014-089-1(0))* Bellwether Media.

Shafer, Susan. Jesse Owens: Fastest Human. 2005. (J). pap. *(978-1-4108-4207-7(X))* Benchmark Education Co.

Shange, Ntozake. Coretta Scott. Nelson, Kadir, illus. (ENG.). 32p. (J). (gr. -1-4). 2011. pap. 6.99 *(978-0-06-125366-9(9))* 2009. 17.99 *(978-0-06-125364-5(2))* HarperCollins Pubs. (Tegen, Katherine Bks).

Shange, Ntozake. Float Like a Butterfly. Rodriguez, Edel, illus. 2017. (ENG.). 40p. (J). (gr. -1-3). 17.99 ***(978-1-368-00827-3(5)***, Jump at the Sun) Hyperion Bks. for Children.

Sharp, Anne Wallace. Coretta Scott King. 2008. (People in the News Ser.). (ENG., Illus.). 128p. (gr. 7-10). lib. bdg. 39.40 *(978-1-4205-0087-5(2)*, LML02109-242091, Lucent Bks.) Cengage Gale.

—Women Civil Rights Leaders. 2012. (Lucent Library of Black History Ser.). (ENG., Illus.). 128p. (J). (gr. 7-10). 39.40 *(978-1-4205-0880-2(6)*, Lucent Bks.) Cengage Gale.

Shea, Therese. CC Sabathia. 2010. (Today's Superstars Ser.). (ENG.). 48p. (J). (gr. 5-8). pap. 14.05 *(978-1-4339-3987-7(8))*; lib. bdg. 31.95 *(978-1-4339-3986-0(X))* Stevens, Gareth Publishing LLLP.

—Rosa Parks, 1 vol. 2015. (ENG., Illus.). 32p. (J). 23.45 *(978-1-62275-697-1(5)*, Britannica Educational Publishing) Rosen Publishing Group, Inc., The.

—Sharon Draper: Author. 2016. (Junior Biographies Ser.). 24p. (J). pap. 9.35 *(978-0-7660-8188-8(5))* Enslow Pubs., Inc.

Sheafer, Silvia Anne. The Life of Aretha Franklin: Queen of Soul. 2015. (Legendary African Americans Ser.). 96p. (J). (gr. 6-12). 27.94 *(978-0-7660-6225-2(2))* Enslow Pubs., Inc.

Shepherd, Jodie. Mae Jemison. 2015. (Rookie Biographies(r) Ser.). (ENG., Illus.). 32p. (J). pap. 5.95 *(978-0-531-20997-4(0))* Scholastic Library Publishing.

—Serena Williams: A Champion on & off the Court. 2016. (Rookie Biographies(tm) Ser.). (ENG., Illus.). 32p. (J). lib. bdg. 25.00 *(978-0-531-21684-2(5)*, Children's Pr.) Scholastic Library Publishing.

Sherrow, Victoria. Wilma Rudolph. Translations.com Staff, tr. Johnson, Larry, illus. 2006. (Yo Solo: Biografías (on My Own Biographies) Ser.). (SPA.). 48p. (gr. 2-4). pap. 6.95 *(978-0-8225-6623-6(0)*, Ediciones Lerner) Lerner Publishing Group.

Shetterly, Margot Lee. Hidden Figures. Freeman, Laura, illus. 2018. (ENG.). 40p. (J). (gr. -1-3). 17.99 ***(978-0-06-274246-9(9))*** HarperCollins Pubs.

—Hidden Figures. 2016. 240p. (J). (gr. 3-7). 16.99 *(978-0-06-266238-5(4))*; (Illus.). pap. 7.99 *(978-0-06-266237-8(6))* HarperCollins Pubs.

—Hidden Figures. 2016. (Illus.). 231p. (J). lib. bdg. 18.40 ***(978-0-606-39623-3(3))*** Turtleback Bks.

Shirley, David. Alex Haley: Author. 2005. (Black Americans of Achievement Ser.). (Illus.). 112p. (gr. 6-12). 35.00 *(978-0-7910-8249-2(0)*, Chelsea Hse.) Facts On File, Inc.

Shone, Rob. Harriet Tubman: The Life of an African-American Abolitionist. 2009. (Graphic Nonfiction Biographies Ser.). (ENG.). 48p. (YA). (gr. 4-5). 58.50 *(978-1-61513-018-4(7)*, Rosen Reference) Rosen Publishing Group, Inc., The.

—Rosa Parks: The Life of a Civil Rights Heroine. 2009. (Graphic Nonfiction Biographies Ser.). (ENG.). 48p. (YA). (gr. 4-5). 58.50 *(978-1-61513-026-9(8)*, Rosen Reference) Rosen Publishing Group, Inc., The.

—Rosa Parks: The Life of a Civil Rights Heroine. Spender, Nick, illus. 2007. (Graphic Nonfiction Biographies Ser.). (ENG.). 48p. (J). (gr. 4-7). lib. bdg. 31.95 *(978-1-4042-0864-3(X))* Rosen Publishing Group, Inc., The.

—Rosa Parks: The Life of a Civil Rights Heroine. Spender, Nik, illus. 2007. (Graphic Biographies Ser.). (ENG.). 48p. (gr. 5-8). pap. 14.05 *(978-1-4042-0927-5(1))* Rosen Publishing Group, Inc., The.

Shoup, Kate & Cunningham, Meghan Engsberg. Serena Williams: International Tennis Superstar. 2016. (Leading Women Ser.). 112p. (J). (gr. 7-7). 39.93 *(978-1-5026-2014-9(6))* Cavendish Square Publishing.

Sickels, Amy. Walter Dean Myers. 2008. (Who Wrote That? Ser.). 128p. (gr. 6-12). 35.00 *(978-0-7910-9524-9(X)*, Chelsea Hse.) Facts On File, Inc.

Siddons, Brian. Crispus Attucks & African American Patriots of the American Revolution. 2015. (Spotlight on American History Ser.). (ENG., Illus.). 24p. (J). (gr. 4-6). pap. 10.00 *(978-1-4994-1739-5(X)*, PowerKids Pr.) Rosen Publishing Group, Inc., The.

Simmons, Matt J. Jackie Robinson: Breaking the Color Line in Baseball. 2014. (ENG., Illus.). 112p. (J). *(978-0-7787-1242-8(7))* Crabtree Publishing Co.

Simons, Lisa M. B. Jerry Pinkney. Byers, Michael, illus. 2017. (Your Favorite Authors Ser.). (ENG.). 24p. (gr. 1-2). lib. bdg. 25.32 *(978-1-5157-3557-1(5))* Capstone Press of Coughlan Cos.

—Nikki Grimes. Byers, Michael, illus. 2017. (Your Favorite Authors Ser.). (ENG.). 24p. (gr. 1-2). lib. bdg. 25.32 *(978-1-5157-3559-5(1))* Capstone Press of Coughlan Cos.

Simons, Lisa M. Bolt. Kadir Nelson. Byers, Michael, illus. 2017. (Your Favorite Authors Ser.). (ENG.). 24p. (gr. 1-2). lib. bdg. 25.32 *(978-1-5157-3556-4(7)*, First Facts) Capstone Press of Coughlan Cos.

Sims, Rudine. Bishop Daniel A. Payne: Great Black Leader. 2009. (Illus.). 70p. (J). (gr. 3-7). pap. 12.95 *(978-1-933491-15-8(9))* Just Us Bks., Inc.

Skelton, Renee. Harriet Tubman A Woman of Courage. 2005. 2005p. (J). lib. bdg. 15.00 *(978-1-4242-0849-4(1))* Fitzgerald Bks.

—A Woman of Courage. 2005. (Time for Kids Ser.). (ENG., Illus.). 48p. (J). (gr. 2-4). pap. 3.99 *(978-0-06-057607-3(3))* HarperCollins Pubs.

Skelton, Renee & Time for Kids Editors. Time for Kids: A Woman of Courage. 2005. (Time for Kids Ser.). (ENG., Illus.). 48p. (J). 16.99 *(978-0-06-057608-0(1))* HarperCollins Pubs.

Skipper, John C. Frank Robinson: A Baseball Biography, 1 vol. 2014. (ENG., Illus.). 220p. pap. 25.00 *(978-0-7864-7561-2(7)*, efd5081f-d54f-4da6-bb69-aad22ed14bb9) McFarland & Co., Inc. Pubs.

Slade, Suzanne. With Books & Bricks: How Booker T. Washington Built a School. Tadgell, Nicole, illus. 2014. (ENG.). 32p. (J). (gr. 2-3). 16.99 *(978-0-8075-0897-8(7))* Whitman, Albert & Co.

Slavicek, Louise Chipley. Harriet Tubman & the Underground Railroad. 2006. (Lucent Library of Black History). (ENG., Illus.). 104p. (J). (gr. 3-7). lib. bdg. 34.80 *(978-1-59018-927-6(2)*, Lucent Bks.) Cengage Gale.

—Paul Robeson. 2011. (Black Americans of Achievement Legacy Edition Ser.). 120p. (YA). (gr. 6-12). 35.00 *(978-1-60413-843-6(2))* Facts On File, Inc.

Sloate, Susan. Ray Charles: Young Musician. Henderson, Meryl, illus. 2007. (Childhood of Famous Americans Ser.). (ENG.). 176p. (J). (gr. 3-7). pap. 6.99 *(978-1-4169-1437-2(4)*, Simon & Schuster/Paula Wiseman Bks.) Simon & Schuster/Paula Wiseman Bks.

Small, Cathleen. Bessie Coleman: First African American & Native American Pilot. 2017. (J). ***(978-1-5026-2753-7(1))*** Cavendish Square Publishing.

Smith, Charles R., Jr. Black Jack: The Ballad of Jack Johnson. Evans, Shane W., illus. 2010. (ENG.). 40p. (J). (gr. -1-1). 16.99 *(978-1-59643-473-8(2)*, 9781596434738) Roaring Brook Pr.

Smith, Pohla. Shaquille O'Neal: Superhero at Center. 2009. (Sports Illustrated for Kids Bks). 176p. (gr. 7-12). 63.90 *(978-1-60853-153-0(8))* Rosen Publishing Group, Inc., The.

Smith, Pohla & Wilson, Steve. Shaquille O'Neal: Superhero at Center. 2005. (Sports Illustrated for Kids Books Ser.). (Illus.). 176p. (YA). (gr. 7-12). lib. bdg. 33.25 *(978-0-8239-3577-2(9))* Rosen Publishing Group, Inc., The.

Smolka, Bo. Jackie Robinson Breaks the Color Barrier, 1 vol. 2014. (Greatest Events in Sports History Ser.). (ENG.). 48p. (gr. 3-6). lib. bdg. 32.79 *(978-1-62403-594-4(9)*, SportsZone) ABDO Publishing Co.

Solomon, Sharon. Cathy Williams, Buffalo Soldier, 1 vol. Lorenzetti, Doreen, illus. 2010. (ENG.). 32p. (J). (gr. k-3). 16.99 *(978-1-58980-801-0(0))* Pelican Publishing Co., Inc.

Somervill, Barbara A. Mary McLeod Bethune: African-American Educator. 2003. (Our People Ser.). (ENG., Illus.). 32p. (J). (gr. 3-6). 29.93 *(978-1-59296-008-8(1)*, 200647) Child's World, Inc., The.

Spence, Kelly. Martin Luther King Jr. & Peaceful Protest. 2016. (Primary Sources of the Civil Rights Movement Ser.). (Illus.). 64p. (J). (gr. 6-6). 34.21 *(978-1-5026-1864-1(8))* Cavendish Square Publishing.

Spencer, Lauren. Hank Aaron. (Baseball Hall of Famers Ser.). 112p. (gr. 5-8). 2009. 63.90 *(978-1-61511-509-9(9))* 2003. (Illus.). lib. bdg. 34.60 *(978-0-8239-3600-7(7))* Rosen Publishing Group, Inc., The. (Rosen Reference).

Stafford, Mark & Davenport, John, texts. W. E. B. Du Bois: Scholar & Activist. 2004. (Black Americans of Achievement Ser.). (Illus.). 112p. (gr. 6-12). 35.00 *(978-0-7910-8158-7(3)*, Chelsea Hse.) Facts On File, Inc.

Staley, Erin. Martin Luther King Jr. & the Speech That Inspired the World. 2014. (Celebration of the Civil Rights Movement Ser.). 80p. (YA). (gr. 7-12). 34.25 *(978-1-4777-7745-9(8))* Rosen Publishing Group, Inc., The.

Staley, Erin. Misty Copeland: Principal Ballerina. 2017. (Influential Lives Ser.). 128p. (J). (gr. 7-8). lib. bdg. 37.27 ***(978-0-7660-8509-1(0))*** Enslow Pubs., Inc.

Stanley, George E. Coretta Scott King: First Lady of Civil Rights. Madsen, Jim & Henderson, Meryl, illus. 2008. (Childhood of Famous Americans Ser.). (ENG.). 224p. (J). (gr. 3-7). pap. 7.99 *(978-1-4169-6800-9(8)*, Simon & Schuster/Paula Wiseman Bks.) Simon & Schuster/Paula Wiseman Bks.

—Frederick Douglass: Abolitionist Hero. Henderson, Meryl, illus. 2008. (Childhood of Famous Americans Ser.). (ENG.). 208p. (J). (gr. 3-7). pap. 6.99 *(978-1-4169-5547-4(X)*, Aladdin) Simon & Schuster Children's Publishing.

Stanmyer, Jackie F. Jesse Owens: Facing down Hitler. 2016. (Game-Changing Athletes Ser.). (ENG., Illus.). 112p. (J). (gr. 9-9). lib. bdg. 42.79 *(978-1-5026-1049-2(3))* Cavendish Square Publishing.

Stanmyre, Jackie. Althea Gibson & Arthur Ashe. 2016. (Game-Changing Athletes Ser.). (ENG., Illus.). 112p. (J). (gr. 9-9). 42.79 *(978-1-5026-1037-9(X))* Cavendish Square Publishing.

Stanmyre, Jackie F. Coretta Scott King & the Center for Nonviolent Social Change. 2016. (Primary Sources of the Civil Rights Movement Ser.). (Illus.). 64p. (J). (gr. 6-6). 34.21 *(978-1-5026-1876-4(1))* Cavendish Square Publishing.

Stearns, Dan. Harriet Tubman & the Underground Railroad. 2006. (In the Footsteps of American Heroes Ser.). (Illus.). 64p. (gr. 5-12). pap. 14.05 *(978-0-8368-6433-5(6))*; lib. bdg. 34.00 *(978-0-8368-6428-1(X))* Stevens, Gareth Publishing LLLP. (Gareth Stevens Secondary Library).

Steenkamer, Paul. Sports Great Donovan Mcnabb. 2003. (Sports Great Bks.). (Illus.). 64p. (J). lib. bdg. 23.94 *(978-0-7660-2114-3(9))* Enslow Pubs., Inc.

Stein, R. Conrad. Harriet Tubman: On My Underground Railroad I Never Ran My Train off the Track. 2010. (Americans—the Spirit of a Nation Ser.). (Illus.). 128p. (J). lib. bdg. 33.27 *(978-0-7660-3481-5(X))* Enslow Pubs., Inc.

Sterling, Kristin. Mary Mcleod Bethune: A Life of Resourcefulness. 2008. (Pull Ahead Books-Biographies Ser.). (ENG., Illus.). 32p. (gr. k-3). lib. bdg. 22.60 *(978-0-8225-8588-6(X)*, Lerner Pubns.) Lerner Publishing Group.

Sterngass, Jon. Jerry Rice. 2008. (Football Superstars Ser.). (Illus.). 144p. (YA). (gr. 7-12). 30.00 *(978-0-7910-9607-9(6))* Facts On File, Inc.

Stevie Wonder: Musician. 2010. (Black Americans of Achievement Legacy Edition Ser.). (Illus.). 112p. (gr. 6-12). 35.00 *(978-1-60413-685-2(5))* Facts On File, Inc.

Stiefel, Chana. Sky High. 2011. (J). *(978-0-531-22558-5(5))* Scholastic, Inc.

Stille, Darlene R. Barack Obama: 44th U.S. President, 1 vol. Stergulz, Richard, illus. 2013. (Beginner Biographies Set 2 Ser.). (ENG.). 32p. (J). (gr. -1-4). 28.50 *(978-1-61641-939-4(3))* Magic Wagon.

—Madam C. J. Walker: The Inspiring Life Story of the Hair Care Entrepreneur. 2016. (Inspiring Stories Ser.). (ENG., Illus.). 112p. (gr. 5-7). lib. bdg. 35.99 *(978-0-7565-5165-0(X)*, CPB Grades 4-8) Compass Point Bks.

Stine, Megan. Who Is Michelle Obama? 2013. (Who Is...? Ser.). lib. bdg. 14.75 *(978-0-606-32131-0(4)*, Turtleback) Turtleback Bks.

Stout, Glenn. Baseball Heroes. 2010. (Good Sports Ser.). (ENG., Illus.). 128p. (J). (gr. 2-5). pap. 6.99 *(978-0-547-41708-0(X))* Houghton Mifflin Harcourt Publishing Co.

Stout, Glenn & Christopher, Matt. Muhammad Ali: Legends in Sports. 2005. (ENG., Illus.). 128p. (J). (gr. 5-8). pap. 15.99 *(978-0-316-10843-0(X))* Little, Brown Bks. for Young Readers.

Stradley, Don. Schooled. 2011. (J). *(978-0-531-22557-8(7))* Scholastic, Inc.

Strazzabosco, Jeanne M. Learning about Responsibility from the Life of Colin Powell. 2009. (Character Building Book Ser.). 24p. (gr. 2-3). 42.50 *(978-1-61511-003-2(8)*, PowerKids Pr.) Rosen Publishing Group, Inc., The.

Streissguth, Tom. Jesse Owens. 2004. (Just the Facts Biographies Ser.). (ENG., Illus.). 112p. (gr. 5-12). lib. bdg. 27.93 *(978-0-8225-2256-0(X))* Lerner Publishing Group.

Sullivan, Laura L. Jacqueline Woodson. 2014. (Spotlight on Children's Authors Ser.). (Illus.). 48p. (J). (gr. 4-6). lib. bdg. 29.93 *(978-1-62712-855-1(7))* Cavendish Square Publishing.

Sullivan, Otha Richard. African American Inventors. Haskins, Jim, ed. 2011. (Black Stars Ser.). (ENG., Illus.). 176p. (J). (gr. 5-9). pap. 27.00 *(978-1-118-11599-2(6)*, Wiley) Wiley, John & Sons, Inc.

Summer, L. S. Rosa Parks. 2009. (Journey to Freedom Ser.). (ENG., Illus.). 32p. (J). (gr. 4-7). 29.93 *(978-1-60253-133-8(1)*, 200399) Child's World, Inc., The.

Summers, Barbara, ed. Open the Unusual Door: True Life Stories of Challenge, Adventure, & Success by Black Americans. 2005. (ENG., Illus.). 224p. (YA). (gr. 7-18). pap. 12.99 *(978-0-618-58531-1(1))* Houghton Mifflin Harcourt Publishing Co.

Sutcliffe, Jane. Jesse Owens. Porter, Janice Lee, illus. 2006. (On My Own Biographies Ser.). 48p. 17.00 *(978-0-7569-6702-4(3))* Perfection Learning Corp.

—Marian Anderson. 2008. pap. 52.95 *(978-0-8225-9394-2(7))*; (ENG., Illus.). 48p. (gr. 3-6). lib. bdg. 27.93 *(978-0-8225-7170-4(6)*, Lerner Pubns.) Lerner Publishing Group.

Sutherland, Adam. Political Leaders. 2012. (Black History Makers Ser.). (ENG., Illus.). 24p. (J). (gr. 3-8). pap. 8.25 *(978-1-4488-7056-1(9))*; lib. bdg. 22.60 *(978-1-4488-6639-7(1))* Rosen Publishing Group, Inc., The. (PowerKids Pr.).

Swain, Gwenyth. Dred & Harriet Scott: A Family's Struggle for Freedom. 2004. (ENG., Illus.). 112p. (J). 22.95 *(978-0-87351-482-8(3))*; pap. 14.95 *(978-0-87351-483-5(1))* Minnesota Historical Society Pr. (Borealis Bk.).

—A Hunger for Learning: A Story about Booker T. Washington. Johnson, Larry, illus. (Creative Minds Biographies Ser.). (ENG.). 64p. (gr. 4-8). 2006. pap. 8.95 *(978-0-8225-3090-9(2))* 2005. lib. bdg. 22.60 *(978-1-57505-754-5(9))* Lerner Publishing Group.

—Sojourner Truth. Archambault, Matthew, illus. 2005. (On My Own Biography Ser.). 48p. (J). (gr. 1-3). pap. 6.95 *(978-1-57505-827-6(8))* Lerner Publishing Group.

—Sojourner Truth. 2005. (On My Own Biography Ser.). (Illus.). 48p. (J). 25.26 *(978-1-57505-651-7(8)*, Carolrhoda Bks.) Lerner Publishing Group.

Swanson, June. Venus & Serena Williams. Burke, Susan S., illus. 2003. (You Must Be Joking! Riddle Bks.). 32p. (J). (gr. 2-5). pap. 5.95 *(978-0-8225-9842-8(6))* Lerner Publishing Group.

Sweeney, Alyse. Easy Reader Biographies: Martin Luther King, Jr: A Man with a Dream. 2007. (ENG.). 16p. pap. 2.99 *(978-0-439-77419-2(5)*, Teaching Resources) Scholastic, Inc.

Szulhan, Rebecca. Contemporary Achievements. 2008. (African American History Ser.). (Illus.). 48p. (YA). (gr. 5-8). pap. 10.95 *(978-1-59036-885-5(1))*; lib. bdg. 29.05 *(978-1-59036-884-8(3))* Weigl Pubs., Inc.

Tapper, Suzanne Cloud. Voices from Slavery's Past: Yearning to Be Heard. 2004. (Slavery in American History Ser.). (Illus.). 128p. (J). lib. bdg. 27.94 *(978-0-7660-2157-0(2))* Enslow Pubs., Inc.

Tarrant-Reid, Linda. Discovering Black America: From the Age of Exploration to the Twenty-First Century. 2012. (ENG., Illus.). 244p. (J). (gr. 3-7). 29.95 *(978-0-8109-7098-4(8)*, Abrams Bks. for Young Readers) Abrams, Inc.

Tate, Don. Poet: The Remarkable Story of George Moses Horton, 1 vol. Tate, Don, illus. 2015. (ENG., Illus.). 36p. (J). (gr. 1-5). 16.95 *(978-1-56145-825-7(2))* Peachtree Pubs.

Taylor-Butler, Christine. Michelle Obama. 2015. (ENG.). 48p. (J). pap. 6.95 *(978-0-531-21206-6(8)*, Orchard Bks.) Scholastic Library Publishing.

—Rosa Parks. 2015. (ENG., Illus.). 48p. (J). pap. 6.95 *(978-0-531-21209-7(2)*, Orchard Bks.) Scholastic Library Publishing.

Taylor, Charlotte. Crispus Attucks: A Hero of the American Revolution. 2016. (Exceptional African Americans Ser.). (ENG., Illus.). 24p. (J). (gr. 3-3). 22.60

(978-0-7660-7187-2(1)); pap. 9.35 (978-0-7660-7185-8(5)) Enslow Pubs., Inc.

—Sojourner Truth: Abolitionist & Activist. 2016. (Exceptional African Americans Ser.). (ENG., Illus.). 24p. (J). (gr. 3-3). 22.60 (978-0-7660-7372-2(6)) Enslow Pubs., Inc.

Taylor, Charlotte & Feinstein, Stephen. Barack Obama: First African-American President. 2015. (Exceptional African Americans Ser.). (ENG.). 24p. (J). (gr. 3-4). pap. 9.35 (978-0-7660-7122-3(7)); (Illus.). 22.60 (978-0-7660-7124-7(3)) Enslow Pubs., Inc.

—Harriet Tubman: Hero of the Underground Railroad. 2015. (Exceptional African Americans Ser.). (ENG.). 24p. (J). (gr. 3-4). pap. 9.35 (978-0-7660-7126-1(X)); (Illus.). 22.60 (978-0-7660-7128-5(6)) Enslow Pubs., Inc.

—Lebron James: Basketball Champion. 2015. (Exceptional African Americans Ser.). (ENG., Illus.). 24p. (J). (gr. 3-4). 22.60 (978-0-7660-6660-1(6)) Enslow Pubs., Inc.

—Mae Jemison: First African-American Woman in Space. 2015. (Exceptional African Americans Ser.). (ENG.). 24p. (J). (gr. 3-4). 22.60 (978-0-7660-6664-9(9)); pap. 9.35 (978-0-7660-6662-5(2)) Enslow Pubs., Inc.

Taylor, Marian. Harriet Tubman. 2004. (Black Americans of Achievement Ser.). (Illus.). 112p. (gr. 6-12). 35.00 (978-0-7910-8166-2(4), Chelsea Hse.) Facts On File, Inc.

Taylor, Yuval, ed. Growing up in Slavery: Stories of Young Slaves as Told by Themselves. Judge, Kathleen, illus. 2007. (ENG.). 256p. (J). (gr. 9). pap. 11.95 (978-1-55652-635-0(0)) Chicago Review Pr., Inc.

Teitelbaum, Michael. Jackie Robinson: Champion for Equality. 2010. (Sterling Biographies(r) Ser.). (ENG., Illus.). 128p. (J). (gr. 5-18). pap. 5.95 (978-1-4027-6362-5(X)) Sterling Publishing Co., Inc.

The Celebrities Arts Center. Beyonce Knowles, the Marvelous Queen. 2007. 76p. pap. 11.00 (978-0-9774483-9-5(8)) International Development Ctr.

Thiel, Kristin. Mae C. Jemison: First African American Woman in Space. 2017. (J). **(978-1-5026-2751-3(5))** Cavendish Square Publishing.

Thomas, Garen. Yes We Can: A Biography of President Barack Obama. 2nd rev. ed. 2008. (ENG., Illus.). 256p. (J). (gr. 3-7). pap. 12.99 (978-0-312-58639-3(6), 9780312586393) Feiwel & Friends.

Thornley, Stew. Super Sports Star Barry Bonds. 2004. (Super Sports Star Ser.). (Illus.). 48p. (J). lib. bdg. 23.93 (978-0-7660-2132-7(7)) Enslow Pubs., Inc.

—Super Sports Star Daunte Culpepper. 2003. (Super Sports Star Ser.). (Illus.). 48p. (J). (gr. 1-4). lib. bdg. 25.27 (978-0-7660-2051-1(7)) Enslow Pubs., Inc.

—Super Sports Star Eddie George. 2003. (Super Sports Star Ser.). (Illus.). 48p. (J). (gr. 1-4). lib. bdg. 25.27 (978-0-7660-2050-4(9)) Enslow Pubs., Inc.

—Super Sports Star Ken Griffey, Jr. 2004. (Super Sports Star Ser.). (Illus.). 48p. (J). lib. bdg. 25.27 (978-0-7660-2133-4(5)) Enslow Pubs., Inc.

—Super Sports Star Randy Moss. 2003. (Super Sports Star Ser.). (Illus.). 48p. (J). (gr. 1-4). lib. bdg. 25.27 (978-0-7660-2049-8(5)) Enslow Pubs., Inc.

Tieck, Sarah. Rosa Parks, 1 vol. 2006. (Buddy Book Ser.). (ENG., Illus.). 32p. (gr. -1-3). 27.07 (978-1-59679-788-8(6), Buddy Bks.) ABDO Publishing Co.

Time for Kids Editors. Rosa Parks: Civil Rights Pioneer. 2007. (Time for Kids Biographies Ser.). (Illus.). 44p. (gr. 2-4). 14.00 (978-0-7569-8110-5(7)) Perfection Learning Corp.

Todd, Anne M. Chris Rock: Comedian & Actor. 2006. (Black Americans of Achievement Legacy Edition Ser.). (Illus.). 100p. (YA). (gr. 7-12). lib. bdg. 35.00 (978-0-7910-9225-5(9)) Facts On File, Inc.

—Tyra Banks. 2009. (Women of Achievement Ser.). (Illus.). 120p. (gr. 6-12). 35.00 (978-1-60413-462-9(3), Chelsea Hse.) Facts On File, Inc.

—Venus & Serena Williams. 2009. (Women of Achievement Ser.). (Illus.). 144p. (gr. 6-12). 35.00 (978-1-60413-461-2(5), Chelsea Hse.) Facts On File, Inc.

Torres, John Albert. Allen Iverson: Never Give Up. 2004. (Sports Leaders Ser.). (Illus.). 104p. (J). lib. bdg. 27.94 (978-0-7660-2174-7(2)) Enslow Pubs., Inc.

—Shaquille O'Neal: Gentle Giant. 2004. (Sports Leaders Ser.). (Illus.). 104p. (J). lib. bdg. 27.94 (978-0-7660-2175-4(0)) Enslow Pubs., Inc.

—Vince Carter: Slam Dunk Artist. 2004. (Sports Leaders Ser.). (Illus.). 104p. (J). lib. bdg. 26.60 (978-0-7660-2173-0(4)) Enslow Pubs., Inc.

Tracy, Kathleen. The Life & Times of Rosa Parks. 2008. (Illus.). 48p. (J). (gr. 4-8). lib. bdg. 29.95 (978-1-58415-666-6(X)) Mitchell Lane Pubs., Inc.

—Queen Latifah. 2004. (Blue Banner Biography Ser.). (Illus.). 32p. (J). (gr. 3-8). lib. bdg. 25.70 (978-1-58415-313-9(X)) Mitchell Lane Pubs., Inc.

Troy, Don. Booker T. Washington. 2009. (Journey to Freedom Ser.). (ENG., Illus.). 32p. (J). (gr. 4-7). 29.93 (978-1-60253-118-5(8), 200384) Child's World, Inc., The.

Trumbull, Jamie. Barney Ford: Pioneer Businessman. 2010. (ENG & SPA., Illus.). 50p. (J). pap. 8.95 (978-0-86541-115-9(8)) Filter Pr., LLC.

Trussell-Cullen, Alan. Jackie Robinson. 2009. pap. 13.25 (978-1-60559-063-9(0)) Hameray Publishing Group, Inc.

Turner, Ann. My Name Is Truth: The Life of Sojourner Truth. Ransome, James, illus. 2015. 40p. (J). (gr. 1-5). (ENG.). 17.99 (978-0-06-075898-1(8)); lib. bdg. 18.89 (978-0-06-075899-8(6)) HarperCollins Pubs.

Turner, Glennette Tilley. Fort Mosé: And the Story of the Man Who Built the First Free Black Settlement in Colonial America. 2010. (ENG., Illus.). 48p. (J). (gr. 3-7). 18.95 (978-0-8109-4056-7(6), Abrams Bks. for Young Readers) Abrams, Inc.

Underwood, Deborah. Nat Love. 2008. pap. 52.95 (978-0-8225-9395-9(5)); (ENG., Illus.). 48p. (gr. 3-6). lib. bdg. 27.93 (978-0-8225-7171-1(4), Lerner Pubns.) Lerner Publishing Group.

Uschan, Michael V. Halle Berry. 2012. (People in the News Ser.). (ENG., Illus.). 128p. (gr. 7-10). lib. bdg. 39.40 (978-1-4205-0817-8(2), Lucent Bks.) Cengage Gale.

—Michelle Obama. 2010. (People in the News Ser.). (Illus.). 128p. (YA). (gr. 8-10). 33.95 (978-1-4205-0209-1(3), Lucent Bks.) Cengage Gale.

—Serena Williams. 2011. (People in the News Ser.). (ENG.). 128p. (gr. 10-10). lib. bdg. 39.40 (978-1-4205-0488-0(6), Lucent Bks.) Cengage Gale.

Vander Hook, Sue. Colin Powell: General & Statesman, 1 vol. 2010. (Military Heroes Ser.). (ENG.). 112p. (J). (gr. 6-12). lib. bdg. 35.64 (978-1-60453-965-3(8)) ABDO Publishing Co.

—Frederick Douglass: Fugitive Slave & Abolitionist, 1 vol. 2010. (Essential Lives Set 5 Ser.). (ENG., Illus.). 112p. (J). (gr. 6-12). lib. bdg. 35.64 (978-1-61613-513-3(1)) ABDO Publishing Co.

Vaughn, Wally G. & Davis, Mattie Campbell, eds. The Selma Campaign, 1963-1965: The Decisive Battle of the Civil Rights Movement. 2006. (ENG., Illus.). 244p. pap. 19.95 (978-0-912469-44-7(7)) Majority Pr., The.

Venezia, Mike. Charles Drew: Doctor Who Got the World Pumped up to Donate Blood. Venezia, Mike, illus. 2009. (Getting to Know the World's Greatest Inventors & Scientists Ser.). (ENG., Illus.). 32p. (J). (gr. 3-4). pap. 6.95 (978-0-531-21334-6(X), Children's Pr.); (gr. 2-5). 28.00 (978-0-531-23725-0(7)) Scholastic Library Publishing.

—Daniel Hale Williams: Surgeon Who Opened Hearts & Minds. 2010. (Getting to Know the World's Greatest Inventors & Scientists Ser.). 32p. (J). (gr. 3-4). pap. 6.95 (978-0-531-22350-5(7), Children's Pr.) Scholastic Library Publishing.

—Faith Ringgold. Venezia, Mike, illus. 2007. (Getting to Know the World's Greatest Artists Ser.). (ENG., Illus.). 32p. (J). (gr. 3-4). 28.00 (978-0-531-18526-1(5), Children's Pr.) Scholastic Library Publishing.

—Horace Pippin. Venezia, Mike, illus. 2007. (Getting to Know the World's Greatest Artists Ser.). (ENG., Illus.). 32p. (J). (gr. 3-4). 28.00 (978-0-531-18527-8(3), Children's Pr.) Scholastic Library Publishing.

Vietze, Andrew. The Life & Death of Malcolm X. 2017. (J). pap. **(978-1-5383-8031-4(5)**, Rosen Young Adult) Rosen Publishing Group, Inc., The.

—The Life & Death of Martin Luther King Jr. 2017. (J). **(978-1-5383-8038-3(2))**; pap. **(978-1-5383-8039-0(0))** Rosen Publishing Group, Inc., The.

Wade, Linda R. Condoleezza Rice. 2004. (Illus.). 32p. (J). lib. bdg. 25.70 (978-1-58415-332-0(6)) Mitchell Lane Pubs., Inc.

Wade, Mary Dodson. Amazing Arctic Explorer Matthew Henson. (Amazing Americans Ser.). (Illus.). 24p. (J). 2013. (gr. k-3). pap. 7.95 (978-0-7660-5974-0(X), Enslow Elementary) 2009. (gr. 1-3). lib. bdg. 22.60 (978-0-7660-3286-6(8)) Enslow Pubs., Inc.

—Amazing Olympic Athlete Wilma Rudolph. (Amazing Americans Ser.). (Illus.). 24p. (J). 2013. (gr. k-3). pap. 7.95 (978-0-7660-5978-8(2), Enslow Elementary) 2009. (gr. 1-3). lib. bdg. 22.60 (978-0-7660-3282-8(5)) Enslow Pubs., Inc.

—Condoleezza Rice. rev. ed. 2005. (Gateway Biography Ser.). (Illus.). 48p. (J). (gr. 4-7). pap. 8.95 (978-0-7613-9549-2(0), First Avenue Editions) Lerner Publishing Group.

—Condoleezza Rice: Being the Best. 2003. (Gateway Biography Ser.: 4). 48p. lib. bdg. 23.90 (978-0-7613-2619-9(7)); (Illus.). (gr. 2-4). pap. 8.95 (978-0-7613-1927-6(1)) Lerner Publishing Group. (Millbrook Pr.).

Wadsworth, Ginger. Benjamin Banneker: Pioneering Scientist. Orback, Craig, illus. 2003. (On My Own Biography Ser.). (ENG.). 48p. (gr. 2-4). 25.26 (978-0-87614-916-4(6)); per. 6.95 (978-0-87614-104-5(1), Carolrhoda Bks.) Lerner Publishing Group.

—Benjamin Banneker: Pioneering Scientist. Orback, Craig, illus. 2006. (On My Own Biographies Ser.). 47p. (gr. 2-5). 17.00 (978-0-7569-6705-5(8)) Perfection Learning Corp.

Wagner, Heather Lehr. Benjamin Banneker. 2010. (Leaders of the Colonial Era Ser.). 104p. (gr. 5-8). 35.00 (978-1-60413-744-6(4), Chelsea Hse.) Facts On File, Inc.

Walker, Sally M. Bessie Coleman: Daring to Fly. Porter, Janice Lee, illus. (On My Own Biographies Ser.). 48p. (gr. 2-5). 2005. lib. bdg. 23.93 (978-0-87614-919-5(0)) 2003. (ENG.). pap. 6.95 (978-0-87614-103-8(3), Carolrhoda Bks.) Lerner Publishing Group.

—Jackie Robinson. Translations.com Staff, tr. Pate, Rodney S., illus. 2005. (Yo Solo: Biografías (on My Own Biographies) Ser.). (SPA & ENG.). 48p. (gr. 2-4). lib. bdg. 25.26 (978-0-8225-3126-5(7), Ediciones Lerner) Lerner Publishing Group.

Wallace, Maurice O. Langston Hughes: The Harlem Renaissance. 2007. (Writers & Their Work Ser.). (Illus.). 144p. (J). (gr. 4-7). lib. bdg. 39.93 (978-0-7614-2591-5(8), Benchmark Bks.) Marshall Cavendish Corp.

Wallenfeldt, Jeff, ed. Black American Biographies: The Journey of Achievement. 2010. (African American History & Culture Ser.). (Illus.). 408p. (YA). 90.00 (978-1-61530-178-2(X)) Rosen Publishing Group, Inc., The.

Wallenfeldt, Jeffrey H., ed. African American History & Culture, 3 vols., Set. Incl. Africa to America: From the Middle Passage Through the 1930s. 272p. lib. bdg. 45.00 (978-1-61530-126-3(7)); Black American Biographies: The Journey of Achievement. 408p. lib. bdg. 45.00 (978-1-61530-137-9(2)); Black Experience in America: From Civil Rights to the Present. 232p. lib. bdg. 45.00 (978-1-61530-146-1(1)); (YA). (gr. 9-12). 2010. (Illus.). 232 - 408p. 2010. Set lib. bdg. 135.00 (978-1-61530-151-5(8)) Rosen Publishing Group, Inc., The.

—Black American Biographies: The Journey of Achievement. 2010. (African American History & Culture Ser.). (Illus.). 408p. (YA). (gr. 9-12). lib. bdg. 45.00 (978-1-61530-137-9(2)) Rosen Publishing Group, Inc., The.

Walsh, Alice. Change of Heart, 1 vol. Banks, Erin, illus. 2016. (ENG.). 32p. (J). (gr. -1-4). 19.95 (978-1-77108-371-3(9)) Nimbus Publishing, Ltd. CAN. Dist: Orca Bk. Pubs. USA.

Ward, Jill. Martin Luther King, Jr: Georgia, My State Biographies. l.t. ed. 2008. (ENG., Illus.). 24p. (J). (gr. k-2). 22.60 (978-1-935077-01-5(5)); pap. 22.60 (978-1-935077-08-4(2)) State Standards Publishing, LLC.

Warren, Nagueyalti. Grandfather of Black Studies: W.E.B. du Bois. 2011. (J). (978-1-59221-821-9(0)); (ENG., Illus.). 258p. pap. (978-1-59221-822-6(9)) Africa World Pr.

Watkins, Angela Farris. My Uncle Martin's Big Heart. Velasquez, Eric, illus. 2010. (ENG.). 32p. (J). (gr. k-2). 19.95 (978-0-8109-8975-7(1), Abrams Bks. for Young Readers) Abrams, Inc.

Watson, Galadriel Findlay. Venus & Serena Williams. 2005. (Great African American Women for Kids Ser.). (Illus.). 24p. (J). (gr. 2-3). lib. bdg. 24.45 (978-1-59036-332-4(9)); (gr. 3-7). per. 8.95 (978-1-59036-338-6(8)) Weigl Pubs., Inc.

Watson, Renée. Harlem's Little Blackbird. Robinson, Christian, illus. 2012. (ENG.). 40p. (J). (gr. -1-2). 17.99 (978-0-375-86973-0(5), Random Hse. Bks. for Young Readers) Random Hse. Children's Bks.

Watson, Stephanie. Cee lo Green: Rapper, Singer, & Record Producer, 1 vol. 2013. (Contemporary Lives Set 2 Ser.). (ENG.). 112p. (J). (gr. 6-12). lib. bdg. 35.64 (978-1-61783-619-0(2), Essential Library) ABDO Publishing Co.

Waxman, Laura Hamilton. Aerospace Engineer Aprille Ericsson. 2015. (STEM Trailblazer Bios Ser.). (ENG., Illus.). 32p. (J). (gr. 2-5). pap. 7.95 (978-1-4677-6118-5(4)); lib. bdg. 26.60 (978-1-4677-5793-5(4)) Lerner Publishing Group. (Lerner Pubns.).

—Colin Powell. 2005. (History Maker Bios Ser.). 48p. (J). pap. 8.95 (978-0-8225-5463-9(1)); (ENG., Illus.). (gr. 3-6). lib. bdg. 27.93 (978-0-8225-2433-5(3), Lerner Pubns.) Lerner Publishing Group.

—Coretta Scott King. 2008. pap. 52.95 (978-0-8225-9387-4(4)); (ENG., Illus.). 48p. (gr. 3-6). lib. bdg. 27.93 (978-0-8225-7168-1(4), Lerner Pubns.) Lerner Publishing Group.

—Sojourner Truth. 2008. pap. 52.95 (978-0-8225-9396-6(3)); (ENG., Illus.). 48p. (gr. 3-6). lib. bdg. 27.93 (978-0-8225-7172-8(2), Lerner Pubns.) Lerner Publishing Group.

Weakland, Mark. When Martin Luther King Jr. Wore Roller Skates. Ballesteros, Patrick, illus. 2017. 31p. (J). (978-1-5158-0141-2(1)) 2016. (ENG.). 32p. (gr. 2-3). lib. bdg. 27.99 (978-1-4795-9685-0(X)) Picture Window Bks.

Weatherford, Carole Boston. Gordon Parks: How the Photographer Captured Black & White America. Christoph, Jamey, illus. 2015. (ENG.). 32p. (J). (gr. k-3). 16.99 (978-0-8075-3017-7(4)) Whitman, Albert & Co.

—Great African-American Lawyers: Raising the Bar of Freedom. 2003. (Collective Biographies Ser.). (Illus.). 112p. (J). (gr. 6-12). lib. bdg. 27.94 (978-0-7660-1837-2(7)) Enslow Pubs., Inc.

—The Legendary Miss Lena Horne. Zunon, Elizabeth, illus. 2017. (ENG.). 48p. (J). (gr. -1-3). 17.99 (978-1-4814-6824-4(3)) Simon & Schuster Children's Publishing.

—Racing Against the Odds: The Story of Wendell Scott, Stock Car Racing's African-American Champion, 0 vols. 2009. (ENG., Illus.). 40p. (J). (gr. -1-2). 17.99 (978-0-7614-5465-6(9), 9780761454656, Amazon Children's Publishing) Amazon Publishing.

Weatherford, Carole Boston. Schomburg: The Man Who Built a Library. Velasquez, Eric, illus. 2017. (ENG.). 48p. (J). (gr. 4-7). 16.99 **(978-0-7636-8046-6(X))** Candlewick Pr.

—Schomburg: The Man Who Built a Library. 2017. (J). 31.99 **(978-1-5200-8717-7(9))**; 31.99 **(978-1-5200-8716-0(0))** Dreamscape Media, LLC.

Weber, Terri Smith. Halle Berry: Fighting for First. 2003. (J). pap. (978-0-9740180-8-9(2)); lib. bdg. (978-0-9740180-7-2(4)) Panda Publishing, L.L.C. (Bios for Kids).

Weerts, Christine. Hero of Faith - Rosa Young. 2011. 64p. pap. 7.99 (978-0-7586-2830-5(7)) Concordia Publishing Hse.

Weidt, Maryann N. Harriet Tubman. 2003. (History Maker Bios Ser.). (Illus.). 47p. (J). 26.60 (978-0-8225-4676-4(0), Lerner Pubns.) Lerner Publishing Group.

—Rosa Parks. (History Maker Bios Ser.). (Illus.). (J). 2004. 48p. pap. 8.95 (978-0-8225-4805-8(4)) 2003. 47p. 26.60 (978-0-8225-4673-3(6)) Lerner Publishing Group. (Lerner Pubns.).

Weidt, Maryann N. & National Geographic Learning Staff. Voice of Freedom: A Story about Frederick Douglass. Reeves, Jeni, illus. 2010. (Rise & Shine Ser.). (ENG.). 64p. (C). (gr. 4-8). pap. 14.95 (978-1-57505-553-4(8)) National Geographic School Publishing, Inc.

Weil, Ann. Medgar Evers, 1 vol. 2012. (American Biographies Ser.). (ENG.). 48p. (gr. 4-6). pap. 9.95 (978-1-4329-6465-8(8), NA-h) Heinemann-Raintree.

—Medgar Evers, 1 vol. Oxford Bible Staff, illus. 2012. (American Biographies Ser.). (ENG.). 48p. (gr. 4-6). lib. bdg. 32.65 (978-1-4329-6454-2(2), NA-h) Heinemann-Raintree.

Weiss, Lynne. Crispus Attucks & the Boston Massacre. 2013. (Jr. Graphic African American History Ser.). 24p. (J). (gr. 3-6). pap. 63.60 (978-1-4777-1456-0(1)); (ENG., Illus.). pap. 10.60 (978-1-4777-1455-3(3)); (ENG., Illus.). lib. bdg. 25.25 (978-1-4777-1315-0(8)) Rosen Publishing Group, Inc., The. (PowerKids Pr.).

—Frederick Douglass & the Abolitionist Movement. 2013. (Jr. Graphic African American History Ser.). (Illus.). 24p. (J). (gr. 3-6). (ENG.). pap. 10.60 (978-1-4777-1451-5(0)); pap. 63.60 (978-1-4777-1452-2(9)); (ENG., lib. bdg. 25.25 (978-1-4777-1313-6(1)) Rosen Publishing Group, Inc., The. (PowerKids Pr.).

Welch, Catherine A. Frederick Douglass. 2003. (History Maker Bios Ser.). (Illus.). 48p. (J). (gr. 4-7). pap. 8.95 (978-0-8225-4802-7(X)); (gr. 3-5). lib. bdg. 26.60 (978-0-8225-4672-6(8)) Lerner Publishing Group.

Westen, Robin. Oprah Winfrey: I Don't Believe in Failure. 2005. (African-American Biography Library). (Illus.). 128p. (J). (gr. 6-12). lib. bdg. 33.27 (978-0-7660-2462-5(8)) Enslow Pubs., Inc.

Weston Woods Staff, creator. Duke Ellington. 2011. 38.75 (978-0-545-02759-5(4)); 18.95 (978-0-545-02757-1(8)) Weston Woods Studios, Inc.

—Martin's Big Words. 2011. 38.75 (978-0-545-15256-3(9)); 18.95 (978-0-545-15251-8(8)) Weston Woods Studios, Inc.

—Rosa. 2011. 38.75 (978-0-545-14963-1(0)); 18.95 (978-0-545-14962-4(2)) Weston Woods Studios, Inc.

Wheeler, Irvin, illus. Justina's Dream. 2005. 30p. (J). (978-1-887302-12-8(3)) Western Images Pubns., Inc.

Wheeler, Jill C. Breaking Barriers Set 3. 2003. (Breaking Barriers Set 3 Ser.). (gr. 3-8). 162.42 (978-1-57765-902-0(3), Abdo & Daughters) ABDO Publishing Co.

—Denzel Washington. 2003. (Star Tracks Ser.). (Illus.). 64p. (J). (gr. 3-8). lib. bdg. 27.07 (978-1-57765-772-9(1)) ABDO Publishing Co.

—Jackie Robinson. 2003. (Breaking Barriers Ser.). 64p. (gr. 3-8). 27.07 (978-1-57765-739-2(X), Abdo & Daughters) ABDO Publishing Co.

—Rosa Parks, Set II. 2003. (Breaking Barriers Ser.). 64p. (gr. 3-8). 27.07 (978-1-57765-640-1(7), Abdo & Daughters) ABDO Publishing Co.

—Walter Dean Myers, 1 vol. 2014. (Children's Authors Set 8 Ser.). (ENG.). 24p. (gr. 3-6). 25.65 (978-1-62403-667-5(8)) ABDO Publishing Co.

Whitehead, Kathy. Art from Her Heart: Folk Artist Clementine Hunter. Evans, Shane W., illus. 2008. (ENG.). 32p. (J). (gr. 1-3). 16.99 (978-0-399-24219-9(8), G.P. Putnam's Sons Books for Young Readers) Penguin Young Readers Group.

Whitelaw, Nancy. Thurgood Marshall. 2011. (Supreme Court Justices Ser.). (Illus.). 128p. 28.95 (978-1-59935-157-5(9)) Reynolds, Morgan Inc.

Whiting, Jim. Booker T. Washington. 2010. (Transcending Race in America Ser.). (Illus.). 64p. (YA). (gr. 4-8). lib. bdg. 22.95 (978-1-4222-1608-8(X)) Mason Crest.

—Frederick Douglass. 2010. (Transcending Race in America: Biographies of Biracial Achievers Ser.). (Illus.). 64p. (YA). (gr. 5-18). lib. bdg. 22.95 (978-1-4222-1611-8(X)) Mason Crest.

—Jim Beckwourth: The Man Who Opened the West. 2007. (Illus.). 144p. (YA). (gr. 6-18). lib. bdg. 25.95 (978-1-59556-027-8(0)) OTTN Publishing.

—Rosa Parks. 2007. (What's So Great About... ? Ser.). (Illus.). 32p. (YA). (gr. 2-4). lib. bdg. 25.70 (978-1-58415-573-7(6)) Mitchell Lane Pubs., Inc.

—W. E. B. du Bois: Civil Rights Activist, Author, Historian. 2009. (Transcending Race in America: Biographies of Biracial Achievers Ser.). 64p. (YA). (gr. 5-18). pap. 9.95 (978-1-4222-1632-3(2)) Mason Crest.

Wiebe, Ruth Lent. African Americans. (Successful Americans Ser.). 64p. (YA). 2009. (gr. 9-12). 22.95 (978-1-4222-0527-3(4)) 2007. (gr. 7-18). pap. 9.95 (978-1-4222-0858-8(3)) Mason Crest.

Wilds, Mary. I Dare Not Fail: Notable African American Women Educators. 2004. (Avisson Young Adult Ser.). 139p. (J). pap. 19.95 (978-1-888105-64-3(X)) Avisson Pr., Inc.

Wilmore, Kathy. Jackie Robinson: With a Discussion of Respect. 2004. (Values in Action Ser.). (J). (978-1-59203-071-2(8)) Learning Challenge, Inc.

—Muhammad Ali: With a Discussion of Honesty. 2003. (Values in Action Ser.). (J). (978-1-59203-065-1(3)) Learning Challenge, Inc.

Wilson, Camilla. Frederick Douglass: A Voice for Freedom in the 1800s. 2003. (Scholastic Biography Ser.). (Illus.). 90p. (J). pap. (978-0-439-38082-9(0)) Scholastic, Inc.

Wilson, Mike. The Williams Sisters: Venus & Serena. 2005. (ENG., Illus.). 32p. pap. 8.50 (978-0-340-84876-0(6)) Cambridge Univ. Pr.

Winget, Mary. Martin Luther King, Jr. 2004. (History Maker Bios Ser.). (Illus.). 48p. (J). pap. 8.95 (978-0-8225-4804-1(6), Lerner Pubns.) Lerner Publishing Group.

Winter, Jonah. Barack. Ford, A. G., illus. 32p. (J). (gr. -1-2). 2010. (ENG.). pap. 7.99 (978-0-06-170396-6(6), Tegen, Katherine Bks) 2008. lib. bdg. 18.89 (978-0-06-170393-5(1)) 2008. (ENG.). 17.99 (978-0-06-170392-8(3), Tegen, Katherine Bks) HarperCollins Pubs.

—Barack, 2 vols. 2009. (J). 38.75 (978-1-4407-3624-7(3)); 40.75 (978-1-4407-3618-6(9)); 38.75 (978-1-4407-3620-9(0)); 40.75 (978-1-4407-3622-3(7)); 222.75 (978-1-4407-3619-3(7)); 1.25 (978-1-4407-3625-4(1)) Recorded Bks., Inc.

Wittrock, Jeni. W. E. B. du Bois. 2014. (Great African-Americans Ser.). (ENG., Illus.). 24p. (gr. k-1). lib. bdg. 21.99 (978-1-4914-0505-5(8), Pebble Bks.) Capstone Press of Coughlan Cos.

Wittrock, Jeni, et al. Great African-Americans, 1 vol. 2014. (Great African-Americans Ser.). (ENG.). 24p. (gr. k-1). pap. 71.40 (978-1-4914-0527-7(9), Pebble Bks.) Capstone Press of Coughlan Cos.

Woelfle, Gretchen. Mumbet's Declaration of Independence. Delinois, Alix, illus. 2014. (ENG.). 32p. (J). (gr. 1-4). 17.95 (978-0-7613-6589-1(3), Carolrhoda Bks.) Lerner Publishing Group.

Woodson, Jacqueline. Brown Girl Dreaming. l.t. ed. 2017. (ENG.). 24.99 **(978-1-4328-4315-1(X))** Cengage Gale.

—Brown Girl Dreaming. (ENG.). (J). (gr. 5). 2016. 368p. pap. 10.99 (978-0-14-751582-7(3), Puffin Books) 2014. (Illus.). 336p. 17.99 (978-0-399-25251-8(7), Nancy Paulsen Books) Penguin Young Readers Group.

—Brown Girl Dreaming. 2016. (ENG.). 368p. (J). (gr. 5). 22.10 (978-0-606-39310-2(2)) Turtleback Bks.

Woog, Dan. Jesse Jackson. 2003. (People in the News Ser.). (ENG., Illus.). 118p. (YA). (gr. 6-9). 33.45 (978-1-56006-631-6(8), Lucent Bks.) Cengage Gale.

Wright, David K. The Life of Arthur Ashe: Smashing the Color Barrier in Tennis. 2015. (Legendary African Americans Ser.). 96p. (J). (gr. 6-12). 27.94 (978-0-7660-6260-3(0)); pap. 10.95 (978-0-7660-6261-0(9)) Enslow Pubs., Inc.

—The Life of Paul Robeson: Actor, Singer, Political Activist. 2014. (Legendary African Americans Ser.). 96p. (J). (gr. 6-12). 27.94 (978-0-7660-6157-6(4)); (Illus.). pap. 10.95 (978-0-7660-6158-3(2)) Enslow Pubs., Inc.

Wright, Simeon & Boyd, Herb. Simeon's Story: An Eyewitness Account of the Kidnapping of Emmett Till. 2011. (ENG.). 160p. (J). (gr. 7). pap. 12.95 (978-1-56976-819-8(6), Hill, Lawrence Bks.) Chicago Review Pr., Inc.

Wyckoff, Edwin Brit. Hair-Care Millionaire: Madam C.J. Walker & Her Amazing Business. 2010. (Genius at Work! Great Inventor Biographies Ser.). 32p. (J). (gr. 2-5). 23.94 (978-0-7660-3449-5(6)) Enslow Pubs., Inc.

Young, Jeff C. Amazing African-American Actors. 2012. (African-American Collective Biographies Ser.). (Illus.). 112p. (J). (gr. 5-18). 33.27 (978-1-59845-135-1(9)) Enslow Pubs., Inc.

—Brilliant African-American Scientists: Nine Exceptional Lives. 2009. (Great Scientists & Famous Inventors Ser.). (Illus.). 128p. (J). (gr. 5-9). lib. bdg. 34.60 (978-1-59845-083-5(2)) Enslow Pubs., Inc.

—Inspiring African-American Inventors: Nine Extraordinary Lives. 2009. (Great Scientists & Famous Inventors Ser.). (Illus.). 128p. (J). (gr. 5-9). lib. bdg. 34.60 (978-1-59845-080-4(8)) Enslow Pubs., Inc.

Zumbusch, Amelie von. Michelle Obama: Our First Lady. 2010. (Making History: the Obamas Ser.). (Illus.). 24p. (J). pap. 8.25 (978-1-4358-9868-4(0)); (gr. 2-3). lib. bdg. 22.60 (978-1-4358-9388-7(3)) Rosen Publishing Group, Inc., The. (PowerKids Pr.).

AFRICAN AMERICANS—CIVIL RIGHTS

Adamson, Heather. The Civil Rights Movement [Scholastic]: An Interactive History Adventure. (You Choose: History Ser.). 112p. 2010. pap. 0.86 *(978-1-4296-5179-0(2))* 2009. (gr. 3-4). pap. 0.86 *(978-1-4296-4047-3(2))* Capstone Press of Coughlan Cos. (You Choose Bks.).

Adler, David A. Heroes for Civil Rights. Farnsworth, Bill, illus. 2007. (ENG.). 32p. (J). (gr. -1-3). 17.95 *(978-0-8234-2008-7(6))* Holiday Hse., Inc.

—A Picture Book of Rosa Parks. Casilla, Robert, illus. 2015. 32p. pap. 8.00 *(978-1-61003-405-0(8))* Center for the Collaborative Classroom.

African American Eras. 2010. *(978-1-4144-3598-5(3)); (978-1-4144-3600-5(9)); (978-1-4144-3597-8(5)); (978-1-4144-3599-2(1))* Cengage Gale. (UXL).

Agins, Donna Brown. Maya Angelou: A Biography of an Award-Winning Poet & Civil Rights Activist. 2013. (African-American Icons Ser.). 104p. (J). (gr. 6-12). lib. bdg. 27.94 *(978-0-7660-3992-6(7))* Enslow Pubs., Inc.

Alexander, Florence. Dare to Be. . . Martin Luther King Jr. Whitmore, Yvette, illus. 2003. (ENG & SPA.). 17p. (J). 3.99 *(978-0-915960-65-1(6))* Ebon Research Systems Publishing, LLC.

Anderson, Wayne. Fighting Racial Discrimination: Treating All Americans Fairly under the Law. (Progressive Movement 1900-1920: Efforts to Reform America's New Industrial Society Ser.). 32p. 2009. (gr. 3-4). 47.90 *(978-1-60854-164-5(9))* 2004. (Illus.). (YA). (gr. 5-9). lib. bdg. 22.50 *(978-1-4042-0189-7(0))* Rosen Publishing Group, Inc., The.

Aretha, David. Black Power. 2011. (Civil Rights Movement Ser.). (Illus.). 128p. (gr. 7-12). 28.95 *(978-1-59935-164-3(1))* Reynolds, Morgan Inc.

—Brown V. Board of Education. 2013. (The Civil Rights Movement Ser.). (Illus.). 128p. (YA). 28.95 *(978-1-59935-370-8(9))* Reynolds, Morgan Inc.

—Freedom Summer. 2007. (Civil Rights Movement Ser.). (Illus.). 128p. (J). (gr. 3-7). lib. bdg. 27.95 *(978-1-59935-059-2(9))* Reynolds, Morgan Inc.

—Martin Luther King Jr. & the 1963 March on Washington. 2014. (Illus.). 112p. (J). 28.95 *(978-1-59935-372-2(5))* Reynolds, Morgan Inc.

—Selma & the Voting Rights Act. 2007. (Civil Rights Movement Ser.). (Illus.). 128p. (J). (gr. 3-7). lib. bdg. 27.95 *(978-1-59935-056-1(4))* Reynolds, Morgan Inc.

—Sit-Ins & Freedom Rides. 2009. (Civil Rights Movement Ser.). 128p. (J). (gr. 4-7). 28.95 *(978-1-59935-098-1(X))* Reynolds, Morgan Inc.

—The Story of Rosa Parks & the Montgomery Bus Boycott in Photographs. 2014. (Story of the Civil Rights Movement in Photographs Ser.). 48p. (J). 25.27 *(978-0-7660-4234-6(0))*; pap. 8.95 *(978-1-4644-0411-5(9))* Enslow Pubs., Inc.

—The Story of the Birmingham Civil Rights Movement in Photographs. 2014. (Story of the Civil Rights Movement in Photographs Ser.). 48p. (J). lib. bdg. 25.27 *(978-0-7660-4237-7(5))* Enslow Pubs., Inc.

—The Story of the Civil Rights Freedom Rides in Photographs. 2014. (Story of the Civil Rights Movement in Photographs Ser.). 48p. (J). lib. bdg. 25.27 *(978-0-7660-4236-0(7))* Enslow Pubs., Inc.

—The Story of the Civil Rights March on Washington for Jobs & Freedom in Photographs. 2014. (Story of the Civil Rights Movement in Photographs Ser.). 48p. (J). lib. bdg. 25.27 *(978-0-7660-4238-4(3))* Enslow Pubs., Inc.

Ashby, Ruth. Rosa Parks: Freedom Rider. 2008. (Sterling Biographies(r) Ser.). (ENG., Illus.). 128p. (J). (gr. 5). pap. 5.95 *(978-1-4027-4865-3(5))* Sterling Publishing Co., Inc.

Bader, Bonnie. Who Was Martin Luther King, Jr.? Wolf, Elizabeth, illus. 2008. (Who Was...? Ser.). 105p. (J). (gr. 2-5). 12.65 *(978-0-7569-8935-4(3))* Perfection Learning Corp.

Banting, Erinn. The Civil Rights Movement. 2008. (African American History Ser.). (Illus.). 48p. (YA). (gr. 5-8). lib. bdg. 29.05 *(978-1-59036-882-4(7))*; pap. 10.95 *(978-1-59036-883-1(5))* Weigl Pubs., Inc.

—Civil Rights Movement. 2013. (J). *(978-1-62127-190-1(0))*; pap. *(978-1-62127-196-3(X))* Weigl Pubs., Inc.

—Rosa Parks. 2005. (Great African American Women for Kids Ser.). (Illus.). 24p. (J). (gr. 2-3). lib. bdg. 26.00 *(978-1-59036-336-2(1))*; (gr. 3-7). per. 8.95 *(978-1-59036-342-3(6))* Weigl Pubs., Inc.

Bass, Hester. Seeds of Freedom: The Peaceful Integration of Huntsville, Alabama. Lewis, E. B., illus. 2015. (ENG.). 32p. (J). (gr. k-3). 16.99 *(978-0-7636-6919-5(9))* Candlewick Pr.

Bausum, Ann & National Geographic Kids Staff. The March Against Fear: The Last Great Walk of the Civil Rights Movement & the Emergence of Black Power. 2017. (ENG., Illus.). 144p. (J). (gr. 7-9). 18.99 *(978-1-4263-2665-3(3))*, National Geographic Children's Bks.) National Geographic Society.

Belinda, Rochelle. Witnesses to Freedom: Young People Who Fought for Civil Rights. 2014. (ENG.). 116p. (J). 12.24 *(978-1-63245-230-6(8))* Lectorum Pubns., Inc.

Benson, Kathleen & Haskins, Jim. John Lewis in the Lead: A Story of the Civil Rights Movement, 1 vol. Andrews, Benny, illus. 2006. (ENG.). 40p. (gr. 2-7). 17.95 *(978-1-58430-250-6(X))* Lee & Low Bks., Inc.

bjornlund, lydia. The Civil Rights Movement. 2012. (Illus.). 96p. (J). lib. bdg. *(978-1-60152-478-2(1))* ReferencePoint Pr., Inc.

Bjornlund, Lydia. Rosa Parks & the Montgomery Bus Boycott. 2007. (Lucent Library of Black History Ser.). (ENG., Illus.). 128p. (gr. 8-12). lib. bdg. 39.40 *(978-1-4205-0010-3(4))*, Lucent Bks.) Cengage Gale.

Bolden, Tonya. M. L. K. The Journey of a King. Adelman, Bob, ed. 2007. (ENG., Illus.). 128p. (J). (gr. 5-9). 27.95 *(978-0-8109-5476-2(1))*, Abrams Bks. for Young Readers) Abrams, Inc.

—W. E. B. du Bois: A Twentieth-Century Life. 2008. (Up Close Ser.). (ENG.). 224p. (YA). (gr. 7-18). 16.99 *(978-0-670-06302-4(9))*, Viking Books for Young Readers) Penguin Young Readers Group.

Boshier, Rosa. How to Analyze the Works of Martin Luther King Jr, 1 vol. 2013. (Essential Critiques Set 4 Ser.). (ENG., Illus.). 112p. (J). (gr. 6-12). lib. bdg. 35.64 *(978-1-61783-647-3(8))*, Essential Library) ABDO Publishing Co.

Brandt, Keith & Mattern, Joanne. Rosa Parks: Freedom Rider. Griffith, Gershom, illus. 2006. 54p. (J). pap. *(978-0-439-66045-7(9))* Scholastic, Inc.

Brimner, Larry Dane. Birmingham Sunday. 2010. (ENG., Illus.). 48p. (J). (gr. 5-18). 17.95 *(978-1-59078-613-0(0))*, Calkins Creek) Boyds Mills Pr.

Brown, Jonatha A. Martin Luther King, Jr. 2005. (People We Should Know Ser.). (Illus.). 24p. (gr. 1-4). pap. 8.15 *(978-0-8368-4474-0(2))*; (ENG & SPA., lib. bdg. 22.00 *(978-0-8368-4583-9(8))*; lib. bdg. 22.00 *(978-0-8368-4467-2(X))* Stevens, Gareth Publishing LLLP. (Weekly Reader Leveled Readers).

—Rosa Parks. 2005. (People We Should Know Ser.). (Illus.). 24p. (gr. 1-4). pap. 8.15 *(978-0-8368-4755-0(5))*; (ENG & SPA., pap. 8.15 *(978-0-8368-4769-7(5))*; (ENG & SPA., lib. bdg. 22.00 *(978-0-8368-4762-8(8))*; lib. bdg. 22.00 *(978-0-8368-4748-2(2))* Stevens, Gareth Publishing LLLP. (Weekly Reader Leveled Readers).

Bull, Angela. The Story of Martin Luther King, Level 4. 2009. (DK Readers Ser.). (ENG.). 48p. (J). (gr. 3-7). 3.99 *(978-0-7566-5615-7(X))*, DK Children) Dorling Kindersley Publishing, Inc.

Burlingame, Jeff. Malcolm X: Fighting for Human Rights. 2017. (Rebels with a Cause Ser.). 128p. (J). (gr. 8-8). lib. bdg. 37.27 ***(978-0-7660-8519-0(8))*** Enslow Pubs., Inc.

Capek, Michael. Civil Rights Movement, 1 vol. 2013. (Essential Library of Social Change Ser.). (ENG.). 112p. (J). (gr. 6-12). lib. bdg. 35.64 *(978-1-61783-885-9(3))*, Essential Library) ABDO Publishing Co.

Caravantes, Peggy. Marcus Garvey: Black Nationalist. 2004. (Twentieth Century Leaders Ser.). (Illus.). 128p. (YA). (gr. 6-12). 23.95 *(978-1-931798-14-3(1))* Reynolds, Morgan Inc.

Cates, David. The Scottsboro Boys, 1 vol. 2012. (Essential Events Set 8 Ser.). (ENG.). 112p. (J). (gr. 6-12). lib. bdg. 35.64 *(978-1-61783-310-6(X))* ABDO Publishing Co.

Civil Rights Leaders, bks. 13, vol. 13. Incl. A. Philip Randolph & the African American Labor Movement. Miller, Calvin Craig. (Illus.). 160p. (YA). (gr. 6-12). 2005. 26.95 *(978-1-931798-50-1(8))*; Eternal Vigilance: The Story of Ida B. Wells-Barnett. Hinman, Bonnie. 128p. (gr. 6-10). 2011. lib. bdg. 28.95 *(978-1-59935-111-7(0))*; Freedom Cannot Rest: Ella Baker & the Civil Rights Movement. Bohannon, Lisa Frederiksen. (Illus.). 176p. (YA). (gr. 6-12). 2005. lib. bdg. 26.95 *(978-1-931798-71-6(0))*; Liberator: The Story of William Lloyd Garrison. Esty, Amos. 144p. 2011. 28.95 *(978-1-59935-137-7(4))*; No Compromise: The Story of Harvey Milk. Aretha, David. 100p. (YA). (gr. 5-9). 2009. lib. bdg. 28.95 *(978-1-59935-129-2(3))*; No Easy Answers: Bayard Rustin & the Civil Rights Movement. (Illus.). 160p. (J). (gr. 6-12). 2005. 26.95 *(978-1-931798-43-3(5))*; Roy Wilkins: Leader of the NAACP. Miller, Calvin Craig. (Illus.). 176p. (YA). (gr. 6-12). 2005. 26.95 *(978-1-931798-49-5(4))*; Stranger in My Own House: The Story of W. E. B. du Bois. Hinman, Bonnie. (Illus.). 176p. (gr. 6-12). 2005. 28.95 *(978-1-931798-45-7(1))*; Unbound & Unbroken: The Story of Frederick Douglass. Esty, Amos. 144p. (gr. 8-10). 2011. 28.95 *(978-1-59935-136-0(6))*; 2008. Set lib. bdg. 376.35 *(978-1-931798-99-0(0))* Reynolds, Morgan Inc.

Coleman, Wim & Perrin, Pat. Martin Luther King, Jr. National Historic Site: A MyReportLinks.com Book. 2005. (Virtual Field Trips Ser.). (Illus.). 48p. (J). (gr. 4-10). lib. bdg. 26.60 *(978-0-7660-5225-3(7))*, MyReportLinks.com Bks.) Enslow Pubs., Inc.

Conklin, Wendy. Civil Rights Movement, 1 vol. 2007. (Primary Source Readers Ser.). (ENG.). 32p. (J). (gr. 5-5). pap. 8.99 *(978-0-7439-0670-8(5))* Shell Educational Publishing.

Connors, Kathleen. The Life of Rosa Parks, Vol. 1. 2014. (Famous Lives Ser.). (ENG.). 24p. (J). (gr. 1-2). 22.60 *(978-1-4824-0419-7(2))* Stevens, Gareth Publishing LLLP.

Corey, Shana. A Time to Act: John F. Kennedy's Big Speech. Christie, R. Gregory, illus. 2017. (ENG.). 56p. (J). (gr. 3). 18.95 *(978-0-7358-4275-5(2))* North-South Bks., Inc.

Crayton, Lisa A. Freedom Riders. 2017. (J). ***(978-1-5383-8027-7(7))***; pap. ***(978-1-5383-8026-0(9))*** Rosen Publishing Group, Inc., The.

Crewe, Sabrina & Ingram, Scott. The 1963 Civil Rights March. 2005. (Events That Shaped America Ser.). (Illus.). 32p. (gr. 3-6). lib. bdg. 26.00 *(978-0-8368-3411-6(9))*, Gareth Stevens Learning Library) Stevens, Gareth Publishing LLLP.

Daly, Ruth. Rosa Parks. 2014. (J). *(978-1-4896-2452-9(X))* Weigl Pubs., Inc.

Davis, W. Harry. Changemaker: W. Harry Davis. Sturdevant, Lori, ed. 2004. (Illus.). 136p. (J). pap. 17.95 *(978-1-890434-60-1(4))* Afton Historical Society Pr.

Deal, Heidi. Perspectives on the Civil Rights Movement. 2018. (ENG.). 32p. (gr. 3-6). ***(978-1-63235-398-6(9))***, 12-Story Library) Pr. Room Editions LLC.

DeRubertis, Barbara. Let's Celebrate Martin Luther King, Jr. Day. Griffith, Gershom, illus. 2013. (Holidays & Heroes Ser.). 32p. (gr. 1-3). pap. 7.95 *(978-1-57565-638-0(8))* Kane Press, Inc.

deRubertis, Barbara. Let's Celebrate Martin Luther King, Jr. Day. Griffith, Gershom, illus. 2014. (Holidays & Heroes Ser.). 32p. (gr. 1-3). lib. bdg. 25.26 *(978-1-57565-724-0(4))* Kane Press, Inc.

—Let's Celebrate Martin Luther King, Jr. Day. 2013. 32p. pap. 16.95 *(978-1-57565-639-7(6))* Kane Press, Inc.

Deutsch, Stacia & Cohon, Rhody. Hot Pursuit: Murder in Mississippi. Orback, Craig, illus. 2010. (ENG.). 40p. (J). (gr. 3-5). pap. 7.95 *(978-0-7613-3956-4(6))*; lib. bdg. 17.95 *(978-0-7613-3955-7(8))* Lerner Publishing Group. (Kar-Ben Publishing).

Dubowski, Cathy East. Rosa Parks: Don't Give In! 2005. (Defining Moments Ser.). (Illus.). 32p. (J). (gr. 2-5). lib. bdg. 25.27 *(978-1-59716-078-0(4))* Bearport Publishing Co., Inc.

Dunn, Joeming W. Martin Luther King, Jr, 1 vol. Allen, Chris, illus. 2008. (Bio-Graphics Ser.). (ENG.). 32p. 28.50 *(978-1-60270-175-5(X))*, Graphic Planet- Nonfiction) ABDO Publishing Co.

Edison, Erin. Rosa Parks, 1 vol. 2013. (Great Women in History Ser.). (ENG., Illus.). 24p. (gr. k-1). lib. bdg. 21.99 *(978-1-62065-071-4(1))*, Pebble Bks.) Capstone Press of Coughlan Cos.

Edwards, Pamela Duncan. The Bus Ride That Changed History: The Story of Rosa Parks. Shanahan, Danny, illus. 2009. (ENG.). 32p. (J). (gr. -1-3). pap. 6.99 *(978-0-547-07674-4(6))* Houghton Mifflin Harcourt Publishing Co.

Ellis, Carol. African American Activists. 2012. (J). pap. *(978-1-4222-2384-0(1))* Mason Crest.

—African American Activists. Hill, Marc Lamont, ed. 2012. (Major Black Contributions from Emancipation to Civil Rights Ser.). 64p. (J). (gr. 5). 22.95 *(978-1-4222-2371-0(X))* Mason Crest.

Fandel, Jennifer. Martin Luther King, Jr: Great Civil Rights Leader, 1 vol. Bascle, Brian, illus. 2006. (Graphic Biographies Ser.). (ENG.). 32p. (gr. 3-4). 30.65 *(978-0-7368-6498-5(9))*, Graphic Library) Capstone Press of Coughlan Cos.

Feinstein, Stephen. Inspiring African-American Civil Rights Leaders. 2012. (African-American Collective Biographies Ser.). (Illus.). 112p. (J). (gr. 5-18). 33.27 *(978-1-59845-136-8(7))* Enslow Pubs., Inc.

—Lee sobre Martin Luther King, Jr. 2006. (I Like Biographies! Bilingual Ser.). Tr. of Read about Martin Luther King, Jr. (ENG & SPA., Illus.). 24p. (J). (gr. 1-3). lib. bdg. 22.60 *(978-0-7660-2745-9(7))*, Enslow Elementary) Enslow Pubs., Inc.

—Read about Martin Luther King, Jr. 2004. (I Like Biographies! Ser.). (Illus.). 24p. (J). lib. bdg. 24.95 *(978-0-7660-2300-0(1))* Enslow Pubs., Inc.

Ferris, Jeri Chase. Demanding Justice: A Story about Mary Ann Shadd Cary. Smith, Kimanne, illus. 2003. (Creative Minds Biographies Ser.). (ENG.). 64p. (gr. 4-8). 22.60 *(978-1-57505-177-2(X))*; pap. 8.95 *(978-0-87614-928-7(X))*, Carolrhoda Bks.) Lerner Publishing Group.

Fine, Edith Hope. Martin Luther King, Jr: Champion of Civil Rights. 2006. (Heroes of American History Ser.). (Illus.). 32p. (J). (gr. 3-7). lib. bdg. 23.94 *(978-0-7660-2466-3(0))*, Enslow Elementary) Enslow Pubs., Inc.

—Rosa Parks: Meet a Civil Rights Hero. 2004. (Meeting Famous People Ser.). (Illus.). 32p. (J). lib. bdg. 23.94 *(978-0-7660-2099-3(1))* Enslow Pubs., Inc.

Finlayson, Reggie. We Shall Overcome: The History of the American Civil Rights Movement. 2005. (People's History Ser.). (Illus.). 96p. (gr. 6-12). lib. bdg. 26.60 *(978-0-8225-0647-8(5))* Lerner Publishing Group.

Fiorelli, June Estep. Fannie Lou Hamer: A Voice for Freedom. 2004. (Avisson Young Adult Ser.). (Illus.). 117p. (J). pap. 19.95 *(978-1-888105-62-9(3))* Avisson Pr., Inc.

Fireside, Harvey & Rauf, Don. Separate but Equal: Plessy V. Ferguson. 2016. (US Supreme Court Landmark Cases Ser.). (Illus.). 128p. (J). 37.27 *(978-0-7660-8434-6(5))* Enslow Pubs., Inc.

Fleming, Alice. Martin Luther King, Jr. A Dream of Hope. 2008. (Sterling Biographies(r) Ser.). (ENG., Illus.). 128p. (J). (gr. 5). pap. 5.95 *(978-1-4027-4439-6(0))* Sterling Publishing Co., Inc.

Flowers, Arthur. I See the Promised Land: A Life of Martin Luther King, Jr., 1 vol. Chitrakar, Manu, illus. rev. ed. 2013. (ENG.). 156p. (J). (gr. 6). 16.95 *(978-1-55498-328-5(2))* Groundwood Bks. CAN. Dist: Publishers Group West (PGW).

Flynn, Riley. Martin Luther King Jr, 1 vol. 2014. (Great African-Americans Ser.). (ENG.). 24p. (gr. k-1). lib. bdg. 21.99 *(978-1-4765-3953-9(7))*, Pebble Bks.) Capstone Press of Coughlan Cos.

Foy, Debbie. Civil-Rights Activists. 2012. (Black History Makers Ser.). (ENG.). 24p. (J). (gr. 3-8). pap. 8.25 *(978-1-4488-7054-7(2))*; lib. bdg. 22.60 *(978-1-4488-6638-0(3))* Rosen Publishing Group, Inc., The. (PowerKids Pr.).

Fradin, Dennis Brindell. The Montgomery Bus Boycott. 2009. (Turning Points in U. S. History Ser.). 48p. (gr. 3-18). 31.36 *(978-0-7614-4258-5(8))* Marshall Cavendish Corp.

Freedman, Russell. Because They Marched: The People's Campaign for Voting Rights That Changed America. 2014. (ENG., Illus.). 96p. (J). (gr. 5-12). 20.00 *(978-0-8234-2921-9(0))* Holiday Hse., Inc.

—Freedom Walkers: The Story of the Montgomery Bus Boycott. (ENG., Illus.). 112p. (J). 2009. (gr. 3-7). pap. 14.95 *(978-0-8234-2195-4(3))* 2006. (gr. 5-10). 18.95 *(978-0-8234-2031-5(0))* Holiday Hse., Inc.

Fremon, David K. The Jim Crow Laws & Racism in United States History. 2014. (In United States History Ser.). (Illus.). 96p. (J). (gr. 5-12). 27.94 *(978-0-7660-6092-0(6))*; pap. 10.95 *(978-0-7660-6093-7(4))* Enslow Pubs., Inc.

Ganeri, Anita. I Have a Dream: Martin Luther King, Jr. & the Fight for Equal Rights. 2013. (Turning Points in History Ser.). (Illus.). 48p. (gr. 5-12). 37.10 *(978-1-59920-972-2(1))* Black Rabbit Bks.

Garbus, Julia. Brown vs the Board of Education Trial. Greenhaven Press Staff, ed. 2014. (Perspectives on Modern World History Ser.). (ENG., Illus.). 224p. (gr. 10-12). lib. bdg. 47.80 *(978-0-7377-7307-1(3))*, Greenhaven Pr., Inc.) Cengage Gale.

Gelfand, Dale Evva. Coretta Scott King: Civil Rights Activist. 2nd rev. ed. 2006. (Black Americans of Achievement Legacy Edition Ser.). (Illus.). 137p. (YA). (gr. 7-12). lib. bdg. 35.00 *(978-0-7910-9522-5(3))* Facts On File, Inc.

George, Enzo. The Civil Rights Movement. 2015. (Primary Sources in U. S. History Ser.). (ENG., Illus.). 48p. (J). (gr. 4-4). 31.36 *(978-1-5026-0496-5(5))* Cavendish Square Publishing.

Giovanni, Nikki. Rosa. Collier, Bryan, illus. rev. ed. 2005. (ENG.). 40p. (J). (gr. -1-3). 17.99 *(978-0-8050-7106-1(7))*, 9780805071061, Holt, Henry & Co. Bks. For Young Readers) Holt, Henry & Co.

—Rosa. Collier, Bryan, illus. 2007. (ENG.). 40p. (J). (gr. -1-3). per. 8.99 *(978-0-312-37602-4(2))*, 9780312376024) Square Fish.

—Rosa. Collier, Bryan, illus. 2011. (J). (gr. 2-5). 29.95 *(978-0-545-04261-1(5))* Weston Woods Studios, Inc.

Gitlin, Martin. The Montgomery Bus Boycott: A History Perspectives Book. 2013. (Perspectives Library). (ENG., Illus.). 32p. (J). (gr. 4-8). 28.50 *(978-1-62431-418-6(X))*, 202792); pap. 14.21 *(978-1-62431-494-0(5))*, 202794) Cherry Lake Publishing.

Gold, Susan Dudley. Brown V. Board of Education: Separate but Equal? 2004. (Supreme Court Milestones Ser.). (Illus.). 143p. (J). 37.07 *(978-0-7614-1842-9(3))*, Benchmark Bks.) Marshall Cavendish Corp.

—The Civil Rights ACT of 1964. 2010. (Landmark Legislation Ser.). 128p. (YA). (gr. 7-12). 39.93 *(978-1-60870-040-0(2))* Marshall Cavendish GBR. Dist: Marshall Cavendish Corp.

Goldsworthy, Steve. Politics: African American History. 2011. (J). (gr. 5-8). pap. 14.95 *(978-1-61690-666-5(9))*, AV2 by Weigl); (Illus.). 48p. (gr. 1-4). 29.99 *(978-1-61690-662-7(6))* Weigl Pubs., Inc.

Gotsch, Patrice. Martin Luther King, Jr: Changing Lives. Arreola, Gil, illus. 2006. 19p. pap. 6.30 *(978-1-55501-779-8(7))* Ballard & Tighe Pubs.

Green, Richard L., et al, eds. A Salute to Black Civil Rights Leaders. Dobson, S. Gaston, illus. (Empak "Black History" Publication). (J). pap. 1.00 *(978-0-9616156-3-5(X))* Empak Publishing Co.

Gregory, Josh. Martin Luther King Jr. 2015. (ENG., Illus.). 48p. (J). pap. 6.95 *(978-0-531-21208-0(4))*, Orchard Bks.) Scholastic Library Publishing.

Haidy, Emma E. Martin Luther King, Jr. Bane, Jeff, illus. 2016. (My Early Library: My Itty-Bitty Bio Ser.). (ENG.). 24p. (J). (gr. k-1). 28.50 *(978-1-63470-477-9(0))*, 207639) Cherry Lake Publishing.

Hall, M. C. Martin Luther King, Jr. Civil Rights Leader, 1 vol. Soud, illus. 2008. (Beginner Biographies Ser.). (ENG.). 32p. (gr. -1-3). 28.50 *(978-1-60270-251-6(9))*, Looking Glass Library- Nonfiction) Magic Wagon.

Hally, Ashleigh. Coretta Scott King. 2012. (Illus.). 24p. (J). *(978-1-935884-78-1(6))*; pap. *(978-1-935884-84-2(0))* State Standards Publishing, LLC.

Hardy, P. Stephen & Hardy, Sheila. Extraordinary People of the Civil Rights Movement. 2006. (Extraordinary People Ser.). (ENG., Illus.). 288p. (J). (gr. 6-18). lib. bdg. 40.00 *(978-0-516-25461-6(8))*, Children's Pr.) Scholastic Library Publishing.

Hasday, Judy L. Women in the Civil Rights Movement. 2012. (J). pap. *(978-1-4222-2366-6(3))* Institute of Physics Publishing.

—Women in the Civil Rights Movement. 2012. 64p. (J). (gr. 5). 22.95 *(978-1-4222-2356-7(6))* Mason Crest.

Haskins, James. Black Stars of the Civil Rights Movement. 2003. (Black Stars Ser.: 2). (ENG., Illus.). 128p. (J). (gr. 5-9). pap. 18.00 *(978-0-471-22068-8(X))*, Wiley) Wiley, John & Sons, Inc.

—Freedom Rides: Journey for Justice. 2005. (Illus.). 88p. (J). (gr. 4-17). per. 10.95 *(978-0-940975-94-1(7))*, Sankofa Bks.) Just Us Bks., Inc.

Haskins, Jim. Delivering Justice: W. W. Law & the Fight for Civil Rights. Andrews, Benny, illus. 2008. (ENG.). 32p. (J). (gr. k-3). pap. 7.99 *(978-0-7636-3880-1(3))* Candlewick Pr.

Haskins, Jim, et al. John Lewis in the Lead: A Story of the Civil Rights Movement, 1 vol. 2006. (ENG., Illus.). 40p. (J). pap. 11.95 *(978-1-60060-849-0(3))* Lee & Low Bks., Inc.

Hermann, Spring. The Struggle for Equality: Women & Minorities in America. 2006. (American Saga Ser.). (Illus.). 128p. (J). (gr. 5-9). lib. bdg. 33.27 *(978-0-7660-2573-8(X))* Enslow Pubs., Inc.

Herr, Melody. Sitting for Equal Service: Lunch Counter Sit-Ins, United States, 1960s. 2010. (Civil Rights Struggles around the World Ser.). (ENG.). 160p. (gr. 9-12). lib. bdg. 38.60 *(978-0-8225-8970-9(2))* Lerner Publishing Group.

Higgins, Nadia. The Split History of the Civil Rights Movement: A Perspectives Flip Book, 1 vol. 2014. (Perspectives Flip Bks.). (ENG.). 64p. (gr. 5-6). lib. bdg. 33.99 *(978-0-7565-4736-3(9))*, CPB Grades 4-8) Compass Point Bks.

Hinman, Bonnie. Eternal Vigilance: The Story of Ida B. Wells-Barnett. 2011. (Civil Rights Leaders Ser.). 128p. (gr. 6-10). lib. bdg. 28.95 *(978-1-59935-111-7(0))* Reynolds, Morgan Inc.

Hinton, KaaVonia. Brown V. Board of Education, Topeka, KS, 1954. 2009. (Monumental Milestones Ser.). 48p. (YA). (gr. 4-7). lib. bdg. 29.95 *(978-1-58415-738-0(0))* Mitchell Lane Pubs., Inc.

—Martin Luther King, Jr. 2008. (What's So Great About...? Ser.). (Illus.). 32p. (YA). (gr. 2-4). lib. bdg. 25.70 *(978-1-58415-724-3(0))* Mitchell Lane Pubs., Inc.

Hinton, Kerry. The Black Power Movement & Civil Unrest. 2017. (J). pap. ***(978-1-5383-8016-1(1))*** Rosen Publishing Group, Inc., The.

—Sit-Ins & Nonviolent Protest. 2017. (J). pap. ***(978-1-5383-8064-2(1))***, Rosen Young Adult) Rosen Publishing Group, Inc., The.

Hoe, Susan C. Rosa Parks. 2009. (Sharing the American Dream Ser.). 64p. (YA). (gr. 7-12). 22.95 *(978-1-4222-0597-6(5))* Mason Crest.

Hooks, Gwendolyn. If You Were a Kid During the Civil Rights Movement. 2017. (If You Were a Kid Ser.). (ENG., Illus.). 32p. (J). lib. bdg. 26.00 *(978-0-531-22384-0(1))*, Children's Pr.) Scholastic Library Publishing.

Hopkinson, Deborah. Sweet Land of Liberty, 1 vol. Jenkins, Leonard, illus. 2007. (ENG.). 32p. (J). (gr. 1-5). 16.95 *(978-1-56145-395-5(1))* Peachtree Pubs.

Houtman, Jacqueline, et al. Bayard Rustin: The Invisible Activist. 2014. (J). pap. *(978-1-937768-58-4(9))* QuakerPress.

Howard, Melanie A. Civil Rights Marches, 1 vol. 2004. (American Moments Ser.). (ENG.). 48p. (gr. 4-8). 27.07 *(978-1-59197-282-2(5))*, Abdo & Daughters) ABDO Publishing Co.

Howell, Izzi. Rosa Parks. 2016. (Fact Cat: History Ser.). (ENG., Illus.). 24p. (J). (gr. k-2). 14.99 *(978-0-7502-9771-4(9))*, Wayland) Hachette Children's Group GBR. Dist: Hachette Bk. Group.

Hull, Mary. Rosa Parks: Civil Rights Leader. 2nd rev. ed. 2006. (Black Americans of Achievement Ser.). (Illus.). 122p. (YA). (gr. 7-12). lib. bdg. 35.00 *(978-0-7910-9523-2(1))* Facts On File, Inc.

Hunter-Gault, Charlayne. To the Mountaintop: My Journey Through the Civil Rights Movement. 2014. (New York Times Ser.). (ENG., Illus.). 224p. (YA). (gr. 7). pap. 12.99 *(978-1-250-04062-6(0))*, 9781250040626) Square Fish.

Hurt, Avery Elizabeth. Rosa Parks: Civil Rights Activist. 2017. (J). pap. ***(978-1-5383-8102-1(8))*** Rosen Publishing Group, Inc., The.

Hussey, Maria. The Rise of the Jim Crow ERA. 2015. (African American Experience: from Slavery to the Presidency Ser.). (ENG., Illus.). 80p. (J). (gr. 7-8). 32.90

(978-1-68048-042-9(1), Britannica Educational Publishing) Rosen Publishing Group, Inc., The.

Hussey, Maria, ed. The Rise of the Jim Crow Era. 2015. (African American Experience: from Slavery to the Presidency Ser.). (ENG.). 80p. (YA). (gr. 7-8). 65.80 (978-1-68048-043-6(X), Britannica Educational Publishing) Rosen Publishing Group, Inc., The.

Jakoubek, Robert E. Martin Luther King, Jr. Civil Rights Leader. 2004. (Black Americans of Achievement Ser.). (Illus.). 112p. (gr. 6-12). 35.00 (978-0-7910-8161-7(3), Chelsea Hse.) Facts On File, Inc.

Jazynka, Kitson. National Geographic Readers: Rosa Parks. 2015. (Readers Bios Ser.). (ENG., Illus.). 32p. (J). (gr. k-3). pap. 3.99 (978-1-4263-2141-2(4), National Geographic Children's Bks.) National Geographic Society.

Jeffrey, Gary. Malcolm X & the Fight for African American Unity. 2012. (Graphic History of the Civil Rights Movement Ser.). (Illus.). 24p. (J). (gr. 3-8). pap. 8.15 (978-1-4339-7488-5(6)); lib. bdg. 23.95 (978-1-4339-7487-8(8)) Stevens, Gareth Publishing LLLP.

—Martin Luther King Jr: The Life of a Civil Rights Leader. 2009. (Graphic Nonfiction Biographies Ser.). (ENG.). 48p. (YA). (gr. 4-5). 58.50 (978-1-61513-021-4(7), Rosen Reference) Rosen Publishing Group, Inc., The.

—Martin Luther King Jr: The Life of a Civil Rights Leader. Forsey, Chris, illus. 2007. (Graphic Nonfiction Biographies Ser.). (ENG.). 48p. (YA). (gr. 4-7). lib. bdg. 31.95 (978-1-4042-0858-2(5)) Rosen Publishing Group, Inc., The.

—Martin Luther King Jr: The Life of a Civil Rights Leader. Forsey, Christopher, illus. 2007. (Graphic Biographies Ser.). (ENG.). 48p. (gr. 5-8). pap. 14.05 (978-1-4042-0921-3(2)) Rosen Publishing Group, Inc., The.

—Martin Luther King Jr. & the March on Washington. 2012. (Graphic History of the Civil Rights Movement Ser.). (Illus.). 24p. (J). (gr. 3-8). pap. 8.15 (978-1-4339-7492-2(4)); lib. bdg. 23.95 (978-1-4339-7491-5(6)) Stevens, Gareth Publishing LLLP.

—Medgar Evers & the NAACP. 2012. (Graphic History of the Civil Rights Movement Ser.). 24p. (J). (gr. 3-8). pap. 8.15 (978-1-4339-7496-0(7)); lib. bdg. 23.95 (978-1-4339-7495-3(9)) Stevens, Gareth Publishing LLLP.

—Rosa Parks & the Montgomery Bus Boycott. 2012. (Graphic History of the Civil Rights Movement Ser.). (Illus.). 24p. (J). (gr. 3-8). pap. 8.15 (978-1-4339-7500-4(9)); lib. bdg. 23.95 (978-1-4339-7499-1(1)) Stevens, Gareth Publishing LLLP.

Johnson, Robin. March on Washington. 2013. (ENG.). 48p. (J). (978-0-7787-1101-8(3)); pap. (978-0-7787-1121-6(8)) Crabtree Publishing Co.

Jones, Rob Lloyd. Martin Luther King, Jr. 2006. (Illus.). 62p. (J). pap. (978-0-439-02299-6(1)) Scholastic, Inc.

Kallen, Stuart A. Marcus Garvey & the Back to Africa Movement. 2006. (Lucent Library of Black History). (ENG., Illus.). 112p. (YA). (gr. 7-10). lib. bdg. 34.80 (978-1-59018-838-5(1), Lucent Bks.) Cengage Gale.

—Women of the Civil Rights Movement. 2005. (Women in History Ser.). (ENG., Illus.). 112p. (YA). (gr. 7-10). lib. bdg. 32.45 (978-1-59018-569-8(2), Lucent Bks.) Cengage Gale.

Kemp, Kristin. Amazing Americans: Rosa Parks, 1 vol. rev. ed. 2014. (Primary Source Readers Content & Literacy Ser.). (ENG., Illus.). 32p. (gr. 3-3). pap. 8.99 (978-1-4333-7375-6(0)) Teacher Created Materials, Inc.

—Amazing Americans: Thurgood Marshall, 1 vol. rev. ed. 2014. (Primary Source Readers Content & Literacy Ser.). (ENG., Illus.). 32p. (gr. 3-3). pap. 8.99 (978-1-4333-7374-9(2)) Teacher Created Materials, Inc.

Kimmel, Allison Crotzer. The Montgomery Bus Boycott. 2015. (We Shall Overcome Ser.). (ENG.). 32p. (gr. 3-4). lib. bdg. 27.32 (978-1-4914-2043-0(X)) Capstone Press of Coughlan Cos.

King, Martin Luther, Jr. I Have a Dream. 2007. (Illus.). 40p. (J). (gr. -1-3). 14.65 (978-0-7569-8119-8(0)) Perfection Learning Corp.

—I Have a Dream, 1 vol. Nelson, Kadir, illus. 2012. (ENG.). 40p. (J). (gr. k-12). 18.99 (978-0-375-85887-1(3), Schwartz & Wade Bks.) Random Hse. Children's Bks.

King, Martin Luther, III. My Daddy, Dr. Martin Luther King, Jr. Ford, A. G., illus. 2013. 32p. (J). (gr. -1-3). 18.89 (978-0-06-028076-5(X)); (ENG.). 17.99 (978-0-06-028075-8(1)) HarperCollins Pubs. (Amistad).

King, Wilma. Children of the Emancipation. 2005. (Picture the American Past Ser.). (Illus.). 48p. (gr. 2-5). 22.60 (978-1-57505-396-7(9)) Lerner Publishing Group.

Kingston, Anna. Respecting the Contributions of African Americans. 2012. (Stop Bullying Now! Ser.). (ENG., Illus.). 24p. (J). (gr. 3-6). 22.60 (978-1-4488-7448-4(3)); pap. 8.25 (978-1-4488-7521-4(8)) Rosen Publishing Group, Inc., The. (PowerKids Pr.).

Kishel, Ann-Marie. Rosa Parks: A Life of Courage. 2006. (Pull Ahead Books-Biographies Ser.). (ENG., Illus.). 32p. (gr. k-3). lib. bdg. 22.60 (978-0-8225-3478-5(9), Lerner Pubns.) Lerner Publishing Group.

—Rosa Parks: Una Vida de Valentia. Translations.com Staff, tr. 2006. (Libros para Avanzar-Biografias (Pull Ahead Books-Biographies) Ser.). (ENG & SPA., Illus.). 32p. (gr. k-3). lib. bdg. 22.60 (978-0-8225-6239-9(1)) Lerner Publishing Group.

Kittinger, Jo S. Rosa's Bus: The Ride to Civil Rights. Walker, Steven, illus. 2010. (ENG.). 40p. (J). (gr. 2-4). 17.95 (978-1-59078-722-9(6)) Boyds Mills Pr.

Krull, Kathleen. What Was the March on Washington? Tomkinson, Tim, illus. 2013. (What Was? Ser.). (ENG.). 112p. (J). (gr. 3-7). pap. 5.99 (978-0-448-46287-5(7), Grosset & Dunlap) Penguin Young Readers Group.

—What Was the March on Washington? 2013. (What Was...? Ser.). lib. bdg. 16.00 (978-0-606-29974-9(2), Turtleback) Turtleback Bks.

Krumm, Brian. The Little Rock Nine: A Primary Source Exploration of the Battle for School Integration, 1 vol. 2014. (We Shall Overcome Ser.). (ENG.). 32p. (gr. 3-4). lib. bdg. 27.32 (978-1-4914-0225-2(3)) Capstone Press of Coughlan Cos.

Kurtz, Jane. Martin's Dream. Bates, Amy June, illus. 2008. (Ready-To-Reads Ser.). (ENG.). 32p. (J). (gr. -1-1). pap. 3.99 (978-1-4169-2774-7(3), Simon Spotlight) Simon Spotlight.

Levinson, Cynthia. We've Got a Job: The 1963 Birmingham Children's March, 1 vol. 2015. (ENG.). 180p. (gr. 5-9). pap. 13.95 (978-1-56145-844-8(9)) Peachtree Pubs.

—The Youngest Marcher: The Story of a Young Civil Rights Activist. Brantley-Newton, Vanessa, illus. 2017. (ENG.). 40p. (J). (gr. k-5). 17.99 (978-1-4814-0070-1(3)) Simon & Schuster, Inc.

Levinson, Cynthia Y. We've Got a Job: The 1963 Birmingham Children's March, 1 vol. 2012. (ENG.). 192p. (J). 19.95 (978-1-56145-627-7(6)) Peachtree Pubs.

Linde, Barbara M. Malcolm X. 2011. (Civil Rights Crusaders Ser.). 24p. (J). (gr. 2-5). pap. 8.15 (978-1-4339-5688-1(8), Gareth Stevens Learning Library); lib. bdg. 22.60 (978-1-4339-5686-7(1)) Stevens, Gareth Publishing LLLP.

—Martin Luther King Jr. 2011. (Civil Rights Crusaders Ser.). (Illus.). 24p. (gr. 2-5). (J). pap. 8.15 (978-1-4339-5692-8(6), Gareth Stevens Learning Library); (YA). lib. bdg. 22.60 (978-1-4339-5690-4(X)) Stevens, Gareth Publishing LLLP.

—Rosa Parks. 2011. (Civil Rights Crusaders Ser.). (Illus.). 24p. (gr. 2-5). (J). pap. 8.15 (978-1-4339-5696-6(9), Gareth Stevens Learning Library); (YA). lib. bdg. 22.60 (978-1-4339-5694-2(2)) Stevens, Gareth Publishing LLLP.

Linney, Susan. Martin Luther King, Jr: With a Discussion of Responsibility. 2004. (Values in Action Ser.). (J). (978-1-59203-069-6(6)) Learning Challenge, Inc.

Lochte, Hilary. W. E. B. du Bois. 2015. (Heroes of Black History Ser.). (ENG., Illus.). 32p. (J). (gr. 3-4). 26.60 (978-1-4824-2922-0(5)) Stevens, Gareth Publishing LLLP.

Loughran, P. J., illus. Turning 15 on the Road to Freedom: My Story of the Selma Voting Rights March. 2015. (ENG.). 128p. (YA). (gr. 7). 19.99 (978-0-8037-4123-2(5), Dial Bks) Penguin Young Readers Group.

Lucas, Eileen. Cracking the Wall: The Struggles of the Little Rock Nine. Anthony, Mark, illus. 2007. pap. 39.95 incl. audio compact disk (978-1-59519-943-0(8)); pap. 37.95 incl. audio (978-1-59519-939-3(X)) Live Oak Media.

Lüsted, Marcia Amidon. Lyndon B. Johnson & the Civil Rights ACT. 2017. (J). pap. **(978-1-5081-7746-3(5))** Rosen Publishing Group, Inc., The.

Mahoney, Emily Jankowski. American Civil Rights Movement. 2016. (Civic Participation: Working for Civil Rights Ser.). 00032p. (J). (gr. 5-5). pap. 10.00 (978-1-4994-2791-2(3), PowerKids Pr.) Rosen Publishing Group, Inc., The.

Maloof, Torrey. Martin Luther King Jr: Destined to Lead. 2016. (Primary Source Readers Ser.). (Illus.). 32p. (gr. 2-2). 8.99 (978-1-4938-2559-2(3)) Teacher Created Materials, Inc.

Maloof, Torrey. You Are There! March on Washington, August 28 1963. 2017. (Time for Kids Nonfiction Readers Ser.). lib. bdg. 19.65 **(978-0-606-40288-0(8))** Turtleback Bks.

Manheimer, Ann S. Martin Luther King Jr: Dreaming of Equality. 2004. (Trailblazer Biographies Ser.). (ENG., Illus.). 112p. (gr. 5-9). 31.93 (978-1-57505-627-2(5), Carolrhoda Bks.) Lerner Publishing Group.

Mara, Wil. Martin Luther King Jr. 2013. (Rookie Biographies(r) Ser.). (ENG.). 32p. (J). pap. 5.95 (978-0-531-24704-4(X)); lib. bdg. 23.00 (978-0-531-24738-9(4)) Scholastic Library Publishing.

—Rosa Parks. (Rookie Biographies Ser.). (ENG., Illus.). 32p. (J). (gr. 1-2). 2004. pap. 4.95 (978-0-516-27916-9(5)) 2007. pap. 4.95 (978-0-531-12592-2(0)) Scholastic Library Publishing. (Children's Pr.).

—Rosa Parks: Mother of the Civil Rights Movement. 2014. (Rookie Biographies(tm) Ser.). (ENG.). 32p. (J). lib. bdg. 25.00 (978-0-531-20561-7(4)); pap. 5.95 (978-0-531-21204-2(1)) Scholastic Library Publishing.

Marsico, Katie. The Montgomery Bus Boycott: Milestone of the Civil Rights Movement. 2011. (Perspectives on 3 Ser.). (Illus.). 112p. (J). (gr. 7). 39.93 (978-1-60870-447-7(5)) Marshall Cavendish Corp.

Martin Luther King Jr. (Illus.). 112p. pap. 9.95 (978-0-8225-5316-8(3)) Lerner Publishing Group.

Mayer, Robert H. When the Children Marched: The Birmingham Civil Rights Movement. 2008. (Prime (Middle/Senior) Ser.). (Illus.). 176p. (J). (gr. 3-7). lib. bdg. 35.94 (978-0-7660-2930-9(1)) Enslow Pubs., Inc.

McKissack, Patricia C. & McKissack, Fredrick L. Martin Luther King, Jr. Civil Rights Leader. 2013. (Famous African Americans Ser.). 24p. (J). (gr. k-3). pap. 7.95 (978-1-4644-0203-6(5)); (Illus.). 22.60 (978-0-7660-4099-1(2)) Enslow Pubs., Inc. (Enslow Elementary).

McNeese, Tim. Brown V. Board of Education: Integrating America's Schools. 2006. (Great Supreme Court Decisions Ser.). (Illus.). 144p. (YA). (gr. 5-9). lib. bdg. 32.95 (978-0-7910-9238-5(0)) Facts On File, Inc.

McPherson, Stephanie Sammartino. Biography Coretta Scott King. 2007. (Biography Ser.). (Illus.). 112p. (YA). (gr. 7-12). lib. bdg. 29.27 (978-0-8225-7156-8(0)) Twenty First Century Bks.

Meltzer, Brad. I Am Martin Luther King, Jr. Eliopoulos, Christopher, illus. 2016. (Ordinary People Change the World Ser.). (ENG.). 40p. (J). (gr. k-3). 14.99 (978-0-525-42852-7(6), Dial Bks) Penguin Young Readers Group.

—I Am Rosa Parks. Eliopoulos, Christopher, illus. 2014. (Ordinary People Change World Ser.). (ENG.). 40p. (J). (gr. -1-k). 14.99 (978-0-8037-4085-3(9), Dial Bks) Penguin Publishing Group.

Michelson, Richard. As Good As Anybody. Colón, Raúl, illus. 2013. (ENG.). 40p. (J). (gr. 1-4). 7.99 (978-0-385-75387-6(X), Dragonfly Bks.) Random Hse. Children's Bks.

Miller, Calvin Craig. A. Philip Randolph & the African American Labor Movement. 2005. (Civil Rights Leaders Ser.). (Illus.). 160p. (YA). (gr. 6-12). 26.95 (978-1-931798-50-1(8)) Reynolds, Morgan Inc.

—Roy Wilkins: Leader of the NAACP. 2005. (Civil Rights Leaders Ser.). (Illus.). 176p. (YA). (gr. 6-12). 26.95 (978-1-931798-49-5(4)) Reynolds, Morgan Inc.

Miller, Connie Colwell. Rosa Parks & the Montgomery Bus Boycott, 1 vol. Kalal, Dan, illus. 2006. (Graphic History Ser.). (ENG.). 32p. (gr. 3-4). 30.65 (978-0-7368-6495-4(4), Graphic Library) Capstone Press of Coughlan Cos.

—Rosa Parks & the Montgomery Bus Boycott, 1 vol. Kalal, Dan, illus. 2006. (Graphic History Ser.). (ENG.). 32p. (gr. 3-4). per. 8.10 (978-0-7368-9658-0(9), Graphic Library) Capstone Press of Coughlan Cos.

Miller, Jake. The March from Selma to Montgomery: African Americans Demand the Vote. (Library of the Civil Rights Movement Ser.). 24p. 2009. (gr. 3-3). 42.50 (978-1-60853-894-2(X)) 2004. (Illus.). (J). lib. bdg. 22.60 (978-0-8239-6254-9(7)) Rosen Publishing Group, Inc., The. (PowerKids Pr.).

—The Montgomery Bus Boycott: Integrating Public Buses. (Library of the Civil Rights Movement Ser.). 24p. 2009. (gr. 3-3). 42.50 (978-1-60853-895-9(8)) 2004. (Illus.). (J). lib. bdg. 22.60 (978-0-8239-6251-8(2)) Rosen Publishing Group, Inc., The. (PowerKids Pr.).

—Sit-Ins & Freedom Rides: The Power of Nonviolent Resistance. (Library of the Civil Rights Movement Ser.). 24p. 2009. (gr. 3-3). 42.50 (978-1-60853-892-8(3)) 2004. (Illus.). (J). lib. bdg. 22.60 (978-0-8239-6253-2(9)) Rosen Publishing Group, Inc., The. (PowerKids Pr.).

—The 1963 March on Washington: Speeches & Songs for Civil Rights. (Library of the Civil Rights Movement Ser.). 24p. 2009. (gr. 3-3). 42.50 (978-1-60853-893-5(1)) 2004. (Illus.). (J). lib. bdg. 22.60 (978-0-8239-6255-6(5)) Rosen Publishing Group, Inc., The. (PowerKids Pr.).

Mis, Melody S. Meet Coretta Scott King. (Civil Rights Leaders Ser.). 24p. (gr. 2-3). 2009. 42.50 (978-1-61511-851-9(9), PowerKids Pr.) 2008. (Illus.). (YA). lib. bdg. 22.60 (978-1-4042-4211-1(2)) Rosen Publishing Group, Inc., The.

—Meet Martin Luther King Jr. 2008. (Civil Rights Leaders Ser.). (Illus.). 24p. (YA). (gr. 2-3). lib. bdg. 22.60 (978-1-4042-4209-8(0)) Rosen Publishing Group, Inc., The.

—Meet Rosa Parks. (Civil Rights Leaders Ser.). 24p. (gr. 2-3). 2009. 42.50 (978-1-61511-855-7(1), PowerKids Pr.) 2008. (Illus.). (YA). lib. bdg. 22.60 (978-1-4042-4210-4(4)) Rosen Publishing Group, Inc., The.

Moore, Johnny Ray. The Story of Martin Luther King Jr. Wummer, Amy, illus. 2016. (J). (978-0-8249-1974-0(2), Ideal Pubns.) Worthy Publishing.

Morris, Roz. Rosa Parks: Mother of the Civil Rights Movement. 2003. (Alabama Roots Biography Ser.). (Illus.). 109p. (J). (978-1-878561-57-2(X)) Seacoast Publishing, Inc.

Mortensen, Lori. Voices of the Civil Rights Movement. 2015. (We Shall Overcome Ser.). (ENG.). 32p. (gr. 3-4). lib. bdg. 27.32 (978-1-4914-2044-7(8)) Capstone Press of Coughlan Cos.

Muldoon, Kathleen M. Jim Crow Era, 1 vol. 2014. (African-American History Ser.). (ENG.). 48p. (gr. 8-12). lib. bdg. 32.79 (978-1-62403-146-5(3)) ABDO Publishing Co.

Nagelhout, Ryan. Martin Luther King Jr. 2015. (Heroes of Black History Ser.). (ENG.). 32p. (J). (gr. 3-4). 26.60 (978-1-4824-2906-0(3)) Stevens, Gareth Publishing LLLP.

Nathan, Amy. Round & Round Together: Taking a Merry-Go-Round Ride into the Civil Rights Movement. 2011. (Nautilus Ser.). (ENG., Illus.). 200p. (gr. 4-10). pap. 14.95 (978-1-58988-071-9(4)) Dry, Paul Bks., Inc.

Nelson, Maria. Coretta Scott King. 2011. (Civil Rights Crusaders Ser.). 24p. (gr. 2-5). (J). pap. 8.15 (978-1-4339-5680-5(2), Gareth Stevens Learning Library); (YA). lib. bdg. 22.60 (978-1-4339-5678-2(0)) Stevens, Gareth Publishing LLLP.

Nichols, Kaitlyn. Martin Luther King. 2009. pap. 13.25 (978-1-60559-065-3(7)) Hameray Publishing Group, Inc.

O'Hern, Kerri & Walsh, Frank. The Montgomery Bus Boycott. 2006. (Graphic Histories Ser.). (Illus.). 32p. (gr. 5-8). pap. 10.50 (978-0-8368-6257-7(0)) Stevens, Gareth Publishing LLLP.

O'Hern, Kerri, et al. El Boicot a los Autobuses de Montgomery. 2007. (Historias gráficas (Graphic Histories) Ser.). (SPA., Illus.). 32p. (gr. 5-8). pap. 10.50 (978-0-8368-7902-5(3)); lib. bdg. 27.00 (978-0-8368-7895-0(7)) Stevens, Gareth Publishing LLLP.

Ollhoff, Jim. The Civil Rights Movement, 1 vol. 2011. (African American History Ser.). (ENG., Illus.). 32p. (YA). (gr. 5-9). 27.07 (978-1-61714-709-8(5)) ABDO Publishing Co.

—Courage & Growth, 1 vol. 2011. (African American History Ser.). (ENG., Illus.). 32p. (YA). (gr. 5-9). lib. bdg. 27.07 (978-1-61714-711-1(7)) ABDO Publishing Co.

Osborne, Linda Barrett. Miles to Go for Freedom: Segregation & Civil Rights in the Jim Crow Years. 2012. (ENG., Illus.). 128p. (J). (gr. 3-7). 25.99 (978-1-4197-0020-0(0), Abrams Bks. for Young Readers) Abrams, Inc.

Partridge, Elizabeth. Marching for Freedom: Walk Together, Children, & Don't You Grow Weary. 2009. (ENG.). 80p. (J). (gr. 5-18). 19.99 (978-0-670-01189-6(4), Viking Books for Young Readers) Penguin Young Readers Group.

Perritano, John. Free at Last! How the Freeing of the Slaves Changed American History. 2008. (Graphic America Ser.). (ENG., Illus.). 32p. (J). (gr. 3-6). pap. (978-0-7787-4212-8(1)) Crabtree Publishing Co.

Perry, M. LaVora. A History of the Civil Rights Movement. 2012. (J). pap. (978-1-4222-2395-6(7)) Mason Crest.

—A History of the Civil Rights Movement. Hill, Marc Lamont, ed. 2012. (Major Black Contributions from Emancipation to Civil Rights Ser.). 64p. (J). (gr. 5). 22.95 (978-1-4222-2382-6(5)) Mason Crest.

Petruccio, Steven James. History of the Civil Rights Movement Coloring Book. 2011. (Dover History Coloring Book Ser.). (ENG., Illus.). 32p. (gr. 3-5). pap. 3.99 (978-0-486-47846-3(7)) Dover Pubns., Inc.

Pierce, Alan. Montgomery Bus Boycott, 1 vol. 2005. (American Moments Ser.). (ENG., Illus.). 48p. (gr. 4-8). 27.07 (978-1-59197-935-7(8), Abdo & Daughters) ABDO Publishing Co.

Pingry, Patricia A. Meet Rosa Parks. Walker, Steven, illus. 2008. (ENG.). 32p. (J). (gr. k-3). per. 7.99 (978-0-8249-5578-6(1), Ideal Pubns.) Worthy Publishing.

—The Story of Coretta Scott King. Walker, Steven, illus. 2007. (ENG.). 26p. (J). (gr. 3-7). bds. 7.69 (978-0-8249-6717-8(8), Ideal Pubns.) Worthy Publishing.

—The Story of Rosa Parks. Walker, Steven, illus. (J). 2016. (978-0-8249-1987-0(4)) 2008. (ENG.). 24p. (gr. 3-7). bds. 7.69 (978-0-8249-6687-4(2)) Worthy Publishing. (Ideal Pubns.).

Pinkney, Andrea Davis. Martin & Mahalia: His Words, Her Song. 2013. (ENG., Illus.). 40p. (J). (gr. 1-17). 18.99 (978-0-316-07013-3(0)) Little Brown & Co.

—Sit-In: How Four Friends Stood up by Sitting Down. 2010. (ENG., Illus.). 40p. (J). (gr. 1-17). 18.99 (978-0-316-07016-4(5)) Little, Brown Bks. for Young Readers.

Ponto, Joanna & Gnojewski, Carol. Martin Luther King Jr. Day. 2016. (Story of Our Holidays Ser.). (Illus.). 32p. (J). pap. 10.52 (978-0-7660-8340-0(3)) Enslow Pubs., Inc.

Randolph, Joanne. African American Politicians & Civil Rights Activists. 2017. (J). **(978-0-7660-9252-5(6))** Enslow Pubs., Inc.

Rappaport, Doreen. Free at Last! Stories & Songs of Emancipation. Evans, Shane W., illus. 2006. (ENG.). 64p. (J). (gr. 4-7). pap. 9.99 (978-0-7636-3147-5(7)) Candlewick Pr.

—Nobody Gonna Turn Me 'Round: Stories & Songs of the Civil Rights Movement. Evans, Shane W., illus. 2006. (ENG.). 64p. (J). (gr. 4-7). 19.99 (978-0-7636-1927-5(2)) Candlewick Pr.

—Nobody Gonna Turn Me 'Round: Stories & Songs of the Civil Rights Movement. Evans, Shane W., illus. 2008. (ENG.). 64p. (J). (gr. 4-7). pap. 9.99 (978-0-7636-3892-4(7)) Candlewick Pr.

Ridley, Sarah. Martin Luther King: ...And the Fight for Equality. 2013. (History Makers Ser.). (Illus.). 24p. (J). (gr. 2-4). 25.65 (978-1-59771-389-4(9)) Sea-To-Sea Pubns.

Rinaldo, Denise. Rosa Parks: With a Discussion of Courage. 2003. (Values in Action Ser.). (J). (978-1-59203-061-3(0)) Learning Challenge, Inc.

Ringgold, Faith. If a Bus Could Talk: The Story of Rosa Parks. Ringgold, Faith, illus. 2003. (ENG., Illus.). 32p. (J). (gr. k-4). pap. 7.99 (978-0-689-85676-1(8), Aladdin) Simon & Schuster Children's Publishing.

Rissman, Rebecca. The Black Power Movement, 1 vol. 2014. (African-American History Ser.). (ENG.). 48p. (gr. 8-12). 32.79 (978-1-62403-144-1(7)) ABDO Publishing Co.

Rodgers, Kelly. Florida's Fight for Equality. 2016. (Primary Source Readers Ser.). 32p. (J). (gr. 4-4). pap. 8.99 (978-1-4938-3544-7(0)) Teacher Created Materials, Inc.

Roome, Hugh. Martin Luther King Jr. 2017. (Rookie Biographies Ser.). (ENG.). 32p. (J). pap. 5.95 **(978-0-531-23861-5(X)**, Children's Pr.) Scholastic Library Publishing.

Rubin, Susan Goldman. Brown V. Board of Education: A Fight for Simple Justice. 2016. (ENG., Illus.). 144p. (J). (gr. 5-8). 18.95 (978-0-8234-3646-0(2)) Holiday Hse., Inc.

—Freedom Summer: The 1964 Struggle for Civil Rights in Mississippi. (ENG.). 144p. (J). 2016. 14.95 (978-0-8234-3557-9(1)) 2014. (Illus.). (gr. 5). 18.95 (978-0-8234-2920-2(2)) Holiday Hse., Inc.

Ruffin, Frances E. Martin Luther King & the March on Washington. 2014. (Penguin Young Readers, L3 Ser.). (ENG.). 48p. (J). (gr. 1-2). 8.24 (978-1-63245-254-2(5)) Lectorum Pubns., Inc.

Rustad, Martha E. H. & Leslie, Tonya. Martin Luther King, Jr: A Life of Fairness. 2007. (People of Character Ser.). (ENG., Illus.). 24p. (J). (gr. 2-5). lib. bdg. 25.95 (978-1-60014-090-7(4)) Bellwether Media.

Saddleback Educational Publishing Staff, ed. Martin Luther King Jr., 1 vol. unabr. ed. 2008. (Graphic Biographies Ser.). (ENG., Illus.). 25p. (YA). (gr. 9-12). pap. 7.95 (978-1-59905-227-4(X)) Saddleback Educational Publishing, Inc.

Sapet, Kerrily. John Lewis. 2009. (Political Profiles Ser.). 100p. (YA). (gr. 5-9). 28.95 (978-1-59935-130-8(7)) Reynolds, Morgan Inc.

Schmermund, Elizabeth. Minority Soldiers Fighting in the Vietnam War. 2017. (J). **(978-1-5026-2666-0(7))** Cavendish Square Publishing.

Schraff, Anne E. Martin Luther King, Jr: We Shall Overcome. 2005. (African-American Biography Library). (Illus.). 128p. (J). (gr. 6-13). lib. bdg. 33.27 (978-0-7660-1774-0(5)) Enslow Pubs., Inc.

—Rosa Parks: Tired of Giving In. 2005. (African-American Biography Library). (Illus.). 128p. (J). (gr. 6-12). lib. bdg. 33.27 (978-0-7660-2463-2(6)) Enslow Pubs., Inc.

Schuetz, Rachael Law. The Long Road to Change: An American Story of Civil Rights & Barack Obama's Journey to the White House. 2009. 36p. (J). 16.00 (978-0-615-27983-1(X)) NRS Enterprises.

Schuldt, Lori Meek. Martin Luther King, Jr: With Profiles of Mohandas K. Gandhi & Nelson Mandela. 2006. (Biographical Connections Ser.). (Illus.). 112p. (J). (978-0-7166-1822-5(2)) World Bk., Inc.

Schuman, Michael A. The Life of Martin Luther King, Jr: Leader for Civil Rights. 2014. (Legendary African Americans Ser.). (Illus.). 96p. (J). (gr. 6-12). 27.94 (978-0-7660-6147-7(7)) Enslow Pubs., Inc.

Schuman, Michael A. & Schraff, Anne E. Martin Luther King Jr: Fighting for Civil Rights. 2017. (Rebels with a Cause Ser.). 128p. (gr. 8-8). lib. bdg. 37.27 **(978-0-7660-8511-4(2))** Enslow Pubs., Inc.

Schwartz, Heather E. Freedom Riders: A Primary Source Exploration of the Struggle for Racial Justice. 2014. (We Shall Overcome Ser.). (ENG.). 32p. (gr. 3-4). lib. bdg. 27.32 (978-1-4914-0222-1(9)) Capstone Press of Coughlan Cos.

—Locked up for Freedom: Civil Rights Protesters at the Leesburg Stockade. 2017. (ENG., Illus.). 64p. (J). (gr. 5-8). lib. bdg. 33.32 **(978-1-4677-8597-6(0)**, Millbrook Pr.) Lerner Publishing Group.

Schwartz, Heather E. The March on Washington: A Primary Source Exploration of the Pivotal Protest, 1 vol. 2014. (We Shall Overcome Ser.). (ENG.). 32p. (gr. 3-4). lib. bdg. 27.32 (978-1-4914-0223-8(7)) Capstone Press of Coughlan Cos.

Sepahban, Lois. 12 Incredible Facts about the Montgomery Bus Boycott. 2015. (Turning Points in US History Ser.). (ENG., Illus.). 32p. (J). (gr. 3-5). (978-1-63235-132-6(3), 12-Story Library) Pr. Room Editions LLC.

Shange, Ntozake. Coretta Scott. Nelson, Kadir, illus. 2011. (ENG.). 32p. (J). (gr. -1-4). pap. 6.99 (978-0-06-125366-9(9), Tegen, Katherine Bks) HarperCollins Pubs.

Sharp, Anne Wallace. Women Civil Rights Leaders. 2012. (Lucent Library of Black History Ser.). (ENG., Illus.). 128p. (J). (gr. 7-10). 39.40 (978-1-4205-0880-2(6), Lucent Bks.) Cengage Gale.

Shea, Therese. Rosa Parks, 1 vol. 2015. (ENG., Illus.). 32p. (J). 23.45 (978-1-62275-697-1(5), Britannica Educational Publishing) Rosen Publishing Group, Inc., The.

Sheinkin, Steve. The Port Chicago 50: Disaster, Mutiny, & the Fight for Civil Rights. 2014. (ENG., Illus.). 208p. (J). (gr. 5-9). 19.99 (978-1-59643-796-8(0), 9781596437968) Roaring Brook Pr.

Shelton, Paula Young. Child of the Civil Rights Movement. Colón, Raúl, illus. 2013. (ENG.). 48p. (J). (gr. -1-3). 7.99

(978-0-385-37606-8(5), Dragonfly Bks.) Random Hse. Children's Bks.

Shone, Rob. Rosa Parks: The Life of a Civil Rights Heroine. 2009. (Graphic Nonfiction Biographies Ser.). (ENG.). 48p. (YA). (gr. 4-5). 58.50 *(978-1-61513-026-9(8),* Rosen Reference) Rosen Publishing Group, Inc., The.

—Rosa Parks: The Life of a Civil Rights Heroine. Spender, Nick, illus. 2007. (Graphic Nonfiction Biographies Ser.). (ENG.). 48p. (J). (gr. 4-7). lib. bdg. 31.95 *(978-1-4042-0864-3(X))* Rosen Publishing Group, Inc., The.

—Rosa Parks: The Life of a Civil Rights Heroine. Spender, Nik, illus. 2007. (Graphic Biographies Ser.). (ENG.). 48p. (gr. 5-8). pap. 14.05 *(978-1-4042-0927-5(1))* Rosen Publishing Group, Inc., The.

Spence, Kelly. Martin Luther King Jr. & Peaceful Protest. 2016. (Primary Sources of the Civil Rights Movement Ser.). (Illus.). 64p. (J). (gr. 6-6). 34.21 *(978-1-5026-1864-1(8))* Cavendish Square Publishing.

Spilsbury, Richard. Who Marched for Civil Rights?, 1 vol. HL Studios Staff, illus. 2014. (Primary Source Detectives Ser.). (ENG.). 64p. (gr. 7-8). lib. bdg. 35.99 *(978-1-4329-9604-8(5))* Heinemann-Raintree.

Staley, Erin. Martin Luther King Jr. & the Speech That Inspired the World. 2014. (Celebration of the Civil Rights Movement Ser.). 80p. (YA). (gr. 7-12). 34.25 *(978-1-4777-7745-9(8))* Rosen Publishing Group, Inc., The.

Stanley, George E. Coretta Scott King: First Lady of Civil Rights. Madsen, Jim & Henderson, Meryl, illus. 2008. (Childhood of Famous Americans Ser.). (ENG.). 224p. (J). (gr. 3-7). pap. 7.99 *(978-1-4169-6800-9(8),* Simon & Schuster/Paula Wiseman Bks.) Simon & Schuster/Paula Wiseman Bks.

Stanmyre, Jackie F. Coretta Scott King & the Center for Nonviolent Social Change. 2016. (Primary Sources of the Civil Rights Movement Ser.). (Illus.). 64p. (J). (gr. 6-6). 34.21 *(978-1-5026-1876-4(1))* Cavendish Square Publishing.

Staton, Hilarie N. Civil Rights. 2015. (ENG.). 48p. (J). *(978-0-7787-1549-8(3))* Crabtree Publishing Co.

Sterling, Kristin. Mary Mcleod Bethune. 2008. pap. 40.95 *(978-0-8225-9474-1(9))* Lerner Publishing Group.

—Mary Mcleod Bethune: A Life of Resourcefulness. 2008. (Pull Ahead Books-Biographies Ser.). (ENG., Illus.). 32p. (gr. k-3). lib. bdg. 22.60 *(978-0-8225-8588-6(X),* Lerner Pubns.) Lerner Publishing Group.

Stotts, Stuart. Father Groppi: Marching for Civil Rights. 2013. (Badger Biographies Ser.). (ENG., Illus.). 160p. (J). pap. 12.95 *(978-0-87020-575-0(7))* Wisconsin Historical Society.

Stroud, Bettye. The Reconstruction Era. 2006. (Drama of African-American History Ser.). (Illus.). 80p. (gr. 6-7). lib. bdg. 35.64 *(978-0-7614-2181-8(5),* Benchmark Bks.) Marshall Cavendish Corp.

Summer, L. S. Rosa Parks. 2009. (Journey to Freedom Ser.). (ENG., Illus.). 32p. (J). (gr. 4-7). 29.93 *(978-1-60253-133-8(1),* 200399) Child's World, Inc., The.

Supples, Kevin. Speaking Out: The Civil Rights Movement 1950-1964. 2005. (Crossroads America Ser.). (ENG., Illus.). 40p. (gr. k-3). 12.95 *(978-0-7922-8279-2(5));* lib. bdg. 21.90 *(978-0-7922-8359-1(7))* National Geographic Society. (National Geographic Children's Bks.).

Supples, Kevin, et al. The Civil Rights Movement. 2006. (Nonfiction Reading & Writing Workshops Ser.). (ENG., Illus.). 40p. (J). pap. 19.95 *(978-0-7922-8628-8(6))* CENGAGE Learning.

Swain, Gwenyth. Riding to Washington. Geister, David, illus. 2007. (Tales of Young Americans Ser.). (ENG.). 32p. (YA). (gr. 6-12). 17.95 *(978-1-58536-324-7(3))* Sleeping Bear Pr.

Taylor-Butler, Christine. Rosa Parks. 2015. (ENG., Illus.). 48p. (J). pap. 6.95 *(978-0-531-21209-7(2),* Orchard Bks.) Scholastic Library Publishing.

Tieck, Sarah. Rosa Parks, 1 vol. 2006. (Buddy Book Ser.). (ENG., Illus.). 32p. (gr. -1-3). 27.07 *(978-1-59679-788-8(6),* Buddy Bks.) ABDO Publishing Co.

Time for Kids Editors. Rosa Parks: Civil Rights Pioneer. 2006. (Time for Kids Ser.). (ENG., Illus.). 48p. (J). (gr. 2-4). pap. 3.99 *(978-0-06-057624-0(3),* Collins) HarperCollins Pubs.

Tisdale, Rachel. The Freedom Riders, 1 vol., 1. 2014. (We Shall Overcome Ser.). (ENG.). 32p. (J). (gr. 3-6). 26.25 *(978-1-4777-6061-1(X),* PowerKids Pr.) Rosen Publishing Group, Inc., The.

—The March on Washington, 1 vol., 1. 2014. (We Shall Overcome Ser.). (ENG.). 32p. (J). (gr. 3-6). 26.25 *(978-1-4777-6069-7(5),* PowerKids Pr.) Rosen Publishing Group, Inc., The.

—The Montgomery Bus Boycott, 1 vol., 1. 2014. (We Shall Overcome Ser.). (ENG., Illus.). 32p. (J). (gr. 3-6). 26.25 *(978-1-4777-6053-6(9),* PowerKids Pr.) Rosen Publishing Group, Inc., The.

—The Woolworth's Sit-In, 1 vol., 1. 2014. (We Shall Overcome Ser.). (ENG.). 32p. (J). (gr. 3-6). 26.25 *(978-1-4777-6065-9(2),* PowerKids Pr.) Rosen Publishing Group, Inc., The.

Toth, Henrietta. The Murder of Emmett Till. 2017. pap. ***(978-1-5383-8054-3(4))*** Rosen Publishing Group, Inc., The.

Tougas, Shelley. Birmingham 1963: How a Photograph Rallied Civil Rights Support, 1 vol. 2011. (Captured History Ser.). (ENG.). 64p. (gr. 5-7). pap. 9.10 *(978-0-7565-4446-1(7));* lib. bdg. 34.65 *(978-0-7565-4398-3(3))* Compass Point Bks. (CPB Grades 4-8).

Turck, Mary C. Freedom Song: Young Voices & the Struggle for Civil Rights. 2008. (ENG., Illus.). 160p. (J). (gr. 4). pap. 18.95 *(978-1-55652-773-9(X))* Chicago Review Pr., Inc.

Uschan, Michael V. The Civil Rights Movement. 2010. (American History Ser.). (ENG.). 128p. 34.80 *(978-1-4205-0261-9(1),* Lucent Bks.) Cengage Gale.

—James Foreman & SNCC. Greenaven Press Staff, ed. 2013. (Lucent Library of Black History Ser.). (ENG., Illus.). 128p. (J). (gr. 7-10). lib. bdg. 39.40 *(978-1-4205-0920-5(9),* Lucent Bks.) Cengage Gale.

—The Scottsboro Case. 2004. (Landmark Events in American History Ser.). (Illus.). 48p. (gr. 5-12). lib. bdg. 31.00 *(978-0-8368-5388-9(1),* Gareth Stevens Secondary Library) Stevens, Gareth Publishing LLLP.

Vaughn, Wally G. & Davis, Mattie Campbell, eds. The Selma Campaign, 1963-1965: The Decisive Battle of the Civil Rights Movement. 2006. (ENG., Illus.). 244p. pap. 19.95 *(978-0-912469-44-7(7))* Majority Pr., The.

Vietze, Andrew. The Life & Death of Malcolm X. 2017. (J). ***(978-1-5383-8032-1(3),*** Rosen Young Adult) Rosen Publishing Group, Inc., The.

—The Life & Death of Martin Luther King Jr. 2017. (J). ***(978-1-5383-8038-3(2));*** pap. ***(978-1-5383-8039-0(0))*** Rosen Publishing Group, Inc., The.

Wallenfeldt, Jeffrey H., ed. African American History & Culture, 3 vols., Set. Incl. Africa to America: From the Middle Passage Through the 1930s. 272p. lib. bdg. 45.00 *(978-1-61530-126-3(7));* Black American Biographies: The Journey of Achievement. 408p. lib. bdg. 45.00 *(978-1-61530-137-9(2));* Black Experience in America: From Civil Rights to the Present. 232p. lib. bdg. 45.00 *(978-1-61530-146-1(1));* (YA). (gr. 9-12). 2010. (Illus.). 232 - 408p. 2010. Set lib. bdg. 135.00 *(978-1-61530-151-5(8))* Rosen Publishing Group, Inc., The.

Walsh, Frank. The Montgomery Bus Boycott. 2003. (Landmark Events in American History Ser.). (Illus.). 48p. (gr. 5-12). pap. 14.05 *(978-0-8368-5403-9(9),* Gareth Stevens Secondary Library) Stevens, Gareth Publishing LLLP.

Walsh, Frank & O'Hern, Kerri. The Montgomery Bus Boycott. McHargue, D., illus. 2006. (Graphic Histories Ser.). 32p. (gr. 5-8). lib. bdg. 27.00 *(978-0-8368-6205-8(8))* Stevens, Gareth Publishing LLLP.

Ward, Jill. Martin Luther King, Jr: Georgia, My State Biographies. l.t. ed. 2008. (ENG., Illus.). 24p. (J). (gr. k-2). 22.60 *(978-1-935077-01-5(5));* pap. 22.60 *(978-1-935077-08-4(2))* State Standards Publishing, LLC.

Watkins, Angela Farris. My Uncle Martin's Big Heart. Velasquez, Eric, illus. 2010. (ENG.). 32p. (J). (gr. k-2). 19.95 *(978-0-8109-8975-7(1),* Abrams Bks. for Young Readers) Abrams, Inc.

—My Uncle Martin's Words for America: Martin Luther King Jr. 's Niece Tells How He Made a Difference. Velasquez, Eric, illus. (ENG.). 40p. (J). (gr. 1-4). 2015. 9.95 *(978-1-4197-1836-6(3))* 2011. 21.95 *(978-1-4197-0022-4(7))* Abrams, Inc. (Abrams Bks. for Young Readers).

Waxman, Laura Hamilton. Coretta Scott King. 2008. (History Maker Biographies Ser.). (ENG., Illus.). 48p. (gr. 3-6). lib. bdg. 27.93 *(978-0-8225-7168-1(4),* Lerner Pubns.) Lerner Publishing Group.

Weakland, Mark. When Martin Luther King Jr. Wore Roller Skates. Ballesteros, Patrick, illus. 2017. 31p. (J). *(978-1-5158-0141-2(1))* 2016. (ENG.). 32p. (gr. 2-3). lib. bdg. 27.99 *(978-1-4795-9685-0(X))* Picture Window Bks.

Weatherford, Carole Boston. The Beatitudes: From Slavery to Civil Rights. Ladwig, Tim, illus. 2009. (ENG.). 36p. (J). (gr. 3-7). 17.00 *(978-0-8028-5352-3(8),* Eerdmans Bks For Young Readers) Eerdmans, William B. Publishing Co.

Weidt, Maryann N. Rosa Parks. (History Maker Bios Ser.). (Illus.). (J). 2004. 48p. pap. 8.95 *(978-0-8225-4805-8(4))* 2003. 47p. 26.60 *(978-0-8225-4673-3(6))* Lerner Publishing Group. (Lerner Pubns.).

Weil, Ann. Medgar Evers, 1 vol. 2012. (American Biographies Ser.). (ENG.). 48p. (gr. 4-6). pap. 9.95 *(978-1-4329-6465-8(8),* NA-h) Heinemann-Raintree.

—Medgar Evers, 1 vol. Oxford Bible Staff, illus. 2012. (American Biographies Ser.). (ENG.). 48p. (gr. 4-6). lib. bdg. 32.65 *(978-1-4329-6454-2(2),* NA-h) Heinemann-Raintree.

Welch, Catherine A. Children of the Civil Rights Era. 2005. (Picture the American Past Ser.). (Illus.). 48p. (J). (gr. 2-5). lib. bdg. 22.60 *(978-1-57505-481-0(7))* Lerner Publishing Group.

Weston Woods Staff, creator. March on! the Day My Brother Martin Changed the World. 2011. 38.75 *(978-0-545-31399-5(6));* 18.95 *(978-0-545-31398-8(8))* Weston Woods Studios, Inc.

—Rosa. 2011. 38.75 *(978-0-545-14963-1(0));* 18.95 *(978-0-545-14962-4(2))* Weston Woods Studios, Inc.

Wheeler, Jill C. Rosa Parks, Set II. 2003. (Breaking Barriers Ser.). 64p. (gr. 3-8). 27.07 *(978-1-57765-640-1(7),* Abdo & Daughters) ABDO Publishing Co.

Whiting, Jim. Rosa Parks. 2007. (What's So Great About... ? Ser.). (Illus.). 32p. (YA). (gr. 2-4). lib. bdg. 25.70 *(978-1-58415-573-7(6))* Mitchell Lane Pubs., Inc.

—W. E. B. du Bois: Civil Rights Activist, Author, Historian. 2009. (Transcending Race in America: Biographies of Biracial Achievers Ser.). 64p. (YA). (gr. 5-18). pap. 9.95 *(978-1-4222-1632-3(2))* Mason Crest.

Winget, Mary. Martin Luther King, Jr. 2004. (History Maker Bios Ser.). (Illus.). 48p. (J). pap. 8.95 *(978-0-8225-4804-1(6),* Lerner Pubns.) Lerner Publishing Group.

Winter, Max. Civil Rights Movement, 1 vol. 2014. (African-American History Ser.). (ENG.). 48p. (gr. 8-12). lib. bdg. 32.79 *(978-1-62403-145-8(5))* ABDO Publishing Co.

Woog, Adam. The Fight Renewed: The Civil Rights Movement. 2005. (Lucent Library of Black History). (ENG., Illus.). 112p. (YA). (gr. 7-10). lib. bdg. 33.45 *(978-1-59018-701-2(6),* Lucent Bks.) Cengage Gale.

World Book, Inc Staff, contrib. by. African American Civil Rights Movement. 2010. (J). *(978-0-7166-1500-2(2))* World Bk., Inc.

Worth, Richard. African Americans During Reconstruction. Schwarz, Philip, ed. 2006. (Slavery in the Americas Ser.). (Illus.). 112p. (gr. 5-8). 35.00 *(978-0-8160-6139-6(4))* Facts On File, Inc.

Zeiger, Jennifer. The Civil Rights Movement. 2011. (Cornerstones of Freedom, Third Ser.). (Illus.). 64p. (J). (ENG.). pap. 8.95 *(978-0-531-26554-3(4));* (ABK., lib. bdg. 30.00 *(978-0-531-25029-7(6))* Scholastic Library Publishing. (Children's Pr.).

Zullo, Allan. 10 True Tales: Young Civil Rights Heroes. 2014. (10 True Tales Ser.). (ENG.). 192p. (J). (gr. 3-7). pap. 5.99 *(978-0-545-76974-7(4))* Scholastic, Inc.

AFRICAN AMERICANS—CIVIL RIGHTS—FICTION

Wiles, Deborah. Revolution. 2014. (Sixties Trilogy Ser.: 2). (ENG., Illus.). 544p. (J). (gr. 3-7). 19.99 *(978-0-545-10607-8(9),* Scholastic Pr.) Scholastic, Inc.

AFRICAN AMERICANS—DICTIONARIES

Rasmussen, R. Kent, ed. The African American Encyclopedia, 10 vols., Set. 2nd rev. ed. (Illus.). 3000p. (J). lib. bdg. 459.95 *(978-1-76147-208-4(9))* Marshall Cavendish Corp.

Wallenfeldt, Jeff, ed. Black American Biographies: The Journey of Achievement. 2010. (African American History & Culture Ser.). (Illus.). 408p. (YA). 90.00 *(978-1-61530-178-2(X))* Rosen Publishing Group, Inc., The.

Wallenfeldt, Jeffrey H., ed. Black American Biographies: The Journey of Achievement. 2010. (African American History & Culture Ser.). (Illus.). 408p. (YA). (gr. 9-12). lib. bdg. 45.00 *(978-1-61530-137-9(2))* Rosen Publishing Group, Inc., The.

AFRICAN AMERICANS—DRAMA

Sanders, Jeff & Sanders, Nancy I. Readers Theatre for African American History, 1 vol. 2008. (Readers Theatre Ser.). (Illus.). 168p. (C). pap. 40.00 *(978-1-59158-693-7(3),* TIP8693, Libraries Unlimited) ABC-CLIO, LLC.

AFRICAN AMERICANS—EDUCATION

Coles, Robert. The Story of Ruby Bridges. 2009. 8.44 *(978-0-7848-3016-1(9),* Everbind) Marco Bk. Co.

—The Story of Ruby Bridges. 2011. 17.00 *(978-1-61383-173-1(0))* Perfection Learning Corp.

—The Story of Ruby Bridges. Ford, George, illus. 50th anniv. ed. 2010. (ENG.). 32p. (J). (gr. -1-3). pap. 6.99 *(978-0-439-47226-5(1),* Scholastic Paperbacks) Scholastic, Inc.

—The Story of Ruby Bridges. 2010. lib. bdg. 17.20 *(978-0-606-23189-3(7),* Turtleback) Turtleback Bks.

Goodman, Susan E. The First Step: How One Girl Put Segregation on Trial. Lewis, E. B., illus. 2016. (J). *(978-0-8027-3741-0(2))* Bloomsbury Pr.

—The First Step: How One Girl Put Segregation on Trial. Lewis, E. B., illus. 2016. (ENG.). 40p. (J). 17.99 *(978-0-8027-3739-7(0),* 9780802737397, Bloomsbury USA Childrens) Bloomsbury Publishing USA.

Jurmain, Suzanne. The Forbidden Schoolhouse: The True & Dramatic Story of Prudence Crandall & Her Students. 2005. (ENG., Illus.). 160p. (J). (gr. 5-7). 19.00 *(978-0-618-47302-1(5))* Houghton Mifflin Harcourt Publishing Co.

Lüsted, Marcia Amidon. The Little Rock Desegregation Crisis. 2017. (J). pap. ***(978-1-5383-8041-3(2))*** Rosen Publishing Group, Inc., The.

Miller, Mara. School Desegregation & the Story of the Little Rock Nine. 2008. (From Many Cultures, One History Ser.). (Illus.). 128p. (J). (gr. 3-7). lib. bdg. 33.27 *(978-0-7660-2835-7(6))* Enslow Pubs., Inc.

Shannon, Ann. The Wilder Kids: I Really Want to Go to College!! 2009. 24p. pap. 13.50 *(978-1-4389-0523-5(8))* AuthorHouse.

Slade, Suzanne. With Books & Bricks: How Booker T. Washington Built a School. Tadgell, Nicole, illus. 2014. (ENG.). 32p. (J). (gr. 2-3). 16.99 *(978-0-8075-0897-8(7))* Whitman, Albert & Co.

Visions: Early Emergent - Complete Kit. (Visions Ser.). (gr. k-18). 319.50 *(978-0-7802-9397-7(5))* Wright Group/McGraw-Hill.

Walker, Paul Robert. Remember Little Rock: The Time, the People, the Stories. (ENG., Illus.). 64p. (J). (gr. 5). 2015. pap. 7.99 *(978-1-4263-2247-1(X))* 2009. 17.95 *(978-1-4263-0402-6(1))* 2009. lib. bdg. 27.90 *(978-1-4263-0403-3(X))* National Geographic Society. (National Geographic Children's Bks.).

AFRICAN AMERICANS—EDUCATION—FICTION

Burton, Jennifer. Princess's Journey. 2003. (Topeka Heights Ser.). (YA). (gr. 9-12). pap. 10.99 *(978-0-9724733-0-9(0))* ALEXZUS Bks.

Griffin, Ramona Rorie. My Mind Looks Back & Wonders ... Tunstel Jr., Robert L., illus. 2009. (ENG.). 28p. pap. 24.95 *(978-1-60813-917-0(4))* America Star Bks.

AFRICAN AMERICANS—EMPLOYMENT

Buckley, Annie. Robert L. Johnson. 2007. (21st Century Skills Library: Life Skills Biographies Ser.). (ENG., Illus.). 48p. (gr. 4-8). lib. bdg. 31.36 *(978-1-60279-072-8(8),* 200046) Cherry Lake Publishing.

Macceca, Stephanie. George Washington Carver: Agriculture Pioneer, 1 vol. 2007. (Science Readers Ser.). (ENG.). 32p. (J). (gr. 3-3). pap. 8.99 *(978-0-7439-0590-9(3))* Shell Educational Publishing.

AFRICAN AMERICANS—FOLKLORE

Currie, Stephen. African-American Folklore. 2008. (Lucent Library of Black History Ser.). (ENG., Illus.). 104p. (YA). (gr. 7-10). 34.80 *(978-1-4205-0082-0(1),* Lucent Bks.) Cengage Gale.

Garcia, Ellen & Benchmark Education Co. Staff. Where There's No Such Thing As Worry & Other African American Folktales. 2014. (Text Connections Ser.). (J). (gr. 6). *(978-1-4900-1521-7(3))* Benchmark Education Co.

Gould, Jane H. John Henry. 2014. (Jr. Graphic American Legends Ser.). (Illus.). 24p. (J). (gr. 3-6). lib. bdg. 26.25 *(978-1-4777-7197-6(2),* PowerKids Pr.) Rosen Publishing Group, Inc., The.

Hamilton, Virginia. The People Could Fly: American Black Folktales. Dillon, Leo & Dillon, Diane, illus. 2009. (American Black Folktales Ser.). (ENG.). 192p. (J). (gr. k-12). 24.99 *(978-0-394-86925-4(7),* Knopf Bks. for Young Readers) Random Hse. Children's Bks.

—The People Could Fly: The Picture Book. Dillon, Leo & Dillon, Diane, illus. movie tie-in ed. 2004. (ENG.). 32p. (J). (gr. k-12). 16.95 *(978-0-375-82405-0(7),* Knopf Bks. for Young Readers) Random Hse. Children's Bks.

Harris, Joel Chandler. Uncle Remus: His Songs & His Sayings. 265p. (J). 18.00 *(978-0-9645990-0-0(7))* Historic Pr.-South.

Kantor, Susan, ed. Read-Aloud African-American Stories: 40 Selections from the World's Best-Loved Stories for Parent & Child to Share. 2012. (ENG., Illus.). 232p. (J). (gr. -1-17). 14.95 *(978-1-57912-922-4(6),* Black Dog & Leventhal Pubs. Inc.) Hachette Bks.

Krensky, Stephen. John Henry. Oldroyd, Mark, illus. 2006. (On My Own Folklore Ser.). (ENG.). 48p. (gr. 2-4). lib. bdg. 25.26 *(978-1-57505-887-0(1),* Millbrook Pr.) Lerner Publishing Group.

Lester, Julius. The Tales of Uncle Remus: The Adventures of Brer Rabbit. Pinkney, Jerry, illus. 2006. (Puffin Modern Classics Ser.). (ENG.). 160p. (J). (gr. 3-7). 7.99 *(978-0-14-240720-2(8),* Puffin Books) Penguin Young Readers Group.

McGill, Alice. Way up & over Everything. Daly, Jude, illus. 2008. (ENG.). 32p. (J). (gr. 2-5). 16.00 *(978-0-618-38796-0(X))* Houghton Mifflin Harcourt Publishing Co.

Schomp, Virginia & Harris, Joel Chandler. Brer Rabbit & the Number-Nine Shoes. 2013. (Illus.). 32p. (J). (gr. 6-9). 28.50 *(978-1-60870-439-2(4))* Cavendish Square Publishing.

Young, Richard & Young, Judy D. African-American Folktales. 2006. (American Storytelling Ser.). (ENG.). 176p. (J). (gr. 3-7). pap. 12.95 *(978-0-87483-309-6(4))* August Hse. Pubs., Inc.

AFRICAN AMERICANS—FICTION

Abdul-Jabbar, Kareem. Streetball Crew Book One Sasquatch in the Paint. 2015. (Streetball Crew Ser.). (ENG.). 288p. (J). (gr. 3-7). pap. 7.99 *(978-1-4231-9254-1(0))* Hyperion Bks. for Children.

Abdul-Jabbar, Kareem & Obstfeld, Raymond. Sasquatch in the Paint. 2013. (Streetball Crew Ser.). (ENG.). 272p. (J). (gr. 3-7). 16.99 *(978-1-4231-7870-5(X))* Hyperion Pr.

Adler, David A. Get a Hit, Mo! Ricks, Sam, illus. (Mo Jackson Ser.: bk.2). (ENG.). 32p. (J). (gr. 1-2). 2017. pap. 3.99 *(978-0-448-48010-7(7))* 2016. 14.99 *(978-0-670-01632-7(2))* Penguin Young Readers Group. (Penguin Young Readers).

Adoff, Arnold. Roots & Blues: A Celebration. Christie, R. Gregory, illus. 2011. (ENG.). 96p. (J). (gr. 5-7). 17.99 *(978-0-547-23554-7(2))* Houghton Mifflin Harcourt Publishing Co.

Albert, Burton. Where Does the Trail Lead? Pinkney, Brian, illus. 2008. (ENG.). 40p. (J). (gr. -1-3). 13.99 *(978-1-4169-7138-2(6),* Aladdin) Simon & Schuster Children's Publishing.

Alexander, Kwame. The Crossover. 2014. (ENG.). (J). (gr. 4-7). E-Book 16.99 *(978-1-306-46985-2(6))* Harcourt Trade Pubs.

—The Crossover. 2014. (ENG.). 240p. (J). (gr. 4-7). 16.99 *(978-0-544-10771-7(3),* HMH Books For Young Readers) Houghton Mifflin Harcourt Publishing Co.

—The Crossover. 2014. lib. bdg. 29.40 *(978-0-606-37975-5(4))* Turtleback Bks.

—He Said, She Said. 2013. 330p. (YA). lib. bdg. *(978-0-06-211897-4(8))* Harper & Row Ltd.

—He Said, She Said. 2013. (ENG.). 336p. (YA). (gr. 9). 17.99 *(978-0-06-211896-7(X),* Amistad) HarperCollins Pubs.

Allen, Crystal. How Lamar's Bad Prank Won a Bubba-Sized Trophy. (ENG.). (J). (gr. 3-7). 2012. 304p. pap. 6.99 *(978-0-06-199273-5(9))* 2011. 288p. 16.99 *(978-0-06-199272-8(0))* HarperCollins Pubs.

—The Laura Line. (J). (gr. 3-7). 2016. 352p. pap. 6.99 *(978-0-06-249021-6(4))* 2013. (ENG.). 336p. 16.99 *(978-0-06-199274-2(7))* HarperCollins Pubs.

Altman, Linda Jacobs & Johnson, Larry. Singing with Momma Lou, 1 vol. 2015. (ENG., Illus.). 28p. (J). pap. 9.95 *(978-1-62014-227-1(9))* Lee & Low Bks., Inc.

Amateau, Gigi. Come August, Come Freedom: The Bellows, the Gallows, & the Black General Gabriel. (ENG.). (YA). (gr. 7). 2014. 256p. pap. 6.99 *(978-0-7636-6870-9(2))* 2012. (Illus.). 240p. 16.99 *(978-0-7636-4792-6(6))* Candlewick Pr.

Anderson, Laurie Halse. Ashes. l.t. ed. 2017. (Seeds of America Ser.: 3). (ENG.). 430p. 23.99 ***(978-1-4104-9607-2(4))*** Cengage Gale.

—Ashes. (Seeds of America Trilogy Ser.: Bk. 3). (ENG., Illus.). (J). (gr. 5). 2017. 320p. pap. 8.99 *(978-1-4169-6147-5(X))* 2016. 304p. 16.99 *(978-1-4169-6146-8(1),* Atheneum/Caitlyn Dlouhy Books) Simon & Schuster Children's Publishing.

—Chains. l.t. ed. 2017. (Seeds of America Ser.). (ENG.). 442p. 22.99 ***(978-1-4104-9917-2(0))*** Cengage Gale.

—Chains. 2014. (Seeds of America Trilogy). (ENG.). 336p. (J). 12.24 *(978-1-63245-094-4(1))* Lectorum Pubns., Inc.

—Chains. 2009. 9.00 *(978-0-7848-3678-1(7),* Everbind) Marco Bk. Co.

—Chains. (Seeds of America Trilogy Ser.). (ENG., Illus.). (J). (gr. 5-9). 2010. 336p. pap. 8.99 *(978-1-4169-0586-8(3))* 2008. 320p. 18.99 *(978-1-4169-0585-1(5))* Simon & Schuster Children's Publishing. (Atheneum Bks. for Young Readers).

—Chains. l.t. ed. 2009. (ENG.). 390p. (YA). 23.95 *(978-1-4104-1425-0(6))* Thorndike Pr.

—Chains. 2010. (Seeds of America Trilogy Ser.: 1). lib. bdg. 19.65 *(978-0-606-14520-6(6),* Turtleback) Turtleback Bks.

—Forge. 2012. 18.00 *(978-1-61383-316-2(4))* Perfection Learning Corp.

—Forge. (Seeds of America Trilogy Ser.). (ENG., Illus.). (J). (gr. 5-9). 2012. 320p. pap. 8.99 *(978-1-4169-6145-1(3))* 2010. 304p. 18.99 *(978-1-4169-6144-4(5))* Simon & Schuster Children's Publishing. (Atheneum Bks. for Young Readers).

—Forge. 2012. (Seeds of America Trilogy Ser.: 2). lib. bdg. 18.40 *(978-0-606-23680-5(5),* Turtleback) Turtleback Bks.

Anderson, M. T. The Kingdom on the Waves. (Astonishing Life of Octavian Nothing, Traitor to the Nation Ser.: Vol. 2). (ENG., Illus.). 592p. 2011. pap. 14.00 *(978-0-7636-5377-4(2))* 2009. (YA). (gr. 9). pap. 12.99 *(978-0-7636-4626-4(1))* Candlewick Pr.

—The Pox Party. (Astonishing Life of Octavian Nothing, Traitor to the Nation Ser.: Vol. 1). (ENG., Illus.). 2006. 368p. (YA). (gr. 9-12). 17.99 *(978-0-7636-2402-6(0))* Vol. I. 2011. 384p. pap. 14.00 *(978-0-7636-5376-7(4))* Candlewick Pr.

Anderson, Pamela Dell. My New School: Afro Boy. Lee, Hanlim & WU, Stacie, illus. 2003. 24p. (J). 12.95 *(978-1-932555-01-1(3))* Watch Me Grow Kids.

—My New School: Afro Girl. Lee, Hanlim & WU, Stacie, illus. 2003. 24p. (J). 12.95 *(978-1-932555-00-4(5))* Watch Me Grow Kids.

Ann, Cameron. The Stories Julian Tells. 2014. (Stepping Stone Book Ser.). (ENG.). 80p. (J). 9.24 *(978-1-63245-217-7(0))* Lectorum Pubns., Inc.

Applegate, Katherine. Home of the Brave. 2008. (ENG.). 272p. (J). (gr. 5-9). pap. 7.99 *(978-0-312-53563-6(5),* 9780312535636) Square Fish.

Armistead, John. The Return of Gabriel. Gregory, Fran, illus. 2004. 218p. (gr. 3-8). 17.45 *(978-0-7569-3460-6(5))* Perfection Learning Corp.

Armstrong, William H. Sounder. l.t. ed. 2005. 111p. (YA). pap. 10.95 *(978-0-7862-7915-9(X))* Thorndike Pr.

Aronson, Marc & Smith, Charles R., Jr., eds. Pick-Up Game: A Full Day of Full Court. Smith, Charles R., Jr., illus. (ENG., Illus.). 176p. (YA). (gr. 9). 2012. pap. 7.99 *(978-0-7636-6068-0(X))* 2011. 15.99 *(978-0-7636-4562-5(1))* Candlewick Pr.

Ashford Frame, Jeron & Christie, R. Gregory. Yesterday I Had the Blues. 2nd rev. ed. 2008. (ENG., Illus.). 32p. (J). (gr. -1-2). pap. 7.99 *(978-1-58246-260-8(7),* Tricycle Pr.) Random Hse. Children's Bks.

Aston, Dianna Hutts. The Moon over Star. Pinkney, Jerry, illus. 2008. (ENG.). 32p. (J). (gr. 1-3). 17.99 *(978-0-8037-3107-3(8),* Dial Bks) Penguin Young Readers Group.

Atkinson, Olympia J. Kendahl's Plans. 2010. 24p. 11.99 *(978-1-4490-8371-7(4))* AuthorHouse.

Baker, Brianna & Hastie, F. Bowman. Little White Lies. 2017. (ENG.). 272p. (YA). (gr. 9). pap. 10.99 *(978-1-61695-707-0(7),* Soho Teen) Soho Pr., Inc.

Bandy, Michael S. & Stein, Eric. Granddaddy's Turn. Ransome, James, illus. 2015. (ENG.). 32p. (J). (gr. 1-4). 16.99 *(978-0-7636-6593-7(2))* Candlewick Pr.

—White Water. Strickland, Shadra, illus. 2011. (ENG.). 40p. (J). (gr. k-3). 16.99 *(978-0-7636-3678-4(9))* Candlewick Pr.

Banks, Jacqueline Turner & Turner Banks, Jacqueline. Egg-Drop Blues. 2003. (ENG.). 128p. (J). (gr. 5-7). pap. 10.95 *(978-0-618-25080-6(8))* Houghton Mifflin Harcourt Publishing Co.

Barber, Barbara E. Allie's Basketball Dream. Ligasan, Darryl, illus. 2013. (ENG.). 32p. (J). (gr. 2-2). pap. 9.95 *(978-1-880000-72-4(5))* Lee & Low Bks., Inc.

—Saturday at the New You. Rich, Anna, illus. 2013. (ENG.). 32p. (J). (gr. -1-3). reprint ed. pap. 9.95 *(978-1-880000-43-4(1))* Lee & Low Bks., Inc.

Barber, Tiki & Barber, Ronde. End Zone. (Barber Game Time Bks.). (ENG., Illus.). (J). (gr. 3-7). 2014. 192p. pap. 7.99 *(978-1-4169-9098-7(4))* 2012. 176p. 15.99 *(978-1-4169-9097-0(6))* Simon & Schuster/Paula Wiseman Bks. (Simon & Schuster/Paula Wiseman Bks.).

—Extra Innings. 2014. (Barber Game Time Bks.). (ENG., Illus.). 160p. (J). (gr. 3-7). 16.99 *(978-1-4424-5726-3(0),* Simon & Schuster/Paula Wiseman Bks.) Simon & Schuster/Paula Wiseman Bks.

—Jump Shot. 2013. (Barber Game Time Bks.). (ENG., Illus.). 160p. (J). (gr. 3-7). 16.99 *(978-1-4424-5729-4(5),* Simon & Schuster/Paula Wiseman Bks.) Simon & Schuster/Paula Wiseman Bks.

Barnes, Derrick. Crown: An Ode to the Fresh Cut. James, Gordon C., illus. 2017. (Denene Millner Bks.). (ENG.). 32p. (J). (gr. -1-3). 17.95 ***(978-1-57284-224-3(5))*** Agate Publishing, Inc.

Barnes, Derrick D. Trivia Queen/Supreme. Newton, Vanessa Brantley, illus. 2008. (Ruby & the Booker Boys Ser.: 2). (ENG.). 144p. (J). (gr. 2-5). pap. 5.99 *(978-0-545-01761-9(0))* Scholastic, Inc.

—We Could Be Brothers. 2010. (J). *(978-0-545-13574-0(5),* Scholastic Pr.) Scholastic, Inc.

Barnwell, Ysaye M. No Mirrors in My Nana's House. Saint James, Synthia, illus. 2005. (ENG.). 32p. (J). (gr. -1-3). reprint ed. 10.99 *(978-0-15-205243-0(7))* Houghton Mifflin Harcourt Publishing Co.

Battle-Lavert, Gwendolyn. The Barber's Cutting Edge. Holbert, Raymond, illus. 2004. (ENG.). 32p. (J). pap. 7.95 *(978-0-89239-196-7(0))* Lee & Low Bks., Inc.

—Papa's Mark. Bootman, Colin, illus. 2003. (ENG.). 32p. (J). (gr. k-3). tchr. ed. 17.95 *(978-0-8234-1650-9(X))* Holiday Hse., Inc.

Bearden, Romare. Li'l Dan the Drummer Boy: A Civil War Story. Bearden, Romare, illus. 2003. (ENG., Illus.). 40p. (J). (gr. -1-3). 24.99 *(978-0-689-86237-3(7),* Simon & Schuster Bks. For Young Readers) Simon & Schuster Bks. For Young Readers.

Beaty, Daniel. Knock Knock: My Dad's Dream for Me. 2013. (ENG.). 40p. (J). (gr. -1-3). 18.99 *(978-0-316-20917-5(1))* Little, Brown Bks. for Young Readers.

Benson, Linda Sue. Hey Latrell, 1 vol. Johnson, Bruce, illus. 2009. 48p. pap. 16.95 *(978-1-60813-961-3(1))* America Star Bks.

Berleth, Richard. Samuel's Choice. Watling, James, illus. 2012. (ENG.). 40p. (J). (gr. 2-3). pap. 6.99 *(978-0-8075-7219-1(5))* Whitman, Albert & Co.

Bildner, Phil. The Hallelujah Flight. Holyfield, John, illus. 2010. (ENG.). 32p. (J). (gr. k-3). 16.99 *(978-0-399-24789-7(0),* G.P. Putnam's Sons Books for Young Readers) Penguin Young Readers Group.

—Marvelous Cornelius: Hurricane Katrina & the Spirit of New Orleans. Parra, John, illus. 2015. (ENG.). 44p. (J). (gr. k-3). 16.99 *(978-1-4521-2578-7(3))* Chronicle Bks. LLC.

Billingsley, ReShonda Tate. Blessings in Disguise. 2007. (Good Girlz Ser.: 2). (ENG.). 192p. (gr. 4-7). pap. 11.00 *(978-1-4165-2561-5(0),* Gallery Bks.) Gallery Bks.

—Eye Candy. 2015. (Rumor Central Ser.). (ENG., Illus.). 202p. (YA). (gr. 9). pap. 9.95 *(978-0-7582-8961-2(8),* Dafina) Kensington Publishing Corp.

—Getting Even: Good Girlz. 2008. (Good Girlz Ser.: 4). (ENG.). 208p. pap. 11.00 *(978-1-4165-5873-6(X),* Gallery Bks.) Gallery Bks.

—Truth or Dare. 2014. (Rumor Central Ser.). (ENG., Illus.). 208p. (YA). (gr. 13). pap. 9.95 *(978-0-7582-8957-5(X),* K-Teen) Kensington Publishing Corp.

—With Friends Like These. 2007. (Good Girlz Ser.: 3). (ENG., Illus.). 256p. (gr. 8-12). pap. 16.99 *(978-1-4165-2562-2(9),* Gallery Bks.) Gallery Bks.

Binns, B. A. Pull. 2010. 310p. (YA). (gr. 9-18). 16.95 *(978-1-934813-43-0(5))* Westside Bks.

Birtha, Becky. Grandmama's Pride. Bootman, Colin, illus. 2005. (ENG.). 32p. (J). (gr. 2-3). 16.99 *(978-0-8075-3028-3(X))* Whitman, Albert & Co.

—Lucky Beans. Tadgell, Nicole, illus. 2012. (J). 34.28 *(978-1-61913-129-3(3))* Weigl Pubs., Inc.

—Lucky Beans. Tadgell, Nicole, illus. 2010. (ENG.). 32p. (J). (gr. 2-3). 16.99 *(978-0-8075-4782-3(4))* Whitman, Albert & Co.

Black, Sonia W. Jumping the Broom. Van Wright, Cornelius & Hu, Ying-Hwa, illus. 2004. 32p. (J). lib. bdg. 15.00 *(978-1-4242-0234-8(5))* Fitzgerald Bks.

Bliss, Harry. Luke on the Loose. 2014. (Toon Books Level 2 Ser.). lib. bdg. 14.75 *(978-0-606-32101-3(2),* Turtleback) Turtleback Bks.

Blue, Rose, et al. Ron's Big Mission. Tate, Don, illus. 2009. (ENG.). 32p. (J). (gr. 1-3). 16.99 *(978-0-525-47849-2(3),* Dutton Books for Young Readers) Penguin Young Readers Group.

Blume, Judy. Iggie's House. 2014. (ENG., Illus.). (J). (gr. 3-7). 160p. 17.99 *(978-1-4814-1410-4(0));* 176p. pap. 7.99 *(978-1-4814-1104-2(7))* Simon & Schuster Children's Publishing. (Atheneum Bks. for Young Readers).

Blythe, Carolita. Revenge of a Not-So-Pretty Girl. 2013. (ENG.). 336p. (YA). (gr. 7). 19.99 *(978-0-375-99081-6(X),* Delacorte Bks. for Young Readers) Random Hse. Children's Bks.

Bolden, Tonya. Crossing Ebenezer Creek. 2017. (ENG.). 240p. (YA). 17.99 *(978-1-59990-319-4(9),* 9781599903194, Bloomsbury USA Childrens) Bloomsbury Publishing USA.

—Finding Family. (ENG., Illus.). 192p. (YA). (gr. 3-12). 2012. pap. 7.99 *(978-1-59990-830-4(1),* 9781599908304) 2010. 15.99 *(978-1-59990-318-7(0),* 9781599903187) Bloomsbury Publishing USA. (Bloomsbury USA Childrens).

Bond, Victoria & Simon, T. R. Zora & Me. (Zora & Me Ser.). (ENG., Illus.). 192p. (J). (gr. 5). 2011. pap. 7.99 *(978-0-7636-5814-4(6))* 2010. 16.99 *(978-0-7636-4300-3(9))* Candlewick Pr.

Booth, Coe. Bronxwood. 2013. (ENG.). 336p. (J). (gr. 9). pap. 10.99 *(978-0-439-92535-8(5),* PUSH) Scholastic, Inc.

—Kinda Like Brothers. 2015. (ENG.). 256p. (J). (gr. 3-7). pap. 6.99 *(978-0-545-22497-0(7),* Scholastic Paperbacks) Scholastic, Inc.

—Tyrell. 2011. 9.04 *(978-0-7848-3385-8(0),* Everbind) Marco Bk. Co.

Bozarth, Jan. Lilu's Book. 2011. (Fairy Godmother Academy Ser.: No. 4). (ENG., Illus.). 192p. (J). (gr. 3-7). 6.99 *(978-0-375-85187-2(9),* Yearling) Random Hse. Children's Bks.

Bradbury, Jennifer. River Runs Deep. 2015. (ENG., Illus.). 336p. (J). (gr. 4-8). 17.99 *(978-1-4424-6824-5(6),* Atheneum Bks. for Young Readers) Simon & Schuster Children's Publishing.

Bradby, Marie. Some Friend. 2007. (ENG.). 240p. (J). (gr. 3-7). pap. 7.99 *(978-1-4169-3452-3(9),* Atheneum Bks. for Young Readers) Simon & Schuster Children's Publishing.

Bradley, John Ed. Call Me by My Name. (ENG.). (YA). (gr. 7). 2015. 288p. pap. 11.99 *(978-1-4424-9794-8(7))* 2014. (Illus.). 272p. 17.99 *(978-1-4424-9793-1(9),* Atheneum Bks. for Young Readers) Simon & Schuster Children's Publishing.

Bradley, Kimberly Brubaker. Jefferson's Sons: A Founding Father's Secret Children. 2013. (ENG.). 400p. (J). (gr. 3-7). pap. 7.99 *(978-0-14-242184-0(7),* Puffin Books) Penguin Young Readers Group.

Brittany's Books, illus. & creator. I Can Too! African American Girls. Brittany's Books, creator. 2006. 44p. (J). lib. bdg. 9.95 *(978-0-9778796-8-7(2))* Brittany's Bks.

Brockenbrough, Martha. The Game of Love & Death. 2015. (ENG.). 336p. (J). (gr. 7). 17.99 *(978-0-545-66834-7(4))* Scholastic, Inc.

Brooks, Bruce. The Moves Make the Man. 2003. (ENG.). 256p. (YA). (gr. 8-18). pap. 8.99 *(978-0-06-447022-3(9),* HarperTeen) HarperCollins Pubs.

Brooks, Gwendolyn. We Are Shining. Gilchrist, Jan Spivey, illus. 2017. 32p. (J). (gr. -1-3). 17.99 *(978-0-06-257066-6(8))* HarperCollins Pubs.

Brown, Marc. D. W. the Big Boss. 2005. (ENG., Illus.). 24p. (J). (gr. -1-1). per. 3.99 *(978-0-316-73395-3(4))* Little, Brown Bks. for Young Readers.

Brown, Margery W. Baby Jesus Like My Brother. 2008. (Illus.). 32p. 6.95 *(978-1-60349-000-9(0),* Marimba Bks.) Hudson Publishing Group, The.

Brown, Tameka Fryer. My Cold Plum Lemon Pie Bluesy Mood. Evans, Shane, illus. 2013. (ENG.). 40p. (J). (gr. -1-2). 16.99 *(978-0-670-01285-5(8),* Viking Books for Young Readers) Penguin Young Readers Group.

Broyles, Anne. Priscilla & the Hollyhocks. Alter, Anna, illus. 2008. (ENG.). 32p. (J). (gr. 1-4). 15.95 *(978-1-57091-675-5(6))* Charlesbridge Publishing, Inc.

Bryan, Ashley. Freedom over Me: Eleven Slaves, Their Lives & Dreams Brought to Life. Bryan, Ashley, illus. 2016. (ENG., Illus.). 56p. (J). (gr. 4-6). 17.99 *(978-1-4814-5690-6(3),* Atheneum/Caitlyn Dlouhy Books) Simon & Schuster Children's Publishing.

Buchanan, Jane. Seed Magic, 1 vol. Riley-Webb, Charlotte, illus. 2012. (ENG.). 32p. (J). 16.95 *(978-1-56145-622-2(5))* Peachtree Pubs.

Bunting, Eve. Flower Garden. Hewitt, Kathryn, illus. 2004. 28p. (gr. -1-2). 17.00 *(978-0-7569-4113-0(X))* Perfection Learning Corp.

Burden-Patmon, Denise. Imani's Gift at Kwanzaa. (J). 48.95 *(978-0-8136-2248-4(4))* Modern Curriculum Pr.

Burg, Ann E. Unbound. 2016. (ENG.). 352p. (J). (gr. 4-6). 16.99 *(978-0-545-93427-5(3),* Scholastic Pr.) Scholastic, Inc.

Burkhart, Kiersi & Keyser, Amber J. One Brave Summer. 2017. (Quartz Creek Ranch Ser.). (ENG.). 224p. (J). (gr. 4-8). 27.99 *(978-1-4677-9254-7(3))* Lerner Publishing Group.

Burney, Claudia Mair. Exorsistah, No. 1. 2008. (ENG.). 272p. (YA). pap. 9.95 *(978-1-4165-6133-0(1),* Gallery Bks.) Gallery Bks.

Cameron, Ann. Gloria Rising. 2004. (Stepping Stone Book Ser.). (ENG.). 112p. (J). (gr. 1-4). 4.99 *(978-0-440-41998-3(0),* Random Hse. Bks. for Young Readers) Random Hse. Children's Bks.

Campbell, Charles K. La Magic Coin. 2004. (YA). (gr. 3-18). per. 15.00 *(978-0-9742064-3-1(1))* Unmistakably C K C.

Capstone Press Staff. Follow the Drinking Gourd: An Underground Railroad Story, 1 vol. Squier, Robert, illus. 2012. (Night Sky Stories Ser.). (ENG.). 24p. (gr. 2-3). lib. bdg. 26.65 *(978-1-4048-7375-9(9))* Picture Window Bks.

—John Henry - Hammerin' Hero. Evergreen, Nelson, illus. 2010. (Graphic Spin Ser.). (ENG.). 40p. (gr. 1-3). lib. bdg. 25.32 *(978-1-4342-1898-8(8),* Graphic Revolve) Stone Arch Bks.

Carbone, Elisa. Stealing Freedom. 2003. (EMC Masterpiece Series Access Editions). (Illus.). xix, 284p. (J). 12.99 *(978-0-8219-2507-2(5))* EMC/Paradigm Publishing.

Carlon, Mick. Riding on Duke's Train. 2011. (LeapKids Ser.). (ENG.). 160p. (J). (gr. k-7). pap. 9.95 *(978-1-935248-06-4(5))* Leapfrog Pr.

—Travels with Louis. 2012. (LeapKids Ser.). (ENG.). 240p. (J). (gr. 2-10). pap. 9.95 *(978-1-935248-35-4(9))* Leapfrog Pr.

Carlson, Nolan. Lame Eagle & Wind Chaser. 2005. (YA). per. *(978-0-9772745-1-2(9))* Mennonite Pr. Inc.

Carroll, Jonathan. Meet Julius Carmichael: First Day Blues. Koltun, Amy, illus. 2003. 96p. (J). (gr. 3-6). pap. 6.95 *(978-0-9724935-0-5(6))* Striking Presence Pubns.

Carter, Dorothy. Wilhe'mina Miles: After the Stork Night. Stevenson, Harvey, illus. 2005. 30p. (J). (gr. k-4). reprint ed. 16.00 *(978-0-7567-9421-7(8))* DIANE Publishing Co.

Carter, Nikki. Doing My Own Thing. 2011. (ENG., Illus.). 240p. (YA). (gr. 9). 9.95 *(978-0-7582-5558-7(6),* K-Teen/Dafina) Kensington Publishing Corp.

—It's All Good: A So for Real Novel. 2009. (ENG., Illus.). 240p. (YA). (gr. 9-18). pap. 9.95 *(978-0-7582-3441-4(4),* K-Teen/Dafina) Kensington Publishing Corp.

—Step to This. 2009. (ENG., Illus.). 240p. (YA). (gr. 9). 9.95 *(978-0-7582-3439-1(2),* K-Teen/Dafina) Kensington Publishing Corp.

Carter, Nikki & Elliott, Kevin. The Break-Up Diaries, Vol. 2. 2011. (ENG.). 288p. (YA). (gr. 9). pap. 9.95 *(978-0-7582-6888-4(2),* K-Teen/Dafina) Kensington Publishing Corp.

Carter, Noni. Good Fortune. (ENG.). 496p. (YA). (gr. 7). 2011. pap. 9.99 *(978-1-4169-8481-8(X))* 2010. 16.99 *(978-1-4169-8480-1(1))* Simon & Schuster Bks. For Young Readers. (Simon & Schuster Bks. For Young Readers).

Certain Signals. 2014. (Gift Ser.). (ENG.). 112p. (YA). (gr. 6-12). lib. bdg. 27.93 *(978-1-4677-3511-7(6))* Lerner Publishing Group.

Childrens Press Staff, ed. Messy Bessey. 2005. (Rookie Reader Ser.). (ENG.). 96p. (J). (gr. -1-2). pap. 9.95 *(978-0-516-25328-2(X),* Children's Pr.) Scholastic Library Publishing.

Chris, Crowe. Mississippi Trial 1955. 2014. (ENG.). 240p. (YA). (gr. 7-12). 10.24 *(978-1-63245-211-5(1))* Lectorum Pubns., Inc.

Christopher, Matt. The Basket Counts. 2008. (New Matt Christopher Sports Library). 96p. (J). (gr. 4-6). lib. bdg. 26.60 *(978-1-59953-212-7(3))* Norwood Hse. Pr.

—Fairway Phenom. 2003. (Matt Christopher Sports Bio Bookshelf Ser.). 132p. (J). (gr. 4-7). 12.65 *(978-0-7569-1605-3(4))* Perfection Learning Corp.

Clark, Henry. The Book That Proves Time Travel Happens. 2015. (ENG., Illus.). 416p. (J). (gr. 3-7). 17.00 *(978-0-316-40617-8(1))* Little Brown & Co.

CLE, Troy. The Marvelous Effect. 2008. (Marvelous World Ser.: 1). (ENG.). 384p. (J). (gr. 5-9). pap. 8.99 *(978-1-4169-4215-3(7),* Simon & Schuster Bks. For Young Readers) Simon & Schuster Bks. For Young Readers.

Cle, Troy. Olivion's Favorites. 2009. (Marvelous World Ser.: 2). (ENG.). 352p. (J). (gr. 5-9). 14.99 *(978-1-4169-4216-0(5),* Simon & Schuster Bks. For Young Readers) Simon & Schuster Bks. For Young Readers.

Cline-Ransome, Lesa. Light in the Darkness: A Story about How Slaves Learned in Secret. Ransome, James E., illus. 2013. (ENG.). 40p. (J). (gr. k-3). 16.99 *(978-1-4231-3495-4(8),* Jump at the Sun) Hyperion Bks. for Children.

Codell, Esmé Raji. Sahara Special. 2003. (ENG., Illus.). 208p. (J). (gr. 3-7). pap. 16.49 *(978-0-7868-2627-8(4))* Hyperion Bks. for Children.

—Sahara Special. 2004. (ENG.). 192p. (J). (gr. 3-7). pap. 6.99 *(978-0-7868-1611-8(2))* Hyperion Pr.

—Vive la Paris. 2006. (ENG.). 224p. (gr. 4-7). 15.99 *(978-0-7868-5124-9(4))* Hyperion Pr.

Colbert, Brandy. Pointe. (ENG.). 352p. (YA). (gr. 9). 2015. pap. 9.99 *(978-0-14-751441-7(X),* Speak) 2014. 17.99 *(978-0-399-16034-9(5),* G.P. Putnam's Sons Books for Young Readers) Penguin Young Readers Group.

Cole, Henry. Unspoken: A Story from the Underground Railroad. Cole, Henry, illus. 2012. (Unspoken Ser.). (ENG., Illus.). 40p. (J). (gr. -1-3). 17.99 *(978-0-545-39997-5(1),* Scholastic Pr.) Scholastic, Inc.

Coleman, Evelyn. Circle of Fire. 2009. (Mysteries Through Time Ser.). 160p. (YA). (gr. 4-8). 31.95 *(978-1-60754-191-2(2));* pap. 15.25 *(978-1-60754-192-9(0))* Windmill Bks.

—Mystery of the Dark Tower. 2009. (Mysteries Through Time Ser.). 160p. (YA). (gr. 4-8). 31.95 *(978-1-60754-188-2(2));* pap. 15.25 *(978-1-60754-189-9(0))* Windmill Bks.

—Shadows on Society Hill. 2007. (American Girl Mysteries Ser.). (ENG., Illus.). 192p. (J). (gr. 4-7). 10.95 *(978-1-59369-163-9(7),* American Girl) American Girl Publishing, Inc.

Collie, Brenda Faye. College Freshman 101. 2014. (ENG.). 282p. pap. 9.99 *(978-0-9840220-2-1(3),* 3c08c3a2-c1e2-4334-9d61-f48276aebfd9) Daylight Bks.

Collier, Bryan. Uptown. unabr. ed. 2007. (J). (gr. k-3). 28.95 incl. audio compact disk *(978-1-4301-0054-6(0))* Live Oak Media.

—Uptown, 4 bks., Set. Collier, Bryan, illus. 2007. (Illus.). (J). (gr. k-3). pap. 39.95 incl. audio compact disk *(978-1-4301-0055-3(9))* Live Oak Media.

—Uptown, 4 bks., Set. unabr. ed. 2007. (J). (gr. k-3). pap. 37.95 incl. audio *(978-1-4301-0052-2(4))* Live Oak Media.

Collier, Bryan & National Geographic Learning Staff. Uptown. Collier, Bryan, illus. rev. ed. 2004. (ENG., Illus.). 32p. (J). (gr. -1-3). pap. 8.99 *(978-0-8050-7399-7(X),* 9780805073997) Square Fish.

Collier, Kristi. Jericho Walls. 2007. (ENG.). 224p. (YA). (gr. 4-9). pap. 10.99 *(978-0-8050-8184-8(4),* 9780805081848, Holt, Henry & Co. Bks. For Young Readers) Holt, Henry & Co.

Cooke, Trish. Full, Full, Full of Love. Howard, Paul, illus. 2008. (ENG.). 32p. (J). (gr. -1-k). pap. 3.99 *(978-0-7636-3883-2(8))* Candlewick Pr.

Cooney, Caroline B. The Lost Songs. 2013. (ENG.). 256p. (YA). (gr. 7). pap. 8.99 *(978-0-385-73967-2(2),* Ember) Random Hse. Children's Bks.

Cooper, Afua. My Name Is Henry Bibb: A Story of Slavery & Freedom. 2009. (ENG., Illus.). 160p. (J). (gr. 5-9). 16.95 *(978-1-55337-813-6(X))* Kids Can Pr., Ltd. CAN. Dist: Hachette Bk. Group.

—My Name Is Phillis Wheatley: A Story of Slavery & Freedom. 2009. (ENG., Illus.). 152p. (J). (gr. 5-9). 16.95 *(978-1-55337-812-9(1))* Kids Can Pr., Ltd. CAN. Dist: Hachette Bk. Group.

Cooper, Floyd. Juneteenth for Mazie. Cooper, Floyd, illus. 2015. (Fiction Picture Bks.). (ENG., Illus.). 40p. (gr. 1-2). lib. bdg. 25.32 *(978-1-4795-5819-3(2),* Fiction Picture Bks.) Picture Window Bks.

Copeland, Misty. Firebird. Myers, Christopher, illus. 2014. (ENG.). 40p. (J). (gr. k-3). 17.99 *(978-0-399-16615-0(7),* G.P. Putnam's Sons Books for Young Readers) Penguin Young Readers Group.

Cousin. My Teacher Helps Me. 2004. 8p. (gr. k-2). 20.95 *(978-0-322-00311-8(3))* Wright Group/McGraw-Hill.

Crawford, Ann Fears. Keechee: The Witch of the Woods. 2005. (J). *(978-1-931823-21-0(9))* Halcyon Pr.

Crowe, Chris. Just as Good: How Larry Doby Changed America's Game. Benny, Mike, illus. 2012. (ENG.). 32p. (J). (gr. 1-4). 16.99 *(978-0-7636-5026-1(9))* Candlewick Pr.

—Mississippi Trial 1955. 2003. (ENG.). 240p. (YA). (gr. 7-18). 5.99 *(978-0-14-250192-4(1),* Speak) Penguin Young Readers Group.

—The Mississippi Trial 1955. 2003. (gr. 7-12). lib. bdg. 16.00 *(978-0-613-86522-7(7),* Turtleback) Turtleback Bks.

Crump Jr., Fred. The Brave Toy Soldier. 2007. (Illus.). 32p. (J). (gr. -1). pap. 9.95 *(978-1-932715-82-8(7))* UMI (Urban Ministries, Inc.).

Curry, Kenneth. The Legend of the Dancing Trees: An African American Folk Tale. 2007. 111p. (J). per. 14.95 *(978-0-9798364-0-4(9))* Curry Brothers Publishing Group.

Curry, Kenneth, et al. The Legend of the Dancing Tees Teachers Resource: The Legend of the Dancing Trees. 2007.Tr. of Teachers Resource. per. 19.95 *(978-0-9798364-1-1(7))* Curry Brothers Publishing Group.

Curtis, Christopher Paul. Bud, Not Buddy. unabr. ed. 2004. 256p. (J). (gr. 4-7). pap. 36.00 incl. audio *(978-0-8072-8210-6(3),* LYA 140 S(, Listening Library) Random Hse. Audio Publishing Group.

—Bud, Not Buddy. 2004. (ENG., Illus.). 288p. (J). (gr. 3-7). mass mkt. 7.99 *(978-0-553-49410-5(4),* Laurel Leaf) Random Hse. Children's Bks.

—The Mighty Miss Malone. (ENG.). 320p. (J). (gr. 4-7). 2013. pap. 7.99 *(978-0-440-42214-3(0),* Yearling) 2012. 15.99 *(978-0-385-73491-2(3),* Lamb, Wendy Bks.) Random Hse. Children's Bks.

—The Mighty Miss Malone. 2013. lib. bdg. 18.40 *(978-0-606-27007-6(8),* Turtleback) Turtleback Bks.

—Mr. Chickee's Funny Money. 2007. (ENG.). 160p. (J). (gr. 3-7). 6.99 *(978-0-440-22919-3(7),* Yearling) Random Hse. Children's Bks.

—Mr. Chickee's Messy Mission. 2008. (ENG., Illus.). 240p. (J). (gr. 3-7). 6.99 *(978-0-440-22922-3(7),* Yearling) Random Hse. Children's Bks.

—The Watsons Go to Birmingham — 1963. 2013. (ENG.). 224p. (J). (gr. 3-7). 7.99 *(978-0-385-38294-6(4),* Yearling) Random Hse. Children's Bks.

—The Watsons Go to Birmingham 1963. 210p. (YA). (gr. 5-18). pap. 5.50 *(978-0-8072-8336-3(3));* 2004. (J). (gr. 4-18). pap. 38.00 incl. audio *(978-0-8072-8335-6(5),* YA166SP) Random Hse. Audio Publishing Group. (Listening Library).

Curtis, Christopher Paul & Jiménez Rioja, Alberto. Me Llamo Bud, No Buddy. 2016. (SPA.). 240p. (J). (gr. 5-12). pap. 12.99 ***(978-1-63245-639-7(7))*** Lectorum Pubns., Inc.

Curtis, Christopher Paul & Vega, Eida de la. Los Watson Van a Birmingham - 1963. 2016. (SPA.). 200p. (J). (gr. 5-12). pap. 12.99 ***(978-1-63245-640-3(0))*** Lectorum Pubns., Inc.

Curtis, Gavin. The Bat Boy & His Violin. Lewis, E. B., illus. 2015. 32p. pap. 8.00 *(978-1-61003-618-4(2))* Center for the Collaborative Classroom.

Cutler, Jane. Susan Marcus Bends the Rules. 2014. (ENG.). 112p. (J). (gr. 3-7). pap. 16.95 *(978-0-8234-3047-5(2))* Holiday Hse., Inc.

Daniels, Babygirl. 16 1/2 on the Block. 2009. (ENG.). 208p. (YA). (gr. 9). 9.95 *(978-1-60162-183-2(3),* Urban Renaissance) Kensington Publishing Corp.

Davis, Tanita S. A la Carte. 2011. (ENG.). 288p. (YA). (gr. 7). pap. 8.99 *(978-0-375-84306-8(X),* Ember) Random Hse. Children's Bks.

—Mare's War. 2011. (ENG.). 352p. (YA). (gr. 7). pap. 9.99 *(978-0-375-85077-6(5),* Knopf Bks. for Young Readers) Random Hse. Children's Bks.

De la Peña, Matt. Last Stop on Market Street. Robinson, Christian, illus. 2015. (ENG.). 32p. (J). 16.99 *(978-0-399-25774-2(8),* G.P. Putnam's Sons Books for Young Readers) Penguin Publishing Group.

Dean, Myers Walter. Fast Sam, Cool Clyde, & Stuff. 2014. (ENG.). 192p. (J). (gr. 12-12). 11.24 *(978-1-63245-241-2(3))* Lectorum Pubns., Inc.

—Monster. 2014. (ENG.). 304p. (J). (gr. 12-12). 14.24 *(978-1-63245-060-9(7))* Lectorum Pubns., Inc.

—Scorpions. 2014. (Trophy Bk Ser.). (ENG.). 240p. (J). (gr. 7-12). 13.24 *(978-1-63245-216-0(2))* Lectorum Pubns., Inc.

Deborah, Wiles. Freedom Summer. 2014. (ENG.). 32p. (J). (gr. k-3). 12.24 *(978-1-63245-316-7(9))* Lectorum Pubns., Inc.

DeGross, Monalisa. Donavan's Double Trouble. Bates, Amy, illus. 192p. (J). (gr. 2-5). 2008. lib. bdg. 16.89 *(978-0-06-077294-9(8))* 2007. (ENG.). 16.99 *(978-0-06-077293-2(X))* HarperCollins Pubs. (Amistad).

Dell, Pamela. Shaky Bones: A Story of the Harlem Renaissance. 2003. (Scrapbooks of America Ser.). (ENG., Illus.). 48p. (J). (gr. 3-6). 32.79 *(978-1-59187-040-1(2),* 200811) Child's World, Inc., The.

Dempsey, Kristy. A Dance Like Starlight: One Ballerina's Dream. Cooper, Floyd, illus. 2014. (ENG.). 32p. (J). (gr. k-3). 16.99 *(978-0-399-25284-6(3),* Philomel Bks.) Penguin Young Readers Group.

Derby, Sally. No Mush Today, 1 vol. Tadgell, Nicole, illus. 2008. (ENG.). 32p. (J). (gr. -1-3). 17.95 *(978-1-60060-238-2(X))* Lee & Low Bks., Inc.

Derby, Sally & Burrowes, Adjoa J. My Steps. 2005. (ENG., Illus.). 32p. (J). (gr. 1-4). pap. 9.95 *(978-1-880000-84-7(9))* Lee & Low Bks., Inc.

Deutsch, Stacia & Cohon, Rhody. King's Courage. Wenzel, David, illus. 2013. (Blast to the Past Ser.: 4). (ENG.). 128p. (J). (gr. 2-5). pap. 5.99 *(978-1-4424-9537-1(5),* Simon & Schuster/Paula Wiseman Bks.) Simon & Schuster/Paula Wiseman Bks.

—Sacagawea's Strength. Wenzel, David T. & Wenzel, David, illus. 2006. (Blast to the Past Ser.: 5). (ENG.). 128p. (J). (gr. 2-5). pap. 9.99 *(978-1-4169-1270-5(3),* Simon & Schuster/Paula Wiseman Bks.) Simon & Schuster/Paula Wiseman Bks.

DeVillers, Julia. Cleared for Takeoff. Pooler, Paige, illus. 2012. (Liberty Porter, First Daughter Ser.: 3). (ENG.). 224p. (J). (gr. 3-7). pap. 7.99 *(978-1-4169-9131-1(X),* Simon & Schuster/Paula Wiseman Bks.) Simon & Schuster/Paula Wiseman Bks.

—New Girl in Town. Pooler, Paige, illus. 2011. (Liberty Porter, First Daughter Ser.: 2). (ENG.). 224p. (J). (gr. 3-7). pap. 6.99 *(978-1-4169-9129-8(8),* Simon & Schuster/Paula Wiseman Bks.) Simon & Schuster/Paula Wiseman Bks.

Diallo, Elishia Shelene. Boogalou: A Boogie down Bronx Tale. 2015. (ENG.). 272p. (YA). pap. 14.99 *(978-1-4951-7655-5(X))* Independent Pub.

Dillon, Leo & Dillon, Diane. Rap a Tap Tap: Here's Bojangles - Think of That! 2005. (J). 28.95 incl. audio compact disk *(978-1-59519-369-8(3))* Live Oak Media.

Divine, L. Drama High - Pushin' 2010. (ENG., Illus.). 256p. (YA). (gr. 9-18). 9.95 *(978-0-7582-3115-4(6)*, K-Teen/Dafina) Kensington Publishing Corp.

—Frenemies. 2008. (ENG., Illus.). 304p. (YA). (gr. 9-12). 15.00 *(978-0-7582-2532-0(6)*, K-Teen/Dafina) Kensington Publishing Corp.

—Frenemies. 2008. (Drama High Ser.: Vol. 4). 218p. (gr. 8-12). 19.95 *(978-0-7569-8832-6(2))* Perfection Learning Corp.

—Holidaze. 2009. (ENG., Illus.). 256p. (YA). (gr. 9-18). pap. 9.95 *(978-0-7582-3109-3(1)*, K-Teen/Dafina) Kensington Publishing Corp.

—Hustlin' 2009. (Drama High Ser.: 7). lib. bdg. 26.95 *(978-0-606-00156-4(5)*, Turtleback) Turtleback Bks.

—Keep It Movin' 2009. (Drama High Ser.: 8). lib. bdg. 20.80 *(978-0-606-00157-1(3)*, Turtleback) Turtleback Bks.

—Lady J. 2008. (Drama High Ser.: Vol. 5). 214p. (gr. 8-12). 19.95 *(978-0-7569-8833-3(0))* Perfection Learning Corp.

Dowell, Frances O'Roark. Trouble the Water. (ENG.). (J). (gr. 4-8). 2017. 304p. pap. 7.99 *(978-1-4814-2464-6(5))* 2016. (Illus.). 288p. 16.99 *(978-1-4814-2463-9(7))* Simon & Schuster Children's Publishing.

—Trouble the Water. 2017. lib. bdg. 18.40 ***(978-0-606-40126-5(1))*** Turtleback Bks.

Doyle, Edwina Ann. The Bless Mark. 2006. (YA). pap. 14.95 *(978-1-58736-674-1(6))* Wheatmark, Inc.

Dragon, Laura. Hurricane Boy, 1 vol. 2014. (ENG., Illus.). 160p. (J). (gr. 3-7). pap. 8.95 *(978-1-4556-1916-0(7))* Pelican Publishing Co., Inc.

Draper, Sharon M. The Backyard Animal Show. Watson, Jesse Joshua, illus. 2012. (Clubhouse Mysteries Ser.: 5). (ENG.). 128p. (J). (gr. 3-7). pap. 5.99 *(978-1-4424-5022-6(3)*, Aladdin) Simon & Schuster Children's Publishing.

—The Backyard Animal Show. Watson, Jesse Joshua, illus. 2012. (Clubhouse Mysteries Ser.: 5). (ENG.). 128p. (J). (gr. 3-7). 15.99 *(978-1-4424-5023-3(1)*, Simon & Schuster/Paula Wiseman Bks.) Simon & Schuster/Paula Wiseman Bks.

—The Buried Bones Mystery. Watson, Jesse Joshua, illus. 2011. (Clubhouse Mysteries Ser.: 1). (ENG.). 112p. (J). (gr. 3-7). pap. 5.99 *(978-1-4424-2709-9(4)*, Aladdin) Simon & Schuster Children's Publishing.

—The Buried Bones Mystery. Watson, Jesse Joshua, illus. 2011. (Clubhouse Mysteries Ser.: 1). (ENG.). 112p. (J). (gr. 3-7). lib. bdg. 15.99 *(978-1-4424-2710-5(8)*, Simon & Schuster/Paula Wiseman Bks.) Simon & Schuster/Paula Wiseman Bks.

—Copper Sun. 2014. (ENG.). 336p. (YA). 14.24 *(978-1-63245-110-1(7))* Lectorum Pubns., Inc.

—Copper Sun. 2011. 11.04 *(978-0-7848-3373-5(7)*, Everbind) Marco Bk. Co.

—Copper Sun. 2008. (ENG.). 336p. (YA). (gr. 9-12). pap. 10.99 *(978-1-4169-5348-7(5)*, Atheneum Bks. for Young Readers) Simon & Schuster Children's Publishing.

—Copper Sun. l.t. ed. 2006. 358p. (YA). (gr. 8-18). 22.95 *(978-0-7862-8948-6(1))* Thorndike Pr.

—Copper Sun. 2008. lib. bdg. 22.10 *(978-1-4177-9702-8(9)*, Turtleback) Turtleback Bks.

—Darkness Before Dawn. 2014. (Hazelwood High Trilogy Ser. 3 Ser.). (ENG.). 288p. (YA). (gr. k-k). 11.24 *(978-1-63245-162-0(X))* Lectorum Pubns., Inc.

—Darkness Before Dawn. 2013. (Hazelwood High Trilogy Ser.: 3). lib. bdg. 20.85 *(978-0-606-32334-5(1)*, Turtleback) Turtleback Bks.

—Double Dutch. 2004. 183p. (gr. 6-9). 17.00 *(978-0-7569-2934-3(2))* Perfection Learning Corp.

—Double Dutch. 2004. (ENG.). 192p. (J). (gr. 5-9). pap. 7.99 *(978-0-689-84231-3(7)*, Atheneum Bks. for Young Readers) Simon & Schuster Children's Publishing.

—Fire from the Rock. 2014. (ENG.). 240p. (YA). (gr. 7-12). 12.24 *(978-1-63245-286-3(3))* Lectorum Pubns., Inc.

—Fire from the Rock. 2008. (ENG.). 240p. (YA). (gr. 7-18). 7.99 *(978-0-14-241199-5(X)*, Speak) Penguin Young Readers Group.

—Forged by Fire. 2013. (Hazelwood High Trilogy Ser.: 2). lib. bdg. 20.85 *(978-0-606-32333-8(3)*, Turtleback) Turtleback Bks.

—Just Another Hero. (Jericho Trilogy Ser.: 3). (ENG., (YA). (gr. 7). 2017. Illus.). 304p. pap. 9.99 ***(978-1-4814-9030-6(3)***, Atheneum/Caitlyn Dlouhy Books) 2009. 288p. 19.99 *(978-1-4169-0700-8(9)*, Atheneum Bks. for Young Readers) Simon & Schuster Children's Publishing.

—Just Another Hero. 2010. (Jericho Trilogy Ser.: 3). lib. bdg. 18.40 *(978-0-606-14725-5(X)*, Turtleback) Turtleback Bks.

—Lost in the Tunnel of Time. Watson, Jesse Joshua, illus. 2011. (Clubhouse Mysteries Ser.: 2). (ENG.). 112p. (J). (gr. 3-7). pap. 5.99 *(978-1-4424-2704-4(3)*, Aladdin) Simon & Schuster Children's Publishing.

—Lost in the Tunnel of Time. Watson, Jesse Joshua, illus. 2011. (Clubhouse Mysteries Ser.: 2). (ENG.). 112p. (J). (gr. 3-7). lib. bdg. 15.99 *(978-1-4424-2703-7(5)*, Simon & Schuster/Paula Wiseman Bks.) Simon & Schuster/Paula Wiseman Bks.

—November Blues. 2011. 9.00 *(978-0-7848-3495-4(4)*, Everbind) Marco Bk. Co.

—November Blues. (Jericho Trilogy Ser.: 2). (ENG., Illus.). (YA). (gr. 7). 2017. 336p. pap. 9.99 ***(978-1-4814-9031-3(1)***, Atheneum/Caitlyn Dlouhy Books) 2007. 320p. 19.99 *(978-1-4169-0698-8(3)*, Atheneum Bks. for Young Readers) Simon & Schuster Children's Publishing.

—Panic. 2013. (ENG., Illus.). 272p. (YA). (gr. 9). 17.99 *(978-1-4424-0896-8(0)*, Atheneum Bks. for Young Readers) Simon & Schuster Children's Publishing.

—Shadows of Caesar's Creek. Watson, Jesse Joshua, illus. 2011. (Clubhouse Mysteries Ser.: 3). (ENG.). 128p. (J). (gr. 3-7). 15.99 *(978-1-4424-2712-9(4))*; pap. 5.99 *(978-1-4424-2711-2(6))* Simon & Schuster Children's Publishing. (Aladdin).

—The Silver Secret. 2010. (J). *(978-0-545-07157-4(7)*, Scholastic Pr.) Scholastic, Inc.

—The Space Mission Adventure. Watson, Jesse Joshua, illus. 2012. (Clubhouse Mysteries Ser.: 4). (ENG.). 112p. (J). (gr. 3-7). 15.99 *(978-1-4424-4225-2(5))*; pap. 5.99 *(978-1-4424-4226-9(3))* Simon & Schuster Children's Publishing. (Aladdin).

—Stars & Sparks on Stage. Watson, Jesse Joshua, illus. 2012. (Clubhouse Mysteries Ser.: 6). (ENG.). 144p. (J). (gr. 3-7). pap. 5.99 *(978-1-4424-5457-6(1)*, Aladdin) Simon & Schuster Children's Publishing.

—Stars & Sparks on Stage. Watson, Jesse Joshua, illus. 2012. (Clubhouse Mysteries Ser.: 6). (ENG.). 144p. (J). (gr. 3-7). 15.99 *(978-1-4424-5459-0(8)*, Simon & Schuster/Paula Wiseman Bks.) Simon & Schuster/Paula Wiseman Bks.

—Tears of a Tiger. 2014. (Hazelwood High Trilogy Ser. 1 Ser.). (ENG.). 192p. (YA). (gr. 12-12). 12.24 *(978-1-63245-075-3(5))* Lectorum Pubns., Inc.

—Tears of a Tiger. 2007. (Hazelwood High Trilogy: Bk. 1). 45p. ring bd. 54.95 *(978-1-60843-737-5(X))* Prestwick Hse., Inc.

—Tears of a Tiger. 2013. (Hazelwood High Trilogy Ser.: 1). (ENG., Illus.). 192p. (J). (gr. 7). pap. 9.99 *(978-1-4424-8913-4(8)*, Atheneum Bks. for Young Readers) Simon & Schuster Children's Publishing.

—Tears of a Tiger. l.t. ed. 2006. (Hazelwood High Trilogy: Bk. 1). 207p. (YA). (gr. 8-12). per. 10.95 *(978-0-7862-8361-3(0))* Thorndike Pr.

—Tears of a Tiger. 2013. (Hazelwood High Trilogy Ser.: 1). lib. bdg. 20.85 *(978-0-606-32332-1(5)*, Turtleback) Turtleback Bks.

Duey, Kathleen & Bale, Karen A. Flood: Mississippi 1927. 2015. (Survivors Ser.). (ENG., Illus.). 176p. (J). (gr. 3-7). pap. 6.99 *(978-1-4814-1642-9(1)*, Aladdin) Simon & Schuster Children's Publishing.

Dukes, LeRoy. The Chill Street Gang. 2005. (Illus.). 40p. (J). 6.99 *(978-0-9664506-1-3(2))* Dukes World, Inc.

Dunagan, Ted M. Secret of the Satilfa. 2010. (ENG.). 208p. (J). (gr. 3-18). 21.95 *(978-1-58838-249-8(4)*, NewSouth Bks.) NewSouth, Inc.

—A Yellow Watermelon. 2014. (ENG.). 240p. (J). pap. 17.95 *(978-1-58838-301-3(6)*, NewSouth Bks.) NewSouth, Inc.

Ehrhardt, Karen. This Jazz Man. Roth, R G, illus. 2006. (ENG.). 32p. (J). (gr. -1-3). 17.99 *(978-0-15-205307-9(7))* Houghton Mifflin Harcourt Publishing Co.

—This Jazz Man. Roth, R. G., illus. 2010. (J). (gr. 1-5). 28.95 incl. audio compact disk *(978-1-4301-0740-8(5))* Live Oak Media.

Elias, Megan J. Stir It Up: Home Economics in American Culture. 2010. (ENG., Illus.). 240p. (C). pap. 22.50 *(978-0-8122-2121-3(4))* Univ. of Pennsylvania Pr.

Elliott, Zetta. Melena's Jubilee, 1 vol. Boyd, Aaron, illus. 2016. (ENG.). 32p. (J). (gr. -1-5). 16.95 *(978-0-88448-443-1(2)*, 884443) Tilbury Hse. Pubs.

—Ship of Souls, 0 vols. 2012. (ENG.). 140p. (gr. 7-9). pap. 9.95 *(978-1-61218-268-1(2)*, 9781612182681, Amazon Children's Publishing) Amazon Publishing.

Elliott, Zetta & Strickland, Shadra. Bird, 1 vol. 2008. (ENG., Illus.). 48p. (J). (gr. 3-7). 19.95 *(978-1-60060-241-2(X))* Lee & Low Bks., Inc.

Elliott, Zetta & Terasaki, Stanley Todd. Bird. Shinjo, Shelly, illus. 2016. (ENG.). 32p. (J). (gr. 2-5). pap. 9.95 ***(978-1-62014-350-6(X))*** Lee & Low Bks., Inc.

Ellison, James W. & Atchison, Doug. Akeelah & the Bee. 2006. (Shooting Script Ser.). (ENG., Illus.). 186p. (gr. 4-6). per. 6.95 *(978-1-55704-729-8(4)*, Dey Street Bks.) HarperCollins Pubs.

Elster, Jean Alicia. The Colored Car. 2013. (Great Lakes Books Ser.). (ENG.). 224p. (YA). pap. 14.99 *(978-0-8143-3606-9(X)*, 2988) Wayne State Univ. Pr.

—I'll Do the Right Thing. Tadgell, Nicole, illus. 2010. (ENG.). 32p. (J). pap. 11.99 *(978-0-8170-1658-6(9))* Judson Pr.

—Who's Jim Hines? 2008. (Great Lakes Books Ser.). (ENG., Illus.). 146p. (J). pap. 14.99 *(978-0-8143-3402-7(4)*, 2162) Wayne State Univ. Pr.

Emerson, Kevin. Carlos Is Gonna Get It. 2008. (J). pap. *(978-0-439-93526-5(1)*, Levine, Arthur A. Bks.) Scholastic, Inc.

England, Linda. The Old Cotton Blues. Flavin, Teresa, illus. 2011. (ENG.). 32p. (J). (gr. -1-2). 14.99 *(978-1-4424-2945-1(3)*, McElderry, Margaret K. Bks.) McElderry, Margaret K. Bks.

English, Karen. Francie. 2007. (ENG.). 208p. (J). (gr. 4-8). per. 8.99 *(978-0-312-37383-2(X)*, 9780312373832) Square Fish.

—It All Comes down to This. 2017. (ENG.). 368p. (J). (gr. 5-7). 16.99 *(978-0-544-83957-1(9)*, Clarion Bks.) Houghton Mifflin Harcourt Trade & Reference Pubs.

—Nikki & Deja: Substitute Trouble. Freeman, Laura, illus. 2014. (ENG.). 112p. (J). (gr. 1-4). pap. 5.99 *(978-0-544-22388-2(8)*, HMH Books For Young Readers) Houghton Mifflin Harcourt Publishing Co.

—Wedding Drama. Freeman, Laura, illus. 2013. (ENG.). 112p. (J). (gr. 1-4). pap. 5.99 *(978-0-544-00324-8(1))* Houghton Mifflin Harcourt Publishing Co.

Evans, Freddi Williams. Hush Harbor: Praying in Secret. Banks, Erin, illus. 2008. (ENG.). 32p. (J). (gr. k-3). 16.95 *(978-0-8225-7965-6(0)*, Carolrhoda Bks.) Lerner Publishing Group.

Evans, Mari. I'm Late: The Story of Laneese & Moonlight & Alisha Who Didn't Have Anyone of Her Own. 2006. (Illus.). 86p. (J). (gr. 7-18). 14.95 *(978-1-933491-00-4(0))* Just Us Bks., Inc.

Evans, Shane W. We March. Evans, Shane W., illus. 2012. (ENG., Illus.). 32p. (J). (gr. -1-3). 16.99 *(978-1-59643-539-1(9)*, 9781596435391) Roaring Brook Pr.

Falwell, Cathryn. Los Dibujos de David. de La Vega, Eida, tr. from ENG. Falwell, Cathryn, illus. 2005. (SPA., Illus.). 32p. (J). (gr. -1-5). pap. 9.95 *(978-1-58430-258-2(5))* Lee & Low Bks., Inc.

—Feast for 10, 1 vol. Falwell, Cathryn, illus. (Read along Book & CD Ser.). (ENG., Illus.). (J). (gr. -1-3). 2008. 32p. audio compact disk 10.99 *(978-0-547-06431-4(4))* 2003. 28p. bds. 4.95 *(978-0-618-38226-2(7))* Houghton Mifflin Harcourt Publishing Co.

—Feast For 10. 2017. (ENG., Illus.). 32p. (J). (gr. -1-3). 26.99 *(978-0-544-93030-8(4)*, HMH Books For Young Readers) Houghton Mifflin Harcourt Publishing Co.

Falwell, Cathryn & National Geographic Learning Staff. David's Drawings. 2010. (Rise & Shine Ser.). (ENG., Illus.). 32p. (C). (gr. -1-2). pap. 14.95 *(978-1-58430-261-2(5))* National Geographic School Publishing, Inc.

Farish, Terry. The Good Braider, 0 vols. 2014. (ENG.). 224p. (YA). (gr. 9-12). pap. 9.99 *(978-1-4778-1628-8(3)*, 9781477816288, Amazon Children's Publishing) Amazon Publishing.

Feiffer, Kate. Which Puppy? Feiffer, Kate & Feiffer, Jules, illus. 2009. (ENG.). 32p. (J). (gr. -1-3). 16.99 *(978-1-4169-9147-2(6)*, Simon & Schuster/Paula Wiseman Bks.) Simon & Schuster/Paula Wiseman Bks.

Feinstein, John. Foul Trouble. (ENG.). (YA). (gr. 7). 2014. 416p. pap. 9.99 *(978-0-375-87169-6(1)*, Ember) 2013. 400p. 16.99 *(978-0-375-86964-8(6)*, Knopf Bks. for Young Readers) Random Hse. Children's Bks.

Figley, Marthy Rhodes & Figley, Marty Rhodes. The Prison-Ship Adventure of James Forten, Revolutionary War Captive. Hammond, Ted & Carbajal, Richard, illus. 2011. (History's Kid Heroes Ser.). (ENG.). 32p. (gr. 3-5). 26.60 *(978-0-7613-6183-1(9))*; pap. 8.95 *(978-0-7613-7075-8(7)*, Graphic Universe™) Lerner Publishing Group.

Figley, Marty Rhodes. The Prison-Ship Adventure of James Forten, Revolutionary War Captive. Hammond, Ted & Carbajal, Richard, illus. 2011. (History's Kid Heroes Ser.). 32p. pap. 51.02 *(978-0-7613-7637-8(2)*, Graphic Universe™) Lerner Publishing Group.

Flake, Sharon. Unstoppable Octobia May. 2014. (ENG.). 288p. (J). (gr. 3-7). 16.99 *(978-0-545-60960-9(7)*, Scholastic Pr.) Scholastic, Inc.

Flake, Sharon G. Bang! 2007. (J). 20.85 *(978-1-4177-7952-9(7)*, Turtleback) Turtleback Bks.

—Begging for Change. rev. ed. 2007. (ENG.). 256p. (J). (gr. 7-12). pap. 7.99 *(978-1-4231-0384-4(X)*, Jump at the Sun) Hyperion Bks. for Children.

—Money Hungry. Disney Press Staff, illus. rev. ed. 2007. (ENG.). 192p. (J). (gr. 5-9). pap. 8.99 *(978-1-4231-0386-8(6)*, Jump at the Sun) Hyperion Bks. for Children.

—Pinned. (ENG.). 240p. (J). 2014. (gr. 9). pap. 9.99 *(978-0-545-05733-2(7))* 2012. (gr. 8-9). 17.99 *(978-0-545-05718-9(3))* Scholastic, Inc. (Scholastic Pr.).

—The Skin I'm In. Disney Press Staff, illus. rev. ed. 2007. (ENG.). 176p. (J). (gr. 5-9). pap. 8.99 *(978-1-4231-0385-1(8)*, Jump at the Sun) Hyperion Bks. for Children.

—The Skin I'm In. 2007. (J). lib. bdg. 19.65 *(978-1-4178-0860-1(8)*, Turtleback) Turtleback Bks.

Fleischner, Jennifer. Nobody's Boy. 2006. (ENG., Illus.). 112p. (gr. 4). per. 12.95 *(978-1-883982-58-4(8))* Missouri Historical Society Pr.

Flood, Pansie Hart. Secret Holes. Marshall, Felicia, illus. 2004. 128p. (J). (gr. 3-6). 15.95 *(978-0-87614-923-2(9)*, Carolrhoda Bks.) Lerner Publishing Group.

—Sometimey Friend. Marshall, Felicia, illus. 2005. 124p. (J). (gr. 3-7). 15.95 *(978-1-57505-866-5(9))* Lerner Publishing Group.

—Sylvia & Miz Lula Maye. Marshall, Felicia, illus. 2003. (Middle Grade Fiction Ser.). 120p. (J). (gr. 3-6). 15.95 *(978-0-87614-204-2(8)*, Carolrhoda Bks.) Lerner Publishing Group.

Flor Ada, Alma. Celebrate Kwanzaa with Boots & Her Kittens. Docampo, Valeria, illus. 2007. (Cuentos para Celebrar / Stories to Celebrate Ser.). 30p. (gr. k-6). per. 11.95 *(978-1-59820-135-2(2))* Santillana USA Publishing Co., Inc.

—Celebrate Martin Luther King, Jr. Day with Mrs. Park's Class. Weiss, Monica, illus. 2006. (Stories to Celebrate Ser.). 30p. (gr. k-6). per. 11.95 *(978-1-59820-125-3(5)*, Alfaguara) Santillana USA Publishing Co., Inc.

Ford, Bernette G. Hurry Up! Kindert, Jennifer C., illus. 2004. (Just for You Ser.). (ENG.). 32p. (gr. k-1). pap. 3.99 *(978-0-439-56849-4(8)*, Teaching Resources) Scholastic, Inc.

Ford, Juwanda G. Shop Talk. Hoston, Jim, illus. 2004. 32p. (J). lib. bdg. 15.00 *(978-1-4242-0236-2(1))* Fitzgerald Bks.

Foster, Cassandra. Do You Know Us? A Collection of Short Stories. 2006. (Illus.). 48p. (YA). per. 8.00 *(978-0-9778641-1-9(1))* Smith, Mildred C.

—A Good Story: A Collection of Short Stories. 2006. (Illus.). 37p. (YA). per. 8.00 *(978-0-9778641-0-2(3))* Smith, Mildred C.

Frank, E. R. Dime. 2015. (ENG., Illus.). 336p. (YA). (gr. 9). 18.99 *(978-1-4814-3160-6(9))* Simon & Schuster Children's Publishing.

Frank, Steven B. Armstrong & Charlie. 2017. (ENG.). 304p. (J). (gr. 5-7). 16.99 *(978-0-544-82608-3(6)*, HMH Books For Young Readers) Houghton Mifflin Harcourt Publishing Co.

Frazier, Sundee T. The Other Half of My Heart. 2011. (ENG.). 304p. (J). (gr. 3-7). 7.99 *(978-0-440-24006-8(9)*, Yearling) Random Hse. Children's Bks.

Fuqua, Jonathon Scott. Darby. 2006. (ENG.). 256p. (J). (gr. 5-7). per. 7.99 *(978-0-7636-2290-9(7))* Candlewick Pr.

—The Reappearance of Sam Webber. 2010. (ENG.). 250p. pap. 12.95 *(978-1-890862-60-2(6))* Bancroft Pr.

Gaines, Ernest J. A Long Day in November. 2013. (ENG., Illus.). 160p. (gr. 2). pap. 11.95 *(978-1-939601-02-5(9))* Ig Publishing, Inc.

Gayle, Sharon Shavers. Emma's Escape: A Story of America's Underground Railroad. Velasquez, Eric, illus. 3rd ed. 2003. (Soundprints' Read-and-Discover Ser.). (ENG.). 48p. (J). (gr. -1-3). pap. 3.95 *(978-1-59249-021-9(2)*, S2009) Soundprints.

George, Olivia. The Bravest Girls in the World. DuBurke, Randy, illus. 2004. 32p. (J). lib. bdg. 15.00 *(978-1-4242-0241-6(8))* Fitzgerald Bks.

Gibney, Shannon. See No Color. 2015. (ENG.). 192p. (YA). (gr. 7-12). 18.99 *(978-1-4677-8814-4(7)*, Carolrhoda Lab™); 18.99 *(978-1-4677-7682-0(3))* Lerner Publishing Group.

Gibson, B. W. Extra Innings: The Diamond Thieves. 2014. 152p. pap. 14.95 *(978-1-4918-5663-5(7))* AuthorHouse.

Gilbert, Julie. Fire & Ice: A Mermaid's Journey. Fagan, Kirbi, illus. 2017. (Dark Waters Ser.). (ENG.). 160p. (gr. 2-4). lib. bdg. 26.65 *(978-1-4965-4168-0(5))* Stone Arch Bks.

—Into the Storm: A Mermaid's Journey. Fagan, Kirbi, illus. 2017. (Dark Waters Ser.). (ENG.). 160p. (gr. 2-4). pap. 6.95 *(978-1-4965-4175-8(8))*; lib. bdg. 26.65 *(978-1-4965-4171-0(5))* Stone Arch Bks.

—Neptune's Trident: A Mermaid's Journey. Fagan, Kirbi, illus. 2017. (Dark Waters Ser.). (ENG.). 160p. (gr. 2-4). lib. bdg. 26.65 *(978-1-4965-4169-7(3))* Stone Arch Bks.

—The Sighting: A Mermaid's Journey. Fagan, Kirbi, illus. 2017. (Dark Waters Ser.). (ENG.). 160p. (gr. 2-4). lib. bdg. 26.65 *(978-1-4965-4170-3(7))* Stone Arch Bks.

Giles, Lamar. Fake ID. 2014. (ENG.). 320p. (YA). (gr. 8). 17.99 *(978-0-06-212184-4(7)*, Amistad) HarperCollins Pubs.

—Overturned. 2017. (ENG.). 352p. (J). (gr. 7). 17.99 *(978-0-545-81250-4(X)*, Scholastic Pr.) Scholastic, Inc.

Glaser, Karina. The Vanderbeekers of 141st Street. 2017. (Vanderbeekers Ser.: 1). (ENG., Illus.). 304p. (J). (gr. 2-5). 16.99 ***(978-0-544-87639-2(3)***, HMH Books For Young Readers) Houghton Mifflin Harcourt Publishing Co.

Glasthal, Jacqueline B. Liberty on 23rd Street. Reingold, Alan, illus. 2006. (Adventures in America Ser.). (gr. 4). 14.95 net. *(978-1-893110-45-8(1))* Silver Moon Pr.

Godin, Thelma Lynne. Hula-Hoopin' Queen. Brantley-Newton, Vanessa, illus. 2014. (ENG.). 40p. (J). 18.95 *(978-1-60060-846-9(9))* Lee & Low Bks., Inc.

Going, K. L. The Liberation of Gabriel King. 2007. (ENG.). 160p. (J). (gr. 3-7). 6.99 *(978-0-14-240766-0(6)*, Puffin Books) Penguin Young Readers Group.

—The Liberation of Gabriel King. 2007. 151p. (gr. 3-7). 17.00 *(978-0-7569-7762-7(2))* Perfection Learning Corp.

Goldberg, Whoopi. Dancing Diva. Roos, Maryn, illus. 2012. (ENG.). 160p. (J). (gr. 1-5). pap. 4.99 *(978-0-7868-5265-9(8)*, Jump at the Sun) Hyperion Bks. for Children.

—Perfectly Prima, No. 3. Roos, Maryn, illus. 2010. (ENG.). 160p. (J). (gr. 1-17). pap. 4.99 *(978-0-7868-5262-8(3)*, Jump at the Sun) Hyperion Bks. for Children.

—Sugar Plum to the Rescue! Roos, Maryn, illus. 2011. (ENG.). 160p. (J). (gr. 1-5). pap. 4.99 *(978-0-7868-5264-2(X)*, Jump at the Sun) Hyperion Bks. for Children.

Goodman, Gabriel. Lightning's Run. 2014. (Bareknuckle Ser.). (ENG.). 104p. (YA). (gr. 6-12). pap. 7.95 *(978-1-4677-2162-2(X)*, Darby Creek) Lerner Publishing Group.

Goodman, Shawn. Something Like Hope. 2010. (ENG.). 208p. (YA). (gr. 9-18). 16.99 *(978-0-385-73939-9(7)*, Delacorte Bks. for Young Readers) Random Hse. Children's Bks.

Gorman, Carol & Findley, Ron J. The Stumptown Kid, 1 vol. 2005. (ENG.). 224p. (J). (gr. 3-7). 15.95 *(978-1-56145-337-5(4))* Peachtree Pubs.

Gottesfeld, Jeff. The Bank of Badness, 1 vol. 2013. (Robinson's Hood Ser.). (ENG.). (gr. 5-8). pap. 8.95 *(978-1-62250-001-7(6))* Saddleback Educational Publishing, Inc.

—The Bank of Badness. 2013. (Robinson's Hood Ser.: 2). lib. bdg. 19.60 *(978-0-606-27019-9(1)*, Turtleback) Turtleback Bks.

—Choices. 2014. (Campus Confessions Ser.: 3). (YA). lib. bdg. 20.80 *(978-0-606-34000-7(9)*, Turtleback) Turtleback Bks.

—Chopped!, 1 vol. 2013. (Robinson's Hood Ser.). (ENG.). (gr. 5-8). pap. 8.95 *(978-1-62250-002-4(4))* Saddleback Educational Publishing, Inc.

—Chopped! 2013. (Robinson's Hood Ser.: 3). lib. bdg. 19.60 *(978-0-606-27020-5(5)*, Turtleback) Turtleback Bks.

—Frenemies. 2014. (Campus Confessions Ser.: 2). (YA). lib. bdg. 20.80 *(978-0-606-33999-5(X)*, Turtleback) Turtleback Bks.

—Robinson's Hood, 1 vol. 2013. (Robinson's Hood Ser.). (ENG.). 128p. (gr. 5-8). pap. 8.95 *(978-1-62250-000-0(8))* Saddleback Educational Publishing, Inc.

—Robinson's Hood. 2013. (Robinson's Hood Ser.: 1). lib. bdg. 19.60 *(978-0-606-27018-2(3)*, Turtleback) Turtleback Bks.

—Xo Ronette. 2013. (Campus Confessions Ser.). (ENG.). 160p. (YA). (gr. 9-12). pap. 9.95 *(978-1-62250-701-6(0))* Saddleback Educational Publishing, Inc.

—Xo Ronette. 2013. (Campus Confessions Ser.: 1). (ENG.). 158p. (YA). (gr. 9-12). lib. bdg. 20.80 *(978-0-606-33998-8(1)*, Turtleback) Turtleback Bks.

Gourley, Robbin. Bring Me Some Apples & I'll Make You a Pie: A Story about Edna Lewis. (ENG., Illus.). 48p. (J). (gr. -1-3). 2016. pap. 6.99 *(978-0-544-80901-7(7)*, HMH Books For Young Readers) 2008. 17.99 *(978-0-618-15836-2(7))* Houghton Mifflin Harcourt Publishing Co.

Graber, Lois, illus. A Song in the Storm. 2012. 32p. (J). *(978-0-7399-2445-7(1))* Rod & Staff Pubs., Inc.

Grant, Karima. Sofie & the City. Montecalvo, Janet, illus. 2006. (ENG.). 32p. (J). (gr. 1-3). 15.95 *(978-1-59078-273-6(9))* Boyds Mills Pr.

Gray, Libba Moore. Miss Tizzy. Rowland, Jada, illus. 2014. 40p. pap. 8.00 *(978-1-61003-356-5(6))* Center for the Collaborative Classroom.

Gray, P. J. The Lab Book 3, 1 vol. 2015. (Trippin' Ser.). (ENG.). 64p. (YA). (gr. 9-12). pap. 8.95 *(978-1-62250-933-1(1))* Saddleback Educational Publishing, Inc.

—Trippin' Book 1, 1 vol. 2015. (Trippin' Ser.). (ENG.). 64p. (YA). (gr. 9-12). 8.95 *(978-1-62250-931-7(5))* Saddleback Educational Publishing, Inc.

Green, Paige. Family over Everything. 2013. (ENG., Illus.). 224p. pap. 15.99 *(978-1-59309-501-7(5)*, Strebor Bks.) Strebor Bks.

Greenberg, David. A Tugging String: A Novel about Growing up During the Civil Rights Era. 2008. (ENG., Illus.). 176p. (J). (gr. 4-7). 17.99 *(978-0-525-47967-3(8)*, Dutton Books for Young Readers) Penguin Young Readers Group.

Greene, Bette. I've Already Forgotten Your Name, Philip Hall! Jenkins, Leonard, illus. 2004. 176p. (J). (gr. 5-18). 15.99 *(978-0-06-051835-6(9))* HarperCollins Pubs.

Greenfield, Eloise. Me & Neesie. Gilchrist, Jan Spivey, illus. anniv. ed. 2005. (Amistad Ser.). 32p. (J). (gr. -1-3). 15.99 *(978-0-06-000701-0(X)*, Amistad) HarperCollins Pubs.

—William & the Good Old Days. Date not set. (Illus.). 32p. (J). (gr. k-3). pap. 4.99 *(978-0-06-443453-9(2))* HarperCollins Pubs.

Griffin, Paul. The Orange Houses. 2011. (ENG.). 176p. (YA). (gr. 9-18). 8.99 *(978-0-14-241982-3(6)*, Speak) Penguin Young Readers Group.

Grigsby, Susan. In the Garden with Dr. Carver. Tadgell, Nicole, illus. 2012. (J). *(978-1-61913-157-6(9))* Weigl Pubs., Inc.

—In the Garden with Dr. Carver. Tadgell, Nicole, illus. 2010. (ENG.). 32p. (J). (gr. 2-3). 16.99 *(978-0-8075-3630-8(X))* Whitman, Albert & Co.

Grimes, Nikki. Almost Zero: A Dyamonde Daniel Book. Christie, R. Gregory, illus. 2010. (Dyamonde Daniel Book Ser.: 3). (ENG.). 128p. (J). (gr. 2-4). 11.99

AB

(978-0-399-25177-1(4), G.P. Putnam's Sons Books for Young Readers) Penguin Young Readers Group.
—Bronx Masquerade. (ENG.). (YA). (gr. 7). 2017. 192p. pap. 8.99 **(978-0-425-28976-1(1))** 2003. 176p. 6.99 (978-0-14-250189-4(1)) Penguin Young Readers Group. (Speak).
—Bronx Masquerade. 2003. (gr. 7-12). lib. bdg. 17.20 (978-0-613-81701-1(X), Turtleback) Turtleback Bks.
—Chasing Freedom: The Life Journeys of Harriet Tubman & Susan B. Anthony, Inspired by Historical Facts. Wood, Michele, illus. 2015. (ENG.). 56p. (J). (gr. 2-5). 18.99 (978-0-439-79338-4(6), Orchard Bks.) Scholastic, Inc.
—Danitra Brown, Class Clown. Lewis, E. B., illus. 2005. 32p. (J). lib. bdg. 17.89 (978-0-688-17291-6(1)); (ENG.). (gr. 3). 16.99 (978-0-688-17290-9(3), Amistad) HarperCollins Pubs.
—Halfway to Perfect: A Dyamonde Daniel Book, 4 vols. Christie, R. Gregory, illus. 2012. (Dyamonde Daniel Book Ser.: 4). (ENG.). 128p. (J). (gr. 2-4). 10.99 (978-0-399-25178-8(2), G.P. Putnam's Sons Books for Young Readers) Penguin Young Readers Group.
—Make Way for Dyamonde Daniel. Christie, R. Gregory, illus. (Dyamonde Daniel Book Ser.: 1). (ENG.). (J). (gr. 2-4). 2010. 112p. pap. 5.99 (978-0-14-241555-9(3), Puffin Books) 2009. 96p. 10.99 (978-0-399-25175-7(8), G.P. Putnam's Sons Books for Young Readers) Penguin Young Readers Group.
—Rich. Christie, R. Gregory, illus. 2009. (Dyamonde Daniel Book Ser.: 2). (ENG.). 112p. (J). (gr. 2-4). 12.99 (978-0-399-25176-4(6), G.P. Putnam's Sons Books for Young Readers) Penguin Young Readers Group.
—The Road to Paris. 2008. 153p. (gr. 3-7). 17.00 (978-0-7569-8932-3(9)) Perfection Learning Corp.
—Road to Paris. 2008. (ENG.). 160p. (J). (gr. 3-7). 6.99 (978-0-14-241082-0(9), Puffin Books) Penguin Young Readers Group.
Grossinger, Tania. Jackie & Me: A Very Special Friendship. Esperanza, Charles George, illus. 2013. (ENG.). 32p. (J). (gr. -1-3). 16.95 (978-1-62087-683-1(3), 620683, Sky Pony Pr.) Skyhorse Publishing Co., Inc.
Gunderson, Jessica. The Songs of Stones River: A Civil War Novel. 2015. (Civil War Ser.). (ENG., Illus.). 96p. (gr. 4-4). lib. bdg. 26.65 (978-1-4342-9703-7(9)) Stone Arch Bks.
Gutman, Dan. Jackie & Me. 2005. (Baseball Card Adventures Ser.). (Illus.). 145p. (YA). (gr. 4-8). reprint ed. 20.00 (978-0-7567-9569-6(9)) DIANE Publishing Co.
—Satch & Me. (Baseball Card Adventures Ser.). (ENG.). 192p. (J). (gr. 5-9). 2009. pap. 5.99 (978-0-06-059493-0(4)) 2006. (Illus.). 16.99 (978-0-06-059491-6(8)) HarperCollins Pubs. (Amistad).
—Satch & Me. 2009. (Baseball Card Adventures Ser.). (J). lib. bdg. 16.00 (978-0-606-00023-9(2), Turtleback) Turtleback Bks.
Hahn, Mary Downing. Promises to the Dead. 2009. (ENG.). 208p. (J). (gr. 5-7). pap. 7.99 (978-0-547-25838-6(0)) Houghton Mifflin Harcourt Publishing Co.
Haislip, Phyllis Hall. Lottie's Courage: A Contraband Slave's Story. 2003. (Illus.). 120p. (J). pap. 7.95 (978-1-57249-311-7(9), White Mane Kids) White Mane Publishing Co., Inc.
Half Baked Sistas-in the Beginning. 2004. 242p. (YA). lib. bdg. 12.99 (978-0-9761819-0-3(8), 002) Smart Publishing.
Hamilton, Patricia Birdsong. Why do you Walk Funny? l.t. ed. 2006. (Ataxia: A Lifestyle Change). 38p. (J). 16.95 (978-1-889826-91-2(X)) Scripts Publishing.
Hamilton, Virginia. The House of Dies Drear. 8.97 (978-0-13-437491-8(6)) Prentice Hall PTR.
—The House of Dies Drear. 2006. (ENG.). 256p. (J). (gr. 6-9). pap. 7.99 (978-1-4169-1405-1(6), Aladdin) Simon & Schuster Children's Publishing.
—M. C. Higgins, the Great. 2006. 271p. (gr. 8-12). 18.00 (978-0-7569-6809-0(7)) Perfection Learning Corp.
—M. C. Higgins, the Great. 3rd ed. (J). pap. 3.95 (978-0-13-800137-7(5)); pap. 23.70 (978-0-13-620220-2(9)) Prentice Hall (Schl. Div.).
—M. C. Higgins, the Great. 2006. (ENG., Illus.). 288p. (J). (gr. 3-7). pap. 7.99 (978-1-4169-1407-5(2), Aladdin) Simon & Schuster Children's Publishing.
—The Planet of Junior Brown. 2006. 210p. (gr. 3-7). 17.00 (978-0-7569-6783-3(X)) Perfection Learning Corp.
—The Planet of Junior Brown. 2006. (ENG., Illus.). 224p. (J). (gr. 3-7). pap. 7.99 (978-1-4169-1410-5(2), Simon & Schuster/Paula Wiseman Bks.) Simon & Schuster/Paula Wiseman Bks.
—Zeely. Shimin, Symeon, illus. 2006. (ENG.). 128p. (J). (gr. 3-7). pap. 6.99 (978-1-4169-1413-6(7), Aladdin) Simon & Schuster Children's Publishing.
—Zeely. 2005. (Illus.). 128p. (J). (gr. 2-6). 21.75 (978-0-8446-7277-9(7), 3592) Smith, Peter Pub., Inc.
Hamilton, Virginia, et al. Plain City. (Barco de Vapor). (SPA.). 176p. (YA). (gr. 5-8). 6.95 (978-84-348-4686-9(1), LEC6861) SM Ediciones ESP. Dist: Continental Bk. Co., Inc.
Hansen, Joyce. The Gift-Giver. 2005. (ENG.). 132p. (J). (gr. 5-7). pap. 7.99 (978-0-618-61123-2(1)) Houghton Mifflin Harcourt Publishing Co.
—The Gift-Giver. 2011. 8.97 (978-0-7848-3614-9(0), Everbind) Marco Bk. Co.
—One True Friend. Giblin, James Cross, ed. 2005. (ENG.). 160p. (J). (gr. 5-7). pap. 11.95 (978-0-618-60991-8(1)) Houghton Mifflin Harcourt Publishing Co.
—Yellow Bird & Me. 2005. (ENG.). 160p. (J). (gr. 5-7). pap. 6.95 (978-0-618-61116-4(9)) Houghton Mifflin Harcourt Publishing Co.
—Yellow Bird & Me. 2005. (163rd Street Ser.). 155p. (gr. 5-9). 16.95 (978-0-7569-6228-9(5)) Perfection Learning Corp.
Harden, Perry Lee. The Percy Hargrove Stories: It's All Elementary. 2012. 160p. pap. 14.95 (978-1-4772-2438-0(6)) AuthorHouse.
Harrington, Janice N. Going North. Lagarrigue, Jerome, illus. 2004. (ENG.). 40p. (J). (gr. k-3). 18.99 (978-0-374-32681-4(9), 9780374326814, Farrar, Straus & Giroux (BYR)) Farrar, Straus & Giroux.
Harris, Frankco. David Saves the Day: An African American Depiction of David & Goliath. 2011. 28p. pap. 15.99 (978-1-4628-4516-3(9)) Xlibris Corp.
Harris, Joel Chandler. Nights with Uncle Remus. 2008. 288p. 29.95 (978-1-60664-915-2(9)) Aegypan.
—Told by Uncle Remus: New Stories of the. 2006. (Illus.). pap. 31.95 (978-1-4254-9964-8(3)) Kessinger Publishing, LLC.
—Uncle Remus His Songs & His Sayings. 2017. (ENG., Illus.). (YA). (gr. 4-12). cd-rom (978-1-892824-57-8(4)) AFCHRON.
Harris, Joel Chandler, et al. The Classic Tales of Brer Rabbit. Daily, Don, illus. 2008. (ENG.). 56p. (J). (gr. 1-17). 9.95 (978-0-7624-3219-6(5)) Running Pr. Bk. Pubs.
Harris, Todd V. Heroes & Haters. 2008. 75p. pap. 19.95 (978-1-60563-157-8(4)) America Star Bks.
Hart, Alison. Gabriel's Horses, 1 vol. 2007. (Racing to Freedom Trilogy). (ENG.). 160p. (J). (gr. 3-7). 14.95 (978-1-56145-398-6(6)) Peachtree Pubs.
—Gabriel's Journey, 1 vol. (Racing to Freedom Ser.). (ENG.). 160p. (J). 2011. pap. 4.99 (978-1-56145-530-0(X)) 2008. (Illus.). (gr. 3-7). 14.95 (978-1-56145-442-6(7)) Peachtree Pubs.
—Gabriel's Triumph, 1 vol. 2007. (Racing to Freedom Trilogy). (ENG.). 160p. (J). (gr. 3-7). 14.95 (978-1-56145-410-5(9)) Peachtree Pubs.
Haskins, James. The March on Washington. 2004. (Illus.). 192p. (J). (gr. 5-18). pap. 10.95 (978-0-940975-93-4(9), Sankofa Bks.) Just Us Bks., Inc.
Hathaway, Barbara. Missy Violet & Me. 2008. (ENG.). 112p. (J). (gr. 2-5). pap. 8.95 (978-0-618-80919-6(8)) Houghton Mifflin Harcourt Publishing Co.
Haugaard, Kay. The Day the Dragon Danced. Barritt, Carolyn Reed, illus. 2004. (Day the Dragon Danced Ser.). 32p. (J). (gr. -1-3). 16.95 (978-1-885008-30-5(9), Shen's Bks.) Lee & Low Bks., Inc.
Havill, Juanita. Jamaica's Blue Marker. O'Brien, Anne Sibley, illus. 2003. (ENG.). 32p. (J). (gr. -1-3). pap. 7.99 (978-0-618-36917-1(1)) Houghton Mifflin Harcourt Publishing Co.
—Jamaica's Find. O'Brien, Anne Sibley, illus. 2009. (ENG.). 32p. (J). (gr. -1-3). audio compact disk 10.99 (978-0-547-11961-8(5)) Houghton Mifflin Harcourt Publishing Co.
Hayes, Sonia. Ms. Thang. 2009. (ENG.). 200p. (YA). per. 9.95 (978-0-9777573-0-5(7)) NUA Multimedia.
—Urban Goddess. 2007. 224p. (YA). per. 9.95 (978-0-9777573-1-2(5)) NUA Multimedia.
Hedstrom-Page, Deborah. From Slavery to Freedom with Harriet Tubman. Martinez, Sergio, illus. 2007. (My American Journey Ser.). 84p. (J). (gr. 3-9). 9.99 (978-0-8054-3268-8(X)) B&H Publishing Group.
Helget, Nicole. Wonder at the Edge of the World. 2015. (ENG., Illus.). 384p. (J). (gr. 3-7). 17.00 (978-0-316-24510-4(0)) Little, Brown Bks. for Young Readers.
Helmso, Candy Grant. Cakewalk. Taylor, Stephen, illus. 2003. (Books for Young Learners). (ENG.). 16p. (J). pap. 5.75 net. (978-1-57274-250-5(X), 2727, Bks. for Young Learners) Owen, Richard C. Pubs., Inc.
Hemphill, Helen. The Adventurous Deeds of Deadwood Jones. (ENG.). 232p. (J). 2011. (gr. 6-9). pap. 7.95 (978-1-59078-896-7(6)) 2008. (gr. 5-18). 16.95 (978-1-59078-637-6(8), Front Street) Boyds Mills Pr.
Hendrickson, David H. Cracking the Ice. 2011. (YA). 365p. (gr. 9-18). 16.95 (978-1-934813-55-3(9)); 366p. (978-1-934813-56-0(7)) Westside Bks.
Hering, Marianne & Sanders, Nancy I. Captured on the High Seas. 2014. (AIO Imagination Station Bks.: 14). (ENG.). 144p. (J). pap. 4.99 (978-1-58997-775-4(0)) Tyndale Hse. Pubs.
Herlong, M. H. Buddy. 2013. (ENG.). 320p. (J). (gr. 5). pap. 7.99 (978-0-14-242544-2(3), Puffin Books) Penguin Young Readers Group.
Hesse, Karen. Come on, Rain! 2004. (J). (gr. k-3). 29.95 (978-1-55592-500-0(6)) Weston Woods Studios, Inc.
Hest, Amy. Mr. George Baker. Muth, Jon J., illus. 2007. (Reading Rainbow Bks.). (ENG.). 32p. (J). (gr. k-3). 6.99 (978-0-7636-3308-0(9)) Candlewick Pr.
—Mr. George Baker. 2007. lib. bdg. 17.20 (978-1-4177-9067-8(9), Turtleback) Turtleback Bks.
Hester, Denia Lewis. Grandma Lena's Big Ol' Turnip. Urbanovic, Jackie, illus. 2005. (ENG.). 32p. (J). (gr. -1-3). 6.99 (978-0-8075-3023-8(9)) Whitman, Albert & Co.
—Grandma Lena's Big Ol'turnip. Urbanovic, Jackie, illus. 2014. (AV2 Fiction Readalong Ser.: Vol. 138). (ENG.). 32p. (J). (gr. -1-3). lib. bdg. 34.28 (978-1-4896-2329-4(9), AV2 by Weigl) Weigl Pubs., Inc.
Hicks, Benjamin. Byron's Tie. Hicks, Benjamin & Hicks, Rosetta, eds. 2013. 35p. pap. 8.95 (978-1-929883-08-0(0)) Ingleside Pr.
Hicks, Clifford B. Alvin Fernald's Incredible Buried Treasure. Bradfield, Roger, illus. 2009. (J). 17.95 (978-1-930900-43-1(0)) Purple Hse. Pr.
Hill, Clarissa. God Deserves Your Best. Hill, Stephanie, illus. 2005. (ENG.). 20p. (J). pap. 11.00 (978-0-9785539-0-6(X)) Hill, Stephanie & Clarissa.
Himes, Rachel. Princess & the Peas. Himes, Rachel, illus. 2017. (ENG., Illus.). 32p. (J). (gr. k-3). 16.99 (978-1-58089-718-1(5)) Charlesbridge Publishing, Inc.
Hines, Thomas, illus. The Bubble Machine. l.t. ed. 2003. 26p. (J). per. (978-1-887636-02-5(1)) Creative Writing & Publishing Co.
Hitchcock, Shannon. Ruby Lee & Me. 2016. (ENG., Illus.). 272p. (J). (gr. 3-7). 16.99 (978-0-545-78230-2(9), Scholastic Pr.) Scholastic, Inc.
Hoena, Blake A. Raw. Cano, Fernando, illus. 2013. (Tony Hawk: Live2Skate Ser.). (ENG.). 72p. (gr. 3-4). pap. 35.70 (978-1-4342-6268-4(5), Tony Hawk's 900 Revolution) Stone Arch Bks.
Hoffman, Mary. Amazing Grace. (Illus.). 32p. (J). (ENG & VIE.). (978-1-85430-340-0(6), 93435); (ARA & ENG.). (978-1-85430-334-9(1), 93433) Little Tiger Pr. Group.
—Princess Grace. Van Wright, Cornelius & Hu, Ying-Hwa, illus. 2008. (ENG.). 32p. (J). (gr. -1-3). 18.99 (978-0-8037-3260-5(0), Dial Bks) Penguin Young Readers Group.
Hooks, Bell. Be Boy Buzz. Raschka, Chris, illus. 2016. (ENG.). 32p. (J). (gr. -1 — 1). bds. 7.99 (978-1-4847-8840-0(0), Jump at the Sun) Hyperion Bks. for Children.
—Happy to Be Nappy (Board Book) Happy to Be Nappy. Raschka, Chris, illus. 2017. (ENG.). 32p. (J). (gr. -1 — 1). bds. 7.99 (978-1-4847-8841-7(9), Jump at the Sun) Hyperion Bks. for Children.
Hooks, Gwendolyn. Three's a Crowd. Walker, Sylvia, illus. 2004. 32p. (J). lib. bdg. 15.00 (978-1-4242-0240-9(X)) Fitzgerald Bks.
Hopkinson, Deborah. From Slave to Soldier: Based on a True Civil War Story. Floca, Brian, illus. (Ready-To-Reads Ser.). (ENG.). 48p. (J). (gr. 1-3). 2007. pap. 3.99 (978-0-689-83966-5(9)) 2005. 16.99 (978-0-689-83965-8(0)) Simon Spotlight. (Simon Spotlight).
—Steamboat School. Husband, Ron, illus. 2016. (ENG.). 40p. (J). (gr. -1-k). 17.99 (978-1-4231-2196-1(1)) Disney Pr.
—Under the Quilt of Night. Ransome, James E., illus. 2005. (gr. k-5). 18.00 (978-0-7569-5077-4(5)) Perfection Learning Corp.
—Under the Quilt of Night. Ransome, James E., illus. 2005. (ENG.). 40p. (J). (gr. k-5). reprint ed. 7.99 (978-0-689-87700-1(5), Aladdin) Simon & Schuster Children's Publishing.
Houston, Julian. New Boy. 2008. (ENG.). 288p. (YA). (gr. 7-12). pap. 7.99 (978-0-618-88405-6(X)) Houghton Mifflin Harcourt Publishing Co.
—New Boy. 2007. 282p. (gr. 7-12). 18.00 (978-0-7569-8139-6(5)) Perfection Learning Corp.
Howard, Annabelle. Keelboat Annie: An American Tall Tale. 2006. (J). pap. (978-1-4108-6169-6(4)) Benchmark Education Co.
Howard, Elizabeth Fitzgerald. Aunt Flossie's Hats (and Crab Cakes Later) Ransome, James, illus. 2015. 32p. pap. 8.00 (978-1-61003-491-3(0)) Center for the Collaborative Classroom.
—Chita's Christmas Tree. 2007. (ENG.). 32p. (J). (gr. -1-3). 13.99 (978-1-4169-6156-7(9), Simon & Schuster/Paula Wiseman Bks.) Simon & Schuster/Paula Wiseman Bks.
—The Train to Lulu's. Casilla, Robert, illus. 2007. (ENG.). 36p. (J). (gr. -1-3). 10.99 (978-1-4169-6161-1(5), Simon & Schuster/Paula Wiseman Bks.) Simon & Schuster/Paula Wiseman Bks.
—Virgie Goes to School with Us Boys. Lewis, E. B., illus. 2005. (gr. k-3). 18.00 (978-0-7569-5088-0(0)) Perfection Learning Corp.
—Virgie Goes to School with Us Boys. Lewis, E. B., illus. 2005. (ENG.). 32p. (J). (gr. k-3). reprint ed. 7.99 (978-0-689-87793-3(5), Aladdin) Simon & Schuster Children's Publishing.
Hru, Dakari. Joshua's Masai Mask. Rich, Anna, illus. 2013. (ENG.). 32p. (J). (gr. -1-5). pap. 9.95 (978-1-880000-32-8(6)) Lee & Low Bks., Inc.
Hubbard, Crystal. Catching the Moon: The Story of a Young Girl's Baseball Dream. DuBurke, Randy, illus. 2005. (ENG.). 32p. (J). pap. 9.95 (978-1-60060-572-7(9)) Lee & Low Bks., Inc.
Hubbell, Patricia. Black All Around! Tate, Don, illus. 2003. (ENG.). 32p. (J). 16.95 (978-1-58430-048-9(5)) Lee & Low Bks., Inc.
Hubler, Marsha. Southern Belle's Special Gift, 1 vol. 2009. (Keystone Stables Ser.). (ENG.). 128p. (J). pap. 7.99 (978-0-310-71794-2(9)) Zonderkidz.
Hudson, Wade. The Two Tyrones. Page, Mark, illus. 2004. 32p. (J). lib. bdg. 15.00 (978-1-4242-0239-3(6)) Fitzgerald Bks.
—The Two Tyrones. Page, Mark, illus. 2004. (Just for You Ser.). (ENG.). 32p. (gr. 2-3). pap. 3.99 (978-0-439-56866-1(8), Teaching Resources) Scholastic, Inc.
Hughes, Langston. Simple Speaks His Mind. (J). (gr. 5-6). reprint ed. lib. bdg. 22.95 (978-0-88411-061-3(3)) Amereon Ltd.
Hurston, Zora Neale. The Six Fools. Tanksley, Ann, illus. 2006. (ENG.). 40p. (J). (gr. 1-5). 15.99 (978-0-06-000646-4(3)) HarperCollins Pubs.
Hurston, Zora Neale & Thomas, Joyce Carol. Lies & Other Tall Tales. Myers, Christopher, illus. 2015. (ENG.). 40p. (J). (gr. -1-3). pap. 6.99 (978-0-06-000657-0(9)) HarperCollins Pubs.
—The Six Fools. Tanksley, Ann, illus. 2005. 40p. (J). (gr. 1-5). lib. bdg. 18.89 (978-0-06-000647-1(1)) HarperCollins Pubs.
I Like Me. 2004. (J). per. (978-1-57657-395-2(8)) Paradise Pr., Inc.
I Like Me. 2004. 8p. (gr. k-2). 20.95 (978-0-322-00630-0(9)) Wright Group/McGraw-Hill.
Imes, Jarod. Age Ain't Nothing but a Number. 2007. 148p. (YA). pap. 10.99 (978-1-934195-04-8(9)) Tinsley Phelps, LLC.
Imes, Jarold. Hold on Be Strong. 2008. (YA). per. 10.99 (978-1-934195-09-3(X)) 2007. 192p. per. 14.99 (978-1-934195-05-5(7)) Tinsley Phelps, LLC.
—Rollin' Wit the Punches. 2008. (YA). per. 10.99 (978-1-934195-08-6(1)) Tinsley Phelps, LLC.
Imes, Jarold, adapted by. U Can't Break Me. 2007. 148p. (YA). pap. 10.99 (978-1-934195-03-1(0)) Tinsley Phelps, LLC.
Irene's Wish. 2014. (ENG., Illus.). 32p. (J). (gr. k-4). 17.99 (978-0-689-86300-4(4), Simon & Schuster/Paula Wiseman Bks.) Simon & Schuster/Paula Wiseman Bks.
Isadora, Rachel. Peekaboo Morning. Isadora, Rachel, illus. 2008. (ENG., Illus.). 24p. (J). (gr. -1 — 1). bds. 7.99 (978-0-399-25153-5(7), G.P. Putnam's Sons Books for Young Readers) Penguin Young Readers Group.
Jack, Keats Ezra. Peter's Chair. 2014. (ENG.). 40p. (J). (gr. k-k). 11.24 (978-1-63245-276-4(6)) Lectorum Pubns., Inc.
—The Snowy Day. 2014. (ENG.). 40p. (J). (gr. 3-7). 12.24 (978-1-63245-154-5(9)) Lectorum Pubns., Inc.
Jackson, Linda. Midnight Without a Moon. 2017. (ENG.). 320p. (J). (gr. 5-7). 16.99 (978-0-544-78510-6(X), HMH Books For Young Readers) Houghton Mifflin Harcourt Publishing Co.
Jackson, Richard. In Plain Sight. Pinkney, Jerry, illus. 2016. (ENG.). 40p. (J). 17.99 (978-1-62672-255-2(2), 9781626722552) Roaring Brook Pr.
Jarman, Benjamin. Tony's Last Touchdown. 2012. (Champion Sports Story Ser.). 104p. (J). (gr. 3-18). pap. 10.95 (978-1-4644-0004-9(0)); 27.94 (978-0-7660-3885-1(8)) Enslow Pubs., Inc.
Jeremiah, Omari. Paperboy 3: The School of Doom. Rollins, Bernie, illus. 2006. 75p. pap. 12.99 (978-1-929188-13-0(7)) Morton Bks.
Johnson, Alaya Dawn. Love Is the Drug. 2014. (YA). pap. (978-0-545-41782-2(1)); (ENG.). 352p. (J). (gr. 9). 17.99 (978-0-545-41781-5(3), Levine, Arthur A. Bks.) Scholastic, Inc.
Johnson, Angela. All This & Heaven Too: Heaven; the First Part Last; Sweet, Hereafter. 2013. (ENG., Illus.). 400p. (YA). (gr. 7). pap. 10.99 (978-1-4424-8719-2(4), Simon & Schuster Bks. For Young Readers) Simon & Schuster Bks. For Young Readers.
—Bird. 2006. 133p. (gr. 3-7). 16.00 (978-0-7569-6660-7(4)) Perfection Learning Corp.
—Daddy Calls Me Man. Mitchell, Rhonda, illus. 2014. 32p. pap. 7.00 (978-1-61003-309-1(4)) Center for the Collaborative Classroom.
—The First Part Last. (ENG.). 144p. (YA). (gr. 7). 2010. pap. 9.99 (978-1-4424-0343-7(8)) 2003. (Illus.). 16.99 (978-0-689-84922-0(2)) Simon & Schuster Bks. For Young Readers. (Simon & Schuster Bks. For Young Readers).
—The First Part Last. 2005. (ENG.). 144p. (YA). (gr. 7). reprint ed. pap. 7.99 (978-0-689-84923-7(0), Simon Pulse) Simon Pulse.
—The First Part Last. l.t. ed. 2005. 241p. pap. 10.95 (978-0-7862-7379-9(8), Large Print Pr.) Thorndike Pr.
—Heaven, 3 vols. 2006. (J). 44.75 (978-1-4281-0237-8(X)) Recorded Bks., Inc.
—Heaven. 2010. (ENG.). 160p. (YA). (gr. 7). pap. 9.99 (978-1-4424-0342-0(X), Simon & Schuster Bks. For Young Readers) Simon & Schuster Bks. For Young Readers.
—Just Like Josh Gibson. Peck, Beth, illus. 2007. (J). 14.65 (978-0-7569-8088-7(7)) Perfection Learning Corp.
—Just Like Josh Gibson. Peck, Beth, illus. (ENG.). 32p. (J). 2004. (gr. -1-2). 17.99 (978-0-689-82628-3(1)) 2007. (gr. k-2). reprint ed. 7.99 (978-1-4169-2728-0(X)) Simon & Schuster Bks. For Young Readers. (Simon & Schuster Bks. For Young Readers).
—Looking for Red. 2003. (ENG., Illus.). 128p. (YA). (gr. 7). pap. 6.99 (978-0-689-86388-2(8), Simon Pulse) Simon Pulse.
—Sweet, Hereafter. 2011. (ENG.). 128p. (YA). (gr. 7). pap. 8.99 (978-0-689-87386-7(7), Simon & Schuster Bks. For Young Readers) Simon & Schuster Bks. For Young Readers.
—Sweet, Hereafter, Bk. 3. 2010. 128p. (YA). (gr. 9-18). pap. 16.99 (978-1-4169-9995-9(7)) Simon & Schuster Children's Publishing.
—A Sweet Smell of Roses. Velasquez, Eric, illus. (ENG.). 32p. (J). 2007. (gr. k-3). 7.99 (978-1-4169-5361-6(2)) 2005. (gr. -1-3). 17.99 (978-0-689-83252-9(4)) Simon & Schuster Bks. For Young Readers. (Simon & Schuster Bks. For Young Readers).
—Wind Flyers. Long, Loren, illus. 2007. (ENG.). 32p. (J). (gr. k-4). 17.99 (978-0-689-84879-7(X), Simon & Schuster Bks. For Young Readers) Simon & Schuster Bks. For Young Readers.
Johnson, Nancy. A Sweet-Sounding Place: A Civil War Story. 2008. (ENG.). 128p. (J). (gr. 3-7). pap. 10.95 (978-0-89272-770-4(5)) Down East Bks.
Jones, Christianne C. John Henry, 1 vol. Robledo, Sol, tr. Peterson, Ben, illus. 2008. (Read-It! Readers en Español: Cuentos Exagerados Ser.). Tr. of John Henry. (SPA.). 32p. (gr. k-3). per. 3.95 (978-1-4048-2174-3(0), Easy Readers) Picture Window Bks.
Jones, Patrick. At the Center. 2016. (Bounce Ser.). (ENG.). 104p. (YA). (gr. 6-12). 26.65 (978-1-5124-1122-5(1)) Lerner Publishing Group.
—Doing Right. 2015. (J). 27.99 (978-1-4677-7691-2(2)); (ENG.). 104p. (gr. 6-12). lib. bdg. 27.99 (978-1-4677-5803-1(5)) Lerner Publishing Group.
—Heart or Mind. 2016. (Unbarred Ser.). (ENG., Illus.). 120p. (YA). (gr. 6-12). lib. bdg. 27.99 (978-1-5124-0003-8(3), Darby Creek) Lerner Publishing Group.
—Heart or Mind. 2016. (Unbarred Ser.). (ENG., Illus.). 120p. (YA). (gr. 6-12). pap. 7.99 (978-1-5124-0091-5(2), Darby Creek) Lerner Publishing Group.
—Heart or Mind. 2016. (Unbarred Ser.). (ENG.). 120p. (YA). (gr. 6-12). 42.65 (978-1-5124-0092-2(0), Darby Creek) Lerner Publishing Group.
—Outburst. 2014. (Alternative Ser.). (ENG.). 104p. (YA). (gr. 6-12). lib. bdg. 27.93 (978-1-4677-3901-6(4)) Lerner Publishing Group.
—Outburst. 2014. (Alternative Ser.). (ENG.). 104p. (YA). (gr. 6-12). pap. 7.95 (978-1-4677-4484-3(0), Darby Creek) Lerner Publishing Group.
—Raising Heaven. 2015. (J). 9.99 (978-1-4677-7697-4(1)); (ENG.). 96p. (gr. 6-12). lib. bdg. 27.99 (978-1-4677-5802-4(7)) Lerner Publishing Group.
—Side Control. 2013. (Dojo Ser.). (ENG.). 136p. (YA). (gr. 6-12). pap. 7.95 (978-1-4677-1488-4(7)); lib. bdg. 27.93 (978-1-4677-0631-5(0)) Lerner Publishing Group. (Darby Creek).
Jones, Patrick & Clark, Marshunna. Duty or Desire. 2016. (Unbarred Ser.). (ENG.). 112p. (YA). (gr. 6-12). lib. bdg. 27.99 (978-1-5124-0002-1(5), Darby Creek) Lerner Publishing Group.
—Duty or Desire. 2016. (Unbarred Ser.). (ENG.). 112p. (YA). (gr. 6-12). pap. 7.99 (978-1-5124-0089-2(0), Darby Creek) Lerner Publishing Group.
—Duty or Desire. 2016. (Unbarred Ser.). (ENG.). 112p. (YA). (gr. 6-12). 42.65 (978-1-5124-0090-8(4), Darby Creek) Lerner Publishing Group.
Jones, Traci L. Silhouetted by the Blue. 2011. (ENG.). 208p. (J). (gr. 5-9). 16.99 (978-0-374-36914-9(3), 9780374369149, Farrar, Straus & Giroux (BYR)) Farrar, Straus & Giroux.
—Standing Against the Wind. 2010. (ENG.). 208p. (YA). (gr. 7-9). pap. 11.99 (978-0-312-62293-0(7), 9780312622930) Square Fish.
Jordan, Brian. I Told You I Can Play! 2008. (Illus.). 32p. 6.95 (978-1-60349-001-6(9), Marimba Bks.) Hudson Publishing Group, The.
Jordan, Dream. Bad Boy. 2012. (ENG.). 208p. (YA). (gr. 6-11). pap. 17.99 (978-0-312-54997-8(0), 9780312549978, St. Martin's Griffin) St. Martin's Pr.
Jordan, Rosa. Lost Goat Lane, 1 vol. 2004. (ENG.). 192p. (J). (gr. 3-7). 14.95 (978-1-56145-325-2(0)) Peachtree Pubs.
Jump Shot. 2014. (Barber Game Time Bks.). (ENG., Illus.). 160p. (J). (gr. 3-7). pap. 7.99 (978-1-4424-5730-0(9), Simon & Schuster/Paula Wiseman Bks.) Simon & Schuster/Paula Wiseman Bks.
Karre, Elizabeth. All You Are. 2014. (Gift Ser.). 120p. (YA). (gr. 6-12). (ENG.). pap. 7.95 (978-1-4677-4477-5(8)); lib. bdg. 27.93 (978-1-4677-3510-0(8)) Lerner Publishing Group. (Darby Creek).

—Certain Signals. 2014. (Gift Ser.). (ENG.). 112p. (YA). (gr. 6-12). pap. 7.95 (978-1-4677-4479-9(4), Darby Creek) Lerner Publishing Group.
—No Regrets. 2014. (Gift Ser.). (ENG.). 120p. (YA). (gr. 6-12). pap. 7.95 (978-1-4677-4480-5(8), Darby Creek); lib. bdg. 27.93 (978-1-4677-3512-4(4)) Lerner Publishing Group.
Karwoski, Gail Langer. When Hurricane Katrina Hit Home. Marshall, Julia, illus. 2013. Orig. Title: When Hurricane Katrina Hit Home. (ENG.). 192p. (gr. 4-7). 15.99 (978-1-62619-083-2(6), History Pr., The) Arcadia Publishing.
Katz, Karen. My First Kwanzaa. Katz, Karen, illus. 2014. (My First Holiday Ser.). (ENG., Illus.). 32p. (J). (gr. -1-k). 7.99 (978-1-250-05046-5(4), 9781250050465) Square Fish.
Keats, Ezra Jack. Peter's Chair. 2015. 40p. pap. 7.00 (978-1-61003-534-7(8)) Center for the Collaborative Classroom.
—Peter's Chair. Keats, Ezra Jack, illus. 2006. (ENG., Illus.). 32p. (J). (gr. -1 — 1). bds. 6.99 (978-0-670-06190-7(5), Viking Books for Young Readers) Penguin Young Readers Group.
—The Snowy Day. (ENG.). (J). 2012. 32p. (gr. -1 — 1). bds. 12.99 (978-0-670-01325-8(0)) 50th anniv. ed. 2011. 48p. (gr. k-3). 19.99 (978-0-670-01270-1(X)) Penguin Young Readers Group. (Viking Books for Young Readers).
—Whistle for Willie. 2015. 32p. pap. 7.00 (978-1-61003-537-8(2)) Center for the Collaborative Classroom.
Kelley, Gloria. Beverly Babes & Guys: Alicia's Thirtee. 2006. 64p. pap. 16.95 (978-1-4241-2610-1(X)) PublishAmerica, Inc.
Kelly, Claire. Nellie in the News. Hicks, Faith, illus. 2007. 48p. (J). lib. bdg. 23.08 (978-1-4242-1631-4(1)) Fitzgerald Bks.
Kelly, Keith. Peace Comes to Ajani. Kelly, Keith, illus. 2009. (Illus.). 56p. (J). pap. 9.95 (978-0-932112-59-0(5)) Carolina Wren Pr.
Kern, Peggy. Little Peach. 2015. (ENG.). 208p. (YA). (gr. 9). 17.99 (978-0-06-226695-8(0)) HarperCollins Pubs.
Keyser, Amber J. & Burkhart, Kiersi. One Brave Summer. 2017. (Quartz Creek Ranch Ser.). (ENG.). 224p. (gr. 4-8). 35.99 **(978-1-5124-0892-8(1)**, Darby Creek) Lerner Publishing Group.
Kidd, Ronald. Night on Fire. 2015. (ENG.). 288p. (J). (gr. 3-7). 16.99 (978-0-8075-7024-1(9)) Whitman, Albert & Co.
Killebrew, Joyce Louise. Triumphant Queen Leah - the Ultimate African American Fairy Tale Picture Book. 2013. 68p. pap. (978-0-9840720-6-4(3)) Roxby Media Ltd.
King, Deja. Ride Wit' Me: A Novel. 2009. 151p. (YA). pap. (978-0-9755811-9-3(8)) King Production, A.
Klein, Adria F. Max Se Queda a Dormir. 1 vol. Robledo, Sol, tr. from ENG. Gallagher-Cole, Mernie, illus. 2007. (Read-It! Readers en Español: la Vida de Max Ser.). (SPA.). 24p. (gr. -1-3). lib. bdg. 21.32 (978-1-4048-3797-3(3), Easy Readers) Picture Window Bks.
—Max's Fun Day. 1 vol. Gallagher-Cole, Mernie, illus. 2007. (Read-It! Readers: the Life of Max Ser.). (ENG.). 24p. (gr. -1-2). lib. bdg. 21.32 (978-1-4048-3150-6(9), 1265797, Easy Readers) Picture Window Bks.
Konigsberg, Bill. The Porcupine of Truth. 2015. (ENG.). 336p. (J). (gr. 9). 17.99 (978-0-545-64893-6(9)) Scholastic, Inc.
Konigsburg, E. L. Jennifer, Hecate, Macbeth, William McKinley, & Me, Elizabeth. (J). (gr. 3-6). 177p. pap. 4.99 (978-0-8072-1524-1(4)); 117p. pap. 4.99 (978-0-8072-1417-6(5)) Random Hse. Audio Publishing Group. (Listening Library).
—Jennifer, Hecate, Macbeth, William Mckinley, & Me, Elizabeth. 2007. (ENG., Illus.). 128p. (J). (gr. 3-7). pap. 7.99 (978-1-4169-3396-0(4), Atheneum Bks. for Young Readers) Simon & Schuster Children's Publishing.
Krensky, Stephen. John Henry. Oldroyd, Mark, illus. 2007. (On My Own Folklore Ser.). (ENG.). 48p. (gr. 2-4). per. 6.95 (978-0-8225-6477-5(7), First Avenue Editions) Lerner Publishing Group.
—Play Ball, Jackie! Morse, Joe, illus. 2011. (Single Titles Ser.). (ENG.). 32p. (J). (gr. 2-5). lib. bdg. 16.95 (978-0-8225-9030-9(1), Millbrook Pr.) Lerner Publishing Group.
Kumara, Mark. The Tr-Youth Truth: Knowledge, Apprehens. 2005. (Illus.). 206p. pap. 24.75 (978-1-4120-6960-1(2)) Trafford Publishing.
Kuskowski, Alex. Tia: Fitting In. 2012. (Juicy Central Ser.: 1). lib. bdg. 20.80 (978-0-606-25132-7(4), Turtleback) Turtleback Bks.
LaFaye, A. Stella Stands Alone. 2010. (ENG.). 256p. (YA). (gr. 7). pap. 7.99 (978-1-4169-8647-8(2), Simon & Schuster Bks. For Young Readers) Simon & Schuster Bks. For Young Readers.
—Walking Home to Rosie Lee. Shepherd, Keith D., illus. 2011. (ENG.). 32p. (J). (gr. 1-6). 16.95 (978-1-933693-97-2(5)) Cinco Puntos Pr.
Lamana, Julie T. Upside down in the Middle of Nowhere. (ENG.). (J). 2015. 328p. (gr. 4-7). pap. 7.99 (978-1-4521-2880-1(4)) 2014. 320p. (gr. 3-7). 16.99 (978-1-4521-2456-8(6)) Chronicle Bks. LLC.
LaMarche, Una & Loftin, Nikki. Don't Fail Me Now. 2015. (ENG.). 288p. (YA). (gr. 7). 17.99 (978-1-59514-817-9(5), Razorbill) Penguin Young Readers Group.
Lane, Marion T. Patriots of African Descent in the Revolutionary War: Part 1. 2011. 56p. 30.00 (978-1-60976-517-0(6), Eloquent Bks.) Strategic Book Publishing & Rights Agency (SBPRA).
Langan, John. Search for Safety. 2012. (Bluford High — Scholastic Ser.: 13). lib. bdg. 16.00 (978-0-606-26204-0(0), Turtleback) Turtleback Bks.
Larson, Kirby. Liberty. 2016. (Dogs of World War II Ser.). (ENG.). 240p. (J). (gr. 3-7). 16.99 (978-0-545-84071-2(6), Scholastic Pr.) Scholastic, Inc.
Latham, Irene. Leaving Gee's Bend. 2017. (ENG.). 192p. (gr. 5). pap. 11.95 (**978-1-58838-332-7(6)**, NewSouth Bks.) NewSouth, Inc.
Latham, Jennifer. Dreamland Burning. 2017.Tr. of s. (ENG.). 384p. (YA). (gr. 9-17). 18.99 (978-0-316-38493-3(3)) Little, Brown Bks. for Young Readers.
Lavonne, Victoria. Twas the Night at the Capitol: A Narrative Featuring the First African American Family. 2012. 28p. pap. 24.95 (978-1-4626-9799-1(2)) America Star Bks.
Lay, Kathryn. Book 4: Time under the Sea. 2016. (Time Twisters Ser.). (ENG.). (J). (gr. 2-6). lib. bdg. 27.07 **(978-1-62402-180-0(8))** ABDO Publishing Co.
LeCraw, Cynthia, retold by. The Tale of the Wonderful Tar Baby. 2007. (J). (978-0-9794203-2-0(6)) Southern Lion Bks.
Lee, Spike & Lee, Tonya Lewis. Please, Baby, Please. Nelson, Kadir, illus. 2007. (Classic Board Bks.). (ENG.). 32p. (J). (gr. -1-k). bds. 7.99 (978-1-4169-4911-4(9), Little Simon) Little Simon.
Lee, Stacey. Under a Painted Sky. 2015. (ENG.). 384p. (YA). (gr. 7). 16.99 (978-0-399-16803-1(6), G.P. Putnam's Sons Books for Young Readers) Penguin Young Readers Group.
—Under a Painted Sky. 2016. lib. bdg. 22.10 (978-0-606-38391-2(3)) Turtleback Bks.
LeFlore, Lyah B. The World Is Mine. Warfield, D. L., illus. 2009. (Come Up Ser.). (ENG.). 304p. (YA). (gr. 9-18). pap. 8.99 (978-1-4169-7963-0(8), Simon Pulse) Simon Pulse.
Leonard, Marcia. Mi Dia de Campamento. Translations.com Staff, tr. from ENG. Handelman, Dorothy, photos by. 2007. (Lecturas para niños de Verdad - Nivel 1 (Real Kids Readers - Level 1) Ser.).Tr. of My Camp-Out. (SPA., Illus.). 32p. (gr. k-2). per. 5.95 (978-0-8225-7798-0(4), Ediciones Lerner) Lerner Publishing Group.
—Mi Dia de Campamento; My Camp Out. 2008. pap. 34.95 (978-0-8225-9496-3(X)) Lerner Publishing Group.
Lester, Julius. Guardian. 2008. (ENG., Illus.). 144p. (YA). (gr. 9-18). 16.99 (978-0-06-155890-0(7), Amistad) HarperCollins Pubs.
Letters from a Slave Girl. 2011. 8.32 (978-0-7848-3635-4(3), Everbind) Marco Bk. Co.
Levine, Ellen. Henry's Freedom Box: A True Story from the Underground Railroad. Nelson, Kadir, illus. 2007. (ENG.). 40p. (J). (gr. -1-3). 17.99 (978-0-439-77733-9(X), Scholastic Pr.) Scholastic, Inc.
—Henry's Freedom Box: A True Story from the Underground Railroad. Nelson, Kadir, illus. 2011. (J). (gr. 2-5). 29.95 (978-0-545-13455-2(2)) Weston Woods Studios, Inc.
Levine, Gail Carson. Dave at Night. 2006. (ENG.). 304p. (J). (gr. 3-7). reprint ed. pap. 7.99 (978-0-06-440747-2(0)) HarperCollins Pubs.
—Dave at Night. 2004. 281p. (gr. 3-7). 17.00 (978-0-7569-4101-7(6)) Perfection Learning Corp.
—Dave at Night. unabr. ed. 2004. 278p. (J). (gr. 4-7). pap. 38.00 incl. audio (978-0-8072-8379-0(7), YA174SP, Listening Library) Random Hse. Audio Publishing Group.
Levine, Kristin. The Lions of Little Rock. (ENG.). (J). (gr. 5-9). 2013. 320p. pap. 7.99 (978-0-14-242435-3(8), Puffin Books) 2012. 304p. 16.99 (978-0-399-25644-8(X), G.P. Putnam's Sons Books for Young Readers) Penguin Young Readers Group.
Life Changing Books, creator. Teenage Bluez 2, 2. 2006. 169p. (J). (gr. -1). per. 10.99 (978-0-9741394-8-7(3)) Power Play Media.
The Lil Dudes. 2006. (YA). per. (978-1-59872-308-3(1)) Instant Pub.
Limb, Lisa. The Wishing Wheelchair. 2009. 40p. pap. 16.99 (978-1-4389-4205-6(2)) AuthorHouse.
Lindbergh, Reeve. Nobody Owns the Sky. Paparone, Pamela, illus. 2004. 32p. (J). (978-1-85269-347-3(9)); (978-1-85269-342-8(8)); (978-1-85269-343-5(6)); (978-1-85269-344-2(4)); (978-1-85269-345-9(2)) Mantra Lingua.
Lindsey, Kathleen D. Sweet Potato Pie. Riley-Webb, Charlotte, illus. 2003. (J). 16.95 (978-1-58430-061-8(2)); (ENG.). 32p. pap. 9.95 (978-1-60060-277-1(0)) Lee & Low Bks., Inc.
Lipsyte, Robert. The Brave. 2003. (Charlotte Zolotow Bk.). (ENG.). 240p. (J). (gr. 8-18). pap. 6.99 (978-0-06-447079-7(2)) HarperCollins Pubs.
—The Contender. 2003. (Trophy Keypoint Bks.). (ENG.). 240p. (YA). (gr. 8-18). pap. 8.99 (978-0-06-447039-1(3), HarperTeen) HarperCollins Pubs.
—The Contender. 2003. (YA). lib. bdg. 19.65 (978-0-88103-014-3(7), Turtleback) Turtleback Bks.
Literature Connections English: The Glory Field. 2004. (Literature Connections Ser.). (gr. 6-12). (978-0-395-78374-0(7), 2-70257) Holt McDougal.
Lombard, Jenny. Drita, My Homegirl. 2008. (ENG.). 144p. (J). (gr. 3-7). 5.99 (978-0-14-240905-3(7), Puffin Books) Penguin Young Readers Group.
Long, Loren & Bildner, Phil. Water, Water Everywhere. Long, Loren, illus. (Sluggers Ser.: 4). (ENG., Illus.). (J). (gr. 3-7). 2010. 288p. pap. 7.99 (978-1-4169-1890-5(6)) 2009. 272p. 14.99 (978-1-4169-1866-0(3)) Simon & Schuster Bks. For Young Readers. (Simon & Schuster Bks. For Young Readers).
Lottie Paris Lives Here. 2014. (Classic Board Bks.). (ENG., Illus.). 34p. (J). (gr. -1-k). bds. 7.99 (978-1-4814-0966-7(2), Little Simon) Little Simon.
Lupica, Mike. True Legend. (ENG.). (J). (gr. 5). 2013. 320p. pap. 7.99 (978-0-14-242650-0(4), Puffin Books) 2012. 304p. 17.99 (978-0-399-25227-3(4), Philomel Bks.) Penguin Young Readers Group.
Luthardt, Kevin. Flying!, 1 vol. Luthardt, Kevin, illus. 2013. (ENG., Illus.). 32p. (J). (gr. -1-1). 7.95 (978-1-56145-724-3(8)) Peachtree Pubs.
Lyon, George Ella. You & Me & Home Sweet Home. Anderson, Stephanie, illus. 2009. (ENG.). 48p. (J). (gr. -1-3). 17.99 (978-0-689-87589-2(4), Atheneum/Richard Jackson Bks.) Simon & Schuster Children's Publishing.
Lyons, Kelly Starling. Ellen's Broom. Minter, Daniel, illus. 2012. (ENG.). 32p. (J). (gr. k-3). 16.99 (978-0-399-25003-3(4), G.P. Putnam's Sons Books for Young Readers) Penguin Young Readers Group.
—Hope's Gift. Tate, Don, illus. 2012. (ENG.). 32p. (J). (gr. 1-3). 16.99 (978-0-399-16001-1(9), G.P. Putnam's Sons Books for Young Readers) Penguin Young Readers Group.
—One Million Men & Me. Ambush, Peter, illus. 2007. 32p. (J). (gr. -1-3). 16.95 (978-1-933491-07-3(8)) Just Us Bks., Inc.
—Tea Cakes for Tosh. Lewis, E. B., illus. 2012. (ENG.). 32p. (J). (gr. k-3). 16.99 (978-0-399-25213-6(4), G.P. Putnam's Sons Books for Young Readers) Penguin Young Readers Group.
Lyons, Mary E. Letters from a Slave Boy: The Story of Joseph Jacobs. 2009. (ENG.). 208p. (YA). (gr. 7). mass mkt. 7.99 (978-0-689-87868-8(0), Simon Pulse) Simon Pulse.
—Letters from a Slave Girl: The Story of Harriet Jacobs. 2008. (Illus.). 175p. (gr. 7-12). 16.00 (978-0-7569-8474-8(2)) Perfection Learning Corp.
—Letters from a Slave Girl: The Story of Harriet Jacobs. 2007. (ENG., Illus.). 192p. (YA). (gr. 7). mass mkt. 6.99 (978-1-4169-3637-4(8), Simon Pulse) Simon Pulse.
Maddox, Jake. Lacrosse Laser. Aburtov, Jesus Aburto, illus. 2016. (Jake Maddox Sports Stories Ser.). (ENG.). 72p. (gr. 2-3). lib. bdg. 25.32 (978-1-4965-3051-6(9)) Stone Arch Bks.
—Slam Dunk Shoes, 1 vol. Tiffany, Sean, illus. 2007. (Jake Maddox Sports Stories Ser.). (ENG.). 72p. (gr. 2-3). 25.32 (978-1-59889-842-2(6)); per. 5.95 (978-1-59889-894-1(9)) Stone Arch Bks.
Maddox, Jake & Anderson, Josh. Second Shot. Aburtov, Jesus Aburto, illus. 2016. (Jake Maddox Sports Stories Ser.). (ENG.). 72p. (gr. 2-3). lib. bdg. 25.32 (978-1-4965-3052-3(7)) Stone Arch Bks.
Magoon, Kekla. Camo Girl. 2012. (ENG.). 224p. (J). (gr. 3-9). pap. 7.99 (978-1-4169-7805-3(4), Aladdin) Simon & Schuster Children's Publishing.
—Camo Girl. 2011. (ENG., Illus.). 224p. (J). (gr. 3-9). 16.99 (978-1-4169-7804-6(6), Simon & Schuster/Paula Wiseman Bks.) Simon & Schuster/Paula Wiseman Bks.
—Fire in the Streets. 2013. (ENG., Illus.). 352p. (J). (gr. 5-9). pap. 7.99 (978-1-4424-2231-5(9), Aladdin) Simon & Schuster Children's Publishing.
—How It Went Down. 2014. (ENG.). 336p. (YA). (gr. 9-12). 18.99 (978-0-8050-9869-3(0), 9780805098693, Holt, Henry & Co. Bks. For Young Readers) Holt, Henry & Co.
—How It Went Down. Barcellona, Christine, ed. 2015. (ENG.). 352p. (YA). (gr. 9). pap. 9.99 (978-1-250-06823-1(1), 9781250068231) Square Fish.
—The Rock & the River. (ENG.). 304p. (J). (gr. 5-9). 2010. pap. 7.99 (978-1-4169-7803-9(8)) 2009. 17.99 (978-1-4169-7582-3(9)) Simon & Schuster Children's Publishing. (Aladdin).
Magoon, Kekla & Keene, Carolyn. Strangers on a Train. 2013. (Nancy Drew Diaries: 2). (ENG.). 208p. (J). (gr. 3-7). pap. 6.99 (978-1-4169-9073-4(9), Aladdin) Simon & Schuster Children's Publishing.
Malaspina, Ann. Finding Lincoln. Bootman, Colin, illus. 2009. (ENG.). 32p. (J). (gr. 2-3). 16.99 (978-0-8075-2435-0(2)) Whitman, Albert & Co.
—The People Could Fly: An African-American Folktale. Otero, Sole, illus. 2013. (Folktales from Around the World Ser.). (ENG.). 24p. (J). (gr. k-3). 28.50 (978-1-62323-617-5(7), 206385) Child's World, Inc., The.
—Touch the Sky: Alice Coachman, Olympic High Jumper. Velasquez, Eric, illus. 2012. (ENG.). 32p. (J). (gr. 1-3). 16.99 (978-0-8075-8035-6(X)) Whitman, Albert & Co.
Maldonado, Torrey. Secret Saturdays. 2012. (ENG.). 208p. (YA). (gr. 7-18). 7.99 (978-0-14-241747-8(5), Puffin Books) Penguin Young Readers Group.
—Secret Saturdays. 2012. lib. bdg. 18.40 (978-0-606-23645-4(7), Turtleback) Turtleback Bks.
Malone, Marianne. The Pirate's Coin.. Call, Greg, illus. 2014. (Sixty-Eight Rooms Adventures Ser.). (ENG.). 240p. (J). (gr. 3-7). 7.99 (978-0-307-97720-5(X), Yearling) Random Hse. Children's Bks.
Manning, Matthew K. U.S. Special Forces: Ghosts of the Night. Enecio, Jeremy, illus. 2016. (U. S. Special Ops Ser.). (ENG.). 96p. (gr. 3-4). E-Book 26.65 (978-1-4965-3477-4(8), Connect) Stone Arch Bks.
Maple, Daphne. Top Dog. Metayer, Annabelle, illus. 2016. (Roxbury Park Dog Club Ser.: 3). 224p. (J). (gr. 3-7). pap. 6.99 (978-0-06-232771-0(2)) HarperCollins Pubs.
Marsh, Carole. The Mystery on the Underground Railroad. 2009. (Real Kids, Real Places Ser.). (Illus.). 146p. (J). lib. bdg. 18.99 (978-0-635-06991-7(1), Marsh, Carole Mysteries) Gallopade International.
—The Mystery on the Underground Railroad (Hardcover) 2003. 160p. (gr. 2-8). 14.95 (978-0-635-02110-6(2)) Gallopade International.
Mason, Margaret H. These Hands. Cooper, Floyd, illus. 2011. (ENG.). 32p. (J). (gr. -1-3). 16.99 (978-0-547-21566-2(5)) Houghton Mifflin Harcourt Publishing Co.
Masters, Susan Rowan. Night Journey to Vicksburg. Killcoyne, Hope L., ed. Smith, Duane A., illus. 2003. (Adventures in America Ser.). 74p. (gr. 4). 14.95 (978-1-893110-30-4(3)) Silver Moon Pr.
Matagrano, Joseph F. Forever Brothers. 2007. 396p. 26.95 (978-1-4327-0963-1(1)); per. 16.95 (978-1-4327-1524-3(0)) Outskirts Pr., Inc.
Mattocks, Kikki. In His Hands. 2011. 24p. pap. 16.99 (978-1-4520-3453-9(2)) AuthorHouse.
May, Eleanor. Keesha's Bright Idea. Wummer, Amy, illus. 2008. (Social Studies Connects Ser.). 32p. (J). (gr. -1-3). pap. 5.95 (978-1-57565-273-3(0)) Kane Press, Inc.
—Keesha's Bright Idea. Wummer, Amy, illus. 2009. (Social Studies Connects (r) Ser.). (ENG.). (gr. 1-3). pap. 33.92 (978-0-7613-4806-1(9)) Lerner Publishing Group.
Mazellan, Ron, illus. We Will Walk. 2005. 16p. (J). pap. (978-0-7367-2919-2(4)) Zaner-Bloser, Inc.
McCully, Emily Arnold. The Escape of Oney Judge: Martha Washington's Slave Finds Freedom. McCully, Emily Arnold, illus. 2007. (ENG., Illus.). 32p. (J). (gr. 1-4). 17.99 (978-0-374-32225-0(2), 9780374322250, Farrar, Straus & Giroux (BYR)) Farrar, Straus & Giroux.
—Wonder Horse: The True Story of the World's Smartest Horse. McCully, Emily Arnold, illus. 2010. (ENG., Illus.). 32p. (J). (gr. -1-3). 17.99 (978-0-8050-8793-2(1), 9780805087932, Holt, Henry & Co. Bks. For Young Readers) Holt, Henry & Co.
Mcgill, Leslie. Hacker. 2014. (Cap Central Ser.: 3). (YA). lib. bdg. 20.80 (978-0-606-35739-5(4)) Turtleback Bks.
McGuigan, Mary Ann. Morning in a Different Place. 2009. (ENG.). 195p. (YA). (gr. 7-18). 17.95 (978-1-59078-551-5(7), Front Street) Boyds Mills Pr.
McKay, Sindy & Johnson, Meredith. We Both Read-Baseball Fever. 2003. (We Both Read Ser.). (Illus.). 44p. (J). (gr. 1-2). 7.99 (978-1-891327-45-2(3)) Treasure Bay, Inc.
McKissack, Fredrick, Jr. Shooting Star. 2010. (ENG.). 288p. (YA). (gr. 7). pap. 9.99 (978-1-4169-9774-0(1), Atheneum Bks. for Young Readers) Simon & Schuster Children's Publishing.
McKissack, Fredrick L. This Generation of Americans. 2004. 150p. (J). lib. bdg. 16.92 (978-1-4242-0769-5(X)) Fitzgerald Bks.
McKissack, Patricia C. Abby Takes a Stand. James, Gordon C., illus. 2007. 104p. (J). (978-0-439-02797-7(7)) Scholastic, Inc.
—Abby Takes a Stand. James, Gordon C. et al, illus. 2006. (Scraps of Time Ser.). (ENG.). 128p. (J). (gr. 3-7). 6.99 (978-0-14-240687-8(2), Puffin Books) Penguin Young Readers Group.
—The All-I'll-Ever-Want Christmas Doll. Pinkney, Jerry, illus. 2007. (J). (978-0-375-83615-2(2), Schwartz & Wade Bks.) Random Hse. Children's Bks.
—The All-I'll-Ever-Want Christmas Doll. Pinkney, Jerry, illus. 2007. (ENG.). 40p. (J). (gr. -1-3). 17.99 (978-0-375-83759-3(0), Schwartz & Wade Bks.) Random Hse. Children's Bks.
—Away West. James, Gordon C. & James, Gordon, illus. 2006. (Scraps of Time Ser.). (ENG.). 144p. (J). (gr. 3-7). 5.99 (978-0-14-240688-5(0), Puffin Books) Penguin Young Readers Group.
—The Dark-Thirty: Southern Tales of the Supernatural. Pinkney, Brian, illus. 2004. 122p. (J). (gr. 5-8). reprint ed. pap. 17.00 (978-0-7567-7601-5(5)) DIANE Publishing Co.
—The Dark-Thirty: Southern Tales of the Supernatural. Pinkney, Brian, illus. 2006. (ENG.). 128p. (J). (gr. 3-7). 18.95 (978-0-679-81863-2(4), Knopf Bks. for Young Readers) Random Hse. Children's Bks.
—A Friendship for Today. 2008. 172p. (J). pap. (978-0-545-06563-4(1)) Scholastic, Inc.
—Goin' Someplace Special. Pinkney, Jerry, illus. 2008. (ENG.). 40p. (J). (gr. -1-3). 7.99 (978-1-4169-2735-8(2), Aladdin) Simon & Schuster Children's Publishing.
—The Home-Run King. 2009. (Scraps of Time Ser.). (ENG.). 112p. (J). (gr. 3-7). 6.99 (978-0-14-241459-0(X), Puffin Books) Penguin Young Readers Group.
—Never Forgotten. Dillon, Leo & Dillon, Diane, illus. 2011. (ENG.). 48p. (J). (gr. k-12). 18.99 (978-0-375-84384-6(1), Schwartz & Wade Bks.) Random Hse. Children's Bks.
—A Picture of Freedom: The Diary of Clotee, a Slave Girl, Belmont Plantation, Virginia, 1859. 2011. (Dear America Ser.). (ENG.). 240p. (J). (gr. 3-7). 14.99 (978-0-545-24253-0(3), Scholastic Pr.) Scholastic, Inc.
—Porch Lies: Tales of Slicksters, Tricksters, & Other Wily Characters. Carrilho, Andre, illus. 2006. (ENG.). 160p. (J). (gr. 3-7). 19.99 (978-0-375-83619-0(5), Schwartz & Wade Bks.) Random Hse. Children's Bks.
—A Song for Harlem. 2008. (Scraps of Time Ser.). (ENG.). 128p. (J). (gr. 3-7). 6.99 (978-0-14-241238-1(4), Puffin Books) Penguin Young Readers Group.
—Stitchin' & Pullin' A Gee's Bend Quilt. Cabrera, Cozbi A., illus. 2016. (ENG.). 48p. (J). (gr. k-4). 8.99 (978-0-399-54950-2(1), Dragonfly Bks.) Random Hse. Children's Bks.
—Tippy Lemmey. Keeter, Susan, illus. 2003. (Ready-for-Chapters Ser.). 59p. (gr. 2-5). lib. bdg. 15.00 (978-0-7569-1432-5(9)) Perfection Learning Corp.
McKissack, Patricia C. & Moss, Onawumi Jean. Precious & the Boo Hag. Brooker, Kyrsten, illus. 2005. (ENG.). 40p. (J). (gr. -1-3). 17.99 (978-0-689-85194-0(4), Atheneum Bks. for Young Readers) Simon & Schuster Children's Publishing.
McKissack, Patricia C., et al. The Honest-to-Goodness Truth. Potter, Giselle, illus. 2003. (ENG.). 40p. (J). (gr. -1-3). 7.99 (978-0-689-85395-1(5), Aladdin) Simon & Schuster Children's Publishing.
McMorrow, T. E. & Hoffmann, E. T. A. Nutcracker in Harlem. Ransome, James, illus. 2017. 32p. (J). (gr. -1-3). 17.99 (978-0-06-117598-5(6)) HarperCollins Pubs.
McQuinn, Anna. Lola at the Library. Beardshaw, Rosalind, illus. 2007. 22p. (gr. -1). 16.95 (978-0-7569-7931-7(5)) Perfection Learning Corp.
—Lola Gets a Cat. Beardshaw, Rosalind, illus. 2017. (ENG.). 28p. (J). (-k). lib. bdg. 15.99 (978-1-58089-736-5(3)) Charlesbridge Publishing, Inc.
—Lola le Lee Al Pequeño Leo. Beardshaw, Rosalind, illus. 2013. (SPA & ENG.). 28p. (J). (-k). pap. 7.95 (978-1-58089-599-6(9)) Charlesbridge Publishing, Inc.
—Lola Loves Stories. Beardshaw, Rosalind, illus. 2010. (ENG.). 28p. (J). (gr. k-3). pap. 6.95 (978-1-58089-259-9(0)) Charlesbridge Publishing, Inc.
—Lola Plants a Garden. Beardshaw, Rosalind, illus. 2014. (ENG.). 28p. (J). (-k). 15.95 (978-1-58089-694-8(4)) Charlesbridge Publishing, Inc.
—Lola Reads to Leo. Beardshaw, Rosalind, illus. 2012. (ENG.). 28p. (J). (-k). 15.95 (978-1-58089-403-6(8)); pap. 6.95 (978-1-58089-404-3(6)) Charlesbridge Publishing, Inc.
—Lola Reads to Leo. 2012. pap. 19.95 incl. audio compact disk (978-0-8045-4236-4(8)) Spoken Arts, Inc.
McQuinn, Anna & Beardshaw, Rosalind. A Lola le Encantan Los Cuentos. Canetti, Yanitzia, tr. from ENG. Beardshaw, Rosalind, illus. 2012. (SPA., Illus.). 28p. (J). (-k). pap. 7.95 (978-1-58089-444-9(5)) Charlesbridge Publishing, Inc.
McQuinn, Anna & Calvo, Carlos E. Lola Planta un Jardin. Beardshaw, Rosalind, illus. 2017. (SPA.). 28p. (J). (-k). pap. 7.99 (978-1-58089-786-0(X)) Charlesbridge Publishing, Inc.
McQuinn, Anna, et al. Lola Plants a Garden: Lola Planta un Jardín. Beardshaw, Rosalind, illus. 2017. (SPA & ENG.). (J). pap. **(978-1-63289-027-6(5))** Charlesbridge Publishing, Inc.
—Lola Reads to Leo: Lola le Lee Al Pequeño Leo. Beardshaw, Rosalind, illus. 2017. (SPA & ENG.). (J). pap. **(978-1-63289-028-3(3))** Charlesbridge Publishing, Inc.
Mead, Alice. Junebug. 2009. (Junebug Ser.). (ENG.). 128p. (J). (gr. 3-7). pap. 7.99 (978-0-312-56126-0(1), 9780312561260) Square Fish.
—Junebug in Trouble. 2003. (ENG., Illus.). 144p. (J). (gr. 3-7). 5.99 (978-0-440-41937-2(9), Yearling) Random Hse. Children's Bks.
Medearis, Angela Shelf. Singing for Dr. King. Hu, Ying-Hwa & Van Wright, Cornelius, illus. 2004. 32p. (J). lib. bdg. 15.00 (978-1-4242-0237-9(X)) Fitzgerald Bks.
Melcher, Rich. A Work in Progress. 2011. 148p. 29.99 (978-1-4568-5192-7(6)); pap. 15.99 (978-1-4568-5191-0(8)) Xlibris Corp.
Meloy, Alice McFeely. As the Crow Flies: Preface to Gettysburg: the Enemy Is Here! 2012. 106p. (J). pap. 8.95 (978-1-57249-411-4(5), White Mane Kids) White Mane Publishing Co., Inc.

Messner, Kate. Long Road to Freedom. McMorris, Kelley, illus. 2015. (Ranger in Time Ser.: 3). (ENG.). 160p. (J). (gr. 2-5). pap. 5.99 (978-0-545-63920-0(4)) Scholastic, Inc.

Meyer, Carolyn. Jubilee Journey. 2007. (ENG., Illus.). 288p. (J). (gr. 5-7). pap. 17.95 (978-0-15-205845-6(1)) Houghton Mifflin Harcourt Publishing Co.

—Jubilee Journey. 2007. 271p. (J). (gr. 5-9). 14.60 (978-0-7569-6682-9(5)) Perfection Learning Corp.

—White Lilacs. 2007. (ENG., Illus.). 256p. (J). (gr. 2-5). pap. 8.99 (978-0-15-205851-7(6)) Houghton Mifflin Harcourt Publishing Co.

—White Lilacs. 2006. (Illus.). 242p. (gr. 4-7). 16.95 (978-0-7569-6683-6(3)) Perfection Learning Corp.

Meyer, Susan Lynn. New Shoes. Velasquez, Eric, illus. (ENG.). 32p. (J). 2016. 7.99 (978-0-8234-3573-9(3)) 2015. (gr. 1-4). 16.95 (978-0-8234-2528-0(2)) Holiday Hse., Inc.

Michelson, Richard. Across the Alley. Lewis, E. B., illus. 2006. (ENG.). 32p. (J). (gr. -1-3). 16.99 (978-0-399-23970-0(7), G.P. Putnam's Sons Books for Young Readers) Penguin Young Readers Group.

Miller, Pat Zietlow. The Quickest Kid in Clarksville. Morrison, Frank, illus. 2016. (ENG.). 40p. (J). (gr. k-3). 16.99 (978-1-4521-2936-5(3)) Chronicle Bks. LLC.

Miller, William. The Bus Ride. Ward, John, illus. 2013. (ENG.). 30p. (J). (gr. -1-18). reprint ed. pap. 9.95 (978-1-58430-026-7(4)) Lee & Low Bks., Inc.

—Joe Louis, My Champion. Pate, Rodney S., illus. 2004. (ENG.). 32p. (J). pap. 10.95 (978-1-60060-426-3(9)) Lee & Low Bks., Inc.

—Joe Louis, My Champion, 1 vol. Pate, Rodney, tr. Pate, Rodney, illus. 2004. (ENG.). 32p. (J). 16.95 (978-1-58430-161-5(9)) Lee & Low Bks., Inc.

—Rent Party Jazz. Riley-Webb, Charlotte, illus. (ENG.). 32p. (J). 2013. (gr. 1-5). 16.95 (978-1-58430-025-0(6)) 2011. pap. 9.95 (978-1-60060-344-0(0)) Lee & Low Bks., Inc.

—Richard Wright y el Carne de Biblioteca. Christie, Gregory R., illus. 2003. (SPA.). (J). 32p. 16.95 (978-1-58430-180-6(5)); pap. 6.95 (978-1-58430-181-3(3)) Lee & Low Bks., Inc.

Mitchell, Margaree King. Uncle Jed's Barbershop. Ransome, James, illus. 2014. 40p. pap. 8.00 (978-1-61003-368-8(X)) Center for the Collaborative Classroom.

Mixon, Donovan. Ahgottahandleonit. 2017. (ENG.). 288p. (J). (gr. 6). 16.95 (978-1-941026-46-5(X)) Cinco Puntos Pr.

Monalisa, DeGross. Donavan's Word Jar. 2014. (Trophy Chapter Bks). (ENG.). 80p. (J). (gr. 2-5). 9.24 (978-1-63245-337-2(1)) Lectorum Pubns., Inc.

Moodley, Ermila. Path to My African Eyes. 2007. 173p. (J). (gr. 6-13). per. 15.95 (978-1-933491-09-7(4)) Just Us Bks., Inc.

Moody Publishing Staff & Lawton, Wendy G. Freedom's Pen: A Story Based on the Life of Freed Slave & Author Phillis Wheatley 2009. (Daughters of the Faith Ser.). (ENG.). 144p. (gr. 3-7). pap. 7.99 (978-0-8024-7639-5(2)) Moody Pubs.

Moore, Shahari. It's Good Sunday. Waddington, Nicole, illus. 2003. (J). (978-0-9743394-0-5(7)) More Pr.

Moore, Stephanie. Better Than Picture Perfect. 2014. (Sharp Sisters Ser.: 2). (ENG.). 160p. (YA). (gr. 6-12). pap. 7.95 (978-1-4677-4486-7(7), Darby Creek) Lerner Publishing Group.

—Make Something of It. 2014. (Sharp Sisters Ser.: 1). (ENG.). 152p. (YA). (gr. 6-12). pap. 7.95 (978-1-4677-4488-1(3), Darby Creek) Lerner Publishing Group.

Moore, Stephanie Perry. Always Upbeat/All That. 2012. (Lockwood Lions Ser.). (YA). lib. bdg. 26.90 (978-0-606-26492-1(2), Turtleback) Turtleback Bks.

—Enjoying True Peace, 1 vol. 2010. (Yasmin Peace Ser.: 5). (ENG.). 176p. pap. 6.99 (978-0-8024-8606-6(1), Lift Every Voice) Moody Pubs.

—Experiencing the Joy, 1 vol. 2009. (Yasmin Peace Ser.: 3). (ENG.). 160p. (gr. 7-10). pap. 7.99 (978-0-8024-8604-2(5), Lift Every Voice) Moody Pubs.

—Forever Hot/Truly Fine. 2013. (Grovehill Giants Ser.). (YA). lib. bdg. 26.90 (978-0-606-31877-8(1), Turtleback) Turtleback Bks.

—Get What You Give. 2010. (ENG., Illus.). 233p. (YA). (gr. 9-18). 16.00 (978-0-7582-3446-9(5), K-Teen/Dafina) Kensington Publishing Corp.

—Icing on the Cake. 2014. (Sharp Sisters Ser.: 5). (ENG.). 160p. (YA). (gr. 6-12). pap. 7.95 (978-1-4677-4487-4(5), Darby Creek); lib. bdg. 27.93 (978-1-4677-3728-9(3)) Lerner Publishing Group.

—Prayed Up, 4 vols. 2008. (ENG., Illus.). 208p. (YA). (gr. 8-12). 15.00 (978-0-7582-2538-2(5), K-Teen/Dafina) Kensington Publishing Corp.

—Problem Solved, 3 vols. 2007. (ENG., Illus.). 208p. (YA). (gr. 9). 15.00 (978-0-7582-1874-2(5), K-Teen/Dafina) Kensington Publishing Corp.

—Sweet Honesty. 2005. (Carmen Browne Ser.: 2). (ENG.). 160p. (YA). (gr. 3-7). per. 6.99 (978-0-8024-8168-9(X), Lift Every Voice) Moody Pubs.

—True Friends. 2005. (Carmen Browne Ser.: 1). (ENG.). 128p. (YA). pap. 6.99 (978-0-8024-8172-6(8), Lift Every Voice) Moody Pubs.

—Truth & Nothing But. 2014. (Sharp Sisters Ser.: 4). (ENG.). 160p. (YA). (gr. 6-12). pap. 7.95 (978-1-4677-4489-8(1), Darby Creek); lib. bdg. 27.93 (978-1-4677-3727-2(5)) Lerner Publishing Group.

—Turn up for Real. 2014. (Sharp Sisters Ser.: 3). (ENG.). 168p. (YA). (gr. 6-12). pap. 7.95 (978-1-4677-4490-4(5), Darby Creek); lib. bdg. 27.93 (978-1-4677-3726-5(7)) Lerner Publishing Group.

—Yell Out/Do You. 2012. (Lockwood Lions Ser.). (YA). lib. bdg. 26.90 (978-0-606-26493-8(0), Turtleback) Turtleback Bks.

Moore, Stephanie Perry & Moody Publishing Staff. Believing in Hope. 2009. (Yasmin Peace Ser.: 2). (ENG.). 176p. (gr. 7-10). pap. 7.99 (978-0-8024-8603-5(7), Lift Every Voice) Moody Pubs.

Moore, Stephanie Perry & Moore, Derrick. Forever Hot/Truly Fine, 1 vol. 2013. (Grovehill Giants Ser.: Bk. 1). (ENG.). 318p. (YA). (gr. 9-12). pap. 14.95 (978-1-62250-683-5(9)) Saddleback Educational Publishing, Inc.

Moore, Wes & Goodman, Shawn. This Way Home. 2015. (ENG.). 256p. (YA). (gr. 9). 20.99 (978-0-375-99019-9(4), Delacorte Pr.) Random Hse. Children's Bks.

Moses, Shelia P. The Baptism. (ENG., 144p. 2008. Illus.). (J). (gr. 5-9). pap. 5.99 (978-1-4169-5833-8(9)) 2007. (YA). (gr. 7-12). 15.99 (978-1-4169-0671-1(1)) McElderry, Margaret K. Bks. (McElderry, Margaret K. Bks.).

—Joseph. (ENG.). (YA). (gr. 7). 2010. 208p. pap. 8.99 (978-1-4169-9442-8(4)) 2008. (Illus.). 176p. 16.99 (978-1-4169-1752-6(7)) McElderry, Margaret K. Bks. (McElderry, Margaret K. Bks.).

—Joseph's Grace. 2011. (ENG.). 160p. (YA). (gr. 7-18). 16.99 (978-1-4169-3942-9(3), McElderry, Margaret K. Bks.) McElderry, Margaret K. Bks.

—The Legend of Buddy Bush. 2004. (ENG., Illus.). 224p. (YA). (gr. 7). 19.99 (978-0-689-85839-0(6), McElderry, Margaret K. Bks.) McElderry, Margaret K. Bks.

—The Legend of Buddy Bush. 2005. (Illus.). 211p. (gr. 7-12). 17.00 (978-0-7569-5459-8(2)) Perfection Learning Corp.

—The Legend of Buddy Bush, 3 vols. unabr. ed. 2005. (YA). (gr. 3-7). 54.75 (978-1-4193-3575-4(8), 42043) Recorded Bks., Inc.

—The Return of Buddy Bush. 2005. (ENG., Illus.). 160p. (J). (gr. 7-12). 15.95 (978-0-689-87431-4(6), McElderry, Margaret K. Bks.) McElderry, Margaret K. Bks.

Moskowitz, Hannah. Not Otherwise Specified: A Novel. 2015. (ENG., Illus.). 304p. (YA). (gr. 9). pap. 11.99 (978-1-4814-0595-9(0), Simon Pulse) Simon Pulse.

Mosley, Walter. 47. 2006. (ENG., Illus.). 240p. (J). (gr. 7-17). reprint ed. per. 10.99 (978-0-316-01635-3(7)) Little, Brown Bks. for Young Readers.

Murray, Victoria Christopher. Aaliyah. 2009. (Divas Ser.). (ENG.). 208p. pap. 14.99 (978-1-4165-6351-8(2), Gallery Bks.) Gallery Bks.

—Diamond. 2008. (Divas Ser.). (ENG.). 256p. (gr. 8-12). pap. 11.00 (978-1-4165-6216-0(8), Gallery Bks.) Gallery Bks.

—India. 2008. (Divas Ser.). (ENG., Illus.). 224p. pap. 15.99 (978-1-4165-6349-5(0), Gallery Bks.) Gallery Bks.

Myers, Walter Dean. All the Right Stuff. (YA). (gr. 8). 2013. (ENG.). 240p. pap. 9.99 (978-0-06-196089-5(6)) 2012. (ENG.). 224p. 17.99 (978-0-06-196087-1(X)) 2012. 224p. lib. bdg. 18.89 (978-0-06-196088-8(8)) HarperCollins Pubs. (Amistad).

—Autobiography of My Dead Brother. Myers, Christopher, illus. 2006. (ENG.). 224p. (YA). (gr. 9). pap. 9.99 (978-0-06-058293-7(6), Amistad) HarperCollins Pubs.

—Autobiography of My Dead Brother. 2006. 20.00 (978-0-7569-6388-0(5)) Perfection Learning Corp.

—The Beast. 2005. 17.00 (978-0-7569-5107-8(0)) Perfection Learning Corp.

—Checkmate. 2015. (News Crew Ser.). (ENG.). 144p. (J). (gr. 5-9). pap. 6.99 (978-0-545-82875-8(9), Scholastic Pr.) Scholastic, Inc.

—The Cruisers. (ENG.). 144p. (J). (gr. 5-9). 2015. (News Crew Ser.). pap. 6.99 (978-0-545-82874-1(0)) 2011. (Cruisers Ser.: 1). pap. 5.99 (978-0-439-91633-2(X)) 2010. (Cruisers Ser.: 1). 15.99 (978-0-439-91626-4(7)) Scholastic, Inc. (Scholastic Pr.).

—Darius & Twig. 2013. 208p. (YA). (gr. 8). (ENG.). 17.99 (978-0-06-172823-5(3)); lib. bdg. 18.89 (978-0-06-172824-2(1)) HarperCollins Pubs. (Amistad).

—Dope Sick. (ENG.). 208p. (YA). (gr. 9). 2010. pap. 9.99 (978-0-06-121479-0(5)) 2009. 17.99 (978-0-06-121477-6(9)) HarperCollins Pubs. (Amistad).

—Down to the Last Out: The Journal of Biddy Owens, the Negro Leagues, Birmingham, Alabama, 1948. 2013. (ENG.). 144p. (J). (gr. 3-7). pap. 6.99 (978-0-545-53050-7(4), Scholastic Paperbacks) Scholastic, Inc.

—The Dream Bearer. (ENG.). 192p. (gr. 5-18). 2003. (J). 15.99 (978-0-06-029521-9(X)) 2003. (J). 15.99 (978-0-06-029521-9(X)) 2004. (YA). reprint ed. pap. 6.99 (978-0-06-447289-0(2)) HarperCollins Pubs. (Amistad).

—The Dream Bearer. 2004. 16.00 (978-0-7569-3242-8(4)) Perfection Learning Corp.

—Fallen Angels. 2008. (ENG.). 336p. (J). (gr. 7). pap. 9.99 (978-0-545-05576-5(8), Scholastic Paperbacks) Scholastic, Inc.

—Game. (ENG.). (YA). (gr. 8). 2009. 240p. pap. 9.99 (978-0-06-058296-8(0)) 2008. 224p. 17.99 (978-0-06-058294-4(4)) HarperCollins Pubs. (HarperTeen).

—Game. 2011. 10.36 (978-0-7848-3476-3(8), Everbind) Marco Bk. Co.

—The Glory Field. 2008. (ENG.). 400p. (J). (gr. 7). pap. 9.99 (978-0-545-05575-8(X), Scholastic Paperbacks) Scholastic, Inc.

—Handbook for Boys. 2003. (Amistad Ser.). (ENG.). 224p. (YA). (gr. 5-18). pap. 8.99 (978-0-06-440930-8(9), Amistad) HarperCollins Pubs.

—Harlem Summer. 2015. (YA). 1.25 (978-1-4906-2986-5(6)) Recorded Bks., Inc.

—Invasion. 2015. (ENG.). 224p. (J). (gr. 6). pap. 8.99 (978-0-545-38429-2(X), Scholastic Pr.) Scholastic, Inc.

—It Ain't All for Nothin' 2003. 226p. (gr. 7-12). 17.00 (978-0-7569-1460-8(4)) Perfection Learning Corp.

—Juba! (Illus.). 208p. (YA). (gr. 8). 2016. pap. 9.99 (978-0-06-211273-6(2)) 2015. (ENG., 17.99 (978-0-06-211271-2(6), HarperTeen) HarperCollins Pubs.

—Lockdown. (YA). (gr. 8). 2011. (ENG.). 272p. pap. 9.99 (978-0-06-121482-0(5)) 2010. 256p. lib. bdg. 17.89 (978-0-06-121481-3(7)) 2010. (ENG.). 256p. 16.99 (978-0-06-121480-6(9)) HarperCollins Pubs. (Amistad).

—Looking Like Me. Myers, Christopher, illus. 2009. (ENG.). 32p. (J). (gr. k-4). 18.99 (978-1-60684-001-6(0), Carolrhoda Bks.) Lerner Publishing Group.

—Monster. Myers, Christopher, illus. 2004. (Monster Ser.). (ENG.). 304p. (YA). (gr. 8). reprint ed. pap. 9.99 (978-0-06-440731-1(4), Amistad) HarperCollins Pubs.

—The Mouse Rap. 3rd ed. (J). pap. 3.95 (978-0-13-800087-5(5)) Prentice Hall (Schl. Div.).

—Oh, Snap! 2013. (Cruisers Ser.: Bk. 4). (ENG.). 128p. (J). (gr. 5-9). 17.99 (978-0-439-91629-5(1), Scholastic Pr.) Scholastic, Inc.

—The Righteous Revenge of Artemis Bonner. 2003. (J). (gr. 5-18). 23.00 (978-0-8446-7250-2(5)) Smith, Peter Pub., Inc.

—Scorpions. 2013. (Trophy Bk.). (ENG.). 240p. (YA). (gr. 8-18). pap. 8.99 (978-0-06-447066-7(0)); 25th anniv. ed. pap. 9.99 (978-0-06-440623-9(7)) HarperCollins Pubs. (Amistad).

—Scorpions. 2013. 216p. (YA). (gr. 7-12). lib. bdg. 19.65 (978-0-8335-4233-5(8), Turtleback) Turtleback Bks.

—Slam! 2008. (Point Signature Ser.). 266p. (gr. 7-12). lib. bdg. 19.65 (978-0-613-12111-8(2), Turtleback) Turtleback Bks.

—A Star Is Born. 2012. (Cruisers Ser.: Bk. 3). (J). (978-0-439-91631-8(3)); (ENG.). 176p. (gr. 5-9). 17.99 (978-0-439-91628-8(3)) Scholastic, Inc.

—Street Love. (ENG.). 2007. 160p. (YA). (gr. 8-18). pap. 9.99 (978-0-06-440732-8(2)) 2006. 144p. (J). (gr. 7-18). 15.99 (978-0-06-028079-6(4)) HarperCollins Pubs. (Amistad).

—Street Love. 2007. 19.00 (978-0-7569-8102-0(6)) Perfection Learning Corp.

—Sunrise over Fallujah. 2011. 9.04 (978-0-7848-3413-8(X), Everbind) Marco Bk. Co.

—Sunrise over Fallujah. (ENG.). (J). (gr. 7). 2009. 320p. 8.99 (978-0-439-91625-7(9)) 2008. (Illus.). 304p. 17.99 (978-0-439-91624-0(0)) Scholastic, Inc. (Scholastic Pr.).

—Sunrise over Fallujah. l.t. ed. 2008. 468p. (YA). 23.95 (978-1-4104-1019-1(6)) Thorndike Pr.

—What They Found: Love on 145th Street. 2011. 10.54 (978-0-7848-3499-2(7)); 10.54 (978-0-7848-3386-5(9)) Marco Bk. Co. (Everbind).

—What They Found: Love on 145th Street. 2009. (ENG.). 256p. (YA). (gr. 9). pap. 8.99 (978-0-375-84545-1(3), Lamb, Wendy Bks.) Random Hse. Children's Bks.

—145th Street: Short Stories. 2012. (ENG.). 192p. (YA). (gr. 7). pap. 9.99 (978-0-307-97610-9(6), Ember) Random Hse. Children's Bks.

Nash, Andy. Melinda & Her Mule: For Kids Blessed with a Strong Will. 2008. (J). (978-0-8127-0453-2(3)) Autumn Hse. Publishing Co.

Nelson, Marilyn. Pemba's Song. 2008. (ENG.). 112p. (J). (gr. 7-18). 16.99 (978-0-545-02076-3(X), Scholastic Pr.) Scholastic, Inc.

Nelson, Vaunda Micheaux. Almost to Freedom. Bootman, Colin, illus. 2003. (Carolrhoda Picture Books Ser.). (ENG.). 40p. (J). (gr. k-3). 16.95 (978-1-57505-342-4(X)) Lerner Publishing Group.

—The Book Itch: Freedom, Truth & Harlem's Greatest Bookstore. Christie, R. Gregory, illus. 2015. (ENG.). 32p. (J). (gr. 2-4). 17.99 (978-1-4677-4618-2(5), Carolrhoda Bks.) Lerner Publishing Group.

—Don't Call Me Grandma. Zunon, Elizabeth, illus. 2016. (ENG.). 32p. (gr. k-3). (J). lib. bdg. 19.99 (978-1-4677-4208-5(2)); (J). 30.65 (978-1-4677-9559-3(3)); 35.99 (978-1-5124-0661-0(9)) Lerner Publishing Group. (Carolrhoda Bks.).

—No Crystal Stair: A Documentary Novel of the Life & Work of Lewis Michaux, Harlem Bookseller. Christie, R. Gregory, illus. 2012. (Carolrhoda YA Ser.). (ENG.). 192p. (YA). (gr. 7-12). 17.95 (978-0-7613-6169-5(3), Carolrhoda Lab™) Lerner Publishing Group.

Neri, G. Ghetto Cowboy. Watson, Jesse Joshua, illus. 2013. (ENG.). 224p. (J). (gr. 5). pap. 6.99 (978-0-7636-6453-4(7)) Candlewick Pr.

Neufeld, John. Edgar Allan. 2007. 136p. (gr. 5-9). per. 11.95 (978-0-595-45039-8(3), Backinprint.com) iUniverse, Inc.

Nichols, Cherrie L. Curtiz Says: I Hate My Shoestrings. 2012. 24p. pap. 17.99 (978-1-4772-7341-8(7)) AuthorHouse.

Nikki, Grimes. Bronx Masquerade. 2014. (ENG.). 176p. (YA). 11.24 (978-1-63245-077-7(1)) Lectorum Pubns., Inc.

Nobody Knows (Africans) 76p. (YA). (gr. 6-12). pap. 9.95 (978-0-8224-3683-6(3)) Globe Fearon Educational Publishing.

Nolan, Han. A Summer of Kings. 2006. 334p. (J). (978-1-4156-7340-9(3)) Harcourt Trade Pubs.

Nolen, Jerdine. Big Jabe. Nelson, Kadir, illus. 2003. (ENG.). 32p. (J). (gr. k-5). pap. 7.99 (978-0-06-054061-6(3), Amistad) HarperCollins Pubs.

—Big Jabe. Nelson, Kadir, illus. 2004. (gr. 1). 17.00 (978-0-7569-3184-1(3)) Perfection Learning Corp.

—Block Party Surprise. Henninger, Michelle, illus. 2015. 41p. (J). (978-1-4806-8574-1(7)) Harcourt.

—Bradford Street Buddies: Block Party Surprise. Henninger, Michelle, illus. 2015. (Green Light Readers Level 3 Ser.). (ENG.). 48p. (J). (gr. 1-4). pap. 3.99 (978-0-544-35863-8(5), HMH Books For Young Readers) Houghton Mifflin Harcourt Publishing Co.

—Bradford Street Buddies: Springtime Blossoms. Henninger, Michelle, illus. 2017. (Green Light Readers Level 3 Ser.). (ENG.). 48p. (J). (gr. 1-4). pap. 3.99 (978-0-544-87390-2(4), HMH Books For Young Readers) Houghton Mifflin Harcourt Publishing Co.

—Calico Girl. 2017. (ENG., Illus.). 192p. (J). (gr. 3-7). 16.99 (978-1-4814-5981-5(3), Simon & Schuster/Paula Wiseman Bks.) Simon & Schuster/Paula Wiseman Bks.

—Eliza's Freedom Road: An Underground Railroad Diary. Strickland, Shadra, illus. 2011. (ENG.). 160p. (J). (gr. 3-7). 16.99 (978-1-4169-5814-7(2), Simon & Schuster/Paula Wiseman Bks.) Simon & Schuster/Paula Wiseman Bks.

—Thunder Rose. Nelson, Kadir, illus. 2007. (ENG.). 32p. (J). (gr. k-3). pap. 7.99 (978-0-15-206006-0(5)) Houghton Mifflin Harcourt Publishing Co.

—Thunder Rose. Nelson, Kadir, illus. 2007. (gr. k-3). 17.00 (978-0-7569-8199-0(9)) Perfection Learning Corp.

Nolen, Jerdine, et al. Bradford Street Buddies: Backyard Camp-Out. Henninger, Michelle, illus. 2015. (Green Light Readers Level 3 Ser.). (ENG.). 48p. (J). (gr. 1-4). pap. 3.99 (978-0-544-36844-6(4), HMH Books For Young Readers) Houghton Mifflin Harcourt Publishing Co.

—Bradford Street Buddies: Backyard Camp-Out. Henninger, Michelle, illus. 2015. (Green Light Readers Level 3 Ser.). (ENG.). 48p. (J). (gr. 1-4). 12.99 (978-0-544-36843-9(6), HMH Books For Young Readers) Houghton Mifflin Harcourt Publishing Co.

Norfleet, Mary Crockett. Hand Me down House. Mallory, Edgar, illus. 2011. 98p. 38.95 (978-1-258-07946-8(1)) Literary Licensing, LLC.

Oakes, Stephanie. The Sacred Lies of Minnow Bly. 2015. (ENG.). 400p. (YA). (gr. 9). 17.99 (978-0-8037-4070-9(0), Dial Bks) Penguin Young Readers Group.

O'Brien, Anne Sibley. I'm New Here. O'Brien, Anne Sibley, illus. 2015. (ENG., Illus.). 32p. (J). (gr. k-3). lib. bdg. 16.95 (978-1-58089-612-2(X)) Charlesbridge Publishing, Inc.

O'Neal, Shaquille. Little Shaq. Taylor, Theodore, illus. 2015. 73p. (J). (978-1-68119-119-5(9)) Bloomsbury Pr.

—Little Shaq. Taylor, Theodore, III, illus. (ENG.). 80p. (J). 2016. 9.99 (978-1-61963-879-2(7), 9781619638792) 2016. 9.99 (978-1-61963-844-0(4), 9781619638440) 2015. 9.99 (978-1-61963-721-4(9), 9781619637214) Bloomsbury Publishing USA. (Bloomsbury USA Childrens).

Osborne, Mary Pope. A Big Day for Baseball. Murdocca, Sal, illus. 2017. (Magic Tree House Ser.: 29). (ENG.). (J). (gr. 1-4). 80p. 13.99 **(978-1-5247-1308-9(2))**; 96p. lib. bdg. 16.99 **(978-1-5247-1309-6(0))** Random Hse. Children's Bks. (Random Hse. Bks. for Young Readers).

Osborne, Mary Pope. A Good Night for Ghosts. 2010. (Magic Tree House Merlin Missions Ser.: No. 14). (Illus.). 157p. (J). pap. (978-4-8401-3411-8(1)) Fukuinkan Shoten.

—A Good Night for Ghosts. Murdocca, Sal, illus. 2011. (Magic Tree House Merlin Mission Ser.: 14). (ENG.). 144p. (J). (gr. 2-5). 5.99 (978-0-375-85649-5(8), Random Hse. Bks. for Young Readers) Random Hse. Children's Bks.

Owen, Rob. Spy Boy, Cheyenne, & Ninety-Six Crayons: A "Mardi Gras" Indian's Story, 1 vol. Owen, Rob, illus. 2013. (ENG., Illus.). 32p. (J). (gr. k-3). 16.99 (978-1-4556-1799-9(7)) Pelican Publishing Co., Inc.

Pace, Lorenzo. Jalani & the Lock, 1 vol. 2015. (ENG.). 48p. (J). 30.25 (978-1-4777-9277-3(5), Windmill Bks.) Rosen Publishing Group, Inc., The.

Paige, D. M. Box-Office Smash. 2015. (Opportunity Ser.). (ENG.). 112p. (YA). (gr. 6-12). 34.65 (978-1-4677-6012-6(9), Lerner Digital) Lerner Publishing Group.

—Size 0. 2015. (Opportunity Ser.). (ENG.). 120p. (YA). (gr. 6-12). 34.65 (978-1-4677-6017-1(X), Lerner Digital) Lerner Publishing Group.

Parsons, Bruce. Siah Carter & the Ship Monitor. 2009. 36p. pap. 16.99 (978-1-4490-3435-1(7)) AuthorHouse.

Paterson, Katherine. Jip: His Story. 2005. (Puffin Modern Classics Ser.). (ENG.). 192p. (J). (gr. 3-7). pap. 6.99 (978-0-14-240411-9(X), Puffin Books) Penguin Young Readers Group.

Patrick, Denise Lewis. Finding Someplace. 2015. (ENG.). 224p. (J). (gr. 3-7). 16.99 (978-0-8050-4716-5(6), 9780805047165, Holt, Henry & Co. Bks. For Young Readers) Holt, Henry & Co.

—Finding Someplace. 2016. (ENG.). 224p. (J). pap. 7.99 (978-1-250-07982-4(9), 9781250079824) Square Fish.

—Finding Someplace. 2016. (J). lib. bdg. 17.20 (978-0-606-38560-2(6)) Turtleback Bks.

—MaDear's Old Green House. Sadler, Sonia Lynn, illus. 2004. 32p. (J). (gr. k-3). 16.95 (978-0-940975-55-2(6), Sankofa Bks.) Just Us Bks., Inc.

—A Matter of Souls. 2014. 192p. (YA). (gr. 6-12). 16.95 (978-0-7613-9280-4(7), Carolrhoda Lab™) Lerner Publishing Group.

Patterson, James. Public School Superhero. 2015. (ENG., Illus.). 304p. (J). (gr. 3-7). 13.99 (978-0-316-32214-0(8), Jimmy Patterson) Little Brown & Co.

Patterson, James & Tebbetts, Chris. Public School Superhero. Thomas, Cory, illus. 2016. (ENG.). 304p. (J). (gr. 3-7). pap. 7.99 (978-0-316-26598-0(5), Jimmy Patterson) Little Brown & Co.

Patterson, James, et al. Public School Superhero. 2015. (978-0-316-34231-5(9)) Little, Brown Bks. for Young Readers.

Paul, Curtis Christopher. Bud, Not Buddy. 2014. (ENG.). 256p. (J). (gr. 12-12). 11.24 (978-1-63245-063-0(1)) Lectorum Pubns., Inc.

—The Watsons Go to Birmingham 1963. 2014. (ENG.). 224p. (J). (gr. 12-12). 11.24 (978-1-63245-108-8(5)) Lectorum Pubns., Inc.

Paul, Volponi. Black & White. 2014. (ENG.). 208p. (YA). 11.24 (978-1-63245-196-5(4)) Lectorum Pubns., Inc.

Pearsall, Shelley. Jump into the Sky. (ENG.). 352p. (J). 2013. (gr. 4-7). pap. 7.99 (978-0-440-42140-5(3), Yearling) 2012. (gr. 5). 16.99 (978-0-375-83699-2(3), Knopf Bks. for Young Readers) Random Hse. Children's Bks.

—The Seventh Most Important Thing. 2015. (ENG., Illus.). 288p. (J). (gr. 5). 16.99 (978-0-553-49728-1(6), Knopf Bks. for Young Readers) Random Hse. Children's Bks.

—Trouble Don't Last. 2003. (ENG.). 256p. (J). (gr. 3-7). reprint ed. 6.99 (978-0-440-41811-5(9), Yearling) Random Hse. Children's Bks.

Pérez, Ashley Hope. Out of Darkness. 2015. (ENG., Illus.). 408p. (YA). (gr. 8-12). 18.99 (978-1-4677-4202-3(3), Carolrhoda Lab™) Lerner Publishing Group.

Philbrick, Rodman. Zane & the Hurricane: A Story of Katrina. (ENG.). 192p. (J). (gr. 5-9). 2015. pap. 6.99 (978-0-545-34239-1(2)) 2014. (Illus.). 16.99 (978-0-545-34238-4(4)) Scholastic, Inc. (Blue Sky Pr., The).

Phillips, Lyda. Mr Touchdown. 2008. 184p. 23.95 (978-1-4401-0976-8(1)); pap. 13.95 (978-1-60528-029-5(1)) iUniverse, Inc. (iUniverse Star).

Pinkney, Andrea Davis. Bird in a Box. Qualls, Sean, illus. 2012. (J). lib. bdg. 18.45 (978-0-606-26157-9(5), Turtleback) Turtleback Bks.

—Boycott Blues: How Rosa Parks Inspired a Nation. Pinkney, Brian, illus. 2008. (ENG.). 40p. (J). (gr. k-3). 16.99 (978-0-06-082118-0(3), Greenwillow Bks.) HarperCollins Pubs.

—Raven in a Dove House. 2014. (ENG.). 224p. (J). (gr. 5-7). pap. 8.99 (978-0-544-23016-3(7), HMH Books For Young Readers) Houghton Mifflin Harcourt Publishing Co.

—Sojourner Truth's Step-Stomp Stride. Pinkney, Brian, illus. 2009. (ENG.). 32p. (J). (gr. k-4). 16.99 (978-0-7868-0767-3(9), Jump at the Sun) Hyperion Bks. for Children.

Pinkney, Brian. Max Found Two Sticks. Pinkney, Brian, illus. 2nd ed. 2005. (Stories to Go! Ser.). (ENG., Illus.). 40p. (J). 4.99 (978-1-4169-0310-9(0), Simon & Schuster/Paula Wiseman Bks.) Simon & Schuster/Paula Wiseman Bks.

Pinkney, Sandra L. Shades of Black: A Celebration of Our Children. Pinkney, Myles C., illus. 2006. (ENG.). 24p. (J). (gr. k — 1). bds. 6.99 (978-0-439-80251-2(2), Cartwheel Bks.) Scholastic, Inc.

Polacco, Patricia. Chicken Sunday. 2015. 32p. pap. 8.00 (978-1-61003-527-9(5)) Center for the Collaborative Classroom.

—January's Sparrow. Polacco, Patricia, illus. 2009. (ENG., Illus.). 96p. (J). (gr. 3-7). 23.99 (978-0-399-25077-4(8), Philomel Bks.) Penguin Young Readers Group.

Powell, GinaMarie. Ayiana & the Hurricane Katrina Classmate. Bray, Pamela, illus. 2008. 28p. pap. 24.95 (978-1-60441-965-8(2)) America Star Bks.

Powell, Patricia Hruby. Loving vs. Virginia: A Documentary Novel of the Landmark Civil Rights Case. Strickland, Shadra, illus. 2017. (ENG.). 260p. (YA). (gr. 7-12). 21.99 *(978-1-4521-2590-9(2))* Chronicle Bks. LLC.

Publications International Ltd. Staff, ed. African American Children's Stories: A Treasury of Tradition & Pride. 2004. (Illus.). 320p. (J). 15.98 *(978-0-7853-5239-6(2),* 7137100) Publications International, Ltd.

Pugliano-Martin, Carol. John Henry: An American Tall Tale. 2006. (J). pap. *(978-1-4108-6170-2(8))* Benchmark Education Co.

Pyrnelle, Louise Clarke. Diddie Dumps & Tot: Or, Plantation Child-life. 2007. 138p. pap. 18.99 *(978-1-4346-0721-8(6));* (ENG.). 150p. pap. 19.99 *(978-1-4346-0781-2(X))* Creative Media Partners, LLC.

Quarles, Bernadict. Chronicles of Maya & Quincy: When I Grow Up. 2013. 28p. pap. 24.95 *(978-1-4626-7832-7(7))* America Star Bks.

Quattlebaum, Mary. Jackson Jones & the Curse of the Outlaw Rose. 2008. (ENG.). 112p. (J). (gr. 3-7). 5.99 *(978-0-440-42138-2(1),* Yearling) Random Hse. Children's Bks.

Queen Latifah. Queen of the Scene. Morrison, Frank, illus. 2006. 32p. (J). (gr. -1-3). 17.89 incl. audio compact disk *(978-0-06-077857-6(1),* Geringer, Laura Book) HarperCollins Pubs.

Quick, Matthew. Boy21. 2013. (ENG.). 272p. (YA). (gr. 7-17). pap. 10.99 *(978-0-316-12796-7(5))* Little, Brown Bks. for Young Readers.

Rabin, Staton. Black Powder. 2005. (ENG.). 256p. (YA). (gr. 7-9). 16.95 *(978-0-689-86876-4(6),* McElderry, Margaret K. Bks.) McElderry, Margaret K. Bks.

Rahim, Rahimah. The Trunk. 2012. 64p. pap. *(978-1-78176-715-3(7))* FeedARead.com.

Rand, Edward A. The Knights of the White Shield: Up-the-Ladder Club Series Round One Play. 2007. 166p. pap. 19.99 *(978-1-4264-8273-1(6));* (ENG.). 184p. pap. 21.99 *(978-1-4264-8310-3(4))* Creative Media Partners, LLC.

—The Knights of the White Shield; or, up-the-Ladder Club Series, Round One Play. 2007. 120p. per. *(978-1-4068-3739-1(3))* Echo Library.

Randall, Alice. The Diary of B. B. Bright, Possible Princess. 2012. (J). *(978-1-61858-016-0(7))* Turner Publishing Co.

Randall, Alice & Williams, Caroline Randall. The Diary of B. B. Bright, Possible Princess. Strickland, Shadra, illus. 2012. (ENG.). 192p. (J). (gr. 2-6). 19.95 *(978-1-61858-015-3(9))* Turner Publishing Co.

Ransom, Candice. The Life-Saving Adventure of Sam Deal, Shipwreck Rescuer. Trover, Zachary, illus. 2010. (History's Kid Heroes Ser.). (ENG.). 32p. (gr. 3-5). pap. 8.95 *(978-0-7613-6196-1(0),* Graphic Universe™); lib. bdg. 26.60 *(978-0-7613-6177-0(4))* Lerner Publishing Group.

Raschka, Chris. Yo! Yes? Raschka, Chris, illus. 2007. (Scholastic Bookshelf Ser.). (ENG., Illus.). 32p. (J). (gr. -1-1). pap. 6.99 *(978-0-439-92185-5(6))* Scholastic, Inc.

Raven, Margot Theis. Circle Unbroken. Lewis, E. B., illus. 2007. (ENG.). 48p. (J). (gr. -1-3). per. 8.99 *(978-0-312-37603-1(0),* 9780312376031) Square Fish.

—Night Boat to Freedom. Lewis, E. B., illus. 2008. (ENG.). 40p. (J). (gr. 1-4). pap. 8.99 *(978-0-312-55018-9(9),* 9780312550189) Square Fish.

Reeves, Dia. Slice of Cherry. 2011. (ENG.). (YA). (gr. 9). 528p. pap. 9.99 *(978-1-4169-8621-8(9));* 512p. 16.99 *(978-1-4169-8620-1(0))* Simon Pulse. (Simon Pulse).

Reid, Kimberly. Sweet 16 to Life. 2013. (ENG., Illus.). 256p. (YA). (gr. 9). pap. 9.95 *(978-0-7582-6742-9(8),* K-Teen/Dafina) Kensington Publishing Corp.

—Sweet 16 to Life. 2013. 233p. (J). lib. bdg. 20.80 *(978-0-606-27166-0(X),* Turtleback) Turtleback Bks.

Reynolds, Aaron. Back of the Bus. Cooper, Floyd, illus. (ENG.). 32p. (J). (gr. 1-3). 2013. 8.99 *(978-0-14-751058-7(9),* Puffin Books) 2010. 16.99 *(978-0-399-25091-0(3),* Philomel Bks.) Penguin Young Readers Group.

—Metal Man. Hoppe, Paul, illus. 2010. (ENG.). 32p. (J). (gr. k-3). pap. 7.95 *(978-1-58089-151-6(9))* Charlesbridge Publishing, Inc.

Reynolds, Jason. As Brave As You. (ENG.). 432p. (J). (gr. 5). 2017. pap. 7.99 *(978-1-4814-1591-0(3),* Atheneum Bks. for Young Readers) 2016. (Illus.). 16.99 *(978-1-4814-1590-3(5),* Atheneum/Caitlyn Dlouhy Books) Simon & Schuster Children's Publishing.

—The Boy in the Black Suit. 2015. (ENG., Illus.). 272p. (YA). (gr. 7). 17.99 *(978-1-4424-5950-2(6))* Simon & Schuster Children's Publishing.

—The Boy in the Black Suit. 2016. (ENG.). (J). lib. bdg. 22.10 *(978-0-606-38272-4(0))* Turtleback Bks.

—Ghost. 2016. (Track Ser.: bk.1). (ENG., Illus.). 192p. (J). (gr. 5). 17.99 *(978-1-4814-5015-7(8),* Atheneum/Caitlyn Dlouhy Books) Simon & Schuster Children's Publishing.

—Patina. 2017. (J). pap. ***(978-1-4814-5019-5(0));*** (Track Ser.: 2). (ENG., Illus.). 240p. (gr. 5). 16.99 ***(978-1-4814-5018-8(2),*** Atheneum/Caitlyn Dlouhy Books) Simon & Schuster Children's Publishing.

Reynolds, Jason. When I Was the Greatest. Frost, Michael, photos by. 2014. (ENG., Illus.). 240p. (YA). (gr. 7). 17.99 *(978-1-4424-5947-2(6),* Atheneum Bks. for Young Readers) Simon & Schuster Children's Publishing.

Reynolds, Jason & Brendan Kiely. All American Boys. 2017. (ENG.). (YA). lib. bdg. 20.85 *(978-0-606-39493-2(1))* Turtleback Bks.

Reynolds, Jason & Kiely, Brendan. All American Boys. 2015. (ENG., Illus.). 320p. (YA). (gr. 7). 19.99 *(978-1-4814-6333-1(0),* Atheneum/Caitlyn Dlouhy Books) Simon & Schuster Children's Publishing.

RH Disney Staff. The Princess & the Frog. RH Disney Staff, illus. 2009. (Little Golden Book Ser.). (ENG., Illus.). 24p. (J). (gr. -1-2). 4.99 *(978-0-7364-2628-2(0),* Golden/Disney) Random Hse. Children's Bks.

Rhodes, Jewell Parker. Bayou Magic. 2015. (ENG., Illus.). 256p. (J). (gr. 3-7). 17.99 *(978-0-316-22484-0(7))* Little Brown & Co.

—Bayou Magic. 2016. (ENG.). 272p. (J). (gr. 3-7). pap. 7.99 *(978-0-316-22485-7(5))* Little, Brown Bks. for Young Readers.

—Ninth Ward. 2010. (ENG.). 224p. (J). (gr. 5-17). 15.99 *(978-0-316-04307-6(9))* Little, Brown Bks. for Young Readers.

—Ninth Ward. 2012. (J). lib. bdg. 18.40 *(978-0-606-26158-6(3),* Turtleback) Turtleback Bks.

—Sugar. 2013. (ENG.). 288p. (J). (gr. 3-7). 16.99 *(978-0-316-04305-2(2))* Little, Brown Bks. for Young Readers.

Rhuday-Perkovich, Olugbemisola. 8th Grade Super Zero. 2011. (ENG.). 336p. (J). (gr. 4-7). pap. 7.99 *(978-0-545-09725-3(8),* Levine, Arthur A. Bks.) Scholastic, Inc.

Rinaldi, Ann. Come Juneteenth. 2009. (ENG., Illus.). 256p. (YA). (gr. 7). pap. 7.99 *(978-0-15-206392-4(7))* Houghton Mifflin Harcourt Publishing Co.

—The Education of Mary: A Little Miss of Color, 1832. 2005. 176p. (J). pap. *(978-0-7868-1377-3(6))* Hyperion Pr.

—Hang a Thousand Trees with Ribbons: The Story of Phillis Wheatley. 2005. (Great Episodes Ser.). (ENG.). 352p. (YA). (gr. 7-8). pap. 8.99 *(978-0-15-205393-2(X))* Houghton Mifflin Harcourt Publishing Co.

—Hang a Thousand Trees with Ribbons: The Story of Phillis Wheatley. 2005. (Great Episodes Ser.). 336p. (gr. 5-9). 18.00 *(978-0-7569-5018-7(X))* Perfection Learning Corp.

—The Letter Writer. 2010. (ENG., Illus.). 224p. (YA). (gr. 7). pap. 8.99 *(978-0-547-32785-3(4))* Houghton Mifflin Harcourt Publishing Co.

—Taking Liberty: The Story of Oney Judge, George Washington's Runaway Slave. Dudash, C. Michael, illus. 2004. (ENG.). 272p. (YA). (gr. 7). mass mkt. 7.99 *(978-0-689-85188-9(X),* Simon Pulse) Simon Pulse.

Ringgold, Faith. Harlem Renaissance. Ringgold, Faith, illus. 2015. (ENG., Illus.). 40p. (J). (gr. -1-3). 17.99 *(978-0-06-057911-1(0),* Amistad) HarperCollins Pubs.

—Tar Beach. 2014. 32p. pap. 7.00 *(978-1-61003-377-0(9))* Center for the Collaborative Classroom.

Ringgold, Faith, et al. Cassie's Word Quilt. Ringgold, Faith, illus. 2004. (Avenues Ser.). (ENG., Illus.). 32p. (J). (gr. -1-2). pap. 6.99 *(978-0-553-11233-7(3),* Dragonfly Bks.) Random Hse. Children's Bks.

Robbins, Jacqui. The New Girl... & Me. Phelan, Matt, illus. 2006. (ENG.). 32p. (J). (gr. -1-2). 17.99 *(978-0-689-86468-1(X),* Atheneum/Richard Jackson Bks.) Simon & Schuster Children's Publishing.

Robert, Lipsyte. The Contender. 2014. (Trophy Keypoint Bks). (ENG.). 240p. (J). 13.24 *(978-1-63245-206-1(5))* Lectorum Pubns., Inc.

Robinet, Harriette Gillem. Walking to the Bus-Rider Blues. 2004. (Jean Karl Bks.). 146p. (gr. 3-7). 16.00 *(978-0-7569-4265-6(9))* Perfection Learning Corp.

Robinson, Sharon. The Hero Two Doors Down: A Story of Friendship Between a Boy & a Baseball Legend. 2017. (ENG.). 208p. (J). (gr. 3-7). pap. 6.99 ***(978-0-545-80452-3(3),*** Scholastic Paperbacks) Scholastic, Inc.

—Testing the Ice: A True Story about Jackie Robinson. Nelson, Kadir, illus. 2009. (ENG.). 40p. (J). (gr. 2-5). 18.99 *(978-0-545-05251-1(3),* Scholastic Pr.) Scholastic, Inc.

—Under the Same Sun. Ford, A. G., illus. 2014. (ENG.). 40p. (J). (gr. -1-3). 17.99 *(978-0-545-16672-0(1),* Scholastic Pr.) Scholastic, Inc.

Rockliff, Mara. Me & Momma & Big John. Low, William, illus. 2012. (ENG.). 32p. (J). (gr. -1-2). 16.99 *(978-0-7636-4359-1(9))* Candlewick Pr.

Rodman, Mary Ann. Yankee Girl. 2008. (ENG.). 240p. (J). (gr. 4-6). pap. 9.99 *(978-0-312-53576-6(7),* 9780312535766) Square Fish.

Roop, Peter. Lead Us to Freedom, Harriet Tubman! 2006. (Illus.). 58p. (J). pap. *(978-0-439-79255-4(X))* Scholastic, Inc.

Ross, Chudney. Lone Bean. 2012. (ENG.). 208p. (J). (gr. 3-7). 16.99 *(978-0-06-166011-5(6),* Amistad) HarperCollins Pubs.

Ross, Jill. The Blake Family Vacation. Pruitt, Gwendolyn, illus. 2010. (ENG.). 130p. (J). (gr. 3-7). pap. 9.95 *(978-1-59825-950-6(4))* Shenanigans Series.

—The Real Nitty-Gritty. Pruitt, Gwendolyn, illus. 2010. (ENG.). 60p. (J). (gr. 3-7). pap. 9.95 *(978-1-59825-949-0(0))* Shenanigans Series.

—What's the Matter, Mr. Ticklebritches? Pruitt, Gwendolyn, illus. 2010. (ENG.). 70p. (J). (gr. 3-7). pap. 9.95 *(978-1-59825-948-3(2))* Shenanigans Series.

Rountree, Wendy. Lost Soul. 2003. 87p. (J). pap. 19.95 *(978-1-59129-975-2(6))* America Star Bks.

Rubright, Lynn. Mama's Window. Smith, Duane, illus. 2005. 89p. (J). 16.95 *(978-1-57480-160-6(0))* Lee & Low Bks., Inc.

Russell, Krista. The Other Side of Free, 1 vol. 2013. (ENG.). 256p. (J). (gr. 5-9). 16.95 *(978-1-56145-710-6(8))* Peachtree Pubs.

Sachar, Louis. Small Steps. 2008. (ENG.). 288p. (YA). (gr. 7-9). pap. 9.99 *(978-0-385-73315-1(1),* Ember) Random Hse. Children's Bks.

—Small Steps. rev. l.t. ed. 2006. 339p. 23.95 *(978-0-7862-8297-5(5))* Thorndike Pr.

San Francisco Shake-Up, 6 Packs. (Greetings Ser.: Vol. 3). (gr. 3-5). 31.00 *(978-0-7635-2075-5(6))* Rigby Education.

Sanders, Dori. Clover. 2013. (ENG.). 208p. pap. 13.95 *(978-1-61620-340-5(4),* 73340) Algonquin Bks. of Chapel Hill.

Sands, Monty. King of Nine Mile Canyon. 2008. 124p. 11.99 *(978-0-615-25788-4(7))* Sands, Monty.

Sanford, William. Margo's Pen, 1 vol. 2009. 324p. pap. 29.95 *(978-1-4489-2616-5(5))* America Star Bks.

Sargent, Dave & Sargent, Pat. Nubbin: (Linebacked Apricot Dun) Freedom, 30 vols., Vol. 43. Lenoir, Jane, illus. 2003. (Saddle up Ser.: Vol. 43). 42p. (J). pap. 10.95 *(978-1-56763-704-5(3));* lib. bdg. 23.60 *(978-1-56763-703-8(5))* Ozark Publishing.

Sarratt, Carla. Freshman Focus Carter G Woodson High Sc. 2006. 292p. pap. 14.95 *(978-1-4327-0109-3(6))* Outskirts Pr., Inc.

Sarratt, Carla R. Just Be. 2008. 312p. pap. 14.95 *(978-1-4327-2212-8(3))* Outskirts Pr., Inc.

Schoberle, Cecile. Morning Sounds, Evening Sounds. 2014. (ENG., Illus.). 24p. (J). (gr. -1-3). 13.99 *(978-1-4814-2538-4(2),* Simon & Schuster Bks. For Young Readers) Simon & Schuster Bks. For Young Readers.

Scholastic, Inc. Staff & Barnes, Derrick D. Low-Down Bad-Day Blues. Boyd, Aaron, illus. 2004. (Just for You Ser.). (ENG.). 32p. (gr. k-1). pap. 3.99 *(978-0-439-56867-8(6),* Teaching Resources) Scholastic, Inc.

Scholastic, Inc. Staff & Bermiss, Aamir Lee. I Hate to Be Sick! Wilson-Max, Ken, illus. 2004. (Just for You Ser.). (ENG.). 32p. (gr. k-3). pap. 3.99 *(978-0-439-56877-7(3),* Teaching Resources) Scholastic, Inc.

Scholastic, Inc. Staff & Black, Sonia. Jumping the Broom. Hu, Ying-Hwa & Van Wright, Cornelius, illus. 2004. (Just for You Ser.). (ENG.). 32p. pap. 3.99 *(978-0-439-56878-4(1),* Teaching Resources) Scholastic, Inc.

—Mommy's Bed. Kindert, Jennifer, illus. 2004. (Just for You Ser.). (ENG.). 32p. pap. 3.99 *(978-0-439-56857-9(9),* Teaching Resources) Scholastic, Inc.

Scholastic, Inc. Staff & Boyd, Dee. Only the Stars. Rich, Anna, illus. 2004. (Just for You Ser.). (ENG.). 32p. pap. 3.99 *(978-0-439-56862-3(5),* Teaching Resources) Scholastic, Inc.

Scholastic, Inc. Staff & Brooks, Regina. Never Finished, Never Done! Borgella, Marjorie, illus. 2004. (Just for You Ser.). (ENG.). 32p. pap. 3.99 *(978-0-439-56863-0(3),* Teaching Resources) Scholastic, Inc.

Scholastic, Inc. Staff & Ford, Juwanda G. Shop Talk. Hoston, Jim, illus. 2004. (Just for You Ser.). (ENG.). 32p. (gr. k-3). pap. 3.99 *(978-0-439-56873-9(0),* Teaching Resources) Scholastic, Inc.

Scholastic, Inc. Staff & Giovanni, Nikki. The Girls in the Circle. Johnson, Cathy Ann, illus. 2004. (Just for You Ser.). (ENG.). 32p. pap. 3.99 *(978-0-439-56861-6(7),* Teaching Resources) Scholastic, Inc.

Scholastic, Inc. Staff & Grimes, Nikki. A Day with Daddy. Tadgell, Nicole, illus. 2004. (Just for You Ser.). (ENG.). 32p. pap. 3.99 *(978-0-439-56850-0(1),* Teaching Resources) Scholastic, Inc.

Scholastic, Inc. Staff & Hooks, Gwendolyn. Three's a Crowd. Walker, Sylvia, illus. 2004. (Just for You Ser.). (ENG.). 32p. (gr. k-3). pap. 3.99 *(978-0-439-56865-4(X),* Teaching Resources) Scholastic, Inc.

Scholastic, Inc. Staff & Hudson, Cheryl Willis. What Do You Know? Snow! Walker, Sylvia, illus. 2004. (Just for You Ser.). (ENG.). 32p. pap. 3.99 *(978-0-439-56851-7(X),* Teaching Resources) Scholastic, Inc.

Scholastic, Inc. Staff & Medearis, Angela Shelf. Singing for Dr. King. Van Wright, Cornelius & Hu, Ying-Hwa, illus. 2004. (Just for You Ser.). (ENG.). 32p. (gr. k-3). pap. 3.99 *(978-0-439-56855-5(2),* Teaching Resources) Scholastic, Inc.

Scholastic, Inc. Staff & Taylor-Butler, Christine. A Mom Like No Other. Devard, Nancy, illus. 2004. (Just for You Ser.). (ENG.). 32p. pap. 3.99 *(978-0-439-56853-1(6),* Teaching Resources) Scholastic, Inc.

—No Boys Allowed! Page, Mark, illus. 2004. (Just for You Ser.). (ENG.). 32p. pap. 3.99 *(978-0-439-56856-2(0),* Teaching Resources) Scholastic, Inc.

Scholastic, Inc. Staff, et al. Don't Hit Me! Grier, Gary, illus. 2004. (Just for You Ser.). (ENG.). 32p. (gr. k-1). pap. 3.99 *(978-0-439-56860-9(9),* Teaching Resources) Scholastic, Inc.

Schraff, Anne. Facing It, 1 vol. 2013. (Urban Underground Ser.). (ENG.). 194p. (YA). (gr. 9-12). pap. 9.95 *(978-1-62250-045-1(8))* Saddleback Educational Publishing, Inc.

—Freedom Knows No Color. 2008. (Passages to History Ser.). 118p. (J). lib. bdg. 13.95 *(978-0-7569-8392-5(4));* (YA). (gr. 7-12). pap. 8.50 *(978-0-7891-7567-0(3))* Perfection Learning Corp.

—If You Really Loved Me, 1 vol. unabr. ed. 2010. (Urban Underground Ser.). (ENG.). 181p. (YA). (gr. 9-12). pap. 9.95 *(978-1-61651-003-9(X))* Saddleback Educational Publishing, Inc.

—If You Were Mine, 1 vol. 2013. (Urban Underground Ser.). (ENG.). 195p. (YA). (gr. 9-12). pap. 9.95 *(978-1-62250-041-3(5))* Saddleback Educational Publishing, Inc.

—Lost & Found. Langan, Paul, ed. 2007. (Bluford High Ser.). 133p. (gr. 8-12). 16.00 *(978-0-7569-8076-4(3))* Perfection Learning Corp.

—Lost & Found. 2007. (Bluford High — Scholastic Ser.: 1). lib. bdg. 16.00 *(978-1-4177-7141-7(0),* Turtleback) Turtleback Bks.

—A Matter of Trust. 2007. (Bluford High — Scholastic Ser.: 2). lib. bdg. 16.00 *(978-1-4177-7142-4(9),* Turtleback) Turtleback Bks.

—The One for Me, 1 vol. 2013. (Urban Underground Ser.). (ENG.). 199p. (YA). (gr. 9-12). pap. 9.95 *(978-1-62250-042-0(3))* Saddleback Educational Publishing, Inc.

—Outrunning the Darkness, 1 vol. unabr. ed. 2010. (Urban Underground Ser.). (ENG.). 191p. (YA). (gr. 9-12). pap. 9.95 *(978-1-61651-000-8(5))* Saddleback Educational Publishing, Inc.

—The Price of Friendship. 2008. (Passages Ser.). 138p. (J). (gr. 4-6). lib. bdg. 13.95 *(978-0-7569-8373-4(8))* Perfection Learning Corp.

—Second Chances, 1 vol. 2013. (Urban Underground Ser.). (ENG.). 192p. (YA). (gr. 9-12). pap. 9.95 *(978-1-62250-044-4(X))* Saddleback Educational Publishing, Inc.

—Secrets in the Shadows. Langan, Paul, ed. 2007. (Bluford High Ser.). 126p. (gr. 8-12). 16.00 *(978-0-7569-8078-8(X))* Perfection Learning Corp.

—Secrets in the Shadows. 2007. (Bluford High — Scholastic Ser.: 3). lib. bdg. 16.00 *(978-1-4177-7149-3(6),* Turtleback) Turtleback Bks.

—Someone to Love Me. 2007. (Bluford High — Scholastic Ser.: 4). lib. bdg. 16.00 *(978-1-4177-7151-6(8),* Turtleback) Turtleback Bks.

—Wildflower. 2011. (Urban Underground — Harriet Tubman High School Ser.). (YA). lib. bdg. 20.80 *(978-0-606-14816-0(7),* Turtleback) Turtleback Bks.

Schraff, Anne E. Don't Think about Tomorrow. 2012. (Urban Underground — Harriet Tubman High School Ser.: 23). (YA). lib. bdg. 20.80 *(978-0-606-23796-3(8),* Turtleback) Turtleback Bks.

—Facing It. 2013. (Urban Underground — Harriet Tubman High School Ser.). (YA). lib. bdg. 20.80 *(978-0-606-31583-8(7),* Turtleback) Turtleback Bks.

—If You Were Mine. 2013. (Urban Underground — Harriet Tubman High School Ser.). (YA). lib. bdg. 20.80 *(978-0-606-31581-4(0),* Turtleback) Turtleback Bks.

—The One for Me. 2013. (Urban Underground — Harriet Tubman High School Ser.). lib. bdg. 20.80 *(978-0-606-31582-1(9),* Turtleback) Turtleback Bks.

—Out of Love for You. 2012. (Urban Underground — Harriet Tubman High School Ser.: 24). (YA). lib. bdg. 20.80 *(978-0-606-23797-0(6),* Turtleback) Turtleback Bks.

—The Outcasts. 2012. (Urban Underground — Harriet Tubman High School Ser.: 21). (YA). lib. bdg. 20.80 *(978-0-606-23794-9(1),* Turtleback) Turtleback Bks.

—The Rescuers. 2012. (Urban Underground — Harriet Tubman High School Ser.: 25). (YA). lib. bdg. 20.80 *(978-0-606-23798-7(4),* Turtleback) Turtleback Bks.

—See No Evil. 2012. (Urban Underground — Harriet Tubman High School Ser.: 22). (YA). lib. bdg. 20.80 *(978-0-606-23795-6(X),* Turtleback) Turtleback Bks.

—Someone to Love Me. 2007. (Bluford High Ser.). 162p. (gr. 8-12). 16.00 *(978-0-7569-8079-5(8))* Perfection Learning Corp.

Scillian, Devin. Pappy's Handkerchief. Ellison, Chris, illus. rev. ed. 2007. (Tales of Young Americans Ser.). (ENG.). 32p. (J). (gr. 3-7). 17.95 *(978-1-58536-316-2(2))* Sleeping Bear Pr.

Scillian, Devin & Young, Judy. Westward Journeys. Ellison, Chris et al, illus. 2013. (American Adventures Ser.). (ENG.). 96p. (J). (gr. 3-6). pap. 6.99 *(978-1-58536-860-0(1),* 202367) Sleeping Bear Pr.

Senzai, N. H. Saving Kabul Corner. 2014. (Kabul Chronicles Ser.). (ENG., Illus.). 288p. (J). (gr. 3-7). 16.99 *(978-1-4424-8494-8(2),* Simon & Schuster/Paula Wiseman Bks.) Simon & Schuster/Paula Wiseman Bks.

Shabazz, Ilyasah & Magoon, Kekla. X. 2015. (ENG., Illus.). 384p. (YA). (gr. 9). 16.99 *(978-0-7636-6967-6(9))* Candlewick Pr.

Sharing Turf. 2004. (Illus.). (YA). mass mkt. 19.95 *(978-0-9753663-0-1(0))* Ballad Productions.

Shaw, Marilyn Bishop. Solomon. 2006. (Florida Historical Fiction for Youth Ser.). (ENG.). 204p. (J). (gr. 4-9). 14.95 *(978-1-56164-349-3(1))* Pineapple Pr., Inc.

Shelton, Rick. Hoggle's Christmas. Gates, Donald, illus. 2007. 80p. (J). pap. 11.95 *(978-1-60306-026-4(X))* NewSouth, Inc.

Sibley, Linda. David Joins the California Gold Rush. 2004. 96p. pap. 6.65 *(978-0-7891-6002-7(1))* Perfection Learning Corp.

Simmons, Clara Ann. Sauncey & Mr. King's Gallery, 1 vol. 2009. (ENG., Illus.). 30p. (J). (gr. 1-4). 10.95 *(978-0-87033-498-6(0),* 9780870334986, Cornell Maritime Pr./Tidewater Pubs.) Schiffer Publishing, Ltd.

Simon, Charnan. Me Gusta Ganar! Translations.com Staff, tr. from ENG. Handelman, Dorothy, photos by. 2007. (Lecturas para niños de Verdad - Nivel 1 (Real Kids Readers - Level 1) Ser.).Tr. of I Like to Win! (SPA., Illus.). 32p. (gr. k-2). per. 5.95 *(978-0-8225-7801-7(8),* Ediciones Lerner) Lerner Publishing Group.

—Me Gusta Ganar; I Like to Win. 2008. pap. 34.95 *(978-0-8225-9499-4(4))* Lerner Publishing Group.

Simone, Ni-Ni. Teenage Love Affair. 2010. lib. bdg. 20.80 *(978-0-606-14705-7(5),* Turtleback) Turtleback Bks.

Simone, Ni-Ni & Abrams, Amir. Get Ready for War. 2013. (Hollywood High Ser.: 2). (ENG., Illus.). 288p. (YA). (gr. 9). pap. 9.95 *(978-0-7582-7355-0(X),* K-Teen/Dafina) Kensington Publishing Corp.

—Get Ready for War. 2013. (Hollywood High Ser.: 2). 423p. (YA). lib. bdg. 20.80 *(978-0-606-27305-3(0),* Turtleback) Turtleback Bks.

Simone, Ni-Ni & London, Kelli. The Break-Up Diaries. 2011. (ENG.). 272p. (YA). (gr. 9-18). 9.95 *(978-0-7582-6316-2(3),* K-Teen/Dafina) Kensington Publishing Corp.

Simpson, Howard, illus. Through Loona's Door: A Tammy & Owen Adventure with Carter G. Woodson. 2009. 80p. (J). per. 14.95 *(978-0-9740212-2-5(9))* Cedar Grove Bks.

Sims, Guy A. & Myers, Walter Dean. Monster. Anyabwile, Dawud, illus. 2015. (Monster Ser.). (ENG.). 160p. (YA). (gr. 8). pap. 9.99 *(978-0-06-227499-1(6))* HarperCollins Pubs.

Sitomer, Alan Lawrence. Hip-Hop High School. 2006. 368p. (J). *(978-0-7868-3831-8(0),* Jump at the Sun) Hyperion Bks. for Children.

—Homeboyz. 2008. (ENG.). 304p. (J). (gr. 5-9). pap. 8.99 *(978-1-4231-0031-7(X),* Jump at the Sun) Hyperion Bks. for Children.

—The Hoopster, 4 vols. unabr. ed. 2005. (GER.). (YA). 57.75 *(978-1-4025-7027-8(9),* 41853) Recorded Bks., Inc.

Slater, Calvin. Hold Me Down. 2015. (Coleman High Ser.: 2). (ENG., Illus.). 328p. (J). (gr. 9). pap. 9.95 *(978-1-61773-134-1(X),* Dafina) Kensington Publishing Corp.

Smalls, Irene. I Can't Take a Bath! Boyd, Aaron, illus. 2004. (Just for You Ser.). (ENG.). 32p. (J). (gr. 1-1). pap. 3.99 *(978-0-439-56852-4(8))* Scholastic, Inc.

Smith, Charles R., Jr. Chameleon. 2010. (ENG., Illus.). 384p. (YA). (gr. 7). pap. 7.99 *(978-0-7636-4660-8(1))* Candlewick Pr.

Smith, Hope Anita. Keeping the Night Watch. Lewis, E. B., illus. 2014. (ENG.). 80p. (J). (gr. 5-8). pap. 9.99 *(978-0-312-65936-3(9),* 9780312659363) Square Fish.

Smith, Ronald L. Hoodoo. 2015. (ENG.). 224p. (J). (gr. 5-7). 16.99 *(978-0-544-44525-3(2),* Clarion Bks.) Houghton Mifflin Harcourt Trade & Reference Pubs.

—Hoodoo. 2017. (ENG.). (J). (gr. 5-7). lib. bdg. 18.40 ***(978-0-606-39820-6(1))*** Turtleback Bks.

Smith, Sarah. The Other Side of Dark. (ENG., 320p. (YA). (gr. 7). 2011. Illus.). pap. 11.99 *(978-1-4424-0281-2(4))* 2010. 16.99 *(978-1-4424-0280-5(6))* Simon & Schuster Children's Publishing. (Atheneum Bks. for Young Readers).

Smith, Sherri L. Flygirl. 2010. (ENG.). 304p. (YA). (gr. 7-18). 9.99 *(978-0-14-241725-6(4),* Speak) Penguin Young Readers Group.

—Flygirl. 2010. lib. bdg. 19.65 *(978-0-606-14999-0(6),* Turtleback) Turtleback Bks.

Smolik, Jane Petrlik. Currents. 2015. (ENG., Illus.). 336p. (YA). (gr. 4-7). lib. bdg. 16.95 *(978-1-58089-648-1(0))* Charlesbridge Publishing, Inc.

Smothers, Ethel Footman. Down in the Piney Woods. 2004. 128p. (J). pap. 7.00 *(978-0-8028-5248-9(3))* Eerdmans, William B. Publishing Co.

Smothers, Ethel Footman & Smothers, Ethel F. Hard-Times Jar. Holyfield, John, illus. 2003. (ENG.). 32p. (J). (gr. k-3). 18.99 *(978-0-374-32852-8(8),* 9780374328528, Farrar, Straus & Giroux (BYR)) Farrar, Straus & Giroux.

A
B

Soentpiet, Chris K., et al. Molly Bannaky. 2009. (ENG., Illus.). 32p. (J). (gr. -1-3). pap. 6.99 (978-0-547-07676-8(2)) Houghton Mifflin Harcourt Publishing Co.

Sosin, Deborah. Charlotte & the Quiet Place. Woolley, Sara, illus. 2015. (ENG.). 40p. (J). (gr. -1-2). 16.95 (978-1-941529-02-7(X), Plum Blossom Bks.) Parallax Pr.

Spears, Jr. Derek's Dilemm. 2009. 148p. pap. 24.95 (978-1-60836-387-2(2)) America Star Bks.

Spruill, Edward L. & Spruill, Sonya. Jordan's Hair. Peringer, Stephen Mercer, illus. 2005. 16p. (J). (gr. -1-3). 8.00 (978-0-8170-1484-1(5)) Judson Pr.

Squier, Robert, illus. Follow the Drinking Gourd: An Underground Railroad Story, 1 vol. 2012. (Night Sky Stories Ser.). (ENG.). 24p. (gr. 2-3). pap. 8.95 (978-1-4048-7714-6(2)) Picture Window Bks.

Stauffacher, Sue & Love, Comfort. Wireman. 2007. (Illus.). 159p. (J). pap. (978-0-9709811-4-1(7)) Grand Valley State Univ.

Steenwyk, Elizabeth Van. Blacksmith's Song. Rich, Anna, illus. 2018. (ENG.). 32p. (J). (gr. 1-5). 17.95 (978-1-56145-580-5(6)) Peachtree Pubs.

Stella M. Reese. The Princess of Topaz: An African American Saga. 2010. 20p. 13.95 (978-1-4269-2432-3(1)) Trafford Publishing.

Stephens, Torrance. A Matter of Attention. 2003. 129p. (YA). pap. 11.95 (978-0-7414-1505-9(4)) Infinity Publishing.

Stone Arch Books Staff. John Henry - Hammerin' Hero. Evergreen, Nelson, illus. 2010. (Graphic Spin Ser.). (ENG.). 40p. (gr. 1-3). pap. 5.95 (978-1-4342-2265-7(9), Graphic Revolve) Stone Arch Bks.

Stoudemire, Amar'e. Most Valuable. 2014. (STAT: Standing Tall & Talented Ser.: 5). lib. bdg. 16.00 (978-0-606-35394-6(1)) Turtleback Bks.

—Standing Tall & Talented - Most Valuable. 2014. (ENG.). 144p. (J). (gr. 3-7). pap. 5.99 (978-0-545-60613-4(6), Scholastic Paperbacks) Scholastic, Inc.

Strasser, Todd. If I Grow Up. (ENG.). 240p. (YA). (gr. 7). 2010. pap. 9.99 (978-1-4169-9443-5(2)) 2009. 17.99 (978-1-4169-2523-1(6)) Simon & Schuster Bks. For Young Readers. (Simon & Schuster Bks. For Young Readers).

Stroud, Bettye & Ramsey, Calvin Alexander. Belle, the Last Mule at Gee's Bend: A Civil Rights Story. Holyfield, John, illus. 2011. (ENG.). 32p. (J). (gr. k-3). 16.99 (978-0-7636-4058-3(1)) Candlewick Pr.

Suen, Anastasia. Loose Tooth. Eitzen, Allan, illus. 2004. 28p. (gr. -1-3). 14.00 (978-0-7569-1955-9(X)) Perfection Learning Corp.

Sullivan, Jacqueline Levering. Annie's War. 2007. (Illus.). 183p. (J). (gr. 3-7). 15.00 (978-0-8028-5325-7(0), Eerdmans Bks For Young Readers) Eerdmans, William B. Publishing Co.

Suter, Lorenzo. TrYouth Truth Knowledge Apprehension Cog. 2005. (Illus.). 206p. 27.55 (978-1-4122-0095-0(4)) Trafford Publishing.

Taddonio, Lea. Book 3: First Fight. 2016. (Head over Heels Ser.). (ENG., Illus.). 46p. (J). (gr. 2-8). lib. bdg. 28.50 **(978-1-62402-194-7(8))** ABDO Publishing Co.

Tarpley, Natasha Anastasia. Bippity Bop Barbershop. Lewis, E. B., illus. 2009. (ENG.). 32p. (gr. -1-3). pap. 7.99 (978-0-316-03382-4(0)) Little, Brown Bks. for Young Readers.

—I Love My Hair! Lewis, E. B., illus. 2014. 32p. pap. 7.00 (978-1-61003-348-0(5)) Center for the Collaborative Classroom.

—I Love My Hair! Lewis, E. B., illus. 2003. (ENG.). 22p. (J). (gr. -1 — 1). bds. 6.99 (978-0-316-52558-9(8)) Little, Brown Bks. for Young Readers.

Tarshis, Lauren. I Survived Hurricane Katrina 2005. 2011. (I Survived Ser.: 3). (ENG.). 112p. (J). (gr. 3-7). pap. 4.99 (978-0-545-20696-9(0), Scholastic Paperbacks) Scholastic, Inc.

—I Survived Hurricane Katrina 2005. 2011. (I Survived ... Ser.: No. 3). lib. bdg. 14.75 (978-0-606-23743-7(7), Turtleback) Turtleback Bks.

Tate, Eleanora E. Celeste's Harlem Renaissance. 2009. (ENG.). 304p. (J). (gr. 3-7). pap. 7.99 (978-0-316-11362-5(X)) Little, Brown Bks. for Young Readers.

—The Minstrel's Melody. 2009. (Mysteries Through Time Ser.). 176p. (gr. 4-8). (YA). pap. 15.25 (978-1-60754-180-6(7)); (Illus.). (J). 31.95 (978-1-60754-179-0(3)) Windmill Bks.

Taylor, Debbie & Morrison, Frank. Sweet Music in Harlem, 1 vol. 2004. (ENG., Illus.). 32p. (J). 17.95 (978-1-58430-165-3(1)) Lee & Low Bks., Inc.

Taylor, Debbie A. Sweet Music in Harlem. Morrison, Frank, illus. 2014. 32p. pap. 9.00 (978-1-61003-220-9(9)) Center for the Collaborative Classroom.

Taylor, Mildred D. The Friendship. 2014. (ENG.). 56p. (J). (gr. 3-7). 11.24 (978-1-63245-342-6(8)) Lectorum Pubns., Inc.

—Roll of Thunder, Hear My Cry. 2004. 276p. (gr. 4-8). reprint ed. pap. 10.00 (978-0-7567-7955-9(3)) DIANE Publishing Co.

—Roll of Thunder, Hear My Cry. 40th anniv. ed. 2016. (ENG., Illus.). 304p. (J). (gr. 3-7). 19.99 (978-1-101-99388-0(X), Dial Bks) Penguin Young Readers Group.

—Roll of Thunder, Hear My Cry. unabr. ed. 2004. 276p. (J). (gr. 5-9). pap. 48.00 incl. audio (978-0-8072-0678-2(4), Listening Library) Random Hse. Audio Publishing Group.

Terrell, Brandon. The Cursed Stage. Epelbaum, Mariano, illus. 2017. (Snoops, Inc Ser.). (ENG.). 112p. (gr. 4-6). lib. bdg. 26.65 (978-1-4965-4346-2(7)) Stone Arch Bks.

—Harmony & Hoops. Max, Iman & Garcia, Eduardo, illus. 2016. (Time Machine Magazine Ser.). (ENG.). 128p. (gr. 3-4). lib. bdg. 22.65 (978-1-4965-2596-3(5)) Capstone Press of Coughlan Cos.

—Science Fair Sabotage. Epelbaum, Mariano, illus. 2017. (Snoops, Inc Ser.). (ENG.). 112p. (gr. 4-6). lib. bdg. 26.65 (978-1-4965-4347-9(5)) Stone Arch Bks.

—Tracking Champ. Epelbaum, Mariano, illus. 2017. (Snoops, Inc Ser.). (ENG.). 112p. (gr. 4-6). lib. bdg. 26.65 (978-1-4965-4348-6(3)) Stone Arch Bks.

—The Undercover Cheerleader. Epelbaum, Mariano, illus. 2017. (Snoops, Inc Ser.). (ENG.). 112p. (gr. 4-6). lib. bdg. 26.65 **(978-1-4965-5061-3(7))** Stone Arch Bks.

Terrell, Brandon. The Vanishing Treasure. Epelbaum, Mariano, illus. 2017. (Snoops, Inc Ser.). (ENG.). 112p. (gr. 4-6). lib. bdg. 26.65 (978-1-4965-4345-5(9)) Stone Arch Bks.

Terry, Chris L. Zero Fade. Knabb, Jacob & Vance, Leonard, eds. 2013. (ENG., Illus.). 294p. (gr. 6). pap. 12.00 (978-0-9884804-3-8(3), 1362831) Curbside Splendor Publishing.

Thomas, Angie. The Hate U Give. 2017. (ENG.). 464p. (YA). (gr. 9). 17.99 (978-0-06-249853-3(3)) HarperCollins Pubs.

Thomas, Jacquelin. Divine Match-Up. 2008. (ENG., Illus.). 304p. (gr. 8-12). pap. 19.99 (978-1-4165-5145-4(X), Gallery Bks.) Gallery Bks.

—It's a Curl Thing. 2009. (Divine & Friends Ser.). (ENG., Illus.). 288p. pap. 18.99 (978-1-4165-9878-7(2)) Pocket Books.

—Simply Divine. 2006. (ENG.). 288p. (gr. 7-12). pap. 18.99 (978-1-4165-2718-3(4), Gallery Bks.) Gallery Bks.

—Split Ends. 2010. (ENG.). 272p. pap. 17.99 (978-1-4165-9879-4(0)) Pocket Books.

Thompson, Brian. Reject High. 2013. 270p. pap. 11.95 (978-0-9891056-0-6(1)) Great Nation Publishing.

Thompson, Tavia. Made by God Wonderfully. 2013. 28p. pap. 24.95 (978-1-63000-403-3(0)) America Star Bks.

Thomson, Melissa. Keena Ford & the Field Trip Mix-Up. 2010. (Keena Ford Ser.). (ENG.). 112p. (J). (gr. 1-3). 5.99 (978-0-14-241572-6(3), Puffin Books) Penguin Young Readers Group.

—Keena Ford & the Secret Journal Mix-Up. Morrison, Frank, illus. 2011. (Keena Ford Ser.). (ENG.). 128p. (J). (gr. 1-3). 5.99 (978-0-14-241937-3(0), Puffin Books) Penguin Young Readers Group.

Tinsley, Helen. Me & My Grandma: A Story for Children about AIDS. 2012.Tr. of 32. (Illus.). 34p. (J). pap. 14.95 (978-1-937622-21-3(5), Nefu Bks.) Africana Homestead Legacy Pubs., Inc.

TJ & the Mysterious Stranger. 2004. (J). bds. 16.95 (978-0-9710487-2-0(X)) Highlights of Chicago Pr.

Toni Eubanks. Journey Home. 2010. 52p. pap. 8.95 (978-1-4401-8246-4(9)) iUniverse, Inc.

Tooke, Wes. King of the Mound: My Summer with Satchel Paige. (ENG.). 160p. (J). (gr. 3-7). 2013. pap. 7.99 (978-1-4424-3347-2(7)) 2012. (Illus.). 17.99 (978-1-4424-3346-5(9)) Simon & Schuster Bks. For Young Readers. (Simon & Schuster Bks. For Young Readers).

Townley, Roderick. Sky. 2010. (ENG.). 272p. (YA). (gr. 7). pap. 12.99 (978-1-4423-3973-6(X), Atheneum Bks. for Young Readers) Simon & Schuster Children's Publishing.

Trees, Annie Mae. The Old Apartment Building: A Tale from the Trees. 2012. 24p. 24.95 (978-1-4626-6093-3(2)) America Star Bks.

Trice, Linda. Kenya's Art. Mitchell, Hazel, illus. 2016. (ENG.). 32p. (J). (gr. -1-3). 16.95 (978-1-57091-848-3(1)) Charlesbridge Publishing, Inc.

—Kenya's Song. Johnson, Pamela, illus. 2013. (ENG.). 32p. (J). (gr. -1-3). pap. 7.95 (978-1-57091-847-6(3)); lib. bdg. 17.95 (978-1-57091-846-9(5)) Charlesbridge Publishing, Inc.

The Troubles of Johnny Cannon. 2014. (ENG., Illus.). 304p. (J). (gr. 3-7). 16.99 (978-1-4814-0003-9(7), Simon & Schuster Bks. For Young Readers) Simon & Schuster Bks. For Young Readers.

Tuck, Pamela M. As Fast As Words Could Fly, 1 vol. Velasquez, Eric, illus. 2013. (ENG.). 40p. (J). 18.95 (978-1-60060-348-8(3)) Lee & Low Bks., Inc.

Turner, Diane D. My Name Is Oney Judge. Massey, Cal, illus. 2010. (J). pap. (978-0-88378-321-4(5)) Third World Press.

—My Name Is Oney Judge. Massey, Call, illus. 2010. (ENG.). 40p. (J). 19.95 (978-0-88378-304-7(5)) Third World Press.

Turner, Morrie. Super Sistahs: Featuring the Accomplishments of African-American Women. 2005. (Illus.). 112p. pap. 14.95 (978-0-9656739-5-2(2)) BYE Publishing Services.

Tyree, Omar R. 12 Brown Boys. 2008. 196p. (J). (gr. 3-7). pap. 9.95 (978-1-933491-12-7(4)) Just Us Bks., Inc.

Uhlberg, Myron. A Storm Called Katrina, 1 vol. Bootman, Colin, illus. (ENG.). 40p. (J). (gr. 2-4). 2015. pap. 8.95 (978-1-56145-887-5(2)) 2011. 17.95 (978-1-56145-591-1(1)) Peachtree Pubs.

—A Storm Called Katrina. 2015. lib. bdg. 19.60 (978-0-606-37467-5(1)) Turtleback Bks.

Underwood, Jamilah. Today's Rain, Tomorrow's Sunshine. 2003. 104p. (YA). pap. 10.00 (978-0-9727201-4-4(6)) Blessed Beginnings Publishing.

van Diepen, Allison. Street Pharm. 2013. (ENG., Illus.). 320p. (YA). (gr. 8). pap. 10.99 (978-1-4424-8166-4(8), Simon Pulse) Simon Pulse.

—Takedown. 2013. (ENG.). 288p. (YA). (gr. 9-9). pap. 11.99 (978-1-4424-6312-7(0), Simon Pulse) Simon Pulse.

Van Wright, Cornelius & Hu, Ying-Hwa, illus. I Told You I Can Play! 2006. (ENM.). 32p. (J). 16.95 (978-1-933491-06-6(X)) Just Us Bks., Inc.

Vander Zee, Ruth. Mississippi Morning. Cooper, Floyd, illus. 2004. 32p. (J). 16.00 (978-0-8028-5211-3(4)) Eerdmans, William B. Publishing Co.

Vanoosting, James. Walking Mary. 2005. 144p. (J). (gr. 7-18). lib. bdg. 16.89 (978-0-06-028472-5(2)) HarperCollins Pubs.

Velasquez, Eric. Grandma's Gift. Velasquez, Eric, illus. 2013. (ENG., Illus.). 32p. (J). (gr. k-1). pap. 9.99 (978-0-8027-3536-2(3), 9780802735362, Bloomsbury USA Childrens) Bloomsbury Publishing USA.

—Grandma's Records. 2014. 32p. pap. 9.00 (978-1-61003-346-6(9)) Center for the Collaborative Classroom.

Velasquez, Gloria. Tyrone's Betrayal. 2006. (Roosevelt High School Series Bks.). 135p. (J). (gr. 3-7). per. 9.95 (978-1-55885-465-9(7), Piñata Books) Arte Publico Pr.

Vision, David & Vision, Mutiya Sahar. Daddy Loves His Baby Girl. Vision, Mutiya Sahar, illus. 2009. (Illus.). 32p. 16.00 (978-0-9659538-7-0(4)) Visor Bks.

—Missing You. Alcantara, Ignacio, illus. 2009. 32p. 17.00 (978-0-9659538-6-3(6)) Von Curtis Publishing.

Vision, David, et al. My Very Best Friend. Alcantara, Ignacio, illus. 2009. (ENG.). 40p. 17.00 (978-0-9659538-5-6(8)) Vitally Important.

Voigt, Cynthia. Come a Stranger. 2012. (Tillerman Cycle Ser.: 5). (ENG., Illus.). 256p. (YA). (gr. 7). 18.99 (978-1-4424-5063-9(0)); pap. 7.99 (978-1-4424-2882-9(1)) Simon & Schuster Children's Publishing. (Atheneum Bks. for Young Readers).

Volponi, Paul. The Final Four. (ENG.). (YA). (gr. 7). 2013. 272p. pap. 9.99 (978-0-14-242385-1(8), Speak) 2012. 256p. 16.99 (978-0-670-01264-0(5), Viking Books for Young Readers) Penguin Young Readers Group.

—Response. 2010. (ENG.). 176p. (YA). (gr. 7-18). 6.99 (978-0-14-241603-7(7), Speak) Penguin Young Readers Group.

—Rikers High. (ENG.). (YA). (gr. 7-18). 2011. 272p. 7.99 (978-0-14-241778-2(5), Speak) 2010. 256p. 16.99 (978-0-670-01107-0(X), Viking Books for Young Readers) Penguin Young Readers Group.

—Rooftop. 2007. (ENG.). 224p. (YA). (gr. 7-18). 6.99 (978-0-14-240844-5(1), Puffin Books) Penguin Young Readers Group.

—Rooftop. 2007. 199p. 17.00 (978-0-7569-7958-4(7)) Perfection Learning Corp.

—Rucker Park Setup. 2008. (ENG.). 160p. (YA). (gr. 7-18). 6.99 (978-0-14-241207-7(4), Speak) Penguin Young Readers Group.

Wagner, Jane. J. T. 125p. (J). (gr. 3-5). pap. 3.00 (978-0-8072-1403-9(5), Listening Library) Random Hse. Audio Publishing Group.

Wahl, Jan. Candy Shop. Wong, Nicole, illus. 2005. (ENG.). 32p. (J). (gr. -1-3). pap. 7.95 (978-1-57091-668-7(3)) Charlesbridge Publishing, Inc.

Waldman, Neil. Starry Night. 2010. (ENG.). 32p. (J). pap. 11.95 (978-1-59078-780-9(3)) Boyds Mills Pr.

Walker, Brian F. Black Boy White School. 2012. (ENG.). 256p. (YA). (gr. 9). 17.99 (978-0-06-191483-6(5), HarperTeen) HarperCollins Pubs.

Walker, Sally M. Freedom Song: The Story of Henry "Box" Brown. Qualls, Sean, illus. 2012. (ENG.). 40p. (J). (gr. -1-3). 17.99 (978-0-06-058310-1(X)) HarperCollins Pubs.

Walter, Jon. My Name Is Not Friday. 2017. (ENG.). 400p. (J). (gr. 7). pap. 9.99 **(978-1-338-16064-2(8))** Scholastic, Inc.

Walter, Jon. My Name's Not Friday. 2016. (ENG.). 384p. (YA). (gr. 7). 18.99 (978-0-545-85522-8(5)) Scholastic, Inc.

Walter, Mildred Pitts. Alec's Primer. Johnson, Larry, illus. 2005. (ENG.). 32p. (J). (gr. -1-3). 15.95 (978-0-916718-20-6(4)) Vermont Folklife Ctr.

—Justin & the Best Biscuits in the World. Stock, Catherine, illus. 2010. (ENG.). 144p. (J). (gr. 3-7). pap. 5.99 (978-0-06-195891-5(3), Amistad) HarperCollins Pubs.

—Justin & the Best Biscuits in the World. 2011. 8.32 (978-0-7848-3586-9(1), Everbind) Marco Bk. Co.

Waltman, Kevin. Next. 2013. (D-Bow High School Hoops Ser.). (ENG.). 216p. (J). 16.95 (978-1-935955-64-1(0)); pap. 11.95 (978-1-935955-65-8(9)) Cinco Puntos Pr.

—Quicks. 2016. (D-Bow High School Hoops Ser.). (ENG.). 216p. (J). (gr. 6). 16.95 (978-1-941026-61-8(3)) Cinco Puntos Pr.

—Slump. 2014. (D-Bow High School Hoops Ser.). (ENG.). 216p. (J). 16.95 (978-1-941026-00-7(1)) Cinco Puntos Pr.

Walvoord, Linda & Walvoord. Rosetta, Rosetta, Sit by Me!, 0 vols. Velasquez, Eric, illus. 2004. (ENG.). 80p. (J). (gr. 3-6). 14.95 (978-0-7614-5171-6(4), 9780761451716, Amazon Children's Publishing) Amazon Publishing.

Warner, Sally. The Dragon Slayer! Biggs, Brian, illus. 2013. (EllRay Jakes Ser.: 4). (ENG.). 144p. (J). (gr. 1-3). 14.99 (978-0-670-78497-4(4), Viking Books for Young Readers) Penguin Young Readers Group.

—EllRay Jakes & the Beanstalk. Biggs, Brian, illus. 2013. (EllRay Jakes Ser.: 5). (ENG.). (J). (gr. 1-3). 128p. 14.99 (978-0-670-78499-8(0), Viking Books for Young Readers); 144p. pap. 5.99 (978-0-14-242359-2(9), Puffin Books) Penguin Young Readers Group.

—EllRay Jakes & the Beanstalk. 2013. (EllRay Jakes Ser.: 5). lib. bdg. 16.00 (978-0-606-32137-2(3), Turtleback) Turtleback Bks.

—Ellray Jakes Is a Rock Star! 2012. (EllRay Jakes Ser.: 2). lib. bdg. 16.00 (978-0-606-23633-1(3), Turtleback) Turtleback Bks.

—EllRay Jakes Is Magic. Biggs, Brian, illus. 2014. (EllRay Jakes Ser.: 6). (ENG.). 160p. (J). (gr. 1-3). 14.99 (978-0-670-78500-1(8), Viking Books for Young Readers) Penguin Young Readers Group.

—Ellray Jakes Is Magic. 2014. (EllRay Jakes Ser.: 6). lib. bdg. 16.00 (978-0-606-34215-5(X), Turtleback) Turtleback Bks.

—EllRay Jakes Is Not a Chicken! 2012. (EllRay Jakes Ser.: 1). lib. bdg. 16.00 (978-0-606-23632-4(5), Turtleback) Turtleback Bks.

—Ellray Jakes Rocks the Holidays! 2014. (EllRay Jakes Ser.: 7). lib. bdg. 16.00 (978-0-606-36188-0(X)) Turtleback Bks.

—EllRay Jakes Stands Tall. Biggs, Brian, illus. 2016. (EllRay Jakes Ser.). (ENG.). (J). (gr. 1-3). 176p. 5.99 (978-0-14-751253-6(0), Puffin Books); 160p. 14.99 (978-0-451-46913-7(5), Viking Books for Young Readers) Penguin Young Readers Group.

—Ellray Jakes Stands Tall. 2016. (EllRay Jakes Ser.: 9). lib. bdg. 16.00 (978-0-606-38420-9(0)) Turtleback Bks.

—EllRay Jakes the Dragon Slayer. 2013. (EllRay Jakes Ser.: 4). lib. bdg. 16.00 (978-0-606-32136-5(5), Turtleback) Turtleback Bks.

—Ellray Jakes the Dragon Slayer, No. 4. Biggs, Brian, illus. 2013. (EllRay Jakes Ser.: 4). (ENG.). 144p. (J). (gr. 1-3). pap. 5.99 (978-0-14-242358-5(0), Puffin Books) Penguin Young Readers Group.

—EllRay Jakes the Recess King! Biggs, Brian, illus. 2015. (EllRay Jakes Ser.: 8). (ENG.). 176p. (J). (gr. 1-3). 5.99 (978-0-14-751252-9(2), Puffin Books); 14.99 (978-0-451-46911-3(9), Viking Books for Young Readers) Penguin Young Readers Group.

—EllRay Jakes Walks the Plank! 2013. (EllRay Jakes Ser.: 3). lib. bdg. 16.00 (978-0-606-30188-6(7), Turtleback) Turtleback Bks.

—Rocks the Holidays! Biggs, Brian, illus. 2014. (EllRay Jakes Ser.: 7). (ENG.). 160p. (J). (gr. 1-3). 14.99 (978-0-451-46909-0(7), Viking Books for Young Readers) Penguin Young Readers Group.

—Walks the Plank! Harper, Jamie, illus. (EllRay Jakes Ser.: 3). (ENG.). 128p. (J). (gr. 1-3). 2013. pap. 5.99 (978-0-14-242409-4(9), Puffin Books) 2012. 14.99 (978-0-670-06306-2(1), Viking Books for Young Readers) Penguin Young Readers Group.

Washington, Kathy. Three Colors of Katie. Farina, Kathy, illus. 2010. (J). (gr. k-2). pap. 9.95 (978-1-932514-18-6(X)) College of DuPage Pr.

Watson, Renée. Piecing Me Together. 2017. (ENG.). 272p. (YA). 17.99 (978-1-68119-105-8(9), 9781681191058, Bloomsbury USA Childrens) Bloomsbury Publishing USA.

—This Side of Home. 2017. (ENG.). 352p. (YA). pap. 9.99 (978-1-61963-930-0(0), 9781619639300, Bloomsbury USA Childrens) Bloomsbury Publishing USA.

—What Momma Left Me. (ENG.). 240p. (YA). 2012. pap. 7.99 (978-1-59990-704-8(6), 9781599907048) 2010. (gr. 5-8). 16.99 (978-1-59990-446-7(2), 9781599904467) Bloomsbury Publishing USA. (Bloomsbury USA Childrens).

Watts, Jeri. Kizzy Ann Stamps. 2013. (ENG., Illus.). 192p. (J). (gr. 4-7). pap. 5.99 (978-0-7636-6976-8(8)) Candlewick Pr.

Watts, Jeri Hanel. Keepers. Marshall, Felicia, illus. 2013. (ENG.). 32p. (J). (gr. -1-5). pap. 9.95 (978-1-58430-013-7(2)) Lee & Low Bks., Inc.

Weatherford, Carole Boston. Becoming Billie Holiday. Cooper, Floyd, illus. 2008. (ENG.). 120p. (YA). (gr. 9-18). 19.95 (978-1-59078-507-2(X), Wordsong) Boyds Mills Pr.

—Celebremos Juneteenth! de La Vega, Eida, tr. from ENG. Buchanan, Yvonne, illus. 2007. (SPA.). 32p. (J). (gr. -1-3). pap. 7.95 (978-1-60060-247-4(9)) Lee & Low Bks., Inc.

—Freedom in Congo Square. Christie, R. Gregory, illus. 2016. (ENG.). 40p. (J). (gr. -1-3). 17.99 (978-1-4998-0103-3(3)) Little Bee Books Inc.

—Freedom on the Menu: The Greensboro Sit-Ins. Lagarrigue, Jerome Lagarrigue, illus. 2007. (ENG.). 32p. (J). (gr. -1-3). pap. 5.99 (978-0-14-240894-0(8), Puffin Books) Penguin Young Readers Group.

—Freedom on the Menu: The Greensboro Sit-Ins. Lagarrigue, Jerome, illus. 2007. (gr. 4-7). 16.00 (978-0-7569-8160-0(3)) Perfection Learning Corp.

—In Your Hands. Pinkney, Brian, illus. 2017. (ENG.). 32p. (J). (gr. -1-3). 17.99 **(978-1-4814-6293-8(8))** Simon & Schuster Children's Publishing.

Weatherford, Carole Boston. Sugar Hill: Harlem's Historic Neighborhood. Christie, R. Gregory, illus. 2014. (ENG.). 32p. (J). (gr. k-3). 16.99 (978-0-8075-7650-2(6)) Whitman, Albert & Co.

Webster-Tyson, Paulette L. I Gotta Get a Nickname! 2011. 32p. (gr. -1-2). pap. 17.25 (978-1-4269-5625-6(8)) Trafford Publishing.

Wesley, Valerie Wilson. How to Almost Ruin Your School Play. 2005. (Illus.). 105p. (J). lib. bdg. 15.00 (978-1-4242-0645-2(6)) Fitzgerald Bks.

—How to Fish for Trouble. Roos, Maryn, illus. 2004. 89p. (J). lib. bdg. 15.00 (978-1-4242-0643-8(X)) Fitzgerald Bks.

Weston Woods Staff, creator. Goggles! 2011. 29.95 (978-0-439-85317-0(6)) 2004. (J). 38.75 (978-1-55592-418-8(2)) 2004. (J). 18.95 (978-1-55592-417-1(4)) Weston Woods Studios, Inc.

—Henry's Freedom Box. 2011. 18.95 (978-0-545-31402-2(X)); 38.75 (978-0-545-31403-9(8)) Weston Woods Studios, Inc.

—Pet Show! 2011. 29.95 (978-0-439-73506-3(8)); 38.75 (978-0-439-72866-9(5)); 18.95 (978-0-439-72865-2(7)) Weston Woods Studios, Inc.

—Peter's Chair. 2011. 29.95 (978-0-439-76006-5(2)) Weston Woods Studios, Inc.

—The Snowy Day. 2004. 29.95 (978-1-55592-853-7(6)) Weston Woods Studios, Inc.

—Whistle for Willie. 2011. 38.75 (978-1-55592-764-6(5)) Weston Woods Studios, Inc.

Westrick, Anne. Brotherhood. 2013. (ENG., Illus.). 368p. (J). (gr. 5). 17.99 (978-0-670-01439-2(7), Viking Books for Young Readers) Penguin Young Readers Group.

Weyn, Suzanne. Beaten. 2011. (Surviving Southside Ser.). (ENG.). 104p. (YA). (gr. 6-12). pap. 7.95 (978-0-7613-6164-0(2)) Lerner Publishing Group.

—Recruited. (Surviving Southside Ser.). (ENG.). 104p. (YA). (gr. 6-12). 2015. 34.65 (978-1-4677-6010-2(2), Lerner Digital) 2011. pap. 7.95 (978-0-7613-6167-1(7)) 2011. lib. bdg. 27.93 (978-0-7613-6153-4(7)) Lerner Publishing Group.

Whelan, Gloria. The Listeners. Benny, Mike, illus. 2009. (Tales of Young Americans Ser.). (ENG.). 32p. (J). (gr. k-6). 17.95 (978-1-58536-419-0(3)) Sleeping Bear Pr.

Whitehouse, Elizabeth. Black Boys. 2005. (J). pap. 5.95 (978-1-933031-93-4(X)) Whitehouse Publishing.

Wiles, Deborah. Freedom Summer. Lagarrigue, Jerome, illus. 50th anniv. ed. 2014. (ENG.). 32p. (J). (gr. -1-3). 17.99 (978-1-4814-2298-7(7), Atheneum Bks. for Young Readers) Simon & Schuster Children's Publishing.

Wiles, Deborah. Revolution. 2017. (Sixties Trilogy Ser.: 2). (ENG.). 544p. (J). (gr. 3-7). pap. 8.99 **(978-0-545-10608-5(7))** Scholastic, Inc.

Wilkins, LaTanya. The Adventures of Dedan & Dylan Jackson: The Second Day of School. 2010. 48p. pap. 13.99 (978-1-4520-5963-1(2)) AuthorHouse.

Wilkins, Verna. Twinkle, Twinkle, Little Star. Kubler, Annie, illus. 2003. (Classic Books with Holes 8x8 Ser.). (ENG.). 16p. (J). (gr. -1-3). pap. (978-0-85953-133-7(3)) Child's Play International Ltd.

Wilkinson, Brenda. Ludell. 2014. (ENG., Illus.). 228p. (J). (-9). pap. 12.95 (978-1-939601-16-2(9)) Ig Publishing, Inc.

William Murray Hogben. Johnny & Mr Reb: A Civil War Tale. 2009. 40p. pap. 18.99 (978-1-4389-4326-8(1)) AuthorHouse.

Williams-Garcia, Rita. Catching the Wild Waiyuuzee. Reed, Mike, illus. 2007. (ENG.). 32p. (J). (gr. -1-1). 12.99 (978-1-4169-6141-3(0), Simon & Schuster/Paula Wiseman Bks.) Simon & Schuster/Paula Wiseman Bks.

—Clayton Byrd Goes Underground. Morrison, Frank, illus. 2017. 176p. (J). (gr. 3-7). 16.99 (978-0-06-221591-8(4)); (ENG.). E-Book (978-0-06-221594-9(9)) HarperCollins Pubs. (Amistad).

—One Crazy Summer. 2009. (KOR.). 272p. (J). pap. (978-89-7199-494-8(0)) Dolbegae Publishing Co.

—One Crazy Summer. (J). (gr. 4-7). 2011. (ENG.). 240p. pap. 7.99 (978-0-06-076090-8(7)) 2010. (ENG.). 224p. 16.99 (978-0-06-076088-5(5)) 2010. 224p. lib. bdg. 16.89 (978-0-06-076089-2(3)) HarperCollins Pubs. (Amistad).

—One Crazy Summer. (J). 2011. 1.25 (978-1-4498-2201-9(0)) 2010. 69.75 (978-1-4498-2197-5(9)) 2010. 67.75 (978-1-4498-2199-9(5)) Recorded Bks., Inc.

—One Crazy Summer. 2011. (J). lib. bdg. 17.20 (978-0-606-23555-6(8), Turtleback) Turtleback Bks.

—P. S. Be Eleven. 2015. (ENG.). 304p. (J). (gr. 3-7). pap. 7.99 (978-0-06-193864-1(5), Amistad) HarperCollins Pubs.

Williams, Julie. Drama Queens in the House. 2014. (ENG.). 432p. (YA). (gr. 7). 17.99 (978-1-59643-735-7(9), 9781596437357) Roaring Brook Pr.

Williams, Lori Aurelia. Broken China. 2006. (ENG., Illus.). 272p. (YA). (gr. 7-12). reprint ed. mass mkt. 7.99 *(978-1-4169-1618-5(0),* Simon Pulse) Simon Pulse.

—Shayla's Double Brown Baby Blues. 2003. (ENG., Illus.). 304p. (YA). (gr. 7). pap. 12.99 *(978-0-689-85670-9(9),* Simon & Schuster Bks. For Young Readers) Simon & Schuster Bks. For Young Readers.

—When Kambia Elaine Flew in from Neptune. unabr. ed. 2004. 246p. (J). (gr. 7-18). pap. 50.00 incl. audio *(978-0-8072-8851-1(9),* Listening Library) Random Hse. Audio Publishing Group.

Williams, Teri. I Got Bank! What My Granddad Taught Me about Money. 2010. (ENG., Illus.). 88p. (J). pap. 14.95 *(978-0-9827943-7-1(1))* Beckham Pubns. Group, Inc.

Wingard, Lucinda. The Turn-Around Bird. 2012. 296p. pap. 16.00 *(978-0-9848400-1-4(X))* Plicata Pr. LLC.

Winston, Sherri. President of the Whole Sixth Grade. 2015. (ENG.). 320p. (J). (gr. 3-7). 17.00 *(978-0-316-37723-2(6))* Little Brown & Co.

—The Sweetest Sound. 2017. (ENG.). 272p. (J). (gr. 3-7). 17.99 *(978-0-316-30295-1(3))* Little Brown & Co.

Winthrop, Elizabeth. Squashed in the Middle. Cummins, Pat, illus. 2008. (J). (gr. k-4). 25.95 incl. audio *(978-1-4301-0440-7(6));* 28.95 incl. audio compact disk *(978-1-4301-0443-8(0))* Live Oak Media.

Wittenstein, Barry & Ladd, London. Waiting for Pumpsie. 2017. (ENG., Illus.). 32p. (J). (gr. k-3). lib. bdg. 16.99 *(978-1-58089-545-3(X))* Charlesbridge Publishing, Inc.

Woods, Brenda. Blossoming Universe of Violet Diamond. 2014. (ENG.). 240p. (J). (gr. 3-7). 16.99 *(978-0-399-25714-8(4),* Nancy Paulsen Books) Penguin Young Readers Group.

—Emako Blue. 2005. (ENG.). 128p. (YA). (gr. 7-18). 6.99 *(978-0-14-240418-8(7),* Speak) Penguin Young Readers Group.

—Emako Blue. 2005. 124p. (gr. 7). 16.00 *(978-0-7569-5495-6(9))* Perfection Learning Corp.

—My Name Is Sally Little Song. 2007. (ENG.). 192p. (J). (gr. 3-7). 7.99 *(978-0-14-240943-5(X),* Puffin Books) Penguin Young Readers Group.

—My Name Is Sally Little Song. 2007. (Illus.). 182p. (gr. 2-7). 17.00 *(978-0-7569-8156-3(5))* Perfection Learning Corp.

Woods, Brenda. Zoe in Wonderland. 2017. (ENG.). 224p. (J). (gr. 3-7). 8.99 ***(978-0-425-28891-7(9)***, Puffin Books) Penguin Young Readers Group.

Woods, Brenda & Airgood, Ellen. Zoe in Wonderland. 2016. (ENG.). 208p. (J). (gr. 3-7). 16.99 *(978-0-399-17097-3(9),* Nancy Paulsen Books) Penguin Young Readers Group.

Woodson, Jacqueline. After Tupac & D Foster. 2008. (ENG.). 160p. (J). (gr. 5-18). 17.99 *(978-0-399-24654-8(1),* G.P. Putnam's Sons Books for Young Readers) Penguin Young Readers Group.

—After Tupac & D Foster. 2010. lib. bdg. 18.40 *(978-0-606-10720-4(7),* Turtleback) Turtleback Bks.

—Behind You. 2010. (ENG.). 176p. (YA). (gr. 7-18). 7.99 *(978-0-14-241554-2(5),* Puffin Books) Penguin Young Readers Group.

—Coming on Home Soon. Lewis, Earl & Lewis, E. B., illus. 2004. (ENG.). 32p. (J). (gr. k-3). 17.99 *(978-0-399-23748-5(8),* G.P. Putnam's Sons Books for Young Readers) Penguin Young Readers Group.

—The Dear One. 2010. (ENG.). 176p. (YA). (gr. 7-18). 7.99 *(978-0-14-241705-8(X),* Puffin Books) Penguin Young Readers Group.

—Feathers. (ENG.). (J). (gr. 5-18). 2010. 160p. 8.99 *(978-0-14-241550-4(2),* Speak) 2007. 128p. 16.99 *(978-0-399-23989-2(8),* G.P. Putnam's Sons Books for Young Readers) Penguin Young Readers Group.

—From the Notebooks of Melanin Sun. 2011. 9.68 *(978-0-7848-3512-8(8))* 2009. 7.84 *(978-0-7848-2356-9(1))* Marco Bk. Co. (Everbind).

—From the Notebooks of Melanin Sun. 2010. (ENG.). 176p. (J). (gr. 5-18). 7.99 *(978-0-14-241641-9(X),* Puffin Books) Penguin Young Readers Group.

—From the Notebooks of Melanin Sun. 2003. (Point Ser.). (ENG.). 141p. (YA). (gr. 7). 13.65 *(978-0-7807-7292-2(X))* Perfection Learning Corp.

—The House You Pass on the Way. 2010. (ENG.). 160p. (YA). (gr. 7-18). 8.99 *(978-0-14-241706-5(8),* Puffin Books) Penguin Young Readers Group.

—Hush. 2011. 9.68 *(978-0-7848-3565-4(9),* Everbind) Marco Bk. Co.

—I Hadn't Meant to Tell You This. 2010. (ENG.). 160p. (YA). (gr. 7-18). 7.99 *(978-0-14-241704-1(1),* Puffin Books) Penguin Young Readers Group.

—I Hadn't Meant to Tell You This. 2006. 114p. (YA). (gr. 7-12). 13.65 *(978-0-7569-6730-7(9))* Perfection Learning Corp.

—If You Come Softly & Behind You. 2010. (ENG.). 352p. (YA). (gr. 7-18). 8.99 *(978-0-14-241918-2(4),* Puffin Books) Penguin Young Readers Group.

—Peace, Locomotion. (ENG.). (J). 2010. 176p. (gr. 5-18). 8.99 *(978-0-14-241512-2(X),* Puffin Books) 2009. 144p. (gr. 4-7). 15.99 *(978-0-399-24655-5(X),* G.P. Putnam's Sons Books for Young Readers) Penguin Young Readers Group.

—Pecan Pie Baby. Blackall, Sophie, illus. 2013. (ENG.). 32p. (J). (gr. k-3). 7.99 *(978-0-14-751128-7(3),* Puffin Books) Penguin Young Readers Group.

—Show Way. Talbott, Hudson, illus. 2005. (ENG.). 48p. (J). (gr. -1-3). 17.99 *(978-0-399-23749-2(6),* G.P. Putnam's Sons Books for Young Readers) Penguin Young Readers Group.

Woolf, Julia. Jack's Room. 2009. (Rookie Preschool Ser.). (ENG.). 24p. (J). (gr. -1). 23.00 *(978-0-531-24400-5(8));* pap. 6.95 *(978-0-531-24575-0(6))* Scholastic Library Publishing. (Children's Pr.).

Wright, Barbara. Crow. 2013. (ENG.). 320p. (J). (gr. 5-7). pap. 7.99 *(978-0-375-87367-6(8),* Yearling) Random Hse. Children's Bks.

Wright, Bil. Sunday You Learn How to Box. 2013. (ENG., Illus.). (YA). (gr. 7). 224p. 16.99 *(978-1-4424-7474-1(2));* 240p. pap. 9.99 *(978-1-4424-7472-7(6))* Simon & Schuster Bks. For Young Readers. (Simon & Schuster Bks. For Young Readers).

Wright, Bill & Wright, Bil. When the Black Girl Sings. 2008. (ENG.). 272p. (YA). (gr. 7-12). 16.99 *(978-1-4169-3995-5(4),* Simon & Schuster Bks. For Young Readers) Simon & Schuster Bks. For Young Readers.

—When the Black Girl Sings. 2009. (ENG.). 272p. (YA). (gr. 7). mass mkt. 6.99 *(978-1-4169-4003-6(0),* Simon Pulse) Simon Pulse.

Wright, Richard. Rite of Passage. 2014. (Trophy Bk Ser.). (ENG.). 160p. (J). (gr. 8-12). 13.24 *(978-1-63245-325-9(8))* Lectorum Pubns., Inc.

Wyeth, Sharon Dennis. Message in the Sky Bk. 3: Corey's Underground Railroad Diary. 2003. (My America Ser.). (ENG.). 112p. (J). 10.95 *(978-0-439-37057-8(4),* Scholastic Pr.) Scholastic, Inc.

Yarbrough, Camille. Tamika & the Wisdom Rings. 2004. (J). pap. 5.95 *(978-0-940975-67-5(X),* Sankofa Bks.) Just Us Bks., Inc.

Yoo, Paula. Lily's New Home. Ng-Benitez, Shirley, illus. 2016. (Confetti Kids Ser.). (ENG.). 32p. (J). (gr. -1-3). 14.95 *(978-1-62014-249-3(X))* Lee & Low Bks., Inc.

Zajac, Kristen. Chasing the Spirit of Service. Tucker, Julie, illus. 2013. 24p. 19.95 *(978-1-61633-393-5(6))* Guardian Angel Publishing, Inc.

AFRICAN AMERICANS—HISTORY

Abolitionism. 2010. (Key Concepts in American History Ser.). (Illus.). 128p. (gr. 6-12). 45.00 *(978-1-60413-220-5(5),* Chelsea Hse.) Facts On File, Inc.

African American Eras. 2010. *(978-1-4144-3598-5(3)); (978-1-4144-3599-2(1)); (978-1-4144-3597-8(5)); (978-1-4144-3600-5(9))* Cengage Gale. (UXL).

African American Eras: Contemporary Times, 4 vols. 2010. (Illus.). (J). *(978-1-4144-3592-3(4)); (978-1-4144-3593-0(2)); (978-1-4144-3594-7(0)); (978-1-4144-3595-4(9))* Cengage Gale. (UXL).

The African American Experience: From Slavery to the Presidency. 2015. (African American Experience: from Slavery to the Presidency Ser.). (ENG.). 80p. (YA). (gr. 7-8). 394.80 *(978-1-68048-200-3(9),* Britannica Educational Publishing) Rosen Publishing Group, Inc., The.

African American Heritage Pictures, Puzzles, & Word Games. 2004. (YA). per. 16.00 *(978-0-9758586-0-8(2))* Jenkins-Simmons, Glenda.

African American History. 2004. (Illus.). lib. bdg. 7.95 *(978-0-8225-4422-7(9));* lib. bdg. 7.95 *(978-0-8225-4418-0(0))* Lerner Publishing Group.

Africans in America: America's Journey Through Slavery. 2004. (gr. 7-18). tchr. ed. 19.95 incl. VHS, cd-rom *(978-1-57807-195-1(X),* WG665) WGBH Boston Video.

American Mosaic: African-American Contributions. (Illus.). (gr. 6-12). lib. bdg. *(978-0-7910-8057-3(9),* Chelsea Hse.) Facts On File, Inc.

Aretha, David. The Middle Passage. 2014. xvi, 585p. (J). *(978-1-59935-408-8(X))* Reynolds, Morgan Inc.

—The Murder of Emmett Till. 2007. (Civil Rights Movement Ser.). (Illus.). 160p. (J). (gr. 3-7). lib. bdg. 27.95 *(978-1-59935-057-8(2))* Reynolds, Morgan Inc.

—Selma & the Voting Rights Act. 2007. (Civil Rights Movement Ser.). (Illus.). 128p. (J). (gr. 3-7). lib. bdg. 27.95 *(978-1-59935-056-1(4))* Reynolds, Morgan Inc.

—Sit-Ins & Freedom Rides. 2009. (Civil Rights Movement Ser.). 128p. (J). (gr. 4-7). 28.95 *(978-1-59935-098-1(X))* Reynolds, Morgan Inc.

Arora, Sabina G. The Great Migration & the Harlem Renaissance. 2015. (African American Experience: from Slavery to the Presidency Ser.). (ENG., Illus.). 80p. (J). (gr. 7-8). 32.90 *(978-1-68048-045-0(6),* Britannica Educational Publishing) Rosen Publishing Group, Inc., The.

Arora, Sabina G., ed. The Great Migration & the Harlem Renaissance. 2015. (African American Experience: from Slavery to the Presidency Ser.). (ENG.). 80p. (YA). (gr. 7-8). 65.80 *(978-1-68048-046-7(4),* Britannica Educational Publishing) Rosen Publishing Group, Inc., The.

Bailer, Darice. African-American Culture, 1 vol. 2014. (African-American History Ser.). (ENG.). 48p. (gr. 8-12). 32.79 *(978-1-62403-143-4(9))* ABDO Publishing Co.

Barile, Mary Collins. J. Milton Turner; an American Hero. Guest, Peggy, illus. 2013. 52p. 24.95 *(978-0-9889643-0-3(9))* MathisJones Communications, LLC.

Bernard-Nollins, Sonya M. Here I Stand: A Musical History of African Americans in Battle Creek, Michigan. 2003. (Illus.). (YA). pap. 15.00 *(978-0-9741611-0-5(1))* Fortitude Graphic Design & Printing.

Blair, Margaret Whitman. Liberty or Death: The Surprising Story of Runaway Slaves Who Sided with the British During the American Revolution. 2010. (ENG., Illus.). 64p. (J). (gr. 5-8). 18.95 *(978-1-4263-0590-0(7));* 27.90 *(978-1-4263-0591-7(5))* National Geographic Society. (National Geographic Children's Bks.).

Boerst, William J. Marching in Birmingham. 2007. (Civil Rights Movement Ser.). (Illus.). 112p. (J). (gr. 3-7). lib. bdg. 27.95 *(978-1-59935-055-4(6))* Reynolds, Morgan Inc.

Burgan, Michael. African Americans in the Thirteen Colonies. 2013. (Cornerstones of Freedom™, Third Ser.). (ENG., Illus.). 64p. (J). pap. 8.95 *(978-0-531-21958-4(5));* lib. bdg. 30.00 *(978-0-531-23600-0(5))* Scholastic Library Publishing.

Byers, Ann. African-American History from Emancipation to Today: Rising above the Ashes of Slavery. 2004. (Slavery in American History Ser.). (Illus.). 128p. (J). lib. bdg. 27.94 *(978-0-7660-2153-2(X))* Enslow Pubs., Inc.

Campbell, Ciara. Slavery in America. 2015. (African American Experience: from Slavery to the Presidency Ser.). (ENG., Illus.). 80p. (J). (gr. 7-8). 32.90 *(978-1-68048-036-8(7),* Britannica Educational Publishing) Rosen Publishing Group, Inc., The.

Campbell, Ciara, ed. Slavery in America. 2015. (African American Experience: from Slavery to the Presidency Ser.). (ENG.). 80p. (YA). (gr. 7-8). 65.80 *(978-1-68048-037-5(5),* Britannica Educational Publishing) Rosen Publishing Group, Inc., The.

Cloud Tapper, Suzanne & Tapper, Suzanne Cloud. Views on Slavery: In the Words of Enslaved Africans, Merchants, Owners, & Abolitionists. 2016. (Slavery & Slave Resistance Ser.). (Illus.). 128p. (J). (gr. 6-6). 37.27 *(978-0-7660-7553-5(2))* Enslow Pubs., Inc.

Colins, Luke & Flynn, Riley. Great African Americans, 1 vol. 2014. (Great African-Americans Ser.). (ENG.). 24p. (gr. k-1). lib. bdg. 109.95 *(978-1-4765-7263-5(1),* Pebble Bks.) Capstone Press of Coughlan Cos.

Cook, Michelle. Our Children Can Soar: A Celebration of Rosa, Barack, & the Pioneers of Change. Ford, A. G. et al, illus. 2009. (ENG.). 32p. (J). (gr. -1-3). 16.99 *(978-1-59990-418-4(7),* 9781599904184, Bloomsbury USA Childrens) Bloomsbury Publishing USA.

Corrick, James A. The Civil War & Emancipation. 2007. (Lucent Library of Black History Ser.). (ENG., Illus.). 128p. (gr. 3-7). lib. bdg. 39.40 *(978-1-4205-0008-0(2),* Lucent Bks.) Cengage Gale.

Cunningham, Kevin. Migration from Africa, 1 vol. 2011. (Children's True Stories: Migration Ser.). (ENG.). 32p. (gr. 3-3). pap. 8.29 *(978-1-4109-4078-0(0));* 30.65 *(978-1-4109-4072-8(1))* Heinemann-Raintree. (Raintree Perspectives).

Currie, Stephen. African-American Literature. 2011. (Lucent Library of Black History Ser.). 128p. (J). lib. bdg. 34.80 *(978-1-4205-0383-8(9),* Lucent Bks.) Cengage Gale.

—The Struggle for Equality: Landmark Court Cases. 2009. (Lucent Library of Black History Ser.). (ENG., Illus.). 128p. (gr. 7-10). 39.40 *(978-1-4205-0122-3(4),* Lucent Bks.) Cengage Gale.

Davidson, Tish. African Americans in Business. 2012. (J). pap. *(978-1-4222-2390-1(6))* Mason Crest.

—African Americans in Business. Hill, Marc Lamont, ed. 2012. (Major Black Contributions from Emancipation to Civil Rights Ser.). 64p. (J). (gr. 5). 22.95 *(978-1-4222-2377-2(9))* Mason Crest.

De Medeiros, James. The Migration North. 2013. (J). 29.99 *(978-1-62127-193-2(5))* 2013. (J). pap. 14.95 *(978-1-62127-199-4(4))* 2008. (Illus.). 48p. (YA). (gr. 5-8). pap. 10.95 *(978-1-59036-881-7(9))* 2008. (Illus.). 48p. (YA). (gr. 5-8). lib. bdg. 29.05 *(978-1-59036-880-0(0))* Weigl Pubs., Inc.

—Slavery. 2013. (J). *(978-1-62127-195-6(1))* 2013. (J). pap. *(978-1-62127-201-4(X))* 2008. (Illus.). 48p. (YA). (gr. 5-8). pap. 10.95 *(978-1-59036-875-6(4))* 2008. (Illus.). 48p. (YA). (gr. 5-8). lib. bdg. 29.05 *(978-1-59036-874-9(6))* Weigl Pubs., Inc.

Donovan, Sandra. The African American Experience. 2010. (USA TODAY Cultural Mosaic Ser.). (ENG., Illus.). 80p. (gr. 6-8). lib. bdg. 33.26 *(978-0-7613-4084-3(X))* Lerner Publishing Group.

Drama of African-American History, 5 bks., Set. Incl. Africa: A Look Back. Haskins, James & Benson, Kathleen. 80p. (J). (gr. 6-7). lib. bdg. 35.64 *(978-0-7614-2148-1(3));* Civil War. Jordan, Anne Devereaux. 72p. (J). (gr. 3-7). lib. bdg. 35.64 *(978-0-7614-2179-5(3));* Reconstruction Era. Stroud, Bettye. 80p. (gr. 6-7). lib. bdg. 35.64 *(978-0-7614-2181-8(5));* Slave Trade & the Middle Passage. Sharp, S. Pearl. 80p. (gr. 6-7). lib. bdg. 35.64 *(978-0-7614-2176-4(9));* Slavery & Resistance. Jordan, Anne Devereaux. 80p. (gr. 6-7). lib. bdg. 35.64 *(978-0-7614-2178-8(5));* (Illus.). 2006. 2007. Set lib. bdg. 178.21 *(978-0-7614-2174-0(2),* Benchmark Bks.) Marshall Cavendish Corp.

Durden, Robert F. The Life of Carter G. Woodson: Father of African-American History. 2014. (Legendary African Americans Ser.). (Illus.). 96p. (J). (gr. 6-12). pap. 10.95 *(978-0-7660-6123-1(X))* Enslow Pubs., Inc.

Durden, Robert Franklin. The Life of Carter G.Woodson: Father of African-American History. 2014. (Legendary African Americans Ser.). 96p. (J). (gr. 6-12). 27.94 *(978-0-7660-6122-4(1))* Enslow Pubs., Inc.

Ellis, Barbara C. Brain Quest Black History. 2004. 131.40 *(978-0-7611-2580-8(9),* 22580) Workman Publishing Co., Inc.

Exceptional African Americans. 2015. (Exceptional African Americans Ser.). (ENG.). 24p. (J). (gr. 3-4). pap., pap., pap. 56.10 *(978-0-7660-7050-9(6));* pap., pap., pap. 336.60 *(978-0-7660-6671-7(1))* Enslow Pubs., Inc.

Fandel, Jennifer. Martin Luther King, Jr. 2005. (Genius Ser.). (Illus.). 48p. (J). (gr. 5-9). lib. bdg. 21.95 *(978-1-58341-329-6(4),* Creative Education) Creative Co., The.

Feinstein, Stephen. Lee sobre Martin Luther King, Jr. 2006. (I Like Biographies! Bilingual Ser.).Tr. of Read about Martin Luther King, Jr. (ENG & SPA., Illus.). 24p. (J). (gr. 1-3). lib. bdg. 22.60 *(978-0-7660-2745-9(7),* Enslow Elementary) Enslow Pubs., Inc.

Fiorelli, June Estep. Fannie Lou Hamer: A Voice for Freedom. 2004. (Avisson Young Adult Ser.). (Illus.). 117p. (J). pap. 19.95 *(978-1-888105-62-9(3))* Avisson Pr., Inc.

Fisher-Shumpert, Sharon Y. Sadie's Hero. 2007. 42p. (J). pap. 10.00 *(978-0-9794871-0-1(2))* SYS Publishing.

Fitts, Leticia. The Black Legacy Learning Series: African American Sheroes & Heroes. 2011. pap. 18.95 *(978-0-7414-6522-1(1))* Infinity Publishing.

Flanagan, Timothy. Reconstruction: A Primary Source History of the Struggle to Unite the North & South after the Civil War. 2005. (Primary Sources in American History Ser.). (Illus.). 64p. (J). (gr. 5-8). lib. bdg. 31.95 *(978-1-4042-0177-4(7))* Rosen Publishing Group, Inc., The.

Ford, Carin T. Lincoln, Slavery, & the Emancipation Proclamation. 2004. (Civil War Library). (Illus.). 48p. (J). lib. bdg. 25.27 *(978-0-7660-2252-2(8))* Enslow Pubs., Inc.

Fremon, David K. The Jim Crow Laws & Racism in United States History. 2014. (In United States History Ser.). (Illus.). 96p. (J). (gr. 5-12). 27.94 *(978-0-7660-6092-0(6));* pap. 10.95 *(978-0-7660-6093-7(4))* Enslow Pubs., Inc.

Giovanni, Nikki. On My Journey Now: Looking at African-American History Through the Spirituals. (ENG., Illus.). 128p. (J). (gr. 7-9). 2009. pap. 9.99 *(978-0-7636-4380-5(7))* 2007. 18.99 *(978-0-7636-2885-7(9))* Candlewick Pr.

Glaser, Jason. The Buffalo Soldiers & the American West. Smith, Tod G. et al, illus. 2005. (Graphic History Ser.). (ENG.). 32p. (gr. 3-4). 30.65 *(978-0-7368-4966-1(1),* Graphic Library) Capstone Press of Coughlan Cos.

Goldsworthy, Steve. Politics: African American History. 2011. (J). (gr. 5-8). pap. 14.95 *(978-1-61690-666-5(9),* AV2 by Weigl); (Illus.). 48p. (gr. 1-4). 29.99 *(978-1-61690-662-7(6))* Weigl Pubs., Inc.

Greene, Meg & Malvasi, Meg Greene. Into the Land of Freedom: African Americans in Reconstruction. 2004. (People's History Ser.). (ENG., Illus.). 96p. (gr. 5-12). lib. bdg. 33.26 *(978-0-8225-4690-0(6))* Lerner Publishing Group.

Halpern, Monica. Moving North: African Americans & the Great Migration 1915-1930. 2005. (Crossroads America Ser.). (ENG., Illus.). 40p. (gr. k-3). 21.90 *(978-0-7922-8358-4(9));* 12.95 *(978-0-7922-8278-5(7))* National Geographic Society. (National Geographic Children's Bks.).

Halpern, Monica & National Geographic Learning Staff. The Great Migration: African Americans Move to the North, 1915-1930. 2006. (Nonfiction Reading & Writing Workshops Ser.). (ENG., Illus.). 40p. (J). pap. 19.95 *(978-0-7922-8677-6(4))* CENGAGE Learning.

Hansen, Joyce & McGowan, Gary. Freedom Roads: Searching for the Underground Railroad. Ransome, James E., illus. 2003. (ENG.). 166p. (J). (gr. 5-9). 18.95 *(978-0-8126-2673-5(7))* Cricket Bks.

Hardy, P. Stephen & Hardy, Sheila. Extraordinary People of the Civil Rights Movement. 2006. (Extraordinary People Ser.). (ENG., Illus.). 288p. (J). (gr. 6-18). lib. bdg. 40.00 *(978-0-516-25461-6(8),* Children's Pr.) Scholastic Library Publishing.

Harkrader, Lisa. Reconstruction & Aftermath of the Civil War: A MyReportLinks. com Book. 2004. (American Civil War Ser.). (Illus.). 48p. (J). lib. bdg. 25.26 *(978-0-7660-5265-9(6),* MyReportLinks.com Bks.) Enslow Pubs., Inc.

Harris, Irene. African American Migrations in North America, 01 vols., 1. 2016. (Spotlight on Immigration & Migration Ser.). (ENG., Illus.). 24p. (J). pap. 10.00 *(978-1-5081-4046-7(4),* PowerKids Pr.) Rosen Publishing Group, Inc., The.

Haskins, James & Benson, Kathleen. Africa: A Look Back. 2006. (Drama of African-American History Ser.). (Illus.). 80p. (J). (gr. 6-7). lib. bdg. 35.64 *(978-0-7614-2148-1(3),* Benchmark Bks.) Marshall Cavendish Corp.

Haskins, Jim. Delivering Justice: W. W. Law & the Fight for Civil Rights. Andrews, Benny, illus. 2008. (ENG.). 32p. (J). (gr. k-3). pap. 7.99 *(978-0-7636-3880-1(3))* Candlewick Pr.

Heroes of Black History. 2015. (Heroes of Black History Ser.). (ENG.). 32p. (J). (gr. 3-4). pap., pap., pap. 63.00 *(978-1-4824-3479-8(2))* Stevens, Gareth Publishing LLLP.

Hinton, Kerry. The Black Power Movement & Civil Unrest. 2017. (J). pap. ***(978-1-5383-8016-1(1))*** Rosen Publishing Group, Inc., The.

Howse, Jennifer. The Civil War. 2008. (African American History Ser.). (Illus.). 48p. (YA). (gr. 5-8). pap. 10.95 *(978-1-59036-877-0(0));* lib. bdg. 29.05 *(978-1-59036-876-3(2))* Weigl Pubs., Inc.

—Civil War. 2013. (J). *(978-1-62127-191-8(9));* pap. *(978-1-62127-197-0(8))* Weigl Pubs., Inc.

—Reconstruction. 2013. (J). *(978-1-62127-194-9(3))* 2013. (J). pap. *(978-1-62127-200-7(1))* 2008. (Illus.). 48p. (YA). (gr. 5-8). pap. 10.95 *(978-1-59036-879-4(7))* 2008. (Illus.). 48p. (YA). (gr. 5-8). lib. bdg. 29.05 *(978-1-59036-878-7(9))* Weigl Pubs., Inc.

Huey, Lois Miner. Forgotten Bones: Uncovering a Slave Cemetery. 2015. (ENG., Illus.). 56p. (gr. 4-8). 30.65 *(978-1-4677-6300-4(4),* Millbrook Pr.) Lerner Publishing Group.

Hussey, Maria. The Rise of the Jim Crow ERA. 2015. (African American Experience: from Slavery to the Presidency Ser.). (ENG., Illus.). 80p. (J). (gr. 7-8). 32.90 *(978-1-68048-042-9(1),* Britannica Educational Publishing) Rosen Publishing Group, Inc., The.

Hussey, Maria, ed. The Rise of the Jim Crow Era. 2015. (African American Experience: from Slavery to the Presidency Ser.). (ENG.). 80p. (YA). (gr. 7-8). 65.80 *(978-1-68048-043-6(X),* Britannica Educational Publishing) Rosen Publishing Group, Inc., The.

Jordan, Anne Devereaux. The Civil War. 2006. (Drama of African-American History Ser.). (Illus.). 72p. (J). (gr. 3-7). lib. bdg. 35.64 *(978-0-7614-2179-5(3),* Benchmark Bks.) Marshall Cavendish Corp.

—Slavery & Resistance. 2006. (Drama of African-American History Ser.). (Illus.). 80p. (gr. 6-7). lib. bdg. 35.64 *(978-0-7614-2178-8(5),* Benchmark Bks.) Marshall Cavendish Corp.

Jr. Graphic African American History. 2013. (Jr. Graphic African American History Ser.). 24p. (J). (gr. 3-6). 151.50 *(978-1-4777-1547-5(9));* pap. 381.60 *(978-1-4777-2672-3(1));* pap. 63.60 *(978-1-4777-2671-6(3))* Rosen Publishing Group, Inc., The. (PowerKids Pr.).

Kallen, Stuart A. A History of Free Blacks in America. 2006. (Lucent Library of Black History). (ENG., Illus.). 112p. (YA). (gr. 7-10). lib. bdg. 33.45 *(978-1-59018-776-0(8),* Lucent Bks.) Cengage Gale.

—Marcus Garvey & the Back to Africa Movement. 2006. (Lucent Library of Black History). (ENG., Illus.). 112p. (YA). (gr. 7-10). lib. bdg. 34.80 *(978-1-59018-838-5(1),* Lucent Bks.) Cengage Gale.

—A Travel Guide to Harlem Renaissance. 2003. (Travel Guide To Ser.). (ENG.). (J). 30.85 *(978-1-59018-358-8(4),* Lucent Bks.) Cengage Gale.

Kimmel, Allison Crotzer. A Primary Source History of Slavery in the United States. 2015. (Primary Source History Ser.). (ENG.). 32p. (gr. 3-4). lib. bdg. 27.32 *(978-1-4914-1839-0(7))* Capstone Press of Coughlan Cos.

Kingston, Anna. Respecting the Contributions of African Americans. 2012. (Stop Bullying Now! Ser.). (ENG., Illus.). 24p. (J). (gr. 3-6). 22.60 *(978-1-4488-7448-4(3));* pap. 8.25 *(978-1-4488-7521-4(8))* Rosen Publishing Group, Inc., The. (PowerKids Pr.).

Kishel, Ann-Marie. Rosa Parks: Una Vida de Valentia. Translations.com Staff, tr. 2006. (Libros para Avanzar-Biografías (Pull Ahead Books-Biographies) Ser.). (ENG & SPA., Illus.). 32p. (gr. k-3). lib. bdg. 22.60 *(978-0-8225-6239-9(1))* Lerner Publishing Group.

Kunjufu, Jawanza & Prescott, Folami. Kindergarten: Self-Esteem Through Culture Leads to Academic Excellence. 2003. (ENG.). 60p. (J). (gr. k). pap. 9.95 *(978-0-913543-85-6(3))* African American Images.

—Self-Esteem Through Culture Leads to Academic Excellence. 2003. (ENG.). 60p. (J). (gr. 8). pap. 9.95 *(978-0-913543-93-1(4));* (gr. 9-12). pap. 14.95 *(978-0-913543-94-8(2))* African American Images.

—SETCLAE, Fifth Grade: Self-Esteem Through Culture Leads to Academic Excellence. 2003. (ENG.). 60p. (J). (gr. 5). pap. 9.95 *(978-0-913543-90-0(X))* African American Images.

—SETCLAE, First Grade: Self-Esteem Through Culture Leads to Academic Excellence. 2003. (ENG.). 60p. (J). (gr. 1). pap. 9.95 *(978-0-913543-86-3(1))* African American Images.

—SETCLAE, Fourth Grade: Self-Esteem Through Culture Leads to Academic Excellence. 2003. (ENG.). 60p. (J). (gr. 4). pap. 9.95 *(978-0-913543-89-4(6))* African American Images.

—SETCLAE, Second Grade: Self-Esteem Through Culture Leads to Academic Excellence. 2003. (ENG.). 60p. (J). (gr. 2). pap. 9.95 (978-0-913543-87-0(X)) African American Images.

—SETCLAE, Seventh Grade: Self-Esteem Through Culture Leads to Academic Excellence. 2003. (ENG.). 60p. (J). (gr. 7). pap. 9.95 (978-0-913543-92-4(6)) African American Images.

—SETCLAE, Sixth Grade: Self-Esteem Through Culture Leads to Academic Excellence. 2003. (ENG.). 60p. (J). (gr. 6). pap. 9.95 (978-0-913543-91-7(8)) African American Images.

—SETCLAE, Third Grade: Self-Esteem Through Culture Leads to Academic Excellence. 2003. (ENG.). 60p. (J). (gr. 3). pap. 9.95 (978-0-913543-88-7(8)) African American Images.

Kurtz, Jane. Martin's Dream. Bates, Amy June, illus. 2008. (Ready-To-Reads Ser.). (ENG.). 32p. (J). (gr. -1-1). pap. 3.99 (978-1-4169-2774-7(3), Simon Spotlight) Simon Spotlight.

Lassieur, Allison. Harlem Renaissance: An Interactive History Adventure. 2013. (You Choose: History Ser.). (ENG.). 112p. (gr. 3-4). pap. 6.95 (978-1-4765-3609-5(0)); 31.99 (978-1-4765-0256-4(0)) Capstone Press of Coughlan Cos. (You Choose Bks.).

Latta, Susan M. Reconstruction Era, 1 vol. 2014. (African-American History Ser.). (ENG.). 48p. (gr. 8-12). lib. bdg. 32.79 (978-1-62403-147-2(1)) ABDO Publishing Co.

Lee, Spike & Lee, Tonya Lewis. Please, Baby, Please. Nelson, Kadir, illus. 2006. (ENG.). 32p. (J). (gr. -1-3). reprint ed. 7.99 (978-0-689-83457-8(8), Simon & Schuster Bks. For Young Readers) Simon & Schuster Bks. For Young Readers.

Leeper, Angela. Juneteenth: A Day to Celebrate Freedom from Slavery. 2004. (Finding Out about Holidays Ser.). (Illus.). 48p. (J). (gr. 3-5). lib. bdg. 25.27 (978-0-7660-2206-5(4)) Enslow Pubs., Inc.

Levin, Judy. A Timeline of the Abolitionist Movement. 2009. (Timelines of American History Ser.). 32p. (gr. 4-4). 47.90 (978-1-60854-381-6(1), Rosen Reference) Rosen Publishing Group, Inc., The.

Levinson, Cynthia Y. We've Got a Job: The 1963 Birmingham Children's March, 1 vol. 2012. (ENG.). 192p. (J). 19.95 (978-1-56145-627-7(6)) Peachtree Pubs.

Lilly, Melinda. San Agustin (St Augustine) Rhine, Karen C., illus. 2005. (Lecturas Historicas Norteamericanas (Reading American Histor Ser.). 24p. (J). (gr. 3-7). lib. bdg. 22.79 (978-1-59515-637-2(2)) Rourke Educational Media.

Linde, Barbara M. Slavery in Early America. 2011. (Story of America Ser.). (Illus.). 32p. (J). (gr. 4-6). lib. bdg. 26.60 (978-1-4339-4776-6(5), Gareth Stevens Learning Library) Stevens, Gareth Publishing LLLP.

Linney, Susan. Martin Luther King, Jr: With a Discussion of Responsibility. 2004. (Values in Action Ser.). (J). (978-1-59203-069-9(6)) Learning Challenge, Inc.

Littlejohn, Randy. A Timeline of the Slave Trade in America. 2009. (Timelines of American History Ser.). 32p. (gr. 4-4). 47.90 (978-1-60854-390-8(0), Rosen Reference) Rosen Publishing Group, Inc., The.

Lowery, Zoe. The African American Experience: From Slavery to the Presidency Set. 2015. (African American Experience: from Slavery to the Presidency Ser.). (ENG.). 80p. (YA). (gr. 7-8). 197.40 (978-1-68048-139-6(8), Britannica Educational Publishing) Rosen Publishing Group, Inc., The.

Magoon, Kekla. Today the World Is Watching You: The Little Rock Nine & the Fight for School Integration 1957. 2011. (Civil Rights Struggles around the World Ser.). (ENG., Illus.). 160p. (gr. 9-12). 38.60 (978-0-7613-5767-4(X)) Lerner Publishing Group.

Main, Mary & Thomason, Cathy. African-Americans in Law & Politics. 2012. (J). pap. (978-1-4222-2391-8(4)) Mason Crest.

—African-Americans in Law & Politics. Hill, Marc Lamont, ed. 2012. (Major Black Contributions from Emancipation to Civil Rights Ser.). 64p. (J). (gr. 5). 22.95 (978-1-4222-2378-9(7)) Mason Crest.

Mara, Wil. Martin Luther King Jr. 2013. (Rookie Biographies(r) Ser.). (ENG.). 32p. (J). pap. 5.95 (978-0-531-24704-4(X)); lib. bdg. 23.00 (978-0-531-24738-9(4)) Scholastic Library Publishing.

Martin, Isabel. Frederick Douglass, 1 vol. 2014. (Great African-Americans Ser.). (ENG., Illus.). 24p. (gr. k-1). pap. 5.95 (978-1-4914-0507-9(4), Pebble Bks.) Capstone Press of Coughlan Cos.

McClaurin, Irma & Schomp, Virginia. Facing the Future. 2007. (Drama of African-American History Ser.). 80p. (gr. 6). lib. bdg. 35.64 (978-0-7614-2644-8(2), Benchmark Bks.) Marshall Cavendish Corp.

McMickle, Marvin Andrew. Profiles in Black: Phat Facts for Teens. Elster, Jean Alicia, ed. 2008. (Illus.). 176p. (J). pap. 22.00 (978-0-8170-1508-4(6)) Judson Pr.

McNeese, Tim. The Rise & Fall of American Slavery: Freedom Denied, Freedom Gained. 2004. (Slavery in American History Ser.). (Illus.). 128p. (J). lib. bdg. 27.94 (978-0-7660-2156-3(4)) Enslow Pubs., Inc.

Meadows, James. Slavery: The Struggle for Freedom. 2009. (Journey to Freedom Ser.). (ENG., Illus.). 32p. (J). (gr. 4-7). 29.93 (978-1-60253-134-5(X), 200400) Child's World, Inc., The.

Media Projects, Inc., Staff, contrib. by. Student Almanac of African American History, 2 vols. 2003. (Middle School Reference Ser.). (Illus.). 144p. (C). (gr. 6-8). 101.00 (978-0-313-32596-0(0), MS2596, Greenwood) ABC-CLIO, LLC.

Metz, Lorijo. The Abolitionist Movement, 1 vol., 1. 2014. (Let's Celebrate Freedom! Ser.). (ENG.). 24p. (J). (gr. 3-6). 23.60 (978-1-4777-2897-0(X), PowerKids Pr.) Rosen Publishing Group, Inc., The.

—El Movimiento Abolicionista / the Abolitionist Movement, 1 vol., 1. Beullens-Maoui, Nathalie, ed. 2014. (¡Celebremos la Libertad! / Let's Celebrate Freedom! Ser.). (SPA & BYN.). 24p. (J). (gr. 3-6). 23.60 (978-1-4777-3249-6(7), PowerKids Pr.) Rosen Publishing Group, Inc., The.

Moreno, Barry. The African Americans. (Major American Immigration Ser.). (YA). 2010. (Illus.). 64p. (gr. 9-12). 22.95 (978-1-4222-0603-4(3)) 2007. pap. 9.95 (978-1-4222-0670-6(X)) Mason Crest.

National Geographic Learning, National Geographic Learning & Rossi, Ann. Reading Expeditions - The Anti-Slavery Movement. 2007. (Rise & Shine Ser.). (ENG.). 40p. pap. 19.95 (978-0-7922-8622-6(7)) National Geographic School Publishing, Inc.

Nelson, Kadir. Heart & Soul: The Story of America & African Americans. Nelson, Kadir, illus. (Illus.). (J). (gr. 1-5). 2013. (ENG.). 112p. pap. 8.99 (978-0-06-173079-5(3)) 2011. (ENG., 108p. 19.99 (978-0-06-173074-0(2)) 2011. 108p. lib. bdg. 20.89 (978-0-06-173076-4(9)) HarperCollins Pubs.

—Heart & Soul: The Story of America & African Americans. 2013. (J). lib. bdg. 19.65 (978-0-606-35050-1(0), Turtleback) Turtleback Bks.

O'Connell, Kim A. Slavery, Emancipation, & the Civil War: A MyReportLinks. com Book. 2004. (American Civil War Ser.). (Illus.). 48p. (J). lib. bdg. 26.60 (978-0-7660-5190-4(0), MyReportLinks.com Bks.) Enslow Pubs., Inc.

Ollhoff, Jim. African-American History, 6 vols., Set. Incl. Civil Rights Movement. 27.07 (978-1-61714-709-8(5)); Civil War. lib. bdg. 27.07 (978-1-61714-710-4(9)); Courage & Growth. lib. bdg. 27.07 (978-1-61714-711-1(7)); Pioneers of Equality. lib. bdg. 27.07 (978-1-61714-712-8(5)); Roots of Humanity. lib. bdg. 27.07 (978-1-61714-713-5(3)); Years of Slavery. lib. bdg. 27.07 (978-1-61714-714-2(1)); (YA). (gr. 5-9). (African-American History Ser.). (Illus.). 32p. 2011. 162.42 (978-1-61714-708-1(7), Abdo & Daughters) ABDO Publishing Co.

—Pioneers of Equality, 1 vol. 2011. (African American History Ser.). (ENG., Illus.). 32p. (YA). (gr. 5-9). lib. bdg. 27.07 (978-1-61714-712-8(5)) ABDO Publishing Co.

—The Roots of Humanity, 1 vol. 2011. (African American History Ser.). (ENG., Illus.). 32p. (YA). (gr. 5-9). lib. bdg. 27.07 (978-1-61714-713-5(3)) ABDO Publishing Co.

—Years of Slavery, 1 vol. 2011. (African American History Ser.). (ENG., Illus.). 32p. (YA). (gr. 5-9). lib. bdg. 27.07 (978-1-61714-714-2(1)) ABDO Publishing Co.

Osborne, Linda Barrett. Miles to Go for Freedom: Segregation & Civil Rights in the Jim Crow Years. 2012. (ENG., Illus.). 128p. (J). (gr. 3-7). 25.99 (978-1-4197-0020-0(0), Abrams Bks. for Young Readers) Abrams, Inc.

—Traveling the Freedom Road: From Slavery & the Civil War Through Reconstruction. 2009. (ENG., Illus.). 128p. (J). (gr. 3-7). 25.95 (978-0-8109-8338-0(9), Abrams Bks. for Young Readers) Abrams, Inc.

Palmer, Kate Salley. Almost Invisible Blk Patriots. Palmer, Kate Salley, illus. 2008. (ENG., Illus.). 56p. (J). pap. 11.95 (978-0-9667114-6-2(7)) Warbranch Pr., Inc.

Peppas, Lynn. Juneteenth. 2010. (Celebrations in My World Ser.). (ENG.). 32p. (J). (gr. k-3). (978-0-7787-4928-8(2)); pap. (978-0-7787-4935-6(5)) Crabtree Publishing Co.

Perritano, John. Free at Last! How the Freeing of the Slaves Changed American History. 2008. (Graphic America Ser.). (ENG., Illus.). 32p. (J). (gr. 3-6). pap. (978-0-7787-4212-8(1)); lib. bdg. (978-0-7787-4185-5(0)) Crabtree Publishing Co.

Pierce, Alan. Montgomery Bus Boycott, 1 vol. 2005. (American Moments Ser.). (ENG., Illus.). 48p. (gr. 4-8). 27.07 (978-1-59197-935-7(8), Abdo & Daughters) ABDO Publishing Co.

Raabe, Emily. Buffalo Soldiers & the Western Frontier. 2009. (Westward Ho! Ser.). 24p. (gr. 2-3). 42.50 (978-1-60854-759-3(0), PowerKids Pr.) Rosen Publishing Group, Inc., The.

Rappaport, Doreen. Free at Last! Stories & Songs of Emancipation. Evans, Shane W., illus. 2006. (ENG.). 64p. (J). (gr. 4-7). pap. 9.99 (978-0-7636-3147-5(7)) Candlewick Pr.

Rissman, Rebecca. Slavery in the United States, 1 vol. 2014. (African-American History Ser.). (ENG.). 48p. (gr. 8-12). 32.79 (978-1-62403-148-9(X)) ABDO Publishing Co.

Robertson, Theda Robinson. Journey to a Free Land: The Story of Nicodemus, the First All Black Town West of the Mississippi. 2006. (Illus.). (J). (978-0-9705721-6-5(6)) Written Images, Inc.

Rosen Publishing Staff. The African American Quartet, 1 vol. 2015. (African American Quartet Ser.). (ENG.). 48p. (J). 121.00 (978-1-4777-9293-3(7), Windmill Bks.) Rosen Publishing Group, Inc., The.

Ruth, Annie. I Can Read. Ruth, Annie, illus. l.t. ed. 2005. (Illus.). 32p. (J). (gr. -1-3). pap. 10.00 (978-0-9656306-7-2(6)) Ruth, A. Creations.

Sanders, Nancy I. A Kid's Guide to African American History: More Than 70 Activities. 2nd ed. 2007. (Kid's Guide Ser.). (ENG., Illus.). 256p. (J). (gr. 2-4). pap. 16.95 (978-1-55652-653-4(9)) Chicago Review Pr., Inc.

Sharp, Anne Wallace, ed. The Freedom Rides. 2012. (Lucent Library of Black History Ser.). (ENG., Illus.). 128p. (gr. 7-10). lib. bdg. 39.40 (978-1-4205-0732-4(X), Lucent Bks.) Cengage Gale.

Shea, Therese. The African Burial Ground. 2016. (Hidden History Ser.). 00032p. (J). pap. 10.50 (978-1-4824-5787-2(3)) Stevens, Gareth Publishing LLLP.

Sioux, Tracee. African American Migration. 2004. (Primary Sources of Immigration & Migration in America Ser.). (ENG., Illus.). 24p. (gr. 4-8). pap. 9.40 (978-0-8239-8953-9(4), PowerKids Pr.) Rosen Publishing Group, Inc., The.

Sirimarco, Elizabeth. The Time of Slavery. 2006. (American Voices Ser.). (Illus.). 114p. (J). (gr. 3-7). lib. bdg. 38.50 (978-0-7614-2169-6(6), Benchmark Bks.) Marshall Cavendish Corp.

Slade, Suzanne. Climbing Lincoln's Steps. Bootman, Colin, illus. 2016. (ENG.). 32p. (J). (gr. -1-3). pap. 6.99 (978-0-8075-1205-0(2)) Whitman, Albert & Co.

Smith, Charles R., Jr. Brick by Brick. Cooper, Floyd, illus. 2015. (ENG.). 32p. (J). (gr. -1-3). pap. 6.99 (978-0-06-192084-4(3), Amistad) HarperCollins Pubs.

—Brick by Brick. 2015. (J). lib. bdg. 17.20 (978-0-606-37371-5(3)) Turtleback Bks.

—28 Days: Moments in Black History That Changed the World. Evans, Shane W., illus. 2015. (ENG.). 56p. (J). (gr. -1-5). 18.99 (978-1-59643-820-0(7), 9781596438200) Roaring Brook Pr.

Sterling, Kristin. Mary Mcleod Bethune: A Life of Resourcefulness. 2008. (Pull Ahead Books-Biographies Ser.). (ENG., Illus.). 32p. (gr. k-3). lib. bdg. 22.60 (978-0-8225-8588-6(X), Lerner Pubns.) Lerner Publishing Group.

Stewart, Gail B. Fighting for Freedom: Blacks in the American Military. 2006. (Lucent Library of Black History Ser.). (ENG., Illus.). 104p. (J). (gr. 3-7). lib. bdg. 34.80 (978-1-59018-952-8(3), Lucent Bks.) Cengage Gale.

Stroud, Bettye. The Reconstruction Era. 2006. (Drama of African-American History Ser.). (Illus.). 80p. (gr. 6-7). lib. bdg. 35.64 (978-0-7614-2181-8(5), Benchmark Bks.) Marshall Cavendish Corp.

Sullivan, Laura L. The Colonial Slave Family. 2015. (Colonial People Ser.). (ENG., Illus.). 48p. (J). (gr. 4-4). 31.36 (978-1-5026-0486-6(8)) Cavendish Square Publishing.

Szulhan, Rebecca. Contemporary Achievements. 2013. (J). (978-1-62127-192-5(7)) 2013. (J). pap. (978-1-62127-198-7(6)) 2008. (Illus.). 48p. (YA). (gr. 5-8). pap. 10.95 (978-1-59036-885-5(1)) 2008. (Illus.). 48p. (YA). (gr. 5-8). lib. bdg. 29.05 (978-1-59036-884-8(3)) Weigl Pubs., Inc.

Tarrant-Reid, Linda. Discovering Black America: From the Age of Exploration to the Twenty-First Century. 2012. (ENG., Illus.). 244p. (J). (gr. 3-7). 29.95 (978-0-8109-7098-4(8), Abrams Bks. for Young Readers) Abrams, Inc.

Taylor, Charlotte & Miller, Mara. The Little Rock Nine & School Desegregation. 2015. (Our Shared History Ser.). (ENG., Illus.). 128p. (J). (gr. 7-7). lib. bdg. 37.27 (978-0-7660-7010-3(7)) Enslow Pubs., Inc.

Taylor, Mildred D. Roll of Thunder, Hear My Cry (Puffin Modern Classics) 25th rev. ed. 2014. (Puffin Modern Classics Ser.). (ENG.). 288p. (J). 12.24 (978-1-63245-097-5(6)) Lectorum Pubns., Inc.

Thornton, Jeremy. Immigration & the Slave Trade: Africans Come to America, 1607-1830. 2004. (Primary Sources of Immigration & Migration in America Ser.). (ENG., Illus.). 24p. (gr. 4-8). pap. 9.40 (978-0-8239-8955-3(0), PowerKids Pr.) Rosen Publishing Group, Inc., The.

Turner, Glennette Tilley. Fort Mosé: And the Story of the Man Who Built the First Free Black Settlement in Colonial America. 2010. (ENG., Illus.). 48p. (J). (gr. 3-7). 18.95 (978-0-8109-4056-7(6), Abrams Bks. for Young Readers) Abrams, Inc.

Uschan, Michael V. Reconstruction. 2007. (Lucent Library of Black History Ser.). (ENG., Illus.). 128p. (gr. 3-7). lib. bdg. 39.40 (978-1-4205-0009-7(0), Lucent Bks.) Cengage Gale.

—The Scottsboro Case. 2004. (Landmark Events in American History Ser.). (Illus.). 48p. (gr. 5-12). lib. bdg. 31.00 (978-0-8368-5388-9(1), Gareth Stevens Secondary Library) Stevens, Gareth Publishing LLLP.

Vaughn, Wally G. & Davis, Mattie Campbell, eds. The Selma Campaign, 1963-1965: The Decisive Battle of the Civil Rights Movement. 2006. (ENG., Illus.). 244p. pap. 19.95 (978-0-912469-44-7(7)) Majority Pr., The.

Wallenfeldt, Jeffrey H., ed. African American History & Culture, 3 vols., Set. Incl. Africa to America: From the Middle Passage Through the 1930s. 272p. lib. bdg. 45.00 (978-1-61530-126-3(7)); Black American Biographies: The Journey of Achievement. 408p. lib. bdg. 45.00 (978-1-61530-137-9(2)); Black Experience in America: From Civil Rights to the Present. 232p. lib. bdg. 45.00 (978-1-61530-146-1(1)); (YA). (gr. 9-12). 2010. (Illus.). 232 - 408p. 2010. Set lib. bdg. 135.00 (978-1-61530-151-5(8)) Rosen Publishing Group, Inc., The.

Walsh, Frank. The Montgomery Bus Boycott. 2003. (Landmark Events in American History Ser.). (Illus.). 48p. (gr. 5-12). pap. 14.05 (978-0-8368-5403-9(9), Gareth Stevens Secondary Library) Stevens, Gareth Publishing LLLP.

Weatherford, Carole Boston. Schomburg: The Man Who Built a Library. Velasquez, Eric, illus. 2017. (ENG.). 48p. (J). (gr. 4-7). 16.99 **(978-0-7636-8046-6(X))** Candlewick Pr.

—Schomburg: The Man Who Built a Library. 2017. (J). 31.99 **(978-1-5200-8717-7(9))**; 31.99 **(978-1-5200-8716-0(0))** Dreamscape Media, LLC.

Wells-Cole, Catherine. Slavery & the Forging of Early America. 2014. (J). (978-1-59935-410-1(1)) Reynolds, Morgan Inc.

West, Lorraine, illus. The Mirror & Me. 2005. 40p. (J). per. 12.95 (978-0-9768674-0-1(0)) Hit Records, LLC.

Whitman Blair, Margaret. Liberty or Death: The Surprising Story of Runaway Slaves Who Sided with the British During the American Revolution (Large Print 16pt) l.t. ed. 2013. 122p. pap. (978-1-4596-6716-7(6)) ReadHowYouWant.com, Ltd.

Wills, Ora, ed. Images in Black: A Pictorial History of Black Pensacola. 2004. (Illus.). 224p. 30.00 (978-0-9659142-6-0(7)) Univ. of West Florida Foundation, Inc.

Wirkner, Linda. Learning about the Settlement of the Americas with Graphic Organizers. 2006. (Graphic Organizers in Science & Social Studies Ser.). (ENG.). 24p. (gr. 4-6). pap. 8.25 (978-1-4042-5057-4(3), Rosen Classroom) Rosen Publishing Group, Inc., The.

Wistrand, Carolyn Nur. Beauty in Black Performance: Plays for African American Youth. 2006. (Illus.). (YA). 151p. (978-1-59221-379-5(0)); (ENG., 158p. pap. (978-1-59221-380-1(4)) Africa World Pr.

Worth, Richard. Africans in America. 2004. (Immigration to the United States Ser.). (Illus.). 96p. (gr. 4-9). 35.00 (978-0-8160-5691-0(9)) Facts On File, Inc.

—The Harlem Renaissance: An Explosion of African-American Culture. 2008. (America's Living History Ser.). (Illus.). 128p. (J). (gr. 5-9). lib. bdg. 33.27 (978-0-7660-2907-1(7)) Enslow Pubs., Inc.

AFRICAN AMERICANS—HISTORY—FICTION

Asim, Jabari. The Road to Freedom: A Story of the Reconstruction. 2004. 131p. (J). lib. bdg. 16.92 (978-1-4242-0765-7(7)) Fitzgerald Bks.

Bandy, Michael S. & Stein, Eric. White Water. Stickland, Shadra, illus. 2015. (ENG.). 40p. (J). (gr. k-3). 7.99 (978-0-7636-7945-3(3)) Candlewick Pr.

Carney-Nunes Charisse. Nappy. Williams, Ann Marie, illus. 2006. (ENG.). 24p. (J). (gr. k-2). 14.99 (978-0-9748142-1-6(0), Brand Nu Words) Nunes Productions, LLC.

Champion, Dionne N., et al. The Spirit of the Baobab Tree. Champion, Dionne N. & Champion, Daryl, illus. 2008. 37p. (J). 31.99 (978-1-4363-7842-0(7)) Xlibris Corp.

Craft, Jerry. Mama's Boyz: Because Learning Shouldn't Stop at 3 o'Clock!: Home Schoolin', 2 vols. 2007. (Illus.). 112p. (YA). per. 9.95 (978-0-9796132-0-3(5)) Mama's Boyz, Inc.

Draper, Sharon M. Copper Sun. 2006. (ENG.). 320p. (YA). (gr. 8-18). 19.99 (978-0-689-82181-3(6), Atheneum Bks. for Young Readers) Simon & Schuster Children's Publishing.

—Stella by Starlight. (ENG., Illus.). (J). (gr. 4-8). 2016. 352p. pap. 8.99 (978-1-4424-9498-5(0)) 2015. 336p. 17.99 (978-1-4424-9497-8(2), Atheneum Bks. for Young Readers) Simon & Schuster Children's Publishing.

—Stella by Starlight. 2016. lib. bdg. 18.40 (978-0-606-38255-7(0)) Turtleback Bks.

Griffin, Ramona Rorie. My Mind Looks Back & Wonders ... Tunstel Jr., Robert L., illus. 2009. (ENG.). 28p. pap. 24.95 (978-1-60813-917-0(4)) America Star Bks.

Kay, Alan. Breaking the Rules. 2007. (Young Heroes of History Ser.: 7). 149p. (J). pap. 7.95 (978-1-57249-389-6(5), White Mane Kids) White Mane Publishing Co., Inc.

Lester, Julius. Day of Tears. 2007. (ENG., Illus.). 192p. (J). (gr. 5-9). pap. 7.99 (978-1-4231-0409-4(9), Jump at the Sun) Hyperion Bks. for Children.

McDougal-Littell Publishing Staff. Literature Connections English: Roll of Thunder, Hear My Cry. 2004. (McDougal Littell Literature Connections Ser.). (ENG.). 288p. (gr. 8-8). stu. ed. 16.90 (978-0-395-77530-1(2), 2-80099) Great Source Education Group, Inc.

McNaught, Maria. Grandma's Ashanti Cloth. 2003. (ENG.). 24p. (J). (gr. -1-5). pap. 8.95 (978-0-913543-83-2(7)) African American Images.

Swain, Gwenyth. Voices for Freedom. Frankenhuyzen, Gijsbert van et al, illus. 2013. (American Adventures Ser.). (ENG.). 72p. (J). (gr. 3-6). 6.99 (978-1-58536-886-0(5), 202900) Sleeping Bear Pr.

Talley, Robin. Lies We Tell Ourselves. 2016. (ENG.). 416p. pap. 9.99 (978-0-373-21204-0(6), Harlequin Teen) Harlequin Enterprises, Ltd. CAN. Dist: HarperCollins Pubs.

Wall, Patricia Q. Child Out of Place: A Story for New England. Ronnquist, Debby, illus. 2003. 116p. (J). (gr. 6-9). pap. 12.00 (978-0-9742185-0-2(2)) Fall Rose Bks.

Winter, Jonah. Lillian's Right to Vote: A Celebration of the Voting Rights Act of 1965. Evans, Shane W., illus. 2015. (ENG.). 40p. (J). (gr. k-4). 17.99 (978-0-385-39028-6(9), Schwartz & Wade Bks.) Random Hse. Children's Bks.

Woodson, Jacqueline. This Is the Rope: A Story from the Great Migration. Ransome, James, illus. (ENG.). 32p. (J). (gr. k-3). 2017. pap. 8.99 **(978-0-425-28894-8(3)**, Puffin Books) 2013. 16.99 (978-0-399-23986-1(3), Nancy Paulsen Books) Penguin Young Readers Group.

AFRICAN AMERICANS IN ART

Gnojewski, Carol. African-American Crafts Kids Can Do! 2006. (Multicultural Crafts Kids Can Do! Ser.). (Illus.). 32p. (J). (gr. 3-4). lib. bdg. 23.94 (978-0-7660-2457-1(1), Enslow Elementary) Enslow Pubs., Inc.

Lace, William W. Blacks in Film. 2008. (Lucent Library of Black History Ser.). (ENG., Illus.). 104p. (J). (gr. 7-10). 34.80 (978-1-4205-0084-4(8), 1284137, Lucent Bks.) Cengage Gale.

AFRICAN AMERICANS IN BUSINESS

see African Americans—Employment

AFRICAN AMERICANS—MUSIC

Grady, Cynthia. Like a Bird: Art of the American Slave Song. Wood, Michele, illus. 2016. (ENG.). 40p. (J). (gr. 3-6). 19.99 (978-1-4677-8550-1(4), Carolrhoda Bks.) Lerner Publishing Group.

—Like a Bird: The Art of the American Slave Song. Wood, Michele, illus. 2016. (ENG.). 40p. (gr. 3-6). 38.65 (978-1-5124-0889-8(1), Millbrook Pr.) Lerner Publishing Group.

Hegel, Claudette. African-American Musicians. 2012. (J). pap. (978-1-4222-2387-1(6)) Mason Crest.

—African-American Musicians. Hill, Marc Lamont, ed. 2012. (Major Black Contributions from Emancipation to Civil Rights Ser.). 64p. (J). (gr. 5). 22.95 (978-1-4222-2374-1(4)) Mason Crest.

Igus, Toyomi. I See the Rhythm. Wood, Michele, illus. 2013. (ENG.). 32p. (J). (gr. 1). pap. 10.95 (978-0-89239-212-4(6)) Lee & Low Bks., Inc.

McKissack, Patricia C. Let's Clap, Jump, Sing & Shout; Dance, Spin & Turn It Out! Games, Songs, & Stories from an African American Childhood. Pinkney, Brian, illus. 2017. (ENG.). 184p. (J). (gr. k-12). 24.99 (978-0-375-87088-0(1), Schwartz & Wade Bks.) Random Hse. Children's Bks.

Turck, Mary C. Freedom Song: Young Voices & the Struggle for Civil Rights. 2008. (ENG., Illus.). 160p. (J). (gr. 4). pap. 18.95 (978-1-55652-773-9(X)) Chicago Review Pr., Inc.

AFRICAN AMERICANS—POETRY

Brooks, Gwendolyn. Bronzeville Boys & Girls. Ringgold, Faith, illus. 2015. (ENG.). 48p. (J). (gr. -1-3). pap. 6.99 (978-0-06-443772-1(8), Amistad) HarperCollins Pubs.

Clinton, Catherine. I, Too, Sing America: Three Centuries of African American Poetry. Alcorn, Stephen, illus. 2017. (ENG.). 128p. (J). (gr. 5-7). 9.99 (978-0-544-58256-9(X), HMH Books For Young Readers) Houghton Mifflin Harcourt Publishing Co.

Greenfield, Eloise. The Great Migration: Journey to the North. Gilchrist, Jan Spivey, illus. 2010. (ENG.). 32p. (J). (gr. -1-3). 16.99 (978-0-06-125921-0(7), Amistad) HarperCollins Pubs.

—Honey, I Love. Gilchrist, Jan Spivey, illus. 2016. 32p. (J). (gr. -1-3). pap. 6.99 (978-0-06-009125-5(8), Amistad) HarperCollins Pubs.

Grimes, Nikki. My Man Blue. Lagarrigue, Jerome, illus. 2015. 32p. pap. 7.00 (978-1-61003-533-0(X)) Center for the Collaborative Classroom.

—One Last Word: Wisdom from the Harlem Renaissance. 2017. (ENG., Illus.). 128p. (J). 18.99 (978-1-61963-554-8(2), 9781619635548, Bloomsbury USA Childrens) Bloomsbury Publishing USA.

Jacqueline, Woodson. Locomotion. 2014. (ENG.). 128p. (YA). (gr. 3-7). 12.24 (978-1-63245-262-7(6)) Lectorum Pubns., Inc.

Lewis, J. Patrick & Lyon, George Ella. Voices from the March on Washington. 2014. (ENG., Illus.). 128p. (J). (gr. 5). 15.95 (978-1-62091-785-5(8), Wordsong) Boyds Mills Pr.

Medina, Tony. Love to Langston, 1 vol. Christie, R., illus. 2005. (ENG.). 40p. (J). (gr. 1-7). pap. 10.95 (978-1-58430-283-4(6)) Lee & Low Bks., Inc.

—Love to Langston. Christie, R. Gregory, illus. 2006. (J). (gr. 1-7). 17.10 (978-0-7569-7016-1(4)) Perfection Learning Corp.

Myers, Walter Dean. Blues Journey. Myers, Christopher A. & Myers, Christopher, illus. 2007. (ENG.). 48p. (J). (gr. -1-3). pap. 8.95 (978-0-8234-2079-7(5)) Holiday Hse., Inc.

Nelson, Marilyn. A Wreath for Emmett Till. Lardy, Philippe, illus. 2009. (ENG.). 48p. (YA). (gr. 7). pap. 8.99 *(978-0-547-07636-2(3))* Houghton Mifflin Harcourt Publishing Co.

Rampersad, Arnold & Blount, Marcellus, eds. Poetry for Young People: African American Poetry. Barbour, Karen, illus. 2013. (Poetry for Young People Ser.). (ENG.). 48p. (J). (gr. 3). 14.95 *(978-1-4027-1689-8(3))* Sterling Publishing Co., Inc.

Roessel, David & Rampersad, Arnold, eds. Poetry for Young People: Langston Hughes. Andrews, Benny, illus. 2013. (Poetry for Young People Ser.). (ENG.). 48p. (J). (gr. 3). 14.95 *(978-1-4549-0328-4(7))* Sterling Publishing Co., Inc.

Shange, Ntozake. Freedom's a-Callin Me. Brown, Rod, illus. 2012. (ENG.). 32p. (J). (gr. 3-7). 16.99 *(978-0-06-133741-3(2),* Amistad) HarperCollins Pubs.

Shore, Diane Z. & Alexander, Jessica. This Is the Dream. Ransome, James E., illus. 2009. (ENG.). 40p. (J). (gr. k-5). pap. 7.99 *(978-0-06-055521-4(1),* Amistad) HarperCollins Pubs.

Smith Turner, Jennifer. Lost & Found: Rhyming Verse Honoring Africa American Heroes. 4th ed. 2006. (Illus.). per. 22.00 *(978-0-9790817-0-5(X))* Smith & Assocs.

Weatherford, Carole Boston. You Can Fly: The Tuskegee Airmen. Weatherford, Jeffery Boston, illus. 2017. (ENG.). 96p. (J). (gr. 4-7). pap. 7.99 *(978-1-4814-4939-7(7))* Simon & Schuster Children's Publishing.

AFRICAN AMERICANS—POLITICS AND GOVERNMENT

Ellis, Carol. African American Activists. 2012. (J). pap. *(978-1-4222-2384-0(1))* Mason Crest.

—African American Activists. Hill, Marc Lamont, ed. 2012. (Major Black Contributions from Emancipation to Civil Rights Ser.). 64p. (J). (gr. 5). 22.95 *(978-1-4222-2371-0(X))* Mason Crest.

Goldsworthy, Steve. Politicians. 2016. (Illus.). 48p. (J). *(978-1-5105-1162-0(8))* SmartBook Media, Inc.

—Politics: African American History. 2011. (J). (gr. 5-8). pap. 14.95 *(978-1-61690-666-5(9),* AV2 by Weigl); (Illus.). 48p. (gr. 1-4). 29.99 *(978-1-61690-662-7(6))* Weigl Pubs., Inc.

Hinton, Kerry. The Black Power Movement & Civil Unrest. 2017. (J). pap. ***(978-1-5383-8016-1(1))*** Rosen Publishing Group, Inc., The.

Ollhoff, Jim. Courage & Growth, 1 vol. 2011. (African American History Ser.). (ENG., Illus.). 32p. (YA). (gr. 5-9). lib. bdg. 27.07 *(978-1-61714-711-1(7))* ABDO Publishing Co.

Sterling, Kristin. Mary Mcleod Bethune. 2008. pap. 40.95 *(978-0-8225-9474-1(9))* Lerner Publishing Group.

Uschan, Michael V. Blacks in Political Office. 2008. (Lucent Library of Black History Ser.). (ENG., Illus.). 128p. (gr. 7-10). 39.40 *(978-1-4205-0085-1(6),* Lucent Bks.) Cengage Gale.

AFRICAN AMERICANS—RELIGION

Robinson, Julia Marie. Race, Religion, & the Pulpit: Rev. Robert L. Bradby & the Making of Urban Detroit. 2015. (Great Lakes Books Ser.). (ENG., Illus.). 216p. 39.99 *(978-0-8143-3291-7(9),* 3073) Wayne State Univ. Pr.

AFRICAN AMERICANS—SEGREGATION

Crayton, Lisa A. Freedom Riders. 2017. (J). ***(978-1-5383-8027-7(7))***; pap. ***(978-1-5383-8026-0(9))*** Rosen Publishing Group, Inc., The.

Fremon, David K. The Jim Crow Laws & Racism in United States History. 2014. (In United States History Ser.). (Illus.). 96p. (J). (gr. 5-12). 27.94 *(978-0-7660-6092-0(6))*; pap. 10.95 *(978-0-7660-6093-7(4))* Enslow Pubs., Inc.

Hoose, Phillip. Claudette Colvin: Twice Toward Justice. 2010. (ENG., Illus.). 160p. (YA). (gr. 8-12). pap. 9.99 *(978-0-312-66105-2(3),* 9780312661052) Square Fish.

Howse, Jennifer. Reconstruction. 2008. (African American History Ser.). (Illus.). 48p. (YA). (gr. 5-8). pap. 10.95 *(978-1-59036-879-4(7))*; lib. bdg. 29.05 *(978-1-59036-878-7(9))* Weigl Pubs., Inc.

Hussey, Maria. The Rise of the Jim Crow ERA. 2015. (African American Experience: from Slavery to the Presidency Ser.). (ENG., Illus.). 80p. (J). (gr. 7-8). 32.90 *(978-1-68048-042-9(1),* Britannica Educational Publishing) Rosen Publishing Group, Inc., The.

Muldoon, Kathleen M. Jim Crow Era, 1 vol. 2014. (African-American History Ser.). (ENG.). 48p. (gr. 8-12). lib. bdg. 32.79 *(978-1-62403-146-5(3))* ABDO Publishing Co.

Osborne, Linda Barrett. Miles to Go for Freedom: Segregation & Civil Rights in the Jim Crow Years. 2012. (ENG., Illus.). 128p. (J). (gr. 3-7). 25.99 *(978-1-4197-0020-0(0),* Abrams Bks. for Young Readers) Abrams, Inc.

Tisdale, Rachel. The Woolworth's Sit-In, 1 vol., 1. 2014. (We Shall Overcome Ser.). (ENG.). 32p. (J). (gr. 3-6). 26.25 *(978-1-4777-6065-9(2),* PowerKids Pr.) Rosen Publishing Group, Inc., The.

AFRICAN AMERICANS—SEGREGATION—FICTION

Coles, Robert. The Story of Ruby Bridges. 2009. 8.44 *(978-0-7848-3016-1(9),* Everbind) Marco Bk. Co.

—The Story of Ruby Bridges. 2011. 17.00 *(978-1-61383-173-1(0))* Perfection Learning Corp.

—The Story of Ruby Bridges. Ford, George, illus. 50th anniv. ed. 2010. (ENG.). 32p. (J). (gr. -1-3). pap. 6.99 *(978-0-439-47226-5(1),* Scholastic Paperbacks) Scholastic, Inc.

—The Story of Ruby Bridges. 2010. lib. bdg. 17.20 *(978-0-606-23189-3(7),* Turtleback) Turtleback Bks.

Draper, Sharon M. Stella by Starlight. (ENG., Illus.). (J). (gr. 4-8). 2016. 352p. pap. 8.99 *(978-1-4424-9498-5(0))* 2015. 336p. 17.99 *(978-1-4424-9497-8(2),* Atheneum Bks. for Young Readers) Simon & Schuster Children's Publishing.

—Stella by Starlight. 2016. lib. bdg. 18.40 *(978-0-606-38255-7(0))* Turtleback Bks.

Mitchell, Margaree King. When Grandmama Sings. Ransome, James E., illus. 2012. (ENG.). 40p. (J). (gr. k-4). 16.99 *(978-0-688-17563-4(5),* Amistad) HarperCollins Pubs.

Wiles, Deborah. Freedom Summer. Lagarrigue, Jerome, illus. 2005. (ENG.). 32p. (J). (gr. -1-3). reprint ed. 7.99 *(978-0-689-87829-9(X),* Aladdin) Simon & Schuster Children's Publishing.

AFRICAN AMERICANS—SOCIAL CONDITIONS

see also African Americans—Suffrage

Anthony, David H. Freedom: Life after Slavery, 1 vol. 2011. (Primary Source Readers Ser.). (ENG.). 32p. (J). (gr. 5-5). pap. 8.99 *(978-1-4333-1521-3(1))* Teacher Created Materials, Inc.

Bausum, Ann. Marching to the Mountaintop: How Poverty, Labor Fights, & Civil Rights Set the Stage for Martin Luther King Jr.'s Final Hours. 2012. (ENG., Illus.). 112p. (J). (gr. 5-9). lib. bdg. 28.90 *(978-1-4263-0940-3(6),* National Geographic Children's Bks.) National Geographic Society.

Bausum, Ann & National Geographic Kids Staff. Marching to the Mountaintop: How Poverty, Labor Fights, & Civil Rights Set the Stage for Martin Luther King Jr.'s Final Hours. 2012. (ENG., Illus.). 112p. (J). (gr. 5-9). 19.95 *(978-1-4263-0939-7(2),* National Geographic Children's Bks.) National Geographic Society.

Bireda, Martha R. & Cummings, Jaha F. Omowali: The Child Returns Home - Reconnecting Our Children with Their True Culture. 2008. 232p. pap. *(978-4-902837-10-0(2))* Aoishima Kenkyusha.

Carosella, Melissa. The Fight for Freedom: Ending Slavery in America, 1 vol. 2011. (Primary Source Readers Ser.). (ENG.). 32p. (J). (gr. 5-5). pap. 8.99 *(978-1-4333-1519-0(X))* Teacher Created Materials, Inc.

Cartlidge, Cherese. Reparations for Slavery. 2007. (Lucent Library of Black History Ser.). (ENG., Illus.). 128p. (gr. 3-7). lib. bdg. 39.40 *(978-1-59018-868-2(3),* Lucent Bks.) Cengage Gale.

Deiters, Erika & Deiters, Jim. The African Community in America. 2003. (J). pap. *(978-1-58417-095-2(6))*; lib. bdg. *(978-1-58417-032-7(8))* Lake Street Pubs.

Dray, Philip. Yours for Justice, Ida B. Wells: The Daring Life of a Crusading Journalist, 1 vol. Alcorn, Stephen, illus. 2008. (ENG.). 48p. (J). (gr. 5-9). 18.95 *(978-1-56145-417-4(6))* Peachtree Pubs.

Dugan, Christine. Between the Wars, 1 vol. 2007. (Primary Source Readers Ser.). (ENG.). 32p. (J). (gr. 5-5). pap. 8.99 *(978-0-7439-0666-1(7))* Shell Educational Publishing.

Forche, Carolyn A. Colors Come from God ... Just Like Me! 2015. 32p. pap. 9.99 *(978-1-5018-0838-8(9))* Abingdon Pr.

Greene, Meg & Malvasi, Meg Greene. Into the Land of Freedom: African Americans in Reconstruction. 2004. (People's History Ser.). (ENG., Illus.). 96p. (gr. 5-12). lib. bdg. 33.26 *(978-0-8225-4690-0(6))* Lerner Publishing Group.

Halpern, Monica. Moving North: African Americans & the Great Migration 1915-1930. 2005. (Crossroads America Ser.). (ENG., Illus.). 40p. (gr. k-3). 12.95 *(978-0-7922-8278-5(7))*; 21.90 *(978-0-7922-8358-4(9))* National Geographic Society. (National Geographic Children's Bks.).

Hinman, Bonnie. Eternal Vigilance: The Story of Ida B. Wells-Barnett. 2011. (Civil Rights Leaders Ser.). 128p. (gr. 6-10). lib. bdg. 28.95 *(978-1-59935-111-7(0))* Reynolds, Morgan Inc.

Holliday, Laurel. Dreaming in Color Living in Black & White: Our Own Stories of Growing up Black in America. 2012. (ENG.). 208p. (YA). (gr. 7). pap. 10.99 *(978-1-4424-7177-1(8),* Simon Pulse) Simon Pulse.

Jackson, Constance L. Over the River: Life of Lydia Maria Child, Abolitionist for Freedom, 1802-1880. 2008. (Illus.). 160p. pap. 18.95 *(978-0-9818204-0-8(9))* Permanent Productions Publishing.

Kallen, Stuart A. A History of Free Blacks in America. 2006. (Lucent Library of Black History). (ENG., Illus.). 112p. (YA). (gr. 7-10). lib. bdg. 33.45 *(978-1-59018-776-0(8),* Lucent Bks.) Cengage Gale.

Kunjufu, Jawanza & Prescott, Folami. Kindergarten: Self-Esteem Through Culture Leads to Academic Excellence. 2003. (ENG.). 60p. (J). (gr. k). pap. 9.95 *(978-0-913543-85-6(3))* African American Images.

—Self-Esteem Through Culture Leads to Academic Excellence. 2003. (ENG.). 60p. (J). (gr. 8). pap. 9.95 *(978-0-913543-93-1(4))*; (gr. 9-12). pap. 14.95 *(978-0-913543-94-8(2))* African American Images.

—SETCLAE, Fifth Grade: Self-Esteem Through Culture Leads to Academic Excellence. 2003. (ENG.). 60p. (J). (gr. 5). pap. 9.95 *(978-0-913543-90-0(X))* African American Images.

—SETCLAE, First Grade: Self-Esteem Through Culture Leads to Academic Excellence. 2003. (ENG.). 60p. (J). (gr. 1). pap. 9.95 *(978-0-913543-86-3(1))* African American Images.

—SETCLAE, Fourth Grade: Self-Esteem Through Culture Leads to Academic Excellence. 2003. (ENG.). 60p. (J). (gr. 4). pap. 9.95 *(978-0-913543-89-4(6))* African American Images.

—SETCLAE, Second Grade: Self-Esteem Through Culture Leads to Academic Excellence. 2003. (ENG.). 60p. (J). (gr. 2). pap. 9.95 *(978-0-913543-87-0(X))* African American Images.

—SETCLAE, Seventh Grade: Self-Esteem Through Culture Leads to Academic Excellence. 2003. (ENG.). 60p. (J). (gr. 7). pap. 9.95 *(978-0-913543-92-4(6))* African American Images.

—SETCLAE, Sixth Grade: Self-Esteem Through Culture Leads to Academic Excellence. 2003. (ENG.). 60p. (J). (gr. 6). pap. 9.95 *(978-0-913543-91-7(8))* African American Images.

—SETCLAE, Third Grade: Self-Esteem Through Culture Leads to Academic Excellence. 2003. (ENG.). 60p. (J). (gr. 3). pap. 9.95 *(978-0-913543-88-7(8))* African American Images.

Lowery, Zoe. Barack Obama & a "Post-Racial Society" 2015. (African American Experience: from Slavery to the Presidency Ser.). (ENG., Illus.). 80p. (J). (gr. 7-8). 32.90 *(978-1-68048-051-1(0),* Britannica Educational Publishing) Rosen Publishing Group, Inc., The.

Lowery, Zoe, ed. Barack Obama & the Idea of a Postracial Society. 2015. (African American Experience: from Slavery to the Presidency Ser.). (ENG.). 80p. (YA). (gr. 7-8). 65.80 *(978-1-68048-052-8(9),* Britannica Educational Publishing) Rosen Publishing Group, Inc., The.

McClaurin, Irma & Schomp, Virginia. Facing the Future. 2007. (Drama of African-American History Ser.). 80p. (gr. 6). lib. bdg. 35.64 *(978-0-7614-2644-8(2),* Benchmark Bks.) Marshall Cavendish Corp.

McKissack, Patricia C. & McKissack, Fredrick L. Ida B. Wells-Barnett: Fighter for Justice. 2013. (Famous African Americans Ser.). (Illus.). 24p. (J). (gr. k-18). 22.60 *(978-0-7660-4108-0(5))* Enslow Pubs., Inc.

Myers, Walter Dean & William Miles. The Harlem Hellfighters: When Pride Met Courage. 2014. (J). lib. bdg. 20.85 *(978-0-606-35507-0(3))* Turtleback Bks.

Ollhoff, Jim. Courage & Growth, 1 vol. 2011. (African American History Ser.). (ENG., Illus.). 32p. (YA). (gr. 5-9). lib. bdg. 27.07 *(978-1-61714-711-1(7))* ABDO Publishing Co.

Pferdehirt, Julia. Blue Jenkins: Working for Workers. 2011. (Badger Biographies Ser.). (ENG., Illus.). 160p. (J). pap. 12.95 *(978-0-87020-427-2(0))* Wisconsin Historical Society.

Shannon, Ann. The Wilder Kids: I Really Want to Go to College!! 2009. 24p. pap. 13.50 *(978-1-4389-0523-5(8))* AuthorHouse.

Sioux, Tracee. African American Migration. 2004. (Primary Sources of Immigration & Migration in America Ser.). (ENG., Illus.). 24p. (gr. 4-8). pap. 9.40 *(978-0-8239-8953-9(4),* PowerKids Pr.) Rosen Publishing Group, Inc., The.

Stone, Tanya Lee. Courage Has No Color - The True Story of the Triple Nickles: America's First Black Paratroopers. 2013. (ENG., Illus.). 160p. (J). (gr. 5). pap. 17.99 *(978-0-7636-6548-7(7))*; 24.99 *(978-0-7636-5117-6(6))* Candlewick Pr.

AFRICAN AMERICANS—SOCIAL LIFE AND CUSTOMS

Aloian, Molly. Kwanzaa. 2008. (Celebrations in My World Ser.). (ENG., Illus.). 32p. (J). (gr. k-3). pap. *(978-0-7787-4302-6(0))* Crabtree Publishing Co.

Bailer, Darice. African-American Culture, 1 vol. 2014. (African-American History Ser.). (ENG.). 48p. (gr. 8-12). 32.79 *(978-1-62403-143-4(9))* ABDO Publishing Co.

Bireda, Martha R. & Cummings, Jaha F. Omowali: The Child Returns Home - Reconnecting Our Children with Their True Culture. 2008. 232p. pap. *(978-4-902837-10-0(2))* Aoishima Kenkyusha.

Bolden, Tonya. Maritcha: A Nineteenth-Century American Girl. 2005. (ENG., Illus.). 48p. (J). (gr. k-4). 19.95 *(978-0-8109-5045-0(6))* Abrams, Inc.

Bullard, Lisa. Kevin's Kwanzaa. Basaluzzo, Constanza, illus. 2012. (Cloverleaf Books (tm) — Fall & Winter Holidays Ser.). (ENG.). 24p. (gr. k-2). 6.95 *(978-0-7613-8588-2(6),* Millbrook Pr.) Lerner Publishing Group.

Donovan, Sandra. The African American Experience. 2010. (USA TODAY Cultural Mosaic Ser.). (ENG., Illus.). 80p. (gr. 6-8). lib. bdg. 33.26 *(978-0-7613-4084-3(X))* Lerner Publishing Group.

Freeman, Dorothy Rhodes & MacMillan, Dianne M. Kwanzaa. rev. ed. 2008. (Best Holiday Bks.). (Illus.). 48p. (J). (gr. 3-7). lib. bdg. 25.27 *(978-0-7660-3042-8(3))* Enslow Pubs., Inc.

Grack, Rachel. Kwanzaa. 2017. (Celebrating Holidays Ser.). 24p. (J). (gr. k-3). pap. 6.99 ***(978-1-61891-275-6(5))***; (ENG., Illus.). lib. bdg. 25.95 *(978-1-62617-596-9(9))* Bellwether Media. (Blastoff! Readers).

Heller, Daryl. Kwanzaa. 2009. (My Library of Holidays Ser.). 24p. (gr. 1-1). 37.50 *(978-1-61514-696-3(2),* PowerKids Pr.) Rosen Publishing Group, Inc., The.

—Kwanzaa. Gonzalez, Tomas, tr. from ENG. 2004. (My Library of Holidays). (ENG & SPA., Illus.). 24p. (J). (gr. k-1). lib. bdg. 16.00 *(978-1-4042-7528-7(2),* PowerKids Pr.) Rosen Publishing Group, Inc., The.

—Kwanzaa / Kwanzaa. 2009. (My Library of Holidays / Mi biblioteca de celebraciones Ser.). (ENG & SPA.). 24p. (gr. 1-1). 37.50 *(978-1-61514-702-1(0),* Editorial Buenas Letras) Rosen Publishing Group, Inc., The.

Levy, Janey. Juneteenth: Celebrating the End of Slavery. (Reading Room Collection 2 Ser.). 24p. 2009. (gr. 3-4). 42.50 *(978-1-60851-976-7(7),* PowerKids Pr.) 2003. (Illus.). (J). lib. bdg. 22.60 *(978-0-8239-3711-0(9))* Rosen Publishing Group, Inc., The.

McKissack, Fredrick L. & McKissack, Lisa Beringer. Kwanzaa-Count & Celebrate! 2009. (Holidays—Count & Celebrate! Ser.). (Illus.). 32p. (J). (gr. k-3). lib. bdg. 23.94 *(978-0-7660-3102-9(0))* Enslow Pubs., Inc.

McKissack, Patricia C. Let's Clap, Jump, Sing & Shout; Dance, Spin & Turn It Out! Games, Songs, & Stories from an African American Childhood. Pinkney, Brian, illus. 2017. (ENG.). 184p. (J). (gr. k-12). 24.99 *(978-0-375-87086-0(1),* Schwartz & Wade Bks.) Random Hse. Children's Bks.

Murray, Julie. Juneteenth, 1 vol. 2011. (Holidays Set 3 Ser.). (ENG., Illus.). 24p. (J). (gr. 1-4). 25.65 *(978-1-61783-039-6(9))* ABDO Publishing Co.

Nelson, Robin. Juneteenth. 2009. (First Step Nonfiction - American Holidays Ser.). (ENG.). 24p. (gr. k-2). 23.93 *(978-0-7613-4934-1(0))* Lerner Publishing Group.

Nelson, Vaunda Micheaux & Nelson, Drew. Juneteenth. Schroder, Mark, illus. 2006. (On My Own Holidays Ser.). 48p. (J). 25.26 *(978-1-57505-876-4(6))*; (ENG.). (gr. 2-4). per. 6.95 *(978-0-8225-5974-0(9),* First Avenue Editions) Lerner Publishing Group.

Otfinoski, Steven. The Story of Juneteenth: An Interactive History Adventure. 2015. (You Choose: History Ser.). (ENG., Illus.). 112p. (gr. 3-4). lib. bdg. 31.99 *(978-1-4914-1802-4(8),* You Choose Bks.) Capstone Press of Coughlan Cos.

Otto, Carolyn B. Celebrate Kwanzaa: With Cadels, a Comminity & the Fruits of the Harvest. 2017. (Holidays Around the World Ser.). (ENG., Illus.). 32p. (J). (gr. 1-4). pap. 7.99 ***(978-1-4263-2849-7(4),*** National Geographic Children's Bks.) National Geographic Society.

—Holidays Around the World: Celebrate Kwanzaa. 2017. (Holidays Around the World Ser.). (ENG.). 32p. (J). (gr. 1-4). lib. bdg. 17.90 ***(978-1-4263-2850-3(8),*** National Geographic Children's Bks.) National Geographic Society.

Otto, Carolyn B. Holidays Around the World: Celebrate Kwanzaa: With Candles, Community, & the Fruits of the Harvest. 2010. (Holidays Around the World Ser.). (ENG., Illus.). 32p. (J). (gr. 1-4). pap. 6.95 *(978-1-4263-0705-8(5),* National Geographic Children's Bks.) National Geographic Society.

Peppas, Lynn. Juneteenth. 2010. (Celebrations in My World Ser.). (ENG.). 32p. (J). (gr. k-3). *(978-0-7787-4928-8(2))*; pap. *(978-0-7787-4935-6(5))* Crabtree Publishing Co.

Robinson, Hilda & Kunkel, Jeff. Didn't We Have Fun! Robinson, Hilda, illus. 2012. (Illus.). 48p. (J). 19.95 *(978-1-933987-17-0(0),* Crickhollow Bks.) Great Lakes Literary, LLC.

Smith, Maximilian. The History of Juneteenth. 2016. (History of Our Holidays Ser.). (ENG.). 24p. (J). (gr. 1-2). pap. 8.15 *(978-1-4824-3894-9(1))* Stevens, Gareth Publishing LLLP.

Worth, Richard. The Harlem Renaissance: An Explosion of African-American Culture. 2008. (America's Living History Ser.). (Illus.). 128p. (J). (gr. 5-9). lib. bdg. 33.27 *(978-0-7660-2907-1(7))* Enslow Pubs., Inc.

AFRICAN AMERICANS—SOUTHERN STATES

Aretha, David. Sit-Ins & Freedom Rides. 2009. (Civil Rights Movement Ser.). 128p. (J). (gr. 4-7). 28.95 *(978-1-59935-098-1(X))* Reynolds, Morgan Inc.

Coles, Robert. The Story of Ruby Bridges. 2009. 8.44 *(978-0-7848-3016-1(9),* Everbind) Marco Bk. Co.

—The Story of Ruby Bridges. 2011. 17.00 *(978-1-61383-173-1(0))* Perfection Learning Corp.

—The Story of Ruby Bridges. Ford, George, illus. 50th anniv. ed. 2010. (ENG.). 32p. (J). (gr. -1-3). pap. 6.99 *(978-0-439-47226-5(1),* Scholastic Paperbacks) Scholastic, Inc.

—The Story of Ruby Bridges. 2010. lib. bdg. 17.20 *(978-0-606-23189-3(7),* Turtleback) Turtleback Bks.

Igus, Toyomi. Going Back Home: An Artist Returns to the South. Wood, Michele, illus. 2013. (ENG.). 32p. (J). (gr. 1-18). pap. 9.95 *(978-0-89239-197-4(9),* Children's Book Press) Lee & Low Bks., Inc.

AFRICAN AMERICANS—SUFFRAGE

Aretha, David. Freedom Summer. 2007. (Civil Rights Movement Ser.). (Illus.). 128p. (J). (gr. 3-7). lib. bdg. 27.95 *(978-1-59935-059-2(9))* Reynolds, Morgan Inc.

—Selma & the Voting Rights Act. 2007. (Civil Rights Movement Ser.). (Illus.). 128p. (J). (gr. 3-7). lib. bdg. 27.95 *(978-1-59935-056-1(4))* Reynolds, Morgan Inc.

—The Story of the Selma Voting Rights Marches in Photographs. 2014. (Story of the Civil Rights Movement in Photographs Ser.). 48p. (J). lib. bdg. 25.27 *(978-0-7660-4239-1(1))* Enslow Pubs., Inc.

Bjornlund, Lydia D. Women of the Suffrage Movement. 2003. (Women in History Ser.). (ENG., Illus.). 112p. (J). 33.45 *(978-1-59018-173-7(5),* Lucent Bks.) Cengage Gale.

Loughran, P. J., illus. Turning 15 on the Road to Freedom: My Story of the Selma Voting Rights March. 2015. (ENG.). 128p. (YA). (gr. 7). 19.99 *(978-0-8037-4123-2(5),* Dial Bks) Penguin Young Readers Group.

Miller, Jake. The March from Selma to Montgomery: African Americans Demand the Vote. 2009. (Library of the Civil Rights Movement Ser.). 24p. (gr. 3-3). 42.50 *(978-1-60853-894-2(X),* PowerKids Pr.) Rosen Publishing Group, Inc., The.

Orr, Tamra. A History of Voting Rights. 2012. (J). lib. bdg. 29.95 *(978-1-61228-262-6(8))* Mitchell Lane Pubs., Inc.

Rubin, Susan Goldman. Freedom Summer: The 1964 Struggle for Civil Rights in Mississippi. (ENG.). 144p. (J). 2016. 14.95 *(978-0-8234-3557-9(1))* 2014. (Illus.). (gr. 5). 18.95 *(978-0-8234-2920-2(2))* Holiday Hse., Inc.

AFRICAN AMERICANS—WEST (U.S.)

Baker, Brynn. Buffalo Soldiers: Heroes of the American West. 2015. (Military Heroes Ser.). (ENG., Illus.). 32p. (gr. 3-4). lib. bdg. 27.32 *(978-1-4914-4838-0(5))* Capstone Press of Coughlan Cos.

Cefrey, Holly. From Slave to Cowboy: The Nat Love Story. 2009. (Great Moments in American History Ser.). 32p. (gr. 3-3). 47.90 *(978-1-61513-142-6(6))* Rosen Publishing Group, Inc., The.

Glaser, Jason. The Buffalo Soldiers & the American West. Smith, Tod G. et al, illus. 2005. (Graphic History Ser.). (ENG.). 32p. (gr. 3-4). 30.65 *(978-0-7368-4966-1(1),* Graphic Library) Capstone Press of Coughlan Cos.

Penn, Sarah. Nat Love: African American Cowboy. 2009. (Primary Sources of Famous People in American History Ser.). 32p. (gr. 2-3). 47.90 *(978-1-60851-706-0(3))* Rosen Publishing Group, Inc., The.

—Nat Love: African American Cowboy / Vaquero Afroamericano. 2009. (Famous People in American History/Grandes personajes en la historia de los Estados Unidos Ser.). (ENG & SPA.). 32p. (gr. 2-3). 47.90 *(978-1-61512-551-7(5),* Editorial Buenas Letras) Rosen Publishing Group, Inc., The.

—Nat Love: Vaquero afroamericano (Nat Love: African American Cowboy) 2009. (Grandes personajes en la historia de los Estados Unidos (Famous People in American History) Ser.). (SPA.). 32p. (gr. 2-3). 47.90 *(978-1-61512-804-4(2),* Editorial Buenas Letras) Rosen Publishing Group, Inc., The.

Raabe, Emily. Buffalo Soldiers & the Western Frontier. (Westward Ho! Ser.). 24p. 2009. (gr. 2-3). 42.50 *(978-1-60854-759-3(0))* 2003. (Illus.). (J). lib. bdg. 22.60 *(978-0-8239-6495-6(7))* Rosen Publishing Group, Inc., The. (PowerKids Pr.).

Randolph, Ryan P. Black Cowboys. 2003. (Library of the Westward Expansion Ser.). (Illus.). 24p. (J). lib. bdg. 22.60 *(978-0-8239-6294-5(6))* Rosen Publishing Group, Inc., The.

Stuckey, Rachel. African Americans in the West. 2015. (True History of the Wild West Ser.). (ENG., Illus.). 32p. (J). (gr. 5-5). pap. 10.00 *(978-1-4994-1172-0(3),* PowerKids Pr.) Rosen Publishing Group, Inc., The.

AFRICAN LANGUAGES

Milet Publishing Staff. Bilingual Visual Dictionary. 2011. (Milet Multimedia Ser.). (ENG & SOM., Illus.). 1p. (J). (gr. k-2). cd-rom 19.95 *(978-1-84059-591-8(4))* Milet Publishing.

—My Bilingual Book-Smell (English-Somali) 2014. (My Bilingual Book Ser.). (ENG & SOM., Illus.). 28p. (J). (gr. -1-k). 9.95 *(978-1-84059-815-5(8))* Milet Publishing.

—My First Bilingual Book-Home (English-Somali) 2011. (My First Bilingual Book Ser.). (ENG., Illus.). 24p. (J). (gr. k — 1). bds. 7.99 *(978-1-84059-651-9(1))* Milet Publishing.

—My First Bilingual Book-Music (English-Somali) 2012. (My First Bilingual Book Ser.). (ENG & SOM., Illus.). 24p. (J). (gr. k — 1). bds. 7.99 *(978-1-84059-727-1(5))* Milet Publishing.

—Sports - My First Bilingual Book. 2012. (My First Bilingual Book Ser.). (ENG & SOM., Illus.). 24p. (J). (gr. k — 1). bds. 7.99 *(978-1-84059-759-2(3))* Milet Publishing.

—Vegetables. 2011. (My First Bilingual Book Ser.). (ENG., Illus.). 24p. (J). (gr. k — 1). bds. 7.99 *(978-1-84059-667-0(8))* Milet Publishing.

NASA Astronauts of Color: African American, Hispanic, Chinese, Japanese & Indian 2nd Edition 2009. 2009. (My Ancestors — My Heroes Ser.: Vol. 3). (ENG., Illus.). 190p. (J). (gr. 3-4). cd-rom 18.95 *(978-1-893091-02-3(3),* My Ancestors, My Heroes) Parker-Wallace Publishing Co., LLC.

National Curriculum Development Centre Staff. Ateso Pupil. 2004. Bk. 1. pap., pupil's gde. ed. *(978-0-521-78928-8(1))*Bk. 2. pap., pupil's gde. ed. *(978-0-521-78929-5(X))*Bk. 3. pap., pupil's gde. ed.

(978-0-521-78930-1(3))Bk. 4. pap., pupil's gde. ed. (978-0-521-78931-8(1)) Cambridge Univ. Pr.
—Luganda. 2004. Bk. 1. pap., pupil's gde. ed. (978-0-521-78932-5(X))Bk. 2. pap., pupil's gde. ed. (978-0-521-78933-2(8))Bk. 4. pap., pupil's gde. ed. (978-0-521-78935-6(4)) Cambridge Univ. Pr.
—Luganda Pupil, Bk. 5. 2004. pap., pupil's gde. ed. (978-0-521-78934-9(6)) Cambridge Univ. Pr.
—Runyankore-Rukiga. 2004. Bk. 1. pap., pupil's gde. ed. (978-0-521-78924-0(9))Bk. 2. pap., pupil's gde. ed. (978-0-521-78925-7(7))Bk. 3. pap., pupil's gde. ed. (978-0-521-78926-4(5))Bk. 4. pap., pupil's gde. ed. (978-0-521-78927-1(3)) Cambridge Univ. Pr.
—Uganda Mother Tongue: Primary 1. 2004. pap., tchr. ed. (978-0-521-78940-0(0)) Cambridge Univ. Pr.
—Uganda Mother Tongue: Primary 2. 2004. pap., tchr. ed. (978-0-521-78941-7(9)) Cambridge Univ. Pr.
—Uganda Mother Tongue: Primary 4. 2004. pap., tchr. ed. (978-0-521-78943-1(5)) Cambridge Univ. Pr.
Turhan, Sedat. New Bilingual Visual Dictionary (English-Somali) 2nd ed. 2017. (New Bilingual Visual Dictionary Ser.). (ENG & SOM., Illus.). 144p. (J). (gr. k-2). 19.95 (978-1-78508-892-6(0)) Milet Publishing.
Welcome to Africa, Swahili & English: Fun & Adventure, a Swahili/English Multicultural Book. 2004. (J). per. 9.95 (978-0-9742688-1-1(X)) Ndegwa, Catherine W.

AFRO-AMERICAN ACTORS
see African American Actors

AFRO-AMERICAN ART
see African American Art

AFRO-AMERICAN ARTISTS
see African American Artists

AFRO-AMERICAN ATHLETES
see African American Athletes

AFRO-AMERICAN AUTHORS
see African American Authors

AFRO-AMERICAN COOKING
see African American Cooking

AFRO-AMERICAN FOLKLORE
see African Americans—Folklore

AFRO-AMERICAN LITERATURE (ENGLISH)
see American Literature—African American Authors

AFRO-AMERICAN MUSIC
see African Americans—Music

AFRO-AMERICAN MUSICIANS
see African American Musicians

AFRO-AMERICAN POETRY (ENGLISH)
see American Poetry—African American Authors

AFRO-AMERICAN SCIENTISTS
see African American Scientists

AFRO-AMERICAN SOLDIERS
see African American Soldiers

AFRO-AMERICAN SONGS
see African Americans—Music

AFRO-AMERICAN SPIRITUALS
see Spirituals (Songs)

AFRO-AMERICANS
see African Americans

AFTERLIFE
see Future Life

AGED
see Older People

AGGREGATES
see Set Theory

AGRICULTURAL BANKS
see Banks and Banking

AGRICULTURAL BOTANY
see Botany, Economic

AGRICULTURAL LABORERS
see also Migrant Labor; Peasants

Adler, David A. & Adler, Michael S. A Picture Book of Cesar Chavez. Olofsdotter, Marie, illus. 2010. (ENG.). 32p. (J). (gr. -1-3). 17.95 (978-0-8234-2202-9(X)) Holiday Hse., Inc.
Berne, Emma Carlson. What's Your Story, Cesar Chavez? 2015. (ENG.). 32p. (J). (gr. k-3). 26.65 (978-1-4677-7967-8(9)) Lerner Publishing Group.
Brimner, Larry Dane. Strike! The Farm Workers' Fight for Their Rights. 2014. (ENG., Illus.). 172p. (J). (gr. 5). 16.95 (978-1-59078-997-1(0), Calkins Creek) Boyds Mills Pr.
Brown, Jonatha A., et al. César Chávez. McHargue, D., illus. 2007. (Biografías Gráficas (Graphic Biographies) Ser.). (SPA.). 32p. (gr. 5-8). lib. bdg. 27.00 (978-0-8368-7879-0(5)) Stevens, Gareth Publishing LLLP.
Brown, Monica. Lado a Lado: La Historia de Dolores Huerta y Cesar Chavez. Cepeda, Joe, illus. 2010.Tr. of Side by Side - The Story of Dolores Huerta & Cesar Chavez. (SPA & ENG.). 32p. (J). (gr. -1-3). 16.99 (978-0-06-122781-3(1), Rayo) HarperCollins Pubs.
Cuesta, Vivian. It Can Be Done: The Life & Legacy of César Chávez. 2003. (ENG., Illus.). 32p. (J). (gr. 6-8). pap. 8.47 net. (978-0-7652-3271-7(5), Celebration Pr.) Pearson Schl.
Dunn, Joeming W. Cesar Chavez, 1 vol. Espinosa, Rod, illus. 2008. (Bio-Graphics Ser.). (ENG.). 32p. (gr. 3-5). 28.50 (978-1-60270-172-4(5), Graphic Planet- Nonfiction) ABDO Publishing Co.
Ebon Research Systems Staff. Dare to Be... A Hero Vol. 3: Cesar Chavez. l.t. ed. 2003.Tr. of Atrevete Ser... Un Heroe Cesar Chavez. (ENG & SPA., Illus.). 16p. (J). 3.99 (978-0-9648313-6-0(8)) Ebon Research Systems Publishing, LLC.
Feinstein, Stephen. Lee Sobre Cesar Chavez. 2006. (I Like Biographies! Bilingual Ser.).Tr. of Read about Cesar Chavez. (ENG & SPA., Illus.). 24p. (J). (gr. -1-3). lib. bdg. 22.60 (978-0-7660-2744-2(9), Enslow Elementary) Enslow Pubs., Inc.
Frey, Wendy. Citizen Heroes. 2007. (Illus.). 68p. (J). (978-1-4105-0887-4(0)); (978-1-4105-0888-1(9)) Johnston, Don Inc.
Gay, Kathlyn. César Chávez: Fighting for Migrant Farmworkers. 2017. (Rebels with a Cause Ser.). 128p. (J). (gr. 8-8). lib. bdg. 37.27 **(978-0-7660-8951-8(7))** Enslow Pubs., Inc.
Gotsch, Patrice. Cesar Chavez: Changing Lives. Arreola, Gil, illus. 2006. 19p. pap. 6.30 (978-1-55501-780-4(0)) Ballard & Tighe Pubs.
Gregory, Josh. Cesar Chavez. 2015. (True Book & Trade; & Mdash;Biographies Ser.). (ENG., Illus.). 48p. (J). pap. 6.95 (978-0-531-21210-3(6)) Scholastic Library Publishing.
Guzman, Lila & Guzman, Rick. Cesar Chavez: Fighting for Fairness. 2006. (Famous Latinos Ser.). (Illus.). 32p. (J). (gr. 3-7). lib. bdg. 22.60 (978-0-7660-2370-3(2), Enslow Elementary) Enslow Pubs., Inc.
Libal, Joyce. Migrant Youth: Falling Between the Cracks. 2009. (Youth in Rural North America Ser.). (Illus.). 96p. (YA). (gr. 3-7). lib. bdg. 22.95 (978-1-4222-0020-9(5)) Mason Crest.
Magoon, Kekla. Cesar Chavez: Crusader for Labor Rights, 1 vol. 2010. (Essential Lives Set 5 Ser.). (ENG., Illus.). 112p. (J). (gr. 6-12). lib. bdg. 35.64 (978-1-61613-512-6(3)) ABDO Publishing Co.
Marsico, Katie. Working on a Farm. 2008. (21st Century Junior Library: Careers Ser.). (ENG.). 24p. (gr. 2-5). lib. bdg. 25.64 (978-1-60279-271-5(2), 200176) Cherry Lake Publishing.
Miklowitz, Gloria. Cesar Chavez. 2009. pap. 13.25 (978-1-60559-056-1(8)) Hameray Publishing Group, Inc.
Miklowitz, Gloria D. César Chávez. 2004. (ENG., Illus.). 29p. (J). (gr. 2-5). pap. 5.97 net. (978-0-7685-1215-1(8), Dominie Elementary) Pearson Schl.
Roome, Anne Ross & Mattern, Joanne. Cesar Chavez. 2016. (Rookie Biographies(tm) Ser.). (ENG., Illus.). 32p. (J). lib. bdg. 25.00 (978-0-531-22546-2(1), Children's Pr.) Scholastic Library Publishing.
Thompson, E. L. Cesar Chavez, with Profiles of Terence V. Powderly & Dolores Huerta. 2006. (Biographical Connections Ser.). (Illus.). 112p. (J). (978-0-7166-1827-0(3)) World Bk., Inc.
Tol, Alex Van & National Geographic Learning Staff. Dolores Huerta: Voice for the Working Poor. 2010. (ENG., Illus.). 112p. (J). pap. (978-0-7787-2545-9(6)) Crabtree Publishing Co.
Van Tol, Alex. Dolores Huerta: Voice for the Working Poor. 2010. (Crabtree Groundbreaker Biographies Ser.). (ENG., Illus.). 112p. (J). (gr. 5-8). lib. bdg. (978-0-7787-2536-7(7)) Crabtree Publishing Co.
Warren, Sarah E. Dolores Huerta: A Hero to Migrant Workers, 0 vols. Casilla, Robert, illus. 2012. (ENG.). 32p. (J). (gr. 2-5). 17.99 (978-0-7614-6107-4(8), 9780761461074, Amazon Children's Publishing) Amazon Publishing.
Youth in Rural North America, 13 vols., Set. Incl. Getting Ready for the Fair: Crafts, Projects, & Prize-Winning Animals. Libal, Joyce. (Illus.). (YA). (gr. 3-7). lib. bdg. 22.95 (978-1-4222-0019-3(1)); Growing up on a Farm: Responsibilities & Issues. Sieling, Peter. (Illus.). (YA). (gr. 3-7). lib. bdg. 22.95 (978-1-4222-0012-4(4)); Migrant Youth: Falling Between the Cracks. Libal, Joyce. (Illus.). (YA). (gr. 3-7). lib. bdg. 22.95 (978-1-4222-0020-9(5)); Rural Crime & Poverty: Violence, Drugs, & Other Issues. Ford, Jean Otto. (Illus.). (YA). (gr. 3-7). lib. bdg. 22.95 (978-1-4222-0016-2(7)); Rural Teens on the Move: Cars, Motorcycles, & off-Road Vehicles. Smith, Roger. (Illus.). (YA). (gr. 7-18). lib. bdg. 22.95 (978-1-4222-0021-6(3)); Teen Life among the Amish & Other Alternative Communities: Choosing a Lifestyle. Hunter, David. (J). (gr. 7-18). lib. bdg. 22.95 (978-1-4222-0017-9(5)); Teen Life on Reservations & in First Nation Communities: Growing up Native. McIntosh, Marsha. (Illus.). (YA). (gr. 3-7). lib. bdg. 22.95 (978-1-4222-0018-6(3)); Teen Minorities in Rural North America: Growing up Different. Bauchner, Elizabeth. (Illus.). (YA). (gr. 3-7). lib. bdg. 22.95 (978-1-4222-0014-8(0)); Teens & Rural Education: Opportunities & Challenges. Stewart, Faith. (Illus.). (YA). (gr. 3-7). lib. bdg. 22.95 (978-1-4222-0015-5(9)); Teens Who Make a Difference in Rural Communities: Youth Outreach Organizations & Community Action. Ford, Jean Otto. (Illus.). (YA). (gr. 7-18). lib. bdg. 22.95 (978-1-4222-0013-1(2)); 96p. 2009. (Youth in Rural North America Ser.). 2007. Set lib. bdg. 298.35 (978-1-4222-0011-7(6)) Mason Crest.

AGRICULTURAL MACHINERY

Alphabet Soup (Firm) Staff, contrib. by. Let's Look at Tractors. 2009. (Let's Go! Ser.). (Illus.). 18p. (J). (gr. -1-k). bds. 12.75 (978-1-60754-418-0(0)) Windmill Bks.
Award, Anna. Picture the World of Farm Machines. 2012. (ENG., Illus.). 16p. (J). pap. 3.95 (978-0-86163-966-3(9)) Award Pubns. Ltd. GBR. Dist: Parkwest Pubns., Inc.
AZ Books, creator. Musical Farm. 2012. (Lively Machines Ser.). (ENG., Illus.). 10p. (J). (gr. -1-k). bds. 10.95 (978-1-61889-326-0(2)) AZ Bks. LLC.
Bell, Samantha. Baler. 2016. (21st Century Basic Skills Library: Welcome to the Farm Ser.). (ENG.). 24p. (J). (gr. k-3). 24.21 (978-1-63471-037-4(1), 208228) Cherry Lake Publishing.
—Combine Harvester. 2016. (21st Century Basic Skills Library: Welcome to the Farm Ser.). (ENG.). 24p. (J). (gr. k-3). 24.21 (978-1-63471-034-3(7), 208216) Cherry Lake Publishing.
—Cotton Picker. 2016. (21st Century Basic Skills Library: Welcome to the Farm Ser.). (ENG.). 24p. (J). (gr. k-3). 24.21 (978-1-63471-035-0(5), 208220) Cherry Lake Publishing.
—Farm Quad. 2016. (21st Century Basic Skills Library: Welcome to the Farm Ser.). (ENG.). 24p. (J). (gr. k-3). 24.21 (978-1-63471-040-4(1), 208240) Cherry Lake Publishing.
—Plow & Ripper. 2016. (21st Century Basic Skills Library: Welcome to the Farm Ser.). (ENG.). 24p. (J). (gr. k-3). 24.21 (978-1-63471-036-7(3), 208224) Cherry Lake Publishing.
—Potato Harvester. 2016. (21st Century Basic Skills Library: Welcome to the Farm Ser.). (ENG.). 24p. (J). (gr. k-3). 24.21 (978-1-63471-039-8(8), 208236) Cherry Lake Publishing.
Borth, Teddy. Machines on the Farm, 1 vol. 2014. (On the Farm Ser.). (ENG., Illus.). 24p. (J). (gr. 4-8). lib. bdg. 28.50 (978-1-62970-054-0(1)) ABDO Publishing Co.
—Tools on the Farm, 1 vol. 2014. (On the Farm Ser.). (ENG.). 24p. (J). (gr. 4-8). lib. bdg. 28.50 (978-1-62970-055-7(X)) ABDO Publishing Co.
Borth, Teddy, et al. Herramientas de la Granja. 2015. (En la Granja Ser.). (SPA., Illus.). 24p. (gr. k-1). pap. 7.95 (978-1-4966-0449-1(0)) Capstone Classroom.
—Maquinaria de la Granja. 2015. (En la Granja Ser.). (SPA & ENG., Illus.). 24p. (gr. k-1). pap. 7.95 (978-1-4966-0451-4(2)) Capstone Classroom.
Clay, Kathryn. Farm Machines. 2015. (Wild about Wheels Ser.). (ENG.). 24p. (gr. k-1). lib. bdg. 26.65 (978-1-4914-2118-5(5), Pebble Plus) Capstone Press of Coughlan Cos.
Collins, Terry. John Deere's Powerful Idea: The Perfect Plow. Pearce, Carl, illus. 2015. (Story Behind the Name Ser.). (ENG.). 32p. (gr. 2-3). lib. bdg. 28.65 (978-1-4795-7138-3(5)) Picture Window Bks.
Daniels, Bethany. How Farming Has Changed. 2013. (InfoMax Readers Ser.). (ENG.). 24p. (J). (gr. 2-3). pap. 49.50 (978-1-4777-2405-7(2)); (Illus.). pap. 8.25 (978-1-4777-2404-0(4)) Rosen Publishing Group, Inc., The. (Rosen Classroom).
Dayton, Connor. Balers. 2012. (Illus.). 24p. (J). 49.50 (978-1-4488-5049-5(5)); pap. 8.25 (978-1-4488-5048-8(7)); lib. bdg. 22.60 (978-1-4488-4949-9(7)) Rosen Publishing Group, Inc., The. (PowerKids Pr.).
—Cultivators. 2012. 24p. (J). 49.50 (978-1-4488-5051-8(7)); pap. 8.25 (978-1-4488-5050-1(9)); lib. bdg. 22.60 (978-1-4488-4950-5(0)) Rosen Publishing Group, Inc., The. (PowerKids Pr.).
—Harvesters. 2012. (J). 49.50 (978-1-4488-5047-1(9)); pap. 8.25 (978-1-4488-5046-4(0)); lib. bdg. 22.60 (978-1-4488-4948-2(9)) Rosen Publishing Group, Inc., The. (PowerKids Pr.).
—Milking Machines/[text by Connor Dayton]. 2012. (Illus.). 24p. (J). 49.50 (978-1-4488-5041-9(X)); pap. 8.25 (978-1-4488-5040-2(1)); lib. bdg. 22.60 (978-1-4488-4945-1(4)) Rosen Publishing Group, Inc., The. (PowerKids Pr.).
—Planters. 2012. (J). 49.50 (978-1-4488-5045-7(2)); pap. 8.25 (978-1-4488-5044-0(4)); lib. bdg. 22.60 (978-1-4488-4947-5(0)) Rosen Publishing Group, Inc., The. (PowerKids Pr.).
Dickmann, Nancy. Farm Machines, 1 vol. 2010. (World of Farming Ser.). (ENG.). 24p. (gr. -1-1). 22.65 (978-1-4329-3928-1(9)); pap. 6.29 (978-1-4329-3942-7(4)) Heinemann-Raintree. (Acorn).
—Las Máquinas de la Granja. 2011. (Mundo de la Granja Ser.). 24p. (gr. -1-1). (SPA & ENG.). 22.65 (978-1-4329-5307-2(9)); (ENG & SPA.). pap. 6.29 (978-1-4329-5314-0(1)) Heinemann-Raintree. (Bellota).
Dufek, Holly. Planters & Cultivators: With Casey & Friends. Nunn, Paul E., illus. 2016. (Casey & Friends Ser.). (ENG.). 32p. (J). (gr. k-3). 14.99 (978-1-937747-55-8(7)) Octane Pr.
Fantastic Farm Machines. 2016. (Fantastic Farm Machines Ser.). 24p. (gr. 2-1). pap. 48.90 (978-1-4824-5280-8(4)); lib. bdg. 135.60 (978-1-4824-4519-0(0)) Stevens, Gareth Publishing LLLP.
Green, Sara. John Deere. 2016. (Brands We Know Ser.). (ENG., Illus.). 24p. (J). (gr. 3-8). lib. bdg. 25.95 (978-1-62617-348-4(6), Pilot Bks.) Bellwether Media.
Kilby, Don. In the Country. Kilby, Don, illus. 2006. (Wheels at Work Ser.). (ENG., Illus.). 24p. (J). (gr. -1-2). 5.95 (978-1-55337-985-0(3)) Kids Can Pr., Ltd. CAN. Dist: Hachette Bk. Group.
LaPadula, Thomas, illus. My Giant Tractor. 2014. (ENG.). 12p. (J). (gr. -1 — 1). bds. 10.99 (978-0-7944-3012-2(0), Reader's Digest Children's Bks.) Studio Fun International.
Marshall, Jane. Trucks & Diggers. 2013. (Wild Rides Ser.). 32p. (J). (gr. k-2). (978-1-84898-623-7(8), TickTock Books) Octopus Publishing Group.
Nelson, Kristin L. Farm Tractors on the Move. 2011. (Lightning Bolt Books Vroom-Vroom Ser.). (ENG.). 32p. (gr. k-2). lib. bdg. 26.60 (978-0-7613-6025-4(5)) Lerner Publishing Group.
North, Dawn. Pull-Alongs: Digger. 2007. 12p. (gr. -1). per. (978-1-84610-446-6(7)) Make Believe Ideas.
Peppas, Lynn. Vehicles on the Farm. 2010. (Vehicles on the Move Ser.). (ENG.). 32p. (J). (gr. k-3). pap. (978-0-7787-3065-1(4)); lib. bdg. (978-0-7787-3051-4(4)) Crabtree Publishing Co.
Peterson, Cris. Fantastic Farm Machines. Lundquist, David R., photos by. 2006. (ENG., Illus.). 32p. (J). (gr. -1-3). 17.95 (978-1-59078-271-2(2)) Boyds Mills Pr.
Randolph, Joanne. Snowplows. 2009. (Road Machines Ser.). 24p. (gr. k-1). 37.50 (978-1-60852-466-2(3), PowerKids Pr.) Rosen Publishing Group, Inc., The.
Rose, Simon. Agricultural Drones. 2017. (Drones Ser.). (ENG., Illus.). 32p. (gr. 3-4). lib. bdg. 27.99 (978-1-5157-3767-4(5), Edge Bks.) Capstone Press of Coughlan Cos.
Smith, Sian. Machines on the Farm, 1 vol. 2013. (Machines at Work Ser.). (ENG.). 24p. (J). (gr. 1-2). pap. 6.95 (978-1-4329-7506-7(4)); 23.32 (978-1-4329-7501-2(3)) Heinemann-Raintree. (Heinemann Read & Learn).
Sutcliffe, Jane. John Deere. 2006. (History Maker Biographies Ser.). (Illus.). 48p. (J). (gr. 3-7). lib. bdg. 26.60 (978-0-8225-6579-6(X), Lerner Pubns.) Lerner Publishing Group.
Vandewièle, Agnès. Monster Machines! on the Farm. Lepretre, Jean-Marc, illus. 2013. (ENG.). 18p. (J). (gr. -1-1). bds. 12.99 (978-1-4022-9247-7(3), Sourcebooks Jabberwocky) Sourcebooks, Inc.
Walter Foster Creative Team. Tractors & Farm Trucks. 2014. (Look, Read, Learn Ser.). (ENG., Illus.). 90p. (J). (gr. -1-1). 12.95 (978-0-7603-4713-3(1), Walter Foster Jr) Quarto Publishing Group USA.
Weingarten, E. T. Planters. 2016. (Fantastic Farm Machines Ser.). 24p. (gr. 2-1). 22.60 (978-1-4824-4585-5(9)) Stevens, Gareth Publishing LLLP.
Wilson, Hannah. Kingfisher Readers L2: Combine Harvesters. 2015. (Kingfisher Readers Ser.). (ENG., Illus.). 32p. (J). (gr. k-3). 12.99 (978-0-7534-7221-7(X), 9780753472217, Kingfisher) Roaring Brook Pr.

AGRICULTURAL PRODUCTS
see Farm Produce

AGRICULTURAL TOOLS
see Agricultural Machinery

AGRICULTURE
see also Botany, Economic; Dairying; Domestic Animals; Farms; Forests and Forestry; Fruit Culture; Gardening; Land Use; Livestock; Organic Farming; Reclamation of Land; Soils
also names of agricultural products e.g. Corn; etc.; and headings beginning with the words Agricultural and Farm

Apte, Sunita. Eating Green. 2009. (Going Green Ser.). (Illus.). 32p. (YA). (gr. 3-6). lib. bdg. 25.27 (978-1-59716-965-3(X)) Bearport Publishing Co., Inc.
Arlon, Penelope. La Granja. 2013. (Scholastic Explora Tu Mundo Ser.). (SPA.). 32p. (J). (gr. -1-3). 7.99 (978-0-545-48874-7(5), Scholastic en Espanol) Scholastic, Inc.
Ayer, Paula & Banyard, Antonia. Eat Up! An Infographic Exploration of Food. Wuthrich, Belle, illus. 2017. (Visual Exploration Ser.). (ENG.). 72p. (gr. 3-7). 22.95 (978-1-55451-884-5(9)) Annick Pr., Ltd. CAN. Dist: Publishers Group West (PGW).
—Eat Up! An Infographic Exploration of Food. Wuthrich, Belle, illus. 2017. (Visual Exploration Ser.). (ENG.). 72p. (gr. 3-7). pap. 12.95 (978-1-55451-883-8(0)) Annick Pr., Ltd. CAN. Dist: Publishers Group West (PGW).
Bailey, Gerry. Farming for the Future. 2011. (Planet SOS Ser.). (Illus.). 48p. (J). (gr. 3-6). pap. 14.05 (978-1-4339-4967-8(9)); lib. bdg. 31.95 (978-1-4339-4966-1(0)) Stevens, Gareth Publishing LLLP. (Gareth Stevens Learning Library).
Baines, John. Food for Life. 2006. (Sustainable Futures Ser.). (Illus.). 48p. (YA). (gr. 5-9). lib. bdg. 32.80 (978-1-58340-978-7(5), 1262622) Black Rabbit Bks.
Baines, John D. Food & Farming. 2009. (J). 32.80 (978-1-59920-103-0(8)) Black Rabbit Bks.
Bodden, Valerie. A Farming Town. 2007. (My First Look at: Communities Ser.). (Illus.). 24p. (J). (gr. -1-3). lib. bdg. 24.25 (978-1-58341-513-9(0), Creative Education) Creative Co., The.
Bontempo, Nancy Rogers. Word of Mouth: The Food You Eat. 2011. (Second Nature Ser.). 48p. (J). (gr. 5-8). 26.60 (978-1-59953-449-7(5)) Norwood Hse. Pr.
Borth, Teddy. Crops on the Farm, 1 vol. 2014. (On the Farm Ser.). (ENG.). 24p. (J). (gr. 4-8). lib. bdg. 28.50 (978-1-62970-052-6(5)) ABDO Publishing Co.
Bright, Michael. From Field to Plate. 2016. (Source to Resource Ser.). (ENG., Illus.). 32p. (J). (gr. 3-6). (978-0-7787-2705-7(X)) Crabtree Publishing Co.
Burgan, Michael. Farming Vegetables & Grains, 1 vol. 2011. (Ethics of Food Ser.). (ENG.). 56p. (gr. 6-6). 34.65 (978-1-4329-5100-9(9)); pap. 9.99 (978-1-4329-6190-9(X)) Heinemann-Raintree.
Carmichael, L. E. How Can We Reduce Agricultural Pollution? 2016. (Searchlight Books — What Can We Do about Pollution? Ser.). (ENG., Illus.). 40p. (J). (gr. 3-5). lib. bdg. 30.65 (978-1-4677-9514-2(3)) Lerner Publishing Group.
Casper, Julie Kerr. Agriculture: The Food We Grow & Animals We Raise. 2007. (Natural Resources Ser.). (Illus.). 210p. (YA). (gr. 7-12). lib. bdg. 39.50 (978-0-8160-6352-9(4)) Facts On File, Inc.
Connelly, Garrett. Construcao Do Tanques Do Ferrocimento. 2nd ed. 2004. (SPA & FRE., Illus.). 80p. per. 22.50 (978-0-9748016-5-0(8)) ferrocement.com.
—Construcción de Tanques de Ferrocemento: Segunda Edición. 2nd ed. 2004.Tr. of Construçao do Tanques do Ferrocimento. (SPA., Illus.). 80p. per. 22.50 (978-0-9748016-2-9(3)) ferrocement.com.
Council for Agricultural Science and Technology Staff, contrib. by. Boundless Science for Bountiful Agriculture: Winning Student Essays, 2003. 2003. viii, 55p. (J). (978-1-887383-24-0(7)) Council for Agricultural Science & Technology (CAST).
Daniels, Bethany. How Farming Has Changed. 2013. (InfoMax Readers Ser.). (ENG.). 24p. (J). (gr. 2-3). pap. 49.50 (978-1-4777-2405-7(2)); (Illus.). pap. 8.25 (978-1-4777-2404-0(4)) Rosen Publishing Group, Inc., The. (Rosen Classroom).
Dickmann, Nancy. Jobs on a Farm, 1 vol. 2010. (World of Farming Ser.). (ENG., Illus.). 24p. (gr. -1-1). 22.65 (978-1-4329-3937-3(8)); pap. 6.29 (978-1-4329-3945-8(9)) Heinemann-Raintree. (Acorn).
—Los Trabajos en la Granja. 2011. (Mundo de la Granja Ser.). 24p. (gr. -1-1). (SPA & ENG.). 22.65 (978-1-4329-5309-6(5)); (ENG & SPA.). pap. 6.29 (978-1-4329-5316-4(8)) Heinemann-Raintree. (Bellota).
Dorling Kindersley Publishing Staff. Follow the Trail: Farm. 2016. (Follow the Trail Ser.). (ENG., Illus.). 14p. (J). (-k). bds. 9.99 (978-1-4654-4480-6(7), DK Children) Dorling Kindersley Publishing, Inc.
—My First Farm. 2016. (ENG., Illus.). 36p. (J). (— 1). bds. 5.99 (978-1-4654-4487-5(4), DK Children) Dorling Kindersley Publishing, Inc.
—Tractor. 2010. (Baby Touch & Feel Ser.). (ENG.). 14p. (J). (gr. -1 — 1). bds. 5.99 (978-0-7566-7132-7(9), DK Children) Dorling Kindersley Publishing, Inc.
Dufek, Holly. Busy on the Farm: With Casey & Friends. Nunn, Paul E. & Kasun, Mike, illus. 2017. (ENG.). 32p. (J). 14.99 (978-1-937747-79-4(4)) Octane Pr.
Dunn, Joeming W. George Washington Carver, 1 vol. Allen, Chris, illus. 2008. (Bio-Graphics Ser.). (ENG.). 32p. 28.50 (978-1-60270-171-7(7), Graphic Planet- Nonfiction) ABDO Publishing Co.
Fajardo, Anika. The Dish on Food & Farming in Colonial America. (Life in the American Colonies Ser.). (ENG.). 32p. (gr. 3-4). 2017. pap. 8.10 **(978-1-5157-9748-7(1))** 2011. pap. 8.10 (978-1-4296-7217-7(X)) 2011. pap. 47.70 (978-1-4296-7218-4(8)) Capstone Press of Coughlan Cos. (Fact Finders).
Flounders, Anne. Growing Good Food. 2014. (Our Green Earth Ser.). (Illus.). 32p. (gr. 2-4). pap. 8.95 (978-1-939656-31-5(1)) Red Chair Pr.
Flour: Level M, 6 vols. (Wonder Worldtm Ser.). 16p. 34.95 (978-0-7802-1998-4(8)) Wright Group/McGraw-Hill.
Gaarder-Juntti, Oona. What in the World Is a Green Garden?, 1 vol. 2010. (Super SandCastle Ser.). (ENG.). 24p. 25.65 (978-1-61613-188-3(8), Super SandCastle) ABDO Publishing Co.
Goodman, Polly. Food, Farming, & the Future. 2011. (Earth Alert! Ser.). 32p. (J). (gr. 3-6). lib. bdg. 26.60 (978-1-4339-6005-5(2)) Stevens, Gareth Publishing LLLP.
Gordon, Sharon. At Home on the Farm. (Bookworms: at Home Ser.). (Illus.). (J). 2007. 31p. (gr. -1-3). pap. 6.99 (978-0-7614-3308-8(2)) 2005. (SPA., 32p. (gr. 3-7). lib. bdg. (978-0-7614-1958-7(6)) Marshall Cavendish Corp. (Benchmark Bks.).
—At Home on the Farm/Mi Casa en la Granja. 2006. (Bookworms Ser.). (ENG & SPA., Illus.). 32p. (gr. k-2). lib. bdg. 15.95 (978-0-7614-2454-3(7)) Marshall Cavendish Corp.
—Mi Casa en la Granja. 2006. (Bookworms Ser.). (SPA & ENG., Illus.). 32p. (gr. k-2). lib. bdg. 15.95 (978-0-7614-2375-1(3)) Marshall Cavendish Corp.

Graham, Ian. Farming & the Future. 2010. (Food & Farming Ser.). (Illus.). 32p. (YA). (gr. 4-7). lib. bdg. 25.25 (978-1-61532-578-8(6)) Rosen Publishing Group, Inc., The.

—Food Technology. 2009. (New Technology Ser.). (YA). (gr. 7-12). 34.25 (978-1-59920-162-7(3)) Black Rabbit Bks.

Gray, Shannon. Growing up Cranberry. Murfield, Anna, illus. 2012. 24p. pap. 9.50 (978-1-937165-27-7(2)) Orange Hat Publishing.

Green, Jen. Food & Farming, 1 vol. 2012. (Impact of Environmentalism Ser.). (ENG.). 64p. (gr. 6-10). pap. 10.95 (978-1-4329-6523-5(9)); lib. bdg. 35.99 (978-1-4329-6517-4(4)) Heinemann-Raintree.

Gregory, Helen. Find Out about Farming, 1 vol. 2011. (Wonder Readers Early Level Ser.). (ENG.). (gr. -1-1). 32p. pap. 5.99 (978-1-4296-7803-2(8)); 16p. pap. 35.94 (978-1-4296-8087-5(3)) Capstone Press of Coughlan Cos. (Wonder Readers).

—Harvest Season, 1 vol. (Wonder Readers Next Steps: Social Studies). (ENG.). (gr. -1-1). 2013. 20p. lib. bdg. 22.65 (978-1-4765-0042-3(8)) 2011. 16p. pap. 35.94 (978-1-4296-8093-6(8)) 2011. 32p. pap. 5.99 (978-1-4296-8058-5(X)) Capstone Press of Coughlan Cos. (Wonder Readers).

Hagen, Debra. Harvest on the Farm - Lapbook. Kinney, Cyndi, ed. 2013. (J). pap. 25.99 (978-1-62472-033-8(1)); cd-rom 19.99 (978-1-62472-032-1(3)) Knowledge Box Central.

—Harvest on the Farm - Lapbook: Assembled. Kinney, Cyndi, ed. 2013. (J). pap. 26.99 (978-1-62472-035-2(8)) Knowledge Box Central.

Hodge, Deborah. Up We Grow! A Year in the Life of a Small, Local Farm. Harris, Brian, illus. 2010. (ENG.). 32p. (J). (gr. -1-2). 16.95 (978-1-55453-561-3(1)) Kids Can Pr., Ltd. CAN. Dist: Hachette Bk. Group.

—Watch Me Grow! A Down-to-Earth Guide to Growing Food in the City. Harris, Brian, illus. 2011. (ENG.). 32p. (J). (gr. -1-2). 16.95 (978-1-55453-618-4(9)) Kids Can Pr., Ltd. CAN. Dist: Hachette Bk. Group.

Holt, Rinehart and Winston Staff. Environmental Science Chptr. 15: Food & Agriculture. 4th ed. Date not set. pap. 11.20 (978-0-03-068076-2(X)) Holt McDougal.

Hord, Colleen. From Farm to Restaurant. 2015. (ENG.). 24p. (gr. k-2). 28.50 (978-1-63430-057-5(2)) Rourke Educational Media.

Jakab, Cheryl. Food Supplies. 2010. (Environment in Focus Ser.). 32p. (gr. 4). 28.50 (978-1-60870-090-5(9)) Marshall Cavendish Corp.

Jeffries, Joyce. Meet the Farmer. 2013. (People Around Town Ser.). (Illus.). 24p. (J). (gr. k-2). pap. 8.15 (978-1-4339-9368-8(6)); pap. 48.90 (978-1-4339-9369-5(4)); (ENG., lib. bdg. 22.60 (978-1-4339-9367-1(8)) Stevens, Gareth Publishing LLLP.

—Meet the Farmer / Conoce a Los Granjeros. 2013. (People Around Town / Gente de Mi Ciudad Ser.). (SPA & ENG., Illus.). 24p. (J). (gr. k-2). 22.60 (978-1-4339-9466-1(6)) Stevens, Gareth Publishing LLLP.

Kalman, Bobbie. Food & Farming Then & Now. 2013. (ENG., Illus.). 24p. (J). (978-0-7787-0126-2(3)); pap. (978-0-7787-0208-5(1)) Crabtree Publishing Co.

King, Zelda. Examining Meadow Habitats. 2009. (Graphic Organizers: Habitats Ser.). 24p. (gr. 2-3). 42.50 (978-1-61513-097-9(7), PowerKids Pr.) Rosen Publishing Group, Inc., The.

Krusinski, Anna. Farm Friends: A Visit to the Local Farm. 2016. (Kubu Ser.). (ENG., Illus.). 34p. (J). (gr. -1-2). pap. 5.99 (978-1-57826-475-9(8), Hatherleigh Pr.) Hatherleigh Co., Ltd., The.

Lascaro, Rita. Down on the Farm. 2003. (Green Light Readers Level 1 Ser.). (ENG., Illus.). 24p. (J). (gr. -1-3). pap. 3.95 (978-0-15-204855-6(3)) Houghton Mifflin Harcourt Publishing Co.

—Down on the Farm. 2003. (Green Light Readers — Level 1 Ser.). (gr. -1-2). lib. bdg. 13.50 (978-0-613-64490-7(5), Turtleback) Turtleback Bks.

Levey, Richard H. & Franck, Daniel H. Dust Bowl! The 1930s Black Blizzards. 2016. (X-Treme Disasters That Changed America Ser.). (ENG.). 32p. (J). (gr. 2-7). pap. 8.95 (978-1-944998-75-2(6)) Bearport Publishing Co., Inc.

Liebman, Daniel. I Want to Be a Farmer. 2016. (I Want to Be Ser.). (ENG., Illus.). 24p. (J). (gr. -1-2). pap. 3.99 (978-1-77085-787-2(7), 9781770857872) Firefly Bks., Ltd.

Liebman, Daniel & Mlawer, Teresa. Quiero Ser Granjero. 2016. (Quiero Ser.). (SPA., Illus.). 24p. (J). (gr. -1-2). pap. 6.99 (978-1-77085-864-0(4), 9781770858640) Firefly Bks., Ltd.

Lindeen, Mary. I Watch Fall Harvests. 2016. (First Step Nonfiction — Observing Fall Ser.). (ENG., Illus.). 24p. (J). (gr. k-2). 23.99 (978-1-5124-0794-5(1)) Lerner Publishing Group.

Lomberg, Michelle. Agriculture. 2017. **(978-1-5105-1929-9(7))** SmartBook Media, Inc.

Macceca, Stephanie. George Washington Carver: Agriculture Pioneer, 1 vol. 2007. (Science Readers Ser.). (ENG.). 32p. (J). (gr. 3-3). pap. 8.99 (978-0-7439-0590-9(3)) Shell Educational Publishing.

Mann, Charles. 1493 for Young People: From Columbus's Voyage to Globalization. 2016. (For Young People Ser.). (ENG., Illus.). 416p. (J). (gr. 7). pap. 18.95 (978-1-60980-663-7(8), Triangle Square) Seven Stories Pr.

Marsh, Carole. Farm Days A-Z Coloring Book. Ford, Yvonne, illus. 2009. 28p. (J). 5.99 (978-0-635-07421-8(4)) Gallopade International.

Marsico, Katie. Working on a Farm. 2008. (21st Century Junior Library: Careers Ser.). (ENG.). 24p. (gr. 2-5). lib. bdg. 25.64 (978-1-60279-271-5(2), 200176) Cherry Lake Publishing.

Martin, Claudia. Farming. 2010. (Working Animals Ser.). 64p. (gr. 5-18). 28.50 (978-1-60870-162-9(X)) Marshall Cavendish Corp.

Martin, Jacqueline Briggs. Farmer Will Allen & the Growing Table. Larkin, Eric, illus. 2013. (ENG.). 32p. (J). (gr. k). 17.95 (978-0-9836615-3-5(7)) READERS to EATERS.

Mason, Paul. How Big Is Your Food Footprint? 2009. (Environmental Footprints Ser.). 32p. (gr. 4). 28.50 (978-0-7614-4413-8(0)) Marshall Cavendish Corp.

Meegan, Britta. Farming Then & Now. 2013. (Rosen Readers Ser.). (ENG.). 24p. (J). (gr. 2-3). pap. 8.25 (978-1-4777-2423-1(0)); pap. 49.50 (978-1-4777-2424-8(9)) Rosen Publishing Group, Inc., The. (Rosen Classroom).

Mickelson, Trina. Free-Range Farming. 2016. (Growing Green Ser.). (ENG., Illus.). 64p. (J). (gr. 6-8). lib. bdg. 34.65 (978-1-4677-9389-6(2)); 51.99 (978-1-4677-9710-8(3), Lerner Pubns.) Lerner Publishing Group.

Moore, David. Expl on Your Own on the Farm. 2009. (Explore on Your Own Ser.). (ENG.). 12p. (C). pap. 7.95 (978-0-7362-5551-6(6)) National Geographic School Publishing, Inc.

Morris, Edmund. Ten Acres Enough: A Practical Experience, Showing How A Very Small Farm May Be Made to Keep A Very Large Family. with Extensive & Profitable Experie. 2006. 260p. per. 23.99 (978-1-4255-2247-6(5)); 268p. per. 23.99 (978-1-4255-2368-8(4)) Michigan Publishing.

Morrison, Heather S. Inventors of Food & Agriculture Technology. 2015. (Designing Engineering Solutions Ser.). (ENG., Illus.). 144p. (J). (gr. 8-8). lib. bdg. 42.79 (978-1-5026-0664-8(X)) Cavendish Square Publishing.

Mortensen, Lori. Working on the Farm. Thompson, Jeffrey, illus. 2010. (First Graphics: My Community Ser.). (ENG.). 24p. (gr. 1-2). pap. 35.70 (978-1-4296-5617-7(4)) Capstone Press of Coughlan Cos.

Netzley, Patricia D. Science & Sustainable Agriculture. 2017. (Science & Sustainability Ser.). (ENG.). 80p. (YA). (gr. 5-12). **(978-1-68282-251-7(6))** ReferencePoint Pr., Inc.

O'Keefe, Emily. Crop Circles. 2015. (Unsolved Mysteries Ser.). (ENG.). 24p. (J). (gr. 1-4). 28.50 (978-1-63407-069-0(0), 208904) Child's World, Inc., The.

Owen, Ruth. How Do Plants Defend Themselves? 2014. (World of Plants Ser.). 32p. (J). (gr. 2-5). lib. bdg. 26.25 (978-1-4777-7157-0(3), PowerKids Pr.) Rosen Publishing Group, Inc., The.

Perritano, John. Agriculture, Vol. 10. 2016. (Stem in Current Events Ser.). 64p. (J). (gr. 7). 23.95 (978-1-4222-3588-1(2)) Mason Crest.

Pettiford, Rebecca. Harvesting. Fretland VanVoorst, Jenny, ed. 2015. (J). lib. bdg. 25.65 (978-1-62031-230-8(1)) Jump! Inc.

Piddock, Charles & Keen, Jared. Future of Farming. 2017. **(978-1-5105-2227-5(1))** SmartBook Media, Inc.

Priddy, Roger. My Big Farm Book. 2011. (My Big Board Bks.). (ENG., Illus.). 12p. (J). (gr. -1 — 1). bds. 8.99 (978-0-312-51082-4(9), 9780312510824, Priddy Bks.) St. Martin's Pr.

Ransom, Candice. The Day of the Black Blizzard. Harden, Laurie, illus. (On My Own History Ser.). 48p. (J). 2016. (ENG.). (gr. 2-4). pap. 6.95 (978-1-5124-1152-2(3)) 2011. pap. 6.95 (978-0-7613-3938-0(8)) Lerner Publishing Group. (First Avenue Editions).

Ready, Dee. Farmers Help, 1 vol. 2014. (Our Community Helpers Ser.). (ENG.). 24p. (gr. k-1). lib. bdg. 21.99 (978-1-4765-3951-5(0), Pebble Bks.) Capstone Press of Coughlan Cos.

Reis, Ronald A. The Dust Bowl. 2008. (Great Historic Disasters Ser.). (Illus.). 128p. (gr. 5-8). lib. bdg. 35.00 (978-0-7910-9737-3(4), Chelsea Hse.) Facts On File, Inc.

Reynolds, Jan. Only the Mountains Do Not Move: A Maasai Story of Culture & Conservation. Reynolds, Jan, photos by. 2011. (ENG., Illus.). 40p. (J). pap. 9.95 (978-1-60060-844-5(2)); (gr. 1-6). pap. 18.95 (978-1-60060-333-4(5)) Lee & Low Bks., Inc.

Rissman, Rebecca. Going to a Farm, 1 vol. 2012. (World of Field Trips Ser.). (ENG.). 24p. (gr. -1-1). pap. 6.29 (978-1-4329-6075-9(X)); lib. bdg. 22.65 (978-1-4329-6066-7(0)) Heinemann-Raintree. (Acorn).

Rose, Simon. Agricultural Drones. 2017. (Drones Ser.). (ENG., Illus.). 32p. (gr. 3-4). pap. 7.95 (978-1-5157-3775-9(6), Edge Bks.) Capstone Press of Coughlan Cos.

Roza, Greg. America's Transition from Agriculture to Industry: Drawing Inferences & Conclusions. (Critical Thinking in American History Ser.). 48p. 2009. (gr. 5-8). 53.00 (978-1-61512-087-1(4), Rosen Reference) 2005. (Illus.). (J). (gr. k-3). lib. bdg. 29.25 (978-1-4042-0410-2(5)) Rosen Publishing Group, Inc., The.

Rustad, Martha E. H. Fall Harvests: Bringing in Food. Enright, Amanda, illus. 2011. (Fall's Here! Ser.). pap. 39.62 (978-0-7613-8645-2(9), Millbrook Pr.); (ENG.). 24p. pap. 6.95 (978-0-7613-8508-0(8), Millbrook Pr.); (ENG.). 24p. lib. bdg. 23.93 (978-0-7613-5067-5(5)) Lerner Publishing Group.

Ryan, Pam Muñoz. How Do You Raise a Raisin? Brown, Craig McFarland & Astrella, Mark, illus. 2003. (ENG.). 32p. (J). (gr. k-3). pap. 7.95 (978-1-57091-398-3(6)) Charlesbridge Publishing, Inc.

Schuh, Mari. Harvest in Fall. 2013. (ENG., Illus.). 24p. (J). lib. bdg. 25.65 (978-1-62031-058-8(9)) Jump! Inc.

Shin, Hye-eun & Cowley, Joy. The Warli People. Jeong, Su-bi, illus. 2017. (J). 10.00 **(978-0-8028-5476-6(1)**, Eerdmans Bks For Young Readers) Eerdmans, William B. Publishing Co.

Shores, Erika L. Harvest Time. 2015. (Celebrate Fall Ser.). (ENG., Illus.). 24p. (gr. k-1). lib. bdg. 21.99 (978-1-4914-6002-3(4), Pebble Bks.) Capstone Press of Coughlan Cos.

Sieling, Peter. Growing up on a Farm: Responsibilities & Issues. 2009. (Youth in Rural North America Ser.). (Illus.). 96p. (YA). (gr. 3-7). lib. bdg. 22.95 (978-1-4222-0012-4(4)) Mason Crest.

Siemens, Jared. Farmer. 2015. (978-1-4896-4225-7(0)) Weigl Pubs., Inc.

Smith, Andrea Claire Harte. The Effects of Farming. 2004. (Earth's Changing Landscape Ser.). (Illus.). 45p. (J). lib. bdg. 28.50 (978-1-58340-475-1(9)) Black Rabbit Bks.

Sobol, Richard. Growing Peace: A Story of Farming, Music, & Religious Harmony, 1 vol. 2016. (ENG., Illus.). 40p. (J). 18.95 (978-1-60060-450-8(1)) Lee & Low Bks., Inc.

Spilsbury, Richard & Spilsbury, Louise. Farming & the Environment. 2010. (Food & Farming Ser.). (Illus.). 32p. (YA). (gr. 4-7). lib. bdg. 25.25 (978-1-61532-577-1(8)) Rosen Publishing Group, Inc., The.

—Feeding the World. 2010. (Food & Farming Ser.). (Illus.). 32p. (YA). (gr. 4-7). lib. bdg. 25.25 (978-1-61532-579-5(4)) Rosen Publishing Group, Inc., The.

Staniford, Linda. From Farm to Fork: Where Does My Food Come From? 2016. (From Farm to Fork: Where Does My Food Come From? Ser.). (ENG.). 24p. (gr. k-2). 95.96 (978-1-4846-3373-1(3), Heinemann Read & Learn) Heinemann-Raintree.

—Where Do Grains Come From? 2016. (From Farm to Fork: Where Does My Food Come From? Ser.). (ENG.). 24p. (gr. k-2). lib. bdg. 23.99 (978-1-4846-3349-6(0)) Capstone Press of Coughlan Cos.

Stewart, Melissa & Young, Allen M. No Monkeys, No Chocolate. Wong, Nicole, illus. 2013. (ENG.). 32p. (J). (gr. k-3). 16.95 (978-1-58089-287-2(6)) Charlesbridge Publishing, Inc.

Stilwell, Debra. Where Does Our Food Come From? 2012. (Everyday Mysteries Ser.). (ENG., Illus.). 24p. (J). (gr. 2-4). pap. 8.15 (978-1-4339-6319-3(1)); lib. bdg. 22.60 (978-1-4339-6317-9(5)) Stevens, Gareth Publishing LLLP.

Syrewicz, Connor. Farming, Ranching, & Agriculture. 2013. (Earning $50,000 - $100,000 with a High School Diploma or Less Ser.: 14). 64p. (J). (gr. 7-18). 22.95 (978-1-4222-2895-1(9)) Mason Crest.

Tan, Richard. Farm Field Trip. 2015. (Rosen REAL Readers: STEM & STEAM Collection). (ENG.). 8p. pap. 5.46 (978-1-4994-9589-8(7), Rosen Classroom) Rosen Publishing Group, Inc., The.

Tate, Nikki. Down to Earth: How Kids Help Feed the World, 1 vol. (Orca Footprints Ser.). (ENG., Illus.). 48p. (J). (gr. 3-7). 2017. pap. 12.95 (978-1-4598-1412-7(6)) 2013. 19.95 (978-1-4598-0423-4(6)) Orca Bk. Pubs. USA.

Taylor, Chad. All about Meadows. 2016. (Rosen REAL Readers: STEM & STEAM Collection). 8p. (gr. 1-k). pap. 5.46 (978-1-5081-2392-7(6), Rosen Classroom) Rosen Publishing Group, Inc., The.

Traini, Agostino, illus. Chef Foody's Field Trip. 2015. (ENG.). 40p. (J). (gr. -1-2). 14.95 (978-0-7892-1241-2(2), Abbeville Kids) Abbeville Pr., Inc.

Urban Gardening & Farming for Teens. 2013. (Urban Gardening & Farming for Teens Ser.). 64p. (YA). (gr. 7-12). 166.25 (978-1-4777-1788-2(9)) Rosen Publishing Group, Inc., The.

Vander Hook, Sue. The Dust Bowl, 1 vol. 2009. (Essential Events Set 3 Ser.). (ENG., Illus.). 112p. (J). (gr. 6-12). lib. bdg. 35.64 (978-1-60453-512-9(1)) ABDO Publishing Co.

Veitch, Catherine. Farms Around the World, 1 vol. 2011. (ENG.). 24p. (gr. -1-1). pap. 9.95 (978-1-4329-5498-7(9)); 25.99 (978-1-4329-5353-9(2)) Heinemann-Raintree. (Acorn Read-Aloud).

Veness, Kimberley. Let's Eat: Sustainable Food for a Hungry Planet, 1 vol. 2017. (Orca Footprints Ser.). (ENG., Illus.). 48p. (J). (gr. 3-7). 19.95 (978-1-4598-0939-0(4)) Orca Bk. Pubs. USA.

Vogel, Julia. Save the Planet: Local Farms & Sustainable Foods. 2010. (Explorer Library: Language Arts Explorer Ser.). (ENG.). 32p. (gr. 4-8). pap. 14.21 (978-1-60279-669-0(6), 200916); lib. bdg. 28.50 (978-1-60279-660-7(2), 200353) Cherry Lake Publishing.

Waldendorf, Kurt. Hooray for Farmers! 2016. (Bumba Books (tm) — Hooray for Community Helpers! Ser.). (ENG.). 24p. (J). (gr. -1-1). 25.32 (978-1-5124-1443-1(3)) Lerner Publishing Group.

Waldendorf, Kurt. ¡Que Vivan los Granjeros! 2017. (Bumba Books (tm) en Español — ¡Que Vivan Los Ayudantes Comunitarios! (Hooray for Community Helpers!) Ser.). (SPA.). 24p. (J). (gr. -1-1). 25.32 **(978-1-5124-4138-3(4))** Lerner Publishing Group.

Welvaert, Scott R. Follow That Crop: From the Farmer's Field to Our Grocery Store. 2003. (From Here to There Ser.). (J). (978-1-58417-194-2(4)); pap. (978-1-58417-195-9(2)) Lake Street Pubs.

When I Grow Up - Farmer. 2016. (When I Grow Up ... Ser.). (ENG., Illus.). 32p. (J). (gr. -1-1). pap. 8.99 **(978-0-7232-9472-6(0))** Penguin Bks., Ltd. GBR. Dist: Independent Pubs. Group.

Whittaker, Helen. Food. 2011. (Living Green Ser.). 32p. (gr. 3). 28.50 (978-1-60870-574-0(9)) Marshall Cavendish GBR. Dist: Marshall Cavendish Corp.

Woods, Michael & Woods, Mary B. Ancient Agricultural Technology: From Sickles to Plows. 2011. (Technology in Ancient Cultures Ser.). (ENG.). 96p. (gr. 6-12). lib. bdg. 31.93 (978-0-7613-6526-6(5)) Lerner Publishing Group.

World Book, Inc. Staff, contrib. by. Foraging to Supermarkets: A Timeline of Food. 2016. (J). (978-0-7166-3547-5(X)) World Bk., Inc.

World Book, Inc Staff, contrib. by. Producing & Obtaining Food. 2008. (Living Green Ser.). (J). (978-0-7166-1409-8(X)) World Bk., Inc.

Wroble, Lisa A. Starving: Can We Feed Everyone? 2016. (End of Life As We Know It Ser.). (ENG.). 128p. (J). (gr. 7-8). 37.27 (978-0-7660-7374-6(2)) Enslow Pubs., Inc.

Wroble, Lisa A. & Library. Food for a Greener Planet: What You Can Do. 2010. (Green Issues in Focus Ser.). (Illus.). 112p. (J). (gr. 7-12). lib. bdg. 33.27 (978-0-7660-3349-8(X)) Enslow Pubs., Inc.

Yasuda, Anita. Eat Green. 2010. (Being Green Ser.). (Illus.). 32p. (YA). (gr. 3-6). lib. bdg. 27.13 (978-1-61690-091-5(1)); (J). (gr. 4-6). pap. 12.95 (978-1-61690-092-2(X)) Weigl Pubs., Inc.

AGRICULTURE—FICTION

Alarid, Carilyn & Markel, Marilyn. Hits With His Fist Gives a Helping Hand: Mimbres Children Learn about Caring. 2012. (Illus.). 113p. (J). pap. 16.95 (978-0-86534-508-9(2)) Sunstone Pr.

Andrews, Andy. The Boy Who Changed the World. 2010. 16.99 (978-1-4003-1718-9(5)) Nelson, Thomas Inc.

—The Kid Who Changed the World, 1 vol. 2014. (ENG.). 40p. (J). 14.99 (978-1-4003-2433-0(5)) Nelson, Thomas Inc.

Apps, Jerry. Eat Rutabagas. Beatty-Anderson, Annika, illus. 2016. (ENG.). 28p. (J). (gr. 1-6). 10.00 (978-1-930596-08-5(1)) Guest Cottage, Incorporated, The.

Bourgeois, Paulette & Clark, Brenda. Franklin's Pumpkin. Southern, Shelley, illus. 2004. (Kids Can Read Ser.). (ENG.). 32p. (J). (gr. 1-2). 3.95 (978-1-55337-496-1(7)); 14.95 (978-1-55337-495-4(9)) Kids Can Pr., Ltd. CAN. Dist: Hachette Bk. Group.

Castillo, Gary D. Quesadilla Moon. 2007. 100p. (J). (gr. 3-7). per. 9.95 (978-1-55885-433-8(9), Piñata Books) Arte Publico Pr.

Clement, Nathan, illus. Big Tractor. 2015. (ENG.). 32p. (J). (gr. k-3). 16.95 (978-1-62091-790-9(4)) Boyds Mills Pr.

Espluga, Maria. I Am a Farmer. 2009. (I Am A... (Alphabet Soup) Ser.). (Illus.). 24p. (J). (gr. k-1). pap. 8.15 (978-1-60754-249-0(8)); lib. bdg. 22.60 (978-1-60754-248-3(X)) Windmill Bks.

Gabel, Stacey. It's Time to Combine. Neuman, Richard, illus. 2009. 24p. pap. 13.95 (978-1-60844-121-1(0)) Dog Ear Publishing, LLC.

Gillingham, Sara & Chronicle Books Staff. In My Meadow. Siminovich, Lorena, illus. 2009. (ENG.). 12p. (J). (gr. -1 — 1). bds. 8.99 (978-0-8118-7338-3(2)) Chronicle Bks. LLC.

Gomi, Taro. Mommy! Mommy! 2013. (ENG., Illus.). 22p. (J). (gr. -1 — 1). bds. 6.99 (978-1-4521-0834-6(X)) Chronicle Bks. LLC.

Hayes, Joe. Don't Say a Word, Mama / No Digas Nada, Mama. 2013. (Illus.). 32p. (gr. -1-3). (ENG & SPA.). 17.95 (978-1-935955-29-0(2)); (SPA & ENG., (J). pap. 8.95 (978-1-935955-45-0(4)) Cinco Puntos Pr.

Hensel, Rita. Humble Stew in Going Country. 2008. 41p. pap. 24.95 (978-1-60563-219-3(8)) America Star Bks.

Hines, Chrissie & Ferreras, Alberto. El Perro y el Gato. Winslow, Justin, illus. 2010.Tr. of Perro y el Gato: la Nieve. (SPA.). 28p. 3.99 (978-0-9828167-1-4(5)) Home Box Office, Inc.

Howard-Parham, Pam. This Is Farmer Greg. Coates, Jennifer, illus. l.t. ed. 2005. (HRL Board Book Ser.). (gr. -1-k). pap. 10.95 (978-1-57332-305-5(5), HighReach Learning, Incorporated) Carson-Dellosa Publishing, LLC.

Hutchinson, Wanda Phillips. The Bee Man. 2009. 24p. pap. 14.49 (978-1-4490-3596-9(5)) AuthorHouse.

Jordan, Mary Ellen & Weldon, Andrew. Lazy Daisy, Cranky Frankie: Bedtime on the Farm. Weldon, Andrew, illus. 2013. (ENG., Illus.). 24p. (J). (gr. -1-3). 15.99 (978-0-8075-4400-6(0)) Whitman, Albert & Co.

Kann, Victoria. Apples, Apples, Apples! Kann, Victoria, illus. 2016. (Pinkalicious Ser.). (ENG., Illus.). 24p. (J). (gr. -1-3). 14.75 (978-0-606-39267-9(X)) Turtleback Bks.

Lamadrid, Enrique R. & Arellano, Juan Estevan. Juan the Bear & the Water of Life: La Acequia de Juan del Oso. Córdova, Amy, illus. 2008. (Paso Por Aqui Ser. in the Nuevomexicano Literary Heritage Ser.). (SPA & ENG.). 48p. (J). (gr. 5-18). 17.95 (978-0-8263-4543-1(3)) Univ. of New Mexico Pr.

Milway, Katie Smith. The Good Garden: How One Family Went from Hunger to Having Enough. Daigneault, Sylvie, illus. 2010. (CitizenKid Ser.). (ENG.). 32p. (J). (gr. 3-7). 18.95 (978-1-55453-488-3(7)) Kids Can Pr., Ltd. CAN. Dist: Hachette Bk. Group.

Pellegrino, Victor. Uncle Kawaiolas Dream. 2010. 32p. 18.95 (978-0-945045-08-3(5)) Maui Arthoughts Co.

Pennypacker, Sara. Sparrow Girl. Tanaka, Yoko, illus. 2009. (ENG.). 40p. (J). (gr. k-4). 16.99 (978-1-4231-1187-0(7)) Hyperion Pr.

Sandburg, Carl. The Huckabuck Family: And How They Raised Popcorn in Nebraska & Quit & Came Back. Small, David, illus. 2006. 30p. (J). (gr. k-4). reprint ed. 16.00 (978-1-4223-5854-2(2)) DIANE Publishing Co.

Sherman, Gisela. An Early Harvest, 1 vol. 2015. (ENG.). 348p. (YA). (gr. 9-12). pap. 12.95 (978-1-927583-64-7(0)) Second Story Pr. CAN. Dist: Orca Bk. Pubs. USA.

Smith Ford, Deborah. The Little Apple. 2009. 32p. pap. 14.62 (978-1-4251-8806-1(0)) Trafford Publishing.

Stanek, Robert, pseud. Visit Garden Box Farms. 2008. (ENG., Illus.). 28p. (J). pap. 5.29 (978-1-57545-190-9(5)) RP Media.

Switzer, Vern. Lucy the Cantaloupe. Connally, Perry L., Sr., illus. 2005. 32p. (J). 15.95 (978-0-9753542-1-6(3)) Rural Farm Productions.

—Puffy the Watermelon. Listokin, David & Connally, Perry L., Sr., illus. 2004. 24p. (J). 15.95 (978-0-9753542-0-9(5)) Rural Farm Productions.

Walker, Lisa & Coyne, Adrian. The Boy Who Brought Thunder. 2012. (Illus.). 40p. pap. 12.95 (978-9987-08-222-3(X)) Mkuki na Nyoka Pubs. TZA. Dist: African Bks. Collective, Ltd.

Williams, Hal G. Qudola's Quest. 2011. 48p. pap. 16.95 (978-1-4560-5167-9(9)) America Star Bks.

Williams, Tad & Beale, Deborah. The Dragons of Ordinary Farm. Swearingen, Greg, illus. 2009. (ENG.). 416p. (J). (gr. 4-7). 16.99 (978-0-06-154345-6(4)) HarperCollins Pubs.

Winfield, Arthur M. The Rover Boys on the Farm. 2006. pap. 27.95 (978-1-4254-9148-2(0)) Kessinger Publishing, LLC.

AGRICULTURE—VOCATIONAL GUIDANCE

Cohn, Jessica. On the Job at a Farm. Scheuer, Lauren, illus. 2016. (Core Content Social Studies — on the Job Ser.). (ENG.). 32p. (J). (gr. 2-5). lib. bdg. 26.65 (978-1-63440-112-8(3)) Red Chair Pr.

Echaore-McDavid, Susan & McDavid, Richard. Agriculture, Food & Natural Resources. 2010. (Career Opportunities Ser.). 352p. pap. 18.95 (978-0-8160-7457-0(7), Checkmark Bks.); 338p. (C). (gr. 9). 49.50 (978-0-8160-7456-3(9), Ferguson Publishing Co.) Facts On File, Inc.

Jeffries, Joyce. Farmers, 01 vols., 1. 2016. (Hands-On Jobs Ser.). (ENG., Illus.). 24p. (J). pap. 8.25 (978-1-5081-4359-8(5), PowerKids Pr.) Rosen Publishing Group, Inc., The.

Johanson, Paula. Jobs in Sustainable Agriculture. 2010. (Green Careers Ser.). 80p. (YA). (gr. 7-12). E-Book 61.20 (978-1-4488-0135-0(4)) Rosen Publishing Group, Inc., The.

Navarre, Gabrielle. Cool Careers Without College for People Who Love Nature. 2013. (New Cool Careers Without College Ser.). (Illus.). 144p. (J). (gr. 7-12). 35.95 (978-1-4777-1821-6(4)) Rosen Publishing Group, Inc., The.

Oleksy, Walter. Choosing a Career in Agriculture. 2009. (World of Work Ser.). 64p. (gr. 5-5). 58.50 (978-1-60854-327-4(7)) Rosen Publishing Group, Inc., The.

Olesky, Walter. Choosing a Career in Agriculture. 2005. (World of Work Ser.). (Illus.). 64p. (YA). (gr. 7-12). lib. bdg. 31.95 (978-0-8239-3332-7(6)) Rosen Publishing Group, Inc., The.

AGRONOMY

see Agriculture

AGUE

see Malaria

AHAB, CAPTAIN (FICTITIOUS CHARACTER)—FICTION

Brook, Henry. Moby Dick. 2010. (Usborne Classics Retold Ser.). 144p. (J). 6.99 (978-0-7945-2761-7(2), Usborne) EDC Publishing.

Dalmatian Press Staff, adapted by. Moby Dick. (J). 9.95 (978-1-56156-308-1(0)) Kidsbooks, LLC.

Eisner, Will & Melville, Herman. Moby Dick. 2003. (ENG., Illus.). 32p. (J). pap. 7.95 (978-1-56163-294-7(5)) NBM Publishing Co.

Melville, Herman. Cities of the Fantastic: Brusel. Eisner, Will, illus. 2003. (Cities of the Fantastic Ser.). (ENG.). 120p. 19.95 (978-1-56163-291-6(0)) NBM Publishing Co.

—Moby Dick. Eisner, Will, illus. 2003. (ENG.). 32p. (J). (gr. 4-7). 15.95 (978-1-56163-293-0(7)) NBM Publishing Co.

—Moby Dick. 2008. (Bring the Classics to Life Ser.). (Illus.). 72p. (gr. 5-12). pap., act. bk. ed. 10.95 (978-1-55576-326-8(X), EDCTR-508B) EDCON Publishing Group.

—Moby Dick. Elphinstone, Katy, illus. 2014. (Travel & Adventure Ser.). (ENG.). 64p. pap. 6.95 (978-1-906230-72-2(2)) Real Reads Ltd. GBR. Dist: Casemate Pubs. & Bk. Distributors, LLC.

—Moby Dick. 2003. (Historias de Siempre Ser.). (SPA., Illus.). 92p. (J). (gr. 5-8). pap. 9.95 (978-84-204-5732-1(9)) Santillana USA Publishing Co., Inc.

—Moby Dick: Or, the Whale. 2010. 528p. pap. 12.95 (978-1-59594-840-3(6), Wingspan Pr.) WingSpan Publishing.

—Moby Dick, Grades 5-12. adapted ed. pap., tchr. ed. 4.95 (978-0-8359-0123-9(8)) Globe Fearon Educational Publishing.

—Moby Dick, or the Whale. 2005. (J). Pt. 1. cd-rom (978-1-4105-0265-0(1))Pt. 2. pap. 9.95 (978-1-4105-0267-4(8)) Vol. 1. pap. 9.95 (978-1-4105-0263-6(5)) Vol. 2. cd-rom (978-1-4105-0269-8(4)) Johnston, Don Inc.

Melville, Herman & Huth, Michael. Moby Dick. 2004. (Veröffentlichung der Maximilian-Gesellschaft für die Jahre 2004/2005 Ser.). (GER., Illus.). 92p. (J). (978-3-921743-52-2(4)) Maximilian-Gesellschaft e. V.

Melville, Herman, et al. Moby Dick. (Classics Illustrated Ser.). (Illus.). 52p. (YA). pap. 4.95 (978-1-57209-003-3(0)) Classics International Entertainment, Inc.

Stevenson, Robert Louis. Moby Dick. 2014. (Graphic Classics Ser.). (Illus.). 48p. (gr. 3-6). 37.10 (978-1-908973-88-7(9)) Book Hse. GBR. Dist: Black Rabbit Bks.

Wakeham, Kate. Moby-Dick, 1 vol. Tempest, Annabel, illus. 2017. (ENG.). 30p. 12.99 **(978-1-4236-4784-3(X))** Gibbs Smith, Publisher.

AIDS (DISEASE)

AIDS. 2005. (Introducing Issues with Opposing Viewpoints Ser.). (Illus.). 144p. (YA). (gr. 7-10). lib. bdg. 34.70 (978-0-7377-3218-4(0), Greenhaven Pr., Inc.) Cengage Gale.

Bardhan-Quallen, Sudipta. AIDS. (Understanding Diseases & Disorders Ser.). (ENG., Illus.). (J). 2005. 48p. (gr. 4-8). lib. bdg. 29.15 (978-0-7377-2638-1(5), Kidhaven) 2004. 112p. (gr. 7-10). 33.45 (978-1-59018-404-2(1)) Cengage Gale.

Berlatsky, Noah. Hiv/aids. 2011. (Global Viewpoints Ser.). (ENG., Illus.). 224p. (gr. 10-12). pap. 31.70 (978-0-7377-5657-9(8), Greenhaven Pr., Inc.) Cengage Gale.

Berlatsky, Noah, ed. Hiv/aids. 2011. (Global Viewpoints Ser.). (Illus.). 224p. (YA). (gr. 9-12). 40.45 (978-0-7377-5656-2(X)) Cengage Gale.

Boberg, C. E. Why Do I Need to Understand AIDS? 2014. (ENG., Illus.). 112p. (YA). 42.79 (978-1-62524-065-1(1), Village Earth Pr.) Harding Hse. Publishing Sebice Inc.

Cefrey, Holly. AIDS. 2009. (Epidemics Ser.). 64p. (gr. 5-5). 58.50 (978-1-61512-272-1(9)) Rosen Publishing Group, Inc., The.

Cefrey, Holly & McPartland, Randall. HIV & AIDS. 2015. (Deadliest Diseases of All Time Ser.). (ENG., Illus.). 64p. (J). (gr. 8-8). lib. bdg. 34.21 (978-1-5026-0642-6(9)) Cavendish Square Publishing.

Chilman-Blair, Kim. Superheroes on a Medical Mission, 6 vols., Set 2. Incl. Medikidz Explain ADHD. Taddeo, John. lib. bdg. 29.25 (978-1-4358-9456-3(1)); Medikidz Explain Autism. Taddeo, John. lib. bdg. 29.25 (978-1-4358-9460-0(X)); Medikidz Explain Depression. Deloache, Shawn. lib. bdg. 29.25 (978-1-4358-9455-6(3)); Medikidz Explain HIV. Taddeo, John. lib. bdg. 29.25 (978-1-4358-9458-7(8)); Medikidz Explain Sleep Apnea. Deloache, Shawn. lib. bdg. 29.25 (978-1-4358-9459-4(6)); Medikidz Explain Swine Flu. lib. bdg. 29.25 (978-1-4358-9457-0(X)); (YA). (gr. 5-8). (Illus.). 40p. 2010. Set lib. bdg. 175.50 (978-1-4358-9570-6(3), Rosen Reference) Rosen Publishing Group, Inc., The.

Chilman-Blair, Kim & Taddeo, John. Medikidz Explain HIV. 2010. (Superheroes on a Medical Mission Ser.). (Illus.). 40p. (YA). pap. 11.75 (978-1-4488-1839-6(7)); (gr. 5-8). lib. bdg. 29.25 (978-1-4358-9458-7(8)) Rosen Publishing Group, Inc., The. (Rosen Reference).

Choosing the Best Path. 3rd ed. 2004. (978-0-9724890-2-7(9)) Choosing The Best Publishing.

Colson, Mary. Fighting AIDS. 2014. (Tiny Battlefields Ser.). 48p. (YA). (gr. 6-8). pap. 84.30 (978-1-4824-1306-9(X)) Stevens, Gareth Publishing LLLP.

Cotts, Nat. How Do AIDS & Science Connect? 2014. (Illus.). 112p. (YA). (978-1-62524-060-6(0), Village Earth Pr.) Harding Hse. Publishing Sebice Inc.

Dicker, Katie. AIDS & HIV. 2011. (Global Issues Ser.). (Illus.). 48p. (YA). (gr. 5-8). lib. bdg. 29.25 (978-1-4488-1876-1(1), Rosen Reference) Rosen Publishing Group, Inc., The.

Dittmer, Lori. HIV/AIDS. 2011. (J). 35.65 (978-1-60818-071-4(9), Creative Education) Creative Co., The.

Ellis, Deborah. Our Stories, Our Songs: African Children Talk about AIDS, 1 vol. 2005. (ENG., Illus.). 104p. (J). (gr. 4-7). (978-1-55041-913-9(7)) Fitzhenry & Whiteside, Ltd.

Espejo, Roman, ed. AIDS. 2012. (Opposing Viewpoints Ser.). (ENG., Illus.). 240p. (J). (gr. 10-12). pap. 29.45 (978-0-7377-5706-4(X), Greenhaven Pr., Inc.); (YA). (gr. 9-12). lib. bdg. 42.95 (978-0-7377-5705-7(1)) Cengage Gale.

Gelletly, LeeAnne. AIDS & Health Issues. Ojakorotu, Victor, ed. 2013. (Africa: Progress & Problems Ser.: 13). (Illus.). 112p. (J). (gr. 7-18). 24.95 (978-1-4222-2935-4(1)) Mason Crest.

Global Issues, 6 vols., Set. Incl. AIDS & HIV. Dicker, Katie. lib. bdg. 29.25 (978-1-4488-1876-1(1)); Fundamentalism. Connolly, Sean. lib. bdg. 29.25 (978-1-4488-1877-8(X)); Globalization. McGregor, Harriet. lib. bdg. 29.25 (978-1-4488-1878-5(8)); Refugees. Senker, Cath & Hachette Children's Group. lib. bdg. 29.25 (978-1-4488-1880-8(X)); Terrorism. Woolf, Alex. lib. bdg. 29.25 (978-1-4488-1881-5(8)); (YA). (gr. 5-8). (Global Issues Ser.). (Illus.). 48p. 2011. Set lib. bdg. 159.00 (978-1-4488-2484-7(2), Rosen Reference) Rosen Publishing Group, Inc., The.

Gutwein, Austin & Hillard, Todd. Take Your Best Shot: Do Something Bigger Than Yourself, 1 vol. 2009. (ENG.). 240p. (gr. 7-12). pap. 14.99 (978-1-4003-1515-4(8)) Nelson, Thomas Inc.

Hinds, Maurene J. Fighting the AIDS & HIV Epidemic: A Global Battle. 2007. (Issues in Focus Today Ser.). (Illus.). 128p. (J). (gr. 3-7). lib. bdg. 33.27 (978-0-7660-2683-4(3)) Enslow Pubs., Inc.

Holt, Rinehart and Winston Staff. A Lifetime of Health Chptr. 21: HIV & AIDS. 4th ed. Date not set. pap. 11.20 (978-0-03-068116-5(2)) Holt McDougal.

Houle, Michelle M. AIDS in the 21st Century: What You Should Know. 2003. (Issues in Focus Ser.). (Illus.). 112p. (J). (gr. 6-12). lib. bdg. 27.94 (978-0-7660-1690-3(0)) Enslow Pubs., Inc.

James, Otto. AIDS. 2010. (Voices Ser.). (YA). (gr. 5-9). 34.25 (978-1-59920-282-2(4)) Black Rabbit Bks.

Johanson, Paula. HIV & AIDS. (Coping in a Changing World Ser.). 112p. (gr. 7-7). 2009. 63.90 (978-1-61512-020-8(3)) 2007. (Illus.). (YA). lib. bdg. 34.60 (978-1-4042-0948-0(4)) Rosen Publishing Group, Inc., The.

Kallen, Stuart A. The Race to Discover the AIDS Virus: Luc Montagnier vs Robert Gallo. 2012. (Scientific Rivalries & Scandals Ser.). (ENG.). 64p. (gr. 6-12). lib. bdg. 33.27 (978-0-7613-5490-1(5)) Lerner Publishing Group.

Marsico, Katie. HIV/AIDS, 1 vol. 2010. (Essential Issues Set 1 Ser.). (ENG.). 112p. (J). (gr. 6-12). lib. bdg. 35.64 (978-1-60453-955-4(0), Essential Library) ABDO Publishing Co.

McIntosh, Kenneth & Walker, Ida. Youth with HIV/AIDS: Living with the Diagnosis. 2009. (Helping Youth with Mental, Physical, & Social Challenges Ser.). (Illus.). 128p. (YA). (gr. 7-18). lib. bdg. 24.95 (978-1-4222-0146-6(5)) Mason Crest.

Raum, Elizabeth. I Know Someone with HIV/AIDS, 1 vol. 2011. (Understanding Health Issues Ser.). (ENG.). 32p. (gr. 1-3). 27.32 (978-1-4329-4554-1(8)); pap. 8.29 (978-1-4329-4570-1(X)) Heinemann-Raintree. (Heinemann First Library).

Reed, Jennifer. The AIDS Epidemic: Disaster & Survival. 2005. (Deadly Disasters Ser.). (Illus.). 48p. (J). lib. bdg. 25.27 (978-0-7660-2382-6(6)) Enslow Pubs., Inc.

Ringbom, Antonia & Wiklund, Alison. The Hiding Hyena. 2nd ed. 2007. (YA). (978-0-9789617-1-8(4)) H.B.P., Inc.

Robinson, Richard. Frequently Asked Questions about AIDS & HIV. (FAQ: Teen Life Ser.). 64p. 2009. (gr. 5-6). 58.50 (978-1-61512-562-3(0)) 2008. (Illus.). (YA). (gr. 7-12). lib. bdg. 31.95 (978-1-4042-1808-6(4)) Rosen Publishing Group, Inc., The.

Routh, Kristina. AIDS. 2004. (21st Century Issues Ser.). (Illus.). 48p. (gr. 5-12). lib. bdg. 31.00 (978-0-8368-5641-5(4), Gareth Stevens Secondary Library) Stevens, Gareth Publishing LLLP.

Schauer, Peter J. AIDS & Other Killer Viruses & Pandemics. 2017. (J). **(978-1-5345-0139-3(8))** Greenhaven Publishing LLC.

Silverstein, Alvin, et al. The AIDS Update. 2007. (Disease Update Ser.). (Illus.). 128p. (J). (gr. 4-7). lib. bdg. 33.27 (978-0-7660-2746-6(5)) Enslow Pubs., Inc.

Winnick, Judd. Pedro & Me. 2011. 14.10 (978-0-7848-3537-1(3), Everbind) Marco Bk. Co.

Yount, Lisa. Luc Montagnier. 2011. (Trailblazers in Science & Technology Ser.). 144p. (gr. 6-12). 35.00 (978-1-60413-661-6(8), Chelsea Hse.) Facts On File, Inc.

AIDS (DISEASE)—FICTION

Albright, Kendra S. & Gavigan, Karen W., eds. AIDS in the Endzone. Petrulis, Sarah, illus. 2014. (Young Palmetto Bks.). (ENG.). 40p. pap. 12.95 (978-1-61117-424-3(4)) Univ. of South Carolina Pr.

Carlson, Melody. Notes from a Spinning Planet: Papua New Guinea. 2007. (Notes from a Spinning Planet Ser.: 2). (ENG.). 240p. (YA). (gr. 7-12). per. 12.99 (978-1-4000-7145-6(3), WaterBrook Pr.) Crown Publishing Group.

Chinodya, Shimmer. Tale of Tamari. 2003. (Illus.). 76p. pap. (978-1-77922-026-4(X)) Weaver Pr.

Kramer, Berri, photos by & text. Mbali: A story from South Africa. Kramer, Berri, text. 2nd ed. 2006. (Illus.). (J). per. (978-0-9706901-1-1(8)) Rotaplast Pr.

Loyie, Larry & Brissenden, Constance. The Gathering Tree. 2nd ed. 2006. (Larry Loyie Ser.). (ENG., Illus.). 48p. pap. 18.95 (978-1-894778-42-8(1)) Theytus Bks., Ltd. CAN. Dist: Univ. of Toronto Pr.

Namukasa, Glaydah. Voice of a Dream. 2006. (Illus.). 97p. (978-1-4050-9592-1(X)) Macmillan/McGraw-Hill Schl. Div.

Odhiambo, Eucabeth. Auma's Long Run. 2017. (ENG.). 304p. (J). (gr. 3-6). 17.99 **(978-1-5124-2784-4(5)**, Carolrhoda Bks.) Lerner Publishing Group.

Olaogbebikan, Michael Olumide. Playmate. 2013. (Illus.). 20p. pap. 19.82 (978-1-4772-4659-7(2)) AuthorHouse.

Oosthuizen, Sarah & Groenewald, Catherine. Nosipho Comes to Stay. 2011. (ENG., Illus.). 24p. (J). (gr. k-2). pap. 8.95 (978-1-77009-834-3(8)) Jacana Media ZAF. Dist: Independent Pubs. Group.

Roman, Annette. Passage 2: HIV/AIDS — First Love. Ng, Leandro, illus. 2005. (1 World Manga Ser.: Vol. 2). (ENG.). 40p. (J). pap. 3.99 (978-0-8213-6406-2(5)) World Bank Pubns.

Sempebwa, Christina. Art of Hope. 2012. 42p. pap. (978-1-908895-47-9(0)) FeedARead.com.

Sheinmel, Courtney. Positively. 2010. (ENG.). 240p. (J). (gr. 4-9). pap. 6.99 (978-1-4424-0622-3(4), Simon & Schuster Bks. For Young Readers) Simon & Schuster Bks. For Young Readers.

The Smartest Thing. 2004. (YA). (978-0-9762904-8-3(0)) Layne Morgan Media, Inc.

Verdi, Jessica. My Life after Now. 2013. (ENG.). 304p. (YA). (gr. 7-12). pap. 9.99 (978-1-4022-7785-6(7), 9781402277856) Sourcebooks, Inc.

AIDS (DISEASE)—PATIENTS

Frey, Wendy. Citizen Heroes. 2007. (Illus.). 68p. (J). (978-1-4105-0888-1(9)); (978-1-4105-0887-4(0)) Johnston, Don Inc.

Hager, Jenna Bush. Ana's Story: A Journey of Hope. Baxter, Mia, illus. 2008. (ENG.). 304p. (YA). (gr. 9-12). pap. 9.99 (978-0-06-137909-3(3)) HarperCollins Pubs.

McIntosh, Kenneth & Walker, Ida. Youth with HIV/AIDS: Living with the Diagnosis. 2007. (Helping Youth with Mental, Physical, & Social Challenges Ser.). (Illus.). 128p. (YA). (gr. 8-12). pap. 14.95 (978-1-4222-0446-7(4)) Mason Crest.

Rawl, Paige, et al. Positive. 2014. (ENG.). 288p. (YA). (gr. 8). 18.99 (978-0-06-234251-5(7)) HarperCollins Pubs.

Sparks, Beatrice & Sparks, B-Ed. It Happened to Nancy: A True Story from the Diary of a Teenager. 2004. (YA). (gr. 7-12). lib. bdg. 19.65 (978-0-7857-2073-7(1), Turtleback) Turtleback Bks.

Upjohn, Rebecca, et al. Patrick's Wish, 1 vol. 2010. (ENG., Illus.). 24p. (J). (gr. 1-3). 7.95 (978-1-897187-70-8(X)) Second Story Pr. CAN. Dist: Orca Bk. Pubs. USA.

Winick, Judd. Pedro & Me: Friendship, Loss, & What I Learned. 2009. (ENG., Illus.). 192p. (YA). (gr. 9-13). pap. 19.99 (978-0-8050-8964-6(0), 9780805089646) Square Fish.

AIR

Here are entered works treating of air as an element and of its chemical and physical properties. Works treating of the body of air surrounding the earth are entered under Atmosphere.

see also Aerodynamics; Atmosphere

Air. (Jump Ser.). (Illus.). 32p. (J). (gr. 2-7). pap. (978-1-882210-26-8(3)) Action Publishing, Inc.

Air. 2014. (Four Elements Ser.). (Illus.). 32p. (J). (gr. k-3). lib. bdg. 26.25 (978-1-4777-9261-2(9)) Windmill Bks.

Branley, Franklyn M. Air Is All Around You. O'Brien, John A., illus. 2006. (Let's-Read-And-Find-Out Science 1 Ser.). (ENG.). 40p. (J). (gr. -1-3). pap. 5.99 (978-0-06-059415-2(2), Collins) HarperCollins Pubs.

Butterfield, M. & Edom, H. Science with Air. rev. ed. 2008. (Science Activities Ser.). 24p. (J). pap. 5.99 (978-0-7945-2331-2(5), Usborne) EDC Publishing.

Davis, Barbara J. Air & Weather. 2007. (Gareth Stevens Vital Science: Earth Science Ser.). (Illus.). 48p. (gr. 5-12). pap. 14.05 (978-0-8368-7871-4(X)); lib. bdg. 27.00 (978-0-8368-7760-1(8)) Stevens, Gareth Publishing LLLP. (Gareth Stevens Secondary Library).

Evans, David & Williams, Claudette. Air & Flying. (Let's Explore Science Ser.). (Illus.). (J). 12.95 (978-0-590-74943-5(9)) Scholastic, Inc.

Flynn, James J. Air. 2003. (Matter & Materials Ser.). (J). pap. (978-1-58417-169-0(3)); lib. bdg. (978-1-58417-163-8(4)) Lake Street Pubs.

Gardner, Robert. Science Fair Projects about the Atmosphere. 2016. (Hands-On Science Ser.). 48p. (J). pap. 11.70 (978-0-7660-8220-5(2)) Enslow Pubs., Inc.

Green, Jen. The Air We Breathe. 2008. (Our Earth Ser.). (Illus.). 24p. (J). (gr. 1-4). lib. bdg. 22.60 (978-1-4042-4274-6(0)) Rosen Publishing Group, Inc., The.

Holt, Rinehart and Winston Staff. Environmental Science Chptr. 12: Air. 4th ed. Date not set. pap. 11.20 (978-0-03-068072-4(7)) Holt McDougal.

Jennings, Terry. Aire (Air) (SPA.). 32p. (J). 6.95 (978-84-348-1743-2(8)) SM Ediciones ESP. Dist: AIMS International Bks., Inc.

Kalman, Bobbie. Rapping about the Air Around Us. 2012. (ENG.). 24p. (J). (978-0-7787-2797-2(1)); pap. (978-0-7787-2804-7(8)) Crabtree Publishing Co.

Katz Cooper, Sharon. Using Air, 1 vol. 2007. (Exploring Earth's Resources Ser.). (ENG., Illus.). 24p. (gr. 3-7). 6.79 (978-1-4034-9323-1(5), Heinemann Read & Learn) Heinemann-Raintree.

Korb, Rena. Awesome Air, 1 vol. Reibeling, Brandon, illus. 2007. (Science Rocks Ser.). (ENG.). 32p. (gr. -1-4). 28.50 (978-1-60270-036-9(2), Looking Glass Library- Nonfiction) Magic Wagon.

Lawrence, Ellen. Air. 2015. (FUN-Damental Experiments Ser.). (ENG.). 24p. (J). (gr. -1-3). lib. bdg. 23.93 (978-1-62724-539-5(1)) Bearport Publishing Co., Inc.

MacAulay, Kelley. Why Do We Need Air? 2014. (ENG., Illus.). 24p. (J). (978-0-7787-0491-1(2)); pap. (978-0-7787-0495-9(5)) Crabtree Publishing Co.

Madgwick, Wendy. Up in the Air: 17 Easy-to-Follow Experiments for Learning Fun - Find Out about Flight & How Weather Works! 2014. (ENG., Illus.). 270p. (J). (gr. -1-12). 8.99 (978-1-86147-350-9(8), Armadillo) Anness Publishing GBR. Dist: National Bk. Network.

Meiani, Antonella. Air. 2003. (Experimenting with Science Ser.). (Illus.). 40p. (J). (gr. 4-8). lib. bdg. 23.93 (978-0-8225-0082-7(5)) Lerner Publishing Group.

Michele, Tracey. Gas & Air. 2011. (Learn-Abouts Ser.). (Illus.). 16p. (J). pap. 7.95 (978-1-59920-644-8(7)) Black Rabbit Bks.

Nunn, Daniel. Air, 1 vol. 2012. (Why Living Things Need Ser.). (ENG.). 24p. (gr. -1-1). pap. 6.29 (978-1-4329-5919-7(0)); lib. bdg. 22.65 (978-1-4329-5913-5(1)) Heinemann-Raintree. (Acorn).

Oxlade, Chris. Experiments with Air & Water, 1 vol. 2015. (ENG., Illus.). 32p. (J). lib. bdg. 27.50 (978-1-4777-5793-2(7), PowerKids Pr.) Rosen Publishing Group, Inc., The.

Paris, Stephanie. Pop! Air & Water Pressure, 1 vol. 2nd rev. ed. 2013. (Nonfiction Readers Ser.). (ENG.). 64p. (J). (gr. 5-5). pap. 10.99 (978-1-4333-4939-3(6)) Teacher Created Materials, Inc.

Parker, Steve. Tabletop Scientist — the Science of Air: Projects & Experiments with Air & Flight. 2013. (ENG., Illus.). 32p. (J). (gr. 3-8). pap. 6.99 (978-0-486-49265-0(6)) Dover Pubns., Inc.

Pluckrose, Henry. Air. 2007. (Let's Explore: Elements Ser.). (Illus.). 32p. (J). (gr. 4-7). lib. bdg. 27.10 (978-1-59771-033-6(4)) Sea-To-Sea Pubns.

Richards, Jon. Air & Flight. (Science Factory Ser.). 32p. (gr. 4-5). 2009. 50.50 (978-1-60853-018-2(3), PowerKids Pr.) 2008. (Illus.). (YA). lib. bdg. 26.50 (978-1-4042-3907-4(3)) Rosen Publishing Group, Inc., The.

Salas, Laura Purdie & Weakland, Mark. Bubbles Float, Bubbles Pop, 1 vol. (Science Starts Ser.). (ENG., 32p. (gr. 1-2). 2011. Illus.). pap. 8.10 (978-1-4296-6141-6(0)) 2010. lib. bdg. 27.32 (978-1-4296-5250-6(0)) Capstone Press of Coughlan Cos. (Aplus Bks.).

Samson, Tess. What Goes Up? 2010. (Sight Word Readers Ser.). (J). 3.49 (978-1-60719-617-4(4)) Newmark Learning LLC.

Sherman, Jill. Clean Air. 2017. (J). pap. **(978-0-7660-9143-6(0))** Enslow Pubs., Inc.

Simon, Seymour & Fauteux, Nicole. Let's Try It Out in the Air. Cushman, Doug, illus. 2003. (Let's Try It Out Ser.). 28p. (J). (gr. -1-3). lib. bdg. 14.65 (978-0-7569-1477-6(9)) Perfection Learning Corp.

Sohn, Emily & Kentor Schmauss, Judy. Air & Weather: Where'd My Hat Go? 2011. (IScience Readers Ser.). 24p. (J). (gr. k-2). lib. bdg. 21.27 (978-1-59953-403-9(7)) Norwood Hse. Pr.

Stille, Darlene R. El Aire: Afuera, Adentro y en Todos Lados, 1 vol. Robledo, Sol, tr. from ENG. Boyd, Sheree, illus. 2007. (Ciencia Asombrosa Ser.). (SPA.). 24p. (gr. k-4). lib. bdg. 26.65 (978-1-4048-3209-1(2)) Picture Window Bks.

Sundance/Newbridge LLC Staff. Bubbles, Bubbles Everywhere. 2007. (Early Science Ser.). (gr. k-3). 18.95 (978-1-4007-6206-4(5)); pap. 6.10 (978-1-4007-6202-6(2)) Sundance/Newbridge Educational Publishing.

Taylor-Butler, Christine. Tiny Life in the Air. 2005. (Rookie Read-About Science Ser.). (ENG., Illus.). 32p. (J). (gr. 1-2). lib. bdg. 20.50 (978-0-516-25273-5(9), Children's Pr.) Scholastic Library Publishing.

Vogel, Julia. Discover Air. Yamada, Jane, illus. 2014. (Science Around Us Ser.). (ENG.). 24p. (J). (gr. -1-2). 25.64 (978-1-62687-300-1(3), 207141) Child's World, Inc., The.

Walker, Kate. Air. 2011. (Investigating Earth Ser.). 32p. (gr. 2). 28.50 (978-1-60870-558-0(7)) Marshall Cavendish Corp.

Weakland, Mark. Las Burbujas Flotan, Las Burbujas Explotan/Bubbles Float, Bubbles Pop. 2012. (Comienza la Ciencia/Science Starts Ser.). 32p. (gr. 1-2). (MUL.). pap. 7.99 (978-1-4765-0065-2(7)); (SPA, ENG & MUL.). lib. bdg. 27.32 (978-1-4296-8257-2(4)) Capstone Press of Coughlan Cos. (A+ Bilingue/Bilingual).

AIR—POLLUTION

Ajmera, Maya & Browning, Dominique. Every Breath We Take. 2016. (ENG., Illus.). 32p. (J). (gr. -1-3). lib. bdg. 16.95 (978-1-58089-616-0(2)) Charlesbridge Publishing, Inc.

Allaby, Michael. Atmosphere: A Scientific History of Air, Weather, & Climate. Garratt, Richard, illus. 2009. (Discovering the Earth Ser.). 242p. (C). (gr. 9-18). 39.95 (978-0-8160-6098-6(3)) Facts On File, Inc.

Amstutz, L. J. & Amstutz, Lisa J. How Can We Reduce Transportation Pollution? 2016. (Searchlight Books — What Can We Do about Pollution? Ser.). (ENG., Illus.). 40p. (J). (gr. 3-5). lib. bdg. 30.65 (978-1-4677-9515-9(1)) Lerner Publishing Group.

Chambers, Catherine. Are Humans Damaging the Atmosphere? 2015. (Earth Debates Ser.). (ENG.). 48p. (gr. 4-6). 33.32 (978-1-4846-0998-9(0), Heinemann InfoSearch) Heinemann-Raintree.

Colson, Mary. What Happens If the Ozone Disappears? 2015. (Unstable Earth Ser.). (Illus.). 32p. (J). 31.35 (978-1-62588-161-8(4)) Black Rabbit Bks.

Feinstein, Stephen & Library. Solving the Air Pollution Problem: What You Can Do. 2010. (Green Issues in Focus Ser.). (Illus.). 128p. (J). (gr. 7-12). lib. bdg. 33.27 (978-0-7660-3347-4(3)) Enslow Pubs., Inc.

Gardner, Robert. Air: Green Science Projects for a Sustainable Planet. 2011. (Team Green Science Projects Ser.). (Illus.). 128p. (J). (gr. 5-9). lib. bdg. 33.27 (978-0-7660-3646-8(4)) Enslow Pubs., Inc.

Green, Jen. Making Air Cleaner. 2016. (Environment Detective Investigates Ser.). (ENG., Illus.). 32p. (J). (gr. 4-6). pap. 11.99 (978-0-7502-9430-0(2), Wayland) Hachette Children's Group GBR. Dist: Hachette Bk. Group.

—Making Air Cleaner. 2011. (Sherlock Bones Looks at the Environment Ser.). (ENG., Illus.). 32p. (YA). (gr. 3-6). lib. bdg. 25.25 (978-1-61533-345-5(2)) Windmill Bks.

—Reducing Air Pollution. 2005. (Improving Our Environment Ser.). (Illus.). 32p. (gr. 3-6). lib. bdg. 26.00 (978-0-8368-4428-3(9), Gareth Stevens Learning Library) Stevens, Gareth Publishing LLLP.

Greene, Carol. I Love Our Air. 2012. (I Love Our Earth Ser.). (Illus.). 24p. (J). (gr. 3-4). 22.60 (978-0-7660-4037-3(2), Enslow Elementary) Enslow Pubs., Inc.

Haynes, Danielle. Chemical Catastrophes. 2017. (Unnatural Disasters Ser.). 32p. (J). (gr. 4-5). pap. 63.00 **(978-1-5382-0417-7(7))** Stevens, Gareth Publishing LLLP.

Higgins, Matt. The Air Out There: How Clean Is Clean? 2011. (Second Nature Ser.). 48p. (J). (gr. 5-8). lib. bdg. 26.60 (978-1-59953-451-0(7)) Norwood Hse. Pr.

Hudak, Heather C. Air Pollution. 2006. (Science Matters Ser.). (Illus.). 24p. (J). (gr. 3-7). lib. bdg. 24.45 (978-1-59036-415-4(5), 1266429); pap. 8.95 (978-1-59036-421-5(X), 1266429) Weigl Pubs., Inc.

—Air Pollution with Code. 2012. (Sky Science Ser.). (ENG., Illus.). 24p. (J). lib. bdg. 27.13 (978-1-61913-096-8(3)); (gr. 3-7). pap. 12.95 (978-1-61913-543-7(4)) Weigl Pubs., Inc. (AV2 by Weigl).

Hustad, Douglas. How Can We Reduce Manufacturing Pollution? 2016. (Searchlight Books — What Can We Do about Pollution? Ser.). (ENG., Illus.). 40p. (J). (gr. 3-5). 30.65 (978-1-4677-9518-0(6), Lerner Pubns.) Lerner Publishing Group.

Kidd, Renee A. Air Pollution: Problems & Solutions. 2nd rev. ed. 2005. (Science & Society Ser.). (Illus.). 176p. (gr. 6-12). 35.00 (978-0-8160-5605-7(6)) Facts On File, Inc.

Lawrence, Ellen. Dirty Air. 2014. (Science Slam: Green World, Clean World Ser.). (Illus.). 24p. (J). (gr. -1-3). lib. bdg. 23.93 (978-1-62724-103-8(5)) Bearport Publishing Co., Inc.

—Fog, Mist, or Haze? 2015. (Weather Wise Ser.). (ENG., Illus.). 24p. (J). (gr. -1-3). lib. bdg. 23.93 (978-1-62724-864-8(1)) Bearport Publishing Co., Inc.

Light, Kate. Smothered in Smog. 2017. (Unnatural Disasters Ser.). 32p. (J). (gr. 4-5). pap. 10.50 **(978-1-5382-0523-5(8))**; lib. bdg. 26.60 **(978-1-5382-0524-2(6))** Stevens, Gareth Publishing LLLP.

Llewellyn, Claire. Fight Air Pollution. 2005. (Illus.). 32p. (YA). (gr. 1-18). lib. bdg. 27.10 (978-1-932333-21-3(5)) Chrysalis Education.

Minden, Cecilia. Kids Can Keep Air Clean. 2010. (21st Century Basic Skills Library: Kids Can Ser.). (ENG.). 24p. (gr. k-3). lib. bdg. 22.79 (978-1-60279-871-7(0), 200608) Cherry Lake Publishing.

Orr, Tamra B. Pondering Pollution. 2014. (Explorer Library: Follow the Clues Ser.). (ENG., Illus.). 32p. (J). (gr. 4-8). 28.50 (978-1-62431-779-8(0), 203312) Cherry Lake Publishing.

Rapp, Val. Protecting Earth's Air Quality. 2009. pap. 58.95 (978-0-7613-4695-1(3)) 2008. 72p. (YA). (gr. 4-7). lib. bdg. 30.60 (978-0-8225-7558-0(2)) Lerner Publishing Group.

Sawyer, Ava. Humans & Earth's Atmosphere: What's in the Air? 2017. (Humans & Our Planet Ser.). (ENG.). 32p. (gr.

3-4). lib. bdg. 27.32 **(978-1-5157-7199-9(7)**, Fact Finders) Capstone Press of Coughlan Cos.

Sechrist, Darren. Air Pollution. 2008. (Saving Our World Ser.). 32p. (gr. 4-18). lib. bdg. 28.50 *(978-0-7614-3220-3(5)*, Benchmark Bks.) Marshall Cavendish Corp.

Smith, Ben. What Makes the Air Dirty? 2014. (Little Books of Answers: Level C Ser.). (Illus.). 16p. (gr. k-2). pap. 7.95 *(978-1-927136-24-9(5))* Three Crows Media NZL. Dist: RiverStream Publishing.

Thomas, Elizabeth. Clean Air. 2011. (Go Green! Ser.). (ENG., Illus.). 32p. (J). (gr. 1-4). lib. bdg. 28.50 *(978-1-60973-170-0(0)*, 201149) Child's World, Inc., The.

Wang, Andrea. How Can We Reduce Fossil Fuel Pollution? 2016. (Searchlight Books — What Can We Do about Pollution? Ser.). (ENG., Illus.). 40p. (J). (gr. 3-5). 30.65 *(978-1-4677-9513-5(5))* Lerner Publishing Group.

AIR BASES

Cernak, Linda. Guarding Fort Knox. 2016. (Highly Guarded Places Ser.). (ENG.). 24p. (J). (gr. 2-5). 28.50 *(978-1-5038-0812-6(2)*, 210646) Child's World, Inc., The.

Haney, Jill. Area 51. 2015. (Red Rhino Nonfiction Ser.). (J). lib. bdg. 20.80 *(978-0-606-37198-8(2))* Turtleback Bks.

Higgins, Nadia. Area 51. 2014. (Unexplained Mysteries Ser.). (ENG., Illus.). 24p. (J). (gr. 3-7). lib. bdg. 25.95 *(978-1-62617-101-5(7)*, Epic Bks.) Bellwether Media.

Karst, Ken. Area 51: Enduring Mysteries. 2014. (Illus.). 48p. (J). pap. *(978-1-60818-399-9(8))* Creative Co., The.

—Enduring Mysteries: Area 51. 2015. (Enduring Mysteries Ser.). (ENG.). 48p. (J). (gr. 5-8). pap. 12.00 *(978-1-62832-070-1(2)*, Creative Paperbacks) Creative Co., The.

Linde, Barbara M. What Happened at Area 51? 2015. (History's Mysteries Ser.). (ENG., Illus.). 32p. (J). (gr. 4-5). pap. 10.50 *(978-1-4824-2102-6(X))* Stevens, Gareth Publishing LLLP.

Lynette, Rachel. Area 51. 2009. (Mysterious Encounters Ser.). (ENG., Illus.). 48p. (J). (gr. 4-8). lib. bdg. 29.00 *(978-0-7377-4410-1(3)*, LML02109-245411, Kidhaven) Cengage Gale.

Martin, Ted. Area 51. 2011. (Unexplained Ser.). (ENG., Illus.). 24p. (YA). (gr. 3-7). lib. bdg. 25.95 *(978-1-60014-642-8(2)*, Torque Bks.) Bellwether Media.

Summers, Portia. The Community of Our Military Base. 2016. (Zoom in on Communities Ser.). (Illus.). 24p. (J). (gr. 2-2). pap. 9.35 *(978-0-7660-7811-6(6))* Enslow Pubs., Inc.

AIR CARGO

see Aeronautics, Commercial

AIR CUSHION VEHICLES

see Ground-Effect Machines

AIR FREIGHT

see Aeronautics, Commercial

AIR HOSTESSES

see Flight Attendants

AIR LINES

see Airlines

AIR PILOTS

see also Astronauts; Women in Aeronautics

Adler, David A. A Picture Book of Amelia Earhart. Fisher, Jeff, illus. 2015. 32p. pap. 8.00 *(978-1-61003-403-6(1))* Center for the Collaborative Classroom.

Airline Pilot. 2008. (Virtual Apprentice Ser.). 64p. (gr. 4-9). 29.95 *(978-0-8160-6755-8(4)*, Ferguson Publishing Co.) Facts On File, Inc.

Alexander, Carol. Bessie Coleman. 2016. (Rookie Biographies(tm) Ser.). (ENG.). 32p. (J). lib. bdg. 25.00 *(978-0-531-22545-5(3)*, Children's Pr.) Scholastic Library Publishing.

Asso, B. & Bergese, F. Cinebook Recounts: Battle of Britain. movie tie-in ed. 2010. (Cinebook Recounts Ser.). (ENG., Illus.). 48p. pap. 11.95 *(978-1-84918-025-2(3))* CineBook GBR. Dist: National Bk. Network.

Asso, Bernard & Bergèse, Francis. Battle of Britain. 2008. (ENG., Illus.). 48p. pap. 11.95 *(978-1-905460-39-7(2))* CineBook GBR. Dist: National Bk. Network.

Asso, Bernard & Rideau, Joel. Biggles Recounts the Falklands War: Volume 1. Chauvin, Daniel & Uderzo, Marcel, illus. 2007. (ENG.). 48p. per. 9.99 *(978-1-905460-22-9(8))* CineBook GBR. Dist: National Bk. Network.

Baker, Brynn. Tuskegee Airmen: Freedom Flyers of World War II. 2015. (Military Heroes Ser.). (ENG., Illus.). 32p. (gr. 3-4). lib. bdg. 27.32 *(978-1-4914-4839-7(3))* Capstone Press of Coughlan Cos.

Barton, Jen. What's Your Story, Amelia Earhart? 2016. (Cub Reporter Meets Famous Americans Ser.). (ENG.). 32p. (J). (gr. k-3). 26.65 *(978-1-4677-8783-3(3))*; (Illus.). pap. 8.99 *(978-1-4677-9645-3(X))* Lerner Publishing Group.

Benge, Janet & Benge, Geoff. Louis Zamperini: Redemption. 2014. (ENG.). 218p. (YA). pap. 9.99 *(978-1-62486-049-2(4))* Emerald Bks.

Bledsoe, Karen E. Daredevils of the Air: Thrilling Tales of Pioneer Aviators. 2003. (Avisson Young Adult Ser.). (Illus.). 155p. (J). pap. 19.95 *(978-1-888105-58-2(5))* Avisson Pr., Inc.

BourkeKenna. LOST: THE MYSTERY OF AMELIA EARHART HIGH BEGINNING BOOK WITH ONLINE ACCESS. 2014. (ENG.). 24p. (J). pap. 9.50 *(978-1-107-69335-7(7))* Cambridge Univ. Pr.

Brown, Jeremy K. Amelia Earhart. 2011. (Women of Achievement Ser.). (Illus.). 132p. (gr. 6-12). 35.00 *(978-1-60413-910-5(2)*, Chelsea Hse.) Facts On File, Inc.

Brown, Jonatha A. Amelia Earhart. 2005. (People to Know Ser.). (Illus.). 24p. (gr. 1-4). pap. 8.15 *(978-0-8368-4472-6(6))*; lib. bdg. 22.00 *(978-0-8368-4465-8(3))* Stevens, Gareth Publishing LLLP. (Weekly Reader Leveled Readers).

Brown, Tami Lewis. Soar, Elinor! Roca, François, illus. 2010. (ENG.). 40p. (J). (gr. -1-3). 16.99 *(978-0-374-37115-9(6)*, 9780374371159, Farrar, Straus & Giroux (BYR)) Farrar, Straus & Giroux.

Buckley, A. M. The Disappearance of Amelia Earhart, 1 vol. 2012. (Unsolved Mysteries (el) Ser.). (ENG.). 112p. (J). (gr. 6-12). lib. bdg. 35.64 *(978-1-61783-302-1(9)*, Essential Library) ABDO Publishing Co.

Burke, John. Amelia Earhart: Flying Solo. 2017. (Great Leaders & Events Ser.). (ENG.). (J). (gr. 4-8). lib. bdg. 35.99 **(978-1-942875-45-1(2))** Quarto Publishing Group USA.

Carpenter, Julie & Omoth, Tyler. Fighter Pilots in Action. 2017. (Dangerous Jobs in Action Ser.). (ENG.). 32p. (J). (gr. 3-6). lib. bdg. 27.07 *(978-1-5038-1629-9(X)*, 211145) Child's World, Inc., The.

The Chocolate Flier: Individual Title Six-Packs. (Action Packs Ser.). 104p. (gr. 3-5). 44.00 *(978-0-7635-3304-5(1))* Rigby Education.

Corrigan, Jim. In the Air: Training. 2013. (Military Experience: in the Air Ser.). (ENG., Illus.). 64p. (YA). (gr. 3-7). 27.45 *(978-1-59935-388-3(1))* Reynolds, Morgan Inc.

Cummins, Julie. Flying Solo: How Ruth Elder Soared into America's Heart. Laugesen, Malene R., illus. 2013. (ENG.). 32p. (J). (gr. 1-3). 17.99 *(978-1-59643-509-4(7)*, 9781596435094) Roaring Brook Pr.

Dakers, Diane. Amelia Earhart: Pioneering Aviator & Force for Women's Rights. 2016. (ENG.). 112p. (J). *(978-0-7787-2562-6(6))* Crabtree Publishing Co.

DeMolay, Jack. The Bermuda Triangle: The Disappearance of Flight 19. (Jr. Graphic Mysteries Ser.). (ENG.). 24p. 2009. (J). (gr. 2-3). 47.90 *(978-1-61513-846-3(3)*, PowerKids Pr.) 2007. (Illus.). (J). (gr. 2-5). lib. bdg. 25.25 *(978-1-4042-3404-8(7))* 2007. (Illus.). (gr. 3-8). pap. 10.60 *(978-1-4042-2157-4(3)*, PowerKids Pr.) Rosen Publishing Group, Inc., The.

—El Triángulo de las Bermudas: La Desaparicion del Vuelo 19. Obregón, José María, tr. 2008. (Historietas Juveniles: Misterios (Jr. Graphic Mysteries) Ser.). (SPA., Illus.). 24p. (J). (gr. 2-5). lib. bdg. 25.25 *(978-1-4358-2535-2(7))* Rosen Publishing Group, Inc., The.

—El Triángulo de las Bermudas: La desaparición del vuelo 19 (the Bermuda Triangle:the Disappearance of Flight 19) 2009. (Historietas Juveniles: Misterios (Jr. Graphic Mysteries) Ser.). (SPA.). 24p. (gr. 2-3). 47.90 *(978-1-61513-348-2(8)*, Editorial Buenas Letras) Rosen Publishing Group, Inc., The.

Doak, Robin S. Amelia Earhart, 1 vol. 2012. (American Biographies Ser.). (ENG.). 48p. (gr. 4-6). pap. 9.95 *(978-1-4329-6462-7(3)*, NA-h) Heinemann-Raintree.

Donelly, Karen. American Women Pilots of World War II. 2009. 112p. (YA). (gr. 7-12). pap. 12.95 *(978-1-4358-3274-9(4))* Rosen Publishing Group, Inc., The.

Dunn, Joeming W. Amelia Earhart, 1 vol. Dunn, Ben, illus. 2008. (Bio-Graphics Ser.). (ENG.). 32p. (gr. 3-5). 28.50 *(978-1-60270-173-1(3)*, Graphic Planet- Nonfiction) ABDO Publishing Co.

Ertle-Rickard, Stephen. Fighter Pilot. 2008. (321 Go! Ser.). (ENG., Illus.). 36p. pap. *(978-1-84167-758-3(2))* Ransom Publishing Ltd.

Famous Flyers. (Illus.). (gr. 6-12). lib. bdg. *(978-0-7910-8058-0(7))*; 2005. 112p. 150.00 *(978-0-7910-7211-0(8))* Facts On File, Inc. (Chelsea Hse.).

Feinstein, Stephen. Read about Amelia Earhart. 2006. (I Like Biographies! Ser.). (Illus.). 24p. (J). (gr. 1-3). lib. bdg. 22.60 *(978-0-7660-2582-0(9)*, Enslow Elementary) Enslow Pubs., Inc.

Fleischman, John. Black & White Airmen: Their True History. 2007. (ENG., Illus.). 160p. (gr. 5-12). 28.80 *(978-1-4287-3953-6(X)*, Follettbound) Follett School Solutions.

—Black & White Airmen: Their True History. 2007. (ENG., Illus.). 160p. (J). (gr. 5-7). 20.00 *(978-0-618-56297-8(4))* Houghton Mifflin Harcourt Publishing Co.

Fleming, Candace. Amelia Lost: The Life & Disappearance of Amelia Earhart. 2011. (ENG., Illus.). 128p. (J). (gr. 3-7). 19.99 *(978-0-375-84198-9(9))*; lib. bdg. 21.99 *(978-0-375-94598-4(9))* Random Hse. Children's Bks. (Schwartz & Wade Bks.).

Flynn, Riley. Bessie Coleman, 1 vol. 2014. (Great African-Americans Ser.). (ENG., Illus.). 24p. (gr. k-1). lib. bdg. 21.99 *(978-1-4765-3955-3(3)*, Pebble Bks.) Capstone Press of Coughlan Cos.

Freedman, Lew. All about Amelia Earhart. 2015. (ENG., Illus.). 128p. (J). pap. 4.99 *(978-1-935628-44-6(5))* Blue River Pr.

Garstecki, Julia. Tuskegee Airmen. 2017. (All-American Fighting Forces Ser.). (ENG.). 32p. (gr. 3-7). 31.35 **(978-1-68072-004-4(X)**, Bolt) Black Rabbit Bks.

Gibson, Karen Bush. Women Aviators: 26 Stories of Pioneer Flights, Daring Missions, & Record-Setting Journeys. 2013. (Women of Action Ser.). (ENG., Illus.). 240p. (YA). (gr. 7). 19.95 *(978-1-61374-540-3(0))* Chicago Review Pr., Inc.

Goldstone, Lawrence. Higher, Steeper, Faster: The Daredevils Who Conquered the Skies. 2017. (ENG., Illus.). 256p. (J). (gr. 3-7). 18.99 *(978-0-316-35023-5(0))* Little Brown & Co.

Golightly, Anne. Amelia Earhart: Female Aviator. 2012. (Beginning Biographies Ser.). (ENG., Illus.). 24p. (J). (gr. 1-3). 22.60 *(978-1-4488-8601-2(5)*, PowerKids Pr.) Rosen Publishing Group, Inc., The.

Graham, Ian. You Wouldn't Want to Be a World War II Pilot! Air Battles You Might Not Survive. Antram, David, illus. 2009. (You Wouldn't Want to Ser.). (ENG.). 32p. (J). 29.00 *(978-0-531-21326-1(9))*; (gr. 3-18). pap. 9.95 *(978-0-531-20517-4(7))* Scholastic Library Publishing.

Graves, Jeseca, illus. Bessie Coleman: The Story of an Aviation Pioneer. 2007. 24p. (J). *(978-0-9745294-1-7(9))* San Diego County Regional Airport Authority.

Gray, Judy Silverstein & Kiland, Taylor Baldwin. Drones: Remote-Controlled Warfare. 2016. (Military Engineering in Action Ser.). 48p. (J). (gr. 6-5). pap. 11.70 *(978-0-7660-7510-8(9))* Enslow Pubs., Inc.

Green, Jen. Audacious Aviators: True Stories of Adventurers' Thrilling Flights, 1 vol. 2014. (Ultimate Adventurers Ser.). (ENG.). 48p. (gr. 6-6). lib. bdg. 29.99 *(978-1-4109-5417-6(X))* Heinemann-Raintree.

Gregory, Josh. Aircraft Pilot. 2012. (21st Century Skills Library: Cool Military Careers Ser.). (ENG.). 32p. (gr. 4-8). 28.50 *(978-1-61080-444-8(9)*, 202054); pap. 14.21 *(978-1-61080-618-3(2)*, 202228) Cherry Lake Publishing.

Haldy, Emma E. Amelia Earhart. Bane, Jeff, illus. 2016. (My Early Library: My Itty-Bitty Bio Ser.). (ENG.). 24p. (J). (gr. k-1). 28.50 *(978-1-63470-480-9(0)*, 207651) Cherry Lake Publishing.

Hally, Ashleigh. Jackie Cochran. 2012. (Illus.). 24p. (J). *(978-1-935884-75-0(1))*; pap. *(978-1-935884-81-1(6))* State Standards Publishing, LLC.

Hamilton, John. Test Pilot. 2015. 32p. pap. 27.07 *(978-1-62403-761-0(5))* ABDO Publishing Co.

Harkins, Susan Sales. Breaking the Sound Barrier: The Story of Chuck Yeager. 2005. (Monumental Milestones Ser.). (Illus.). 48p. (YA). (gr. 4-7). lib. bdg. 29.95 *(978-1-58415-398-6(9)*, 1244924) Mitchell Lane Pubs., Inc.

Harmon, Daniel E. Amelia Earhart: Aviation Pioneer. 2017. (J). **(978-1-5383-0020-6(6))** Rosen Publishing Group, Inc., The.

Hart, Phillip S. Bessie Coleman. 2005. (Just the Facts Biographies Ser.). (ENG., Illus.). 112p. (gr. 5-12). 27.93 *(978-0-8225-2469-4(4))* Lerner Publishing Group.

Holden, Henry M. American Women of Flight: Pilots & Pioneers. 2003. (Collective Biographies Ser.). (Illus.). 112p. (J). (gr. 6-12). lib. bdg. 26.60 *(978-0-7660-2005-4(3))* Enslow Pubs., Inc.

Homan, Lynn M. & Reilly, Thomas. Women Who Fly, 1 vol. Shepherd, Rosalie M., illus. 2004. (ENG.). 104p. (J). (gr. 3-7). 14.95 *(978-1-58980-160-8(1))* Pelican Publishing Co., Inc.

Hopkins, Ellen H. Storming the Skies: The Story of Katherine & Marjorie Stinson: Pioneer Women Aviators. 2003. (Avisson Young Adult Ser.). (Illus.). 75p. (J). pap. 18.95 *(978-1-888105-56-8(9))* Avisson Pr., Inc.

Horn, Geoffrey M. Test Pilot. 2008. (Cool Careers: Adventure Careers Ser.). (Illus.). 32p. (gr. 5-8). pap. 10.50 *(978-0-8368-8891-1(X))*; lib. bdg. 26.00 *(978-0-8368-8884-3(7))* Stevens, Gareth Publishing LLLP.

Houran, Lori Haskins. The $25,000 Flight. Lowe, Wesley, illus. 2014. (Totally True Adventures Ser.). (ENG.). 112p. (J). (gr. 2-5). 4.99 *(978-0-385-38284-7(7)*, Random Hse. Bks. for Young Readers) Random Hse. Children's Bks.

Inventions & Discovery, Set. 2006. (Inventions & Discovery Ser.). (ENG., Illus.). 32p. (gr. 3-4). pap. 89.10 *(978-0-7368-7532-5(8)*, Graphic Library) Capstone Press of Coughlan Cos.

Irving, Barrington & Peppe, Holly. Touch the Sky. 2012. (J). *(978-0-531-22525-7(9))* Scholastic, Inc.

Jeffries, Joyce. Meet the Pilot. 2013. (People Around Town Ser.). 24p. (J). (gr. k-2). 22.60 *(978-1-4339-9382-4(1))*; pap. 48.90 *(978-1-4339-9384-8(8))*; pap. 8.15 *(978-1-4339-9383-1(X))* Stevens, Gareth Publishing LLLP.

—Meet the Pilot / Conoce a Los Pilotos. 2013. (People Around Town / Gente de Mi Ciudad Ser.). (SPA.). 24p. (J). (gr. k-2). 22.60 *(978-1-4339-9472-2(0))* Stevens, Gareth Publishing LLLP.

Jones, Victoria Garrett. Amelia Earhart: A Life in Flight. 2009. (Sterling Biographies(r) Ser.). (ENG., Illus.). 128p. (J). (gr. 5-18). pap. 5.95 *(978-1-4027-5157-8(5))* Sterling Publishing Co., Inc.

Kiland, Taylor Baldwin & Bledsoe, Glen. Military Helicopters: Heroes of the Sky. 2015. (Military Engineering in Action Ser.). (ENG., Illus.). 48p. (J). (gr. 6-6). 27.93 *(978-0-7660-6912-1(5))* Enslow Pubs., Inc.

Kiland, Taylor Baldwin, et al. Fighter Planes: Masters of the Sky. 2015. (Military Engineering in Action Ser.). (ENG.). 48p. (J). (gr. 6-6). 27.93 *(978-0-7660-6910-7(9))*; pap. 11.70 *(978-0-7660-7061-5(1))* Enslow Pubs., Inc.

The Knights of Avalon: Seaplanes of Catalina Island. 2004. 207p. per. 22.00 *(978-0-9749426-0-5(X))* Horizon Line Pr.

Koestler-Grack, Rachel A. Spirit of St. Louis, 1 vol. 2005. (American Moments Ser.). (ENG., Illus.). 48p. (gr. 4-8). 27.07 *(978-1-59197-940-1(4)*, Abdo & Daughters) ABDO Publishing Co.

Lakin, Patricia, et al. Amelia Earhart: More Than a Flier. Daniel, Alan & Daniel, Lea, illus. 2003. (Ready-To-read SOFA Ser.). (ENG.). 48p. (J). (gr. 1-3). pap. 3.99 *(978-0-689-85575-7(3)*, Simon Spotlight) Simon Spotlight.

Landmann, Bimba, illus. In Search of the Little Prince: The Story of Antoine de Saint-Exupéry. 2014. (ENG.). 34p. (J). 17.00 *(978-0-8028-5435-3(4)*, Eerdmans Bks For Young Readers) Eerdmans, William B. Publishing Co.

Langley, Wanda. Women of the Wind: Early Women Aviators. 2006. (Women Adventurers Ser.). (Illus.). 160p. (J). (gr. 6-12). lib. bdg. 26.95 *(978-1-931798-81-5(8))* Reynolds, Morgan Inc.

Leavitt, Amie Jane. Amelia Earhart. 2007. (What's So Great About...? Ser.). (Illus.). 32p. (J). (gr. 2-4). lib. bdg. 25.70 *(978-1-58415-576-8(0))* Mitchell Lane Pubs., Inc.

Lenski, Lois. The Little Airplane. Lenski, Lois, illus. 2003. (Lois Lenski Bks.). (ENG., Illus.). 56p. (J). (gr. -1-k). reprint ed. 11.95 *(978-0-375-81079-4(X)*, Random Hse. Bks. for Young Readers) Random Hse. Children's Bks.

Lewis, Simon. Adventures in the Air. 2009. (Difficult & Dangerous Ser.). (J). 28.50 *(978-1-59920-161-0(5))* Black Rabbit Bks.

Liebman, Dan. Pilote. Lior, Tsipora, tr. from ENG. 2006. (Je Veux Etre Ser.). (FRE., Illus.). 24p. (J). (gr. -1-2). pap. 5.95 *(978-1-55407-106-7(2)*, 9781554071067) Firefly Bks., Ltd.

—Piloto. 2003. (Quiero Ser.). (SPA., Illus.). 24p. (J). (gr. -1-2). pap. 5.99 *(978-1-55297-745-3(5)*, 9781552977453) Firefly Bks., Ltd.

Lindbergh, Charles A., Jr. The Spirit of St Louis. 2003. 562p. pap. 29.00 *(978-0-7581-3991-7(8))* Textbook Pubs.

Linde, Barbara. Heroes of the Us Air Force. 2012. (Heroes of the US Military Ser.). (Illus.). 32p. (gr. 3-6). 26.60 *(978-1-4339-7232-4(8))*; pap. 10.50 *(978-1-4339-7233-1(6))* Stevens, Gareth Publishing LLLP. (Gareth Stevens Learning Library).

Loveless, Antony. Apache Helicopter Pilot. 2009. (World's Most Dangerous Jobs Ser.). (ENG., Illus.). 32p. (J). (gr. 3-6). pap. *(978-0-7787-5112-0(0))* Crabtree Publishing Co.

—Apache Helicopter Pilots. 2009. (World's Most Dangerous Jobs Ser.). (ENG., Illus.). 32p. (J). (gr. 3-6). lib. bdg. *(978-0-7787-5098-7(1))* Crabtree Publishing Co.

—Test Pilots. 2009. (World's Most Dangerous Jobs Ser.). (ENG., Illus.). 32p. (J). (gr. 3-6). pap. *(978-0-7787-5113-7(9))*; lib. bdg. *(978-0-7787-5099-4(X))* Crabtree Publishing Co.

Lowell, Barbara. Daring Amelia. Tuya, Jez, illus. 2016. (J). *(978-0-451-53373-9(9)*, Warne, Frederick Pubs.) Penguin Bks., Ltd.

Lynch, Christopher. Albert Bond Lambert: Aviation Pioneer. 2015. (ENG., Illus.). 48p. (J). pap. 24.00 *(978-1-61248-155-5(8))* Truman State Univ. Pr.

Mallory, Mark. Amelia Earhart: Queen of the Sky. 2009. (Real Life Readers Ser.). 16p. (gr. 2-3). pap. 7.05 *(978-1-4358-0053-3(2)*, Rosen Classroom) Rosen Publishing Group, Inc., The.

Mara, Wil. Amelia Earhart. 2014. (Rookie Biographies(tm) Ser.). (ENG.). 32p. (J). lib. bdg. 25.00 *(978-0-531-21059-8(6))* Scholastic Library Publishing.

Marsh, Carole. Amelia Earhart. 2003. 12p. (gr. k-4). 2.95 *(978-0-635-02131-1(5))* Gallopade International.

—Charles Lindbergh. 2003. 12p. (gr. k-4). 2.95 *(978-0-635-02130-4(7))* Gallopade International.

—Charles W. Dryden: Tuskegee Airman. 2004. (1000 Readers Ser.). (Illus.). 12p. (J). (gr. k-4). pap. 2.95 *(978-0-635-02493-0(4))* Gallopade International.

Masters, Nancy Robinson. Drone Pilot. 2012. (21st Century Skills Library: Cool Military Careers Ser.). (ENG.). 32p. (gr. 4-8). 28.50 *(978-1-61080-448-6(1)*, 202058); pap. 14.21 *(978-1-61080-622-0(0)*, 202232) Cherry Lake Publishing.

Mattern, Joanne. Pilotos. 2004. (Trabajo en Grupo (Working Together) Ser.). (SPA & ENG., Illus.). 24p. (J). (gr. 3-6). lib. bdg. 22.60 *(978-0-8239-6840-4(5)*, Editorial Buenas Letras) Rosen Publishing Group, Inc., The.

—Pilotos (Pilots) 2009. (Trabajo en grupo (Working Together) Ser.). (SPA.). 24p. (gr. 1-2). 42.50 *(978-1-60854-577-3(6)*, Editorial Buenas Letras) Rosen Publishing Group, Inc., The.

—Pilots. 2009. (Working Together Ser.). 24p. (gr. 1-2). 42.50 *(978-1-60854-832-3(5)*, PowerKids Pr.) Rosen Publishing Group, Inc., The.

McCarthy, Meghan. Daredevil: The Daring Life of Betty Skelton. McCarthy, Meghan, illus. 2013. (ENG., Illus.). 48p. (J). (gr. -1-3). 17.99 *(978-1-4424-2262-9(9)*, Simon & Schuster/Paula Wiseman Bks.) Simon & Schuster/Paula Wiseman Bks.

McNeil, Tom & Benchmark Education Co. Staff. Take-Off: A Pilot's Memoir. 2014. (Text Connections Ser.). (J). (gr. 6). *(978-1-4900-1536-1(1))* Benchmark Education Co.

Micklos, John & Micklos, John, Jr. Unsolved: What Really Happened to Amelia Earhart? 2006. (Prime (Middle/Senior) Ser.). (Illus.). 144p. (J). (gr. 5-9). lib. bdg. 34.60 *(978-0-7660-2365-9(6))* Enslow Pubs., Inc.

Miklowitz, Gloria D. Amelia Earhart. 2004. (ENG., Illus.). 31p. (J). (gr. 2-5). pap. 7.33 *(978-0-7685-1213-7(1)*, Dominie Elementary) Pearson Schl.

Mills, Nathan & Golightly, Anne. Amelia Earhart: Female Aviator. 2012. (Rosen Readers Ser.). (ENG., Illus.). 24p. (J). (gr. 1-2). pap. 8.25 *(978-1-4488-8854-2(9)*, Rosen Classroom) Rosen Publishing Group, Inc., The.

Minden, Cecilia & Minden-Zins, Mary. Pilots. 2014. (People in Our Community Ser.). (ENG.). 24p. (J). (gr. k-3). 27.07 *(978-1-62687-016-1(0)*, 206806) Child's World, Inc., The.

Morris, Neil. Air Pioneers. (Illus.). 48p. (YA). (gr. 5-18). lib. bdg. 29.95 *(978-1-932333-81-7(9))* Chrysalis Education.

Moss, Marissa. Brave Harriet. Payne, C. F., illus. 2015. 32p. pap. 8.00 *(978-1-61003-492-0(9))* Center for the Collaborative Classroom.

Niver, Heather Moore. Breaking the Sound Barrier. 2015. (Incredible True Adventures Ser.). (ENG.). 32p. (J). (gr. 3-4). pap. 10.50 *(978-1-4824-2030-2(9))* Stevens, Gareth Publishing LLLP.

Orr, Tamra. What's So Great about the Tuskegee Airmen. 2009. (What's So Great About...? Ser.). 32p. (J). (gr. 2-4). lib. bdg. 25.70 *(978-1-58415-832-5(8))* Mitchell Lane Pubs., Inc.

Orr, Tamra B. Amelia Earhart. 2015. (ENG., Illus.). 48p. (J). pap. 6.95 *(978-0-531-21207-3(6)*, Orchard Bks.) Scholastic Library Publishing.

Parkes, Elle. Hooray for Pilots! 2016. (Bumba Books (tm) — Hooray for Community Helpers! Ser.). (ENG., Illus.). 24p. (J). (gr. -1-1). lib. bdg. 25.32 *(978-1-5124-1442-4(5))* Lerner Publishing Group.

Parkes, Elle. ¡Que Vivan Los Pilotos! (Hooray for Pilots!) 2017. (Bumba Books (tm) en Español — ¡Que Vivan Los Ayudantes Comunitarios! (Hooray for Community Helpers!) Ser.). (SPA.). 24p. (J). (gr. -1-1). pap. 6.99 **(978-1-5124-5388-1(9))**; (Illus.). 25.32 **(978-1-5124-4137-6(6))** Lerner Publishing Group. (Ediciones Lerner).

Petrick, Neila S. Katherine Stinson Otero: High Flyer, 1 vol. Wallace, Daggi, illus. 2006. (ENG.). 32p. (J). (gr. k-3). 16.99 *(978-1-58980-368-8(X))* Pelican Publishing Co., Inc.

Pflueger, Lynda. Amelia Earhart: Legend of Flight. 2003. (Historical American Biographies Ser.). (Illus.). 128p. (J). lib. bdg. 27.94 *(978-0-7660-1976-8(4))* Enslow Pubs., Inc.

Pimm, Nancy Roe. The Jerrie Mock Story: The First Woman to Fly Solo Around the World. 2016. (Biographies for Young Readers Ser.). (ENG., Illus.). 168p. (J). (gr. 1-6). 28.95 *(978-0-8214-2215-1(4))* Ohio Univ. Pr.

Plantz, Connie. The Life of Bessie Coleman: First African-American Woman Pilot. 2014. (Legendary African Americans Ser.). (Illus.). 96p. (J). (gr. 6-12). 27.94 *(978-0-7660-6117-0(5))* Enslow Pubs., Inc.

Provensen, Alice. Glorius Flight. 2014. 17.00 *(978-1-63419-702-1(X))* Perfection Learning Corp.

Purcell, Martha Sias. Pioneer Pilots & Flying Aces of World War I. 2003. (Reading Essentials in Social Studies). (Illus.). 48p. (J). 9.00 *(978-0-7891-5881-9(7))* Perfection Learning Corp.

Rauf, Don & Vescia, Monique. Airline Pilot. 2008. (Virtual Apprentice Ser.). (Illus.). 64p. (gr. 4-9). pap. 9.95 *(978-0-8160-7549-2(2)*, Checkmark Bks.) Facts On File, Inc.

Reed, Jennifer. Daring American Heroes of Flight: Nine Brave Fliers. 2009. (Great Scientists & Famous Inventors Ser.). (Illus.). 128p. (J). (gr. 5-9). lib. bdg. 34.60 *(978-1-59845-081-1(6))* Enslow Pubs., Inc.

Reyburn, Susan. Amelia Earhart. 2006. (Women Who Dare Ser.). (Illus.). 64p. 12.95 *(978-0-7649-3545-9(3)*, A111) Pomegranate Communications, Inc.

Rideau, J. & Asso, B. The Falklands War. Chauvin, D. & Uderzo, M., illus. 2011. (Cinebook Recounts Ser.). (ENG.). 48p. pap. 11.95 *(978-1-84918-056-6(3))* CineBook GBR. Dist: National Bk. Network.

Rinaldo, Denise. Amelia Earhart: With a Discussion of Courage. 2004. (Values in Action Ser.). (J). *(978-1-59203-068-2(8))* Learning Challenge, Inc.

Robbins, Trina. Bessie Coleman: Daring Stunt Pilot, 1 vol. Steacy, Ken, illus. 2007. (Graphic Biographies Ser.). (ENG.). 32p. (gr. 3-4). per. 8.10 *(978-0-7368-7903-3(X)*, Graphic Library) Capstone Press of Coughlan Cos.

Rowell, Rebecca. Charles Lindbergh: Groundbreaking Aviator, 1 vol. 2010. (Essential Lives Set 5 Ser.). (ENG.). 112p. (J).

(gr. 6-12). lib. bdg. 35.64 (978-1-61613-516-4(6)) ABDO Publishing Co.

Royston, Angela. Diary of a Pilot, 1 vol. 2013. (Diary of A... Ser.). (ENG.). 32p. (gr. 1-3). 27.32 (978-1-4329-7584-5(6)); pap. 8.95 (978-1-4329-7591-3(9)) Heinemann-Raintree. (Heinemann First Library).

Roza, Greg. Famous Flights: Understanding & Using Variables. (Math for the Real World Ser.). 32p. 2009. (ENG., Illus.). (gr. 6-7). pap. 10.00 (978-1-4042-6087-0(0)) 2009. (gr. 5-5). 47.90 (978-1-60851-354-3(8), PowerKids Pr.) 2006. (Illus.). (YA). (gr. 5-9). lib. bdg. 25.25 (978-1-4042-3367-6(9)) Rosen Publishing Group, Inc., The.

Saddleback Educational Publishing Staff, ed. Amelia Earhart, 1 vol. unabr. ed. 2008. (Graphic Biographies Ser.). (ENG., Illus.). 25p. (YA). (gr. 9-12). pap. 7.95 (978-1-59905-214-4(8)) Saddleback Educational Publishing, Inc.

—Charles Lindbergh, 1 vol. unabr. ed. 2008. (Graphic Biographies Ser.). (ENG., Illus.). 25p. (YA). (gr. 9-12). pap. 7.95 (978-1-59905-218-2(0)) Saddleback Educational Publishing, Inc.

Sanchez Vegara, Ma Isabel. Amelia Earhart. Mariadiamantes, illus. 2016. (Little People, Big Dreams Ser.). (ENG.). 32p. (J). (gr. k-3). 14.99 (978-1-84780-888-2(3), Frances Lincoln Children's Bks.) Quarto Publishing Group UK GBR. Dist: Hachette Bk. Group.

Schraff, Anne. Daredevil American Heroes of Exploration & Flight. 2013. (Inspiring Collective Biographies Ser.). 112p. (J). (gr. 5-12). pap. 10.95 (978-1-4644-0247-0(7)) Enslow Pubs., Inc.

Schraff, Anne E. Daredevil American Heroes of Exploration & Flight. 2013. (Inspiring Collective Biographies Ser.). (Illus.). 112p. (J). (gr. 5-18). 33.27 (978-0-7660-4163-9(8)) Enslow Pubs., Inc.

Shea, John M. The Tuskegee Airmen. 2015. (Heroes of Black History Ser.). (ENG., Illus.). 32p. (J). (gr. 3-4). 26.60 (978-1-4824-2918-3(7)) Stevens, Gareth Publishing LLLP.

Simons, Lisa M. Bolt. Airmen of the U. S. Air Force [Scholastic]. 2010. (People of the U. S. Armed Forces Ser.). (ENG.). 24p. pap. 0.49 (978-1-4296-5804-1(5), Pebble Plus) Capstone Press of Coughlan Cos.

Simons, Lisa M. Bolt. The U. S. WASP: Trailblazing Women Pilots of World War II. 2017. (Women & War Ser.). (ENG.). 32p. (gr. 3-4). pap. 8.19 **(978-1-5157-7944-5(0)**, Snap Bks.) Capstone Press of Coughlan Cos.

Sís, Peter. The Pilot & the Little Prince: The Life of Antoine de Saint-Exupéry. Sís, Peter, illus. 2014. (ENG., Illus.). 48p. (J). (gr. k-3). 18.99 (978-0-374-38069-4(4), 9780374380694, Farrar, Straus & Giroux (BYR)) Farrar, Straus & Giroux.

Sisson, Kathryn Cleven. Eddie Rickenbacker: Boy Pilot & Racer, 6 vols. Underdown, Harold D., ed. Morrison, Cathy, illus. rev. ed. 2003. (Young Patriots Ser.: 6). (ENG.). 120p. (J). (gr. 4-7). 15.95 (978-1-882859-12-2(X)) Patria Pr., Inc.

—Eddie Rickenbacker: Boy Pilot & Racer, 6 vols. Morrison, Cathy, illus. rev. ed. 2003. (Young Patriots Ser.: 6). (ENG.). 120p. (J). (gr. 4-7). pap. 9.95 (978-1-882859-13-9(8)) Patria Pr., Inc.

Small, Cathleen. Bessie Coleman: First African American & Native American Pilot. 2017. (J). **(978-1-5026-2753-7(1))** Cavendish Square Publishing.

Snedden, Robert. Air Force. 2016. (Defend & Protect Ser.). (ENG.). 48p. (J). (gr. 4-5). pap. 14.05 (978-1-4824-4106-2(3)) Stevens, Gareth Publishing LLLP.

Sofer, Barbara. Ilan Ramon: Israel's Space Hero. 2003. (Illus.). 64p. (J). (gr. 3-6). 16.95 (978-1-58013-115-5(8)); pap. 6.95 (978-1-58013-116-2(6)) Lerner Publishing Group. (Kar-Ben Publishing).

Speregen, Debra Newberger. Ilan Ramon: Jewish Star. 2004. (ENG., Illus.). 120p. (J). pap. 13.00 (978-0-8276-0769-9(5)) Jewish Pubn. Society.

Stiefel, Chana. Sky High. 2011. (J). (978-0-531-22558-5(5)) Scholastic, Inc.

Stone, Tanya Lee & Dorling Kindersley Publishing Staff. Amelia Earhart. 2007. (DK Biography Ser.). (ENG., Illus.). 128p. (J). (gr. 5-12). pap. 6.99 (978-0-7566-2552-8(1), DK Children) Dorling Kindersley Publishing, Inc.

Strom, Laura Layton. Racing on the Wind: Steve Fossett. 2008. (Illus.). 36p. (J). pap. (978-0-531-15541-7(2)) Children's Pr., Ltd.

Sutcliffe, Jane. Amelia Earhart. 2003. (History Maker Bios Ser.). (Illus.). 48p. (J). (gr. 3-5). lib. bdg. 26.60 (978-0-8225-0396-5(4)) Lerner Publishing Group.

Tetrick, Byron. Choosing a Career as a Pilot. 2009. (World of Work Ser.). 64p. (gr. 5-5). 58.50 (978-1-60854-325-0(0)) Rosen Publishing Group, Inc., The.

Thiel, Kristin. Amelia Earhart: First Woman to Fly Solo Across the Atlantic. 2017. (J). **(978-1-5026-2749-0(3))** Cavendish Square Publishing.

Thomas, William. Wilderness Rescue Pilot. 2010. (Benchmark Rockets: Dirty & Dangerous Jobs Ser.). 32p. (J). (gr. 3-6). 28.50 (978-1-60870-180-3(8)) Marshall Cavendish Corp.

Tunnell, Michael O. Candy Bomber: The Story of the Berlin Airlift's Chocolate Pilot. 2010. (ENG., Illus.). 120p. (J). (gr. 4-7). pap. 9.95 (978-1-58089-337-4(6)) Charlesbridge Publishing, Inc.

Valentin, Jean. The Bravery of Amelia Earhart. 2012. (InfoMax Readers Ser.). (ENG., Illus.). 24p. (J). (gr. 1-2). pap. 8.25 (978-1-4488-9067-5(5), Rosen Classroom) Rosen Publishing Group, Inc., The.

Vansant, Wayne. The Red Baron: The Graphic History of Richthofen's Flying Circus & the Air War in WWI. Vansant, Wayne, illus. 2015. (Graphic Histories Ser.). (ENG., Illus.). 104p. (J). (gr. 8-12). 34.65 (978-1-939581-80-8(X)) Quarto Publishing Group USA.

—The Red Baron: The Graphic History of Richthofen's Flying Circus & the Air War in WWI. 2014. (Zenith Graphic Histories Ser.). (ENG., Illus.). 104p. pap. 19.99 (978-0-7603-4602-0(X), 076034602X, Zenith Pr.) Quarto Publishing Group USA.

Walker, Sally M. Bessie Coleman: Daring to Fly. Porter, Janice Lee, illus. (On My Own Biographies Ser.). 48p. (gr. 2-5). 2005. lib. bdg. 23.93 (978-0-87614-919-5(0)) 2003. (ENG.). pap. 6.95 (978-0-87614-103-8(3), Carolrhoda Bks.) Lerner Publishing Group.

Watson, Marilyn Myrick. Frank Luke, the Arizona Balloon Buster. 2007. (978-0-9790826-3-4(3)); (978-0-9790826-4-1(1)) Acacia Publishing, Inc.

Weakland, Mark. When Amelia Earhart Built a Roller Coaster. Grivina, Oksana, illus. 2017. 31p. (J). (978-1-5158-0142-9(X)) 2016. (ENG.). 32p. (gr. 2-3). lib. bdg. 27.99 (978-1-4795-9686-7(8)) Picture Window Bks.

Wearing, Judy. Amelia Earhart. 2010. pap. 9.95 (978-1-61690-060-1(1)); 24p. (J). (gr. 2-4). lib. bdg. 25.70 (978-1-61690-059-5(8)) Weigl Pubs., Inc.

West, David. Fighter Pilots. 2009. (Graphic Careers Ser.). (ENG.). 48p. (YA). (gr. 5-5). 58.50 (978-1-61512-880-8(8), Rosen Reference) Rosen Publishing Group, Inc., The.

—Ten of the Best Adventures in the Sky. 2015. (Ten of the Best: Stories of Exploration & Adventure Ser.). (ENG., Illus.). 24p. (J). (gr. 3-6). lib. bdg. (978-0-7787-1838-3(7)) Crabtree Publishing Co.

Whitaker, Suzanne George. The Daring Miss Quimby. Stock, Catherine, illus. 2009. (ENG.). 32p. (J). (gr. -1-3). 16.95 (978-0-8234-1996-8(7)) Holiday Hse., Inc.

Williams, Brian. Pilots in Peril, 1 vol. 2011. (War Stories Ser.). (ENG.). 32p. (gr. 3-6). 30.65 (978-1-4329-4830-6(X), NA-h) Heinemann-Raintree.

Williams, Colleen Madonna Flood. Chuck Yeager. 2006. (Illus.). 106p. (J). (gr. 4-8). reprint ed. 20.00 (978-1-4223-5543-5(8)) DIANE Publishing Co.

Winegarten, Debra L. Katherine Stinson: The Flying Schoolgirl. 2004. (Illus.). 133p. (gr. 4-7). 26.95 (978-1-57168-459-2(X)) Eakin Pr.

Wood, Alix. Test Pilot, 1 vol., 1. 2014. (World's Coolest Jobs Ser.). (ENG.). 32p. (J). (gr. 3-6). 26.25 (978-1-4777-6019-2(9), PowerKids Pr.) Rosen Publishing Group, Inc., The.

Woods, Bob. A Day with a Pilot. 2008. (Reading Rocks! Ser.). (ENG., Illus.). 32p. (J). (gr. 2-5). 28.50 (978-1-60253-097-3(1), 200755) Child's World, Inc., The.

AIR POLLUTION

see Air—Pollution

AIR RAIDS—PROTECTIVE MEASURES

see Aeronautics, Military

AIR STATIONS, MILITARY

see Air Bases

AIR STATIONS, NAVAL

see Air Bases

AIR STEWARDESSES

see Flight Attendants

AIR TRAFFIC CONTROL

Gish, Melissa. An Airport. 2003. 24p. (J). lib. bdg. 21.35 (978-1-58340-322-8(1)) Black Rabbit Bks.

Labrecque, Ellen. Air Traffic Controller. 2016. (21st Century Skills Library: Cool Vocational Careers Ser.). (ENG., Illus.). 32p. (J). (gr. 4-7). 29.93 (978-1-63471-057-2(6), 208308) Cherry Lake Publishing.

Masters, Nancy Robinson. Air Traffic Controller. 2010. (21st Century Skills Library: Cool Careers Ser.). (ENG.). 32p. (gr. 4-8). lib. bdg. 28.50 (978-1-60279-940-0(7), 200625) Cherry Lake Publishing.

AIR TRANSPORT

see Aeronautics, Commercial

AIR WARFARE

see Aeronautics, Military; Airplanes, Military

see names of wars with the subdivision Aerial Operations, e.g. World War, 1939-1945—Aerial Operations; etc.

AIRCRAFT ACCIDENTS

see also Survival

Benoit, Peter. The Hindenburg Disaster. 2011. (Illus.). 48p. (J). pap. (978-0-531-29025-5(5)) Children's Pr., Ltd.

—The Hindenburg Disaster. 2011. (True Book(tm), A — Disasters Ser.). (ENG.). 48p. (J). (gr. 3-5). lib. bdg. 31.00 (978-0-531-20626-3(2)); pap. 6.95 (978-0-531-28995-2(8)) Scholastic Library Publishing. (Children's Pr.).

Bowman, Chris. The Hindenburg Disaster. 2014. (Disaster Stories Ser.). (ENG., Illus.). 24p. (J). (gr. 3-8). 29.95 (978-1-62617-153-4(X), Black Sheep) Bellwether Media.

Buckley, A. M. The Disappearance of Amelia Earhart, 1 vol. 2012. (Unsolved Mysteries (el) Ser.). (ENG.). 112p. (J). (gr. 6-12). lib. bdg. 35.64 (978-1-61783-302-1(9), Essential Library) ABDO Publishing Co.

Burgan, Michael. The Hindenburg in Flames: How a Photograph Marked the End of the Airship. 2016. (Captured World History Ser.). (ENG.). 64p. (gr. 5-7). lib. bdg. 34.65 (978-0-7565-5441-5(1), CPB Grades 4-8) Compass Point Bks.

Byers, Ann. The Crash of the Concorde. 2009. (When Disaster Strikes! Ser.). 48p. (gr. 5-8). 53.00 (978-1-60854-779-1(5), Rosen Reference) Rosen Publishing Group, Inc., The.

—The Crash of the Concorde: When Disaster Strikes! 2005. (When Disaster Strikes! Ser.). (Illus.). 48p. (J). (gr. 5-8). lib. bdg. 29.25 (978-0-8239-3673-1(2)) Rosen Publishing Group, Inc., The.

Cheney, Glenn. Shot Down, 1 vol. unabr. ed. 2012. (Astonishing Headlines Ser.). (ENG.). 92p. (YA). (gr. 9-12). 8.95 (978-1-61651-924-7(X)) Saddleback Educational Publishing, Inc.

DeMolay, Jack. The Bermuda Triangle: The Disappearance of Flight 19. (Jr. Graphic Mysteries Ser.). (ENG.). 24p. 2009. (J). (gr. 2-3). 47.90 (978-1-61513-846-3(3), PowerKids Pr.) 2007. (Illus.). (J). (gr. 2-5). lib. bdg. 25.25 (978-1-4042-3404-8(7)) 2007. (Illus.). (gr. 3-8). pap. 10.60 (978-1-4042-2157-4(3), PowerKids Pr.) Rosen Publishing Group, Inc., The.

—El Triángulo de las Bermudas: La Desaparicíon del Vuelo 19. Obregón, José María, tr. 2008. (Historietas Juveniles: Misterios (Jr. Graphic Mysteries) Ser.). (SPA., Illus.). 24p. (J). (gr. 2-5). lib. bdg. 25.25 (978-1-4358-2535-2(7)) Rosen Publishing Group, Inc., The.

—El Triángulo de las Bermudas: La desaparición del vuelo 19 (the Bermuda Triangle:the Disappearance of Flight 19) 2009. (Historietas Juveniles: Misterios (Jr. Graphic Mysteries) Ser.). (SPA.). 24p. (gr. 2-3). 47.90 (978-1-61513-348-2(8), Editorial Buenas Letras) Rosen Publishing Group, Inc., The.

Doeden, Matt. The Hindenburg Disaster, 1 vol. Erwin, Steve et al, illus. 2006. (Disasters in History Ser.). (ENG.). 32p. (gr. 3-4). 30.65 (978-0-7368-5481-8(9), Graphic Library) Capstone Press of Coughlan Cos.

Feigenbaum, Aaron. The Hindenburg Disaster. 2007. (Code Red Ser.). (Illus.). 32p. (YA). (gr. 2-5). lib. bdg. 25.27 (978-1-59716-361-3(9)) Bearport Publishing Co., Inc.

Goldberg, Jan. James Lovell: The Rescue of Apollo 13. 2004. (Library of Astronaut Biographies Ser.). (Illus.). 112p. (gr. 5-8). lib. bdg. 34.60 (978-0-8239-4459-0(X), Rosen Reference) Rosen Publishing Group, Inc., The.

Hamilton, Sue. Air & Sea Mysteries, 1 vol. 2007. (Unsolved Mysteries Ser.). (ENG.). 32p. (gr. 3-7). 27.07 (978-1-59928-837-6(0), Abdo & Daughters) ABDO Publishing Co.

Hasday, Judy L. The Apollo 13 Mission: Overcoming Adversity. 2006. (Illus.). 120p. (J). (gr. 4-8). reprint ed. 25.00 (978-1-4223-5546-6(2)) DIANE Publishing Co.

Hatch, Andrew. Examining Airplane Crashes. 2015. (ENG., Illus.). 48p. (J). lib. bdg. 24.95 net. (978-1-934545-61-4(9)) Oliver Pr., Inc.

Hawkins, John. Air Disasters. 2011. (Catastrophe! Ser.). (ENG., Illus.). 48p. (J). (gr. 5-9). lib. bdg. 29.25 (978-1-4488-6006-7(7)) Rosen Publishing Group, Inc., The.

Holden, Henry M. The Tragedy of the Space Shuttle Challenger: A MyReportLinks. com Book. 2004. (Space Flight Adventures & Disasters Ser.). (Illus.). 48p. (J). lib. bdg. 25.26 (978-0-7660-5165-2(X), MyReportLinks.com Bks.) Enslow Pubs., Inc.

Koestler-Grack, Rachel A. Space Shuttle Columbia Disaster, 1 vol. 2004. (American Moments Ser.). (ENG.). 48p. (gr. 4-8). 27.07 (978-1-59197-659-2(6), Abdo & Daughters) ABDO Publishing Co.

Lace, William W. The Hindenburg Disaster Of 1937. 2008. (Great Historic Disasters Ser.). (Illus.). 120p. (gr. 5-8). lib. bdg. 35.00 (978-0-7910-9739-7(0), Chelsea Hse.) Facts On File, Inc.

Leavitt, Amie Jane. Anatomy of a Plane Crash. (Disasters Ser.). (ENG.). 48p. (gr. 3-4). 2011. pap. 59.70 (978-1-4296-7362-4(1)) 2010. lib. bdg. 31.99 (978-1-4296-4796-0(5)) Capstone Press of Coughlan Cos.

Nagelhout, Ryan. The Hindenburg Disaster. 2015. (Doomed! Ser.). (ENG., Illus.). 32p. (J). (gr. 4-5). 26.60 (978-1-4824-2938-1(1)) Stevens, Gareth Publishing LLLP.

O'Brien, Patrick. The Hindenburg. Date not set. (J). pap. 6.95 (978-0-8050-7264-8(0), Holt, Henry & Co. Bks. For Young Readers) Holt, Henry & Co.

Olson, Tod. Lost in the Pacific, 1942: Not a Drop to Drink. 2016. (J). (978-0-545-92808-3(7)); (Lost Ser.: 1). (ENG., Illus.). 176p. (gr. 4-7). 12.99 (978-0-545-92811-3(7), Scholastic Nonfiction) Scholastic, Inc.

Otfinoski, Steven. The Hindenburg Explosion: Core Events of a Disaster in the Air, 1 vol. 2014. (What Went Wrong? Ser.). (ENG.). 32p. (gr. 3-4). pap. 7.95 (978-1-4765-5133-3(2)); lib. bdg. 27.32 (978-1-4765-4184-6(1)) Capstone Press of Coughlan Cos.

Pascal, Janet B. What Was the Hindenburg? Groff, David & McVeigh, Kevin, illus. 2014. (What Was? Ser.). (ENG.). 112p. (J). (gr. 3-7). 5.99 (978-0-448-48119-7(7), Penguin Workshop) Penguin Young Readers Group.

—What Was the Hindenburg? 2014. (What Was... ? Ser.). lib. bdg. 16.00 (978-0-606-36186-6(3)) Turtleback Bks.

Perish, Patrick. Survive a Plane Crash. 2017. (Survival Zone Ser.). (ENG., Illus.). 24p. (J). (gr. 3-7). lib. bdg. 25.95 (978-1-62617-582-2(9), Torque Bks.) Bellwether Media.

The Science of a Plane Crash. 2014. (21st Century Skills Library: Disaster Science Ser.). (ENG., Illus.). 32p. (J). (gr. 4-8). 28.50 (978-1-63137-626-9(8), 205287) Cherry Lake Publishing.

Sherman, Jill. The Hindenburg Disaster, 1 vol. 2010. (Essential Events Set 4 Ser.). (ENG.). 112p. (J). (gr. 6-12). lib. bdg. 35.64 (978-1-60453-944-8(5)) ABDO Publishing Co.

Sofer, Barbara. Ilan Ramon: Israel's Space Hero. 2003. (Illus.). 64p. (J). (gr. 3-6). 16.95 (978-1-58013-115-5(8)); pap. 6.95 (978-1-58013-116-2(6)) Lerner Publishing Group. (Kar-Ben Publishing).

Spalding, Frank. Plane Crash: True Stories of Survival. (Survivor Stories Ser.). 48p. (gr. 5-5). 2009. 53.00 (978-1-60853-255-1(0), Rosen Reference) 2006. (Illus.). (YA). lib. bdg. 29.25 (978-1-4042-0999-2(9), 1267009) Rosen Publishing Group, Inc., The.

Verstraete, Larry. Surviving the Hindenburg. 2012. (ENG., Illus.). 40p. (J). (gr. k-5). 16.95 (978-1-58536-787-0(7)) Sleeping Bear Pr.

Vogel, Carole Garbuny & Leshem, Yossi. The Man Who Flies with Birds. 2009. (Israel Ser.). (ENG., Illus.). 64p. (J). (gr. 5-12). 18.95 (978-0-8225-7643-3(0), Kar-Ben Publishing) Lerner Publishing Group.

Walker, Kathryn. The Mystery of the Ghosts of Flight 401. 2008. (ENG., Illus.). 32p. (J). (gr. 3-7). pap. (978-0-7787-4155-8(9)); lib. bdg. (978-0-7787-4142-8(7)) Crabtree Publishing Co.

Werther, Scott P. Alive! Airplane Crash in the Andes Mountains. 2003. (Survivor Ser.). (Illus.). 48p. (J). 24.50 (978-0-516-24329-0(2), Children's Pr.) Scholastic Library Publishing.

Wicker, R. Doug. The Bombing of Pan Am Flight 103. 2009. (Terrorist Attacks Ser.). 64p. (gr. 5-5). 58.50 (978-1-60853-315-2(8)) Rosen Publishing Group, Inc., The.

Woods, Michael & Woods, Mary B. Air Disasters. 2008. (Disasters up Close Ser.). (ENG., Illus.). 64p. (gr. 4-8). lib. bdg. 27.93 (978-0-8225-6772-1(5), Lerner Pubns.) Lerner Publishing Group.

AIRCRAFT CARRIERS

Allen, Kenny. Aircraft Carriers. 2012. (Monster Machines Ser.). (Illus.). 24p. (J). (gr. 1-3). pap. 8.15 (978-1-4339-7160-0(7)); lib. bdg. 22.60 (978-1-4339-7159-4(3)) Stevens, Gareth Publishing LLLP.

Amato, William. Aircraft Carriers. 2009. (High-Tech Vehicles Ser.). 24p. (gr. 2-3). 42.50 (978-1-61513-303-1(8), PowerKids Pr.) Rosen Publishing Group, Inc., The.

—Portaaviones. 2004. (Vehículos de Alta Tecnología (High-Tech Vehicles) Ser.). (SPA & ENG., Illus.). 24p. (J). (gr. 3-6). lib. bdg. 22.60 (978-0-8239-6883-1(9), Editorial Buenas Letras) Rosen Publishing Group, Inc., The.

—Portaaviones (Aircraft Carriers) 2009. (Vehículos de alta tecnología (High-Tech Vehicles) Ser.). (SPA.). 24p. (gr. 2-3). 42.50 (978-1-60854-719-7(1), Editorial Buenas Letras) Rosen Publishing Group, Inc., The.

Arnold, Quinn M. Nimitz Aircraft Carrier. 2016. (Illus.). 24p. (J). (978-1-60818-712-6(8), Creative Education) Creative Co., The.

Beyer, Mark. Aircraft Carriers: Inside & Out. 2005. (Technology: Blueprints of the Future Ser.). (Illus.). 48p. (YA). (gr. 4-8). lib. bdg. 29.25 (978-0-8239-6111-5(7)) Rosen Publishing Group, Inc., The.

Beyer, Mark T. Aircraft Carriers: Inside & Out. 2009. (Technology: Blueprints of the Future Ser.). 48p. (gr. 4-4). 53.00 (978-1-60853-281-0(X)) Rosen Publishing Group, Inc., The.

Biello, David. Portaaviones: Por dentro y por fuera (Aircraft Carriers: Inside & Out) 2009. (Tecnología: Mapas para el Futuro Ser.). (SPA.). 48p. (gr. 4-4). 53.00 (978-1-60853-287-2(9), Editorial Buenas Letras) Rosen Publishing Group, Inc., The.

Bodden, Valerie. Aircraft Carriers. 2011. (J). 25.65 (978-1-60818-122-3(7), Creative Education) Creative Co., The.

Doeden, Matt. Aircraft Carriers. 2005. (Pull Ahead Books-Mighty Movers Ser.). (ENG., Illus.). 32p. (gr. k-3). lib. bdg. 22.60 (978-0-8225-2666-7(2)); per. 7.95 (978-0-8225-2872-2(X)) Lerner Publishing Group. (Lerner Pubns.).

Doyle, Kevin. Aircraft Carriers. 2003. (Military Hardware in Action Ser.). (ENG., Illus.). 48p. (gr. 5-9). lib. bdg. 25.26 (978-0-8225-4702-0(3)) Lerner Publishing Group.

Farndon, John. Stickmen's Guide to Watercraft. Paul de Quay, John, illus. 2016. (Stickmen's Guides to How Everything Works). (ENG.). 32p. (J). (gr. 3-6). 30.65 (978-1-4677-9594-4(1)); 30.65 (978-1-5124-0699-3(6)) Lerner Publishing Group.

Finn, Denny Von. Nimitz Aircraft Carriers. 2013. (Military Vehicles Ser.). (ENG., Illus.). 24p. (J). (gr. 3-7). lib. bdg. 25.95 (978-1-60014-887-3(5), Epic Bks.) Bellwether Media.

Hamilton, John. Aircraft Carriers. 2012. (Military Ships Ser.). 32p. (J). (gr. 3-9). 27.07 (978-1-61783-519-3(6)) ABDO Publishing Co.

Loh-Hagan, Virginia. Aircraft Carriers. 2017. (21st Century Junior Library: Extraordinary Engineering Ser.). (ENG., Illus.). 24p. (J). (gr. 2-5). lib. bdg. 27.07 (978-1-63472-161-5(6), 209216) Cherry Lake Publishing.

Mavrikis, Peter. Battleships & Aircraft Carriers. 2014. (Illus.). 48p. (J). (978-1-4351-5367-7(7)) Barnes & Noble, Inc.

Niver, Heather Moore. Life on an Aircraft Carrier. 2013. (Extreme Jobs in Extreme Places Ser.). (Illus.). 32p. (J). (gr. 3-6). pap. 10.50 (978-1-4339-8493-8(8)); lib. bdg. 26.60 (978-1-4339-8492-1(X)) Stevens, Gareth Publishing LLLP.

Oxlade, Chris & Farndon, John. Stickmen's Guide to Watercraft. Pyke, Jerry & Quay, John Paul de, illus. 2016. (Stickmen's Guides to How Everything Works). (ENG.). 32p. (J). (gr. 3-6). lib. bdg. 26.65 (978-1-4677-9362-9(0)) Lerner Publishing Group.

Patchett, F. Plane Fun. 2009. (Kid Kits Ser.). 32p. (J). 11.99 (978-1-60130-162-8(6), Usborne) EDC Publishing.

Peppas, Lynn. Aircraft Carriers: Runways at Sea. 2011. (ENG.). 32p. (J). pap. (978-0-7787-2752-1(1)); lib. bdg. (978-0-7787-2747-7(5)) Crabtree Publishing Co.

Roza, Greg. The Incredible Story of Aircraft Carriers. (Kid's Guide to Incredible Technology Ser.). 24p. 2009. (gr. 3-4). 42.50 (978-1-61511-170-1(0)) 2004. (Illus.). (J). lib. bdg. 22.60 (978-0-8239-6714-8(X)) Rosen Publishing Group, Inc., The. (PowerKids Pr.).

Stone, Lynn M. Aircraft Carriers. 2005. (Fighting Forces Ser.). (Illus.). 32p. (J). (gr. 4-8). lib. bdg. 19.95 (978-1-59515-459-0(0), 1244401) Rourke Educational Media.

Strazzabosco, John. Aircraft Carriers, Supplies for a City at Sea: Multiplying Multidigit Numbers with Regrouping. (PowerMath Ser.). (Illus.). 32p. 2009. (gr. 4-5). pap. 10.00 (978-0-8239-8919-5(4), PowerKids Pr.) 2004. (YA). (gr. 5-9). lib. bdg. 25.25 (978-0-8239-8995-9(X)) Rosen Publishing Group, Inc., The.

—Aircraft Carriers Supplies for a City at Sea: Multiplying Multidigit Numbers with Regrouping. 2009. (PowerMath: Proficiency Ser.). 32p. (gr. 4-5). 47.90 (978-1-60851-389-5(0), PowerKids Pr.) Rosen Publishing Group, Inc., The.

Tagliaferro, Linda. Who Lands Planes on a Ship? Working on an Aircraft Carrier. 2010. (Wild Work Ser.). (ENG.). 32p. (gr. 1-2). 29.99 (978-1-4109-3853-4(0), Read Me!) Heinemann-Raintree.

Tripp, Will. Water Adventures. 2005. (Real Deal Ser.). (Illus.). 32p. (J). pap. (978-0-7608-9636-5(4)) Sundance/Newbridge Educational Publishing.

Zobel, Derek. Nimitz Aircraft Carriers. 2008. (Military Machines Ser.). (ENG., Illus.). 24p. (YA). (gr. 3-7). lib. bdg. 25.95 (978-1-60014-222-2(2)) Bellwether Media.

AIRLINE CRASHES

see Aircraft Accidents

AIRLINES

Larson, Kirsten W. Federal Air Marshals. 2016. (Protecting Our People Ser.). (ENG., Illus.). 32p. (J). (gr. 1-4). 20.95 (978-1-60753-984-1(5)) Amicus Publishing.

Murray, Laura K. Southwest Airlines. 2015. (Illus.). 48p. (J). (978-1-60818-559-7(1), Creative Education) Creative Co., The.

—Southwest Airlines: Built for Success. 2016. (Built for Success Ser.). (ENG., Illus.). 48p. (J). (gr. 5-9). pap. 12.00 (978-1-62832-160-9(1), Creative Paperbacks) Creative Co., The.

Rogers, Kate. Air Marshals, 01 vols., 1. 2016. (Careers for Heroes Ser.). (ENG., Illus.). 24p. (J). pap. 8.25 (978-1-5081-4387-1(0), PowerKids Pr.) Rosen Publishing Group, Inc., The.

AIRLINES—HOSTESSES

see Flight Attendants

AIRPLANE ACCIDENTS

see Aircraft Accidents

AIRPLANE CARRIERS

see Aircraft Carriers

AIRPLANE CRASHES

see Aircraft Accidents

AIRPLANE RACING

Dorling Kindersley Publishing Staff. Disney Planes. 2013. (ENG., Illus.). 64p. (J). (gr. 2-5). 12.99 (978-1-4654-0268-4(3), DK Children) Dorling Kindersley Publishing, Inc.

Hamilton, S. L. Reno Air Races. 2013. (Xtreme Races Ser.). (Illus.). 32p. (J). (gr. 3-9). lib. bdg. 27.07

(978-1-61783-696-1(6), Abdo & Daughters) ABDO Publishing Co.

AIRPLANES

see also Aeronautics; Gliders (Aeronautics)

also types of airplanes, e.g. Bombers; Vertically Rising Airplanes; etc.

Adams, C. Planes Go Places: Learning the PL Sound. 2009. (PowerPhonics Ser.). 24p. (gr. 1-1). 39.90 *(978-1-60851-468-7(4),* PowerKids Pr.) Rosen Publishing Group, Inc., The.

Adamson, Thomas K. Airplanes. 2017. (Mighty Machines in Action Ser.). (ENG., Illus.). 24p. (J). (gr. k-3). lib. bdg. 25.95 *(978-1-62617-599-0(3),* Blastoff! Readers) Bellwether Media.

Aircraft, 14 bks., Set. Incl. Air Force Aircraft. Holden, Henry M. (J). 2001. lib. bdg. 23.93 *(978-0-7660-1714-6(1));* Air Show Pilots & Airplanes. Gaffney, Timothy R. (YA). 2001. lib. bdg. 23.93 *(978-0-7660-1570-8(X));* Amazing Agricultural Aircraft. Gaffney, Timothy R. (J). 2001. lib. bdg. 23.93 *(978-0-7660-1608-8(0));* Black Hawk Helicopter. Holden, Henry M. (J). 2002. lib. bdg. 23.93 *(978-0-7660-1568-5(8));* Hurricane Hunters. Gaffney, Timothy R. (J). 2001. lib. bdg. 25.27 *(978-0-7660-1569-2(6));* Stealth Fighters & Bombers. Berliner, Don. (YA). 2001. lib. bdg. 23.93 *(978-0-7660-1567-8(X));* 48p. (gr. 4-10). (Illus.). Set lib. bdg. 227.40 *(978-0-7660-1799-3(0))* Enslow Pubs., Inc.

Allen, Kenny. Jumbo Jets. 2012. (Monster Machines Ser.). (Illus.). 24p. (J). (gr. 1-3). pap. 8.15 *(978-1-4339-7176-1(3));* lib. bdg. 22.60 *(978-1-4339-7175-4(5))* Stevens, Gareth Publishing LLLP.

Alvarez, Carlos. V-22 Ospreys. 2010. (Military Machines Ser.). (ENG., Illus.). 24p. (J). (gr. 3-7). lib. bdg. 25.95 *(978-1-60014-333-5(4))* Bellwether Media.

Amoroso, Cynthia. Airplanes. 2014. (Big Machines at Work Ser.). (ENG.). 24p. (J). (gr. -1-2). 25.64 *(978-1-62323-961-9(3),* 206736) Child's World, Inc., The.

Ard, Catherine. Origami Planes. 2015. (Amazing Origami Ser.). (ENG.). 32p. (J). (gr. 2-3). 26.60 *(978-1-4824-2203-0(4))* Stevens, Gareth Publishing LLLP.

Ardagh, Philip. Up in the Air. (Mighty Machines Ser.). (Illus.). 32p. lib. bdg. 24.25 *(978-1-931983-03-7(8))* Chrysalis Education.

Ashley, Susan. Por Avión. 2003. (Weekly Reader Early Learning Library). (SPA., Illus.). 24p. (gr. 1-4). pap. 8.15 *(978-0-8368-3841-1(6),* Weekly Reader Leveled Readers) Stevens, Gareth Publishing LLLP.

AZ Books Staff. Flying Planes. Tulup, Natasha, ed. 2012. (Workshop Ser.). (ENG.). 10p. (J). (gr. -1-k). 10.95 *(978-1-61889-159-4(6))* AZ Bks. LLC.

B-29 Superfortress Pilot's Manual Collection. 2005. (YA). cd-rom 69.95 *(978-0-9742781-6-2(5))* Rhode, Steve Inc.

Baines, Francesca. Planes. 2015. (Wonderwise Ser.). (Illus.). 32p. (gr. 2-6). 31.35 *(978-1-62588-361-2(7))* Black Rabbit Bks.

Bender, Lionel. Airplanes & Helicopters. 2006. (J). *(978-1-59389-261-6(6))* Chrysalis Education.

Berger, Melvin. How Do Airplanes Fly? (Discovery Readers Ser.). (ENG.). 48p. (J). pap. 3.95 *(978-0-8249-5317-1(7),* Ideal Pubns.) Worthy Publishing.

Berger, Melvin & Berger, Gilda. Can You Fly High, Wright Brothers? Dorman, Brandon, illus. 2007. (Scholastic Science Supergiants Ser.: Vol. 1). (ENG.). 48p. (J). (gr. 2-5). pap. 4.99 *(978-0-439-83378-3(7))* Scholastic, Inc.

Bergin, Mark. How to Draw Planes. 2009. (How to Draw Ser.). (Illus.). 32p. (gr. 4-6). pap. 11.75 *(978-1-4358-2648-9(5),* Rosen Classroom) Rosen Publishing Group, Inc., The.

—Planes. 2012. (You Can Draw Ser.). (Illus.). 32p. (J). (gr. 1-3). pap. 10.50 *(978-1-4339-7472-4(X));* lib. bdg. 26.60 *(978-1-4339-7471-7(1))* Stevens, Gareth Publishing LLLP.

Bethea, Nikole Brooks. The Dynamic World of Drones: Max Axiom STEM Adventures. 2017. (STEM Adventures Ser.). (ENG.). 32p. (gr. 3-4). lib. bdg. 30.65 ***(978-1-5157-7390-0(6),*** Graphic Library) Capstone Press of Coughlan Cos.

Beyer, Mark. Aviones Del Pasado. 2004. (Transporte Ayer y Hoy (Transportation Through the Ages) Ser.). (SPA & ENG., Illus.). 24p. (J). (gr. 2-4). lib. bdg. 22.60 *(978-0-8239-6905-0(3))* Rosen Publishing Group, Inc., The.

—Aviones del pasado (Planes of the Past) 2009. (transporte ayer y hoy (Transportation Through the Ages) Ser.). (SPA.). 24p. (gr. 1-2). 42.50 *(978-1-61512-252-3(4),* Editorial Buenas Letras) Rosen Publishing Group, Inc., The.

—Planes of the Past. 2009. (Transportation Through the Ages Ser.). 24p. (gr. 1-1). 42.50 *(978-1-60854-590-2(3),* PowerKids Pr.) Rosen Publishing Group, Inc., The.

Biesty, Stephen. Look Inside Cross-Sections: Planes. (ENG., Illus.). 32p. (J). mass mkt. 8.99 *(978-0-590-24341-4(1))* Scholastic, Inc.

Bowman, Chris. Monster Airplanes. 2014. (Monster Machines Ser.). (ENG., Illus.). 24p. (J). (gr. k-3). lib. bdg. 25.95 *(978-1-62617-052-0(5),* Blastoff! Readers) Bellwether Media.

Brasch, Nicolas. Machines of Speed & Flight. 2011. (Technology Behind Ser.). 32p. (YA). (gr. 3-6). 28.50 *(978-1-59920-568-7(8))* Black Rabbit Bks.

Brown, Jordan. How Airplanes Get from Here... to There! Borgions, Mark, illus. 2016. 48p. (J). ***(978-1-5182-1871-2(7),*** Simon Spotlight) Simon Spotlight.

Brown, Jordan D. How Airplanes Get from Here ... to There! Borgions, Mark, illus. 2016. (Science of Fun Stuff Ser.). (ENG.). 48p. (J). (gr. 1-3). pap. 3.99 *(978-1-4814-6164-1(8),* Simon Spotlight) Simon Spotlight.

Burch, Lynda S. Wicky Wacky Things that Go! Airplanes 1. Roberts, MarySue, photos by. 2004. (Illus.). 28p. (J). E-Book 9.95 incl. cd-rom *(978-1-933090-07-8(3))* Guardian Angel Publishing, Inc.

Carrière, Nicholle. Planes, 1 vol. 2017. (Super Explorers Ser.). (ENG., Illus.). 64p. (J). pap. 6.99 ***(978-1-926700-74-8(0),*** 9781926700748) Blue Bike Bks. CAN. Dist: Lone Pine Publishing USA.

Catala, Ellen. Up, up, & Away. 2005. (Yellow Umbrella Fluent Level Ser.). (ENG., Illus.). 16p. (gr. k-1). pap. 35.70 *(978-0-7368-5301-9(4),* Yellow Umbrella Bks.) Capstone Press of Coughlan Cos.

Chandler, Matt. Military Drones. 2017. (Drones Ser.). (ENG., Illus.). 32p. (gr. 3-4). pap. 7.95 *(978-1-5157-3777-3(2),* Edge Bks.) Capstone Press of Coughlan Cos.

—Recreational Drones. 2017. (Drones Ser.). (ENG., Illus.). 32p. (gr. 3-4). pap. 7.95 *(978-1-5157-3770-4(5));* lib. bdg. 27.99 *(978-1-5157-3766-7(7))* Capstone Press of Coughlan Cos. (Edge Bks.).

Channing, Margot. Space & Other Flying Machines. 2015. (Inside Eye Ser.). (Illus.). 32p. (gr. 3-6). 31.35 *(978-1-906370-79-4(6))* Book Hse. GBR. Dist: Black Rabbit Bks.

Christiansen, Jennifer. Get to Know Inclined Planes. 2009. (ENG., Illus.). 32p. (J). (gr. 2-4). lib. bdg. *(978-0-7787-4466-5(3))* Crabtree Publishing Co.

Civardi, Anne. Going on a Plane. Bates, Michelle, ed. Cartwright, Stephen, illus. rev. ed. 2005. (Usborne First Experiences Ser.). 16p. (J). pap. 4.99 *(978-0-7945-1005-3(1),* Usborne) EDC Publishing.

Clark, Willow. Planes on the Move. 2010. (Transportation Station Ser.). 24p. (J). (ENG.). pap. 8.25 *(978-1-4358-9752-6(8));* (Illus.). (gr. 2-5). lib. bdg. 22.60 *(978-1-4358-9332-0(8))* Rosen Publishing Group, Inc., The. (PowerKids Pr.).

Coffin, Rebecca J. Airplanes: The Work They Do & How They Do It. Coffin, Rebecca J. et al, eds. 2011. 28p. 35.95 *(978-1-258-06643-7(2))* Literary Licensing, LLC.

Cudeyro, Erica M. American History for Young Minds - Volume 1, Looking Towards the Sky, Book 1, the First Airplane. Butler, Lindsay L., illus. 2008. 20p. pap. 11.95 *(978-1-934925-34-8(9),* Eloquent Bks.) Strategic Book Publishing & Rights Agency (SBPRA).

Curry, Peter, illus. Trains, Boats, & Planes. 2016. (ENG.). 12p. (J). (gr. -1 — 1). bds. 4.99 *(978-1-4998-0262-7(5))* Little Bee Books Inc.

David West. Jet Plane. 2006. (Illus.). 32p. (J). pap. *(978-1-4109-2563-3(3))* Steck-Vaughn.

Dawson, Emily C. Airplanes. 2012. (ENG., Illus.). 24p. (J). lib. bdg. 25.65 *(978-1-62031-021-2(X))* Jump! Inc.

Demand, Carlo. Airplanes of World War I Coloring Book. 2013. (Dover History Coloring Book Ser.). (ENG., Illus.). 48p. (J). (gr. 3-12). pap. 4.99 *(978-0-486-23807-4(5))* Dover Pubns., Inc.

deMarin, Layne. To Fly in the Sky. 2011. (Wonder Readers Fluent Level Ser.). (ENG.). (gr. -1-2). 16p. pap. 35.94 *(978-1-4296-8189-6(6));* 32p. pap. 5.99 *(978-1-4296-7943-5(3))* Capstone Press of Coughlan Cos. (Wonder Readers).

Dewar, Andrew. Ultimate Paper Airplanes for Kids: The Best Guide to Paper Airplanes - Complete Instructions + 48 Colorful Paper Planes! Vints, Kostya, illus. 2015. (ENG.). 160p. pap. 14.95 *(978-4-8053-1363-3(3))* Tuttle Publishing.

Doman, Mary Kate. Airplanes. 2011. (All about Big Machines Ser.). (Illus.). 24p. (J). (gr. -1-18). pap. 7.95 *(978-1-59845-240-2(1),* Enslow Elementary); (gr. k-3). lib. bdg. 22.60 *(978-0-7660-3933-9(1))* Enslow Pubs., Inc.

Dorling Kindersley Publishing Staff. Airplanes. 2013. (Eye Wonder Ser.). (ENG.). 56p. (J). (gr. k-4). 10.99 *(978-1-4654-0251-6(9),* DK Children) Dorling Kindersley Publishing, Inc.

—Big Book of Airplanes. 2016. (ENG., Illus.). 32p. (J). (gr. k-4). 14.99 *(978-1-4654-4507-0(2),* DK Children) Dorling Kindersley Publishing, Inc.

—Disney Planes. 2013. (ENG., Illus.). 64p. (J). (gr. 2-5). 12.99 *(978-1-4654-0268-4(3),* DK Children) Dorling Kindersley Publishing, Inc.

Dorling Kindersley Publishing Staff & Nahum, Andrew. Flight. 2011. (DK Eyewitness Bks.). (ENG.). 72p. (J). (gr. 3-7). 16.99 *(978-0-7566-7317-8(8),* DK Children) Dorling Kindersley Publishing, Inc.

Dos Santos, Julie. Aircraft. 2009. (Amazing Machines Ser.). 32p. (gr. 2). 28.50 *(978-0-7614-4404-6(1))* Marshall Cavendish Corp.

Dubowski, Mark. Superfast Planes. 2005. (Ultimate Speed Ser.). (Illus.). 32p. (YA). (gr. 3-6). lib. bdg. 25.27 *(978-1-59716-082-7(2))* Bearport Publishing Co., Inc.

Eden, Paul. The World's Most Powerful Civilian Aircraft. 2016. (World's Most Powerful Machines Ser.). 00224p. (J). (gr. 9-9). 45.10 *(978-1-4994-6588-4(2),* Rosen Young Adult) Rosen Publishing Group, Inc., The.

Eden, Paul E. Weird & Wonderful Aircraft. 2006. (Aircraft of the World Ser.). (Illus.). 32p. (gr. 2-6). lib. bdg. 26.00 *(978-0-8368-6906-4(0),* Gareth Stevens Learning Library) Stevens, Gareth Publishing LLLP.

Enz, Tammy. Batplanes & Batcopters: The Engineering Behind Batman's Wings, 1 vol. 2014. (Batman Science Ser.). (ENG.). 32p. (gr. 3-4). 27.32 *(978-1-4765-3941-6(3),* DC Super Heroes) Stone Arch Bks.

—Building Vehicles That Fly. 2017. (Young Engineers Ser.). (ENG., Illus.). 32p. (gr. 1-2). lib. bdg. 27.32 *(978-1-4846-3747-0(X),* Heinemann First Library) Heinemann-Raintree.

—The Science Behind Batman's Flying Machines. Vecchio, Luciano, illus. 2016. (Science Behind Batman Ser.). (ENG.). 24p. (gr. 1-2). lib. bdg. 25.32 *(978-1-5157-2036-2(5),* DC Super Heroes) Stone Arch Bks.

Faber, Harold. The Airplane. 2005. (Great Inventions Ser.). (Illus.). 128p. (J). (gr. 3-7). lib. bdg. *(978-0-7614-1876-4(8),* Benchmark Bks.) Marshall Cavendish Corp.

Farndon, John. Megafast Planes. Edwards, Mat & Pyke, Jeremy, illus. 2016. (Megafast Ser.). (ENG.). 32p. (J). (gr. 3-6). lib. bdg. 26.65 *(978-1-4677-9365-0(5))* Lerner Publishing Group.

—Stickmen's Guide to Aircraft. Paul de Quay, John, illus. 2016. (Stickmen's Guides to How Everything Works). (ENG.). 32p. (J). (gr. 3-6). 30.65 *(978-1-4677-9592-0(5));* 30.65 *(978-1-5124-0690-0(2))* Lerner Publishing Group.

A Fifty Year Affair: Living with Light Planes. l.t. ed. 2004. (Illus.). 208p. (YA). pap. 18.95 *(978-0-9746564-0-3(2))* Julson, D. K.

Finn, Denny Von. U-2 Planes. 2013. (Military Vehicles Ser.). (ENG., Illus.). 24p. (J). (gr. 3-7). lib. bdg. 25.95 *(978-1-60014-944-3(8),* Epic Bks.) Bellwether Media.

Flight Sets: 1 Each of 3 Big Books. (Sunshinetm Science Ser.). (gr. 1-2). 111.50 *(978-0-7802-2816-0(2))* Wright Group/McGraw-Hill.

Flight Sets: 1 Each of 3 Student Books. (Sunshinetm Science Ser.). (gr. 1-2). 20.95 *(978-0-7802-2817-7(0))* Wright Group/McGraw-Hill.

French, Cathy. Make a Paper Airplane & Haz un avión de Papel: 6 English, 6 Spanish Adaptations. 2011. (ENG & SPA.). (J). 75.00 net. *(978-1-4108-5631-9(3))* Benchmark Education Co.

Gabrielson, Curt. Kinetic Contraptions: Build a Hovercraft, Airboat, & More with a Hobby Motor. 2010. (ENG., Illus.). 192p. (J). (gr. 7-18). pap. 16.95 *(978-1-55652-957-3(0))* Chicago Review Pr., Inc.

Galvin, Laura Gates. First Look at Aircraft. Eaddy, Susan, illus. 2008. (ENG.). 16p. (J). (gr. -1-k). bds. 6.95 *(978-1-59249-862-8(0))* Soundprints.

Gamble, Adam & Jasper, Mark. Good Night Planes. Kelly, Cooper, illus. 2015. (Good Night Our World Ser.). (ENG.). 26p. (J). (— 1). bds. 9.95 *(978-1-60219-218-8(9))* Good Night Bks.

Ganeri, Anita. Flip the Flaps: Things That Go! Humphries, Tudor, illus. 2014. (Flip the Flaps Ser.). (ENG.). 32p. (J). (gr. -1-1). pap. 6.99 *(978-0-7534-7133-3(7),* 9780753471333, Kingfisher) Roaring Brook Pr.

Gifford, Clive. Planes & Helicopters. 2012. (ENG.). 24p. (J). *(978-0-7787-7476-1(7));* (Illus.). pap. *(978-0-7787-7481-5(3))* Crabtree Publishing Co.

Glaser, Rebecca Stromstad. Planes Soar. 2016. (ENG., Illus.). 14p. (J). (gr. -1 — 1). bds. 7.99 *(978-1-68152-122-0(9))* Amicus.

Glover, David & Glover, Penny. Planes in Action. 2008. (On the Go Ser.). (Illus.). 24p. (J). (gr. 3-7). lib. bdg. 22.60 *(978-1-4042-4308-8(9),* PowerKids Pr.) Rosen Publishing Group, Inc., The.

Goldish, Meish. Freaky-Big Airplanes. 2009. (World's Biggest Ser.). (Illus.). 24p. (J). (gr. 1-6). lib. bdg. 22.61 *(978-1-59716-959-2(5))* Bearport Publishing Co., Inc.

Goldish, Meish & Geddry, Mike, Sr. Freaky-Big Airplanes. 2016. (World's Biggest Ser.). (ENG.). 24p. (J). (gr. 1-6). pap. 7.95 *(978-1-944998-54-7(3))* Bearport Publishing Co., Inc.

Graham, Ian. Aircraft. 2009. (Mighty Machines Ser.). (Illus.). 31p. (J). (gr. 4-7). pap. 7.95 *(978-1-59920-254-9(9))* Black Rabbit Bks.

—In the Air. 2008. (QEB Machines at Work Ser.). (Illus.). 36p. (YA). (gr. 4-7). 19.95 *(978-1-59566-315-3(0))* QEB Publishing Inc.

—You Wouldn't Want to Be on the First Flying Machine! A High-Soaring Ride You'd Rather Not Take. Antram, David, illus. 2013. (You Wouldn't Want to... Ser.). (ENG.). 32p. (J). 29.00 *(978-0-531-25945-0(5));* pap. 9.95 *(978-0-531-23042-8(2))* Scholastic Library Publishing. (Watts, Franklin).

—You Wouldn't Want to Be on the First Flying Machine! A High-Soaring Ride You'd Rather Not Take. 2013. (You Wouldn't Want To... Ser.). lib. bdg. 20.80 *(978-0-606-31631-6(0),* Turtleback) Turtleback Bks.

Graham, Ian & Salariya, David. Planes, Rockets — And Other — Flying Machines. Hewetson, N. J., illus. 2014. (Time Shift Speed Ser.). 32p. (gr. 3-6). 31.35 ***(978-1-908973-95-5(1))*** Book Hse. GBR. Dist: Black Rabbit Bks.

Grant, Donald. El Avion. (Coleccion Mundo Maravilloso). (SPA., Illus.). 40p. (J). (gr. 2-4). *(978-84-348-3536-8(3),* AV9291) SM Ediciones.

Gregory, Josh. From Birds to... Aircraft. 2012. (21st Century Skills Innovation Library: Innovations from Nature Ser.). (ENG.). 32p. (gr. 4-8). 28.50 *(978-1-61080-497-4(X),* 202107); pap. 14.21 *(978-1-61080-671-8(9),* 202281) Cherry Lake Publishing.

Grist, Julie. Flying: Just Plane Fun. Grist, Julie, illus. 2006. (ENG., Illus.). 24p. (J). (gr. k-7). pap. 8.95 *(978-0-9725750-2-7(2))* Spoonbender Bks.

Gunston, Bill Tudor & Parker, Steve. Fasten Your Seatbelt! Mind-Boggling Machines. 2010. (ENG.). 96p. (J). (gr. 2-4). pap. 9.95 *(978-1-84696-205-9(6),* TickTock Books) Octopus Publishing Group GBR. Dist: Independent Pubs. Group.

Hamilton, John. UAVs: Unmanned Aerial Vehicles. 2012. 32p. 27.07 *(978-1-61783-271-0(5),* Abdo & Daughters) ABDO Publishing Co.

Hamilton, Robert M. On a Plane. 2012. (Going Places Ser.). (ENG.). 24p. (J). (gr. k-2). pap. 8.15 *(978-1-4339-6279-0(9));* lib. bdg. 22.60 *(978-1-4339-6277-6(2))* Stevens, Gareth Publishing LLLP.

Hammelef, Danielle S. Building an Airplane, 1 vol. 2014. (See How It's Made Ser.). (ENG.). 32p. (gr. 1-2). lib. bdg. 26.65 *(978-1-4765-3978-2(2),* Blazers) Capstone Press of Coughlan Cos.

Hansen, Ole Steen. Weird & Wonderful Aircraft. 2003. (Story of Flight Ser.). (ENG., Illus.). 32p. (J). (gr. 4). pap. *(978-0-7787-1226-8(5));* lib. bdg. *(978-0-7787-1210-7(9))* Crabtree Publishing Co.

Hanson, Anders. Let's Go by Airplane, 1 vol. 2008. (Let's Go Ser.). (ENG., Illus.). 24p. (J). (gr. k-3). lib. bdg. 24.21 *(978-1-59928-893-2(1),* SandCastle) ABDO Publishing Co.

Harbo, Christopher L. Co-Pilot, Level 2. 2010. (Paper Airplanes Ser.). (ENG.). 32p. (gr. 3-4). lib. bdg. 27.99 *(978-1-4296-4742-7(6),* Edge Bks.) Capstone Press of Coughlan Cos.

—Paper Airplanes, Flight School Level 1, 1 vol. 2010. (Paper Airplanes Ser.). (ENG.). 32p. (gr. 3-4). lib. bdg. 27.99 *(978-1-4296-4741-0(8),* Edge Bks.) Capstone Press of Coughlan Cos.

—Pilot, Level 3. 2010. (Paper Airplanes Ser.). (ENG.). 32p. (gr. 3-4). lib. bdg. 27.99 *(978-1-4296-4743-4(4),* Edge Bks.) Capstone Press of Coughlan Cos.

—The Ultimate Guide to Paper Airplanes: 35 Amazing Step-by-Step Designs! 2010. (Paper Airplanes Ser.). (ENG., Illus.). 112p. (gr. 3-4). pap. 9.95 *(978-1-4296-5648-1(4),* Edge Bks.) Capstone Press of Coughlan Cos.

Harding, Les. McCurdy & the Silver Dart, 1 vol. 2nd ed. 2014. (ENG., Illus.). 96p. pap. *(978-1-927492-77-2(7))* Cape Breton Univ. Pr.

Harrison, Paul. Superplanes. 2013. (Illus.). 32p. (J). *(978-1-84858-565-2(9))* Arcturus Pubs., Inc.

Hawcock, David. Fantastic Press-Out Flying Airplanes: Includes 18 Flying Models. Montgomery, Lee & Pastor, Terry, illus. 2015. (ENG.). 76p. (J). (gr. 2-4). 14.99 *(978-0-486-80127-8(6))* Dover Pubns., Inc.

Hayes, Amy. How a Plane Is Made. 2016. (Engineering Our World Ser.). (ENG., Illus.). 24p. (J). (gr. 2-3). pap. 8.15 *(978-1-4824-3931-1(X))* Stevens, Gareth Publishing LLLP.

Hewitt, Sally. Planes. 2006. (Illus.). 24p. (YA). (gr. 1-18). lib. bdg. 22.80 *(978-1-931983-54-9(2))* Chrysalis Education.

Hicks, Kelli. Airplanes. 2014. (ENG.). 24p. (gr. k-3). 28.50 *(978-1-62717-649-1(7))* Rourke Educational Media.

High Flying: Level P, 6 vols., Vol. 3. (Explorers Ser.). 32p. (gr. 3-6). 44.95 *(978-0-7699-0619-5(2))* Shortland Pubns. (U. S. A.) Inc.

Hofer, Charles. Airplanes. (World's Fastest Machines Ser.). 24p. 2009. (gr. 2-3). 42.50 *(978-1-60854-851-4(1))* 2008. (Illus.). (J). (gr. 3-7). lib. bdg. 22.60 *(978-1-4042-4173-2(6))* Rosen Publishing Group, Inc., The. (PowerKids Pr.).

Holzer, David. Make & Play Airplanes. Galvani, Maureen, illus. 2005. (Fun Kits (Top That!) Ser.). 48p. (J). (gr. -1-3). *(978-1-84510-549-5(4))* Top That! Publishing PLC.

Hosley, Maria. Airplanes, 1 vol. 2007. (First Drawings Ser.). (ENG., Illus.). 24p. (J). (gr. -1-3). 25.65 *(978-1-59679-799-4(1),* Buddy Bks.) ABDO Publishing Co.

How Airplanes Fly: 6 Each of 1 Student Book, 6 vols. (Sunshinetm Science Ser.). 24p. (gr. 1-2). 41.95 *(978-0-7802-2716-3(6))* Wright Group/McGraw-Hill.

How Airplanes Fly: Big Book. (Sunshinetm Science Ser.). 24p. (gr. 1-2). 37.50 *(978-0-7802-2792-7(1))* Wright Group/McGraw-Hill.

Hutchison, Patricia. The Invention of the Airplane. 2017. (Engineering That Made America Ser.). (ENG.). 32p. (J). (gr. 3-6). lib. bdg. 28.50 *(978-1-5038-1639-8(7),* 211155) Child's World, Inc., The.

In the Air: Drones. 2013. (Military Experience: in the Air Ser.). (ENG., Illus.). 64p. (YA). (gr. 3-7). 27.45 *(978-1-59935-384-5(9))* Reynolds, Morgan Inc.

Ivanoff, George. Meet the Flying Doctors. 2017. (Meet... Ser.). (ENG.). 32p. (J). (gr. 2-4). pap. 22.99 ***(978-0-14-378068-7(9))*** Random Hse. Australia AUS. Dist: Independent Pubs. Group.

Jackson, Tom. Aircraft. 2015. (Technology Timelines Ser.). (Illus.). 32p. (gr. 3-6). 31.35 *(978-1-78121-236-3(8))* Brown Bear Bks.

January, Brendan. Air Force One. (Cornerstones of Freedom Ser.). (ENG.). 48p. 2008. (J). pap. 5.95 *(978-0-531-20826-7(5),* Children's Pr.) 2004. (Illus.). (YA). (gr. 4-7). 26.00 *(978-0-516-24236-1(9))* Scholastic Library Publishing.

Jefferis, David. Planes. 2007. (Extreme Machines/Watts Ser.). (Illus.). 32p. (YA). (gr. 4-7). lib. bdg. 28.50 *(978-1-59920-042-2(2))* Black Rabbit Bks.

Kelley, K. C. Ultralight Aircraft. 2012. (Extreme Sports Ser.). (ENG., Illus.). 32p. (J). (gr. 2-5). lib. bdg. 28.50 *(978-1-60973-209-7(X),* 201136) Child's World, Inc., The.

Kids Can Press Staff. This Is Daniel Cook on a Plane. 2006. (This Is Daniel Cook Ser.). (ENG., Illus.). 24p. (J). (gr. -1-1). 4.95 *(978-1-55453-082-3(2))* Kids Can Pr., Ltd. CAN. Dist: Hachette Bk. Group.

Kirk, Ellen. My Plane Book. 2006. (Smithsonian Ser.). (ENG., Illus.). 16p. (J). (gr. -1-k). bds. 5.99 *(978-0-06-089941-7(7),* Collins) HarperCollins Pubs.

Kuskowski, Alex & Craig, Diane. Super Simple Aircraft Projects: Inspiring & Educational Science Activities, 1 vol. 2016. (ENG., Illus.). 32p. (J). *(978-1-62403-728-3(3))* ABDO Publishing Co.

Langley, Andrew. Planes. 2010. (Machines on the Move Ser.). 32p. (J). 28.50 *(978-1-60753-061-9(9))* Amicus Publishing.

—Planes. 2012. (Illus.). 32p. (gr. 1-3). pap. 8.95 *(978-1-926722-71-9(X))* Saunders Bk. Co. CAN. Dist: RiverStream Publishing.

Leavitt, Amie Jane. Experimental Drones. 2017. (Drones Ser.). (ENG., Illus.). 32p. (gr. 3-4). pap. 7.95 *(978-1-5157-3776-6(4),* Edge Bks.) Capstone Press of Coughlan Cos.

Let's Look at Planes. 2009. (Let's Go! Ser.). (Illus.). 18p. (J). (gr. -1-k). bds. 12.75 *(978-1-60754-416-6(4))* Windmill Bks.

Lindeen, Mary. Airplanes. 2007. (Mighty Machines Ser.). (ENG., Illus.). 24p. (J). (gr. k-3). lib. bdg. 25.95 *(978-1-60014-058-7(0))* Bellwether Media.

Loewen, Nancy. Airplanes. 2003. 24p. (J). lib. bdg. 21.35 *(978-1-58340-321-1(3))* Black Rabbit Bks.

Mackey, Dean. Paper Planes That Really Fly. 2012. 128p. (J). pap. 10.99 *(978-1-74308-787-9(X))* Hinkler Bks. Pty, Ltd. AUS. Dist: Ideals Pubns.

Mahaney, Ian F. Extreme Aircraft. 2015. (Extreme Machines Ser.). (ENG.). 32p. (J). (gr. 3-4). pap. 10.00 *(978-1-4994-1183-6(9),* PowerKids Pr.) Rosen Publishing Group, Inc., The.

Masters, Nancy Robinson. The Airplane. 2006. (Inventions That Shaped the World Ser.). (Illus.). 80p. (gr. 4-7). 19.95 *(978-0-7569-6852-6(6))* Perfection Learning Corp.

—Airplanes. 2008. (21st Century Skills Innovation Library: Innovation in Transportation Ser.). (ENG., 32p. (gr. 4-8). Illus.). lib. bdg. 28.50 *(978-1-60279-235-7(6),* 200165); lib. bdg. 28.50 *(978-1-60279-119-0(8),* 200091) Cherry Lake Publishing.

—How Does It Fly? Propeller Plane. 2011. (Community Connections: How Does It Fly? Ser.). (ENG.). 24p. (gr. 2-5). lib. bdg. 25.64 *(978-1-61080-070-9(2),* 201066) Cherry Lake Publishing.

Masters, Neil. Aircrafts Coloring Book. 2013. (ENG.). 42p. 12.92 *(978-1-62884-652-2(6),* Baby Professor (Education Kids)) Speedy Publishing LLC.

Mattern, Joanne. Air Force One: The President's Plane. 2014. (Rookie Read-About(r) American Symbols Ser.). (ENG.). 32p. (J). pap. 5.95 *(978-0-531-21841-9(4));* lib. bdg. *(978-0-531-21568-5(7))* Scholastic Library Publishing.

McAneney, Caitlin. The First Flight Across the Atlantic. 2015. (Incredible True Adventures Ser.). (ENG., Illus.). 32p. (J). (gr. 3-4). pap. 10.50 *(978-1-4824-2034-0(1))* Stevens, Gareth Publishing LLLP.

McCurry, Kristen. How to Draw Amazing Airplanes & Spacecraft. Edwards, Mat, illus. 2012. (Smithsonian Drawing Bks.). (ENG.). 64p. (gr. 3-4). pap. 41.70 *(978-1-4296-9449-0(1))* Capstone Press of Coughlan Cos.

Meredith, Susan Markowitz, et al. How Do Aircraft Fly? 2009. (Science in the Real World Ser.). (Illus.). 32p. (gr. 4-6). 28.00 *(978-1-60413-464-3(X),* Chelsea Clubhouse) Facts On File, Inc.

Micro Planes. 2004. (Whizz Kits Ser.). (Illus.). 48p. (J). *(978-1-84229-946-3(8))* Top That! Publishing PLC.

Miller, Amanda. What Is Air Force One? 2009. (Scholastic News Nonfiction Readers Ser.). (ENG.). 24p. (J). (gr. 1-2). pap. 6.95 *(978-0-531-22426-7(0))* Scholastic Library Publishing.

A
B

Miller, Amanda & Falk, Laine. What is Air Force One? 2009. (Scholastic News Nonfiction Readers Ser.). 24p. (J). (gr. 1-2). 22.00 *(978-0-531-21089-5(8))* Scholastic Library Publishing.

Miller, Reagan. High-Flying Airplanes. 2010. (Vehicles on the Move Ser.). (ENG.). 32p. (J). (gr. k-3). pap. *(978-0-7787-3061-3(1))*; lib. bdg. *(978-0-7787-3047-7(6))* Crabtree Publishing Co.

Mills, Lois. Three Together: Story of the Wright Brothers & Their Sister. Moyers, William, illus. 2011. 160p. 41.95 *(978-1-258-05968-2(1))* Literary Licensing, LLC.

Mitton, Tony. Amazing Airplanes. Parker, Ant, illus. 2005. (Amazing Machines Ser.). (ENG.). (J). (gr. -1-k). lib. bdg. 15.60 ***(978-1-68065-291-8(5))*** Perfection Learning Corp.

—Amazing Airplanes. Parker, Ant, illus. 2016. (Amazing Machines Ser.). (ENG.). 24p. pap., act. bk. ed. 4.99 *(978-0-7534-7255-2(4)*, 9780753472552, Kingfisher) Roaring Brook Pr.

Mitton, Tony & Parker, Ant. Amazing Airplanes. 2005. (Amazing Machines Ser.). (ENG., Illus.). 24p. (J). (gr. -1-k). 4.99 *(978-0-7534-5915-7(9)*, 9780753459157, Kingfisher) Roaring Brook Pr.

Molzahn, Arlene Bourgeois. Airplanes. 2003. (Transportation & Communication Ser.). (Illus.). 48p. (J). (gr. 1-4). lib. bdg. 25.27 *(978-0-7660-2026-9(6))* Enslow Pubs., Inc.

Mott, Professor. Flight: First Vehicles. Lenehan, Mary & Weber, Rich, illus. 8p. (J). (gr. -1-3). 14.99 *(978-1-890647-36-0(5))* TOMY International, Inc.

Murray, Julie. Planes, 1 vol. 2014. (Transportation Ser.). (ENG.). 24p. (J). (gr. 4-8). lib. bdg. 28.50 *(978-1-62970-080-9(0))* ABDO Publishing Co.

Murray, Julie, et al. Aviones. 2015. (Medios de Transporte Ser.). (SPA., Illus.). 24p. (gr. k-1). pap. 7.95 *(978-1-4966-0485-9(7))* Capstone Classroom.

Nagelhout, Ryan. Drones. 2013. (Military Machines Ser.). (Illus.). 32p. (J). (gr. 3-6). pap. 10.50 *(978-1-4339-8458-7(X))*; lib. bdg. 26.60 *(978-1-4339-8457-0(1))* Stevens, Gareth Publishing LLLP.

National Geographic. Things That Go! Collection. 2015. (Readers Ser.). (ENG., Illus.). 120p. (J). (gr. k-3). lib. bdg. 16.90 *(978-1-4263-1973-0(8)*, National Geographic Children's Bks.) National Geographic Society.

Nelson, Robin. From Metal to Airplane. 2004. (Start to Finish Ser.). (J). 18.60 *(978-0-8225-1388-9(9)*, Lerner Pubns.); pap. 4.95 *(978-0-8225-2145-7(8))* Lerner Publishing Group.

Oxlade, Chris. Airplanes Inside & Out. 2009. (Machines Inside Out Ser.). (ENG.). 32p. (J). (gr. 4-6). pap. 10.00 *(978-1-4358-2941-1(7)*, PowerKids Pr.); (YA). (gr. 3-6). lib. bdg. 25.25 *(978-1-4358-2863-6(1))* Rosen Publishing Group, Inc., The.

—Plane. (Take It Apart Ser.). (Illus.). 32p. (J). (gr. 4-6). lib. bdg. 24.25 *(978-1-930643-95-6(0))* Chrysalis Education.

Oxlade, Chris & Farndon, John. Stickmen's Guide to Aircraft. Pyke, Jerry & Quay, John Paul de, illus. 2016. (Stickmen's Guides to How Everything Works). (ENG.). 32p. (J). (gr. 3-6). lib. bdg. 26.65 *(978-1-4677-9359-9(0))* Lerner Publishing Group.

P-47B, P-47C & P-47D Airplanes - Erection & Maintenance Instructions. 2005. (YA). cd-rom 29.95 *(978-0-9742781-9-3(X))* Rhode, Steve Inc.

Parker, Steve. Aircraft. 2010. (How It Works Ser.). 40p. (J). (gr. 3-18). lib. bdg. 19.95 *(978-1-4222-1791-7(4))* Mason Crest.

—In the Air. 2010. (J). 28.50 *(978-1-59920-284-6(0))* Black Rabbit Bks.

Parker, Steve & Parker, Vic. My First Trip on an Airplane, 1 vol. 2011. (Growing Up Ser.). (ENG.). 24p. (gr. k-2). 23.32 *(978-1-4329-4801-6(6))*; pap. 6.79 *(978-1-4329-4811-5(3))* Heinemann-Raintree. (Heinemann Read & Learn).

Patchett, F. Planes. 2004. (Beginners Ser.). (Illus.). 32p. (J). (gr. 1-18). lib. bdg. 12.95 *(978-1-58086-484-8(8))* EDC Publishing.

Patchett, F. & King, Colin. Planes. King, Colin, illus. 2004. (Beginners Ser.). (ENG., Illus.). 32p. (J). (gr. 1-18). pap. 4.95 *(978-0-7945-0319-2(5)*, Usborne) EDC Publishing.

Perritano, John. Planes. 2013. (Machines in Motion Ser.). 48p. (J). (gr. 3-5). pap. 84.30 *(978-1-4339-9610-8(3))*; pap. 14.05 *(978-1-4339-9609-2(X))*; (ENG., Illus.). lib. bdg. 31.95 *(978-1-4339-9608-5(1))* Stevens, Gareth Publishing LLLP.

Peterson, Megan Cooley & Rustad, Martha E. H. The First Airplanes, 1 vol. 2014. (Famous Firsts Ser.). (ENG., Illus.). 24p. (gr. k-1). 26.65 *(978-1-4914-0573-4(2)*, Pebble Plus) Capstone Press of Coughlan Cos.

Petrie, Kristin. Airplanes, 1 vol. 2009. (Everyday Inventions Ser.). (ENG., Illus.). 32p. (gr. 3-6). 27.07 *(978-1-60453-082-7(0)*, Checkerboard Library) ABDO Publishing Co.

Planes That Fly. 2008. (Build it now Ser.). 16p. pap. *(978-1-4075-2248-7(5))* Parragon, Inc.

Prior, Jennifer. Take Off! All about Airplanes, 1 vol. 2nd rev. ed. 2011. (Nonfiction Readers Ser.). (ENG.). 28p. (J). (gr. 3-3). pap. 8.99 *(978-1-4333-3655-3(3))* Teacher Created Materials, Inc.

—Take Off! All about Airplanes, 1 vol. 2nd rev. ed. 2014. (TIME for KIDS(r) Nonfiction Readers Ser.). (ENG., Illus.). 28p. (J). (gr. 3-3). pap. 25.96 *(978-1-4807-1070-2(9))* Shell Educational Publishing.

Provensen, Alice. Glorius Flight. 2014. 17.00 *(978-1-63419-702-1(X))* Perfection Learning Corp.

Publications International Ltd. Staff, ed. Airplanes! 2013. 12p. (J). bds. 9.98 *(978-1-4508-1133-0(7)*, 1450811337) Publications International, Ltd.

Rare B-17 Flying Fortress Document & Photo Collection. 2004. (YA). cd-rom 89.95 *(978-0-9742781-4-8(9))* Rhode, Steve Inc.

Rau, Dana Meachen. Planes. 2009. (Bookworms Ser.). 24p. (gr. k-1). 15.95 *(978-0-7614-4080-2(1))* Marshall Cavendish Corp.

—Planes/En Aviones. 2009. (Bookworms Ser.). (SPA & ENG.). 24p. (gr. k-1). lib. bdg. 15.95 *(978-0-7614-4772-6(5))* Marshall Cavendish Corp.

Red Bird Press Staff. Flying Machines. 2004. (Mission Xtreme 3D Ser.). 18p. (J). pap. 5.95 *(978-1-902626-63-5(X))* Red Bird Publishing GBR. Dist: Weatherhill, Inc.

—High Flyers. 2004. (Build Your Own Ser.). 20p. (J). pap. 5.95 *(978-1-902626-69-7(9))* Red Bird Publishing GBR. Dist: Weatherhill, Inc.

Rose, Simon. Drones. 2017. (J). ***(978-1-5105-2225-1(5))*** SmartBook Media, Inc.

Ruck, Colleen. Planes. 2011. (My Favorite Machines Ser.). 24p. (gr. 2-5). 28.50 *(978-1-59920-677-6(3))* Black Rabbit Bks.

Rustad, Martha E. H. Airplanes, 1 vol. 2013. (Little Scientist Ser.). (ENG., 32p. (gr. 1-2). Illus.). 6.95 *(978-1-4765-3542-5(6))*; pap. 6.95 *(978-1-4765-3548-7(5))*; lib. bdg. 27.99 *(978-1-4765-0248-9(X))* Capstone Press of Coughlan Cos.

Sage, Alison. Going on a Plane Purple Band. 2016. (Cambridge Reading Adventures Ser.). (ENG.). 24p. pap. 7.19 *(978-1-316-50088-0(8))* Cambridge Univ. Pr.

Salzmann, Mary Elizabeth. Aircraft, 1 vol. 2016. (ENG., Illus.). 24p. (J). *(978-1-62403-707-8(0))* ABDO Publishing Co.

Sandler, Martin W. Flying over the USA: Airplanes in American Life. 2006. (Illus.). 61p. (J). (gr. 4-8). reprint ed. 20.00 *(978-1-4223-5623-4(X))* DIANE Publishing Co.

Santella, Andrew. Air Force One. 2003. (Illus.). 48p. (gr. 4-18). (J). pap. 8.95 *(978-0-7613-1926-9(3))*; (Women at War Ser.: up). lib. bdg. 24.90 *(978-0-7613-2617-5(0))* Lerner Publishing Group. (Millbrook Pr.).

Scarry, Richard. Richard Scarry's Planes. Scarry, Richard, illus. 2015. (ENG., Illus.). 24p. (J). (— 1). bds. 4.99 *(978-0-385-39270-9(2)*, Golden Bks.) Random Hse. Children's Bks.

Schaefer, Lola M. Airplanes in Action. 2012. (Transportation Zone Ser.). (ENG.). 24p. (gr. 1-2). pap. 41.70 *(978-1-4296-8392-0(9))*; lib. bdg. 25.32 *(978-1-4296-7688-5(4))* Capstone Press of Coughlan Cos. (First Facts).

Schmidt, Norman. Best Ever Paper Airplanes. 2007. (ENG., Illus.). 96p. (J). (gr. 5). pap. 7.95 *(978-1-895569-83-4(4))* Tamos Bks., Inc. CAN. Dist: Sterling Publishing Co., Inc.

Schuh, Mari. Aircraft. 2013. (Aircraft Ser.). (ENG.). 24p. (gr. k-1). lib. bdg. 79.95 *(978-1-62065-115-5(7)*, Pebble Plus) Capstone Press of Coughlan Cos.

—Airplanes. 2017. (Transportation Ser.). (ENG.). 24p. (gr. k-1). lib. bdg. 21.99 ***(978-1-5157-7305-4(1)***, Pebble Bks.) Capstone Press of Coughlan Cos.

Schuh, Mari. Seaplanes, 1 vol. 2013. (Aircraft Ser.). (ENG.). 24p. (gr. k-1). lib. bdg. 26.65 *(978-1-62065-114-8(9)*, Pebble Plus) Capstone Press of Coughlan Cos.

Schulz, Walter A. Johnny Moore & the Wright Brothers' Flying Machine. Bowles, Doug, illus. 2011. (History Speaks: Picture Books Plus Reader's Theater Ser.). (ENG.). 48p. (gr. 2-4). lib. bdg. 27.93 *(978-0-7613-5876-3(5)*, Millbrook Pr.) Lerner Publishing Group.

Shields, Amy. Planes. 2010. (Readers Ser.). (ENG., Illus.). 32p. (J). (gr. -1-1). pap. 3.99 *(978-1-4263-0712-6(8))*; lib. bdg. 13.90 *(978-1-4263-0713-3(6))* National Geographic Society. (National Geographic Children's Bks.).

Silverman, Buffy. How Do Jets Work? 2013. (Lightning Bolt Books (tm) — How Flight Works). (ENG., Illus.). 32p. (gr. k-2). pap. 7.95 *(978-1-4677-0786-2(4))* Lerner Publishing Group.

Sodomka, Martin & Lacey, Saskia. How to Build a Plane. 2015. (Technical Tales Ser.). (ENG., Illus.). 64p. (J). (gr. 1-3). 14.95 *(978-1-63322-041-6(9)*, Walter Foster Jr) Quarto Publishing Group USA.

Solway, Andrew. Aircraft, 1 vol. 2011. (Sci-Hi: Science & Technology Ser.). (ENG., Illus.). 48p. (gr. 4-4). 33.32 *(978-1-4109-4270-8(8)*, Sci-Hi) Heinemann-Raintree.

Soundprints Staff & Galvin, Laura Gates. First Look at Aircraft. 2009. (ENG.). 16p. (J). 6.95 *(978-1-60727-118-5(4))* Soundprints.

Spilsbury, Louise & Spilsbury, Richard. The Airplane, 1 vol. 2010. (Tales of Invention Ser.). (ENG.). 32p. (gr. 3-5). 30.65 *(978-1-4329-3830-7(4))*; pap. 8.95 *(978-1-4329-3837-6(1))* Heinemann-Raintree. (NA-h).

Spilsbury, Richard. Great Aircraft Designs 1900-Today. 2015. (Iconic Designs Ser.). (ENG., Illus.). 48p. (gr. 4-6). pap. 8.99 *(978-1-4846-2621-4(4)*, Heinemann InfoSearch) Heinemann-Raintree.

Stillinger, Doug. Aviones de Papel. 2005. (SPA., Illus.). 56p. (J). spiral bd. 19.95 *(978-987-1078-44-8(7))* Klutz Latino MEX. Dist: Independent Pubs. Group.

Suen, Anastasia. Air Show. Mariniello, Cecco, illus. 2006. 30p. (J). (gr. k-4). reprint ed. 16.00 *(978-1-4223-5669-2(8))* DIANE Publishing Co.

Summers, Alex. Airplane. 2017. (Transportation & Me! Ser.). (ENG.). (J). (gr. k-1). 28.51 ***(978-1-68342-162-7(0))*** Rourke Educational Media.

Tatge, Cathy. Airplanes. 2007. (My First Look at: Vehicles Ser.). (Illus.). 24p. (J). (gr. -1-3). lib. bdg. 24.25 *(978-1-58341-525-2(4)*, Creative Education) Creative Co., The.

Tiner, John Hudson. Airplanes. (Illus.). 32p. 2004. pap. 8.95 *(978-0-89812-387-6(9)*, Creative Paperbacks) 2003. (J). lib. bdg. 18.95 *(978-1-58341-258-9(1)*, Creative Education) Creative Co., The.

Top That Publishing Staff, ed. Aircraft. 2005. (Illus.). 24p. *(978-1-84510-537-2(0))* Top That! Publishing PLC.

—Ultimate Micro Fliers. 2005. 48p. *(978-1-84510-659-1(8))* Top That! Publishing PLC.

van Lieshout, Maria. Flight 1-2-3. 2015. (ENG., Illus.). 32p. (J). (gr. -1 — 1). bds. 7.99 *(978-1-4521-4291-3(2))* Chronicle Bks. LLC.

VanVoorst, Jenny Fretland. Paper Airplanes. 2016. (Early Physics Fun). 24p. (J). (gr. 2-5). lib. bdg. 25.65 *(978-1-62031-317-6(0)*, Pogo) Jump! Inc.

Walker, Sally M. & Feldmann, Roseann. Planos Inclinados. King, Andy, photos by. 2005. (Libros de Física para Madrugadores (Early Bird Physics) Ser.). (SPA & ENG., Illus.). 48p. (gr. 3-6). lib. bdg. 26.60 *(978-0-8225-2970-5(X)*, Ediciones Lerner) Lerner Publishing Group.

Watt, Fiona. Planes: Internet-Referenced. 2009. (Beginner's Science Ser.). 32p. (J). 4.99 *(978-0-7945-1480-8(4)*, Usborne) EDC Publishing.

Waxman, Laura Hamilton. Terrific Transportation Inventions. 2013. (Awesome Inventions You Use Every Day Ser.). (ENG., Illus.). 32p. (gr. 3-6). lib. bdg. 26.60 *(978-1-4677-1096-1(2)*, Lerner Pubns.) Lerner Publishing Group.

Weitzman, David. Jenny: The Airplane That Taught America to Fly. Weitzman, David, illus. 2006. (Illus.). 27p. (J). (gr. k-4). reprint ed. 19.00 *(978-1-4223-5582-4(9))* DIANE Publishing Co.

West, David, illus. Planes. 2017. (What's Inside? Ser.). 24p. (gr. k-3). lib. bdg. 28.50 *(978-1-62588-401-5(X))* Black Rabbit Bks.

White, Nancy. Aviation Firefighters. 2014. (Fire Fight! the Bravest Ser.). 32p. (J). (gr. 2-7). lib. bdg. 26.60 *(978-1-62724-096-3(9))* Bearport Publishing Co., Inc.

Williams, Zachary. How Do Airplanes Fly? 2009. (Reading Room Collection 2 Ser.). 24p. (gr. 3-4). 42.50 *(978-1-60851-969-9(4)*, PowerKids Pr.) Rosen Publishing Group, Inc., The.

Winchester, Jim. Civil Aircraft. 2006. (Aircraft of the World Ser.). (Illus.). 32p. (gr. 2-6). lib. bdg. 26.00 *(978-0-8368-6903-3(6)*, Gareth Stevens Learning Library) Stevens, Gareth Publishing LLLP.

—World's Worst Aircraft. (World's Worst: from Innovation to Disaster Ser.). 80p. 2009. (gr. 8-8). 61.20 *(978-1-60854-857-6(0))* 2008. (Illus.). (J). lib. bdg. 33.25 *(978-1-4042-1837-6(8))* Rosen Publishing Group, Inc., The.

Winters, Pierre. Traveling by Airplane. Meinink, Tineke, illus. 2012. (Want to Know Ser.). (ENG.). 30p. (J). (gr. -1-k). 16.95 *(978-1-60537-137-5(8))* Cobblestone Publishing Co.

Wiseman, Blaine. Boeing. 2017. (J). ***(978-1-5105-2360-9(X))*** SmartBook Media, Inc.

—Jumbo Jets. 2010. (World of Wonder Ser.). 24p. (J). (gr. 2-4). lib. bdg. 25.70 *(978-1-61690-136-3(5))* Weigl Pubs., Inc.

—Jumbo Jets: WOW: Big Machines. 2010. (J). pap. 9.95 *(978-1-61690-137-0(3))* Weigl Pubs., Inc.

Wood, Alix. Test Pilot, 1 vol., 1. 2014. (World's Coolest Jobs Ser.). (ENG.). 32p. (J). (gr. 3-6). 26.25 *(978-1-4777-6019-2(9)*, PowerKids Pr.) Rosen Publishing Group, Inc., The.

Woodroffe, David. Making Paper Airplanes: Make Your Own Aircraft & Watch Them Fly! 2012. (ENG., Illus.). 192p. (J). (gr. 4-7). pap. 12.95 *(978-1-62087-168-3(8)*, 620168, Sky Pony Pr.) Skyhorse Publishing Co., Inc.

Yaun, Katherine. Drones in the Classroom. 2016. (Inside the World of Drones Ser.). 00064p. (J). (gr. 7-7). 34.45 *(978-1-5081-7345-8(1)*, Rosen Young Adult) Rosen Publishing Group, Inc., The.

AIRPLANES—ACCIDENTS

see Aircraft Accidents

AIRPLANES—FICTION

Adair, Amy. Jay Jay's Special Delivery. 2003. (Illus.). (J). 15.98 *(978-0-7853-8625-4(4))* Publications International, Ltd.

Adams, Eustace L. The Plane Without a Pilot. 2011. 226p. 44.95 *(978-1-258-10181-7(5))* Literary Licensing, LLC.

Adan, Jennifer. I Don't See Heaven. 2013. 24p. pap. 10.99 *(978-1-4808-0307-7(3))* Archway Publishing.

Adler, David A. The Mystery of Flight 427: Inside a Crash Investigation. Natti, Susanna, illus. 2004. (Cam Jansen Ser.: No. 12). 56p. (J). pap. *(978-0-439-13384-5(X)*, Puffin) Penguin Publishing Group.

Afetian, "Uncle Ted". The Adventures of Midas & the Little Red Airplane. 2005. (Illus.). 32p. (J). 16.95i *(978-0-9752749-0-3(2))* Snyder-Winston Pr.

Altsheler, Joseph A. The Hosts of the Air: The Story of a Quest in the Great War. 2006. (World War I Ser.: Vol. 2). 288p. (J). reprint ed. 28.95 *(978-1-4218-1773-6(X))*; pap. 13.95 *(978-1-4218-1873-3(6))* 1st World Publishing, Inc. (1st World Library - Literary Society).

—The Hosts of the Air: The Story of a Quest in the Great War. (World War I Ser.: Vol. 2). 327p. (J). reprint ed. lib. bdg. 25.95 *(978-0-88411-947-0(5))* Amereon Ltd.

—The Hosts of the Air: The Story of a Quest in the Great War. 2010. 352p. pap. 32.75 *(978-1-142-69983-3(8))* 2007. (World War I Ser.: Vol. 2). 258p. (J). reprint ed. pap. 23.99 *(978-1-4264-9850-3(0))* 2010. (World War I Ser.: Vol. 2). 356p. (J). (gr. 3-7). reprint ed. pap. 32.75 *(978-1-149-41015-8(9)*, Nabu Pr.) 2008. (World War I Ser.: Vol. 2). 260p. (J). reprint ed. 25.99 *(978-0-554-35041-7(6))* 2008. (World War I Ser.: Vol. 2). 260p. (J). reprint ed. 28.99 *(978-0-554-25738-9(6))* 2007. (World War I Ser.: Vol. 2). 232p. (J). reprint ed. pap. 20.99 *(978-1-4264-9469-7(6))* Creative Media Partners, LLC.

—The Hosts of the Air: The Story of a Quest in the Great War. 2006. (World War I Ser.: Vol. 2). (Illus.). (J). reprint ed. pap. *(978-1-4065-0814-7(4))* Dodo Pr.

—The Hosts of the Air: The Story of a Quest in the Great War. 2007. (World War I Ser.: Vol. 2). 168p. (J). reprint ed. per. *(978-1-4068-1679-2(5))* Echo Library.

—The Hosts of the Air: The Story of a Quest in the Great War. (World War I Ser.: Vol. 2). (J). reprint ed. 2010. 152p. (gr. 4-7). pap. 19.99 *(978-1-4432-1323-3(3))* 2009. 170p. pap. 9.39 *(978-1-150-51448-7(5))* General Bks. LLC.

—The Hosts of the Air: The Story of a Quest in the Great War. Wrenn, Charles, illus. (World War I Ser.: Vol. 2). (J). reprint ed. 2010. 346p. (gr. 4-7). 37.56 *(978-1-164-36346-0(8))* 2010. 346p. (gr. 4-7). pap. 25.56 *(978-1-163-98051-4(X))* 2008. 344p. 46.95 *(978-0-548-98763-6(7))* 2007. 348p. per. 31.95 *(978-0-548-65961-8(3))* Kessinger Publishing, LLC.

—The Hosts of the Air: The Story of a Quest in the Great War. 2011. (World War I Ser.: Vol. 2). 252p. (J). (gr. 4-7). reprint ed. pap. *(978-3-8424-7804-6(6))* Tredition GmbH.

Amerikaner, Susan. Dusty Flies High. Random House Disney Staff, illus. 2013. (Step into Reading Ser.). (ENG.). 32p. (J). (gr. -1-1). pap. 3.99 *(978-0-7364-3018-0(0)*, RH/Disney) Random Hse. Children's Bks.

Amery, Heather. Wind-up Plane. 2009. (Wind-up Bks). 14p. (J). bds. 29.99 *(978-0-7945-2534-7(2)*, Usborne) EDC Publishing.

Anderson, David. Emily's Imaginary Airplane. 2013. 24p. pap. 10.99 *(978-1-4808-0347-3(2))* Archway Publishing.

Appleton, Victor. Tom Swift & His Aerial Warship: Or the Naval Terror of the Seas. l.t. ed. 2007. (ENG.). 156p. pap. 21.99 *(978-1-4346-1578-7(2))* Creative Media Partners, LLC.

—Tom Swift & His Airship. 2007. 224p. 29.95 *(978-1-4344-9460-3(8))*; per. 19.95 *(978-1-4344-9459-7(4))* Wildside Pr., LLC.

—Tom Swift in the Caves of Ice. 2005. 27.95 *(978-1-4218-1509-1(5))*; 204p. pap. 12.95 *(978-1-4218-1609-8(1))* 1st World Publishing, Inc. (1st World Library - Literary Society).

Atlas. The Antarctic Express. 2009. 32p. 19.95 *(978-1-58978-111-5(2)*, Atlas Games) Trident, Inc.

Baker, Kane. Bobby the Bush Pilot. Swain, Alison Campbell, illus. 2003. (J). pap. *(978-1-932046-02-1(X))* Pastime Pr.

Barber, Elaine R. Billy's First Flight Lesson. 2010. 36p. (J). 16.95 *(978-1-4507-0620-9(7))* Independent Pub.

Bardwell, Harrison. Roberta's Flying Courage. 2003. (ENG.). 248p. pap. 13.95 *(978-1-55753-335-7(0)*, 9e38e2dc-8c18-49c1-8447-1205f9e2b108) Purdue Univ. Pr.

Bartholomew, Carl R. Plane Phenomenon: The Pawnshop Mysteries. 2006. (ENG., Illus.). 44p. (J). (gr. 4-7). per. *(978-1-933255-24-8(2))* DNA Pr.

Beach, Charles Amory. Air Service Boys over the Atlantic. rev. ed. 2006. 180p. 26.95 *(978-1-4218-1718-7(7))*; pap. 11.95 *(978-1-4218-1818-4(3))* 1st World Publishing, Inc. (1st World Library - Literary Society).

Bently, Peter. Those Magnificent Sheep in Their Flying Machine. Bently, Peter, illus. 2014. (ENG., Illus.). 32p. (J). (gr. -1-3). 16.95 *(978-1-4677-4935-0(4))* Lerner Publishing Group.

Berenstain, Jan, et al. Kindness Counts, 1 vol. 2010. (Berenstain Bears/Living Lights Ser.). (ENG.). 32p. (J). (gr. -1-2). pap. 3.99 *(978-0-310-71257-2(2))* Zonderkidz.

Berrios, Frank. Plane Pals. 2014. (Step into Reading Level 1 Ser.). lib. bdg. 13.55 *(978-0-606-35202-4(3))* Turtleback Bks.

Biggs, Brian. Everything Goes - What Flies in the Air? Biggs, Brian, illus. 2013. (ENG., Illus.). 24p. (J). (gr. -1 — 1). bds. 7.99 *(978-0-06-195816-8(6))* HarperCollins Pubs.

Billy & Baxter at the Airport, 4 vols. 2005. (Illus.). 24p. (J). (gr. -1-7). 8.95 *(978-1-58087-100-6(3))* Stampley, C. D. Enterprises, Inc.

Blake, Jocelyn. Mama Is on an Airplane. Blake, Jocelyn, illus. 2006. (Illus.). (J). per. 9.99 *(978-0-9790572-0-5(5))* Kreativ Kaos.

Bowen, Carl & Fuentes, Benny. Phantom Sun, 1 vol. Tortosa, Wilson, illus. 2014. (Shadow Squadron Ser.). (ENG.). 112p. (gr. 4-8). 26.65 *(978-1-4342-6399-5(1))* Stone Arch Bks.

Brooks, Felicity. Construction Sites. Newell, Keith, illus. 2010. (Lift & Look Board Bks.). 12p. (J). bds. 9.99 *(978-0-7945-2728-0(0)*, Usborne) EDC Publishing.

—Planes. 2010. (Lift & Look Board Bks.). 12p. (J). bds. 9.99 *(978-0-7945-2669-6(1)*, Usborne) EDC Publishing.

Brown, Amanda C. Flying Courage. Archeval, Jose, illus. 2012. (ENG.). 26p. (J). pap. 9.99 *(978-1-62006-121-3(X))* Sunbury Press, Inc.

Carbone, Courtney. Rescue Buddies! (Disney Planes: Fire & Rescue) Random House Disney Staff, illus. 2015. (Friendship Box Ser.). (ENG.). 48p. (J). (-k). bds. 10.99 *(978-0-7364-3333-4(3)*, RH/Disney) Random Hse. Children's Bks.

Catran, Ken. Dawn Hawk. 96p. pap. *(978-0-7344-0468-8(9)*, Lothian Children's Bks.) Hachette Australia.

Cole, Henry. The Somewhat True Adventures of Sammy Shine, 1 vol. Cole, Henry, illus. 2016. (ENG., Illus.). 272p. (J). (gr. 3-6). 16.95 *(978-1-56145-866-0(X))* Peachtree Pubs.

Coleman-Woolslayer, Mary. A Biplane & Her Boy. 2010. (Illus.). 45p. (J). 24.95 *(978-0-9844785-0-7(7))* Tigermoth Pubns.

Cotter, Bill. Hello, Airplane! 2014. (ENG., Illus.). 32p. (J). (-3). 16.99 *(978-1-4926-0353-5(8)*, Sourcebooks Jabberwocky) Sourcebooks, Inc.

Cousins, Lucy. Maisy Goes on a Plane. Cousins, Lucy, illus. 2015. (Maisy Ser.). (ENG., Illus.). 32p. (J). (-k). 12.99 *(978-0-7636-7825-8(2))* Candlewick Pr.

Craine, E. J. Airplane Boys at Belize. 2003. (ENG.). 224p. (J). pap. 13.95 *(978-1-55753-323-4(7)*, 451f8175-099e-4a08-95b9-2fe962b09c95) Purdue Univ. Pr.

—Airplane Boys at Platinum River. 2003. (ENG.). 200p. (J). pap. 13.95 *(978-1-55753-320-3(2)*, b9d659a0-68ba-48a1-a242-99e8f0499774) Purdue Univ. Pr.

—Airplane Boys Discover the Secrets of Cuzco. 2003. (ENG.). 246p. (J). pap. 13.95 *(978-1-55753-318-0(0)*, c2a914a5-1d24-4220-b51b-b0f6d6ddfdfe) Purdue Univ. Pr.

—Airplane Boys Flying to Amy-Ran Fastness. 2003. (ENG.). 245p. (J). pap. 13.95 *(978-1-55753-319-7(9)*, dace6a4f-5096-44da-9d37-8e4e29b8bd1c) Purdue Univ. Pr.

—Airplane Boys in the Black Woods. 2003. (ENG.). 209p. (J). pap. 13.95 *(978-1-55753-322-7(9)*, d34bb521-9c84-4a95-a288-d1a9a2b27b27) Purdue Univ. Pr.

—Airplane Boys on the Border Line. 2003. (ENG.). 246p. (J). pap. 13.95 *(978-1-55753-316-6(4)*, d264e88f-e170-4467-b25f-1696b7278137) Purdue Univ. Pr.

—Airplane Boys with the Revolutionists in Bolivia. 2003. (ENG.). 201p. (J). pap. 13.95 *(978-1-55753-321-0(0)*, 0bc79ba3-a232-40ec-b30c-db35be518b4d) Purdue Univ. Pr.

Cuniffe, John. Postman Pat Makes an Aeroplane. (Illus.). 20p. (J). pap. *(978-0-340-73716-3(6))* Hodder & Stoughton.

Daval, Josie. The Wright Twist. 2006. (Illus.). 151p. (J). (gr. 3-7). 14.95 *(978-1-933197-19-7(6))* Orange Frazer Pr.

Davis, Richard A. Spinner's Secret. 2007. 52p. per. 24.95 *(978-1-4241-8339-5(1))* America Star Bks.

Disney. Dusty to the Rescue. 2014. lib. bdg. 14.75 *(978-0-606-35999-3(0))* Turtleback Bks.

Disney Planes, Disney. Disney Planes Fire & Rescue to the Rescue: Build 6 Planes That Really Fly! 2014. (Build It Ser.: 3). (ENG.). 24p. (J). (gr. -1-1). 14.99 *(978-0-7944-3139-6(9))* Reader's Digest Assn., Inc., The.

Downs, Mike. The Noisy Airplane Ride. Gordon, David, illus. 2005. (ENG.). 32p. (J). (gr. -1-2). pap. 6.99 *(978-1-58246-157-1(0)*, Tricycle Pr.) Random Hse. Children's Bks.

Duble, Kathleen Benner. Bravo Zulu, Samantha!, 1 vol. 2007. (ENG.). 144p. (J). (gr. 3-7). 14.95 *(978-1-56145-401-3(X))* Peachtree Pubs.

Eastman, Peter. Fred & Ted Like to Fly. 2011. (Bright & Early Board Books Ser.). (ENG., Illus.). 24p. (J). (— 1). bds. 4.99 *(978-0-375-86802-3(X)*, Random Hse. Bks. for Young Readers) Random Hse. Children's Bks.

—Fred & Ted Like to Fly. Eastman, Peter, illus. 2007. (Beginner Books Ser.). (ENG., Illus.). 48p. (J). (gr. -1-2). 8.99 *(978-0-375-84064-7(8)*, Random Hse. Bks. for Young Readers) Random Hse. Children's Bks.

Feldman, Thea. Things That Go. 2006. 3p. 5.99 *(978-1-932915-31-0(1))* Sandvik Publishing.

Ferrari, Michael. Born to Fly. 2011. (ENG.). 224p. (J). (gr. 3-7). 6.99 *(978-0-375-84607-6(7)*, Yearling) Random Hse. Children's Bks.

Fields, Trisha A. Eggbert, the Hero. 2012. 44p. pap. 21.99 *(978-1-4771-3548-8(0))* Xlibris Corp.

Forde, Winston. Airborne Soldiers. 2010. (Illus.). 120p. 29.99 *(978-1-4535-6451-6(9))* Xlibris Corp.

Fraser, Chelsea Curtis. Around the World in Ten Days. 2007. (ENG.). 192p. pap. 19.99 *(978-1-4346-3412-2(4))*; 208p. pap. 22.99 *(978-1-4346-3413-9(2))* Creative Media Partners, LLC.

Garis, Howard R. Dick Hamilton's Airship. 2008. 160p. 25.95 *(978-1-60664-781-3(4))* Aegypan.

Garis, Howard Roger. Dick Hamiltons Airship. 2005. 28.95 *(978-1-4218-1463-6(3))*; 260p. pap. 13.95 *(978-1-4218-1563-3(X))* 1st World Publishing, Inc. (1st World Library - Literary Society).

Gillespie, Hollis. Unaccompanied Minor. 2014. (ENG.). 256p. (YA). 17.99 *(978-1-4405-6773-5(5))* Adams Media Corp.

Gordon, David. The Ugly Truckling. Gordon, David, illus. 2004. (Illus.). 32p. (J). (gr. -1-2). lib. bdg. 16.89 *(978-0-06-054601-4(8),* Geringer, Laura Book) HarperCollins Pubs.

Grimm, Kristi. Mommy, Tell Me a Story about a Plane, 2nd Edition. Grimm, Dave, illus. 2nd ed. 2013. 36p. pap. 13.99 *(978-0-9855699-8-3(0))* Richer Life, LLC.

Guy, Ginger Foglesong. Mi Abuelita. Escrivá, Viví, illus. 2007.Tr. of My Grandma. (ENG & SPA.). 24p. (J). (gr. -1-k). 16.99 *(978-0-06-079098-1(9),* Rayo) HarperCollins Pubs.

Harrison, Sarah. A Day at an Airport. 2009. (Time Goes By Ser.). (ENG.). 24p. (J). (gr. k-3). pap. 6.95 *(978-1-58013-801-7(2),* First Avenue Editions) Lerner Publishing Group.

Hawksley, Gerald, illus. Quacky Duck's Plane: Press Out Parts Make an Airplane Carrying Quacky Duck! 2009. (Toddler Make & Play Ser.). 10p. bds. 6.95 *(978-1-59496-185-4(9))* Teora USA LLC.

Henry, Heather French. Flying Away. Henry, Heather French, illus. 2004. (Claire's Everyday Adventures Ser.). (Illus.). 32p. (J). (gr. k-4). pap. 8.95 *(978-0-9706341-8-4(8),* 1231610); (ENG., 15.95 *(978-0-9706341-4-6(5),* 1231610) Cubbie Blue Publishing.

—Volando. 2007. (Claire's Everyday Adventures Ser Ser.). (SPA & ENG., Illus.). 32p. (J). (gr. k-4). pap. 9.95 *(978-1-932824-04-9(9))* Cubbie Blue Publishing.

Hilton, Fern A. Jesse & Henry Save the Day. 2012. 24p. pap. 14.50 *(978-1-4772-9282-2(9))* AuthorHouse.

—Jesse & Wee. 2012. 20p. pap. 12.99 *(978-1-4685-7613-9(5))* AuthorHouse.

Hoffman, Mary Ann. Elbert Takes a Trip. 2006. (Neighborhood Readers Ser.). (ENG., Illus.). 12p. (gr. 1-3). pap. 5.90 *(978-1-4042-6847-0(2),* Rosen Classroom) Rosen Publishing Group, Inc., The.

Ingram, W. J. Evelyn. Saint Crispin & Other Quaint Conceits. 2005. pap. 24.95 *(978-1-4179-6255-6(0))* Kessinger Publishing, LLC.

Ivanoff, George. Royal Flying Doctor Service 1: Remote Rescue. 2016. (Royal Flying Doctor Service Ser.). (ENG.). 192p. (J). (gr. 3-6). pap. 12.99 *(978-0-85798-876-8(X))* Random Hse. Australia AUS. Dist: Independent Pubs. Group.

—Royal Flying Doctor Service 2: Emergency Echo. 2016. (Royal Flying Doctor Service Ser.). (ENG.). 192p. (J). (gr. 3-6). pap. 12.99 *(978-0-85798-878-2(6))* Random Hse. Australia AUS. Dist: Independent Pubs. Group.

Jackson, Ciandress. Chloe the Jumbo Jet: First Class to Seoul! Let's Rock & Roll. 2013. 26p. pap. 9.99 *(978-1-61286-196-8(2))* Avid Readers Publishing Group.

Kalep, Elvy. Air Babies. 2011. (ENG., Illus.). 24p. (J). (gr. -1-k). pap. 12.95 *(978-1-55709-391-2(1))* Applewood Bks.

Kinerk, Robert. Clorinda Takes Flight. Kellogg, Steven, illus. 2007. (ENG.). 40p. (J). (gr. -1-3). 17.99 *(978-0-689-86864-1(2),* Simon & Schuster/Paula Wiseman Bks.) Simon & Schuster/Paula Wiseman Bks.

Kuhlmann, Torben. Lindbergh: The Tale of a Flying Mouse. 2014. (ENG., Illus.). 96p. (J). (gr. k-k). 19.95 *(978-0-7358-4167-3(5))* North-South Bks., Inc.

Lagasse, Paul. Seeing Through Clouds: The Story of an Airship Apprentice. 2006. 180p. per. 11.95 *(978-1-59858-115-7(5))* Dog Ear Publishing, LLC.

LeapFrog Staff & Partnership Staff, compiled by. Jay Jay the Jet Plane: U.K. 2003. (J). spiral bd. 8.99 *(978-1-58605-072-6(9))* LeapFrog Enterprises, Inc.

LeSourd, Nancy. Attack at Pearl Harbor, 1 vol. 2008. (Liberty Letters Ser.). (ENG.). 224p. (J). pap. 7.99 *(978-0-310-71389-0(7))* Zonderkidz.

Light, Steve. Planes Go. 2014. (ENG., Illus.). 16p. (J). (gr. -1 — 1). bds. 9.99 *(978-1-4521-2899-3(5))* Chronicle Bks. LLC.

Lund, Deb. Dinosoaring. Fine, Howard, illus. 2012. (ENG.). 40p. (J). (gr. -1-3). 16.99 *(978-0-15-206016-9(2))* Houghton Mifflin Harcourt Publishing Co.

Lyon, George Ella. Planes Fly! Wiggins, Mick, illus. 2013. (ENG.). 40p. (J). (gr. -1-2). 17.99 *(978-1-4424-5025-7(8))* Simon & Schuster Children's Publishing.

Maguire, Thomas Aquinas. Three Little Dreams, 3 vols. 2010. (ENG., Illus.). 36p. (J). (gr. -1). 16.95 *(978-1-894965-79-8(5))* Simply Read Bks. CAN. Dist: Ingram Publisher Services.

Manushkin, Fran. Fly High, Katie, 1 vol. Lyon, Tammie, illus. 2014. (Katie Woo Ser.). (ENG.). 32p. (gr. k-2). lib. bdg. 21.32 *(978-1-4795-2175-3(2))* Picture Window Bks.

Marsh, Carole. The Mystery at Kill Devil Hills. 2009. (Real Kids, Real Places Ser.). (Illus.). 145p. (J). lib. bdg. 18.99 *(978-0-635-06999-3(7),* Marsh, Carole Mysteries) Gallopade International.

Mayhar, Ardath. Medicine Walk. 2007. (ENG.). 96p. (YA). (gr. 9). pap. 7.95 *(978-1-4169-6846-7(6),* Simon Pulse) Simon Pulse.

McCarty, Peter. Moon Plane. McCarty, Peter, illus. 2006. (ENG., Illus.). 40p. (J). (gr. -1-1). 18.99 *(978-0-8050-7943-2(2),* 9780805079432, Holt, Henry & Co. Bks. For Young Readers) Holt, Henry & Co.

McCormick, Scott. Trick or Feet! Lazzell, R. H., illus. 2015. (Mr. Pants Ser.: 3). (ENG.). 128p. (J). (gr. k-3). 12.99 *(978-0-525-42811-4(9),* Dial Bks) Penguin Young Readers Group.

McInnes, Dawn Daniels. I Want off This Stinkin' Plane, 1 vol. Daniels, Greg, illus. 2010. 18p. pap. 24.95 *(978-1-4489-7809-0(2))* PublishAmerica, Inc.

Meister, Cari. Airplane Adventure, 1 vol. Jaworski, Marilyn, illus. 2010. (My First Graphic Novel Ser.). 32p. (gr. k-2). (ENG.). pap. 6.25 *(978-1-4342-2286-2(1))*; pap. 4.95 *(978-1-4342-3602-9(1))* Stone Arch Bks. (My First Graphic Novel).

Mikaelsen, Ben. Sparrow Hawk Red. 2010. (ENG.). 192p. (J). (gr. 3-7). pap. 5.99 *(978-1-4231-3361-2(7))* Hyperion Pr.

Mills, Charles. Wings over Oshkosh. 2005. (Honors Club Story Ser.: Vol. 5). 127p. (J). 7.99 *(978-0-8163-2089-9(6))* Pacific Pr. Publishing Assn.

Moyer, Bess. Gypsies of the Air. 2004. reprint ed. pap. 19.95 *(978-1-4179-9112-9(7))* Kessinger Publishing, LLC.

Newcomb, Ambrose. Flying the Coast Skyways or Jack Ralston. 2005. pap. 26.95 *(978-1-4179-8975-1(0))* Kessinger Publishing, LLC.

Once upon a Time- Fantasy Flight. 2005. (J). bds. *(978-1-4194-0095-7(9))* Paradise Pr., Inc.

Oppel, Kenneth. Skybreaker. 2007. (Illus.). 544p. (YA). (gr. 8-12). lib. bdg. 20.85 *(978-1-4177-8130-0(0),* Turtleback) Turtleback Bks.

Paulson, Gary. Hatchet. unabr. ed. 2004. 195p. (J). (gr. 5-9). pap. 36.00 incl. audio *(978-0-8072-8319-6(3),* YA161SP, Listening Library) Random Hse. Audio Publishing Group.

Pearson, Peter. How to Eat an Airplane. Catusanu, Mircea, illus. 2016. (Bad Idea Book Club Ser.). 40p. (J). (gr. -1-3). 17.99 *(978-0-06-232062-9(9))* HarperCollins Pubs.

Penn, Linda M. Is Kentucky in the Sky? 2012. 36p. pap. 9.95 *(978-0-9852488-0-2(7))* Racing to Joy Pr. LLC.

Porchlight Entertainment Staff, ed. You Are Special. 2004. (Jay Jay the Jet Plane Ser.: Vol. 1). (Illus.). 12p. (J). (gr. -1-1). bds. 6.99 *(978-0-8499-7550-9(6))* Nelson, Thomas Inc.

Ralphson, G. Harvey. Boy Scouts in an Airship. 2007. 104p. per. *(978-1-4068-3727-8(X))* Echo Library.

Random House Disney Staff. Disney Planes. Random House Disney Staff, illus. 2013. (Big Golden Book Ser.). (ENG., Illus.). 64p. (J). (gr. -1-2). 9.99 *(978-0-7364-3019-7(9),* Golden/Disney) Random Hse. Children's Bks.

—Dusty to the Rescue (Disney Planes: Fire & Rescue) Random House Disney Staff, illus. 2014. (Pictureback Ser.). (ENG., Illus.). 24p. (J). (gr. -1-2). 4.99 *(978-0-7364-3255-9(8),* RH/Disney) Random Hse. Children's Bks.

—Fast! Random House Disney Staff, illus. 2013. (Disney Chapters Ser.). (ENG., Illus.). 80p. (J). (gr. 1-4). 4.99 *(978-0-7364-3017-3(2),* RH/Disney) Random Hse. Children's Bks.

—Planes: Fire & Rescue (Disney Planes: Fire & Rescue) Random House Disney Staff, illus. 2014. (Little Golden Book Ser.). (ENG., Illus.). 24p. (J). (-k). 4.99 *(978-0-7364-3166-8(7),* Golden/Disney) Random Hse. Children's Bks.

Reedy, Trent. Stealing Air. 2012. (ENG.). 288p. (J). (gr. 3-7). 16.99 *(978-0-545-38307-3(2),* Levine, Arthur A. Bks.) Scholastic, Inc.

Reid, Charles. Chasing the Arrow. 2006. (ENG.). 144p. (J). (gr. 7). pap., tchr. ed. 6.95 *(978-0-88878-439-1(2))* Dundurn CAN. Dist: Ingram Publisher Services.

Reynolds, Peter H. I'm Here. Reynolds, Peter H., illus. 2011. (ENG., Illus.). 32p. (J). (gr. -1-3). 16.99 *(978-1-4169-9649-1(4),* Atheneum Bks. for Young Readers) Simon & Schuster Children's Publishing.

RH Disney Staff & Hall, Klay. Disney Planes. Golden Books Staff & Hand, Jason, illus. 2013. (Little Golden Book Ser.). (ENG.). 24p. (J). (-k). 4.99 *(978-0-7364-2974-0(3),* Golden/Disney) Random Hse. Children's Bks.

RH Disney Staff & Scollon, Bill. Wings Around the Globe. RH Disney Staff & Disney Storybook Artists Staff, illus. 2013. (Pictureback(R) Ser.). (ENG.). 24p. (J). (gr. -1-2). pap. 3.99 *(978-0-7364-3016-6(4),* RH/Disney) Random Hse. Children's Bks.

Rigsby, Annelle & Raffa, Edwina. Race to Kitty Hawk. 2003. (Adventures in America Ser.). (Illus.). 84p. (gr. 4). 14.95 *(978-1-893110-33-5(8))* Silver Moon Pr.

Rohen, Sean. Unprincess Nermine. 2009. 84p. pap. 26.99 *(978-1-4490-3592-1(2))* AuthorHouse.

Samson, Don. Teenage Aviation Stories. 2005. reprint ed. pap. 26.95 *(978-1-4191-1624-7(X))* Kessinger Publishing, LLC.

Sander, Sonia. LEGO City Reader Collection: LEGO City Emergency. 2012. (Illus.). 127p. (J). *(978-1-4351-3985-5(2))* Scholastic, Inc.

Savage, Stephen. Little Plane Learns to Write. Savage, Stephen, illus. 2017. (ENG., Illus.). 32p. (J). 16.99 *(978-1-62672-436-5(9),* 9781626724365) Roaring Brook Pr.

Saviola, Erin. Airplane Jane. 2006. (Neighborhood Readers Ser.). (ENG., Illus.). 16p. (gr. 1-3). pap. 6.50 *(978-1-4042-7236-1(4),* Rosen Classroom) Rosen Publishing Group, Inc., The.

Sayres, Brianna Caplan. Where Do Jet Planes Sleep at Night? Slade, Christian, illus. 2017. (ENG.). 32p. (J). (gr. -1-2). 16.99 *(978-0-399-55448-3(3))*; lib. bdg. 19.99 ***(978-0-399-55449-0(1))*** Random Hse. Children's Bks. (Random Hse. Bks. for Young Readers).

Scholastic, Inc. Staff. Ready for Takeoff! 2010. (LEGO City Adventures Scholastic Readers Level 1 Ser.: 5). lib. bdg. 13.55 *(978-0-606-15057-6(9),* Turtleback) Turtleback Bks.

Scholastic, Inc. Staff & Sander, Sonia. Ready for Takeoff! 2010. (Lego City Ser.). (ENG.). 32p. (J). (gr. -1-k). pap. 3.99 *(978-0-545-21986-0(8))* Scholastic, Inc.

Shakespeare, Nancy. Benjamin the Bear Rides on an Airplane. Clouette, Katie, illus. 2013. (Benjamin the Bear Ser.). (ENG.). (J). (gr. -1-3). 14.95 *(978-1-62086-318-3(9))* Mascot Bks., Inc.

Simmons, J. A. Hannah's First Airplane Ride. 2013. 32p. pap. 24.95 *(978-1-63004-197-7(1))* America Star Bks.

Singhose, Rose & StGermain, Annetta. Gramma's Sure Fire Cure for Insomnia in the Very Young. 2010. 67p. pap. 27.50 *(978-0-557-08697-9(3))* Lulu Pr., Inc.

Smith, Sherri L. Flygirl. 2010. (ENG.). 304p. (YA). (gr. 7-18). 9.99 *(978-0-14-241725-6(4),* Speak) Penguin Young Readers Group.

Snape, Emily. Motor Mix, Flight: Invent Your Own Mix-And-Match Vehicles! Alexander, Rilla, illus. 2017. (ENG.). 16p. (J). (gr. -1 — 1). bds. 9.99 *(978-1-4521-4839-7(2))* Chronicle Bks. LLC.

Snell, Roy F. Wings for Victory. 2005. pap. 26.95 *(978-1-4191-6999-1(8))* Kessinger Publishing, LLC.

Stamp, Jørgen & Buckley, William F., Jr. Flying High. 2009. (ENG., Illus.). 32p. (J). (gr. -1-2). 16.95 *(978-1-59270-089-6(9))* Enchanted Lion Bks., LLC.

Steele, Michael Anthony. The Case of the Fright Flight. Neely, Scott, illus. 2016. (You Choose Stories: Scooby-Doo Ser.). (ENG.). 112p. (gr. 2-3). lib. bdg. 32.65 *(978-1-4965-2662-5(7),* You Choose Bks.) Capstone Press of Coughlan Cos.

Sterling Children's, Sterling. Airport. Finn, Rebecca, illus. 2015. (Busy Bks.). (ENG.). 10p. (J). (— 1). bds. 8.95 *(978-1-4549-1732-8(6))* Sterling Publishing Co., Inc.

Sutton, Felix. We Were There at the First Airplane Flight. Matulay, Laszlo, illus. 2013. (ENG.). 192p. (J). (gr. 3-8). pap. 6.99 *(978-0-486-49258-2(3))* Dover Pubns., Inc.

Sykes, Harold S. The Beacon of Airport Seven. 2004. reprint ed. pap. 1.99 *(978-1-4192-5375-1(1))* Kessinger Publishing, LLC.

Urish, J. D. The Adventures of Rex Bolton Volume 1. 2010. 60p. pap. 9.98 *(978-0-578-03676-2(2))* Jentmedia.

van Lieshout, Maria. Flight 1-2-3. van Lieshout, Maria, illus. 2013. (ENG., Illus.). 40p. (J). (gr. -1 — 1). 14.99 *(978-1-4521-1662-4(8))* Chronicle Bks. LLC.

Van Straaten, Harmen. TIM & the FLYING MACHINE. 2008. (ENG.). 28p. (J). (gr. 1-7). 12.95 *(978-1-60136-003-8(7))* Audio Holdings, LLC.

Vasquez, Elisa Irene. My Little Piggy: A Bilingual English-Spanish Children's Book. 2010. 28p. 14.95 *(978-1-4490-8716-6(7))* AuthorHouse.

Velazquez, Anna. Stewart's Airplane Adventure. 2008. 40p. pap. 24.95 *(978-1-60441-486-8(3))* America Star Bks.

Victor, Appleton. Tom Swift & His Aerial Warship: Or the Naval Terror of the Seas. 2007. (ENG.). 144p. pap. 18.99 *(978-1-4346-1484-1(0))* Creative Media Partners, LLC.

Walker, Peter. The Magic Airplane. 2006. (ENG.). 160p. per. 12.95 *(978-1-59526-416-9(7))* Aeon Publishing Inc.

Watt, Fiona. That's Not My Plane. rev. ed. 2012. (Touchy-Feely Board Bks). 10p. (J). bds. 8.99 *(978-0-7945-3294-9(2),* Usborne) EDC Publishing.

Weeks, Kermit. All of Life Is a School. Project Firefly, illus. 2007. 64p. (J). 19.95 *(978-0-9790267-0-6(9))* KWIP, Inc.

Weiland, Peter. So Big yet So Small. Coffey, Kevin, illus. 2012. (J). 14.95 *(978-1-937406-16-5(4))* Mascot Bks., Inc.

White, Howard. The Airplane Ride. Guzek, Greta, illus. unabr. ed. 2006. (ENG.). 32p. (J). bds. 16.95 *(978-0-88971-224-9(7))* Harbour Publishing Co., Ltd. CAN. Dist: Midpoint Trade Bks., Inc.

Wilson, David Lloyd. Some Dogs Fly, 1 vol. 2009. 89p. pap. 19.95 *(978-1-61582-968-2(7))* America Star Bks.

Woodbury, Mary. Flight of the Tiger Moth, 1 vol. 2007. (ENG.). 240p. (YA). (gr. 7-11). per. 8.95 *(978-1-55050-364-7(2))* Coteau Bks. CAN. Dist: Orca Bk. Pubs. USA.

Wrecks, Billy. In the Lead! (Disney Planes) Random House Disney Staff, illus. 2014. (3-D Pictureback Ser.). (ENG.). 16p. (J). (gr. -1-2). 4.99 *(978-0-7364-2992-4(1),* RH/Disney) Random Hse. Children's Bks.

AIRPLANES—FLIGHT TESTING

see Airplanes—Testing

AIRPLANES, JET PROPELLED

see Jet Planes

AIRPLANES, MILITARY

see also types of military airplanes, e.g. Bombers

Abramovitz, Melissa. Military Airplanes. 2012. (Military Machines Ser.). (ENG.). 24p. (gr. k-1). pap. 41.70 *(978-1-4296-8312-8(0))*; lib. bdg. 26.65 *(978-1-4296-7571-0(3))* Capstone Press of Coughlan Cos. (Pebble Plus).

—Military Helicopters, 1 vol. 2012. (Military Machines Ser.). (ENG.). 24p. (gr. k-1). lib. bdg. 26.65 *(978-1-4296-7574-1(8),* Pebble Plus) Capstone Press of Coughlan Cos.

Adams, Simon. Warplanes. 2009. (J). 28.50 *(978-1-59920-223-5(9))* Black Rabbit Bks.

Aircraft, 14 bks., Set. Incl. Air Force Aircraft. Holden, Henry M. (J). 2001. lib. bdg. 23.93 *(978-0-7660-1714-6(1))*; Air Show Pilots & Airplanes. Gaffney, Timothy R. (YA). 2001. lib. bdg. 23.93 *(978-0-7660-1570-8(X))*; Amazing Agricultural Aircraft. Gaffney, Timothy R. (J). 2001. lib. bdg. 23.93 *(978-0-7660-1608-8(0))*; Black Hawk Helicopter. Holden, Henry M. (J). 2002. lib. bdg. 23.93 *(978-0-7660-1568-5(8))*; Hurricane Hunters. Gaffney, Timothy R. (J). 2001. lib. bdg. 25.27 *(978-0-7660-1569-2(6))*; Stealth Fighters & Bombers. Berliner, Don. (YA). 2001. lib. bdg. 23.93 *(978-0-7660-1567-8(X))*; 48p. (gr. 4-10). (Illus.). Set lib. bdg. 227.40 *(978-0-7660-1799-3(0))* Enslow Pubs., Inc.

Alvarez, Carlos. EA-6B Prowlers. 2009. (Military Machines Ser.). (ENG., Illus.). 24p. (J). (gr. 3-7). lib. bdg. 25.95 *(978-1-60014-292-5(3))* Bellwether Media.

—MH-53E Sea Dragons. 2010. (Military Machines Ser.). (ENG., Illus.). 24p. (J). (gr. 3-7). lib. bdg. 25.95 *(978-1-60014-495-0(0),* Torque Bks.) Bellwether Media.

Braun, Eric. Trapped Behind Enemy Lines: The Story of the U. S. Army Air Force 807th Medical Evacuation Squadron. 2016. (Encounter: Narrative Nonfiction Stories Ser.). (ENG.). 224p. (gr. 4-6). 14.95 *(978-1-62370-605-0(X))*; (Illus.). lib. bdg. 32.65 *(978-1-4914-8042-7(4),* 1400082) Encounter Bks.

Byers, Ann. America's Star Wars Program. 2009. (Library of Weapons of Mass Destruction Ser.). 64p. (gr. 5-5). 58.50 *(978-1-60853-950-5(4))* Rosen Publishing Group, Inc., The.

Chandler, Matt. Military Drones. 2017. (Drones Ser.). (ENG., Illus.). 32p. (gr. 3-4). lib. bdg. 27.99 *(978-1-5157-3769-8(1),* Edge Bks.) Capstone Press of Coughlan Cos.

Cohn, Jessica. Military Machines. 2013. (Machines in Motion Ser.). 48p. (J). (gr. 3-5). pap. 84.30 *(978-1-4339-9606-1(5))*; pap. 14.05 *(978-1-4339-9605-4(7))*; (ENG., Illus.). lib. bdg. 31.95 *(978-1-4339-9604-7(9))* Stevens, Gareth Publishing LLLP.

Cornish, Geoff. Battleground Support. 2004. (Military Hardware in Action Ser.). (Illus.). 48p. (J). (gr. 4-9). lib. bdg. 25.26 *(978-0-8225-4708-2(2))* Lerner Publishing Group.

Corrigan, Jim. In the Air: Cargo Planes. 2013. (Military Experience: in the Air Ser.). (ENG., Illus.). 64p. (YA). (gr. 3-7). 27.45 *(978-1-59935-380-7(6))* Reynolds, Morgan Inc.

Cunningham, Anne C., ed. Drones, Surveillance, & Targeted Killings. 2017. (Current Controversies Ser.). 224p. (J). (gr. 10-12). pap. 32.00 ***(978-1-5345-0036-5(7))***; lib. bdg. 46.40 ***(978-1-5345-0020-4(0))*** Greenhaven Publishing LLC. (Greenhaven Publishing).

Dartford, Mark. Bombers. 2003. (Military Hardware in Action Ser.). (ENG., Illus.). 48p. (gr. 5-9). lib. bdg. 25.26 *(978-0-8225-4705-1(8))* Lerner Publishing Group.

—Fighter Planes. 2003. (Military Hardware in Action Ser.). (ENG., Illus.). 48p. (gr. 5-9). lib. bdg. 25.26 *(978-0-8225-4706-8(6))* Lerner Publishing Group.

David, Jack. Air Force Air Commandos. 2009. (Armed Forces Ser.). (ENG., Illus.). 24p. (J). (gr. 3-7). lib. bdg. 25.95 *(978-1-60014-262-8(1))* Bellwether Media.

—AV-8B Harrier Jump Jets. 2008. (Military Machines Ser.). (ENG., Illus.). 24p. (J). (gr. 3-7). lib. bdg. 25.95 *(978-1-60014-233-8(8))* Bellwether Media.

—F-14 Tomcats. 2008. (Military Machines Ser.). (ENG., Illus.). 24p. (YA). (gr. 3-7). lib. bdg. 25.95 *(978-1-60014-202-4(8))* Bellwether Media.

—F-15 Eagles. 2008. (Military Machines Ser.). (ENG., Illus.). 24p. (J). (gr. 3-7). lib. bdg. 25.95 *(978-1-60014-203-1(6))* Bellwether Media.

—U-2 Planes. 2007. (Military Machines Ser.). (ENG., Illus.). 24p. (J). (gr. 3-7). lib. bdg. 25.95 *(978-1-60014-106-5(4))* Bellwether Media.

Dell, Pamela & Delmar, Peter. The Science of Military Vehicles, 1 vol. 2012. (Science of War Ser.). (ENG.). 48p. (gr. 5-6). pap. 9.10 *(978-0-7565-4525-3(0),* CPB Grades 4-8) Compass Point Bks.

Doman, Mary Kate. Big Military Machines. 2011. (All about Big Machines Ser.). (Illus.). 24p. (J). (gr. -1-18). pap. 7.95 *(978-1-59845-243-3(6),* Enslow Elementary) Enslow Pubs., Inc.

Dowswell. Military Aircraft, 6 pack. 2004. (Mean Machines Ser.). (Illus.). (J). pap. 48.30 *(978-1-4109-1201-5(9))* Harcourt Schl. Pubs.

Ellis, Catherine. Planes. 2009. (Mega Military Machines Ser.). 24p. (gr. 1-1). 42.50 *(978-1-61514-636-9(9),* PowerKids Pr.) Rosen Publishing Group, Inc., The.

—Planes/Aviones. 2009. (Mega Military Machines/Megamaquinas militares Ser.). (ENG & SPA.). 24p. (gr. 1-1). 42.50 *(978-1-61514-641-3(5),* Editorial Buenas Letras) Rosen Publishing Group, Inc., The.

—Planes/Aviones. Brusca, Maria Cristina, tr. 2007. (Mega Military Machines / Megamaquinas Militares Ser.). (ENG & SPA., Illus.). 24p. (J). lib. bdg. 22.60 *(978-1-4042-7622-2(X),* PowerKids Pr.) Rosen Publishing Group, Inc., The.

Farndon, John. Megafast Planes. Edwards, Mat & Pyke, Jeremy, illus. 2016. (Megafast Ser.). (ENG.). 32p. (J). (gr. 3-6). lib. bdg. 26.65 *(978-1-4677-9365-0(5))* Lerner Publishing Group.

Faust, Daniel R. Military Drones, 01 vols., 1. 2016. (Drones: Eyes in the Skies Ser.). (ENG., Illus.). 32p. (J). pap. 11.75 *(978-1-5081-4496-0(6),* PowerKids Pr.) Rosen Publishing Group, Inc., The.

Finn, Denny Von. B-2 Stealth Bombers. 2013. (Military Vehicles Ser.). (ENG., Illus.). 24p. (J). (gr. 3-7). lib. bdg. 25.95 *(978-1-60014-883-5(2),* Epic Bks.) Bellwether Media.

—Military Helicopters. 2010. (World's Fastest Ser.). (ENG., Illus.). 24p. (J). (gr. 3-7). lib. bdg. 25.95 *(978-1-60014-336-6(9))* Bellwether Media.

—Predator Drones. 2012. (Military Vehicles Ser.). (ENG., Illus.). 24p. (J). (gr. 3-7). lib. bdg. 25.95 *(978-1-60014-821-7(2),* Epic Bks.) Bellwether Media.

Gilpin, Daniel & Pang, Alex. Modern Military Aircraft. 2010. (Machines Close-Up Ser.). 32p. (J). (gr. 4-7). 28.50 *(978-1-60870-108-7(5))* Marshall Cavendish Corp.

Goldberg, Jan. The C-130 Hercules. 2009. (U. S. Warplanes Ser.). 48p. (gr. 5-8). 53.00 *(978-1-60854-595-7(4),* Rosen Reference) Rosen Publishing Group, Inc., The.

Graham, Ian. Military Planes: Model Maker. 2006. (Illus.). 48p. (J). (gr. 4-8). reprint ed. 13.00 *(978-1-4223-5180-2(7))* DIANE Publishing Co.

Hamilton, John. A-10 Thunderbolt Ii. 2013. (Xtreme Military Aircraft Set 2 Ser.). 32p. (J). (gr. 3-9). lib. bdg. 27.07 *(978-1-61783-685-5(0),* Abdo & Daughters) ABDO Publishing Co.

—Ac-130H/U Gunship. 2013. (Xtreme Military Aircraft Set 2 Ser.). 32p. (J). (gr. 3-9). lib. bdg. 27.07 *(978-1-61783-686-2(9),* Abdo & Daughters) ABDO Publishing Co.

—Aircraft of World War I, 1 vol. 2004. (World War I Ser.). (ENG.). 32p. (gr. 4-8). 27.07 *(978-1-57765-912-9(0),* Abdo & Daughters) ABDO Publishing Co.

—B-52 Stratofortress. 2013. (Xtreme Military Aircraft Set 2 Ser.). 32p. (J). (gr. 3-9). lib. bdg. 27.07 *(978-1-61783-687-9(7),* Abdo & Daughters) ABDO Publishing Co.

—F-22 Raptor. 2013. (Xtreme Military Aircraft Set 2 Ser.). 32p. (J). (gr. 3-9). lib. bdg. 27.07 *(978-1-61783-688-6(5),* Abdo & Daughters) ABDO Publishing Co.

—V-22 Osprey. 2013. (Xtreme Military Aircraft Set 2 Ser.). 32p. (J). (gr. 3-9). lib. bdg. 27.07 *(978-1-61783-690-9(7),* Abdo & Daughters) ABDO Publishing Co.

Harasymiw, Mark. Military Helicopters. 2013. (Military Machines Ser.). (Illus.). 32p. (gr. 3-6). pap. 10.50 *(978-1-4339-8468-6(7))*; lib. bdg. 26.60 *(978-1-4339-8467-9(9))* Stevens, Gareth Publishing LLLP.

In the Air: Helicopters. 2013. (Military Experience: in the Air Ser.). (ENG., Illus.). 64p. (YA). (gr. 3-7). 27.45 *(978-1-59935-382-1(2))* Reynolds, Morgan Inc.

Jackson, Kay. Military Helicopters in Action. 2009. (Amazing Military Vehicles Ser.). 24p. (gr. 3-3). 42.50 *(978-1-61511-312-5(6),* PowerKids Pr.); (YA). lib. bdg. 22.60 *(978-1-4358-2748-6(1))* Rosen Publishing Group, Inc., The.

—Military Planes in Action. 2009. (Amazing Military Vehicles Ser.). 24p. (J). (gr. 3-5). pap. 8.25 *(978-1-4358-3157-5(8),* PowerKids Pr.); lib. bdg. 22.60 *(978-1-4358-2747-9(3))* Rosen Publishing Group, Inc., The.

Jackson, Robert. Warplanes of World War II up Close, 01 vols., 1. Pearson, Colin, illus. 2016. (Military Technology: Top Secret Clearance Ser.). (ENG.). 224p. (YA). 43.60 *(978-1-5081-7078-5(9),* Rosen Young Adult) Rosen Publishing Group, Inc., The.

Kids' Guides Spring 2011. 2010. (Kids' Guides). (ENG.). 32p. (gr. 3-4). lib. bdg. 111.96 *(978-1-4296-5445-6(7),* Edge Bks.) Capstone Press of Coughlan Cos.

Littlejohn, Randy. Air Warfare of the Future. (Library of Future Weaponry Ser.). 64p. 2009. (gr. 6-6). 58.50 *(978-1-60853-635-1(1))* 2006. (Illus.). (J). (gr. 2-7). lib. bdg.

31.95 *(978-1-4042-0523-9(3))* Rosen Publishing Group, Inc., The.

Loveless, Antony. Air War. 2008. (ENG., Illus.). 32p. (J). (gr. 6-10). lib. bdg. *(978-0-7787-3812-1(4))* Crabtree Publishing Co.

Meister, Cari. Totally Amazing Facts about Military Sea & Air Vehicles. 2017. (Mind Benders Ser.). (ENG., Illus.). 112p. (gr. 1-3). lib. bdg. 23.32 *(978-1-5157-4526-6(0))* Capstone Press of Coughlan Cos.

Mooney, Carla. Pilotless Planes. 2010. (Great Idea Ser.). 48p. (J). (gr. 4-6). lib. bdg. 26.60 *(978-1-59953-381-0(2))* Norwood Hse. Pr.

Murray, Aaron R. Aircraft of World War II. 2014. (Illus.). 48p. (J). *(978-1-4351-5366-0(9))* Barnes & Noble, Inc.

—Aircraft of World War II, 01 vols., 1. 2016. (What's Inside? Ser.). (ENG.). 48p. (J). pap. 11.75 *(978-1-5081-4599-8(7),* PowerKids Pr.) Rosen Publishing Group, Inc., The.

—Modern Military Aircraft, 01 vols., 1. 2016. (What's Inside? Ser.). (ENG.). 48p. (J). pap. 11.75 *(978-1-5081-4611-7(X),* PowerKids Pr.) Rosen Publishing Group, Inc., The.

—Modern Military Aircraft/[author, Aaron R. Murray]. 2014. (Illus.). 48p. (J). *(978-1-4351-5370-7(7))* Barnes & Noble, Inc.

Myhra, David. The Horten Ho 9/Ho 229 Vol. 1: Retrospective, 1 vol. 2003. (ENG., Illus.). 224p. (gr. 10-13). 49.95 *(978-0-7643-1666-1(4),* 9780764316661) Schiffer Publishing, Ltd.

Nardo, Don. Invisible Weapons: The Science of Biological & Chemical Warfare, 1 vol. 2010. (Headline Science Ser.). (ENG.). 48p. (gr. 7-8). lib. bdg. 29.32 *(978-0-7565-4217-7(0),* Headline Science) Compass Point Bks.

Parker, Steve. Military Machines. 2010. (How It Works Ser.). 40p. (J). (gr. 3-18). lib. bdg. 19.95 *(978-1-4222-1797-9(3))* Mason Crest.

Seidman, David. The F/A-18 Hornet. (U. S. Warplanes Ser.). 48p. (gr. 5-8). 2009. 53.00 *(978-1-60854-596-4(2),* Rosen Reference) 2005. (Illus.). (YA). lib. bdg. 29.25 *(978-0-8239-3874-2(3))* Rosen Publishing Group, Inc., The.

Stark, William N. Mighty Military Aircraft. 2016. (Military Machines on Duty Ser.). (ENG., Illus.). 24p. (gr. 1-2). lib. bdg. 25.32 *(978-1-4914-8845-4(X),* First Facts) Capstone Press of Coughlan Cos.

Stone, Lynn M. A-10 Thunderbolt II. 2004. (Fighting Forces Ser.). (Illus.). 32p. (gr. 4-8). lib. bdg. *(978-1-59515-178-0(8))* Rourke Educational Media.

US Warplanes. 2005. (Illus.). (gr. 5-8). lib. bdg. 159.00 *(978-0-8239-4057-8(8))* Rosen Publishing Group, Inc., The.

Wood, Alix. Drone Operator, 1 vol., 1. 2014. (World's Coolest Jobs Ser.). (ENG.). 32p. (J). (gr. 3-6). 26.25 *(978-1-4777-6023-9(7),* PowerKids Pr.) Rosen Publishing Group, Inc., The.

—Drones, 01 vols., 1. 2016. (Today's High-Tech Weapons Ser.). (ENG.). 32p. (J). pap. 10.00 *(978-1-5081-4683-4(7),* PowerKids Pr.) Rosen Publishing Group, Inc., The.

Xtreme Military Aircraft Set 2. 2013. (Xtreme Military Aircraft Set 2 Ser.: 6). 32p. (J). (gr. 3-9). lib. bdg. 162.42 *(978-1-61783-684-8(2),* Abdo & Daughters) ABDO Publishing Co.

Zobel, Derek. A-10 Thunderbolts. 2008. (Military Machines Ser.). (ENG., Illus.). 24p. (J). (gr. 3-7). lib. bdg. 25.95 *(978-1-60014-201-7(X))* Bellwether Media.

—F-117A Nighthawks. 2008. (Military Machines Ser.). (ENG., Illus.). 24p. (J). (gr. 3-7). lib. bdg. 25.95 *(978-1-60014-221-5(4))* Bellwether Media.

—F-22 Raptors. 2008. (Military Machines Ser.). (ENG., Illus.). 24p. (YA). (gr. 3-7). lib. bdg. 25.95 *(978-1-60014-204-8(4))* Bellwether Media.

AIRPLANES—MODELS

Chandler, Matt, et al. Drones. 2017. (Drones Ser.). (ENG.). 32p. (gr. 3-4). 111.96 *(978-1-5157-3798-8(5),* Edge Bks.) Capstone Press of Coughlan Cos.

Collins, Francis. The Boys' Book of Model Aeroplanes: How to Build & Fly Them: with the Story of the Evolution of the Flying Machine. 2004. (Illus.). 308p. (YA). per. 16.95 *(978-0-9758914-3-8(X))* Gustav's Library.

—The Second Boys' Book of Model Aeroplanes. 2004. (Illus.). 262p. per. 16.95 *(978-0-9758914-4-5(8))* Gustav's Library.

Kinmont, Ritchie. Every Kid Needs Things That Fly, 1 vol. Casey, Robert, photos by. 2005. (ENG., Illus.). 136p. (J). pap. 14.95 *(978-1-58685-509-3(3),* 1241179) Gibbs Smith, Publisher.

Leavitt, Amie Jane. Experimental Drones. 2017. (Drones Ser.). (ENG., Illus.). 32p. (gr. 3-4). lib. bdg. 27.99 *(978-1-5157-3768-1(3),* Edge Bks.) Capstone Press of Coughlan Cos.

Mattern, Joanne. Remote Control Planes. 2015. (Rookie Read-About(tm) Science: How Things Work Ser.). (ENG.). 32p. (J). lib. bdg. 25.00 *(978-0-531-21369-8(2),* Children's Pr.) Scholastic Library Publishing.

Rauf, Don. Getting the Most Out of Makerspaces to Build Unmanned Aerial Vehicles. 2014. (Makerspaces Ser.). (Illus.). 64p. (J). (gr. 6-12). 32.95 *(978-1-4777-7827-2(6))* Rosen Publishing Group, Inc., The.

Rudy, Lisa Jo. Micro Spies: Spy Planes the Size of Birds! 2007. (24/7: Science Behind the Scenes Ser.). (ENG., Illus.). 64p. (J). (gr. 8-12). 29.00 *(978-0-531-12083-5(X),* Watts, Franklin) Scholastic Library Publishing.

Storey, Rita. How to Build Aircraft. 2017. (Illus.). 32p. (J). ***(978-0-7787-3384-3(X))*** Crabtree Publishing Co.

Stunt Planes. 2004. (Fantastic Fliers Ser.). (Illus.). 48p. (J). pap. *(978-1-84229-726-1(0))* Top That! Publishing PLC.

Supercool Fliers. 2004. (Fantastic Fliers Ser.). (Illus.). 48p. (J). pap. *(978-1-84229-729-2(5))* Top That! Publishing PLC.

AIRPLANES, NAVAL

see Airplanes, Military

AIRPLANES—OPERATION

see Airplanes—Piloting

AIRPLANES—PILOTING

Airline Pilot. 2008. (Virtual Apprentice Ser.). 64p. (gr. 4-9). 29.95 *(978-0-8160-6755-8(4),* Ferguson Publishing Co.) Facts On File, Inc.

Boothroyd, Jennifer. How Do Hang Gliders Work? 2013. (Lightning Bolt Books (tm) — How Flight Works). (ENG., Illus.). 32p. (gr. k-2). lib. bdg. 26.60 *(978-0-7613-8970-5(9))* Lerner Publishing Group.

Loveless, Antony. Fighter Pilots. 2009. (World's Most Dangerous Jobs Ser.). (ENG., Illus.). 32p. (J). (gr. 3-6). pap. *(978-0-7787-5110-6(4));* lib. bdg. *(978-0-7787-5096-3(5))* Crabtree Publishing Co.

Mattern, Joanne. Pilots. 2009. (Working Together Ser.). 24p. (gr. 1-2). 42.50 *(978-1-60854-832-3(5),* PowerKids Pr.) Rosen Publishing Group, Inc., The.

Minden, Cecilia & Minden-Zins, Mary. Pilots. 2014. (People in Our Community Ser.). (ENG.). 24p. (J). (gr. k-3). 27.07 *(978-1-62687-016-1(0),* 206806) Child's World, Inc., The.

Parks, Peggy J. Fighter Pilot. 2005. (Exploring Careers Ser.). (ENG., Illus.). 48p. (J). (gr. 4-8). lib. bdg. 29.15 *(978-0-7377-3079-1(X),* Kidhaven) Cengage Gale.

Perish, Patrick. Wilderness Rescue Pilot. 2015. (Dangerous Jobs Ser.). (ENG., Illus.). 24p. (J). (gr. 3-7). lib. bdg. 25.95 *(978-1-62617-199-2(8),* Torque Bks.) Bellwether Media.

Pilot's Flight Operating Instructions for P-47B, P-47C, P-47D & P-47G Airplanes. 2005. (YA). cd-rom 29.95 *(978-0-9742781-8-6(1))* Rhode, Steve Inc.

Rauf, Don & Vescia, Monique. Airline Pilot. 2008. (Virtual Apprentice Ser.). (Illus.). 64p. (gr. 4-9). pap. 9.95 *(978-0-8160-7549-2(2),* Checkmark Bks.) Facts On File, Inc.

Schorr, Titus. My Mother Is a Pilot, 01 vols., 1. 2016. (Rosen REAL Readers: Social Studies Nonfiction / Fiction: Family, Community, & the World Ser.). (ENG.). 12p. (J). pap. 6.33 *(978-1-5081-1731-5(4),* Rosen Classroom) Rosen Publishing Group, Inc., The.

Silverman, Buffy. How Do Jets Work? 2013. (Lightning Bolt Books (tm) — How Flight Works). (ENG., Illus.). 32p. (gr. k-2). lib. bdg. 26.60 *(978-0-7613-8967-5(9),* Lerner Pubns.) Lerner Publishing Group.

Tetrick, Byron. Choosing a Career as a Pilot. (World of Work Ser.). 64p. 2009. (gr. 5-5). 58.50 *(978-1-60854-325-0(0))* 2005. (Illus.). (YA). (gr. 7-12). lib. bdg. 31.95 *(978-0-8239-3571-0(X))* Rosen Publishing Group, Inc., The.

Thomas, William. Wilderness Rescue Pilot. 2010. (Benchmark Rockets: Dirty & Dangerous Jobs Ser.). 32p. (J). (gr. 3-6). 28.50 *(978-1-60870-180-3(8))* Marshall Cavendish Corp.

West, David. Fighter Pilots. Field, James, illus. 2008. (Graphic Careers Ser.). (ENG.). 48p. (gr. 5-8). per. 14.05 *(978-1-4042-1456-9(9));* (YA). lib. bdg. 31.95 *(978-1-4042-1455-2(0))* Rosen Publishing Group, Inc., The.

—Fighter Pilots. 2008. 52p. (gr. 5-8). pap. 29.25 *(978-1-4358-3785-0(1))* Rosen Publishing Group, Inc., The.

Wolfe, Hillary & Rice, William B. Blast off to Space Camp, 1 vol. 2nd rev. ed. 2014. (TIME for KIDS(r) Nonfiction Readers Ser.). (ENG., Illus.). 32p. (J). (gr. 3-3). pap. 25.96 *(978-1-4807-1082-5(2))* Shell Educational Publishing.

AIRPLANES—PILOTS

see Air Pilots

AIRPLANES—RACING

see Airplane Racing

AIRPLANES—TESTING

Hamilton, John. Test Pilot. 2015. 32p. pap. 27.07 *(978-1-62403-761-0(5))* ABDO Publishing Co.

Horn, Geoffrey M. Test Pilot. 2008. (Cool Careers: Adventure Careers Ser.). (Illus.). 32p. (gr. 5-8). pap. 10.50 *(978-0-8368-8891-1(X));* lib. bdg. 26.00 *(978-0-8368-8884-3(7))* Stevens, Gareth Publishing LLLP.

Loveless, Antony. Test Pilots. 2009. (World's Most Dangerous Jobs Ser.). (ENG., Illus.). 32p. (J). (gr. 3-6). pap. *(978-0-7787-5113-7(9));* lib. bdg. *(978-0-7787-5099-4(X))* Crabtree Publishing Co.

AIRPORTS

see also Air Bases

The Airport 2 packs: Individual Title. (Chiquilibros Ser.). (gr. -1-1). 12.00 *(978-0-7635-8537-2(8))* Rigby Education.

Brown, Lisa. The Airport Book. 2016. (ENG., Illus.). 40p. (J). 17.99 *(978-1-62672-091-6(8),* 9781626720916) Roaring Brook Pr.

Broyles, Matthew. U. S. Air Marshals. (Extreme Careers Ser.). 64p. 2009. (gr. 5-5). 58.50 *(978-1-61512-416-9(0),* Rosen Reference) 2007. (Illus.). (J). (gr. 3-7). lib. bdg. 31.95 *(978-1-4042-0942-8(5))* Rosen Publishing Group, Inc., The.

Daynes, Katie. Flip Flap Airport. 2009. (Flip Flap Board Bks). 13p. (J). (gr. -1). bds. 14.99 *(978-0-7945-2401-2(X),* Usborne) EDC Publishing.

Gish, Melissa. An Airport. 2003. 24p. (J). lib. bdg. 21.35 *(978-1-58340-322-8(1))* Black Rabbit Bks.

Goldsmith, Mike. The Airport. Daubney, Kate, illus. 2015. (I Explore Ser.). (ENG.). 12p. (J). (gr. -1-k). bds. 6.95 *(978-1-4549-1495-2(5))* Sterling Publishing Co., Inc.

Gonzales, Sharon, illus. Airport Explorers: 2008 Activity Book. 2008. 32p. (J). 6.95 *(978-0-9745294-2-4(7))* San Diego County Regional Airport Authority.

Haerens, Margaret. US Airport Security. Zott, Lynn, ed. 2013. (Opposing Viewpoints Ser.). (ENG., Illus.). 224p. (gr. 10-12). pap. 33.80 *(978-0-7377-6041-5(9),* Greenhaven Pr., Inc.) Cengage Gale.

Harrison, Sarah. A Day at an Airport. 2008. (Time Goes By Ser.). (ENG.). (gr. k-3). pap. 39.62 *(978-0-7613-4709-5(7));* (Illus.). 24p. (J). lib. bdg. 22.60 *(978-1-58013-551-1(X))* Lerner Publishing Group.

Hill, Mary. Signs at the Airport. 2003. (Signs in My World Ser.). (ENG., Illus.). 24p. (J). 19.00 *(978-0-516-24272-9(5));* (gr. -1-2). pap. 4.95 *(978-0-516-24364-1(0))* Scholastic Library Publishing. (Children's Pr.).

Hutchings, Amy. What Happens at an Airport? 2009. (Where People Work Ser.). 24p. (J). (gr. -1-3). lib. bdg. 22.00 *(978-1-4339-0072-3(6),* Weekly Reader Leveled Readers) Stevens, Gareth Publishing LLLP.

—What Happens at an Airport? (¿Qué pasa en un Aeropuerto?) 2009. (Where People Work Ser.). 24p. (gr. -1-3). pap. 8.15 *(978-1-4339-0136-2(6),* Weekly Reader Leveled Readers) Stevens, Gareth Publishing LLLP.

Hutchings, Amy & Nations, Susan. What Happens at an Airport? (?¿Qué pasa en un Aeropuerto?) 2009. (Where People Work/Dónde Trabaja la Gente? Ser.). (SPA & ENG.). 24p. (gr. -1-3). pap. 8.15 *(978-1-4339-0144-7(7),* Weekly Reader Leveled Readers) Stevens, Gareth Publishing LLLP.

—What Happens at an Airport?/¿Qué Pasa en un Aeropuerto? 2009. (Where People Work/Dónde Trabaja la Gente? Ser.). (SPA & ENG.). 24p. (J). (gr. -1-3). lib. bdg. 22.00 *(978-1-4339-0080-8(7),* Weekly Reader Leveled Readers) Stevens, Gareth Publishing LLLP.

Jones, Rob Lloyd. Look Inside an Airport. rev. ed. 2012. (Look Inside Board Bks). 14p. (J). ring bd. 15.99 *(978-0-7945-3234-5(9),* Usborne) EDC Publishing.

Martin, Isabel. An Airport Field Trip. 2015. (Let's Take a Field Trip Ser.). (ENG.). 24p. (gr. k-1). pap. 6.95 *(978-1-4914-2313-4(7),* Pebble Plus) Capstone Press of Coughlan Cos.

Mullins, Matt. How Did They Build That? Airport. 2009. (Community Connections: How Did They Build That? Ser.). (ENG.). 24p. (gr. 2-5). lib. bdg. 25.64 *(978-1-60279-486-3(3),* 200253) Cherry Lake Publishing.

Parker, Steve & Parker, Vic. My First Trip on an Airplane, 1 vol. 2011. (Growing Up Ser.). (ENG.). 24p. (gr. k-2). 23.32 *(978-1-4329-4801-6(6));* pap. 6.79 *(978-1-4329-4811-5(3))* Heinemann-Raintree. (Heinemann Read & Learn).

Parragon Publishing Staff. Busy Day at the Airport. (Busy Books Large Ser.). *(978-1-4054-7873-1(X))* Parragon, Inc.

Priddy, Roger. Airport. rev. ed. 2016. (ENG., Illus.). 14p. (J). bds. 9.99 *(978-0-312-52170-7(7),* 9780312521707, Priddy Bks.) St. Martin's Pr.

—Playtown: Airport. 2015. (Playtown Ser.). (ENG., Illus.). 16p. (J). (gr. -1-k). bds. 12.99 *(978-0-312-51803-5(X),* 9780312518035, Priddy Bks.) St. Martin's Pr.

Ready for School: Individual Title Six-Packs. (gr. 1-2). 22.00 *(978-0-7635-9188-5(2))* Rigby Education.

Rhatigan, Joe. Get a Job at the Airport. 2016. (Bright Futures Press: Get a Job Ser.). (ENG., Illus.). 32p. (J). (gr. 4-6). 29.93 *(978-1-63471-903-2(4),* 208933) Cherry Lake Publishing.

Roby, Cynthia. Discovering STEM at the Airport. 2015. (STEM in the Real World Ser.). (ENG., Illus.). 24p. (J). (gr. 2-3). pap. 8.25 *(978-1-4994-0907-9(9),* PowerKids Pr.) Rosen Publishing Group, Inc., The.

Sarver, Amy. Science at the Airport. 2007. (Reading Expeditions Ser.). (ENG., Illus.). 24p. (J). pap. 14.95 *(978-0-7922-4568-1(7))* CENGAGE Learning.

Sermons, Faye. My Granma Lives at the Airport. 2012. 20p. pap. 12.00 *(978-1-4490-1893-1(9))* AuthorHouse.

Smith, S. & Robins, W. Airport Sticker Book. 2015. (First Sticker Bks.). (ENG.). 16+8p. (J). pap. 6.99 *(978-0-7945-3566-7(6),* Usborne) EDC Publishing.

Smith, Sian. Machines at the Airport, 1 vol. 2013. (Machines at Work Ser.). (ENG., Illus.). 24p. (gr. 1-2). pap. 6.95 *(978-1-4329-7504-3(8));* 23.32 *(978-1-4329-7499-2(8))* Heinemann-Raintree. (Heinemann Read & Learn).

Souter, Janet. Air Marshal: And Careers in Transportation Security. 2006. (Homeland Security & Counterterrorism Careers Ser.). (Illus.). 128p. (J). (gr. 6). lib. bdg. 33.27 *(978-0-7660-2647-6(7))* Enslow Pubs., Inc.

Steffora, Tracey. Math at the Airport, 1 vol. 2013. (Math on the Job Ser.). (ENG., Illus.). 24p. (gr. k-2). pap. 6.29 *(978-1-4329-7158-8(1));* lib. bdg. 22.65 *(978-1-4329-7151-9(4))* Heinemann-Raintree. (Acorn).

Tam-McMillan, Gianni. Your Journey Through the Airport. 2012. 28p. pap. 21.99 *(978-1-4797-2112-2(3))* Xlibris Corp.

White, Nancy. Aviation Firefighters. 2014. (Fire Fight! the Bravest Ser.). 32p. (J). (gr. 2-7). lib. bdg. 26.60 *(978-1-62724-096-3(9))* Bearport Publishing Co., Inc.

Willis, John. Airport. 2016. (J). ***(978-1-5105-1877-3(0))*** SmartBook Media, Inc.

Wright, John. The U. S. Transportation Security Administration. 2004. (Rescue & Prevention Ser.). (Illus.). 96p. (YA). (gr. 7-18). lib. bdg. 22.95 *(978-1-59084-412-0(2))* Mason Crest.

Zott, Lynn, ed. US Airport Security. 2013. (Opposing Viewpoints Ser.). (ENG., Illus.). 240p. (gr. 10-12). lib. bdg. 42.95 *(978-0-7377-6040-8(0),* Greenhaven Pr., Inc.) Cengage Gale.

AIRSHIPS

see also Aeronautics; Balloons

Benoit, Peter. The Hindenburg Disaster. 2011. (Illus.). 48p. (J). pap. *(978-0-531-29025-5(5))* Children's Pr., Ltd.

—The Hindenburg Disaster. 2011. (True Book(tm), A — Disasters Ser.). (ENG.). 48p. (J). (gr. 3-5). lib. bdg. 31.00 *(978-0-531-20626-3(2));* pap. 6.95 *(978-0-531-28995-2(8))* Scholastic Library Publishing. (Children's Pr.).

Bowman, Chris. The Hindenburg Disaster. 2014. (Disaster Stories Ser.). (ENG., Illus.). 24p. (J). (gr. 3-8). 29.95 *(978-1-62617-153-4(X),* Black Sheep) Bellwether Media.

Burgan, Michael. The Hindenburg in Flames: How a Photograph Marked the End of the Airship. 2016. (Captured World History Ser.). (ENG.). 64p. (gr. 5-7). lib. bdg. 34.65 *(978-0-7565-5441-5(1),* CPB Grades 4-8) Compass Point Bks.

Doeden, Matt. The Hindenburg Disaster, 1 vol. Erwin, Steve et al, illus. 2006. (Disasters in History Ser.). (ENG.). 32p. (gr. 3-4). 30.65 *(978-0-7368-5481-8(9),* Graphic Library) Capstone Press of Coughlan Cos.

Dykema, Owen Wood & Dykema, Owen W., eds. Warbird History Part II: Fighter, Attack & Support Aircraft of WWII. 2003. 190p. per. 7.00 *(978-0-9701538-1-4(3))* Dykema Publishing Co.

Feigenbaum, Aaron. The Hindenburg Disaster. 2007. (Code Red Ser.). (Illus.). 32p. (YA). (gr. 2-5). lib. bdg. 25.27 *(978-1-59716-361-3(9))* Bearport Publishing Co., Inc.

Graham, Ian. Be on the Hindenburg! A Transatlantic Trip You'd Rather Skip. 2009. (You Wouldn't Want to Ser.). (ENG., Illus.). 32p. (J). (gr. 3-18). 29.00 *(978-0-531-20823-6(0),* Watts, Franklin) Scholastic Library Publishing.

—You Wouldn't Want to Be on the Hindenburg! A Transatlantic Trip You'd Rather Skip. 2009. (You Wouldn't Want to... Ser.). (ENG., Illus.). 32p. (J). (gr. 3-18). pap. 9.95 *(978-0-531-21049-9(9),* Children's Pr.) Scholastic Library Publishing.

Icanberry, Mark & Mount, Arthur. Picnic on a Cloud. 2010. (Look, Learn & Do Ser.). (Illus.). 48p. (J). (gr. 3-5). 14.95 *(978-1-893327-00-9(0))* Look, Learn & Do Pubns.

Lace, William W. The Hindenburg Disaster Of 1937. 2008. (Great Historic Disasters Ser.). (Illus.). 120p. (gr. 5-8). lib. bdg. 35.00 *(978-0-7910-9739-7(0),* Chelsea Hse.) Facts On File, Inc.

Nagelhout, Ryan. The Hindenburg Disaster. 2015. (Doomed! Ser.). (ENG., Illus.). 32p. (J). (gr. 4-5). 26.60 *(978-1-4824-2938-1(1))* Stevens, Gareth Publishing LLLP.

Nittinger, Sharon. How Does It Fly? Blimp. 2011. (Community Connections: How Does It Fly? Ser.). (ENG.). 24p. (gr. 2-5). lib. bdg. 25.64 *(978-1-61080-071-6(0),* 201068) Cherry Lake Publishing.

O'Brien, Patrick. The Hindenburg. Date not set. (J). pap. 6.95 *(978-0-8050-7264-8(0),* Holt, Henry & Co. Bks. For Young Readers) Holt, Henry & Co.

Otfinoski, Steven. The Hindenburg Explosion: Core Events of a Disaster in the Air, 1 vol. 2014. (What Went Wrong? Ser.). (ENG.). 32p. (gr. 3-4). pap. 7.95 *(978-1-4765-5133-3(2));* lib. bdg. 27.32 *(978-1-4765-4184-6(1))* Capstone Press of Coughlan Cos.

Pascal, Janet B. What Was the Hindenburg? Groff, David & McVeigh, Kevin, illus. 2014. (What Was? Ser.). (ENG.). 112p. (J). (gr. 3-7). 5.99 *(978-0-448-48119-7(7),* Penguin Workshop) Penguin Young Readers Group.

—What Was the Hindenburg? 2014. (What Was... ? Ser.). lib. bdg. 16.00 *(978-0-606-36186-6(3))* Turtleback Bks.

Sherman, Jill. The Hindenburg Disaster, 1 vol. 2010. (Essential Events Set 4 Ser.). (ENG.). 112p. (J). (gr. 6-12). lib. bdg. 35.64 *(978-1-60453-944-8(5))* ABDO Publishing Co.

Verstraete, Larry. Surviving the Hindenburg. 2012. (ENG., Illus.). 40p. (J). (gr. k-5). 16.95 *(978-1-58536-787-0(7))* Sleeping Bear Pr.

AKHENATEN, KING OF EGYPT

Villa, Jaime Valencia. Akhenatón. 2005. (SPA.). 132p. (YA). *(978-958-30-1981-4(X))* Panamericana Editorial.

ALABAMA

Aretha, David. The Story of Rosa Parks & the Montgomery Bus Boycott in Photographs. 2014. (Story of the Civil Rights Movement in Photographs Ser.). 48p. (J). pap. 8.95 *(978-1-4644-0411-5(9))* Enslow Pubs., Inc.

—The Story of the Birmingham Civil Rights Movement in Photographs. 2014. (Story of the Civil Rights Movement in Photographs Ser.). 48p. (J). lib. bdg. 25.27 *(978-0-7660-4237-7(5))* Enslow Pubs., Inc.

—The Story of the Selma Voting Rights Marches in Photographs. 2014. (Story of the Civil Rights Movement in Photographs Ser.). 48p. (J). lib. bdg. 25.27 *(978-0-7660-4239-1(1))* Enslow Pubs., Inc.

Ashby, Ruth. Rosa Parks: Freedom Rider. 2008. (Sterling Biographies(r) Ser.). (ENG., Illus.). 128p. (J). (gr. 5). pap. 5.95 *(978-1-4027-4865-3(5))* Sterling Publishing Co., Inc.

Asim, Jabari. Preaching to the Chickens: The Story of Young John Lewis. Lewis, E. B., illus. 2016. (ENG.). 32p. (J). (gr. k-3). 17.99 *(978-0-399-16856-7(7),* Nancy Paulsen Books) Penguin Young Readers Group.

Bailey, Tom. Raphael Semmes: Commander of the Alabama. 2011. (Illus.). 120p. (J). *(978-1-59421-062-4(4))* Seacoast Publishing, Inc.

—Red Eagle: Legendary Creek Warrior. 2009. (Illus.). 104p. (J). pap. *(978-1-59421-047-1(0))* Seacoast Publishing, Inc.

Bass, Hester. Seeds of Freedom: The Peaceful Integration of Huntsville, Alabama. Lewis, E. B., illus. 2015. (ENG.). 32p. (J). (gr. k-3). 16.99 *(978-0-7636-6919-5(9))* Candlewick Pr.

Bednar, Chuck. Rosa Parks. 2010. (Transcending Race in America Ser.). (Illus.). 64p. (YA). (gr. 5-18). lib. bdg. 22.95 *(978-1-4222-1615-6(2))* Mason Crest.

Blackshear, Sue, illus. Tuskaloosa Tales: Stories of Tuscaloosa & Its People. 2011. 95p. (J). *(978-0-9801113-2-3(3))* Look Again Pr., LLC.

Brown, Dottie. Alabama. 2012. (J). lib. bdg. 25.26 *(978-0-7613-4186-4(2),* Lerner Pubns.) Lerner Publishing Group.

Brown, Vanessa. Alabama. (Bilingual Library of the United States of America Ser.). 32p. 2009. (gr. 2-2). 47.90 *(978-1-60853-341-1(7),* Editorial Buenas Letras) 2005. (ENG & SPA., Illus.). (J). (gr. 3-6). lib. bdg. 25.25 *(978-1-4042-3065-1(3))* Rosen Publishing Group, Inc., The.

Cates, David. The Scottsboro Boys, 1 vol. 2012. (Essential Events Set 8 Ser.). (ENG.). 112p. (J). (gr. 6-12). lib. bdg. 35.64 *(978-1-61783-310-6(X))* ABDO Publishing Co.

Crane, Carol. Y Is for Yellowhammer: An Alabama Alphabet. Bum, Ted, illus. 2003. (Discover America State by State Ser.). (ENG.). 40p. (J). 17.95 *(978-1-58536-118-2(6))* Sleeping Bear Pr.

Crewe, Sabrina & Uschan, Michael V. The Scottsboro Case. 2004. (Events That Shaped America Ser.). (Illus.). 32p. (gr. 3-6). lib. bdg. 26.00 *(978-0-8368-3407-9(0),* Gareth Stevens Learning Library) Stevens, Gareth Publishing LLLP.

Durrie, Karen. Alabama: The Yellowhammer State. 2012. (J). *(978-1-61913-321-1(0));* pap. *(978-1-61913-322-8(9))* Weigl Pubs., Inc.

Feeney, Kathy. Alabama. 2008. (ENG.). 80p. (J). pap. 7.95 *(978-0-531-20800-7(1),* Children's Pr.) Scholastic Library Publishing.

Gamble, Adam & Jasper, Mark. Good Night Alabama. Veno, Joe, illus. 2015. (Good Night Our World Ser.). (ENG.). 20p. (J). (— 1). bds. 9.95 *(978-1-60219-220-1(0))* Good Night Bks.

Gosman, Gillian. Rosa Parks. 2011. (Life Stories Ser.). (Illus.). 24p. (J). pap. 8.25 *(978-1-4488-2757-2(4),* PowerKids Pr.); (ENG & SPA., (gr. 1-4). lib. bdg. 22.60 *(978-1-4488-3218-7(7));* (gr. 1-4). lib. bdg. 22.60 *(978-1-4488-2584-4(9),* PowerKids Pr.) Rosen Publishing Group, Inc., The.

Hart, Joyce. Alabama. 2014. (J). lib. bdg. *(978-1-62712-221-4(4))* Cavendish Square Publishing.

—Alabama. 2007. (It's My State! Ser.). (Illus.). 80p. (J). (gr. 4-7). lib. bdg. 29.93 *(978-0-7614-1925-9(X),* Benchmark Bks.) Marshall Cavendish Corp.

Hart, Joyce & Bass, Elissa. Alabama. 2016. (ENG., Illus.). 80p. (J). 34.21 *(978-1-62713-235-0(X))* Cavendish Square Publishing.

Heos, Bridget. Alabama: Past & Present. 2010. (United States: Past & Present Ser.). (ENG., Illus.). 48p. (J). pap. 11.75 *(978-1-4358-8486-1(8));* lib. bdg. 29.25 *(978-1-4358-3518-4(2))* Rosen Publishing Group, Inc., The. (Rosen Reference).

Hurt, Avery Elizabeth. Rosa Parks: Civil Rights Activist. 2017. (J). ***(978-1-5383-8105-2(2))*** Rosen Publishing Group, Inc., The.

Jazynka, Kitson. National Geographic Readers: Rosa Parks. 2015. (Readers Bios Ser.). (ENG., Illus.). 32p. (J). (gr. k-3). pap. 3.99 *(978-1-4263-2141-2(4),* National Geographic Children's Bks.) National Geographic Society.

Jerome, Kate B. Lucky to Live in Alabama. 2017. (Arcadia Kids Ser.). (ENG., Illus.). 32p. (J). 16.99 ***(978-0-7385-2789-5(0))*** Arcadia Publishing.

Johnston, Lissa Jones. Alabama. 2006. (Portraits of the States Ser.). (Illus.). 32p. (gr. 2-6). pap. 10.50

(978-0-8368-4678-2(8)); lib. bdg. 26.00 *(978-0-8368-4659-1(1))* Stevens, Gareth Publishing LLLP. (Gareth Stevens Learning Library).

Kallio, Jamie. What's Great about Alabama? 2014. (Our Great States Ser.). (ENG., 32p. (gr. 2-5). Illus.). pap. 7.95 *(978-1-4677-4531-4(6))*; lib. bdg. 26.60 *(978-1-4677-3343-4(1)*, Lerner Pubns.) Lerner Publishing Group.

Kimmel, Allison Crotzer. The Montgomery Bus Boycott. 2015. (We Shall Overcome Ser.). (ENG.). 32p. (gr. 3-4). lib. bdg. 27.32 *(978-1-4914-2043-0(X))* Capstone Press of Coughlan Cos.

Kirchner, Jason. Alabama. 2016. (States Ser.). (ENG., Illus.). 32p. (gr. 3-4). lib. bdg. 27.32 *(978-1-5157-0386-0(X))* Next Page Pr., The.

Kjelle, Marylou Morano. Alabama: A MyReportLinks. Com Book. 2003. (States Ser.). (Illus.). 48p. (J). lib. bdg. 25.26 *(978-0-7660-5151-5(X)*, MyReportLinks.com Bks.) Enslow Pubs., Inc.

Levinson, Cynthia. We've Got a Job: The 1963 Birmingham Children's March, 1 vol. 2015. (ENG.). 180p. (gr. 5-9). pap. 13.95 *(978-1-56145-844-8(9))* Peachtree Pubs.

—The Youngest Marcher: The Story of a Young Civil Rights Activist. Brantley-Newton, Vanessa, illus. 2017. (ENG.). 40p. (J). (gr. k-5). 17.99 *(978-1-4814-0070-1(3))* Simon & Schuster, Inc.

Lusted, Marcia Amidon. Alabama: The Heart of Dixie. 2010. (Our Amazing States Ser.). (Illus.). 24p. (J). pap. 8.25 *(978-1-4358-9792-2(7))*; lib. bdg. 22.60 *(978-1-4358-9349-8(2))* Rosen Publishing Group, Inc., The. (PowerKids Pr.).

Marsh, Carole. Alabama Current Events Projects: 30 Cool, Activities, Crafts, Experiments & More for Kids to Do to Learn about Your State! 2003. (Alabama Experience Ser.). 32p. (gr. k-8). pap. 5.95 *(978-0-635-02020-8(3)*, Marsh, Carole Bks.) Gallopade International.

—Alabama Geography Projects: 30 Cool, Activities, Crafts, Experiments & More for Kids to Do to Learn about Your State! 2003. (Alabama Experience Ser.). 32p. (gr. k-5). pap. 5.95 *(978-0-635-01820-5(9)*, Marsh, Carole Bks.) Gallopade International.

—Alabama Government Projects: 30 Cool, Activities, Crafts, Experiments & More for Kids to Do to Learn about Your State! 2003. (Alabama Experience Ser.). 32p. (gr. k-5). pap. 5.95 *(978-0-635-01920-2(5)*, Marsh, Carole Bks.) Gallopade International.

—Alabama History Projects: 30 Cool, Activities, Crafts, Experiments & More for Kids to Do to Learn about Your State! 2003. (Alabama Experience Ser.). 32p. (gr. k-5). pap. 5.95 *(978-0-635-01770-3(9)*, Marsh, Carole Bks.) Gallopade International.

—Alabama Symbols & Facts Projects: 30 Cool, Activities, Crafts, Experiments & More for Kids to Do to Learn about Your State! 2003. (Alabama Experience Ser.). 32p. (gr. k-5). pap. 5.95 *(978-0-635-01869-4(1)*, Marsh, Carole Bks.) Gallopade International.

—Exploring Alabama Through Project-Based Learning. 2016. (Alabama Experience Ser.). (ENG.). (J). pap. 9.99 *(978-0-635-12325-1(8))* Gallopade International.

Mayer, Robert H. When the Children Marched: The Birmingham Civil Rights Movement. 2008. (Prime (Middle/Senior) Ser.). (Illus.). 176p. (J). (gr. 3-7). lib. bdg. 35.94 *(978-0-7660-2930-9(1))* Enslow Pubs., Inc.

McCormick, Anita Louise. Rosa Parks & the Montgomery Bus Boycott. 2017. (J). pap. ***(978-1-5383-8062-8(5))*** Rosen Publishing Group, Inc., The.

Miller, Jake. The March from Selma to Montgomery: African Americans Demand the Vote. 2009. (Library of the Civil Rights Movement Ser.). 24p. (gr. 3-3). 42.50 *(978-1-60853-894-2(X)*, PowerKids Pr.) Rosen Publishing Group, Inc., The.

Morretta, Alison. Rosa Parks & Civil Disobedience. 2016. (Primary Sources of the Civil Rights Movement Ser.). (Illus.). 64p. (J). (gr. 6-6). 34.21 *(978-1-5026-1870-2(2))* Cavendish Square Publishing.

Murray, Julie. Alabama, 1 vol. 2006. (Buddy Book Ser.). (ENG., Illus.). 32p. (gr. k-4). 27.07 *(978-1-59197-660-8(X)*, Buddy Bks.) ABDO Publishing Co.

Orr, Tamra. What's So Great about the Tuskegee Airmen. 2009. (What's So Great About... ? Ser.). 32p. (J). (gr. 2-4). lib. bdg. 25.70 *(978-1-58415-832-5(8))* Mitchell Lane Pubs., Inc.

Parker, Janice. Alabama. 2011. (Guide to American States Ser.). (Illus.). 48p. (YA). (gr. 3-6). 29.99 *(978-1-61690-773-0(8))*; (J). 29.99 *(978-1-61690-448-7(8))* Weigl Pubs., Inc.

—Alabama: The Heart of Dixie. 2016. (J). *(978-1-5105-0647-3(0))* SmartBook Media, Inc.

—Alabama: The Heart of Dixie. 2016. (J). *(978-1-4896-4815-0(1))* Weigl Pubs., Inc.

Pierce, Alan. Montgomery Bus Boycott, 1 vol. 2005. (American Moments Ser.). (ENG., Illus.). 48p. (gr. 4-8). 27.07 *(978-1-59197-935-7(8)*, Abdo & Daughters) ABDO Publishing Co.

Quasha, J. How to Draw Alabama's Sights & Symbols. 2009. (Kid's Guide to Drawing America Ser.). 32p. (gr. k-k). 50.50 *(978-1-61511-043-8(7)*, PowerKids Pr.) Rosen Publishing Group, Inc., The.

Ruiz, Rachel. When Rosa Parks Went Fishing. Fedele, Chiara, illus. 2017. (Leaders Doing Headstands Ser.). (ENG.). 32p. (gr. 2-3). lib. bdg. 27.99 ***(978-1-5158-1574-7(9))*** Picture Window Bks.

Shirley, David & Hart, Joyce. Alabama. 2nd rev. ed. 2008. (Celebrate the States Ser.). 144p. (gr. 6-18). lib. bdg. 42.79 *(978-0-7614-3397-2(X)*, Benchmark Bks.) Marshall Cavendish Corp.

Shofner, Shawndra. Alabama. 2008. (This Land Called America Ser.). 32p. (YA). (gr. 3-6). 22.95 *(978-1-58341-626-6(9))* Creative Co., The.

Smith, Rich. Alabama, 1 vol. 2009. (United States Ser.). (ENG., Illus.). 48p. (YA). (gr. 2-5). 27.07 *(978-1-60453-636-2(5))* ABDO Publishing Co.

Somervill, Barbara A. Alabama. 2014. (America the Beautiful Ser.: 3). (ENG.). 144p. (J). lib. bdg. 40.00 *(978-0-531-24875-1(5))* Scholastic Library Publishing.

Sullivan, E. J. A Is for Alabama. Eldredge, Ernie, illus. 2006. (State Alphabet Bks.). 24p. (J). *(978-1-58173-523-9(5))* Sweetwater Pr.

Summy, Rachel C. Good Night Sweet Home. 2011. 28p. pap. 13.59 *(978-1-4634-0164-1(7))* AuthorHouse.

Tieck, Sarah. Alabama, 1 vol. 2012. (Explore the United States Ser.). (ENG.). 32p. (J). (gr. 2-5). 28.50 *(978-1-61783-339-7(8))* ABDO Publishing Co.

Turnipseed, Nancy. Dixie's Big Heart: A Story about Alabama, 1 vol. Doucet, Bob, illus. 2011. (Fact & Fable: State Stories Set 3 Ser.). (ENG.). 24p. (J). (gr. -1-2). lib. bdg. 25.65 *(978-1-61714-680-0(3))* ABDO Publishing Co.

Vaughn, Wally G. & Davis, Mattie Campbell, eds. The Selma Campaign, 1963-1965: The Decisive Battle of the Civil Rights Movement. 2006. (ENG., Illus.). 244p. pap. 19.95 *(978-0-912469-44-7(7))* Majority Pr., The.

Yeager, Alice. George C. Wallace: Alabama Political Power. 2003. (Alabama Roots Biography Ser.). (Illus.). 104p. (J). pap. *(978-1-59421-003-7(9))* Seacoast Publishing, Inc.

—Lurleen B. Wallace: Alabama's First Woman Governor. 2003. (Alabama Roots Biography Ser.). (ENG., Illus.). 104p. (J). pap. 7.95 *(978-1-59421-002-0(0))* Seacoast Publishing, Inc.

Zangas, Sherri. A Is for Alabama: Roll Tide Roll. Williams, Tim, illus. 2009. (J). lib. bdg. 17.95 *(978-0-692-00093-9(3))* Mascot Bks., Inc.

Ziff, John. Gulf States: Alabama, Louisiana, Mississippi, Vol. 19. 2015. (Let's Explore the States Ser.). (Illus.). 64p. (J). (gr. 5). 23.95 *(978-1-4222-3324-5(3))* Mason Crest.

ALABAMA—FICTION

Armistead, John & Gregory, Fran. The $66 Summer: A Novel of the Segregated South. 2nd ed. 2006. (Milkweed Prize for Children's Literature Ser.). (ENG., Illus.). 240p. (J). (gr. 3-8). reprint ed. per. 8.00 *(978-1-57131-663-9(9))* Milkweed Editions.

Banks, Sara Harrell. The Everlasting Now, 1 vol. 2010. (ENG.). 168p. (J). (gr. 3-7). 15.95 *(978-1-56145-525-6(3)*, Peachtree Junior) Peachtree Pubs.

Beasley, Kate. Gertie's Leap to Greatness. Tamaki, Jillian, illus. 2016. (ENG.). 256p. (J). 16.99 *(978-0-374-30261-0(8)*, 9780374302610, Farrar, Straus & Giroux (BYR)) Farrar, Straus & Giroux.

Belisle, Barbara J. The Red Hills of Alabama. 2010. 36p. 15.49 *(978-1-4490-9848-3(7))* AuthorHouse.

Butler, Darren J. The Secret of Crybaby Hollow. 2004. (YA). mass mkt. 6.99 *(978-0-9753367-5-5(4))* Onstage Publishing, LLC.

Campbell, Isaiah. The Struggles of Johnny Cannon. 2015. 322p. (J). pap. *(978-1-4814-2632-9(X)*, Simon & Schuster Bks. For Young Readers) Simon & Schuster Bks. For Young Readers.

Collard, Sneed B., III. Double Eagle, 1 vol. 2011. (ENG.). 256p. pap. 7.95 *(978-1-56145-599-7(7)*, Peachtree Junior) Peachtree Pubs.

Collier, Kristi. Jericho Walls. 2007. (ENG.). 224p. (YA). (gr. 4-9). pap. 10.99 *(978-0-8050-8184-8(4)*, 9780805081848, Holt, Henry & Co. Bks. For Young Readers) Holt, Henry & Co.

Cottrell, Laura. Introducing: Honey Gem Sheasby, 1 vol. 2010. 48p. pap. 16.95 *(978-1-4489-7874-8(2))* America Star Bks.

Counts, Monika, illus. Alabama Countdown to Touchdown. 2010. (Countdown to Touchdown Ser.). 20p. (J). 14.95 *(978-1-61524-080-7(2)*, Intervisual/Piggy Toes) Bendon, Inc.

Curtis, Christopher Paul. The Watsons Go to Birmingham 1963. 210p. (YA). (gr. 5-18). pap. 5.50 *(978-0-8072-8336-3(3))*; 2004. (J). (gr. 4-18). pap. 38.00 incl. audio *(978-0-8072-8335-6(5)*, YA166SP) Random Hse. Audio Publishing Group. (Listening Library).

Daniels, Darla. Carrie Goes Camping. 2011. 24p. pap. 16.95 *(978-1-4626-0642-9(3))* America Star Bks.

Davis, Tanita S. Mare's War. 2011. (ENG.). 352p. (YA). (gr. 7). pap. 9.99 *(978-0-375-85077-6(5)*, Knopf Bks. for Young Readers) Random Hse. Children's Bks.

Dion, Elayne. The Brass Button. 2008. 72p. pap. 9.95 *(978-0-557-01210-7(4))* Lulu Pr., Inc.

Dunagan, Ted M. Secret of the Satilfa. 2010. (ENG.). 208p. (J). (gr. 3-18). 21.95 *(978-1-58838-249-8(4)*, NewSouth Bks.) NewSouth, Inc.

—A Yellow Watermelon. 2014. (ENG.). 240p. (J). pap. 17.95 *(978-1-58838-301-3(6)*, NewSouth Bks.) NewSouth, Inc.

Duncan Gurley, Ann. Esbe's Halo. 2009. 108p. (J). pap. 15.95 *(978-1-4327-3453-4(9))* Outskirts Pr., Inc.

Echols, Jennifer. Going Too Far. 2009. (ENG.). 256p. pap. 16.99 *(978-1-4165-7173-5(6)*, MTV Bks.) MTV Books.

Garris, Rebekah. Whither Thou Goest, I Will Go. 2005. pap. 24.95 *(978-1-4137-8823-5(8))* PublishAmerica, Inc.

Glines, Abbi. Breathe. 2013. (Sea Breeze Ser.). (ENG., Illus.). 352p. (YA). (gr. 11). 17.99 *(978-1-4424-8870-0(0))*; pap. 9.99 *(978-1-4424-8869-4(7))* Simon Pulse. (Simon Pulse).

—Breathe. 2011. 166p. (gr. 8-12). pap. 9.99 *(978-1-61798-004-6(8))* Wild Child Publishing.

—Just for Now. 2013. (Sea Breeze Ser.). (ENG., Illus.). 336p. (YA). (gr. 11). 17.99 *(978-1-4424-8861-8(1))*; pap. 9.99 *(978-1-4424-8860-1(3))* Simon Pulse. (Simon Pulse).

—Misbehaving. 2014. (Sea Breeze Ser.). (ENG., Illus.). 352p. (YA). (gr. 11). 17.99 *(978-1-4814-0674-1(4))*; pap. 11.99 *(978-1-4814-0673-4(6))* Simon Pulse. (Simon Pulse).

—The Sea Breeze Collection: Breathe; Because of Low; While It Lasts; Just for Now. 2013. (Sea Breeze Ser.). (ENG., Illus.). 1312p. (YA). (gr. 11-11). pap. 39.99 *(978-1-4424-9606-8(8)*, Simon Pulse) Simon Pulse.

—Under the Lights. 2016. (Field Party Ser.: 2). (ENG., Illus.). 336p. (YA). (gr. 9). 17.99 *(978-1-4814-3889-6(1)*, Simon Pulse) Simon Pulse.

Golden, Laura. Every Day After. 2013. (ENG.). 224p. (J). (gr. 4-7). 15.99 *(978-0-385-74326-6(2)*, Delacorte Bks. for Young Readers) Random Hse. Children's Bks.

Green, John. Looking for Alaska. 2009. 11.04 *(978-0-7848-1838-1(X)*, Everbind) Marco Bk. Co.

—Looking for Alaska. 2014. *(978-0-525-42728-5(7)*, Dutton Adult) 2006. 20.00 *(978-0-7569-6726-0(0))* Penguin Publishing Group.

—Looking for Alaska. (ENG.). (YA). 2006. 256p. (gr. 9-18). pap. 10.99 *(978-0-14-240251-1(6)*, Speak) 2005. 160p. (gr. 8-12). 18.99 *(978-0-525-47506-4(0)*, Dutton Books for Young Readers) 10th anniv. ed. 2015. 368p. (gr. 9). 19.99 *(978-0-525-42802-2(X)*, Dutton Books for Young Readers) Penguin Young Readers Group.

—Looking for Alaska. l.t. ed. 2016. (ENG.). pap. 13.99 *(978-1-59413-982-6(2)*, Large Print Pr.) Thorndike Pr.

—Looking for Alaska. 2006. 221p. (gr. 7-12). lib. bdg. 20.85 *(978-1-4177-2915-9(5)*, Turtleback) Turtleback Bks.

Hanna, James Milton, Sr. Once upon a Time in the South. l.t. ed. 2004. (Illus.). 235p. per. 12.95 *(978-1-930052-15-4(4))* Cherokee Bks.

Hardegree, Maureen. Haint She Sweet. 2013. 206p. pap. 12.95 *(978-1-61194-325-2(6)*, Bell Bridge Bks.) BelleBks., Inc.

Harrington, Janice N. Catching a Story Fish. 2016. (ENG.). 224p. (J). (gr. 2-7). 17.95 *(978-1-62979-429-7(5)*, Wordsong) Boyds Mills Pr.

Harris, Rita & Long, Paul. The 19 Cats of Alabama. 2004. (ENG.). 35p. 24.95 *(978-1-4137-3006-7(X))* America Star Bks.

Herren, Greg. Dark Tide. 2014. (ENG.). 264p. (J). (gr. 7). pap. 11.95 *(978-1-62639-197-0(1))* Bold Strokes Bks.

Hopkins, Nicolia. What was Grandma Doing? Wiggins, Margaret W., illus. 2007. (J). per. 9.99 *(978-0-9768579-8-3(7))* eVision, LLC.

Jacobs, Lily. The Littlest Bunny in Alabama: An Easter Adventure. 2015. (ENG.). 32p. (J). (-3). 9.99 *(978-1-4926-1015-1(1)*, Sourcebooks Jabberwocky) Sourcebooks, Inc.

James, Eric. A Halloween Scare in Alabama. Le Ray, Marina, illus. 2015. (ENG.). 32p. (J). (-5). 9.99 *(978-1-4926-2359-5(8)*, 9781492623595, Sourcebooks Jabberwocky) Sourcebooks, Inc.

—Santa's Sleigh Is on Its Way to Alabama. Dunn, Robert, illus. 2015. (ENG.). 32p. (J). (-2). 12.99 *(978-1-4926-2763-0(1)*, Sourcebooks Jabberwocky) Sourcebooks, Inc.

Johnson, Allen, Jr. My Brother's Story. McMorris, Kelley, illus. 2014. (Blackwater Novels Ser.: Vol. 1). (ENG.). 191p. (J). (gr. 4-7). 14.99 *(978-1-933725-37-6(0))* Premium Pr. America.

Johnson, Angela. Bird. 2006. (ENG.). 144p. (YA). (gr. 7-18). reprint ed. 6.99 *(978-0-14-240544-4(2)*, Puffin Books) Penguin Young Readers Group.

—Bird. 2006. 133p. (gr. 3-7). 16.00 *(978-0-7569-6660-7(4))* Perfection Learning Corp.

Key, Watt. Alabama Moon. (Alabama Moon Ser.: 1). (ENG.). (J). (gr. 5-9). 2008. 304p. pap. 8.99 *(978-0-312-38428-9(9)*, 9780312384289) 2010. 320p. pap. 8.99 *(978-0-312-64480-2(9)*, 9780312644802) Square Fish.

—Dirt Road Home. 2011. (Alabama Moon Ser.: 2). (ENG.). 240p. (J). (gr. 5-9). pap. 8.99 *(978-0-312-67435-9(X)*, 9780312674359) Square Fish.

—Fourmile, 1 vol. 2012. (ENG.). 240p. (J). (gr. 4-7). 24.99 *(978-0-374-35095-6(7)*, 9780374350956, Farrar, Straus & Giroux (BYR)) Farrar, Straus & Giroux.

—Fourmile. 2014. (ENG.). 256p. (J). (gr. 4-7). pap. 8.99 *(978-1-250-03995-8(9)*, 9781250039958) Square Fish.

Lai, Thanhhà. Inside Out & Back Again. (ENG.). (J). (gr. 3-7). 2013. 288p. pap. 8.99 *(978-0-06-196279-0(1))* 2011. 272p. 16.99 *(978-0-06-196278-3(3))* HarperCollins Pubs.

—Inside Out & Back Again. 2014. (ENG.). 288p. (J). (gr. 3-7). 12.24 *(978-1-63245-350-1(9))* Lectorum Pubns., Inc.

—Inside Out & Back Again. 2009. 9.68 *(978-0-7848-3867-7(9)*, Everbind) Marco Bk. Co.

—Inside Out & Back Again. 2013. 18.00 *(978-1-61383-970-6(7))* Perfection Learning Corp.

—Inside Out & Back Again. 2013. (J). lib. bdg. 18.40 *(978-0-606-27126-4(0)*, Turtleback) Turtleback Bks.

Lai, Thanhha. Inside Out & Back Again: a Harper Classic. 2017. (Harper Classic Ser.). 288p. (J). (gr. 3-7). 16.99 ***(978-0-06-257402-2(7))*** HarperCollins Pubs.

Latham, Irene. Leaving Gee's Bend. 2017. (ENG.). 192p. (gr. 5). pap. 11.95 ***(978-1-58838-332-7(6)***, NewSouth Bks.) NewSouth, Inc.

Les Becquets, Diane. The Stones of Mourning Creek, 0 vols. 2005. (ENG.). 320p. (YA). (gr. 7-9). reprint ed. pap. 9.99 *(978-0-7614-5238-6(9)*, 9780761452386, Amazon Children's Publishing) Amazon Publishing.

Levine, Kristin. The Best Bad Luck I Ever Had. 2010. (ENG.). 272p. (J). (gr. 5-18). 7.99 *(978-0-14-241648-8(7)*, Puffin Books) Penguin Young Readers Group.

Lough, Erin & Duke, Mave Lough. The Spirit Tree at Toomer's Corner. 2012. (J). 19.95 *(978-1-62086-122-6(4))* Mascot Bks., Inc.

Lyon, George Ella. Sonny's House of Spies. 2007. (ENG.). 304p. (J). (gr. 6-9). pap. 14.95 *(978-1-4169-6815-3(6)*, Simon & Schuster/Paula Wiseman Bks.) Simon & Schuster/Paula Wiseman Bks.

Malaspina, Ann. Finding Lincoln. Bootman, Colin, illus. 2009. (ENG.). 32p. (J). (gr. 2-3). 16.99 *(978-0-8075-2435-0(2))* Whitman, Albert & Co.

Mayfield, Jamie. Choices. 2016. (ENG., Illus.). (J). 27.99 ***(978-1-63477-953-1(3))*** 2013. 304p. pap. 17.99 *(978-1-62380-720-7(4))* Dreamspinner Pr. (Harmony Ink Pr.).

Mayfield, Jamie. Choices [Library Edition]. 2013. 304p. pap. 17.99 *(978-1-62380-928-7(2)*, Harmony Ink Pr.) Dreamspinner Pr.

Medearis, Angela Shelf. Singing for Dr. King. Hu, Ying-Hwa & Van Wright, Cornelius, illus. 2004. 32p. (J). lib. bdg. 15.00 *(978-1-4242-0237-9(X))* Fitzgerald Bks.

Miller, Sarah. Miss Spitfire: Reaching Helen Keller. (ENG.). (J). (gr. 5-7). 2010. 256p. pap. 7.99 *(978-1-4424-0851-7(0))* 2007. 240p. 17.99 *(978-1-4169-2542-2(2))* Simon & Schuster Children's Publishing. (Atheneum Bks. for Young Readers).

Molock, Anthony. The Adventures of Cocoa Pelou: Cocoa Pelou Meets Alabama Black. 2011. 24p. pap. 14.00 *(978-1-4634-4118-0(5))* AuthorHouse.

Nelson, R. A. Breathe My Name. 2008. (ENG.). 320p. (YA). (gr. 7-18). 9.99 *(978-1-59514-186-6(3)*, Razorbill) Penguin Young Readers Group.

Neri, G. Tru & Nelle. (ENG., Illus.). (J). (gr. 3-5). 2017. 352p. pap. 7.99 ***(978-1-328-74095-3(1))*** 2016. 336p. 16.99 *(978-0-544-69960-1(2))* Houghton Mifflin Harcourt Publishing Co. (HMH Books For Young Readers).

Nolan, Han. Send Me down a Miracle. 2003. (ENG.). 276p. (YA). (gr. 7-12). pap. 15.95 *(978-0-15-204680-4(1))* Houghton Mifflin Harcourt Publishing Co.

O'Dell, Scott. 290. 2008. (ENG.). 128p. (J). (gr. 4-7). pap. 8.99 *(978-1-4022-1326-7(3)*, Sourcebooks Jabberwocky) Sourcebooks, Inc.

Phillips, Gin. A Little Bit of Spectacular. 2015. (ENG.). 176p. (J). (gr. 5). 16.99 *(978-0-8037-3837-9(4)*, Dial Bks) Penguin Young Readers Group.

Pink, Randi. Wearing White. 2016. (ENG.). 288p. (YA). 17.99 *(978-1-250-07021-0(X)*, 9781250070210) Feiwel & Friends.

Pinkney, Andrea Davis. Boycott Blues: How Rosa Parks Inspired a Nation. Pinkney, Brian, illus. 2008. (ENG.). 40p. (J). (gr. k-3). 16.99 *(978-0-06-082118-0(3)*, Greenwillow Bks.) HarperCollins Pubs.

Reid, Roger. Space. 2008. (ENG.). 160p. (J). 19.95 *(978-1-58838-230-6(3)*, NewSouth Bks.) NewSouth, Inc.

—Time. 2011. (ENG.). 152p. (J). 19.95 *(978-1-58838-262-7(1)*, NewSouth Bks.) NewSouth, Inc.

Reisz, Kristopher. The Drowned Forest. 2014. (ENG.). 240p. (YA). pap. 9.99 *(978-0-7387-3910-6(3)*, Flux) North Star Editions.

Reynolds, Aaron. Back of the Bus. Cooper, Floyd, illus. 2013. (ENG.). 32p. (J). (gr. 1-3). 8.99 *(978-0-14-751058-7(9)*, Puffin Books) Penguin Young Readers Group.

Robinet, Harriette Gillem. Walking to the Bus-Rider Blues. 2004. (Jean Karl Bks.). 146p. (gr. 3-7). 16.00 *(978-0-7569-4265-6(9))* Perfection Learning Corp.

Rocky Porch Moore. It's Farm Market Day! 2009. 24p. pap. 12.99 *(978-1-4490-2854-1(3))* AuthorHouse.

Scholastic, Inc. Staff & Medearis, Angela Shelf. Singing for Dr. King. Van Wright, Cornelius & Hu, Ying-Hwa, illus. 2004. (Just for You Ser.). (ENG.). 32p. (gr. k-3). pap. 3.99 *(978-0-439-56855-5(2)*, Teaching Resources) Scholastic, Inc.

Sharpe, Cathy. Jayne Sullivan, Army Brat. 2010. 96p. pap. 9.95 *(978-1-4502-6158-6(2))* iUniverse, Inc.

Silvano, Wendi. Love Is All Around Alabama. Czernichowska, Joanna, illus. 2016. (ENG.). 32p. (J). (-6). 12.99 *(978-1-4926-2900-9(6)*, Sourcebooks Jabberwocky) Sourcebooks, Inc.

Smallman, Steve. Santa Is Coming to Alabama. Dunn, Robert, illus. 2013. (ENG.). 32p. (J). (-3). 9.99 *(978-1-4022-8821-0(2)*, Sourcebooks Jabberwocky) Sourcebooks, Inc.

Smith, Ronald L. Hoodoo. 2015. (ENG.). 224p. (J). (gr. 5-7). 16.99 *(978-0-544-44525-3(2)*, Clarion Bks.) Houghton Mifflin Harcourt Trade & Reference Pubs.

—Hoodoo. 2017. (ENG.). (J). (gr. 5-7). lib. bdg. 18.40 ***(978-0-606-39820-6(1))*** Turtleback Bks.

Sorrells, Walter. Fake ID. 2007. (Hunted Ser.). (ENG.). 336p. (YA). (gr. 7-18). 9.99 *(978-0-14-240762-2(3)*, Puffin Books) Penguin Young Readers Group.

Spurlock, Jefferson. Clemente's Dream. 2007. 108p. per. 19.95 *(978-1-4241-7483-6(X))* America Star Bks.

Stewart, Chuck. Angels at Rickwood. 2009. (J). pap. 10.00 *(978-1-61584-842-3(8))* Independent Pub.

Stewart III, Freddie Leonard. Night Night Birmingham. 2009. 24p. 12.00 *(978-0-557-08775-4(9))* Lulu Pr., Inc.

Stroud, Bettye & Ramsey, Calvin Alexander. Belle, the Last Mule at Gee's Bend: A Civil Rights Story. Holyfield, John, illus. 2011. (ENG.). 32p. (J). (gr. k-3). 16.99 *(978-0-7636-4058-3(1))* Candlewick Pr.

Thompson, Shannon Raines. Mad about Miller. Stone, Kathrine Thompson, ed. Shehan, Terece, illus. 2006. 24p. (YA). 12.95 *(978-1-59971-853-8(7))* Aardvark Global Publishing.

—Nuts about Neal. Stone, Kathrine Thompson, ed. Shehan, Terece, illus. 2006. 24p. (YA). 12.95 *(978-1-59971-852-1(9))* Aardvark Global Publishing.

The Troubles of Johnny Cannon. 2014. (ENG., Illus.). 304p. (J). (gr. 3-7). 16.99 *(978-1-4814-0003-9(7)*, Simon & Schuster Bks. For Young Readers) Simon & Schuster Bks. For Young Readers.

Tunks, Karyn. Jubilee!, 1 vol. Buckner, Julie, illus. 2012. (ENG.). 32p. (J). (gr. k-3). 16.99 *(978-1-58980-880-5(0))* Pelican Publishing Co., Inc.

Williams-Garcia, Rita. Gone Crazy in Alabama. (J). (gr. 3-7). 2016. 320p. pap. 6.99 *(978-0-06-221589-5(2)*, Amistad) 2015. (ENG., Illus.). 304p. 16.99 *(978-0-06-221587-1(6))* HarperCollins Pubs.

Wilson, Martin. What They Always Tell Us. 2010. (ENG.). 304p. (YA). (gr. 9). pap. 8.99 *(978-0-385-73508-7(1)*, Delacorte Bks. for Young Readers) Random Hse. Children's Bks.

Yeager, Paugh Paugh Tom. The 26th of June. 2008. 34p. pap. 24.95 *(978-1-60563-822-5(6))* America Star Bks.

ALADDIN (LEGENDARY CHARACTER)—FICTION

Aladdin: Here Comes a Parade. unabr. ed. (My First Read Along Ser.). (Illus.). (J). 7.99 incl. audio *(978-1-55723-748-4(4))* Walt Disney Records.

Baruzzi, Agnese. Aladdin: A Cut-Paper Book. 2014. (ENG., Illus.). 14p. (J). (gr. k-2). 19.99 *(978-1-85707-873-2(X))* Tango Bks. GBR. Dist: Independent Pubs. Group.

Braswell, Liz. A Whole New World. 2016. (Twisted Tale Ser.). (YA). lib. bdg. 20.85 *(978-0-606-38511-4(8))* Turtleback Bks.

—A Whole New World: A Twisted Tale. 2015. (Twisted Tale Ser.). (ENG.). 384p. (YA). (gr. 7-12). 17.99 *(978-1-4847-0729-6(X))* Disney Pr.

Chronicle Books Staff. Aladdin & the Magic Lamp (Aladino y la Lampara Maravillosa) Montserrat, Pep, illus. 2006. (Bilingual Fairy Tales Ser.: BILI). (ENG & SPA.). 32p. (J). (gr. -1-3). 14.95 *(978-0-8118-5061-2(7))* Chronicle Bks. LLC.

Cloke, Rene, illus. Aladdin & His Magical Lamp. 2012. (ENG.). 24p. pap. 6.50 *(978-1-84135-534-4(8))* Award Pubns. Ltd. GBR. Dist: Parkwest Pubns., Inc.

Deighton, Jo, adapted by. Scheherezade Presents. (Scheherezade Presents Ser.: No. 1). (Illus.). 48p. (J). pap. *(978-1-85964-091-3(5))*; pap. *(978-1-85964-100-2(8))*; pap. *(978-1-85964-092-0(3))*; pap. *(978-1-85964-093-7(1))*; pap. *(978-1-85964-094-4(X))*; pap. *(978-1-85964-095-1(8))*; pap. *(978-1-85964-096-8(6))*; pap. *(978-1-85964-097-5(4))*; pap. *(978-1-85964-098-2(2))*; pap. *(978-1-85964-099-9(0))* Garnet Publishing, Ltd. (Ithaca Pr.).

Disney Book Group Staff. Aladdin Read-Along Storybook & CD. Disney Storybook Artists Staff, illus. 2015. (Read-Along Storybook & CD Ser.). (ENG.). 32p. (J). (gr. -1-k). pap. 6.99 *(978-1-4231-4688-9(3))* Disney Pr.

Disney Staff. Aladdin. (FRE.). 96p. (J). (gr. k-5). pap. 9.95 *(978-0-7859-8852-6(1))* French & European Pubns., Inc.

Fairy Tale- Aladdin. 2005. (J). bds. *(978-1-4194-0037-7(1))* Paradise Pr., Inc.

A
B

French, Vivian, et al. Aladdin & the Genies. 2016. (ENG., Illus.). 48p. (J). pap. 9.95 (978-0-00-814720-4(5)) HarperCollins Pubs. Ltd. GBR. Dist: Independent Pubs. Group.

Khoury, Jessica. The Forbidden Wish. (ENG.). 352p. (YA). (gr. 7). 2017. pap. 9.99 (978-1-59514-768-4(3)) 2016. 17.99 (978-1-59514-767-7(5)) Penguin Young Readers Group. (Razorbill).

—The Forbidden Wish. 2017. lib. bdg. 20.85 **(978-0-606-40000-8(1))** Turtleback Bks.

Kreider, Karen. Aladdin. Baker, Darrell, illus. 2015. (Little Golden Book Ser.). (ENG.). 24p. (J). (gr. -1-2). 4.99 (978-0-7364-2259-8(5), Golden/Disney) Random Hse. Children's Bks.

Landes, William-Alan. Aladdin n' His Magic Lamp. rev. ed. 2003. (Wondrawhopper Ser.). 51p. (J). (gr. 3-12). pap. 6.00 (978-0-88734-102-1(0)) Players Pr., Inc.

Lawrence, C. H., illus. Aladdin or, the Wonderful Lamp. 2012. (Shape Bks.). (ENG.). 16p. pap. 9.95 (978-1-59583-454-6(0), 9781595834546, Green Tiger Pr.) Laughing Elephant.

Lewis, Jan. First Fairy Tales Aladdin & the Lamp. 2013. (ENG., Illus.). 24p. (J). (gr. -1-12). bds. 6.99 (978-1-86147-337-0(0), Armadillo) Anness Publishing GBR. Dist: National Bk. Network.

Montserrat, Pep, illus. Aladdin & the Magic Lamp/(Aladino y la Lampara Maravillosa) 2006. (Bilingual Fairy Tales Ser.: BILI). (ENG & SPA.). 32p. (J). (gr. -1-3). pap. 6.95 (978-0-8118-5062-9(5)) Chronicle Bks. LLC.

Mounter, Paddy. Aladdin & His Magical Lamp. 2004. (Young Reading Ser.: Vol. 1). 48p. (J). (gr. 2-18). pap. 5.95 (978-0-7945-0582-0(1)); lib. bdg. 13.95 (978-1-58086-559-3(3), Usborne) EDC Publishing.

Nazran, Govinder, illus. Aladdin. (ENG.). 2017. 24p. pap. 7.99 (978-1-86147-819-1(4)) 2014. 48p. (J). (gr. 2-5). pap. 7.99 (978-1-84322-790-8(8)) Anness Publishing GBR. (Armadillo). Dist: National Bk. Network.

Ohtaka, Shinobu. Magi: The Labyrinth of Magic, Vol. 1. 2013. (ENG., Illus.). 200p. pap. 9.99 (978-1-4215-5951-3(X)) Viz Media.

O'Ryan, Ellie. Jasmine: The Jewel Orchard. 2013. (Disney Princess Early Chapter Bks.). (J). lib. bdg. 14.75 (978-0-606-27068-7(X), Turtleback) Turtleback Bks.

Ransome, Arthur. Aladdin & His Wonderful Lamp in Rhyme. Mackenzie, Thomas, illus. 2011. (Calla Editions Ser.). (ENG.). 160p. (gr. 5). 30.00 (978-1-60660-002-3(8)) Dover Pubns., Inc.

Robinson, Hilary & Catling, Andy. Aladdin & the Lamp. 2009. (Hopscotch Adventures Ser.). (Illus.). 31p. (J). (gr. 1). lib. bdg. 25.65 (978-1-59771-181-4(0)) Sea-To-Sea Pubns.

Rossi, Francesca, illus. Aladdin. 2015. (Fairy Tale Adventures Ser.). (ENG.). 64p. (J). (gr. 2-6). 7.95 (978-1-4549-1506-5(4)) Sterling Publishing Co., Inc.

Squillace, Elisa, illus. Aladdin. 2007. (Flip-Up Fairy Tales Ser.). (ENG.). 24p. (J). (gr. 2-2). (978-1-84643-113-5(1)) Child's Play International Ltd.

Stempleski. Aladdin & the Magic Lamp. Date not set. (Illus.). 23p. pap. 72.95 (978-0-582-03043-5(9)) Addison-Wesley Longman, Ltd. GBR. Dist: Trans-Atlantic Pubns., Inc.

Wells, H. G. The War of the Worlds. Gorey, Edward, illus. 2005. (New York Review Books Classics). (ENG.). 260p. 17.95 (978-1-59017-158-5(6), NYRB Classics) New York Review of Bks., Inc., The.

—The War of the Worlds. 2005. (Aladdin Classics Ser.). (ENG.). 336p. (J). (gr. 4-7). pap. 6.99 (978-1-4169-0368-0(2), Aladdin) Simon & Schuster Children's Publishing.

ALAMO (SAN ANTONIO, TEX.)

Adams, Colleen. The True Story of the Battle of the Alamo. 2009. (What Really Happened? Ser.). 24p. (gr. 2-3). 42.50 (978-1-60854-768-5(X), PowerKids Pr.); (Illus.). (YA). (gr. 3-6). lib. bdg. 22.60 (978-1-4042-4477-1(8)) Rosen Publishing Group, Inc., The.

Allen, Charles F. David Crockett: Scout, Small Boy, Pilgrim, Mountaineer, Soldier, Bear-Hunter, & Congressman, Defender of the Alamo. (Illus.). 308p. reprint ed. lib. bdg. 98.00 (978-0-7222-4856-0(3)) Library Reprints, Inc.

Belviso, Meg & Pollack, Pam. What Was the Alamo? Groff, David, illus. 2013. (What Was? Ser.). (ENG.). 112p. (J). (gr. 3-7). 5.99 (978-0-448-46710-8(0), Penguin Workshop) Penguin Young Readers Group.

Belviso, Meg & Pollack, Pamela. What Was the Alamo? 2013. (What Was... ? Ser.). lib. bdg. 16.00 (978-0-606-32129-7(2), Turtleback) Turtleback Bks.

Brown, Susan Taylor. Enrique Esparza & the Battle of the Alamo. 2010. pap. 56.72 (978-0-7613-6926-4(0)) Lerner Publishing Group.

Capek, Michael. Davy Crockett. 2017. 25.70 (978-1-61228-974-8(6)) Mitchell Lane Pubs., Inc.

Caravantes, Peggy. The Battle of the Alamo: A History Perspectives Book. 2014. (Perspectives Library). (ENG., Illus.). 32p. (J). (gr. 4-8). 28.50 (978-1-62431-664-7(6), 203220) Cherry Lake Publishing.

Chemerka, William R. The Alamo from A to Z, 1 vol. Dillon, Wade, illus. 2011. (ENG.). 32p. (J). (gr. k-3). 16.99 (978-1-4556-1461-5(0)) Pelican Publishing Co., Inc.

Chemerka, William R. & Collins, Don. Gregorio Esparza: Alamo Defender. Collins, Don, illus. 2009. (ENG., Illus.). 80p. (J). (gr. 4-7). 16.95 (978-1-933979-36-6(4), 9781933979366) Bright Sky Pr.

Coddington, Andrew. Davy Crockett. Lapegüe, Matias, illus. 2016. (American Legends & Folktales Ser.). 32p. (J). 28.50 (978-1-5026-2193-1(2)) Cavendish Square Publishing.

Coleman, Wim & Perrin, Pat. The Alamo: A MyReportLinks.com Book. 2005. (Virtual Field Trips Ser.). (Illus.). 48p. (J). (gr. 4-10). lib. bdg. 26.60 (978-0-7660-5221-5(4), MyReportLinks.com Bks.) Enslow Pubs., Inc.

Copeland, Peter F. The Story of the Alamo. 2005. (Dover History Coloring Book Ser.). (ENG., Illus.). 32p. (gr. 3-8). 3.99 (978-0-486-44459-8(7)) Dover Pubns., Inc.

Doeden, Matt. The Battle of the Alamo, 1 vol. Barnett, Charles, III & Miller, Phil, illus. 2005. (Graphic History Ser.). (ENG.). 32p. (gr. 3-4). per. 8.10 (978-0-7368-5242-5(5), Graphic Library) Capstone Press of Coughlan Cos.

—The Battle of the Alamo, 1 vol. Barnett, Charles et al, illus. 2005. (Graphic History Ser.). (ENG.). 32p. (gr. 3-4). 30.65 (978-0-7368-3832-0(5), Graphic Library) Capstone Press of Coughlan Cos.

Edmondson, J. R. Jim Bowie: Frontier Legend, Alamo Hero. (Library of American Lives & Times Ser.). 112p. 2009. (gr. 5-5). 69.20 (978-1-60853-488-3(X)) 2005. (Illus.). (YA). (gr. 4-8). lib. bdg. 34.60 (978-0-8239-5734-7(9)) Rosen Publishing Group, Inc., The.

Fein, Eric. Outnumbered: Davy Crockett's Final Battle at the Alamo. 2009. (Great Moments in American History Ser.). 32p. (gr. 3-3). 47.90 (978-1-61513-148-8(5)) Rosen Publishing Group, Inc., The.

Fradin, Dennis Brindell. The Alamo. 2006. (Turning Points in U. S. History Ser.). (Illus.). 46p. (J). (gr. 3-7). lib. bdg. 29.93 (978-0-7614-2127-6(0), Benchmark Bks.) Marshall Cavendish Corp.

Gaines, Ann. Jim Bowie: Legendary Hero of the Alamo. 2015. (Legendary American Biographies Ser.). 96p. (J). (gr. 6-12). pap. 10.95 (978-0-7660-6471-3(9)) Enslow Pubs., Inc.

Gaines, Ann Graham. Jim Bowie: Legendary Hero of the Alamo. 2015. (Legendary American Biographies Ser.). 96p. (J). (gr. 6-12). 27.94 (978-0-7660-6470-6(0)) Enslow Pubs., Inc.

Garland, Sherry. Voices of the Alamo, 1 vol. Himler, Ronald, illus. 2017. (Voices of History Ser.). (ENG.). 40p. (J). (gr. 3-3). 17.99 (978-1-58980-222-3(5)) Pelican Publishing Co., Inc.

Goldsworthy, Steve. El Alamo. 2013. (Iconos Americanos Ser.). (SPA., Illus.). 24p. (J). (gr. k-2). lib. bdg. 27.13 (978-1-62127-615-9(5), AV2 by Weigl) Weigl Pubs., Inc.

—Alamo with Code. 2012. (AV2 American Icons Ser.). (ENG., Illus.). 24p. (J). pap. 12.95 (978-1-61913-299-3(0)); lib. bdg. 27.13 (978-1-61913-080-7(7)) Weigl Pubs., Inc. (AV2 by Weigl).

Gunderson, Cory Gideon. Battle of the Alamo, 1 vol. 2004. (American Moments Ser.). (ENG.). 48p. (gr. 4-8). 27.07 (978-1-59197-278-5(7), Abdo & Daughters) ABDO Publishing Co.

Gunderson, Jessica. The Alamo: Myths, Legends, & Facts, 1 vol. 2014. (Monumental History Ser.). (ENG.). 32p. (gr. 3-4). lib. bdg. 27.32 (978-1-4914-0204-7(0)) Capstone Press of Coughlan Cos.

Hale, Nathan. Alamo All-Stars. 2016. (Nathan Hale's Hazardous Tales Ser.: 6). (ENG., Illus.). 128p. (J). (gr. 3-7). 12.95 (978-1-4197-1902-8(5), Amulet Bks.) Abrams, Inc.

—Alamo All-Stars. 2017. (Nathan Hale's Hazardous Tales Ser.). (J). lib. bdg. 24.45 **(978-0-606-40709-0(X))** Turtleback Bks.

Jeffrey, Gary. The Battle of the Alamo. Spender, Nick, illus. 2012. (Graphic History of the American West Ser.). (ENG.). 24p. (J). (gr. 3-8). pap. 8.15 (978-1-4339-6729-0(4), Gareth Stevens Learning Library); (gr. 4-7). lib. bdg. 23.95 (978-1-4339-6727-6(8)) Stevens, Gareth Publishing LLLP.

Keller, Susanna & Levy, Janey. A Primary Source Investigation of the Alamo. 2015. (Uncovering American History Ser.). (ENG., Illus.). 64p. (J). (gr. 5-6). 32.95 (978-1-4994-3507-8(X), Rosen Central) Rosen Publishing Group, Inc., The.

Landau, Elaine. The Alamo: Would You Join the Fight? 2014. (What Would You Do? Ser.). (Illus.). 48p. (J). (gr. 3-4). lib. bdg. 25.27 (978-0-7660-4226-1(X), Enslow Elementary) Enslow Pubs., Inc.

Leavitt, Amie Jane. The Battle of the Alamo: An Interactive History Adventure. 2016. (You Choose: History Ser.). (ENG.). 112p. (gr. 3-4). pap. 6.95 (978-1-5157-4257-9(1), You Choose Bks.) Capstone Press of Coughlan Cos.

Levy, Janey. The Battle of the Alamo. 2009. (Real Life Readers Ser.). 32p. (gr. 4-5). pap. 10.00 (978-1-4358-0167-7(9), Rosen Classroom); (gr. 4-4). 47.90 (978-1-61511-369-9(X), PowerKids Pr.); (J). (gr. 3-4). lib. bdg. 25.25 (978-1-4358-2991-6(3), PowerKids Pr.) Rosen Publishing Group, Inc., The.

Marcovitz, Hal. The Alamo. 2004. (American Symbols & Their Meanings Ser.). (Illus.). 48p. (J). (gr. 4-18). lib. bdg. 19.95 (978-1-59084-037-5(2)) Mason Crest.

—The Alamo: Symbol of Freedom. Moreno, Barry, ed. 2014. (Patriotic Symbols of America Ser.: 20). 48p. (J). (gr. 4-18). 20.95 (978-1-4222-3118-0(6)) Mason Crest.

Mattern, Joanne. The Alamo. 2014. (ENG.). 32p. (gr. 3-6). 32.79 (978-1-62717-740-5(X)) Rourke Educational Media.

Micklos, John, Jr. To the Last Man: The Battle of the Alamo. 2015. (Adventures on the American Frontier Ser.). (ENG., Illus.). 32p. (gr. 3-4). pap. 7.95 (978-1-4914-4911-0(X)) Capstone Press of Coughlan Cos.

Moriarty, J. T. Davy Crockett: Frontier Hero. 2009. (Primary Sources of Famous People in American History Ser.). 32p. (gr. 2-3). 47.90 (978-1-60851-670-4(9)) Rosen Publishing Group, Inc., The.

Mountjoy, Shane. The Alamo: The Battle for Texas. 2009. (Milestones in American History Ser.). (Illus.). 144p. (gr. 6-12). 35.00 (978-1-60413-056-0(3), Chelsea Hse.) Facts On File, Inc.

Nardo, Don. The Alamo. 2012. (World History Ser.). (ENG., Illus.). 128p. (gr. 7-10). lib. bdg. 39.90 (978-1-4205-0861-1(X), Lucent Bks.) Cengage Gale.

Nelson, Kristin L. The Alamo. 2010. pap. 45.32 (978-0-7613-6991-2(0)) 2010. (ENG.). 32p. pap. 7.95 (978-0-7613-6050-6(6)) 2003. (ENG., Illus.). 32p. pap. 7.95 (978-0-8225-3760-1(5)) 2003. (ENG., Illus.). 32p. lib. bdg. 22.60 (978-0-8225-3599-7(8)) Lerner Publishing Group.

Nichols, Kaitlyn. Davey Crockett. 2009. pap. 13.25 (978-1-60559-057-8(6)) Hameray Publishing Group, Inc.

O'Hern, Kerri & Riehecky, Janet. The Battle of the Alamo. 2006. (Graphic Histories Ser.). (Illus.). 32p. (gr. 5-8). pap. 10.50 (978-0-8368-6253-9(8)) Stevens, Gareth Publishing LLLP.

O'Hern, Kerri, et al. La Batalla de el Álamo. 2007. (Historias Graficas (Graphic Histories) Ser.). (SPA., Illus.). 32p. (gr. 5-8). pap. 10.50 (978-0-8368-7900-1(7)); lib. bdg. 27.00 (978-0-8368-7893-6(0)) Stevens, Gareth Publishing LLLP.

Peppas, Lynn. The Battle of the Alamo. 2017. 48p. (J). **(978-0-7787-3940-1(6))** Crabtree Publishing Co.

Riehecky, Janet & O'Hern, Kerri. The Battle of the Alamo. McHargue, D., illus. 2006. (Graphic Histories Ser.). 32p. (gr. 5-8). lib. bdg. 27.00 (978-0-8368-6201-0(5)) Stevens, Gareth Publishing LLLP.

RJF Publishing Staff & Burgan, Michael. The Alamo. 2009. (Symbols of American Freedom Ser.). 48p. (gr. 4-6). 30.00 (978-1-60413-512-1(3), Chelsea Clubhouse) Facts On File, Inc.

Ruffin, Frances E. The Alamo. 2006. (Places in American History Ser.). (Illus.). 24p. (gr. 1-4). pap. 8.15 (978-0-8368-6414-4(X)); lib. bdg. 22.00 (978-0-8368-6407-6(7)) Stevens, Gareth Publishing LLLP. (Weekly Reader Leveled Readers).

Sanford, William R. & Green, Carl R. Davy Crockett: Courageous Hero of the Alamo. 2012. (Courageous Heroes of the American West Ser.). (Illus.). 48p. (J). (gr. 5-18). 22.60 (978-0-7660-4005-2(4)) Enslow Pubs., Inc.

Sipe, Antoinette Leonard. The Alamo. 2004. (American Forts & Their Strategic Importance Ser.). (J). 19.95 (978-1-59084-708-4(3)) Mason Crest.

Smith, Andrea P. Jim Bowie. 2012. (Illus.). 24p. (J). 63.60 (978-1-4488-5231-4(5)); pap. 10.60 (978-1-4488-5230-7(7)); lib. bdg. 25.25 (978-1-4488-5196-6(3)) Rosen Publishing Group, Inc., The. (PowerKids Pr.).

Sorrels, Roy. The Legend of the Alamo. 2012. (Stories in American History Ser.). (Illus.). 128p. (J). (gr. 5-18). 33.27 (978-0-7660-3952-0(8)) Enslow Pubs., Inc.

—The Legend of the Alamo: Stories in American History. 2012. (Stories in American History Ser.). (Illus.). 128p. (J). (gr. 5-18). pap. 10.95 (978-1-4644-0022-3(9)) Enslow Pubs., Inc.

South, Victor. Remember the Alamo: Americans Fight for Texas, 1820-1845. 2012. (J). pap. (978-1-4222-2416-8(3)) Mason Crest.

—Remember the Alamo: Americans Fight for Texas, 1820-1845. Rakove, Jack N., ed. 2012. (How America Became America Ser.). 48p. (J). (gr. 3-4). 19.95 (978-1-4222-2402-1(3)) Mason Crest.

Tanaka, Shelley. A Day That Changed America - The Alamo: Surrounded & Outnumbered,They Chose to Make a Defiant Last Stand. Craig, David, illus. 2003. (ENG.). 48p. (gr. 3-17). 16.99 (978-0-7868-1923-2(5)) Hyperion Pr.

Walker, Paul Robert. Remember the Alamo: Texians, Tejanos, & Mexicans Tell Their Stories. (ENG., Illus.). 64p. (J). (gr. 5). 2015. pap. 7.99 (978-1-4263-2249-5(6)) 2007. 17.95 (978-1-4263-0010-3(7)) National Geographic Society. (National Geographic Children's Bks.).

Warrick, Karen Clemens. Alamo: Victory or Death on the Texas Frontier. 2008. (America's Living History Ser.). (Illus.). 128p. (J). (gr. 5-9). lib. bdg. 33.27 (978-0-7660-2937-8(9)) Enslow Pubs., Inc.

Yomtov, Nel. Defend until Death! Nickolas Flux & the Battle of the Alamo, 1 vol. Ginevra, Dante, illus. 2014. (Nickolas Flux History Chronicles Ser.). (ENG.). 32p. (gr. 3-4). lib. bdg. 30.65 (978-1-4765-3945-4(6), Graphic Library) Capstone Press of Coughlan Cos.

ALAMO (SAN ANTONIO, TEX.)—FICTION

Altsheler, Joseph A. The Texan Scouts. 2007. (Texan Ser.: Vol. 2). 272p. reprint ed. per. 10.45 (978-1-60424-305-5(8), Book Jungle) Standard Pubns., Inc.

—The Texan Scouts: A Story of the Alamo & Goliad. 2006. (Texan Ser.). 352p. (J). reprint ed. pap. 15.95 (978-1-4218-1881-8(7), 1st World Library - Literary Society) 1st World Publishing, Inc.

—The Texan Scouts: A Story of the Alamo & Goliad. l.t. ed. (Texan Ser.: Vol. 2). (J). reprint ed. 2007. (ENG.). 316p. pap. 24.99 (978-1-4264-3365-8(4)) 2010. 376p. (gr. 4-7). pap. 33.75 (978-1-177-24805-1(0)) 2008. 320p. 29.99 (978-0-554-22920-1(X)) 2008. 320p. 28.99 (978-0-554-32223-0(4)) 2007. (ENG.). 282p. pap. 21.99 (978-1-4264-3310-8(7)) Creative Media Partners, LLC.

—The Texan Scouts: A Story of the Alamo & Goliad. 2006. (Texan Ser.: Vol. 2). (J). reprint ed. pap. (978-1-4065-0826-0(8)) Dodo Pr.

—The Texan Scouts: A Story of the Alamo & Goliad. 2007. (Texan Ser.: Vol. 2). 208p. (J). reprint ed. per. (978-1-4068-1691-4(4)) Echo Library.

—The Texan Scouts: A Story of the Alamo & Goliad. 2010. (Texan Ser.: Vol. 2). (Illus.). 184p. (J). (gr. 4-7). reprint ed. pap. 19.99 (978-1-4432-3075-9(8)) General Bks. LLC.

—The Texan Scouts: A Story of the Alamo & Goliad. (Texan Ser.: Vol. 2). (J). reprint ed. 2012. 380p. (gr. 4-7). pap. (978-1-290-32714-5(9)) 2010. 258p. pap. (978-1-4076-1525-7(4)) HardPr.

—The Texan Scouts: A Story of the Alamo & Goliad. (Texan Ser.: Vol. 2). (J). reprint ed. 2011. 362p. (gr. 4-7). 46.95 (978-1-169-83723-2(9)) 2010. 362p. (gr. 4-7). 37.56 (978-1-163-21368-1(3)) 2010. 362p. (gr. 4-7). pap. 25.56 (978-1-162-64067-9(7)) 2004. 360p. 46.95 (978-1-4326-1538-3(6)) 2004. pap. 31.95 (978-1-4179-1479-1(3)) Kessinger Publishing, LLC.

—The Texan Scouts: A Story of the Alamo & Goliad. 2008. (Texan Ser.: Vol. 2). 364p. (J). reprint ed. per. (978-1-4086-5013-4(4)) Read Bks.

—The Texan Scouts: A Story of the Alamo & Goliad. 2011. (Texan Ser.: Vol. 1). 290p. (J). (gr. 4-7). reprint ed. pap. (978-3-8424-7933-3(6)) Tredition GmbH.

Barr, Amelia E. Remember the Alamo. 2005. 156p. pap. (978-1-84637-856-0(7)) Echo Library.

Brown, Jeff. Flat Stanley's Worldwide Adventures #10: Showdown at the Alamo. Pamintuan, Macky, illus. 2013. (Flat Stanley's Worldwide Adventures Ser.: 10). (ENG.). 112p. (J). (gr. 1-5). 15.99 (978-0-06-218988-2(3)) HarperCollins Pubs.

—Showdown at the Alamo. Pamintuan, Macky, illus. 2013. (Flat Stanley's Worldwide Adventures Ser.: 10). (ENG.). 112p. (J). (gr. 1-5). pap. 4.99 (978-0-06-218987-5(5)) HarperCollins Pubs.

—Showdown at the Alamo. 2013. (Flat Stanley's Worldwide Adventures Ser.: 10). (J). lib. bdg. 14.75 (978-0-606-35046-4(2), Turtleback) Turtleback Bks.

Cuate, Melodie A. Journey to the Alamo. 2006. (Mr. Barrington's Mysterious Trunk Ser.). (Illus.). 144p. (J). (gr. 4-7). 18.95 (978-0-89672-592-8(8)) Texas Tech Univ. Pr.

MacGregor, Roy. Face-Off at the Alamo. 2013. (Screech Owls Ser.). (ENG.). 176p. (J). (gr. 4-7). pap. 8.95 (978-1-77049-418-3(9), Tundra Bks.) Tundra Bks. CAN. Dist: Penguin Random Hse. LLC.

Marsh, Carole. The Mystery of the Alamo Ghost. (Real Kids, Real Places Ser.). (J). 2009. (Illus.). 146p. lib. bdg. 18.99 (978-0-635-06993-1(8), Marsh, Carole Mysteries) 2003. 160p. (gr. 2-8). 14.95 (978-0-635-01654-6(0)) 2003. 160p. (gr. 2-8). pap. 7.99 (978-0-635-01652-2(4)) Gallopade International.

Sibley, Linda & Marks, Dea. David Takes Part in the Battle of the Alamo. 2004. (Cover-To-Cover Books). (Illus.). 84p. pap. 6.65 (978-0-7891-6044-7(7)) Perfection Learning Corp.

Smith, Roland & Spradlin, Michael P. The Windy City, Bk.5. 2014. (I, Q Ser.). (ENG.). 240p. (YA). (gr. 5-7). 9.99 (978-1-58536-823-5(7), 202902) Sleeping Bear Pr.

ALASKA

Bugni, Alice. Beluga Whales, Grizzly Tales, & More Alaska Kidsnacks: Fun Recipes for Cooking with Kids. Brooks, Erik, illus. 2016. (Paws IV Ser.). (ENG.). 32p. (J). (gr. -1-2). pap. 10.99 (978-1-57061-999-1(9), Little Bigfoot) Sasquatch Bks.

Chamberlin-Calamar, Pat. Alaska's 12 Days of Summer. Cartwright, Shannon, illus. 2003. (Paws IV Ser.). (ENG.). 32p. (J). (gr. -1-2). pap. 10.99 (978-1-57061-341-8(9), Little Bigfoot) Sasquatch Bks.

Elavgak, Vernon. Life at the Top of the World. 2017. (Text Connections Guided Close Reading Ser.). (J). (gr. 2). (978-1-4900-1857-7(3)) Benchmark Education Co.

Feinstein, Stephen. Alaska: A MyReportLinks.com Book. 2003. (States Ser.). (Illus.). 48p. (J). (gr. 4-10). lib. bdg. 25.26 (978-0-7660-5025-9(4), MyReportLinks.com Bks.) Enslow Pubs., Inc.

Freedman, Russell. Because They Marched: The People's Campaign for Voting Rights That Changed America. 2014. (ENG., Illus.). 96p. (J). (gr. 5-12). 20.00 (978-0-8234-2921-9(0)) Holiday Hse., Inc.

Gill, Shelley. Alaska. Endres, Patrick J., photos by. 2007. (ENG., Illus.). 32p. (J). (gr. 1-4). pap. 7.99 (978-0-88106-293-9(6)) Charlesbridge Publishing, Inc.

HarrisNic. ALASKA: WILD AND FREE HIGH BEGINNING BOOK WITH ONLINE ACCESS. 2014. (ENG., Illus.). 24p. (J). pap. 9.50 (978-1-107-67464-6(6)) Cambridge Univ. Pr.

Harrison, Ted. A Northern Alphabet. 2009. (ABC Our Country Ser.). (ENG., Illus.). 32p. (J). (gr. 1-4). pap. 7.99 (978-0-88776-960-3(8), Tundra Bks.) Tundra Bks. CAN. Dist: Penguin Random Hse. LLC.

Johnston, Joyce. Alaska. (J). 2012. lib. bdg. 25.26 (978-0-7613-4520-6(5), Lerner Pubns.) 2nd rev. exp. ed. 2003. (Illus.). 84p. (gr. 3-6). pap. 6.95 (978-0-8225-4157-8(2)) Lerner Publishing Group.

Kupperberg, Paul. The Alaska Highway. 2009. (Building America Ser.). (Illus.). 144p. (gr. 5-8). 35.00 (978-1-60413-074-4(1), Chelsea Hse.) Facts On File, Inc.

Leacock, Elspeth. Exxon Valdez Oil Spill. 2005. (Environmental Disasters Ser.). (Illus.). 112p. (J). (gr. 6-12). 35.00 (978-0-8160-5754-2(0)) Facts On File, Inc.

Lusted, Marcia Amidon. Alaska: The Last Frontier. 2010. (Our Amazing States Ser.). (Illus.). 24p. (J). 22.60 (978-1-4488-0666-9(6), PowerKids Pr.) Rosen Publishing Group, Inc., The.

Marsh, Carole. Alaska Current Events Projects: 30 Cool, Activities, Crafts, Experiments & More for Kids to Do to Learn about Your State! 2003. (Alaska Experience Ser.). 32p. (gr. k-5). pap. 5.95 (978-0-635-02021-5(1), Marsh, Carole Bks.) Gallopade International.

—Alaska Geography Projects: 30 Cool, Activities, Crafts, Experiments & More for Kids to Do to Learn about Your State! 2003. (Alaska Experience Ser.). 32p. (gr. k-5). pap. 5.95 (978-0-635-01821-2(7), Marsh, Carole Bks.) Gallopade International.

—Alaska Government Projects: 30 Cool, Activities, Crafts, Experiments & More for Kids to Do to Learn about Your State! 2003. (Alaska Experience Ser.). 32p. (gr. k-5). pap. 5.95 (978-0-635-01921-9(3), Marsh, Carole Bks.) Gallopade International.

—Alaska People Projects: 30 Cool, Activities, Crafts, Experiments & More for Kids to Do to Learn about Your State! 2003. (Alaska Experience Ser.). 32p. (gr. k-5). pap. 5.95 (978-0-635-01971-4(X), Marsh, Carole Bks.) Gallopade International.

—Alaska Symbols & Facts Projects: 30 Cool, Activities, Crafts, Experiments & More for Kids to Do to Learn about Your State! 2003. (Alaska Experience Ser.). 32p. (gr. k-5). pap. 5.95 (978-0-635-01870-0(5), Marsh, Carole Bks.) Gallopade International.

Marsico, Katie. The Darkest & the Brightest. 2015. (True Book(tm), a — Extreme Places Ser.). (ENG., Illus.). 48p. (J). lib. bdg. 31.00 (978-0-531-21848-8(1), Children's Pr.) Scholastic Library Publishing.

Miller, Debbie S. & Eiler, John H. A King Salmon Journey. Van Zyle, Jon, illus. 2014. 44p. 15.95 (978-1-60223-230-3(X)); 32p. pap. 12.95 (978-1-60223-231-0(8)) Univ. of Alaska Pr.

Mis, Melody S. Exploring Glaciers. 2009. (Geography Zone: Landforms Ser.). (J). lib. bdg. 22.60 (978-1-4358-2714-1(7), PowerKids Pr.) Rosen Publishing Group, Inc., The.

Morgan, Marilyn. Alaska Alphabet CD-ROM. 2007. cd-rom 29.95 (978-1-878051-56-1(3)) Circumpolar Pr.

Muir, John. Stickeen. Buell, Carl Dennis, illus. Date not set. 94p. (J). 16.95 (978-0-8488-2803-5(8)) Amereon Ltd.

Murray, Julie. Alaska, 1 vol. 2006. (Buddy Book Ser.). (ENG., Illus.). 32p. (gr. k-4). 27.07 (978-1-59197-661-5(8), Buddy Bks.) ABDO Publishing Co.

Obregon, Jose Maria. Alaska. 2005. (Bilingual Library of the United States of America Ser.: Set 1). (ENG & SPA., Illus.). 32p. (J). (gr. 3-6). lib. bdg. 25.25 (978-1-4042-3066-8(1)) Rosen Publishing Group, Inc., The.

Obregón, José María. Alaska. 2009. (Bilingual Library of the United States of America Ser.). (SPA.). 32p. (gr. 2-2). 47.90 (978-1-60853-342-8(5), Editorial Buenas Letras) Rosen Publishing Group, Inc., The.

Ollhoff, Jim. Alaska, 1 vol. 2009. (United States Ser.). (ENG., Illus.). 48p. (YA). (gr. 2-5). 27.07 (978-1-60453-637-9(3)) ABDO Publishing Co.

Orr, Tamra B. Alaska (Revised Edition) 2014. (America the Beautiful Ser.: 3). (ENG.). 144p. (J). lib. bdg. 40.00 (978-0-531-24876-8(3)) Scholastic Library Publishing.

Petechuk, David. Non-Continental: Alaska, Hawaii, Vol. 19. 2015. (Let's Explore the States Ser.). (Illus.). 64p. (J). (gr. 5). 23.95 (978-1-4222-3328-3(6)) Mason Crest.

Peterson, Sheryl. Alaska. 2008. (This Land Called America Ser.). 32p. (YA). (gr. 3-6). lib. bdg. 22.95 (978-1-58341-627-3(7)) Creative Co., The.

Petrillo, Lisa. Sarah Palin. 2009. (Political Profiles Ser.). 100p. (YA). (gr. 6-9). 28.95 (978-1-59935-133-9(1)) Reynolds, Morgan Inc.

Quasha, J. How to Draw Alaska's Sights & Symbols. 2009. (Kid's Guide to Drawing America Ser.). 32p. (gr. k-k). 50.50

(978-1-61511-044-5(5), PowerKids Pr.) Rosen Publishing Group, Inc., The.
Richter, Bernd & Richter, Susan. Discover Alaskas Denali Park. 2008. (Illus.). 48p. (J). pap. 9.95 (978-1-931353-37-3(9)) Saddle Pal Creations, Inc.
—Listen to Alaskas Animals. Richter, Bernd, illus. 2003. (Illus.). 12p. bds. 12.95 (978-1-931353-12-0(3)) Saddle Pal Creations, Inc.
—Touch & Feel Alaskas Animals. 2003. (Illus.). 12p. bds. 9.95 (978-1-931353-13-7(1)) Saddle Pal Creations, Inc.
—Traveling Alaska. 2008. (Illus.). 48p. (J). pap. 9.95 (978-1-931353-36-6(0)) Saddle Pal Creations, Inc.
Rickus, John. The Animals of Alaska. 2008. (Real Readers - Upper Emergent Ser.). (ENG., Illus.). 12p. (gr. 1-2). pap. 5.90 (978-0-8239-6361-4(6)) Rosen Publishing Group, Inc., The.
Seder, Isaac. Alaska: The Last Frontier. 2003. (World Almanac Library of the States). (Illus.). 48p. (gr. 4-9). pap. 14.05 (978-0-8368-5318-6(0)); lib. bdg. 31.00 (978-0-8368-5147-2(1)) Stevens, Gareth Publishing LLLP. (Gareth Stevens Learning Library).
Stefoff, Rebecca. Alaska. 2nd rev. ed. 2006. (Celebrate the States Ser.). (Illus.). 144p. (gr. 6-7). lib. bdg. 42.79 (978-0-7614-2153-5(X), Benchmark Bks.) Marshall Cavendish Corp.
Stone, Sandra & Stone, James. The Alaska We Love. Stone, Sandra & Stone, James, photos by. Irby, Rob, photos by. 2007. (Illus.). 70p. (978-0-9800019-0-7(0)) Blue Skies Above Texas Co.
Strudwick, Leslie. Alaska: The Last Frontier. 2016. (J). (978-1-5105-0650-3(0)) SmartBook Media, Inc.
—Alaska: The Last Frontier. 2016. (J). (978-1-4896-4818-1(6)) Weigl Pubs., Inc.
Thomas, William David. Alaska. 2006. (Portraits of the States Ser.). 32p. (gr. 2-6). pap. 10.50 (978-0-8368-4714-7(8), Gareth Stevens Learning Library) Stevens, Gareth Publishing LLLP.
—Alaska. 2006. (Portraits of the States Ser.). (Illus.). 32p. (gr. 2-6). lib. bdg. 26.00 (978-0-8368-4697-3(4), Gareth Stevens Learning Library) Stevens, Gareth Publishing LLLP.
The Trail to the Iditarod Trail. 2003. (Illus.). 166p. per. 24.95 (978-0-9741254-0-4(7), Dynagraphix) Elliott, Jane.
Winner, Cherie. Life in the Tundra. 2003. (Ecosystems in Action Ser.). (ENG., Illus.). 72p. (gr. 5-9). lib. bdg. 26.60 (978-0-8225-4686-3(8)) Lerner Publishing Group.

ALASKA—FICTION

AaronG, Driftin'. Claude Henry, the Iditarod Mouse: The Adventures Begin. 2007. 108p. (J). per. 9.95 (978-0-595-44990-3(5)) iUniverse, Inc.
Adams, Andy. Alaska Ghost Glacier Mystery: A Biff Brewster Mystery Adventure. 2011. 184p. 42.95 (978-1-258-06473-0(1)) Literary Licensing, LLC.
Amos, Muriel & Olrun, Prudy. Animals of Nunivak Island. Amos, Muriel & Olrun, Prudy, illus. 2006. (Animal Story Collection Ser.). (Illus.). 16p. (J). (gr. 2-6). pap. 9.00 (978-1-58084-238-9(0)) Lower Kuskokwim Schl. District.
Appleton, Victor. Tom Swift in the Caves of Ice. 2005. 27.95 (978-1-4218-1509-1(5)); 204p. pap. 12.95 (978-1-4218-1609-8(1)) 1st World Publishing, Inc. (1st World Library - Literary Society).
—Tom Swift in the Caves of Ice or the Wre. 2006. pap. (978-1-4065-0915-1(9)) Dodo Pr.
Ayagalria, Julia, et al. Animals of the River. Ayagalria, Julia et al, illus. 2006. (Animal Story Collection Ser.). 24p. (J). (gr. 2-6). pap. 9.00 (978-1-58084-236-5(4)) Lower Kuskokwim Schl. District.
Babcock, Lee L. Ghost of Sunday Creek. 2006. (Illus.). 104p. per. 13.95 (978-1-4251-0162-6(3)) Trafford Publishing.
Barrett, Cheryl. Andy Goes Crab Fishin' 2010. 32p. pap. 12.99 (978-1-4490-7459-3(6)) AuthorHouse.
Blake, Robert J. Akiak. 2004. (Illus.). 28p. (gr. -1-3). 17.00 (978-0-7569-3207-7(6)) Perfection Learning Corp.
—Painter & Ugly. Blake, Robert J., illus. 2011. (ENG., Illus.). 48p. (J). (gr. k-3). 16.99 (978-0-399-24323-3(2), Philomel Bks.) Penguin Young Readers Group.
Boochever, Annie. Bristol Bay Summer. 2014. (ENG., Illus.). 258p. (J). (gr. 3-7). 28.99 (978-1-941821-27-5(8)); pap. 12.99 (978-0-88240-994-8(8)) Graphic Arts Ctr. Publishing Co. (Alaska Northwest Bks.).
Bowen, Carl. Bone Yard. Lee, Marc, illus. 2016. (Firestormers Ser.). (ENG.). 112p. (gr. 4-8). lib. bdg. 26.65 (978-1-4965-3306-7(2)) Stone Arch Bks.
Brown, Tricia. Charlie & the Blanket Toss. Martinsen, Sarah, illus. 2015. (ENG.). 32p. (J). pap. 10.99 (978-1-941821-66-4(9), Alaska Northwest Bks.) Graphic Arts Ctr. Publishing Co.
—Groucho's Eyebrows: An Alaskan Cat Tale. Lavallee, Barbara, illus. 2012. (ENG.). 32p. (J). (gr. -1-1). pap. 9.99 (978-0-88240-892-7(5), Alaska Northwest Bks.) Graphic Arts Ctr. Publishing Co.
—Musher's Night Before Christmas, 1 vol. Dubac, Debra, illus. 2011. (Night Before Christmas Ser.). (ENG.). 32p. (J). (gr. k-3). 16.99 (978-1-58980-843-0(6)) Pelican Publishing Co., Inc.
Bryson, Jamie S. The War Canoe. 2nd ed. 2009. (ENG., Illus.). 180p. (YA). (gr. 8-12). pap. 9.95 (978-0-88240-758-6(9), Alaska Northwest Bks.) Graphic Arts Ctr. Publishing Co.
Burchett, Jan & Vogler, Sara. Polar Meltdown, 1 vol. Le Feyer, Diane, illus. 2012. (Wild Rescue Ser.). (ENG.). 152p. (gr. 3-6). 9.95 (978-1-4342-4594-6(2)); lib. bdg. 25.32 (978-1-4342-3769-9(9)) Stone Arch Bks.
Carlstrom, Nancy White. Raven & River. Van Zyle, Jon, illus. 2011. (ENG.). 32p. pap. 11.95 (978-1-60223-150-4(8)) Univ. of Alaska Pr.
Chase, Anita, et al. Tundra Adventures. Chase, Anita et al, illus. 2006. (Adventure Story Collection Ser.). 28p. (J). (gr. 2-6). pap. 10.00 (978-1-58084-254-9(2)) Lower Kuskokwim Schl. District.
Claflin, Willy. The Uglified Ducky. Stimson, James, illus. 2011. (ENG.). 32p. (J). (gr. -1-3). pap. 9.95 (978-0-87483-953-1(X)) August Hse. Pubs., Inc.
Clarke, Tom E. The Puddle Jumper: The Adventures of A Young Flyer in Alaska. 2011. 190p. 42.95 (978-1-258-05006-1(4)) Literary Licensing, LLC.
Clements, Becky. A Picnic with Friends: Alaska Adventure Bears. 2003. (Alaska Adventure Bears Ser.). 16p. (J). pap. 9.95 (978-1-888125-87-0(X)) Publication Consultants.
Corwin, Jeff. The Great Alaska Adventure!, 2 vols., Bk. 2. 2010. (Jeff Corwin Ser.: 2). (ENG.). 112p. (J). (gr. 1-3). 4.99 (978-0-14-241409-5(3), Puffin Books) Penguin Young Readers Group.
Cosgrove, Stephen. Gnome from Nome. James, Robin, illus. 2012. (Paws IV Ser.). (ENG.). 32p. (J). (gr. -1-2). pap. 10.99 (978-1-57061-777-5(5), Little Bigfoot) Sasquatch Bks.
Dagg, Carole Estby. Sweet Home Alaska. 2016. (ENG.). 304p. (J). (gr. 5). 16.99 (978-0-399-17203-8(3), Nancy Paulsen Books) Penguin Young Readers Group.
Dawn, Nyrae, et al. Out of Play. 2013. (Entangled Teen Ser.). (ENG.). 320p. (YA). pap. 9.99 (978-1-62266-010-0(2), 9781622660100) Entangled Publishing, LLC.
Denucci, Sharon. Ava Goes to Alask: Grammie & the Gecko Series. 2012. 32p. pap. 19.99 (978-1-4685-6157-9(X)) AuthorHouse.
Dillingham, Mike. Rivers Book Two: Through the Eyes of a Blind Sled Dog. 2003. (YA). pap. 13.95 (978-1-59433-004-9(2)) Publication Consultants.
Dirkes, Craig. Sucktown, Alaska. 2017. (ENG.). 352p. (gr. 9-12). 17.95 (978-1-63079-055-4(9)) Switch Pr.
Dwyer, Mindy. The Salmon Princess: An Alaska Cinderella Story. 2004. (Paws IV Ser.). (ENG., Illus.). 32p. (J). (gr. -1-2). pap. 10.99 (978-1-57061-355-5(9), Little Bigfoot) Sasquatch Bks.
Earhart, Kristin. Arctic Freeze. 2015. (Race the Wild Ser.: 3). lib. bdg. 14.75 (978-0-606-37773-7(5)) Turtleback Bks.
Edward, J. P. The Outsider. 2012. 24p. pap. 24.95 (978-1-4626-7213-4(2)) America Star Bks.
Edwardson, Debby Dahl. My Name Is Not Easy, 0 vols. 2013. (ENG.). 256p. (YA). (gr. 7-9). pap. 9.99 (978-1-4778-1629-5(1), 9781477816295, Amazon Children's Publishing) Amazon Publishing.
Fincher, Cecilia. Chandra's Adventure. 2012. 28p. pap. 19.99 (978-1-4772-0137-4(8)) AuthorHouse.
Forbush, Kyle. The Sourdoughs' Five Children. Forbush, Lisa, illus. 2004. (J). bds. 6.95 (978-1-57833-258-8(3)) Todd Communications.
—Who Is Alaska's Favorite Bear? Forbush, Lisa, illus. 2003. (J). bds. 6.95 (978-1-57833-211-3(7)) Todd Communications.
Frost, Helen. Diamond Willow. 2011. (ENG.). 144p. (J). (gr. 5-9). pap. 7.99 (978-0-312-60383-0(5), 9780312603830) Square Fish.
Giles, Gail. Right Behind You. 2008. (ENG.). 320p. (J). (gr. 10-17). pap. 10.99 (978-0-316-16637-9(5)) Little, Brown Bks. for Young Readers.
Gill, Shelley. Kiana's Iditarod. Cartwright, Shannon, illus. 2008. (Paws IV Ser.). (ENG.). 32p. (J). (gr. -1-3). pap. 10.99 (978-1-57061-589-4(6), Little Bigfoot) Sasquatch Bks.
—Prickly Rose. Cartwright, Shannon & Love, Judy, illus. 2014. (ENG.). 32p. (J). (gr. -1-3). pap. 7.95 (978-1-57091-357-0(9)); lib. bdg. 17.95 (978-1-57091-356-3(0)) Charlesbridge Publishing, Inc.
—Sitka Rose. Cartwright, Shannon, illus. 2005. (ENG.). 32p. (J). (gr. -1-3). per. 7.95 (978-1-57091-364-8(1)) Charlesbridge Publishing, Inc.
Glaser, Linda. Alask. 2012. 28p. pap. 21.99 (978-1-4797-3781-9(X)) Xlibris Corp.
Herron, Edward A. The Return of the Alaskan: Mailboat in the Outpost. Langley, Gene, illus. 2011. 190p. 42.95 (978-1-258-09093-7(7)) Literary Licensing, LLC.
Higgins, Kitty. Mushing in Alaska. 2005. (J). pap. (978-1-4108-4228-2(2)) Benchmark Education Co.
Hill, Kirkpatrick. Bo at Ballard Creek. Pham, LeUyen, illus. 2013. (ENG.). 288p. (J). (gr. 3-7). 16.99 (978-0-8050-9351-3(6), 9780805093513, Holt, Henry & Co. Bks. For Young Readers) Holt, Henry & Co.
—Bo at Ballard Creek. Pham, LeUyen, illus. 2014. (ENG.). 304p. (J). (gr. 3-7). pap. 7.99 (978-1-250-04425-9(1), 9781250044259) Square Fish.
—Bo at Iditarod Creek. Pham, LeUyen, illus. 2014. (ENG.). 288p. (J). (gr. 3-7). 15.99 (978-0-8050-9352-0(4), 9780805093520, Holt, Henry & Co. Bks. For Young Readers) Holt, Henry & Co.
—Dancing at the Odinochka. 2010. (ENG.). 272p. (J). (gr. 5-9). pap. 12.99 (978-1-4424-1352-8(2), McElderry, Margaret K. Bks.) McElderry, Margaret K. Bks.
—Do Not Pass Go. 2011. (ENG.). 240p. (J). (gr. 4-9). pap. 6.99 (978-1-4424-2122-6(3), McElderry, Margaret K. Bks.) McElderry, Margaret K. Bks.
—Winter Camp. 2007. (ENG.). 192p. (J). (gr. 3-7). pap. 10.99 (978-1-4169-6455-1(X), Simon & Schuster/Paula Wiseman Bks.) Simon & Schuster/Paula Wiseman Bks.
—The Year of Miss Agnes. 2003. (Aladdin Historical Fiction Ser.). 115p. (gr. 3-7). 17.00 (978-0-7569-1407-3(8)) Perfection Learning Corp.
Hitchcock, Bonnie-Sue. The Smell of Other People's Houses. 2016. (ENG., Illus.). 240p. (YA). (gr. 7). 17.99 (978-0-553-49778-6(2), Lamb, Wendy Bks.) Random Hse. Children's Bks.
Hobbs, Will. Leaving Protection. 2005. (ENG.). 192p. (J). (gr. 5-18). pap. 8.99 (978-0-380-73312-5(9)) HarperCollins Pubs.
—Leaving Protection. 2005. 178p. (gr. 5-9). 19.00 (978-0-7569-5121-4(6)) Perfection Learning Corp.
Hobbs, Will & Hobbs, William. Wild Man Island. 2003. (ENG.). 192p. (J). (gr. 5-18). pap. 5.99 (978-0-380-73310-1(2)) HarperCollins Pubs.
Jacobs, Lily. The Littlest Bunny in Alaska: An Easter Adventure. 2015. (ENG.). 32p. (J). (-3). 9.99 (978-1-4926-1018-2(6), Sourcebooks Jabberwocky) Sourcebooks, Inc.
James, Arthur. Jason & the Kodikats. 2013. 118p. pap. (978-0-9918166-2-0(5)) Flower Pr.
James, Eric. A Halloween Scare in Alaska. Le Ray, Marina, illus. 2015. (ENG.). 32p. (J). (-5). 9.99 (978-1-4926-2360-1(1), 9781492623601, Sourcebooks Jabberwocky) Sourcebooks, Inc.
—Santa's Sleigh Is on Its Way to Alaska: A Christmas Adventure. Dunn, Robert, illus. 2016. (ENG.). 32p. (J). (-2). 12.99 (978-1-4926-4314-2(9), 9781492643142, Sourcebooks Jabberwocky) Sourcebooks, Inc.
Jefford, Nikki. Aurora Sky: Vampire Hunter, Vol. 1. 2013. 260p. pap. 10.99 (978-1-939997-48-7(8)) Boyce, S. M.
Johannes, Avril & Branham, Jan. Bunny an Alaskan Hare. 2006. 32p. 7.95 (978-0-9749360-3-1(0)) Icicle Falls Publishing Co.
—Eeny, Meeny, Miney, Moe, Four Alaskan Ravens. Tessama, C., illus. 2003. 32p. (J). 7.95 (978-0-9749360-0-0(6)) Icicle Falls Publishing Co.
Johnson, Christine. Deep in Alaska. Johnson, Gary R., illus. 2013. 42p. pap. 12.95 (978-1-60223-215-0(6)) Univ. of Alaska Pr.
K/H (Pathways). Kindergarten Stepping Stones: Kindergarten the Bravest Dog Ever - The True Story of Balto Trade Book. rev. ed. 2010. (ENG.). 48p. pap. 9.00 (978-0-7575-8646-0(5)) Kendall Hunt Publishing Co.
Keene, Carolyn. Curse of the Arctic Star. 2013. (Nancy Drew Diaries: 1). (ENG.). 208p. (J). (gr. 3-7). 15.99 (978-1-4424-6610-4(3)); pap. 6.99 (978-1-4169-9072-7(0)) Simon & Schuster Children's Publishing. (Aladdin).
—Nancy Drew Diaries: Curse of the Arctic Star; Strangers on a Train; Mystery of the Midnight Rider; Once upon a Thriller. 2013. (Nancy Drew Diaries). (ENG., Illus.). 768p. (J). (gr. 3-7). pap. 27.99 (978-1-4424-8896-0(4), Aladdin) Simon & Schuster Children's Publishing.
—Nancy Drew Diaries 3-Books-In-1! Curse of the Arctic Star; Strangers on a Train; Mystery of the Midnight Rider. 2016. (Nancy Drew Diaries). (ENG., Illus.). 592p. (J). (gr. 3-7). pap. 8.99 (978-1-4814-8554-8(7), Aladdin) Simon & Schuster Children's Publishing.
—Once upon a Thriller. 2013. (Nancy Drew Diaries: 4). (ENG., Illus.). 144p. (J). (gr. 3-7). 15.99 (978-1-4424-6612-8(X)); pap. 6.99 (978-1-4169-9074-1(7)) Simon & Schuster Children's Publishing. (Aladdin).
—Strangers on a Train. 2013. (Nancy Drew Diaries: 2). (ENG.). 208p. (J). (gr. 3-7). 15.99 (978-1-4424-6611-1(1), Simon & Schuster/Paula Wiseman Bks.) Simon & Schuster/Paula Wiseman Bks.
Kennedy, Marlane. Volcano Blast. 2015. (Disaster Strikes Ser.: 4). (ENG.). 128p. (J). (gr. 2-5). pap. 4.99 (978-0-545-53047-7(4), Scholastic Paperbacks) Scholastic, Inc.
Kerr, Mike. Mike & a Lynx Named Kitty. Vitt, Karren, illus. 2nd rev. ed. 2006. 112p. per. 13.50 (978-1-931195-36-2(6)) KiwE Publishing, Ltd.
Kimmel, Elizabeth Cody. Legend of the Ghost Dog. (J). 2014. (ENG.). 208p. (gr. 3-7). pap. 6.99 (978-0-545-39128-3(8)) 2012. (ENG.). 208p. (gr. 3-7). 16.99 (978-0-545-39127-6(X)) 2012. 200p. pap. (978-0-545-50705-9(7)) Scholastic, Inc. (Scholastic Pr.).
Kirsch, Amanda. Honor Bound. 2013. pap. 11.95 (978-1-59433-375-0(0)) Publication Consultants.
Kita, Suzanne. Three Whales: Who Won the Heart of the World. Sundram, Steve, illus. 2010. (ENG.). 40p. (J). (gr. 3). (978-1-59700-761-0(7)) Island Heritage Publishing.
Kittredge, Frances. Neeluk: An Eskimo Boy in the Days of the Whaling Ships. Rock, Howard, illus. 2005. 88p. (J). (gr. 3-7). 18.95 (978-0-88240-545-2(4)) Graphic Arts Ctr. Publishing Co.
Lawrence, Iain. The Skeleton Tree. 2016. (ENG.). 288p. (J). (gr. 3-7). 16.99 (978-0-385-73378-6(X), Delacorte Bks. for Young Readers) Random Hse. Children's Bks.
Leinberger, Judy. The Man Who Talks with Eagles. 2010. 60p. pap. 14.00 (978-1-4269-3396-7(7)) Trafford Publishing.
Lindoff, Hannah. Mary's Wild Winter Feast. Koch, Nobu & Rizal, Clarissa, illus. 2014. 40p. pap. 14.95 (978-1-60223-232-7(6)) Univ. of Alaska Pr.
London, Jack. The Call of the Wild. Green, John, illus. abr. l.t. ed. 2011. (Dover Children's Thrift Classics Ser.). (ENG.). 64p. (J). (gr. 3-8). pap. 3.00 (978-0-486-40551-3(6)) Dover Pubns., Inc.
London, Jonathan. Little Puffin's First Flight. Van Zyle, Jon, illus. 2016. (ENG.). 32p. (J). (gr. -1-3). 10.99 (978-0-88240-924-5(7), Alaska Northwest Bks.) Graphic Arts Ctr. Publishing Co.
Marsh, Carole. The Gosh Awful! Gold Rush Mystery. (Real Kids, Real Places Ser.). (Illus.). 146p. (J). 2009. lib. bdg. 18.99 (978-0-635-07026-5(X), Marsh, Carole Mysteries) 2007. (gr. 2-8). 14.95 (978-0-635-06390-8(5)) Gallopade International.
—The Mystery on Alaska's Iditarod Trail. 2009. (Real Kids, Real Places Ser.). 145p. (J). 18.99 (978-0-635-06997-9(0), Marsh, Carole Mysteries) Gallopade International.
McCracken, Harold. Pirate of the North. Tonk, Ernest, illus. 2011. 224p. 44.95 (978-1-258-09631-1(5)) Literary Licensing, LLC.
McKinley, Mary. Rusty Summer. 2015. (Rusty Winters Ser.: 2). (ENG.). 352p. (YA). (gr. 9). pap. 9.95 (978-1-61773-257-7(5)) Kensington Publishing Corp.
McKittrick, Erin. My Coyote Nose & Ptarmigan Toes: An Almost-True Alaskan Adventure. Higman, Valisa, illus. 2016. (Paws IV Ser.). (ENG.). 32p. (J). (gr. -1-2). 17.99 (978-1-63217-052-1(3)); pap. 10.99 (978-1-63217-031-6(0)) Sasquatch Bks. (Little Bigfoot).
Mcpherson, Missie & O'Neill, Elizabeth. Alfred Visits Alaska. 2006. (Illus.). 24p. (J). pap. 12.00 (978-0-9771836-3-0(7)) Global Business Information Strategies, Inc.
Merrill, Karen Grill. Oh, What a State I'm In: The USA in Rhyme & Riddle, 1 vol. Grill, Gerald, illus. 2010. 48p. pap. 24.95 (978-1-4489-7979-0(X)) PublishAmerica, Inc.
Monninger, Joseph. Crash. 2014. (Stay Alive Ser.: 1). lib. bdg. 16.00 (978-0-606-35392-2(5)) Turtleback Bks.
—Stay Alive #1: Crash. 2014. (Stay Alive Ser.: 1). (ENG.). 208p. (J). (gr. 3-7). pap. 5.99 (978-0-545-56348-2(8), Scholastic Paperbacks) Scholastic, Inc.
Murphy, Gold Rush Dog, 1 vol. 2014. (Dog Chronicles Ser.). (ENG., Illus.). 160p. (J). (gr. 2-5). 12.95 (978-1-56145-769-4(8)) Peachtree Pubs.
Myers, Hortense & Burnett, Ruth. Carl Ben Eielson: Young Alaskan Pilot. Morrow, Gray, illus. 2011. 200p. 44.95 (978-1-258-01949-5(3)) Literary Licensing, LLC.
Nolting, Anne Carse. Pythagoras Eagle & the Music of the Spheres. 2003. (ENG.). 172p. (YA). 23.95 (978-1-878044-94-5(X)) Mayhaven Publishing, Inc.
Orenstein, Denise Gosliner. Unseen Companion. 2003. 368p. (J). 15.99 (978-0-06-052056-4(6)); lib. bdg. 16.89 (978-0-06-052057-1(4)) HarperCollins Pubs.
Orenstein, Denise Gosliner & Orenstein, Denise G. Unseen Companion. 2005. (ENG.). 368p. (YA). (gr. 8). reprint ed. pap. 7.99 (978-0-06-052058-8(2), Tegen, Katherine Bks) HarperCollins Pubs.
Ostow, Micol. What Would My Cell Phone Do? 2011. (ENG.). 272p. (YA). (gr. 7-18). 7.99 (978-0-14-241469-9(7), Speak) Penguin Young Readers Group.
Papish, Ram. The Little Fox: An Alaska Adventure. Papish, Ram & Papish, Ram, illus. 2008. (ENG., Illus.). 38p. (gr. 3-7). 15.95 (978-1-889963-87-7(9)) Univ. of Alaska Pr.
—The Little Seal: An Alaska Adventure. 2009. (ENG., Illus.). 24p. (J). 15.95 (978-1-60223-068-2(4)) Univ. of Alaska Pr.
Peratrovich, Roy A., Jr. Little Whale: A Story of the Last Tlingit War Canoe. 2016. (ENG., Illus.). 64p. (J). pap. 16.95 (978-1-60223-295-2(4)) Univ. of Alaska Pr.
Perry, Jolene. Has to Be Love. 2015. (ENG.). 272p. (YA). (gr. 8-12). 16.99 (978-0-8075-6557-5(1)) Whitman, Albert & Co.
Peterson, Sara Budinger. The Journey of Perm. Kaufman, Mary Bee, illus. 2004. 96p. pap. 11.95 (978-0-9665282-3-7(9)) Saranjon Publishing.
Plum, Amy. After the End. 2014. (After the End Ser.: 1). (ENG.). 336p. (YA). (gr. 8). 17.99 (978-0-06-222560-3(X), HarperTeen) HarperCollins Pubs.
Poulsen, David A. The Book of Vampire. 4th rev. ed. 2007. (Salt & Pepper Chronicles). (ENG., Illus.). 160p. (J). (gr. 4-7). 6.95 (978-1-55263-805-7(7)) Leaf Storm Pr.
Renae, Cameo. Hidden Wings. 2013. 270p. pap. 13.99 (978-1-939769-21-3(3)) Crushing Hearts and Black Butterfly Publishing.
Renfrew, Regan. Orphans of the Heart: A Young Girl & a Paint Filly Heal Each Other's Broken Hearts. 2013. (ENG.). 163p. (YA). pap. 12.95 (978-1-4787-1686-0(X)) Outskirts Pr., Inc.
Richardson, Nikki. A Beautiful Lie, 1 vol. 2009. 168p. pap. 24.95 (978-1-61582-927-9(X)) America Star Bks.
Richter, Bernd & Richter, Susan. Cruising Alaska's Inside Passage. 2003. (ENG., Illus.). 56p. pap. 9.95 (978-1-931353-09-0(3)) Saddle Pal Creations, Inc.
—Gandma & Grandpa Cruise Alaska Inside Passage. 2008. (Illus.). 52p. (J). pap. 9.95 (978-1-931353-35-9(2)) Saddle Pal Creations, Inc.
—Grandma & Grandpa Ride Alaska Train. 2008. (Illus.). 48p. (J). pap. 9.95 (978-1-931353-34-2(4)) Saddle Pal Creations, Inc.
—Grandma & Grandpa Visit Denali. Drashner, Diane, illus. 2008. 48p. (J). pap. 9.95 (978-1-931353-33-5(6)) Saddle Pal Creations, Inc.
—Listen to Alaskas Animals. Richter, Bernd, illus. 2006. (Illus.). 12p. (J). act. bk. ed. 12.95 (978-1-931353-25-0(5)) Saddle Pal Creations, Inc.
—When Grandma & Grandpa Cruised Through Alaska. 2008. (ENG., Illus.). 18p. (J). bds. 8.95 (978-1-931353-39-7(5)) Saddle Pal Creations, Inc.
—When Grandma & Grandpa Rode the Alaska Train. 2008. (ENG., Illus.). 16p. (J). bds. 8.95 (978-1-931353-40-3(9)) Saddle Pal Creations, Inc.
Rockwood, Roy. On a Torn-Away World. 2008. 136p. pap. 12.95 (978-1-60664-174-3(3)) Aegypan.
Roddy, Lee. Hunted in the Alaskan Wilderness. 2008. (Ladd Family Adventure Ser.: Vol. 13). (Illus.). 149p. (Orig.). (J). (gr. 3-7). per. 7.99 (978-0-88062-262-2(8)) Mott Media.
—Tracked by the Wolf Pack. 2006. (Ladd Family Adventure Ser.: Vol. 15). (J). 7.99 (978-0-88062-264-6(4)) Mott Media.
Rose, Caroline Starr. Jasper & the Riddle of Riley's Mine. 2017. (ENG.). 288p. (J). (gr. 5). 16.99 (978-0-399-16811-6(7), G.P. Putnam's Sons Books for Young Readers) Penguin Young Readers Group.
Rouse, Betty Munn. The Adventures of the Phillyfab Family. 2011. 68p. pap. 12.95 (978-1-4567-3005-5(3)) AuthorHouse.
Roy, Ron. Operation Orca. Gurney, John Steven, illus. 2015. (to Z Mysteries Ser.). (ENG.). 144p. (J). (gr. 1-4). 12.99 (978-0-553-52397-3(X), Random Hse. Bks. for Young Readers) Random Hse. Children's Bks.
Sargent, Daina. Alaska: Be Brave, 4 vols. Lenoir, Jane, illus. l.t. ed. 2004. (Double Trouble Ser.: 4). 48p. (J). pap. 10.95 (978-1-59381-121-7(7)); lib. bdg. 23.60 (978-1-59381-120-4(9)) Ozark Publishing.
Sharp, Lydia. Whenever I'm with You. 2017. (ENG.). 304p. (J). (gr. 7). 17.99 (978-1-338-04749-3(3), Scholastic Pr.) Scholastic, Inc.
Sherman, V. T. The Call of the Beaver Patrol: Or A Break in the Glacier. 2007. (ENG.). 238p. pap. 20.99 (978-1-4346-3570-9(8)) Creative Media Partners, LLC.
—The Call of the Beaver Patrol: Or a Break in the Glacier. l.t. ed. 2007. (ENG.). 270p. pap. 23.99 (978-1-4346-3571-6(6)) Creative Media Partners, LLC.
Silvano, Wendi. Love Is All Around Alaska. Czernichowska, Joanna, illus. 2016. (ENG.). 32p. (J). (-6). 12.99 (978-1-4926-2901-6(4), Sourcebooks Jabberwocky) Sourcebooks, Inc.
Simmons, Lynn Sheffield. Bo, the Famous Retriever, 1 vol. Hampton, Lin, illus. 2003. (Bo Ser.). (ENG.). 128p. (J). (gr. 3-6). 10.95 (978-1-58980-217-9(9)) Pelican Publishing Co., Inc.
Skurzynski, Gloria & Ferguson, Alane. Buried Alive! 2008. (Mysteries in Our National Park Ser.). (ENG., Illus.). 160p. (J). (gr. 3-7). pap. 4.99 (978-1-4263-0252-7(5), National Geographic Children's Bks.) National Geographic Society.
Slim, Lillian, et al. Subsistence Adventures. Slim, Lillian et al, illus. 2006. (Adventure Story Collection Ser.). 28p. (J). (gr. 2-6). pap. 10.00 (978-1-58084-252-5(6)) Lower Kuskokwim Schl. District.
Smallman, Steve. Santa Is Coming to Alaska. Dunn, Robert, illus. 2013. (ENG.). 32p. (J). (-3). 9.99 (978-1-4022-9517-1(0), Sourcebooks Jabberwocky) Sourcebooks, Inc.
Smelcer, John. Edge of Nowhere. 2014. (ENG.). 194p. (J). (gr. 6). pap. 9.99 (978-1-935248-57-6(X)) Leapfrog Pr.
—The Great Death. 2009. (ENG.). 176p. (YA). (gr. 5-9). 17.99 (978-0-8050-8100-8(3), 9780805081008, Holt, Henry & Co. Bks. For Young Readers) Holt, Henry & Co.
—Savage Mountain. 2015. (ENG., Illus.). 160p. (J). (gr. 6). pap. 12.00 (978-1-935248-65-1(0)) Leapfrog Pr.
—The Trap. 2007. (ENG.). 176p. (YA). (gr. 7-9). per. 9.99 (978-0-312-37755-7(X), 9780312377557) Square Fish.
Smith, Stephanie Harms. For Everything There Is a Season in God's Time. 2007. 84p. per. 11.99 (978-1-60477-224-1(7)) Salem Author Services.

A
B

Snell, Roy J. The Blue Envelope. 2009. 112p. 22.95 *(978-1-60664-675-5(3))*; pap. 9.95 *(978-1-60664-304-4(5))* Rodgers, Alan Bks.
Souders, Taryn. How to (Almost) Ruin Your Summer. 2016. (ENG.). 240p. (J). (gr. 3-7). pap. 7.99 *(978-1-4926-3774-5(2)*, 9781492637745, Sourcebooks Jabberwocky) Sourcebooks, Inc.
Springer, Susan Woodward. Seldovia Sam & Wildfire Escape. Meissner, Amy, illus. 2005. (Misadventures of Seldovia Sam Ser.: Bk. 3). (ENG.). 64p. (J). (gr. -1-4). per. 6.95 *(978-0-88240-601-5(9))* Graphic Arts Ctr. Publishing Co.
Starr, Barbara May. A Home for Finn: The Tail of an Alaska Rescue Dog, 1 vol. 2009. 23p. pap. 24.95 *(978-1-60749-679-3(8))* America Star Bks.
Stevens, Beverly. This Dog Team Lives in the House. 2005. (Illus.). 32p. (J). pap. 9.95 *(978-1-57833-317-2(2))* Todd Communications.
Stihler, Chérie B. The Sourdough Man: An Alaska Folktale. Lavallee, Barbara, illus. 2010. (Paws IV Ser.). (ENG.). 32p. (J). (gr. -1-2). pap. 10.99 *(978-1-57061-594-8(2)*, Little Bigfoot) Sasquatch Bks.
—Wiggle-Waggle Woof: Counting Sled Dogs in Alaska. Bania, Michael, illus. 2009. (Paws IV Ser.). (ENG.). 32p. (J). (gr. -1-2). pap. 10.99 *(978-1-57061-559-7(4)*, Little Bigfoot) Sasquatch Bks.
Taylor, Richard B. Chispita Service Dog Extraordinaire: Volume 3. Alaskan Cruise. 2010. 52p. pap. 20.49 *(978-1-4490-5563-9(X))* AuthorHouse.
—Chispita Service Dog Extraordinaire: Volume 4. Alaskan Land Cruise. 2010. 68p. pap. 23.49 *(978-1-4490-5613-1(X))* AuthorHouse.
Thomas, Terri. The Barge Ghost, 1 vol. unabr. ed. 2010. (Q Reads Ser.). (ENG.). 32p. (YA). (gr. 9-12). pap. 6.95 *(978-1-61651-211-8(3))* Saddleback Educational Publishing, Inc.
Thompson, Louise. Cold Weather Readers. 2010. 206p. pap. 21.95 *(978-0-557-38162-3(2))* Lulu Pr., Inc.
Trout, Richard. Czar of Alaska: The Cross of Charlemagne, 1 vol. 2005. (MacGregor Family Adventure Ser.: 4). (ENG.). 256p. (YA). (gr. k-3). 16.99 *(978-1-58980-328-2(0))* Pelican Publishing Co., Inc.
Vanasse, Deb. Cold Spell. 2014. (Alaska Literary Ser.). 224p. pap. 15.95 *(978-1-60223-242-6(3))* Univ. of Alaska Pr.
—Lucy's Dance. 2011. (ENG., Illus.). 29p. 16.95 *(978-1-60223-127-6(3))*; 32p. pap. 10.95 *(978-1-60223-126-9(5))* Univ. of Alaska Pr.
—Under Alaska's Midnight Sun. Trammell, Jeremiah, illus. 2005. (Paws IV Ser.). (ENG.). 32p. (J). (gr. -1-2). pap. 10.99 *(978-1-57061-422-4(9)*, Little Bigfoot) Sasquatch Bks.
Viano, Hannah. Arrow to Alaska: A Pacific Northwest Adventure. 2015. (ENG., Illus.). 32p. (J). (gr. k-4). 16.99 *(978-1-57061-949-6(2)*, Little Bigfoot) Sasquatch Bks.
Walker, Dan. Secondhand Summer. 2016. (ENG.). 184p. (YA). 23.99 *(978-1-943328-79-6(X)*, Alaska Northwest Bks.) Graphic Arts Ctr. Publishing Co.
Walker, Lane. Terror at Deadwood Lake. 2014. (Hometown Hunters Collection: Vol. 3). (ENG.). 137p. (YA). (gr. 7-13). pap. 9.99 *(978-1-58169-519-9(5)*, Evergreen Pr.) Genesis Communications, Inc.
Walluk, Wilbur, illus. The Alaskan Ten-Footed Bear & Other Legends. 2013. 44p. pap. 9.95 *(978-1-61646-201-7(9))* Coachwhip Pubns.
Wassillie, Eliza, et al. Four Legged Adventures. Wassillie, Eliza et al, illus. 2006. (Adventure Story Collection Ser.). 28p. (J). (gr. 2-6). pap. 10.00 *(978-1-58084-250-1(X))* Lower Kuskokwim Schl. District.
Weaver, Jenny. Following the Raven. 2003. (ENG.). 113p. (YA). (gr. 5-8). pap. 14.95 *(978-1-878044-91-4(5))* Mayhaven Publishing, Inc.
Whelan, Gloria. Silver. Marchesi, Stephen, illus. 2004. (Stepping Stone Book(TM) Ser.). (ENG.). 64p. (J). (gr. 1-4). 3.99 *(978-0-394-89611-3(4)*, Random Hse. Bks. for Young Readers) Random Hse. Children's Bks.
Wilderness, Dale. Drift in Your Pillow's Eyes. 2013. pap. 9.95 *(978-1-59433-155-8(3))* Publication Consultants.
Winfield, Arthur M. Rover Boys in Alaska or Lost in the Fiel. 2006. pap. 30.95 *(978-1-4286-4107-5(6))* Kessinger Publishing, LLC.
Young, Judy. The Missing Grizzly Cubs. 2016. (Wild World of Buck Bray Ser.). (ENG.). 240p. (J). (gr. 3-6). 16.99 *(978-1-58536-970-6(5)*, 204107) Sleeping Bear Pr.

ALASKA—HISTORY

Alaska Boys and Girls Clubs Staff. A Is for Alaska. McCann, Michelle, ed. 2015. (See-My-State Alphabet Ser.). (ENG., Illus.). 32p. (J). (gr. -1-3). 13.99 *(978-1-941821-41-1(3)*, West Winds Pr.) Graphic Arts Ctr. Publishing Co.
Alaskan Iditarod Adventure: Represent & Solve Problems Involving Multiplication. 2014. (Rosen Common Core Math Readers Ser.). (ENG., Illus.). 24p. (J). (gr. 3-4). pap. 8.25 *(978-1-4777-4962-3(4)*, PowerKids Pr.) Rosen Publishing Group, Inc., The.
Beech, Linda Ward. The Exxon Valdez's Deadly Oil Spill. 2007. (Code Red Ser.). (Illus.). 32p. (YA). (gr. 2-5). lib. bdg. 25.27 *(978-1-59716-366-8(X))* Bearport Publishing Co., Inc.
Benoit, Peter. The Exxon Valdez Oil Spill. 2011. (J). pap. *(978-0-531-29028-6(X))* Children's Pr., Ltd.
—The Exxon Valdez Oil Spill. 2011. (True Bks.). 48p. (J). (gr. 3-5). 29.00 *(978-0-531-20629-4(7)*, Children's Pr.) Scholastic Library Publishing.
—The EXXON Valdez Oil Spill. 2011. (True Bk Ser.). (ENG., Illus.). 48p. (J). pap. 6.95 *(978-0-531-28998-3(2)*, Children's Pr.) Scholastic Library Publishing.
Bjorklund, Ruth, et al. Alaska. 2016. (ENG., Illus.). 80p. (J). 34.21 *(978-1-62713-154-4(X))* Cavendish Square Publishing.
Blake, Kevin. Balto's Story. 2014. (Dog Heroes Ser.). (ENG.). 32p. (J). (gr. 2-7). lib. bdg. 25.27 *(978-1-62724-286-8(4))* Bearport Publishing Co., Inc.
Carpenter, Chad. Tundra Alaska Coloring Book. (J). pap. 3.00 *(978-1-878100-32-0(7))* Todd Communications.
Cartwright, Shannon. Alaska 1 2 3: Colors & Numbers. 2005. (Illus.). (J). *(978-0-9772297-0-3(X))* Taku Graphics.
Chipman-Sullivan, Lois. What Does Love Mean, God? 2013. 36p. pap. 10.50 *(978-1-61286-141-8(5))* Avid Readers Publishing Group.
Cobb, Vicki. This Place Is Cold. Lavallee, Barbara, illus. 2013. (Imagine Living Here Ser.). (ENG.). 32p. (J). (gr. k-4). pap. 8.99 *(978-0-8027-3401-3(4)*, 9780802734013, Bloomsbury USA Childrens) Bloomsbury Publishing USA.
Durrie, Karen. Alaska: The Last Frontier. 2012. (J). *(978-1-61913-323-5(7))*; pap. *(978-1-61913-324-2(5))* Weigl Pubs., Inc.
Dyan, Penelope. Do You Know Juneau? a Kid's Guide to Juneau, Alaska. Weigand, John D., photos by. 2013. (Illus.). 34p. pap. 11.95 *(978-1-61477-105-0(7))* Bellissima Publishing, LLC.
—Movin' on! a Kid's Guide to Skagway, Alaska. Weigand, John D., photos by. 2013. (Illus.). 34p. pap. 11.95 *(978-1-61477-106-7(5))* Bellissima Publishing, LLC.
—Totems & More! a Kid's Guide to Ketchikan, Alaska. Weigand, John D., photos by. 2013. (Illus.). 34p. pap. 11.95 *(978-1-61477-107-4(3))* Bellissima Publishing, LLC.
Felix, Rebecca. What's Great about Alaska? 2015. (ENG., Illus.). 32p. (J). (gr. 2-5). 26.65 *(978-1-4677-3888-0(3))* Lerner Publishing Group.
Forbush, Kyle & Forbush, Kyle. A Is for Alaska - an ABC Book. Forbush, Lisa, illus. 2004. (J). bds. 6.95 *(978-1-57833-287-8(7))* Todd Communications.
Gamble, Adam & Jasper, Mark. Good Night Alaska. Kelly, Cooper, illus. 2015. (Good Night Our World Ser.). (ENG.). 20p. (J). (— 1). bds. 9.95 *(978-1-60219-219-5(7))* Good Night Bks.
Gregory, Josh. Alaska. 2017. (True Book — My United States Ser.). (ENG.). 48p. (J). pap. 7.95 ***(978-0-531-23281-1(6)***, Children's Pr.) Scholastic Library Publishing.
Hengel, Katherine. Monty's Ice Pick: A Story about Alaska, 1 vol. Doucet, Bob, illus. 2010. (Fact & Fable: State Stories Set 2 Ser.). (ENG.). 24p. (J). (gr. -1-2). 25.65 *(978-1-60453-925-7(9))* ABDO Publishing Co.
Howse, Jennifer. Alaska & Hawaii. 2016. (Illus.). 48p. (J). *(978-1-5105-1134-7(2))* SmartBook Media, Inc.
Hyde, Michelle Hazelwood, illus. Night Night, Birmingham. 2011. (J). *(978-1-59421-074-7(8))* Seacoast Publishing, Inc.
Jans, Nick. Once upon Alaska: A Kid's Photo Book. Kelley, Mark, photos by. 2013. (ENG., Illus.). 56p. (J). 15.95 *(978-1-880865-20-0(3))* Kelley, Mark.
Jerome, Kate B. Lucky to Live in Alaska. 2017. (Arcadia Kids Ser.). (ENG., Illus.). 32p. (J). 16.99 ***(978-0-7385-2807-6(2))*** Arcadia Publishing.
King, Elaine. Alaskan Honeymoon Adventure. 2004. per. *(978-0-9758654-0-8(4))* Adventure Pr.
Kirchner, Jason. Alaska. 2016. (States Ser.). (ENG., Illus.). 32p. (gr. 3-4). lib. bdg. 27.32 *(978-1-5157-0387-7(8))* Next Page Pr., The.
Kleinmartin, Hex. Seward's Folly & Alaska. 2016. (Expanding America Ser.). (ENG., Illus.). 96p. (J). (gr. 8-8). 42.79 *(978-1-5026-0970-0(3))* Cavendish Square Publishing.
Lusted, Marcia Amidon. Alaska: The Last Frontier. 2010. (Our Amazing States Ser.). (ENG.). 24p. (J). pap. 8.25 *(978-1-4488-0769-7(7)*, PowerKids Pr.) Rosen Publishing Group, Inc., The.
Marsh, Carole. Alaska History Projects: 30 Cool, Activities, Crafts, Experiments & More for Kids to Do to Learn about Your State! 2003. (Alaska Experience Ser.). 32p. (gr. k-5). pap. 5.95 *(978-0-635-01771-0(7)*, Marsh, Carole Bks.) Gallopade International.
—Exploring Alaska Through Project-Based Learning. 2016. (Alaska Experience Ser.). (ENG.). (J). pap. 9.99 *(978-0-635-12326-8(6))* Gallopade International.
—I'm Reading about Alaska. 2014. (ENG., Illus.). (J). pap., pap. 8.99 *(978-0-635-11278-1(7))* Gallopade International.
Mattern, Joanne. Alaska: Past & Present. 2010. (United States: Past & Present Ser.). (ENG.). 48p. (YA). pap. 11.75 *(978-1-4358-9503-4(7))*; lib. bdg. 29.25 *(978-1-4358-9475-4(8))* Rosen Publishing Group, Inc., The. (Rosen Reference).
Maxwell, Noel. Kid's Alaska; Workbook of Alaska & its History. 2005. 60p. (gr. 6-18). 12.95 *(978-0-9745187-0-1(0))* Good Roots Publishing.
McGehee, Claudia. My Wilderness. 2017. (ENG.). 32p. (J). (gr. k-4). 10.99 *(978-1-57061-951-9(4)*, Little Bigfoot) Sasquatch Bks.
—My Wilderness: An Alaskan Adventure. 2015. (ENG., Illus.). 32p. (J). (gr. k-4). 16.99 *(978-1-57061-950-2(6)*, Little Bigfoot) Sasquatch Bks.
Miller, Debbie S. A Caribou Journey. 2010. (ENG., Illus.). 32p. (J). 15.95 *(978-1-60223-097-2(8))* Univ. of Alaska Pr.
Miller, Debbie S. & Van Zyle, Jon. The Great Serum Race: Blazing the Iditarod Trail. Van Zyle, Jon, illus. 2006. (ENG., Illus.). 40p. (J). (gr. 2-7). pap. 9.99 *(978-0-8027-7723-2(6)*, 9780802777232, Bloomsbury USA Childrens) Bloomsbury Publishing USA.
Mossy Moose Alaska: Coloring & Activity Book. (J). pap. 5.00 *(978-0-9677477-2-9(4))* "Grandma's Hope Notes".
Murphy, Claire Rudolf. A Child's Alaska. Mason, Charles, photos by. 2012. (ENG., Illus.). 48p. (J). (gr. 2-8). pap. 10.95 *(978-0-88240-859-0(3)*, Alaska Northwest Bks.) Graphic Arts Ctr. Publishing Co.
Olson, Marie. Tlingit Coloring Book. 24p. (J). pap. 6.00 *(978-1-57833-051-5(3))* Todd Communications.
Olson, Robert. Alaska - Hints of Paradise: Photographs & Essays by Robert Olson. Olson, Robert, photos by. 2004. (Illus.). 160p. 39.95 *(978-0-9749570-0-5(3))* Visions Of Nature.
O'Neill, Dan. The Stubborn Gal: The True Story of an Undefeated Sled Dog Racer. Maisch, Klara, illus. 2015. 48p. 15.95 *(978-1-60223-272-3(5))* Univ. of Alaska Pr.
Parker, Lewis K. Russian Colonies in the Americas. 2003. (European Colonies in the Americas Ser.). (Illus.). 24p. (J). lib. bdg. 22.60 *(978-0-8239-6470-3(1)*, PowerKids Pr.) Rosen Publishing Group, Inc., The.
Rajczak, Kristen. Racing the Iditarod. 2014. (Illus.). 32p. (J). *(978-1-4824-3292-3(7)*, 1368191) Stevens, Gareth Publishing LLLP.
Rudd, Brandon Kyle. Cooper's Pack Travel Guide to Alaska. McCann, Martin, illus. 2011. (Cooper's Pack Ser.). (ENG.). 72p. (J). (gr. 1-6). pap. 12.95 *(978-0-9794882-3-8(0))* Cooper's Pack.
Sandler, Martin W. The Impossible Rescue: The True Story of an Amazing Arctic Adventure. (ENG.). 176p. (J). (gr. 5). 2014. pap. 15.99 *(978-0-7636-7093-1(6))* 2012. (Illus.). 22.99 *(978-0-7636-5080-3(3))* Candlewick Pr.
Skewes, John & Mullin, Michael. Larry Gets Lost in Alaska. Skewes, John, illus. 2013. (Larry Gets Lost Ser.). (ENG., Illus.). 32p. (J). (gr. -1-2). pap. 10.99 *(978-1-57061-859-8(3)*, Little Bigfoot) Sasquatch Bks.
Strudwick, Leslie. Alaska. 2011. (Guide to American States Ser.). (Illus.). 48p. (YA). (gr. 3-6). 29.99 *(978-1-61690-774-7(6))*; (J). *(978-1-61690-449-4(6))* Weigl Pubs., Inc.
Swimow, Linda. Take on Alaska! a Photophonics Reader. 2009. 28p. pap. 12.99 *(978-1-4389-1394-0(X))* AuthorHouse.
Tieck, Sarah. Alaska, 1 vol. 2012. (Explore the United States Ser.). (ENG.). 32p. (J). (gr. 2-5). 28.50 *(978-1-61783-340-3(1))* ABDO Publishing Co.
Yomtov, Nel. Sarah Palin: Political Rebel, 1 vol. D'Ottavi, Francesca, illus. 2011. (American Graphic Ser.). (ENG.). 32p. (gr. 3-4). pap. 8.10 *(978-1-4296-7341-9(9))*; pap. 47.70 *(978-1-4296-7342-6(7))* Capstone Press of Coughlan Cos. (Graphic Library).
Yomtov, Nelson. Sarah Palin: Political Rebel, 1 vol. D'Ottavi, Francesca, illus. 2011. (American Graphic Ser.). (ENG.). 32p. (gr. 3-4). lib. bdg. 30.65 *(978-1-4296-6018-1(X)*, Graphic Library) Capstone Press of Coughlan Cos.

ALBERTA

Baker, Brynn. Tuskegee Airmen: Freedom Flyers of World War II. 2015. (Military Heroes Ser.). (ENG., Illus.). 32p. (gr. 3-4). lib. bdg. 27.32 *(978-1-4914-4839-7(3))* Capstone Press of Coughlan Cos.
Genereux, Andy. Yamnuska Rock: The Crown Jewel of Canadian Rockies Traditional Climbing, 1 vol. 2010. (ENG., Illus.). 320p. pap. *(978-1-894765-74-9(5))* RMB Rocky Mountain Bks.
Johnson, Allen L. Willmore Horseback Adventure: Adventures with Grandchildren 2004. (Illus.). 190p. 15.00 *(978-1-880675-08-3(0))* Creative Enterprises.

ALBERTA—FICTION

Asnong, Jocey, illus. Nuptse & Lhotse Go to the Rockies. rev. ed. 2016. (ENG.). 40p. (J). (gr. k-4). 18.00 *(978-1-77160-152-8(3))* Road West Publishing Co.
Barr, Gordon. The Beginning. 2005. 67p. (J). (gr. 3-8). pap. *(978-0-9730093-2-3(2))* Barr, Gordon Ltd.
Clay, Ian. Coyote Lake. 2007. 104p. per. 9.95 *(978-0-595-44590-5(X))* iUniverse, Inc.
Coe, Mary E. The Prince of Betherland A Wonderful World of Fantasy. 2009. 66p. pap. 9.95 *(978-0-557-08499-9(7))* Lulu Pr., Inc.
Cook, Gerri. Christmas in the Badlands. 2003. (Dinosaur Soup Ser.). (Illus.). 120p. (YA). (gr. 3-5). pap. 9.95 *(978-1-895836-94-3(8))* River Bks. CAN. Dist: Fitzhenry & Whiteside, Ltd.
—A Penny for Albert. 2005. (Illus.). 64p. (J). 9.95 *(978-1-895836-93-6(X))* River Bks. CAN. Dist: Fitzhenry & Whiteside, Ltd.
Draper, Penny. Terror at Turtle Mountain, 1 vol. 2006. (Disaster Strikes! Ser.: 1). (ENG., Illus.). 168p. (J). (gr. 4-7). per. 7.95 *(978-1-55050-343-2(X))* Coteau Bks. CAN. Dist: Orca Bk. Pubs. USA.
Gamble, Adam & Jasper, Mark. Good Night Alberta. Chan, Suwin, illus. 2017. (Good Night Our World Ser.). (ENG.). 20p. (J). (— 1). bds. 9.95 *(978-1-60219-442-7(4))* Good Night Bks.
Glaze, Dave. Danger in Dead Man's Mine, 1 vol. 2009. (1912: the Mackenzie Davis Files Ser.). (ENG., Illus.). 176p. (J). (gr. 4-7). pap. 8.95 *(978-1-55050-416-3(9))* Coteau Bks. CAN. Dist: Orca Bk. Pubs. USA.
Guest, Jacqueline. Outcasts of River Falls, 1 vol. Peetoom, Laura, ed. 2012. (ENG.). 248p. (J). (gr. 4-7). pap. 9.95 *(978-1-55050-480-4(0))* Coteau Bks. CAN. Dist: Orca Bk. Pubs. USA.
—War Games, 1 vol. 2008. (Lorimer SideStreets Ser.). (ENG.). 184p. (YA). (gr. 9-12). 9.95 *(978-1-55277-035-1(4)*, 9781552770351); 16.95 *(978-1-55277-036-8(2)*, 9781552770368) Lorimer, James & Co., Ltd., Pubs. CAN. Dist: Casemate Pubs. & Bk. Distributors, LLC.
Heidbreder, Robert. Drumheller Dinosaur Dance. Slavin, Bill et al, illus. 2006. (ENG.). 32p. (J). (gr. -1-2). pap. 7.95 *(978-1-55337-982-9(9))* Kids Can Pr., Ltd. CAN. Dist: Hachette Bk. Group.
Holubitsky, Katherine. The Mountain That Walked, 1 vol. 2005. (ENG.). 224p. (J). (gr. 5-8). lib. bdg. 9.95 *(978-1-55143-392-9(3))* Orca Bk. Pubs. USA.
Jacobs, Lily. The Littlest Bunny in Calgary: An Easter Adventure. Dunn, Robert, illus. 2015. (ENG.). 32p. (J). (-3). 11.99 *(978-1-4926-1039-7(9)*, Sourcebooks Jabberwocky) Sourcebooks, Inc.
—The Littlest Bunny in Edmonton: An Easter Adventure. Dunn, Robert, illus. 2015. (ENG.). 32p. (J). (-3). 11.99 *(978-1-4926-1066-3(6)*, Sourcebooks Jabberwocky) Sourcebooks, Inc.
James, Eric. A Halloween Scare in Calgary. Le Ray, Marina, illus. 2015. (ENG.). 32p. (J). (-5). 11.99 *(978-1-4926-2367-0(9)*, 9781492623670, Sourcebooks Jabberwocky) Sourcebooks, Inc.
—A Halloween Scare in Edmonton. Le Ray, Marina, illus. 2015. (ENG.). 32p. (J). (-5). 11.99 *(978-1-4926-2372-4(5)*, 9781492623724, Sourcebooks Jabberwocky) Sourcebooks, Inc.
—Santa's Sleigh Is on Its Way to Calgary: A Christmas Adventure. Dunn, Robert, illus. 2016. (ENG.). 32p. (J). (-2). 12.99 *(978-1-4926-4320-3(3)*, 9781492643203, Sourcebooks Jabberwocky) Sourcebooks, Inc.
—Santa's Sleigh Is on Its Way to Edmonton: A Christmas Adventure. Dunn, Robert, illus. 2016. (ENG.). 32p. (J). (-2). 12.99 *(978-1-4926-4327-2(0)*, 9781492643272, Sourcebooks Jabberwocky) Sourcebooks, Inc.
Lottridge, Celia. Ticket to Curlew, 1 vol. 2nd ed. 2007. (ENG.). 144p. (J). (gr. 2-7). pap. 8.95 *(978-0-88899-843-9(0))* Groundwood Bks. CAN. Dist: Publishers Group West (PGW).
Maes, Nicholas. Locksmith. 2008. (Felix Taylor Adventure Ser.: 1). (ENG.). 240p. (J). (gr. 5-8). pap. 11.99 *(978-1-55002-791-4(3)*, Sandcastle Bks.) Dundurn CAN. Dist: Ingram Publisher Services.
Molnar, Gwen. Hate Cell: A Casey Templeton Mystery. 2009. (Casey Templeton Mystery Ser.: 1). (ENG.). 184p. (YA). (gr. 5). pap. 11.99 *(978-1-55002-850-8(2))* Dundurn CAN. Dist: Ingram Publisher Services.
Schillow, Ned W. and Schillow. Titanic Hearts. 2007. 100p. per. 10.00 *(978-1-4257-3842-6(7))* Xlibris Corp.
Silvano, Wendi. Love Is All Around Calgary. Czernichowska, Joanna, illus. 2016. (ENG.). 32p. (J). (-6). 12.99 *(978-1-4926-2908-5(1)*, Sourcebooks Jabberwocky) Sourcebooks, Inc.
—Love Is All Around Edmonton. Czernichowska, Joanna, illus. 2016. (ENG.). 32p. (J). (-6). 12.99 *(978-1-4926-2917-7(0)*, Sourcebooks Jabberwocky) Sourcebooks, Inc.
Smallman, Steve. Santa Is Coming to Calgary. Dunn, Robert, illus. 2013. (ENG.). 32p. (J). (-3). 11.99 *(978-1-4022-8988-0(X)*, Sourcebooks Jabberwocky) Sourcebooks, Inc.
—Santa Is Coming to Edmonton. Dunn, Robert, illus. 2013. (ENG.). 32p. (J). (-3). 11.99 *(978-1-4022-8991-0(X)*, Sourcebooks Jabberwocky) Sourcebooks, Inc.
Truckey, Don. The Adventures of Caraway Kim... Southpaw. MacIntyre, R P, ed. 2006. (ENG.). 192p. pap. 10.95 *(978-1-894345-90-3(8))* Thistledown Pr., Ltd. CAN. Dist: Univ. of Toronto Pr.
Wierenga, Emily Theresa. Save My Children: The Story of a Father's Love. 2008. *(978-1-897213-35-3(2))* BayRidge Bks.
Woodson, Marion. Dinosaur Fever. 2008. (ENG.). 160p. (J). (gr. 4). pap. 11.99 *(978-1-55002-690-0(9)*, Sandcastle Bks.) Dundurn CAN. Dist: Ingram Publisher Services.

ALCHEMY

Place, Robert M. Magic & Alchemy. 2009. (Mysteries, Legends, & Unexplained Phenomena Ser.). (Illus.). 144p. (YA). (gr. 7-12). 29.95 *(978-0-7910-9390-0(5))* Facts On File, Inc.
Stefoff, Rebecca. Alchemy & Chemistry. 2014. 48p. pap. 29.93 *(978-1-62712-509-3(4))* Cavendish Square Publishing.

ALCINDOR, LEW, 1947-

see Abdul-Jabbar, Kareem, 1947-

ALCOHOLICS

see Alcoholism

ALCOHOLISM

Alagna, Magdalena. Everything You Need to Know about the Dangers of Binge Drinking. 2009. (Need to Know Library). 64p. (gr. 5-5). 58.50 *(978-1-60854-091-4(X))* Rosen Publishing Group, Inc., The.
Ambrose, Marylou & Deisler, Veronica. Investigate Alcohol. 2014. (Investigate Drugs Ser.). (Illus.). 112p. (J). (gr. 5-12). lib. bdg. 33.27 *(978-0-7660-4253-7(7))* Enslow Pubs., Inc.
Aretha, David. On the Rocks: Teens & Alcohol. 2006. (ENG., Illus.). 144p. (YA). (gr. 9-13). 30.50 *(978-0-531-16792-2(5)*, Watts, Franklin) Scholastic Library Publishing.
Auer, Jim. Know How to Say No to Drugs & Alcohol: A Kid's Guide. 2007. (Elf-Help Books for Kids Ser.). (Illus.). (J). (gr. -1-3). per. 7.95 *(978-0-87029-407-5(5))* Abbey Pr.
Benton, John. New Hope Series, 10 bks., Set. 2004p. (J). (gr. 3-12). 35.00 *(978-0-9635411-1-6(0))* Benton, John Bks.
Bjornlund, Lydia D. Alcohol. 2008. (21st Century Skills Library: Health at Risk Ser.). (ENG., Illus.). 32p. (gr. 4-8). lib. bdg. 28.50 *(978-1-60279-280-7(1)*, 200129) Cherry Lake Publishing.
Bow, James. Binge Drinking. 2015. (ENG., Illus.). 48p. (J). *(978-0-7787-2200-7(7))* Crabtree Publishing Co.
Burlingame, Jeff. Alcohol. 2013. 64p. (J). (gr. 6-9). 34.21 *(978-1-60870-822-2(5))*; pap. 15.28 *(978-1-62712-058-6(0))* Cavendish Square Publishing.
Centore, Michael. Intervention & Recovery, Vol. 13. Becker, Sara, ed. 2016. (Drug Addiction & Recovery Ser.). (Illus.). 64p. (J). (gr. 7). 23.95 *(978-1-4222-3605-5(6))* Mason Crest.
Clayton, Lawrence. Barbiturates & Other Depressants. (Drug Abuse Prevention Library). 64p. 2009. (gr. 5-5). 58.50 *(978-1-60853-427-2(8))* 2005. (Illus.). (YA). (gr. 7-12). lib. bdg. 31.95 *(978-0-8239-3442-3(X))* Rosen Publishing Group, Inc., The.
Connolly, Sean. Alcohol. 2006. (Straight Talking Ser.). (Illus.). 46p. (YA). (gr. 4-7). lib. bdg. 32.80 *(978-1-58340-923-7(8))* Black Rabbit Bks.
—Alcohol. 2009. (Straight Talking Ser.). (Illus.). 46p. (YA). (gr. 8-12). pap. *(978-1-895058-51-2(1))* Saunders Bk. Co.
Crist, James J. When Someone You Love Abuses Alcohol or Drugs - a Guide for Kids. 2003. 112p. pap. 12.95 *(978-1-58741-119-9(9))* Wellness Institute/Self-Help Bks., LLC.
Cross, David B., ed. Book of Stories & Study Guide. 2nd exp. ed. 2005. 116p. (YA). per. 4.95 *(978-0-9759988-1-6(1))* Lockman, James Consulting.
currie-mcghee, leanne. Teenage Alcoholism. 2011. (Compact Research Ser.). 96p. (YA). (gr. 7-12). lib. bdg. 27.95 *(978-1-60152-164-4(2))* ReferencePoint Pr., Inc.
Decoded. Hooked: When Addiction Hits Home. Shantz-Hilkes, Chloe, ed. 2013. (ENG., Illus.). 128p. (YA). (gr. 7-12). pap. 12.95 *(978-1-55451-474-8(6)*, 9781554514748) Annick Pr., Ltd. CAN. Dist: Publishers Group West (PGW).
Diconsiglio, John. True Confessions: Real Stories about Drinking & Drugs. 2008. (Scholastic Choices Ser.). (ENG., Illus.). 112p. (J). (gr. 7-13). pap. 8.95 *(978-0-531-14773-3(8)*, Watts, Franklin) Scholastic Library Publishing.
Drug & Alcohol Prevention. (J). (gr. 2-3). 3.80 *(978-0-8374-1262-7(5)*, 211); (gr. 3). 3.80 *(978-0-8374-0120-1(8)*, 212); (gr. 4). 3.80 *(978-0-8374-0121-8(6)*, 213); (gr. 5-6). 5.95 *(978-0-8374-1266-5(8)*, 267); (gr. 7-9). 3.80 *(978-0-8374-0080-8(5)*, 411) Weekly Reader Corp.
Esherick, Joan. Drug - & Alcohol-Related Health Issues. McDonnell, Mary Ann & Forman, Sara, eds. 2013. (Young Adult's Guide to the Science of Health Ser.: 15). 128p. (J). (gr. 7-18). 24.95 *(978-1-4222-2808-1(8))* Mason Crest.
—Dying for Acceptance: A Teen's Guide to Drug- & Alcohol-Related Health Issues. 2006. (Science of Health Ser.). (Illus.). 128p. (YA). lib. bdg. 24.95 *(978-1-59084-847-0(0))* Mason Crest.
Espejo, Roman, ed. Alcohol. 2013. (Teen Rights & Freedoms Ser.). (ENG., Illus.). 176p. (gr. 10-12). lib. bdg. 37.45 *(978-0-7377-6398-0(1)*, Greenhaven Pr., Inc.) Cengage Gale.
Fatal Decision, Grade 8. (YA). pap., tchr. ed. 195.00 incl. VHS *(978-0-8068-0614-3(1))* AIMS Multimedia.
Friedman, Lauri S. Drunk Driving. Nasso, Christine & Des Chenes, Elizabeth, eds. 2007. (Writing the Critical Essay Ser.). (ENG., Illus.). 128p. (gr. 10-12). lib. bdg. 38.30 *(978-0-7377-3581-9(3)*, Greenhaven Pr., Inc.) Cengage Gale.

Friedman, Lauri S. & Scherer, Lauri S., eds. Underage Drinking. 2013. (Issues That Concern You Ser.). (ENG., Illus.). 144p. (gr. 7-10). lib. bdg. 36.95 *(978-0-7377-6300-3(0))* Cengage Gale.

Gass, Justin T. Alcohol. 2010. (Understanding Drugs Ser.). (Illus.). 120p. (YA). (gr. 9-12). 34.95 *(978-1-60413-529-9(8))* Facts On File, Inc.

Gottfried, Ted & Follett, Katherine. The Facts about Alcohol. 2009. (Benchmark Rockets Ser.). 32p. (YA). (gr. 5-9). 28.50 *(978-0-7614-4348-3(7))* Marshall Cavendish Corp.

Green, Carl R. Alcohol: A MyReportLinks.com Book. 2005. (Drugs Ser.). (Illus.). 48p. (J). (gr. 4-10). lib. bdg. 26.60 *(978-0-7660-5282-6(6)*, MyReportLinks.com Bks.) Enslow Pubs., Inc.

Haney, Johannah. Alcohol: Rules, Regulations, & Responsibilities. 2014. (J). lib. bdg. *(978-1-62712-407-2(1))* Cavendish Square Publishing.

Henneberg, Susan. Defeating Addiction & Alcoholism, 01 vols., 1. 2016. (Effective Survival Strategies Ser.). (ENG., Illus.). 64p. (J). 32.95 *(978-1-4994-6179-4(8)*, Rosen Young Adult) Rosen Publishing Group, Inc., The.

Holt, Rinehart and Winston Staff. Decisions for Health Blue, Chptr. 15: Alcohol. 4th ed. 2004. pap. 11.20 *(978-0-03-068049-6(2))* Holt McDougal.

—Decisions for Health Green Chptr. 14: Tobacco & Alcohol. 4th ed. 2004. pap. 11.20 *(978-0-03-068036-6(0))* Holt McDougal.

—Decisions for Health Red Chptr. 12: Teens & Alcohol. 4th ed. 2004. pap. 11.20 *(978-0-03-068038-0(7))* Holt McDougal.

Horsfield, Alan & Horsfield, Elaine. Talking about the Dangers of Alcohol, Tobacco, & Caffeine. 2010. (Healthy Living Ser.). (Illus.). 32p. (YA). (gr. 3-6). lib. bdg. 26.00 *(978-1-4339-3661-6(5))* Stevens, Gareth Publishing LLLP.

Human Relations Media. Kidsdom: An Alcohol Prevention Curriculum. 2005. (J). cd-rom 119.95 *(978-1-55548-059-2(4))* Human Relations Media.

Kelley, R. A. Why Doesn't Daddy Feel so Well? 2011. 48p. pap. 18.99 *(978-1-4520-9750-3(X))* AuthorHouse.

Landau, Elaine. Alcohol. 2003. (Watts Library). (ENG.). 64p. (J). (gr. 5-7). pap. 8.95 *(978-0-531-16665-9(1)*, Watts, Franklin) Scholastic Library Publishing.

Landau, Jennifer. Helping a Friend with an Alcohol Problem. 2016. (How Can I Help? Friends Helping Friends Ser.). 00064p. (J). (gr. 6-6). pap. 12.95 *(978-1-4994-6448-1(7))* Rosen Publishing Group, Inc., The.

Lessa, Nicholoas & Lessa, M. S. W. Living with Alcoholism & Drug Addiction. 2009. (Teen's Guides). 192p. (gr. 6-12). 34.95 *(978-0-8160-7326-9(0))* Facts On File, Inc.

Libal, Joyce. Drug Therapy an Substance-Related Disorders. 2003. (Psychiatric Disorders: Drugs & Psychology for the Mind & Bod Ser.). (Illus.). 124p. (YA). (gr. 8-12). pap. 14.95 *(978-1-4222-0401-6(4))* Mason Crest.

Macaulay, John. Alcoholism. 2007. (Illus.). 244p. (gr. 10-12). 24.95 *(978-0-7377-2473-8(0))*; pap. 36.20 *(978-0-7377-2472-1(2))* Cengage Gale. (Greenhaven Pr., Inc.).

Marcovitz, Hal. Drug & Alcohol Abuse. 2008. (Gallup Major Trends & Events Ser.). (Illus.). 120p. (YA). (gr. 7-18). lib. bdg. 22.95 *(978-1-59084-963-7(9))* Mason Crest.

Marsico, Katie. Alcohol Abuse. 2013. 80p. (YA). (gr. 7-12). 34.21 *(978-1-60870-848-2(9))*; pap. 17.64 *(978-1-62712-125-5(0))* Cavendish Square Publishing.

Mason, Paul. Know the Facts about Drinking & Smoking. 2009. (J). 70.50 *(978-1-4358-5463-5(2)*, Rosen Reference); (ENG.). 48p. (YA). pap. 11.75 *(978-1-4358-5462-8(4)*, Rosen Reference); (ENG., Illus.). 48p. (YA). (gr. 5-9). lib. bdg. 29.25 *(978-1-4358-5339-3(3))* Rosen Publishing Group, Inc., The.

McClellan, Marilyn. The Big Deal about Alcohol: What Teens Need to Know about Drinking. 2004. (Issues in Focus Ser.). (Illus.). 128p. (J). lib. bdg. 27.94 *(978-0-7660-2163-1(7))* Enslow Pubs., Inc.

McIntosh, Kenneth & Livingston, Phyllis. Youth with Alcohol & Drug Addiction: Escape from Bondage. 2009. (Helping Youth with Mental, Physical, & Social Challenges Ser.). (Illus.). 128p. (YA). (gr. 7-18). lib. bdg. 24.95 *(978-1-4222-0143-5(0))* Mason Crest.

Merino, Noël. Gateway Drugs. 2008. (Opposing Viewpoints Ser.). (ENG., Illus.). (gr. 10-12). 224p. 48.80 *(978-0-7377-4002-8(7))*; 198p. (YA). 29.45 *(978-0-7377-4003-5(5))* Cengage Gale. (Greenhaven Pr., Inc.).

Meyer, Terry Teague. I Have an Alcoholic Parent. Now What?, 1 vol. 2015. (ENG.). 112p. (YA). 35.60 *(978-1-4777-7982-8(5)*, Rosen Young Adult) Rosen Publishing Group, Inc., The.

Miller, Andrew. Alcohol & Your Liver: The Incredibly Disgusting Story. 2005. (Incredibly Disgusting Drugs Ser.). (Illus.). 48p. (YA). (gr. 5-9). lib. bdg. 29.25 *(978-0-8239-3254-2(0)*, DDALLI) Rosen Publishing Group, Inc., The.

Mintzer, Richard. Alcohol = Busted! 2005. (Busted! Ser.). (Illus.). 104p. (J). (gr. 6-12). lib. bdg. 33.27 *(978-0-7660-2552-3(7))* Enslow Pubs., Inc.

Nakaya, Andrea C. Alcohol. 2007. (Opposing Viewpoints Ser.). (ENG., Illus.). 219p. (gr. 10-12). 29.45 *(978-0-7377-3734-9(4)*, Greenhaven Pr., Inc.); (YA). (gr. 9-12). pap. 42.95 *(978-0-7377-3733-2(6))* Cengage Gale.

—Alcohol. 2007. (Compact Research Ser.). (ENG., Illus.). 112p. (YA). (gr. 7-12). lib. bdg. 25.95 *(978-1-60152-007-4(7))* ReferencePoint Pr., Inc.

Newell, Ella. The Hidden Story of Alcoholism. 2013. (Undercover Story Ser.). 48p. (J). (gr. 5-8). 29.95 *(978-1-4777-2793-5(0)*, Rosen Reference) Rosen Publishing Group, Inc., The.

Olson, Karen W. Healthy Choices, Healthy Lives. Hamelin, Marie-Micheline, illus. 2009. (Caring for Me Ser.). (ENG.). 20p. pap. 9.95 *(978-1-894778-53-4(7))* Theytus Bks., Ltd. CAN. Dist: Univ. of Toronto Pr.

Parks, Peggy J. The Dangers of Alcohol. 2016. (ENG.). 80p. (YA). (gr. 5-12). *(978-1-68282-012-4(2))* ReferencePoint Pr., Inc.

—Driving under the Influence. 2007. (Ripped from the Headlines Ser.). (YA). (gr. 7-12). 23.95 *(978-1-60217-013-1(4))* Erickson Pr.

Piehl, Norah. Underage Drinking. 2010. (Social Issues Firsthand Ser.). (Illus.). 192p. (J). 33.75 *(978-0-7377-4799-7(4)*, Greenhaven Pr., Inc.) Cengage Gale.

Poole, H. W. Alcohol & Tobacco, Vol. 13. Becker, Sara, ed. 2016. (Drug Addiction & Recovery Ser.). (Illus.). 64p. (J). (gr. 7). 23.95 *(978-1-4222-3599-7(8))* Mason Crest.

—Drug & Alcohol Dependence, Vol. 13. Walters, Anne S., ed. 2015. (Mental Illnesses & Disorders: Awareness & Understanding Ser.). (Illus.). 48p. (J). (gr. 5). 20.95 *(978-1-4222-3371-9(5))* Mason Crest.

Powell, Jillian & Samanich, John G. Alcohol & Drug Abuse. 2008. (Emotional Health Issues Ser.). (Illus.). 48p. (YA). (gr. 7-12). lib. bdg. 31.00 *(978-0-8368-9199-7(6))* Stevens, Gareth Publishing LLLP.

Rodger, Ellen. Fetal Alcohol Spectrum Disorder. 2013. (ENG., Illus.). 48p. (J). *(978-0-7787-0083-8(6))* Crabtree Publishing Co.

Rodger, Ellen & Gowsell, Rosie. Fetal Alcohol Spectrum Disorder. 2013. (ENG., Illus.). 48p. (J). pap. *(978-0-7787-0089-0(5))* Crabtree Publishing Co.

Roleff, Tamara. Alcoholism. 2010. (Issues That Concern You Ser.). (Illus.). 144p. (J). 36.95 *(978-0-7377-4742-3(0))* Cengage Gale.

Shantz-Hilkes, Chloe, ed. Hooked: When Addiction Hits Home. 2013. (ENG., Illus.). 128p. (YA). (gr. 7-12). 21.95 *(978-1-55451-475-5(4)*, 9781554514755) Annick Pr., Ltd. CAN. Dist: Publishers Group West (PGW).

Sheen, Barbara. Teen Alcoholism. 2003. (Illus.). 112p. 29.95 *(978-1-59018-501-8(3)*, Lucent Bks.) Cengage Gale.

Smith, Terri Peterson, et al. Junior Drug Awareness: Alcohol. 2008. (Junior Drug Awareness Ser.). (Illus.). 112p. (gr. 5-8). 30.00 *(978-0-7910-9764-9(1)*, Chelsea Hse.) Facts On File, Inc.

Snyder, Gail. Teens & Alcohol. Developed in Association with the Gallup Organization Staff, ed. 2013. (Gallup Youth Survey: Major Issues & Trends Ser.: 14). 112p. (J). (gr. 7-18). 24.95 *(978-1-4222-2949-1(1))* Mason Crest.

Stewart, Gail B. Fetal Alcohol Syndrome. 2004. (Diseases & Disorders Ser.). (Illus.). 112p. (YA). (gr. 7-12). lib. bdg. 32.45 *(978-1-59018-591-9(9)*, Lucent Bks.) Cengage Gale.

Stewart, Jan. How Drugs & Alcohol Affect Us. 2004. (ENG., Illus.). 32p. (J). pap. 9.95 *(978-0-89793-314-8(1)*, Hunter Hse.) Turner Publishing Co.

Stewart, Sheila. Sometimes My Mom Drinks Too Much. (Kids Have Troubles Too Ser.). (Illus.). 48p. (YA). (gr. 5-18). 2010. lib. bdg. 19.95 *(978-1-4222-1704-7(3))* 2009. pap. 7.95 *(978-1-4222-1917-1(8))* Mason Crest.

Watkins, Christine, ed. Alcohol Abuse. 2012. (At Issue Ser.). (ENG.). 128p. (gr. 10-12). pap. 24.45 *(978-0-7377-5543-5(1)*, Greenhaven Pr., Inc.); (YA). (gr. 9-12). lib. bdg. 34.45 *(978-0-7377-5542-8(3))* Cengage Gale.

Watson, Stephanie. Binge Drinking, 1 vol. 2011. (Essential Issues Set 3 Ser.). (ENG., Illus.). 112p. (J). (gr. 6-12). lib. bdg. 35.64 *(978-1-61783-131-7(X))* ABDO Publishing Co.

Wyborny, Sheila. Alcoholism. 2007. (Diseases & Disorders Ser.). (ENG., Illus.). 128p. (gr. 7-12). lib. bdg. 39.90 *(978-1-59018-996-2(5))* Cengage Gale.

ALCOHOLISM—FICTION

Adams, Mark. A Boy Named Bucky, Vol. 1. Dolan, Amy, illus. 2006. 17p. (J). pap. 5.00 *(978-0-9670245-5-4(2))* Enthusi Adams, Inc.

Airgood, Ellen. The Education of Ivy Blake. 2015. (ENG.). 240p. (J). (gr. 5). 16.99 *(978-0-399-16278-7(X)*, Nancy Paulsen Books) Penguin Young Readers Group.

Anderson, Jessica Lee. Border Crossing. 2009. (ENG.). 160p. (J). (gr. 5-10). pap. 8.00 *(978-1-57131-691-2(4))* Milkweed Editions.

Auth, Jeannine. Emmy's Question. 2010. 155p. pap. 11.99 *(978-0-9790395-3-9(3))* 2007. 151p. (J). (gr. 4-7). 16.99 *(978-0-9790395-2-2(5))* Morningtide Pr.

Barnes, John. Tales of the Madman Underground. 2011. (ENG.). 544p. (YA). (gr. 9-18). 9.99 *(978-0-14-241702-7(5)*, Speak) Penguin Young Readers Group.

Bauer, Joan. Rules of the Road. 2005. (ENG.). 208p. (YA). (gr. 7-7). pap. 8.99 *(978-0-14-240425-6(X)*, Speak) Penguin Young Readers Group.

Bauman, Beth Ann. Rosie & Skate. 2011. (ENG.). 224p. (YA). (gr. 9). pap. 8.99 *(978-0-385-73736-4(X)*, Ember) Random Hse. Children's Bks.

Beauty of the Broken. 2014. (ENG., Illus.). 368p. (YA). (gr. 9). 17.99 *(978-1-4814-0709-0(0)*, Simon Pulse) Simon Pulse.

Bo, Ben. Skullcrack. 2003. (ENG.). 168p. (YA). (gr. 5-12). pap. 6.95 *(978-0-8225-3311-5(1))* Lerner Publishing Group.

Bollendorf, Robert F. & Makely, William. Flight of the Loon: One Family's Battle with Recovery. Donlon, Eleanor, ed. 2007. 8.95 *(978-1-932514-15-5(5))* College of DuPage Pr.

Brooks, Kevin. Martyn Pig. 2003. 230p. (J). (gr. 5-9). 15.65 *(978-0-7569-7217-2(5))* Perfection Learning Corp.

Bruchac, Joseph. The Heart of a Chief. 2007. 153p. (gr. 4-7). 17.00 *(978-0-7569-7805-1(X))* Perfection Learning Corp.

Buffie, Margaret. Out of Focus. 2006. (ENG.). 240p. (J). (gr. 7-9). 6.95 *(978-1-55337-956-0(X))* Kids Can Pr., Ltd. CAN. Dist: Hachette Bk. Group.

Carlson, Melody. Lost in Las Vegas, 1 vol. 2014. (Carter House Girls Ser.). (ENG.). 208p. (YA). pap. 9.99 *(978-0-310-74716-1(3))* Zondervan.

—New York Debut, 1 vol. 2014. (Carter House Girls Ser.). (ENG.). 224p. (YA). pap. 9.99 *(978-0-310-74779-6(1))* Zondervan.

—Notes from a Spinning Planet - Mexico. 2007. (Notes from a Spinning Planet Ser.). (ENG.). 256p. (YA). (gr. 7). pap. 12.99 *(978-1-4000-7146-3(1)*, WaterBrook Pr.) Crown Publishing Group.

Carter, Alden R. Up Country. 2004. (ENG.). 256p. (YA). (gr. 7-5). 7.99 *(978-0-14-240243-6(5)*, Speak) Penguin Young Readers Group.

—Walkaway. 2008. (ENG.). 192p. (YA). (gr. 7-18). 16.95 *(978-0-8234-2106-0(6))* Holiday Hse., Inc.

Cormier, Robert. We All Fall Down. 22.75 *(978-0-8446-7217-5(3))* Smith, Peter Pub., Inc.

Cousins, Dave. 15 Days Without a Head. 2013. (ENG.). 312p. (YA). pap. 9.99 *(978-0-7387-3642-6(2)*, Flux) North Star Editions.

Cuchna, Reed. Out of Love, 1 vol. 2009. 327p. pap. 29.95 *(978-1-60836-345-2(7))* America Star Bks.

Dean, Carolee. Comfort. 2004. (ENG.). 256p. (YA). (gr. 7-18). pap. 14.95 *(978-0-618-43912-6(9))* Houghton Mifflin Harcourt Publishing Co.

Desir, C. Other Broken Things. 2016. (ENG., Illus.). 256p. (YA). (gr. 9). 17.99 *(978-1-4814-3739-4(9)*, Simon Pulse) Simon Pulse.

Deuker, Carl & Perry, Thomas. Runner. 2007. (ENG.). 224p. (YA). (gr. 7-12). pap. 8.99 *(978-0-618-73505-1(4))* Houghton Mifflin Harcourt Publishing Co.

Ehrenhaft, Daniel. The After Life. 2006. (ENG.). 272p. (YA). (gr. 7-12). 8.99 *(978-1-59514-080-7(8)*, Razorbill) Penguin Young Readers Group.

Encyclopaedia Britannica, Inc. Staff, compiled by. I Wish Daddy Didn't Drink So Much. 2008. 49.95 *(978-1-59339-667-1(8))* Encyclopaedia Britannica, Inc.

—If Your Parents Drink. 2008. 49.95 *(978-1-59339-649-7(X))* Encyclopaedia Britannica, Inc.

Fogelin, Adrian. The Sorta Sisters, 1 vol. 2007. (ENG., Illus.). 224p. (J). (gr. 3-7). 15.95 *(978-1-56145-424-2(9))* Peachtree Pubs.

—Sorta Sisters, 1 vol. Fogelin, Adrian, illus. 2011. (ENG., Illus.). 288p. pap. 7.95 *(978-1-56145-592-8(X)*, Peachtree Junior) Peachtree Pubs.

Gantos, Jack. Joey Pigza Loses Control. braille ed. 2003. (Joey Pigza Ser.: Bk. 2). (J). (gr. 2). spiral bd. *(978-0-616-15268-3(X))* Canadian National Institute for the Blind/Institut National Canadien pour les Aveugles.

—Joey Pigza Loses Control. unabr. ed. 2004. (Joey Pigza Ser.: Bk. 2). 195p. (J). (gr. 5-9). pap. 36.00 incl. audio *(978-0-8072-8726-2(1)*, LyA 248 SP, Listening Library) Random Hse. Audio Publishing Group.

—Joey Pigza Loses Control. 2014. (Joey Pigza Ser.: 2). (J). lib. bdg. 18.40 *(978-0-606-36561-1(3))* Turtleback Bks.

Garsee, Jeannine. Before, after, & Somebody in Between. 2008. (ENG., Illus.). 368p. (YA). (gr. 9-12). pap. 8.99 *(978-1-59990-292-0(3)*, 9781599902920, Bloomsbury USA Childrens) Bloomsbury Publishing USA.

Hankins, M. Lil' Mikie Tells It Like It Is. 2007. 20p. per. 24.95 *(978-1-4137-0168-5(X))* America Star Bks.

Hodges, Jean A. Drinking Dragon Sam Learns Drinking Doesn't Pay. 2011. 40p. pap. 24.95 *(978-1-4560-5507-3(0))* America Star Bks.

Hogan, Mary. The Serious Kiss. 2005. (ENG.). 256p. (YA). (gr. 8). pap. 7.99 *(978-0-06-072208-1(8)*, HarperTeen); (gr. 7-18). 16.99 *(978-0-06-072206-7(1))* HarperCollins Pubs.

Hopkins, Ellen. Burned. 2013. (ENG., Illus.). 560p. (YA). (gr. 9). pap. 12.99 *(978-1-4424-9461-9(1)*, McElderry, Margaret K. Bks.) McElderry, Margaret K. Bks.

Hulet, Debra. Independence Rock. 2011. 208p. pap. 13.99 *(978-1-59955-441-9(0)*, Bonneville Bks.) Cedar Fort, Inc./CFI Distribution.

Hyde, Catherine Ryan. The Year of My Miraculous Reappearance. 2009. (ENG.). 240p. (YA). (gr. 7). pap. 8.99 *(978-0-375-83261-1(0)*, Knopf Bks. for Young Readers) Random Hse. Children's Bks.

Jacobus, Ann. Romancing the Dark in the City of Light: A Novel. 2015. (ENG.). 288p. (YA). (gr. 7-12). 18.99 *(978-1-250-06443-1(0)*, 9781250064431) St. Martin's Pr.

Johnson, Maureen. The Key to the Golden Firebird. 2004. (ENG.). 304p. (J). (gr. 7-18). 15.99 *(978-0-06-054138-5(5))* HarperCollins Pubs.

Jones, Patrick. Triangle Choke. 2013. (Dojo Ser.). (ENG.). 136p. (YA). (gr. 6-12). pap. 7.95 *(978-1-4677-1487-7(9))*; lib. bdg. 27.93 *(978-1-4677-0630-8(2))* Lerner Publishing Group. (Darby Creek).

Konigsberg, Bill. The Porcupine of Truth. 2015. (ENG.). 336p. (J). (gr. 9). 17.99 *(978-0-545-64893-6(9))* Scholastic, Inc.

Laurie, Victoria. When. 2016. (ENG.). 336p. (YA). (gr. 7-12). pap. 9.99 *(978-1-4847-0149-2(6))* Hyperion Bks. for Children.

—When. 2015. (ENG.). 336p. (YA). (gr. 7-12). 17.99 *(978-1-4847-0008-2(2))* Hyperion Pr.

Luddy, Karon. Spelldown: The Big-Time Dreams of a Small-Town Word Whiz. 2008. (Mix Ser.). (ENG.). 224p. (J). (gr. 4-8). pap. 10.99 *(978-1-4169-5452-1(X)*, Simon & Schuster/Paula Wiseman Bks.) Simon & Schuster/Paula Wiseman Bks.

Luedeke, Lisa. Smashed. (ENG., 336p. (YA). (gr. 9). 2013. Illus.). pap. 10.99 *(978-1-4424-2780-8(9))* 2012. 16.99 *(978-1-4424-2779-2(5))* McElderry, Margaret K. Bks. (McElderry, Margaret K. Bks.).

Lynch, Chris. Inexcusable. 2005. (ENG., Illus.). 176p. (YA). (gr. 7-18). 19.99 *(978-0-689-84789-9(0)*, Atheneum Bks. for Young Readers) Simon & Schuster Children's Publishing.

Mangum, Kay Lynn. When the Bough Breaks. 2007. 352p. (YA). pap. 15.95 *(978-1-59038-748-1(1))* Deseret Bk. Co.

Martinez, Victor. Parrot in the Oven. Scott, Steve, illus. rev. ed. 2004. (ENG.). 240p. (YA). (gr. 8-18). pap. 8.99 *(978-0-06-447186-2(1)*, Rayo) HarperCollins Pubs.

Mason, Jane B. Without Annette. 2016. (ENG.). 336p. (YA). (gr. 7). 18.99 *(978-0-545-81995-4(4)*, Scholastic Pr.) Scholastic, Inc.

McMann, Lisa. Gone. (Wake Ser.: Bk. 3). (ENG.). (YA). (gr. 9). 2011. 240p. pap. 9.99 *(978-1-4169-7921-0(2))* 2010. 224p. 17.99 *(978-1-4169-7918-0(2))* Simon Pulse. (Simon Pulse).

The Misadventures of Wags & Freckles. (J). 4.00 *(978-1-56230-043-2(1))* Syndistar, Inc.

Moses, Shelia P. Joseph. (ENG.). (YA). (gr. 7). 2010. 208p. pap. 8.99 *(978-1-4169-9442-8(4))* 2008. (Illus.). 176p. 16.99 *(978-1-4169-1752-6(7))* McElderry, Margaret K. Bks. (McElderry, Margaret K. Bks.).

—Joseph's Grace. 2011. (ENG.). 160p. (YA). (gr. 7-18). 16.99 *(978-1-4169-3942-9(3)*, McElderry, Margaret K. Bks.) McElderry, Margaret K. Bks.

Murray, Jaye. Bottled Up. 2004. (ENG.). 224p. (YA). (gr. 7-12). reprint ed. 6.99 *(978-0-14-240240-5(0)*, Speak) Penguin Young Readers Group.

Owens, L. L. Kendra's Big Decision. 2004. (Illus.). 26p. pap. *(978-1-57021-031-0(4))* Comprehensive Health Education Foundation.

Paratore, Coleen Murtagh. Dreamsleeves. 2012. (ENG.). 288p. (J). (gr. 5-9). 16.99 *(978-0-545-31020-8(2)*, Scholastic Pr.) Scholastic, Inc.

Pearson, Mary E. A Room on Lorelei Street. 2008. (ENG.). 288p. (YA). (gr. 9-13). pap. 19.99 *(978-0-312-38019-9(4)*, 9780312380199) Square Fish.

Plum-Ucci, Carol. What Happened to Lani Garver. 2004. (ENG.). 336p. (YA). (gr. 9). reprint ed. pap. 9.99 *(978-0-15-205088-7(4))* Houghton Mifflin Harcourt Publishing Co.

Reed, Amy. Clean. (ENG.). (YA). (gr. 9). 2012. 304p. pap. 10.99 *(978-1-4424-1345-0(X))* 2011. 288p. 16.99 *(978-1-4424-1344-3(1))* Simon Pulse. (Simon Pulse).

Sanchez, Alex. Rainbow Boys. 2003. (ENG., Illus.). 262p. (YA). (gr. 7). pap. 9.99 *(978-0-689-85770-6(5)*, Simon & Schuster Bks. For Young Readers) Simon & Schuster Bks. For Young Readers.

Scott, Elizabeth. Love You Hate You Miss You. (ENG.). (YA). (gr. 8). 2010. 304p. pap. 8.99 *(978-0-06-112285-9(8))* 2009. 288p. 16.99 *(978-0-06-112283-5(1))* HarperCollins Pubs. (HarperTeen).

Scott, Mindi. Freefall. 2010. (ENG.). 336p. (YA). (gr. 9-18). pap. 8.99 *(978-1-4424-0278-2(4)*, Simon Pulse) Simon Pulse.

Sherrard, Brent R. Wasted, 1 vol. 2009. (Lorimer SideStreets Ser.). (ENG.). 144p. (YA). (gr. 9-12). 16.95 *(978-1-55277-420-5(1)*, 9781552774205); 9.95 *(978-1-55277-419-9(8)*, 9781552774199) Lorimer, James & Co., Ltd., Pubs. CAN. Dist: Casemate Pubs. & Bk. Distributors, LLC.

Smith, Heather. Baygirl, 1 vol. 2013. (ENG.). 288p. (YA). (gr. 8-12). pap. 12.95 *(978-1-4598-0274-2(8))* Orca Bk. Pubs. USA.

Stoehr, Shelley. Crosses. 2003. 161p. (YA). pap. 13.95 *(978-0-595-26952-5(4)*, Writers Club Pr.) iUniverse, Inc.

Suzuma, Tabitha. Forbidden. (ENG.). 464p. (YA). (gr. 11). 2012. pap. 11.99 *(978-1-4424-1996-4(2))* 2011. 17.99 *(978-1-4424-1995-7(4))* Simon Pulse. (Simon Pulse).

Tony's Sobering Lesson. (J). 39.50 *(978-1-56230-075-3(X))* Syndistar, Inc.

Velasquez, Gloria. Tyrone's Betrayal. 2006. (Roosevelt High School Series Bks.). 135p. (J). (gr. 3-7). per. 9.95 *(978-1-55885-465-9(7)*, Piñata Books) Arte Publico Pr.

Vrettos, Adrienne Maria. Burnout. (ENG., 208p. (YA). (gr. 7). 2012. Illus.). pap. 8.99 *(978-1-4169-9470-1(X))* 2011. 16.99 *(978-1-4169-9469-5(6))* McElderry, Margaret K. Bks. (McElderry, Margaret K. Bks.).

Woodson, Jacqueline. The Dear One. 2010. (ENG.). 176p. (YA). (gr. 7-18). 7.99 *(978-0-14-241705-8(X)*, Puffin Books) Penguin Young Readers Group.

Wright, Julie. My Not-So-Fairytale Life. 2005. 256p. (YA). pap. 15.95 *(978-1-59038-476-3(8))* Deseret Bk. Co.

ALCOTT, LOUISA MAY, 1832-1888

Aller, Susan Bivin. Beyond Little Women: A Story about Louisa May Alcott. Wang, Qi Z., illus. 2004. (Creative Minds Biographies Ser.). (ENG.). 64p. (J). (gr. 4-8). pap. 8.95 *(978-1-57505-636-4(4))*; lib. bdg. 22.60 *(978-1-57505-602-9(X))* Lerner Publishing Group.

Ditchfield, Christin. Louisa May Alcott: Author of Little Women. 2005. (Great Life Stories Ser.). (ENG., Illus.). 111p. (J). (gr. 6-8). 30.50 *(978-0-531-12403-1(7)*, Watts, Franklin) Scholastic Library Publishing.

Fromowitz, Lori. Louisa May Alcott. 2013. (ENG.). 48p. (J). pap. 15.64 *(978-1-61783-765-4(2))*; (gr. 3-6). lib. bdg. 32.79 *(978-1-61783-715-9(6))* ABDO Publishing Co.

Herweck Rice, Dona. Stepping into Louisa May Alcott's World (Grade 7) 2017. (TIME for KIDS(r) Nonfiction Readers Ser.). (Illus.). 48p. (J). (gr. 7-7). pap. 9.99 ***(978-1-4938-3619-2(6))*** Teacher Created Materials, Inc.

McDonough, Yona Zeldis. Louisa. Andersen, Bethanne, illus. 2014. (ENG.). 48p. (J). (gr. 1-5). pap. 7.99 *(978-1-250-05047-2(2)*, 9781250050472) Square Fish.

Meigs, Cornelia. Invincible Louisa. 2005. 216p. (J). (gr. 4-7). 21.50 *(978-0-8446-7268-7(8)*, 3584) Smith, Peter Pub., Inc.

Silverthorne, Elizabeth. Louisa May Alcott. 2nd rev. ed. 2011. (Who Wrote That? Ser.). (Illus.). 120p. (gr. 6-12). 35.00 *(978-1-60413-760-6(6)*, Chelsea Hse.) Facts On File, Inc.

ALCOTT, LOUISA MAY, 1832-1888—FICTION

Archer, Nick & McDonald, Megan. Rule of Three. 2010. (Sisters Club Ser.: 2). (ENG., Illus.). 240p. (J). (gr. 3-7). pap. 5.99 *(978-0-7636-4830-5(2))* Candlewick Pr.

—Rule of Three. Consolazio, Pamela A., illus. 2009. (Sisters Club Ser.: 2). (ENG.). 240p. (J). (gr. 3-7). 15.99 *(978-0-7636-4153-5(7))* Candlewick Pr.

Baratz-Logsted, Lauren. Little Women & Me. 2013. (ENG., Illus.). 336p. (YA). (gr. 7). pap. 9.99 *(978-1-61963-033-8(8)*, 9781619630338, Bloomsbury USA Childrens) Bloomsbury Publishing USA.

Carpenter, Nan. Louisa May Alcott & Thoreau's Flute, Two Letters: The Huntington Library Quarterly V24, No. 1, November 1960. 2011. 8p. pap. 35.95 *(978-1-258-09228-3(X))* Literary Licensing, LLC.

Frederick, Heather Vogel. The Mother-Daughter Book Club. (Mother-Daughter Book Club Ser.). (ENG.). (J). 2008. 288p. (gr. 4-7). pap. 7.99 *(978-1-4169-7079-8(7))* 2007. (Illus.). 256p. (gr. 5-7). 17.99 *(978-0-689-86412-4(4))* Simon & Schuster Bks. For Young Readers. (Simon & Schuster Bks. For Young Readers).

MacColl, Michaela. The Revelation of Louisa May. 2015. (ENG.). 272p. (J). (gr. 7-12). 16.99 *(978-1-4521-3357-7(3))* Chronicle Bks. LLC.

ALDRIDGE, IRA FREDERICK, -1867

Armand, Glenda & Cooper, Floyd. Ira's Shakespeare Dream, 1 vol. 2015. (ENG., Illus.). 40p. (J). 18.95 *(978-1-62014-155-7(8)*, 9781620000000) Lee & Low Bks., Inc.

ALEUTIAN ISLANDS (ALASKA)—FICTION

Villoldo, Alberto. Skeleton Woman. 2008. (ENG.). 36p. (J). (gr. -1-3). 12.99 *(978-1-4169-8962-2(5)*, Simon & Schuster Bks. For Young Readers) Simon & Schuster Bks. For Young Readers.

ALEUTS

Doak, Robin S. Arctic Peoples, 1 vol. 2011. (First Nations of North America Ser.). (ENG.). 48p. (gr. 3-3). pap. 9.95 *(978-1-4329-4956-3(X)*, Heinemann InfoSearch) Heinemann-Raintree.

Goldsworthy, Steve. Aleuts. 2014. (Illus.). 32p. (J). *(978-1-62127-511-4(6))* Weigl Pubs., Inc.

ALEUTS—FICTION

Hesse, Karen. Aleutian Sparrow. McGillivray, Kim & Zerbetz, Evon, illus. 2005. (ENG.). 160p. (J). (gr. 4-9). reprint ed. pap. 7.99 *(978-1-4169-0327-7(5)*, McElderry, Margaret K. Bks.) McElderry, Margaret K. Bks.

—Aleutian Sparrow. Zerbetz, Evon, illus. 2005. 156p. (J). (gr. 5-9). 13.65 *(978-0-7569-5589-2(0))* Perfection Learning Corp.

A B

ALEXANDER, THE GREAT, 356 B.C.-323 B.C.

Abbott, Jacob. Alexander the Great. 2009. (J). pap. 12.00 *(978-1-59128-058-3(3))* Canon Pr.

—Alexander the Great. 2004. (Illus.). (J). pap. 9.99 *(978-1-887159-97-5(5))* Preston-Speed Pubns.

—Alexander the Great. 2009. 212p. pap. 10.95 *(978-1-59915-132-8(4))* Yesterday's Classics.

Adams, Simon. Alexander: The Boy Soldier Who Conquered the World. 2005. (National Geographic World History Biographies Ser.). (ENG., Illus.). 64p. (J). (gr. 3-7). 17.95 *(978-0-7922-3660-3(2)*, National Geographic Children's Bks.) National Geographic Society.

—World History Biographies: Alexander: The Boy Soldier Who Conquered the World. 2013. (National Geographic World History Biographies Ser.). (ENG., Illus.). 64p. (J). (gr. 3-7). pap. 7.99 *(978-1-4263-1449-0(3)*, National Geographic Children's Bks.) National Geographic Society.

Adams, Simon & National Geographic Learning Staff. Alexander: The Boy Soldier Who Conquered the World. 2006. (Nonfiction Reading & Writing Workshops Ser.). (ENG., Illus.). 64p. (C). (gr. 3-7). lib. bdg. 45.95 *(978-0-7922-3661-0(0))* National Geographic School Publishing, Inc.

Bankston, John. Alexander the Great. 2013. (ENG.). 48p. (J). (gr. 3-6). lib. bdg. 29.95 *(978-1-61228-431-6(0))* Mitchell Lane Pubs., Inc.

—The Life & Times of Alexander the Great. (Biography from Ancient Civilizations Ser.). (Illus.). 48p. (J). 2005. (gr. 4-8). lib. bdg. 29.95 *(978-1-58415-283-5(4))* 2004. lib. bdg. *(978-1-58415-235-4(4))* Mitchell Lane Pubs., Inc.

Behnke, Alison. The Conquests of Alexander the Great. 2007. (Pivotal Moments in History Ser.). (ENG., Illus.). 160p. (gr. 9-12). lib. bdg. 38.60 *(978-0-8225-5920-7(X))* Lerner Publishing Group.

Caper, William. Alexander the Great: Set Of 6. 2011. (Navigators Ser.). (J). pap. 50.00 net. *(978-1-4108-5116-1(8))* Benchmark Education Co.

—Alexander the Great: Text Pairs. 2008. (Bridges/Navigators Ser.). (J). (gr. 6). 89.00 *(978-1-4108-8427-5(9))* Benchmark Education Co.

Crompton, Samuel Willard. Alexander the Great. 2003. (Ancient World Leaders Ser.). (Illus.). 112p. (J). (gr. 6-12). 30.00 *(978-0-7910-7219-6(3)*, Chelsea Hse.) Facts On File, Inc.

Demi Staff & Marshall Cavendish Corporation Staff. Alexander the Great, 0 vols. 2010. (ENG., Illus.). 64p. (J). (gr. 3-7). 19.99 *(978-0-7614-5700-8(3)*, 9780761457008, Amazon Children's Publishing) Amazon Publishing.

Doleac, Miles. Alexander the Great. 2016. (Conquerors & Combatants Ser.). 224p. (YA). lib. bdg. 55.00 *(978-1-5026-2453-6(2))* Cavendish Square Publishing.

Ganeri, Anita. Alexander the Great: The Life of a King & Conqueror. 2005. (Graphic Nonfiction Biographies Ser.). (ENG., Illus.). 48p. (J). (gr. 4-7). lib. bdg. 31.95 *(978-1-4042-0238-2(2)*, 1241094) Rosen Publishing Group, Inc., The.

Marsico, Katie. Alexander the Great: Ancient King & Conqueror, 1 vol. 2009. (Essential Lives Set 3 Ser.). (ENG., Illus.). 112p. (J). (gr. 6-12). lib. bdg. 35.64 *(978-1-60453-520-4(2))* ABDO Publishing Co.

McGowen, Tom. Alexander the Great: Conqueror of the Ancient World. 2006. (Rulers of the Ancient World Ser.). (Illus.). 160p. (YA). (gr. 6-12). lib. bdg. 29.27 *(978-0-7660-2560-8(8))* Enslow Pubs., Inc.

Morley, Jacqueline. You Wouldn't Want to Be in Alexander the Great's Army! Miles You'd Rather Not March. Antram, David, illus. 2005. (You Wouldn't Want to... Ser.). (ENG.). 32p. (J). (gr. 2-5). 29.00 *(978-0-531-12410-9(X))*; (gr. 4-7). pap. 9.95 *(978-0-531-12390-4(1))* Scholastic Library Publishing. (Watts, Franklin).

Nardo, Don. Alexander the Great: Conqueror of the Known World. 2009. (World Leaders Ser.). (Illus.). 100p. (J). 28.95 *(978-1-59935-126-1(9))* Reynolds, Morgan Inc.

Santillian, Beatriz & Randall, Bernard. Alexander the Great: Macedonian King & Conqueror. 2017. (Leaders of the Ancient World Ser.). 112p. (J). (gr. 12-11). 37.10 ***(978-1-5081-7482-0(2)***, Rosen Young Adult) Rosen Publishing Group, Inc., The.

Shecter, Vicky Alvear. Alexander the Great Rocks the World. Naughton, Terry, illus. 2006. 128p. (J). (gr. 5-7). lib. bdg. 18.95 *(978-1-58196-045-7(X)*, Darby Creek) Lerner Publishing Group.

Shone, Rob. Alexander the Great: The Life of a King & Conqueror. 2009. (Graphic Nonfiction Biographies Ser.). (ENG.). 48p. (YA). (gr. 4-5). 58.50 *(978-1-61513-012-2(8)*, Rosen Reference) Rosen Publishing Group, Inc., The.

Waterfield, Robin H., et al. Who Was Alexander the Great? Thomson, Andrew, illus. 2016. (Who Was? Ser.). (ENG.). 112p. (J). (gr. 3-7). lib. bdg. 15.99 *(978-0-399-54235-0(3)*, Grosset & Dunlap) Penguin Young Readers Group.

Wilhelm, Doug. Alexander the Great. rev. ed. 2015. (Wicked History Ser.). (ENG., Illus.). 144p. (J). lib. bdg. 33.00 *(978-0-531-22124-2(5)*, Children's Pr.) Scholastic Library Publishing.

—Alexander the Great: Master of the Ancient World. (Wicked History Ser.). (ENG.). 128p. (J). 2010. (gr. 6-12). pap. 5.95 *(978-0-531-22821-0(5)*, Watts, Franklin) 2009. (gr. 5-9). 31.00 *(978-0-531-21275-2(0))* Scholastic Library Publishing.

ALEXANDER, THE GREAT, 356 B.C.-323 B.C.—FICTION

Johnson, Vargie. Alexander the Great the All-Powerful: What Made Them Famous? 2006. 156p. (J). per. 15.00 *(978-1-931195-93-5(5))* KiwE Publishing, Ltd.

Osborne, Mary Pope. Stallion by Starlight. Murdocca, Sal, illus. (Magic Tree House Merlin Mission Ser.: No. 21). (ENG.). (J). (gr. 2-5). 2014. 144p. pap. 5.99 *(978-0-307-98044-1(8))* 2013. 128p. lib. bdg. 15.99 *(978-0-307-98042-7(1))* Random Hse. Children's Bks. (Random Hse. Bks. for Young Readers).

—Stallion by Starlight. 2014. (Magic Tree House Merlin Missions Ser.: 21). lib. bdg. 16.00 *(978-0-606-36411-9(0))* Turtleback Bks.

ALFRED, KING OF ENGLAND, 849-899

Abbott, Jacob. King Alfred of England. 2006. pap. *(978-1-4068-0240-5(9))* Echo Library.

—King Alfred of England, Makers of Histor. 2006. pap. *(978-1-4065-0359-3(2))* Dodo Pr.

ALGAE

Deep Sea Invasion. 2004. (NOVA Ser.). (gr. 4-18). 19.95 *(978-1-57807-980-3(2)*, WG36733) WGBH Boston Video.

Douglas, Lloyd G. Kelp. 2005. (Ocean Life Ser.). (ENG., Illus.). 24p. (J). (gr. -1-2). per. 4.95 *(978-0-516-23742-8(X)*, Children's Pr.) Scholastic Library Publishing.

Encyclopedia Britannica Staff, creator. Plants, Algae, & Fungi. 2011. (Britannica Illustrated Science Library Ser.). 104p. (J). 37.44 *(978-1-61535-461-0(1))* Encyclopaedia Britannica, Inc.

Hollar, Sherman. A Closer Look at Bacteria, Algae, & Protozoa. 2011. (Illus.). 88p. (J). lib. bdg. 31.70 *(978-1-61530-534-6(3))* Rosen Publishing Group, Inc., The.

Murphy, Daniel. Seaweed Soup. 2003. (J). pap., tchr. ed. *(978-0-7398-6546-0(3))* Steck-Vaughn.

Murphy, Stuart J. Seaweed Soup. Remkiewicz, Frank, illus. 2003. (Mathstart Ser.). 31p. (J). (gr. -1-3). pap. *(978-0-7398-6790-7(3))* Steck-Vaughn.

Westerskov, Kim, photos by. Forests in the Sea. 2004. (Illus.). 32p. (J). *(978-0-7685-2387-4(7))* Dominie Pr., Inc.

Zabludoff, Marc. The Protoctist Kingdom. 2005. (Family Trees Ser.). (Illus.). 96p. (gr. 6-7). lib. bdg. 34.21 *(978-0-7614-1818-4(0)*, Benchmark Bks.) Marshall Cavendish Corp.

ALGEBRA

see also Number Theory; Probabilities

Accelerated Math Learning Cards - Algebra I. 2004. 199.00 *(978-1-59455-121-5(9))* Renaissance Learning, Inc.

Accelerated Math West Virginia State Tagged Algebra I Library. 2004. cd-rom 1199.00 *(978-1-59455-113-0(8))* Renaissance Learning, Inc.

Accelerated Math West Virginia State Tagged Algebra II Library. 2004. cd-rom 1199.00 *(978-1-59455-114-7(6))* Renaissance Learning, Inc.

Accelerated Math West Virginia State Tagged Pre-Calculus Library. 2004. cd-rom 1199.00 *(978-1-59455-116-1(2))* Renaissance Learning, Inc.

Ace Academics & Burchard, Elizabeth R., eds. Algebra 1: A Whole Course in a Box! 2007. (Exambusters Ser.). 384p. (gr. 7-18). 12.95 *(978-1-881374-92-3(0)*, Exambusters) Ace Academics, Inc.

Adler, David A. Mystery Math: A First Book of Algebra. Miller, Edward, illus. 2011. (ENG.). 32p. (J). 17.95 *(978-0-8234-2289-0(5))* Holiday Hse., Inc.

—Mystery Math: A First Book of Algebra. Miller, Edward, illus. 2012. (ENG.). 32p. (J). (gr. 2-5). pap. 7.99 *(978-0-8234-2548-8(7))* Holiday Hse., Inc.

AIMS Education Foundation. Looking at Lines: Interesting Objects & Linear Functions. 2005. (ENG.). 320p. pap. 24.95 *(978-1-881431-91-6(6))* AIMS Education Foundation.

Algebra 1: Concepts & Skills. 2004. (gr. 6-12). wbk. ed. *(978-0-618-07867-7(3)*, 2-61259); wbk. ed. *(978-0-618-07865-3(7)*, 2-61257) Holt McDougal.

Algebra 2. 2004. (gr. 6-12). stu. ed. *(978-0-618-02031-7(4)*, 2-99720); stu. ed., wbk. ed. *(978-0-618-02033-1(0)*, 2-99744); stu. ed., wbk. ed. *(978-0-618-02034-8(9)*, 2-99745) Holt McDougal.

Algebra & Trigonometry: Complete Solutions Guide. 6th ed. 2004. (gr. 11-12). *(978-0-618-31785-1(6)*, 3-32723) CENGAGE Learning.

Algebra & Trigonometry: Learning Tools. 6th ed. 2004. (gr. 11-12). stu. ed. incl. cd-rom *(978-0-618-31794-3(5)*, 3-32732) CENGAGE Learning.

Algebra & Trigonometry: Test Item File. 6th ed. 2004. (gr. 11-12). *(978-0-618-31786-8(4)*, 3-32724) CENGAGE Learning.

Algebraic Thinking Algebra I Supplement. 2005. *(978-1-57290-068-4(7))* National Training Network, Inc.

Analysis I: Grundlagen: Zahlenfolgen und Reelle Funktionen. (Duden Abiturhilfen Ser.). (GER.). 112p. (YA). (gr. 11). *(978-3-411-70122-3(6))* Bibliographisches Institut & F. A. Brockhaus AG DEU. Dist: International Bk. Import Service, Inc.

Arvoy, Marsha & Nardi, Dorianne. Rounding. 2010. (My Path to Math Ser.). (ENG.). 24p. (J). (gr. k-3). *(978-0-7787-6786-2(8))*; pap. *(978-0-7787-6795-4(7))* Crabtree Publishing Co.

Aufmann, Richard N., et al. Beginning Algebra with Applications Student Solutions Manual. 6th ed. 2003. (Illus.). 324p. stu. ed., per. 49.56 *(978-0-618-30607-7(2)*, 301493) CENGAGE Learning.

Barden, Cindy & Mark Twain Media Staff. Pre-Algebra, Grades 6+ Short Daily Warm-Ups for the Classroom. 2005. (Jumpstarters Ser.). (ENG., Illus.). 48p. (gr. 6-8). pap. 8.99 *(978-1-58037-303-6(8))* Twain, Mark Media, Inc. Pubs.

Barker, Lori. Land Animals. rev. ed. 2012. (Mathematics Readers Ser.). (ENG.). 32p. (J). (gr. 6-6). pap. 8.99 *(978-1-4333-3456-6(9))* Teacher Created Materials, Inc.

—Sea Creatures. rev. ed. 2012. (Mathematics Readers Ser.). (ENG.). 32p. (J). (gr. 6-6). pap. 8.99 *(978-1-4333-3457-3(7))* Teacher Created Materials, Inc.

—Where Germs Lurk. rev. ed. 2012. (Mathematics Readers Ser.). (ENG.). 32p. (J). (gr. 6-6). pap. 8.99 *(978-1-4333-3455-9(0))* Teacher Created Materials, Inc.

Basher, Simon. Algebra & Geometry: Anything but Square! Basher, Simon, illus. 2011. (Basher Science Ser.). (ENG., Illus.). 128p. (J). (gr. 5-9). pap. 8.99 *(978-0-7534-6597-4(3)*, 9780753465974, Kingfisher) Roaring Brook Pr.

Beck, Ray, et al. Practicing Basic Skills in Algebra. 2004. (One-Minute Fluency Builders Ser.). 248p. per. 44.95 *(978-1-59318-005-8(5)*, 234ALG) Cambium Education, Inc.

Benchmark Education Company, LLC Staff, compiled by. Algebra. 2005. spiral bd. 255.00 *(978-1-4108-5861-0(8))*; spiral bd. 375.00 *(978-1-4108-5860-3(X))*; spiral bd. 295.00 *(978-1-4108-5450-6(7))*; spiral bd. 440.00 *(978-1-4108-4510-8(9))*; spiral bd. 365.00 *(978-1-4108-5449-0(3))*; spiral bd. 35.00 *(978-1-4108-3913-8(3))*; spiral bd. 105.00 *(978-1-4108-3900-8(1))*; spiral bd. 255.00 *(978-1-4108-3899-5(4))*; spiral bd. 215.00 *(978-1-4108-3892-6(7))*; spiral bd. 245.00 *(978-1-4108-3891-9(9))*; spiral bd. 105.00 *(978-1-4108-3883-4(8))*; spiral bd. 55.00 *(978-1-4108-3884-1(6))* Benchmark Education Co.

BJU Staff. Algebra 1 Student Text Grd 9. 2004. 32.00 *(978-1-57924-325-8(8))* BJU Pr.

Boswell, Kelly. Diagrams, Diagrams, Diagrams!, 1 vol. 2013. (Displaying Information Ser.). (ENG.). 32p. (gr. 1-2). 27.32 *(978-1-4765-0260-1(9))*; pap. 8.95 *(978-1-4765-3337-7(7))* Capstone Press of Coughlan Cos. (Aplus Bks.).

Bradsby, Larry, et al. Algebra 1 Rescue! Student Book: Chapters 1-6. 2003. 190p. (YA). per. *(978-1-57035-935-4(0)*, 169ALG) Cambium Education, Inc.

—Algebra 1 Rescue! Student Book: Chapters 7-12. 2003. 192p. (YA). per. *(978-1-57035-936-1(9)*, 169ALG) Cambium Education, Inc.

Burnett, James & i, Calvin. A Simple Stew: A Book about Growing Number Patterns. 2012. (J). *(978-1-921358-99-9(8))* Origo Education.

Campbell, Sarah C. Growing Patterns: Fibonacci Numbers in Nature. Campbell, Richard P., photos by. 2010. (ENG., Illus.). 32p. (J). (gr. k-6). 17.95 *(978-1-59078-752-6(8))* Boyds Mills Pr.

Canavan, Thomas. Symbols & Algebra: 50 Math Super Puzzles. 2011. (Math Standards Workout Ser.). (ENG., Illus.). 48p. (YA). (gr. 5-8). pap. 11.75 *(978-1-4488-6685-4(5)*, Rosen Reference); lib. bdg. 29.25 *(978-1-4488-6678-6(2))* Rosen Publishing Group, Inc., The.

Caron, Lucille & St. Jacques, Philip M. Pre-Algebra & Algebra Smarts! 2011. (Math Smarts! Ser.). (Illus.). 64p. (J). (gr. 5-18). pap. 8.95 *(978-1-59845-319-5(X))* Enslow Pubs., Inc.

Caron, Lucille, et al. Pre-Algebra & Algebra Smarts! 2011. (Math Smarts! Ser.). (Illus.). 64p. (J). (gr. 5-18). lib. bdg. 29.27 *(978-0-7660-3938-4(2))* Enslow Pubs., Inc.

Christopher, Nick. Janey Adds: Understanding Addition. 2013. (Rosen Math Readers Ser.). (ENG.). 16p. (J). (gr. k-1). pap. 7.00 *(978-1-4777-1602-1(5))*; pap. 42.00 *(978-1-4777-1603-8(3))* Rosen Publishing Group, Inc., The. (Rosen Classroom).

CMSP Projects Staff. Prealgebra. rev. ed. (Illus.). 101p. (YA). reprint ed. pap. *(978-0-942851-00-7(5))* CMSP Projects.

Concentrate on! Algebra I. 2003. (J). spiral bd. 15.95 *(978-1-58123-336-0(1))* Larson Learning, Inc.

Core Math Skills: Operations & Algebraic Thinking. 2013. (Core Math Skills: Operations & Algebraic Thinking Ser.). 24p. (J). (gr. 1-2). 135.60 *(978-1-4777-2233-6(5)*, Rosen Classroom) Rosen Publishing Group, Inc., The.

Davenport, Jefferson. Let's Help the Librarian! 2013. (InfoMax Math Readers Ser.). (ENG.). 24p. (J). (gr. 1-2). pap. 8.25 *(978-1-4777-2121-6(5)*, Rosen Classroom) Rosen Publishing Group, Inc., The.

—Let's Help the Librarian! Subtract Within 20. 2013. (InfoMax Math Readers Ser.). (ENG.). 24p. (J). (gr. 1-2). pap. 49.50 *(978-1-4777-2122-3(3)*, Rosen Classroom) Rosen Publishing Group, Inc., The.

Davis, Karen Lyn. Coolmath Algebra, Pt. 2. 2007. (YA). per. 19.95 *(978-0-9791628-1-7(5))* Coolmath.com, Inc.

—Coolmath Algebra Part 1. 2007. (YA). per. 19.95 *(978-0-9791628-0-0(7))* Coolmath.com, Inc.

Deen, Marilyn. The Right Place, 1 vol. 2011. (Wonder Readers Fluent Level Ser.). (ENG.). 32p. (gr. -1-2). pap. 5.99 *(978-1-4296-7937-4(9)*, Wonder Readers) Capstone Press of Coughlan Cos.

Diggory, Nikki. Jacob Counts Down: Understanding Subtraction. 2013. (InfoMax Math Readers Ser.). (ENG.). 16p. (J). (gr. k-1). pap. 42.00 *(978-1-4777-2004-2(9))*; pap. 7.00 *(978-1-4777-2003-5(0))* Rosen Publishing Group, Inc., The. (Rosen Classroom).

Downey, Tika. How the Arabs Invented Algebra: The History of the Concept of Variables. (Powermath Ser.). (ENG., 32p. (gr. 4-5). 2009. Illus.). pap. 10.00 *(978-0-8239-8879-2(1)*, PowerKids Pr.) 2004. 47.50 *(978-0-8239-7650-8(5))* Rosen Publishing Group, Inc., The.

Dressler, Isidore. Algebra I. 2nd rev. ed. 2005. pap. *(978-1-56765-575-9(0)*, R27P) AMSCO Schl. Pubns., Inc.

Edgar, Sherra G. Graphing Story Problems. 2013. (21st Century Basic Skills Library: Let's Make Graphs Ser.). (ENG., Illus.). 24p. (J). (gr. k-3). 22.79 *(978-1-62431-391-2(4)*, 202684); pap. 12.79 *(978-1-62431-467-4(8)*, 202686) Cherry Lake Publishing.

Encyclopaedia Britannica Publishers, Inc. Staff. Math in Context: Algebra Rules! 6th ed. 2005. (Math in Context Ser.). pap. 10.60 *(978-0-03-038574-2(1))* Harcourt Schl. Pubs.

Faulkner, Nicholas & Hosch, William L. Algebra & Trigonometry. 2017. (J). lib. bdg. ***(978-1-68048-774-9(4))*** Rosen Publishing Group, Inc., The.

Flip over Math: Algebraic Thinking. 2004. (J). spiral bd. 14.95 *(978-1-56911-539-8(7))* Learning Resources, Inc.

Francis, Jo. Diego Goes to the Beach: Represent & Solve Addition Problems. 2013. (InfoMax Math Readers Ser.). (ENG.). 24p. (J). (gr. 1-2). pap. 49.50 *(978-1-4777-2113-1(4))*; (Illus.). pap. 8.25 *(978-1-4777-2112-4(6))* Rosen Publishing Group, Inc., The. (Rosen Classroom).

Gateways to Algebra & Geometry, an Integrated Approach: Multi-Language Glossary. 2003. *(978-0-618-10650-9(2)*, 2-61315) Holt McDougal.

Glencoe McGraw-Hill Staff. Interactive Student Edition CD-ROM. 2006. (Johnson: Gregg Micro Keyboard Ser.). (ENG.). (gr. 9-12). cd-rom 115.04 *(978-0-07-875710-5(X)*, 007875710X) McGraw-Hill Higher Education.

Glencoe McGraw-Hill Staff, creator. Algebra 1: Volume Two: Integration Applications Connections, Vol. 2. 2006. (Illus.). 862p. stu. ed. 89.00 *(978-0-07-822849-0(2))* McGraw-Hill Cos., The.

Gregories, Rachel. Connor Goes to Camp: Subtract Within 20. 2013. (Rosen Math Readers Ser.). (ENG.). 24p. (J). (gr. 1-2). pap. 49.50 *(978-1-4777-2086-8(3))*; (Illus.). pap. 8.25 *(978-1-4777-2085-1(5))* Rosen Publishing Group, Inc., The. (Rosen Classroom).

Harcourt Brace Staff. Astro Algebra: Grades 6-8 Net Version Software Package. 99th ed. 2003. (Mighty Mathtm Ser.). (gr. 6-8). cd-rom 851.80 *(978-0-15-313212-4(4))* Harcourt Schl. Pubs.

Hamadek, Anita. Algebra Word Problems, Bk. 1. 2013. (Algebra Word Problems Ser.). (ENG.). 272p. (gr. 7-12). pap. 29.99 *(978-0-89455-799-6(8))* Critical Thinking Co., The.

Hesse, Leah. Let's Count Down: Understanding Subtraction. 2013. (Rosen Math Readers Ser.). (ENG.). 16p. (J). (gr. k-1). pap. 7.00 *(978-1-4777-1617-5(3)*, Rosen Classroom) Rosen Publishing Group, Inc., The.

Holliday, Berchie, et al. Algebra 1. 2005. (Merrill Algebra 1 Ser.). (ENG., Illus.). 884p. (gr. 8-12). stu. ed. 108.08 *(978-0-07-865113-7(1)*, 0078651131) McGraw-Hill Higher Education.

—Algebra 2. 2004. (Merrill Algebra 2 Ser.). (ENG., Illus.). 1024p. (gr. 10-12). stu. ed. 121.76 *(978-0-07-865609-5(5)*, 0078656095) McGraw-Hill Higher Education.

HOLT MCDOUGAL. Holt Mcdougal Algebra 1: Student Interactive Worktext 2014. 2013. (Holt Mcdougal Algebra 1 Ser.). (ENG.). 928p. (gr. 9-9). pap. 23.30 *(978-0-544-10215-6(0))* Big Ideas Learning, LLC.

Holt, Rinehart and Winston Staff. Pre-Algebra. 4th ed. 2003. (Holt Pre-Algebra Ser.). (ENG.). 116p. (gr. 8-8). pap., wbk. ed., pupil's gde. ed. 14.00 *(978-0-03-069714-2(X))* Houghton Mifflin Harcourt Publishing Co.

—Pre-Algebra: Are You Ready: Intervention. 4th ed. Date not set. pap. 74.40 *(978-0-03-070803-9(6))* Holt McDougal.

—Pre-Algebra: Chapter Resources. 4th ed. Date not set. pap. 367.00 *(978-0-03-070828-2(1))* Holt McDougal.

—Pre-Algebra: Homework & Practice Workbook Answer Key. 4th ed. Date not set. pap., wbk. ed. 11.00 *(978-0-03-069701-2(8))* Holt McDougal.

—Pre-Algebra: Interactive Problem Solving with Answer Key. 4th ed. 2003. pap. 30.53 *(978-0-03-069702-9(6))* Holt McDougal.

—Pre-Algebra: Interactive Study Guide with Answer Key. 4th ed. 2003. pap., stu. ed. 13.20 *(978-0-03-069703-6(4))* Holt McDougal.

—Pre-Algebra: Math: Reading, Writing & Content Areas. 4th ed. 2003. pap. 30.45 *(978-0-03-069801-9(4))* Holt McDougal.

—Pre-Algebra: Multilingual Glossary. 4th ed. Date not set. pap. 26.00 *(978-0-03-070804-6(4))* Holt McDougal.

—Pre-Algebra: Readiness Activities with Answer Key. 4th ed. 2003. pap. 13.20 *(978-0-03-069803-3(0))* Holt McDougal.

—Pre-Algebra: Standard Test Preparation. 4th ed. 2004. (Holt Pre-Algebra Ser.). (ENG.). 136p. (gr. 8-8). pap., wbk. ed. 4.90 *(978-0-03-070801-5(X))* Houghton Mifflin Harcourt Publishing Co.

—Pre-Algebra: Standard Test Preparation with Answer Key. 4th ed. Date not set. pap., wbk. ed. 12.60 *(978-0-03-070802-2(8))* Holt McDougal.

—Pre-Algebra: Success for English Language Learners. 4th ed. 2003. pap. 80.66 *(978-0-03-069859-0(6))* Holt McDougal.

—Pre-Algebra Chptr. 2: Resource Book with Answer Key. 4th ed. 2003. pap. 38.86 *(978-0-03-069681-7(X))* Holt McDougal.

—Pre-Algebra Chptr. 9: Resource Book with Answer Key. 4th ed. 2003. pap. 38.86 *(978-0-03-069689-3(5))* Holt McDougal.

—Pre-Algebra Chptr. 10: Resource Book with Answer Key. 4th ed. 2003. pap. 38.86 *(978-0-03-069691-6(7))* Holt McDougal.

—Pre-Algebra Chptr. 11: Resource Book with Answer Key. 4th ed. 2003. pap. 38.86 *(978-0-03-069692-3(5))* Holt McDougal.

—Pre-Algebra Chptr. 12: Resource Book with Answer Key. 4th ed. 2003. pap. 38.86 *(978-0-03-069693-0(3))* Holt McDougal.

—Pre-Algebra Chptr. 13: Resource Book with Answer Key. 3rd ed. 2003. pap. 38.86 *(978-0-03-069694-7(1))* Holt McDougal.

—Pre-Algebra Chptr. 14: Resource Book with Answer Key. 4th ed. 2003. pap. 38.86 *(978-0-03-069696-1(8))* Holt McDougal.

—Pre-Algebra Know-It Notebook. 4th ed. 2004. (Holt Pre-Algebra Ser.). pap. 13.93 *(978-0-03-038014-3(6))* Holt McDougal.

—Standard Test Practice Workbook: South Carolina Edition - Algebra. 3rd ed. 2003. pap. 13.26 *(978-0-03-069033-4(1))* Holt McDougal.

Hungerford, Thomas W. Contemporary College Algebra & Trigonometry: A Graphing Approach. 2nd ed. 2004. (ENG.). 496p. (C). pap. 111.95 *(978-0-534-46792-0(X))* Brooks/Cole.

In Step with the Standards - Algebra Concepts. 2005. (J). spiral bd. 15.95 *(978-1-58123-380-3(9))* Larson Learning, Inc.

Integrating Grade 10 TAKS Algebra I Objectives into Geometry, A Graphing Calculator Approach - Student Approach. 2005. (Region IV ESC Resources for Mathematics Ser.). pap. *(978-1-932797-69-5(6))* Region IV Education Service Ctr.

Interactive Mathematics - Elementary Algebra: Personal Academic Notebook. rev. ed. Date not set. (Illus.). 492p. (YA). (gr. 6-18). pap. 68.50 *(978-1-928962-01-4(7)*, MP-502-010) Academic Systems Corp.

Jacobson, Fiona. Lindsey Helps at the Library: Subtract Within 20. 2013. (Rosen Math Readers Ser.). (ENG.). 24p. (J). (gr. 1-2). pap. 49.50 *(978-1-4777-2029-5(4))*; (Illus.). pap. 8.25 *(978-1-4777-2028-8(6))* Rosen Publishing Group, Inc., The. (Rosen Classroom).

The Journey of Al & Gebra to the Land of Algebra PPT. 2006. (YA). cd-rom 20.00 *(978-1-929229-72-7(0))* aha! Process, Inc.

Karapetian, Marjam. Bilingual Content Dictionary: English to Spanish. 2004. (SPA & ENG., Illus.). 4.95 *(978-0-9764829-1-8(6))* WizdomInc.

King, Julie & Rasmussen, Peter. Graphs, 8. 2012. (Key To... workbooks Ser.: Bk. 8). (ENG., Illus.). 40p. (gr. 6-8). spiral bd. 5.64 *(978-1-55953-008-8(1)*, 1559530081) McGraw-Hill Education.

—Multiplying & Dividing Rational Expressions, 6. 2012. (Key To... workbooks Ser.: Bk. 6). (ENG., Illus.). 40p. (gr. 6-8). spiral bd. 5.64 *(978-1-55953-006-4(5)*, 1559530065) McGraw-Hill Education.

—Operations on Integers, Bk. 1. 2012. (Key To... workbooks Ser.: Bk. 1). (ENG.). 40p. (gr. 6-8). pap. 5.64 *(978-1-55953-001-9(4)*, 1559530014) McGraw-Hill Education.

—Rational Numbers, 5. 2012. (Key To... workbooks Ser.: Bk. 5). (ENG., Illus.). 40p. (gr. 6-8). spiral bd. 5.64 *(978-1-55953-005-7(7)*, 1559530057) McGraw-Hill Education.

King, Julie, et al. Equations, Bk. 3. 2012. (Key To... workbooks Ser.: Bk. 3). (ENG.). 40p. (gr. 6-8). spiral bd. 5.64 *(978-1-55953-003-3(0)*, 1559530030) McGraw-Hill Education.

—Polynomials, Bk. 4. 2012. (Key To... workbooks Ser.: Bk. 4). (ENG.). 40p. (gr. 6-8). spiral bd. 5.64 *(978-1-55953-004-0(9)*, 1559530049) McGraw-Hill Education.

—Square Roots & Quadratic Equations, Bk. 10. 2012. (Key To... workbooks Ser.: Bk. 10). (ENG., Illus.). 40p. (gr. 6-8). spiral bd. 5.64 *(978-1-55953-010-1(3)*, 1559530103) McGraw-Hill Education.

—Systems of Equations, Bk. 9. 2012. (Key To... workbooks Ser.: Bk. 9). (ENG., Illus.). 40p. (gr. 6-8). spiral bd. 5.64 *(978-1-55953-009-5(X)*, 155953009X) McGraw-Hill Education.

Kizlik, S. B. & BarCharts Inc., Staff. Algebra, Pt. 2. 2005. (ENG., Illus.). 6p. 6.95 *(978-1-57222-922-8(5))* Barcharts, Inc.

Kopp, Jaine. Algebraic Reasoning: Professor Arbegla Introduces Variables & Functions. 2003. (Great Explorations in Math & Science Ser.). (Illus.). 148p. (Orig.). (J). (gr. 3-5). pap. 18.00 *(978-0-924886-70-6(6)*, GEMS) Univ. of California, Berkeley, Lawrence Hall of Science.

Krech, Bob & Grabell, Jeff. Algebra Readiness: Mini-Lessons, Games, & Activities to Review & Reinforce Essential Math Concepts & Skills. 2008. (Reteaching Math Ser.). (ENG.). 96p. pap. 14.99 *(978-0-439-52966-2(2)*, Teaching Resources) Scholastic, Inc.

Krech, Bob & Novelli, Joan. Algebra: Engaging Story Problems for Students to Read, Fill-In, Solve, & Sharpen Their Math Skills. 2009. (50 Fill-in Math Word Problems Ser.). (ENG.). 64p. (gr. 4-6). pap. 11.99 *(978-0-545-07487-2(8)*, Teaching Resources) Scholastic, Inc.

—50 Fill-In Math Word Problems - Algebra Readiness: Engaging Story Problems for Students to Read, Fill-In, Solve, & Sharpen Their Math Skills. 2009. (50 Fill-in Math Word Problems Ser.). (ENG.). 64p. (gr. 2-3). pap. 11.99 *(978-0-545-07484-1(3)*, Teaching Resources) Scholastic, Inc.

Lane County Mathematics Project Staff. Problem Solving in Mathematics. (YA). (gr. 9). pap. 27.95 *(978-0-86651-186-5(5)*, DSO1412) Globe Fearon Educational Publishing.

Larson, Roland E. Passport to Algebra & Geometry: (c)2004. I.t. ed. 2004. (McDougal Littell Math Ser.). (YA). (gr. 6-9). stu. ed. *(978-0-618-37422-9(1)*, 2-05530) Holt McDougal.

Larson, Ron. Precalculus. 6th ed. 2003. (ENG.). 184p. (C). (gr. 11-12). pap., stu. ed. 18.95 *(978-0-618-31440-9(7)*, 332746) CENGAGE Learning.

—Study & Solutions Guide: Used with ... Larson-Precalculus. 6th ed. 2003. (YA). (gr. 11-12). stu. ed. 54.36 *(978-0-618-31437-9(7)*, 332743) CENGAGE Learning.

Larson, Ron, et al. Algebra 1. 2006. (Illus.). 870p. (gr. 6-12). *(978-0-618-25018-9(2)*, 2-06008) Holt McDougal.

—Algebra 2. 2006. (gr. 6-12). incl. cd-rom *(978-0-618-40097-3(4)*, 2-05667) Holt McDougal.

—Geometry: Applying, Reasoning, Measuring. 2003. (McDougal Littell High School Math Ser.). (ENG.). 992p. (gr. 9-12). stu. ed. 114.95 *(978-0-618-25022-6(0)*, 2-06012) Great Source Education Group, Inc.

—Precalculus with Limits: A Graphing Approach. 4th ed. 2004. (ENG.). 1104p. (C). 199.95 *(978-0-618-39478-4(8)*, 333050) CENGAGE Learning.

Lawler, Graham. Introducing Algebra 2: Specialising & Generalising. 2010. (Illus.). 60p. (J). spiral bd. *(978-1-84285-080-0(6))* GLMP Ltd. GBR. Dist: NBN International.

Lawrence, David P. Skill & Practice Masters in Algebra Using the Ti-84. 2004. 50p. pap. 14.95 net. *(978-1-58108-050-6(6))* Pencil Point Pr., Inc.

—Ti-84 Easy Warm Ups in Algebra One. 2004. 32p. pap. 14.95 net. *(978-1-58108-049-0(2)*, 1-58108-049-2) Pencil Point Pr., Inc.

Lay, Steven R. & Lay, L. Clark. Prelude to Algebra. 2007. 338p. 60.00 *(978-0-9793087-0-3(4))* Cross Product Pubns.

Lechner, Judith. Our New Fish Tank: Learning to Estimate & Round Numbers to the Nearest Ones, Tens, & Hundreds Places. 2004. (Math Big Bookstm Ser.). (ENG.). 16p. (gr. 2-3). 37.95 *(978-0-8239-7640-9(8))* Rosen Publishing Group, Inc., The.

Lineare Algebra und Analytische Geometrie I: Leistungskurs. (Duden Abiturhilfen Ser.). (GER.). 96p. (YA). (gr. 12-13). *(978-3-411-04601-0(5))* Bibliographisches Institut & F. A. Brockhaus AG DEU. Dist: International Bk. Import Service, Inc.

Lineare Algebra und Analytische Geometrie II: Leistungskurs. (Duden Abiturhilfen Ser.). (GER.). 96p. (YA). (gr. 12-13). *(978-3-411-04631-7(7))* Bibliographisches Institut & F. A. Brockhaus AG DEU. Dist: International Bk. Import Service, Inc.

Low, Yvonne. Kyoodoz Pre-Algebra Maven. 2007. (Illus.). 200p. (YA). per. 16.50 *(978-0-9771172-2-7(7))* Kyoodoz.

Marks, Jennifer L. Clasificar Dinero/Sorting Money, 1 vol. 2012. (Vamos a Ordenar / Sorting Ser.). (ENG, SPA & MUL., Illus.). 32p. (gr. 1-2). lib. bdg. 27.32 *(978-1-4296-8255-8(8)*, A+ Bilingue/Bilingual) Capstone Press of Coughlan Cos.

—Clasificar Juguetes/Sorting Toys, 1 vol. 2012. (Vamos a Ordenar / Sorting Ser.). (ENG, SPA & MUL.). 32p. (gr. 1-2). lib. bdg. 27.32 *(978-1-4296-8254-1(X)*, A+ Bilingue/Bilingual) Capstone Press of Coughlan Cos.

—Clasificar por Tamaño. 2012. (Vamos a Ordenar / Sorting Ser.). (MUL & SPA., Illus.). 32p. (gr. 1-2). lib. bdg. 27.32 *(978-1-4296-8253-4(1)*, A+ Bilingue/Bilingual) Capstone Press of Coughlan Cos.

Math Forum Staff. Dr. Math Explains Algebra: Learning Algebra Is Easy! Just Ask Dr. Math! 2003. (ENG., Illus.). 192p. pap. 14.95 *(978-0-471-22555-3(X)*, Jossey-Bass) Wiley, John & Sons, Inc.

Mathematical Models with Applications: Algebra II Alignment Student Handbook. 2003. per. *(978-1-932524-01-7(0))* Region IV Education Service Ctr.

McConnell, Cara. We Can Recycle: Represent & Solve Addition Problems. 2013. (InfoMax Math Readers Ser.). (ENG.). 24p. (J). (gr. 1-2). pap. 8.25 *(978-1-4777-2178-0(9))*; pap. 49.50 *(978-1-4777-2179-7(7))* Rosen Publishing Group, Inc., The. (Rosen Classroom).

McDougal Littell Algebra 1: Exercises in Spanish. 2004. (McDougal Littell Math Ser.). (gr. 6-12). *(978-0-618-37048-1(X)*, 2-06532) Holt McDougal.

McDougal Littell Algebra 1: Functions Sourcebook. 2004. (gr. 6-12). *(978-0-618-39081-6(2)*, K-51303) Holt McDougal.

McDougal Littell Algebra 1: Notetaking Guide, PE. 2004. (gr. 6-12). *(978-0-618-41021-7(X)*, 2-05710) Holt McDougal.

McDougal Littell Algebra 1: Personal Student Tutor. 2004. (gr. 6-12). cd-rom *(978-0-618-38108-1(2)*, 2-05537); cd-rom *(978-0-618-39631-3(4)*, 2-05623); cd-rom *(978-0-618-35333-0(X)*, 2-91224) Holt McDougal.

McDougal Littell Algebra 2: EEdition. 2004. (gr. 6-12). cd-rom *(978-0-618-43978-2(1)*, 2-05467) Holt McDougal.

McDougal Littell Algebra 2: Exercises in Spanish. 2004. (McDougal Littell Math Ser.). (gr. 6-12). *(978-0-618-37050-4(1)*, 2-06534) Holt McDougal.

McDougal Littell Algebra 2: Personal Student Tutor. 2004. (gr. 6-12). cd-rom *(978-0-618-38109-8(0)*, 2-05538); cd-rom *(978-0-618-39639-9(X)*, 2-05626); cd-rom *(978-0-618-35340-8(2)*, 2-91231) Holt McDougal.

McDougal Littell Algebra 2: Pupil's Edition (c) 2004. 2004. (gr. 6-12). *(978-0-618-25020-2(4)*, 2-06010) Holt McDougal.

McDougal Littell Geometry: Notetaking Guide, PE. 2004. (gr. 6-12). *(978-0-618-41023-1(6)*, 2-05712) Holt McDougal.

McKeague. Ssm Elementary Algebra. 7th ed. 2003. (C). pap. 34.95 *(978-0-534-42311-7(6))* Brooks/Cole.

—Ssm Intermediate Algebra. 7th ed. 2003. (C). pap. 36.95 *(978-0-534-42291-2(8))* Brooks/Cole.

Mercer, Susan. Pathway to Pre-Algebra Proficiency. 2008. 76p. per. 14.95 *(978-1-4327-1719-3(7))* Outskirts Pr., Inc.

Michele, Angela. Books at the Library: Understanding Addition. 2013. (Rosen Math Readers Ser.). (ENG.). 16p. (J). (gr. k-1). pap. 42.00 *(978-1-4777-1630-4(0))*; (Illus.). pap. 7.00 *(978-1-4777-1629-8(7))* Rosen Publishing Group, Inc., The. (Rosen Classroom).

Muschla, Erin. Practice Makes Perfect Pre-Algebra. 2012. (ENG.). 160p. pap. 17.00 *(978-0-07-177278-5(2)*, 0071772782) McGraw-Hill Education.

Nathan, Kris. Kris's Key - Math & Pre-Algebra Concepts. 2004. pap. 8.95 *(978-0-9755341-0-6(6)*, 20) Abccurate Business Ventures.

Nichols, Susan. Al-Karaji: Tenth Century Mathematician & Engineer. 2016. (Physicians, Scientists, & Mathematicians of the Islamic World Ser.). 112p. (J). (gr. 6-6). 37.10 *(978-1-5081-7143-0(2))* Rosen Publishing Group, Inc., The.

O'Donnell, Kerri. The Ancient Civilizations of Greece & Rome: Solving Algebraic Equations. 2009. (PowerMath: Proficiency Plus Ser.). 32p. (gr. 4-5). 47.90 *(978-1-60851-417-5(X)*, PowerKids Pr.) Rosen Publishing Group, Inc., The.

Passport to Algebra & Geometry. 2004. (gr. 6-12). stu. ed. *(978-0-395-87988-7(4)*, 2-77610); stu. ed. *(978-0-618-18596-2(8)*, 2-05508) Holt McDougal.

Passport to Algebra & Geometry: Practice Workbook. 2004. (gr. 6-12). (SPA.). *(978-0-395-90160-1(X)*, 2-77865); stu. ed., wbk. ed. *(978-0-395-89670-9(3)*, 2-77742) Holt McDougal.

Peppas, Lynn. Symmetry. 2009. (ENG., Illus.). 24p. (J). lib. bdg. *(978-0-7787-4351-4(9)*, 1302766); pap. *(978-0-7787-4369-9(1)*, 1302766) Crabtree Publishing Co.

Piddock, Claire. Regrouping. 2010. (ENG.). 24p. (J). *(978-0-7787-6785-5(X))* Crabtree Publishing Co.

Potter, Kevin. Frugal Bear's Algebra Boot Camp. 2004. (YA). per. *(978-0-9678694-5-2(5)*, FrugalBear.com) Frugal Bear Communications.

Precalculus: Complete Solutions Guide. 6th ed. 2004. (gr. 11-12). *(978-0-618-31438-6(5)*, 3-32744) CENGAGE Learning.

Precalculus: HM MathSpace Technology Package. 3rd ed. 2004. (gr. 6-12). tchr. ed. *(978-0-618-35699-7(1)*, 3-02981) Holt McDougal.

Precalculus with Limits: a Graphing Approach: Learning Tools. 6th ed. 2004. (gr. 11-12). stu. ed. incl. cd-rom *(978-0-618-31447-8(4)*, 3-32754) CENGAGE Learning.

Puritz, Christian. Venture Mathematics Worksheets: Algebra & Arithmetic. 2007. (ENG.). 32p. (J). pap. 21.00 *(978-1-899618-70-5(8))* Parkwest Pubns., Inc.

Reeves, Brian & Robinson, Craig. Pre-Calculus Student Activity Book. Matthews, Douglas L., ed. 2003. (Illus.). stu. ed., per., wbk. ed. *(978-1-931680-24-0(8)*, Expert Systems for Teachers) Teaching Point, Inc.

Robinson, C. L. MATH1on1 Algebra Foundation. 2006. (YA). per. 9.99 *(978-0-9786767-5-9(0))* Robinson, Consuelo.

Roza, Greg. Famous Flights: Understanding & Using Variables. (Math for the Real World Ser.). 32p. 2009. (ENG., Illus.). (gr. 6-7). pap. 10.00 *(978-1-4042-6087-0(0))* 2009. (gr. 5-5). 47.90 *(978-1-60851-354-3(8)*, PowerKids Pr.) 2006. (Illus.). (YA). (gr. 5-9). lib. bdg. 25.25 *(978-1-4042-3367-6(9))* Rosen Publishing Group, Inc., The.

—Inside the Human Body: Using Scientific & Exponential Notation. (Math for the Real World Ser.). 32p. 2009. (ENG., Illus.). (gr. 6-7). pap. 10.00 *(978-1-4042-6077-1(3))* 2009. (gr. 5-5). 47.90 *(978-1-60851-359-8(9)*, PowerKids Pr.) 2006. (Illus.). (YA). (gr. 5-9). lib. bdg. 25.25 *(978-1-4042-3362-1(8))* Rosen Publishing Group, Inc., The.

Sandall, Barbara R., et al. Algebra Practice: Examples & Practice. 2006. (ENG., Illus.). 128p. (gr. 7-8). per. 13.99 *(978-1-58037-325-8(9))* Twain, Mark Media, Inc. Pubs.

Sanders, Sammy. Bryce's Bike Race: Add Within 20. 2013. (InfoMax Math Readers Ser.). (ENG.). 24p. (J). (gr. 1-2). pap. 49.50 *(978-1-4777-2116-2(9))*; (Illus.). pap. 8.25 *(978-1-4777-2115-5(0))* Rosen Publishing Group, Inc., The. (Rosen Classroom).

Santana, Rachel. Who's Older? Understand & Apply Properties of Operations. 2013. (Rosen Math Readers Ser.). (ENG.). 24p. (J). (gr. 1-2). pap. 49.50 *(978-1-4777-2083-7(9))*; (Illus.). pap. 8.25 *(978-1-4777-2082-0(0))* Rosen Publishing Group, Inc., The. (Rosen Classroom).

Saxon Algebra 1/2 Answer Key & Test. 2004. 18.00 *(978-0-01-205182-5(9))* Saxon Pubs., Inc.

Saxon Algebra 1/2 Home Study Kit. 2004. 60.25 *(978-0-01-204722-4(8))* Saxon Pubs., Inc.

Saxon, John H., Jr. Algebra 2: An Incremental Development. 3rd ed. 2003. (Saxon Algebra 2 Ser.). (ENG., Illus.). 600p. (gr. 9-12). stu. ed. 83.10 *(978-1-56577-140-6(0)*, 140-0) Houghton Mifflin Harcourt Publishing Co.

Simpson, Jeff. Access to Algebra, Vol. 2. Simpson, Marilyn, ed. 2006. (Count, Notice, & Remember Ser.: 514). ring bd. 100.00 *(978-1-888976-35-9(7)*, 514); ring bd. 100.00 *(978-1-888976-36-6(5)*, 514) Mastery Learning Systems.

Sky, Lucinda. At the Amusement Park: Understand & Apply Properties of Operations. 2013. (InfoMax Math Readers Ser.). (ENG.). 24p. (J). (gr. 1-2). pap. 49.50 *(978-1-4777-2152-0(5))*; (Illus.). pap. 8.25 *(978-1-4777-2151-3(7))* Rosen Publishing Group, Inc., The. (Rosen Classroom).

Ssm Precalc: Func/Graphs. 10th ed. 2005. (C). pap. 37.95 *(978-0-534-99995-7(6))* Brooks/Cole.

Steck-Vaughn Staff. Top Line Math: Algebra. 2005. pap. 5.49 *(978-1-4190-0372-1(0))* Steck-Vaughn.

Teacher Created Materials Staff, ed. Crash Course: Guide: Active Algebra. 2008. (Active Algebra Ser.). 280p. tchr. ed., ring bd. 59.99 *(978-1-4333-0002-8(8))* Teacher Created Materials, Inc.

Tent, M. B. W. Emmy Noether: The Mother of Modern Algebra. 2008. (ENG., Illus.). 184p. (C). 35.95 *(978-1-56881-430-8(5)*, K00391) AK Peters, Ltd.

Tobin, Jason. Algebra, 1 vol. 2015. (ENG.). 64p. (YA). 31.70 *(978-1-62275-521-9(9)*, Britannica Educational Publishing) Rosen Publishing Group, Inc., The.

Vanderbilt, David. Up & down on the Elevator: Add & Subtract Within 20. 2013. (Rosen Math Readers Ser.). (ENG.). 24p. (J). (gr. 1-2). pap. 49.50 *(978-1-4777-2032-5(4))*; (Illus.). pap. 8.25 *(978-1-4777-2031-8(6))* Rosen Publishing Group, Inc., The. (Rosen Classroom).

Visto, Joy. Why Do Math with Letters? 2015. (Illus.). 48p. (J). *(978-1-60818-577-1(X)*, Creative Education) Creative Co., The.

—Why Do Math with Letters? Making Math Work. 2016. (Making Math Work Ser.). (ENG.). 48p. (J). (gr. 5-9). pap. 12.00 *(978-1-62832-178-4(4)*, Creative Paperbacks) Creative Co., The.

Webber, Berryl & Barnes, Terry. How to Dazzle at Algebra. 2004. (Illus.). 48p. pap. 30.00 *(978-1-903853-12-2(5))* Brilliant Pubns. GBR. Dist: Parkwest Pubns., Inc.

Weir, Ben. Maggie's Money: Understanding Addition & Subtraction. 2013. (InfoMax Math Readers Ser.). (ENG.). 16p. (J). (gr. k-1). pap. 42.00 *(978-1-4777-1959-6(8))*; (Illus.). pap. 7.00 *(978-1-4777-1958-9(X))* Rosen Publishing Group, Inc., The. (Rosen Classroom).

Williams, Zella & Wingard-Nelson, Rebecca. Word Problems Using Operations & Algebraic Thinking. 2016. (Mastering Math Word Problems Ser.). 48p. (J). pap. 11.70 *(978-0-7660-8268-7(7))* Enslow Pubs., Inc.

Wingard-Nelson, Rebecca. Algebra & Pre-Algebra: It's Easy. 2014. (Easy Genius Math Ser.). 64p. (J). (gr. 4-18). lib. bdg. 29.27 *(978-0-7660-4251-3(0))* Enslow Pubs., Inc.

—Algebra I & Algebra II. 2004. (Math Success Ser.). (Illus.). 64p. (J). lib. bdg. 23.94 *(978-0-7660-2566-0(7))* Enslow Pubs., Inc.

—Algebra I & Algebra II Smarts! 2011. (Math Smarts! Ser.). (Illus.). 64p. (J). (gr. 5-18). pap. 8.95 *(978-1-59845-322-5(X))*; lib. bdg. 29.27 *(978-0-7660-3941-4(2))* Enslow Pubs., Inc.

—Algebra Word Problems: No Problem! 2010. (Math Busters Word Problems Ser.). 64p. (J). 29.27 *(978-0-7660-3367-2(8))* Enslow Pubs., Inc.

—Amusement Park Word Problems Starring Pre-Algebra: Math Word Problems Solved. 2009. (Math Word Problems Solved Ser.). (Illus.). 48p. (J). (gr. 2-5). lib. bdg. 25.27 *(978-0-7660-2922-4(0))* Enslow Pubs., Inc.

—Pre-Algebra & Algebra: Ace Your Math Test. 2012. (Ace Your Math Test Ser.). (Illus.). 104p. (J). (gr. 5-18). pap. 10.95 *(978-1-4644-0009-4(1))* Enslow Pubs., Inc.

—Problem Solving & Word Problems. 2004. (Math Success Ser.). (Illus.). 64p. (J). lib. bdg. 23.94 *(978-0-7660-2565-3(9))* Enslow Pubs., Inc.

Woods, Michael. Factoring. 2005. 28p. 8.84 *(978-1-4116-6014-4(5))* Lulu Pr., Inc.

ALGERIA

DiPiazza, Francesca Davis. Algeria in Pictures. 2007. (Visual Geography (Lerner) Ser.). (Illus.). 80p. (YA). (gr. 7-12). lib. bdg. 31.93 *(978-0-8225-7144-5(7))* Twenty First Century Bks.

Hintz, Martin. Algeria. 2017. (Enchantment of the World(tm) Ser.). (ENG., Illus.). 144p. (J). lib. bdg. 40.00 *(978-0-531-22081-8(8)*, Children's Pr.) Scholastic Library Publishing.

Kagda, Falaq & Latif, Zawiah Abdul. Algeria. 2nd rev. ed. 2007. (Cultures of the World Ser.). 144p. (gr. 6). lib. bdg. 42.79 *(978-0-7614-2085-9(1)*, Benchmark Bks.) Marshall Cavendish Corp.

Kagda, Falaq, et al. Algeria. 2017. (Illus.). (J). ***(978-1-5026-2742-1(6))*** Cavendish Square Publishing.

Marston, Elsa. The Compassionate Warrior: Abd el-Kader of Algeria. 2013. (ENG., Illus.). 184p. (J). (gr. 8-12). pap. 16.95 *(978-1-937786-10-6(2)*, Wisdom Tales) World Wisdom, Inc.

McManus, Lori. Algeria, 1 vol. 2012. (Countries Around the World Ser.). (ENG.). 48p. (gr. 3-6). pap. 8.99 *(978-1-4329-6119-0(5))*; lib. bdg. 33.32 *(978-1-4329-6093-3(8))* Heinemann-Raintree. (NA-h).

Morrow, James. Algeria. 2010. (Major Muslim Nations Ser.). 112p. (YA). (gr. 5-18). lib. bdg. 25.95 *(978-1-4222-1392-6(7))* Mason Crest.

Wagner, Heather Lehr. The Algerian War. 2012. (Milestones in Modern World History Ser.). 120p. (C). (gr. 9). 35.00 *(978-1-60413-923-5(4)*, Chelsea Hse.) Facts On File, Inc.

ALGERIA—FICTION

Fequiere, Marie A. Devil Rain & the Bearded Child of the Desert. 2007. (J). pap. 8.00 *(978-0-8059-7366-2(4))* Dorrance Publishing Co., Inc.

ALHAMBRA (GRANADA, SPAIN)

Crossling, Nick. Alhambra Stained Glass Coloring Book. 2008. (Dover Design Stained Glass Coloring Book Ser.). (ENG., Illus.). 32p. (gr. 3-8). per. 7.99 *(978-0-486-46531-9(4))* Dover Pubns., Inc.

ALI, MUHAMMAD, 1942-2016

Ali: An American Champion. 2014. (ENG., Illus.). 96p. (J). (gr. 3-7). 17.99 *(978-1-4814-0141-8(6)*, Simon & Schuster Bks. For Young Readers) Simon & Schuster Bks. For Young Readers.

Barretta, Gene. Muhammad Ali & the Stolen Bicycle. Morrison, Frank, illus. 2017. 40p. (J). (gr. -1-3). 17.99 *(978-0-06-243016-8(5)*, Tegen, Katherine Bks) HarperCollins Pubs.

Bolden, Tonya. The Champ. Christie, R. Gregory, illus. 2007. (gr. k-3). 17.00 *(978-0-7569-7940-9(4))* Perfection Learning Corp.

—The Champ: The Story of Muhammad Ali. Christie, R. Gregory, illus. 2007. (ENG.). 40p. (J). (gr. 1-4). pap. 7.99 *(978-0-440-41782-8(1)*, Dragonfly Bks.) Random Hse. Children's Bks.

Brown, Jonatha A. Muhammad Ali. 2005. (People We Should Know Ser.). (Illus.). 24p. (J). (gr. 1-4). (SPA.). pap. 8.15 *(978-0-8368-4764-2(4))*; (SPA., lib. bdg. 22.00 *(978-0-8368-4757-4(1))*; lib. bdg. 22.00 *(978-0-8368-4743-7(1))* Stevens, Gareth Publishing LLLP. (Weekly Reader Leveled Readers).

Buckley, James, Jr. Muhammad Ali. 2004. (Trailblazers of the Modern World Ser.). (Illus.). 48p. (J). (gr. 5-12). pap. 14.05 *(978-0-8368-5256-1(7))*; lib. bdg. 31.00 *(978-0-8368-5096-3(3))* Stevens, Gareth Publishing LLLP. (Gareth Stevens Secondary Library).

—Who Is Muhammad Ali? Marchesi, Stephen & Harrison, Nancy, illus. 2014. (Who Was? Ser.). (ENG.). 112p. (J). (gr. 3-7). 5.99 *(978-0-448-47955-2(9)*, Grosset & Dunlap) Penguin Young Readers Group.

Buckley, James. Who Is Muhammad Ali? 2014. (Who Was... ? Ser.). lib. bdg. 16.00 *(978-0-606-35696-1(7))* Turtleback Bks.

Burgan, Michael. Ali's Knockout Punch: How a Photograph Stunned the Boxing World. 2017. (Captured History Sports Ser.). (ENG., Illus.). 64p. (gr. 5-7). lib. bdg. 34.65 *(978-0-7565-5527-6(2)*, CPB Grades 4-8) Compass Point Bks.

—Muhammad Ali: American Champion, 1 vol. Bascle, Brian, illus. 2008. (Graphic Biographies Ser.). (ENG.). 32p. (gr. 3-4). per. 8.10 *(978-1-4296-1771-0(3)*, Graphic Library) Capstone Press of Coughlan Cos.

Doeden, Matt. Muhammad Ali: The Greatest. 2017. (Gateway Biographies Ser.). (ENG.). 48p. (J). (gr. 4-8). 12.99 ***(978-1-5124-4433-9(2)***, Lerner Pubns.); 39.99 ***(978-1-5124-4434-6(0)***, Lerner Pubns.); (Illus.). 26.65 *(978-1-5124-4431-5(6))*; 39.99 ***(978-1-5124-4432-2(4)***, Lerner Pubns.) Lerner Publishing Group.

Down, Susan. Muhammad Ali: The Greatest. 2013. (ENG., Illus.). 112p. (J). pap. *(978-0-7787-1043-1(2))* Crabtree Publishing Co.

Down, Susan Brophy. Muhammad Ali: The Greatest. 2013. (ENG., Illus.). 112p. (J). *(978-0-7787-1034-9(3))* Crabtree Publishing Co.

Feinstein, Stephen. Muhammad Ali. 2007. (African-American Heroes Ser.). (Illus.). 24p. (J). (gr. 1-3). lib. bdg. 22.60 *(978-0-7660-2763-3(5)*, Enslow Elementary) Enslow Pubs., Inc.

Ford, Carin T. Muhammad Ali: I Am the Greatest. 2006. (African-American Biography Library). (Illus.). 128p. (J). (gr. 6-12). lib. bdg. 33.27 *(978-0-7660-2460-1(1))* Enslow Pubs., Inc.

Golus, Carrie. Muhammad Ali. 2006. (Sports Heroes & Legends Ser.). (ENG., Illus.). 120p. (J). (gr. 5-12). lib. bdg. 30.60 *(978-0-8225-5960-3(9))* Lerner Publishing Group.

Graham, Tim. Muhammad Ali: Conscientious Objector. 2016. (Game-Changing Athletes Ser.). (ENG., Illus.). 112p. (J). (gr. 9-9). lib. bdg. 42.79 *(978-1-5026-1051-5(5))* Cavendish Square Publishing.

Gregory, Josh. Muhammad Ali. 2017. (True Book(tm), A — Biographies Ser.). (ENG., Illus.). 48p. (J). lib. bdg. 31.00 *(978-0-531-22170-9(9)*, Children's Pr.) Scholastic Library Publishing.

Healy, Nick. Muhammad Ali. 2005. (Genius Ser.). (Illus.). 48p. (J). (gr. 5-9). lib. bdg. 21.95 *(978-1-58341-333-3(2)*, Creative Education) Creative Co., The.

Helfand, Lewis. Muhammad Ali: The King of the Ring. Sharma, Lalit Kumar, illus. 2012. (Campfire Graphic Novels Ser.). (ENG.). 92p. (YA). (gr. 5-12). pap. 12.99 *(978-93-80741-23-9(5)*, Campfire) Steerforth Pr.

Hord, Colleen. Muhammad Ali. 2013. (ENG., Illus.). 24p. (J). (gr. k-3). pap. 8.95 *(978-1-61810-285-0(0))* Rourke Educational Media.

Jordan, Denise M. Muhammad Ali: Meet the Champion. 2003. (Meeting Famous People Ser.). (Illus.). 32p. (J). lib. bdg. 22.60 *(978-0-7660-2272-0(2))* Enslow Pubs., Inc.

Kent, Daniel T. Muhammad Ali & Laila Ali. 2004. (Famous Families Ser.). (Illus.). 48p. (J). lib. bdg. 29.25 *(978-1-4042-0261-0(7))* Rosen Publishing Group, Inc., The.

Latimer, Clay. Muhammad Ali. 2009. (Journey to Freedom Ser.). (ENG., Illus.). 32p. (J). (gr. 4-7). 29.93 *(978-1-60253-132-1(3)*, 200398) Child's World, Inc., The.

Mattern, Joanne. Muhammad Ali: The Greatest. 2017. (Rookie Biographies(tm) Ser.). (ENG., Illus.). 32p. (J). lib. bdg. 25.00 *(978-0-531-22117-4(2)*, Children's Pr.) Scholastic Library Publishing.

Micklos, John. Muhammad Ali: "I Am the Greatest" 2010. (American Rebels Ser.). 160p. (J). (gr. 7-12). 35.94 *(978-0-7660-3381-8(3))* Enslow Pubs., Inc.

Myers, Walter Dean. Muhammad Ali: The People's Champion. Delinois, Alix, illus. 40p. (J). (gr. -1-3). 2016. pap. 6.99 *(978-0-06-443718-9(3)*, Amistad) 2009. (ENG.). 16.99 *(978-0-06-029131-0(1)*, Collins) HarperCollins Pubs.

—Muhammad Ali: The People's Champion. 2016. (J). lib. bdg. 17.20 *(978-0-606-38179-6(1))* Turtleback Bks.

Owens, Thomas. Muhammad Ali: Boxing Champ & Role Model, 1 vol. 2011. (Legendary Athletes Ser.). (ENG., Illus.). 112p. (YA). (gr. 7-12). 34.22 *(978-1-61714-752-4(4)*, 1324107) ABDO Publishing Co.

Peters, Gregory N. Muhammad Ali-Boxing Legend, 1 vol. 2014. (Sports & Recreation Ser.). (ENG., Illus.). 48p. (gr. 4-12). 31.99 *(978-1-4765-8439-3(7))* Capstone Press of Coughlan Cos.

Schulman, Arlene. Muhammad Ali. (Just the Facts Biographies Ser.). (Illus.). (J). (gr. 6-12). 2005. 112p. 27.93 *(978-0-8225-2448-9(1))* 2003. 128p. pap. 7.95 *(978-0-8225-9693-6(8)*, Lerner Pubns.) Lerner Publishing Group.

Shange, Ntozake. Float Like a Butterfly. Rodriguez, Edel, illus. 2017. (ENG.). 40p. (J). (gr. -1-3). 17.99 ***(978-1-368-00827-3(5)***, Jump at the Sun) Hyperion Bks. for Children.

Shone, Rob. Muhammad Ali: The Life of a Boxing Hero. 2009. (Graphic Nonfiction Biographies Ser.). (ENG.). 48p. (YA). (gr. 4-5). 58.50 *(978-1-61513-022-1(5)*, Rosen Reference) Rosen Publishing Group, Inc., The.

—Muhammad Ali: The Life of a Boxing Hero. Spender, Nick, illus. 2007. (Graphic Nonfiction Biographies Ser.). (ENG.). 48p. (J). (gr. 4-7). lib. bdg. 31.95 *(978-1-4042-0856-8(9))*; (gr. 5-8). pap. 14.05 *(978-1-4042-0919-0(0))* Rosen Publishing Group, Inc., The.

Smith, Charles R., Jr. Twelve Rounds to Glory: The Story of Muhammad Ali. Collier, Bryan, illus. (ENG.). 80p. (J). (gr. 5). 2010. pap. 10.99 *(978-0-7636-5002-5(1))* 2007. 19.99 *(978-0-7636-1692-2(3))* Candlewick Pr.

Stout, Glenn & Christopher, Matt. Muhammad Ali: Legends in Sports. 2005. (ENG., Illus.). 128p. (J). (gr. 5-8). pap. 15.99 *(978-0-316-10843-0(X))* Little, Brown Bks. for Young Readers.

Streissguth, Tom. Clay V. United States & How Muhammad Ali Fought the Draft: Debating Supreme Court Decisions. 2006. (Debating Supreme Court Decisions Ser.). (Illus.). 112p. (J). (gr. 6-12). lib. bdg. 27.94 *(978-0-7660-2393-2(1))* Enslow Pubs., Inc.

Wilmore, Kathy. Muhammad Ali: With a Discussion of Honesty. 2003. (Values in Action Ser.). (J). *(978-1-59203-065-1(3))* Learning Challenge, Inc.

ALICE (FICTITIOUS CHARACTER: CARROLL)—FICTION

Adair, Gilbert. Alice Through the Needle's Eye: The Further Adventures of Lewis Carroll's Alice. Thorne, Jenny, illus. 4th ed. 2012. 150p. pap. *(978-1-78201-000-5(9))* Evertype.

Alexander, Jason, illus. Alice's Adventures in Wonderland. 2009. (ENG.). 12p. (J). 8.95 *(978-1-58117-855-5(7),* Intervisual/Piggy Toes) Bendon, Inc.

Alice in Wonderland. Alice in Wonderland Storybook & CD 8x8. 2009. pap. 6.99 *(978-1-4231-3331-5(5))* Disney Pr.

Alice in Wonderland. 2003. (Illus.). 288p. (J). 9.98 *(978-1-4054-1674-0(2))* Parragon, Inc.

Aris, Mary. Bartholomew. 2010. 86p. pap. 36.95 *(978-1-4457-8958-3(2));* pap. 36.50 *(978-1-4457-5351-5(0))* Lulu Pr., Inc.

Bobowicz, Pamela. Alice in Wonderland (Disney Alice in Wonderland) Disney Storybook Artists Staff, illus. 2013. (Step into Reading Ser.). (ENG.). 32p. (J). (gr. -1-1). pap. 3.99 *(978-0-7364-3027-2(X),* RH/Disney) Random Hse. Children's Bks.

—Disney Alice in Wonderland. 2013. (Step into Reading Level 2 Ser.). lib. bdg. 13.55 *(978-0-606-26972-8(X),* Turtleback) Turtleback Bks.

Brown, Michele. New Tales from Alice's Wonderland: Dinah Plays Hide & Seek. Martyr, Paula, illus. 24p. (J). pap. 7.99 *(978-0-233-99535-9(8))* Andre Deutsch GBR. Dist: Trafalgar Square Publishing.

But I Knew Better: Individual Title, 6 pack. (gr. k-1). 23.00 *(978-0-7635-9033-8(9))* Rigby Education.

Carroll, Lewis, pseud. AILICE'S ANTERS IN FERLIELANN. 2012. (GER., Illus.). 144p. pap. *(978-1-78201-016-6(5))* Evertype.

—AILICE'S AVENTURS IN WUNNERLAND. 2011. (GER., Illus.). 140p. pap. *(978-1-904808-64-0(6))* Evertype.

—AILIS'S ANTERINS I THE LAUN O FERLIES. 2013. (GER., Illus.). 138p. pap. *(978-1-78201-026-5(2))* Evertype.

—Alice. 2004. (ENG., Illus.). 112p. (J). pap. 8.95 *(978-0-9716338-3-4(5),* 9780971633834) About Comics.

—DER ALICE IHRE OBMTEIER IM WUNDERLAUND: ALICE'S ADVENTURES IN WONDERLAND IN VIENNESE GERMAN. 2012. (GER., Illus.). 150p. pap. *(978-1-78201-020-3(3))* Evertype.

—Alice in Wonderland. Steadman, Ralph, illus. 2010. (ENG.). 128p. pap. 19.95 *(978-1-55407-203-3(4),* 9781554072033) Firefly Bks., Ltd.

—Alice in Wonderland. 2009. (Stepping Stone Book Ser.). (ENG.). 112p. (J). (gr. 1-4). 4.99 *(978-0-375-86641-8(8),* Random Hse. Bks. for Young Readers) Random Hse. Children's Bks.

—Alice in Wonderland & Through the Looking-Glass. Andreasen, Dan, illus. 2009. (Classic Starts(tm) Ser.). (ENG.). 160p. (J). (gr. 2-4). 6.95 *(978-1-4027-5422-7(1))* Sterling Publishing Co., Inc.

—Alice in Wonderland Giant Poster & Coloring Book. Tenniel, John, illus. 2012. (ENG.). 48p. (gr. -1-17). pap. 12.95 *(978-1-4197-0089-7(8),* Abrams Image) Abrams, Inc.

—Alice in Wonderland Made Simple for Kids. Sloan, Peter, illus. 2007. 126p. (J). per. 19.95 net. *(978-0-923891-91-6(9))* Ishi Pr. International.

—Alice's Abenteuer im Wunderland. Zimmermann, Antonie, tr. Tenniel, John, illus. 2012. (Dover Dual Language German Ser.).Tr. of Alice's Adventures in Wonderland. (GER & ENG.). 192p. (J). reprint ed. pap. 8.95 *(978-0-486-20668-4(8))* Dover Pubns., Inc.

—ALICE'S ADVENTIRS IN WONDERLAAND. 2012. (GER., Illus.). 140p. pap. *(978-1-78201-008-1(4))* Evertype.

—Alice's Adventures in Wonderland. 2004. 124p. pap. 10.95 *(978-1-59540-442-8(2),* 1st World Library - Literary Society) 1st World Publishing, Inc.

—Alice's Adventures in Wonderland. Date not set. (J). lib. bdg. 16.95 *(978-0-8488-1262-1(X))* Amereon Ltd.

—Alice's Adventures in Wonderland. Robinson, Gordon, illus. 2009. 118p. (gr. 3-18). pap. 4.50 *(978-1-60450-761-4(6),* Serenity Pubs.) Arc Manor.

—Alice's Adventures in Wonderland. Tenniel, John, illus. Date not set. 248p. (YA). 14.95 *(978-1-884807-19-0(4))* Blushing Rose Publishing.

—Alice's Adventures in Wonderland. Oxenbury, Helen, illus. 2003. (ENG.). 208p. (J). (gr. 3-7). pap. 16.99 *(978-0-7636-2049-3(1))* Candlewick Pr.

—Alice's Adventures in Wonderland. Tenniel, John, illus. 2007. 204p. (J). 24.95 *(978-1-58218-791-4(6));* (ENG.). (YA). per. 14.95 *(978-1-58218-790-7(8))* Digital Scanning, Inc.

—Alice's Adventures in Wonderland. Rountree, Harry, illus. 2011. (Calla Editions Ser.). (ENG.). 248p. (gr. 3). 40.00 *(978-1-60660-014-6(1))* Dover Pubns., Inc.

—Alice's Adventures in Wonderland. Lornie, June, illus. 2013. 104p. pap. *(978-1-78201-037-1(8))* Evertype.

—Alice's Adventures in Wonderland. Bloom, Harold, ed. 2006. (Bloom's Modern Critical Interpretations Ser.). (Illus.). 150p. (C). (gr. 9). lib. bdg. 45.00 *(978-0-7910-8586-8(4),* Chelsea Hse.) Facts On File, Inc.

—Alice's Adventures in Wonderland. 2009. 80p. pap. 14.14 *(978-1-4590-2482-3(6));* 78p. (gr. 4-18). pap. 14.14 *(978-1-4590-2479-3(6))* General Bks. LLC.

—Alice's Adventures in Wonderland. 2008. (Green Apple Starter Ser.). 64p. (J). (gr. 4). pap. 24.95 incl. cd-rom *(978-88-530-0768-1(0),* Black Cat) Grove/Atlantic, Inc.

—Alice's Adventures in Wonderland. Date not set. 192p. (YA). (gr. 3-18). mass mkt. 8.99 *(978-0-06-440929-2(5));* (ENG., Illus.). 176p. (J). 14.95 *(978-0-06-095770-4(0))* HarperCollins Pubs.

—Alice's Adventures in Wonderland. Sabuda, Robert, illus. 2003. (ENG.). 12p. (J). (gr. -1-3). 34.99 *(978-0-689-84743-1(2),* Little Simon) Little Simon.

—Alice's Adventures in Wonderland. 2010. 208p. pap. 24.95 *(978-0-557-01173-5(6))* 2009. 67p. pap. 12.36 *(978-0-557-15604-7(1))* Lulu Pr., Inc.

—Alice's Adventures in Wonderland. 2009. pap. 2.95 *(978-1-61600-010-3(4))* Mizzou Publishing - The Mizzou Store.

—Alice's Adventures in Wonderland. 2015. (Macmillan Classics Ser.). (ENG., Illus.). 192p. (J). (gr. 2-4). 16.99 *(978-1-4472-7308-0(7),* Macmillan Children's Bks.) Pan Macmillan GBR. Dist: Independent Pubs. Group.

—Alice's Adventures in Wonderland. (Charm Book Classics Ser.). 26p. *(978-1-4054-9107-5(8))* Parragon, Inc.

—Alice's Adventures in Wonderland. (J). 2006. 34.75 *(978-1-4193-1123-9(9))* 2004. 36.75 *(978-1-4025-8106-9(8))* Recorded Bks., Inc.

—Alice's Adventures in Wonderland. Ingpen, Robert R., illus. 2009. (Sterling Illustrated Classics Ser.). (ENG.). 192p. (J). (gr. 5-18). 19.95 *(978-1-4027-6835-4(4))* Sterling Publishing Co., Inc.

—Alice's Adventures in Wonderland. McKowen, Scott, illus. 2005. (Sterling Unabridged Classics Ser.). (ENG.). 136p. (J). (gr. 5-9). 9.95 *(978-1-4027-2502-9(7))* Sterling Publishing Co., Inc.

—Alice's Adventures in Wonderland. Lipchenko, Oleg, illus. 2009. (ENG.). 104p. (J). (gr. k-12). 22.95 *(978-0-88776-932-0(2),* Tundra Bks.) Tundra Bks. CAN. Dist: Penguin Random Hse. LLC.

—Alice's Adventures in Wonderland. Wiley, Nancy, illus. 2009. 88p. 35.00 *(978-0-615-29492-6(8))* OBrien, Wiley Workspace.

—Alice's Adventures in Wonderland. Ghiuselev, Iassen, illus. rev. ed. 2012. (ENG.). 120p. (J). (gr. 3). 29.95 *(978-1-897476-42-0(6))* Simply Read Bks. CAN. Dist: Ingram Publisher Services.

—Alice's Adventures in Wonderland. 2008. (Puffin Classics Ser.). (gr. 5-8). lib. bdg. 16.00 *(978-0-613-63916-3(2),* Turtleback) Turtleback Bks.

—Alice's Adventures in Wonderland. D'Aquino, Andrea, illus. unabr. ed. 2015. (Classics Reimagined Ser.). (ENG.). 248p. 25.00 *(978-1-63159-075-7(8),* Rockport Publishers) Quarto Publishing Group USA.

—Alice's Adventures in Wonderland, 1. Tenniel, John, illus. 2011. (Macmillan Alice Ser.). (ENG.). 208p. (J). (gr. 2). 26.99 *(978-0-230-75538-3(0))* Pan Macmillan GBR. Dist: Independent Pubs. Group.

—Alice's Adventures in Wonderland. Bond, Anna, illus. 150th anniv. ed. 2015. (ENG.). 192p. (J). (gr. 5). 30.00 *(978-0-14-751587-2(4),* Puffin Books) Penguin Young Readers Group.

—Alice's Adventures in Wonderland & Other Tales. 2015. (Knickerbocker Classics Ser.). (ENG., Illus.). 1060p. (gr. 4-17). 35.00 *(978-1-63106-068-7(6),* Knickerbocker Pr.) Book Sales, Inc.

—Alice's Adventures in Wonderland, & Through the Looking Glass, 1bk. Bachelier, Anne, illus. 2005. (J). *(978-0-9728620-8-0(0)); (978-0-9769071-0-7(0));* per. *(978-0-9769071-1-4(9));* im. lthr. *(978-0-9728620-9-7(9))* CFM.

—Alice's Adventures in Wonderland & Through the Looking Glass. Tenniel, John & Bickford-smith, Coralie, illus. 2010. (Penguin Classics Hardcover Ser.). (ENG.). 448p. (gr. 12). 24.00 *(978-0-14-119246-8(1),* Penguin Classics) Penguin Publishing Group.

—Alice's Adventures in Wonderland & Through the Looking Glass. 2010. (Enriched Classics Ser.). (ENG.). 336p. mass mkt. 5.99 *(978-1-4391-6947-6(0))* Simon & Schuster.

—ALICE'S CARRÀNTS IN WUNNERLAN: ALICE'S ADVENTURES IN WONDERLAND IN ULSTER SCOTS. 2nd ed. 2013. (GER., Illus.). 140p. pap. *(978-1-78201-011-1(4))* Evertype.

—Alicia en el Pais de las Maravillas. Aranguren, Dolores, tr. 2010.Tr. of Alice's Adventures in Wonderland. (SPA.). 264p. (YA). (gr. 5-8). pap. *(978-607-07-0359-1(6))* Editorial Planeta Mexicana.

—Alicia en el País de las Maravillas. 2011. (Vintage Espanol Ser.). (SPA.). 384p. pap. 15.00 *(978-0-307-74514-9(7),* Vintage Espanol) Knopf Doubleday Publishing Group.

—Las Aventuras de Alicia. (Coleccion Clasicos de la Juventud).Tr. of Alice's Adventures in Wonderland. (SPA., Illus.). 240p. (J). 12.95 *(978-84-7189-060-3(7),* ORT308) Ortells, Alfredo Editorial S.L. ESP. Dist: Continental Bk. Co., Inc.

—LA AVENTURAS DE ALISIA EN LA PAIS DE MERVELIAS. 2012. (GER., Illus.). 136p. pap. *(978-1-904808-88-6(3))* Evertype.

—La Aventuroj de Alicio en Mirlando: Alice's Adventures in Wonderland in Esperanto. 2012. (Illus.). 134p. pap. *(978-1-904808-86-2(7))* Evertype.

—DEE ERLAWNISSE VON ALICE EM WUNDALAUND. 2012. (GER., Illus.). 152p. pap. *(978-1-904808-83-1(2))* Evertype.

—Eachdraidh Ealasaid Ann an Tir Nan Iongantas. Watson, Moray, tr. from ENG. Tenniel, John, illus. 2012. 156p. pap. *(978-1-78201-015-9(7))* Evertype.

—L'AVENTUROS D'ALIS IN MARVOLAND. 2013. (GER., Illus.). 134p. pap. *(978-1-78201-019-7(X))* Evertype.

—LES-AVENTURES D'ALICE O PEYIS DES MERVEY. 2012. (GER., Illus.). 150p. pap. *(978-1-904808-87-9(5))* Evertype.

—MA LOKO O KE ANIANI K A ME KA MEA I LOA A I LEKA MA LAILA. 2012. (HAW., Illus.). 184p. pap. *(978-1-78201-022-7(X))* Evertype.

—Michael Foreman's Alice's Adventures in Wonderland. Foreman, Michael, illus. 2010. (ENG.). 176p. (J). (gr. 2-7). 19.99 *(978-1-84365-142-0(4),* Pavilion) Pavilion Bks. GBR. Dist: Independent Pubs. Group.

—NA HANA KUPANAHA A'ALEKA MA KA 'AINA KAMAHA'O. 2012. (HAW., Illus.). 148p. pap. *(978-1-904808-97-8(2))* Evertype.

—The Nursery Alice. 2013. 425p. reprint ed. lthr. 69.00 *(978-0-7426-2289-0(4))* Classic Bks.

—The Nursery Alice. Tenniel, Sir John & Thomson, E. Gertrude, illus. 2014. 64p. *(978-1-907960-09-3(0))* English Rose Publishing.

—The Nursery Alice. Tenniel, John & Thomson, E. Gertrude, illus. 2010. 64p. pap. *(978-1-907960-00-0(7))* English Rose Publishing.

—The Nursery Alice. Tenniel, John, illus. 2010. 86p. pap. *(978-1-904808-42-8(5))* Evertype.

—The Nursery Alice. Tenniel, John, illus. 2013. 74p. (J). pap. 18.58 *(978-1-939652-68-3(5))* Lire Bks.

—The Nursery Alice. Tenniel, John, illus. 2009. 56p. *(978-973-88826-8-3(0))* Mediamorphosis.

—The Nursery Alice. Tenniel, John, illus. 2015. (Macmillan Alice Ser.). (ENG.). 72p. (J). (-k). 19.99 *(978-1-4472-8711-7(8))* Pan Macmillan GBR. Dist: Independent Pubs. Group.

—'O Tafaoga a 'Alise I Le Nu'o O Mea Ofoofogia. Simanu-Klutz, Luafata, tr. from ENG. Tenniel, John, illus. 2013. 152p. pap. *(978-1-78201-023-4(8))* Evertype.

—Through the Looking Glass. Tenniel, John, illus. 2012. *(978-1-897093-65-8(9))* Qualitas Publishing.

—Through the Looking-Glass. Date not set. 176p. (J). 19.95 *(978-0-8488-2629-1(9))* Amereon Ltd.

—Through the Looking-Glass. l.t. ed. 2006. 176p. pap. *(978-1-84637-329-9(8))* Echo Library.

—Trans la Spegulo Kaj Kion Alico Trovis Tie. Broadribb, Donald, tr. from ENG. Tenniel, John, illus. 2012. 180p. pap. *(978-1-78201-001-2(7))* Evertype.

Carroll, Lewis, pseud & Baker, Kyle. Through the Looking-Glass. (Classics Illustrated Ser.). (Illus.). 52p. (YA). pap. 4.95 *(978-1-57209-002-6(2))* Classics International Entertainment, Inc.

Carroll, Lewis, pseud & Bué, Henri. Les Adventures D'Alice Au Pays des Merveilles. 2010. (FRE., Illus.). 138p. pap. *(978-1-904808-52-7(2))* Evertype.

Carroll, Lewis, pseud & Burstein, Mark. Sonja in a Kingdom of Wonder. 2013. (RUS., Illus.). 206p. pap. *(978-1-78201-040-1(8))* Evertype.

Carroll, Lewis, pseud & Everson, Michael. Alice's Adventures in Wonderland: Retold in Words of One Syllable. 2010. (Illus.). 108p. pap. *(978-1-904808-44-2(1))* Evertype.

Carroll, Lewis, pseud & Frith, Barbara. Alice's Adventures in Wonderland & Through the Looking-Glass. Tenniel, John, illus. 2013. (ENG.). 288p. *(978-1-907360-36-7(0),* Collector's Library, The) Pan Macmillan.

Carroll, Lewis, pseud & Kearney, Elfric Leofwine. La Aventuroj de Alicio en Mirlando: Alice's Adventures in Wonderland in Esperanto. 2009. (Illus.). 128p. *(978-1-904808-20-6(4))* Evertype.

Carroll, Lewis, pseud & Ladybird Books Staff. Alice in Wonderland. García-Cortés, Ester, illus. 2015. (Ladybird Classics Ser.). (ENG.). 72p. (J). (gr. k-3). 8.99 *(978-1-4093-1123-2(6))* Penguin Bks., Ltd. GBR. Dist: Independent Pubs. Group.

Carroll, Lewis, pseud & Nonnen, Emily. Alices äfventyr I Sagolandet. 2010. (SWE., Illus.). 134p. pap. *(978-1-904808-61-9(1))* Evertype.

Carroll, Lewis, pseud & Roberts, Selyf. Anturiaethau Alys Yng Ngwlad Hud. 2010.Tr. of Alice in Wonderland. (WEL., Illus.). 126p. pap. *(978-1-904808-46-6(8))* Evertype.

Carroll, Lewis, pseud & Ross, Tony. Alice - Through the Looking-Glass. Ross, Tony, illus. 2016. (ENG., Illus.). 116p. (J). (-k). pap. 14.99 *(978-1-78344-412-0(6))* Andersen Pr. GBR. Dist: Independent Pubs. Group.

Carroll, Lewis, pseud & Stowell, Brian. Contoyryssyn Ealish Ayns Cheer Ny Yindyssyn. 2010. (Illus.). 144p. pap. *(978-1-904808-48-0(4))* Evertype.

Carroll, Lewis, pseud & Sweeney, Kevin. Exeunt Alice. 2009. 87p. pap. *(978-0-9556938-1-6(0))* Black Rainbow Pr.

Carroll, Lewis, pseud & Williams, Nicholas. Alys in POW an Anethow: Alice's Adventures in Wonderland in Cornish. 2009. (COR., Illus.). vi, 134p. pap. *(978-1-904808-19-0(0))* Evertype.

Carroll, Lewis, pseud & Þórarinn Eldjárn. Ævintýri Lísu Undralandi. 2nd ed. 2013. (ICE., Illus.). 142p. pap. *(978-1-78201-025-8(4))* Evertype.

Carter, R. J. Alices Journey Beyond Moon, 1 vol. Wright, Lucy, illus. 2004. (ENG.). 98p. *(978-1-903889-76-3(6))* Telos Publishing, Ltd. GBR. Dist: Fitzhenry & Whiteside, Ltd.

Cowley, Joseph. Alice's Adventures in Wonderland by Lewis Carroll: (Adapted by Joseph Cowley) 2012. 102p. pap. 9.95 *(978-1-4759-3276-8(6))* iUniverse, Inc.

Dorling Kindersley Publishing Staff. Alice Through the Looking Glass. 2016. (Ultimate Sticker Bks.). (ENG.). 16p. (J). (gr. 3-7). pap. 6.99 *(978-1-4654-5254-2(0),* DK Children) Dorling Kindersley Publishing, Inc.

Gauthier, Gilles. La Petite Lili Est un Genie. Derome, Pierre-André, illus. 2004. (Premier Roman Ser.). (FRE.). 64p. (J). (gr. 1-4). pap. *(978-2-89021-686-0(1))* Diffusion du livre Mirabel (DLM).

Hughes, Shirley. Alfie Wins a Prize. Hughes, Shirley, illus. rev. ed. 2010. (Alfie Ser.). (ENG., Illus.). 32p. (J). (gr. k-k). pap. 12.99 *(978-1-86230-788-9(1),* Red Fox) Random House Children's Books GBR. Dist: Independent Pubs. Group.

Imholtz, August & Tannenbaum, Alison. Alice Eats Wonderland. Carr, A. E. K., illus. 2009. (ENG.). 120p. pap. 14.95 *(978-1-4290-9106-0(1))* Applewood Bks.

Kaishaku. Eternal Alice Rondo, Vol. 4. 2007. (ENG., Illus.). 192p. pap. 9.95 *(978-1-59796-123-3(X))* DrMaster Pubns. Inc.

Landes, William-Alan. Alice n' Wonderland. 2003. (Wondrawhopper Ser.). 32p. (Orig.). (YA). (gr. 3-18). pap. 6.00 *(978-0-88734-112-0(8))* Players Pr., Inc.

Larson, Abigail. Alice's Wonderfilled Adventures: Coloring Pages for Adults up for a Wonderfilled Exploration of Wonderland. 2016. (ENG.). 144p. pap. 14.99 *(978-1-4403-4668-2(2),* Impact) F&W Media, Inc.

Linn, Susie. Alice in Wonderland. Ball, Alexandra, illus. 2017. (ENG.). 32p. (J). (gr. -1-k). pap. 9.99 ***(978-1-78445-246-9(7))*** Top That! Publishing PLC GBR. Dist: Independent Pubs. Group.

Maconie, Robin. Alice & Her Fabulous Teeth! Fruisen, Catherine Myler, illus. 2004. 32p. (J). per. *(978-1-893974-21-0(9),* Design Pr. Bks.) Savannah College of Art & Design Exhibitions.

Maraja, illus. Alice in Wonderland Picture Book. 2013. (Shape Bks.). (ENG.). 16p. (J). pap. 9.95 *(978-1-59583-701-1(9))* Laughing Elephant.

Parragon Staff. Alice in Wonderland: The Magical Story. 2010. (Disney Padded Magical Storybks.). (Illus.). 32p. (J). (gr. -1-1). *(978-1-4075-8455-3(3))* Parragon, Inc.

—Disney's Alice in Wonderland. 2010. (Disney Diecut Classics). 72p. (J). (gr. -1-1). *(978-1-4075-8934-3(2))* Parragon, Inc.

Peabody, Richard. Alice Redux: New Stories of Alice, Lewis, & Wonderland. 2006. (Illus.). xvi, 319p. pap. *(978-0-931181-22-1(4))* Paycock Pr.

Rae, John & Carroll, Lewis. New Adventures of Alice: A Sequel to Lewis Carroll's Wonderland. 2010. (Illus.). 152p. pap. *(978-1-904808-53-4(0))* Evertype.

RH Disney Staff. Walt Disney's Alice in Wonderland. RH Disney Staff, illus. 2010. (Little Golden Book Ser.). (ENG., Illus.). 24p. (J). (gr. -1-2). 4.99 *(978-0-7364-2670-1(1),* Golden/Disney) Random Hse. Children's Bks.

Richards, Anna Matlack & Carroll, Lewis. A New Alice in the Old Wonderland. 2009. (Illus.). 178p. *(978-1-904808-35-0(2))* Evertype.

Salisbury, Mark. Walt Disney's Alice in Wonderland: An Illustrated Journey Through Time. 2016. (Disney Editions Deluxe Ser.). (ENG., Illus.). 176p. pap. 29.99 *(978-1-4847-3769-9(5),* Disney Editions) Disney Pr.

Sanrio Company, LTD. Hello Kitty Presents the Storybook Collection: Alice's Adventures in Wonderland. 2017. (Hello Kitty Storybook Ser.). (ENG., Illus.). 32p. (J). (gr. -1-k). pap. 6.95 *(978-1-4197-2488-6(6),* Abrams Appleseed) Abrams, Inc.

Scieszka, Jon. Walt Disney's Alice in Wonderland (Reissue) Blair, Mary, illus. 2016. (ENG.). 64p. (J). (gr. -1-k). 16.99 *(978-1-4847-3041-6(0))* Disney Pr.

Sewell, Byron W. & Carroll, Lewis. Álbok's Adventures in Goatland. 2011. (Illus.). 140p. pap. *(978-1-904808-76-3(X))* Evertype.

Sewell, Byron W. & Everson, Michael. Alice's Bad Hair Day in Wonderland: A Tangled Tale. 2013. (Illus.). 112p. pap. *(978-1-78201-009-8(2))* Evertype.

Shannon, David. Alice the Fairy. Shannon, David, illus. 2009. (ENG., Illus.). (J). (gr. -1-k). pap. 9.95 incl. audio compact disk *(978-0-545-11758-6(5))* Scholastic, Inc.

Sheppard, Keith. Wonderland Revisited & the Games Alice Played There. 2009. (Illus.). 128p. (gr. 3-7). pap. *(978-1-904808-34-3(4))* Evertype.

Through the Looking Glass. (Read-Along Ser.). (YA). pap., stu. ed. 34.95 incl. audio *(978-0-88432-971-8(2),* S23946) Pavilion Pubs.

Werner, Jane. Mad Hatter's Tea Party (Disney Alice in Wonderland) RH Disney, illus. 2016. (Little Golden Book Ser.). (ENG.). 24p. (J). (-k). 4.99 *(978-0-7364-3627-4(8),* Golden/Disney) Random Hse. Children's Bks.

Wilson, Gerrard. Alice on Top of the World. 2009. 159p. pap. 17.50 *(978-0-9561553-0-6(8))* Wilson, Gerrard IRL. Dist: Lulu Pr., Inc.

Yuki, Kaori. Alice in Murderland, Vol. 5. 2017. (Alice in Murderland Ser.: 5). (ENG., Illus.). 176p. (gr. 11-17). 17.00 *(978-0-316-50279-5(0),* Yen Pr.) Orbit.

ALIENS (EXTRATERRESTRIALS)

see Extraterrestrial Beings; Life on Other Planets

ALIENS, ILLEGAL

see Illegal Aliens

ALL FOOLS' DAY

see April Fools' Day

ALL HALLOWS' EVE

see Halloween

ALLEGORIES

see also Fables; Parables

Black, Chuck. Sir Dalton & the Shadow Heart. 2009. (Knights of Arrethtrae Ser.). (ENG., Illus.). 176p. (YA). (gr. 7-9). pap. 9.99 *(978-1-60142-126-5(5),* Multnomah Bks.) Crown Publishing Group.

Canfield, Andrea. Sassy the Seahag. Hallinan, Susan, illus. 2003. Orig. Title: Sassy the Seahag. (J). per. *(978-0-9721327-3-2(2))* Bad Choices Media.

Hunt, Susan. Sammy & His Shepherd. Godbey, Corey, illus. 2008. (J). *(978-1-56769-109-2(9))* Reformation Pubs.

Nobisso, Josephine. Take It to the Queen. 2009. 32p. 17.95 *(978-0-8146-3288-8(2),* Liturgical Pr. Bks.) Liturgical Pr.

ALLEN, ETHAN, 1738-1789

Ades, Audrey. Ethan Allen & the Green Mountain Boys. 2017. 25.70 *(978-1-61228-952-6(5))* Mitchell Lane Pubs., Inc.

ALLERGY

Ballard, Carol. Explaining Food Allergies. 2010. (J). 34.25 *(978-1-59920-316-4(2))* Black Rabbit Bks.

Boothroyd, Jennifer. Caution in the Kitchen! Germs, Allergies, & Other Health Concerns. 2016. (Lightning Bolt Books — Healthy Eating Ser.). (ENG., Illus.). 32p. (J). (gr. 1-3). 26.65 *(978-1-4677-9473-2(2),* Lerner Pubns.) Lerner Publishing Group.

Chilman-Blair, Kim, et al. Medikidz Explain Food Allergy: What's up with Paulina? 2009. (Illus.). 32p. (J). pap. *(978-1-906935-06-1(8))* Medikidz Ltd.

A Day at the Playground. 2004. (J). pap. 12.95 *(978-1-59526-606-4(2))* Aeon Publishing Inc.

Dickmann, Nancy. What You Need to Know about Allergies. 2016. (Focus on Health Ser.). (ENG., Illus.). 32p. (gr. 3-4). lib. bdg. 27.32 *(978-1-4914-8048-9(3))* Capstone Press of Coughlan Cos.

Edwards, Nicola. My Friend Has Allergies. 2004. (J). lib. bdg. 27.10 *(978-1-59389-169-5(5))* Chrysalis Education.

Ehrlich, Paul. Living with Allergies. 2008. (Teen's Guides). 176p. (gr. 6-12). pap. 14.95 *(978-0-8160-7742-7(8),* Checkmark Bks.) Facts On File, Inc.

Ford, Jean. Allergies & Asthma. Bridgemohan, Carolyn & Forman, Sara, eds. 2013. (Young Adult's Guide to the Science of Health Ser.: 15). 128p. (J). (gr. 7-18). 24.95 *(978-1-4222-2804-3(5))* Mason Crest.

—Breathe Easy! A Teen's Guide to Allergies & Asthma. 2006. (Science of Health Ser.). (Illus.). 128p. (YA). 24.95 *(978-1-59084-842-5(X))* Mason Crest.

Gillard, Arthur. Food Allergies. Greenhaven Press Editors, ed. 2013. (Perspectives on Diseases & Disorders Ser.). (ENG., Illus.). 144p. (gr. 10-12). lib. bdg. 44.30 *(978-0-7377-6354-6(X),* Greenhaven Pr., Inc.) Cengage Gale.

Gordon, Sharon. Allergies. 2003. (Rookie Read-About Health Ser.). (ENG., Illus.). 32p. (J). (gr. k-2). pap. 5.95 *(978-0-516-27394-5(9)*, Children's Pr.) Scholastic Library Publishing.

Gordon, Sherri Mabry. Are You at Risk for Food Allergies? Peanut Butter, Milk, & Other Deadly Threats. 2014. (Got Issues? Ser.). (Illus.). 112p. (J). (gr. 6-12). lib. bdg. 33.27 *(978-0-7660-6045-6(4))* Enslow Pubs., Inc.

—Peanut Butter, Milk, & Other Deadly Threats: What You Should Know about Food Allergies. 2006. (Issues in Focus Today Ser.). (Illus.). 112p. (J). (gr. 6-12). lib. bdg. 33.27 *(978-0-7660-2529-5(2))* Enslow Pubs., Inc.

Hand, Carol. Living with Food Allergies, 1 vol. 2012. (Living with Health Challenges Set 1 Ser.). (ENG.). 112p. (J). (gr. 6-12). lib. bdg. 35.64 *(978-1-61783-128-7(X)*, Essential Library) ABDO Publishing Co.

Herbst, Benjamin. What Happens When I Cough? 2013. (My Body Does Strange Stuff! Ser.). (ENG., Illus.). 24p. (J). (gr. 1-3). pap. 8.15 *(978-1-4339-9334-3(1))*; lib. bdg. 22.60 *(978-1-4339-9333-6(3))* Stevens, Gareth Publishing LLLP.

Hicks, Terry Allan. Allergies. 2005. (Health Alert Ser.). (Illus.). 64p. (YA). (gr. 4-7). lib. bdg. 32.79 *(978-0-7614-1918-1(7))* Marshall Cavendish Corp.

I'm Allergic. 2014. (I'm Allergic Ser.). 24p. (J). (gr. 1-3). 135.60 *(978-1-4824-0973-4(9))*; pap. 48.90 *(978-1-4824-1571-1(2))* Stevens, Gareth Publishing LLLP.

Johnson, Rebecca L. Daring Cell Defenders. 2008. pap. 52.95 *(978-0-8225-9381-2(5))* Lerner Publishing Group.

—Daring Cell Defenders. Desrocher, Jack & Fairman, Jennifer, illus. 2007. (Microquests Ser.). 48p. (J). (gr. 4-7). lib. bdg. 29.27 *(978-0-8225-7140-7(4)*, Millbrook Pr.) Lerner Publishing Group.

Jorgensen, Katrina. This Is Not Cheesy! Easy & Delecious Dairy-Free Recipes for Kids with Allergies. 2016. (Allergy Aware Cookbooks Ser.). (ENG., Illus.). 32p. (gr. 3-4). lib. bdg. 27.99 *(978-1-4914-8053-3(X)*, Edge Bks.) Capstone Press of Coughlan Cos.

Kolpin, Molly. Why Do I Sneeze? 2015. (My Silly Body Ser.). (ENG.). 24p. (gr. k-1). lib. bdg. 26.65 *(978-1-4914-2108-6(8)*, Pebble Plus) Capstone Press of Coughlan Cos.

Landau, Elaine. Food Allergies. 2009. (Head-to-Toe Health Ser.). 32p. (gr. 2-3). 28.50 *(978-0-7614-3500-6(X))* Marshall Cavendish Corp.

—Head Lice. 2009. (Head-to Toe Health 2 Ser.). 32p. (gr. 2). 28.50 *(978-0-7614-3501-3(8))* Marshall Cavendish Corp.

Latta, Sara L. What You Can Do about Allergies. 2015. (Contemporary Diseases & Disorders Ser.). (ENG.). 128p. (J). (gr. 7-7). lib. bdg. 37.27 *(978-0-7660-7030-1(1))* Enslow Pubs., Inc.

Lerner, Carol. Plants that Make You Sniffle & Sneeze. 2004. (Illus.). 32p. (J). (gr. k-4). reprint ed. 15.00 *(978-0-7567-8288-7(0))* DIANE Publishing Co.

Levine, Michelle. Allergies. 2015. (Living With... Ser.). (Illus.). 32p. (J). 28.50 *(978-1-60753-477-8(0))* Amicus Publishing.

McAneney, Caitlin. Peanut & Other Food Allergies, 1 vol. 2015. (ENG., Illus.). 24p. (J). pap. 8.25 *(978-1-4777-5807-6(0)*, PowerKids Pr.) Rosen Publishing Group, Inc., The.

McCune, Susan. I'm Allergic to Nuts, 01 vols., 1. 2016. (Rosen REAL Readers: Social Studies Nonfiction / Fiction: Family, Community, & the World Ser.). (ENG.). 12p. (J). pap. 6.33 *(978-1-5081-1809-1(4)*, Rosen Classroom) Rosen Publishing Group, Inc., The.

Miller, Madison. What Happens When I Sneeze? 2013. (My Body Does Strange Stuff! Ser.). (ENG., Illus.). 24p. (J). (gr. 1-3). pap. 8.15 *(978-1-4339-9343-5(0))*; lib. bdg. 22.60 *(978-1-4339-9342-8(2))* Stevens, Gareth Publishing LLLP.

Moragne, Wendy. Allergies. 2011. (USA TODAY Health Reports: Diseases & Disorders Ser.). (ENG., Illus.). 128p. (gr. 6-12). lib. bdg. 34.60 *(978-0-7613-6089-6(1))* Lerner Publishing Group.

Naff, Clayton Farris. Allergies. 2009. (Perspectives on Diseases & Disorders Ser.). (Illus.). 144p. (YA). (gr. 10-12). lib. bdg. 37.10 *(978-0-7377-4377-7(8)*, LML02109-245382, Greenhaven Pr., Inc.) Cengage Gale.

Nelson, Maria. I'm Allergic to Milk. 2014. (I'm Allergic Ser.). 24p. (J). (gr. 1-3). 22.60 *(978-1-4824-0968-0(2))* Stevens, Gareth Publishing LLLP.

—I'm Allergic to Peanuts. 2014. 24p. (J). (gr. 1-3). pap. 8.15 *(978-1-4824-0975-8(5))* Stevens, Gareth Publishing LLLP.

—I'm Allergic to Pets. 2014. (I'm Allergic Ser.). 24p. (J). (gr. 1-3). 22.60 *(978-1-4824-0979-6(8))* Stevens, Gareth Publishing LLLP.

—I'm Allergic to Strawberries. 2014. (I'm Allergic Ser.). 24p. (J). (gr. 1-3). 22.60 *(978-1-4824-0984-0(4))* Stevens, Gareth Publishing LLLP.

—I'm Allergic to Wheat. 2014. (I'm Allergic Ser.). 24p. (J). (gr. 1-3). 22.60 *(978-1-4824-0989-5(5))* Stevens, Gareth Publishing LLLP.

Parker, Vic. I Know Someone with Allergies, 1 vol. 2011. (Understanding Health Issues Ser.). (ENG.). 32p. (gr. 1-3). 27.32 *(978-1-4329-4555-8(6)*, Heinemann First Library) Heinemann-Raintree.

Peterson, Judy Monroe. I Have a Food Allergy, Now What?, 1 vol. 2015. (ENG.). 112p. (YA). 35.60 *(978-1-4777-7974-3(4)*, Rosen Young Adult) Rosen Publishing Group, Inc., The.

Rajczak, Kristen. I'm Allergic to Bees. 2014. (I'm Allergic Ser.). (Illus.). 24p. (J). (gr. 1-3). 22.60 *(978-1-4824-0787-7(6))* Stevens, Gareth Publishing LLLP.

Ribke, Simone T. I Have Allergies. 2016. (Rookie Read-About Health Ser.). (ENG., Illus.). 32p. (J). pap. 5.95 *(978-0-531-22580-6(1)*, Children's Pr.) Scholastic Library Publishing.

Richards, Tanya Dawn. Squirrel's Peanut Allergy: A Peanut-Free Story. 2012. 48p. pap. 21.99 *(978-1-4685-8512-4(6))* AuthorHouse.

Robbins, Lynette. How to Deal with Allergies. 2009. (Kids' Health Ser.). (ENG.). 24p. (J). pap. 8.25 *(978-1-4358-3414-9(3)*, PowerKids Pr.) Rosen Publishing Group, Inc., The.

Rogers, Robyn. No Lobster, Please! A Story of a Child with a Severe Seafood Allergy. 2003. (Illus.). 30p. (J). 19.95 *(978-0-9726408-0-0(0))* Heartsome Publishing.

Royston, Angela. Allergies. 2009. (How's Your Health? Ser.). (YA). (gr. 1-4). 28.50 *(978-1-59920-220-4(4))* Black Rabbit Bks.

Schuh, Mari C. Nut-Free Diets, 1 vol. 2014. (Special Diets Ser.). (ENG.). 24p. (gr. k-1). lib. bdg. 26.65 *(978-1-4914-0591-8(0)*, Pebble Plus) Capstone Press of Coughlan Cos.

Sherman, Rebecca. Allergies & Other Immune System Disorders. 2017. (J). ***(978-1-4222-3749-6(4))*** Mason Crest.

Squire, Ann O. Allergies. 2015. (ENG., Illus.). 48p. (J). lib. bdg. *(978-0-531-21470-1(2)*, Orchard Bks.) Scholastic, Inc.

What Happens When I Cough? 2013. (My Body Does Strange Stuff! Ser.). 24p. (J). (gr. 1-3). pap. 48.90 *(978-1-4339-9335-0(X))* Stevens, Gareth Publishing LLLP.

ALLEYS

see Streets

ALLIGATORS

Alligator: Killer King of the Swamp. 2013. (Top of the Food Chain Ser.). 32p. (J). (gr. k-5). pap. 60.00 *(978-1-61533-802-3(0)*, PowerKids Pr.) Rosen Publishing Group, Inc., The.

Alligator Alley. (Sails Literacy Ser.). 24p. (gr. 1-18). 27.00 *(978-0-7635-5928-1(8))*;Pack. 57.00 *(978-0-7578-3203-1(2))* Rigby Education.

Alligators Are Not Pets! 2013. (When Pets Attack! Ser.). 32p. (J). (gr. 3-6). pap. 63.00 *(978-1-4339-9280-3(9))* Stevens, Gareth Publishing LLLP.

Avett, Harper. Watch Out for Alligators!, 01 vols., 1. 2016. (Wild Backyard Animals Ser.). (ENG., Illus.). 24p. (J). 23.60 *(978-1-5081-4257-7(2)*, PowerKids Pr.) Rosen Publishing Group, Inc., The.

Borgert-Spaniol, Megan. American Alligators. 2016. (North American Animals Ser.). (ENG., Illus.). 24p. (J). (gr. k-3). 25.95 *(978-1-62617-399-6(0)*, Blastoff! Readers) Bellwether Media.

Bredeson, Carmen. Fun Facts about Alligators! 2007. (I Like Reptiles & Amphibians! Ser.). (Illus.). 24p. (J). (gr. 1-3). lib. bdg. 22.60 *(978-0-7660-2786-2(4)*, Enslow Elementary) Enslow Pubs., Inc.

Crocodiles & Alligators. 2005. (J). per. 4.99 *(978-1-933581-23-1(9))* Byeway Bks.

Daly, Timothy M. Alligators. 2013. (Nature's Children Ser.). (ENG., Illus.). 48p. (J). pap. 6.95 *(978-0-531-24301-5(X))*; lib. bdg. 28.00 *(978-0-531-20975-2(X))* Scholastic Library Publishing.

Dennard, Deborah. Alligators & Crocodiles. Dewey, Jennifer Owings, illus. (Our Wild World Ser.). (ENG.). 48p. (J). (gr. 2-5). 2008. pap. 8.95 *(978-1-55971-859-2(5))* 2003. 10.95 *(978-1-55971-860-8(9))* Cooper Square Publishing Llc.

Durrie, Karen. I Am an Alligator. 2012. (J). *(978-1-61913-221-4(4))*; pap. *(978-1-61913-222-1(2))* Weigl Pubs., Inc.

—Yo Soy el Caimán. 2014. (SPA., Illus.). 24p. (J). *(978-1-62127-563-3(9))* Weigl Pubs., Inc.

Feeney, Kathy. Those Amazing Alligators. Weaver, Steve, illus. 2006. (Those Amazing Animals Ser.). (ENG.). 55p. (J). (gr. 3-7). per. 9.95 *(978-1-56164-356-1(4))* Pineapple Pr., Inc.

Feigenbaum, Aaron. American Alligators: Freshwater Survivors. 2007. (America's Animal Comebacks Ser.). (Illus.). 32p. (YA). (gr. 2-5). lib. bdg. 25.27 *(978-1-59716-503-7(4))* Bearport Publishing Co., Inc.

Friesen, Helen Lepp. Scaly & Scary. 2008. (Discovering & Exploring Science Ser.). (Illus.). 15p. (J). (gr. -1-3). lib. bdg. 12.95 *(978-0-7569-8410-6(6))* Perfection Learning Corp.

Furstinger, Nancy. Alligators, 1 vol. 2014. (Amazing Reptiles Ser.). (ENG.). 48p. (gr. 8-12). lib. bdg. 32.79 *(978-1-62403-368-1(7))* ABDO Publishing Co.

Gallagher, Debbie. Alligators & Crocodiles. 2009. (Zoo Animals 2 Ser.). 32p. (gr. 2). lib. bdg. 18.56 *(978-0-7614-4743-6(1))* Marshall Cavendish GBR. Dist: Marshall Cavendish Corp.

Garver, Lorie. Alligators. 2003. (Animals Attack Ser.). (Illus.). 48p. (J). 23.70 *(978-0-7377-1524-8(3)*, Greenhaven Pr., Inc.) Cengage Gale.

George, Jean Craighead. Autumn Moon. 2003. (J). (gr. 3-7). 20.75 *(978-0-8446-7241-0(6))* Smith, Peter Pub., Inc.

Gibbons, Gail. Alligators & Crocodiles. Gibbons, Gail, illus. (ENG., Illus.). 32p. (J). 2011. pap. 7.99 *(978-0-8234-2343-9(3))* 2010. (gr. -1-3). 17.95 *(978-0-8234-2234-0(8))* Holiday Hse., Inc.

Gish, Melissa. Alligators. (J). 2017. ***(978-1-60818-817-8(5)***, Creative Education) 2011. (ENG., Illus.). 48p. (gr. 4-7). pap. 12.00 *(978-0-89812-550-4(2)*, Creative Paperbacks) Creative Co., The.

Gish, Melissa. Living Wild - Alligators. 2010. (Living Wild Ser.). 46p. (YA). (gr. 5-18). 23.95 *(978-1-58341-967-0(5)*, Creative Education) Creative Co., The.

Gray, Susan H. American Alligator. 2007. (21st Century Skills Library: Road to Recovery Ser.). (ENG.). 32p. (gr. 4-8). lib. bdg. 29.93 *(978-1-60279-035-3(3)*, 200076) Cherry Lake Publishing.

Halfmann, Janet. Alligator at Saw Grass Road. Anzalone, Lori, illus. 2011. (Smithsonian's Backyard Ser.). (ENG.). 32p. (J). (gr. -1-3). 8.95 *(978-1-60727-631-9(3))*; 19.95 *(978-1-60727-630-2(5))* Soundprints.

Hansen, Grace. Alligators, 1 vol. 2014. (Reptiles Ser.). (ENG.). 24p. (J). (gr. 4-8). lib. bdg. 28.50 *(978-1-62970-057-1(6))* ABDO Publishing Co.

Hansen, Grace, et al. Caimanes. 2015. (Reptiles Ser.). (SPA., Illus.). 24p. (gr. k-1). pap. 7.95 *(978-1-4966-0499-6(7))* Capstone Classroom.

Harasymiw, Mark. Alligators Are Not Pets! 2013. (When Pets Attack! Ser.). 32p. (J). (gr. 3-6). pap. 10.50 *(978-1-4339-9279-7(5))* Stevens, Gareth Publishing LLLP.

Harasymiw, Mark & Harasymiw, Mark J. Alligators Are Not Pets! 2013. 32p. (J). (gr. 3-6). 26.60 *(978-1-4339-9278-0(7))* Stevens, Gareth Publishing LLLP.

Harris, Tim. Alligators. 2008. (Nature's Children Ser.). (Illus.). 52p. (J). *(978-0-7172-6215-1(4))* Grolier, Ltd.

—Crocodiles & Alligators. 2010. (Slimy, Scaly, Deadly Reptiles & Amphibians Ser.). (Illus.). 32p. (J). (gr. 2-6). pap. 10.50 *(978-1-4339-3436-0(1))*; lib. bdg. 26.00 *(978-1-4339-3435-3(3))* Stevens, Gareth Publishing LLLP. (Gareth Stevens Learning Library).

Herrington, Lisa M. Crocodiles & Alligators. 2015. (Rookie Read-About(tm) Science: What's the Difference? Ser.). (ENG., Illus.). 32p. (J). lib. bdg. 25.00 *(978-0-531-21483-1(4)*, Children's Pr.) Scholastic Library Publishing.

Hirsch, Rebecca E. American Alligators: Armored Roaring Reptiles. 2015. (ENG., Illus.). 32p. (J). (gr. 2-4). 26.65 *(978-1-4677-7984-5(9)*, Lerner Pubns.) Lerner Publishing Group.

Holden, Henry M. The American Alligator: A MyReportLinks. Com Book. 2003. (Endangered & Threatened Animals Ser.). (Illus.). 48p. (J). lib. bdg. 26.60 *(978-0-7660-5117-1(X)*, MyReportLinks.com Bks.) Enslow Pubs., Inc.

Hudak, Heather C. Alligators. 2008. (Backyard Animals Ser.). (Illus.). 24p. (J). (gr. 4-7). lib. bdg. 24.45 *(978-1-60596-001-2(2))* Weigl Pubs., Inc.

Hudak, Heather C., ed. Alligators. 2008. (Backyard Animals Ser.). (Illus.). 24p. (J). (gr. 4-7). pap. 8.95 *(978-1-60596-007-4(1))* Weigl Pubs., Inc.

Johnson, Jinny. Alligator. Rosewarne, Graham, illus. 2007. (Zoo Animals in the Wild Ser.). 32p. (J). (gr. -1-3). lib. bdg. 28.50 *(978-1-58340-902-2(5))* Black Rabbit Bks.

Kralovansky, Susan. Crocodile or Alligator?, 1 vol. 2014. (This or That? Ser.). (ENG.). 24p. (gr. 5-10). lib. bdg. 25.65 *(978-1-62403-285-1(0)*, Super SandCastle) ABDO Publishing Co.

Landau, Elaine. Alligators & Crocodiles: Hunters of the Night. 2007. (Animals after Dark Ser.). (Illus.). 32p. (J). (gr. 2-4). lib. bdg. 23.94 *(978-0-7660-2771-8(6)*, Enslow Elementary) Enslow Pubs., Inc.

—Fearsome Alligators. 2003. (Fearsome, Scary, & Creepy Animals Ser.). (Illus.). 48p. (J). (gr. 1-4). lib. bdg. 23.93 *(978-0-7660-2060-3(6))* Enslow Pubs., Inc.

Lawrence, Ellen. American Alligator. 2016. (Swamp Things: Animal Life in a Wetland Ser.). (ENG.). 24p. (J). (gr. -1-3). lib. bdg. 17.95 *(978-1-944102-51-7(5))* Bearport Publishing Co., Inc.

Lawrence, Ellen. Black Caiman. 2017. (Apex Predators of the Amazon Rain Forest Ser.). (ENG., Illus.). 24p. (J). (gr. -1-3). 17.95 ***(978-1-68402-032-4(8))*** Bearport Publishing Co., Inc.

Marsh, Laura. National Geographic Readers: Alligators & Crocodiles. 2015. (Readers Ser.). (ENG., Illus.). 32p. (J). (gr. k-3). pap. 3.99 *(978-1-4263-1947-1(9)*, National Geographic Children's Bks.) National Geographic Society.

Misconish Tyler, Darlene. Amazing Animals: Alligators: Multiplication (Grade 4) 2017. (Mathematics Readers Ser.). (Illus.). 32p. (gr. 4-4). 9.99 ***(978-1-4258-5548-2(2))*** Teacher Created Materials, Inc.

Moore, David. Expl on Your Own the Muddy Dragon. 2009. (Explore on Your Own Ser.). (ENG.). (C). pap. 7.95 *(978-0-7362-5513-4(3))* National Geographic School Publishing, Inc.

Morgan, Sally. Alligators & Crocodiles. 2011. (Amazing Animal Hunters Ser.). (Illus.). 32p. (J). 28.50 *(978-1-60753-043-5(0))* Amicus Publishing.

—Alligators & Crocodiles. 2006. (QEB Animal Lives Ser.). (Illus.). 32p. (J). (gr. 4-7). lib. bdg. 19.95 *(978-1-59566-205-7(7))* QEB Publishing Inc.

—Alligators & Crocodiles. 2012. (Illus.). 32p. (gr. 3-5). pap. 8.95 *(978-1-926722-47-4(7))* Saunders Bk. Co. CAN. Dist: RiverStream Publishing.

Morgan, Sally & Teacher Created Resources Staff. Alligators & Crocodiles. 2007. (Animal Lives (QEB Publishing) Ser.). (ENG., Illus.). 32p. (gr. 2-9). pap. 7.99 *(978-1-4206-8114-7(1))* Teacher Created Resources, Inc.

Muñoz, William. Waiting Alligators. 2003. (Pull Ahead Bks.). (ENG., Illus.). 32p. (J). (gr. k-2). pap. 6.95 *(978-0-8225-3621-5(8))* Lerner Publishing Group.

Murray, Julie. Alligators, 1 vol. 2003. (Buddy Book Ser.). (ENG.). 24p. (J). (gr. 1-4). 25.65 *(978-1-57765-716-3(0))* ABDO Publishing Co.

Nagle, Jeanne. Saving the Endangered American Alligator, 01 vols., 1. 2016. (Conservation of Endangered Species Ser.). (ENG., Illus.). 32p. (J). pap. 12.90 *(978-1-5081-0057-7(8)*, Britannica Educational Publishing) Rosen Publishing Group, Inc., The.

O'Brien, Bridget. Alligators: Level 1. 2014. (Magic Readers Ser.). (ENG.). 24p. (J). (gr. 5-9). lib. bdg. 24.21 *(978-1-62402-054-4(2))* Magic Wagon.

—Alligators Eat & Grow: Level 2. 2014. (Magic Readers Ser.). (ENG.). 24p. (J). (gr. 5-9). lib. bdg. 24.21 *(978-1-62402-055-1(0))* Magic Wagon.

—Alligators in the Swamp: Level 3. 2014. (Magic Readers Ser.). (ENG.). 24p. (J). (gr. 5-9). lib. bdg. 24.21 *(978-1-62402-056-8(9))* Magic Wagon.

Omoth, Tyler. American Alligators. 2017. (Animals of North America (hardcover) Ser.). (ENG., Illus.). 32p. (J). (gr. 3-5). lib. bdg. 28.50 ***(978-1-63517-027-6(3)***, Focus Readers) North Star Editions.

O'Shaughnessy, Ruth. Crocodiles & Alligators after Dark. 2015. (Animals of the Night Ser.). (ENG.). 32p. (J). (gr. 3-4). pap. 10.52 *(978-0-7660-6754-7(8))*; (Illus.). 25.27 *(978-0-7660-6756-1(4))* Enslow Pubs., Inc.

Otfinoski, Steven. Alligators. 2008. (Animals Animals Ser.). (Illus.). 48p. (J). (gr. 3-18). lib. bdg. 29.93 *(978-0-7614-2930-2(1)*, Benchmark Bks.) Marshall Cavendish Corp.

Pafford, Nancy McIntosh. Oscar: Legendary Alligator of the Okefenokee Swamp. 2009. (Illus.). 54p. (J). pap. 12.95 *(978-0-9815702-8-0(3)*, Catch the Spirit of Appalachia) Ammons Communications, Ltd.

Pearl, Norman. Alligators: Fast & Fierce. 2009. (Powerful Predators Ser.). 24p. (gr. 2-3). 42.50 *(978-1-60851-345-1(9))*; (Illus.). (J). lib. bdg. 22.60 *(978-1-4042-4505-1(7))* Rosen Publishing Group, Inc., The. (PowerKids Pr.).

Plattner, Josh. Alligator: Master of Might, 1 vol. 2016. (ENG., Illus.). 24p. (J). *(978-1-62403-735-1(6))* ABDO Publishing Co.

Pohl, Kathleen. Alligators. 2007. (Animals I See at the Zoo Ser.). 24p. (gr. k-3). pap. 8.15 *(978-0-8368-8224-7(5))*; (Illus.). lib. bdg. 22.00 *(978-0-8368-8217-9(2))* Stevens, Gareth Publishing LLLP. (Weekly Reader Leveled Readers).

—Alligators (Caimanes) 2007. (Animals I See at the Zoo/ Animales que veo en el zoologico Ser.). (SPA.). 24p. (gr. k-3). pap. 8.15 *(978-0-8368-8238-4(5)*, Weekly Reader Leveled Readers) Stevens, Gareth Publishing LLLP.

—Alligators/Caimanes. 2007. (Animals I See at the Zoo/Animales que Veo en el Zoológico Ser.). (SPA & ENG., Illus.). 24p. (gr. k-3). lib. bdg. 22.00 *(978-0-8368-8231-5(8)*, Weekly Reader Leveled Readers) Stevens, Gareth Publishing LLLP.

Potts, Steve. American Alligators, 1 vol. 2012. (North American Animals Ser.). (ENG.). 24p. (gr. k-1). pap. 7.29 *(978-1-4296-7918-3(2))*; pap. 41.70 *(978-1-4296-8356-2(2))*; lib. bdg. 26.65 *(978-1-4296-7703-5(1))* Capstone Press of Coughlan Cos. (Pebble Plus).

Pringle, Laurence. Alligators & Crocodiles! Henderson, Meryl, illus. 2009. (Strange & Wonderful Ser.). (ENG.). 32p. (J). (gr. 2-4). 16.95 *(978-1-59078-256-9(9))* Boyds Mills Pr.

Read, Tracy. Exploring the World of Alligators & Crocodiles. 2017. (Exploring the World Of Ser.). (ENG., Illus.). 24p. (J). (gr. 4-7). 16.95 ***(978-1-77085-942-5(X)***, 9781770859425); pap. 6.95 ***(978-1-77085-943-2(8)***, 9781770859432) Firefly Bks., Ltd.

Riggs, Kate. Alligators. 2012. (J). 25.65 *(978-1-60818-104-9(9)*, Creative Education) Creative Co., The.

—Amazing Animals: Alligators. 2012. (Amazing Animals Ser.). (ENG., Illus.). 24p. (J). (gr. 1-3). pap. 8.99 *(978-0-89812-689-1(4)*, Creative Paperbacks) Creative Co., The.

Rockwell, Anne F. Who Lives in an Alligator Hole? Rockwell, Lizzy, illus. 2006. (Let's-Read-and-Find-Out Science Ser.). 33p. (gr. k-4). 16.00 *(978-0-7569-6953-0(0))* Perfection Learning Corp.

Rockwell, Anne F. & Rockwell. Who Lives in an Alligator Hole? Rockwell, Lizzy, illus. 2006. (Let's-Read-and-Find-Out Science Ser.). (ENG.). 40p. (J). (gr. k-4). 15.99 *(978-0-06-028530-2(3))*; pap. 5.99 *(978-0-06-445200-7(X))* HarperCollins Pubs.

Rockwood, Leigh. Tell Me the Difference Between an Alligator & a Crocodile. 2013. (How Are They Different? Ser.). (ENG., Illus.). 24p. (J). (gr. k-5). pap. 8.25 *(978-1-4488-9728-5(9))*; lib. bdg. 22.60 *(978-1-4488-9635-6(5))* Rosen Publishing Group, Inc., The. (PowerKids Pr.).

Royston, Angela. Alligator. 2013. (Top of the Food Chain Ser.). 32p. (J). (gr. k-5). 25.25 *(978-1-61533-742-2(3))*; pap. 10.00 *(978-1-61533-801-6(2))* Rosen Publishing Group, Inc., The. (PowerKids Pr.).

—Alligators & Crocodiles. (Amazing Animals Ser.). (Illus.). 24p. (J). 2009. (gr. 2-4). pap. 8.95 *(978-1-60596-153-8(1))* 2009. (gr. 2-4). lib. bdg. 24.45 *(978-1-60596-152-1(3))* 2003. lib. bdg. 24.45 *(978-1-58340-225-2(X))* Weigl Pubs., Inc.

Ryndak, Rob. Alligator or Crocodile? 2015. (Animal Look-Alikes Ser.). (ENG., Illus.). 24p. (J). (gr. 1-2). pap. 8.15 *(978-1-4824-2708-0(7))* Stevens, Gareth Publishing LLLP.

Salzmann, Mary Elizabeth. Baby Alligators, 1 vol. 2014. (Baby Animals Set 2 Ser.). (ENG.). 24p. (J). (gr. -1-3). 24.21 *(978-1-62403-507-4(8))* ABDO Publishing Co.

Shea, Therese. Crocodiles & Alligators. (Big Bad Biters Ser.). 24p. 2009. (gr. 2-3). 42.50 *(978-1-61511-562-4(5))* 2006. (Illus.). (J). (gr. 3-7). lib. bdg. 22.60 *(978-1-4042-3523-6(X))* Rosen Publishing Group, Inc., The. (PowerKids Pr.).

Silverman, Buffy. Can You Tell an Alligator from a Crocodile? 2011. (Lightning Bolt Books (tm) — Animal Look-Alikes Ser.). (ENG.). 32p. (gr. k-2). pap. 7.95 *(978-0-7613-7846-4(4))*; (Illus.). 26.60 *(978-0-7613-6733-8(0))* Lerner Publishing Group.

—Can You Tell an Alligator from A Crocodile? 2011. (Animal Look-Alikes Ser.). pap. 45.32 *(978-0-7613-8381-9(6))* Lerner Publishing Group.

Stewart, Melissa. Alligator or Crocodile? How Do You Know? 2011. (Which Animal Is Which? Ser.). (Illus.). 24p. (J). (gr. k-18). pap. 7.95 *(978-1-59845-234-1(7)*, Enslow Elementary); lib. bdg. 22.60 *(978-0-7660-3677-2(4))* Enslow Pubs., Inc.

Turnbull, Stephanie. Alligator. 2013. (Big Beasts Ser.). (Illus.). 24p. (gr. k-3). 28.50 *(978-1-59920-831-2(8))* Black Rabbit Bks.

Twine, Alice. Alligators. (Baby Animals Ser.). 24p. 2009. (gr. 1-1). 42.50 *(978-1-61511-485-6(8))* 2008. (Illus.). (J). (gr. -1-3). lib. bdg. 22.60 *(978-1-4042-4146-6(9))* Rosen Publishing Group, Inc., The. (PowerKids Pr.).

—Alligators/Caimanes. 2009. (Baby Animals/Animales bebé Ser.). (SPA.). 24p. (gr. 1-1). 42.50 *(978-1-61511-497-9(1)*, Editorial Buenas Letras) Rosen Publishing Group, Inc., The.

—Alligators/Caimanes. Obregon, Jose Maria, tr. from ENG. 2008. (Baby Animals / Animales Bebé Ser.). (SPA., Illus.). 24p. (J). (gr. k-3). lib. bdg. 22.60 *(978-1-4042-7682-6(3))* Rosen Publishing Group, Inc., The.

Wexo, John Bonnett. Alligators & Crocodiles. rev. ed. 2003. (Illus.). 24p. (J). (gr. 1-7). 10.95 *(978-1-932396-03-4(9)*, Zoo Bks.) Wildlife Education, Ltd.

Wildlife Education, compiled by. Alligators. 2007. (Illus.). 12p. (J). 5.99 *(978-1-932396-39-3(X)*, Critters Up Close) Wildlife Education, Ltd.

Wong, Angi Ma, illus. My Story: Reggie: The L.A. Gator. 2007. 25p. *(978-1-928753-12-4(4))* Pacific Heritage Bks.

Zobel, Derek. Alligators. 2011. (Animal Safari Ser.). (ENG., Illus.). 24p. (J). (gr. k-3). lib. bdg. 25.95 *(978-1-60014-601-5(5)*, Blastoff! Readers) Bellwether Media.

ALLIGATORS—FICTION

Alexander, Lestat. The Blue-Eyed Alligator. 2011. 24p. pap. 12.56 *(978-1-4269-5467-2(0))* Trafford Publishing.

Anderson, Airlie. Momo & Snap. 2013. (Child's Play Library). (ENG., Illus.). 32p. (J). *(978-1-84643-603-1(6))* Child's Play International Ltd.

Armstrong, Cindy. Boudreaux & His Buddies. 2006. 98p. pap. 16.95 *(978-1-4241-3906-4(6))* PublishAmerica, Inc.

Asch, Frank. Monsieur Saguette & His Baguette. Asch, Frank, illus. 2006. (ENG., Illus.). 32p. (J). (gr. -1-2). 6.95 *(978-1-55337-978-2(0))* Kids Can Pr., Ltd. CAN. Dist: Hachette Bk. Group.

Baker, Keith. At the Park: A Mr. & Mrs. Green Adventure. 2016. (Green Light Readers Level 2 Ser.). (ENG., Illus.). 32p. (J). (gr. 1-4). pap. 3.99 *(978-0-544-55556-3(2)*, HMH Books For Young Readers) Houghton Mifflin Harcourt Publishing Co.

—Camping: A Mr. & Mrs. Green Adventure. 2012. (Green Light Readers Level 2 Ser.). (ENG., Illus.). 24p. (J). (gr. -1-3). 12.99 *(978-0-547-74961-7(9))*; pap. 3.99 *(978-0-547-74559-6(1))* Houghton Mifflin Harcourt Publishing Co.

—Cookies: A Mr. & Mrs. Green Adventure. 2012. (Green Light Readers Level 2 Ser.). (ENG., Illus.). 24p. (J). (gr. -1-3). pap. 3.99 *(978-0-547-74561-9(3))* Houghton Mifflin Harcourt Publishing Co.

—Gumballs: A Mr. & Mrs. Green Adventure. 2014. (Green Light Readers Level 2 Ser.). (ENG., Illus.). 24p. (J). (gr. -1-3). 12.99 *(978-0-544-23605-9(X)*, HMH Books For Young Readers) Houghton Mifflin Harcourt Publishing Co.

—Lucky Days with Mr. & Mrs. Green, 1 vol. Baker, Keith, illus. 2007. (Mr. & Mrs. Green Ser.). (ENG., Illus.). 72p. (gr. 2-4). 27.07 *(978-1-59961-300-0(X))* Spotlight.

—Meet Mr. & Mrs. Green. 2004. (Mr. & Mrs. Green Ser.: 1). (ENG., Illus.). 72p. (J). (gr. -1-3). pap. 5.95 *(978-0-15-204955-3(X))* Houghton Mifflin Harcourt Publishing Co.

—Meet Mr. & Mrs. Green, 1 vol. Baker, Keith, illus. 2007. (Mr. & Mrs. Green Ser.). (ENG., Illus.). 71p. (gr. 2-4). 27.07 *(978-1-59961-301-7(8))* Spotlight.

—More Mr. & Mrs. Green, 1 vol. Baker, Keith, illus. 2007. (Mr. & Mrs. Green Ser.). (ENG., Illus.). 68p. (gr. 2-4). 27.07 *(978-1-59961-302-4(6))* Spotlight.

—On the Go with Mr. & Mrs. Green, 1 vol. Baker, Keith, illus. 2007. (Mr. & Mrs. Green Ser.). (ENG., Illus.). 72p. (gr. 2-4). 27.07 *(978-1-59961-303-1(4))* Spotlight.

—Sometimes. 2003. (Green Light Readers Level 1 Ser.). (ENG., Illus.). 24p. (J). (gr. -1-3). pap. 3.95 *(978-0-15-204847-1(2))* Houghton Mifflin Harcourt Publishing Co.

—Sometimes. 2003. (Green Light Readers — Level 1 Ser.). (gr. -1-2). lib. bdg. 13.50 *(978-0-613-64597-3(9),* Turtleback) Turtleback Bks.

—Sometimes/Algunas Veces. Flor Ada, Alma & Campoy, F. Isabel, trs. from ENG. 2007. (Green Light Readers Level 1 Ser.). (ENG & SPA., Illus.). 28p. (J). (gr. -1-3). pap. 3.95 *(978-0-15-205961-3(X))* Houghton Mifflin Harcourt Publishing Co.

Beasley, Cassie. Tumble & Blue. 2017. (ENG.). 400p. (J). (gr. 3-7). 17.99 ***(978-0-525-42844-2(5)***, Dial Bks) Penguin Young Readers Group.

Beaudoin, Liliana F. Alton the Unique Alligator: Alton, el Caimán único. 2011. 32p. pap. 13.25 *(978-1-4634-2025-3(0))* AuthorHouse.

Beckenstein, Cara. The True Story of Federico Fish & Ana Alligator. Tanchak, Diane, illus. 2003. 32p. 11.95 *(978-0-9726699-0-0(6))* Laughing Gull Pr.

Bergman, Mara. Snip Snap! What's That? Maland, Nick, illus. 2005. (ENG.). 32p. (J). (gr. -1-3). 16.99 *(978-0-06-077754-8(0),* Greenwillow Bks.) HarperCollins Pubs.

Berkes, Marianne. The Swamp Where Gator Hides, 1 vol. Baird, Roberta, illus. 2014. (ENG.). 32p. (J). (gr. k-4). 16.95 *(978-1-58469-470-0(X))*; pap. 8.95 *(978-1-58469-471-7(8))* Dawn Pubns.

Brooks, Erik. Later, Gator! 2016. (ENG., Illus.). 40p. (J). (gr. -1). 14.95 *(978-1-4549-1816-5(0))* Sterling Publishing Co., Inc.

Bryan, Sean. A Girl & Her Gator. Murphy, Tom, illus. 2011. (ENG.). 32p. (J). (gr. -1-k). 14.95 *(978-1-61145-032-3(2),* 611032, Arcade Publishing) Skyhorse Publishing Co., Inc.

Cole, Dina. Are There Alligators at the Equator? An Eddie the Equator Adventure. 2012. 40p. pap. 20.99 *(978-1-4772-6819-3(7))* AuthorHouse.

Conlon, Mara, adapted by. Bill Hatches an Egg. 2005. (Sitting Ducks Ser.). (J). *(978-0-8431-1343-3(X),* Price Stern Sloan) Penguin Publishing Group.

Coronado, Mark & Jackson, Dominic. Swamp Life. 2012. 16p. pap. 15.99 *(978-1-4772-1042-0(3))* AuthorHouse.

Couch, Caroline. Ally Gator & Her Search for a Rainbow, 1 vol. 2009. 19p. pap. 24.95 *(978-1-60836-182-3(9))* America Star Bks.

Creghan, Brian C. Pauly: The alligator who wore tennis Shoes. 2010. 48p. pap. 24.00 *(978-1-4269-3614-2(1))* Trafford Publishing.

Cronin, Susan L. Gidget Goes Away. 2006. 54p. pap. 16.95 *(978-1-4137-9878-4(0))* PublishAmerica, Inc.

Dadey, Debbie. Great Green Gator Graduation. Lucas, Margeaux, illus. 2006. (Swamp Monster in Third Grade Ser.). 58p. (J). pap. *(978-0-439-79401-5(3))* Scholastic, Inc.

Dillard, Sarah. First Day at Zoo School. Dillard, Sarah, illus. 2014. (ENG., Illus.). 40p. (J). (gr. k-2). 14.99 *(978-1-58536-890-7(3),* 203670) Sleeping Bear Pr.

Dixon, Kirstie. Pickles Helps a Friend. 2012. 16p. pap. 15.99 *(978-1-4772-6445-4(0))* AuthorHouse.

Eastman, P. D. Aaron Has a Lazy Day. 2015. (Step into Reading Ser.). (ENG., Illus.). 32p. (J). (gr. -1-1). lib. bdg. 12.99 *(978-0-375-97411-3(3),* Random Hse. Bks. for Young Readers) Random Hse. Children's Bks.

—Aaron Is Cool. 2015. (Step into Reading Ser.). (ENG., Illus.). 32p. (J). (gr. -1-1). 12.99 *(978-0-553-51238-0(2),* Random Hse. Bks. for Young Readers) Random Hse. Children's Bks.

—Aaron Loves Apples & Pumpkins. 2015. (Step into Reading Ser.). (ENG., Illus.). 32p. (J). (gr. -1-1). 12.99 *(978-0-553-51235-9(8),* Random Hse. Bks. for Young Readers) Random Hse. Children's Bks.

Emde, Nicole. Alabaster the Albino Alligator. 2008. 40p. per. 24.95 *(978-1-4241-9778-1(3))* America Star Bks.

Engram, Teta. Baxter & the Sidewalk Alligator. Holland, Lisa Tomms, illus. 2009. 32p. pap. 12.99 *(978-1-4389-9367-6(6))* AuthorHouse.

Falatko, Julie. Snappsy the Alligator (Did Not Ask to Be in This Book) Miller, Tim J., illus. 2016. (ENG.). 40p. (J). (gr. -1-3). 16.99 *(978-0-451-46945-8(3),* Viking Books for Young Readers) Penguin Young Readers Group.

Fisher, Valorie. Ellsworth's Extraordinary Electric Ears: And Other Amazing Alphabet Anecdotes. Fisher, Valorie, illus. 2009. (ENG., Illus.). 36p. (J). (gr. -1-3). 10.99 *(978-1-4424-0658-2(5),* Atheneum Bks. for Young Readers) Simon & Schuster Children's Publishing.

Fleming, Candace. Gator Gumbo: A Spicy-Hot Tale. Lambert, Sally Anne, illus. 2004. (ENG.). 32p. (J). (gr. -1-3). 18.99 *(978-0-374-38050-2(3),* 9780374380502, Farrar, Straus & Giroux (BYR)) Farrar, Straus & Giroux.

Foust, Cindy G. Austin Alligator: I'll See You Guys Later. Revoir, Joyce, illus. 2003. (J). 12.95 *(978-0-9749220-0-3(5))* Alpha-kidZ.

Geringswald, Rita T. The Adventures of Ali Alligator. 2007. (Illus.). 33p. (J). 6.95 *(978-0-9797566-1-0(8))* R & D Publishing of Lakeland, Florida.

Gibson, Cay. Cajun 'Ti Beau & the Cocodries. D'Antoni, Colleen, illus. 2014. (ENG.). 32p. (J). (gr. k-3). 16.99 *(978-1-4556-1947-4(7))* Pelican Publishing Co., Inc.

Golde, Justin F. Yes, My Dear, Alligators Do Belong on the Moon. 2012. 24p. pap. 11.50 *(978-1-62212-188-5(0),* Strategic Bk. Publishing) Strategic Book Publishing & Rights Agency (SBPRA).

Gray, Susannah. Alligators Coming! Jones, Zach, illus. 2012. 20p. pap. 15.00 *(978-1-4575-1316-9(1))* Dog Ear Publishing, LLC.

Green, Kevin M. Livy Bug & Ally Gator in Best Friends. 2008. 16p. per. 24.95 *(978-1-4241-9385-1(0))* America Star Bks.

Hannigan, Katherine. Gwendolyn Grace. Hannigan, Katherine, illus. 2015. (ENG., Illus.). 32p. (J). (gr. -1-3). 17.99 *(978-0-06-234519-6(2),* Greenwillow Bks.) HarperCollins Pubs.

Hayes, Geoffrey. The Mystery of the Riverboat Robber. 2016. (Step into Reading Ser.). (ENG., Illus.). 48p. (J). (gr. k-3). lib. bdg. 12.99 *(978-0-375-97470-0(9),* Random Hse. Bks. for Young Readers) Random Hse. Children's Bks.

Hersey, Jodi. Achy Ali. Peabody, Rob, illus. 2011. pap. 5.00 *(978-1-4276-5272-0(4))* Aardvark Global Publishing.

Hiaasen, Carl. Hoot. 2014. 17.00 *(978-1-63419-707-6(0))* Perfection Learning Corp.

Himes, John. The Adventures of an Alligator Named Ally. 2012. 24p. pap. 17.99 *(978-1-4772-9676-9(X))* AuthorHouse.

Hoffman, Beth Greiner. Animal Gym. Gergely, Tibor, illus. 2009. (Little Golden Book Ser.). (ENG.). 24p. (J). (gr. -1-2). 4.99 *(978-0-375-84751-6(0),* Golden Bks.) Random Hse. Children's Bks.

How the Gator's Snout Grew Out. Date not set. 5.95 *(978-0-89868-359-2(9))* ARO Publishing Co.

Hurd, Thacher. Mama Don't Allow. 2003. (Illus.). (J). (gr. -1-2). pap. 35.95 incl. audio compact disk *(978-1-59112-605-8(3))* Live Oak Media.

Hurd, Thacher & Hurd. Mama Don't Allow. Hurd, Thacher, illus. 25th anniv. ed. 2008. (Trophy Picture Bks.). (ENG., Illus.). 40p. (J). (gr. -1-3). pap. 6.99 *(978-0-06-443078-4(2))* HarperCollins Pubs.

Hurd, Thacher & Hurd, T. Mama Don't Allow. 2008. (Illus.). (J). (gr. -1-2). 17.20 *(978-0-8085-3698-7(2),* Turtleback) Turtleback Bks.

Jarvis. Alan's Big, Scary Teeth. Jarvis, illus. 2016. (ENG., Illus.). 32p. (J). (-k). 16.99 *(978-0-7636-8120-3(2))* Candlewick Pr.

Kasza, Keiko. My Lucky Birthday. Kasza, Keiko, illus. 2013. (ENG., Illus.). 32p. (J). (gr. -1-k). 16.99 *(978-0-399-25763-6(2),* G.P. Putnam's Sons Books for Young Readers) Penguin Young Readers Group.

Ketteman, Helen. The Three Little Gators. Terry, Will, illus. 2009. (ENG.). 32p. (J). (gr. -1-3). 16.99 *(978-0-8075-7824-7(X))* Whitman, Albert & Co.

Kimball, Michael D. Alligator Bay: A Beary Tale. 2009. 132p. pap. 11.95 *(978-1-4401-1804-3(3))* iUniverse, Inc.

Knapp, Rene & Berger, Marjorie B. The Little Lost Allygator. 2012. 44p. pap. 24.95 *(978-1-4626-9717-5(8))* America Star Bks.

—The Little Lost Allygator. Kurt D Williams and Jeff Baker, illus. 2012. 44p. pap. 24.95 *(978-1-4626-8155-6(7))* America Star Bks.

Krepela, Rebecca. Vernon, Drake & Chomp. 2013. 20p. pap. 24.95 *(978-1-62709-841-0(0))* America Star Bks.

Kuehnel, Judy Lyons. Archie & Abigail. 2008. 64p. per. 17.95 *(978-1-4327-0565-7(2))* Outskirts Pr., Inc.

Lamson, Martha. Oliver. 2008. 28p. pap. 15.99 *(978-1-4363-5100-3(6))* Xlibris Corp.

Lane, Alison Hoffman. Uncle Arnel & the Awful, Angry Alligator. 2009. (Uncle Arnel Ser.). (Illus.). 32p. (J). 15.95 *(978-1-58980-645-0(X))* Pelican Publishing Co., Inc.

Langlois, Annie. Mia, Matt & the Lazy Gator. Cummins, Sarah, tr. from FRE. Beaulieu, Jimmy, illus. 2010. (Formac First Novels Ser.). (ENG.). 64p. (J). (gr. 1-4). 14.95 *(978-0-88780-938-5(3),* 9780887809385); pap. 5.95 *(978-0-88780-936-1(7),* 9780887809361) Formac Publishing Co., Ltd. CAN. Dist: Casemate Pubs. & Bk. Distributors, LLC.

Larsen, Alison. Thomas the Turtle. 2006. (Illus.). 21p. (J). per. 14.95 *(978-1-60002-097-1(6),* 3961) Mountain Valley Publishing, LLC.

Leah. The Alligator Named Ally, 1 vol. 2009. 20p. pap. 24.95 *(978-1-60749-726-4(3))* America Star Bks.

Lee, Dennis. Alligator Pie. Newfeld, Frank & Hilb, Nora, illus. rev. ed. 2008. (ENG.). 16p. (J). (gr. k-k). bds. *(978-1-55263-674-9(7))* Me to We.

Lehrhaupt, Adam. Warning: Do Not Open This Book! Forsythe, Matthew, illus. 2013. (ENG.). 40p. (J). (gr. -1-3). 17.99 *(978-1-4424-3582-7(8),* Simon & Schuster Bks. For Young Readers) Simon & Schuster Bks. For Young Readers.

Lewin, Betsy. You Can Do It! Lewin, Betsy, illus. 2014. (I Like to Read(r) Ser.). (ENG., Illus.). 24p. (J). (gr. -1-3). 6.99 *(978-0-8234-3055-0(3))* Holiday Hse., Inc.

—You Can Do It! 2013. (I Like to Read(r) Ser.). (ENG.). 24p. (J). 14.95 *(978-0-8234-2522-8(3))* Holiday Hse., Inc.

Lies, Brian. Gator Dad. 2016. (ENG., Illus.). 32p. (J). (gr. -1-3). 17.99 *(978-0-544-53433-9(6),* HMH Books For Young Readers) Houghton Mifflin Harcourt Publishing Co.

Lionni, Leo. An Extraordinary Egg. 2014. (ENG., Illus.). 40p. (J). (gr. -1-2). 17.99 *(978-0-679-85840-9(7),* Knopf Bks. for Young Readers) Random Hse. Children's Bks.

Lo, Yer Jenny. The Disobedient Ducklings. Lo, Talthau, photos by. 2008. (Illus.). 44p. pap. 24.95 *(978-1-60441-576-6(2))* America Star Bks.

Macalino, Damien. What If an Alligator Ate an Avalanche. Paj, Eduardo, illus. 2013. 32p. pap. 10.00 *(978-0-9836303-8-8(0))* Crystal Mosaic Bks.

Mallory, Nicole. I Wish I Was an Alligator. 2013. (ENG.). 29p. (J). pap. 15.95 *(978-1-4787-1066-0(7))* Outskirts Pr., Inc.

Marsalis, Dustin S. The Alligator Astronauts Go to the Zipper Zoo. 2013. 36p. pap. 15.99 *(978-1-4624-0678-4(5),* Inspiring Voices) Author Solutions, Inc.

Mcallister, Herb West. Doo West to Toadstool. 2011. 44p. pap. 21.99 *(978-1-4628-5530-8(X))* Xlibris Corp.

Mckenzie, Precious. Now or Later Alligator. Snape, Jenny, illus. 2012. (ENG.). 24p. (gr. k-1). pap. 8.95 *(978-1-61810-305-5(9))* Rourke Educational Media.

McLaughlin, Julie. Hungry Mr. Gator. McKay, Ann Marie, illus. 2005. (J). 15.99 *(978-0-933101-24-1(4))* Legacy Pubns.

McMilin, Jack D. The Water Dog. Nevarez, Lisa D., illus. 2011. 24p. pap. 24.95 *(978-1-4626-0544-6(3))* America Star Bks.

Minarik, Else Holmelund. No Fighting, No Biting! Sendak, Maurice, illus. 2004. 63p. (J). (gr. k-4). reprint ed. pap. 17.00 *(978-0-7567-7235-2(4))* DIANE Publishing Co.

Morris, Jennifer E. May I Please Have a Cookie? Morris, Jennifer E., illus. (ENG., Illus.). (J). 2015. 30p. (— 1). bds. 6.99 *(978-0-545-81502-4(9))* 2005. 32p. (gr. -1-3). per. 4.99 *(978-0-439-73819-4(9))* Scholastic, Inc. (Cartwheel Bks.).

Morrow, Dj. The Good Ol' Boys. 2012. 28p. pap. 24.95 *(978-1-4626-9533-1(7))* America Star Bks.

Mozelle, Shirley. Zack's Alligator & the First Snow. Watts, James, illus. 2011. (I Can Read Level 2 Ser.). (ENG.). 32p. (J). (gr. k-3). pap. 3.99 *(978-0-06-147372-2(3))* HarperCollins Pubs.

Mrs O'Malley in Alligator Alley: 3-in-1 Package. (Sails Literacy Ser.). 24p. (gr. 1-18). 57.00 *(978-0-7578-3209-3(1))* Rigby Education.

Munsch, Robert. Alligator Baby. 2004. (Illus.). (J). (gr. k-3). spiral bd. *(978-0-616-01730-2(8))*; spiral bd. *(978-0-616-01731-9(6))* Canadian National Institute for the Blind/Institut National Canadien pour les Aveugles.

—Un Bébé Alligator? 2004.Tr. of Alligator Baby. (FRE., Illus.). (J). (gr. k-3). spiral bd. *(978-0-616-01839-2(8))* Canadian National Institute for the Blind/Institut National Canadien pour les Aveugles.

Nanette. The Black Alligator. 2004. (Life on Granny's Farm Ser.). (J). 12.95 *(978-0-9741269-3-7(4))* St. Bernard Publishing, LLC.

Nesci, Andrea Lynn & Nesci, Jim. Bubba: A True Story about an Amazing Alligator. Kostelyk, Jason, illus. l.t. ed. 2003. 24p. (J). pap. 12.50 *(978-0-9713197-6-9(6))* ECO Herpetological Pub. & Dist.

Palatini, Margie. No Biting, Louise. Reinhart, Matthew, illus. 2007. 32p. (J). (gr. -1-3). 16.99 *(978-0-06-052627-6(0))*; lib. bdg. 17.89 *(978-0-06-052628-3(9))* HarperCollins Pubs. (Tegen, Katherine Bks).

Parsley, Elise. If You Ever Want to Bring an Alligator to School, Don't! Parsley, Elise, illus. 2015. (ENG., Illus.). 40p. (J). (gr. -1-1). 17.00 *(978-0-316-37657-0(4))* Little Brown & Co.

Perret, Delphine. Pedro & George. Perret, Delphine, illus. 2015. (ENG., Illus.). 32p. (J). (gr. -1-3). 17.99 *(978-1-4814-2925-2(6))* Simon & Schuster Children's Publishing.

Rice, James. Gaston(r) Goes to Texas, 1 vol. Rice, James, illus. 2007. (Gaston(r) Ser.). (ENG., Illus.). 32p. (J). (gr. 1-3). 16.99 *(978-1-58980-531-6(3))* Pelican Publishing Co., Inc.

—Gaston(r) Lays an Offshore Pipeline, 1 vol. Rice, James, illus. 2007. (Gaston(r) Ser.). (ENG., Illus.). 32p. (J). (gr. k-3). 16.99 *(978-1-58980-510-1(0))* Pelican Publishing Co., Inc.

Rice, James, illus. Gaston Joins the Circus, 1 vol. 2015. (ENG.). 32p. (J). (gr. k-3). pap. 9.95 *(978-1-4556-2092-0(0))* Pelican Publishing Co., Inc.

—Gaston(r) Joins the Circus, 1 vol. 2015. (ENG.). 32p. (J). (gr. k-3). 16.99 *(978-1-4556-2129-3(3))* Pelican Publishing Co., Inc.

Ripley's Believe It or Not Editors & Ripley's Believe It Or Not! Staff. A Scaly Tale. 2010. (Rbi Ser.: 1). (ENG.). 128p. (J). pap. 4.99 *(978-1-893951-52-5(9))* Ripley Entertainment, Inc.

Rowe, Ben. Can an Alligator Drive a Nail with His Tail? 2008. 18p. pap. 24.95 *(978-1-60610-625-9(2))* America Star Bks.

Ryan, Connie. Gary the Gator. 2009. 36p. pap. 15.49 *(978-1-4490-3329-3(6))* AuthorHouse.

Samoun, Abigail. How Gator Says Good-Bye! Watts, Sarah, illus. 2014. (Little Traveler Ser.). (ENG.). 22p. (J). (gr. -1-k). bds. 6.95 *(978-1-4549-0821-0(1))* Sterling Publishing Co., Inc.

Sargent, Dave & Sargent, Pat. I Can Read, Too/Puedo Leer, Tambien, 10 vols. Robinson, Laura, illus. 2003. (Puedo Leer Ser.). (SPA.). 24p. (J). Vol. 1. lib. bdg. 20.95 *(978-1-56763-943-8(7))* Vol. 3. pap. 10.95 *(978-1-56763-948-3(8))* Vol. 3. lib. bdg. 20.95 *(978-1-56763-947-6(X))* Vol. 4. pap. 10.95 *(978-1-56763-950-6(X))* Vol. 5. lib. bdg. 20.95 *(978-1-56763-951-3(8))* Vol. 6. pap. 6.95 *(978-1-56763-954-4(2))* Vol. 6. lib. bdg. 20.95 *(978-1-56763-953-7(4))* Vol. 7. pap. 6.95 *(978-1-56763-956-8(9))* Vol. 8. pap. 10.95 *(978-1-56763-958-2(5))* Vol. 9. pap. 10.95 *(978-1-56763-960-5(7))* Vol. 9. lib. bdg. 20.95 *(978-1-56763-959-9(3))* Vol. 10. pap. 10.95 *(978-1-56763-962-9(3))* Vol. 10. lib. bdg. 20.95 *(978-1-56763-961-2(5))* Ozark Publishing.

Schmid, Paul. Oliver & His Alligator. Schmid, Paul, illus. 2013. (ENG., Illus.). 40p. (J). (gr. -1-k). 15.99 *(978-1-4231-7437-0(2))* Disney Pr.

Schnetzler, Pattie L. Fast 'n Snappy. Manning, Jane K., tr. Manning, Jane K., illus. 2004. (Carolrhoda Picture Books Ser.). 32p. (J). (gr. k-3). 16.95 *(978-1-57505-539-8(2))* Lerner Publishing Group.

Sendak, Maurice. Alligators All Around Board Book: An Alphabet. Sendak, Maurice, illus. 2017. (Illus.). 32p. (J). (gr. -1-3). bds. 7.95 *(978-0-06-266807-3(2))* HarperCollins Pubs.

Shaffert, Charles. Googus, the Toothless Alligator. Stringer, Margaret, illus. l.t. ed. 2003. 30p. (J). per. 7.95 *(978-1-932338-27-0(6))* Lifevest Publishing, Inc.

Shaffert, Charles F. Googus to the Rescue. Stringer, Margaret, illus. l.t. ed. 2005. 31p. (J). per. 10.00 *(978-1-59879-043-6(9))* Lifevest Publishing, Inc.

Sherlock, Philip. Anansi & the Alligator Eggs y Los Huevos Del Caimán. Rickham, Elethia, tr. Judah, Susan, illus. 2nd ed. 2013. 42p. pap. 15.00 *(978-976-95510-6-0(6))* Minna Pr.

Spaht-Gill, Janie. Gator's Out, Said the Trout. Reese, Bob, illus. (J). (gr. k-2). 5.95 *(978-0-89868-305-9(X))* ARO Publishing Co.

Sparkes, Ali. Alligator Action. Collins, Ross, illus. 2014. (S. W. I. T. C. H. Ser.: 14). (ENG.). 112p. (J). (gr. 2-5). lib. bdg. 27.93 *(978-1-4677-2117-2(4),* Darby Creek) Lerner Publishing Group.

Stauffacher, Sue. Animal Rescue Team: Gator on the Loose! Lamont, Priscilla, illus. 2011. (Animal Rescue Team Ser.). (ENG.). 160p. (J). (gr. 3-7). 5.99 *(978-0-375-85131-5(3),* Yearling) Random Hse. Children's Bks.

Sweet, George M. The Old Alligator & the Young Bird. 2011. 52p. pap. 19.39 *(978-1-4269-5357-6(7))* Trafford Publishing.

Thomas, Jason. The Adventures of Bird & Gator: Best Friends. 2012. 24p. pap. 12.56 *(978-1-4669-4973-7(2))* Trafford Publishing.

Urbanovic, Jackie. Duck & Cover. Urbanovic, Jackie, illus. 2009. (Max the Duck Ser.: 3). (ENG., Illus.). 32p. (J). (gr. -1-2). 17.99 *(978-0-06-121444-8(2))* HarperCollins Pubs.

Verrett, Michael. The White Alligator Crown Quatro. 2010. 147p. pap. 13.95 *(978-0-557-58121-4(4))* Lulu Pr., Inc.

—The White Alligator (paper Back) 2010. 116p. pap. 17.30 *(978-0-557-28042-1(7))* Lulu Pr., Inc.

—The White Alligator (paperback full Color) 2010. 116p. pap. 42.00 *(978-0-557-36924-9(X))* Lulu Pr., Inc.

Viviani, Luisa. There Is Something Special Inside of Me. 2004. 25p. pap. 24.95 *(978-1-4137-2372-4(1))* PublishAmerica, Inc.

Walker, Anna. Alfie's Lost Sharkie. 2016. (ENG., Illus.). 24p. (J). (gr. -1-3). 14.99 *(978-0-544-58656-7(5))* Houghton Mifflin Harcourt Publishing Co.

—Hurry up, Alfie! 2016. (ENG., Illus.). 24p. (J). (gr. -1-3). 14.99 *(978-0-544-58654-3(9))* Houghton Mifflin Harcourt Publishing Co.

Watts, Jane & Nobel, DeAnna. The Adventures of Alligator Tater. 2007. 64p. per. 10.95 *(978-1-4327-0228-1(9))* Outskirts Pr., Inc.

Wells, Rosemary. Hands Off, Harry! Wells, Rosemary, illus. 2011. (ENG., Illus.). 40p. (J). (gr. -1-1). 14.99 *(978-0-06-192112-4(2),* Tegen, Katherine Bks) HarperCollins Pubs.

—Miracle Melts Down. Wells, Rosemary, illus. 2012. (ENG., Illus.). 40p. (J). (gr. -1-3). 14.99 *(978-0-06-192115-5(7),* Tegen, Katherine Bks) HarperCollins Pubs.

West, Shawna Makala. Is There an Alligator at Kaipapau? 2004.Tr. of Aia Ka Alakeka Ma Kaipapau? (ENG & HAW.). (J). lib. bdg. 12.95 *(978-0-9760892-1-6(1),* Ho'ulu Hou Project: Stories Told by Us) Na Kamalei Koolauloa Early Education Program.

Willems, Mo. Hooray for Amanda & Her Alligator! Willems, Mo, illus. 2011. (ENG., Illus.). 72p. (J). (gr. -1-3). 17.99 *(978-0-06-200400-0(X))* HarperCollins Pubs.

Wilsdon, Christina. An Alligator Adventure in Florida. Mayo, Frank, illus. 2006. 26p. (J). 7.99 *(978-1-59939-010-9(8))* Cornerstone Pr.

Wilson, Karma. A Frog in the Bog. Rankin, Joan, illus. (ENG.). 32p. (J). (gr. -1-3). 2007. 7.99 *(978-1-4169-2727-3(1))* 2003. 17.99 *(978-0-689-84081-4(0))* McElderry, Margaret K. Bks. (McElderry, Margaret K. Bks.).

Yeoman, John. Quentin Blake's Amazing Animal Stories. Blake, Quentin, illus. 2012. (ENG.). 124p. (J). (gr. 2-4). 19.99 *(978-1-84365-195-6(5),* Pavilion Children's Books) Pavilion Bks. GBR. Dist: Independent Pubs. Group.

Zabel, Randy & Broesch, Valerie, illus. Al-the-Gator & Freddy Frog. 2007. 48p. (J). per. 18.99 *(978-0-9797513-0-1(6))* 4RV Publishing, LLC.

ALLOYS

Gray, Leon. Zinc. 2005. (Elements Ser.). (Illus.). 32p. (gr. 4-7). lib. bdg. 28.50 *(978-0-7614-1922-8(5),* Benchmark Bks.) Marshall Cavendish Corp.

ALLUSIONS

Fandel, Jennifer. Puns, Allusions, & Other Word Secrets. 2005. (Understanding Poetry Ser.). (Illus.). 48p. (YA). (gr. 4-7). lib. bdg. 21.95 *(978-1-58341-341-8(3))* Creative Co., The.

ALMANACS

see also Calendars; Yearbooks

Almanac, Old Farmer's. The Old Farmer's Almanac for Kids, Vol. 7. 2017. (ENG., Illus.). 192p. pap. 9.95 ***(978-1-57198-743-3(6)***, Old Farmer's Almanac) Yankee Publishing, Inc.

El Nabli, Dina. Henry Ford - Putting the World on Wheels. Time for Kids Editors, ed. 2008. (Time for Kids Ser.). (ENG., Illus.). 48p. (J). (gr. 2-4). pap. 3.99 *(978-0-06-057630-1(8),* Collins) HarperCollins Pubs.

Hopkins, Lee Bennett. Days to Celebrate: A Full Year of Poetry, People, Holidays, History, Fascinating Facts, & More. Alcorn, Stephen, illus. 2004. (ENG.). 112p. (J). (gr. 2-7). 18.99 *(978-0-06-000765-2(6),* Greenwillow Bks.) HarperCollins Pubs.

Howes, Kelly King & Baker, Lawrence W. Almanac, Reconstruction Era. 2004. (Reconstruction Era Reference Library). (ENG., Illus.). 272p. (J). lib. bdg. 106.00 *(978-0-7876-9217-9(4),* UXL) Cengage Gale.

Howes, Kelly King & Carnagie, Julie L. The Roaring Twenties Almanac & Primary Sources. 2005. (Roaring 20's Reference Library). (ENG., Illus.). 352p. (J). (gr. 3-7). 106.00 *(978-1-4144-0212-3(0),* UXL) Cengage Gale.

Media Projects, Inc., Staff. Almanac of Asian American History, 2 vols., Vol. 1. 2004. (Illus.). 144p. (C). (gr. 6-8). stu. ed. 97.00 *(978-0-313-32602-8(9),* MS2602, Greenwood) ABC-CLIO, LLC.

Media Projects, Inc., Staff, contrib. by. Student Almanac of African American History, 2 vols. 2003. (Middle School Reference Ser.). (Illus.). 144p. (C). (gr. 6-8). 101.00 *(978-0-313-32596-0(0),* MS2596, Greenwood) ABC-CLIO, LLC.

National Geographic. National Geographic Kids Almanac 2016. 2015. lib. bdg. 26.95 *(978-0-606-36424-9(2))* Turtleback Bks.

National Geographic Kids. National Geographic Kids Almanac 2018. 2017. lib. bdg. 26.95 ***(978-0-606-40080-0(X))*** Turtleback Bks.

National Geographic Kids Staff. National Geographic Kids Almanac 2012. 2011. (ENG.). 352p. (J). (gr. 2-4). pap. 13.99 *(978-1-4263-0783-6(7))*; (Illus.). 21.95 *(978-1-4263-0784-3(5))* National Geographic Society. (National Geographic Children's Bks.).

—National Geographic Kids Almanac 2013. 2012. (ENG., Illus.). 352p. (J). (gr. 3-7). 21.95 *(978-1-4263-0925-0(2),* National Geographic Children's Bks.) National Geographic Society.

—National Geographic Kids Almanac 2017. 2016. (ENG., Illus.). 352p. (J). (gr. 3-7). pap. 14.99 *(978-1-4263-2417-8(0),* National Geographic Children's Bks.) National Geographic Society.

—National Geographic Kids Almanac 2018. 2017. (National Geographic Almanacs Ser.). (ENG., Illus.). 352p. (J). (gr. 3-7). pap. 14.99 *(978-1-4263-2772-8(2),* National Geographic Children's Bks.) National Geographic Society.

Old Farmer's Almanac Staff. The Old Farmer's Almanac for Kids, Vol. 5. 2013. (ENG., Illus.). 192p. (J). pap. 9.95 *(978-1-57198-613-9(8))* Yankee Publishing, Inc.

—The Old Farmer's Almanac for Kids, Volume 6. 2015. (ENG., Illus.). 192p. (J). pap. 9.95 *(978-1-57198-683-2(9))* Yankee Publishing, Inc.

Old Farmer's Almanac Staff, ed. The Old Farmer's Almanac for Kids, 4 vols., Vol. 4. 2011. (ENG., Illus.). 192p. pap. 9.95 *(978-1-57198-554-5(9))* Yankee Publishing, Inc.

Pendergast, Tom & Pendergast, Sara. Almanac. 2004. (Sixties in America Reference Library). (ENG., Illus.). 288p. (J). lib. bdg. 106.00 *(978-0-7876-9246-9(3),* UXL) Cengage Gale.

Polidoro, J. Lavatory 101-A Bathroom Book of Knowledge. 2004. 408p. pap. 24.99 *(978-1-4134-8374-1(7))* Xlibris Corp.

Scholastic Editors. Scholastic Almanac for Kids 2016. 2015. lib. bdg. 25.75 *(978-0-606-37770-6(0))* Turtleback Bks.

Scholastic, Inc. Staff. Scholastic Almanac for Kids 2015. 2014. (ENG.). 352p. (J). (gr. 3-7). pap. 13.99 *(978-0-545-67949-7(4)*, Scholastic Paperbacks) Scholastic, Inc.

The Sixties in America, 3 vols. 2004. (ENG.). 600p. 286.00 *(978-0-7876-9249-0(2)*, UXL) Cengage Gale.

TIME for Kids Almanac 2009. 2008. (Time Inc. Home Entertainment Library-Bound Titles Ser.). 256p. (YA). (gr. 5-12). lib. bdg. 39.93 *(978-0-7613-4052-2(1)*, Twenty-First Century Bks.) Lerner Publishing Group.

Time For Kids Editors. Time for Kids Almanac 2017. 2016. (J). lib. bdg. 26.95 *(978-0-606-38564-0(9))* Turtleback Bks.

U. S. National Geographic Society Staff. National Geographic Kids Almanac 2011. 2010. 352p. (J). pap. 13.99 *(978-1-4263-0684-6(9)*, National Geographic Children's Bks.) National Geographic Society.

Willard, Nancy. Cracked Corn & Snow Ice Cream: A Family Almanac. Dyer, Jane, illus. 2005. 56p. (YA). (gr. 4-8). 18.00 *(978-0-7567-8835-3(8))* DIANE Publishing Co.

World Almanac Editors. The World Almanac(r) for Kids 2012. Janssen, Sarah, ed. 2011. (World Almanac Ser.). 352p. (gr. 4-9). 24.95 *(978-1-60057-152-7(2))*; pap. 13.99 *(978-1-60057-153-4(0))* Facts On File, Inc. (World Almanac Bks.).

—The World Almanac(r) for Kids 2013. 2012. (World Almanac Ser.). (gr. 4-9). 24.95 *(978-1-60057-166-4(2)*, World Almanac Bks.) Facts On File, Inc.

—The World Almanac(r) for Kids 2013 Trivia Game. 2012. (World Almanac Ser.). (gr. 4-9). pap. 26.95 *(978-1-60057-170-1(0)*, World Almanac Bks.) Facts On File, Inc.

World Almanac Puzzler Deck for Kids: Math (BoMC) World Almanac Deck: Math, 11-13. 2007. 9.95 *(978-0-8118-6243-1(7))* Chronicle Bks. LLC.

World Almanac Puzzler Deck for Kids: Science (BoMC) World Almanac Deck: Science, 9-11. 2007. 9.95 *(978-0-8118-6242-4(9))* Chronicle Bks. LLC.

World Almanac Puzzler Deck for Kids: U. S. History (BoMC) World Almanac U. S. History, 9-11. 2007. 9.95 *(978-0-8118-6241-7(0))* Chronicle Bks. LLC.

ALPHABET

see also Writing

Active Minds, 6 bks. (Illus.). (J). (gr. -1-3). lib. bdg. 71.70 *(978-1-56674-926-8(3))* Forest Hse. Publishing Co., Inc.

Alexander, Nicole "Nikki". Nicole's Rules of Life. 2012. 32p. pap. 14.99 *(978-1-4669-5488-5(4))* Trafford Publishing.

Allen, Susan & Lindaman, Jane. Read Anything Good Lately? Enright, Vicky, illus. 2003. 32p. 22.90 *(978-0-7613-2322-8(8))*; (J). (gr. -1-3). 14.95 *(978-0-7613-1889-7(5))* Lerner Publishing Group. (Millbrook Pr.).

Alphabet. 2004. (J). ring bd. 29.95 *(978-1-56911-525-1(7))* Learning Resources, Inc.

Alphabet Books. 2010. (Alphabet Bks.). 32p. lib. bdg. 129.95 *(978-1-4296-5200-1(4)*, Aplus Bks.) Capstone Press of Coughlan Cos.

Alphabet Fun. 2010. (Alphabet Fun Ser.). 32p. lib. bdg. 155.94 *(978-1-4296-5838-6(X))*; (ENG.). (gr. 1-2). lib. bdg. 54.64 *(978-1-4296-4431-0(1))* Capstone Press of Coughlan Cos. (Aplus Bks.).

Alphabet Sack Puppets. 2004. (J). ring bd. *(978-0-9749844-0-7(X))* Sunshine Publishing.

Alphabet Sack Puppets: Colored Edition. 2004. (J). ring bd. *(978-0-9749844-1-4(8))* Sunshine Publishing.

Alphabet Zoo. (Padded Large Learners Ser.). (Illus.). (J). bds. *(978-0-7525-9888-8(0))* Parragon, Inc.

Alvarez, Lourdes M. Mi Primer Libro Alfabeto. Brooks, David, illus. 2005. (Mi primer libro Ser.). (SPA.). 9p. (J). (gr. -1 — 1). bds. 3.95 *(978-1-933050-02-7(0))* Sweetwater Pr.

—My First Book Alphabet. Brooks, David, illus. 2005. (My First Book Ser.). 9p. (J). (gr. -1-17). bds. 3.95 *(978-1-933050-08-9(X))* Sweetwater Pr.

American Museum of Natural History. ABC Universe. 2015. (AMNH ABC Board Bks.). (ENG., Illus.). 18p. (J). (gr. -1-k). bds. 7.95 *(978-1-4549-1409-9(2))* Sterling Publishing Co., Inc.

American Museum of Natural History Staff. ABC Dinosaurs. Hartman, Scott, illus. 2011. (AMNH ABC Board Bks.). (ENG.). 18p. (J). (gr. -1-k). bds. 7.95 *(978-1-4027-7715-8(9))* Sterling Publishing Co., Inc.

Astroword: Module 10-Vowel Digraphs & Diphthongs (1-3) 2003. 166.95 net. *(978-0-7652-0831-6(8))*; 55.50 net. *(978-0-7652-0587-2(4))* Modern Curriculum Pr.

Astroword: Module 11-R-Controlled Vowels (1-3) 2003. 55.50 net. *(978-0-7652-0588-9(2))* Modern Curriculum Pr.

Astroword: Module 12-Base Words & Endings (2-6) 2003. 55.50 net. *(978-0-7652-0589-6(0))* Modern Curriculum Pr.

Astroword: Module 13-Compound Words (2-6) 2003. 55.50 net. *(978-0-7652-0590-2(4))* Modern Curriculum Pr.

Astroword: Module 3-Short Vowels A, I (1-2) 2003. 55.50 net. *(978-0-7652-0579-7(3))* Modern Curriculum Pr.

Astroword: Module 4-Short Vowels I, O (1-2) 2003. 55.50 net. *(978-0-7652-0580-3(7))* Modern Curriculum Pr.

Astroword: Module 5-Short Vowels E, U (1-2) 2003. 55.50 net. *(978-0-7652-0581-0(5))* Modern Curriculum Pr.

Astroword: Module 6-Consonant Blends & Digraphs (1-2) 2003. 55.50 net. *(978-0-7652-0582-7(3))*; 166.95 net. *(978-0-7652-0825-5(3))* Modern Curriculum Pr.

Astroword: Module 7-Long Vowels A, I (1-3) 2003. 166.95 net. *(978-0-7652-0826-2(1))*; 55.50 net. *(978-0-7652-0583-4(1))* Modern Curriculum Pr.

Astroword: Module 8-Long Vowels I, O (1-3) 2003. 55.50 net. *(978-0-7652-0585-8(8))*; 166.95 net. *(978-0-7652-0828-6(8))* Modern Curriculum Pr.

Astroword: Module 9-Long Vowels E, U (1-3) 2003. 166.95 net. *(978-0-7652-0829-3(6))*; 55.50 net. *(978-0-7652-0586-5(6))* Modern Curriculum Pr.

Autumn Publishing Staff, illus. Learn the Alphabet. 2004. (Wall Charts Ser.). (J). pap. 4.99 *(978-1-85997-290-8(X))* Byeway Bks.

Award Publications Limited Staff, creator. My First Bumper Colouring Fun: ABC & 1 2 3. 2013. (ENG., Illus.). 32p. (J). (gr. -1-3). pap. 6.50 *(978-1-84135-997-7(1))* Award Pubns. Ltd. GBR. Dist: Parkwest Pubns., Inc.

Aylesworth, Jim. Naughty Little Monkeys. Cole, Henry, illus. 2006. (ENG.). 32p. (J). (gr. -1-2). reprint ed. 6.99 *(978-0-14-240562-8(0)*, Puffin Books) Penguin Young Readers Group.

Azarian, Mary. A Gardener's Alphabet. 2005. (ENG., Illus.). 32p. (J). (gr. -1-3). reprint ed. 7.99 *(978-0-618-54881-1(5))* Houghton Mifflin Harcourt Publishing Co.

Baby's First ABC Book. 2004. 10p. (J). bds. 4.99 *(978-1-85854-923-1(X))* Brimax Books Ltd. GBR. Dist: Byeway Bks.

Balsley, Tilda. ABC Passover Hunt. Poole, Helen, illus. 2016. (ENG.). 32p. (gr. -1-3). 17.99 *(978-1-4677-7843-5(5)*, 1401803, Kar-Ben Publishing) Lerner Publishing Group.

Bar-el, Dan. Alphabetter, 1 vol. Ross, Graham, illus. 2007. (ENG.). 32p. (J). (gr. -1-3). 8.95 *(978-1-55143-861-0(5))* Orca Bk. Pubs. USA.

Bataille, Marion. ABC3D. 2008. (ENG.). 36p. (J). (gr. -1 — 1). 24.99 *(978-1-59643-425-7(2)*, 9781596434257) Roaring Brook Pr.

Bates, John, et al. My First Buddhist Alphabet. 2004. (Illus.). 32p. (J). *(978-0-915678-79-2(9))* World Tribune Pr.

Belgrave, Joanne. Go, Go, Go! ABC: Text & Illustrations. 2009. (Illus.). *(978-0-9811981-0-1(4))* Nakita Publishing.

Bell-Myers, Darcy. The Animal Babies ABC Book of Princesses. 2013. (ENG.). 32p. (J). (gr. -1-3). pap. 3.99 *(978-0-486-49811-9(5))* Dover Pubns., Inc.

Bellefontaine, Kim. ABC of Canada. Gürth, Per-Henrik, illus. 2004. (ENG.). 32p. (J). (gr. -1-1). 7.95 *(978-1-55337-685-9(4))* Kids Can Pr., Ltd. CAN. Dist: Hachette Bk. Group.

Benzwie, Teresa. Alphabet Movers. Bender, Robert, illus. 30p. (J). (gr. -1-6). pap. *(978-1-930798-08-3(3))* National Dance Education Organization.

Beveridge, Dorothy. Belize Living Alphabet. Beveridge, Jim, photos by. 2013. (Illus.). 38p. pap. *(978-976-8142-51-1(0))* Producciones de la Hamaca.

Birnbaumi, Ricki Korey. Alphabet Jingles. 2005. (Illus.). 26p. (J). 15.95 *(978-0-9706094-2-7(6))* Effective Literacy Methods.

Bluedorn, Harvey. A Greek Alphabetarion: A Primer for Teaching How to Read, Write & Pronounce Ancient & Biblical Greek. 5th ed. 2004. (ENG & GEC.). 158p. pap. 25.00 incl. cd-rom *(978-0-9743616-9-7(0))* Trivium Pursuit.

Body, Wendy. Azio's ABC. 2006. (Qeb Fun with Phonics Ser.). (Illus.). 24p. (J). (gr. -1-3). lib. bdg. 15.95 *(978-1-59566-222-4(7))* QEB Publishing Inc.

Bonder, Dianna. An Accidental Alphabet. 2003. (Illus.). 32p. (J). *(978-1-55285-394-8(2))* Whitecap Bks., Ltd.

Book Company Staff. Alphabet Flash Cards. 2004. (Novelty Bks.). (Illus.). 16p. (J). (gr. 3-5). bds. *(978-1-74047-473-3(2))* Book Co. Publishing Pty, Ltd., The.

Brame, Kimberly. My Abc & Color Bible Book. 2009. 16p. pap. 12.24 *(978-1-4389-4174-5(9))* AuthorHouse.

Bruce, Lisa. Amazing Alphabets. Gliori, Debi, illus. 2003. 24p. (J). pap. 9.95 *(978-0-7112-2129-1(4))* Fleming, Randall.

Buckingham, Melinda. The Christian Alphabet for Children. 2012. 32p. pap. 19.99 *(978-1-4772-8500-8(8))* AuthorHouse.

Bumpers, Katrina. Alphabet Fun, Book 2: Coloring & Activity Book. 2008. (Illus.). 64p. (gr. -1-3). pap. 10.95 *(978-0-9797208-1-9(8))* K's Kids Publishing.

Byckowski, Mark. Animals Know Their Abc's a to Z So Can You! 2013. (ENG.). 30p. (J). pap. 24.95 *(978-1-4327-8841-4(8))* Outskirts Pr., Inc.

Calfee, Susan. St. Augustine a to Z: A Young Reader's Guide to America's Oldest City. Senn, Oscar, illus. 2016. (ENG.). (J). pap. 12.95 *(978-0-9895487-1-7(6))* Wordwhittler Bks.

Cameron, Eileen. G Is for Garden State: A New Jersey Alphabet. Ettlinger, Doris, illus. 2004. (Discover America State by State Ser.). (ENG.). 40p. (J). 17.95 *(978-1-58536-152-6(6))* Sleeping Bear Pr.

A Can of Gas: Consonant g: Level A, 6 vols. (Wright Skills Ser.). 12p. (gr. k-3). 17.95 *(978-0-322-03111-1(7))* Wright Group/McGraw-Hill.

Carson-Dellosa Publishing Staff. Alphabet, Grades PK - K: Dot-to-Dot. 2010. (Home Workbooks Ser.). (ENG.). 64p. (gr. -1-k). pap. 4.49 *(978-1-60418-759-5(X))* Carson-Dellosa Publishing, LLC.

—Alphabet, Grades PK - K: Sounds & Pictures. 2010. (Home Workbooks Ser.). (ENG.). 64p. (gr. -1-k). pap. 4.49 *(978-1-60418-758-8(1))* Carson-Dellosa Publishing, LLC.

Cave, Kathryn. W Is for World Big Book: A Round-the-World ABC. Oxfam Staff, illus. 2004. 32p. (J). pap. *(978-1-84507-026-7(7)*, Frances Lincoln) Quarto Publishing Group UK.

Chaley, Dimitry, illus. Marty the Martian Learns ABC. 2005. 24p. (J). bds. 6.99 *(978-0-9747387-1-0(9))* EKADOO Publishing Group.

Cheney, Lynne. A Is for Abigail: An Almanac of Amazing American Women. Glasser, Robin Preiss, illus. 2003. (ENG.). 48p. (J). (gr. 1-7). 19.99 *(978-0-689-85819-2(1)*, Simon & Schuster Bks. For Young Readers) Simon & Schuster Bks. For Young Readers.

Chorao, Kay. D Is for Drums: A Colonial Williamsburg A. B. C. 2004. (J). 16.95 *(978-0-87935-197-7(7))* Colonial Williamsburg Foundation.

Chronicle Books Staff. My Favorite Things Flash Cards. Siminovich, Lorena, illus. 2010. (ENG.). 26p. (J). (gr. -1 — 1). 14.95 *(978-0-8118-6799-3(4))* Chronicle Bks. LLC.

Chwast, Seymour & Moskof, Martin. Still Another Alphabet Book. 2014. (ENG., Illus.). 64p. (J). (gr. -1). pap. 9.99 *(978-0-486-49200-1(1))* Dover Pubns., Inc.

Clark, M. H. ABC Menagerie. 2012. (ENG., Illus.). (J). (gr. -1-3). 17.95 *(978-1-932319-54-5(9))* Compendium, Inc., Publishing & Communications.

Clark, Rosalynn. World of Alphabets. 2013. 48p. pap. 24.95 *(978-1-4626-9594-2(9))* America Star Bks.

Clarke, Jacqueline. Shoe Box Learning Centers: Alphabet: 30 Instant Centers with Reproducible Templates & Activities That Help Kids Practice Important Literacy Skills-Independently! 2012. (ENG.). 80p. (gr. k-1). pap. 12.99 *(978-0-545-46871-8(X)*, Teaching Resources) Scholastic, Inc.

Claussen-Schoolmeester, Wendy. Police Car Abc's. 2009. 32p. pap. 14.99 *(978-1-4389-6276-4(2))* AuthorHouse.

Clay, Kathryn & Vonne, Mira. Signing Around Town: Sign Language for Kids, 1 vol. Reid, Mick, illus. 2013. (Time to Sign Ser.). (ENG.). 32p. (gr. 1-2). 27.32 *(978-1-62065-053-0(3)*, Aplus Bks.) Capstone Press of Coughlan Cos.

—Signing at Home: Sign Language for Kids, 1 vol. Chewning, Randy, illus. 2013. (Time to Sign Ser.). (ENG.). 32p. (gr. 1-2). 27.32 *(978-1-62065-051-6(7)*, Aplus Bks.) Capstone Press of Coughlan Cos.

—Signing at School: Sign Language for Kids, 1 vol. Lucas, Margeaux, illus. 2013. (Time to Sign Ser.). (ENG.). 32p. (gr. 1-2). 27.32 *(978-1-62065-052-3(5)*, Aplus Bks.) Capstone Press of Coughlan Cos.

—Signing in My World: Sign Language for Kids, 1 vol. Griffo, Daniel, illus. 2013. (Time to Sign Ser.). (ENG.). 32p. (gr. 1-2). 27.32 *(978-1-62065-054-7(1)*, Aplus Bks.) Capstone Press of Coughlan Cos.

Coerr, Eleanor. S Is for Silver: A Nevada Alphabet. Park, Darcie, illus. 2004. (State Ser.). (ENG.). 40p. (J). 17.95 *(978-1-58536-117-5(8))* Sleeping Bear Pr.

Collard, Sneed B., III. B Is for Big Sky Country. Yardley, Joanna, illus. 2003. (Discover America State by State Ser.). (ENG.). 40p. (J). 17.95 *(978-1-58536-098-7(8))* Sleeping Bear Pr.

Concepcion, Patrick & Concepcion, Traci. Alphabetics: An Aesthetically Awesome Alliterated Alphabet Anthology. Ryski, Dawid, illus. 2014. (ENG.). 64p. (J). (gr. -1-2). 16.95 ***(978-3-89955-728-2(X))*** Die Gestalten Verlag DEU. Dist: Penguin Random Hse. LLC.

Cook, Bob. A Is for Anteater! Greenhalgh, Rachel, illus. 2011. 36p. pap. 24.95 *(978-1-4626-4035-5(4))* America Star Bks.

Country ABCs, 12 bks. Incl. Australia ABCs: A Book about the People & Places of Australia. Heiman, Sarah. Avila, Arturo, illus. 2002. 27.99 *(978-1-4048-0018-2(2))*; Egypt ABCs: A Book about the People & Places of Egypt. Heiman, Sarah. Ouren, Todd, illus. 2002. 27.99 *(978-1-4048-0019-9(0))*; Germany ABCs: A Book about the People & Places of Germany. Heiman, Sarah. Millet, Jason, illus. 2002. 27.99 *(978-1-4048-0020-5(4))*; Japan ABCs: A Book about the People & Places of Japan. Heiman, Sarah. Ouren, Todd, illus. 2002. 27.99 *(978-1-4048-0021-2(2))*; Kenya ABCs: A Book about the People & Places of Kenya. Heiman, Sarah. Avila, Arturo, illus. 2002. 27.99 *(978-1-4048-0022-9(0))*; Mexico ABCs: A Book about the People & Places of Mexico. Heiman, Sarah. Ouren, Todd, illus. 2002. 27.99 *(978-1-4048-0023-6(9))*; New Zealand ABCs: A Book about the People & Places of New Zealand. Schroeder, Holly. Wolf, Claudia, illus. 2004. 27.99 *(978-1-4048-0178-3(2)*, 1229507); United States ABCs: A Book about the People & Places of the United States. Schroeder, Holly. Yesh, Jeff, illus. 2004. 27.99 *(978-1-4048-0181-3(2)*, 1229509); (gr. k-5). (Country ABCs Ser.). (ENG.). 32p. 2004. 335.88 o.p. *(978-1-4048-0177-6(4))* Picture Window Bks.

Crane, Carol. F Is for First State: A Delaware Alphabet. Traynor, Elizabeth, illus. 2005. (State Ser.). (ENG.). 40p. (J). (gr. -1-3). 17.95 *(978-1-58536-154-0(2))* Sleeping Bear Pr.

—Y Is for Yellowhammer: An Alabama Alphabet. Burn, Ted, illus. 2003. (Discover America State by State Ser.). (ENG.). 40p. (J). 17.95 *(978-1-58536-118-2(6))* Sleeping Bear Pr.

Crawford, Laura. The Pilgrims' Thanksgiving from A to Z, 1 vol. Hierstein, Judith, illus. 2005. (ENG.). 32p. (J). (gr. k-3). per. 8.99 *(978-1-58980-238-4(1))* Pelican Publishing Co., Inc.

Crazy Miss Majsey's Alphabet Pets: Level N, 6 vols. 128p. (gr. 2-3). 49.95 *(978-0-7699-1018-5(1))* Shortland Pubns. (U. S. A.) Inc.

Cruz, Alexandra. Abc's Around the World. 2012. 32p. pap. 19.99 *(978-1-4772-7287-9(9))* AuthorHouse.

D'Angelo, Gus. New York ABCs. 2013. (ENG.). 30p. (J). (-k). bds. 9.95 *(978-0-615-70443-2(3))* DAngelo, Gus.

Das, Prodeepta. I Is for India. Das, Prodeepta, illus. rev. ed. 2016. (World Alphabets Ser.). (ENG., Illus.). 32p. (J). (gr. -1-2). pap. 9.99 *(978-1-84780-757-1(7)*, Frances Lincoln Children's Bks.) Quarto Publishing Group UK GBR. Dist: Hachette Bk. Group.

Davis, Caroline. First Abc. 2012. (ENG., Illus.). 10p. (J). (gr. k-1). bds. 7.99 *(978-1-84322-772-4(X))* Anness Publishing GBR. Dist: National Bk. Network.

Demarest, Chris L. Alpha Bravo Charlie: The Military Alphabet. Demarest, Chris L., illus. 2005. (ENG., Illus.). 40p. (J). (gr. 1-5). 18.99 *(978-0-689-86928-0(2)*, McElderry, Margaret K. Bks.) McElderry, Margaret K. Bks.

—Firefighters A to Z. Demarest, Chris L., illus. 2003. (ENG., Illus.). 32p. (J). (gr. -1-3). 7.99 *(978-0-689-85999-1(6)*, McElderry, Margaret K. Bks.) McElderry, Margaret K. Bks.

Dinosaur Alphabet Dinosaur Alphabet. bds. *(978-1-58394-099-0(5))* North Atlantic Bks.

Disney Staff, contrib. by. Write, Slide & Learn Disney Winnie the Pooh: ABC. 2011. (Disney Write, Slide & Learn Ser.). 12p. (J). bds. 9.99 *(978-1-74183-853-4(3))* Hinkler Bks. Pty, Ltd. AUS. Dist: Ideals Pubns.

Domeniconi, David. M Is for Majestic: A National Parks Alphabet. Carroll, Pam, illus. 2003. (ENG.). 40p. (J). (gr. k-6). 17.95 *(978-1-58536-138-0(0))* Sleeping Bear Pr.

Dompierre, Judith. Strange Passions. 2011. 32p. pap. 24.95 *(978-1-4512-6963-5(3))* America Star Bks.

Donahue, Peter. Build a Poster Coloring Book — ABC & 123. 2010. (Dover Build a Poster Coloring Book Ser.). (ENG., Illus.). 48p. (J). (gr. 3-5). pap. 4.99 *(978-0-486-47946-0(3))* Dover Pubns., Inc.

Dorling Kindersley Publishing Staff. Animal Alphabet. 2014. (ENG.). 14p. (J). (gr. -1-k). bds. 7.99 *(978-1-4654-1754-1(0)*, DK Children) Dorling Kindersley Publishing, Inc.

Dot-to-Dot Alphabet (Gr. K-1) 2003. (J). *(978-1-58232-067-0(5))* ECS Learning Systems, Inc.

Dragonwagon, Crescent. All the Awake Animals Are Almost Asleep. McPhail, David, illus. 2012. (ENG.). 40p. (J). (gr. -1-3). 16.99 *(978-0-316-07045-4(9))* Little Brown & Co.

A Dress for Fran: R-Family Blends: Level B, 6 vols. (Wright Skills Ser.). 16p. (gr. k-3). 17.95 *(978-0-322-01460-2(3))* Wright Group/McGraw-Hill.

Drews, Judith. The Zoo's Grand Opening: An ABC & Counting Book. 2014. (ENG., Illus.). 64p. 16.95 *(978-3-89955-714-5(X))* Die Gestalten Verlag DEU. Dist: Penguin Random Hse. LLC.

Duke, Cooper & Duke, Nell K. Animal Alphabet. 2016. (Illus.). 56p. (J). *(978-0-87659-711-8(8))* Gryphon Hse., Inc.

Dunn, James & Quarto Generic Staff. ABC London. Slater, Kate, illus. rev. ed. 2014. (ENG.). 40p. (J). (gr. k-3). pap. 8.99 *(978-1-84780-495-2(0)*, Frances Lincoln) Quarto Publishing Group UK GBR. Dist: Hachette Bk. Group.

Dwell Studio Staff & Forss, Sarah. Alphabet Wall Cards. 2011. (ENG., Illus.). 27p. (J). (gr. k-12). 24.99 *(978-1-60905-103-7(3))* Blue Apple Bks.

Eakle, Janice. 3 A's & 3 B's All the Way to Z, 1 vol. Eakle, Tayah, illus. 2009. 36p. pap. 24.95 *(978-1-60813-739-8(2))* America Star Bks.

Edwards, Pamela Duncan. O Is for Old Dominion: A Virginia Alphabet. Howell, Troy, illus. 2005. (State Ser.). (ENG.). 40p. (J). (gr. -1-3). 17.95 *(978-1-58536-161-8(5))* Sleeping Bear Pr.

Ehlert, Lois. Eating the Alphabet: Fruits & Vegetables from A to Z. alt. ed. 2006. (ENG., Illus.). 28p. (J). (gr. -1 — 1). bds. 11.99 *(978-0-15-205688-9(2))* Houghton Mifflin Harcourt Publishing Co.

Einhorn, Kama. Letter of the Week Flip Chart: Write-On/Wipe-Off Activity Pages That Introduce Each Letter from A to Z. 2010. (ENG.). 26p. (gr. -1-1). pap. 24.99 *(978-0-545-22417-8(9)*, Teaching Resources) Scholastic, Inc.

Elissa, Grodin. N Is for Nutmeg: A Connecticut Alphabet. Brookfield, Maureen, illus. 2003. (Discover America State by State Ser.). (ENG.). 40p. (J). 17.95 *(978-1-58536-124-3(0))* Sleeping Bear Pr.

Ernst, Lisa Campbell. The Turn-Around, Upside-Down Alphabet Book. Ernst, Lisa Campbell, illus. 2004. (ENG., Illus.). 32p. (J). (gr. -1-3). 17.99 *(978-0-689-85685-3(7)*, Simon & Schuster Bks. For Young Readers) Simon & Schuster Bks. For Young Readers.

Esparza, Thomas, Jr., prod. Esther's Playhouse, Disk A. 2004. (Illus.). (J). cd-rom *(978-1-879817-42-5(X)*, Children) Star Light Pr.

Eubank, Patti Reeder, tr. ABCs of Halloween. 2003. (ENG., Illus.). 30p. (J). (gr. -1-k). 8.95 *(978-0-8249-5467-3(X)*, Ideal Pubns.) Worthy Publishing.

Evers, Betty Jo. Alphabet: Instant Manipulatives That Teach Each Letter of the Alphabet. 2011. (ENG.). 48p. (gr. k-1). pap. 10.99 *(978-0-545-28077-8(X)*, Teaching Resources) Scholastic, Inc.

Falconer, Ian, illus. Olivia Alphabet Flash Cards. 2013. (ENG.). 26p. (J). (gr. -1 — 1). 14.99 *(978-1-4521-1179-7(0))* Chronicle Bks. LLC.

Fans: Consonant f: Level A, 6 vols. (Wright Skills Ser.). 12p. (gr. k-3). 17.95 *(978-0-322-03107-4(9))* Wright Group/McGraw-Hill.

Fay & Kay by the Bay: Long a Digraphs: Level B, 6 vols. (Wright Skills Ser.). 16p. (gr. k-3). 26.50 *(978-0-322-01478-7(6))* Wright Group/McGraw-Hill.

Feldman, Jean. Action Alphabet Lap Book. 2009. pap. 6.99 *(978-1-60689-096-7(4))* Creative Teaching Pr., Inc.

Felix, Monique. The Alphabet. Felix, Monique, illus. 2012. (Mouse Book Ser.). (ENG., Illus.). 32p. (J). (gr. -1-k). 12.99 *(978-1-56846-226-4(3)*, Creative Editions) Creative Co., The.

Ferris, Julie Alfriend. Badges, Egg Salad, & Green Jackets: The Masters a to Z. 2012. (Illus.). (J). 14.95 *(978-1-62086-149-3(6))* Mascot Bks., Inc.

Fine, Jil. Writing in Ancient India. 2003. (Writing in the Ancient World Ser.). (Illus.). 24p. (J). lib. bdg. 22.60 *(978-0-8239-6508-3(2)*, PowerKids Pr.) Rosen Publishing Group, Inc., The.

—Writing in Ancient Phoenicia. 2003. (Writing in the Ancient World Ser.). (Illus.). 24p. (J). lib. bdg. 22.60 *(978-0-8239-6507-6(4)*, PowerKids Pr.) Rosen Publishing Group, Inc., The.

Fisher, Henry. ABC Dreams. Fisher, Henry, illus. 2014. (ENG., Illus.). 12p. (J). (gr. -1-k). 7.99 *(978-1-78244-535-7(8))* Top That! Publishing PLC GBR. Dist: Independent Pubs. Group.

Fisher, Valorie. Everything I Need to Know Before I'm Five. Fisher, Valorie, illus. 2011. (ENG., Illus.). 40p. (J). (gr. k-k). 17.99 *(978-0-375-86865-8(8)*, Schwartz & Wade Bks.) Random Hse. Children's Bks.

Flash Kids Editors, ed. Alphabet Activities: Grade PreK-K (Flash Skills) 2010. (Flash Skills Ser.). (ENG.). 64p. (J). pap. 3.95 *(978-1-4114-3439-4(0)*, Spark Publishing Group) Sterling Publishing Co., Inc.

—Alphabet Puzzles & Games: Grade Pre-K-K (Flash Skills) 2010. (Flash Skills Ser.). (ENG.). 64p. (J). pap. 3.95 *(978-1-4114-3465-3(X)*, Spark Publishing Group) Sterling Publishing Co., Inc.

—Letter Dot-to-Dot. 2010. (Flash Skills Ser.). (ENG.). 64p. (J). pap. 3.95 *(978-1-4114-3462-2(5)*, Spark Publishing Group) Sterling Publishing Co., Inc.

Flor Ada, Alma. Gathering the Sun. (ENG & SPA.). (J). (gr. k-2). 12.95 net. *(978-1-58186-202-7(4)*, DSP8805) Del Sol Publishing.

Focus on Prephonics Kits: Focus on Prephonics Complete Kit. (Wright Skillstm Ser.). 397.50 *(978-0-322-01636-1(3))* Wright Group/McGraw-Hill.

Focus on Prephonics Kits: Focus on Prephonics Core Kit. (Wright Skillstm Ser.). 312.50 *(978-0-322-01637-8(1))* Wright Group/McGraw-Hill.

Focus on Prephonics Write-on Rhyme Charts Kit. (gr. k-3). 158.50 *(978-0-322-01638-5(X))* Wright Group/McGraw-Hill.

Forbush, Kyle & Forbush, Kyle. A Is for Alaska - an ABC Book. Forbush, Lisa, illus. 2004. (J). bds. 6.95 *(978-1-57833-287-8(7))* Todd Communications.

Franceschelli, Christopher. Alphablock. Peskimo, illus. 2013. (Alphablock Ser.). (ENG.). 104p. (J). (gr. -1 — 1). bds. 16.95 *(978-1-4197-0936-4(4)*, Abrams Appleseed) Abrams, Inc.

French, Karen. Dr. Frenchy's Pet Training from a to Z: A Fun, Colorful, Stimulating Alphabet Pattern Book. 2003. (J). per. 9.95 *(978-1-888125-07-8(1))* Publication Consultants.

Gág, Wanda. ABC Bunny. 2004. (Fesler-Lampert Minnesota Heritage Ser.). (Illus.). 40p. 14.95 *(978-0-8166-4416-2(0))* Univ. of Minnesota Pr.

Gagliano, Eugene. C Is for Cowboy: A Wyoming Alphabet. Guy, Susan, illus. 2003. (Discover America State by State Ser.). (ENG.). 40p. (J). 17.95 *(978-1-58536-097-0(X))* Sleeping Bear Pr.

Galloway, Fhiona, illus. ABC Alphabet Sticker Book. 2014. (My Little World Ser.). (ENG.). 14p. (J). (gr. -1). pap. 3.99 *(978-1-58925-445-9(7))* Tiger Tales.

Galvin, Laura Gates. Alphabet of African Animals. Denman, Michael et al, illus. 2008. (ENG.). 40p. (J). (gr. -1-2). 17.95 *(978-1-59249-854-3(X))* Soundprints.

Gaydos, Nora. Snack Attack, Level 2. Sams, B. B., illus. 2004. (NIR! Leveled Readers Ser.). (ENG.). 128p. (J). (gr. -1-3). 16.99 *(978-1-58476-264-5(0),* Now I'm Reading!) Random Hse. Children's Bks.

Golenbock, Peter. ABCs of Baseball. Andreasen, Dan, illus. 2012. (ENG.). 48p. (J). (gr. 1-3). 16.99 *(978-0-8037-3711-2(4),* Dial Bks) Penguin Young Readers Group.

Gregorich, Barbara, et al. Lowercase Alphabet. rev. ed. 2004. (ENG., Illus.). 64p. (J). pap., wbk. ed. 3.99 *(978-1-58947-345-4(0),* 02272) School Zone Publishing Co.

—Uppercase Alphabet. deluxe ed. 2004. (ENG., Illus.). 64p. (J). pap., wbk. ed. 3.99 *(978-1-58947-344-7(2),* 02221) School Zone Publishing Co.

Grodin, Elissa. D Is for Democracy: A Citizen's Alphabet. Juhasz, Victor, illus. 2004. (ENG.). 40p. (J). (gr. 1-4). 16.95 *(978-1-58536-234-9(4),* 202059) Sleeping Bear Pr.

Grose, Crystal. Eat & Drink Your ABCs. 2005. 57p. (J). pap. 15.64 *(978-1-4116-0098-0(3))* Lulu Pr., Inc.

Group/McGraw-Hill, Wright. The Wright Skills: Level A Sets - 1 Each of 40 Titles (includes Short Vowels) (Wright Skills Ser.). (gr. k-3). *(978-0-322-03873-8(1))* Wright Group/McGraw-Hill.

—The Wright Skills: Level A Sets - 6 Each of 40 Titles (includes Short Vowels) (Wright Skills Ser.). (gr. k-3). 730.50 *(978-0-322-03874-5(X))* Wright Group/McGraw-Hill.

—The Wright Skills: Level A Sets - Short Vowels only: 1 Each of 19 Titles. (Wright Skills Ser.). (gr. k-3). 56.95 *(978-0-322-06473-7(2))* Wright Group/McGraw-Hill.

—The Wright Skills: Level A Sets - Short Vowels only: 6 Each of 19 Titles. (Wright Skills Ser.). (gr. k-3). 122.95 *(978-0-322-06474-4(0))* Wright Group/McGraw-Hill.

—The Wright Skills: Level B Sets - 1 Each of 40 Titles (includes long Vowels) (Wright Skills Ser.). (gr. k-3). 143.95 *(978-0-322-03878-3(2))* Wright Group/McGraw-Hill.

—The Wright Skills: Level B Sets - 6 Each of 40 Titles (includes long Vowels) (gr. k-3). 860.50 *(978-0-322-03880-6(4))* Wright Group/McGraw-Hill.

Gunzi, Christiane. ABC. 2015. (ENG., Illus.). 34p. (J). 7.99 *(978-1-906572-17-4(8))* Award Pubns. Ltd. GBR. Dist: Parkwest Pubns., Inc.

Gutiérrez, Elisa & Owlkids Books Inc. Staff. Letter Lunch, 0 vols. 2014. (ENG., Illus.). 32p. (J). (gr. -1-2). 16.95 *(978-1-77147-000-1(3),* Owlkids) Owlkids Bks. Inc. CAN. Dist: Publishers Group West (PGW).

Hall, Eve D. Dontay's Alphabet Book of Color. Hale, J. P., illus. 2004. 46p. (J). per. 13.00 *(978-0-9758899-1-6(5))* Imagine Publishing.

Hall, Rebecca. A Is for Arches: A Utah Alphabet. Larson, Katherine & Langton, Bruce, illus. 2003. (Discover America State by State Ser.). (ENG.). 40p. (J). (gr. 1-3). 17.95 *(978-1-58536-096-3(1),* 201976) Sleeping Bear Pr.

Hands on Alphabet Skills (Gr. K-1) 2003. (J). *(978-1-58232-114-1(0))* ECS Learning Systems, Inc.

Harcourt School Publishers Staff. Alphabet Construction. 3rd ed. 2003. (Harcourt School Publishers Trophies Ser.). (ENG.). 32p. (gr. -1 — 1). pap. 62.95 *(978-0-15-340894-6(4))* Harcourt Schl. Pubs.

Hardy, Joshua O. The A B C Book on Protecting Yourself from Strangers: A-z. 2011. 76p. (gr. 2-4). pap. 30.00 *(978-1-4269-6987-4(2))* Trafford Publishing.

Harper, Marrisa and Normita. ABC Book. 2005. 58p. 8.19 *(978-1-4116-2660-7(5))* Lulu Pr., Inc.

Harris, Sue. ABC: A Busy Fingers Book. Chrystall, Claire, illus. 2003. 10p. (J). bds. 10.95 *(978-1-57145-936-7(7),* Silver Dolphin Bks.) Readerlink Distribution Services, LLC.

Harte, May. ABCs in My House. 2004. (Look-And-Learn Books). (Illus.). (J). lib. bdg. 8.95 *(978-1-4042-2824-5(1),* PowerKids Pr.) Rosen Publishing Group, Inc., The.

Hasselius, Michelle M., et al. Alphabet Connection: The ABCs of Prehistoric Beasts! Loram, James & Jevons, Chris, illus. 2016. (Alphabet Connection Ser.). (ENG.). 32p. (gr. k-1). pap. 31.80 *(978-1-5158-0403-1(8))* Picture Window Bks.

Hausmann, Gisela. Obvious Letters: The Alphabet Every Child Will Remember. 2nd ed. 2004. (Illus.). 60p. (J). cd-rom 18.00 *(978-0-9664217-1-2(X))* Educ-Easy Bks.

Heller, Lora. Sign Language ABC. 2014. (ENG., Illus.). 28p. (J). (— 1). bds. 6.95 *(978-1-4549-1145-6(X))* Sterling Publishing Co., Inc.

Herzog, Brad. H Is for Home Run: A Baseball Alphabet. Rose, Melanie, illus. 2004. (Sports Ser.). (ENG.). 40p. (J). (gr. -1-5). 16.95 *(978-1-58536-219-6(0))* Sleeping Bear Pr.

—Little Basketball. Bowles, Doug, illus. 2011. (Little Sports Ser.). (ENG.). 22p. 9.95 *(978-1-58536-181-6(X))* Sleeping Bear Pr.

Hidden Pictures Alphabet (Gr. K-1) 2003. (J). *(978-1-58232-062-5(4))* ECS Learning Systems, Inc.

Hoffman, Joan. ABC Dot-To-Dots. deluxe ed. 2004. (ENG., Illus.). 64p. (J). pap., wbk. ed. 3.99 *(978-1-58947-347-8(7),* 02274) School Zone Publishing Co.

Horcasitas, Barbara. My Pet Alphabet. 2012. 56p. pap. 31.99 *(978-1-4691-4984-4(2))* Xlibris Corp.

Hot Off the Press Staff. Alphabet Tiles. 2003. 24p. pap. 8.99 *(978-1-56231-841-3(1))* Hot off the Pr.

—Alphabet Tiles #2. 2003. 24p. pap. 8.99 *(978-1-56231-897-0(7))* Hot off the Pr.

Howell, Theresa. A Is for Airplane. Brooks, David, illus. 2003. (SPA, ENG & MUL.). 28p. (J). (gr. -1-k). bds. 6.95 *(978-0-87358-831-7(2))* Cooper Square Publishing Llc.

Hruby, Patrick. ABC Is for Circus (Chunky) 2010. (ENG.). 56p. (gr. -1). bds. 14.95 *(978-1-934429-61-7(9))* AMMO Bks., LLC.

I'm Learning My ABCs. 2004. (Flash Card + Music CD Learning Kits Ser.). 20p. 18.99 *(978-1-894677-60-8(9))* Kidzup Productions.

Ipcar, Dahlov. Dahlov Ipcar's Maine Alphabet. 2012. (ENG., Illus.). 24p. (J). bds. 10.95 *(978-1-934031-87-2(9),* e93823ef-f4cd-45da-bc3f-2f7da4f8dc56) Islandport Pr., Inc.

Is Nan In? Consonant n: Level A, 6 vols. (Wright Skills Ser.). 12p. (gr. k-3). 17.95 *(978-0-322-03106-7(0))* Wright Group/McGraw-Hill.

Ishikawa, Shiho. AlphaPets. 2010. (ENG., Illus.). 60p. (gr. k). spiral bd. 12.95 *(978-1-934734-44-5(6))* Seven Footer Pr.

Iversen, Sandra. Alphabet Book Ff. 2009. (Quick60 Alphabet Bks.). (ENG., Illus.). 12p. (J). pap. *(978-1-77540-005-9(0))* Iversen Publishing Ltd.

—Alphabet Book Kk. 2009. (Quick60 Alphabet Bks.). (ENG., Illus.). 12p. (J). pap. *(978-1-77540-010-3(7))* Iversen Publishing Ltd.

—Alphabet Book Ll. 2009. (Quick60 Alphabet Bks.). (ENG., Illus.). 12p. (J). pap. *(978-1-77540-011-0(5))* Iversen Publishing Ltd.

—Alphabet Book Mm. 2009. (ENG., Illus.). 12p. (J). pap. *(978-1-77540-012-7(3))* Iversen Publishing Ltd.

—Alphabet Book Nn. 2009. (Quick60 Alphabet Bks.). (ENG., Illus.). 12p. (J). pap. *(978-1-77540-013-4(1))* Iversen Publishing Ltd.

—Alphabet Book Oo. 2009. (Quick60 Alphabet Bks.). (ENG., Illus.). 12p. (J). pap. *(978-1-77540-014-1(X))* Iversen Publishing Ltd.

—Alphabet Book Pp. 2009. (Quick60 Alphabet Bks.). (ENG., Illus.). 12p. (J). pap. *(978-1-77540-015-8(8))* Iversen Publishing Ltd.

—Alphabet Book Zz. 2009. (Quick60 Alphabet Bks.). (ENG., Illus.). 12p. (J). pap. *(978-1-77540-025-7(5))* Iversen Publishing Ltd.

James, Helen Foster. E Is for Enchantment: A New Mexico Alphabet. Twinem, Neecy, illus. 2004. (State Ser.). (ENG.). 40p. (J). 17.95 *(978-1-58536-153-3(4),* 1235984) Sleeping Bear Pr.

James, Setria. Doodles: Alphabet Coloring Fun. 2010. 32p. (gr. -1 — 1). 14.49 *(978-1-4520-9085-6(8))* AuthorHouse.

Jamison, Kathy. Looking for the Alphabet. 2011. 16p. (gr. -1). pap. 9.36 *(978-1-4567-0145-1(2))* AuthorHouse.

Jocelyn, Marthe. ABC X 3: English - Español - Français. Slaughter, Tom, illus. 2005. (ENG, SPA & FRE.). 32p. (J). (gr. k-k). 15.99 *(978-0-88776-707-4(9),* Tundra Bks.) Tundra Bks. CAN. Dist: Penguin Random Hse. LLC.

Johnson, Annie P. & Johnson, Russell. My Florida Alphabet. Hume, John, illus. 2014. (ENG.). 64p. (J). pap. 15.95 *(978-1-56164-729-3(2))* Pineapple Pr., Inc.

Jones, Linda. Alphabet Anatomy: Meet the Capital Letters. Jones, Branson & Mikle, Toby, illus. 2012. 32p. pap. *(978-1-4602-0047-6(0))* FriesenPress.

Jones-Taylor, Audree V. All about Me & My Abc's. 2013. 30p. pap. 13.99 *(978-1-4525-6458-6(2))* Balboa Pr.

Jordan, Christopher. ABC. 2012. (My First NASCAR Racing Ser.). (ENG., Illus.). 30p. (J). (gr. k-k). bds. 7.95 *(978-1-77049-429-9(4),* Fenn-Tundra) Tundra Bks. CAN. Dist: Penguin Random Hse. LLC.

—Hockey ABC. 2011. (My First NHL Book Ser.). (ENG.). 30p. (J). (gr. k-k). bds. 6.95 *(978-1-77049-346-9(8),* Fenn-Tundra) Tundra Bks. CAN. Dist: Penguin Random Hse. LLC.

Kalman, Bobbi. The ABCs of Endangered Animals. 2014. 32p. pap. 9.00 *(978-1-61003-364-0(7))* Center for the Collaborative Classroom.

Kalman, Bobbie. The ABCs of Oceans. 2007. (ABCs of the Natural World Ser.). (ENG., Illus.). 32p. (J). (gr. 1-4). lib. bdg. *(978-0-7787-3412-3(9))* Crabtree Publishing Co.

Kane, Kristen. K Is for Keystone: A Pennsylvania Alphabet. Knorr, Laura, illus. 2003. (Discover America State by State Ser.). (ENG.). 40p. (J). 17.95 *(978-1-58536-104-5(6))* Sleeping Bear Pr.

Kelley, Gerald. M Is for Monster: A Fantastic Creatures Alphabet. 2014. (ENG., Illus.). 32p. (J). (gr. 2-5). 16.99 *(978-1-58536-818-1(0),* 203669) Sleeping Bear Pr.

Kenney, Sean. Amazing ABC: An Alphabet Book of Lego Creations. Kenney, Sean, illus. 2012. (ENG., Illus.). 30p. (J). (gr. -1-k). bds. 7.99 *(978-0-8050-9464-0(4),* 9780805094640, Holt, Henry & Co. Bks. For Young Readers) Holt, Henry & Co.

Kent, Lorna, illus. Baby's First ABC Book. 2004. 12p. (J). bds. 7.99 *(978-1-85854-659-9(1))* Brimax Books Ltd. GBR. Dist: Byeway Bks.

Kids Can Press Staff & Shannon, Rosemarie. Alphabet Mazes. 2003. (Kids Can Learn with Franklin Ser.). (ENG., Illus.). 32p. (J). (gr. -1-1). pap. 3.95 *(978-1-55337-592-0(0))* Kids Can Pr., Ltd. CAN. Dist: Hachette Bk. Group.

Kidzup Productions Staff. ABC Theater. 2003. (Interactive Learning Kits Ser.). (Illus.). 24p. (J). (gr. k-2). 13.99 incl. audio *(978-1-894281-00-3(4))* Kidzup Productions.

Kim, Maria. JookaPooka & Friends ABC. 2010. 60p. pap. 27.00 *(978-0-557-46635-1(0))* Lulu Pr., Inc.

The Kitty: Long Vowels e, y, CVCe & Final y Patterns: Level B, 6 vols. (Wright Skills Ser.). 16p. (gr. k-3). 17.95 *(978-0-322-03130-2(3))* Wright Group/McGraw-Hill.

Klein, Fredrick C. For the Love of the Yankees: An A-to-Z Primer for Yankees Fans of All Ages. Anderson, Mark, illus. 2003. 48p. (J). 19.95 *(978-1-57243-579-7(8))* Triumph Bks.

Klutz Editors, creator. Magnetic A to Z. 2005. (Chicken Socks Ser.). (ENG., Illus.). 12p. (J). (gr. -1-3). 12.95 *(978-1-59174-359-0(1))* Klutz.

Kratky, Lada Josefa. Alfarrimas: Guía Del Maestro. 2005. (Alfarrimas Ser.). (SPA & ENG., Illus.). 8p. (C). pap. 36.95 *(978-0-7362-2659-2(1))* CENGAGE Learning.

Lane, Larry. Alphabet Soup. 2012. 48p. pap. 21.99 *(978-1-4772-5277-2(0))* AuthorHouse.

Langley, Judy. God's World & Me from A to Z. Coker, Carla, illus. 2004. 32p. (gr. -1). 8.99 *(978-1-56309-367-8(7))* New Hope Pubs.

Laurence, Jo. How to Sparkle at Alphabet Skills. 2004. (Illus.). 48p. pap. 30.00 *(978-1-897675-17-5(8))* Brilliant Pubns. GBR. Dist: Parkwest Pubns., Inc.

Law, Felicia. Alphabet. Knight, Paula, illus. 2015. (Patchwork Ser.). (ENG.). 24p. (J). (gr. k-3). lib. bdg. 22.60 *(978-1-59953-715-3(X))* Norwood Hse. Pr.

LD COACH. TEH Learns to Read: Beginning Words & Written Characters, Volume One. 2004. (Illus.). 40p. (J). 34.95 *(978-0-9745938-1-4(8))* LD Coach, LLC.

Learning Made Easy LLC. Learn to Write the Alphabet. 2012. (ENG.). (J). pap. 13.95 *(978-1-4675-4876-2(6))* Independent Pub.

Lennon, Pat. A Is for Ark. 2009. 32p. pap. 21.99 *(978-1-4415-6262-3(1))* Xlibris Corp.

Leonard, Barry, ed. & illus. Alphabet Connections: English-Spanish: 26 Picture Cards. Leonard, Barry, illus. 2004. 26p. (J). (gr. k-4). reprint ed. *(978-0-7567-7825-5(5))* DIANE Publishing Co.

Letter Clusters Big Book, 6 vols. 32p. (gr. k-3). 38.50 *(978-0-7802-7194-4(7))* Wright Group/McGraw-Hill.

Lewis, Jan, illus. ABC: Turn the Wheels; Find the Words. 2016. (ENG.). 10p. bds. 14.99 *(978-1-86147-712-5(0),* Armadillo) Anness Publishing GBR. Dist: National Bk. Network.

—My First ABC. 2014. (ENG.). 24p. (J). (gr. -1-k). bds. 6.99 *(978-1-86147-372-1(9),* Armadillo) Anness Publishing GBR. Dist: National Bk. Network.

—My First ABC: Learn the Alphabet with 300 Words & Pictures. 2016. (ENG.). 48p. (J). (gr. -1-12). pap. 9.99 *(978-1-86147-728-6(7),* Armadillo) Anness Publishing GBR. Dist: National Bk. Network.

Litchfield, Jo, illus. First Picture Abc. 2005. (First Picture Board Books Ser.). 16p. (J). 11.95 *(978-0-7945-0907-1(X),* Usborne) EDC Publishing.

little bee books, little bee & Blake, Carly. Baby's First ABC. Max and Sid Staff, illus. 2015. (Baby's First Ser.). (ENG.). 12p. (J). (gr. -1 — 1). bds. 4.99 *(978-1-4998-0052-4(5))* Little Bee Books Inc.

Litton, Jonathan. ABC Alphabet Fun. 2014. (My First Touch & Feel Bks.). (ENG., Illus.). 24p. (J). bds. 12.99 *(978-1-58925-592-0(5))* Tiger Tales.

Lluch, Alex A. Animal Alphabet: Slide & Seek the ABCs. Defenbaugh, David, illus. 2013. (ENG.). 13p. (J). (-k). bds. 12.99 *(978-1-61351-041-4(1))* WS Publishing.

—Let's Leap Ahead Alphabet. 2012. (ENG.). 80p. (J). (gr. -1). spiral bd. 9.95 *(978-1-936061-59-4(7))* WS Publishing.

Lobel, Anita. Animal Antics: A to Z. Lobel, Anita, illus. 2005. (Illus.). 32p. (J). lib. bdg. 16.89 *(978-0-06-051815-8(4))* HarperCollins Pubs.

Long Vowels & Inflections Big Book: Level C, set. (Sing-along Songs Ser.). (gr. -1-2). 48.46 incl. audio compact disk *(978-0-7362-0421-7(0))* CENGAGE Learning.

Long Vowels, R-Controlled Vowels, Inflections Big Book: Level E, set. (Sing-along Songs Ser.). (gr. -1-2). 48.46 incl. audio compact disk *(978-0-7362-0635-8(3))* CENGAGE Learning.

Luebs Shepherd, Rajean. C Is for Cornhusker: A Nebraska Alphabet. Appleoff, Sandy, illus. 2004. (State Ser.). (ENG.). 40p. (J). 17.95 *(978-1-58536-147-2(X))* Sleeping Bear Pr.

Magsamen, Sandra. I Love Minnesota. 2016. (ENG.). 40p. (J). (-5). 12.99 *(978-1-4926-2838-5(7),* Sourcebooks Jabberwocky) Sourcebooks, Inc.

Major, Sarah. Alphabet Tales. Major, Sarah, illus. 2010. (Illus.). 139p. (J). pap. 19.95 *(978-0-9829873-3-9(1))* Child1st Pubns., LLC.

Make Believe Ideas, creator. Touch & Learn ABC. 2007. (Illus.). (gr. -1). per. *(978-1-84610-506-7(4))* Make Believe Ideas.

Mangrum, Kaylea J. How to Draw Step-By-Step Using the Alphabet. Mangrum, Kaylea J., illus. 2013. (Illus.). 38p. pap. 12.49 *(978-0-9883009-4-1(X))* Mangrum, Kaylea J.

Martin, Susi. Animal ABC. 2014. (ENG., Illus.). 32p. (J). (gr. -1-2). 9.95 *(978-1-77085-456-7(8),* 9781770854567) Firefly Bks., Ltd.

Martins, Isabel Minhós & Kono, Yara. Abzzzz... A Bedtime Alphabet. 2016. (ENG., Illus.). 28p. (J). (gr. -1-2). 14.95 *(978-0-500-65077-6(2),* 565077) Thames & Hudson.

Marzollo, Jean. I Spy Letters. 2012. (I Spy — Scholastic Ser.). lib. bdg. 13.55 *(978-0-606-23970-7(7),* Turtleback) Turtleback Bks.

McKay, Sindy. Can You Find? An ABC Book. Loveridge, Matt, illus. 2016. 41p. (J). ***(978-1-4844-8052-6(X))*** Treasure Bay, Inc.

McKay, Sindy. Can You Find? (We Both Read - Level Pk-K) An ABC Book. 2015. (We Both Read - Level Pk -K Ser.). (ENG., Illus.). 41p. (J). 9.95 *(978-1-60115-279-4(5))* Treasure Bay, Inc.

McLimans, David. Gone Wild. McLimans, David, illus. 2016. (ENG., Illus.). 32p. (J). bds. 7.99 *(978-1-61963-954-6(8),* 9781619639546, Bloomsbury USA Childrens) Bloomsbury Publishing USA.

Medcalf, Carol & Hempstock, Becky. Letts Monster Skills Practice e Alphabet Age 3-5. 2014. (Letts Monster Practice Ser.). (ENG.). 32p. (J). (gr. -1-k). pap. 6.99 *(978-1-84419-768-2(9))* HarperCollins Pubs. Ltd. GBR. Dist: Independent Pubs. Group.

Mein Erstes Lexikon A-Z. 3rd ed. 2005. (GER., Illus.). 104p. (J). (gr. -1-3). pap. 27.75 *(978-3-411-05453-4(0))* Langenscheidt Publishing Group.

Melvin E., Meggan & Wiliams, Cornelius. Learn to Read with M. C. Ant Tanna. 2009. (J). pap. 50.00 *(978-1-61623-533-8(0));* pap. 50.00 *(978-1-61623-532-1(2))* Independent Pub.

Menendez, Shirley. B Is for Blue Crab: A Maryland Alphabet. Stutzman, Laura, illus. 2004. (Discover America State by State Ser.). (ENG.). 40p. (J). (gr. 1-3). 17.95 *(978-1-58536-160-1(7),* 202020) Sleeping Bear Pr.

Meyers, Nancy. Doodles ABC: Alphabet Fun with Dots to Join & Doodles to Do. Meyers, Nancy, illus. 2012. (Doodles Ser.). (ENG., Illus.). 64p. (J). (gr. -1-1). pap. 7.95 *(978-1-61608-666-4(1),* 608666, Sky Pony Pr.) Skyhorse Publishing Co., Inc.

Midda, Sara. How to Build an A. 2008. (ENG., Illus.). 56p. (J). (gr. -1-3). 19.95 *(978-1-57965-378-1(2),* 85378) Artisan.

Morice, Dave. A Visit from St. Alphabet. Morice, Dave, illus. 2005. (ENG., Illus.). 24p. (Orig.). (J). (gr. -1-3). 9.95 *(978-1-56689-179-0(5))* Coffee Hse. Pr.

Munari, Bruno. Bruno Munari's ABC: Semplice Lezione Di Inglese. 2003. (J). 60.00 *(978-0-8118-4119-1(7))* Chronicle Bks. LLC.

My Abc. 32p. (gr. k-3). 38.50 *(978-0-7802-4191-6(6))* Wright Group/McGraw-Hill.

My Abc Student Book: 6 Each of 1 Student Book, 6 vols. 32p. (gr. k-3). 31.95 *(978-0-7802-9032-7(1))* Wright Group/McGraw-Hill.

Nagara, Innosanto. A de Activista. 2014. (SPA.). (J). *(978-1-60980-570-8(4))* Seven Stories Pr.

— A Is for Activist. Nagara, Innosanto, illus. 2012. (ENG., Illus.). 28p. bds. 15.00 *(978-0-9883448-9-1(0))* Kupu Kupu Pr.

No, not Yet: Consonants k, v, y; Short Vowel e word families: Level A, 6 vols. (Wright Skills Ser.). 12p. (gr. k-3). 17.95 *(978-0-322-01455-8(7))* Wright Group/McGraw-Hill.

Novick, Mary. Double Delight Pop up Alphabet. Harlin, Sybel, illus. 2009. (ENG.). 20p. (J). (gr. -1 — 1). 12.99 *(978-1-921272-61-5(9))* Little Hare Bks. AUS. Dist: Independent Pubs. Group.

Novick, Mary & Miesen, Christina. Alphabet. 2006. (Illus.). 16p. *(978-1-921049-60-6(X))* Little Hare Bks. AUS. Dist: HarperCollins Pubs. Australia.

O'Kane, George & Weikert, Dana, illus. Baldwin's Colorful Campus Tour - Boston College A-Z. 2004. (J). 9.99 *(978-1-933069-00-5(7))* Odd Duck Ink, Inc.

Open Court Staff. Breaking Code Cursive Alphabet. (J). pap. *(978-0-87548-599-7(5),* 1210) Open Court Publishing Co.

Page, Stefan. ABC Farmers' Market Flash Cards. 2014. (ENG., Illus.). 26p. (J). (gr. -1-17). 14.99 *(978-1-4521-1835-2(3))* Chronicle Bks. LLC.

Pallotta, Jerry. The Beetle Alphabet Book. Biedrzycki, David, illus. 2004. (ENG.). 32p. (J). (gr. -1-3). 17.95 *(978-1-57091-551-2(2))* Charlesbridge Publishing, Inc.

—The Beetle Alphabet Book. Biedrzycki, David, tr. Biedrzycki, David, illus. 2004. (ENG.). 32p. (J). (gr. -1-3). pap. 7.95 *(978-1-57091-552-9(0))* Charlesbridge Publishing, Inc.

—F Is for Fenway Park: America's Oldest Major League Ballpark. 2012. (Discover the World Ser.). (ENG., Illus.). 40p. (YA). (gr. 2-5). 16.95 *(978-1-58536-788-7(5))* Sleeping Bear Pr.

Paré, Roger. L' Alphabet. (Livres-jeux Ser.). (FRE., Illus.). (J). (gr. -1). 2004. 12p. pap. *(978-2-89021-655-6(1))* 2003. 24p. pap. *(978-2-89021-224-4(6))* Diffusion du livre Mirabel (DLM).

Parmley, Dave & Ruffing, Eric. Alternative ABCs. 2010. (Illus.). 58p. bds. 14.95 *(978-1-934429-39-6(2))* AMMO Bks., LLC.

Phillips, Vivian A. The Biblical Alphabets Book. Date not set. (Illus.). 32p. (Orig.). (J). pap. *(978-1-888413-01-4(8))* Seasoning Quilting (Arts & Crafts).

Pierce, Patricia A. H Is for Hawkeye: An Iowa Alphabet. Langton, Bruce, tr. Langton, Bruce, illus. 2003. (Discover America State by State Ser.). (ENG.). 40p. (J). 17.95 *(978-1-58536-114-4(3))* Sleeping Bear Pr.

Poelman, Heidi. A Is for Abinadi: An Alphabet Book of Scripture Heroes. 2014. pap. 14.99 *(978-1-4621-1369-9(9),* Horizon Pubs.) Cedar Fort, Inc./CFI Distribution.

Preece, Bronwyn. Gulf Islands Alphabet. Walton, Alex, illus. 2016. (ENG.). 56p. (J). (gr. k-3). 8.99 *(978-1-77229-011-0(4))* Simply Read Bks. CAN. Dist: Ingram Publisher Services.

Priddy, Roger. ABC: Easy Learning Fun, for the Very Young. rev. ed. 2004. (Play & Learn Ser.). (ENG., Illus.). 12p. (J). (gr. -1-k). 8.95 *(978-0-312-49395-0(9),* Priddy Bks.) St. Martin's Pr.

—Alphaprints: ABC. 2013. (Alphaprints Ser.). (ENG.). 28p. (J). (gr. -1 — 1). bds. 9.99 *(978-0-312-51646-8(0),* 9780312516468, Priddy Bks.) St. Martin's Pr.

—Happy Baby ABC. rev. ed. 2003. (Happy Baby Ser.). (ENG., Illus.). 28p. (J). (gr. -1 — 1). bds. 6.99 *(978-0-312-49169-7(7),* 9780312491697, Priddy Bks.) St. Martin's Pr.

—Mi Libro Pequeño de Palabras. 2005. (My Little Bks.). (ENG & SPA., Illus.). 28p. (J). (gr. -1-k). bds. 9.95 *(978-0-312-49462-9(9),* 9780312494629, Priddy Bks.) St. Martin's Pr.

—Play & Learn ABC. 2013. (Play & Learn Ser.). (ENG.). 10p. (J). (gr. -1-k). bds. 12.99 *(978-0-312-51638-3(X),* 9780312516383, Priddy Bks.) St. Martin's Pr.

—Slide & Surprise Alphabet. 2010. (ENG., Illus.). 16p. (J). (gr. -1-k). bds. 6.99 *(978-0-312-50948-4(0),* 9780312509484, Priddy Bks.) St. Martin's Pr.

Prieto, Anita C. P Is for Pelican: A Louisiana Alphabet. Knorr, Laura, illus. 2004. (Discover America State by State Ser.). (ENG.). 40p. (J). 17.95 *(978-1-58536-137-3(2))* Sleeping Bear Pr.

Publications International Ltd. Staff, ed. Alphabet. 2011. 12p. (J). spiral bd. *(978-1-4508-1448-5(4))* Publications International, Ltd.

—Alphabet Wipe off Learning Board. 2011. 1p. (J). spiral bd. *(978-1-4508-1430-0(1))* Publications International, Ltd.

—My Alphabet Book. 2011. 32p. (J). bds. 5.98 *(978-1-4508-1020-3(9))* Publications International, Ltd.

Random House. Elmo's ABC Song (Sesame Street) 2015. (Pictureback(R) Ser.). (ENG., Illus.). 24p. (J). (gr. -1-2). pap. 4.99 *(978-0-553-53672-0(9),* Random Hse. Bks. for Young Readers) Random Hse. Children's Bks.

Raschka, Chris & Radunsky, Vladimir. Alphabetabum: An Album of Rare Photographs & Medium Verses. 2014. (ENG., Illus.). 80p. (J). (gr. -1-3). 19.95 *(978-1-59017-817-1(3),* NYR Children's Collection) New York Review of Bks., Inc., The.

Reading Rods Alphabet Books. 2003. (J). pap. 24.95 *(978-1-56911-120-8(0))* Learning Resources, Inc.

Really Big Coloring Books Staff. ABC 123 Learn My Letters & Numbers. l.t. ed. 2003. Orig. Title: 123-ABC Learn My Letters & Numbers. (Illus.). 321p. (J). *(978-0-9729753-1-5(4))* Really Big Coloring Bks., Inc.

Rhodes, Immacula A. Alphabet Trees: 50+ Practice Pages That Help Kids Master the Letters a to Z & Build a Foundation for Reading Success. 2013. (ENG.). 64p. (gr. -1-1). pap. 11.99 *(978-0-545-53832-9(7),* Teaching Resources) Scholastic, Inc.

Rhodes, Immacula A. Write-N-Seek: Alphabet: Motivating Practice Pages to Help Kids Master Their ABCs. 2017. (Write-N-Seek: Ser.). (ENG.). 64p. (gr. -1-2). pap. 10.99 ***(978-1-338-18018-3(5))*** Scholastic, Inc.

Riehle, Mary Ann McCabe. M Is for Mountain State: A West Virginia Alphabet. Bryant, Laura J., illus. 2004. (State Ser.). (ENG.). 40p. (J). 17.95 *(978-1-58536-151-9(8))* Sleeping Bear Pr.

Roberson, Bobby. Lillie Boy Willie Thompson. 2006. 178p. pap. 8.57 *(978-1-4116-2271-5(5))* Lulu Pr., Inc.

Rosas, Heather. ABC What Will I Be? Rosas, Heather, illus. 2008. (ENG., Illus.). 16p. (J). 12.95 *(978-1-58117-681-0(3),* Intervisual/Piggy Toes) Bendon, Inc.

Ross, Richhi. After the Alphabet. 2012. 36p. pap. 14.62 *(978-1-4251-8669-2(6))* Trafford Publishing.

Rossi, Renzo. The Revolution of the Alphabet. Baldanzi, Alessandro, illus. 2008. (Reading & Writing Ser.). 32p. (gr. 4-7). 28.50 *(978-0-7614-4320-9(7),* Benchmark Bks.) Marshall Cavendish Corp.

Rush, Elizabeth. H Is for Hanoi. Nguyen, Nghia Cuong, illus. 2013. (Alphabetical World Ser.). (ENG & VIE.). 48p. (gr. k-4). 12.95 *(978-1-934159-42-2(5))* ThingsAsian Pr.

Ruurs, Margriet. A Mountain Alphabet. Kiss, Andrew, illus. 2009. (ABC Our Country Ser.). (ENG.). 32p. (J). (gr. 1-4).

pap. 7.95 *(978-0-88776-940-5(3),* Tundra Bks.) Tundra Bks. CAN. Dist: Penguin Random Hse. LLC.

Saffer, Barbara. ABC Science Riddles. Johnson, Jennifer, illus. 2004. (ABC Riddles Ser.). 32p. (J). (gr. -1-3). 13.95 *(978-0-939217-55-7(4))* Peel Productions, Inc.

Salas, Laura Purdie. S Is for Score! A Sports Alphabet, 1 vol. 2010. (Alphabet Fun Ser.). (ENG.). 32p. (gr. 1-2). lib. bdg. 27.32 *(978-1-4296-3915-6(6),* Aplus Bks.) Capstone Press of Coughlan Cos.

Salzmann, Mary Elizabeth. Angling to Zorbing: Sports from A to Z, 1 vol. 2007. (Let's See A to Z Ser.). (ENG., Illus.). 32p. (gr. 3-7). 27.07 *(978-1-59928-881-9(8),* Super SandCastle) ABDO Publishing Co.

Santillo, LuAnn. A Sights & Sounds - Level, 36 vols. Santillo, LuAnn, ed. 2003. (Half-Pint Kids Readers Ser.). (Illus.). 7p. (J). (gr. -1-1). pap. 39.95 *(978-1-59256-126-1(8))* Half-Pint Kids, Inc.

Scarry, Richard. Richard Scarry's ABC Word Book. 2011. (ENG., Illus.). 60p. (J). (gr. -1-2). 12.95 *(978-1-4027-7221-4(1))* Sterling Publishing Co., Inc.

Schemenauer, Patty Ann. Alphabet Fun at the Zoo. 2011. 32p. 14.39 *(978-1-4567-0146-8(0))* AuthorHouse.

Scholastic, Inc. Staff, contrib. by. ABC. 2012. (Rookie Toddler Ser.). (ENG., Illus.). 12p. (J). (gr. -1 — 1). bds. 6.95 *(978-0-531-20850-2(8),* Children's Pr.) Scholastic Library Publishing.

Scholastic Teaching Resources Staff. Kindergarten Basic Skills: Alphabet & Fine-Motor Skills. 2012. (Kindergarten Basic Skills Ser.). (ENG.). 48p. pap. 6.99 *(978-0-545-42964-1(1))* Teacher's Friend Pubns., Inc.

School Zone Interactive Staff. Flash Action Software Go Fish / Old Maid. 2005. (ENG.). (J). cd-rom 12.99 *(978-1-58947-830-5(4))* School Zone Publishing Co.

School Zone Publishing Company Staff. Alphabet Fun! Hours of Reusable Fun! rev. ed. 2005. (ENG.). 26p. (J). (gr. k-1). pap. 3.99 *(978-1-58947-781-0(2))* School Zone Publishing Co.

—Bilingual ABC Dot to Dots. 2007. (ENG.). 64p. (J). pap. 3.99 *(978-1-58947-972-2(6))* School Zone Publishing Co.

—Lowercase Alphabet. 2007. (ENG.). 64p. (J). pap., wbk. ed. 2.69 *(978-1-58947-970-8(X))* School Zone Publishing Co.

School Zone Staff. Alphabet Match. rev. ed. 2005. (ENG.). 56p. (J). 2.99 *(978-1-58947-477-2(5))* School Zone Publishing Co.

—Bilingual Alphabet. 2004. (ENG.). 56p. (J). 2.99 *(978-1-58947-981-4(5))* School Zone Publishing Co.

—Go Fish. rev. ed. 2004. (ENG.). 56p. (J). 2.79 *(978-1-58947-991-3(2))* School Zone Publishing Co.

Schroeder, Holly. New Zealand ABCs: A Book about the People & Places of New Zealand. Wolf, Claudia, illus. 2004. (Country ABCs Ser.). (ENG.). 32p. (gr. k-5). 27.99 *(978-1-4048-0178-3(2),* 1229507) Picture Window Bks.

—The United States ABCs: A Book about the People & Places of the United States. Yesh, Jeff, illus. 2004. (Country ABCs Ser.). (ENG.). 32p. (gr. k-5). 27.99 *(978-1-4048-0181-3(2),* 1229509) Picture Window Bks.

Schumacher, Bev. Letters Aa to Zz. 2005. 8p. (J). bds. 4.95 net. *(978-0-9741549-9-2(7))* Learning Props.

Schwartz, David & Schwartz, David M. Q Is for Quark: A Science Alphabet Book. Doner, Kim, illus. 2009. (ENG.). 64p. (J). (gr. 3-7). pap. 9.99 *(978-1-58246-303-2(4),* Tricycle Pr.) Random Hse. Children's Bks.

Scillian, Devin. P Is for Passport: A World Alphabet. Rose, Melanie, illus. 2003. (Discover the World Ser.). (ENG.). 48p. (J). (gr. 1-3). 19.95 *(978-1-58536-157-1(7),* 202017) Sleeping Bear Pr.

—S Is for Sooner: An Oklahoma Alphabet. Doner, Kim & Radzinski, Kandy, illus. 2003. (Discover America State by State Ser.). (ENG.). 40p. (J). 17.95 *(978-1-58536-062-8(7))* Sleeping Bear Pr.

Scott, Donald Iain. Letters of the Alphabet - Celtic Art Designs. 2012. 162p. pap. 28.03 *(978-1-4797-6313-9(6))* Xlibris Corp.

Scott, Karen. Endangered Species & Friends in the U. S. A. Seamans, Amanda, illus. unabr. ed. Date not set. (J). (gr. -1-6). 16.95 *(978-1-889667-00-3(5))* Second Ark Pubns.

Scott, Linda. How to Be the Best Bubblewriter in the World Ever! 2011. (ENG., Illus.). 160p. (J). (gr. 3-7). pap. 14.95 *(978-1-85669-761-3(4))* King, Laurence Publishing GBR. Dist: Hachette Bk. Group.

Sevaly, Karen, ed. Vowel Puzzles: 20 Activities. 2006. (Scholastic Hands-on Learning Ser.). (ENG., Illus.). (gr. k-2). 12.99 *(978-0-439-82389-0(7),* Teaching Resources) Scholastic, Inc.

Severe, Doreese. ABC's See What They Say. alt. ed. 2006. (J). spiral bd. *(978-1-890566-06-7(3))* See abc's LC.

—Beginning See ABC'S Package. 2006. (J). per. *(978-1-890566-00-5(4))* See abc's LC.

Seymour, Gloria, told to. ABC Sing-along. 2004. (J). pap. 8.00 *(978-0-8059-6473-8(8))* Dorrance Publishing Co., Inc.

Shaw-Russell, Susan. Animal ABC. 2011. (Dover Sticker Bks.). (ENG., Illus.). 4p. (J). (gr. 1-5). 7.99 *(978-0-486-48396-2(7))* Dover Pubns., Inc.

Sheldon, Ken. The Alphabet: Easy Learning Songs & Instant Activities That Teach Each Letter of the Alphabet. 2006. (Sing along & Learn Ser.). (ENG., Illus.). 32p. 9.99 *(978-0-439-80497-4(3),* Teaching Resources) Scholastic, Inc.

Short Vowels Set: Level B. (Sing-along Songs Ser.). (gr. -1-2). 48.46 incl. audio compact disk *(978-0-7362-0420-0(2))* CENGAGE Learning.

Shoulders, Debbie & Shoulders, Michael. T Is for Titanic: A Titanic Alphabet. van Frankenhuyzen, Gijsbert, illus. 2011. (ENG.). 32p. (gr. k-5). 17.95 *(978-1-58536-176-2(3))* Sleeping Bear Pr.

Shoulders, Michael. N Is for Natural State: An Arkansas Alphabet. Anderson, Rick, illus. 2003. (Discover America State by State Ser.). (ENG.). 40p. (J). (gr. k-6). 17.95 *(978-1-58536-067-3(8))* Sleeping Bear Pr.

Singh, Lee. ABC & Do. Wall, Karen, illus. 2013. (ENG.). 24p. (J). (gr. -1-k). 19.99 *(978-1-4052-6532-4(9))* Egmont Bks., Ltd. GBR. Dist: Independent Pubs. Group.

Smart Kidz, creator. The ABC's of How I Love You: You're My Alphabet of Love! 2013. (Parent Love Letters Ser.). (ENG., Illus.). 12p. (gr. -1). bds. 12.99 *(978-1-891100-30-7(0),* Smart Kids) Penton Overseas, Inc.

Smith, Lynn & Faust Kalscheur, Jann. ABC's Naturally: A Child's Guide to the Alphabet Through Nature. Faust Kalscheur, Jann, photos by. 2003. (Illus.). (J). 16.95 *(978-1-931599-27-6(0),* Trails Bks.) Bower Hse.

Smith, Marie & Smith, Roland. W Is for Waves: An Ocean Alphabet. Megahan, John & Rose, Melanie, illus. 2008. (ENG.). 32p. (J). (gr. k-6). 17.95 *(978-1-58536-254-7(9))* Sleeping Bear Pr.

Smith, Roland & Smith, Marie. E Is for Evergreen: A Washington State Alphabet. Holt Ayriss, Linda, illus. 2004. (State Ser.). (ENG.). 40p. (J). 17.95 *(978-1-58536-143-4(7))* Sleeping Bear Pr.

Smyth, Jennifer. Abc's for Silver Spoon Babies: A Couture Alphabet Learning Book. 2009. 32p. pap. 19.99 *(978-1-4490-1162-8(4))* AuthorHouse.

Soman, Pascal K. & Soman, Vickie A. A-B-C for Alex, Bash, & Company: A to Z Animal Tales from Around the World. 2012. 68p. (gr. -1). pap. 9.95 *(978-1-4759-3087-0(9))* iUniverse, Inc.

Somerville, Louisa. Alphabet & First Words, Ages 6-7. Tulip, Jenny, illus. 2016. (ENG.). 32p. (J). (gr. -1-12). pap. 6.99 *(978-1-86147-680-7(9),* Armadillo) Anness Publishing GBR. Dist: National Bk. Network.

Sounding Out the Alphabet. 2004. (J). cd-rom, audio compact disk 9.95 *(978-1-930006-62-1(4),* Reading Co., The) Rhoades & Assocs.

Spieker, Diana. Alphabetica: Odes to the Alphabet. Skehan, Krista, illus. 2009. (ENG.). 26p. 16.95 *(978-0-9797491-0-0(7))* Personify Pr.

Steck-Vaughn Staff. At-Home Workbooks: The Alphabet. 2004. (Illus.). pap., wbk. ed. *(978-0-7398-8528-4(6))* Steck-Vaughn.

Strother, Ruth. W Is for Woof: A Dog Alphabet. van Frankenhuyzen, Gijsbert, illus. 2008. (ENG.). 40p. (J). (gr. k-6). 17.95 *(978-1-58536-343-8(X))* Sleeping Bear Pr.

Sunshine Tool Box: Alphabet Books. (gr. k-3). 73.50 *(978-0-7802-4559-4(8));* 127.50 *(978-0-7802-6760-2(5))* Wright Group/McGraw-Hill.

Sylvan Learning Staff. Pre-K Page per Day: Letters. 2012. (Sylvan Page per Day Series, Language Arts Ser.). (ENG.). 64p. (J). (gr. -1-2). pap. 6.99 *(978-0-307-94455-9(7),* Sylvan Learning Publishing) Random Hse. Children's Bks.

Tabletop Pocket Chart Alphabet Photo Cards. 2004. (J). 8.95 *(978-1-56911-199-4(5))* Learning Resources, Inc.

Tam on Sam: Consonants m, s, t; Short Vowel a; -am, -at word families: Level A, 6 vols. (Wright Skills Ser.). 12p. (gr. k-3). 17.95 *(978-0-322-01445-9(X))* Wright Group/McGraw-Hill.

Taylor, Jacqui. African ABC. 2005. (ENG., Illus.). 96p. 14.95 *(978-1-86872-703-2(3))* Penguin Random House Grupo Editorial ESP. Dist: Casemate Pubs. & Bk. Distributors, LLC.

Taylor, Trace. B. 2010. (ICP Beginning Letter Ser.). (ENG.). 16p. (J). (gr. k-1). pap. 5.99 *(978-1-61541-089-7(9))* American Reading Co.

—C. 2010. (ICP Beginning Letter Ser.). (ENG.). 16p. (J). (gr. k-1). pap. 5.99 *(978-1-61541-101-6(1))* American Reading Co.

—D. 2010. (ICP Beginning Letter Ser.). (ENG.). 16p. (J). (gr. k-1). pap. 5.99 *(978-1-61541-087-3(2))* American Reading Co.

—F. 2010. (ICP Beginning Letter Ser.). (ENG.). 16p. (J). (gr. k-1). pap. 5.99 *(978-1-61541-104-7(6))* American Reading Co.

—G. 2010. (ICP Beginning Letter Ser.). (ENG.). 16p. (J). (gr. k-1). pap. 5.99 *(978-1-61541-106-1(2))* American Reading Co.

—H. 2010. (ICP Beginning Letter Ser.). (ENG.). 16p. (J). (gr. k-1). pap. 5.99 *(978-1-61541-108-5(9))* American Reading Co.

—J. 2010. (ICP Beginning Letter Ser.). (ENG.). 16p. (J). (gr. k-1). pap. 5.99 *(978-1-61541-110-8(0))* American Reading Co.

—K. 2010. (ICP Beginning Letter Ser.). (ENG.). 16p. (J). (gr. k-1). pap. 5.99 *(978-1-61541-112-2(7))* American Reading Co.

—L. 2010. (ICP Beginning Letter Ser.). (ENG.). 16p. (J). (gr. k-1). pap. 5.99 *(978-1-61541-086-6(4))* American Reading Co.

—M. 2010. (ICP Beginning Letter Ser.). (ENG.). 16p. (J). (gr. k-1). pap. 5.99 *(978-1-61541-078-1(3))* American Reading Co.

—N. 2010. (ICP Beginning Letter Ser.). (ENG.). 16p. (J). (gr. k-1). pap. 5.99 *(978-1-61541-114-6(3))* American Reading Co.

—P. 2010. (ICP Beginning Letter Ser.). (ENG.). 16p. (J). (gr. k-1). pap. 5.99 *(978-1-61541-116-0(X))* American Reading Co.

—R. 2010. (ICP Beginning Letter Ser.). (ENG.). 16p. (J). (gr. k-1). pap. 5.99 *(978-1-61541-118-4(6))* American Reading Co.

—S. 2010. (ICP Beginning Letter Ser.). (ENG.). 16p. (J). (gr. k-1). pap. 5.99 *(978-1-61541-098-9(8))* American Reading Co.

—T. 2010. (ICP Beginning Letter Ser.). (ENG.). 16p. (J). (gr. k-1). pap. 5.99 *(978-1-61541-100-9(3))* American Reading Co.

Teaching Resources Staff. AlphaTales Interactive E-Storybooks: 26 e-Books with Engaging Interactive Whiteboard Activities for Systematic Alphabet Instruction. 2013. (ENG., Illus.). 192p. (-2). pap. 129.99 *(978-0-545-45951-8(6),* Teaching Resources) Scholastic, Inc.

Teal, Joyce Willard. Learning A, B, C's with Seth. 2011. 36p. pap. 21.32 *(978-1-4628-2944-6(9))* Xlibris Corp.

Tedder, Elizabeth, illus. Alphabet & Numbers in a New Way. 2011. 32p. pap. 35.95 *(978-1-258-06357-3(3))* Literary Licensing, LLC.

Tekiela, Stan. C Is for Cardinal, 1 vol. 2016. (ENG., Illus.). 64p. (J). (-k). 8.95 *(978-1-59193-533-9(4))* Adventure Pubns.

Thomas, Isabel. Alphabet Fun: Making Letters with Your Body, 1 vol. 2014. (ENG.). 32p. (gr. k-k). lib. bdg. 25.99 *(978-1-4329-8802-9(6))* Heinemann-Raintree.

Thomas, Scott. Angry Aardvark to Zealous Zebra-Curious Creatures ABC. 2012. 32p. (J). pap. 6.99 *(978-1-62267-000-0(0))* Bright Connections Media.

Top That Publishing Staff, ed. Magnetic Play & Learn ABC. 2005. (Illus.). 12p. *(978-1-84510-727-7(6))* Top That! Publishing PLC.

Tropical ABC's. 2004. (J). 12.95 *(978-0-9763907-0-1(1))* Ola's Hanalei LTD.

Tunes for June: Long Vowel u: Level B, 6 vols. (Wright Skills Ser.). 16p. (gr. k-3). 17.95 *(978-0-322-01468-8(9))* Wright Group/McGraw-Hill.

Ulmer, Michael. H Is for Horse: An Equestrian Alphabet. vanFrankenhuyze, Gijsbert, illus. rev. ed. 2004. (Sports Ser.). (ENG.). 40p. (J). (gr. -1-5). 17.95 *(978-1-58536-213-4(1))* Sleeping Bear Pr.

Ulmer, Mike. M Is for Maple: A Canadian Alphabet. Rose-Popp, Melanie, illus. rev. ed. 2004. (Discover the World Ser.). (ENG.). 48p. (J). (gr. -1-1). pap. 8.95 *(978-1-58536-235-6(2),* 202276) Sleeping Bear Pr.

University Games Staff. I Have. 2007. 32p. (J). *(978-1-57528-888-8(5))* Univ. Games.

Vassar, Michael. Learning the Alphabet Can Be Easy A-Z. 2003. (Illus.). 27p. (J). (gr. -1-18). 12.95 *(978-0-9741043-1-7(0))* Mike-Mike Distribution.

Viano, Hannah. S Is for Salmon: A Pacific Northwest Alphabet. Viano, Hannah, illus. 2014. (ENG., Illus.). 32p. (J). (-k). 16.99 *(978-1-57061-873-4(9),* Little Bigfoot) Sasquatch Bks.

Vidrine, Beverly Barras. Halloween Alphabet, 1 vol. Lyne, Alison Davis, illus. 2004. (ENG.). 32p. (J). (gr. k-1). pap. 8.95 *(978-1-58980-242-1(X))* Pelican Publishing Co., Inc.

Viggers, Katie. Almost an Animal Alphabet. 2013. (ENG., Illus.). 56p. (J). (gr. -1-2). 19.95 *(978-1-57687-643-5(8),* powerHouse Bks.) powerHouse Cultural Entertainment, Inc.

Vitali, Daniela, illus. Play with My Animals ABCs. 2003. 16p. (J). bds. 5.99 *(978-1-931722-34-6(X),* Sixth Avenue Bks.) Grand Central Publishing.

Walker, Sylvia. Halloween ABC Coloring Book. 2011. (Dover Holiday Coloring Book Ser.). (ENG.). 32p. (J). (gr. -1-3). pap. 3.99 *(978-0-486-48175-3(1))* Dover Pubns., Inc.

Walling, Sandy Seeley, illus. & text. ABC's at the Zoo! The Fun Way to Teach Your Child the Relationship between Upper Case & Lower Case Letters Walling, Sandy Seeley, text. I.t. ed. 2004. 36p. (J). per. 7.95 *(978-0-9741940-1-1(8))* Abernathy Hse. Publishing.

Walter Foster Creative Team. Marvel's Avengers ABC: Learn Letters with Reusable Chalkboard Pages! 2017. (ENG., Illus.). 14p. (J). (gr. -1-1). bds. 12.95 ***(978-1-63322-253-3(5),*** Walter Foster Jr) Quarto Publishing Group USA.

Ware, Claudia. The Day the Alphabet Rebelled. 2012. 38p. 19.99 *(978-0-9858899-1-3(8))* For Him Pr.

Wargin, Kathy-jo. B Is for Badger: A Wisconsin Alphabet. Graef, Renee, illus. 2004. (Discover America State by State Ser.). (ENG.). 40p. (J). 17.95 *(978-1-58536-135-9(6))* Sleeping Bear Pr.

—L Is for Lincoln: An Illinois Alphabet. van Frankenhuyzen, Gijsbert, illus. 2004. (Discover America State by State Ser.). (ENG.). 40p. (J). (gr. 1-3). pap. 7.95 *(978-1-58536-250-9(6),* 202283) Sleeping Bear Pr.

—M Is for Melody: A Music Alphabet. Larson, Katherine, illus. 2006. (Art & Culture Ser.). (ENG.). 40p. (J). (gr. 1-4). 16.95 *(978-1-58536-215-8(8),* 202129) Sleeping Bear Pr.

Welykochy, Dawn. C Is for Chinook: An Alberta Alphabet. Bennett, Lorna, illus. rev. ed. 2004. (Discover Canada Province by Province Ser.). (ENG.). 40p. (J). 17.95 *(978-1-58536-223-3(9))* Sleeping Bear Pr.

Whitney, Gleaves & Whitney, Louise Doak. B Is for Buckaroo: A Cowboy Alphabet. Guy, Sue & Guy, Susan, illus. rev. ed. 2003. (Sports Ser.). (ENG.). 40p. (J). (gr. 1-4). 17.95 *(978-1-58536-139-7(9),* 202000) Sleeping Bear Pr.

Wilbur, Helen L. M Is for Meow: A Cat Alphabet. Papp, Robert, illus. rev. ed. 2006. (ENG.). 40p. (J). (gr. k-6). 17.95 *(978-1-58536-304-9(9))* Sleeping Bear Pr.

Willeford, Tammy Jean. Alphabear. Hopkins, Emily, illus. 2013. 32p. pap. 8.00 *(978-1-62080-998-3(2))* Hopkins Publishing.

Wimbrey, Crystal M. Alphascripts: The ABC's of the Bible. Mozley, Peggy, illus. 2006. 56p. 14.95 *(978-1-933285-63-4(X))* Brown Books Publishing Group.

The Wright Skills: Level B Sets - Long vowels only: 1 Each of 6 Titles. (gr. k-3). 17.95 *(978-0-322-01934-8(6))* Wright Group/McGraw-Hill.

The Wright Skills: Level B Sets - Long vowels only: 6 Each of 6 Titles. (gr. k-3). 109.50 *(978-0-322-01935-5(4))* Wright Group/McGraw-Hill.

The Wright Skills: Level C Sets - 1 Each of 16 Titles. (gr. k-3). 69.95 *(978-0-322-00734-5(8))* Wright Group/McGraw-Hill.

The Wright Skills: Level C Sets - 6 Each of 16 Titles. (gr. k-3). 322.95 *(978-0-322-00813-7(1))* Wright Group/McGraw-Hill.

Young, Dawn. The Abcs of Making Good Choices. Keaggy, Sarah, illus. 2013. 34p. 17.00 *(978-0-9860244-8-1(1))* O'More Publishing.

Yoyo Books Staff. ABC: Mini Baby's First Library. 2005. 42p. bds. *(978-90-5843-806-5(6))* YoYo Bks.

Zuckerman, Andrew, photos by. Creature ABC Flash Cards. 2014. (ENG., Illus.). 26p. (J). (gr. -1-17). 14.99 *(978-1-4521-1181-0(2))* Chronicle Bks. LLC.

Zuravicky, Orli. C Is for City: An Alphabet Book. Castellano, Giuseppe, illus. 2011. (Mister Doodle Ser.). (ENG.). 40p. (J). (gr. -1-k). bds. 7.99 *(978-1-4424-2049-6(9),* Little Simon) Little Simon.

ALPHABET BOOKS

Here are entered A B C books.

A, B, C Senang. 2013. (Illus.). 36p. (J). pap. 12.00 *(978-0-9828492-4-8(9))* Conscience Studio. A to Z with Noah. 2006. (J). bds. *(978-0-9771117-3-2(3))* JMG Studio.

ABC Atlantic City: An Alphabet Book, Travel Guide & Souvenir for Kids! 2006. (J). 8.95 *(978-0-9760047-1-4(2))* Rosenberger, Matthew.

ABC Order (Gr. 1-2) 2003. (J). *(978-1-58232-041-0(1))* ECS Learning Systems, Inc.

ABDO Publishing Company Staff. Let's See A to Z. 2007. (Let's See A to Z Ser.). 162.42 *(978-1-59928-878-9(8),* Super SandCastle) ABDO Publishing Co.

Aboff, Marcie. Guatemala ABCs: A Book about the People & Places of Guatemala, 1 vol. Trover, Zachary, illus. 2006. (Country ABCs Ser.). (ENG.). 32p. (gr. k-5). 27.99 *(978-1-4048-1570-4(8))* Picture Window Bks.

—India ABCs: A Book about the People & Places of India, 1 vol. Moore, Frances, illus. 2006. (Country ABCs Ser.). (ENG.). 32p. (gr. k-5). 27.99 *(978-1-4048-1571-1(6))* Picture Window Bks.

Abrams, Pam. Now I Eat My ABC's. Wolf, Bruce, illus. 2004. (ENG.). 8p. (J). (gr. k — 1). bds. 7.99 *(978-0-439-64942-1(0),* Cartwheel Bks.) Scholastic, Inc.

Addington, Judith. A-Z Leader Alphabook. 2012. (ENG.). (J). spiral bd. 14.95 *(978-1-4675-3105-4(7))* Independent Pub.

Adhikary, Anita B. My Daughters Are Smart! D Is for Daughters & S Is for Smart. Russo, Blythe, illus. 2014. (ENG.). 24p. (J). (gr. -1-3). 14.95 *(978-1-62086-429-6(0))* Mascot Bks., Inc.

Aery, Roxanne. The ABC's of Kids (Paperback) 2009. 32p. pap. 14.94 *(978-0-557-04415-3(4))* Lulu Pr., Inc.

Aiken, Zora & Aiken, David. A to Z: Pick What You'll Be. Aiken, David, illus. 2011. (ENG., Illus.). 32p. (J). 14.99 *(978-0-7643-3701-7(7),* 9780764337017, Schiffer Publishing Ltd) Schiffer Publishing, Ltd.

—Camp ABC: A Place for Outdoor Fun, 1 vol. Aiken, David, illus. 2013. (ENG., Illus.). 32p. (J). 16.99 *(978-0-7643-4423-7(4),* 9780764344237) Schiffer Publishing, Ltd.

Aksomitis, Linda. L Is for Land of Living Skies: A Saskatchewan Alphabet. Bennett, Lorna, illus. 2010. (Discover Canada Province by Province Ser.). (ENG.). 32p. (J). (gr. 1-3). 17.95 *(978-1-58536-490-9(8),* 202194) Sleeping Bear Pr.

Al-Ghani, K. I. Bertie Bumble Bee: Troubled by the Letter "B", 1 vol. Al-Ghani, Haitham, illus. 2012. (ENG.). 44p. (J). 16.99 *(978-0-7643-3993-6(1),* 9780764339936) Schiffer Publishing, Ltd.

Al-Kinani, Maarja. Arabic alphabet III. 2010. (ARA.). 100p. pap. 77.95 *(978-1-4461-6517-1(5))* Lulu Pr., Inc.

Alaska Boys and Girls Clubs Staff. A Is for Alaska. McCann, Michelle, ed. 2015. (See-My-State Alphabet Ser.). (ENG., Illus.). 32p. (J). (gr. -1-3). 13.99 *(978-1-941821-41-1(3),* West Winds Pr.) Graphic Arts Ctr. Publishing Co.

Albee, Sarah. Halloween ABC. Woolf, Julia, illus. 2009. (Little Golden Book Ser.). (ENG.). 24p. (J). (gr. -1-k). 4.99 *(978-0-375-84823-0(1),* Golden Bks.) Random Hse. Children's Bks.

Alberti, Theresa. Vietnam ABCs: A Book about the People & Places of Vietnam, 1 vol. Blanks, Natascha Alex, illus. 2007. (Country ABCs Ser.). (ENG.). 32p. (gr. k-5). lib. bdg. 27.99 *(978-1-4048-2251-1(8))* Picture Window Bks.

Alko, Selina. B Is for Brooklyn. Alko, Selina, illus. 2012. (ENG., Illus.). 40p. (J). (gr. -1-1). 17.99 *(978-0-8050-9213-4(7),* 9780805092134, Holt, Henry & Co. Bks. For Young Readers) Holt, Henry & Co.

Allaway, Al. Laughing Flowers & Blooming Animals. 2009. 32p. pap. 17.95 *(978-0-557-04195-4(3))* Lulu Pr., Inc.

Allen, Susan & Lindaman, Jane. Read Anything Good Lately? Enright, Vicky, illus. 2006. (ENG.). 32p. (J). (gr. k-3). per. 6.95 *(978-0-8225-6470-6(X),* First Avenue Editions) Lerner Publishing Group.

Allio, Mark R. R Is for Rhode Island Red: A Rhode Island Alphabet. Begin, Mary Jane, illus. 2005. (Discover America State by State Ser.). (ENG.). 40p. (J). (gr. k-5). 17.95 *(978-1-58536-149-6(6))* Sleeping Bear Pr.

Allred, Sylvester. The ForestAlphabet: Encyclopedia. Iverson, Diane, illus. unabr. ed. 2005. (Naturencyclopedia Ser.). 48p. (J). (gr. k-3). pap. 24.95 *(978-0-88045-155-0(6))* Stemmer Hse. Pubs.

—The Freshwater Alphabet. Iverson, Diane, illus. 2009. 48p. (J). (gr. 4-7). pap. 8.95 *(978-0-916144-48-7(8))* Stemmer Hse. Pubs.

Alpers, Jody. T Is for Tortilla: A Southwestern Alphabet Book. Johnson, Celeste, illus. 2006. (J). (gr. -1-3). *(978-1-929115-14-3(8))* Azro Pr., Inc.

Alphabet & Phonemic Awareness Activity Cards (OCR) 2004. (J). 14.95 *(978-1-56911-192-5(8))* Learning Resources, Inc.

Alphabet Book. 2006. (YA). per. *(978-1-59872-350-2(2))* Instant Pub.

Alphabet Book Classroom Library Set. 2004. (J). pap. 139.95 *(978-1-56911-190-1(1))* Learning Resources, Inc.

Alphabet Dot-to-Dot. 2004. (Play & Learn Pads Ser.). 48p. (J). 3.99 *(978-1-85997-717-0(0))* Byeway Bks.

Alphabet Fun. 2010. (Alphabet Fun Ser.). (ENG.). 32p. (gr. k-1). lib. bdg. 109.28 *(978-1-4296-5567-5(4));* (gr. 1-2). lib. bdg. 109.28 *(978-1-4296-4726-7(4))* Capstone Press of Coughlan Cos. (Aplus Bks.).

Alphabet (Gr. K-1) 2003. (J). *(978-1-58232-029-8(2))* ECS Learning Systems, Inc.

Alphabet Recognition (Gr. K-1) 2003. (J). *(978-1-58232-036-6(5))* ECS Learning Systems, Inc.

Alphabet Sorting Box. (gr. -1-12). 22.40 *(978-0-7362-1095-9(4))* CENGAGE Learning.

Alphasnaps & Snapphonics: Snapphonics Big Book: The Big & Little Alphabet Book. 2003. 46.95 *(978-0-673-60205-3(2))* Celebration Pr.

Alvarez, Juan. José Rabbit's Southwest Adventures: An ABC Coloring Book with Spanish Words. Alvarez, Juan, illus. 2004. (ENG., Illus.). 32p. (Orig.). (gr. -1-3). pap. 3.95 *(978-1-878610-00-3(7))* Red Crane Bks., Inc.

American Museum of Natural History Staff. ABC Insects. 2014. (AMNH ABC Board Bks.). (ENG., Illus.). 18p. (J). (gr. -1-k). bds. 7.95 *(978-1-4549-1194-4(8))* Sterling Publishing Co., Inc.

Amery, H. & Cartwright, S. Alphabet Lotto. 2004. (Encyclopedia of World Religions Ser.). (Illus.). (J). 12.95 *(978-0-7945-0314-7(4),* Usborne) EDC Publishing.

Amft, Robert. Peter's ABC Book: Peter Learns about Animals, Birds, Fishes, & Insects. 2006. (ENG., Illus.). 56p. pap. 12.00 *(978-0-945323-08-2(5))* WhiteWalls, Inc.

Amoroso, Cynthia. A Day with George: The Sound of Soft G. 2016. (Consonants Ser.). (ENG.). 24p. (J). (gr. -1-2). 25.64 *(978-1-5038-0931-4(5),* 210766) Child's World, Inc., The.

Anders, Isabel. Easter ABCs. 2007. (Illus.). 32p. (J). (gr. -1-1). per. 6.49 *(978-0-7586-1204-5(4))* Concordia Publishing Hse.

—Easter ABCs. Rasche, Shelly, illus. 2004. 32p. (J). tchr. ed. 9.49 *(978-0-570-07020-7(1),* 56-2040) Concordia Publishing Hse.

Anders, Shirley. The Land of Alphabet: Adventures of Mr. Scribe. 2011. 32p. pap. 21.99 *(978-1-4568-9724-6(1))* Xlibris Corp.

Anderson, Rodney P. The Invisible ABC's: Exploring the World of Microbes..., 1 vol. 2006. (ENG., Illus.). 64p. (gr. 3-7). 19.95 *(978-1-55581-386-4(0),* 9781555813864) ASM Pr.

Anderson, William. V Is for Von Trapp: A Musical Family Alphabet. Graves, Linda, illus. 2010. (ENG.). 32p. (J). (gr. 1-4). 16.95 *(978-1-58536-531-9(9),* 202214) Sleeping Bear Pr.

Animal ABCs. 2003. (Wipe-Off Activity Bks.). 16p. (J). (gr. 2). 3.79 *(978-1-58792-047-9(6))* Trend Enterprises, Inc.

Animal Alphabet. (J). pap. 6.95 incl. audio *(978-0-86545-096-7(X))* Spizzirri Pr., Inc.

A
B

Anjou, Colette. Olga's Cats: An ABC Book. Linville, S. Olga, illus. 2005. 28p. (J). (gr. -1-3). per. 15.95 *(978-0-9748933-5-8(8))* E & E Publishing.

Anonymous & Laughing Elephant Staff. Kitty's A. B. C. Shape Book. 2011. (Shape Bks.). (ENG., Illus.). 16p. (J). (gr. -1-k). pap. 9.95 *(978-1-59583-448-5(6)*, Green Tiger Pr.) Laughing Elephant.

Apseloff, Stanford S. African Animals Alphabet Book. 2010. (Illus.). (J). *(978-0-9647934-8-4(2))* Ohio Distinctive Publishing, Inc.

Archambault, John & Martin, Bill, Jr. Chicka Chicka ABC. Ehlert, Lois, illus. 2005. (Chicka Chicka Book Ser.). (ENG.). 16p. (J). (gr. -1 — 1). bds. 9.99 *(978-0-689-87820-6(6)*, Little Simon) Little Simon.

Armstrong, Moses K. Orthodox Christian Alphabet Coloring Book. Date not set. 35p. (J). (gr. k-3). pap. 5.00 *(978-1-879038-45-5(5)*, 9013) Synaxis Pr.

Arnaldo, Monica. The Little Book of Big Fears. 2015. (ENG., Illus.). 40p. (J). (gr. k-4). 16.95 *(978-1-77147-047-6(X)*, Owlkids) Owlkids Bks. Inc. CAN. Dist: Publishers Group West (PGW).

Arsenault, Elaine. F Is for French: Un Livre d'Alphabet Sur le Quebec - A Quebec Alphabet. Benoit, Renne, illus. 2013. (Discover Canada Province by Province Ser.). (FRE, ENG & MUL.). 40p. (J). (gr. 1-4). 17.95 *(978-1-58536-435-0(5)*, 202351) Sleeping Bear Pr.

Artell, Mike. Awesome Alphabets. 2nd ed. 2004. 88p. pap. 13.95 *(978-1-59647-030-9(5))* Good Year Bks.

Arthur, Felix. A Little Book of Alliterations. Capon, Jenny, illus. 2011. (Inside Pocket Single Titles Ser.). (ENG.). 64p. (J). (gr. k-3). 7.99 *(978-0-9562315-5-0(1))* Lerner Publishing Group.

Artist Collection Staff. The Dog from Arf! Arf! to Zzzzzz. Artist Collection Staff, illus. 2007. (Artist Collection: the Dog Ser.). (Illus.). 40p. (J). (gr. -1-3). 6.99 *(978-0-06-059859-4(X))* HarperCollins Pubs.

Asbury, Terri. Josh's Book of ABC's: Events at the Powwow. 2008. 29p. pap. 24.95 *(978-1-60672-378-4(2))* America Star Bks.

Asnong, Jocey, illus. Rocky Mountain ABCs. 2016. (ENG.). 28p. (— 1). bds. 12.00 *(978-1-77160-163-4(9))* Road West Publishing Co.

Aspinall, Sarah. Penguins Love Their ABC's. Aspinall, Sarah, illus. 2017. (ENG., Illus.). 40p. (J). (gr. -1-k). 17.99 ***(978-1-338-13420-9(5)**, Blue Sky Pr., The)* Scholastic, Inc.

Astroword: Module 11-r-Controlled Vowels (1-3) 2003. 158.95 net. *(978-0-7652-0832-3(6))* Modern Curriculum Pr.

Auerbach, Annie. Junkyard Dig! Building from A to Z. Shannon, David et al, illus. 2010. (Jon Scieszka's Trucktown Ser.). (ENG.). 26p. (J). (gr. -1-k). bds. 5.99 *(978-1-4169-4187-3(8)*, Little Simon) Little Simon.

Aunt Julie. Paddleduck # ABC. 2011. 60p. pap. *(978-1-4269-9393-0(5))* Trafford Publishing (UK) Ltd.

Autumn Publishing Staff, illus. ABC Learning. 2004. (Wall Charts Ser.). (J). pap. 4.99 *(978-1-85997-302-8(7))* Byeway Bks.

Award, Anna. My First ABC. 2012. (ENG., Illus.). 10p. (J). bds. 6.50 *(978-1-84135-418-7(X))*; bds. 9.95 *(978-1-84135-501-6(1))* Award Pubns. Ltd. GBR. Dist: Parkwest Pubns., Inc.

Azarian, Mary. A Farmer's Alphabet. (Illus.). (J). (gr. -1-1). pap. 14.95 *(978-0-9673268-8-7(5))* Learning Fasten-Ations, Inc.

—Farmers Alphabet. Azarian, Mary, illus. 2012. (ENG., Illus.). 32p. (J). (gr. -1-2). pap. 15.95 *(978-0-87923-397-6(4))* Godine, David R. Pub.

Babypants, Caspar. Augie to Zebra: An Alphabet Book! Endle, Kate, illus. 2012. (ENG.). 32p. (J). (gr. -1-2). 16.99 *(978-1-57061-750-8(3)*, Little Bigfoot) Sasquatch Bks.

Bagley, Val. My Gospel ABCs. 2004. cd-rom 5.98 *(978-1-57734-762-0(5))*; (Illus.). (J). 9.95 *(978-1-57734-669-2(6))* Covenant Communications, Inc.

Bagley, Val Chadwick & Mullins, Amy. Book of Mormon ABC Book. 2007. (Illus.). (J). 14.95 *(978-1-59811-458-4(1))* Covenant Communications, Inc.

Bajaj, Varsha. T Is for Taj Mahal: An India Alphabet. Crawford, Robert, illus. 2011. (Discover the World Ser.). (ENG.). 40p. (J). (gr. k-6). 17.95 *(978-1-58536-504-3(1))* Sleeping Bear Pr.

—T Is for Taj Mahal: An India Alphabet. 2016. (Av2 Fiction Readalong 2017 Ser.). (ENG.). (J). (gr. k-6). 34.28 ***(978-1-4896-5227-0(2)**, AV2 by Weigl)* Weigl Pubs., Inc.

Baker, Alan. Black & White Rabbit's ABC. 2017. (Little Rabbit Bks.). (ENG.). 24p. 12.99 *(978-0-7534-7322-1(4)*, 9780753473221, Kingfisher) Roaring Brook Pr.

Baker, Keith. LMNO Peas. Baker, Keith, illus. 2010. (Peas Ser.). (ENG., Illus.). 40p. (J). (gr. -1-3). 17.99 *(978-1-4169-9141-0(7)*, Beach Lane Bks.) Beach Lane Bks.

—LMNO Peas. Baker, Keith, illus. 2014. (Peas Ser.). (ENG., Illus.). 36p. (J). (gr. -1-k). bds. 7.99 *(978-1-4424-8978-3(2)*, Little Simon) Little Simon.

Ballard, Peg & Amoroso, Cynthia. Fun! The Sound of Short U. 2015. (Long & Short Vowels Ser.). (ENG.). 24p. (J). (gr. -1-2). 25.64 *(978-1-63407-022-5(4)*, 208857) Child's World, Inc., The.

Balsley, Tilda. ABC Hanukkah Hunt. Poole, Helen, illus. 2013. (Hanukkah Ser.). (ENG.). 32p. (J). (gr. -1-2). lib. bdg. 17.95 *(978-1-4677-0420-5(2)*, Kar-Ben Publishing) Lerner Publishing Group.

Bannatyne-Cugnet, Jo. A Prairie Alphabet. Moore, Yvette, illus. 2009. (ABC Our Country Ser.). (ENG.). 32p. (J). (gr. 1-4). pap. 7.95 *(978-0-88776-937-5(3)*, Tundra Bks.) Tundra Bks. CAN. Dist: Penguin Random Hse. LLC.

Banner, Angela. More & More Ant & Bee. 2014. (Ant & Bee Ser.: 3). (ENG., Illus.). 112p. (J). (gr. -1-k). 7.99 *(978-1-4052-6673-4(2))* Egmont Bks., Ltd. GBR. Dist: Independent Pubs. Group.

Bar-el, Dan. Alphabetter, 1 vol. Ross, Graham, illus. 2007. (ENG.). 32p. (J). (gr. -1-3). 8.95 *(978-1-55143-861-0(5))* Orca Bk. Pubs. USA.

Barber, Shirley, illus. The Fairies Alphabet Puzzle Tray: With Five 6-Piece Jigsaw Puzzles. 2004. 10p. (J). *(978-1-74124-437-3(4))* Bonnier Publishing Australia.

Barker, Cicely Mary. Flower Fairies Alphabet Coloring Book. 2010. (Flower Fairies Ser.). (ENG.). 24p. (J). (gr. -1-2). 4.99 *(978-0-7232-6496-5(1)*, Warne) Penguin Young Readers Group.

—Flower Fairies Library: A Flower Fairy Alphabet. 2007. 16.99 *(978-0-7232-5975-6(5))* Penguin Publishing Group.

Barlow, Amanda. Apple Bird ABC. 2004. (Baby Board Bks.). (ENG., Illus.). 1p. (J). (gr. -1-18). bds. 4.95 *(978-0-7460-4100-0(4))* EDC Publishing.

Barnes, Wiley. C is for Chickasaw. 2014. (Illus.). 40p. (J). 19.95 *(978-1-935684-19-0(1))* White Dog Pr., Ltd.

Barrett, Judi. An Excessive Alphabet: Avalanches of As to Zillions of Zs. Barrett, Ron, illus. 2016. (ENG.). 40p. (J). (gr. -1-3). 17.99 *(978-1-4814-3986-2(3)*, Atheneum/Caitlyn Dlouhy Books) Simon & Schuster Children's Publishing.

Batten, Scott A. Johnny the Phoenix. 2008. 64p. pap. 23.95 *(978-1-4343-7297-0(9))* AuthorHouse.

Bauer, Patricia. B Is for Battle Cry: A Civil War Alphabet. Geister, David, illus. 2009. (History Ser.). (ENG.). 40p. (J). (gr. 2-5). 17.95 *(978-1-58536-356-8(1))* Sleeping Bear Pr.

Bauley, Thomas K. Williamsburg A-Z: An Alphabetical Journey, 1 vol. 2010. (ENG., Illus.). 32p. 19.99 *(978-0-7643-3671-3(1)*, 9780764336713) Schiffer Publishing, Ltd.

Baum, L. Frank. Navy Alphabet Book. 2004. (ENG., Illus.). 60p. (J). (gr. -1-3). per. 14.95 *(978-1-55709-570-1(1))* Applewood Bks.

Bayley, Kimberly & Lawton, Caroline. Bugs A to Z. 2011. (ENG., Illus.). 32p. (J). (gr. -1-3). pap. 4.99 *(978-0-545-27330-5(7)*, Scholastic Paperbacks) Scholastic, Inc.

Behrens, Janice. Let's Make Letters: ABC Kids. Michael, Joan, illus. 2007. (Let's Find Out Early Learning Bks.). (ENG.). 32p. (J). (gr. -1-3). 18.00 *(978-0-531-14867-9(X)*, Children's Pr.) Scholastic Library Publishing.

—Letters/Numbers, 4 bks., Set. Michael, Joan, illus. Incl. Let's Make Letters: ABC Kids. (Illus.). 32p. (J). (gr. -1-3). 2007. 18.00 *(978-0-531-14867-9(X)*, Children's Pr.); (Let's Find Out Early Learning Bks.). 2007. 72.00 o.p. *(978-0-531-17599-6(5)*, Children's Pr.) Scholastic Library Publishing.

Bell, Liz. A to Z We Write the Words You See. 2011. 16p. pap. 24.95 *(978-1-4512-7220-8(0))* America Star Bks.

Belle, Jennifer. Animal Stackers. McPhail, David, illus. 2005. (ENG.). 40p. (J). (gr. k-4). 15.99 *(978-0-7868-1834-1(4))* Hyperion Pr.

Bellefontaine, Kim. ABC of Canada. Gürth, Per-Henrik, illus. 2006. (ENG.). 30p. (J). (gr. -1 — 1). bds. 8.95 *(978-1-55337-979-9(9))* Kids Can Pr., Ltd. CAN. Dist: Hachette Bk. Group.

Bennett, Andrea T. & Kessler, James H. Apples, Bubbles, & Crystals: Your Science ABCs. Sarecky, Melody, illus. 2004. (J). *(978-0-8412-3944-9(4))* American Chemical Society.

Bess Press, creator. From Aloha to Zippy's: A Keiki Alphabet Book. 2007. (Illus.). 32p. (J). (gr. -1-k). bds. 14.95 *(978-1-57306-255-8(3))* Bess Pr., Inc.

Bethea, Nikole Brooks. G Is for Grits: A Southern Alphabet, 1 vol. Lyne, Alison Davis, illus. 2012. (ENG.). 32p. (J). (gr. k-3). 16.99 *(978-1-4556-1698-5(2))* Pelican Publishing Co., Inc.

Bevan, C. Scott. Aa-Zz. 2013. 56p. pap. *(978-1-4602-3358-0(1))* FriesenPress.

Bianchi, Mike & Novak, Marisol. Gator Alphabet ABC. Marlette, Andy, illus. 2004. 32p. (J). (gr. -1-k). 6.95 *(978-1-58261-403-8(2))* Sports Publishing, LLC.

Bill, Martin & John, Archambault. Chicka Chicka Boom Boom. 2014. (Chicka Chicka Book Ser.). (ENG.). 40p. (J). (gr. k-3). 12.24 *(978-1-63245-294-8(4))* Lectorum Pubns., Inc.

Billmayer, Stephanie Joy. Apples to Zebras. 2012. 32p. pap. *(978-1-84903-151-6(7))* Schiel & Denver Publishing Ltd.

Bingham, Kelly. Z Is for Moose. Zelinsky, Paul O., illus. 2012. 32p. (J). (gr. -1-2). (ENG.). 16.99 *(978-0-06-079984-7(6))*; lib. bdg. 17.89 *(978-0-06-079985-4(4))* HarperCollins Pubs. (Greenwillow Bks.).

Bird, Benjamin. Scooby-Doo's ABC Mystery. 2015. (Scooby-Doo! Little Mysteries Ser.). (ENG., Illus.). 20p. (gr. -1 — 1). bds. 7.99 *(978-1-62370-175-8(9))* Capstone Press of Coughlan Cos.

Bird, Nicky & Duncan, Peter. Canada Alphabet Book, 1 vol. 2016. (IThink Ser.: 1). (ENG., Illus.). 64p. (J). pap. 6.99 ***(978-1-897206-03-4(8)**, 9781897206034)* Folklore Publishing CAN. Dist: Lone Pine Publishing USA.

Biskup, Agnieszka. Awesome Animals ABC. Brooks, David, illus. 2005. (J). *(978-1-58987-095-6(6))* Kindermusik International.

Bixley, Donovan, illus. The Great Kiwi ABC Book. 2017. (ENG.). 24p. (J). (gr. -1-k). pap. 9.99 ***(978-1-927262-71-9(2))*** Upstart Pr. NZL. Dist: Independent Pubs. Group.

Bjorklund, Shawn. G Is for Goat's Groovy Galoshes: Silly ABCs & Other Oddities. 2009. (ENG.). 24p. (J). 12.95 *(978-1-58117-783-1(6)*, Intervisual/Piggy Toes) Bendon, Inc.

Blackstone, Stella. Alligator Alphabet. Bauer, Stephanie, illus. (ENG.). (J). (gr. -1-k). 2007. 32p. 8.99 *(978-1-84686-073-7(3))* 2005. 48p. 16.99 *(978-1-84148-494-5(6))* Barefoot Bks., Inc.

Blackstone, Stella & Mockford, Caroline. Cleo's Alphabet Book. 2003. (Cleo the Cat Ser.). (ENG., Illus.). 32p. (J). 15.99 *(978-1-84148-008-4(8))*; pap. 6.99 *(978-1-84148-165-4(3))* Barefoot Bks., Inc.

Blake, Quentin. Quentin Blake's ABC. 2014. lib. bdg. 24.50 *(978-0-606-31770-2(8)*, Turtleback) Turtleback Bks.

Blue Lantern Studio Staff, creator. The Green Tiger's Illustrated ABC. 2006. (ENG., Illus.). 72p. (J). (gr. -1-3). 12.95 *(978-1-59583-041-8(3)*, Green Tiger Pr.) Laughing Elephant.

Blyton, Enid, et al. My First Abc. 2013. (ENG., Illus.). 20p. (J). bds. 11.50 *(978-1-84135-757-7(X))* Award Pubns. Ltd. GBR. Dist: Parkwest Pubns., Inc.

Bodleian Library Staff & F., Warner. Father Christmas' ABC: A Fascimile. 2005. (Illus.). 24p. (gr. -1-3). 11.99 *(978-1-85124-325-9(9))* Bodleian Library GBR. Dist: Chicago Distribution Ctr.

Boehnert, Ernest. The Great Alphabet Reminder Book. 2009. 56p. (gr. 2-2). pap. 10.82 *(978-1-4269-1256-6(0))* Trafford Publishing.

Bond, Susan. Ride with Me Through ABC. Lemke, Horst, illus. 32p. (J). (gr. -1). 14.95 *(978-0-87592-043-6(8))* Scroll Pr., Inc.

Bonder, Dianna. A, B, Sea: A Deep Sea Symphony, 1 vol. 2013. (ENG.). 32p. (J). 11.95 *(978-1-77050-043-3(X))* Whitecap Bks., Ltd.

—Dogabet, 1 vol. Bonder, Dianna, illus. 2008. (ENG., Illus.). 32p. (J). (gr. -1-2). pap. 6.95 *(978-1-55285-922-3(3)*, Walrus Bks.) Whitecap Bks., Ltd.

Bonnet, Rosalinde, illus. Alphabet Picture Book. 2011. (Alphabet Picture Book Ser.). 26p. (J). ring bd. 11.99 *(978-0-7945-2954-3(2)*, Usborne) EDC Publishing.

Borja, Richard. Flash! Alphabet Enigma. 2009. 48p. pap. 14.92 *(978-1-84728-659-8(3))* Lulu Pr., Inc.

Bousquet, Anthea. Lucy's St. Lucian Alphabet: The ABCs of Caribbean Culture in Upbeat Rhyming Verse. Sandiford, Ted, illus. 2012. 20p. (J). pap. *(978-976-8238-02-3(X))* Maryli Pubs.

BOWE, Andi. Alphabet book 2: a to z in song & Verse. 2009. 44p. pap. 27.95 *(978-0-557-02784-2(5))* Lulu Pr., Inc.

Bowman, Crystal. My ABC Bible, 1 vol. Lamb, Stacey, illus. 2012. (ENG.). 56p. (J). 5.99 *(978-0-310-73037-8(6))* Zonderkidz.

—My ABC Prayers, 1 vol. Lamb, Stacey, illus. 2012. (ENG.). 56p. (J). 5.99 *(978-0-310-73039-2(2))* Zonderkidz.

Bowman, Crystal & McKinley, Teri. A Is for Ark. Flowers, Luke, illus. 2017. (Our Daily Bread for Little Hearts Ser.). (ENG.). 18p. (J). (— 1). bds. 9.99 *(978-1-62707-599-2(2))* Discovery Hse. Pubs.

—M Is for Manger. Keay, Claire, illus. 2015. (ENG.). 64p. (J). 7.99 *(978-1-4964-0195-3(6))* Tyndale Hse. Pubs.

Boyden, Linda. Giveaways: An ABC Book of Loanwords from the Americas. 2010. (ENG., Illus.). 74p. (J). (gr. 3-6). 19.95 *(978-0-8263-4726-8(6))* Univ. of New Mexico Pr.

Boynton, Sandra. A Is for Angry: An Animal & Adjective Alphabet. 2016. (ENG.). (J). (gr. -1-1). lib. bdg. 24.45 ***(978-0-606-39769-8(8))*** Turtleback Bks.

Boys & Girls Club of Downtown Toronto Staff. C Is for Colorado. 2012. (See My State Ser.). (ENG., Illus.). 32p. (J). (gr. -1-3). 14.99 *(978-0-88240-776-0(7)*, West Winds Pr.) Graphic Arts Ctr. Publishing Co.

Boys and Girls Club of Oklahoma County. O Is for Oklahoma: Written by Kids for Kids. McCann, Michelle, ed. 2013. (See My State Ser.). (ENG., Illus.). 32p. (J). (gr. -1-3). 14.99 *(978-0-88240-911-5(5)*, West Winds Pr.) Graphic Arts Ctr. Publishing Co.

Brainy Baby Quad Book. 2005. (Brainy Baby Ser.). 40p. (J). bds. 10.39 *(978-1-59394-240-3(0))* Bendon, Inc.

Branch, Jennifer. The Inspired ABC's. Smith, Jenni, illus. 2008. 60p. (J). per. 16.99 *(978-0-615-18948-2(2))* Laughing Baby Pubns.

Breaking the Code Cursive Alphabet. (J). pap. *(978-0-87548-954-4(0)*, 8512) Open Court Publishing Co.

BrickHouse Education & Colón, Priscilla. Wild ABC's. 2009. 40p. (J). 8.99 *(978-1-59835-116-3(8))* Cambridge BrickHouse, Inc.

Bright Sky Press, Bright Sky, et al. H Is for Howdy: And Other Lone Star Letters. Little, James, illus. 2016. (ENG.). 24p. (J). 15.95 *(978-1-942945-34-5(5)*, 9781942945345) Bright Sky Pr.

Bringhurst, Nancy J. A Is for Alligator. Stark, Mindy C., illus. 2004. 32p. (J). 17.95 *(978-1-883991-96-8(X))* White Cloud Pr.

British Broadcasting Corporation Children's Books Staff. T Is for Tardis. Howling, Adam, illus. 2017. (ENG.). 60p. (J). 9.99 ***(978-1-4059-2998-1(7)**, 9781405929981)* Penguin Bks., Ltd. GBR. Dist: Diamond Comic Distributors, Inc.

Brock Bryant, Anita. Abcs of Advent. 2009. 40p. pap. 16.99 *(978-1-4490-3151-0(X))* AuthorHouse.

Brown, Jr. Jimmy's Alphabet Garden. 2013. 32p. pap. 13.50 *(978-1-4575-1797-6(3))* Dog Ear Publishing, LLC.

Brown, Kate. Sleepy ABC. Date not set. 32p. (J). (gr. -1-2). pap. 4.99 *(978-0-06-443370-9(6))* HarperCollins Pubs.

Brown, Margaret Wise. Goodnight Moon ABC: An Alphabet Book. Hurd, Clement, illus. 2010. (ENG.). (J). (gr. -1-k). 30p. bds. 8.99 *(978-0-06-189490-9(7)*, HarperFestival); 32p. 16.99 *(978-0-06-189484-8(2))* HarperCollins Pubs.

—Goodnight Moon ABC Padded Board Book: An Alphabet Book. Hurd, Clement, illus. 2013. (ENG.). 30p. (J). (gr. -1-k). bds. 9.99 *(978-0-06-224404-8(3)*, HarperFestival) HarperCollins Pubs.

—Sleepy ABC. Katz, Karen, illus. 2009. (ENG.). 40p. (J). (gr. -1-3). 16.99 *(978-0-06-128863-0(2))* HarperCollins Pubs.

Brown, Michelle Haney. My First Book of Japanese Words: An ABC Rhyming Book. Padron, Aya, illus. 2013. (ENG & JPN.). 32p. (J). (gr. -1-3). 12.95 *(978-4-8053-1201-8(7))* Tuttle Publishing.

Browning, Kurt. A Is for Axel: An Ice Skating Alphabet. Rose, Melanie, illus. rev. ed. 2005. (Sports Ser.). (ENG.). 40p. (J). (gr. -1-5). 17.95 *(978-1-58536-280-6(8))* Sleeping Bear Pr.

—A Is for Axel: An Ice Skating Alphabet. Rose, Melanie, illus. 2015. (Av2 Fiction Readalong 2016 Ser.). (ENG.). (J). (gr. 1-4). lib. bdg. 34.28 *(978-1-4896-3732-1(X)*, AV2 by Weigl) Weigl Pubs., Inc.

Bruchac, Joseph. Many Nations. Goetzl, Robert F., illus. 2004. (ENG.). 32p. (J). (gr. 5-9). pap. 6.99 *(978-0-439-63590-5(X))* Scholastic, Inc.

Bruel, Nick. Bad Kitty. Bruel, Nick, illus. 2nd ed. 2007. (Bad Kitty Ser.). (ENG., Illus.). 40p. (J). (gr. -1-3). 17.99 *(978-1-59643-299-4(3)*, 9781596432994) Roaring Brook Pr.

Bryant, Megan E. Alphasaurus. Powell, Luciana Navarro, illus. 2012. (ENG.). 20p. (J). (gr. -1 — 1). bds. 9.99 *(978-1-4521-0748-6(3))* Chronicle Bks. LLC.

Buck, Bryant. My First Christian Abc Bk. 2009. 32p. 14.95 *(978-1-58169-322-5(2)*, Evergreen Pr.) Genesis Communications, Inc.

Bugbird, T. My Pretty Pink School Purse. Horne, J., illus. 2010. 16p. (J). 12.99 *(978-1-84879-379-8(0))* Make Believe Ideas GBR. Dist: Nelson, Thomas Inc.

Bullard, Lisa. Not Enough Beds! A Christmas Alphabet Book. Oeltjenbruns, Joni, illus. 2004. (Picture Bks.). 32p. (J). (gr. -1-3). 15.95 *(978-1-57505-356-1(X)*, Carolrhoda Bks.); per. 6.95 *(978-1-57505-797-2(2))* Lerner Publishing Group.

Bulloch, Ivan & James, Diane. Learn with Me ABC. Pangbourne, Daniel, photos by. 2007. (ENG., Illus.). 45p. (J). (gr. -1-3). pap. 6.95 *(978-1-58728-599-8(1))* Cooper Square Publishing Llc.

Bumpers, Katrina B. Alphabet Fun, Book 1: Coloring & Activity Book. Lopez, Eddie, ed. Bourrouet, Jonathan, illus. 2008. 64p. pap. 10.95 *(978-0-9797208-0-2(X))* K's Kids Publishing.

Bunting, Jane. My First ABC. (Illus.). (J). (gr. -1). pap. 15.95 *(978-0-590-24127-4(3))* Scholastic, Inc.

Burmeff, Marian. How the Short Vowel Club Got Started. 2013. 40p. pap. 19.57 *(978-1-4669-8199-7(7))* Trafford Publishing.

Burr, Holly. An a-Bee-Sea Book. Abremski, Kathy, illus. 2012. 28p. pap. 14.95 *(978-1-61493-040-2(6))* Peppertree Pr., The.

Burris, Andrea & Schad, Anna. A Dog Lover's Alphabet Book. Burris, Andrea, illus. 2007. (ENG., Illus.). 32p. (J). (gr. k-2). 14.95 *(978-0-9743294-1-3(X))* A & D Bks.

Burris, Andrea M. & Schad, Anna M. The Kitty Cat Alphabet Book. Burris, Andrea M., illus. 2004. (ENG., Illus.). 32p. (J). 14.95 *(978-0-9743294-0-6(1)*, 1230444) A & D Bks.

Butler, Darnell. ABC's of People in the Bible. Uto-Uko, Iniobong, illus. 2006. 56p. (J). (gr. -1-3). per. 28.95 *(978-1-59299-163-1(7))* Inkwater Pr.

Butler, Dori Hillestad. P Is for Police, 1 vol. Waites, Joan, illus. 2009. (ENG.). 32p. (J). (gr. k-3). 16.99 *(978-1-58980-652-8(2))* Pelican Publishing Co., Inc.

Butzer, Anna. A Pirate Alphabet: The ABCs of Piracy! Jevons, Chris, illus. 2016. (Alphabet Connection Ser.). (ENG.). 32p. (gr. k-1). lib. bdg. 27.32 *(978-1-4795-6886-4(4))* Picture Window Bks.

Buzzeo, Toni. R Is for Research. Wong, Nicole, illus. 2008. 17.95 *(978-1-60213-032-6(9))*; (J). (gr. 2-4). 17.95 *(978-1-60213-030-2(2))* Highsmith Inc. (Upstart Bks.).

Byckowski, Mark. Animals Know Their Abc's a to Z So Can You! 2013. 32p. (J). pap. 14.95 *(978-1-4327-9915-1(0))* Outskirts Pr., Inc.

Cabanillas, Laura Sabin. The Abc's of Character. Sebastian, illus. 2009. 60p. pap. 12.95 *(978-0-9818488-2-2(6))* Ajoyin Publishing, Inc.

Cabat, Erni. Erni Cabat's Magical ABC: Animals Around the Farm. Date not set. (Illus.). 64p. (Orig.). (J). (gr. -1-2). 23.00 *(978-0-943173-73-3(6))* Cabat Studio Pubns.

Cabatingan, Erin. A Is for Musk Ox. Myers, Matthew, illus. 2012. (Musk Ox Ser.: 1). (ENG.). 40p. (J). (gr. k-2). 18.99 *(978-1-59643-676-3(X)*, 9781596436763) Roaring Brook Pr.

Calino & Abbeville Press Staff. ABC Snake. Calino, illus. 2008. (ENG., Illus.). 30p. (J). (gr. k-k). 8.95 *(978-0-7892-0303-8(0)*, Abbeville Kids) Abbeville Pr., Inc.

Callen, Sharon. The Curious Café, 1 vol. rev. ed. 2013. (Fiction Readers Ser.). (ENG., Illus.). 32p. (J). (gr. 3-3). pap. 8.99 *(978-1-4333-5609-4(0))* Shell Educational Publishing.

—The Curious Café. rev. ed. 2013. (Fiction Readers Ser.). (ENG., Illus.). 32p. (gr. 3-3). pap. 19.96 *(978-1-4807-1731-2(2))* Teacher Created Materials, Inc.

Canetti, Yanitzia. ABC's of Plants. 2010. (ENG.). 40p. (J). pap. 8.99 *(978-1-59835-118-7(4)*, BrickHouse Education) Cambridge BrickHouse, Inc.

—ABCs of School. 2010. (J). 8.99 *(978-1-59835-277-1(6)*, BrickHouse Education) Cambridge BrickHouse, Inc.

—Abecedario de Plantas. 2010. (SPA.). 40p. (J). pap. 8.99 *(978-1-59835-119-4(2)*, BrickHouse Education) Cambridge BrickHouse, Inc.

—Abecedario de Profesiones y Oficios. 2009. (SPA.). 40p. (J). pap. 8.99 *(978-1-59835-122-4(2)*, BrickHouse Education) Cambridge BrickHouse, Inc.

—Abecedario Escolar. 2010. (SPA.). 40p. (J). pap. 8.99 *(978-1-59835-275-7(X)*, BrickHouse Education) Cambridge BrickHouse, Inc.

—Abecedario Nutritivo. 2009. (SPA.). 40p. (J). pap. 8.99 *(978-1-59835-115-6(X)*, BrickHouse Education) Cambridge BrickHouse, Inc.

—ABeCedario Salvaje. 2009. (SPA.). 40p. (J). (gr. -1-3). pap. 7.99 *(978-1-59835-117-0(6))* Cambridge BrickHouse, Inc.

—Yummy ABC's. 2010. (ENG.). 40p. (J). pap. 8.99 *(978-1-59835-114-9(1)*, BrickHouse Education) Cambridge BrickHouse, Inc.

Capstone Press. Alphabet Fun. 2010. (Alphabet Fun Ser.). (ENG.). 32p. lib. bdg. 259.90 *(978-1-4296-5922-2(X)*, Aplus Bks.) Capstone Press of Coughlan Cos.

Capucilli, Alyssa Satin. Biscuit's ABC Adventure. Wenzel, David T. & Schories, Pat, illus. 2008. (Biscuit Ser.). 32p. (J). (gr. -1-2). pap. 3.99 *(978-0-06-112841-7(4)*, HarperFestival) HarperCollins Pubs.

Carle, Eric. Eric Carle's ABC. 2007. (World of Eric Carle Ser.). (ENG., Illus.). 16p. (J). (gr. -1-k). 7.99 *(978-0-448-44564-9(6)*, Grosset & Dunlap) Penguin Young Readers Group.

Carlson, Nancy & McCool, Barry. T Is for Twin Cities: A Minneapolis/St. Paul Alphabet. Geister, David, illus. 2012. (City Alphabet Ser.). (ENG.). 32p. (J). (gr. 1-5). 16.95 *(978-1-58536-583-8(1))* Sleeping Bear Pr.

Carluccio, Maria. D Is for Dress Up: The ABCs of What We Wear. 2016. (ENG., Illus.). 36p. (J). (gr. -1-k). 15.99 *(978-1-4521-4025-4(1))* Chronicle Bks. LLC.

Carolan. B Is for Beach: An Alphabet Book. 64p. 2007. 18.95 incl. audio compact disk *(978-0-9715333-8-7(5))* 2005. (Illus.). (J). 16.95 *(978-0-9715333-1-8(8))* Banana Patch Pr.

Carson-Dellosa Publishing Staff. El Alfabeto. 2006.Tr. of Alphabet. (SPA & ENG., Illus.). 54p. (gr. -1-3). 2.99 *(978-0-7696-4759-3(6)*, Brighter Child) Carson-Dellosa Publishing, LLC.

—Alphabet. 2006. (ENG., Illus.). 54p. (gr. -1-1). 2.99 *(978-0-7696-4679-4(4)*, Brighter Child) Carson-Dellosa Publishing, LLC.

—Alphabet Animals, Grades PK - K. 2010. (Home Workbooks Ser.). (ENG.). 64p. (gr. -1-k). pap. 4.49 *(978-1-60418-760-1(3))* Carson-Dellosa Publishing, LLC.

—Letters & Sounds, Grades K - 1. 2010. (Home Workbooks Ser.). (ENG.). 64p. (gr. k-1). pap. 4.49 *(978-1-60418-779-3(4))* Carson-Dellosa Publishing, LLC.

—Letters, Grades PK - K: Uppercase & Lowercase. 2010. (Home Workbooks Ser.). (ENG.). 64p. (gr. -1-k). pap. 4.49 *(978-1-60418-757-1(3))* Carson-Dellosa Publishing, LLC.

Carter, David A. Alpha Bugs: A Pop-Up Alphabet. Carter, David A., illus. 2006. (David Carter's Bugs Ser.). (ENG., Illus.). 28p. (J). (gr. -1-2). 12.99 *(978-1-4169-0973-6(7)*, Little Simon) Little Simon.

—Yellow Square: A Pop-Up Book for Children of All Ages. Carter, David A., illus. 2008. (ENG., Illus.). 20p. (J). (gr. -1-3). 19.99 *(978-1-4169-4093-7(6)*, Little Simon) Little Simon.

Cartwright, Stephen. Abc Floor. Cartwright, Stephen, illus. 2006. (Illus.). 16p. (J). bds. 15.99 *(978-0-7945-1367-2(0)*, Usborne) EDC Publishing.

Castaneda, Ana Zelaya. The Animal Alphabet. 2012. 32p. pap. 21.99 *(978-1-4691-4947-9(8))* Xlibris Corp.

Castella, Krystina & Boyl, Brian. Discovering Nature's Hidden Alphabet. 2017. (J). ***(978-1-59714-358-5(8))*** Heyday.

Castleden, James, illus. The Cockney Alphabet. 2014. (ENG.). 56p. pap. 14.00 *(978-1-909470-50-7(3))* Triarchy Press GBR. Dist: ISBS Publisher Services.

Catalanotto, Peter. Matthew A. B. C. Catalanotto, Peter, illus. 2005. (ENG., Illus.). 32p. (J). (gr. -1-3). reprint ed. 7.99 *(978-1-4169-0330-7(5),* Atheneum Bks. for Young Readers) Simon & Schuster Children's Publishing.

Chapman, Todd & Judge, Lita. D Is for Dinosaur: A Prehistoric Alphabet. Judge, Lita, illus. 2007. (Science Alphabet Ser.). (ENG., Illus.). 48p. (J). (gr. 1-4). 19.99 *(978-1-58536-242-4(5),* 202065) Sleeping Bear Pr.

Charlesworth, Liza. Nonfiction Alphabet Readers: A Big Collection of Just-Right Informational Books for Teaching the Letters a to Z. 2013. (ENG.). (gr. -1-1). 139.99 *(978-0-545-55426-8(8),* Teaching Resources) Scholastic, Inc.

Chemerka, William R. The Alamo from A to Z, 1 vol. Dillon, Wade, illus. 2011. (ENG.). 32p. (J). (gr. k-3). 16.99 *(978-1-4556-1461-5(0))* Pelican Publishing Co., Inc.

Chen, E. C. Bad Alphabet. 2013. 62p. 15.99 *(978-0-9891510-0-9(X))* Zebra Ginkgo.

Cheney, Lynne. A Is for Abigail: An Almanac of Amazing American Women. Glasser, Robin Preiss, illus. 2003. (ENG.). 48p. (J). (gr. 1-7). 19.99 *(978-0-689-85819-2(1),* Simon & Schuster Bks. For Young Readers) Simon & Schuster Bks. For Young Readers.

Chin, Foo Swee. Zeet. Chin, Foo Swee, illus. 2003. (Illus.). 32p. (Orig.). pap. 2.95 *(978-0-943151-75-5(9))* Slave Labor Bks.

Chorao, Kay. D Is for Drums: A Colonial Williamsburg ABC. 2004. (ENG., Illus.). 32p. (J). (gr. -1-1). 16.95 *(978-0-8109-4927-0(X))* Abrams, Inc.

—D Is for Drums: A Colonial Williamsburg ABC. Chorao, Kay, illus. 2006. (Illus.). 30p. (J). (gr. k-4). reprint ed. 17.00 *(978-1-4223-5240-3(4))* DIANE Publishing Co.

Clark, Isabel. Sticker & Colour- in Playbook: On the Farm. Tulip, Jenny, illus. 2016. (ENG.). 16p. (J). (gr. -1-12). pap. 4.99 *(978-1-86147-748-4(1))* Anness Publishing, Inc.

Clark, Judy. I Spy Disney: An ABC Book. 2008. (Illus.). 32p. 12.99 *(978-0-7868-3185-2(5))* Disney Pr.

Clary, Margie Willis. A Gullah Alphabet. Brown, Dennis L., illus. 2007. (J). *(978-0-87844-184-6(0))* Sandlapper Publishing Co., Inc.

Clement, Janet. Jewish Alphabet, 1 vol. Rodriguez, Albert G., illus. 2006. (ENG.). 32p. (J). (gr. k-3). 16.99 *(978-1-58980-414-2(7))* Pelican Publishing Co., Inc.

Coburn, Claudia. Did the Aardvarks Say "No Ark"? Hoard, Angela, illus. 2004. 32p. (J). *(978-0-9759343-1-9(7))* Purfect Promises.

Cohn, Tricia L. Beobi & the Magic Coloring Book ABC First Words. 2003. (J). *(978-0-9743847-0-2(4))* Cohn, Tricia.

Coirault, Christine. Alphabet. 2008. (Gymboree Play & Music Ser.). (ENG., Illus.). 26p. (gr. -1). bds. *(978-1-55470-031-8(0))* Magma.

Cole, Quinn. Alphabet Puke: Monsters' Medicine A-Z. Eubanks, Charles, illus. 2013. 32p. pap. 6.99 *(978-1-936214-94-5(6))* Wyatt-MacKenzie Publishing.

Colello, Nicholas. Architecture Alphabet. 2010. 61p. pap. 10.95 *(978-0-557-40226-7(3))* Lulu Pr., Inc.

Collier, photos by. ABCs of South African Animals. Collier, . 2015. (Illus.). 32p. (gr. -1-1). pap. 12.99 *(978-0-692-59277-9(6))* Educational Consulting by Design, LLC.

Collins Easy Learning, Collins Easy. Lower-Case Letters - Wipe-Clean. 2017. (Collins Easy Learning Preschool Ser.). (ENG.). 24p. (J). (gr. -1-k). 7.99 ***(978-0-00-821292-6(9))*** HarperCollins Pubs. Ltd. GBR. Dist: Independent Pubs. Group.

—Upper-Case Letters - Wipe Clean. 2017. (Collins Easy Learning Preschool Ser.). (ENG.). 24p. (J). (gr. -1-k). act. bk. ed. 7.99 ***(978-0-00-821291-9(0))*** HarperCollins Pubs. Ltd. GBR. Dist: Independent Pubs. Group.

Collison, Cathy & Campbell, Janis. G Is for Galaxy: An Out of This World Alphabet. Stacy, Alan, illus. (World/Country Alphabet Ser.). (ENG.). 40p. (J). (gr. k-5). 2005. 16.95 *(978-1-58536-255-4(7))* 2006. pap. 7.95 *(978-1-58536-335-3(9))* Sleeping Bear Pr.

Collison, Shauna. Heavenites Angels to Zebras Board Book with Audio CD. Nelson, Christine, illus. 2007. 26p. (J). 15.95 *(978-0-9792510-0-9(1))* Revelation Products LLC.

Color All About: A Giant Coloring Book about the Alphabet: the Alphabet. 2004. (SPA & ENG., Illus.). 36p. (J). *(978-1-59949-000-7(5))* Food Marketing Consultants, Inc.

Compestine, Ying Chang. D Is for Dragon Dance. Xuan, YongSheng, illus. 2005. (ENG.). 32p. (J). (gr. -1-3). 17.95 *(978-0-8234-1887-9(1))* Holiday Hse., Inc.

Conley, Connie. The Alphabet Doggie Style. 2007. (Illus.). 31p. (J). 18.00 *(978-0-9800898-0-6(8))* Conley, Connie.

Connelly, Neil O. Alphabet. Thornburgh, Rebecca, illus. 10p. (J). (gr. -1). bds. 3.95 *(978-1-58989-004-6(3))* Thurman Hse., LLC.

Cook, Jane Hampton. B Is for Baylor. Dobbins, Erin & Connally, Erin, illus. 2010. (Big Bear Bks.). (ENG.). 64p. (gr. 17). 29.95 *(978-1-60258-270-5(X))* Baylor Univ. Pr.

Cooper, Elisha. 8: An Animal Alphabet. 2015. (ENG., Illus.). 40p. (J). (gr. -1-k). 17.99 *(978-0-545-47083-4(8))* Scholastic, Inc.

Cooper, Sharon Katz. Costa Rica ABCs: A Book about the People & Places of Costa Rica, 1 vol. Eitzen, Allan, illus. 2007. (Country ABCs Ser.). (ENG.). 32p. (gr. k-5). lib. bdg. 27.99 *(978-1-4048-2249-8(6))* Picture Window Bks.

—A Is for Albatross: ABCs of Endangered Birds. 2016. (E for Endangered Ser.). (ENG., Illus.). 32p. (gr. 1-2). lib. bdg. 27.32 *(978-1-4914-8032-8(7),* Aplus Bks.) Capstone Press of Coughlan Cos.

Cordero, Flor de Maria, photos by. M Is for Mexico. 2008. (World Alphabets Ser.). (ENG., Illus.). 32p. (J). (gr. -1-2). 16.95 *(978-1-84507-593-4(5),* Frances Lincoln) Quarto Publishing Group UK GBR. Dist: Hachette Bk. Group.

Cormack, Malcolm & Twiggs, Ruth. Tigers & Sails & ABC Tales. 2006. (ENG., Illus.). 64p. (gr. 17). 14.95 *(978-0-917046-65-0(X))* University of Virginia Pr.

Corporate Contibutor Staff. Dinosaur Alphabet. 2012. (ENG.). 24p. (J). *(978-0-7787-7453-2(8))* Crabtree Publishing Co.

Corporate Contibutor Staff & West, David. Dinosaur Alphabet. 2012. (ENG.). 24p. (J). pap. *(978-0-7787-7458-7(9))* Crabtree Publishing Co.

Corrigan, Kathleen. ABC, 1 vol. 2014. (Canadian Board Bks.). (ENG & FRE.). 20p. bds. 7.99 *(978-1-62370-223-6(2))* Capstone Young Readers of Coughlan Cos.

Cousins, Lucy. Maisy's Amazing Big Book of Words. Cousins, Lucy, illus. 2007. (Maisy Ser.). (ENG., Illus.). 64p. (J). (gr. k-k). 14.99 *(978-0-7636-0794-4(0))* Candlewick Pr.

Covello, Paul. Canada ABC. 2016. 30p. (J). bds. 10.50 *(978-1-4434-4884-0(2))* HarperCollins Pubs.

—Toronto ABC. 2014. (ENG., Illus.). 15p. (J). bds. 10.50 *(978-1-4434-3144-6(3),* Harper Trophy) HarperCollins Pubs.

Cox, Katie. Learn on the Go Sticker Activity - Abc. 2010. 20p. pap. *(978-1-84879-395-8(2))* Make Believe Ideas.

Cox, Katie, des. Little Hands First Words. 2009. (Little Hands (Make Believe Ideas) Ser.). (ENG., Illus.). 24p. (gr. -1-k). 6.99 *(978-1-84610-957-7(4))* Make Believe Ideas GBR. Dist: Nelson, Thomas Inc.

Cox-Sands, Angela. The Missing Vowel. Piscopo, Samantha, illus. 2008. 20p. pap. 24.95 *(978-1-60813-028-3(2))* America Star Bks.

Cox, Tracey M. Arachnabet- an Alphabet of Spiders. 2013. 20p. pap. 9.95 *(978-1-61633-362-1(6))* Guardian Angel Publishing, Inc.

Crane, Carol. Discover Florida, 2 bks. Monroe, Michael Glenn & Monroe Donovan, Jane, illus. 2003. (ENG.). 40p. (J). 27.95 *(978-1-58536-226-4(3))* Sleeping Bear Pr.

—Discover Texas, 2 bks. Stacy, Alan, illus. 2003. (ENG.). 40p. (J). 27.95 *(978-1-58536-227-1(1))* Sleeping Bear Pr.

—P Is for Pilgrim: A Thanksgiving Alphabet. Urban, Helle, illus. rev. ed. 2007. (ENG.). 40p. (J). (gr. k-6). 7.95 *(978-1-58536-353-7(7))* Sleeping Bear Pr.

—T Is for Tar Heel: A North Carolina Alphabet. Palmer, Gary, illus. 2003. (Discover America State by State Ser.). (ENG.). 40p. (J). 17.95 *(978-1-58536-082-6(1))* Sleeping Bear Pr.

Crawford, Laura. The American Revolution from A to Z, 1 vol. Hierstein, Judith, illus. 2009. (ENG.). 32p. (J). (gr. k-3). 16.99 *(978-1-58980-515-6(1))* Pelican Publishing Co., Inc.

—Benjamin Franklin from A to Z, 1 vol. Hierstein, Judith, illus. 2013. (ENG.). 32p. (J). (gr. k-3). 16.99 *(978-1-4556-1713-5(X))* Pelican Publishing Co., Inc.

Cronin, Doreen. Click, Clack, ABC. Lewin, Betsy, illus. 2010. (Click, Clack Book Ser.). (ENG.). 24p. (J). (gr. -1 — 1). bds. 7.99 *(978-1-4169-9124-3(7),* Little Simon) Little Simon.

—Click, Clack, Quackity-Quack: A Typing Adventure. Lewin, Betsy, illus. 2008. (Click, Clack Book Ser.). (ENG.). 14p. (J). (gr. -1-k). 14.99 *(978-1-4169-5517-7(8),* Little Simon) Little Simon.

Cronin, Doreen & Lewin, Betsy. Click, Clack, Quackity-Quack: An Alphabetical Adventure. 2006. (Doreen Cronin: Click-Clack & More Ser.). (ENG.). (gr. -1-3). lib. bdg. 24.21 *(978-1-59961-089-4(2))* Spotlight.

Crum, Nate. Abc. 2013. 36p. pap. 14.99 *(978-1-4808-0223-0(9))* Archway Publishing.

Cruz, Ginny Wilson. E Is for Ellisville. 2011. (Illus.). (J). pap. *(978-0-615-55095-4(9))* Pioneer Poet Publishing.

Cyr, Lynne G. Drako's ABC Adventures as an Iguana. 2006. (Illus.). 37p. (J). spiral bd. 21.95 *(978-0-9774543-0-3(4))* Cyr Design Publishing.

Czekaj, Jef. A Call for a New Alphabet. Czekaj, Jef, illus. 2011. (ENG., Illus.). 48p. (J). (gr. 1-4). pap. 5.95 *(978-1-58089-229-2(9))* Charlesbridge Publishing, Inc.

Dahlen, Noelle. My Christmas Alphabet Coloring Book. 2015. (Dover Holiday Coloring Book Ser.). (ENG.). 32p. (J). (gr. -1-2). pap. 3.99 *(978-0-486-79244-6(7))* Dover Pubns., Inc.

Dalmatian Press Staff. The Alphabet Song Book. 2008. (ENG.). 5p. (J). bds. 4.95 *(978-1-58117-726-8(7),* Intervisual/Piggy Toes) Bendon, Inc.

Daly, Gael. Hopkinton & the Boston Marathon from, a Tp Z. 2013. 38p. pap. 14.95 *(978-0-9910923-0-7(9))* CONVERPAGE.

Daste, Larry. Alphabet Search: Activity & Coloring Book. 2007. (Dover Children's Activity Bks.). (ENG., Illus.). 48p. (J). (gr. k-3). 4.99 *(978-0-486-46196-0(3))* Dover Pubns., Inc.

David C. Cook Publishing Company Staff. ABC's. 2003. (My Jesus Pocket Bks.). (Illus.). 32p. (J). pap., pap. 8.90 *(978-1-55513-091-6(7),* 1555130917) Cook, David C.

Davidow, Shelley. The Wise Enchanter: A Journey through the Alphabet. Kurzyca, Krystyna Emilia, illus. 2005. (ENG.). 159p. (J). (gr. 3-7). per. 17.95 *(978-0-88010-562-0(3))* SteinerBooks, Inc.

Davids, Tom & Davids, Veronica. Wrestling the ABCs: Creating Character & Fostering Fitness. 2009. (ENG.). 32p. (J). 17.95 *(978-1-933916-33-0(8));* pap. 11.95 *(978-1-933916-34-7(6))* Nelson Publishing & Marketing.

Davies, Becky. Peekaboo Pals a to Z. Lucas, Gareth, illus. 2016. (Peekaboo Pals Ser.). (ENG.). 20p. (J). (gr. -1). bds. 14.95 *(978-1-62686-520-4(5),* Silver Dolphin Bks.) Readerlink Distribution Services, LLC.

de Brunhoff, Laurent. B Is for Babar: An Alphabet Book. 2012. (ENG., Illus.). 30p. (J). (gr. -1 — 1). bds. 7.95 *(978-1-4197-0298-3(X),* Abrams Appleseed) Abrams, Inc.

—Babar's ABC. 2012. (ENG., Illus.). 40p. (J). (gr. k-2). 16.95 *(978-1-4197-0382-9(X),* Abrams Bks. for Young Readers) Abrams, Inc.

Deborah Wanda. Wanda's Wittle Wunders. 2009. 32p. pap. 14.49 *(978-1-4389-4862-1(X))* AuthorHouse.

Demarest, Chris L. & Mayer, Bill. All Aboard! A Traveling Alphabet. 2008. (ENG., Illus.). 40p. (J). (gr. -1-2). 17.99 *(978-0-689-85249-7(5),* McElderry, Margaret K. Bks.) McElderry, Margaret K. Bks.

Demeo, Kristen. Sounds Like This ... 2007. (J). per. 7.95 *(978-1-59872-819-4(9))* Instant Pub.

Deneux, Xavier. ABC: TouchThinkLearn. 2016. (ENG., Illus.). 32p. (J). (gr. -1-k). bds. 24.99 *(978-1-4521-4503-7(2))* Chronicle Bks. LLC.

Dennis, Penny Ruth. How I Learn My ABC's Through Sights & Sounds Around Me. 2007. (J). pap. 14.99 *(978-0-9796130-6-7(X))* Kingdom Publishing Group, Inc.

deRubertis, Barbara. Alexander Anteater's Amazing Act. Alley, R. W., illus. 2010. (Animal Antics A to Z Ser.). 32p. (J). (ENG.). (gr. -1-3). pap. 7.95 *(978-1-57565-300-6(1));* (gr. k-1). lib. bdg. 22.60 *(978-1-57565-304-4(4))* Kane Press, Inc.

—Bobby Baboon's Banana Be-Bop. Alley, R. W., illus. 2010. (Animal Antics A to Z Ser.). 32p. (J). lib. bdg. 22.60 *(978-1-57565-305-1(2));* (ENG.). (gr. -1-3). pap. 7.95 *(978-1-57565-301-3(X))* Kane Press, Inc.

—Corky Cub's Crazy Caps. Alley, R. W., illus. 2010. (Animal Antics A to Z Ser.). 32p. (J). lib. bdg. 22.60 *(978-1-57565-306-8(0));* (ENG.). (gr. -1-3). pap. 7.95 *(978-1-57565-302-0(8))* Kane Press, Inc.

—Dilly Dog's Dizzy Dancing. Alley, R. W., illus. 2010. (Animal Antics A to Z Ser.). 32p. (J). lib. bdg. 22.60 *(978-1-57565-307-5(9));* (ENG.). (gr. -1-3). pap. 7.95 *(978-1-57565-303-7(6))* Kane Press, Inc.

—Eddie Elephant's Exciting Egg-Sitting. Alley, R. W., illus. 2010. (Animal Antics A to Z Ser.). 32p. (J). (gr. -1-3). pap. 7.95 *(978-1-57565-309-9(5));* lib. bdg. 22.60 *(978-1-57565-316-7(8))* Kane Press, Inc.

—Frances Frog's Forever Friend. Alley, R. W., illus. 2010. (Animal Antics A to Z Ser.). 32p. (J). (gr. -1-3). (ENG.). pap. 7.95 *(978-1-57565-310-5(9));* lib. bdg. 22.60 *(978-1-57565-317-4(6))* Kane Press, Inc.

—Gertie Gorilla's Glorious Gift. Alley, R. W., illus. 2010. (Animal Antics A to Z Ser.). 32p. (J). (gr. -1-3). pap. 7.95 *(978-1-57565-311-2(7));* lib. bdg. 22.60 *(978-1-57565-318-1(4))* Kane Press, Inc.

—Hanna Hippo's Horrible Hiccups. Alley, R. W., illus. 2010. (Animal Antics A to Z Ser.). 32p. (J). (gr. -1-3). pap. 7.95 *(978-1-57565-312-9(5));* lib. bdg. 22.60 *(978-1-57565-319-8(2))* Kane Press, Inc.

—Izzy Impala's Imaginary Illnesses. Alley, R. W., illus. 2010. (Animal Antics A to Z Ser.). 32p. (J). (gr. -1-3). pap. 7.95 *(978-1-57565-313-6(3));* lib. bdg. 22.60 *(978-1-57565-320-4(6))* Kane Press, Inc.

—Jeremy Jackrabbit's Jumping Journey. Alley, R. W., illus. 2010. (Animal Antics A to Z Ser.). 32p. (J). (gr. -1-3). pap. 7.95 *(978-1-57565-314-3(1));* lib. bdg. 22.60 *(978-1-57565-321-1(4))* Kane Press, Inc.

—Kylie Kangaroo's Karate Kickers. Alley, R. W., illus. 2011. (Animal Antics A to Z Ser.). 32p. (J). pap. 45.32 *(978-0-7613-7657-6(7));* (ENG.). lib. bdg. 22.60 *(978-1-57565-332-7(X));* (gr. -1-3). pap. 7.95 *(978-1-57565-323-5(0))* Kane Press, Inc.

—Lana Llama's Little Lamb. Alley, R. W., illus. 2011. (Animal Antics A to Z Ser.). 32p. (J). pap. 45.32 *(978-0-7613-7658-3(5))* Kane Press, Inc.

—Maxwell Moose's Mountain Monster. Alley, R. W., illus. 2011. (Animal Antics A to Z Ser.). 32p. (J). pap. 45.32 *(978-0-7613-7659-0(3))* Kane Press, Inc.

—Nina Nandu's Nervous Noggin. Alley, R. W., illus. 2011. (Animal Antics A to Z Ser.). 32p. (J). pap. 45.32 *(978-0-7613-7660-6(7));* (gr. -1-3). pap. 7.95 *(978-1-57565-326-6(5))* Kane Press, Inc.

—Oliver Otter's Own Office. Alley, R. W., illus. 2011. (Animal Antics A to Z Ser.). 32p. (J). pap. 45.32 *(978-0-7613-7661-3(5));* lib. bdg. 22.60 *(978-1-57565-336-5(2));* (gr. -1-3). pap. 7.95 *(978-1-57565-327-3(3))* Kane Press, Inc.

—Polly Porcupine's Painting Prize. Alley, R. W., illus. 2011. (Animal Antics A to Z Ser.). 32p. (J). pap. 45.32 *(978-0-7613-7662-0(3));* lib. bdg. 22.60 *(978-1-57565-337-2(0))* Kane Press, Inc.

—Polly Porcupine's Painting Prizes. Alley, R. W., illus. 2011. (Animal Antics A to Z Ser.). (ENG.). 32p. (J). (gr. -1-3). pap. 7.95 *(978-1-57565-328-0(1))* Kane Press, Inc.

—Quentin Quokka's Quick Questions. Alley, R. W., illus. 2011. (Animal Antics A to Z Ser.). 32p. (J). pap. 45.32 *(978-0-7613-7663-7(1));* lib. bdg. 22.60 *(978-1-57565-338-9(9));* (gr. -1-3). pap. 7.95 *(978-1-57565-329-7(X))* Kane Press, Inc.

—Rosie Raccoon's Rock & Roll Raft. Alley, R. W., illus. 2011. (Animal Antics A to Z Ser.). 32p. (J). pap. 45.32 *(978-0-7613-7664-4(X));* lib. bdg. 22.60 *(978-1-57565-339-6(7));* (gr. -1-3). pap. 7.95 *(978-1-57565-330-3(3))* Kane Press, Inc.

Derubertis, Barbara. Sammy Skunk's Super Sniffer. Alley, R. W., illus. 2011. (Animal Antics A to Z Set III Ser.). pap. 45.32 *(978-0-7613-8428-1(6))* Kane Press, Inc.

deRubertis, Barbara. Sammy Skunk's Super Sniffer. Alley, R. W., illus. 2011. (Animal Antics A to Z Ser.). pap. 7.95 *(978-1-57565-344-0(3));* lib. bdg. 22.60 *(978-1-57565-352-5(4))* Kane Press, Inc.

Derubertis, Barbara. Tessa Tiger's Temper Tantrums. Alley, R. W., illus. 2011. (Animal Antics A to Z Set III Ser.). pap. 45.32 *(978-0-7613-8429-8(4))* Kane Press, Inc.

deRubertis, Barbara. Tessa Tiger's Temper Tantrums. Alley, R. W., illus. 2011. (Animal Antics A to Z Ser.). 32p. (J). pap. 7.95 *(978-1-57565-345-7(1));* lib. bdg. 22.60 *(978-1-57565-353-2(2))* Kane Press, Inc.

Derubertis, Barbara. Umma Ungka's Unusual Umbrella. Alley, R. W., illus. 2011. (Animal Antics A to Z Set III Ser.). pap. 45.32 *(978-0-7613-8430-4(8))* Kane Press, Inc.

deRubertis, Barbara. Umma Ungka's Unusual Umbrella. Alley, R. W., illus. 2011. (Animal Antics A to Z Ser.). pap. 7.95 *(978-1-57565-346-4(X));* lib. bdg. 22.60 *(978-1-57565-354-9(0))* Kane Press, Inc.

Derubertis, Barbara. Victor Vicuna's Volcano Vacation. Alley, R. W., illus. 2011. (Animal Antics A to Z Set III Ser.). pap. 45.32 *(978-0-7613-8431-1(6))* Kane Press, Inc.

deRubertis, Barbara. Victor Vicuna's Volcano Vacation. Alley, R. W., illus. 2011. (Animal Antics A to Z Ser.). 32p. (J). (ENG.). pap. 7.95 *(978-1-57565-347-1(8));* lib. bdg. 22.60 *(978-1-57565-355-6(9))* Kane Press, Inc.

Derubertis, Barbara. Walter Warthog's Wonderful Wagon. Alley, R. W., illus. 2011. (Animal Antics A to Z Set III Ser.). pap. 45.32 *(978-0-7613-8432-8(4))* Kane Press, Inc.

deRubertis, Barbara. Walter Warthog's Wonderful Wagon. Alley, R. W., illus. 2011. (Animal Antics A to Z Ser.). 32p. (J). (ENG.). pap. 7.95 *(978-1-57565-348-8(6));* lib. bdg. 22.60 *(978-1-57565-356-3(7))* Kane Press, Inc.

Derubertis, Barbara. Xavier Ox's Xylophone Experiment. Alley, R. W., illus. 2011. (Animal Antics A to Z Set III Ser.). pap. 45.32 *(978-0-7613-8433-5(2))* Kane Press, Inc.

deRubertis, Barbara. Xavier Ox's Xylophone Experiment. Alley, R. W., illus. 2011. (Animal Antics A to Z Ser.). 32p. (J). (ENG.). pap. 7.95 *(978-1-57565-349-5(4));* lib. bdg. 22.60 *(978-1-57565-357-0(5))* Kane Press, Inc.

—Yoko Yak's Yakety Yakking. Alley, R. W., illus. 2011. (Animal Antics A to Z Ser.). pap. 7.95 *(978-1-57565-350-1(8));* lib. bdg. 22.60 *(978-1-57565-358-7(3))* Kane Press, Inc.

Derubertis, Barbara. Zachary Zebra's Zippity Zooming. Alley, R. W., illus. 2011. (Animal Antics A to Z Set III Ser.). pap. 45.32 *(978-0-7613-8435-9(9))* Kane Press, Inc.

deRubertis, Barbara. Zachary Zebra's Zippity Zooming. Alley, R. W., illus. 2011. (Animal Antics A to Z Ser.). 32p. (J). pap. 7.95 *(978-1-57565-351-8(6));* lib. bdg. 22.60 *(978-1-57565-359-4(1))* Kane Press, Inc.

deRubertis, Barbara & DeRubertis, Barbara. Alexander Anteater's Amazing Act. Alley, R. W., illus. 2012. (Animal Antics A to Z Ser.). 32p. (J). (gr. 2 — 1). cd-rom 7.95 *(978-1-57565-394-5(X))* Kane Press, Inc.

—Bobby Baboon's Banana Be-Bop. Alley, R. W., illus. 2012. (Animal Antics A to Z Ser.). 32p. (J). (gr. 2 — 1). cd-rom 7.95 *(978-1-57565-395-2(8))* Kane Press, Inc.

—Corky Cub's Crazy Caps. Alley, R. W., illus. 2012. (Animal Antics A to Z Ser.). 32p. (J). (gr. 2 — 1). cd-rom 7.95 *(978-1-57565-396-9(6))* Kane Press, Inc.

—Dilly Dog's Dizzy Dancing. Alley, R. W., illus. 2012. (Animal Antics A to Z Ser.). 32p. (J). (gr. 2 — 1). cd-rom 7.95 *(978-1-57565-397-6(4))* Kane Press, Inc.

—Eddie Elephant's Exciting Egg-Sitting. Alley, R. W., illus. 2012. (Animal Antics A to Z Ser.). 32p. (J). (gr. 2 — 1). cd-rom 7.95 *(978-1-57565-398-3(2))* Kane Press, Inc.

—Frances Frog's Forever Friend. Alley, R. W., illus. 2012. (Animal Antics A to Z Ser.). 32p. (J). (gr. 2 — 1). cd-rom 7.95 *(978-1-57565-399-0(0))* Kane Press, Inc.

—Gertie Gorilla's Glorious Gift. Alley, R. W., illus. 2012. (Animal Antics A to Z Ser.). 32p. (J). (gr. 2 — 1). cd-rom 7.95 *(978-1-57565-400-3(8))* Kane Press, Inc.

—Hanna Hippo's Horrible Hiccups. Alley, R. W., illus. 2012. (Animal Antics A to Z Ser.). 32p. (J). (gr. 2 — 1). cd-rom 7.95 *(978-1-57565-401-0(6))* Kane Press, Inc.

—Izzy Impala's Imaginary Illnesses. Alley, R. W., illus. 2012. (Animal Antics A to Z Ser.). 32p. (J). (gr. 2 — 1). cd-rom 7.95 *(978-1-57565-402-7(4))* Kane Press, Inc.

—Jeremy Jackrabbit's Jumping Journey. Alley, R. W., illus. 2012. (Animal Antics A to Z Ser.). 32p. (J). (gr. 2 — 1). cd-rom 7.95 *(978-1-57565-403-4(2))* Kane Press, Inc.

—Kylie Kangaroo's Karate Kickers. Alley, R. W., illus. 2012. (Animal Antics A to Z Ser.). 32p. (J). (gr. 2 — 1). cd-rom 7.95 *(978-1-57565-404-1(0))* Kane Press, Inc.

—Lana Llama's Little Lamb. Alley, R. W., illus. 2012. (Animal Antics A to Z Ser.). 32p. (J). (gr. 2 — 1). cd-rom 7.95 *(978-1-57565-405-8(9))* Kane Press, Inc.

—Maxwell Moose's Mountain Monster. Alley, R. W., illus. 2012. (Animal Antics A to Z Ser.). 32p. (J). (gr. 2 — 1). cd-rom 7.95 *(978-1-57565-406-5(7))* Kane Press, Inc.

—Nina Nandu's Nervous Noggin. Alley, R. W., illus. 2012. (Animal Antics A to Z Ser.). 32p. (J). (gr. 2 — 1). cd-rom 7.95 *(978-1-57565-407-2(5))* Kane Press, Inc.

—Oliver Otter's Own Office. Alley, R. W., illus. 2012. (Animal Antics A to Z Ser.). 32p. (J). (gr. 2 — 1). cd-rom 7.95 *(978-1-57565-408-9(3))* Kane Press, Inc.

—Polly Porcupine's Painting Prizes. Alley, R. W., illus. 2012. (Animal Antics A to Z Ser.). 32p. (J). (gr. 2 — 1). cd-rom 7.95 *(978-1-57565-409-6(1))* Kane Press, Inc.

—Quentin Quokka's Quick Questions. Alley, R. W., illus. 2012. (Animal Antics A to Z Ser.). 32p. (J). (gr. 2 — 1). cd-rom 7.95 *(978-1-57565-410-2(5))* Kane Press, Inc.

—Rosie Raccoon's Rock & Roll Raft. Alley, R. W., illus. 2012. (Animal Antics A to Z Ser.). 32p. (J). (gr. 2 — 1). cd-rom 7.95 *(978-1-57565-411-9(3))* Kane Press, Inc.

—Sammy Skunk's Super Sniffer. Alley, R. W., illus. 2012. (Animal Antics A to Z Ser.). 32p. (J). (gr. 2 — 1). cd-rom 7.95 *(978-1-57565-412-6(1))* Kane Press, Inc.

—Tessa Tiger's Temper Tantrums. Alley, R. W., illus. 2012. (Animal Antics A to Z Ser.). 32p. (J). (gr. 2 — 1). cd-rom 7.95 *(978-1-57565-413-3(X))* Kane Press, Inc.

—Umma Ungka's Unusual Umbrella. Alley, R. W., illus. 2012. (Animal Antics A to Z Ser.). 32p. (J). (gr. 2 — 1). cd-rom 7.95 *(978-1-57565-414-0(8))* Kane Press, Inc.

—Victor Vicuna's Volcano Vacation. Alley, R. W., illus. 2012. (Animal Antics A to Z Ser.). 32p. (J). (gr. 2 — 1). cd-rom 7.95 *(978-1-57565-415-7(6))* Kane Press, Inc.

—Walter Warthog's Wonderful Wagon. Alley, R. W., illus. 2012. (Animal Antics A to Z Ser.). 32p. (J). (gr. 2 — 1). cd-rom 7.95 *(978-1-57565-416-4(4))* Kane Press, Inc.

—Xavier Ox's Xylophone Experiment. Alley, R. W., illus. 2012. (Animal Antics A to Z Ser.). 32p. (J). (gr. 2 — 1). cd-rom 7.95 *(978-1-57565-417-1(2))* Kane Press, Inc.

—Yoko Yak's Yakety Yakking. Alley, R. W., illus. 2012. (Animal Antics A to Z Ser.). 32p. (J). (gr. 2 — 1). cd-rom 7.95 *(978-1-57565-418-8(0))* Kane Press, Inc.

—Zachary Zebra's Zippity Zooming. Alley, R. W., illus. 2012. (Animal Antics A to Z Ser.). 32p. (J). (gr. 2 — 1). cd-rom 7.95 *(978-1-57565-419-5(9))* Kane Press, Inc.

Diaz-Cubero, Jose H. Practicas de Ortografia: 5 Grado. (SPA & ENG.). (J). (gr. 5). 9.95 *(978-84-357-0125-9(5),* CPR92) Ediciones y Distribuciones Codice, S.A. ESP. Dist: Continental Bk. Co., Inc.

Dillon-Hreha, Denise. The Wedding of Q & U. 2007. (Illus.). 48p. per. 16.99 *(978-1-4259-8040-5(6))* AuthorHouse.

Disney Book Group. Lion Guard Kion's Animal Alphabet. Disney Storybook Art Team, illus. 2016. (ENG.). 10p. (J). (gr. -1-k). bds. 12.99 *(978-1-4847-2949-6(8))* Disney Pr.

Disney Book Group Staff & Kelman, Marcy. Animal ABCs. Disney Storybook Art Team, illus. 2014. (ENG.). 10p. (J). (gr. -1-k). bds. 10.99 *(978-1-4231-8488-1(2))* Disney Pr.

Disney Mickey Mouse Clubhouse, ed. Clubhouse ABCs: Mickey Mouse Clubhouse. 2009. (ENG.). 24p. 7.99 *(978-1-59069-771-9(5))* Studio Mouse LLC.

DiTerlizzi, Tony. G Is for One Gzonk! An Alpha-Number-Bet Book. DiTerlizzi, Tony, illus. 2006. (ENG., Illus.). 80p. (J). (gr. -1-2). 29.99 *(978-0-689-85290-9(8),* Simon & Schuster Bks. For Young Readers) Simon & Schuster Bks. For Young Readers.

Doak, Angela K. Atlantic Animal ABCs, 1 vol. 2017. (ENG., Illus.). 26p. (J). (gr. -1-k). bds. 14.95 ***(978-1-77108-463-5(4))*** Nimbus Publishing, Ltd. CAN. Dist: Orca Bk. Pubs. USA.

Dodd, Marion. Mystic by the A,B, Sea. Dodd, Marion, illus. 2006. (Illus.). (J). 17.95 *(978-0-9773725-2-2(9))* Flat Hammock Pr.

Dodson, Peter. An Alphabet of Dinosaurs. Barlowe, Wayne D. & Meaker, Michael, illus. 2016. (ENG.). (gr. k-5). 29.95 ***(978-1-59687-512-8(7),*** ipicturebooks) ibooks, Inc.

Dog Artist Collection Staff. The Dog from Arf! Arf! to Zzzzzz. Dog Artist Collection Staff, illus. 2004. (ENG., Illus.). 40p. (J). 14.99 *(978-0-06-059857-0(3))* HarperCollins Pubs.

Dolphin, Colleen. April Fools' Day to Z Day: Holidays from A to Z, 1 vol. 2009. (Let's Learn A to Z Ser.). (ENG., Illus.). 32p. (J). (gr. -1-2). 27.07 *(978-1-60453-495-5(8))* ABDO Publishing Co.

A
B

—Armadillos to Zorillas: Animals from A to Z, 1 vol. 2007. (Let's See A to Z Ser.). (ENG., Illus.). 32p. (gr. -1-3). 27.07 *(978-1-59928-883-3(4),* Super SandCastle) ABDO Publishing Co.

—It's E!, 1 vol. 2010. (It's the Alphabet! Ser.). (ENG., Illus.). 24p. (gr. k-4). 25.65 *(978-1-60453-592-1(X),* Super SandCastle) ABDO Publishing Co.

Domeniconi, David. M Is for Majestic: A National Parks Alphabet. Carroll, Pam, illus. 2007. (ENG.). 48p. (J). (gr. k-6). per. 7.95 *(978-1-58536-333-9(2))* Sleeping Bear Pr.

Dompierre, Judith. Strange Passions. 2012. 32p. 29.95 *(978-1-4626-9273-6(7))* America Star Bks.

Dompierre, Judith E. Jennie's New Adventure Looking for Letters. 2012. 28p. 24.95 *(978-1-4626-6486-3(5))* America Star Bks.

—Strange Passions. 2012. 32p. pap. 24.95 *(978-1-4626-9326-9(1))* America Star Bks.

Donenfeld, Deborah. Baby ABC. 2013. (ENG.). 24p. (J). (— 1). bds. 6.99 *(978-0-8037-3973-4(7),* Dial Bks) Penguin Young Readers Group.

Doodler, Todd H. The Zoo I Drew. 2009. (ENG., Illus.). 56p. (J). (gr. -1-k). 14.99 *(978-0-375-85201-5(8),* Random Hse. Bks. for Young Readers) Random Hse. Children's Bks.

Dorling Kindersley Publishing Staff. ABC - Fun Flaps, Plus Touch & Feel! 2014. (ENG.). 12p. (J). (gr. -1 — 1). bds. 6.99 *(978-1-4654-3258-2(2),* DK Children) Dorling Kindersley Publishing, Inc.

—My First ABC. 2015. (My First Bks.). (ENG.). 36p. (J). (gr. -1 — 1). bds. 5.99 *(978-1-4654-2900-1(X),* DK Children) Dorling Kindersley Publishing, Inc.

Doudna, Kelly. Emma & Eddie, 1 vol. 2005. (First Sounds Ser.). (Illus.). (J). (gr. k-3). (ENG.). 24p. lib. bdg. 24.21 *(978-1-59679-144-2(6),* SandCastle); 23p. pap. 48.42 *(978-1-59679-145-9(4))* ABDO Publishing Co.

—It's K !, 1 vol. 2010. (It's the Alphabet! Ser.). (ENG., Illus.). 24p. (gr. k-4). 25.65 *(978-1-60453-598-3(9),* Super SandCastle) ABDO Publishing Co.

—It's T !, 1 vol. 2010. (It's the Alphabet! Ser.). (ENG., Illus.). 24p. (gr. k-4). 25.65 *(978-1-60453-607-2(1),* Super SandCastle) ABDO Publishing Co.

Douglas, Lisa Jo. Active Animals A Thru Z. 2008. (ENG., Illus.). 30p. (J). per. 12.99 *(978-1-59879-311-6(X),* Lifevest) Lifevest Publishing, Inc.

Downie, Mary Alice. A Pioneer Alphabet. Gerber, Mary Jane, illus. 2009. (ABC Our Country Ser.). (ENG.). 32p. (J). (gr. k-3). pap. 7.95 *(978-0-88776-961-0(6),* Tundra Bks.) Tundra Bks. CAN. Dist: Penguin Random Hse. LLC.

DuBois, Juli. The Happiness of Being Me: An A-Z Owners Manual, 1 vol. Zitnak, Allison Day, illus. 2009. 47p. pap. 24.95 *(978-1-60749-613-7(5))* America Star Bks.

Duchesne, Christiane. W Is for Wapiti! An Alphabet Songbook. Côté, Geneviève, illus. 2012. (ENG.). 48p. (J). (gr. -1-k). 16.95 *(978-2-923163-83-3(4))* La Montagne Secrete CAN. Dist: Independent Pubs. Group.

Dugan, Joanne. ABC Nyc: A Book about Seeing New York City. 2005. (ENG., Illus.). 56p. (J). (gr. -1-1). 17.95 *(978-0-8109-5854-8(6))* Abrams, Inc.

Dunlop, Cliff. Flights of Fancy: An Anthology. 2009. 224p. pap. *(978-1-932252-56-9(8))* Creative Continuum, Inc.

Durber, Matt, illus. First ABC. 2007. (Usborne Look & Say Ser.). 22p. (J). (gr. -1-k). bds. 14.99 *(978-0-7945-1435-8(9),* Usborne) EDC Publishing.

Duris, Joan & Jones, Gillian. B Is for Berkshires. 2015. (ENG.). 32p. 17.95 *(978-1-939017-51-2(3),* e79df012-d55f-4ec1-9a59-318cc001d57e) Islandport Pr., Inc.

DuTemple, Lesley A. R Is for Raccoon. 2007. 32p. pap. 11.95 *(978-1-892384-42-3(6))* Avery Color Studios, Inc.

Duvernay, Sharon. My Alphabet Book: Mi Libro Alfabeto Flash Cards. 2013. (J). 9.95 *(978-0-9888644-8-1(7))* Knowledge Power Communications.

Dyan, Penelope. Go to Rat House, Go to Cat House — Even Though Houses Are Not People. Dyan, Penelope, illus. 2008. (Illus.). 44p. pap. 11.95 *(978-1-935118-14-5(5))* Bellissima Publishing, LLC.

—Jump Frog, Funny Frog — -Because Frogs Are Funny. Dyan, Penelope, illus. 2008. (Illus.). 44p. pap. 11.95 *(978-1-935118-19-0(6))* Bellissima Publishing, LLC.

—That Fat Elephant — -Because Everyone Likes Elephants. Dyan, Penelope, illus. 2008. (Illus.). 44p. pap. 11.95 *(978-1-935118-16-9(1))* Bellissima Publishing, LLC.

—That Fat Rat Family — Because All Families Aren't Rats. Dyan, Penelope, illus. 2008. (Illus.). 44p. pap. 11.95 *(978-1-935118-17-6(X))* Bellissima Publishing, LLC.

—Who Cut the Cheese? a for Boys Only Book. Dyan, Penelope, illus. 2008. (Illus.). 44p. pap. 11.95 *(978-1-935118-22-0(6))* Bellissima Publishing, LLC.

Ebin, Matthew, illus. The Wonderfully Ridiculous Alphabet Book. 2007. 27p. (J). 10.00 *(978-0-9787628-0-3(0))* MEAR LLC.

Editors of Ulysses Press. A Is for America Letter Tracing. 2017. (ENG., Illus.). 112p. (gr. -1-k). pap. 6.95 *(978-1-61243-665-4(X))* Ulysses Pr.

Edwards, Pamela Duncan. B Is for Big Ben: An England Alphabet. Rose, Melanie, illus. 2008. (Discover the World Ser.). (ENG.). 40p. (J). (gr. -1-3). 17.95 *(978-1-58536-305-6(7))* Sleeping Bear Pr.

—The Wacky Wedding: A Book of Alphabet Antics. 2005. 32p. (J). pap. *(978-0-7868-1172-4(2))* Hyperion Bks. for Children.

Edwards, Wallace. Alphabeasts. Edwards, Wallace, illus. 2008. (ENG., Illus.). 32p. (J). (gr. 1-4). pap. 9.95 *(978-1-55453-227-8(2))* Kids Can Pr., Ltd. CAN. Dist: Hachette Bk. Group.

Edwards-Wright, Tracy. Meet Angel & All Her Friends. Shekailo, Pamela, illus. 2012. 48p. pap. 24.95 *(978-1-4512-8280-1(X))* America Star Bks.

Ellerson, Terryann. The Rappin' Tappin Alphabet. 2011. 24p. pap. 11.99 *(978-1-4567-6733-4(X))* AuthorHouse.

Ellis, Belinda. Giant See-a-Shape My Giant ABC Book. 2005. (Giant See a Shape Ser.). (Illus.). 52p. (gr. -1-k). bds. *(978-1-905051-92-2(1))* Make Believe Ideas.

—Touch & Learn: Fairy Tale ABC. 2006. (Illus.). 12p. (J). (gr. -1). per. *(978-1-84610-090-1(9))* Make Believe Ideas.

Engelbreit, Mary. Mary Engelbreit's A Merry Little Christmas: Celebrate from A to Z. Engelbreit, Mary, illus. 2006. (Illus.). 40p. (J). (gr. -1-3). lib. bdg. 17.89 *(978-0-06-074159-4(7))* HarperCollins Pubs.

—Mary Engelbreit's a Merry Little Christmas: Celebrate from A to Z. Engelbreit, Mary, illus. 2010. (ENG., Illus.). 40p. (J). (gr. -1-3). pap. 6.99 *(978-0-06-074160-0(0))* HarperCollins Pubs.

Entrekin, Allison Weiss. For the Love of Dogs: An A-to-Z Primer for Dog Lovers of All Ages. Anderson, Mark, illus. 2011. (For the Love Of... Ser.). (ENG.). 48p. 16.95 *(978-1-60078-371-5(6))* Triumph Bks.

epstein, brad M., et al. Dogs ABC: My First Alphabet Book. 2013. (Illus.). 32p. (J). *(978-1-60730-400-5(7),* ABC Bk.) Michaelson Entertainment.

Eubank, Patricia Reeder. ABCs of Easter. 2010. 40p. (J). (gr. k-3). 8.99 *(978-0-8249-5617-2(6),* Ideal Pubns.) Worthy Publishing.

—Valentine ABCs. Eubank, Patricia Reeder, illus. 2009. (Illus.). 32p. (J). (gr. -1-3). 9.99 *(978-0-8249-5597-7(8),* Ideal Pubns.) Worthy Publishing.

Evans, Nate & Brown, Stephanie Gwyn. Bang! Boom! Roar! A Busy Crew of Dinosaurs. Santoro, Christopher, illus. 2012. (ENG.). 40p. (J). (gr. -1-2). 15.99 *(978-0-06-087960-0(2))* HarperCollins Pubs.

—Dinosaur ABC. Santoro, Christopher, illus. 2011. (J). lib. bdg. 16.89 *(978-0-06-087962-4(9))* HarperCollins Pubs.

Farmer, Bonnie. Abc Letters in the Library. l.t. ed. 2012. 60p. (J). pap. *(978-1-4596-3446-6(2))* ReadHowYouWant.com, Ltd.

Fay, Nicole. Andy & Armadillio Are Astronauts. 2008. 20p. pap. 10.49 *(978-1-4389-1057-4(6))* AuthorHouse.

Fazio, Maria R. Block Party! 2013. 28p. pap. 24.95 *(978-1-4241-2603-3(7))* America Star Bks.

Feit, Maureen. Letters & Laughs from a to Z. 2009. (Illus.). 52p. pap. 22.50 *(978-1-4490-2527-4(7))* AuthorHouse.

Feldman, Jean. Highway Letters, Numbers & Shapes: PreK-1. 2010. 80p. pap. 22.99 *(978-1-61601-036-2(3))* Creative Teaching Pr., Inc.

Feldman, Jean R. & Karapetkova, Holly. Deck the Room (Tune, Deck the Halls) Lap Book. 2010. (ENG., Illus.). 12p. (gr. -1-k). 9.95 *(978-1-61590-184-5(1))* Rourke Educational Media.

Ferrie, Chris. ABC's of Science. 2017. (Baby University Ser.: 0). (ENG.). 26p. (J). bds. 9.99 ***(978-1-4926-5631-9(3),*** Sourcebooks Jabberwocky) Sourcebooks, Inc.

Finley, Thomas Murray. Alphapet City. 2012. (ENG.). 32p. pap. 9.99 *(978-1-4675-2587-9(1))* Independent Pub.

First Words. 2007. (Early Days Ser.). (Illus.). 16p. (gr. -1-k). bds. *(978-1-84666-365-9(2))* Top That! Publishing PLC.

Fisher, Henry. When I Dream of ABC. 2014. (Illus.). 64p. (J). *(978-1-84956-102-0(8))* Barnes & Noble, Inc.

Fisher, Valorie. Ellsworth's Extraordinary Electric Ears: And Other Amazing Alphabet Anecdotes. Fisher, Valorie, illus. 2009. (ENG., Illus.). 36p. (J). (gr. -1-3). 10.99 *(978-1-4424-0658-2(5),* Atheneum Bks. for Young Readers) Simon & Schuster Children's Publishing.

Fitzgerald, Paula. The ABCs of How I Love You! 2011. 16p. (J). (gr. -1-1). bds. 12.99 *(978-0-8249-1495-0(3),* Ideal Pubns.) Worthy Publishing.

Fitzsimmons, Kakie. Bur Bur's Boating ABC's: Learn the Most Amazing Things with the ABCs of Boating! 2007. (Bur Bur & Friends Ser.). (Illus.). (J). (gr. 3-7). lib. bdg. *(978-0-9777121-2-0(5))* IGI Pr.

Flanagan, Alice K. A Pet: The Sound of P. 2016. (Consonants Ser.). (ENG.). 24p. (J). (gr. -1-2). 25.64 *(978-1-5038-0910-9(2),* 210746) Child's World, Inc., The.

Fleming, Denise. Shout! Shout It Out! Fleming, Denise, illus. 2011. (ENG., Illus.). 40p. (J). (gr. -1-1). 16.99 *(978-0-8050-9237-0(4),* 9780805092370, Holt, Henry & Co. Bks. For Young Readers) Holt, Henry & Co.

Flett, Julie. Li Yiiboo Miyo-Waapamik LII Swer: L'Alfabet Di Michif. 2010.Tr. of Owls See Clearly at Night - A Michif Alphabet. (CRP & ENG., Illus.). 56p. (J). (gr. -1-3). 16.95 *(978-1-897476-28-4(0))* Simply Read Bks. CAN. Dist: Ingram Publisher Services.

Floca, Brian. The Racecar Alphabet. Floca, Brian, illus. 2003. (ENG., Illus.). 40p. (J). (gr. -1-2). 18.99 *(978-0-689-85091-2(3),* Atheneum/Richard Jackson Bks.) Simon & Schuster Children's Publishing.

Flora, Sherrill B. Alphabet: Signs, Letters, Sounds. 2010. (ENG.). 26p. (gr. -1-k). 11.99 *(978-1-60268-087-6(6),* Key Education Publishing Company, LLC) Carson-Dellosa Publishing, LLC.

Florida, Boys and Girls Clubs of Central. F Is for Florida. 2017. (See My State Ser.). (ENG., Illus.). 32p. (J). (gr. -1-3). 14.99 *(978-1-5132-6049-5(9),* West Winds Pr.) Graphic Arts Ctr. Publishing Co.

Foam Magnetic Letters in Spanish. (gr. -1-12). 26.20 *(978-0-7362-1530-5(1))* CENGAGE Learning.

Folsom, Michael & Elting, Mary. Q Is for Duck: An Alphabet Guessing Game. Kent, Jack & Kent, June K., illus. 2005. (ENG.). 64p. (J). (gr. -1-3). pap. 6.95 *(978-0-618-57412-4(3))* Houghton Mifflin Harcourt Publishing Co.

—Q Is for Duck: An Alphabet Guessing Game. Kent, Jack, illus. 2007. 60p. (gr. -1-k). 16.95 *(978-0-7569-7871-6(8))* Perfection Learning Corp.

Fortman, Susie. Lakota's Alphabet Walk. 2009. 36p. pap. 15.99 *(978-1-4389-8399-8(9))* AuthorHouse.

Foust, Cindy. Elephant emma Lou. 2006. (J). 12.94 *(978-0-9749220-4-1(8))* Alpha-kidZ.

—Harry, harry Hippo. 2006. (J). 12.94 *(978-0-9749220-8-9(0))* Alpha-kidZ.

—Kristy Kangaroo. 2008. (J). 12.94 *(978-0-9749220-6-5(4))* Alpha-kidZ.

—Louis Lion. 2008. (J). 12.94 *(978-0-9749220-7-2(2))* Alpha-kidZ.

Franceschelli, Christopher. Red Apple, Yellow Banana & the Blue Cockatoo: An Alphabet Adventure. 2012. (ConceptTheater Ser.). 12p. (J). 8.99 *(978-0-8249-1458-5(9),* Ideal Pubns.) Worthy Publishing.

Frasier, Debra. A Fabulous Fair Alphabet. Frasier, Debra, illus. 2010. (ENG., Illus.). 40p. (J). (gr. k-6). 16.99 *(978-1-4169-9817-4(9),* Beach Lane Bks.) Beach Lane Bks.

Fredericks, Anthony D. A Is for Anaconda: A Rainforest Alphabet. Regan, Laura, illus. 2009. (Science Ser.). (ENG.). 40p. (J). (gr. 1-5). 17.95 *(978-1-58536-317-9(0))* Sleeping Bear Pr.

—P Is for Prairie Dog: A Prairie Alphabet. Bowles, Doug, illus. 2011. (Sleeping Bear Alphabets Ser.). (ENG.). 32p. (J). (gr. k-6). 16.95 *(978-1-58536-508-1(4))* Sleeping Bear Pr.

Freeburn, Eva & Gow, Lawson. H Is for Howdy: the Coloring Book: And Other Lone Star Letters. Little, James, illus. 2016. (ENG.). 24p. (J). pap. 9.95 *(978-1-942945-45-1(0),* 9781942945451) Bright Sky Pr.

Freyou, Lerin. The Adventures of Piston the Puppy: A Journey Through the Alphabet as Piston Discovers the World Around Him. 2009. 31p. 15.80 *(978-0-557-12597-5(9))* Lulu Pr., Inc.

Fried, Miriam. My Jelly Bean Book. 2005. (Illus.). (J). *(978-1-57400-049-8(7))* Data Trace Publishing, Co.

Fuertes, Gloria. Abecedario - Don Hilario (Don Hillario's Alphabet) (SPA.). 40p. (J). 10.50 *(978-84-305-7195-6(7))* Susaeta Ediciones, S.A. ESP. Dist: AIMS International Bks., Inc.

Fujikawa, Gyo. Gyo Fujikawa's A to Z Picture Book. 2010. (ENG., Illus.). 72p. (J). (gr. -1-2). 9.95 *(978-1-4027-6818-7(4),* 1318769) Sterling Publishing Co., Inc.

Gaarder-Juntti, Oona. It's C!, 1 vol. 2010. (It's the Alphabet! Ser.). (ENG.). 24p. (gr. k-4). 25.65 *(978-1-60453-590-7(3),* Super SandCastle) ABDO Publishing Co.

—It's D!, 1 vol. 2010. (It's the Alphabet! Ser.). (ENG.). 24p. (gr. k-4). 25.65 *(978-1-60453-591-4(1),* Super SandCastle) ABDO Publishing Co.

—It's L!, 1 vol. 2010. (It's the Alphabet! Ser.). (ENG., Illus.). 24p. (gr. k-4). 25.65 *(978-1-60453-599-0(7),* Super SandCastle) ABDO Publishing Co.

—It's N!, 1 vol. 2010. (It's the Alphabet! Ser.). (ENG., Illus.). 24p. (gr. k-4). 25.65 *(978-1-60453-601-0(2),* Super SandCastle) ABDO Publishing Co.

—It's O!, 1 vol. 2010. (It's the Alphabet! Ser.). (ENG., Illus.). 24p. (gr. k-4). 25.65 *(978-1-60453-602-7(0),* Super SandCastle) ABDO Publishing Co.

—It's S!, 1 vol. 2010. (It's the Alphabet! Ser.). (ENG., Illus.). 24p. (gr. k-4). 25.65 *(978-1-60453-606-5(3),* Super SandCastle) ABDO Publishing Co.

—It's Y!, 1 vol. 2010. (It's the Alphabet! Ser.). (ENG., Illus.). 24p. (gr. k-4). 25.65 *(978-1-60453-612-6(8),* Super SandCastle) ABDO Publishing Co.

Gagliano, Eugene. V Is for Venus Flytrap: A Plant Alphabet. Traynor, Elizabeth, illus. 2009. (Science Ser.). (ENG.). 40p. (J). (gr. k-8). 17.95 *(978-1-58536-350-6(2))* Sleeping Bear Pr.

Gagnon, Lauren. An Exeter Alphabet: Learning about Exeter from A to Z. 2005. (Illus.). 44p. (J). (gr. 3-7). per. *(978-1-933002-05-7(0))* PublishingWorks.

Gaiman, NEil. The Dangerous Alphabet. Grimly, Gris, illus. 2008. (ENG.). 32p. (J). (gr. k-3). 17.99 *(978-0-06-078333-4(8))* HarperCollins Pubs.

Gallardo, Yuri, ed. Houses & Apartments under 1000 Square Feet. 2013. (ENG., Illus.). 256p. pap. 24.95 *(978-1-77085-214-3(X),* 9781770852143) Firefly Bks., Ltd.

Galvin, Laura. Oh Where, Oh Where Has My Little Dog Gone? Villnave, Erica Pelton, illus. 2008. (ENG.). 32p. (J). (gr. -1-2). 9.95 *(978-1-59249-860-4(4))* Soundprints.

Galvin, Laura Gates. ABCDEarth. 2010. (Sesame Street Alphabet Bks.). (Illus.). 40p. (J). (gr. -1). 17.95 *(978-1-59069-875-4(4));* 17.95 *(978-1-59069-874-7(6))* Studio Mouse LLC.

—Alphabet of African Animals. Leeper, Christopher J. et al, illus. 2011. (Alphabet Bks.). (ENG.). 40p. (J). (gr. -1-3). 17.95 *(978-1-60727-574-9(0))* Soundprints.

—Alphabet of Animals. Kest, Kristin, illus. (Alphabet Bks.). (ENG.). 40p. 2011. (J). (gr. -1-3). 9.95 *(978-1-60727-443-8(4))* 2009. 9.95 *(978-1-59249-991-5(0))* 2006. (J). (gr. -1-k). 15.95 *(978-1-59249-655-6(5))* Soundprints.

—Alphabet of Ocean Animals. Petruccio, Steven James et al, illus. 2009. (ENG.). 40p. 9.95 *(978-1-60727-024-9(2))* Soundprints.

—Alphabet of Ocean Animals. Petruccio, Steven James et al, illus. 2007. (ENG.). 40p. (J). (gr. k-2). 15.95 *(978-1-59249-690-7(3))* Soundprints.

—Alphabet of Space. Bond, Higgins, illus. (ENG.). 40p. 2009. 9.95 *(978-1-59249-990-8(2))* 2007. (J). (gr. -1-k). 15.95 *(978-1-59249-656-3(3))* Soundprints.

—Angry, Brave & Cheerful: An Alphabet of Feelings. 123 Sesame Street, ed. 2009. 20p. (J). (gr. -1). 8.99 incl. audio compact disk *(978-1-59069-833-4(9))* Studio Mouse LLC.

—Princess ABCs. 2004. (ENG., Illus.). 36p. (J). 12.99 *(978-1-59069-412-1(0),* 1A107) Studio Mouse LLC.

—Take-with-Me Alphabet. 2006. (ENG., Illus.). 36p. (J). (gr. -1). 12.99 *(978-1-59069-480-0(5))* Studio Mouse LLC.

—Winnie the Pooh Bedtime ABCs. 2008. (ENG.). 20p. (J). (gr. -1-3). 9.99 *(978-1-59069-656-9(5))* Studio Mouse LLC.

Galvin, Laura Gates & Soundprints Editorial Staff. Animals A to Z. Schwaeber, Barbie H. & Williams, Tracee, eds. Kest, Kristin, illus. 2008. (ENG.). 36p. (J). (gr. 3-7). 12.99 *(978-1-59069-672-9(7))* Studio Mouse LLC.

Galvin, Laura Gates & Studio Mouse Staff. Disney Marie A Is for Adorable: A Fabulous Alphabet. Schwaeber, Barbie H., ed. rev. ed. 2007. (ENG., Illus.). 36p. (J). 12.99 *(978-1-59069-569-2(0))* Studio Mouse LLC.

—Write-with-Me Alphabet. Giblin, Brian E., ed. (Write-with-Me Ser.). (Illus.). 28p. (J). 2011. 15.99 *(978-1-59069-921-8(1))* 2008. (ENG., 14.99 *(978-1-59069-618-7(2))* Studio Mouse LLC.

Gant, Robert, illus. My Big Box of Letters. gif. ed. 2005. 64p. (J). cd-rom 24.95 *(978-1-57791-193-7(8))* Brighter Minds Children's Publishing.

Garcia, Juliet. Joshua's Abc Book. 2011. 32p. pap. 24.95 *(978-1-61546-992-5(3))* America Star Bks.

Garnett, Sammie & Pallotta, Jerry. U. S. Army Alphabet Book. 2012. (ENG., Illus.). (J). pap. 7.95 *(978-0-9852032-2-1(6))* Bald Eagle Bks.

—U. S. Navy Alphabet Book. Bolster, Rob, illus. 2004. (ENG.). 32p. (J). (gr. -1-3). pap. 7.95 *(978-1-57091-587-1(3))* Charlesbridge Publishing, Inc.

Gates Galvin, Laura. Alphabet of Art. Tabbutt, Steven, illus. 2011. (ENG.). 40p. (J). 9.95 *(978-1-60727-196-3(6))* Soundprints.

—A de Adorable: Un Abecedario Fabuloso. Schwaeber, Barbie Heit, ed. 2009. (Zip & Carry Ser.). (SPA., Illus.). 24p. (J). (gr. -1-3). bds. 12.99 incl. audio compact disk *(978-1-59069-694-1(8))* Studio Mouse LLC.

Gates, Valerie. The Alphabet of Bugs: An ABC Book. Cutting, Ann, photos by. 2015. (ENG., Illus.). 56p. (J). (gr. -1-k). 14.99 *(978-1-63220-407-3(X),* Sky Pony Pr.) Skyhorse Publishing Co., Inc.

—The Other Colors: An ABC Book. Cutting, Ann, photos by. 2013. (ENG., Illus.). 56p. (J). (gr. -1-k). 14.95 *(978-1-62087-537-7(3),* 620537, Sky Pony Pr.) Skyhorse Publishing Co., Inc.

Gaydos, Nora. All about the ABC's. Sams, B. B., illus. 2006. (ENG.). 112p. (J). (gr. -1-1). 16.99 *(978-1-58476-410-6(4),* IKIDS) Innovative Kids.

—Word Play: Sight Words. Sullivan, Mary, illus. 2008. (NIR! Leveled Readers Ser.). (ENG.). 120p. (J). (gr. -1-2). 16.99 *(978-1-58476-725-1(1),* Now I'm Reading!) Random Hse. Children's Bks.

Gelber, Lisa & Roberts, Jody. P Is for Peanut: A Photographic A-B-C. 2007. (ENG., Illus.). 58p. (J). (gr. -1-3). 9.95 *(978-0-89236-878-5(0))* Oxford Univ. Pr., Inc.

George, Pamela & Brown, Walter M. The North Carolina Alphabet. 2005. 60p. (J). *(978-0-932112-50-7(1))* Carolina Wren Pr.

Ghigna, Charles. The Alphabet Parade. Jatkowska, Ag, illus. 2014. 24p. (J). pap. *(978-1-4795-1930-9(8))* Picture Window Bks.

—Alphabet Parade. Jatkowska, Ag, illus. 2013. (My Little School House Ser.). (ENG.). 24p. (gr. -1-2). 21.99 *(978-1-4048-8310-9(X))* Picture Window Bks.

Gibeau, Claire Janvier. Active Alphabet. 2009. 16p. pap. 8.49 *(978-1-4490-3828-1(X))* AuthorHouse.

Gilbert, Drexel. H Is for Heaven: The Bible Alphabet Book. Spradlin, Leslie, illus. 2011. 36p. (J). pap. *(978-0-9818464-3-9(2))* Gilbert, Drexel Enterprises, Inc.

Gillespie, Jane. G Is for Gecko: An Alphabet Adventure in Hawai'i. Robinson, Don, illus. 2013. (ENG.). 26p. (J). (gr. -1-1). 12.95 *(978-1-933067-51-3(9))* Beachhouse Publishing, LLC.

—S Went Surfing in Hawai'i. Moen, Ruth, illus. 2013. (ENG.). 32p. (J). (gr. -1-1). 12.95 *(978-1-933067-50-6(0))* Beachhouse Publishing, LLC.

Gillian, Chelsea, et al. Princess ABCs And 123s. rev. ed. 2007. (Illus.). 24p. (J). (gr. -1-1). 4.99 *(978-1-59069-560-9(7))* Studio Mouse LLC.

Giordano, Jean. Alphabet for Young Eckists. Epps, SArah, illus. 2nd ed. 2007. (J). pap. *(978-1-57043-245-3(7))* Eckankar.

Glastetter, KC & Hollman, Jeremie. Glacier National Park: An ABC Adventure. 2008. (J). pap. *(978-0-87842-552-5(7))* Mountain Pr. Publishing Co., Inc.

Glastetter, KC & Hollman, Jeremie, photos by. Yellowstone Natl Park Abc Adv. 2010. (Illus.). 64p. (J). pap. 12.00 *(978-0-87842-572-3(1))* Mountain Pr. Publishing Co., Inc.

Glover, Maria Robinson. Who Do I Want to Be? Contemporary Black Women from A to Z. Glover, Maria Robinson, illus. 2006. (Illus.). (J). 16.95 *(978-0-9787990-0-2(1))* HotComb Pr.

Goldeen, Ruth & Goldeen, Bill. Alef-Bet Yoga for Kids. Goldeen, Bill, photos by. 2009. (Israel Ser.). (ENG., Illus.). 32p. (J). (gr. -1-2). pap. 7.95 *(978-0-7613-4506-0(X),* Kar-Ben Publishing) Lerner Publishing Group.

Goldsberry, U'ilani. A Is for Aloha: A Hawaii Alphabet. Yee, Tammy, illus. 2005. (Discover America State by State Ser.). (ENG.). 40p. (J). (gr. k-5). 17.95 *(978-1-58536-146-5(1))* Sleeping Bear Pr.

Gonyea, Mark. Counting on Letters: From A to Z & 1 to 26. 2014. (ENG., Illus.). 28p. (J). (gr. -1-1). bds. 10.95 *(978-1-57687-702-9(7),* powerHouse Bks.) powerHouse Cultural Entertainment, Inc.

Gordon, Bob. Carry-Me ABC. 2009. (Carry-Me Ser.). (ENG., Illus.). 12p. (gr. -1-k). 7.99 *(978-1-84610-873-0(X))* Make Believe Ideas GBR. Dist: Nelson, Thomas Inc.

Gorey, Edward. Thoughtful Alphabets: The Just Dessert / The Deadly Blotter. 2012. 64p. 14.95 *(978-0-7649-6336-0(8))* Pomegranate Communications, Inc.

Gorman, Lovenia. A Is for Algonquin: An Ontario Alphabet. Rose, Melanie, illus. rev. ed. 2005. (Discover Canada Province by Province Ser.). (ENG.). 40p. (J). (gr. k-5). 17.95 *(978-1-58536-263-9(8))* Sleeping Bear Pr.

Gowan, Barbara. D Is for Desert: A World Deserts Alphabet. 2012. (ENG., Illus.). 32p. (J). (gr. 1-5). 16.95 *(978-1-58536-501-2(7))* Sleeping Bear Pr.

Graham, Judith A. The Didley-Doo's, 1 vol. 2009. 36p. pap. 24.95 *(978-1-60836-035-2(0))* America Star Bks.

Granny Says. 2005. (Illus.). (J). pap. 11.00 *(978-0-9764198-0-8(7))* Allecram Publishing.

Grassby, Donna. A Seaside Alphabet. Tooke, Susan, illus. 2009. (ABC Our Country Ser.). (ENG.). 32p. (J). (gr. 1-4). pap. 7.95 *(978-0-88776-938-2(1),* Tundra Bks.) Tundra Bks. CAN. Dist: Penguin Random Hse. LLC.

Greco, Theresa. ABC Town. 2008. (Illus.). (J). (gr. -1-3). pap. 10.95 *(978-1-934666-16-6(5))* High-Pitched Hum Inc.

Grierson, Ruth. A Is for Acadia: Mount Desert Island from A to Z. Johnson, Richard, illus. 2007. (ENG.). 32p. (J). 15.95 *(978-1-934031-03-2(8),* 5605501a-a510-48b1-a5fb-bed4fcf85688) Islandport Pr., Inc.

Griffin, Sandra. The Big & Little ABC Book. 2016. (ENG., Illus.). 32p. (J). 16.95 *(978-0-9744446-7-3(7))* All About Kids Publishing.

Grobler, Piet. Little Bird's ABC. Grobler, Piet, illus. 2005. (ENG., Illus.). 52p. (J). (gr. -1-3). 8.95 *(978-1-932425-52-9(7),* Lemniscaat) Boyds Mills Pr.

Grocki, Jennifer. From A to Zamboni, the Alphabet Hockey Style! Flyers Edition. Lendway, Andy, illus. 2007. 32p. (J). 16.95 *(978-0-9793833-0-4(7))* Team Kidz, Inc.

Grodin, Elissa. D Is for Democracy: A Citizen's Alphabet. Juhasz, Victor, illus. 2006. (ENG.). 40p. (J). (gr. 1-4). per. 7.95 *(978-1-58536-328-5(6),* 203807) Sleeping Bear Pr.

Grodin, Elissa D., et al. C Is for Ciao: An Italy Alphabet. Ventura, Marco, illus. 2008. (Discover the World Ser.). (ENG.). 40p. (J). (gr. 1-5). 17.95 *(978-1-58536-361-2(8))* Sleeping Bear Pr.

Grosset and Dunlap Staff & dePaola, Tomie. My ABC Book. Seiden, Art, illus. 2015. (G&d Vintage Ser.). (ENG.). 24p. (J). (gr. -1-k). bds. 7.99 *(978-0-448-48215-6(0),* Grosset & Dunlap) Penguin Young Readers Group.

Grossman, Bill. My Little Sister Hugged an Ape. Hawkes, Kevin, illus. 2008. (ENG.). 40p. (J). (gr. -1-2). pap. 6.99 *(978-0-385-73660-2(6),* Dragonfly Bks.) Random Hse. Children's Bks.

Group/McGraw-Hill, Wright. Sign Language Alphabet Cards. (Professional Resources Ser.). 19.50 *(978-0-7802-4383-5(8))* Wright Group/McGraw-Hill.

Guéry, Anne & Dussutour, Olivier. Alphab'art: Find the Letters Hidden in the Paintings. Parkin, Antonia, tr. from FRE. 2009. (ENG., Illus.). 64p. (J). (gr. -1-k). (978-1-84780-013-8(0)) Rough Guides, Ltd.

Gürth, Per-Henrik. ABC of Toronto. Gürth, Per-Henrik, illus. 2013. (ENG., Illus.). 32p. (J). (gr. -1-k). 15.95 (978-1-77138-037-9(3)) Kids Can Pr., Ltd. CAN. Dist: Hachette Bk. Group.

Guy, Pauline & Pierre-Louis, Jerry. The Alphabet Rocks: Happy Kids Rock. 2006. (Illus.). 26p. (J). (gr. -1-k). 12.99 (978-0-9769364-0-4(2)) Golden Eagle Publishing Hse., Inc.

Hagin, Randall S. Awesome ABC. 2011. 56p. pap. 21.68 (978-1-4567-1573-1(9)) AuthorHouse.

Haile, Carol J. Christmas Cows. Haile, Carol J., illus. 2012. (ENG., Illus.). 40p. (J). 19.95 (978-0-9711236-5-6(9)) Firenze Pr.

Hall, Michael. Little I. Hall, Michael, illus. 2017. (Illus.). 48p. (J). (gr. -1-3). 17.99 **(978-0-06-238300-6(0)**, Greenwillow Bks.) HarperCollins Pubs.

Hall, Pamela. ELEMENOPEE, the Day I, M, N, O & P Left the Abc's. Williamson, James, illus. 2005. 16p. (J). 12.95 (978-1-58117-209-6(5), Intervisual/Piggy Toes) Bendon, Inc.

Hallinan, P. K. ABC I Love You. 2003. (ENG., Illus.). 24p. (J). bds. 7.95 (978-0-8249-5458-1(0), Ideal Pubns.) Worthy Publishing.

Hanson, Anders. Elephants Are Not Little! 2005. (Illus.). 23p. (J). pap. 48.42 (978-1-59679-371-2(6)) ABDO Publishing Co.

—Elephants Are Not Little, 1 vol. 2006. (First Words Ser.). (ENG., Illus.). 24p. (J). (gr. k-3). lib. bdg. 24.21 (978-1-59679-370-5(8), SandCastle) ABDO Publishing Co.

—Liz & Len. 2005. (First Sounds Ser.). (Illus.). 23p. (J). pap. 48.42 (978-1-59679-173-2(X)) ABDO Publishing Co.

—Meg & Mark, 1 vol. 2005. (First Sounds Ser.). (Illus.). (J). (gr. k-3). (ENG.). 24p. lib. bdg. 24.21 (978-1-59679-174-9(8), SandCastle); 23p. pap. 48.42 (978-1-59679-175-6(6)) ABDO Publishing Co.

—Nan & Nick. 2005. (First Sounds Ser.). (Illus.). 23p. (J). pap. 48.42 (978-1-59679-177-0(2)) ABDO Publishing Co.

—Olga & Olaf. 2005. (First Sounds Ser.). (Illus.). 23p. pap. 48.42 (978-1-59679-179-4(9)) ABDO Publishing Co.

—Olive & Oscar. 2005. (First Sounds Ser.). (Illus.). 23p. pap. 48.42 (978-1-59679-181-7(0)) ABDO Publishing Co.

—Pam & Pete. 2005. (First Sounds Ser.). (Illus.). 23p. (J). pap. 48.42 (978-1-59679-183-1(7)) ABDO Publishing Co.

—Quinn & Quenton. 2005. (First Sounds Ser.). (Illus.). 23p. (J). pap. 48.42 (978-1-59679-185-5(3)) ABDO Publishing Co.

—Ruth & Rob. 2005. (First Sounds Ser.). 23p. (J). pap. 48.42 (978-1-59679-187-9(X)) ABDO Publishing Co.

—Sara & Sam. 2005. (First Sounds Ser.). (Illus.). 23p. (J). pap. 48.42 (978-1-59679-189-3(6)) ABDO Publishing Co.

Harper, Charles. Alphabet Children Puzzle Book. 2013. 40p. pap. 19.57 (978-1-4907-0660-3(7)) Trafford Publishing.

Harper, Charley. ABC's. 2008. (ENG., Illus.). 62p. (J). (gr. -1-3). bds. 14.95 (978-1-934429-07-5(4)) AMMO Bks., LLC.

Harris, Stephen. Ballroom Bonanza: A Hidden Pictures ABC Book. Rycroft, Nina, illus. 2010. (ENG.). 40p. (J). (gr. k-2). 16.95 (978-0-8109-8842-2(9), Abrams Bks. for Young Readers) Abrams, Inc.

Harrison, Ted. A Northern Alphabet. (ABC Our Country Ser.). (ENG., Illus.). (J). 2017. 28p. (— 1). bds. 8.99 (978-1-101-91896-8(9)) 2009. 32p. (gr. 1-4). pap. 7.99 (978-0-88776-960-3(8)) Tundra Bks. CAN. (Tundra Bks.). Dist: Penguin Random Hse. LLC.

Harte, May. ABC's in My House. 2009. (Board Bks.). 16p. (gr. k-1). 23.90 (978-1-61511-638-6(9), PowerKids Pr.) Rosen Publishing Group, Inc., The.

Hasselfeldt, Lori. The under the Ocean Alphabet Book. Hasselfeldt, Lori, illus. 2013. (Illus.). 32p. 24.95 (978-1-61493-155-3(0)); pap. 14.95 (978-1-61493-154-6(2)) Peppertree Pr., The.

Hasselius, Michelle M. A Dinosaur Alphabet: The ABCs of Prehistoric Beasts! Rossiter, Clair, illus. 2016. (Alphabet Connection Ser.). (ENG.). 32p. (gr. k-1). lib. bdg. 27.32 (978-1-4795-6884-0(8)) Picture Window Bks.

Hatanaka, Kellen. Work: An Occupational ABC, 1 vol. 2014. (ENG., Illus.). 40p. (J). (gr. -1-2). 16.95 (978-1-55498-409-1(2)) Groundwood Bks. CAN. Dist: Publishers Group West (PGW).

Hayashi, Leslie Ann. A Fishy Alphabet in Hawaii. Bishop, Kathleen Wong, illus. 2007. (J). 13.95 (978-1-56647-830-4(8)) Mutual Publishing LLC.

Hayes, Larry E. My Name Starts with J. Anderson, Airlie, illus. 2004. (My Name Starts With Ser.). 31p. (J). spiral bd. 12.95 (978-0-9725292-2-8(5)) Inspire Pubns.

—My Name Starts with M. Anderson, Airlie, illus. Hayes, Larry E., photos by. 2004. (My Name Starts With Ser.). 31p. (J). spiral bd. 12.95 (978-0-9725292-3-5(3), 1) Inspire Pubns.

—My Name Starts with S. Anderson, Airlie, illus. Hayes, Larry E., photos by. 2003. (My Name Starts With Ser.). 31p. spiral bd. 10.95 (978-0-9725292-1-1(7)) Inspire Pubns.

Hayes, Trudie L. & Perkins, Kenneth B. Of All the People in the World to Be I Am Glad That I Am Me! 2008. 24p. pap. 14.95 (978-1-59858-853-8(2)) Dog Ear Publishing, LLC.

Hays, Ethel. One, Two, Buckle My Shoe: An Alphabet & Counting Book. 2012. (Shape Bks.). (ENG., Illus.). 16p. (J). pap. 9.95 (978-1-59583-624-3(1)) Laughing Elephant.

HealthTeacher. HealthTeacher: K-1. 2006. (Illus.). 334p. lib. bdg. 99.95 (978-0-9785578-5-0(9)) HealthTeacher.

Heit Schwaeber, Barbie. Alphabet of Dogs. 2011. (ENG.). 40p. (J). 9.95 (978-1-60727-198-7(2)) Soundprints.

Hell-Höflinger, Philippa. My First Coloring Dictionary from a to Z. 2012. 56p. pap. (978-3-8482-0712-1(5)) Books on Demand GmbH.

Helman, Andrea. O Is for Orca: An Alphabet Book. Wolfe, Art, photos by. 2003. (ENG., Illus.). 32p. (J). (gr. -1-2). pap. 10.99 (978-1-57061-392-0(3), Little Bigfoot) Sasquatch Bks.

HELMAN, Wolfe Jecan. C Is for Coyote: A Southwest Alphabet Book, Vol. 2017. (ENG., Illus.). 32p. (J). (gr. k-3). 7.95 (978-1-63076-300-8(4)) Muddy Boots Pr.

Henderson, Kris. Animalimericks! Burt, Kelly, illus. 2009. 32p. pap. 14.99 (978-1-4389-4333-6(4)) AuthorHouse.

Hengel, Katherine. It's B!, 1 vol. 2010. (It's the Alphabet! Ser.). (ENG.). 24p. (gr. k-4). 25.65 (978-1-60453-589-1(X), Super SandCastle) ABDO Publishing Co.

—It's G!, 1 vol. 2010. (It's the Alphabet! Ser.). (ENG.). 24p. (gr. k-4). 25.65 (978-1-60453-594-5(6), Super SandCastle) ABDO Publishing Co.

—It's H!, 1 vol. 2010. (It's the Alphabet! Ser.). (ENG.). 24p. (gr. k-4). 25.65 (978-1-60453-595-2(4), Super SandCastle) ABDO Publishing Co.

—It's M!, 1 vol. 2010. (It's the Alphabet! Ser.). (ENG., Illus.). 24p. (gr. k-4). 25.65 (978-1-60453-600-3(4), Super SandCastle) ABDO Publishing Co.

—It's Q!, 1 vol. 2010. (It's the Alphabet! Ser.). (ENG., Illus.). 24p. (gr. k-4). 25.65 (978-1-60453-604-1(7), Super SandCastle) ABDO Publishing Co.

—It's R!, 1 vol. 2010. (It's the Alphabet! Ser.). (ENG., Illus.). 24p. (gr. k-4). 25.65 (978-1-60453-605-8(5), Super SandCastle) ABDO Publishing Co.

—It's V!, 1 vol. 2010. (It's the Alphabet! Ser.). (ENG., Illus.). 24p. (gr. k-4). 25.65 (978-1-60453-609-6(8), Super SandCastle) ABDO Publishing Co.

—It's X!, 1 vol. 2010. (It's the Alphabet! Ser.). (ENG., Illus.). 24p. (gr. k-4). 25.65 (978-1-60453-611-9(X), Super SandCastle) ABDO Publishing Co.

Henley, Ivan. Kitty Milo Says the Alphabet (A Read-Aloud Book for Children) 2008. 68p. pap. 34.50 (978-1-4357-1423-6(7)) Lulu Pr., Inc.

Henry, Marcia. Madeline Island ABC Coloring Book. Parsons, Sally, illus. 2008. (ENG.). 32p. (J). (gr. k-6). pap. 6.95 (978-0-9817723-0-1(7)) Univ. of Wisconsin Pr.

Henry, Marcia Kierland. Madeline Island ABC Book. Parsons, Sally, illus. 2008. (ENG.). 52p. (J). (gr. -1-4). pap. 18.95 (978-1-4243-3753-8(4)) Univ. of Wisconsin Pr.

Hernandez, Annette. Captain Holo's Journey through the Alphabet: An ABC Book. 2010. (Illus.). 30p. (J). pap. 19.95 (978-1-4327-5261-3(8)) Outskirts Pr., Inc.

Hershenhorn, Esther. S Is for Story: A Writer's Alphabet. Pullen, Zachary, illus. 2009. (ENG.). 40p. (J). (gr. 1-4). 17.95 (978-1-58536-439-8(8), 202167) Sleeping Bear Pr.

Herzog, Brad. E Is for Extreme: An Extreme Sports Alphabet. Rose, Melanie, illus. 2015. (Av2 Fiction Readalong 2016 Ser.). (ENG.). (J). (gr. 1-4). lib. bdg. 34.28 (978-1-4896-3735-2(4), AV2 by Weigl) Weigl Pubs., Inc.

—G Is for Gold Medal: An Olympics Alphabet. Bowles, Doug, illus. 2015. (Av2 Fiction Readalong 2016 Ser.). (ENG.). (J). (gr. 1-4). lib. bdg. 34.28 (978-1-4896-3738-3(9), AV2 by Weigl) Weigl Pubs., Inc.

—H Is for Home Run: A Baseball Alphabet. Rose, Melanie, illus. 2009. (Alphabet-Sports Ser.). (ENG.). 40p. (gr. k-6). pap. 7.95 (978-1-58536-475-6(4)) Sleeping Bear Pr.

—H Is for Home Run: A Baseball Alphabet. Rose, Melanie, illus. 2015. (Av2 Fiction Readalong 2016 Ser.). (ENG.). (J). (gr. 1-4). lib. bdg. 34.28 (978-1-4896-3744-4(3), AV2 by Weigl) Weigl Pubs., Inc.

—A Is for Amazing Moments: A Sports Alphabet. Rose, Melanie, illus. 2008. (Sports Ser.). (ENG.). 40p. (J). (gr. -1-5). 17.95 (978-1-58536-360-5(X)) Sleeping Bear Pr.

—A Is for Amazing Moments: A Sports Alphabet. Rose, Melanie, illus. 2015. (Av2 Fiction Readalong 2016 Ser.). (ENG.). (J). (gr. 1-4). lib. bdg. 34.28 (978-1-4896-3729-1(X), AV2 by Weigl) Weigl Pubs., Inc.

—K Is for Kick: A Soccer Alphabet. Rose, Melanie, illus. rev. ed. (Sports Ser.). (ENG.). 40p. (J). (gr. -1-3). 2006. pap. 7.95 (978-1-58536-339-1(1)) 2003. 16.95 (978-1-58536-130-4(5)) Sleeping Bear Pr.

—K Is for Kick: A Soccer Alphabet. Rose, Melanie, illus. 2015. (Av2 Fiction Readalong 2016 Ser.). (ENG.). (J). (gr. 1-4). lib. bdg. 34.28 (978-1-4896-3756-7(7), AV2 by Weigl) Weigl Pubs., Inc.

—P Is for Putt: A Golf Alphabet. Langton, Bruce, illus. (Alphabet-Sports Ser.). (ENG.). 40p. 2009. (gr. k-6). pap. 7.95 (978-1-58536-476-3(2)) 2005. (J). (gr. -1-5). 16.95 (978-1-58536-252-3(2)) Sleeping Bear Pr.

—P Is for Putt: A Golf Alphabet. Langton, Bruce, illus. 2015. (Av2 Fiction Readalong 2016 Ser.). (ENG.). (J). (gr. 1-4). lib. bdg. 34.28 (978-1-4896-3759-8(1), AV2 by Weigl) Weigl Pubs., Inc.

—R Is for Race: A Stock Car Alphabet. Bready, Jane Gilltrap, illus. 2006. (Sports Ser.). (ENG.). 40p. (J). (gr. -1-5). 16.95 (978-1-58536-272-1(7)) Sleeping Bear Pr.

—T Is for Touchdown: A Football Alphabet. Braught, Mark, illus. 2006. (Sports Alphabet Ser.). (ENG.). 40p. (J). (gr. 1-4). pap. 7.95 (978-1-58536-337-7(5), 202300) Sleeping Bear Pr.

—T Is for Touchdown: A Football Alphabet. Stacy, Alan & Braught, Mark, illus. 2004. (Sports Ser.). (ENG.). 40p. (J). (gr. -1-5). 16.95 (978-1-58536-233-2(6)) Sleeping Bear Pr.

—W Is for Wrigley: A Friendly Confines Alphabet. Hanley, John, illus. 2013. (ENG.). (J). (978-1-58536-816-7(4)) Sleeping Bear Pr.

Herzog, Brad & Bowles, Doug. G Is for Gold Medal: An Olympics Alphabet. Bowles, Doug, illus. 2011. (ENG., Illus.). 32p. (gr. k-5). 15.95 (978-1-58536-462-6(2)) Sleeping Bear Pr.

Herzog, Joyce. Exploring the Alphabet: Student Activity Book. Sinclair, Angie & Sinclair, Dan, eds. 2005. (J). spiral bd. 15.00 (978-1-887225-42-7(0)) Herzog, Joyce.

—LetterMaster: Comic Book. 2004. (J). 6.00 (978-1-887225-17-5(X)) Herzog, Joyce.

Heshka, Ryan. Ryan Heshka's ABC Spookshow. 2007. (ENG., Illus.). 58p. (J). (gr. k-3). 12.95 (978-1-894965-68-2(X)) Simply Read Bks. CAN. Dist: Ingram Publisher Services.

Hicks, Rob & Hicks, Kim. Amelia, A to Z. Bolton-Eells, Sharon, illus. 2011. (J). (978-0-9829908-0-3(4)) Island Media Publishing, LLC.

Highlights for Children Editorial Staff, creator. My First ABC. 2016. (Highlights(tm) My First Write-On Wipe-off Board Bks.). (ENG.). 28p. (J). (gr. -1-k). bds. 9.99 (978-1-62979-706-9(5), Highlights) Boyds Mills Pr.

Hill, Cheryl E. R Is for Reading Books. Pierce, Dave G., illus. 2012. 56p. pap. 17.99 (978-0-9859770-0-9(0)) N.O.A.H Bks.

Hill, Kevin. A - Z Animal Coloring & Activity Book: English & Spanish. 2012. 60p. (gr. -1). pap. 12.95 (978-1-4772-0407-8(5)) AuthorHouse.

Hillert, Margaret. Dear Dragon's A Is for Apple. Schimmell, David, illus. 2008. (BeginningtoRead Ser.). 32p. (J). (gr. k-2). lib. bdg. 22.60 (978-1-59953-158-8(5)) Norwood Hse. Pr.

Hinkler Books Staff. ABC. rev. ed. 2006. (Slide & Learn Ser.). (ENG., Illus.). 12p. (J). (gr. -1-1). bds. 7.95 (978-1-74157-602-3(4)) Hinkler Bks. Pty, Ltd. AUS. Dist: Penton Overseas, Inc.

Ho, Jane. ABC Alphabet Book, No. 1. 29p. (J). (gr. -1). 20.00 (978-0-9619126-0-4(X)) Ho's, Jane Children Bks.

Hodge, Deborah. West Coast Wild: A Nature Alphabet, 1 vol. Reczuch, Karen, illus. 2015. (ENG.). 48p. (J). (gr. -1-2). 18.95 (978-1-55498-440-4(8)) Groundwood Bks. CAN. Dist: Publishers Group West (PGW).

Hoffman, Joan. Alphabet Stickers. Boyer, Robin, illus. 2006. (ENG.). 64p. (J). (gr. -1-k). 7.99 (978-1-58947-746-9(4)) School Zone Publishing Co.

Holden, Pam. Naughty Goldilocks, 6 pack. Holt, Richard, illus. 2009. (Red Rocket Readers Ser.). (ENG.). 16p. (gr. -1-1). pap. (978-1-877363-08-5(1), Red Rocket Readers) Flying Start Bks.

—Red Riding Hood, 6 pack. Hawley, Kelvin, illus. 2009. (Red Rocket Readers Ser.). (ENG.). 16p. (gr. -1-1). pap. (978-1-877363-09-2(X), Red Rocket Readers) Flying Start Bks.

—Three Billy Goats Gruff, 6 pack. Hawley, Kelvin, illus. 2009. (Red Rocket Readers Ser.). (ENG.). 16p. (gr. -1-1). pap. (978-1-877363-10-8(3), Red Rocket Readers) Flying Start Bks.

—Three Little Pigs, 6 pack. Storey, Jim, illus. 2009. (Red Rocket Readers Ser.). (ENG.). 16p. (gr. -1-1). pap. (978-1-877363-11-5(1), Red Rocket Readers) Flying Start Bks.

Holland, Trish. Build It from A to Z. 2010. (J). (978-1-60617-136-3(4)) Teaching Strategies, LLC.

Holliday, Patricia. A Is for Anjelina. 2009. 32p. pap. 18.60 (978-1-4357-4402-8(0)) Lulu Pr., Inc.

—A Is for Anjelina: an Introduction to ABC's And 123's. 2005. 29p. (J). 12.26 (978-1-4116-4471-7(9)) Lulu Pr., Inc.

Holmes, Stephen. Alphabet Zoo. 2003. (J). bds. 5.98 (978-0-7525-8922-0(9)) Parragon, Inc.

Hoover, Nadine. A, B, C Awal. Bardo, Yuyun, illus. 2013. 36p. (J). pap. 12.00 (978-0-9828492-1-7(4)) Conscience Studio.

HOP, LLC. Hooked on ABCs Super Activity Kit. 2006. (J). (gr. -1). 9.99 (978-1-933863-16-0(1)) HOP, LLC.

Hopkins, Lee Bennett & Boyds Mills Press Staff. Alphathoughts: Alphabet Poems. Baggetta, Marla, illus. 2003. (ENG.). 32p. (J). (gr. 1-3). 16.95 (978-1-56397-979-8(9)) Boyds Mills Pr.

Hopkins, Mary Rice. Animal Alphabet: On the Land, in the Sky or Sea, Meet God's Creatures from a to Z. Francisco, Wendy, illus. 2003. 32p. (J). (gr. -1-1). 12.99 (978-0-89107-968-2(8)) Crossway.

Horne, Jane. Busy Baby Sparklies 4 Volume Boxed Set: Baby's First Box of Books. 2007. (Illus.). 12p. (gr. -1-k). bds., bds. (978-1-84610-565-4(X)) Make Believe Ideas.

—Flip & Find Abc. 2008. (Illus.). 12p. (J). (gr. -1-3). bds. (978-1-84610-730-6(X)) Make Believe Ideas.

Hosford, William. ABalloonC. Hosford, William, illus. 2007. (Illus.). 32p. (J). per. 10.00 (978-0-9776562-1-9(7)) WGH Arts LLC.

Hosta, Dar. I Love the Alphabet. 2004. (Illus.). (J). 16.95 (978-0-9721967-1-0(4)) Brown Dog Bks.

Howarth, Jill, illus. The ABCs of Christmas. 2016. (ENG.). 26p. (J). (gr. -1-17). bds. 7.95 (978-0-7624-6125-7(X), Running Pr. Kids) Running Pr. Bk. Pubs.

Howell, Des. The Abcs of Good Manners. 2009. 20p. pap. 13.00 (978-1-4389-1837-2(2)) AuthorHouse.

Hruby, Patrick. ABC Is for Circus: Hardcover Popular Edition. 2017. (ENG., Illus.). 56p. 9.95 (978-1-62326-107-8(4)) AMMO Bks., LLC.

Hu, Lorna. Pili the 'Iwa Bird Shares the Letter B: Book #1 in the Gift of Reading Series. Omoto, Garrett, illus. 2013. (J). pap. 9.95 (978-1-933835-28-0(1)) Partners in Development Foundation.

Hutchcraft, Steve. B Is for Bufflehead: Flying Through the ABC's with Fun Feathered Friends. Hutchcraft, Steve, photos by. 2009. (Illus.). 80p. (J). (gr. -1-4). 19.95 (978-0-9824925-0-5(2)) PhotoHutch.

Hylton, Adlyn. The A-B-C Smarts: Book 1. 2010. 56p. pap. 23.99 (978-1-4520-2283-3(6)) AuthorHouse.

Hyperion Staff. First Signing ABC. Williams, Sam, illus. 2007. (ENG.). 64p. (J). (gr. -1-3). 16.99 (978-1-4231-0248-9(7)) Hyperion Pr.

I Love to Read (Spanish) 2007. (Illus.). bds. 15.95 (978-1-59572-064-1(2)) Star Bright Bks., Inc.

In Our Words. Korean Letter Story. 2012.Tr. of 한글나라 이야기. (KOR., Illus.). 66p. (J). 29.99 (978-1-938040-00-9(7)) In Our Words Inc.

Inkpen, Mick. A to Z: An Alphabet Adventure. 2005. (Kipper Ser.). (ENG., Illus.). 64p. (J). (gr. -1-3). pap. 7.99 (978-0-15-205441-0(3)) Houghton Mifflin Harcourt Publishing Co.

—Kipper's A to Z: An Alphabet Adventure. 2006. (Kipper Ser.). (Illus.). 54p. (gr. -1-2). 18.00 (978-0-7569-6557-0(8)) Perfection Learning Corp.

Inthof, Marian. Aunt Marian's Abc Book, 1 vol. 2009. 32p. pap. 24.95 (978-1-60813-704-6(X)) America Star Bks.

Ipcar, Dahlov. Dahlov Ipcar's Farmyard Alphabet, 1 vol. 2010. (ENG., Illus.). 18p. (J). bds. 10.95 (978-1-934031-43-8(7), 322cba51-66de-4792-9574-ca10ba745057) Islandport Pr., Inc.

Ipcizade, Catherine. T Is for Tiara: A Princess Alphabet, 1 vol. 2010. (Alphabet Fun Ser.). (ENG.). 32p. (gr. 1-2). lib. bdg. 27.32 (978-1-4296-4462-4(1), Aplus Bks.) Capstone Press of Coughlan Cos.

A Is for Adam: An Alphabet Book of Bible Heroes. 2017. (ENG.). (J). (gr. -1-1). 14.99 **(978-1-4621-2024-6(5))** Cedar Fort, Inc./CFI Distribution.

Jackaman, Philippa. ABC Kaleidoscope Book. Walsh, Mike, illus. 16p. (J). bds. (978-1-84322-126-5(8)) Alligator Bks. Ltd.

Jackson, Nikki. Georgia & Reeds: The AL-PHA-BET Book. 2012. 20p. pap. 17.99 (978-1-4772-2939-2(6)) AuthorHouse.

James, Helen Foster. S Is for S'Mores: A Camping Alphabet. Judge, Lita, illus. rev. ed. 2007. (ENG.). 40p. (J). (gr. k-6). 17.95 (978-1-58536-302-5(2)) Sleeping Bear Pr.

Jansen, Karen. Mardi Gras in New Orleans: An Alphabet Book. 2008. 32p. pap. 13.99 (978-1-4389-1543-2(8)) AuthorHouse.

Jarboe, Tracy & Sadler, Stefani. Cut, Paste & Write ABC Activity Pages: 26 Lessons That Use Art & Alliterative Poetry to Build Phonemic Awareness, Teach Letter Sounds, & Help Children Really Learn the Alphabet. 2006. (ENG., Illus.). 80p. pap. 12.99 (978-0-439-57630-7(X), Teaching Resources) Scholastic, Inc.

Jarvis, Natalie. An Alphabet in Silhouette. 2016. (ENG., Illus.). 24p. (J). (gr. -1-k). bds. 14.99 (978-1-76012-511-0(3)) Hardie Grant Egmont Pty, Ltd. AUS. Dist: Independent Pubs. Group.

Jay, Alison. ABC: A Child's First Alphabet Book. Jay, Alison, illus. 2005. (ENG., Illus.). 32p. (J). (gr. -1 — 1). bds. 10.99 (978-0-525-47524-8(9), Dutton Books for Young Readers) Penguin Young Readers Group.

Jaycox, Jaclyn. A Princess Alphabet: The ABCs of Royalty! Eriza, Gustavo, illus. 2016. (Alphabet Connection Ser.). (ENG.). 32p. (gr. k-1). lib. bdg. 27.32 (978-1-4795-6885-7(6)) Picture Window Bks.

Jaycox, Jaclyn, et al. Alphabet Connection. Loram, James & Jevons, Chris, illus. 2016. (Alphabet Connection Ser.). (ENG.). 32p. (gr. k-1). 109.28 (978-1-4795-8005-7(8)) Picture Window Bks.

Jeffers, Oliver. Once upon an Alphabet: Short Stories for All the Letters. Jeffers, Oliver, illus. 2014. (ENG., Illus.). 112p. (J). (gr. -1-k). 26.99 (978-0-399-16791-1(9), Philomel Bks.) Penguin Publishing Group.

—Once upon an Alphabet: Short Stories for All the Letters. Jeffers, Oliver, illus. 2017. (ENG., Illus.). 26p. (J). (— 1). bds. 8.99 (978-0-399-54542-9(5), Philomel Bks.) Penguin Young Readers Group.

Jenkins, Merryann. Nehemiah the Postman: Journey Through the Alphabet. 2010. 32p. pap. 14.95 (978-1-4389-3344-3(4)) AuthorHouse.

Jensen, Sydell A. Christian Alphabet. 2010. 32p. pap. 14.99 (978-1-4490-0631-0(0)) AuthorHouse.

Johnson, Florence. The Christmas ABC. Wilkin, Eloise, illus. 2013. (Little Golden Book Ser.). (ENG.). 24p. (J). (-k). 4.99 (978-0-307-97891-2(5), Golden Bks.) Random Hse. Children's Bks.

Johnson, Michael. Iroquois: People of the Longhouse. 2013. (ENG., Illus.). 160p. 35.00 (978-1-77085-218-1(2), 9781770852181) Firefly Bks., Ltd.

Johnson, Odette & Johnson, Bruce. Apples, Alligators & Also Alphabets, 1 vol. (ENG., Illus.). 26p. (978-1-55005-077-6(X)) Fitzhenry & Whiteside, Ltd.

Johnson, Stephen T. A Is for Art: An Abstract Alphabet. Johnson, Stephen T., illus. 2008. (ENG., Illus.). 40p. (J). (gr. k-4). 18.99 (978-0-689-86301-1(2), Simon & Schuster/Paula Wiseman Bks.) Simon & Schuster/Paula Wiseman Bks.

—Alphabet School. Johnson, Stephen T., illus. 2015. (ENG., Illus.). 32p. (J). (gr. -1-3). 17.99 (978-1-4169-2521-7(X), Simon & Schuster Bks. For Young Readers) Simon & Schuster Bks. For Young Readers.

Johnson, Tasha A. & Johnson, Jeff A. The Child Care Alphabet Book of Early Learning. 2007. 60p. pap. 9.95 (978-0-615-15718-4(1)) Explorations Early Learning.

—The Child Care Alphabet Book of Manipulatives. 2007. 60p. pap. 9.95 (978-0-615-15719-1(X)) Explorations Early Learning.

Johnston, Coleen. Unusual Mammals from A to Z. 2009. 36p. pap. 19.95 (978-1-4357-5566-6(9)) Lulu Pr., Inc.

Johnston, Tony. P Is for Pinata. Parra, John, illus. 2008. (Discover the World Ser.). (ENG.). 40p. (J). (gr. 1-5). 17.95 (978-1-58536-144-1(5)) Sleeping Bear Pr.

Jones, Karen. Around the World from a to Z. 2011. 56p. pap. 21.95 (978-1-4567-6145-5(5)) AuthorHouse.

Jordan, Christopher. Hockey ABC. 2010. (My First NHL Bks.). (ENG., Illus.). 30p. (J). (gr. -1). bds. (978-1-55168-365-2(2)) Me to We.

Joseph, Patricia. Animals from Aa to Zz. 2009. 40p. pap. 18.50 (978-1-4490-2419-2(X)) AuthorHouse.

Josiah, Iris. Tiny Goat's Alphabet Book. 2015. (Illus.). 40p. (J). pap. (978-0-9572728-7-3(1)) Tiny Island Pr.

—Tiny Hen's Alphabet Book. 2015. (Illus.). 40p. (J). pap. (978-0-9572728-8-0(X)) Tiny Island Pr.

—Tiny Pig's Alphabet Book. 2015. (Illus.). 40p. (J). pap. (978-0-9572728-6-6(3)) Tiny Island Pr.

—Tiny Rabbit's Alphabet Book. 2015. (Illus.). 40p. (J). pap. (978-0-9572728-5-9(5)) Tiny Island Pr.

Joubert, Beverly & Joubert, Dereck. African Animal Alphabet. 2011. (ENG., Illus.). 48p. (J). (gr. -1-k). 26.90 (978-1-4263-0782-9(9), National Geographic Children's Bks.) National Geographic Society.

Journeys: Animal Alphabet Book. (Journeys Ser.). pap. 46.60 (978-1-4042-5413-8(7), Rosen Classroom) Rosen Publishing Group, Inc., The.

Joy, Susan. My 1st Wacky ABCs. 2008. 32p. pap. 24.95 (978-1-4241-9955-6(7)) America Star Bks.

Joyce, Susan. ABC Nature Riddles. DuBosque, Doug, illus. 2004. (ABC Riddles Ser.). 32p. (J). (gr. -1-k). 13.95 (978-0-939217-53-3(8)) Peel Productions, Inc.

Joyce, William. The Numberlys. Joyce, William & Ellis, Christina, illus. 2014. (ENG.). 56p. (J). (gr. -1-2). 17.99 (978-1-4424-7343-0(6), Atheneum Bks. for Young Readers) Simon & Schuster Children's Publishing.

J.s., Monroe-Daley. A Is for Arizona. 2009. (J). 14.95 (978-1-934878-65-1(0)) Mascot Bks., Inc.

Kalman, Bobbie. The ABCs of Animals. 2007. (ABCs of the Natural World Ser.). (ENG., Illus.). 32p. (J). (gr. 1-5). pap. (978-0-7787-3430-7(7)) Crabtree Publishing Co.

—The ABCs of Continents. 2009. (ABCs of the Natural World Ser.). (ENG., Illus.). 32p. (J). (gr. 1-5). pap. (978-0-7787-3434-5(X)); (gr. 2-4). lib. bdg. (978-0-7787-3414-7(5)) Crabtree Publishing Co.

—The ABCs of Endangered Animals. 2009. (ABCs of the Natural World Ser.). (ENG., Illus.). 32p. (J). (gr. 1-5). pap. (978-0-7787-3435-2(8)); (gr. 2-4). lib. bdg. (978-0-7787-3415-4(3)) Crabtree Publishing Co.

—The ABCs of Habitats. 2007. (ABCs of the Natural World Ser.). (ENG., Illus.). 32p. (J). (gr. 1-4). pap. (978-0-7787-3431-4(5)) Crabtree Publishing Co.

—The ABCs of Insects. 2009. (ABCs of the Natural World Ser.). (ENG., Illus.). 32p. (J). (gr. 1-5). pap. (978-0-7787-3436-9(6)); (gr. 2-4). lib. bdg. (978-0-7787-3416-1(1)) Crabtree Publishing Co.

—The ABCs of Oceans. 2007. (ABCs of the Natural World Ser.). (ENG., Illus.). 32p. (J). (gr. 1-5). pap. (978-0-7787-3432-1(3)) Crabtree Publishing Co.

—The ABCs of Plants. 2007. (ABCs of the Natural World Ser.). (ENG., Illus.). 32p. (J). (gr. 1-4). pap. (978-0-7787-3433-8(1)) Crabtree Publishing Co.

AB

—The ABCs of the Environment. 2009. (ABCs of the Natural World Ser.). (ENG., Illus.). 32p. (J). (gr. 1-5). pap. (978-0-7787-3437-6(4)); (gr. 2-4). lib. bdg. (978-0-7787-3417-8(X)) Crabtree Publishing Co.

Kalman, Maira. What Pete Ate from A to Z. 2003. (ENG., Illus.). 48p. (J). (gr. -1-2). pap. 6.99 (978-0-14-250159-7(X), Puffin Books) Penguin Young Readers Group.

Kann, Victoria. Pinkalicious ABC: An Alphabet Book. Kann, Victoria, illus. 2016. (Pinkalicious Ser.). (Illus.). 32p. (J). (gr. -1 — 1). bds. 7.99 (978-0-06-243755-6(0), HarperFestival) HarperCollins Pubs.

Kaufman, Elliott, photos by. Alphabet Everywhere. 2012. (ENG., Illus.). 60p. (J). (gr. -1). 14.95 (978-0-7892-1115-6(7), Abbeville Kids) Abbeville Pr., Inc.

Kehl, Esther. The Amazing Action Alphabet Activities. Carlson, Andy, illus. 2009. 40p. (J). spiral bd. 12.50 (978-0-9788089-1-4(6)) SeeHearDo Co., LLC, The.

Keith, Barbara Benson. Mosaic Zoo: An ABC Book. Keith, Barbara Benson, illus. 2008. (Illus.). 32p. (J). per. 8.99 (978-0-9789688-1-6(6)) Brownian Bee Pr.

Keith, Doug, illus. B Is for Baseball: Alphabet Cards. 2011. (ENG.). 26p. (J). 12.95 (978-1-897476-55-0(8)) Simply Read Bks. CAN. Dist: Ingram Publisher Services.

Kelly Edwards Elementary School (Williston, S.C.) Staff, contrib. by. The ABCs of Williston History. 2007. (J). pap. (978-0-87844-185-3(9)) Sandlapper Publishing Co., Inc.

Keman, Martin James. Danger Dolphin. Finley, Thomas Murray, illus. 2012. 28p. pap. 14.95 (978-1-4675-2428-5(X)) Independent Pub.

Kertell, Lynn Maslen. Alphabet. Maslen, John R. & Hendra, Sue, illus. 2008. (Bob Bks.). (ENG.). 144p. (J). (gr. -1-3). pap. 16.99 (978-0-545-01921-7(4), Cartwheel Bks.) Scholastic, Inc.

Kesselman, Robin & Kesselman, Marc. Nerdel's ABC Book. Martinez, Natali, illus. 2009. 38p. (J). 16.99 (978-0-9823357-2-7(5)) Nerdel Co., The.

Kiehm, Eve Begley. B Is for Bagpipes: A Scotland Alphabet. Rutherford, Alexa, illus. 2010. (Discover the World Ser.). (ENG.). 40p. (J). 17.95 (978-1-58536-453-4(3)) Sleeping Bear Pr.

Kinast, Susan. Play from A to Z. 2006. (J). lib. bdg. 19.95 (978-1-933732-11-4(3)) Big Ransom Studio.

King, Emiliya. Amy Uses the Alphabet: Step by Step. 2017. (Computer Science for the Real World Ser.). 12p. (gr. 6-7). pap. 7.05 **(978-1-5383-5142-0(0)**, Rosen Classroom) Rosen Publishing Group, Inc., The.

Klement, Jon. Smerd's Book of ABC's. 2009. 32p. pap. 19.85 (978-0-557-19030-0(4)) Lulu Pr., Inc.

Kline, Trish & Donev, Mary. The Busy Preschooler's Guide to Learning. 2007. (Illus.). 128p. (J). per. 60.00 (978-1-934307-17-5(3)) Ghost Hunter Productions.

—Celebration of Letters A & B: Busy Preschoolers. 2007. (Illus.). 16p. (J). per. 20.00 (978-1-934307-04-5(1)) Ghost Hunter Productions.

—Celebration of Letters C & D: Busy Preschoolers. 2007. (Illus.). 16p. (J). per. 20.00 (978-1-934307-05-2(X)) Ghost Hunter Productions.

—Celebration of Letters E & F: Busy Preschoolers. 2007. (Illus.). 16p. (J). per. 20.00 (978-1-934307-06-9(8)) Ghost Hunter Productions.

—Celebration of Letters G & H: Busy Preschoolers. 2007. (Illus.). 16p. (J). per. 20.00 (978-1-934307-07-6(6)) Ghost Hunter Productions.

—Celebration of Letters I & J: Busy Preschoolers. 2007. (Illus.). 16p. (J). per. 20.00 (978-1-934307-08-3(4)) Ghost Hunter Productions.

—Celebration of Letters K & L: Busy Preschoolers. 2007. (Illus.). 16p. (J). per. 20.00 (978-1-934307-09-0(2)) Ghost Hunter Productions.

—Celebration of Letters M & N: Busy Preschoolers. 2007. (Illus.). 16p. (J). per. 20.00 (978-1-934307-10-6(6)) Ghost Hunter Productions.

—Celebration of Letters O & Q: Busy Preschoolers. 2007. (Illus.). 16p. (J). per. 20.00 (978-1-934307-11-3(4)) Ghost Hunter Productions.

—Celebration of Letters P & R: Busy Preschoolers. 2007. (Illus.). 16p. (J). per. 20.00 (978-1-934307-12-0(2)) Ghost Hunter Productions.

—Celebration of Letters S & T: Busy Preschoolers. 2007. (Illus.). 16p. (J). per. 20.00 (978-1-934307-13-7(0)) Ghost Hunter Productions.

—Celebration of Letters U & V: Busy Preschoolers. 2007. (Illus.). 16p. (J). per. 20.00 (978-1-934307-14-4(9)) Ghost Hunter Productions.

—Celebration of Letters W & X: Busy Preschoolers. 2007. (Illus.). 16p. (J). per. 20.00 (978-1-934307-15-1(7)) Ghost Hunter Productions.

—Celebration of Letters Y & Z: Busy Preschoolers. 2007. (Illus.). 16p. (J). per. 20.00 (978-1-934307-16-8(5)) Ghost Hunter Productions.

Knowlton, Laurie Lazzaro. Cowgirl Alphabet, 1 vol. Knowlton, Charlotte & Coates, Kathy, illus. 2011. (ENG.). 32p. (J). (gr. k-3). 16.99 (978-1-58980-669-6(7)) Pelican Publishing Co., Inc.

Koenigsberg, Phyllis & Winkler, Ziporah, creators. Color My Alef Bet. 2004. (J). 2.99 (978-965-90462-5-6(1)) Mazo Pubs.

Kontis, Alethea. Alpha Oops! The Day Z Went First. Kolar, Bob, illus. 2012. (ENG.). 48p. (J). (gr. -1-3). pap. 6.99 (978-0-7636-6084-0(1)) Candlewick Pr.

—AlphaOops! H Is for Halloween. Kolar, Bob, illus. 2010. (ENG.). 40p. (J). (gr. -1-3). 15.99 (978-0-7636-3966-2(4)) Candlewick Pr.

Kowalski, Gary A. Earth Day: An Alphabet Book. Baviera, Rocco, illus. 2009. (ENG.). 32p. (J). (gr. -1-4). 12.00 (978-1-55896-542-3(4), 1297770, Skinner Hse. Bks.) Unitarian Universalist Assn.

Krans, Kim. ABC Dream. 2016. (ENG., Illus.). 48p. (J). (gr. -1-2). 16.99 (978-0-553-53929-5(9), Random Hse. Bks. for Young Readers) Random Hse. Children's Bks.

Kratter, Paul. The Living Rain Forest: An Animal Alphabet. Kratter, Paul, illus. rev. ed. 2010. (ENG., Illus.). 32p. (J). (gr. 1-4). pap. 7.95 (978-1-58089-393-0(7)) Charlesbridge Publishing, Inc.

Krull, Kathleen. M Is for Music. Innerst, Stacy, illus. 2003. (ENG.). 56p. (J). (gr. -1-3). 17.00 (978-0-15-201438-4(1)) Houghton Mifflin Harcourt Publishing Co.

Kumon. My First Book of Lowercase Letters. 2004. (Kumon Ser.). (ENG., Illus.). 80p. (J). per. 6.95 (978-4-7743-0706-0(8)) Kumon Publishing North America, Inc.

—My First Book of Uppercase Letters. 2004. (Kumon Ser.). (ENG., Illus.). 80p. (J). per. 6.95 (978-4-7743-0705-3(X)) Kumon Publishing North America, Inc.

Kumon Publishing, creator. My Book of Alphabet Games Ages 4, 5, 6. 2007. (Kumon Workbooks Ser.). (Illus.). 80p. per. 7.95 (978-1-933241-36-4(5)) Kumon Publishing North America, Inc.

Kumon Publishing North America, creator. ABC's Write & Wipe! Uppercase Letters. 2006. (Kumon Flash Cards Ser.). (ENG., Illus.). 32p. (J). pap. 9.95 (978-1-933241-10-4(1)) Kumon Publishing North America, Inc.

Kusugak, Michael. T Is for Territories: A Yukon, Northwest Territories, & Nunavut Alphabet. 2013. (Discover Canada Province by Province Ser.). (ENG., Illus.). 40p. (J). (gr. 1-4). 17.95 (978-1-58536-207-3(7), 202273) Sleeping Bear Pr.

Kutner, Richard, tr. from FRE. The Wild Piano. Fred, illus. 2015. (Philemon Adventures Ser.). (ENG.). 48p. (J). (gr. 2-7). 16.95 (978-1-935179-83-2(7)) TOON Books / RAW Junior, LLC.

Lagrange, Tiffany. My Abc Blue Book. LaGrange, Tiffany, illus. 2008. 32p. pap. 12.95 (978-1-934246-38-2(7)) Peppertree Pr., The.

—My Abc Pink Book. LaGrange, Tiffany, illus. 2008. 32p. pap. 12.95 (978-0-9814894-3-8(5)) Peppertree Pr., The.

Lakeshore Learning Materials Staff, contrib. by. Read-along Alphabet Chants: Big Book. 2007. (J). pap. 19.95 (978-1-59746-013-2(3)) Lakeshore Learning Materials.

—Read-along Alphabet Chants: Student Books. 2007. (J). pap. 16.95 (978-1-59746-012-5(5)) Lakeshore Learning Materials.

—Spanish Alphabet Big Book. 2006. (SPA.). (J). pap. 19.95 (978-1-59746-000-2(1)) Lakeshore Learning Materials.

Lamb, Stacey. ABC Coloring Book with Stickers. 2010. (Sticker Coloring Bks). 16p. (J). pap. 5.99 (978-0-7945-2786-0(8), Usborne) EDC Publishing.

Lamb, Stacey, illus. ABC. 2009. (Sticker Bks). 24p. (J). pap. 6.99 (978-0-7945-2362-6(5), Usborne) EDC Publishing.

—Wipe Clean Alphabet Book. 2011. (Wipe-Clean Bks). 20p. (J). pap. 7.99 (978-0-7945-3099-0(0), Usborne) EDC Publishing.

Larousse Color ABC y 123 (Amarillo), Vol. 1. 2003. (SPA., Illus.). 6p. (J). 2.98 (978-970-22-0163-2(2)) Larousse, Ediciones, S. A. de C. V. MEX. Dist: Giron Bks.

Larson, Elaine M., et al. I Am Utterly Unique: Celebrating the Strengths of Children with Asperger Syndrome & High-Functioning Autism. Strand, Vivian, illus. 2006. 56p. (J). (gr. -1-3). 18.95 (978-1-931282-89-5(7)) Autism Asperger Publishing Co.

Law, Felicia. Alphabet. Knight, Paula, illus. 2015. (Patchwork Ser.). (ENG.). 24p. (J). (gr. k-3). pap. 11.94 (978-1-60357-805-9(6)) Norwood Hse. Pr.

Layne, Deborah & Layne, Steven. P Is for Princess: A Royal Alphabet. Papp, Robert & Papp, Lisa, illus. rev. ed. 2007. (ENG.). 40p. (J). (gr. k-6). 17.95 (978-1-58536-306-3(5)) Sleeping Bear Pr.

Layne, Steven, et al. W Is for Windy City: A Chicago City Alphabet. Hays, Michael, illus. 2010. (Sleeping Bear City Alphabet Ser.). (ENG.). 40p. (J). 17.95 (978-1-58536-420-6(7)) Sleeping Bear Pr.

Layne, Steven L. & Layne, Deborah Dover. T Is for Teacher: A School Alphabet. Ettlinger, Doris, illus. 2007. (ENG.). 40p. (J). (gr. 1-4). per. 7.95 (978-1-58536-331-5(6), 202294) Sleeping Bear Pr.

Learn the Alphabet. 2004. (Alphabet & Counting Ser.). 12p. (J). bds. 5.99 (978-1-85997-809-2(6)) Byeway Bks.

Learn to Write: ABC. (Disney Princess Ser.). (Illus.). 20p. (J). bds. (978-2-7643-0216-3(9)) Phidal Publishing, Inc./Editions Phidal, Inc.

Learning Company Books Staff, ed. Reader Rabbit: ABC Order. 2003. (Illus.). 32p. (J). pap., wbk. ed. (978-0-7630-7644-3(9)) Magma.

—Reader Rabbit: Alphabet. 2003. (Illus.). 32p. (J). pap., wbk. ed. (978-0-7630-7577-4(9)) Magma.

—Reader Rabbit Fun with ABC's. 2004. (Illus.). 32p. (J). pap. (978-0-7630-7737-2(2)) Magma.

Leedom, Karen L. A Is for Astoria. Bailey, Sally, illus. 2010. 32p. 15.00 (978-0-9826252-0-0(0)) Rivertide Publishing.

LeMaistre, Gretchen, photos by. Boo ABC: A to Z with the World's Cutest Dog. 2013. (ENG., Illus.). 32p. (J). (gr. -1-1). 12.99 (978-1-4521-0919-0(2)) Chronicle Bks. LLC.

Leman, Nora. The Alpha Building Crew. Hartmann, April, illus. 2005. (J). (978-1-58987-110-6(3)) Kindermusik International.

Lersch, N. Scrantz. Bob Loves Letters. 2013. 26p. pap. 9.99 (978-0-615-79740-3(7)) Studio 37 Pubns.

Lester, Vivian & Luhrs, Jeannece Jackson. Alphabet Alive Lesson Plans Books. 78p. (J). pap. 9.95 (978-1-929785-03-2(8)) Connexions Unlimited.

Letters & Numbers. 2004. 12.99 incl. audio compact disk (978-1-57583-300-2(X)) Twin Sisters IP, LLC.

Leuck, Laura. Jeepers Creepers: A Monstrous ABC. Parkins, David, illus. 2003. (ENG.). 32p. (J). (gr. -1-7). 15.95 (978-0-8118-3509-1(X), 53408263) Chronicle Bks. LLC.

Levison, Jesse. U Is for Underwear. 2014. (ENG., Illus.). 28p. (J). (-k). bds. 9.95 (978-1-57687-690-9(X), powerHouse Bks.) powerHouse Cultural Entertainment, Inc.

Lichtenheld, Tom. E-Mergency! Lichtenheld, Tom, illus. 2011. (ENG., Illus.). 40p. (J). (gr. -1-17). 16.99 (978-0-8118-7898-2(8)) Chronicle Bks. LLC.

Linda, Winder. Glitter: My First Book of Shapes Numbers Colors & the Alphabet Gods Way. 2003. (978-1-892354-85-3(3)) Educational Publishing Concepts, Inc.

Lindsay, Courtney B. ABC Scream, It's Halloween! 2010. 48p. 17.99 (978-1-4520-3889-6(9)) AuthorHouse.

Lionni, Leo. Colors, Numbers, Letters. 2010. (ENG., Illus.). 40p. (J). (gr. k — 1). bds. 10.99 (978-0-375-85474-3(6), Knopf Bks. for Young Readers) Random Hse. Children's Bks.

Lisa LeLeu, 6th. Alphie's Alphabet Act. 2007. (Lisa Leleu Puppet Show Books Ser.: 6). (J). (978-0-9770299-0-7(5), W12348) LeLeu, Lisa Studios! Inc.

Litchfield, Jo. Very First ABC. 2010. (Very First Words Board Bks). 10p. (J). bds. 6.99 (978-0-7945-2709-9(4), Usborne) EDC Publishing.

Lluch, Alex A. Alphabet: I Like to Learn the ABCs! Defenbaugh, David, illus. 2014. (ENG.). 30p. (J). bds. 8.95 (978-1-61351-077-3(2)) WS Publishing.

—Animal Alphabet: Slide & Seek the ABCs. 2011. (Animal Alphabet Ser.). (ENG.). 13p. (J). (gr. -1-k). bds. 7.95 (978-1-936061-49-5(X)) WS Publishing.

—Let's Leap Ahead - Alphabet Play & Learn! 2013. (ENG., Illus.). 126p. (J). (gr. -1). pap. 7.95 (978-1-61351-069-8(1)) WS Publishing.

—Trace & Learn the ABCs: And Have Fun Playing Peek-A-Boo Who? Defenbaugh, David, illus. 2014. (ENG.). 26p. (J). bds. 8.95 (978-1-61351-082-7(9)) WS Publishing.

—Zoo Clues Animal Alphabet. 2011. (ENG.). 52p. (J). (gr. -1-k). bds. 6.95 (978-1-936061-50-1(3)) WS Publishing.

Lobel, Arnold. On Market Street. Lobel, Anita, illus. 25th anniv. ed. 2006. (ENG.). 40p. (J). (gr. -1-3). pap. 6.99 (978-0-688-08745-6(0), Greenwillow Bks.) HarperCollins Pubs.

Lohnes, Marilyn. ABC Literacy Storytimes: Storytimes to Promote Literacy & Learning. Neu, Debra, illus. 2008. 251p. pap. 19.95 (978-1-60213-023-4(X), Upstart Bks.) Highsmith Inc.

—F Is for Fiddlehead: A New Brunswick Alphabet. Tooke, Susan, illus. rev. ed. 2007. (Discover Canada Province by Province Ser.). (ENG.). 40p. (J). (gr. 1-7). 17.95 (978-1-58536-318-6(9)) Sleeping Bear Pr.

Lovelace, Victoria. Animal Crackers & Alphabet Soup. 2014. (ENG.). 84p. pap. 19.95 (978-1-4670-3532-3(7), b9230d6d-2918-4b50-9842-302a1082f149) AuthorHouse.

Lowrie, Paul. Hooray for Minnesota Winters. 2008. 19.95 (978-0-9755801-9-6(1)) Questmarc Publishing.

Lozano, José. Once Around the Block (Una Vuelta a la Manzana) Crosthwaite, Luis Humberto, tr. 2009. (SPA & ENG., Illus.). 32p. (J). (gr. -1-4). 16.95 (978-1-933693-57-6(6)) Cinco Puntos Pr.

Lucia Kemp, Henry. Now I Know My Alphabet & Phonics. 2014. (Now I Know My Ser.). (ENG.). 224p. (gr. -1-1). pap. 8.99 (978-0-545-77684-4(8), Teaching Resources) Scholastic, Inc.

Luevano, Richard. Uncle Bun Bun's Abc's of the Animal World. 2012. 34p. pap. 24.99 (978-1-61904-921-5(X)) Salem Author Services.

Lund, Evelyn. It Happened on Alphabet Street. 2003. (ENG., Illus.). 32p. (J). pap. 12.95 (978-1-878044-50-1(8), Wild Rose) Mayhaven Publishing, Inc.

Lynch, Wayne. Arctic Alphabet: Exploring the North from A to Z. Lynch, Wayne, photos by. 2006. (Illus.). 32p. (J). (gr. k-4). reprint ed. 20.00 (978-1-4223-5190-1(4)) DIANE Publishing Co.

Lyons, Theresa. Eating My ABC's. 2008. 18p. pap. 24.95 (978-1-60474-946-5(6)) America Star Bks.

Lyver, Patti. Did You Ever See Gulls? 2012. (ENG.). (J). pap. 12.95 (978-1-4675-3549-6(4)) Independent Pub.

Maass, Robert. A Is for Autumn. Maass, Robert, photos by. 2011. (ENG., Illus.). 32p. (J). (gr. -1-1). 16.99 (978-0-8050-9093-2(2), 9780805090932, Holt, Henry & Co. Bks. For Young Readers) Holt, Henry & Co.

Macalino, Damien. What If an Alligator Ate an Avalanche. Paj, Eduardo, illus. 2013. 32p. pap. 10.00 (978-0-9836303-8-8(0)) Crystal Mosaic Bks.

Maccarone, Grace. The Three Bears ABC. Hibbert, Hollie, illus. 2013. (ENG.). 32p. (J). (gr. -1-3). 16.99 (978-0-8075-7904-6(1)) Whitman, Albert & Co.

MacCuish, Al. Operation Alphabet. Lozano, Luciano, illus. 2011. (Ministry of Letters Ser.: 0). (ENG.). 64p. (J). (gr. -1-k). 19.95 (978-0-500-51584-6(0), 551584) Thames & Hudson.

MacDonald, Hugh. I Is for Island: A Prince Edward Island Alphabet. Jones, Brenda, illus. 2012. (ENG.). 40p. (J). (gr. 1-5). 16.95 (978-1-58536-367-4(7)) Sleeping Bear Pr.

MacDonald, Suse. Alphabet Animals: A Slide-and-Peek Adventure. MacDonald, Suse, illus. 2008. (ENG., Illus.). 28p. (J). (gr. -1-k). 12.99 (978-1-4169-5045-5(1), Little Simon) Little Simon.

MacKey, Cindy. A Curious Abc's: An Alphabet for Non Linear Thinkers. 2013. 32p. pap. 12.99 (978-0-9892699-8-8(1)) Cyrano Bks.

MacKey, Cindy K. A Curious Abc's: An Alphabet for Non Linear Thinkers. 2012. 30p. pap. 15.00 (978-0-615-55618-5(3)) Cyrano Bks.

MacKinnon, Mairi. The Usborne Animal Alphabet Activity Book. Horne, Sarah & Barker, Vicky, illus. 2014. (ENG.). (J). pap. 9.99 (978-0-7945-3274-1(8), Usborne) EDC Publishing.

Magnetic Alphabet Tiles & Magnetic Lapboard: Magnetic Alphabet Tiles (130 Letters) (gr. -1-12). 8.36 (978-0-7362-1097-3(0)) CENGAGE Learning.

Magnetic Alphabet Tiles & Magnetic Lapboard: Magnetic Lapboard 12 9. (gr. -1-12). 8.74 (978-0-7362-0850-5(X)) CENGAGE Learning.

Magsamen, Sandra. I Love America - An ABC Adventure. 2016. (ENG.). 40p. (J). (-5). 12.99 (978-1-4926-2854-5(9), Sourcebooks Jabberwocky) Sourcebooks, Inc.

—I Love Florida. 2016. (ENG.). 40p. (J). (-5). 12.99 (978-1-4926-2843-9(3), 9781492628439, Sourcebooks Jabberwocky) Sourcebooks, Inc.

—I Love Wisconsin. 2016. (ENG.). 40p. (J). (-5). 12.99 (978-1-4926-2840-8(9), Sourcebooks Jabberwocky) Sourcebooks, Inc.

Mahr, Aryeh. Mysteries of the Aleph Beis. 2008. 54p. 17.99 (978-1-59826-211-7(4)) Feldheim Pubs.

Main, Judith Lang. A Is for Altar, B Is for Bible. 2003. (Illus.). 65p. (J). 10.00 (978-1-56854-458-8(8), Catechesis of the Good Shepherd) Liturgy Training Pubns.

Major, Kevin. Eh? To Zed: A Canadian Abecedarium. 2004. (Illus.). (J). (gr. -1-3). spiral bd. (978-0-616-11120-8(7)); spiral bd. (978-0-616-11119-2(3)) Canadian National Institute for the Blind/Institut National Canadien pour les Aveugles.

Make Believe Ideas. B Is for Breakdancing Bear Alphabet Sticker Activity Book. 2015. (ENG.). 110p. (J). pap. 9.99 (978-1-78393-442-3(5)) Make Believe Ideas GBR. Dist: Nelson, Thomas Inc.

—Bubble Buddies ABC. 2014. (ENG.). 12p. (J). bds. 9.99 (978-1-78235-971-5(0)) Make Believe Ideas GBR. Dist: Nelson, Thomas Inc.

—My Best Ever: ABC Alphabet Book. 2013. (ENG.). 16p. (J). bds. 12.99 (978-1-78235-611-0(8)) Make Believe Ideas GBR. Dist: Nelson, Thomas Inc.

Make Believe Ideas, creator. Alphabet Book. 2014. (ENG., Illus.). 20p. (J). (gr. -1). bds. 9.99 (978-1-78235-969-2(9)) Make Believe Ideas GBR. Dist: Nelson, Thomas Inc.

—Busy Baby ABC: First Concepts. 2007. (Busy Baby Ser.). (Illus.). 12p. (gr. -1-k). per., bds. (978-1-84610-467-1(X)) Make Believe Ideas.

—Trace, Stick & Learn Wipe Clean ABC Activity Book. 2007. (Trace, Stick & Learn Ser.). (Illus.). 12p. (J). (gr. -1-3). pap. (978-1-84610-430-5(0)) Make Believe Ideas.

Makeeff, Cyndi Sue. Inky Winky Spider ABC's. Riley, Kevin, illus. 2006. 32p. (J). pap. 7.99 (978-0-9778310-0-5(0)) New Vision Entertainment, LLC.

Marchetti, Matt. Annabel Aardvark Arrives at an Avalanche. 2008. 32p. pap. 24.95 (978-1-60703-219-9(8)) America Star Bks.

Markle, Sandra & Markle, William. Gone Forever: An Alphabet of Extinct Animals. Davalos, Felipe, illus. 2007. (ENG.). 40p. (J). (gr. 4-6). 14.99 (978-1-4169-6138-3(0), Simon & Schuster/Paula Wiseman Bks.) Simon & Schuster/Paula Wiseman Bks.

Marsell-Jones, Connie. Abc's of Angels. 2010. 32p. pap. 15.99 (978-1-4520-4859-8(2)) AuthorHouse.

Martin, Bill, Jr. & Archambault, John. Chicka Chicka ABC. Ehlert, Lois, illus. 2009. (Chicka Chicka Book Ser.). (ENG.). 16p. (J). (gr. -1-1). bds. 10.99 (978-1-4169-8447-4(X), Little Simon) Little Simon.

—Chicka Chicka Boom Boom. Ehlert, Lois, illus. anniv. ed. 2009. (Chicka Chicka Book Ser.). (ENG.). 40p. (J). (gr. -1-3). 17.99 (978-1-4169-9091-8(7), Beach Lane Bks.) Beach Lane Bks.

—Chicka Chicka Boom Boom. Ehlert, Lois, illus. (Chicka Chicka Book Ser.). (ENG.). (J). (gr. -1-1). 2010. 36p. bds. 12.99 (978-1-4169-9999-7(X)) 2006. 40p. 10.99 (978-1-4169-2718-1(2)) Little Simon. (Little Simon).

Martin, Bill, Jr., et al. Chicka Chicka Boom Boom. Ehlert, Lois, illus. 2008. (J). 13.99 (978-1-59319-935-7(X)) LeapFrog Enterprises, Inc.

Martin, Steve & Chast, Roz. The Alphabet from A to Y with Bonus Letter Z! 2007. (ENG., Illus.). 64p. (J). (gr. k-k). 17.95 (978-0-385-51662-4(2), Flying Dolphin Pr.) Knopf Doubleday Publishing Group.

Martin, Susi. Animal ABC. 2014. (ENG., Illus.). 32p. (J). (gr. -1-2). 9.95 (978-1-77085-456-7(8), 9781770854567) Firefly Bks., Ltd.

Masu. Levi's Look'n for Things to Do in the Fall. 2009. 13p. pap. 24.95 (978-1-60836-233-2(7)) America Star Bks.

Mathieu, Joe, et al. Big Bird's Big Book: Counting Colors Country City Opposites Playing. Mathieu, Joe, illus. 2009. (Sesame Street Ser.). (ENG., Illus.). 14p. (J). (gr. k — 1). bds. 45.00 (978-0-394-89128-6(7), Random Hse. Bks. for Young Readers) Random Hse. Children's Bks.

Mayer, Marvin. The Day X Ran Away. 2013. (ENG., Illus.). 38p. (gr. -1-3). pap. 12.00 (978-1-936205-87-5(4)) Austin, Stephen F. State Univ. Pr.

Mayer, Nicole & Mayer, Ryan. Hannah's Homework. Simmons, Russell, illus. 2012. 36p. (J). 14.95 (978-0-9849293-0-6(4)) Beaner Bks.

Maze, Stephanie, ed. Healthy Foods from A to Z: Comida Sana de la a a la Z. Comet, Renee, photos by. 2012. (SPA & ENG., Illus.). 32p. (J). (gr. -1-k). 15.95 (978-0-9834983-1-5(8)) Moonstone Pr., LLC.

Mazurkiewicz, Jessica. Alphascapes. 2013. (Dover Design Coloring Bks.). (ENG.). 32p. (J). (gr. 1-5). pap. 3.99 (978-0-486-49010-6(6)) Dover Pubns., Inc.

Mazxzeo, J. L. Xavia's X Book (BL) el libro X de Xavia (PB), 24 vols. 2007. (My Letter Library Ser.: 24). (SPA., Illus.). (J). pap. 10.95 (978-1-59646-558-9(1)) Dingles & Co.

Mazza, Barbara. How the Short Vowels Got Their Sound. 2007. 28p. per. 17.32 (978-1-4257-2721-5(2)) Xlibris Corp.

Mazzeo, J. L. Aimee's A Book, 1. 2007. (My Letter Library Ser.: 1). (Illus.). 32p. (J). lib. bdg. 23.60 (978-1-59646-416-2(X)) Dingles & Co.

—Aimee's A Book (PB), 1. 2007. (My Letter Library Ser.: 1). (J). pap. 10.95 (978-1-59646-417-9(8)) Dingles & Co.

—Bebe's B Book, 26 vols. 2007. (My Letter Library Ser.: 2). (J). pap. 10.95 (978-1-59646-423-0(2)); 32p. lib. bdg. 23.60 (978-1-59646-422-3(4)) Dingles & Co.

—Bebe's B Book/ el libro B de Bebé, 2 vols. 2007. (My Letter Library Ser.: 2). (SPA & ENG., Illus.). (J). pap. 10.95 (978-1-59646-426-1(7)); lib. bdg. 23.60 (978-1-59646-425-4(9)) Dingles & Co.

—Cassie's C Book. 2007. (My Letter Library Ser.: 3). (J). lib. bdg. 23.60 (978-1-59646-428-5(3)) Dingles & Co.

—Cassie's C Book (PB), 3 vols. 2007. (My Letter Library Ser.: 3). (J). pap. 10.95 (978-1-59646-429-2(1)) Dingles & Co.

—Delia's D Book, 4 vols. 2007. (My Letter Library Ser.: 4). (J). pap. 10.95 (978-1-59646-435-3(6)); lib. bdg. 23.60 (978-1-59646-434-6(8)) Dingles & Co.

—Delia's D Book /el libro D de Delia, 4 vols. 2007. (My Letter Library Ser.: 4). (SPA., Illus.). (J). pap. 10.95 (978-1-59646-438-4(0)); lib. bdg. 23.60 (978-1-59646-437-7(2)) Dingles & Co.

—Emma's E Book, 5 vols. 2007. (My Letter Library Ser.: 5). (J). lib. bdg. 23.60 (978-1-59646-440-7(2)) Dingles & Co.

—Emma's E-Book / El Libro E de Emma, 5 vols. 2007. (My Letter Library Ser.: 5). (SPA & ENG.). (J). pap. 10.95 (978-1-59646-444-5(5)); lib. bdg. 23.60 (978-1-59646-443-8(7)) Dingles & Co.

—Emma's E Book (PB), 5 vols. 2007. (My Letter Library Ser.: 5). (J). pap. 10.95 (978-1-59646-441-4(0)) Dingles & Co.

—Faye's F Book, 6 vols. 2007. (My Letter Library Ser.: 6). (J). lib. bdg. 23.60 (978-1-59646-446-9(1)) Dingles & Co.

—Faye's F Book (BL) el libro F de Faye (PB), 6 vols. 2007. (My Letter Library Ser.: 6). (SPA.). (J). pap. 10.95 (978-1-59646-450-6(X)) Dingles & Co.

—Faye's F Book (PB), 6 vols. 2007. (My Letter Library Ser.: 6). (J). pap. 10.95 (978-1-59646-447-6(X)) Dingles & Co.

—George's G Book, 7 vols. 2007. (My Letter Library Ser.: 7). (J). lib. bdg. 23.60 (978-1-59646-452-0(6)) Dingles & Co.

—George's G Book (BL) el libro G de George, 7 vols. 2007. (My Letter Library Ser.: 7). (J). lib. bdg. 23.60 (978-1-59646-455-1(0)) Dingles & Co.

—George's G Book (BL) el libro G de George (PB), 7 vols. 2007. (My Letter Library Ser.: 7). (SPA.). (J). pap. 10.95 (978-1-59646-456-8(9)) Dingles & Co.
—George's G Book (PB), 7 vols. 2007. (My Letter Library Ser.: 7). (J). pap. 10.95 (978-1-59646-453-7(4)) Dingles & Co.
—Henry's H Book, 8 vols. 2007. (My Letter Library Ser.: 8). (Illus.). (J). lib. bdg. 23.60 (978-1-59646-458-2(5)) Dingles & Co.
—Henry's H Book (BL) el libro H de Henry, 8 vols. 2007. (My Letter Library Ser.: 8). (J). lib. bdg. 23.60 (978-1-59646-461-2(5)) Dingles & Co.
—Henry's H Book (BL) el libro H de Henry (PB), 8 vols. 2007. (My Letter Library Ser.: 8). (SPA.). (J). pap. 10.95 (978-1-59646-462-9(3)) Dingles & Co.
—Henry's H Book (PB), 8 vols. 2007. (My Letter Library Ser.: 8). (J). pap. 10.95 (978-1-59646-459-9(3)) Dingles & Co.
—Izzy's I Book, 9 vols. 2007. (My Letter Library Ser.: 9). (J). lib. bdg. 23.60 (978-1-59646-464-3(X)) Dingles & Co.
—Izzy's I Book (BL) el libro I de Izzy, 9 vols. 2007. (My Letter Library Ser.: 9). (SPA.). (J). lib. bdg. 23.60 (978-1-59646-467-4(4)) Dingles & Co.
—Izzy's I Book (BL) el libro I de Izzy (PB), 9 vols. 2007. (My Letter Library Ser.: 9). (SPA.). (J). pap. 10.95 (978-1-59646-468-1(2)) Dingles & Co.
—Izzy's I Book (PB), 9 vols. 2007. (My Letter Library Ser.: 9). (J). pap. 10.95 (978-1-59646-465-0(8)) Dingles & Co.
—Jade's J Book, 10 vols. 2007. (My Letter Library Ser.: 10). (J). lib. bdg. 23.60 (978-1-59646-470-4(4)) Dingles & Co.
—Jade's J Book (BL) el libro J de Jade, 10 vols. 2007. (My Letter Library Ser.: 10). (SPA.). (J). lib. bdg. 23.60 (978-1-59646-473-5(9)) Dingles & Co.
—Jade's J Book (BL) el libro J de Jade (PB), 10 vols. 2007. (My Letter Library Ser.: 10). (SPA.). (J). pap. 10.95 (978-1-59646-474-2(7)) Dingles & Co.
—Jade's J Book (PB), 10 vols. 2007. (My Letter Library Ser.: 10). (J). pap. 10.95 (978-1-59646-471-1(2)) Dingles & Co.
—Kelsey's K Book, 11 vols. 2007. (My Letter Library Ser.: 11). (J). lib. bdg. 23.60 (978-1-59646-476-6(3)) Dingles & Co.
—Kelsey's K Book (BL) el libro K de Kelsey, 11 vols. 2007. (My Letter Library Ser.: 11). (SPA.). (J). lib. bdg. 23.60 (978-1-59646-479-7(8)) Dingles & Co.
—Kelsey's K Book (BL) el libro K de Kelsey (PB), 11 vols. 2007. (My Letter Library Ser.: 11). (SPA.). (J). pap. 10.95 (978-1-59646-480-3(1)) Dingles & Co.
—Kelsey's K Book (PB), 11 vols. 2007. (My Letter Library Ser.: 11). (J). pap. 10.95 (978-1-59646-477-3(1)) Dingles & Co.
—El Libro F de Faye, 5 vols. 2007. (My Letter Library Ser.: 6).Tr. of Faye's F Book. (SPA.). (J). lib. bdg. 23.60 (978-1-59646-449-0(6)) Dingles & Co.
—Logan's L Book, 12 vols. 2007. (My Letter Library Ser.: 12). (J). lib. bdg. 23.60 (978-1-59646-482-7(8)) Dingles & Co.
—Logan's L Book (BL) el libro L de Logan, 12 vols. 2007. (My Letter Library Ser.: 12). (SPA.). (J). lib. bdg. 23.60 (978-1-59646-485-8(2)) Dingles & Co.
—Logan's L Book (BL) el libro L de Logan (PB), 12 vols. 2007. (My Letter Library Ser.: 12). (SPA.). (J). pap. 10.95 (978-1-59646-486-5(0)) Dingles & Co.
—Logan's L Book (PB), 12 vols. 2007. (My Letter Library Ser.: 12). (J). pap. 10.95 (978-1-59646-483-4(6)) Dingles & Co.
—Mia's M Book, 13 vols. 2007. (My Letter Library Ser.: 13). (J). lib. bdg. 23.60 (978-1-59646-488-9(7)) Dingles & Co.
—Mia's M Book (BL) el libro M de Mia, 13 vols. 2007. (My Letter Library Ser.: 13). (SPA.). (J). lib. bdg. 23.60 (978-1-59646-491-9(7)) Dingles & Co.
—Mia's M Book (BL) el libro M de Mia (PB), 13 vols. 2007. (My Letter Library Ser.: 13). (SPA.). (J). pap. 10.95 (978-1-59646-492-6(5)) Dingles & Co.
—Mia's M Book (PB), 13 vols. 2007. (My Letter Library Ser.: 13). (J). pap. 10.95 (978-1-59646-489-6(5)) Dingles & Co.
—Nate's N Book, 14 vols. 2007. (My Letter Library Ser.: 14). (J). lib. bdg. 23.60 (978-1-59646-494-0(1)) Dingles & Co.
—Nate's N Book (BL) el libro N de Nate, 14 vols. 2007. (My Letter Library Ser.: 14). (SPA.). (J). lib. bdg. 23.60 (978-1-59646-497-1(6)) Dingles & Co.
—Nate's N Book (BL) el libro N de Nate (PB), 14 vols. 2007. (My Letter Library Ser.: 14). (SPA.). (J). pap. 10.95 (978-1-59646-498-8(4)) Dingles & Co.
—Nate's N Book (PB), 14 vols. 2007. (My Letter Library Ser.: 14). (J). pap. 10.95 (978-1-59646-495-7(X)) Dingles & Co.
—Owen's O Book, 15 vols. 2007. (My Letter Library Ser.: 15). (J). lib. bdg. 23.60 (978-1-59646-500-8(X)) Dingles & Co.
—Owen's O Book (BL) el libro O de Owen, 15 vols. 2007. (My Letter Library Ser.: 15). (SPA.). (J). lib. bdg. 23.60 (978-1-59646-503-9(4)) Dingles & Co.
—Owen's O Book (BL) el libro O de Owen (PB), 15 vols. 2007. (My Letter Library Ser.: 15). (SPA.). (J). pap. 10.95 (978-1-59646-504-6(2)) Dingles & Co.
—Owen's O Book (PB), 15 vols. 2007. (My Letter Library Ser.: 15). (J). pap. 10.95 (978-1-59646-501-5(8)) Dingles & Co.
—Perer's P Book, 16 vols. 2007. (My Letter Library Ser.: 16). (J). lib. bdg. 23.60 (978-1-59646-506-0(9)) Dingles & Co.
—Peter's P Book (BL) el libro P de Peter, 16 vols. 2007. (My Letter Library Ser.: 16). (SPA.). (J). lib. bdg. 23.60 (978-1-59646-509-1(3)) Dingles & Co.
—Peter's P Book (BL) el libro P de Peter (PB), 16 vols. 2007. (My Letter Library Ser.: 16). (SPA.). (J). pap. 10.95 (978-1-59646-510-7(7)) Dingles & Co.
—Peter's P Book (PB), 16 vols. 2007. (My Letter Library Ser.: 16). (J). pap. 10.95 (978-1-59646-507-7(7)) Dingles & Co.
—Quinn's Q Book, 17 vols. 2007. (My Letter Library Ser.: 17). (J). lib. bdg. 23.60 (978-1-59646-512-1(3)) Dingles & Co.
—Quinn's Q Book (BL) el libro Q de Quinn, 17 vols. 2007. (My Letter Library Ser.: 17). (SPA.). (J). lib. bdg. 23.60 (978-1-59646-515-2(8)) Dingles & Co.
—Quinn's Q Book (BL) el libro Q de Quinn (PB), 17 vols. 2007. (My Letter Library Ser.: 17). (SPA.). (J). pap. 10.95 (978-1-59646-516-9(6)) Dingles & Co.
—Quinn's Q Book (PB), 17 vols. 2007. (My Letter Library Ser.: 17). (J). lib. bdg. 10.95 (978-1-59646-513-8(1)) Dingles & Co.
—Rosie's R Book, 18 vols. 2007. (My Letter Library Ser.: 18). (J). lib. bdg. 23.60 (978-1-59646-518-3(2)) Dingles & Co.
—Rosie's R Book (BL) el libro R de Rosie, 18 vols. 2007. (My Letter Library Ser.: 18). (SPA.). (J). lib. bdg. 23.60 (978-1-59646-521-3(2)) Dingles & Co.
—Rosie's R Book (BL) el libro R de Rosie (PB), 18 vols. 2007. (My Letter Library Ser.: 18). (SPA.). (J). pap. 10.95 (978-1-59646-522-0(0)) Dingles & Co.
—Rosie's R Book (PB), 18 vols. 2007. (My Letter Library Ser.: 18). (J). pap. 10.95 (978-1-59646-519-0(0)) Dingles & Co.
—Sofie's S Book, 19 vols. 2007. (My Letter Library Ser.: 19). (J). lib. bdg. 23.60 (978-1-59646-524-4(7)) Dingles & Co.
—Sofie's S Book (BL) el libro S de Sofie, 19 vols. 2007. (My Letter Library Ser.: 19). (SPA.). (J). lib. bdg. 23.60 (978-1-59646-527-5(1)) Dingles & Co.
—Sofie's S Book (BL) el libro S de Sofie (PB), 19 vols. 2007. (My Letter Library Ser.: 19). (SPA.). (J). pap. 10.95 (978-1-59646-528-2(X)) Dingles & Co.
—Sofie's S Book (PB), 19 vols. 2007. (My Letter Library Ser.: 19). (J). pap. 10.95 (978-1-59646-525-1(5)) Dingles & Co.
—Tad's T Book, 20 vols. 2007. (My Letter Library Ser.: 20). (J). lib. bdg. 23.60 (978-1-59646-530-5(1)) Dingles & Co.
—Tad's T Book (BL) el libro T de Tad, 20 vols. 2007. (My Letter Library Ser.: 20). (SPA.). (J). lib. bdg. 23.60 (978-1-59646-533-6(6)) Dingles & Co.
—Tad's T Book (BL) el libro T de Tad (PB), 20 vols. 2007. (My Letter Library Ser.: 20). (SPA.). (J). pap. 10.95 (978-1-59646-534-3(4)) Dingles & Co.
—Tad's T Book (PB), 20 vols. 2007. (My Letter Library Ser.: 20). (J). pap. 10.95 (978-1-59646-531-2(X)) Dingles & Co.
—Uri's U Book, 21 vols. 2007. (My Letter Library Ser.: 21). (Illus.). (J). lib. bdg. 23.60 (978-1-59646-536-7(0)) Dingles & Co.
—Uri's U Book (BL) el libro U de Uri, 21 vols. 2007. (My Letter Library Ser.: 21). (SPA.). (J). lib. bdg. 23.60 (978-1-59646-539-8(5)) Dingles & Co.
—Uri's U Book (BL) el libro U de Uri (PB), 21 vols. 2007. (My Letter Library Ser.: 21). (SPA.). (J). pap. 10.95 (978-1-59646-540-4(9)) Dingles & Co.
—Uri's U Book (PB), 21 vols. 2007. (My Letter Library Ser.: 21). (Illus.). (J). pap. 10.95 (978-1-59646-537-4(9)) Dingles & Co.
—Vera's V Book, 22 vols. 2007. (My Letter Library Ser.: 22). (J). lib. bdg. 23.60 (978-1-59646-542-8(5)) Dingles & Co.
—Vera's V Book (BL) el libro V de Vera, 22 vols. 2007. (My Letter Library Ser.: 22). (SPA & ENG., Illus.). (J). lib. bdg. 23.60 (978-1-59646-545-9(X)) Dingles & Co.
—Vera's V Book (BL) el libro V de Vera (PB), 22 vols. 2007. (My Letter Library Ser.: 22). (SPA & ENG., Illus.). (J). pap. 10.95 (978-1-59646-546-6(8)) Dingles & Co.
—Vera's V Book (PB), 22 vols. 2007. (My Letter Library Ser.: 22). (J). pap. 10.95 (978-1-59646-543-5(3)) Dingles & Co.
—Will's W Book, 23 vols. 2007. (My Letter Library Ser.: 23). (J). lib. bdg. 23.60 (978-1-59646-548-0(4)) Dingles & Co.
—Will's W Book (BL) el libro W de Will, 23 vols. 2007. (My Letter Library Ser.: 23). (SPA.). (J). lib. bdg. 23.60 (978-1-59646-551-0(4)) Dingles & Co.
—Will's W Book (BL) el libro W de Will (PB), 23 vols. 2007. (My Letter Library Ser.: 23). (SPA.). (J). pap. 10.95 (978-1-59646-552-7(2)) Dingles & Co.
—Will's W Book (PB), 23 vols. 2007. (My Letter Library Ser.: 23). (J). pap. 10.95 (978-1-59646-549-7(2)) Dingles & Co.
—Xavia's X Book, 24 vols. 2007. (My Letter Library Ser.: 24). (J). lib. bdg. 23.60 (978-1-59646-554-1(9)) Dingles & Co.
—Xavia's X Book (BL) el libro X de Xavia, 24 vols. 2007. (My Letter Library Ser.: 24). (SPA., Illus.). (J). lib. bdg. 23.60 (978-1-59646-557-2(3)) Dingles & Co.
—Xavia's X Book (PB), 24 vols. 2007. (My Letter Library Ser.: 24). (J). pap. 10.95 (978-1-59646-555-8(7)) Dingles & Co.
—Yola's Y Book, 25 vols. 2007. (My Letter Library Ser.: 25). (Illus.). (J). lib. bdg. 23.60 (978-1-59646-560-2(3)) Dingles & Co.
—Yola's Y Book (BL) el libro Y de Yola, 25 vols. 2007. (My Letter Library Ser.: 25). (SPA.). (J). lib. bdg. 23.60 (978-1-59646-563-3(8)) Dingles & Co.
—Yola's Y Book (BL) el libro Y de Yola (PB), 25 vols. 2007. (My Letter Library Ser.: 25). (SPA.). (J). pap. 10.95 (978-1-59646-564-0(6)) Dingles & Co.
—Yola's Y Book (PB), 25 vols. 2007. (My Letter Library Ser.: 25). (Illus.). (J). pap. 10.95 (978-1-59646-561-9(1)) Dingles & Co.
—Zach's Z Book. 2007. (My Letter Library Ser.: 26). (J). lib. bdg. 23.60 (978-1-59646-566-4(2)) Dingles & Co.
—Zach's Z Book (PB), 26 vols. 2007. (My Letter Library Ser.: 26). (J). pap. 10.95 (978-1-59646-567-1(0)) Dingles & Co.
McArthur, Meher. An ABC of What Art Can Be. Watson, Esther Pearl, illus. 2010. (ENG.). 32p. (J). (gr. -1-3). 17.95 (978-0-89236-999-7(X), J. Paul Getty Museum) Getty Pubns.
McAtee, Rick. Alphabetland the Beginning. Hammons, Barbara, illus. 2005. 48p. (J). 12.95 (978-0-9762030-0-1(6)) Turning a New Page.
—Alphabetland the Story of R. Hammons, Barbara, illus. 2005. (J). 14.95 (978-0-9762030-1-8(4), 1000) Turning a New Page.
McCurdy, Michael. Walden Then & Now: An Alphabetical Tour of Henry Thoreau's Pond. McCurdy, Michael, illus. 2010. (ENG., Illus.). 32p. (J). (gr. k-12). 16.95 (978-1-58089-253-7(1)) Charlesbridge Publishing, Inc.
McDonnell, Patrick. The Little Red Cat Who Ran Away & Learned His ABC's (the Hard Way) 2017. (ENG.). 48p. (J). (gr. -1-1). 17.99 **(978-0-316-50246-7(4))** Little, Brown Bks. for Young Readers.
McGehee, Claudia. A Tallgrass Prairie Alphabet. McGehee, Claudia, illus. 2004. (Bur Oak Book Ser.). (Illus.). 32p. (J). 17.95 (978-0-87745-897-5(9)) Univ. of Iowa Pr.
McGuirk, Leslie. If Rocks Could Sing: A Discovered Alphabet. 2011. (ENG., Illus.). 48p. (J). (gr. -1-2). 15.99 (978-1-58246-370-4(0), Tricycle Pr.) Random Hse. Children's Bks.
McKay, Chelsea. A Tangram ABC: Shaping the Alphabet from an Ancient Chinese Puzzle. Firos, Daphne, illus. 2013. 60p. (J). pap. 13.95 (978-1-939431-04-2(2)) MathWord Pr., LLC.
McKay, Sindy. Can You Find?/Puedes Hallarlo? Spanish/English Bilingual (We Both Read - Level Pk-K) An ABC Book. Loveridge, Matt, illus. 2016. (We Both Read - Level Pk -K Ser.). (ENG & SPA.). (J). pap. 4.99 (978-1-60115-072-1(5)) Treasure Bay, Inc.
McKinley, Teri & Bowman, Crystal. M Is for Manger. Keay, Claire, illus. 2016. (ENG.). 32p. (J). bds. 6.99 (978-1-4964-2004-6(7), Tyndale Kids) Tyndale Hse. Pubs.
Mckinsey, Michelle. Weird O. 2007. (ENG., Illus.). 44p. (J). 9.95 (978-0-9788092-0-1(3)) McGab Publishing.
McLeod, Bob. SuperHero ABC. McLeod, Bob, illus. 2008. (ENG., Illus.). 40p. (J). (gr. -1-3). pap. 7.99 (978-0-06-074516-5(9)) HarperCollins Pubs.
—Superhero ABC. McLeod, Bob, illus. 2006. (ENG., Illus.). 40p. (J). (gr. -1-3). 17.99 (978-0-06-074514-1(2)) HarperCollins Pubs.
McMillan, Jenna. East Tennessee from a to Z. Patients from East Tennessee Children's Hospital, illus. 2013. (ENG.). 26p. 20.00 (978-0-9830954-2-2(6)) Books by Kids LLC.
McTaggart, Stephen & McTaggart, Debra. ABC Talking Book Adventures. Nord, Mary, illus. (Talking Book Adventures Ser.). 12p. (J). (gr. -1-18). 16.95 (978-0-9627001-2-5(6)) Futech Educational Products, Inc.
Medina Rosas, Juana. ABC Pasta. 2017. (ENG., Illus.). 40p. (J). (— 1). 17.99 (978-1-101-99978-3(0), Viking Books for Young Readers) Penguin Young Readers Group.
Mehta, Poonam V. A-B-C in Action. Kurup, Prakash, illus. 2012. 36p. pap. 22.12 (978-1-4669-2687-5(2)) Trafford Publishing.
Melmed, Laura Krauss. New York, New York! The Big Apple from A to Z. Lessac, Frané, illus. 2008. (ENG.). 48p. (J). (gr. 1-6). pap. 6.99 (978-0-06-054877-3(0), Collins) HarperCollins Pubs.
—New York, New York City: The Big Apple from A to Z. Lessac, Frané, illus. 2005. (ENG.). 48p. (J). (gr. 1-6). 16.99 (978-0-06-054874-2(6)) HarperCollins Pubs.
Messenger, Norman. An Artist's Alphabet. Messenger, Norman, illus. 2016. (ENG., Illus.). 48p. (J). (gr. k-12). 17.99 (978-0-7636-8123-4(7)) Candlewick Pr.
Meza, Martin. Martin Meza's story time Volume 5. 2007. 54p. pap. 25.95 (978-0-615-16571-4(0)) Meza, Marti.
Michaels, Pat. W Is for Wind: A Weather Alphabet. Rose, Melanie, illus. rev. ed. (Science Ser.). (ENG.). 40p. (J). 2006. (gr. -1-3). pap. 7.95 (978-1-58536-330-8(8)) 2005. 16.95 (978-1-58536-237-0(9)) Sleeping Bear Pr.
Michelson, Richard. S Is for Sea Glass: A Beach Alphabet. Ettlinger, Doris, illus. 2014. (ENG.). 32p. (J). (gr. 2-5). 15.95 (978-1-58536-862-4(8), 203010) Sleeping Bear Pr.
Miller, Brandy. My First Abc Poem, 1 vol. 2009. 29p. pap. 24.95 (978-1-60703-490-2(5)) America Star Bks.
Miller, Bryan. Dinosaur Fun: With Letters. 2008. (Illus.). 24p. (J). (gr. -1). bds. 11.99 (978-0-89051-488-7(7)) Master Bks.
Miller, Tiwana Mutch. You Can Learn from Any Level. 2007. 60p. (J). per. 10.00 (978-0-9788937-4-3(3)) Amani Publishing, LLC.
Mills, Wynette. Nana's Backyard Alphabet. 2012. 36p. pap. 15.99 (978-1-4771-4061-1(1)) Xlibris Corp.
Milne, A. A. ABC. Shepard, Ernest H., illus. 2004. (Winnie-The-Pooh Ser.). (ENG.). 26p. (J). (gr. -1-k). bds. 8.99 (978-0-525-47280-3(0), Dutton Books for Young Readers) Penguin Young Readers Group.
Minneapolis, Jewish Family and Children's Service of. M Is for Minnesota. 2016. (See My State Ser.). (ENG., Illus.). 32p. (J). 13.99 (978-1-943328-07-9(2), West Winds Pr.) Graphic Arts Ctr. Publishing Co.
Minor, Wendell. Yankee Doodle Alphabet: The Spirit of 1776 from a to Z. 2016. (J). (978-1-56792-566-1(9)) Godine, David R. Pub.
Mischel, Jenny Ann. Animal Alphabet. Bell-Myers, Darcy, illus. 2006. (J). bds. (978-0-9769239-0-9(4)) Perfect 4 Preschool.
Mitchell, Cynthia. A Big & Beastly Alphabet. 2006. pap. (978-1-84401-716-4(8)) Athena Pr.
Mitchell-Tulloss, Delores. ABCs of Character for People Around the World. Hardison, Brian, illus. 2007. 32p. (J). pap. (978-0-9670712-6-8(7)) zReyomi Publishing.
Mock, Jean. The Amazing Animal ABC Book. Martin, Joyce, illus. 2005. (J). (978-0-9767210-1-7(5)) JM2 Publishing Co.
—The Amazing Animal ABC Book (big Format) 2005. (J). (978-0-9767210-0-0(7)) JM2 Publishing Co.
—The Amazing Animal ABC Book the Study Guide. Martin, Joyce, illus. 2005. (978-0-9767210-2-4(3)) JM2 Publishing Co.
Mockford, Caroline & Blackstone, Stella. Cleo's Alphabet Book. 2007. (Cleo Ser.). (ENG., Illus.). 24p. (J). (gr. -1-k). bds. 7.99 (978-1-84686-046-1(6)) Barefoot Bks., Inc.
Moncure, Jane Belk. My 'j' Sound Box. Thornburgh, Rebecca, illus. 2009. (Sound Box Bks.). (ENG.). 32p. (J). (gr. -1-2). 25.64 (978-1-60253-150-5(1), 200831) Child's World, Inc., The.
—My 'm' Sound Box. Thornburgh, Rebecca, illus. 2009. (Sound Box Bks.). (ENG.). 32p. (J). (gr. -1-2). 25.64 (978-1-60253-153-6(6), 200834) Child's World, Inc., The.
Monroe, Judith W. The Gypsy Chickens Alphabet. Montague, Ruth, illus. 2006. (J). 7.00 (978-0-9768370-2-2(1)) Seastory Pr.
Moon, Jo, illus. Making Letters. 2006. (Making... Ser.). 14p. (J). (gr. -1-3). bds. 7.95 (978-1-57791-248-4(9)) Brighter Minds Children's Publishing.
Moore, Sheila. Abadaba Alphabet: Learning Letter Sounds. Holsinger, Carol, illus. 2006. 31p. (gr. -1-3). 19.95 (978-0-9789473-0-9(4)) Abadaba Reading LLC.
Morales, Yuyi. Just in Case: A Trickster Tale & Spanish Alphabet Book. Morales, Yuyi, illus. 2008. (ENG., Illus.). 40p. (J). (gr. -1-3). 18.99 (978-1-59643-329-8(9), 9781596433298) Roaring Brook Pr.
Morgan, Marilyn. Alaska Alphabet CD-ROM. 2007. cd-rom 29.95 (978-1-878051-56-1(3)) Circumpolar Pr.
Morgan, Michelle. Colorsaurus ABC. 2009. 32p. pap. 18.00 (978-0-557-07782-3(6)) Lulu Pr., Inc.
Morstad, Julie. T Is for Tumbling. 2014. (ENG., Illus.). 26p. (J). (gr. -1 — 1). 14.95 (978-1-927018-44-6(7), 9781927018446) Simply Read Bks. CAN. Dist: Ingram Publisher Services.
Moseley, Christopher & Campbell, George L. The Routeldge Handbook of Scripts & Alphabets. 2nd rev. ed. 2009. (ENG., Illus.). 200p. (C). 170.00 (978-0-415-56098-6(5), Y105116) Routledge.
Most, Bernard. ABC T-Rex. 2004. (ENG., Illus.). 40p. (J). (gr. -1-3). pap. 7.99 (978-0-15-205028-3(0)) Houghton Mifflin Harcourt Publishing Co.
Mount, Jane. 26 Animals! 2009. 32p. pap. 17.98 (978-0-557-17908-4(4)) Lulu Pr., Inc.
Msmh. Learning to Count, Alphabets a-J & Colours. 2013. 16p. pap. 12.68 (978-1-4669-7416-6(8)) Trafford Publishing.
Mukherjee, Aiswarya & S., Bijan, illus. My Family! ABCs with Keesha. 2011. (J). pap. 2.99 (978-0-9767273-9-2(0)) Dodi Pr.
Mullin, Rene. Aibitir. 2014. (ENG., Illus.). 40p. (J). 13.95 (978-0-85640-917-2(0)) Blackstaff Pr., Ltd. GBR. Dist: Dufour Editions, Inc.
Munari, Bruno. Bruno Munari's ABC. 6th ed. 2006. (ENG., Illus.). 48p. (J). (gr. -1-1). 19.99 (978-0-8118-5463-4(9)) Chronicle Bks. LLC.
Murphy, Chuck. Animal Babies A to Z. 2007. (ENG.). 8p. (J). bds. 16.95 (978-1-58117-652-0(X), Intervisual/Piggy Toes) Bendon, Inc.
My Awesome Alphabet Book. 2015. (ENG., Illus.). 56p. (gr. -1). bds. (978-1-78393-822-3(6)) Make Believe Ideas.
My First A B C. Date not set. (Illus.). (J). bds. 5.98 (978-0-7525-7984-9(3)) Parragon, Inc.
My Nativity ABCs. 2017. (ENG.). (J). (gr. -1-k). 14.99 **(978-1-4621-2027-7(X))** Cedar Fort, Inc./CFI Distribution.
Nadal, Gloria. No No Foca Loca. 2007. (SPA.). 40p. per. 13.95 (978-1-59526-450-3(7), Llumina Kids) Aeon Publishing Inc.
Nagara, Innosanto. A Is for Activist. 2016. (ENG., Illus.). 32p. (J). (gr. -1-2). 17.95 (978-1-60980-693-4(X), Triangle Square) Seven Stories Pr.
Napier, Matt. Hat Tricks Count: A Hockey Number Book. Rose, Melanie, illus. rev. ed. 2005. (Sports Ser.). (ENG.). 40p. (J). (gr. k-5). 16.95 (978-1-58536-163-2(1)) Sleeping Bear Pr.
—Z Is for Zamboni: A Hockey Alphabet. Rose, Melanie, illus. 2015. (Av2 Fiction Readalong 2016 Ser.). (ENG.). (J). (gr. -1-1). lib. bdg. 34.28 (978-1-4896-3771-0(0), AV2 by Weigl) Weigl Pubs., Inc.
—Z Is for Zamboni: A Hockey Alphabet. Rose, Melanie, illus. rev. ed. 2006. (Sports Alphabet Ser.). (ENG.). 32p. (J). (gr. -1-1). 8.99 (978-1-58536-303-2(0), 202288) Sleeping Bear Pr.
Napier, Matt & Rose, Melanie. Z Is for Zamboni: A Hockey Alphabet. Rose, Melanie, illus. rev. ed. 2003. (Sports Alphabet Ser.). (ENG., Illus.). 40p. (J). (gr. -1-1). pap. 8.99 (978-1-58536-238-7(7), 202277) Sleeping Bear Pr.
Nash, Ogden. Lineup for Yesterday. Payne, C. F., illus. 2011. (ENG.). 56p. (J). (gr. 1-3). 24.99 (978-1-56846-212-7(3), Creative Editions) Creative Co., The.
Neely, Wilma F. Aaron & Abbey Go to School: Trevor Tutors His Friends. 2009. 28p. pap. 12.49 (978-1-4389-5420-2(4)) AuthorHouse.
Newman-D'Amico, Fran. Alphabet Mazes. 2006. (Dover Children's Activity Bks.). (ENG., Illus.). 32p. (J). (gr. -1-2). 3.99 (978-0-486-44894-7(0)) Dover Pubns., Inc.
Nguyen, An Mai. Let's Learn the Vietnamese Alphabet. 2006. (VIE & ENG., Illus.). (J). bds. 6.95 (978-0-9776482-0-7(6)) Viet Baby, LLC.
Nichols, Stephen J. & Bustard, Ned. The Church History ABCs: Augustine & 25 Other Heroes of the Faith. 2010. 32p. (J). 16.99 (978-1-4335-1472-2(9)) Crossway.
Nickelodeon Staff, ed. ABC, Dora the Explorer. 2010. (Write, Slide & Learn Ser.). 14p. (J). (gr. -1-1). 9.99 (978-1-74184-522-8(X), Ideal Pubns.) Worthy Publishing.
—Phonics - Spongebob Squarepants. 2010. (Write, Slide & Learn Ser.). 14p. (J). (gr. -1-1). 9.99 (978-1-74184-520-4(3), Ideal Pubns.) Worthy Publishing.
Noble, Ron. Letter Beasties. 2013. 34p. 19.95 (978-1-4575-1931-4(3)); pap. 12.95 (978-1-4575-1893-5(7)) Dog Ear Publishing, LLC.
Nogueras, Paola. ABC de Puerto Rico. 2006. (SPA.). (J). (gr. k-1). 12.00 (978-0-9721888-2-1(7), GP33485) Gabriel Pr.
Nosy Crow Staff. Halloween ABC. Ho, Jannie, illus. 2017. (ENG.). 26p. (J). (— 1). bds. 6.99 **(978-0-7636-9527-9(0)**, Nosy Crow) Candlewick Pr.
November, Deborah. Elmo's ABC Book. Nicklaus, Carol, illus. 2007. (Big Bird's Favorites Board Bks.). (ENG.). 24p. (J). (gr. k — 1). bds. 4.99 (978-0-375-84037-1(0), Random Hse. Bks. for Young Readers) Random Hse. Children's Bks.
Novick, Mary, et al. Alphabet. Hale, Jenny, illus. 2006. (Princess Poppets Ser.). (ENG.). 16p. (J). (gr. k-k). 10.95 (978-1-921049-03-3(0)) Little Hare Bks. AUS. Dist: Independent Pubs. Group.
Novit, Renee Z. Alphabet Aa to Zz. R. Z. Novit Graphic Design Staff, illus. (Kidz & Katz Educational Learning Book Ser.). 16p. (J). (gr. -1). pap. 7.95 (978-1-883371-00-5(7)) Kidz & Katz Publishing Co.
Ogwang, Evelynn. My Alphabet Safari. 2012. 60p. pap. 21.99 (978-1-4567-5621-5(4)) AuthorHouse.
Ohanesian, Diane. The ABCs of Thanks & Please. Chamberlain, Margaret, illus. 2011. (J). (978-0-545-37962-5(8)) Scholastic, Inc.
Olivares, Katie Lydon. ABC Book of Shadows. l.t. ed. 2005. (Illus.). 30p. (J). bds. 9.99 (978-0-9768573-0-3(8)) Itty Bitty Witch Works.
Olivera, Ramon. ABCs on Wheels. Olivera, Ramon, illus. 2016. (ENG., Illus.). 40p. (J). (gr. -1-k). 17.99 (978-1-4814-3244-3(3), Little Simon) Little Simon.
—ABCs on Wings. Olivera, Ramon, illus. 2015. (ENG., Illus.). 40p. (J). (gr. -1-2). 17.99 (978-1-4814-3242-9(7), Little Simon) Little Simon.
Olivia's ABC. 2014. (ENG., Illus.). 30p. (J). (gr. -1-k). bds. 7.99 (978-1-4814-2192-8(1), Atheneum Bks. for Young Readers) Simon & Schuster Children's Publishing.
Olson, Gillia M. A Monster Alphabet: The ABCs of Screams! Loram, James, illus. 2016. (Alphabet Connection Ser.). (ENG.). 32p. (gr. k-1). lib. bdg. 27.32 (978-1-4795-6887-1(2)) Picture Window Bks.
Open Court Staff. Breaking Code Manuscript Alphabet. (J). pap. (978-0-87548-955-1(9), 8514) Open Court Publishing Co.
Oquendo, Lisa, illus. Abecedario. 2006. (SPA.). bds. 5.99 (978-1-934113-04-2(2)) Little Cubans, LLC.
Orca Book Publishers, ed. Baby's First Bookshelf, 3 vols. 2013. (ENG.). 72p. (J). (gr. -1-k). bds. 24.95 (978-1-4598-0447-0(3)) Orca Bk. Pubs. USA.
Osornio, Catherine L. The Declaration of Independence from A to Z, 1 vol. Johnson, Layne, illus. 2010. (ENG.). 32p. (J). (gr. 1-7). 16.99 (978-1-58980-676-4(X)) Pelican Publishing Co., Inc.
O'Toole, Patrick. Alphabetimals — in the Wild! 2013. (Dover Coloring Bks.). (ENG., Illus.). 32p. (J). (gr. -1-5). pap. 3.99 (978-0-486-49914-7(6)) Dover Pubns., Inc.
—Alphabetimals Picture Dictionary. 2014. (ENG.). 144p. (J). (gr. -1). pap. 6.99 (978-0-486-49180-6(3)) Dover Pubns., Inc.

Outside Your Back Door. 2004. (J). bds. 12.00 net. *(978-0-9747081-0-2(0))* Cohen, Deanna Moreau.

Owens, Mary Beth. The Caribou Alphabet: A Tilbury House Nature Book. Owens, Mary Beth, illus. exp. ed. 2015. (Tilbury House Nature Book Ser.: 0). (ENG., Illus.). 36p. (gr. -1-3). pap. 8.95 *(978-0-88448-446-2(7),* 884446) Tilbury Hse. Pubs.

P. N. Alphabet Country: A Read-Together ABC Game. P. N., illus. 2012. (ENG., Illus.). 26p. (J). spiral bd. 9.00 *(978-0-615-59362-3(3))* Easy Reach Corp.

Pack, Linda Hager. A Is for Appalachia: The Alphabet Book of Appalachian Heritage. Banks, Pat, illus. 2009. (ENG.). 44p. 16.95 *(978-0-8131-2556-5(1))* Univ. Pr. of Kentucky.

Paigerac, Patricia. Chimmy '5 in 1' Language Alphabet Book. Choi, Allan Jai-Ho, illus. 2007. 56p. (J). 23.00 *(978-0-9801137-0-9(9))* Paigerac, Patricia M.

Pain, Catherine. Alphabet for Colouring In. 2008. 112p. pap. 16.95 *(978-1-4092-1024-5(3))* Lulu Pr., Inc.

Pallotta, Jerry. The Construction Alphabet Book. Bolster, Rob, illus. 2006. (Jerry Pallotta's Alphabet Bks.). (ENG.). 32p. (J). (gr. -1-3). lib. bdg. 17.95 *(978-1-57091-437-9(0));* per. 7.95 *(978-1-57091-438-6(9))* Charlesbridge Publishing, Inc.

—The Icky Bug Alphabet Book. Masiello, Ralph, photos by. (Illus.). 32p. (J). (gr. -1-1). 10.95 *(978-0-933341-95-1(4))* Quinlan Pr.

—Sea Mammal Alphabet Book. 2012. (ENG.). (J). 16.95 *(978-0-9852032-5-2(0))* Bald Eagle Bks.

Pallotta, Jerry & Bolster, Rob. The Construction Alphabet. 2017. (ENG., Illus.). 28p. (J). (— 1). bds. 7.99 *(978-1-57091-799-8(X))* Charlesbridge Publishing, Inc.

Pallotta, Jerry & Garnett, Sammie. U. S. Army Alphabet Book. 2012. (ENG., Illus.). 32p. (J). 16.95 *(978-0-9852032-3-8(4))* Bald Eagle Bks.

Paprocki, Greg. Halloween Alphabet, 1 vol. 2017. (ENG.). 32p. (J). bds. 9.99 ***(978-1-4236-4780-5(7))*** Gibbs Smith, Publisher.

Paprocki, Greg, illus. C Is for Castle: A Medieval Primer, 1 vol. 2016. (ENG.). 32p. (J). bds. 9.99 *(978-1-4236-4281-7(3))* Gibbs Smith, Publisher.

—A Is for Atom: a Midcentury Alphabet, 1 vol. 2016. (ENG.). 32p. (J). bds. 9.99 *(978-1-4236-4426-2(3))* Gibbs Smith, Publisher.

—J Is for Jazz: a Roaring Twenties Alphabet, 1 vol. 2017. (ENG.). 32p. (J). bds. 9.99 *(978-1-4236-4604-4(5))* Gibbs Smith, Publisher.

—M Is for Monocle - Victorian Alphabet, 1 vol. 2016. (ENG.). 32p. (J). bds. 9.99 *(978-1-4236-4284-8(8))* Gibbs Smith, Publisher.

—R Is for Railway: An Industrial Revolution Alphabet, 1 vol. 2016. (ENG.). 32p. bds. 9.99 *(978-1-4236-4423-1(9))* Gibbs Smith, Publisher.

—S Is for Sabertooth: a Stone Age Alphabet, 1 vol. 2016. (ENG.). 32p. (J). bds. 9.99 *(978-1-4236-4420-0(4))* Gibbs Smith, Publisher.

—Swinging Sixties Alphabet (tentative), 1 vol. 2017. (ENG.). 32p. (J). bds. 9.99 *(978-1-4236-4667-9(3))* Gibbs Smith, Publisher.

—Wild West Alphabet, 1 vol. 2016. (ENG.). 32p. (J). bds. 9.99 *(978-1-4236-4251-0(1))* Gibbs Smith, Publisher.

Parent, Lauren A. Alphabet Kingdom. McGee, Mo, illus. 2009. (ENG.). 40p. (J). (gr. -1-1). pap. 8.95 *(978-1-55591-643-5(0))* Fulcrum Publishing.

Parker, Laurie. A for Angels: A Bible Alphabet. 2010. (Illus.). 56p. (J). 18.50 *(978-1-934193-48-8(8))* Quail Ridge Pr., Inc.

Pasda Diedwardo, Maryann & Pasda, Patricia J. Pennsylvania Voices Book Xi: The Marvelous Nature Alphabet Book. 2008. (Illus.). 68p. pap. 11.99 *(978-1-4389-0641-6(2))* AuthorHouse.

Patterson, James & Patterson, Susan. Big Words for Little Geniuses. Pan, Hsinping, illus. 2017. (ENG.). 32p. (J). (gr. -1-1). 17.99 ***(978-0-316-50293-1(6),*** Jimmy Patterson) Little Brown & Co.

Pattullo, Alice. An Animal ABC. 2017. (ENG., Illus.). 64p. (J). (gr. -1-1). 17.99 ***(978-1-84365-313-4(3),*** Pavilion) Pavilion Bks. GBR. Dist: Independent Pubs. Group.

Peanuckle. Mrs. Peanuckle's Vegetable Alphabet. Ford, Jessie, illus. 2017. (Mrs. Peanuckle's Alphabet Library: 1). (ENG.). 28p. (J). bds. 7.99 ***(978-1-62336-870-8(7),*** 9781623368708, Rodale Kids) Rodale Pr., Inc.

Pearson, Debora. Alphabeep! A Zipping, Zooming ABC. Miller, Edward, illus. 2007. (ENG.). 36p. (J). (gr. -1-3). 6.95 *(978-0-8234-2076-6(0))* Holiday Hse., Inc.

Pelikan, Judy. All Around the Block: An Alphabet. 2008. (ENG., Illus.). 64p. (J). 16.95 *(978-1-56792-343-8(7))* Godine, David R. Pub.

Penguin Books Staff, ed. My Alphabet Book. (Early Readers Ser.: No. S8711-5). (Illus.). 24p. (J). (gr. -1-2). 3.95 *(978-0-7214-5145-9(4),* Dutton Juvenile) Penguin Publishing Group.

Perrett, Lisa, illus. Sparkling Princess ABC. 2013. (Sparkling Stories Ser.). (ENG.). 14p. (J). bds. 5.95 *(978-1-4027-8886-4(X))* Sterling Publishing Co., Inc.

Perry, Marcia. Here on Earth: An Animal Alphabet. 2013. (ENG., Illus.). 60p. (J). 15.95 *(978-0-7649-6452-7(6))* Pomegranate Communications, Inc.

Peters, Rob, illus. Kansas City Chiefs ABCs And 1-2-3s. 2015. (ENG.). 26p. (J). bds. 18.95 *(978-0-9961944-0-2(1))* Ascend Bks., LLC.

Petrey, Ashley. The Abc's Game. 2013. 36p. pap. 24.95 *(978-1-62709-707-9(4))* America Star Bks.

Phillips, Lori. Carolinian Alphabet. 2004. (Island Alphabet Books). (Illus.). 80p. (J). 4.95 *(978-1-57306-220-6(0))* Bess Pr., Inc.

—Chamorro Alphabet. 2004. (Island Alphabet Books). (Illus.). 56p. 4.95 *(978-1-57306-213-8(8))* Bess Pr., Inc.

—Chuukese Alphabet. 2004. (Island Alphabet Books). (Illus.). 56p. 4.95 *(978-1-57306-222-0(7))* Bess Pr., Inc.

—English Alphabet. 2004. (Island Alphabet Books). (Illus.). 56p. (J). 9.95 *(978-1-57306-219-0(7))* Bess Pr., Inc.

—Hawaiian Alphabet. 2004. (Island Alphabet Books). (Illus.). 32p. (J). 9.95 *(978-1-57306-218-3(9))* Bess Pr., Inc.

—Kosraean Alphabet. 2004. (Island Alphabet Books). (Illus.). 48p. 4.95 *(978-1-57306-217-6(0))* Bess Pr., Inc.

—Marshallese Alphabet. 2004. (Island Alphabet Books). (Illus.). 56p. 4.95 *(978-1-57306-221-3(9))* Bess Pr., Inc.

—Palauan Alphabet. 2004. (Island Alphabet Books). (Illus.). 40p. 4.95 *(978-1-57306-216-9(2))* Bess Pr., Inc.

—Pohnpeian Alphabet. 2004. (Island Alphabet Books). (Illus.). 40p. (J). 4.95 *(978-1-57306-215-2(4))* Bess Pr., Inc.

—Samoan Alphabet. 2004. (Island Alphabet Books). (Illus.). 40p. (J). 4.95 *(978-1-57306-214-5(6))* Bess Pr., Inc.

Phillips, Sarah. Lift & Learn ABC. Snaith, Andy, photos by. 2006. (Illus.). 24p. (gr. -1). per., bds. *(978-1-84610-029-1(1))* Make Believe Ideas.

—Magnet Matching ABC: Match the Magnets & Learn Your Alphabet. 2006. (Illus.). 12p. (J). (gr. k-2). *(978-1-84610-121-2(2))* Make Believe Ideas.

—Touch & Learn: ABC. 2007. (Touch & Learn (Make Believe Ideas) Ser.). (Illus.). 12p. (gr. -1). per., bds. *(978-1-84610-461-9(0))* Make Believe Ideas.

—Touch & Learn ABC. 2005. (Illus.). 12p. (J). (gr. -1-1). per., bds. *(978-1-905051-75-5(1))* Make Believe Ideas.

Pike, Katy. Funny Photo Alphabet. Jurevicius, Luke, photos by. 2006. (Funny Photo Alphabet Ser.). (Illus.). 32p. (J). lib. bdg. 26.95 *(978-0-8225-6076-0(3),* Lerner Pubns.) Lerner Publishing Group.

Pilobolus. The Human Alphabet. Pilobolus. Kane, John, photos by. 2003. (Illus.). 40p. (J). *(978-1-58717-225-0(9));* lib. bdg. *(978-1-58717-226-7(7))* Chronicle Bks. LLC. (SeaStar Bks.).

Pirog, Kristen T. An Army ABC Book. Pierce, Julie A., illus. 2007. 32p. (J). per. 14.99 *(978-1-59879-324-6(1))* Lifevest Publishing, Inc.

—A Marine ABC Book. Pierce, Julie A., illus. l.t. ed. 2006. 32p. (J). per. 16.99 *(978-1-59879-221-8(0))* Lifevest Publishing, Inc.

Pittman, Rickey E. Confederate Alphabet, 1 vol. Ford, Stephanie A., illus. 2011. (ENG.). 32p. (J). (gr. k-3). 16.99 *(978-1-58980-760-0(X))* Pelican Publishing Co., Inc.

—Irish Alphabet, 1 vol. 2011. (ENG., Illus.). 32p. (J). (gr. k-3). 16.99 *(978-1-58980-745-7(6))* Pelican Publishing Co., Inc.

Polacco, Patricia. G Is for Goat. Polacco, Patricia, illus. 2006. (ENG., Illus.). 32p. (J). (gr. -1-k). reprint ed. pap. 7.99 *(978-0-14-240550-5(7),* Puffin Books) Penguin Young Readers Group.

Polark, Kelly. Rockabet: Classic Edition. Little, Kelli Ann, illus. 2013. 32p. pap. 10.49 *(978-0-9888462-0-3(9))* Big Smile Pr., LLC.

Pollock, Valerie. Alpha's Alphabet. 2010. 32p. pap. 15.95 *(978-1-4520-5760-6(5))* AuthorHouse.

Popper, Carol. David, Mormor, Homo & the Yak: An Alphabet Mystery. 2008. 24p. pap. 24.95 *(978-1-4241-8772-0(9))* America Star Bks.

Porter, Matthew & Morstad, Julie. ABC. 2006. (ENG., Illus.). 28p. (J). (gr. -1 — 1). bds. 8.95 *(978-1-894965-38-5(8))* Simply Read Bks. CAN. Dist: Ingram Publisher Services.

Powell, Consie. A Bold Carnivore: An Alphabet of Predators. 2007. (Illus.). 32p. (J). (gr. -1-k). 12.95 *(978-0-9766264-8-0(9))* Raven Productions, Inc.

Practice Pals Bilingual Practice Book: Cursive Letters. 2006. (ENG & FRE., Illus.). 16p. (J). (gr. k-2). spiral bd. *(978-1-930355-54-5(8))* Bright of America.

Practice Pals Bilingual Practice Book: Manuscript Letters. 2006. (ENG & FRE., Illus.). 16p. (J). (gr. -1-1). spiral bd. *(978-1-930355-56-9(4))* Bright of America.

Pratico, Ariel R. Do You Know Where Z Is? 2011. 36p. pap. 24.95 *(978-1-4626-2560-4(6))* America Star Bks.

Pratt-Serafini, Kristin Joy. A Walk in the Rainforest. Pratt-Serafini, Kristin Joy, illus. 2007. (Simply Nature Book Ser.). (Illus.). 26p. (J). (gr. -1 — 1). bds. 7.95 *(978-1-58469-088-7(7))* Dawn Pubns.

Pratt Serafini, Kristin Joy, illus. A Swim Through the Sea, 1 vol. 2006. (Simply Nature Bks.). (ENG.). 26p. (J). (gr. -1). bds. 7.95 *(978-1-58469-080-1(1))* Dawn Pubns.

Preece, Mary Ellen Goble. The ABC Cousins & Fun from A to Z. 2007. (J). per. 12.00 *(978-1-60458-005-1(4))* Instant Pub.

Prescott, Brian. Chloe Knows Her Alphabet. 2013. 20p. pap. *(978-1-909192-51-5(1))* Beaten Track Publishing.

Priddy Books Staff & Priddy, Roger. Dinosaur A-Z: For Kids Who Really Love Dinosaurs! l.t. rev. ed. 2004. (Smart Kids Ser.). (ENG., Illus.). 32p. (J). (gr. -1-2). bds. 9.99 *(978-0-312-49254-0(5),* 9780312492540, Priddy Bks.) St. Martin's Pr.

Priddy, Roger. ABC 123. 2014. (Hello Kitty Ser.). (ENG.). 60p. (J). (gr. -1-1). pap., wbk. ed. 12.99 *(978-0-312-51764-9(5),* 9780312517649, Priddy Bks.) St. Martin's Pr.

—Alphaprints. 2017. (Wipe Clean Activity Bks.). (ENG.). 56p. (J). spiral bd. 12.99 *(978-0-312-52152-3(9),* 9780312521523, Priddy Bks.) St. Martin's Pr.

—First Words / Primeras Palabras. 2007. (Bright Baby Ser.). (ENG & SPA., Illus.). 12p. (J). (gr. -1 — 1). bds. 4.95 *(978-0-312-50300-0(8),* 9780312503000, Priddy Bks.) St. Martin's Pr.

—A Is for Animal. 2013. (ABC Bks.). (ENG.). 24p. (J). (gr. -1 — 1). bds. 12.99 *(978-0-312-51637-6(1),* 9780312516376, Priddy Bks.) St. Martin's Pr.

—Learn to Write Your - Letters ABC. rev. ed. 2004. (Wipe Clean Learning Bks.). (ENG., Illus.). 24p. (J). (gr. -1-1). 8.95 *(978-0-312-49251-9(0),* 9780312492519, Priddy Bks.) St. Martin's Pr.

—Learn to Write Your Letters ABC. 2006. (Wipe Clean Activity Flash Cards Ser.). (ENG.). 30p. (J). (gr. -1-1). bds. 9.99 *(978-0-312-49816-0(0),* 9780312498160, Priddy Bks.) St. Martin's Pr.

—Lowercase Alphabet. 2010. (ENG.). 28p. (J). (gr. -1-1). spiral bd., wbk. ed. 6.99 *(978-0-312-50868-5(9),* 9780312508685, Priddy Bks.) St. Martin's Pr.

—My First Alphabet Touch & Feel. 2016. (ENG.). 20p. (J). bds. 12.99 *(978-0-312-52012-0(3),* 9780312520120, Priddy Bks.) St. Martin's Pr.

—Sticker Activity ABC. 2008. (Sticker Activity Fun Ser.). (ENG.). 20p. (J). (gr. -1-1). pap. 4.99 *(978-0-312-50483-0(7),* 9780312504830, Priddy Bks.) St. Martin's Pr.

—Trace, Write, & Learn ABC. 2017. (Alphaprints Ser.). (ENG.). 14p. (J). bds. 9.99 *(978-0-312-52149-3(9),* 9780312521493, Priddy Bks.) St. Martin's Pr.

—Uppercase Alphabet. 2010. (ENG.). 28p. (J). (gr. -1-1). spiral bd., wbk. ed. 7.99 *(978-0-312-50867-8(0),* 9780312508678, Priddy Bks.) St. Martin's Pr.

Priest, Jerry and Beverly. ABC Memory Verse Program. 2003. (Illus.). 60p. (J). spiral bd. 15.95 *(978-0-9743871-0-9(X))* Priest, Gerald L.

Prieto, Anita C. B Is for Bookworm: A Library Alphabet. Graef, Renee, illus. 2007. (J). (gr. k-7). 16.10 *(978-0-7569-6657-7(4))* Perfection Learning Corp.

—B Is for Bookworm: A Library Alphabet. Graef, Renee, illus. 2007. (ENG.). 40p. (J). (gr. 1-4). per. 7.95 *(978-1-58536-326-1(X),* 202290) Sleeping Bear Pr.

Pringle, Cindy & Pringle, Kirby. Happy Tails: Earl & Pearl on the Farm. l.t. ed. 2006. (ENG., Illus.). 32p. (J). (gr. k-2). *(978-0-9777126-0-1(5))* Dogtown Artworks.

Privateer, Mark & Dunlap, Jennifer. Sharks Don't Eat Peanut Butter. 2013. 62p. pap. 12.95 *(978-0-9896220-6-6(1))* No Frills Buffalo.

Prochovnic, Dawn Babb. A to Z Sign with Me: Sign Language for the Alphabet, 1 vol. Bauer, Stephanie, illus. 2012. (ENG.). 32p. 28.50 *(978-1-61641-835-9(4),* Looking Glass Library) Magic Wagon.

Prus, Jennifer. A Toddler's Abc of Blessings. McIlhany, illus. 2012. 20p. pap. 9.95 *(978-1-61633-256-3(5))* Guardian Angel Publishing, Inc.

Publications International Ltd. Staff, creator. Dora the Explorer Learn to Write. 2007. (Play-A-Sound Bks.). (Illus.). (J). (gr. -1-3). 19.98 *(978-1-4127-6659-3(1))* Publications International, Ltd.

—Tonka Wipe-off Activity Kit: ABCs And 123s. 2007. (Wipe off Activity Kit Ser.). 14.98 *(978-1-4127-7443-7(8))* Publications International, Ltd.

Publications International Ltd. Staff, ed. Disney Pixar ABC Board Books. 2010. 10p. (J). 23.98 *(978-1-4508-0370-0(9))* Phoenix International Publications, Inc.

—Dora the Explorer: Let's Write Letters. 2010. 16p. (J). bds. 16.98 *(978-1-60553-618-7(0))* Phoenix International Publications, Inc.

—Play-a-Puzzle trade; Book: Alphabet. 2010. 12p. (J). bds. 10.98 *(978-1-60553-799-3(3))* Publications International, Ltd.

Publishing, Chouette. Caillou, My First ABC: The Alphabet Soup. Brignaud, Pierre, illus. 2015. (ENG.). 32p. (J). (gr. -1-k). 9.99 *(978-2-89718-201-4(6))* Caillouet, Gerry.

Puck. My Foodie ABC: A Little Gourmet's Guide. Lemay, Violet, illus. 2010. (ENG.). 22p. (J). (gr. -1-k). bds. 8.95 *(978-0-9825295-2-2(X))* Duo Pr. LLC.

Pulver, Robin. The Case of the Incapacitated Capitals. Reed, Lynn Rowe, illus. 2013. (ENG.). 32p. (J). (gr. -1-3). pap. 7.99 *(978-0-8234-2914-1(8))* Holiday Hse., Inc.

Q. Dani-L's Counting Alphabet Book. 2009. 28p. pap. 14.99 *(978-1-4343-7927-6(2))* AuthorHouse.

Raczka, Bob. 3-D ABC: A Sculptural Alphabet. 2006. (Bob Raczka's Art Adventures Ser.). (ENG., Illus.). 32p. (J). (gr. k-12). lib. bdg. 25.26 *(978-0-7613-9456-3(7),* Millbrook Pr.) Lerner Publishing Group.

Ramey, Kathy. The Animal Alphabet. 2007. (Illus.). (J). pap. 12.95 *(978-1-931334-96-9(X))* Pieces of Learning.

Random, Melanie, des. The Alphabet Song Book. 2006. (ENG., Illus.). 16p. (J). (gr. -1-3). 12.95 *(978-1-58117-444-1(6),* Intervisual/Piggy Toes) Bendon, Inc.

Reid, Demetra. Alice's ABC's: Version 2. Deffenbaugh, Dena, illus. 2010. 66p. pap. 14.00 *(978-0-9802275-8-1(5))* Candalyse Publishing.

Rey, H. A. Curious George Curious about Learning Boxed Set. 2012. (Curious George Ser.). (ENG., Illus.). 144p. (J). (gr. -1-3). 16.99 *(978-0-547-58209-2(9))* Houghton Mifflin Harcourt Publishing Co.

Rey, H. A. & Rey, Margret. Curious George Learns the Alphabet. 50th ed. 2013. (Curious George Ser.). (ENG., Illus.). 80p. (J). (gr. -1-3). 12.99 *(978-0-544-10523-2(0))* Houghton Mifflin Harcourt Publishing Co.

Rey, H. A., et al. Curious George Discovery Day. 2007. (Curious George Ser.). (ENG., Illus.). 14p. (J). (gr. k — 1). bds. 13.95 *(978-0-618-73761-1(8))* Houghton Mifflin Harcourt Publishing Co.

Reyes, Jose & Reyes, Rhonda. The I AM Alphabet Book. 2007. (J). per. 14.95 *(978-0-9794731-0-4(1))* Reyes, Jose.

Richard, Lolita Louise. Walking with a B C Big Book Adventure. 2009. 60p. pap. 31.99 *(978-1-4415-3719-5(8))* Xlibris Corp.

Richard Scott Morris. Alphabet Soup with Anchovies. 2009. 32p. pap. 18.00 *(978-1-4389-5379-3(8))* AuthorHouse.

Richardson, Bill. The Alphabet Thief, 1 vol. Bikadoroff, Roxanna, illus. 2017. (ENG.). 40p. (J). (gr. k-4). 16.95 *(978-1-55498-877-8(2))* Groundwood Bks. CAN. Dist: Publishers Group West (PGW).

Rigby Education Staff. Animals: A Is for Animal. (Pebble Soup Explorations Ser.). 16p. (gr. -1-18). 5.00 *(978-0-7635-7047-7(8))* Rigby Education.

Ripley's Believe It Or Not! Staff, compiled by. Oddphabet. 2017. (Little Bks.: 2). (ENG.). 26p. (J). bds. 6.99 *(978-1-60991-170-6(9))* Ripley Entertainment, Inc.

Risley, Jacqueline & Tim. Alpha's ABC's Games: Spanish & English Ages 2-6. Risley, Jacqueline & Tim, illus. 2007.Tr. of Alfa y sus Juegos de la A a la Z. (SPA & ENG., Illus.). 32p. (J). 6.99 *(978-0-9791680-0-0(7))* Alpha Learning World, Inc.

Roach, Sandra & Torowski, Dave. Alina's Options: Careers from A to Z. 2008. (ENG., Illus.). 52p. pap. 12.99 *(978-0-9801426-0-0(1))* Options Galore.

Robb, Don. Ox, House, Stick: The History of Our Alphabet. Smith, Anne, illus. 2007. (Junior Library Guild Selection (Charlesbridge Paper) Ser.). (ENG.). 48p. (J). (gr. 3-7). pap. 7.95 *(978-1-57091-610-6(1))* Charlesbridge Publishing, Inc.

Roberts, G. Gregory. S Is for Spirit Bear: A British Columbia Alphabet. Doucet, Bob, illus. rev. ed. 2006. (Discover Canada Province by Province Ser.). (ENG.). 40p. (J). (gr. 3-7). 18.95 *(978-1-58536-291-2(3))* Sleeping Bear Pr.

Robins, Sandy. For the Love of Cats: An A-to-Z Primer for Cat Lovers of All Ages. Anderson, Mark, illus. 2011. (For the Love Of... Ser.). (ENG.). 48p. 16.95 *(978-1-60078-581-8(6))* Triumph Bks.

Rodriguez, Sonia & Browning, Kurt. T Is for Tutu: A Ballet Alphabet. Ong, Wilson, illus. 2011. (ENG.). 32p. (gr. k-5). 16.95 *(978-1-58536-312-4(X))* Sleeping Bear Pr.

Rogers, Brandy. It's Big, It's Little. 2008. 12p. pap. 24.95 *(978-1-60474-585-6(1))* America Star Bks.

Ronay, Laura. Kids Like Me... Learn ABCs. Kishimoto, Jon Wayne, illus. 2008. (ENG.). 32p. (J). (gr. -1-1). 12.95 *(978-1-60613-000-1(5))* Woodbine Hse.

Rosa-Mendoza, Gladys. The Alphabet. Cifuentes, Carolina, ed. Noiset, Michele, illus. 2004. (English-Spanish Foundations Ser.).Tr. of El Alfabeto. (ENG & SPA.). 32p. (J). bds. 6.95 *(978-0-9679748-0-4(1))* Me+Mi Publishing.

Rosario, Sherwin, illus. Meet the Letters. 2005. 26p. (J). 9.99 *(978-0-9767008-0-7(8))* Preschool Prep Co.

Rosenthal, Amy Krouse. Al Pha's Bet. Durand, Delphine, illus. 2011. (ENG.). 32p. (J). (gr. -1-k). 16.99 *(978-0-399-24601-2(0),* G.P. Putnam's Sons Books for Young Readers) Penguin Young Readers Group.

—Awake Beautiful Child. Lam, Gracia, illus. 2015. (ENG.). 32p. (J). (gr. -1-k). 17.95 *(978-1-938073-92-2(4))* McSweeney's Publishing.

Ross, Barbara & Beatty, Nicholas. The Goops Circus: A Whimsical Telling of Do-Good Tales. Camille, Diana, illus. 2010. (Goops Ser.). 58p. (J). 19.95 incl. audio compact disk *(978-0-9712368-4-4(4))* Goops Unlimited.

Rossi, Joe, photos by. Minnesota's Hidden Alphabet. 2010. (ENG., Illus.). 48p. (J). (gr. -1-1). 16.95 *(978-0-87351-808-6(X))* Minnesota Historical Society Pr.

Rossi, Michelle. Letters & sounds in Loveland. 2005. 28p. (J). 6.95 *(978-1-4116-3185-4(4))* Lulu Pr., Inc.

Roth, Ruby. V Is for Vegan: The ABCs of Being Kind. Roth, Ruby, illus. 2013. (ENG., Illus.). 32p. (J). (gr. -1-2). 12.95 *(978-1-58394-649-7(7))* North Atlantic Bks.

Rowe, Jodye P. & Pileggi, Steven. Once upon a Time a Fairy Tale ABC Book. 2006. (Illus.). 56p. pap. 9.99 *(978-0-9671344-3-7(9))* Joewolf Pubs.

Rupp, Dain Chistopher. The Greatest Saint Stories A-Z: (Book 1 of 2: A-M) 2008. 32p. per. 24.95 *(978-1-60441-067-9(1))* America Star Bks.

Saaf, Donald. The ABC Animal Orchestra. Saaf, Donald, illus. 2015. (ENG., Illus.). 40p. (J). (gr. -1 — 1). 16.99 *(978-0-8050-9072-7(X),* 9780805090727, Holt, Henry & Co. Bks. For Young Readers) Holt, Henry & Co.

Salas, Laura Purdie. C Is for Cake! A Birthday Alphabet. 2010. (Alphabet Fun Ser.). (ENG.). 32p. (gr. 1-2). pap. 47.70 *(978-1-4296-5086-1(9));* lib. bdg. 27.32 *(978-1-4296-3914-9(8))* Capstone Press of Coughlan Cos. (Aplus Bks.).

—S Is for Score! A Sports Alphabet. 2010. (Alphabet Fun Ser.). (ENG.). 32p. (gr. 1-2). pap. 47.70 *(978-1-4296-5087-8(7),* Aplus Bks.) Capstone Press of Coughlan Cos.

—Y Is for Yak: A Zoo Alphabet, 1 vol. 2010. (Alphabet Fun Ser.). (ENG.). 32p. (gr. 1-2). lib. bdg. 27.32 *(978-1-4296-4465-5(6),* Aplus Bks.) Capstone Press of Coughlan Cos.

Salonen, Roxane B. P Is for Peace Garden: A North Dakota Alphabet. Yardley, Joanna, illus. 2005. (Discover America State by State Ser.). (ENG.). 40p. (J). (gr. -1-7). 17.95 *(978-1-58536-142-7(9))* Sleeping Bear Pr.

Salzmann, Mary Elizabeth. Accordion to Zeppelin: Inventions from A to Z, 1 vol. 2008. (Let's Look A to Z Ser.). (ENG., Illus.). 32p. (gr. k-4). 27.07 *(978-1-60453-008-7(1),* Super SandCastle) ABDO Publishing Co.

—Airedale to Zuchon: Dogs from A to Z, 1 vol. 2009. (Let's Learn A to Z Ser.). (ENG., Illus.). 32p. (J). (gr. -1-2). 27.07 *(978-1-60453-491-7(5))* ABDO Publishing Co.

—Albatross to Zebra Finch: Birds from A to Z, 1 vol. 2008. (Let's Look A to Z Ser.). (ENG., Illus.). 32p. (gr. k-4). 27.07 *(978-1-60453-009-4(X),* Super SandCastle) ABDO Publishing Co.

—Amy & Abe. 2005. (First Sounds Ser.). (Illus.). 23p. (J). pap. 48.42 *(978-1-59679-125-1(X))* ABDO Publishing Co.

—Ann & Alan. 2005. (First Sounds Ser.). (Illus.). (J). (gr. k-3). (ENG.). 24p. lib. bdg. 24.21 *(978-1-59679-126-8(8),* SandCastle); 23p. pap. 48.42 *(978-1-59679-127-5(6))* ABDO Publishing Co.

—Ant Farm to Zebra Fish: Pets from A to Z, 1 vol. 2009. (Let's Learn A to Z Ser.). (ENG., Illus.). 32p. (J). (gr. -1-2). 27.07 *(978-1-60453-494-8(X))* ABDO Publishing Co.

—Appleseed to Zamboni: Famous Men from A to Z, 1 vol. 2008. (Let's Look A to Z Ser.). (ENG., Illus.). 32p. (gr. k-4). 27.07 *(978-1-60453-012-4(X),* Super SandCastle) ABDO Publishing Co.

—Arctic Ocean to Zimbabwe: Geography from A to Z, 1 vol. 2008. (Let's Look A to Z Ser.). (ENG., Illus.). 32p. (gr. k-4). 27.07 *(978-1-60453-013-1(8),* Super SandCastle) ABDO Publishing Co.

—Bess & Bill, 1 vol. 2005. (First Sounds Ser.). (Illus.). (J). (gr. k-3). (ENG.). 24p. lib. bdg. 24.21 *(978-1-59679-216-6(7),* SandCastle); 23p. pap. 48.42 *(978-1-59679-217-3(5))* ABDO Publishing Co.

—Blair & Blaine, 1 vol. 2005. (First Sounds Ser.). (Illus.). (J). (gr. k-3). (ENG.). 24p. lib. bdg. 24.21 *(978-1-59679-128-2(4),* SandCastle); 23p. pap. 48.42 *(978-1-59679-129-9(2))* ABDO Publishing Co.

—Brandi & Brent, 1 vol. 2005. (First Sounds Ser.). (Illus.). (J). (gr. k-3). (ENG.). 24p. lib. bdg. 24.21 *(978-1-59679-130-5(6),* SandCastle); 23p. pap. 48.42 *(978-1-59679-131-2(4))* ABDO Publishing Co.

—Cassie & Carl, 1 vol. 2005. (First Sounds Ser.). (Illus.). (J). (gr. k-3). (ENG.). 24p. lib. bdg. 24.21 *(978-1-59679-132-9(2),* SandCastle); 23p. pap. 48.42 *(978-1-59679-133-6(0))* ABDO Publishing Co.

—Chelsey & Chad, 1 vol. 2005. (First Sounds Ser.). (J). (gr. k-3). (ENG.). 24p. lib. bdg. 24.21 *(978-1-59679-134-3(9),* SandCastle); 23p. pap. 48.42 *(978-1-59679-135-0(7))* ABDO Publishing Co.

—Cindy & Cecil, 1 vol. 2005. (First Sounds Ser.). (Illus.). (J). (gr. k-3). (ENG.). 24p. lib. bdg. 24.21 *(978-1-59679-136-7(5),* SandCastle); 23p. pap. 48.42 *(978-1-59679-137-4(3))* ABDO Publishing Co.

—Cristy & Craig, 1 vol. 2005. (First Sounds Ser.). (Illus.). (J). (gr. k-3). (ENG.). 24p. lib. bdg. 24.21 *(978-1-59679-138-1(1),* SandCastle); 23p. pap. 48.42 *(978-1-59679-139-8(X))* ABDO Publishing Co.

—Deb & Dan, 1 vol. 2005. (First Sounds Ser.). (Illus.). (J). (gr. k-3). (ENG.). 24p. lib. bdg. 24.21 *(978-1-59679-140-4(3),* SandCastle); 23p. pap. 48.42 *(978-1-59679-141-1(1))* ABDO Publishing Co.

—Drew & Drake, 1 vol. 2005. (First Sounds Ser.). (Illus.). (J). (gr. k-3). (ENG.). 24p. lib. bdg. 24.21 *(978-1-59679-142-8(X),* SandCastle); 23p. pap. 48.42 *(978-1-59679-143-5(8))* ABDO Publishing Co.

—It's A!, 1 vol. 2010. (It's the Alphabet! Ser.). (ENG.). 24p. (gr. k-4). 25.65 *(978-1-60453-588-4(1),* Super SandCastle) ABDO Publishing Co.

—It's F!, 1 vol. 2010. (It's the Alphabet! Ser.). (ENG.). 24p. (gr. k-4). 25.65 *(978-1-60453-593-8(8)*, Super SandCastle) ABDO Publishing Co.
—It's I!, 1 vol. 2010. (It's the Alphabet! Ser.). (ENG., Illus.). 24p. (gr. k-4). 25.65 *(978-1-60453-596-9(2)*, Super SandCastle) ABDO Publishing Co.
—It's J!, 1 vol. 2010. (It's the Alphabet! Ser.). (ENG., Illus.). 24p. (gr. k-4). 25.65 *(978-1-60453-597-6(0)*, Super SandCastle) ABDO Publishing Co.
—It's P!, 1 vol. 2010. (It's the Alphabet! Ser.). (ENG., Illus.). 24p. (gr. k-4). 25.65 *(978-1-60453-603-4(9)*, Super SandCastle) ABDO Publishing Co.
—It's U!, 1 vol. 2010. (It's the Alphabet! Ser.). (ENG., Illus.). 24p. (gr. k-4). 25.65 *(978-1-60453-608-9(X)*, Super SandCastle) ABDO Publishing Co.
—It's W!, 1 vol. 2010. (It's the Alphabet! Ser.). (ENG., Illus.). 24p. (gr. k-4). 25.65 *(978-1-60453-610-2(1)*, Super SandCastle) ABDO Publishing Co.
—It's Z!, 1 vol. 2010. (It's the Alphabet! Ser.). (ENG., Illus.). 24p. (gr. 1-4). 25.65 *(978-1-60453-613-3(6)*, Super SandCastle) ABDO Publishing Co.
Sandage, Charley. Big Bear's Arkansas ABCs Big Book. 2005. (Illus.). (J). pap. *(978-0-9794044-1-2(X))* Archeological Assessments, Inc.
Sanders, Nancy I. D Is for Drinking Gourd: An African American Alphabet. Lewis, E. B., illus. 2007. (ENG.). 40p. (J). (gr. k-6). 17.95 *(978-1-58536-293-6(X))* Sleeping Bear Pr.
Sanders, Sandy. Ms. Goozenpopa's Crazy Alphabet Show & Tell. 2010. 41p. 18.80 *(978-0-557-24222-1(3))* Lulu Pr., Inc.
Sandoval, Anthony J. Unusual Animals from A to Z. 2008. 30p. pap. 24.95 *(978-1-60672-184-1(4))* America Star Bks.
Sandy Marie Russell. The Abc's of Fun Activities. 2009. 32p. pap. 15.99 *(978-1-4389-8024-9(8))* AuthorHouse.
Saviola, Ava. Dinosaur ABCs. 2012. (Dinosaur School Ser.). (Illus.). 24p. (J). (gr. -1-1). pap. 8.15 *(978-1-4339-7136-5(4))*; lib. bdg. 22.60 *(978-1-4339-7135-8(6))* Stevens, Gareth Publishing LLLP.
Sayles, Alayne. Alphie & the Alphabets: A Fun Way to Learn to Read. Platt, Greg, illus. 2005. 44p. (J). spiral bd. 79.95 incl. audio compact disk *(978-0-9767506-0-4(0))* Reading Studio Pr.
Scarry, Richard. Best Little Board Book Ever. Random House Staff, illus. 2013. (ENG.). 24p. (J). (—1). bds. 4.99 *(978-0-449-81901-2(9)*, Golden Bks.) Random Hse. Children's Bks.
Schaefer, Lola M. & Miller, Heather Lynn. Look Behind! Tales of Animal Ends. Manning, Jane K., illus. 2008. 32p. (J). (gr. -1-3). lib. bdg. 17.89 *(978-0-06-088394-2(4)*, Greenwillow Bks.) HarperCollins Pubs.
Schafer, Kevin. Penguins ABC. 2004. (Penguins Ser.). (ENG., Illus.). 32p. (J). (gr. -1 — 1). bds. 6.95 *(978-1-55971-905-6(2))* Cooper Square Publishing Llc.
Scholastic, Inc. Staff. Modern Manuscript Alphabet. 2005. (ENG.). 5.99 *(978-0-439-73278-9(6)*, Teaching Resources) Scholastic, Inc.
—Touch & Feel ABC (Scholastic Early Learners) 2015. (Scholastic Early Learners Ser.). (ENG.). 26p. (J). (—1). bds. 12.99 *(978-0-545-90317-2(3)*, Cartwheel Bks.) Scholastic, Inc.
Scholastic, Inc. Staff, contrib. by. ABC. 2013. (Rookie Toddler(r) Ser.). (ENG.). 12p. (J). bds. 6.95 *(978-0-531-21576-0(8)*, Children's Pr.) Scholastic Library Publishing.
Scholastic, Inc. Staff, et al. Alphabet: 10 Ready-to-Go Games That Help Children Learn & Practice Letter-Recognition Skills-Independently. 2009. (File-Folder Games in Color Ser.). (ENG.). 144p. pap. 19.99 *(978-0-439-46591-5(5)*, Teaching Resources) Scholastic, Inc.
Schonberg, Marcia. Discover Ohio, 2 bks. Langton, Bruce, illus. 2003. (ENG.). 40p. (J). 27.95 *(978-1-58536-225-7(5))* Sleeping Bear Pr.
—I Is for Idea: An Inventions Alphabet. Radzinski, Kandy, illus. (Science Ser.). (ENG.). (J). 2006. 40p. (gr. -1-3). pap. 7.95 *(978-1-58536-327-8(8))* 2005. 48p. (gr. k-5). 16.95 *(978-1-58536-257-8(3))* Sleeping Bear Pr.
School Zone Publishing Co. Alphabet Bingo Game. rev. ed. 2006. (ENG.). (J). (gr. -1-k). 5.99 *(978-1-58947-494-9(5))* School Zone Publishing Co.
School Zone Publishing Company Staff. El Alfabeto Mayusculas Uppercase Alphabet. 2007. (ENG.). 64p. (J). pap. 2.69 *(978-1-58947-969-2(6))* School Zone Publishing Co.
—Big Alphabet. 2008. (ENG.). 30p. (J). pap. 12.99 *(978-1-60159-016-9(4))* School Zone Publishing Co.
—3D Think & Blink Alphabet. 2007. (ENG.). (J). 7.99 *(978-1-60159-101-2(2))* School Zone Publishing Co.
School Zone Staff. My First Smart Art Alphabet. 2009. pap. 2.99 *(978-1-60159-250-7(7))* School Zone Publishing Co.
Schroeder, Alan. Abe Lincoln: His Wit & Wisdom from A to Z. O'brien, John, illus. 2015. (ENG.). 32p. (J). (gr. 1-5). 17.95 *(978-0-8234-2420-7(0))* Holiday Hse., Inc.
—Abe Lincoln: His Wit & Wisdom from A-Z. O'brien, John, illus. 2016. (ENG.). 32p. (J). 7.99 *(978-0-8234-3575-3(X))* Holiday Hse., Inc.
—Ben Franklin: His Wit & Wisdom from A to Z. O'brien, John, illus. 2011. (ENG.). 32p. (J). (gr. 1-5). 16.95 *(978-0-8234-1950-0(9))* Holiday Hse., Inc.
—Ben Franklin: His Wit & Wisdom from A-Z. O'brien, John, illus. 2012. (ENG.). 32p. (J). pap. 7.95 *(978-0-8234-2435-1(9))* Holiday Hse., Inc.
Schwacber, Barbie Helt. Alphabet of Earth. Vitsky, Sally, illus. 2009. (ENG.). 40p. (J). 9.95 *(978-1-59249-997-7(X))* Soundprints.
Schwaeber, Barbie. Alphabet of Earth. Vitsky, Sally, illus. 2009. (ENG.). 40p. 17.95 *(978-1-59249-996-0(1))* Soundprints.
Schwaeber, Barbie Helt. Alphabet of Bears. Nelson, Will et al, illus. 2011. (Alphabet Bks.). (ENG.). 40p. (J). (gr. -1-3). 17.95 *(978-1-60727-668-5(2))* Soundprints.
—Alphabet of Bears. Nelson, Will et al, illus. 2007. (Alphabet Of... Ser.). (ENG.). 40p. (J). 15.95 *(978-1-59249-689-1(X))* Soundprints.
—Alphabet of Dance. Ward, Damian, illus. 2009. (Smithsonian Alphabet Books). (ENG.). 40p. (J). (gr. -1-k). 17.95 *(978-1-60727-110-9(9))* Soundprints.
—Alphabet of Dance. Wood, Damian, illus. 2009. (Smithsonian Alphabet Books). (ENG.). 40p. (J). (gr. -1-k). 9.95 *(978-1-60727-111-6(7))* Soundprints.
—Alphabet of Dinosaurs. Buchs, Thomas et al, illus. 2011. (Alphabet Bks.). (ENG.). 40p. (J). (gr. -1-3). 17.95 *(978-1-60727-671-5(2))*; 9.95 *(978-1-60727-444-5(2))* Soundprints.
—Alphabet of Dinosaurs. Buchs, Thomas, illus. (ENG.). 40p. 2009. 9.95 *(978-1-59249-993-9(7))* 2007. (J). (gr. -1-2). 15.95 *(978-1-59249-724-9(1))* Soundprints.
—Alphabet of Insects. Buchs, Thomas, illus. 2009. (ENG.). 40p. 9.95 *(978-1-59249-992-2(9))* Soundprints.
—Alphabet of Insects. Bratun, Katy et al, illus. 2007. (ENG.). 40p. (J). (gr. -1-3). 15.95 *(978-1-59249-725-6(X))* Soundprints.
—Alphabet of Music. Santillan, Jorge & Clark, Debbie, illus. 2011. (Alphabet Bks.). (ENG.). 40p. (J). (gr. -1-3). 9.95 *(978-1-60727-445-2(0))* Soundprints.
—Alphabet of Music. Clark, Debbie, illus. 2009. (ENG.). 40p. 9.95 *(978-1-59249-995-3(3))* Soundprints.
—Alphabet of Music. Santillan, Jorge, illus. 2008. (ENG.). 40p. (J). (gr. k-2). 15.95 *(978-1-59249-770-6(5))* Soundprints.
—Alphabet of Sports. Lowe, David, illus. (Alphabet Bks.). (ENG.). 40p. 2011. (J). (gr. -1-3). 9.95 *(978-1-60727-446-9(9))* 2009. 9.95 *(978-1-59249-994-6(5))* 2008. (J). (gr. k-2). 15.95 *(978-1-59249-769-0(1))* Soundprints.
Schwartz, Barry L. Adam's Animals. Doneva, Steliyana, illus. 2017. (J). ***(978-1-68115-530-2(3))*** Behrman Hse., Inc.
Scillian, Devin. D Is for down Under: An Australia Alphabet. Cook, Geoff, illus. 2010. (Discover the World Ser.). (ENG.). 40p. (J). (gr. 1-3). 17.95 *(978-1-58536-445-9(2)*, 202170) Sleeping Bear Pr.
—D Is for down Under: An Australia Alphabet. 2016. (Av2 Fiction Readalong 2017 Ser.). (ENG.). (J). (gr. k-6). 34.28 ***(978-1-4896-5206-5(X)***, AV2 by Weigl) Weigl Pubs., Inc.
Scillian, Devin. H Is for Honor: A Military Family Alphabet. Juhasz, Victor, illus. 2006. (ENG.). 40p. (J). (gr. k-6). 17.95 *(978-1-58536-292-9(1))* Sleeping Bear Pr.
Scillian, Devin & Scillian, Corey. S Is for Sunflower: A Kansas Alphabet. Bowles, Doug, illus. 2004. (State Ser.). (ENG.). 40p. (J). 17.95 *(978-1-58536-061-1(9)*, 1235980) Sleeping Bear Pr.
Segal, Robin. ABC in Albuquerque. 2009. (All 'Bout Cities Ser.). (ENG.). 32p. (J). (gr. -1-k). *(978-1-935139-01-0(0))* Murray Hill Bks., LLC.
—ABC in Boston. 2008. (All 'Bout Cities Ser.). (ENG.). 32p. (J). (gr. -1-k). *(978-0-9719697-1-1(X))* Murray Hill Bks., LLC.
—ABC in Chicago. 2007. (All 'Bout Cities Ser.). (ENG.). 32p. (J). (gr. -1-k). *(978-0-9719697-8-0(7))* Murray Hill Bks., LLC.
—ABC in Miami: And the Beaches. 2008. (All 'Bout Cities Ser.). (ENG & SPA.). 32p. (J). (gr. -1-k). *(978-0-9719697-2-8(8))* Murray Hill Bks., LLC.
—ABC in San Antonio. 2009. (All 'Bout Cities Ser.). (ENG.). 32p. (J). (gr. -1-k). *(978-1-935139-04-1(5))* Murray Hill Bks., LLC.
—ABC in San Francisco. 2008. (All 'Bout Cities Ser.). (ENG.). 32p. (J). (gr. -1-k). *(978-0-9719697-9-7(5))* Murray Hill Bks., LLC.
—ABC in the City. 2008. (All 'Bout Cities Ser.). (ENG.). 32p. (J). (gr. -1-k). *(978-0-9719697-3-5(6))* Murray Hill Bks., LLC.
—ABC in Tulsa. 2009. (All 'Bout Cities Ser.). (ENG.). 32p. (J). (gr. -1-k). *(978-1-935139-03-4(7))* Murray Hill Bks., LLC.
—ABC in Washington, DC. 2007. (All 'Bout Cities Ser.). (ENG.). 32p. (J). (gr. k — 1). 12.95 *(978-0-9719697-7-3(9))* Murray Hill Bks., LLC.
Segal, Robin & Adler, Tasha. ABC in Los Angeles: And la County. 2009. (All 'Bout Cities Ser.). (ENG.). 32p. (J). (gr. -1-k). *(978-1-935139-02-7(9))* Murray Hill Bks., LLC.
Sesame Street Staff, creator. Sesame Street: Early Learning Boxed Set. 2011. 72p. (J). bds. 12.99 *(978-1-60745-237-9(5))* Flying Frog Pubs.
Sesame Workshop. The Messy Alphabet Book! 2017. (Sesame Street Scribbles Ser.: 0). (ENG.). 40p. (J). (-3). 10.99 *(978-1-4926-4140-7(5)*, Sourcebooks Jabberwocky) Sourcebooks, Inc.
Sesame Workshop, ed. ABC Sesame Street Flash Cards. 2009. (ENG.). 30p. 9.95 *(978-1-74185-997-3(2)*, Ideal Pubns.) Worthy Publishing.
Sesame's: A Giant Coloring Book that Introduces Kids to the Alphabet: the ABCs of Sesame Street. 2006. (J). 6.99 *(978-1-59949-498-2(1))* Food Marketing Consultants, Inc.
Seuss, Dr. Hooper Humperdink...? Not Him! Nash, Scott, illus. 2006. (Bright & Early Books(R) Ser.). (ENG.). 48p. (J). (gr. -1-k). 9.99 *(978-0-679-88129-2(8)*, Random Hse. Bks. for Young Readers) Random Hse. Children's Bks.
Sevaly, Karen, ed. Alphabet Mats. 2006. (Scholastic Hands-on Learning Ser.). (ENG.). (gr. -1-1). 14.99 *(978-0-439-82377-7(3)*, Teaching Resources) Scholastic, Inc.
Seykora, Teresa M. Peanut Butter Bob's Alphabet Book: The Adventures of Peanut Butter Bob. 2010. 36p. pap. 15.49 *(978-1-4520-4184-1(9))* AuthorHouse.
Shan Shan, Kathryn Velikanje. E Is for Elephant. Wilson, Lynda Farrington, illus. 2013. 36p. pap. 9.87 *(978-1-939896-17-9(7))* Levity Pr.
—A Is for Alligator. Wilson, Lynda Farrington, illus. 2013. 34p. pap. 9.97 *(978-1-939896-13-1(4))* Levity Pr.
Shanddaramon. A Pagan Book of ABCs. 2009. 60p. pap. 24.95 *(978-0-557-09532-2(8))* Lulu Pr., Inc.
Sharpe, Jesse. Pictures Poetry & ABCs: My alphabet Learning Book. 2005. 69p. spiral bd. 9.95 *(978-1-4116-2461-0(0))* Lulu Pr., Inc.
Shaw-Russell, Susan. Seek, Sketch & Color — Alphabet. 2013. (Dover Children's Activity Bks.). (ENG.). 64p. (J). (gr. 1-3). pap. 5.99 *(978-0-486-49772-3(0))* Dover Pubns., Inc.
Shea, Kevin. H Is for Hockey. 2013. (ENG.). (J). pap. *(978-1-58536-891-4(1))* Sleeping Bear Pr.
Shearin, Mary A. A Is for All of Us: Earth Friendly ABC's. 2008. (Illus.). 32p. (J). 16.95 *(978-0-9800263-0-6(X))* D H Publishing LLC.
Sheldon. Not Just Another Alphabet Book. (J). 15.95 *(978-0-8118-4329-4(7))* Chronicle Bks. LLC.
Shoulders, Debbie & Shoulders, Michael. G Is for Gladiators: An Ancient Rome Alphabet. Juhasz, Victor, illus. 2010. (Sleeping Bear Alphabets Ser.). (ENG.). 40p. (J). (gr. 1-4). 19.99 *(978-1-58536-457-2(6)*, 202180) Sleeping Bear Pr.
Shoulders, Michael. Discover Tennessee: Count on Us; V is for Volunteer, 2 bks. Langton, Bruce, illus. 2003. (ENG.). 40p. (J). 27.95 *(978-1-58536-228-8(X))* Sleeping Bear Pr.
—Little Tennessee. 2012. (My Little State Ser.). (ENG., Illus.). 22p. (J). 9.95 *(978-1-58536-201-1(8))* Sleeping Bear Pr.
—M Is for Magnolia: A Mississippi Alphabet. Anderson, Rick, illus. 2003. (Discover America State by State Ser.). (ENG.). 40p. (J). 17.95 *(978-1-58536-129-8(1))* Sleeping Bear Pr.
Shoulders, Michael & Shoulders, Debbie. D Is for Drum: A Native American Alphabet. Toddy, Irving, illus. rev. ed. 2006. (ENG.). 40p. (J). (gr. k-6). 16.95 *(978-1-58536-274-5(3))* Sleeping Bear Pr.
—M Is for Money: An Economics Alphabet. Kelley, Marty, illus. 2015. (Science Alphabet Ser.). (ENG.). 32p. (J). (gr. 3-6). 16.99 *(978-1-58536-817-4(2)*, 203953) Sleeping Bear Pr.
Showalter, Sarah Evelyn, illus. Animals of the Bible from A to Z. 2007. (J). (gr. -1-3). 16.95 *(978-0-87946-331-1(7))* ACTA Pubns.
Sickman, Kari. Sounds & Letters. 2003. (Full-Color Literacy Activities Ser.). (ENG., Illus.). 176p. (gr. -1-1). pap. 24.99 *(978-0-7439-3235-6(8))* Teacher Created Resources, Inc.
Sierra, Judy. Sleepy Little Alphabet: A Bedtime Story from Alphabet Town. Sweet, Melissa, illus. 2009. (ENG.). 40p. (J). (gr. -1 — 1). 16.99 *(978-0-375-84002-9(8)*, Knopf Bks. for Young Readers) Random Hse. Children's Bks.
—The Sleepy Little Alphabet: A Bedtime Story from Alphabet Town. Sweet, Melissa, illus. 2014. (ENG.). 34p. (J). (— 1). bds. 6.99 *(978-0-385-75400-2(0)*, Knopf Bks. for Young Readers) Random Hse. Children's Bks.
Signing Time Flash Cards 5: ABC's. 2006. (J). 10.99 *(978-1-933543-12-3(4))* Two Little Hands Productions LLC.
Skafish, Brad. Red Letter Day: The Bad Cats Learn about Letters! 2012. 20p. pap. 11.95 *(978-1-62141-260-1(1))* Booklocker.com, Inc.
Skewes, John. Chicago ABC. 2016. (Larry Gets Lost Ser.). (ENG., Illus.). 32p. (J). (-k). 14.99 *(978-1-57061-993-9(X)*, Little Bigfoot) Sasquatch Bks.
—San Francisco ABC. 2016. (Larry Gets Lost Ser.). (ENG., Illus.). 32p. (J). (-k). 14.99 *(978-1-57061-994-6(8)*, Little Bigfoot) Sasquatch Bks.
—Seattle ABC: a Larry Gets Lost Book. 2017. (Larry Gets Lost Ser.). (ENG., Illus.). 32p. (J). (-k). 14.99 *(978-1-63217-093-4(0)*, Little Bigfoot) Sasquatch Bks.
Skewes, John, illus. Portland ABC. 2014. (Larry Gets Lost Ser.). (ENG.). 32p. (J). (gr. -1-k). 14.99 *(978-1-57061-920-5(4)*, Little Bigfoot) Sasquatch Bks.
Skirving, Janet. P Is for Puffin: A Newfoundland & Labrador Alphabet. Archibald, Odell, illus. rev. ed. 2006. (Discover Canada Province by Province Ser.). (ENG.). 40p. (J). (gr. 1-3). 17.95 *(978-1-58536-287-5(5)*, 202098) Sleeping Bear Pr.
Smith, Marie & Smith, Roland. B Is for Beaver: An Oregon Alphabet. Roydon, Michael, illus. 2003. (Discover America State by State Ser.). (ENG.). 40p. (J). 17.95 *(978-1-58536-071-0(6))* Sleeping Bear Pr.
Smith, R. M. An A to Z Walk in the Park (Animal Alphabet Book) Smith, R. M., illus. 2008. (ENG., Illus.). 32p. (J). per. 7.95 *(978-0-615-19572-8(5))* Clarence-Henry Bks.
Smith, Roland & Smith, Marie. S Is for Smithsonian: America's Museum Alphabet. Frankenhuyzen, Gijsbert van, illus. 2010. (Sleeping Bear Alphabets Ser.). (ENG.). 32p. (J). (gr. 1-5). 17.95 *(978-1-58536-314-8(6))* Sleeping Bear Pr.
—Z Is for Zookeeper: A Zoo Alphabet. Cole, Henry, illus. (ENG.). 40p. (J). (gr. k-6). 2005. 16.95 *(978-1-58536-158-8(5))* 2007. pap. 7.95 *(978-1-58536-329-2(4))* Sleeping Bear Pr.
Smith, Sherri. Mike the Tiger Teaches the Alphabet. Walsh, D. T., illus. 2013. (ENG.). (J). (gr. -1-k). 14.95 *(978-1-62086-348-0(0))* Mascot Bks., Inc.
Smith, Sherri Graves. UGA Teaches the Alphabet. Walsh, D. T., illus. 2013. (ENG.). 28p. (J). (gr. -1-3). 14.95 *(978-1-62086-450-0(9))* Mascot Bks., Inc.
Smithsonian Institution, ed. Dinosaurs & More! Write-with-Me Alphabet. 2009. (ENG.). 28p. 15.99 *(978-1-59069-826-6(6))* Studio Mouse LLC.
Snavlin, Joyce Burgess. Adirondack ABCs. Reed, Linda Davis, illus. 2009. 32p. (J). 9.95 *(978-1-59531-028-6(2))* North Country Bks., Inc.
Snow, Peggy. My Favorite Places from a to Z. Barber, Brian, illus. 2007. (My Favorites Ser.). (ENG.). 32p. (J). (gr. -1). lib. bdg. 15.99 *(978-1-934277-03-4(7))* Marn Green Publishing, Inc.
—My Favorite Sounds from a to Z. 2007. (ENG.). 32p. (J). lib. bdg. 15.99 *(978-1-934277-02-7(9))* Marn Green Publishing, Inc.
Snow, Todd & Snow, Peggy. Feelings to Share from a to Z. Hartman, Carrie, illus. 2007. (ENG.). 32p. (J). pap. 9.99 *(978-1-934277-00-3(2))* Marn Green Publishing, Inc.
Sobel, June. B Is for Bulldozer: A Construction ABC. Iwai, Melissa, illus. 2006. 28p. (gr. -1-k). 17.00 *(978-0-7569-7037-6(7))* Perfection Learning Corp.
—B Is for Bulldozer: A Construction ABC. Iwai, Melissa, illus. 2006. (ENG.). 32p. (J). (gr. -1-3). pap. 7.99 *(978-0-15-205774-9(9))* Houghton Mifflin Harcourt Publishing Co.
Sobel, June & Iwai, Melissa. B Is for Bulldozer: A Construction ABC. Iwai, Melissa, illus. 2013. (ENG., Illus.). 32p. (J). (— 1). bds. 7.99 *(978-0-544-10808-0(6))* Houghton Mifflin Harcourt Publishing Co.
Soffer, Ruth. Birds Alphabet Coloring Book. 2005. (Dover Nature Coloring Book Ser.). (ENG., Illus.). 32p. (J). (gr. -1-5). 3.99 *(978-0-486-44035-4(4))* Dover Pubns., Inc.
—Garden Flowers Alphabet. 2004. (Dover Design Coloring Bks.). (ENG., Illus.). 32p. (J). (gr. -1-5). pap. 3.99 *(978-0-486-43595-4(4))* Dover Pubns., Inc.
—Nature Alphabets Coloring Book. 2006. (Dover Nature Coloring Book Ser.). (ENG., Illus.). 96p. (J). (gr. -1-5). 7.95 *(978-0-486-45921-9(7))* Dover Pubns., Inc.
Somme, Kate. A Very Active Alphabet & Other Alphabet Rhymes. 2006. (ENG., Illus.). 32p. (J). (gr. 4-7). pap. 8.95 *(978-0-7145-3304-9(1))* Boyars, Marion Pubs., Ltd. GBR. Dist: Consortium Bk. Sales & Distribution.
Sonday, Arlene. The Sonday System - Let's Play Learn: Alphabet Book. Breckman, Cindy, ed. l.t. ed. 2004. (Illus.). 53p. (J). per. *(978-1-891602-11-5(X))* Winsor Learning, Inc.
Sounds & Letters, 26 bks., Level A. (Phonics & Friends Ser.). (gr. -1-2). suppl. ed. 1260.39 *(978-0-7362-0354-8(0)*, PH3000) CENGAGE Learning.
Sperber, Susie. 'Geee' Giggles My Grammy Who Glides down Giraffes. 2008. 36p. pap. 15.49 *(978-1-4389-1526-5(8))* AuthorHouse.
Spieker, Diana. Alphabetica: Odes to the Alphabet. Skehan, Krista, illus. 2009. (ENG.). 26p. 16.95 *(978-0-9797491-0-0(7))* Personify Pr.
Spinelli, Patti. Alphabet Book with Mackenzie & Emma. Spinelli, Patti, illus. 2003. (Illus.). 32p. (Orig.). (J). (gr. k-4). pap. 11.95 *(978-1-892066-00-8(9))* Nicolin Fields Publishing, Inc.
Spooner, Joe. N Is for Nostril — and Other Alphabet Silliness. 2007. (ENG., Illus.). 32p. (J). 14.95 *(978-0-9794771-1-9(5))* ACS, LLC Amica Creative Services.
Spradlin, Michael P. Baseball from A to Z. Pamintuan, Macky, illus. 2010. (ENG.). 32p. (J). (gr. -1-3). 16.99 *(978-0-06-124081-2(8))* HarperCollins Pubs.
Spray, Michelle. My ABCs: An ABC Book for Any Age. Pasternack, Susan, ed. Martines, Donna, illus. l.t. ed. 2006. 64p. (J). per. 8.95 *(978-0-9714160-4-8(4))* Bk. Shelf.
Square Cat ABC. 2014. (ENG., Illus.). 32p. (J). (gr. -1-3). 15.99 *(978-1-4424-9895-2(1)*, Aladdin) Simon & Schuster Children's Publishing.
Staker, Sara. My Baptism Keepsake. 2009. (Illus.). (J). *(978-1-59811-837-7(4))* Covenant Communications, Inc.
Stanek, Robert, pseud. Buster Bee's Adventures with Letters & Words. 2007. (ENG., Illus.). 28p. (J). pap. 9.99 *(978-1-57545-156-5(5))* RP Media.
Steiner, Stan, et al. P Is for Potato: An Idaho Alphabet. Slack, Jocelyn, illus. 2005. (Discover America State by State Ser.). (ENG.). 40p. (J). 17.95 *(978-1-58536-155-7(0))* Sleeping Bear Pr.
Steps To Literacy Staff, compiled by. Alphabet Books: Alphabet Picture Books Set 1 (5 Titles) 2005.Tr. of Alc025. (J). pap. 34.95 *(978-1-59564-988-1(3))* Steps To Literacy, LLC.
Stevens, Dave. Weirdly Wonderful a to Z: Exotic, Aquatic Creatures from the West Coast of British Columbia, Canada. Stevens, Dave, illus. 2016. (ENG., Illus.). 32p. (J). *(978-0-9950594-0-5(3))* Treewind Publishing.
Stone, Tanya Lee. A Is for America: A Patriotic Alphabet Book. Kelley, Gerald, illus. 2011. (ENG.). 24p. (J). (gr. -1-k). mass mkt. 4.99 *(978-0-8431-9877-5(X)*, Price Stern Sloan) Penguin Young Readers Group.
—T Is for Turkey: A True Thanksgiving Story. Kelley, Gerald, illus. 2009. (ENG.). 24p. (J). (gr. -1-k). mass mkt. 4.99 *(978-0-8431-2570-2(5)*, Price Stern Sloan) Penguin Young Readers Group.
Stortz, Diane. Adam Named the Animals from a to Z. Reed, Lisa, illus. 2012. (Roma Downey's Little Angels Ser.). 24p. (J). bds. 7.99 *(978-0-8249-5642-4(7)*, Ideal Pubns.) Worthy Publishing.
Strother, Ruth. W Is for Woof: A Dog Alphabet. Frankenhuyzen, Gijsbert van, illus. 2009. (ENG.). 40p. (J). (gr. k-6). pap. 7.95 *(978-1-58536-477-0(0))* Sleeping Bear Pr.
Stuart, Natalie. Monster Alphabet. 2013. (ENG.). 54p. 13.00 *(978-1-62884-649-2(6)*, Baby Professor (Education Kids)) Speedy Publishing LLC.
Studio Mouse, creator. My Clubhouse Alphabet. 2011. (Disney Mickey Mouse Clubhouse (Studio Mouse) Ser.). (ENG., Illus.). 24p. (J). (gr. -1-3). 8.99 *(978-1-60727-287-8(3))* Studio Mouse LLC.
—Tracing ABCs. rev. ed. 2005. (Trace & Learn Ser.). (ENG., Illus.). 28p. (J). (gr. -1-3). 16.49 *(978-1-59069-447-3(3)*, 1A602) Studio Mouse LLC.
Studio Mouse Staff. First Concepts, Pack. rev. ed. 2003. (ENG., Illus.). 60p. (J). (gr. -1-k). 12.99 *(978-1-59069-363-6(9)*, 1A502) Studio Mouse LLC.
—Take-with-Me-Alphabet. rev. ed. 2007. (ENG., Illus.). 36p. (J). (gr. -1-3). 12.99 *(978-1-59069-570-8(4))* Studio Mouse LLC.
Stutson, Caroline. Prairie Primer: A to Z. Lamb, Susan Condie, illus. 2006. 29p. (J). (gr. -1-2). reprint ed. 16.00 *(978-1-4223-5585-5(3))* DIANE Publishing Co.
Sullivan, E. J. F Is for Florida. Eldredge, Ernie, illus. 2006. (State Alphabet Bks.). 24p. (J). *(978-1-58173-525-3(1))* Sweetwater Pr.
—G Is for Georgia. Cross, Neal, illus. 2006. 24p. (J). *(978-1-58173-524-6(3))* Sweetwater Pr.
—A Is for Alabama. Eldredge, Ernie, illus. 2006. (State Alphabet Bks.). 24p. (J). *(978-1-58173-523-9(5))* Sweetwater Pr.
—N Is for North Carolina. Eldredge, Ernie, illus. 2007. (State Alphabet Bks.). 20p. *(978-1-58173-625-0(8))* Sweetwater Pr.
—S Is for South Carolina. Eldredge, Ernie, illus. 2007. (State Alphabet Bks.). 20p. *(978-1-58173-626-7(6))* Sweetwater Pr.
—T Is for Tennessee. Cross, Neal, illus. 2007. (State Alphabet Bks.). 24p. (J). (gr. -1-3). *(978-1-58173-527-7(8))* Sweetwater Pr.
—V Is for Virginia. Eldredge, Ernie, illus. 2006. 24p. (J). lib. bdg. *(978-1-58173-526-0(X))* Sweetwater Pr.
Sunshine Alphabet Book. (gr. k-3). 13.95 *(978-0-7802-6169-3(0))* Wright Group/McGraw-Hill.
Taylor, Gwen. Exploring Idaho from A to Z. Harvey, Robin, illus. 2003. (J). pap. *(978-1-930043-35-0(X))* Scott Publishing Co.
Taylor, Maxwell. Fun with Letters. Mshindu, illus. Date not set. (Fun with Ser.: Vol. 3). (J). (gr. -1-1). pap. 3.95 *(978-1-881316-42-8(4))* A & B Distributors & Pubs. Group.
Teach-Me-Bears Learn Letters. 2003. (J). per. *(978-1-884907-63-0(6))* Paradise Pr., Inc.
Thomas Nelson. Daring Dinosaur Alphabet. 2016. (ENG.). 14p. (gr. -1). bds. *(978-1-78598-466-2(7))* Make Believe Ideas.
—First 100 Words. 2016. (ENG.). 15p. (gr. -1). bds. *(978-1-78598-467-9(5))* Make Believe Ideas.
—My Awesome Alphabet Book. 2015. (ENG., Illus.). 160p. (gr. -1). bds. *(978-1-78393-754-7(8))* Make Believe Ideas.
Thomas Nelson. Petite Boutique Alphabet. 2017. (ENG.). (J). (gr. -1-7). bds. ***(978-1-78692-111-6(1))*** Make Believe Ideas.
Thompson, Gabrielle. The ABCs of Childhood Cancer. 2008. (Illus.). (J). *(978-1-59298-247-9(6))* Beaver's Pond Pr., Inc.
Thompson, Kim & Carder, Ken. Phonics. Billman, Dave et al, illus. 2009. 96p. (J). (gr. -1-3). pap. 10.99 incl. audio compact disk *(978-1-57583-820-5(6))* Twin Sisters IP, LLC.

Thompson, Kim Mitzo & Hilderbrand, Karen Mitzo. Alphabet. 2010. 12p. (J). (gr. k-2). bds. 8.99 *(978-1-59922-569-2(7))* Twin Sisters IP, LLC.

Thompson, Lauren. Little Quack's ABC's. Anderson, Derek, illus. 2010. (Super Chubbies Ser.). (ENG.). 26p. (J). (gr. -1 — 1). bds. 5.99 *(978-1-4169-6091-1(0),* Little Simon) Little Simon.

Thornhill, Jan. The Wildlife ABC: A Nature Alphabet Book. Thornhill, Jan, illus. 2012. (ENG., Illus.). 32p. (J). (gr. -1-2). pap. 7.95 *(978-1-926973-08-1(9),* Owlkids) Owlkids Bks. Inc. CAN. Dist: Publishers Group West (PGW).

Thurlby, Paul. Paul Thurlby's Alphabet. Thurlby, Paul, illus. 2011. (ENG., Illus.). 64p. (J). (gr. -1-2). 16.99 *(978-0-7636-5565-5(1),* Templar) Candlewick Pr.

Tiger Tales, ed. A Is for Apple. Birkett, Georgie, illus. 2011. (ENG.). 26p. (J). bds. 7.95 *(978-1-58925-872-3(X))* Tiger Tales.

Tiger Tales Staff. First ABC. 2013. (My First Touch & Trace Ser.). (ENG.). 26p. bds. 7.99 *(978-1-58925-626-2(3))* Tiger Tales Pubns.

Toliver, Marilyn. Marcellus Alphabet Book: One, Two, Three What a Words Do You See? 2012. 32p. pap. 17.25 *(978-1-4669-0035-6(0))* Trafford Publishing.

Tonderum, Angela. Kaycee Kangaroo Lost in Alphabet Forest: Adventures of Kaycee Kangaroo. Carlson, Christine, illus. 2008. 41p. pap. 24.95 *(978-1-60672-601-3(3))* America Star Bks.

Tooke, Susan. B Is for Bluenose: A Nova Scotia Alphabet. Tooke, Susan, illus. 2008. (Discover Canada Province by Province Ser.). (ENG., Illus.). 40p. (J). 17.95 *(978-1-58536-362-9(6))* Sleeping Bear Pr.

Top That Publishing Staff, ed. Alphabet Farm. Parry, Jo, illus. 2007. (Magnetic - Alphabet Ser.). 10p. (J). (gr. -1). bds. *(978-1-84666-272-0(9),* Tide Mill Pr.) Top That! Publishing PLC.

Top That! Alphabet Farm (large Version) Parry, Jo, illus. 2007. 10p. (J). (gr. -1). *(978-1-84666-553-0(1),* Tide Mill Pr.) Top That! Publishing PLC.

Top That!, creator. ABC Train. 2007. (Jigsaw Book Ser.). (Illus.). 18p. (J). (gr. -1-3). bds. *(978-1-84666-095-5(5))* Top That! Publishing PLC.

Torma, Patrick. Alphabet for American Children Coloring Book. 2010. 88p. pap. 12.99 *(978-1-4520-5231-1(X))* AuthorHouse.

Touch, Trace & Write Lowercase. 2005. (J). pap. *(978-1-60015-001-2(2))* Steps To Literacy, LLC.

Transparent Letter Tiles. (gr. -1-12). 21.95 *(978-0-7362-1289-2(2))* CENGAGE Learning.

Travers, P. L. Mary Poppins from A to Z. Shepard, Mary, illus. 2006. (Mary Poppins Ser.). (ENG.). 64p. (J). (gr. 5-7). 16.99 *(978-0-15-205834-0(6))* Houghton Mifflin Harcourt Publishing Co.

Tripp, Analisa. A Is for Acorn: A California Indian ABC. Risling, Lyn, illus. 2015. (J). *(978-1-59714-316-5(2))* Heyday.

Tudor, Tasha. A Is for Annabelle: A Doll's Alphabet. Tudor, Tasha, illus. 2004. (ENG., Illus.). 64p. (J). (gr. -1-3). reprint ed. 7.99 *(978-0-689-86996-9(7),* Simon & Schuster/Paula Wiseman Bks.) Simon & Schuster/Paula Wiseman Bks.

Twin Sisters(r) Staff, prod. Alphabet & Counting: Songs That Teach. 2009. (J). per. 10.99 *(978-1-57583-819-9(2))* Twin Sisters IP, LLC.

—Preschool: Songs That Teach. 2009. (J). per. 10.99 *(978-1-57583-817-5(6))* Twin Sisters IP, LLC.

Twin Sisters(r) Staff, et al. Trace & Learn Sticker Fun: ABCs. 2015. (I'm Learning the Bible Activity Book Ser.). (ENG.). 16p. (J). (gr. -1-k). pap. 6.99 *(978-1-63058-895-3(4))* Barbour Publishing, Inc.

Uchiyama, Akira & Kodaira, Hiromi. Yubisashi Yubinazori Aiueo. 2011. (JPN., Illus.). 96p. (J). (gr. -1-3). *(978-4-564-00493-3(X))* Hikari no Kuni.

Ulmer, Michael. H Is for Horse: An Equestrian Alphabet. Frankenhuyzen, Gijsbert van, illus. 2015. (Av2 Fiction Readalong 2016 Ser.). (ENG.). (J). (gr. 1-4). lib. bdg. 34.28 *(978-1-4896-3750-5(8),* AV2 by Weigl) Weigl Pubs., Inc.

—J Is for Jump Shot: A Basketball Alphabet. Braught, Mark, illus. 2005. (Sports Alphabet Ser.). (ENG.). 40p. (J). (gr. -1-5). 16.95 *(978-1-58536-229-5(8))* Sleeping Bear Pr.

—J Is for Jump Shot: A Basketball Alphabet. Braught, Mark, illus. 2015. (Av2 Fiction Readalong 2016 Ser.). (ENG.). (J). (gr. 1-4). lib. bdg. 34.28 *(978-1-4896-3753-6(2),* AV2 by Weigl) Weigl Pubs., Inc.

—M Is for Maple Leafs. Rose, Melanie, illus. 2014. (ENG.). 32p. (J). 19.95 *(978-1-77049-798-6(6),* Tundra Bks.) Tundra Bks. CAN. Dist: Penguin Random Hse. LLC.

Ulmer, Mike. J Is for Jump Shot: A Basketball Alphabet. Braught, Mark, illus. rev. ed. 2006. (Sports Ser.). (ENG.). 40p. (J). (gr. k-5). pap. 7.95 *(978-1-58536-338-4(3))* Sleeping Bear Pr.

Ulmer, Mike & Ulmer, Michael. M Is for Maple: A Canadian Alphabet. Rose, Melanie, illus. rev. abr. ed. 2007. (Discover the World Ser.). (ENG.). 32p. (J). (gr. -1-1). 8.99 *(978-1-58536-345-2(6),* 202380) Sleeping Bear Pr.

Ulmer, Wendy. A Isn't for Fox: An Isn't Alphabet. Knorr, Laura, illus. rev. ed. 2007. (ENG.). 32p. (J). (gr. k-6). 16.95 *(978-1-58536-319-3(7))* Sleeping Bear Pr.

Valério, Geraldo, illus. Moose, Goose, Animals on the Loose! A Canadian Wildlife ABC. 2016. (ENG.). 40p. (J). (gr. -1-1). 16.95 *(978-1-77147-174-9(3),* Owlkids) Owlkids Bks. Inc. CAN. Dist: Publishers Group West (PGW).

Vamos, Samantha R. Alphabet Trains. O'Rourke, Ryan, illus. 2015. (ENG.). 32p. (J). (gr. -1-2). lib. bdg. 14.95 *(978-1-58089-592-7(1))* Charlesbridge Publishing, Inc.

—Alphabet Trucks. O'Rourke, Ryan, illus. 2016. (J). *(978-1-58089-740-2(1))* Charlesbridge Publishing, Inc.

Van Fleet, Matthew. Alphabet. Skwarek, Skip, ed. Van Fleet, Matthew, illus. 2008. (ENG., Illus.). 20p. (J). (gr. -1-1). 19.99 *(978-1-4169-5565-8(8),* Simon & Schuster/Paula Wiseman Bks.) Simon & Schuster/Paula Wiseman Bks.

—Van Fleet Alphabet Heads: Alphabet; Heads. Van Fleet, Matthew, illus. 2013. (ENG., Illus.). 38p. (J). (gr. -1-2). 39.99 *(978-1-4424-8448-1(9),* Simon & Schuster/Paula Wiseman Bks.) Simon & Schuster/Paula Wiseman Bks.

van Lieshout, Maria. Backseat A-B-See. 2014. (ENG., Illus.). 26p. (J). (gr. -1-k). bds. 7.99 *(978-1-4521-3732-2(3))* Chronicle Bks. LLC.

Velikanje, Kathryn. B Is for Boys & Bees. Wilson, Lynda Farrington, illus. 2013. 34p. pap. 9.13 *(978-1-939896-05-6(3))* Levity Pr.

—A Bike of Bees. Hovhannisyan, Nune, illus. 2013. 58p. (J). pap. 12.28 *(978-1-939896-03-2(7))* Levity Pr.

—C Is for Crazy Cats. Wilson, Lynda Farrington, illus. 2013. (ENG.). 40p. pap. 9.13 *(978-1-939896-06-3(1))* Levity Pr.

—D Is for Dragon. Wilson, Lynda Farrington, illus. 2013. 34p. pap. 9.13 *(978-1-939896-07-0(X))* Levity Pr.

—E Is for Elephant. Wilson, Lynda Farrington, illus. 2013. 36p. pap. 9.13 *(978-1-939896-08-7(8))* Levity Pr.

—F Is for Face. Wilson, Lynda Farrington, illus. 2013. 40p. pap. 9.13 *(978-1-939896-09-4(6))* Levity Pr.

—G Is for Girly Girls. Wilson, Lynda Farrington, illus. 2013. 36p. pap. 9.13 *(978-1-939896-10-0(X))* Levity Pr.

—H Is for Horse. Wilson, Lynda Farrington, illus. 2013. 38p. pap. 9.13 *(978-1-939896-11-7(8))* Levity Pr.

—I Is for Ice Cream. Wilson, Lynda Farrington, illus. 2013. (ENG.). 36p. pap. 9.13 *(978-1-939896-12-4(6))* Levity Pr.

—A Is for Alligator. Wilson, Lynda Farrington, illus. 2013. (ENG.). 34p. pap. 9.13 *(978-1-939896-04-9(5))* Levity Pr.

Verma, Dinesh, et al. Hindi Alphabet Activity Book International Edition. 2009. 112p. pap. 25.00 *(978-0-557-10678-3(8))* Lulu Pr., Inc.

Verstraete, Larry. S Is for Scientists: A Discovery Alphabet. Geister, David, illus. 2010. (Science Alphabet Ser.). (ENG & ABK.). 40p. (J). (gr. 1-4). 16.95 *(978-1-58536-470-1(3),* 202189) Sleeping Bear Pr.

Viano, Hannah. B Is for Bear: A Natural Alphabet. Viano, Hannah, illus. 2015. (ENG., Illus.). 32p. (J). (-k). 16.99 *(978-1-63217-039-2(6),* Little Bigfoot) Sasquatch Bks.

Vidrine, Beverly Barras. Easter Day Alphabet, 1 vol. Lyne, Alison Davis, illus. 2003. (ENG.). 32p. (J). (gr. k-k). pap. 8.95 *(978-1-58980-076-2(1))* Pelican Publishing Co., Inc.

—Halloween Alphabet, 1 vol. Lyne, Alison Davis, illus. 2004. (ENG.). 32p. (J). (gr. k-1). pap. 8.95 *(978-1-58980-242-1(X))* Pelican Publishing Co., Inc.

—Thanksgiving Day Alphabet, 1 vol. Lyne, Alison D., illus. 2006. (ENG.). 32p. (J). (gr. k-3). 8.95 *(978-1-58980-338-1(8))* Pelican Publishing Co., Inc.

Voiland, Adam. ABCs from Space: A Discovered Alphabet. 2017. (ENG., Illus.). 40p. (J). (gr. -1-3). 18.99 ***(978-1-4814-9428-1(7),*** Simon & Schuster Bks. For Young Readers) Simon & Schuster Bks. For Young Readers.

Wadhwa, Vick. A New Take on ABCs - S Is for Smiling Sunrise: An Alphabet Book of Goodness, Beauty, & Wonder [Free Audio-Book Download Included]. Artists, Various, illus. l.t. ed. 2014. 32p. (J). 16.95 *(978-1-940229-12-6(X))* WordsBright.

Walch, Michelle E. & Maddin, John. Letters of the West. Maddin, John, illus. 2014. (Little Naturalist Ser.). (ENG., Illus.). 32p. (J). (gr. -1-k). 17.99 *(978-1-940052-10-6(6))* Craigmore Creations.

Wallace, Melissa. It's Great to Be a NOLA Kid: An a-Z Coloring Book, 1 vol. 2015. (ENG., Illus.). 32p. (J). pap. 4.95 *(978-1-4556-2052-4(1))* Pelican Publishing Co., Inc.

Walling, Sandy Seeley, illus. & text. ABC's at the Zoo! The Fun Way to Teach Your Child the Relationship between Upper Case & Lower Case Letters Walling, Sandy Seeley, text. l.t. ed. 2004. 36p. (J). per. 7.95 *(978-0-9741940-1-1(8))* Abernathy Hse. Publishing.

Walters, Eric. An African Alphabet, 1 vol. Todd, Sue, illus. 2017. (ENG.). 32p. (J). (gr. -1-k). bds. 9.95 *(978-1-4598-1070-9(8))* Orca Bk. Pubs. USA.

Ware, Claudia. The Day the Alphabet Rebelled. 2012. 38p. 19.99 *(978-0-9858899-1-3(8))* For Him Pr.

Wargin, Kathy-jo. D Is for Dala Horse: A Nordic Countries Alphabet. Graef, Renee, illus. 2010. (Discover the World Ser.). (ENG.). 40p. (J). (gr. 1-3). 17.95 *(978-1-58536-510-4(6),* 202203) Sleeping Bear Pr.

—D Is for Dala Horse: A Nordic Countries Alphabet. 2016. (Av2 Fiction Readalong 2017 Ser.). (ENG.). (J). (gr. k-6). 34.28 ***(978-1-4896-5200-3(0),*** AV2 by Weigl) Weigl Pubs., Inc.

—F Is for Fireflies: God's Summertime Alphabet, 1 vol. Bronson, Linda, illus. 2011. (ENG.). 40p. (J). (gr. -1-2). 15.99 *(978-0-310-71663-1(2))* Zonderkidz.

—M Is for Melody: A Music Alphabet. Larson, Katherine, illus. rev. ed. 2006. (Art & Culture Ser.). (ENG.). 40p. (J). (gr. 1-4). pap. 9.99 *(978-1-58536-332-2(4),* 202295) Sleeping Bear Pr.

—P Is for Pumpkin: God's Harvest Alphabet, 1 vol. Pang, YaWen Ariel, illus. 2008. (ENG.). 40p. (J). (gr. -1-3). 15.99 *(978-0-310-71180-3(0))* Zonderkidz.

—S Is for Sleeping Bear Dunes: A National Lakeshore Alphabet. Frankenhuyzen, Gijsbert van, illus. 2015. (ENG.). 32p. (J). (gr. 2-4). 16.99 *(978-1-58536-917-1(9),* 203818) Sleeping Bear Pr.

—V Is for Viking: A Minnesota Alphabet. Latham, Karen & Latham, Rebecca, illus. 2003. (Discover America State by State Ser.). (ENG.). 40p. (J). 17.95 *(978-1-58536-125-0(9))* Sleeping Bear Pr.

Warner, Roxie & Warner, Christian. Land of the Free, A to Z. Schartup, Adam, illus. 2014. (J). *(978-1-62086-801-0(6))* Mascot Bks., Inc.

Watkins, Adam F. R Is for Robot: A Noisy Alphabet. Watkins, Adam F., illus. 2014. (ENG., Illus.). 32p. (J). (gr. -1-k). 16.99 *(978-0-8431-7237-9(1),* Price Stern Sloan) Penguin Young Readers Group.

Watt, Fiona. ABC. Elkerton, Andy, illus. 2009. (Luxury Touchy-Feely Board Bks). 10p. (J). (gr. -1). bds. 15.99 *(978-0-7945-2094-6(4),* Usborne) EDC Publishing.

Watt, Mélanie. The Alphabet. Watt, Mélanie, illus. 2005. (Learning with Animals Ser.). (ENG., Illus.). 30p. (J). (gr. -1 — 1). bds. 5.95 *(978-1-55337-829-7(6))* Kids Can Pr., Ltd. CAN. Dist: Hachette Bk. Group.

Waunsch, John. My Very, Very First Weather Book. 2013. 56p. 23.99 *(978-1-62697-903-1(0));* pap. 12.99 *(978-1-62697-764-8(X))* Salem Author Services.

Weakland, Mark. Football ABC. 1 vol. 2013. (SI Kids Rookie Bks.). (ENG.). 20p. (gr. 1-2). bds. 7.95 *(978-1-4296-9965-5(5))* Capstone Press of Coughlan Cos.

Webb, Anne Aldridge. Appalachian State, A to Z. Bostian, Laurie, illus. 2010. (J). 18.95 *(978-1-933251-69-1(7))* Parkway Pubs., Inc.

Weidknecht, Lisa. E Is for Emotions. 2009. 56p. pap. 21.99 *(978-1-4343-9260-2(0))* AuthorHouse.

Weill, Cynthia. ABeCedarios: Mexican Folk Art ABCs in English & Spanish. Basseches, K. B., photos by. 2008. (First Concepts in Mexican Folk Art Ser.). (SPA & ENG., Illus.). 32p. (J). (gr. k — 1). 14.95 *(978-1-933693-13-2(4))* Cinco Puntos Pr.

—ABeCedarios - Mexican Folk Art ABCs in English & Spanish. Basseches, K. B., photos by. 2017. (First Concepts in Mexican Folk Art Ser.). (ENG., Illus.). 32p. (J). (— 1). bds. 9.95 *(978-1-941026-66-3(4))* Cinco Puntos Pr.

—Opuestos. 2017. (First Concepts in Mexican Folk Art Ser.). (ENG.). 32p. (J). (— 1). bds. 9.95 *(978-1-941026-68-7(0))* Cinco Puntos Pr.

Weisenfluh, Craig. ABC's in the Trees, a LittleWeeds Adventure: A book for Little Ones. 2007. (Illus.). (J). 11.95 *(978-0-9746782-1-4(X))* B'Squeak Productions.

Wells, Rosemary. Max's ABC. 2006. (Max & Ruby Ser.). (ENG., Illus.). 32p. (J). (gr. -1-k). 16.99 *(978-0-670-06074-0(7),* Viking Books for Young Readers) Penguin Young Readers Group.

—Max's ABC. 2008. (Max & Ruby Ser.). (Illus.). 26p. (gr. -1-k). 17.00 *(978-0-7569-8924-8(8))* Perfection Learning Corp.

Wenatchee High School Staff. W Is for Washington. 2008. (See My State Ser.). (ENG., Illus.). 32p. (J). (gr. -1-3). 13.95 *(978-0-88240-748-7(1),* West Winds Pr.) Graphic Arts Ctr. Publishing Co.

Werner, Sharon, et al. Alphabeasties. Nelson, Sarah, illus. 2010. (ENG.). 26p. (J). (gr. k-12). 15.99 *(978-1-60905-003-0(7))* Blue Apple Bks.

Wertz, Michael. ABC Oakland. 2017. (J). *(978-1-59714-371-4(5))* Heyday.

Whelan, Gloria & Nolan, Jenny. K Is for Kabuki: A Japan Alphabet. Han, Oki S., illus. 2009. (Discover the World Ser.). (ENG.). 40p. (J). (gr. 1-3). 17.95 *(978-1-58536-444-2(4),* 202169) Sleeping Bear Pr.

White, Teagan. Adventures with Barefoot Critters. (ENG., Illus.). (J). 2017. 30p. (— 1). bds. 7.99 *(978-1-101-91913-2(2))* 2014. 32p. (gr. -1-3). 16.99 *(978-1-77049-624-8(6))* Tundra Bks. CAN. (Tundra Bks.). Dist: Penguin Random Hse. LLC.

Whitney, Gleaves & Whitney, Louise Doak. B Is for Buckaroo: A Cowboy Alphabet. Guy, Susan, illus. 2006. (Sleeping Bear Alphabets Ser.). (ENG.). 40p. (J). (gr. -1-3). pap. 7.95 *(978-1-58536-336-0(7))* Sleeping Bear Pr.

Wigington, Patti. Pirate's Alphabet. Umscheid, Kit, illus. 2007. (ENG.). 32p. (J). (gr. -1-3). lib. bdg. 15.95 *(978-0-9766805-8-1(0))* Keene Publishing.

Wilbur, Helen & L Wilbur, Helen. E Is for Eiffel Tower: A France Alphabet. 2016. (Av2 Fiction Readalong 2017 Ser.). (ENG.). (J). (gr. k-6). 34.28 ***(978-1-4896-5209-6(4),*** AV2 by Weigl) Weigl Pubs., Inc.

Wilbur, Helen L. B Is for Beacon: A Great Lakes Lighthouse Alphabet. Graef, Renee, illus. 2016. (ENG.). 32p. (J). (gr. 1-4). 16.99 *(978-1-58536-916-4(0),* 204025) Sleeping Bear Pr.

—D Is for Derby: A Kentucky Derby Alphabet. Corum, Jaime, illus. 2014. (ENG.). 38p. (J). (gr. 3-6). 16.95 *(978-1-58536-813-6(X),* 203008) Sleeping Bear Pr.

—E Is for Eiffel Tower: A France Alphabet. Nascimbene, Yan, illus. 2010. (Discover the World Ser.). (ENG.). 40p. (J). (gr. 1-3). 17.95 *(978-1-58536-505-0(X),* 202199) Sleeping Bear Pr.

—F Is for Friendship: A Quilt Alphabet. van Frankenhuyzen, Gijsbert, illus. 2011. (Sleeping Bear Alphabets Ser.). (ENG.). 32p. (J). (gr. 1-4). lib. bdg. 16.95 *(978-1-58536-532-6(7),* 202215) Sleeping Bear Pr.

—Z Is for Zeus: A Greek Mythology Alphabet. Juhasz, Victor, illus. rev. ed. 2008. (Art & Culture Ser.). (ENG.). 40p. (J). (gr. 1-7). 17.95 *(978-1-58536-341-4(3))* Sleeping Bear Pr.

Wildman, Dale. Do You Know the Way to Find an A? A Rhyming ABC Book. Sisung, Peter, illus. 2006. 24p. (J). per. 2.99 *(978-1-59958-002-9(0))* Journey Stone Creations, LLC.

Wildsmith, Brian. Brian Wildsmith's Amazing Animal Alphabet Book, 1 vol. 2009. (ENG., Illus.). 32p. (J). pap. 7.95 *(978-1-59572-185-3(1))* Star Bright Bks., Inc.

—Brian Wildsmith's Amazing Animal Alphabet Book. Wildsmith, Brian, illus. 2007. (Illus.). 32p. (J). pap. 8.95 *(978-1-59572-111-2(8))* Star Bright Bks., Inc.

Wildsmith, Brian, illus. Brian Wildsmith's Amazing Animal Alphabet Book, 1 vol. 2008. (ENG.). 32p. (J). 17.95 *(978-1-59572-104-4(5))* Star Bright Bks., Inc.

Wilkens, Karen & Johnson, Tiffany. ABC - I - I Like: StartUp Unit 1 Lap Book. Litwin, Mike, illus. 2015. (Start up Core Phonics Ser.). (J). (gr. k). *(978-1-4900-2590-2(1))* Benchmark Education Co.

Williams, Tracee, ed. Dinosaurs Write-with-Me Alphabet. 2011. (Write-with-Me Ser.). (ENG., Illus.). 10p. (J). 15.99 *(978-1-59069-922-5(X))* Studio Mouse LLC.

Williamson, Chet. Pennsylvania Dutch Alphabet, 1 vol. Stacy, Alan, illus. 2007. (ENG.). 32p. (J). (gr. k-3). 16.99 *(978-1-58980-496-8(1))* Pelican Publishing Co., Inc.

Wilson, Kris E. & Maurer, Toby. How Putter Learned His ABC's: An alphabet Book for Your Littlest Golfer. 2010. 17.00 *(978-0-578-05153-6(2))* Sandy Putter Pr.

Wilson, Veronica B. Aswald's ABC Adventure. 2008. 28p. pap. 24.95 *(978-1-60441-691-6(2))* America Star Bks.

Winterhaven Elementary Staff. O Is for Oregon. 2008. (See My State Ser.). (ENG., Illus.). 32p. (J). (gr. -1-3). 13.95 *(978-0-88240-747-0(3),* West Winds Pr.) Graphic Arts Ctr. Publishing Co.

Winters, Kari-Lynn. Runaway Alphabet. Frey, Ben, illus. 2010. (ENG.). 32p. (J). (gr. -1-3). 17.95 *(978-1-897476-24-6(8))* Simply Read Bks. CAN. Dist: Ingram Publisher Services.

Wishinsky, Frieda. Where Are You, Bear? A Canadian Alphabet Adventure. Moore, Sean L. & Owlkids Books Inc. Staff, illus. 2010. (ENG.). 32p. (J). (gr. -1-2). 17.95 *(978-1-897349-91-5(2),* Owlkids) Owlkids Bks. Inc. CAN. Dist: Publishers Group West (PGW).

Wisniewski, Lori. The Importance of Being Uu. 2013. 28p. pap. 14.97 *(978-1-61897-464-8(5),* Strategic Bk. Publishing) Strategic Book Publishing & Rights Agency (SBPRA).

Witty Bit World Book: Letters A-E & Music CD. 2005. (J). 19.95 *(978-0-9770548-1-7(0))* Witty Bit World, Inc.

Witty Bit World Book: Letters F-J & Music CD. 2005. (J). 19.95 *(978-0-9770548-2-4(9))* Witty Bit World, Inc.

Witty Bit World Book: Letters K-O & Music CD. 2005. (J). 1995.00 *(978-0-9770548-3-1(7))* Witty Bit World, Inc.

Witty Bit World Book: Letters P-T & Music CD. 2005. (J). 19.95 *(978-0-9770548-4-8(5))* Witty Bit World, Inc.

Witty Bit World Book: Letters U-Z & Music CD. 2005. (J). 19.95 *(978-0-9770548-5-5(3))* Witty Bit World, Inc.

Witty Bit World Complete Alphabet & Music Collection. 2005. (J). 79.95 *(978-0-9770548-0-0(2))* Witty Bit World, Inc.

Witty One Restickable Framed ABC Book. 2003. per. *(978-1-932435-07-8(7));* per. *(978-1-932435-01-6(8))* Cardinal Brands, Inc.

Wood, A. J. My First Animal ABC. Pledger, Maurice, illus. 2017. (ENG.). 32p. (J). (gr. -1). 17.99 *(978-1-62686-776-5(3),* Silver Dolphin Bks.) Readerlink Distribution Services, LLC.

Woods, Linda J. Dino-Alphabet Book. 2008. 48p. pap. 19.49 *(978-1-4343-9588-7(X))* AuthorHouse.

The World of Eric Carle My Alphabet Activity Kit. 2007. (J). 16.99 *(978-0-9794445-0-0(0))* Loew-Cornell, Inc.

Wright, Ralph. Wild. 2008. 76p. 19.95 *(978-0-9799482-1-3(5))* MathisJones Communications, LLC.

Wynne Pechter, Lesley. Alligator, Bear, Crab: A Baby's ABC, 1 vol. (ENG., Illus.). (J). (gr. -1-k). 2017. 28p. 6.95 *(978-1-4598-1507-0(6))* 2011. 24p. bds. 9.95 *(978-1-55469-360-3(8))* Orca Bk. Pubs. USA.

Yates, Gene. The Elephant Alphabet Book. 2003. (Illus.). (J). *(978-1-58865-106-8(1))* Kidsbooks, LLC.

Yates, Gene, illus. The Elephant Alphabet Book. 2006. (J). *(978-1-58865-363-5(3))* Kidsbooks, LLC.

Yost-Filgate, Susan. Rip Squeak's A to Z Book. Filgate, Leonard, illus. 2009. (ENG.). 22p. (J). (gr. -1-12). 7.95 *(978-1-934960-44-8(6),* Raven Tree Pr.,Csi) Continental Sales, Inc.

Young, Judy. H Is for Hook: A Fishing Alphabet. Palmer, Gary, illus. 2008. (Sports Alphabet Ser.). (ENG.). 40p. (J). (gr. 1-4). 17.95 *(978-1-58536-347-6(2),* 202305) Sleeping Bear Pr.

—H Is for Hook: A Fishing Alphabet. Palmer, Gary, illus. 2015. (Av2 Fiction Readalong 2016 Ser.). (ENG.). (J). (gr. 1-4). lib. bdg. 34.28 *(978-1-4896-3747-5(8),* AV2 by Weigl) Weigl Pubs., Inc.

—R Is for Rhyme: A Poetry Alphabet. Juhasz, Victor, illus. rev. ed. 2006. (Art & Culture Ser.). (ENG.). 40p. (J). (gr. -1-3). 17.95 *(978-1-58536-240-0(9))* Sleeping Bear Pr.

Zangas, Sherri. A Is for Alabama: Roll Tide Roll. Williams, Tim, illus. 2009. (J). lib. bdg. 17.95 *(978-0-692-00093-9(3))* Mascot Bks., Inc.

Zocchi, Judith Mazzeo. Uri's "U" Book. Revutsky, Helen Ross, illus. 2007. (J). *(978-1-59646-538-1(7))* Dingles & Co.

—Yola's "Y" Book. Revutsky, Helen Ross, illus. 2007. (J). *(978-1-59646-562-6(X))* Dingles & Co.

Zocchi, Judith Mazzeo, et al. Zach's "Z" Book: El Libro "Z" de Zach. Revutsky, Helen Ross, illus. 2005. (SPA & ENG.). (J). *(978-1-59646-571-8(9))* Dingles & Co.

Zolty, Howard. Mountain View A through Z. A Colorful Reader for Children of All Ages. 2006. 28p. 14.99 *(978-1-4116-5708-3(X))* Lulu Pr., Inc.

Zonneveld, Famke, illus. Waldorf Alphabet Book. 2005. (ENG.). 54p. (J). (gr. 4-7). per. 12.95 *(978-0-88010-559-0(3),* Bell Pond Bks.) SteinerBooks, Inc.

Zook, Melinda. L-E-t-t-e-r-s. 2012. 24p. pap. 24.95 *(978-1-4626-7175-5(6))* America Star Bks.

Zschock, Martha Day. Journey Around Maine from A to Z. 2007. (Journeys Ser.). (ENG., Illus.). 32p. (J). (gr. 1-6). 17.95 *(978-1-933212-31-9(4),* Commonwealth Editions) Applewood Bks.

—Journey Around Nantucket from A to Z. Zschock, Martha Day, illus. 2008. (Journeys Ser.). (Illus.). 32p. (J). (gr. 1-6). 17.95 *(978-1-933212-82-1(9),* Commonwealth Editions) Applewood Bks.

Zuckerman, Rory. Alphabetical Sleepy Sheep. Roos, Maryn, illus. 2007. (Sleepy Sheep Ser.). (J). (gr. -1-k). bds. 7.95 incl. audio compact disk *(978-0-9796393-1-9(X))* Little Lion Pr.

ALPS

Maynard, Charles W. The Alps. (Great Mountain Ranges of the World Ser.). 24p. (gr. 3-3). 2009. 42.50 *(978-1-61513-167-9(1),* PowerKids Pr.) 2004. (Illus.). (YA). lib. bdg. 22.60 *(978-0-8239-6697-4(6))* Rosen Publishing Group, Inc., The.

Peppas, Lynn. The Alps. 2011. (ENG., Illus.). 48p. (J). pap. *(978-0-7787-7566-9(6));* (gr. 4-7). lib. bdg. *(978-0-7787-7559-1(3))* Crabtree Publishing Co.

Somervill, Barbara A. The Awesome Alps. 2004. (Geography of the World Ser.). (ENG., Illus.). 32p. (J). (gr. 3-6). 28.50 *(978-1-59296-330-0(7),* 200262) Child's World, Inc., The.

ALPS—FICTION

Cullen, Seán. Hamish X & the Hollow Mountain. 2008. (ENG.). 288p. (J). (gr. 7-18). 9.99 *(978-0-14-305312-5(4),* Puffin Canada) Penguin Random House Canada Young Readers CAN. Dist: Penguin Random Hse. LLC.

Horowitz, Anthony. Point Blanc. 2004. (Alex Rider Ser.: Bk. 2). (SPA.). 264p. pap. 7.95 *(978-84-414-1410-5(6))* Editorial Edaf, S.L. ESP. Dist: Spanish Pubs., LLC.

—Point Blank. 2006. (Alex Rider Ser.). (ENG.). 320p. (J). (gr. 5-18). 8.99 *(978-0-14-240612-0(0),* Puffin Books) Penguin Young Readers Group.

Toska, Mary Lou. Ernest's Dream: A Young Boy Wanting to Spend the Summer in the High Alps. 2012. 20p. pap. 24.95 *(978-1-4626-8662-9(1))* America Star Bks.

ALSACE (FRANCE)—FICTION

Fitzgugh, Percy Keese. Tom Slade with the Boys over There. 2007. (ENG.). 140p. pap. 18.99 *(978-1-4264-9511-3(0));* 150p. pap. 19.99 *(978-1-4264-9892-3(6))* Creative Media Partners, LLC.

ALTITUDE, INFLUENCE OF

see Human Beings—Effect of Environment on

ALUMINUM

Blaxland, Wendy. Cans. 2009. (How Are They Made? 2 Ser.). 32p. (gr. 4). lib. bdg. 18.56 *(978-0-7614-4753-5(9))* Marshall Cavendish Corp.

Csiszar, John. Aluminum. 2017. (Chemistry of Everyday Elements Ser.). (ENG.). (YA). (gr. 7-12). 23.95 ***(978-1-4222-3838-7(5))*** Mason Crest.

Hasan, Heather. Aluminum. 2009. (Understanding the Elements of the Periodic Table Ser.). 48p. (gr. 6-6). 53.00 *(978-1-60854-629-9(2),* Rosen Reference) Rosen Publishing Group, Inc., The.

MacGregor, Cynthia. Recycling a Can. 2009. (Reading Room Collection 2 Ser.). 24p. (gr. 3-4). 42.50

(978-1-60851-984-2(8), PowerKids Pr.) Rosen Publishing Group, Inc., The.

ALZHEIMER'S DISEASE

Kelly, Evelyn B. Alzheimer's Disease. 2008. (Genes & Disease Ser.). (Illus.). 128p. (YA). (gr. 7-12). 35.00 *(978-0-7910-9588-1(6))* Facts On File, Inc.

McAuliffe, Bill. Alzheimer's Disease. 2011. 48p. (J). 35.65 *(978-1-60818-072-1(7)*, Creative Education) Creative Co., The.

Poole, H. W. Alzheimer's Disease, Vol. 13. Walters, Anne S., ed. 2015. (Mental Illnesses & Disorders: Awareness & Understanding Ser.). (Illus.). 48p. (J). (gr. 5). 20.95 *(978-1-4222-3365-8(0))* Mason Crest.

Schnurbush, Barbara. Striped Shirts & Flowered Pants: A Story about Alzheimer's Disease for Young Children. Pillo, Cary, illus. 2006. 32p. (J). (gr. -1-3). 14.95 *(978-1-59147-475-3(2))*; per. 9.95 *(978-1-59147-476-0(0))* American Psychological Assn. (Magination Pr.).

Tarnow, Georgette H. Special Secret Hearts: A Child's Introduction to Dementia & Pink Curls - a Santa Claus Story. 2012. 60p. pap. 11.95 *(978-1-61434-719-4(0))* Booklocker.com, Inc.

Voight, Joseph. My Grandma Has Alzheimer's Too. 2008. 26p. (J). (gr. 2-7). pap. 12.95 *(978-1-933255-44-6(7))* DNA Pr.

Weitzman, Elizabeth. Let's Talk about When Someone You Love Has Alzheimer's Disease. 2009. (Let's Talk Library). 24p. (gr. 2-3). 42.50 *(978-1-60853-453-1(7)*, PowerKids Pr.) Rosen Publishing Group, Inc., The.

Wood, Charlotte B. Remembering for Both of Us: A Child Learns about Alzheimer's. Auth, Dennis, illus. 2014. 32p. (J). (gr. k-3). 18.95 *(978-1-939930-38-5(3))* Brandylane Pubs., Inc.

ALZHEIMER'S DISEASE—FICTION

Acheson, Alison. Grandpa's Music: A Story about Alzheimer's. Farnsworth, Bill, illus. 2009. (ENG.). 32p. (J). (gr. 3-3). 16.99 *(978-0-8075-3052-8(2))* Whitman, Albert & Co.

Altman, Linda Jacobs & Johnson, Larry. Singing with Momma Lou, 1 vol. 2015. (ENG., Illus.). 28p. (J). pap. 9.95 *(978-1-62014-227-1(9))* Lee & Low Bks., Inc.

Bachus, Margaret Trimm. A Is for Awful! 2012. 40p. pap. 20.99 *(978-1-4772-8457-5(5))* AuthorHouse.

Bell, Ossie S. When Grandma Is Not Grandma: Alzheimer's Steals Family's Treasures. 2006. 51p. pap. 16.95 *(978-1-4241-2920-1(6))* PublishAmerica, Inc.

Broome, Errol. The Judas Donkey. Thompson, Sharon, illus. 2003. 144p. pap. 13.50 *(978-1-920731-18-2(0))* Fremantle Pr. AUS. Dist: Independent Pubs. Group.

Downham, Jenny. Unbecoming. (ENG.). 384p. (J). (gr. 9-9). 2017. pap. 9.99 ***(978-1-338-16072-7(9))*** 2016. 17.99 *(978-0-545-90717-0(9))* Scholastic, Inc.

—Unbecoming. 2017. lib. bdg. 20.85 ***(978-0-606-40147-0(4))*** Turtleback Bks.

Gerdner, Linda & Langford, Sarah. Grandfather's Story Cloth. Loughridge, Stuart, illus. 2008. (Grandfather's Story Cloth Ser.). 32p. (J). (gr. 2-4). 16.95 *(978-1-885008-34-3(1)*, Shen's Bks.) Lee & Low Bks., Inc.

Kiely, Brendan. The Last True Love Story. 2016. (ENG., Illus.). 288p. (YA). (gr. 9). 17.99 *(978-1-4814-2988-7(4)*, McElderry, Margaret K. Bks.) McElderry, Margaret K. Bks.

—Last True Love Story. 2017. (ENG., Illus.). 288p. (YA). (gr. 9). pap. 11.99 *(978-1-4814-2989-4(2)*, McElderry, Margaret K. Bks.) McElderry, Margaret K. Bks.

Korman, Gordon. Pop. 272p. (YA). (gr. 8). 2011. pap. 9.99 *(978-0-06-174261-3(9))* 2009. 16.99 *(978-0-06-174228-6(7))* HarperCollins Pubs.

Law, Ingrid. Switch. 2015. (ENG.). 368p. (J). (gr. 3-7). 16.99 *(978-0-8037-3862-1(5)*, Dial Bks) Penguin Young Readers Group.

McIntyre, Connie. Flowers for Grandpa Dan: A Gentle Story to Help Children Understand Alzheimer's Disease. McIntyre, Louise, illus. 2004. 20p. (J). 12.95 *(978-0-9677685-5-7(1))*; lib. bdg. 17.95 *(978-0-9677685-6-4(X))* Grannie Annie Family Story Celebration, The.

Richards, Josie Aleardi. Grandma's Just Not Herself. Rowland, Lauri, illus. 2010. 36p. pap. 13.95 *(978-1-60911-236-3(9)*, Eloquent Bks.) Strategic Book Publishing & Rights Agency (SBPRA).

Rivard, Émilie & Quinn, Sarah. Really & Truly. Delisle, Anne-Claire & Owlkids Books Inc. Staff, illus. 2012. (ENG.). 24p. (J). (gr. -1-3). 15.95 *(978-1-926973-40-1(2))* Owlkids Bks. Inc. CAN. Dist: Publishers Group West (PGW).

Scacco, Linda. Always My Grandpa: A Story for Children about Alzheimer's Disease. Wong, Nicole, illus. 2005. 48p. (J). (gr. -1-3). 14.95 *(978-1-59147-311-4(X))*; per. 9.95 *(978-1-59147-312-1(8))* American Psychological Assn. (Magination Pr.).

Shawver, Margaret. What's Wrong with Grandma? A Family's Experience with Alzheimer's. Bagby, Jeffrey K., illus. 2003. (ENG.). 62p. (J). (gr. -1-3). pap. 16.99 *(978-1-59102-174-2(X))* Prometheus Bks., Pubs.

Simard, Danielle. Little Word Catcher, 1 vol. Côté, Geneviève & Second Story Press Staff, illus. 2008. (ENG.). 32p. (J). (gr. 1-3). 14.95 *(978-1-897187-44-9(0))* Second Story Pr. CAN. Dist: Orca Bk. Pubs. USA.

Smith, Brian, Brian. Memory. 2014. (ENG.). 216p. (C). pap. 49.95 *(978-1-138-87117-5(6)*, Y178984) Routledge.

Sonnenblick, Jordan. Curveball: The Year I Lost My Grip. 304p. 2014. (ENG.). (J). (gr. 7). pap. 9.99 *(978-0-545-32070-2(4)*, Scholastic Paperbacks) 2012. pap. 17.99 *(978-0-545-39311-9(6))* Scholastic, Inc.

Stang, Debra L. Visiting Grandma. 2003. 136p. (YA). pap. 12.95 *(978-1-59113-322-3(X))* Booklocker.com, Inc.

Steinkellner, Elisabeth. My New Granny. Roher, Michael, illus. 2012. (ENG.). 32p. (J). (gr. -1-3). 16.95 *(978-1-62087-223-9(4)*, 620223, Sky Pony Pr.) Skyhorse Publishing Co., Inc.

Swallow, Pamela. It Only Looks Easy. 2009. (ENG.). 192p. (J). (gr. 3-7). pap. 9.99 *(978-0-312-56114-7(8)*, 9780312561147) Square Fish.

Van Den Abeele, Veronique. Still My Grandma. Dubois, Claude K., illus. 2007. (ENG.). 28p. (J). (gr. -1-5). 16.00 *(978-0-8028-5323-3(4)*, Eerdmans Bks For Young Readers) Eerdmans, William B. Publishing Co.

Van Laan, Nancy. Forget Me Not. Graegin, Stephanie, illus. 2014. (ENG.). 40p. (J). (gr. -1-3). 16.99 *(978-0-449-81543-4(9)*, Schwartz & Wade Bks.) Random Hse. Children's Bks.

Velásquez, Gloria. Rudy's Memory Walk. 2009. (Roosevelt High School Ser.). 140p. (YA). (gr. 6-18). pap. 9.95 *(978-1-55885-593-9(X))* Arte Publico Pr.

Wiersbitzky, Shannon. What Flowers Remember. 2014. 158p. (J). 18.95 *(978-1-60898-166-3(5))* namelos llc.

Wolf, Mária. An Extraordinary Ordinary Day. 2012. 20p. pap. 17.99 *(978-1-4772-8638-8(1))* AuthorHouse.

Zafrilla, Marta. Grandpa Monty's Muddles. 2012. (ENG., Illus.). 32p. (J). (gr. 2-4). *(978-84-15241-17-1(8))* D P & G Military Pubs.

AMATEUR FILMS

Anniss, Matthew. Create Your Own Movie or TV Show. 2016. (Media Genius Ser.). (ENG.). 48p. (gr. 5-8). lib. bdg. 33.32 *(978-1-4109-8110-3(X))* Heinemann-Raintree.

Bamford, Donna & Farrell, Dan. The Movie Making Book: Skills & Projects to Learn & Share. 2017. (ENG.). 144p. (J). (gr. 2-7). pap. 18.99 ***(978-1-61373-915-0(X))*** Chicago Review Pr., Inc.

AMATEUR MOVING-PICTURES

see Amateur Films

AMAZON RIVER

Aloian, Molly. The Amazon: River in a Rain Forest. 2010. (Rivers Around the World Ser.). (ENG., Illus.). 32p. (J). (gr. 5-8). pap. *(978-0-7787-7465-5(1))*; lib. bdg. *(978-0-7787-7442-6(2))* Crabtree Publishing Co.

The Amazon. 2011. (River Journey Ser.). (ENG.). 48p. (YA). (gr. 5-8). 27.95 *(978-1-4488-6010-4(5)*, Rosen Reference) Rosen Publishing Group, Inc., The.

Arnold, Caroline. A Day & Night in the Rain Forest. Arnold, Caroline, illus. 2015. (Caroline Arnold's Habitats Ser.). (ENG., Illus.). 24p. (gr. 2-3). lib. bdg. 27.99 *(978-1-4795-6074-5(X))* Picture Window Bks.

Bingham, Jane. The Amazon, 1 vol. 2012. (Explorer Tales Ser.). (ENG.). 32p. (gr. 1-3). 29.99 *(978-1-4109-4780-2(7)*, Read Me!) Heinemann-Raintree.

Bodden, Valerie. Amazon River. 2010. (Big Outdoors Ser.). 24p. (J). (gr. k-3). 16.95 *(978-1-58341-814-7(8))* Creative Co., The.

Clarke, Ginjer L. & dePaola, Tomie. What's up in the Amazon Rainforest. 2015. (What's Up Ser.). (ENG., Illus.). 144p. (J). (gr. 3-7). bds. 8.99 *(978-0-448-48103-6(0)*, Grosset & Dunlap) Penguin Young Readers Group.

deMarin, Layne. Amazon Adventure, 1 vol. 2011. (Wonder Readers: Science Ser.). (ENG.). (gr. -1-2). 20p. lib. bdg. 22.65 *(978-1-4296-8634-1(0))*; 32p. pap. 5.99 *(978-1-4296-7907-7(7))*; 16p. pap. 35.94 *(978-1-4296-8069-1(5))* Capstone Press of Coughlan Cos. (Wonder Readers).

Dorling Kindersley Publishing Staff. The Amazon. 2015. (DK Eyewitness Bks.). (ENG., Illus.). 72p. (J). (gr. 3-7). 19.99 *(978-1-4654-3567-5(0)*, DK Children) Dorling Kindersley Publishing, Inc.

Fitzpatrick, Anne. Amazon River. 2004. (Natural Wonders of the World Ser.). (Illus.). 32p. (J). lib. bdg. 27.10 *(978-1-58341-322-7(7)*, Creative Education) Creative Co., The.

Franchino, Vicky. Amazon Rain Forest. 2016. (Community Connections: Getting to Know Our Planet Ser.). (ENG., Illus.). 24p. (J). (gr. 2-5). lib. bdg. 27.07 *(978-1-63470-513-4(0)*, 207783) Cherry Lake Publishing.

Gibson, Karen. The Amazon River. 2012. 48p. (J). (gr. 3-6). lib. bdg. 29.95 *(978-1-61228-293-0(8))* Mitchell Lane Pubs., Inc.

Hyde, Natalie. Amazon Rainforest Research Journal. 2017. (Illus.). 32p. (J). ***(978-0-7787-3467-3(6))***; pap. ***(978-0-7787-3492-5(7))*** Crabtree Publishing Co.

Lonely Planet Publications Staff, et al. Unfolding Journeys Amazon Adventure, 1 vol. 2016. (Lonely Planet Kids Ser.). (ENG., Illus.). 16p. (J). pap. 17.99 *(978-1-78657-106-9(4)*, 5246) Lonely Planet Pubns.

Maimone, Sofia. Exploring the Amazon River. 2009. (Real Life Readers Ser.). 32p. (gr. 4-6). pap. 10.00 *(978-1-4358-0234-6(9)*, Rosen Classroom) Rosen Publishing Group, Inc., The.

Manning, Paul. Amazon River. 2014. (River Adventures Ser.). (J). 31.35 *(978-1-59920-914-2(4))* Black Rabbit Bks.

Rice, William B. La Selva Amazónica. 2017. (TIME for Kids en Español - Level 3 Ser.). (SPA.). 32p. (gr. 3-3). lib. bdg. 31.99 ***(978-1-5157-5178-6(3))*** Capstone Press of Coughlan Cos.

Schulte, Mary. The Amazon River. 2006. (Rookie Read-About Geography Ser.). (ENG., Illus.). 32p. (J). (gr. 1-2). pap. 5.95 *(978-0-516-29700-2(7)*, Children's Pr.) Scholastic Library Publishing.

Simon, Charnan. The Mysterious Amazon. 2004. (Geography of the World Ser.). (ENG., Illus.). 32p. (J). (gr. 3-6). 28.50 *(978-1-59296-336-2(6)*, 200271) Child's World, Inc., The.

Watson, Galadriel Findlay. Amazon Rain Forest. 2012. (J). *(978-1-61913-522-2(1))* Weigl Pubs., Inc.

Woolf, Alex. Journey along the Amazon. 2014. (Traveling Wild Ser.). 32p. (J). (gr. 3-6). pap. 63.00 *(978-1-4824-1251-2(9))* Stevens, Gareth Publishing LLLP.

Zuravicky, Orli. The Amazon & the Sahara: Using Double Line Graphs & Double Bar Graphs. (PowerMath Ser.). (Illus.). 32p. 2009. (ENG.). (gr. 4-5). pap. 10.00 *(978-0-8239-8868-6(6))* 2004. (J). lib. bdg. 23.95 *(978-0-8239-8981-2(X))* Rosen Publishing Group, Inc., The. (PowerKids Pr.).

AMAZON RIVER—FICTION

Allen, Nancy Kelly. On the Banks of the Amazon/en las orillas del Amazonas. de la Vega, Eida, tr. Driessen, Elizabeth, illus. 2003.Tr. of En las orillas del Amazonas. (SPA & ENG.). 32p. (J). (gr. -1-3). 16.95 *(978-0-9720192-7-9(8)*, 626999, Raven Tree Pr.,Csi) Continental Sales, Inc.

Allende, Isabel. A Cidade das Feras. 2006.Tr. of Ciudad de las Bestias. (POR.). 280p. (YA). pap. 26.95 *(978-85-286-0977-6(4))* Bertrand Brasil Editora SA BRA. Dist: Distribooks, Inc.

—City of the Beasts. 2009. (P. S. Ser.: Bk. 1). (ENG.). 448p. pap. 14.99 *(978-0-06-182511-8(5)*, Harper Perennial) 2005. 464p. (J). (gr. 7-17). pap. 7.99 *(978-0-06-077645-9(5)*, Rayo) HarperCollins Pubs.

—City of the Beasts. Peden, Margaret Sayers, tr. from SPA. 2004. (City of the Beasts Ser.: Bk. 1). (ENG.). 432p. (J). (gr. 5-18). reprint ed. pap. 7.99 *(978-0-06-053503-2(2)*, Rayo) HarperCollins Pubs.

Angello, Mary L. The Legend of the Crystal Skull. 2008. 147p. pap. 15.50 *(978-1-4357-3194-3(8))* Lulu Pr., Inc.

Avalos, Francisco. Amazon Tale. 2013. 124p. 29.99 *(978-1-4797-6689-5(5))*; pap. 19.99 *(978-1-4797-6688-8(7))* Xlibris Corp.

Borgenicht, David & Khan, Hena. Amazon: You Decide How to Survive! 2015. (WorstCase Scenario Ultimate Adventure Ser.). (ENG., Illus.). 204p. (gr. 3-8). 47.10 *(978-1-59920-980-7(2)*, 1389530) Black Rabbit Bks.

Cherry, Lynne. The Great Kapok Tree: A Tale of the Amazon Rain Forest. 2010. (Rise & Shine Ser.). (ENG., Illus.). 40p. (C). (gr. -1-3). pap. 13.95 *(978-0-15-202614-1(2))* National Geographic School Publishing, Inc.

Guillain, Charlotte. The Tree of Life: An Amazonian Folk Tale, 1 vol. Dorado, Steve, illus. 2014. (Folk Tales from Around the World Ser.). (ENG.). 24p. (gr. 1-3). pap. 6.95 *(978-1-4109-6698-8(4)*, NA-r) Heinemann-Raintree.

Hanson, Ed. Amazon Adventure. 2003. (Barclay Family Adventure Ser.: Bk. 1). 64p. (J). (gr. k-6). per. 3.95 *(978-1-56254-550-5(7)*, SP 5507) Saddleback Educational Publishing, Inc.

Hapka, Catherine, pseud. One Big Blue Family. 2014. (I Can Read! Level 2 Ser.). (J). lib. bdg. 13.55 *(978-0-606-35063-1(2)*, Turtleback) Turtleback Bks.

—Vacation in the Wild. 2014. (I Can Read! Level 2 Ser.). (J). lib. bdg. 13.55 *(978-0-606-35064-8(0)*, Turtleback) Turtleback Bks.

Hussey, Charmian. The Valley of Secrets. Crump, Christopher, illus. 2006. (ENG.). 400p. (J). (gr. 7-12). per. 17.99 *(978-1-4169-0015-3(2)*, Simon Pulse) Simon Pulse.

Ibbotson, Eva. Journey to the River Sea. 5th unabr. ed. 2008. (ENG.). 304p. (J). (gr. 10-14). 14.95 *(978-0-330-39715-5(X)*, Macmillan) Pan Macmillan GBR. Dist: Trans-Atlantic Pubns., Inc.

—Journey to the River Sea. Hawkes, Kevin, illus. 2003. 298p. (gr. 3-7). 18.00 *(978-0-7569-1552-0(X))* Perfection Learning Corp.

Kerr, P. B., pseud. The Eye of the Forest. 2009. (Children of the Lamp Ser.: 5). (ENG.). 432p. (J). (gr. 3-7). 17.99 *(978-0-439-93215-8(7)*, Orchard Bks.) Scholastic, Inc.

Khoury, Jessica. Origin. 2013. (ENG., Illus.). 432p. (YA). (gr. 7). pap. 9.99 *(978-1-59514-596-3(6)*, Razorbill) Penguin Young Readers Group.

Krebs, Laurie. We're Roaming in the Rainforest. Wilson, Anne, illus. 2010. 40p. (J). (ENG.). (gr. k-5). 8.99 *(978-1-84686-545-9(X))*; (SPA.). (gr. k-5). pap. 8.99 *(978-1-84686-551-0(4))*; (ENG.). (gr. -1-5). 16.99 *(978-1-84686-331-8(7))* Barefoot Bks., Inc.

Kuhl, Debra. Sammy's Magic Carpet Ride, 1 vol. 2009. 73p. pap. 14.95 *(978-1-4489-9204-1(4))* PublishAmerica, Inc.

Kuijpers, Justin. The Dragon Myth & the Mysterious Eyeball. 2010. 58p. pap. 7.90 *(978-3-8391-5033-7(7))* Bks. on Demand.

London, C. Alexander. We Dine with Cannibals. 2013. (Accidental Adventure Ser.: 2). (ENG.). 384p. (J). (gr. 3-7). pap. 7.99 *(978-0-14-242474-2(9)*, Puffin Books) Penguin Young Readers Group.

Marsh, Carole. The Mystery in the Amazon Rainforest: South America. (Around the World in 80 Mysteries Ser.). (Illus.). 131p. (J). 2009. lib. bdg. 18.99 *(978-0-635-07017-3(0)*, Marsh, Carole Mysteries) 2007. (gr. 3-5). 14.95 *(978-0-635-06212-3(7))* 2007. (gr. 3-5). per. 7.99 *(978-0-635-06208-6(9))* Gallopade International.

Montgomery, R. A. Lost on the Amazon. 2007. 144p. (J). pap. *(978-1-86504-931-1(X))* Chooseco LLC.

—Lost on the Amazon. Millet, Jason, illus. 2006. (Choose Your Own Adventure Ser.: No. 9). 144p. (J). (gr. 4-8). per. 6.99 *(978-1-933390-09-3(3)*, CHCL09) Chooseco LLC.

—Lost on the Amazon. 2005. (Choose Your Own Adventure Ser.). (Illus.). 114p. (gr. 4-8). pap. 5.50 *(978-0-7608-9697-6(6))* Sundance/Newbridge Educational Publishing.

Nelson, N. A. Bringing the Boy Home. 2008. (ENG.). 224p. (J). (gr. 3-7). 16.99 *(978-0-06-088698-1(6))* HarperCollins Pubs.

Stilton, Geronimo. The Temple of the Ruby of Fire. Wolf, Matt, illus. 2004. (Geronimo Stilton Ser.: No. 14). 109p. (J). lib. bdg. 10.00 *(978-1-4242-0283-6(3))* Fitzgerald Bks.

Thomas, Debbie. Jungle Tangle. MacDonald, Stella, illus. 2013. (ENG.). 320p. (J). pap. 14.95 *(978-1-78117-116-5(5))* Mercier Pr., Ltd., The IRL. Dist: Dufour Editions, Inc.

Turner, Tracey. Lost in the Jungle of Doom. 2014. (ENG., Illus.). 128p. (J). *(978-0-7787-0727-1(X))* Crabtree Publishing Co.

Wilkerson, Dawn. Katie & Katoa Travel down the River. 2009. 48p. pap. 16.95 *(978-1-61582-862-3(1))* America Star Bks.

AMAZON VALLEY

Rice, William B. Amazon Rainforest, 1 vol. 2nd rev. ed. 2012. (Nonfiction Readers Ser.). (ENG.). 32p. (J). (gr. 3-3). pap. 8.99 *(978-1-4333-3671-3(5))* Teacher Created Materials, Inc.

World Book, Inc Staff, contrib. by. The Mysteries of the Amazon Rain Forest. 2015. (Illus.). 48p. (J). *(978-0-7166-2671-8(3))* World Bk., Inc.

AMBASSADORS

see Diplomats

AMELIA-BEDELIA (FICTITIOUS CHARACTER)—FICTION

Amelia Bedelia. 2005. (J). *(978-1-59564-833-4(X))* Steps To Literacy, LLC.

De Uribe, Maria L. Senorita Amelia (Miss Amelia) (SPA.). 24p. (J). 16.95 *(978-84-233-1245-0(3))* Ediciones Destino ESP. Dist: AIMS International Bks., Inc.

Moss, Marissa. Amelia's Must-Keep Resolutions for the Best Year Ever! Moss, Marissa, illus. 2006. (Amelia Ser.). (ENG., Illus.). 40p. (J). (gr. 4-7). 12.99 *(978-1-4169-3361-8(1)*, Simon & Schuster/Paula Wiseman Bks.) Simon & Schuster/Paula Wiseman Bks.

Parish, Herman. Amelia Bedelia. Avril, Lynne, illus. (Amelia Bedelia Ser.: No. 2). (J). (gr. 1-5). 2013. (ENG.). 160p. pap. 5.99 *(978-0-06-209499-5(8))*Set. 2016. 1600p. pap. 49.99 *(978-0-06-256981-3(3))* HarperCollins Pubs. (Greenwillow Bks.).

—Amelia Bedelia Bakes Off. Sweat, Lynn, illus. 2010. (Amelia Bedelia Ser.). 64p. (J). (gr. k-3). (ENG.). 17.99 *(978-0-06-084358-8(6))*; lib. bdg. 18.89 *(978-0-06-084359-5(4))* HarperCollins Pubs. (Greenwillow Bks.).

—Amelia Bedelia, Bookworm. Sweat, Lynn, illus. 2005. (I Can Read Level 2 Ser.). (ENG.). 64p. (J). (gr. k-3). pap. 3.99 *(978-0-06-051892-9(8)*, Greenwillow Bks.) HarperCollins Pubs.

—Amelia Bedelia Chapter Book #10: Amelia Bedelia Ties the Knot. Avril, Lynne, illus. 2016. (Amelia Bedelia Ser.). 160p. (J). (gr. 1-5). pap. 4.99 *(978-0-06-233416-9(6)*, Greenwillow Bks.) HarperCollins Pubs.

—Amelia Bedelia Chapter Book #8: Amelia Bedelia Dances Off. Avril, Lynne, illus. 2015. (Amelia Bedelia Ser.). (ENG.). 160p. (J). (gr. 1-5). 15.99 *(978-0-06-233409-1(3)*, Greenwillow Bks.) HarperCollins Pubs.

—Amelia Bedelia Dances Off. Avril, Lynne, illus. 2015. (Amelia Bedelia Ser.). (ENG.). 160p. (J). (gr. 1-5). pap. 4.99 *(978-0-06-233408-4(5)*, Greenwillow Bks.) HarperCollins Pubs.

—Amelia Bedelia Goes Back to School. Sweat, Lynn, illus. 2004. (Amelia Bedelia Ser.). (ENG.). 20p. (J). (gr. -1-3). pap. 6.99 *(978-0-06-051873-8(1)*, Greenwillow Bks.) HarperCollins Pubs.

—Amelia Bedelia Goes Wild! 2014. (Amelia Bedelia Chapter Book Ser.: 4). (J). lib. bdg. 14.75 *(978-0-606-35077-8(2)*, Turtleback) Turtleback Bks.

—Amelia Bedelia Hits the Trail. Avril, Lynne, illus. 2013. (I Can Read Level 1 Ser.). (ENG.). 32p. (J). (gr. -1-3). 16.99 *(978-0-06-209527-5(7)*, Greenwillow Bks.) HarperCollins Pubs.

—Amelia Bedelia Joins the Club. 2014. (Amelia Bedelia: I Can Read! Ser.). (J). lib. bdg. 13.55 *(978-0-606-35051-8(9)*, Turtleback) Turtleback Bks.

—Amelia Bedelia Means Business. Avril, Lynne, illus. (Amelia Bedelia Ser.). (ENG.). (J). (gr. 1-5). 2015. 320p. 12.99 *(978-0-06-240367-4(2))* 2013. 160p. 15.99 *(978-0-06-209497-1(1))* 2013. 149p. pap. 5.99 *(978-0-06-209496-4(3))* HarperCollins Pubs. (Greenwillow Bks.).

—Amelia Bedelia Means Business. Avril, Lynne, illus. 2013. (Amelia Bedelia Chapter Book Ser.: 1). (J). lib. bdg. 14.75 *(978-0-606-27137-0(6)*, Turtleback) Turtleback Bks.

—Amelia Bedelia Road Trip! Avril, Lynne, illus. 2013. (Amelia Bedelia Ser.: No. 3). (ENG.). 160p. (J). (gr. 1-5). 15.99 *(978-0-06-209503-9(X))*; pap. 5.99 *(978-0-06-209502-2(1))* HarperCollins Pubs. (Greenwillow Bks.).

—Amelia Bedelia Road Trip! 2013. (Amelia Bedelia Chapter Book Ser.: 3). (J). lib. bdg. 14.75 *(978-0-606-32453-3(4)*, Turtleback) Turtleback Bks.

—Amelia Bedelia, Rocket Scientist? Sweat, Lynn, illus. (I Can Read Level 2 Ser.). 64p. (J). 2007. (ENG.). (gr. k-3). pap. 3.99 *(978-0-06-051889-9(8)*, Greenwillow Bks.) 2005. (gr. 1-18). 15.99 *(978-0-06-051887-5(1))* 2005. (gr. k-4). lib. bdg. 17.89 *(978-0-06-051888-2(X)*, Greenwillow Bks.) HarperCollins Pubs.

—Amelia Bedelia Sleeps Over. 2012. (Amelia Bedelia: I Can Read! Ser.). (J). lib. bdg. 13.55 *(978-0-606-26849-3(9)*, Turtleback) Turtleback Bks.

—Amelia Bedelia Storybook Treasury. Sweat, Lynn, illus. 2016. (Amelia Bedelia Ser.). 192p. (J). (gr. 1-5). 11.99 *(978-0-06-246908-3(8)*, Greenwillow Bks.) HarperCollins Pubs.

—Amelia Bedelia Storybook Treasury: Amelia Bedelia's First Day of School; Amelia Bedelia's First Field Trip; Amelia Bedelia Makes a Friend; Amelia Bedelia Sleeps over; Amelia Bedelia Hits the Trail. Avril, Lynne, illus. 2013. (ENG.). 192p. (J). (gr. -1-3). 11.99 *(978-0-06-228714-4(1)*, Greenwillow Bks.) HarperCollins Pubs.

—Amelia Bedelia Takes the Cake. Avril, Lynne, illus. 2016. (I Can Read Level 1 Ser.). 32p. (J). (gr. -1-3). pap. 3.99 *(978-0-06-233430-5(1)*, Greenwillow Bks.) HarperCollins Pubs.

—Amelia Bedelia Tries Her Luck. Avril, Lynne, illus. 2013. (I Can Read Level 1 Ser.). (ENG.). 32p. (J). (gr. -1-3). 16.99 *(978-0-06-222128-5(0))*; pap. 3.99 *(978-0-06-222127-8(2))* HarperCollins Pubs. (Greenwillow Bks.).

—Amelia Bedelia Tries Her Luck. 2013. (Amelia Bedelia: I Can Read! Ser.). (J). lib. bdg. 13.55 *(978-0-606-32445-8(3)*, Turtleback) Turtleback Bks.

—Amelia Bedelia Unleashed. Avril, Lynne, illus. 2013. (Amelia Bedelia Ser.: No. 2). (ENG.). 160p. (J). (gr. 1-5). 15.99 *(978-0-06-209500-8(5)*, Greenwillow Bks.) HarperCollins Pubs.

—Amelia Bedelia Unleashed. Avril, Lynne, illus. 2013. (Amelia Bedelia Chapter Book Ser.: 2). (J). lib. bdg. 14.75 *(978-0-606-27138-7(4)*, Turtleback) Turtleback Bks.

—Amelia Bedelia's Backpack Bundle. Sweat, Lynn, illus. 2012. 192p. (J). *(978-1-4351-4392-0(2)*, Greenwillow Bks.) HarperCollins Pubs.

—Amelia Bedelia's First Apple Pie. Avril, Lynne, illus. 2010. (Amelia Bedelia Ser.). 32p. (J). (gr. -1-3). (ENG.). 16.99 *(978-0-06-196409-1(3))*; lib. bdg. 17.89 *(978-0-06-196410-7(7))* HarperCollins Pubs. (Greenwillow Bks.).

—Amelia Bedelia's First Day of School. Avril, Lynne, illus. (Amelia Bedelia Ser.). (ENG.). 32p. (J). (gr. -1-3). 2015. pap. 6.99 *(978-0-06-154457-6(4))* 2011. 9.99 *(978-0-06-203274-4(7))* 2009. 16.99 *(978-0-06-154455-2(8))* HarperCollins Pubs. (Greenwillow Bks.).

—Amelia Bedelia's First Field Trip. Avril, Lynne, illus. 2013. (Amelia Bedelia Ser.). (ENG.). 32p. (J). (gr. -1-3). pap. 6.99 *(978-0-06-196415-2(8)*, Greenwillow Bks.) HarperCollins Pubs.

—Amelia Bedelia's First Field Trip. 2013. (Amelia Bedelia Picture Bks.). (J). lib. bdg. 17.20 *(978-0-606-31818-1(6)*, Turtleback) Turtleback Bks.

—Amelia Bedelia's First Valentine. Avril, Lynne, illus. (Amelia Bedelia Ser.). (ENG.). 32p. (J). (gr. -1-3). 2014. pap. 6.99 *(978-0-06-154460-6(4))* 2011. 9.99 *(978-0-06-203275-1(5))* 2009. 16.99 *(978-0-06-154458-3(2))* HarperCollins Pubs. (Greenwillow Bks.).

—Amelia Bedelia's First Valentine. 2014. (Amelia Bedelia Picture Bks.). (J). lib. bdg. 17.20 *(978-0-606-35971-9(0))* Turtleback Bks.

—Amelia Bedelia's Masterpiece. Sweat, Lynn, illus. (I Can Read Level 2 Ser.). (ENG.). 64p. (J). (gr. k-3). 2008. pap. 3.99 *(978-0-06-084357-1(8))* 2007. 16.99 *(978-0-06-084355-7(1))* HarperCollins Pubs. (Greenwillow Bks.).

—Be My Valentine, Amelia Bedelia. Sweat, Lynn, illus. 2004. (Amelia Bedelia Ser.). (ENG.). 20p. (J). (gr. -1-3). pap. 6.99

(978-0-06-051886-8(3), Greenwillow Bks.) HarperCollins Pubs.

—Calling Doctor Amelia Bedelia. Sweat, Lynn, illus. 2004. (I Can Read Level 2 Ser.). (ENG.). 64p. (J). (gr. k-3). pap. 3.99 (978-0-06-008780-7(3), Greenwillow Bks.) HarperCollins Pubs.

—Happy Haunting, Amelia Bedelia. Sweat, Lynn, illus. (I Can Read Level 2 Ser.). 64p. (J). (gr. k-3). 2006. (ENG.). pap. 3.99 (978-0-06-051895-0(2)) 2004. (ENG.). 16.99 (978-0-06-051893-6(6)) 2004. lib. bdg. 16.89 (978-0-06-051894-3(4)) HarperCollins Pubs. (Greenwillow Bks.).

Parish, Peggy. Amelia Bedelia. Siebel, Fritz, illus. 50th ed. 2012. (I Can Read Level 2 Ser.). (ENG.). 64p. (J). (gr. k-3). pap. 3.99 (978-0-06-444155-1(5), Greenwillow Bks.) HarperCollins Pubs.

—Amelia Bedelia. 50th anniv. ed. 2012. (I Can Read Level 2 Ser.). (Illus.). 96p. (J). (gr. k-3). pap. 11.99 (978-0-06-054238-2(1), Greenwillow Bks.) HarperCollins Pubs.

—Amelia Bedelia. Siebel, Fritz, illus. 2012. (Amelia Bedelia: I Can Read! Ser.: 1). (J). (gr. 1-3). lib. bdg. 13.55 (978-0-88103-916-0(0), Turtleback) Turtleback Bks.

—Amelia Bedelia & the Baby. Sweat, Lynn, illus. 2004. (I Can Read Level 2 Ser.). (ENG.). 64p. (J). (gr. k-3). pap. 3.99 (978-0-06-051105-0(2), Greenwillow Bks.) HarperCollins Pubs.

—Amelia Bedelia Goes Camping. Sweat, Lynn, illus. 2003. (I Can Read Level 2 Ser.). (ENG.). 64p. (J). (gr. k-3). pap. 3.99 (978-0-06-051106-7(0), Greenwillow Bks.) HarperCollins Pubs.

—Amelia Bedelia Goes Camping. 2003. (Amelia Bedelia: I Can Read! Ser.: 10). (J). (gr. k-3). lib. bdg. 13.55 (978-0-613-62664-4(8), Turtleback) Turtleback Bks.

—Amelia Bedelia's Family Album. Sweat, Lynn, illus. 2003. (I Can Read Level 2 Ser.). (ENG.). 48p. (J). (gr. k-3). pap. 3.99 (978-0-06-051116-6(8), Greenwillow Bks.) HarperCollins Pubs.

—Amelia Bedelia's Family Album. 2003. (Amelia Bedelia: I Can Read! Ser.: 12). (J). (gr. k-3). lib. bdg. 13.55 (978-0-613-62129-8(8), Turtleback) Turtleback Bks.

—Good Work, Amelia Bedelia. Sweat, Lynn, illus. 2003. (I Can Read Level 2 Ser.). (ENG.). 64p. (J). (gr. k-3). pap. 3.99 (978-0-06-051115-9(X), Greenwillow Bks.) HarperCollins Pubs.

—Good Work, Amelia Bedelia. 2003. (Amelia Bedelia: I Can Read! Ser.: 6). (J). (gr. k-3). lib. bdg. 13.55 (978-0-613-68343-2(9), Turtleback) Turtleback Bks.

AMENHETEP IV, KING OF EGYPT

see Akhenaten, King of Egypt

AMERICA

see also Central America; Latin America; North America; South America

Benchmark Education Company, LLC Staff, compiled by. Social Studies Theme: Civilizations of the Americas. 2005. spiral bd. 115.00 (978-1-4108-5323-3(3)) Benchmark Education Co.

McNeese, Tim. John Smith. 2010. (Leaders of the Colonial Era Ser.). 128p. (gr. 5-8). 35.00 (978-1-60413-742-2(8), Chelsea Hse.) Facts On File, Inc.

Rappaport, Doreen. In the Promised Land: Lives of Jewish Americans. Van Wright, Cornelius, illus. 2005. 32p. (J). (gr. k-4). lib. bdg. 16.89 (978-0-06-059395-7(4)) HarperCollins Pubs.

Rice, Dona Herweck. American Through & Through, 1 vol. 2011. (Early Childhood Themes Ser.). (ENG.). 16p. (J). (gr. -1-2). pap. 6.99 (978-1-4333-2362-1(1)) Teacher Created Materials, Inc.

—American Through & Through Lap Book, 1 vol. 2011. (Early Childhood Themes Ser.). (ENG.). 16p. (J). (gr. -1-2). pap. 19.99 (978-1-4333-2363-8(X)) Teacher Created Materials, Inc.

Taylor, Isaac. Scenes in America, for the Amusement & Instruction of Little Tarry-at-Home Travellers by the Rev Isaac Taylor. 2006. 156p. per. 18.99 (978-1-4255-1143-2(0)) Michigan Publishing.

Toler, Pamela D. Transatlantic Slave Networks. 2017. (J). **(978-1-5026-2696-7(9))** Cavendish Square Publishing.

AMERICA—ANTIQUITIES

Anderson, Michael. Early Civilizations of the Americas. 2011. (J). lib. bdg. 31.70 (978-1-61530-525-4(4)) Rosen Publishing Group, Inc., The.

Aveni, Anthony. Buried Beneath Us: Discovering the Ancient Cities of the Americas. Roy, Katherine, illus. 2013. (ENG.). 96p. (J). (gr. 4-8). 18.99 (978-1-59643-567-4(4), 9781596435674) Roaring Brook Pr.

Benson, Sonia & Baker, Deborah J. Early Civilizations in the, 2.0. 2005. (Early Civilizations in the Americas Ser.). (ENG., Illus.). xli, 551p. (J). 191.00 (978-0-7876-9252-0(2), UXL) Cengage Gale.

Discovering Ancient America: Set 2. 2017. (Discovering Ancient America Ser.). 200p. (gr. 12-14). 119.25 **(978-1-4994-6660-7(9)**, Rosen Young Adult) Rosen Publishing Group, Inc., The.

Haze, Xaviant. Ancient America's Lost Giants. 2017. (Discovering Ancient America Ser.). 200p. (J). (gr. 12-14). 39.75 **(978-1-4994-6676-8(5)**, Rosen Young Adult) Rosen Publishing Group, Inc., The.

Joseph, Frank. Archaeological Discoveries of Ancient America, 1 vol., 1. 2014. (Discovering Ancient America Ser.). (ENG.). 296p. (YA). (gr. 7-12). 38.25 (978-1-4777-2809-3(0)) Rosen Publishing Group, Inc., The.

Mann, Charles C. Before Columbus: The Americas of 1491. 2009. (ENG., Illus.). 128p. (J). (gr. 3-7). 24.99 (978-1-4169-4900-8(3), Atheneum Bks. for Young Readers) Simon & Schuster Children's Publishing.

The New World: Prehistory To 1542. 2010. (Discovering U. S. History Ser.). (Illus.). 128p. (gr. 5-8). 35.00 (978-1-60413-348-6(1), Chelsea Hse.) Facts On File, Inc.

Wyatt, Valerie. Who Discovered America? Woo, Howie, illus. 2008. (ENG.). 40p. (J). (gr. 3-7). 17.95 (978-1-55453-128-8(4)); pap. 8.95 (978-1-55453-129-5(2)) Kids Can Pr., Ltd. CAN. Dist: Hachette Bk. Group.

AMERICA—CIVILIZATION

Benchmark Education Company, LLC Staff, compiled by. Civilizations of the Americas. 2006. spiral bd. 330.00 (978-1-4108-7008-7(1)) 2005. (J). spiral bd. 265.00 (978-1-4108-5768-2(9)) Benchmark Education Co.

—Civilizations of the Americas: Theme Set. 2006. (J). 173.00 (978-1-4108-7110-7(X)) Benchmark Education Co.

Cooper, Debbie, illus. The Garifuna: Cultures of the Caribbean & Central America l.t. ed. 2005. 32p. (J). 9.99 (978-0-9760406-0-6(3), 6-0-3, A Kidz World) ABUAA, Inc.

Discovering Ancient America: Set 2. 2017. (Discovering Ancient America Ser.). 200p. (gr. 12-14). 119.25 **(978-1-4994-6660-7(9)**, Rosen Young Adult) Rosen Publishing Group, Inc., The.

Samuels, Charlie. Technology in the Ancient Americas. 2013. (Technology in the Ancient World Ser.). 48p. (J). (gr. 4-6). pap. 14.05 (978-1-4339-9621-4(9)); pap. 84.30 (978-1-4339-9622-1(7)); (ENG., Illus.). lib. bdg. 31.95 (978-1-4339-9620-7(0)) Stevens, Gareth Publishing LLLP.

AMERICA—DISCOVERY AND EXPLORATION

see also Explorers; Northwest Passage

Abnett, Dan. Christopher Columbus & the Voyage of 1492. Q2A Staff, illus. 2007. (Jr. Graphic Biographies Ser.). (ENG.). 24p. (gr. 3-8). pap. 10.60 (978-1-4042-2143-7(3), PowerKids Pr.) Rosen Publishing Group, Inc., The.

—Christopher Columbus & the Voyage Of 1492. (Jr. Graphic Biographies Ser.). (ENG.). 24p. (J). (gr. 2-3). 2009. 47.90 (978-1-61513-810-4(2), PowerKids Pr.) 2007. (Illus.). lib. bdg. 25.25 (978-1-4042-3390-4(3)) Rosen Publishing Group, Inc., The.

—Cristóbal Colón y el Viaje de 1942. 2009. (Historietas Juveniles: Biografías (Jr. Graphic Biographies) Ser.). (SPA & ENG., Illus.). 24p. (J). (gr. 2-5). 25.25 (978-1-4358-8559-2(7)); (gr. 3-8). pap. 10.60 (978-1-4358-3312-8(0)) Rosen Publishing Group, Inc., The.

Abrams, Dennis. El Dorado. 2012. (Lost Worlds & Mysterious Civilizations Ser.). (Illus.). 109p. (gr. 6-12). 35.00 (978-1-60413-975-4(7), Chelsea Hse.) Facts On File, Inc.

Allen, Kathy & Krueger, Jennifer. When Did Columbus Arrive in the Americas? And Other Questions about Columbus's Voyages. 2012. (Six Questions of American History Ser.). (ENG.). 48p. (gr. 4-6). pap. 56.72 (978-0-7613-9240-8(8)); pap. 9.95 (978-0-7613-7127-4(3)); lib. bdg. 30.60 (978-0-7613-5327-0(5)) Lerner Publishing Group.

Aller, Susan Bivin. Christopher Columbus. 2003. (History Maker Bios Ser.). (Illus.). 48p. (J). (gr. 3-5). lib. bdg. 26.60 (978-0-8225-0398-9(0)) Lerner Publishing Group.

Aloian, Molly. Columbus Day. 2010. (ENG., Illus.). 32p. (J). (978-0-7787-4760-4(3)); pap. (978-0-7787-4778-9(6)) Crabtree Publishing Co.

Anderson, Michael. Biographies of the New World: From Leif Eriksson to Charles Darwin. 2012. (Impact on America: Collective Biographies Ser.). (ENG., Illus.). 136p. (J). (gr. 7-12). lib. bdg. 32.90 (978-1-61530-672-5(2)) Rosen Publishing Group, Inc., The.

Anderson, Michael, ed. Biographies of the New World: Leif Eriksson, Henry Hudson, Charles Darwin, & More. 2012. (Impact on America: Collective Biographies Ser.). (ENG., Illus.). 112p. (YA). (gr. 7-12). 65.80 (978-1-61530-803-3(2)) Rosen Publishing Group, Inc., The.

Anderson, Zachary. John Cabot: Searching for a Westward Passage to Asia. 2015. (Incredible Explorers Ser.). (ENG., Illus.). 64p. (J). (gr. 7-7). 34.21 (978-1-5026-0173-5(7)) Cavendish Square Publishing.

—Samuel de Champlain: Exploring the Great Lakes. 2015. (J). lib. bdg. (978-1-62713-423-1(9)) Cavendish Square Publishing.

Aretha, David. La Salle: French Explorer of the Mississippi. 2009. (Great Explorers of the World Ser.). (Illus.). 112p. (J). (gr. 7-12). lib. bdg. 33.27 (978-1-59845-098-9(0)) Enslow Pubs., Inc.

Asselin, Kristine Carlson. Who Really Discovered America?, 1 vol. (Race for History Ser.). (ENG., 32p. (gr. 3-4). 2011. Illus.). pap. 8.10 (978-1-4296-6247-5(6)) 2011. pap. 47.70 (978-1-4296-6415-8(0)) 2010. lib. bdg. 27.32 (978-1-4296-3342-0(5)) Capstone Press of Coughlan Cos. (Fact Finders).

Bader, Bonnie. Who Was Christopher Columbus? Harrison, Nancy, illus. 2013. (Who Was? Ser.). (ENG.). 112p. (J). (gr. 3-7). pap. 5.99 (978-0-448-46333-9(4), Grosset & Dunlap) Penguin Young Readers Group.

—Who Was Christopher Columbus? 2013. (Who Was...? Ser.). lib. bdg. 16.00 (978-0-606-31684-2(1), Turtleback) Turtleback Bks.

Bailey, Gerry & Foster, Karen. Columbus's Chart. Radford, Karen & Noyes, Leighton, illus. 2008. (Stories of Great People Ser.). (ENG.). 40p. (J). (gr. 3-8). pap. (978-0-7787-3708-7(X)); lib. bdg. (978-0-7787-3686-8(5)) Crabtree Publishing Co.

Bell, Robin. My Adventure Discovering America. 2007. 44p. (J). 8.99 (978-1-59092-415-0(0)) Blue Forge Pr.

Benchmark Education Company. Spain Explores the Americas (Teacher Guide) 2005. (978-1-4108-4645-7(8)) Benchmark Education Co.

Berne, Emma Carlson. Did Christopher Columbus Really Discover America? And Other Question about the New World. 2015. (Good Question! Ser.). (ENG., Illus.). 32p. (J). (gr. 2). pap. 5.95 (978-1-4549-1259-0(6)) Sterling Publishing Co., Inc.

—Did Christopher Columbus Really Discover America? And Other Questions about the New World. 2015. (Good Question! Ser.). (ENG., Illus.). 40p. (J). (gr. 2). 12.95 (978-1-4549-1258-3(8)) Sterling Publishing Co., Inc.

Bodden, Valerie. Conquistadors. 2017. (J). (978-1-60818-812-3(4), Creative Education) 2013. 24p. pap. (978-1-60818-467-5(6)) Creative Co., The.

Brown, Janet Hubbard. Hernando de Soto & His Expeditions Across the Americas. Goetzmann, William H., ed. 2005. (Explorers of New Lands Ser.). (Illus.). 100p. (gr. 5-8). lib. bdg. 30.00 (978-0-7910-8610-0(0)) Facts On File, Inc.

Burgan, Michael. The Story of North America's First Explorers. 2016. (Discovering the New World Ser.). (ENG., Illus.). 48p. (gr. 3-4). lib. bdg. 29.32 (978-1-5157-1868-0(9)) Capstone Press of Coughlan Cos.

Cohen, Robert Z. Hernando de Soto. 2016. (Spotlight on Explorers & Colonization Ser.). 00048p. (J). (gr. 6-6). pap. 11.75 (978-1-5081-7210-9(2)) Rosen Publishing Group, Inc., The.

Collier, James Lincoln. Christopher Columbus: To the New World. 2006. (Great Explorations Ser.). (Illus.). 80p. (J). (gr. 3-7). lib. bdg. 32.79 (978-0-7614-2221-1(8), Benchmark Bks.) Marshall Cavendish Corp.

Conklin, Wendy. Exploring the New World, 1 vol. 2004. (Primary Source Readers Ser.). (ENG.). 24p. (J). (gr. 5-5). 8.99 (978-0-7439-8740-0(3)) Shell Educational Publishing.

—Finding Florida: Exploration & Its Legacy. 2016. (Primary Source Readers Ser.). 32p. (J). (gr. 4-4). pap. 8.99 (978-1-4938-3536-2(X)) Teacher Created Materials, Inc.

Connelly, Jack. Christopher Columbus: Discovering the Americas. 2015. (Incredible Explorers Ser.). (ENG., Illus.). 64p. (J). (gr. 7-7). 34.21 (978-1-5026-0171-1(0)) Cavendish Square Publishing.

Conquistadors: Hernan Cortes; Francisco Pizarro; Inca Rebellion, 3 cass.; set. 2003. (YA). (gr. 7-12). tchr. ed. 129.95 (978-1-58738-433-2(7)) Discovery Education.

Cook, Diane. Pathfinders of the American Frontier. 2004. (Exploration & Discovery Ser.). (Illus.). 64p. (YA). (gr. 5-18). lib. bdg. 19.95 (978-1-59084-045-0(3)) Mason Crest.

Cooke, Tim. The Exploration of North America. 2013. (Explorers Discovering the World Ser.). (Illus.). 48p. (J). (gr. 4-6). pap. 14.05 (978-1-4339-8624-6(8)) Stevens, Gareth Publishing LLLP.

—The Exploration of North America. 2013. (Explorers Discovering the World Ser.). (Illus.). 48p. (J). (gr. 4-6). lib. bdg. 31.95 (978-1-4339-8623-9(X)) Stevens, Gareth Publishing LLLP.

—Explore with Henry Hudson. 2014. (ENG., Illus.). 32p. (J). (978-0-7787-1246-6(X)); pap. (978-0-7787-1258-9(3)) Crabtree Publishing Co.

Corrigan, Jim. Europeans & Native Americans. Johnson, Troy, ed. 2013. (Native American Life Ser.: 15). 64p. (J). (gr. 5-18). 19.95 (978-1-4222-2964-4(5)) Mason Crest.

Cosson, M. J. Three Worlds Meet. 2011. (Explorer Library: Language Arts Explorer Ser.). (ENG.). 32p. (gr. 4-8). pap. 14.21 (978-1-61080-281-9(0), 201204) Cherry Lake Publishing.

Craats, Rennay. Columbus Day. (American Celebrations Ser.). (Illus.). 24p. (J). 2010. (gr. 3-5). pap. 11.95 (978-1-60596-933-6(8)) 2010. (gr. 3-5). lib. bdg. 25.70 (978-1-60596-775-2(0)) 2004. lib. bdg. 24.45 (978-1-59036-106-1(7)) 2004. (gr. 1-3). per. 8.95 (978-1-59036-164-1(4)) Weigl Pubs., Inc.

—Exploration of North America. (Great Journeys Ser.). (Illus.). 32p. (J). 2005. (gr. 3-7). per. 9.95 (978-1-59036-258-7(6)) 2004. lib. bdg. 26.00 (978-1-59036-206-8(3)) Weigl Pubs., Inc.

Crompton, Samuel Willard. Lewis & Clark. 2009. (Great Explorers Ser.). (Illus.). 120p. (J). (gr. 6-12). 30.00 (978-1-60413-418-6(6), Chelsea Hse.) Facts On File, Inc.

Currie, Stephen & National Geographic Learning Staff. Expeditions in the Americas, 1492-1700. 2007. (Nonfiction Reading & Writing Workshops Ser.). (ENG., Illus.). 32p. (J). pap. 17.95 (978-0-7922-4544-5(X)) CENGAGE Learning.

Dalrymple, Lisa & O'Brien, Cynthia. Explore with John Cabot. 2015. (Travel with the Great Explorers Ser.). (ENG., Illus.). 32p. (J). (gr. 3-6). (978-0-7787-1702-7(X)) Crabtree Publishing Co.

Daly, Ruth. French Explorers. 2016. (J). **(978-1-5105-1873-5(8))** SmartBook Media, Inc.

D'Aulaire, Ingri & D'Aulaire, Edgar Parin. Leif the Lucky. 2014. (ENG., Illus.). 60p. 16.95 (978-0-8166-9545-4(8)) Univ. of Minnesota Pr.

Davenport, John. Juan Ponce de Leon & His Lands of Discovery. Goetzmann, William H., ed. 2005. (Explorers of New Lands Ser.). (Illus.). 110p. (gr. 5-8). lib. bdg. 30.00 (978-0-7910-8607-0(0)) Facts On File, Inc.

Dawson, Patricia A. First Peoples of the Americas & the European Age of Exploration. 2015. (Exploring the Ancient & Medieval Worlds Ser.). (ENG., Illus.). 160p. (J). (gr. 8-8). lib. bdg. 45.64 (978-1-5026-0685-3(2)) Cavendish Square Publishing.

Dayton, Connor. Columbus Day. 2012. (American Holidays Ser.). (ENG., Illus.). 24p. (J). (gr. k-3). pap. 8.25 (978-1-4488-6248-1(5)); lib. bdg. 22.60 (978-1-4488-6145-3(4)) Rosen Publishing Group, Inc., The. (PowerKids Pr.).

—Columbus Day: Día de la Raza. Alamán, Eduardo, tr. from ENG. 2012. (American Holidays / Celebraciones en los Estados Unidos Ser.). (SPA & ENG., Illus.). 24p. (J). (gr. k-3). lib. bdg. 22.60 (978-1-4488-6711-0(8), PowerKids Pr.) Rosen Publishing Group, Inc., The.

Demi. Columbus, 0 vols. Demi, illus. 2012. (ENG., Illus.). 64p. (J). (gr. 3-7). 19.99 (978-0-7614-6167-8(1), 9780761461678, Amazon Children's Publishing) Amazon Publishing.

DePietro, Frank. Spain Arrives in the Americas. Limón, José E., ed. 2012. (Hispanic Americans: Major Minority Ser.). 64p. (J). (gr. 4). 22.95 (978-1-4222-2330-7(2)) Mason Crest.

DeRubertis, Barbara. Let's Celebrate Columbus Day. Sperling, Thomas, illus. 2014. (Holidays & Heroes Ser.). 32p. (J). (gr. 1-3). pap. 7.95 (978-1-57565-634-2(5)) Kane Press, Inc.

Ditchfield, Christin. The Lewis & Clark Expedition. 2006. (True Bks.). (ENG., Illus.). 48p. (J). (gr. 3-7). pap. 6.95 (978-0-516-25222-3(4), Children's Pr.) Scholastic Library Publishing.

Donaldson-Forbes, Jeff. Jacques Cartier. 2009. (Primary Source Library of Famous Explorers Ser.). 24p. (gr. 4-4). 42.50 (978-1-60854-126-3(6), PowerKids Pr.) Rosen Publishing Group, Inc., The.

—Jacques Marquette & Louis Jolliet. 2009. (Primary Source Library of Famous Explorers Ser.). 24p. (gr. 4-4). 42.50 (978-1-60854-127-0(4), PowerKids Pr.) Rosen Publishing Group, Inc., The.

—La Salle. 2009. (Primary Source Library of Famous Explorers Ser.). 24p. (gr. 4-4). 42.50 (978-1-60854-129-4(0), PowerKids Pr.) Rosen Publishing Group, Inc., The.

Donohue, Moira Rose. Christopher Columbus. 2013. (Illus.). 24p. (J). (978-1-938813-04-7(9)); pap. (978-1-938813-08-5(1)) State Standards Publishing, LLC.

—Henry Hudson. 2014. (Illus.). 24p. (J). (978-1-938813-16-0(2)) State Standards Publishing, LLC.

—Hernando de Soto. 2015. (Illus.). 24p. (J). (978-1-938813-20-7(0)) State Standards Publishing, LLC.

—Jacques Cartier. 2013. (Illus.). 24p. (J). (978-1-938813-03-0(0)) State Standards Publishing, LLC.

—John Cabot. 2014. (Illus.). 24p. (J). (978-1-938813-15-3(4)) State Standards Publishing, LLC.

—Juan Ponce de León. 2013. (Illus.). 24p. (J). (978-1-938813-06-1(5)) State Standards Publishing, LLC.

Eagen, Rachel. Ponce de Leon: Exploring Florida & Puerto Rico. 2005. (In the Footsteps of Explorers Ser.). (ENG., Illus.). 32p. (J). (gr. 4-5). pap. (978-0-7787-2448-3(4)) Crabtree Publishing Co.

Elliott, Lynne. Exploration in the Renaissance. 2009. (Renaissance World Ser.). (ENG., Illus.). 32p. (J). (gr. 5-8). pap. (978-0-7787-4613-3(5)); lib. bdg. (978-0-7787-4593-8(7)) Crabtree Publishing Co.

Evan-Moor & McFarren, Kathleen. History Pockets: Explorers of North America, Grades 4-6. 2003. (History Pockets Ser.). (ENG., Illus.). 96p. (J). (gr. 4-6). pap., suppl. ed. 14.99 (978-1-55799-905-4(8), EMC 3708) Evan-Moor Educational Pubs.

Exploring North America, 1800-1900, Revised Edition. 2nd rev. ed. 2009. (Discovery & Exploration Ser.). (Illus.). 152p. (YA). (gr. 7-12). 35.00 (978-1-60413-194-9(2)) Facts On File, Inc.

Feinstein, Stephen. Columbus: Opening up the New World. 2009. (Great Explorers of the World Ser.). (Illus.). 112p. (J). (gr. 7-12). lib. bdg. 33.27 (978-1-59845-101-6(4)) Enslow Pubs., Inc.

Freedman, Russell. Who Was First? Discovering the Americas. 2007. (ENG., Illus.). 96p. (J). (gr. 5-7). 19.00 (978-0-618-66391-0(6)) Houghton Mifflin Harcourt Publishing Co.

George, Enzo. The Expanding Frontier. 2015. (Primary Sources in U. S. History Ser.). (ENG.). 48p. (J). (gr. 4-4). lib. bdg. 31.36 (978-1-5026-0248-0(2)) Cavendish Square Publishing.

Gleason, Carrie. Henry Hudson: Seeking the Northwest Passage. 2005. (In the Footsteps of Explorers Ser.). (ENG., Illus.). 32p. (J). (gr. -1-9). pap. (978-0-7787-2444-5(1)) Crabtree Publishing Co.

Goldberg, Jan. Hernando de Soto: Trailblazer of the American Southeast. (Library of Explorers & Exploration Ser.). 112p. (gr. 5-8). 2009. 66.50 (978-1-60853-607-8(6)) 2003. (Illus.). lib. bdg. 34.60 (978-0-8239-3623-6(6)) Rosen Publishing Group, Inc., The. (Rosen Reference).

Gondosch, Linda. Where Did Sacagawea Join the Corps of Discovery? And Other Questions about the Lewis & Clark Expedition. 2011. (Six Questions of American History Ser.). (ENG.). 48p. (gr. 4-6). lib. bdg. 30.60 (978-0-7613-5226-6(0)) Lerner Publishing Group.

Gould, Jane H. Henry Hudson. 2013. (Jr. Graphic Famous Explorers Ser.). (ENG., Illus.). 24p. (J). (gr. 3-6). pap. 10.60 (978-1-4777-0127-0(3)); lib. bdg. 25.25 (978-1-4777-0071-6(4)) Rosen Publishing Group, Inc., The. (PowerKids Pr.).

Greenway, Shirley. Exploration of North America. 2010. (History of Exploration Ser.). 48p. 32.80 (978-1-84898-301-4(8)) Black Rabbit Bks.

Gunderson, Jessica. Christopher Columbus: New World Explorer or Fortune Hunter?, 1 vol. 2013. (Perspectives on History Ser.). (ENG.). 32p. (gr. 3-4). 27.32 (978-1-4765-0242-7(0)); pap. 7.95 (978-1-4765-3406-0(3)) Capstone Press of Coughlan Cos. (Fact Finders).

—Conquistadors. 2012. (Fearsome Fighters Ser.). 48p. (gr. 5-12). 23.95 (978-1-60818-183-4(9), Creative Education) Creative Co., The.

—Your Life As a Private on the Lewis & Clark Expedition, 1 vol. Madden, Colleen, illus. 2012. (Way It Was Ser.). (ENG.). 32p. (gr. 2-3). lib. bdg. 26.65 (978-1-4048-7370-4(8)) Picture Window Bks.

Gunderson, Jessica Sarah. Your Life As a Private on the Lewis & Clark Expedition, 1 vol. Madden, Colleen, illus. 2012. (Way It Was Ser.). (ENG.). 32p. (gr. 2-3). pap. 8.95 (978-1-4048-7746-7(0)) Picture Window Bks.

Hakim, Joy. The First Americans: Prehistory-1600. 2nd rev. ed. 2007. (History of US Ser.: 1). (ENG., Illus.). 192p. (gr. 4-7). per. 15.95 (978-0-19-532715-1(2)) Oxford Univ. Pr., Inc.

—The First Americans Prehistory 1600. 3rd rev. ed. 2006. (History of US Ser.: 1). (ENG., Illus.). 192p. (gr. 4-7). 24.95 (978-0-19-518894-3(2)) Oxford Univ. Pr., Inc.

Harkins, Susan Sales & Harkins, William H. The Life & Times of Father Jacques Marquette. 2008. (Profiles in American History Ser.). (Illus.). 48p. (J). (gr. 4-8). lib. bdg. 29.95 (978-1-58415-528-7(0)) Mitchell Lane Pubs., Inc.

Hazelton, Amie. Henry Hudson: An Explorer of the Northwest Passage. 2017. (World Explorers Ser.). (ENG., Illus.). 32p. (gr. 3-4). lib. bdg. 27.32 (978-1-5157-4205-0(9)) Capstone Press of Coughlan Cos.

—Hernando de Soto: An Explorer of the Southeast. 2017. (World Explorers Ser.). (ENG., Illus.). 32p. (gr. 3-4). lib. bdg. 27.32 (978-1-5157-4204-3(0)) Capstone Press of Coughlan Cos.

Hazleton, Amie. Francisco Vasquez de Coronado: An Explorer of the Southwest. 2017. (World Explorers Ser.). (ENG., Illus.). 32p. (gr. 3-4). lib. bdg. 27.32 (978-1-5157-4203-6(2)) Capstone Press of Coughlan Cos.

Hernández, Roger E. Early Explorations: The 1500s. 2008. (Hispanic America Ser.). 80p. (gr. 5-18). lib. bdg. 34.21 (978-0-7614-2937-1(9), Benchmark Bks.) Marshall Cavendish Corp.

Herr, Melody. Exploring the New World: An Interactive History Adventure. 2016. (You Choose: History Ser.). (ENG.). 112p. (gr. 3-4). pap. 6.95 (978-1-5157-4258-6(X), You Choose Bks.) Capstone Press of Coughlan Cos.

Hill, Christina. Racing to Colonize the New World. 2016. (Primary Source Readers Ser.). (Illus.). 32p. (J). (gr. 4-5). 8.99 (978-1-4938-3074-9(0)) Teacher Created Materials, Inc.

Hoogenboom, Lynn. Amerigo Vespucci. 2009. (Primary Source Library of Famous Explorers Ser.). 24p. (gr. 4-4). 42.50 (978-1-60854-118-8(5), PowerKids Pr.) Rosen Publishing Group, Inc., The.

—Amerigo Vespucci: A Primary Source Biography. 2005. (Primary Source Library of Famous Explorers Ser.). (Illus.). 24p. (J). (gr. 3-7). lib. bdg. 21.25 (978-1-4042-3037-8(8), PowerKids Pr.) Rosen Publishing Group, Inc., The.

—Christopher Columbus. 2009. (Primary Source Library of Famous Explorers Ser.). 24p. (gr. 4-4). 42.50 (978-1-60854-119-5(3), PowerKids Pr.) Rosen Publishing Group, Inc., The.

—Christopher Columbus: A Primary Source Biography. 2006. (Primary Source Library of Famous Explorers Ser.). (Illus.). 24p. (YA). (gr. 2-5). lib. bdg. 22.60 (978-1-4042-3036-1(X)) Rosen Publishing Group, Inc., The.

—Francisco Pizarro. 2009. (Primary Source Library of Famous Explorers Ser.). 24p. (gr. 4-4). 42.50 *(978-1-60854-121-8(5),* PowerKids Pr.) Rosen Publishing Group, Inc., The.

—Francisco Pizarro: A Primary Source Biography. 2006. (Primary Source Library of Famous Explorers Ser.). (Illus.). 24p. (YA). (gr. 2-5). lib. bdg. 22.60 *(978-1-4042-3038-5(6))* Rosen Publishing Group, Inc., The.

—Juan Ponce de Leon. 2009. (Primary Source Library of Famous Explorers Ser.). 24p. (gr. 4-4). 42.50 *(978-1-60854-128-7(2),* PowerKids Pr.) Rosen Publishing Group, Inc., The.

—Juan Ponce de Leon: A Primary Source Biography. 2006. (Primary Source Library of Famous Explorers Ser.). (Illus.). 24p. (YA). (gr. 2-5). lib. bdg. 22.60 *(978-1-4042-3040-8(8))* Rosen Publishing Group, Inc., The.

—Sir Francis Drake. 2009. (Primary Source Library of Famous Explorers Ser.). 24p. (gr. 4-4). 42.50 *(978-1-60854-131-7(2),* PowerKids Pr.) Rosen Publishing Group, Inc., The.

—Sir Francis Drake: A Primary Source Biography. 2006. (Primary Source Library of Famous Explorers Ser.). (Illus.). 24p. (YA). (gr. 2-5). lib. bdg. 22.60 *(978-1-4042-3035-4(1))* Rosen Publishing Group, Inc., The.

Huey, Lois Miner. American Archaeology Uncovers the Earliest English Colonies. 2009. (American Archaeology Ser.). 64p. (gr. 5-6). 31.36 *(978-0-7614-4264-6(2))* Marshall Cavendish Corp.

—American Archaeology Uncovers the Vikings. 2009. (American Archaeology Ser.). 64p. (gr. 5-6). 31.36 *(978-0-7614-4270-7(7))* Marshall Cavendish Corp.

—The Search for el Dorado (Totally True Adventures) 2016. (Totally True Adventures Ser.). (ENG., Illus.). 112p. (J). (gr. 2-5). 4.99 *(978-0-553-53614-0(1),* Random Hse. Bks. for Young Readers) Random Hse. Children's Bks.

Hunter, Nick. Christopher Columbus & Neil Armstrong. 2015. (Comparing People from the Past Ser.). (ENG., Illus.). 32p. (gr. 3-3). pap. 6.49 *(978-1-4846-0920-0(4),* Heinemann First Library) Heinemann-Raintree.

Hyde, Natalie. Explore with Leif Eriksson. 2014. (ENG., Illus.). 32p. (J). *(978-0-7787-1427-9(6))* Crabtree Publishing Co.

Isserman, Maurice. Across America: The Lewis & Clark Expedition, Revised Edition. 2nd rev. ed. 2009. (Discovery & Exploration Ser.). (Illus.). 128p. (gr. 5-8). 35.00 *(978-1-60413-192-5(6),* Chelsea Hse.) Facts On File, Inc.

Jeffrey, Gary. The Explorations of Lewis & Clark. Riley, Terry, illus. 2012. (Graphic History of the American West Ser.). (ENG.). 24p. (J). (gr. 3-8). pap. 8.15 *(978-1-4339-6737-5(5),* Gareth Stevens Learning Library); (gr. 4-7). lib. bdg. 23.95 *(978-1-4339-6735-1(9))* Stevens, Gareth Publishing LLLP.

Johnston, Charles H. Famous Discoverers & Explorers of Amer. 2006. pap. 38.95 *(978-1-4254-9677-7(6))* Kessinger Publishing, LLC.

Johnston, Lissa J. & Núñez Cabeza de Vaca, Alvar. Crossing a Continent: The Incredible Journey of Cabeza de Vaca. 2005. 82p. (J). pap. 9.95 *(978-1-57168-183-6(3),* Eakin Pr.) Eakin Pr.

Jones, Charlotte Foltz. Westward Ho! Eleven Explorers of the American West. 2005. (ENG., Illus.). 240p. (J). (gr. 4-6). tchr. ed. 22.95 *(978-0-8234-1586-1(4))* Holiday Hse., Inc.

Jones, Stephen A. So What Did the People Find? 2009. 24p. pap. 11.50 *(978-1-4389-2736-7(3))* AuthorHouse.

Joseph, Frank. Archaeological Discoveries of Ancient America, 1 vol., 1. 2014. (Discovering Ancient America Ser.). (ENG.). 296p. (YA). (gr. 7-12). 38.25 *(978-1-4777-2809-3(0))* Rosen Publishing Group, Inc., The.

—Legends & Lore of Ancient America, 1 vol., 1. 2014. (Discovering Ancient America Ser.). (ENG.). 296p. (YA). (gr. 7-12). lib. bdg. 38.25 *(978-1-4777-2807-9(4))* Rosen Publishing Group, Inc., The.

Kachurek, Sandra J. Francisco Pizarro: Explorer of South America. 2004. (Explorers! Ser.). (Illus.). 48p. (J). lib. bdg. 23.93 *(978-0-7660-2178-5(5))* Enslow Pubs., Inc.

Kallen, Stuart A. A Journey with Christopher Columbus. 2017. (Primary Source Explorers Ser.). (ENG.). 40p. (J). (gr. 3-5). lib. bdg. 30.65 *(978-1-5124-0772-3(0))* Lerner Publishing Group.

—A Journey with Francisco Vázquez de Coronado. 2017. (Primary Source Explorers Ser.). (ENG.). 40p. (J). (gr. 3-5). 30.65 *(978-1-5124-0773-0(9))* Lerner Publishing Group.

Keller, Susanna. The Age of Exploration, 01 vols., 1. 2016. (Early American History Ser.). (ENG., Illus.). 80p. (J). 32.90 *(978-1-68048-267-6(X),* Britannica Educational Publishing) Rosen Publishing Group, Inc., The.

—The True Story of Christopher Columbus. 2013. (What Really Happened? Ser.). (ENG., Illus.). 24p. (J). (gr. 3-6). pap. 8.25 *(978-1-4488-9842-8(0));* lib. bdg. 22.60 *(978-1-4488-9692-9(4))* Rosen Publishing Group, Inc., The. (PowerKids Pr.).

Kneib, Martha. Christopher Columbus: Master Italian Navigator in the Court of Spain. 2009. (Library of Explorers & Exploration Ser.). 112p. (gr. 5-8). 66.50 *(978-1-60853-601-6(7),* Rosen Reference) Rosen Publishing Group, Inc., The.

Knudsen, Shannon. Leif Eriksson. Oldroyd, Mark, illus. 2005. (On My Own Biography Ser.). (ENG.). 48p. (gr. 2-4). pap. 6.95 *(978-1-57505-828-3(6));* lib. bdg. 25.26 *(978-1-57505-649-4(6),* Carolrhoda Bks.) Lerner Publishing Group.

Kramer, Sydelle. Who Was Daniel Boone? Ulrich, George, illus. 2006. (Who Was... ? Ser.). 108p. (gr. 2-6). 15.00 *(978-0-7569-6951-6(4))* Perfection Learning Corp.

Kudlinski, Kathleen. Christopher Columbus: Young Explorer. 2005. 199p. (J). lib. bdg. 18.46 *(978-1-4242-1727-4(X))* Fitzgerald Bks.

Lackey, Jennifer. Jacques Cartier: Exploring the St. Lawrence River. 2006. (In the Footsteps of Explorers Ser.). (ENG., Illus.). 32p. (J). (gr. 4-7). pap. *(978-0-7787-2466-7(2))* Crabtree Publishing Co.

Lambert, Lorene & Mickle, Jed. The Forgotten Explorer? The Story of Amerigo Vespucci. 2005. (Who in the World Ser.: 0). (ENG., Illus.). 48p. (gr. 2-4). per. 9.50 *(978-0-9728603-8-3(X),* 86038) Well-Trained Mind Pr.

Landau, Elaine. Celebrating Columbus Day. 2012. (Celebrating Holidays Ser.). 48p. (J). (gr. 3-4). (Illus.). pap. 8.95 *(978-1-59845-400-0(5));* 25.27 *(978-0-7660-4033-5(X))* Enslow Pubs., Inc. (Enslow Elementary).

—Discovering a New World: Would You Sail with Columbus? 2014. (What Would You Do? Ser.). (Illus.). 48p. (J). (gr. 3-4). lib. bdg. 25.27 *(978-0-7660-4222-3(7),* Enslow Elementary) Enslow Pubs., Inc.

Larkin, Tanya. Jacques Marquette & Louis Jolliet: Explorers of the Mississippi. 2009. (Library of Explorers & Exploration Ser.). 112p. (gr. 5-8). 66.50 *(978-1-60853-608-5(4),* Rosen Reference) Rosen Publishing Group, Inc., The.

Leavitt, Amie Jane. Christopher Columbus. 2007. (What's So Great About... ? Ser.). (Illus.). 32p. (J). (gr. 2-4). lib. bdg. 25.70 *(978-1-58415-578-2(7))* Mitchell Lane Pubs., Inc.

Levy, Janey. Mapping America's Westward Expansion: Applying Geographic Tools & Interpreting Maps. 2009. (Critical Thinking in American History Ser.). 48p. (gr. 5-8). 53.00 *(978-1-61512-095-6(5),* Rosen Reference) Rosen Publishing Group, Inc., The.

Macdonald, Fiona. You Wouldn't Want to Sail with Christopher Columbus! (Revised Edition) 2014. (You Wouldn't Want to... Ser.). (ENG.). 32p. (J). lib. bdg. 29.00 *(978-0-531-21177-9(0),* Watts, Franklin) Scholastic Library Publishing.

MacLeod, Elizabeth. Samuel de Champlain. Mantha, John, illus. 2008. (Kids Can Read Ser.). (ENG.). 32p. (J). (gr. 1-3). 14.95 *(978-1-55453-049-6(0));* pap. 3.95 *(978-1-55453-050-2(4))* Kids Can Pr., Ltd. CAN. Dist: Hachette Bk. Group.

Marsh, Carole. Alvar Nunez Cabeza de Vaca:Explorer & Survivor: Explorer & Survivor. 2003. 12p. (gr. k-4). 2.95 *(978-0-635-02135-9(8))* Gallopade International.

—Meriwether Lewis & William Clark: Explorers of the Uncharted West: Explorers of the Uncharted West. 2003. 12p. (gr. k-4). 2.95 *(978-0-635-02133-5(1))* Gallopade International.

Mattern, Joanne. Celebrate Columbus Day. 2006. (Celebrate Holidays Ser.). (Illus.). 104p. (J). (gr. 5-6). lib. bdg. 33.27 *(978-0-7660-2580-6(2))* Enslow Pubs., Inc.

Matthews, Rupert. Conquistadors. 2015. (History's Fearless Fighters Ser.). (ENG., Illus.). 48p. (J). (gr. 5-6). pap. 14.05 *(978-1-4824-3161-2(0))* Stevens, Gareth Publishing LLLP.

Maynard, Charles W. John Wesley Powell: Soldier, Scientist, & Explorer. 2009. (Famous Explorers of the American West Ser.). 24p. (gr. 3-4). 42.50 *(978-1-61512-505-0(1),* PowerKids Pr.) Rosen Publishing Group, Inc., The.

McCormick, Lisa Wade. Christopher Columbus. 2005. (Scholastic News Nonfiction Readers Ser.). (ENG., Illus.). 24p. (J). (gr. 1-2). lib. bdg. 22.00 *(978-0-516-24938-4(X))* Scholastic Library Publishing.

McNeese, Tim. Christopher Columbus & the Discovery of the Americas, Explorers of New Lands. Goetzmann, William H., ed. 2005. (Explorers of New Lands Ser.). (Illus.). 100p. (gr. 5-8). lib. bdg. 30.00 *(978-0-7910-8613-1(5))* Facts On File, Inc.

Micklos, John, Jr. A Wilderness of Experiences - Explorers & American Indians on the Frontier. 2016. (Discovering the New World Ser.). (ENG., Illus.). 48p. (gr. 3-4). lib. bdg. 29.32 *(978-1-5157-1866-6(2))* Capstone Press of Coughlan Cos.

Micklos, John, Jr., et al. Discovering the New World. 2016. (Discovering the New World Ser.). (ENG.). 48p. (gr. 3-4). 114.61 *(978-1-5157-1885-7(9),* Connect) Stone Arch Bks.

Mitchell, Mark. Raising la Belle. Mitchell, Mark, illus. (Professor Wigglestix & the Weather Ser.). (Illus.). 112p. 10.95 *(978-1-57168-703-6(3))* Eakin Pr.

Molzahn, Arlene Bourgeois. Henry Hudson: Explorer of the Hudson River. 2003. (Explorers! Ser.). (Illus.). 48p. (J). lib. bdg. 25.27 *(978-0-7660-2070-2(3))* Enslow Pubs., Inc.

—Ponce de Leon: Explorer of Florida. 2003. (Explorers! Ser.). (Illus.). 48p. (J). lib. bdg. 23.93 *(978-0-7660-2071-9(1))* Enslow Pubs., Inc.

Morganelli, Adrianna. Christopher Columbus: Sailing to a New World. 2005. (In the Footsteps of Explorers Ser.). (ENG., Illus.). 32p. (J). (gr. -1-9). pap. *(978-0-7787-2445-2(X));* lib. bdg. *(978-0-7787-2409-4(3))* Crabtree Publishing Co.

—Samuel de Champlain: From New France to Cape Cod. 2005. (In the Footsteps of Explorers Ser.). (ENG., Illus.). 32p. (J). (gr. 4-5). pap. *(978-0-7787-2450-6(6))* Crabtree Publishing Co.

Mountjoy, Shane. Francisco Coronado & the Seven Cities of Gold. Goetzmann, William H., ed. 2005. (Explorers of New Lands Ser.). (Illus.). 160p. (gr. 5-8). lib. bdg. 30.00 *(978-0-7910-8631-5(3))* Facts On File, Inc.

Murray, Julie. Columbus Day, 1 vol. 2005. (Holidays Ser.). (ENG.). 24p. (gr. k-4). 25.65 *(978-1-59197-587-8(5),* Buddy Bks.) ABDO Publishing Co.

Nagelhout, Ryan. Vasco Núñez de Balboa. 2016. (Spotlight on Explorers & Colonization Ser.). 48p. (J). (gr. 6-6). pap. 11.75 *(978-1-4777-8828-8(X))* Rosen Publishing Group, Inc., The.

Nardo, Don. The European Exploration of America. 2011. (World History Ser.). (Illus.). 122p. (J). 28.95 *(978-1-59935-141-4(2))* Reynolds, Morgan Inc.

—The Spanish Conquistadors. 2009. (World History Ser.). (ENG.). 128p. (J). (gr. 7-10). 34.95 *(978-1-4205-0133-9(X),* Lucent Bks.) Cengage Gale.

Nelson, Robin. Columbus Day. 2009. (First Step Nonfiction - American Holidays Ser.). (J). (gr. k-2). 19.93 *(978-0-7613-4928-0(6))* Lerner Publishing Group.

The New World: Prehistory To 1542. 2010. (Discovering U. S. History Ser.). (Illus.). 128p. (gr. 5-8). 35.00 *(978-1-60413-348-6(1),* Chelsea Hse.) Facts On File, Inc.

Nextext Staff, contrib. by. The Ancient Americas: 30,000 B.C.-A.D.1600. 2004. (Stories in History Ser.). (Illus.). 192p. (gr. 6-12). tchr. ed. *(978-0-618-25525-2(7),* 2-00331) Holt McDougal.

Nichols, Susan. Conquistadors. 2016. (Warriors Around the World Ser.). 00048p. (J). (gr. 5-5). lib. bdg. 26.85 *(978-1-5081-0378-3(X))* Rosen Publishing Group, Inc., The.

O'Brien, Cynthia. Explore with Christopher Columbus. 2014. (ENG., Illus.). 32p. (J). *(978-0-7787-1245-9(1));* pap. *(978-0-7787-1257-2(5))* Crabtree Publishing Co.

—Explore with Ponce de León. 2014. (ENG., Illus.). 32p. (J). *(978-0-7787-1429-3(2))* Crabtree Publishing Co.

—Explore with Samuel de Champlain. 2014. (ENG., Illus.). 32p. (J). *(978-0-7787-1256-5(7));* pap. *(978-0-7787-1260-2(5))* Crabtree Publishing Co.

—Explore with Sieur de la Salle. 2014. (ENG., Illus.). 32p. (J). *(978-0-7787-1430-9(6))* Crabtree Publishing Co.

O'Donnell, Kerri. Explorers in North America: Solving Addition & Subtraction Problems Using Timelines. 2009. (PowerMath Ser.). (ENG., Illus.). 32p. (gr. 4-5). pap. 10.00 *(978-0-8239-8898-3(8),* PowerKids Pr.) Rosen Publishing Group, Inc., The.

Ollhoff, Jim. Christopher Columbus. 2013. (Great Explorers Ser.). 32p. (J). (gr. 5-9). lib. bdg. 27.07 *(978-1-61783-964-1(7),* Abdo & Daughters) ABDO Publishing Co.

—The Conquistadors, 1 vol. 2011. (Hispanic American History Ser.). (ENG., Illus.). 32p. (YA). (gr. 5-9). 27.07 *(978-1-61783-055-6(0))* ABDO Publishing Co.

Opening up North America, 1497-1800, Revised Edition. 2nd rev. ed. 2009. (Discovery & Exploration Ser.). (Illus.). 144p. (gr. 5-8). 35.00 *(978-1-60413-196-3(9),* Chelsea Hse.) Facts On File, Inc.

Otfinoski, Steven. Henry Hudson: In Search of the Northwest Passage. 2006. (Great Explorations Ser.). (Illus.). 80p. (J). (gr. 3-7). lib. bdg. 32.79 *(978-0-7614-2225-9(0),* Benchmark Bks.) Marshall Cavendish Corp.

—Juan Ponce de Leon: Discoverer of Florida. 2004. (Great Explorations Ser.). 80p. (gr. 6). 22.95 *(978-0-7614-1610-4(2),* Benchmark Bks.) Marshall Cavendish Corp.

Owens, Ann-Maureen & Yealland, Jane. Canadian Exploration. Mantha, John, illus. 2008. (Kids Book Of Ser.). (ENG.). 56p. (J). (gr. 3-7). pap. 14.95 *(978-1-55453-257-5(4))* Kids Can Pr., Ltd. CAN. Dist: Hachette Bk. Group.

Parker, Lewis K. French Colonies in the Americas. 2009. (European Colonies in the Americas Ser.). 24p. (gr. 2-2). 42.50 *(978-1-61512-318-6(0),* PowerKids Pr.) Rosen Publishing Group, Inc., The.

—Russian Colonies in the Americas. 2009. (European Colonies in the Americas Ser.). 24p. (gr. 2-2). 42.50 *(978-1-61512-319-3(9),* PowerKids Pr.) Rosen Publishing Group, Inc., The.

—Spanish Colonies in the Americas. 2009. (European Colonies in the Americas Ser.). 24p. (gr. 2-2). 42.50 *(978-1-61512-320-9(2),* PowerKids Pr.) Rosen Publishing Group, Inc., The.

Payment, Simone. La Salle: Claiming the Mississippi River for France. (Library of Explorers & Exploration Ser.). 112p. (gr. 5-8). 2009. 66.50 *(978-1-60853-610-8(6))* 2004. (Illus.). lib. bdg. 34.60 *(978-0-8239-3628-1(7))* Rosen Publishing Group, Inc., The. (Rosen Reference).

Pelleschi, Andrea. Juan Ponce de Leon. 2013. (Jr. Graphic Famous Explorers Ser.). (ENG., Illus.). 24p. (J). (gr. 3-6). pap. 10.60 *(978-1-4777-0131-7(1));* lib. bdg. 25.25 *(978-1-4777-0073-0(0))* Rosen Publishing Group, Inc., The. (PowerKids Pr.).

Peppas, Lynn. Why Francisco Coronado Matters to Texas. 2014. (Illus.). 32p. (J). lib. bdg. 26.25 *(978-1-4777-0909-2(6))* Rosen Publishing Group, Inc., The.

—Why Sieur de La Salle Matters to Texas. 2014. (Illus.). 32p. (J). lib. bdg. 26.25 *(978-1-4777-0917-7(7))* Rosen Publishing Group, Inc., The.

Perritano, John. Colonization & Settlement. 2016. (Illus.). 48p. (J). *(978-1-5105-1284-9(5))* SmartBook Media, Inc.

Peterson, Cris. Birchbark Brigade: A Fur Trade History. 2009. (ENG.). 136p. (J). (gr. 4-18). 18.95 *(978-1-59078-426-6(X),* Calkins Creek) Boyds Mills Pr.

Petrie, Kristin. Christopher Columbus, 1 vol. 2004. (Explorers Set 1 Ser.). (ENG., Illus.). 32p. (gr. k-6). 27.07 *(978-1-59197-595-3(6),* Checkerboard Library) ABDO Publishing Co.

—Daniel Boone, 1 vol. 2004. (Explorers Set 1 Ser.). (ENG.). 32p. (gr. k-6). 27.07 *(978-1-59197-592-2(1),* Checkerboard Library) ABDO Publishing Co.

—Francisco Vasquez de Coronado, 1 vol. 2004. (Explorers Set 1 Ser.). (ENG.). 32p. (gr. k-6). 27.07 *(978-1-59197-597-7(2),* Checkerboard Library) ABDO Publishing Co.

—Henry Hudson, 1 vol. 2007. (Explorers Set 2 Ser.). (ENG., Illus.). 32p. (gr. 4-7). 27.07 *(978-1-59679-741-3(X),* Checkerboard Library) ABDO Publishing Co.

—Hernando de Soto, 1 vol. 2004. (Explorers Set 1 Ser.). (ENG.). 32p. (gr. k-6). 27.07 *(978-1-59197-600-4(6),* Checkerboard Library) ABDO Publishing Co.

—Jacques Cartier, 1 vol. 2004. (Explorers Set 1 Ser.). (ENG., Illus.). 32p. (gr. k-6). 27.07 *(978-1-59197-594-6(8),* Checkerboard Library) ABDO Publishing Co.

—John Cabot, 1 vol. 2004. (Explorers Set 1 Ser.). (ENG.). 32p. (gr. k-6). 27.07 *(978-1-59197-593-9(X),* Checkerboard Library) ABDO Publishing Co.

—Juan Ponce de Leon, 1 vol. 2007. (Explorers Set 2 Ser.). (ENG., Illus.). 32p. (gr. 4-7). 27.07 *(978-1-59679-742-0(8),* Checkerboard Library) ABDO Publishing Co.

—Marquette & Jolliet, 1 vol. 2007. (Explorers Set 2 Ser.). (ENG., Illus.). 32p. (gr. 4-7). 27.07 *(978-1-59679-745-1(2),* Checkerboard Library) ABDO Publishing Co.

—La Salle, 1 vol. 2007. (Explorers Set 2 Ser.). (ENG., Illus.). 32p. (gr. 4-7). 27.07 *(978-1-59679-750-5(9),* Checkerboard Library) ABDO Publishing Co.

—Vasco Núñez de Balboa, 1 vol. 2007. (Explorers Set 2 Ser.). (ENG., Illus.). 32p. (gr. 4-7). 27.07 *(978-1-59679-740-6(1),* Checkerboard Library) ABDO Publishing Co.

Ponto, Joanna. Columbus Day. 2016. (Story of Our Holidays Ser.). (Illus.). 32p. (J). (gr. 3-3). pap. 10.52 *(978-0-7660-7654-9(7))* Enslow Pubs., Inc.

Ramen, Fred. Francisco Pizarro: The Exploration of Peru & the Conquest of the Inca. 2009. (Library of Explorers & Exploration Ser.). 112p. (gr. 5-8). 66.50 *(978-1-60853-603-0(3),* Rosen Reference) Rosen Publishing Group, Inc., The.

Ransom, Candice. Daniel Boone. 2005. (History Maker Biographies Ser.). (ENG., Illus.). 48p. (gr. 3-6). lib. bdg. 27.93 *(978-0-8225-2941-5(6),* Lerner Pubns.) Lerner Publishing Group.

Redmond, Shirley Raye. Lewis & Clark: A Prairie Dog for the President. Manders, John, illus. 2003. (Step into Reading Ser.). 48p. 14.00 *(978-0-7569-1697-8(6))* Perfection Learning Corp.

Reis, Ronald A. Christopher Columbus & the Age of Exploration for Kids: With 21 Activities. 2013. (For Kids Ser.). (ENG., Illus.). 160p. (J). (gr. 4). pap. 16.95 *(978-1-61374-674-5(1))* Chicago Review Pr., Inc.

Rengel, Marian. John Cabot: The Ongoing Search for a Westward Passage to Asia. 2003. (Library of Explorers & Exploration Ser.). (Illus.). 112p. (J). (gr. 5-8). lib. bdg. 34.60 *(978-0-8239-3626-7(0),* Rosen Reference) Rosen Publishing Group, Inc., The.

Rice, Earle. The Life & Times of Erik the Red. 2008. (Biography from Ancient Civilizations Ser.). (Illus.). 48p. (J). (gr. 4-8). lib. bdg. 29.95 *(978-1-58415-701-4(1))* Mitchell Lane Pubs., Inc.

—The Life & Times of Leif Eriksson. 2008. (Biography from Ancient Civilizations Ser.). (Illus.). 48p. (J). (gr. 4-8). lib. bdg. 29.95 *(978-1-58415-702-1(X))* Mitchell Lane Pubs., Inc.

Roberts, Steven. John Cabot. 2013. (Jr. Graphic Famous Explorers Ser.). (ENG., Illus.). 24p. (J). (gr. 3-6). pap. 10.60 *(978-1-4777-0129-4(X));* lib. bdg. 25.25 *(978-1-4777-0072-3(2))* Rosen Publishing Group, Inc., The. (PowerKids Pr.).

Rossi, Ann. Cultures Collide: Native American & Europenas 1492-1700. 2004. (Crossroads America Ser.). (ENG., Illus.). 40p. (J). (gr. 5-9). 21.90 *(978-0-7922-7198-7(X),* National Geographic Children's Bks.) National Geographic Society.

Safari. 2003. (J). per. *(978-1-57657-957-2(3))* Paradise Pr., Inc.

Sanders, Walter. England Explores the Americas. 2005. (J). pap. *(978-1-4108-4611-2(3))* Benchmark Education Co.

—Spain Explores the Americas. 2005. (J). pap. *(978-1-4108-4597-9(4))* Benchmark Education Co.

Shafer, Susan. Ponce de Leon & the Fountain of Youth. 2005. (J). pap. *(978-1-4108-4231-2(2))* Benchmark Education Co.

Shardlow, Tom & Wysotski, Chrissie. Mapping the Wilderness: The Story of David Thompson. 2006. (Stories of Canada Ser.: 9). (ENG., Illus.). 72p. (J). 18.95 *(978-0-929141-85-5(7),* Napoleon & Co.) Dundurn CAN. Dist: Ingram Publisher Services.

Sherman, Josepha. Henry Hudson: English Explorer of the Northwest Passage. (Library of Explorers & Exploration Ser.). 112p. (gr. 5-8). 2009. 66.50 *(978-1-60853-605-4(X))* 2003. (Illus.). (J). lib. bdg. 34.60 *(978-0-8239-3620-5(1))* Rosen Publishing Group, Inc., The. (Rosen Reference).

—Henry Hudson: Exploring the Northwest Passage. 2015. (Incredible Explorers Ser.). (ENG., Illus.). 64p. (J). (gr. 7-7). 34.21 *(978-1-5026-0127-8(3))* Cavendish Square Publishing.

—Samuel de Champlain: Explorer of the Great Lakes Region & Founder of Quebec. 2009. (Library of Explorers & Exploration Ser.). 112p. (gr. 5-8). 66.50 *(978-1-60853-611-5(4),* Rosen Reference) Rosen Publishing Group, Inc., The.

Smalley, Carol Parenzan. Henry Hudson. 2006. (What's So Great About... ? Ser.). (Illus.). 32p. (J). (gr. 2-4). lib. bdg. 25.70 *(978-1-58415-479-2(9))* Mitchell Lane Pubs., Inc.

Smith, Tom. Discovery of the Americas, 1492-1800. 2nd rev. ed. 2009. (Discovery & Exploration Ser.). (Illus.). 136p. (gr. 5-8). 35.00 *(978-1-60413-195-6(0),* Chelsea Hse.) Facts On File, Inc.

Sonneborn, Liz. Pizarro: Conqueror of the Mighty Incas. 2010. (Great Explorers of the World Ser.). (Illus.). 112p. (J). (gr. 7-12). 33.27 *(978-1-59845-128-3(6))* Enslow Pubs., Inc.

Spotlight on Explorers & Colonization: Set 1. 2016. (Spotlight on Explorers & Colonization Ser.). 48p. (gr. 6-6). 381.00 *(978-1-4777-8955-1(3));* pap. 141.00 *(978-1-4994-6413-9(4))* Rosen Publishing Group, Inc., The. (Rosen Young Adult).

Stanley, George Edward. The European Settlement of North America (1492-1754) 2005. (Primary Source History of the United States Ser.). (Illus.). 48p. (gr. 5-12). pap. 14.05 *(978-0-8368-5833-4(6));* lib. bdg. 31.00 *(978-0-8368-5824-2(7))* Stevens, Gareth Publishing LLLP. (Gareth Stevens Secondary Library).

Staunton, Ted. The Northwest Passage. 2007. (Dreadful Truth Ser.). (ENG., Illus.). 96p. (J). (gr. 3-8). *(978-0-88780-735-0(6))* Formac Publishing Co., Ltd.

Stefoff, Rebecca. Exploration & Settlement. 2007. (ENG., Illus.). 96p. (C). (gr. 6-18). lib. bdg. 158.00 *(978-0-7656-8108-9(0),* Y182272) Routledge.

Stein, R. Conrad. The Conquistadors: Building a Spanish Empire in the Americas. 2004. (Proud Heritage: the Hispanic Library). (ENG., Illus.). 40p. (J). (gr. 3-6). 29.93 *(978-1-59296-144-3(4),* 200016) Child's World, Inc., The.

Stuckey, Rachel. Explore with Hernando de Soto. 2016. (Travel with the Great Explorers Ser.). (ENG., Illus.). 32p. (J). (gr. 3-6). *(978-0-7787-2849-8(8))* Crabtree Publishing Co.

—Explore with Lewis & Clark. 2014. (ENG., Illus.). 32p. (J). *(978-0-7787-1247-3(8));* pap. *(978-0-7787-1259-6(1))* Crabtree Publishing Co.

Sutcliffe, Jane. Juan Ponce de Leon. 2005. (History Maker Bios Ser.). (Illus.). 48p. (J). (gr. 3-7). lib. bdg. 26.60 *(978-0-8225-2944-6(0),* Lerner Pubns.) Lerner Publishing Group.

Swanson, Jennifer. Lewis & Clark. 2016. (Spotlight on Explorers & Colonization Ser.). 00048p. (J). (gr. 6-6). pap. 11.75 *(978-1-5081-7237-6(4))* Rosen Publishing Group, Inc., The.

Taylor-Butler, Christine. Explorers of North America. (True Bks.). (ENG., Illus.). 48p. (J). (gr. 3-5). 2008. pap. 6.95 *(978-0-531-14782-5(7))* 2007. lib. bdg. 29.00 *(978-0-531-12632-5(3))* Scholastic Library Publishing. (Children's Pr.).

Toth, Henrietta. Henry Hudson. 2016. (Spotlight on Explorers & Colonization Ser.). 00048p. (J). (gr. 6-6). pap. 11.75 *(978-1-5081-7222-2(6))* Rosen Publishing Group, Inc., The.

Uhl, Xina M. Francisco de Vasquez Coronado. 2016. (Spotlight on Explorers & Colonization Ser.). 00048p. (J). (gr. 6-6). pap. 11.75 *(978-1-5081-7214-7(5))* Rosen Publishing Group, Inc., The.

Van Loon, Hendrik Willem. A Short History of Discovery: From the Earliest Times to the Founding of Colonies in the American Continent. 2007. 132p. per. 16.99 *(978-1-59605-799-9(8))* Cosimo, Inc.

Van Meter, Larry A. Yerba Buena. 2007. (Colonial Settlements in America Ser.). (Illus.). 100p. (YA). (gr. 5-9). lib. bdg. 30.00 *(978-0-7910-9338-2(7))* Facts On File, Inc.

Vietze, Andrew. Samuel de Champlain. 2016. (Spotlight on Explorers & Colonization Ser.). 00048p. (J). (gr. 6-6). 31.75 *(978-1-5081-7230-7(7));* pap. 11.75 *(978-1-5081-7227-7(7))* Rosen Publishing Group, Inc., The.

Wade, Mary Dodson. Christopher Columbus. 2014. (Rookie Biographies(r) Ser.). (ENG., Illus.). 32p. (J). lib. bdg. *(978-0-531-20559-4(2));* pap. 5.95 *(978-0-531-21202-8(5))* Scholastic Library Publishing.

Wade, Mary Dodson & Capstone Press Staff. Christopher Columbus: Famous Explorer, 1 vol. Whigham, Rod & Barnett, Charles, III, illus. 2007. (Graphic Biographies Ser.). (ENG.). 32p. (gr. 3-4). 30.65 *(978-0-7368-6853-2(4),* 1264941, Graphic Library) Capstone Press of Coughlan Cos.

Waldman, Stuart. We Asked for Nothing. McNally, Tom, illus. 2014. (ENG.). 208p. (J). (gr. 5-7). pap. 8.95 *(978-1-931414-50-0(5),* 9781931414500) Mikaya Pr.

Ward, Nancy. Sir Walter Raleigh: Founding the Virginia Colony. 2006. (In the Footsteps of Explorers Ser.). (ENG., Illus.). 32p. (J). (gr. 4-7). lib. bdg. *(978-0-7787-2424-7(7),* 1253445) Crabtree Publishing Co.

Warrick, Karen Clemens. The Perilous Search for the Fabled Northwest Passage in American History. 2004. (In American History Ser.). (Illus.). 128p. (J). lib. bdg. 26.60 *(978-0-7660-2148-8(3))* Enslow Pubs., Inc.

Waxman, Laura Hamilton. A Journey with Henry Hudson. 2017. (Primary Source Explorers Ser.). (ENG.). 40p. (J). (gr. 3-5). 30.65 *(978-1-5124-0774-7(7))* Lerner Publishing Group.

—A Journey with Juan Ponce de León. 2017. (Primary Source Explorers Ser.). (ENG.). 40p. (J). (gr. 3-5). 30.65 *(978-1-5124-0776-1(3))* Lerner Publishing Group.

Weaver, Janice. Hudson. Craig, David, illus. 2010. (ENG.). 48p. (J). (gr. 3-7). 22.95 *(978-0-88776-814-9(8),* Tundra Bks.) Tundra Bks. CAN. Dist: Penguin Random Hse. LLC.

Webb, Sarah Powers. When They Came: A Chronology of North American Exploration. 2016. (Discovering the New World Ser.). (ENG., Illus.). 48p. (gr. 3-4). lib. bdg. 29.32 *(978-1-5157-1867-3(0),* Connect) Stone Arch Bks.

Weisberg, Barbara & Haley, Alex. Coronado's Golden Quest. Eagle, Mike, illus. 2009. (Steck-Vaughn Stories of America Ser.). (ENG.). 88p. (gr. 3-8). pap. 14.20 *(978-0-8114-8072-7(0))* Houghton Mifflin Harcourt Publishing Co.

West, David. Christopher Columbus: The Life of a Master Navigator & Explorer. 2009. (Graphic Nonfiction Biographies Ser.). (ENG.). 48p. (YA). (gr. 4-5). 58.50 *(978-1-61513-014-6(4),* Rosen Reference) Rosen Publishing Group, Inc., The.

West, David & Gaff, Jackie. Christopher Columbus: The Life of a Master Navigator & Explorer. 2005. (Graphic Nonfiction Biographies Ser.). (ENG., Illus.). 48p. (J). (gr. 4-7). lib. bdg. 31.95 *(978-1-4042-0243-6(9))* Rosen Publishing Group, Inc., The.

Whiting, Jim. The Life & Times of Hernando Cortes. 2006. (Profiles in American History Ser.). (Illus.). 48p. (J). (gr. 3-7). lib. bdg. 29.95 *(978-1-58415-449-5(7))* Mitchell Lane Pubs., Inc.

Wirkner, Linda. Learning about the Settlement of the Americas with Graphic Organizers. 2006. (Graphic Organizers in Science & Social Studies Ser.). (ENG.). 24p. (gr. 4-6). pap. 8.25 *(978-1-4042-5057-4(3),* Rosen Classroom) Rosen Publishing Group, Inc., The.

Woog, Adam. Jacques Cartier. 2009. (Great Explorers Ser.). (Illus.). 112p. (gr. 6-12). 30.00 *(978-1-60413-430-8(5),* Chelsea Hse.) Facts On File, Inc.

Worth, Richard. Ponce de Leon & the Age of Spanish Exploration in World History. 2003. (In World History Ser.). (Illus.). 112p. (J). (gr. 5-12). lib. bdg. 26.60 *(978-0-7660-1940-9(3))* Enslow Pubs., Inc.

Wyatt, Valerie. Who Discovered America? Woo, Howie, illus. 2008. (ENG.). 40p. (J). (gr. 3-7). 17.95 *(978-1-55453-128-8(4));* pap. 8.95 *(978-1-55453-129-5(2))* Kids Can Pr., Ltd. CAN. Dist: Hachette Bk. Group.

Young, Jeff C. Henry Hudson: Discoverer of the Hudson River. 2009. (Great Explorers of the World Ser.). (Illus.). 112p. (J). (gr. 7-12). lib. bdg. 33.27 *(978-1-59845-123-8(5))* Enslow Pubs., Inc.

—Hernando de Soto: Spanish Conquistador in the Americas. 2009. (Great Explorers of the World Ser.). (Illus.). 112p. (J). (gr. 7-12). lib. bdg. 33.27 *(978-1-59845-104-7(9))* Enslow Pubs., Inc.

AMERICA—DISCOVERY AND EXPLORATION—FICTION

Adler, David A. & Adler, Michael S. A Picture Book of Daniel Boone. Collins, Matt, illus. 2013. (ENG.). 32p. (J). (gr. -1-3). 17.95 *(978-0-8234-2748-2(X))* Holiday Hse., Inc.

Coatsworth, Elizabeth. Door to the North: A Saga of 14th Century America. Chapman, Frederick T., illus. 2013. 245p. (YA). pap. 15.95 *(978-1-932350-39-5(X))* Bethlehem Bks.

Dorris, Michael. Morning Girl. 2005. 80p. (J). (gr. 3-18). 20.50 *(978-0-8446-7272-4(6),* 3587) Smith, Peter Pub., Inc.

Duble, Kathleen Benner. Quest. 2008. (ENG.). 256p. (J). (gr. 5-9). 17.99 *(978-1-4169-3386-1(7),* McElderry, Margaret K. Bks.) McElderry, Margaret K. Bks.

Mangum, Ariana. Carlos, the Mouse Who Discovered Americ. 2008. 272p. pap. 17.99 *(978-1-4343-6344-2(9))* AuthorHouse.

Mattern, Joanne. Leif Eriksson: Viking Explorer. 2004. (Explorers! Ser.). (Illus.). 48p. (J). lib. bdg. 25.27 *(978-0-7660-2146-4(7))* Enslow Pubs., Inc.

McCall, Edith. Heroes of American Explorations: Frontiers of America Series. Borja, Robert, illus. 2011. 124p. 40.95 *(978-1-258-03255-5(4))* Literary Licensing, LLC.

McCall, Edith S. Adventures of the American Colonies. Rogers, Carol, illus. 2011. 126p. 40.95 *(978-1-258-06470-9(7))* Literary Licensing, LLC.

Whittier, Mary Ann. Tales from 1492. (YA). (gr. 7-18). lib. bdg. 19.99 *(978-0-89824-981-1(3))* Royal Fireworks Publishing Co.

AMERICAN ABORIGINES

see Indians of North America; Indians of South America

AMERICAN ARTISTS

see Artists, American

AMERICAN AUTHORS

see Authors, American

AMERICAN BISON

Here are entered works on the American buffalo. Works on buffaloes of the eastern hemisphere are entered under Buffaloes.

Arnold, Quinn M. Bison. 2016. (Illus.). 24p. (J). *(978-1-60818-795-9(0),* Creative Education) Creative Co., The.

Beer, Amy-Jane. Bison. 2008. (Nature's Children Ser.). (Illus.). 52p. (J). *(978-0-7172-6249-6(9))* Grolier, Ltd.

Berman, Ruth. American Bison. rev. ed. 2008. (Nature Watch Ser.). (ENG., Illus.). 48p. (gr. 4-8). 27.93 *(978-0-8225-7513-9(2),* Lerner Pubns.) Lerner Publishing Group.

Bowman, Chris. American Bison. 2015. (North American Animals Ser.). (ENG., Illus.). 24p. (J). (gr. k-3). lib. bdg. 25.95 *(978-1-62617-184-8(X),* Blastoff! Readers) Bellwether Media.

Bruchac, Joseph. Buffalo Song. Farnsworth, Bill, illus. 2008. (J). Lee & Low Bks., Inc.

—Buffalo Song. Farnsworth, Bill, illus. 2013. (ENG.). 40p. (C). pap. 15.95 *(978-1-60060-990-9(2))* National Geographic School Publishing, Inc.

Carr, Aaron. Bison. 2014. (Illus.). 24p. (J). *(978-1-62127-230-4(3))* Weigl Pubs., Inc.

Cimarusti, Marie Torres & George, Jean Craighead. The Buffalo Are Back. Peterson, Stephanie & Minor, Wendell, illus. 2010. (ENG.). 32p. (J). (gr. k-3). 16.99 *(978-0-525-42215-0(3),* Dutton Books for Young Readers) Penguin Young Readers Group.

Dyan, Penelope. The Comeback Kids — Book 10 — The American Bison. Weigand, John, photos by. 2012. (Illus.). 34p. pap. 14.95 *(978-1-61477-063-3(8))* Bellissima Publishing, LLC.

Elston, Heidi M. D. Buffaloes: Level 1. Keimig, Candice, illus. 2014. (Magic Readers Ser.). (ENG.). 24p. (J). (gr. 5-9). 24.21 *(978-1-62402-060-5(7))* ABDO Publishing Co.

—Buffaloes Eat & Grow: Level 2. Keimig, Candice, illus. 2014. (Magic Readers Ser.). (ENG.). 24p. (J). (gr. 5-9). 24.21 *(978-1-62402-061-2(5))* ABDO Publishing Co.

—Buffaloes on the Prairie: Level 3. Keimig, Candice, illus. 2014. (Magic Readers Ser.). (ENG.). 24p. (J). (gr. 5-9). 24.21 *(978-1-62402-062-9(3))* ABDO Publishing Co.

Gish, Melissa. Bison. 2011. (Illus.). 46p. (J). 35.65 *(978-1-60818-077-6(8),* Creative Education) Creative Co., The.

Grant, Debbie. American Bison. 2005. (Voices Reading Ser.). (Illus.). 32p. (J). pap. *(978-0-7367-4526-0(2))* Zaner-Bloser, Inc.

Graubart, Norman D. Bison in American History. 2014. (How Animals Shaped History Ser.). (Illus.). 24p. (J). (gr. k-5). 23.60 *(978-1-4777-6757-3(6),* PowerKids Pr.) Rosen Publishing Group, Inc., The.

Herrington, Lisa M. Totally Fierce Animals. 2017. (Rookie Amazing America(tm) Ser.). (ENG., Illus.). 32p. (J). pap. 5.95 *(978-0-531-22590-5(9),* Children's Pr.) Scholastic Library Publishing.

Hirsch, Rebecca. Buffalo Migration. 2012. (Animal Migrations Ser.). (ENG., Illus.). 32p. (J). (gr. 2-5). lib. bdg. 29.93 *(978-1-60973-617-0(6),* 201194) Child's World, Inc., The.

Omoth, Tyler. American Bison. 2017. (Animals of North America (paperback) Ser.). (ENG., Illus.). 32p. (J). (gr. 3-5). pap. 9.95 ***(978-1-63517-085-6(0),*** Focus Readers) North Star Editions.

Patent, Dorothy Hinshaw. Camas & Sage: A Story of Bison Life on the Prairie, 1 vol. Wald, Christina, illus. 2015. (ENG.). 48p. (J). pap. *(978-0-87842-641-6(8))* Mountain Pr. Publishing Co., Inc.

Perry, Phyllis J. Buffalo. 2005. (Animals Animals Ser.). (Illus.). 48p. (gr. 3-7). lib. bdg. 29.93 *(978-0-7614-1866-5(0),* Benchmark Bks.) Marshall Cavendish Corp.

Potts, Steve. American Bison, 1 vol. 2012. (North American Animals Ser.). (ENG.). 24p. (gr. k-1). pap. 7.29 *(978-1-4296-7920-6(4));* pap. 41.70 *(978-1-4296-8357-9(0));* (Illus.). lib. bdg. 26.65 *(978-1-4296-7702-8(3))* Capstone Press of Coughlan Cos. (Pebble Plus).

Randolph, Ryan P. Following the Great Herds: The Plains Indians & the American Buffalo. (Library of the Westward Expansion Ser.). 24p. 2009. (gr. 3-4). 42.50 *(978-1-60853-934-5(2))* 2003. (Illus.). (J). lib. bdg. 22.60 *(978-0-8239-6296-9(2))* Rosen Publishing Group, Inc., The. (PowerKids Pr.).

Somervill, Barbara A. American Bison. 2007. (21st Century Skills Library: Road to Recovery Ser.). (ENG., Illus.). 32p. (gr. 4-8). lib. bdg. 29.93 *(978-1-60279-031-5(0),* 200077) Cherry Lake Publishing.

Stockland, Patricia M. In the Buffalo Pasture, 1 vol. Ouren, Todd, illus. 2009. (Barnyard Buddies Set 2 Ser.). (ENG.). 24p. (gr. -1-2). 27.07 *(978-1-60270-641-5(7),* Looking Glass Library- Nonfiction) Magic Wagon.

Tomljanovic, Tatiana. Bison. 2010. (Backyard Animals Ser.). (Illus.). 24p. (gr. 2-4). (J). pap. 11.95 *(978-1-60596-956-5(7));* (YA). lib. bdg. 25.70 *(978-1-60596-955-8(9))* Weigl Pubs., Inc.

AMERICAN CIVIL WAR, 1861-1865

see United States—History—Civil War, 1861-1865

AMERICAN COLONIES

see United States—History—Colonial Period, ca. 1600-1775

AMERICAN DRAMA—COLLECTIONS

Marx, Pamela. Practical Plays: Grades 1-5. Moore, Cyd, illus. 2nd rev. ed. 2007. 170p. (J). (gr. 1-6). per. 17.95 *(978-1-59647-196-2(4))* Good Year Bks.

Messer, Kimberly. Patriotic Program Builder: Creative Resources for Program Directors. 2005. (ENG.). 36p. pap. 5.99 *(978-0-8341-7408-5(1),* MP-506) Lillenas Publishing Co.

AMERICAN DRAMA—HISTORY AND CRITICISM

Blair, Cathy. About 100 Years of American Musical Theatre in about 100 Minutes: Ten Short Units Covering Broadway Shows from 1900-2000 (CD Enclosed) 2006. (J). 29.95 *(978-0-89328-244-8(8))* Heritage Music Pr.

Hermann, Spring. A Student's Guide to Tennessee Williams. 2007. (Understanding Literature Ser.). (Illus.). 160p. (YA). (gr. 8-12). lib. bdg. 29.27 *(978-0-7660-2706-0(6))* Enslow Pubs., Inc.

Wiener, Gary. Gender in Lorraine Hansberry's a Raisin in the Sun. 2011. (Social Issues in Literature Ser.). (ENG.). 224p. (gr. 12-12). pap. 32.00 *(978-0-7377-5023-2(5));* (Illus.). 40.95 *(978-0-7377-5022-5(7))* Cengage Gale. (Greenhaven Pr., Inc.).

AMERICAN ESSAYS—COLLECTIONS

Why Is Your Best Friend Your Best Friend. 2006. (YA). per. 16.95 *(978-0-9661256-7-2(3))* Youth Communication - New York Center.

AMERICAN FICTION—HISTORY AND CRITICISM

Angel, Ann. A Reader's Guide to Sandra Cisneros's the House on Mango Street. 2010. (Multicultural Literature Ser.). (Illus.). 128p. (YA). 33.27 *(978-0-7660-3167-8(5))* Enslow Pubs., Inc.

Bloom, Harold. A Farewell to Arms - Ernest Hemingway. 2nd rev. ed. 2009. (Modern Critical Interpretations Ser.). 244p. (C). (gr. 9). 45.00 *(978-0-7910-9624-6(6),* Chelsea Hse.) Facts On File, Inc.

Bloom, Harold, ed. Harper Lee's To Kill a Mockingbird. 2nd rev. ed. 2006. (Bloom's Modern Critical Interpretations Ser.). 216p. (C). (gr. 9-18). lib. bdg. 45.00 *(978-0-7910-9308-5(5),* Chelsea Hse.) Facts On File, Inc.

—Herman Melville's Moby-Dick. 2nd rev. ed. 2007. (Bloom's Modern Critical Interpretations Ser.). 256p. (C). (gr. 9-12). 45.00 *(978-0-7910-9363-4(8),* Chelsea Hse.) Facts On File, Inc.

—Miss Lonelyhearts. 2005. (Bloom's Modern Critical Interpretations Ser.). (Illus.). 144p. (C). (gr. 9-13). 45.00 *(978-0-7910-8123-5(0),* Chelsea Hse.) Facts On File, Inc.

Bryfonski, Dedria. Political Issues in J. K. Rowling's Harry Potter Series. 2008. (Social Issues in Literature Ser.). (ENG., Illus.). 224p. (gr. 10-12). 46.40 *(978-0-7377-4022-6(1),* LML02109-239997, Greenhaven Pr., Inc.) Cengage Gale.

Hinds, Maurene J. A Reader's Guide to Richard Wright's Black Boy. 2009. (Multicultural Literature Ser.). (Illus.). 128p. (YA). (gr. 9-12). lib. bdg. 33.27 *(978-0-7660-3165-4(9))* Enslow Pubs., Inc.

Jones, Jen. A Reader's Guide to Gary Soto's Taking Sides. 2010. (Multicultural Literature Ser.). (Illus.). 128p. (YA). (gr. 8-18). 33.27 *(978-0-7660-3168-5(3))* Enslow Pubs., Inc.

Litwin, Laura Baskes. A Reader's Guide to Zora Neale Hurston's Their Eyes Were Watching God. 2010. (Multicultural Literature Ser.). (Illus.). 128p. (YA). (gr. 8-18). 33.27 *(978-0-7660-3164-7(0))* Enslow Pubs., Inc.

McArthur, Debra. A Student's Guide to Edgar Allan Poe. 2006. (Understanding Literature Ser.). (Illus.). 160p. (YA). (gr. 8-12). lib. bdg. 27.93 *(978-0-7660-2437-3(7))* Enslow Pubs., Inc.

A Prayer for Owen Meany: Response Journal. 2003. 28p. (YA). *(978-1-58049-982-8(1),* RJ82) Prestwick Hse., Inc.

AMERICAN INDIANS

see Indians; Indians of North America; Indians of South America

AMERICAN LITERATURE

Crow, Anne & Miller, Arthur. Death of a Salesman. 2011. (Philip Allan Literature Guide for A-Level Ser.). (Illus.). 96p. (gr. 10-12). pap. 39.50 *(978-1-4441-2158-2(8))* Hodder Education Group GBR. Dist: Trans-Atlantic Pubns., Inc.

Dandelion & Other Stories: Individual Title, 6 packs. (Story Steps Ser.). (gr. k-2). 48.00 *(978-0-7635-9838-9(0))* Rigby Education.

Johnson, Claudia Durst. Race in the Poetry of Langston Hughes. Greenhaven Press Editors, ed. 2013. (Social Issues in Literature Ser.). (ENG., Illus.). 224p. (gr. 10-12). pap. 32.00 *(978-0-7377-6981-4(5));* lib. bdg. 46.40 *(978-0-7377-6980-7(7))* Cengage Gale. (Greenhaven Pr., Inc.).

Martz, Sandra, ed. When I Am an Old Woman I Shall Wear Purple: Petite Version. 2nd gif. rev. ed. 2006. (Illus.). 64p. (C). pap. 47.70 *(978-1-57601-093-8(7))* Nodin Pr.

Publishers, Chelsea House, creator. Decades of American History Set. 2005. (Decades of American History Ser.). (gr. 5-8). 350.00 *(978-0-8160-6489-2(X))* Facts On File, Inc.

Ray, Deborah Kogan. Paiute Princess: The Story of Sarah Winnemucca, 1 vol. Ray, Deborah Kogan, illus. 2012. (ENG., Illus.). 48p. (J). (gr. 3-7). 17.99 *(978-0-374-39897-2(6),* 9780374398972, Farrar, Straus & Giroux (BYR)) Farrar, Straus & Giroux.

Saddleback Educational Publishing Staff, ed. Adventures of Huckleberry Finn. 2011. (Timeless Classics Ser.). (ENG.). 48p. (YA). (gr. 9-12). pupil's gde. ed. 19.95 incl. cd-rom *(978-1-61651-125-8(7))* Saddleback Educational Publishing, Inc.

—Adventures of Tom Sawyer. 2011. (Timeless Classics Ser.). (ENG.). 48p. (YA). (gr. 9-12). pupil's gde. ed. 19.95 incl. cd-rom *(978-1-61651-126-5(5))* Saddleback Educational Publishing, Inc.

—A Call of the Wild. 2011. (Timeless Classics Ser.). (ENG.). 48p. (YA). (gr. 9-12). pupil's gde. ed. 19.95 incl. cd-rom *(978-1-61651-128-9(1))* Saddleback Educational Publishing, Inc.

—The Jungle Book. 2011. (Timeless Classics Ser.). (ENG.). 48p. (YA). (gr. 9-12). pupil's gde. ed. 19.95 incl. cd-rom *(978-1-61651-140-1(0))* Saddleback Educational Publishing, Inc.

—The Last of the Mohicans. 2011. (Timeless Classics Ser.). (ENG.). 48p. (YA). (gr. 9-12). pupil's gde. ed. 19.95 incl. cd-rom *(978-1-61651-142-5(7))* Saddleback Educational Publishing, Inc.

—Moby Dick. 2011. (Timeless Classics Ser.). (ENG.). 48p. (YA). (gr. 9-12). cd-rom 19.95 *(978-1-61651-144-9(3))* Saddleback Educational Publishing, Inc.

—Prince & the Pauper. 2011. (Timeless Classics Ser.). (ENG.). 48p. (YA). (gr. 9-12). pupil's gde. ed. 19.95 incl. cd-rom *(978-1-61651-147-0(8))* Saddleback Educational Publishing, Inc.

—Scarlet Letter. 2011. (Timeless Classics Ser.). (ENG.). 48p. (YA). (gr. 9-12). pupil's gde. ed. 19.95 incl. cd-rom *(978-1-61651-150-0(8))* Saddleback Educational Publishing, Inc.

AMERICAN LITERATURE—AFRICAN AMERICAN AUTHORS

see also African American Authors

Currie, Stephen. African-American Literature. 2011. (Lucent Library of Black History Ser.). 128p. (J). lib. bdg. 34.80 *(978-1-4205-0383-8(9),* Lucent Bks.) Cengage Gale.

Herringshaw, DeAnn. The Harlem Renaissance, 1 vol. 2011. (Essential Events Set 7 Ser.). (ENG., Illus.). 112p. (J). (gr. 6-12). lib. bdg. 35.64 *(978-1-61783-101-0(8))* ABDO Publishing Co.

Mangrum, Allison. African American Writers Who Inspired Change. 2005. (Illus.). 79p. 17.00 *(978-1-55501-650-0(2))* Ballard & Tighe Pubs.

Price, Hope Lynne. The Jump at the Sun Treasury: An African American Picture Book Collection. Collier, Bryan, illus. 2004. 205p. (J). (gr. 4-8). reprint ed. 17.00 *(978-0-7567-7328-1(8))* DIANE Publishing Co.

Samuels, Wilfred D. Encyclopedia of African-American Literature. Woodard, Loretta Gilchrist & Guzzio, Tracie Church, eds. 2007. (Encyclopedia of Multi-Cultural Literature Ser.). 448p. (C). (gr. 9). 75.00 *(978-0-8160-5073-4(2))* Facts On File, Inc.

AMERICAN LITERATURE—BIBLIOGRAPHY

Crosetto, Alice & Garcha, Rajinder. Native North Americans in Literature for Youth: A Selective Annotated Bibliography for K-12. 2013. (Literature for Youth Ser.: 14). (ENG.). 286p. 110.00 *(978-0-8108-9189-0(1))* Scarecrow Pr., Inc.

Marcus, Leonard S., ed. Funny Business: Conversations with Writers of Comedy. 2009. (ENG., Illus.). 224p. (J). (gr. 5-18). 24.99 *(978-0-7636-3254-0(6))* Candlewick Pr.

AMERICAN LITERATURE—BIOGRAPHY

see Authors, American

AMERICAN LITERATURE—COLLECTIONS

Cofer, Judith Ortiz, ed. Riding Low on the Streets of Gold: Latino Literature for Young Adults. 2003. (Illus.). 192p. (J). pap. 14.95 *(978-1-55885-380-5(4),* Piñata Books) Arte Publico Pr.

The Collector's Anthology. (Illus.). 48.50 *(978-0-8359-0100-0(9))* Globe Fearon Educational Publishing.

Dureke, Chidinma & Dureke, Angel. Arts, Poems & Stories of the Heart. 2003. (Illus.). 70p. (YA). pap. 9.95 *(978-0-9701144-8-8(6))* Jahs Publishing Group.

Haynes, David & Landsman, Julie, eds. Welcome to Your Life: Writings for the Heart of Young America. tchr. ed. 4.95 *(978-1-57131-291-4(9))* Milkweed Editions.

Lynn, Steve & Rogers, Aida, eds. Writing South Carolina. 2015. (Young Palmetto Bks.). (ENG.). 96p. (YA). pap. 14.95 *(978-1-61117-519-6(4))* Univ. of South Carolina Pr.

Milkweed Editions Staff. The South Atlantic Coast & Piedmont: A Literary Field Guide. St. Antoine, Sara, ed. Nicholson, Trudy & Mirocha, Paul, illus. 2006. (Stories from Where We Live Ser.). (ENG.). 256p. (J). (gr. 4-7). per. 10.95 *(978-1-57131-664-6(7))* Milkweed Editions.

AMERICAN LITERATURE—HISTORY AND CRITICISM

Abrams, Dennis. S. E. Hinton. 2009. (Who Wrote That? Ser.). (Illus.). 104p. (gr. 6-12). 35.00 *(978-1-60413-088-1(1),* Chelsea Hse.) Facts On File, Inc.

American Literature, 6 vols., Set. 2004. (Illus.). (YA). (gr. 9-18). stu. ed., wbk. ed. 38.95 *(978-0-7403-0134-6(9),* EL9415, Lifepac) Alpha Omega Pubns., Inc.

Bickerstaff, Linda. The Red Badge of Courage & the Civil War. 2009. (Looking at Literature Through Primary Sources Ser.). 64p. (gr. 5-8). 58.50 *(978-1-61514-307-8(6))* Rosen Publishing Group, Inc., The.

Bloom, Harold, ed. The House on Mango Street - Sandra Cisneros. 2009. (Bloom's Modern Critical Interpretations Ser.). 192p. (C). (gr. 9-18). 45.00 *(978-1-60413-586-2(7),* Chelsea Hse.) Facts On File, Inc.

—John Knowles's a Separate Peace. 2008. (Bloom's Guides). 162p. (YA). (gr. 9-12). 30.00 *(978-0-7910-9785-4(4))* Facts On File, Inc.

—John Steinbeck's of Mice & Men. 2006. (Bloom's Guides). 80p. (YA). (gr. 9-12). lib. bdg. 30.00 *(978-0-7910-8581-3(3))* Facts On File, Inc.

—Long Day's Journey into Night - Eugene O'Neill, New Edition. 2nd rev. ed. 2009. (Bloom's Modern Critical Interpretations Ser.). 248p. (C). (gr. 9-18). 45.00 *(978-1-60413-390-5(2),* Chelsea Hse.) Facts On File, Inc.

Bloom, Harold, ed. & intro. Sylvia Plath's The Bell Jar. Bloom, Harold, intro. 2009. (Bloom's Guides). 176p. (C). (gr. 9-18). 30.00 *(978-1-60413-203-8(5),* Chelsea Hse.) Facts On File, Inc.

Bloom, Harold, intro. Nick Adams. 2004. (Bloom's Major Literary Characters Ser.). (Illus.). 177p. (C). (gr. 9-13). 40.00 *(978-0-7910-7885-3(X),* Chelsea Hse.) Facts On File, Inc.

Bloom, Harold & Hayes, Kevin J., eds. Benjamin Franklin. 2008. (Bloom's Classic Critical Views Ser.). 264p. (YA). (gr. 9-12). 45.00 *(978-1-60413-135-2(7))* Facts On File, Inc.

Bodden, Valerie. Poetry Basics - Nursery Rhymes. 2009. (Poetry Basics Ser.). 32p. 19.95 *(978-1-58341-778-2(8),* Creative Education) Creative Co., The.

Borus, Audrey. Reading & Interpreting the Works of Amy Tan. 2016. (Lit Crit Guides). (Illus.). 176p. (J). (gr. 6-6). 39.93 *(978-0-7660-7916-8(3))* Enslow Pubs., Inc.

Clare, Cassandra, ed. Shadowhunters & Downworlders: A Mortal Instruments Reader. 2013. (ENG.). 256p. (J). (gr. 6). pap. 12.95 *(978-1-937856-22-9(4))* BenBella Bks.

Clinton, Greg. Reading & Interpreting the Works of Cormac McCarthy. 2016. (Lit Crit Guides). 176p. (gr. 6-6). 39.93 *(978-0-7660-7915-1(5))* Enslow Pubs., Inc.

Collins, Carolyn Strom & Eriksson, Christina Wyss. Inside the Secret Garden: A Treasury of Crafts, Recipes, & Activities. Tudor, Tasha, illus. 2004. 130p. (J). (gr. 2-8). reprint ed. 25.00 *(978-0-7567-7630-5(9))* DIANE Publishing Co.

Combs, Maggie. How to Analyze the Works of F. Scott Fitzgerald, 1 vol. 2011. (Essential Critiques Set 2 Ser.). (ENG., Illus.). 112p. (J). (gr. 6-12). lib. bdg. 35.64 *(978-1-61783-092-1(5))* ABDO Publishing Co.

Crayton, Lisa A. Reading & Interpreting the Works of Alice Walker. 2016. (Lit Crit Guides). (Illus.). 176p. (J). 39.93 *(978-0-7660-8359-2(4))* Enslow Pubs., Inc.

Dunkleberger, Amy. A Student's Guide to Arthur Miller. 2005. (Understanding Literature Ser.). (Illus.). 160p. (YA). (gr. 7-13). lib. bdg. 29.27 *(978-0-7660-2432-8(6))* Enslow Pubs., Inc.

Hinds, Maurene J. How to Analyze the Works of Toni Morrison, 1 vol. 2012. (Essential Critiques Set 3 Ser.). (ENG.). 112p. (J). (gr. 6-12). lib. bdg. 35.64 *(978-1-61783-458-5(0),* Essential Library) ABDO Publishing Co.

Holt, Rinehart and Winston Staff. Elements of Literature: Family Involvement Activities. 5th ed. 2003. (SPA & ENG., Illus.). pap. 38.80 *(978-0-03-073854-8(7))* Holt McDougal.

—Elements of Literature: Supporting Instructions. 5th ed. 2003. (SPA.). pap. 29.20 *(978-0-03-073826-5(1));* pap. 29.20 *(978-0-03-073824-1(5));* (Illus.). pap. 29.20 *(978-0-03-073823-4(7))* Holt McDougal.

—Elements of Literature, Grade 6: Holt Reader. 4th ed. 2003. pap., tchr. ed. 23.20 *(978-0-03-068398-5(X))* Holt McDougal.

—Elements of Literature, Grade 7: Holt Reader. 5th ed. 2003. pap., tchr. ed. 23.20 *(978-0-03-068399-2(8))* Holt McDougal.

—Elements of Literature, Grade 8: Holt Reader. 5th ed. 2003. pap., tchr. ed. 23.20 *(978-0-03-068401-2(3))* Holt McDougal.
Ishizuka, Kathy. John Grisham: Best-Selling Author. 2003. (People to Know Ser.). (Illus.). 112p. (J). lib. bdg. 26.60 *(978-0-7660-2102-0(5))* Enslow Pubs., Inc.
Johnson, Claudia, ed. Women's Issues in Nathaniel Hawthorne's The Scarlett Letter. 2008. (Social Issues in Literature Ser.). (ENG., Illus.). 224p. (gr. 10-12). 46.40 *(978-0-7377-4262-6(3),* LML02109-243172); pap. 32.00 *(978-0-7377-4263-3(1),* LML02109-243176) Cengage Gale. (Greenhaven Pr., Inc.).
Llanas, Sheila Griffin. How to Analyze the Works of Suzanne Collins, 1 vol. 2012. (Essential Critiques Set 3 Ser.). (ENG.). 112p. (J). (gr. 6-12). lib. bdg. 35.64 *(978-1-61783-456-1(4),* Essential Library) ABDO Publishing Co.
Owen, James A., ed. Secrets of the Dragon Riders: Your Favorite Authors on Christopher Paolini's Inheritance Cycle: Completely Unauthorized. 2010. (ENG., Illus.). 192p. (J). (gr. 7-11). pap. 12.95 *(978-1-933771-97-7(6))* BenBella Bks.
Peterson-Hilleque, Victoria & Llanas, Sheila Griffin. How to Analyze the Works of Sylvia Plath, 1 vol. 2012. (Essential Critiques Set 3 Ser.). (ENG.). 112p. (J). (gr. 6-12). lib. bdg. 35.64 *(978-1-61783-457-8(2),* Essential Library) ABDO Publishing Co.
Riordan, Rick, ed. Demigods & Monsters: Your Favorite Authors on Rick Riordan's Percy Jackson & the Olympians Series. rev. ed. 2013. (ENG.). 288p. (J). (gr. 5). pap. 12.95 *(978-1-937856-36-6(4))* BenBella Bks.
Saddleback Educational Publishing Staff, ed. White Fang. 2011. (Timeless Classics Ser.). (ENG.). 48p. (YA). (gr. 9-12). pupil's gde. ed. 19.95 incl. cd-rom *(978-1-61651-158-6(3))* Saddleback Educational Publishing, Inc.
Schmermund, Elizabeth. Reading & Interpreting the Works of Harper Lee. 2016. (Lit Crit Guides). 176p. (gr. 6-6). 39.93 *(978-0-7660-7914-4(7))* Enslow Pubs., Inc.
Stobaugh, James. American Literature Student. 2005. (Broadman & Holman Literature Ser.). 368p. stu. ed. 24.99 *(978-0-8054-5900-5(6))* B&H Publishing Group.
Welsch, Gabe. Philip Roth. 2003. (Bloom's Modern Critical Views Ser.). (Illus.). 200p. (C). (gr. 9-13). 45.00 *(978-0-7910-7446-6(3),* Chelsea Hse.) Facts On File, Inc.

AMERICAN MUSEUM OF NATURAL HISTORY

Wynne, Patricia J. Exploring the American Museum of Natural History: A Children's Guide with Pictures to Color. 2004. (Dover Nature Coloring Book Ser.). (ENG., Illus.). 32p. (J). (gr. 3-8). pap. 4.99 *(978-0-486-43714-9(0))* Dover Pubns., Inc.

AMERICAN MUSIC

see Music, American

AMERICAN MUSICIANS

see Musicians—United States

AMERICAN NATIONAL RED CROSS

Crompton, Samuel Williard. Clara Barton. 2009. (Women of Achievement Ser.). (Illus.). 144p. (J). (gr. 6-12). 35.00 *(978-1-60413-492-6(5),* Chelsea Hse.) Facts On File, Inc.
Devillier, Christy. Clara Barton, 1 vol. 2004. (First Biographies Set Iv Ser.). (ENG., Illus.). 32p. (gr. k-4). 27.07 *(978-1-59197-511-3(5),* Buddy Bks.) ABDO Publishing Co.
Ditchfield, Christin. Clara Barton: Founder of the American Red Cross. 2004. (Great Life Stories Ser.). (ENG., Illus.). 111p. (J). 30.50 *(978-0-531-12276-1(X),* Watts, Franklin) Scholastic Library Publishing.
Edison, Erin. Clara Barton. 2013. (Great Women in History Ser.). (ENG.). 24p. (gr. k-1). pap. 35.70 *(978-1-62065-858-1(5));* (Illus.). lib. bdg. 21.99 *(978-1-62065-076-9(2))* Capstone Press of Coughlan Cos. (Pebble Bks.).
Hamen, Susan E. Clara Barton: Civil War Hero & American Red Cross Founder, 1 vol. 2010. (Military Heroes Ser.). (ENG.). 112p. (J). (gr. 6-12). lib. bdg. 35.64 *(978-1-60453-960-8(7))* ABDO Publishing Co.
Harkins, Susan Sales & Harkins, William H. The Life & Times of Clara Barton. 2008. (Profiles in American History Ser.). (Illus.). 48p. (J). (gr. 4-8). lib. bdg. 29.95 *(978-1-58415-667-3(8))* Mitchell Lane Pubs., Inc.
Lakin, Patricia. Clara Barton: Spirit of the American Red Cross. Sullivan, Simon, illus. 2004. (Ready-To-read SOFA Ser.). (ENG.). 48p. (J). (gr. 1-3). pap. 3.99 *(978-0-689-86513-8(9),* Simon Spotlight) Simon Spotlight.
Marsico, Katie. The Red Cross. 2014. (Community Connections: How Do They Help? Ser.). (ENG.). 24p. (J). (gr. 2-5). 25.64 *(978-1-63188-028-5(4),* 205519) Cherry Lake Publishing.
Nardo, Don. Clara Barton: Face Danger, but Never Fear It. 2008. (Americans—the Spirit of a Nation Ser.). (Illus.). 128p. (J). (gr. 3-7). lib. bdg. 33.27 *(978-0-7660-3024-4(5))* Enslow Pubs., Inc.
Wade, Mary Dodson. Amazing Civil War Nurse Clara Barton. 2009. (Amazing Americans Ser.). (Illus.). 24p. (J). (gr. 1-3). lib. bdg. 22.60 *(978-0-7660-3281-1(7))* Enslow Pubs., Inc.

AMERICAN POETRY

Appelt, Kathi. I See the Moon. Jenkins, Reid Debra, illus. 2009. (ENG.). 12p. (J). (gr. -1). 8.00 *(978-0-8028-5358-5(7),* Eerdmans Bks For Young Readers) Eerdmans, William B. Publishing Co.
—I See the Moon. Jenkins, Debra Reid, illus. 2004. 24p. (J). (gr. -1-2). 15.00 *(978-0-8028-5118-5(5))* Eerdmans, William B. Publishing Co.
Bates, Katharine Lee. America the Beautiful. Gall, Chris, illus. 2010. (ENG.). 32p. (J). (gr. -1-3). pap. 7.99 *(978-0-316-08338-6(0))* Little, Brown Bks. for Young Readers.
Bates, Katharine Lee & Bates, Katharine. America the Beautiful. Minor, Wendell & Howell, Troy, illus. 2003. (ENG.). 32p. (J). (gr. -1-2). 18.99 *(978-0-399-23885-7(9),* G.P. Putnam's Sons Books for Young Readers) Penguin Young Readers Group.
Berquist, Laura M. The Harp & Laurel Wreath: Poetry & Dictation for the Classical Curriculum. 2011. (Illus.). 493p. pap. *(978-1-58617-691-4(9))* Ignatius Pr.
Brown, Calef. Flamingos on the Roof. 2006. (ENG., Illus.). 64p. (J). (gr. 5-7). 16.99 *(978-0-618-56298-5(2))* Houghton Mifflin Harcourt Publishing Co.
—We Go Together! A Curious Selection of Affectionate Verse. 2013. (ENG., Illus.). 40p. (J). (gr. -1-3). 9.99 *(978-0-547-72128-6(5))* Houghton Mifflin Harcourt Publishing Co.
Brown, Margaret Wise. Nibble Nibble. Minor, Wendell, illus. 2007. (ENG.). 32p. (J). (gr. -1-3). 17.99 *(978-0-06-059208-0(7))* HarperCollins Pubs.
Brown, Michael R. Susquehanna. 2003. 80p. per. 12.00 *(978-0-9633092-3-5(4))* Ragged Sky Pr.
Buckwalter, Stephanie. Early American Poetry: "Beauty in Words" 2009. (Poetry Rocks! Ser.). (Illus.). 160p. (YA). (gr. 9-12). lib. bdg. 35.94 *(978-0-7660-3277-4(9))* Enslow Pubs., Inc.
—Early American Poetry- Beauty in Words. 2011. (Poetry Rocks! Ser.). (Illus.). 160p. (YA). (gr. 9-18). pap. 10.95 *(978-1-59845-378-2(5))* Enslow Pubs., Inc.
Bulion, Leslie. At the Sea Floor Café: Odd Ocean Critter Poems, 1 vol. Evans, Leslie, illus. 2011. (ENG.). 48p. (J). (gr. 3-7). 14.95 *(978-1-56145-565-2(2))* Peachtree Pubs.
Carlson, Lori Marie. Red Hot Salsa: Bilingual Poems on Being Young & Latino in the United States. rev. ed. 2005. (ENG & SPA.). 160p. (YA). (gr. 7). 18.99 *(978-0-8050-7616-5(6),* 9780805076165, Holt, Henry & Co. Bks. For Young Readers) Holt, Henry & Co.
Carlstrom, Nancy White. Glory. Jenkins, Debra Reid, illus. 2004. 32p. (J). (gr. -1-3). 17.00 *(978-0-8028-5143-7(6))* Eerdmans, William B. Publishing Co.
Carpenter, Stephen, illus. If Kids Ruled the School: More Kids' Favorite Funny School Poems. 2004. 73p. (J). 8.95 *(978-0-88166-468-3(5))* Meadowbrook Pr.
—Mary Had a Little Jam, & Other Silly Rhymes. 2004. 32p. (J). *(978-0-88166-470-6(7))* Meadowbrook Pr.
Child, L. Maria. Over the River & Through the Wood: The New England Boy's Song about Thanksgiving Day. Tavares, Matt, illus. 2013. (ENG.). 32p. (J). (gr. -1-2). 8.99 *(978-0-7636-6696-5(3))* Candlewick Pr.
Child, Lydia Maria. Over the River & Through the Wood. Manson, Christopher, illus. 2014. (ENG.). 32p. (J). 14.95 *(978-0-7358-4191-8(8))* North-South Bks., Inc.
Cleary, Brian. Ode to a Commode: Concrete Poems. Rowland, Andy, illus. 2014. (Poetry Adventures Ser.). (ENG.). 32p. (gr. 2-5). pap. 6.95 *(978-1-4677-4454-6(9),* Millbrook Pr.) Lerner Publishing Group.
Cleary, Brian P. Rainbow Soup: Adventures in Poetry. Layton, Neal, tr. Layton, Neal, illus. 2004. (ENG.). 88p. (gr. 3-6). 26.60 *(978-1-57505-597-8(X))* Lerner Publishing Group.
—Rhyme & Punishment: Adventures in Wordplay. Sandy, J. P., illus. 2006. (ENG.). 48p. (gr. 4-6). 26.60 *(978-1-57505-849-8(9),* Millbrook Pr.) Lerner Publishing Group.
Damanda, Lori. The Story of the "Star-Spangled Banner" 2009. (Real Life Readers Ser.). 32p. (J). (ENG., Illus.). (gr. 5-6). pap. 10.00 *(978-1-4358-0205-6(5));* (gr. 4-6). lib. bdg. 25.25 *(978-1-4358-3015-8(6))* Rosen Publishing Group, Inc., The. (PowerKids Pr.).
—The Story of the Star-Spangled Banner. 2009. (American History Milestones Ser.). 32p. (gr. 5-5). 47.90 *(978-1-61511-375-0(4),* PowerKids Pr.) Rosen Publishing Group, Inc., The.
Di Pasquale, Emanuel, et al. Cartwheel to the Moon: My Sicilian Childhood. 2003. (ENG., Illus.). 64p. (J). (gr. 3-7). 16.95 *(978-0-8126-2679-7(6))* Cricket Bks.
Diggory, Terence. Encyclopedia of the New York School Poets. 2009. (Literary Movements Ser.). (Illus.). 560p. (C). (gr. 9). 75.00 *(978-0-8160-5743-6(5))* Facts On File, Inc.
Dunbar, Polly, illus. Here's a Little Poem: A Very First Book of Poetry. 2007. (ENG.). 112p. (J). (gr. k-12). 21.99 *(978-0-7636-3141-3(8))* Candlewick Pr.
Ehrmann, Max. Desiderata: Words to Live By. Tauss, Marc, illus. 2003. (Desiderata Ser.). (ENG.). 48p. (J). 15.95 *(978-0-439-37293-0(3),* Scholastic Pr.) Scholastic, Inc.
Esbensen, Barbara Juster. Swing Around the Sun. Chee, Cheng-Khee et al, illus. 2003. (ENG.). 48p. (J). (gr. k-3). 17.95 *(978-0-87614-143-4(2),* Carolrhoda Bks.) Lerner Publishing Group.
Florian, Douglas. Autumnblings. Florian, Douglas, illus. 2003. (ENG., Illus.). 48p. (J). (gr. k-5). 16.99 *(978-0-06-009278-8(5),* Greenwillow Bks.) HarperCollins Pubs.
—Laugh-Eteria. Florian, Douglas, illus. 2008. (ENG., Illus.). 160p. (J). (gr. 1-4). pap. 8.99 *(978-0-15-206148-7(7))* Houghton Mifflin Harcourt Publishing Co.
Foxworthy, Jeff. Dirt on My Shirt. Björkman, Steve, illus. (I Can Read Book 2 Ser.). 32p. (J). 2009. (gr. -1-3). 16.99 *(978-0-06-176525-4(2))* 2009. (ENG.). (gr. k-3). pap. 3.99 *(978-0-06-176524-7(4))* 2008. (gr. -1-2). lib. bdg. 17.89 *(978-0-06-120847-8(7))* 2008. (ENG.). (gr. -1-3). 17.99 *(978-0-06-120846-1(9))* HarperCollins Pubs.
Franco, Betsy. Counting Our Way to the 100th Day! Salerno, Steven, illus. 2004. (ENG.). 48p. (J). (gr. -1-3). 17.99 *(978-0-689-84793-6(9),* McElderry, Margaret K. Bks.) McElderry, Margaret K. Bks.
Franco, Betsy & Salerno, Steven. Mathematickles! 2006. (Illus.). (gr. k-5). 18.00 *(978-0-7569-6709-3(0))* Perfection Learning Corp.
Freese, Susan M. Bees to Trees: Reading, Writing, & Reciting Poems about Nature, 1 vol. Westberg, Jan, illus. 2008. (Poetry Power Ser.). (ENG.). 32p. (J). (gr. 1-4). 27.07 *(978-1-60453-001-8(4))* ABDO Publishing Co.
—Buses to Books: Reading, Writing, & Reciting Poems about School, 1 vol. Westberg, Jan, illus. 2008. (Poetry Power Ser.). (ENG.). 32p. (J). (gr. 1-4). 27.07 *(978-1-60453-002-5(2))* ABDO Publishing Co.
—Carrots to Cupcakes: Reading, Writing, & Reciting Poems about Food, 1 vol. Westberg, Jan, illus. 2008. (Poetry Power Ser.). (ENG.). 32p. (J). (gr. 1-4). 27.07 *(978-1-60453-003-2(0))* ABDO Publishing Co.
—Fireworks to Fruitcake: Reading, Writing, & Reciting Poems about Holidays, 1 vol. Westberg, Jan, illus. 2008. (Poetry Power Ser.). (ENG.). 32p. (J). (gr. 1-4). 27.07 *(978-1-60453-004-9(9))* ABDO Publishing Co.
Frost, Robert. The Runaway. Lang, Glenna, illus. Date not set. (ENG.). 32p. pap. 9.95 *(978-1-56792-243-1(0))* Godine, David R. Pub.
Gage, Amy Glaser & McIntyre, Connie. Upside Downside Inside Out: Poems about Being a Kid. Gage, Amy Glaser & McIntyre, Connie, illus. 2nd rev. ed. 2003. (Illus.). 49p. (J). per. 9.95 *(978-0-9677685-4-0(3))* Grannie Annie Family Story Celebration, The.
George, Kristine O'Connell. Fold Me a Poem. Stringer, Lauren, illus. 2005. (ENG.). 56p. (J). (gr. 1-4). 17.99 *(978-0-15-202501-4(4))* Houghton Mifflin Harcourt Publishing Co.
Graham, Joan Bransfield, et al. Flicker Flash. Davis, Nancy, illus. 2003. (Avenues Ser.). (ENG.). 32p. (C). (gr. -1-3). pap. 11.95 *(978-0-618-31102-6(5))* National Geographic School Publishing, Inc.
Grandits, John. Technically, It's Not My Fault: Concrete Poems. 2004. (ENG., Illus.). 48p. (J). (gr. 5-7). pap. 6.99 *(978-0-618-50361-2(7))* Houghton Mifflin Harcourt Publishing Co.
Greenberg, David. Don't Forget Your Etiquette! The Essential Guide to Misbehavior. Westcott, Nadine Bernard, illus. 2006. (ENG.). 40p. (J). (gr. 1-4). 17.99 *(978-0-374-34990-5(8),* 9780374349905, Farrar, Straus & Giroux (BYR)) Farrar, Straus & Giroux.
Greenfield, Eloise & Greenfield. In the Land of Words: New & Selected Poems. Gilchrist, Jan Spivey, illus. 2003. (ENG.). 48p. (J). (gr. -1-3). 17.99 *(978-0-06-028993-5(7),* Amistad) HarperCollins Pubs.
Grimes, Nikki. Tai Chi Morning: Snapshots of China. Young, Ed, illus. 2004. (ENG.). 64p. (J). 15.95 *(978-0-8126-2707-7(5))* Cricket Bks.
—What Is Goodbye? 2005. (Illus.). (J). lib. bdg. *(978-0-7868-2623-0(1),* Jump at the Sun) Hyperion Bks. for Children.
Hess, Paul. Polar Animals. Hess, Paul, illus. 2009. (Animal Verse Ser.). (ENG., Illus.). 24p. (J). (gr. -1-k). pap. *(978-1-84089-561-2(6))* Zero to Ten, Ltd.
Hillert, Margaret. Come Play with Me. (J). 4.95 *(978-0-87895-629-6(8))* Modern Curriculum Pr.
Hoberman, Mary Ann. Forget-Me-Nots: Poems to Learn by Heart. Emberley, Michael, illus. 2012. (ENG.). 144p. (J). (gr. -1-3). 19.99 *(978-0-316-12947-3(X),* Tingley, Megan Bks.) Little, Brown Bks. for Young Readers.
—You Read to Me, I'll Read to You: Very Short Mother Goose Tales to Read Together. Emberley, Michael, illus. 3rd rev. ed. 2005. (ENG.). 32p. (J). (gr. -1-3). 16.99 *(978-0-316-14431-5(2))* Little, Brown Bks. for Young Readers.
—You Read to Me, I'll Read to You: Very Short Stories to Read Together. Emberley, Michael, illus. 2006. 28p. (gr. -1-1). 17.00 *(978-0-7569-6581-5(0))* Perfection Learning Corp.
Holbrook, Sara. By Definition: Poems of Feelings. Mattern, Scott, illus. 2003. (ENG.). 48p. (J). (gr. 4-6). 15.95 *(978-1-59078-060-2(4));* pap. 8.95 *(978-1-59078-085-5(X))* Boyds Mills Pr.
Hopkins, Lee Bennett. Mother Goose Through the Seasons. Fehlau, Dagmar et al, illus. 2005. (Lee Bennett Hopkins Mother Goose Ser.). (YA). (gr. -1-1). 76.50 *(978-0-8215-0480-2(0))* Sadlier, William H. Inc.
—A Pet for Me. Manning, Jane, illus. 2003. (I Can Read Bks.). (ENG.). 48p. (J). (gr. k-3). 15.99 *(978-0-06-029111-2(7))* HarperCollins Pubs.
—Valentine Hearts: Holiday Poetry. Adinolfi, JoAnn, illus. 2004. (I Can Read Bks.). 32p. (J). (gr. k-3). 15.99 *(978-0-06-008057-0(4))* HarperCollins Pubs.
Hubbell, Patricia & Hubbell. Boo! Halloween Poems & Limericks, 1 vol. Spackman, Jeff, illus. 2005. (ENG.). 32p. (YA). pap. 5.95 *(978-0-7614-5151-8(X))* Marshall Cavendish Corp.
Janeczko, Paul B. Requiem: Poems of the Terezin Ghetto. 2013. (ENG.). 112p. (YA). (gr. 7). pap. 7.99 *(978-0-7636-6465-7(0))* Candlewick Pr.
Janeczko, Paul B., ed. A Poke in the I: A Collection of Concrete Poems. Raschka, Chris, illus. 2005. (ENG.). 48p. (J). (gr. 1-4). reprint ed. pap. 7.99 *(978-0-7636-2376-0(8))* Candlewick Pr.
Keane, Sarah. Around the World in Twenty-Eight Pages, 1 vol. rev. ed. 2013. (Fiction Readers Ser.). (ENG., Illus.). 28p. (J). (gr. 3-3). pap. 8.99 *(978-1-4333-5600-1(7))* Shell Educational Publishing.
Kennedy, Caroline. Poems to Learn by Heart. Muth, Jon J., illus. 2013. (ENG.). 194p. (J). (gr. 5-9). 21.99 *(978-1-4231-0805-4(1))* Hyperion Pr.
Kennedy, Caroline & Sampson, Ana. Poems to Learn by Heart. Muth, Jon J., illus. 2014. (ENG.). 224p. 22.95 *(978-1-78243-145-9(4))* O'Mara, Michael Bks., Ltd. GBR. Dist: Independent Pubs. Group.
Kinerk, Robert. Oh, How Sylvester Can Pester! And Other Poems More or Less about Manners. Kozjan, Drazen, illus. 2011. (ENG.). 32p. (J). (gr. -1-3). 16.99 *(978-1-4169-3362-5(X),* Simon & Schuster/Paula Wiseman Bks.) Simon & Schuster/Paula Wiseman Bks.
Lansky, Bruce. Rolling in the Aisles: A Collection of Laugh-Out-Loud Poems. Carpenter, Stephen, illus. 2004. 116p. (J). *(978-0-88166-473-7(1))* Meadowbrook Pr.
Lansky, Bruce. A Bad Case of the Giggles. Carpenter, Stephen, illus. 2013. (Giggle Poetry Ser.). (ENG.). 128p. (J). (gr. 1-6). per. 9.95 *(978-1-4169-5197-1(0))* Meadowbrook Pr.
Lewis, J. Patrick. Galileo's Universe. Curry, Tom, illus. 2005. (Creative Editions Ser.). 18p. (YA). (gr. 4-7). 24.95 *(978-1-56846-183-0(6))* Creative Co., The.
—Please Bury Me in the Library. Stone, Kyle M., illus. 2005. (ENG.). 32p. (J). (gr. -1-3). 16.99 *(978-0-15-216387-7(5))* Houghton Mifflin Harcourt Publishing Co.
—Swan Song. Wormell, Christopher, illus. 2003. (ENG.). 32p. (J). (gr. 3-17). 18.95 *(978-1-56846-175-5(5),* Creative Editions) Creative Co., The.
Lewis, Patrick J. Heroes & She-Roes: Poems of Amazing & Everyday Heroes. Lewis, J. Patrick & Cooke, Jim, trs. Cooke, Jim, illus. 2005. (ENG.). 40p. (J). (gr. -1-3). 17.99 *(978-0-8037-2925-4(1),* Dial Bks) Penguin Young Readers Group.
Llanas, Sheila Griffin. Contemporary American Poetry: Not the End, but the Beginning. 2010. (Poetry Rocks! Ser.). (Illus.). 160p. (YA). (gr. 9-12). 35.94 *(978-0-7660-3279-8(5))* Enslow Pubs., Inc.
—Contemporary American Poetry- Not the End, but the Beginning. 2011. (Poetry Rocks! Ser.). (Illus.). 160p. (YA). (gr. 9-18). pap. 10.95 *(978-1-59845-380-5(7))* Enslow Pubs., Inc.
—Modern American Poetry: Echoes & Shadows. 2009. (Poetry Rocks! Ser.). (Illus.). 160p. (YA). (gr. 9-12). lib. bdg. 35.94 *(978-0-7660-3275-0(2))* Enslow Pubs., Inc.
—Modern American Poetry- Echoes & Shadows. 2011. (Poetry Rocks! Ser.). (Illus.). 160p. (YA). (gr. 9-18). pap. 10.95 *(978-1-59845-379-9(3))* Enslow Pubs., Inc.
Longfellow, Henry Wadsworth & Remington, Frederic. The Song of Hiawatha. 2004. (Nonpareil Book Ser.). (ENG., Illus.). 304p. pap. 14.95 *(978-1-56792-258-5(9));* 23.95 *(978-1-56792-273-8(2))* Godine, David R. Pub.
Mannis, Celeste Davidson. One Leaf Rides the Wind. Hartung, Susan Kathleen, illus. 2005. (ENG.). 32p. (J). (gr. k-3). pap. 6.99 *(978-0-14-240195-8(1),* Puffin Books) Penguin Young Readers Group.
Medina, Tony. Love to Langston. Christie, R. Gregory, illus. 2006. (J). (gr. 1-7). 17.10 *(978-0-7569-7016-1(4))* Perfection Learning Corp.
Miller, Kate. Poems in Black & White. 2007. (ENG., Illus.). 40p. (J). (gr. 1-3). 17.95 *(978-1-59078-412-9(X),* Front Street) Boyds Mills Pr.
Moore, Clement C. The Night Before Christmas. Engelbreit, Mary, illus. 2011. (ENG.). 40p. (J). (gr. -1-3). 9.99 *(978-0-06-208944-1(7))* HarperCollins Pubs.
—The Night Before Christmas. Whatley, Bruce, illus. 2004. (ENG.). 32p. (J). (gr. -1 — 1). bds. 6.99 *(978-0-06-073917-1(7),* HarperFestival) HarperCollins Pubs.
—The Night Before Christmas. Malvern, Corinne, illus. 2011. (Little Golden Book Ser.). (ENG.). 24p. (J). (gr. -1-k). 4.99 *(978-0-375-86359-2(1),* Golden Bks.) Random Hse. Children's Bks.
—The Night Before Christmas. Bell, Bill, illus. 2011. (ENG.). 32p. (J). (gr. k-2). 6.95 *(978-1-61608-470-7(7),* 608470, Sky Pony Pr.) Skyhorse Publishing Co., Inc.
—The Night Before Christmas. 2010. (Illus.). 32p. (J). 9.99 *(978-0-8249-5627-1(3),* Ideal Pubns.) Worthy Publishing.
Moore, Clement C., ed. & illus. The Night Before Christmas. Moore, Clement C., illus. Gorsline, Douglas, illus. 32p. (J). Random Hse. Children's Bks.
—The Night Before Christmas. Moore, Clement C., illus. Porfirio, Guy, illus. 2004. 20p. (J). 9.95 *(978-0-8249-6553-2(1),* Ideal Pubns.) Worthy Publishing.
Mora, Pat. The Desert Is My Mother/el Desierto Es Mi Madre. Lechon, Daniel, illus. 97th ed. 2008. (SPA & ENG.). 32p. (J). (gr. -1-2). pap. 7.95 *(978-1-55885-158-0(5),* Piñata Books) Arte Publico Pr.
Morice, Dave. A Visit from St. Alphabet. Morice, Dave, illus. 2005. (ENG., Illus.). 24p. (Orig.). (J). (gr. -1-3). 9.95 *(978-1-56689-179-0(5))* Coffee Hse. Pr.
Myers, Walter Dean. Here in Harlem: Poems in Many Voices. 2004. (ENG., Illus.). 96p. (J). (gr. 7-18). tchr. ed. 18.95 *(978-0-8234-1853-4(7))* Holiday Hse., Inc.
Nikola-Lisa, W. Bein' with You This Way. Bryant, Michael, illus. 97th ed. 2013. (ENG.). 32p. (J). (gr. -1-3). 9.95 *(978-1-880000-26-7(1))* Lee & Low Bks., Inc.
Nye, Naomi Shihab. A Maze Me: Poems for Girls. Maher, Terre, illus. 2005. (ENG.). 128p. (YA). (gr. 8-18). 17.99 *(978-0-06-058189-3(1),* Greenwillow Bks.) HarperCollins Pubs.
One from the Willow. 2003. (Illus.). 99p. (J). bds. 17.95 *(978-1-929416-67-7(9))* Magner Publishing & American Binding & Publishing.
Perdomo, Willie. Visiting Langston. Collier, Bryan, illus. 2006. (gr. -1-3). 19.00 *(978-0-7569-6802-1(X))* Perfection Learning Corp.
Perry, Andrea J. & Perry, Andrea. Here's What You Do When You Can't Find Your Shoe: Ingenious Inventions for Pesky Problems. Snow, Alan, illus. 2003. (ENG.). 40p. (J). (gr. -1-3). 18.99 *(978-0-689-83067-9(X),* Atheneum Bks. for Young Readers) Simon & Schuster Children's Publishing.
Perry, Rex, illus. Over the River & Through the Woods. 2004. 24p. (J). lib. bdg. 8.00 *(978-1-4242-0640-7(5))* Fitzgerald Bks.
Pinz, Shelley. Holly, Bear & Coty, & the Very First Angel of Christmas. (Illus.). 18p. (J). pap. 12.95 incl. cd-rom *(978-0-9700251-3-5(0))* Pinz, Shelley Music.
Poe, Edgar Allen. The Raven. Price, Ryan, illus. 2014. (Visions in Poetry Ser.). (ENG.). 48p. (J). (gr. 5-9). pap. 9.95 *(978-1-55453-459-3(3))* Kids Can Pr., Ltd. CAN. Dist: Hachette Bk. Group.
Pomerantz, Charlotte. Thunderboom! Poems for Everyone. Shepperson, Rob, illus. 2006. (ENG.). 48p. (J). (gr. -1). 17.95 *(978-1-932425-40-6(3),* Lemniscaat) Boyds Mills Pr.
Prelutsky, Jack. Awful Ogre's Awful Day. Zelinsky, Paul O., illus. 2005. (ENG.). 40p. (J). (gr. k-5). reprint ed. pap. 6.99 *(978-0-06-077459-2(2),* Greenwillow Bks.) HarperCollins Pubs.
—If Not for the Cat. Rand, Ted, illus. 2004. (ENG.). 40p. (J). (gr. -1-3). 17.99 *(978-0-06-059677-4(5),* Greenwillow Bks.) HarperCollins Pubs.
—The New Kid on the Block. Stevenson, James, illus. 2013. (ENG.). 160p. (J). (gr. k-5). pap. 9.99 *(978-0-06-223950-1(3),* Greenwillow Bks.) HarperCollins Pubs.
—What a Day It Was at School! Cushman, Doug, illus. 2006. 40p. (J). (gr. k). 16.99 *(978-0-06-082335-1(6))* HarperCollins Pubs.
Rose, Deborah Lee. The Twelve Days of Kindergarten: A Counting Book. Armstrong-Ellis, Carey F., illus. 2017. (ENG.). 32p. (J). (gr. -1-1). pap. 4.95 ***(978-1-4197-2742-9(7),*** Abrams Bks. for Young Readers) Abrams, Inc.
—The Twelve Days of Kindergarten: A Counting Book. Armstrong-Ellis, Carey, illus. 2003. (ENG.). 30p. (J). (gr. -1-1). 16.95 *(978-0-8109-4512-8(6))* Abrams, Inc.
Ross, Mandy. Animal Lullabies. Nagy, Krisztina, tr. Nagy, Krisztina & Kallai Nagy, Krisztina, illus. 2003. (Poems for the Young Ser.). (ENG.). 32p. (J). (gr. 2-3). *(978-0-85953-116-0(3))* Child's Play International Ltd.
Rowden, Justine. Paint Me a Poem: Poems Inspired by Masterpieces of Art. 2005. (ENG., Illus.). 32p. (J). (gr. 1-4). 18.95 *(978-1-59078-289-7(5),* Wordsong) Boyds Mills Pr.
Santore, Charles, illus. The Night Before Christmas. 2011. (Classic Edition Ser.). (ENG.). 44p. (J). (gr. -1). 19.95 *(978-1-60433-237-7(9),* Applesauce Pr.) Cider Mill Pr. Bk. Pubs., LLC.
Scanlon, Elizabeth Garton. A Sock Is a Pocket for Your Toes. Glasser, Robin Preiss, illus. 2004. (ENG.). 32p. (J). (gr. -1-2). 16.99 *(978-0-06-029526-4(0))* HarperCollins Pubs.
Scanlon, Liz Garton. All the World. Frazee, Marla, illus. 2009. (ENG.). 40p. (J). (gr. -1-3). 17.99 *(978-1-4169-8580-8(8),* Beach Lane Bks.) Beach Lane Bks.

—All the World. Frazee, Marla, illus. 2015. (Classic Board Bks.). (ENG.). 44p. (J). (gr. -1-k). bds. 7.99 *(978-1-4814-3121-7(8)*, Little Simon) Little Simon.
—All the World. Frazee, Marla, illus. 2011. (J). (gr. -1-2). 29.95 *(978-0-545-32716-9(4))* Weston Woods Studios, Inc.
Sendak, Maurice. My Brother's Book. Sendak, Maurice, illus. 2013. (ENG., Illus.). 32p. 18.95 *(978-0-06-223489-6(7))* HarperCollins Pubs.
Shange, Ntozake. Ellington Was Not a Street. Nelson, Kadir, illus. 2004. (ENG.). 40p. (J). (gr. k-6). 18.99 *(978-0-689-82884-3(5)*, Simon & Schuster Bks. For Young Readers) Simon & Schuster Bks. For Young Readers.
—Ellington Was Not a Street. Nelson, Kadir, illus. 2005. (J). 29.95 *(978-0-439-77582-3(5)*, WHCD672) Weston Woods Studios, Inc.
Sidman, Joyce. Dark Emperor & Other Poems of the Night. Allen, Rick, illus. 2010. (ENG.). 32p. (J). (gr. 1-4). 16.99 *(978-0-547-15228-8(0))* Houghton Mifflin Harcourt Publishing Co.
—Song of the Water Boatman & Other Pond Poems. Prange, Beckie, illus. 2005. (ENG.). 32p. (J). (gr. -1-3). 17.99 *(978-0-618-13547-9(2))* Houghton Mifflin Harcourt Publishing Co.
Silverstein, Shel. Falling Up: Poems & Drawings. Silverstein, Shel, illus. 2006. (ENG., Illus.). 184p. (J). (gr. -1-3). 19.99 *(978-0-06-024802-4(5))* HarperCollins Pubs.
—Falling Up: Poems & Drawings. 2006. (CHI., Illus.). 171p. (J). *(978-7-5442-3557-0(2))* Nanhai Publishing Co.
—Falling up Special Edition. Silverstein, Shel, illus. 2015. (ENG., Illus.). 200p. (J). (gr. -1-3). 19.99 *(978-0-06-232133-6(1))* HarperCollins Pubs.
—Runny Babbit: A Billy Sook. Silverstein, Shel, illus. (ENG., Illus.). 96p. (J). (gr. -1-3). 2015. 18.99 *(978-0-06-025653-1(2))* 2006. 22.99 *(978-0-06-113047-2(8))* HarperCollins Pubs.
Singer, Marilyn. Fireflies at Midnight. Robbins, Ken, illus. 2003. (ENG.). 32p. (J). (gr. k-4). 17.99 *(978-0-689-82492-0(0)*, Atheneum Bks. for Young Readers) Simon & Schuster Children's Publishing.
—Follow Follow: A Book of Reverso Poems. Masse, Josée, illus. 2013. (ENG.). 32p. (J). (gr. 1-4). 16.99 *(978-0-8037-3769-3(6)*, Dial Bks) Penguin Young Readers Group.
—Mirror Mirror. Masse, Josée, illus. 2010. (ENG.). 32p. (J). (gr. 1-4). 17.99 *(978-0-525-47901-7(5)*, Dutton Books for Young Readers) Penguin Young Readers Group.
Snyder, Betsy E. I Haiku You. 2012. (ENG., Illus.). 32p. (J). (gr. -1-3). 9.99 *(978-0-375-86750-7(3)*, Random Hse. Bks. for Young Readers) Random Hse. Children's Bks.
Spinelli, Eileen. Polar Bear, Arctic Hare: Poems of the Frozen North. Fernandes, Eugenie, illus. 2007. (ENG.). 32p. (J). (gr. -1-3). 16.95 *(978-1-59078-344-3(1))* Boyds Mills Pr.
—Song for the Whooping Crane. Warnick, Elsa, illus. 2004. 32p. (J). (gr. 3-6). 16.00 *(978-0-8028-5172-7(X))* Eerdmans, William B. Publishing Co.
Testa, Maria. Becoming Joe Dimaggio. Hunt, Scott, illus. 2006. 51p. (gr. 5-9). 17.00 *(978-0-7569-6576-1(4))* Perfection Learning Corp.
Thayer, Ernest L. Casey at the Bat. Morse, Joe, illus. 2010. (Visions in Poetry Ser.). (ENG.). 48p. (J). (gr. 5-9). pap. 9.95 *(978-1-55453-458-6(5))* Kids Can Pr., Ltd. CAN. Dist: Hachette Bk. Group.
—Casey at the Bat: A Ballad of the Republic Sung in the Year 1888. Payne, C. F., illus. 2003. (ENG.). 40p. (J). (gr. -1-3). 17.99 *(978-0-689-85494-1(3)*, Simon & Schuster Bks. For Young Readers) Simon & Schuster Bks. For Young Readers.
Thayer, Ernest Lawrence. Casey at the Bat: A Ballad of the Republic, Sung in the Year 1888. 2009. 30p. 17.00 *(978-1-4379-6644-2(6))* DIANE Publishing Co.
Trapani, Iza. Twinkle, Twinkle, Little Star. Trapani, Iza, illus. 2008. (ENG., Illus.). 26p. (J). (gr. -1 — 1). bds. 7.95 *(978-1-58089-015-1(6))* Charlesbridge Publishing, Inc.
Turley, LuAnn & Whiteman, Rita. A View, a Clue, & You: Poetry & American Art at the Museum of Fine Arts, Houston. 2010. (Illus.). 56p. pap. *(978-0-89090-172-4(4))* Museum of Fine Arts, Houston.
Viorst, Judith. What Are You Glad About? What Are You Mad About? White, Lee, illus. 2017. (ENG.). 112p. (J). (gr. 1-4). pap. 7.99 *(978-1-4814-2356-4(8))* Simon & Schuster Children's Publishing.
—What Are You Glad About? What Are You Mad About? Poems for When a Person Needs a Poem. White, Lee, illus. 2016. (ENG.). 112p. (J). (gr. 1-4). 17.99 *(978-1-4814-2355-7(X)*, Atheneum/Caitlyn Dlouhy Books) Simon & Schuster Children's Publishing.
Whitman, Walt. I Hear America Singing. Sabuda, Robert, illus. 2004. 30p. (J). (gr. k-4). reprint ed. 15.00 *(978-0-7567-8097-5(7))* DIANE Publishing Co.
Williams, Vera B. Amber Was Brave, Essie Was Smart. Williams, Vera B., illus. 2003. (Illus.). (J). (gr. k-3). 25.95 incl. audio *(978-1-59112-186-2(8))* Live Oak Media.
—Amber Was Brave, Essie Was Smart. 2003. (Illus.). (J). (gr. 4-7). 28.95 incl. audio compact disk *(978-1-59112-339-2(9))* Live Oak Media.
Wilson, Edwin Graves, ed. Poetry for Young People: Maya Angelou. Lagarrigue, Jerome, illus. 2013. (Poetry for Young People Ser.). (ENG.). 48p. (J). (gr. 3). 14.95 *(978-1-4549-0329-1(5))* Sterling Publishing Co., Inc.
Wolf, Allan. The Blood-Hungry Spleen & Other Poems about Our Parts. Clarke, Greg, illus. 2008. (ENG.). 56p. (J). (gr. 3-7). per. 9.99 *(978-0-7636-3806-1(4))* Candlewick Pr.
Wong, Janet S. & Paschkis, Julie. Knock on Wood: Poems about Superstitions. Paschkis, Julie, illus. 2003. (ENG., Illus.). 40p. (J). (gr. 2-5). 19.99 *(978-0-689-85512-2(5)*, McElderry, Margaret K. Bks.) McElderry, Margaret K. Bks.
Woodson, Jacqueline. Locomotion. (ENG.). (J). (gr. 5-18). 2010. 144p. 8.99 *(978-0-14-241552-8(9)*, Speak) 2003. 112p. 16.99 *(978-0-399-23115-5(3)*, G.P. Putnam's Sons Books for Young Readers) Penguin Young Readers Group.
Young, Gary. More Than Two: Under the Sea. 2014. (ENG., Illus.). 80p. (J). (gr. 2-3). 9.99 *(978-1-74257-539-1(0))* New Holland Pubs. Pty, Ltd. AUS. Dist: Midpoint Trade Bks., Inc.

AMERICAN POETRY—AFRICAN AMERICAN AUTHORS

Brooks, Gwendolyn & Brooks. Bronzeville Boys & Girls. Ringgold, Faith, illus. 2006. (ENG.). 48p. (J). (gr. -1-3). 16.99 *(978-0-06-029505-9(8)*, Amistad) HarperCollins Pubs.
Marsalis, Wynton. Jazz A-B-Z: An A to Z Collection of Jazz Portraits. Rogers, Paul, illus. 2005. (ENG.). 76p. (J). (gr. 4-7). 24.99 *(978-0-7636-2135-3(8))* Candlewick Pr.
Myers, Walter Dean. Here in Harlem: Poems in Many Voices. 2004. (ENG., Illus.). 96p. (J). (gr. 7-18). tchr. ed. 18.95 *(978-0-8234-1853-4(7))* Holiday Hse., Inc.
Shange, Ntozake. Ellington Was Not a Street. Nelson, Kadir, illus. 2004. (ENG.). 40p. (J). (gr. k-6). 18.99 *(978-0-689-82884-3(5)*, Simon & Schuster Bks. For Young Readers) Simon & Schuster Bks. For Young Readers.
—Ellington Was Not a Street. Nelson, Kadir, illus. 2005. (J). 29.95 *(978-0-439-77582-3(5)*, WHCD672) Weston Woods Studios, Inc.

AMERICAN POETRY—COLLECTIONS

Baxter, Jennifer. Turned Inside Out. 2003. (YA). per. 10.00 *(978-0-9741294-3-3(7))* Main St Publishing, Inc.
Carpenter, Stephen, illus. If Kids Ruled the School: More Kids' Favorite Funny School Poems. 2004. 73p. (J). 8.95 *(978-0-88166-468-3(5))* Meadowbrook Pr.
A Celebration of Young Poets - New Jersey Spring 2006. 2006. (J). 21.95 *(978-978-160-050-0(0))* Univ. Publishing Co.
Cole, Joanna & Calmenson, Stephanie. Yours till Banana Splits: 201 Autograph Rhymes. Tiegreen, Alan, illus. 2004. 64p. (J). (gr. 6-8). reprint ed. pap. 7.00 *(978-0-7567-7349-6(0))* DIANE Publishing Co.
Creative Communication Staff, ed. Celebrate! Young Poets Speak Out - Appalachia Spring 2006. 2006. (YA). 21.95 *(978-1-60050-039-8(0))* Creative Communication.
—Celebrate! Young Poets Speak Out - California Spring 2006. 2006. (YA). 21.95 *(978-1-60050-057-2(9))* Creative Communication.
—Celebrate! Young Poets Speak Out - Canada Spring 2006. 2006. (YA). 21.95 *(978-1-60050-037-4(4))* Creative Communication.
—Celebrate! Young Poets Speak Out - Illinois/Indiana Spring 2006. 2006. (YA). 21.95 *(978-1-60050-043-5(9))* Creative Communication.
—Celebrate! Young Poets Speak Out - Michigan Spring 2006. 2006. (YA). 21.95 *(978-1-60050-048-0(X))* Creative Communication.
—Celebrate! Young Poets Speak Out - Midwest Spring 2006. 2006. (YA). 21.95 *(978-1-60050-045-9(5))* Creative Communication.
—Celebrate! Young Poets Speak Out - New Jersey Spring 2006. 2006. (YA). 21.95 *(978-1-60050-033-6(1))* Creative Communication.
—Celebrate! Young Poets Speak Out - New York Spring 2006. 2006. (YA). 21.95 *(978-1-60050-031-2(5))* Creative Communication.
—Celebrate! Young Poets Speak Out - Northeast Spring 2006. 2006. (YA). 21.95 *(978-1-60050-028-2(5))* Creative Communication.
—Celebrate! Young Poets Speak Out - Pennsylvania Spring 2006. 2006. (YA). 21.95 *(978-1-60050-032-9(3))* Creative Communication.
—Celebrate! Young Poets Speak Out - Rocky Mountain Spring 2006. 2006. (YA). 21.95 *(978-1-60050-053-4(6))* Creative Communication.
—Celebrate! Young Poets Speak Out - South Spring 2006. 2006. (YA). 21.95 *(978-1-60050-038-1(2))* Creative Communication.
—Celebrate! Young Poets Speak Out - Texas Spring 2006. 2006. (YA). 21.95 *(978-1-60050-055-8(2))* Creative Communication.
—Celebrate! Young Poets Speak Out - West Spring 2006. 2006. (YA). 21.95 *(978-1-60050-052-7(8))* Creative Communication.
—Celebrate! Young Poets Speak Out - Wisconsin/Minnesota Spring 2006. 2006. (YA). 21.95 *(978-1-60050-047-3(1))* Creative Communication.
—Celebrate! Young Poets Speak Out - Heartland Spring 2006. 2006. (YA). 21.95 *(978-1-60050-041-1(2))* Creative Communication.
—Celebrating Poetry - East Spring 2006. 2006. (J). 21.95 *(978-1-60050-034-3(X))* Creative Communication.
—Celebrating Poetry - Midwest Spring 2006. 2006. (J). 21.95 *(978-1-60050-050-3(1))* Creative Communication.
—Celebrating Poetry - Spring 2006. 2006. (J). 21.95 *(978-1-60050-035-0(8))* Creative Communication.
—Celebrating Poetry - West Spring 2006. 2006. (J). 21.95 *(978-1-60050-058-9(7))* Creative Communication.
—A Celebration of Young Poets - California Spring 2006. 2006. (J). 21.95 *(978-1-60050-056-5(0))* Creative Communication.
—A Celebration of Young Poets - Canada Spring 2006. 2006. (J). 21.95 *(978-1-60050-025-1(0))* Creative Communication.
—A Celebration of Young Poets - Heartland Spring 2006. 2006. (J). 21.95 *(978-1-60050-040-4(4))* Creative Communication.
—A Celebration of Young Poets - Illinois/Indiana Spring 2006. 2006. (J). 21.95 *(978-1-60050-042-8(0))* Creative Communication.
—A Celebration of Young Poets - Midwest Spring 2006. 2006. (J). 21.95 *(978-1-60050-044-2(7))* Creative Communication.
—A Celebration of Young Poets - New Jersey Spring 2006. 2006. (J). 21.95 *(978-1-60050-027-5(7))* Creative Communication.
—A Celebration of Young Poets - New York Spring 2006. 2006. (J). 21.95 *(978-1-60050-029-9(3))* Creative Communication.
—A Celebration of Young Poets - Northeast Spring 2006. 2006. (J). 21.95 *(978-1-60050-026-8(9))* Creative Communication.
—A Celebration of Young Poets - Ohio Spring 2006. 2006. (J). 21.95 *(978-1-60050-049-7(8))* Creative Communication.
—A Celebration of Young Poets - Pennsylvania Spring 2006. 2006. (J). 21.95 *(978-1-60050-030-5(7))* Creative Communication.
—A Celebration of Young Poets - South Spring 2006. 2006. (J). 21.95 *(978-1-60050-036-7(6))* Creative Communication.
—A Celebration of Young Poets - Texas Spring 2006. 2006. (J). 21.95 *(978-1-60050-054-1(4))* Creative Communication.
—A Celebration of Young Poets - West Spring 2006. 2006. (J). 21.95 *(978-1-60050-051-0(X))* Creative Communication.
—A Celebration of Young Poets - Wisconsin/Michigan Spring 2006. 2006. (J). 21.95 *(978-1-60050-046-6(3))* Creative Communication.
Davis, David. A Southern Child's Garden of Verses, 1 vol. Leonhard, Herb, illus. 2010. (ENG.). 40p. (J). (gr. k-k). 17.99 *(978-1-58980-764-8(2))* Pelican Publishing Co., Inc.
Feldman, Thea. First Foil Poetry Love, 2 vols. Berg, Michelle, illus. 2005. (First Foil Poetry Haikus Ser.). 10p. (J). 6.95 *(978-1-58117-189-1(7)*, Intervisual/Piggy Toes) Bendon, Inc.
Hamilton, Meredith, illus. They're Poets & They Know It! A Collection of 30 Timeless Poems. 2007. 31p. (J). pap. *(978-0-545-03017-5(X))* Scholastic, Inc.
Hopkins, Lee Bennett. Hanukkah Lights: Holiday Poetry. Hall, Melanie, illus. 2004. (I Can Read Bks.). (J). (gr. k-3). 15.99 *(978-0-06-008051-8(5))*; 32p. lib. bdg. 16.89 *(978-0-06-008052-5(3))* HarperCollins Pubs.
Lewis, J. Patrick. Castles: Old Stone Poems. 2006. (ENG., Illus.). 48p. (J). (gr. 4-7). 18.95 *(978-1-59078-380-1(8))* Boyds Mills Pr.
—Swan Song. Wormell, Chris, illus. 2005. 32p. (J). reprint ed. 17.00 *(978-0-7567-8662-5(2))* DIANE Publishing Co.
Rachel, T. Cole & Costello, Rita D., eds. Bend, Don't Shatter: Poets on the Beginning of Desire. 2004. (ENG., Illus.). 120p. (YA). pap. 11.95 *(978-1-932360-17-2(4))* Cricket Bks.
Roche, Judith, ed. The Bottom of Heaven: Artwork & Poetry of the Remann Hall Women's Project. 2003. (J). per. 19.95 *(978-0-9726649-0-5(4))* Museum of Glass.
Weston Woods Staff, creator. Antarctic Antics. 2004. (J). 38.75 *(978-1-55592-616-8(9))*; 18.95 *(978-1-55592-615-1(0))* Weston Woods Studios, Inc.
Williamson, Melanie, illus. Drift upon a Dream: Poems for Sleepy Babies. 2004. 32p. (J). 16.95 *(978-1-57091-577-2(6))* Charlesbridge Publishing, Inc.

AMERICAN SOCIETY FOR THE PREVENTION OF CRUELTY TO ANIMALS

Furstinger, Nancy & Pipe, Sheryl L. Kids Making a Difference for Animals. 2009. (ASPCA Kids Ser.: 4). (ENG., Illus.). 108p. 12.99 *(978-0-470-41086-8(8)*, Howell Bk. Hse.) Wiley, John & Sons, Inc.
Miller-Schroeder, Patricia. The ASPCA. 2003. (International Organizations Ser.). (Illus.). 32p. (J). (gr. 4-7). lib. bdg. 26.00 *(978-1-59036-024-8(9))* Weigl Pubs., Inc.
Suen, Anastasia. Asociación para la prevención de la crueldad de los animales, ASPCA (the Association for the Prevention of Cruelty to Animals) 2009. (Organizaciones de ayuda (Helping Organizations) Ser.). (SPA.). 24p. (gr. 2-2). 42.50 *(978-1-60851-143-3(X)*, Editorial Buenas Letras) Rosen Publishing Group, Inc., The.

AMERICAN WIT AND HUMOR

Bathroom Readers' Institute Staff. Uncle John's Totally Quacked Bathroom Reader for Kids Only! 2014. (ENG., Illus.). 288p. (J). (gr. 2-7). 14.95 *(978-1-62686-175-6(7)*, Portable Pr.) Readerlink Distribution Services, LLC.
Graham, Joan Claire. Minnesota Memories 3. 2003. (Illus.). 192p. per. 13.95 *(978-0-9711971-2-1(1))* Megyeri, Graham Bks.
Hample, Stuart E. & Hample, Stoo. The Silly Book. Hample, Stuart E. & Hample, Stoo, illus. 2010. (ENG., Illus.). 32p. (J). (gr. -1-3). 16.99 *(978-0-7636-4124-5(3))* Candlewick Pr.
—The Silly Book. Hample, Stoo, illus. 2004. (ENG., Illus.). 32p. (J). (gr. k-12). 15.99 *(978-0-7636-2256-5(7))* Candlewick Pr.
Heimberg, Justin & Gomberg, David. Doubly Disgusting: Over 300 All New Crazy Questions Plus Extra Pages to Make up Your Own! 2009. (Would You Rather... ? Ser.). (ENG., Illus.). 224p. (gr. 2). pap. 9.95 *(978-1-934734-00-1(4))* Seven Footer Pr.
—Extra Extremely Extreme: Over 1,200 Positively Preposterous Dilemmas to Ponder. 2009. (Would You Rather... ? Ser.). (ENG.). 418p. pap. 14.95 *(978-1-934734-07-0(1))* Seven Footer Pr.
—Would You Rather... ? for Kids! 2007. (Would You Rather... ? Ser.). (ENG., Illus.). 184p. (J). (gr. 2-7). pap. 9.95 *(978-0-9788178-2-4(6))* Seven Footer Pr.
Heimberg, Justin & Gomberg, David, eds. Would You Rather... ? BFF: Over 300 Fiercely Fascinating Questions to Ask Your Friends. 2009. (Would You Rather... ? Ser.). (ENG.). 184p. pap. 9.95 *(978-1-934734-08-7(X))* Seven Footer Pr.
Levy, Elizabeth & Havlan, J. R. Westward, Ha-Ha!, 1800-1850. McFeeley, Dan, illus. 2003. 160p. (J). pap. *(978-0-590-12257-3(6))* Scholastic, Inc.
Rosenbloom, Joseph. Jokes. Hoffman, Sanford, illus. 2007. (ENG.). 352p. (J). (gr. 2-5). pap. 6.95 *(978-1-4027-4973-5(2))* Sterling Publishing Co., Inc.
Schultz, Sam. Animal Antics: The Beast Jokes Ever! 2004. (Make Me Laugh! Ser.). (Illus.). 32p. (J). (gr. k-3). lib. bdg. 19.93 *(978-1-57505-640-1(2))* Lerner Publishing Group.
Schulz, Charles. Security Is a Thumb & a Blanket. 2006. (Peanuts(r) Ser.). (ENG., Illus.). 72p. 5.95 *(978-1-933662-09-1(3))* Cider Mill Pr. Bk. Pubs., LLC.
Scieszka, Jon. Knucklehead: Tall Tales & Almost True Stories about Growing up Scieszka. 2008. (ENG., Illus.). 96p. (J). (gr. 3-7). 12.99 *(978-0-670-01138-4(X)*, Viking Books for Young Readers) Penguin Young Readers Group.
St. George, Judith. So You Want to Be President? Small, David, illus. rev. ed. 2004. (ENG.). 56p. (J). (gr. 2-5). 17.99 *(978-0-399-24317-2(8)*, Philomel Bks.) Penguin Young Readers Group.
Van Wagenen, Maya. Popular: A Memoir. 2014. (ENG., Illus.). 272p. (YA). (gr. 7). 18.99 *(978-0-525-42681-3(7)*, Dutton Books for Young Readers) Penguin Young Readers Group.

AMERICAN WIT AND HUMOR, PICTORIAL

Barrett, Judi. Animals Should Definitely Not Act Like People. Barrett, Ron, illus. pap. 35.95 incl. audio compact disk *(978-1-59112-827-4(7))*; (J). pap. 33.95 incl. audio *(978-0-87499-232-8(X))* Live Oak Media.
Pastis, Stephan. Beginning Pearls. 2013. (Pearls Before Swine Kids Ser.: 1). (ENG., Illus.). 224p. (J). pap. 9.99 *(978-1-4494-2303-2(5))* Andrews McMeel Publishing.

AMERICANISMS

Cobuild Basic American English Dictionary. 2nd rev. ed. 2016. (ENG., Illus.). 608p. pap. 29.95 *(978-0-00-813579-9(7))* HarperCollins Pubs. Ltd. GBR. Dist: Independent Pubs. Group.

AMERICANS—AFRICA—FICTION

Nuckolls, Les. Chester the Chimpanzee. 2012. 14.99 *(978-1-4621-1131-2(9))* Cedar Fort, Inc./CFI Distribution.
Vickie A. Soman. The Sahara Desert Angel: Education & Nature Folktales 2. 2010. 208p. pap. 14.95 *(978-1-4502-1465-0(7))* iUniverse, Inc.

AMERICANS—EUROPE

Katz, William Loren & Crawford, Marc. The Lincoln Brigade: A Picture History. 2013. 96p. pap. 12.00 *(978-1-62032-901-6(8)*, Wipf and Stock) Wipf & Stock Pubs.

AMERICANS—EUROPE—FICTION

Archer, E. Geek Fantasy Novel. 2011. (ENG.). 320p. (J). (gr. 7-7). 17.99 *(978-0-545-16040-7(5)*, Scholastic Pr.) Scholastic, Inc.
Gerdner, Linda & Langford, Sarah. Grandfather's Story Cloth. Loughridge, Stuart, illus. 2008. (Grandfather's Story Cloth Ser.). 32p. (J). (gr. 2-4). 16.95 *(978-1-885008-34-3(1)*, Shen's Bks.) Lee & Low Bks., Inc.
Jacobus, Ann. Romancing the Dark in the City of Light: A Novel. 2015. (ENG.). 288p. (YA). (gr. 7-12). 18.99 *(978-1-250-06443-1(0)*, 9781250064431) St. Martin's Pr.
Kolosov, Jacqueline. Along the Way. 2015. (ENG.). 300p. (YA). (gr. 7). 24.95 *(978-1-941311-47-9(4))* Luminis Bks., Inc.
Sheldon, Dyan. I Conquer Britain. 2007. (ENG., Illus.). 208p. (YA). (gr. 7). 15.99 *(978-0-7636-3300-4(3))* Candlewick Pr.

AMISH

Hess, Ingrid. An Amish Alphabet. 2012. (ENG., Illus.). 32p. (J). 17.99 *(978-0-8361-9645-0(7))* Herald Pr.
Hunter, David. Teen Life among the Amish & Other Alternative Communities: Choosing a Lifestyle. 2009. (Youth in Rural North America Ser.). 96p. (J). (gr. 7-18). lib. bdg. 22.95 *(978-1-4222-0017-9(5))* Mason Crest.
Therrien, Patricia. Amish & Mennonite Cooking. (American Regional Cooking Library). (Illus.). 72p. 2006. (YA). lib. bdg. 19.95 *(978-1-59084-612-4(5))* 2005. (J). lib. bdg. 299.25 *(978-1-59084-609-4(5))* Mason Crest.

AMISH—FICTION

Bender, Carrie. Hemlock Hill Hideaway: Whispering Brook Series #4. 2007. (Illus.). 168p. pap. 8.99 *(978-1-60126-022-2(9))* Masthof Pr.
—Summerville Days: Whispering Brook Series #2. 2007. (Illus.). 224p. pap. 8.99 *(978-1-60126-023-9(7))* Masthof Pr.
—Timber Lane Cove. 2003. (ENG.). 144p. (YA). pap. 8.99 *(978-0-8361-9202-5(8))* Herald Pr.
Bickle, Laura. The Outside. (ENG.). 320p. (YA). (gr. 7). 2014. pap. 8.99 *(978-0-544-33635-3(6)*, HMH Books For Young Readers) 2013. 16.99 *(978-0-544-00013-1(7))* Houghton Mifflin Harcourt Publishing Co.
Bomtrager, Mary Christner. Andy. 2015. (Ellie's People Ser.: Vol. 6). (ENG.). 200p. (YA). (gr. 7-18). pap. 9.99 *(978-0-8361-3633-3(0))* Herald Pr.
—Ellie. 2014. (Ellie's People, Book One Ser.: Vol. 1). (ENG.). 193p. (J). (gr. 3-7). pap. 9.99 *(978-0-8361-3468-1(0))* Herald Pr.
—Polly. 2015. (ENG.). 176p. (YA). (gr. 4-7). pap. 9.99 *(978-0-8361-3670-8(5))* Herald Pr.
—Rebecca. 2014. (Ellie's People, Book Two Ser.: Vol. 2). (ENG.). 234p. (J). (gr. 4-7). pap. 9.99 *(978-0-8361-3500-8(8))* Herald Pr.
Byler, Linda. Becky Meets Her Match: An Amish Christmas Romance. 2016. (ENG.). 240p. 14.99 *(978-1-68099-178-9(7)*, Good Bks.) Skyhorse Publishing Co., Inc.
—Big Decisions: A Novel Based on True Experiences from an Amish Writer!, 1 vol. 2011. (ENG.). 345p. pap. 13.99 *(978-1-56148-700-4(7)*, Good Bks.) Skyhorse Publishing Co., Inc.
—The Little Amish Matchmaker: A Christmas Romance. 2012. (ENG.). 187p. 14.95 *(978-1-56148-776-9(7)*, Good Bks.) Skyhorse Publishing Co., Inc.
—Running Around (And Such) 2010. (ENG.). 345p. pap. 13.99 *(978-1-56148-688-5(4)*, Good Bks.) Skyhorse Publishing Co., Inc.
—When Strawberries Bloom: A Novel Based on True Experiences from an Amish Writer! 2010. (ENG.). 297p. pap. 13.99 *(978-1-56148-699-1(X)*, Good Bks.) Skyhorse Publishing Co., Inc.
Good, Merle. Reuben & the Balloon. Moss, P. Buckley, illus. rev. ed. 2016. (ENG.). 32p. (J). (gr. -1-3). 16.99 *(978-1-68099-149-9(3)*, Good Bks.) Skyhorse Publishing Co., Inc.
—Reuben & the Blizzard. Moss, P. Buckley, illus. rev. ed. 2016. (ENG.). 32p. (J). (gr. -1-3). 16.99 *(978-1-68099-147-5(7)*, Good Bks.) Skyhorse Publishing Co., Inc.
—Reuben & the Fire. Moss, P. Buckley, illus. rev. ed. 2016. (ENG.). 32p. (J). (gr. -1-3). 16.99 *(978-1-68099-153-6(1)*, Good Bks.) Skyhorse Publishing Co., Inc.
—Reuben & the Quilt. Moss, P. Buckley, illus. rev. ed. 2016. (ENG.). 32p. (J). (gr. -1-3). 16.99 *(978-1-68099-151-2(5)*, Good Bks.) Skyhorse Publishing Co., Inc.
The Journey. 2003. 170p. (YA). per. 10.95 *(978-0-9713292-8-7(1))* Aim Higher Bks.
Kjellberg, B. Apple Acres: The Farm. 2006. (J). per. 7.95 *(978-0-912868-10-3(4))* Kjellberg, Inc.
Kjellberg Publishers. Courtnee: A Farm Girl, 6 vols., bk. 1. 2nd ed. 2005. (ENG., Illus.). 84p. (J). 7.95 *(978-0-912868-06-6(6)*, Kjellberg Pubs.) Kjellberg, Inc.
—Sandy: A City Girl, 6 bks., bk. 1. 2nd ed. 2005. (ENG., Illus.). 94p. (J). 7.95 *(978-0-912868-08-0(2)*, 8080, Kjellberg Pubs.) Kjellberg, Inc.
Kjellberg Publishing. Abe: A Farm Boy, 6 vols., vol. 1. 2nd l.t. ed. 2006. (Illus.). 96p. (J). 7.95 *(978-0-912868-07-3(4)*, Kjellberg Pubs.) Kjellberg, Inc.
Lewis, Beverly. SummerHill Secrets. 2007. (Summerhill Secrets Ser.: Vols. 1-5). (ENG.). Vol. 1. 560p. (gr. 6-9). pap. 17.00 *(978-0-7642-0445-6(9))* Vol. 2. (Illus.). 544p. (gr. 11-12). pap. 17.00 *(978-0-7642-0452-4(1))* Bethany Hse. Pubs.
Martin, Rebecca. The Treasure Hunt. 2015. (Amish Frontier Ser.). (ENG., Illus.). 160p. (J). (gr. 2-7). pap. 8.99 *(978-0-7369-6369-5(3))* Harvest Hse. Pubs.
Munro, Sandie. Karlee's Other Family. 2006. 84p. pap. 8.95 *(978-1-60126-000-0(8))* Masthof Pr.
Seyfert, Ella Maie. Amish Moving Day. Jones, Henrietta, illus. 2011. 132p. 40.95 *(978-1-258-01315-8(0))* Literary Licensing, LLC.
Stewart, Sarah. The Journey. Smalls, David, illus. pap. incl. audio compact disk *(978-1-59112-556-3(1))*; pap. 18.95 incl. audio compact disk *(978-1-59112-344-6(5))*; pap. incl. audio *(978-0-87499-924-2(3))*; pap. 16.95 incl. audio *(978-0-87499-922-8(7))* Live Oak Media.

—The Journey. Small, David, illus. 2006. (ENG.). 40p. (J). (gr. k-4). reprint ed. pap. 8.99 *(978-0-374-40010-1(5),* 9780374400101) Square Fish.

AMISTAD (SCHOONER)

Apte, Sunita & Hess, Debra. Amistad: Fight for Freedom. 2007. (Read on! Special Edition: Level RA Ser.). (Illus.). 23p. pap. 18.51 *(978-1-4190-3507-4(X))* Steck-Vaughn.

Azarian, Melissa Eisen. The Amistad Mutiny: From the Court Case to the Movie. 2009. (Famous Court Cases That Became Movies Ser.). (Illus.). 128p. (J). (gr. 6-18). lib. bdg. 33.27 *(978-0-7660-3054-1(7))* Enslow Pubs., Inc.

Baumann, Susan K. The Middle Passage & the Revolt on the Amistad. 2013. (Jr. Graphic African American History Ser.). (ENG., Illus.). 24p. (J). (gr. 3-6). pap. 10.60 *(978-1-4777-1447-8(2))*; lib. bdg. 25.25 *(978-1-4777-1311-2(5))* Rosen Publishing Group, Inc., The. (PowerKids Pr.).

Gold, Susan Dudley. United States V. Amistad: Slave Ship Mutiny. 2006. (Supreme Court Milestones Ser.). (Illus.). 128p. (gr. 7-7). lib. bdg. 42.79 *(978-0-7614-2143-6(2),* Benchmark Bks.) Marshall Cavendish Corp.

Grayson, Robert. The Amistad, 1 vol. 2011. (Essential Events Set 6 Ser.). (ENG., Illus.). 112p. (J). (gr. 6-12). lib. bdg. 35.64 *(978-1-61714-761-6(3))* ABDO Publishing Co.

McKissack, Patricia C. Amistad: The Story of a Slave Ship. Stanley, Sanna, illus. 2005. (Penguin Young Readers, Level 4 Ser.). (ENG.). 48p. (J). (gr. 3-4). mass mkt. 3.99 *(978-0-448-43900-6(X),* Penguin Young Readers) Penguin Young Readers Group.

The Middle Passage & the Revolt on the Amistad. 2013. (Jr. Graphic African American History Ser.). 24p. (J). (gr. 3-6). pap. 63.60 *(978-1-4777-1448-5(0),* PowerKids Pr.) Rosen Publishing Group, Inc., The.

Roxburgh, Ellis. The Amistad Revolt. 2017. (Rebellions, Revolts, & Uprisings Ser.). 48p. (gr. 5-5). pap. 84.30 ***(978-1-5382-0752-9(4))*** Stevens, Gareth Publishing LLLP.

Worth, Richard. The Amistad Revolt & the Transatlantic Slave Trade. 2016. (People & Events That Changed the World Ser.). (ENG., Illus.). 128p. (J). (gr. 7-8). lib. bdg. 37.27 *(978-0-7660-7378-4(5))* Enslow Pubs., Inc.

AMNESIA

Holtje, Bert & Collins, Christine. Amnesia & Related Disorders. 2011. (Psychological Disorders Ser.). (YA). (gr. 7-12). 37.50 *(978-1-60413-937-2(4))* Facts On File, Inc.

MacKay, Jennifer. Amnesia. 2009. (Diseases & Disorders Ser.). (ENG., Illus.). 128p. (gr. 7-10). lib. bdg. 39.90 *(978-1-4205-0040-0(6),* LML02109-240027, Lucent Bks.) Cengage Gale.

AMNESIA—FICTION

Armentrout, Jennifer L. Don't Look Back. 2014. (Novel Ser.: 1). (ENG.). 384p. (YA). (gr. 9-17). 16.99 *(978-1-4231-7512-4(3))* Hyperion Bks. for Children.

Armistead, Cal. Being Henry David. (ENG.). 312p. (YA). (gr. 8-12). 2014. pap. 9.99 *(978-0-8075-0616-5(8))* 2013. 16.99 *(978-0-8075-0615-8(X))* Whitman, Albert & Co.

Ashley, Bernard. Solitaire. 2012. (Fiction Ser.). 338p. (J). pap. 6.99 *(978-0-7945-3031-0(1),* Usborne) EDC Publishing.

Barr, Emily. The One Memory of Flora Banks. 2017. (ENG.). 304p. (YA). (gr. 7). 15.99 *(978-0-399-54701-0(0),* Philomel Bks.) Penguin Young Readers Group.

Bayle, B. J. Perilous Passage. 2007. (ENG.). 184p. (YA). (gr. k-7). pap. 11.99 *(978-1-55002-689-4(5),* Sandcastle Bks.) Dundurn CAN. Dist: Ingram Publisher Services.

Brody, Jessica. Unchanged. 2015. (Unremembered Trilogy Ser.: 3). (ENG.). 432p. (YA). (gr. 7). 17.99 *(978-0-374-37969-6(0),* 9780374379896, Farrar, Straus & Giroux (BYR)) Farrar, Straus & Giroux.

—Unremembered. 2013. (Unremembered Trilogy Ser.: 1). (ENG.). 320p. (YA). (gr. 7). 17.99 *(978-0-374-37991-9(2),* 9780374379919, Farrar, Straus & Giroux (BYR)) Farrar, Straus & Giroux.

—Unremembered. 2014. (Unremembered Trilogy Ser.: 1). (ENG.). 352p. (YA). (gr. 7). pap. 9.99 *(978-1-250-04002-2(7),* 9781250040022) Square Fish.

Cameron, Sharon. The Forgetting. (ENG.). 416p. (gr. 7-7). 2017. (J). pap. 9.99 ***(978-1-338-16071-0(0))*** 2016. (YA). 18.99 *(978-0-545-94521-9(6))* Scholastic, Inc. (Scholastic Pr.).

Carey, Anna. Blackbird. (Blackbird Ser.: 1). (ENG.). (YA). (gr. 9). 2015. 272p. pap. 9.99 *(978-0-06-229974-1(3))* 2014. 256p. 17.99 *(978-0-06-229973-4(5))* HarperCollins Pubs. (HarperTeen).

—Blackbird. 2015. (SPA.). 240p. (YA). (gr. 9-12). pap. 17.99 *(978-987-612-909-1(0))* Lectorum Pubns., Inc.

—Deadfall. 2015. 256p. (J). pap. 9.99 *(978-0-06-242788-5(1))* HarperCollins Pubs.

Coley, Liz. Pretty Girl-13. 2013. (ENG.). 352p. (YA). (gr. 9). 17.99 *(978-0-06-212737-2(3),* Tegen, Katherine Bks) HarperCollins Pubs.

Cremer, Andrea. The Inventor's Secret. (Inventor's Secret Ser.). (ENG.). (YA). (gr. 7). 2015. 416p. pap. 10.99 *(978-0-14-751438-7(X),* Speak) 2014. 336p. 18.99 *(978-0-399-15962-6(2),* Philomel Bks.) Penguin Young Readers Group.

Dashner, James. The Maze Runner, 4 vols. (ENG.). (YA). (gr. 7). 2015. 75.96 *(978-1-101-93213-1(9),* Delacorte Pr.) 2010. (Maze Runner Ser.: 1). 416p. pap. 9.99 *(978-0-385-73795-1(5),* Delacorte Pr.) 2009. (Maze Runner Ser.: Bk. 1). 384p. 18.99 *(978-0-385-73794-4(7),* Delacorte Pr.) 2014. (Maze Runner Ser.: 1). 400p. pap. 10.99 *(978-0-385-38520-6(X),* Delacorte Pr.)Bk. 1. 2014. (Maze Runner Ser.). 400p. 17.99 *(978-0-553-51153-6(X),* Delacorte Bks. for Young Readers) Random Hse. Children's Bks.

—The Maze Runner. 2010. (Maze Runner Ser.: 1). lib. bdg. 20.85 *(978-0-606-15077-4(3),* Turtleback) Turtleback Bks.

—The Maze Runner; The Scorch Trials; The Death Cure; The Kill Order, 4 vols. 2014. (ENG.). (YA). (gr. 7). pap., pap., pap. 39.96 *(978-0-385-38889-4(6),* Delacorte Pr.) Random Hse. Children's Bks.

—The Maze Runner Trilogy, 3 vols. 2013. (Maze Runner Ser.). (ENG.). (YA). pap., pap., pap. 29.97 *(978-0-385-37379-1(1),* Ember) Random Hse. Children's Bks.

Griffin, Adele. Loud Awake & Lost. (ENG.). 304p. (YA). (gr. 7). 2015. pap. 9.99 *(978-0-385-75275-6(X),* Ember) 2013. lib. bdg. 19.99 *(978-0-385-75273-2(3),* Knopf Bks. for Young Readers) Random Hse. Children's Bks.

Hargreaves, Roger. Mr. Nobody. Hargreaves, Adam, illus. 2011. (Mr. Men & Little Miss Ser.). (ENG.). 32p. (J). (gr. -1-2). mass mkt. 4.99 *(978-0-8431-9876-8(1),* Price Stern Sloan) Penguin Young Readers Group.

Herren, Greg. Sleeping Angel. 2011. (ENG.). 288p. (J). (gr. 7). pap. 13.95 *(978-1-60282-214-6(X))* Bold Strokes Bks.

Houck, Colleen. Tiger's Destiny. 2015. (Tiger's Curse Ser.: Bk. 4). (ENG.). 464p. (J). (gr. 7). pap. 9.95 *(978-1-4549-0356-7(2))* Sterling Publishing Co., Inc.

—Tiger's Voyage. (Tiger's Curse Ser.: Bk. 3). (ENG.). (J). (gr. 7). 2014. 568p. pap. 9.95 *(978-1-4549-0357-4(0))*Bk. 3. 2011. 560p. 17.95 *(978-1-4027-8405-7(8))* Sterling Publishing Co., Inc.

Keaney, Brian. Jacob's Ladder. 2007. (ENG., Illus.). 224p. (J). (gr. 5-9). 15.99 *(978-0-7636-3071-3(3))* Candlewick Pr.

Klavan, Andrew. The Last Thing I Remember, 1 vol. 2010. (Homelanders Ser.: 1). (ENG.). 352p. (YA). pap. 9.99 *(978-1-59554-586-2(7))* Nelson, Thomas Inc.

Kleyla, Mary Pat. Identity Unknown. 2003. 154p. (YA). 22.95 *(978-0-595-65812-1(1))*; pap. 12.95 *(978-0-595-28473-3(6))* iUniverse, Inc.

Korman, Gordon. Restart. 2017. (ENG.). 256p. (J). (gr. 3-7). 16.99 ***(978-1-338-05377-7(9),*** Scholastic Pr.) Scholastic, Inc.

Kuehn, Stephanie. Complicit. (ENG.). 256p. (YA). 2016. pap. 10.99 *(978-1-250-04460-0(X),* 9781250044600) 2014. (gr. 8-12). 19.99 *(978-1-250-04459-4(6),* 9781250044594) St. Martin's Pr. (St. Martin's Griffin).

Lockhart, E. We Were Liars. 2014. (Illus.). 227p. (YA). *(978-0-385-39009-5(2),* Delacorte Pr) Random House Publishing Group.

—We Were Liars. (ENG., (YA). (gr. 7). 2014. Illus.). 240p. 17.99 *(978-0-385-74126-2(X))* 2017. 272p. 18.99 ***(978-1-5247-6458-6(2))*** Random Hse. Children's Bks. (Delacorte Pr.).

Matthews, L. S. Lexi. 2008. 200p. (J). pap. *(978-0-385-73575-9(8),* Delacorte Pr) Random House Publishing Group.

McBride, Kristina. One Moment. 2017. (ENG.). 272p. (YA). (gr. 8). pap. 9.99 *(978-1-5107-1455-7(3),* Sky Pony Pr.) Skyhorse Publishing Co., Inc.

Messenger, Shannon. Let the Sky Fall. 2013. (Sky Fall Ser.: 1). (ENG., (YA). (gr. 7). Illus.). 432p. pap. 10.99 *(978-1-4424-5042-4(8))*; 416p. 17.99 *(978-1-4424-5041-7(X))* Simon Pulse. (Simon Pulse).

Mlynowski, Sarah. Beauty Queen. (Whatever After Ser.: 7). (ENG.). 176p. (J). (gr. 3-7). 2016. pap. 5.99 *(978-0-545-74657-1(4))* 2015. 14.99 *(978-0-545-74654-0(X))* Scholastic, Inc. (Scholastic Pr.).

Oswald, Pete & Thompson, Justin K. Mingo the Flamingo. Oswald, Pete & Thompson, Justin K., illus. 2017. (Illus.). 40p. (J). (gr. -1-3). 17.99 *(978-0-06-239198-8(4))* HarperCollins Pubs.

Paquette, Ammi-Joan. Paradox. 2014. (ENG.). 240p. (YA). (gr. 7). pap. 9.99 *(978-0-375-87163-4(2),* Ember) Random Hse. Children's Bks.

Quinn, Kate Karyus. Another Little Piece. 2013. (ENG.). 432p. (YA). (gr. 9). 17.99 *(978-0-06-213595-7(3),* HarperTeen) HarperCollins Pubs.

Reed, Jaime. Keep Me in Mind. 2016. (ENG.). 336p. (J). (gr. 7). 17.99 *(978-0-545-88381-8(4))* Scholastic, Inc.

Searles, Rachel. The Lost Planet. 2014. (Lost Planet Ser.: 1). (ENG.). 384p. (YA). (gr. 4-8). 16.99 *(978-1-250-03879-1(0),* 9781250038791) Feiwel & Friends.

—The Stolen Moon. 2015. (Lost Planet Ser.: 2). (ENG.). 368p. (YA). (gr. 4-9). 15.99 *(978-1-250-03880-7(4),* 9781250038807) Feiwel & Friends.

Sigler, Scott. Alight. 2016. (Generations Trilogy Ser.: 2). (ENG.). 464p. (gr. 9). pap. 10.00 *(978-0-553-39317-0(0),* Del Rey) Random House Publishing Group.

—Alive. 2016. (Generations Trilogy Ser.: 1). (ENG.). 384p. (gr. 9). pap. 12.00 *(978-0-553-39312-5(X),* Del Rey) Random House Publishing Group.

Sirowy, Alexandra. The Creeping: If You Hunt for Monsters, You'll Find Them. 2015. (ENG., Illus.). 400p. (YA). (gr. 7). 17.99 *(978-1-4814-1886-7(6))* Simon & Schuster Children's Publishing.

St. Jean, Trina. Blank, 1 vol. 2015. (ENG.). 312p. (YA). (gr. 8-12). pap. 12.95 *(978-1-4598-0807-2(X))* Orca Bk. Pubs. USA.

Stanley, Malaika Rose. Miss Bubble's Troubles. Smith, Jan, illus. 2010. (ENG.). 40p. (J). (gr. 2-4). pap. 10.99 *(978-1-84853-024-9(2))* Transworld Publishers Ltd. GBR. Dist: Independent Pubs. Group.

Ward, Rachel. The Drowning. 2014. (ENG.). 272p. (J). (gr. 9). 17.99 *(978-0-545-62771-9(0),* Chicken Hse., The) Scholastic, Inc.

Wells, Helen. Cherry Ames at Hilton Hospital: Book 13. 2007. (Cherry Ames Nurse Stories Ser.). 224p. (J). (gr. 3-7). 14.95 *(978-0-8261-0421-2(5))* Springer Publishing Co., Inc.

Winick, Judd. The Boy Who Crashed to Earth. 2015. (Hilo Ser.: 1). (ENG., Illus.). 208p. (J). (gr. 3-7). 16.99 *(978-0-385-38618-0(4),* Random Hse. Bks. for Young Readers) Random Hse. Children's Bks.

Zevin, Gabrielle. Memoirs of a Teenage Amnesiac. 2011. 9.46 *(978-0-7848-3492-3(X),* Everbind) Marco Bk. Co.

—Memoirs of a Teenage Amnesiac. 2009. (ENG.). 304p. (YA). (gr. 9-13). pap. 10.99 *(978-0-312-56128-4(8),* 9780312561284) Square Fish.

AMPHIBIANS

see also names of amphibians, e.g. Frogs; Salamanders; etc.

Amphibians. 2010. (Amphibians Ser.). (ENG.). 24p. (gr. k-1). pap. 14.58 *(978-1-4296-4986-5(0))*; pap. 14.58 *(978-1-4296-5172-1(5))*; lib. bdg. 79.95 *(978-1-4296-4437-2(0))* Capstone Press of Coughlan Cos. (Pebble Plus).

Amphibians & Reptiles. 2005. (World of Animals Ser.: Vols. 41-50). (J). 499.00 *(978-0-7172-5916-8(1))* Scholastic Library Publishing.

Amphibians [Capstone Sole Source]. 2010. (Amphibians Ser.). 24p. lib. bdg. 119.95 *(978-1-4296-5840-9(1),* Pebble Plus) Capstone Press of Coughlan Cos.

Basic Domestic Reptiles & Amphibians. 2005. (Basic Domestic Reptiles & Amphibians Ser.). 64p. (gr. 6-12). 137.50 *(978-0-7910-8062-7(5),* Chelsea Hse.) Facts On File, Inc.

Bell, Samantha S. 12 Amphibians Back from the Brink. 2015. (ENG., Illus.). 32p. (J). pap. 9.95 *(978-1-63235-060-2(2))* RiverStream Publishing.

Berne, Emma Carlson. Amphibians. 2017. (My First Animal Kingdom Encyclopedias Ser.). (ENG., Illus.). 32p. (gr. 1-2). lib. bdg. 27.32 *(978-1-5157-3926-5(0),* Aplus Bks.) Capstone Press of Coughlan Cos.

Bulletpoints Reptiles & Amphibians. 2005. (Illus.). (J). per. 4.99 *(978-1-933581-05-7(0))* Byeway Bks.

Bumstead, Pat & Worsley, Norman H. Canadian Skin & Scales. 2003. (Illus.). 168p. (YA). (gr. 5-6). pap. *(978-0-9689278-1-6(5))* Simply Wild Pubns., Inc.

Caputo, Christine A. Reptiles & Amphibians. 2012. (Illus.). 32p. (J). *(978-0-545-46701-8(2))* Scholastic, Inc.

Clarke, Barry & Dorling Kindersley Publishing Staff. Amphibian. Brightling, Geoff & Greenaway, Frank, photos by. 2005. (DK Eyewitness Bks.). (ENG., Illus.). 72p. (J). (gr. 3-7). 16.99 *(978-0-7566-1380-8(9),* DK Children) Dorling Kindersley Publishing, Inc.

Cleary, Brian P. Salamander, Frog, & Polliwog: What Is an Amphibian? Goneau, Martin, illus. 2012. (Animal Groups Are CATegorical (tm) Ser.). (ENG.). 32p. (gr. k-3). pap. 7.95 *(978-1-4677-0339-0(7))*; lib. bdg. 26.60 *(978-0-7613-6209-8(6))* Lerner Publishing Group. (Millbrook Pr.).

Crump, Marty. Amphibians & Reptiles: An Introduction to Their Natural History & Conservation, 1 vol. 2011. (ENG., Illus.). 272p. (J). 29.95 *(978-1-935778-20-2(X))* McDonald & Woodward Publishing Co., The.

De la Bédoyère, Camilla. The Wild Life of Frogs, 1 vol. 2015. (ENG., Illus.). 24p. (J). lib. bdg. 23.60 *(978-1-4777-5518-1(7),* Windmill Bks.) Rosen Publishing Group, Inc., The.

Dorling Kindersley Publishing Staff. DK Findout! Reptiles & Amphibians. 2017. (DK Find Out! Ser.). (ENG.). 64p. (J). (gr. 1-4). pap. 10.99 ***(978-1-4654-6310-4(0),*** DK Children) Dorling Kindersley Publishing, Inc.

Dorling Kindersley Publishing Staff. Everything You Need to Know about Frogs & Other Slippery Creatures. 2011. (Everything You Need to Know Ser.). (ENG., Illus.). 80p. (J). (gr. 2-5). 15.99 *(978-0-7566-8232-3(0),* DK Children) Dorling Kindersley Publishing, Inc.

Dowling, Lucy. Why Why Why... Do Lizards Stick to Walls? 2010. (Why Why Why Ser.). 32p. (J). (gr. 1-3). lib. bdg. 18.95 *(978-1-4222-1582-1(2))* Mason Crest.

Duke, Shirley Smith. Reptiles & Amphibians Explained. 2016. (Distinctions in Nature Ser.). 32p. (J). (gr. 3-3). 28.50 *(978-1-5026-1746-0(3))* Cavendish Square Publishing.

Encyclopaedia Britannica, Inc. Staff, compiled by. Britannica Illustrated Science Library: Fish & Amphibians, 16 vols. 2008. (Illus.). (J). 29.95 *(978-1-59339-389-2(X))* Encyclopaedia Britannica, Inc.

Fisher, Diana. Reptiles & Amphibians: Step by Step Intsructions for 29 Reptiles & Amphibians. 2006. (Learn to Draw Ser.). (ENG., Illus.). 40p. (J). (gr. 1-17). per. 4.95 *(978-1-56010-994-5(7),* 1560109947) Quarto Publishing Group USA.

Fletcher, Patricia. Why Do Frogs Have Teeth? And Other Curious Amphibian Adaptations. 2017. (Odd Adaptations Ser.). 32p. (J). (gr. 3-4). pap. 10.50 ***(978-1-5382-0389-7(8))*** Stevens, Gareth Publishing LLLP.

Gaines, Ann. Kids Top 10 Pet Reptiles & Amphibians. 2015. (American Humane Association Top 10 Pets for Kids Ser.). 48p. (J). (gr. 3-4). 25.27 *(978-0-7660-6645-8(2))* Enslow Pubs., Inc.

Gaines, Ann Graham. Kids Top 10 Pet Reptiles & Amphibians. 2015. (American Humane Association Top 10 Pets for Kids Ser.). 48p. (J). (gr. 3-4). pap. 8.95 *(978-0-7660-6646-5(0),* Enslow Elementary) Enslow Pubs., Inc.

—Top 10 Reptiles & Amphibians for Kids. 2008. (Top Pets for Kids with American Humane Ser.). (Illus.). 48p. (J). (gr. 2-5). lib. bdg. 25.27 *(978-0-7660-3074-9(1))* Enslow Pubs., Inc.

Galindo-Leal, Carlos. De dos mundos = of Two Worlds: Las ranas, sapos y salamandras de la Península de Yucatán, México = the Frogs, Toads & Salamanders of the Yucatan Peninsula, Mexico. Arreola Alemón, Roberto, illus. 2003. (SPA & ENG.). 152p. pap. 19.95 *(978-1-929165-52-0(8))* PANGAEA.

Hall, Julie. Reptiles & Amphibians: Grades 2 & 3. (Illus.). (J). pap., wbk. ed. 4.99 *(978-0-88743-964-3(0))* School Zone Publishing Co.

Hall, Katharine. Amphibians & Reptiles, 1 vol. 2015. (Compare & Contrast Ser.). (ENG., Illus.). 32p. (J). (gr. k-3). pap. 9.95 *(978-1-62855-560-8(2))* Arbordale Publishing.

—Amphibians & Reptiles: A Compare & Contrast Book, 1 vol. 2015. (SPA & ENG.). 32p. (J). (gr. k-3). pap. 9.95 *(978-1-62855-569-1(6))* Arbordale Publishing.

Harrington, Jane. Extreme Pets. 2007. (ENG., Illus.). 164p. (J). (gr. 2-5). pap., instr.'s hndbk. ed. 12.99 *(978-0-439-82948-9(8))* Scholastic, Inc.

Harris, Tim. Amphibians. 2010. (Slimy, Scaly, Deadly Reptiles & Amphibians Ser.). (Illus.). 32p. (J). (gr. 2-6). pap. 10.50 *(978-1-4339-3442-1(6))*; lib. bdg. 26.00 *(978-1-4339-3441-4(8))* Stevens, Gareth Publishing LLLP. (Gareth Stevens Learning Library).

Harris, Tim, ed. Reptiles & Amphibians. 2011. (FAYFT: Endangered Animals Ser.). 64p. (gr. 4-10). lib. bdg. 39.95 *(978-1-936333-36-3(8))* Brown Bear Bks.

Holt, Rinehart and Winston Staff. Holt Science & Technology Chapter 16: Life Science: Fishes, Amphibians, & Reptiles. 5th ed. 2004. (Illus.). pap. 12.86 *(978-0-03-030221-3(8))* Holt McDougal.

Housel, Debra J. Reptiles y Anfibios Reptantes. 2017. (TIME for Kids en Español - Level 3 Ser.). (SPA & ENG.). 32p. (gr. 3-3). lib. bdg. 31.99 ***(978-1-5157-5172-4(4))*** Time for Kids Inc AUS. Dist: Capstone Pub.

Housel, Debra J. Slithering Reptiles & Amphibians, 1 vol. 2nd rev. ed. 2013. (Nonfiction Readers Ser.). (ENG., Illus.). 28p. (J). (gr. 3-3). pap. 25.96 *(978-1-4807-1074-0(1))* Shell Educational Publishing.

—Slithering Reptiles & Amphibians, 1 vol. 2nd rev. ed. 2011. (Nonfiction Readers Ser.). (ENG.). 28p. (J). (gr. 3-3). pap. 8.99 *(978-1-4333-3659-1(6))* Teacher Created Materials, Inc.

Howell, Catherine Herbert. Ultimate Explorer Field Guide: Reptiles & Amphibians: Find Adventure! Go Outside! Have Fun! Be a Backyard Ranger & Amphibian Adventurer. 2016. (ENG., Illus.). 160p. (J). (gr. 3-7). pap. 12.99 *(978-1-4263-2544-1(4),* National Geographic Children's Bks.) National Geographic Society.

—Ultimate Explorer Field Guide: Reptiles & Amphibians: Find Adventure! Go Outside! Have Fun! Be a Backyard Ranger & Amphibian Adventurer! 2016. (ENG., Illus.). 160p. (J). (gr. 3-7). lib. bdg. 22.90 *(978-1-4263-2545-8(2),* National Geographic Children's Bks.) National Geographic Society.

Hudak, Heather C. Reptiles & Amphibians. (Animal Facts Ser.). (Illus.). 24p. (J). 2005. (gr. 2-3). per. 8.95 *(978-1-59036-246-4(2))* 2004. lib. bdg. 24.45 *(978-1-59036-204-4(7))* Weigl Pubs., Inc.

Hughes, Sarah Anne. Reptiles & Amphibians. Peterson, Roger Tory, ed. Hughes, Sarah Anne, illus. 2nd ed. 2013. (Peterson Field Guide Color-In Bks.). (ENG., Illus.). 64p. (J). 8.95 *(978-0-544-02695-7(0))* Houghton Mifflin Harcourt Publishing Co.

Kalman, Bobbie. Frogs & Other Amphibians. 2005. (What Kind of Animal Is It? Ser.). (Illus.). 32p. (J). *(978-978-077-872-9(1))*; (ENG., pap. *(978-0-7787-2217-5(1))* Crabtree Publishing Co.

—Les Grenouilles et Autres Amphibiens. 2010. (Petit Monde Vivant Ser.). (FRE., Illus.). 32p. (J). pap. 9.95 *(978-2-89579-319-9(0))* Bayard Canada Livres CAN. Dist: Crabtree Publishing Co.

—Ranas y Otros Anfibios. 2007. (Que Tipo de Animal Es? Ser.). (SPA., Illus.). 32p. (J). (gr. 1-2). lib. bdg. *(978-0-7787-8837-9(7))*; (gr. k-4). pap. *(978-0-7787-8873-7(3))* Crabtree Publishing Co.

Kalman, Bobbie & Langille, Jacqueline. ?Que Son los Anfibios? 2005. (Ciencia de los Seres Vivos Ser.). (SPA., Illus.). 32p. (J). (gr. 3-4). pap. *(978-0-7787-8807-2(5))* Crabtree Publishing Co.

—¿Qué Son los Anfibios? 2005. (Serie la Ciencia de los Seres Vivos Ser.). (SPA., Illus.). 32p. (J). (gr. 3-4). lib. bdg. *(978-0-7787-8761-7(3))* Crabtree Publishing Co.

Kaspar, Anna. What's an Amphibian? 2012. (All about Animals Ser.). (ENG.). 24p. (J). (gr. k-3). pap. 8.25 *(978-1-4488-6234-4(5))*; lib. bdg. 22.60 *(978-1-4488-6138-5(1))* Rosen Publishing Group, Inc., The. (PowerKids Pr.).

—What's an Amphibian? Qué Es un Anfibio? 2012. (All about Animals / Todo sobre los animales Ser.). (SPA & ENG.). 24p. (J). (gr. k-3). lib. bdg. 22.60 *(978-1-4488-6705-9(3),* PowerKids Pr.) Rosen Publishing Group, Inc., The.

Levine, Michelle. Amphibians. 2015. (Animal Kingdom Ser.). (Illus.). 32p. (J). 28.50 *(978-1-60753-471-6(1))* Amicus Publishing.

Lewis, Clare. Amphibian Body Parts. 2015. (Animal Body Parts Ser.). (ENG., Illus.). 24p. (gr. k-2). 23.32 *(978-1-4846-2557-6(9))* Heinemann-Raintree.

Little & Large Sticker Activity - Reptiles & Amphibians. 2006. (J). 3.99 *(978-1-933581-35-4(2))* Byeway Bks.

Markle, Sandra. Hip-Pocket Papa. Marks, Alan, illus. 2010. (ENG.). 32p. (J). (gr. -1-3). 15.95 *(978-1-57091-708-0(6))* Charlesbridge Publishing, Inc.

Martin, Isabel. Amphibians: A Question & Answer Book, 1 vol. 2014. (Animal Kingdom Questions & Answers Ser.). (ENG.). 24p. (gr. k-1). 26.65 *(978-1-4914-0562-8(7))*; (Illus.). pap. 6.95 *(978-1-4914-0630-4(5))* Capstone Press of Coughlan Cos. (Pebble Plus).

Mathewson, Robert F. The How & Why Wonder Book of Reptiles & Amphibians. Sweet, Darrell & Allen, Douglas, illus. 2011. 48p. pap. 35.95 *(978-1-258-09940-4(3))* Literary Licensing, LLC.

Mattern, Joanne. Reptiles & Amphibians. 2009. (Reading Room Collection 2 Ser.). 24p. (gr. 3-4). 42.50 *(978-1-60851-986-6(4),* PowerKids Pr.) Rosen Publishing Group, Inc., The.

—Reptiles y anfibios (Reptiles & Amphibians) 2009. (Reading Room Collection: Spanish Ser.). (SPA.). 24p. (gr. 3-4). 42.50 *(978-1-60854-179-9(7),* Editorial Buenas Letras) Rosen Publishing Group, Inc., The.

Mattison, Christopher. Reptiles & Amphibians. 2007. (Facts at Your Fingertips Ser.). (Illus.). 64p. (YA). (gr. 7-12). lib. bdg. 35.65 *(978-1-933834-04-7(8))* Brown Bear Books.

McDowell, Pamela. Salamander Rescue, 1 vol. Charko, Kasia, illus. 2016. (Orca Echoes Ser.). (ENG.). 80p. (J). (gr. 2-3). pap. 6.95 *(978-1-4598-1123-2(2))* Orca Bk. Pubs. USA.

Meadows, Graham & Vial, Claire. Amphibians. 2004. (ENG., Illus.). 24p. (J). (gr. 2-3). pap. 7.47 net. *(978-0-7685-1631-9(5),* Dominie Elementary) Pearson Schl.

Mertz, Leslie A., et al. Amphibians, 3.0, Vol. 3. 2005. (Grzimek's Student Animal Life Resource Ser.). (ENG., Illus.). 600p. (J). 286.00 *(978-0-7876-9407-4(X),* UXL) Cengage Gale.

—Grzimek's Student Animal Life Resource, 3 vols. 2005. (Illus.). (J). *(978-0-7876-9409-8(6))*; *(978-0-7876-9408-1(8))*; *(978-0-7876-9410-4(X))* Cengage Gale. (UXL).

Morgan, Sally. Frogs & Toads: Animal Lives Series. 2008. 32p. (J). lib. bdg. 18.95 *(978-1-59566-538-6(2))* QEB Publishing Inc.

Munro, Alice. Friend of My Youth. 2012. (Vintage International Ser.). (ENG., Illus.). 288p. E-Book *(978-0-307-81459-3(9),* Vintage) Knopf Doubleday Publishing Group.

National Geographic Editors. Creepy, Crawly Collection. 2012. (Readers Ser.). (ENG., Illus.). 128p. (J). (gr. -1-1). pap. 7.99 *(978-1-4263-1197-0(4),* National Geographic Children's Bks.) National Geographic Society.

National Geographic Kids. National Geographic Kids Reptiles & Amphibians Sticker Activity Book. 2017. (NG Sticker Activity Bks.). (ENG.). 56p. (J). (gr. -1-3). pap. 6.99 *(978-1-4263-2777-3(3),* National Geographic Children's Bks.) National Geographic Society.

Niven, Felicia Lowenstein & Library Association Staff. Learning to Care for Reptiles & Amphibians. 2010. (Beginning Pet Care with American Humane Ser.). 48p. (J). 25.27 *(978-0-7660-3194-4(2),* Enslow Elementary) Enslow Pubs., Inc.

O'Hare, Ted. Amphibians. 2005. (What Is an Animal? (Discovery Library) Ser.). (Illus.). 24p. (J). (gr. 1-4). per. 5.45 *(978-1-59515-729-4(8))*; lib. bdg. 14.95 *(978-1-59515-415-6(9))* Rourke Educational Media.

O'Reilly, Wenda. GO FISH WILDLIFE REPTILES & AMPHIBIANS. 2007. n/ap. pap. 119.40 *(978-1-59960-018-5(8))* Birdcage Pr.

A
B

Phillips, Dee. Reptiles & Amphibians. 2006. (Blue Zoo Guides). (ENG., Illus.). 96p. (J). (gr. -1-2). 18.95 *(978-1-58728-561-5(4))* Cooper Square Publishing Llc.

Ransom, Candice. Endangered & Extinct Amphibians. 2014. (Lightning Bolt Books Animals in Danger Ser.). (ENG., Illus.). 32p. (gr. k-2). lib. bdg. 26.60 *(978-1-4677-1332-0(5)*, Lerner Pubns.) Lerner Publishing Group.

Reference, Brown. Exploring the World of Reptiles & Amphibians, 6-Volume Set, 6 vols. 2009. (Exploring the World of Reptiles & Amphibians Ser.). (Illus.). 480p. (gr. 5-8). 210.00 *(978-1-60413-256-4(6)*, Chelsea Hse.) Facts On File, Inc.

Reptiles & Amphibians. 2014. (Animal Q & A Ser.). (Illus.). 24p. (J). (gr. k-3). lib. bdg. 23.60 *(978-1-4777-9194-3(9))* Windmill Bks.

Reptiles & Amphibians: Level P, 6 vols., Vol. 3. (Explorers Ser.). 32p. (gr. 3-6). 44.95 *(978-0-7699-0614-0(1))* Shortland Pubns. (U. S. A.) Inc.

Royston, Angela. Amphibians. (Illus.). 32p. (YA). (gr. 2-18). lib. bdg. 27.10 *(978-1-932333-33-6(9))* Chrysalis Education.

—Amphibians. 2015. (Animal Classifications Ser.). (ENG., Illus.). 32p. (gr. 1-3). 27.32 *(978-1-4846-0749-7(X)*, Heinemann First Library) Heinemann-Raintree.

Savage, Stephen. Focus on Amphibians. 2011. (Animal Watch Ser.). 32p. (YA). (gr. 3-6). lib. bdg. 26.60 *(978-1-4339-5978-3(X))* Stevens, Gareth Publishing LLLP.

Schafer, Susan. Invasive Reptiles & Amphibians. 2016. (Invasive Species Ser.). 48p. (J). (gr. 4-4). 31.36 *(978-1-5026-1830-6(3))* Cavendish Square Publishing.

School Zone Publishing Company Staff. Reptiles & Amphibians. (Illus.). (J). 19.99 incl. audio compact disk *(978-0-88743-978-0(0))* School Zone Publishing Co.

Schuetz, Kari. Amphibians. 2012. (Animal Classes Ser.). (ENG., Illus.). 24p. (J). (gr. k-3). lib. bdg. 25.95 *(978-1-60014-771-5(2)*, Blastoff! Readers) Bellwether Media.

Schuh, Mari. The World's Biggest Amphibians. 2015. (Illus.). 24p. (J). lib. bdg. 25.65 *(978-1-62031-209-4(3))* Jump! Inc.

Shea, Nicole. Creepy Amphibians. 2012. (Nature's Creepiest Creatures Ser.). (ENG.). 24p. (J). (gr. 2-5). pap. 8.15 *(978-1-4339-6483-1(X))*; lib. bdg. 22.60 *(978-1-4339-6481-7(3))* Stevens, Gareth Publishing LLLP. (Gareth Stevens Learning Library).

Shofner, Melissa Raé. Really Strange Amphibians. 2016. (Really Strange Adaptations Ser.). 00032p. (J). (gr. 5-5). pap. 10.00 *(978-1-4994-2740-0(9)*, PowerKids Pr.) Rosen Publishing Group, Inc., The.

Sill, Cathryn, et al. About Amphibians: A Guide for Children. Sill, John, illus. 2006. (Avenues Ser.). (ENG.). 48p. (C). (gr. k-3). pap. 13.95 *(978-1-56145-312-2(9))* National Geographic School Publishing, Inc.

Silverman, Buffy. Do You Know about Amphibians? 2009. (Lightning Bolt Books — Meet the Animal Groups Ser.). (ENG., Illus.). 32p. (gr. k-2). pap. 7.95 *(978-1-58013-856-7(X))*; lib. bdg. 26.60 *(978-0-8225-7543-6(4)*, Lerner Pubns.) Lerner Publishing Group.

—¿Sabes Algo Sobre Anfibios? (Do You Know about Amphibians?) 2012. (Libros Rayo — Conoce Los Grupos de Animales (Lightning Bolt Books — Meet the Animal Groups) Ser.). (SPA., Illus.). 32p. (gr. k-2). (J). lib. bdg. 26.60 *(978-0-7613-9333-7(1))*; pap. 7.95 *(978-0-7613-9363-4(3))* Lerner Publishing Group. (Ediciones Lerner).

Smalley, Carol. A Project Guide to Fishes & Amphibians. 2010. (Life Science Projects for Kids Ser.). (Illus.). 48p. (J). (gr. 4-8). lib. bdg. 29.95 *(978-1-58415-873-8(5))* Mitchell Lane Pubs., Inc.

Snedden, Robert. Amphibians. (Living Things Ser.). (Illus.). 32p. 2009. (J). (gr. -1-3). pap. 7.95 *(978-1-59920-192-4(5))* 2007. (YA). (gr. 3-6). lib. bdg. 28.50 *(978-1-59920-075-0(9))* Black Rabbit Bks.

Spim, Michele. Ripley's Cold-Blooded Creatures. 2004. (Illus.). 60p. (J). *(978-0-439-63362-8(1))* Scholastic, Inc.

Stefoff, Rebecca. The Amphibian Class. 2007. (Family Trees Ser.). (Illus.). 96p. (gr. 6-7). lib. bdg. 34.21 *(978-0-7614-2692-9(2)*, Benchmark Bks.) Marshall Cavendish Corp.

Stille, Darlene R. The Life Cycle of Amphibians, 1 vol. 2011. (Life Cycles Ser.). (ENG.). 48p. (gr. 3-5). pap. 9.95 *(978-1-4329-4985-3(3))*; 33.32 *(978-1-4329-4978-5(0))* Heinemann-Raintree. (Heinemann InfoSearch).

Taylor-Butler, Christine. Amphibians. 2013. (True Book(tm), a — Animal Kingdom Ser.). (ENG.). 48p. (J). 31.00 *(978-0-531-21750-4(7))*; pap. 6.95 *(978-0-531-22335-2(3))* Scholastic Library Publishing.

Twist, Clint. Reptiles & Amphibians Dictionary. 2005. (Illus.). 64p. (J). pap. *(978-0-439-66828-6(X))* Scholastic, Inc.

Veitch, Catherine. Amphibian Babies, 1 vol. 2013. (Animal Babies Ser.). (ENG.). 24p. (gr. -1-1). 22.65 *(978-1-4329-7491-6(2))*; pap. 6.95 *(978-1-4329-8416-8(0))*; pap. 35.94 *(978-1-4329-8423-6(3))* Heinemann-Raintree. (Acorn).

Wilkes, Sarah. Amphibians. 2006. (World Almanac Library of the Animal Kingdom Ser.). (Illus.). 48p. (gr. 5-12). lib. bdg. 31.00 *(978-0-8368-6208-9(2)*, World Almanac Library) Stevens, Gareth Publishing LLLP.

Williams, Brian. Amazing Reptiles & Amphibians. 2008. (Amazing Life Cycles Ser.). (Illus.). 32p. (gr. 2-6). lib. bdg. 26.00 *(978-0-8368-8898-0(7)*, Gareth Stevens Learning Library) Stevens, Gareth Publishing LLLP.

Williams, Dinah. Slithery, Slimy, Scaly Treats. 2009. (Extreme Cuisine Ser.). (Illus.). 24p. (J). (gr. 1-4). lib. bdg. 22.61 *(978-1-59716-762-8(2))* Bearport Publishing Co., Inc.

World Book, Inc Staff, contrib. by. Amphibians. 2009. (J). *(978-0-7166-0402-0(7))* World Bk., Inc.

World Book, Inc. Staff, contrib. by. Amphibians & Reptiles of the United States & Canada. 2004. (World Book's Science & Nature Guides Ser.). (Illus.). 80p. (J). *(978-0-7166-4209-1(3))* World Bk., Inc.

—Frogs & Other Amphibians. 2005. (World Book's Animals of the World Ser.). (Illus.). 64p. (J). *(978-0-7166-1269-8(0))* World Bk., Inc.

Zayarny, Jack. Amphibians. 2016. (J). *(978-1-5105-1108-8(3))* SmartBook Media, Inc.

AMPHIBIANS—FICTION

Andrews McMeel Publishing Staff, et al. Happy, Sad, Silly, Mad: My World Makes Me Feel. 2009. (ENG., Illus.). 28p. (J). (gr. -1-3). 12.99 *(978-0-7407-8430-9(7))* Andrews McMeel Publishing.

Braddock, Paige. Stinky Cecil in Operation Pond Rescue. 2015. (Stinky Cecil Ser.: 1). (ENG.). 128p. (J). pap. 9.99 *(978-1-4494-5711-2(8))* Andrews McMeel Publishing.

—Stinky Cecil in Terrarium Terror. 2016. (Stinky Cecil Ser.: 2). (ENG.). 128p. (J). pap. 9.99 *(978-1-4494-7186-6(2))* Andrews McMeel Publishing.

Edmonds, Lin. Patric the Pony & the Golden Salamander. 2009. 32p. pap. 13.99 *(978-1-4389-8021-8(3))* AuthorHouse.

Heydt, Scott. Mice Don't Taste Like Chicken. Aaron, Rich, illus. 2011. 188p. pap. 13.00 *(978-0-9830109-2-0(7))* Helm Publishing.

Hood, Karen Jean Matsko. There's a Toad in the Hole: A Big Fat Toad in the Hole, Bk.2. Whispering Pine Press International, ed. Artistic Design Service Staff, illus. 2014. (Hood Poetry Ser.). (J). per. 19.95 *(978-1-59649-298-1(8))* Whispering Pine Pr. International, Inc.

Lamstein, Sarah Marwil. Big Night for Salamanders. Benioff, Carol, illus. 2010. (ENG.). 40p. (J). (gr. 3-7). 17.95 *(978-1-932425-98-7(5))* Boyds Mills Pr.

Leedy, Loreen. The Great Graph Contest. Leedy, Loreen, illus. (ENG., Illus.). 32p. (J). (gr. -1-3). 2006. 7.99 *(978-0-8234-2029-2(9))* 2005. 17.95 *(978-0-8234-1710-0(7))* Holiday Hse., Inc.

Munton, Gill. Who Ate All the Lettuce? Top That Publishing Staff, ed. Elliott, Rebecca, illus. 2007. 12p. (gr. -1-k). bds. *(978-1-84666-177-8(3)*, Tide Mill Pr.) Top That! Publishing PLC.

Sazaklis, John. Salamander Smackdown. Baltazar, Art, illus. 2011. (DC Super-Pets Ser.). (ENG.). 56p. (gr. 2-2). pap. 4.95 *(978-1-4048-6844-1(5)*, DC Super-Pets) Picture Window Bks.

—Salamander Smackdown!, 1 vol. Baltazar, Art, illus. 2011. (DC Super-Pets Ser.). (ENG.). 56p. (gr. 2-2). lib. bdg. 23.99 *(978-1-4048-6478-8(4)*, DC Super-Pets) Picture Window Bks.

Small, David. Eulalie & the Hopping Head. 2003. (Illus.). (J). 25.95 incl. audio *(978-1-59112-217-3(1))* Live Oak Media.

Sparkes, Ali. Newt Nemesis. Collins, Ross, illus. 2014. (S. W. I. T. C. H. Ser.: 8). (ENG.). 88p. (J). (gr. 2-5). lib. bdg. 27.93 *(978-1-4677-3233-8(8)*, Darby Creek) Lerner Publishing Group.

Vernon, Ursula. Attack of the Ninja Frogs. 2nd ed. (Dragonbreath Ser.: 2). (ENG.). 208p. (J). (gr. 3-7). 2012. pap. 6.99 *(978-0-14-242066-9(2)*, Puffin Books) 2010. 12.99 *(978-0-8037-3365-7(8)*, Dial Bks) Penguin Young Readers Group.

—Attack of the Ninja Frogs. 2012. (Dragonbreath Ser.: 2). lib. bdg. 17.20 *(978-0-606-26666-6(6)*, Turtleback) Turtleback Bks.

AMUNDSEN, ROALD, 1872-1928

Bodden, Valerie. To the South Pole. (Great Expeditions Ser.). 48p. (J). 2012. (ENG.). (gr. 4-7). pap. 12.00 *(978-0-89812-667-9(3)*, Creative Paperbacks) 2011. (Illus.). 35.65 *(978-1-60818-069-1(7)*, Creative Education) Creative Co., The.

Karner, Julie. Roald Amundsen: The Conquest of the South Pole. 2006. (In the Footsteps of Explorers Ser.). (ENG., Illus.). 32p. (J). (gr. 3-7). pap. *(978-0-7787-2468-1(9))*; lib. bdg. *(978-0-7787-2432-2(8))* Crabtree Publishing Co.

Llanas, Sheila Griffin. Who Reached the South Pole First? (Race for History Ser.). (ENG.). 32p. (gr. 3-4). 2011. pap. 47.70 *(978-1-4296-6413-4(4))* 2010. lib. bdg. 27.32 *(978-1-4296-3344-4(1))* Capstone Press of Coughlan Cos. (Fact Finders).

McNeil, Niki, et al. HOCPP 1102 Roald Amundsen. 2006. spiral bd. 18.50 *(978-1-60308-102-3(X))* In the Hands of a Child.

Thompson, Gare. Roald Amundsen & Robert Scott Race to the South Pole. 2007. (History Chapters Ser.). (ENG., Illus.). 48p. (J). (gr. 1-4). lib. bdg. 17.90 *(978-1-4263-0187-2(1)*, National Geographic Children's Bks.) National Geographic Society.

Yomtov, Nel. Roald Amundsen Explores the South Pole. 2015. (Extraordinary Explorers Ser.). (ENG., Illus.). 24p. (J). (gr. 3-7). lib. bdg. 29.95 *(978-1-62617-295-1(1)*, Black Sheep) Bellwether Media.

AMUNDSEN SCOTT SOUTH POLE STATION (ANTARCTICA)

Hao, K. T. & Fulla, Monserrat. Scott y Amundsen: La Conquista del Polo Sur. Ingpen, Robert R., illus. 2006.Tr. of Scott & Amundsen, The Conquest of the South Pole. (SPA.). (J). (gr. 6-8). 9.60 *(978-84-316-7172-3(6)*, W32815) Vicens-Vives, Editorial, S.A. ESP. Dist: Lectorum Pubns., Inc.

AMUSEMENT PARKS—FICTION

Adams, Diane. Zoom!, 1 vol. Luthardt, Kevin, illus. 2005. (ENG.). 32p. (J). (gr. k-1). 15.95 *(978-1-56145-332-0(3))* Peachtree Pubs.

Adler, David A. Bones & the Roller Coaster Mystery, 7 vols. Newman, Barbara Johansen, illus. 2010. (Bones Ser.: 7). (ENG.). 32p. (J). (gr. 1-3). mass mkt. 3.99 *(978-0-14-241687-7(8)*, Penguin Young Readers) Penguin Young Readers Group.

Arena, Felice & Kettle, Phil. Wet World. Vane, Mitch, illus. 2004. (J). pap. *(978-1-59336-356-7(7))* Mondo Publishing.

Brezenoff, Steve. The Carnival Caper: An Interactive Mystery Adventure. Calo, Marcos, illus. 2017. (You Choose Stories: Field Trip Mysteries Ser.). (ENG.). 112p. (gr. 3-7). lib. bdg. 32.65 *(978-1-4965-2645-8(7))* Stone Arch Bks.

—The Ride That Was Really Haunted, 1 vol. Calo, Marcos, illus. 2011. (Field Trip Mysteries Ser.). (ENG.). 88p. (gr. 2-3). pap. 6.10 *(978-1-4342-3427-8(4))*; lib. bdg. 25.32 *(978-1-4342-3224-3(7))* Stone Arch Bks.

Child, Lauren. I Want to Be Much More Bigger Like You. 2008. (Charlie & Lola Ser.). (ENG.). 24p. (J). (gr. -1-k). mass mkt. 3.99 *(978-0-448-44867-1(X)*, Grosset & Dunlap) Penguin Young Readers Group.

Childs, Mark. Jaloopa: Home of the Poobah Baloo. 2009. (Illus.). (J). 25.99 *(978-1-4415-0481-4(8))* Xlibris Corp.

Chin, Oliver. Baltazar & the Flying Pirates. Roth, Justin, illus. 2009. (ENG.). 36p. (J). (gr. -1-3). 15.95 *(978-1-59702-018-3(4))* Immedium.

Corlett, William. The Tunnel Behind the Waterfall. 2010. (Magician's House Quartet Ser.: 3). (ENG.). 320p. (YA). (gr. 5-8). pap. 14.99 *(978-1-4424-1413-6(8)*, Simon Pulse) Simon Pulse.

Cozzo, Karole. The Truth about Happily Ever After. 2017. (ENG.). 320p. (YA). 17.99 *(978-1-250-12797-6(1)*, 9781250127976) Feiwel & Friends.

Crespo, Ana. JP & the Bossy Dinosaur: Feeling Unhappy. Sirotich, Erica, illus. 2016. (My Emotions & Me Ser.). (ENG.). 32p. (J). (gr. -1-3). 16.99 *(978-0-8075-3981-1(3))* Whitman, Albert & Co.

Cummings, Troy. Rumble of the Coaster Ghost. Cummings, Troy, illus. 2016. (Notebook of Doom Ser.: 9). (ENG., Illus.). 96p. (J). (gr. 1-3). pap. 4.99 *(978-0-545-86497-8(6))* Scholastic, Inc.

Demeritt, Mary Anne. The Twilight Ride of the Pink Fairy. Daniel, Ellen, illus. 2006. 36p. (J). pap. 17.95 *(978-1-58597-410-8(2))* Leathers Publishing.

Dixon, Franklin W. Thrill Ride. 2005. 154p. (J). lib. bdg. 16.92 *(978-1-4242-0366-4(4))* Fitzgerald Bks.

Doherty, Dave, illus. There Once Was a Place Called P.O.P. 2008. 93p. (J). 61.99 *(978-1-4363-6190-3(7))* Xlibris Corp.

Dubisch, Mike & Bloodworth, Mark, illus. The Amusement Park Mystery. 2010. (Boxcar Children Graphic Novels Ser.: 10). (ENG.). 32p. (J). (gr. 1-5). pap. 6.99 *(978-0-8075-0321-8(5))* Whitman, Albert & Co.

Elrod, Julie. Splitting Hares. 2008. 36p. pap. 16.50 *(978-1-60693-484-5(8)*, Eloquent Bks.) Strategic Book Publishing & Rights Agency (SBPRA).

Ewart, Franzeska G. & Quarto Generic Staff. Sita, Snake-Queen of Speed. Bate, Helen, illus. 2012. (ENG.). 96p. (J). (gr. 3-6). pap. 8.99 *(978-1-84780-330-6(X)*, Frances Lincoln) Quarto Publishing Group UK GBR. Dist: Hachette Bk. Group.

Finelli, S. Life's Amusement Park: A Whimsical Perspective on the Rides of Life! 2009. 36p. pap. 16.99 *(978-1-4389-3648-2(6))* AuthorHouse.

Fontes, Justine. Cheerios Action Park Adventure. 2005. (Picture Clue Math Reader Ser.). (Illus.). 28p. (J). pap. *(978-0-439-70343-7(3))* Scholastic, Inc.

Harkrader, Lisa. Ruby Makes It Even! Odd/Even Numbers. Wummer, Amy, illus. 2015. (ENG.). 32p. (gr. k-2). (J). pap. 5.95 *(978-1-57565-805-6(4))*; 11.99 *(978-1-57565-806-3(2))* Kane Press, Inc.

Horse, Harry. Little Rabbit Lost. Horse, Harry, illus. 2005. (ENG., Illus.). 32p. (J). (gr. k-1). bds. 9.95 *(978-1-56145-345-0(5))* Peachtree Pubs.

Hurtado, Patricia. The Magical Feline & the White Haven. 2009. 142p. pap. 10.95 *(978-1-60594-325-1(8)*, Llumina Pr.) Aeon Publishing Inc.

Jack Stanley. The Coaster Cats Go to the Amusement Park. Breuer, Paul, illus. 2006. 19p. (J). pap. 5.99 *(978-0-9776284-0-7(X))* Forbes Literary Ltd. Inc.

Jessell, Tim. The Boardwalk Mystery. Dunn, Robert, illus. 2013. (Boxcar Children Mysteries Ser.: 131). (ENG.). 144p. (J). (gr. 1-5). 15.99 *(978-0-8075-0802-2(0))*; pap. 5.99 *(978-0-8075-0803-9(9))* Whitman, Albert & Co.

Kapai, Tommy. Cuzzies Find the Rainbow's End. Henry, Mike, illus. 2004. (Cuzzies Adventures Ser.). (MAO & ENG.). 32p. (J). (gr. -1-3). pap. 9.00 *(978-0-9582517-0-9(3)*, Kina) Huia Pubs. NZL. Dist: Univ. of Hawaii Pr.

Keene, Carolyn. Candy Kingdom Chaos. Francis, Peter, illus. 2017. (Nancy Drew Clue Book Ser.: 7). (ENG.). 96p. (J). (gr. 1-4). pap. 5.99 *(978-1-4814-5826-9(4)*, Simon & Schuster/Paula Wiseman Bks.) Simon & Schuster/Paula Wiseman Bks.

Krosoczka, Jarrett J. Platypus Police Squad: The Ostrich Conspiracy. Krosoczka, Jarrett J., illus. 2014. (Platypus Police Squad Ser.: 2). (ENG., Illus.). 240p. (J). (gr. 3-7). 12.99 *(978-0-06-207166-8(1)*, Walden Pond Pr.) HarperCollins Pubs.

Krulik, Nancy. Holly's Jolly Christmas. John and Wendy Staff, illus. 2009. (Katie Kazoo, Switcheroo Ser.: No. 8). (ENG.). 160p. (J). (gr. 2-4). pap. 4.99 *(978-0-448-45218-0(9)*, Grosset & Dunlap) Penguin Young Readers Group.

—Wet & Wild! #5, 5 vols. Blecha, Aaron, illus. 2011. (George Brown, Class Clown Ser.: 5). (ENG.). 128p. (J). (gr. 2-4). pap. 4.99 *(978-0-448-45570-9(6)*, Grosset & Dunlap) Penguin Young Readers Group.

Lerangis, Peter. Whoa! Amusement Park Gone Wild! Talbot, Jim, illus. 2003. (Abracadabra Ser.: No. 7). (ENG.). 112p. (J). pap. 3.99 *(978-0-439-38938-9(0)*, Scholastic Paperbacks) Scholastic, Inc.

Lord, Cynthia. Hot Rod Hamster Meets His Match! Anderson, Derek, illus. 2016. (Scholastic Reader, Level 2 Ser.). (ENG.). 32p. (J). (gr. -1-2). pap. 3.99 *(978-0-545-82591-7(1)*, Scholastic Pr.) Scholastic, Inc.

Loyd, Todd. Dark Ride. 2012. (ENG.). 320p. (YA). (gr. 7-9). pap. 15.00 *(978-1-936487-22-6(5)*, 1936487225) Franklin Green Publishing.

May, Eleanor. Albert Is Not Scared. Melmon, Deborah, illus. 2013. (Mouse Math Ser.). (ENG.). 32p. (J). (gr. -1-1). pap. 7.95 *(978-1-57565-629-8(9))*; lib. bdg. 22.60 *(978-1-57565-628-1(0))* Kane Press, Inc.

—Albert Is Not Scared. 2013. 32p. 22.60 *(978-1-57565-630-4(2))* Kane Press, Inc.

McMullan, Kate. Pearl & Wagner: Three Secrets. 2013. (Penguin Young Readers Level 3 Ser.). lib. bdg. 13.55 *(978-0-606-31708-5(2)*, Turtleback) Turtleback Bks.

—Three Secrets. Alley, R. W., illus. 2013. (Pearl & Wagner Ser.: 3). (ENG.). 48p. (J). (gr. 1-3). pap. 3.99 *(978-0-448-46472-5(1)*, Penguin Young Readers) Penguin Young Readers Group.

Meister, Cari. Beat Bugs. 2017. (I Can Read Level 1 Ser.). 32p. (J). (gr. -1-3). pap. 3.99 *(978-0-06-264069-7(0))* HarperCollins Pubs.

Mezrich, Ben. Bringing down the Mouse. 2014. (ENG., Illus.). 336p. (J). (gr. 3-7). 16.99 *(978-1-4424-9626-2(6)*, Simon & Schuster Bks. For Young Readers) Simon & Schuster Bks. For Young Readers.

Morgan, Ruth. Behind You! Glyn, Chris, tr. Glyn, Chris, illus. 2003. (ENG.). 48p. pap. 11.95 *(978-1-84323-269-8(3))* Beekman Bks., Inc.

Morgan, Winter. The Return of the Rainbow Griefers: League of Griefers Series, Book Four. 2015. (League of Griefers Ser.: 4). (ENG.). 112p. (J). (gr. 1-7). pap. 7.99 *(978-1-63450-599-4(9)*, Sky Pony Pr.) Skyhorse Publishing Co., Inc.

Nickel, Scott. Blastoff to the Secret Side of the Moon!, 1 vol. Bradley, Jessica, illus. 2013. (Comics Land Ser.). (ENG.). 32p. (gr. k-2). 7.95 *(978-1-4342-4273-0(0))*; lib. bdg. 25.32 *(978-1-4342-4031-6(2))* Stone Arch Bks.

Nuño, Fran. Fairground Lights. 2013. (ENG., Illus.). 24p. (J). (gr. k-2). 16.95 *(978-84-15784-20-3(1))* Eastern National.

Ogilvy, Ian. Measle & the Dragodon. 2006. 344p. (J). (gr. 3-8). per. 6.99 *(978-0-06-058690-4(7)*, Harper Trophy) HarperCollins Pubs.

Osterhold, Jared, illus. OLIVIA Measures Up. 2013. (Olivia TV Tie-In Ser.). (ENG.). 24p. (J). (gr. -1-1). 15.99 *(978-1-4424-5974-8(3))*; pap. 3.99 *(978-1-4424-5973-1(5))* Simon Spotlight. (Simon Spotlight).

Pearson, Ridley. Disney after Dark. 2005. (Kingdom Keepers Ser.: Bk. 1). 324p. *(978-1-4156-2836-2(X))* Disney Pr.

—Disney after Dark. Elwell, Tristan, illus. 2009. (Kingdom Keepers Ser.: Bk. 1). (ENG.). 336p. (J). (gr. 5-9). pap. 8.99 *(978-1-4231-2311-8(5))* Hyperion Pr.

—Disney at Dawn. Elwell, Tristan, illus. 2009. (Kingdom Keepers Ser.: Bk. 2). (ENG.). 384p. (J). (gr. 5-9). pap. 8.99 *(978-1-4231-0708-8(X))* Hyperion Pr.

—Disney in Shadow. Elwell, Tristan, illus. 2011. (Kingdom Keepers Ser.: Bk. 3). (ENG.). 576p. (J). (gr. 5-17). pap. 8.99 *(978-1-4231-3856-3(2))* Hyperion Pr.

—Power Play. Elwell, Tristan, illus. 2011. (Kingdom Keepers Ser.: Bk. 4). (ENG.). 448p. (J). (gr. 5-9). 17.99 *(978-1-4231-3857-0(0))* Hyperion Pr.

Ponti, Jamie. Animal Attraction. 2012. (Romantic Comedies Ser.). (ENG.). 272p. (YA). (gr. 9). pap. 12.99 *(978-1-4424-6059-1(8)*, Simon Pulse) Simon Pulse.

Powell, Jillian. Roller Coaster Fun!, 1 vol. Colnaghi, Stefania, illus. 2013. (Start Reading Ser.). (ENG.). 24p. (gr. k-1). pap. 7.95 *(978-1-4765-4135-8(3))* Capstone Press of Coughlan Cos.

Preller, James. I Scream, You Scream! Bruno, Iacopo, illus. 2013. (Scary Tales Ser.: 2). (ENG.). 112p. (J). (gr. 2-5). 14.99 *(978-1-250-01888-5(9)*, 9781250018885); pap. 5.99 *(978-1-250-01889-2(7)*, 9781250018892) Feiwel & Friends.

Pugliano-Martin, Carol. Little Cat Goes Fast. 2011. (Early Connections Ser.). (J). *(978-1-61672-358-3(0))* Benchmark Education Co.

Random House & Shealy, Dennis R. The Park Is Open. Random House, illus. 2015. (Pictureback(R) Ser.). (ENG., Illus.). 16p. (J). (gr. -1-2). 4.99 *(978-0-553-53692-8(3)*, Random Hse. Bks. for Young Readers) Random Hse. Children's Bks.

Reeve, Philip. Carnival in a Fix. McIntyre, Sarah, illus. 2017. (Not-So-Impossible Tale Ser.). (ENG.). 224p. (J). (gr. 2-5). 12.99 *(978-0-385-38800-9(4)*, Random Hse. Bks. for Young Readers) Random Hse. Children's Bks.

Rey, H. A. & Rey, Margret. Roller Coaster. 2007. (Curious George Ser.). (ENG., Illus.). 24p. (J). (gr. -1-3). pap. 3.99 *(978-0-618-80040-7(9))* Houghton Mifflin Harcourt Publishing Co.

Romano, Ray. Raymie, Dickie, & the Bean: Why I Love & Hate My Brothers. Locke, Gary, illus. 2007. 30p. (J). 18.00 *(978-1-4223-6806-0(8))* DIANE Publishing Co.

Rosen, Michael. Bear Flies High. Reynolds, Adrian, illus. 2009. (ENG.). 32p. (J). (gr. -1-1). 16.99 *(978-1-59990-386-6(5)*, 9781599903866, Bloomsbury USA Childrens) Bloomsbury Publishing USA.

Rutch, Joe. Grampa & the Roller Coaster. 2010. 28p. 13.99 *(978-1-4490-9152-1(0))* AuthorHouse.

Simonson, Walter. Jurassic Park: Danger: Vol. 1, 1 vol. 2013. (Jurassic Park Ser.). (ENG.). 32p. (J). (gr. 4-8). lib. bdg. 24.21 *(978-1-61479-183-6(X))* Spotlight.

Smith, Lane. Return to Augie Hobble. 2015. (ENG., Illus.). 288p. (J). (gr. 3-7). 16.99 *(978-1-62672-054-1(1)*, 9781626720541) Roaring Brook Pr.

—Return to Augie Hobble. 2017. (J). lib. bdg. 18.40 *(978-0-606-38550-3(9))* Turtleback Bks.

Stine, R. L. Claws! 2011. (Goosebumps Hall of Horrors Ser.: 1). (ENG.). 160p. (J). (gr. 3-7). pap. 6.99 *(978-0-545-28933-7(5)*, Scholastic Paperbacks) Scholastic, Inc.

—Creep from the Deep. 2008. (Goosebumps HorrorLand Ser.: No. 2). 137p. (gr. 4-7). 17.00 *(978-0-7569-8815-9(2))* Perfection Learning Corp.

—Creep from the Deep. 2008. (Goosebumps Horrorland Ser.: 2). (ENG.). 160p. (J). (gr. 3-7). 6.99 *(978-0-439-91870-1(7)*, Scholastic Paperbacks) Scholastic, Inc.

—Dr. Maniac vs. Robby Schwartz. 2008. (Goosebumps Horrorland Ser.: 5). (ENG.). 160p. (J). (gr. 3-7). pap. 6.99 *(978-0-439-91873-2(1)*, Scholastic Paperbacks) Scholastic, Inc.

—Escape from Horrorland. 2009. (Goosebumps HorrorLand Ser.: 11). lib. bdg. 17.20 *(978-0-606-05355-6(7)*, Turtleback) Turtleback Bks.

—Espanto Marino. 2009. (Goosebumps Horrorland Ser.: 2). (SPA.). 160p. (J). (gr. 3-7). pap. 6.99 *(978-0-545-15408-6(1)*, Scholastic en Espanol) Scholastic, Inc.

—Heads, You Lose. 2010. (Goosebumps HorrorLand Ser.: No. 15). 160p. (J). pap. *(978-1-4071-1636-5(3))* Scholastic, Inc.

—The Horror at Chiller House. 2011. (Goosebumps Horrorland Ser.: 19). (ENG.). 160p. (J). (gr. 3-7). pap. 6.99 *(978-0-545-16200-5(9)*, Scholastic Paperbacks) Scholastic, Inc.

—One Day at Horrorland. 2008. (Classic Goosebumps Ser.: 5). (ENG.). 144p. (J). (gr. 3-7). 6.99 *(978-0-545-03522-4(8)*, Scholastic Paperbacks) Scholastic, Inc.

—Revenge of the Lawn Gnomes. 2011. (Classic Goosebumps Ser.: 19). (ENG.). 160p. (J). (gr. 3-7). pap. 6.99 *(978-0-545-29835-3(0)*, Scholastic Paperbacks) Scholastic, Inc.

—Revenge of the Living Dummy. 2008. (Goosebumps HorrorLand Ser.: No. 1). 128p. (J). (gr. 4-7). 13.65 *(978-0-7569-8816-6(0))* Perfection Learning Corp.

—Revenge of the Living Dummy. 2008. (Goosebumps Horrorland Ser.: 1). (ENG.). 144p. (J). (gr. 3-7). 6.99 *(978-0-439-91869-5(3)*, Scholastic Paperbacks) Scholastic, Inc.

—Revenge of the Living Dummy. 2008. (Goosebumps HorrorLand Ser.: 1). 128p. (gr. 4-7). lib. bdg. 17.20 *(978-1-4178-1891-4(3)*, Turtleback) Turtleback Bks.

—Say Cheese - And Die Screaming! 2008. (Goosebumps HorrorLand Ser.: No. 8). (Illus.). 125p. lib. bdg. 17.00 (978-1-60686-344-2(4)) Perfection Learning Corp.

—Say Cheese & Die Screaming! 2009. (Goosebumps HorrorLand Ser.: 8). lib. bdg. 17.20 (978-0-606-06886-4(4), Turtleback) Turtleback Bks.

—The Scream of the Haunted Mask. 2008. (Goosebumps HorrorLand Ser.: No. 4). (Illus.). 139p. (J). (gr. 4-7). 13.65 (978-0-7569-8818-0(7)) Perfection Learning Corp.

—The Streets of Panic Park. 2009. (Goosebumps HorrorLand Ser.: No. 10). (Illus.). 136p. 16.00 (978-1-60686-405-0(X)) Perfection Learning Corp.

—The Streets of Panic Park. 2009. (Goosebumps HorrorLand Ser.: 12). lib. bdg. 17.20 (978-0-606-05366-2(2), Turtleback) Turtleback Bks.

—Terror Trips. Thompson, Jill et al, illus. 2007. (Goosebumps Graphix Ser.: 2). (ENG.). 144p. (J). (gr. 3-7). pap. 9.99 (978-0-439-85780-2(5), Graphix) Scholastic, Inc.

—Welcome to Camp Slither. 2009. (Goosebumps HorrorLand Ser.: 9). lib. bdg. 17.20 (978-0-606-05345-7(X), Turtleback) Turtleback Bks.

—When the Ghost Dog Howls. 2010. (Goosebumps HorrorLand Ser.: 13). lib. bdg. 17.20 (978-0-606-07124-6(5), Turtleback) Turtleback Bks.

—Who's Your Mummy? 2009. (Goosebumps HorrorLand Ser.: No. 7). 160p. (J). pap. (978-1-4071-0755-4(0)) Scholastic, Inc.

—Who's Your Mummy? 2009. (Goosebumps HorrorLand Ser.: 6). lib. bdg. 17.20 (978-0-606-05328-0(X), Turtleback) Turtleback Bks.

Stolarz, Laurie Faria. Welcome to the Dark House. 2014. (Dark House Ser.). (ENG., Illus.). 368p. (YA). (gr. 7-12). 16.99 (978-1-4231-8172-9(7)) Hyperion Bks. for Children.

Storrie, Paul D. Peril at Summerland Park. Carruthers, Sandy, illus. 2012. (Twisted Journeys Ser.: 20). (ENG.). 112p. (J). (gr. 4-7). pap. 45.32 (978-0-7613-9290-3(4)); pap. 7.95 (978-0-7613-8551-6(7)); lib. bdg. 27.93 (978-0-7613-4935-8(9)) Lerner Publishing Group. (Graphic Universe™).

Strohmeyer, Sarah. How Zoe Made Her Dreams (Mostly) Come True. 2013. (ENG.). 320p. (YA). (gr. 8). pap. 9.99 (978-0-06-218745-1(7)) HarperCollins Pubs.

Tatulli, Mark. Desmond Pucket & the Mountain Full of Monsters. 2015. (Desmond Pucket Ser.: 2). lib. bdg. 20.85 (978-0-606-38232-8(1)) Turtleback Bks.

—Desmond Pucket Makes Monster Magic. 2015. (Desmond Pucket Ser.: 1). lib. bdg. 20.85 (978-0-606-38231-1(3)) Turtleback Bks.

Thaler, Mike. The Amusement Park from the Black Lagoon. Lee, Jared D., illus. 2014. 64p. (J). (978-0-545-61641-6(7)) Scholastic, Inc.

Thung, Diana. Captain Long Ears. 2010. (ENG., Illus.). 168p. (J). pap. 12.95 (978-1-59362-187-2(6), 9781593621872) Slave Labor Bks.

Viguié, Debbie. The Spring of Candy Apples, 1 vol. 2009. (Sweet Seasons Novel Ser.). (ENG.). 208p. (YA). (gr. 8-11). pap. 9.99 (978-0-310-71753-9(1)) Zondervan.

—The Summer of Cotton Candy, 1 vol. 2008. (Sweet Seasons Novel Ser.). (ENG., Illus.). 224p. (YA). (gr. 8-11). pap. 9.99 (978-0-310-71558-0(X)) Zondervan.

Williams, Mandi Tillotson. The Many Adventures of Mortimer Crump: Mortimer's Sweet Retreat. 2011. 28p. pap. 13.83 (978-1-4634-2637-8(2)) AuthorHouse.

Wilsdon, Christina. An Amusement Park Mystery in Ohio. Ebert, Len, illus. 2006. 26p. (J). 7.99 (978-1-59939-013-0(2)) Cornerstone Pr.

Yasuda, Anita. The Haunted House, 1 vol. Harpster, Steve, illus. 2013. (Dino Detectives Ser.). (ENG.). 32p. (gr. 1-2). lib. bdg. 22.65 (978-1-4342-5970-7(6)) Stone Arch Bks.

—Haunted House. Harpster, Steve, illus. 2013. (Dino Detectives Ser.). (ENG.). 32p. (gr. 1-2). pap. 5.95 (978-1-4342-6199-1(9)) Stone Arch Bks.

Yasuda, Anita & Harpster, Steve. The Haunted House. 2013. (Dino Detectives Ser.). (ENG.). 32p. (gr. 1-2). pap. 29.70 (978-1-4342-6227-1(8)) Stone Arch Bks.

AMUSEMENTS

see also Circus; Concerts; Dance; Entertaining; Fortune-Telling; Games; Hobbies; Magic; Mathematical Recreations; Play; Puzzles; Recreation; Riddles; Scientific Recreations; Sports; Theater; Toys

American Heritage Dictionary Editors, ed. What Can I Do When It Rains? (Qué Puedo Hacer Cuando Llueve?) Zagarenski, Pamela, illus. 2004. (Good Beginnings Ser.). (SPA & ENG.). 8p. (J). (gr. k — 1). bds. 3.95 (978-0-618-44376-5(2)) Houghton Mifflin Harcourt Publishing Co.

Angel's Christmas Party Activity Fun. 2003. (Christmas Activity Bks.). (Illus.). 128p. (J). 3.98 (978-0-7525-6499-9(4)) Parragon, Inc.

Anness Publishing Staff, et al. The Great Big Book of Things to Make & Do: Cooking, Painting, Crafts, Science, Gardening, Magic, Music & Having a Party - Simple & Fun Step-by-Step Projects for Young Children. 2013. (ENG., Illus.). 256p. (J). (gr. -1-12). pap. 18.99 (978-1-84038-552-6(9), Hermes House) Anness Publishing GBR. Dist: National Bk. Network.

Appelt, Kathi. Incredible Me! Date not set. 32p. (J). (gr. -1-1). pap. 5.99 (978-0-06-443609-0(8)) HarperCollins Pubs.

—Incredible Me! Karas, G. Brian, illus. 2003. 32p. (J). (gr. -1-1). lib. bdg. 16.89 (978-0-06-028623-1(7)) HarperCollins Pubs.

Arnold, Laurie B. Hello There, We've Been Waiting for You! 2013. (ENG.). 176p. (J). (gr. 3-8). pap. 9.95 (978-1-935212-51-5(6), Prospecta Pr.) Easton Studio Pr., LLC.

Balloon Books Staff. I Can Draw. 2003. (ENG., Illus.). 18p. (J). pap., wbk. ed. 3.95 (978-1-4027-0494-9(1), Balloon Bks.) Sterling Publishing Co., Inc.

Beard, Daniel. The American Boy's Handy Book: Turn-of-the-Century Classic of Crafts & Activities. unabr. ed. 2003. (Dover Children's Activity Bks.). (ENG., Illus.). 464p. (J). pap. 12.95 (978-0-486-43138-3(X)) Dover Pubns., Inc.

Beard, Daniel C. American Boy's Handy Book. 2014. (ENG., Illus.). 320p. (J). (gr. -1-3). pap. 12.95 (978-0-8048-4403-1(8)) Tuttle Publishing.

Beard, Lina & Beard, Adelia B. The American Girl's Handy Book: Turn-of-the-Century Classic of Crafts & Activities. 2008. (Dover Children's Activity Bks.). (ENG., Illus.). 496p. (J). (gr. 6-8). pap. 12.99 (978-0-486-46772-6(4)) Dover Pubns., Inc.

Beaton, Clare. Easter Activity Book. 2011. (Seasonal Activity Ser.). (ENG., Illus.). 24p. (J). (gr. 1-4). reprint ed. pap., act. bk. ed. 7.99 (978-1-874735-46-5(8)) B Small Publishing GBR. Dist: Independent Pubs. Group.

—My Book of Things to Make & Do. 2007. (ENG., Illus.). 96p. (J). (gr. 1-4). pap. 15.99 (978-1-902915-95-1(X)) B Small Publishing GBR. Dist: Independent Pubs. Group.

Bell-Rehwoldt, Sheri. Maya: Amazing Inventions You Can Build Yourself. Casteel, Tom, illus. 2nd ed. 2011. (Build It Yourself Ser.). (ENG.). 128p. (J). (gr. 3-7). 21.95 (978-1-936749-61-4(0)); pap. 15.95 (978-1-936749-60-7(2)) Open City Bks.

Beylon, Cathy. Kits Cuts Sticker Activity Book. 2003. (Dover Little Activity Bks.). (ENG., Illus.). 4p. (J). (gr. -1-5). act. bk. ed. 1.50 (978-0-486-43011-9(1)) Dover Pubns., Inc.

Bidder, Jane. Inventions We Use for Information & Entertainment. 2006. (Everyday Inventions Ser.). (Illus.). 32p. (gr. 1-4). lib. bdg. 26.00 (978-0-8368-6899-9(4), Gareth Stevens Learning Library) Stevens, Gareth Publishing LLLP.

Big Fun Learning Workbook. 2003. (Bumper Gold Stars Ser.). (Illus.). 256p. (J). 9.98 (978-1-4054-1718-1(8)); 9.98 (978-1-4054-1717-4(X)) Parragon, Inc.

Bingham, Jane. Fairgrounds. 2017. (Explore! Ser.). (ENG., Illus.). 32p. (J). (gr. 4-6). pap. 11.99 (978-0-7502-8406-6(4), Wayland) Hachette Children's Group GBR. Dist: Hachette Bk. Group.

Bodden, Valerie. Roller Coasters. 2012. (Illus.). 24p. (J). 25.65 (978-1-60818-114-8(6), Creative Education) Creative Co., The.

—Water Rides. 2012. (Illus.). 24p. (J). 25.65 (978-1-60818-115-5(4), Creative Education) Creative Co., The.

Boys Town Press Staff. Time to Enrich: Activity Kit. 2004. (Illus.). 134p. (gr. k-6). pap., spiral bd. 99.95 (978-1-889322-50-6(4), 45-502); 187p. (gr. 7-12). pap., spiral bd. 99.95 (978-1-889322-51-3(2), 45-503) Boys Town Pr.

Brian, Sarah Jane. Brainiac's Secret Agent: Fun Activities for Spies of All Ages. 2005. (Activity Journal Ser.). 128p. act. bk. ed. 12.99 (978-0-88088-446-4(0)) Peter Pauper Pr. Inc.

Carlson, Nancy. Harriet & the Roller Coaster. Carlson, Nancy, illus. unabr. ed. (Illus.). (J). (gr. k-3). 24.95 incl. audio (978-0-941078-56-6(6)); pap. 15.95 incl. audio (978-0-941078-54-2(X)); pap., tchr. ed. 31.95 incl. audio (978-0-941078-55-9(8)) Live Oak Media.

Carmichael, Lindsey. Innovations in Entertainment. 2016. (Problem Solved! Your Turn to Think Big Ser.). (ENG.). 32p. (J). (gr. 3-6). (978-0-7787-2671-5(1)) Crabtree Publishing Co.

Catlow, Nikalas, illus. Mind Your Own Business: A File of Super Secret Stuff. 2007. (ENG.). 224p. (J). 8.00 (978-1-84046-763-5(0), Wizard Books) Icon Bks., Ltd. GBR. Dist: Publishers Group Canada.

Chandler, Matt. Recreational Drones. 2017. (Drones Ser.). (ENG., Illus.). 32p. (gr. 3-4). pap. 7.95 (978-1-5157-3770-4(5), Edge Bks.) Capstone Press of Coughlan Cos.

Chastain, Zachary. Passing the Time: Entertainment in The 1800s. 2009. (Daily Life in America in the 1800s Ser.). 64p. (YA). (gr. 7-18). pap. 9.95 (978-1-4222-1858-7(9)); lib. bdg. 22.95 (978-1-4222-1785-6(X)) Mason Crest.

Christian Virtues Series Kindness, Contains Bible Based Activities, Puzzles, Raps, Poem. (J). (gr. -1). 4.95 (978-0-382-30739-3(9)) Cobblestone Publishing Co.

Colich, Abby. A Babysitter's Guide to Keeping the Kids Entertained. 2017. (Go-To Guides). (ENG., Illus.). 32p. (gr. 3-4). lib. bdg. 27.99 (978-1-5157-3664-6(4), Snap Bks.) Capstone Press of Coughlan Cos.

Cook, David C. Publishing Staff. God Made It Gook: Pencil Fun Book. Date not set. pap. 0.79 (978-1-55513-262-0(6)) Cook, David C.

Cox, Catherine. Go-Carts, Catapults & Midnight Feasts: 101 Vintage Pastimes for Modern Kids. 2015. (ENG., Illus.). 224p. (J). (gr. k-5). pap. 14.99 (978-0-7509-6429-6(4)) History Pr. Ltd.,The GBR. Dist: Independent Pubs. Group.

Creative Team of Weldon Owen. 101 Things to Do Before You Grow Up: Fun Activities for You to Check off Your List. 2015. (101 Things Ser.). (ENG.). 144p. (J). (gr. 3-7). spiral bd. 12.95 (978-1-63322-003-4(6)) Quarto Publishing Group USA.

Cullen, Ruth. Brainiac's Giant Book of Gross Outs. 2005. (Activity Journal Ser.). 128p. 14.99 (978-0-88088-448-8(7)) Peter Pauper Pr. Inc.

Cunningham, Kevin. Roller Coasters: From Concept to Consumer. 2013. (Calling All Innovators). (ENG.). 64p. (J). pap. 8.95 (978-0-531-22009-2(5)); lib. bdg. 30.00 (978-0-531-26521-5(8)) Scholastic Library Publishing. (Children's Pr.).

Daniel in the Lion's Den. Date not set. (J). stu. ed., act. bk. ed. 1.49 (978-0-88271-233-8(0), 1749) Regina Pr., Malhame & Co.

Danks, Fiona & Schofield, Jo. The Wild Weather Book: Loads of Things to Do Outdoors in Rain, Wind & Snow. 2013. (Going Wild Ser.). (ENG., Illus.). 128p. pap. 14.95 (978-0-7112-3255-6(5), 0711232555, Frances Lincoln) Quarto Publishing Group UK GBR. Dist: Hachette Bk. Group.

Dyan, Penelope. On the Way to Rome —- a Kid's Guide to Civitavecchia , Italy. Weigand, John D., photos by. 2011. (Illus.). 34p. pap. 11.95 (978-1-935630-59-3(8)) Bellissima Publishing, LLC.

Dymock, Melissa. Sliding in the Snow: Winter Activities for Kids, 1 vol. Lee, Frances Cook, illus. 2015. (ENG.). 64p. (J). pap. 9.99 (978-1-4236-3893-3(X)) Gibbs Smith, Publisher.

Elliott, Lynne. Children & Games in the Middle Ages. 2004. (Medieval World Ser.). (ENG., Illus.). 32p. (J). pap. (978-0-7787-1381-4(4)); lib. bdg. (978-0-7787-1349-4(0)) Crabtree Publishing Co.

Encarnacion, Elizabeth. Cat's Cradle & Other Fantastic String Figures: Over 20 String Games. [BURST] Includes DVD & 2 Strings. 2010. (ENG., Illus.). 58p. (J). (gr. 3). 14.95 (978-1-60433-105-9(4), Applesauce Pr.) Cider Mill Pr. Bk. Pubs., LLC.

Fancy Friendship Bracelets. 2009. (ENG., Illus.). 60p. (J). (gr. 3). spiral bd. 19.95 (978-1-59174-692-8(2)) Klutz.

Faust, Daniel R. Entertainment Drones, 01 vols., 1. 2016. (Drones: Eyes in the Skies Ser.). (ENG.). 32p. (J). pap. 11.75 (978-1-5081-4493-9(1), PowerKids Pr.) Rosen Publishing Group, Inc., The.

Fernandez, Caroline. More Boredom Busters: Over 50 Awesome Activities for Children Aged 7 Years + 2015. (ENG., Illus.). 128p. (J). (gr. 7-11). pap. 14.95 (978-1-78249-199-6(6), CICO Books) Ryland Peters & Small GBR. Dist: WIPRO.

Folmer, A. P. Fabulous Rainy Day Fun Book. (FRE., Illus.). (Orig.). (J). pap. 7.99 (978-0-590-74412-6(7)) Scholastic, Inc.

Foster, Juliana. The Girls' Book: How to Be the Best at Everything. Wingate, Philippa, ed. Enright, Amanda, illus. 2007. (Best at Everything Ser.). (ENG.). 128p. (J). (gr. 3-7). 9.99 (978-0-545-01629-2(0), Scholastic Pr.) Scholastic, Inc.

Francis, Suzanne. How to Survive When (You Think) There's Nothing to Do. 2004. (Illus.). 80p. (J). pap. (978-0-439-57906-3(6)) Scholastic, Inc.

Garrett, Joseph. Stampy's Lovely Book. 2016. (ENG., Illus.). 72p. (J). (gr. 2-5). 9.99 (978-0-399-55543-5(9), Random Hse. Bks. for Young Readers) Random Hse. Children's Bks.

Gifford, Clive. Teenage Kicks: 101 Things to Do Before You're 16. 2008. (ENG., Illus.). 160p. (J). (gr. 7-17). pap. 9.99 (978-0-340-95061-6(7)) Hodder & Stoughton GBR. Dist: Hachette Bk. Group.

Gilpin, Rebecca. Fairy Things to Make & Do Kid Kit. McCafferty, Jan, illus. 2004. (Kid Kits Ser.). 32p. (J). 15.99 (978-1-58086-727-6(8)); 15.99 (978-1-58086-731-3(6)) EDC Publishing. (Usborne).

—Travel Activity Book. 2013. (Doodle Bks). 96p. (J). pap. 12.99 (978-0-7945-3287-1(X), Usborne) EDC Publishing.

Givens, David, ed. For the Kids! A Family-Friendly Guide to Outings & Activities. 2003. (ENG., Illus.). 220p. pap. 24.95 (978-1-904148-27-2(1)) Liffey Pr., The IRL. Dist: Dufour Editions, Inc.

Glenn, Joshua & Larsen, Elizabeth Foy. UNBORED Adventure. Leone, Tony et al, illus. 2015. (ENG.). 176p. pap. 16.00 (978-1-63286-096-5(1), 9781632860965) Bloomsbury Publishing USA.

—Unbored Games: Serious Fun for Everyone. Leone, Tony et al, illus. 2014. (ENG.). 176p. pap. 16.00 (978-1-62040-706-6(X), 9781620407066) Bloomsbury Publishing USA.

Goes, Peter. Timeline: Activity Book Create Your Own Journey Through Time. Goes, Peter, illus. 2017. (ENG., Illus.). 72p. (gr. 5-12). 12.99 **(978-1-77657-128-4(2))** Gecko Pr. NZL. Dist: Lerner Publishing Group.

Goldish, Meish. Amazing Amusement Park Rides. 2011. (So Big Compared to What? Ser.). 24p. (YA). (gr. 1-4). lib. bdg. 22.61 (978-1-61772-304-9(5)) Bearport Publishing Co., Inc.

—Heart-Stopping Roller Coasters. 2009. (World's Biggest Ser.). (Illus.). 24p. (J). (gr. 1-6). lib. bdg. 22.61 (978-1-59716-956-1(0)) Bearport Publishing Co., Inc.

Goldish, Meish & Gieszl, Eric. Heart-Stopping Roller Coasters. 2016. (World's Biggest Ser.). (ENG.). 24p. (J). (gr. 1-6). pap. 7.95 (978-1-944998-55-4(1)) Bearport Publishing Co., Inc.

Golosi, Rosanne. Best Friends Forever! Martini, Angela, illus. 2005. 64p. (J). (978-0-439-80072-3(2)) Scholastic, Inc.

Goodlett, Liza. Getting Ready for the Show. 2007. 50p. pap. 21.50 (978-1-4357-0520-3(3)) Lulu Pr., Inc.

Gordon, Lynn. 52 Christmas Activities. Johnson, Karen, illus. 2004. (52 Ser.: 52SE). (ENG.). 52p. (J). (gr. k-4). 6.95 (978-0-8118-4123-8(5)) Chronicle Bks. LLC.

Gordon, Sherri Mabry. Using Technology. 2011. (Life—a How-To Guide Ser.). (Illus.). 128p. (J). lib. bdg. 33.27 (978-0-7660-3441-9(0)); (gr. 6-18). pap. 10.95 (978-1-59845-311-9(4)) Enslow Pubs., Inc.

Green, Rod. The Naughty Kid's Handbook. 2015. (ENG., Illus.). 192p. (J). (gr. 3-7). pap. 8.99 (978-1-78418-338-7(5)) Blake, John Publishing, Ltd. GBR. Dist: Independent Pubs. Group.

Groening, Matt. The Simpsons Ultra-Jumbo Rain-or-Shine Fun Book. 2006. (Simpsons Ser.). (ENG., Illus.). 128p. pap. 14.95 (978-0-06-095006-4(4), Collins Design) HarperCollins Pubs.

Handford, Martin. Where's Waldo? the Coloring Book. Handford, Martin, illus. 2016. (Where's Waldo? Ser.). (ENG., Illus.). 64p. (J). (gr. -1-3). pap. 12.00 (978-0-7636-8844-8(4)) Candlewick Pr.

Hanneman, Monika, et al. Gardening with Children. Tomasello, Sam, illus. 2011. (BBG Guides for a Greener Planet Ser.). (ENG.). 120p. pap. 12.95 (978-1-889538-78-5(7)) Brooklyn Botanic Garden.

Hawes, Alison. Go Greek! (ENG.). 32p. (J). (gr. 3-5). 2011. (978-0-7787-9894-1(1)) 2010. (Crabtree Connections Ser.: No. 2). pap. (978-0-7787-9915-3(8)) Crabtree Publishing Co.

Higgins, Melissa. Let's Play! Awesome Activities Every Babysitter Needs to Know, 1 vol. 2014. (Babysitter's Backpack Ser.). (ENG., Illus.). 32p. (gr. 3-4). lib. bdg. 27.99 (978-1-4914-0763-9(8), Snap Bks.) Capstone Press of Coughlan Cos.

Hughes, Shirley. A Year of Stories: And Things to Do. 2015. (ENG., Illus.). 288p. (J). (gr. k-2). 34.99 (978-0-370-33248-2(2)) Transworld Publishers Ltd. GBR. Dist: Independent Pubs. Group.

Hull, Robert. Entertainment & the Arts. 2007. (World of Ancient Greece Ser.). (Illus.). 32p. (YA). (gr. 3-6). lib. bdg. 27.10 (978-1-59771-061-9(X)) Sea-To-Sea Pubns.

Hurley, Jo. Scooby-Doo's Super Fun Book. 2005. (Illus.). 64p. (J). (978-0-439-70864-7(8)) Scholastic, Inc.

—Slumber-Ific! Great Sleepover Ideas for You & Your Friends. Morley, Taia, illus. 2007. 63p. (J). (978-0-439-02015-2(8)) Scholastic, Inc.

Hutchings, Amy & Nations, Susan. What Happens at an Amusement Park? 2009. (Where People Work Ser.). 24p. (gr. -1-3). pap. 8.15 (978-1-4339-0137-9(4), Weekly Reader Leveled Readers) Stevens, Gareth Publishing LLLP.

Hyde, Andrew. Experience the Point: Unofficial Guidebook to Cedar Point. 2nd ed. 2003. 87p. (YA). pap. 10.95 (978-0-7414-1499-1(6)) Infinity Publishing.

Ipcizade, Catherine. BIG Roller Coasters. 2016. (Big Ser.). (ENG.). 24p. pap. 6.95 (978-1-5157-6212-6(2), Pebble Plus) Capstone Press of Coughlan Cos.

Jacobson, Ryan. Exciting Entertainment Inventions. 2013. (Awesome Inventions You Use Every Day Ser.). (ENG., Illus.). 32p. (gr. 3-6). lib. bdg. 26.60 (978-1-4677-1094-7(6), Lerner Pubns.) Lerner Publishing Group.

Jenkins, Sandra. My Play & Learn Book. (Illus.). (J). (gr. -1). pap. 19.99 (978-0-590-24537-1(6)) Scholastic, Inc.

Jolly Jungle. Date not set. (Sticker Shapes Ser.). (Illus.). 16p. (J). 2.98 (978-0-7525-8140-8(6)) Parragon, Inc.

The Journey's of Paul. Date not set. (J). stu. ed., act. bk. ed. 1.49 (978-0-88271-232-1(2), 1748) Regina Pr., Malhame & Co.

Jovinelly, Joann. The Crafts & Culture of the Ancient Greeks. 2009. (Crafts of the Ancient World Ser.). 48p. (gr. 5-8). 58.50 (978-1-61512-063-5(7), Rosen Reference) Rosen Publishing Group, Inc., The.

Jumbo Activity. Date not set. (Illus.). 256p. (J). 5.98 (978-1-4054-0698-7(4)) Parragon, Inc.

Jungle Fun. 2003. 32p. 12.98 (978-1-4054-2004-4(9)) Parragon, Inc.

Kallen, Stuart A. Careers If You Like the Outdoors. 2017. (ENG.). 80p. (YA). (gr. 5-12). 39.93 **(978-1-68282-140-4(4))** ReferencePoint Pr., Inc.

Kallen, Stuart A. Cutting Edge Entertainment Technology. 2016. (ENG.). 80p. (J). (gr. 5-12). lib. bdg. (978-1-68282-040-7(8)) ReferencePoint Pr., Inc.

Kalz, Jill. Amusement Park Adventure. Cerato, Mattia, illus. 2010. (A-MAZE-Ing Adventures Ser.). (ENG.). 32p. (gr. 1-2). lib. bdg. 26.65 (978-1-4048-6023-0(1)) Picture Window Bks.

Karr, Susan Schott. Scream Machines: All about Roller Coasters. Ruben, Paul L., photos by. 2004. (Illus.). 32p. (J). (978-0-7652-3264-9(2)) Celebration Pr.

Kawai, Ritsuko. Hamtaro Pop-Up Playset. Kawai, Ritsuko, illus. 2003. (Hamtaro Ser.). (ENG., Illus.). 20p. (J). pap. 16.95 (978-1-56931-846-1(8)) Viz Media.

Kemp, Marion, et al. All Together. Barnes-Murphy, Rowan, illus. Date not set. (Whizz Bang Bumper Bk.). 63p. (J). 129.15 (978-0-582-18259-2(X)) Addison-Wesley Longman, Ltd. GBR. Dist: Trans-Atlantic Pubns., Inc.

Kennedy, Michelle. The Big Book of Happy: 500 Games & Activities for Ages 2 to 6. 2008. (Illus.). 360p. (J). (978-1-4351-0544-7(3)) Metro Bks.

King, Bart. Bart's King Sized Book of Fun, 1 vol. 2010. (ENG., Illus.). 304p. (J). (gr. 5-6). pap. 19.99 (978-1-4236-0641-3(8)) Gibbs Smith, Publisher.

Kissock, Heather, ed. Entertainment. 2011. 48p. (gr. 5-8). (978-1-77071-673-5(4)); pap. (978-1-77071-676-6(9)) Weigl Educational Pubs. Ltd.

Klutz Editors. The Encyclopedia of Immaturity, Vol. 2. 2009. (ENG., Illus.). 200p. (J). (gr. 3). 19.95 (978-1-59174-689-8(2)) Klutz.

Klutz Editors, ed. The Most Incredible, Outrageous, Packed-to-The Gills, Bulging-at-the-Seams Sticker Book You've Ever Seen. 2010. (ENG., Illus.). 30p. (J). (gr. -1-3). 12.99 (978-1-57054-117-9(5)) Klutz.

Knapman, Timothy & Collins UK Staff. Leisure & Entertainment since 1900. 2016. (ENG.). 32p. (J). (gr. 2-3). pap. 8.95 (978-0-00-816382-2(0)) HarperCollins Pubs. Ltd. GBR. Dist: Independent Pubs. Group.

Kroll, Jennifer. A la Vanguardia: Adelantos en Tecnología. 2016. (TIME for Kids en Español - Level 5 Ser.). (SPA.). 64p. (gr. 5-5). lib. bdg. 31.99 (978-1-5157-2927-3(3)) Time for Kids Inc AUS. Dist: Capstone Pub.

Laliberte, Mario, illus. Match, Sort & Play. 2007. (Hands-on Bks.). 48p. (J). (gr. -1-k). spiral bd. (978-2-7641-1936-5(4)) Tormont Pubns.

Lane, Sheila Mary & Kemp, Marion. Start Here. Birch, Linda, illus. Date not set. (Whizz Bang Bumper Bk.). 64p. (J). pap. 129.15 (978-0-582-19331-4(1)) Addison-Wesley Longman, Ltd. GBR. Dist: Trans-Atlantic Pubns., Inc.

Larsen, Elizabeth Foy & Glenn, Joshua. Unbored: The Essential Field Guide to Serious Fun. Leone, Tony et al, illus. 2012. (ENG.). 352p. 28.00 (978-1-60819-641-8(0), 9781608196418) Bloomsbury Publishing USA.

Lewis, Clare. Entertainment Through the Years: How Having Fun Has Changed in Living Memory. 2015. (History in Living Memory Ser.). (ENG.). 24p. (gr. k-2). 23.32 (978-1-4846-0923-1(9), Heinemann Read & Learn) Heinemann-Raintree.

Loh-Hagan, Virginia. Scavenger Hunt. 2016. (D. I. Y. Make It Happen Ser.). (ENG.). 32p. (J). (gr. 4-8). 29.93 (978-1-63471-103-6(3), 208523, 45th Parallel Press) Cherry Lake Publishing.

Martin, Isabel. Let's Take a Field Trip. 2015. (Let's Take a Field Trip Ser.). (ENG.). 24p. (gr. k-1). lib. bdg. 106.60 (978-1-4914-2596-1(2), Pebble Plus) Capstone Press of Coughlan Cos.

Marzollo, Jean. C'est Moi l'Espion: Défis Suprêmes! Duchesne, Lucie, tr. Wick, Walter, photos by. (I Spy Bks.).Tr. of I Spy Fantasy. (FRE., Illus.). 37p. (J). (gr. -1-3). pap. 16.99 (978-0-590-24340-7(3)) Scholastic, Inc.

Masters, Nancy Robinson. How Did They Build That? Water Park. 2011. (Community Connections: How Did They Build That? Ser.). (ENG.). 24p. (gr. 2-5). lib. bdg. 25.64 (978-1-60279-983-7(0), 200956) Cherry Lake Publishing.

McCullagh, Sheila K. & Myers, Lois. Galapagos. Date not set. (Whizz Bang Bumper Bk.). (Illus.). 32p. (J). pap. 129.15 (978-0-582-19338-3(9)) Addison-Wesley Longman, Ltd. GBR. Dist: Trans-Atlantic Pubns., Inc.

Meachen Rau, Dana. Juegos y Diversiones en la Historia de América. 2006. (Como era la vida en America (How People Lived in America) Ser.). (SPA., Illus.). 24p. (gr. 1-4). lib. bdg. 22.00 (978-0-8368-7429-7(3), Weekly Reader Leveled Readers) Stevens, Gareth Publishing LLLP.

—Juegos y diversiones en la historia de America (Toys, Games, & Fun in American History) 2006. (Como era la vida en America (How People Lived in America) Ser.). (SPA.). 24p. (gr. 1-4). pap. 8.15 (978-0-8368-7436-5(6), Weekly Reader Leveled Readers) Stevens, Gareth Publishing LLLP.

—Toys, Games, & Fun in American History. 2006. (How People Lived in America Ser.). (Illus.). 24p. (gr. 1-4). pap. 8.15 (978-0-8368-7216-3(9)); lib. bdg. 22.00 (978-0-8368-7209-5(6)) Stevens, Gareth Publishing LLLP. (Weekly Reader Leveled Readers).

Mercado, Nancy E. Boredom Busters! Activities to Do for Kids Like You! 2003. (Illus.). 38p. (J). (978-0-439-52312-7(5)) Scholastic, Inc.

Michael O'Mara Books UK Staff. The Gift for Boys. 2010. (ENG., Illus.). 64p. (J). (gr. 1-7). 4.95 (978-1-84317-423-3(5)) O'Mara, Michael Bks., Ltd. GBR. Dist: Independent Pubs. Group.

Miller, Karen. Children & the Entertainment Industry. 2010. (Opposing Viewpoints Ser.). (Illus.). 240p. (J). 42.95 *(978-0-7377-4763-8(3))*; pap. 29.45 *(978-0-7377-4764-5(1))* Cengage Gale. (Greenhaven Pr., Inc.).

Mitchell, Susan. Amusement Park Rides. 2009. (Ultimate 10: Entertainment Ser.). (ENG.). 48p. (J). (gr. 4-8). pap. 10.50 *(978-1-4339-2210-7(X))*; (YA). (gr. 5-9). lib. bdg. 31.00 *(978-0-8368-9162-1(7))* Stevens, Gareth Publishing LLLP.

Mulcahy, Lisa, et al. Bye Bye Boredom! The Girl's Life Big Book of Fun. 2003. (Illus.). 124p. (J). *(978-0-439-44976-2(6))* Scholastic, Inc.

My Big Creepy Sticker. 2003. (Illus.). 48p. (J). 5.98 *(978-1-4054-1218-6(6))* Parragon, Inc.

My Big Spooky Sticker Activity Book. 2003. (Illus.). 48p. (J). 5.98 *(978-1-4054-1219-3(4))* Parragon, Inc.

My Pocket Dot to Dot Boat. 2003. (Illus.). 192p. (J). 1.49 *(978-1-4054-0884-4(7))* Parragon, Inc.

National Geographic Kids Staff & Gerry, Lisa. 100 Things to Do Before You Grow Up. 2014. (ENG., Illus.). 256p. (J). (gr. 4-7). pap. 9.99 *(978-1-4263-1558-9(9))*, National Geographic Children's Bks.) National Geographic Society.

Newman-D'Amico, Fran. Travel Fun. 2004. (Dover Little Activity Bks.). (ENG., Illus.). 64p. (J). (gr. k-3). pap., act. bk. ed. 1.99 *(978-0-486-43532-9(6))* Dover Pubns., Inc.

Newton, Joan. Gravity in Action: Roller Coasters! 2009. (Amazing Science Ser.). 24p. (J). (gr. 2-5). lib. bdg. 22.60 *(978-1-4358-2976-3(X))*, PowerKids Pr.) Rosen Publishing Group, Inc., The.

Okido Staff. My Animal Book: Facts & Fun, Questions & Answers, Things to Make & Do. 2014. (ENG., Illus.). 64p. (J). (gr. k-2). 18.95 *(978-0-500-65024-0(1))*, 565024) Thames & Hudson.

Painter, Lucy. The Really Big Book of Amazing Things to Make & Do: With 2000 Step-By-Step Photos! 2017. (ENG., Illus.). 256p. (J). (gr. -1-12). pap. 11.99 ***(978-1-78214-226-3(6)***, Armadillo) Anness Publishing GBR. Dist: National Bk. Network.

Painter, Lucy. 100 Fantastic Things to Make, Do & Play: Simple, Fun Projects That Use Easy Everyday Materials - Cooking, Growing, Science, Music, Painting, Crafts & Party Games! 2014. (ENG., Illus.). 256p. (J). (gr. -1 — 1). pap. 16.99 *(978-1-84322-941-4(2))*, Armadillo) Anness Publishing GBR. Dist: National Bk. Network.

Peirce, Lincoln. Big Nate: Fun Blaster: Cheezy Doodles, Crazy Comix, & Loads of Laughs! Peirce, Lincoln, illus. 2012. (Big Nate Activity Book Ser.: 2). (ENG., Illus.). 224p. (J). (gr. 3-7). 10.99 *(978-0-06-209045-4(3))* HarperCollins Pubs.

—Big Nate Boredom Buster. Peirce, Lincoln, illus. 2014. (Big Nate Activity Book Ser.: 1). (ENG., Illus.). 224p. (J). (gr. 3-7). pap. 6.99 *(978-0-06-233800-6(5))* HarperCollins Pubs.

—Big Nate Boredom Buster: Super Scribbles, Cool Comix, & Lots of Laughs. Peirce, Lincoln, illus. 2011. (Big Nate Activity Book Ser.: 1). (ENG., Illus.). 224p. (J). (gr. 3-7). 10.99 *(978-0-06-206094-5(5))* HarperCollins Pubs.

—Big Nate Fun Blaster. 2012. (Illus.). 198p. (J). 6.99 *(978-0-06-219962-1(5))* HarperCollins Pubs.

Peters, Rosalind. Midnight Feast Magic: Sleepover Fun & Food. Pankhurst, Kate, illus. Boursnell, Clive, photos by. 2009. (ENG.). 64p. (J). (gr. 3-6). pap. 15.95 *(978-1-84507-783-9(0))*, Frances Lincoln) Quarto Publishing Group UK GBR. Dist: Hachette Bk. Group.

Peterson, Megan Cooley, et al. How to Build Hair-Raising Haunted Houses, 1 vol. 2010. (Halloween Extreme Ser.). (ENG.). 32p. (gr. 3-4). lib. bdg. 27.99 *(978-1-4296-5421-0(X))*, Edge Bks.) Capstone Press of Coughlan Cos.

Pettiford, Rebecca. Roller Coasters. 2015. (Illus.). 24p. (J). lib. bdg. 25.65 *(978-1-62031-215-5(8))* Jump! Inc.

Platt, Richard. A Circus Horse Could Count?! And Other Extraordinary Entertainments. 2015. (ENG., Illus.). 48p. pap. 12.95 *(978-0-19-911871-7(X))* Oxford Univ. Pr., Inc.

PRESS, Celebration. Scream Machines: All about Roller Coasters. 2003. (ENG.). (J). (gr. 6-8). pap. 37.95 *(978-0-7652-3244-1(8))*, Celebration Pr.) Pearson Schl.

Priddy, Roger. Easter Egg Hunt. 2014. (Shaped Board Bks.). (ENG.). 6p. (J). (gr. -1-k). bds. 6.99 *(978-0-312-51669-7(X))*, 9780312516697, Priddy Bks.) St. Martin's Pr.

Puzzles Sparkly Sticker Book. Date not set. (Illus.). 16p. (J). 3.98 *(978-1-4054-0995-7(9))* Parragon, Inc.

Rau, Dana Meachen. Roller Coasters. 2010. (Bookworms Chapter Books: Surprising Science Ser.). 24p. (gr. 2-3). 22.79 *(978-0-7614-4872-3(1))* Marshall Cavendish Corp.

Rauchwerger, Lisa. Chocolate Chip Challah. Rauchwerger, Lisa, illus. 2004. (Illus.). (gr. k-3). pap., act. bk. ed. 9.95 *(978-0-8074-0736-3(4))*, 104035) URJ Pr.

Really Horrible Facts. 2013. (Really Horrible Facts Ser.). 32p. (J). (gr. k-3). 101.00 *(978-1-61533-868-9(3))*; pap. 40.00 *(978-1-61533-876-4(4))*; pap. 240.00 *(978-1-61533-877-1(2))* Windmill Bks.

Roby, Cynthia. Discovering STEM at the Amusement Park. 2015. (STEM in the Real World Ser.). (ENG., Illus.). 24p. (J). (gr. 2-3). pap. 8.25 *(978-1-4994-0910-9(9))*, PowerKids Pr.) Rosen Publishing Group, Inc., The.

Rosen, Michael J. & Kassoy, Ben. Wacky Sports. Jones, Doug, illus. 2013. (No Way! Ser.). (ENG.). 32p. (gr. 3-5). lib. bdg. 26.60 *(978-0-7613-8982-8(2))*, Millbrook Pr.) Lerner Publishing Group.

Salzmann, Mary Elizabeth. Money for Entertainment, 1 vol. 2010. (Your Piggy Bank: A Guide to Spending & Saving for Kids! Ser.). (ENG., Illus.). 24p. (J). (gr. k-3). 27.07 *(978-1-61641-028-5(0))* Magic Wagon.

Savage, Jeff. Thrill Rides! All about Roller Coasters. 2006. 48p. (J). pap. *(978-1-59336-727-5(9))* Mondo Publishing.

Scratch & Sketch Funny Faces. 2005. (Activity Journal Ser.). (Illus.). 60p. (J). 12.99 *(978-0-88088-487-7(8))* Peter Pauper Pr. Inc.

Sharky & George. Don't You Dare. 2013. (Sharky & George Ser.). (ENG., Illus.). 96p. (J). (gr. -1). pap. 19.99 *(978-1-4052-5829-6(2))* Egmont Bks., Ltd. GBR. Dist: Independent Pubs. Group.

Sheep. Date not set. (Old MacDonald Stickers Ser.). (Illus.). 16p. (J). 5.98 *(978-0-7525-9969-4(0))* Parragon, Inc.

Siomades, Lorianne, ed. Look What You Can Make with Boxes: Creative Crafts from Everyday Objects. Schneider, Hank, photos by. 2013. (Look What You Can Make Ser.). (ENG., Illus.). 48p. (J). (gr. k-7). pap. 6.95 *(978-1-56397-704-6(4))* Boyds Mills Pr.

Smith, Keri. Tear up This Book! The Sticker, Stencil, Stationery, Games, Crafts, Doodle, & Journal Book for Girls! Magruder, Trula, ed. Smith, Keri, illus. 2005. (ENG., Illus.). 96p. (J). (gr. 3-7). spiral bd. 10.95 *(978-1-58485-977-2(6))*, American Girl) American Girl Publishing, Inc.

Stewart, Trenton Lee. Mr. Benedict's Book of Perplexing Puzzles, Elusive Enigmas, & Curious Conundrums. Sudyka, Diana, illus. 2011. (Mysterious Benedict Society Ser.). (ENG.). 176p. (J). (gr. 3-7). 15.99 *(978-0-316-18193-8(5))* Little, Brown Bks. for Young Readers.

Stillerman, Robbie. Amusement Park Stickers. 2004. (Dover Little Activity Books Stickers Ser.). (ENG., Illus.). 8p. (J). (gr. -1-5). pap. 1.50 *(978-0-486-43305-9(6))* Dover Pubns., Inc.

—Princess the Pony Sticker Activity Book. 2003. (Dover Little Activity Books Stickers Ser.). (ENG., Illus.). 4p. (J). (gr. k-3). pap. 1.99 *(978-0-486-43020-1(2))* Dover Pubns., Inc.

Stotter, Ruth. A Loop of String: String Stories & String Stunts: Traditional & Original String Figures & Stories. Coffey, Kevin, illus. 2009. 110p. (J). pap. 22.95 *(978-1-58790-170-6(6))* Regent Pr.

TerKeurst, Lysa. The Sweetest Story Ever Told Activity Kit. Sparks, Michal, illus. 2003. 14.99 *(978-0-8024-7093-5(9))* Moody Pubs.

Things to Make & Do. (Get Crafty Ser.). (J). Date not set. 48p. pap. 4.98 *(978-0-7525-8411-9(1))* 64p. 5.98 *(978-1-4054-0412-9(4))* 2003. (Illus.). 64p. 12.98 *(978-1-4054-1220-9(8))* Parragon, Inc.

Thomas, Keith A. Cross-Lengua Coloring Book for Kids. Thomas, Keith A., illus. l.t. ed. 2004. (ENG & SPA., Illus.). 22p. (J). (gr. 3-18). pap. *(978-0-9617451-2-7(6))* KALEXT Productions, LLC.

Thrills & Spills, Bk. 3/2. (J). (gr. 3). 34.40 *(978-0-673-72656-8(8))*, Scott Foresman) Addison Wesley Schl.

Today's Superstars: Entertainment, 6 bks., Set. Incl. Jessica Simpson. Mitchell, Susan K. lib. bdg. 31.95 *(978-0-8368-8201-8(6))*; Jim Carrey. Stone, Amy. lib. bdg. 31.95 *(978-0-8368-8197-4(4))*; Kenny Chesney. Thomas, William David. lib. bdg. 31.95 *(978-0-8368-8198-1(2))*; Olsen Twins. Gorman, Jacqueline Laks. lib. bdg. 31.95 *(978-0-8368-8199-8(0))*; Tyra Banks. Mitchell, Susan K. lib. bdg. 31.95 *(978-0-8368-8196-7(6))*; (Illus.). 32p. (gr. 5-8). 2007. 2007. Set lib. bdg. 143.58 o.p. *(978-0-8368-8195-0(8))*; Set lib. bdg. 143.58 o.p. *(978-0-8368-8120-2(6))* Stevens, Gareth Publishing LLLP.

Treasure Chest. 2003. (J). per. *(978-1-57657-978-7(6))* Paradise Pr., Inc.

A Treasury for One Year Olds. Date not set. 96p. (J). 7.98 *(978-1-4054-0021-3(8))* Parragon, Inc.

A Treasury for Two Year Olds. Date not set. (Illus.). 96p. (J). 7.98 *(978-1-4054-0022-0(6))* Parragon, Inc.

Walton, Sally & Painter, Lucy. 100 Fantastic Things to Make, Do & Play: Simple, Fun Projects That Use Easy Everyday Materials. 2008. (ENG., Illus.). 256p. (J). (gr. -1-2). pap. 24.99 *(978-1-84476-473-0(7))* Anness Publishing GBR. Dist: National Bk. Network.

Walton, Sally, et al. Fun Projects & Amazing Things to Make, Do, Play & Give: Two Fantastic Books in a Box - the Ultimate Rainy-Day Collection with 220 Exciting Step-By-Step Projects Shown in over 3000 Photographs, 2 vols. 2013. (ENG., Illus.). 265p. 25.00 *(978-1-84322-960-5(9))* Anness Publishing GBR. Dist: National Bk. Network.

Weekly Reader Early Learning Library Staff. Things I Play With. 2006. (Things in My World Ser.). (Illus.). 16p. (gr. -1-2). lib. bdg. 19.00 *(978-0-8368-6811-1(0))*, Weekly Reader Leveled Readers) Stevens, Gareth Publishing LLLP.

Where's Henry? (J). 21.95 *(978-0-8136-4327-4(9))*; pap. 13.15 *(978-0-8136-4326-7(0))* Modern Curriculum Pr.

Williams, Colleen Madonna Flood. My Adventure at the Water Park. 2009. (ENG.). 44p. (J). 8.99 *(978-1-59092-579-9(3))* Blue Forge Pr.

Williams, Dinah. Abandoned Amusement Parks. 2013. (Scary Places Ser.). 32p. (J). (gr. 4-8). lib. bdg. 25.27 *(978-1-61772-884-6(5))* Bearport Publishing Co., Inc.

Wilmes, Liz & Wilmes, Dick. Felt Board Fun: For Everyday & Holidays. Dane, Donna, illus. 2004. 244p. (J). pap. 16.95 *(978-0-943452-02-9(3))* Building Blocks, LLC.

Wingard-Nelson, Rebecca. Amusement Park Word Problems Starring Pre-Algebra: Math Word Problems Solved. 2009. (Math Word Problems Solved Ser.). (Illus.). 48p. (J). (gr. 2-5). lib. bdg. 25.27 *(978-0-7660-2922-4(0))* Enslow Pubs., Inc.

Zimmerman Rutledge, Jill S. Prom Parade. 2017. (ENG., Illus.). 80p. (J). (gr. 8-12). 35.99 *(978-1-5124-0267-4(2))*, Twenty-First Century Bks.) Lerner Publishing Group.

100s of Fun Things to Make & Do. Date not set. 256p. (J). 12.98 *(978-1-4054-0452-5(3))* Parragon, Inc.

365 Things to Make & Do. Date not set. (Illus.). 256p. (J). 12.98 *(978-1-4054-0023-7(4))* Parragon, Inc.

ANALYSIS (CHEMISTRY)

see Chemistry, Analytic

ANALYSIS, MICROSCOPIC

see Microscopy

ANALYTICAL CHEMISTRY

see Chemistry, Analytic

ANALYTICAL GEOMETRY

see Geometry, Analytic

ANARCHISM

see also Socialism

Croce, Nicholas, ed. Anarchism, Revolution, & Terrorism. 2014. (Political & Economic Systems Ser.). 312p. (J). (gr. 9-12). 45.00 *(978-1-62275-353-6(4))* Rosen Publishing Group, Inc., The.

ANARCHISM AND ANARCHISTS

see Anarchism

ANATOLE (FICTITIOUS CHARACTER)—FICTION

Titus, Eve. Anatole. 2010. (ENG., Illus.). 32p. (J). (gr. k-3). pap. 7.99 *(978-0-375-85546-7(7))*, Dragonfly Bks.) Random Hse. Children's Bks.

—Anatole & the Cat. 2010. (ENG., Illus.). 32p. (J). (gr. k-3). pap. 7.99 *(978-0-375-85547-4(5))*, Dragonfly Bks.) Random Hse. Children's Bks.

ANATOMY

Here are entered general treatises and works on human anatomy. General works on animal anatomy are entered under Anatomy, Comparative.

see also Anatomy, Comparative; Bones; Nervous System; Physiology; Plant Anatomy

also subjects with the subdivision Anatomy, e.g. Birds—Anatomy; Botany—Anatomy; etc.; and names of organs and regions of the body, e.g. Heart

Acampora, Courtney. Heads & Tails. Tinarelli, Beatrice, illus. 2016. (ENG.). 22p. (J). (gr. -1). bds. 12.99 *(978-1-62686-748-2(8))*, Silver Dolphin Bks.) Readerlink Distribution Services, LLC.

Andrews, Barbara. The Nervous & Digestive Systems. 2006. (J). pap. *(978-1-4108-6512-0(6))* Benchmark Education Co.

Apel, Melanie Ann. Let's Talk about When You Have to Have Your Appendix Out. 2009. (Let's Talk Library). 24p. (gr. 2-3). 42.50 *(978-1-60853-448-7(0))*, PowerKids Pr.) Rosen Publishing Group, Inc., The.

Axelrod-Contrada, Joan & Klepeis, Alicia Z. Real-Life Zombies. 2016. (Real-Life Zombies Ser.). (ENG.). 32p. (gr. 3-4). 111.96 *(978-1-5157-2517-6(0))*, Edge Bks.) Capstone Press of Coughlan Cos.

Bailey, Gerry & Way, Steve. Body & Health. 2009. (Simply Science Ser.). (Illus.). 32p. (YA). (gr. 3-6). lib. bdg. 26.00 *(978-1-4339-0030-3(0))* Stevens, Gareth Publishing LLLP.

Ballard, Carol. Keeping Fit: Body Systems. 2016. (Do It Yourself Ser.). (ENG.). 48p. pap. 8.99 *(978-1-4846-3815-6(8))*, NA-h) Heinemann-Raintree.

Barraclough, Sue. The Circulatory System: Why Does My Heart Beat? 2016. (Body Systems Ser.). (ENG.). 32p. pap. 8.29 *(978-1-4846-3825-5(5))*, Heinemann First Library) Heinemann-Raintree.

—My Body. 2009. (Me & My World Ser.). (Illus.). 24p. (J). (gr. -1-2). pap. 8.15 *(978-1-60754-062-5(2))*; lib. bdg. 22.60 *(978-1-60754-057-1(6))* Windmill Bks.

Bauer, Marion Dane. Toes, Ears, & Nose! Katz, Karen, illus. 2003. (ENG.). 16p. (J). (gr. -1 — 1). bds. 6.99 *(978-0-689-84712-7(2))*, Little Simon) Little Simon.

Beevor, Lucy. Understanding Our Head. 2017. (Brains, Body, Bones! Ser.). (ENG., Illus.). 32p. (gr. 3-5). lib. bdg. 30.65 *(978-1-4109-8580-4(6))*, Raintree Perspectives) Heinemann-Raintree.

—Understanding Our Muscles. 2017. (Brains, Body, Bones! Ser.). (ENG., Illus.). 32p. (gr. 3-5). lib. bdg. 30.65 *(978-1-4109-8581-1(4))*, Raintree Perspectives) Heinemann-Raintree.

—Understanding Our Organs. 2017. (Brains, Body, Bones! Ser.). (ENG., Illus.). 32p. (gr. 3-5). lib. bdg. 30.65 *(978-1-4109-8579-8(2))*, Raintree Perspectives) Heinemann-Raintree.

—Understanding Our Skeleton. 2017. (Brains, Body, Bones! Ser.). (ENG., Illus.). 32p. (gr. 3-5). lib. bdg. 30.65 *(978-1-4109-8578-1(4))*, Raintree Perspectives) Heinemann-Raintree.

Bell, Samantha. My Fingernails Grow. 2014. (Tell Me Why Library). (ENG., Illus.). 24p. (J). (gr. 2-5). 25.64 *(978-1-63188-009-4(8))*, 205443) Cherry Lake Publishing.

Berne, Emma Carlson. Nail Care Tips & Tricks. Heschke, Elena, illus. 2015. (ENG.). 32p. (J). (gr. 4-8). lib. bdg. 26.65 *(978-1-4677-6221-3(5))*, Lerner Pubns.) Lerner Publishing Group.

Body. (Make it Work Ser.). 42p. (J). (gr. 4-8). pap. *(978-1-882210-42-8(5))* Action Publishing, Inc.

The Body. (J). (gr. k-1). *(978-84-342-2399-8(6))*, PR30569) Parramon Ediciones S.A. ESP. Dist: Lectorum Pubns., Inc.

Boynton, Sandra. The Going to Bed Book. Boynton, Sandra, illus. 2004. (ENG., Illus.). 14p. (J). (gr. -1 — 1). bds. 9.99 *(978-0-689-87028-6(0))*, Little Simon) Little Simon.

Bozzo, Linda. Amazing Animal Tails. 2009. (Creature Features Ser.). 24p. (gr. 2-3). 42.50 *(978-1-61512-068-0(8))*, PowerKids Pr.) Rosen Publishing Group, Inc., The.

—Amazing Beaks. (Creature Features Ser.). 24p. 2009. (gr. 2-3). 42.50 *(978-1-61512-071-0(8))* 2008. (Illus.). (J). (gr. 3-7). lib. bdg. 22.60 *(978-1-4042-4169-5(8))* Rosen Publishing Group, Inc., The. (PowerKids Pr.).

Bradley, Timothy. Increíble pero Real - Anatomías Asquerosas. 2017. (TIME for Kids en Español - Level 4 Ser.). (SPA.). 48p. (gr. 4-4). lib. bdg. 31.99 *(978-1-5157-5141-0(4))* Time for Kids Inc AUS. Dist: Capstone Pub.

—Strange but True: Gross Anatomy, 1 vol. 2nd rev. ed. 2013. (Nonfiction Readers Ser.). (ENG., Illus.). 48p. (J). (gr. 4-4). pap. 29.96 *(978-1-4807-1112-9(8))* Shell Educational Publishing.

Bradley, Timothy J. Strange but True: Gross Anatomy, 1 vol. 2nd rev. ed. 2012. (Nonfiction Readers Ser.). (ENG.). 48p. (J). (gr. 4-4). pap. 9.99 *(978-1-4333-4860-0(8))* Teacher Created Materials, Inc.

Brett, Flora. Your Digestive System Works! 2015. (Your Body Systems Ser.). (ENG.). 24p. (gr. 1-2). lib. bdg. 25.32 *(978-1-4914-2064-5(2))* Capstone Press of Coughlan Cos.

—Your Respiratory System Works! 2015. (Your Body Systems Ser.). (ENG.). 24p. (gr. 1-2). lib. bdg. 25.32 *(978-1-4914-2067-6(7))* Capstone Press of Coughlan Cos.

Brezina, Corona. Organ Donation: Risks, Rewards, & Research. 2009. (J). 77.70 *(978-1-4358-5557-1(4))*; (ENG.). 64p. (YA). pap. 12.95 *(978-1-4358-5556-4(6))*; (Illus.). 64p. (YA). (gr. 7-12). lib. bdg. 31.95 *(978-1-4358-5275-4(3))* Rosen Publishing Group, Inc., The.

Burstein, John. The Dynamic Digestive System: How Does My Stomach Work? 2009. (Slim Goodbody's Body Buddies Ser.). (ENG., Illus.). 32p. (J). (gr. 3-5). lib. bdg. *(978-0-7787-4415-3(9))* Crabtree Publishing Co.

Canavan, Thomas. Fighting Illness & Injury: The Immune System. 2015. (How Your Body Works). (ENG.). 32p. (J). (gr. 4-4). pap. 10.00 *(978-1-4994-1223-9(1))*, PowerKids Pr.) Rosen Publishing Group, Inc., The.

—Fit & Healthy: Heart, Lungs, & Hormones. 2015. (How Your Body Works). (ENG.). 32p. (J). (gr. 4-4). pap. 10.00 *(978-1-4994-1224-6(X))*, PowerKids Pr.) Rosen Publishing Group, Inc., The.

—Why Do X-Rays Show Your Bones? Questions about Bones & the Skeleton. 2016. (Human Body FAQ Ser.). 00032p. (J). (gr. 3-3). pap. 10.00 *(978-1-4994-3173-5(2))*, PowerKids Pr.) Rosen Publishing Group, Inc., The.

Canetti, Yanitzia. La Adaptación, ¡qué Sensación! 2010. (SPA.). (J). *(978-1-59835-175-0(3))* Cambridge BrickHouse, Inc.

—La Adaptación, Qué Sensación Alas. 2010. (SPA.). (J). *(978-1-59835-190-3(7))* Cambridge BrickHouse, Inc.

—Amazing Adaptations! 2010. (J). *(978-1-59835-199-6(0))* Cambridge BrickHouse, Inc.

Capaccio, George. Digestive Disorders. 2010. (Health Alert 7 Ser.). 64p. (YA). (gr. 4-7). 32.79 *(978-0-7614-4822-8(5))* Marshall Cavendish GBR. Dist: Marshall Cavendish Corp.

Caster, Shannon. Kidneys. 2010. (Body Works Ser.). (Illus.). 24p. (J). pap. 8.25 *(978-1-4358-9832-5(X))*, PowerKids Pr.); (YA). (gr. 2-5). lib. bdg. 22.60 *(978-1-4358-9372-6(7))* Rosen Publishing Group, Inc., The.

—Lungs. 2010. (Body Works Ser.). (Illus.). 24p. (J). pap. 8.25 *(978-1-4358-9830-1(3))*, PowerKids Pr.); (YA). (gr. 2-5). lib. bdg. 22.60 *(978-1-4358-9371-9(9))* Rosen Publishing Group, Inc., The.

Clark, Katie Lea. A Tour of Your Muscular & Skeletal Systems, 1 vol. Jones, Chris B., illus. 2012. (First Graphics: Body Systems Ser.). (ENG.). 24p. (gr. 1-2). pap. 6.29 *(978-1-4296-9326-4(6))* Capstone Press of Coughlan Cos.

Close, Edward. Body Basics, 1 vol., 1. 2014. (Discovery Education: How It Works). (ENG.). 32p. (gr. 3-6). 26.25 *(978-1-4777-6309-4(0))*, PowerKids Pr.) Rosen Publishing Group, Inc., The.

Cohen, Robert Z. The Stomach & Intestines in Your Body, 1 vol. 2015. (ENG.). 32p. (J). 23.45 *(978-1-62275-632-2(0))*, Britannica Educational Publishing) Rosen Publishing Group, Inc., The.

Collins, Katie. Anatomy Academy: Respiration, Circulation & Digestion, Vol. 2. 2005. 64p. 11.95 *(978-1-59363-050-8(6))* Prufrock Pr.

—Anatomy Academy Bk. 1: Cells, Muscles & Bones. 2005. 64p. 11.95 *(978-1-59363-049-2(2))* Prufrock Pr.

Cuerpo Humano. 2003. (Fun Non-Fiction Ser.). (SPA.). (J). *(978-970-690-135-4(3))* Planeta Mexicana Editorial S. A. de C. V.

Daniels, Patricia, et al. Ultimate Bodypedia: An Amazing Inside-Out Tour of the Human Body. 2014. (ENG.). 272p. (J). (gr. 2-5). lib. bdg. 33.90 *(978-1-4263-1722-4(0))*, National Geographic Children's Bks.) National Geographic Society.

Davies, Nicola. Just the Right Size: Why Big Animals Are Big & Little Animals Are Little. Layton, Neal, illus. 2011. (Animal Science Ser.). (ENG.). 64p. (J). (gr. 3-7). pap. 7.99 *(978-0-7636-5300-2(4))* Candlewick Pr.

Dawson, Emily C. Animal Clothing. 2010. (Our Animal World Ser.). 24p. (J). 25.65 *(978-1-60753-006-0(6))* Amicus Publishing.

Daynes, Katie & King, Colin. Tu Cuerpo: Conoce Por Dentro. 2007. (Titles in Spanish Ser.). (Illus.). 15p. (J). (gr. -1). bds. 12.99 *(978-0-7460-8386-4(6))*, Usborne) EDC Publishing.

de la Bédoyere, Camilla. 3-D Explorer: Human Body. 2015. (3D Explorers Ser.). (ENG., Illus.). 32p. (J). (gr. 1). 19.95 *(978-1-62686-433-7(0))*, Silver Dolphin Bks.) Readerlink Distribution Services, LLC.

Dolphin, Colleen. Armpits to Zits: The Body from A to Z, 1 vol. Craig, Diane, ed. 2007. (Let's See A to Z Ser.). (ENG., Illus.). 32p. (gr. -1-3). 27.07 *(978-1-59928-884-0(2))*, Super SandCastle) ABDO Publishing Co.

Dompierre, Judith. Body & Body Functions. 2012. 30p. 29.95 *(978-1-4626-9274-3(5))*; 32p. pap. 25.00 *(978-1-4626-9327-6(X))* America Star Bks.

Dorling Kindersley Publishing Staff. DK Adventures: a Trip Through the Body: A Trip Through the Body. 2015. (DK Adventures Ser.). (ENG.). 128p. (J). (gr. 3-7). 16.99 *(978-1-4654-2932-2(8))*, DK Children) Dorling Kindersley Publishing, Inc.

—Human Body! 2017. (ENG.). 208p. (J). (gr. 4-7). 24.99 ***(978-1-4654-6239-8(2)***, DK Children) Dorling Kindersley Publishing, Inc.

—Pocket Genius: Human Body. 2016. (Pocket Genius Ser.). (ENG., Illus.). 160p. (J). (gr. 3-7). pap. 4.99 *(978-1-4654-4588-9(9))*, DK Children) Dorling Kindersley Publishing, Inc.

—A Trip Through the Body. 2015. (DK Adventures Ser.). (ENG.). 128p. (J). (gr. 3-7). pap. 5.99 *(978-1-4654-2933-9(6))*, DK Children) Dorling Kindersley Publishing, Inc.

Dorling Kindersley Publishing Staff, creator. My First Spanish Body Board Book/Mi Primer Libro del Cuerpo. 2005. (My First Bks.). (SPA & ENG., Illus.). 36p. (J). (gr. -1 — 1). bds. 5.99 *(978-0-7566-1501-7(1))*, DK Children) Dorling Kindersley Publishing, Inc.

Dowdy, Penny. Body Math. 2008. (Math Alive! Ser.). 32p. (gr. 4-18). lib. bdg. 28.50 *(978-0-7614-3215-9(9))*, Benchmark Bks.) Marshall Cavendish Corp.

Duke, Shirley Smith. Vertebrates & Invertebrates Explained. 2016. (Distinctions in Nature Ser.). (Illus.). 32p. (J). (gr. 3-3). pap. 10.58 *(978-1-5026-1779-8(X))* Cavendish Square Publishing.

Easton, Marilyn. Big & Little. 2011. (Illus.). 62p. (J). pap. *(978-0-545-38782-8(5))* Scholastic, Inc.

Encyclopaedia Britannica, Inc. Staff, compiled by. The Respiratory System. 2008. 49.95 *(978-1-59339-558-2(2))* Encyclopaedia Britannica, Inc.

Feldman, Jean R. & Karapetkova, Holly. Arms Are for Hugging (Tune, the Girl I Left Behind Me) Lap Book. 2010. (ENG., Illus.). 12p. (gr. -1-k). 9.95 *(978-1-61590-200-2(7))* Rourke Educational Media.

Figorito, Christine. The Lungs in Your Body, 1 vol. 2015. (ENG.). 32p. (J). 23.45 *(978-1-62275-628-5(2))*, Britannica Educational Publishing) Rosen Publishing Group, Inc., The.

Fornari, Giuliano, illus. Panoramas Human Body. 2006. (J). *(978-0-7607-8155-5(9))* backpackbooks.

Ganeri, Anita. The Inside & Out Guide to Animals, 1 vol. 2006. (Inside & Out Guides To Ser.). (ENG., Illus.). 32p. pap. 7.99 *(978-1-4034-9091-9(0))*, NA-h) Heinemann-Raintree.

Gardner, Jane P. Take a Closer Look at Your Lungs. 2013. (Take a Closer Look Ser.). (ENG.). 24p. (J). (gr. 2-5). 28.50 *(978-1-62323-548-2(0))*, 206353) Child's World, Inc., The.

—Take a Closer Look at Your Stomach. 2013. (Take a Closer Look Ser.). (ENG.). 24p. (J). (gr. 2-5). 28.50 *(978-1-62323-553-6(7))*, 206357) Child's World, Inc., The.

Gardner, Robert & Conklin, Joshua. Experiments for Future Doctors. 2016. (Experiments for Future STEM Professionals Ser.). 128p. (J). (gr. 6-6). 37.27 *(978-0-7660-7854-3(X))* Enslow Pubs., Inc.

Gibson, Brylee. Tails, Tails, Tails. 2003. (Rigby Sails Early Ser.). (ENG., Illus.). 16p. (gr. 1-2). pap. 6.95 *(978-0-7578-8904-2(2))* Houghton Mifflin Harcourt Publishing Co.

Gold, Susan Dudley. Learning about the Digestive & Excretory Systems. 2013. (Learning about the Human Body Systems Ser.). 48p. (J). (gr. 5-12). pap. 8.95 *(978-1-4644-0235-7(3))*; 25.27 *(978-0-7660-4157-8(3))* Enslow Pubs., Inc.

—Learning about the Respiratory System. 2013. (Learning about the Human Body Systems Ser.). 48p. (J). (gr. 5-12). pap. 8.95 *(978-1-4644-0243-2(4))*; 25.27 *(978-0-7660-4161-5(1))* Enslow Pubs., Inc.

Gray, Susan H. Camels Have Humps. 2014. (Tell Me Why Library). (ENG.). 24p. (J). (gr. 2-5). 25.64 *(978-1-63188-001-8(2)*, 205411) Cherry Lake Publishing.

Green, Jen. Inside Animals. 2010. (Invisible Worlds Ser.). 48p. (gr. 4). 28.50 *(978-0-7614-4195-3(6))* Marshall Cavendish Corp.

Gregory, Helen. Wings, 1 vol. (Wonder Readers Next Steps: Science Ser.). (ENG.). (gr. -1-1). 2013. 20p. 22.65 *(978-1-4765-2373-6(8))* 2011. 32p. pap. 5.99 *(978-1-4296-7812-4(7))* 2011. 16p. pap. 35.94 *(978-1-4296-8208-4(6))* Capstone Press of Coughlan Cos. (Wonder Readers).

Guillain, Charlotte. Nuestros Pulmones, 1 vol. 2010. (Nuestros Cuerpos Ser.).Tr. of Our Lungs. (SPA.). 24p. (gr. -1-1). pap. 6.29 *(978-1-4329-4308-0(1))*; (Illus.). 22.65 *(978-1-4329-4299-1(9))* Heinemann-Raintree. (Bellota).

Haerens, Margaret. Organ Donation. 2012. (Global Viewpoints Ser.). (ENG., Illus.). 224p. (gr. 10-12). pap. 31.70 *(978-0-7377-6445-1(7)*, Greenhaven Pr., Inc.) Cengage Gale.

Haerens, Margaret, ed. Organ Donation. 2012. (Global Viewpoints Ser.). (ENG., Illus.). 224p. (gr. 10-12). lib. bdg. 40.45 *(978-0-7377-6269-3(1)*, Greenhaven Pr., Inc.) Cengage Gale.

Halvorson, Karin. Inside the Kidneys, 1 vol. 2016. (Super Simple Body Set 2 Ser.). (ENG., Illus.). 32p. (J). (gr. k-4). 27.07 *(978-1-62403-943-0(X))* ABDO Publishing Co.

—Inside the Skin, Hair, & Nails, 1 vol. 2016. (Super Simple Body Set 2 Ser.). (ENG., Illus.). 32p. (J). (gr. k-4). 27.07 *(978-1-62403-942-3(1))* ABDO Publishing Co.

Hengel, Katherine. Senses Are for Everything: The Five Senses, 1 vol. 2012. (All about Your Senses Ser.). (ENG.). 24p. (J). (gr. k-3). lib. bdg. 24.21 *(978-1-61783-201-7(4)*, SandCastle) ABDO Publishing Co.

Higginson, Mel. Beaks & Bills. 2006. (Let's Look at Animals Discovery Library). (Illus.). 24p. (J). (gr. 3-7). lib. bdg. 22.79 *(978-1-60044-169-1(6))* Rourke Educational Media.

—Picos/Beaks & Bills. Sarfatti, Esther, tr. 2007. (Miremos A los Animales Ser.). (ENG & SPA., Illus.). 24p. lib. bdg. 22.79 *(978-1-60044-267-4(6))* Rourke Educational Media.

Hixson, Bryce. Anatomy Academy. Hixson, Bryce, illus. 2003. (Illus.). (J). per. 14.95 *(978-1-931801-03-4(7))* Loose In The Lab.

Holland, Mary. Animal Legs, 1 vol. 2016. (Animal Adaptations Ser.). (ENG., Illus.). 32p. (J). (gr. k-3). 17.95 *(978-1-62855-843-2(1))* Arbordale Publishing.

—Patas de Los Animales, 1 vol. 2016. (SPA., Illus.). 32p. (J). (gr. k-3). pap. 9.95 *(978-1-62855-845-6(8))* Arbordale Publishing.

Hulbert, Laura. Who Has This Tail? Brooks, Erik, illus. 2012. (ENG.). 40p. (J). (gr. -1-2). 17.99 *(978-0-8050-9429-9(6)*, 9780805094299, Holt, Henry & Co. Bks. For Young Readers) Holt, Henry & Co.

Human Body. 2014. (DK Eyewitness Bks.). (ENG.). 72p. (J). (gr. 3-7). lib. bdg. 19.99 *(978-1-4654-2620-8(5)*, DK Children) Dorling Kindersley Publishing, Inc.

Human Body Experiments. 2010. (Facts on File Science Experiments Ser.). (Illus.). 192p. (gr. 6-12). 40.00 *(978-0-8160-8171-4(9))* Facts On File, Inc.

Ipcizade, Catherine. BIG Mouths, 1 vol. 2010. (Big Ser.). (ENG.). 24p. (gr. k-1). lib. bdg. 26.65 *(978-1-4296-3996-5(2)*, Pebble Plus) Capstone Press of Coughlan Cos.

Jankowski, Connie. Investigating the Human Body, 1 vol. 2007. (Science Readers Ser.). (ENG., Illus.). 32p. (J). (gr. 4-4). pap. 8.99 *(978-0-7439-0595-4(4))* Shell Educational Publishing.

Jenkins, Pete. Hands. Quintanilla, Hazel, illus. 2017. (I See, I Saw Ser.). (ENG.). (J). (gr. k-1). 28.51 ***(978-1-68342-150-4(7))*** Rourke Educational Media.

Jenkins, Steve & Page, Robin. Creature Features: Twenty-Five Animals Explain Why They Look the Way They Do. Jenkins, Steve, illus. 2014. (ENG., Illus.). 32p. (J). (gr. -1-3). 17.99 *(978-0-544-23351-5(4)*, HMH Books For Young Readers) Houghton Mifflin Harcourt Publishing Co.

Johnson, Rebecca L. Daring Cell Defenders. 2008. pap. 52.95 *(978-0-8225-9381-2(5))* Lerner Publishing Group.

—Ultra-Organized Cell Systems. 2008. pap. 52.95 *(978-0-8225-9384-3(X))* Lerner Publishing Group.

—Ultra-Organized Cell Systems. Desrocher, Jack & Fairman, Jennifer, illus. 2007. (Microquests Ser.). (ENG.). 48p. (gr. 3-5). lib. bdg. 29.27 *(978-0-8225-7138-4(2)*, Millbrook Pr.) Lerner Publishing Group.

—Your Muscular System. 2012. (Searchlight Books — How Does Your Body Work? Ser.). (ENG., Illus.). 40p. (gr. 3-5). lib. bdg. 27.93 *(978-0-7613-7449-7(3)*, Lerner Pubns.) Lerner Publishing Group.

Jones, Peter. The Complete Guide to the Human Body. 2015. (Illus.). 144p. (J). *(978-1-4351-6167-2(X))* Barnes & Noble, Inc.

Kalman, Bobbie. Arms & Legs, Fingers & Toes. 2010. (ENG., Illus.). 16p. (J). (gr. k-2). *(978-0-7787-9416-5(4))*; pap. *(978-0-7787-9460-8(1))* Crabtree Publishing Co.

—Arms & Legs, Fingers & Toes: Brazos, Piernas y Dedos. 2010. (SPA, ENG & MUL.). 16p. (J). pap. *(978-0-7787-8264-3(6))*; lib. bdg. *(978-0-7787-8271-1(9))* Crabtree Publishing Co.

—Brazos, Piernas y Dedos. 2010. (SPA & ENG.). 16p. (J). pap. *(978-0-7787-8579-8(3))*; lib. bdg. *(978-0-7787-8553-8(X))* Crabtree Publishing Co.

—What Kind of Coverings Do Animals Have? 2015. (ENG., Illus.). 24p. (J). *(978-0-7787-1466-8(7))* Crabtree Publishing Co.

Kauffman, Dorothy. How the Earth Gets Its Shape. 2005. (Oxford Picture Dictionary for the Content Areas Ser.). (ENG., Illus.). 22p. (J). pap. 7.56 *(978-0-19-430956-1(8))* Oxford Univ. Pr., Inc.

—Inside the Human Body. 2005. (Oxford Picture Dictionary for the Content Areas Ser.). (ENG., Illus.). 24p. pap. 7.56 *(978-0-19-430953-0(3))* Oxford Univ. Pr., Inc.

Know Your Body. 2016. (Know Your Body Ser.). 24p. (gr. 2-1). pap. 48.90 *(978-1-4824-4512-1(3))*; lib. bdg. 135.60 *(978-1-4824-4372-1(4))* Stevens, Gareth Publishing LLLP.

Kolpin, Molly Erin. A Tour of Your Digestive System, 1 vol. Jones, Chris B., illus. 2012. (First Graphics: Body Systems Ser.). (ENG.). 24p. (gr. 1-2). pap. 6.29 *(978-1-4296-9324-0(X))* Capstone Press of Coughlan Cos.

Lambeth, Amy. The Body. 2009. 20p. pap. 12.50 *(978-1-4490-1995-2(1))* AuthorHouse.

Lee, Justin. The Respiratory System. 2009. (Insider's Guide to the Body Ser.). 48p. (gr. 5-8). 53.00 *(978-1-61513-585-1(5)*, Rosen Reference) Rosen Publishing Group, Inc., The.

Leech, Christopher & Pattison, Mark. Your 'Body Bitz' & What They Are Doing Right Now. 2009. (Illus.). 20p. pap. 10.49 *(978-1-4490-0109-4(2))* AuthorHouse.

Levete, Sarah. Understanding the Heart, Lungs, & Blood. 2010. (Understanding the Human Body Ser.). (Illus.). 48p. (YA). pap. 11.75 *(978-1-4358-9690-1(4))*; (gr. 5-8). lib. bdg. 29.25 *(978-1-4358-9684-0(X))* Rosen Publishing Group, Inc., The. (Rosen Reference).

Lew, Kristi. The Respiratory System. 2009. (Amazing Human Body 2 Ser.). (Illus.). 80p. (gr. 5). 34.21 *(978-0-7614-4042-0(9))* Marshall Cavendish Corp.

Lewis, Wendy. Sabrina the Girl with A Hole in Her Heart. Lucas, Diane, illus. 2011. (ENG.). 34p. pap. 10.95 *(978-1-4663-3473-1(8))* CreateSpace Independent Publishing Platform.

Liflander, Pamela. Gray's Anatomy. 2004. (Start Exploring Ser.). (Illus.). 16p. (J). pap. 19.95 *(978-0-7624-1590-8(8))* Running Pr. Bk. Pubs.

Lukeman, Noah. You're Growing. 2015. (ENG., Illus.). 20p. (J). pap. 5.99 *(978-1-63291-387-6(9))* Morgan Rice Bks.

Lundgren, Julie K. Eating & the Digestive System. 2012. (ENG.). 24p. (gr. 4-5). pap. 8.95 *(978-1-61810-234-8(6))* Rourke Educational Media.

—Skeletons & Exoskeletons. 2012. (ENG.). 24p. (gr. 3-4). pap. 8.95 *(978-1-61810-221-8(4))* Rourke Educational Media.

Macnair, Patricia. Everything You Need to Know about the Human Body. 2014. (Everything You Need to Know Ser.). (ENG., Illus.). 160p. (J). (gr. k-4). pap. 10.99 *(978-0-7534-7168-5(X)*, 9780753471685, Kingfisher) Roaring Brook Pr.

Manolis, Kay. The Digestive System. 2009. (Blastoff! Readers Ser.). (ENG., Illus.). 24p. (J). (gr. k-3). 20.00 *(978-0-531-21702-3(7)*, Children's Pr.) Scholastic Library Publishing.

—The Respiratory System. 2009. (Blastoff! Readers Ser.). (ENG., Illus.). 24p. (J). (gr. k-3). 20.00 *(978-0-531-21705-4(1)*, Children's Pr.) Scholastic Library Publishing.

Marcovitz, Hal. Organ & Body Donation, 1 vol. 2010. (Essential Viewpoints Set 5 Ser.). (ENG.). 112p. (J). (gr. 6-12). lib. bdg. 35.64 *(978-1-61613-524-9(7)*, Essential Library) ABDO Publishing Co.

Marshall Cavendish Corporation Staff. Mammal Anatomy: An Illustrated Guide. 2009. (Illus.). 287p. (YA). (gr. 7-18). 99.93 *(978-0-7614-7882-9(5))* Marshall Cavendish Corp.

Marsico, Katie. I Throw Up. 2014. (Tell Me Why Library). (ENG., Illus.). 24p. (J). (gr. 2-5). 25.64 *(978-1-63188-006-3(3)*, 205431) Cherry Lake Publishing.

Martin, Bobi. The Muscles in Your Body, 1 vol. 2015. (ENG.). 32p. (J). 23.45 *(978-1-62275-651-3(7)*, Britannica Educational Publishing) Rosen Publishing Group, Inc., The.

Martin, Ruth. Little Explorers: My Amazing Body. Sanders, Allan, illus. 2015. (Little Explorers Ser.). (ENG.). 18p. (J). (gr. -1-3). 9.99 *(978-1-4998-0040-1(1))* Little Bee Books Inc.

Mason, Paul. Your Breathtaking Lungs & Rocking Respiratory System: Find Out How Your Body Works! 2015. (Your Brilliant Body! Ser.). (ENG., Illus.). 32p. (J). (gr. 3-7). lib. bdg. *(978-0-7787-2195-6(7))* Crabtree Publishing Co.

Masters, Nancy Robinson. I Get the Hiccups. 2015. (Tell Me Why Library). (ENG., Illus.). 24p. (J). (gr. 2-5). 27.07 *(978-1-63362-611-9(3)*, 206628) Cherry Lake Publishing.

Maynard, Christopher & Martin, Terry. Why Do We Laugh? Questions Children Ask about the Human Body. (Why Bks.). (Illus.). 24p. (J). pap. 10.99 *(978-0-590-24955-3(X))* Scholastic, Inc.

Maynard, Christopher, et al. How Your Body Works. 2004. (Knowledge Masters Plus Ser.). (Illus.). 32p. (YA). pap. incl. cd-rom *(978-1-903954-44-7(4)*, Pavilion Children's Books) Pavilion Bks.

McDowell, Pamela. Flight. 2015. (Illus.). 24p. (J). *(978-1-4896-3671-3(4))* Weigl Pubs., Inc.

McManus, Lori. Cell Systems, 1 vol. 2012. (Investigating Cells Ser.). (ENG., Illus.). 48p. (gr. 3-6). 33.32 *(978-1-4329-3879-6(7)*, Heinemann InfoSearch) Heinemann-Raintree.

Meister, Cari. Totally Wacky Facts about the Human Body. 2016. (Mind Benders Ser.). (ENG.). 112p. (gr. 1-3). lib. bdg. 23.32 *(978-1-4914-8359-6(8))* Capstone Press of Coughlan Cos.

—Totally Wacky Facts about YOU! 2016. (Mind Benders Ser.). (ENG., Illus.). 240p. (gr. 1-3). pap. 7.95 *(978-1-4914-8376-3(8))* Capstone Press of Coughlan Cos.

Midthun, Joseph & Hiti, Samuel. The Endocrine & Reproductive Systems. 2014. (Illus.). 32p. (J). *(978-0-7166-1840-9(0))* World Bk., Inc.

Mitchell, Melanie S. Mouths. 2004. (First Step Nonfiction - Animal Traits Ser.). (ENG., Illus.). 8p. (gr. -1-1). pap. 4.95 *(978-0-8225-3913-1(6)*, Lerner Pubns.) Lerner Publishing Group.

Movement. (Jump Ser.). (Illus.). 32p. (J). (gr. 2-7). pap. *(978-1-882210-24-4(7))* Action Publishing, Inc.

Murphy, Julie. I've Got Feet!: Fantastical Feet of the Animal World. Tolson, Hannah, illus. 2017. (ENG.). 32p. (J). (gr. -1-1). 17.99 ***(978-1-68152-195-4(4))*** Amicus.

Nathan, Jacintha & Oleksy, Walter G. The Head & Neck in 3D. 2015. (Human Body In 3D Ser.). (ENG.). 64p. (J). (gr. 5-6). 32.95 *(978-1-4994-3593-1(2)*, Rosen Central) Rosen Publishing Group, Inc., The.

Omoto, Garrett, illus. Tutu Books Preschool Library, 3 bks. 2006. (ENG & HAW.). 48p. (YA). 29.95 *(978-1-933835-04-4(4))* Partners in Development Foundation.

Orr, Tamra B. Super Cool Science Experiments: Digestion. 2009. (Explorer Library: Science Explorer Ser.). (ENG., Illus.). 32p. (gr. 4-8). lib. bdg. 28.50 *(978-1-60279-518-1(5)*, 200303) Cherry Lake Publishing.

—Super Cool Science Experiments: Respiration. 2009. (Explorer Library: Science Explorer Ser.). (ENG., Illus.). 32p. (gr. 4-8). lib. bdg. 28.50 *(978-1-60279-519-8(3)*, 200292) Cherry Lake Publishing.

Osburn, Mary Rose. I Know Body Parts. 2016. (What I Know Ser.). 00024p. (J). pap. 8.15 *(978-1-4824-5453-6(X))* Stevens, Gareth Publishing LLLP.

Owen, Ruth. What Happens When I Eat? 2013. (My Body: Inside & Out! Ser.). 24p. (J). (gr. -1-3). lib. bdg. 23.93 *(978-1-909673-26-7(9))* Ruby Tuesday Books Limited GBR. Dist: Bearport Publishing Co., Inc.

—What Happens When I Grow? 2013. (My Body: Inside & Out! Ser.). 24p. (J). (gr. -1-3). lib. bdg. 23.93 *(978-1-909673-32-8(3))* Ruby Tuesday Books Limited GBR. Dist: Bearport Publishing Co., Inc.

—What Happens When I Move? 2013. (My Body: Inside & Out! Ser.). 24p. (J). (gr. -1-3). lib. bdg. 23.93 *(978-1-909673-28-1(5))* Ruby Tuesday Books Limited GBR. Dist: Bearport Publishing Co., Inc.

—What Happens When I Sleep? 2013. (My Body: Inside & Out! Ser.). 24p. (J). (gr. -1-3). lib. bdg. 23.93 *(978-1-909673-30-4(7))* Ruby Tuesday Books Limited GBR. Dist: Bearport Publishing Co., Inc.

Parker, Steve. Atlas Visual del Cuerpo Humano. (Colección Atlas Visual). (SPA., Illus.). 64p. (YA). (gr. 5-8). *(978-84-216-2056-4(8)*, BU5680) Bruño, Editorial ESP. Dist: Lectorum Pubns., Inc.

—Human Body. 2013. (Illus.). 48p. (J). *(978-1-4351-5091-1(0))* Barnes & Noble, Inc.

—What about the Human Body. 2008. 40p. pap. *(978-1-84810-070-1(1))* Miles Kelly Publishing, Ltd.

Penguin Books Staff, ed. Your Body. (Information Activity Ser.). 24p. (J). 3.50 *(978-0-7214-3441-4(X)*, Dutton Juvenile) Penguin Publishing Group.

Peterson, Megan Cooley & Rustad, Martha E. H. The Smallest Animals, 1 vol. 2012. (Extreme Animals Ser.). (ENG., Illus.). 24p. (gr. k-1). pap. 7.29 *(978-1-4296-7903-9(4)*, Pebble Plus) Capstone Press of Coughlan Cos.

Prior, Jennifer. The Digestive System, 1 vol. 2nd rev. ed. 2013. (Nonfiction Readers Ser.). (ENG., Illus.). 32p. (J). (gr. 3-3). pap. 25.96 *(978-1-4807-1086-3(5))* Shell Educational Publishing.

Pryor, Kimberley Jane. Amazing Armor. 2009. (Animal Attack & Defense Ser.). 32p. (gr. 3). 28.50 *(978-0-7614-4424-4(6))* Marshall Cavendish Corp.

Rabe, Tish. Inside Your Outside! All about the Human Body. Ruiz, Aristides, illus. 2003. (Cat in the Hat's Learning Library). (ENG.). 48p. (J). (gr. -1-3). 9.99 *(978-0-375-81100-5(1)*, Random Hse. Bks. for Young Readers) Random Hse. Children's Bks.

—A Tale about Tails (Dr. Seuss/Cat in the Hat) Brannon, Tom, illus. 2014. (Step into Reading Ser.). (ENG.). 48p. (J). (gr. k-3). 3.99 *(978-0-385-37117-9(9)*, Random Hse. Bks. for Young Readers) Random Hse. Children's Bks.

Randolph, Joanne. Whose Back Is This? 2009. (Animal Clues Ser.). 24p. (gr. 1-1). 42.50 *(978-1-61511-431-3(9)*, PowerKids Pr.); (Illus.). (J). lib. bdg. 22.60 *(978-1-4042-4454-2(9))* Rosen Publishing Group, Inc., The.

—Whose Back Is This? De Quién Es Esta Espalda? 2009. (Animal Clues / ¿Adivina de Quién Es? Ser.). (SPA & ENG., Illus.). 24p. (J). lib. bdg. 22.60 *(978-1-4358-2531-4(4)*, PowerKids Pr.) Rosen Publishing Group, Inc., The.

—Whose Back Is This? / ¿de quién es esta Espalda? 2009. (Animal Clues / ¿Adivina de Quién Es? Ser.). (ENG & SPA.). 24p. (gr. 1-1). 42.50 *(978-1-61511-437-5(8)*, Editorial Buenas Letras) Rosen Publishing Group, Inc., The.

Rau, Dana Meachen. My Bones & Muscles. 2007. (J). pap. 6.99 *(978-0-7614-3351-4(1))* Marshall Cavendish Corp.

—My Lungs. 2007. (J). pap. 6.99 *(978-0-7614-3355-2(4))* Marshall Cavendish Corp.

Reina, Mary. A Tour of Your Respiratory System, 1 vol. Jones, Chris B., illus. 2012. (First Graphics: Body Systems Ser.). (ENG.). 24p. (gr. 1-2). pap. 6.29 *(978-1-4296-9330-1(4))*; lib. bdg. 23.99 *(978-1-4296-8652-5(9))* Capstone Press of Coughlan Cos.

Ribke, Simone T. I Have a Skeleton. 2016. (Rookie Read-About Health Ser.). (ENG., Illus.). 32p. (J). pap. 5.95 *(978-0-531-22579-0(8)*, Children's Pr.) Scholastic Library Publishing.

Ripley's Believe It or Not Editors & Ripley's Believe It Or Not! Staff. Ripley Twists: Human Body PORTRAIT EDN. 2014. (Twist Ser.). (ENG.). 48p. (J). 12.95 *(978-1-893951-84-6(7))* Ripley Entertainment, Inc.

Rissman, Rebecca. Beaks, 1 vol. 2011. (Animal Spikes & Spines Ser.). (ENG.). 24p. (gr. -1-1). pap. 6.29 *(978-1-4329-5045-3(2))*; 22.65 *(978-1-4329-5038-5(X))* Heinemann-Raintree. (Acorn).

Rose, Simon. Digestive System. 2014. (J). *(978-1-4896-1166-6(5))* Weigl Pubs., Inc.

—Respiratory System. 2014. (J). *(978-1-4896-1178-9(9))* Weigl Pubs., Inc.

—Skeletal System. 2014. (J). *(978-1-4896-1182-6(7))* Weigl Pubs., Inc.

Rotner, Shelley. Whose Eye Am I? Rotner, Shelley, photos by. 2016. (ENG., Illus.). 32p. (J). 16.95 *(978-0-8234-3558-6(X))* Holiday Hse., Inc.

Roza, Greg. The Muscular System. 2012. (Human Body Ser.). (ENG., Illus.). 32p. (J). (gr. 4-6). pap. 10.50 *(978-1-4339-6586-9(0)*, Gareth Stevens Learning Library); lib. bdg. 26.60 *(978-1-4339-6584-5(4))* Stevens, Gareth Publishing LLLP.

Rushworth, Gary. Body Systems: Human Cells: Text Pairs. 2008. (Bridges/Navigators Ser.). (J). (gr. 5). 81.00 *(978-1-4108-8406-0(6))* Benchmark Education Co.

—Body Systems: Skeletal & Muscular: Text Pairs. 2008. (Bridges/Navigators Ser.). (J). (gr. 5). 81.00 *(978-1-4108-8408-4(2))* Benchmark Education Co.

Saddleback, creator. Human Body. 2008. (Factoscope Ser.). (Illus.). 64p. (YA). (gr. 8-12). per. 10.95 *(978-1-59905-234-2(2))* Saddleback Educational Publishing, Inc.

Scaly Things: Level N, 6 vols. (Explorers Ser.). 32p. (gr. 3-6). 44.95 *(978-0-7699-0594-5(3))* Shortland Pubns. (U. S. A.) Inc.

Scarry, Richard. Richard Scarry's This Is Me. 2008. (ENG., Illus.). 18p. (J). (gr. -1-k). bds. 6.95 *(978-1-4027-6234-5(8))* Sterling Publishing Co., Inc.

Scholastic, Inc. Staff, contrib. by. Ears, Eyes, Nose. 2013. (ENG.). 12p. (J). bds. 6.95 *(978-0-531-27254-1(0))* Scholastic Library Publishing.

Schumacher, Bev. Body Parts (Chinese-English) 2008. 20p. (J). lib. bdg. 9.95 *(978-1-935292-01-2(3))* Learning Props.

Schumacher, Bev, creator. Body Parts. 2005. 20p. (J). lib. bdg. 9.95 *(978-0-9768706-0-9(6))* Learning Props.

Shea, John M. The Digestive System. 2012. (Human Body Ser.). (ENG.). 32p. (J). (gr. 4-6). pap. 10.50 *(978-1-4339-6582-1(8)*, Gareth Stevens Learning Library); lib. bdg. 26.60 *(978-1-4339-6624-8(7))* Stevens, Gareth Publishing LLLP.

Silver, Donald M. & Wynne, Patricia J. The Body Book: Easy-To-Make Hands-on Models That Teach. 2008. (ENG.). 128p. (gr. 3-6). pap. 18.99 *(978-0-545-04873-6(7)*, Teaching Resources) Scholastic, Inc.

Silverman, Buffy. Body Parts: Double-Jointedness, Hitchhiker's Thumb, & More. 2012. (Lightning Bolt Books (tm) — What Traits Are in Your Genes? Ser.). (ENG., Illus.). 32p. (gr. k-2). lib. bdg. 26.60 *(978-0-7613-8942-2(3)*, Lerner Pubns.) Lerner Publishing Group.

Simpson, Kathleen. Genetics: From DNA to Designer Dogs. 2008. (National Geographic Investigates Science Ser.). (ENG., Illus.). 64p. (J). (gr. 5). 27.90 *(978-1-4263-0327-2(0)*, National Geographic Children's Bks.) National Geographic Society.

Simpson, Kathleen & National Geographic Kids Staff. Genetics: From DNA to Designer Dogs. 2008. (National Geographic Investigates Science Ser.). (ENG., Illus.). 64p. (J). (gr. 5). 17.95 *(978-1-4263-0361-6(0)*, National Geographic Children's Bks.) National Geographic Society.

Smith, Sian & Guillain, Charlotte. How Does My Body Work?, 1 vol. 2011. (ENG.). 24p. (gr. -1-1). 25.99 *(978-1-4329-5349-2(4)*, Acorn Read-Aloud) Heinemann-Raintree.

Solway, Andrew. Heart & Lungs. 2011. (Your Body Inside & Out Ser.). (Illus.). 32p. (J). (gr. 3-6). lib. bdg. 28.50 *(978-1-59771-266-8(3))* Sea-To-Sea Pubns.

Spilsbury, Louise. What Is the Structure of an Animal?, 1 vol., 1. 2014. (Let's Find Out! Ser.). (ENG.). 32p. (gr. 3-6). 23.45 *(978-1-62275-246-1(5))* Rosen Publishing Group, Inc., The.

Spilsbury, Louise & Spilsbury, Richard. The Science of the Digestive System. 2017. (Flowchart Smart Ser.). 48p. (gr. 4-5). pap. 84.30 ***(978-1-5382-0682-9(X))*** Stevens, Gareth Publishing LLLP.

—The Science of the Lungs & Respiratory System. 2017. (Flowchart Smart Ser.). 48p. (gr. 4-5). pap. 84.30 ***(978-1-5382-0684-3(6))*** Stevens, Gareth Publishing LLLP.

Steele, Philip. My Body. 2009. (Now We Know About... Ser.). (ENG., Illus.). 24p. (J). (gr. k-3). pap. *(978-0-7787-4738-3(7))* Crabtree Publishing Co.

Steele, Philip & Goldsmith, Mike. My Body. 2009. (ENG., Illus.). 24p. (J). (gr. k-4). lib. bdg. *(978-0-7787-4721-5(2))* Crabtree Publishing Co.

Stewart, Gregory J. The Immune System. 2009. (Human Body: How It Works Ser.). (Illus.). 128p. (C). (gr. 9-18). 35.00 *(978-1-60413-372-1(4)*, Chelsea Hse.) Facts On File, Inc.

Stewart, Melissa. Give Me a Hand: The Secrets of Hands, Feet, Arms, & Legs. Hamlin, Janet, illus. 2010. (Gross & Goofy Body 2 Ser.). 48p. (gr. 3). lib. bdg. 29.93 *(978-0-7614-4158-8(1))* Marshall Cavendish Corp.

—Nifty Noses up Close. 2012. (Animal Bodies up Close Ser.). (Illus.). 24p. (J). (gr. k-3). pap. 7.95 *(978-1-4644-0079-7(2)*, Enslow Elementary) Enslow Pubs., Inc.

—The Skin You're In: The Secrets of Skin. 2010. (Gross & Goofy Body 2 Ser.). 48p. (gr. 3). 29.93 *(978-0-7614-4169-4(7))* Marshall Cavendish Corp.

—Talented Tails up Close. 2012. (Animal Bodies up Close Ser.). 24p. (J). (gr. k-3). (Illus.). pap. 7.95 *(978-1-4644-0082-7(2))*; 22.60 *(978-0-7660-3893-6(9))* Enslow Pubs., Inc. (Enslow Elementary).

—Up Your Nose! The Secrets of Schnozes & Snouts. Hamlin, Janet, illus. 2009. (Gross & Goofy Body Ser.). 48p. (gr. 3-4). 29.93 *(978-0-7614-4170-0(0))* Marshall Cavendish Corp.

Stone, Lynn M. Horns, Humps, & Hooks. 2008. (Illus.). 24p. (J). 22.79 *(978-1-60472-309-0(2))* Rourke Educational Media.

Swanson, Diane. You Are Weird: Your Body's Peculiar Parts & Funny Functions. Boake, Kathy, illus. 2009. (ENG.). 40p. (J). (gr. 3-7). 16.95 *(978-1-55453-282-7(5))*; pap. 7.95 *(978-1-55453-283-4(3))* Kids Can Pr., Ltd. CAN. Dist: Hachette Bk. Group.

Tieck, Sarah. Respiratory System, 1 vol. 2011. (Body Systems Ser.). (ENG., Illus.). 32p. (J). (gr. 2-5). lib. bdg. 27.07 *(978-1-61613-501-0(8))* ABDO Publishing Co.

Troupe, Thomas Kingsley. Why Does My Body Make Bubbles? Learning about the Digestive System with the Garbage Gang. Toye, Derek, illus. 2014. (Garbage Gang's Super Science Questions Ser.). (ENG.). 24p. (gr. k-2). lib. bdg. 26.65 *(978-1-4795-5480-5(4))* Picture Window Bks.

TUXWORTH NICOLA. Bodies. 2014. (ENG., Illus.). 20p. (J). (gr. k-2). bds. 6.99 *(978-1-84322-860-8(2)*, Armadillo) Anness Publishing GBR. Dist: National Bk. Network.

Ventura, Marne. Take a Closer Look at Your Bladder. 2013. (Take a Closer Look Ser.). (ENG.). 24p. (J). (gr. 2-5). 28.50 *(978-1-62323-550-5(2)*, 206347) Child's World, Inc., The.

von Mackensen, Manfred, et al. Uprightness, Weight, & Balance: Human Biology in Grade Eight. Mitchell, David S., ed. Allgoewer, Claudia, tr. 2004. (YA). per. 12.00 *(978-1-888365-53-5(6))* Waldorf Publications.

Waldron, Melanie. Your Digestive System: Understand It with Numbers, 1 vol. 2014. (Your Body by Numbers Ser.). (ENG.). 48p. (gr. 3-5). lib. bdg. 32.65 *(978-1-4109-5982-9(1))* Heinemann-Raintree.

—Your Respiration & Circulation: Understand Them with Numbers, 1 vol. 2014. (Your Body by Numbers Ser.). (ENG.). 48p. (gr. 3-5). lib. bdg. 32.65 *(978-1-4109-5983-6(X))* Heinemann-Raintree.

Ward, Jennifer. Feathers & Hair, What Animals Wear. Tsong, Jing Jing, illus. 2017. (ENG.). 48p. (J). (gr. -1-3). 17.99 *(978-1-4814-3081-4(5)*, Beach Lane Bks.) Beach Lane Bks.

Weber, Valerie J. Why Animals Live in Shells. 2008. (Where Animals Live Ser.). (Illus.). 24p. (gr. 1-4). lib. bdg. 22.00 *(978-0-8368-8797-6(2)*, Weekly Reader Leveled Readers) Stevens, Gareth Publishing LLLP.

Williams, Ben. Look Inside: Your Heart & Lungs, 1 vol. 2nd rev. ed. 2013. (Nonfiction Readers Ser.). (ENG., Illus.). 28p. (J). (gr. 2-2). pap. 23.96 *(978-1-4807-1057-3(1))* Shell Educational Publishing.

Winston, Robert. My Amazing Body Machine. Gildersleeve, Owen, illus. 2017. (ENG.). 128p. (J). (gr. 2-4). 19.99 *(978-1-4654-6185-8(X)*, DK Children) Dorling Kindersley Publishing, Inc.

Woodward, John. What Lives on Your Body? 2007. (What Lives in... ? Ser.). (Illus.). 48p. (gr. 2-6). lib. bdg. 27.00 *(978-0-8368-7861-5(2)*, Gareth Stevens Learning Library) Stevens, Gareth Publishing LLLP.

World Book, Inc Staff, contrib. by. Explore & Learn-Me & My Body. 2008. (J). *(978-0-7166-3021-0(4))* World Bk., Inc.

World Book Staff. Cells to Organ Systems. 2014. (Illus.). 32p. (J). *(978-0-7166-1848-5(6))* World Bk., Inc.

—The Circulatory System. 2014. 32p. *(978-0-7166-1841-6(9))* World Bk., Inc.

Young, Thomas. How Do Hair & Nails Grow?, Vol. 1. 2014. (My Body Does Strange Stuff! Ser.). (ENG.). 24p. (J). (gr. 1-2). pap. 8.15 *(978-1-4824-0250-6(5))* Stevens, Gareth Publishing LLLP.

Zoehfeld, Kathleen Weidner. What Lives in a Shell? Davie, Helen K., illus. 2015. (Let's-Read-And-Find-Out Science 1 Ser.). (ENG.). 32p. (J). (gr. -1-3). pap. 6.99 *(978-0-06-238196-5(2))* HarperCollins Pubs.

ANATOMY, ARTISTIC

see also Figure Drawing

Anatomy for the Artist. 2003. (Essential Art Ser.). (Illus.). 160p. 9.98 *(978-0-7525-8668-7(8))* Parragon, Inc.

ANATOMY, COMPARATIVE

see also Human Beings—Origin

ABDO Publishing Company Staff. Creature Features. 2007. (Creature Features Ser.). 307.80 *(978-1-59928-877-2(X)*, Super SandCastle) ABDO Publishing Co.

Boothroyd, Jennifer. Feathers. 2011. (First Step Nonfiction / Body Coverings Ser.). (ENG., Illus.). 24p. (gr. k-2). lib. bdg. 23.93 *(978-0-7613-5785-8(8)*, 1331168) Lerner Publishing Group.

Cardenas, Ernesto A. Legs. 2009. 23.95 *(978-1-60698-038-5(6))*; pap. 4.95 *(978-1-60698-036-1(X))* Milo Educational Bks. & Resources.

Eason, Sarah, ed. Animals & Humans. 2011. (FAYFT: Introducing Biology Ser.). 64p. (gr. 4-10). lib. bdg. 39.95 *(978-1-936333-03-5(1))* Brown Bear Bks.

Ganeri, Anita. Orangutan. Incl. Anaconda. pap. 6.79 *(978-1-4329-4123-9(2))*; Capybara. (Illus.). pap. 6.79 *(978-1-4329-4121-5(6))*; Howler Monkey. pap. 6.79 *(978-1-4329-4124-6(0))*; Jaguar. (Illus.). pap. 6.79 *(978-1-4329-4117-8(8))*; Lemur. pap. 6.79 *(978-1-4329-4122-2(4))*; Macaw. pap. 6.79 *(978-1-4329-4116-1(X))*; pap. 6.79 *(978-1-4329-4118-5(6))*; Poison Dart Frog. pap. 6.79 *(978-1-4329-4115-4(1))*; (gr. k-2). (Day in the Life: Rain Forest Animals Ser.). (ENG.). 24p. 2010. Set pap. 54.32 *(978-1-4329-4125-3(9)*, Heinemann Read & Learn) Heinemann-Raintree.

James, Emily. Do Whales Have Whiskers? A Question & Answer Book about Animal Body Parts. 2016. (Animals, Animals! Ser.). (ENG., Illus.). 32p. (gr. 1-2). lib. bdg. 27.32 *(978-1-5157-2664-7(9)*, Aplus Bks.) Capstone Press of Coughlan Cos.

Kalman, Bobbie. What Are Natural Structures? 2008. (Looking at Nature Ser.). (ENG., Illus.). 24p. (J). (gr. -1-2). pap. *(978-0-7787-3343-0(2))*; lib. bdg. *(978-0-7787-3323-2(8))* Crabtree Publishing Co.

Legg, Gerald. The X-Ray Picture Book of Incredible Creatures. Salariya, David & Scrace, Carolyn, illus. 2004. 48p. (J). (gr. 4-8). pap. 9.00 *(978-0-7567-7406-6(3))* DIANE Publishing Co.

Levine, Sara. Tooth by Tooth. Spookytooth, T. S., illus. 2016. (ENG.). 32p. (J). (gr. k-4). 26.65 *(978-1-4677-5215-2(0)*, Millbrook Pr.) Lerner Publishing Group.

—Tooth by Tooth: Comparing Fangs, Tusks, & Chompers. Spookytooth, T. S., illus. 2016. (ENG.). 32p. (gr. k-4). 39.99 *(978-1-4677-9727-6(8)*, Millbrook Pr.) Lerner Publishing Group.

Levine, Sara C. Bone by Bone: Comparing Animal Skeletons. Spookytooth, T. S., illus. 2013. (ENG.). 32p. (J). (gr. k-4). lib. bdg. 26.60 *(978-0-7613-8464-9(2)*, Millbrook Pr.) Lerner Publishing Group.

—Tooth by Tooth: Comparing Fangs, Tusks, & Chompers. Spookytooth, T. S., illus. 2016. (Millbrook Picture Bks). (ENG.). 32p. (gr. k-4). 39.99 *(978-1-5124-0732-7(1))* Lerner Publishing Group.

Lewis, Clare. Animal Body Parts. 2015. (Animal Body Parts Ser.). (ENG.). 24p. (gr. k-2). lib. bdg. 116.60 *(978-1-4846-2558-3(7)*, Heinemann Read & Learn) Heinemann-Raintree.

Patkau, Karen. Creatures Great & Small. 2012. (ENG., Illus.). 32p. (J). (gr. 1-4). pap. 8.95 *(978-1-77049-309-4(3)*, Tundra Bks.) Tundra Bks. CAN. Dist: Penguin Random Hse. LLC.

Rice, Dona Herweck. Animal Eyes, 1 vol. 2nd rev. ed. 2014. (TIME for KIDS(r) Nonfiction Readers Ser.). (ENG., Illus.). 12p. (J). (gr. 1-1). pap. 15.96 *(978-1-4807-1017-7(2))* Shell Educational Publishing.

Rotner, Shelley. Body Bones. White, David, illus. Rotner, Shelley, photos by. 2014. (ENG.). 32p. (J). (gr. k-5). 16.95 *(978-0-8234-3162-5(2))* Holiday Hse., Inc.

—Body Bones. 2014. pap. *(978-0-8234-3249-3(1))* Holiday Hse., Inc.

Sideri, Simona. Let's Look at Mouths. Noble, Sheilagh, illus. 2003. (Let's Look at Ser.). 24p. (J). *(978-1-84089-147-8(5))* Zero to Ten, Ltd.

Spilsbury, Louise. Octopus Set. Incl. Dolphin. pap. 6.79 *(978-1-4329-4006-5(6))*; Jellyfish. pap. 6.79 *(978-1-4329-4007-2(4))*; Octopus. pap. 6.79 *(978-1-4329-4011-9(2))*; Sea Turtle. pap. 6.79 *(978-1-4329-4008-9(2))*; Seal. pap. 6.79 *(978-1-4329-4009-6(0))*; Shark. pap. 6.79 *(978-1-4329-4010-2(4))*; (gr. k-2). (Day in the Life: Sea Animals Ser.). (ENG.). 24p. 2010. Set pap. 40.74 *(978-1-4329-4012-6(0)*, Heinemann Read & Learn) Heinemann-Raintree.

Stone, Lynn. Como Usan Los Animales Sus Alas?/How Do Animals Use Their Wings ? Serafini, Estela, tr. from ENG. 2008. (Como Usan los Animales (Bilingual How Do Animals Use) Ser.). (ENG & SPA., Illus.). 24p. (J). (gr. 3-7). lib. bdg. 22.79 *(978-1-60044-741-9(4))* Rourke Educational Media.

Weber, Valerie J. Por qué Algunos Animales Tienen Caparazón. 2008. (Donde viven los animales (Where Animals Live) Ser.). (SPA., Illus.). 24p. (gr. 1-4). lib. bdg. 22.00 *(978-0-8368-8811-9(1)*, Weekly Reader Leveled Readers) Stevens, Gareth Publishing LLLP.

Weber, Valerie J. & Weber, Valerie J. Why Animals Live in Shells. 2008. (Where Animals Live Ser.). (SPA.). 24p. (gr. 1-4). pap. 8.15 *(978-0-8368-8804-1(9)*, Weekly Reader Leveled Readers) Stevens, Gareth Publishing LLLP.

ANATOMY, DENTAL

see Teeth

ANCIENT ART

see Art, Ancient

ANCIENT CIVILIZATION

see Civilization, Ancient

ANCIENT HISTORY

see History, Ancient

ANCIENT PHILOSOPHY

see Philosophy, Ancient

ANDERSEN, H. C. (HANS CHRISTIAN), 1805-1875

Bloom, Harold. Hans Christian Andersen. 2004. (Bloom's Modern Critical Views Ser.). (Illus.). 252p. (C). (gr. 9-13). 45.00 *(978-0-7910-8129-7(X)*, Chelsea Hse.) Facts On File, Inc.

Carew-Miller, Anna. Hans Christian Andersen: Denmark's Famous Author. 2004. (Great Names Ser.). (Illus.). 32p. (J). (gr. 3-18). lib. bdg. 19.95 *(978-1-59084-160-0(3))* Mason Crest.

Fischel, Emma. Hans Christian Andersen. Ward, Nick, illus. 2010. (Famous People, Famous Lives Ser.). 38p. (J). *(978-89-491-8824-9(4))* Biryongso Publishing Co.

Fradin, Dennis Brindell. Tell Us a Tale, Hans! The Life of Hans Christian Andersen. von Buhler, Cynthia, illus. 2006. (J). *(978-1-59336-681-0(7))*; pap. *(978-1-59336-682-7(5))* Mondo Publishing.

Hesse, Karen. The Young Hans Christian Andersen. Blegvad, Erik, illus. 2005. (ENG.). 48p. (J). (gr. 2-5). 16.99 *(978-0-439-67990-9(7))* Scholastic, Inc.

ANDERSON, ELIZABETH GARRETT, 1836-1917

Klobuchar, Lisa. Elizabeth Blackwell: With Profiles of Elizabeth Garrett Anderson & Susan la Flesche Picotte. 2006. (Biographical Connections Ser.). (Illus.). 112p. *(978-0-7166-1826-3(5))* World Bk., Inc.

Thomas, Isabel. Collins Big Cat - The World's First Women Doctors: Elizabeth Blackwell & Elizabeth Garrett Anderson: Band 16/Sapphire. 2015. (Collins Big Cat Ser.). (ENG., Illus.). 56p. (J). (gr. 4-5). pap. 9.95 *(978-0-00-812789-3(1))* HarperCollins Pubs. Ltd. GBR. Dist: Independent Pubs. Group.

ANDERSON, MARIAN, 1897-1993

Broadwater, Andrea. The Life of Marian Anderson: Diva & Humanitarian. 2015. (Legendary African Americans Ser.). 96p. (J). (gr. 6-12). 27.94 *(978-0-7660-6285-6(6))*; pap. 10.95 *(978-0-7660-6286-3(4))* Enslow Pubs., Inc.

Freedman, Russell. The Voice That Challenged a Nation: Marian Anderson & the Struggle for Equal Rights. (ENG., Illus.). 128p. (J). (gr. 5-7). 2011. pap. 10.99 *(978-0-547-48034-3(2))* 2004. tchr. ed. 18.00 *(978-0-618-15976-5(2))* Houghton Mifflin Harcourt Publishing Co.

—The Voice That Challenged a Nation: Marian Anderson & the Struggle for Equal Rights, 2 vols. 2005. (J). 45.75 *(978-1-4193-3970-7(2))* Recorded Bks., Inc.

Haldy, Emma E. Marian Anderson. Bane, Jeff, illus. 2016. (My Early Library: My Itty-Bitty Bio Ser.). (ENG.). 24p. (J). (gr. k-1). 28.50 *(978-1-63471-023-7(1)*, 208172) Cherry Lake Publishing.

Hopkinson, Deborah. Sweet Land of Liberty, 1 vol. Jenkins, Leonard, illus. 2007. (ENG.). 32p. (J). (gr. 1-5). 16.95 *(978-1-56145-395-5(1))* Peachtree Pubs.

Kramer, Candice. Eleanor Roosevelt & Marian Anderson. 2005. (J). pap. *(978-1-4108-4537-5(0))* Benchmark Education Co.

McKissack, Patricia C. & McKissack, Fredrick L. Marian Anderson: Amazing Opera Singer. 2013. (Famous African Americans Ser.). (Illus.). 24p. (J). (gr. k-18). 22.60 *(978-0-7660-4101-1(8))*; pap. 7.95 *(978-1-4644-0202-9(7))* Enslow Pubs., Inc. (Enslow Elementary).

Ryan, Pam Muñoz. When Marian Sang: The True Recital of Marian Anderson. Selznick, Brian, illus. pap. incl. audio compact disk *(978-1-59112-949-3(4))*; pap. 18.95 incl. audio compact disk *(978-1-59112-947-9(8))*; pap. 16.95 incl. audio *(978-1-59112-943-1(5))*; pap. incl. audio *(978-1-59112-945-5(1))*; 2004. (J). 28.95 incl. audio compact disk *(978-1-59112-948-6(6))* Live Oak Media.

Sutcliffe, Jane. Marian Anderson. 2008. pap. 52.95 *(978-0-8225-9394-2(7))*; (ENG., Illus.). 48p. (gr. 3-6). lib. bdg. 27.93 *(978-0-8225-7170-4(6)*, Lerner Pubns.) Lerner Publishing Group.

ANDES

Aloian, Molly. The Andes. 2011. (ENG., Illus.). 48p. (J). pap. *(978-0-7787-7567-6(4))*; (gr. 4-7). lib. bdg. *(978-0-7787-7560-7(7))* Crabtree Publishing Co.

Marsico, Katie. The Darkest & the Brightest. 2015. (True Book(tm), a — Extreme Places Ser.). (ENG., Illus.). 48p. (J). lib. bdg. 31.00 *(978-0-531-21848-8(1)*, Children's Pr.) Scholastic Library Publishing.

Maynard, Charles W. The Andes. (Great Mountain Ranges of the World Ser.). 24p. (gr. 3-3). 2009. 42.50 *(978-1-61513-168-6(X)*, PowerKids Pr.) 2004. (Illus.). (YA). lib. bdg. 22.60 *(978-0-8239-6696-7(8))* Rosen Publishing Group, Inc., The.

Somervill, Barbara A. The Land of the Andes. 2004. (Geography of the World Ser.). (ENG., Illus.). 32p. (J). (gr. 3-6). 28.50 *(978-1-59296-331-7(5)*, 200263) Child's World, Inc., The.

ANDES—FICTION

Alvarado, Beatriz. Juliana: A girl from the Andes. 2008. 44p. pap. 16.95 *(978-1-4327-0253-3(X))* Outskirts Pr., Inc.

Ballantyne, Robert Michael. The Rover of the Andes: A Tale of Adventure in South America. 2007. (ENG.). 266p. pap. 21.99 *(978-1-4346-3753-6(0))*; 296p. pap. 23.99 *(978-1-4346-3767-3(0))* Creative Media Partners, LLC.

Silvano, Wendi. Just One More. Gamboa, Ricardo, illus. 2007. (ENG.). 36p. (J). reprint ed. pap. 11.95 *(978-0-9744446-5-9(0))* All About Kids Publishing.

Suits, Patti J. Topa & the Path of the Pum. 2008. 112p. pap. 10.99 *(978-1-4343-9520-7(0))* AuthorHouse.

ANDORRA

Augustin, Byron. Andorra. 2008. (Cultures of the World Ser.). (Illus.). 144p. (gr. 6-18). lib. bdg. 42.79 *(978-0-7614-3122-0(5)*, Benchmark Bks.) Marshall Cavendish Corp.

ANESTHETICS—HISTORY

Apel, Melanie Ann. Virginia Apgar: Innovative Female Physician & Inventor of the Apgar Score. 2004. (Women Hall of Famers in Mathematics & Science Ser.). (Illus.). 112p. (gr. 5-8). lib. bdg. 34.60 *(978-0-8239-3880-3(8)*, Rosen Reference) Rosen Publishing Group, Inc., The.

Burgdorf, Stephen. Anesthetics, 1 vol. 2013. (Medical Marvels Ser.). (ENG., Illus.). 112p. (YA). (gr. 6-12). lib. bdg. 35.64 *(978-1-61783-900-9(0)*, Essential Library) ABDO Publishing Co.

Kovacs, Vic. Anesthetics. 2016. (Miracles of Medicine Ser.). 00048p. (J). pap. 14.05 ***(978-1-4824-6093-3(9))*** Stevens, Gareth Publishing LLLP.

ANGEL (FICTITIOUS CHARACTER)—FICTION

Gage, Christos. What You Want, Not What You Need. Allie, Scott & Hahn, Sierra, eds. 2014. (ENG., Illus.). 136p. pap. 17.99 *(978-1-61655-253-4(0))* Dark Horse Comics.

ANGELS

Cooper, Diana. Angel Cards for Children. 2004. (ENG., Illus.). 33p. (J). (gr. -1-3). 15.99 *(978-1-84409-027-3(2))* Flying Elephants Pr.

Dittmer, Cherie Pless. Angel! Angel! 2004. (Illus.). 24p. (J). (gr. -1-k). bds. 7.49 *(978-0-7586-0687-7(7))* Concordia Publishing Hse.

Dockrey, Donna. Tell Me about A Place Called Heaven. 2010. 32p. pap. 14.50 *(978-0-557-23820-0(X))* Lulu Pr., Inc.

Dodd, Sarah J. Christmas Stories for Little Angels. Kolanovic, Dubravka, illus. 2010. (Little Angels Ser.). (ENG.). 32p. (J). (gr. -1-k). 12.99 *(978-0-7459-6917-6(8))* Lion Hudson PLC GBR. Dist: Independent Pubs. Group.

Donaghy, Thomas J. Angels All Around Us. 2004. (Illus.). (J). *(978-0-89942-717-1(0))* Catholic Bk. Publishing Corp.

Glavich, Mary Kathleen. God's Angels, Our Friends: Stories & Activities about Angels. 2005. (Illus.). 44p. (J). pap. 15.00 *(978-1-893757-42-4(0)*, 42-0, E T Nedder) Paulist Pr.

Halpin, D. My Guardian Angel Col/Act Bk. 24p. pap. 1.25 *(978-0-8198-4825-3(5)*, 332-216) Pauline Bks. & Media.

Hunt, Marigold. A Book of Angels: Stories of Angels in the Bible. 2006. (Illus.). 167p. (J). (gr. 3-7). per. 14.95 *(978-1-933184-00-5(0))* Sophia Institute Pr.

Hydeck, Michelle A. R. Wings Up: All with a Little Help from Our Angels. 2012. 40p. pap. 12.95 *(978-1-4525-5595-9(8))* Balboa Pr.

Joslin, Mary. The Paraclete Treasury of Angel Stories. Temporin, Elena, illus. 2008. (ENG.). 48p. (J). (gr. -1-6). 18.95 *(978-1-55725-572-3(5))* Paraclete Pr., Inc.

Lane, Leena. Angels among Us. Baboni, Elena, illus. 2007. 29p. (J). (gr. k-5). 17.00 *(978-0-8028-5321-9(8)*, Eerdmans Bks For Young Readers) Eerdmans, William B. Publishing Co.

Llewellyn, Claire. Saints & Angels. 2003. (ENG., Illus.). 64p. (J). (gr. 5-9). tchr. ed. 16.99 *(978-0-7534-5588-3(9)*, 9780753455883, Kingfisher) Roaring Brook Pr.

Macrae, Tammy Vallieres & Lucente-Rizzo, Susan. Jeffrey Finds His Way. 2012. 72p. pap. 8.99 *(978-1-4525-4724-4(6))* Balboa Pr.

Martin, Debra & Landfair, Barton. Me & My Angels. 2008. 32p. pap. 12.99 *(978-1-4389-2918-7(8))* AuthorHouse.

Miller, Jocelyn. My Carry-Along Angel Activity Book: Christmas Fun with Stickers. Hughes, Cathy, illus. 2013. (ENG.). 32p. (J). (gr. k-2). pap. 9.99 *(978-0-7459-6418-8(4))* Lion Hudson PLC GBR. Dist: Independent Pubs. Group.

Murray, Laura K. Angels, Are They Real? 2017. (Illus.). 24p. (J). *(978-1-60818-760-7(8)*, Creative Education) Creative Co., The.

Murray, Laura K. Are They Real?: Angels. 2017. (Are They Real? Ser.). (ENG., Illus.). 24p. (J). (gr. 1-3). pap. 8.99 ***(978-1-62832-368-9(X)***, Creative Paperbacks) Creative Co., The.

Nolan, Allia Zobel. Angels in the Bible for Little Ones, 1 vol. Massari, Alida, illus. 2017. (ENG.). 32p. (J). bds. 9.99 *(978-0-310-75043-7(1))* Zonderkidz.

—Angels in the Bible Storybook, 1 vol. Massari, Alida, illus. 2016. (ENG.). 224p. (J). 16.99 *(978-0-310-74365-1(6))* Zonderkidz.

O'Brien, Joan. Littlest Angels Stickers. 2003. (Dover Little Activity Books Stickers Ser.). (ENG., Illus.). 4p. (J). (gr. -1-5). pap. 1.50 *(978-0-486-43007-2(3))* Dover Pubns., Inc.

Oral, Osman. I Believe in the Angels. 2013. (J). *(978-1-59784-303-4(2))* Tughra Bks.

Osborne, Rick & Strauss, Ed. Angels & Demons, 1 vol. 2004. (2:52 Ser.). (ENG., Illus.). 112p. (J). pap. 7.99 *(978-0-310-70775-2(7))* Zonderkidz.

Rayburn, Cathy & Stone, Elaine Murray. Angels in the Bible. 2006. (Illus.). 76p. (J). (gr. 3-7). per. 7.95 *(978-0-8091-6729-6(8)*, 6729-8) Paulist Pr.

Romero Gutiérrez, Astrid. Cuentos de Angeles Para Ninos. 2011. (SPA., Illus.). 160p. (YA). (gr. -1-3). pap. *(978-970-643-065-6(2))* Selector, S.A. de C.V.

Ross, Melissa. Angels Watching over Us. 2012. 132p. pap. 9.95 *(978-1-61633-249-5(2))* Guardian Angel Publishing, Inc.

Rostrom, Laura Lee. My First Book of Mormon Activity Book, Vol. 1. 2011. 64p. pap. 3.99 *(978-1-59955-957-5(9))* Cedar Fort, Inc./CFI Distribution.

Sotnik, Katherine, illus. Choir of Angels Coloring Book. 2012. (Holy Imitation Ser.). (ENG.). 72p. (J). (gr. -1-3). 4.95 *(978-1-58617-588-7(2))* Ignatius Pr.

Strong, Cynda. Where Do Angels Sleep? Denos, Julia, illus. 2007. 24p. (J). (gr. -1-3). 14.99 *(978-0-7586-1298-4(2))* Concordia Publishing Hse.

Tebo, Mary Elizabeth. Angel of God, My Guardian Dear. Slade, Christian, illus. 2008. 14p. (J). (gr. -1). 8.95 *(978-0-8198-0784-7(2))* Pauline Bks. & Media.

Turner, Patrenia. A Christmas Carol For Keeng Troyius. 2016. (Illus.). pap. *(978-0-578-18261-2(0))* Royalty Patrenia Turner Publications.

Virtue, Doreen. Thank You, Angels! Keeler, Patricia, illus. 2007. (ENG.). 32p. (gr. -1-3). 16.99 *(978-1-4019-1846-0(8))* Hay Hse., Inc.

Wenman, Alexandra. Ariel. 2015. (ENG., Illus.). 29p. (J). (gr. k-8). pap. 9.95 *(978-1-78099-319-5(6)*, Our Street Bks.) Hunt, John Publishing Ltd. GBR. Dist: National Bk. Network.

ANGELS—FICTION

Adams, Denise H. Annabelle's Angels. Adams, Denise H., illus. 2007. (Illus.). 24p. (J). (gr. -1-3). 11.99 *(978-1-59879-386-4(1))* Lifevest Publishing, Inc.

Adornetto, Alexandra. Hades. 2011. (Halo Trilogy Ser.: 2). (ENG.). 432p. (J). (gr. 7-12). 17.99 *(978-0-312-65627-0(0))* Feiwel & Friends.

—Hades. 2012. (Halo Trilogy Ser.: 2). (ENG.). 448p. (YA). (gr. 7-12). pap. 10.99 *(978-1-250-01030-8(6))* Square Fish.

—HADES. 2011. (SPA.). 360p. (YA). pap. 21.95 *(978-84-9918-290-2(9))* Roca Editorial ESP. Dist: Spanish Pubs., LLC.

—Halo. 2010. (Halo Trilogy Ser.: 1). (ENG.). 496p. (YA). (gr. 7-12). 16.99 *(978-0-312-65626-3(2))* Feiwel & Friends.

—Halo. 2011. (Halo Trilogy Ser.: 1). (ENG.). 512p. (YA). (gr. 7-12). pap. 10.99 *(978-0-312-67436-6(8)*, 9780312674366) Square Fish.

—HALO. 2010. (SPA.). 416p. (YA). pap. 22.95 *(978-84-9918-173-8(2))* Roca Editorial ESP. Dist: Spanish Pubs., LLC.

—Heaven. 2012. (Halo Trilogy Ser.: 3). (ENG.). 432p. (YA). (gr. 7-12). 17.99 *(978-0-312-65628-7(9))* Feiwel & Friends.

—Heaven. 2013. (Halo Trilogy Ser.: 3). (ENG.). 448p. (YA). (gr. 7-12). pap. 10.99 *(978-1-250-02941-6(4)*, 9781250029416) Square Fish.

Agresti, Aimee. Illuminate: A Gilded Wings Novel, Book One. 2013. (ENG.). 544p. (YA). (gr. 7). pap. 9.99 *(978-0-544-02222-5(X))* Houghton Mifflin Harcourt Publishing Co.

—Infatuate: A Gilded Wings Novel, Book Two. (ENG.). 416p. (YA). (gr. 7). 2014. pap. 9.99 *(978-0-544-23291-4(7)*, HMH Books For Young Readers) 2013. 17.99 *(978-0-547-62615-4(0))* Houghton Mifflin Harcourt Publishing Co.

Akainy, Boma. Angel Legn. 2011. 28p. pap. 15.99 *(978-1-4628-8214-4(5))* Xlibris Corp.

Alexandria, Chris. Pick-A-Woowoo: Have You Ever Wondered about Angels? Levitas, Alex, illus. 2013. 34p. *(978-1-921883-50-7(2))* Pick-a-Woo Woo Pubs.

—Pick-A-Woowoo - Have You Ever Wondered about Angels? Levitas, Alex, illus. 2013. 34p. pap. *(978-1-921883-36-1(7))* Pick-a-Woo Woo Pubs.

Almond, David. Skellig. 2009. 9.14 *(978-0-7848-2973-8(X)*, Everbind) Marco Bk. Co.

Angels for Little People. 2006. (ENG., Illus.). 36p. (J). pap. 11.95 *(978-1-85390-908-5(4))* Send The Light Distribution LLC.

Appelhans, Lenore. Level 2 Bk. 1: There Has to Be More to the Afterlife Than This. 2013. (Memory Chronicles Ser.: 1). (ENG.). 288p. (YA). (gr. 7). 17.99 *(978-1-4424-4185-9(2)*, Simon & Schuster Bks. For Young Readers) Simon & Schuster Bks. For Young Readers.

—Memory of After. 2013. (Memory Chronicles Ser.: 1). (ENG.). 304p. (YA). (gr. 7). pap. 9.99 *(978-1-4424-4186-6(0)*, Simon & Schuster Bks. For Young Readers) Simon & Schuster Bks. For Young Readers.

Arrigan, Mary. Mario's Angels: A Story about the Artist Giotto. McClure, Gillian, illus. 2006. (ENG.). 32p. (J). (gr. k-3). 15.95 *(978-1-84507-404-3(1)*, Frances Lincoln) Quarto Publishing Group UK GBR. Dist: Hachette Bk. Group.

Avia. Sunshine & Ladybug: In Angel Balloons. 2013. 32p. pap. 17.25 *(978-1-4669-6380-1(8))* Trafford Publishing.

Ayasta, Ayasta. Star. 2007. 117p. pap. 17.96 *(978-1-4303-1809-5(0))* Lulu Pr., Inc.

Ayers, Michelle. Michael. 2011. 134p. pap. 9.99 *(978-0-557-78630-5(4))* Lulu Pr., Inc.

Baker, Gabi. Angels of Hope. 2012. 112p. pap. 10.95 *(978-1-935993-32-2(1))* Nightengale Pr.

Bankow, Henriette. Alfie's Angels: Big Book English Only. Garson, Sarah, illus. 2004. 30p. (J). *(978-1-84444-119-8(9))* Mantra Lingua.

Barkow, Henriette. Alfie's Angels. 2004. (Illus.). 32p. (J). pap. *(978-1-85269-903-1(5))*; pap. *(978-1-85269-938-3(8))*; pap. *(978-1-85269-943-7(4))*; pap. *(978-1-85269-947-5(7))*; pap. *(978-1-85269-948-2(5))*; pap. *(978-1-85269-952-9(3))*; pap. *(978-1-85269-967-3(1))*; pap. *(978-1-85269-972-7(8))*; (GER & ENG., pap. *(978-1-85269-982-6(5))*; pap. *(978-1-85269-992-5(2))*; pap. *(978-1-85269-913-0(2))*; (POR & ENG., pap. *(978-1-85269-908-6(6))*; pap. *(978-1-85269-919-2(3))*; pap. *(978-1-85269-933-8(7))*; pap. *(978-1-85269-928-4(0))*; (SOM & ENG., pap. *(978-1-85269-923-9(X))* Mantra Lingua.

—Alfie's Angels. Garson, Sarah, illus. 2004. 32p. (J). (FRE & ENG.). pap. *(978-1-85269-977-2(9))*; (ENG & PAN.). pap. *(978-1-85269-997-0(3))* Mantra Lingua.

Basye, Dottie. The Angel with Big Feet. 2012. 32p. pap. 13.95 *(978-1-4497-3595-1(9)*, WestBow Pr.) Author Solutions, Inc.

The Beautiful & the Damned. 2014. (ENG., Illus.). 288p. (YA). (gr. 7). pap. 11.99 *(978-1-4424-8836-6(0)*, Simon Pulse) Simon Pulse.

Bell, G. F. Angel Wings & S'Mores. 2008. 152p. 29.99 *(978-1-4257-7491-2(1))*; pap. 19.99 *(978-1-4257-7489-9(X))* Xlibris Corp.

Bennett, Marilyn J. The Poinsettia Adventure. 2010. 60p. pap. 21.99 *(978-1-4490-7108-0(2))* AuthorHouse.

Bergren, Lisa T. God Gave Us Angels. Bryant, Laura J., illus. 2014. (ENG.). 40p. (J). (gr. -1-2). 10.99 *(978-1-60142-661-1(5)*, WaterBrook Pr.) Crown Publishing Group.

Berkeley, Jon. Between the Light. Dorman, Brandon, illus. 2008. (Julie Andrews Collection). (J). lib. bdg. 17.89 *(978-0-06-075514-0(8))* HarperCollins Pubs.

—The Palace of Laughter. Dorman, Brandon, illus. 2007. (Wednesday Tales Ser.: No. 1). (ENG.). 464p. (J). (gr. 3-7). pap. 8.99 *(978-0-06-075509-6(1))* HarperCollins Pubs.

—The Tiger's Egg. Dorman, Brandon, illus. (Wednesday Tales Ser.: No. 2). (J). 2009. (ENG.). 432p. pap. 7.99 *(978-0-06-075512-6(1)*, Harper Trophy) 2007. 416p. (gr.

3-7). 16.99 *(978-0-06-075510-2(5)*, Julie Andrews Collection) HarperCollins Pubs.

Berni, K. S. Angels of Children: Sarafina Teaches the Importance of Prayer. 2012. 40p. pap. 20.99 *(978-1-4772-7708-9(0))* AuthorHouse.

Berry, Ron. My Guardian Angel. Sharp, Chris, illus. 2008. 12p. (J). (gr. -1-k). bds. 12.99 *(978-0-8249-1819-4(3)*, Ideal Pubns.) Worthy Publishing.

Bethany: Adventures of the Mighty Mustard Seed. 2004. Orig. Title: Bethany in Beulah Land. (J). mass mkt. 12.95 *(978-0-9745440-0-7(0))* McKatlib Pr.

Billington, Rachel. Poppy's Angel. 2014. (ENG., Illus.). 288p. (J). (gr. 5-17). pap. 8.99 *(978-1-84780-362-7(8)*, Frances Lincoln) Quarto Publishing Group UK GBR. Dist: Hachette Bk. Group.

Birch, Manuel James. Dudley the Angel & His Buddy Gabby the Elf. 2009. 40p. pap. 18.49 *(978-1-4490-1704-0(5))* AuthorHouse.

Black, Chuck. The Light of the Last, Bk. 3. 2016. (Wars of the Realm Ser.). (ENG.). 368p. (YA). (gr. 7). pap. 11.99 *(978-1-60142-506-5(6)*, Multnomah Bks.) Crown Publishing Group.

—Rise of the Fallen: Wars of the Realm, Book 2. 2015. (Wars of the Realm Ser.). (ENG.). 320p. (YA). (gr. 7). pap. 11.99 *(978-1-60142-504-1(X)*, Multnomah Bks.) Crown Publishing Group.

Blacker, Terence. The Angel Factory. 2012. (ENG., Illus.). 224p. (J). (gr. 5-9). pap. 10.99 *(978-0-689-86413-1(2)*, Simon & Schuster/Paula Wiseman Bks.) Simon & Schuster/Paula Wiseman Bks.

Blanco, Alberto. Angel's Kite (La estrella de Angel) Bellm, Dan, tr. Morales, Rodolfo, illus. 2014. (ENG & SPA.). 32p. (J). (gr. 1-4). pap. 9.95 *(978-0-89239-156-1(1))* Lee & Low Bks., Inc.

Block, Francesca Lia. Dangerous Angels. 2010. (Weetzie Bat Ser.). (ENG.). 496p. (YA). (gr. 9). pap. 9.99 *(978-0-06-200740-7(8)*, HarperTeen) HarperCollins Pubs.

Bock, Suzanne, illus. In the Beginning: Angels with Attitudes 2004. 32p. (J). 12.99 *(978-0-9758709-0-7(4)*, 11412) Journey Stone Creations, LLC.

—Meet the Angels l.t. ed. 2004. 10p. (J). bds. 12.99 *(978-0-9758709-4-5(7)*, 13401) Journey Stone Creations, LLC.

Boggs, Patdee. Island of Angels. 2006. 55p. pap. 16.95 *(978-1-4241-3758-9(6))* PublishAmerica, Inc.

Bornstein, Laurie. Angel Cloud. 2003. pap. 9.00 *(978-0-8059-6083-9(X))* Dorrance Publishing Co., Inc.

Boylan, Jennifer Finney. Falcon Quinn & the Black Mirror. Dorman, Brandon, illus. (Falcon Quinn Ser.: 1). (ENG.). (J). (gr. 5-9). 2011. 512p. pap. 7.99 *(978-0-06-172834-1(9))* 2010. 496p. 16.99 *(978-0-06-172832-7(2))* HarperCollins Pubs. (Tegen, Katherine Bks).

—Falcon Quinn & the Crimson Vapor. 2011. (Falcon Quinn Ser.: 2). (ENG.). 384p. (J). (gr. 5-9). 16.99 *(978-0-06-172835-8(7)*, Tegen, Katherine Bks) HarperCollins Pubs.

Bradford, Bruce. An Angel Named Herald. 2011. 32p. pap. 12.77 *(978-1-4634-0407-9(7))* AuthorHouse.

Brannon, Dj. The Angelic Soldiers: The Way Back. 2012. 138p. (gr. 4-6). 28.95 *(978-1-4497-5971-1(8))*; pap. 11.95 *(978-1-4497-5972-8(6))* Author Solutions, Inc. (WestBow Pr.).

Bray, Libba. Going Bovine. 2010. (ENG.). 496p. (YA). (gr. 9). pap. 10.99 *(978-0-385-73398-4(4)*, Ember) Random Hse. Children's Bks.

Brockenbrough, Martha. Devine Intervention. 2012. (YA). pap. *(978-0-545-38214-4(9))*; (ENG.). 304p. (J). (gr. 7-7). 17.99 *(978-0-545-38213-7(0))* Scholastic, Inc. (Levine, Arthur A. Bks.).

Brothers, Marilee. Moonstone. 2008. 236p. (YA). pap. 14.95 *(978-0-9802453-4-9(6)*, Bell Bridge Bks.) BelleBks., Inc.

Brown, Cornelia. Constance the Little Angel Wants Curls. 2009. 28p. pap. 15.99 *(978-1-4490-3962-2(6))* AuthorHouse.

Bucheimer, Melissa. Matthew the Little Angel. 2008. 35p. pap. 24.95 *(978-1-60441-335-9(2))* America Star Bks.

Bunton, M. Star Girl. 2005. 100p. pap. 9.95 *(978-1-59526-109-0(5)*, Llumina Pr.) Aeon Publishing Inc.

Burton, Jeffery. Whispering to Lilly. 2007. 52p. per. 16.95 *(978-1-4241-3891-3(4))* PublishAmerica, Inc.

Capozzola, Christine. Angel from Heaven. Nguyen, Cindy, illus. 2014. (ENG.). 28p. pap. 9.95 *(978-1-63047-189-7(5))* Morgan James Publishing.

Cauley, Phil. The Adventures of Io, the Little Angel: Sticks & Stones. 2012. 52p. pap. 20.95 *(978-1-4497-3614-9(9)*, WestBow Pr.) Author Solutions, Inc.

Causton, Linda. Lester's Rainy Lake Pony. l.t. ed. 2004. (Illus.). 32p. (J). 12.00 *(978-1-930374-09-6(7))* DeForest Pr.

Chandler, Elizabeth. Everafter. (Kissed by an Angel Ser.). (ENG., 272p. (YA). (gr. 9). 2014. Illus.). pap. 11.99 *(978-1-4424-0919-4(3))* 2013. 16.99 *(978-1-4424-0918-7(5))* Simon Pulse. (Simon Pulse).

—Evercrossed. (Kissed by an Angel Ser.). (ENG.). (YA). (gr. 7). 2012. 304p. pap. 9.99 *(978-1-4424-0915-6(0))* 2011. 288p. 16.99 *(978-1-4424-0914-9(2))* Simon Pulse. (Simon Pulse).

—Everlasting. (Kissed by an Angel Ser.). (ENG.). (YA). (gr. 7). 2013. 336p. pap. 9.99 *(978-1-4424-0917-0(7))* 2012. 320p. 16.99 *(978-1-4424-0921-7(5))* Simon Pulse. (Simon Pulse).

—Kissed by an Angel: Evercrossed; Everlasting; Everafter. 2014. (Kissed by an Angel Ser.). (ENG., Illus.). 912p. (YA). (gr. 9). pap. 29.99 *(978-1-4424-9494-7(8)*, Simon Pulse) Simon Pulse.

—Kissed by an Angel: Kissed by an Angel; the Power of Love; Soulmates. 2008. (Kissed by an Angel Ser.: Bks. 1-3). (ENG.). 704p. (YA). (gr. 9). pap. 12.99 *(978-1-4169-7883-1(6)*, Simon Pulse) Simon Pulse.

Chase, et al. Angel in a Gum Tree. (Illus.). 32p. pap. 13.95 *(978-1-86368-222-0(8))* Fremantle Pr. AUS. Dist: Independent Pubs. Group.

Chasing Before. 2014. (Memory Chronicles Ser.: 2). (ENG., Illus.). 368p. (YA). (gr. 7). 19.99 *(978-1-4424-4188-0(7)*, Simon & Schuster Bks. For Young Readers) Simon & Schuster Bks. For Young Readers.

Chelsea, David. Snow Angel. Chelsea, David, illus. 2016. (ENG., Illus.). 112p. (J). (gr. 3-7). pap. 9.99 *(978-1-61655-940-3(3))* Dark Horse Comics.

The Children's Book of Angels. 2005. (J). pap. *(978-0-9769166-6-6(5))* Living Life Publishing Co.

The Children's Book of Angels. 2005. (J). per. *(978-0-9769166-5-9(7))* Living Life Publishing Co.

Clark, Debbie. Amberleigh's Christmas Angel: An Adolescent's Story of Love, Loss, & Renewed Hope for the Future. 2004. 48p. pap. 16.95 *(978-1-4137-4528-3(8))* America Star Bks.

Clark, Steven & Clark, Justin. The Golden Knight #1: The Boy Is Summoned. Gibson, Taylor, illus. 2011. (ENG.). 80p. (J). pap. 5.99 *(978-0-9647933-9-2(3))* New Horizons Pr.

Clay, Judith L. Mansfield. "ABE" the Chumsy Angel. (Illus.). 18p. (J). (gr. -1-k). pap. 8.95 *(978-0-9707428-0-3(0))* Mansfield, J. Hse. Publishing Co.

Cleofas-Moore, Ramona. Tiffany. 2008. 60p. pap. 16.95 *(978-1-60474-238-1(0))* America Star Bks.

Clifford, Leah. A Touch Menacing. 2013. (Touch Mortal Trilogy Ser.: 3). (ENG.). 320p. (YA). (gr. 9). 17.99 *(978-0-06-200505-2(7)*, Greenwillow Bks.) HarperCollins Pubs.

—A Touch Morbid. 2012. (Touch Mortal Trilogy Ser.: 2). (ENG.). 304p. (YA). (gr. 9). 16.99 *(978-0-06-200502-1(2)*, Greenwillow Bks.) HarperCollins Pubs.

—A Touch Mortal. 2011. (Touch Mortal Trilogy Ser.: 1). (ENG.). 432p. (YA). (gr. 8-18). 17.99 *(978-0-06-200499-4(9)*, Greenwillow Bks.) HarperCollins Pubs.

Conyers, Miranda Parbhoo. Daddy Please Don't Cry. 2009. (J). *(978-1-61623-310-5(9))* Independent Pub.

Cooper, Diana. Tara & the Talking Kitten Meet Angels & Fairies. Shannon, Kate, illus. 2011. (Tara & Ash-ting Ser.). (ENG.). 80p. (J). (gr. k-4). 8.95 *(978-1-84409-551-3(7))* Innovation Pr., The.

corjanjamnic. Angels on Earth, 1 vol. 2010. 48p. pap. 16.95 *(978-1-4512-0050-8(1))* America Star Bks.

Cox, Tracey M. Angels Do That. Movshina, Marina, illus. 2012. 16p. pap. 9.95 *(978-1-61633-299-0(9))* Guardian Angel Publishing, Inc.

Craft, Mahlon. Christmas Moon. Craft, K. Y., illus. 2003. 32p. (J). 15.95 *(978-1-58717-056-0(6))*; lib. bdg. *(978-1-58717-057-7(4))* Chronicle Bks. LLC. (SeaStar Bks.).

Crayon, Paula. An Angel in My Pocket. 2010. 44p. (J). pap. 17.99 *(978-1-4490-9921-3(1))* AuthorHouse.

Creech, Sharon. The Unfinished Angel. 2013. (ENG.). 160p. (J). (gr. 3-7). pap. 6.99 *(978-0-06-143097-8(8))* HarperCollins Pubs.

Curley, Marianne. Broken. 2014. (Avena Ser.). (ENG.). 384p. (YA). (gr. 7). 17.99 *(978-1-61963-168-7(7)*, 9781619631687, Bloomsbury USA Childrens) Bloomsbury Publishing USA.

Cushway, Rosemary Lester. The Angel & the Elephant. 2015. (ENG.). 94p. (J). (gr. 2-3). mass mkt. 11.95 *(978-1-78612-047-2(X)*, 14a88a22-ec2b-4701-9a84-b4fc34b4a6b4) Austin, Stan AUS. Dist: Bookmasters Distribution.

Dahl, Regina. Love Is Not Selfish. 2013. 32p. pap. 13.95 *(978-1-4497-9289-3(8)*, WestBow Pr.) Author Solutions, Inc.

Dahl, Steven. Harold Angel. Cotta-Flood, Stephanie, illus. 2012. 40p. (J). *(978-0-9883420-0-2(6))* Thotsup LLC.

Dalton, Annie. Budding Star: Mission - Rescue a Pop Princess. 2008. (Mel Beeby Agent Angel Ser.). (ENG.). 208p. (J). (gr. 4-7). pap. 6.95 *(978-0-00-720478-6(7))* HarperCollins Pubs. Ltd. GBR. Dist: Independent Pubs. Group.

—The Divine Collection: Three Amazing Missions in One Book! 2008. (Mel Beeby Agent Angel Ser.). (ENG., Illus.). 608p. (J). (gr. 4-7). pap. 19.95 *(978-0-00-719074-4(3))* HarperCollins Pubs. Ltd. GBR. Dist: Independent Pubs. Group.

—Feeling the Vibes: Babysit a Buddha! 2008. (Mel Beeby Agent Angel Ser.). (ENG.). 208p. (J). (gr. 4-7). pap. 6.95 *(978-0-00-716140-9(9))* HarperCollins Pubs. Ltd. GBR. Dist: Independent Pubs. Group.

—Fighting Fit: Mission - Get into the Gladiator Groove! 2009. (Mel Beeby, Agent Angel Ser.: 6). (ENG.). 192p. (J). (gr. 4-7). pap. 7.99 *(978-0-00-720476-2(0))* HarperCollins Pubs. Ltd. GBR. Dist: HarperCollins Pubs.

—Flying High: Mission - Prepare to Party! 2010. (Mel Beeby, Agent Angel Ser.: 3). (ENG.). 144p. (J). (gr. 4-7). pap. 7.99 *(978-0-00-720473-1(6))* HarperCollins Pubs. Ltd. GBR. Dist: HarperCollins Pubs.

—Fogging Over: Mission - Take a Trip down Under. 2010. (Mel Beeby, Agent Angel Ser.: 5). (ENG.). 160p. (J). (gr. 4-7). pap. 7.99 *(978-0-00-720475-5(2))* HarperCollins Pubs. Ltd. GBR. Dist: HarperCollins Pubs.

—The Heavenly Collection: Three Amazing Missions in One Book! (Angels Unlimited Ser.). (ENG.). 400p. (J). 2010. pap., pap., pap. 14.99 *(978-0-00-714406-8(7)*, HarperCollins Children's Bks.) 2008. (gr. 4-7). pap. 19.95 *(978-0-00-723307-6(8))* HarperCollins Pubs. Ltd. GBR. Dist: HarperCollins Pubs., Independent Pubs. Group.

—Losing the Plot: Mission: Rescue a Teenage Trio! 2008. (Mel Beeby Agent Angel Ser.). (ENG.). 160p. (J). (gr. 4-7). pap. 6.95 *(978-0-00-720472-4(8))* HarperCollins Pubs. Ltd. GBR. Dist: Independent Pubs. Group.

—Making Waves: Mission - Foil the Pirates. 2010. (Mel Beeby, Agent Angel Ser.: 7). (ENG.). 208p. (J). (gr. 4-7). pap. 9.99 *(978-0-00-720477-9(9))* HarperCollins Pubs. Ltd. GBR. Dist: HarperCollins Pubs.

—Winging It: Mission: Enrol at Angel School! 2008. (Mel Beeby Agent Angel Ser.). (ENG.). 144p. (J). (gr. 4-7). pap. 6.95 *(978-0-00-720471-7(X))* HarperCollins Pubs. Ltd. GBR. Dist: Independent Pubs. Group.

Davies, Jocelyn. A Beautiful Dark. 2012. (ENG.). 416p. (YA). (gr. 8). pap. 9.99 *(978-0-06-199066-3(3)*, HarperTeen) HarperCollins Pubs.

—A Fractured Light. 2013. (ENG.). 368p. (YA). (gr. 8). pap. 9.99 *(978-0-06-199068-7(X)*, HarperTeen) HarperCollins Pubs.

—A Radiant Sky. 2014. (ENG.). 384p. (YA). (gr. 8). pap. 9.99 *(978-0-06-199070-0(1)*, HarperTeen) HarperCollins Pubs.

Davis, Christine. For Every Dog an Angel. 2nd ed. 2004. (Illus.). 32p. (J). 9.95 *(978-0-9659225-2-4(9))* Lighthearted Pr., Inc.

Dean Wafstet, Cindi. Wings of Light. 2005. 31p. 15.00 *(978-1-4116-5567-6(2))* Lulu Pr., Inc.

Desrochers, Lisa. Original Sin. 2011. (Personal Demons Ser.: 2). (ENG.). 400p. (YA). (gr. 9-18). pap. 25.99 *(978-0-7653-2809-0(7)*, 9780765328090, Tor Teen) Doherty, Tom Assocs., LLC.

Diamond, Kathryn. Rachel's Magic Swing. 2009. 80p. pap. 11.00 *(978-0-557-06497-7(X))* Lulu Pr., Inc.

Dickson, Diane. Daisy & the Dust Angel. 2010. 35p. pap. 20.50 *(978-1-4452-1375-0(3))* Lulu Pr., Inc.

Disner, R. M. Angel Feather. 2012. 32p. pap. 14.50 *(978-1-4669-4874-7(4))* Trafford Publishing.

Doman, Regina. Angel in the Waters. Hatke, Ben, illus. 2004. 48p. (J). (gr. -1-3). pap. 6.95 *(978-1-928832-81-2(4))* Sophia Institute Pr.

—Mi Angelito en Las Aguas. Hatke, Ben, illus. 2006. (SPA.). 40p. (J). (gr. -1-3). pap. 6.95 *(978-1-933184-22-7(1))* Sophia Institute Pr.

Donna, Gelsinger, ed. In My Father's Garden. 2007. (ENG.). 10p. (J). bds. 6.99 *(978-1-4037-3625-3(1)*, Spirit Pr.) Bendon, Inc.

Dorothy Disanto-Morrell. Dorotea & Friends Visit the Hospital. 2010. 20p. pap. 7.31 *(978-1-4269-2557-3(3))* Trafford Publishing.

Dorsey, Angela. Spring of Secrets. 2012. 122p. pap. *(978-1-927100-26-4(7))* Enchanted Pony Bks.

Dudek, V. A. Soldiers of Fate. 2009. 94p. pap. 15.99 *(978-1-4415-2702-8(8))* Xlibris Corp.

Dyan, Penelope. Why Angels Sing! Dyan, Penelope, illus. 2012. (Illus.). 34p. pap. 11.95 *(978-1-61477-065-7(4))* Bellissima Publishing, LLC.

Dyer, Heather. The Girl with the Broken Wing. Bailey, Peter, illus. 2005. 147p. (J). *(978-1-4156-3468-4(8))* Scholastic, Inc.

Ee, Susan. Angelfall, 0 vols. 2012. (Penryn & the End of Days Ser.: 1). (ENG.). 288p. (YA). (gr. 9-12). pap. 7.99 *(978-0-7614-6327-6(5)*, 9780761463276, Amazon Children's Publishing) Amazon Publishing.

—Angelfall. 2012. 256p. pap. 12.99 *(978-0-9835970-1-8(4))* Dream, Feral LLC.

—World After, 0 vols. 2013. (Penryn & the End of Days Ser.: 2). (ENG.). 320p. (YA). (gr. 9-12). pap. 7.99 *(978-1-4778-1728-5(X)*, 9781477817285, Amazon Children's Publishing) Amazon Publishing.

Erwin, Kay. A Sheepdog's Christmas. 2008. 56p. pap. 10.99 *(978-1-60647-698-7(X))* Salem Author Services.

Essig, Helene & Perez, Victoria. Angela's Angel. 2007. 112p. per. 11.95 *(978-1-4327-1348-5(5))* Outskirts Pr., Inc.

Eubanks, Sandra. Carina the Angel. 2005. 17.00 *(978-0-8059-9793-4(8))* Dorrance Publishing Co., Inc.

Evangel - the Smallest Angel. 2006. (J). 14.95 *(978-0-9790210-0-8(6))* Evening Star Enterprise, Inc.

Eyuboglu, Melisa, illus. Angel in a Bubble. Eyuboglu, Melisa, . 2007. 28p. (J). 10.95 *(978-1-933090-48-1(0))* Guardian Angel Publishing, Inc.

Falzon, Adrienne. What Is an Angel? Salzberg, Helen, illus. 2012. 32p. 18.99 *(978-0-9855562-2-8(6))* Blue Note Pubns.

Farnsworth-Simpson, Patricia Ann. The Wonderful Butterbee Angel's. 2010. 125p. pap. 14.50 *(978-1-4092-8762-9(9))* Lulu Pr., Inc.

Feliciano, Luis. The Adventures of the Three Angels. 2005. (J). pap. 8.00 *(978-0-8059-6676-3(5))* Dorrance Publishing Co., Inc.

Fitzpatrick, Becca. The Complete Hush, Hush Saga: Hush, Hush; Crescendo; Silence; Finale. 2012. (Hush, Hush Saga Ser.: Bks. 1-4). (ENG.). 1744p. (YA). (gr. 9). 74.99 *(978-1-4424-7372-0(X)*, Simon & Schuster Bks. For Young Readers) Simon & Schuster Bks. For Young Readers.

—Crescendo. 2011. (Hush, Hush Saga: Bk. 2). (SPA.). 408p. (YA). pap. 20.95 *(978-84-666-4639-0(6))* Ediciones B ESP. Dist: Spanish Pubs., LLC.

—Crescendo. (Hush, Hush Saga Ser.: Bk. 2). (ENG.). (YA). (gr. 9). 2012. 464p. pap. 12.99 *(978-1-4169-8944-8(7))* 2010. 432p. 18.99 *(978-1-4169-8943-1(9))* Simon & Schuster Bks. For Young Readers. (Simon & Schuster Bks. For Young Readers).

—Finale. (Hush, Hush Saga Ser.). (ENG., (YA). (gr. 9). 2013. Illus.). 480p. pap. 12.99 *(978-1-4424-2668-9(3))* 2012. 464p. 19.99 *(978-1-4424-2667-2(5))* Simon & Schuster Bks. For Young Readers. (Simon & Schuster Bks. For Young Readers).

—Hush, Hush. (SPA.). 368p. 2010. (Hush, Hush Saga: Bk. 1). (YA). pap. 20.95 *(978-84-666-4417-4(2))* pap. 13.95 *(978-84-9872-932-0(7))* Ediciones B ESP. Dist: Spanish Pubs., LLC.

—Hush, Hush, 3 vols. Ruiz, Derek, ed. 2012. (Hush, Hush Saga: Bk. 1). (Illus.). 120p. (YA). 19.95 *(978-0-9836131-1-4(7))* Sea Lion Bks.

—Hush, Hush. (Hush, Hush Saga Ser.: Bk. 1). (ENG.). (YA). (gr. 9-18). 2010. 432p. pap. 11.99 *(978-1-4169-8942-4(0))* 2009. 400p. 21.99 *(978-1-4169-8941-7(2))* Simon & Schuster Bks. For Young Readers. (Simon & Schuster Bks. For Young Readers).

Fleischman, Marcia C. Angels Everywhere. 2008. 36p. pap. 15.49 *(978-1-4389-2531-8(X))* AuthorHouse.

Fletcher, Christopher. The Guardian Angel. 2008. 212p. pap. *(978-1-84923-031-5(5))* YouWriteOn.

Flora, B. David. An Angel's Day on Earth. Alexander, Johnna A., illus. 2011. 24p. pap. 24.95 *(978-1-4560-9851-3(9))* PublishAmerica, Inc.

Foster, Katy. The Most Important Job. 2013. 40p. pap. 15.99 *(978-1-4497-9887-1(X)*, WestBow Pr.) Author Solutions, Inc.

Fox, Sabrina. Who Can Help Me Sleep? Rothan, Ann, illus. 2004. 32p. (gr. -1-3). 16.95 *(978-1-885394-36-1(5))* Amber Lotus Publishing.

Fuchs, Michael. Keniff & Kieff. 2013. 28p. pap. 13.95 *(978-1-4908-0002-8(6)*, WestBow Pr.) Author Solutions, Inc.

Fujimoto, Yoshie. The Ninjas & Goblins. 2008. pap. 13.00 *(978-0-8059-8638-9(3))* Dorrance Publishing Co., Inc.

Gano, Debra. Beauty's Secret. Pitre, Dawn, illus. 2008. (Heartlight Girls Ser.). 54p. (J). 17.95 *(978-0-9787689-0-4(6))* Heartlight Girls.

Gentilin, Isabella. Whispers of an Angel. 2010. 32p. pap. 13.00 *(978-1-60911-778-8(6)*, Eloquent Bks.) Strategic Book Publishing & Rights Agency (SBPRA).

Glowacki, Helen. God's Plan of Salvation. 2013. 152p. pap. 17.50 *(978-0-9893807-4-4(2))* Glowacki, Helen.

Gooch-Anderson, Stacy. The Legend of the Star. 2009. (Illus.). (J). 15.99 *(978-1-59955-243-9(4))* Cedar Fort, Inc./CFI Distribution.

Gordon, Andrew. Andy's Book. 2012. 56p. pap. 11.00 *(978-1-4349-7317-7(4)*, RoseDog Bks.) Dorrance Publishing Co., Inc.

Goring, Ruth & Meza, Erika. Los Angeles de Adriana (Spanish Edition) Meza, Erika, illus. 2017. (SPA., Illus.). (J). 16.99 *(978-1-5064-2507-8(0)*, Sparkhouse Family) Augsburg Fortress, Pubs.

Granata, Nancy. The Perfect Porch for Witch Watching. 2008. 52p. pap. 22.49 *(978-1-4389-0107-7(0))* AuthorHouse.

Grant, Eleanor. Ministering Angels. 2003. 32p. (J). pap. 9.00 *(978-0-8059-5611-5(5))* Dorrance Publishing Co., Inc.

Greenlee, Don. This Countryboy Guardian Was Heaven Sent. 2007. (Illus.). 114p. (YA). per. 14.95 net. *(978-0-9795574-0-8(2))* Country Boy Publishing Co.

Guest, Charlotte. Peredur the Son of Evrawc. 2004. reprint ed. pap. 15.95 *(978-1-4191-4086-0(8))*; pap. 1.99 *(978-1-4192-4086-7(2))* Kessinger Publishing, LLC.

Guiffre, William. Angelita's Song. Baron, Cheri Ann, illus. 2008. 32p. (J). (gr. -1-3). pap. 9.95 *(978-1-931650-36-6(5))* Bks. for Children Publishing.

Guiffre, William A. Angelita's Song. Baron, Cheri Ann, illus. 2008. 32p. (J). (gr. -1-3). lib. bdg. 17.95 *(978-1-931650-30-4(6))* Bks. for Children Publishing.

Gustke, Carol Davis. An Angel's First Job. 2008. (Illus.). 24p. (J). lib. bdg. *(978-0-9801376-2-0(4))*; per. *(978-0-9801376-3-7(2))* Dragonfly Publishing, Inc.

Gutteridge, Alex. Last Chance Angel. 2013. (ENG.). 368p. (YA). (gr. 8). pap. 11.99 *(978-1-84877-299-1(8))* Bonnier Publishing GBR. Dist: Independent Pubs. Group.

Hamilton, Annie. The Unforgettable Night. 2013. (Illus.). 70p. pap. *(978-1-78148-617-7(4))* Grosvenor Hse. Publishing Ltd.

Hamilton, John. Dog Friday. 2010. (Illus.). 60p. pap. 21.99 *(978-1-4490-9468-3(6))* AuthorHouse.

Hand, Cynthia. Boundless. 2013. (Unearthly Ser.: 3). (ENG.). 448p. (YA). (gr. 8). pap. 9.99 *(978-0-06-199621-4(1))*; 17.99 *(978-0-06-199620-7(3))* HarperCollins Pubs. (HarperTeen).

—Hallowed. 2012. (Unearthly Ser.: 2). (ENG.). (YA). (gr. 8). 432p. pap. 9.99 *(978-0-06-199619-1(X))*; 416p. 17.99 *(978-0-06-199618-4(1))* HarperCollins Pubs. (HarperTeen).

—Unearthly. 2011. (Unearthly Ser.: 1). (ENG.). 464p. (YA). (gr. 8). pap. 9.99 *(978-0-06-199617-7(3)*, HarperTeen) HarperCollins Pubs.

Harbridge, Paul. Helena's Voyage: A Mystic Adventure. 2008. (HEB, ARA & ENG., Illus.). 48p. (J). (gr. -1-2). pap. 9.95 *(978-1-84694-114-6(8)*, Our Street Bks.) Hunt, John Publishing Ltd. GBR. Dist: National Bk. Network.

Harold & I. 2007. (ENG., Illus.). 291p. (J). (gr. 3-8). per. 13.99 *(978-0-7684-2432-4(1))* Send The Light Distribution LLC.

Harper, Stephan J. One Christmas Story. Steuerwald, Joy, illus. 2003. 32p. (J). lib. bdg. 16.95 *(978-0-9741800-0-7(9))* Inspire Press, Inc.

Hartman, Bob. Easter Angels. Williams, Sophy, illus. 2010. (ENG.). 32p. (J). (gr. 2-4). 14.99 *(978-0-7459-6922-0(4))* Lion Hudson PLC GBR. Dist: Independent Pubs. Group.

Healer, Stephanie A. My Angel Michael. 2013. 24p. pap. 10.95 *(978-1-4525-7498-1(7)*, Balboa Pr.) Author Solutions, Inc.

Hendry, Diana. Harvey Angel y la Nina Fantasma. Alban, Rafael Segovia, tr. Morin, Mauricio Gomez, illus. 2003. (la Orilla Del Viento Ser.). (SPA.). 166p. (J). reprint ed. pap., pap. 7.50 *(978-968-16-6723-8(9))* Fondo de Cultura Economica USA.

Higgins, Wendy. Sweet Evil. 2012. (Sweet Evil Ser.: 1). (ENG.). 464p. (YA). (gr. 8). pap. 9.99 *(978-0-06-208561-0(1)*, HarperTeen) HarperCollins Pubs.

—Sweet Peril. 2013. (Sweet Evil Ser.: 2). (ENG.). 384p. (YA). (gr. 8). pap. 9.99 *(978-0-06-226594-4(6)*, HarperTeen) HarperCollins Pubs.

—Sweet Reckoning. 2014. (Sweet Evil Ser.: 3). (ENG.). 400p. (YA). (gr. 8). pap. 9.99 *(978-0-06-226597-5(0)*, HarperTeen) HarperCollins Pubs.

—Sweet Temptation. 2015. (Sweet Evil Ser.: 4). (ENG.). 512p. (YA). (gr. 8). pap. 9.99 *(978-0-06-238142-2(3)*, HarperTeen) HarperCollins Pubs.

Hill, Judith J. Champion for Grace. 2012. 128p. pap. 15.00 *(978-1-936688-22-7(0))* AKA:yoLa.

Hoban, Russell. A Birthday for Frances. Hoban, Lillian, illus. 2012. (I Can Read Level 2 Ser.). (ENG.). 48p. (J). (gr. k-3). pap. 3.99 *(978-0-06-083797-6(7))* HarperCollins Pubs.

Holman, Donna Buckman. Little Angel Friends. 2013. 24p. pap. 10.95 *(978-1-4525-8494-2(X)*, Balboa Pr.) Author Solutions, Inc.

Holthaus, Abbey. The Treasures of Christmas. Downs, Braden, illus. 2008. 126p. pap. 19.95 *(978-1-60672-152-0(6))* America Star Bks.

Hood, Karen Jean Matsko. Angels, Angels Way up High. Whispering Pine Press International, ed. Alexandra Dzhiganskaya, illus. 2017. (Hood Picture Book Ser.). (J). bk. 2. pap. 15.95 *(978-1-930948-09-9(3))* Vol. 2. 24.95 *(978-1-930948-81-5(6))* Whispering Pine Pr. International, Inc.

Hooper, Mary. Down to Earth. Harker, Lesley, illus. 2008. (Two Naughty Angels Ser.). (ENG.). 96p. (J). (gr. 2-4). pap. 11.95 *(978-0-7475-9061-3(3))* Bloomsbury Publishing Plc GBR. Dist: Independent Pubs. Group.

—The Ghoul at School. Harker, Lesley, illus. 2008. (Two Naughty Angels Ser.). (ENG.). 96p. (J). (gr. 2-4). pap. 11.95 *(978-0-7475-9060-6(5))* Bloomsbury Publishing Plc GBR. Dist: Independent Pubs. Group.

—Round the Rainbow. Harker, Lesley, illus. 2008. (Two Naughty Angels Ser.). (ENG.). 96p. (J). (gr. 2-4). pap. 11.95 *(978-0-7475-9062-0(1))* Bloomsbury Publishing Plc GBR. Dist: Independent Pubs. Group.

Horner, Susan. The Mission: An Angel's Most Important Assignment. Allen, Joe, illus. 2006. pap. 10.99 *(978-1-59317-148-3(X))* Warner Pr., Inc.

Howe, Norma. Angel in Vegas: The Chronicles of Noah Sark. 2009. (ENG., Illus.). 256p. (YA). (gr. 7-18). 16.99 *(978-0-7636-3985-3(0))* Candlewick Pr.

Hutchings, Harriet Anne. Amanda & the Angel. Cragg, Marcelyn Martin, illus. 2010. 24p. pap. 9.95 *(978-1-936051-81-6(8))* Peppertree Pr., The.

I Have Feelings. 2004. (J). per. *(978-1-57657-393-8(1))* Paradise Pr., Inc.

I Like You: (a little book of friendship) 2004. (J). per. *(978-1-57657-394-5(X))* Paradise Pr., Inc.

Itty-Bitty/The Mission/Easter Storybook 1-6. 2006. pap. 11.99 *(978-1-59317-152-0(8))* Warner Pr., Inc.

Jacques, Brian. The Angel's Command. Elliot, David & Schoenherr, Ian, illus. 2005. (ENG.). 384p. (J). (gr. 3-7). 7.99 *(978-0-14-240285-6(0)*, Firebird) Penguin Young Readers Group.

—The Angel's Command. 2003. (Castaways of the Flying Dutchman Ser.: No. 2). 1.00 *(978-1-4175-5393-8(6))* Recorded Bks., Inc.
James, Syrie & James, Ryan M. Forbidden. 2012. (ENG.). 416p. (YA). (gr. 8). pap. 9.99 *(978-0-06-202789-4(1),* HarperTeen) HarperCollins Pubs.
Jenkins, Barbie. The Legend of the Christmas Kiss. 2010. (ENG.). 32p. pap. 11.99 *(978-1-4391-9623-6(0),* Howard Bks.) Howard Books.
Johnson, Marsha Deveaux. Power Angels on Assignment: Cinnamon Comes to Earth. 2003. (Illus.). 48p. (J). lib. bdg. 14.95 *(978-1-59094-022-8(9),* 1590940229) Jawbone Publishing Corp.
Johnson, Susana M. Our Very Special Brother. 2010. 28p. pap. 15.99 *(978-1-4500-4394-6(1))* Xlibris Corp.
Jones, H. Lena. Trapped on Planet Liska. 2006. 180p. pap. 19.95 *(978-1-4241-0989-0(2))* America Star Bks.
Karchut, Darby. Griffin Rising. 2011. 176p. (YA). pap. 15.95 *(978-1-60619-210-8(8))* Twilight Times Bks.
Karol, Leslee. Sylvie the Littlest Guardian Angel: Cassie Makes a Friend. 2013. 48p. pap. 21.99 *(978-1-4817-0864-7(3))* AuthorHouse.
Kate, Lauren. Fallen. (Fallen Ser.: Bk. 1). (ENG.). (YA). (gr. 7). 2010. 480p. pap. 10.99 *(978-0-385-73913-9(3),* Ember) 2009. 464p. 17.99 *(978-0-385-73893-4(5),* Delacorte Pr.) Random Hse. Children's Bks.
—Fallen. 2010. (Fallen Ser.: 1). lib. bdg. 22.10 *(978-0-606-15168-9(0),* Turtleback) Turtleback Bks.
—Fallen in Love. 2012. (Fallen Ser.). (ENG.). (YA). (gr. 7). 224p. pap. 8.99 *(978-0-385-74262-7(2),* Ember); 256p. 15.99 *(978-0-385-74261-0(4),* Delacorte Pr.) Random Hse. Children's Bks.
—Oscuros. 2011. (Vintage Espanol Ser.: Bk. 1).Tr. of Fallen. (SPA.). 416p. (YA). (gr. 5). pap. 9.95 *(978-0-307-74500-2(7),* Vintage Espanol) Knopf Doubleday Publishing Group.
—Pasión. 2011. (Vintage Espanol Ser.: Bk. 3).Tr. of Passion. (SPA.). 384p. (YA). (gr. 7). pap. 9.95 *(978-0-307-74523-1(6),* Vintage Espanol) Knopf Doubleday Publishing Group.
—Passion. (Fallen Ser.: Bk. 3). (ENG.). (YA). (gr. 7). 2012. 448p. pap. 10.99 *(978-0-385-73917-7(6),* Ember) 2011. 432p. 17.99 *(978-0-385-73916-0(8),* Delacorte Pr.) Random Hse. Children's Bks.
—Passion. 2012. (Fallen Ser.: 3). lib. bdg. 22.10 *(978-0-606-26410-5(8),* Turtleback) Turtleback Bks.
—Rapture. 2012. (Fallen Ser.: Bk. 4). (ENG.). 464p. (YA). (gr. 7). 17.99 *(978-0-385-73918-4(4),* Delacorte Pr.) Random Hse. Children's Bks.
—Torment. (Fallen Ser.: Bk. 2). (ENG.). (YA). (gr. 7). 2011. 480p. pap. 10.99 *(978-0-385-73915-3(X),* Ember) 2010. 464p. 17.99 *(978-0-385-73914-6(1),* Delacorte Pr.) Random Hse. Children's Bks.
—Torment. 2011. (Fallen Ser.: 2). lib. bdg. 22.10 *(978-0-606-22247-1(2),* Turtleback) Turtleback Bks.
—Tormento. 2011. (Vintage Espanol Ser.: Bk. 2).Tr. of Torment. (SPA.). 416p. (YA). (gr. 7). pap. 9.95 *(978-0-307-74512-5(0),* Vintage Espanol) Knopf Doubleday Publishing Group.
—Unforgiven. (Fallen Ser.). (ENG.). 368p. (YA). (gr. 7). 2016. pap. 10.99 *(978-0-385-74264-1(9),* Ember) 2015. 18.99 *(978-0-385-74263-4(0),* Delacorte Pr.) 2015. lib. bdg. 21.99 *(978-0-375-99068-7(2),* Delacorte Pr.) Random Hse. Children's Bks.
Keeble, Helen. No Angel. 2013. (ENG.). 384p. (YA). (gr. 8). pap. 9.99 *(978-0-06-208227-5(2),* HarperTeen) HarperCollins Pubs.
Kelly, Karen. Angel Tree. 2012. (Illus.). 24p. pap. 19.82 *(978-1-4678-9637-5(3))* AuthorHouse.
Kelly, Nikki. Gabriel. 2015. (Styclar Saga Ser.: 2). (ENG.). 384p. (YA). (gr. 7). 17.99 *(978-1-250-05153-0(3),* 9781250051530) Feiwel & Friends.
—Lailah. 2014. (Styclar Saga Ser.: 1). (ENG.). 416p. (YA). (gr. 7). 17.99 *(978-1-250-05151-6(7),* 9781250051516) Feiwel & Friends.
Kensley, Karen. Gods in Pods. 2008. (ENG., Illus.). 122p. (J). (gr. 4-7). pap. *(978-1-85756-682-6(3))* Janus Publishing Co.
Kinde, Christa. The Hidden Deep, 1 vol. 2013. (Threshold Ser.). (ENG.). 272p. (J). 14.99 *(978-0-310-72489-6(9))* Zonderkidz.
Klein, Janet A. Angelic Beginnings: What are Angels? 2011. 24p. pap. 12.99 *(978-1-4520-7131-2(4))* AuthorHouse.
Knight, Jovannah. A Heavenly Message. 2011. 20p. pap. 16.95 *(978-1-61204-430-9(1),* Strategic Bk. Publishing) Strategic Book Publishing & Rights Agency (SBPRA).
Knights, Harry B. Angel's Star. 2006. (J). lib. bdg. 20.00 *(978-0-9632248-8-0(3))* Synergetic Pubns., Inc.
Knipe, Sally J. The Angel with the Broken Wings. 2012. 28p. pap. 16.95 *(978-1-4497-5865-3(7),* WestBow Pr.) Author Solutions, Inc.
—The Angel with the Broken Wings. 2012. 28p. pap. 15.99 *(978-1-4691-4896-0(X))* Xlibris Corp.
Kraszewski. Surf Angel. 2009. 40p. *(978-0-9821989-0-2(6))* Kraszewski, Terry.
Kress, Adrienne. Outcast. 2013. (ENG.). 326p. pap. 18.99 *(978-1-62681-092-1(3))* Diversion Publishing Corp.
Kuplenk, Martina. The Angelettes. 2012. 28p. pap. 18.95 *(978-1-4525-5256-9(8))* Balboa Pr.
LaMothe, Karin Elaine. The Angels' Lullaby. 2003. (Illus.). 8p. (J). pap. 9.95 *(978-0-9728763-0-8(8))* LaMothe, Karin.
Lancett, Peter. The Dark Waters of Time, 1 vol. unabr. ed. 2010. (Dark Man Ser.). (ENG.). 34p. (YA). (gr. 9-12). pap. 7.95 *(978-1-61651-020-6(X))* Saddleback Educational Publishing, Inc.
Lane, Nickel. The Ferret Crusaders: Quest of the Wish A Pod. 2nd ed. 2004. 73p. (J). per. 8.49 *(978-1-4116-0459-9(8))* Lulu Pr., Inc.
Law, Jerel. Spirit Fighter, 1 vol. 2012. (Son of Angels, Jonah Stone Ser.). (ENG.). 256p. (J). pap. 9.99 *(978-1-4003-1843-8(2))* Nelson, Thomas Inc.
Lethcoe, Jason. Der Geheimnisvolle Mr. Spines - Wings. Altmann, Scott, illus. 2009. (Mysterious Mr. Spines Ser.: 1). (ENG.). 256p. (J). (gr. 5-18). pap. 7.99 *(978-0-448-44653-0(7),* Grosset & Dunlap) Penguin Young Readers Group.
Lim, Rebecca. Exile (Mercy, Book 2) 2016. (Mercy Ser.: 2). (ENG.). 304p. (J). pap. 9.99 *(978-0-00-816904-6(7),* HarperCollins Children's Bks.) HarperCollins Pubs. Ltd. GBR. Dist: HarperCollins Pubs.
—Fury (Mercy, Book 4) 2016. (Mercy Ser.: 4). (ENG.). 384p. (YA). pap. 9.99 *(978-0-00-816906-0(3),* HarperCollins Children's Bks.) HarperCollins Pubs. Ltd. GBR. Dist: HarperCollins Pubs.
—Mercy (Mercy, Book 1) 2016. (Mercy Ser.: 1). (ENG.). 288p. (J). pap. 9.99 *(978-0-00-816903-9(9),* HarperCollins Children's Bks.) HarperCollins Pubs. Ltd. GBR. Dist: HarperCollins Pubs.
Liz Smith And Kate Spohrer. Jangelle the Adhd Angel - Training the Dunelm Way. 2010. 56p. pap. 8.95 *(978-1-4502-0879-6(7))* iUniverse, Inc.
Lockhart, Linda J. A Little Angel Dressed in Red. 2006. (J). pap. 8.00 *(978-0-8059-6923-8(3))* Dorrance Publishing Co., Inc.
Loeffler, Sherry. The Guardian Angel. 2012. 70p. pap. 10.99 *(978-1-62230-792-0(5))* Salem Author Services.
Lorenz Guest, Donna. The Enchanted Ride. 2009. 32p. pap. 14.99 *(978-1-4389-8116-1(3))* AuthorHouse.
Lunsford, Gary. Georgia Is on My Mind: A Tale of a Guardian Angel. 2010. 374p. 30.50 *(978-1-60911-164-9(8),* Eloquent Bks.) Strategic Book Publishing & Rights Agency (SBPRA).
Magni, Aurora. The 10 Marys & the Little Gabriel. Vignaga, Francesca Dafne, illus. 2011. (J). *(978-0-8091-6764-7(6))* Paulist Pr.
Magnier, Thierry & Hallenleben, Georg. Babel y el Angel. (CAT., Illus.). 40p. (J). 14.95 *(978-84-8488-051-6(6))* Serres, Ediciones, S. L. ESP. Dist: Lectorum Pubns., Inc.
Mallory, Barbara. Shantelle: Angels, Stars & Faith. 2008. pap. 16.95 *(978-1-60563-038-0(1))* America Star Bks.
Mancil, Arlene. The Angel Explains Christmas Blessings. McKinnon, Joy, illus. 2008. 16p. pap. 24.95 *(978-1-60813-297-3(8))* America Star Bks.
Marino, Kellie A. Marcella's Angel. 2011. 20p. 10.95 *(978-1-4520-9519-6(1))* AuthorHouse.
Marks, Graham. How It Works: Everyone Gets the Angel They Deserve. (ENG.). 240p. (J). pap. 12.99 *(978-0-7475-7015-8(9))* Bloomsbury Publishing Plc GBR. Dist: Trafalgar Square Publishing.
Marrero Laurano, Edward A. Aliens & Angels: Secrets & Mysteries. 2011. 48p. pap. 8.95 *(978-1-4620-6122-8(2))* iUniverse, Inc.
Martinez, Roland. The Angel with Red Wings. Graphic Manufacture, illus. 2008. 27p. pap. 24.95 *(978-1-60672-713-3(3))* America Star Bks.
Mason, Kerry. Angel Baby. 2010. 28p. pap. 28.03 *(978-1-4500-2605-5(2))* Xlibris Corp.
Matsuura, Richard & Matsuura, Ruth. Angels Masquerading on Earth. Chao, Linus, illus. (J). 7.95 *(978-1-887916-07-3(5))* Orchid Isle Publishing Co.
Matuszak, Pat. Angela's Answer, 2 vols, Bk 1. 2008. (Angel Light Ser.: 1). (ENG.). 256p. (YA). (gr. 5-12). pap. 12.99 *(978-0-89957-875-0(6))* AMG Pubs.
—Simone's Secret, 2, Bk 2. 2009. (Angel Light Ser.: 2). (ENG.). 192p. (gr. 11). pap. 12.99 *(978-0-89957-876-7(4))* AMG Pubs.
McCorkle, Denise. On Angels Wings - Softball. 2008. 32p. pap. 17.95 *(978-1-4327-3102-1(5))* Outskirts Pr., Inc.
McGurk, Monica. Dark Hope: Book 1 of the Archangel Prophecies. 2014. 410p. (YA). pap. *(978-1-938416-67-5(8))* River Grove Bks.
McHay, Micki. The Ugly Snowflake (children's hard cover book with musical C. D.) 2006. (J). 15.95 *(978-0-9786826-0-6(2))* McHay, Micki.
Mcintyre, Sharyn. Christmas Tea with the Angels. 2007. 112p. 24.95 *(978-1-4327-1457-4(0))* Outskirts Pr., Inc.
McNaney, Jeanne. Miracle in Sumatra: The Story of Gutsy Gus. Cochard, David, illus. 2009. (ENG.). 32p. (J). (gr. -1-3). 16.95 *(978-0-9814534-6-0(5))* Ovation Bks.
McNish, Cliff. Angel. (Exceptional Reading & Language Arts Titles for Intermediate Grades Ser.). (YA). 2012. (ENG.). 312p. (gr. 7-12). pap. 9.95 *(978-0-7613-8501-1(0),* Carolrhoda Lab™) 2008. 311p. (gr. 8-12). 16.95 *(978-0-8225-8900-6(1))* Lerner Publishing Group.
Mear, Shirley A. Feathers from Heaven. 2013. 24p. (J). pap. *(978-1-78148-567-5(4))* Grosvenor Hse. Publishing Ltd.
Melendez-Shafe, Yvette. The Adventures of Mudpie. 2009. 100p. pap. 28.99 *(978-1-4389-6616-8(4))* AuthorHouse.
Menard, Michele R. The Cherub in the Lily Field. 2013. 50p. pap. 13.50 *(978-0-9887969-3-5(7))* Four Menards, The.
Menear, Linda. The Little Groundhog Discovers the True Meaning of Christmas. 2011. 24p. pap. 24.95 *(978-1-4626-3288-6(2))* America Star Bks.
Messer, Celeste M. Angel Experiment J134 Bk #1. 2004. (Adventures of Andi O'Malley Ser.). (Illus.). 82-92p. (J). (gr. 4-7). 4.95 *(978-0-9702171-0-3(2))* AshleyAlan Enterprises.
—The Broken Wing: The Adventures of Andi O'Malley. Hoeffner, Deb, illus. 2004. (Adventures of Andi O'Malley Ser.). 82-92p. (J). (gr. 4-7). 4.95 *(978-0-9702171-1-0(0))* AshleyAlan Enterprises.
—The Circle of Light. 2004. (Adventures of Andi O'Malley Ser.). (Illus.). 82-92p. (J). (gr. 4-7). 4.95 *(978-0-9702171-2-7(9))* AshleyAlan Enterprises.
—The Gift. 2004. (Adventures of Andi O'Malley Ser.). (Illus.). 82-92p. (J). (gr. 4-7). 4.95 *(978-0-9702171-3-4(7))* AshleyAlan Enterprises.
—Three Miracles. 2004. (Adventures of Andi O'Malley Ser.). (Illus.). 82-92p. (J). (gr. 4-7). 4.95 *(978-0-9702171-4-1(5))* AshleyAlan Enterprises.
Michaels, M. J. The Snow Angels' Christmas. Nausley, Kathy, illus. 2016. (ENG.). 24p. (J). (gr. -1-1). 14.95 *(978-1-63322-124-6(5),* Seagrass) Quarto Publishing Group USA.
Mims, Melanie. Not All Angels Have Wings. Floyd, John, Jr., illus. 2006. (Fruit of the Spirit Ser.). 24p. (J). (gr. -1-1). 6.95 *(978-0-9752860-6-7(4))* OurRainbow Pr., LLC.
Misra, Michelle. Birthday Surprise. Chaffey, Samantha, illus. 2016. (Angel Wings Ser.: 2). (ENG.). 128p. (J). (gr. 1-4). pap. 5.99 *(978-1-4814-5800-9(0),* Aladdin) Simon & Schuster Children's Publishing.
—Secrets & Sapphires. Chaffey, Samantha, illus. 2016. (Angel Wings Ser.: 3). (ENG.). 128p. (J). (gr. 1-4). pap. 5.99 *(978-1-4814-5803-0(5),* Aladdin) Simon & Schuster Children's Publishing.
—Secrets & Sapphires. Chaffey, Samantha, illus. 2016. (Angel Wings Ser.: 3). (ENG.). 128p. (J). (gr. 1-4). 16.99 *(978-1-4814-5804-7(3),* Simon & Schuster/Paula Wiseman Bks.) Simon & Schuster/Paula Wiseman Bks.
Molinari, Laurice E. Pillars of Fire, 1 vol. 2016. (Ether Novel Ser.). (ENG.). 368p. (J). pap. 8.99 *(978-0-310-73562-5(9))* Zonderkidz.
Molinari, Laurice Elehwany. The Ether: Vero Rising, 1 vol. 2014. (Ether Novel Ser.). (ENG.). 368p. (J). pap. 8.99 *(978-0-310-73561-8(0))* Zonderkidz.
—Pillars of Fire, 1 vol. 2015. (Ether Novel Ser.). (ENG.). 368p. (J). 16.99 *(978-0-310-73556-4(4))* Zonderkidz.
Moore, Karen. Everybody Counts. Reed, Lisa, illus. 2012. (Roma Downey's Little Angels Ser.). 24p. (J). bds. 7.99 *(978-0-8249-5643-1(5),* Ideal Pubns.) Worthy Publishing.
Morgan, Pamela. The Great Game of Angels. 2013. 28p. pap. 13.95 *(978-1-4525-8651-9(9),* Balboa Pr.) Author Solutions, Inc.
Morrill, Madge Haines. Angel Stories of the Bible. 2011. 136p. 40.95 *(978-1-258-01514-5(5))* Literary Licensing, LLC.
Moulton, Courtney Allison. Angelfire. 2011. (Angelfire Ser.: 1). (ENG.). 464p. (YA). (gr. 8-18). 17.99 *(978-0-06-200232-7(5),* Tegen, Katherine Bks) HarperCollins Pubs.
—My Soul to Reap. 2011. (YA). lib. bdg. 17.89 *(978-0-06-200234-1(1))* HarperCollins Pubs.
—Wings of the Wicked. 2012. (Angelfire Ser.: 2). (ENG.). 528p. (YA). (gr. 9). 17.99 *(978-0-06-200236-5(8),* Tegen, Katherine Bks) HarperCollins Pubs.
Moulton, Mark Kimball. Everyday Angels. Winget, Susan, illus. 2003. (ENG.). 32p. (J). 14.95 *(978-0-8249-5479-6(3),* Ideal Pubns.) Worthy Publishing.
Moyston, Connaelia. God's Faith Is Real. 2013. 44p. pap. 21.99 *(978-1-4817-0155-6(X))* AuthorHouse.
Musgrave, Sugin. Butterfly in the Sky: Daddy's Little Girl. 2008. 32p. 14.00 *(978-1-4389-2218-8(3))* AuthorHouse.
Myers, Bill. The Enemy Closes In, 1 vol. 2009. (Elijah Project Ser.). (ENG.). 128p. (J). (gr. 4-7). pap. 6.99 *(978-0-310-71194-0(0))* Zonderkidz.
Myers, Bill & Riordan, James. On the Run, 1 vol. 2009. (Elijah Project Ser.). (ENG.). 128p. (J). (gr. 4-7). pap. 4.99 *(978-0-310-71193-3(2))* Zonderkidz.
Myers, Janice Limb. Carolee Sings in the Christmas Choir: A Christmas Story for Children of All Ages. Velica, Teodora, illus. 2013. 48p. pap. 13.77 *(978-0-9897175-1-9(8))* LJM Publishing.
Nieto, Nancy. My Angel & Me. Nieto, Gina L., illus. 2003. 19p. (J). *(978-1-932046-04-5(6))* Pastime Pr.
Nishimori, Hiroyuki. Cheeky Angel. Nishimori, Hiroyuki, illus. (Cheeky Angel Ser.). (ENG., Illus.). Vol. 8. 2005. 192p. pap. 9.99 *(978-1-59116-979-6(8))* Vol. 13. 2006. 208p. pap. 9.99 *(978-1-4215-0447-6(2))* Viz Media.
Nora, David, Jr. Happy Balloon to You. 2005. 9.00 *(978-0-8059-9870-2(5))* Dorrance Publishing Co., Inc.
Nowell, Daphne A. Juana Meets Gabriel, the Small Business Angel: What if you Don't Want to Wait Around for a Prince Charming? 2008. (Illus.). 24p. (J). 17.95 *(978-0-9798909-1-8(8))* Business Angel Pr.
Pashley, Hilton. Gabriel's Clock. 2014. (ENG.). 304p. (J). (gr. 5-7). 16.99 *(978-0-544-30176-4(5),* HMH Books For Young Readers) Houghton Mifflin Harcourt Publishing Co.
Pasquali, Elena. Safely Through the Night. Kolanovic, Dubravka, illus. 2008. (ENG.). 32p. (J). (gr. k — 1). pap. 9.95 *(978-0-7459-6047-0(2))* Lion Hudson PLC GBR. Dist: Independent Pubs. Group.
—Safely Through the Night. Kolanovic, Dubravka, illus. 2008. (ENG.). 32p. (J). (gr. k-k). 16.95 *(978-0-7459-6048-7(0))* Lion Hudson PLC GBR. Dist: Independent Pubs. Group.
Patsakos, Julienne. Angel, Angel Where are You? 2004. 20p. pap. 16.95 *(978-1-4137-3350-1(6))* America Star Bks.
Patterson, Barbara A. The Sweetest Angel. 2008. 16p. per. 24.95 *(978-1-4241-9722-4(8))* America Star Bks.
Pearl, B. B. Poerava's Heaven. 2011. (Illus.). 88p. pap. 12.85 *(978-1-4567-8985-5(6))* AuthorHouse.
Penley, Janet. Boo Boo Kisses from the Littlest Angel, 1 vol. Bartlett, Alyssa Joy, illus. 2010. 34p. 24.95 *(978-1-4489-4539-9(9))* PublishAmerica, Inc.
Perez, Olga. Sitting on Cloud 9 at the 50-Yard Line. 2012. (Illus.). 28p. pap. 19.99 *(978-1-4772-9225-9(X))* AuthorHouse.
Perugini, Donna. Do Angels Go Camping? 2010. 32p. (Orig.). pap. 9.99 *(978-0-88144-536-7(3))* Yorkshire Publishing Group.
Pesca, Jodi. Angels Angels Everywhere. 2013. 20p. pap. 24.95 *(978-1-63000-001-1(9))* America Star Bks.
Phillips, Shirley. The Best Gift. 2012. 20p. pap. 10.95 *(978-1-4497-4229-4(7),* WestBow Pr.) Author Solutions, Inc.
Pickard, W. Raymond. When an Angel Cries: (but I Don't Want to Be an Angel) 2006. 67p. pap. 16.95 *(978-1-4241-0243-3(X))* PublishAmerica, Inc.
Pilkey, Dav. God Bless the Gargoyles. 2016. (ENG., Illus.). 40p. (J). (gr. -1-3). 17.99 *(978-0-545-93514-2(8))* Scholastic, Inc.
Pohl, Dora & Kremer, Kevin. Maggie's Christmas Miracle. Ely, Dave, illus. 2010. 78p. (J). pap. 4.99 *(978-0-9824611-2-9(7))* Snow In Sarasota Publishing.
Politi, Leo. Pedro: The Angel of Olvera Street. 2009. (ENG., Illus.). 32p. 14.95 *(978-0-89236-990-4(6))* Oxford Univ. Pr., Inc.
Porpora, Donnamarie. Grampa's Wings. 2013. 32p. pap. *(978-1-4602-1366-7(1))* FriesenPress.
Powell, Inez. Sparkle, My Angel. 2003. (Illus.). 30p. per. 8.95 *(978-1-932344-24-0(1),* Profitable Publishing) Thornton Publishing, Inc.
Quarles, Jean Marie. Not Quite Angels of Icicle Lap. 2004. 204p. 14.00 *(978-1-58961-093-4(8))* PageFree Publishing, Inc.
Randall, Angel. Snow Angels. 2011. (Illus.). 32p. (J). 17.99 *(978-1-60641-046-2(6),* Shadow Mountain) Shadow Mountain Publishing.
Ras, J. J. The Ketchup Story. 2007. 48p. pap. 19.94 *(978-1-84728-470-9(1))* Lulu Pr., Inc.
Reavis, Laura. An Angel to Watch Over. 2008. (ENG., Illus.). 32p. (J). pap. 9.99 *(978-0-9800091-0-1(3))* Stop N Go Fitness.
Renae, Cameo. Hidden Wings. 2013. 270p. pap. 13.99 *(978-1-939769-21-3(3))* Crushing Hearts and Black Butterfly Publishing.
Repicci, Albert. The Littlest Angel: A Christmas Story. 2012. 36p. pap. 21.99 *(978-1-4691-9547-6(X))* Xlibris Corp.
Reynolds, Peter H., illus. Star Bright: A Christmas Story. 2014. (ENG.). 40p. (J). (gr. -1-3). 17.99 *(978-1-4169-5858-1(4),* Atheneum Bks. for Young Readers) Simon & Schuster Children's Publishing.
Riley, Christine. Chester's Field O'Brien, Laurel, illus. 2004. 296p. (J). per. 17.50 *(978-0-9740683-6-7(5))* Authors & Artists Publishers of New York, Inc.
Robbins, Trina. A Match Made in Heaven. Ota, Yuko & Studio, Xian Nu, illus. 2013. (My Boyfriend Is a Monster Ser.: 8). (ENG.). 128p. (YA). (gr. 7-12). pap. 9.95 *(978-1-4677-0732-9(5),* Graphic Universe™) Lerner Publishing Group.
—A Match Made in Heaven. Xian Nu Studio Staff, illus. 2013. (My Boyfriend Is a Monster Ser.: 8). (ENG.). 128p. (YA). (gr. 7-12). lib. bdg. 29.27 *(978-0-7613-6857-1(4),* Graphic Universe™) Lerner Publishing Group.
Roberts, Heather H. Raven & the Forest Angels. 2012. 66p. pap. 27.95 *(978-1-4525-5739-7(X))* Balboa Pr.
Roberts, Roxanne. Angel Wings, Faery Dust & Other Magical Things: A Story about Guardian Angels. 2012. 16p. pap. 10.00 *(978-1-61897-252-1(9),* Eloquent Bks.) Strategic Book Publishing & Rights Agency (SBPRA).
—Angel Wings, Faery Dust & Other Magical Things: A Story about Merpeople. 2011. 24p. pap. 11.50 *(978-1-61204-588-7(X),* Strategic Bk. Publishing) Strategic Book Publishing & Rights Agency (SBPRA).
—Angel Wings, Faery Dust & Other Magical Things: A Story about Witches, Warlocks & Such. 2011. 24p. pap. 11.50 *(978-1-61204-072-1(1),* Eloquent Bks.) Strategic Book Publishing & Rights Agency (SBPRA).
Roesti, Delores. Mareena Maree Mulligan & the Flying Wheel Chair: Book 1: School Days. 2007. 81p. pap. 9.95 *(978-0-7414-4048-8(2))* Infinity Publishing.
Rogers-Busboom, Kimberly. The Angel Who Didn't Fit In. LeBlanc, Marc, illus. 2010. 32p. (J). lib. bdg. 16.99 *(978-0-9823145-3-1(1))* Dirks Publishing, LLC.
Rose, Lynda J. Assignment Earth. 2008. (ENG.). 160p. (J). (gr. 4-7). pap. 8.95 *(978-0-7459-6063-0(4))* Lion Hudson PLC GBR. Dist: Independent Pubs. Group.
Rose, Robin. Reaching for the Stars. 2008. 24p. pap. 11.95 *(978-1-4389-2299-7(X))* AuthorHouse.
Rossi, Veronica. Riders. (ENG.). (YA). 2017. (Riders Ser.: 1). 384p. pap. 9.99 *(978-0-7653-8255-9(5),* 9780765382559) 2016. 368p. 17.99 *(978-0-7653-8254-2(7),* 9780765382542) Doherty, Tom Assocs., LLC. (Tor Teen).
Rowe, Anne Burgess, illus. The Newest Angel. 2015. 47p. (J). pap. *(978-1-63293-039-2(0))* Sunstone Pr.
Royce Conant, Jan. Children of Light. Royce Conant, Jan, illus. 2005. (Illus.). (J). per. 20.00 *(978-0-9740683-7-4(3),* Ithaca Pr.) Authors & Artists Publishers of New York, Inc.
Rucinski, Sandra. The Story of Jesus According to Tobin. 2009. 32p. pap. 14.50 *(978-1-60860-372-5(5),* Eloquent Bks.) Strategic Book Publishing & Rights Agency (SBPRA).
Ruiz, Joseph J. Angel on Daniel's Shoulder. 2004. (SPA & ENG., Illus.). 108p. (J). pap. 12.95 *(978-0-86534-402-0(7))* Sunstone Pr.
Satera, Diane. The Angel of Wild Springs: Jaiden & the Sacred Stones. 2010. 168p. 23.99 *(978-1-4520-3460-7(5));* pap. 11.99 *(978-1-4520-3461-4(3))* AuthorHouse.
Sauls, Debra A. Angel Quest. 2008. 84p. pap. 19.95 *(978-1-60703-890-0(0))* America Star Bks.
Scheer, Ruth D. The Mouse & the Angel. 2003. (J). lib. bdg. 15.95 *(978-0-9671761-3-0(1))* Scheer Delight Publishing.
Schwab, Victoria. New Beginnings. 2014. (Everyday Angel Ser.: 1). (J). (ENG.). 208p. (gr. 3-7). pap. 6.99 *(978-0-545-52846-7(1),* Scholastic Paperbacks); 195p. pap. *(978-0-545-68443-9(9))* Scholastic, Inc.
—Second Chances. 2014. (Everyday Angel Ser.: 2). (ENG.). 208p. (J). (gr. 3-7). pap. 6.99 *(978-0-545-52847-4(X),* Scholastic Paperbacks) Scholastic, Inc.
Schweitzer, C. V. The Making of an Angel. 2012. 48p. (-18). pap. 31.99 *(978-1-4797-3502-0(7))* Xlibris Corp.
Shelton, Dierdre A. Angels Surrounding Me. 2009. 32p. pap. 16.49 *(978-1-4389-4407-4(1))* AuthorHouse.
Shirvington, Jessica. Emblaze. 2013. (Embrace Ser.: 3). (ENG.). 464p. (YA). (gr. 7-12). pap. 14.99 *(978-1-4022-7131-1(X));* 16.99 *(978-1-4022-6846-5(7))* Sourcebooks, Inc.
—Embrace. 2012. (Embrace Ser.: 1). (ENG.). 400p. (YA). (gr. 7-12). pap. 9.99 *(978-1-4022-7125-0(5))* Sourcebooks, Inc.
—Empower. 2014. (Embrace Ser.: 5). (ENG.). 496p. (YA). (gr. 7-12). 16.99 *(978-1-4022-9460-0(3))* Sourcebooks, Inc.
—Endless. 2014. (Embrace Ser.: 4). (ENG.). 480p. (YA). (gr. 7-12). pap. 9.99 *(978-1-4022-8945-3(6))* Sourcebooks, Inc.
—Entice. 2013. (Embrace Ser.: 2). (ENG.). 464p. (YA). (gr. 7-12). pap. 10.99 *(978-1-4022-7128-1(X))* Sourcebooks, Inc.
Showers, Barbara. Angel Jubilee. 2008. 28p. pap. 12.95 *(978-1-4327-2084-1(8))* Outskirts Pr., Inc.
Sigal, Maxine Handelman. Shabbat Angels. Rothenberg, Joani, illus. 2003. (gr. k-3). 13.95 *(978-0-8074-0865-0(4),* 164051) URJ Pr.
Smith, Barbara Maxine. God Loves You & You Love Yourself -To God You Are Special. 2013. 38p. pap. 12.99 *(978-0-578-11939-7(0))* Smith, Barbara Maxine.
Smith, Cynthia Leitich. Diabolical. 2012. (Tantalize Ser.). (ENG., Illus.). 368p. (YA). (gr. 9). 17.99 *(978-0-7636-5118-3(4))* Candlewick Pr.
—Eternal. (Tantalize Ser.). (ENG., Illus.). 320p. (YA). (gr. 9). 2010. pap. 8.99 *(978-0-7636-4773-5(X))* 2009. 17.99 *(978-0-7636-3573-2(1))* Candlewick Pr.
Smith, Molly K. Cassie's Guardian Angel. 2009. 24p. pap. 17.50 *(978-1-4490-4065-9(9))* AuthorHouse.
Sniegoski, Thomas E. Aerie & Reckoning. 2010. (Fallen Ser.: 2). (ENG.). 576p. (YA). (gr. 11-18). pap. 9.99 *(978-1-4424-0863-0(4),* Simon Pulse) Simon Pulse.
—End of Days Vol. 3. 2011. (Fallen Ser.: 3). (ENG.). 384p. (YA). (gr. 9). pap. 9.99 *(978-1-4424-2349-7(8),* Simon Pulse) Simon Pulse.
—The Fallen 5: Armageddon. 2013. (Fallen Ser.: 5). (ENG., Illus.). 592p. (YA). (gr. 9). pap. 9.99 *(978-1-4424-6005-8(9),* Simon Pulse) Simon Pulse.
—The Fallen & Leviathan. 2010. (Fallen Ser.: 1). (ENG.). 544p. (YA). (gr. 11). pap. 11.99 *(978-1-4424-0862-3(6),* Simon Pulse) Simon Pulse.
—Forsaken. 2012. (Fallen Ser.: 4). (ENG.). 416p. (YA). (gr. 9). pap. 9.99 *(978-1-4424-4699-1(4),* Simon Pulse) Simon Pulse.
Snorradottir, Asthildur Bj. Raphael: The Angel Who Decided to Visit Earth. Bjarnason, Bjarni Thor, illus. 2011. 74p. pap.

21.50 (978-1-60976-683-2(0), Strategic Bk. Publishing) Strategic Book Publishing & Rights Agency (SBPRA).

Speak, Steven. Skip & L, Guardian Angel. 2011. 20p. pap. 12.45 (978-1-4525-3643-9(0)) Get Published.

Stein, Tammar. Kindred. 2012. (ENG.). 276p. (YA). (gr. 7). pap. 8.99 (978-0-375-85349-4(9), Ember) Random Hse. Children's Bks.

Stentiford, Tyler Michael. A Darker Secret. 2009. (ENG.). 128p. (YA). pap. 9.99 (978-1-60138-315-0(0)) Atlantic Publishing Group, Inc.

Stinnett, Leia A. The Other Me. Date not set. (Little Angel Bks.). (Illus.). (J). (gr. k-8). pap. (978-1-880737-18-7(3)) Crystal Journeys Publishing.

Stortz, Diane. Adam Named the Animals from a to Z. Reed, Lisa, illus. 2012. (Roma Downey's Little Angels Ser.). 24p. (J). bds. 7.99 (978-0-8249-5642-4(7), Ideal Pubns.) Worthy Publishing.

Strickland, James R. Lincoln's Lost Papers. 2008. 131p. (J). pap. 11.95 (978-0-7414-4601-5(4)) Infinity Publishing.

Stromberg, Ronica. The Time-for-Bed Angel. Stephenson, Kristina, illus. 2010. (ENG.). 32p. (J). (gr. -1-k). pap. 9.99 (978-0-7459-6066-1(9)) Lion Hudson PLC GBR. Dist: Independent Pubs. Group.

Sunkuli, O. The Hero & the Dream. 2004. (Illus.). 28p. pap. (978-9966-25-161-9(8)) Heinemann Kenya, Limited (East African Educational Publishers Ltd E.A.E.P.) KEN. Dist: Michigan State Univ. Pr.

Sylvester, Sr. Land of the Angels, 1 vol. Morrison, Nancy, illus. 2009. 32p. pap. 24.95 (978-1-60836-888-4(2)) America Star Bks.

Sylvester Sr, John S. Our Day on the Farm, 1 vol. 2010. 44p. pap. 24.95 (978-1-4489-7139-8(X)) PublishAmerica, Inc.

Taylor, Laini. Daughter of Smoke & Bone. 2011. (ENG.). 432p. (YA). (gr. 10-17). 20.00 (978-0-316-13402-6(3)) Little Brown & Co.

—Daughter of Smoke & Bone. 2012. (ENG.). (YA). (gr. 10-17). 448p. pap. 12.99 (978-0-316-13399-9(X)); 624p. pap. 28.99 (978-0-316-22435-2(9)) Little, Brown Bks. for Young Readers.

—Daughter of Smoke & Bone. 2012. (Daughter of Smoke & Bone Ser.: 1). (YA). lib. bdg. 24.50 (978-0-606-26704-5(2), Turtleback) Turtleback Bks.

—Days of Blood & Starlight. (ENG.). (YA). (gr. 10-17). 2014. 544p. pap. 12.99 (978-0-316-13398-2(1)) 2012. (Illus.). 528p. 18.99 (978-0-316-13397-5(3)) 2012. 688p. 39.99 (978-0-316-22433-8(2)) Little, Brown Bks. for Young Readers.

Tazewell, Charles. The Littlest Angel. lthr. 29.95 (978-0-8249-5333-1(9), Ideal Pubns.) Worthy Publishing.

—The Littlest Angel. Micich, Paul, illus. (ENG.). 32p. (J). (gr. -1-3). 2008. 8.99 (978-0-8249-5575-5(7)) 2007. pap. 3.99 (978-0-8249-5549-6(8)) Worthy Publishing. (Ideal Pubns.).

—The Littlest Angel. Porfirio, Guy, illus. 2004. 32p. (J). 16.95 (978-0-8249-5473-4(4), Ideal Pubns.) Worthy Publishing.

Telles, Cecilia R. & Heinerke, Kristina. Soar with the Angels. 2004. pap. 14.95 (978-1-889743-30-1(5)) Robbie Dean Pr.

Terrell, Heather. Eternity. 2011. (Fallen Angel Ser.: 2). (ENG.). 304p. (YA). (gr. 8). pap. 8.99 (978-0-06-196571-5(5), HarperTeen) HarperCollins Pubs.

Toffler-Corrie, Laura. My Totally Awkward Supernatural Crush. 2013. (ENG.). 352p. (J). (gr. 7). 17.99 (978-1-59643-733-3(2)) Roaring Brook Pr.

Towbin, Meredith. Straightjacket. 2013. (ENG.). 272p. pap. 12.99 (978-1-939194-70-1(9)) Etopia Pr.

Valenzuela, Anabelle. The Day an Angel Ran into My Room. Latham, Sarah, illus. 2012. 56p. 30.50 (978-1-61897-794-6(6), Strategic Bk. Publishing) Strategic Book Publishing & Rights Agency (SBPRA).

Verday, Jessica. The Beautiful & the Damned. 2013. (ENG., Illus.). 272p. (YA). (gr. 7). 17.99 (978-1-4424-8835-9(2), Simon Pulse) Simon Pulse.

Villa, Leesan. The Angel on Top of the Tree. 2011. 68p. pap. 31.99 (978-1-4628-7837-6(7)) Xlibris Corp.

Visser, Joan. Angel Messages: Stories of Inspiration & Healing for Children. 2012. 24p. pap. 10.95 (978-1-4624-0044-7(2), Inspiring Voices) Author Solutions, Inc.

Von Dornheim, Curt H. The Children's Angel Clock. Date not set. (Illus.). 64p. (YA). (gr. 5-18). 12.95 (978-0-89404-225-6(4)) Aztex Corp.

Walker, Crystal. Do Angels Like Chocolate? 2010. 32p. 12.99 (978-1-4520-4824-6(X)) AuthorHouse.

Walker, Kagon. Amber Wings. 2009. 16p. pap. 9.99 (978-1-4490-4266-0(X)) AuthorHouse.

Walley, Keith. An Angel to Guide Me. 2012. 62p. pap. 12.99 (978-1-105-68254-4(4)) Lulu Pr., Inc.

Wangerin, Walter, Jr. Probity Jones & the Fear Not Angel. Ladwig, Tim, illus. 2005. 32p. (J). (gr. 1-4). 16.95 (978-1-55725-457-3(5)) Paraclete Pr., Inc.

Warstler, Mary Lu. Michael's Angel, 1 vol. 2009. 227p. pap. 24.95 (978-1-61546-723-5(8)) PublishAmerica, Inc.

Watt, Fiona. Sparkly Christmas Angel. Kightley, Rosalinda, illus. 2007. (Luxury Touchy-Feely Board Bks). 10p. (J). (gr. -1-k). bds. 15.99 (978-0-7945-1477-8(4), Usborne) EDC Publishing.

—That's Not My Angel. 2009. (Touchy-Feely Board Bks). 10p. (J). bds. 9.99 (978-0-7945-2428-9(1), Usborne) EDC Publishing.

Weatherly, L. A. Angel Burn. 2011. (Angel Ser.: 1). (ENG., Illus.). 464p. (YA). (gr. 9). pap. 9.99 (978-0-7636-5846-5(4)); 17.99 (978-0-7636-5652-2(6)) Candlewick Pr.

—Angel Fever. (Angel Ser.). (ENG.). 496p. (gr. 9). 2014. (YA). pap. 8.99 (978-0-7636-7173-0(8)) 2013. (J). 17.99 (978-0-7636-5680-5(1)) Candlewick Pr.

—Angel Fire. 2012. (Angel Ser.: 2). (ENG., Illus.). (YA). (gr. 9). pap. 8.99 (978-0-7636-6064-2(7)); 17.99 (978-0-7636-5679-9(8)) Candlewick Pr.

Wheatley, Steven. Jack's Little Angel. 2012. 32p. pap. 19.99 (978-1-4685-9445-4(1)) AuthorHouse.

Whelan, Daniel. The Box of Demons. 2016. (ENG.). 256p. (YA). (gr. 7). pap. 10.99 (978-1-4472-7373-8(7)) Pan Macmillan GBR. Dist: Independent Pubs. Group.

Whitedove, Michelle. My Invisible Friends. Poynter, Linda, illus. l.t. ed. 2005. 30p. (gr. -1-3). spiral bd. 18.95 (978-0-9714908-4-0(8)) Whitedove Pr.

Wickham, Kimberly, illus. Angels & Horses. 2007. 128p. per. 12.85 (978-1-4251-0215-9(8)) Trafford Publishing.

Williams, Rachel. Alex & the Archangel. Konopka, Jan, illus. 2005. (ENG.). 56p. pap. (978-1-84401-614-3(5)) Athena Pr.

Wilson, Agy. From Heaven to Earth - Angel on My Shoulder. Wilson, Agy, illus. 2004. (From Heaven to Earth Ser.). (Illus.). 150p. (J). (gr. 2-7). pap. 5.95 (978-0-9718348-1-1(4)) Blooming Tree Pr.

Winnette, Sandy. A Snow Angel Story Book: Little Beth & the Snow Angel. 2008. 108p. pap. 11.99 (978-1-4343-8133-0(1)) AuthorHouse.

Winstead, V. L. Wings. 2010. 12p. 12.99 (978-1-4520-3115-6(0)) AuthorHouse.

Wondra, Ashley E. Kelsey's Coat. 2008. 28p. pap. 15.99 (978-1-4363-2987-3(6)) Xlibris Corp.

Yang, Gene Luen & Pham, Thien. Level Up. 2016. (YA). lib. bdg. 20.85 (978-0-606-38563-3(0)) Turtleback Bks.

Yolen, Jane. Stone Angel. Green, Katie May, illus. 2015. (ENG.). 40p. (J). (gr. k-3). 16.99 (978-0-399-16741-6(2), Philomel Bks.) Penguin Young Readers Group.

York Lumbard, Alexis. Angels. Weedn, Flavia, illus. 2013. (ENG.). 28p. (J). (gr. -1-1). 14.95 (978-1-937786-15-1(3), Wisdom Tales) World Wisdom, Inc.

Zink, Michelle. A Temptation of Angels. 2013. (ENG.). 448p. (YA). (gr. 7). pap. 9.99 (978-0-14-242423-0(4), Speak) Penguin Young Readers Group.

ANGINA PECTORIS

see Heart—Diseases

ANGLING

see Fishing

ANGLO-SAXONS

Bingham, Jane. Anglo-Saxons. 2017. (Explore! Ser.). (ENG., Illus.). 32p. (J). (gr. 4-6). pap. 12.99 (978-0-7502-9734-9(4), Wayland) Hachette Children's Group GBR. Dist: Hachette Bk. Group.

Butterfield, Moira. Religion & Saints. 2016. (Discover the Anglo-Saxons Ser.). (ENG., Illus.). 32p. (J). (gr. 4-6). pap. 11.99 (978-1-4451-3339-3(3), Franklin Watts) Hachette Children's Group GBR. Dist: Hachette Bk. Group.

Clark, Connie & Weiss, Jim. Who in the World Was the Unready King? The Story of Ethelred. unabr. ed. 2008. (ENG.). 1p. 12.95 (978-1-933339-28-3(4), 333928) Well-Trained Mind Pr.

Howell, Izzi. Anglo Saxons. 2016. (Fact Cat: History: Early Britons Ser.). (ENG., Illus.). 24p. (J). (gr. k-2). pap. 9.99 (978-0-7502-9939-8(8), Wayland) Hachette Children's Group GBR. Dist: Hachette Bk. Group.

McNeil, Niki, et al. HOCPP 1097 Anglo-Saxons. 2006. spiral bd. 24.50 (978-1-60308-097-2(X)) In the Hands of a Child.

ANGLO-SAXONS—FICTION

Bond, Douglas. Hand of Vengeance. 2012. (J). pap. (978-1-59638-215-2(5)) P & R Publishing.

Farmer, Nancy. The Islands of the Blessed. Foster, Jon, illus. 2009. (ENG.). 496p. (YA). (gr. 7-9). 18.99 (978-1-4169-0737-4(8), Atheneum/Richard Jackson Bks.) Simon & Schuster Children's Publishing.

—The Islands of the Blessed. l.t. ed. 2010. (Sequel to the Land of the Silver Apples Ser.). (ENG.). 520p. (J). 23.95 (978-1-4104-2253-8(4)) Thorndike Pr.

—The Land of the Silver Apples. 2009. (ENG., Illus.). 528p. (YA). (gr. 7). pap. 11.99 (978-1-4169-0736-7(X), Atheneum Bks. for Young Readers) Simon & Schuster Children's Publishing.

—The Land of the Silver Apples. Sardinha, Rick, illus. 2007. (ENG.). 512p. (J). (gr. 5-9). 18.99 (978-1-4169-0735-0(1), Atheneum/Richard Jackson Bks.) Simon & Schuster Children's Publishing.

—The Sea of Trolls. 2006. (ENG., Illus.). 480p. (YA). (gr. 9-8). reprint ed. pap. 11.99 (978-0-689-86746-0(8), Atheneum Bks. for Young Readers) Simon & Schuster Children's Publishing.

Jones, Frewin. Destiny's Path. 2009. (Warrior Princess Ser.: 2). (ENG.). 352p. (YA). (gr. 8-18). 16.99 (978-0-06-087146-8(6), HarperTeen) HarperCollins Pubs.

—The Emerald Flame. 2010. (Warrior Princess Ser.: 3). (ENG.). 352p. (YA). (gr. 8-18). 16.99 (978-0-06-087149-9(0), HarperTeen) HarperCollins Pubs.

—Warrior Princess. 2009. (YA). 346p. lib. bdg. 17.89 (978-0-06-087144-4(X)); (ENG.). 352p. (gr. 7-18). 16.99 (978-0-06-087143-7(1)) HarperCollins Pubs. (Eos).

—Warrior Princess #2: Destiny's Path. 2010. (Warrior Princess Ser.: 2). (ENG.). 352p. (YA). (gr. 8). pap. 8.99 (978-0-06-087148-2(2), HarperTeen) HarperCollins Pubs.

Scott, Walter, ed. Ivanhoe. 2008. (Bring the Classics to Life Ser.). (Illus.). 72p. (gr. 5-12). pap., act. bk. ed. 10.95 (978-1-55576-099-1(6), EDN506B) EDCON Publishing Group.

ANIMAL BABIES

see Animals—Infancy

ANIMAL BEHAVIOR

see Animals—Habits and Behavior

ANIMAL COMMUNICATION

Baines, Becky. What Did One Elephant Say to the Other? 2008. (ZigZag Ser.). (ENG., Illus.). 32p. (J). (gr. k-3). lib. bdg. 19.90 (978-1-4263-0308-1(4), National Geographic Children's Bks.) National Geographic Society.

Baines, Becky & National Geographic Learning Staff. What Did One Elephant Say to the Other? 2008. (ZigZag Ser.). (ENG., Illus.). 32p. (J). (gr. k-3). 14.95 (978-1-4263-0307-4(6), National Geographic Children's Bks.) National Geographic Society.

Brynie, Faith Hickman. Do Animals Work Together? 2010. (I Like Reading about Animals! Ser.). (Illus.). 32p. (J). (gr. k-3). 23.94 (978-0-7660-3328-3(7)); pap. 7.95 (978-0-7660-3749-6(5), Enslow Elementary) Enslow Pubs., Inc.

Carmichael, L. E. Fox Talk. Bronson, Jody, illus. 2013. 62p. (978-0-9881638-5-0(3)); pap. (978-0-9881638-6-7(1)) Ashby-BP Publishing.

Chrustowski, Rick. Bee Dance. Chrustowski, Rick, illus. 2015. (ENG., Illus.). 32p. (J). (gr. -1-3). 17.99 (978-0-8050-9919-5(0), 9780805099195, Holt, Henry & Co. Bks. For Young Readers) Holt, Henry & Co.

Davies, Nicola. Talk, Talk, Squawk! 2015. (Animal Science Ser.). lib. bdg. 18.40 (978-0-606-37413-2(2)) Turtleback Bks.

Downer, Ann. Elephant Talk: The Surprising Science of Elephant Communication. 2015. (ENG., Illus.). 112p. (gr. 6-12). 34.65 (978-1-4677-5988-5(0), Lerner Digital) Lerner Publishing Group.

Downer, Anna. Elephant Talk: The Surprising Science of Elephant Communication. 2011. (Single Titles Ser.). (ENG.). 112p. (gr. 6-12). 33.26 (978-0-7613-5766-7(1)) Lerner Publishing Group.

Dunne, Abbie. Animal Communication. 2016. (Life Science Ser.). (ENG., Illus.). 24p. (gr. k-1). lib. bdg. 26.65 (978-1-5157-0943-5(4), Pebble Plus) Capstone Press of Coughlan Cos.

Gibson, Brylee. Keeping in Touch. 2007. (Connectors Ser.). (gr. 2-5). pap. (978-1-877453-05-2(6)) Global Education Systems Ltd.

Gray, Leon. Amazing Animal Communicators. 2015. (Animal Scientists Ser.). (ENG., Illus.). 32p. (gr. 3-4). lib. bdg. 27.32 (978-1-4914-6981-1(1), Fact Finders) Capstone Press of Coughlan Cos.

Howell, Sara. How Do Animals Communicate? 2015. (Let's Find Out! Animal Life Ser.). (ENG., Illus.). 32p. (J). (gr. 2-3). 23.45 (978-1-68048-005-4(7), Britannica Educational Publishing) Rosen Publishing Group, Inc., The.

Jenkins, Steve & Page, Robin. How to Clean a Hippopotamus: A Look at Unusual Animal Partnerships. 2013. lib. bdg. 18.40 (978-0-606-31663-7(9), Turtleback) Turtleback Bks.

Jennings, Terry Catasús. Sounds of the Savanna, 1 vol. Saroff, Phyllis, illus. 2015. 32p. (J). (gr. k-3). (SPA & ENG.). pap. 9.95 (978-1-62855-642-1(0)); (ENG.). pap. 9.95 (978-1-62855-637-7(4)) Arbordale Publishing.

Judge, Lita. Bird Talk: What Birds Are Saying & Why. Judge, Lita, illus. 2012. (ENG., Illus.). 48p. (J). (gr. 1-4). 18.99 (978-1-59643-646-6(8), 9781596436466) Roaring Brook Pr.

Kalman, Bobbie. How & Why Do Animals Communicate? 2015. (ENG., Illus.). 24p. (J). (978-0-7787-1464-4(0)) Crabtree Publishing Co.

—How Do Animals Communicate? 2009. (Big Science Ideas Ser.). (ENG., Illus.). 32p. (J). (gr. 1-4). pap. (978-0-7787-3302-7(5)); (gr. 2-4). (978-0-7787-3282-2(7)) Crabtree Publishing Co.

Katz, Jon. Lenore Finds a Friend: A True Story from Bedlam Farm. Katz, Jon, photos by. 2012. (My Readers Ser.). (ENG., Illus.). 32p. (J). (gr. -1-3). 15.99 (978-0-8050-9220-2(X), 9780805092202, Holt, Henry & Co. Bks. For Young Readers) Holt, Henry & Co.

Klepeis, Alicia. The Language of Cats & Other Felines. 2016. (Call of the Wild Ser.). (ENG., Illus.). 32p. (J). (gr. 3-3). 28.50 (978-1-5026-1724-8(2)) Cavendish Square Publishing.

Koontz, Robin Michal. Screams & Songs: How Animals Communicate to Survive. 2011. (Amazing Animal Skills Ser.). 48p. (gr. 4). 29.93 (978-0-7614-4907-2(8)) Marshall Cavendish Corp.

Kopp, Megan. The Language of Dogs & Other Canines. 2016. (Call of the Wild Ser.). (ENG.). 32p. (J). (gr. 3-3). 28.50 (978-1-5026-1725-5(0)) Cavendish Square Publishing.

LernerClassroom Editors, ed. Teaching Guide for Fsn / Animal Adaptations. 2010. pap. 5.95 (978-0-7613-6681-2(4)) Lerner Publishing Group.

Lindeen, Mary. Dancing Bees & Other Amazing Communicators. 2017. (Searchlight Books (tm) — Animal Superpowers Ser.). (ENG.). 40p. (J). (gr. 3-5). 16.99 **(978-1-5124-3657-0(7)**, Lerner Pubns.); 46.65 **(978-1-5124-2821-6(3)**, Lerner Pubns.); 46.65 **(978-1-5124-3656-3(9)**, Lerner Pubns.); (Illus.). 30.65 (978-1-5124-2545-1(1)) Lerner Publishing Group.

Muldrow, Diane. How Do Lions Say I Love You? Walker, David, illus. 2013. (Little Golden Book Ser.). (ENG.). 24p. (J). (-k). 4.99 (978-0-449-81256-3(1), Golden Bks.) Random Hse. Children's Bks.

National Wildlife Federation Staff. My First Book of Animal Hugs & Kisses. 2016. (ENG., Illus.). 22p. (J). (— 1). bds. 6.95 (978-1-62354-061-6(5)) Charlesbridge Publishing, Inc.

Newman, Aline Alexander & Weitzman, Gary. How to Speak Dog: A Guide to Decoding Dog Language. 2013. (ENG.). 176p. (J). (gr. 3-7). lib. bdg. 21.90 (978-1-4263-1559-6(7)); (Illus.). pap. 12.95 (978-1-4263-1373-8(X)) National Geographic Society. (National Geographic Children's Bks.).

Page, Robin & Jenkins, Steve. How to Clean a Hippopotamus: A Look at Unusual Animal Partnerships. Jenkins, Steve, illus. 2013. (ENG., Illus.). 32p. (J). (gr. 1-4). pap. 7.99 (978-0-547-99484-0(2)) Houghton Mifflin Harcourt Publishing Co.

Radford, Tracey. Animal Fun! What Sound Do I Make? Press the Button! 2016. (ENG., Illus.). 10p. (J). (gr. 1-4). 6.95 (978-1-78249-398-3(0), 1782493980, CICO Books) Ryland Peters & Small GBR. Dist: WIPRO.

Scheunemann, Pam. Animal Sounds Set 2, 1 vol., Vol. 2. Incl. Dolphins Click! lib. bdg. 24.21 (978-1-61613-570-6(0)); Elephants Trumpet! lib. bdg. 24.21 (978-1-61613-571-3(9)); Frogs Croak! lib. bdg. 24.21 (978-1-61613-572-0(7)); Mice Squeak! lib. bdg. 24.21 (978-1-61613-573-7(5)); Parrots Talk! lib. bdg. 24.21 (978-1-61613-574-4(3)); Snakes Hiss! lib. bdg. 24.21 (978-1-61613-575-1(1)); (J). (gr. k-3). (Animal Sounds Set 2 Ser.: 6). (ENG., Illus.). 24p. 2011. Set lib. bdg. 145.26 (978-1-61613-569-0(7), SandCastle) ABDO Publishing Co.

Schlein, Miriam. Hello, Hello! Kirk, Daniel, illus. 2011. (ENG.). 32p. (J). (gr. -1-1). pap. 16.99 (978-1-4424-5229-9(3), Simon & Schuster Bks. For Young Readers) Simon & Schuster Bks. For Young Readers.

Stefoff, Rebecca. How Animals Communicate. 2013. (Animal Behavior Revealed Ser.). 80p. (J). (gr. 6-9). pap. 17.64 (978-1-62712-021-0(1)); (Illus.). 34.21 (978-1-60870-510-8(2)) Cavendish Square Publishing.

Stewart, Gail B. Cesar Milan. 2010. (People in the News Ser.). (Illus.). 128p. (J). 33.95 (978-1-4205-0231-2(X), Lucent Bks.) Cengage Gale.

Stewart, Melissa, Melissa. Can an Aardvark Bark? Jenkins, Steve, illus. 2017. (ENG.). 32p. (J). (gr. -1-3). 17.99 **(978-1-4814-5852-8(3)**, Beach Lane Bks.) Beach Lane Bks.

Stonehouse, Bernard. & Bertram, Esther. The Truth about Animal Communication. Francis, John, illus. 2003. (Animals Exposed! Ser.). 48p. (J). 11.99 (978-0-439-54329-3(0)) Scholastic, Inc.

Tiger Tales Staff, ed. Animals Talk. Emily, Bolam, illus. 2010. (Touch, Look, & Learn! Ser.). (ENG.). 10p. (J). (gr. -1). bds. 5.95 (978-1-58925-855-6(X)) Tiger Tales.

Tomecek, Stephen M. Animal Communication. 2009. (Animal Behavior Ser.). (Illus.). 136p. (gr. 5-8). lib. bdg. 32.95 (978-1-60413-091-1(1), Chelsea Hse.) Facts On File, Inc.

Townsend, John. Amazing Animal Communicators, 1 vol. 2012. (Animal Superpowers Ser.). (ENG.). 32p. (gr. 1-3). pap. 8.29 (978-1-4109-4751-2(3)); lib. bdg. 29.99 (978-1-4109-4744-4(0)) Heinemann-Raintree. (Read Me!).

Troupe, Thomas Kingsley. Do Ants Get Lost? Learning about Animal Communication with the Garbage Gang, 1 vol. Toye, Derek, illus. 2014. (Garbage Gang's Super Science Questions Ser.). (ENG.). 24p. (gr. k-2). lib. bdg. 26.65 (978-1-4795-5478-2(2)) Picture Window Bks.

Webster, Maureen. Cat Speak: Revealing Answers to the Strangest Cat Behaviors. 2016. (Cats Rule! Ser.). (ENG., Illus.). 32p. (gr. 3-4). lib. bdg. 27.99 (978-1-4914-8400-5(4), Snap Bks.) Capstone Press of Coughlan Cos.

Wolfe, Jane. Who Says Moo? Toy Box Staff, illus. 2013. (ENG.). 8p. bds. 6.99 (978-1-84322-679-6(0), Armadillo) Anness Publishing GBR. Dist: National Bk. Network.

—Who's Hiding? Toy Box Staff, illus. 2013. (ENG.). 8p. bds. 6.99 (978-1-84322-657-4(X), Armadillo) Anness Publishing GBR. Dist: National Bk. Network.

Wolfe, Jane & Baxter, Nicola. Who's on the Farm? Lawson, Peter, illus. 2013. (ENG.). 8p. bds. 6.99 (978-1-84322-652-9(9), Armadillo) Anness Publishing GBR. Dist: National Bk. Network.

Yaw, Valerie. Color-Changing Animals. (Animals with Super Powers Ser.). 24p. 2016. (ENG.). (J). (gr. 1-6). pap. 7.95 **(978-1-944998-68-4(3))** 2011. (YA). (gr. 2-5). lib. bdg. 22.61 (978-1-61772-122-9(0)) Bearport Publishing Co., Inc.

ANIMAL DISTRIBUTION

see also Animals—Migration

Dawson, Emily C. Where Animals Live. 2010. (Our Animal World Ser.). 24p. (J). 25.65 (978-1-60753-015-2(5)) Amicus Publishing.

Dorling Kindersley Publishing Staff. Children's Illustrated Animal Atlas. 2017. (ENG.). 96p. (J). (gr. 1-3). 15.99 **(978-1-4654-6203-9(1)**, DK Children) Dorling Kindersley Publishing, Inc.

Hammond, Paula. Atlas of the World's Strangest Animals. 2010. 224p. (J). 99.93 (978-0-7614-7940-6(6), Marshall Cavendish Reference Bks.) Marshall Cavendish Corp.

Johnson, Jinny. Animal Planet - Atlas of Animals. 2013. (ENG., Illus.). 128p. (gr. 4-8). lib. bdg. 35.93 (978-1-4677-1327-6(9), Millbrook Pr.) Lerner Publishing Group.

Salariya, David & Williams, Mark. Animal Atlas. 2014. (Where on Earth? Ser.). (ENG., Illus.). 16p. (J). (gr. -1). bds. 8.95 (978-1-905638-43-7(4), Scribblers) Book Hse. GBR. Dist: Sterling Publishing Co., Inc.

World Book, Inc Staff, contrib. by. Wildlife & Climate Change. 2015. (Illus.). 44p. (J). (978-0-7166-2709-8(4)) World Bk., Inc.

ANIMAL DRAWING

see Animal Painting and Illustration

ANIMAL HOMES

see Animals—Habitations

ANIMAL-HUMAN RELATIONSHIPS

see Human-animal Relationships

ANIMAL INDUSTRY

see Domestic Animals; Livestock

ANIMAL INTELLIGENCE

see also Animals—Habits and Behavior; Psychology, Comparative

Castaldo, Nancy F. Beastly Brains: Exploring How Animals Think, Talk, & Feel. 2017. (ENG., Illus.). 160p. (YA). (gr. 5-7). 16.99 (978-0-544-63335-3(0), HMH Books For Young Readers) Houghton Mifflin Harcourt Publishing Co.

Clarke, Ginjer L. Far Out! Animals That Do Amazing Things. Mueller, Pete, illus. 2009. (Penguin Young Readers, Level 3 Ser.). (ENG.). 48p. (J). (gr. 1-3). mass mkt. 3.99 (978-0-448-44826-8(2), Penguin Young Readers) Penguin Young Readers Group.

De la Bédoyère, Camilla. Smartest & Silliest. 2010. (Animal Opposites Ser.). (ENG., Illus.). 32p. (J). (gr. -1-3). pap. 5.95 (978-1-55407-819-6(9), 9781554078196) Firefly Bks., Ltd.

Driscoll, Laura. Do Dolphins Really Smile? Wald, Christina, illus. 2006. (Penguin Young Readers, Level 3 Ser.). (ENG.). 48p. (J). (gr. 1-3). mass mkt. 3.99 (978-0-448-44341-6(4), Penguin Young Readers) Penguin Young Readers Group.

Farndon, John. Amazing Land Animals. Portolano, Cristina, illus. 2016. (Animal Bests Ser.). (ENG.). 32p. (J). (gr. 3-6). 26.65 (978-1-5124-0627-6(9)) Lerner Publishing Group.

Franchino, Vicky. Animal Brainiacs. 2015. (ENG., Illus.). 48p. (J). lib. bdg. (978-0-531-21543-2(1), Orchard Bks.) Scholastic, Inc.

Ingram, Scott. Dolphins. 2006. (Smart Animals! Ser.). (Illus.). 32p. (YA). (gr. 2-5). lib. bdg. 25.27 (978-1-59716-161-9(6)) Bearport Publishing Co., Inc.

Markle, Sandra. Snow School. Marks, Alan, illus. 2013. (ENG.). 32p. (J). (gr. -1-3). lib. bdg. 16.95 (978-1-58089-410-4(0)) Charlesbridge Publishing, Inc.

Marsico, Katie. Therapy Horses. 2013. 48p. (J). (gr. 4-8). 29.93 (978-1-60870-839-0(X)) Cavendish Square Publishing.

Meister, Cari. Electric Animals. Fretland VanVoorst, Jenny, ed. 2016. (Back off! Animal Defenses). 24p. (J). (gr. 2-5). lib. bdg. 25.65 (978-1-62031-309-1(X), Pogo) Jump! Inc.

National Geographic Kids Staff. To the Rescue! Collection: Amazing Stories of Courageous Animals & Animal Rescues. 2015. (NGK Chapters Ser.). (ENG.). 336p. (J). (gr. 2-5). pap. 14.99 (978-1-4263-2023-1(X), National Geographic Children's Bks.) National Geographic Society.

Ritchey, Kate & Bader, Bonnie. Lion, Tiger, & Bear, Level 4. 2015. (Penguin Young Readers, Level 4 Ser.). (ENG., Illus.). 48p. (J). (gr. 3-4). pap. 3.99 (978-0-448-48336-8(X), Penguin Young Readers) Penguin Young Readers Group.

Searl, Duncan. Elephants. 2006. (Smart Animals! Ser.). (Illus.). 32p. (J). (gr. 2-5). lib. bdg. 25.27 (978-1-59716-162-6(4)) Bearport Publishing Co., Inc.

—Pigs. 2006. (Smart Animals! Ser.). (Illus.). 32p. (J). (gr. 2-5). lib. bdg. 25.27 (978-1-59716-164-0(0)) Bearport Publishing Co., Inc.

Spirn, Michele. Octopuses. 2006. (Smart Animals! Ser.). (Illus.). 32p. (YA). (gr. 2-5). lib. bdg. 25.27 (978-1-59716-250-0(7)) Bearport Publishing Co., Inc.

Stefoff, Rebecca. How Animals Think. 2013. (Animal Behavior Revealed Ser.). 80p. (J). (gr. 6-9). pap. 17.64

(978-1-62712-024-1(6)); (Illus.). 34.21 *(978-1-60870-513-9(7))* Cavendish Square Publishing.
Turner, Pamela S. Crow Smarts: Inside the Brain of the World's Brightest Bird. Comins, Andy, photos by. 2016. (Scientists in the Field Ser.). (ENG., Illus.). 80p. (J). (gr. 5-7). 18.99 *(978-0-544-41619-2(8))*, HMH Books For Young Readers) Houghton Mifflin Harcourt Publishing Co.

ANIMAL KINGDOM

see Zoology

ANIMAL LANGUAGE

see Animal Communication

ANIMAL LIGHT

see Bioluminescence

ANIMAL LORE

see Animals, Mythical; Natural History

ANIMAL MAGNETISM

see Hypnotism

ANIMAL MIGRATION

see Animals—Migration

ANIMAL PAINTING AND ILLUSTRATION

see also Animals in Art; Photography of Animals

Ard, Catherine. Drawing Zentangle Animals. Geddes, Hannah, illus. 2017. (How to Draw Zentangle Art Ser.). 32p. (gr. 3-3). pap. 63.00 ***(978-1-5382-0705-5(2))*** Stevens, Gareth Publishing LLLP.
Davies, Jacqueline. The Boy Who Drew Birds: A Story of John James Audubon. Sweet, Melissa, illus. 2004. (ENG.). 32p. (J). (gr. -1-3). tchr. ed. 16.99 *(978-0-618-24343-3(7))* Houghton Mifflin Harcourt Publishing Co.
Flying Frog Publishing, ed. Farm Animals. 2012. (Drawing in Color Ser.). 96p. (J). 12.99 *(978-1-60745-373-4(8))* Flying Frog Publishing, Inc.
—Jungle Animals. 2012. (Drawing in Color Ser.). 96p. (J). 12.99 *(978-1-60745-374-1(6))* Flying Frog Publishing, Inc.
—Ocean Animals. 2012. (Drawing in Color Ser.). 96p. (J). 12.99 *(978-1-60745-375-8(4))* Flying Frog Publishing, Inc.
Green, John. Big Book of Horses to Color. 2006. (Dover Nature Coloring Book Ser.). (ENG., Illus.). 160p. (gr. 3-8). 7.95 *(978-0-486-45178-7(X))* Dover Pubns., Inc.
—Horse Scenes to Paint or Color. 2006. (Dover Art Coloring Book Ser.). (ENG., Illus.). 48p. (gr. 3-5). 5.99 *(978-0-486-45209-8(3))* Dover Pubns., Inc.
Heller, Elaine. Half 'n Half Animals A1: Think, Draw, & Color. 2010. (Half 'n Half Animals Ser.). 48p. (gr. k-1). pap. 8.99 *(978-0-89455-867-2(6))* Critical Thinking Co., The.
Huancai, Yang, et al. Drawing Fun: Animals. Liu, Xuemei & Henderson, Ann, eds. Noad, Sarah, tr. from CHI. (Illus.). 55p. *(978-90-806752-1-6(0))* Merry Star Pr.
Pratt, Leonie & Stowell, Louie. How to Draw Animals. Figg, Non, illus. 2006. (Usborne Activities Ser.). 32p. (J). (gr. 1-4). pap. 8.99 *(978-0-7945-1241-5(0)*, Usborne) EDC Publishing.
Sherman, Patrice & Wood, Elaine. John James Audubon. 2011. (Conservation Heroes Ser.). (Illus.). 152p. (YA). (gr. 6-12). 35.00 *(978-1-60413-953-2(6)*, Chelsea Hse.) Facts On File, Inc.
Smith, Lucy. How to Draw Horses. Chapman, Chris et al, illus. rev. ed. 2006. (Kid Kits Ser.). 32p. (J). (gr. 4). pap. 13.99 *(978-1-58086-969-0(6))* EDC Publishing.
Staple, Sandra. Drawing Dragons: Learn How to Create Fantastic Fire-Breathing Dragons. 2008. (ENG., Illus.). 144p. (gr. 4-18). pap. 16.95 *(978-1-56975-641-6(4))* Ulysses Pr.

ANIMAL PHOTOGRAPHY

see Photography of Animals

ANIMAL PHYSIOLOGY

see Zoology

ANIMAL PRODUCTS

see Dairy Products

see names of special products, e.g. Hides and Skins; Ivory; etc

ANIMAL PSYCHOLOGY

see also Psychology, Comparative

Bright, Michael. Behavior in Living Things, 1 vol. 2012. (Web of Life Ser.). (ENG.). 48p. (gr. 3-3). pap. 9.49 *(978-1-4109-4432-0(8)*, Raintree Freestyle Express); (gr. 3-3). lib. bdg. 34.65 *(978-1-4109-4425-2(5)*, Raintree Freestyle Express); (Illus.). (gr. 6-10). pap. 9.49 *(978-1-4109-4405-4(0)*, Raintree Freestyle); (Illus.). (gr. 6-10). lib. bdg. 34.65 *(978-1-4109-4398-9(4)*, Raintree Freestyle) Heinemann-Raintree.
Ritchey, Kate & Bader, Bonnie. Lion, Tiger, & Bear, Level 4. 2015. (Penguin Young Readers, Level 4 Ser.). (ENG., Illus.). 48p. (J). (gr. 3-4). pap. 3.99 *(978-0-448-48336-8(X)*, Penguin Young Readers) Penguin Young Readers Group.
Santomauro, Josie. The ASD Zoo of Kalamazoo. 2014. (ENG., Illus.). 52p. (J). lib. bdg. 10.77 net. *(978-1-937473-98-3(8))* Autism Asperger Publishing Co.

ANIMAL WELFARE

see Animals—Treatment

ANIMALS

see also Desert Animals; Domestic Animals; Forest Animals; Freshwater Animals; Game and Game Birds; Human-animal Relationships; Marine Animals; Natural History; Pets; Zoology; Zoos

also names of orders and classes of the animal kingdom (e.g. Birds; Insects; etc.); and names of animals, e.g. Dogs; Bears; etc.

The ABC of Animals. (Illus.). 44p. 9.95 *(978-1-55285-421-1(3)*, Walrus Bks.) Whitecap Bks., Ltd. CAN. Dist: Graphic Arts Ctr. Publishing Co.
Abdo Publishing. Animal Icons, 1 vol. 2013. (Animal Icons Ser.: 6). (ENG.). 32p. (J). (gr. 3-6). lib. bdg. 162.42 *(978-1-61783-566-7(8)*, Checkerboard Library) ABDO Publishing Co.
—Asian Animals, 1 vol. 2013. (Asian Animals Ser.: 6). (ENG.). 32p. (J). (gr. 2-5). lib. bdg. 171.00 *(978-1-61783-552-0(8)*, Big Buddy Bks.) ABDO Publishing Co.
ABDO Publishing. Bioindicator Species. 2016. (Bioindicator Species Ser.: 6). (ENG.). 48p. (J). (gr. 3-6). lib. bdg. 196.74 *(978-1-68078-007-9(7))* ABDO Publishing Co.
ABDO Publishing Company. Animal Kingdom Set 2, Set II. 2005. (Animal Kingdom Set II Ser.). (gr. k-4). 1026.00 *(978-1-59197-300-3(7)*, Buddy Bks.) ABDO Publishing Co.
—Great Predators: Set Of 8. 2013. (Great Predators Ser.: 8). 48p. (J). (gr. 3-6). lib. bdg. 262.32 *(978-1-61783-944-3(2))* ABDO Publishing Co.
ABDO Publishing Company Staff. Animals: Resource Guide. 2006. (Animals: Resource Guide Ser.). *(978-1-59679-977-6(3)*, Checkerboard Library) ABDO Publishing Co.
—Australian Animals, 1 vol. 2011. (Australian Animals Ser.). (ENG., Illus.). 32p. 171.00 *(978-1-61783-009-9(7)*, Big Buddy Bks.) ABDO Publishing Co.
—Critter Chronicles. 2007. (Critter Chronicles Ser.: 24). (ENG.). 24p. (J). (gr. k-3). lib. bdg. 581.04 *(978-1-59928-428-6(6)*, SandCastle) ABDO Publishing Co.
—South American Animals. 2014. (South American Animals Ser.: 6). (ENG.). 32p. (gr. 2-5). lib. bdg. 171.00 *(978-1-62403-188-5(9)*, Big Buddy Bks.) ABDO Publishing Co.
—This or That? 2014. (This or That? Ser.: 6). (ENG.). 24p. (gr. 5-10). lib. bdg. 153.90 *(978-1-62403-284-4(2)*, Super SandCastle) ABDO Publishing Co.
Ablow, Gail. A Horse in the House & Other Strange but True Animal Stories. Osborn, Kathy, illus. 2007. (ENG.). 40p. (J). (gr. 1-4). 17.99 *(978-0-7636-2838-3(7))* Candlewick Pr.
Accord Publishing Staff & Andrews McMeel Publishing, LLC Staff. Numbers: A Silly Slider Book. Cole, Jeff, illus. 2011. (ENG.). 12p. (J). (gr. -1-k). bds. 10.99 *(978-1-4494-0174-0(0))* Andrews McMeel Publishing.
Ackland, Nick. Animals. Bradley, Jennie, illus. 2017. (Busy Baby Ser.). (ENG.). 10p. (J). (gr. -1 — 1). bds. 6.99 *(978-0-7641-6892-5(4))* Barron's Educational Series, Inc.
—Animals. 2015. (Bright Beginnings Ser.). (ENG., Illus.). 20p. (J). (gr. -1 — 1). bds. 6.99 *(978-0-7641-6741-6(3))* Barron's Educational Series, Inc.
—Woof! Bradley, Jennie, illus. 2016. (Baby Sparkler Ser.). (ENG.). 10p. (J). (gr. -1 — 1). bds. 5.99 *(978-0-7641-6848-2(7))* Barron's Educational Series, Inc.
Acredolo, Linda & Goodwyn, Susan. Baby Signs for Animals. Gentieu, Penny, illus. 2003. (ENG.). 24p. (J). (gr. -1 — 1). bds. 6.99 *(978-0-06-009075-3(8)*, HarperFestival) HarperCollins Pubs.
—I Can Sign! Animals. 2007. (Baby Signs (Ideals) Ser.). (ENG., Illus.). 12p. (gr. -1). 9.99 *(978-0-8249-6709-3(7)*, Ideal Pubns.) Worthy Publishing.
Adams, Emma. Animals. 2016. (ENG.). 96p. pap. 17.95 *(978-1-78319-880-1(X))* Oberon Bks., Ltd. GBR. Dist: Consortium Bk. Sales & Distribution.
Adams, Simon, et al. Discover the Savage World. 2013. (Illus.). 224p. (J). *(978-1-4351-4990-8(4))* Barnes & Noble, Inc.
Adamson, Heather. Animals with Speed. 2010. (Our Animal World Ser.). 24p. (J). 25.65 *(978-1-60753-007-7(4))* Amicus Publishing.
—Big Animals. 2010. (Our Animal World Ser.). 24p. (J). 25.65 *(978-1-60753-008-4(2))* Amicus Publishing.
Africa. 2015. (FAYFT: the World of Endangered Animals Ser.). 64p. (gr. 4-10). lib. bdg. 39.95 *(978-1-78121-079-6(9))* Windmill Bks. Ltd. GBR. Dist: Black Rabbit Bks.
Alaina, Maria. Adding Animals, 1 vol. (Wonder Readers Next Steps: Math Ser.). (ENG.). (gr. -1-1). 2013. 20p. lib. bdg. 22.65 *(978-1-4765-0032-4(0))* 2011. 32p. pap. 5.99 *(978-1-4296-7832-2(1))* 2011. 16p. pap. 35.94 *(978-1-4296-8064-6(4))* Capstone Press of Coughlan Cos. (Wonder Readers).
Alexander, Florence & Alexander, Stanley. Come with Me & See... Animals of the World. 2003. (Illus.). 32p. 9.99 *(978-0-915960-60-6(5))* Ebon Research Systems Publishing, LLC.
Alexander, Florence, et al. Come with Me & See... A Total Eclipse in Africa. Alexander, Florence et al, illus. 2003. (ENG & SPA.). 40p. (J). 3.99 *(978-0-915960-50-7(8))* Ebon Research Systems Publishing, LLC.
Algarra, Alejandro & Bonilla, Rocio. How Do Animals Use Their Five Senses? 2016. (Curious Young Minds Ser.). (ENG., Illus.). 36p. (J). (gr. -1-2). pap. 7.99 *(978-1-4380-0891-2(0))* Barron's Educational Series, Inc.
All about Wild Animals, 10 bks. Incl. Chimpanzees. Gareth Stevens Publishing Staff, contrib. by. lib. bdg. 26.00 *(978-0-8368-4171-8(9))*; Dolphins. Gareth Stevens Editorial Staff. lib. bdg. 26.00 *(978-0-8368-4115-2(8))*; Giraffes. Gareth Stevens Publishing Staff, contrib. by. lib. bdg. 26.00 *(978-0-8368-4116-9(6))*; Hippos. Gareth Stevens Editorial Staff. lib. bdg. 26.00 *(978-0-8368-4118-3(2))*; Kangaroos. Gareth Stevens Publishing Staff, contrib. by. lib. bdg. 26.00 *(978-0-8368-4119-0(0))*; Pandas. Gareth Stevens Editorial Staff. lib. bdg. 26.00 *(978-0-8368-4121-3(2))*; Parrots. Gareth Stevens Editorial Staff. lib. bdg. 26.00 *(978-0-8368-4122-0(0))*; Spiders. Gareth Stevens Publishing Staff, contrib. by. lib. bdg. 26.00 *(978-0-8368-4172-5(7))*; Turtles. Gareth Stevens Publishing Staff, contrib. by. lib. bdg. 26.00 *(978-0-8368-4123-7(9))*; Wolves. Gareth Stevens Editorial Staff. lib. bdg. 26.00 *(978-0-8368-4124-4(7))*; 32p. (gr. k-4)., Gareth Stevens Learning Library (Illus.). 2004. Set lib. bdg. 226.00 o.p. *(978-0-8368-4114-5(X))* Stevens, Gareth Publishing LLLP.
Allaire, Caroline. Let's Look at the Stream. Hugo, Pierre de, illus. 2012. (ENG.). 38p. (J). (gr. 1-4). pap. 11.99 *(978-1-85103-359-1(9))* Moonlight Publishing, Ltd. GBR. Dist: Independent Pubs. Group.
Allgor, Marie. Endangered Grassland Animals. 2012. (Save Earth's Animals! Ser.). (ENG., Illus.). 24p. (J). (gr. k-5). pap. 8.25 *(978-1-4488-7498-9(X))*; lib. bdg. 22.60 *(978-1-4488-7425-5(4))* Rosen Publishing Group, Inc., The. (PowerKids Pr.).
—Endangered Tundra Animals. 2012. (Save Earth's Animals! Ser.). (ENG., Illus.). 24p. (J). (gr. k-5). pap. 8.25 *(978-1-4488-7494-1(7))*; lib. bdg. 22.60 *(978-1-4488-7421-7(1))* Rosen Publishing Group, Inc., The. (PowerKids Pr.).
Allman, Toney. Life in a Cave. 2004. (Ecosystems Ser.). (Illus.). 48p. (J). (gr. 4-7). 29.15 *(978-0-7377-3014-2(5)*, Greenhaven Pr., Inc.) Cengage Gale.
Aloian, Molly & Kalman, Bobbie. Des Animaux de Toutes Sortes. 2011. (Petit Monde Vivant (Small Living World) Ser.: No. 75). (FRE., Illus.). 32p. (J). pap. 10.95 *(978-2-89579-369-4(7))* Bayard Canada Livres CAN. Dist: Crabtree Publishing Co.
—Habitats Subterráneos. 2007. (Introduccion A los Habitats Ser.). (SPA., Illus.). 32p. (J). (gr. -1-3). lib. bdg. *(978-0-7787-8331-2(6))* Crabtree Publishing Co.
—Hábitats Subterráneos. rev. ed. 2007. (Introduction a Los Habitats Ser.). (SPA., Illus.). 32p. (J). (gr. k-3). pap. *(978-0-7787-8355-8(3))* Crabtree Publishing Co.
—Many Kinds of Animals. 2005. (What Kind of Animal Is It? Ser.). (ENG., Illus.). 32p. (J). lib. bdg. *(978-0-7787-2156-7(6))*; *(978-0-7787-7597-3(6))*; pap. *(978-0-7787-2214-4(7))* Crabtree Publishing Co.
—Muchos Tipos de Animales. 2006. (?Qui Tipo de Animal Es? Ser.). (SPA., Illus.). 32p. (J). (gr. 3-7). pap. *(978-0-7787-8868-3(7))*; lib. bdg. *(978-0-7787-8832-4(6))* Crabtree Publishing Co.
Altson, John. The A to Z of Forgotten Animals. 2010. 48p. pap. 19.99 *(978-1-4520-7891-5(2))* AuthorHouse.
Alvarez, Lourdes M. Mi Primer Libro Animales. Brooks, David, illus. 2005. (Mi primer libro Ser.). (SPA.). 9p. (J). (gr. -1 — 1). bds. 3.95 *(978-1-933050-04-1(7))* Sweetwater Pr.
—Mi Primer Libro Cosas. Brooks, David, illus. 2005. (Mi primer libro Ser.). (SPA.). 9p. (J). (gr. -1 — 1). bds. 3.95 *(978-1-933050-03-4(9))* Sweetwater Pr.
—Mi Primer Libro Formas. Brooks, David, illus. 2005. (Mi primer libro Ser.). (SPA.). 9p. (J). (gr. -1 — 1). bds. 3.95 *(978-1-933050-05-8(5))* Sweetwater Pr.
Amazing Animals. Date not set. (Illus.). 12p. (J). 3.98 *(978-1-4054-0496-9(5))* Parragon, Inc.
Amazing Eggs: Individual Title Six-Packs. (Discovery World Ser.). 16p. (gr. 1-2). 28.00 *(978-0-7635-8455-9(X))* Rigby Education.
American Animals: Set 2. 2013. (American Animals Ser.). 24p. (J). (gr. k-5). 135.60 *(978-1-4777-1146-0(5)*, PowerKids Pr.) Rosen Publishing Group, Inc., The.
American Animals: Sets 1 - 2. 2013. (American Animals Ser.). 24p. (J). (gr. k-5). 271.20 *(978-1-4777-1152-1(X))*; pap. 99.00 *(978-1-4777-2559-7(8))*; pap. 594.00 *(978-1-4777-2561-0(X))* Rosen Publishing Group, Inc., The. (PowerKids Pr.).
American Museum of Natural History. ABC Rainforest. 2016. (AMNH ABC Board Bks.). (ENG., Illus.). 18p. (J). (gr. -1-k). bds. 7.95 *(978-1-4549-1746-5(6))* Sterling Publishing Co., Inc.
American Museum of Natural History Staff. Spot the Animals: A Lift-the-Flap Book of Colors. 2012. (ENG., Illus.). 16p. (J). (gr. -1-2). bds. 6.95 *(978-1-4027-7723-3(X))* Sterling Publishing Co., Inc.
Amstutz, L. J. Investigating Animal Life Cycles. 2015. (ENG., Illus.). 40p. (J). (gr. 3-5). 29.32 *(978-1-4677-8057-5(X)*, Lerner Pubns.) Lerner Publishing Group.
Amstutz, Lisa J. Polar Animal Adaptations, 1 vol. 2011. (Amazing Animal Adaptations Ser.). (ENG.). 32p. (gr. 1-2). pap. 8.10 *(978-1-4296-7031-9(2))*; pap. 47.70 *(978-1-4296-7039-5(8))*; lib. bdg. 27.32 *(978-1-4296-6031-0(7))* Capstone Press of Coughlan Cos. (Aplus Bks.).
—Show Me Polar Animals: My First Picture Encyclopedia, 1 vol. 2013. (My First Picture Encyclopedias Ser.). (ENG.). 32p. (gr. 1-2). pap. 8.10 *(978-1-4765-3791-7(7))*; (Illus.). 7.95 *(978-1-62065-920-5(4))*; lib. bdg. 27.32 *(978-1-62065-059-2(2))* Capstone Press of Coughlan Cos. (Aplus Bks.).
—Thorny Devil Lizards & Other Extreme Reptile Adaptations, 1 vol. 2014. (Extreme Adaptations Ser.). (ENG.). 32p. (gr. 3-4). lib. bdg. 27.32 *(978-1-4914-0168-2(0))* Capstone Press of Coughlan Cos.
Amstutz, Lisa J., et al. Awesome African Animals. 2015. (Awesome African Animals! Ser.). (ENG.). 32p. (gr. 1-2). lib. bdg. 163.92 *(978-1-4914-1783-6(8)*, Aplus Bks.) Capstone Press of Coughlan Cos.
Anderson, Jill, ed. Let's Go on Safari!/Vamos de Safari! Utton, Peter, illus. 2005. (Word Play/Juegos con Pala Ser.). (ENG & SPA.). 20p. (J). (gr. -1-17). bds. 6.95 *(978-1-58728-522-6(3))* Cooper Square Publishing Llc.
Anderson, Melissa & Elrazky, Sumaiyah. Animals A-Z in Arabic - an Arabic / English Easy Reader. 2004. (ARA.). 23p. (J). per. 17.95 *(978-1-4116-0752-1(X))* Lulu Pr., Inc.
Anderson, Sheila. What Can Live in a Grassland? 2010. (First Step Nonfiction - Animal Adaptations Ser.). (ENG.). 24p. (gr. k-2). pap. 6.95 *(978-0-7613-5678-3(9))* Lerner Publishing Group.
—What Can Live in A Grassland? 2010. pap. 33.92 *(978-0-7613-6911-0(2))* Lerner Publishing Group.
—What Can Live in a Lake? 2010. (First Step Nonfiction - Animal Adaptations Ser.). (ENG., Illus.). 24p. (J). (gr. k-2). lib. bdg. 23.93 *(978-0-7613-4573-2(6))* Lerner Publishing Group.
—What Can Live in A Lake? 2010. pap. 33.92 *(978-0-7613-6910-3(4))* Lerner Publishing Group.
—What Can Live in the Mountains? 2010. pap. 33.92 *(978-0-7613-6909-7(0))*; (ENG.). 24p. pap. 6.95 *(978-0-7613-5676-9(2))*; (ENG., Illus.). 24p. (J). lib. bdg. 23.93 *(978-0-7613-4572-5(8))* Lerner Publishing Group.
Andreae, Giles. Mad about Mega Beasts! Wojtowycz, David, illus. 2015. (ENG.). 32p. (J). (gr. -1-k). pap. 9.99 *(978-1-4083-2936-8(0))* Hodder & Stoughton GBR. Dist: Hachette Bk. Group.
Andrus, Aubre. Now You See It! Small to Scary Animals. 2015. (ENG.). 64p. (J). (gr. 1-3). pap. 5.99 *(978-0-545-88960-5(X)*, Scholastic Paperbacks) Scholastic, Inc.
Animal 911: Environmental Threats. 2013. (Animal 911: Environmental Threats Ser.). 48p. (J). (gr. 3-5). 191.70 *(978-1-4339-9726-6(6))*; pap. 505.80 *(978-1-4339-9799-0(1))*; pap. 84.30 *(978-1-4339-9798-3(3))* Stevens, Gareth Publishing LLLP.
Animal ABCs. 2003. (Wipe-Off Activity Bks.). 16p. (J). (gr. 2). 3.79 *(978-1-58792-047-9(6))* Trend Enterprises, Inc.
Animal Adventures/Aventuras De Animales. 2005. 64p. (J). pap. 3.99 *(978-0-9762071-3-9(3))* Big City Publishing.
Animal Attack! Set 2, Vol. 1. 2014. (Animal Attack! Ser.). 32p. (J). (gr. 2-5). 135.60 *(978-1-4824-0537-8(7))* Stevens, Gareth Publishing LLLP.
Animal Attack! Sets 1 - 2, Vol. 1. 2014. (Animal Attack! Ser.). 32p. (J). (gr. 2-5). 271.20 *(978-1-4824-0611-5(X))* Stevens, Gareth Publishing LLLP.
Animal Builders. 2016. (Animal Builders Ser.). 24p. (J). pap. 49.32 *(978-1-5026-2423-9(0))* Cavendish Square Publishing.
Animal Camouflage [Scholastic]. 2010. (Hidden in Nature Ser.). pap. 2.08 *(978-1-4296-5050-2(8)*, Pebble Plus) Capstone Press of Coughlan Cos.
Animal Classifying Cards: Grasslands. 2004. (J). 9.95 *(978-1-56911-537-4(0))* Learning Resources, Inc.
Animal Clues: 6 Small Books. (gr. k-1). 35.00 *(978-0-7635-6226-7(2))* Rigby Education.
Animal Faces. 16p. (J). 1.89 *(978-0-7847-1020-3(1))* Standard Publishing.
Animal Facts, 4 vols., Set. 2005. (Animal Facts Ser.). (Illus.). 24p. (gr. 2-4). 92.00 *(978-0-7910-7279-0(7)*, Chelsea Hse.) Facts On File, Inc.
An Animal Family: Set 2. 2017. (Animal Family Ser.). 24p. (gr. k-k). pap. 48.90 ***(978-1-4824-6489-4(6))***; lib. bdg. 135.60 ***(978-1-4824-6487-0(X))*** Stevens, Gareth Publishing LLLP.
Animal Friends. 2009. 64p. (J). pap. *(978-0-7666-3562-3(7))* Modern Publishing.
The Animal Kingdom. 2005. (Animals, Animals, Animals Ser.). (YA). (gr. k-3). 178.20 *(978-0-7368-4207-5(1)*, Pebble Bks.) Capstone Press of Coughlan Cos.
The Animal Kingdom Series, 8 bks., Set 1. 2004. pap. 68.40 *(978-1-4109-1358-6(9))* Harcourt Schl. Pubs.
Animal Legs 6 Packs: Individual Title. (Discovery World Ser.). 12p. (gr. k-1). 28.00 *(978-0-7635-8449-8(5))* Rigby Education.
Animal Life Cycles. 2009. (Illus.). pap. 7.95 *(978-0-8225-4757-0(0))*Set. 2006. (J). 20.95 *(978-0-8225-4754-9(6))* Lerner Publishing Group.
Animal Lives: Animal Lives: Orang Utans, Bears, Eagles, Sharks, Crocodiles & Alligators, Tortoises, Giraffes, Bees & Wasps. 2007. (QEB Animal Lives Ser.). (J). per. *(978-1-59566-489-1(0))* QEB Publishing Inc.
Animal Look-Alikes. 2015. (Animal Look-Alikes Ser.). (ENG.). 24p. (J). (gr. 1-2). 135.60 *(978-1-4824-2544-4(0))*; pap., pap., pap. 48.90 *(978-1-4824-3437-8(7))*; pap., pap., pap. 293.40 *(978-1-4824-3436-1(9))* Stevens, Gareth Publishing LLLP.
Animal Mechanicals. 2016. (Animal Mechanicals Ser.). 32p. (gr. 3-3). 157.50 *(978-1-4994-2248-1(2))*; pap. 60.00 *(978-1-4994-2442-3(6))* Rosen Publishing Group, Inc., The. (PowerKids Pr.).
Animal Planet Staff. Finding Bigfoot: Everything You Need to Know. 2013. (ENG., Illus.). 160p. (J). (gr. 2-7). 19.99 *(978-1-250-04089-3(2)*, 9781250040893); pap. 14.99 *(978-1-250-04090-9(6)*, 9781250040909) Feiwel & Friends.
Animal Planet Staff, et al. Animals: A Visual Encyclopedia. 2015. (ENG., Illus.). 304p. (J). (gr. 3-7). 24.95 *(978-1-61893-153-5(9))* Time Inc. Bks.
Animal Predators: Complete Set. Incl. Animal Predators: Classroom Set. Lerner Publishing Group Staff. (Illus.). (J). 2005. 54.95 *(978-0-8225-5487-5(9))*; Crocodiles. (Illus.). 40p. (J). 2005. pap. 46.95 *(978-0-8225-5493-6(3))*; Great White Sharks. (Illus.). 40p. (J). 2005. pap. 46.95 *(978-0-8225-5488-2(7))*; Killer Whales. (Illus.). 40p. (J). 2005. pap. 46.95 *(978-0-8225-5492-9(5))*; Lions. (Illus.). 40p. (J). 2005. pap. 46.95 *(978-0-8225-5491-2(7))*; Owls. (Illus.). 40p. (J). 2005. pap. 46.95 *(978-0-8225-5490-5(9))*; Polar Bears. (Illus.). 40p. (J). 2005. pap. 46.95 *(978-0-8225-5489-5(5))*; Teaching Animal Predators. LernerClassroom Editors, ed. 2008. pap., tchr. ed. 7.95 *(978-0-8225-4044-1(4))*; Wolves: Easyreads - Level 1. (Illus.). 40p. (J). 2005. pap. 46.95 *(978-0-8225-5494-3(1))*; (gr. 3-6). 2005. 327.95 *(978-0-8225-3885-1(7))* Lerner Publishing Group.
Animal Q & A. 2014. (Animal Q & A Ser.). 24p. (J). (gr. k-3). 141.60 *(978-1-4777-9110-3(8))* Windmill Bks.
Animal Secrets Revealed! 2017. (Animal Secrets Revealed! Ser.). 48p. (gr. 4-4). pap. 70.20 ***(978-0-7660-8889-4(8))***; lib. bdg. 167.58 ***(978-0-7660-8589-3(9))*** Enslow Pubs., Inc.
Animal Stickers. 2004. (Art Rom Create Your Own... Ser.). (Illus.). 24p. (J). pap. incl. audio compact disk *(978-1-84229-736-0(8))* Top That! Publishing PLC.
Animal Superpowers. 2013. (Animal Superpowers Ser.). 24p. (J). (gr. k-5). 135.60 *(978-1-4777-1140-8(6))*; pap. 49.50 *(978-1-4777-1239-9(9))*; pap. 297.00 *(978-1-4777-1240-5(2))* Rosen Publishing Group, Inc., The. (PowerKids Pr.).
Animal Teamwork. 2017. (Animal Teamwork Ser.). 24p. (gr. 7-8). 141.60 ***(978-1-4994-3495-8(2))***; pap. 49.50 ***(978-1-5081-5371-9(X))*** Rosen Publishing Group, Inc., The. (PowerKids Pr.).
Animal Tracks: Level C, 6 vols. (Wonder Worldtm Ser.). 16p. 24.95 *(978-0-7802-1211-4(8))* Wright Group/McGraw-Hill.
Animales: Individual Title-Six Packs. (Chiquilibros Ser.). (SPA.). (gr. k-1). 23.00 *(978-0-7635-8607-2(2))* Rigby Education.
Animales, animales, animales Interactive Packages: Animales grandes y Pequeños. (Pebble Soup Exploraciones Ser.). (SPA.). (gr. -1-18). 52.00 *(978-0-7578-5261-9(0))* Rigby Education.
Animales, animales, animales Interactive Packages: Donde viven los Animales. (Pebble Soup Exploraciones Ser.). (SPA.). (gr. -1-18). 52.00 *(978-0-7578-5260-2(2))* Rigby Education.
Animales Con Escamas, 6 vols. (Explorers. Exploradores Nonfiction Sets Ser.). (SPA.). 32p. (gr. 3-6). 44.95 *(978-0-7699-0630-0(3))* Shortland Pubns. (U. S. A.) Inc.
Animales de la Granja. 2005. (Collection Abre Tus Ojos, Collection Eye Openers Ser.).Tr. of Barnyard Animals. (SPA.). (J). (gr. k-2). 6.95 *(978-950-11-0901-6(1))* Sigmar ARG. Dist: Iaconi, Mariuccia Bk. Imports.
Animales Del Zoologico. 2005. (Collection Abre Tus Ojos, Collection Eye Openers Ser.).Tr. of Zoo Animals. (SPA.). (J). (gr. k-2). 6.95 *(978-950-11-0898-9(8))* Sigmar ARG. Dist: Iaconi, Mariuccia Bk. Imports.
Animales Peligrosos, 6 vols., Vol. 3. (Explorers. Exploradores Nonfiction Sets Ser.). (SPA.). (gr. 3-6). *(978-0-7699-0649-2(4))* Shortland Pubns. (U. S. A.) Inc.
Animals. 2010. (Discovering the Earth Ser.). (Illus.). 224p. (C). (gr. 9-18). 39.95 *(978-0-8160-6101-3(7))* Facts On File, Inc.
Animals: Individual Title-Six Packs. (Chiquilibros Ser.). (gr. k-1). 23.00 *(978-0-7635-0428-1(9))* Rigby Education.
Animals: KinderFacts Individual Title Six-Packs. (Kinderstarters Ser.). 8p. (gr. -1-1). 21.00 *(978-0-7635-8739-0(7))* Rigby Education.
Animals & Their Sounds. 2004. (J). per. 15.99 *(978-0-9759122-2-5(4))* Golden Eagle Publishing Hse., Inc.
Animals Animals, 6 bks., Group 6. Incl. Buffalo. Perry, Phyllis J. lib. bdg. 29.93 *(978-0-7614-1866-5(0))*; Kangaroos.

Jango-Cohen, Judith. (J). lib. bdg. 29.93 (978-0-7614-1869-6(5)); Moose. Estigarribia, Diana. lib. bdg. 29.93 (978-0-7614-1870-2(9)); Porcupines. Jango-Cohen, Judith. (J). lib. bdg. (978-0-7614-1868-9(7)); Zebras. Noble-Goodman, Katherine. lib. bdg. 29.93 (978-0-7614-1871-9(7)); (Illus.). 48p. (gr. 3-7). 2005. 179.57 (978-0-7614-1865-8(2), Benchmark Bks.) Marshall Cavendish Corp.

Animals Animals, 6 vols., Group 8. Incl. Beavers. Mara, Wil. (Illus.). lib. bdg. 29.93 (978-0-7614-2524-3(1), Benchmark Bks.); Koalas. Otfinoski, Steven. (Illus.). lib. bdg. 29.93 (978-0-7614-2526-7(8), Benchmark Bks.); Otters. Mara, Wil. lib. bdg. 29.93 (978-0-7614-2527-4(6), Benchmark Bks.); Rabbits. Stewart, Melissa. (Illus.). lib. bdg. 29.93 (978-0-7614-2528-1(4)); Seahorses. Otfinoski, Steven. (Illus.). lib. bdg. 29.93 (978-0-7614-2529-8(2)); Swans. Stewart, Melissa. (Illus.). lib. bdg. 29.93 (978-0-7614-2530-4(6)); 48p. (gr. 3-7). (Animals Animals 8 Ser.). 2007. Set lib. bdg. 179.58 (978-0-7614-2523-6(3), Benchmark Bks.) Marshall Cavendish Corp.

Animals, Animals, Animals Interactive Packages: Animals Big & Little. (Pebble Soup Explorations Ser.). (gr. -1-18). 52.00 (978-0-7578-5237-4(8)) Rigby Education.

Animals, Animals, Animals Interactive Packages: Where Animals Live. (Pebble Soup Explorations Ser.). (gr. -1-18). 52.00 (978-0-7578-5236-7(X)) Rigby Education.

Animals Animals Group 7, 6 bks., Set. Incl. Anteaters. Rebman, Renee C. (J). lib. bdg. 29.93 (978-0-7614-2234-1(X)); Bees. Jango-Cohen, Judith. lib. bdg. 29.93 (978-0-7614-2235-8(8)); Eagles. Nobleman, Marc Tyler. (J). lib. bdg. 28.50 (978-0-7614-2236-5(6)); Foxes. Nobleman, Marc Tyler. lib. bdg. 29.93 (978-0-7614-2237-2(4)); Hippopotamuses. Jango-Cohen, Judith. lib. bdg. 29.93 (978-0-7614-2238-9(2)); Turtles & Tortoises. Rebman, Renee C. lib. bdg. 29.93 (978-0-7614-2239-6(0)); (Illus.). 48p. (gr. 3-7). 2006. 2006. Set lib. bdg. 171.00 (978-0-7614-2233-4(1), Benchmark Bks.) Marshall Cavendish Corp.

Animals Animals Group 9, 6 bks., Set. Incl. Alligators. Otfinoski, Steven. (Illus.). lib. bdg. 29.93 (978-0-7614-2930-2(1)); Coyotes. Mara, Wil. (Illus.). (J). lib. bdg. 29.93 (978-0-7614-2928-9(X)); Deer. Mara, Wil. (Illus.). lib. bdg. 29.93 (978-0-7614-2926-5(3)); Ducks. Mara, Wil. (Illus.). lib. bdg. 29.93 (978-0-7614-2927-2(1)); Hummingbirds. Otfinoski, Steven. lib. bdg. 29.93 (978-0-7614-2932-6(8)); Skunks. Otfinoski, Steven. lib. bdg. 29.93 (978-0-7614-2929-6(8)); 48p. (gr. 3-18). (Animals Animals 9 Ser.). 2008. Set lib. bdg. 179.58 (978-0-7614-2925-8(5), Benchmark Bks.) Marshall Cavendish Corp.

Animals Animals Series - Group 3, 6 bks., Set. 153.86 (978-0-7614-1442-1(8), Benchmark Bks.) Marshall Cavendish Corp.

Animals Are Wild! 2016. (Animals Are Wild! Ser.). 40p. (gr. 4-3). pap. 84.30 (978-1-4824-5307-2(X)); lib. bdg. 191.70 (978-1-4824-4971-6(4)) Stevens, Gareth Publishing LLLP.

Animals at Work: Individual Title Six-Packs. (gr. k-1). 23.00 (978-0-7635-9060-4(6)) Rigby Education.

Animals Classroom Library. (gr. k-2). lib. bdg. 90.95 (978-0-7368-7135-8(7)) Red Brick Learning.

Animals Far & Wide. (Magnets on the Move Ser.). 8p. (J). bds. (978-2-7643-0102-9(2)) Phidal Publishing, Inc./Editions Phidal, Inc.

Animals from Head to Tail. 2016. (Animals from Head to Tail Ser.). 24p. (gr. k-k). pap. 48.90 (978-1-4824-5309-6(6)); lib. bdg. 135.60 (978-1-4824-4516-9(6)) Stevens, Gareth Publishing LLLP.

Animals (Gr. 1-2) 2003. (J). (978-1-58232-073-1(X)) ECS Learning Systems, Inc.

Animals II Classroom Library. (gr. k-2). lib. bdg. 54.95 (978-0-7368-9127-1(7)) Red Brick Learning.

Animals II Complete Unit. (gr. k-2). 311.95 (978-0-7368-9128-8(5)) Red Brick Learning.

Animals in My World. 2017. (Animals in My World Ser.). 24p. (gr. 4-6). 141.60 **(978-1-5081-6173-8(9))**; pap. 49.50 **(978-1-5081-6174-5(7))** Rosen Publishing Group, Inc., The. (PowerKids Pr.).

Animals of Mass Destruction. 2014. (Animals of Mass Destruction Ser.). 32p. (J). (gr. 2-5). 151.50 (978-1-4824-1045-7(1)); pap. 63.00 (978-1-4824-1551-3(8)) Stevens, Gareth Publishing LLLP.

Animals of the Night. 2015. (Animals of the Night Ser.). (ENG.). 32p. (J). (gr. 3-4). 151.62 (978-0-7660-6676-2(2)); pap., pap., pap. 378.72 (978-0-7660-6677-9(0)) Enslow Pubs., Inc.

Animals of the Night: Set 3. 2016. (Animals of the Night Ser.). 32p. (gr. 3-3). pap. 63.12 (978-0-7660-7965-6(1)); lib. bdg. 151.62 (978-0-7660-7495-8(1)) Enslow Pubs., Inc.

Animals on the Edge. 2010. (Animals on the Edge Ser.). (ENG.). 32p. (gr. 3-4). lib. bdg. 136.60 (978-1-4296-5404-3(X), Fact Finders) Capstone Press of Coughlan Cos.

Animals on the Go! (Flip Flap Fun Book Ser.). (Illus.). 10p. (J). bds. (978-2-7643-0041-1(7)) Phidal Publishing, Inc./Editions Phidal, Inc.

Animals Set 1: Cats, Dogs & Other Pets. 2005. (J). spiral bd. 23.40 (978-0-9770248-7-2(3)) Sidedoor Publishing LLC.

Animals Who Help Us: Chapters Indigo QEB Canadian Edition. 2007. (J). per. (978-1-59566-465-5(3)) QEB Publishing Inc.

Animals with Super Powers, 4 vols., Set. Incl. Color-Changing Animals. Yaw, Valerie. lib. bdg. 22.61 (978-1-61772-122-9(0)); Electric Animals. Lunis, Natalie. lib. bdg. 22.61 (978-1-61772-121-2(2)); Glow-in-the-Dark Animals. Lunis, Natalie. lib. bdg. 22.61 (978-1-61772-119-9(0)); See-Through Animals. Lunis, Natalie. lib. bdg. 22.61 (978-1-61772-120-5(4)); (YA). (gr. 2-5). 2011. (Animals with Super Powers Ser.). 24p. 2014. 135.68 (978-1-61772-118-2(2)) Bearport Publishing Co., Inc.

Animals Working Together. 2011. (Animals Working Together Ser.). (ENG.). 24p. (gr. k-1). pap. 166.80 (978-1-4296-6370-0(7), Pebble Plus) Capstone Press of Coughlan Cos.

AnimalWays, 5 bks., Group 5. Incl. Butterflies. Schlaepfer, Gloria G. 104p. (J). (gr. 4-7). lib. bdg. 24.95 (978-0-7614-1745-3(1)); Hawks. Warhol, Tom. 104p. (gr. 6-7). lib. bdg. 24.95 (978-0-7614-1744-6(3), Benchmark Bks.); Lions. Stefoff, Rebecca. 104p. (gr. 6-7). lib. bdg. 24.95 (978-0-7614-1746-0(X), Benchmark Bks.); Penguins. Stefoff, Rebecca. 112p. (J). (gr. 3-7). lib. bdg. (978-0-7614-1743-9(5), Benchmark Bks.); Spiders. Zabludoff, Marc. 112p. (J). (gr. 3-7). lib. bdg. (978-0-7614-1747-7(8), Benchmark Bks.); (Illus.). 2005. o.p. (978-0-7614-1742-2(7), Benchmark Bks.) Marshall Cavendish Corp.

AnimalWays - Group 3. 156.79 (978-0-7614-1388-2(X), Benchmark Bks.) Marshall Cavendish Corp.

Animaux de la Savane. 16.95 (978-2-03-553030-1(X)) Librairie Larousse FRA. Dist: Distribooks, Inc.

Annino, J. G. Florida's Famous Animals: True Stories of Sunset Sam the Dolphin, Snooty the Manatee, Big Guy the Panther, & Others. 2008. (ENG., Illus.). 160p. per. 9.95 (978-0-7627-4136-6(8)) Globe Pequot Pr., The.

Apseloff, Stanford S. African Animals Alphabet Book. 2010. (Illus.). (J). (978-0-9647934-8-4(2)) Ohio Distinctive Publishing, Inc.

Arita, Vera. Animals Sing Aloha. Louie, Ron, illus. 2009. (ENG.). 20p. (J). (gr. -1-1). bds. 7.95 (978-1-933067-29-2(2)) Beachhouse Publishing, LLC.

Arlon, Penelope. Animal Faces. 2014. (Scholastic Discover More Ser.). (ENG.). 32p. (J). (gr. -1-3). 7.99 (978-0-545-79121-2(9)) Scholastic, Inc.

—Big Book of Animals. 2017. (LEGO Nonfiction Ser.). (ENG.). 128p. (J). (gr. -1-3). 14.99 (978-1-338-13007-2(2)) Scholastic, Inc.

Arlon, Penelope & Hayes, Susan. Polar Animals. 2014. (Scholastic Discover More Ser.). (ENG., Illus.). 80p. (J). (gr. 3-7). 12.99 (978-0-545-66777-7(1), Scholastic Reference) Scholastic, Inc.

Arlon, Penelope & Tuchman, Gail. Scholastic Discover More Reader Level 1: Petting Zoo. 2013. (Scholastic Discover More Reader Level 1 Ser.). (ENG.). 32p. (J). (gr. -1-2). pap. 3.99 (978-0-545-63631-5(0), Scholastic Reference) Scholastic, Inc.

Armadillo. Let's Look & See: Animals. 2014. (ENG., Illus.). 24p. (J). (gr. k-2). bds. 6.99 (978-1-86147-376-9(1), Armadillo) Anness Publishing GBR. Dist: National Bk. Network.

Armentrout, David & Armentrout, Patricia. Animals That Fly & Birds That Don't. 2008. (Illus.). 32p. (J). 28.50 (978-1-60472-300-7(9)) Rourke Educational Media.

—Crafty Critters. 2008. (Illus.). 32p. (J). 28.50 (978-1-60472-302-1(5)) Rourke Educational Media.

—Speed Demons. 2008. (Illus.). 32p. (J). 28.50 (978-1-60472-305-2(X)) Rourke Educational Media.

Arnold, Caroline. Caroline Arnold's Animals, 8 vols., Set. Arnold, Caroline, illus. Incl. Penguin's World. 2006. 27.99 (978-1-4048-1323-6(3), 1253185); Wombat's World. 2008. lib. bdg. 27.99 (978-1-4048-3986-1(0)); (Illus.). (J). (gr. k-2). (Caroline Arnold's Animals Ser.). (ENG.). 24p. 2008. Set lib. bdg. 55.98 (978-1-4048-4364-6(7)) Picture Window Bks.

—A Walrus' World, 1 vol. Arnold, Caroline, illus. 2010. (Caroline Arnold's Animals Ser.). (ENG., Illus.). 24p. (gr. k-2). lib. bdg. 27.99 (978-1-4048-5744-5(3)) Picture Window Bks.

—A Warmer World. Hogan, Jamie, illus. 2012. (ENG.). 32p. (J). (gr. 2-5). pap. 7.95 (978-1-58089-267-4(1)) Charlesbridge Publishing, Inc.

Arnold, Nick & ARNOLD, NICK. Esa Repelente Naturaleza. 2003. (Coleccion Esa Horrible Cienca). (SPA., Illus.). 158p. (YA). (978-84-272-2053-9(7), ML8314) Molino, Editorial ESP. Dist: Lectorum Pubns., Inc.

Arnosky, Jim. The Frozen Wild: How Animals Survive in the Coldest Places on Earth. 2015. (ENG., Illus.). 40p. (J). (gr. 1-5). 14.95 (978-1-4549-1025-1(9), 1394159) Sterling Publishing Co., Inc.

—Tooth & Claw: The Wild World of Big Predators. 2014. (ENG., Illus.). 32p. (J). (gr. 1-5). 14.95 (978-1-4027-8624-2(7)) Sterling Publishing Co., Inc.

Aronin, Miriam. Black-Footed Ferrets: Back from the Brink. 2007. (America's Animal Comebacks Ser.). (Illus.). 32p. (YA). (gr. 2-5). lib. bdg. 25.27 (978-1-59716-506-8(9)) Bearport Publishing Co., Inc.

—Saving Animals from Volcanoes. 2011. (Rescuing Animals from Disasters Ser.). 32p. (YA). (gr. 2-5). lib. bdg. 25.27 (978-1-61772-291-2(X)) Bearport Publishing Co., Inc.

Arrhenius, Ingela P. Animals. Arrhenius, Ingela P., illus. 2016. (ENG., Illus.). 40p. (J). (gr. -1-2). 22.00 (978-0-7636-9268-1(9)) Candlewick Pr.

Art with Animals! (Learning Ser.). 22p. (J). bds. (978-2-7643-0164-7(2)) Phidal Publishing, Inc./Editions Phidal, Inc.

Artell, Mike. Backyard Bloodsuckers: Questions, Facts & Tongue Twisters about Creepy Crawlers. 2004. (Illus.). 80p. pap. 14.95 (978-0-673-59248-4(0)) Good Year Bks.

Asian Animals. 2010. (Asian Animals Ser.). (ENG.). 24p. (gr. k-1). pap. 36.45 (978-1-4296-5170-7(9)); pap. 36.45 (978-1-4296-4987-2(9)); lib. bdg. 53.30 (978-1-4296-4413-6(3)) Capstone Press of Coughlan Cos. (Pebble Plus).

Asian Animals [Capstone Sole Source]. 2010. (Asian Animals Ser.). 24p. lib. bdg. 143.94 (978-1-4296-5842-3(8), Pebble Plus) Capstone Press of Coughlan Cos.

Asper-Smith, Sarah. Have You Ever Seen a Smack of Jellyfish? An Alphabet Book. 2010. (ENG., Illus.). 32p. (J). (gr. -1-2). 16.99 (978-1-57061-687-7(6), Little Bigfoot) Sasquatch Bks.

Australian Animals [Capstone Sole Source]. 2010. (Australian Animals Ser.). 24p. lib. bdg. 191.92 (978-1-4296-5843-0(6), Pebble Plus) Capstone Press of Coughlan Cos.

Awa, Simon, et al. Uumajut: Learn about Arctic Wildlife, 1 vol. Caron, Romi, illus. 2010. (ENG.). 32p. (J). (gr. 1-3). pap. 9.95 (978-1-926569-08-6(3)) Inhabit Media Inc. CAN. Dist: Independent Pubs. Group.

—Uumajut Vol. 2: Learn More about Arctic Wildlife!, 1 vol., Vol. 2. Otak, Leah, tr. Caron, Romi, illus. 2011. (ENG.). 32p. (J). (gr. 1-3). pap. 9.95 (978-1-926569-22-2(9)) Inhabit Media Inc. CAN. Dist: Independent Pubs. Group.

Awesome Animal Trivia. 2013. (Ultimate Trivia Challenge Ser.). 32p. (J). (gr. 2-5). pap. 63.00 (978-1-4339-8290-3(0)) Stevens, Gareth Publishing LLLP.

Awesome Animals. 2013. (J). pap. (978-1-4222-2789-3(8)) Mason Crest.

Awesome Armored Animals. 2013. (Awesome Armored Animals Ser.). 24p. (J). (gr. k-5). 135.60 (978-1-4777-1147-7(3)); pap. 297.00 (978-1-4777-1534-5(7)); pap. 49.50 (978-1-4777-1533-8(9)) Rosen Publishing Group, Inc., The. (PowerKids Pr.).

Axelrod-Contrada, Joan. Animal Debate: A Rip-Roaring Game of Either-Or Questions. 2012. (This or That? Ser.). (ENG.). 32p. (gr. 3-4). lib. bdg. 27.99 (978-1-4296-8593-1(X)) Capstone Press of Coughlan Cos.

—Animal Debate: A Rip-Roaring Game of Either/Or Questions. 2012. (This or That? Ser.). (ENG.). 32p. (gr. 3-4). pap. 8.29 (978-1-4296-9272-4(3)) Capstone Press of Coughlan Cos.

—This or That Animal Debate: A Rip-Roaring Game of Either/or Questions. 2012. (This or That? Ser.). (ENG.). 32p. (gr. 3-4). pap. 47.70 (978-1-4296-9273-1(1), Edge Bks.) Capstone Press of Coughlan Cos.

Ayers, Amy. Contando en el Zoologico. 2007. (Las matematicas en nuestro mundo (Spanish- Math in Our World) Ser.). (SPA.). 8p. (gr. 1-2). pap. 8.15 (978-0-8368-8496-8(5), Weekly Reader Leveled Readers) Stevens, Gareth Publishing LLLP.

—Counting at the Zoo. 2007. (Math in Our World Ser.). (Illus.). 24p. (gr. 1-2). lib. bdg. 22.00 (978-0-8368-8469-2(8), Weekly Reader Leveled Readers) Stevens, Gareth Publishing LLLP.

AZ Books, creator. Farm Animals. 2012. (Touch & Feel Ser.). (ENG., Illus.). 10p. (J). (gr. -1 — 1). bds. 12.95 (978-1-61889-223-2(1)) AZ Bks. LLC.

—In the Noisy Forest. 2013. (Talking Flaps Ser.). (ENG., Illus.). 10p. (J). (gr. -1-k). bds. 9.95 (978-1-61889-086-3(7)) AZ Bks. LLC.

—Pond Animals. 2013. (Touch & Feel Ser.). (ENG., Illus.). 10p. (J). (gr. -1-k). bds. 12.95 (978-1-61889-224-9(X)) AZ Bks. LLC.

AZ Books Staff. Animals. Slusar, Julia, ed. 2012. (Pull It Out Ser.). (ENG.). 10p. (J). (gr. -1 — 1). 7.95 (978-1-61889-195-2(2)) AZ Bks. LLC.

—Discovering the Savanna. Gorojan, Elena, ed. 2012. (Wild Theater Ser.). (ENG.). 8p. (J). (gr. -1-3). bds. 17.95 (978-1-61889-017-7(4)) AZ Bks. LLC.

—Visiting Africa. Zuk, Valentina, ed. 2012. (Lively Pictures Ser.). (ENG.). 10p. (J). (gr. -1-k). bds. 9.95 (978-1-61889-179-2(0)) AZ Bks. LLC.

—Visiting the Forest. Zuk, Valentina, ed. 2012. (Lively Pictures Ser.). (ENG.). 10p. (J). (gr. -1-k). bds. 9.95 (978-1-61889-178-5(2)) AZ Bks. LLC.

B&H Kids Editorial Staff. Mix & Match: Fun with God's Animals. 2017. (ENG.). 32p. (J). (gr. -1 — 1). 12.99 (978-1-4336-4315-6(4), B&H Kids) B&H Publishing Group.

Baby's First Animal Book. 2004. 10p. (J). bds. 4.99 (978-1-85854-921-7(3)) Brimax Books Ltd. GBR. Dist: Byeway Bks.

Backpack Books (Firm) Staff, contrib. by. My Big Animal Book: Includes Touch-And-Feel, Flaps, Pull-Out Tabs, & a Puzzle! 2005. (Illus.). (J). (978-0-7607-6966-9(4)) backpackbook.

Backshall, Steve. Steve Backshall Annual 2017. 2016. (Steve Backshall Ser.). (ENG.). 64p. (J). (gr. 4-6). 10.99 (978-1-5101-0156-2(X), Orion Children's Bks.) Hachette Children's Group GBR. Dist: Hachette Bk. Group.

Backyard Wildlife Level 1: Early Emergent, 4 vols., Set. Incl. Beavers. Green, Emily K. (Illus.). lib. bdg. 22.00 (978-0-531-20136-7(8)); Opossums. Green, Emily. lib. bdg. 22.00 (978-0-531-20137-4(6)); Porcupines. Green, Emily. lib. bdg. 22.00 (978-0-531-20488-7(X)); Wolves. Green, Emily. lib. bdg. 22.00 (978-0-531-20489-4(8)); 24p. (J). (gr. k-1). 2011. Set lib. bdg. 88.00 (978-0-531-23925-4(X), Children's Pr.) Scholastic Library Publishing.

Bad to the Bone: Nastiest Animals. 2015. (Bad to the Bone: Nastiest Animals Ser.). (ENG.). 24p. (J). (gr. 2-3). 135.60 (978-1-4824-1643-5(3)) Stevens, Gareth Publishing LLLP.

Baggott, Stella. Baby's Very First Touchy-Feely Animals Book. 2011. (Baby's Very First Ser.). 10p. (J). ring bd. 7.99 (978-0-7945-2895-9(3), Usborne) EDC Publishing.

Bailey, Diane. Arctic Wildlife. 2017. (J). **(978-1-4222-3863-9(6))** Mason Crest.

Baillie, Marilyn, et al. How to Save a Species. 2014. (ENG.). 48p. (J). (gr. 3-7). 17.95 (978-1-77147-063-6(1), Owlkids) Owlkids Bks. Inc. CAN. Dist: Publishers Group West (PGW).

Baines, Becky. National Geographic Kids Funny Fill-In: My Safari Adventure. 2014. (NG Kids Funny Fill In Ser.). (ENG.). 48p. (J). (gr. 3-7). pap. 4.99 (978-1-4263-1708-8(5), National Geographic Children's Bks.) National Geographic Society.

Baker, Charles F., ed. Wild Animals: Lions, Tigers, Bears, & More! 2005. (ENG., Illus.). 32p. (J). (gr. 1-5). 17.95 (978-0-8126-7928-1(8)) Cobblestone Publishing Co.

Baker, Robin J., et al. Awesome Animal Designs. 2012. (Adult Coloring Ser.). (ENG., Illus.). 64p. (gr. 3). pap. 5.99 (978-0-486-49135-6(8)) Dover Pubns., Inc.

Ballard, Carol. Animal Animal Variation & Classification. 2017. (Living Processes Ser.). (ENG., Illus.). 48p. (J). (gr. 7-11). pap. 11.99 (978-0-7502-9633-5(X), Wayland) Hachette Children's Group GBR. Dist: Hachette Bk. Group.

Balloon Books Staff, ed. Wild Animals Board Book. 2003. (Animal Bring-Along Bks.). (Illus.). 32p. (J). bds. 5.95 (978-0-8069-8965-5(3)) Sterling Publishing Co., Inc.

Baltazar, Art, illus. DC Super-Pets, 12 vols., Set. Incl. Attack of the Invisible Cats. Sonneborn, Scott. lib. bdg. 23.99 (978-1-4048-6481-8(4)); Backward Bowwow. Stephens, Sarah Hines. lib. bdg. 23.99 (978-1-4048-6480-1(6)); Battle Bugs of Outer Space. Mason, Jane B. lib. bdg. 23.99 (978-1-4048-6482-5(2)); Fastest Pet on Earth. Bright, J. E. lib. bdg. 23.99 (978-1-4048-6264-7(1)); Heroes of the High Seas. Bright, J. E. 23.99 (978-1-4048-6263-0(3)); Hopping Hero. Sazaklis, John. lib. bdg. 23.99 (978-1-4048-6477-1(6)); Midway Monkey Madness. Stephens, Sarah. lib. bdg. 23.99 (978-1-4048-6305-7(2)); Pooches of Power! Stephens, Sarah. lib. bdg. 23.99 (978-1-4048-6306-4(0)); Royal Rodent Rescue. Sazaklis, John. lib. bdg. 23.99 (978-1-4048-6307-1(9)); Salamander Smackdown! Sazaklis, John. lib. bdg. 23.99 (978-1-4048-6478-8(4)); Super Hero Splash Down. Mason, Jane B. lib. bdg. 23.99 (978-1-4048-6357-6(5)); Superpowered Pony. Stephens, Sarah Hines. lib. bdg. 23.99 (978-1-4048-6479-5(2)); (gr. 2-2). (DC Super-Pets Ser.). (ENG., Illus.). 56p. 2011. Set lib. bdg. 287.88 (978-1-4048-6774-1(0), DC Super-Pets) Picture Window Bks.

Bampton, Bob, illus. Animals in the Wild. 2004. (Look & Learn about Ser.). 18p. (J). bds. 5.99 (978-1-85854-351-2(7)) Brimax Books Ltd. GBR. Dist: Byeway Bks.

Barbaresi, Nina. Animal Firefighters Stickers. 2004. (Dover Little Activity Books Stickers Ser.). (ENG., Illus.). 4p. (J). (gr. k-3). pap. 1.50 (978-0-486-43451-3(6)) Dover Pubns., Inc.

Barlowe, Dot. Grand Canyon Plants & Animals. 2010. (Dover Nature Coloring Book Ser.). (ENG., Illus.). 32p. (gr. 3-8). pap. 3.99 (978-0-486-47294-2(9)) Dover Pubns., Inc.

Barman, Adrienne. Creaturepedia. 2015. (Creaturepedia Ser.). (ENG., Illus.). 216p. (J). 22.99 (978-1-84780-634-5(1), Wide Eyed Editions) Quarto Publishing Group UK GBR. Dist: Littlehampton Bk Services, Ltd.

Barner, Bob. Animals! Matching Game. 2011. (ENG.). 72p. (J). (gr. -1-17). bds. 14.99 (978-1-4521-0055-5(1)) Chronicle Bks. LLC.

Barnham, Kay. Animal Rights. 2004. (21st Century Issues Ser.). (Illus.). 48p. (gr. 5-12). lib. bdg. 31.00 (978-0-8368-5642-2(2), Gareth Stevens Secondary Library) Stevens, Gareth Publishing LLLP.

Barnhill, Kelly. Animals with No Eyes: Cave Adaptation. 2016. (Extreme Life Ser.). (ENG.). 32p. pap. 8.10 (978-1-5157-6283-6(1), Fact Finders) Capstone Press of Coughlan Cos.

Barr, Brady. Chomp! Fierce Facts about the BITE FORCE, CRUSHING JAWS, & MIGHTY TEETH of Earth's Champion Chewers. 2017. (ENG.). 96p. (J). (gr. 2-5). lib. bdg. 22.90 (978-1-4263-2840-4(0), National Geographic Children's Bks.) National Geographic Society.

Barraclough, Sue. Animal Characteristics. 2016. (Investigate! Ser.). (ENG.). 32p. pap. 7.99 (978-1-4846-4019-7(5), NA-h) Heinemann-Raintree.

Barrett, Jennifer & Barrett, Judi. The Snake Is Totally Tail. 2007. (ENG.). 32p. (J). (gr. -1-2). 8.99 (978-1-4169-6845-0(8), Aladdin) Simon & Schuster Children's Publishing.

Barrett, Judi. Los Animales No Deven Actuar Como la Gente. (SPA., Illus.). (J). (gr. k-1). pap. (978-950-515-807-2(6), FL5250) De La Flor ARG. Dist: Lectorum Pubns., Inc.

—Animals Should Definitely Not Act Like People. Barrett, Ron, illus. pap. 35.95 incl. audio compact disk (978-1-59112-827-4(7)); (J). pap. 33.95 incl. audio (978-0-87499-232-8(X)) Live Oak Media.

Base, Graeme. The Water Hole. Base, Graeme, illus. 2004. (ENG., Illus.). 32p. (J). (gr. k-3). reprint ed. pap. 8.99 (978-0-14-240197-2(8), Puffin Books) Penguin Young Readers Group.

Bateman, Donna M. Deep in the Swamp. Lies, Brian, illus. 2007. (ENG.). 32p. (J). (gr. -1-3). 16.95 (978-1-57091-596-3(2)); pap. 7.95 (978-1-57091-597-0(0)) Charlesbridge Publishing, Inc.

Batten, Mary. Aliens from Earth: When Animals & Plants Invade Other Ecosystems, 1 vol. Doyle, Beverly, illus. 2003. (ENG.). 32p. (J). (gr. 3-7). 15.95 (978-1-56145-236-1(X)) Peachtree Pubs.

Bauer, David. Adding Arctic Animals, 6 vols., Set. 2003. (Yellow Umbrella Early Level Ser.). (ENG.). 16p. (gr. k-1). pap. 35.70 (978-0-7368-2990-8(3), Yellow Umbrella Bks.) Capstone Press of Coughlan Cos.

Be a Plant Scientist: Level L, 6 vols. (Take-Twostm Ser.). 16p. 36.95 (978-0-322-03403-7(5)) Wright Group/McGraw-Hill.

Beach, Stewart. Good Morning-Sun's Up. Sugita, Yataka, illus. 32p. (J). (gr. -1-3). 13.95 (978-0-87592-021-4(7)) Scroll Pr., Inc.

Beaton, Clare. Animals Count Dominoes. gif. ed. (J). 14.99 (978-0-7353-1811-3(5)) Galison.

Beaumont, Holly. Why Do Snails & Other Animals Have Shells? 2015. (Animal Body Coverings Ser.). (ENG., Illus.). 24p. (gr. 1-3). 23.32 (978-1-4846-2536-1(6)) Heinemann-Raintree.

Los Bebes Animales y Sus Mamas.Tr. of Animal Babies & Their Moms. (SPA.). (J). 2.50 (978-970-607-744-8(8)) Larousse, Ediciones, S. A. de C. V. MEX. Dist: Continental Bk. Co., Inc.

Beck, Paul. Calls of the Wild: Nighttime Animals. 2016. (Calls of the Wild Ser.). (ENG., Illus.). 32p. (J). (gr. k). 24.95 (978-1-62686-425-2(X), Silver Dolphin Bks.) Readerlink Distribution Services, LLC.

—Extreme Animals: Predators. 2016. (Extreme Animals Ser.). (ENG., Illus.). 48p. (J). (gr. 3). 17.95 (978-1-62686-384-2(9), Silver Dolphin Bks.) Readerlink Distribution Services, LLC.

Belback, Elsie. Hidden in Plain Sight: Animal Camouflage. 2014. (ENG.). 24p. (gr. k-3). 28.50 (978-1-62717-635-4(7)) Rourke Educational Media.

Bell, Jessica. My Wild New Yard. 2017. (Text Connections Guided Close Reading Ser.). (J). (gr. 1). (978-1-4900-1801-0(8)) Benchmark Education Co.

Bell-Myers, Darcy. The Animal Babies ABC Book of Ballet. 2013. (Dover Coloring Bks.). (ENG.). 32p. (J). (gr. -1-3). pap. 3.99 (978-0-486-49814-0(X)) Dover Pubns., Inc.

Bellamy, Rufus. Backyard Encyclopedia. 2010. (Crabtree Connections Ser.). (ENG., Illus.). 24p. (J). (gr. 3-6). (978-0-7787-9945-0(X)); pap. (978-0-7787-9967-2(0)) Crabtree Publishing Co.

—Backyard Heroes. 2010. (Crabtree Connections Ser.). (ENG., Illus.). 24p. (J). (gr. 3-6). (978-0-7787-9953-5(0), 1317277); pap. (978-0-7787-9975-7(1), 1317277) Crabtree Publishing Co.

Benbow, Ann & Mably, Colin. Nature's Secret Habitats Science Projects. LaBaff, Tom, illus. 2009. (Real Life Science Experiments Ser.). 48p. (J). (gr. 2-5). lib. bdg. 25.27 (978-0-7660-3150-0(0)) Enslow Pubs., Inc.

Benchmark Education Company, LLC Staff. Relationships in Nature Teacher's Guide. 2004. (978-1-4108-2585-8(X)) Benchmark Education Co.

Benchmark Education Company, LLC Staff, compiled by. Animal Adaptation. 2006. (J). 240.00 (978-1-4108-7057-5(X)) Benchmark Education Co.

—Plants & Animal Life: Theme Set. 2006. (J). 178.00 (978-1-4108-7083-4(9)) Benchmark Education Co.

—Plants & Animals: Theme Set. 2006. (J). 173.00 (978-1-4108-7137-4(1)); spiral bd. 174.00 (978-1-4108-7063-6(4)) Benchmark Education Co.

Benefield, James. Carnivores. 2015. (What Animals Eat Ser.). (ENG., Illus.). 24p. (gr. k-2). 23.32 (978-1-4846-0847-0(X), Heinemann Read & Learn) Heinemann-Raintree.

—Herbivores. 2015. (What Animals Eat Ser.). (ENG., Illus.). 24p. (gr. k-2). 23.32 (978-1-4846-0848-7(8), Heinemann Read & Learn) Heinemann-Raintree.

A B

—Omnivores. 2015. (What Animals Eat Ser.). (ENG., Illus.). 24p. (gr. k-2). 23.32 *(978-1-4846-0849-4(6),* Heinemann Read & Learn) Heinemann-Raintree.

—What Animals Eat. 2015. (What Animals Eat Ser.). (ENG.). 24p. (gr. k-2). lib. bdg. 69.96 *(978-1-4846-0850-0(X),* Heinemann Read & Learn) Heinemann-Raintree.

Benjamin, Tina. Let's Go to a Pond. 2015. (Let's Go Outdoors! Ser.). (ENG., Illus.). 24p. (J). (gr. k-k). pap. 8.15 *(978-1-4824-2617-5(X))* Stevens, Gareth Publishing LLLP.

Bennett, Doraine. Coastal Plain. 2009. (J). *(978-1-935077-51-0(1));* pap. *(978-1-935077-52-7(X))* State Standards Publishing, LLC.

—Marsh & Swamp. 2009. (J). *(978-1-935077-36-7(8));* pap. *(978-1-935077-41-1(4))* State Standards Publishing, LLC.

—Mountains. 2009. (J). *(978-1-935077-37-4(6));* pap. *(978-1-935077-42-8(2))* State Standards Publishing, LLC.

Berger, Gilda & Berger, Melvin. Dangerous Animals. 2009. (Scholastic True or False Ser.: 5). (ENG.). 48p. (J). (gr. 2-5). pap. 4.99 *(978-0-545-00395-7(4),* Scholastic Reference) Scholastic, Inc.

—Scholastic Reader Level 2: Ugly Cute Animals. 2014. (Scholastic Reader Level 2 Ser.). (ENG.). 32p. (J). (gr. 1-3). pap. 3.99 *(978-0-545-60976-0(3))* Scholastic, Inc.

—101 Animal Secrets. 2009. (ENG.). 112p. (J). (gr. 2-5). pap. 8.99 *(978-0-545-05122-4(3),* Scholastic Reference) Scholastic, Inc.

Berger, Melvin. What Do Animals Do in Winter? (Discovery Readers Ser.). (ENG.). 48p. (J). pap. 3.95 *(978-0-8249-5314-0(2),* Ideal Pubns.) Worthy Publishing.

Berger, Melvin & Berger, Gilda. Animales Polares en Peligro: Polar Animals in Danger. 2006. (SPA & ENG., Illus.). (J). *(978-0-439-87987-3(6))* Scholastic, Inc.

—Penguins Swim but Don't Get Wet: And Other Amazing Facts about Polar Animals. 2004. (Speedy Facts Ser.). (Illus.). 48p. (J). *(978-0-439-32783-1(0))* Scholastic, Inc.

—Polar Animals in Danger. 2006. (Scholastic Reader Ser.). (Illus.). (J). *(978-0-439-81535-2(5))* Scholastic, Inc.

—Supersize Animals. 2015. (Illus.). 32p. (J). *(978-1-4806-8787-5(1))* Scholastic, Inc.

—Supersize Animals. 2015. (Scholastic Reader Level 2 Ser.). lib. bdg. 13.55 *(978-0-606-37756-0(5))* Turtleback Bks.

—Supersize Animals (Scholastic Reader, Level 2) 2015. (Scholastic Reader, Level 2 Ser.). (ENG., Illus.). 32p. (J). (gr. 1-3). pap. 3.99 *(978-0-545-80857-6(X))* Scholastic, Inc.

—The Wacky World of Living Things! 273 Facts! Miller, Ed, illus. 2017. (Fact Attack Ser.: 1). (ENG.). 96p. (J). (gr. 1-3). pap. 7.99 ***(978-1-338-03839-2(7))*** Scholastic, Inc.

—101 Animal Super Powers. 2015. (ENG., Illus.). 112p. (J). (gr. 2-5). pap. 8.99 *(978-0-545-82624-2(1),* Scholastic Paperbacks) Scholastic, Inc.

—101 Animal Super Powers. 2015. lib. bdg. 19.65 *(978-0-606-37752-2(2))* Turtleback Bks.

—101 Hidden Animals. 2014. (ENG.). 112p. (J). (gr. 2-5). pap. 8.99 *(978-0-545-67016-6(0),* Scholastic Paperbacks) Scholastic, Inc.

—101 Hidden Animals. 2014. lib. bdg. 19.65 *(978-0-606-36041-8(7))* Turtleback Bks.

Berkes, Marianne Collins. Animalogy: Animal Analogies, 1 vol. Morrison, Cathy, illus. 2011. (ENG.). 32p. (J). (gr. -1-3). 16.95 *(978-1-60718-127-9(4),* 9781607181279); pap. 8.95 *(978-1-60718-137-8(1))* Arbordale Publishing.

Berne, Emma Carlson. Crustaceans. 2017. (My First Animal Kingdom Encyclopedias Ser.). (ENG., Illus.). 32p. (gr. 1-2). lib. bdg. 27.32 *(978-1-5157-3923-4(6),* Aplus Bks.) Capstone Press of Coughlan Cos.

Berne, Emma Carlson, et al. My First Animal Kingdom Encyclopedias. 2017. (My First Animal Kingdom Encyclopedias Ser.). (ENG.). 32p. (gr. 1-2). 218.56 *(978-1-5157-3971-5(6),* Aplus Bks.) Capstone Press of Coughlan Cos.

Besson, Agnès. My First 1000 Animals. Surein, Manuel, illus. 2016. (ENG.). 64p. (J). (gr. -1 — 1). 19.95 *(978-1-77085-796-4(6),* 9781770857964) Firefly Bks., Ltd.

Bethune, Helen. Why Do Monkeys Chatter? 2010. (Solving Science Mysteries Ser.). (Illus.). 24p. (J). pap. 8.25 *(978-1-4488-0395-8(0),* PowerKids Pr.); (YA). (gr. 3-6). lib. bdg. 22.60 *(978-1-4488-0394-1(2))* Rosen Publishing Group, Inc., The.

—Why Do Monkeys Chatter? All about Animals. 2010. (Illus.). 24p. (J). 49.50 *(978-1-4488-0396-5(9),* 1307171, PowerKids Pr.) Rosen Publishing Group, Inc., The.

Beullens, Nathalie, ed. Our Wonderful World (Cantonese-Chinese) Set. 2016. (Our Wonderful World (Cantonese-Chinese) Ser.). (ENG.). 8p. pap. 56.10 *(978-1-5081-1265-5(7),* Rosen Classroom) Rosen Publishing Group, Inc., The.

Beveridge, Dorothy. Belize Living Alphabet. Beveridge, Jim, photos by. 2013. (Illus.). 38p. pap. *(978-976-8142-51-1(0))* Producciones de la Hamaca.

Beylon, Cathy. Animal Opposites. 2008. (Dover Coloring Bks.). (ENG., Illus.). 32p. (J). (gr. -1-2). pap. 3.99 *(978-0-486-46197-7(1))* Dover Pubns., Inc.

Bickel, Karla. The Animals' Debate. Bickel, Karla, illus. I.t. ed. 2004. (Illus.). 16p. (J). (gr. -1-6). pap. 5.00 *(978-1-891452-16-1(9),* 10) Heart Arbor Bks.

Bicknell, Joanna. My Animal Book. 2005. (Shimmer & Shine Books Ser.). 12p. (gr. -1-k). per., bds. *(978-1-905051-28-1(X))* Make Believe Ideas.

Big & Little: KinderWords Individual Title Six-Packs. (Kinderstarters Ser.). 8p. (gr. -1-1). 21.00 *(978-0-7635-8700-0(1))* Rigby Education.

Big Book of Animals. rev. ed. 2007. (ENG., Illus.). 26p. (J). (gr. -1-1). 16.99 *(978-1-59069-504-3(6),* 1S1000) Studio Mouse LLC.

Big Picture Press, Big Picture. Animalium Activity Book. Scott, Katie, illus. 2016. (ENG.). 72p. (J). (gr. 2-5). 14.99 *(978-0-7636-8919-3(X),* Big Picture Press) Candlewick Pr.

Bingham, Jane. Great Prehistoric Search. 2004. (Great Searches Ser.). 32p. (J). lib. bdg. 16.95 *(978-1-58086-641-5(7),* Usborne) EDC Publishing.

—Great Prehistoric Search. Jackson, Ian, illus. 2004. (Great Searches Ser.). 32p. (J). pap. 8.95 *(978-0-7945-0663-6(1),* Usborne) EDC Publishing.

Bird, Nicky & Duncan, Peter. Canadian Animals Alphabet Book, 1 vol. 2016. (Think Ser.: 2). (ENG., Illus.). 64p. (J). pap. 6.99 ***(978-1-897206-07-2(0),*** 9781897206072) Folklore Publishing CAN. Dist: Lone Pine Publishing USA.

Bishop, Nic. Weird Little Monsters. Bishop, Nic, illus. 2007. (Collins Big Cat Ser.). (ENG., Illus.). 1p. (J). (gr. 2-4). pap. 7.99 *(978-0-00-723080-8(X))* HarperCollins Pubs. Ltd. GBR. Dist: Independent Pubs. Group.

BishopRoby, Joshua. The World of Animals, 1 vol. 2007. (Science Readers Ser.). (SPA & ENG.). 32p. (J). (gr. 4-4). pap. 8.99 *(978-0-7439-0593-0(8))* Shell Educational Publishing.

Biskup, Agnieszka. Awesome Animals ABC. Brooks, David, illus. 2005. (J). *(978-1-58987-095-6(6))* Kindermusik International.

Bizarre Beast Battles. 2015. (Bizarre Beast Battles Ser.). (ENG.). 24p. (J). (gr. 2-3). 135.60 *(978-1-4824-2547-5(5))* Stevens, Gareth Publishing LLLP.

Blacker, Sharnika. Big Cats, 1 vol. 2012. (Engage Literacy Green Ser.). (ENG.). 32p. (gr. k-2). pap. 5.99 *(978-1-4296-8839-0(4),* Engage Literacy) Capstone Press of Coughlan Cos.

Blackstone, Stella. Counting Cockatoos. Bauer, Stephanie, illus. 2007. (ENG.). 32p. (J). (gr. -1-k). 8.99 *(978-1-84686-061-4(X))* Barefoot Bks., Inc.

Blackstone, Stella & Bauer, Stephanie. Counting Cockatoos. 2006. (ENG., Illus.). 32p. (J). (gr. -1-3). 16.99 *(978-1-905236-31-2(X))* Barefoot Bks., Inc.

—Octopus Opposites. Bauer, Stephanie, illus. 2011. (ENG., Illus.). 32p. (J). (gr. -1-k). 8.99 *(978-1-84686-591-6(3))* Barefoot Bks., Inc.

Blake, Carly. Why Why Why... Do Fish Bite? 2010. (Why Why Why Ser.). 32p. (J). (gr. 1-3). lib. bdg. 18.95 *(978-1-4222-1585-2(7))* Mason Crest.

Blashfield, Jean F. Animal Life. 2007. (Gareth Stevens Vital Science Ser.). (Illus.). 48p. (gr. 5-12). lib. bdg. 27.00 *(978-0-8368-8436-4(1),* Gareth Stevens Secondary Library) Stevens, Gareth Publishing LLLP.

Blashfield, Jean F. & Ryback, Carol. Animal Life. 2007. (Gareth Stevens Vital Science- Life Science Ser.). (Illus.). 48p. (gr. 5-12). pap. 14.05 *(978-0-8368-8445-6(0),* Gareth Stevens Secondary Library) Stevens, Gareth Publishing LLLP.

Blomgren, Jennifer. Why Do I Sing? Animal Songs of the Pacific Northwest. Gabriel, Andrea, illus. 2013. (ENG.). 32p. (J). (gr. -1-2). 16.99 *(978-1-57061-845-1(3),* Little Bigfoot) Sasquatch Bks.

Bloom, Steve. Polar Animals: In Search of Polar Bears, Penguins, Whales & Seals. 2012. (ENG., Illus.). 48p. (J). 15.95 *(978-0-500-65011-0(X),* 565011) Thames & Hudson.

Bloomsbury USA. Baby's First Words: Animals. 2016. (ENG., Illus.). 10p. (J). bds. 5.99 *(978-1-61963-994-2(7),* 9781619639942, Bloomsbury Activity Bks.) Bloomsbury Publishing USA.

Blyton, Enid, et al. My First Animals. 2013. (ENG., Illus.). 20p. (J). bds. 11.50 *(978-1-84135-758-4(8))* Award Pubns. Ltd. GBR. Dist: Parkwest Pubns., Inc.

Boardworks Learning Centers: Amazing Animals. 2006. (J). bds. *(978-0-9755252-3-4(9))* Evergreen Pr. of Brainerd, LLC.

Bogart, Jon. Animals & Oil Spills. 2013. (Animal 911: Environmental Threats Ser.). 48p. (J). (gr. 3-5). pap. 14.05 *(978-1-4339-9711-2(8));* pap. 84.30 *(978-1-4339-9712-9(6));* (ENG., Illus.). lib. bdg. 31.95 *(978-1-4339-9710-5(X))* Stevens, Gareth Publishing LLLP.

Bogue, Gary. Raccoon Next Door: And Other Creatures of the Urban Wilderness. Todd, Chuck, illus. 2003. 196p. pap. 16.95 *(978-1-890771-71-3(6))* Heyday.

Bond, Rebecca. Out of the Woods: A True Story of an Unforgettable Event. 2015. (ENG., Illus.). 40p. (J). (gr. k-4). 17.99 *(978-0-374-38077-9(5),* 9780374380779, Farrar, Straus & Giroux (BYR)) Farrar, Straus & Giroux.

Bonnet, Rosalind. Animals. rev. ed. 2013. (First Words Board Bks). 12p. (J). ring bd. 6.99 *(978-0-7945-3389-2(2),* Usborne) EDC Publishing.

Books Are Fun 8 Title Animal Lives Set. 2006. (J). mass mkt. *(978-1-59566-305-4(3))* QEB Publishing Inc.

Books Are Fun Exclusive Animal Lives 4 Set. 2005. lib. bdg. *(978-1-59566-166-1(2))* QEB Publishing Inc.

Boos, Andre, illus. Amazing Animal Puzzle Stickers: #1. 2005. (Amazing Animal Puzzle Stickers Ser.). 10p. (J). pap. 5.99 *(978-1-59496-063-5(1))* Teora USA LLC.

—Amazing Animal Puzzle Stickers: #2, Vol. 2. 2005. (Amazing Animal Puzzle Stickers Ser.). 10p. (J). pap. 5.99 *(978-1-59496-064-2(X))* Teora USA LLC.

—Amazing Animal Puzzle Stickers: #3, Vol. 3. 2005. (Amazing Animal Puzzle Stickers Ser.). 10p. (J). pap. 5.99 *(978-1-59496-065-9(8))* Teora USA LLC.

—Hi! Read, Stick & Learn about Animals. Little Bears are Brown. 2004. 20p. (J). pap. 6.99 *(978-1-59496-003-1(8))* Teora USA LLC.

—Hi! Read, Stick & Learn about Animals. Little rabbits have Fur. 2004. 20p. (J). pap. 6.99 *(978-1-59496-002-4(X))* Teora USA LLC.

Booth, Edison. Awesome Animal Tails. 2017. (Animals in My World Ser.). 24p. (gr. 4-6). pap. 8.25 ***(978-1-5383-2144-7(0),*** PowerKids Pr.) Rosen Publishing Group, Inc., The.

—Awesome Animal Tales. 2017. (J). ***(978-1-5081-5921-6(1),*** PowerKids Pr.) Rosen Publishing Group, Inc., The.

Boothroyd, Jennifer. Animals & the Environment. 2008. (First Step Nonfiction - Ecology Ser.). (ENG., Illus.). 24p. (gr. k-2). lib. bdg. 23.93 *(978-0-8225-8602-9(9),* Lerner Pubns.) Lerner Publishing Group.

—In a Cave. (First Step Nonfiction - Animal Homes Ser.). (ENG., Illus.). 8p. (gr. -1-1). 2015. 11.99 *(978-1-5124-1031-0(4))* 2006. pap. 4.95 *(978-0-8225-5662-6(6),* Lerner Pubns.) Lerner Publishing Group.

—Let's Visit the Tundra. 2016. (Lightning Bolt Books (tm) — Biome Explorers Ser.). (ENG., Illus.). 32p. (J). (gr. 1-3). 26.65 *(978-1-5124-1196-6(5))* Lerner Publishing Group.

—On the Ground. 2015. (First Step Nonfiction - Animal Homes Ser.). (ENG., Illus.). 8p. (gr. -1-1). 11.99 *(978-1-5124-1034-1(9))* Lerner Publishing Group.

—Under the Ground. (First Step Nonfiction - Animal Homes Ser.). (ENG., Illus.). 8p. (gr. -1-1). 2015. 11.99 *(978-1-5124-1035-8(7))* 2006. pap. 4.95 *(978-0-8225-5661-9(8),* Lerner Pubns.) Lerner Publishing Group.

Borando, Silvia. Near, Far: A Minibombo Book. Borando, Silvia, illus. 2016. (Minibombo Ser.). (ENG., Illus.). 48p. (J). (-k). 14.00 *(978-0-7636-8783-0(9))* Candlewick Pr.

—Now You See Me, Now You Don't: A Minibombo Book. Borando, Silvia, illus. 2016. (Minibombo Ser.). (ENG., Illus.). 28p. (J). (-k). 14.00 *(978-0-7636-8782-3(0))* Candlewick Pr.

Borene, Mark R. Welcome to the Ground. 2009. (Illus.). 20p. pap. 10.49 *(978-1-4389-8268-7(2))* AuthorHouse.

Borgert-Spaniol, Megan. Ticks. 2016. (Creepy Crawlies Ser.). (ENG., Illus.). 24p. (J). (gr. k-3). lib. bdg. 25.95 *(978-1-62617-302-6(8),* Blastoff! Readers) Bellwether Media.

Borth, Teddy. Blue Animals, 1 vol. 2014. (Animal Colors Ser.). (ENG.). 24p. (J). (gr. 2-4). lib. bdg. 28.50 *(978-1-62970-694-8(9))* ABDO Publishing Co.

—Green Animals, 1 vol. 2014. (Animal Colors Ser.). (ENG.). 24p. (J). (gr. 2-4). lib. bdg. 28.50 *(978-1-62970-695-5(7))* ABDO Publishing Co.

—Orange Animals, 1 vol. 2014. (Animal Colors Ser.). (ENG.). 24p. (J). (gr. 2-4). lib. bdg. 28.50 *(978-1-62970-696-2(5))* ABDO Publishing Co.

—Red Animals, 1 vol. 2014. (Animal Colors Ser.). (ENG.). 24p. (J). (gr. 2-4). lib. bdg. 28.50 *(978-1-62970-697-9(3))* ABDO Publishing Co.

—White Animals, 1 vol. 2014. (Animal Colors Ser.). (ENG.). 24p. (J). (gr. 2-4). lib. bdg. 28.50 *(978-1-62970-698-6(1))* ABDO Publishing Co.

—Yellow Animals, 1 vol. 2014. (Animal Colors Ser.). (ENG.). 24p. (J). (gr. 2-4). lib. bdg. 28.50 *(978-1-62970-699-3(X))* ABDO Publishing Co.

Bosch, Sammy. Super Simple Backyard Critter Crafts: Fun & Easy Animal Crafts. 2016. (ENG., Illus.). 32p. (J). *(978-1-68078-160-1(X))* ABDO Publishing Co.

Botham, Noel. Do Turtles Really Breathe Out of Their Bums? 2015. (Dr. Dino's Learnatorium Ser.). (ENG., Illus.). 160p. (J). (gr. 4-7). pap. 8.99 *(978-1-78219-774-4(5))* Blake, John Publishing, Ltd. GBR. Dist: Independent Pubs. Group.

Bourke, Kenna. Deadly Animals High Beginning Book with Online Access. 2014. (ENG., Illus.). 24p. (J). pap. 9.50 *(978-1-107-69371-5(3))* Cambridge Univ. Pr.

Bow, James. Animal Mysteries Revealed. 2010. (ENG., Illus.). 32p. (J). pap. *(978-0-7787-7427-3(9));* (gr. 4-7). lib. bdg. *(978-0-7787-7412-9(0))* Crabtree Publishing Co.

—Mountains Inside Out. 2015. (ENG.). 32p. (J). *(978-0-7787-1498-9(5))* Crabtree Publishing Co.

—Wetlands Inside Out. 2014. (ENG.). 32p. (J). *(978-0-7787-0641-0(9))* Crabtree Publishing Co.

Bowman, Chris. Animal Control Officer. 2014. (Dangerous Jobs Ser.). (ENG., Illus.). 24p. (J). (gr. 3-7). lib. bdg. 25.95 *(978-1-62617-109-1(2),* Torque Bks.) Bellwether Media.

Bowman, Crystal & McKinley, Teri. Do Baby Bears Have Mommies? Busby, Ailie, illus. 2017. (I've Got Questions Ser.). (ENG.). 32p. (J). 9.99 *(978-1-4964-1740-4(2))* Tyndale Hse. Pubs.

Boyle, L. D. Pegram. Trever's Biscuit. 2010. 48p. pap. 19.49 *(978-1-4490-8266-6(1))* AuthorHouse.

Boynton, Sandra. Fifteen Animals! 2008. (ENG., Illus.). 24p. (J). (gr. k — 1). 6.95 *(978-0-7611-3066-6(7),* 13066) Workman Publishing Co., Inc.

Bozzo, Linda. Amazing Animal Tails. 2008. (Creature Features Ser.). (Illus.). 24p. (J). (gr. 3-7). lib. bdg. 22.60 *(978-1-4042-4171-8(X))* Rosen Publishing Group, Inc., The.

Bradley, Timothy. Increíble pero Real: Animales Extraños. 2017. (TIME for Kids en Español - Level 4 Ser.). (SPA., Illus.). 48p. (gr. 4-4). lib. bdg. 31.99 *(978-1-5157-5142-7(2))* Time for Kids Inc AUS. Dist: Capstone Pub.

—Increíble pero Real: Criaturas Diminutas. 2017. (TIME for Kids en Español - Level 4 Ser.). (SPA., Illus.). 48p. (gr. 4-4). lib. bdg. 31.99 *(978-1-5157-5143-4(0))* Time for Kids Inc AUS. Dist: Capstone Pub.

—Strange but True: Tiny Creatures, 1 vol. 2nd rev. ed. 2013. (Nonfiction Readers Ser.). (ENG., Illus.). 48p. (J). (gr. 4-4). pap. 29.96 *(978-1-4807-1114-3(4))* Shell Educational Publishing.

—Terror en Los Trópicos. 2016. (TIME for Kids en Español - Level 5 Ser.). (SPA.). 64p. (gr. 5-5). lib. bdg. 31.99 *(978-1-5157-2939-6(7))* Time for Kids Inc AUS. Dist: Capstone Pub.

Bradley, Timothy J. Animal Architects, 1 vol. 2nd rev. ed. 2013. (Nonfiction Readers Ser.). (ENG., Illus.). 48p. (J). (gr. 4-4). pap. 29.96 *(978-1-4807-1098-6(9))* Shell Educational Publishing.

—Strange but True: Bizarre Animals, 1 vol. 2nd rev. ed. 2013. (Nonfiction Readers Ser.). (ENG., Illus.). 48p. (J). (gr. 4-4). pap. 29.96 *(978-1-4807-1113-6(6))* Shell Educational Publishing.

—Strange but True: Bizarre Animals, 1 vol. 2nd rev. ed. 2012. (Nonfiction Readers Ser.). (ENG.). 48p. (J). (gr. 4-4). pap. 9.99 *(978-1-4333-4861-7(6))* Teacher Created Materials, Inc.

Braidich, Victoria. Animals on the Farm: Learning to Compare Size. 2009. (Math for the REAL World Ser.). 12p. (gr. 1-2). pap. 5.90 *(978-0-8239-8847-1(3),* Rosen Classroom) Rosen Publishing Group, Inc., The.

Brainy Baby Animals. 2004. *(978-1-59394-234-2(6))* Bendon, Inc.

Braun, Sebastien, illus. The Tiger Prowls: A Pop-Up Book of Wild Animals. 2016. (ENG.). 12p. (J). 16.99 *(978-1-4711-2215-6(8),* Simon & Schuster Children's) Simon & Schuster, Ltd. GBR. Dist: Simon & Schuster, Inc.

Brayley, Genevieve. Noah Saves the Tigers. 2010. 28p. pap. 28.03 *(978-1-4500-3077-9(7))* Xlibris Corp.

Bre, Norman H. Fehr. Animals in Canad. 2011. 176p. pap. 81.99 *(978-1-4628-5606-0(3))* Xlibris Corp.

Bredeson, Carmen. Boa Constrictors up Close. 2006. (Zoom in on Animals! Ser.). (Illus.). 24p. (J). (gr. 1-3). lib. bdg. 22.60 *(978-0-7660-2498-4(9),* Enslow Elementary) Enslow Pubs., Inc.

Brenneman, Kimberly. Let's Visit a Coral Reef. 2016. (Illus.). 32p. (J). pap. *(978-0-87659-708-8(8))* Gryphon Hse., Inc.

Brett, Jessica. Animals on the Go. Cowdrey, Richard, illus. 2003. (Green Light Readers Level 2 Ser.). (ENG.). 24p. (J). (gr. -1-3). pap. 3.95 *(978-0-15-204827-3(8))* Houghton Mifflin Harcourt Publishing Co.

Brian Wildsmith's Box of Books. 2004. (Illus.). (J). 24.95 *(978-1-59572-016-0(2))* Star Bright Bks., Inc.

BrickHouse Education. Guess Who: Whose Silhouette Is This? 2010. (J). pap. 8.99 *(978-1-59835-139-2(7))* Cambridge BrickHouse, Inc.

Bridges, Taylor. Animals Tall & Short: Describe & Compare Measurable Attributes. 2013. (Rosen Math Readers Ser.). (ENG.). 16p. (J). (gr. k-1). pap. 42.00

(978-1-4777-1633-5(5)); (Illus.). pap. 7.00 *(978-1-4777-1632-8(7))* Rosen Publishing Group, Inc., The. (Rosen Classroom).

Bright & Beautiful. (J). (gr. 6). 43.50 *(978-0-673-72659-9(2),* Scott Foresman) Addison Wesley Schl.

Brim, Warren & Eglitis, Anna. Creatures of the Rainforest: Two Artists Explore Djabugay Country. Brim, Warren & Eglitis, Anna, illus. 2005. (ENG., Illus.). 64p. (J). (gr. k). 19.95 *(978-1-875641-99-4(8))* Magabala Bks. AUS. Dist: Independent Pubs. Group.

Brischke, D. Wake Up Zoo. 2005. 28p. (J). pap. *(978-0-9752878-9-7(3))* Dream-Catcher Pubns.

Britannica, Learning Library. Wildlife Wonders. 2003. (Illus.). 64p. 14.95 *(978-1-59339-046-4(7))* Encyclopaedia Britannica, Inc.

Britannica Learning Library Staff. Familiar Animals. 2003. (Illus.). 64p. 14.95 *(978-1-59339-047-1(5))* Encyclopaedia Britannica, Inc.

Brocklehurst, Ruth. Animal Sticker Atlas. Turnbull, Stephanie, ed. 2004. (Sticker Atlas Ser.). (Illus.). 24p. (J). pap. 8.95 *(978-0-7945-0670-4(4),* Usborne) EDC Publishing.

—Animales: Atlas con Pegatinas. Lucas, Ana Cristina Llompart, tr. 2006. (Illus.). 24p. (J). (gr. 1-4). pap. 8.99 *(978-0-7460-6649-2(X),* Usborne) EDC Publishing.

—1001 Animals Que Buscar. Gower, Teri, illus. 2003. (Facts & Lists Internet-Linked Ser.). (SPA.). 64p. (J). (gr. 4-7). lib. bdg. 14.95 *(978-1-58086-493-0(7))* EDC Publishing.

—1001 Animals to Spot. 2004. (1001 Things to Spot Ser.). (SPA., Illus.). 32p. (J). lib. bdg. 14.95 *(978-1-58086-424-4(4));* (gr. -1-18). pap. 6.95 *(978-0-7945-0149-5(4),* Usborne) EDC Publishing.

Brook-Piper, Holly. Animal Shapes: A Touch-and-Feel Book. 2015. (ENG., Illus.). 12p. (J). (gr. -1 — 1). bds. 6.99 *(978-1-4998-0039-5(8))* Little Bee Books Inc.

Brookes, Olivia. An Animal. 2009. (Ask Ser.). (Illus.). 32p. (J). lib. bdg. 26.50 *(978-1-4358-2512-3(8),* PowerKids Pr.) Rosen Publishing Group, Inc., The.

Brooks, Brody. How Animals Survive. 2013. (Rosen Readers Ser.). (ENG.). 24p. (J). (gr. 3-4). pap. 49.50 *(978-1-4777-2523-8(7));* pap. 8.25 *(978-1-4777-2522-1(9))* Rosen Publishing Group, Inc., The. (Rosen Classroom).

Brooks, Felicity. Very First Animals Board Book. 2010. (Very First Words Board Bks). 10p. (J). bds. 6.99 *(978-0-7945-2479-1(6),* Usborne) EDC Publishing.

Brooks, Felicity & Litchfield, Jo. First Picture Animals. Van Wyk, Hanri, illus. 2008. (First Picture Board Bks.). 12p. (J). (gr. -1). bds. 11.99 *(978-0-7945-1831-8(1),* Usborne) EDC Publishing.

Broom, Jenny. Color Create: Animals. Nój, Nahta, illus. 2012. (ENG.). 32p. (J). (gr. k). 16.95 *(978-0-60710-493-3(8),* Silver Dolphin Bks.) Readerlink Distribution Services, LLC.

Brown, Carron. Secrets of Animal Camouflage. Robins, Wesley, illus. 2016. (ENG.). 36p. (J). 12.99 *(978-1-61067-466-9(9))* Kane Miller.

—Secrets of the Rain Forest. Nassner, Alyssa, illus. 2015. (ENG.). 36p. (J). 12.99 *(978-1-61067-325-9(5))* Kane Miller.

Brown, Jonatha A. Animal Tails. 2006. (Why Animals Look Different Ser.). (Illus.). 24p. (J). (gr. 1-4). lib. bdg. 22.00 *(978-0-8368-6863-0(3),* Weekly Reader Leveled Readers) Stevens, Gareth Publishing LLLP.

—Las patas y los pies de los animales. 2006. (En que se diferencian los animales (Why Animals Look Different) Ser.). (SPA., Illus.). 24p. (J). (gr. 1-4). lib. bdg. 22.00 *(978-0-8368-7414-3(5),* Weekly Reader Leveled Readers) Stevens, Gareth Publishing LLLP.

—La Piel y el Pelo de los Animales. 2006. (En que se diferencian los animales (Why Animals Look Different) Ser.). (SPA., Illus.). 24p. (J). (gr. 1-4). lib. bdg. 22.00 *(978-0-8368-7415-0(3),* Weekly Reader Leveled Readers) Stevens, Gareth Publishing LLLP.

Brown, Martin. Lesser Spotted Animals. 2016. (ENG.). 56p. (J). (gr. 2-5). 18.99 *(978-1-338-08934-9(X))* Scholastic, Inc.

Browne, Philippa-Alys. "Bushbaby blinks" (African Animals ABC) (Illus.). 14.99 *(978-1-84148-756-4(2))* Barefoot Bks., Inc.

—"Giraffe dozes" (African Animals ABC) (Illus.). 14.99 *(978-1-84148-758-8(9))* Barefoot Bks., Inc.

—"Hippo sleeps" (African Animals ABC) (Illus.). 14.99 *(978-1-84148-754-0(6))* Barefoot Bks., Inc.

Brusha, Joe, et al. Worlds Most Dangerous Animals. 2012. (ENG., Illus.). 120p. pap. 9.99 *(978-0-9827507-3-5(0),* 9780982750735) Zenescope Entertainment.

Brynie, Faith Hickman. Do Animals Migrate? 2010. (I Like Reading about Animals! Ser.). (Illus.). 32p. (J). 23.94 *(978-0-7660-3325-2(2))* Enslow Pubs., Inc.

—Which Animals Are the Best Athletes? 2010. (I Like Reading about Animals! Ser.). (Illus.). 32p. (J). (gr. k-3). 23.94 *(978-0-7660-3329-0(5));* pap. 7.95 *(978-0-7660-3751-9(7),* Enslow Elementary) Enslow Pubs., Inc.

Buchanan, Shelly. Animal Senses. 2015. (Science Readers: Content & Literacy Ser.). (ENG.). 32p. (J). (gr. 4-4). pap. 8.99 *(978-1-4807-4678-7(9))* Teacher Created Materials, Inc.

Buckley, Arabella B. Wild Life in Woods & Fields (Yesterday's Classics) 2008. (Illus.). 60p. pap. 9.95 *(978-1-59915-271-4(1))* Yesterday's Classics.

Buckley, James. Antarctic Wildlife. 2017. (Exploring the Polar Regions Today Ser.). (ENG.). (YA). (gr. 7-12). 23.95 ***(978-1-4222-3864-6(4))*** Mason Crest.

Bugbird, Tim. Peek a Boo Perfect Pets. 2009. (ENG., Illus.). 12p. (J). (gr. -1-k). bds. *(978-1-84610-907-2(8))* Make Believe Ideas.

Bugler, Matt. My First Encyclopedia of Animals: A First Encyclopedia with Supersize Pictures. 2016. (ENG.). 24p. pap. 7.99 *(978-1-86147-822-1(4),* Armadillo) Anness Publishing GBR. Dist: National Bk. Network.

Built for Cold: Arctic Animals, 6 vols., Set. Incl. Arctic Wolf: The High Arctic. DeLallo, Laura. lib. bdg. 25.27 *(978-1-61772-132-8(8));* Caribou: And Reindeer, Too. Markovics, Joyce L. lib. bdg. 25.27 *(978-1-61772-130-4(1));* Polar Bear: Shrinking Ice. Person, Stephen. lib. bdg. 25.27 *(978-1-61772-129-8(8));* Sled Dog: Powerful Miracle. Person, Stephen. lib. bdg. 25.27 *(978-1-61772-134-2(4));* Walrus: Tusk, Tusk. Person, Stephen. lib. bdg. 25.27 *(978-1-61772-133-5(6));* Wolverine: Super Strong. Markovics, Joyce L. lib. bdg. 25.27 *(978-1-61772-131-1(X));* (YA). (gr. 1-4). 32p. 2011. Set lib. bdg. 151.62

(978-1-61772-128-1(X)); Set lib. bdg., E-Book 295.28 (978-1-61772-218-9(9)) Bearport Publishing Co., Inc.

Built to Survive: Animal Adaptations. 2007. (Illus.). 32p. (J). pap. (978-0-545-04074-7(4)) Scholastic, Inc.

Bull, Andrea & Bull, Robert J. Animal Appetites: A Book of Unusual ABCs. Bull, Andrea & Bull, Robert J., illus. 2015. (ENG., Illus.). 40p. pap. 10.95 (978-0-9948622-0-4(2)) Bk.Baby Print.

Bullard, Lisa. Fast & Slow [Scholastic]: An Animal Opposites Book. 2009. (Animal Opposites Ser.). 32p. (gr. 1-2). pap. 1.00 (978-1-4296-4231-6(9), Aplus Bks.) Capstone Press of Coughlan Cos.

—Loud & Quiet [Scholastic]: An Animal Opposites Book. 2009. (Animal Opposites Ser.). 32p. (gr. 1-2). pap. 1.00 (978-1-4296-4232-3(7), Aplus Bks.) Capstone Press of Coughlan Cos.

Burke, Frank. Animal Antics. Burke, Frank, illus. (Illus.). (Orig.). (J). pap. 3.59 (978-0-927206-05-1(6)) Author's Connection Pr.

Burklow, Shan Williams. Learn to Draw with Quacker & Friends. 2012. (ENG.). (J). pap. 12.99 (978-1-4675-4791-8(3)) Independent Pub.

Burns, Diane L. Horsing Around: Jokes to Make Ewe Smile. Gable, Brian, illus. 2005. (Make Me Laugh! Ser.). 32p. (J). (gr. k-3). lib. bdg. 19.93 (978-1-57505-662-3(3)) Lerner Publishing Group.

Burns, Diane L. & Scholten, Dan. Horsing Around: Jokes to Make Ewe Smile. Gable, Brian, illus. 2004. (Make Me Laugh! Ser.). 32p. (J). (gr. -1-3). per. 4.95 (978-1-57505-737-8(9)) Lerner Publishing Group.

Burns, Loree Griffin. Citizen Scientists: Be a Part of Scientific Discovery from Your Own Backyard. Harasimowicz, Ellen, photos by. 2012. (ENG., Illus.). 80p. (J). (gr. 3-7). 19.99 (978-0-8050-9062-8(2), 9780805090628, Holt, Henry & Co. Bks. For Young Readers) Holt, Henry & Co.

—Citizen Scientists: Be a Part of Scientific Discovery from Your Own Backyard. Harasimowicz, Ellen, photos by. 2012. (ENG., Illus.). 80p. (J). (gr. 3-7). pap. 14.99 (978-0-8050-9517-3(9), 9780805095173) Square Fish.

Burr, Debora. In the Wild. (Animal Families Board Bks.). (Illus.). (J). bds. 4.00 net. (978-1-56021-389-5(2)) W.J. Fantasy, Inc.

Burton, Margie, et al. Animal Groups. 2011. (Early Connections Ser.). (J). (978-1-61672-515-0(X)) Benchmark Education Co.

—Endangered Animals. 2011. (Early Connections Ser.). (J). (978-1-61672-522-8(2)) Benchmark Education Co.

—How Do Animals Stay Alive? 2011. (Early Connections Ser.). (J). (978-1-61672-523-5(0)) Benchmark Education Co.

—Look at the Animals. 2011. (Early Connections Ser.). (J). (978-1-61672-298-2(3)) Benchmark Education Co.

Busquets, Carlos, illus. Los Animales Cuentan 365 Historias. 2nd ed. 2004. (SPA.). 193p. (J). (gr. -1-7). 14.50 (978-970-22-0445-9(3)) Larousse, Ediciones, S. A. de C. V. MEX. Dist: Giron Bks.

Butterfield, Moira. Wild Animals. 2006. (Illus.). 24p. (YA). (gr. 1-18). lib. bdg. 22.80 (978-1-931983-60-0(7)) Chrysalis Education.

Butterfield, Moira & Jacobs, Pat. Animals. 2016. (Know It All Ser.). (ENG., Illus.). 32p. (J). (gr. 5-5). pap. 10.58 (978-1-5026-0890-1(1), 1398895) Cavendish Square Publishing.

Byerly, Robbie. We Are All Animals. 2016. (1G Science Ser.). (ENG., Illus.). 32p. (J). pap. 5.99 **(978-1-63437-677-8(3))** American Reading Co.

Byerly, Robbie. Who Eats What? - on the Prairie. 2016. (1G Science Ser.). (ENG., Illus.). 32p. (J). pap. 5.99 (978-1-63437-484-2(3)) American Reading Co.

Cabat, Erni. Erni Cabat's Magical ABC: Animals Around the Farm. Date not set. (Illus.). 64p. (Orig.). (J). (gr. -1-2). 23.00 (978-0-943173-73-3(6)) Cabat Studio Pubns.

Cain, Marie Mowery. Feathers or Fur. 2013. (Big Books, Red Ser.). (ENG & SPA., Illus.). 16p. pap. 33.00 (978-1-59246-216-2(2)) Big Books, by George!

—Very, Very Big. 2013. (Big Books, Blue Ser.). (ENG & SPA., Illus.). 16p. pap. 33.00 (978-1-59246-016-8(X)) Big Books, by George!

Calino & Abbeville Press Staff. ABC Snake. Calino, illus. 2008. (ENG., Illus.). 30p. (J). (gr. k-k). 8.95 (978-0-7892-0303-8(0), Abbeville Kids) Abbeville Pr., Inc.

—123 Caterpillar. Calino, illus. 2008. (ENG., Illus.). 30p. (J). (gr. k-k). 8.95 (978-0-7892-0304-5(9), Abbeville Kids) Abbeville Pr., Inc.

Callery, Sean. Life Cycles: Grassland. 2012. (ENG., Illus.). 32p. (J). (gr. 2-5). 6.99 (978-0-7534-6895-1(6), 9780753468951, Kingfisher) Roaring Brook Pr.

—Life Cycles: Polar Lands. 2012. (Lifecycles Ser.). (ENG., Illus.). 32p. (J). (gr. 2-5). 6.99 (978-0-7534-6896-8(4), 9780753468968, Kingfisher) Roaring Brook Pr.

Cameron, Shanda. Feathered & Furry Friends. 2010. 16p. 8.49 (978-1-4520-6909-8(3)) AuthorHouse.

Campbell, Rod. Wild Animals. (Pop-Up Paperback Bk.). (Illus.). 16p. (J). (gr. -1-k). pap. (978-1-56021-356-7(6), 207) W.J. Fantasy, Inc.

Canavan, Thomas. Why Do Zebras Have Stripes? Questions & Answers about Animals. 2013. (Science F. A. Q. Ser.). 32p. (gr. 3-6). 31.35 (978-1-78212-397-2(0)) Arcturus Publishing GBR. Dist: Black Rabbit Bks.

Canetti, Yanitzia. La Adaptación, ¡qué Sensación! 2010. (SPA.). (J). (978-1-59835-172-9(9)); (978-1-59835-167-5(2)); (978-1-59835-169-9(9)); (978-1-59835-171-2(0)); (978-1-59835-176-7(1)); (978-1-59835-174-3(5)); (978-1-59835-170-5(2)); (978-1-59835-175-0(3)) Cambridge BrickHouse, Inc.

—La adaptación, ¡qué Sensación! Lenguas. 2010. (SPA.). 24p. (J). pap. (978-1-59835-188-0(5), BrickHouse Education) Cambridge BrickHouse, Inc.

—La Adaptación, Qué Sensación Alas. 2010. (SPA.). (J). (978-1-59835-190-3(7)) Cambridge BrickHouse, Inc.

—Amazing Adaptations! 2010. (J). (978-1-59835-191-0(5)); (978-1-59835-195-8(8)); (978-1-59835-196-5(6)); (978-1-59835-193-4(1)); (978-1-59835-199-6(0)); (978-1-59835-194-1(X)); (978-1-59835-198-9(2)); (978-1-59835-200-9(8)) Cambridge BrickHouse, Inc.

—Amazing Adaptations! Tongues. 2010. 24p. (J). pap. (978-1-59835-213-9(X), BrickHouse Education) Cambridge BrickHouse, Inc.

—Colors on Colors/Colores Sobre Colores: A World of Color. 2010. (SPA & ENG.). 24p. (J). pap. 6.99 (978-1-59835-276-4(8), BrickHouse Education) Cambridge BrickHouse, Inc.

—De quien es esta Sombra? Adivina Adivinador. 2010. (J). pap. 8.99 (978-1-59835-129-3(X), BrickHouse Education) Cambridge BrickHouse, Inc.

—Rhyming Tongue Twisters Animals. 2010. 32p. (J). 6.99 (978-1-59835-269-6(5), BrickHouse Education) Cambridge BrickHouse, Inc.

—Say What? 2010. 32p. 8.99 (978-1-59835-255-9(5), BrickHouse Education) Cambridge BrickHouse, Inc.

—Trabalenguas Zoológicos. 2010. (SPA.). 32p. (J). pap. 6.99 (978-1-59835-159-0(1), BrickHouse Education) Cambridge BrickHouse, Inc.

Canfield, Michael. Freaky Animal Stories. 2015. (Freaky True Science Ser.). (ENG., Illus.). 32p. (J). (gr. 4-5). pap. 10.50 (978-1-4824-2948-0(9), 1390462) Stevens, Gareth Publishing LLLP.

Carbone, Courtney. Amazing Animals (the World of Eric Carle) 2014. (Deluxe Reusable Sticker Book Ser.). (ENG.). 24p. (J). (gr. -1-2). pap. 6.99 (978-0-385-38787-3(3), Golden Bks.) Random Hse. Children's Bks.

Cardenas, Ernesto A. Amazing Animals. 2009. 23.95 (978-1-60698-035-4(1)); pap. 4.95 (978-1-60698-033-0(5)) Milo Educational Bks. & Resources.

—Textures. 2009. 23.95 (978-1-60698-047-7(5)); pap. 4.95 (978-1-60698-045-3(9)) Milo Educational Bks. & Resources.

Carle, Eric. El Canguro Tiene Mama?, 1 vol. Mlawer, Teresa, tr. Carle, Eric, illus. 2008.Tr. of Does a Kangaroo Have a Mother, Too? (SPA., Illus.). 32p. (J). (gr. -1-1). pap. 6.99 (978-0-06-001111-6(4)) HarperCollins Pubs.

—Does a Kangaroo Have a Mother, Too? Carle, Eric, illus. 2005. (ENG., Illus.). 32p. (J). (gr. -1-3). reprint ed. pap. 6.99 (978-0-06-443642-7(X)) HarperCollins Pubs.

—My Very First Book of Animal Sounds. Carle, Eric, illus. 2007. (ENG., Illus.). 40p. (J). (gr. -1 — 1). bds. 5.99 (978-0-399-24648-7(7), Philomel Bks.) Penguin Young Readers Group.

Carlton Publishing Group, illus. Fabulous Animals. 2016. (Cool & Calm Coloring for Kids Ser.). (ENG.). 48p. (J). (gr. 2-6). pap. 6.99 (978-1-4380-0926-1(7)) Barron's Educational Series, Inc.

Carnelos, Melissa. The 10 Most Amazing Animal Heroes. 2008. 14.99 (978-1-55448-516-1(9)) Scholastic Library Publishing.

Carnovsky, illus. Illuminature: A Search & Find Extravaganza That Illuminates Nature Night & Day with a Magical Viewing Lens. 2016. (ENG.). 64p. (J). (gr. 3-6). 30.00 (978-1-84780-887-5(5), Wide Eyed Editions) Quarto Publishing Group UK GBR. Dist: Hachette Bk. Group.

Carpenter, Tad. Arctic Animals. 2015. (Who's That? Ser.). (ENG., Illus.). 16p. (J). (— 1). bds. 7.95 (978-1-4549-1227-9(8)) Sterling Publishing Co., Inc.

Carr, Aaron. The Great Seal. 2013. (J). (978-1-62127-204-5(4)); pap. (978-1-62127-208-3(7)) Weigl Pubs., Inc.

—Magents with Code. 2012. (Science Kids Ser.). (ENG., Illus.). 24p. (J). (gr. -1-3). lib. bdg. 27.13 (978-1-61913-086-9(6), AV2 by Weigl) Weigl Pubs., Inc.

—Magnets, with Code. 2012. (Science Kids Ser.). (ENG., Illus.). 24p. (J). (gr. -1-1). pap. 12.95 (978-1-61913-756-1(9), AV2 by Weigl) Weigl Pubs., Inc.

—Números. 2013. (SPA.). (J). (978-1-62127-609-8(0)) Weigl Pubs., Inc.

Carr, Joaquin. Habitats of South America: Text Pairs. 2008. (Bridges/Navigators Ser.). (J). (gr. 3). 81.00 (978-1-4108-8361-2(2)) Benchmark Education Co.

Carson-Dellosa Publishing Staff. Alphabet Animals, Grades PK - K. 2010. (Home Workbooks Ser.). (ENG.). 64p. (gr. -1-k). pap. 4.49 (978-1-60418-760-1(3)) Carson-Dellosa Publishing, LLC.

Cartwright, Shannon. Alaska 1 2 3: Colors & Numbers. 2005. (Illus.). (J). (978-0-9772297-0-3(X)) Taku Graphics.

Cartwright, Stephen. Animal Noises. 2004. (Usborne Farmyard Tales Ser.). (ENG., Illus.). 1p. (J). (gr. -1-k). bds. 4.99 (978-0-7460-4104-8(7)) EDC Publishing.

—Noisy Animals Board Bk. Cartwright, Stephen, illus. 2007. (Illus.). 12p. (J). bds. 18.99 (978-0-7945-1551-5(7), Usborne) EDC Publishing.

Casado, Dami & Casado, Alicia. Los Ruidos Del Bosque. 2005. (SPA.). 12p. 7.99 (978-84-272-8292-6(3)) Molino, Editorial ESP. Dist: Santillana USA Publishing Co., Inc.

—Ruidos de la Selva. 2005. (SPA.). 12p. 7.99 (978-84-272-8294-0(X)) Molino, Editorial ESP. Dist: Santillana USA Publishing Co., Inc.

Catt, Thessaly. Animal Journeys, 6 vols., Set. Incl. Migrating with the Arctic Tern. (J). lib. bdg. 22.60 (978-1-4488-2542-4(3)); Migrating with the Caribou. (YA). 22.60 (978-1-4488-2541-7(5)); Migrating with the Humpback Whale. (J). lib. bdg. 22.60 (978-1-4488-2543-1(1)); Migrating with the Monarch Butterfly. (YA). lib. bdg. 22.60 (978-1-4488-2546-2(6)); Migrating with the Salmon. (YA). lib. bdg. 22.60 (978-1-4488-2545-5(8)); Migrating with the Wildebeest. (J). lib. bdg. 22.60 (978-1-4488-2544-8(X)); (gr. 1-4). (Animal Journeys Ser.). (Illus.). 24p. 2011. Set lib. bdg. 127.50 (978-1-4488-2781-7(7), PowerKids Pr.) Rosen Publishing Group, Inc., The.

Chamberlin-Calamar, Pat. Alaska's 12 Days of Summer. Cartwright, Shannon, illus. 2003. (Paws IV Ser.). (ENG.). 32p. (J). (gr. -1-2). pap. 10.99 (978-1-57061-341-8(9), Little Bigfoot) Sasquatch Bks.

Channing, Margot. Amazing Animals. 2015. (Inside Eye Ser.). (Illus.). 32p. (gr. 3-6). 31.35 (978-1-906370-73-2(7)) Book Hse. GBR. Dist: Black Rabbit Bks.

—Animals. Claude, Jean, illus. 2017. (First Words & Pictures Ser.). (ENG.). 14p. (J). (gr. -1 — 1). bds. 9.99 (978-1-68152-200-5(4)) Amicus.

—Incredible Creatures. 2015. (Inside Eye Ser.). (Illus.). 32p. (gr. 3-6). 31.35 (978-1-906370-80-0(X)) Book Hse. GBR. Dist: Black Rabbit Bks.

Charlesworth, Liza. Amazing Animals: A Spin & Spot Book. Reese, Brandon, illus. 2017. (ENG.). 16p. (J). (— 1). 8.99 (978-0-545-78383-5(6), Cartwheel Bks.) Scholastic, Inc.

—Guided Science Readers Super Set: Animals: A BIG Collection of High-Interest Leveled Books for Guided Reading Groups. 2012. (ENG.). 144p. (gr. -1-1). 129.99 (978-0-545-44272-5(9), Teaching Resources) Scholastic, Inc.

Charner, Kathy, ed. Learn Every Day about Animals. 2010. (Learn Every Day Ser.). (ENG., Illus.). 128p. pap. 12.95 (978-0-87659-126-0(8), Gryphon House Inc) Gryphon Hse., Inc.

Cherry Lake Publishing Staff, compiled by. Road to Recovery. 2009. 32p. lib. bdg. 319.20 (978-1-60279-106-0(6), 200075) Cherry Lake Publishing.

Cheshire, Gerald. Living World. 2013. (World of Wonder Ser.). (ENG., Illus.). 32p. (gr. 1-3). lib. bdg. 31.35 (978-1-908973-99-3(4)) Book Hse. GBR. Dist: Black Rabbit Bks.

Cheshire, Gerard. Scary Creatures of the Soil. Antram, David et al, illus. 2009. (Scary Creatures Ser.). (ENG.). 32p. (J). (gr. 2-4). 27.00 (978-0-531-21821-1(X), Watts, Franklin); pap. 8.95 (978-0-531-22226-3(8), Children's Pr.) Scholastic Library Publishing.

Chesire, Gerald. Living Things. Baker, Janet, illus. 2008. (World of Wonder Ser.). (ENG.). 32p. (J). (gr. 1-4). pap. 9.95 (978-0-531-23822-6(9), Children's Pr.) Scholastic Library Publishing.

—Living World. Baker, Janet et al, illus. 2008. (World of Wonder Ser.). (ENG.). 32p. (J). (gr. 1-4). 29.00 (978-0-531-24026-7(6), Children's Pr.) Scholastic Library Publishing.

Children's Nature Library: Animals, Animals, Animals. (Illus.). (J). (gr. k-4). lib. bdg. 104.65 (978-1-56674-930-5(1)) Forest Hse. Publishing Co., Inc.

Child's World Staff, The & Watson, S. B. Weird Animal Sports. 2011. (Weird Sports Ser.). (ENG., Illus.). 24p. (J). (gr. 2-5). lib. bdg. 28.50 (978-1-60954-375-4(0), 201053) Child's World, Inc., The.

Chinery, Michael. Animal Kingdom: Life in the Wild. 2011. (ENG., Illus.). 512p. (J). (gr. 4-7). 35.00 (978-0-7548-1963-9(9)) Anness Publishing GBR. Dist: National Bk. Network.

—Animales Salvajes. (Enciclopedias Everest Internacional Ser.). (SPA., Illus.). 320p. (J). (gr. 3-5). (978-84-241-9399-7(7), EV1502) Everest Editora ESP. Dist: Lectorum Pubns., Inc.

Chinery, Michael, ed. The Children's Encyclopedia of Animals: Life in the Wild. 2013. (ENG., Illus.). 512p. pap. 17.99 (978-1-84322-863-9(7), Armadillo) Anness Publishing GBR. Dist: National Bk. Network.

Christian, Cheryl. How Many? (Portuguese/English), 1 vol. Dwight, Laura, photos by. 2009. (ENG & POR., Illus.). 12p. (J). 5.95 (978-1-59572-190-7(8)) Star Bright Bks., Inc.

Christopher, Garrett. Look at These Animals: A Content Area Reader-science. 2005. (Sadlier Phonics Reading Program). (Illus.). 16p. (gr. k-2). 25.20 (978-0-8215-7812-4(X)) Sadlier, William H. Inc.

Chronicle Books Staff & Carle, Eric. Animal Place Mats: The World of Eric Carle Animal Place Mats. 2013. (ENG., Illus.). 96p. (J). (gr. -1-4). 12.99 (978-1-4521-1543-6(5)) Chronicle Bks. LLC.

Ciletti, Barbara. Asian Carp. 2016. (Invasive Species Takeover Ser.). (ENG., Illus.). 32p. (J). pap. 9.95 (978-1-68072-277-2(8)) RiverStream Publishing.

Ciovacco, Justine. Meerkats. 2007. (J). (978-1-59939-129-8(5), Reader's Digest Young Families, Inc.) Studio Fun International.

Clark, Katie. Animal Actors. 2013. (We Work! Animals with Jobs Ser.). (Illus.). 24p. (J). (gr. -1-3). lib. bdg. 21.32 (978-1-61772-897-6(7)) Bearport Publishing Co., Inc.

Clark Sawyer, J. Patterns in the Snow. 2015. (J). lib. bdg. (978-1-62724-340-7(2)) Bearport Publishing Co., Inc.

Clark, Willow. Animal Families, 6 vols., Set. Incl. Dolphins: Life in the Pod. lib. bdg. 22.60 (978-1-4488-2512-7(1)); Gorillas: Life in the Troop. lib. bdg. 22.60 (978-1-4488-2514-1(8)); Lions: Life in the Pride. lib. bdg. 22.60 (978-1-4488-2513-4(X)); Meerkats: Life in the Mob. lib. bdg. 22.60 (978-1-4488-2511-0(3)); Penguins: Life in the Colony. lib. bdg. 22.60 (978-1-4488-2510-3(5)); Wolves: Life in the Pack. lib. bdg. 22.60 (978-1-4488-2515-8(6)); (J). (gr. k-1). (Animal Families Ser.). (Illus.). 24p. 2011. 127.50 (978-1-4488-2777-0(9), PowerKids Pr.) Rosen Publishing Group, Inc., The.

—Yaks. 2012. (Animals of Asia Ser.). (ENG., Illus.). 24p. (J). (gr. 1-5). pap. 8.25 (978-1-4488-7488-0(2)); lib. bdg. 22.60 (978-1-4488-7415-6(7)) Rosen Publishing Group, Inc., The. (PowerKids Pr.).

Clarke, Ginjer L. Fake Out! Animals That Play Tricks. Mueller, Pete, illus. 2007. (Penguin Young Readers, Level 3 Ser.). (ENG.). 48p. (J). (gr. 1-3). mass mkt. 3.99 (978-0-448-44656-1(1), Penguin Young Readers) Penguin Young Readers Group.

—Freak Out! Animals Beyond Your Wildest Imagination. Mueller, Pete, illus. 2006. (Penguin Young Readers, Level 4 Ser.). (ENG.). 48p. (J). (gr. 3-4). mass mkt. 3.99 (978-0-448-44308-9(2), Penguin Young Readers) Penguin Young Readers Group.

—Freak Out! Animals Beyond Your Wildest Imagination. Mueller, Pete, illus. 2007. (All Aboard Science Reader Ser.). 48p. (gr. 1-3). 14.00 (978-0-7569-8173-0(5)) Perfection Learning Corp.

—Watch Out! The World's Most Dangerous Creatures. Mueller, Pete, illus. 2012. (Penguin Young Readers, Level 3 Ser.). (ENG.). 48p. (J). (gr. 1-3). pap. 3.99 (978-0-448-45108-4(5), Penguin Young Readers) Penguin Young Readers Group.

Clarke, Penny. The Arctic. 2008. (Scary Creatures Ser.). (ENG., Illus.). 32p. (J). (gr. 2-4). 27.00 (978-0-531-20449-8(9), Children's Pr.) Scholastic Library Publishing.

—Scary Creatures of the Arctic. 2008. (Scary Creatures Ser.). (ENG., Illus.). 32p. (J). (gr. 2-4). pap. 8.95 (978-0-531-21008-6(1), Watts, Franklin) Scholastic Library Publishing.

—Scary Creatures of the City. Baker, Janet et al, illus. 2009. (Scary Creatures Ser.). (ENG.). 32p. (J). (gr. 2-4). 27.00 (978-0-531-21820-4(1), Watts, Franklin); pap. 8.95 (978-0-531-22225-6(X), Children's Pr.) Scholastic Library Publishing.

—Scary Creatures of the Mountains. 2008. (Scary Creatures Ser.). (ENG.). 32p. (J). 27.00 (978-0-531-21748-1(5)); (gr. 2-4). pap. 8.95 (978-0-531-21902-7(X)) Scholastic Library Publishing. (Watts, Franklin).

—Scary Creatures of the Rain Forest. 2008. (Scary Creatures Ser.). (ENG., Illus.). 32p. (J). (gr. 2-7). 27.00 (978-0-531-20544-0(4), Children's Pr.); pap. 8.95 (978-0-531-21010-9(3), Watts, Franklin) Scholastic Library Publishing.

—Scary Creatures of the Wetlands. 2008. (Scary Creatures Ser.). (ENG.). 32p. (J). 27.00 (978-0-531-21749-8(3)); (gr. 2-4). pap. 8.95 (978-0-531-21903-4(8)) Scholastic Library Publishing. (Watts, Franklin).

Clarke, Phillip & Khan, Sarah. Facts & Records - Internet Linked: Combined Volume. 2004. (Facts & Lists Internet-Linked Ser.). 256p. (J). pap. 12.95 (978-0-7945-0679-7(8), Usborne) EDC Publishing.

Claybourne, Anna. Animal Atlas. Gwinn, Saskia, ed. Wald, Christina, illus. 2014. (ENG.). 64p. (J). (gr. -1-3). 17.99 (978-1-4088-4218-8(1), 9781408842188, Bloomsbury USA Childrens) Bloomsbury Publishing USA.

—Deadly Animals. 2016. (Animals Are Wild! Ser.). 40p. (gr. 4-3). pap. 14.05 (978-1-4824-5014-9(3)) Stevens, Gareth Publishing LLLP.

—Scanorama: Amazing Animals. 2016. (Scanorama Ser.). (ENG., Illus.). 32p. (J). (gr. 1). 18.99 (978-1-62686-631-7(7), Silver Dolphin Bks.) Readerlink Distribution Services, LLC.

—Scanorama: Deadly Predators. 2016. (Scanorama Ser.). (ENG., Illus.). 32p. (J). (gr. 1). 18.99 (978-1-62686-632-4(5), Silver Dolphin Bks.) Readerlink Distribution Services, LLC.

—100 Deadliest Things on the Planet. 2012. (ENG.). 112p. (J). (gr. 3-7). pap. 7.99 (978-0-545-43437-9(8), Scholastic Paperbacks) Scholastic, Inc.

—100 Deadliest Things on the Planet. 2012. (100 Most Ser.). lib. bdg. 18.40 (978-0-606-26744-1(1), Turtleback) Turtleback Bks.

Close, Edward. Endangered Animals. 2013. (Discovery Education: Habitats Ser.). 32p. (J). (gr. 3-6). 25.25 (978-1-4777-1325-9(5)); pap. 60.00 (978-1-4777-1486-7(3)); pap. 10.00 (978-1-4777-1485-0(5)) Rosen Publishing Group, Inc., The. (PowerKids Pr.).

Cloverfield, James. At Home with Animals. 2012. (InfoMax Readers Ser.). (ENG., Illus.). 24p. (J). (gr. 1-2). pap. 8.25 (978-1-4488-9007-1(1), Rosen Classroom) Rosen Publishing Group, Inc., The.

Cohen, Fiona. Curious Kids Nature Guide: Explore the Amazing Outdoors of the Pacific Northwest. Fylling, Marni, illus. 2017. (ENG.). 96p. (J). (gr. k-4). 19.99 (978-1-63217-083-5(3), Little Bigfoot) Sasquatch Bks.

Cohn, Scotti. Animal Partners, 1 vol. Bersani, Shennen, illus. 2015. (ENG.). 32p. (J). (gr. 2-5). 17.95 (978-1-62855-448-9(7)) Arbordale Publishing.

Coldiron, Deborah. Coral, 1 vol. 2007. (Underwater World Ser.). (ENG.). 32p. (gr. 3-7). 27.07 (978-1-59928-811-6(7), Buddy Bks.) ABDO Publishing Co.

Cole, Joanna. Polar Animals. 2014. (Magic School Bus Presents Ser.). lib. bdg. 17.20 (978-0-606-36331-0(9)) Turtleback Bks.

Cole, Joanna & O'Brien, Cynthia. Polar Animals. Degen, Bruce & Bracken, Carolyn, illus. 2014. (Magic School Bus Presents Ser.). (ENG.). 32p. (J). (gr. 1-3). pap. 6.99 (978-0-545-68586-3(9), Scholastic Paperbacks) Scholastic, Inc.

Colella, O. Animales de la Selva (Jungle Animals) 2005. (Collection Abre Tus Ojos, Collection Eye Openers Ser.). (SPA.). (J). (gr. k-2). 6.95 (978-950-11-0900-9(3)) Sigmar ARG. Dist: Iaconi, Mariuccia Bk. Imports.

Coleman, Michelle, compiled by. My Pets. 2012. (Touch & Feel Ser.). (ENG., Illus.). 10p. (J). (— 1). bds. 12.95 (978-1-61889-221-8(5)) AZ Bks. LLC.

—Wild Animals. 2013. (Touch & Feel Ser.). (ENG., Illus.). 10p. (J). (— 1). bds. 12.95 (978-1-61889-209-6(6)) AZ Bks. LLC.

Coleman, William L. The Big Book of Animal Devotions: 250 Daily Readings about God's Amazing Creation, 1 vol. 2009. (ENG.). 394p. (J). pap. 17.00 (978-0-7642-0669-6(9)) Bethany Hse. Pubs.

Collard, Sneed B., III. In the Wild. 2005. (Science Adventures Ser.). (Illus.). 48p. (gr. 4-7). lib. bdg. 29.93 (978-0-7614-1955-6(1), Benchmark Bks.) Marshall Cavendish Corp.

—Smart Survivors. 2004. (It's Nature! Ser.). (Illus.). 32p. (J). (gr. 3-6). pap. 7.95 (978-1-55971-750-2(5), Creative Publishing International) Quarto Publishing Group USA.

Collier, photos by. ABCs of South African Animals. Collier, . 2015. (Illus.). 32p. (gr. -1-1). pap. 12.99 (978-0-692-59277-9(6)) Educational Consulting by Design, LLC.

Collins. Collins Fascinating Facts - Animals. rev. ed. 2016. (Collins Fascinating Facts Ser.). (ENG., Illus.). 72p. (J). (gr. 1-3). pap. 10.99 (978-0-00-816929-9(2)) HarperCollins Pubs. Ltd. GBR. Dist: Independent Pubs. Group.

Collins, Stan. Animal Signs. 2003. (ENG.). 10p. (J). (gr. -1-k). spiral bd. 19.95 (978-1-930820-37-1(2)) Garlic Pr.

Collisin, Shauna. Heavenites Learning to Count on God Board Book with audio CD. Nelson, Christine, illus. 2007. 22p. (J). 15.95 (978-0-9792510-1-6(X)) Revelation Products LLC.

Colvin, L. Living World Encyclopedia. 2009. pap. 14.99 (978-0-7945-2784-6(1)) EDC Publishing.

¿Como Hablan los Animales? (Coleccion Primeros Pasos en la Ciencia). (SPA., Illus.). (J). (gr. 1-3). pap. (978-950-724-220-5(1), LMA8224) Lumen ARG. Dist: Lectorum Pubns., Inc.

Confusing Creature Names. 2014. (Confusing Creature Names Ser.). 24p. (J). (gr. 1-3). 135.60 (978-1-4824-0940-6(2)); pap. 48.90 (978-1-4824-1555-1(0)) Stevens, Gareth Publishing LLLP.

Cooper, Elisha. 8: An Animal Alphabet. 2015. (ENG., Illus.). 40p. (J). (gr. -1-k). 17.99 (978-0-545-47083-4(8)) Scholastic, Inc.

Cooper, Jayda. Food for Animals. 2016. (Rosen REAL Readers: STEM & STEAM Collection). 8p. (gr. 1-k). pap. 5.46 (978-1-5081-2374-3(8), Rosen Classroom) Rosen Publishing Group, Inc., The.

Cooper, Wade. Night Creatures. 2008. (Scholastic Reader Level 2 Ser.). (ENG.). 32p. (J). (gr. -1-3). pap. 3.99 (978-0-545-05797-4(3), Cartwheel Bks.) Scholastic, Inc.

—Polar Animals. 2009. (Scholastic Reader Level 1 Ser.). (ENG.). 32p. (J). (gr. -1-3). pap. 3.99 (978-0-545-05766-0(3), Cartwheel Bks.) Scholastic, Inc.

Corcorane, Ann. Big & Small Animals, 1 vol. 2011. (Wonder Readers Emergent Level Ser.). (ENG.). (gr. -1-1). 32p. pap.

5.99 *(978-1-4296-7840-7(2))*; 8p. pap. 35.94 *(978-1-4296-8220-6(5))* Capstone Press of Coughlan Cos. (Wonder Readers).

Corderoy, Tracey. Now! Warnes, Tim, illus. 2016. (ENG.). 32p. (J). (gr. -1-2). 16.99 *(978-1-68010-033-4(5))* Tiger Tales.

Coss, Lauren. Life in Estuaries. 2014. (Life in Water Biomes Ser.). (ENG.). 24p. (J). (gr. 2-5). 28.50 *(978-1-62687-294-3(5)*, 207135) Child's World, Inc., The.

Coste, Marion. Hawaii's Animals Do the Most Amazing Things! Ekmanis, Rena, illus. 2014. 47p. (J). *(978-0-8248-3962-8(5))* Univ. of Hawaii Pr.

Crazy Animals. 2014. (Ripleys Believe It or Not! Download the Weird Ser.: 8). 36p. (J). (gr. 4-18). lib. bdg. 20.95 *(978-1-4222-3149-4(6))* Mason Crest.

Creature Scene Investigation, 6 vols., Set. 2010. (Creature Scene Investigation Ser.). (gr. 5-8). 197.70 *(978-0-7910-9934-6(2)*, Chelsea Hse.) Facts On File, Inc.

Creature's Corner. (Super Sticker Book Ser.). (Illus.). 64p. (J). pap. *(978-2-7643-0129-6(4))* Phidal Publishing, Inc./Editions Phidal, Inc.

Creatures We Can't Live Without. 2015. (Creatures We Can't Live Without Ser.). (ENG.). 24p. (J). (gr. 3-4). pap., pap., pap. 297.00 *(978-1-4994-1280-2(0)*, PowerKids Pr.) Rosen Publishing Group, Inc., The.

Creese, Sarah. Extreme Animals: I-Explore Reader. 2013. (ENG.). 32p. (J). pap. 4.99 *(978-1-78235-158-0(2))* Make Believe Ideas GBR. Dist: Nelson, Thomas Inc.

Criaturas Increibles, 6 vols. (Explorers. Exploradores Nonfiction Sets Ser.). (SPA.). 32p. (gr. 3-6). 44.95 *(978-0-7699-0625-6(7))* Shortland Pubns. (U. S. A.) Inc.

Cricket Magazine Editors. Oink-Oink: And Other Animal Sounds. Conteh-Morgan, Jane, illus. 2007. (ENG.). 20p. (J). (gr. k-k). bds. 7.95 *(978-0-8126-7934-2(2))* Cricket Bks.

Crispiels, Giada, illus. Wildlife of New York Coloring Book: A Five-Borough Coloring Book. 2016. (ENG.). 60p. 14.95 *(978-0-7892-1255-9(2))* Abbeville Pr., Inc.

Critters & Bugs of the Tropical Rainforest. 2003. (J). spiral bd. 12.95 *(978-1-931334-33-4(1))* Pieces of Learning.

Cromarty, Jim. Great Barrier Reef Adventures. 2005. (Adventure Ser.). (ENG., Illus.). 96p. (J). (gr. 3-7). per. 8.99 *(978-1-84550-068-9(7)*, 3ec344eb-b5a7-45bd-8d58-a6ba056815cc) Christian Focus Pubns. GBR. Dist: Bookmasters Distribution.

Cuddy, Robbin. Learn to Draw Exotic Animals: Step-By-step Instructions for More Than 25 Unusual Animals. 2016. (Learn to Draw Ser.). (ENG., Illus.). 64p. (J). (gr. 1-3). pap. 8.95 *(978-1-63322-065-2(6)*, Walter Foster Jr) Quarto Publishing Group USA.

Cundy, David. Animals Spell Love. 2016. (Illus.). 40p. (J). *(978-1-56792-586-9(3))* Godine, David R. Pub.

Cusick, Dawn. Animal Snacks. 2012. (ENG., Illus.). 96p. (J). (gr. -1-3). 15.95 *(978-0-9832014-5-8(5))* EarlyLight Bks., Inc.

—Animal Tongues. 2017. (ENG., Illus.). 36p. (J). (gr. -1-3). pap. 7.99 ***(978-1-58089-687-0(1))*** Charlesbridge Publishing, Inc.

—Animals That Make Me Say Ewww! 2016. (ENG., Illus.). 80p. (J). (gr. 2-5). 14.95 *(978-1-62354-063-0(1))* Charlesbridge Publishing, Inc.

—Cool Animal Names. 2011. (ENG., Illus.). 80p. (J). (gr. 2-5). 14.95 *(978-1-936140-39-8(X))* Charlesbridge Publishing, Inc.

—Get the Scoop on Animal Poop: From Lions to Tapeworms: 251 Cool Facts about Scat, Frass, Dung, & More! 2013. (ENG., Illus.). 80p. (J). (gr. 2-5). pap. 9.95 *(978-1-62354-014-2(3))* Charlesbridge Publishing, Inc.

—Get the Scoop on Animal Puke! From Zombie Ants to Vampire Bats, 251 Cool Facts about Vomit, Regurgitation, & More! 2014. (ENG., Illus.). 80p. (J). (gr. 2-5). 14.95 *(978-1-62354-045-6(3))* Charlesbridge Publishing, Inc.

Cusick, Dawn & National Wildlife Federation Staff. Animals That Make Me Say Ouch! 2014. (ENG., Illus.). 80p. (J). (gr. 2-5). 14.95 *(978-1-62354-042-5(9))* Charlesbridge Publishing, Inc.

—Animals That Make Me Say Wow! 2014. (ENG., Illus.). 80p. (J). (gr. 2-5). 14.95 *(978-1-62354-041-8(0))* Charlesbridge Publishing, Inc.

Cutest Animals... That Could Kill You! 2016. (Cutest Animals... That Could Kill You! Ser.). 24p. (gr. 3-2). pap. 48.90 *(978-1-4824-5315-7(0))*; lib. bdg. 135.60 *(978-1-4824-4597-8(2))* Stevens, Gareth Publishing LLLP.

Cuxart, Bernadette. Modeling Clay with 3 Basic Shapes: Model More Than 40 Animals with Drops, Balls, & Worms. 2016. (ENG.). 96p. (J). (gr. -1-3). pap. 11.99 *(978-1-4380-0908-7(9))* Barron's Educational Series, Inc.

Dahl, Michael & Jensen, Brian. Rápido, Más Rápido, Muy Rápido: Animales Que se Muevan a Grandes Velocidades. Translations.com Staff, tr. from ENG. Dahl, Michael & Jensen, Brian, illus. 2012. (Los Extremos y Los Animales/Animal Extremes Ser.).Tr. of Fast, Faster, Fastest-Animals That Move at Great Speeds. (MUL & SPA., Illus.). 24p. (gr. k-2). lib. bdg. 26.65 *(978-1-4048-7317-9(1))* Picture Window Bks.

Dalmatian Press Staff. Say Moo! 2008. (ENG.). 5p. (J). bds. 4.95 *(978-1-58117-722-0(4)*, Intervisual/Piggy Toes) Bendon, Inc.

Dangerous Animals: Level P, 6 vols., Vol. 3. (Explorers Ser.). 32p. (gr. 3-6). 44.95 *(978-0-7699-0613-3(3))* Shortland Pubns. (U. S. A.) Inc.

D'Aulaire, Ingri & D'Aulaire, Edgar Parin. D'Aulaires' Book of Animals. 2007. (New York Review Children's Collection). (ENG., Illus.). 30p. (J). (gr. k-k). 18.95 *(978-1-59017-226-1(4)*, NYR Children's Collection) New York Review of Bks., Inc., The.

David C. Cook Publishing Company Staff. Land of Milk & Honey. 2007. (LMH Ser.). 16p. (J). (gr. 1-3). Bk. 3. 6.99 *(978-0-7814-4526-9(4))*Bk. 4. 6.99 *(978-0-7814-4527-6(2))* Cook, David C.

Davidson, Susanna. World of Animals: Internet-Linked. Unwin, Mike, illus. 2009. (Nature Encyclopedias Ser.). 144p. (YA). (gr. 3-18). pap. 16.99 *(978-0-7945-2033-5(2)*, Usborne) EDC Publishing.

Davidson, Susanna & Unwin, Mike. The Usborne World of Animals. Montgomery, Lee & Jackson, Ian, illus. 2005. 128p. (J). pap. *(978-0-439-86321-6(X))* Scholastic, Inc.

Davies, Becky. Peekaboo Pals a to Z. Lucas, Gareth, illus. 2016. (Peekaboo Pals Ser.). (ENG.). 20p. (J). (gr. -1). bds. 14.95 *(978-1-62686-520-4(5)*, Silver Dolphin Bks.) Readerlink Distribution Services, LLC.

—Peekaboo Pals Opposites. Lucas, Gareth, illus. 2016. (Peekaboo Pals Ser.). (ENG.). 20p. (J). (gr. -1). bds. 14.95 *(978-1-62686-522-8(1)*, Silver Dolphin Bks.) Readerlink Distribution Services, LLC.

Davies, Monika. Adaptations. 2015. (Science Readers: Content & Literacy Ser.). (ENG., Illus.). 32p. (gr. 4-4). pap. 8.99 *(978-1-4807-4679-4(7))* Teacher Created Materials, Inc.

Davies, Nicola. Deadly! The Truth about the Most Dangerous Creatures on Earth. Layton, Neal, illus. 2013. (Animal Science Ser.). (ENG.). 64p. (J). (gr. 3-7). 14.99 *(978-0-7636-6231-8(3))* Candlewick Pr.

—Deadly! the Truth about the Most Dangerous Creatures on Earth. 2015. (Animal Science Ser.). lib. bdg. 18.40 *(978-0-606-37412-5(4))* Turtleback Bks.

—Everything You Need to Know about Animals: A First Enyclopedia for Budding Zoologists. 2013. (Everything You Need to Know Ser.). (ENG., Illus.). 160p. (J). (gr. k-4). pap. 12.99 *(978-0-7534-6975-0(8)*, 9780753469750, Kingfisher) Roaring Brook Pr.

—Just the Right Size: Why Big Animals Are Big & Little Animals Are Little. Layton, Neal, illus. 2011. (Animal Science Ser.). (ENG.). 64p. (J). (gr. 3-7). pap. 7.99 *(978-0-7636-5300-2(4))* Candlewick Pr.

—What Happens Next? Boutavant, Marc, illus. 2012. (Flip the Flap & Find Out Ser.). (ENG.). 24p. (J). (gr. -1-2). 9.99 *(978-0-7636-6264-6(X))* Candlewick Pr.

—What Will I Be? Boutavant, Marc, illus. 2012. (Flip the Flap & Find Out Ser.). (ENG.). 32p. (J). (gr. -1-2). 9.99 *(978-0-7636-5803-8(0))* Candlewick Pr.

Davis, Lee. The Lifesize Animal Opposites Book. (Illus.). 32p. (J). pap. 16.95 *(978-0-590-24372-8(1))* Scholastic, Inc.

Day, Trevor. Pets Parents Hate! [Scholastic]: Animal Life Cycles. 2011. (Extreme! Ser.). 32p. pap. 1.00 *(978-1-4296-6487-5(8)*, Fact Finders) Capstone Press of Coughlan Cos.

Dayton, Connor. Mountain Animals. 2009. (American Habitats Ser.). (gr. 2-5). (ENG., Illus.). 24p. (J). pap. 8.25 *(978-1-4358-3194-0(2)*, PowerKids Pr.); 24p. 42.50 *(978-1-61511-354-5(1)*, PowerKids Pr.); (J). lib. bdg. 22.60 *(978-1-4358-2765-3(1))* Rosen Publishing Group, Inc., The.

—Prairie Animals. 2009. (American Habitats Ser.). 24p. (gr. 2-3). 42.50 *(978-1-61511-357-6(6)*, PowerKids Pr.) Rosen Publishing Group, Inc., The.

—Tundra Animals. 2009. (American Habitats Ser.). 24p. (gr. 2-5). (ENG., Illus.). (J). pap. 8.25 *(978-1-4358-3197-1(7)*, PowerKids Pr.); 42.50 *(978-1-61511-360-6(6)*, PowerKids Pr.); (YA). lib. bdg. 22.60 *(978-1-4358-2768-4(6))* Rosen Publishing Group, Inc., The.

—Wetland Animals. 2009. (American Habitats Ser.). 24p. (gr. 2-5). (ENG., Illus.). (J). pap. 8.25 *(978-1-4358-3198-8(5)*, PowerKids Pr.); (YA). lib. bdg. 22.60 *(978-1-4358-2769-1(4))* Rosen Publishing Group, Inc., The.

A de Animales: Big Book. (Pebble Soup Exploraciones Ser.). (SPA.). 16p. (gr. -1-18). 31.00 *(978-0-7578-1681-9(9))* Rigby Education.

A de Animales: Small Book. (Pebble Soup Exploraciones Ser.). (SPA.). 16p. (gr. -1-18). 5.00 *(978-0-7578-1721-2(1))* Rigby Education.

De la Bédoyère, Camilla. Biggest & Smallest. 2010. (Animal Opposites Ser.). (ENG., Illus.). 32p. (J). (gr. -1-3). pap. 5.95 *(978-1-55407-805-9(9)*, 9781554078059) Firefly Bks., Ltd.

—The Complete Guide to Deadly Predators. 2016. (Illus.). 144p. (J). ***(978-1-4351-6353-9(2))*** Barnes & Noble, Inc.

—Deadly Creatures. 2010. (Unpredictable Nature Ser.). (Illus.). 48p. (J). (gr. 3-18). lib. bdg. 19.95 *(978-1-4222-1996-6(8))* Mason Crest.

—I Love Hugs & Kisses. 2014. (Illus.). (J). *(978-1-4351-5942-6(X))* Barnes & Noble, Inc.

De La Bédoyère, Camilla. Mega Spot the Difference: Rainforest. 2016. (ENG., Illus.). 80p. (J). (gr. 3). pap. 9.95 *(978-1-78312-165-6(3))* Carlton Kids GBR. Dist: Sterling Publishing Co., Inc.

De la Bédoyère, Camilla. My Little Book of Animals. 2014. (Illus.). 64p. (J). ***(978-1-4351-5526-8(2))*** Barnes & Noble, Inc.

—Smartest & Silliest. 2010. (Animal Opposites Ser.). (ENG., Illus.). 32p. (J). (gr. -1-3). pap. 5.95 *(978-1-55407-819-6(9)*, 9781554078196) Firefly Bks., Ltd.

—Strongest & Weakest. 2010. (Animal Opposites Ser.). (ENG., Illus.). 32p. (J). (gr. -1-3). pap. 5.95 *(978-1-55407-823-3(7)*, 9781554078233) Firefly Bks., Ltd.

—Wild Animals. 2010. (Ripley Twists Ser.). 48p. (J). (gr. 3-18). lib. bdg. 19.95 *(978-1-4222-1835-8(X))* Mason Crest.

De La Bédoyère, Camilla. The Wild Side, 1 vol. 2015. (Wild Side Ser.). (ENG.). 24p. (J). 66.00 *(978-1-4994-8027-6(X)*, Windmill Bks.) Rosen Publishing Group, Inc., The.

de Lambilly-Bresson, Elisabeth. Animales Sorprendentes. 2007. (Los animales nos cuentan su vida (Animal Show & Tell) Ser.). (SPA., Illus.). 16p. (gr. -1-3). lib. bdg. 19.00 *(978-0-8368-8108-0(7)*, Gareth Stevens Learning Library) Stevens, Gareth Publishing LLLP.

—Animals in Polar Regions. 2007. (Animal Show & Tell Ser.). (Illus.). 16p. (gr. -1-3). lib. bdg. 19.00 *(978-0-8368-8203-2(2)*, Gareth Stevens Learning Library) Stevens, Gareth Publishing LLLP.

—Animals in the Field. 2007. (Animal Show & Tell Ser.). (Illus.). 16p. (gr. -1-3). lib. bdg. 19.00 *(978-0-8368-7831-8(0)*, Gareth Stevens Learning Library) Stevens, Gareth Publishing LLLP.

—Animals in the Garden. 2007. (Animal Show & Tell Ser.). (Illus.). 16p. (gr. -1-3). lib. bdg. 19.00 *(978-0-8368-7832-5(9)*, Gareth Stevens Learning Library) Stevens, Gareth Publishing LLLP.

—Animals of the Mountains. 2007. (Animal Show & Tell Ser.). (Illus.). 16p. (gr. -1-3). lib. bdg. 19.00 *(978-0-8368-8207-0(5)*, Gareth Stevens Learning Library) Stevens, Gareth Publishing LLLP.

—Unusual Animals. 2007. (Animal Show & Tell Ser.). (Illus.). 16p. (gr. -1-3). lib. bdg. 19.00 *(978-0-8368-7836-3(1)*, Gareth Stevens Learning Library) Stevens, Gareth Publishing LLLP.

Deen, Marilyn. Big, Bigger, Biggest, 1 vol. 2011. (Wonder Readers: Mathematics Ser.). (ENG.). (gr. -1-2). 20p. lib. bdg. 22.65 *(978-1-4296-8629-7(4))*; 16p. pap. 35.94 *(978-1-4296-8071-4(7))*; 32p. pap. 5.99 *(978-1-4296-7909-1(3))* Capstone Press of Coughlan Cos. (Wonder Readers).

Del Moral, S., tr. Animales. 2006. (Disney Learning (Silver Dolphin en Espanol) Ser.). (Illus.). 22p. (J). (gr. -1). *(978-970-718-431-2(0)*, Silver Dolphin en Español) Advanced Marketing, S. de R. L. de C. V.

del Moral Zavariz, Susana. Donde Viven? 2007. (Baby Einstein Ser.). (Illus.). 8p. (J). (gr. -1). *(978-970-718-395-7(0)*, Silver Dolphin en Español) Advanced Marketing, S. de R. L. de C. V.

Delacre, Lulu. ¡Olinguito, de la A a la Z!: Descubriendo el Bosque Nublado: Olinguito, from A to Z!: Unveiling the Cloud Forest. Delacre, Lulu, illus. 2016. (ENG & SPA., Illus.). 40p. (J). 18.95 *(978-0-89239-327-5(0))* Lee & Low Bks., Inc.

Los Desiertos. (Coleccion Planeta Vivo).Tr. of Deserts. (SPA.). (J). (gr. 5-8). 12.00 *(978-84-342-1947-2(6))* Parramon Ediciones S.A. ESP. Dist: Distribuidora Norma, Inc.

Diamant, Vlasta. This Really Happened. 2010. (ENG.). (J). pap. *(978-1-4507-3132-4(5))* Independent Pub.

Diaz, Joanne Ruelos. Animals All Day!, 1 vol. Mendez, Simon, illus. 2014. (Animals All Day! Ser.). (ENG.). 32p. (gr. k-2). 109.08 *(978-1-4795-5702-8(1))* Picture Window Bks.

—Animals on the African Savanna, 1 vol. Mendez, Simon, illus. 2014. (Animals All Day! Ser.). (ENG.). 32p. (gr. k-2). 27.27 *(978-1-4795-5701-1(3))* Picture Window Bks.

Dickmann, Nancy. Food from Farms, 1 vol. 2010. (World of Farming Ser.). (ENG.). 24p. (gr. -1-k). pap. 6.29 *(978-1-4329-3943-4(2)*, Acorn) Heinemann-Raintree.

—Watch It Grow, 1 vol., Set. Incl. Apple's Life. (Illus.). pap. 6.29 *(978-1-4329-4150-5(X))*; Bean's Life. (Illus.). pap. 6.29 *(978-1-4329-4151-2(8))*; Bee's Life. (Illus.). pap. 6.29 *(978-1-4329-4146-8(1))*; Butterfly's Life. (Illus.). pap. 6.29 *(978-1-4329-4147-5(X))*; Chicken's Life. (Illus.). pap. 6.29 *(978-1-4329-4148-2(8))*; Dog's Life. pap. 6.29 *(978-1-4329-4232-8(8))*; Frog's Life. pap. 6.29 *(978-1-4329-4149-9(6))*; Oak Tree's Life. (Illus.). pap. 6.29 *(978-1-4329-4152-9(6))*; Penguin's Life. (Illus.). pap. 6.29 *(978-1-4329-4233-5(6))*; Sunflower's Life. (Illus.). pap. 6.29 *(978-1-4329-4153-6(4))*; Turtle's Life. pap. 6.29 *(978-1-4329-4234-2(4))*; (gr. -1-1). (Watch It Grow Ser.). (ENG.). 24p. 2010. Set pap. 69.19 *(978-1-4329-4154-3(2)*, Acorn) Heinemann-Raintree.

—World of Farming, 1 vol., Set. Incl. Farm Animals. pap. 6.29 *(978-1-4329-3941-0(6))*; Farm Machines. pap. 6.29 *(978-1-4329-3942-7(4))*; Food from Farms. pap. 6.29 *(978-1-4329-3943-4(2))*; Jobs on a Farm. (Illus.). pap. 6.29 *(978-1-4329-3945-8(9))*; Plants on a Farm. pap. 6.29 *(978-1-4329-3950-2(5))*; Seasons on a Farm. pap. 6.29 *(978-1-4329-3953-3(X))*; (gr. -1-1). (World of Farming Ser.). (ENG.). 24p. 2010. Set pap. 35.94 *(978-1-4329-3935-9(1)*, Acorn) Heinemann-Raintree.

Discovery Education: Animals. 2014. (Discovery Education: Animals Ser.). 32p. (J). (gr. 3-6). 210.00 *(978-1-4777-6984-3(6))*; pap. 80.00 *(978-1-4777-7258-4(8))* Rosen Publishing Group, Inc., The. (PowerKids Pr.).

DiSiena, Laura Lyn & Eliot, Hannah. Chickens Don't Fly: And Other Fun Facts. Oswald, Pete, illus. 2014. (Did You Know? Ser.). (ENG.). 32p. (J). (gr. -1-3). 17.99 *(978-1-4424-9353-7(4))*; pap. 6.99 *(978-1-4424-9326-1(7))* Little Simon. (Little Simon).

—Did You Know? Hippos Can't Swim; Chickens Don't Fly; Rainbows Never End; Trains Can Float. Oswald, Pete & Spurgeon, Aaron, illus. 2014. (Did You Know? Ser.). (ENG.). 128p. (J). (gr. -1-3). pap. 23.99 *(978-1-4814-3032-6(7)*, Little Simon) Little Simon.

Disiena, Laura Lyn & Eliot, Hannah. Hippos Can't Swim. 2014. (Did You Know? Ser.). lib. bdg. 16.00 *(978-0-606-35424-0(7))* Turtleback Bks.

DiSiena, Laura Lyn & Eliot, Hannah. Hippos Can't Swim: And Other Fun Facts. Oswald, Pete, illus. 2014. (Did You Know? Ser.). (ENG.). 32p. (J). (gr. -1-3). 17.99 *(978-1-4424-9352-0(6))*; pap. 5.99 *(978-1-4424-9324-7(0))* Little Simon. (Little Simon).

Disney Book Group. Lion Guard Kion's Animal Alphabet. Disney Storybook Art Team, illus. 2016. (ENG.). 10p. (J). (gr. -1-k). bds. 12.99 *(978-1-4847-2949-6(8))* Disney Pr.

Dlugos, Jenn & Hatton, Charlie. Crooked Critters. 2016. (Things That Make You Go Yuck! Ser.: 0). (ENG., Illus.). 88p. (J). (gr. 4-7). pap. 7.95 *(978-1-61821-609-0(0)*, 9781618216090) Prufrock Pr.

—Extreme Living. 2016. (Things That Make You Go Yuck! Ser.: 0). (ENG., Illus.). 88p. (J). (gr. 4-7). pap. 7.95 *(978-1-61821-568-0(X)*, 9781618215680) Prufrock Pr.

—Mystifying Mutants. 2016. (Things That Make You Go Yuck! Ser.: 0). (ENG., Illus.). 88p. (J). (gr. 4-7). pap. 7.95 *(978-1-61821-564-2(7)*, 9781618215642) Prufrock Pr.

Dodson, Emma & Woodward, John. Wow, I Didn't Know That! Surprising Facts about Animals. Aspinall, Marc, illus. 2013. (Wow! Ser.). (ENG.). 32p. (J). (gr. k-3). 8.99 *(978-0-7534-7166-1(3)*, 9780753471661, Kingfisher) Roaring Brook Pr.

Doeden, Matt. Deadly Venomous Animals. 2013. (ShockZone — Deadly & Dangerous Ser.). (ENG., Illus.). 32p. (gr. 5-8). pap. 8.95 *(978-1-4677-0892-0(5))*; lib. bdg. 26.60 *(978-1-4677-0599-8(3)*, Lerner Pubns.) Lerner Publishing Group.

—Real-World Dragons, 1 vol. Pellegrino, Rich, illus. 2013. (World of Dragons Ser.). (ENG.). 32p. (gr. 1-2). lib. bdg. 26.65 *(978-1-62065-146-9(7)*, Blazers) Capstone Press of Coughlan Cos.

Doherty, Gillian. 1001 Animals, Farm, Town & Long Ago. 2004. (1001 Things to Spot Ser.). 132p. (J). pap. 12.95 *(978-0-7945-0352-9(7))* EDC Publishing.

—1001 Animals to Spot. 2010. (1001 Things to Spot Ser.). 32p. (J). 9.99 *(978-0-7945-2704-4(3)*, Usborne) EDC Publishing.

Doherty, Gillian, et al. The Usborne Big Book of Things to Spot. Gower, Teri, illus. 2006. (1001 Things to Spot Ser.). 132p. (J). (gr. 1). lib. bdg. 20.95 *(978-1-58086-496-1(1))* EDC Publishing.

Dolphin, Colleen. Armadillos to Zorillas: Animals from A to Z, 1 vol. 2007. (Let's See A to Z Ser.). (ENG., Illus.). 32p. (gr. -1-3). 27.07 *(978-1-59928-883-3(4)*, Super SandCastle) ABDO Publishing Co.

Dompierre, Judith E. No More Than Four of a Kind. 2012. 36p. pap. 24.95 *(978-1-4626-9329-0(6))* America Star Bks.

Donahue, Peter. All Aboard! Trains Stained Glass Coloring Book. 2011. (Dover Stained Glass Coloring Book Ser.). (ENG., Illus.). 32p. (J). (gr. -1-2). pap. 6.99 *(978-0-486-47896-8(3))* Dover Pubns., Inc.

Donaldson, Julia. My First Animal Fun Sticker Book. Sharratt, Nick, illus. 2016. (ENG.). 30p. (J). (gr. -1-2). pap. 8.99 *(978-1-5098-1622-4(4))* Pan Macmillan GBR. Dist: Independent Pubs. Group.

Donovan, Barbara A. A World of Animals, 6 vols., Set. 2004. (Phonics Readers Books 37-72 Ser.). (ENG.). 8p. (gr. k-1). pap. 35.70 *(978-0-7368-4059-0(1)*, Phonics Readers) Capstone Press of Coughlan Cos.

Donovan, Sandy. Until the Cows Come Home: And Other Expressions about Animals. Blecha, Aaron, illus. 2012. (It's Just an Expression Ser.). (ENG.). 32p. (gr. 4-6). lib. bdg. 26.60 *(978-0-7613-7890-7(1)*, Lerner Pubns.) Lerner Publishing Group.

Donovan, Tristan. Feral Cities: Adventures with Animals in the Urban Jungle. 2015. (ENG.). 256p. pap. 16.95 *(978-1-56976-067-3(5))* Chicago Review Pr., Inc.

Dorling Kindersley Publishing Staff. Amazing Giant Wild Animals. 2013. (Amazing Giant Ser.). (ENG.). 16p. (J). (gr. k-4). 19.99 *(978-1-4654-0915-7(7)*, DK Children) Dorling Kindersley Publishing, Inc.

—Animal. 2015. (DK Eyewitness Bks.). (ENG., Illus.). 72p. (J). (gr. 3-7). 19.99 *(978-1-4654-3571-2(9)*, DK Children) Dorling Kindersley Publishing, Inc.

—Animal Alphabet. 2014. (ENG.). 14p. (J). (gr. -1-k). bds. 7.99 *(978-1-4654-1754-1(0)*, DK Children) Dorling Kindersley Publishing, Inc.

—The Animal Book. 2013. (ENG.). 304p. (J). (gr. 3-7). 24.99 *(978-1-4654-1457-1(6)*, DK Children) Dorling Kindersley Publishing, Inc.

—Animal Face Book. 2012. (ENG.). 64p. (J). (gr. 2-7). 12.99 *(978-0-7566-9050-2(1))* Dorling Kindersley Publishing, Inc.

—Animals. Quasha, Jennifer, ed. 2008. (Baby Touch & Feel Ser.). (ENG., Illus.). 14p. (J). (gr. -1 — 1). bds. 5.99 *(978-0-7566-3468-1(7)*, DK Children) Dorling Kindersley Publishing, Inc.

—Animals. (DK Braille Ser.). (ENG.). (J). 2016. 32p. (gr. 2-4). 22.99 *(978-1-4654-3611-5(1))* 2005. 16p. (gr. -1 — 1). 9.99 *(978-0-7566-1515-4(1))* 3rd ed. 2012. (Illus.). 304p. (gr. k-4). 19.99 *(978-0-7566-9170-7(2))* Dorling Kindersley Publishing, Inc. (DK Children).

—Animals. 2004. (Illus.). lib. bdg. 7.95 *(978-0-8225-3624-6(2))* Lerner Publishing Group.

—Animals. 2003. (J). per. *(978-1-884907-42-5(3))*; per. *(978-1-884907-46-3(6))* Paradise Pr., Inc.

—Animals. Date not set. (Illus.). (J). 40p. 3.98 *(978-1-4054-0176-0(1))*; 176p. 7.98 *(978-0-7525-9623-5(3))*; bds. 5.98 *(978-0-7525-8558-1(4))* Parragon, Inc.

—Animals. (J). (gr. k-1). *(978-84-342-2417-9(8)*, PR30571) Parramon Ediciones S.A. ESP. Dist: Lectorum Pubns., Inc.

—Baby Faces Peekaboo! 2009. (ENG.). 12p. (J). (gr. -1 — 1). bds. 9.99 *(978-0-7566-5506-8(4)*, DK Children) Dorling Kindersley Publishing, Inc.

—Baby Roar! Roar! 2015. (ENG.). 14p. (J). (gr. -1 — 1). bds. 5.99 *(978-1-4654-3554-5(9)*, DK Children) Dorling Kindersley Publishing, Inc.

—Children's Book of Mythical Beasts & Magical Monsters. 2011. (ENG.). 144p. (J). (gr. 2-5). 24.99 *(978-0-7566-8605-5(9)*, DK Children) Dorling Kindersley Publishing, Inc.

—Cuddly Animals. 2011. (Baby Touch & Feel Ser.). (ENG.). 14p. (J). (gr. -1 — 1). bds. 5.99 *(978-0-7566-8688-8(1)*, DK Children) Dorling Kindersley Publishing, Inc.

—Deadly Animals. 2016. (Ultimate Sticker Bks.). (ENG.). 32p. (J). (gr. k-3). pap. 6.99 *(978-1-4654-5087-6(4)*, DK Children) Dorling Kindersley Publishing, Inc.

—Did You Know? Animals. 2016. (ENG., Illus.). 144p. (J). (gr. k-4). 21.99 *(978-1-4654-4759-3(8)*, DK Children) Dorling Kindersley Publishing, Inc.

—DK Eyewitness Books: Animal: Animal. 2015. (DK Eyewitness Bks.). (ENG., Illus.). 72p. (J). (gr. 3-7). pap. 9.99 *(978-1-4654-3570-5(0)*, DK Children) Dorling Kindersley Publishing, Inc.

—DK Findout! Animals. 2016. (DK Find Out! Ser.). (ENG., Illus.). 64p. (J). (gr. 1-4). pap. 10.99 *(978-1-4654-5426-3(8)*, DK Children) Dorling Kindersley Publishing, Inc.

—Farm. 2013. (ENG.). 12p. (J). (gr. -1 — 1). bds. 9.99 *(978-1-4654-0924-9(6)*, DK Children) Dorling Kindersley Publishing, Inc.

—First Animal Encyclopedia. 2015. (ENG., Illus.). 168p. (J). (gr. 1-4). 16.99 *(978-1-4654-3552-1(2)*, DK Children) Dorling Kindersley Publishing, Inc.

—Follow the Trail: Winter Wonderland. 2017. (Follow the Trail Ser.). (ENG.). 14p. (J). (-k). bds. 9.99 ***(978-1-4654-6136-0(1)***, DK Children) Dorling Kindersley Publishing, Inc.

—Garden Friends, Pre-Level 1. 2010. (DK Readers Ser.). (ENG.). 32p. (J). (gr. -1-1). 3.99 *(978-0-7566-6167-0(6)*, DK Children) Dorling Kindersley Publishing, Inc.

—Growl! Howl! Animals. 2015. (ENG.). 12p. (J). (— 1). bds. 14.99 *(978-1-4654-3830-0(0)*, DK Children) Dorling Kindersley Publishing, Inc.

—Little Hide & Seek Animals. 2012. (ENG.). 16p. (J). (gr. -1 — 1). bds. 7.99 *(978-0-7566-9273-5(3)*, DK Children) Dorling Kindersley Publishing, Inc.

—My Encyclopedia of Very Important Animals. 2017. (ENG.). 224p. (J). (gr. -1-3). 16.99 ***(978-1-4654-6198-8(1)***, DK Children) Dorling Kindersley Publishing, Inc.

—My First Animals: Let's Squeak & Squawk! 2010. (Tab Board Bks.). (ENG., Illus.). 28p. (J). (gr. -1 — 1). bds. 9.99 *(978-0-7566-6301-8(6)*, DK Children) Dorling Kindersley Publishing, Inc.

—Pocket Genius: Animals. 2016. (Pocket Genius Ser.). (ENG., Illus.). 160p. (J). (gr. 3-7). pap. 4.99 *(978-1-4654-4526-1(9)*, DK Children) Dorling Kindersley Publishing, Inc.

—Pull the Tab - Animals. 2014. (ENG., Illus.). 10p. (J). (gr. -1 — 1). bds. 6.99 *(978-1-4654-1686-5(2)*, DK Children) Dorling Kindersley Publishing, Inc.

—Roar! Roar! 2013. (Baby Touch & Feel Ser.). (ENG.). 14p. (J). (gr. -1 — 1). bds. 5.99 *(978-1-4654-1671-1(4)*, DK Children) Dorling Kindersley Publishing, Inc.

—Smithsonian Super Nature Encyclopedia. 2012. (ENG., Illus.). 256p. (J). (gr. 3-7). 24.99 *(978-0-7566-9793-8(X)*, DK Children) Dorling Kindersley Publishing, Inc.

—Sticker Encyclopedia - Animals. 2008. (ENG.). 96p. (J). (gr. k-4). pap. 12.99 *(978-0-7566-3899-3(2)*, DK Children) Dorling Kindersley Publishing, Inc.

—Touch & Feel: Animal Library: Animal Library. 2014. (Touch & Feel Ser.). (ENG., Illus.). 36p. (J). (gr. -1-k). bds. 19.99 *(978-1-4654-2766-3(X)*, DK Children) Dorling Kindersley Publishing, Inc.
—Wild Animals. (ENG., (J). 2016. Illus.). 14p. (-k). bds. 9.99 *(978-1-4654-5125-5(0))* 2012. 12p. (gr. -1-k). bds. 6.99 *(978-0-7566-9803-4(0))* 2009. (Illus.). 14p. (gr. -1 — 1). bds. 5.99 *(978-0-7566-5150-3(6))* Dorling Kindersley Publishing, Inc. (DK Children).
—Woodland & Forests. 2017. (ENG., Illus.). 64p. (J). (gr. 1-3). 9.99 *(978-1-4654-5754-7(2)*, DK Children) Dorling Kindersley Publishing, Inc.
Dorling Kindersley Publishing Staff & Buckley, Jim. Spiders & Other Deadly Animals. 2016. (DK Readers Ser.). (ENG., Illus.). 96p. (J). (gr. 3-7). pap. 3.99 *(978-1-4654-5209-2(5)*, DK Children) Dorling Kindersley Publishing, Inc.
Dorling Kindersley Publishing Staff & Lock, Deborah. African Adventure. 2014. (DK Readers Ser.). (ENG.). 48p. (J). (gr. 2-4). pap. 3.99 *(978-1-4654-1719-0(2)*, DK Children) Dorling Kindersley Publishing, Inc.
Dorling Kindersley Publishing Staff & Mack, Lorrie. Big Babies, Little Babies. 2010. (ENG.). 64p. (J). (gr. 2-5). 12.99 *(978-0-7566-6165-6(X)*, DK Children) Dorling Kindersley Publishing, Inc.
Doucet, Bob, illus. Fact & Fable: State Stories, 6 vols., Set 2. Incl. Buster's Trip to Cape Cod: A Story about Massachusetts. Gaarder-Juntti, Oona. 25.65 *(978-1-60453-921-9(6))*; Frenchy's Float: A Story about Louisiana. Scheunemann, Pam. 25.65 *(978-1-60453-922-6(4))*; Great Lei Race: A Story about Hawaii. Salzmann, Mary Elizabeth. 25.65 *(978-1-60453-923-3(2))*; Leaping Lily: A Story about Georgia. Dolphin, Colleen. 25.65 *(978-1-60453-924-0(0))*; Monty's Ice Pick: A Story about Alaska. Hengel, Katherine. 25.65 *(978-1-60453-925-7(9))*; Rupert & the Liberty Bell: A Story about Pennsylvania. Hengel, Katherine. 25.65 *(978-1-60453-926-4(7))*; (J). (gr. -1-3). (Fact & Fable: State Stories Set 2 Ser.). (Illus.). 24p. 2010. 153.90 *(978-1-60453-920-2(8))*; 153.90 *(978-1-61714-678-7(1))* ABDO Publishing Co. (Super SandCastle).
Douglas, Lisa Jo. Active Animals A Thru Z. 2008. (ENG., Illus.). 30p. (J). per. 12.99 *(978-1-59879-311-6(X)*, Lifevest) Lifevest Publishing, Inc.
Doward, Jan S. Grandpa's Furry & Feathered Friends: Meet Stubbytail, Hop-Hops, & All Other Birds & Animals at Grandpa's Place. 2003. (Illus.). 95p. (J). pap. 7.99 *(978-0-8163-1952-7(9))* Pacific Pr. Publishing Assn.
Dowley, Tim. Bible Animals Stencil Activity Pack, 1 vol. Smallman, Steve, illus. 2017. (ENG.). 12p. (J). 9.99 ***(978-1-78128-315-8(X)***, Candle Bks.) Lion Hudson PLC GBR. Dist: Kregel Pubns.
Downer, Ann. Wild Animal Neighbors: Sharing Our Urban World. 64p. 2015. (ENG., Illus.). (YA). (gr. 5-12). 34.65 *(978-1-4677-5934-2(1)*, Lerner Digital) 2013. pap. 24.95 *(978-1-4677-1663-5(4))* 2013. (ENG., Illus.). (gr. 5-12). 33.27 *(978-0-7613-9021-3(9)*, Twenty-First Century Bks.) Lerner Publishing Group.
Downey, Glen R. The 10 Smartest Animals. 2007. 14.99 *(978-1-55448-512-3(6))* Scholastic Library Publishing.
Dowswell, Paul. The Usborne Little Book of Animals. rev. ed. 2007. (Miniature Editions Ser.). (Illus.). 61p. (J). (gr. 4-7). 6.99 *(978-0-7945-1872-1(9)*, Usborne) EDC Publishing.
Duke, Cooper & Duke, Nell K. Animal Alphabet. 2016. (Illus.). 56p. (J). *(978-0-87659-711-8(8))* Gryphon Hse., Inc.
Duke, Shirley. STEM Jobs with Animals. 2014. (ENG., Illus.). 48p. (gr. 4-8). 35.64 *(978-1-62717-698-9(5))* Rourke Educational Media.
Duke, Shirley Smith. Herbivores & Carnivores Explained. 2016. (Distinctions in Nature Ser.). 32p. (J). (gr. 3-3). 28.50 *(978-1-5026-1745-3(5))* Cavendish Square Publishing.
—Reptiles & Amphibians Explained. 2016. (Distinctions in Nature Ser.). 32p. (J). (gr. 3-3). 28.50 *(978-1-5026-1746-0(3))* Cavendish Square Publishing.
—Vertebrates & Invertebrates Explained. 2016. (Distinctions in Nature Ser.). (Illus.). 32p. (J). (gr. 3-3). pap. 10.58 *(978-1-5026-1779-8(X))* Cavendish Square Publishing.
Dunn, Phoebe, illus. Guess Who I Am... gif. ed. 2005. 10p. (J). (gr. -1). per., bds. 7.99 *(978-1-57791-175-3(X))* Brighter Minds Children's Publishing.
Dunphy, Madeleine. Here Is Antarctica. Leonard, Tom, illus. 2008. (Web of Life Ser.). (ENG.). 32p. (J). (gr. -1-3). 16.95 *(978-0-9777539-4-9(8))* Web of Life Children's Bks.
Dunton, Blair. Where the Animals Are King: Ranthambore National Park. Dunton, Blair, illus. 2016. (ENG., Illus.). (J). 12.95 *(978-1-934159-29-3(8))* ThingsAsian Pr.
Earley, Chris. Falcons in the City: The Story of a Peregrine Family. Massey, Luke, photos by. 2016. (ENG., Illus.). 48p. (J). (gr. 4-8). pap. 9.95 *(978-1-77085-803-9(2)*, 9781770858039) Firefly Bks., Ltd.
Earth's Grossest Animals. 2013. (Earth's Grossest Animals Ser.). 32p. (J). (gr. k-5). 151.50 *(978-1-4777-1542-0(8))*; pap. 360.00 *(978-1-61533-875-7(6))*; pap. 60.00 *(978-1-61533-874-0(8))* Windmill Bks.
Eason, Sarah, ed. Animals & Humans. 2011. (FAYFT: Introducing Biology Ser.). 64p. (gr. 4-10). lib. bdg. 39.95 *(978-1-936333-03-5(1))* Brown Bear Bks.
Easy-To-Make Spool Knit Animals: Simple & Charming Projects to Make with Spool Knitting! 2013. (Craft Box Kids Ser.). (ENG., Illus.). 48p. (J). *(978-1-77132-025-2(7))* SpiceBox Products Ltd.
Edgren, David. The Lamb Scroll. 2010. (J). pap. 11.99 *(978-0-8163-2375-3(5))* Pacific Pr. Publishing Assn.
Editors of TIME For Kids Magazine. Animal Adventures 3D. 2015. (ENG., Illus.). 80p. (J). (gr. 3-17). 19.95 *(978-1-61893-145-0(8))* Time Inc. Bks.
Editors of Time for Kids Magazine, Editors of. Awesome Animal Kingdom, 1 vol. 2014. (Little Kids Books of Why Ser.). (ENG.). 48p. (gr. 5-6). pap. 8.95 *(978-1-4914-1931-1(8))* Capstone Press of Coughlan Cos.
Edwards, Wallace. Alphabeasts. Edwards, Wallace, illus. 2008. (ENG., Illus.). 32p. (J). (gr. 1-4). pap. 9.95 *(978-1-55453-227-8(2))* Kids Can Pr., Ltd. CAN. Dist: Hachette Bk. Group.
Edwards-Wright, Tracy. Meet Angel & All Her Friends. Shekailo, Pamela, illus. 2012. 48p. pap. 24.95 *(978-1-4512-8280-1(X))* America Star Bks.
Eggleton, Jill. Creatures of the Extreme. 2007. (Connectors Ser.). (gr. 2-5). pap. *(978-1-877453-10-6(2))* Global Education Systems Ltd.
Elgar, Rebecca. Is That an Elephant over There? (Illus.). 10p. (J). (gr. -1-k). bds. 7.99 *(978-0-590-24917-1(7))* Scholastic, Inc.
Elmore, Amber. Betsy Beansprout Camping Guide. Hickey, Josh, illus. 2013. 50p. pap. 13.99 *(978-1-937331-37-5(7))* ShadeTree Publishing, LLC.
Elphick, Jonathan, et al. Encyclopedia of Animals. 2006. (ENG., Illus.). 376p. (J). (gr. 5-12). pap. 21.99 *(978-0-7566-1972-5(6)*, DK Children) Dorling Kindersley Publishing, Inc.
Encyclopaedia Britannica, Inc. Staff, compiled by. Wildlife Wonders. 2003. (Britannica Learning Library). (Illus.). (gr. 2-5). 14.95 *(978-1-59339-015-0(7)*, 049909-EN-REF) Encyclopaedia Britannica, Inc.
An Encyclopedia of Animals: Fourth Grade Guided Comprehension Level M. (On Our Way to English Ser.). (gr. 4-18). 34.50 *(978-0-7578-7158-0(5))* Rigby Education.
Encyclopedia Prehistorica Set. 2006. (J). 55.98 *(978-0-7636-3507-7(3))* Candlewick Pr.
Endres, Hollie J. The Letter Bb Set: What Animals Do, 6 vols. 2004. (Letter Bks.). (ENG.). 8p. (gr. k-1). pap. 29.70 *(978-0-7368-4101-6(6)*, Letter Bks.) Capstone Press of Coughlan Cos.
—The Letter Kk Set: Animals, 6 vols. 2004. (Letter Bks.). (ENG.). 8p. (gr. k-1). pap. 29.70 *(978-0-7368-4110-8(5)*, Letter Bks.) Capstone Press of Coughlan Cos.
English, June. Let's Talk Tails. Regan, Dana, illus. 2004. 14p. (J). (gr. k-4). reprint ed. 4.00 *(978-0-7567-7832-3(8))* DIANE Publishing Co.
Equipo Staff & Andrew, Charman. El Dodo Desaparecio. 2003. (Enciclopedia Me Pregunto Por Que). (SPA., Illus.). 32p. (J). (gr. 3-5). 12.99 *(978-84-241-1963-8(0)*, EV6618) Everest Editora ESP. Dist: Lectorum Pubns., Inc.
Ertner, Jim & Lederer, Richard. Super Funny Animal Jokes. 2011. (Animal Cracker Uppers Ser.). (ENG.). 96p. (J). (gr. 4-7). pap. 7.95 *(978-1-933338-88-0(1))* Marion Street Pr., LLC.
Esbaum, Jill. Angry Birds Playground - Animals: An Around-the-World Habitat Adventure. 2012. (ENG.). 128p. (J). (gr. -1-3). lib. bdg. 21.90 *(978-1-4263-1323-3(3)*, National Geographic Children's Bks.) National Geographic Society.
—Animal Groups. Lanting, Frans, illus. 2015. (ENG.). 32p. (J). (gr. -1-3). 16.99 *(978-1-4263-2060-6(4)*, National Geographic Children's Bks.) National Geographic Society.
Esbaum, Jill & National Geographic Kids Staff. Animals: An Around-the-World Habitat Adventure. 2012. (ENG., Illus.). 128p. (J). (gr. -1-3). 14.95 *(978-1-4263-1266-3(0)*, National Geographic Children's Bks.) National Geographic Society.
Eszterhas, Suzi. Moto & Me: My Year As a Wildcat's Foster Mom. 2017. (ENG., Illus.). 40p. (J). (gr. 2-6). 17.95 *(978-1-77147-242-5(1))* Owlkids Bks. Inc. CAN. Dist: Publishers Group West (PGW).
Evento, Susan & Jaffe, Elizabeth Dana. The World's Deadliest Creatures. 2007. (Illus.). 40p. (J). *(978-0-696-23826-0(8))* Meredith Bks.
Evento, Susan, et al. The World's Deadliest Creatures. 2008. (Illus.). 40p. (J). per. 6.99 *(978-0-696-23981-6(7))* Meredith Bks.
Extreme Animals. (Extreme Animals Ser.). (ENG.). 24p. (gr. k-1). 2011. pap. 250.20 *(978-1-4296-6383-0(9))* 2010. pap. 21.87 *(978-1-4296-6382-3(0))* Capstone Press of Coughlan Cos. (Pebble Plus).
Fact Finders: Animals. 2017. (Fact Finders: Animals Ser.). 24p. (gr. 7-7). 123.00 ***(978-1-4994-8270-6(1))***; pap. 41.25 ***(978-1-4994-8380-2(5))*** Rosen Publishing Group, Inc., The. (Windmill Bks.).
Facts on File, Inc. Staff, ed. Invasive Species Set, 5 Vols. 2007. (Invasive Species Ser.). 100p. (gr. 6-12). 120.00 *(978-0-7910-9455-6(3)*, Chelsea Hse.) Facts On File, Inc.
Falchetta, Drew. Here Are My Eggs. 2016. (1-3Y Animals Ser.). (ENG., Illus.). 24p. (J). pap. 5.99 ***(978-1-63437-613-6(7))*** American Reading Co.
Family Trees, 5 bks., Set. Incl. Flowering Plant Division. Stefoff, Rebecca. lib. bdg. 34.21 *(978-0-7614-1817-7(2))*; Insect Class. Zabludoff, Marc. lib. bdg. 34.21 *(978-0-7614-1819-1(9))*; Primate Order. Stefoff, Rebecca. lib. bdg. 34.21 *(978-0-7614-1816-0(4))*; Protoctist Kingdom. Zabludoff, Marc. lib. bdg. 34.21 *(978-0-7614-1818-4(0))*; Reptile Class. Zabludoff, Marc. lib. bdg. 34.21 *(978-0-7614-1820-7(2))*; (Illus.). 96p. (gr. 6-7). (Family Trees Ser.). 2005. 171.07 *(978-0-7614-1815-3(6)*, Benchmark Bks.) Marshall Cavendish Corp.
Famous Animals: Individual Title, 6 pack. (Action Packs Ser.). 104p. (gr. 3-5). 44.00 *(978-0-7635-8409-2(6))* Rigby Education.
Farndon, John. Wild Animals. 2008. (1000 Things You Should Know about Ser.). (Illus.). 61p. (J). pap. *(978-1-84236-627-1(0))* Miles Kelly Publishing, Ltd.
—1000 Things You Should Know about Wild Animals. 2004. (1000 Things You Should Know about Ser.). (Illus.). 64p. (YA). (gr. 5-18). lib. bdg. 19.95 *(978-1-59084-473-1(4))* Mason Crest.
Fecher, Sarah. Animales Salvajes: Wild Animals. 2004. (Ladders Ser.). (SPA & ENG., Illus.). 32p. (J). (gr. -1-3). 12.95 *(978-1-58728-164-8(3))* Cooper Square Publishing Llc.
Feldman, Thea & American Museum of Natural History Staff. Strangest Animals: (Level 2) 2013. (Amer Museum of Nat History Easy Readers Ser.: 1). (ENG., Illus.). 32p. (J). (gr. k-1). pap. 3.95 *(978-1-4027-7790-5(6))* Sterling Publishing Co., Inc.
Felix, Rebecca. What Do Animals Do in Summer? 2014. (21st Century Basic Skills Library: Let's Look at Summer Ser.). (ENG., Illus.). 24p. (J). (gr. k-3). pap. 12.79 *(978-1-63137-645-0(4)*, 205184) Cherry Lake Publishing.
—What Do Animals Do in Winter? 2014. (21st Century Basic Skills Library: Let's Look at Winter Ser.). (ENG., Illus.). 24p. (J). (gr. k-3). 22.79 *(978-1-63137-607-8(1)*, 205211) Cherry Lake Publishing.
Fennell, Clare, illus. Playtime Pond. 2017. (Push & Pull Ser.). (ENG.). 8p. (J). (gr. -1 — 1). bds. 5.99 *(978-0-7641-6890-1(8))* Barron's Educational Series, Inc.
Ferguson. Animal Care. 4th rev. ed. 2011. (Careers in Focus Ser.). 236p. (gr. 6-12). 32.95 *(978-0-8160-8037-3(2)*, Ferguson Publishing Co.) Facts On File, Inc.
Fetty, Margaret. Seizure-Alert Dogs. 2009. (Dog Heroes Ser.). (Illus.). 32p. (YA). (gr. 2-5). lib. bdg. 25.27 *(978-1-59716-865-6(3))* Bearport Publishing Co., Inc.
Fiedler, Julie. Pit Bulls. 2006. (Tough Dogs Ser.). (Illus.). 24p. (J). (gr. 3-7). lib. bdg. 21.25 *(978-1-4042-3117-7(X)*, PowerKids Pr.) Rosen Publishing Group, Inc., The.
Fields, Terri. Los Más Peligrosos, 1 vol. Jacques, Laura, illus. 2012. (SPA.). 32p. (J). (gr. -1-3). 17.95 *(978-1-60718-677-9(2))* Arbordale Publishing.
—The Most Dangerous, 1 vol. Jacques, Laura, illus. 2012. (ENG.). 32p. (J). (gr. -1-3). 17.95 *(978-1-60718-526-0(1))* Arbordale Publishing.
—The Most Dangerous, 1 vol. Jaques, Laura, illus. 2012. (ENG.). 32p. (J). (gr. -1-3). pap. 9.95 *(978-1-60718-535-2(0))* Arbordale Publishing.
—The Most Dangerous, 1 vol. Jacques, Laura, illus. 2012. (SPA.). 32p. (J). (gr. -1-3). pap. 9.95 *(978-1-62855-424-3(X))* Arbordale Publishing.
Filipek, Nina. Animals. O'Toole, Jeanette, illus. 2009. (Bright Basics Ser.). 12p. (J). (gr. -1-k). bds. 11.40 *(978-1-60754-688-7(4))* Windmill Bks.
Fink, Courtney. Wings, Shells, & Fur: Surviving in the Wild. 2013. (InfoMax Readers Ser.). (ENG.). 24p. (J). (gr. 3-4). pap. 8.25 *(978-1-4777-2519-1(9))*; pap. 49.50 *(978-1-4777-2520-7(2))* Rosen Publishing Group, Inc., The. (Rosen Classroom).
Fischer, Amelia S. E. Roo's Cat Tales: The Cat Who Didn't Know First in a Series. 2012. 24p. pap. 12.55 *(978-1-4269-7178-5(8))* Trafford Publishing.
Fisher, Diana. Animals: Step-by-Step Instructions for 26 Captivating Creatures. 2005. (Learn to Draw Ser.). (ENG., Illus.). 40p. (gr. 1-3). per. 4.95 *(978-1-56010-864-1(9)*, 1560108649) Quarto Publishing Group USA.
"Fisher" Suedmeyer, Paul A. The 12 Eternals on the Great Voyage. 2013. 40p. pap. *(978-1-4602-1731-3(4))* FriesenPress.
Fishy Tales. 12p. (J). *(978-2-7643-0193-7(6))* Phidal Publishing, Inc./Editions Phidal, Inc.
Flad, Antje, illus. Oops! Who's Been Nibbling? 2016. (Mini Movers Ser.). (ENG.). 12p. (J). (gr. -1 — 1). bds. 4.99 *(978-0-7641-6867-3(3))* Barron's Educational Series, Inc.
Fleisher, Paul. Forest Food Webs in Action. 2013. (Searchlight Books What Is a Food Web Ser.). (ENG., Illus.). 40p. (gr. 3-5). pap. 8.95 *(978-1-4677-1553-9(0))* Lerner Publishing Group.
—Grassland Food Webs in Action. 2013. (Searchlight Books What Is a Food Web Ser.). (ENG., Illus.). 40p. (gr. 3-5). pap. 8.95 *(978-1-4677-1554-6(9))*; lib. bdg. 27.93 *(978-1-4677-1293-4(0)*, Lerner Pubns.) Lerner Publishing Group.
—Lake & Pond Food Webs in Action. 2013. (Searchlight Books What Is a Food Web Ser.). (ENG., Illus.). 40p. (gr. 3-5). pap. 8.95 *(978-1-4677-1555-3(7))*; lib. bdg. 27.93 *(978-1-4677-1256-9(6)*, Lerner Pubns.) Lerner Publishing Group.
—Tundra Food Webs in Action. 2013. (Searchlight Books What Is a Food Web Ser.). (ENG., Illus.). 40p. (gr. 3-5). pap. 8.95 *(978-1-4677-1557-7(3))*; lib. bdg. 27.93 *(978-1-4677-1295-8(7)*, Lerner Pubns.) Lerner Publishing Group.
Fleming, Sally. Rapid Runners. Underwood, Kay Povelite, illus. 2004. (It's Nature! Ser.). 32p. (J). (gr. 3-6). pap. 7.95 *(978-1-55971-789-2(0)*, NorthWord Bks. for Young Readers) T&N Children's Publishing.
Flowerpot Press, creator. Animals Coloring Book. 2013. (Sockheadz Ser.). (ENG., Illus.). 72p. (J). (gr. -1-3). 4.99 *(978-1-77093-546-4(0))* Flowerpot Pr.
Follen, Eliza Lee. What the Animals Do & Say. 2004. reprint ed. pap. 15.95 *(978-1-4191-9359-0(7))* Kessinger Publishing, LLC.
Follow It!, 6 vols., Set. Incl. Bill's Journey into Law. Slade, Suzanne. Trimmer, Tony, illus. 2011. lib. bdg. 26.65 *(978-1-4048-6831-1(3))*; Dollar Bill's Journey. Slade, Suzanne. Swan, Susan, illus. 2010. lib. bdg. 26.65 *(978-1-4048-6265-4(X))*; Germ's Journey. Rooke, Thom. Trimmer, Tony, illus. 2010. lib. bdg. 26.65 *(978-1-4048-6268-5(4))*; Monarch Butterfly's Journey. Slade, Suzanne. Swan, Susan, illus. 2011. lib. bdg. 26.65 *(978-1-4048-6655-3(8))*; Raindrop's Journey. Slade, Suzanne. Conger, Holli, illus. 2010. lib. bdg. 26.65 *(978-1-4048-6266-1(8))*; (gr. 1-3). (Follow It! Ser.). (ENG.). 24p. 2011. Set lib. bdg. 159.90 *(978-1-4048-6833-5(X))* Picture Window Bks.
Folsom, Michael & Elting, Mary. Q Is for Duck: An Alphabet Guessing Game. Kent, Jack, illus. 2007. 60p. (gr. -1-k). 16.95 *(978-0-7569-7871-6(8))* Perfection Learning Corp.
Foran, Jill. Herbivores. (J). 2016. ***(978-1-4896-5773-2(8))*** 2011. (gr. 4-6). pap. 12.95 *(978-1-61690-714-3(2)*, AV2 by Weigl) 2011. (Illus.). 24p. (J). (gr. 2-5). 27.13 *(978-1-61690-708-2(8))* 2005. (Illus.). 24p. (gr. -1-3). per. 8.95 *(978-1-59036-264-8(0))* 2004. (Illus.). 24p. lib. bdg. 8.95 *(978-1-59036-240-2(3))* Weigl Pubs., Inc.
Forbush, Kyle. Alaska's Wild Animals Coloring Book. Forbush, Lisa, illus. 2003. (J). 3.95 *(978-1-57833-232-8(X))* Todd Communications.
Forest Trail. 2008. (Fold Out Pop-Ups Ser.). 6p. bds. *(978-1-4075-1301-0(X))* Parragon, Inc.
Franceschelli, Christopher. The Big Green Square. 2012. (ConceptTheater Ser.). 12p. (J). 8.99 *(978-0-8249-1521-6(6)*, Ideal Pubns.) Worthy Publishing.
—Red Apple, Yellow Banana & the Blue Cockatoo: An Alphabet Adventure. 2012. (ConceptTheater Ser.). 12p. (J). 8.99 *(978-0-8249-1458-5(9)*, Ideal Pubns.) Worthy Publishing.
Franchino, Vicky. Animal Mash-Ups. 2015. (True Book(tm), a — Amazing Animals Ser.). (ENG., Illus.). 48p. (J). lib. bdg. 31.00 *(978-0-531-21544-9(X)*, Children's Pr.) Scholastic Library Publishing.
Francis, Suzanne. Dangerous & Deadly Toxic Animals. 2007. (Illus.). 32p. *(978-0-439-02571-3(0))* Scholastic, Inc.
—On the Prowl: Animal Hunters. 2007. (Illus.). 32p. (J). *(978-0-439-02575-1(3))* Scholastic, Inc.
Freaky Flying Animals. 2013. (Earth's Grossest Animals Ser.). 32p. (J). (gr. k-5). pap. 60.00 *(978-1-61533-790-3(3)*, PowerKids Pr.) Rosen Publishing Group, Inc., The.
Fredericks, Anthony D. Near One Cattail: Turtles, Logs, & Leaping Frogs. DiRubbio, Jennifer, illus. 2005. (Sharing Nature with Children Book Ser.). 32p. (J). 16.95 *(978-1-58469-070-2(4))*; pap. 7.95 *(978-1-58469-071-9(2))* Dawn Pubns.
—Under One Rock: Bugs, Slugs, & Other Ughs. DiRubbio, Jennifer, illus. 2004. (Sharing Nature with Children Book Ser.). 32p. (J). 16.95 *(978-1-58469-028-3(3))* Dawn Pubns.
—Weird Walkers. 2004. (It's Nature! Ser.). (Illus.). 32p. (J). (gr. 3-6). pap. 7.95 *(978-1-55971-630-7(4)*, Creative Publishing International) Quarto Publishing Group USA.
Freed, Kira. Classifying Animals. 2017. (Text Connections Guided Close Reading Ser.). (J). (gr. 1). *(978-1-4900-1799-0(2))* Benchmark Education Co.
La Fresa. (Coleccion Ciclos Vitales). (SPA., Illus.). (J). (gr. 3-5). pap. *(978-84-236-2653-3(9)*, ED4700) Edebé ESP. Dist: Lectorum Pubns., Inc.
Fretland VanVoorst, Jenny. Animal Classification, 1 vol. 2014. (Science of Life Ser.). (ENG.). 48p. (gr. 3-6). lib. bdg. 32.79 *(978-1-62403-157-1(9))* ABDO Publishing Co.
—Animals in Spring. 2015. (Illus.). 24p. (J). lib. bdg. *(978-1-62031-234-6(4)*, Bullfrog Bks.) Jump! Inc.
Friddell, Claudia. Goliath: Hero of the Great Baltimore Fire. Howell, Troy, illus. 2010. (True Stories Ser.). (ENG.). 32p. (J). (gr. 1-4). 17.95 *(978-1-58536-455-8(X)*, 202179) Sleeping Bear Pr.
Friedman, Sharon. Grin & Bear It: Zoo Jokes to Make You Roar. Gable, Brian, illus. 2005. (Make Me Laugh! Ser.). 32p. (J). (gr. k-3). lib. bdg. 19.93 *(978-1-57505-660-9(7))* Lerner Publishing Group.
Frisch-Schmoll, Joy & Higgins, Melissa. Ice Age Animals. 2015. (Ice Age Animals Ser.). (ENG.). 24p. (gr. k-1). lib. bdg. 159.90 *(978-1-4914-2589-3(X)*, Pebble Plus) Capstone Press of Coughlan Cos.
Froman, Craig. How Many Animals Were on the Ark? Understanding the Animal Kinds. 2016. (ENG.). 64p. (J). 15.99 *(978-0-89051-935-6(8))* Master Bks.
Frydenborg, Kay. Animal Therapist. 2005. (Weird Careers in Science Ser.). (Illus.). 88p. (gr. 5-8). lib. bdg. 25.00 *(978-0-7910-8704-6(2)*, Chelsea Hse.) Facts On File, Inc.
Fuentes, Marco. At Home with Animals. 2016. (Spring Forward Ser.). (J). (gr. 2). *(978-1-4900-6023-1(5))* Benchmark Education Co.
Fuertes, Gloria. El Gran Libro de los Animales. 2003. (SPA.). 168p. 17.56 *(978-84-305-8755-1(1)*, SU3119) Susaeta Ediciones, S.A. ESP. Dist: Lectorum Pubns., Inc.
Fuhr, Ute & Allaire, Caroline. Let's Look at the Rainforest. Sautai, Raoul, illus. 2012. (ENG.). 38p. (J). (gr. 1-4). pap. 11.99 *(978-1-85103-360-7(2))* Moonlight Publishing, Ltd. GBR. Dist: Independent Pubs. Group.
Fulbright, Jeannie. Exploring Creation with Zoology 3: Land Animals of the Sixth Day. Wile, Jay L., ed. 2008. (ENG., Illus.). 35.00 *(978-1-932012-85-9(0))* Apologia Educational Ministries, Inc.
Fun Fact File: Animal Adaptations. 2016. (Fun Fact File: Animal Adaptations Ser.). 32p. (gr. 3-2). pap. 63.00 *(978-1-4824-5285-3(5))*; lib. bdg. 151.50 *(978-1-4824-4440-7(2))* Stevens, Gareth Publishing LLLP.
Fun Fact File (January 2014), Vol. 1. 2013. (Fun Fact File Ser.). 32p. (J). (gr. 3-6). 757.50 *(978-1-4824-0608-5(X))*; pap. 1890.00 *(978-1-4824-0706-8(X))*; pap. 315.00 *(978-1-4824-0707-5(8))* Stevens, Gareth Publishing LLLP.
Fur, Feathers, or Skin: Early Level Satellite Individual Title Six-Packs. (Sails Literacy Ser.). 16p. (gr. 1-2). 27.00 *(978-0-7578-3165-2(6))* Rigby Education.
Fyne, Olga M. My Abc Animal Book of Rhymes & Jingles. 2011. 56p. pap. 14.95 *(978-1-61286-052-7(4))* Avid Readers Publishing Group.
G., Ashley. Critter Colors. G., Ashley, illus. 2015. (ENG., Illus.). 28p. (J). (gr. -1-k). bds. 7.99 *(978-1-4814-4218-3(X)*, Little Simon) Little Simon.
Gaarder- Juntti, Oona. What Lives in the Wetlands?, 1 vol. 2008. (Animal Habitats Ser.). (ENG., Illus.). 24p. (J). (gr. k-3). 25.65 *(978-1-60453-180-0(0))* ABDO Publishing Co.
Gaarder-Juntti, Oona. What Lives in Antarctica?, 1 vol. 2008. (Animal Habitats Ser.). (ENG., Illus.). 24p. (J). (gr. k-3). 25.65 *(978-1-60453-169-5(X))* ABDO Publishing Co.
—What Lives in the Arctic?, 1 vol. 2008. (Animal Habitats Ser.). (ENG., Illus.). 24p. (J). (gr. k-3). 25.65 *(978-1-60453-172-5(X))* ABDO Publishing Co.
—What Lives in the Prairie?, 1 vol. 2008. (Animal Habitats Ser.). (ENG., Illus.). 24p. (J). (gr. k-3). 25.65 *(978-1-60453-176-3(2))* ABDO Publishing Co.
—What Lives in the Rain Forest?, 1 vol. 2008. (Animal Habitats Ser.). (ENG., Illus.). 24p. (J). (gr. k-3). 25.65 *(978-1-60453-177-0(0))* ABDO Publishing Co.
—What Lives in the Savanna?, 1 vol. 2008. (Animal Habitats Ser.). (ENG., Illus.). 24p. (J). (gr. k-3). 25.65 *(978-1-60453-178-7(9))* ABDO Publishing Co.
—What Lives in the Tundra?, 1 vol. 2008. (Animal Habitats Ser.). (ENG., Illus.). 24p. (J). (gr. k-3). 25.65 *(978-1-60453-179-4(7))* ABDO Publishing Co.
Gagne, Tammy. All about Animals. 2015. (All about Animals Ser.). (ENG.). 24p. (gr. 1-2). lib. bdg. 101.28 *(978-1-4914-2491-9(5)*, First Facts) Capstone Press of Coughlan Cos.
—Backyard Jungle Safari Raccoons: Racoons. 2015. (ENG., Illus.). 32p. (J). 26.50 *(978-1-62469-102-7(1))* Purple Toad Publishing, Inc.
—Predator Profiles. 2016. (Predator Profiles Ser.). (ENG.). 24p. (gr. 1-2). 253.20 *(978-1-4914-8263-6(X)*, First Facts) Capstone Press of Coughlan Cos.
—The Strangest Animals in the World. 2015. (All about Animals Ser.). (ENG.). 24p. (gr. 1-2). pap. 6.95 *(978-1-4914-2240-3(8))* Capstone Press of Coughlan Cos.
Gagne, Tammy, et al. Big Cats. 2012. (Big Cats Ser.). (ENG.). 32p. (gr. 3-4). lib. bdg. 111.96 *(978-1-4296-8186-5(1)*, Edge Bks.) Capstone Press of Coughlan Cos.
Galloway, Fhiona. Look Through: Animals. 2016. (Look Through Ser.). (ENG., Illus.). 10p. (J). bds. 8.99 *(978-1-62686-578-5(7)*, Silver Dolphin Bks.) Readerlink Distribution Services, LLC.
Galvin, Laura Gates. Alphabet of African Animals. Leeper, Christopher J. et al, illus. 2011. (Alphabet Bks.). (ENG.). 40p. (J). (gr. -1-3). 17.95 *(978-1-60727-574-9(0))* Soundprints.
—Alphabet of African Animals. Denman, Michael et al, illus. 2008. (ENG.). 40p. (J). (gr. -1-2). 17.95 *(978-1-59249-854-3(X))* Soundprints.

—Alphabet of Animals. Kest, Kristin, illus. (Alphabet Bks.). (ENG.). 40p. 2011. (J). (gr. -1-3). 9.95 (978-1-60727-443-8(4)) 2009. 9.95 (978-1-59249-991-5(0)) 2006. (J). (gr. -1-k). 15.95 (978-1-59249-655-6(5)) Soundprints.

—Is That You, Piglet? 2009. (Disney Friends Carry-a-Tune Ser.). 24p. (J). (gr. -1). 4.99 (978-1-59069-855-6(X)) Studio Mouse LLC.

—Peep's Nature. 2006. (ENG., Illus.). 24p. (J). (gr. -1-k). 15.99 (978-1-59249-519-1(2), 1C301) Soundprints.

—Who Am I? 2010. (Explore & Grow Ser.). (ENG., Illus.). 16p. (J). (gr. -1). 6.95 (978-1-60727-154-3(0)) Soundprints.

Galvin, Laura Gates & Soundprints Editorial Staff. Animals A to Z. Schwaeber, Barbie H. & Williams, Tracee, eds. Kest, Kristin, illus. 2008. (ENG.). 36p. (J). (gr. 3-7). 12.99 (978-1-59069-672-9(7)) Studio Mouse LLC.

Ganeri, Anita. Astonishing Animals. Dogi, Fiammetta & Cole, Dan, illus. 2015. (Record Breakers Ser.: 1). (ENG.). 18p. (J). (gr. k-5). 12.99 (978-1-4998-0016-6(9)) Little Bee Books Inc.

—Colorful Creatures. 2016. (Illus.). 79p. (J). **(978-1-4351-6383-6(4))** Barnes & Noble, Inc.

—Discover the Okapi. 2016. (Fabulous Animals Ser.). (ENG., Illus.). 32p. (gr. 1-3). lib. bdg. 27.32 (978-1-4846-2712-9(1), Heinemann First Library) Heinemann-Raintree.

—Exploring Coasts: A Benjamin Blog & His Inquisitive Dog Investigation, 1 vol. 2014. (Exploring Habitats with Benjamin Blog & His Inquisitive Dog Ser.). (ENG., Illus.). 32p. (gr. 1-3). lib. bdg. 29.99 (978-1-4329-8777-0(1), NA-h) Heinemann-Raintree.

—Exploring Coral Reefs: A Benjamin Blog & His Inquisitive Dog Investigation, 1 vol. 2014. (Exploring Habitats with Benjamin Blog & His Inquisitive Dog Ser.). (ENG., Illus.). 32p. (gr. 1-3). pap. 8.95 (978-1-4329-8787-9(9)); lib. bdg. 29.99 (978-1-4329-8780-0(1)) Heinemann-Raintree. (NA-h).

—Exploring Mountains: A Benjamin Blog & His Inquisitive Dog Investigation, 1 vol. 2014. (Exploring Habitats with Benjamin Blog & His Inquisitive Dog Ser.). (ENG.). 32p. (gr. 1-3). lib. bdg. 29.99 (978-1-4329-8776-3(3), NA-h) Heinemann-Raintree.

—Exploring Rain Forests: A Benjamin Blog & His Inquisitive Dog Investigation, 1 vol. 2014. (Exploring Habitats with Benjamin Blog & His Inquisitive Dog Ser.). (ENG., Illus.). 32p. (gr. 1-3). pap. 8.95 (978-1-4329-8786-2(0)); lib. bdg. 29.99 (978-1-4329-8779-4(8)) Heinemann-Raintree. (NA-h).

—Exploring Rivers: A Benjamin Blog & His Inquisitive Dog Investigation, 1 vol. 2014. (Exploring Habitats with Benjamin Blog & His Inquisitive Dog Ser.). (ENG., Illus.). 32p. (gr. 1-3). lib. bdg. 29.99 (978-1-4329-8775-6(5), NA-h) Heinemann-Raintree.

—Fabulous Animals. 2016. (Fabulous Animals Ser.). (ENG.). 32p. (gr. 1-3). 109.28 (978-1-4846-2725-9(3), Heinemann First Library) Heinemann-Raintree.

—First Animal Encyclopedia. 2014. (First Animal Encyclopedia Ser.). (ENG., Illus.). 64p. (J). (gr. -1-3). 13.99 (978-1-4088-4252-2(1), 9781408842522, Bloomsbury USA Childrens) Bloomsbury Publishing USA.

—The Inside & Out Guide to Animals, 1 vol. 2006. (Inside & Out Guides To Ser.). (ENG., Illus.). 32p. pap. 7.99 (978-1-4034-9091-9(0), NA-h) Heinemann-Raintree.

Ganeri, Anita & West, David. Creatures of Myths & Legends. 2012. (J). 70.50 (978-1-4488-5235-2(8)); pap. 11.75 (978-1-4488-5234-5(X)); lib. bdg. 26.50 (978-1-4488-5198-0(X)) Rosen Publishing Group, Inc., The. (PowerKids Pr.).

Gangemi, Alphia. Hunting with Wolves. 2012. (Animal Attack! Ser.). (Illus.). 24p. (J). (gr. 2-5). 22.60 (978-1-4339-7083-2(X)); pap. 8.15 (978-1-4339-7084-9(8)) Stevens, Gareth Publishing LLLP. (Gareth Stevens Learning Library).

Gannij, Joan. Hidden Hippo. Beaton, Clare, illus. 2011. (ENG.). 32p. (J). (gr. -1-2). pap. 6.99 (978-1-84686-533-6(6)) Barefoot Bks., Inc.

Garcia, Gloria. Los Animales. (SPA.). 8p. 9.95 (978-84-272-7272-9(3)) Molino, Editorial ESP. Dist: Distribooks, Inc.

Gardeski, Christina Mia. Pet Fish: Questions & Answers. 2016. (Pet Questions & Answers Ser.). (ENG., Illus.). 24p. (gr. k-1). lib. bdg. 26.65 (978-1-5157-0353-2(3), Pebble Plus) Capstone Press of Coughlan Cos.

Gardiner, Lisa. Creatures Great & Small. Flowerpot Press, ed. 2012. (Illus.). 20p. (J). (978-1-926988-07-8(8)) Flowerpot Children's Pr. Inc.

Gardner, Robert & Conklin, Joshua. A Kid's Book of Experiments about Animals. 2016. (Surprising Science Experiments Ser.). (ENG., Illus.). 48p. (J). (gr. 4-4). 27.93 (978-0-7660-7266-4(5)) Enslow Pubs., Inc.

—A Kid's Book of Experiments with Animals. 2016. (Surprising Science Experiments Ser.). (ENG.). 48p. (J). (gr. 4-4). pap. 11.70 (978-0-7660-7264-0(9)) Enslow Pubs., Inc.

Gaspar, Joe. The Bald Eagle. 2013. (PowerKids Readers: American Symbols Ser.). (Illus.). 24p. (J). (gr. k-2). pap. 8.25 (978-1-4777-0815-6(4)); pap. 49.50 (978-1-4777-0816-3(2)); lib. bdg. 22.60 (978-1-4777-0737-1(9)) Rosen Publishing Group, Inc., The. (PowerKids Pr.).

—The Bald Eagle / el Guila Calva. Alamn, Eduardo, ed. 2013. (PowerKids Readers: American Symbols / Smbolos de Amrica Ser.). (ENG & SPA.). 24p. (J). (gr. k-2). 22.60 (978-1-4777-1205-4(4), PowerKids Pr.) Rosen Publishing Group, Inc., The.

Gee, Allison. Animal Dreams: Coloring Book. 2009. 52p. pap. 14.99 (978-1-4389-9014-9(6)) AuthorHouse.

Geltrich, Brigitta, ed. In the Love of Animals. Baldwin, Christopher, illus. Date not set. (Animals Ser.). 96p. (J). pap. 6.00 (978-0-936945-64-4(8)) Creative with Words Pubns.

George, Bobby, et al. Montessori: Map Work. 2014. (Montessori Ser.). (ENG., Illus.). 20p. (J). (gr. -1-k). bds. 9.95 (978-1-4197-0934-0(8), Abrams Appleseed) Abrams, Inc.

George, Joshua. Animals: Sticker Book Fun for Little Ones! 2017. (My First Sticker Book Ser.). (ENG.). 36p. (J). (gr. -1-k). pap. 8.99 **(978-1-78700-068-1(0))** Top That! Publishing PLC GBR. Dist: Independent Pubs. Group.

George, Joshua. Opposites with Animals. 2016. (ENG.). 10p. (J). (gr. -1-k). 9.99 (978-1-78445-648-1(9)) Top That! Publishing PLC GBR. Dist: Independent Pubs. Group.

Gerard Clark. Crickley Meadow. 2010. 124p. pap. 13.89 (978-1-4251-6956-5(2)) Trafford Publishing.

Gerbracht, Edie. Especially Me! Stoner, Alexis, illus. 2012. 34p. pap. 11.77 (978-0-9843855-5-3(X)) aBASK Publishing.

Gibson. Sail Yel Nf Colorful Animals. 2003. (Rigby Sails Early Ser.). (ENG.). 16p. (gr. 1-2). pap. 6.95 (978-0-7578-8895-3(X)) Rigby Education.

Gibson, Brylee. Tails, Tails, Tails. 2003. (Rigby Sails Early Ser.). (ENG., Illus.). 16p. (gr. 1-2). pap. 6.95 (978-0-7578-8904-2(2)) Houghton Mifflin Harcourt Publishing Co.

Gifford, Clive. Animal Survivors. Horne, Sarah, illus. 2017. (Reading Ladder Ser.). (ENG.). 32p. (J). (gr. 1-3). pap. 6.99 **(978-1-4052-8492-9(7))** Egmont Bks., Ltd. GBR. Dist: Independent Pubs. Group.

Gifford, Clive. The Ultimate Animal Criminals. Horne, Sarah, illus. 2016. (ENG.). 48p. (J). (gr. 2-4). 14.99 (978-1-4052-7381-7(X)) Egmont Bks., Ltd. GBR. Dist: Independent Pubs. Group.

Gigliotti, Jim. Animal Sports, 1 vol. 2011. (Extreme Sports Ser.). (ENG., Illus.). 32p. (gr. 1-2). pap. 8.29 (978-1-4109-4223-4(6)); 29.99 (978-1-4109-4216-6(3)) Heinemann-Raintree. (Read Me!).

Gillenwater, Chadwick & Dunn, Mary R. South American Animals. 2012. (South American Animals Ser.). (ENG.). 24p. (gr. k-1). lib. bdg. 53.30 (978-1-4296-9175-8(1)); lib. bdg. 133.25 (978-1-4296-8114-8(4)) Capstone Press of Coughlan Cos. (Pebble Plus).

Gilpin, Daniel. Record-Breaking Animals. 2012. (Record Breakers Ser.). (Illus.). 32p. lib. bdg. 26.50 (978-1-4488-5287-1(0), PowerKids Pr.) Rosen Publishing Group, Inc., The.

Gilpin, Rebecca. Animal Things to Make & Do. 2009. (Activity Bks). 32p. (J). pap. 6.99 (978-0-7945-2349-7(8), Usborne) EDC Publishing.

—Dangerous Animals (Level 1) - Internet Referenced. 2008. (Beginners Nature Ser.). 32p. (J). 4.99 (978-0-7945-2060-1(X), Usborne) EDC Publishing.

Gleisner, Jenna Lee. Animals in Fall. 2017. (Welcome, Fall! Ser.). (ENG.). 24p. (J). (gr. -1-2). lib. bdg. 27.07 (978-1-5038-1659-6(1), 211495) Child's World, Inc., The.

Golden Books Staff. Animal Sounds. Battaglia, Aurelius, illus. 2005. (Golden Sturdy Book Ser.). (ENG.). 26p. (J). (gr. k — 1). bds. 7.99 (978-0-375-83278-9(5), Golden Bks.) Random Hse. Children's Bks.

Goldman, Phyllis, ed. Monkeyshines on What's up down There: Exploring the World Underground. 2003. (Illus.). 122p. (YA). per. 32.95 (978-1-888325-23-2(2)) Allosaurus Pubs.

Goldsworthy, Steve. Physical Characteristics. 2016. (Illus.). 24p. (J). (978-1-5105-0933-7(X)) SmartBook Media, Inc.

Gómez Cerdá, Alfredo. NOCHE DE ALACRANES. (Coleccion Mundo Maravilloso). (SPA.). 48p. (J). (gr. 3-5). (978-84-348-4431-5(1)) SM Ediciones.

Goodwyn, Susan. My First Spoken Words: Animals. 2007. (Smart Kids Talking Bks.). (ENG., Illus.). 12p. (gr. -1-k). bds. 12.99 (978-0-8249-6718-5(6), Ideal Pubns.) Worthy Publishing.

Gordon, Anne. Animals of the Ice & Snow. 2007. (Literacy 2000 Ser.). (Illus.). 24p. (J). (gr. 4-7). pap. (978-0-7327-0888-7(5), Rigby) Pearson Education Australia.

Gordon, Sharon. Animales de la Montaña. Victory Productions, Inc. Staff, tr. from ENG. 2008. (Animales Salvajes Ser.). (SPA.). 24p. (gr. k-1). lib. bdg. 15.95 (978-0-7614-3429-0(1), Benchmark Bks.) Marshall Cavendish Corp.

—Animales de las Planicies. Victory Productions, Inc. Staff, tr. from ENG. 2008. (Animales Salvajes Ser.). (SPA.). 24p. (gr. k-1). lib. bdg. 15.95 (978-0-7614-3430-6(5), Benchmark Bks.) Marshall Cavendish Corp.

—Animales de los Humedales. 2008. (Animales Salvajes Ser.). (SPA.). 24p. (gr. k-1). lib. bdg. 15.95 (978-0-7614-3433-7(X), Benchmark Bks.) Marshall Cavendish Corp.

—Animals in the Wild, 6 bks., Set. Incl. Desert Animals. lib. bdg. 15.95 (978-0-7614-2898-5(4)); Mountain Animals. (Illus.). lib. bdg. 15.95 (978-0-7614-2900-5(X)); Ocean Animals. lib. bdg. 15.95 (978-0-7614-2903-6(4)); Plains Animals. lib. bdg. 15.95 (978-0-7614-2902-9(6)); Rainforest Animals. lib. bdg. 15.95 (978-0-7614-2899-2(2)); Wetland Animals. lib. bdg. 15.95 (978-0-7614-2904-3(2)); 24p. (gr. k-1). (Benchmark Rebus: Animals in the Wild Ser.). 2008. Set lib. bdg. 95.70 (978-0-7614-2897-8(6), Benchmark Bks.) Marshall Cavendish Corp.

—Mountain Animals. 2008. (Animals in the Wild Ser.). (Illus.). 24p. (gr. k-1). lib. bdg. 15.95 (978-0-7614-2900-5(X), Benchmark Bks.) Marshall Cavendish Corp.

—Plains Animals. 2008. (Animals in the Wild Ser.). 24p. (gr. k-1). lib. bdg. 15.95 (978-0-7614-2902-9(6), Benchmark Bks.) Marshall Cavendish Corp.

—Rainforest Animals. 2008. (Animals in the Wild Ser.). 24p. (gr. k-1). lib. bdg. 15.95 (978-0-7614-2899-2(2), Benchmark Bks.) Marshall Cavendish Corp.

—Wetland Animals. 2008. (Animals in the Wild Ser.). 24p. (gr. k-1). lib. bdg. 15.95 (978-0-7614-2904-3(2), Benchmark Bks.) Marshall Cavendish Corp.

Gottlieb. Land Animals. 2004. (Wonders of Science Ser.). (ENG., Illus.). 144p. (gr. 7-12). pap., stu. ed. 24.55 (978-0-7398-9177-3(4)) Houghton Mifflin Harcourt Publishing Co.

Grandlic, Miha. Tasmanian Devil. 2013. 16p. pap. 7.95 (978-1-4525-8255-9(6), Balboa Pr.) Author Solutions, Inc.

Gray, Leon. Amazing Animal Engineers. 2015. (Animal Scientists Ser.). (ENG., Illus.). 32p. (gr. 3-4). lib. bdg. 27.32 (978-1-4914-6980-4(3), Fact Finders) Capstone Press of Coughlan Cos.

—Amazing Animal Shape-Shifters. 2015. (Animal Scientists Ser.). (ENG., Illus.). 32p. (gr. 3-4). lib. bdg. 27.32 (978-1-4914-6983-5(8), Fact Finders) Capstone Press of Coughlan Cos.

—Amazing Animal Super-Sleuths. 2015. (Animal Scientists Ser.). (ENG., Illus.). 32p. (gr. 3-4). lib. bdg. 27.32 (978-1-4914-6982-8(X), Fact Finders) Capstone Press of Coughlan Cos.

—Polar Lands. 2015. (Amazing Biomes Ser.). (Illus.). 32p. (gr. 3-6). 31.35 (978-1-78121-245-5(7), 1389655) Brown Bear Bks.

Gray, Rita. Flowers Are Calling. Pak, Kenard, illus. 2015. (ENG.). 32p. (J). (gr. -1-3). 16.99 (978-0-544-34012-1(4), HMH Books For Young Readers) Houghton Mifflin Harcourt Publishing Co.

Grayson, Robert. Transportation. 2010. (Working Animals Ser.). 64p. (gr. 5-18). 28.50 (978-1-60870-167-4(0)) Marshall Cavendish Corp.

Graziano, Claudia. Meerkat's Safari. Barbera, Michelle, illus. 2007. 36p. (J). 15.99 (978-0-9778072-0-8(7)) Meerkat's Adventures Bks.

Great Big Animals. 2013. (Great Big Animals Ser.). 24p. (J). (gr. k-2). 135.50 (978-1-4339-9671-9(5)); pap. 293.40 (978-1-4339-9829-4(7)); pap. 48.90 (978-1-4339-9828-7(9)) Stevens, Gareth Publishing LLLP.

Great Big Animals / Superanimales. 2013. (Great Big Animals / Superanimales Ser.). (SPA.). 24p. (J). (gr. k-2). 135.60 (978-1-4339-9672-6(3)) Stevens, Gareth Publishing LLLP.

Greathead, Helen. Wicked Wildlife. 2016. (What Would You Choose? Ser.). 00032p. (J). pap. 10.50 **(978-1-4824-6120-6(X))** Stevens, Gareth Publishing LLLP.

Green, Gail. Animals & Teens: The Ultimate Teen Guide. 2009. (It Happened to Me Ser.: 22). (ENG., Illus.). 272p. (gr. 7-18). 55.00 (978-0-8108-5769-8(3)) Scarecrow Pr., Inc.

Green, Jen. Frozen Extremes. 2008. (Extreme Nature Ser.). (ENG., Illus.). 32p. (J). (gr. 2-3). pap. (978-0-7787-4519-8(8)) Crabtree Publishing Co.

—Life in a Backyard. 2010. (Nature in Focus Ser.). (Illus.). 32p. (gr. 2-5). (J). pap. 10.50 (978-1-4339-3415-5(9), Gareth Stevens Learning Library); (YA). lib. bdg. 26.00 (978-1-4339-3414-8(0), 1309267) Stevens, Gareth Publishing LLLP.

Green, Kate. A Number of Animals Nesting Blocks. Wormell, Christopher, illus. 2013. (ENG.). (J). (gr. -1-k). 24.99 (978-1-56846-248-6(4), Creative Editions) Creative Co., The.

Greenaway, Theresa. Animals: Foldout Book. 2005. (Illus.). 12p. (J). (gr. k-4). reprint ed. 10.00 (978-0-7567-8778-3(5)) DIANE Publishing Co.

Greene, Carol. I Love Our Animals. 2012. (I Love Our Earth Ser.). (Illus.). 24p. (J). pap. 7.95 (978-1-4644-0139-8(X)); (gr. 3-4). 22.60 (978-0-7660-4038-0(0)) Enslow Pubs., Inc. (Enslow Elementary).

Greenwell, Jessica. Animal Coloring Book with Stickers. 2009. (Sticker Coloring Bks). 16p. (J). pap. 5.99 (978-0-7945-2506-4(7), Usborne) EDC Publishing.

Greenwell, Jessica & Taplin, Sam. Big Sticker Book of Animals. 2012. (First Sticker Bks). 64p. (J). pap. 17.99 (978-0-7945-3132-4(6), Usborne) EDC Publishing.

Gregory, Josh. African Savanna. 2016. (Community Connections: Getting to Know Our Planet Ser.). (ENG., Illus.). 24p. (J). (gr. 2-5). 27.07 (978-1-63470-512-7(2), 207779) Cherry Lake Publishing.

—Animal Predators. 2015. (ENG., Illus.). 48p. (J). lib. bdg. (978-0-531-21546-3(6), Orchard Bks.) Scholastic, Inc.

Grolier (Firm) Staff, contrib. by. Amazing Animals of the the World 3. 2006. (978-0-7172-6189-5(1)); (978-0-7172-6188-8(3)); (978-0-7172-6187-1(5)); (978-0-7172-6186-4(7)); (978-0-7172-6185-7(9)); (978-0-7172-6184-0(0)); (978-0-7172-6183-3(2)); (978-0-7172-6182-6(4)); (978-0-7172-6180-2(8)); (978-0-7172-6181-9(6)) Grolier, Ltd.

Grolier Educational (Firm) Staff, contrib. by. Nature's Children. 2007. (J). (978-0-7172-8079-7(9)) Grolier, Ltd.

Grolier Educational Staff, contrib. by. Amazing Animals of the the World 2, 10 vols. 2005. (Illus.). (J). 199.00 (978-0-7172-6112-3(3), Grolier) Scholastic Library Publishing.

Group/McGraw-Hill, Wright. Animal Advocates, 6 vols. (Wildcats Ser.). 32p. (gr. 2-8). (978-0-322-05861-3(9)) Wright Group/McGraw-Hill.

—Las Crias de Los Animales, 6 vols. (First Explorers. Primeros Exploradores Nonfiction Sets Ser.). (SPA.). (gr. 1-2). 29.95 (978-0-7699-1467-1(5)) Shortland Pubns. (U. S. A.) Inc.

—Donde Viven Algunos Animales, 6 vols. (First Explorers. Primeros Exploradores Nonfiction Sets Ser.). (SPA.). (gr. 1-2). 29.95 (978-0-7699-1472-5(1)) Shortland Pubns. (U. S. A.) Inc.

—Lights Out! 6 Each of 1 Anthology, 6 vols. (Wildcats Ser.). 32p. (gr. 2-8). (978-0-322-05858-3(9)) Wright Group/McGraw-Hill.

—Take-Twos Animals: Early Fluency - Complete Kit, Vol. 4. (gr. 2-18). 420.50 (978-0-322-09175-7(6)) Wright Group/McGraw-Hill.

—Take-Twos Animals Vol. 4: Early Fluency - Student Book Set - 1 Each of 12 Titles. (gr. 2-18). 69.95 (978-0-322-09303-4(1)) Wright Group/McGraw-Hill.

Guess That Animal! 2016. (Guess That Animal! Ser.). 24p. (gr. 2-1). pap. 48.90 (978-1-4824-5288-4(X)); lib. bdg. 135.60 (978-1-4824-4587-9(5)) Stevens, Gareth Publishing LLLP.

Guest, John. Amazing True Facts. 2012. (Illus.). 224p. (978-1-4351-4353-1(1)) Barnes & Noble, Inc.

Guiberson, Brenda Z. The Deadliest Creature in the World. Spirin, Gennady, illus. 2016. (ENG.). 32p. (J). 17.99 (978-1-62779-198-4(1), 9781627791984, Holt, Henry & Co. Bks. For Young Readers) Holt, Henry & Co.

Guile, Gill, illus. In My Garden. 20p. (J). (978-1-932209-38-9(7)) Bendon, Inc.

Guillain, Charlotte. Animal Life Stories, 1 vol. 2014. (Animal Life Stories Ser.). (ENG.). 32p. (gr. 1-3). 81.96 (978-1-4846-0491-5(1), Heinemann First Library) Heinemann-Raintree.

—Walk on the Wild Side. 2013. (Walk on the Wild Side Ser.). (ENG.). 32p. (gr. 1-3). pap. 47.94 (978-1-4109-5228-8(2)); lib. bdg. 179.94 (978-1-4109-5221-9(5)) Heinemann-Raintree. (Read Me!).

Guillain, Charlotte & Claybourne, Anna. Animal Abilities. 2013. (Animal Abilities Ser.). (ENG.). 32p. (gr. 2-4). pap. 47.94 (978-1-4109-5249-3(5)); lib. bdg. 179.94 (978-1-4109-5242-4(8)) Heinemann-Raintree. (Raintree Perspectives).

Guillain, Charlotte & Mason, Paul. Animal Family Albums. Elsom, Clare, illus. 2013. (Animal Family Albums Ser.). (ENG.). 32p. (gr. 2-4). pap. 31.96 (978-1-4109-4944-8(3)); lib. bdg. 122.60 (978-1-4109-4939-4(7)) Heinemann-Raintree. (Raintree Perspectives).

Hacohen, Dean. Who's Hungry? Scharschmidt, Sherry, illus. 2015. (ENG.). 40p. (J). (— 1). 9.99 (978-0-7636-6586-9(X)) Candlewick Pr.

Haddon, Jean. It's a Beautiful Day! Enright, Vicky, tr. Enright, Vicky, illus. 2005. (Silly Millies Level 2 Ser.). (ENG.). 32p. (J). (gr. 1-3). lib. bdg. 21.27 (978-0-7613-2834-6(3), Millbrook Pr.) Lerner Publishing Group.

Hall, Katharine. Osos Polares y Pingüinos: Un Libro de Comparación y Contraste. 2014.Tr. of Polar Bears & Penguins: a Compare & Contrast Book. (SPA.). 32p. (J). (gr. -1-3). pap. 9.95 (978-1-62855-227-0(1)) Arbordale Publishing.

Hall, Katherine. Polar Bears & Penguins: A Compare & Contrast Book, 1 vol. 2014. (Compare & Contrast Ser.). (ENG., Illus.). 32p. (J). (gr. -1-3). 17.95 (978-1-62855-209-6(3)) Arbordale Publishing.

Hall, Susan T. Happy Halloween Coloring Book. 2013. (Dover Holiday Coloring Book Ser.). (ENG., Illus.). 32p. (J). (gr. -1-8). pap. 3.99 (978-0-486-49218-6(4)) Dover Pubns., Inc.

Halls, Kelly Milner. Albino Animals. 2004. (Junior Library Guild Selection Ser.). (Illus.). 72p. (J). (gr. 4-18). 18.95 (978-1-58196-012-9(3)); pap. 8.95 (978-1-58196-019-8(0)) Lerner Publishing Group. (Darby Creek).

—Animals. Cosgrove, Lee, illus. 2015. (Lie Detector Ser.). (ENG.). 32p. (gr. k-3). pap. 5.95 (978-1-4795-8513-7(0)) Picture Window Bks.

—National Geographic Kids Chapters: Courageous Canine: And More True Stories of Amazing Animal Heroes. 2013. (NGK Chapters Ser.). (ENG., Illus.). 112p. (J). (gr. 2-5). pap. 5.99 (978-1-4263-1396-7(9), National Geographic Children's Bks.) National Geographic Society.

—Wild Horses: Galloping Through Time. Hallett, Mark, illus. 2008. (Darby Creek Exceptional Titles Ser.). 72p. (J). (gr. 1-7). 18.95 (978-1-58196-065-5(4), Darby Creek) Lerner Publishing Group.

Halsey, Megan. 3 Pandas Planting, 0 vols. Halsey, Megan, illus. rev. ed. 2011. (ENG., Illus.). 34p. (J). (gr. -1-3). pap. 6.99 (978-0-7614-5844-9(1), 9780761458449, Amazon Children's Publishing) Amazon Publishing.

Hamilton, Sue. Close Encounters of the Wild Kind, 6 vols., Set. Incl. Ambushed by a Cougar. 27.07 (978-1-60453-928-8(3)); Attacked by a Crocodile. 27.07 (978-1-60453-929-5(1)); Bitten by a Rattlesnake. 27.07 (978-1-60453-930-1(5)); Eaten by a Shark. 27.07 (978-1-60453-931-8(3)); Mauled by a Bear. 27.07 (978-1-60453-932-5(1)); Swarmed by Bees. 27.07 (978-1-60453-933-2(X)); (YA). (gr. 4-7). (Close Encounters of the Wild Kind Ser.). 32p. 2010. 162.42 (978-1-60453-927-1(5), Abdo & Daughters) ABDO Publishing Co.

Hamilton, Sue L. Nature on the Rampage, 1 vol. 2007. (World of Horror Ser.). (ENG.). 32p. (gr. 4-8). 27.07 (978-1-59928-773-7(0), Abdo & Daughters) ABDO Publishing Co.

Hamilton, Tisha. Animals of Asia: Set Of 6. 2011. (Navigators Ser.). (J). pap. 48.00 net. (978-1-4108-5075-1(7)) Benchmark Education Co.

—Animals of Asia: Text Pairs. 2008. (Bridges/Navigators Ser.). (J). (gr. 5). 89.00 (978-1-4108-8379-7(5)) Benchmark Education Co.

Hammersmith, Craig. Life in the Pond, 1 vol. 2011. (Habitats Around the World Ser.). (ENG.). 24p. (gr. k-1). pap. 7.29 (978-1-4296-7149-1(1), Pebble Plus) Capstone Press of Coughlan Cos.

Hansen, Grace. Animal Facts to Make You Smile!, 1 vol. 2014. (Seeing Is Believing Ser.). (ENG.). 24p. (J). (gr. 2-4). lib. bdg. 28.50 (978-1-62970-731-0(7)) ABDO Publishing Co.

—Animals of North America. 2016. (Animals of North America Ser.: 6). (ENG.). 24p. (J). (gr. k-2). lib. bdg. 171.00 (978-1-68080-106-4(6)) ABDO Publishing Co.

—Weird Animals to Shock You!, 1 vol. 2014. (Seeing Is Believing Ser.). (ENG.). 24p. (J). lib. bdg. 28.50 (978-1-62970-735-8(X)) ABDO Publishing Co.

Hansen, Keli. Nala's Story. 2009. 130p. pap. 19.95 (978-1-60749-816-2(2)) America Star Bks.

Hansen, Rosanna. Caring Animals. (True Tales Ser.). (ENG.). 48p. (J). 2004. (gr. 2-4). pap. 4.95 (978-0-516-24603-1(8)) 2003. (Illus.). 22.50 (978-0-516-22912-6(5)) Scholastic Library Publishing. (Children's Pr.).

Hanson, Anders. Giant Animals. 2014. (Giant Animals Ser.: 6). (ENG.). 24p. (J). (gr. -1-3). lib. bdg. 145.26 (978-1-62403-056-7(4), SandCastle) ABDO Publishing Co.

Hanson, Anders & Mann, Elissa. Biggest, Baddest Book of Beasts, 1 vol. 2012. (Biggest, Baddest Books for Boys Ser.). (ENG., Illus.). 24p. (J). (gr. k-4). 25.65 (978-1-61783-404-2(1)) ABDO Publishing Co.

Harasymiw, Therese. Meerkats. 2010. (Animals That Live in the Grasslands Ser.). (ENG.). 24p. (J). (gr. -1-3). pap. 8.15 (978-1-4339-3876-4(6)); lib. bdg. 22.60 (978-1-4339-3875-7(8)) Stevens, Gareth Publishing LLLP.

Harmon, Minnie P. Golden's Animal Friends. 2011. 36p. pap. 21.99 (978-1-4568-6486-6(6)) Xlibris Corp.

Harrington, Daniel. What Am I. 2009. 32p. 12.95 (978-1-56647-913-4(4)) Mutual Publishing LLC.

—What Am I? A Hawai'i Animal Guessing Game. Brandt, Susan, illus. 2006. (J). (978-1-56647-813-7(8)) Mutual Publishing LLC.

Harrington, Fred H. The Gray Wolf. 2009. (Library of Wolves & Wild Dogs Ser.). 24p. (gr. 3-3). 42.50 (978-1-60853-973-4(3), PowerKids Pr.) Rosen Publishing Group, Inc., The.

Harris, Monica. My First Book of Animals. 2005. (My First Ser.). (Illus.). 128p. 7.98 (978-0-7853-8372-7(7), 7183700) Publications International, Ltd.

Harris, Tim. The Animal Kingdom. 2015. (Science Q & A Ser.). (ENG., Illus.). 32p. (J). (gr. 5-5). pap. 10.58 (978-1-5026-0618-1(6), 1389983) Cavendish Square Publishing.

—Europe. 2015. (FAYFT: the World of Endangered Animals Ser.). (Illus.). 64p. (gr. 4-10). lib. bdg. 39.95 (978-1-78121-076-5(4), Brown Bear Bks.) Windmill Bks. Ltd. GBR. Dist: Black Rabbit Bks.

—North & South America. 2015. (FAYFT: the World of Endangered Animals Ser.). (Illus.). 64p. (gr. 4-10). lib. bdg. 39.95 (978-1-78121-075-8(6), Brown Bear Bks.) Windmill Bks. Ltd. GBR. Dist: Black Rabbit Bks.

—South & Central Asia. 2015. (FAYFT: the World of Endangered Animals Ser.). (Illus.). 64p. (gr. 4-10). lib. bdg. 39.95 (978-1-78121-077-2(2), Brown Bear Bks.) Windmill Bks. Ltd. GBR. Dist: Black Rabbit Bks.

Harrod-Eagles, Cynthia. Cave Homes. 2007. (Illus.). 16p. (J). (978-0-545-00712-2(7)) Scholastic, Inc.

Hartman, Eve & Meshbesher, Wendy. Animal Classification: Do Cats Have Family Trees?, 1 vol. 2014. (Show Me

Science Ser.). (ENG.). 32p. (gr. 3-5). lib. bdg. 30.65 *(978-1-4329-8752-7(6)*, Raintree Perspectives) Heinemann-Raintree.

Hartsell, Sandra. Let's Go Feed the Animals. 2012. 36p. pap. 24.95 *(978-1-4626-7398-8(8))* America Star Bks.

Harvey, Bev. Animal Kingdom, 6 vols., Set. 2005. (Animal Kingdom Ser.). (Illus.). 32p. (gr. 2-4). 92.00 *(978-0-7910-7056-7(5)*, Chelsea Hse.) Facts On File, Inc.

Harvey, Derek. Super Nature Encyclopedia: The 100 Most Incredible Creatures on the Planet. 2012. (Illus.). 255p. (J). *(978-1-4654-0270-7(5))* Dorling Kindersley Publishing, Inc.

Haus, Robyn. Create a Year-Round Wildlife Habitat: For Urban & Suburban Small Spaces. 2004. (Quick Starts for Kids! Ser.). (Illus.). 64p. (J). pap. 8.95 *(978-1-885593-97-9(X)*, Ideal Pubns.) Worthy Publishing.

Hawkins, Jay. Really Horrible Animal Facts. 2013. (Really Horrible Facts Ser.). 32p. (J). (gr. k-3). 25.25 *(978-1-61533-744-6(X))*; pap. 10.00 *(978-1-61533-805-4(5))*; pap. 60.00 *(978-1-61533-806-1(3))* Windmill Bks.

Hawksworth, Lorraine. The Masked Intruder. 2011. 16p. 8.32 *(978-1-4389-6571-0(0))* AuthorHouse.

Hawthorn, Philip & Tyler, Jenny. Who's Making That Mess? Cartwright, Stephen, illus. 2008. (Luxury Flap Bks). (gr. -1-k). 9.99 *(978-0-7945-1694-9(7))* EDC Publishing.

Healy, Shay. Beastly Jokes. 2005. (ENG., Illus.). 96p. (J). pap. 10.00 *(978-0-86278-923-7(0))* O'Brien Pr., Ltd., The IRL. Dist: Dufour Editions, Inc.

—More Beastly Jokes. 2005. (ENG., Illus.). 96p. (J). pap. 10.00 *(978-0-86278-924-4(9))* O'Brien Pr., Ltd., The IRL. Dist: Dufour Editions, Inc.

Hearst, Michael. Unusual Creatures: A Mostly Accurate Account of Earth's Strangest Animals. 2014. (ENG., Illus.). 112p. (J). (gr. 3-7). pap. 9.99 *(978-1-4521-3645-5(9))* Chronicle Bks. LLC.

Helberg, Berit. Sniffer & Tinni: A True Tale of Amazing Animal Friendship. Berge, Torgeir, photos by. 2016. (ENG., Illus.). 40p. (J). (gr. -1-3). 14.95 *(978-1-4549-1870-7(5))* Sterling Publishing Co., Inc.

Helbrough, Emma. 1001 Bugs to Spot. Gower, Teri, illus. 2005. 32p. (J). pap. 6.95 *(978-0-7945-1000-8(0)*, Usborne) EDC Publishing.

Held, George. Neighbors: The Yard Critters Too. Kim, Joung Un, illus. 2013. (ENG.). 32p. 20.00 *(978-0-916754-26-6(X))* Filsinger & Co., Ltd.

Heller, Ruth. Animals Born Alive & Well. (FRE., Illus.). (J). 6.99 *(978-0-590-73030-3(4))* Scholastic, Inc.

—Nous Ne Sommes Pas Nes/Oeuf! l.t. ed. (FRE., Illus.). (J). bds. 29.99 *(978-0-590-73029-7(0))* Scholastic, Inc.

Henry, Claire. The World's Deadliest Animals, 1 vol., 1. 2014. (World's Deadliest Ser.). (ENG.). 32p. (J). (gr. 3-6). 26.25 *(978-1-4777-6150-2(0)*, PowerKids Pr.) Rosen Publishing Group, Inc., The.

Heos, Bridget. Do You Really Want a Hamster? Longhi, Katya, illus. 2013. (Do You Really Want a Pet? Ser.). (ENG.). 24p. (gr. 1-4). 27.10 *(978-1-60753-206-4(9))* Amicus Publishing.

—Do You Really Want a Rabbit? Longhi, Katya, illus. 2013. (Do You Really Want a Pet? Ser.). (ENG.). 24p. (gr. 1-4). 27.10 *(978-1-60753-208-8(5))* Amicus Publishing.

Herkimer, Barbara. Our New Neighbors. 2009. 28p. pap. 12.49 *(978-1-4490-0615-0(9))* AuthorHouse.

Hernandez, Christopher. Animal Superpowers. 2012. (Scholastic Reader Level 3 Ser.). (ENG.). 32p. (J). (gr. 2-5). pap. 3.99 *(978-0-545-41564-4(0)*, Scholastic Paperbacks) Scholastic, Inc.

Herrington, Lisa M. The Bald Eagle. 2014. (Rookie Read-About(r) American Symbols Ser.). (ENG., Illus.). 32p. (J). pap. 5.95 *(978-0-531-21837-2(6))*; lib. bdg. *(978-0-531-21564-7(4))* Scholastic Library Publishing.

Hesper, Sam. Animal Cannibals, 1 vol. 2015. (Animal Cannibals Ser.). (ENG.). 24p. (J). 49.50 *(978-1-4994-0305-3(4)*, PowerKids Pr.) Rosen Publishing Group, Inc., The.

Hess, Nina. Whose Feet? Kanzler, John, tr. Kanzler, John, illus. 2004. (Step into Reading Ser.). (ENG.). 32p. (J). (gr. -1-1). pap. 3.99 *(978-0-375-82623-8(8)*, Random Hse. Bks. for Young Readers) Random Hse. Children's Bks.

Hess, Paul. Animal Worlds. 2006. (Animal Verse Ser.). (ENG., Illus.). 96p. (J). (gr. -1-k). pap. *(978-1-84089-408-0(3))* Zero to Ten, Ltd.

Hess, Paul, illus. Rainforest Animals. 2003. (Animals Ser.). 24p. (J). pap. *(978-1-84089-172-0(6))* Zero to Ten, Ltd.

Hibbert, Clare. Pond Wildlife, 01 vols., 1. 2016. (Adventures in Nature Ser.). (ENG.). 32p. (J). pap. 10.00 *(978-1-5081-4587-5(3)*, PowerKids Pr.) Rosen Publishing Group, Inc., The.

Hickman, Pamela. Animals & Their Mates: How Animals Attract, Fight for & Protect Each Other. Stephens, Pat, illus. 2004. (Animal Behavior Ser.). (ENG.). 40p. (J). (gr. 2-6). 5.95 *(978-1-55337-546-3(7))* Kids Can Pr., Ltd. CAN. Dist: Hachette Bk. Group.

—How Animals Eat. Stephens, Pat, illus. 2007. (Kids Can Read Ser.). (ENG.). 32p. (J). (gr. 1-3). 3.95 *(978-1-55453-032-8(6))*; 14.95 *(978-1-55453-031-1(8))* Kids Can Pr., Ltd. CAN. Dist: Hachette Bk. Group.

—How Animals Move. Stephens, Pat, illus. 2007. (Kids Can Read Ser.). (ENG.). 32p. (J). (gr. 1-3). 14.95 *(978-1-55453-029-8(6))* Kids Can Pr., Ltd. CAN. Dist: Hachette Bk. Group.

Hicks, Kelli. Companion & Therapy Animals. 2015. (ENG.). 24p. (gr. 1-4). 28.50 *(978-1-63430-068-1(8))* Rourke Educational Media.

—Let's Classify Organisms. 2012. (ENG.). 24p. (gr. 3-4). pap. 8.95 *(978-1-61810-231-7(1))* Rourke Educational Media.

Hide to Survive, 6 Packs. (gr. k-1). 23.00 *(978-0-7635-8857-1(1))* Rigby Education.

Hile, Kevin. Animal Rights. 2004. (Point/Counterpoint Ser.). (Illus.). 120p. (C). (gr. 9-13). 35.00 *(978-0-7910-7922-5(8)*, Chelsea Hse.) Facts On File, Inc.

Hile, Lori. Animal Survival. 2011. (Extreme Survival Ser.). (ENG.). 56p. (gr. 5-5). pap. 9.49 *(978-1-4109-3980-7(4)*, Raintree Freestyle) Heinemann-Raintree.

Hill, Emma. My First Book of Animals: A Pull-Out Toddler Book. 2014. (My First Book Ser.). (ENG., Illus.). 12p. (J). (gr. -1 — 1). bds. 6.99 *(978-1-77085-313-3(8)*, 9781770853133) Firefly Bks., Ltd.

Himmelman, John. Frog in a Bog. Himmelman, John, illus. 2004. (ENG., Illus.). 32p. (J). (gr. -1-2). pap. 7.95 *(978-1-57091-518-5(0))* Charlesbridge Publishing, Inc.

Hinkler Books, creator. 101 First Words: Animals. 2011. (101 First Words Ser.). (Illus.). 16p. (J). (gr. -1). bds. 7.99 *(978-1-74184-817-5(2))* Hinkler Bks. Pty, Ltd. AUS. Dist: Ideals Pubns.

Hirsch, Rebecca E. Trap-Door Spiders & Other Amazing Predators. 2017. (Searchlight Books (tm) — Animal Superpowers Ser.). (ENG.). 40p. (J). (gr. 3-5). 30.65 *(978-1-5124-2548-2(6))*; 16.99 ***(978-1-5124-3669-3(0)***, Lerner Pubns.); 46.65 ***(978-1-5124-2823-0(X)***, Lerner Pubns.); 46.65 ***(978-1-5124-3668-6(2)***, Lerner Pubns.) Lerner Publishing Group.

Hirschmann, Kris. Real Life Zombies. 2013. (Illus.). 32p. (J). *(978-0-545-53563-2(8))* Scholastic, Inc.

Hnatov, Catherine. Hip, Hop (Arabic/English), 1 vol. 2012. (ENG., Illus.). 12p. (J). 5.95 *(978-1-59572-366-6(8))* Star Bright Bks., Inc.

—Hip, Hop (Hmong/English), 1 vol. 2012. (ENG., Illus.). 12p. (J). 5.95 *(978-1-59572-367-3(6))* Star Bright Bks., Inc.

—Hip, Hop (Portuguese/English), 1 vol. Icibaci, Neusa, tr. from ENG. 2010. (POR & ENG., Illus.). 12p. (J). 5.95 *(978-1-59572-271-3(8))* Star Bright Bks., Inc.

—Hip, Hop (Spanish/English), 1 vol. Del Risco, Eida, tr. 2010. (SPA & ENG., Illus.). 32p. (J). bds. 5.95 *(978-1-59572-270-6(X))* Star Bright Bks., Inc.

—Yum, Yum (Spanish/English), 1 vol. 2011. (ENG., Illus.). 32p. (J). bds. 5.95 *(978-1-59572-276-8(9))* Star Bright Bks., Inc.

Hodge, Deborah. Polar Animals. Stephens, Pat, illus. 2008. (Who Lives Here? Ser.). (ENG.). 24p. (J). (gr. -1-2). 14.95 *(978-1-55453-043-4(1))*; pap. 5.95 *(978-1-55453-044-1(X))* Kids Can Pr., Ltd. CAN. Dist: Hachette Bk. Group.

—Savanna Animals. Stephens, Pat, illus. 2009. (Who Lives Here? Ser.). (ENG.). 24p. (J). (gr. -1-2). 5.95 *(978-1-55453-073-1(3))*; 14.95 *(978-1-55453-072-4(5))* Kids Can Pr., Ltd. CAN. Dist: Hachette Bk. Group.

—Wetland Animals. Stephens, Pat, illus. 2008. (Who Lives Here? Ser.). (ENG.). 24p. (J). (gr. -1-2). 14.95 *(978-1-55453-045-8(8))*; pap. 5.95 *(978-1-55453-046-5(6))* Kids Can Pr., Ltd. CAN. Dist: Hachette Bk. Group.

Hodgkins, Fran. Who's Been Here? A Tale in Tracks. Hayes, Karel, illus. 2008. (ENG.). 32p. (J). (gr. -1-3). 15.95 *(978-0-89272-714-8(4))* Down East Bks.

Hoena, Blake A. If an Egg Hatches... & Other Animal Predictions. 2012. (If Bks.). (ENG.). 32p. (gr. 1-2). pap. 47.70 *(978-1-4296-9246-5(4)*, Aplus Bks.); (Illus.). pap. 8.10 *(978-1-4296-9245-8(6))* Capstone Press of Coughlan Cos.

Hoff, Mary. Metamorphosis. 2003. (World of Wonder Ser.). (Illus.). 32p. (J). lib. bdg. *(978-1-58341-268-8(9)*, Creative Education) Creative Co., The.

Hoffman, Mary Ann. Animal Features. 2009. (Real Life Readers Ser.). 8p. (gr. k-1). pap. 5.15 *(978-1-4042-7967-4(9)*, Rosen Classroom) Rosen Publishing Group, Inc., The.

Hogan, Martina, illus. Rainbow Zoo. 2016. (Early Birds Ser.). (ENG.). 12p. (J). (gr. -1 — 1). bds. 6.99 *(978-1-4998-0209-2(9))* Little Bee Books Inc.

Holden, Pam. Animal Defenses. 2015. (ENG., Illus.). 16p. (-1). pap. *(978-1-77654-146-1(4)*, Red Rocket Readers) Flying Start Bks.

—On the Outside - BIG BOOK. 2016. (ENG.). 16p. (-1). Beta *(978-1-77654-163-8(4)*, Red Rocket Readers) Flying Start Bks.

Holland-Boatwright, Terry. God's Animals, My Friends. 2009. (Illus.). 24p. pap. 12.99 *(978-1-4389-9722-3(1))* AuthorHouse.

Hollar, Sherman. A Closer Look at the Animal Kingdom. 2011. (J). lib. bdg. 31.70 *(978-1-61530-531-5(9))* Rosen Publishing Group, Inc., The.

Holloway, Jamie. Adding with Animals. 2015. (Rosen REAL Readers: STEM & STEAM Collection). (ENG.). 8p. pap. 5.46 *(978-1-4994-9639-0(7)*, Rosen Classroom) Rosen Publishing Group, Inc., The.

Holt, Jane E. In Madera Canyon. 2009. pap. 15.95 *(978-1-60494-002-2(6))* Wheatmark, Inc.

Home in a Tree. (J). pap. 13.15 *(978-0-8136-4256-7(6))* Modern Curriculum Pr.

HOP, LLC. Hooked on Animals in the Wild Super Activity Kit. 2006. (J). (gr. -1). 9.99 *(978-1-933863-17-7(X))* HOP, LLC.

—Super Activity 3-pack - Hooked on Animals. 2006. (J). (gr. -1). 24.99 *(978-1-933863-97-9(8))* HOP, LLC.

Hopgood, Sally & Graham, Oakley. Safari Wonders. Wood, Hannah, illus. 2012. (Sparkling Slide Nature Bks.). (ENG.). 12p. (J). (gr. -1-k). 9.99 *(978-1-84956-676-6(3))* Top That! Publishing PLC GBR. Dist: Independent Pubs. Group.

Hopkins, Andy & Potter, Joc. Animals in Danger, Level 1. Lindop, Christine, ed. 3rd ed. 2008. (ENG., Illus.). 64p. pap. 9.38 *(978-0-19-423379-8(0))* Oxford Univ. Pr., Inc.

Hopkins, Mary Rice. Animal Alphabet: On the Land, in the Sky or Sea, Meet God's Creatures from a to Z. Francisco, Wendy, illus. 2003. 32p. (J). (gr. -1-1). 12.99 *(978-0-89107-968-2(8))* Crossway.

Hoppner, Gabi. Fun with Animals. 2004. (What A Series of Fun! Ser.). (Illus.). 10p. (J). bds. 3.99 *(978-1-59384-052-5(7))* Parklane Publishing.

Horácek, Petr. Animal Opposites. Horácek, Petr, illus. 2013. (ENG., Illus.). 20p. (J). (gr. -1-2). 15.99 *(978-0-7636-6776-4(5))* Candlewick Pr.

Hort, Lenny. Seals on the Bus. Karas, G. Brian & Karas, G., illus. 2008. (ENG.). 32p. (J). (gr. -1-k). pap. 26.99 *(978-0-8050-8678-2(1)*, 9780805086782, Holt, Henry & Co. Bks. For Young Readers) Holt, Henry & Co.

Houghton, Sarah. Bloodsuckers: Bats, Bugs, & Other Bloodthirsty Creatures, 6 vols. 2003. (High Five Reading - Green Ser.). (ENG.). 48p. (gr. 3-4). pap. 54.00 *(978-0-7368-2844-4(3))*; (Illus.). per. 9.00 *(978-0-7368-2834-5(6))* Capstone Press of Coughlan Cos. (High Five Reading (RBL)).

How Animals Hide: Level G, 6 vols. (Wonder Worldtm Ser.). 16p. 29.95 *(978-0-7802-4581-5(4))* Wright Group/McGraw-Hill.

How Animals Move: Individual Title Six-Packs. (Discovery World Ser.). 24p. (gr. 1-2). 33.00 *(978-0-7635-8473-3(8))* Rigby Education.

How Animals Shaped History. 2014. (How Animals Shaped History Ser.). 24p. (J). (gr. k-5). 141.60 *(978-1-4777-6618-7(9))*; pap. 49.50 *(978-1-4777-7224-9(3))* Rosen Publishing Group, Inc., The. (PowerKids Pr.).

Hudak, Heather C. Carnivores. (J). 2016. ***(978-1-4896-5785-5(1))*** 2005. (Illus.). 24p. (gr. -1-3). per. 8.95 *(978-1-59036-262-4(4))* 2004. (Illus.). 24p. lib. bdg. 24.45 *(978-1-59036-238-9(1))* Weigl Pubs., Inc.

Hudak, Heather C. Omnivores. (J). 2016. ***(978-1-4896-5788-6(6))*** 2011. (gr. 4-6). pap. 12.95 *(978-1-61690-715-0(0)*, AV2 by Weigl) 2005. (Illus.). 24p. (gr. -1-3). per. 8.95 *(978-1-59036-265-5(9))* 2004. (Illus.). 24p. lib. bdg. 8.95 *(978-1-59036-241-9(1))* Weigl Pubs., Inc.

Hughes, Catherine D. Little Kids Big Book of Animals. 2010. (ENG., Illus.). 128p. (J). (gr. -1-3). lib. bdg. 21.90 *(978-1-4263-0721-8(7)*, National Geographic Children's Bks.) National Geographic Society.

Hughes, Catherine D. & National Geographic Kids Staff. Little Kids First Big Book of Animals. 2010. (National Geographic Little Kids First Big Bks.). (ENG., Illus.). 128p. (J). (gr. -1-3). 14.95 *(978-1-4263-0704-1(7)*, National Geographic Children's Bks.) National Geographic Society.

Hughes, Mónica. Carry Me. 2005. (Big Cat Ser.). (gr. k-2). pap. 6.50 *(978-1-59055-964-2(9))* Pacific Learning, Inc.

Hunt, Jilly. Saving Endangered Animals. 2017. (Beyond the Headlines! Ser.). (ENG.). 48p. (gr. 4-6). lib. bdg. 33.32 ***(978-1-4846-4140-8(X)***, Heinemann InfoSearch) Heinemann-Raintree.

Hurwitz, Jane. Choosing a Career in Animal Care. 2005. (World of Work Ser.). (Illus.). 64p. (YA). (gr. 7-12). lib. bdg. 31.95 *(978-0-8239-3356-3(3))* Rosen Publishing Group, Inc., The.

Hussl Krassnig, Gloria. What a Family. 2006. (Illus.). 114p. 23.95 *(978-0-9791468-0-0(1))* Hussl, Gloria.

Hutt, Sarah. Animals Are Delicious. Ladd, David & Anderson, Stephanie, illus. 2016. (ENG.). 48p. 17.95 *(978-0-7148-7123-3(0))* Phaidon Pr., Inc.

Hyland, Tony & Scarborough, Kate. Killer Pets. 2012. (Fast Facts Ser.). 32p. (gr. 4-6). pap. 28.50 *(978-1-59771-327-6(9))* Sea-To-Sea Pubns.

Icky Animals! Small & Gross. 2015. (Icky Animals! Small & Gross Ser.). (ENG.). 24p. (J). (gr. 1-1). pap., pap., pap. 297.00 *(978-1-4994-1298-7(3)*, PowerKids Pr.) Rosen Publishing Group, Inc., The.

Ideals Children's Books Staff, creator. My Big Book of Wild Animals. 2007. (ENG., Illus.). 224p. (J). (gr. 4-7). pap. 19.99 *(978-0-8249-5543-4(9)*, Ideal Pubns.) Worthy Publishing.

Ideals Publications Inc. Staff, creator. Hands-on Highlights Rebus Fun: Animal Tales. 2007. (Hands-on Ser.). (ENG., Illus.). 16p. (J). (gr. k-3). 16.99 *(978-0-8249-1501-8(1)*, Ideal Pubns.) Worthy Publishing.

Idee, Ari. What's Your Snack? 2013. 28p. pap. 9.49 *(978-0-9798991-2-6(5))* Technology & Imagination Pr.

legg, Gerard. Minibeasts. 2006. (Illus.). 24p. (YA). (gr. 1-18). lib. bdg. 22.80 *(978-1-931983-59-4(3))* Chrysalis Education.

Ikids Staff. Animals Everywhere. Phillips, Jillian, illus. 2010. (ENG.). 20p. (J). (gr. -1-17). 6.99 *(978-1-60169-006-7(1))* Innovative Kids.

Ikids Staff & Schimel, Lawrence. Is a Spider an Insect? Perez, Sara, illus. 2009. (ENG.). 22p. (J). (gr. -1-1). 9.99 *(978-1-58476-820-3(7)*, IKIDS) Innovative Kids.

Imbriaco, Alison. The Otter: A MyReportLinks. com Book. 2005. (Endangered & Threatened Animals Ser.). (Illus.). 48p. (J). lib. bdg. 26.60 *(978-0-7660-5067-9(X)*, MyReportLinks.com Bks.) Enslow Pubs., Inc.

In Danger, 6 Packs. (gr. k-1). 23.00 *(978-0-7635-8841-0(5))* Rigby Education.

Incredible Creatures: Level N, 6 vols. (Explorers Ser.). 32p. (gr. 3-6). 44.95 *(978-0-7699-0589-1(7))* Shortland Pubns. (U. S. A.) Inc.

Inky. Dottie Goes to the Circus. 2011. 28p. pap. 14.99 *(978-1-4634-4403-7(6))* AuthorHouse.

Innovative Kids Staff, creator. Soft Shapes - Animals. 2010. (ENG.). 8p. (J). (gr. -1 — 1). 10.99 *(978-1-58476-964-4(5))* Innovative Kids.

Inside Animal Homes. 2015. (Inside Animal Homes Ser.). (ENG.). 24p. (J). (gr. 2-3). pap., pap., pap. 297.00 *(978-1-4994-1300-7(9)*, PowerKids Pr.) Rosen Publishing Group, Inc., The.

Invasive Species. 2016. (Invasive Species Ser.). 48p. (gr. 4-4). lib. bdg. 156.80 *(978-1-5026-1820-7(6))* Cavendish Square Publishing.

Ipcar, Dahlov. Animal Hide & Seek, 1 vol. 2013. (ENG., Illus.). 32p. (J). 17.95 *(978-1-934031-80-3(1)*, d6d51255-f6fd-4100-9abb-cbebfc8ccecf) Islandport Pr., Inc.

Ipcar, Dahlov, illus. Wild & Tame Animals. 2015. (Dahlov Ipcar Collection). (ENG.). 48p. (J). (gr. -1-2). 19.95 *(978-1-909263-64-2(8))* Flying Eye Bks. GBR. Dist: Consortium Bk. Sales & Distribution.

Ipcizade, Catherine. BIG Predators. 2016. (Big Ser.). (ENG.). 24p. pap. 6.95 *(978-1-5157-6218-8(1)*, Pebble Plus) Capstone Press of Coughlan Cos.

—Extreme Animals, 6 vols., Set. Incl. Fastest Animals. lib. bdg. 26.65 *(978-1-4296-5311-4(6))*; Slowest Animals. lib. bdg. 26.65 *(978-1-4296-5310-7(8))*; (gr. k-1). (Extreme Animals Ser.). (ENG.). 24p. 2010. Set lib. bdg. 53.30 *(978-1-4296-5313-8(2)*, Pebble Plus) Capstone Press of Coughlan Cos.

—The Fastest Animals, 1 vol. (Extreme Animals Ser.). (ENG., 24p. (gr. k-1). 2011. Illus.). pap. 7.29 *(978-1-4296-6208-6(5))* 2011. pap. 41.70 *(978-1-4296-6377-9(4))* 2010. lib. bdg. 26.65 *(978-1-4296-5311-4(6))* Capstone Press of Coughlan Cos. (Pebble Plus).

—The Slowest Animals, 1 vol. 2011. (Extreme Animals Ser.). (ENG., 24p. (gr. k-1). Illus.). pap. 7.29 *(978-1-4296-6209-3(3))*; pap. 41.70 *(978-1-4296-6379-3(0))* Capstone Press of Coughlan Cos. (Pebble Plus).

—The Strongest Animals. 2011. (Extreme Animals Ser.). (ENG.). 24p. (gr. k-1). pap. 41.70 *(978-1-4296-6381-6(2)*, Pebble Plus) Capstone Press of Coughlan Cos.

Ireland, Karin. Wonderful Nature, Wonderful You, 1 vol. Canyon, Christopher, illus. 2017. (ENG.). 32p. (J). (gr. k-3). 16.95 *(978-1-58469-582-0(X))* Dawn Pubns.

Issa, Joanna. What Can I See?, 1 vol. 2014. (These Are My Senses Ser.). (ENG., Illus.). 24p. (gr. -1-1). pap. 5.99 *(978-1-4846-0431-1(8)*, Acorn) Heinemann-Raintree.

It's Amazing: It's Amazing Package. 2003. 125.95 *(978-0-673-61613-5(4))* Celebration Pr.

Iversen, Sandra. What Is It? 2009. (ENG., Illus.). 12p. (J). pap. *(978-1-77540-046-2(8))* Iversen Publishing Ltd.

Jackson, Tom. The Complete Book of Animals: A World Encyclopedia of Amphibians, Reptiles & Mammals with over 500 Detailed Illustrations. 2014. (ENG., Illus.). 256p. pap. 9.99 *(978-1-84322-734-2(7)*, Armadillo) Anness Publishing GBR. Dist: National Bk. Network.

—An Illustrated Guide to the Animals of America: A Visual Encyclopedia of Amphibians, Reptiles & Mammals in the United States, Canada & South America, with over 350 Illustrations. 2013. (ENG., Illus.). 96p. (J). (gr. -1-12). pap. 9.99 *(978-1-84322-769-4(X)*, Armadillo) Anness Publishing GBR. Dist: National Bk. Network.

—Musk Ox. 2008. (Nature's Children Ser.). (Illus.). 52p. (J). *(978-0-7172-6259-5(6))* Grolier, Ltd.

—Piranhas & Other Small Deadly Creatures. 2008. (ENG., Illus.). 32p. (J). (gr. 5-9). lib. bdg. *(978-0-7787-3770-4(5))* Crabtree Publishing Co.

—Saving Animal Species. 2015. (Animal Trackers Ser.). (ENG., Illus.). 32p. (gr. 3-4). lib. bdg. 27.32 *(978-1-4914-6989-7(7)*, Fact Finders) Capstone Press of Coughlan Cos.

—Tracking Animal Identity. 2015. (Animal Trackers Ser.). (ENG., Illus.). 32p. (gr. 3-4). lib. bdg. 27.32 *(978-1-4914-6986-6(2)*, Fact Finders) Capstone Press of Coughlan Cos.

Jacobs, Pat. I Wonder Why Penguins Can't Fly. 2014. 32p. pap. 7.00 *(978-1-61003-350-3(7))* Center for the Collaborative Classroom.

—I Wonder Why Penguins Can't Fly: And Other Questions about Polar Lands. 2011. (I Wonder Why Ser.). (ENG., Illus.). 32p. (J). (gr. k-3). pap. 6.99 *(978-0-7534-6530-1(2)*, 9780753465301, Kingfisher) Roaring Brook Pr.

Jacobson, Ryan. Super Animal Powers. Tekiela, Stan, photos by. 2016. (Wildlife Picture Bks.). (ENG., Illus.). 32p. (J). (gr. -1-3). 12.95 *(978-1-59193-648-0(9))* Adventure Pubns.

Jacobson, Ryan. What Eats That? Tekiela, Stan, photos by. 2017. (Wildlife Picture Bks.). (ENG., Illus.). 32p. (J). (gr. -1-3). 14.95 ***(978-1-59193-749-4(3))*** Adventure Pubns.

Jaeger, Pamela. Fiona No No. 2005. 32p. (J). 8.95 *(978-0-9704876-4-3(9))* First Mom's Club, The.

James, Emily. Animals, Animals! 2016. (Animals, Animals! Ser.). (ENG.). 32p. (gr. 1-2). 109.28 *(978-1-5157-2685-2(1)*, Aplus Bks.) Capstone Press of Coughlan Cos.

—Do Goldfish Fly? A Question & Answer Book about Animal Movements. 2016. (Animals, Animals! Ser.). (ENG., Illus.). 32p. (gr. 1-2). lib. bdg. 27.32 *(978-1-5157-2666-1(5)*, Aplus Bks.) Capstone Press of Coughlan Cos.

—Do Whales Have Whiskers? A Question & Answer Book about Animal Body Parts. 2016. (Animals, Animals! Ser.). (ENG., Illus.). 32p. (gr. 1-2). lib. bdg. 27.32 *(978-1-5157-2664-7(9)*, Aplus Bks.) Capstone Press of Coughlan Cos.

Jango-Cohen, Judith. El Aguila Calva. 2005. (Libros para Avanzar (Pull Ahead Bks.)). (SPA., Illus.). 32p. (J). (gr. k-3). per. 5.95 *(978-0-8225-3135-7(6)*, Ediciones Lerner) Lerner Publishing Group.

Jaworski, Sarah. Gabe's Garden Food Chain. 2013. (Rosen Readers Ser.). (ENG.). 24p. (J). (gr. 2-3). pap. 49.50 *(978-1-4777-2369-2(2))*; pap. 8.25 *(978-1-4777-2368-5(4))* Rosen Publishing Group, Inc., The. (Rosen Classroom).

Jenkins, Jennifer Meghan. The 10 Deadliest Predators. 2008. 14.99 *(978-1-55448-502-4(9))* Scholastic Library Publishing.

Jenkins, Steve. Actual Size. (ENG., Illus.). (J). (gr. 1-4). 2011. 28p. pap. 7.99 *(978-0-547-51291-4(0))* 2004. 34p. tchr. ed. 17.99 *(978-0-618-37594-3(5))* Houghton Mifflin Harcourt Publishing Co.

—The Animal Book: A Collection of the Fastest, Fiercest, Toughest, Cleverest, Shyest - And Most Surprising - Animals on Earth. Jenkins, Steve, illus. 2013. (ENG., Illus.). 208p. (J). (gr. 1-4). 24.99 *(978-0-547-55799-1(X))* Houghton Mifflin Harcourt Publishing Co.

—Apex Predators: The World's Deadliest Hunters, Past & Present. 2017. (ENG., Illus.). 32p. (J). (gr. 1-4). 17.99 *(978-0-544-67160-7(0)*, HMH Books For Young Readers) Houghton Mifflin Harcourt Publishing Co.

Jenkins, Steve. Trickiest! 19 Sneaky Animals. 2017. (Extreme Animals Ser.). (ENG., Illus.). 40p. (J). (gr. 1-4). 14.99 ***(978-0-544-93716-1(3)***, HMH Books For Young Readers) Houghton Mifflin Harcourt Publishing Co.

Jerome, Kate B. The Wise Animal Handbook. 2017. (Arcadia Kids Ser.). (ENG., Illus.). 32p. (J). 16.99 ***(978-0-7385-2765-9(3))*** Arcadia Publishing.

—The Wise Animal Handbook Alabama. 2017. (Arcadia Kids Ser.). (ENG., Illus.). 32p. (J). 16.99 ***(978-0-7385-2809-0(9))*** Arcadia Publishing.

—The Wise Animal Handbook Alaska. 2017. (Arcadia Kids Ser.). (ENG., Illus.). 32p. (J). 16.99 ***(978-0-7385-2810-6(2))*** Arcadia Publishing.

—The Wise Animal Handbook Arizona. 2017. (Arcadia Kids Ser.). (ENG., Illus.). 32p. (J). 16.99 ***(978-0-7385-2811-3(0))*** Arcadia Publishing.

—The Wise Animal Handbook Arkansas. 2017. (Arcadia Kids Ser.). (ENG., Illus.). 32p. (J). 16.99 ***(978-0-7385-2767-3(X))*** Arcadia Publishing.

—The Wise Animal Handbook Colorado. 2017. (Arcadia Kids Ser.). (ENG., Illus.). 32p. (J). 16.99 ***(978-0-7385-2812-0(9))*** Arcadia Publishing.

—The Wise Animal Handbook Connecticut. 2017. (Arcadia Kids Ser.). (ENG., Illus.). 32p. (J). 16.99 ***(978-0-7385-2813-7(7))*** Arcadia Publishing.

—The Wise Animal Handbook Florida. 2017. (Arcadia Kids Ser.). (ENG., Illus.). 32p. (J). 16.99 ***(978-0-7385-2814-4(5))*** Arcadia Publishing.

—The Wise Animal Handbook Georgia. 2017. (Arcadia Kids Ser.). (ENG., Illus.). 32p. (J). 16.99 ***(978-0-7385-2815-1(3))*** Arcadia Publishing.

—The Wise Animal Handbook Idaho. 2017. (Arcadia Kids Ser.). (ENG., Illus.). 32p. (J). 16.99 ***(978-0-7385-2817-5(X))*** Arcadia Publishing.

—The Wise Animal Handbook Illinois. 2017. (Arcadia Kids Ser.). (ENG., Illus.). 32p. (J). 16.99 ***(978-0-7385-2818-2(8))*** Arcadia Publishing.

—The Wise Animal Handbook Indiana. 2017. (Arcadia Kids Ser.). (ENG., Illus.). 32p. (J). 16.99 ***(978-0-7385-2819-9(6))*** Arcadia Publishing.

—The Wise Animal Handbook Iowa. 2017. (Arcadia Kids Ser.). (ENG., Illus.). 32p. (J). 16.99 *(978-0-7385-2820-5(X))* Arcadia Publishing.

—The Wise Animal Handbook Kansas. 2017. (Arcadia Kids Ser.). (ENG., Illus.). 32p. (J). 16.99 *(978-0-7385-2821-2(8))* Arcadia Publishing.

—The Wise Animal Handbook Kentucky. 2017. (Arcadia Kids Ser.). (ENG., Illus.). 32p. (J). 16.99 *(978-0-7385-2822-9(6))* Arcadia Publishing.

—The Wise Animal Handbook Louisiana. 2017. (Arcadia Kids Ser.). (ENG., Illus.). 32p. (J). 16.99 *(978-0-7385-2823-6(4))* Arcadia Publishing.

Jocelyn, Marthe. Eats. Slaughter, Tom, illus. (ENG.). (J). (gr. k-k). 2010. 16p. bds. 7.95 *(978-0-88776-988-7(8))* 2007. 24p. 16.99 *(978-0-88776-820-0(2))* Tundra Bks. CAN. (Tundra Bks.). Dist: Penguin Random Hse. LLC.

Johnson, Bruce. We Read Phonics-A Day at the Zoo. Johnson, Meredith, illus. 2012. 32p. (J). 9.95 *(978-1-60115-349-4(X))*; pap. 4.99 *(978-1-60115-350-0(3))* Treasure Bay, Inc.

Johnson, Bruce & Johnson, Meredith, illus. A Day at the Zoo. 2012. 27p. (J). *(978-1-60115-595-5(6))* Treasure Bay, Inc.

Johnson-Farris, Nancy. Critters & Bugs of the Great Sonoran Desert. 2003. (J). spiral bd. 12.95 *(978-1-931334-32-7(3))* Pieces of Learning.

Johnson, Jinny. Animal Planet - Wild World: An Encyclopedia of Animals. 2013. (ENG., Illus.). 132p. (gr. 4-8). lib. bdg. 35.93 *(978-1-4677-1597-3(2)*, Millbrook Pr.) Lerner Publishing Group.

—Armored Dinosaurs. 2014. (Discovering Dinosaurs Ser.). (Illus.). 24p. (gr. 3-6). 28.50 *(978-1-62588-012-3(X))* Black Rabbit Bks.

—Mighty Killers. 2014. (Discovering Dinosaurs Ser.). (Illus.). 24p. (gr. 3-6). 28.50 *(978-1-62588-015-4(4))* Black Rabbit Bks.

—Speedy Dinosaurs. 2014. (Discovering Dinosaurs Ser.). (Illus.). 24p. (gr. 3-6). 28.50 *(978-1-62588-017-8(0))* Black Rabbit Bks.

—Tyrannosaurus & Other Mighty Hunters. Rosewarne, Graham, illus. 2007. (Dinosaurs Alive! Ser.). 32p. (J). (gr. -1-3). lib. bdg. 28.50 *(978-1-59920-063-7(5))* Black Rabbit Bks.

Johnson, Jinny & Humphries, Tudor. How Fast Is a Cheetah? (Illus.). (J). pap. 18.99 *(978-0-590-24630-9(5))* Scholastic, Inc.

Johnson, Rebecca. When Lunch Fights Back: Wickedly Clever Animal Defenses. 2014. (Illus.). 48p. (gr. 4-8). lib. bdg. 26.60 *(978-1-4677-2109-7(3)*, Millbrook Pr.) Lerner Publishing Group.

Johnson, Rebecca L. Journey into the Deep: Discovering New Ocean Creatures. 2015. (ENG., Illus.). 64p. (gr. 4-8). 34.65 *(978-1-4677-5923-6(6)*, Lerner Digital) Lerner Publishing Group.

Johnson, Virginia, illus. Don't, 1 vol. 2014. (ENG.). 24p. (J). (— 1). bds. 9.95 *(978-1-55498-355-1(X))* Groundwood Bks. CAN. Dist: Publishers Group West (PGW).

Jones, Cathy & Amos, Janine. Dangerous Animals. 2012. (Illus.). 116p. *(978-1-4351-4155-1(5))* Barnes & Noble, Inc.

Jones, Frankie. Faces: A Follow-the-Trail Book. Galloway, Fhiona, illus. 2016. (ENG.). 10p. (J). (gr. -1 — 1). bds. 7.99 *(978-1-4998-0268-9(4))* Little Bee Books Inc.

Jones, Jennifer Berry. Who Lives in the Snow? Powell, Consie, illus. 2012. (ENG.). 32p. (gr. -1-3). pap. 8.95 *(978-1-57098-444-0(1))* Rinehart, Roberts Pubs.

Jordan, Christopher. Baseball Animals. 2014. (Major League Baseball: First Base Bks.). (ENG., Illus.). 24p. (gr. -1-2). 12.99 *(978-1-77049-474-9(X)*, Fenn-Tundra) Tundra Bks. CAN. Dist: Penguin Random Hse. LLC.

—Hockey Animals. 2011. (My First NHL Book Ser.). (ENG., Illus.). 24p. (J). (-k). bds. 8.99 *(978-1-77049-317-9(4))*; bds. 6.95 *(978-1-77049-344-5(1)*, Fenn-Tundra) Tundra Bks. CAN. Dist: Random Hse., Inc., Penguin Random Hse. LLC.

Joseph, Patricia. Animals from Aa to Zz. 2009. 40p. pap. 18.50 *(978-1-4490-2419-2(X))* AuthorHouse.

Joubert, Beverly & Joubert, Dereck. African Animal Alphabet. 2011. (ENG., Illus.). 48p. (J). (gr. -1-k). 16.95 *(978-1-4263-0781-2(0))*; 26.90 *(978-1-4263-0782-9(9))* National Geographic Society. (National Geographic Children's Bks.).

Judson, Karen. Animal Testing. 2005. (Open for Debate Ser.). (Illus.). 128p. (gr. 7-7). lib. bdg. 42.79 *(978-0-7614-1882-5(2)*, Benchmark Bks.) Marshall Cavendish Corp.

Jungle Animals. Date not set. (Question & Answers of the Natural World Ser.). 32p. 4.98 *(978-0-7525-4319-2(9))* Parragon, Inc.

Junor, Amy. My Giant Fold-Out Wild Animals. 2014. (My Giant Fold-Outs Ser.). (ENG.). 10p. (J). (gr. -1 — 1). 6.99 *(978-0-7641-6669-3(7))* Barron's Educational Series, Inc.

Justine, Ciovacco. Meerkats. 2009. (Amazing Animals Ser.). 48p. (gr. 2-6). pap. 10.50 *(978-1-4339-2015-8(8)*, Gareth Stevens Learning Library) Stevens, Gareth Publishing LLLP.

Kaiser, Amy L. If I Lived in the Ocean. 2012. 12p. pap. 12.68 *(978-1-4669-4864-8(7))* Trafford Publishing.

Kallio, Jamie. 12 Things to Know about Invasive Species. 2015. (ENG., Illus.). 32p. (J). *(978-1-63235-030-5(0))* Pr. Room Editions LLC.

Kalman, Bobbie. The ABCs of Animals. 2007. (ABCs of the Natural World Ser.). (ENG., Illus.). 32p. (J). (gr. 1-5). pap. *(978-0-7787-3430-7(7))* Crabtree Publishing Co.

—Animal Families. 2007. (Introducing Living Things Ser.). (ENG., Illus.). 24p. (J). (gr. 1-4). pap. *(978-0-7787-3250-1(9))* Crabtree Publishing Co.

—Animal Life Cycles: Growing & Changing. 2006. (Nature's Changes Ser.). (ENG., Illus.). 32p. (J). (gr. 3-7). pap. *(978-0-7787-2312-7(7))* Crabtree Publishing Co.

—Animals Grow & Change. 2007. (Introducing Living Things Ser.). (ENG., Illus.). 24p. (J). (gr. 1-4). pap. *(978-0-7787-3251-8(7))* Crabtree Publishing Co.

—Big Science Ideas. 2008. (J). pap. *(978-0-7787-3292-1(4))* Crabtree Publishing Co.

—El Ciclo de Vida de la Rana. 2005. (Serie Ciclos de Vida Ser.). (SPA., Illus.). 32p. (J). lib. bdg. *(978-0-7787-8663-4(3))* Crabtree Publishing Co.

—Ciclos de Vida de Los Animales: Crecimiento y Cambios. 2006. (Cambios Que Suceden en la Naturaleza Ser.). (SPA., Illus.). 32p. (J). (gr. 1-4). pap. *(978-0-7787-8389-3(8))* Crabtree Publishing Co.

—Ciclos de Vida de los Animales: Crecimiento y Cambios. 2006. (Cambios Que Suceden en la Naturaleza Ser.). (SPA., Illus.). 32p. (J). (gr. 1-4). lib. bdg. *(978-0-7787-8375-6(8))* Crabtree Publishing Co.

—Como Se Adaptan los Animales? 2006. (Libro de Bobbie Kalman Ser.). (SPA., Illus.). 32p. (J). (gr. 3-7). pap. *(978-0-7787-8813-3(X))*; lib. bdg. *(978-0-7787-8767-9(2))* Crabtree Publishing Co.

—¿Cómo Se Mueve? 2009. (SPA.). 24p. (J). *(978-0-7787-8704-4(4))*; pap. *(978-0-7787-8743-3(5))* Crabtree Publishing Co.

—¿Es Igual O Diferente? 2008. (SPA.). 24p. (J). pap. *(978-0-7787-8734-1(6))*; lib. bdg. *(978-0-7787-8725-9(7))* Crabtree Publishing Co.

—Hogares de los Seres Vivos. 2008.Tr. of Living Things Need Water. (SPA.). 24p. (J). pap. *(978-0-7787-8687-0(0))* Crabtree Publishing Co.

—How & What Do Animals Eat? 2014. (ENG., Illus.). 24p. (J). *(978-0-7787-0543-7(9))* Crabtree Publishing Co.

—How & Why Do Animals Adapt? 2015. (ENG., Illus.). 24p. (J). *(978-0-7787-1463-7(2))* Crabtree Publishing Co.

—How & Why Do Animals Change As They Grow? 2014. (ENG., Illus.). 24p. (J). *(978-0-7787-0545-1(5))* Crabtree Publishing Co.

—How Are They the Same? 2011. (ENG.). 16p. (J). pap. *(978-0-7787-9581-0(0))* Crabtree Publishing Co.

—How Do Animals Change? 2011. (ENG.). 24p. (J). pap. *(978-0-7787-9593-3(4))*; lib. bdg. *(978-0-7787-9568-1(3))* Crabtree Publishing Co.

—How Do Living Things Find Food? 2010. (Introducing Living Things Ser.). (ENG.). 24p. (J). (gr. 1-4). pap. *(978-0-7787-3258-7(4))*; lib. bdg. *(978-0-7787-3234-1(7))* Crabtree Publishing Co.

—I Can Count. 2010. (ENG., Illus.). 16p. (J). (gr. k-2). *(978-0-7787-9411-0(3))*; pap. *(978-0-7787-9455-4(5))* Crabtree Publishing Co.

—I Can Count: Sé Contar. 2010. (SPA, ENG & MUL.). 16p. (J). pap. *(978-0-7787-8262-9(X))*; lib. bdg. *(978-0-7787-8269-8(7))* Crabtree Publishing Co.

—Invasive Animal Species. 2016. (ENG., Illus.). 32p. (J). *(978-0-7787-2783-5(1))* Crabtree Publishing Co.

—Las Plantas Son Seres Vivos. 2008. (SPA.). 24p. (J). pap. *(978-0-7787-8692-4(7))* Crabtree Publishing Co.

—Living Things in My Back Yard. 2007. (Introducing Living Things Ser.). (ENG., Illus.). 24p. (J). (gr. 1-4). pap. *(978-0-7787-3255-6(X))* Crabtree Publishing Co.

—Los Seres Vivos Necesitan Agua. 2008.Tr. of Animals Grow & Change. (SPA.). 24p. (J). pap. *(978-0-7787-8691-7(9))* Crabtree Publishing Co.

—Metamorphosis: Changing Bodies. 2005. (Nature's Changes Ser.). (ENG., Illus.). 32p. (J). (gr. 1-5). pap. *(978-0-7787-2307-3(0))* Crabtree Publishing Co.

—¿Qué Es el Reino Animal? 2005. (Ciencia de los Seres Vivos Ser.). (SPA., Illus.). 32p. (J). (gr. 2-4). pap. *(978-0-7787-8803-4(2))* Crabtree Publishing Co.

—¿Qué Son los Biomas? 2005. (Ciencia de los Seres Vivos Ser.). (SPA., Illus.). 32p. (J). (gr. 2-4). pap. *(978-0-7787-8801-0(6))* Crabtree Publishing Co.

—Le Regne Animal. 2004. (Petit Monde Vivant Ser.). (FRE., Illus.). 32p. (J). pap. 10.95 *(978-2-89579-025-9(6))* Bayard Canada Livres CAN. Dist: Crabtree Publishing Co.

—Sé Contar. 2010. (SPA.). 16p. (J). pap. *(978-0-7787-8577-4(7))*; lib. bdg. *(978-0-7787-8551-4(3))* Crabtree Publishing Co.

—Seres Vivos de Mi Jardín. 2008. (SPA.). 24p. (J). lib. bdg. *(978-0-7787-8683-2(8))* Crabtree Publishing Co.

—Warm-Blooded or Cold-Blooded? 2008. (Big Science Ideas Ser.). (ENG., Illus.). 32p. (J). (gr. 1-4). pap. *(978-0-7787-3301-0(7))* Crabtree Publishing Co.

—What Is a Carnivore? (ENG., Illus.). 32p. (J). 2008. *(978-0-7787-7663-5(8))* 2007. (gr. 1-5). pap. *(978-0-7787-3294-5(0))* Crabtree Publishing Co.

—What Is a Herbivore? (ENG.). 32p. (J). 2008. *(978-0-7787-7667-3(0))* 2008. *(978-0-7787-7666-6(2))* 2007. (Illus.). (gr. 1-4). lib. bdg. *(978-0-7787-3275-4(4))* 2007. (Illus.). (gr. 1-5). pap. *(978-0-7787-3295-2(9))* Crabtree Publishing Co.

—What Is a Top Predator? 2012. (ENG.). 32p. (J). *(978-0-7787-2772-9(6))*; pap. *(978-0-7787-2777-4(7))* Crabtree Publishing Co.

—What Is an Omnivore? (ENG., Illus.). 32p. (J). 2008. *(978-0-7787-7669-7(7))* 2007. (gr. 1-5). pap. *(978-0-7787-3296-9(7))* Crabtree Publishing Co.

Kalman, Bobbie, intro. Les Bébés Tamias. 2012. (FRE.). 24p. (J). pap. 9.95 *(978-2-89579-476-9(6))* Bayard Canada CAN. Dist: Crabtree Publishing Co.

Kalman, Bobbie & Aloian, Molly. Polar Oceans. 2003. (Living Ocean Ser.). (ENG., Illus.). 32p. (J). (gr. 2-9). lib. bdg. *(978-0-7787-1297-8(4))* Crabtree Publishing Co.

Kalman, Bobbie & Langille, Jacqueline. ¿Que Son Las Redes y Cadenas Alimentarias? 2005. (Ciencia de los Seres Vivos Ser.). (SPA., Illus.). 32p. (J). pap. *(978-0-7787-8802-7(4))* Crabtree Publishing Co.

Kalman, Bobbie & Larin, Allison. Les Poissons. Briere, Marie-Josee, tr. from ENG. rev. ed. 2007. (Petit Monde Vivant Ser.). (FRE., Illus.). 32p. (J). (gr. 1-7). pap. 9.95 *(978-2-89579-126-3(0))* Bayard Canada Livres CAN. Dist: Crabtree Publishing Co.

Kalman, Bobbie & Sjonger, Rebecca. Animal Life Cycles: Growing & Changing. 2008. (ENG.). 32p. (J). *(978-0-7787-7722-9(7))* Crabtree Publishing Co.

—Metamorphosis: Changing Bodies. 2008. (ENG.). 32p. (J). *(978-0-7787-7713-7(8))* Crabtree Publishing Co.

Kalman, Bobbie & Smithyman, Kathryn. El Ciclo de Vida de la Rana. Rouse, Bonna, illus. 2005. (Serie Ciclos de Vida Ser.). (SPA.). 32p. (J). (gr. 1-4). pap. *(978-0-7787-8709-9(5))* Crabtree Publishing Co.

Kaner, Etta. And the Winner Is... Amazing Animal Athletes. Anderson, David, illus. 2013. (ENG.). 32p. (J). (gr. -1-3). 16.95 *(978-1-55453-904-8(8))* Kids Can Pr., Ltd. CAN. Dist: Hachette Bk. Group.

—Have You Ever Seen a Duck in a Raincoat? Szuc, Jeff, illus. 2009. (Have You Ever Seen Ser.). (ENG.). 32p. (J). (gr. -1-2). 14.95 *(978-1-55453-246-9(9))* Kids Can Pr., Ltd. CAN. Dist: Hachette Bk. Group.

—Have You Ever Seen a Hippo with Sunscreen? Szuc, Jeff, illus. 2010. (Have You Ever Seen Ser.). (ENG.). 32p. (J). (gr. -1-2). 14.95 *(978-1-55453-337-4(6))* Kids Can Pr., Ltd. CAN. Dist: Hachette Bk. Group.

—How Animals Defend Themselves. Stephens, Pat, illus. 2006. (Kids Can Read Ser.). (ENG.). 32p. (J). (gr. 1-3). 14.95 *(978-1-55337-904-1(7))* Kids Can Pr., Ltd. CAN. Dist: Hachette Bk. Group.

Kapchinske, Pam. Hey Diddle Diddle: A Food Chain Tale, 1 vol. Rogers, Sherry, illus. 2011. (ENG.). 32p. (J). (gr. -1-3). 16.95 *(978-1-60718-130-9(4))*; pap. 8.95 *(978-1-60718-140-8(1))* Arbordale Publishing.

Katz, Julie & Merberg, Julie. Turn the Key: Who Do You See? McQueen, Lucinda, illus. 2011. (ENG.). 12p. (J). (gr. -1). bds. 11.99 *(978-1-935703-11-2(0))* Downtown Bookworks.

Kavanagh, James. African Wildlife Nature Activity Book. Leung, Raymond, illus. 2nd ed. 2011. (Nature Activity Book Ser.). (ENG.). 32p. (J). (gr. 4-7). 6.95 *(978-1-58355-574-3(9))* Western National Parks Assn.

—Arctic Wildlife Nature Activity Book. Leung, Raymond, illus. 2nd ed. 2011. (Nature Activity Book Ser.). (ENG.). 32p. (J). (gr. 4-7). 6.95 *(978-1-58355-575-0(7))* Western National Parks Assn.

—Australian Wildlife. Leung, Raymond, illus. 2nd ed. 2011. (Nature Activity Book Ser.). (ENG.). 32p. (J). (gr. 4-7). act. bk. ed. 6.95 *(978-1-58355-576-7(5))* Western National Parks Assn.

—Great Lakes Wildlife Nature Activity Book. Leung, Raymond, illus. 2nd ed. 2011. (Nature Activity Book Ser.). (ENG.). 32p. (J). (gr. 4-7). 6.95 *(978-1-58355-580-4(3))* Western National Parks Assn.

—Mammals Nature Activity Book. Leung, Raymond, illus. 2nd ed. 2011. (Nature Activity Book Ser.). (ENG.). 32p. (J). (gr. 4-7). 6.95 *(978-1-58355-581-1(1))* Western National Parks Assn.

—My First Arctic Nature. Leung, Raymond, illus. 2011. (Nature Activity Book Ser.). (ENG.). 32p. (J). (gr. 2-4). act. bk. ed. 6.95 *(978-1-58355-586-6(2))* Western National Parks Assn.

Kavanagh, James & Waterford Press Staff. Pond Life Nature Activity Book. Leung, Raymond, illus. 2nd ed. 2011. (Nature Activity Book Ser.). (ENG.). 32p. (J). (gr. 4-7). 6.95 *(978-1-58355-582-8(X))* Western National Parks Assn.

Kavanagh, Shannon & Davie, Rob. Safari Jeff & Shannon Visit Africa. 2004. (Great Green Adventure Ser.). (Illus.). 46p. 14.95 incl. audio compact disk *(978-0-9734409-0-4(2))* Croctalk Publishing CAN. Dist: Hushion Hse. Publishing, Ltd.

Kearney, Brendan, illus. The Amazing Animal Adventure: An Around-The-World Spotting Expedition. 2016. (ENG.). 64p. (J). (gr. 1-5). 19.95 *(978-1-78067-845-0(2))* King, Laurence Publishing GBR. Dist: Hachette Bk. Group.

Kennedy, Pamela. My Big Book of 5-Minute Devotions: Celebrating God's World. Wummer, Amy, illus. 2006. (ENG.). 96p. (J). (gr. 3-7). pap. 12.99 *(978-0-8249-5556-4(0)*, Ideal Pubns.) Worthy Publishing.

Kenney, Karen Latchana. The Bald Eagle, 1 vol. Hunt, Judith A., illus. 2011. (Our Nation's Pride Set 2 Ser.). (ENG.). 32p. (J). (gr. 1-4). 28.50 *(978-1-61641-149-7(X))* Magic Wagon.

Kennst du Das? Die Tiere. (Duden Ser.). (GER., Illus.). 16p. (J). *(978-3-411-70441-5(1))* Bibliographisches Institut & F. A. Brockhaus AG DEU. Dist: International Bk. Import Service, Inc.

Kent, Lorna, illus. Baby's First Animal Book. 2004. 12p. (J). bds. 7.99 *(978-1-85854-884-5(5))* Brimax Books Ltd. GBR. Dist: Byeway Bks.

Khan, S. Amazing Animal Facts & Lists. 2004. (Facts & Lists Internet-Linked Ser.). 64p. (J). lib. bdg. 15.95 *(978-1-58086-577-7(1))*; (ENG.). pap. 7.95 *(978-0-7945-0543-1(0))* EDC Publishing.

Khanduri, K. The Usborne Book of World Wildlife. 2004. (World Wildlife Ser.). 128p. (J). lib. bdg. 26.95 *(978-1-58086-034-5(6)*, Usborne) EDC Publishing.

KidsLabel Staff, creator. Spot 7 Animals. 2007. (ENG., Illus.). 40p. (J). (gr. -1-17). 12.95 *(978-0-8118-5722-2(0))* Chronicle Bks. LLC.

Killen, Nicola. Animal Noises. 2014. (Nicola Killen Animals Ser.). (ENG., Illus.). 10p. (J). (— 1). bds. 8.99 *(978-1-4052-6287-3(7))* Egmont Bks., Ltd. GBR. Dist: Independent Pubs. Group.

Kingfisher Editors. Who's That? Eating. 2013. (Who's That? Ser.). (ENG.). 14p. (J). (gr. -1-k). bds. 5.99 *(978-0-7534-7070-1(5)*, 9780753470701, Kingfisher) Roaring Brook Pr.

Kinsner, Kathy. Animals at the Extremes: Set Of 6. 2011. (Navigators Ser.). (J). 48.00 net. *(978-1-4108-0425-9(9))* Benchmark Education Co.

—Animals at the Extremes & Animales en los Extremos: 6 English, 6 Spanish Adaptations. 2011. (ENG & SPA.). (J). 97.00 net. *(978-1-4108-5694-4(1))* Benchmark Education Co.

Kipling, Rudyard. Just So Stories, 1 vol., Vol. 1. Wallace, Ian, illus. 2013. (ENG.). 64p. (J). (gr. k). 19.95 *(978-1-55498-212-7(X))* Groundwood Bks. CAN. Dist: Publishers Group West (PGW).

Kisner, Kathy. Relationships in Nature: Set Of 6. 2011. (Navigators Ser.). (J). pap. 50.00 net. *(978-1-4108-2570-4(1))* Benchmark Education Co.

Klepeis, Alicia. Warm-Blooded & Cold-Blooded Animals Explained. 2016. (Distinctions in Nature Ser.). 32p. (J). pap. 10.58 *(978-1-5026-2181-8(9))* Cavendish Square Publishing.

Klepeis, Alicia Z. Brain Eaters: Creatures with Zombielike Diets. 2016. (Real-Life Zombies Ser.). (ENG., Illus.). 32p. (gr. 3-4). lib. bdg. 27.99 *(978-1-5157-2479-7(4)*, Edge Bks.) Capstone Press of Coughlan Cos.

—Praying Mantis vs. Giant Hornet: Battle of the Powerful Predators. 2016. (Bug Wars Ser.). (ENG., Illus.). 32p. (gr. 3-4). lib. bdg. 27.99 *(978-1-4914-8067-0(X)*, Edge Bks.) Capstone Press of Coughlan Cos.

Klevanksy, Rhonda, ed. 999 Amazing Animal Facts: Featuring Whales, Elephants, Bears, Wolves, Monkeys, Turtles, Snakes, Birds, Bees, Ants & Many, Many More. 2013. (ENG., Illus.). 512p. (J). (gr. 3-7). pap. 17.99 *(978-1-84322-989-6(7)*, Armadillo) Anness Publishing GBR. Dist: National Bk. Network.

Knapp, Ron. Bloodsucking Creatures. 2011. (Bizarre Science Ser.). (Illus.). 48p. (J). (gr. 5-18). pap. 8.95 *(978-1-59845-219-8(3))*; lib. bdg. 25.27 *(978-0-7660-3671-0(5))* Enslow Pubs., Inc.

Knowlton, Laurie Lazzaro. African Giants. Tusan, Stan, illus. Prebeg, Rick, photos by. 2005. (J). *(978-1-933248-08-0(4))* World Quest Learning.

—Come on Down. Brown, Kevin, illus. 2005. (J). *(978-1-933248-07-3(6))* World Quest Learning.

KociendaGenevieve. WEIRD ANIMALS LOW INTERMEDIATE BOOK WITH ONLINE ACCESS. 2014. (ENG.). 24p. (J). pap. 9.50 *(978-1-107-65664-2(8))* Cambridge Univ. Pr.

Koeppel, Ruth. In the Wild. McBee, Scott, illus. 2009. (ENG.). 10p. (J). (gr. -1-1). 15.99 *(978-1-58476-816-6(9))* Innovative Kids.

Koontz, Robin Michal. Sniffs & Stinks: How Animals Use Odor to Survive. 2011. (Amazing Animal Skills Ser.). (Illus.). 48p. (J). (gr. 4). 29.93 *(978-0-7614-4908-9(6))* Marshall Cavendish GBR. Dist: Marshall Cavendish Corp.

—Spits & Squirts: How Animals Squirt to Survive. 2011. (Amazing Animal Skills Ser.). (Illus.). 48p. (J). (gr. 4). 29.93 *(978-0-7614-4909-6(4))* Marshall Cavendish Corp.

Kopp, Megan. Real-Life Vampires, 1 vol. 2010. (Vampires Ser.). (ENG.). 32p. (gr. 3-4). lib. bdg. 27.99 *(978-1-4296-4578-2(4)*, Edge Bks.) Capstone Press of Coughlan Cos.

—What Do You Find in a Backyard? 2016. (ENG., Illus.). 24p. (J). *(978-0-7787-2255-7(4))* Crabtree Publishing Co.

—What Do You Find in a Coral Reef? 2016. (ENG., Illus.). 24p. (J). *(978-0-7787-2257-1(0))* Crabtree Publishing Co.

Korb, Rena B. Discovering Pteranodon, 1 vol. Dawson, Ted, illus. 2008. (Dinosaur Digs Ser.). (ENG.). 32p. (gr. -1-4). 28.50 *(978-1-60270-108-3(3)*, Looking Glass Library-Nonfiction) Magic Wagon.

Kramer, Nash. Night Animals. 2008. (Discovering & Exploring Science Ser.). (Illus.). 16p. (J). (gr. -1-3). lib. bdg. 12.95 *(978-0-7569-8254-6(5))* Perfection Learning Corp.

—Why Do You Change in Winter? 2014. (Little Books of Answers: Level F Ser.). (Illus.). 16p. (gr. k-2). pap. 7.95 *(978-1-927136-57-7(1))* Three Crows Media NZL. Dist: RiverStream Publishing.

Kratt, Chris & Kratt, Martin. Go, Creature Powers! (Wild Kratts) Random House, illus. 2016. (Pictureback(R) Ser.). (ENG.). 24p. (J). (gr. -1-2). 5.99 *(978-1-101-93306-0(2)*, Random Hse. Bks. for Young Readers) Random Hse. Children's Bks.

—Wild Predators (Wild Kratts) Random House, illus. 2015. (Step into Reading Ser.). (ENG.). 32p. (J). (gr. -1-1). 3.99 *(978-0-553-52472-7(0)*, Random Hse. Bks. for Young Readers) Random Hse. Children's Bks.

Krebs, Laurie. Nos Fuimos Todos de Safari: Una Aventura de Números Por Tanzania. Cairns, Julia, illus. 2005. (SPA & ESP.). 32p. (J). (gr. k-5). pap. 8.99 *(978-1-905236-08-4(5))* Barefoot Bks., Inc.

Kroll, Virginia. Let There Be Llamas! Lombardo, Irina, illus. 2006. 31p. (J). pap. 11.95 *(978-0-8198-4519-1(1))* Pauline Bks. & Media.

Kudlinski, Kathleen V. The Sunset Switch. Burnett, Lindy, illus. 2005. (Picture Book Ser.). (ENG.). 32p. (J). (gr. k-3). 15.95 *(978-1-55971-916-2(8))* Cooper Square Publishing Llc.

Kuskowski, Alex. Mini Animal Marvels. 2014. (Mini Animal Marvels Ser.: 6). (ENG.). 24p. (J). (gr. -1-3). lib. bdg. 145.26 *(978-1-62403-063-5(7)*, SandCastle) ABDO Publishing Co.

Kvatum, Lia. Saving Yasha: The Incredible True Story of an Adopted Moon Bear. Pokrovskaya, Liya, photos by. 2012. (ENG., Illus.). 32p. (J). (gr. -1-3). lib. bdg. 25.90 *(978-1-4263-1076-8(5)*, National Geographic Children's Bks.) National Geographic Society.

Kvatum, Lia & National Geographic Kids Staff. Saving Yasha: The Incredible True Story of an Adopted Moon Bear. Pokrovskaya, Liya, photos by. 2012. (ENG., Illus.). 32p. (J). (gr. -1-3). 16.95 *(978-1-4263-1051-5(X)*, National Geographic Children's Bks.) National Geographic Society.

La Coccinella. Look & See: What Am I? 2008. (Look & See! Ser.). (ENG., Illus.). 24p. (J). (gr. -1-1). bds. 6.95 *(978-1-4027-5828-7(6))* Sterling Publishing Co., Inc.

LaBaff, Stephanie. Draw Animals in 4 Easy Steps: Then Write a Story. LaBaff, Tom, illus. 2012. (Drawing in 4 Easy Steps Ser.). 48p. (J). (gr. 3-18). 25.27 *(978-0-7660-3840-0(8))* Enslow Pubs., Inc.

Labaff, Stephanie. Draw Animals in 4 Easy Steps: Then Write a Story. LaBaff, Tom, illus. 2012. (Drawing in 4 Easy Steps Ser.). 48p. (J). (gr. 3-18). pap. 8.95 *(978-1-4644-0013-1(X)*, Enslow Elementary) Enslow Pubs., Inc.

Lacey, Saskia. Showdown: Alpha Animals (Level 3) 2017. (Exploring Reading Ser.). (Illus.). 32p. (J). (gr. 3-3). pap. 8.99 *(978-1-4258-4976-4(8))* Teacher Created Materials, Inc.

Lachner, Elizabeth. Herbivores & Carnivores. 2009. (Real Life Readers Ser.). 32p. (gr. 5-6). pap. 10.00 *(978-1-4358-0183-7(0)*, Rosen Classroom) Rosen Publishing Group, Inc., The.

Lalley, Kristine. How Many Legs? Learning to Multiply Using Repeated Addition. (PowerMath: Beginning Ser.). 16p. 2009. (gr. 2-2). 37.50 *(978-1-60851-373-4(4))* 2006. (Illus.). (J). (gr. 3-7). lib. bdg. 18.75 *(978-1-4042-3336-2(9))* Rosen Publishing Group, Inc., The. (PowerKids Pr.).

—How Many Legs? Learning to Multiply Using Repeated Action. 2009. (Math for the REAL World Ser.). 16p. (gr. 2-3). pap. 7.05 *(978-0-8239-8929-4(1)*, Rosen Classroom) Rosen Publishing Group, Inc., The.

Laman, Judi-Lynn. The 10 Most Bizarre Animal Habits. 2008. 14.99 *(978-1-55448-542-0(8))* Scholastic Library Publishing.

Lambert, Nat. Animals. Hinton, Steph, illus. 2017. (Wipe Clean Dot-To-dot Ser.). (ENG.). 24p. (J). (gr. -1-k). bds. 9.99 *(978-1-78700-001-8(X))* Top That! Publishing PLC GBR. Dist: Independent Pubs. Group.

—Magnetic Silly Animals. 2007. (ENG., Illus.). 10p. (J). (gr. -1-k). 9.99 *(978-1-84666-346-8(6))* Top That! Publishing PLC GBR. Dist: Independent Pubs. Group.

Landau, Elaine. Bites & Stings. 2008. (Head-to-Toe Health Ser.). 32p. (gr. 2-7). lib. bdg. 28.50 *(978-0-7614-2850-3(X)*, Benchmark Bks.) Marshall Cavendish Corp.

Landstrom, Lee Ann & Shragg, Karen I. Nature's Yucky! 3: The Eastern United States. Rogge, Rachel, illus. 2013. 48p. (J). pap. 12.00 *(978-0-87842-601-0(9))* Mountain Pr. Publishing Co., Inc.

Landstrom, Lee Ann, et al. Nature's Yucky! Gross Stuff That Helps Nature Work, 1 vol. rev. ed. (ENG., Illus.). 48p. (J). (gr. k-5). pap. 10.00 *(978-0-87842-474-0(1)*, 338) Mountain Pr. Publishing Co., Inc.

Lantz, Peggy Sias & Hale, Wendy A. The Coastlines of Florida. 2014. (Florida Water Story Ser.). (ENG., Illus.). 34p. (J). (gr. 4). pap. 6.95 *(978-1-56164-702-6(0))* Pineapple Pr., Inc.

—The Wetlands of Florida. 2014. (Florida Water Story Ser.). (ENG., Illus.). 34p. (J). (gr. 4). pap. 6.95 *(978-1-56164-705-7(5))* Pineapple Pr., Inc.

Laplante, Walter. Plants & Animals of the Great Lakes. 2014. (Exploring the Great Lakes Ser.). 32p. (J). (gr. 3-6). pap. 63.00 *(978-1-4824-1193-5(8))* Stevens, Gareth Publishing LLLP.

Larranaga, Ana, illus. Matching Puzzle Cards - Animals. 2012. (ENG.). 36p. (J). (gr. k-12). 9.99 *(978-1-60905-225-6(0))* Blue Apple Bks.

Larson, Kirsten W. Vampires in Nature. 2015. (Freaky Nature Ser.). (ENG., Illus.). 32p. (J). (gr. 2-4). 19.95 *(978-1-60753-782-3(6))* Amicus Publishing.

Latou, Pierre. Who Eats Who in A Food Chain? 2014. (Little Books of Answers: Level F Ser.). (Illus.). 16p. (gr. k-2). pap. 7.95 *(978-1-927136-58-4(X))* Three Crows Media NZL. Dist: RiverStream Publishing.

Latta, Sara L., et al. Nature's Invaders. 2013. (Nature's Invaders Ser.). (ENG.). 32p. (gr. 3-4). lib. bdg. 111.96 *(978-1-4765-0320-2(6)*, Edge Bks.) Capstone Press of Coughlan Cos.

Laval, Thierry. Look & Find Nature. 2016. (Look & Find Ser.). (ENG., Illus.). 14p. (J). 18.99 *(978-0-531-22238-6(1)*, Children's Pr.) Scholastic Library Publishing.

Law, Felicia. Lost in the Cave. 2015. (Science to the Rescue Ser.). (ENG., Illus.). 32p. (J). (gr. 3-6). *(978-0-7787-1677-8(5))* Crabtree Publishing Co.

Lawrence, Ellen. Poop Cures. 2017. (Scoop on Poop Ser.). (ENG.). (J). (gr. -1-3). lib. bdg. 17.95 ***(978-1-68402-249-6(5))*** Bearport Publishing Co., Inc.

Lawrence, Ellen. Roseate Spoonbill. 2016. (Swamp Things: Animal Life in a Wetland Ser.). (ENG.). 24p. (J). (gr. -1-3). lib. bdg. 17.95 *(978-1-944102-53-1(1))* Bearport Publishing Co., Inc.

Lawrence, Riley. Snowy Owls of the Tundra. 2017. (J). ***(978-1-5345-2216-9(6)***, KidHaven Publishing) Greenhaven Publishing LLC.

Lazoo Publishing Staff. Hidden Animals! 2010. (ENG., Illus.). 30p. (J). bds. 6.99 *(978-1-934734-57-5(8))* Seven Footer Pr.

Leake, Diyan. Ponds, 1 vol. 2014. (Water, Water Everywhere! Ser.). (ENG., Illus.). 24p. (gr. -1-1). 22.65 *(978-1-4846-0452-6(0)*, Acorn) Heinemann-Raintree.

Leber, Nancy. Rain Forest Animals, 6 vols., Set. 2003. (Phonics Readers 1-36 Ser.). (ENG.). 8p. (gr. k-1). pap. 29.70 *(978-0-7368-3198-7(3)*, Phonics Readers) Capstone Press of Coughlan Cos.

Lee Follen, Eliza. What the Animals Do & Say. 2004. reprint ed. pap. 1.99 *(978-1-4192-9359-7(1))* Kessinger Publishing, LLC.

Legg, Gerald. The X-Ray Picture Book of Incredible Creatures. Salariya, David & Scrace, Carolyn, illus. 2004. 48p. (J). (gr. 4-8). pap. 9.00 *(978-0-7567-7406-6(3))* DIANE Publishing Co.

Legg, Gerald & Weston, Steve. The World of Animal Life. 2012. (ENG., Illus.). 48p. (J). 15.00 *(978-1-899762-71-2(X))* Award Pubns. Ltd. GBR. Dist: Parkwest Pubns., Inc.

Legs: Big Book: Level C. 8p. 20.95 *(978-0-322-00343-9(1))* Wright Group/McGraw-Hill.

Legs: Individual Title Six-Packs. (Literatura 2000 Ser.). (gr. 1-2). 28.00 *(978-0-7635-0094-8(1))* Rigby Education.

Legs: Level C, 6 vols. 8p. 24.95 *(978-0-7802-9120-1(4))* Wright Group/McGraw-Hill.

Leigh, Autumn. Flying Without Wings: Amazing Animal Adaptations. 2009. (Real Life Readers Ser.). 16p. (gr. 2-3). pap. 7.05 *(978-1-4358-0089-2(3)*, Rosen Classroom) Rosen Publishing Group, Inc., The.

—Spots & Stripes. 2006. (Rosen Real Readers Big Bookstm Ser.). (ENG.). 8p. (gr. k-1). 29.95 *(978-1-4042-6209-6(1))* Rosen Publishing Group, Inc., The.

Lemu, B.Aisha. Animals in Islam. 2005. (Illus.). 52p. pap. *(978-978-2462-33-6(0))* Spectrum Bks., Ltd. NGA. Dist: Michigan State Univ. Pr.

Lerner Publishing Group Staff. Animal Predators: Classroom Set. 2005. (Illus.). (J). (gr. 3-6). 54.95 *(978-0-8225-5487-5(9))* Lerner Publishing Group.

LernerClassroom Editors. First Step Nonfiction-Animal Families Teaching Guide. 2009. pap. 7.95 *(978-0-8225-5658-9(8))* Lerner Publishing Group.

LernerClassroom Editors, ed. Teaching Animal Predators. 2008. (Animal Predators Ser.). (gr. 3-6). pap., tchr. ed. 7.95 *(978-0-8225-4044-1(4))* Lerner Publishing Group.

—Teaching Guide for Fsn / Animal Adaptations. 2010. pap. 5.95 *(978-0-7613-6681-2(4))* Lerner Publishing Group.

Leroy-Bennett, Veronique. Les Animaux: First French. 2016. (ENG & FRE., Illus.). 64p. 12.99 *(978-1-86147-632-6(9)*, Armadillo) Anness Publishing GBR. Dist: National Bk. Network.

Let's Find Out! Animal Life. 2015. (Let's Find Out! Animal Life Ser.). (ENG.). 32p. (J). (gr. 2-3). 281.40 *(978-1-68048-203-4(3))*; pap., pap., pap. 464.40 *(978-1-68048-150-1(9))* Rosen Publishing Group, Inc., The. (Britannica Educational Publishing).

Levine, Julia Pimsleur. Little Pim: Animals. 2012. (ENG.). 10p. (J). (gr. -1-k). bds. 8.95 *(978-1-4197-0174-0(6))* Abrams, Inc.

Levine, Shar. Animals. 2010. (Class of Their Own Ser.). (ENG., Illus.). 48p. (J). (gr. 5-8). pap. *(978-0-7787-5386-5(7))*; lib. bdg. *(978-0-7787-5372-8(7))* Crabtree Publishing Co.

Levine, Stuart P. Animals. 2009. (21st Century Skills Library: Real World Science Ser.). (ENG.). 32p. (J). (gr. 4-8). lib. bdg. 28.50 *(978-1-60279-456-6(1)*, 200227) Cherry Lake Publishing.

Levy, Barbara Soloff. Drawing on the Go! Animals. 2010. (Dover Doodle Bks.). (ENG., Illus.). 64p. (J). (gr. k-3). pap. 1.99 *(978-0-486-47944-6(7))* Dover Pubns., Inc.

—Who's Who in the Zoo? Dot-to-Dot Fun. 2007. (Dover Children's Activity Bks.). (ENG., Illus.). 32p. (J). (gr. 1-3). per. 3.99 *(978-0-486-46181-6(5))* Dover Pubns., Inc.

Levy, Barbara Soloff & Drawing Staff. You Can Draw Animals. 2003. (Dover How to Draw Ser.). (ENG., Illus.). 132p. (J). (gr. k-4). pap. 8.95 *(978-0-486-42899-4(0))* Dover Pubns., Inc.

Levy, Duncan. Happy about Animals: An 8-Year-Old's View on Sharing the Earth. 2007. (Illus.). 54p. (J). per. 21.95 *(978-1-60005-019-0(0))* Happy About.

Levy, Janey. Life in a Rain Forest Ecosystem. 2009. (Real Life Readers Ser.). (J). (ENG., Illus.). 32p. (gr. 5-6). pap. 10.00 *(978-1-4358-0189-9(X))*; lib. bdg. 25.25 *(978-1-4358-2997-8(2))* Rosen Publishing Group, Inc., The. (PowerKids Pr.).

—What Lives on a Prairie? (Reading Room Collection 2 Ser.). 24p. 2009. (gr. 3-4). 42.50 *(978-1-60852-001-5(3)*, PowerKids Pr.) 2003. (Illus.). (J). lib. bdg. 22.60 *(978-0-8239-3701-1(1))* Rosen Publishing Group, Inc., The.

Lewin, Ted. Look! Lewin, Ted, illus. (I Like to Read(r) Ser.). (ENG., Illus.). 24p. (J). (gr. -1-3). 2014. 6.99 *(978-0-8234-3059-8(6))* 2013. 14.95 *(978-0-8234-2607-2(6))* Holiday Hse., Inc.

—What Am I? Where Am I? Lewin, Ted, illus. 2014. (I Like to Read(r) Ser.). (ENG., Illus.). 24p. (J). (gr. -1-3). 6.99 *(978-0-8234-3180-9(0))* Holiday Hse., Inc.

—What Am I? Where Am I? 2013. (I Like to Read(r) Ser.). (ENG.). 24p. (J). (gr. -1-3). 14.95 *(978-0-8234-2856-4(7))* Holiday Hse., Inc.

Lewis, Brenda Ralph. Prehistoric Creatures in the Sea & Sky. 2006. (Nature's Monsters Ser.). (Illus.). 32p. (gr. 2-6). lib. bdg. 26.00 *(978-0-8368-6845-6(5)*, Gareth Stevens Learning Library) Stevens, Gareth Publishing LLLP.

Lewis, Kelly. Animals by Day, Animals by Night. 2016. (Spring Forward Ser.). (J). (gr. 1). *(978-1-4900-3727-1(6))* Benchmark Education Co.

Limon, Daniel, illus. The Colossal Creature Count: Add up All of the Animals to Solve Each Scene. 2017. (ENG.). 48p. (J). (gr. 1-4). pap. 9.99 *(978-1-4380-0992-6(5))* Barron's Educational Series, Inc.

Litchfield, Jo. Animals. 2004. (First Words Board Bks.). (SPA & ENG., Illus.). 1p. (J). (gr. -1-18). bds. 4.95 *(978-0-7460-4093-5(8))* EDC Publishing.

Little & Large Sticker Activity - Big Animals. 2006. (J). 3.99 *(978-1-933581-30-9(1))* Byeway Bks.

Little & Large Sticker Activity Big Animals. 2008. 24p. pap. *(978-1-84810-056-5(6))* Miles Kelly Publishing, Ltd.

Liu, Li. Who Am I? 2016. (1-3Y Animals Ser.). (ENG., Illus.). 28p. (J). pap. 5.99 ***(978-1-63437-584-9(X))*** American Reading Co.

Llewellyn, Claire. City Animals. 2005. (Illus.). 24p. (YA). (gr. 1-18). lib. bdg. 22.80 *(978-1-932889-31-4(0))* Sea-To-Sea Pubns.

—Looking after Animals. 2016. (Cambridge Reading Adventures Ser.). (ENG., Illus.). 16p. pap. 6.56 *(978-1-316-60582-0(5))* Cambridge Univ. Pr.

Llewellyn, Claire & Feldman, Thea. Kingfisher Readers L2: Amazing Animal Senses. 2014. (Kingfisher Readers Ser.). (ENG., Illus.). 32p. (J). (gr. k-3). 12.99 *(978-0-7534-7173-9(6)*, 9780753471739, Kingfisher) Roaring Brook Pr.

Lluch, Alex A. Animal Alphabet: Slide & Seek the ABCs. Defenbaugh, David, illus. 2013. (ENG.). 13p. (J). (-k). bds. 12.99 *(978-1-61351-041-4(1))* WS Publishing.

—Animal Alphabet: Slide & Seek the ABCs. 2011. (Animal Alphabet Ser.). (ENG.). 13p. (J). (gr. -1-k). bds. 7.95 *(978-1-936061-49-5(X))* WS Publishing.

—I Like to Learn Numbers: Hungry Chameleon. 2011. (ENG.). 32p. (J). (gr. -1-k). bds. 4.95 *(978-1-934386-01-9(4))* WS Publishing.

—Zoo Clues Animal Alphabet. 2011. (ENG.). 52p. (J). (gr. -1-k). bds. 6.95 *(978-1-936061-50-1(3))* WS Publishing.

Loh-Hagan, Virginia. Top 10: Oddities. 2016. (Illus.). 32p. (J). *(978-1-63470-504-2(1))* Cherry Lake Publishing.

—Top 10: Venom. 2016. (Illus.). 32p. (J). *(978-1-63470-507-3(6))* Cherry Lake Publishing.

—Top 10 - Horrors. 2016. (Wild Wicked Wonderful Ser.). (ENG., Illus.). 32p. (J). (gr. 4-8). 29.93 *(978-1-63471-099-2(1)*, 208507, 45th Parallel Press) Cherry Lake Publishing.

—Top 10: Body Parts. 2017. (Wild Wicked Wonderful Ser.). (ENG., Illus.). 32p. (J). (gr. 4-8). lib. bdg. 29.93 *(978-1-63472-140-0(3)*, 209132, 45th Parallel Press) Cherry Lake Publishing.

—Top 10: Super Senses. 2017. (Wild Wicked Wonderful Ser.). (ENG., Illus.). 32p. (J). (gr. 4-8). lib. bdg. 29.93 *(978-1-63472-141-7(1)*, 209136, 45th Parallel Press) Cherry Lake Publishing.

Lonely Planet Publications Staff. The Animal Book, 1 vol. 2017. (Lonely Planet Kids Ser.). (ENG., Illus.). 164p. (J). 19.99 ***(978-1-78657-434-3(9)***, 5372) Lonely Planet Pubns.

—How Animals Build: Lift the Flaps to Discover Amazing Animal Homes, 1 vol. 2017. (Lonely Planet Kids Ser.). (ENG., Illus.). 24p. (J). 18.99 ***(978-1-78657-663-7(5)***, 5633) Lonely Planet Pubns.

Lonely Planet Publications Staff. World Search - Incredible Animals, 1 vol. 2014. (Lonely Planet Kids Ser.). (ENG., Illus.). 16p. (J). 14.99 *(978-1-74321-922-5(9)*, 4643) Lonely Planet Pubns.

Long, Matthew & Long, Thomas. Any Bear Can Wear Glasses: The Spectacled Bear & other Curious Creatures. Long, Sylvia, illus. 2005. 24p. (J). (gr. k-4). reprint ed. 17.00 *(978-0-7567-9763-8(2))* DIANE Publishing Co.

Loomis, Jennifer A. Wildlife in the Rocky Mountains. Loomis, Jennifer A., photos by. unabr. ed. 2005. (Illus.). 100p. (J). 24.95 *(978-0-88045-159-8(9))* Stemmer Hse. Pubs.

Lord, Michelle. Animal School: What Class Are You? Garland, Michael, illus. 2014. (ENG.). 32p. (J). (gr. -1-3). 16.95 *(978-0-8234-3045-1(6))* Holiday Hse., Inc.

Lorimer, Janet. Beasts. 2005. (Quickreads Ser.). (Illus.). 32p. (J). pap. 2.95 *(978-1-56254-738-7(0)*, SP7380) Saddleback Educational Publishing, Inc.

Lovejoy, Sharon. The Little Green Island with a Little Red House: A Book of Colors & Critters. 2015. (ENG., Illus.). 32p. (J). (gr. -1-2). 10.95 *(978-1-60893-464-5(0))* Down East Bks.

Lowery, Lawrence F. Animals Two by Two. 2015. (I Wonder Why Ser.). (ENG., Illus.). 36p. (J). (gr. k-3). pap. 11.95 *(978-1-941316-28-3(X))* National Science Teachers Assn.

—What Can an Animal Do? Pfloog, Jan, illus. 2012. (I Wonder Why Ser.). (ENG.). 32p. (J). (gr. k-3). pap. 11.95 *(978-1-936959-45-7(3))* National Science Teachers Assn.

—What Does an Animal Eat? Reusswig, William, illus. 2012. (I Wonder Why Ser.). (ENG.). 32p. (J). (gr. k-3). pap. 11.95 *(978-1-936959-46-4(1))* National Science Teachers Assn.

Loy, Jessica. Weird & Wild Animal Facts. Loy, Jessica, illus. 2015. (ENG., Illus.). 40p. (J). (gr. -1-3). 17.99 *(978-0-8050-7945-6(9)*, 9780805079456, Holt, Henry & Co. Bks. For Young Readers) Holt, Henry & Co.

Luevano, Richard. Uncle Bun Bun's Abc's of the Animal World. 2012. 34p. 34.99 *(978-1-61904-922-2(8))*; pap. 24.99 *(978-1-61904-921-5(X))* Salem Author Services.

Lunde, Darrin. Meet the Meerkat. Wynne, Patricia J., illus. 2007. (ENG.). 32p. (J). (gr. -1-2). pap. 7.95 *(978-1-58089-154-7(3))* Charlesbridge Publishing, Inc.

Lunde, Darrin P. After the Kill. Stock, Catherine, illus. 2011. (ENG.). 32p. (J). (gr. 1-4). 16.95 *(978-1-57091-743-1(4))*; pap. 7.95 *(978-1-57091-744-8(2))* Charlesbridge Publishing, Inc.

Lundgren, Julie K. Animal Adaptations. 2011. (ENG., Illus.). 24p. (gr. 1-2). pap. 8.95 *(978-1-61741-935-5(4))* Rourke Educational Media.

—Run, Swim, Fly. 2011. (ENG., Illus.). 24p. (gr. k-1). pap. 8.95 *(978-1-61741-922-5(2))* Rourke Educational Media.

—Squirrels. 2010. (ENG., Illus.). 24p. (gr. 1-4). pap. 8.95 *(978-1-61590-549-2(9))* Rourke Educational Media.

Lunis, Natalie. Comfort Dogs. 2014. (Dog Heroes Ser.). (ENG., Illus.). 32p. (J). (gr. 2-7). lib. bdg. 25.27 *(978-1-62724-287-5(2))* Bearport Publishing Co., Inc.

—Shape-Shifting Animals. 2014. (Animals with Super Powers Ser.). 24p. (J). (gr. 1-6). lib. bdg. 22.61 *(978-1-62724-079-6(9))* Bearport Publishing Co., Inc.

Lynch, Wayne. The Arctic. Lynch, Wayne, photos by. 2007. (Our Wild World Ser.). (ENG., Illus.). 64p. (J). (gr. 3-7). pap. 8.95 *(978-1-55971-961-2(3))* Cooper Square Publishing Llc.

—Wayne Lynch's Canadian Rockies Wildlife for Kids. 2011. 22.95 *(978-1-926983-05-9(X))* Summerthought Publishing Ltd. CAN. Dist: Alpen Bks.

Lynette, Rachel. Who Lives in a Deep, Dark Cave? 2010. (Exploring Habitats Ser.). (ENG.). 24p. (J). pap. 8.25 *(978-1-4488-1277-6(1))*; lib. bdg. 22.60 *(978-1-4488-0676-8(3))* Rosen Publishing Group, Inc., The. (PowerKids Pr.).

—Who Lives on a Towering Mountain? 2010. (Exploring Habitats Ser.). (ENG.). 24p. (J). pap. 8.25 *(978-1-4488-1287-5(9))*; lib. bdg. 22.60 *(978-1-4488-0680-5(1))* Rosen Publishing Group, Inc., The. (PowerKids Pr.).

—Who Lives on the Icy, Cold Tundra? 2010. (Exploring Habitats Ser.). (ENG.). 24p. (J). pap. 8.25 *(978-1-4488-1279-0(8))*; lib. bdg. 22.60 *(978-1-4488-0675-1(5))* Rosen Publishing Group, Inc., The. (PowerKids Pr.).

Lyons, Eric. God Made Animals. 2006. (ENG., Illus.). (J). (gr. -1-3). 3.00 *(978-0-932859-70-9(4))* Apologetics Pr., Inc.

M, Patty. Seven Beagles. 2013. 24p. pap. *(978-1-4602-2674-2(7))* FriesenPress.

Macdonald, Fiona. Killer Animals: You Wouldn't Want to Meet! 2010. (Top 10 Worst Ser.). (Illus.). 32p. (J). (gr. 3-6). (ENG.). pap. 10.50 *(978-1-4339-4077-4(9))*; lib. bdg. 26.60 *(978-1-4339-4076-7(0))* Stevens, Gareth Publishing LLLP. (Gareth Stevens Learning Library).

MacDonald, Mercia. Mammals on a Mission: 1. the Big Cat... 2. the Little Lamb... 3. the Cheeky Colt... 2010. (Illus.). 32p. 12.99 *(978-1-4520-0418-1(8))* AuthorHouse.

Mack, B. P. Animalphabet. 2011. 56p. pap. 19.50 *(978-1-61204-172-8(6)*, Eloquent Bks.) Strategic Book Publishing & Rights Agency (SBPRA).

Mackall, Dandi Daley. God Made Polliwogs & Puppy Dogs. 2015. (ENG., Illus.). 32p. (J). 12.99 *(978-0-7369-5873-8(8))* Harvest Hse. Pubs.

Macken, JoAnn Early. Animals That Live in... Complete Series, 38 vols. 2009. (Animals That Live in... Ser.). (ENG.). 24p. (J). (gr. 1-1). pap. 226.10 *(978-1-4339-2455-2(2)*, Weekly Reader Leveled Readers) Stevens, Gareth Publishing LLLP.

—Rivers. 2005. (Water Habitats Ser.). (Illus.). 24p. (gr. k-3). pap. 8.15 *(978-0-8368-4893-9(4))*; lib. bdg. 22.00 *(978-0-8368-4886-1(1))* Stevens, Gareth Publishing LLLP. (Weekly Reader Leveled Readers).

Macken, JoAnn Early & Early Macken, JoAnn. Rivers/Rios. 2005. (Water Habitats/ Habitats acuaticos Ser.). (ENG & SPA., Illus.). 24p. (gr. k-3). lib. bdg. 22.00 *(978-0-8368-6031-3(4)*, Weekly Reader Leveled Readers) Stevens, Gareth Publishing LLLP.

MacKenzie, Catherine. Scottish Highland. 2007. (Adventure Ser.). (ENG., Illus.). 96p. (J). per. 8.99 *(978-1-84550-281-2(7)*, beeaf3cf-4408-4d2c-89dc-81ff3e31e46b) Christian Focus Pubns. GBR. Dist: Bookmasters Distribution.

Maclay, Elise. Reading the Wild. Doolittle, Bev, illus. 2005. 32p. (J). (gr. k-4). reprint ed. 17.00 *(978-0-7567-9649-5(0))* DIANE Publishing Co.

Madema, Victoria. Playful Pictures — Animals. 2013. (ENG., Illus.). 32p. (J). (gr. -1-8). pap. 3.99 *(978-0-486-49268-1(0))* Dover Pubns., Inc.

Madgwick, Wendy. Animals & Plants: 10 Easy-to-Follow Experiments for Learning Fun - Find Out about Nature & How Things Live! 2014. (ENG., Illus.). 270p. (J). (gr. -1-12). 8.99 *(978-1-86147-349-3(4)*, Armadillo) Anness Publishing GBR. Dist: National Bk. Network.

—My Book of Animals. Rosewarne, Graeme, illus. 2016. (ENG.). 48p. (J). (gr. -1-12). bds. 9.99 *(978-1-86147-768-2(6)*, Armadillo) Anness Publishing GBR. Dist: National Bk. Network.

Madison, Amelia. Predators of Asia & Australia. 2015. (J). lib. bdg. *(978-1-62713-556-6(1))* Cavendish Square Publishing.

—Predators of Europe & Africa. 2015. (J). lib. bdg. *(978-1-62713-553-5(7))*; (ENG.). 32p. (gr. 3-3). 28.50 *(978-1-5026-0179-7(6))* Cavendish Square Publishing.

Magic Wagon Staff & ABDO Publishing Company Staff. Famous Firsts: Animals Making History, 1 vol. 2011. (Famous Firsts: Animals Making History Ser.). (ENG., Illus.). 32p. 171.00 *(978-1-61641-636-2(X)*, Graphic Planet) Magic Wagon.

Maher, Jack. Animal Instincts. 2011. (J). pap. *(978-0-531-22560-8(7))* Scholastic, Inc.

Maile, Ruby. What Do Animals Eat? 2014. (Little Books of Answers: Level d Ser.). (Illus.). 16p. (gr. k-2). pap. 7.95 *(978-1-927136-37-9(7))* Three Crows Media NZL. Dist: RiverStream Publishing.

Maj, Laure. 365 Incredible Animals. 2016. (ENG., Illus.). 376p. (J). (gr. 4-7). pap. 14.95 *(978-1-77085-755-1(9)*, 9781770857551) Firefly Bks., Ltd.

Make Believe Ideas. First 100 Animals. 2015. (ENG.). 16p. (J). bds. 8.99 *(978-1-78393-529-1(4))* Make Believe Ideas GBR. Dist: Nelson, Thomas Inc.

Make Believe Ideas, Ltd., creator. Animals & Kittens Pack. 2007. (Touch & Sparkle Ser.). (Illus.). (gr. -1-k). per., bds. *(978-1-84610-691-0(5))* Make Believe Ideas.

Malam, John. Of the Night. 2008. (Scary Creatures Ser.). (ENG., Illus.). 32p. (J). (gr. 2-4). 27.00 *(978-0-531-20424-5(3)*, Children's Pr.) Scholastic Library Publishing.

—Prehistoric Scary Creatures. 2008. (Scary Creatures Ser.). (ENG.). 32p. (J). 27.00 *(978-0-531-21747-4(7))*; (gr. 2-4). pap. 8.95 *(978-0-531-21901-0(1))* Scholastic Library Publishing. (Watts, Franklin).

—Scary Creatures of the Night. 2008. (Scary Creatures Ser.). (ENG., Illus.). 32p. (J). pap. 8.95 *(978-0-531-21009-3(X)*, Watts, Franklin) Scholastic Library Publishing.

Maldonado, Premier. Animales. 2006. (SPA.). 14.99 *(978-0-9727886-5-6(4))* Osmosis, LLC.

Manchas y Rayas. 2006. (Real Readers en español Ser.). (J). pap. 24.95 *(978-1-4042-2487-2(4)*, Rosen Classroom) Rosen Publishing Group, Inc., The.

Mangor, Jodie. Animal Myths, Busted! 2017. (Science Myths, Busted! Ser.). (ENG., Illus.). 32p. (J). (gr. 3-6). 21.95 *(978-1-63235-300-9(8))* Pr. Room Editions LLC.

El Manzano. (Coleccion Ciclos Vitales). (SPA., Illus.). (J). (gr. 3-5). pap. 7.96 *(978-84-236-2659-5(8)*, ED4704) Edebé ESP. Dist: Lectorum Pubns., Inc.

Mara, Wil. What Should I Do? If I See a Stray Animal. 2011. (Community Connections: What Should I Do? Ser.). (ENG., Illus.). 24p. (J). (gr. 2-5). lib. bdg. 25.64 *(978-1-61080-050-1(8)*, 1330905) Cherry Lake Publishing.

Mara, Wil, et al. Real-Life Dragons. 2017. (Real-Life Dragons Ser.). (ENG.). 32p. (gr. 3-4). 111.96 *(978-1-5157-5089-5(2)*, Edge Bks.) Capstone Press of Coughlan Cos.

Marchesani, Laura & Grosset and Dunlap Staff. Who Says? Aikins, Dave, illus. 2013. (Sassy Ser.). (ENG.). 12p. (J). (gr. -1 — 1). bds. 6.99 *(978-0-448-47789-3(0)*, Grosset & Dunlap) Penguin Young Readers Group.

Marcovitz, Hal. Bald Eagle: The Story of Our National Bird. Moreno, Barry, ed. 2014. (Patriotic Symbols of America Ser.: 20). 48p. (J). (gr. 4-18). 20.95 *(978-1-4222-3120-3(8))* Mason Crest.

La Mariposa y la Oruga. (Coleccion Ciclos Vitales). (SPA., Illus.). (J). (gr. 3-5). pap. 7.96 *(978-84-236-2663-2(6)*, ED4702) Edebé ESP. Dist: Lectorum Pubns., Inc.

La Mariquita. (Coleccion Ciclos Vitales). (SPA., Illus.). (J). (gr. 3-5). pap. 7.96 *(978-84-236-2661-8(X)*, ED4701) Edebé ESP. Dist: Lectorum Pubns., Inc.

Mark R. Borene, R. Borene & Mark R Borene. Welcome to the Sky. 2009. (Illus.). 20p. pap. 10.49 *(978-1-4389-7088-2(9))* AuthorHouse.

Markle, Sandra. Animal Scavengers, 6 bks., Set. Incl. Army Ants. (J). lib. bdg. 25.26 *(978-0-8225-3196-8(8))*; Hyenas. lib. bdg. 25.26 *(978-0-8225-3194-4(1))*; Jackals. lib. bdg. 25.26 *(978-0-8225-3197-5(6))*; Tasmanian Devils. lib. bdg. 25.26 *(978-0-8225-3199-9(2))*; Vultures. lib. bdg. 25.26 *(978-0-8225-3195-1(X))*; Wolverines. (J). lib. bdg. 25.26 *(978-0-8225-3198-2(4))*; (Illus.). 40p. (gr. 3-6). 2005. Set lib. bdg. 151.56 *(978-0-8225-3210-1(7)*, Lerner Pubns.) Lerner Publishing Group.

—Animales Carroneros; Animal Scavengers: Classroom Set. 2008. pap. 30.95 *(978-0-8225-9906-7(6))* Lerner Publishing Group.

—Animales Carroneros; Animal Scavengers: Complete Set. 2008. pap. 186.95 *(978-1-58013-300-5(2))* Lerner Publishing Group.

—Animales Depredadores; Animal Predators: Classroom Set. 2008. pap. 30.95 *(978-0-8225-7086-8(6))* Lerner Publishing Group.

—Animales Depredadores; Animal Predators: Complete Set. 2008. pap. 186.95 *(978-0-8225-7087-5(4))* Lerner Publishing Group.

—Los Demonios de Tasmania. 2007. (Animales carroñeros (Animal Scavengers) Ser.). (SPA., Illus.). 39p. (J). (gr. -1-3). per. 7.95 *(978-0-8225-7737-9(2)*, Ediciones Lerner) Lerner Publishing Group.

—Los Demonios de Tasmania. Translations.com Staff, tr. from ENG. 2007. (Animales carroñeros (Animal Scavengers) Ser.). (SPA., Illus.). 40p. (gr. 3-6). lib. bdg. 25.26 *(978-0-8225-7733-1(X))* Lerner Publishing Group.

—Jackals. 2006. (Animal Scavengers Ser.). (ENG., Illus.). 40p. (gr. 3-6). pap. 7.95 *(978-0-8225-3469-3(X)*, First Avenue Editions) Lerner Publishing Group.

—What If You Had Animal Ears? McWilliam, Howard, illus. 2016. (ENG.). 32p. (J). (gr. -1-3). pap. 4.99 *(978-0-545-85926-4(3)*, Scholastic Nonfiction) Scholastic, Inc.

Markle, Sandra. What If You Had Animal Eyes? McWilliam, Howard, illus. 2017. (ENG.). 32p. (J). (gr. -1-3). pap. 4.99 ***(978-1-338-10108-9(0))***; lib. bdg. 19.99 ***(978-1-338-20645-6(1))*** Scholastic, Inc.

Marsh, Laura. National Geographic Readers: Ugly Animals. 2015. (Readers Ser.). (ENG., Illus.). 32p. (J). (gr. k-3). pap. 3.99 *(978-1-4263-2129-0(5)*, National Geographic Children's Bks.) National Geographic Society.

Marshall Cavendish Corporation Staff, contrib. by. Wildlife & Plants, 20 Vols., Set. 3rd ed. 2007. (Illus.). 1280p. (J). (gr. 4-8). lib. bdg. 514.21 *(978-0-7614-7693-1(8))* Marshall Cavendish Corp.

Marshall Cavendish Reference Staff. North American Wildlife. 2010. 240p. (J). 99.93 *(978-0-7614-7938-3(4)*, Marshall Cavendish Reference Bks.) Marshall Cavendish Corp.

Marsico, Katie. How Do We Live Together? Rabbits. 2010. (Community Connections: How Do We Live Together? Ser.). (ENG.). 24p. (gr. 2-5). lib. bdg. 25.64 *(978-1-60279-622-5(X)*, 200329) Cherry Lake Publishing.

—A Kangaroo Joey Grows Up. 2007. (Scholastic News Nonfiction Readers Ser.). (ENG., Illus.). 24p. (J). (gr. 1-2). 22.00 *(978-0-531-17476-0(X))* Scholastic Library Publishing.

—Step-by-Step Experiments with Life Cycles. Ostrom, Bob, illus. 2012. (Step-By-Step Experiments Ser.). (ENG.). 32p. (J). (gr. 1-4). lib. bdg. 29.93 *(978-1-60973-587-6(0)*, 201232) Child's World, Inc., The.

Martin, Bill, Jr. Brown Bear, Brown Bear, What Do You See? Carle, Eric, illus. 2010. (ENG.). 22p. (J). (-1). bds. 12.99

(978-0-312-50926-2(X), 9780312509262, Priddy Bks.) St. Martin's Pr.

Martin, Claudia. Helpers. 2010. (Working Animals Ser.). 64p. (gr. 5-18). lib. bdg. 28.50 *(978-1-60870-163-6(8))* Marshall Cavendish Corp.

Martin, Isabel. Animal Kingdom Questions & Answers, 1 vol. 2014. (Animal Kingdom Questions & Answers Ser.). (ENG.). 24p. (gr. k-1). 159.90 *(978-1-4914-0659-5(3)*, Pebble Plus) Capstone Press of Coughlan Cos.

Martin, Kathy. Animals, Birds & the Alphabets. 2011. 32p. 14.39 *(978-1-4567-3302-5(8))* AuthorHouse.

Martin, Ruth. Little Explorers: the Animal World. Sanders, Allan, illus. 2016. (Little Explorers Ser.). (ENG.). 18p. (J). (gr. -1-3). 9.99 *(978-1-4998-0249-8(8))* Little Bee Books Inc.

Marzollo, Jean. I Spy Animals. Wick, Walter, illus. 2012. (I Spy Ser.). (ENG.). 32p. (J). (gr. -1-k). pap. 3.99 *(978-0-545-41583-5(7))* Scholastic, Inc.

Maskell, Hazel. Big Book of Big Animals. 2011. (Big Books Ser.). 16p. (J). ring bd. 13.99 *(978-0-7945-3051-8(6)*, Usborne) EDC Publishing.

Mason, Adrienne. Skunks. Ogle, Nancy Gray & Ogle, Nancy, illus. 2006. (Kids Can Press Wildlife Ser.). (ENG.). 32p. (J). (gr. k-5). 6.95 *(978-1-55337-734-4(6))* Kids Can Pr., Ltd. CAN. Dist: Hachette Bk. Group.

Mason, Paul. Could a Walrus Play the Saxophone? And Other Questions about Animals, 1 vol. 2013. (Questions You Never Thought You'd Ask Ser.). (ENG.). 32p. (gr. 1-3). 29.99 *(978-1-4109-5197-7(9))*; pap. 8.95 *(978-1-4109-5203-5(7))* Heinemann-Raintree. (Read Me!).

—The Fact or Fiction Behind Animals. 2016. (Fact or Phony? Ser.). (ENG.). 96p. (J). (gr. 5-6). lib. bdg. 33.25 *(978-1-4824-4276-2(0))* Stevens, Gareth Publishing LLLP.

Massey, Kay. What Do Animals Eat for Lunch? Canals, Sonia, illus. 2009. (Little Green Footprints Ser.). 12p. (J). (gr. -1-k). bds. 11.40 *(978-1-60754-697-9(3))* Windmill Bks.

—What Is a Flower's Special Power? Canals, Sonia & O'Toole, Jeanette, illus. 2009. (Little Green Footprints Ser.). 12p. (J). (gr. -1-k). bds. 11.40 *(978-1-60754-695-5(7))* Windmill Bks.

Masters, Neil. Wild Animals Coloring Book. 2013. (ENG.). 42p. 12.92 *(978-1-62884-653-9(4)*, Baby Professor (Education Kids)) Speedy Publishing LLC.

Mattern, Joanne. Animals of the Tropical Rain Forest. (Reading Room Collection 1 Ser.). 16p. 2009. (gr. 2-3). 37.50 *(978-1-60851-941-5(4))* 2006. (Illus.). (J). (gr. 3-7). lib. bdg. 17.25 *(978-1-4042-3341-6(5))* Rosen Publishing Group, Inc., The. (PowerKids Pr.).

—Perfect Predators. 2012. (ENG., Illus.). 24p. (J). (gr. 2-5). pap. 8.95 *(978-1-61810-251-5(6))* Rourke Educational Media.

—Super Pets: True Tales of Animal Heroes. 2012. (Illus.). 82p. (J). pap. *(978-0-545-46042-2(5))* Scholastic, Inc.

—What Grassland Animals Eat. 2006. (Nature's Food Chains Ser.). (Illus.). 24p. (gr. k-3). lib. bdg. 22.00 *(978-0-8368-6872-2(2)*, Weekly Reader Leveled Readers) Stevens, Gareth Publishing LLLP.

—What Grassland Animals Eat: Qué Comen los Animales de Las Praderas? 2006. (Nature's Food Chains/ Las cadenas alimentarias en la naturaleza Ser.). (ENG & SPA., Illus.). 24p. (gr. k-3). pap. 8.15 *(978-0-8368-7380-1(7)*, Weekly Reader Leveled Readers) Stevens, Gareth Publishing LLLP.

—What Grassland Animals Eat (¿Qué Comen Los Animales de Las Praderas?) 2006. (Nature's Food Chains/ Las cadenas alimentarias en la naturaleza Ser.). (SPA., Illus.). 24p. (gr. k-3). lib. bdg. 22.00 *(978-0-8368-7373-3(4)*, Weekly Reader Leveled Readers) Stevens, Gareth Publishing LLLP.

—What Polar Animals Eat. 2006. (Nature's Food Chains Ser.). (Illus.). 24p. (gr. k-3). pap. 8.15 *(978-0-8368-6880-7(3))*; lib. bdg. 22.00 *(978-0-8368-6873-9(0))* Stevens, Gareth Publishing LLLP. (Weekly Reader Leveled Readers).

—What Polar Animals Eat: Qué Comen los Animales de los Polos? 2006. (Nature's Food Chains/ Las cadenas alimentarias en la naturaleza Ser.). (ENG & SPA., Illus.). 24p. (gr. k-3). pap. 8.15 *(978-0-8368-7381-8(5)*, Weekly Reader Leveled Readers) Stevens, Gareth Publishing LLLP.

—What Polar Animals Eat/¿Qué Comen los Animales de los Polos? 2006. (Nature's Food Chains/ Las cadenas alimentarias en la naturaleza Ser.). (SPA., Illus.). 24p. (gr. k-3). lib. bdg. 22.00 *(978-0-8368-7374-0(2)*, Weekly Reader Leveled Readers) Stevens, Gareth Publishing LLLP.

—What River Animals Eat. 2006. (Nature's Food Chains Ser.). (Illus.). 24p. (gr. k-3). pap. 8.15 *(978-0-8368-6881-4(1))*; lib. bdg. 22.00 *(978-0-8368-6874-6(9))* Stevens, Gareth Publishing LLLP. (Weekly Reader Leveled Readers).

Mattern, Joanne & Herndon, Ryan, compiled by. Guinness World Records. 2005. (Illus.). 47p. pap. *(978-0-439-71568-3(7))* Scholastic, Inc.

Mattern, Joanne, et al. North American Animals. 2012. (North American Animals Ser.). (ENG.). 24p. (gr. k-1). lib. bdg. 53.30 *(978-1-4296-9171-0(9))*; pap. 250.20 *(978-1-4296-8363-0(5))* Capstone Press of Coughlan Cos. (Pebble Plus).

Matthews, Derek. Animales de la Granja. 2005. (Escucha y Aprende Ser.). (SPA., Illus.). 10p. (J). (gr. -1-1). *(978-970-718-300-1(4)*, Silver Dolphin en Español) Advanced Marketing, S. de R. L. de C. V.

—Animales de la Selva. 2005. (Escucha y Aprende Ser.). (SPA., Illus.). 10p. (J). (gr. -1-1). *(978-970-718-298-1(9)*, Silver Dolphin en Español) Advanced Marketing, S. de R. L. de C. V.

Max and Sid Staff, illus. My First Animals. 2016. (My First Ser.). (ENG.). 12p. (J). (gr. -1 — 1). bds. 5.99 *(978-1-4998-0185-9(8))* Little Bee Books Inc.

May, Suellen. Invasive Terrestrial Animals. 2006. (Invasive Species Ser.). (Illus.). 100p. (gr. 6-12). 30.00 *(978-0-7910-9127-2(9)*, Chelsea Hse.) Facts On File, Inc.

Mazurkiewicz, Jessica. Animals Mosaics Coloring Book. 2014. (Adult Coloring Ser.). (ENG., Illus.). 64p. (gr. 3). pap. 5.99 *(978-0-486-78177-8(1))* Dover Pubns., Inc.

McAlpine, Margaret. Working with Animals. 2004. (My Future Career Ser.). (Illus.). 64p. (gr. 3-7). lib. bdg. 27.00 *(978-0-8368-4240-1(5)*, Gareth Stevens Learning Library) Stevens, Gareth Publishing LLLP.

McCann, Emily. Animal Doodles. McCann, Emily, illus. 2011. (Doodle On! Ser.). (ENG., Illus.). 160p. (J). (gr. k-4). 15.99 *(978-0-230-74485-1(0))* Pan Macmillan GBR. Dist: Independent Pubs. Group.

McCarthy, Cecilia Pinto. Mandrill Monkeys, 1 vol. 2013. (Monkeys Ser.). (ENG., Illus.). 24p. (gr. k-1). lib. bdg. 26.65 *(978-1-62065-106-3(8)*, Pebble Plus) Capstone Press of Coughlan Cos.

McCarthy, Cecilia Pinto & Marx, Mandy R. Colorful World of Animals. 2011. (Colorful World of Animals Ser.). (ENG.). 24p. (gr. k-1). lib. bdg. 79.95 *(978-1-4296-6053-2(8)*, Pebble Plus) Capstone Press of Coughlan Cos.

McCurry, Kristen & Hilton, Jennifer. Dios No Creo Todos. Garton, Michael, illus. 2016. (SPA.). (J). ***(978-1-5064-2092-9(3))*** Augsburg Fortress, Pubs.

McDowell, Barbara. Animals. 2004. (Illus.). 24p. (J). act. bk. ed. 3.99 *(978-1-85997-696-8(4))* Byeway Bks.

McGehee, Claudia. A Tallgrass Prairie Alphabet. McGehee, Claudia, illus. 2004. (Bur Oak Book Ser.). (Illus.). 32p. (J). 17.95 *(978-0-87745-897-5(9))* Univ. of Iowa Pr.

McKendry, Sam. Are You Ticklish?/Tienes Cosquillas? Mitchell, Melanie, illus. 2005. (ENG.). 12p. (gr. -1-k). 10.95 *(978-1-58117-472-4(1)*, Intervisual/Piggy Toes) Bendon, Inc.

McKenzie, Precious. Search & Rescue Animals. 2015. (ENG.). 24p. (gr. 1-4). 28.50 *(978-1-63430-067-4(X))* Rourke Educational Media.

McKissack, Fredrick L. & McKissack, Lisa Beringer. Counting in the Grasslands. 2008. (Counting in the Biomes Ser.). (Illus.). 32p. (J). (gr. 1-3). lib. bdg. 23.94 *(978-0-7660-2991-0(3)*, Enslow Elementary) Enslow Pubs., Inc.

—Counting in the Taiga. 2009. (Counting in the Biomes Ser.). (Illus.). 32p. (J). (gr. 1-3). lib. bdg. 23.94 *(978-0-7660-2995-8(6)*, Enslow Elementary) Enslow Pubs., Inc.

—Counting in the Tundra. 2008. (Counting in the Biomes Ser.). (Illus.). 32p. (J). (gr. 3-7). lib. bdg. 23.94 *(978-0-7660-2989-7(1)*, Enslow Elementary) Enslow Pubs., Inc.

—Counting in the Wetlands. 2008. (Counting in the Biomes Ser.). (Illus.). 32p. (J). (gr. 1-3). lib. bdg. 23.94 *(978-0-7660-2993-4(X)*, Enslow Elementary) Enslow Pubs., Inc.

McLachlan, Brian, illus. What Noise Do I Make? 2016. (ENG.). 64p. (J). (gr. -1-5). 16.95 *(978-1-77147-150-3(6)*, Owlkids) Owlkids Bks. Inc. CAN. Dist: Publishers Group West (PGW).

McMahon, Sharon. Animals Can Work. 2016. (1-3Y Animals Ser.). (ENG., Illus.). 16p. (J). pap. 5.99 ***(978-1-63437-666-2(8))*** American Reading Co.

McNicholas, June. Ferrets, 1 vol. 2nd ed. 2010. (Keeping Unusual Pets Ser.). (ENG., Illus.). 48p. (gr. 3-6). 32.65 *(978-1-4329-3848-2(7)*, NA-h) Heinemann-Raintree.

McRae, Anne. The Animal Atlas. De Luca, Daniela, illus. 2008. (ENG.). 29p. (J). (gr. -1-3). 16.95 *(978-88-88166-38-4(6))* McRae Bks. Srl ITA. Dist: Independent Pubs. Group.

McRae, Anne & Morris, Neil. Josh the Anteater. De Luca, Daniela, illus. 2017. (J). ***(978-0-7166-3525-3(9))*** World Bk., Inc.

Meachen Rau, Dana. Una Veterinaria. 2007. (En el Trabajo Ser.). (SPA., Illus.). 24p. (gr. k-1). lib. bdg. 15.95 *(978-0-7614-2787-2(2)*, Benchmark Bks.) Marshall Cavendish Corp.

—Veterinarian. 2007. (Jobs in Town Ser.). (SPA., Illus.). 24p. (gr. k-1). lib. bdg. 15.95 *(978-0-7614-2622-6(1)*, Benchmark Bks.) Marshall Cavendish Corp.

Media, Cont. Animal Kingdom: The World of Mammals. 2008. 96p. (YA). 17.99 *(978-1-931703-04-8(3))* Creative Publishing Consultants.

—Greatest Inventions. 2008. (ENG., Illus.). 48p. (YA). 12.99 *(978-1-931703-22-2(1))* Creative Publishing Consultants.

Meeuwissen, Tony. Remarkable Animals: Mix & Match to Create 100 Crazy Creatures. Meeuwissen, Tony, illus. rev. ed. 2016. (ENG., Illus.). 24p. (J). (gr. -1-k). 7.99 *(978-1-84780-762-5(3)*, Frances Lincoln Children's Bks.) Quarto Publishing Group UK GBR. Dist: Hachette Bk. Group.

Meister, Cari. Totally Wacky Facts about Animals. 2015. (Mind Benders Ser.). (ENG., Illus.). 240p. (gr. 1-3). pap. 7.95 *(978-1-4914-6525-7(5))* Capstone Press of Coughlan Cos.

—Totally Wacky Facts about Land Animals. 2015. (Mind Benders Ser.). (ENG., Illus.). 112p. (gr. 1-3). lib. bdg. 23.32 *(978-1-4914-6522-6(0))* Capstone Press of Coughlan Cos.

—Venomous Animals. Fretland VanVoorst, Jenny, ed. 2016. (Back off! Animal Defenses). 24p. (J). (gr. 2-5). lib. bdg. 25.65 *(978-1-62031-313-8(8)*, Pogo) Jump! Inc.

Menon, Sujatha. Mountain Creatures. (Wild Creatures Ser.). 48p. 2009. (gr. 4-5). 53.00 *(978-1-60854-790-6(6)*, PowerKids Pr.) 2007. (Illus.). (YA). (gr. 3-6). lib. bdg. 29.25 *(978-1-4042-3877-0(8))* Rosen Publishing Group, Inc., The.

—Safari Creatures. (Wild Creatures Ser.). 48p. 2009. (gr. 4-5). 53.00 *(978-1-60854-792-0(2)*, PowerKids Pr.) 2007. (Illus.). (YA). (gr. 3-6). lib. bdg. 29.25 *(978-1-4042-3894-7(8))* Rosen Publishing Group, Inc., The.

Meredith, S. Night Animals. 2004. (Beginners Ser.). 32p. (J). (gr. 1-18). lib. bdg. 12.95 *(978-1-58086-510-4(0))* EDC Publishing.

Meredith, Susan Markowitz. Bitsy the Beaver. 2011. (Early Connections Ser.). (J). *(978-1-61672-574-7(5))* Benchmark Education Co.

Meyers, Phyllis. Animals! Animals! Animals! 2013. 56p. pap. 10.00 *(978-1-4575-2286-4(1))* Dog Ear Publishing, LLC.

Michele, Tracey. How Can You Group Animals? 2014. (Little Books of Answers: Level e Ser.). (Illus.). 16p. (gr. k-2). pap. 7.95 *(978-1-927136-47-8(4))* Three Crows Media NZL. Dist: RiverStream Publishing.

Milbourne, Anna. In the Nest. 2005. (First Discovery Ser.). 24p. (J). 9.95 *(978-0-7945-0735-0(2)*, Usborne) EDC Publishing.

Miles Kelly Staff. Animals. 2003. (Info Bank Ser.). (Illus.). 96p. (J). 7.95 *(978-1-84236-153-5(8))* Miles Kelly Publishing, Ltd. GBR. Dist: Independent Pubs. Group.

—Animals: Flip Quiz. 2003. (Flip Quiz Ser.). (Illus.). 38p. (J). spiral bd. 5.95 *(978-1-84236-079-8(5))*; spiral bd. 5.95 *(978-1-84236-078-1(7))*; spiral bd. 5.95 *(978-1-84236-076-7(0))*; spiral bd. 5.95 *(978-1-84236-077-4(9))* Miles Kelly Publishing, Ltd. GBR. Dist: Independent Pubs. Group.

Miles, Lisa. Origami Wild Animals. 2013. (Amazing Origami Ser.). 32p. (J). (gr. 2-5). pap. 63.00 *(978-1-4339-9666-5(9))*; pap. 10.50 *(978-1-4339-9665-8(0))*; (ENG., Illus.). lib. bdg. 26.60 *(978-1-4339-9664-1(2))* Stevens, Gareth Publishing LLLP.

Milet Publishing Staff. Animals. 2011. (My First Bilingual Book Ser.). (Illus.). 24p. (J). (gr. k — 1). (FRE & ENG.). bds. 8.99 *(978-1-84059-612-0(0))*; (ENG., bds. 8.99 *(978-1-84059-617-5(1))*; (ENG., bds. 7.99 *(978-1-84059-622-9(8))*; (ENG & ITA., bds. 7.99 *(978-1-84059-614-4(7))*; (ENG & POR., bds. 7.99 *(978-1-84059-616-8(3))*; (ENG., bds. 8.99 *(978-1-84059-613-7(9))*; (ENG., bds. 8.99 *(978-1-84059-615-1(5))* Milet Publishing.

—Animals - My First Bilingual Book. 2011. (My First Bilingual Book Ser.). (Illus.). 24p. (J). (gr. k — 1). (ENG.). bds. 8.99 *(978-1-84059-623-6(6))*; (ENG., bds. 7.99 *(978-1-84059-618-2(X))*; (ENG., bds. 7.99 *(978-1-84059-608-3(2))*; (SPA & ENG., bds. 8.99 *(978-1-84059-620-5(1))* Milet Publishing.

—My First Bilingual Book - Animals. 2011. (My First Bilingual Book Ser.). (ENG., Illus.). 24p. (J). (gr. k — 1). bds. 7.99 *(978-1-84059-611-3(2))*; bds. 8.99 *(978-1-84059-610-6(4))*; bds. 7.99 *(978-1-84059-609-0(0))*; bds. 7.99 *(978-1-84059-621-2(X))* Milet Publishing.

—My First Bilingual Book - Animals (English-Somali) 2011. (My First Bilingual Book Ser.). (ENG., Illus.). 24p. (J). (gr. k — 1). bds. 8.99 *(978-1-84059-619-9(8))* Milet Publishing.

Miller, Connie Colwell. The Creepiest Animals, 1 vol. 2011. (Extreme Animals Ser.). (ENG., 24p. (gr. k-1). Illus.). pap. 7.29 *(978-1-4296-6207-9(7))*; pap. 41.70 *(978-1-4296-6376-2(6))* Capstone Press of Coughlan Cos. (Pebble Plus).

—The Most Dangerous Animals. 2011. (Extreme Animals Ser.). (ENG.). 24p. (gr. k-1). pap. 41.70 *(978-1-4296-6378-6(2)*, Pebble Plus) Capstone Press of Coughlan Cos.

—The Stinkiest Animals. 2011. (Extreme Animals Ser.). (ENG.). 24p. (gr. k-1). pap. 41.70 *(978-1-4296-6380-9(4)*, Pebble Plus) Capstone Press of Coughlan Cos.

—Therapy Animals. 2013. (Animals with Jobs Ser.). (ENG.). 32p. (gr. 1-4). 28.50 *(978-1-60753-381-8(2))* Amicus Publishing.

Miller, J. Tiburones. 2004. (Discovery Program Ser.).Tr. of Sharks. (SPA., Illus.). 64p. (J). (gr. 3-18). lib. bdg. 16.95 *(978-1-58086-348-3(5))* EDC Publishing.

Miller, Sara Swan. Secret Lives of Burrowing Beasts. 2010. (Secret Lives Ser.). 48p. (gr. 4). 29.93 *(978-0-7614-4221-9(9))* Marshall Cavendish GBR. Dist: Marshall Cavendish Corp.

—Secret Lives of Cave Creatures. 2010. (Secret Lives Ser.). 48p. (gr. 4). 29.93 *(978-0-7614-4224-0(3))* Marshall Cavendish Corp.

Miller, Tori & Lynette, Rachel. Who Lives in a Colorful Coral Reef? 2010. (Exploring Habitats Ser.). (ENG.). 24p. (J). pap. 8.25 *(978-1-4488-1281-3(X))*; lib. bdg. 22.60 *(978-1-4488-0677-5(1))* Rosen Publishing Group, Inc., The. (PowerKids Pr.).

Mills, Nathan & Swan, Henry. How Animals Live & Grow. 2012. (Rosen Readers Ser.). (ENG., Illus.). 24p. (J). (gr. 1-2). pap. 8.25 *(978-1-4488-8764-4(X)*, Rosen Classroom) Rosen Publishing Group, Inc., The.

Milner Halls, Kelly. National Geographic Kids Chapters: Courageous Canine: And More True Stories of Amazing Animal Heroes. 2013. (National Geographic Kids Everything Ser.). (ENG., Illus.). 112p. (J). (gr. 2-5). lib. bdg. 14.90 *(978-1-4263-1397-4(7)*, National Geographic Children's Bks.) National Geographic Society.

Minden, Cecilia. Big & Small. 2016. (21st Century Basic Skills Library: Animal Opposites Ser.). (ENG., Illus.). 24p. (J). (gr. k-3). 24.21 *(978-1-63470-471-7(1)*, 207615) Cherry Lake Publishing.

—Fast & Slow. 2016. (21st Century Basic Skills Library: Animal Opposites Ser.). (ENG., Illus.). 24p. (J). (gr. k-3). 24.21 *(978-1-63470-472-4(X)*, 207619) Cherry Lake Publishing.

—Hard & Soft. 2016. (21st Century Basic Skills Library: Animal Opposites Ser.). (ENG., Illus.). 24p. (J). (gr. k-3). 24.21 *(978-1-63470-469-4(X)*, 207607) Cherry Lake Publishing.

—Hot & Cold. 2016. (21st Century Basic Skills Library: Animal Opposites Ser.). (ENG.). 24p. (J). (gr. k-3). 24.21 *(978-1-63470-473-1(8)*, 207623) Cherry Lake Publishing.

—In & Out. 2016. (21st Century Basic Skills Library: Animal Opposites Ser.). (ENG., Illus.). 24p. (J). (gr. k-3). 24.21 *(978-1-63470-470-0(3)*, 207611) Cherry Lake Publishing.

—Push & Pull. 2016. (21st Century Basic Skills Library: Animal Opposites Ser.). (ENG., Illus.). 24p. (J). (gr. k-3). 24.21 *(978-1-63470-474-8(6)*, 207627) Cherry Lake Publishing.

—Sit & Stand. 2016. (21st Century Basic Skills Library: Animal Opposites Ser.). (ENG., Illus.). 24p. (J). (gr. k-3). 24.21 *(978-1-63470-475-5(4)*, 207631) Cherry Lake Publishing.

—Up & Down. 2016. (21st Century Basic Skills Library: Animal Opposites Ser.). (ENG., Illus.). 24p. (J). (gr. k-3). 24.21 *(978-1-63470-468-7(1)*, 207603) Cherry Lake Publishing.

Mini Animals. 2016. (Mini Animals Ser.). 00032p. (J). (gr. 2-3). 163.50 *(978-1-4994-8146-4(2)*, Windmill Bks.) Rosen Publishing Group, Inc., The.

Mis, Melody S. Exploring Canyons. 2009. (Geography Zone: Landforms Ser.). (Illus.). 24p. (J). (gr. 2-4). pap. 8.25 *(978-1-4358-3114-8(4))*; 24p. (gr. 2-3). 42.50 *(978-1-61512-692-7(9))*; (J). lib. bdg. 22.60 *(978-1-4358-2716-5(3))* Rosen Publishing Group, Inc., The. (PowerKids Pr.).

Misterios de Oceano. (Colección Ventana Transparente). (SPA., Illus.). (J). (gr. 3-5). *(978-950-11-1247-4(0)*, SG5233) Sigmar ARG. Dist: Lectorum Pubns., Inc.

Mitchell Lane Publishers Inc. Staff. How to Convince Your Parents You Can..., 10 vols., Set. 2009. (J). (gr. 1-4). lib. bdg. 257.00 *(978-1-58415-664-2(3))* Mitchell Lane Pubs., Inc.

Mitchell, Melanie S. Ears. 2008. (First Step Nonfiction - Animal Traits Ser.). (ENG., Illus.). 8p. (gr. -1-1). pap. 4.95 *(978-0-8225-3910-0(1)*, Lerner Pubns.) Lerner Publishing Group.

Mitchell, Susan K. Animals with Awesome Armor: Shells, Scales, & Exoskeletons. 2008. (Amazing Animal Defenses Ser.). (Illus.). 48p. (J). (gr. 5-9). lib. bdg. 25.27 *(978-0-7660-3296-5(5))* Enslow Pubs., Inc.

Mitton, Jacqueline. Zoo in the Sky. 2014. 17.95 *(978-1-63419-754-0(2))* Perfection Learning Corp.

—Zoo in the Sky: A Book of Animal Constellations. Balit, Christina, illus. 2006. (ENG.). 32p. (J). (gr. 1-4). pap. 7.95 *(978-0-7922-5935-0(1)*, National Geographic Children's Bks.) National Geographic Society.

Miura, Taro. Bum, Bum. Miura, Taro, illus. 2016. (ENG., Illus.). 24p. (J). (— 1). bds. 8.99 *(978-0-7636-8784-7(7))* Candlewick Pr.

Monroe, Tyler. Bald Eagle. 2013. (U. S. Symbols Ser.). (ENG.). 24p. (gr. k-1). 26.65 *(978-1-4765-3089-5(0))*; pap. 7.95 *(978-1-4765-3538-8(8))* Capstone Press of Coughlan Cos. (Pebble Plus).

Montgomery, Heather L. The Case of the Missing Arctic Fox & Other True Animal Mysteries for You to Solve, 1 vol. 2012. (Seriously True Mysteries Ser.). (ENG., Illus.). 32p. (gr. 3-4). lib. bdg. 27.32 *(978-1-4296-7625-0(6)*, Fact Finders) Capstone Press of Coughlan Cos.

Montgomery, Kelly. SPARK Wildlife Designs Coloring Book. 2016. (Dover Coloring Bks.). (ENG., Illus.). 64p. (J). (gr. 1-4). pap. 5.99 *(978-0-486-81092-8(5))* Dover Pubns., Inc.

Montgomery, Sy & Bishop, Nic. The Tapir Scientist: Saving South America's Largest Mammal. 2017. (Scientists in the Field Ser.). (ENG., Illus.). 80p. (J). (gr. 5-7). pap. 9.99 *(978-0-544-80908-6(4)*, HMH Books For Young Readers) Houghton Mifflin Harcourt Publishing Co.

Morey, Allan. 12 Scary Animals. 2017. (Scary & Spooky Ser.). (ENG.). 32p. (J). (gr. 3-6). 21.95 *(978-1-63235-295-8(8))* Pr. Room Editions LLC.

Morgan, Sally. In the Ground & Other Landscapes. 2006. (Hidden Habitats Ser.). (J). *(978-1-59389-281-4(0))* Chrysalis Education.

Moriuchi, Mique, illus. Mix & Match Animals: Over 20 Different Animal Combinations! 2007. (ENG.). 10p. (gr. -1). 10.95 *(978-1-58117-603-2(1)*, Intervisual/Piggy Toes) Bendon, Inc.

Morlock, Lisa. Track that Scat! 2012. (ENG., Illus.). 32p. (J). (gr. k-5). 15.95 *(978-1-58536-536-4(X))* Sleeping Bear Pr.

Morog, Joyce Jo. Boots A Fireside Critter: A Fireside Critter. 2004. (Illus.). 32p. (J). *(978-0-9753248-0-6(2))* Fireside Critters.

Morrison, Cathy, illus. The Prairie That Nature Built, 1 vol. 2014. (ENG.). 32p. (J). (gr. k-4). pap. 8.95 *(978-1-58469-492-2(0))* Dawn Pubns.

Mortensen, Lori. Animals in Winter. 2016. (Spring Forward Ser.). (J). (gr. 2). *(978-1-4900-9452-6(0))* Benchmark Education Co.

Mostue, Trude. Wild about Animals: A Book of Beastly Behaviour. (Illus.). 108p. (J). (gr. 4-6). 24.95 *(978-0-233-99684-4(2))* Andre Deutsch GBR. Dist: Trafalgar Square Publishing.

Munnerlyn, Cindy, ed. Investigating Science - Animals. 2003. 48p. 9.95 *(978-1-56234-567-9(2)*, Mailbox Bks., The) Education Ctr., Inc.

Munro, Fiona & Phillipson, Fiona. Whose Nose? Moon, Jo, illus. 2011. (ENG.). 10p. (J). (gr. -1-k). bds. 6.99 *(978-0-8431-9811-9(7)*, Price Stern Sloan) Penguin Young Readers Group.

—Whose Stripes? Garden, Jo, illus. 2011. (ENG.). 10p. (J). (gr. -1-k). bds. 6.99 *(978-0-8431-9812-6(5)*, Price Stern Sloan) Penguin Young Readers Group.

Murphy, Glenn. Predators: The Whole Tooth-and-Claw Story. 2015. (Science Sorted Ser.). (ENG., Illus.). 192p. (J). (gr. 4-6). pap. 8.99 *(978-1-4472-8504-5(2))* Pan Macmillan GBR. Dist: Independent Pubs. Group.

Murphy, Julie. I've Got Feet!: Fantastical Feet of the Animal World. Tolson, Hannah, illus. 2017. (ENG.). 32p. (J). (gr. -1-1). 17.99 ***(978-1-68152-195-4(4))*** Amicus.

Murphy, Julie & Amstutz, Lisa J. Amazing Animal Adaptations. 2011. (Amazing Animal Adaptations Ser.). (ENG.). 32p. (gr. 1-2). pap. 31.80 *(978-1-4296-7040-1(1))*; pap. 190.80 *(978-1-4296-7041-8(X))*; lib. bdg. 109.28 *(978-1-4296-6032-7(5))* Capstone Press of Coughlan Cos. (Aplus Bks.).

Murphy, Patricia J. Why Do Some Animals Shed. 2004. (Library of Why Ser.). (Illus.). 24p. (J). lib. bdg. 22.60 *(978-0-8239-6237-2(7))* Rosen Publishing Group, Inc., The.

—Why Do Some Animals Shed Their Skin? 2009. (Library of Why Ser.). 24p. (gr. 3-4). 42.50 *(978-1-60853-964-2(4)*, PowerKids Pr.) Rosen Publishing Group, Inc., The.

Murray, Aaron R. Counting in the Tundra 1-2-3. 2012. (All about Counting in the Biomes Ser.). (Illus.). (J). 24p. pap. 7.95 *(978-1-4644-0064-3(4))*; 24p. (gr. -1-1). 22.60 *(978-0-7660-4056-4(9))*; 23p. E-Book *(978-1-4645-0971-1(9))* Enslow Pubs., Inc.

Murray, Julie. Backyard, 1 vol. 2009. (That's Gross!:A Look at Science Ser.). (ENG., Illus.). 32p. (J). (gr. 2-5). 28.50 *(978-1-60453-553-2(9))* ABDO Publishing Co.

—Everyday Animals. 2016. (Everyday Animals Ser.: 6). (ENG.). 24p. (J). (gr. k-2). lib. bdg. 162.42 *(978-1-68080-113-2(9))* ABDO Publishing Co.

—Fastest Animals, 1 vol. 2010. (That's Wild!: A Look at Animals Ser.). (ENG.). 32p. (J). (gr. 2-5). 28.50 *(978-1-60453-978-3(X))* ABDO Publishing Co.

—Strongest Animals, 1 vol. 2010. (That's Wild!: A Look at Animals Ser.). (ENG.). 32p. (J). (gr. 2-5). 28.50 *(978-1-60453-981-3(X))* ABDO Publishing Co.

—Therapy Animals, 1 vol. 2009. (Going to Work:Animal Edition Ser.). (ENG., Illus.). 32p. (J). (gr. 2-5). 27.07 *(978-1-60453-565-5(2))* ABDO Publishing Co.

Murugarren Barrio, Miguel María. ANIMALARIO UNIVERSAL DEL PROFESOR REVILLOD: FABULOSO ALMANAQUE DE LA FAUNA MUNDIAL. 2003. (Los Especials de A la Orilla Del Viento Ser.). (SPA., Illus.). 40p. (J). (gr. -1-3). 12.99 *(978-968-16-7048-1(5))* Fondo de Cultura Economica USA.

Musgrave, Ruth. Funny Fill-In: My Animal Adventure. Tharp, Jason, illus. 2013. (ENG.). 48p. (J). (gr. 3-7). pap. 4.99 *(978-1-4263-1355-4(1)*, National Geographic Children's Bks.) National Geographic Society.

My Little Box of Animals. Date not set. (Illus.). (J). bds. 6.98 *(978-1-4054-0810-3(3))* Parragon, Inc.

My World of Animals.Tr. of Yo y los animales. (ENG & SPA., Illus.). (gr. 1-2). (J). 96.00 *(978-1-4042-7533-1(9))*; 2004. 24p. spiral bd. 23.95 *(978-0-8239-7533-4(9))* Rosen Publishing Group, Inc., The. (Editorial Buenas Letras).

Myers, Jack. The Puzzle of the Platypus: And Other Explorations of Science in Action. Rice, John, illus. 2008. (ENG.). 64p. (J). (gr. 4-7). 17.95 *(978-1-59078-556-0(8))* Boyds Mills Pr.

Mystifying Mammals. 2016. (Illus.). 32p. (J). *(978-1-4222-3523-2(8))* Mason Crest.

Nagle, Jeanne. How Do Animals Hunt & Feed? 2015. (Let's Find Out! Animal Life Ser.). (ENG., Illus.). 32p. (J). (gr. 2-3).

23.45 *(978-1-68048-015-3(4),* Britannica Educational Publishing) Rosen Publishing Group, Inc., The.

Napier, Lauren. All My Animals. Ryski, Dawid, illus. 2016. (ENG.). 48p. (J). (gr. -1-2). 24.95 *(978-3-89955-777-0(8))* Die Gestalten Verlag DEU. Dist: Penguin Random Hse. LLC.

National Geographic. Predators Collection: Readers That Grow with You. 2013. (Readers Ser.). (ENG.). 128p. (J). (gr. -1-1). pap. 7.99 *(978-1-4263-1406-3(X));* lib. bdg. 16.90 *(978-1-4263-1610-4(0))* National Geographic Society. (National Geographic Children's Bks.).

—125 Cute Animals. 2015. lib. bdg. 24.50 *(978-0-606-36423-2(4))* Turtleback Bks.

National Geographic Editors. Creepy Crawly Collection. 2012. lib. bdg. 18.40 *(978-0-606-26822-6(7),* Turtleback) Turtleback Bks.

National Geographic Kids. National Geographic Kids Adorable Animals Super Sticker Activity Book: 2,000 Stickers! 2015. (NG Sticker Activity Bks.). (ENG.). 112p. (J). (gr. -1-3). pap. 12.99 *(978-1-4263-2108-5(2),* National Geographic Children's Bks.) National Geographic Society.

—National Geographic Kids Amazing Animals Super Sticker Activity Book: 2,000 Stickers! 2015. (NG Sticker Activity Bks.). (ENG.). 112p. (J). (gr. -1-3). pap. 12.99 *(978-1-4263-2107-8(4),* National Geographic Children's Bks.) National Geographic Society.

—National Geographic Kids Ferocious Animals Super Sticker Activity Book: 2,000 Stickers! 2015. (NG Sticker Activity Bks.). (ENG.). 112p. (J). (gr. -1-3). pap. 12.99 *(978-1-4263-2109-2(0),* National Geographic Children's Bks.) National Geographic Society.

—National Geographic Kids Look & Learn: Peek-A-boo. 2016. (Look & Learn Ser.). (ENG., Illus.). 24p. (J). (-k). bds. 6.99 *(978-1-4263-2455-0(3),* National Geographic Children's Bks.) National Geographic Society.

National Geographic Kids. National Geographic Kids Wild Adventures Super Sticker Activity Book. 2017. (NG Sticker Activity Bks.). (ENG.). 112p. (J). (gr. -1-3). pap. 12.99 ***(978-1-4263-2851-0(6),*** National Geographic Children's Bks.) National Geographic Society.

National Geographic Kids & Delano, Marfe Ferguson. Explore My World: Ducklings. 2017. (Explore My World Ser.). (ENG., Illus.). 32p. (J). (gr. -1-2). pap. 4.99 *(978-1-4263-2715-5(3),* National Geographic Children's Bks.) National Geographic Society.

National Geographic Kids & Donohue, Moira Rose. National Geographic Kids Chapters: Dog on a Bike. 2017. (NGK Chapters Ser.). (ENG., Illus.). 112p. (J). (gr. 2-5). pap. 5.99 *(978-1-4263-2705-6(6),* National Geographic Children's Bks.) National Geographic Society.

National Geographic Kids & Hoena, Blake. National Geographic Kids Everything Predators. 2016. (National Geographic Kids Everything Ser.). (ENG., Illus.). 64p. (J). (gr. 3-7). pap. 12.99 *(978-1-4263-2534-2(7),* National Geographic Children's Bks.) National Geographic Society.

National Geographic Kids Staff. Animals, Dinosaurs, Why? - National Geographic Kids, Set. 2014. (National Geographic Little Kids First Big Bks.). (ENG.). 384p. (J). (gr. -1-3). pap. 44.85 *(978-1-4263-2010-1(8),* National Geographic Children's Bks.) National Geographic Society.

—Fierce Animals. 2015. (NG Sticker Activity Bks.). (ENG.). 56p. (J). (gr. -1-3). pap., act. bk. ed. 6.99 *(978-1-4263-1901-3(0),* National Geographic Children's Bks.) National Geographic Society.

—National Geographic Kids 125 True Stories of Amazing Animals: Inspiring Tales of Animal Friendship & Four-Legged Heroes, Plus Crazy Animal Antics. 2012. (ENG., Illus.). 112p. (J). (gr. 3-7). lib. bdg. 21.90 *(978-1-4263-0919-9(8),* National Geographic Children's Bks.) National Geographic Society.

—National Geographic Kids: Animal Creativity Book: Cut-Outs, Games, Stencils, Stickers. 2013. (ENG.). 80p. (J). (gr. 1-4). pap. 12.99 *(978-1-4263-1402-5(7),* National Geographic Children's Bks.) National Geographic Society.

—National Geographic Kids Cool Animals Sticker Activity Book: Over 1,000 Stickers! 2013. (ENG., Illus.). 56p. (J). (gr. -1-3). pap. 6.99 *(978-1-4263-1113-0(3),* National Geographic Children's Bks.) National Geographic Society.

—National Geographic Kids Cutest Animals Sticker Activity Book: Over 1,000 Stickers! 2013. (ENG., Illus.). 56p. (J). (gr. -1-3). pap. 6.99 *(978-1-4263-1112-3(5),* National Geographic Children's Bks.) National Geographic Society.

—125 Cute Animals: Meet the Cutest Critters on the Planet, Including Animals You Never Knew Existed, & Some So Ugly They're Cute. 2015. (ENG., Illus.). 112p. (J). (gr. 3-7). pap. 12.99 *(978-1-4263-1887-0(1),* National Geographic Children's Bks.) National Geographic Society.

—125 Pet Rescues: From Pound to Palace: Homeless Pets Made Happy. 2017. (ENG.). 112p. (J). (gr. 3-7). pap. 12.99 *(978-1-4263-2736-0(6),* National Geographic Children's Bks.) National Geographic Society.

—125 True Stories of Amazing Animals. 2012. lib. bdg. 24.45 *(978-0-606-23887-8(5),* Turtleback) Turtleback Bks.

—125 True Stories of Amazing Animals: Inspiring Tales of Animal Friendship & Four-Legged Heroes, Plus Crazy Animal Antics. 2012. (ENG., Illus.). 112p. (J). (gr. 3-7). pap. 12.95 *(978-1-4263-0918-2(X),* National Geographic Children's Bks.) National Geographic Society.

—125 True Stories of Amazing Pets: Inspiring Tales of Animal Friendship & Four-Legged Heroes, Plus Crazy Animal Antics. 2014. (ENG., Illus.). 112p. (J). (gr. 3-7). pap. 12.99 *(978-1-4263-1459-9(0),* National Geographic Children's Bks.) National Geographic Society.

National Geographic Learning Staff. Taking Care of Earth, Level 3. 2011. (World Windows Ser.). (ENG., Illus.). 16p. (J). stu. ed. 9.95 *(978-1-133-56615-1(4))* Cengage Heinle.

National Geographic Staff. Animal Pop! With 5 Incredible, Life Size Fold-Outs. 2010. (In Your Face Ser.). (ENG., Illus.). 20p. (J). (gr. 2-5). 14.95 *(978-1-4263-0716-4(0),* National Geographic Children's Bks.) National Geographic Society.

—Awesome Animals: With Games, Facts, & 10 Pull-Out Posters! 2011. (ENG., Illus.). 64p. (J). (gr. 3-7). pap. 9.95 *(978-1-4263-0754-6(3),* National Geographic Children's Bks.) National Geographic Society.

—True or False Animal Cards. 2011. (ENG., Illus.). 44p. (J). (gr. k-3). 9.95 *(978-1-4263-0794-2(2),* National Geographic Children's Bks.) National Geographic Society.

National Science Resources Center, creator. Science & Technology for Children Books: Animal Studies. 2004. (J). *(978-1-933008-00-4(8))* Smithsonian Science Education Ctr. (SSEC).

National Wildlife Federation Staff. My First Book of Animal Opposites. 2016. (ENG., Illus.). 22p. (J). (— 1). bds. 6.95 *(978-1-62354-062-3(3))* Charlesbridge Publishing, Inc.

—My First Book of Wild Animals (National Wildlife Federation) 2014. (ENG., Illus.). 22p. (J). (— 1). bds. 6.95 *(978-1-62354-029-6(1))* Charlesbridge Publishing, Inc.

National Wildlife Federation Staff & Bové, Jennifer. Ranger Rick Jr: Animal Opposites. 2017. (Ranger Rick: Animal Fun for Young Children Ser.). (ENG., Illus.). 32p. (J). (gr. -1-1). pap. 5.99 *(978-1-63076-292-6(X))* Muddy Boots Pr.

Nature's Children (Fall 2014 Set Of 6) 2014. (Nature's Children Ser.). (J). lib. bdg. 168.00 *(978-0-531-24357-2(5))* Scholastic Library Publishing.

Nature's Grossest. 2015. (Nature's Grossest Ser.). (ENG.). 24p. (J). (gr. 1-2). 135.60 *(978-1-4824-1634-3(4))* Stevens, Gareth Publishing LLLP.

Nelson, Esther & Hirsch, Davida. Riggeldy Jiggeldy Joggeldy Jam: Can You Guess Who I Am? Ellis, Libby, illus. 2003. (J). bds. 5.95 *(978-0-7607-3278-6(7))* Barnes & Noble, Inc.

—Riggeldy Jiggeldy Joggeldy Roo: Can You Guess What I Do? Ellis, Libby, illus. 2003. (J). bds. 5.95 *(978-0-7607-3279-3(5))* Barnes & Noble, Inc.

Newhouse, Maxwell. Counting on Snow. 2010. (ENG., Illus.). 24p. (J). (gr. k-k). 14.99 *(978-0-88776-985-6(3),* Tundra Bks.) Tundra Bks. CAN. Dist: Penguin Random Hse. LLC.

Newland, Sonya. Mountain Animals. 2011. (Saving Wildlife Ser.). 32p. (gr. 4-7). lib. bdg. 31.35 *(978-1-59920-657-8(9))* Black Rabbit Bks.

—Polar Animals. 2011. (Saving Wildlife Ser.). 32p. (gr. 4-7). lib. bdg. 31.35 *(978-1-59920-659-2(5))* Black Rabbit Bks.

Newman, Aline Alexander. Animal Superstars: And More True Stories of Amazing Animal Talents. 2013. (NGK Chapters Ser.). (ENG., Illus.). 112p. (J). (gr. 2-5). pap. 5.99 *(978-1-4263-1091-1(9));* lib. bdg. 14.90 *(978-1-4263-1092-8(7))* National Geographic Society. (National Geographic Children's Bks.).

—Animal Superstars: And More True Stories of Amazing Animal Talents. 2013. (National Geographic Kids Chapters Ser.). lib. bdg. 16.00 *(978-0-606-27013-7(2),* Turtleback) Turtleback Bks.

Newman-D'Amico, Fran. Animal Spot-the-Differences. 2007. (Dover Little Activity Bks.). (ENG., Illus.). 64p. (J). (gr. k-3). per. 1.99 *(978-0-486-45649-2(8))* Dover Pubns., Inc.

Nguyen, An Mai. Let's Learn Animals in Vietnamese. 2006. (VIE & ENG., Illus.). (J). bds. 6.95 *(978-0-9776482-3-8(0))* Viet Baby, LLC.

Nichols, Catherine & National Geographic Learning Staff. Animal Masterminds. 2010. (Rise & Shine Ser.). (ENG.). 48p. (C). (gr. 2-4). pap. 8.95 *(978-0-516-24601-7(1))* National Geographic School Publishing, Inc.

Nicola. The Lost Boomerang. 2012. 36p. pap. 22.00 *(978-1-61933-546-2(8))* FastPrncil, Inc.

El Nido del Pajaro. (Coleccion Ciclos Vitales). (SPA., Illus.). (J). (gr. 3-5). pap. 7.96 *(978-84-236-2651-9(2),* ED4699) Edebé ESP. Dist: Lectorum Pubns., Inc.

The Noises Animals Make. Date not set. 5.95 *(978-0-89868-313-4(0))* ARO Publishing Co.

Nolan, Joy. Animals of North America: Set Of 6. 2011. (Navigators Ser.). (J). pap. 48.00 net. *(978-1-4108-5076-8(5))* Benchmark Education Co.

—Animals of North America: Text Pairs. 2008. (Bridges/Navigators Ser.). (J). (gr. 4). 81.00 *(978-1-4108-8380-3(9))* Benchmark Education Co.

Noll, Katherine. Animal Jam: Official Insider's Guide. 2014. (ENG., Illus.). 240p. (J). (gr. 2-5). pap. 9.99 *(978-1-4263-1778-1(6),* National Geographic Children's Bks.) National Geographic Society.

Norby, Lisa. Animals of Africa: Set Of 6. 2011. (Navigators Ser.). (J). pap. 48.00 net. *(978-1-4108-5077-5(3))* Benchmark Education Co.

—Animals of Africa: Text Pairs. 2008. (Bridges/Navigators Ser.). (J). (gr. 4). 81.00 *(978-1-4108-8378-0(7))* Benchmark Education Co.

NorthWord Books for Young Readers Editors, ed. Forest Babies. 2003. (Animal Babies Ser.). (ENG., Illus.). 22p. (J). (gr. -1 — 1). bds. 5.95 *(978-1-55971-874-5(9))* Cooper Square Publishing Llc.

Novick, Mary & Hale, Jenny. Zoo Animals Jigsaw Book. 2007. bds. *(978-1-921272-00-4(7))* Little Hare Bks. AUS. Dist: HarperCollins Pubs. Australia.

Nunn, Daniel. Food, 1 vol. 2012. (Why Living Things Need Ser.). (ENG.). 24p. (gr. -1-1). pap. 6.29 *(978-1-4329-5920-3(4));* lib. bdg. 22.65 *(978-1-4329-5914-2(X))* Heinemann-Raintree. (Acorn).

O'Brady, Terry, et al. Count the Animals. 2007. (Windows on Literacy Ser.). (ENG., Illus.). 12p. (J). pap. 10.95 *(978-0-7922-8484-0(4))* CENGAGE Learning.

O'Brien, Lindsy. The World's Weirdest Animals. 2015. (Library of Weird Ser.). (ENG., Illus.). 32p. (gr. 3-4). lib. bdg. 27.99 *(978-1-4914-2019-5(7))* Capstone Press of Coughlan Cos.

Los Oceanos.Tr. of Oceans. (SPA.). (J). (gr. 5-8). 12.00 *(978-84-342-1949-6(2))* Parramon Ediciones S.A. ESP. Dist: Distribuidora Norma, Inc.

O'Donnell, Liam & Dorling Kindersley Publishing Staff. Amazing Animal Journeys, Level 3. 2008. (DK Readers Ser.). (ENG., Illus.). 48p. (J). (gr. 2-4). 3.99 *(978-0-7566-4085-9(7),* DK Children) Dorling Kindersley Publishing, Inc.

O'Donnell, Sallie. Animals, Vegetables & Minerals from A to Z. Plumley, Alea, illus. l.t. ed. 2005. 60p. pap. 9.95 *(978-0-9764982-5-4(1))* Legacy Publishing Services, Inc.

O'Hare, Ted. Animals of the Rain Forest. 2004. (Rain Forest Today Discovery Library Ser.). (Illus.). 24p. (gr. 1-4). lib. bdg. 22.79 *(978-1-59515-152-0(4))* Rourke Educational Media.

O'Hearn, Michael. This or That History Debate: A Rip-Roaring Game of Either/or Questions. 2012. (This or That? Ser.). (ENG.). 32p. (gr. 3-4). pap. 47.70 *(978-1-4296-9275-5(8),* Edge Bks.) Capstone Press of Coughlan Cos.

Okido Staff. My Animal Book: Facts & Fun, Questions & Answers, Things to Make & Do. 2014. (ENG., Illus.). 64p. (J). (gr. k-2). 18.95 *(978-0-500-65024-0(1),* 565024) Thames & Hudson.

Oliver, Narelle. Twilight Hunt, 1 vol. Oliver, Narelle, illus. 2007. (Seek-and-Find Bks.). (ENG., Illus.). 32p. (J). (gr. k-3). 16.95 *(978-1-59572-107-5(X))* Star Bright Bks., Inc.

One, Two, Three, Four: KinderWords Individual Title Six-Packs. (Kinderstarters Ser.). 8p. (gr. -1-1). 21.00 *(978-0-7635-8705-5(2))* Rigby Education.

Orme, David. Strange Creatures. 2010. (Fact to Fiction Grafx Ser.). (Illus.). 36p. (J). lib. bdg. 16.95 *(978-1-60686-469-2(6))* Perfection Learning Corp.

Orozco, Rebeca. It's Our Nature. Cottin, Menena, illus. 2012. (ENG.). 24p. (J). (gr. k-3). 12.95 *(978-1-77049-283-7(6),* Tundra Bks.) Tundra Bks. CAN. Dist: Penguin Random Hse. LLC.

Osborne, Mary Pope & Boyce, Natalie Pope. Animal Games & Puzzles. Murdocca, Sal, illus. 2015. (Magic Tree House Ser.). (ENG.). 256p. (J). (gr. 2-5). 6.99 *(978-0-553-50840-6(7),* Random Hse. Bks. for Young Readers) Random Hse. Children's Bks.

—Sharks & Other Predators. Molinari, Carlo, illus. 2015. (Magic Tree House - Fact Tracker Ser.: 32). (ENG.). 128p. (J). (gr. 2-5). 12.99 *(978-0-385-38642-5(7),* Random Hse. Bks. for Young Readers) Random Hse. Children's Bks.

Osborne, Rick, et al. Creepy Creatures & Bizarre Beasts from the Bible, 1 vol. Carpenter, Anthony, illus. 2004. (2:52 Ser.). (ENG.). 128p. (J). pap. 7.99 *(978-0-310-70654-0(8))* Zonderkidz.

Oswald, Nina. Saving Endangered Animals: Develop Understanding of Fractions & Numbers, 1 vol. 2015. (InfoMax Common Core Math Readers Ser.). (ENG.). 24p. (J). pap. 8.25 *(978-1-4777-4612-7(9),* Rosen Classroom) Rosen Publishing Group, Inc., The.

Ottina, Laura. In the Arctic. Ranchetti, Sebastiano, illus. 2009. (Learn with Animals Ser.). (ENG.). 24p. (J). (gr. -1-2). pap. 8.15 *(978-1-4339-2088-2(3));* lib. bdg. 22.00 *(978-1-4339-1911-4(7))* Stevens, Gareth Publishing LLLP. (Weekly Reader Leveled Readers).

—On the Savanna. Ranchetti, Sebastiano, illus. 2009. (Learn with Animals Ser.). (ENG.). 24p. (J). (gr. -1-2). pap. 8.15 *(978-1-4339-2093-6(X));* lib. bdg. 22.00 *(978-1-4339-1916-9(8))* Stevens, Gareth Publishing LLLP. (Weekly Reader Leveled Readers).

Owen, Ruth. Mountain Animals. 2014. (Origami Safari Ser.). (Illus.). 32p. (J). (gr. 3-6). lib. bdg. 27.50 *(978-1-4777-9257-5(0))* Windmill Bks.

—Science & Craft Projects with Wildlife. 2013. (Get Crafty Outdoors Ser.). (ENG., Illus.). 32p. (J). (gr. k-3). 26.50 *(978-1-4777-0243-7(1),* PowerKids Pr.) Rosen Publishing Group, Inc., The.

—Wild Baby Animals, 8 vols., Set. Incl. Arctic Fox Pups. lib. bdg. 19.96 *(978-1-61772-156-4(5));* Beaver Kits. lib. bdg. 19.96 *(978-1-61772-155-7(7));* Lion Cubs. lib. bdg. 19.96 *(978-1-61772-159-5(X));* Polar Bear Cubs. lib. bdg. 19.96 *(978-1-61772-157-1(3));* Raccoon Cubs. lib. bdg. 19.96 *(978-1-61772-154-0(9));* Skunk Kits. lib. bdg. 19.96 *(978-1-61772-161-8(1));* Squirrel Kits. lib. bdg. 19.96 *(978-1-61772-160-1(3));* Tiger Cubs. lib. bdg. 19.96 *(978-1-61772-158-8(1));* (J). (gr. k-3). 24p. 2011. Set lib. bdg. 159.68 *(978-1-61772-153-3(0))* Bearport Publishing Co., Inc.

Oxlade, Chris. Animal Infographics, 1 vol. 2014. (Infographics Ser.). (ENG.). 32p. (gr. 1-3). lib. bdg. 29.99 *(978-1-4109-6216-4(4),* Read Me!) Heinemann-Raintree.

Page, Nick & Page, Claire. Quick Smarts Dangerous Animals. 2009. 64p. (J). pap. 7.99 *(978-1-84610-971-3(X))* Make Believe Ideas GBR. Dist: Nelson, Thomas Inc.

Page, Robin. Sisters & Brothers: Sibling Relationships in the Animal World. 2012. lib. bdg. 18.40 *(978-0-606-23994-3(4),* Turtleback) Turtleback Bks.

—What Do You Do with a Tail Like This? Jenkins, Steve, illus. 2011. (J). (gr. -1-3). 29.95 *(978-0-545-10698-6(2))* Weston Woods Studios, Inc.

Page, Robin & Jenkins, Steve. Animals in Flight. Jenkins, Steve, illus. 2005. (ENG., Illus.). 32p. (J). (gr. -1-3). pap. 6.99 *(978-0-618-54882-8(3))* Houghton Mifflin Harcourt Publishing Co.

—What Do You Do with a Tail Like This? 2003. (ENG., Illus.). 32p. (J). (gr. -1-3). 17.99 *(978-0-618-25628-0(8))* Houghton Mifflin Harcourt Publishing Co.

Paige, Joy. Record-Breaking Animals, 6 bks. Incl. Blue Whale: World's Largest Mammal. (gr. 2-4). lib. bdg. 22.60 *(978-0-8239-5962-4(7));* Giraffe: World's Tallest Animal. (gr. 1). lib. bdg. 22.60 *(978-0-8239-5964-8(3),* PowerKids Pr.); Hummingbird: World's Smallest Bird. (gr. 1). lib. bdg. 22.60 *(978-0-8239-5960-0(0),* PowerKids Pr.); Sloth: The World's Slowest Mammal. (gr. 1). lib. bdg. 22.60 *(978-0-8239-5961-7(9),* PowerKids Pr.); Stick Insect: World's Longest Insect. (gr. 1). lib. bdg. 22.60 *(978-0-8239-5963-1(5),* PowerKids Pr.); 24p. (J). 2002. (Illus.). Set lib. bdg. 96.00 *(978-0-8239-7119-0(8),* PowerKids Pr.) Rosen Publishing Group, Inc., The.

Paine, Penelope C. Gift of Love. Maeno, Itoko, illus. 2006. 24p. per. 5.95 *(978-0-7909-7443-9(6))* Paper Posie.

El Paisaje. (Coleccion Planeta Vivo).Tr. of Topography. (SPA.). (YA). (gr. 5-8). 10.36 *(978-84-342-1948-9(4))* Parramon Ediciones S.A. ESP. Dist: Lectorum Pubns., Inc.

Paiva, Johannah Gilman, ed. Crazy Critters. Gardiner, Lisa M., illus. 2013. (Big Padded Lift-The-Flap Ser.). (ENG.). 20p. (J). (gr. -1-2). 8.99 *(978-1-77093-630-0(0))* Flowerpot Children's Pr. Inc. CAN. Dist: Cardinal Pubs. Group.

Pajaros. 2005. (Collection Abre Tus Ojos, Collection Eye Openers Ser.).Tr. of Birds. (SPA.). (J). (gr. k-2). 6.95 *(978-950-11-0965-8(8))* Sigmar ARG. Dist: Iaconi, Mariuccia Bk. Imports.

Palacios, Vicente. Origami Animals. 2012. (Dover Origami Papercraft Ser.). (ENG., Illus.). 64p. (gr. 7). pap. 9.95 *(978-0-486-47874-6(2))* Dover Pubns., Inc.

Palika, Liz & Miller, Katherine A. Animals at Work. 2009. (ASPCA Kids Ser.: 2). (ENG., Illus.). 108p. 12.99 *(978-0-470-41084-4(1),* Howell Bk. Hse.) Wiley, John & Sons, Inc.

Pang, Hannah. Wilderness. Wren, Jenny, illus. 2016. (360 Degrees Ser.). (ENG.). 28p. (J). (gr. 3-6). 22.99 *(978-1-944530-03-7(7),* 360 Degrees) Tiger Tales.

A Park Ecosystem. 2012. (Nature Trail Ser.). (ENG., Illus.). 32p. (J). (gr. k-5). 23.95 *(978-1-4488-6626-7(X),* PowerKids Pr.) Rosen Publishing Group, Inc., The.

Parker, Andy. Mekanimals: Clockwork Safari, Spanish-Language Edition. 2005. (Mekanimals Ser.). (SPA., Illus.). 8p. (J). bds. *(978-970-718-322-3(5),* Silver Dolphin en Español) Advanced Marketing, S. de R. L. de C. V.

Parker, Marjorie Blain. A Paddling of Ducks: Animals in Groups from A to Z. Kelly, Joseph, illus. 2010. (ENG.). 32p. (J). (gr. -1-2). 16.95 *(978-1-55337-682-8(X))* Kids Can Pr., Ltd. CAN. Dist: Hachette Bk. Group.

Parker, Steve. Animal Life. 2010. (Science Library). 40p. (J). (gr. 3-18). lib. bdg. 19.95 *(978-1-4222-1547-0(4))* Mason Crest.

—Bugs. 2010. (Remarkable Man & Beast Ser.). (Illus.). 48p. (J). (gr. 3-18). lib. bdg. 19.95 *(978-1-4222-1967-6(4))* Mason Crest.

—Do Animals Go to School? And Other Questions & Answers about Animal Survival. Rosewarne, Graham, illus. 2016. (ENG.). 32p. 7.99 *(978-1-86147-479-7(2),* Armadillo) Anness Publishing GBR. Dist: National Bk. Network.

—Do Animals Need Umbrellas? And Other Questions & Answers about Life in the Wild. Rosewarne, Graham, illus. 2016. (ENG.). 32p. 7.99 *(978-1-86147-478-0(4),* Armadillo) Anness Publishing GBR. Dist: National Bk. Network.

—Extreme Animals. 2016. (Animals Are Wild! Ser.). 40p. (gr. 4-3). pap. 14.05 *(978-1-4824-5010-1(0))* Stevens, Gareth Publishing LLLP.

—Fierce Predators. 2016. (Animals Are Wild! Ser.). 40p. (gr. 4-3). pap. 14.05 *(978-1-4824-5006-4(2))* Stevens, Gareth Publishing LLLP.

—Weird Animals. 2016. (Animals Are Wild! Ser.). 40p. (gr. 4-3). pap. 14.05 *(978-1-4824-4998-3(6))* Stevens, Gareth Publishing LLLP.

Parker, Steve & Dewan, Ted. Inside the Whale & Other Animals. (Illus.). (J). 18.95 *(978-0-590-73869-9(0))* Scholastic, Inc.

Parragon, creator. Growl with the Animals! 2014. (Discovery Kids 10 Button Ser.). (ENG., Illus.). (J). (gr. -1). bds. *(978-1-4723-6108-0(3))* Parragon Bk. Service Ltd.

Party Animals: Individual Title Six-Packs. (Story Steps Ser.). (gr. k-2). 32.00 *(978-0-7635-9820-4(8))* Rigby Education.

Pascoe, Elaine. The Ecosystem of an Apple Tree. 2003. (Library of Small Ecosystems Ser.). (Illus.). 24p. (J). lib. bdg. 25.25 *(978-0-8239-6304-1(7),* PowerKids Pr.) Rosen Publishing Group, Inc., The.

Pasques, Patrick. Savanna Animals. 2013. (3D Paper Craft Ser.). (ENG & ITA., Illus.). 48p. (J). (gr. k). 14.95 *(978-84-92810-75-8(0))* Promotora de prensa internacional S.A ESP. Dist: Consortium Bk. Sales & Distribution.

Pat Them Gently w/ Plush. 2007. 14.95 *(978-1-58117-626-1(0),* Intervisual/Piggy Toes) Bendon, Inc.

La Patata. (Coleccion Ciclos Vitales). (SPA., Illus.). pap. 7.96 *(978-84-236-2657-1(1),* ED4698) Edebé ESP. Dist: Lectorum Pubns., Inc.

Patkau, Karen. Creatures Great & Small. (ENG., Illus.). 32p. (J). (gr. 1-4). 2012. pap. 8.95 *(978-1-77049-309-4(3))* 2006. 17.95 *(978-0-88776-754-8(0))* Tundra Bks. CAN. (Tundra Bks.). Dist: Penguin Random Hse. LLC.

—Creatures Yesterday & Today. Patkau, Karen, illus. 2012. (ENG., Illus.). 32p. (J). (gr. 1-4). pap. 8.95 *(978-1-77049-310-0(7),* Tundra Bks.) Tundra Bks. CAN. Dist: Penguin Random Hse. LLC.

Patrick, B. & Schotz, Leo D. Is That Funny? Ruell, L J, illus. 2006. (ENG.). 32p. (J). (gr. -1-3). 15.95 *(978-0-9741319-6-2(2))* 4N Publishing LLC.

Pattison, Darcy. Prairie Storms, 1 vol. Rietz, Kathleen, illus. 2011. (ENG.). 32p. (J). (gr. -1-4). 16.95 *(978-1-60718-129-3(0));* pap. 8.95 *(978-1-60718-139-2(8))* Arbordale Publishing.

Pavitte, Thomas. Querkles: Animals. 2016. (ENG., Illus.). 48p. pap. 14.99 *(978-1-62686-791-8(7),* Thunder Bay Pr.) Readerlink Distribution Services, LLC.

Pearson, Carrie A. A Cool Summer Tail, 1 vol. Wald, Christina, illus. 2014. (ENG.). 32p. (J). (gr. -1-3). 17.95 *(978-1-62855-205-8(0));* pap. 9.95 *(978-1-62855-214-0(X))* Arbordale Publishing.

—Un Invierno Muy Abrigador, 1 vol. Wald, Christina, illus. 2012. (SPA & ENG.). 32p. (J). (gr. -1-3). 17.95 *(978-1-60718-680-9(2))* Arbordale Publishing.

—A Warm Winter Tail, 1 vol. Wald, Christina, illus. 2012. (SPA & ENG.). 32p. (J). (gr. -1-3). 17.95 *(978-1-60718-529-1(6));* pap. 9.95 *(978-1-60718-538-3(5))* Arbordale Publishing.

Pearson, Deborah. Animachines. Hilb, Nora, illus. 2016. (ENG.). 16p. (J). (— 1). bds. 7.99 *(978-1-55451-831-9(8))* Annick Pr., Ltd. CAN. Dist: Publishers Group West (PGW).

Pearson, Maria, illus. Animal Stencil Cards. 2008. (Stencil Cards Ser.). 16p. (J). 9.99 *(978-0-7945-1961-2(X),* Usborne) EDC Publishing.

Pebble Books: Animals, Animals, Animals. 2005. (YA). (gr. k-3). 683.10 *(978-0-7368-4221-1(7),* Pebble Bks.) Capstone Press of Coughlan Cos.

Peers, Jill. Rainbow Cottage. 2011. 24p. pap. 12.96 *(978-1-4490-6199-9(0))* AuthorHouse.

Penguin Books Staff, ed. Animals. (Learners Ser.). (Illus.). 48p. (J). 3.50 *(978-0-7214-1705-9(1),* Dutton Juvenile) Penguin Publishing Group.

Pequena Historia de Mi Gatito, Conejito, Perrito. 2003. (SPA.). 3.98 *(978-968-855-202-5(X))* Suromex, Ediciones, S.A. MEX. Dist: Giron Bks.

Percy, J.P. Animals. 2013. (Can You Guess What I Am? Ser.). 24p. (gr. k-3). 28.50 *(978-1-59920-892-3(X))* Black Rabbit Bks.

Pero, Denis & Auzou Publishing Staff. My Book of Animals: A Walk Through the National Parks. 2013. (ENG., Illus.). 96p. (J). (gr. 2). 16.95 *(978-2-7338-2315-6(9))* Auzou, Philippe Editions FRA. Dist: Consortium Bk. Sales & Distribution.

Perry, Marcia. Here on Earth: An Animal Alphabet. 2013. (ENG., Illus.). 60p. (J). 15.95 *(978-0-7649-6452-7(6))* Pomegranate Communications, Inc.

Person, Stephen. Saving Animals from Hurricanes. 2011. (Rescuing Animals from Disasters Ser.). 32p. (YA). (gr. 2-5). lib. bdg. 25.27 *(978-1-61772-290-5(1))* Bearport Publishing Co., Inc.

—Saving Animals from Oil Spills. 2011. (Rescuing Animals from Disasters Ser.). 32p. (YA). (gr. 2-5). lib. bdg. 25.27 *(978-1-61772-288-2(X))* Bearport Publishing Co., Inc.

Peterson, Megan Cooley. Extreme Animals. 2012. (Extreme Animals Ser.). (ENG.). 24p. (gr. k-1). pap. 333.60 *(978-1-4296-8344-9(9),* Pebble Plus) Capstone Press of Coughlan Cos.

Peterson, Megan Cooley & Rustad, Martha E. H. Chimpanzees Are Awesome! 2015. (Awesome African

Animals! Ser.). (ENG.). 32p. (gr. 1-2). lib. bdg. 27.32 (978-1-4914-1759-1(5)) Capstone Press of Coughlan Cos.

—Extreme Animals. 2012. (Extreme Animals Ser.). (ENG.). 24p. (gr. k-1). pap. 36.45 (978-1-4296-8343-2(0)); pap. 13.90 (978-1-4296-8342-5(2)); lib. bdg. 53.30 (978-1-4296-8117-9(9)); lib. bdg. 106.60 (978-1-4296-8118-6(7)) Capstone Press of Coughlan Cos. (Pebble Plus).

—The Smallest Animals, 1 vol. 2012. (Extreme Animals Ser.). (ENG., Illus.). 24p. (gr. k-1). pap. 7.29 (978-1-4296-7903-9(4)); lib. bdg. 26.65 (978-1-4296-7600-7(0)) Capstone Press of Coughlan Cos. (Pebble Plus).

—This Book Might Bite: A Collection of Wacky Animal Trivia, 1 vol. 2012. (Super Trivia Collection). (ENG., Illus.). 32p. (gr. 3-4). 27.99 (978-1-4296-7655-7(8), Edge Bks.) Capstone Press of Coughlan Cos.

—Zebras Are Awesome! 2015. (Awesome African Animals! Ser.). (ENG.). 32p. (gr. 1-2). lib. bdg. 27.32 (978-1-4914-1764-5(1)) Capstone Press of Coughlan Cos.

Petrie, Kristin. Backyard Animals, 1 vol. 2014. (Backyard Animals Ser.: 6). (ENG.). 32p. (gr. 3-6). lib. bdg. 162.42 (978-1-62403-657-6(0), Checkerboard Library) ABDO Publishing Co.

Petz, Moritz. The Day Everything Went Wrong. Jackowski, Amélie, illus. 2015. (ENG.). 32p. (J). 17.95 (978-0-7358-4209-0(4)) North-South Bks., Inc.

Peyrols, Sylvaine. La Historia de la Vida: Los Animales. (SPA., Illus.). 64p. (J). (gr. 3-5). (978-84-261-3149-2(2), JV30157) Juventud, Editorial ESP. Dist: Lectorum Pubns., Inc.

Pfister, Marcus. Animal ABC. 2013. (ENG., Illus.). 32p. (J). (gr. -1-3). 17.95 (978-0-7358-4136-9(5)) North-South Bks., Inc.

Phillips, Dee. Find It in the Park. 2006. (Can You Find It? Ser.). (Illus.). 24p. (gr. k-3). lib. bdg. 23.00 (978-0-8368-6301-7(1), Gareth Stevens Learning Library) Stevens, Gareth Publishing LLLP.

Phillips, Jillian. What to Doodle? - Jr. Animals! 2011. (Dover Doodle Bks.). (ENG.). 128p. (J). (gr. k-3). pap. 3.99 (978-0-486-47822-7(X)) Dover Pubns., Inc.

Phillips, Sara & Running Press Staff. Animals. 2003. (Illus.). 8p. (J). pap. 4.95 (978-0-7624-1650-9(5)) Running Pr. Bk. Pubs.

Pickering, Fran. The Illustrated Encyclopedia of Animals in Nature & Myth. 2003. (Illus.). 144p. (YA). (978-1-903954-53-9(3), Pavilion Children's Books) Pavilion Bks.

Picthall & Gunzi Ltd, creator. In the Jungle. 2006. (Feels Real Bks.). (ENG., Illus.). 10p. (J). (gr. -1). bds. 6.99 (978-0-7641-5949-7(6)) Barron's Educational Series, Inc.

Pierson, Clara Dillingham. Among the Forest People (Yesterday's Classics) 2005. (Illus.). 148p. (J). per. 8.95 (978-1-59915-018-5(2)) Yesterday's Classics.

—Among the Meadow People (Yesterday's Classics) 2005. (Illus.). 136p. (J). per. 8.95 (978-1-59915-019-2(0)) Yesterday's Classics.

—Among the Night People (Yesterday's Classics) 2005. (Illus.). 164p. (J). per. 8.95 (978-1-59915-020-8(4)) Yesterday's Classics.

—Among the Pond People (Yesterday's Classics) 2005. (Illus.). 160p. (J). per. 8.95 (978-1-59915-021-5(2)) Yesterday's Classics.

Pitzer, Marjorie. Animal Fun for Everyone! 2014. (ENG., Illus.). 14p. (J). pap. (978-1-60613-188-6(5)) Woodbine Hse.

Pledger, Maurice, illus. Into the Wild. 2014. (ENG.). 120p. (J). (gr. -1). act. bk. ed. 12.95 (978-1-62686-107-7(2), Silver Dolphin Bks.) Readerlink Distribution Services, LLC.

—Jungles & Oceans. 2015. (Animal Kingdom Ser.). (ENG.). 120p. (gr. -1). act. bk. ed. 12.95 (978-1-62686-108-4(0), Silver Dolphin Bks.) Readerlink Distribution Services, LLC.

Poisonous Predators. 2008. (Predator Sticker Books Ser.). 16p. pap. (978-1-4075-1265-5(X)) Parragon, Inc.

Polydoros, Lori. Killer Animals: On the Hunt. 2016. (Killer Animals Ser.). (ENG.). 32p. pap. 55.65 **(978-1-5157-9073-0(8)**, Blazers) Capstone Press of Coughlan Cos.

Polydoros, Lori, et al. Predator Profiles. 2015. (Predator Profiles Ser.). (ENG.). 24p. (gr. 1-2). 151.92 (978-1-4914-6811-1(4), First Facts) Capstone Press of Coughlan Cos.

Pomaska, Anna. 3-D Coloring Book — My First Animal Mandalas. 2011. (Dover 3-D Coloring Book Ser.). (ENG., Illus.). 32p. (J). (gr. -1-2). pap. 5.99 (978-0-486-48103-6(4)) Dover Pubns., Inc.

Pomerance, Diane. Animal Companions: In Our Hearts, Our Lives, & Our World. Mier, Vanessa, illus. 2004. (YA). per. 9.95 (978-0-9708500-3-4(4)) Polaire Pubns.

Porter, Matthew. Calling All Animals. 2010. (ENG., Illus.). 28p. (J). (gr. -1 — 1). bds. 8.95 (978-1-897476-34-5(5)) Simply Read Bks. CAN. Dist: Ingram Publisher Services.

Posada, Mia. Who Was Here? Discovering Wild Animal Tracks. Posada, Mia, illus. 2014. (ENG., Illus.). 32p. (J). (gr. k-3). 16.95 (978-1-4677-1871-4(8), Millbrook Pr.) Lerner Publishing Group.

Post, Lee. Texas Animals Big & Small. POST, L. E. E., illus. 2008. 32p. pap. 9.95 (978-1-934443-33-0(6)) ExpandingBooks.com.

Potts, Steve, et al. North American Animals. 2012. (North American Animals Ser.). (ENG.). 24p. (gr. k-1). pap. 41.70 (978-1-4296-8362-3(7)); lib. bdg. 159.90 (978-1-4296-8142-1(X)) Capstone Press of Coughlan Cos. (Pebble Plus).

Pountney, Beth. My Books of Animal Fun Slipcase. 2007. (Illus.). 12p. (gr. -1-k). per. (978-1-84610-563-0(3)) Make Believe Ideas.

PowerPhonics Skill Set I: Includes Animals I, Self I & Growing Things, 18 bks. (Illus.). (J). (gr. 1). lib. bdg. 324.00 (978-0-8239-7204-3(6), PowerKids Pr.) Rosen Publishing Group, Inc., The.

Prap, Lila. Whyld Animals Kid Kit. 2010. (Kid Kits Ser.). 32p. (J). pap. 9.99 (978-1-60130-219-9(3), Usborne) EDC Publishing.

Prasadam-Halls, Smriti. In the Garden. Scobie, Lorna, illus. 2017. (Pairs Ser.). (ENG.). 12p. (J). (gr. -1-k). bds. 9.99 (978-1-84780-883-7(2), Frances Lincoln Children's Bks.) Quarto Publishing Group UK GBR. Dist: Hachette Bk. Group.

Prasadam, Smriti & Mitchell, Melanie. Peepo Paw Printes. 2008. (ENG., Illus.). 14p. (J). bds. 13.95 (978-0-7475-9535-9(6)) Bloomsbury Publishing Plc GBR. Dist: Independent Pubs. Group.

Pratt-Serafini, Kristin Joy. Salamander Rain: A Lake & Pond Journal. 2004. (Sharing Nature with Children Book Ser.). (Illus.). 32p. (YA). (gr. 4-7). 16.95 (978-1-58469-018-4(6)) Dawn Pubns.

Prentice-Hall, Inc. Staff, creator. Science Explorer - Animals. 2006. (ENG., Illus.). 214p. (J). (gr. 6-8). lib. bdg., stu. ed. 14.97 (978-0-13-201144-0(1)) Prentice Hall (Schl. Div.).

PRESS, Celebration. Communicating with Animals. 2003. (ENG.). (J). (gr. 6-8). pap. 37.95 (978-0-7652-3247-2(2), Celebration Pr.) Pearson Schl.

Price, Nick, illus. Animal Legends. 2004. 48p. (J). (gr. 2-18). (Young Reading Series One Ser.). pap. 5.95 (978-0-7945-0408-3(6)); (Young Reading Ser.: Vol. 1). lib. bdg. 13.95 (978-1-58086-660-6(3)) EDC Publishing. (Usborne).

—Magical Animals. 2004. (Young Reading Series One Ser.). 48p. (J). (gr. 2-18). pap. 5.95 (978-0-7945-0454-0(X), Usborne) EDC Publishing.

Price, Roger & Stern, Leonard. Mad about Animals Mad Libs. 2009. (Mad Libs Ser.). (ENG.). 48p. (J). (gr. 3-7). 4.99 (978-0-8431-3713-2(4), Mad Libs) Penguin Young Readers Group.

Price, Sean Stewart. The World's Deadliest Animals. 2016. (World Record Breakers Ser.). (ENG., Illus.). 32p. (gr. 3-4). lib. bdg. 27.99 (978-1-4914-8176-9(5), Edge Bks.) Capstone Press of Coughlan Cos.

Priddy Books Staff & Priddy, Roger. Animals. rev. ed. 2004. (Bright Baby Ser.). (ENG., Illus.). 26p. (J). (gr. -1 — 1). bds. 4.99 (978-0-312-49248-9(0), 9780312492489, Priddy Bks.) St. Martin's Pr.

—Wipe Clean Animals. rev. ed. 2004. (Wipe Clean Learning Bks.). (ENG., Illus.). 24p. (J). (gr. -1-1). bds., act. bk. ed. 8.99 (978-0-312-49401-8(7), 9780312494018, Priddy Bks.) St. Martin's Pr.

Priddy, Roger. Alphaprints: ABC. 2013. (Alphaprints Ser.). (ENG.). 28p. (J). (gr. -1 — 1). bds. 9.99 (978-0-312-51646-8(0), 9780312516468, Priddy Bks.) St. Martin's Pr.

—Animales. 2007. (Bright Baby Ser.).Tr. of Animals. (ENG & SPA., Illus.). 12p. (J). (gr. -1 — 1). bds. 4.95 (978-0-312-50298-0(2), 9780312502980, Priddy Bks.) St. Martin's Pr.

—Animals. (Bright Baby Ser.). (ENG., (J). 2013. Illus.). 16p. (gr. -1 — 1). bds. 8.99 (978-0-312-51622-2(3), 9780312516222) 2013. (Illus.). 16p. (gr. -1 — 1). bds. 4.99 (978-0-312-51597-3(9), 9780312515973) 2005. 12p. bds. 0.97 (978-0-312-49610-4(9)) St. Martin's Pr. (Priddy Bks.).

—At the Zoo. 2006. (Bright Baby Touch & Feel Ser.). (ENG., Illus.). 10p. (J). (gr. -1 — 1). bds. 4.95 (978-0-312-49857-3(8), 9780312498573, Priddy Bks.) St. Martin's Pr.

—Baby Basics Animals. 2013. (Baby Basics Ser.). (ENG., Illus.). 10p. (J). (gr. -1 — 1). bds. 4.99 (978-0-312-51553-9(7), 9780312515539, Priddy Bks.) St. Martin's Pr.

—Baby Basics My First Animals. 2013. (Baby Basics Ser.). (ENG., Illus.). 28p. (J). (gr. -1 — 1). bds. 8.99 (978-0-312-51634-5(7), 9780312516345, Priddy Bks.) St. Martin's Pr.

—Baby's First Animals. 2016. (Baby's First Ser.). (ENG., Illus.). 8p. (J). bds. 7.99 (978-0-312-51952-0(4), 9780312519520, Priddy Bks.) St. Martin's Pr.

—Busy Babies Farm Animals. 2010. 8p. (J). bds. 4.99 (978-0-312-50857-9(3), Priddy Bks.) St. Martin's Pr.

—First 100 Animals. (First 100 Ser.). (ENG., Illus.). (J). (gr. -1 — 1). 2011. 26p. bds. 5.99 (978-0-312-51079-4(9), 9780312510794) 2006. 14p. bds. 8.99 (978-0-312-49676-0(1), 9780312496760) St. Martin's Pr. (Priddy Bks.).

—First 100 Animals Lift-The-Flap. 2014. (First 100 Ser.). (ENG., Illus.). 14p. (J). (gr. -1 — 1). bds. 9.99 (978-0-312-51752-6(1), 9780312517526, Priddy Bks.) St. Martin's Pr.

—First 100 Animals Sticker Book. 2016. (First 100 Ser.). (ENG.). 80p. (J). pap. 9.99 (978-0-312-52011-3(5), 9780312520113, Priddy Bks.) St. Martin's Pr.

—Let's Go Learning: I Love Animals. 2013. (Let's Go Learning Ser.). (ENG.). 104p. (J). (gr. -1-1). pap. 6.99 (978-0-312-51069-5(1), 9780312510695, Priddy Bks.) St. Martin's Pr.

—Let's Pretend: Animal Rescue. 2015. (Let's Pretend Ser.). (ENG.). 6p. (J). 14.99 (978-0-312-51907-0(9), 9780312519070, Priddy Bks.) St. Martin's Pr.

—Little Alphaprints: Animals. 2015. (Alphaprints Ser.). (ENG., Illus.). 10p. (J). (gr. -1 — 1). bds. 5.99 (978-0-312-51828-8(5), 9780312518288, Priddy Bks.) St. Martin's Pr.

—My Big Animal Book. 2011. (My Big Board Bks.). (ENG., Illus.). 12p. (J). (gr. -1 — 1). bds. 7.99 (978-0-312-51107-4(8), 9780312511074, Priddy Bks.) St. Martin's Pr.

—My Giant Fold-Out Book of Animals. 2009. (ENG.). 16p. (J). (gr. -1 — 1). bds. 9.99 (978-0-312-50712-1(7), 9780312507121, Priddy Bks.) St. Martin's Pr.

—My Little Animal Book. 2nd rev. ed. 2012. (My Little Bks.). (ENG., Illus.). 24p. (J). (gr. -1-k). bds. 8.99 (978-0-312-51461-7(1), 9780312514617, Priddy Bks.) St. Martin's Pr.

—Picture Fit Board Books: a Parade of Animals (Large) A Counting Book. 2017. (Picture Fit Ser.). (ENG., Illus.). 14p. (J). bds. 12.99 (978-0-312-52174-5(X), 9780312521745, Priddy Bks.) St. Martin's Pr.

—Playtime. 2013. (Hello Baby Ser.). (ENG., Illus.). 12p. (J). (gr. -1 — 1). bds. 14.99 (978-0-312-51603-1(7), 9780312516031, Priddy Bks.) St. Martin's Pr.

—Predators: The World's Deadliest Hunters. 2013. (Smart Kids Ser.). (ENG., Illus.). 30p. (J). (gr. -1-2). 9.99 (978-0-312-51623-9(1), 9780312516239, Priddy Bks.) St. Martin's Pr.

—1000 Animal Stickers. 2010. (ENG., Illus.). 128p. (J). (gr. -1-2). pap. 9.99 (978-0-312-50941-5(3), 9780312509415, Priddy Bks.) St. Martin's Pr.

Privateer, Mark & Dunlap, Jennifer. Sharks Don't Eat Peanut Butter. 2013. 62p. pap. 12.95 (978-0-9896220-6-6(1)) No Frills Buffalo.

Probst, Jeff. Outrageous Animals: Weird Trivia & Unbelievable Facts to Test Your Knowledge about Mammals, Fish, Insects & More! 2015. (Challenge Yourself Ser.: 1). (ENG., Illus.). 176p. (J). (gr. 3-7). 8.99 (978-0-14-751375-5(8), Puffin Books) Penguin Young Readers Group.

Pryor, Kimberley Jane. Venom, Poison, & Electricity. 2009. (Animal Attack & Defense Ser.). 32p. (gr. 3). 28.50 (978-0-7614-4422-0(X)) Marshall Cavendish GBR. Dist: Marshall Cavendish Corp.

Publications International Ltd. Staff, ed. My First Book Block Set Animals. 2011. 12p. (J). bds. 14.98 (978-1-4508-1244-3(9)) Publications International, Ltd.

—The World of Eric Carle - Baby Animals. 2011. 10p. (J). bds. 7.98 (978-1-4508-0508-7(6)) Phoenix International Publications, Inc.

Publishers, Hancock House Publishers. Wildlife Coloring Book. 2004. (Illus.). 24p. (J). pap. 4.95 (978-0-88839-599-3(X)) Hancock Hse. Pubs.

Publishing, Sterling. Look at Me! 2008. (Illus.). 10p. (J). bds. (978-1-934618-41-7(1)) Begin Smart LLC.

Puchta, Herbert & Gerngross, Günter. SUPER SAFARI LEVEL 1 BIG BOOK. 2015. (ENG., Illus.). 32p. 27.50 (978-1-107-53925-9(0)) Cambridge Univ. Pr.

Pugliano-Martin, Carol. Cats of the Serengeti. 2011. (Early Connections Ser.). (J). (978-1-61672-575-4(3)) Benchmark Education Co.

Pyers, Greg. How to Behave in the Animal Kingdom. 2007. 96p. (J). (978-1-4207-0739-7(6)) Sundance/Newbridge Educational Publishing.

Quarto Books, Quarto, ed. Amazing Animals: A Collection of Creatures Great & Small. 2015. (ENG., Illus.). 62p. (J). (gr. -1-k). 14.95 (978-1-4549-1458-7(0)) Sterling Publishing Co., Inc.

Quinlan, Julia J. Dingoes. 2013. (Ferocious Fighting Animals Ser.). (ENG., Illus.). 24p. (J). (gr. k-5). 22.60 (978-1-4488-9675-2(4)); pap. 8.25 (978-1-4488-9808-4(0)) Rosen Publishing Group, Inc., The. (PowerKids Pr.).

—Tasmanian Devils. 2013. (Ferocious Fighting Animals Ser.). (ENG., Illus.). 24p. (J). (gr. k-5). 22.60 (978-1-4488-9674-5(6)); pap. 8.25 (978-1-4488-9806-0(4)) Rosen Publishing Group, Inc., The. (PowerKids Pr.).

—Wild Boars. 2013. (Ferocious Fighting Animals Ser.). (ENG., Illus.). 24p. (J). (gr. k-5). 22.60 (978-1-4488-9676-9(2)); pap. 8.25 (978-1-4488-9810-7(2)) Rosen Publishing Group, Inc., The. (PowerKids Pr.).

—Wolverines. 2013. (Ferocious Fighting Animals Ser.). (ENG., Illus.). 24p. (J). (gr. k-5). 22.60 (978-1-4488-9672-1(X)); pap. 8.25 (978-1-4488-9802-2(1)) Rosen Publishing Group, Inc., The. (PowerKids Pr.).

Quinton, Sasha. Go-Go-Goat: A Phonics Reader. 2009. (Illus.). pap. (978-1-936199-09-9(2)) Book Shop, Ltd., The.

—I-Spy: A Phonics Reader. 2009. (Illus.). (978-1-936199-06-8(8)) Book Shop, Ltd., The.

—Ring-A-Ding: A Phonics Reader. 2009. (Illus.). pap. (978-1-936199-00-6(9)) Book Shop, Ltd., The.

—Rub-A-Dub: A Phonics Reader. 2009. (Illus.). (978-1-936199-03-7(3)) Book Shop, Ltd., The.

Raatma, Lucia. How Do We Live Together? Raccoons. 2010. (Community Connections: How Do We Live Together? Ser.). (ENG.). 24p. (gr. 2-5). lib. bdg. 25.64 (978-1-60279-619-5(X), 200330) Cherry Lake Publishing.

Rabe, Tish. Out of Sight till Tonight! All about Nocturnal Animals. 2015. (Cat in the Hat's Learning Library). (ENG., Illus.). 48p. (J). (gr. k-3). 9.99 (978-0-375-87076-7(8), Random Hse. Bks. for Young Readers) Random Hse. Children's Bks.

Racanelli, Marie. Animals with Armor. 2010. (Crazy Nature Ser.). 24p. (J). (gr. 1-5). lib. bdg., E-Book 42.50 (978-1-4488-0157-2(5)); (Illus.). pap. 8.25 (978-1-4358-9864-6(8), PowerKids Pr.); (Illus.). (gr. 1-4). lib. bdg. 22.60 (978-1-4358-9386-3(7)) Rosen Publishing Group, Inc., The.

—Underground Animals. 24p. (J). 2011. (Illus.). pap. 8.25 (978-1-4358-9860-8(5), PowerKids Pr.) 2011. (Illus.). (gr. 1-4). lib. bdg. 22.60 (978-1-4358-9384-9(0)) 2010. (gr. 1-5). lib. bdg., E-Book 42.50 (978-1-4488-0153-4(2)) 2010. (Illus.). 49.50 (978-1-4358-9861-5(3), PowerKids Pr.) Rosen Publishing Group, Inc., The.

Radford, Tracey. Animal Fun! Touch & Feel: Stroke the Animals! 2016. (ENG., Illus.). 10p. (J). (gr. 1-4). 6.95 (978-1-78249-401-0(4), 1782494014, CICO Books) Ryland Peters & Small GBR. Dist: WIPRO.

—Animal Fun Where Do I Live? 2016. (ENG., Illus.). 10p. (J). (gr. 1-4). 6.95 (978-1-78249-399-0(9), 1782493999, CICO Books) Ryland Peters & Small GBR. Dist: WIPRO.

Rafferty, John P., ed. Carnivores: Meat-Eating Mammals. 2011. (Britannica Guide to Predators & Prey Ser.). (Illus.). 320p. (YA). 103.40 (978-1-61530-430-1(4)) Rosen Publishing Group, Inc., The.

Raintree Steck-Vaughn Staff. Biomes Animals: Arkansas Edition, 36 bks., Set. 2003. (Illus.). 1062.48 (978-1-4109-0142-2(4)) Harcourt Schl. Pubs.

Rake, Jody Sullivan. Bloodsuckers of the Animal World. 2015. (Disgusting Creature Diets Ser.). (ENG., Illus.). 32p. (gr. 1-2). 26.65 (978-1-4914-1997-7(0)) Capstone Press of Coughlan Cos.

—Carcass Chewers of the Animal World. 2015. (Disgusting Creature Diets Ser.). (ENG.). 32p. (gr. 1-2). 26.65 (978-1-4914-1998-4(9)) Capstone Press of Coughlan Cos.

—Speed, Strength, & Stealth: Animal Weapons & Defenses. 2012. (Animal Weapons & Defenses Ser.). (ENG.). 32p. (gr. 1-2). pap. 47.70 (978-1-4296-8503-0(4), Blazers) Capstone Press of Coughlan Cos.

—Spines, Horns, & Armor: Animal Weapons & Defenses, 1 vol. 2012. (Animal Weapons & Defenses Ser.). (ENG., Illus.). 32p. (gr. 1-2). 26.65 (978-1-4296-6505-6(X)); pap. 8.10 (978-1-4296-8011-0(3)) Capstone Press of Coughlan Cos. (Blazers).

—Star-Nosed Moles & Other Extreme Mammal Adaptations, 1 vol. 2014. (Extreme Adaptations Ser.). (ENG.). 32p. (gr. 3-4). lib. bdg. 27.32 (978-1-4914-0167-5(2)) Capstone Press of Coughlan Cos.

—Underground Safari. 2015. (Underground Safari Ser.). (ENG.). 24p. (gr. 1-2). 101.28 (978-1-4914-6912-5(9), First Facts) Capstone Press of Coughlan Cos.

Rake, Matthew. Prehistoric Ancestors of Modern Animals. Mendez, Simon, illus. 2017. (If Extinct Beasts Came to Life Ser.). (ENG.). 32p. (J). (gr. 3-6). 7.99 (978-1-5124-1159-1(0)); 7.99 **(978-1-5124-3609-9(7))**; 39.99 **(978-1-5124-0906-2(5))**; 39.99 **(978-1-5124-3608-2(9))** Lerner Publishing Group.

Rake, Matthew. Prehistoric Predators. Mendez, Simon, illus. 2017. (If Extinct Beasts Came to Life Ser.). (ENG.). 32p. (J). (gr. 3-6). 26.65 (978-1-5124-0633-7(3)); 7.99 **(978-1-5124-3615-0(1))**; 39.99 **(978-1-5124-0907-9(3))**; 39.99 **(978-1-5124-3614-3(3))** Lerner Publishing Group.

Ramey, Kathy. The Animal Alphabet. 2007. (Illus.). (J). pap. 12.95 (978-1-931334-96-9(X)) Pieces of Learning.

Ranchetti, Sebastiano. Animal Opposites. 2008. (Learn with Animals Ser.). (Illus.). 24p. (gr. -1-2). pap. 8.15 (978-0-8368-8827-0(8)); lib. bdg. 22.00 (978-0-8368-8822-5(7)) Stevens, Gareth Publishing LLLP. (Weekly Reader Leveled Readers).

—Animal Opposites/Opuestos Animales. 2008. (Learn with Animals/Aprende con los Animales Ser.). (SPA & ENG., Illus.). 24p. (gr. -1-2). lib. bdg. 22.00 (978-0-8368-9038-9(8), Weekly Reader Leveled Readers) Stevens, Gareth Publishing LLLP.

—Shapes in Animals. 2008. (Learn with Animals;Aprende con los animales Ser.). 24p. (gr. -1-2). (SPA & ENG.). pap. 8.15 (978-0-8368-9045-7(0)); (Illus.). pap. 8.15 (978-0-8368-8829-4(4)); (Illus.). lib. bdg. 22.00 (978-0-8368-8824-9(3)) Stevens, Gareth Publishing LLLP. (Weekly Reader Leveled Readers).

—Shapes in Animals/Figuras en los Animales. 2008. (Learn with Animals/Aprende con los Animales Ser.). (SPA & ENG., Illus.). 24p. (gr. -1-2). lib. bdg. 22.00 (978-0-8368-9040-2(X), Weekly Reader Leveled Readers) Stevens, Gareth Publishing LLLP.

Rappoport, Bernice. Habitats of Africa: Text Pairs. 2008. (Bridges/Navigators Ser.). (J). (gr. 3). 81.00 (978-1-4108-8359-9(0)) Benchmark Education Co.

Rau, Dana Meachen. Animals. 2009. (Bookworms Ser.). 32p. (gr. 1-2). 15.95 (978-0-7614-4093-2(3)) Marshall Cavendish Corp.

—Animals/Los Animales. 2009. (Bookworms Ser.). (SPA & ENG.). 32p. (gr. 1-2). lib. bdg. 15.95 (978-0-7614-4787-0(3)) Marshall Cavendish Corp.

Rauen, Amy & Ayers, Amy. Counting at the Zoo. Andersen, Gregg, photos by. 2007. (Math in Our World Ser.). (Illus.). 24p. (gr. 1-2). pap. 8.15 (978-0-8368-8478-4(7), Weekly Reader Leveled Readers) Stevens, Gareth Publishing LLLP.

Rauker, Lucy. Awesome Animal Trivia. 2013. (Ultimate Trivia Challenge Ser.). (Illus.). 32p. (J). (gr. 2-5). pap. 10.50 (978-1-4339-8289-7(7)); lib. bdg. 25.25 (978-1-4339-8288-0(9)) Stevens, Gareth Publishing LLLP.

Rayburn, Scooter. Animal Friends for You! Let's Be Friends! 2011. 16p. pap. (978-1-4269-8944-5(X)) Trafford Publishing (UK) Ltd.

Raymos, Rick. Fighting for Survival: Predators & Prey. 2014. (ENG.). 24p. (gr. k-3). 28.50 (978-1-62717-638-5(1)) Rourke Educational Media.

Read, Nicholas. City Critters: Wildlife in the Urban Jungle, 1 vol. 2012. (ENG.). 144p. (J). (gr. 3-7). pap. 19.95 (978-1-55469-394-8(2)) Orca Bk. Pubs. USA.

Reade, Clara. Meerkats. 2012. (PowerKids Readers: Safari Animals Ser.). (ENG., Illus.). 24p. (J). (gr. k-2). pap. 8.25 (978-1-4488-7474-3(2)); lib. bdg. 22.60 (978-1-4488-7394-4(0)) Rosen Publishing Group, Inc., The. (PowerKids Pr.).

Reader dsm-3 plant&animal population Ea. 2004. (J). (978-1-59242-524-2(0)) Delta Education, LLC.

Reasoner, Charles. Brrrr! 2009. (Lift & Learn Ser.). (Illus.). 10p. (J). (gr. -1-k). 10.99 (978-1-934650-09-7(9)) Just For Kids Pr., LLC.

—Whooo? 2009. (Lift & Learn Ser.). (Illus.). 10p. (J). (gr. -1-k). 10.99 (978-1-934650-11-0(0)) Just For Kids Pr., LLC.

Record Breaking Animals: Campeones Del Mundo Animal Series, 6 bks., Set. 2003. (Campeones Del Mundo Animal Ser.). (SPA & ENG., Illus.). (J). lib. bdg. 103.50 (978-0-8239-6912-8(6), Editorial Buenas Letras) Rosen Publishing Group, Inc., The.

Reed, Janet. Animal Patterns, 6 vols., Set. 2003. (Yellow Umbrella Early Level Ser.). (ENG.). 16p. (gr. k-1). pap. 35.70 (978-0-7368-2991-5(1), Yellow Umbrella Bks.) Capstone Press of Coughlan Cos.

Reeve, Penny. Himalayan Adventures. 2005. (Adventure Ser.). (ENG., Illus.). 96p. (J). (gr. 3-7). per. 8.99 (978-1-84550-080-1(6), 9781845500801, CF4Kids) Christian Focus Pubns. GBR. Dist: Bookmasters Distribution.

Regan, Lisa. Animal Riddles. 2014. (Riddle Me This! Ser.). 32p. (J). (gr. 1-5). lib. bdg. 27.50 (978-1-4777-9157-8(4)) Windmill Bks.

Reher, Matt. Animals & Tools. 2015. (1B Zoology Magazine Ser.). (ENG., Illus.). 24p. (J). pap. 5.99 (978-1-63437-179-7(8)) American Reading Co.

—Are You in My Family? 2017. (1G Science Ser.). (ENG.). 28p. pap. 5.99 **(978-1-63437-842-0(3))** American Reading Co.

—Savanna Teeth. 2016. (1G Science Ser.). (ENG., Illus.). 28p. (J). pap. 5.99 **(978-1-63437-665-5(X))** American Reading Co.

Reilly, Cherie Brooks, et al. Animal Tales & Tracks: The Feathered & Furry Friends at Reilly's Summer Seat Farm. 2009. (Illus.). 106p. 13.17 (978-1-4251-4734-1(8)) Trafford Publishing.

Remarkable Man & Beast: Facing Survival, 15 vols., Set. Incl. Big Cats. De la Bédoyère, Camilla. (Illus.). lib. bdg. 19.95 (978-1-4222-1965-2(8)); Birds of Prey. De la Bédoyère, Camilla. (Illus.). lib. bdg. 19.95 (978-1-4222-1966-9(6)); Bugs. Parker, Steve. (Illus.). lib. bdg. 19.95 (978-1-4222-1967-6(4)); Elephants. De la Bédoyère, Camilla. (Illus.). lib. bdg. 19.95 (978-1-4222-1968-3(2)); Explorers. North, Dan. (Illus.). lib. bdg. 19.95 (978-1-4222-1969-0(0)); Gladiators. Matthews, Rupert. lib. bdg. 19.95 (978-1-4222-1970-6(4)); Mummies. Malam, John. lib. bdg. 19.95 (978-1-4222-1971-3(2)); Penguins. De la Bédoyère, Camilla. (Illus.). lib. bdg. 19.95 (978-1-4222-1972-0(0)); Samurai. Malam, John. (Illus.). lib. bdg. 19.95 (978-1-4222-1973-7(9)); Sharks. Parker, Steve. (Illus.). lib. bdg. 19.95 (978-1-4222-1974-4(7)); Snakes. Taylor, Barbara. (Illus.). lib. bdg. 19.95 (978-1-4222-1975-1(5)); Special Forces. Farndon, John.

(Illus.). lib. bdg. 19.95 *(978-1-4222-1976-8(3))*; Vikings. Macdonald, Fiona. (Illus.). lib. bdg. 19.95 *(978-1-4222-1977-5(1))*; Wales & Dolphins. Parker, Steve. (Illus.). lib. bdg. 19.95 *(978-1-4222-1978-2(X))*; Warriors. Malam, John. (Illus.). lib. bdg. 19.95 *(978-1-4222-1979-9(8))*. 48p. (J). (gr. 3-18). 2010. 2011. Set lib. bdg. 299.25 *(978-1-4222-1964-5(X))* Mason Crest.

Reyes, Blanca Matilde. Wild Animals. 2006. (Illus.). 16p. (J). act. bk. ed. 0.75 *(978-1-933984-01-8(5))* Two Lands.

Reynolds, Toby & Calver, Paul. Predators. 2015. (Visual Explorers Ser.). (ENG.). 32p. (J). (gr. 3-7). pap. 6.99 *(978-1-4380-0580-5(6))* Barron's Educational Series, Inc.

Rhodes, Lisa. Animals of Africa. 2010. (Pruett Ser.). (ENG.). 32p. (J). pap. 3.95 *(978-0-87108-953-3(X))* Pruett Publishing Co.

—Animals of Mountain West Region. 2010. (Pruett Ser.). (ENG.). 32p. (J). pap. 3.95 *(978-0-87108-956-4(4))* Pruett Publishing Co.

Rice, David L. & Calvert, Trudy L. Do Animals Have Feelings Too? 2004. (Sharing Nature with Children Book Ser.). (Illus.). 32p. (YA). (gr. -1-7). 16.95 *(978-1-58469-003-0(8))* Dawn Pubns.

—Do Animals Have Feelings Too? 2010. (Rise & Shine Ser.). (ENG., Illus.). 32p. (C). (gr. 4-5). pap. 14.95 *(978-1-58469-004-7(6))* National Geographic School Publishing, Inc.

Rice, Dona. Please Don't Feed the Animals. 2015. (Building Fluency Through Reader's Theater Ser.). (ENG., Illus.). 32p. (gr. 3-3). pap. 7.99 *(978-1-4938-1288-2(2))* Teacher Created Materials, Inc.

—Traits for Survival, 1 vol. 2015. (Science Readers: Content & Literacy Ser.). (ENG., Illus.). 32p. (gr. 3-3). pap. 8.99 *(978-1-4807-4639-8(8))* Teacher Created Materials, Inc.

Rice, Dona Herweck. Animal Eyes, 1 vol. 2nd rev. ed. 2011. (TIME for KIDS(r) Nonfiction Readers Ser.). (ENG.). 12p. (J). (gr. 1-1). 4.99 *(978-1-4333-3578-5(6))* Teacher Created Materials, Inc.

—Ojos de Animales, 1 vol. 2nd rev. ed. 2011. (Nonfiction Readers Ser.). (SPA.). 12p. (J). (gr. 1-1). pap. 4.99 *(978-1-4333-4417-6(3))* Teacher Created Materials, Inc.

—Things with Wings, 1 vol. 2nd rev. ed. 2013. (Nonfiction Readers Ser.). (ENG., Illus.). 20p. (J). (gr. 1-1). pap. 19.96 *(978-1-4807-1022-1(9))* Shell Educational Publishing.

Richards, Jon & Simkins, Ed. Record-Breaking Animals. 2015. (Infographic Top 10s Ser.). (ENG., Illus.). 32p. (J). (gr. 4-6). pap. 7.99 *(978-1-4677-9379-7(5)*, Lerner Pubns.) Lerner Publishing Group.

Richter, Bernd & Richter, Susan. Listen to Alaskas Animals. Richter, Bernd, illus. 2003. (Illus.). 12p. bds. 12.95 *(978-1-931353-12-0(3))* Saddle Pal Creations, Inc.

—Touch & Feel Alaskas Animals. 2003. (Illus.). 12p. bds. 9.95 *(978-1-931353-13-7(1))* Saddle Pal Creations, Inc.

Rickus, John. The Animals of Alaska. 2008. (Real Readers - Upper Emergent Ser.). (ENG., Illus.). 12p. (gr. 1-2). pap. 5.90 *(978-0-8239-6361-4(6))* Rosen Publishing Group, Inc., The.

Rieger, Linda. Flying Animals. Bianchi, John, illus. 2006. 20p. (J). *(978-0-9779427-1-8(6))* Pathways into Science.

Riehecky, Janet. Carnotaurus & Other Odd Meat-Eaters: The Need-To-Know Facts. Hughes, Jon, illus. 2016. (Dinosaur Fact Dig Ser.). (ENG.). 32p. (gr. 1-2). lib. bdg. 27.32 *(978-1-5157-2695-1(9))* Capstone Press of Coughlan Cos.

—Poisons & Venom: Animal Weapons & Defenses, 1 vol. 2012. (Animal Weapons & Defenses Ser.). (ENG.). 32p. (gr. 1-2). 26.65 *(978-1-4296-6504-9(1))*; pap. 47.70 *(978-1-4296-8500-9(X))*; pap. 8.10 *(978-1-4296-8008-0(3))* Capstone Press of Coughlan Cos. (Blazers).

—Slime, Poop, & Other Wacky Animal Defenses, 1 vol. 2012. (Animal Weapons & Defenses Ser.). (ENG., Illus.). 32p. (gr. 1-2). 26.65 *(978-1-4296-6509-4(2))*; pap. 8.10 *(978-1-4296-8009-7(1))* Capstone Press of Coughlan Cos. (Blazers).

Rigby Education Staff. Animals: A Is for Animal. (Pebble Soup Explorations Ser.). 16p. (gr. -1-18). 5.00 *(978-0-7635-7047-7(8))* Rigby Education.

—At the Big & Small Zoo. (Illus.). (J). suppl. ed. 20.00 *(978-0-7635-6469-8(9)*, 764699C99) Rigby Education.

—Bugs on the Menu. (Sails Literacy Ser.). (Illus.). 16p. (gr. 2-3). 27.00 *(978-0-7635-9954-6(9)*, 699549C99) Rigby Education.

—Discovery World Yel Animl Leg. (Discovery World Ser.). (Illus.). 12p. (gr. k-1). 23.00 *(978-0-7635-2696-2(7))* Rigby Education.

—The Hiders. (Sails Literacy Ser.). (Illus.). 16p. (gr. 2-3). 27.00 *(978-0-7635-9957-7(3)*, 699573C99) Rigby Education.

—In the Jungle River. (Sails Literacy Ser.). (Illus.). 16p. (gr. 1-2). 27.00 *(978-0-7635-9921-8(2)*, 699212C99) Rigby Education.

—Peekaboo. (Illus.). 8p. (J). bds. 3.95 *(978-0-7635-6464-3(8)*, 764648C99) Rigby Education.

—Spikes, Scales & Armor. (Sails Literacy Ser.). (Illus.). 16p. (gr. 1-2). 27.00 *(978-0-7635-9919-5(0)*, 699190C99) Rigby Education.

—Stomachs. (Sails Literacy Ser.). (Illus.). 16p. (gr. 2-3). 27.00 *(978-0-7635-9960-7(3)*, 699603C99) Rigby Education.

—Using a Tail. (Sails Literacy Ser.). (Illus.). 16p. (gr. 2-3). 27.00 *(978-0-7635-9950-8(6)*, 699506C99) Rigby Education.

Rigg, Jo & Priddy, Roger. My Little Animal Book. 2006. (My Little Bks.). (ENG., Illus.). 28p. (J). (gr. -1-k). bds. 9.95 *(978-0-312-49807-8(1)*, 9780312498078, Priddy Bks.) St. Martin's Pr.

Riggs, Kate. Crowds of Creatures. Dogi, Fiammetta, illus. 2017. (ENG.). 14p. (J). (gr. -1 — 1). bds. 7.99 *(978-1-56846-301-8(4)*, Creative Education) Creative Co., The.

—Wild Backyard. Dogi, Fiammetta, illus. 2016. (ENG.). 14p. (J). (gr. -1 — 1). bds. 7.99 *(978-1-56846-287-5(5)*, Creative Editions) Creative Co., The.

Riggs, Sandy. Habitats of Australia: Text Pairs. 2008. (Bridges/Navigators Ser.). (J). (gr. 3). 94.00 *(978-1-4108-8360-5(4))* Benchmark Education Co.

Riley, Cooper. Absolutely Awesome Island Animals. 2009. 24p. pap. 9.95 *(978-0-9740582-4-5(6))* Tiki Tales.

Riley, Peter. What Animal Is It? 2016. (Ways into Science Ser.). (ENG., Illus.). 32p. (J). (gr. k-2). pap. 11.99 *(978-1-4451-3478-9(0)*, Franklin Watts) Hachette Children's Group GBR. Dist: Hachette Bk. Group.

Ringstad, Arnold. True Stories of Animal Antics. 2014. (True Animal Stories Ser.). (ENG.). 24p. (J). (gr. 1-4). 28.50 *(978-1-62687-356-8(9)*, 207196) Child's World, Inc., The.

—True Stories of Animal Friends. 2014. (True Animal Stories Ser.). (ENG.). 24p. (J). (gr. 1-4). 28.50 *(978-1-62687-357-5(7)*, 207197) Child's World, Inc., The.

—True Stories of Animal Heroes. 2014. (True Animal Stories Ser.). (ENG.). 24p. (J). (gr. 1-4). 28.50 *(978-1-62687-358-2(5)*, 207198) Child's World, Inc., The.

—True Stories of Animal Oddities. 2014. (True Animal Stories Ser.). (ENG.). 24p. (J). (gr. 1-4). 28.50 *(978-1-62687-359-9(3)*, 207199) Child's World, Inc., The.

—True Stories of Animals at Work. 2014. (True Animal Stories Ser.). (ENG.). 24p. (J). (gr. 1-4). 28.50 *(978-1-62687-361-2(5)*, 207201) Child's World, Inc., The.

Ripley's Believe It or Not Editors. Expect the Unexpected: Amazing Animals. 2010. (Ripley's Remarkable & Unexpected Ser.). 36p. (J). (gr. 3-18). lib. bdg. 19.95 *(978-1-4222-2015-3(X))* Mason Crest.

—The Remarkable Revealed: Incredible Animals. (Ripley's Remarkable & Unexpected Ser.). 36p. (J). (gr. 3-18). 2010. lib. bdg. 19.95 *(978-1-4222-2022-1(2))* 2009. pap. 8.95 *(978-1-4222-2056-6(7))* Mason Crest.

Ripley's Believe It or Not Editors & Ripley's Believe It Or Not! Staff. Brutal Beasts. 2013. (Twist Ser.: 9). (ENG.). 48p. (J). (gr. 1-4). 12.95 *(978-1-60991-084-6(2))* Ripley Entertainment, Inc.

Ripley's Believe It Or Not! Staff. Animal Stories. 2013. (Ripley's Believe It or Not! Enter If You Dare Ser.: 8). 36p. (J). (gr. 4-18). 19.95 *(978-1-4222-2771-8(5))* Mason Crest.

—Awesome Animals. 2013. (Ripley's Believe It or Not! Strikingly True Ser.: 8). 36p. (J). (gr. 4-18). 19.95 *(978-1-4222-2772-5(3))* Mason Crest.

—Curious Creatures. 2012. (Ripley's Disbelief & Shock Ser.). 36p. (J). (gr. 3-4). 19.95 *(978-1-4222-2565-3(8))* Mason Crest.

—Fun Animals. 2012. (Ripley's Disbelief & Shock Ser.). 36p. (J). (gr. 3-4). 19.95 *(978-1-4222-2569-1(0))* Mason Crest.

—Ripley Twists: Wild Animals PORTRAIT EDN. 2014. (Twist Ser.). (ENG., Illus.). 48p. (J). 12.95 *(978-1-893951-86-0(3))* Ripley Entertainment, Inc.

Ripley's Believe It Or Not! Staff & Ripley's Believe It Or Not! Editors, compiled by. Crazy Pets & Cute Animals. 2015. (Fun Facts Ser.: 1). (ENG., Illus.). 224p. (J). pap. 8.99 *(978-1-60991-120-1(2))* Ripley Entertainment, Inc.

Ripley's Inc. Staff. Roar! Graziano, John, illus. 2012. (Ripley's Shout Outs Ser.: 1). (ENG.). 96p. (J). (gr. 2-5). pap. 4.99 *(978-0-545-38075-1(8))* Scholastic, Inc.

Rissman, Rebecca. Animals, 1 vol. 2013. (Say What You See Ser.). (ENG.). 24p. (gr. -1-1). 22.65 *(978-1-4109-5046-8(8))*; pap. 7.10 *(978-1-4109-5051-2(4))* Heinemann-Raintree.

—Claws, 1 vol. 2011. (Animal Spikes & Spines Ser.). (ENG.). 24p. (gr. -1-1). 22.65 *(978-1-4329-5039-2(8)*, Acorn) Heinemann-Raintree.

—Horns, 1 vol. 2011. (Animal Spikes & Spines Ser.). (ENG.). 24p. (gr. -1-1). pap. 6.29 *(978-1-4329-5047-7(9))*; 22.65 *(978-1-4329-5040-8(1))* Heinemann-Raintree. (Acorn).

Rivera, Sheila. Wetland. 2005. (First Step Nonfiction Ser.). (Illus.). 23p. (J). (gr. 3-7). lib. bdg. 18.60 *(978-0-8225-2598-1(4)*, Lerner Pubns.) Lerner Publishing Group.

RiverStream Readers - Level 1. 2013. (RiverStream Readers Ser.: 1). 124p. (gr. -1-2). 11.49 *(978-1-62588-901-0(1))* Black Rabbit Bks.

RiverStream Readers - Level 2. 2013. (RiverStream Readers Ser.: 2). 124p. (gr. -1-2). 11.49 *(978-1-62588-902-7(X))* Black Rabbit Bks.

RiverStream Readers - Level 3. 2013. (RiverStream Readers Ser.: 3). 124p. (gr. -1-2). 11.49 *(978-1-62588-903-4(8))* Black Rabbit Bks.

Roachford, Deidre. Rights for Animals? 2005. (Viewpoints (Sea to Sea) Ser.). (Illus.). 32p. (YA). (gr. 5-9). lib. bdg. 27.10 *(978-1-932889-55-0(8))* Sea-To-Sea Pubns.

Roberts, Christa. Guinness World Records: Incredible Animals: Amazing Animals & Their Awesome Feats! 2016. (J). lib. bdg. 16.00 *(978-0-606-38191-8(0))* Turtleback Bks.

Robinson, Francesca. Defenseless World. 2011. 28p. pap. 15.99 *(978-1-4568-8945-6(1))* Xlibris Corp.

Robleda, Margarita. Quien Soy? Adivinanzas Animales. Gurovich, Natalia, illus. 2003. (SPA.). 32p. (J). 12.95 *(978-970-690-805-6(6))* Planeta Mexicana Editorial S. A. de C. V. MEX. Dist: Lectorum Pubns., Inc.

Robson, Gary D. Who Pooped in the Black Hills? Scats & Tracks for Kids. Rath, Robert, illus. 2006. (Who Pooped in the Park? Ser.). 48p. (J). (gr. 3-7). pap. 11.95 *(978-1-56037-387-2(3))* Farcountry Pr.

—Who Pooped in the Park? Yellowstone. 2004. (Illus.). 48p. (J). pap. 11.95 *(978-1-56037-273-8(7))* Farcountry Pr.

—Who Pooped in the Park? Acadia National Park. Rath, Robert, illus. 2006. (Who Pooped in the Park? Ser.). 48p. (J). (gr. -1-3). pap. 11.95 *(978-1-56037-338-4(5))* Farcountry Pr.

—Who Pooped in the Park? Red Rock Canyon National Conservation Area: Scats & Tracks for Kids. Rath, Robert, illus. 2005. (Who Pooped in the Park? Ser.). 48p. (J). (gr. -1-3). pap. 9.95 *(978-1-56037-371-1(7))* Farcountry Pr.

—Who Pooped in the Park? Sequoia & Kings Canyon National Parks: Scats & Tracks for Kids. 2006. (Who Pooped in the Park? Ser.). (Illus.). 48p. (J). (gr. -1-3). pap. 9.95 *(978-1-56037-327-8(X))* Farcountry Pr.

—Who Pooped in the Park? Shenandoah National Park: Scats & Tracks for Kids. Rath, Robert, illus. 2006. (Who Pooped in the Park? Ser.). 48p. (J). (gr. -1-3). pap. *(978-1-56037-339-1(3))* Farcountry Pr.

—Who Pooped in the Sonoran Desert? Scats & Tracks for Kids. Rath, Robert, illus. 2006. (Who Pooped in the Park? Ser.). 48p. (J). (gr. -1-3). pap. 11.95 *(978-1-56037-349-0(0))* Farcountry Pr.

Rockett, Paul. Ten Thousand, Eight Hundred & Twenty Endangered Species in the Animal Kingdom. Ruffle, Mark, illus. 2015. (Big Countdown Ser.). (ENG.). 32p. (gr. 3-5). 29.99 *(978-1-4109-6879-1(0)*, Raintree Perspectives) Heinemann-Raintree.

—30 Million Different Insects in the Rain Forest. Ruffle, Mark, illus. 2015. (Big Countdown Ser.). (ENG.). 32p. (gr. 3-5). 29.99 *(978-1-4109-6876-0(6)*, Raintree Perspectives) Heinemann-Raintree.

Rockwood, Leigh. Creepy Crawlies, 6 vols., Set. Incl. Centipedes & Millipedes Are Gross! Clark, Willow. (J). lib. bdg. 22.60 *(978-1-4488-0701-7(8))*; Flies & Maggots Are Gross! (J). lib. bdg. 22.60 *(978-1-4488-0703-1(4))*; Salamanders Are Gross! Clark, Willow. (J). lib. bdg. 22.60 *(978-1-4488-0702-4(6))*; Slugs Are Gross! (YA). 22.60 *(978-1-4488-0704-8(2))*; Snails Are Gross! Clark, Willow. (J). lib. bdg. 22.60 *(978-1-4488-0699-7(2))*; Worms Are Gross! Clark, Willow. (YA). lib. bdg. 22.60 *(978-1-4488-0700-0(X))*; (gr. k-2). (Illus.). 24p. 2010. Set lib. bdg. 127.50 *(978-1-4488-0778-9(6)*, PowerKids Pr.) Rosen Publishing Group, Inc., The.

RodríGuez, Ana María. Polar Bears, Penguins, & Other Mysterious Animals of the Extreme Cold. 2012. (Extreme Animals in Extreme Environments Ser.). (Illus.). 48p. (J). (gr. 5-18). pap. 8.95 *(978-1-4644-0017-9(2))* Enslow Pubs., Inc.

Rodríguez, Ana María. Polar Bears, Penguins, & Other Mysterious Animals of the Extreme Cold. 2012. (Extreme Animals in Extreme Environments Ser.). (Illus.). 48p. (J). (gr. 5-18). 25.27 *(978-0-7660-3695-6(2))* Enslow Pubs., Inc.

RodríGuez, Ana María. Vampire Bats, Giant Insects, & Other Mysterious Animals of the Darkest Caves. 2012. (Extreme Animals in Extreme Environments Ser.). (Illus.). 48p. (J). (gr. 5-18). 25.27 *(978-0-7660-3698-7(7))* Enslow Pubs., Inc.

Rodríguez, Ana María. Vampire Bats, Giant Insects, & Other Mysterious Animals of the Darkest Caves. 2012. (Extreme Animals in Extreme Environments Ser.). (Illus.). 48p. (J). (gr. 5-18). pap. 8.95 *(978-1-4644-0018-6(0))* Enslow Pubs., Inc.

Rogers, Simon. Information Graphics: Animal Kingdom. Blechman, Nicholas, illus. 2014. (ENG.). 80p. (J). (gr. 1-4). 17.99 *(978-0-7636-7122-8(3)*, Big Picture Press) Candlewick Pr.

Rogge, Robie & Smith, Dian G. Animals in the Stars Lacing Cards. 2014. (ENG., Illus.). 10p. (J). (gr. -1-k). 16.99 *(978-1-4521-3741-4(2))* Chronicle Bks. LLC.

Rohr, Ian. Biggest, Highest, Fastest. 2005. 32p. (J). lib. bdg. 13.95 *(978-0-7608-6689-4(9))* Sundance/Newbridge Educational Publishing.

Rohrer, Martha. Animals, Animals, Animals. 2004. (Illus.). 32p. (gr. -1-5). 1.70 *(978-0-7399-2348-1(X)*, 2950) Rod & Staff Pubs., Inc.

Romero, Libby. Characteristics of Animals. 2006. (J). pap. *(978-1-4108-6481-9(2))* Benchmark Education Co.

—Discover Animals. 2006. (J). pap. *(978-1-4108-6484-0(7))* Benchmark Education Co.

Rooney, Anne. Layer by Layer: into the Wild. Carpenter, Suzanne, illus. 2016. (Layer by Layer Ser.). (ENG.). 32p. (J). (gr. k). 19.99 *(978-1-62686-751-2(8)*, Silver Dolphin Bks.) Readerlink Distribution Services, LLC.

—A Math Journey Through the Animal Kingdom. 2014. (ENG.). 32p. (J). *(978-0-7787-0732-5(6))* Crabtree Publishing Co.

Roop, Peter & Roop, Connie. Down East in the Ocean: A Maine Counting Book. 2011. (ENG., Illus.). 32p. (J). (gr. -1-3). 16.95 *(978-0-89272-709-4(8))* Down East Bks.

Rose, Elizabeth. Animal Adaptations for Survival. 2006. (Life Science Library). (Illus.). 24p. (YA). (gr. 3-6). lib. bdg. 22.60 *(978-1-4042-2817-7(9))* Rosen Publishing Group, Inc., The.

Rose, Naomi C. Where Snow Leopard Prowls: Wild Animals of Tibet. Rose, Naomi C., illus. 2013. (ENG., Illus.). 32p. (J). 17.95 *(978-0-9836333-0-3(4))* Dancing Dakini Pr.

Rosen Publishing Staff. Animal Cannibals, 1 vol. 2015. (Animal Cannibals Ser.). (ENG.). 24p. (J). 141.60 *(978-1-4777-5734-5(1)*, PowerKids Pr.) Rosen Publishing Group, Inc., The.

—Glow-In-the-Dark Animals, 1 vol. 2015. (Glow-In-the-Dark Animals Ser.). (ENG.). 24p. (J). 141.60 *(978-1-4777-5735-2(X)*, PowerKids Pr.) Rosen Publishing Group, Inc., The.

—The Wild Side, 1 vol. 2015. (Wild Side Ser.). (ENG.). 24p. (J). 188.80 *(978-1-4777-5456-6(3)*, Windmill Bks.) Rosen Publishing Group, Inc., The.

Rosenberg, Pam. Ack! Icky, Sticky, Gross Stuff Underground. Ramos, Beatriz Helena, illus. 2007. (Icky, Sticky, Gross-Out Bks.). (ENG.). 24p. (J). (gr. 3-6). 27.07 *(978-1-59296-900-5(3)*, 200353) Child's World, Inc., The.

—Yuck! Icky, Sticky, Gross Stuff in Your Garden. Ramos, Beatriz Helena, illus. 2007. (Icky, Sticky, Gross-Out Bks.). (ENG.). 24p. (J). (gr. 3-6). 27.07 *(978-1-59296-896-1(1)*, 200359) Child's World, Inc., The.

Rosewarne, Graham, et al, illus. Discover the Amazing World of Animals. 87p. (J). *(978-1-902272-27-6(7))* Tucker Slingsby, Ltd.

Ross, Samuel B., Jr. The Extraordinary Spirit of Green Chimneys: Connecting Children & Animals to Create Hope. 2011. (ENG., Illus.). 268p. 24.95 *(978-1-55753-580-1(9)*, f4620000-a1e9-429e-8b9a-e198a58f775f) Purdue Univ. Pr.

Roth, Ruby. Vegan Is Love: Having Heart & Taking Action. Roth, Ruby, illus. 2012. (ENG., Illus.). 44p. (J). (gr. 2-5). 16.95 *(978-1-58394-354-0(4))* North Atlantic Bks.

Rowe, Brooke. What's Your Spirit Animal? 2016. (Illus.). 32p. (J). *(978-1-63470-510-3(6))* Cherry Lake Publishing.

Royston, Angela. Adapted to Survive: Animals That Climb, 1 vol. 2014. (Adapted to Survive Ser.). (ENG., Illus.). 32p. (gr. 1-3). lib. bdg. 29.99 *(978-1-4109-6148-8(6)*, Read Me!) Heinemann-Raintree.

—Adapted to Survive: Animals That Fly, 1 vol. 2014. (Adapted to Survive Ser.). (ENG., Illus.). 32p. (gr. 1-3). lib. bdg. 29.99 *(978-1-4109-6147-1(8)*, Read Me!) Heinemann-Raintree.

—Amphibians. 2015. (Animal Classifications Ser.). (ENG., Illus.). 32p. (gr. 1-3). 27.32 *(978-1-4846-0749-7(X)*, Heinemann First Library) Heinemann-Raintree.

—Animal Classification. 2013. (Life Science Stories Ser.). (Illus.). 32p. (J). (gr. 3-5). pap. 10.50 *(978-1-4339-8704-5(X))*; lib. bdg. 26.60 *(978-1-4339-8703-8(1))* Stevens, Gareth Publishing LLLP.

—Animal Classifications. 2015. (Animal Classifications Ser.). (ENG.). 32p. (gr. 1-3). lib. bdg. 163.92 *(978-1-4846-0755-8(4)*, Heinemann First Library) Heinemann-Raintree.

—Birds. 2015. (Animal Classifications Ser.). (ENG., Illus.). 32p. (gr. 1-3). 27.32 *(978-1-4846-0750-3(3)*, Heinemann First Library) Heinemann-Raintree.

—Fish. 2015. (Animal Classifications Ser.). (ENG., Illus.). 32p. (gr. 1-3). 27.32 *(978-1-4846-0751-0(1)*, Heinemann First Library) Heinemann-Raintree.

—Grassland Food Chains, 1 vol. 2014. (Food Chains & Webs Ser.). (ENG., Illus.). 32p. (gr. 1-3). 27.32 *(978-1-4846-0522-6(5)*, Heinemann First Library) Heinemann-Raintree.

—Invertebrates. 2015. (Animal Classifications Ser.). (ENG.). 32p. (gr. 1-3). 27.32 *(978-1-4846-0752-7(X)*, Heinemann First Library) Heinemann-Raintree.

—Mammals. 2015. (Animal Classifications Ser.). (ENG., Illus.). 32p. (gr. 1-3). 27.32 *(978-1-4846-0753-4(8)*, Heinemann First Library) Heinemann-Raintree.

—Mountain Food Chains, 1 vol. 2014. (Food Chains & Webs Ser.). (ENG., Illus.). 32p. (gr. 1-3). 27.32 *(978-1-4846-0519-6(5)*, Heinemann First Library) Heinemann-Raintree.

—Reptiles. 2015. (Animal Classifications Ser.). (ENG., Illus.). 32p. (gr. 1-3). 27.32 *(978-1-4846-0754-1(6)*, Heinemann First Library) Heinemann-Raintree.

Roza, Greg. Armed & Dangerous, 6 vols., Set. Incl. Chomp! The Great White Shark & Other Animals That Bite. (J). lib. bdg. 22.60 *(978-1-4488-2551-6(2))*; Phew! The Skunk & Other Stinky Animals. (YA). lib. bdg. 22.60 *(978-1-4488-2549-3(0))*; Poison! The Spitting Cobra & Other Venomous Animals. (YA). lib. bdg. 22.60 *(978-1-4488-2550-9(4))*; Poke! The Sea Urchin & Other Animals with Spikes. (YA). lib. bdg. 22.60 *(978-1-4488-2552-3(0))*; Sting! The Scorpion & Other Animals That Sting. (J). 22.60 *(978-1-4488-2548-6(2))*; Zap! The Electric Eel & Other Electric Animals. (YA). 22.60 *(978-1-4488-2547-9(4))*; (gr. 1-4). (Armed & Dangerous Ser.). (Illus.). 24p. 2011. Set lib. bdg. 127.50 *(978-1-4488-2780-0(9)*, PowerKids Pr.) Rosen Publishing Group, Inc., The.

—Chomp! The Great White Shark & Other Animals That Bite. 2011. (Armed & Dangerous Ser.). (Illus.). 24p. (J). pap. 8.25 *(978-1-4488-2686-5(1)*, PowerKids Pr.); (gr. 1-4). lib. bdg. 22.60 *(978-1-4488-2551-6(2))* Rosen Publishing Group, Inc., The.

RSPB Wild Nature Colouring Book. 2013. (ENG., Illus.). 48p. pap. 7.95 *(978-1-4081-9249-8(7)*, 9781408192498, A&C Black Childrens & Educational) Bloomsbury Publishing Plc GBR. Dist: Macmillan.

Runnells, Treesha. Forest Friends: A Fold-Out Fun Book. Runnells, Treesha, illus. 2005. (Fold-Out Fun Ser.). (Illus.). 10p. (J). 4.95 *(978-1-58117-275-1(3)*, Intervisual/Piggy Toes) Bendon, Inc.

—Safari Friends: Fold-Out Fun. Runnells, Treesha, illus. 2005. (Fold-Out Fun Ser.). (Illus.). 10p. (J). 4.95 *(978-1-58117-276-8(1)*, Intervisual/Piggy Toes) Bendon, Inc.

Rushworth, Gary. What Makes a Human a Human: Text Pairs. 2008. (Bridges/Navigators Ser.). (J). (gr. 4). 89.00 *(978-1-4108-8399-5(X))* Benchmark Education Co.

—What Makes an Animal an Animal: Text Pairs. 2008. (Bridges/Navigators Ser.). (J). (gr. 4). 89.00 *(978-1-4108-8401-5(5))* Benchmark Education Co.

Rustad, Martha E. H. All about Animals in Winter. 2015. (Celebrate Winter Ser.). (ENG., Illus.). 24p. (gr. k-1). lib. bdg. 21.99 *(978-1-4914-6005-4(9)*, Pebble Bks.) Capstone Press of Coughlan Cos.

—Animal Camouflage in the Snow [Scholastic]. 2010. (Hidden in Nature Ser.). pap. 0.52 *(978-1-4296-5049-6(4)*, Pebble Plus) Capstone Press of Coughlan Cos.

—Animals in Spring. 2012. (All about Spring Ser.). (ENG.). 24p. (gr. k-1). pap. 41.70 *(978-1-4296-9360-8(6))*; (Illus.). 26.65 *(978-1-4296-8655-6(3))*; (Illus.). pap. 7.29 *(978-1-4296-9358-5(4))* Capstone Press of Coughlan Cos. (Pebble Plus).

—Animals Working Together, 4 vols., Set. Incl. Clown Fish & Sea Anemones Work Together. lib. bdg. 26.65 *(978-1-4296-5297-1(7))*; Moray Eels & Cleaner Shrimp Work Together. lib. bdg. 26.65 *(978-1-4296-5299-5(3))*; (gr. k-1). (Animals Working Together Ser.). (ENG.). 24p. 2010. Set lib. bdg. 53.30 *(978-1-4296-5301-5(9)*, Pebble Plus) Capstone Press of Coughlan Cos.

—Do Trees Get Hungry? Noticing Plant & Animal Traits. Moran, Mike, illus. 2015. (Cloverleaf Books (tm) — Nature's Patterns Ser.). (ENG.). 24p. (gr. k-2). pap. 6.99 *(978-1-4677-8605-8(5)*, Millbrook Pr.) Lerner Publishing Group.

—Elephants Are Awesome! 2015. (Awesome African Animals! Ser.). (ENG.). 32p. (gr. 1-2). lib. bdg. 27.32 *(978-1-4914-1760-7(9))* Capstone Press of Coughlan Cos.

—On a Safari 5, 10, 15: A Counting by Fives Book. 2017. (1, 2, 3 Count with Me Ser.). (ENG., Illus.). 24p. (J). (gr. k-2). pap. 8.99 *(978-1-68152-113-8(X))* Amicus.

—On a Safari 5, 10, 15: A Counting by Fives Book. 2016. (1, 2, 3 Count with Me Ser.). (ENG., Illus.). 24p. (J). (gr. k-3). 20.95 *(978-1-60753-922-3(5))* Amicus Publishing.

—What's in a Cave? 2015. (What's in There? Ser.). (ENG., Illus.). 24p. (gr. k-1). lib. bdg. 21.99 *(978-1-4914-6009-2(1)*, Pebble Bks.) Capstone Press of Coughlan Cos.

—What's in a Pond? 2015. (What's in There? Ser.). (ENG., Illus.). 24p. (gr. k-1). lib. bdg. 21.99 *(978-1-4914-6010-8(5)*, Pebble Bks.) Capstone Press of Coughlan Cos.

—What's in the Dirt? 2015. (What's in There? Ser.). (ENG., Illus.). 24p. (gr. k-1). lib. bdg. 21.99 *(978-1-4914-6012-2(1)*, Pebble Bks.) Capstone Press of Coughlan Cos.

—What's in There? 2015. (What's in There? Ser.). (ENG.). 24p. (gr. k-1). 87.96 *(978-1-4914-6919-4(6)*, Pebble Bks.) Capstone Press of Coughlan Cos.

—World's Longest Snake & Other Animal Records. 2013. (Wow! Ser.). (ENG.). 24p. (gr. k-1). 26.65 *(978-1-4765-0258-8(7)*, Pebble Plus) Capstone Press of Coughlan Cos.

Rustad, Martha E. H. & Morey, Allan. Awesome Asian Animals. 2015. (Awesome Asian Animals Ser.). (ENG.). 32p. (gr. 1-2). 163.92 *(978-1-4914-6631-5(6)*, Aplus Bks.) Capstone Press of Coughlan Cos.

Ruurs, Margriet. In My Backyard. Broda, Ron, illus. 2007. (ENG.). 32p. (J). (gr. -1-3). 18.95 *(978-0-88776-775-3(3)*, Tundra Bks.) Tundra Bks. CAN. Dist: Penguin Random Hse. LLC.

Ryals, Katherine. Storytime Stickers: Baby Animals at Play. Berlin, Rose Mary, illus. 2010. (Storytime Stickers Ser.). (ENG.). 16p. (J). (gr. k-2). pap. 5.95 *(978-1-4027-5933-8(9))* Sterling Publishing Co., Inc.

Saaf, Donald. The ABC Animal Orchestra. Saaf, Donald, illus. 2015. (ENG., Illus.). 40p. (J). (gr. -1 — 1). 16.99

(978-0-8050-9072-7(X), 9780805090727, Holt, Henry & Co. Bks. For Young Readers) Holt, Henry & Co.

Sabatino, Chris. Animal Doodles for Kids, 1 vol. 2013. (ENG., Illus.). 240p. pap. 9.99 *(978-1-4236-3457-7(8))* Gibbs Smith, Publisher.

Sadan, Dana. Animals of the Rain Forest. 2008. (Reading Rocks! Ser.). (ENG., Illus.). 32p. (J). (gr. 2-5). 28.50 *(978-1-60253-094-2(7)*, 200757) Child's World, Inc., The.

Saddleback, creator. Animal World. 2008. (Factoscope Ser.). (Illus.). 64p. (YA). (gr. 8-12). per. 10.95 *(978-1-59905-232-8(6))* Saddleback Educational Publishing, Inc.

Salas, Laura Purdie. Many Creatures: A Song about Animal Classifications, 1 vol. De Giorgi, Sergio, illus. 2010. (Science Songs Ser.). (ENG.). 24p. (gr. 1-3). lib. bdg. 26.65 *(978-1-4048-5763-6(X))* Picture Window Bks.

—Y Is for Yak: A Zoo Alphabet, 1 vol. 2010. (Alphabet Fun Ser.). (ENG.). 32p. (gr. 1-2). lib. bdg. 27.32 *(978-1-4296-4465-5(6)*, Aplus Bks.) Capstone Press of Coughlan Cos.

Salzano, Tammi J., et al. Animal Friends. 2009. (Illus.). 32p. (J). *(978-0-545-13901-4(5))* Scholastic, Inc.

Salzmann, Mary Elizabeth. Know Your Numbers: Animals, 1 vol. 2014. (Numbers 1-20 Ser.). (ENG.). 24p. (J). (gr. k-3). lib. bdg. 24.21 *(978-1-62403-264-6(8)*, SandCastle) ABDO Publishing Co.

—What Has a Tail?, 1 vol. 2007. (Creature Features Ser.). (ENG., Illus.). 24p. (gr. -1-3). 25.65 *(978-1-59928-874-1(5)*, Super SandCastle) ABDO Publishing Co.

—What Has Claws?, 1 vol. 2007. (Creature Features Ser.). (ENG., Illus.). 24p. (gr. -1-3). 25.65 *(978-1-59928-865-9(6)*, Super SandCastle) ABDO Publishing Co.

—What Has Fur?, 1 vol. 2007. (Creature Features Ser.). (ENG., Illus.). 24p. (gr. -1-3). 25.65 *(978-1-59928-866-6(4)*, Super SandCastle) ABDO Publishing Co.

—What Has Hooves?, 1 vol. 2007. (Creature Features Ser.). (ENG., Illus.). 24p. (gr. -1-3). 25.65 *(978-1-59928-867-3(2)*, Super SandCastle) ABDO Publishing Co.

—What Has Webbed Feet?, 1 vol. 2007. (Creature Features Ser.). (ENG., Illus.). 24p. (gr. -1-3). 25.65 *(978-1-59928-875-8(3)*, Super SandCastle) ABDO Publishing Co.

Samoun, Abigail. Little Traveler's Library: Four Adventures in Eight Languages. Watts, Sarah, illus. 2016. (Little Traveler Ser.). (ENG.). 88p. (J). (gr. -1-k). 12.95 *(978-1-4549-2006-9(8))* Sterling Publishing Co., Inc.

Samson, Tess. Animals on the Farm. 2010. (Sight Word Readers Ser.). (J). 3.49 *(978-1-60719-619-8(0))* Newmark Learning LLC.

San Diego Zoo Staff. Animal ABC's San Diego Zoo. 2004. (ENG., Illus.). 20p. (J). 7.95 *(978-0-8249-6551-8(5)*, Ideal Pubns.) Worthy Publishing.

Sanchez, Richard. Animales (Animals) (SPA.). (J). 4.95 *(978-84-243-2173-4(1))* Publicaciones Fher, S.A. ESP. Dist: AIMS International Bks., Inc.

Sargent, Daina. Colors & the Number 2, 11 vols. Lenoir, Jane, illus. 2004. (Learn to Read Ser.: 11). 24p. (J). pap. 10.95 *(978-1-59381-033-7(4))* Ozark Publishing.

Scarry, Richard. Richard Scarry's the Rooster Struts. 2015. (ENG., Illus.). 26p. (J). (— 1). bds. 7.99 *(978-0-553-50852-9(0)*, Golden Bks.) Random Hse. Children's Bks.

Scary Creatures, 4 vols., Set. Incl. Scary Creatures of the City. Clarke, Penny. Baker, Janet, illus. 27.00 *(978-0-531-21820-4(1))*; Scary Creatures of the Deep. Pipe, Jim. Bergin, Mark, illus. 27.00 *(978-0-531-21822-8(8))*; Scary Creatures of the River. Cheshire, Gerard. Francis, John et al, illus. 27.00 *(978-0-531-21823-5(6))*; Scary Creatures of the Soil. Cheshire, Gerard. Antram, David, illus. 27.00 *(978-0-531-21821-1(X))*; 32p. (J). (gr. 2-4). 2009. 2009. Set lib. bdg. 104.00 *(978-0-531-26139-2(5)*, Watts, Franklin) Scholastic Library Publishing.

Schaefer, Lola M. Hidden Dangers: Seek & Find 13 of the World's Deadliest Animals. Armstrong, Tymn, illus. 2017. (ENG.). 40p. (J). (gr. k-3). 16.99 *(978-1-4521-3429-1(4))* Chronicle Bks. LLC.

—Lifetime: The Amazing Numbers in Animal Lives. Neal, Christopher Silas, illus. 2016. (ENG.). 40p. (J). (gr. k-3). 7.99 *(978-1-4521-5210-3(1))* Chronicle Bks. LLC.

Schaefer, Lola M. & Miller, Heather Lynn. Look Behind! Tales of Animal Ends. Manning, Jane K., illus. 2008. 32p. (J). (gr. -1-3). lib. bdg. 17.89 *(978-0-06-088394-2(4)*, Greenwillow Bks.) HarperCollins Pubs.

Schafer, Susan. Invasive Mammals. 2016. (Invasive Species Ser.). (ENG.). 48p. (J). (gr. 4-4). 31.36 *(978-1-5026-1832-0(X))* Cavendish Square Publishing.

Schemenauer, Patty Ann. Alphabet Fun at the Zoo. 2011. 32p. 14.39 *(978-1-4567-0146-8(0))* AuthorHouse.

Schieber, Jennifer. Animals in Motion. 2004. (Shared Connections Ser.). (J). instr.'s gde. ed. 27.00 *(978-1-4108-1606-1(0))* Benchmark Education Co.

—Animals in Motion: Small Book. 2004. (Shared Connections Ser.). (J). pap. *(978-1-4108-1630-6(3))* Benchmark Education Co.

Scholastic Clubs US Animal Kingdom Pack #2: Animal Lives. 2006. (J). 44.75 *(978-1-59566-324-5(X))* QEB Publishing Inc.

Scholastic Clubs US Animal Kingdom Pack #3: Animal Lives. 2007. (J). 44.75 *(978-1-59566-327-6(4))* QEB Publishing Inc.

Scholastic Inc, contrib. by. Amazing Animals. 2017. (Words Are Fun Ser.). (ENG.). 12p. (J). bds. 8.95 *(978-0-531-23722-9(2)*, Children's Pr.) Scholastic Library Publishing.

Scholastic Inc. (US) Staff, contrib. by. Amazing Animals/ Animales Increíbles. 2017. (Words Are Fun/ Diverpalabras (Bilingual) Ser.). (ENG.). 12p. (J). bds. 8.95 *(978-0-531-23072-5(4)*, Children's Pr.) Scholastic Library Publishing.

Scholastic, Inc. Staff. Carry & Learn Colors. Ward, Sarah G., illus. 2015. (ENG.). 10p. (J). (gr. -1 — 1). bds. 7.99 *(978-0-545-78385-9(2)*, Cartwheel Bks.) Scholastic, Inc.

—Carry & Learn Numbers. Ward, Sarah G., illus. 2015. (ENG.). 10p. (J). (— 1). bds. 7.99 *(978-0-545-79790-0(X)*, Cartwheel Bks.) Scholastic, Inc.

—First 100 Animals. 2016. (Scholastic Early Learners Ser.). (ENG.). 12p. (J). (gr. -1 — 1). bds. 6.99 *(978-0-545-90342-4(4))* Scholastic, Inc.

—Slide & Find ABC Animals. 2016. (Scholastic Early Learners Ser.). (ENG.). 10p. (J). (gr. -1 — 1). bds. 9.99 *(978-0-545-90344-8(0))* Scholastic, Inc.

—Woof! 2016. (Scholastic Early Learners Ser.). (ENG.). 12p. (J). (gr. -1-k). bds. 9.99 *(978-0-545-90340-0(8))* Scholastic, Inc.

School Zone. Animal Alphabet. 2008. (ENG.). 26p. (J). 5.99 *(978-1-58947-932-6(7))* School Zone Publishing Co.

School Zone Staff. Animals of All Kinds. 2004. (ENG.). 32p. (J). 12.99 *(978-1-58947-473-4(2)*, 03604) School Zone Publishing Co.

—Bilingual Animals of All Kinds. 2004. (ENG.). 56p. (J). 2.99 *(978-1-58947-989-0(0))* School Zone Publishing Co.

Schrier, Allyson Valentine. Fast as a Cheetah, Slow as a Sloth. 2008. (Discovering & Exploring Science Ser.). (Illus.). 16p. (J). (gr. -1-3). lib. bdg. 12.95 *(978-0-7569-8417-5(3))* Perfection Learning Corp.

—How Many in All? 2008. (Discovering & Exploring Science Ser.). (Illus.). 16p. (J). (gr. -1-3). lib. bdg. 12.95 *(978-0-7569-8423-6(8))* Perfection Learning Corp.

Schubert, Dieter. Opposites. Schubert, Dieter, illus. 2013. (ENG., Illus.). 32p. (J). (gr. -1). 17.95 *(978-1-935954-26-2(1)*, 9781935954262) Lemniscaat USA.

Schuetz, Kari. Life in a Tropical Rain Forest. 2016. (Biomes Alive! Ser.). (ENG., Illus.). 24p. (J). (gr. k-3). lib. bdg. 25.95 *(978-1-62617-320-0(6)*, Blastoff! Readers) Bellwether Media.

Schuh, Mari. Animals in the Garden. 2010. (Gardens Ser.). (ENG.). 24p. (gr. k-1). pap. 35.70 *(978-1-4296-5152-3(0))*; lib. bdg. 21.99 *(978-1-4296-3982-8(2))* Capstone Press of Coughlan Cos. (Pebble Bks.).

—Backyard Animals. 2015. (Backyard Animals Ser.). (ENG.). 24p. (gr. k-1). lib. bdg. 106.60 *(978-1-4914-2562-6(8)*, Pebble Plus) Capstone Press of Coughlan Cos.

Schumacher, Bev. Critters. 2007. 20p. (J). lib. bdg. 9.95 *(978-0-9768706-6-1(5))* Learning Props.

—Critters (Chinese/English) 2012. 20p. (J). pap. 8.95 *(978-1-935292-46-3(3))* Learning Props.

Schur, Maxine Rose. There's a Babirusa in My Bathtub: Fact & Fancy about Curious Creatures, 1 vol. Maydak, Michael S., illus. 2009. (ENG.). 32p. (J). (gr. 2-7). 16.95 *(978-1-58469-117-4(4))* Dawn Pubns.

—There's a Babirusa in My Bathtub: Fact & Fancy about Curious Creatures. Maydak, Michael, illus. 2009. 32p. (J). (gr. 2-7). pap. 8.95 *(978-1-58469-118-1(2))* Dawn Pubns.

Schwartz, David M. & Schy, Yael. Where Else in the Wild? Kuhn, Dwight, illus. Kuhn, Dwight, photos by. 2009. (ENG.). 50p. (J). (gr. -1-2). 16.99 *(978-1-58246-283-7(6)*, Tricycle Pr.) Random Hse. Children's Bks.

Schy, Yael & Schwartz, David. What in the Wild? Mysteries of Nature Concealed... And Revealed. Kuhn, Dwight, photos by. 2010. (ENG., Illus.). 44p. (J). (gr. 1-4). 16.99 *(978-1-58246-310-0(7)*, Tricycle Pr.) Random Hse. Children's Bks.

Science & Technology for Children's Books, Animal Studies Set, 8 vols. 2004. (Illus.). 64p. (J). *(978-1-933008-12-7(1))* Smithsonian Science Education Ctr. (SSEC).

Scollen, Chris. Busy Kids Baby Animals Sticker Activity Book. 2008. (Busy Kids Ser.). (Illus.). 12p. (J). (gr. -1-3). pap. *(978-1-84610-636-1(2))* Make Believe Ideas.

Scott, Peter David, illus. Amazing Animals: A Nature Adventure. 2015. (Peter David Scott Ser.). (ENG.). 64p. (gr. -1). 16.95 *(978-1-62686-323-1(7)*, Silver Dolphin Bks.) Readerlink Distribution Services, LLC.

Scott-Royce, Brenda & Roth, Megan. Smithsonian Readers: Ultimate Predators Level 3. 2016. (Smithsonian Readers Ser.). (ENG., Illus.). 132p. (J). (gr. k). pap. 7.99 *(978-1-62686-761-1(5)*, Silver Dolphin Bks.) Readerlink Distribution Services, LLC.

Sebastiani, Laura, creator. Penny & Drew's Penciltips: Animal Alliteration. 2006. 80p. (J). 4.95 *(978-0-9766793-1-8(0))* ThoughtRockets, Inc.

Seder, Rufus Butler. ABC Animals!: a Scanimation Picture Book. 2016. (Scanimation Ser.). (ENG., Illus.). 16p. (J). 16.95 *(978-0-7611-7782-1(5))* Workman Publishing Co., Inc.

Seidensticker, John & Lumpkin, Susan. Predators. 2008. (Insiders Ser.). Orig. Title: Thinning the Predators. (ENG., Illus.). 64p. (J). (gr. 3-7). 17.99 *(978-1-4169-3863-7(X)*, Simon & Schuster Bks. For Young Readers) Simon & Schuster Bks. For Young Readers.

Seidlitz, Lauri. Animals. 2007. (Life Science (Weigl Hardcover) Ser.). (Illus.). 32p. (J). (gr. 4-7). lib. bdg. 26.00 *(978-1-59036-701-8(4))*; per. 9.95 *(978-1-59036-702-5(2))* Weigl Pubs., Inc.

Selwyn, Josephine. How Do I Move? 2014. (Little Books of Answers: Level a Ser.). (Illus.). 16p. (gr. k-2). pap. 7.95 *(978-1-927136-09-6(1))* Three Crows Media NZL. Dist: RiverStream Publishing.

Sen, Benita. Polar Creatures. (Wild Creatures Ser.). 48p. 2009. (gr. 4-5). 53.00 *(978-1-60854-791-3(4)*, PowerKids Pr.) 2007. (Illus.). (YA). (gr. 3-6). lib. bdg. 29.25 *(978-1-4042-3892-3(1))* Rosen Publishing Group, Inc., The.

—Rainforest Creatures. 2007. (Wild Creatures Ser.). (Illus.). 48p. (J). (gr. 3-7). lib. bdg. 29.25 *(978-1-4042-3893-0(X)*, PowerKids Pr.) Rosen Publishing Group, Inc., The.

Serafini, Frank. The Garden. Serafini, Frank, illus. 2008. (Looking Closely Ser.). (ENG., Illus.). 40p. (J). (gr. -1-2). 16.95 *(978-1-55453-210-0(8))* Kids Can Pr., Ltd. CAN. Dist: Hachette Bk. Group.

Sesame Street Staff, creator. Sesame Street: Early Learning Boxed Set. 2011. 72p. (J). bds. 12.99 *(978-1-60745-237-9(5))* Flying Frog Pubs.

Sesame Workshop. Toddler Time Explore Animals with Elmo. 2011. (J). (gr. k-1). pap. 3.99 *(978-1-59922-882-2(3))* Twin Sisters IP, LLC.

Seto, Alex. What Do You See? Touch My Nose, It Feels Funny. 2006. (Illus.). 14p. bds. *(978-0-9734496-4-8(0))* ADVAN Pr., Inc.

Seton, Ernest Thompson. The Trail of the Sandhill Stag. Seton, Ernest Thompson, illus. 2007. (Illus.). 94p. (YA). pap. 16.95 *(978-1-60355-055-0(0))* Juniper Grove.

Seton, Ernest Thompson, et al. Books about Animals. 2004. cd-rom 25.00 *(978-0-931968-83-9(6))* Samizdat Express.

Seuling, Barbara. Cows Sweat Through Their Noses: And Other Freaky Facts about Animal Habits, Characteristics, & Homes. Skeens, Matthew, illus. 2010. (Freaky Facts Ser.). 40p. pap. 0.50 *(978-1-4048-6200-5(5)*, Nonfiction Picture Bks.) Picture Window Bks.

Shannon, Jason. Three Things about Animals... And Only One of Them's True! Hartter, Sean, illus. 2nd rev. ed. 2008. (J). per. 12.95 *(978-0-9790889-4-0(1))* CatsCurious Pr.

Shaw-Russell, Susan. Animal ABC. 2011. (Dover Sticker Bks.). (ENG., Illus.). 4p. (J). (gr. 1-5). 7.99 *(978-0-486-48396-2(7))* Dover Pubns., Inc.

—Seek, Sketch & Color — Animals. 2013. (Dover Children's Activity Bks.). (ENG.). 64p. (J). (gr. 1-3). pap. 5.99 *(978-0-486-49773-0(9))* Dover Pubns., Inc.

Shea, Nicole. Animals & Climate Change. 2013. (Animal 911: Environmental Threats Ser.). 48p. (J). (gr. 3-5). pap. 84.30 *(978-1-4339-9704-4(5))*; pap. 14.05 *(978-1-4339-9703-7(7))*; (ENG., Illus.). lib. bdg. 31.95 *(978-1-4339-9702-0(9))* Stevens, Gareth Publishing LLLP.

—Poaching & Illegal Trade. 2013. (Animal 911: Environmental Threats Ser.). 48p. (J). (gr. 3-5). pap. 84.30 *(978-1-4339-9720-4(7))*; (ENG., Illus.). lib. bdg. 31.95 *(978-1-4339-9718-1(5))* Stevens, Gareth Publishing LLLP.

Shea, Therese. Do Cows Have Two Stomachs? And Other FAQs about Animals. 2016. (Q & a: Life's Mysteries Solved! Ser.). 32p. (J). (gr. 4-3). lib. bdg. 26.60 *(978-1-4824-4778-1(9))* Stevens, Gareth Publishing LLLP.

Sheehan, Jennifer E. Miss Bumples Lands on Earth. 2003. (Illus.). 31p. (J). *(978-0-9700952-6-8(0))* Bumples.

Sheikh-Miller, J. & Turnbull, S. Big Cats. 2004. (Discovery Program Ser.). (Illus.). 48p. (J). pap. 8.99 *(978-0-7945-0143-3(5)*, Usborne) EDC Publishing.

Sherman, Janice. Colorful Critters. 2007. (ENG., Illus.). 10p. (J). pap. 4.99 *(978-0-9797139-2-7(7))* Jan's Bks.

—Colorful Critters Color Match Coloring Book. 2007. (ENG., Illus.). 10p. (J). pap. 1.99 *(978-0-9797139-3-4(5))* Jan's Bks.

—Counting Critters. 2007. (ENG., Illus.). 10p. (J). pap. 4.99 *(978-0-9797139-1-0(9))* Jan's Bks.

—Critter Zoo. 2007. (ENG., Illus.). 10p. (J). pap. 4.99 *(978-0-9797139-8-9(6))* Jan's Bks.

—Critters A-Z. 2007. (ENG., Illus.). 26p. (J). pap. 5.99 *(978-0-9797139-0-3(0))* Jan's Bks.

—Ocean Critters. 2007. (ENG., Illus.). 13p. (J). pap. 4.99 *(978-0-9797139-9-6(4))* Jan's Bks.

—Rainforest Critters. 2007. (ENG., Illus.). 10p. (J). pap. 4.99 *(978-0-9797139-4-1(3))* Jan's Bks.

—Where Critters Live. 2007. (ENG., Illus.). 10p. (J). pap. 4.99 *(978-0-9797139-7-2(8))* Jan's Bks.

Shields, Amy. Best Friends Forever! And More True Stories of Animal Friendships. 2013. (NGK Chapters Ser.). (ENG., Illus.). 112p. (J). (gr. 2-5). pap. 5.99 *(978-1-4263-0935-9(X)*, National Geographic Children's Bks.) National Geographic Society.

Shkhyan, Maria. Funny Day. 2010. 28p. pap. 15.99 *(978-1-4500-9203-6(9))* Xlibris Corp.

Shores, Erika L. The Deadliest Animals on Earth. 2010. (World's Deadliest Ser.). (ENG.). 32p. (gr. 1-2). lib. bdg. 26.65 *(978-1-4296-3929-3(6)*, Blazers) Capstone Press of Coughlan Cos.

—The Deadliest Bugs on Earth. 2010. (World's Deadliest Ser.). (ENG.). 32p. (gr. 1-2). lib. bdg. 26.65 *(978-1-4296-3930-9(X)*, Blazers) Capstone Press of Coughlan Cos.

Showalter, Sarah Evelyn, illus. Animals of the Bible from A to Z. 2007. (J). (gr. -1-3). 16.95 *(978-0-87946-331-1(7))* ACTA Pubns.

Silate, Jennifer. The Bald Eagle. 2009. (Primary Sources of American Symbols Ser.). 24p. (gr. 3-3). 42.50 *(978-1-60851-508-0(7)*, PowerKids Pr.) Rosen Publishing Group, Inc., The.

Sill, Cathryn. About Habitats: Polar Regions, 1 vol. Sill, John, illus. 2015. (About Habitats Ser.). (ENG.). 48p. (J). (gr. -1-2). 16.95 *(978-1-56145-832-5(5))* Peachtree Pubs.

Sill, Cathryn & Sill, John. Seashores, 1 vol. Sill, John, illus. 2017. (About Habitats Ser.). (ENG., Illus.). 48p. (J). (gr. -1-2). 16.95 *(978-1-56145-968-1(2))* Peachtree Pubs.

Silverman, Buffy. Can an Old Dog Learn New Tricks? And Other Questions about Animals. 2010. (Is That a Fact? Ser.). (ENG., Illus.). 40p. (J). (gr. 4-6). lib. bdg. 26.60 *(978-0-8225-9083-5(2)*, 1306467) Lerner Publishing Group.

—Lightning Bolt Books: Meet the Animal Groups, 6 vols., Set. Incl. Do You Know about Amphibians? (Illus.). lib. bdg. 26.60 *(978-0-8225-7543-6(4))*; Do You Know about Birds? (Illus.). lib. bdg. 26.60 *(978-0-8225-7541-2(8))*; Do You Know about Fish? (J). 25.26 *(978-0-8225-7540-5(X))*; Do You Know about Insects? (Illus.). lib. bdg. 26.60 *(978-0-8225-7544-3(2))*; Do You Know about Mammals? (Illus.). 26.60 *(978-0-8225-7539-9(6))*; Do You Know about Reptiles? (Illus.). 26.60 *(978-0-8225-7542-9(6))*; 32p. (gr. k-2). 2009. Set lib. bdg. 151.56 *(978-0-8225-7538-2(8)*, Lerner Pubns.) Lerner Publishing Group.

—Lightning Bolt Books#8482; - Animal Look-Alikes: 6Pack Set. 2012. (Animal Look-Alikes Ser.). 32p. (gr. k-2). pap. 271.89 *(978-0-7613-9260-6(2))* Lerner Publishing Group.

—Lightning Bolt Books#8482; - Animal Look-Alikes: Single Copy Set. 2012. (Animal Look-Alikes Ser.). 32p. (gr. k-2). pap. 45.32 *(978-0-7613-9259-0(9))* Lerner Publishing Group.

—Lightning Bolt Books#8482; - Animal Look-Alikes: Spring 2012 New Releases. 2012. (Animal Look-Alikes Ser.). 32p. (gr. k-2). lib. bdg. 151.56 *(978-0-7613-8906-4(7)*, Lerner Pubns.) Lerner Publishing Group.

Silverstein, Virginia B. & Nunn, Laura Silverstein. Handy Health Guide to Bites & Stings. 2013. (Handy Health Guides). 48p. (J). 25.27 *(978-0-7660-4271-1(5))* Enslow Pubs., Inc.

Simon, Seymour. Creepy Creatures. 2006. (Illus.). 24p. (J). *(978-0-439-77703-2(8))* Scholastic, Inc.

—Deadly Ants. Downey, William, illus. 2012. (Dover Children's Science Bks.). (ENG.). 64p. (J). (gr. 3-5). pap. 5.99 *(978-0-486-48468-6(8))* Dover Pubns., Inc.

—Poisonous Animals. 2007. (Illus.). 31p. (J). pap. *(978-0-439-79600-2(8))* Scholastic, Inc.

Singer, Marilyn. Animales a Tu Alrededor. Zaidi, Nadeem, illus. 2004. (Baby Einstein Ser.). (SPA.). 16p. (J). bds. *(978-970-718-152-6(4)*, Silver Dolphin en Español) Advanced Marketing, S. de R. L. de C. V.

—Fun with Animals Friendship Box. Zaidi, Nadeem, illus. 2009. (J). *(978-1-4231-2799-4(4))*; *(978-1-4231-2797-0(8))*; *(978-1-4231-2798-7(6))* Disney Pr.

—Venom. 2014. (ENG., Illus.). 96p. (gr. 5-12). pap. *(978-1-4677-4909-1(5)*, Millbrook Pr.) Lerner Publishing Group.

Sipp, Leora Janson. Nathan & Tori Visit Ohio: And Learn about Wild Animals. 2012. 40p. pap. 14.50 *(978-1-4669-3822-9(6))* Trafford Publishing.

Sirota, Lyn A. & Koran, Maria. Rhodesian Ridgebacks. 2016. (J). **(978-1-4896-5614-8(6))** Weigl Pubs., Inc.

Skwarck, Skip, ed. Tails: An Interactive Book. 2006. (Illus.). 18p. (gr. -1-3). reprint ed. 13.00 *(978-1-4223-5439-1(3))* DIANE Publishing Co.

Slade, Suzanne. What Do You Know about Animal Adaptations? 2008. (20 Questions: Science Ser.). (Illus.). 24p. (J). (gr. 2-5). lib. bdg. 22.60 *(978-1-4042-4199-2(X))* Rosen Publishing Group, Inc., The.

—What Do You Know about Life Cycles? 2008. (20 Questions: Science Ser.). (Illus.). 24p. (YA). (gr. 2-5). lib. bdg. 22.60 *(978-1-4042-4201-2(5))* Rosen Publishing Group, Inc., The.

Small World Creations. Woodland Animals. 2016. (Crinkle Cloth Bks.). (ENG.). 8p. (J). (gr. -1 — 1). 9.99 *(978-1-4380-7754-3(8))* Barron's Educational Series, Inc.

Smith, Alastair. Nighttime Lift-the-flap. Butler, John, illus. 2005. 16p. (J). (gr. 1-18). 11.95 *(978-0-7945-0967-5(3)*, Usborne) EDC Publishing.

Smith, Jodene Lynn & Rice, Dona. Los Hogares de los Animales, 1 vol. rev. ed. 2010. (Early Childhood Themes Ser.). (SPA., Illus.). 16p. (J). (gr. -1-2). pap. 19.99 *(978-1-4333-2097-2(5))* Shell Educational Publishing.

Smith, Jodene Lynn & Rice, Dona Herweck. Los Hogares de los Animales, 1 vol. rev. ed. 2010. (Early Childhood Themes Ser.). (SPA., Illus.). 16p. (J). (gr. -1-2). pap. 6.99 *(978-1-4333-2096-5(7))* Shell Educational Publishing.

Smith, Naniloa. The Children Are Happy Activity Book with Animals from the Southwest. 2003. (J). 11.00 *(978-0-9744005-0-1(5))* In the Desert.

Smith, Penny & Dorling Kindersley Publishing Staff. Animal Hide & Seek. 2006. (DK Readers Ser.). (ENG., Illus.). 32p. (J). (gr. k-2). pap. 3.99 *(978-0-7566-1961-9(0)*, DK Children) Dorling Kindersley Publishing, Inc.

Smith, R. M. An A to Z Walk in the Park (Animal Alphabet Book) Smith, R. M., illus. 2008. (ENG., Illus.). 32p. (J). per. 7.95 *(978-0-615-19572-8(5))* Clarence-Henry Bks.

Smith Sr., Ernest Lee. Which Animal Am I? 2013. 28p. pap. 24.95 *(978-1-4626-6343-9(5))* America Star Bks.

Smith, Tim. Buck Wilder's Animal Wisdom. Herrick, Mark, illus. 2006. 32p. (J). (gr. 3-7). *(978-1-934133-02-6(7)*, Mackinac Island Press, Inc.) Charlesbridge Publishing, Inc.

Snow, Virginia Brimhall. Winter Walk, 1 vol. 2014. (ENG., Illus.). 32p. (J). 16.99 *(978-1-4236-3747-9(X))* Gibbs Smith, Publisher.

Soffer, Ruth. Swampland Plants & Animals Coloring Book. 2011. (Dover Nature Coloring Book Ser.). (ENG., Illus.). 48p. (J). (gr. 3-5). pap. 4.99 *(978-0-486-29625-8(3))* Dover Pubns., Inc.

Solway, Andrew. Secrets of Animal Life Cycles. 2010. (Science Secrets Ser.). 32p. (gr. 4). 28.50 *(978-1-60870-135-3(2))* Marshall Cavendish Corp.

Souza, D. M. Packed with Poison! Deadly Animal Defenses. Harris, Jack, illus. 2006. (On My Own Science Ser.). 48p. (J). (gr. -1-3). per. 6.95 *(978-0-8225-6448-5(3)*, First Avenue Editions); (ENG.). (gr. 2-4). lib. bdg. 25.26 *(978-1-57505-877-1(4)*, Millbrook Pr.) Lerner Publishing Group.

Souza, Dorothy M. Look What Tails Can Do. 2006. (Look What Animals Can Do Ser.). (Illus.). 48p. (J). (gr. -1-3). lib. bdg. 22.60 *(978-0-7613-9458-7(3)*, Lerner Pubns.) Lerner Publishing Group.

Sovak, Jan. Deadly Creatures Coloring Book. 2011. (Dover Nature Coloring Book Ser.). (ENG., Illus.). 32p. (J). (gr. 3-8). pap. 3.99 *(978-0-486-47655-1(3))* Dover Pubns., Inc.

—3-D Coloring Book — Dangerous Animals. 2012. (Dover 3-D Coloring Book Ser.). (ENG., Illus.). 32p. (J). (gr. 2-6). pap. 5.99 *(978-0-486-48419-8(X))* Dover Pubns., Inc.

Spilsbury, Louise. Animal Bodies: Extreme Anatomies. 2015. (Extreme Biology Ser.). (ENG.). 48p. (J). (gr. 4-4). lib. bdg. 31.95 *(978-1-4824-2230-6(1))* Stevens, Gareth Publishing LLLP.

—A Day in the Life Set: Grassland Animals, 6 vols. Incl. Baboon. pap. 6.79 *(978-1-4329-4737-8(0))*; Coyote. pap. 6.79 *(978-1-4329-4739-2(7))*; Hyena. pap. 6.79 *(978-1-4329-4742-2(7))*; Ostrich. pap. 6.79 *(978-1-4329-4740-8(0))*; (Illus.). (gr. k-2). (Day in the Life: Grassland Animals Ser.). (ENG.). 24p. 2011. Set pap. 25.96 *(978-1-4329-4746-0(X)*, Heinemann Read & Learn) Heinemann-Raintree.

—What Is the Structure of an Animal?, 1 vol., 1. 2014. (Let's Find Out! Ser.). (ENG.). 32p. (gr. 3-6). 23.45 *(978-1-62275-246-1(5))* Rosen Publishing Group, Inc., The.

—Wildebeest, 6 vols. Incl. Baboon. 23.32 *(978-1-4329-4727-9(3))*; Coyote. 23.32 *(978-1-4329-4729-3(X))*; Kori Bustard. 23.32 *(978-1-4329-4733-0(8))*; Ostrich. 23.32 *(978-1-4329-4730-9(3))*; 23.32 *(978-1-4329-4735-4(4))*; (gr. k-2). (Day in the Life: Grassland Animals Ser.). (ENG., Illus.). 24p. 2011. Set lib. bdg. 139.92 *(978-1-4329-4736-1(2)*, Heinemann Read & Learn) Heinemann-Raintree.

—Zoologists in the Field. 2010. (Big Picture: People & Culture Ser.). (ENG.). 24p. (gr. 1-2). pap. 41.70 *(978-1-4296-5822-5(3)*, First Facts) Capstone Press of Coughlan Cos.

Spilsbury, Louise & Spilsbury, Richard. A Nature Walk in the City, 1 vol. 2014. (Nature Walks Ser.). (ENG., Illus.). 24p. (gr. k-2). 23.32 *(978-1-4846-0401-4(6)*, Heinemann Read & Learn) Heinemann-Raintree.

—A Nature Walk on the Beach, 1 vol. 2014. (Nature Walks Ser.). (ENG., Illus.). 24p. (gr. k-2). 23.32 *(978-1-4846-0400-7(8)*, Heinemann Read & Learn) Heinemann-Raintree.

Spilsbury, Louise and Richard & Spilsbury, Richard. Animal Adaptations. 2017. (Engineered by Nature Ser.). (ENG., Illus.). 32p. (J). (gr. 3-8). lib. bdg. 25.95 *(978-1-62617-585-3(3)*, Pilot Bks.) Bellwether Media.

Spilsbury, Richard. Animal Variation & Classification. 2010. (Living Processes Ser.). (Illus.). 48p. (J). pap. 11.75 *(978-1-61532-347-0(3))*; (YA). (gr. 5-8). lib. bdg. 29.25 *(978-1-61532-344-9(9))* Rosen Publishing Group, Inc., The. (Rosen Reference).

—Born Survivors. 2017. (Engineered by Nature Ser.). (ENG., Illus.). 32p. (J). (gr. 3-8). lib. bdg. 25.95 *(978-1-62617-588-4(8)*, Pilot Bks.) Bellwether Media.

—Burrow. Hanna, Gary, illus. 2013. (Look Inside Ser.). (ENG.). 32p. (gr. 1-3). 27.32 *(978-1-4329-7193-9(X))*; pap. 8.29 *(978-1-4329-7200-4(6))* Heinemann-Raintree. (Heinemann First Library).

Spilsbury, Richard & Spilsbury, Louise. At Home in a Coral Reef, 01 vols., 1. 2016. (Home in the Biome Ser.). (ENG.). 32p. (J). pap. 10.00 *(978-1-5081-4552-3(0)*, PowerKids Pr.) Rosen Publishing Group, Inc., The.

—At Home in the Mountains, 01 vols., 1. 2016. (Home in the Biome Ser.). (ENG.). 32p. (J). pap. 10.00 *(978-1-5081-4563-9(6)*, PowerKids Pr.) Rosen Publishing Group, Inc., The.

—At Home in the Wetlands, 01 vols., 1. 2016. (Home in the Biome Ser.). (ENG.). 32p. (J). pap. 10.00 *(978-1-5081-4569-1(5)*, PowerKids Pr.) Rosen Publishing Group, Inc., The.

—Lion Prides. 2013. (Animal Armies Ser.). (ENG., Illus.). 32p. (J). (gr. k-5). pap. 10.00 *(978-1-4777-0334-2(9))*; lib. bdg. 25.25 *(978-1-4777-0306-9(3))* Rosen Publishing Group, Inc., The. (PowerKids Pr.).

Spurgeon, Maureen. The Big Book of Animals. 192p. *(978-0-7097-1636-5(2))* Brown Watson Ltd.

Squire, Ann O. Animals Helping with Healing. 2015. (ENG.). 48p. (J). pap. 6.95 *(978-0-531-20534-1(7)*, Orchard Bks.) Scholastic Library Publishing.

St. James, Cassidy. Finding a Mate: Animal Companions. 2014. (ENG.). 24p. (gr. k-3). 28.50 *(978-1-62717-632-3(2))* Rourke Educational Media.

St. John, Sally. Polar Regions. 2010. (Illus.). 16p. *(978-0-545-24809-9(4))* Scholastic, Inc.

Steck-Vaughn Staff. Animal Eyes. 2003. pap. 4.10 *(978-0-7398-7638-1(4))* Steck-Vaughn.

—Creepy Creatures. 2003. pap. 4.10 *(978-0-7398-7629-9(5))* Steck-Vaughn.

Steffora, Tracey. Animal Math. 2013. (Animal Math Ser.). (ENG.). 24p. (gr. -1-1). pap. 29.95 *(978-1-4329-7571-5(4))*; lib. bdg. 113.25 *(978-1-4329-7564-7(1))* Heinemann-Raintree. (NA-h).

Stephens, Catherine. Classification Clues. 2007. (Nonfiction Reading & Writing Workshops Ser.). (ENG., Illus.). 32p. (J). pap. 17.95 *(978-0-7922-4576-6(8))* CENGAGE Learning.

Stephens, Catherine & National Geographic Learning Staff. Life Cycles. 2006. (Nonfiction Reading & Writing Workshops Ser.). (ENG., Illus.). 32p. (J). pap. 17.95 *(978-0-7922-4579-7(2))* CENGAGE Learning.

Stephens, William R. Finding Food in the Wild. 2003. (Extreme Animals Ser.). (J). pap. *(978-1-58417-247-5(9))*; lib. bdg. *(978-1-58417-246-8(0))* Lake Street Pubs.

Sterling Children's, Sterling. Meow, Moo, Cock-A-Doodle-Doo: A Book of Animals. 2016. (ENG., Illus.). 28p. (J). (— 1). bds. 6.95 *(978-1-4114-7586-1(0)*, Spark Publishing Group) Sterling Publishing Co., Inc.

Sterling Publishing Co., Inc. Begin Smart(tm) Look at Me! 2016. (Begin Smart(tm) Ser.). (ENG., Illus.). 10p. (J). (— 1). bds. 8.95 *(978-1-4549-1755-7(5))* Sterling Publishing Co., Inc.

—Begin Smart(tm) Who Am I? 2016. (Begin Smart(tm) Ser.). (ENG., Illus.). 10p. (J). (— 1). bds. 8.95 *(978-1-4549-1756-4(3))* Sterling Publishing Co., Inc.

—Oink, Moo, Meow - Oink, Muu, Miau. 2013. (Say & Play Ser.). (ENG & SPA., Illus.). 28p. (J). (— 1). bds. 4.95 *(978-1-4549-1041-1(0))* Sterling Publishing Co., Inc.

Sterling Publishing Company Staff & Ward, Adam. Endangered Animals. 2004. (Pocket Factfiles Ser.). (Illus.). 256p. (J). 4.98 *(978-1-4027-1850-2(0))* Sterling Publishing Co., Inc.

Stevens, Kathryn. Night Creatures. 2007. (Reading Rocks! Ser.). (ENG., Illus.). 32p. (J). (gr. 2-5). 28.50 *(978-1-59296-855-8(4)*, 200746) Child's World, Inc., The.

Stewart, Melissa. Deadliest Animals. U. S. National Geographic Society Staff, photos by. 2011. (Readers Ser.). (ENG., Illus.). 48p. (J). (gr. 1-4). pap. 3.99 *(978-1-4263-0757-7(8)*, National Geographic Children's Bks.) National Geographic Society.

—National Geographic Readers: Deadly Predators. 2013. (Readers Ser.). (ENG.). 32p. (J). (gr. k-3). pap. 3.99 *(978-1-4263-1346-2(2))*; lib. bdg. 13.90 *(978-1-4263-1347-9(0))* National Geographic Society. (National Geographic Children's Bks.).

—National Geographic Readers: Predator Face-Off. 2017. (Readers Ser.). (ENG., Illus.). 32p. (J). (gr. -1-1). lib. bdg. 13.90 ***(978-1-4263-2812-1(5)***, National Geographic Children's Bks.) National Geographic Society.

—Predator Face-Off. 2017. (Readers Ser.). (ENG., Illus.). 32p. (J). (gr. -1-1). pap. 3.99 ***(978-1-4263-2811-4(7)***, National Geographic Children's Bks.) National Geographic Society.

Stewart, Melissa & American Museum of Natural History Staff. World's Fastest Animals, Level 2. 2014. (Amer Museum of Nat History Easy Readers Ser.). (ENG., Illus.). 32p. (J). (gr. k-1). pap. 3.95 *(978-1-4027-7793-6(0))* Sterling Publishing Co., Inc.

Stockdale, Susan. Stripes of All Types: Rayas de Todas Las Tallas. 2014. (SPA & ENG.). (J). *(978-1-56145-798-4(1))* Peachtree Pubs.

Stockland, Patricia M. Barnyard Buddies, 6 vols., Set 2. Ouren, Todd, illus. Incl. In the Buffalo Pasture. 27.07 *(978-1-60270-641-5(7))*; In the Goat Yard. 27.07 *(978-1-60270-642-2(5))*; In the Goose Pen. 27.07 *(978-1-60270-643-9(3))*; In the Llama Yard. 27.07 *(978-1-60270-644-6(1))*; In the Rabbit Hutch. 27.07 *(978-1-60270-645-3(X))*; In the Turkey Pen. 27.07 *(978-1-60270-646-0(8))*; (gr. -1-2). (Barnyard Buddies Set 2 Ser.). (Illus.). 24p. 2009. 162.42 *(978-1-60270-640-8(9)*, Looking Glass Library- Nonfiction) Magic Wagon.

Stone, Kate, illus. Heads & Tails. 2013. (ENG.). 20p. (J). bds. 10.99 *(978-1-4494-3246-1(8))* Andrews McMeel Publishing.

Stone, Lynn. How Do Animals Use Their Ears? 2007. (How Do Animals Use (Discovery Library) Ser.). (Illus.). 24p. (J). (gr. -1-3). lib. bdg. 22.79 *(978-1-60044-503-3(9))* Rourke Educational Media.

Stone, Lynn M. Border Collies. 2006. (Eye to Eye with Dogs Ser.). (Illus.). 24p. (J). (gr. -1-k). lib. bdg. 27.07 *(978-1-60044-237-7(4))* Rourke Educational Media.

—Pugs. 2006. (Eye to Eye with Dogs Ser.). (Illus.). 24p. (J). (gr. -1-k). lib. bdg. 27.07 *(978-1-60044-242-1(0))* Rourke Educational Media.

Storey Publishing Editors. The Petting Farm Poster Book. 2005. (ENG., Illus.). 64p. (J). (gr. 2-8). pap. 9.95 *(978-1-58017-597-5(X)*, 67597) Storey Publishing, LLC.

Storey, Rita. Animals. 2013. (Have Fun with Arts & Crafts Ser.). 32p. (gr. 4-7). 31.35 *(978-1-59920-896-1(2))* Black Rabbit Bks.

Stout, Frankie. Extreme Animals. 2008. (J). (gr. k-5). lib. bdg. 127.50 *(978-1-4042-4245-6(7))* Rosen Publishing Group, Inc., The.

—Nature's Best Jumpers. (Extreme Animals Ser.). 24p. 2009. (gr. 2-3). 42.50 *(978-1-61512-377-3(6))* 2008. (Illus.). (J). (gr. 3-7). lib. bdg. 22.60 *(978-1-4042-4155-8(8))* Rosen Publishing Group, Inc., The. (PowerKids Pr.).

—Nature's Deadliest Animals. (Extreme Animals Ser.). 24p. 2009. (gr. 2-3). 42.50 *(978-1-61512-378-0(4))* 2008. (Illus.). (J). (gr. 3-7). lib. bdg. 22.60 *(978-1-4042-4159-6(0))* Rosen Publishing Group, Inc., The. (PowerKids Pr.).

—Nature's Fastest Animals. (Extreme Animals Ser.). 24p. 2009. (gr. 2-3). 42.50 *(978-1-61512-379-7(2))* 2008. (Illus.). (J). (gr. 3-7). lib. bdg. 22.60 *(978-1-4042-4156-5(6))* Rosen Publishing Group, Inc., The. (PowerKids Pr.).

—Nature's Nastiest Biters. 2008. (Extreme Animals Ser.). (Illus.). 24p. (J). (gr. 3-7). lib. bdg. 22.60 *(978-1-4042-4157-2(4)*, PowerKids Pr.) Rosen Publishing Group, Inc., The.

—Nature's Slowest Animals. 2009. (Extreme Animals Ser.). 24p. (gr. 2-3). 42.50 *(978-1-61512-381-0(4)*, PowerKids Pr.) Rosen Publishing Group, Inc., The.

—Nature's Strongest Animals. (Extreme Animals Ser.). 24p. 2009. (gr. 2-3). 42.50 *(978-1-61512-382-7(2))* 2008. (Illus.). (J). (gr. 3-7). lib. bdg. 22.60 *(978-1-4042-4158-9(2))* Rosen Publishing Group, Inc., The. (PowerKids Pr.).

Strain, Connie Rae. Perfect Imperfections: For Animal lovers of all Ages collector's ed. 2003. (Illus.). 257p. (YA). 27.95 *(978-0-9741321-0-5(1))* Isle of Dogs Publishing, Co.

Suen, Anastasia. Asociacion Para la Prevencion de la Crueldad de los Animales, (ASPCA) 2004. (Organizaciones de Ayuda (Helping Organizations) Ser.). (SPA & ENG., Illus.). 24p. (J). (gr. 2-4). lib. bdg. 22.60 *(978-0-8239-6861-9(8))* Rosen Publishing Group, Inc., The.

Summers, Portia & Grady, Colin. The Grassland Biome. 2016. (Zoom in on Biomes Ser.). 24p. (J). (gr. 2-2). pap. 9.35 *(978-0-7660-7778-2(0))* Enslow Pubs., Inc.

—The Tundra Biome. 2016. (Zoom in on Biomes Ser.). 24p. (J). (gr. 2-2). pap. 9.35 *(978-0-7660-7794-2(2))* Enslow Pubs., Inc.

Sundance/Newbridge LLC Staff. Animal Life Cycles. 2004. (Reading PowerWorks Ser.). (gr. 1-3). 37.50 *(978-0-7608-9233-6(4))*; pap. 6.10 *(978-0-7608-9234-3(2))* Sundance/Newbridge Educational Publishing.

—Animals & Their Babies. 2007. (Early Science Ser.). (gr. k-3). 18.95 *(978-1-4007-6215-6(4))*; pap. 6.10 *(978-1-4007-6211-8(1))* Sundance/Newbridge Educational Publishing.

—How Animals Survive. 2004. (Reading PowerWorks Ser.). (gr. 1-3). 37.50 *(978-0-7608-8892-6(2))*; pap. 6.10 *(978-0-7608-8893-3(0))* Sundance/Newbridge Educational Publishing.

Sutton, Lynn Parrish. Animally. Mitchell, Hazel, illus. 2016. (ENG.). 30p. (J). 11.99 *(978-1-61067-345-7(X))* Kane Miller.

Swanson, Diane. Animals Can Be So Playful, 1 vol. 2003. (Animals Can Be So — Ser.). (ENG., Illus.). 22p. (J). *(978-1-55041-328-1(7))* Fitzhenry & Whiteside, Ltd.

—Animals Can Be So Speedy, 1 vol. 2003. (Animals Can Be So — Ser.). (ENG., Illus.). 22p. (J). *(978-1-55041-334-2(1))* Fitzhenry & Whiteside, Ltd.

—Feet That Suck & Feed. 2003. (Up Close Ser.). (Illus.). 32p. (J). (gr. k-2). 5.95 *(978-1-55054-769-6(0))* Da Capo Pr., Inc.

—Teeth That Stab & Grind. 2003. (Up Close Ser.). (Illus.). 32p. (J). (gr. 2-4). 5.95 *(978-1-55054-770-2(4))* Da Capo Pr., Inc.

—Welcome to the World of Animals, 23 bks. Incl. Beavers. 2002. lib. bdg. 24.00 *(978-0-8368-3560-1(3))*; Coyotes. (J). 2002. lib. bdg. 24.00 *(978-0-8368-3313-3(9))*; Eagles. 2002. lib. bdg. 24.00 *(978-0-8368-3561-8(1))*; Elephants. 2004. lib. bdg. 24.00 *(978-0-8368-4022-3(4))*; Foxes. 2002. lib. bdg. 24.00 *(978-0-8368-3562-5(X))*; Frogs & Toads. 2004. lib. bdg. 24.00 *(978-0-8368-4023-0(2))*; Octopuses. (J). 2002. lib. bdg. 24.00 *(978-0-8368-3314-0(7))*; Penguins. 2004. lib. bdg. 24.00 *(978-0-8368-4025-4(9))*; Porcupines. (J). 2002. lib. bdg. 24.00 *(978-0-8368-3315-7(5))*; Rabbits & Hares. 2002. lib. bdg. 24.00 *(978-0-8368-3316-4(3))*; Sharks. 2002. lib. bdg. 24.00 *(978-0-8368-3563-2(8))*; Skunks. 2002. lib. bdg. 24.00 *(978-0-8368-3317-1(1))*; Snakes. 2002. lib. bdg. 24.00 *(978-0-8368-3318-8(X))*; Squirrels. 2002. lib. bdg. 24.00 *(978-0-8368-3564-9(6))*; Wild Horses. 2004. lib. bdg. 24.00 *(978-0-8368-4026-1(7))*; (gr. 1-4)., Gareth Stevens Learning Library (Welcome to the World of Animals Ser.). (Illus.). 32p. 430.74 o.p. *(978-0-8368-4170-1(0))* Stevens, Gareth Publishing LLLP.

Swanson, Maggie. Awesome Animals Coloring Book. 2016. (Dover Coloring Bks.). (ENG.). 32p. (J). (gr. k-2). pap. 3.99 *(978-0-486-80496-5(8))* Dover Pubns., Inc.

Swimow, Linda. Take on Yellowstone! 2011. 32p. pap. 12.99 *(978-1-4490-2219-8(7))* AuthorHouse.

Takeuchi, Mayuko. Circle, Triangle, Elephant! A Book of Shapes & Surprises. 2017. (ENG., Illus.). 22p. (gr. -1 — 1). bds. 9.95 ***(978-0-7148-7411-1(6))*** Phaidon Pr., Inc.

Tang, Sanmu. Chinese Zodiac Animals. Jingwen, Zhu, tr. 2011. (ENG., Illus.). 56p. (J). (gr. 4-6). pap. 8.95 *(978-1-60220-977-0(4))* BetterLink Pr., Inc.

Taplin, Sam. Animal. 2009. (Sticker Bks). 24p. (J). pap. 6.99 *(978-0-7945-2475-3(3)*, Usborne) EDC Publishing.

Tarakson, Stella. Bizarre Animals. 2017. (Gross & Frightening Animal Facts Ser.: Vol. 6). (ENG.). (YA). (gr. 5-8). 20.95 ***(978-1-4222-3924-7(1))*** Mason Crest.

—Disgusting Animals. 2017. (Gross & Frightening Animal Facts Ser.: Vol. 6). (ENG.). (YA). (gr. 5-8). 20.95 ***(978-1-4222-3925-4(X))*** Mason Crest.

—Freaky Animals. 2017. (Gross & Frightening Animal Facts Ser.: Vol. 6). (ENG.). (YA). (gr. 5-8). 20.95 ***(978-1-4222-3926-1(8))*** Mason Crest.

—Stinky Animals. 2017. (Gross & Frightening Animal Facts Ser.: Vol. 6). (ENG.). (YA). (gr. 5-8). 20.95 ***(978-1-4222-3929-2(2))*** Mason Crest.

Taylor, Barbara. My Big Animal World: Essential Facts from the Amazing World of Animals. 2007. (Illus.). 60p. (J). *(978-1-84332-358-7(3)*, Priddy Bks.) St. Martin's Pr.

—Slide & Discover: Animal Atlas. 2013. (Slide & Discover Ser.). (ENG., Illus.). 24p. (J). (gr. 2). 19.95 *(978-1-60710-586-2(1)*, Silver Dolphin Bks.) Readerlink Distribution Services, LLC.

—Urban Wildlife Habitats. 2006. (Exploring Habitats Ser.). (Illus.). 36p. (J). (gr. 3-7). lib. bdg. 26.00 *(978-0-8368-7259-0(2)*, Gareth Stevens Learning Library) Stevens, Gareth Publishing LLLP.

—3-D Explorer: Predators. Veres, Laszlo, illus. 2014. (3D Explorers Ser.). (ENG.). 32p. (J). (gr. 1). 19.95 *(978-1-60710-882-5(8)*, Silver Dolphin Bks.) Readerlink Distribution Services, LLC.

Taylor, Barbara & Parker, Steve. Animals. 2013. (Illus.). 48p. (J). *(978-1-4351-5084-3(8))* Barnes & Noble, Inc.

Taylor, Barbara, et al. Wild Animals the Best-Ever Box of Books: A Fabulous Collection of Eight Wildlife Books with Fascinating Facts & over 1600 Amazing Photographs, 8 vols. 2012. (ENG., Illus.). 64p. (J). (gr. 3-7). pap. 20.00 *(978-1-84322-798-4(3))* Anness Publishing GBR. Dist: National Bk. Network.

Taylor, David Conrad. Animal Olympians: Sporting Champions of the Animal World. (Illus.). 48p. (J). (gr. 4-18). reprint ed. 5.95 *(978-0-8225-9576-2(1)*, Lerner Pubns.) Lerner Publishing Group.

Teeth Sets: 1 Each of 3 Big Books. (Sunshinetm Science Ser.). (gr. 1-2). 111.50 *(978-0-7802-1449-1(8))* Wright Group/McGraw-Hill.

Tekavec, Heather. Different? Same! Curnick, Pippa, illus. 2017. (ENG.). 32p. (J). (gr. -1-1). 16.95 *(978-1-77138-565-7(0))* Kids Can Pr., Ltd. CAN. Dist: Hachette Bk. Group.

Tekiela, Stan. Do Beavers Need Blankets?, 1 vol. 2015. (Wildlife Picture Bks.). (ENG.). 32p. (J). 12.95 *(978-1-59193-467-7(2))* Adventure Pubns.

—Floppers & Loppers, 1 vol. 2013. (Adventure Boardbook Ser.). (ENG.). 22p. (J). (gr. -1-k). bds. 6.95 *(978-1-59193-424-0(9))* Adventure Pubns.

—Paws & Claws, 1 vol. 2013. (Adventure Boardbook Ser.). (ENG.). 22p. (J). (gr. -1-k). bds. 6.95 *(978-1-59193-425-7(7))* Adventure Pubns.

—Peepers & Peekers, 1 vol. 2013. (Adventure Boardbook Ser.). (ENG.). 22p. (J). (gr. -1-k). bds. 6.95 *(978-1-59193-423-3(0))* Adventure Pubns.

—Whose Butt?, 1 vol. 2012. (Wildlife Picture Bks.). (ENG., Illus.). 48p. (J). (gr. -1-3). 14.95 *(978-1-59193-374-8(9))* Adventure Pubns.

Tell Me Why, Tell Me How, 6 vols., Group 3. Incl. How Do Caterpillars Become Butterflies? Bailer, Darice. 29.93 *(978-0-7614-3987-5(0))*; How Do Mountains Form? Hicks, Terry Allan. 29.93 *(978-0-7614-3992-9(7))*; Why Do Bears Hibernate? Bailer, Darice. 29.93 *(978-0-7614-3990-5(0))*; Why Do Volcanoes Erupt? Mara, Wil. 29.93 *(978-0-7614-3989-9(7))*; Why Does It Rain? Mara, Wil. 29.93 *(978-0-7614-3991-2(9))*; Why Does the Sun Set? Hicks, Terry Allan. 29.93 *(978-0-7614-3993-6(5))*; 32p. (gr. 3-18). (Tell Me Why, Tell Me How 3 Ser.). 2009. Set lib. bdg. 179.58 o.p. *(978-0-7614-3986-8(2))* Marshall Cavendish Corp.

Teora, creator. Let's Get to Know the Animals! 2005. (Illus.). 48p. (J). pap. 9.95 *(978-1-59496-081-9(X))* Teora USA LLC.

—Wild Animals. 2007. (My First Sticker Encyclopedia Ser.). (Illus.). 18p. (J). (gr. -1-3). pap. 5.95 *(978-1-59496-141-0(7))* Teora USA LLC.

Terry, Paul. Top 10 for Kids Deadly Animals. 2015. (ENG., Illus.). 96p. (J). (gr. 3-6). pap. 9.95 *(978-1-77085-526-7(2)*, 9781770855267) Firefly Bks., Ltd.

Testa, Fulvio & Aesop Enterprise Inc. Staff. Aesop's Fables. Testa, Fulvio, illus. 2011. (ENG., Illus.). 128p. (J). (gr. 2-4). 24.99 *(978-1-84939-049-1(5))* Andersen Pr. GBR. Dist: Independent Pubs. Group.

Thanner, Eric. Leaping Lengths! Relate Addition & Subtraction to Length, 1 vol. 2015. (InfoMax Common Core Math Readers Ser.). (ENG.). 24p. (J). pap. 8.25 *(978-1-4777-4760-5(5)*, Rosen Classroom) Rosen Publishing Group, Inc., The.

Things That Sting. 2015. (Things That Sting Ser.). (ENG.). 24p. (J). (gr. 2-3). pap., pap., pap. 48.90 *(978-1-4824-3499-6(7))* Stevens, Gareth Publishing LLLP.

Thomas, Isabel. Animal Athletics. 2016. (Animalympics Ser.). (ENG., Illus.). 32p. (gr. 1-3). lib. bdg. 29.99 *(978-1-4109-8090-8(1)*, Read Me!) Heinemann-Raintree.

—Animal Gymnastics. 2016. (Animalympics Ser.). (ENG., Illus.). 32p. (gr. 1-3). lib. bdg. 29.99 *(978-1-4109-8093-9(6)*, Read Me!) Heinemann-Raintree.

—Animalympics. 2016. (Animalympics Ser.). (ENG.). 32p. (gr. 1-3). 119.96 *(978-1-4109-8106-6(1)*, Read Me!) Heinemann-Raintree.

Thomas, Louis, illus. A Walk on the Wild Side: Filled with Facts & over 60 Creatures. 2016. (ENG.). 80p. (J). (gr. k-3). 19.99 *(978-1-84780-914-8(6)*, Frances Lincoln Children's Bks.) Quarto Publishing Group UK GBR. Dist: Hachette Bk. Group.

Thomas Nelson. Flip Flap Fun Animals. 2015. (ENG.). 62p. (J). (gr. -1-7). *(978-1-78393-711-0(4))* Make Believe Ideas.

—Meow! 2016. (ENG.). 34p. (J). (gr. k-4). pap. *(978-1-78598-137-1(4))* Make Believe Ideas.

—Touch & Sparkle Wild Animals. 2016. (ENG.). 12p. (gr. -1). bds. *(978-1-78598-134-0(X))* Make Believe Ideas.

—Woof! 2016. (ENG.). 34p. (J). (gr. k-4). pap. *(978-1-78598-138-8(2))* Make Believe Ideas.

Thomas, Scott. Angry Aardvark to Zealous Zebra-Curious Creatures ABC. 2012. 32p. (J). pap. 6.99 *(978-1-62267-000-0(0))* Bright Connections Media.

Thompson, Gare. Serengeti Journey: On Safari in Africa. 2006. (Science Chapters Ser.). (ENG., Illus.). 48p. (J). (gr. 1-4). 17.90 *(978-0-7922-5952-7(1)*, National Geographic Children's Bks.) National Geographic Society.

Thornborough, Kathy. Animals. Petelinsek, Kathleen, illus. 2014. (Talking Hands Ser.). (ENG.). 24p. (J). (gr. k-3). 25.64 *(978-1-62687-314-8(3)*, 207154) Child's World, Inc., The.

Thornhill, Jan. I Am Josephine: (and I Am a Living Thing) Lee, Jacqui, illus. 2016. (ENG.). 32p. (J). (gr. -1-2). 16.95 *(978-1-77147-156-5(5)*, Owlkids) Owlkids Bks. Inc. CAN. Dist: Publishers Group West (PGW).

—The Wildlife 123: A Nature Counting Book. 2012. (ENG., Illus.). 32p. (J). (gr. -1-2). pap. 7.95 *(978-1-926973-46-3(1)*, Owlkids) Owlkids Bks. Inc. CAN. Dist: Publishers Group West (PGW).

—The Wildlife ABC: A Nature Alphabet Book. Thornhill, Jan, illus. 2012. (ENG., Illus.). 32p. (J). (gr. -1-2). pap. 7.95 *(978-1-926973-08-1(9)*, Owlkids) Owlkids Bks. Inc. CAN. Dist: Publishers Group West (PGW).

Those Tricky Animals, 6 Packs. (Literatura 2000 Ser.). (gr. 2-3). 33.00 *(978-0-7635-0211-9(1))* Rigby Education.

TickTock Books Ltd. Fierce Predators. 2010. (Top Tens Ser.). (ENG.). 32p. (J). (gr. 1-3). pap. 6.95 *(978-1-84898-198-0(8)*, TickTock Books) Octopus Publishing Group GBR. Dist: Independent Pubs. Group.

Ticktock Media, Ltd. Staff. Deadly Animals. 2009. (ENG.). 112p. (J). (gr. 2-4). pap. 9.95 *(978-1-84696-836-5(4)*, TickTock Books) Octopus Publishing Group GBR. Dist: Independent Pubs. Group.

—Living Planet: Uncovering the Wonders of the Natural World. 2008. (ENG.). 128p. (J). (gr. 4-7). pap. 12.95 *(978-1-84696-816-7(X)*, TickTock Books) Octopus Publishing Group GBR. Dist: Independent Pubs. Group.

—Who Am I? Wild Animal Babies. 2008. (Mini Flap Ser.). (ENG.). 10p. (J). (gr. k — 1). bds. 5.95 *(978-1-84696-820-4(8)*, TickTock Books) Octopus Publishing Group GBR. Dist: Independent Pubs. Group.

Tidey, John & Tidey, Jackie. Wildlife. 2008. (China Ser.). 32p. (gr. 4-18). lib. bdg. 18.56 *(978-0-7614-3161-9(6)*, Benchmark Bks.) Marshall Cavendish Corp.

Tiger Tales Staff, creator. Farm. 2013. (My First Touch & Feel Ser.). (ENG., Illus.). 10p. (gr. -1). bds. 7.99 *(978-1-58925-634-7(4))* Tiger Tales.

—Pets. 2013. (My First Touch & Feel Ser.). (ENG., Illus.). 10p. (gr. -1). bds. 7.99 *(978-1-58925-631-6(X))* Tiger Tales.

—Savanna Animals: Fun Facts & Stuff to Do. 2006. (Tiger Tales Ser.). (Illus.). 22p. (J). (gr. 3-7). bds. 7.95 *(978-1-58925-798-6(7))* Tiger Tales.

—100 First Animals. 2013. (My Big Book of Lift & Learn Ser.). (ENG., Illus.). 12p. (gr. -1). bds. 9.99 *(978-1-58925-608-8(5))* Tiger Tales.

Tildes, Phyllis Limbacher. Eye Guess: A Foldout Guessing Game. Tildes, Phyllis Limbacher, illus. 2005. (ENG., Illus.). 36p. (J). (gr. -1-2). 11.95 *(978-1-57091-650-2(0))* Charlesbridge Publishing, Inc.

Toft, Kim Michelle. The World That We Want. Toft, Kim Michelle, illus. 2005. (Illus.). 32p. (J). pap. *(978-0-7022-3482-8(6))* Univ. of Queensland Pr.

Toms, Kate. Animal Tails. 2006. (Illus.). 12p. (gr. -1-k). per., bds. *(978-1-84610-098-7(4))* Make Believe Ideas.

Top of the Food Chain. 2013. (Top of the Food Chain Ser.). 32p. (J). (gr. k-5). 151.50 *(978-1-4777-1544-4(4))* Windmill Bks.

Top That Publishing, ed. Mixed up Animals. 2007. 144p. pap. *(978-1-84666-403-8(9))* Top That! Publishing PLC.

Top That Publishing Staff. What Am I. 2006. 10p. *(978-1-84666-101-3(3))* Top That! Publishing PLC.

Top That Publishing Staff, ed. Animal Fun. 2006. (Illus.). 16p. *(978-1-84666-012-2(2))* Top That! Publishing PLC.

—Animals. 2005. (Illus.). 12p. *(978-1-84510-728-4(4))* Top That! Publishing PLC.

—Arctic Animals. 2005. (Illus.). 24p. *(978-1-84510-533-4(8))* Top That! Publishing PLC.

Tomio, Stacy & Keffer, Ken. The Secret Lives of Animals: 1,001 Tidbits, Oddities, & Amazing Facts about North America's Coolest Animals. 2015. (ENG., Illus.). 264p. (J). (gr. -1-5). pap. 19.95 *(978-1-4930-1191-9(X)*, Falcon Guides) Globe Pequot Pr., The.

Toufexis, George. History's Mysteries! Animals: Activity Book. 2012. (Dover Children's Activity Bks.). (ENG.). 48p. (J). (gr. 3-8). pap. 4.99 *(978-0-486-48699-4(0))* Dover Pubns., Inc.

Tourville, Amanda Doering. Animal Invaders. 2010. (ENG., Illus.). 48p. (gr. 4-6). pap. 10.95 *(978-1-61590-558-4(8))* Rourke Educational Media.

Townsend, Emily Rose. Polar Animals, 4 bks. Incl. Seals. (ENG., Illus.). 24p. (gr. k-1). 2004. 21.32 *(978-0-7368-2359-3(X)*, Pebble Bks.); (Polar Animals Ser.). (ENG.). Illus.). 24p. 2004. Set lib. bdg. 87.96 o.p. *(978-0-7368-2532-0(0)*, Pebble Bks.) Capstone Press of Coughlan Cos.

Townsend, John. Amazing Animal Movers, 1 vol. 2012. (Animal Superpowers Ser.). (ENG.). 32p. (gr. 1-3). lib. bdg. 29.99 *(978-1-4109-4746-8(7)*, Read Me!) Heinemann-Raintree.

—Amazing Predators, 1 vol. 2012. (Animal Superpowers Ser.). (ENG.). 32p. (gr. 1-3). pap. 8.29 *(978-1-4109-4756-7(4))*; lib. bdg. 29.99 *(978-1-4109-4749-9(1))* Heinemann-Raintree. (Read Me!).

Traeger, Heather. Rabbiting on Nowingi - A Coloring Book: A Bush Kid Loving the Red Soil, Australian Bush Animals & Starry Nights! 2011. 48p. (gr. 1-2). pap. 9.89 *(978-1-4269-9510-1(5))* Trafford Publishing.

Travis, Joelle & Figueras, Ligaya, eds. Los Animales y los Verbos. Hazan, Maurice, illus. 2003. (SPA.). 89p. (J). per. 20.00 *(978-1-932770-16-2(X)*, SWLB1) Symtalk, Inc.

Tripp, Penny. Animal Rights. 2003. (World Issues Ser.). (Illus.). 57p. (J). (gr. 5-18). lib. bdg. 29.95 *(978-1-931983-80-8(1))* Chrysalis Education.

Trueba, Jose Luis. Descubre... Los Animales. Cortes, Osvaldo, illus. 2004. (Ser. Descubre). 96p. (J). (gr. 3-5). pap. 18.95 *(978-970-29-0510-3(9))* Santillana USA Publishing Co., Inc.

Tuchman, Gail. Safari. 2015. (National Geographic Readers: Pre-Reader Ser.). (ENG.). (gr. -1-k). 19.95 *(978-1-4301-1889-3(X))* Live Oak Media.

—Safari. 2010. (Readers Ser.). (ENG., Illus.). 24p. (J). (gr. -1-k). pap. 3.99 *(978-1-4263-0614-3(8))*; lib. bdg. 13.90 *(978-1-4263-0615-0(6))* National Geographic Society. (National Geographic Children's Bks.).

Tumaš, Tomás. Animal Atlas. 2015. (ENG., Illus.). 28p. (J). (gr. 1-3). 16.95 *(978-1-4549-1742-7(3))* Sterling Publishing Co., Inc.

Turner, F. Bernadette. Faith of Little Creatures. (J). (gr. 1-3). pap. 5.00 *(978-0-8315-0138-9(3))* Speller, Robert & Sons, Pubs., Inc.

Tweet, Jonathan. Grandmother Fish: A Child's First Book of Evolution. Lewis, Karen, illus. 2016. (ENG.). 40p. (J). 17.99 *(978-1-250-11323-8(7)*, 9781250113238) Feiwel & Friends.

Twist, Clint. A Little Book of Slime: Everything That Oozes, from Killer Slime to Living Mold. 2012. (ENG., Illus.). 80p. (J). (gr. 4-18). 9.95 *(978-1-77085-006-4(6)*, 9781770850064) Firefly Bks., Ltd.

Tye, Laurie. The Animal in Me: Is Very Plain to See. Mangelsen, Thomas D., photos by. 2005. (ENG., Illus.). 32p. (J). (gr. -1-k). per. 8.95 *(978-1-55868-898-6(6),* West Winds Pr.) Graphic Arts Ctr. Publishing Co.

Tyler, Michael. Predators of North America. 2015. (J). lib. bdg. *(978-1-62713-547-4(2));* (ENG.). 32p. (gr. 3-3). pap. 10.58 *(978-1-5026-0184-1(2))* Cavendish Square Publishing.

—Predators of South America & Antarctica. 2015. (J). lib. bdg. *(978-1-62713-550-4(2))* Cavendish Square Publishing.

U. S. National Geographic Society Staff & Stewart, Melissa. Deadliest Animals. 2011. (Readers Ser.). (ENG., Illus.). 48p. (J). (gr. 1-4). lib. bdg. 13.90 *(978-1-4263-0758-4(6),* National Geographic Children's Bks.) National Geographic Society.

Underwood, Deborah. Hiding in Grasslands, 1 vol. 2010. (Creature Camouflage Ser.). (ENG.). 32p. (gr. 1-3). 27.32 *(978-1-4329-4024-9(4));* pap. 8.29 *(978-1-4329-4033-1(3))* Heinemann-Raintree. (Heinemann First Library).

—Hiding in Mountains, 1 vol. 2010. (Creature Camouflage Ser.). (ENG.). 32p. (gr. 1-3). 27.32 *(978-1-4329-4023-2(6));* pap. 8.29 *(978-1-4329-4032-4(5))* Heinemann-Raintree. (Heinemann First Library).

—Hiding in the Polar Regions, 1 vol. 2010. (Creature Camouflage Ser.). (ENG., Illus.). 32p. (gr. 1-3). 27.32 *(978-1-4329-4027-0(9));* pap. 8.29 *(978-1-4329-4036-2(8))* Heinemann-Raintree. (Heinemann First Library).

—Hiding in Wetlands, 1 vol. 2010. (Creature Camouflage Ser.). (ENG., Illus.). 32p. (gr. 1-3). pap. 8.29 *(978-1-4329-4034-8(1),* Heinemann First Library) Heinemann-Raintree.

Unglik, Richard. Animals of the World. 2016. (Playmobil Ser.). (ENG., Illus.). 96p. (J). (gr. 1-7). 19.95 *(978-1-63322-184-0(9),* Walter Foster Jr) Quarto Publishing Group USA.

Up Close, 6 bks., Set. Incl. Dinosaurs. Amery, Heather. lib. bdg. 25.25 *(978-1-4042-3759-9(3));* Micro Bugs. Harrison, Paul. lib. bdg. 25.25 *(978-1-4042-3760-5(7));* Mummies. Fleury, Kevin. lib. bdg. 25.25 *(978-1-4042-3761-2(5));* Reptiles. Harrison, Paul. lib. bdg. 25.25 *(978-1-4042-3763-6(1));* Sharks. Gibbons, Lynn & Coode, Chris. lib. bdg. 25.25 *(978-1-4042-3762-9(3));* Snakes. Harrison, Paul. lib. bdg. 25.25 *(978-1-4042-3764-3(X));* (Illus.). 24p. (J). (gr. 3-7). 2007. 2007. Set lib. bdg. 143.70 *(978-1-4042-3765-0(8),* PowerKids Pr.) Rosen Publishing Group, Inc., The.

Usborne Books Staff, ed. Los Animales del Mundo. 2004.Tr. of Great Animal Search. (SPA., Illus.). 48p. (J). (gr. -1-3). lib. bdg. 17.95 *(978-1-58086-228-8(4))* EDC Publishing.

Valat, Pierre-Marie. Animal Faces: 15 Punch-Out Masks. 3rd ed. 2007. (ENG., Illus.). 32p. (J). (gr. -1-7). per. 16.95 *(978-1-59354-196-5(1),* Handprint Bks.) Chronicle Bks. LLC.

Valer, Frantisek, illus. The Buffalo & the Boat: Thathánka na Wáta. 2004. (DAK, ENG & SIO.). 18p. (J). 9.95 *(978-0-9761082-3-8(2))* Lakota Language Consortium, Inc.

—Pispíza WAN Wayawa Iyaye/Prairie Dog Goes to School. 2006. (DAK, ENG & SIO.). 24p. (J). (gr. -1-3). pap. 9.95 *(978-0-9761082-4-5(0))* Lakota Language Consortium, Inc.

Valério, Geraldo. Jump, Leap, Count Sheep! A Canadian Wildlife 123. 2017. (ENG., Illus.). 24p. (J). (gr. -1-2). 16.95 ***(978-1-77147-289-0(8))*** Owlkids Bks. Inc. CAN. Dist: Publishers Group West (PGW).

Van Der Linden, Elly. The Prickly Hedgehog. Lavreys, Debbie, illus. 2007. 12p. (J). (gr. -1-k). *(978-0-86315-603-8(7))* Floris Bks.

—The Woolly Sheep. Lavreys, Debbie, illus. 2007. 12p. (gr. -1-k). *(978-0-86315-604-5(5))* Floris Bks.

Van Eerbeek, Ton. The World of Wild Animals: An Early Encyclopedia for Beginning Readers. Balloon Books Staff, ed. 2003. (Animal Bring-Along Bks.). (Illus.). 24p. (J). (gr. -1-1). 4.95 *(978-0-8069-8452-0(X),* 019720, Balloon Bks.) Sterling Publishing Co., Inc.

van Genechten, Guido. Guess What? 2012. (Guess Along Ser.). (ENG.). 16p. (J). (gr. k — 1). 9.95 *(978-1-60537-116-0(5))* Cobblestone Publishing Co.

Veitch, Catherine. Learning about Animals, 1 vol. 2013. (Natural World Ser.). (ENG.). 24p. (gr. -1-1). 22.65 *(978-1-4109-5404-6(8));* pap. 6.95 *(978-1-4109-5409-1(9))* Heinemann-Raintree. (NA-r).

—The Natural World. 2013. (Natural World Ser.). (ENG.). 24p. (gr. -1-1). lib. bdg. 90.60 *(978-1-4109-5405-3(6),* NA-r) Heinemann-Raintree.

Velikanje, Kathryn. Zebras Paint Themselves Rainbow. Hovhannisyan, Nune, illus. 2013. 58p. pap. 12.28 *(978-1-939896-02-5(9))* Levity Pr.

Vickers, Roy Henry & Budd, Robert. Hello Humpback! Vickers, Roy Henry, illus. 2017. (ENG., Illus.). 20p. (J). pap. 9.95 ***(978-1-55017-799-2(0))*** Harbour Publishing Co., Ltd. CAN. Dist: Midpoint Trade Bks., Inc.

Viggers, Katie. Almost an Animal Alphabet. 2013. (ENG., Illus.). 56p. (J). (gr. -1-2). 19.95 *(978-1-57687-643-5(8),* powerHouse Bks.) powerHouse Cultural Entertainment, Inc.

—1 to 20 Animals Aplenty. 2014. (ENG., Illus.). 48p. (J). (gr. -1-2). 17.95 *(978-1-57687-680-0(2),* powerHouse Bks.) powerHouse Cultural Entertainment, Inc.

Voake, Steve. Insect Detective. Voake, Charlotte, illus. (Read & Wonder Ser.). (J). 2012. (ENG.). 32p. (gr. -1-3). pap. 6.99 *(978-0-7636-5816-8(2))* 2010. 28p. *(978-1-4063-1051-1(4))* Candlewick Pr.

Vogel, Elizabeth. Big Cats, 6 bks. Incl. Cheetahs. (gr. -1-2). lib. bdg. 18.75 *(978-0-8239-6023-1(4));* Jaguars. (gr. 1). lib. bdg. 18.75 *(978-0-8239-6024-8(2),* PowerKids Pr.); Leopards. (gr. 1). lib. bdg. 18.75 *(978-0-8239-6019-4(6),* PowerKids Pr.); Lions. (gr. 1). lib. bdg. 18.75 *(978-0-8239-6021-7(8),* PowerKids Pr.); Pumas. (gr. 1). lib. bdg. 18.75 *(978-0-8239-6022-4(6),* PowerKids Pr.); Tigers. (gr. 1). lib. bdg. 18.75 *(978-0-8239-6020-0(X),* PowerKids Pr.); 24p. (J). 2002. (Illus.). Set lib. bdg. 88.50 *(978-0-8239-7112-1(0),* PowerKids Pr.) Rosen Publishing Group, Inc., The.

Von Zumbusch, Amelie. Safari Animals, 6 bks., Set. Incl. Cheetahs. lib. bdg. 22.60 *(978-1-4042-3614-1(7),* 1266066); Elephants. lib. bdg. 22.60 *(978-1-4042-3616-5(3));* Giraffes. lib. bdg. 22.60 *(978-1-4042-3615-8(5));* Hippos. lib. bdg. 22.60 *(978-1-4042-3617-2(1));* Lions. lib. bdg. 22.60 *(978-1-4042-3612-7(0));* Zebras. lib. bdg. 22.60 *(978-1-4042-3613-4(9),* 1266071); (Illus.). 24p. (J). (gr. 3-7). 2007., PowerKids Pr. 2007. Set lib. bdg. 127.50 *(978-1-4042-3597-7(3))* Rosen Publishing Group, Inc., The.

Votaw, Carol. Waking up down Under. Banta, Susan, illus. 2007. (ENG.). 32p. (J). (gr. k-3). 15.95 *(978-1-55971-976-6(1))* Cooper Square Publishing Llc.

Votaw, Carol J. Good Morning, Little Polar Bear. Banta, Susan, illus. 2005. (ENG.). 32p. (J). (gr. k-3). 15.95 *(978-1-55971-932-2(X))* Cooper Square Publishing Llc.

Vous, Nous. Show + Tell: Animal Activities: With 3 Posters, 40 Stickers & Coloring + Activity Book. 2017. (ENG.). 18p. (J). (gr. -1-k). pap. 9.99 *(978-1-84780-775-5(5),* Wide Eyed Editions) Quarto Publishing Group UK GBR. Dist: Hachette Bk. Group.

Voz, Samuel. Exploring the Great Basin. 2013. (InfoMax Readers Ser.). (ENG.). 24p. (J). (gr. 3-4). pap. 49.50 *(978-1-4777-2492-7(3));* pap. 8.25 *(978-1-4777-2491-0(5))* Rosen Publishing Group, Inc., The. (Rosen Classroom).

Wadsworth, Pamela. Golwg Gyntaf Ar Bethau Byw. Owen, Ken & Owen, Siân, illus. 2005. (WEL.). 24p. pap. *(978-1-85596-250-7(0))* Dref Wen.

—Golwg Gyntaf Ar Wahanol Blanhigion AC Anifeiliaid. 2005. (WEL., Illus.). 24p. pap. *(978-1-85596-254-5(3))* Dref Wen.

—Gwahanol Blanhigion AC Anifeiliaid. Owen, Ken & Owen, Siân, illus. 2005. (WEL.). 24p. pap. *(978-1-85596-223-1(3))* Dref Wen.

—Rhagor Am Bethau Byw Ar Waith. 2005. (WEL., Illus.). 24p. pap. *(978-1-85596-234-7(9))* Dref Wen.

—Rhagor Am Wahanol Blanhigion Ac Anifeiliaid. 2005. (WEL., Illus.). 24p. pap. *(978-1-85596-224-8(1))* Dref Wen.

Walden, Libby. Search & Find: Animals. Solis, Fermin, illus. 2016. (Search & Find Ser.). (ENG.). 12p. (J). (gr. -1). 9.99 *(978-1-62686-771-0(2),* Silver Dolphin Bks.) Readerlink Distribution Services, LLC.

Waldron, Melanie. Variation & Classification, 1 vol. 2014. (Essential Life Science Ser.). (ENG.). 48p. (gr. 4-6). lib. bdg. 33.32 *(978-1-4329-7813-6(6),* Heinemann InfoSearch) Heinemann-Raintree.

Waldron, Melanie, et al. Essential Life Science, 1 vol. 2014. (Essential Life Science Ser.). (ENG.). 48p. (gr. 4-6). lib. bdg. 133.28 *(978-1-4329-7814-3(4),* Heinemann InfoSearch) Heinemann-Raintree.

Walker, Colin, et al. Los Pajaros Son Animales. (Coleccion Conceptos de Ciencia en Big Books). (SPA., Illus.). (J). (gr. k-3). 12.00 *(978-0-8136-6751-5(8),* MD7208) Modern Curriculum Pr.

—Los Peces Son Animales. (Coleccion Conceptos de Ciencia en Big Books). (SPA., Illus.). (J). (gr. k-3). 12.00 net. *(978-0-8136-6750-8(X),* MD7213) Modern Curriculum Pr.

Walker, Theo. Swing, Slither, Swim Low Intermediate Book with Online Access. 2014. (ENG., Illus.). 24p. pap. 9.50 *(978-1-107-69242-8(3))* Cambridge Univ. Pr.

Wallace, Bruce. Wild Animals. 2005. (Touch & Sparkle Ser.). (Illus.). 12p. (gr. -1-k). per., bds. *(978-1-905051-00-7(X))* Make Believe Ideas.

Wallace, Marianne D. America's Seashores: Guide to Plants & Animals. 2005. (America's Ecosystems Ser.). (ENG., Illus.). 48p. (J). (gr. 3-7). pap. 11.95 *(978-1-55591-483-7(7),* 1250708) Fulcrum Publishing.

Walsh, Kieran. Animal Math. 2005. (Math & My World Ser.). (Illus.). 48p. (J). (gr. 4-6). lib. bdg. 20.95 *(978-1-59515-491-0(4))* Rourke Educational Media.

Walter Foster Creative Team. Animals: 30+ Fun & Relaxing Color-by-Number Projects to Engage & Entertain. 2016. (Color by Number Ser.). (ENG.). 112p. pap. 17.95 *(978-1-63322-099-7(0),* Walter Foster) Quarto Publishing Group USA.

Walter Foster Jr. Creative Team. 50 Wacky Things Animals Do: Unbelievable Things That Animals Do That Seem Too Crazy to Be Real! Ballesteros, Carles, illus. 2017. (Wacky Ser.). (ENG.). 104p. (J). (gr. 2-6). 14.95 *(978-1-63322-295-3(0),* Walter Foster Jr) Quarto Publishing Group USA.

Walters, Martin & Johnson, Jinny. The World of Animals. 2011. 256p. (YA). lib. bdg. 24.99 *(978-0-89051-617-1(0))* Master Bks.

Wanjie, Anne, ed. The Basics of Animal Systems. 2013. (Core Concepts Ser.). (ENG., Illus.). 96p. (YA). (gr. 7-12). lib. bdg. 34.60 *(978-1-4777-0556-8(2),* Rosen Classroom) Rosen Publishing Group, Inc., The.

Ward, Jennifer. Forest Bright, Forest Night. Henterly, Jamichael, illus. 2005. (Sharing Nature with Children Book Ser.). 32p. (J). (gr. k-3). 16.95 *(978-1-58469-066-5(6));* (ENG.). pap. 8.95 *(978-1-58469-067-2(4))* Dawn Pubns.

Warnau, Genevieve. The Encyclopedia of Animals. 2005. (Illus.). 301p. (J). (gr. 3-7). *(978-1-59496-035-2(6))* Teora USA LLC.

Wassner, Sarah & Furgang, Kathy. Animal Records - National Geographic Kids: The Biggest, Fastest, Grossest, Tiniest, Slowest, & Smelliest Creatures on the Planet. 2015. (ENG., Illus.). 208p. (J). (gr. 3-7). pap. 14.99 *(978-1-4263-1873-3(1),* National Geographic Children's Bks.) National Geographic Society.

—National Geographic Kids Animal Records: The Biggest, Fastest, Weirdest, Tiniest, Slowest, & Deadliest Creatures on the Planet. 2015. (ENG., Illus.). 208p. (J). (gr. 3-7). lib. bdg. 24.90 *(978-1-4263-1874-0(X),* National Geographic Children's Bks.) National Geographic Society.

Watch Them Grow! 2015. (Watch Them Grow! Ser.). (ENG.). 24p. (J). (gr. 1-1). pap., pap., pap. 297.00 *(978-1-4994-1329-8(7),* PowerKids Pr.) Rosen Publishing Group, Inc., The.

Watson, Richar, illus. My Book of Letters: For Ages 3+ 2016. (ENG.). (J). pap. ***(978-1-78209-799-0(6))*** Miles Kelly Publishing, Ltd.

Watson, Stephanie. Animal Testing: Issues & Ethics. 2009. (Science & Society Ser.). (Illus.). 64p. (YA). (gr. 7-12). lib. bdg. 31.95 *(978-1-4358-5022-4(X))* Rosen Publishing Group, Inc., The.

Watt, Mélanie. The Alphabet. Watt, Mélanie, illus. 2005. (Learning with Animals Ser.). (ENG., Illus.). 30p. (J). (gr. -1 — 1). bds. 5.95 *(978-1-55337-829-7(6))* Kids Can Pr., Ltd. CAN. Dist: Hachette Bk. Group.

—Colors. Watt, Mélanie, illus. 2005. (Learning with Animals Ser.). (ENG., Illus.). 24p. (J). (gr. -1 — 1). bds. 5.95 *(978-1-55337-830-3(X))* Kids Can Pr., Ltd. CAN. Dist: Hachette Bk. Group.

—Numbers. Watt, Mélanie, illus. 2005. (Learning with Animals Ser.). (ENG., Illus.). 24p. (J). (gr. -1 — 1). bds. 5.95 *(978-1-55337-831-0(8))* Kids Can Pr., Ltd. CAN. Dist: Hachette Bk. Group.

—Opposites. Watt, Mélanie, illus. 2005. (Learning with Animals Ser.). (ENG., Illus.). 24p. (J). (gr. -1 — 1). bds. 5.95 *(978-1-55337-832-7(6))* Kids Can Pr., Ltd. CAN. Dist: Hachette Bk. Group.

—Shapes. Watt, Mélanie, illus. 2005. (Learning with Animals Ser.). (ENG., Illus.). 24p. (J). (gr. -1 — 1). bds. 5.95 *(978-1-55337-833-4(4))* Kids Can Pr., Ltd. CAN. Dist: Hachette Bk. Group.

Watts, Barrie. El Hámster. (Coleccion Ciclos Vitales). (SPA., Illus.). 32p. (J). (gr. 3-5). *(978-84-236-2665-6(2),* ED4704) Edebé ESP. Dist: Lectorum Pubns., Inc.

Waxman, Laura Hamilton. Life in a Grassland. 2016. (Biomes Alive! Ser.). (ENG., Illus.). 24p. (J). (gr. k-3). lib. bdg. 25.95 *(978-1-62617-318-7(4),* Blastoff! Readers) Bellwether Media.

—Life in a Wetland. 2016. (Biomes Alive! Ser.). (ENG., Illus.). 24p. (J). (gr. k-3). lib. bdg. 25.95 *(978-1-62617-322-4(2),* Blastoff! Readers) Bellwether Media.

We Can Read! Series, 4 bks., Set. 85.43 *(978-0-7614-1509-1(2),* Benchmark Bks.) Marshall Cavendish Corp.

Weber, Belinda. I Wonder Why Animals Are Amazing Sticker Activity Book. 2013. (I Wonder Why Ser.). (ENG., Illus.). 24p. (J). (gr. k-3). 6.99 *(978-0-7534-6830-2(1),* 9780753468302, Kingfisher) Roaring Brook Pr.

Weber, Rebecca. How Many Legs? 2011. (Early Connections Ser.). (J). *(978-1-61672-323-1(8))* Benchmark Education Co.

Weekly Reader Editorial Staff. Things at the Park. 2006. (Things in My World Ser.). (Illus.). 16p. (J). (gr. -1-2). lib. bdg. 19.00 *(978-0-8368-6809-8(9),* Weekly Reader Leveled Readers) Stevens, Gareth Publishing LLLP.

—Things at the Park (Las Cosas Del Parque) 2006. (Things in My World/ Las cosas de mi mundo Ser.). (ENG & SPA., Illus.). 16p. (gr. -1-2). pap. 5.30 *(978-0-8368-7228-6(2),* Weekly Reader Leveled Readers) Stevens, Gareth Publishing LLLP.

—Things at the Park/Las Cosas del Parque. 2006. (Things in My World/ Las cosas de mi mundo Ser.). (ENG & SPA., Illus.). 16p. (gr. -1-2). lib. bdg. 19.00 *(978-0-8368-7221-7(5),* Weekly Reader Leveled Readers) Stevens, Gareth Publishing LLLP.

Weekly Reader Editorial Staff, contrib. by. Things at the Park. 2006. (Things in My World Ser.). (Illus.). 16p. (gr. -1-2). pap. 5.30 *(978-0-8368-6816-6(1),* Weekly Reader Leveled Readers) Stevens, Gareth Publishing LLLP.

Wegerif, Gay. Up Close. 2013. (ENG., Illus.). 30p. (J). (gr. -1 — 1). bds. 13.95 *(978-1-4197-0391-1(9))* Abrams, Inc.

Weingarten, E. T. Hunting with Killer Whales, Vol. 1. 2014. (Animal Attack! Ser.). (ENG.). 32p. (J). (gr. 2-3). 22.60 *(978-1-4824-0496-8(6))* Stevens, Gareth Publishing LLLP.

Weird Animals in the Wild. 2013. (Earth's Grossest Animals Ser.). 32p. (J). (gr. k-5). pap. 60.00 *(978-1-61533-788-0(1),* PowerKids Pr.) Rosen Publishing Group, Inc., The.

Wendorff, Anne. Blastoff! Readers - Watch Animals Grow, 4 vols., Set. Incl. Bear Cubs. 20.00 *(978-0-531-21626-2(8));* Eaglets. 20.00 *(978-0-531-21627-9(6));* Fawns. 20.00 *(978-0-531-21628-6(4));* Lambs. 20.00 *(978-0-531-21629-3(2));* (Illus.). 24p. (J). (gr. k-3). 2009. (Blastoff! Readers Ser.). 2009. Set lib. bdg. 80.00 *(978-0-531-26129-3(8),* Children's Pr.) Scholastic Library Publishing.

West, David. Garden Animals. (Nora the Naturalist's Animals Ser.). 24p. (gr. k-3). 2014. pap. 8.95 *(978-1-62588-050-5(2))* 2013. (Illus.). 28.50 *(978-1-62588-003-1(0))* Black Rabbit Bks.

—Mountain Animals. 2016. (Safari Sam's Wild Animals Ser.). 24p. (gr. k-3). 28.50 *(978-1-62588-073-4(1),* Smart Apple Media) Black Rabbit Bks.

—Polar Animals. 2016. (Safari Sam's Wild Animals Ser.). 24p. (gr. k-3). 28.50 *(978-1-62588-074-1(X),* Smart Apple Media) Black Rabbit Bks.

What Can Fly?, 6 Packs. (Literatura 2000 Ser.). (gr. k-1). 28.00 *(978-0-7635-0073-3(9))* Rigby Education.

What's That Sound? (Peek A Boo Pockets Ser.). (Illus.). 12p. (J). bds. *(978-2-89393-877-6(9))* Phidal Publishing, Inc./Editions Phidal, Inc.

Whelon, Chuck. What to Doodle? Amazing Animals! 2009. (Dover Doodle Bks.). (ENG., Illus.). 64p. (J). (gr. 2-5). pap. 5.99 *(978-0-486-47266-9(3))* Dover Pubns., Inc.

White, Teagan. Counting with Barefoot Critters. 2016. (ENG., Illus.). 32p. (J). (gr. -1-3). 16.99 *(978-1-101-91771-8(7),* Tundra Bks.) Tundra Bks. CAN. Dist: Penguin Random Hse. LLC.

Whitfield, Philip. Firefly Encyclopedia of Animals. 2014. (ENG., Illus.). 256p. (J). (gr. 4-7). pap. 19.95 *(978-1-77085-457-4(6),* 9781770854574) Firefly Bks., Ltd.

Whittaker, Andrea. All-Star Animals: Pets who'd rather play than Stay. 2004. (YA). 3.99 *(978-1-930623-35-4(6))* Sports Illustrated For Kids.

Who's Hiding Inside? Animals. 2005. (Who's Hiding Inside Ser.). 12p. (J). bds. 7.95 *(978-1-58117-306-2(7),* Intervisual/Piggy Toes) Bendon, Inc.

Whos Who at the Zoo. 2004. pap. 9.99 *(978-0-307-14272-6(8))* Random Hse., Inc.

Wicks, Maris. Science Comics: Coral Reefs. 2016. (Science Comics Ser.). (ENG., Illus.). 128p. (J). pap. 12.99 *(978-1-62672-145-6(9),* 9781626721456, First Second Bks.) Roaring Brook Pr.

A Wild Animal. 2005. (The Fawn Chapter Ser.). (ENG., Illus.). (J). pap. 7.67 *(978-1-58453-312-2(9))* Pioneer Valley Bks.

Wild Animals. (First Facts about Ser.). 24p. (J). (gr. 3-7). pap. *(978-1-882210-18-3(2))* Action Publishing, Inc.

Wild Animals, Level 2. 2016. (Ladybird Readers Ser.). (ENG.). 48p. (J). (gr. 2-4). pap. 9.99 *(978-0-241-25445-5(0))* Penguin Bks., Ltd. GBR. Dist: Independent Pubs. Group.

Wild, Anne S. Wildlife Pop-Ups: A Collection of 3-D Greetings Cards on Wildlife Themes to Cut Out & Make. 2004. (Illus.). 36p. (J). 12.00 *(978-1-899618-48-4(1))* Tarquin Pubns. GBR. Dist: Parkwest Pubns., Inc.

A Wild Time! Individual Title Six-Packs. (Bookweb Ser.). 32p. (gr. 6-18). 34.00 *(978-0-7578-0904-0(9))* Rigby Education.

Wild World. 2016. (Wild World Ser.). 00032p. (J). (gr. 1-2). 218.00 *(978-1-4994-8134-1(9),* Windmill Bks.) Rosen Publishing Group, Inc., The.

Wildlife Education, Ltd. Staff, contrib. by. Spanish Hardcover Set, 12 vols. 2003. (Zoobooks Ser.). (SPA., Illus.). 24p. (J). (gr. k-6). 191.40 *(978-1-932396-06-5(3))* Wildlife Education, Ltd.

Wildlife of North America Classroom Library. (gr. 4-18). lib. bdg. 74.95 *(978-0-7368-7092-4(X))* Red Brick Learning.

Wildlife Safari Africa, Swahili & English: Who's Who in the African Jungle & Savanna, a Swahili/English Multicultural Book. 2004. (J). per. 9.95 *(978-0-9742688-2-8(8))* Ndegwa, Catherine W.

Wildlife Watching: Level R, 6 vols. (Wonder Worldtm Ser.). 48p. 44.95 *(978-0-7802-7076-3(2))* Wright Group/McGraw-Hill.

Wildlife Wonders. 2016. (Wildlife Wonders Ser.). 00032p. (J). (gr. 3-3). pap. 60.00 *(978-1-4994-3191-9(0),* PowerKids Pr.) Rosen Publishing Group, Inc., The.

Wildsmith, Brian. Animals to Count. Wildsmith, Brian, illus. (Illus.). 16p. (J). 2004. (PER.). bds. 4.99 *(978-1-932065-43-5(1))* 2003. (CHI., bds. 4.99 *(978-1-932065-17-6(2),* 1718-784-9112) Star Bright Bks., Inc.

—Brian Wildsmith's Amazing Animal Alphabet Book, 1 vol. 2009. (ENG., Illus.). 32p. (J). pap. 7.95 *(978-1-59572-185-3(1))* Star Bright Bks., Inc.

—Brian Wildsmith's Amazing Animal Alphabet Book. Wildsmith, Brian, illus. 2007. (Illus.). 32p. (J). pap. 8.95 *(978-1-59572-111-2(8))* Star Bright Bks., Inc.

—Brian Wildsmith's Animal Colors, 1 vol. 2007. (ENG., Illus.). 16p. (J). (gr. -1). bds. 4.99 *(978-1-59572-118-1(5))* Star Bright Bks., Inc.

—Brian Wildsmith's Animal Colors, 1 vol. Wildsmith, Brian, illus. (Illus.). 16p. (J). 2004. (NAV.). 4.99 *(978-1-932065-34-3(2),* 718-784-9112) 2003. (TAG., 4.99 *(978-1-932065-30-5(X),* 1-718-784-9112) 2003. (KOR., 4.99 *(978-1-932065-28-2(8),* 1-718-784-9112) Star Bright Bks., Inc.

—Brian Wildsmith's Animal Colors (Simplified Mandarin) Wildsmith, Brian, illus. 2004. (CHI., Illus.). 16p. (J). bds. 4.95 *(978-1-932065-52-7(0),* 7187849112) Star Bright Bks., Inc.

—Brian Wildsmith's Animal Colors (Traditional Cantonese) Wildsmith, Brian, illus. 2004. (CHI., Illus.). 16p. (J). bds. 4.99 *(978-1-932065-53-4(9))* Star Bright Bks., Inc.

—Brian Wildsmith's Animals to Count, 1 vol. Wildsmith, Brian, illus. 2009. (ENG., Illus.). 32p. (J). bds. 4.99 *(978-1-59572-128-0(2))* Star Bright Bks., Inc.

—Brian Wildsmith's Animals to Count, 1 vol. 2004. (NAV., Illus.). 16p. (J). 4.99 *(978-1-932065-25-1(3))* Star Bright Bks., Inc.

—Brian Wildsmith's Animals to Count, 1 vol. Wildsmith, Brian, illus. 2003. (Illus.). 16p. (J). (KOR.). 4.99 *(978-1-932065-13-8(X),* 1718-784-9112); (TAG., 4.99 *(978-1-932065-31-2(8),* 1-718-784-9112); (POR., bds. 4.95 *(978-1-932065-15-2(6),* 17187849112) Star Bright Bks., Inc.

—Los Colores de los Animales/Animal Colors. 2005. (SPA & ENG., Illus.). 16p. (J). (gr. -1 — 1). per., bds. 5.95 *(978-1-59572-023-8(5))* Star Bright Bks., Inc.

Wildsmith, Brian, illus. Brian Wildsmith's Amazing Animal Alphabet Book, 1 vol. 2008. (ENG.). 32p. (J). 17.95 *(978-1-59572-104-4(5))* Star Bright Bks., Inc.

—Brian Wildsmith's Animal Colors. 16p. (J). 2004. (ARA.). bds. 4.95 *(978-1-932065-44-2(X),* 718-784-9112) 2004. (VIE.). bds. 4.95 *(978-1-932065-51-0(2))* 2003. (POR.). bds. 4.95 *(978-1-932065-27-5(X),* 1-718-784-9112) Star Bright Bks., Inc.

—Brian Wildsmith's Animals to Count. 2003. (VIE.). 16p. (J). bds. 4.95 *(978-1-932065-16-9(4),* 17187849112) Star Bright Bks., Inc.

Wildsmith, Brian, illus. Brian Wildsmith's Animals to Count (Traditional Cantonese), 1 vol. Wildsmith, Brian, . 2003. (CHI & ENG.). 16p. (J). 4.99 *(978-1-932065-18-3(0),* 1-718-784-9112) Star Bright Bks., Inc.

Wiley, Paula. Groove with the Animals. 2003. 29p. spiral bd. 14.59 *(978-1-4116-0160-4(2))* Lulu Pr., Inc.

Wilkes, Angela. Discover Science: Animal Homes. 2017. (Discover Science Ser.). (ENG.). 56p. (J). pap. 7.99 *(978-0-7534-7331-3(3),* 9780753473313, Kingfisher) Roaring Brook Pr.

Wilkins, John-Paul. What Can Live in the Snow?, 1 vol. 2014. (What Can Live There? Ser.). (ENG., Illus.). 24p. (gr. -1-1). 22.65 *(978-1-4846-0577-6(2),* Heinemann Read & Learn) Heinemann-Raintree.

Wilkins, Mary-Jane. Frozen Lands. 2017. (Fast Track: Who Lives Here? Ser.). (Illus.). 24p. (gr. k-3). 28.50 ***(978-1-78121-347-6(X))*** Brown Bear Bks.

—Grasslands. 2017. (Fast Track: Who Lives Here? Ser.). (Illus.). 24p. (gr. k-3). 28.50 ***(978-1-78121-362-9(3))*** Brown Bear Bks.

—Mountains. 2017. (Fast Track: Who Lives Here? Ser.). (Illus.). 24p. (gr. k-3). 28.50 ***(978-1-78121-348-3(8))*** Brown Bear Bks.

—Rain Forests. 2017. (Fast Track: Who Lives Here? Ser.). (Illus.). 24p. (gr. k-3). 28.50 ***(978-1-78121-349-0(6))*** Brown Bear Bks.

William H. Sadlier Staff. Amazing Blue Animals, Vol. 2. 2005. (Early Library). (gr. k-2). 24.00 net. *(978-0-8215-8948-9(2))* Sadlier, William H. Inc.

Winbolt-Lewis, Martin. Never Rely on a Lion. 2013. (Illus.). 60p. pap. *(978-1-78222-158-6(1))* Paragon Publishing, Rothersthorpe.

Wingard-Nelson, Rebecca. Animal Word Problems Starring Addition & Subtraction. LaBaff, Tom, illus. 2009. (Math Word Problems Solved Ser.). 48p. (J). (gr. 2-5). lib. bdg. 25.27 *(978-0-7660-2917-0(4))* Enslow Pubs., Inc.

Winkler, Peter & National Geographic Learning Staff. Animal Adaptations. 2007. (Nonfiction Reading & Writing Workshops Ser.). (ENG., Illus.). 32p. (J). pap. 17.95 *(978-0-7922-4577-3(6))* CENGAGE Learning.

Winner, Cherie. Animal Minis! What Kids Really Want to Know about Tiny Animals. 2006. (Kids Faqs Ser.). (ENG., Illus.). 64p. (J). (gr. 3-6). pap. 7.95 *(978-1-55971-934-6(6))* Cooper Square Publishing Llc.

Winsten, Martha Raleigh. Awesome Elijah. 2007. (Illus.). 32p. 14.95 *(978-1-57258-476-1(9))* TEACH Services, Inc.

Winter Survival: Individual Title Six-Packs. (Action Packs Ser.). 104p. (gr. 3-5). 44.00 *(978-0-7635-8400-9(2))* Rigby Education.

Wiseman, Blaine. The Midwest. 2014. (Illus.). 32p. (J). *(978-1-4896-1226-7(2))* Weigl Pubs., Inc.

—The Northeast. 2014. (Illus.). 32p. (J). *(978-1-4896-1230-4(0))* Weigl Pubs., Inc.

—The Southeast. 2014. (Illus.). 32p. (J). (978-1-4896-1234-2(3)) Weigl Pubs., Inc.

—The Southwest. 2014. (Illus.). 32p. (J). (978-1-4896-1238-0(6)) Weigl Pubs., Inc.

—The West. 2014. (Illus.). 32p. (J). (978-1-4896-1242-7(4)) Weigl Pubs., Inc.

Wittrock, Jeni & Rustad, Martha E. H. Baby Animals. 2011. (Baby Animals Ser.). (ENG.). 24p. (gr. k-1). pap. 250.20 (978-1-4296-7104-0(1), Pebble Plus) Capstone Press of Coughlan Cos.

Wojahn, Rebecca Hogue & Wojahn, Donald. A Coral Reef Food Chain: A Who-Eats-What Adventure in the Caribbean Sea. 2009. (Follow That Food Chain Ser.). (ENG.). 64p. (gr. 3-5). 30.60 (978-0-8225-7611-2(2)) Lerner Publishing Group.

The Wolf, 6 vols. (gr. 4-18). 39.95 (978-0-7368-8503-4(X)) Red Brick Learning.

Wolfe, Jane. Pull the Lever: Who Are You? The Toy Box, illus. 2014. (ENG.). 8p. (J). (gr. -1-2). bds. 6.99 (978-1-86147-391-2(5), Armadillo) Anness Publishing GBR. Dist: National Bk. Network.

Wollman, Neil & Fuller, Abigail. What Animal Needs a Wig?, 1 vol. Fuller Baldwin, Fran, illus. 2014. (ENG.). 32p. (J). pap. 6.99 (978-1-59572-677-3(2)) Star Bright Bks., Inc.

Wood, A. J. My First Animal ABC. Pledger, Maurice, illus. 2017. (ENG.). 32p. (J). (gr. -1). 17.99 (978-1-62686-776-5(3), Silver Dolphin Bks.) Readerlink Distribution Services, LLC.

Wood, Alix. Amazing Animal Life Cycles. 2012. (Wow! Wildlife Ser.). (ENG., Illus.). 24p. (J). (gr. k-5). 22.60 (978-1-4488-8100-0(5)); pap. 8.25 (978-1-4488-8167-3(6)) Windmill Bks.

—Freaky Flying Animals. 2013. (Earth's Grossest Animals Ser.). 32p. (J). (gr. k-5). 25.25 (978-1-61533-736-1(9)); pap. 10.00 (978-1-61533-789-7(X)) Rosen Publishing Group, Inc., The. (PowerKids Pr.).

—Gruesome Animals in the Ground. 2013. (Earth's Grossest Animals Ser.). 32p. (J). (gr. k-5). pap. 10.00 (978-1-61533-785-9(7)); pap. 60.00 (978-1-61533-786-6(5)); (ENG., Illus.). lib. bdg. 25.25 (978-1-61533-734-7(2)) Windmill Bks.

—Weird Animals in the Wild. 2013. (Earth's Grossest Animals Ser.). 32p. (J). (gr. k-5). 25.25 (978-1-61533-735-4(0)); pap. 10.00 (978-1-61533-787-3(3)) Rosen Publishing Group, Inc., The. (PowerKids Pr.).

—Yucky Animals in the Yard. 2013. (Earth's Grossest Animals Ser.). 32p. (J). (gr. k-5). 25.25 (978-1-61533-731-6(8)); pap. 10.00 (978-1-61533-779-8(2)) Rosen Publishing Group, Inc., The. (PowerKids Pr.).

Woods, Bob. Animal Testing: Attacking a Controversial Problem. 2017. (J). **(978-1-4222-3872-1(5))** Mason Crest.

Woodward, John. What Lives in the Garden? 2007. (What Lives in... ? Ser.). (Illus.). 48p. (gr. 2-6). lib. bdg. 27.00 (978-0-8368-7859-2(0), Gareth Stevens Learning Library) Stevens, Gareth Publishing LLLP.

—What Lives under the Carpet? 2007. (What Lives in... ? Ser.). (Illus.). 48p. (gr. 2-6). lib. bdg. 27.00 (978-0-8368-7862-2(0), Gareth Stevens Learning Library) Stevens, Gareth Publishing LLLP.

Woop Studios Staff. A Zeal of Zebras: An Alphabet of Collective Nouns. 2011. (ENG.). 64p. (J). (gr. -1-17). 17.99 (978-1-4521-0492-8(1)) Chronicle Bks. LLC.

Working Animals, 6 vols., Set. Incl. Farming. Martin, Claudia. 28.50 (978-1-60870-162-9(X)); Helpers. Martin, Claudia. lib. bdg. 28.50 (978-1-60870-163-6(8)); Military. Grayson, Robert. 28.50 (978-1-60870-164-3(6)); Police. Mezzanotte, Jim. 28.50 (978-1-60870-166-7(2)); Transportation. Grayson, Robert. 28.50 (978-1-60870-167-4(0)); 64p. (gr. 5-18). (Working Animals Ser.). 2010. Set lib. bdg. 171.00 o.p. (978-1-60870-161-2(1)) Marshall Cavendish Corp.

Workman Publishing Company Staff. Wild Animals. 2014. (Eyelike Stickers Ser.). (ENG.). 12p. (J). pap. 6.95 (978-0-7611-7964-1(X), 17964) Workman Publishing Co., Inc.

World Book, Inc Staff, contrib. by. Animal Life Cycles. 2014. (Illus.). 32p. (J). (978-0-7166-2824-8(4)) World Bk., Inc.

—Animal Structure & Classification. 2014. (Illus.). 32p. (J). (978-0-7166-2822-4(8)) World Bk., Inc.

—Endangered & Threatened Species of Africa. 2014. (J). (978-0-7166-5621-0(3)) World Bk., Inc.

—Grasslands. 2012. (J). (978-0-7166-0446-4(9)) World Bk., Inc.

—Learning about Animals. 2011. (J). (978-0-7166-0231-6(8)) World Bk., Inc.

—Miniature Schnauzers & Other Terriers. 2009. (J). (978-0-7166-1366-4(2)) World Bk., Inc.

—Mountains & Polar Regions. 2012. (J). (978-0-7166-0448-8(5)) World Bk., Inc.

—Rain Forest Animals. 2007. (J). (978-0-7166-7729-1(6)) World Bk., Inc.

—Resources & Cumulative Index. 2005. (World Book's Science & Nature Guides Ser.). 80p. (J). (978-0-7166-4216-9(6)) World Bk., Inc.

—Savannas. 2012. (J). (978-0-7166-0443-3(4)) World Bk., Inc.

—Wild Animals. 2007. (J). (978-0-7166-7733-8(4)) World Bk., Inc.

—Wildlife & Climate Change. (Illus.). 44p. (J). 2016. (978-0-7166-2719-7(1)) 2015. (978-0-7166-2709-8(4)) World Bk., Inc.

World Book's Animals of the World. 2005. 569.00 (978-0-7166-1284-1(4), 60107) World Bk., Inc.

World Book's Animals of the World Set 2, 10 vols. 2005. (gr. 2-8). 189.00 (978-0-7166-1249-0(6), 20125) World Bk., Inc.

World of Animals. 2003. (Illus.). 256p. (J). 12.98 (978-1-4054-1704-4(8)) Parragon, Inc.

The World of Animals. (Children's Reference Ser.). 224p. (978-1-4054-9926-2(5)) Parragon, Inc.

The World of Eric Carle My Animals Activity Kit. 2007. (J). 16.99 (978-0-9794445-4-8(3)) Loew-Cornell, Inc.

World's Longest-Living Animals. 2016. (World's Longest-Living Animals Ser.). 00024p. (J). pap. 48.90 **(978-1-4824-5842-8(X))** Stevens, Gareth Publishing LLLP.

World's Scariest Predators. 2015. (World's Scariest Predators Ser.). (ENG.). 32p. (J). (gr. 3-3). 42.32 (978-1-5026-0332-6(2)); 114.00 (978-1-5026-0318-0(7)) Cavendish Square Publishing.

Worth, Bonnie. Safari, So Good! All about African Wildlife. Ruiz, Aristides & Mathieu, Joe, illus. 2011. (Cat in the Hat's Learning Library). (ENG.). 48p. (J). (gr. -1-3). 9.99 (978-0-375-86681-4(7), Random Hse. Bks. for Young Readers) Random Hse. Children's Bks.

Wright, Anna. A Tower of Giraffes: Animal Bunches. Wright, Anna, illus. 2015. (ENG., Illus.). 32p. (J). (gr. -1-2). lib. bdg. 17.95 (978-1-58089-707-5(X)) Charlesbridge Publishing, Inc.

Wright, Russell G. Survive? Investigations in Animal Diversity. (Event-Based Science Ser.). (gr. 5-9). 38p. pap., tchr.'s training gde. ed. 25.95 incl. VHS (978-0-7690-2353-3(3)); 66p. (YA). pap., stu. ed. 11.50 (978-0-7690-2352-6(5)) Seymour, Dale Pubns.

Wright, Shannon. Wild Wild Animals Coloring Book. 2013. (ENG.). 30p. 8.89 (978-1-62884-680-5(1), Baby Professor (Education Kids)) Speedy Publishing LLC.

Wynne, Patricia J. Wild Animals Activity Book. 2008. (Dover Children's Activity Bks.). (ENG., Illus.). 48p. (J). (gr. k-3). pap. 4.95 (978-0-486-46564-7(0)) Dover Pubns., Inc.

Wynne Pechter, Lesley. Alligator, Bear, Crab: A Baby's ABC, 1 vol. 2011. (ENG., Illus.). 24p. (J). (gr. -1-k). bds. 9.95 (978-1-55469-360-3(8)) Orca Bk. Pubs. USA.

Yolen, Jane. Animal Stories: Heartwarming True Tales from the Animal Kingdom. Ishida, Jui, illus. 2014. (ENG.). 160p. (J). (gr. 2-12). 24.99 (978-1-4263-1725-5(5), National Geographic Children's Bks.) National Geographic Society.

Yoon, Salina. Do Crocs Kiss? 2012. (Lift-The-Flap Book Ser.). (ENG., Illus.). 18p. (J). (gr. k — 1). bds. 9.95 (978-1-4027-8955-7(6)) Sterling Publishing Co., Inc.

Yoon, Salina, illus. Peek-a-Boo Farm Animals. 2005. (Peek-a-Boo Guess Who Book Ser.: Vol. 2). 10p. (J). 7.95 (978-1-58117-158-7(7), Intervisual/Piggy Toes) Bendon, Inc.

—Peek-a-Boo Wild Animals. 2005. (Peek-a-Boo Guess Who Book Ser.: Vol. 1). 10p. (J). (gr. -1-k). 7.95 (978-1-58117-157-0(9), Intervisual/Piggy Toes) Bendon, Inc.

York, M. J. Animals in Spring. 2017. (Welcome, Spring! Ser.). (ENG.). 24p. (J). (gr. -1-2). lib. bdg. 27.07 (978-1-5038-1651-0(6), 211503) Child's World, Inc., The.

Young, Caroline. The Great Animal Search. Jackson, Ian, illus. 2006. (Great Searches New Format Ser.). 48p. (J). (gr. 3). lib. bdg. 15.99 (978-1-58086-965-2(3)); (gr. -1-3). pap. 8.99 (978-0-7945-1028-2(0), Usborne) EDC Publishing.

Yoyo Books, creator. Baby Animals. 2011. (ENG., Illus.). 10p. (gr. -1-k). bds. (978-94-6151-209-3(0)) YoYo Bks.

—Wild Animals. 2011. (ENG., Illus.). 10p. (gr. -1-k). bds. (978-94-6151-207-9(4)) YoYo Bks.

Yoyo Books Staff. Animals: Mini Baby's First Library. 2005. 42p. bds. (978-90-5843-805-8(8)) YoYo Bks.

—Animals Around Me: Animal Jigsaw Fun. 2004. 12p. bds. (978-90-5843-550-7(4)) YoYo Bks.

—Baby Animals: Animal Jigsaw Fun. 2004. 12p. bds. (978-90-5843-551-4(2)) YoYo Bks.

—Wild Animals: Animal Jigsaw Fun. 2004. 12p. bds. (978-90-5843-552-1(0)) YoYo Bks.

Yucky Animals in the Yard. 2013. (Earth's Grossest Animals Ser.). 32p. (J). (gr. k-5). pap. 60.00 (978-1-61533-780-4(6), PowerKids Pr.) Rosen Publishing Group, Inc., The.

Zarin, Cynthia. Saints among the Animals. Gore, Leonid, illus. 2012. (ENG.). 96p. (J). (gr. 2-7). pap. 6.99 (978-1-4424-7296-9(0), Atheneum Bks. for Young Readers) Simon & Schuster Children's Publishing.

Zollman, Pam. Animal Life Cycles. 2006. (ENG.). 144p. (J). (gr. 1-2). pap. 8.95 (978-0-516-24555-3(4), Children's Pr.) Scholastic Library Publishing.

Zombie Animals: Parasites Take Control! 2015. (Zombie Animals: Parasites Take Control! Ser.). (ENG.). 24p. (J). (gr. 2-3). 135.60 (978-1-4824-2549-9(1)) Stevens, Gareth Publishing LLLP.

Zommer, Yuval & Taylor, Barbara. The Big Book of Beasts. 2017. (ENG., Illus.). 64p. (gr. -1-2). 19.95 (978-0-500-65106-3(X), 565106) Thames & Hudson.

Zondervan Staff. Polar Pals, 1 vol. 2011. (I Can Read! / Made by God Ser.). (ENG.). 32p. (J). pap. 3.99 (978-0-310-72188-8(1)) Zonderkidz.

—Weird & Wonderful Creations, 1 vol. 2014. (Made by God Ser.). (ENG., Illus.). 128p. (J). 9.99 (978-0-310-73124-5(0)) Zonderkidz.

—Wilderness Discoveries, Volume 1: Sand, Snakes, & Screeching Birds, 1 vol. 2013. (Nature of God Ser.). (ENG.). (J). 7.99 (978-0-310-88834-5(4)) Zonderkidz.

Zondervan Staff & Schriemer, Peter. Wilderness Discoveries, Volume 2: Forest, Frogs, & Feisty Critters, 1 vol. 2013. (Nature of God Ser.). (ENG.). (J). 7.99 (978-0-310-88835-2(2)) Zonderkidz.

—Wilderness Discoveries, Volume 3: Bugs, Bogs, & Spiky Beasts, 1 vol. 2013. (Nature of God Ser.). (ENG.). (J). 7.99 (978-0-310-88836-9(0)) Zonderkidz.

Zoo Animals. (Puzzle Shapes Ser.). 10p. (J). bds. (978-2-89393-788-5(8)) Phidal Publishing, Inc./Editions Phidal, Inc.

Zoobooks, 56 bks., Set. Incl. Animal Champions. Wexo, John Bonnett. 32p. (gr. 1-4). lib. bdg. 19.95 (978-0-88682-409-9(5)); Animal Champions 2. Shaw, Marjorie B. & Elwood, Ann. 24p. (gr. 1-4). lib. bdg. 19.95 (978-0-88682-774-8(4)); Animal Wonders. Wexo, John Bonnett. 32p. (gr. 1-4). lib. bdg. 14.95 (978-0-88682-407-5(9)); Apes. Wexo, John Bonnett. 24p. (gr. 2-12). lib. bdg. 19.95 (978-0-88682-265-1(3)); Baby Animals. Wexo, John Bonnett. 24p. (gr. 1-4). lib. bdg. 19.95 (978-0-88682-270-5(X)); Bats. Wood, Linda C. & Rink, Deane. 24p. (gr. 2-12). lib. bdg. 19.95 (978-0-88682-337-5(4)); Bears. Wexo, John Bonnett. 24p. (gr. 3-12). lib. bdg. 19.95 (978-0-88682-221-7(1)); Birds of Prey. Wexo, John Bonnett. 24p. (gr. 2-12). lib. bdg. 19.95 (978-0-88682-332-0(3)); Butterflies. Brust, Beth Wagner. 32p. (gr. 3-12). lib. bdg. 19.95 (978-0-88682-421-1(4)); Camels. Wexo, John Bonnett. 32p. (gr. 2-12). lib. bdg. 19.95 (978-0-88682-222-4(X)); Cheetahs. Wood, Linda C. & Jenson, Cynthia L. 32p. (gr. 2-12). lib. bdg. 19.95 (978-0-88682-417-4(6)); Chimpanzees & Bonobos. Elwood, Ann. 24p. (gr. 2-12). lib. bdg. 19.95 (978-0-88682-340-5(4)); Deer Family. Biel, Timothy Levi. 24p. (gr. 2-12). lib. bdg. 19.95 (978-0-88682-775-5(2)); Dinosaurs. Wexo, John Bonnett. 24p. (gr. 2-12). lib. bdg. 19.95 (978-0-88682-223-1(8)); Dolphins & Porpoises. Brust, Beth Wagner. 24p. (gr. 2-12). lib. bdg. 19.95 (978-0-88682-339-9(0)); Ducks, Geese & Swans. Wexo, John Bonnett. 24p. (gr. 3-12). lib. bdg. 19.95 (978-0-88682-224-8(6)); Eagles. Richardson, Adele D. 24p. (gr. 2-12). lib. bdg. 19.95 (978-0-88682-225-5(4)); Elephants. Wexo, John Bonnett. 24p. (gr. 2-12). lib. bdg. 19.95 (978-0-88682-226-2(2)); Endangered Animals. Wexo, John Bonnett. 24p. (gr. 2-12). lib. bdg. 19.95 (978-0-88682-269-9(6)); Giant Pandas. Wexo, John Bonnett. 24p. (gr. 2-12). lib. bdg. 19.95 (978-0-88682-228-6(9)); Giraffes. Wexo, John Bonnett. 24p. (gr. 2-12). lib. bdg. 19.95 (978-0-88682-334-4(X)); Gorillas. Wexo, John Bonnett. 32p. (gr. 2-12). lib. bdg. 19.95 (978-0-88682-423-5(0)); Hippos. Brust, Beth Wagner. 32p. (gr. 2-12). lib. bdg. 19.95 (978-0-88682-424-2(9)); Hummingbirds. Biel, Timothy Levi. 24p. (gr. 2-12). lib. bdg. 19.95 (978-0-88682-336-8(6)); Insects. Wexo, John Bonnett. 24p. (gr. 2-12). lib. bdg. 19.95 (978-0-88682-335-1(8)); Insects 2. Wexo, John Bonnett. 24p. (gr. 2-12). lib. bdg. 19.95 (978-0-88682-776-2(0)); Kangaroos. Brust, Beth Wagner. 32p. (gr. 2-12). lib. bdg. 19.95 (978-0-88682-425-9(7)); Koalas. Wexo, John Bonnett. 24p. (gr. 2-12). lib. bdg. 19.95 (978-0-88682-227-9(0)); Lions. Elwood, Ann & Estrada, Jackie. 32p. (gr. 2-12). lib. bdg. 19.95 (978-0-88682-422-8(2)); Little Cats. Wexo, John Bonnett. 32p. (gr. 2-12). lib. bdg. 19.95 (978-0-88682-413-6(3)); Night Animals. Wexo, John Bonnett. 24p. (gr. 2-12). lib. bdg. 19.95 (978-0-88682-777-9(9)); Old World Monkeys. Elwood, Ann. 32p. (gr. 3-12). lib. bdg. 19.95 (978-0-88682-419-8(2)); Orangutans. Wexo, John Bonnett. 32p. (gr. 2-12). lib. bdg. 19.95 (978-0-88682-412-9(5)); Ostriches, Emus, Rheas, Kiwis & Cassowaries. Elwood, Ann. 24p. (gr. 2-12). lib. bdg. 19.95 (978-0-88682-338-2(2)); Owls. Biel, Timothy Levi. 24p. (gr. 3-12). lib. bdg. 19.95 (978-0-88682-268-2(8)); Parrots. Wexo, John Bonnett. 32p. (gr. 2-12). lib. bdg. 19.95 (978-0-88682-408-2(7)); Penguins. Wexo, John Bonnett. 24p. (gr. 2-12). lib. bdg. 19.95 (978-0-88682-263-7(7)); Polar Bears. Biel, Timothy Levi. 32p. (gr. 2-12). lib. bdg. 19.95 (978-0-88682-414-3(1)); Rattlesnakes. Brust, Beth Wagner & Dorn, Bob. 32p. (gr. 2-12). lib. bdg. 19.95 (978-0-88682-426-6(5)); Rhinos. Wexo, John Bonnett. 24p. (gr. 2-12). lib. bdg. 19.95 (978-0-88682-333-7(1)); Sea Birds. Brust, Beth Wagner. 32p. (gr. 2-12). lib. bdg. 19.95 (978-0-88682-416-7(8)); Sea Otters. Brust, Beth Wagner. 32p. (gr. 2-12). lib. bdg. 19.95 (978-0-88682-415-0(X)); Seals, Sea Lions & Walruses. Wexo, John Bonnett. 24p. (gr. 2-12). lib. bdg. 19.95 (978-0-88682-271-2(8)); Sharing the World with Animals. Shaw, Marjorie B. & Elwood, Ann. 24p. (gr. 1-4). lib. bdg. 19.95 (978-0-88682-778-6(7)); Sharks. Wexo, John Bonnett. 24p. (gr. 2-12). lib. bdg. 19.95 (978-0-88682-229-3(7)); Skunks & Their Relatives. Biel, Timothy Levi. 24p. (gr. 2-12). lib. bdg. 19.95 (978-0-88682-779-3(5)); Snakes. Wexo, John Bonnett. 24p. (gr. 2-12). lib. bdg. 19.95 (978-0-88682-331-3(5)); Spiders. Biel, Timothy Levi. 32p. (gr. 2-12). lib. bdg. 19.95 (978-0-88682-410-5(9)); Tigers. Biel, Timothy Levi. 24p. (gr. 2-12). lib. bdg. 19.95 (978-0-88682-266-8(1)); Turtles. Biel, Timothy Levi. 32p. (gr. 2-12). lib. bdg. 19.95 (978-0-88682-411-2(7)); Whales. Wexo, John Bonnett. 24p. (gr. 2-12). lib. bdg. 19.95 (978-0-88682-272-9(6)); Wolves. Wexo, John Bonnett. 24p. (gr. 2-12). lib. bdg. 19.95 (978-0-88682-267-5(X)); Zebras. Wood, Linda C. 32p. (gr. 2-12). lib. bdg. 19.95 (978-0-88682-420-4(6)); (J). 1995. (Illus.). 1157.10 (978-0-88682-238-5(6), Creative Education) Creative Co., The.

Zorzi, Gina & Sánchez, Lucía M. Desiertos: This Is a Desert. 2011. (2G Ecosistemas Ser.). (SPA.). 36p. (J). (gr. k-2). pap. 6.99 (978-1-61541-424-6(X)) American Reading Co.

Zourelias, Diana. A Barrel of Monkeys & Other Animal Groups. 2015. (Dover Coloring Bks.). (ENG.). 32p. (J). (gr. 1-5). pap. 3.99 (978-0-486-78465-6(7)) Dover Pubns., Inc.

Zuchora-Walske, Christine. That Bull Is Seeing Red! Science's Biggest Mistakes about Animals & Plants. 2014. (Science Gets It Wrong Ser.). (Illus.). 32p. (gr. 4-6). pap. 7.95 (978-1-4677-4550-5(2)); (ENG., lib. bdg. 26.60 (978-1-4677-3660-2(0), Lerner Pubns.) Lerner Publishing Group.

Zuckerman, Andrew, photos by. Creature ABC Flash Cards. 2014. (ENG., Illus.). 26p. (J). (gr. -1-17). 14.99 (978-1-4521-1181-0(2)) Chronicle Bks. LLC.

—Creature Colors. 2014. (ENG., Illus.). 20p. (J). (gr. -1 — 1). bds. 7.99 (978-1-4521-1668-6(7)) Chronicle Bks. LLC.

—Creature Matching Game. 2014. (ENG., Illus.). 36p. (J). (gr. -1-k). bds. 14.99 (978-1-4521-1723-2(3)) Chronicle Bks. LLC.

Zuravicky, Orli. Amazing Animals: Multiplying Multidigit Numbers by a One-Digit Number with Regrouping. 2009. (PowerMath Ser.). (Illus.). 24p. (gr. 3-4). pap. 8.25 (978-0-8239-8861-7(9), PowerKids Pr.) Rosen Publishing Group, Inc., The.

100 Facts You Should Know: Set 3. 2015. (100 Facts You Should Know Ser.). (ENG.). 48p. (J). (gr. 4-5). pap., pap., pap. 84.30 (978-1-4824-3429-3(6)) Stevens, Gareth Publishing LLLP.

ANIMALS—ANATOMY

see Anatomy, Comparative

ANIMALS, AQUATIC

see Freshwater Animals; Marine Animals

ANIMALS—COLOR

Algarra, Alejandro & Bonilla, Rocio. Why Are Animals Different Colors? 2016. (Curious Young Minds Ser.). (ENG., Illus.). 36p. (J). (gr. -1-2). pap. 7.99 (978-1-4380-0893-6(7)) Barron's Educational Series, Inc.

Borth, Teddy. Animal Colors, 1 vol. 2014. (Animal Colors Ser.: 6). (ENG.). 24p. (J). (gr. 2-4). lib. bdg. 171.00 (978-1-62970-693-1(0)) ABDO Publishing Co.

Clark Sawyer, J. Animal Colors: What They Mean. 2014. (Little Bits: Colors Tell a Story Ser.). (ENG.). 24p. (J). (gr. -1-3). lib. bdg. 23.93 (978-1-62724-321-6(6)) Bearport Publishing Co., Inc.

—Los Colores de Los Animales: Qué Significan. 2014. (Los Colores Cuentan una Historia Ser.). (SPA., Illus.). 24p. (J). (gr. -1-3). lib. bdg. 23.93 (978-1-62724-463-3(8)) Bearport Publishing Co., Inc.

de Lambilly-Bresson, Elisabeth. Animales de Vivos Colores. 2007. (Los animales nos cuentan su vida (Animal Show & Tell) Ser.). (SPA., Illus.). 16p. (gr. -1-3). lib. bdg. 19.00 (978-0-8368-8161-5(3), Gareth Stevens Learning Library) Stevens, Gareth Publishing LLLP.

—Colorful Animals. 2007. (Animal Show & Tell Ser.). (Illus.). 16p. (gr. -1-3). lib. bdg. 19.00 (978-0-8368-8159-2(1), Gareth Stevens Learning Library) Stevens, Gareth Publishing LLLP.

Dorling Kindersley Publishing Staff. Animal Colors. (ENG., (J). (gr. -1-k). 2015. Illus.). 14p. bds. 7.99 (978-1-4654-2946-9(8)) 2012. 12p. bds. 6.99 (978-1-4654-0164-9(4)) Dorling Kindersley Publishing, Inc. (DK Children).

Feldman, Thea. Kingfisher Readers L1: Animal Colors. 2014. (Kingfisher Readers Ser.). (ENG., Illus.). 32p. (J). (gr. k-3). 12.99 (978-0-7534-7134-0(5), 9780753471340, Kingfisher) Roaring Brook Pr.

Fielding, Beth. Animal Colors. 2010. (ENG., Illus.). 24p. (J). (— 1). bds. 7.99 (978-0-9797455-6-0(X)) EarlyLight Bks., Inc.

—Animal Colors: A Rainbow of Colors from Animals Around the World. (ENG.). 32p. (J). (gr. -1-3). 2010. pap. 8.95 (978-0-9832014-8-9(X)) 2009. 14.95 (978-0-9797455-4-6(3)) EarlyLight Bks., Inc.

Gibbs, Edward. I Spy with My Little Eye. Gibbs, Edward, illus. 2014. (ENG., Illus.). 22p. (J). (-k). bds. 7.99 (978-0-7636-7163-1(0), Templar) Candlewick Pr.

Keating, Jess. Pink Is for Blobfish. 2016. (World of Weird Animals Ser.). (ENG., Illus.). 48p. (J). (gr. k-3). 16.99 (978-0-553-51227-4(7), Knopf Bks. for Young Readers) Random Hse. Children's Bks.

Lawler, Janet. Rain Forest Colors. Laman, Tim, photos by. 2014. (ENG., Illus.). 32p. (J). (-k). 16.99 (978-1-4263-1733-0(6), National Geographic Children's Bks.) National Geographic Society.

little bee books, little bee. Animal Colors. Max & Sid, Max &, illus. 2015. (Tiny Touch Ser.). (ENG.). 12p. (J). (gr. -1 — 1). bds. 4.99 (978-1-4998-0057-9(6)) Little Bee Books Inc.

Lunde, Darrin P. Monkey Colors. Wynne, Patricia J., illus. 2012. (ENG.). 32p. (J). (gr. -1-2). 15.95 (978-1-57091-741-7(8)); pap. 7.99 (978-1-57091-742-4(6)) Charlesbridge Publishing, Inc.

Maze, Stephanie, ed. Beautiful Moments in the Wild: Animals & Their Colors. 2006. (Moments in the Wild Ser.). (Illus.). 36p. (J). (gr. -1-k). pap. 8.00 (978-0-9769542-5-5(7)) Moonstone Pr., LLC.

—Momentos Hermosos en el Reino Animal: Los Animales y Sus Colores. 2006. (Momentos en el reino Animal Ser.). (SPA., Illus.). 28p. (J). (gr. -1-k). pap. 8.00 (978-0-9769542-7-9(3)) Moonstone Pr., LLC.

Rabe, Tish. High? Low? Where Did It Go? All about Animal Camouflage. Ruiz, Aristides & Mathieu, Joe, illus. 2016. (Cat in the Hat's Learning Library). (ENG.). 48p. (J). (gr. k-3). 9.99 (978-0-449-81496-3(3), Random Hse. Bks. for Young Readers) Random Hse. Children's Bks.

Racanelli, Marie. Albino Animals. 2010. (Crazy Nature Ser.). 24p. (J). (gr. 1-5). lib. bdg., E-Book 42.50 (978-1-4488-0149-7(4)); (Illus.). pap. 8.25 (978-1-4358-9854-7(0), PowerKids Pr.); (Illus.). (gr. 1-4). lib. bdg. 22.60 (978-1-4358-9381-8(6)) Rosen Publishing Group, Inc., The.

Salzmann, Mary Elizabeth. What Has Spots?, 1 vol. 2007. (Creature Features Ser.). (ENG., Illus.). 24p. (gr. -1-3). 25.65 (978-1-59928-872-7(9), Super SandCastle) ABDO Publishing Co.

—What Has Stripes?, 1 vol. 2007. (Creature Features Ser.). (ENG., Illus.). 24p. (gr. -1-3). 25.65 (978-1-59928-873-4(7), Super SandCastle) ABDO Publishing Co.

Schuh, Mari. Black & White Animals. 2017. (Black & White Animals Ser.). (ENG.). 24p. (gr. k-1). 131.94 (978-1-5157-3398-0(X), Pebble Bks.) Capstone Press of Coughlan Cos.

—Zebras. 2017. (Black & White Animals Ser.). (ENG., Illus.). 24p. (gr. k-1). lib. bdg. 21.99 (978-1-5157-3374-4(2), Pebble Bks.) Capstone Press of Coughlan Cos.

Shepherd, Jodie. Black-And-White Animals. 2016. (Rookie Toddlers Ser.). (ENG.). 12p. (J). bds. 6.95 (978-0-531-22452-6(X), Children's Pr.) Scholastic Library Publishing.

Stewart, Melissa. Blue Animals. 2012. (All about a Rainbow of Animals Ser.). (Illus.). 24p. (J). (gr. -1-1). pap. 7.95 (978-1-4644-0041-4(5), Enslow Elementary); 22.60 (978-0-7660-3999-5(4)) Enslow Pubs., Inc.

—Green Animals. 2012. (All about a Rainbow of Animals Ser.). 24p. (J). (gr. -1-1). (Illus.). pap. 7.95 (978-1-4644-0044-5(X), Enslow Elementary); 22.60 (978-0-7660-3998-8(6)) Enslow Pubs., Inc.

—Orange Animals. 2012. (All about a Rainbow of Animals Ser.). 24p. (J). (gr. -1-1). (Illus.). pap. 7.95 (978-1-4644-0043-8(1), Enslow Elementary); 22.60 (978-0-7660-3996-4(X)) Enslow Pubs., Inc.

—Purple Animals. 2012. (All about a Rainbow of Animals Ser.). 24p. (J). (gr. -1-1). (Illus.). pap. 7.95 (978-1-4644-0040-7(7)); 22.60 (978-0-7660-4000-7(3)) Enslow Pubs., Inc. (Enslow Elementary).

—A Rainbow of Animals. 2010. (Rainbow of Animals Ser.). (Illus.). 128p. (J). (gr. k-3). pap. 11.99 (978-0-7660-3706-9(1)) Enslow Pubs., Inc.

—Red Animals. 2012. (All about a Rainbow of Animals Ser.). 24p. (J). (gr. -1-1). (Illus.). pap. 7.95 (978-1-4644-0042-1(3), Enslow Elementary); 22.60 (978-0-7660-3995-7(1)) Enslow Pubs., Inc.

—Why Are Animals Blue? 2009. (Rainbow of Animals Ser.). (Illus.). 32p. (J). (gr. k-3). lib. bdg. 23.94 (978-0-7660-3251-4(5)) Enslow Pubs., Inc.

—Why Are Animals Green? 2009. (Rainbow of Animals Ser.). (Illus.). 32p. (J). (gr. k-3). lib. bdg. 23.94 (978-0-7660-3252-1(3)) Enslow Pubs., Inc.

—Why Are Animals Orange? 2009. (Rainbow of Animals Ser.). (Illus.). 32p. (J). (gr. k-3). lib. bdg. 23.94 (978-0-7660-3250-7(7)) Enslow Pubs., Inc.

—Why Are Animals Purple? 2009. (Rainbow of Animals Ser.). (Illus.). 32p. (J). (gr. k-3). lib. bdg. 23.94 (978-0-7660-3254-5(X)) Enslow Pubs., Inc.

—Why Are Animals Red? 2009. (Rainbow of Animals Ser.). (Illus.). 32p. (J). (gr. k-3). lib. bdg. 23.94 (978-0-7660-3249-1(3)) Enslow Pubs., Inc.

—Why Are Animals Yellow? 2009. (Rainbow of Animals Ser.). (Illus.). 32p. (J). (gr. k-3). lib. bdg. 23.94 (978-0-7660-3253-8(1)) Enslow Pubs., Inc.

—Yellow Animals. 2012. (All about a Rainbow of Animals Ser.). 24p. (J). (gr. -1-1). (Illus.). pap. 7.95 (978-1-4644-0045-2(8),

Enslow Elementary); 22.60 *(978-0-7660-3997-1(8))* Enslow Pubs., Inc.

Stockdale, Susan. Spectacular Spots, 1 vol. Stockdale, Susan, illus. 2015. (ENG & SPA., Illus.). 32p. (J). (gr. 1-1). 15.95 *(978-1-56145-817-2(1))* Peachtree Pubs.

—Spectacular Spots / Magníficas Manchas, 1 vol. Stockdale, Susan, illus. rev. ed. 2017. (ENG & SPA., Illus.). 32p. (J). (gr. -1-1). pap. 8.95 *(978-1-56145-978-0(X))* Peachtree Pubs.

—Stripes of All Types, 1 vol. Stockdale, Susan, illus. 2013. (About Habitats Ser.). (ENG., Illus.). 32p. (J). (gr. -1-1). 16.95 *(978-1-56145-695-6(0))* Peachtree Pubs.

—Stripes of All Types / Rayas de Todas Las Tallas, 1 vol. Stockdale, Susan, illus. 2014. (SPA & ENG., Illus.). 32p. (J). (gr. -1-1). pap. 8.95 *(978-1-56145-793-9(0))* Peachtree Pubs.

Stone, Lynn M. Códigos de Color: Color Codes. 2008. (SPA & ENG.). (J). 22.79 *(978-1-60472-509-4(5))* Rourke Educational Media.

Sundance/Newbridge LLC Staff. Animals in Hiding. 2007. (Early Science Ser.). (gr. k-3). 18.95 *(978-1-4007-6350-4(9))*; pap. 6.10 *(978-1-4007-6346-7(0))* Sundance/Newbridge Educational Publishing.

Tildes, Phyllis Limbacher. Baby Animals Spots & Stripes. Tildes, Phyllis Limbacher, illus. 2015. (ENG., Illus.). 10p. (J). (— 1). bds. 6.95 *(978-1-58089-608-5(1))* Charlesbridge Publishing, Inc.

Waxman, Laura Hamilton. Walking Sticks & Other Amazing Camouflage. 2017. (Searchlight Books (tm) — Animal Superpowers Ser.). (ENG.). 40p. (J). (gr. 3-5). 16.99 ***(978-1-5124-3672-3(0)***, Lerner Pubns.); 46.65 ***(978-1-5124-2824-7(8)***, Lerner Pubns.); 46.65 ***(978-1-5124-3671-6(2)***, Lerner Pubns.); (Illus.). 30.65 *(978-1-5124-2549-9(4))* Lerner Publishing Group.

Wildsmith, Brian, illus. Les Couleurs des Animaux. 2005. (FRE & ENG.). 16p. (J). (gr. -1). per., bds. 5.95 *(978-1-59572-031-3(6))* Star Bright Bks., Inc.

Yaw, Valerie. Color-Changing Animals. 2016. (Animals with Super Powers Ser.). (ENG.). 24p. (J). (gr. 1-6). pap. 7.95 ***(978-1-944998-68-4(3))*** Bearport Publishing Co., Inc.

Yontz-Oetting, Carolyn. Black & White Animals Color the World. 2008. 48p. pap. 21.99 *(978-1-4363-1160-1(8))* Xlibris Corp.

ANIMALS, CRUELTY TO

see Animals—Treatment

ANIMALS—DICTIONARIES

ABDO Publishing Company. Animal Kingdom Set 1, Set. 2003. (Animal Kingdom Set 1 Ser.). (gr. k-4). 1026.00 *(978-1-57765-531-2(1)*, Buddy Bks.) ABDO Publishing Co.

Amstutz, Lisa J., et al. My First Picture Encyclopedias. 2013. (My First Picture Encyclopedias Ser.). (ENG.). 32p. (gr. 1-2). pap. 31.80 *(978-1-62065-769-0(4)*, Aplus Bks.) Capstone Press of Coughlan Cos.

Barman, Adrienne. Creaturepedia: Welcome to the Greatest Show on Earth. 2015. (Creaturepedia Ser.). (ENG.). 216p. (J). (gr. k-3). 22.99 *(978-1-84780-696-3(1)*, Wide Eyed Editions) Quarto Publishing Group UK GBR. Dist: Hachette Bk. Group.

—Creaturepedia Activity Book. 2016. (Creaturepedia Ser.). (ENG.). 40p. (J). pap. 9.99 *(978-1-84780-793-9(3)*, Wide Eyed Editions) Quarto Publishing Group UK GBR. Dist: Littlehampton Bk Services, Ltd.

Claybourne, Anna, et al. My First Animal Encyclopedia. 2015. (Illus.). 184p. (J). *(978-1-4351-5933-4(0))* Barnes & Noble, Inc.

Dowswell, Paul. First Encyclopedia of Animals. 2004. (First Encyclopedias Ser.). (SPA & ENG., Illus.). (J). (gr. 3-18). 1p. pap. 9.95 *(978-0-7945-0215-7(6)*, Usborne); 64p. lib. bdg. 17.95 *(978-1-58086-426-8(0))* EDC Publishing.

—Little Encyclopedia of Animals. 2005. (Illus.). 64p. (J). (gr. -1-3). 6.95 *(978-0-7945-1093-0(0)*, Usborne) EDC Publishing.

French, Mary. Animal Gazetteer. 2nd ed. 2011. (Illus.). 569p. (J). *(978-1-934669-05-1(9))* Dictionary Project, Inc., The.

Ganeri, Anita. First Animal Encyclopedia Rainforests. 2014. (First Animal Encyclopedia Ser.). (ENG., Illus.). 64p. (J). (gr. -1-3). 13.99 *(978-1-4088-4308-6(0)*, 9781408843086, Bloomsbury USA Childrens) Bloomsbury Publishing USA.

Grolier Incorporated Staff, contrib. by. Amazing Animals of the World. 2007. (J). *(978-0-7172-6229-8(4))*; *(978-0-7172-6228-1(6))*; *(978-0-7172-6227-4(8))*; *(978-0-7172-6226-7(X))*; *(978-0-7172-6235-9(9))*; *(978-0-7172-6234-2(0))*; *(978-0-7172-6233-5(2))*; *(978-0-7172-6230-4(8))*; *(978-0-7172-6231-1(6))*; *(978-0-7172-6232-8(4))* Grolier, Ltd.

—Amazing Animals of the World, 10 vols., Set 1. rev. ed. 2007. (J). (gr. 3-9). lib. bdg. 199.00 *(978-0-7172-6225-0(1)*, Grolier) Scholastic Library Publishing.

Holland, Simon. First Animal Encyclopedia Polar Animals. 2015. (First Animal Encyclopedia Ser.). (ENG., Illus.). 64p. (J). (gr. -1-3). 13.99 *(978-1-4729-1344-9(2)*, 9781472913449, Bloomsbury USA Childrens) Bloomsbury Publishing USA.

Howell, Laura & Rogers, Kirsteen. Animal World. 2004. (Internet-Linked Library of Science). 64p. (J). pap. 9.95 *(978-0-7945-0083-2(8)*, Usborne); lib. bdg. 17.95 *(978-1-58086-372-8(8))* EDC Publishing.

Jackson, Tom. The World Encyclopedia of Animals: An Expert Reference Guide to 350 Amphibians, Reptiles & Mammals from Every Continent, with over 500 Illustrations & photographs. 2016. (ENG., Illus.). 256p. 10.99 *(978-1-84681-852-3(4)*, Lorenz Bks.) Anness Publishing GBR. Dist: National Bk. Network.

Johnson, Jinny, ed. Animal Planet Wild World: An Encyclopedia of Animals. 2013. 132p. pap. 35.93 *(978-1-4677-1692-5(8))* Lerner Publishing Group.

Kingfisher Editors. First Encyclopedia of Animals. 2nd ed. 2011. (Kingfisher First Reference Ser.). (ENG., Illus.). 144p. (J). (gr. k-3). pap. 10.99 *(978-0-7534-6588-2(4)*, 9780753465882, Kingfisher) Roaring Brook Pr.

Morgan, Sally. Children's Animal Encyclopedia. 2011. (Illus.). 224p. (J). *(978-1-4351-3676-2(4))* Barnes & Noble, Inc.

My First Animal Encyclopedia. (Children's Reference Ser.). 224p. *(978-1-4054-9454-0(9))*; 2008. 256p. *(978-1-4075-3203-5(0))* Parragon, Inc.

My First Picture Encyclopedias. 2013. (My First Picture Encyclopedias Ser.). (ENG.). 32p. (gr. 1-2). pap. 63.60 *(978-1-62065-770-6(8)*, Aplus Bks.) Capstone Press of Coughlan Cos.

Pet Dictionary: An a to Z of Animal Companions. 2005. (Illus.). 64p. (J). pap. *(978-0-439-75459-0(3))* Scholastic, Inc.

Taplin, Sam. Little Encyclopedia of Dinosaurs. 2005. (Illus.). 64p. (J). (gr. -1-3). 6.95 *(978-0-7945-1087-9(6)*, Usborne) EDC Publishing.

Toft, Barbara. Complete Guides Animals. 2012. (ENG.). 144p. (J). *(978-1-4351-4403-3(1))* Barnes & Noble, Inc.

U. S. National Geographic Society Staff & Spelman, Lucy H. Animal Encyclopedia: 2,500 Animals with Photos, Maps, & More! 2012. (ENG., Illus.). 304p. (J). (gr. 3-7). 24.95 *(978-1-4263-1022-5(6))*; lib. bdg. 33.90 *(978-1-4263-1023-2(4))* National Geographic Society. (National Geographic Children's Bks.).

Wild Wild World. Date not set. (Illus.). (J). 48p. 5.98 *(978-1-4054-0208-8(3))*; 256p. *(978-1-4054-1541-5(X))* Parragon, Inc.

Wooster, Patricia & Dell, Pamela. My First Picture Encyclopedias. 2013. (My First Picture Encyclopedias Ser.). (ENG.). 32p. (gr. 1-2). lib. bdg. 109.28 *(978-1-62065-967-0(0)*, Aplus Bks.) Capstone Press of Coughlan Cos.

World Book, Inc Staff, contrib. by. Encyclopedia of Animals. 2013. (Illus.). (J). *(978-0-7166-7518-1(8))* World Bk., Inc.

Young, Carol. Los Animales del Mundo. 2004.Tr. of Great Animal Search. (SPA., Illus.). 48p. (J). (gr. -1-3). pap. 9.95 *(978-0-7460-3656-3(6))* EDC Publishing.

ANIMALS—DISEASES

see Veterinary Medicine

ANIMALS, DOMESTIC

see Domestic Animals

ANIMALS, EXTINCT

see Extinct Animals

ANIMALS—FICTION

see also Fables

Abraham, Arnetta. Miss Robbie's House. 2009. 64p. pap. 23.49 *(978-1-4490-4571-5(5))* AuthorHouse.

Abrams, Penny. The Calabash Tales. Mikki, illus. 2011. 66p. 28.00 *(978-1-4349-1169-8(1))* Dorrance Publishing Co., Inc.

Absolutely Not! Individual Title Six-Packs. (Story Steps Ser.). (gr. k-2). 29.00 *(978-0-7635-9613-2(2))* Rigby Education.

Ackerman, Tova. Group Soup. Gorbachev, Valeri, illus. (Orig.). pap. 6.95 *(978-0-9720183-0-2(1))* Puppetry in Practice.

Adams, Jesse. Farmer Dillo Paints His Barn. Speer, Julie & Davis, Christopher Owen, illus. 2007. (J). (gr. -1-3). pap. 12.95 *(978-1-59166-808-4(5))* BJU Pr.

Adams, Michelle Medlock. The Sparrow's Easter Song. Eldridge, Marion, illus. 2003. (ENG.). 32p. (J). 14.95 *(978-0-8249-5470-3(X)*, Ideal Pubns.) Worthy Publishing.

Adams, Najla. The Adventures of Mama Deer. 2012. 48p. pap. 21.99 *(978-1-4691-6155-6(9))* Xlibris Corp.

Adeleke, Abraham Ajibade. Beauty Contest in the Animal Kingdom. 2011. 40p. pap. 16.46 *(978-1-4269-5773-4(4))* Trafford Publishing.

Adler, Naomi. The Barefoot Book of Animal Tales. Hall, Amanda, illus. 2004. 80p. (J). 9.99 *(978-1-84148-547-8(0))* Barefoot Bks., Inc.

The adventures of officer Byrd. 2007. (J). 16.99 *(978-0-9787322-0-2(0))* Officer Byrd Publishing Co.

Aesop Enterprise Inc. Staff & Baruzzi, Agnese. Aesop's Fables. Baruzzi, Agnese, illus. 2012. (ENG., Illus.). 16p. (J). (gr. k-2). 18.99 *(978-1-85707-895-4(0))* Tango Bks. GBR. Dist: Independent Pubs. Group.

Agatha Jane. Ces Mignonnes Autres Créatures: L'Histoire de Ben. Mais Est-Elle Vraie ? 2012. 64p. (-18). pap. 27.45 *(978-1-4772-4306-6(0))* AuthorHouse.

Ahearn, Dan & Ahearn, Janet. Animal Adventures. 2011. (Navigators Ser.). (J). pap. *(978-1-61672-967-7(8))* Benchmark Education Co.

Ahlberg, Allan. Chicken, Chips & Peas, Vol. 1. Amstutz, Andre, illus. (ENG.). 32p. (J). pap. 9.95 *(978-0-14-056397-9(0))* Penguin Publishing Group.

Ahmed, Said Salah. The Lion's Share/Qayb Libaax: A Somali Folktale. Dupre, Kelly, illus. 2006. 32p. (J). (gr. -1-3). pap. 7.95 *(978-1-931016-13-1(5))* Minnesota Humanities Ctr.

Ahrens, Albrecht. Simply Out in the Woods: An Inspirational Children's Story. 2013. 232p. pap. *(978-1-4602-0688-1(6))* FriesenPress.

Aigner-Clark, Julie. Baby Einstein: on the Farm. Zaidi, Nadeem, illus. 2007. (Baby Einstein Ser.). (ENG.). *(978-0-7634-2150-2(2))* Walt Disney Records.

Aiken, Zora & Aiken, David. Busy Bodies: Play Like the Animals, 1 vol. 2011. (ENG., Illus.). 32p. (J). 14.99 *(978-0-7643-3832-8(3)*, 9780764338328, Schiffer Publishing Ltd) Schiffer Publishing, Ltd.

Aikins, Dave, illus. Race to the Tower of Power. 2005. (Backyardigans Ser.: Vol. 1). (ENG.). 24p. (J). pap. 3.99 *(978-1-4169-0799-2(8)*, Simon Spotlight/Nickelodeon) Simon Spotlight/Nickelodeon.

Albee, Sarah. Max Can Fix That. Schick, Joel, illus. 2006. (Step-By-Step Readers Ser.). (J). pap. *(978-1-59939-055-0(8)*, Reader's Digest Young Families, Inc.) Studio Fun International.

Alborough, Jez. Billy the Goat's Big Breakfast. Alborough, Jez, illus. 2014. (ENG., Illus.). 32p. (J). 12.99 *(978-1-61067-190-3(2))* Kane Miller.

Albuquerque, Jessica. Jessica & the Caramuri. 2012. 32p. pap. 19.99 *(978-1-4772-7916-8(4))* AuthorHouse.

Alemagna, Beatrice, creator. The Wonderful Fluffy Little Squishy. 2015. (ENG., Illus.). 48p. (J). (gr. -1-3). 18.95 *(978-1-59270-180-3(9))* Enchanted Lion Bks., LLC.

Alexander, Brad. Antiniak: A Different Kind of Village. 2011. 76p. pap. 15.50 *(978-1-257-10163-4(3))* Lulu Pr., Inc.

Alexander, Claire. Lucy & the Bully, 1 vol. Alexander, Claire, illus. 2008. (ENG., Illus.). 32p. (J). (gr. -1-3). 16.99 *(978-0-8075-4786-1(7))* Whitman, Albert & Co.

Alexander, Claire, illus. Back to Front & Upside Down. 2012. (ENG.). 26p. (J). 16.00 *(978-0-8028-5414-8(1)*, Eerdmans Bks For Young Readers) Eerdmans, William B. Publishing Co.

Alexander, Heather. Wallace & Grace & the Cupcake Caper. Zarrin, Laura, illus. 2017. (Wallace & Grace Ser.). (ENG.). 80p. (J). 9.99 *(978-1-68119-010-5(9)*, 9781681190105, Bloomsbury USA Childrens) Bloomsbury Publishing USA.

Alexander, Heather. Wallace & Grace & the Lost Puppy. Zarrin, Laura, illus. 2017. (Wallace & Grace Ser.). (ENG.). 80p. (J). 9.99 ***(978-1-68119-012-9(5)***, 9781681190129, Bloomsbury USA Childrens) Bloomsbury Publishing USA.

Alexander, Janice Marie. Princess Panny - Not Princess Nobody. Arkanov, Elvira, illus. 2013. 46p. pap. 21.95 *(978-0-9890410-1-0(8))* Artistic Angels Corp.

Alexander, Mark. Whose Toes Are Those? 2006. (Neighborhood Readers Ser.). (ENG.). 12p. (gr. 1-3). pap. 5.90 *(978-1-4042-7042-8(6)*, Rosen Classroom) Rosen Publishing Group, Inc., The.

Allaway, Al. Laughing Flowers & Blooming Animals. 2009. 32p. pap. 17.95 *(978-0-557-04195-4(3))* Lulu Pr., Inc.

Allen, Alejandro & Rountree, Benjamin. El Jirafante Luis: The Giraffephant Luis. 2011. (SPA.). 40p. (gr. 1-2). pap. 18.99 *(978-1-4567-3903-4(4))* AuthorHouse.

Allen, Teresa R. Laura, the Bichon Frise: My New Home. 2004. 31p. pap. 24.95 *(978-1-4137-3525-3(8))* PublishAmerica, Inc.

Almeida, Jose-Gabriel. Lodiville: Adventure Land. 2008. 52p. pap. 16.95 *(978-1-60563-989-5(3))* America Star Bks.

Alter, Anna. Sprout Street Neighbors - A New Arrival. 2016. (Sprout Street Neighbors Ser.). (ENG., Illus.). 128p. (J). (gr. 1-4). 12.99 *(978-0-385-75562-7(7)*, Knopf Bks. for Young Readers) Random Hse. Children's Bks.

—Sprout Street Neighbors: a New Arrival. 2017. (Sprout Street Neighbors Ser.: 2). (ENG.). 128p. (J). (gr. 1-4). pap. 6.99 ***(978-0-385-75564-1(3)***, Yearling) Random Hse. Children's Bks.

—Sprout Street Neighbors: Bon Voyage. 2017. (Sprout Street Neighbors Ser.: 3). (ENG., Illus.). 96p. (J). (gr. 1-4). pap. 6.99 ***(978-1-5247-0053-9(3)***, Yearling) Random Hse. Children's Bks.

Alvarez, Jennifer Lynn. The Guardian Herd: Windborn. McClellan, David, illus. 2017. (Guardian Herd Ser.: 4). 432p. (J). (gr. 3-7). pap. 6.99 ***(978-0-06-228616-1(1))*** HarperCollins Pubs.

Alvarez, Jennifer Lynn. Starfire. 2014. (Guardian Herd Ser.: 1). (ENG., Illus.). 272p. (J). (gr. 3-7). 16.99 *(978-0-06-228606-2(4))* HarperCollins Pubs.

Amateau, Gigi. Chancey of the Maury River. 2010. (ENG., Illus.). 256p. (J). (gr. 4-7). pap. 6.99 *(978-0-7636-4523-6(0))* Candlewick Pr.

Amma, Jill. The Indaba Tree Odyssey: An African Tale. 2006. 360p. pap. 18.95 *(978-0-7414-3172-1(6))* Infinity Publishing.

Amos, Muriel & Olrun, Prudy. Animals of Nunivak Island. Amos, Muriel & Olrun, Prudy, illus. 2006. (Animal Story Collection Ser.). (Illus.). 16p. (J). (gr. 2-6). pap. 9.00 *(978-1-58084-238-9(0))* Lower Kuskokwim Schl. District.

Anastas, Margaret. Mommy's Best Kisses. Winter, Susan, illus. 2003. (ENG.). 32p. (J). (gr. -1-1). 17.99 *(978-0-06-623601-8(0))* HarperCollins Pubs.

Anaya, Hector. Cuenta Cuenta. Moreno, Sergio, illus. 2nd rev. ed. 2005. (Castillo de la Lectura Verde Ser.). (SPA & ENG.). 184p. (J). (gr. -1-7). pap. 7.95 *(978-970-20-0135-5(8))* Castillo, Ediciones, S. A. de C. V. MEX. Dist: Macmillan.

Andersen, Hans Christian. The Racers: A Tale about Fairness. Goodell, Jon, illus. 2007. (J). *(978-1-59939-090-1(6)*, Reader's Digest Young Families, Inc.) Studio Fun International.

Andersen, Hans Christian & Falloon, Jane. Thumbelina. Chichester Clark, Emma, illus. 2006.Tr. of Tommelise. 38p. (J). (gr. k-4). reprint ed. 16.00 *(978-1-4223-5373-8(7))* DIANE Publishing Co.

Andersen, Hans Christian & White, Mus. For Sure! for Sure! Czernecki, Stefan, illus. 2005. (ENG.). 32p. (J). (gr. k-3). 16.95 *(978-0-87483-742-1(1))* August Hse. Pubs., Inc.

Anderson, Airlie. A Very Furry Flap Book. 2004. (Illus.). 10p. (J). bds. 5.95 *(978-1-58925-701-6(4))* Tiger Tales.

Anderson, Airlie, illus. A Very Patchy Flap Book. 2004. 10p. (J). bds. 5.95 *(978-1-58925-702-3(2))* Tiger Tales.

—A Very Stripy Flap Book. 2004. 10p. (J). bds. 5.95 *(978-1-58925-704-7(9))* Tiger Tales.

Anderson, Jane. Anansi the Spider & the Sky King: A Tale from Africa. 2006. (J). pap. *(978-1-4108-6175-7(9))* Benchmark Education Co.

Anderson, Laurie Halse. Acting Out, 14 vols. 2012. (Vet Volunteers Ser.: 14). (ENG.). 144p. (J). (gr. 3-7). pap. 6.99 *(978-0-14-241676-1(2)*, Puffin Books) Penguin Young Readers Group.

—Helping Hands. 2013. (Vet Volunteers Ser.: 15). (ENG.). 144p. (J). (gr. 3-7). pap. 6.99 *(978-0-14-241677-8(0)*, Puffin Books) Penguin Young Readers Group.

—Masks, 11 vols. 2012. (Vet Volunteers Ser.: 11). (ENG.). 128p. (J). (gr. 3-7). 6.99 *(978-0-14-241257-2(0)*, Puffin Books) Penguin Young Readers Group.

Andreae, Giles. Giraffes Can't Dance: Number Rumba. Parker-Rees, Guy, illus. 2014. (ENG.). 12p. (J). (gr. -1 — 1). bds. 7.99 *(978-0-545-63996-5(4)*, Cartwheel Bks.) Scholastic, Inc.

Andrew, Carol B. Animal Alphabet: An Interactive Book to Learn about Letters. 2005. (Illus.). (J). *(978-1-933577-00-5(2))* Learning Wood, LLC.

Andrews, Charlie J. Tales of Animals on Farmer Brown's Farm: Children Stories. 2007. 60p. per. 10.95 *(978-1-4327-0138-3(X))* Outskirts Pr., Inc.

Andrews, Julie. The Little Grey Men: A Story for the Young in Heart. Watkins-Pitchford, Denys, illus. 2004. 304p. (J). 17.89 *(978-0-06-055449-1(5)*, Julie Andrews Collection) HarperCollins Pubs.

Andrews McMeel Publishing Staff & Moore, Clement C. Twas the Night Before Christmas. Goodell, Jon, illus. deluxe ed. 2009. (ENG.). 26p. (J). (gr. -1-3). 19.99 *(978-0-7407-8432-3(3))* Andrews McMeel Publishing.

Andrews McMeel Publishing Staff, et al. Happy, Sad, Silly, Mad: My World Makes Me Feel. 2009. (ENG., Illus.). 28p. (J). (gr. -1-3). 12.99 *(978-0-7407-8430-9(7))* Andrews McMeel Publishing.

Angelo, Tony. Just Inn Time. Freeman, Angela, illus. 2011. 24p. pap. 24.95 *(978-1-4560-6828-8(8))* America Star Bks.

Angers, Michelle. The Animal Garden. 2004. 31p. pap. 24.95 *(978-1-4137-5270-0(5))* PublishAmerica, Inc.

Angleberger, Tom. Inspector Flytrap. Bell, Cece, illus. 2016. (Inspector Flytrap Ser.). (ENG.). 112p. (J). (gr. 1-4). 14.95 *(978-1-4197-0948-7(8))*; 14.95 *(978-1-4197-0955-5(0))*; pap. 5.95 *(978-1-4197-0965-4(8))* Abrams, Inc. (Amulet Bks.).

Angus, Jennifer. In Search of Goliathus Hercules. 2013. (ENG.). 352p. (J). (gr. 3-7). 17.99 *(978-0-8075-2990-4(7))* Whitman, Albert & Co.

Animal Friends Squeaky. 2005. (J). bds. *(978-1-4194-0094-0(0))* Paradise Pr., Inc.

Animal Friends Squeaky - Cat. 2005. (J). bds. *(978-1-4194-0092-6(4))* Paradise Pr., Inc.

Animal Parade. (J). 26.20 *(978-0-8136-8441-3(2))* Modern Curriculum Pr.

The Animal Parade. (J). 59.50 *(978-0-8136-8002-6(6))* Modern Curriculum Pr.

Animal Tales from Indian Mythology - 1. 2010. 70p. pap. 4.00 *(978-81-7806-186-3(4))* Unicorn Bks. Pvt Ltd. IND. Dist: Mahal, Pustak Pubs., Booksellers & Order Suppliers.

Animal Tales from Indian Mythology - 2. 2010. 70p. pap. 4.00 *(978-81-7806-187-0(2))* Unicorn Bks. Pvt Ltd. IND. Dist: Mahal, Pustak Pubs., Booksellers & Order Suppliers.

The Animals, 6 vols., Pack. (Sails Literacy Ser.). 16p. (gr. k-18). 27.00 *(978-0-7635-4398-3(5))* Rigby Education.

The Animals Went to Bed: Individual Title-Six Packs. (Chiquilibros Ser.). (gr. k-1). 23.00 *(978-0-7635-0457-1(2))* Rigby Education.

Antony, Steve. I'll Wait, Mr. Panda. Antony, Steve, illus. 2016. (ENG., Illus.). 32p. (J). (gr. -1-k). 16.99 *(978-1-338-02836-2(7)*, Scholastic Pr.) Scholastic, Inc.

Anza, Ana Luisa. El Misterio de la Casa Chueca (y el Bulto Color Mugre) The Mystery of the Crooked House. Escobar, Antonio Rocha, illus. rev. ed. 2006. (Castillo de la Lectura Naranja Ser.). (SPA & ENG.). 120p. (J). (gr. 4-7). pap. 7.95 *(978-970-20-0200-0(1))* Castillo, Ediciones, S. A. de C. V. MEX. Dist: Macmillan.

Aoki, Hisako. Santa's Favorite Story: Santa Tells the Story of the First Christmas. Gantschev, Ivan, illus. 2007. (ENG.). 28p. (J). (gr. -1-3). 9.99 *(978-1-4169-5029-5(X)*, Simon & Schuster Bks. For Young Readers) Simon & Schuster Bks. For Young Readers.

Appelt, Kathi. The True Blue Scouts of Sugar Man Swamp. Bricking, Jennifer, illus. 2013. (ENG.). 336p. (J). (gr. 3-7). 16.99 *(978-1-4424-2105-9(3))* Simon & Schuster Children's Publishing.

Apps Ltd, Colossi. The Wild Bed Time Stories. 2011. 62p. pap. 12.95 *(978-1-4466-1546-1(4))* Lulu Pr., Inc.

Apted, Violet. Tommy & Jacqui: Laughing with Kookaburras. 2011. 32p. pap. 13.00 *(978-1-61204-118-6(3)*, Eloquent Bks.) Strategic Book Publishing & Rights Agency (SBPRA).

Aqkay. Jungle Olympics-800 Metres Sprint. 2013. 36p. pap. 24.95 *(978-1-62709-117-6(3))* America Star Bks.

Archambault, John. By the Baobab Tree. Bender, Robert, illus. 2005. (J). *(978-1-58669-164-6(3))* Childcraft Education Corp.

Archbold, David M. The Amazing Adventures of Chumley, Robin, Snickers & Mac. 2011. 48p. (gr. 4-6). pap. 19.26 *(978-1-4634-1518-1(4))* AuthorHouse.

Archer, Dosh. Big Bad Wolf. Archer, Dosh, illus. (Urgency Emergency! Ser.). (ENG., Illus.). 48p. (J). (gr. -1-3). 2015. pap. 9.99 *(978-0-8075-8351-7(0))* 2013. 12.99 *(978-0-8075-8352-4(9))* Whitman, Albert & Co.

—Humpty's Fall. Archer, Dosh, illus. (Urgency Emergency! Ser.). (ENG., Illus.). 48p. (J). (gr. -1-3). 2016. pap. 9.99 *(978-0-8075-8362-3(6))* 2015. 12.99 *(978-0-8075-8356-2(1))* Whitman, Albert & Co.

—Itsy Bitsy Spider. Archer, Dosh, illus. (Urgency Emergency! Ser.). (ENG., Illus.). 48p. (J). (gr. -1-3). 2015. pap. 9.99 *(978-0-8075-8360-9(X))* 2013. 12.99 *(978-0-8075-8358-6(8))* Whitman, Albert & Co.

—Little Elephant's Blocked Trunk. Archer, Dosh, illus. 2014. (Urgency Emergency! Ser.). (ENG., Illus.). 48p. (J). (gr. -1-3). 12.99 *(978-0-8075-8354-8(5))* Whitman, Albert & Co.

Archer, Micha. Daniel Finds a Poem. Archer, Micha, illus. 2016. (ENG., Illus.). 32p. (J). (gr. k-3). 16.99 *(978-0-399-16913-7(X)*, Nancy Paulsen Books) Penguin Young Readers Group.

Ardagh, Philip. High in the Clouds. Dunbar, Geoff, illus. 2007. 93p. (J). 20.00 *(978-1-4223-6720-9(7))* DIANE Publishing Co.

Arena, Jen. Marta! Big & Small. Dominguez, Angela, illus. 2016. (ENG & SPA.). 32p. (J). 16.99 *(978-1-62672-243-9(9)*, 9781626722439) Roaring Brook Pr.

Arenstam, Peter. Nicholas: A New Hampshire Tale. Holman, Karen Busch, illus. 2009. (Nicholas Northeastern Ser.: 3). (ENG.). 144p. (J). (gr. k-7). 14.95 *(978-1-58726-521-1(4)*, Mitten Pr.) Ann Arbor Editions LLC.

—Nicholas: A Vermont Tale. Holman, Karen Busch, illus. 2010. (Nicholas Northeastern Ser.: 4). (ENG.). 144p. (J). (gr. k-7). 14.95 *(978-1-58726-522-8(2)*, Mitten Pr.) Ann Arbor Editions LLC.

Arias, Carlos Ballesteros. The Magic Forest. 2006. (J). pap. 8.00 *(978-0-8059-7022-7(3))* Dorrance Publishing Co., Inc.

Aristizabal, Nora. La Selva Maravillosa/the Wonderful Jungle. Reyes, Maria Margarita, illus. 2005. (Bilingual Collection). (SPA.). 31p. (J). *(978-958-30-1966-1(6))* Panamericana Editorial.

Ariye, Shirley. Our Georgia School: A Wildlife Habitat. 2012. 24p. pap. 11.95 *(978-1-60976-608-5(3)*, Strategic Bk. Publishing) Strategic Book Publishing & Rights Agency (SBPRA).

Arline-Hicks, Patience & Hicks, Wendi N. Old Mean Molly, 1 vol. Bouthyette, Valerie, illus. 2009. 38p. pap. 24.95 *(978-1-60749-678-6(X))* America Star Bks.

Armstrong, Alan W. Whittington. 2006. (ENG., Illus.). 208p. (J). (gr. 3-7). 7.99 *(978-0-375-82865-2(6)*, Yearling) Random Hse. Children's Bks.

Armstrong, Luanne. Jeannie & the Gentle Giants. 2005. (ENG., Illus.). 154p. (J). (gr. 3-7). pap., tchr. ed. 8.95 *(978-0-921870-91-3(4))* Ronsdale Pr. CAN. Dist: General Distribution Services, Inc.

Armstrong, Robert W. The Big Blue Lake. Broxon, Janet, illus. 2015. (ENG.). 32p. (J). (gr. -1). 13.95 *(978-0-9801468-3-7(6))* All About Kids Publishing.

Arnauld, D. S. Zertelo & the Road of Fire: Book Two. Scott, Sara, ed. 2007. 210p. (J). per. 9.95 *(978-0-9801408-1-1(1))* Heroes & Leaders.

Arnold, Connie & Grady, Kit. Animal Sound -up. 2010. 16p. pap. 9.95 *(978-1-61633-083-5(X))* Guardian Angel Publishing, Inc.

Arnold, Marsha Diane. Lost. Found. Cordell, Matthew, illus. 2015. (ENG.). 32p. (J). (gr. -1-3). 16.99 *(978-1-62672-017-6(7)*, 9781626720176) Roaring Brook Pr.

—Waiting for Snow. Liwska, Renata, illus. 2016. (ENG.). 32p. (J). (gr. -1-3). 14.99 *(978-0-544-41687-1(2)*, HMH Books For Young Readers) Houghton Mifflin Harcourt Publishing Co.

Arnold, Tedd. Vincent Paints His House. (ENG.). 32p. (J). (gr. -1-3). 2016. 6.99 *(978-0-8234-3686-6(1))* 2015. (Illus.). 16.95 *(978-0-8234-3210-3(6))* Holiday Hse., Inc.

Arnosky, Jim. The Pirates of Crocodile Swamp. 2009. (ENG.). 240p. (J). (gr. 4-7). 15.99 *(978-0-399-25068-2(9))*, G.P. Putnam's Sons Books for Young Readers) Penguin Young Readers Group.

Aroner, Miriam. Clink Clank Clunk! Catalano, Dominic, illus. 2006. (ENG.). 32p. (J). (gr. -1-1). 15.95 *(978-1-59078-270-5(4))* Boyds Mills Pr.

Asch, Frank. Moongame. Asch, Frank, illus. 2014. (Moonbear Ser.). (ENG., Illus.). 32p. (J). (gr. -1-3). 7.99 *(978-1-4424-9406-0(9))*, Aladdin) Simon & Schuster Children's Publishing.

Ashman, Linda. Rock-a-Bye Romp. Mulazzani, Simona, illus. 2016. (ENG.). 36p. (J). (— 1). 16.99 *(978-0-399-17150-5(9))*, Nancy Paulsen Books) Penguin Young Readers Group.

Asper-Smith, Sarah. I Would Tuck You In. Watley, Mitchell, illus. (ENG.). (J). 2014. 20p. (— 1). bds. 9.99 *(978-1-57061-944-1(1))* 2012. 32p. (gr. -1-2). 16.99 *(978-1-57061-844-4(5))* Sasquatch Bks. (Little Bigfoot).

Atamer, Bilie. A Christmas Party for Santa. 2013. 36p. pap. 13.95 *(978-1-61244-187-0(4))* Halo Publishing International.

Atherton, Isabel & Straker, Bethany. Springy Chicken. Straker, Bethany, illus. 2014. (ENG., Illus.). 32p. (J). (gr. -1-k). 14.95 *(978-1-62636-161-4(4))*, Sky Pony Pr.) Skyhorse Publishing Co., Inc.

Atkins, Jill. Toad Swims for his Life! Mostyn, David, illus. 2004. (ENG.). 24p. (J). lib. bdg. 23.65 *(978-1-59646-712-5(6))* Dingles & Co.

Atlas, Ron. Ten Pigs Fiddling. Flint, Stacie, illus. 2nd rev. ed. 2006. (ENG.). 32p. (J). (gr. -1-k). 17.95 *(978-0-9630243-3-6(7))* Amberwood Pr.

Auch, Mary Jane. Chickerella. Auch, Herm, illus. 2006. (ENG.). 32p. (J). (gr. -1-3). 6.95 *(978-0-8234-2015-5(9))* Holiday Hse., Inc.

Auntie Annie. Knute: Dreams of Africa. 2013. 32p. pap. 17.25 *(978-1-4669-7519-4(9))* Trafford Publishing.

Avery, Terry, illus. Who Will Save Mr Squeaky? 2004. 29p. (J). *(978-1-929115-11-2(3))* Azro Pr., Inc.

Avi. The Good Dog. 2003. (ENG.). 256p. (J). (gr. 3-7). mass mkt. 7.99 *(978-0-689-83825-5(5))*, Atheneum Bks. for Young Readers) Simon & Schuster Children's Publishing.

—The Mayor of Central Park. Floca, Brian, illus. 2003. (ENG.). 208p. (J). (gr. 3-6). 15.99 *(978-0-06-000682-2(X))* HarperCollins Pubs.

—The Mayor of Central Park. Floca, Brian, illus. 2005. 193p. (J). (gr. 3-7). 13.65 *(978-0-7569-5125-2(9))* Perfection Learning Corp.

—Poppy & Rye. Floca, Brian, illus. 2006. (Poppy Stories Ser.). (ENG.). 240p. (J). (gr. 3-7). pap. 6.99 *(978-0-380-79717-2(8))* HarperCollins Pubs.

—Poppy & Rye. Floca, Brian, illus. 2006. (Poppy Stories Ser.: 3). 182p. (J). (gr. 3-7). lib. bdg. 17.20 *(978-0-613-17447-3(X))*, Turtleback) Turtleback Bks.

—Poppy's Return. Floca, Brian, illus. (Poppy Stories Ser.). (J). 2006. (ENG.). 256p. (gr. 3-7). pap. 6.99 *(978-0-06-000014-1(7))* 2005. 240p. lib. bdg. 16.89 *(978-0-06-000013-4(9))* HarperCollins Pubs.

Avignone, June. A Peek into the Secret Little Ones of Turtle Back Island. My Wolf Dog, illus. 2004. 40p. (J). pap. *(978-0-9654628-2-2(X))* Mill Street Forward, The.

Award Staff & Award, Anna. Meerkat Mayhem. 2015. (ENG., Illus.). 32p. (J). pap. 9.99 *(978-1-78270-050-0(1))* Award Pubns. Ltd. GBR. Dist: Parkwest Pubns., Inc.

Awdry, W. Animals Everywhere! Courtney, Richard, illus. 2011. (Step into Reading Ser.). (ENG.). 32p. (J). (gr. -1-1). pap. 3.99 *(978-0-375-86812-2(7))*, Random Hse. Bks. for Young Readers) Random Hse. Children's Bks.

Awdry, Wilbert V. & Awdry, W. Thomas & the Hide & Seek Animals. Bell, Owain, illus. 2007. (Thomas & Friends Ser.). (ENG.). 24p. (J). (gr. -1-k). 5.99 *(978-0-375-84173-6(3))*, Random Hse. Bks. for Young Readers) Random Hse. Children's Bks.

Ayagalria, Julia, et al. Animals of the River. Ayagalria, Julia et al, illus. 2006. (Animal Story Collection Ser.). 24p. (J). (gr. 2-6). pap. 9.00 *(978-1-58084-236-5(4))* Lower Kuskokwim Schl. District.

AZ Books. In Hot Africa. 2013. (Talking Flaps Ser.). (ENG.). 10p. (J). (gr. -1-k). bds. 9.95 *(978-1-61889-087-0(5))* AZ Bks. LLC.

AZ Books Staff. Bear's Forest. Potapenko, Olga, ed. 2012. (Talking Plush Animals Ser.). (ENG.). 10p. (J). (gr. -1-k). bds. 10.95 *(978-1-61889-111-2(1))* AZ Bks. LLC.

—Colores - Colorful Animals: Colorful Animals. Gorbachenok, Ekaterina, ed. 2012. (Spanish for Kids Ser.). (ENG & SPA.). 10p. (J). (gr. -1-k). bds. 11.95 *(978-1-61889-136-5(7))* AZ Bks. LLC.

—Merry Orchestra. Tulup, Natalia, ed. 2012. (Tra-La-la Ser.). (ENG.). 14p. (J). (-k). bds. 10.95 *(978-1-61889-056-6(5))* AZ Bks. LLC.

—Musical Animals. Tulup, Natalia, ed. 2012. (Tra-La-la Ser.). (ENG.). 14p. (J). (-k). bds. 10.95 *(978-1-61889-057-3(3))* AZ Bks. LLC.

—My Pond. Yaroshevich, Angelica, ed. 2012. (Open the Book-I Am Alive Ser.). (ENG.). 8p. (J). (— 1). bds. 5.95 *(978-1-61889-046-7(8))* AZ Bks. LLC.

—Who Is the Bear Looking For? Sharipovas, Alesja, ed. 2012. (Who Is There Ser.). (ENG.). 10p. (J). (-k). bds. 11.95 *(978-1-61889-039-9(5))* AZ Bks. LLC.

—Who Is the Hare Looking For? Zajceva, Ira, ed. 2012. (Who Is There Ser.). (ENG.). 10p. (J). (-k). bds. 11.95 *(978-1-61889-040-5(9))* AZ Bks. LLC.

—Who Is the Lion Looking For? Shestakova, Anna, ed. 2012. (Who Is There Ser.). (ENG.). 10p. (J). (-k). bds. 11.95 *(978-1-61889-041-2(7))* AZ Bks. LLC.

—Who Is the Puppy Looking For? Gridina, Anna, ed. 2012. (Who Is There Ser.). (ENG.). 10p. (J). (-k). bds. 11.95 *(978-1-61889-038-2(7))* AZ Bks. LLC.

—Who Is the Tiger Looking For? Gridina, Anna, ed. 2012. (Who Is There Ser.). (ENG.). 10p. (J). (-k). bds. 11.95 *(978-1-61889-037-5(9))* AZ Bks. LLC.

—Who Lives in the Pond? Gridina, Anna, ed. 2012. (Funny Animals Ser.). (ENG.). 10p. (J). (-k). bds. 8.95 *(978-1-61889-049-8(2))* AZ Bks. LLC.

—Who Lives in the Savanna? Gridina, Anna, ed. 2012. (Funny Animals Ser.). (ENG.). 10p. (J). (-k). bds. 8.95 *(978-1-61889-050-4(6))* AZ Bks. LLC.

Azman, Hacer. The Adventures of Kyle. 2011. (ENG.). 96p. (J). (gr. k-1). 14.95 *(978-1-59784-231-0(1))* Tughra Bks.

Babypants, Caspar. Augie to Zebra: An Alphabet Book! Endle, Kate, illus. 2012. (ENG.). 32p. (J). (gr. -1-2). 16.99 *(978-1-57061-750-8(3))*, Little Bigfoot) Sasquatch Bks.

Bach, Annie. Night-Night, Forest Friends. Bach, Annie, illus. 2013. (ENG., Illus.). 24p. (J). (gr. -1-k). bds. 8.99 *(978-0-8431-7278-2(9))*, Grosset & Dunlap) Penguin Young Readers Group.

Baggott, Stella, illus. Baby's Very First Stroller Book Animals. 2015. (Baby's Very First Stroller Bks.). (ENG.). 8p. (J). 7.99 *(978-0-7945-3535-3(6))*, Usborne) EDC Publishing.

Baglio, Ben M. Help Find Honey! 2006. (Pet Finders Club Ser.: Vol. 10). (Illus.). 157p. (J). *(978-0-439-87143-3(3))* Scholastic, Inc.

—Lost in the Snow. Ettinger, Doris, illus. 2007. 153p. (J). *(978-0-439-87144-0(1))* Scholastic, Inc.

Baiker, Karen. Barnyard Friends. (Felt Read-and-Play Ser.). (Illus.). 14p. (J). 17.95 *(978-1-59354-052-4(3))* Handprint Bks.

Bailey, Arthur Scott. Sleepy Time Tales the Tale of Fatty Coon. 2004. reprint ed. pap. 1.99 *(978-1-4192-4779-8(4))*; pap. 15.95 *(978-1-4191-4779-1(X))* Kessinger Publishing, LLC.

—The Tale of Benny Badger. 2005. reprint ed. pap. 20.95 *(978-1-4179-0197-5(7))* Kessinger Publishing, LLC.

—The Tale of Peter Mink. 2005. pap. 20.95 *(978-0-7661-9699-5(2))* Kessinger Publishing, LLC.

Bailey, Carla R. A. Inner Beauty. 2013. 24p. pap. *(978-1-4602-1535-7(4))* FriesenPress.

Bailey, Scott. The Tales of Billy Woodchuck. 2007. 128p. per. 16.95 *(978-1-60466-000-5(7))* Capricorn Hse. Publishing.

Baker, Alan, illus. Two Tiny Mice: A Mouse-Eye Exploration of Nature. rev. ed. 2014. (ENG.). 40p. (J). (gr. -1-3). 16.95 *(978-1-62914-627-0(7))*, Sky Pony Pr.) Skyhorse Publishing Co., Inc.

Baker, E. D. Magic Animal Rescue 3: Maggie & the Unicorn. 2017. (ENG., Illus.). 128p. (J). pap. 5.99 ***(978-1-68119-488-2(0))***, 9781681194882, Bloomsbury USA Childrens) Bloomsbury Publishing USA.

Baker, Harriet Li. Book I: Boyduck Goose: His Life & Times. 2004. pap. 9.00 *(978-0-8059-6541-4(6))* Dorrance Publishing Co., Inc.

Baker, Keith. Hickory Dickory Dock. 2007. (ENG., Illus.). 32p. (J). (gr. -1-3). 17.99 *(978-0-15-205818-0(4))* Houghton Mifflin Harcourt Publishing Co.

Baker, Ken. Old MacDonald Had a Dragon, 0 vols. Santoro, Christopher, illus. 2012. (ENG.). 32p. (J). (gr. k-3). 16.99 *(978-0-7614-6175-3(2))*, 9780761461753, Amazon Children's Publishing) Amazon Publishing.

Bakos, Lisa M. Wrong Side of the Bed. Raff, Anna, illus. 2016. (ENG.). 40p. (J). (-k). 16.99 *(978-0-399-16572-6(X))*, G.P. Putnam's Sons Books for Young Readers) Penguin Young Readers Group.

Balchin, Lance. Mechanica. 2016. (ENG., Illus.). 40p. (J). (gr. 3-7). 17.99 *(978-1-4998-0343-3(5))* Little Bee Books Inc.

Baldry, Cherith. The Emerald Throne. Wyatt, David, illus. 2003. (Eaglesmount Ser.). (J). 144p. 15.95 *(978-1-59034-584-9(3))*; 141p. pap. *(978-1-59034-585-6(1))* Mondo Publishing.

—The Lake of Darkness. Wyatt, David, illus. 2004. (Eaglesmount Ser.). 144p. (J). 15.95 *(978-1-59034-586-3(X))*; pap. *(978-1-59034-587-0(8))* Mondo Publishing.

Baldwin, Christopher. Little Dee & the Penguin. 2016. (ENG., Illus.). 128p. (J). (gr. 3-7). pap. 10.99 *(978-0-8037-4108-9(1))*, Dial Bks) Penguin Young Readers Group.

Baley, Arthur. The Tale of Brownie Beaver. 2007. 128p. per. 16.95 *(978-1-60466-001-2(5))* Capricorn Hse. Publishing.

Ball, Pauline E. Chubsey Tucker Tales. 2005. (Illus.). 98p. pap. *(978-1-84401-211-4(5))* Athena Pr.

Ballantyne, R. M. Hunting the Lions. 2005. reprint ed. pap. 15.95 *(978-1-4191-2501-0(X))*; pap. 1.99 *(978-1-4192-2501-7(4))* Kessinger Publishing, LLC.

Ballinger, Bryan. Animal Gas. 2015. (ENG., Illus.). 32p. (J). (gr. -1-2). 12.95 *(978-1-4549-1616-1(8))* Sterling Publishing Co., Inc.

Banana-Tail. 2003. lib. bdg. 13.95 *(978-0-9727681-0-8(6))* Active Media Publishing, LLC.

Banks, Kate. El Pajaro, el Mono y la Serpiente en la Selva. Bogacki, Tomek, illus. (SPA.). 24p. (J). (gr. k-2). *(978-84-261-3129-4(8))*, JV2823) Juventud, Editorial ESP. Dist: Lectorum Pubns., Inc.

Banks, Kate & Sheldrake, Rupert. Boy's Best Friend. 2015. (ENG.). 224p. (J). (gr. 3-7). 15.99 *(978-0-374-38008-3(2))*, 9780374380083, Farrar, Straus & Giroux (BYR)) Farrar, Straus & Giroux.

Banks, Lynne Reid. I, Houdini. Riley, Terry, illus. 2003. (ENG.). 126p. (J). (gr. 3-7). pap. 5.99 *(978-0-440-41924-2(7))*, Yearling) Random Hse. Children's Bks.

Banner, Angela. Ant & Bee & the Secret. 2015. (Ant & Bee Ser.). (ENG., Illus.). 84p. (J). (gr. -1-k). 7.99 *(978-1-4052-7515-6(4))* Egmont Bks., Ltd. GBR. Dist: Independent Pubs. Group.

Bansch, Helga. Petra. 2010. (SPA., Illus.). 48p. (J). 15.95 *(978-84-9871-003-8(0))* OQO, Editora ESP. Dist: Baker & Taylor Bks.

Barberis, France. Would You Like a Parrot? Barberis, Franco, illus. 32p. (J). (gr. -1). 16.95 *(978-0-87592-060-3(8))* Scroll Pr., Inc.

Barklem, Jill. Spring Story. Barklem, Jill, illus. 2011. (Brambly Hedge Ser.). (ENG., Illus.). 32p. (J). 9.99 *(978-0-00-183922-9(5))*, HarperCollins Children's Bks.) HarperCollins Pubs. Ltd. GBR. Dist: HarperCollins Pubs.

Barkley, Callie. Amy Is a Little Bit Chicken. Bishop, Tracy, illus. 2015. (Critter Club Ser.: 13). (ENG.). 128p. (J). (gr. k-4). pap. 5.99 *(978-1-4814-5174-1(X))*, Little Simon) Little Simon.

—Liz Learns a Lesson. 2013. (Critter Club Ser.: 3). lib. bdg. 16.00 *(978-0-606-32032-0(6))*, Turtleback) Turtleback Bks.

—Marion Takes a Break. 2013. (Critter Club Ser.: 4). lib. bdg. 16.00 *(978-0-606-32045-0(8))*, Turtleback) Turtleback Bks.

Barkow, Henriette. Don't Cry, Sly! Ne Pleure Pas Sly! Johnson, Richard, illus. 2004. (ENG & FRE.). 32p. (J). pap. *(978-1-85269-654-2(0))* Mantra Lingua.

Barnard, Lucy, illus. Squirrel's Busy Day. 2014. 24p. (J). ***(978-1-4351-5602-9(1))*** Barnes & Noble, Inc.

Barnes, Derrick D. Trivia Queen/Supreme. Newton, Vanessa Brantley, illus. 2008. (Ruby & the Booker Boys Ser.: 2). (ENG.). 144p. (J). (gr. 2-5). pap. 5.99 *(978-0-545-01761-9(0))* Scholastic, Inc.

Barnes, Kenneth Edward. A Children's Story Collection. 2011. 216p. (gr. -1). pap. 15.95 *(978-1-4634-2863-1(4))*; (gr. 1-2). 24.59 *(978-1-4634-2864-8(2))* AuthorHouse.

—Invasion of the Dregs. 2011. 164p. (gr. 10-12). pap. 13.50 *(978-1-4634-0745-2(9))*; (gr. 4-6). 22.23 *(978-1-4634-0726-1(2))* AuthorHouse.

Barnes, Laura T. Ernest & Elston. Camburn, Carol A., illus. 2005. (Ernest Ser.). 32p. (J). (gr. -1-3). 15.95 *(978-0-9674681-6-7(7))* Barnesyard Bks.

Barnhill, Carla. Rufus & the Very Special Baby: A Frolic Christmas Story. Barnhill, Carla, illus. 2016. (Frolic First Faith Ser.). (ENG., Illus.). 32p. (J). (gr. -1-3). 12.99 *(978-1-5064-1762-2(0))*, Sparkhouse Family) Augsburg Fortress, Pubs.

Barnum, P. T. Dick Broadhead: A Story of Perilous Adve. 2006. pap. 30.95 *(978-1-4286-1959-3(3))* Kessinger Publishing, LLC.

—Jack in the Jungle: A Tale of Land & S. 2006. pap. 33.95 *(978-1-4286-0764-4(1))* Kessinger Publishing, LLC.

Barnum, Richard. Mappo the Merry Monkey Illustrated Editi. 2006. (Illus.). pap. *(978-1-4065-0920-5(5))* Dodo Pr.

Barraclough, Sue, et al. Springtime Tales: A Collection of Animal Stories. 2005. (ENG., Illus.). 68p. (J). *(978-1-55168-273-0(7))* Fenn, H. B. & Co., Ltd.

Barrett, Granny Rita. The Adventures on Granny's Fun-Ee Farm: Book 1. 2012. 20p. pap. 14.00 *(978-1-4772-8356-1(0))* AuthorHouse.

Barrett, Judi. Los Animales No Se Visten. 2004.Tr. of Animals Should Definely Not Wear Clothes. (SPA.). (gr. k-3). lib. bdg. 23.30 *(978-0-8335-7297-4(0))*, Turtleback) Turtleback Bks.

—Never Take a Shark to the Dentist: And Other Things Not to Do. Nickle, John, illus. 2008. (ENG.). 34p. (J). (gr. -1-3). 17.99 *(978-1-4169-0724-4(6))*, Atheneum Bks. for Young Readers) Simon & Schuster Children's Publishing.

Barretta, Gene. Zoola Palooza: A Book of Homographs. Barretta, Gene, illus. 2011. (ENG., Illus.). 40p. (J). (gr. k-3). 16.99 *(978-0-8050-9107-6(6))*, 9780805091076, Holt, Henry & Co. Bks. For Young Readers) Holt, Henry & Co.

Barroux. Where's the Elephant? Barroux, illus. 2016. (ENG., Illus.). 32p. (J). (gr. -1-2). 14.99 *(978-0-7636-8110-4(5))* Candlewick Pr.

Bartlett, Lorrie & Bartlett, Helen. Kicker & the Iron Horse: Book Ii. 2013. 24p. pap. 24.95 *(978-1-4626-9246-0(X))* America Star Bks.

—Kicker & the Lost Mine: Book Iii. 2013. 28p. pap. 24.95 *(978-1-4626-9286-6(9))* America Star Bks.

—Kicker & the Missing Water: Book I. 2013. 28p. pap. 24.95 *(978-1-4626-9245-3(1))* America Star Bks.

Bartlett, T. C. Tuba Lessons. Felix, Monique, illus. (ENG.). 32p. (J). (gr. 1-17). 2011. pap. 9.95 *(978-0-89812-522-1(7))*, Creative Paperbacks) 2009. 17.95 *(978-1-56846-209-7(3))* Creative Co., The.

Barto, Jean S. Critter Chronicles. 2010. pap. 9.95 *(978-0-7414-6289-3(3))* Infinity Publishing.

Bartoletti, Susan Campbell. Naamah & the Ark at Night. Meade, Holly, illus. 2011. (ENG.). 32p. (J). (gr. -1-3). 16.99 *(978-0-7636-4242-6(8))* Candlewick Pr.

Barton, Byron. La Gallinita Roja. 2003. (SPA.). 40p. (J). (gr. -1-k). 15.99 *(978-84-8470-077-7(1))* Corimbo, Editorial S.L. ESP. Dist: Lectorum Pubns., Inc.

Barwood, Lee & Barwood, Lee. Klassic Koalas: Ancient Aboriginal Tales in New Retellings. 2007. (Illus.). 64p. (J). pap. 28.99 *(978-0-9764698-1-0(2))* Koala Jo Publishing.

Basora, Bettye. Pride's Pride. 2003. 32p. (J). pap. 9.00 *(978-0-8059-5833-1(9))* Dorrance Publishing Co., Inc.

Bauer, Marion Dane. Crinkle, Crackle, Crack: It's Spring! Shelley, John, illus. 2015. (ENG.). 32p. (J). (gr. -1-3). 16.95 *(978-0-8234-2952-3(0))* Holiday Hse., Inc.

—If Frogs Made the Weather. Donohue, Dorothy, illus. 2005. (ENG.). 32p. (J). 16.95 *(978-0-8234-1622-6(4))* Holiday Hse., Inc.

—The Longest Night. Lewin, Ted, illus. 2009. (ENG.). 40p. (J). (gr. -1-3). 17.95 *(978-0-8234-2054-4(X))* Holiday Hse., Inc.

—My Mother Is Mine. Elwell, Peter, illus. 2009. (Classic Board Bks.). (ENG.). 36p. (J). (gr. -1-k). bds. 7.99 *(978-1-4169-6090-4(2))*, Little Simon) Little Simon.

—My Mother Is Mine. Elwell, Peter, illus. 2004. (ENG.). 40p. (J). (gr. -1-k). reprint ed. 7.99 *(978-0-689-86695-1(X))*, Simon & Schuster Bks. For Young Readers) Simon & Schuster Bks. For Young Readers.

—The Very Best Daddy of All. Wu, Leslie, illus. 2011. (Classic Board Bks.). (ENG.). 34p. (J). (gr. -1 — 1). bds. 7.99 *(978-1-4169-8517-4(4))*, Little Simon) Little Simon.

—The Very Best Daddy of All. Wu, Leslie, illus. 2007. (ENG.). 40p. (J). (gr. -1-3). 6.99 *(978-1-4169-2736-5(0))*, Simon & Schuster Bks. For Young Readers) Simon & Schuster Bks. For Young Readers.

Bauer, Marion Dane. Winter Dance. Jones, Richard, illus. 2017. (ENG.). 40p. (J). (gr. -1-3). 16.99 ***(978-0-544-31334-7(8))***, HMH Books For Young Readers) Houghton Mifflin Harcourt Publishing Co.

Baum, L. Frank. Ozma of Oz. 2007. 108p. (gr. 4-7). per. 9.95 *(978-1-60312-150-7(1))* Aegypan.

Baum, L. Frank & Bancroft, Laura. Twinkle & Chubbins. 2011. 106p. 22.95 *(978-1-4638-9604-1(2))* Rodgers, Alan Bks.

Baumann, Kurt. Joachim. (SPA.). 32p. (YA). (gr. 5-8). *(978-84-264-3551-4(3))*, LM1740) Editorial Lumen ESP. Dist: Lectorum Pubns., Inc.

Baxter, Nicola. Josie the Giraffe & the Starry Night. Fox, Lisa, illus. 2016. (ENG.). 16p. (J). (gr. -1-12). 7.99 *(978-0-85723-526-8(5))*, Armadillo) Anness Publishing GBR. Dist: National Bk. Network.

—Old MacDonald's: Barnyard Tales. Davis, Caroline, illus. 256p. (J). *(978-0-7525-8771-4(4))* Parragon Bk. Service Ltd.

—3-Minute Animal Stories. Everitt-Stewart, Andy, illus. 2013. (ENG.). 80p. (J). (gr. -1-k). pap. 9.99 *(978-1-84322-978-0(1))*, Armadillo) Anness Publishing GBR. Dist: National Bk. Network.

Bayless, Julie. Roar! 2015. (ENG., Illus.). 32p. (J). (gr. -1-17). 16.95 *(978-0-7624-5750-2(3))*, Running Pr. Kids) Running Pr. Bk. Pubs.

Baylor, Byrd & Parnall, Peter. Desert Voices. 2014. 32p. pap. 8.00 *(978-1-61003-343-5(4))* Center for the Collaborative Classroom.

The Bean Bag that Mom Made: 6 Small Books. (gr. k-3). 24.00 *(978-0-7635-6241-0(6))* Rigby Education.

Beard, Alex. The Jungle Grapevine. 2009. (ENG., Illus.). 48p. (J). (gr. k-2). 17.95 *(978-0-8109-8001-3(0))*, Abrams Bks. for Young Readers) Abrams, Inc.

Beaton, Clare & Blackstone, Stella. Un Alce, Veinte Ratones. Beaton, Clare, illus. 2006.Tr. of One Moose, Twenty Mice. (ENG., Illus.). 32p. (J). (gr. -1-k). bds. 6.99 *(978-1-84686-019-5(9))* Barefoot Bks., Inc.

Beaty, Noel. The Legend of Snowy the Shrew. 2007. 168p. per. *(978-0-7552-0295-9(3))* Authors OnLine, Ltd.

Beaumont, Karen. Move over, Rover! Dyer, Jane, illus. 2016. (ENG.). 40p. (J). (gr. -1-3). 7.99 *(978-0-544-80900-0(9))*, HMH Books For Young Readers) Houghton Mifflin Harcourt Publishing Co.

—Who Ate All the Cookie Dough? Yelchin, Eugene, illus. 2008. (ENG.). 32p. (J). (gr. -1-k). 18.99 *(978-0-8050-8267-8(0))*, 9780805082678, Holt, Henry & Co. Bks. For Young Readers) Holt, Henry & Co.

Beauregard, Lynda. The Werewolf Chase: A Mystery about Adaptations. Torres, German, illus. 2012. (Summer Camp Science Mysteries Ser.: 4). (ENG.). 48p. (gr. 3-6). pap. 39.62 *(978-0-7613-9271-2(8))*, Graphic Universe™); pap. 6.95 *(978-0-7613-8542-4(8))*, Graphic Universe™); lib. bdg. 29.27 *(978-0-7613-5691-2(6))* Lerner Publishing Group.

Beck, Ernie. Skinni Mini & Friends in the Valley of Hope. Beck, Blaze, illus. 2012. 74p. pap. 13.99 *(978-0-9858398-5-7(6))* Mindstir Media.

Beck, W. H. Malcolm at Midnight. Lies, Brian, illus. (ENG.). 272p. (J). (gr. 2-5). 2015. pap. 7.99 *(978-0-544-33666-7(6))*, HMH Books For Young Readers) 2012. 16.99 *(978-0-547-68100-9(3))* Houghton Mifflin Harcourt Publishing Co.

—Malcolm under the Stars. Lies, Brian, illus. (ENG.). 272p. (J). (gr. 2-5). 2016. pap. 7.99 *(978-0-544-81312-0(X))* 2015. 16.99 *(978-0-544-39267-0(1))* Houghton Mifflin Harcourt Publishing Co. (HMH Books For Young Readers).

A Bed for Bear. 2014. (ENG., Illus.). 32p. (J). (gr. -1-3). 17.99 *(978-0-06-223705-7(5))* HarperCollins Pubs.

Bedford, David. Mole's in Love. Beardshaw, Rosalind, illus. 2009. 32p. (J). (gr. -1-2). 15.95 *(978-1-58925-084-0(2))*; pap. 6.95 *(978-1-58925-417-6(1))* Tiger Tales.

Bedore, Bernie. Mythical Mufferaw. (Illus.). 96p. (J). pap. 10.95 *(978-1-55082-087-4(7))* Quarry Pr. CAN. Dist: LPC/InBook.

Beecher, Elizabeth. Roy Rogers' Bullet & Trigger: Wild Horse Roundup. Lenox, August, illus. 2011. 28p. pap. 35.95 *(978-1-258-03850-2(1))* Literary Licensing, LLC.

Beeny, Emily. Hector the Collector. Graegin, Stephanie, illus. 2017. (ENG.). 40p. (J). 17.99 *(978-1-62672-296-5(X))*, 9781626722965) Roaring Brook Pr.

Beighey, Carole La Flamme. The Waddodles of Hollow Lake: Ruffed Grouse Courtship Ceremony. 2010. 284p. (gr. 4-7). 25.99 *(978-1-4490-7766-2(8))* AuthorHouse.

Beiser, Tim. Bradley McGogg: The Very Fine Frog. Berman, Rachel, illus. 2011. (ENG.). 24p. (J). (gr. k-k). pap. 7.95 *(978-1-77049-276-9(3))*, Tundra Bks.) Tundra Bks. CAN. Dist: Penguin Random Hse. LLC.

Beitler, Stacey Ann. Willy Goes to School. 2011. 28p. pap. 14.50 *(978-1-61204-397-5(6))*, Strategic Bk. Publishing) Strategic Book Publishing & Rights Agency (SBPRA).

—Willy Helps a Friend. 2010. 30p. pap. 14.50 *(978-1-60911-355-1(1))*, Eloquent Bks.) Strategic Book Publishing & Rights Agency (SBPRA).

Bell, Anthea. Frog in Love. Velthuijs, Max, illus. 2015. (J). *(978-1-4351-5750-7(8))* Barnes & Noble, Inc.

Bell, Debora. Lyssa Lamb. Ronda, Gilger, illus. 2005. 32p. (J). 4.95 *(978-0-9768465-0-5(0))* Frontier Pr.

Bell, Jaime R. Terra. 2011. 68p. pap. 27.68 *(978-1-4269-6115-1(4))* Trafford Publishing.

Bell, Johanna. Go Home, Cheeky Animals! Beasley, Dion, illus. 2016. (ENG.). 32p. (J). (-1). 18.99 *(978-1-76029-165-5(X))* Allen & Unwin AUS. Dist: Independent Pubs. Group.

Bell, Karen. Cookie's Victorian. 2010. 84p. pap. 31.95 *(978-1-4497-0558-9(8))*, WestBow Pr.) Author Solutions, Inc.

Bell, Lucy J. God Made Feelings. Rimmington, Natasha, illus. 2017. 10p. (J). 6.99 ***(978-1-5064-1782-0(5))***, Sparkhouse Family) Augsburg Fortress, Pubs.

—Uri & the Busy Day. Garton, Michael, illus. 2017. (J). 12.99 ***(978-1-5064-1787-5(6))***, Sparkhouse Family) Augsburg Fortress, Pubs.

Bell, Samantha. The Perfect Pet, 1 vol. 2013. (SPA.). 32p. (J). (gr. -1-3). pap. 9.95 *(978-1-60718-701-1(9))* Arbordale Publishing.

Bellamy, Marian Meredith. Goldie & Androcles — A Fable for the 21st Century. Bellamy, Marian Meredith, illus. 2005. (Illus.). 91p. (YA). per. 20.00 *(978-0-9765341-0-5(X))* Meredith Group Ltd., The.

Belle, Jennifer. Animal Stackers. McPhail, David, illus. 2005. (ENG.). 40p. (gr. k-4). 15.99 *(978-0-7868-1834-1(4))* Hyperion Pr.

Benchmark Education Co., LLC. Happy Hippo Holiday Big Book. 2014. (Shared Reading Foundations Ser.). (J). (gr. -1). *(978-1-4509-9425-5(3))* Benchmark Education Co.

Bender, Carrie, compiled by. Betty Girl & Other Animal Stories. 2004. pap. 8.99 *(978-1-930353-96-1(0))* Masthof Pr.

Benjamin, A. H. I'm Taller Than You! O'Kif, illus. 2008. (Tadpoles Ser.). (ENG.). 24p. (J). (gr. -1-3). lib. bdg. *(978-0-7787-3854-1(X))* Crabtree Publishing Co.

Bennett, Dean. Everybody Needs a Hideaway. 2004. (ENG., Illus.). 32p. (J). (gr. k-17). 15.95 *(978-0-89272-645-5(8))* Down East Bks.

Bennett, Steven. The Adventures of Super Dad: Colossal Encounters (Book #1) 2005. 98p. pap. 10.49 *(978-1-4116-5947-6(3))* Lulu Pr., Inc.

Bentley, Dawn. Saber-Tooth Trap. (Smithsonian's Prehistoric Pals Ser.). (ENG., Illus.). 36p. (J). (gr. -1-2). 9.95 *(978-1-59249-457-6(9))*, PS2456) Soundprints.

—Saber-Tooth Trap. Reavely, Trever, illus. (Smithsonian's Prehistoric Pals Ser.). (ENG.). 36p. (J). (gr. -1-2). 2.95 *(978-1-59249-456-9(0))*, S2456) Soundprints.

—Saber-Tooth Trap. Reavely, Trevor, illus. 2005. (Smithsonian's Prehistoric Pals Ser.). (ENG.). 36p. (J). (gr. k-2). 14.95 *(978-1-59249-453-8(6))*, H2406); pap. 6.95 *(978-1-59249-454-5(4))*, S2406) Soundprints.

—Three Stretchy Frogs. Wallis, Becky, illus. 2010. (Stretchies Book Ser.). 16p. (J). 8.99 *(978-0-8249-1459-2(7))* Hinkler Bks. Pty, Ltd. AUS. Dist: Ideals Pubns.

—Velociraptor: Small & Speedy. Carr, Karen, illus. 2005. (ENG.). 36p. (J). (gr. -1-2). 9.95 *(978-1-59249-164-3(2),* PS2452) Soundprints.

Bently, Peter. The Great Balloon Hullaballoo. Matsuoka, Mei, illus. 2014. (ENG.). 32p. (J). (gr. -1-3). 16.95 *(978-1-4677-3449-3(7))* Lerner Publishing Group.

Bentorah, Chaim. Biblical Truths from Uncle Otto's Farm. 2012. 108p. 28.95 *(978-1-4497-6170-7(4));* pap. 11.95 *(978-1-4497-6168-4(2))* Author Solutions, Inc. (WestBow Pr.).

ber, Gail. Time of the Cats. 2013. 132p. pap. 11.99 *(978-1-4582-1232-0(7),* Abbott Pr.) Author Solutions, Inc.

Beres, Nancy. The Night the Animals Spoke. Schirack, Timm, illus. 2012. (J). 12.95 *(978-0-9752801-3-3(9))* Beres, Nancy.

Berg, Laurna L. The Adventures of Lynx & Cheetah: The Unconditional Love of a Beloved Pet Gives Us a Glimpse into the Heart of God. 2012. 62p. pap. 23.95 *(978-1-4497-6021-2(X),* WestBow Pr.) Author Solutions, Inc.

Berger, Samantha. Snoozefest. Litten, Kristyna, illus. 2015. (ENG.). 34p. (J). (gr. -1-k). 16.99 *(978-0-8037-4046-4(8),* Dial Bks) Penguin Young Readers Group.

Bergman, Mara. Yum Yum! What Fun! Maland, Nick, illus. 2009. (ENG.). 32p. (J). (gr. -1-2). 17.99 *(978-0-06-168860-7(6),* Greenwillow Bks.) HarperCollins Pubs.

Bergmann, Andy. The Starry Giraffe. Bergmann, Andy, illus. 2017. (ENG., Illus.). 40p. (J). (gr. -1-3). 15.99 ***(978-1-4814-9100-6(8),*** Aladdin) Simon & Schuster Children's Publishing.

Berkes, Marianne. Hay Alguien en Casa?, 1 vol. Dickinson, Rebecca, illus. 2013. (SPA.). 32p. (J). (gr. -1-3). 17.95 *(978-1-60718-714-1(0))* Arbordale Publishing.

—Over in the Grasslands: On an African Savanna, 1 vol. Dubin, Jill, illus. 2016. (ENG.). 32p. (J). (gr. -1-2). 16.95 *(978-1-58469-567-7(6))* Dawn Pubns.

—The Swamp Where Gator Hides, 1 vol. Baird, Roberta, illus. 2014. (ENG.). 32p. (J). (gr. k-4). 16.95 *(978-1-58469-470-0(X));* pap. 8.95 *(978-1-58469-471-7(8))* Dawn Pubns.

Bernal, Mitchell. Skelanimals: Dead Animals Need Love Too Bernal, Mitchell, illus. l.t. ed. 2005. (Illus.). 22p. (J). per. 12.95 *(978-0-9766621-0-5(8),* 818 554-8965) Kreations.

Bernasconi, Pablo. El Zoo de Joaquin. 2006. (Illus.). 32p. (YA). (gr. 7-9). 15.99 *(978-84-96388-36-9(0))* Lectorum Pubns., Inc.

Berne, Jennifer. Nighty-Night, Sleep Tight. Walker, David, illus. 2015. (Snuggle Time Stories Ser.). (ENG.). 24p. (J). (gr. -1-k). bds. 6.95 *(978-1-4549-1390-0(8))* Sterling Publishing Co., Inc.

Bernstrom, Daniel. One Day in the Eucalyptus, Eucalyptus Tree. Wenzel, Brendan, illus. 2016. 32p. (J). (gr. -1-3). 17.99 *(978-0-06-235485-3(X),* Tegen, Katherine Bks) HarperCollins Pubs.

Berry, Carolyn. Buster Tells It All: Stories from Pony Creek Ranch. Cash, Eric, illus. 2011. 24p. (J). 16.95 *(978-1-61254-011-5(2))* Brown Books Publishing Group.

Berry, Ron. The Silly Safari Bus! Sharp, Chris, illus. 2008. (ENG.). 12p. (J). bds. 12.99 *(978-0-8249-6736-9(4),* Ideal Pubns.) Worthy Publishing.

Bersani, Shennen. Achoo! Why Pollen Counts, 1 vol. 2015. (ENG., Illus.). 32p. (J). (gr. k-3). 17.95 *(978-1-62855-550-9(5))* Arbordale Publishing.

Between the Lions for QVC Only, 6 vols. 2003. (Between the Lions Presents the Vowels Ser.). (J). lib. bdg. 30.00 incl. VHS *(978-1-59375-029-9(3))* WGBH Boston Video.

Beyers, Andrea. Johnny Joins the Army. LeTourneau, Anthony Alex, illus. 2008. (Flower Kingdom Ser.: Vol. 2). 40p. (J). 16.95 *(978-0-9800754-1-0(6))* RockTuff.

Bhandari, D. Growing Wings: Parrot's Day Out. 2010. 28p. 17.99 *(978-1-4520-1102-8(8))* AuthorHouse.

Biddulph, Rob. Blown Away. Biddulph, Rob, illus. 2015. (ENG., Illus.). 40p. (J). (gr. -1-3). 17.99 *(978-0-06-236724-2(2))* HarperCollins Pubs.

Bidoli, Katie. Karate Adventures of Kisho, Hana, & Nobu: Karate Is for Everyone! 2006. (Illus.). 16p. (J). 10.00 *(978-1-60243-029-7(2))* Keen's Martial Arts Academy.

The Big, Bad Cook: Individual Title Six-Packs. (Literatura 2000 Ser.). (gr. 2-3). 33.00 *(978-0-7635-0252-2(9))* Rigby Education.

Bigham, Madge A. Little Folks' Land. Ripperton, Lisa M., ed. 2009. 452p. pap. 15.95 *(978-1-59915-375-9(0))* Yesterday's Classics.

Billet, Marion. Littleland. Billet, Marion, illus. 2013. (ENG., Illus.). 32p. (J). (gr. k-k). 14.99 *(978-0-7636-6550-0(9),* Nosy Crow) Candlewick Pr.

Billingsley, Victoria. Happy Hoppy's Orchestra & Other Stories. 2010. 44p. 16.99 *(978-1-4520-6753-7(8))* AuthorHouse.

Bill's Baby: 6 Small Books. (gr. k-3). 24.00 *(978-0-7635-6242-7(4))* Rigby Education.

Binks. The Girl with Chipmunk Hands. Begonia, Ruby, illus. 2013. 24p. (J). 15.95 *(978-1-935448-20-4(X))* Lost Coast Pr.

Birnbaum, A. Green Eyes. Birnbaum, A., illus. 2011. (Family Storytime Ser.). (ENG., Illus.). 48p. (J). (gr. -1-2). pap. 7.99 *(978-0-375-86201-4(3),* Dragonfly Bks.) Random Hse. Children's Bks.

Bissett, Josie. Boogie Monster. Atteberry, Kevan J., illus. 2011. 36p. (J). (gr. -1-3). 16.95 *(978-1-935414-10-0(0))* Compendium, Inc., Publishing & Communications.

Blabey, Aaron. The Bad Guys. (Bad Guys Ser.: bk.4). (ENG.). 144p. (J). (gr. 2-5). 2017. pap. 5.99 ***(978-1-338-08753-6(3),*** Scholastic Paperbacks) 2017. pap. 5.99 *(978-0-545-91241-9(5),* Scholastic Pr.) 2016. pap. 5.99 *(978-0-545-91240-2(7),* Scholastic Pr.) Scholastic, Inc.

—The Bad Guys. 2016. (Bad Guys Ser.: 1). lib. bdg. 16.00 ***(978-0-606-40039-8(7))*** Turtleback Bks.

—Mission Unpluckable. 2017. (Bad Guys Ser.: 2). lib. bdg. 16.00 ***(978-0-606-40154-8(7))*** Turtleback Bks.

Black, Birdie. Warthog. Beardshaw, Rosalind, illus. 2017. (ENG.). 24p. (J). (gr. -1-2). 14.99 *(978-0-7636-9323-7(5),* Nosy Crow) Candlewick Pr.

Black, Cuyler. The Goat of Many Colors, 1 vol. 2010. (ENG.). 32p. (J). (gr. k-3). pap. 4.99 *(978-0-310-71634-1(9))* Zonderkidz.

Black, Michael Ian. Chicken Cheeks. Hawkes, Kevin, illus. 2009. (ENG.). 40p. (J). (gr. -1-3). 17.99 *(978-1-4169-4864-3(3),* Simon & Schuster Bks. For Young Readers) Simon & Schuster Bks. For Young Readers.

Blackford, Cheryl. Hungry Coyote. Caple, Laurie, illus. 2015. (ENG.). 32p. (J). (gr. -1-2). 16.95 *(978-0-87351-964-9(7))* Minnesota Historical Society Pr.

Blackstone, Stella. Alligator Alphabet. Bauer, Stephanie, illus. (ENG.). (J). (gr. -1-k). 2007. 32p. 8.99 *(978-1-84686-073-7(3))* 2005. 48p. 16.99 *(978-1-84148-494-5(6))* Barefoot Bks., Inc.

—A Dragon on the Doorstep. Harter, Debbie, illus. (ENG.). 32p. (J). 2012. (gr. -1-2). 9.99 *(978-1-84686-826-9(2))* 2006. pap. 9.99 *(978-1-905236-66-4(2))* 2006. (gr. -1-k). pap. 6.99 *(978-1-84686-032-4(6))* 2005. (gr. -1-1). 15.99 *(978-1-84148-227-9(7))* Barefoot Bks., Inc.

—Storytime: First Tales for Sharing. Wilson, Anne, illus. 2005. (ENG.). 96p. (J). (gr. -1-3). 19.99 *(978-1-84148-345-0(1))* Barefoot Bks., Inc.

—Walk with Me! Mockford, Caroline, illus. 2009. (ENG.). 14p. (J). (gr. -1). bds. 7.99 *(978-1-84686-179-6(9))* Barefoot Bks., Inc.

—Walking Through the Jungle. Harter, Debbie, illus. 2004. (ENG.). 32p. (J). (gr. -1-k). pap. 6.99 *(978-1-84148-548-5(9))* Barefoot Bks., Inc.

—Walking Through the Jungle. Harter, Debbie, illus. 32p. (J). 2006. (ENG.). 9.99 *(978-1-905236-99-2(9))* 2004. 9.99 *(978-1-84148-182-1(3))* Barefoot Bks., Inc.

—Who Are You, Baby Kangaroo? Beaton, Clare, illus. 2004. 32p. (J). 14.99 *(978-1-84148-217-0(X))* Barefoot Bks., Inc.

Blackstone, Stella & Bass, Jules. Hay una Vaca Entre las Coles. Beaton, Clare, illus. 2003.Tr. of There's a Cow in the Cabbage Patch. (SPA.). 32p. (J). (gr. k-2). pap. 6.99 *(978-1-84148-965-0(4))* Barefoot Bks., Inc.

Blackstone, Stella & Bauer, Stephanie. Octopus Opposites. Bauer, Stephanie, illus. 2010. (ENG., Illus.). 32p. (J). (gr. -1). 16.99 *(978-1-84686-328-8(7))* Barefoot Bks., Inc.

Blackstone, Stella & Broadbent, Jim. Storytime: First Tales for Sharing. Wilson, Anne, illus. 2008. (ENG.). 96p. (J). pap. 12.99 *(978-1-84686-165-9(9))* Barefoot Bks., Inc.

Blackstone, Stella & Harter, Debbie. Who Are You? Harter, Debbie, illus. 2003. (ENG., Illus.). 24p. (J). (gr. k-2). bds. 6.99 *(978-1-84148-609-3(4))* Barefoot Bks., Inc.

Blackstone, Stella, et al. Walking Through the Jungle. 2011. (ENG., Illus.). 32p. (J). (gr. -1-2). 9.99 *(978-1-84686-660-9(X))* Barefoot Bks., Inc.

Blaha-Black, Caroline. Anika & the Magic Top. 2008. 60p. pap. 11.95 *(978-1-4357-1194-5(7))* Lulu Pr., Inc.

Blair, Eric. The Bremen Town Musicians: A Retelling of the Grimm's Fairy Tale, 1 vol. Dickson, Bill, illus. 2013. (My First Classic Story Ser.). (ENG.). 32p. (gr. k-3). pap. 7.10 *(978-1-4795-1848-7(4),* My First Classic Story) Picture Window Bks.

—Pecos Bill, 1 vol. Chambers-Goldberg, Micah, illus. 2013. (My First Classic Story Ser.).Tr. of Pecos Bill. (ENG.). 32p. (gr. k-3). pap. 7.10 *(978-1-4795-1860-9(3),* My First Classic Story) Picture Window Bks.

Blake-Garrett, Andrea. The Adventures of Izzy & Juju: Twin Detective Investigators (T. D. I.) 2012. 28p. pap. 19.99 *(978-1-4685-0683-9(8))* AuthorHouse.

Bland, Nick. Some Dads. 2017. (ENG., Illus.). 24p. (J). (gr. -1-1). 9.95 *(978-0-7624-6199-8(3),* Running Pr.) Running Pr. Bk. Pubs.

—The Very Cranky Bear. Bland, Nick, illus. 2014. (ENG., Illus.). 32p. (J). (gr. -1-k). 16.99 *(978-0-545-61269-2(1),* Orchard Bks.) Scholastic, Inc.

Blazin' Hot: Coloring/Activity Book (English) 2005. (Illus.). (J). 2.99 *(978-0-9770455-0-1(1))* Mighty Kids Media.

Blazin' Hot: Picture Book (English) 8x8. 2006. (J). 5.99 *(978-1-933934-29-7(8))* Mighty Kids Media.

Blazin' Hot Picture Book (English) 2005. (Illus.). (J). 5.99 *(978-0-9765953-9-7(7))* Mighty Kids Media.

Blevins, Wiley. Duck, Duck, Goose. Kreloff, Elliott, illus. 2016. (Basic Concepts Ser.). (ENG.). 24p. (J). (gr. -1-1). lib. bdg. 14.99 *(978-1-63440-084-8(4))* Red Chair Pr.

Blom, Jen K. Possum Summer. Rayyan, Omar, illus. 2011. (ENG.). 256p. (J). (gr. 3-7). 17.95 *(978-0-8234-2331-6(X))* Holiday Hse., Inc.

Blomgren, Jennifer. Where Do I Sleep? A Pacific Northwest Lullaby. Gabriel, Andrea, illus. 2015. (ENG.). 20p. (J). (—1). bds. 9.99 *(978-1-63217-019-4(1),* Little Bigfoot) Sasquatch Bks.

Bloom, Suzanne. Feeding Friendsies. 2011. (ENG., Illus.). 32p. (J). (gr. -1-1). 16.95 *(978-1-59078-529-4(0))* Boyds Mills Pr.

—A Mighty Fine Time Machine. Bloom, Suzanne, illus. 2014. (ENG., Illus.). 32p. (J). (gr. k-2). pap. 6.95 *(978-1-62091-605-6(3))* Boyds Mills Pr.

—A Mighty Fine Time Machine. 2009. (ENG., Illus.). 32p. (J). (gr. -1-2). 16.95 *(978-1-59078-527-0(4))* Boyds Mills Pr.

Bloomer, Nancy Clark. Through the Glass Bottom Boat. 2012. 36p. pap. 18.60 *(978-1-4772-4789-1(0))* AuthorHouse.

BlueWolf, James Don. Speaking for Fire. Greenlee, Carolyn Wing, illus. 2007. (ENG.). 44p. (gr. 2-7). per. 12.95 *(978-1-887400-31-2(1))* Earthen Vessel Production, Inc.

Blume, Judy. The One in the Middle Is the Green Kangaroo. 39p. (J). (gr. k-3). pap. 3.99 *(978-0-8072-1337-7(3),* Listening Library) Random Hse. Audio Publishing Group.

Blumenthal, Bliss & Alarcon, Claudia. Wiley's Way: El Camino de Wiley. Gonzalez, Ricky & Gonzalez, Crysol, illus. 2004. (ENG & SPA.). 96p. mass mkt. 9.95 *(978-0-292-70615-6(4))* Univ. of Texas Pr.

Blyton, Enid. Children of Green Meadows. 2013. (ENG.). 240p. (J). pap. 9.99 *(978-1-84135-645-7(X))* Award Pubns. Ltd. GBR. Dist: Parkwest Pubns., Inc.

Bock, Danuta. The Flying Turtle: A Test of Friendship & Understanding. 2007. 56p. per. 12.95 *(978-1-4327-0918-1(6))* Outskirts Pr., Inc.

Bodenstein, Dan. Steven the Vegan. Ronald, Robrahn, illus. 2012. 38p. (J). pap. 12.99 *(978-0-9843228-9-3(2))* Totem Tales Publishing.

Bodoh, Tony. Hannah's Animal Farm. 2008. 28p. pap. 14.95 *(978-1-4327-2046-9(5))* Outskirts Pr., Inc.

Bohlken, Bob. How the Rabbit Became the Easter Bunny. Hogue, Ann, illus. 2016. (ENG.). 32p. (J). pap. 10.95 *(978-0-930643-36-2(4),* Snaptail Pr.) Images Unlimited Publishing.

Bolam, Emily, illus. In the Jungle. 2013. (Peekabooks Ser.). (ENG.). 8p. (J). (gr. -1 — 1). bds. 5.99 *(978-0-7641-6629-7(8))* Barron's Educational Series, Inc.

Boldt, Claudia. Uugghh! Boldt, Claudia, illus. 2011. (Child's Play Library). (ENG., Illus.). 32p. (J). (gr. 2-2). *(978-1-84643-372-6(X))* Child's Play International Ltd.

Boldt, Mike. The Gophers in Farmer Burrows' Field. 2009. (Illus.). 30p. (J). 15.99 *(978-0-88144-472-8(3))* Yorkshire Publishing Group.

—123 Versus ABC. Boldt, Mike, illus. 2013. (ENG., Illus.). 32p. (J). (gr. -1-3). 17.99 *(978-0-06-210299-7(0))* HarperCollins Pubs.

Bond, Felicia. Big Hugs Little Hugs. Bond, Felicia, illus. 2013. (ENG., Illus.). 30p. (J). (gr. -1-k). bds. 6.99 *(978-0-399-16206-0(2),* Philomel Bks.) Penguin Young Readers Group.

Bondanella Filutze, Ann M. On Gramma's Rocker: Animal Tales & Other Short Stories. 2013. 84p. pap. 27.95 *(978-1-4624-0498-8(7),* Inspiring Voices) Author Solutions, Inc.

Bonnell, Kris. We Like the Beach. 2007. (J). pap. 5.95 *(978-1-933727-55-4(1))* Reading Reading Bks., LLC.

—The White, White Snow. 2007. (J). pap. 5.95 *(978-1-933727-44-8(6))* Reading Reading Bks., LLC.

—Who Has a Hump? 2007. (J). pap. 5.95 *(978-1-933727-58-5(6))* Reading Reading Bks., LLC.

Bonnett-Rampersaud, Louise. How Do You Sleep?, 1 vol. Kest, Kristin, illus. 2008. (ENG.). 34p. (J). (gr. -1). 6.99 *(978-0-7614-5449-6(7))* Marshall Cavendish Corp.

Book Company Staff. Animal Friends. 2003. (Sparkle Bks.). (Illus.). (J). bds. 14.95 *(978-1-74047-322-4(1))* Book Co. Publishing Pty, Ltd., The AUS. Dist: Penton Overseas, Inc.

—Our Precious World Stationery Set. Schimmel, Schim, illus. 2003. (Stationery Ser.). (J). pap. 15.95 *(978-1-74047-215-9(2))* Book Co. Publishing Pty, Ltd., The AUS. Dist: Penton Overseas, Inc.

Booth, Chrissie. Don't Even Think about It. McMurry, Marena, illus. 2011. 24p. pap. 24.95 *(978-1-4560-8289-5(2))* America Star Bks.

Booth, Tom. Don't Blink! Booth, Tom, illus. 2017. (ENG., Illus.). 40p. (J). 17.99 *(978-1-250-11736-6(4),* 9781250117366) Feiwel & Friends.

Borando, Silvia & Clerici, Lorenzo. Open up, Please! A Minibombo Book. 2016. (Minibombo Ser.). (ENG., Illus.). 24p. (J). (-k). 14.00 *(978-0-7636-9037-3(6))* Candlewick Pr.

Borgo, Lacy Finn. Big Mama's Baby. Cote, Nancy, illus. 2007. (ENG.). 32p. (J). (gr. k-2). 15.95 *(978-1-59078-187-6(2))* Boyds Mills Pr.

Bostrom, Kathleen Long. The View at the Zoo. Francis, Guy, illus. 2011. 32p. (J). (gr. -1-3). 14.99 *(978-0-8249-5629-5(X),* Ideal Pubns.) Worthy Publishing.

Botelho, R. J. G. A. R. T. H. Book IV: A Whale of a Tale. 2007. 104p. per. 19.95 *(978-1-4241-8799-7(0))* America Star Bks.

Bourgeois, Paulette & Clark, Brenda. Franklin's Trading Cards. 2003. (Kids Can Read Ser.). (ENG., Illus.). 32p. (J). (gr. 1-2). 3.95 *(978-1-55337-464-0(9));* 14.95 *(978-1-55337-463-3(0))* Kids Can Pr., Ltd. CAN. Dist: Hachette Bk. Group.

Bourke, Debra. First Day at Bouddi School. Cowley, Ray B., illus. 2012. 32p. pap. 18.00 *(978-1-4349-8469-2(9),* RoseDog Bks.) Dorrance Publishing Co., Inc.

Bourne, Sylvia. Animal Tales. 2009. 49p. pap. 31.50 *(978-1-4452-1311-8(7))* Lulu Pr., Inc.

Bowen, Gary. Maren's Nest. Date not set. (ENG.). 48p. (J). pap. 6.99 *(978-0-06-440790-8(X))* HarperCollins Pubs.

Bowler, Ann Martin & Bowler, Anna. Gecko's Complaint: A Balinese Folktale. Sukanada, I. Gusti Made, illus. 2009. (ENG & IND.). 32p. (J). (gr. k-3). 14.95 *(978-0-7946-0484-4(6))* Tuttle Publishing.

Bowlin, Serina. Wandering Sam. Thrasher, Brian, illus. 2011. 20p. pap. 9.97 *(978-1-61204-280-0(5),* Eloquent Bks.) Strategic Book Publishing & Rights Agency (SBPRA).

Boyd, Lizi. Big Bear Little Chair. 2015. (ENG., Illus.). 36p. (J). (gr. -1-k). 16.99 *(978-1-4521-4447-4(8))* Chronicle Bks. LLC.

—I Wrote You a Note. 2017. (ENG., Illus.). 36p. (J). 16.99 *(978-1-4521-5957-7(2))* Chronicle Bks. LLC.

Boyle, Bob. Rosie & Rex: A Nose for Fun! Boyle, Bob, illus. 2014. (ENG., Illus.). 40p. (J). (gr. -1-3). 15.99 *(978-0-06-221131-6(5))* HarperCollins Pubs.

Boynton, Sandra. Are You a Cow? Boynton, Sandra, illus. 2012. (ENG., Illus.). 16p. (J). (gr. -1-k). bds. 5.99 *(978-1-4424-1733-5(1),* Little Simon) Little Simon.

—Azul el Sombrero, Verde el Sombrero. Boynton, Sandra, illus. 2003.Tr. of Blue Hat, Green Hat. (SPA., Illus.). 14p. (J). (gr. -1 — 1). bds. 5.99 *(978-0-689-86304-2(7),* Libros Para Ninos) Libros Para Ninos.

—Bath Time! 2007. (ENG., Illus.). 10p. (J). (gr. k — 1). 9.95 *(978-0-7611-4708-4(X),* 14708) Workman Publishing Co., Inc.

—Big Box of Boynton. Boynton, Sandra, illus. 2005. (ENG., Illus.). 24p. (J). (gr. k — 1). bds. 21.00 *(978-0-7611-3989-8(3),* 13989) Workman Publishing Co., Inc.

—The Bunny Rabbit Show! Boynton, Sandra, illus. 2014. (ENG., Illus.). 24p. (J). (gr. -1). bds. 6.95 *(978-0-7611-8060-9(5),* 18060) Workman Publishing Co., Inc.

—Fuzzy Fuzzy Fuzzy! A Touch, Skritch, & Tickle Book. Boynton, Sandra, illus. 2003. (ENG., Illus.). 12p. (J). (gr. -1-k). bds. 14.99 *(978-0-689-86363-9(2),* Little Simon) Little Simon.

—The Going to Bed Book. Boynton, Sandra, illus. (ENG., Illus.). (J). 2006. 14p. bds. 12.95 *(978-1-4169-2794-5(8))* 30th anniv. ed. 2012. 18p. (gr. -1-3). bds. 7.99 *(978-1-4424-5409-5(1))* Little Simon. (Little Simon).

—Happy Hippo, Angry Duck: A Book of Moods. Boynton, Sandra, illus. 2011. (ENG., Illus.). 16p. (J). (gr. -1-k). bds. 5.99 *(978-1-4424-1731-1(5),* Little Simon) Little Simon.

—Hey! Wake Up! 2004. (Illus.). (J). (gr. -1-18). spiral bd., bds. *(978-0-616-14611-8(6))* Canadian National Institute for the Blind/Institut National Canadien pour les Aveugles.

—Moo, Baa, la la La! Boynton, Sandra, illus. (ENG., Illus.). (J). (gr. -1 — 1). 2004. 16p. bds. 9.99 *(978-0-689-87027-9(2))* 2012. 18p. bds. 7.99 *(978-1-4424-5410-1(5))* Little Simon. (Little Simon).

—Moo, Baa, La La La! braille ed. 2004. (J). (gr. 1). spiral bd., bds. *(978-0-616-03082-0(7))* Canadian National Institute for the Blind/Institut National Canadien pour les Aveugles.

—Muu - Beee - ¡Asi Fue! Boynton, Sandra, illus. 2003. (SPA., Illus.). 14p. (J). (gr. -1 — 1). bds. 5.99 *(978-0-689-86302-8(0),* Libros Para Ninos) Libros Para Ninos.

—Opuestos. Ziegler, Argentina Palacios, tr. Boynton, Sandra, illus. 2004.Tr. of Opposites. (SPA., Illus.). 16p. (J). (gr. -1 — 1). bds. 5.99 *(978-0-689-86978-5(9),* Libros Para Ninos) Libros Para Ninos.

—Pajama Time! (Lap Edition) 2011. (ENG., Illus.). 20p. (J). (gr. k — 1). bds. 11.95 *(978-0-7611-6617-7(3),* 16617) Workman Publishing Co., Inc.

—Sandra Boynton's Moo, Baa, la la La! Boynton, Sandra, illus. 2009. (ENG., Illus.). 16p. (J). bds. 16.99 *(978-1-4169-5035-6(4),* Little Simon) Little Simon.

Bracken, Beth. Terrible, Awful, Horrible Manners, 1 vol. Watson, Richard, illus. 2012. (Little Boost Ser.). (ENG.). 32p. (gr. k-3). 7.95 *(978-1-4048-7419-0(4),* Little Boost) Picture Window Bks.

—Too Shy for Show-And-Tell, 1 vol. Bell, Jennifer A., illus. 2012. (Little Boost Ser.). (ENG.). 32p. (gr. k-3). 7.95 *(978-1-4048-7418-3(6),* Little Boost) Picture Window Bks.

Bradley, Kathleen. The Boy Who Cried Wolf, 1 vol. 2008. (Building Fluency Through Reader's Theater Ser.). (ENG.). 24p. (J). (gr. 1-3). pap. 6.99 *(978-1-4333-0297-8(7))* Teacher Created Materials, Inc.

Bradley, Matthew J. O! Who Ate My Dinner! & Other Colin the Cat Stories. 2010. (ENG., Illus.). 98p. pap. *(978-1-84748-766-7(1))* Athena Pr.

Bradley, Timothy J. Time Jump, Bk. 3. 2014. (Sci Hi Ser.). (ENG.). 232p. (J). (gr. 3-6). lib. bdg. 26.96 *(978-1-4807-4217-8(1))* Teacher Created Materials, Inc.

Brandon, Anthony G. Moving Day. Yee, Wong Herbert, illus. 2005. (Green Light Readers Level 2 Ser.). (ENG.). 32p. (J). (gr. -1-3). pap. 3.95 *(978-0-15-205652-0(1))* Houghton Mifflin Harcourt Publishing Co.

Braun, Sebastien. One Sleepy Night. 2013. (Padded Board Books Ser.). (ENG.). 20p. (J). bds. 8.95 *(978-1-58925-619-4(0))* Tiger Tales Pubns.

Brazauski, Vickie. Tweeter the Peachick A True Story, 1 vol. 2010. 26p. 24.95 *(978-1-4489-4257-2(8))* PublishAmerica, Inc.

Breen, Steve. Woodpecker Wants Waffles. Breen, Steve, illus. 2016. (Illus.). 32p. (J). (gr. -1-3). 17.99 *(978-0-06-234257-6(6))* HarperCollins Pubs.

Brenda, Jones. No, I Don't Want to Play Today: An African Tale about Bullying. 2010. 40p. pap. 14.95 *(978-1-60911-387-2(X),* Eloquent Bks.) Strategic Book Publishing & Rights Agency (SBPRA).

Brenner, Emily. On the First Day of Grade School. Whatley, Bruce, illus. 2004. 32p. (J). (gr. -1-1). lib. bdg. 16.89 *(978-0-06-051041-1(2))* HarperCollins Pubs.

Brett, Jan. The Animals' Santa. Brett, Jan, illus. 2014. (ENG., Illus.). 32p. (J). (gr. -1-k). 17.99 *(978-0-399-25784-1(5),* G.P. Putnam's Sons Books for Young Readers) Penguin Young Readers Group.

—Annie & the Wild Animals. 2006. (ENG., Illus.). 32p. (J). (gr. -1-3). bds. 7.95 *(978-0-618-74786-3(9))* Houghton Mifflin Harcourt Publishing Co.

—Armadillo Rodeo. Brett, Jan, illus. 2004. (ENG., Illus.). 32p. (J). (gr. -1-3). pap. 6.99 *(978-0-14-240125-5(0),* Puffin Books) Penguin Young Readers Group.

—Little Library, 3 vols. Brett, Jan, illus. 2003. (ENG., Illus.). 98p. (J). (gr. -1 — 1). bds. 23.99 *(978-0-399-24183-3(3),* G.P. Putnam's Sons Books for Young Readers) Penguin Young Readers Group.

—On Noah's Ark. Brett, Jan, illus. (ENG., Illus.). (J). (gr. -1 — 1). 2009. 34p. bds. 7.99 *(978-0-399-25220-4(7))* 2003. 32p. 17.99 *(978-0-399-24028-7(4))* Penguin Young Readers Group. (G.P. Putnam's Sons Books for Young Readers).

—El Sombrero. (Buenas Noches Ser.).Tr. of Hat. (SPA.). (J). *(978-958-04-4169-4(3))* Norma S.A.

—The Umbrella. Brett, Jan, illus. (ENG., Illus.). (J). (gr. -1 — 1). 2011. 34p. bds. 7.99 *(978-0-399-25540-3(0))* 2004. 32p. 18.99 *(978-0-399-24215-1(5))* Penguin Young Readers Group. (G.P. Putnam's Sons Books for Young Readers).

—The Umbrella. 2005. (Illus.). (J). (gr. k-3). 27.95 incl. audio *(978-0-8045-6931-6(2),* SAC6931) Spoken Arts, Inc.

Brett, Jan & McPike, Elizabeth. The Turnip. Brett, Jan, illus. 2015. (ENG., Illus.). 32p. (J). (-k). bds. 17.99 *(978-0-399-17070-6(7),* G.P. Putnam's Sons Books for Young Readers) Penguin Young Readers Group.

Bricker, Sherry A. Simon & Salina: The Journey Has Begun. 2006. 108p. pap. 19.95 *(978-1-4241-1283-8(4))* PublishAmerica, Inc.

Bright, J. E. Best Friends - Continental Drift. 2012. (I Can Read Level 2 Ser.). (ENG.). 32p. (J). (gr. k-3). pap. 3.99 *(978-0-06-210483-0(7))* HarperCollins Pubs.

—Continental Drift: Manny's Big Adventure. 2012. (I Can Read Level 2 Ser.). (ENG.). 32p. (J). (gr. k-3). pap. 3.99 *(978-0-06-210481-6(0))* HarperCollins Pubs.

Bright, Paul. There's a Bison Bouncing on the Bed! Chatterton, Chris, illus. 2016. (ENG.). 32p. (J). (gr. -1-2). 16.99 *(978-1-68010-006-8(8))* Tiger Tales.

Bright, Rachel. Side by Side. Glori, Debi, illus. 2015. (ENG.). 32p. (J). (gr. -1-k). 17.99 *(978-0-545-81326-6(3),* Scholastic Pr.) Scholastic, Inc.

Brightwell, Beverly. Pea Key & Sam Go to the State Fair. 2013. 24p. pap. 24.95 *(978-1-62709-261-6(7))* America Star Bks.

Brightwood, Laura, illus. Mousanga Bira Mousa. Brightwood, Laura, . 2006. (J). *(978-0-9789871-1-4(X))* 3-C Institute for Social Development.

Brignaud, Pierre, illus. Baby Caillou Looks Around: Animals (A Toddler's Search & Find Book) 2014. (Baby Caillou Ser.). (ENG.). 10p. (J). bds. 6.99 *(978-2-89718-150-5(8))* Caillouet, Gerry.

Brimner, Larry Dane. Trick or Treat, Old Armadillo. Catalano, Dominic, illus. 2010. (ENG.). 32p. (J). (gr. k-2). 16.95 *(978-1-59078-758-8(7))* Boyds Mills Pr.

Brockway, Bettina Chevalier. Muff & the Mushroom Forest. 2010. 32p. pap. 23.50 *(978-1-4520-7426-9(7))* AuthorHouse.

Brook-Piper, Holly. Animal Friends: A Touch-and-Feel Book. 2015. (ENG.). 12p. (J). (gr. -1 — 1). bds. 6.99 *(978-1-4998-0038-8(X))* Little Bee Books Inc.

Brooke, Samantha & S. I. International. Go Go Goes to the Doctor. 2009. (Playskool Ser.). (ENG.). 24p. (J). (gr. -1). pap.

3.99 *(978-1-4169-8295-1(7)*, Simon Spotlight) Simon Spotlight.
Brooks, Walter R. Freddy & Simon the Dictator. Wiese, Kurt, illus. (ENG.). (gr. 4-13). 2014. 256p. pap. 10.99 *(978-1-4683-0976-8(5)*, 460976) 2003. 220p. (J). 23.95 *(978-1-58567-359-9(5))* Overlook Pr., The.
—Freddy & the Ignormus. Wiese, Kurt, illus. 2011. (ENG.). 288p. (gr. 4-13). pap. 10.99 *(978-1-59020-467-2(0)*, 902467) Overlook Pr., The.
—The Story of Freginald. Wiese, Kurt, illus. 2014. (ENG.). 256p. pap. 10.99 *(978-1-4683-0975-1(7)*, 460975) Overlook Pr., The.
Broutin & Stehr. Baldomero Va A la Escuela. (SPA.). 26p. *(978-84-95150-47-9(6))* Corimbo, Editorial S.L.
Broutin, Christian. In the Jungle. Broutin, Christian, illus. 2013. (ENG., Illus.). 36p. (J). (gr. -1-k). 12.99 *(978-1-85103-417-8(X))* Moonlight Publishing, Ltd. GBR. Dist: Independent Pubs. Group.
Brown, Daniel. Chipper Learns a Lesson. 2013. 28p. pap. 5.99 *(978-0-9897549-4-1(4))* Story and Logic Media Group.
Brown, Heather. Big Chomp. 2013. (ENG.). 20p. (J). bds. 8.99 *(978-1-4494-3553-0(X))* Andrews McMeel Publishing.
Brown, Jo. Where's My Mommy? Brown, Jo, illus. 2006. (Storytime Board Bks.). (Illus.). 18p. (J). (gr. -1-3). bds. 6.95 *(978-1-58925-795-5(2))* Tiger Tales.
—Where's My Mommy? 2004. (Illus.). 32p. (J). tchr. ed. 14.95 *(978-1-58925-019-2(2))* Tiger Tales.
Brown, Kathryn. Adventures at Aaron Loch Farm. 2009. 50p. pap. 23.50 *(978-1-4092-6961-8(2))* Lulu Pr., Inc.
Brown, Ken. What's the Time, Grandma Wolf?, 1 vol. Brown, Ken, illus. 2015. (ENG., Illus.). 32p. (J). (gr. -1-2). pap. 7.95 *(978-1-56145-891-2(0))* Peachtree Pubs.
Brown, Lisa. How to Be. Brown, Lisa, illus. 2006. (ENG., Illus.). 32p. (J). (gr. -1 — 1). 17.99 *(978-0-06-054635-9(2))* HarperCollins Pubs.
Brown, Marc. Arthur & the 1,001 Dads, Bk. 28. Brown, Marc, illus. 2003. (ENG., Illus.). 64p. (J). (gr. 1-4). pap. 4.25 *(978-0-316-12280-1(7))* Little, Brown Bks. for Young Readers.
—Arthur & the Bad-Luck Brain. 2003. (Marc Brown Arthur Chapter Bks.). (Illus.). 55p. (gr. 2-4). 14.25 *(978-0-7569-1701-2(8))* Perfection Learning Corp.
—Arthur & the Bad-Luck Brain, Bk. 30. 2003. (ENG., Illus.). 64p. (J). (gr. 1-4). pap. 4.25 *(978-0-316-12377-8(3))* Little, Brown Bks. for Young Readers.
—Arthur & the Nerves of Steal. 32nd ed. 2004. (ENG., Illus.). 64p. (J). (gr. 1-4). pap. 4.25 *(978-0-316-12618-2(7)*, Tingley, Megan Bks.) Little, Brown Bks. for Young Readers.
—Arthur & the Popularity Test. (Arthur Chapter Bks.: Bk. 12). 58p. (J). (gr. 3-6). pap. 3.95 *(978-0-8072-1308-7(X))*; 2004. (gr. 2-4). pap. 17.00 incl. audio *(978-0-8072-0413-9(7)*, FTR204SP) Random Hse. Audio Publishing Group. (Listening Library).
—Arthur Jumps into Fall. 2006. (ENG., Illus.). 24p. (J). (gr. -1-1). pap. 3.99 *(978-0-316-05775-2(4))* Little, Brown Bks. for Young Readers.
—Arthur Lost & Found. 2004. (Arthur Adventure Ser.). (J). (gr. k-3). spiral bd. *(978-0-616-11102-4(9))* Canadian National Institute for the Blind/Institut National Canadien pour les Aveugles.
—Arthur to the Rescue. 13th ed. 2006. (ENG., Illus.). 24p. (J). (gr. -1-1). pap. 3.99 *(978-0-316-05773-8(8))* Little, Brown Bks. for Young Readers.
—Arthur's Birthday Surprise. 2004. (ENG., Illus.). 24p. (J). (gr. -1-1). pap. 3.99 *(978-0-316-73379-3(2))* Little, Brown Bks. for Young Readers.
—Arthur's Classroom Fib. 2007. (Arthur Step into Reading Ser.). lib. bdg. 13.55 *(978-1-4177-7281-0(6)*, Turtleback) Turtleback Bks.
—Arthur's Heart Mix-Up. 2004. (ENG., Illus.). 24p. (J). (gr. -1-1). pap. 3.99 *(978-0-316-73381-6(4))* Little, Brown Bks. for Young Readers.
—Arthur's Jelly Beans. 2004. (ENG., Illus.). 24p. (J). (gr. -1-1). pap. 3.99 *(978-0-316-73382-3(2))* Little, Brown Bks. for Young Readers.
—Arthur's off to School. 2004. (ENG., Illus.). 24p. (J). (gr. -1-1). pap. 3.99 *(978-0-316-73378-6(4))* Little, Brown Bks. for Young Readers.
—Arthur's Tooth. Brown, Marc, illus. 2005. (ENG., Illus.). 32p. (J). (gr. -1-3). pap. 10.99 *(978-0-316-05960-2(9))* Little, Brown Bks. for Young Readers.
—La Visita del Senor Rataquemada. Sarfatti, Esther, tr. from ENG. 2003.Tr. of Arthur's Teacher Moves In. (SPA.). (J). (gr. k-2). pap. 6.95 *(978-1-930332-41-6(6))* Lectorum Pubns., Inc.
Brown, Marc & Sarfatti, Esther. Arturo y la Navidad. 2004. (SPA.). (J). pap. 6.95 *(978-1-930332-48-5(3))* Lectorum Pubns., Inc.
Brown, Margaret Wise. A Child's Good Morning Book. Katz, Karen, illus. 2009. 32p. (J). (gr. -1-3). lib. bdg. 18.89 *(978-0-06-128861-6(6))* HarperCollins Pubs.
—The Dirty Little Boy, 1 vol. Salerno, Steven, illus. 2005. (ENG.). 32p. (J). (gr. -1-1). pap. 5.95 *(978-0-7614-5180-8(3))* Marshall Cavendish Corp.
—Little Fur Family. Williams, Garth, illus. deluxe ed. 2003. (ENG.). 32p. (J). (gr. -1-1). pap. 17.99 *(978-0-06-051898-1(7)*, HarperFestival) HarperCollins Pubs.
—Where Have You Been? Dillon, Leo & Dillon, Diane, illus. 2004. 32p. (J). (gr. -1-1). (ENG.). 16.99 *(978-0-06-028378-0(5))*; lib. bdg. 16.89 *(978-0-06-028379-7(3))* HarperCollins Pubs.
Brown, Pamela. Barnyard Buddies II. Hutchins, Annie H., illus. 2004. 90p. (J). pap. 16.00 *(978-1-928589-21-1(9))* Gival Pr., LLC.
Brown, Peter. Chowder. 2012. (Chowder Book Ser.). (ENG., Illus.). 32p. (J). (gr. -1-3). pap. 7.99 *(978-0-316-20088-2(3))* Little, Brown Bks. for Young Readers.
—Chowder. 2012. (J). lib. bdg. 18.40 *(978-0-606-26146-3(X)*, Turtleback) Turtleback Bks.
—The Wild Robot. 2016. (ENG., Illus.). 288p. (J). (gr. 3-7). 16.99 *(978-0-316-38199-4(3))* Little, Brown Bks. for Young Readers.
—You Will Be My Friend! 2011. (Starring Lucille Beatrice Bear Ser.). (ENG., Illus.). 40p. (J). (gr. -1-3). 18.00 *(978-0-316-07030-0(0))* Little, Brown Bks. for Young Readers.
Brown, Rena Cherry. Otter Lee Brave, 1 vol. Maidment, Mikaila, illus. 2012. (ENG.). 48p. (J). 16.99 *(978-0-7643-4155-7(3)*, 9780764341557) Schiffer Publishing, Ltd.
Brown, Ron. Three-Toes the Raccoon Visits the Farm. 2009. 24p. pap. 10.49 *(978-1-4389-9035-4(9))* AuthorHouse.
Browne, Anthony. One Gorilla. Browne, Anthony, illus. 2013. (ENG., Illus.). 32p. (J). (gr. -1-2). 17.99 *(978-0-7636-6352-0(2))* Candlewick Pr.
Browne, Eileen. Handa's Surprise. Browne, Eileen, illus. 2011. (Reading & Math Together Ser.). (ENG., Illus.). 32p. (J). (gr. -1-2). pap. 24.99 *(978-0-7636-5385-9(3))* Candlewick Pr.
—Handa's Surprise: Read & Share. Browne, Eileen, illus. 2004. (ENG & URD., Illus.). 32p. (J). pap. *(978-1-85269-478-4(5))*; pap. *(978-1-85269-514-9(5))*; pap. *(978-1-85269-476-0(9))*; pap. *(978-1-85269-472-2(6))*; pap. *(978-1-85269-473-9(4))*; pap. *(978-1-85269-474-6(2))*; pap. *(978-1-85269-475-3(0))*; pap. *(978-1-85269-477-7(7))*; pap. *(978-1-85269-507-1(2))*; pap. *(978-1-85269-508-8(0))*; pap. *(978-1-85269-509-5(9))*; pap. *(978-1-85269-510-1(2))* Mantra Lingua.
—Handa's Surprise: Read & Share. 2004. (ENG., Illus.). 32p. (J). pap. *(978-1-85269-511-8(0))* Mantra Lingua.
—Handa's Surprise: Read & Share. Browne, Eileen, illus. 2004. (ENG & TAM., Illus.). 32p. (J). pap. *(978-1-85269-512-5(9))*; pap. *(978-1-85269-513-2(7))*; pap. *(978-1-85269-515-6(3))* Mantra Lingua.
Browne, Eileen & Habashi, Azza. Handa's Surprise: Read & Share. 2004. (ENG & ARA., Illus.). 32p. (J). pap. *(978-1-85269-471-5(8))* Mantra Lingua.
Brug, Sandra Gilbert. Soccer Beat. Moseng, Elisabeth, illus. 2012. (ENG.). 32p. (J). (gr. -1-1). 16.99 *(978-1-4424-8610-2(4)*, McElderry, Margaret K. Bks.) McElderry, Margaret K. Bks.
Bruna, Dick. Miffy Dances. 2004. (Illus.). 24p. pap. 4.99 *(978-1-59226-010-2(1))* Big Tent Entertainment, Inc.
—Miffy Says, I Love You! 2004. (Illus.). 12p. bds. 5.99 *(978-1-59226-187-1(6))* Big Tent Entertainment, Inc.
Bryant, Sara Cone. Stories to Tell Children: Fifty-Four Stories with Some Suggestions for Telling. 2007. (ENG.). 186p. pap. 19.99 *(978-1-4346-0234-3(6))*; 206p. pap. 22.99 *(978-1-4346-0308-1(3))* Creative Media Partners, LLC.
Budge, Donald. Where Is My Butt? Parton, Daron, illus. 2016. (ENG.). 32p. (J). (gr. -1-2). 14.95 *(978-1-4549-1697-0(4))* Sterling Publishing Co., Inc.
Budic, Hannah Purdy. Ebenezer Flea & the Right Thing to Do, 1 vol. Rosendahl, Melissa M., illus. 2008. (ENG.). 30p. 24.95 *(978-1-60441-750-0(1))* America Star Bks.
Bugbird, Tim. Peek a Boo Baby Animals. 2008. (Peek A Boo Ser.). (Illus.). 12p. (gr. -1-k). 7.99 *(978-1-84610-858-7(6))* Make Believe Ideas GBR. Dist: Nelson, Thomas Inc.
—Peek a Boo Wacky Wild Animals. 2008. (Peek A Boo Ser.). (Illus.). 12p. (gr. -1-k). 7.99 *(978-1-84610-860-0(8))* Make Believe Ideas GBR. Dist: Nelson, Thomas Inc.
The Bull & the Tramp. 2005. (J). *(978-0-9746600-1-1(9))* Scott, Josephine.
Bunting, Eve. The Baby Shower. Love, Judy, illus. 2007. (ENG.). 28p. (J). (gr. -1-2). 15.95 *(978-1-58089-139-4(X))* Charlesbridge Publishing, Inc.
—Frog & Friends. 2012. (I AM a READER! Frog & Friends Ser.: 4). (ENG., Illus.). 48p. (J). (gr. 1-3). pap. 3.99 *(978-1-58536-806-8(7))* Sleeping Bear Pr.
—Frog & Friends. Masse, Josée, illus. 2011. (I Am A Reader! Ser.). (ENG.). 40p. (J). (gr. k-3). pap. 3.99 *(978-1-58536-689-7(7))*; lib. bdg. 9.95 *(978-1-58536-548-7(3))* Sleeping Bear Pr.
—Frog & Friends: Frog's Flying Adventure. 2012. (I AM a READER! Frog & Friends Ser.: 4). (ENG., Illus.). 48p. (J). (gr. 1-3). 9.95 *(978-1-58536-805-1(9))* Sleeping Bear Pr.
—Frog & Friends: Outdoor Surprises. Masse, Josée, illus. 2013. (I AM a READER!: Frog & Friends Ser.). (ENG.). 48p. (J). (gr. 1-2). 9.95 *(978-1-58536-807-5(5)*, 202361); pap. 3.99 *(978-1-58536-808-2(3)*, 202370) Sleeping Bear Pr.
—Frog & Friends: The Best Summer Ever. 2012. (I Am A Reader!, Frog & Friends Ser.). (ENG., Illus.). 48p. (J). (gr. k-3). pap. 3.99 *(978-1-58536-691-0(9))*; lib. bdg. 9.95 *(978-1-58536-550-0(5))* Sleeping Bear Pr.
—Frog & Friends Celebrate Thanksgiving, Christmas, & New Year's Eve. Masse, Josée, illus. 2015. (I AM a READER!: Frog & Friends Ser.). (ENG.). 40p. (J). (gr. 1-2). 9.99 *(978-1-58536-897-6(0)*, 203949) Sleeping Bear Pr.
—Frog's Lucky Day. Masse, Josée, illus. 2014. (I Am a Reader!: Frog & Friends Ser.). (ENG.). 40p. (J). (gr. 1-2). 9.99 *(978-1-58536-892-1(X)*, 203014) Sleeping Bear Pr.
—Have You Seen My New Blue Socks? Ruzzier, Sergio, illus. 2013. (ENG.). 32p. (J). (gr. -1-3). 16.99 *(978-0-547-75267-9(9))* Houghton Mifflin Harcourt Publishing Co.
—Hey Diddle Diddle. Fraser, Mary Ann, illus. 2011. (ENG.). 32p. (J). (gr. -1-k). 16.95 *(978-1-59078-768-7(4))* Boyds Mills Pr.
—Whose Shoe? Ruzzier, Sergio, illus. 2015. (ENG.). 32p. (J). (gr. -1-3). 16.99 *(978-0-544-30210-5(9))* Houghton Mifflin Harcourt Publishing Co.
Burach, Ross. There's a Giraffe in My Soup. Burach, Ross, illus. 2016. (Illus.). 32p. (J). (gr. -1-3). 17.99 *(978-0-06-236014-4(0))* HarperCollins Pubs.
Burgess, Linda, text. Mount Vernon's Magnificent Menagerie: And the Very Mysterious Guest. 2012. (ENG., Illus.). 48p. (J). 15.95 *(978-0-931917-31-8(X))* Mount Vernon Ladies' Assn. of the Union.
Burgess, Lisa Maria. Juma on Safari. Gugu, Abdul M., illus. 2013. 32p. 19.95 *(978-1-939604-07-1(9))*; pap. 9.99 *(978-1-939604-03-3(6))* Barranca Pr.
Burgess, Thornton W. The Adventures of Bob White. (J). 18.95 *(978-0-88411-776-6(6))* Amereon Ltd.
—Adventures of Bob White. Cady, Harrison, illus. 2011. (Dover Children's Thrift Classics Ser.). (ENG.). 96p. (J). (gr. k-3). pap. 3.00 *(978-0-486-48109-8(3))* Dover Pubns., Inc.
—The Adventures of Buster Bear. 2008. 108p. per. 9.95 *(978-1-60312-500-0(0))* Aegypan.
—The Adventures of Buster Bear. 2011. 108p. 23.95 *(978-1-4638-9555-6(0))* Rodgers, Alan Bks.
—The Adventures of Buster Bear. 2007. 192p. (gr. 4-7). 29.95 *(978-1-4344-8855-8(1))*; per. 14.95 *(978-1-4344-8854-1(3))* Wildside Pr., LLC.
—The Adventures of Danny Meadow Mouse. 2009. (gr. 4-7). 108p. 22.95 *(978-1-60664-649-6(4))*; 104p. pap. 9.95 *(978-1-60664-274-0(X))* Rodgers, Alan Bks.
—The Adventures of Grandfather Frog. 2007. 108p. (gr. -1-3). per. 9.95 *(978-1-60312-154-5(4))*; 22.95 *(978-1-60312-837-7(9))* Aegypan.
—The Adventures of Grandfather Frog. (J). (gr. 5-6). 18.95 *(978-0-88411-777-3(4))* Amereon Ltd.
—The Adventures of Grandfather Frog. 2011. 108p. 23.95 *(978-1-4638-9570-9(4))* Rodgers, Alan Bks.
—The Adventures of Happy Jack. 2004. (Dover Children's Thrift Classics Ser.). (ENG., Illus.). 128p. (J). (gr. 3-8). pap. 4.00 *(978-0-486-43321-9(8))* Dover Pubns., Inc.
—The Adventures of Jerry Muskrat. 2007. 108p. (gr. 2-5). per. 9.95 *(978-1-60312-336-5(9))*; 22.95 *(978-1-60312-674-8(0))* Aegypan.
—The Adventures of Jerry Muskrat. (J). (gr. 5-6). 18.95 *(978-0-88411-782-7(0))* Amereon Ltd.
—The Adventures of Jerry Muskrat. 2004. reprint ed. pap. 1.99 *(978-1-4192-5151-1(1))*; pap. 15.95 *(978-1-4191-5151-4(7))* Kessinger Publishing, LLC.
—The Adventures of Jerry Muskrat. 2011. 108p. 23.95 *(978-1-4638-9564-8(X))* Rodgers, Alan Bks.
—The Adventures of Jimmy Skunk. 2007. 112p. 22.95 *(978-1-60312-594-9(9))* Aegypan.
—The Adventures of Jimmy Skunk. 2016. (ENG., Illus.). (J). 22.95 ***(978-1-358-39350-1(8))*** Creative Media Partners, LLC.
—The Adventures of Jimmy Skunk. 2011. 110p. 23.95 *(978-1-4638-9560-0(7))* Rodgers, Alan Bks.
—The Adventures of Johnny Chuck. 2007. 108p. (gr. 2-5). per. 9.95 *(978-1-60312-257-3(5))*; 22.95 *(978-1-60312-755-4(0))* Aegypan.
—The Adventures of Johnny Chuck. 2004. reprint ed. pap. 15.95 *(978-1-4191-5154-5(1))*; pap. 1.99 *(978-1-4192-5154-2(6))* Kessinger Publishing, LLC.
—The Adventures of Johnny Chuck. 2011. 108p. 23.95 *(978-1-4638-9568-6(2))* Rodgers, Alan Bks.
—The Adventures of Lightfoot the Deer. 2008. 104p. per. 9.95 *(978-1-60312-501-7(9))* Aegypan.
—The Adventures of Lightfoot the Deer. 2011. 108p. 23.95 *(978-1-4638-9556-3(9))* Rodgers, Alan Bks.
—The Adventures of Mr. Mocker. (J). 18.95 *(978-0-8488-0378-0(7))* Amereon Ltd.
—The Adventures of Mr. Mocker. Cady, Harrison, illus. 2011. (Dover Children's Thrift Classics Ser.). (ENG.). 96p. (J). (gr. k-3). pap. 3.00 *(978-0-486-48101-2(8))* Dover Pubns., Inc.
—The Adventures of Mr Mocker. 2007. 108p. per. 9.95 *(978-1-60312-296-2(6))*; (gr. 4-7). 22.95 *(978-1-60312-714-1(3))* Aegypan.
—The Adventures of Mr Mocker. 2011. 108p. 23.95 *(978-1-4638-9565-5(8))* Rodgers, Alan Bks.
—The Adventures of Ol' Mistah Buzzard. (J). (gr. 5-6). 18.95 *(978-0-88411-784-1(7))* Amereon Ltd.
—The Adventures of Ol' Mistah Buzzard. 2005. reprint ed. pap. 22.95 *(978-1-4179-2352-6(0))* Kessinger Publishing, LLC.
—The Adventures of Old Man Coyote. (J). (gr. 5-6). 18.95 *(978-0-88411-781-0(2))* Amereon Ltd.
—The Adventures of Old Mr. Toad. (J). (gr. 5-6). 18.95 *(978-0-88411-785-8(5))* Amereon Ltd.
—The Adventures of Old Mr Toad. 2007. 140p. (gr. 4-7). 24.95 *(978-1-60312-637-3(6))*; per. 11.95 *(978-1-60312-379-2(2))* Aegypan.
—The Adventures of Old Mr Toad. 2011. 138p. 25.95 *(978-1-4638-9561-7(5))* Rodgers, Alan Bks.
—The Adventures of Paddy the Beaver. 2008. 108p. (gr. 4-7). 22.95 *(978-1-60664-952-7(3))* Aegypan.
—The Adventures of Paddy the Beaver. 2011. 108p. 23.95 *(978-1-4638-9557-0(7))* Rodgers, Alan Bks.
—The Adventures of Poor Mrs Quack. 2007. 124p. 23.95 *(978-1-60312-595-6(7))* Aegypan.
—The Adventures of Poor Mrs Quack. 2011. 124p. 24.95 *(978-1-4638-9562-4(3))* Rodgers, Alan Bks.
—The Adventures of Poor Mrs. Quack. 2004. reprint ed. pap. 15.95 *(978-1-4191-5160-6(6))*; pap. 1.99 *(978-1-4192-5160-3(0))* Kessinger Publishing, LLC.
—The Adventures of Prickly Porky. 2007. 140p. (gr. 4-7). per. 11.95 *(978-1-60312-048-7(3))*; 24.95 *(978-1-60312-953-4(7))* Aegypan.
—The Adventures of Prickly Porky. (J). (gr. 5-6). 18.95 *(978-0-88411-783-4(9))* Amereon Ltd.
—The Adventures of Prickly Porky. 2011. 138p. 25.95 *(978-1-4638-9572-3(0))* Rodgers, Alan Bks.
—The Adventures of Reddy Fox. 2005. 84p. pap. 10.95 *(978-1-59540-695-8(6)*, 1st World Library - Literary Society) 1st World Publishing, Inc.
—The Adventures of Reddy Fox. 2007. 108p. (gr. 4-7). per. 9.95 *(978-1-60312-155-2(2))*; 22.95 *(978-1-60312-838-4(7))* Aegypan.
—The Adventures of Reddy Fox. Frost, Maddie, illus. 2017. (Thornton Burgess Library). (ENG.). 128p. (J). (gr. -1-2). pap. 9.95 ***(978-1-63322-368-4(X)***, Seagrass) Quarto Publishing Group USA.
—The Adventures of Reddy Fox. 2011. 108p. 23.95 *(978-1-4638-9571-6(2))* Rodgers, Alan Bks.
—The Adventures of Unc' Billy Possum. 2007. 140p. (gr. 4-7). per. 13.95 *(978-1-60312-337-2(7))*; 24.95 *(978-1-60312-675-5(9))* Aegypan.
—The Adventures of Unc' Billy Possum. Cady, Harrison & Stewart, Pat Ronson, trs. Cady, Harrison & Stewart, Pat Ronson, illus. 2003. (Dover Children's Thrift Classics Ser.). (ENG.). 96p. (J). (gr. 3-8). pap. 3.00 *(978-0-486-43031-7(6))* Dover Pubns., Inc.
—The Adventures of Unc' Billy Possum. 2011. 140p. 24.95 *(978-1-4638-9563-1(1))* Rodgers, Alan Bks.
—Big Book of Animal Stories. 2011. (Dover Children's Classics Ser.). (ENG., Illus.). 272p. (J). (gr. 3-8). 9.95 *(978-0-486-41980-0(0))* Dover Pubns., Inc.
—Blacky the Crow. 2006. 136p. per. 10.95 *(978-1-59818-116-6(5))*; 24.95 *(978-1-59818-470-9(9))* Aegypan.
—Bowser the Hound. 2010. (Dover Children's Thrift Classics Ser.). (ENG., Illus.). 96p. (J). (gr. 3-8). pap. 4.00 *(978-0-486-42847-5(8))* Dover Pubns., Inc.
—Bowser the Hound. 2004. reprint ed. pap. 24.95 *(978-1-4179-2323-6(7))* Kessinger Publishing, LLC.
—The Burgess Seashore Book for Children. Sutton, George Miksch, illus. 2005. (Dover Children's Classics Ser.). (ENG.). 288p. (J). (gr. k-3). per. 12.95 *(978-0-486-44253-2(5))* Dover Pubns., Inc.
—Dear Old Briar Patch. (J). 18.95 *(978-0-8488-0402-2(3))* Amereon Ltd.
—Fifty Favorite Burgess Stories. Cady, Harrison, illus. 2011. 376p. 53.95 *(978-1-258-07354-1(4))* Literary Licensing, LLC.
—Happy Jack. (J). 19.95 *(978-0-8488-0389-6(2))* Amereon Ltd.
—Longlegs the Heron. (J). 19.95 *(978-0-8488-0400-8(7))* Amereon Ltd.
—Mother West Wind 'How' Stories. 2008. 108p. (gr. -1-3). 22.95 *(978-1-60664-893-3(4))*; pap. 9.95 *(978-1-60664-012-8(7))* Aegypan.
—Mother West Wind 'Where' Stories. 2009. 108p. 22.95 *(978-1-60664-597-0(8))*; 104p. pap. 9.95 *(978-1-60664-326-6(6))* Rodgers, Alan Bks.
—Mother West Wind 'Why' Stories. 108p. (gr. -1-3). 2007. per. 9.95 *(978-1-60312-004-3(1))* 2006. 22.95 *(978-1-59818-467-9(9))* Aegypan.
—Mother West Wind 'Why' Stories. 2011. 108p. 23.95 *(978-1-4638-9574-7(7))* Rodgers, Alan Bks.
—Mother West Wind's Animal Friends. Kerr, George, tr. Kerr, George & Stewart, Pat Ronson, illus. 2003. (Dover Children's Thrift Classics Ser.). (ENG.). 128p. (J). (gr. 3-8). pap. 4.00 *(978-0-486-43030-0(8))* Dover Pubns., Inc.
—Mother West Wind's Children. 2007. 116p. (gr. 2-13). per. 9.95 *(978-1-60312-156-9(0))*; 22.95 *(978-1-60312-836-0(0))* Aegypan.
—Mother West Wind's Children. Kerr, George, illus. 2013. (Dover Children's Classics Ser.). (ENG.). 144p. (J). (gr. 1-5). pap. 3.00 *(978-0-486-49724-2(0))* Dover Pubns., Inc.
—Mother West Wind's Children. 2011. 114p. 23.95 *(978-1-4638-9569-3(0))* Rodgers, Alan Bks.
—Mother West Wind's Neighbors. Kerr, George & Stewart, Pat, illus. 2003. (Dover Children's Thrift Classics Ser.). (ENG.). 96p. (J). (gr. 3-8). pap. 4.00 *(978-0-486-42846-8(X))* Dover Pubns., Inc.
—Mrs Peter Rabbit. 2007. 120p. (gr. -1-3). per. 10.95 *(978-1-60312-005-0(X))* Aegypan.
—Mrs. Peter Rabbit. 2004. reprint ed. pap. 15.95 *(978-1-4191-3581-1(3))*; pap. 1.99 *(978-1-4192-3581-8(8))* Kessinger Publishing, LLC.
—The National Review Treasury of Classic Bedtime Stories. Cady, Harrison, illus. 2004. 368p. (J). 29.95 *(978-0-9627841-8-7(4))* ISI Bks.
—Old Granny Fox. 2007. 124p. 23.95 *(978-1-60312-593-2(0))* Aegypan.
—Old Granny Fox. 2004. reprint ed. pap. 1.99 *(978-1-4192-3801-7(9))*; pap. 15.95 *(978-1-4191-3801-0(4))* Kessinger Publishing, LLC.
—Old Granny Fox. 2011. 122p. 24.95 *(978-1-4638-9559-4(3))* Rodgers, Alan Bks.
—Old Mother West Wind. Kerr, George, illus. annot. ed. 2011. (Dover Children's Classics Ser.). (ENG.). 336p. (J). (gr. 1-5). 20.00 *(978-0-486-48051-0(8))* Dover Pubns., Inc.
—Old Mother West Wind. 2011. 110p. 23.95 *(978-1-4638-9554-9(2))* Rodgers, Alan Bks.
—Old Mother West Wind's Children. (J). 18.95 *(978-0-8488-0386-5(8))* Amereon Ltd.
—Old Mother West Wind's "Where" Stories. (J). 18.95 *(978-0-8488-0388-9(4))* Amereon Ltd.
—Short Works of Thornton W. Burgess. 2007. (ENG.). 282p. pap. 21.99 *(978-1-4346-1957-0(5))*; 340p. pap. 24.99 *(978-1-4346-1981-5(8))* Creative Media Partners, LLC.
—Thornton Burgess Bedtime Stories: Includes Downloadable MP3s. Hauge, Carl & Hauge, Mary, illus. 2013. (Dover Read & Listen Ser.). (ENG.). 112p. (J). (gr. 1). pap. 14.99 *(978-0-486-49189-9(7))* Dover Pubns., Inc.
—Whitefoot the Wood Mouse. Cady, Harrison, illus. 2006. (Dover Children's Thrift Classics Ser.). (ENG.). 112p. (J). (gr. 3-8). per. 4.00 *(978-0-486-44944-9(0))* Dover Pubns., Inc.
—Whitefoot the Woodmouse. 2011. 118p. 23.95 *(978-1-4638-9567-9(4))* Rodgers, Alan Bks.
Burgess, W. Thornton. Old Mother West Wind. 2007. 72p. per. 87.99 *(978-1-4280-7713-3(8))* IndyPublish.com.
Burke, Christina. Melvin et le Grand Match de Hockey. Minguet, Anne, tr. Franfou, illus. 2013. 52p. *(978-0-9918561-3-8(9))*; pap. *(978-0-9918561-2-1(0))* Stars Aligned Publishing.
Burke, Zoe. Charley Harper's What's in the Coral Reef? A Nature Discovery Book. 2014. 3. (ENG., Illus.). 34p. (J). 14.95 *(978-0-7649-6846-4(7))* Pomegranate Communications, Inc.
—Charley Harper's What's in the Rain Forest? A Nature Discovery Book. Harper, Charley, illus. 2013. 34p. (J). 14.95 *(978-0-7649-6584-5(0))* Pomegranate Communications, Inc.
—Charley Harper's What's in the Woods? A Nature Discovery Book. Harper, Charley, illus. 2013. (ENG.). 32p. (J). 14.95 *(978-0-7649-6453-4(4))* Pomegranate Communications, Inc.
Burnford, Sheila. The Incredible Journey. (J). (gr. 6-8). 18.95 *(978-0-88411-099-6(0))* Amereon Ltd.
—The Incredible Journey. unabr. ed. 2004. 145p. (J). (gr. 5-9). pap. 29.00 incl. audio *(978-0-8072-8322-6(3)*, YA162SP, Listening Library) Random Hse. Audio Publishing Group.
Burningham, John. Picnic. Burningham, John, illus. 2014. (ENG., Illus.). 32p. (J). (-k). 16.99 *(978-0-7636-6945-4(8))* Candlewick Pr.
Burr, Avril. Naughty Art. 2012. (Illus.). 66p. pap. *(978-1-78281-017-9(X))* Athena Pr.
Burwitz, Patrick. Mia's Dogcow. 2009. 28p. pap. 13.00 *(978-1-4343-8580-2(9))* AuthorHouse.
Busch, Miriam. Lion, Lion. Day, Larry, illus. 2014. (ENG.). 32p. (J). (gr. -1-3). 17.99 *(978-0-06-227104-4(0))* HarperCollins Pubs.
Bush, John & Geraghty, Paul. The Bungle in the Jungle. (Illus.). 32p. (J). 17.95 *(978-0-09-174056-6(8))* Random Hse. GBR. Dist: Trafalgar Square Publishing.
Bushman, Janet. A Shiny Red Apple. 2010. 16p. 8.95 *(978-1-4389-7861-1(8))* AuthorHouse.
Butler, Craig. Possum's Christmas. 2009. 16p. pap. 11.50 *(978-1-60693-715-0(4)*, Eloquent Bks.) Strategic Book Publishing & Rights Agency (SBPRA).
Butler, John. Can You Cuddle Like a Koala? Butler, John, illus. (Illus.). (J). (gr. k-1). 2005. (ENG.). 20p. bds. 6.95

(978-1-56145-347-4(1)) 2003. 32p. 15.95 (978-1-56145-298-9(X)) Peachtree Pubs.

—Can You Growl Like a Bear? Butler, John, illus. (Illus.). (J). 2012. 20p. bds. 6.95 (978-1-56145-667-3(5)) 2007. (ENG., 32p. 15.95 (978-1-56145-396-2(X), Peachtree Junior) Peachtree Pubs.

—If You See a Kitten. 1 vol. Butler, John, illus. 2015. (ENG., Illus.). 24p. (J). (gr. 1-2). pap. 7.95 (978-1-56145-838-7(4)) Peachtree Pubs.

—Ten in the Meadow. Butler, John, illus. 2006. (ENG., Illus.). 32p. (J). (gr. k-1). 15.95 (978-1-56145-372-6(2)) Peachtree Pubs.

Butler, Kristi T. A Big Surprise. Paparone, Pamela, illus. 2005. (Green Light Readers Level 1 Ser.). (ENG.). 24p. (J). (gr. -1-3). pap. 3.95 (978-0-15-205141-9(4)) Houghton Mifflin Harcourt Publishing Co.

Butler, M. Christina. One Special Christmas. Macnaughton, Tina, illus. 2013. (ENG.). 32p. (J). (978-1-58925-145-8(8)) Tiger Tales.

Butterfield, Moira. Wake up, Magic Duck! Child, Jeremy, illus. 2010. (Magic Bath Bks.). (ENG.). 8p. (J). (gr. -1-k). 5.99 (978-0-7641-9792-5(4)) Barron's Educational Series, Inc.

Butterworth, Nick. After the Storm. Butterworth, Nick, illus. 2003. (Percy the Park Keeper Ser.). (ENG., Illus.). 32p. (J). (gr. k-2). pap. 11.00 (978-0-00-715515-6(8), HarperCollins Children's Bks.) HarperCollins Pubs. Ltd. GBR. Dist: Independent Pubs. Group.

—One Snowy Night. Butterworth, Nick, illus. 2008. (Tales from Percy's Park Ser.). (ENG., Illus.). 32p. (J). (gr. k-2). pap. 12.95 incl. audio compact disk (978-0-00-726024-9(5)) HarperCollins Pubs.

—One Snowy Night. Butterworth, Nick, illus. 2007. (ENG., Illus.). 32p. (J). 24.00 (978-0-00-725942-7(5)) HarperCollins Pubs. Ltd. GBR. Dist: Independent Pubs. Group.

—Percy's Bumpy Ride. Butterworth, Nick, illus. 2011. (Tales from Percy's Park Ser.). (ENG., Illus.). 32p. (J). pap. 11.00 (978-0-00-715514-9(X), HarperCollins Children's Bks.) HarperCollins Pubs. Ltd. GBR. Dist: HarperCollins Pubs.

—Q Pootle 5. Butterworth, Nick, illus. 2009. (ENG., Illus.). 32p. (J). (gr. -1-k). pap. 11.95 (978-0-00-717235-1(4), HarperCollins Children's Bks.) HarperCollins Pubs. Ltd. GBR. Dist: HarperCollins Pubs.

—The Secret Path. Butterworth, Nick, illus. 2011. (Tales from Percy's Park Ser.). (ENG., Illus.). 32p. (J). pap. 11.95 (978-0-00-715518-7(2), HarperCollins Children's Bks.) HarperCollins Pubs. Ltd. GBR. Dist: HarperCollins Pubs.

Byars, Betsy. Bingo Brown, Amante Gitano. 2003. (Survival Ser.).Tr. of Bingo Brown, Gypsy Lover. (SPA., Illus.). 168p. (J). (gr. 4-7). 10.95 (978-84-239-7158-9(9), EC6469) Espasa Calpe, S.A. ESP. Dist: Planeta Publishing Corp.

Caballero, Erica. Mount Mole. 2006. pap. 10.00 (978-1-4257-2301-9(2)) Xlibris Corp.

Cabrera, Jane. Kitty's Cuddles. 2007. (ENG., Illus.). 32p. (J). (gr. -1-k). 16.95 (978-0-8234-2066-7(3)) Holiday Hse., Inc.

—Mommy, Carry Me Please! Cabrera, Jane, illus. (Jane Cabrera Board Bks.). (ENG., Illus.). (J). 2008. 24p. (gr. -1-k). bds. 6.95 (978-0-8234-2131-2(7)) 2006. 32p. (gr. 3-6). 16.95 (978-0-8234-1935-7(5)) Holiday Hse., Inc.

—The 12 Days of Christmas. 2013. (ENG., Illus.). 32p. (J). (gr. -1-k). 16.95 (978-0-8234-2870-0(2)) Holiday Hse., Inc.

Cail, Carol. It's a Zoo Around Here. 2012. (Illus.). 36p. pap. 8.99 (978-1-60820-567-7(3)) MLR Pr., LLC.

Cain, Sheridan. Donde Dormiras Pequena Liebre? Percy, Sally, illus. (SPA.). (J). (gr. k-2). pap. 16.95 (978-84-488-0869-3(X), BS3556) Beascoa, Ediciones S.A. ESP. Dist: Lectorum Pubns., Inc.

Calhoun, Terry. The Muggwapps. 2007. (J). pap. 8.00 (978-0-8059-7223-8(4)) Dorrance Publishing Co., Inc.

Callahan, Sean. A Wild Day with Dad. Howarth, Daniel, illus. 2012. (ENG.). 18p. (J). (gr. -1 — 1). bds. 7.99 (978-0-8075-2295-0(3)) Whitman, Albert & Co.

Callahan, Susan. Always Right. 2012. 20p. pap. 15.99 (978-1-4772-0424-5(5)) AuthorHouse.

Callen, Sharon. The Lovely One. 1 vol. rev. ed. 2013. (Fiction Readers Ser.). (ENG., Illus.). 32p. (J). (gr. 3-3). pap. 8.99 (978-1-4333-5649-0(X)) Shell Educational Publishing.

Calmenson, Stephanie. Birthday at the Panda Palace. Cushman, Doug, illus. 2007. 32p. (J). (gr. -1-3). 15.99 (978-0-06-052663-4(7)) HarperCollins Pubs.

—Jazzmatazz! Degen, Bruce, illus. 2008. 32p. (J). (gr. -1). lib. bdg. 17.89 (978-0-06-077290-1(5)) HarperCollins Pubs.

—There Are No Moose on This Island. 1 vol. Thermes, Jennifer, illus. 2013. (ENG.). 32p. (J). 17.95 (978-1-934031-34-6(8), a2b39bfc-ad16-4e21-bc2e-5db5168164a8) Islandport Pr., Inc.

El Camaleon. (Coleccion Animalitos Exoticos). (SPA., Illus.). 16p. (J). 16.95 (978-84-7630-370-2(X), SAN370) Editorial Libsa, S.A. ESP. Dist: Continental Bk. Co., Inc.

Camp, Lindsay. Keeping up with Cheetah. Newton, Jill, illus. 2004. 28p. (J). (gr. -1-2). (978-1-85269-150-9(6)) Mantra Lingua.

Campbell, Lori. The Adventures of Tinkerbelle & Peanut. 2012. 36p. pap. 21.99 (978-1-4771-4835-8(3)) Xlibris Corp.

Campbell, S Q. Animals. 2006. (Picture Me Ser.). (Illus.). (J). (978-1-57151-769-2(3)) Playhouse Publishing.

Campbell, Shirlene. Ook Ook the Monkey. 2013. 24p. pap. 24.95 (978-1-63004-355-1(9)) America Star Bks.

Can I Come Too?, 1 vol. 2014. (ENG., Illus.). 32p. (J). (gr. -1-3). pap. 16.95 (978-1-56145-796-0(5)) Peachtree Pubs.

Candlewick Press Editors. Peppa Pig & the Busy Day at School. 2014. (Peppa Pig Ser.). lib. bdg. 16.00 (978-0-606-35154-6(X)) Turtleback Bks.

Candlewick Press Staff. Peppa Pig & the Great Vacation. 2014. (Peppa Pig Ser.). (ENG.). 32p. (J). (-k). 12.99 (978-0-7636-6986-7(5), Candlewick Entertainment) Candlewick Pr.

—Peppa Pig & the Lost Christmas List. Candlewick Press Staff, illus. 2014. (Peppa Pig Ser.). (ENG., Illus.). 32p. (J). (-k). 5.99 (978-0-7636-7456-4(7), Candlewick Entertainment) Candlewick Pr.

—Peppa Pig & the Lost Christmas List. 2014. (Peppa Pig Ser.). lib. bdg. 16.00 (978-0-606-35868-2(4)) Turtleback Bks.

Cannon, Janell. Pinduli. Cannon, Janell, illus. 2004. (ENG., Illus.). 48p. (J). (gr. -1-3). 17.99 (978-0-15-204668-2(2)) Houghton Mifflin Harcourt Publishing Co.

Caplan, Frank A. The Donkey Who Lost His Tail. 2010. (Illus.). 20p. 12.49 (978-1-4520-2778-4(1)) AuthorHouse.

Caple, Kathy. Duck & Company Christmas. Caple, Kathy, illus. 2011. (ENG., Illus.). 48p. (J). 15.95 (978-0-8234-2239-5(9)) Holiday Hse., Inc.

Capozzi, Suzy & Finnegan, Delphine. Lady & the Tramp. Random House Disney Staff, illus. 2012. (Step into Reading Ser.). (ENG.). 32p. (J). (gr. -1-1). pap. 3.99 (978-0-7364-3026-5(1), RH/Disney) Random Hse. Children's Bks.

Capstone Press. Jelly Bear Christmas Surprise, 1 vol. 2015. (Jelly Bear Ser.). (ENG.). 10p. (gr. -1 — 1). bds. 12.99 (978-1-62370-247-2(X)) Capstone Young Readers of Coughlan Cos.

Capucilli, Alyssa Satin. Biscuit. Schories, Pat, illus. 2006. (My First I Can Read Ser.). (ENG.). 32p. (J). (gr. -1 — 1). reprint ed. pap. 3.99 (978-0-06-444212-1(8)) HarperCollins Pubs.

—Biscuit in the Garden. Schories, Pat, illus. 2013. (My First I Can Read Ser.). (ENG.). 32p. (J). (gr. -1-3). 16.99 (978-0-06-193505-3(0)); pap. 3.99 (978-0-06-193504-6(2)) HarperCollins Pubs.

Carey, Catherine Elaine. The Colorful & Playful Animal Friends, 1 vol. 2009. 73p. pap. 16.95 (978-1-60749-480-5(9)) PublishAmerica, Inc.

Carey, Janet Lee. The Beast of Noor. (ENG., Illus.). 512p. (J). (gr. 5-9). 2011. pap. 7.99 (978-1-4424-4338-9(3)) 2006. 19.99 (978-0-689-87644-8(0)) Simon & Schuster Children's Publishing. (Atheneum Bks. for Young Readers).

Carkhuff Jr., Sam. The Ranch Race. Crow, Katie, illus. 2012. 36p. 16.99 (978-1-939054-03-6(6)); pap. 11.99 (978-1-939054-02-9(8)) Rowe Publishing and Design.

Carle, Eric. Animal Stories: 8 Animal Stories over 35 Sounds. 2014. 36p. (J). bds. 24.98 (978-1-4508-8529-4(2), 1450885292) Publications International, Ltd.

—The Artist Who Painted a Blue Horse. Carle, Eric, illus. (ENG., Illus.). (J). (gr. -1 — 1). 2013. 22p. bds. 7.99 (978-0-399-16402-6(2)) 2011. 32p. 17.99 (978-0-399-25713-1(6)) Penguin Young Readers Group. (Philomel Bks.).

—The Eric Carle Gift Set: The Tiny Seed; Pancakes, Pancakes!; a House for Hermit Crab; Rooster's off to See the World. Carle, Eric, illus. 2013. (World of Eric Carle Ser.). (ENG., Illus.). 124p. (J). (gr. -1 — 1). bds. 34.99 (978-1-4424-8885-4(9), Little Simon) Little Simon.

—How Things Grow. 2015. (ENG.). 14p. (J). (gr. -1-k). 7.99 (978-0-448-48768-7(3), Grosset & Dunlap) Penguin Young Readers Group.

—My First Busy Book. Carle, Eric, illus. 2015. (World of Eric Carle Ser.). (ENG., Illus.). 12p. (J). bds. 14.99 (978-1-4814-5791-0(8), Little Simon) Little Simon.

—Rooster Is off to See the World. Carle, Eric, illus. 2013. (World of Eric Carle Ser.). (ENG., Illus.). 24p. (J). (gr. -1-1). 16.99 (978-1-4424-7270-9(7)); pap. 3.99 (978-1-4424-7269-3(3)) Simon Spotlight. (Simon Spotlight).

—Rooster Is off to See the World. 2013. (Eric Carle Ready-To-Read Ser.). lib. bdg. 13.55 (978-0-606-32063-4(6), Turtleback) Turtleback Bks.

Carle, Eric & Chronicle Books Staff. Stage & Play: Brown Bear, Brown Bear, What Do You See? 2015. (ENG., Illus.). 8p. (J). (gr. -1-1). 16.99 (978-1-4521-4320-0(X)) Chronicle Bks. LLC.

Carlson, Martin D. Rfaud Tastes Wisdom. Oketch, Alphonce Omondi, illus. 2013. 36p. pap. 11.00 (978-0-9848791-2-0(9)) BoCook Publishing.

Carlson, Nancy. Arnie & the Skateboard Gang. Carlson, Nancy, illus. 2012. (Nancy Carlson Picture Bks.). (Illus.). 32p. (J). (gr. k-2). (ENG.). 9.95 (978-0-7613-8948-4(2)); 56.72 (978-0-7613-9303-0(X)) Lerner Publishing Group. (Carolrhoda Bks.).

—Arnie Goes to Camp. Carlson, Nancy, illus. 2012. (Nancy Carlson Picture Bks). (Illus.). 32p. (J). (gr. k-2). (ENG.). 9.95 (978-0-7613-8947-7(4)); 56.72 (978-0-7613-9302-3(1)) Lerner Publishing Group. (Carolrhoda Bks.).

—Get up & Go! 2008. (Illus.). (gr. -1-3). 16.00 (978-0-7569-8922-4(1)) Perfection Learning Corp.

—Henry & the Bully. 2012. (ENG.). 32p. (J). (gr. -1-1). pap. 6.99 (978-0-14-242120-8(0), Puffin Books) Penguin Young Readers Group.

—Henry's Show & Tell. Carlson, Nancy, illus. 2012. (Nancy Carlson Picture Bks.). (Illus.). 32p. (J). (gr. k-2). 56.72 (978-0-7613-9308-5(0)); (ENG., 9.95 (978-0-7613-8953-8(9)) Lerner Publishing Group. (Carolrhoda Bks.).

—Louanne Pig in the Talent Show. 2005. (Louanne Pig Ser.). (Illus.). 32p. (J). (gr. -1-3). lib. bdg. 15.95 (978-1-57505-915-0(0)) Lerner Publishing Group.

—Louanne Pig in Witch Lady. 2006. (Illus.). 32p. (J). (gr. -1-3). lib. bdg. 15.95 (978-0-8225-6196-5(4), Carolrhoda Bks.) Lerner Publishing Group.

—Louanne Pig in Witch Lady. Carlson, Nancy, illus. rev. ed. 2006. (ENG., Illus.). 32p. (J). (gr. k-2). per. 9.95 (978-0-8225-6197-2(2), First Avenue Editions) Lerner Publishing Group.

Carlstrom, Nancy White. Raven & River. Van Zyle, Jon, illus. 2011. (ENG.). 32p. pap. 11.95 (978-1-60223-150-4(8)) Univ. of Alaska Pr.

Carmichael, Bruce. The Little Path by Shadow Mountain. 2003. (J). per. 10.95 (978-1-58597-198-5(7)) Leathers Publishing.

Carmody, Isobelle. A Fox Called Sorrow. 2008. (Little Fur Ser.: Bk. 2). (ENG., Illus.). 272p. (J). (gr. 3-7). 5.99 (978-0-375-83857-6(0), Yearling) Random Hse. Children's Bks.

—A Mystery of Wolves. 2009. (Little Fur Ser.: Bk. 3). (ENG., Illus.). 256p. (J). (gr. 3-7). 6.99 (978-0-375-83859-0(7), Yearling) Random Hse. Children's Bks.

—A Riddle of Green. 2009. (Little Fur Ser.: Bk. 4). (J). (978-0-375-83860-6(0)) Random House Children's Books.

Carney, Karin. Prince Braden's Animal Kingdom. 2011. 40p. pap. 18.95 (978-1-4357-9406-1(0)) Lulu Pr., Inc.

—Princess Bailey & Her Animal Friends. 2011. (Illus.). 46p. pap. 18.95 (978-0-557-95745-3(1)) Lulu Pr., Inc.

Carol, Light. Chickensing Story Book Board. Carol, Light, illus. 2003. (Illus.). 60p. (J). (978-0-9745803-0-2(9)) Little Big Tomes.

Carol Muller-Funk. Proxmire & the Exodus of Prairieville. 2009. 400p. pap. 17.99 (978-1-4389-4013-7(0)) AuthorHouse.

Carolan, Joanna F. Old Makana Had a Taro Farm. Carolan, Joanna F., illus. 2008. (Illus.). 48p. 17.95 (978-0-9715333-9-4(3)) Banana Patch Pr.

Carr, Elias. Jo y la Sopa Lenta. Garton, Michael, illus. 2016. (SPA.). (J). **(978-1-5064-2097-4(4)**, Sparkhouse Pr.) Spark Hse.

Carre, Lilli. Tippy & the Night Parade. Carre, Lilli, illus. 2014. (ENG., Illus.). 32p. (J). (gr. -1-3). 12.95 (978-1-935179-57-3(8)) TOON Books / RAW Junior, LLC.

Carrick, Valery. Tales of Wise & Foolish Animals. 2015. (ENG., Illus.). 112p. (J). (gr. 2-5). reprint ed. pap. 6.99 (978-0-486-21997-4(6)) Dover Pubns., Inc.

Carriger, Candace. Inside My Garden. Allen, Cassandra, illus. 2011. 46p. (J). pap. 11.95 (978-0-9816047-5-6(7)) Sadie Bks.

Carris, Joan. Magic at the Bed & Biscuit. Jones, Noah Z., illus. 2012. (ENG.). 112p. (J). (gr. 1-4). pap. 5.99 (978-0-7636-5849-6(9)) Candlewick Pr.

—Welcome to the Bed & Biscuit. Jones, Noah Z., illus. 2009. (ENG.). 128p. (J). (gr. 1-4). 5.99 (978-0-7636-4621-9(0)) Candlewick Pr.

—Wild Times at the Bed & Biscuit. Jones, Noah Z., illus. (ENG.). 128p. (J). (gr. 1-4). 2011. pap. 5.99 (978-0-7636-5294-4(6)) 2009. 15.99 (978-0-7636-3705-7(X)) Candlewick Pr.

Carris, Joan Davenport. Magic at the Bed & Biscuit. Meserve, Jessica & Jones, Noah Z., illus. 2011. (Daisy Dawson Ser.). (ENG.). 128p. (J). (gr. 1-4). 15.99 (978-0-7636-4306-5(8)) Candlewick Pr.

Carroll, James Christopher. The Boy & the Moon. Carroll, James Christopher, illus. 2010. (ENG., Illus.). 32p. (J). (gr. 1-4). 19.99 (978-1-58536-521-0(1), 202209) Sleeping Bear Pr.

Carter, Aimée. Simon Thorn & the Viper's Pit. 2017. (Simon Thorn Ser.). (ENG.). 304p. (J). 16.99 (978-1-61963-715-3(4), 9781619637153, Bloomsbury USA Childrens) Bloomsbury Publishing USA.

—Simon Thorn & the Wolf's Den. 2016. (Simon Thorn Ser.). (ENG.). 320p. (YA). (gr. 3-6). 16.99 (978-1-61963-704-7(9), 9781619637047, Bloomsbury USA Childrens) Bloomsbury Publishing USA.

—Simon Thorn & the Wolf's Den. 2017. (Simon Thorn Ser.). (ENG.). 336p. (J). pap. 7.99 (978-1-61963-706-1(5), 9781619637061, Bloomsbury USA Childrens) Bloomsbury Publishing USA.

Carter, David A. Builder Bugs: A Busy Pop-Up Book. Carter, David A., illus. 2012. (David Carter's Bugs Ser.). (ENG., Illus.). 16p. (J). (gr. -1-2). 12.99 (978-1-4424-2648-1(9), Little Simon) Little Simon.

—Winter. 2015. (Seasons Pop-Up Ser.). (ENG., Illus.). 12p. (J). (gr. -1-k). 14.95 (978-1-4197-1823-6(1), Abrams Appleseed) Abrams, Inc.

Carter, Liane. The Chronicles of Joy. 2008. 244p. pap. (978-1-84923-001-8(3)) YouWriteOn.

Carter, Russell Gordon. Teenage Animal Stories. Osborne, Richard, illus. 2011. 252p. 46.95 (978-1-258-09864-3(4)) Literary Licensing, LLC.

Casad, Patricia E. Bubbykins: (Life on the Farm) 2008. 46p. pap. 24.95 (978-1-4241-9140-6(8)) America Star Bks.

Casanova, Mary. One-Dog Canoe. Hoyt, Ard, illus. 2003. (ENG.). 32p. (J). (gr. -1-1). 18.99 (978-0-374-35638-5(6), 9780374356385, Farrar, Straus & Giroux (BYR)) Farrar, Straus & Giroux.

—One-Dog Canoe. Hoyt, Ard, illus. 2009. (ENG.). 32p. (J). (gr. -1-1). pap. 7.99 (978-0-312-56118-5(0), 9780312561185) Square Fish.

—One-Dog Sleigh. Hoyt, Ard, illus. 2013. (ENG.). 32p. (J). (gr. k-3). 16.99 (978-0-374-35639-2(4), 9780374356392, Farrar, Straus & Giroux (BYR)) Farrar, Straus & Giroux.

Casello-Atassi, Rosemarie. Camel's Tales: The Journey to Bethlehem. 2013. 86p. pap. 15.99 (978-1-4797-7565-1(7)) Xlibris Corp.

Casey, Barbara. Two Dogs & a Tail. 2004. (Illus.). 30p. (J). 7.95 (978-1-932162-25-7(9)) Benoy Publishing.

Casey, Dawn. The Great Race: The Story of the Chinese Zodiac. Wilson, Anne, illus. 2008. (ENG.). 32p. (J). (gr. -1-2). 8.99 (978-1-84686-202-1(7)) Barefoot Bks., Inc.

Casey, Mark. An African Princess: Deasha's Wild Adventure. 2010. (Illus.). 54p. pap. 11.95 (978-1-4327-3864-8(X)) Outskirts Pr., Inc.

Catchpool, Michael. Where There's a Bear, There's Trouble. Cabban, Vanessa, illus. 2004. 32p. (J). pap. 6.95 (978-1-58925-389-6(2)) Tiger Tales.

Cazet, Denys, reader. Minnie & Moo: Will You Be My Valentine? 2004. (Read-Alongs for Beginning Readers Ser.). (Illus.). (J). (gr. -1-3). 25.95 incl. audio (978-1-59112-892-2(7)); pap. 29.95 incl. audio (978-1-59112-893-9(5)); pap. 31.95 incl. audio compact disk (978-1-59112-897-7(8)) Live Oak Media.

Cebollero, Julie. The Lion That Roared. 2012. (ENG.). 61p. pap. 9.95 (978-1-4327-8067-8(0)) Outskirts Pr., Inc.

Cendrars, Blaise. Petits Contes Negres pour les Enfants. (FRE.). (J). pap. 19.95 (978-2-07-051787-9(X)) Gallimard, Editions FRA. Dist: Distribooks, Inc.

Centeio, Tara Jaye. Mommy Loves Her Baby. Date not set. 32p. (J). (gr. -1-1). pap. 5.99 (978-0-06-443715-8(9)) HarperCollins Pubs.

Chadwick, Robert. Vengeful Impulse. 2003. 70p. pap. 8.95 (978-0-595-27876-3(0)) iUniverse, Inc.

Chambers, Bev R. Bouncer & Friends. 2012. (ENG., Illus.). 40p. (J). 14.99 (978-1-937008-14-7(2)) Heart to Heart Publishing, Inc.

Chambers, Melinda. We Are Whoooo We Are. Spiker, Sue Ann, illus. 2006. 32p. (J). 16.95 (978-0-929915-46-3(1)) Headline Bks., Inc.

Chambers, Whittaker, tr. from GER. The City Jungle. 2014. (Bambi's Classic Animal Tales Ser.). (ENG., Illus.). 288p. (J). (gr. 3-7). pap. 7.99 (978-1-4424-8751-2(8), Aladdin) Simon & Schuster Children's Publishing.

Chan, Ruth. Georgie's Best Bad Day. 2017. (Georgie & Friends Ser.). (ENG., Illus.). 40p. (J). 17.99 (978-1-62672-270-5(6), 9781626722705) Roaring Brook Pr.

—Where's the Party? 2016. (Georgie & Friends Ser.). (ENG., Illus.). 40p. (J). 17.99 (978-1-62672-269-9(2), 9781626722699) Roaring Brook Pr.

Chang, Grace. Jin Jin & Rain Wizard. Chang, Chong, illus. 2009. (ENG.). 48p. (J). (gr. -1-3). 16.95 (978-1-59270-086-8(1)) Enchanted Lion Bks., LLC.

—Jin Jin the Dragon. Chang, Chong, illus. 2008. (ENG.). 48p. (J). (gr. -1-3). 16.95 (978-1-59270-102-5(7)) Enchanted Lion Bks., LLC.

Chapman, Cheryl. Pass the Fritters, Critters. Roth, Susan L., illus. 2007. (ENG.). 40p. (J). (gr. -1-2). 11.99 (978-1-4169-6160-4(7), Simon & Schuster/Paula Wiseman Bks.) Simon & Schuster/Paula Wiseman Bks.

Chapman, Helen. How the Animals Got Their Colours: Tales from the Australian Dreamland. 2017. (ENG.). 32p. (J). (gr. 2-3). pap. 8.99 (978-0-00-817934-2(4)) HarperCollins Pubs. Ltd. GBR. Dist: Independent Pubs. Group.

Chapman, Jane. Hands off My Honey! Warnes, Tim, illus. 2013. (ENG.). 32p. (J). (gr. -1-1). 12.95 (978-1-58925-142-7(3)) Tiger Tales.

Chapman, Jason. Who's That Snoring? A Pull-the-Tab Bedtime Book. Chapman, Jason, illus. 2010. (ENG., Illus.). 12p. (J). (gr. -1-1). bds. 9.99 (978-1-4169-8937-0(4), Little Simon) Little Simon.

Charlesworth, Liza. Night on the Farm: An Animal Friends Reader. Smith, Ian, illus. 2015. 16p. (J). pap. **(978-0-545-85964-6(6))** Scholastic, Inc.

—Wake up, Rooster! An Animal Friends Reader. Smith, Ian, illus. 2015. 16p. (J). pap. **(978-0-545-85971-4(9))** Scholastic, Inc.

Chartier, Doris E. Ben's Desert Journey. 2009. 32p. pap. 14.49 (978-1-4389-7756-0(5)) AuthorHouse.

Chase, Kit. Charlie's Boat. Chase, Kit, illus. 2017. (ENG., Illus.). 32p. (J). (-k). 16.99 (978-0-399-25702-5(0), G.P. Putnam's Sons Books for Young Readers) Penguin Young Readers Group.

—Lulu's Party. Chase, Kit, illus. 2015. (ENG., Illus.). 32p. (J). (gr. -1-k). 16.99 (978-0-399-25701-8(2), G.P. Putnam's Sons Books for Young Readers) Penguin Young Readers Group.

Chen, Sam. A Real Meal Table Fable. Peschel, Georgia, illus. 2007. 60p. (J). (978-0-9800764-0-0(4)) Uncle Jim's Publishing.

Chew, Ruth. No Such Thing as a Witch. 2013. (Matter-Of-Fact Magic Book Ser.). (ENG., Illus.). 128p. (J). (gr. 2-5). 5.99 (978-0-449-81562-5(5)); 15.99 (978-0-449-81559-5(5)) Random Hse. Children's Bks. (Random Hse. Bks. for Young Readers).

Chick, Bryan. The Secret Zoo. 2010. (Secret Zoo Ser.: 1). (ENG.). 304p. (J). (gr. 3-7). 16.99 (978-0-06-198750-2(6), Greenwillow Bks.) HarperCollins Pubs.

—The Secret Zoo: Traps & Specters. 2012. (Secret Zoo Ser.: 4). (ENG.). 320p. (J). (gr. 3-7). 16.99 (978-0-06-219222-6(1), Greenwillow Bks.) HarperCollins Pubs.

Chiew, Suzanne. Friends to the Rescue. Pedler, Caroline, illus. 2016. (ENG.). 32p. (J). (gr. -1-2). 16.99 (978-1-68010-007-5(6)) Tiger Tales.

Child, Lauren. I Am Going to Save a Panda! 2010. (Charlie & Lola Ser.). lib. bdg. 13.55 (978-0-606-10628-3(6), Turtleback) Turtleback Bks.

—I Am Not Sleepy & I Will Not Go to Bed. 2004. (J). (gr. k-3). spiral bd. (978-0-616-11105-5(3)); spiral bd. (978-0-616-11104-8(5)) Canadian National Institute for the Blind/Institut National Canadien pour les Aveugles.

—I Am Not Sleepy & I Will Not Go to Bed. Child, Lauren, illus. 2005. (Charlie & Lola Ser.). (ENG., Illus.). 32p. (J). (gr. -1-2). reprint ed. pap. 8.99 (978-0-7636-2970-0(7)) Candlewick Pr.

Children's Press, contrib. by. The Frog in the Pond & Other Animal Stories. 2008. (Rookie Reader Treasury Ser.). (ENG., Illus.). 128p. (J). 11.95 (978-0-531-21727-6(2), Children's Pr.) Scholastic Library Publishing.

Chin, Oliver. The Year of the Dragon: Tales from the Chinese Zodiac. 2012. (Tales from the Chinese Zodiac Ser.: 7). (ENG., Illus.). 36p. (J). (gr. -1-3). 15.95 (978-1-59702-028-2(1)) Immedium.

—The Year of the Horse: Tales from the Chinese Zodiac. Wood, Jennifer, illus. 2013. (Tales from the Chinese Zodiac Ser.: 8). (ENG.). 36p. (J). (gr. -1-3). 15.95 (978-1-59702-080-0(X)) Immedium.

—The Year of the Monkey: Tales from the Chinese Zodiac. Ono, Kenji, illus. 2015. (Tales from the Chinese Zodiac Ser.: 11). (ENG & CHI.). 36p. (J). (gr. -1). 15.95 (978-1-59702-118-0(0)) Immedium.

—The Year of the Ox: Tales from the Chinese Zodiac. Alcorn, Miah, illus. 2009. (Tales from the Chinese Zodiac Ser.). (ENG.). 36p. (J). (gr. -1-3). 15.95 (978-1-59702-015-2(X)) Immedium.

—Year of the Rooster. Calle, Juan, illus. 2016. (Tales from the Chinese Zodiac Ser.: 12). (ENG.). 40p. (J). (gr. -1). 15.95 (978-1-59702-125-8(3)) Immedium.

Chin, Oliver, ed. The Year of the Snake: Tales from the Chinese Zodiac. Wood, Jennifer, illus. 2012. (Tales from the Chinese Zodiac Ser.: 8). (ENG.). 36p. (J). (gr. -1-3). 15.95 (978-1-59702-038-1(9)) Immedium.

Chin, Oliver Clyde. The Year of the Rabbit: Tales from the Chinese Zodiac. Roth, Justin, illus. 2010. (Tales from the Chinese Zodiac Ser.). (ENG.). 36p. (J). (gr. -1-3). 15.95 (978-1-59702-023-7(0)) Immedium.

Chinery, Michael & Michael, Chinery. Enciclopedia de los Animales Salvajes, 8 vols.Tr. of Wild World of Animals. (SPA.). 346p. (J). (gr. 3-5). 100.00 (978-84-241-2059-7(0)) Everest Editora ESP. Dist: Lectorum Pubns., Inc.

Chocolate, Debbi. Pigs Can Fly! The Adventures of Harriet Pig & Friends. Tryon, Leslie, illus. 2004. (ENG.). 64p. (J). 15.95 (978-0-8126-2706-0(7)) Cricket Bks.

The Chocolate Moose. 2007. (Illus.). 48p. (J). per. 13.00 (978-0-9767189-5-6(2)) Better Day Publishing LLC.

Christie, Donna. Bobby & the Well. 2013. 28p. pap. 16.09 (978-1-4669-6667-3(X)) Trafford Publishing.

Christie, Jacqueline. Alphabet Animals. 2012. 60p. pap. 37.37 (978-1-4797-1567-1(0)) Xlibris Corp.

Christine Battuz, Christine, illus. Goodnight, Sleepy Animals: A Nightlight Book. 2016. (Nightlight Ser.). (ENG.). 14p. (J). (gr. -1-k). 12.99 (978-2-89718-338-7(1)) CrackBoom! Bks. CAN. Dist: Publishers Group West (PGW).

Christmas Is Coming. 2003. (J). 6.99 (978-1-59384-012-9(8)) Parklane Publishing.

Christopher, Neil. Way Back Then, 1 vol. Amaktauyok, Germaine, illus. 2015. (ENG.). 40p. (J). (gr. -1-k). 16.95 (978-1-77227-021-1(0)) Inhabit Media Inc. CAN. Dist: Independent Pubs. Group.

Chronicle Books Staff & Leuck, Laura. For Just One Day. Boutavant, Marc, illus. 2009. (ENG.). 32p. (J). (gr. -1 — 1). 16.99 (978-0-8118-5610-2(0)) Chronicle Bks. LLC.

Chwast, Seymour & Lofting, Hugh. Dr. Dolittle. Chwast, Seymour, illus. 2015. (ENG., Illus.). 40p. (J). (gr. 4-7). 18.99 (978-1-56846-258-5(1), Creative Editions) Creative Co., The.

Ciminera, Siobhan. Farm Animal Friends. Collection/Jupiterimages Unlimited, illus. 2009. (ENG.). 48p. (J). (gr. -1-2). 12.99 (978-1-4169-6786-6(9), Simon Scribbles) Simon Scribbles.

Civardi, Anna. Farm Magnet Book. Cartwright, Stephen, illus. 2009. (Magnet Bks). 10p. (J). bds. 19.99 (978-0-7945-2231-5(9), Usborne) EDC Publishing.

Clapp. Eloy the Elk & His Desert Friends. Clapp, ed. Drotar, illus. 2009. (J). pap. 9.95 (978-0-9825181-0-6(2)) Arizona Elk Society.

Clark, Gloria. The Little Candy Breathing Dragons. 2008. 36p. per. 12.95 (978-1-4327-1510-6(0)) Outskirts Pr., Inc.

Clark, Sarah Kartchner. ¡En Equipo Con el Sr. Supercoyote!, 1 vol. rev. ed. 2007. (Building Fluency Through Reader's Theater Ser.).Tr. of Teaming with Mr. Cool! (SPA., Illus.). 24p. (J). (gr. 3-4). pap. 6.99 (978-1-4333-0025-7(7)) Teacher Created Materials, Inc.

Clarke, Jacqueline A. Moose's Loose Tooth. McNally, Bruce, illus. 2003. (J). (978-0-439-41183-7(1)) Scholastic, Inc.

Clarke, Jane. Clover the Bunny. 2016. (Dr. KittyCat Ser.: 2). (ENG.). 96p. (J). (gr. 2-5). pap. 4.99 (978-0-545-87336-9(3), Scholastic Paperbacks) Scholastic, Inc.

Clarkson, Kelly. River Rose & the Magical Lullaby. Hughes, Laura, illus. 2016. 32p. (J). (gr. -1-3). 18.99 (978-0-06-242756-4(3)) HarperCollins Pubs.

Clary, Julian. The Bolds to the Rescue. Roberts, David, illus. 2017. (Bolds Ser.: 2). (ENG.). 288p. (J). (gr. 3-6). 16.99 (978-1-5124-1022-8(5), Carolrhoda Bks.) Lerner Publishing Group.

Classic Tales: Based on the Originals by Beatrix Potter, 12 bks. (Illus.). (J). (gr. 2-4). lib. bdg. 143.40 (978-1-56674-923-7(9)) Forest Hse. Publishing Co., Inc.

Clement-Davies, David. The Sight. 2007. (ENG.). 480p. (YA). (gr. 7-18). 8.99 (978-0-14-240874-2(3), Firebird) Penguin Young Readers Group.

Cleveland, Rob. The Archer & the Sun: A Tale from China. Hoffmire, Baird, illus. 2007. (Story Cove Ser.). (ENG.). 24p. (J). (gr. -1-3). pap. 3.95 (978-0-87483-878-7(9)) August Hse. Pubs., Inc.

Clifton-Brown, Holly. Annie Hoot & the Knitting Extravaganza. Clifton-Brown, Holly, illus. 2010. (Andersen Press Picture Bks). (ENG., Illus.). 32p. (J). (gr. -1-3). 16.95 (978-0-7613-6444-3(7)) Lerner Publishing Group.

Cloke, Rene, illus. Storytime Classics. 2012. (ENG.). 144p. (J). 12.50 (978-1-84135-521-4(6)) Award Pubns. Ltd. GBR. Dist: Parkwest Pubns., Inc.

Cloke, Rene & Cloke, Rene. Woodland Stories. 2013. (ENG., Illus.). 104p. (J). 16.50 (978-1-84135-931-1(9)) Award Pubns. Ltd. GBR. Dist: Parkwest Pubns., Inc.

Clynes, Kate. Not Again, Red Riding Hood! Daykin, Louise, illus. 2004. 32p. (J). (HIN & ENG.). (978-1-85269-998-7(1)); (ENG & SPA.). pap. (978-1-85269-939-0(6)); (ENG & SOM.). pap. (978-1-85269-934-5(5)); (POR & ENG.). pap. (978-1-85269-919-2(1)); (ENG & POL.). pap. (978-1-85269-914-7(0)); (ENG & PAN.). pap. (978-1-85269-909-3(4)); (ENG & ITA.). pap. (978-1-85269-904-8(3)); (ENG & GUJ.). pap. (978-1-85269-993-2(0)); (GER & ENG.). pap. (978-1-85269-988-8(4)); (ENG & RUS.). pap. (978-1-85269-924-6(8)); (FRE & ENG.). pap. (978-1-85269-983-3(3)); (ENG & PER.). pap. (978-1-85269-978-9(7)); (ENG & CZE.). pap. (978-1-85269-973-4(6)); (ENG & CHI.). pap. (978-1-85269-968-0(X)); (ENG & VIE.). pap. (978-1-85269-959-8(0)); (ENG & ARA.). pap. (978-1-85269-958-1(2)); (ENG & URD.). pap. (978-1-85269-954-3(X)); (ENG & ALB.). pap. (978-1-85269-953-6(1)); (ENG & TUR.). pap. (978-1-85269-949-9(3)); (ENG & TAM.). pap. (978-1-85269-944-4(2)); (ENG & SER.). pap. (978-1-85269-929-1(9)) Mantra Lingua.

Coates, Theresa. Imaginary Time of Life. 2007. 102p. pap. 10.95 (978-0-7414-4067-9(9)) Infinity Publishing.

Coats, Vivian. His Special Love. 2009. 32p. pap. 12.99 (978-1-4490-1915-0(3)) AuthorHouse.

Cochran, Jean M. If a Monkey Jumps onto Your School Bus. Morris, Jennifer & Morris, Jennifer E., illus. 2008. (ENG.). 32p. (J). (gr. -1-k). 16.95 (978-0-9792035-2-7(X)) Pleasant St. Pr.

Cochran, Randy. Critter Golf: The Adventures at Owl's Nest. 2013. (ENG.). 84p. (YA). pap. 8.95 (978-1-4787-1263-3(5)) Outskirts Pr., Inc.

Cofer, Judith Ortiz. Animal Jamboree / La Fiesta de los Animales: Latino Folktales / Leyendas Latinas. Rosales-Yeomans, Natalia, tr. 2012. (SPA & ENG.). (J). pap. 9.95 (978-1-55885-743-8(5), Piñata Books) Arte Publico Pr.

Coffelt, Nancy. Aunt Ant Leaves Through the Leaves. Coffelt, Nancy, illus. 2013. (ENG., Illus.). 32p. (J). pap. 7.99 (978-0-8234-2761-1(7)) Holiday Hse., Inc.

—Aunt Ant Leaves Through the Leaves: A Story with Homophones & Homonyms. Coffelt, Nancy, illus. 2012. (ENG., Illus.). 32p. (J). 16.95 (978-0-8234-2353-8(0)) Holiday Hse., Inc.

Cohen, Jerianne. Max A. Million's Birthday Party. 2008. 193p. pap. 24.95 (978-1-60672-844-4(X)) America Star Bks.

Cohen, Lee. The Surprise Party. Neuville, Loyal de, illus. 2010. (ENG.). 32p. (J). (gr. -1-12). lib. bdg. 16.95 (978-1-934960-85-1(3), Raven Tree Pr.,Csi) Continental Sales, Inc.

Cohn, Marvin. Tell Me A Story Gramps. 2007. 52p. pap. 16.95 (978-1-4241-5075-5(2)) America Star Bks.

Cohn, Scott M. Daddy Sat on a Duck. 2015. (Daddy Ser.: 1). (ENG., Illus.). 32p. (J). (gr. -1-3). 15.00 (978-0-316-40749-6(6)) Little Brown & Co.

Cole, Babette. Los Animales Me Aterrorizan. 2003. (Babette Cole Ser.).Tr. of Animals Scare Me Stiff. (SPA.). 28p. (J). (gr. -1-3). 15.95 (978-84-233-3234-2(9)) Ediciones Destino ESP. Dist: Planeta Publishing Corp., Lectorum Pubns., Inc.

Cole, Henry. Bayberry Island. Cole, Henry, illus. 2017. (Brambleheart Ser.: 2). (Illus.). 176p. (J). (gr. 3-7). 16.99 (978-0-06-224551-9(1), Tegen, Katherine Bks) HarperCollins Pubs.

—Brambleheart. Cole, Henry, illus. 2016. (Brambleheart Ser.: 1). (Illus.). 272p. (J). (gr. 3-7). 16.99 (978-0-06-224546-5(5)) HarperCollins Pubs.

—The Somewhat True Adventures of Sammy Shine, 1 vol. Cole, Henry, illus. 2016. (ENG., Illus.). 272p. (J). (gr. 3-6). 16.95 (978-1-56145-866-0(X)) Peachtree Pubs.

Coles, Michael Joseph, et al. The Land of Caring Bou. Banks, Timothy, illus. 2006. (J). (978-0-87483-814-5(2)) August Hse. Pubs., Inc.

Coll, Ivar Da. El Senor Joser Tomillo. (SPA.). (J). bds. (978-958-04-4906-5(6)) Norma S.A. COL. Dist: Lectorum Pubns., Inc.

Colleen, Marcie. Super Happy Party Bears: Knock Knock on Wood. James, Steve, illus. 2016. (Super Happy Party Bears Ser.: 2). (ENG.). 144p. (J). pap. 5.99 (978-1-250-09808-5(4), 9781250098085) Imprint IND. Dist: Macmillan.

Collier, Kevin Scott. Tales from Kensington Forest. l.t. ed. 2006. (Illus.). 26p. (J). E-Book 5.00 incl. cd-rom (978-1-933090-26-9(X)) Guardian Angel Publishing, Inc.

Collier, Kristen & Collier, Kevin. Natalie's Ark. 2009. 84p. pap. 8.95 (978-1-61633-007-1(4)) Guardian Angel Publishing, Inc.

Collins, Charles. Hover for a Day. Seltzer, Jerry, illus. 2006. (ENG.). 56p. (J). 19.95 (978-1-60131-004-0(8), Castlebridge Bks.) Big Tent Bks.

Collins, Suzanne. Gregor, Set, Nos. 1-5. 2009. (Underland Chronicles Ser.). (ENG.). (J). (gr. 3-7). pap., pap., pap. 39.95 (978-0-545-16681-2(0)) Scholastic, Inc.

—Gregor & the Code of Claw. 2008. (Underland Chronicles Ser.: 5). (ENG., Illus.). 416p. (J). (gr. 3-7). pap. 7.99 (978-0-439-79144-1(8), Scholastic Paperbacks) Scholastic, Inc.

—Gregor & the Code of Claw. l.t. ed. 2007. (Underland Chronicles: Bk. 5). 413p. (YA). (gr. 8-12). 22.95 (978-0-7862-9696-5(8)) Thorndike Pr.

—Gregor & the Curse of the Warmbloods. 2006. (Underland Chronicles: Bk. 3). 358p. (gr. 4-7). 17.00 (978-0-7569-6766-6(X)) Perfection Learning Corp.

—Gregor & the Curse of the Warmbloods, Bk. 3. 2006. (Underland Chronicles Ser.: 3). (ENG.). 368p. (J). (gr. 3-7). pap. 7.99 (978-0-439-65624-5(9), Scholastic Paperbacks) Scholastic, Inc.

—Gregor & the Marks of Secret. 2007. (Underland Chronicles Ser.: 4). (ENG., Illus.). 352p. (J). (gr. 3-7). 7.99 (978-0-439-79146-5(4), Scholastic Paperbacks) Scholastic, Inc.

—Gregor & the Marks of Secret. 2007. (Underland Chronicles Ser.: 4). 343p. (gr. 4-7). lib. bdg. 18.40 (978-1-4177-8358-8(3), Turtleback) Turtleback Bks.

—Gregor & the Prophecy of Bane. 2005. (Underland Chronicles Ser.: 2). (ENG.). 320p. (J). (gr. 3-7). pap. 7.99 (978-0-439-65076-2(3)) Scholastic, Inc.

Colón, Raúl. Draw! Colón, Raúl, illus. 2014. (ENG., Illus.). 40p. (J). (gr. -1-3). 17.99 (978-1-4424-9492-3(1), Simon & Schuster/Paula Wiseman Bks.) Simon & Schuster/Paula Wiseman Bks.

Come & Play: Individual Title Six-Packs. (Story Steps Ser.). (gr. k-2). 29.00 (978-0-7635-9595-1(0)) Rigby Education.

Compo-Pratt, Paula. BooBoo & the Land of Mists & Dreams. 2012. (J). (gr. k-1). 14.95 (978-1-57197-513-3(6), Ivy House Publishing Group) Pentland Pr., Inc.

Confederated Salish and Kootenai Tribes Staff. Beaver Steals Fire: A Salish Coyote Story. Sandoval, Sam, illus. 2008. (ENG.). 64p. (YA). (gr. k-3). pap. 14.95 (978-0-8032-1640-2(8), Bison Bks.) Univ. of Nebraska Pr.

Conway, David. Errol & His Extraordinary Nose. Angaramo, Roberta, illus. 2010. (ENG.). 32p. (J). (gr. -1-3). 16.95 (978-0-8234-2262-3(3)) Holiday Hse., Inc.

Conway, Jill Ker, et al. El Flamingo Felipe. Millis, Lokken, illus. 2009. (SPA & ENG.). 32p. (J). (gr. -1-3). pap. 9.95 (978-1-55591-714-2(3)) Fulcrum Publishing.

Cook, Eileen. Fourth Grade Fairy. 2011. (Fourth Grade Fairy Ser.: 1). (ENG.). 176p. (J). (gr. 3-7). pap. 7.99 (978-1-4169-9811-2(X), Aladdin) Simon & Schuster Children's Publishing.

—Wishes for Beginners. 2011. (Fourth Grade Fairy Ser.: 2). (ENG.). 160p. (J). (gr. 3-7). pap. 6.99 (978-1-4169-9812-9(8), Aladdin) Simon & Schuster Children's Publishing.

Cook, Gerri. Where the Buffalo Jump. Yu, Chao & Wang, Jue, illus. 2003. (Dinosaur Soup Ser.). 120p. (YA). (gr. 3-5). pap. 9.95 (978-1-895836-95-0(6)) River Bks. CAN. Dist: Fitzhenry & Whiteside, Ltd.

Cook, Sherry & Johnson, Terri. Jazzy Jet, 26 vols. Kuhn, Jesse, illus. l.t. ed. 2006. (Quirkles — Exploring Phonics through Science Ser.: 10). 32p. (J). 7.99 (978-1-933815-09-1(4), Quirkles, The) Creative 3, LLC.

—Ollie Oxygen, 26 vols. Kuhn, Jesse, illus. l.t. ed. 2006. (Quirkles — Exploring Phonics through Science Ser.: 15). 32p. (J). 7.99 (978-1-933815-14-5(0), Quirkles, The) Creative 3, LLC.

Cook, Sherry & Terri, Johnson. Yawning Yolanda, 26. l.t. ed. 2006. (Quirkles — Exploring Phonics through Science Ser.: 25). (Illus.). 32p. (J). 7.99 (978-1-933815-24-4(8), Quirkles, The) Creative 3, LLC.

Cooke, Brandy. My Valentine. Wilkinson, Annie, illus. 2010. (ENG.). 12p. (J). (gr. -1 — 1). bds. 4.99 (978-1-4424-0779-4(4), Little Simon) Little Simon.

Cool by the Pool: Coloring/Activity Book. 2005. (Illus.). (J). 2.99 (978-0-9770455-2-5(8)) Mighty Kids Media.

Cool by the Pool: Picture Book (English) 2005. (Illus.). 47p. (J). 5.99 (978-0-9770455-3-2(6)) Mighty Kids Media.

Cooper, Doris Marie. Ben Bear's Eventful Day. 2010. (Illus.). 40p. 20.99 (978-1-4389-0839-7(3)) AuthorHouse.

Cooper, Helen S. & Butterworth, Ian. Pinsiaid o Bupur. Williams, Dylan, tr. from ENG. 2005. (WEL., Illus.). 36p. (978-1-84512-022-1(1)) Cymdeithas Lyfrau Ceredigion.

Cooper, Nelle. Princess Lil. 2013. 82p. (J). pap. 9.00 (978-1-936442-16-4(7)) Fresh Ink Group.

Cooper, Page. Amigo, Circus Horse. Pitz, Henry, illus. 2011. 240p. 46.95 (978-1-258-06394-8(8)) Literary Licensing, LLC.

Cooper, Polly. The Adventures of Sir George & His Friends. 2008. (Illus.). 48p. pap. 17.49 (978-1-4343-4057-3(0)) AuthorHouse.

Correa, Shan. Gaff, 1 vol. 2010. (ENG.). 224p. (J). (gr. 3-7). 15.95 (978-1-56145-526-3(1), Peachtree Junior) Peachtree Pubs.

Cortright, Angel. The Miss Adventure of Animals & Their Short Stories. 2013. 28p. pap. 24.95 (978-1-62709-063-6(0)) America Star Bks.

Corum, Stephanie J. Goats with Coats. 2008. 32p. pap. 12.99 (978-1-4343-9302-9(X)) AuthorHouse.

Corwin, Jeff. The Wild, Wild Southwest!, 3 vols. 2010. (Jeff Corwin Ser.: 3). (ENG.). 112p. (J). (gr. 1-3). 4.99 (978-0-14-241440-8(9), Puffin Books) Penguin Young Readers Group.

Costello, David Hyde. I Can Help. Costello, David Hyde, illus. 2010. (ENG., Illus.). 32p. (J). (gr. -1-1). 15.99 (978-0-374-33526-7(5), 9780374335267, Farrar, Straus & Giroux (BYR)) Farrar, Straus & Giroux.

Cote, Jenny. The Ark, the Reed & the Fire Cloud: The Amazing Tales of Max & Liz Book One, 2 bks, Bk 1. 2008. (Amazing Tales of Max & Liz Ser.: 1). (ENG., Illus.). 432p. (J). (gr. 5-11). pap. 16.99 (978-0-89957-198-0(0), Living Ink Bks.) AMG Pubs.

Councilman, Janet H. Rocky the Respectful Raccoon & His Red Sunglasses. 2008. 16p. pap. 24.95 (978-1-60813-100-6(9)) America Star Bks.

Courter, John. The Cheetah & the Turtle. 2011. 28p. pap. 15.99 (978-1-4628-2952-1(X)) Xlibris Corp.

Courtin, Thierry. Decouvre les animaux avec T. (FRE.). pap. (978-2-09-202274-0(1)) Editions Rouge et Or.

Cousins, Lucy. I'm the Best. Cousins, Lucy, illus. 2013. (ENG., Illus.). 32p. (J). (-k). 6.99 (978-0-7636-6348-3(4)) Candlewick Pr.

—Maisy, Charley, & the Wobbly Tooth. Cousins, Lucy, illus. 2009. (Maisy Ser.). (ENG., Illus.). 32p. (J). (gr. k-k). pap. 6.99 (978-0-7636-4369-0(6)) Candlewick Pr.

—Maisy Goes Camping. Cousins, Lucy, illus. 2009. (Maisy Ser.). (ENG., Illus.). 32p. (J). (gr. k-k). pap. 6.99 (978-0-7636-4368-3(8)) Candlewick Pr.

—Maisy Goes Camping. 2009. (Maisy First Experiences Ser.). lib. bdg. 17.20 (978-0-606-06667-9(5), Turtleback) Turtleback Bks.

—Maisy Goes on a Sleepover. Cousins, Lucy, illus. 2016. (Maisy Ser.). (ENG., Illus.). 32p. (J). (gr. -1-2). 6.99 (978-0-7636-8947-6(5)) Candlewick Pr.

—Maisy Goes to Preschool: A Maisy First Experiences Book. Cousins, Lucy, illus. 2010. (Maisy Ser.). (ENG., Illus.). 32p. (J). (gr. k-k). pap. 6.99 (978-0-7636-5086-5(2)) Candlewick Pr.

—Maisy Goes to the Hospital. Cousins, Lucy, illus. 2009. (Maisy Ser.). (ENG., Illus.). 32p. (J). (gr. k-k). pap. 6.99 (978-0-7636-4372-0(6)) Candlewick Pr.

—Maisy Goes to the Hospital. 2009. (Maisy First Experiences Ser.). lib. bdg. 17.20 (978-0-606-06686-0(1), Turtleback) Turtleback Bks.

—Maisy Goes to the Library. 2009. (Maisy First Experiences Ser.). lib. bdg. 17.20 (978-0-606-06687-7(X), Turtleback) Turtleback Bks.

—Maisy's Amazing Big Book of Learning. 2011. (Maisy Ser.). (ENG., Illus.). 48p. (J). (gr. k-k). 14.99 (978-0-7636-5481-8(7)) Candlewick Pr.

—Maisy's Animals (Los Animales de Maisy) Cousins, Lucy, illus. 2009. (Maisy Ser.). (SPA & ENG., Illus.). 16p. (J). (gr. -1-2). bds. 5.99 (978-0-7636-4517-5(6)) Candlewick Pr.

—Maisy's Fire Engine. Cousins, Lucy, illus. 2009. (Maisy Ser.). (ENG., Illus.). 16p. (J). (gr. k-k). bds. 5.99 (978-0-7636-4252-5(5)) Candlewick Pr.

—Maisy's First Numbers: A Maisy Concept Book. Lucy Cousins, illus. 2013. (Maisy Ser.). (ENG.). 14p. (J). (-k). bds. 6.99 (978-0-7636-6805-1(2)) Candlewick Pr.

—Maisy's Pool. 2015. 24p. pap. 4.00 (978-1-61003-408-1(2)) Center for the Collaborative Classroom.

—Maisy's Train. Cousins, Lucy, illus. 2009. (Maisy Ser.). (ENG., Illus.). 16p. (J). (gr. k-k). bds. 5.99 (978-0-7636-4251-8(7)) Candlewick Pr.

—Where Is Maisy? Cousins, Lucy, illus. 2010. (Maisy Ser.). (ENG., Illus.). 14p. (J). (gr. k-k). bds. 5.99 (978-0-7636-4673-8(3)) Candlewick Pr.

Covas Sadriwalla, Deborah. Top Secret. 2009. 40p. pap. 16.99 (978-1-4389-8182-6(1)) AuthorHouse.

Covey, S. K. The Road to Rincon, 1 vol. 2010. 40p. 24.95 (978-1-4489-4929-8(7)) PublishAmerica, Inc.

Covey, Sean. Goob & His Grandpa. Curtis, Stacy, illus. 2013. (7 Habits of Happy Kids Ser.: 7). (ENG.). 32p. (J). (gr. -1-1). 7.99 (978-1-4424-7653-0(2), Simon & Schuster Bks. For Young Readers) Simon & Schuster Bks. For Young Readers.

—A Place for Everything: Habit 3. Curtis, Stacy, illus. 2010. (7 Habits of Happy Kids Ser.: 3). (ENG.). 32p. (J). (gr. -1-1). 7.99 (978-1-4169-9425-1(4), Simon & Schuster Bks. For Young Readers) Simon & Schuster Bks. For Young Readers.

—Sophie & the Perfect Poem. Curtis, Stacy, illus. 2013. (7 Habits of Happy Kids Ser.: 6). (ENG.). 32p. (J). (gr. -1-1). 7.99 (978-1-4424-7651-6(6), Simon & Schuster Bks. For Young Readers) Simon & Schuster Bks. For Young Readers.

Cowan, Catherine. My Life with the Wave. Buehner, Mark, illus. 2004. (J). (gr. k-3). spiral bd. (978-0-616-11863-4(5)) Canadian National Institute for the Blind/Institut National Canadien pour les Aveugles.

Cowan, Charlotte. Sadie's Sore Throat. Bratun, Katy, illus. 2007. (Dr. Hippo Ser.). (ENG.). 32p. (J). (gr. 3-7). 17.95 (978-0-9753516-4-2(8)) Hippocratic Pr., The.

Cowley, Joy. Mrs. WishyWashy & the Big Farm Fair. 2009. pap. 8.25 (978-1-60559-231-2(5)) Hameray Publishing Group, Inc.

—Mrs. WishyWashy & the Big Tub. 2009. pap. 8.25 (978-1-60559-233-6(1)) Hameray Publishing Group, Inc.

—Mrs. WishyWashy & the Big Wash. 2009. pap. 8.25 (978-1-60559-235-0(8)) Hameray Publishing Group, Inc.

Cox, Joseph J. Grobar & the Mind Control Potion. Becker, Rebecca J., illus. 2005. 168p. (J). per. 9.95 (978-0-9764659-3-5(0)) Suckerfish Bks.

Cox, Judy. Sheep Won't Sleep: Counting by 2s, 5s, And 10s. Cuneo, Nina, illus. 2017. (ENG.). 32p. (J). 16.95 (978-0-8234-3701-6(9)) Holiday Hse., Inc.

Cox, Katie & Make Believe Ideas Staff. Little Hands Animals. 2009. (Little Hands Ser.). (Illus.). 24p. (gr. -1-k). 6.99 (978-1-84610-958-4(2)) Make Believe Ideas GBR. Dist: Nelson, Thomas Inc.

Cox, Michael. Johnny Catbiscuit & the Stolen Secrets! Dunn, Gary, illus. 2008. (Johnny Catbiscuit Ser.). (ENG.). 160p. (J). (gr. 2-4). pap. 9.95 (978-1-4052-3739-0(2)) Egmont Bks., Ltd. GBR. Dist: Independent Pubs. Group.

Cox, Phil Roxbee. Curly's Friends. Cartwright, Stephen, illus. rev. ed. 2005. (Usborne Farmyard Tales Touchy-Feely Ser.). 10p. (J). (gr. -1-k). bds. 7.95 (978-0-7945-1180-7(5), Usborne) EDC Publishing.

Cox, Tammy Parker. The Not So Ordinary Farm. 2011. 20p. pap. 14.99 (978-1-257-03319-5(0)) Lulu Pr., Inc.

Coyle, Carmela Lavigna. Do Princesses Count? Gordon, Mike & Gordon, Carl, illus. 2006. (ENG.). 24p. (J). (gr. -1-3). bds. 6.95 (978-0-87358-916-1(5)) Cooper Square Publishing Llc.

Craddock, Erik. Dragon Boogie. Craddock, Erik, illus. 2012. (Stone Rabbit Ser.: Vol. 7). (ENG., Illus.). 96p. (J). (gr. 2-5). pap. 6.99 (978-0-375-86912-9(3), Random Hse. Bks. for Young Readers) Random Hse. Children's Bks.

—Dragon Boogie. 2012. (Stone Rabbit Ser.: 7). lib. bdg. 17.20 (978-0-606-23868-7(9), Turtleback) Turtleback Bks.

—Ninja Slice. Craddock, Erik, illus. 2010. (Stone Rabbit Ser.: No. 5). (ENG., Illus.). 96p. (J). (gr. 3-7). pap. 6.99 (978-0-375-86723-1(6), Random Hse. Bks. for Young Readers) Random Hse. Children's Bks.

—Robot Frenzy. 2013. (Stone Rabbit Ser.: 8). lib. bdg. 17.20 (978-0-606-27004-5(3), Turtleback) Turtleback Bks.

—Stone Rabbit #6: Night of the Living Dust Bunnies. Craddock, Erik, illus. 2011. (Stone Rabbit Ser.: 6). (ENG., Illus.). 96p. (J). (gr. 3-7). pap. 6.99 (978-0-375-86724-8(4), Random Hse. Bks. for Young Readers) Random Hse. Children's Bks.

—Stone Rabbit #8: Robot Frenzy. Craddock, Erik, illus. 2013. (Stone Rabbit Ser.). (ENG., Illus.). 96p. (J). (gr. 2-5). pap. 6.99 (978-0-375-86913-6(1)); lib. bdg. 12.99 (978-0-375-96913-3(6)) Random Hse. Children's Bks. (Random Hse. Bks. for Young Readers).

Craig, Lindsey. Dancing Feet! Brown, Marc, illus. 2010. (ENG.). 40p. (J). (gr. -1-2). 16.99 (978-0-375-86181-9(5), Knopf Bks. for Young Readers) Random Hse. Children's Bks.

Craik, Maria Dinah. The Little Lame Prince. 2008. 120p. 24.99 (978-0-554-21709-3(0)) 2006. 118p. pap. 19.99 (978-1-4264-0739-0(4)) Creative Media Partners, LLC.

Crawford, Ann Fears. Keechee: The Witch of the Woods. 2005. (J). (978-1-931823-21-0(9)) Halcyon Pr.

Crawford, Deborah Kay. Pity & the Princess. Turner, Aubrey, illus. 2013. 40p. pap. 24.95 (978-1-62709-695-9(7)) America Star Bks.

Crawford, Joanne. Bilby & the Bushfire. Fielding, Grace, illus. 2007. 28p. (J). pap. (978-1-921248-30-6(0)) Magabala Bks.

—A Home for Bilby. Fielding, Grace, illus. 2004. 28p. (J). pap. (978-1-875641-91-8(2)) Magabala Bks.

Crawford, Ken. Cappy, the Arctic Tern. 2016. (Illus.). 64p. (J). pap. (978-0-8163-6108-3(8)) Pacific Pr. Publishing Assn.

Crayton, Tina. The Wolf. 2010. 36p. pap. 15.50 (978-1-4520-7219-7(1)) AuthorHouse.

Cregan, Mairin. Old John. Sewell, Helen, illus. 2012. 198p. 44.95 (978-1-258-23306-8(1)); pap. 29.95 (978-1-258-24727-0(5)) Literary Licensing, LLC.

Crimi, Carolyn. Dear Tabby. Roberts, David, illus. 2011. (ENG.). 32p. (J). (gr. -1-3). 16.99 (978-0-06-114245-1(X)) HarperCollins Pubs.

The Critter Club Collection: A Purrfect Four-Book Boxed Set: Amy & the Missing Puppy; All about Ellie; Liz Learns a Lesson; Marion Takes a Break. 2014. (Critter Club Ser.). (ENG., Illus.). 512p. (J). (gr. k-4). pap. 23.99 (978-1-4814-0664-2(7), Little Simon) Little Simon.

Crofoot, Betty & Arledge, Roo. The Great Celebration Ceremony - My Genie & Me Series Book 2. 2012. 84p. pap. 8.95 (978-1-60862-430-0(7)) E-BookTime LLC.

Cronin, Doreen. Boom Snot Twitty. Liwska, Renata, illus. 2014. (ENG.). 32p. (J). (gr. -1-k). 16.99 (978-0-670-78575-9(X), Viking Books for Young Readers) Penguin Young Readers Group.

—Boom Snot Twitty This Way That Way. Liwska, Renata, illus. 2015. (ENG.). 32p. (J). (-k). 16.99 (978-0-670-78577-3(6), Viking Books for Young Readers) Penguin Young Readers Group.

—Clic, Clac, Plif, Plaf: Una Aventura de Contar. Lewin, Betsy, illus. 2006. (J). (gr. -1-k). per. 6.99 (978-1-933032-03-0(0)) Lectorum Pubns., Inc.

—Clic, Clac, Plif, Plaf: Una Aventura de Contar. Rioja, Alberto Jimenez, tr. from ENG. Lewin, Betsy, illus. 2006. (J). (gr. 5-6). 12.99 (978-1-933032-11-5(1)) Lectorum Pubns., Inc.

—Click, Clack, Ho! Ho! Ho! Lewin, Betsy, illus. 2015. (Click, Clack Book Ser.). (ENG.). 40p. (J). (gr. -1-2). 17.99 (978-1-4424-9673-6(8)) Simon & Schuster Children's Publishing.

—Click, Clack, Quackity-Quack: A Typing Adventure. Lewin, Betsy, illus. 2008. (Click, Clack Book Ser.). (ENG.). 14p. (J). (gr. -1-k). 14.99 (978-1-4169-5517-7(8), Little Simon) Little Simon.

—Click, Clack, Quackity-Quack: An Alphabetical Adventure. Lewin, Betsy, illus. 2005. (Click, Clack Book Ser.). (ENG.). 24p. (J). (gr. -1-3). 17.99 (978-0-689-87715-5(3), Atheneum Bks. for Young Readers) Simon & Schuster Children's Publishing.

—Click, Clack, Splish, Splash: A Counting Adventure. Lewin, Betsy, illus. 2006. (Click, Clack Book Ser.). (ENG.). 24p. (J). (gr. -1-3). 17.99 (978-0-689-87716-2(1), Atheneum Bks. for Young Readers) Simon & Schuster Children's Publishing.

—The Legend of Diamond Lil. Cornell, Kevin, illus. 2013. (ENG.). 144p. (J). (gr. 1-5). pap. 5.99 (978-0-06-177997-8(0)) HarperCollins Pubs.

—Wiggle, 1 vol. Menchin, Scott, illus. 2006. (Doreen Cronin: Click-Clack & More Ser.). (ENG.). 36p. (gr. -1-3). lib. bdg. 24.21 (978-1-59961-093-1(0)) Spotlight.

Cronin, Doreen & Lewin, Betsy. Click, Clack, Quackity-Quack: An Alphabetical Adventure. 2006. (Doreen Cronin: Click-Clack & More Ser.). (ENG.). (gr. -1-3). lib. bdg. 24.21 (978-1-59961-089-4(2)) Spotlight.

—Click, Clack, Splish, Splash: A Counting Adventure, 1 vol. 2006. (Doreen Cronin: Click-Clack & More Ser.). (ENG.). 24p. (gr. -1-3). lib. bdg. 24.21 (978-1-59961-090-0(6)) Spotlight.

Crook, M. J. Village on Crooked Hill. 2008. 168p. pap. 11.99 (978-1-4389-0486-3(X)) AuthorHouse.

Crow, Marilee. A Short Tale about a Long Tail. Snider, K. C., illus. 2010. 16p. pap. 10.95 (978-1-61633-067-5(8)) Guardian Angel Publishing, Inc.

Crow, Nosy. Can You Say It, Too? Moo! Moo! Braun, Sebastien, illus. 2014. (Can You Say It, Too? Ser.). (ENG.). 10p. (J). (— 1). bds. 8.99 (978-0-7636-7066-5(9), Nosy Crow) Candlewick Pr.

—Flip Flap Farm. Scheffler, Axel, illus. 2014. (ENG.). 26p. (J). (gr. -1-2). 11.99 (978-0-7636-7067-2(7), Nosy Crow) Candlewick Pr.

Crowe, Ellie. Go to Sleep, Hide & Seek. Wu, Julie, illus. 2009. 10p. (J). bds. 11.95 (978-1-59700-759-7(5)) Island Heritage Publishing.

Crowson, Andrew. Flip Flap Farm. 2003. (Illus.). 12p. bds. (978-1-85602-430-3(X), Pavilion Children's Books) Pavilion Bks.

Crozon, Alain. All Shook Up! 2015. (ENG., Illus.). 12p. (J). (gr. -1 — 1). bds. 10.99 (978-1-4521-4013-1(8)) Chronicle Bks. LLC.

Crummel, Susan Stevens. Ten-Gallon Bart, 0 vols. Donohue, Dorothy, illus. 2010. (ENG.). 32p. (J). (gr. k-3). pap. 9.99 (978-0-7614-5719-0(4), 9780761457190, Amazon Children's Publishing) Amazon Publishing.

—Ten-Gallon Bart Beats the Heat, 0 vols. Donohue, Dorothy, illus. 2010. (ENG.). 40p. (J). (gr. k-3). 17.99 (978-0-7614-5634-6(1), 9780761456346, Amazon Children's Publishing) Amazon Publishing.

Crummel, Susan Stevens & Stevens, Janet. Shoe Town. 2003. (Green Light Readers Level 2 Ser.). (ENG., Illus.). 32p. (J). (gr. -1-3). pap. 3.95 (978-0-15-204842-6(1)) Houghton Mifflin Harcourt Publishing Co.

Cuentos de Animales Fantasticos para Ninos (Fantastic Animal Tales for Children) (SPA.). 72p. (J). 9.95 (978-958-04-0960-1(9), 103378519) Norma S.A. COL. Dist: Distribuidora Norma, Inc.

Cullum, A. A. Rugly Puffs: The Bear Detective. 2008. 80p. pap. (978-1-84923-248-7(2)) YouWriteOn.

Cummins, Lucy Ruth. A Hungry Lion or a Dwindling Assortment of Animals. Cummins, Lucy Ruth, illus. 2016. (ENG., Illus.). 40p. (J). (gr. -1-3). 16.99 (978-1-4814-4889-5(7)) Simon & Schuster Children's Publishing.

Currie, Robin. The Baby Bible Animals, 1 vol. Basaluzzo, Constanza, illus. 2009. (Baby Bible Ser.). (ENG.). 48p. (J). bds. 12.99 (978-1-4347-6541-3(5)) Cook, David C.

—Tuktuk: Tundra Tale, 1 vol. Saroff, Phyllis, illus. 2016. (ENG & SPA.). 32p. (J). (gr. k-3). 17.95 (978-1-62855-879-1(2)) Arbordale Publishing.

—Tuktuk: Un Cuento Sobre la Tundra. Saroff, Phyllis, illus. 2016. (SPA.). 32p. (J). (gr. k-3). pap. 9.95 (978-1-62855-881-4(4)) Arbordale Publishing.

Curtis, Jennifer Keats. Saving Squeak: The Otter Tale, 1 vol. Ramsey, Marcy Dunn, illus. 2010. (ENG.). 31p. (J). 14.99 (978-0-7643-3588-4(X), 9780764335884) Schiffer Publishing, Ltd.

Cuyler, Margery. Please Say Please! Penguin's Guide to Manners. Hillenbrand, Will, illus. 2005. (J). (978-0-439-67874-2(9)) Scholastic, Inc.

Cvetkovic, Judith Lynn. A Special Love for Twelve Border Collies. 2011. 76p. pap. 19.95 (978-1-4560-7749-5(X)) America Star Bks.

Cynthia, Rylant. Every Living Thing. 2014. (ENG.). 96p. (J). (gr. 5-9). 10.24 (978-1-63245-336-5(3)) Lectorum Pubns., Inc.

D C Thomson Staff, ed. Animals & You Annual 2004. 2003. (Illus.). 128p. (J). 9.95 (978-0-85116-840-1(X)) Thomson, D.C. & Co., Ltd. GBR. Dist: APG Sales & Distribution Services.

da Pavlova, Chrisi È. Animal Stories from Green Lane Estate: Series Six. 2013. (Illus.). 283p. pap. 20.49 (978-1-78035-553-5(X), Fastprint Publishing) Upfront Publishing Ltd. GBR. Dist: Printondemand-worldwide.com.

—Animal Stories from Green Lane Estate Series 5. 2012. (Illus.). 290p. pap. 22.00 (978-1-78035-452-1(5), Fastprint Publishing) Upfront Publishing Ltd. GBR. Dist: Printondemand-worldwide.com.

Dahl, Michael. Hippo Says "Excuse Me" Vidal, Oriol, illus. 2011. (Hello Genius Ser.). (ENG.). 20p. (gr. 1-2). bds. 7.99 (978-1-4048-6787-1(2)) Picture Window Bks.

Dahl, Roald. Agu Trot. Blake, Quentin, illus. 2003.Tr. of Esio Trot. (SPA.). 64p. (J). (gr. 3-5). pap. 9.95 (978-84-204-4436-9(7)) Santillana USA Publishing Co., Inc.

Daily, Don. The Classic Treasury of Aesop's Fables. 2007. (ENG., Illus.). 56p. (J). (gr. 1-17). 9.95 (978-0-7624-2876-2(7)) Running Pr. Bk. Pubs.

Daisy, April. The Crazy 8 Diner. 2004. (Illus.). 28p. (J). per. 7.95 (978-1-59466-023-8(9), Little Ones) Port Town Publishing.

Dale, Elizabeth. Little Red Hen's Great Escape. 2016. (ENG., Illus.). 32p. (J). (978-0-7787-2461-2(1)) Crabtree Publishing Co.

Dale, Hannah, illus. Mr. Hare's Big Secret. 2016. (ENG.). 32p. (J). (gr. -1-2). 16.99 (978-0-553-53856-4(X), Doubleday Bks. for Young Readers) Random Hse. Children's Bks.

Dale, Jay. What Is the Matter, Mrs. Long?, 1 vol. Diggory, Nick, illus. 2012. (Engage Literacy Green Ser.). (ENG.). 32p. (gr. k-2). pap. 5.99 (978-1-4296-9030-0(5), Engage Literacy) Capstone Press of Coughlan Cos.

—Who Is under There?, 1 vol. Webb, Philip, illus. 2012. (Wonder Words Ser.). (ENG.). 32p. (gr. k-2). pap. 5.99 (978-1-4296-8924-3(2), Engage Literacy) Capstone Press of Coughlan Cos.

Dale, Jenny. Forever Sam. Reid, Mick, illus. 2003. 104p. (J). (978-0-439-33801-1(8)) Scholastic, Inc.

Daley, Michael J. Pinch & Dash & the Terrible Couch. Yezerski, Thomas F., illus. 2013. (ENG.). 48p. (J). (gr. k-3). 12.95 (978-1-58089-379-4(1)); pap. 5.95 (978-1-58089-380-0(5)) Charlesbridge Publishing, Inc.

—Pinch & Dash Make Soup. Yezerski, Thomas F., illus. 2012. (ENG.). 48p. (J). (gr. k-3). 12.95 (978-1-58089-346-6(5)); pap. 5.95 (978-1-58089-347-3(3)) Charlesbridge Publishing, Inc.

Dalmatian Press Staff. The Alphabet Song Book. 2008. (ENG.). 5p. (J). bds. 4.95 (978-1-58117-726-8(7), Intervisual/Piggy Toes) Bendon, Inc.

Daly, Kathleen. Howdy Doody's Animal Friends. Seiden, Art, illus. 2011. 26p. 35.95 (978-1-258-02771-1(2)) Literary Licensing, LLC.

D'Amico, Carmela. Ella Sets the Stage. D'Amico, Steven, illus. 2006. 41p. (J). pap. 16.99 (978-0-439-83153-6(9), Levine, Arthur A. Bks.) Scholastic, Inc.

D'Amico, Carmela & D'Amico, Steven. Ella Sets Sail. 2008. (J). (978-0-439-83156-7(3), Levine, Arthur A. Bks.) Scholastic, Inc.

Damjan, Mischa. The Clown Said No. 2004. (Illus.). (J). (gr. k-3). spiral bd. (978-0-616-14569-2(1)) Canadian National Institute for the Blind/Institut National Canadien pour les Aveugles.

Damschroder, Scott. Pinky's Rainy Day: Pinky Padooka takes a trip to Imaginationville. Faust, Laurie, illus. 2004. 36p. (J). lib. bdg. 19.95 (978-0-9754728-0-4(1)) Big Ransom Studio.

Dana, Barbara. Spencer & His Friends. 2014. (ENG., Illus.). 128p. (J). (gr. 3-7). pap. 13.99 (978-1-4814-3754-7(2), Atheneum Bks. for Young Readers) Simon & Schuster Children's Publishing.

Daniel, Claire. The Chick That Wouldn't Hatch. Ernst, Lisa Campbell, illus. 2003. (Green Light Readers Level 2 Ser.). (ENG.). 24p. (J). (gr. -1-3). pap. 3.95 (978-0-15-204831-0(6)) Houghton Mifflin Harcourt Publishing Co.

Daniel, Claire & Ernst, Lisa Campbell. El Pollito Que No Quería Salir del Huevo. Flor Ada, Alma & Campoy, F. Isabel, trs. from ENG. Ernst, Lisa Campbell, illus. 2009. (Green Light Readers Level 2 Ser.).Tr. of Chick That Wouldn't Hatch. (SPA & ENG., Illus.). 28p. (J). (gr. -1-3). pap. 3.99 (978-0-15-206446-4(X)) Houghton Mifflin Harcourt Publishing Co.

Daniels, Kimberly. Animal Bible Stories - AbraHAM, 1 vol. 2009. 20p. pap. 24.95 (978-1-60749-382-2(9)) America Star Bks.

Dann, Colin. The Animals of Farthing Wood. 2014. (ENG.). 400p. (J). (gr. k-2). 16.99 (978-1-4052-6733-5(X)) Egmont Bks., Ltd. GBR. Dist: Independent Pubs. Group.

—The Animals of Farthing Wood. Tettmar, Jacqueline, illus. 2007. (ENG.). 302p. (J). (gr. 4-7). per. 12.99 (978-1-4052-2552-6(1)) Egmont Bks., Ltd. GBR. Dist: Independent Pubs. Group.

Danylyshyn, Greg. A Crash of Rhinos. Lomp, Stephan, illus. 2016. (ENG.). 40p. (J). (gr. -1-3). 16.99 (978-1-4814-3150-7(1), Little Simon) Little Simon.

Darden, Floyd. Drumdee makes a Drum. 2007. 15.95 (978-1-59526-711-5(5)) Aeon Publishing Inc.

Dasilva, Kiko. Moncho y la Mancha. 2004. (SPA.). 40p. (J). 15.99 (978-84-8464-078-3(7)) Kalandraka Editora, S.L. ESP. Dist: Lectorum Pubns., Inc.

David, Juliet. The Midnight Visitors, 1 vol. Parry, Jo, illus. 2015. 32p. (J). 14.99 (978-1-78128-233-5(1), Candle Bks.) Lion Hudson PLC GBR. Dist: Kregel Pubns.

Davidson, Alice Joyce. St. Francis & the Animals. Swanson, Maggie, illus. 2006. 24p. (J). 7.95 (978-0-88271-003-7(6)) Regina Pr., Malhame & Co.

Davidson, Susanna. The Musicians of Bremen. Gordon, Mike & Gordon, Carl, illus. 2007. (Usborne First Reading: Level 3 Ser.). 48p. (J). 8.99 (978-0-7945-1911-7(3), Usborne) EDC Publishing.

—Treasury of Animal Stories. 2008. (Stories for Young Children Ser.). 96p. (J). 16.99 (978-0-7945-2095-3(2), Usborne) EDC Publishing.

Davies, Caroline & Martin, Sharon. Chwarae Cuddio. 2005. (WEL., Illus.). 12p. pap. (978-1-86101-080-3(X)) Acen Limited.

—Y Frech Goch. 2005. (WEL., Illus.). 12p. pap. (978-1-86101-079-7(6)) Acen Limited.

Davies, Kate, ed. Old Woman Who Swallowed a Fly. Home, Sarah, illus. 2009. (First Reading Level 3 Ser.). 48p. (J). (gr. 2). 6.99 (978-0-7945-2267-4(X), Usborne) EDC Publishing.

Davis, Caroline. Animals on the Farm. 2009. (My First Noisy Bath Bks.). (ENG.). 8p. (J). (gr. -1). 4.99 (978-0-7641-9592-1(1)) Barron's Educational Series, Inc.

—Sparkly Garden. Davis, Caroline, illus. 2008. (Tiger Tales Ser.). (Illus.). 8p. (J). (gr. -1). bds. 6.95 (978-1-58925-830-3(4)) Tiger Tales.

Davis, Eleanor. Stinky. 2008. (ENG., Illus.). 40p. (J). (gr. -1-3). 12.95 (978-0-9799238-4-5(0)) TOON Books / RAW Junior, LLC.

Davis, Izzy. The Croaks at Roaring River, 1 vol. 2009. 40p. pap. 24.95 (978-1-60813-245-4(5)) America Star Bks.

Davis, Jacky & Soman, David. Ladybug Girl Visits the Farm. Soman, David, illus. 2011. (Ladybug Girl Ser.). (ENG., Illus.). 16p. (J). (gr. -1-k). pap. 6.99 (978-0-448-45598-3(6), Grosset & Dunlap) Penguin Young Readers Group.

Davis, Katie & DAvis, Kate. Who Hops? Davis, Katie, illus. 2010. (Rise & Shine Ser.). (ENG., Illus.). 36p. (C). (gr. -1 — 1). pap. 11.95 (978-0-15-216412-6(X)) National Geographic School Publishing, Inc.

Davis, Nancy & Davis, Kathryn Lynn. Wake Up! Wake Up! Davis, Nancy & Davis, Kathryn Lynn, illus. 2011. (ENG., Illus.). 14p. (J). (gr. -1 — 1). bds. 5.99 (978-1-4424-1217-0(8), Little Simon) Little Simon.

Davis, Peg. Napoleon & Marigold. 2008. 24p. pap. 13.50 (978-1-60693-114-1(8), Eloquent Bks.) Strategic Book Publishing & Rights Agency (SBPRA).

The Day the Class Chameleon Disappeared: Word Study: Prefixes dis-, un-, ex-, re-, Level B. 2003. ("Plaid" Phonics & Stories Libraries). (gr. 2-3). 38.50 (978-0-8136-9154-1(0)) Modern Curriculum Pr.

De Beaumont, Leprince. La Belle et la Bete.Tr. of Beauty & the Beast. (FRE.). (J). pap. 14.95 (978-2-07-052101-2(X)) Gallimard, Editions FRA. Dist: Distribooks, Inc.

de Las Casas, Dianne. The Gigantic Sweet Potato, 1 vol. Gentry, Marita, illus. 2010. (ENG.). 32p. (J). (gr. k-3). 16.99 (978-1-58980-755-6(3)) Pelican Publishing Co., Inc.

De Los Heros, Luis & Wilson, Elizabeth. Chifa Chi's Little Adventure in New York City. 2011. 44p. pap. 21.99 (978-0-557-91842-3(1)) Lulu Pr., Inc.

—Chifa Chi's Little Adventure in Washington Dc. 2010. 40p. pap. 21.99 (978-0-557-23085-3(3)) Lulu Pr., Inc.

De Luca, Daniela. Ben the Beaver. 2008. (It's a Wildlife, Buddy! Ser.). (ENG., Illus.). 30p. (J). (gr. -1-1). 12.95 (978-88-89272-24-4(4)) McRae Bks. Srl ITA. Dist: Independent Pubs. Group.

de Moüy, Iris. Naptime, 1 vol. Tanaka, Shelley, tr. from FRE. 2014. (ENG., Illus.). 28p. (J). (-k). 16.95 (978-1-55498-487-9(4)) Groundwood Bks. CAN. Dist: Publishers Group West (PGW).

De Paolo, Tom. Paddy Platypus & the Ring-Tail Squatteroo. 2012. 36p. pap. 19.99 (978-1-4772-7243-5(7)) AuthorHouse.

de Pavlova, Chrisi É. Animal Stories from Green Lane Estate: Series Four. 2012. (Illus.). 290p. pap. 22.00 (978-1-78035-357-9(X), Fastprint Publishing) Upfront Publishing Ltd. GBR. Dist: Printondemand-worldwide.com.

—Animal Stories from Green Lane Estate: Series Three. 2012. (Illus.). 254p. pap. 22.00 (978-1-78035-292-3(1), Fastprint Publishing) Upfront Publishing Ltd. GBR. Dist: Printondemand-worldwide.com.

De Regniers, Beatrice Schenk. What Did You Put in Your Pocket? Date not set. 32p. (J). (gr. -1-1). pap. 5.95 (978-0-06-443700-4(0)) HarperCollins Pubs.

De Serres, Michelle. The Gecko Ball. 2011. (Illus.). 28p. pap. (978-1-905553-78-5(1)) BookPublishingWorld.

De Valdenebro, Eladio. Tono y los Animales Cautivos. (SPA.). (J). 8.95 (978-958-04-6021-3(3)) Norma S.A. COL. Dist: Distribuidora Norma, Inc.

Dean, James & Dean, Kimberly. Pete the Cat & the Bedtime Blues. Dean, James, illus. 2015. (Pete the Cat Ser.). (Illus.). 40p. (J). (gr. -1-3). (ENG.). 17.99 (978-0-06-230430-8(5)); lib. bdg. 18.89 (978-0-06-230431-5(3)) HarperCollins Pubs.

—Pete the Cat & the New Guy. Dean, James, illus. 2014. (Pete the Cat Ser.). (ENG., Illus.). 40p. (J). (gr. -1-3). 17.99 (978-0-06-227560-8(7)); lib. bdg. 18.89 (978-0-06-227561-5(5)) HarperCollins Pubs.

Dean, Richard B. The Bear & the Ox. 2005. 28p. (YA). pap. 8.95 (978-0-7414-2855-4(5)) Infinity Publishing.

Debecker, Benoit & Benoît, Debecker. La Primera Navidad de los Animales. 2005. (Montana Encantada Ser.). (SPA., Illus.). 48p. (J). (gr. k-2). pap. 8.50 (978-84-241-1675-0(5)) Lectorum Pubns., Inc.

Debnam, Mio. Animalympics, 5 BK Set. 2010. (ENG.). 140p. (J). (gr. -1-3). pap. 23.00 (978-988-98819-0-0(X)) Haven Bks.

Deborah Wanda. Wanda's Wittle Wunders. 2009. 32p. pap. 14.49 (978-1-4389-4862-1(X)) AuthorHouse.

Debowksi, Sharon. The Grape Escape: Call 9-1-1, the Grapes Are on the Run! Fonseca-Hughes, Sarah, illus. 2007. 32p. (J). 14.95 (978-1-60227-472-3(X)) Above the Clouds Publishing.

Décary, Marie. Adam's Tropical Adventure. Cummins, Sarah, tr. from FRE. Beshwaty, Steve, illus. 2005. (Formac First Novels Ser.: 56). (ENG.). 64p. (gr. 2-5). 14.95 (978-0-88780-687-2(2), 9780887806872); (J). 4.95 (978-0-88780-686-5(4), 9780887806865) Formac Publishing Co., Ltd. CAN. Dist: Casemate Pubs. & Bk. Distributors, LLC.

Deen, Ron. Annabelle Rides Her Bike on an Iowa Farm. 2005. (J). 6.95 (978-1-57166-261-3(8)) Quixote Pr.

Defreitas, Henrietta. Henratty Mortimer: We Were Only Strawberry Picking. 2011. (Illus.). 176p. (gr. -1). pap. 15.66 (978-1-4567-8911-4(2)) AuthorHouse.

deGroat, Diane. Brand-New Pencils, Brand-New Books. deGroat, Diane, illus. 2007. (ENG., Illus.). 32p. (J). (gr. -1-3). pap. 6.99 (978-0-06-072616-4(4)) HarperCollins Pubs.

—Brand-New Pencils, Brand-New Books. deGroat, Diane, illus. 2007. (Gilbert & Friends Ser.). (Illus.). (J). (gr. -1-3). 14.65 (978-0-7569-8087-0(9)) Perfection Learning Corp.

—Jingle Bells, Homework Smells. deGroat, Diane, illus. 2003. (ENG., Illus.). 32p. (J). (gr. -1-3). pap. 6.99 (978-0-688-17545-0(7)) HarperCollins Pubs.

—Jingle Bells, Homework Smells. deGroat, Diane, illus. 2008. (Illus.). (J). (gr. -1-3). pap. 16.95 incl. audio (978-1-4301-0419-3(8)) Live Oak Media.

Dehm, Debbie. Animal Stories of the Desert. 2009. (Illus.). 41p. (J). pap. 20.95 (978-1-4327-3461-9(X)) Outskirts Pr., Inc.

Del Moral, Susana. Un Paseo Por la Selva. Zaidi, Nadeem, illus. 2005. (Baby Einstein: Libros de Carton Ser.). (SPA.). 10p. (J). (gr. -1). bds. (978-970-718-306-3(3), Silver Dolphin en Español) Advanced Marketing, S. de R. L. de C. V.

Delessert, Etienne. Fuzzy, Furry Hat. Delessert, Etienne, illus. 2016. (ENG., Illus.). 32p. (J). (gr. 1-3). 18.99 (978-1-56846-296-7(4), Creative Editions) Creative Co., The.

—Yok-Yok, 12 bks., Set. Delessert, Etienne, illus. Incl. At Home. lib. bdg. 14.60 (978-0-88682-646-8(2), 97934-098); Best Friends. lib. bdg. 14.60 (978-0-88682-639-0(X), 97927-098); For the Birds. lib. bdg. 14.60 (978-0-88682-638-3(1), 97926-098); Moonlight. lib. bdg. 14.60 (978-0-88682-648-2(9), 97936-098); Nonsense. lib. bdg. 14.60 (978-0-88682-641-3(1), 97929-098); Nuts! lib. bdg. 14.60 (978-0-88682-644-4(6), 97932-098); Surprises. lib. bdg. 14.60 (978-0-88682-643-7(8), 97931-098); Weird? lib. bdg. 14.60 (978-0-88682-645-1(4), 97933-098); What a Circus! lib. bdg. 14.95 (978-0-88682-640-6(3), 97928-098); 32p. (J). (gr. 1-5). 1993. (Illus.). lib. bdg. o.p. (978-0-88682-637-6(3), Creative Education) Creative Co., The.

Dell'orco, Antonio. The Wolf Lion & Whistle: Two Children's Stories. 2013. 68p. 22.95 (978-0-9755471-8-2(6)) Divine Mercy Pr.

Deluna, Alicia C. Tippy Gets a Friend. 2012. 20p. pap. 17.99 (978-1-4685-5513-4(8)) AuthorHouse.

Demarte, Lisa Marie. I Can See. 2011. (Illus.). 12p. pap. 14.95 (978-1-4461-1507-7(0)) Lulu Pr., Inc.

Dembicki, Carol & Dembicki, Matt. Mr. Big: A Tale of Pond Life. 2012. (ENG., Illus.). 160p. (J). (gr. 1-7). pap. 12.95 (978-1-61608-967-2(9), 608967, Sky Pony Pr.) Skyhorse Publishing Co., Inc.

Demers, Karen. My Love of the Animals in the Town of St Jovite: Our Beautiful Laurentians. 2012. 32p. pap. 21.99 (978-1-4771-3700-0(9)) Xlibris Corp.

Dempsey, Kristy. Mini Racer. Strevens-Marzo, Bridget, illus. 2011. (ENG.). 32p. (J). (gr. -1-k). 16.99 (978-1-59990-170-1(6), 9781599901701); 17.89 (978-1-59990-591-4(4), 9781599905914) Bloomsbury Publishing USA. (Bloomsbury USA Childrens).

DePalma, Mary Newell. The Perfect Gift. 2010. (J). pap. (978-0-545-15403-1(0), Levine, Arthur A. Bks.) Scholastic, Inc.

dePaola, Tomie. Four Friends at Christmas. dePaola, Tomie, illus. 2009. (ENG., Illus.). 32p. (J). (gr. -1-1). 12.99 (978-1-4169-9175-5(1), Aladdin) Simon & Schuster Children's Publishing.

—Four Friends in Autumn. dePaola, Tomie, illus. 2004. (ENG., Illus.). 32p. (J). (gr. -1-3). 17.99 (978-0-689-85980-9(5), Simon & Schuster Bks. For Young Readers) Simon & Schuster Bks. For Young Readers.

—Four Friends in Summer. dePaola, Tomie, illus. 2003. (ENG., Illus.). 32p. (J). (gr. -1-3). reprint ed. 17.99 (978-0-689-85693-8(8), Simon & Schuster Bks. For Young Readers) Simon & Schuster Bks. For Young Readers.

—Jack. dePaola, Tomie, illus. 2014. (ENG., Illus.). 40p. (J). (gr. -1-k). 17.99 (978-0-399-16154-4(6), Nancy Paulsen Books) Penguin Young Readers Group.

Depken, Kristen L. & Jackson, Kathryn. Tawny Scrawny Lion. DiCicco, Sue, illus. 2016. (Step into Reading Ser.). (ENG.). 32p. (J). (gr. -1-1). pap. 3.99 (978-1-101-93424-1(7), Random Hse. Bks. for Young Readers) Random Hse. Children's Bks.

Depken, Kristen L. & Schurr, Cathleen. The Shy Little Kitten. DiCicco, Sue, illus. 2015. (Step into Reading Ser.). (ENG.). 32p. (J). (gr. -1-1). 12.99 (978-0-375-97377-2(X), Random Hse. Bks. for Young Readers) Random Hse. Children's Bks.

DePrisco, Dorothea. Lullaby & Good Night: Music & Lights. 2006. (ENG., Illus.). 12p. (gr. -1-k). 12.95 (978-1-58117-450-2(0), Intervisual/Piggy Toes) Bendon, Inc.

—Pig-a-Boo! A Farmyard Peekaboo Book. Runnells, Patricia & Runnells, Treesha, illus. 2009. (ENG.). 14p. (J). (gr. -1-k). 9.99 (978-1-4169-7226-6(9), Little Simon) Little Simon.

Derrick, Patricia. Mr. Walrus & the Old School Bus. Martinez, J-P Loppo, illus. 2007. 32p. 18.95 incl. audio compact disk (978-1-933818-13-9(1)) Animalations.

deRubertis, Barbara. Alexander Anteater's Amazing Act. Alley, R. W., illus. 2010. (Animal Antics A to Z Ser.). 32p. (J). (ENG.). (gr. -1-3). pap. 7.95 (978-1-57565-300-6(1)); (gr. k-1). lib. bdg. 22.60 (978-1-57565-304-4(4)) Kane Press, Inc.

—Bobby Baboon's Banana Be-Bop. Alley, R. W., illus. 2010. (Animal Antics A to Z Ser.). 32p. (J). lib. bdg. 22.60 (978-1-57565-305-1(2)); (ENG.). (gr. -1-3). pap. 7.95 (978-1-57565-301-3(X)) Kane Press, Inc.

—Corky Cub's Crazy Caps. Alley, R. W., illus. 2010. (Animal Antics A to Z Ser.). 32p. (J). lib. bdg. 22.60 (978-1-57565-306-8(0)); (ENG.). (gr. -1-3). pap. 7.95 (978-1-57565-302-0(8)) Kane Press, Inc.

—Dilly Dog's Dizzy Dancing. Alley, R. W., illus. 2010. (Animal Antics A to Z Ser.). 32p. (J). lib. bdg. 22.60 (978-1-57565-307-5(9)); (ENG.). (gr. -1-3). pap. 7.95 (978-1-57565-303-7(6)) Kane Press, Inc.

—Jeremy Jackrabbit's Jumping Journey. Alley, R. W., illus. 2010. (Animal Antics A to Z Ser.). 32p. (J). (gr. -1-3). pap. 7.95 (978-1-57565-314-3(1)); lib. bdg. 22.60 (978-1-57565-321-1(4)) Kane Press, Inc.

—Lana Llama's Little Lamb. Alley, R. W., illus. 2011. (Animal Antics A to Z Ser.). 32p. (J). pap. 45.32 (978-0-7613-7658-3(5)); (ENG.). lib. bdg. 22.60 (978-1-57565-333-4(8)); (gr. -1-3). pap. 7.95 (978-1-57565-324-2(9)) Kane Press, Inc.

—Nina Nandu's Nervous Noggin. Alley, R. W., illus. 2011. (Animal Antics A to Z Ser.). 32p. (J). pap. 45.32 (978-0-7613-7660-6(7)); (ENG.). lib. bdg. 22.60 (978-1-57565-335-8(4)); (gr. -1-3). pap. 7.95 (978-1-57565-326-6(5)) Kane Press, Inc.

Derubertis, Barbara. Sammy Skunk's Super Sniffer. Alley, R. W., illus. 2011. (Animal Antics A to Z Set III Ser.). pap. 45.32 (978-0-7613-8428-1(6)) Kane Press, Inc.

deRubertis, Barbara. Sammy Skunk's Super Sniffer. Alley, R. W., illus. 2011. (Animal Antics A to Z Ser.). pap. 7.95 (978-1-57565-344-0(3)); lib. bdg. 22.60 (978-1-57565-352-5(4)) Kane Press, Inc.

Derubertis, Barbara. Tessa Tiger's Temper Tantrums. Alley, R. W., illus. 2011. (Animal Antics A to Z Set III Ser.). pap. 45.32 (978-0-7613-8429-8(4)) Kane Press, Inc.

deRubertis, Barbara. Tessa Tiger's Temper Tantrums. Alley, R. W., illus. 2011. (Animal Antics A to Z Ser.). 32p. (J). pap. 7.95 (978-1-57565-345-7(1)); lib. bdg. 22.60 (978-1-57565-353-2(2)) Kane Press, Inc.

Derubertis, Barbara. Umma Ungka's Unusual Umbrella. Alley, R. W., illus. 2011. (Animal Antics A to Z Set III Ser.). pap. 45.32 (978-0-7613-8430-4(8)) Kane Press, Inc.

deRubertis, Barbara. Umma Ungka's Unusual Umbrella. Alley, R. W., illus. 2011. (Animal Antics A to Z Ser.). pap. 7.95 (978-1-57565-346-4(X)); lib. bdg. 22.60 (978-1-57565-354-9(0)) Kane Press, Inc.

Derubertis, Barbara. Victor Vicuna's Volcano Vacation. Alley, R. W., illus. 2011. (Animal Antics A to Z Set III Ser.). pap. 45.32 (978-0-7613-8431-1(6)) Kane Press, Inc.

deRubertis, Barbara. Victor Vicuna's Volcano Vacation. Alley, R. W., illus. 2011. (Animal Antics A to Z Ser.). 32p. (J). (ENG.). pap. 7.95 (978-1-57565-347-1(8)); lib. bdg. 22.60 (978-1-57565-355-6(9)) Kane Press, Inc.

Derubertis, Barbara. Walter Warthog's Wonderful Wagon. Alley, R. W., illus. 2011. (Animal Antics A to Z Set III Ser.). pap. 45.32 (978-0-7613-8432-8(4)) Kane Press, Inc.

deRubertis, Barbara. Walter Warthog's Wonderful Wagon. Alley, R. W., illus. 2011. (Animal Antics A to Z Ser.). 32p. (J). (ENG.). pap. 7.95 (978-1-57565-348-8(6)); lib. bdg. 22.60 (978-1-57565-356-3(7)) Kane Press, Inc.

Derubertis, Barbara. Xavier Ox's Xylophone Experiment. Alley, R. W., illus. 2011. (Animal Antics A to Z Set III Ser.). pap. 45.32 (978-0-7613-8433-5(2)) Kane Press, Inc.

deRubertis, Barbara. Xavier Ox's Xylophone Experiment. Alley, R. W., illus. 2011. (Animal Antics A to Z Ser.). 32p. (J). (ENG.). pap. 7.95 (978-1-57565-349-5(4)); lib. bdg. 22.60 (978-1-57565-357-0(5)) Kane Press, Inc.

—Yoko Yak's Yakety Yakking. Alley, R. W., illus. 2011. (Animal Antics A to Z Ser.). pap. 7.95 (978-1-57565-350-1(8)); lib. bdg. 22.60 (978-1-57565-358-7(3)) Kane Press, Inc.

Derubertis, Barbara. Zachary Zebra's Zippity Zooming. Alley, R. W., illus. 2011. (Animal Antics A to Z Set III Ser.). pap. 45.32 (978-0-7613-8435-9(9)) Kane Press, Inc.

deRubertis, Barbara. Zachary Zebra's Zippity Zooming. Alley, R. W., illus. 2011. (Animal Antics A to Z Ser.). 32p. (J). pap. 7.95 (978-1-57565-351-8(6)); lib. bdg. 22.60 (978-1-57565-359-4(1)) Kane Press, Inc.

deRubertis, Barbara & DeRubertis, Barbara. Alexander Anteater's Amazing Act. Alley, R. W., illus. 2012. (Animal Antics A to Z Ser.). 32p. (J). (gr. 2 — 1). cd-rom 7.95 (978-1-57565-394-5(X)) Kane Press, Inc.

—Bobby Baboon's Banana Be-Bop. Alley, R. W., illus. 2012. (Animal Antics A to Z Ser.). 32p. (J). (gr. 2 — 1). cd-rom 7.95 *(978-1-57565-395-2(8))* Kane Press, Inc.

—Corky Cub's Crazy Caps. Alley, R. W., illus. 2012. (Animal Antics A to Z Ser.). 32p. (J). (gr. 2 — 1). cd-rom 7.95 *(978-1-57565-396-9(6))* Kane Press, Inc.

—Dilly Dog's Dizzy Dancing. Alley, R. W., illus. 2012. (Animal Antics A to Z Ser.). 32p. (J). (gr. 2 — 1). cd-rom 7.95 *(978-1-57565-397-6(4))* Kane Press, Inc.

—Jeremy Jackrabbit's Jumping Journey. Alley, R. W., illus. 2012. (Animal Antics A to Z Ser.). 32p. (J). (gr. 2 — 1). cd-rom 7.95 *(978-1-57565-403-4(2))* Kane Press, Inc.

—Lana Llama's Little Lamb. Alley, R. W., illus. 2012. (Animal Antics A to Z Ser.). 32p. (J). (gr. 2 — 1). cd-rom 7.95 *(978-1-57565-405-8(9))* Kane Press, Inc.

—Nina Nandu's Nervous Noggin. Alley, R. W., illus. 2012. (Animal Antics A to Z Ser.). 32p. (J). (gr. 2 — 1). cd-rom 7.95 *(978-1-57565-407-2(5))* Kane Press, Inc.

—Sammy Skunk's Super Sniffer. Alley, R. W., illus. 2012. (Animal Antics A to Z Ser.). 32p. (J). (gr. 2 — 1). cd-rom 7.95 *(978-1-57565-412-6(1))* Kane Press, Inc.

—Tessa Tiger's Temper Tantrums. Alley, R. W., illus. 2012. (Animal Antics A to Z Ser.). 32p. (J). (gr. 2 — 1). cd-rom 7.95 *(978-1-57565-413-3(X))* Kane Press, Inc.

—Umma Ungka's Unusual Umbrella. Alley, R. W., illus. 2012. (Animal Antics A to Z Ser.). 32p. (J). (gr. 2 — 1). cd-rom 7.95 *(978-1-57565-414-0(8))* Kane Press, Inc.

—Victor Vicuna's Volcano Vacation. Alley, R. W., illus. 2012. (Animal Antics A to Z Ser.). 32p. (J). (gr. 2 — 1). cd-rom 7.95 *(978-1-57565-415-7(6))* Kane Press, Inc.

—Walter Warthog's Wonderful Wagon. Alley, R. W., illus. 2012. (Animal Antics A to Z Ser.). 32p. (J). (gr. 2 — 1). cd-rom 7.95 *(978-1-57565-416-4(4))* Kane Press, Inc.

—Xavier Ox's Xylophone Experiment. Alley, R. W., illus. 2012. (Animal Antics A to Z Ser.). 32p. (J). (gr. 2 — 1). cd-rom 7.95 *(978-1-57565-417-1(2))* Kane Press, Inc.

—Yoko Yak's Yakety Yakking. Alley, R. W., illus. 2012. (Animal Antics A to Z Ser.). 32p. (J). (gr. 2 — 1). cd-rom 7.95 *(978-1-57565-418-8(0))* Kane Press, Inc.

—Zachary Zebra's Zippity Zooming. Alley, R. W., illus. 2012. (Animal Antics A to Z Ser.). 32p. (J). (gr. 2 — 1). cd-rom 7.95 *(978-1-57565-419-5(9))* Kane Press, Inc.

Desbordes, Astrid. Edmond, the Moonlit Party. Boutavant, Marc, illus. 2015. (ENG.). 32p. (J). (gr. -1-3). 17.95 *(978-1-59270-174-2(4))* Enchanted Lion Bks., LLC.

Desbordes, Astrid. The Thing. Boutavant, Marc, illus. 2017. (ENG.). 32p. (J). (gr. -1-3). 17.95 ***(978-1-59270-217-6(1))*** Enchanted Lion Bks., LLC.

Desbordes, Astrid & Martin, Pauline. Daydreams of a Solitary Hamster. 2010. (ENG., Illus.). 56p. (J). (gr. 1-2). 17.95 *(978-1-59270-093-6(4))* Enchanted Lion Bks., LLC.

El desfile de Animales, 6 Pack. (Literatura 2000 Ser.). (SPA.). (gr. -1-1). 28.00 *(978-0-7635-1190-6(0))* Rigby Education.

Devine, Ginger. The Missing Pencils: A Sam the Lamb Mystery. 2009. 36p. pap. 17.99 *(978-1-4389-5313-7(5))* AuthorHouse.

Dewdney, Anna. Llama Llama & the Bully Goat. 2013. (Llama Llama Ser.). (ENG., Illus.). 40p. (J). (gr. -1-k). 17.99 *(978-0-670-01395-1(1)*, Viking Books for Young Readers) Penguin Young Readers Group.

Dhariwal, Radhika R. The Tale of a No-Name Squirrel. Benjaminsen, Audrey, illus. 2016. (ENG.). 384p. (J). (gr. 3-7). 16.99 *(978-1-4814-4475-0(1)*, Simon & Schuster Bks. For Young Readers) Simon & Schuster Bks. For Young Readers.

Díaz, Katacha. Badger at Sandy Ridge Road. Kest, Kristin, illus. 2005. (Smithsonian's Backyard Ser.). (ENG.). 32p. (J). (gr. -1-2). 4.95 *(978-1-59249-421-7(8)*, B5078); 15.95 *(978-1-59249-420-0(X)*, B5028); pap. 6.95 *(978-1-59249-422-4(6)*, S5028) Soundprints.

Diaz, Katacha. Badger at Sandy Ridge Road. Kest, Kristin, illus. 2005. (Smith Sonian's Backyard Ser.). (ENG.). 32p. (J). (gr. 2-2). 19.95 *(978-1-59249-424-8(2)*, BC5028); 8.95 *(978-1-59249-423-1(4)*, SC5028) Soundprints.

DiCamillo, Kate. Great Joy. Ibatoulline, Bagram, illus. 2007. (ENG.). 32p. (J). (gr. -1-3). 16.99 *(978-0-7636-2920-5(0))* Candlewick Pr.

Dickens, Charles. A Christmas Carol: Being a Ghost Story of Christmas. 2013. (Cambridge Library Collection - Fiction & Poetry Ser.). (ENG., Illus.). 186p. pap. 28.99 *(978-1-108-05714-1(4))* Cambridge Univ. Pr.

Dickson, Robert. Sam Ferret Mysteries. 2010. 88p. pap. 14.95 *(978-1-4259-2741-7(6))* AuthorHouse.

DiGuardo, Maggie & Leventis, Kelly. Celly. 2012. (J). 14.95 *(978-1-937406-17-2(2))* Mascot Bks., Inc.

Dillingham Pierson, Clara. Among the Farmyard People. 2008. 112p. pap. 8.15 *(978-1-60459-505-5(1))* Wilder Pubns., Corp.

—Among the Meadow People. 2008. 84p. pap. 8.15 *(978-1-60459-504-8(3))* Wilder Pubns., Corp.

—Among the Night People. 2008. 96p. pap. 8.15 *(978-1-60459-503-1(5))* Wilder Pubns., Corp.

—Among the Pond People. 2008. 96p. pap. 8.15 *(978-1-60459-502-4(7))* Wilder Pubns., Corp.

—Clara Dillingham Pierson's Complete among the People Series. 2008. 352p. pap. 19.99 *(978-1-60459-528-4(0))* Wilder Pubns., Corp.

Ding, Sean. Monkey Ming & the Dream Team. 2013. 34p. pap. *(978-981-07-0631-9(6))* Lukano Publishing Pte, Ltd.

Dingman, Matthew. The Very Different Animal from Mars. 2013. 24p. pap. 24.95 *(978-1-63000-730-0(7))* America Star Bks.

Dinner: Individual Title Six-Packs. (Sails Literacy Ser.). 16p. (gr. k-18). 27.00 *(978-0-7635-4445-4(0))* Rigby Education.

Dipucchio, Kelly. Gilbert Goldfish Wants a Pet. Shea, Bob, illus. 2011. (ENG.). 32p. (J). (gr. -1-k). 16.99 *(978-0-8037-3394-7(1)*, Dial Bks) Penguin Young Readers Group.

Disney Book Group. Doc Mcstuffins Smitten with a Kitten. Disney Storybook Art Team, illus. 2016. (ENG.). 24p. (J). (gr. -1-k). pap. 4.99 *(978-1-4847-6203-5(7))* Disney Pr.

—The Lion Guard Babysitter Bunga. Disney Storybook Art Team, illus. 2017. (ENG.). 24p. (J). (gr. -1-k). pap. 4.99 *(978-1-4847-8868-4(0))* Disney Pr.

—Lion Guard Meet the New Guard. Disney Storybook Art Team, illus. 2016. (ENG.). 10p. (J). (gr. -1-k). bds. 8.99 *(978-1-4847-1914-5(X))* Disney Pr.

—Zootopia Picture Book: A Day in the Life of Judy Hopps. 2016. (ENG.). 40p. (J). (gr. -1-k). 16.99 *(978-1-4847-2102-5(0))* Disney Pr.

—Zootopia Read-Along Storybook & CD. Disney Storybook Art Team, illus. 2016. (Read-Along Storybook & CD Ser.). (ENG.). 32p. (J). (gr. 1-3). pap. 6.99 *(978-1-4847-2104-9(7))* Disney Pr.

Disney Book Group Staff. Guess Who! Disney Storybook Artists Staff, illus. 2012. (ENG.). 14p. (J). (gr. -1-k). bds. 6.99 *(978-1-4231-6008-3(8))* Disney Pr.

Disney Book Group Staff & Hapka, Catherine. Sofia the First. Lee, Grace, illus. 2012. (ENG.). 40p. (J). (gr. -1-k). 15.99 *(978-1-4231-6986-4(7))* Disney Pr.

Disney Pixar Editors. Disney Pixar Finding Nemo Movie Comic. 2017. lib. bdg. 18.40 *(978-0-606-39082-8(0))* Turtleback Bks.

Disney Press Editors. Lion Guard: Bunga the Wise. 2016. (World of Reading Ser.). (J). lib. bdg. 13.55 *(978-0-606-37539-9(2))* Turtleback Bks.

Disney Press Staff & Disney Book Group Staff. Furry Friends! Disney Storybook Artists Staff, illus. 2011. (Touch-And-feel Book Ser.). (ENG.). 16p. (J). (gr. -1-k). bds. 7.99 *(978-1-4231-4183-9(0))* Disney Pr.

Disney, Rh. Zootopia Deluxe Junior Novelization. 2016. 128p. *(978-0-7364-3550-5(6))* Random Hse., Inc.

Disney Staff. Rox & Rouky. (FRE.). 96p. (J). (gr. k-5). pap. 9.95 *(978-0-7859-8851-9(3))* French & European Pubns., Inc.

Disney Storybook Art Team, illus. Legend of the Neverbeast. 2015. (Read-Along Storybook & CD Ser.). (ENG.). 32p. (J). (gr. 1-3). pap. 6.99 *(978-1-4847-1075-3(4))* Disney Pr.

—Whisker Haven Tales - Halloween in Whisker Haven. 2016. (Read-Along Storybook & CD Ser.). (ENG.). 32p. (J). (gr. -1-k). pap. 6.99 *(978-1-4847-4707-0(0))* Disney Pr.

DiTerlizzi, Angela. Some Pets. Wenzel, Brendan, illus. 2016. (ENG.). 32p. (J). (gr. -1-3). 17.99 *(978-1-4814-4402-6(6)*, Beach Lane Bks.) Beach Lane Bks.

DiTerlizzi, Tony. G Is for One Gzonk! An Alpha-Number-Bet Book. DiTerlizzi, Tony, illus. 2006. (ENG., Illus.). 80p. (J). (gr. -1-2). 29.99 *(978-0-689-85290-9(8))*; 150.00 *(978-1-4169-2471-5(X))* Simon & Schuster Bks. For Young Readers. (Simon & Schuster Bks. For Young Readers).

Dittman, Jeffery. Jungle Heroes. 2013. 36p. pap. 15.95 *(978-1-4327-9935-9(5))* Outskirts Pr., Inc.

Divenuto, John. Scruffy Hawk & Freddy Ferret. 2011. 32p. pap. 13.00 *(978-1-60976-702-0(0)*, Eloquent Bks.) Strategic Book Publishing & Rights Agency (SBPRA).

Dixon, Amy. Sophie's Animal Parade. Wish, Katia, illus. 2015. (ENG.). 32p. (J). (gr. -1-k). 16.99 *(978-1-63220-403-5(7)*, Sky Pony Pr.) Skyhorse Publishing Co., Inc.

Dixon, Andy. Dragon Quest. Brooks, Felicity, ed. Harris, Nick, illus. rev. ed. 2005. (Usborne Fantasy Puzzle Bks.). 32p. (J). (gr. 3-7). per. 7.99 *(978-0-7945-1098-5(1)*, Usborne) EDC Publishing.

Dixon, Franklin W. The Great Escape. Burroughs, Scott, illus. 2015. (Hardy Boys: the Secret Files Ser.: 17). (ENG.). 112p. (J). (gr. 1-4). pap. 4.99 *(978-1-4814-2267-3(7)*, Aladdin) Simon & Schuster Children's Publishing.

Dobbins, Jan. Driving My Tractor Puzzle. Sim, David, illus. 2011. (ENG.). (J). (gr. -1-1). 14.99 *(978-1-84686-573-2(5))* Barefoot Bks., Inc.

Docherty, Helen. The Snatchabook. Docherty, Helen, illus. 2013. (ENG., Illus.). 32p. (J). (-2). 16.99 *(978-1-4022-9082-4(9)*, 9781402290824, Sourcebooks Jabberwocky) Sourcebooks, Inc.

Dodson, Merilee. Kids from Critter Cove. Gregor, Terril, illus. 2007. 48p. per. 24.95 *(978-1-4137-2644-2(5))* America Star Bks.

Dolan, Elys. Nuts in Space. Dolan, Elys, illus. 2015. (ENG., Illus.). 32p. (J). (gr. k-3). 17.99 *(978-0-7636-7609-4(8)*, Nosy Crow) Candlewick Pr.

Dompierre, Judith. Little Bear's & Friend's Summer Trip. 2012. 32p. 29.95 *(978-1-4626-9272-9(9))* America Star Bks.

Dompierre, Judith E. Little Bear's & Friend's Summer Trip. 2012. 32p. pap. 24.95 *(978-1-4626-9325-2(3))* America Star Bks.

—Wow, What's That? 2012. 48p. pap. 24.95 *(978-1-4626-9332-0(6))* America Star Bks.

Don, Lari. The Tortoise's Gift: A Story from Zambia. Williamson, Melanie, illus. 2012. (Animal Stories Ser.). (ENG.). 48p. (J). (gr. 1-4). pap. 8.99 *(978-1-84686-774-3(6))* Barefoot Bks., Inc.

Donaldson, Julia. The Giant Jumperee. Oxenbury, Helen, illus. 2017. (ENG.). 32p. (J). (-k). 17.99 *(978-0-7352-2797-2(7)*, Dial Bks) Penguin Young Readers Group.

—El Grufalo. Scheffler, Axel, illus. 2003. (SPA.). 32p. (J). (gr. k-2). 7.96 *(978-84-233-3145-1(8)*, DS4478) Ediciones Destino ESP. Dist: Lectorum Pubns., Inc.

—The Gruffalo. Harris, Ben, tr. from ENG. Scheffler, Axel, illus. 2012. (LAT, SPA & ENG.). 32p. (J). (gr. -1-2). 19.99 *(978-0-230-75932-9(7))* Pan Macmillan GBR. Dist: Independent Pubs. Group.

—The Gruffalo. Scheffler, Axel, illus. (ENG.). (J). (gr. -1-2). 2006. 32p. pap. 7.99 *(978-0-14-240387-7(3)*, Puffin Books) 2005. 26p. bds. 8.99 *(978-0-8037-3047-2(0)*, Dial Bks) Penguin Young Readers Group.

—The Gruffalo. Scheffler, Axel, illus. 2005. (ENG.). 32p. (J). (gr. -1-2). 17.99 *(978-0-8037-3109-7(4)*, Dial Bks) Penguin Young Readers Group.

—The Gruffalo. 2006. lib. bdg. 18.40 *(978-0-606-23141-1(2)*, Turtleback) Turtleback Bks.

—The Gruffalo's Child. Scheffler, Axel, illus. 2007. (ENG.). 32p. (J). (gr. -1-2). pap. 7.99 *(978-0-14-240754-7(2)*, Puffin Books) Penguin Young Readers Group.

—The Highway Rat. Scheffler, Axel, illus. 2013. (ENG.). 32p. (J). (gr. -1-3). 16.99 *(978-0-545-47758-1(1)*, Levine, Arthur A. Bks.) Scholastic, Inc.

—One Mole Digging a Hole, 2. Sharratt, Nick, illus. 2010. (ENG.). 32p. (J). (gr. k-k). pap. 8.99 *(978-0-230-70647-7(9))* Macmillan Pubs., Ltd. GBR. Dist: Independent Pubs. Group.

—Room on the Broom. Scheffler, Axel, illus. 2003. (ENG.). 32p. (J). (gr. -1-2). pap. 6.99 *(978-0-14-250112-2(3)*, Puffin Books) Penguin Young Readers Group.

—The Spiffiest Giant in Town. Scheffler, Axel, illus. 2005. (ENG.). 32p. (J). (gr. -1-2). reprint ed. pap. 6.99 *(978-0-14-240275-7(3)*, Puffin Books) Penguin Young Readers Group.

Donovan, Dan. A Christmas Tail! 2008. 28p. pap. 14.50 *(978-1-4389-1220-2(X))* AuthorHouse.

Dorling Kindersley Publishing Staff. Baby Cheep! Cheep! 2015. (ENG.). 14p. (J). (gr. -1 — 1). bds. 5.99 *(978-1-4654-3184-4(5)*, DK Children) Dorling Kindersley Publishing, Inc.

—Noisy Animal Peekaboo! 2015. (ENG., Illus.). 12p. (J). (gr. -1 — 1). bds. 12.99 *(978-1-4654-3182-0(9)*, DK Children) Dorling Kindersley Publishing, Inc.

—Woof! Woof! 2009. (ENG.). 12p. (J). (gr. -1 — 1). bds. 12.99 *(978-0-7566-5236-4(7)*, DK Children) Dorling Kindersley Publishing, Inc.

Dormer, Frank W. Firefighter Duckies! Dormer, Frank W., illus. 2017. (ENG., Illus.). 40p. (J). (gr. -1-3). 17.99 *(978-1-4814-6090-3(0)*, Atheneum Bks. for Young Readers) Simon & Schuster Children's Publishing.

Dornan, Rae. Sunbuddy Fables. 2013. 108p. pap. 9.99 *(978-0-9896218-3-0(9))* Sunraehealing.

Doupe, Pauline Wood. My Arctic Circle of Friends. Fawcett, Vicki, illus. Belair, Brenda Brousseau, photos by. 2009. 24p. pap. 16.98 *(978-1-4251-8097-3(3))* Trafford Publishing.

Down on Piggy Farm. 2005. (J). bds. 12.95 *(978-0-9764114-2-0(3))* Little People Bks.

Down, Reg. The Magic Knot: And other Tangles. 2007. (Illus.). 100p. (J). per. 14.95 *(978-0-9794452-0-0(5))* Lightly Pr.

Downard, Barry. The Race of the Century. Downard, Barry, illus. 2008. (ENG., Illus.). 40p. (J). (gr. -1-3). 17.99 *(978-1-4169-2509-5(0)*, Simon & Schuster Bks. For Young Readers) Simon & Schuster Bks. For Young Readers.

Downing, Johnette. Down in Louisiana, 1 vol. Kadair, Deborah Ousley, illus. 2007. (ENG.). 32p. (J). (gr. k-3). 16.99 *(978-1-58980-451-7(1))* Pelican Publishing Co., Inc.

—Down in Mississippi, 1 vol. Zecca, Katherine, illus. 2016. (ENG.). 32p. (J). 16.99 *(978-1-4556-2098-2(X))* Pelican Publishing Co., Inc.

—Petit Pierre & the Floating Marsh, 1 vol. Stanley, Heather, illus. 2016. (ENG.). 32p. (J). (gr. k-3). 16.99 *(978-1-4556-2279-5(6))* Pelican Publishing Co., Inc.

Doyle, Roddy. Brilliant. Hughes, Emily, illus. 2015. (ENG.). 192p. (J). (gr. 3-7). 16.95 *(978-1-4197-1479-5(1)*, Amulet Bks.) Abrams, Inc.

Dragonwagon, Crescent. All the Awake Animals Are Almost Asleep. McPhail, David, illus. 2012. (ENG.). 40p. (J). (gr. -1-3). 16.99 *(978-0-316-07045-4(9))* Little Brown & Co.

—All the Awake Animals Are Almost Asleep. McPhail, David, illus. 2016. (ENG.). 30p. (J). (gr. -1 — 1). bds. 7.99 *(978-0-316-33627-7(0))* Little, Brown Bks. for Young Readers.

DreamWorks. Kung Fu Panda: Po's Tasty Training. 2008. (J). 13.99 *(978-1-59319-981-4(3))* LeapFrog Enterprises, Inc.

DreamWorks & DreamWorks / LeapFrog. Kung Fu Panda: L'Entrainement Gourmand. 2008. (J). 20.79 *(978-1-59319-946-3(5))* LeapFrog Enterprises, Inc.

Dreher, Gidge. Gus, Scruffy, Clara & Friends. 2007. 80p. per. 9.95 *(978-1-933912-24-0(3))* Westview Publishing Co., Inc.

Driscoll, Amanda. Duncan the Story Dragon. 2015. (ENG., Illus.). 40p. (J). (gr. -1-2). 16.99 *(978-0-385-75507-8(4)*, Knopf Bks. for Young Readers) Random Hse. Children's Bks.

Drummond, Ree. Charlie Goes to School. deGroat, Diane, illus. 2013. (Charlie the Ranch Dog Ser.). (ENG.). 40p. (J). (gr. -1-3). 17.99 *(978-0-06-221920-6(0))* HarperCollins Pubs.

Dubosarsky, Ursula. The Terrible Plop. Joyner, Andrew, illus. 2009. (ENG.). 40p. (J). (gr. -1-1). 17.99 *(978-0-374-37428-0(7)*, 9780374374280, Farrar, Straus & Giroux (BYR)) Farrar, Straus & Giroux.

Dubuc, Marianne & Ghione, Yvette. The Bus Ride. Dubuc, Marianne, illus. 2015. (ENG., Illus.). 40p. (J). (gr. -1-2). 15.95 *(978-1-77138-209-0(0))* Kids Can Pr., Ltd. CAN. Dist: Hachette Bk. Group.

Ducharme, P. J. The Adventures of Jungle Foot Rot, 1 vol. 2009. 17p. pap. 24.95 *(978-1-60813-918-7(2))* America Star Bks.

Dudley, Blanche R. Siggy's Parade: Helping Kids with Disabilities Find Their Strengths. 2014. (ENG., Illus.). 48p. (J). (gr. -1-2). 9.95 *(978-0-88282-469-7(4))* New Horizon Pr. Pubs., Inc.

Dudley, Rebecca. Hank Finds an Egg. Dudley, Rebecca, photos by. 2013. (ENG., Illus.). 40p. (J). 16.99 *(978-1-4413-1158-0(0))* Peter Pauper Pr. Inc.

Duey, Kathleen. Ella the Baby Elephant: A Baby Elephant's Story. Gurin, Lara, illus. 2008. (My Animal Family Ser.). (ENG.). 32p. (J). (gr. -1-3). 12.99 *(978-0-8249-5584-7(6)*, Ideal Pubns.) Worthy Publishing.

Dufresne, Didier, et al. Solamente un Poco de Gripe. Vinent, Julia, tr. Modéré, Armelle, illus. 2003. (SPA.). 32p. (J). (gr. k-2). 15.99 *(978-84-8470-123-1(9))* Corimbo, Editorial S.L. ESP. Dist: Lectorum Pubns., Inc.

Dufris, William, reader. The Case of the Climbing Cat. 2004. (High-Rise Private Eyes Ser.: No. 2). (Illus.). (J). (gr. -1-2). pap. 31.95 incl. audio compact disk *(978-1-59112-612-6(6))* Live Oak Media.

Dugan, Karen. Ms. April & Ms. Mae: A Fable. 2009. (ENG., Illus.). 40p. (J). (gr. 3-6). 17.95 *(978-0-940719-07-1(X))* Gryphon Pr., The.

Duggleby, Sue & Duggleby, Ross. Narrative. (ENG., Illus.). 48p. *(978-0-86388-549-5(7)*, 003-5294, Routledge) Taylor & Francis Group.

Dumbleton, Mike. Muddled-Up Farm, 1 vol. Murphy, Jobi, illus. 2013. (ENG.). 32p. (J). pap. 6.99 *(978-1-59572-631-5(4))* Star Bright Bks., Inc.

Dumesnil, Phil & Sanchez, Asa. The Woollyhoodwinks: Vs. the Dark Patch. Root, Jeff & Runcorn, Scott, illus. 2008. (ENG.). 36p. (J). (gr. -1-3). 15.95 *(978-1-59702-012-1(5))* Immedium.

Dumortier, Marjorie. Zoe & Her Zany Animals. 2006. (ENG., Illus.). 32p. (J). (gr. -1-3). 14.99 *(978-0-7145-3306-3(8))* Boyars, Marion Pubs., Ltd. GBR. Dist: Consortium Bk. Sales & Distribution.

Dunbar, Geoff & Ardagh, Philip. High in the Clouds. 2005. (Illus.). 91p. (J). *(978-1-4156-2820-1(3)*, Dutton Juvenile) Penguin Publishing Group.

Dunbar, Polly. Goodnight, Tiptoe. Dunbar, Polly, illus. 2009. (Tilly & Friends Ser.). (ENG., Illus.). 32p. (J). (gr. -1-2). 12.99 *(978-0-7636-4328-7(9))* Candlewick Pr.

—Pretty Pru: A Tilly & Friends Book. Dunbar, Polly, illus. 2009. (Tilly & Friends Ser.). (ENG., Illus.). 32p. (J). (gr. -1-2). 12.99 *(978-0-7636-4272-3(X))* Candlewick Pr.

Duncan, Jodi. Happy Flowers. 2009. 24p. pap. 14.50 *(978-1-60693-519-4(4)*, Eloquent Bks.) Strategic Book Publishing & Rights Agency (SBPRA).

Duncan, Tisha Admire. Myrtle the Blue Eyed Turtle: A My Dirty Cat Mutt Adventure. 2012. 28p. pap. 14.95 *(978-1-4497-5727-4(8)*, WestBow Pr.) Author Solutions, Inc.

Dunlap, Sonya. Responza the Bull Learns the Ropes of Friendship. Snider, Sharon, illus. 2009. 32p. pap. 17.95 *(978-0-9815245-8-0(3))* Accelerator Bks.

Dunn, Carolyn. A Pie Went By. Date not set. 32p. (J). (gr. -1-1). pap. 4.99 *(978-0-06-443649-6(7))* HarperCollins Pubs.

Dunrea, Olivier. Gideon. 2012. (Gossie & Friends Ser.). (ENG., Illus.). 32p. (J). (gr. k — 1). 9.99 *(978-0-618-43661-3(8))* Houghton Mifflin Harcourt Publishing Co.

—Gideon: It's Play Time, Not Naptime! 2013. (Gossie & Friends Ser.). (ENG., Illus.). 32p. (J). (— 1). bds. 6.99 *(978-0-547-98399-8(9))* Houghton Mifflin Harcourt Publishing Co.

—Me & Annie McPhee. Hillenbrand, Will, illus. 2016. (ENG.). 32p. (J). (gr. -1-2). 16.99 *(978-0-399-16808-6(7)*, Philomel Bks.) Penguin Young Readers Group.

Dunsany, Taylor. The Little Witch Who Lost Her Broom & Other Stories. 2008. 48p. pap. 8.95 *(978-0-595-52506-5(7))* iUniverse, Inc.

Duplaix, Georges & Golden Books Staff. The Merry Shipwreck. Gergely, Tibor, illus. 2011. (Little Golden Book Ser.). (ENG.). 24p. (J). (gr. -1-2). 4.99 *(978-0-375-86800-9(3)*, Golden Bks.) Random Hse. Children's Bks.

Duroux, Mary. The Rain Flower. Briggs, Karen, illus. 2005. (ENG.). 48p. pap. 13.45 *(978-0-85575-467-9(2))* Aboriginal Studies Pr. AUS. Dist: Independent Pubs. Group.

DuTemple, Leslie A. One Little Balsam Fir: A Northwoods Counting Book. Robinson, Susan, illus. 2006. 32p. (J). per. *(978-1-892384-37-9(X))* Avery Color Studios, Inc.

Duvoisin, Roger. Favorite Stories of Roger Duvoisin: Including the Crocodile in the Tree, See What I Am, Periwinkle, & Snowy & Woody. 2016. (ENG., Illus.). 128p. (J). (gr. 2-4). pap. 14.99 *(978-0-486-79888-2(7))* Dover Pubns., Inc.

Dwyer, Mindy. Sweet Dreams, Polar Bear. 2004. (ENG., Illus.). 32p. (J). 15.95 *(978-0-88240-554-4(3))*; pap. 8.99 *(978-0-88240-555-1(1))* Graphic Arts Ctr. Publishing Co.

Dyan, Penelope. Adam. 2011. 34p. pap. 11.96 *(978-1-935630-94-4(6))* Bellissima Publishing, LLC.

—Animal Rescue, Book 2, Hanauma Bay, Hawaii. Weigand, John D., photos by. 2008. (Illus.). 56p. pap. 15.95 *(978-1-935118-43-5(9))* Bellissima Publishing, LLC.

—Hush! 2011. 34p. pap. 11.95 *(978-1-935630-53-1(9))* Bellissima Publishing, LLC.

—New Shoes for Hand Me down Rose. Dyan, Penelope, illus. 2012. (Illus.). 34p. pap. 11.95 *(978-1-61477-041-1(7))* Bellissima Publishing, LLC.

Dyan, Peneope. Bunny Ears. Dyan, Penelope, illus. 2011. 34p. pap. 11.95 *(978-1-935630-68-5(7))* Bellissima Publishing, LLC.

Dyckman, Ame. Tea Party Rules. Campbell, K. G., illus. 2013. (ENG.). 36p. (J). (gr. -1-k). 16.99 *(978-0-670-78501-8(6)*, Viking Books for Young Readers) Penguin Young Readers Group.

Eaddy, Susan. Poppy's Best Paper. Bonnet, Rosalinde, illus. 2015. (ENG.). 40p. (J). (gr. k-3). lib. bdg. 15.95 *(978-1-58089-614-6(6))* Charlesbridge Publishing, Inc.

—Poppy's Best Paper (1 Hardcover/1 CD) Bonnet, Rosalinde, illus. 2016. (ENG.). (J). (gr. 1-4). audio compact disk 29.95 *(978-1-4301-2187-9(4))* Live Oak Media.

Earhart, Kristin. Mountain Mission. 2016. (Race the Wild Ser.: 6). (ENG.). 144p. (J). (gr. 2-5). 14.75 *(978-0-606-39139-9(8))* Turtleback Bks.

—Outback All-Stars (Race the Wild #5) 2016. (Race the Wild Ser.: 5). (ENG., Illus.). 144p. (J). (gr. 2-5). pap. 4.99 *(978-0-545-94064-1(8)*, Scholastic Paperbacks) Scholastic, Inc.

—Savanna Showdown. (Illus.). (J). 2016. 138p. ***(978-1-5182-0302-2(7))*** 2015. (Race the Wild Ser.: 4). (ENG., 144p. (gr. 2-5). pap. 4.99 *(978-0-545-77356-0(3)*, Scholastic Paperbacks) Scholastic, Inc.

—Savanna Showdown. 2015. (Race the Wild Ser.: 4). (ENG., Illus.). 144p. (J). (gr. 2-5). lib. bdg. 14.75 *(978-0-606-38080-5(9))* Turtleback Bks.

Earl, Cheri Pray & Williams, Carol Lynch. The Rescue Begins in Delaware. Oliphant, Manelle, illus. 2013. (Just in Time Ser.: 1). (ENG.). 144p. (J). (gr. 3-7). pap. 9.95 *(978-1-938301-74-2(9))* Familius LLC.

Eash, Sara. Adeline. 2011. 28p. pap. 15.99 *(978-1-4568-7099-7(8))* Xlibris Corp.

Eastman, Charles A. & Eastman, Elaine Goodale. The Raccoon & the Bee Tree. Susan, Turnbull, illus. 2013. 32p. (J). *(978-0-9860355-4-8(8))* South Dakota State Historical Society Pr.

Eastman, P. D. Are You My Mother? deluxe ed. 2005. (Bright & Early Cloth Book Ser.). (ENG., Illus.). 8p. (J). (gr. k — 1). 16.99 *(978-0-375-81599-7(6)*, Random Hse. Bks. for Young Readers) Random Hse. Children's Bks.

—Big Blue Book of Beginner Books. 2008. (Beginner Books(R) Ser.). (ENG., Illus.). 368p. (J). (gr. -1-2). 16.99 *(978-0-375-85552-8(1)*, Random Hse. Bks. for Young Readers) Random Hse. Children's Bks.

Eberhart, Nancy. The Adventures of Granny: Granny Goes to the Zoo. Pyers, Kelsey, illus. 2007. (J). 24p. per. 10.99 *(978-1-59879-372-7(1))*; (gr. -1-3). 13.99 *(978-1-59879-373-4(X))* Lifevest Publishing, Inc.

Ecton, Emily. The Curse of Cuddles McGee. 2008. (ENG.). 272p. (J). (gr. 3-7). pap. 12.99 *(978-1-4169-6450-6(9)*, Simon & Schuster/Paula Wiseman Bks.) Simon & Schuster/Paula Wiseman Bks.

Eddy, Randon T. The Mysterious Creature. Eddy, Randon T., illus. 2007. (Illus.). 32p. (J). per. 15.95 *(978-0-9769332-2-9(5))* Jungle Hse. Pubns.

Edmonds, Lin. Patric the Pony & the Flash of Lightning. 2009. 34p. pap. 13.99 *(978-1-4389-6302-0(5))* AuthorHouse.

Edmondson, Frank. Mr. Frank's Magic School Bus: Rainbow's End Adventure. Edmondson, Brad, illus. 2007. 20p. per. 24.95 *(978-1-4241-8617-4(X))* America Star Bks.

Edward S. Ellis. The Cave in the Mountain: A Sequel to in the Pecos Country by Lieut. R. H. J. l.t. ed. 2007. (ENG.). 186p. pap. 21.99 *(978-1-4264-8202-1(7))* Creative Media Partners, LLC.

Edwards, Cory, et al. Hoodwinked! The True Story of Little Red Riding Hood. 2005. (ENG., Illus.). 32p. (J). (gr. k-2). per. 9.95 *(978-1-57178-188-8(9))* Council Oak Bks.
Edwards, Gareth. Never Ask a Dinosaur to Dinner. Parker-Rees, Guy, illus. 2015. (ENG.). 32p. (J). (gr. -1-k). 17.99 *(978-0-545-81296-2(8),* Scholastic Pr.) Scholastic, Inc.
Edwards, Jamee-Marie. But I Am a Cat! 2013. 44p. pap. 20.00 *(978-1-4772-8231-1(9))* AuthorHouse.
Edwards, Marnie. Pets & Parties. Hodgkinson, Leigh, illus. 2013. (Magical Mix-Ups Ser.). (ENG.). 96p. (J). (gr. 2-5). pap. 6.99 *(978-0-7636-6371-1(9),* Nosy Crow) Candlewick Pr.
Edwards, Pamela Duncan. Teddy Bear Hide-and-Seek. Birkett, Georgie, illus. 2008. (ENG.). 20p. (J). (gr. 2-5). 14.95 *(978-0-230-01442-8(9),* Macmillan) Pan Macmillan GBR. Dist: Trans-Atlantic Pubns., Inc.
—The Wacky Wedding: A Book of Alphabet Antics. 2005. 32p. (J). pap. *(978-0-7868-1172-4(2))* Hyperion Bks. for Children.
Edwards, Richard. The Forest Child. Malone, Peter, illus. 2004. 28p. (J). reprint ed. *(978-0-7567-7850-7(6))* DIANE Publishing Co.
Edwards, Sherri L. Sally the Platypus. 2009. 48p. pap. 18.95 *(978-1-4389-5930-6(3))* AuthorHouse.
EEBOO Staff, creator. Circus Animals' Adventures Write Me a Story - #WSADV. 2008. (J). pap. *(978-1-59461-282-4(X))* eeBoo Corp.
Egmont UK, Egmont. Peekaboo! Snow. 2014. (Animaru Ser.). (ENG., Illus.). 12p. (J). (— 1). bds. 9.99 *(978-1-4052-6775-5(5))* Egmont Bks., Ltd. GBR. Dist: Independent Pubs. Group.
Ehlert, Lois. Lots of Spots. Ehlert, Lois, illus. 2014. (Classic Board Bks.). (ENG., Illus.). 40p. (J). (gr. -1 — 1). bds. 7.99 *(978-1-4424-8927-1(8),* Little Simon) Little Simon.
—Oodles of Animals. 2008. (ENG., Illus.). 56p. (J). (gr. -1-2). 18.99 *(978-0-15-206274-3(2))* Houghton Mifflin Harcourt Publishing Co.
Eiden, T. J. The Little Guine. 2012. 28p. pap. 15.99 *(978-1-4691-8487-6(7))* Xlibris Corp.
Eirug Wyn. Powdwr Rhech! 2005. (WEL.). 64p. pap. *(978-0-86243-571-4(4))* Y Lolfa.
Eisele, Barbara. Miss Thistle & Friends. 2009. 48p. pap. 12.99 *(978-1-4490-2007-1(0))* AuthorHouse.
Eliason, Scott. Andy's Magic Marble. 2008. 40p. per. 24.95 *(978-1-4241-8774-4(5))* America Star Bks.
Elliott, David. And Here's to You! Cecil, Randy, illus. (ENG.). 32p. (J). (gr. -1-2). 2009. pap. 6.99 *(978-0-7636-4126-9(X))* 2004. 15.99 *(978-0-7636-1427-0(0))* Candlewick Pr.
Elliott, Laura Malone. Thanksgiving Day Thanks. Munsinger, Lynn, illus. 2013. (ENG.). 32p. (J). (gr. -1-3). 17.99 *(978-0-06-000236-7(0))* HarperCollins Pubs.
Ellis, Brian. The Web at Dragonfly Pond. Maydak, Michael S., illus. 2006. (Sharing Nature with Children Book Ser.). 32p. (J). (gr. 1-7). 16.95 *(978-1-58469-078-8(X));* pap. 8.95 *(978-1-58469-079-5(8))* Dawn Pubns.
Ellis, Elina. The Big Adventure. 2015. (ENG., Illus.). 32p. (J). (gr. -1-3). 16.99 *(978-1-4998-0109-5(2))* Little Bee Books Inc.
Ells, Marcia Louise. Glips, Snodagers & Wallywogs. Ells, Marcia Louise, illus. l.t. ed. 2006. (Illus.). 44p. (J). 6.99 *(978-0-9777359-0-7(7))* Marcia's Menagerie.
Emerson, Carl. Animal Underdogs, 6 vols., Set. Trover, Zachary, illus. Incl. Falling Freddy the Fainting Goat. 28.50 *(978-1-60270-015-4(X));* Nosy Amie the Anteater. 28.50 *(978-1-60270-016-1(8));* Opie the Opossum Wakes Up. 28.50 *(978-1-60270-017-8(6));* Sally the Salamander's Lost Tail. 28.50 *(978-1-60270-018-5(4));* Speed up, Sammy the Tree Sloth! 28.50 *(978-1-60270-019-2(2));* What Are You, Patty? A Platypus Tale. 28.50 *(978-1-60270-020-8(6));* 32p. (gr. -1-4). (Animal Underdogs Ser.). (Illus.). 2007. 171.00 *(978-1-60270-014-7(1),* Looking Glass Library) ABDO Publishing Co.
Emmett, Jonathan. The Best Gift of All. Cabban, Vanessa, illus. 2008. (ENG.). 32p. (J). (gr. -1-2). 15.99 *(978-0-7636-3860-3(9))* Candlewick Pr.
—Through the Heart of the Jungle. Gomez, Elena, illus. 2003. 32p. (J). tchr. ed. 15.95 *(978-1-58925-029-1(X));* pap. 5.95 *(978-1-58925-380-3(9))* Tiger Tales.
Enderle, Dotti. The Fat Stock Stampede at the Houston Livestock Show & Rodeo, 1 vol. Galey, Chuck, illus. 2008. (ENG.). 32p. (J). (gr. 1-3). 16.99 *(978-1-58980-443-2(0))* Pelican Publishing Co., Inc.
Endredy, James. The Journey of Tunuri & the Blue Deer: A Huichol Indian Story. Cruz, María Hernández de la & López, Casimiro de la Cruz, trs. Cruz, María Hernández de la & López, Casimiro de la Cruz, illus. 2003. (ENG.). 32p. (J). (gr. -1-6). 15.95 *(978-1-59143-016-2(X))* Bear & Co.
England-Lord, Susan. The Adventures of Andrew: Breezy's Day Out. 2004. 23p. pap. 24.95 *(978-1-4137-3285-6(2))* PublishAmerica, Inc.
Engle, Janice. Rainbows Stories & Poetry for Children. 2004. 277p. (J). pap. 15.08 *(978-1-4116-8612-0(8))* Lulu Pr., Inc.
Epner, Paul. Herbert Hilligan & His Magical Adventure. Kuon, Vuthy & Nguyen, Duke, illus. 2003. 32p. (J). 15.95 *(978-0-9743335-0-2(6))* Imaginative Publishing, Ltd.
Epps, Lawrence. Stomping on Toad Stools. 2011. 40p. pap. 24.95 *(978-1-4560-3702-4(1))* America Star Bks.
Epstein, Adam Jay & Jacobson, Andrew. Circle of Heroes. (Familiars Ser.: 3). (ENG.). 336p. (J). (gr. 3-7). 2013. pap. 6.99 *(978-0-06-196116-8(7))* 2012. (Illus.). 16.99 *(978-0-06-196114-4(0))* HarperCollins Pubs.
—Palace of Dreams. Phillips, Dave, illus. (Familiars Ser.: 4). (ENG.). 336p. (J). (gr. 3-7). 2015. pap. 6.99 *(978-0-06-212031-1(X))*No. 4. 2013. 16.99 *(978-0-06-212029-8(8))* HarperCollins Pubs.
—Secrets of the Crown. (Familiars Ser.: 2). (ENG.). (J). (gr. 3-7). 2012. 400p. pap. 6.99 *(978-0-06-196113-7(2))* 2011. 384p. 16.99 *(978-0-06-196111-3(6))* HarperCollins Pubs.
Equidna. (Coleccion Animalitos Exoticos). (SPA., Illus.). 166p. (J). 16.95 *(978-84-7630-368-9(8),* SAN688) Editorial Libsa, S.A. ESP. Dist: Continental Bk. Co., Inc.
Eriksen, Craig A. Nollie Gnome & Friends: 1. Return from Holiday. 2008. 52p. pap. 10.50 *(978-1-4092-0497-8(9))* Lulu Pr., Inc.
Ernst, Lisa Campbell. Wake up, It's Spring! Ernst, Lisa Campbell, illus. 2004. (ENG., Illus.). 40p. (J). (gr. -1-3). 16.99 *(978-0-06-008985-6(7))* HarperCollins Pubs.
Erwin, Kay. A Sheepdog's Christmas. 2008. 56p. pap. 10.99 *(978-1-60647-698-7(X))* Salem Author Services.
Esbaum, Jill, et al. Adorable Animals Collection. 2017. (Explore My World Ser.). (ENG., Illus.). 96p. (J). (gr. -1-2). pap. 9.99 ***(978-1-4263-2949-4(0),*** National Geographic Children's Bks.) National Geographic Society.
Ets, Marie Hall. Just Me. Ets, Marie Hall, illus. unabr. ed. (Illus.). (J). (gr. k-3). pap., stu. ed. 33.95 *(978-0-941078-74-0(4));* pap. 15.95 incl. audio *(978-0-941078-73-3(6))* Live Oak Media.
Eubank, Patricia Reeder. The Leprechaun's Big Pot of Gold. Eubank, Patricia Reeder, illus. 2012. (Illus.). 20p. (J). bds. 6.99 *(978-0-8249-1877-4(0),* Ideal Pubns.) Worthy Publishing.
Eubank, Patti Reeder, illus. Just Where You Belong. 2004. 32p. (J). 8.95 *(978-0-8249-5481-9(5),* Ideal Pubns.) Worthy Publishing.
Evangelista, Susan. Tommy's New Shell, 2nd in series. Coke, Sherrie, illus. 2005. 24p. (J). bds. 19.95 *(978-0-9769602-0-1(6))* Evangelista, Susan.
Evans, Dan C. The High Peaks Paradigm Shift: A Canine Agent Teabo Adventure, 1 vol. 2010. 362p. pap. 29.95 *(978-1-61582-712-1(9))* America Star Bks.
Evert, Lori. The Brave Little Puppy. Breiehagen, Per, illus. 2016. (ENG.). 28p. (J). (-k). bds. 8.99 *(978-0-399-54945-8(5),* Random Hse. Bks. for Young Readers) Random Hse. Children's Bks.
—The Christmas Wish. Breiehagen, Per, illus. Breiehagen, Per, photos by. 2013. (ENG.). 48p. (J). (gr. -1-2). 17.99 *(978-0-449-81681-3(8),* Random Hse. Bks. for Young Readers) Random Hse. Children's Bks.
—The Christmas Wish. Breiehagen, Per, illus. Breiehagen, Per, photos by. 2013. (J). *(978-0-449-81942-5(6))* Random Hse., Inc.
—The Tiny Wish. Breiehagen, Per, illus. 2015. (ENG.). 48p. (J). (gr. -1-2). lib. bdg. 20.99 *(978-0-375-97336-9(2),* Random Hse. Bks. for Young Readers) Random Hse. Children's Bks.
Everyday Signs of Zoo Animals. 2007. (J). bds. *(978-0-9791059-1-3(9))* Dakitab, Inc.
Ewing, Juliana Horatia. Brothers of Pity & Other Tales of Beasts & Men. 2007. (ENG.). 152p. pap. 19.99 *(978-1-4264-9205-1(7));* 168p. pap. 21.99 *(978-1-4264-9262-4(6))* Creative Media Partners, LLC.
Exactly Like Me. 2003. (J). per. 8.95 *(978-0-9746151-0-3(2))* Alta Retreat Ctr.
Eyuboglu, Melisa, illus. Angel in a Bubble. Eyuboglu, Melisa, . 2007. 28p. (J). 10.95 *(978-1-933090-48-1(0))* Guardian Angel Publishing, Inc.
Eze-Offormezie, Ngozika. An Invitation from the Fairy. 2008. 64p. pap. 23.49 *(978-1-4343-9784-3(X))* AuthorHouse.
Faber, Toni Tuso. The Poodle Tales: Book Eight. Rudd, Benton, illus. 2013. 24p. 16.99 *(978-0-9897168-0-2(5));* pap. 10.99 *(978-0-9897168-1-9(3))* Mindstir Media.
—The Poodle Tales: Book Seven. Rudd, Benton, illus. 2013. 26p. 16.99 *(978-0-9894748-6-3(0));* pap. 10.99 *(978-0-9894748-7-0(9))* Mindstir Media.
Fallon, Jimmy. Your Baby's First Word Will Be Dada. Ordóñez, Miguel, illus. 2015. (ENG.). (J). (gr. -1 — 1). 40p. 16.99 *(978-1-250-00934-0(0),* 9781250009340); 16p. bds. 7.99 *(978-1-250-07181-1(X),* 9781250071811) Feiwel & Friends.
Fallon, Karla. Rainforest Moon. 2005. 102p. pap. 9.98 *(978-1-4116-3776-4(3))* Lulu Pr., Inc.
Farber, Erica. Kooky Campout. Scarry, Huck, illus. 2015. (Richard Scarry's Great Big Schoolhouse Ser.). (ENG.). 24p. (J). (gr. 1-2). 12.95 *(978-1-4027-9914-3(4))* Sterling Publishing Co., Inc.
—Richard Scarry's Readers (Level 1): Snow Dance. Scarry, Huck, illus. 2014. (Richard Scarry's Great Big Schoolhouse Ser.). (ENG.). 24p. (J). (gr. -1 — 1). pap. 3.95 *(978-1-4027-9896-2(2));* 12.95 *(978-1-4027-9895-5(4))* Sterling Publishing Co., Inc.
Farley, Robin. Adventures of MIA. Ivanov, A. & Ivanov, O., illus. 2013. 158p. (J). *(978-1-4351-5061-4(9))* Barnes & Noble, Inc.
—Mia & the Big Sister Ballet. 2012. (Mia I Can Read Bks.). (J). lib. bdg. 13.55 *(978-0-606-26282-8(2),* Turtleback) Turtleback Bks.
—Mia & the Daisy Dance. 2012. (Mia I Can Read Bks.). (J). lib. bdg. 13.55 *(978-0-606-23595-2(7),* Turtleback) Turtleback Bks.
—Mia & the Girl with a Twirl. 2013. (Mia I Can Read Bks.). (J). lib. bdg. 13.55 *(978-0-606-31811-2(9),* Turtleback) Turtleback Bks.
—Mia & the Tiny Toe Shoes. 2012. (Mia I Can Read Bks.). (J). lib. bdg. 13.55 *(978-0-606-26863-9(4),* Turtleback) Turtleback Bks.
—Mia Sets the Stage. 2013. (Mia I Can Read Bks.). (J). lib. bdg. 13.55 *(978-0-606-27160-8(0),* Turtleback) Turtleback Bks.
—Time to Trick or Treat! Ivanov, Olga & Ivanov, Aleksey, illus. 2012. (Mia Ser.). (ENG.). 24p. (J). (gr. -1-3). pap. 4.99 *(978-0-06-210011-5(4),* HarperFestival) HarperCollins Pubs.
Farm Animal Board Books 800654, 7. 2005. (J). bds. *(978-1-59794-006-1(2))* Environments, Inc.
Farmer, Tom. Once upon a Daydream: The Story of Patrick & the Clumsy Camel. 2013. 44p. pap. 17.44 *(978-1-4669-6912-4(1))* Trafford Publishing.
Farshtey, Greg. Fire & Ice. 2014. (LEGO Legends of Chima Chapter Bks.: 6). lib. bdg. 14.75 *(978-0-606-36069-2(7))* Turtleback Bks.
Fatus, Sophie, illus. A Hen, a Chick & a String Guitar. 2005. 32p. (J). 17.99 incl. audio compact disk *(978-1-84148-796-0(1))* Barefoot Bks., Inc.
Faul, Nicole. The Great Animal Race & Trap the Angry Elephant Finds a Friend. 2009. (Illus.). 44p. pap. 18.49 *(978-1-4389-3320-7(7))* AuthorHouse.
Faulkner, Michael H. The Pearl Necklace: Miss Kitty Mysteries. 2006. (Illus.). 43p. (J). per. 21.95 *(978-1-59858-150-8(3))* Dog Ear Publishing, LLC.
Favorite Animals Book Set 800892, 3 vols. 2005. (J). *(978-1-59794-067-2(4))* Environments, Inc.
Fearnley, Jan. Mr Wolf & the Enormous Turnip. Fearnley, Jan, illus. 2005. (ENG., Illus.). 40p. (J). (gr. k-2). pap. 10.99 *(978-1-4052-1580-0(1))* Egmont Bks., Ltd. GBR. Dist: Independent Pubs. Group.
Feiffer, Jules. A Room with a Zoo. Feiffer, Jules, illus. 2007. (ENG., Illus.). 192p. (gr. 2-7). per. 7.99 *(978-0-7868-3703-8(9),* di Capua, Michael Bks.) Hyperion Bks. for Children.
Felix, Erica. Jay-Bee & Me. 2013. 20p. pap. 24.95 *(978-1-62709-205-0(6))* America Star Bks.
Felix, Monique. The Rumor. Felix, Monique, illus. 2011. (ENG., Illus.). 24p. (J). (gr. 1-3). 19.99 *(978-1-56846-219-6(0),* Creative Editions) Creative Co., The.
Fernandes, Eugenie. Kitten's Autumn. Fernandes, Eugenie, illus. 2010. (ENG., Illus.). 24p. (J). (gr. -1 — 1). 14.95 *(978-1-55453-341-1(4))* Kids Can Pr., Ltd. CAN. Dist: Hachette Bk. Group.
—Kitten's Summer. Fernandes, Eugenie, illus. 2013. (ENG., Illus.). 24p. (J). (gr. -1 — 1). bds. 7.95 *(978-1-55453-721-1(5))* Kids Can Pr., Ltd. CAN. Dist: Hachette Bk. Group.
—Kitten's Winter. Fernandes, Eugenie, illus. 2011. (ENG., Illus.). 24p. (J). (gr. -1 — 1). 14.95 *(978-1-55453-343-5(0))* Kids Can Pr., Ltd. CAN. Dist: Hachette Bk. Group.
Ferrara-Lester, Lisa. The Sky's the Limit. 2012. 24p. pap. 10.99 *(978-1-937829-60-5(X),* Total Publishing & Media) Yorkshire Publishing Group.
Ferri, Francesca, illus. Peek-A-Boo Jungle. 2006. (ENG.). 10p. (J). (gr. -1). 8.99 *(978-0-7641-5940-4(2))* Barron's Educational Series, Inc.
Ferri, Giuliano, illus. Illustrated Stories from Aesop. 2014. (ENG.). 272p. (J). 19.99 *(978-0-7945-2917-8(8),* Usborne) EDC Publishing.
Ferrier, Florian, et al. The Ghosts in the Clouds. Ferrier, Katherine, illus. 2017. (Hotel Strange Ser.: 4). (ENG.). 40p. (gr. 2-5). 26.65 *(978-1-4677-8587-7(3),* Graphic Universe™) Lerner Publishing Group.
Fessahaye, Miss Mehret. Layla the Animals' Friend. 2012. (Illus.). 40p. pap. 22.81 *(978-1-4772-5086-0(7))* AuthorHouse.
Few, Valerie. Filbert & Friends. 2008. 56p. pap. *(978-1-84748-346-1(1))* Athena Pr.
Fields, Jan. Hunt the Ozark Howler, 1 vol. Brundage, Scott, illus. 2016. (ENG.). 80p. (J). lib. bdg. *(978-1-62402-152-7(2))* Magic Wagon.
Fields, Terri. El Domador de Tornados, 1 vol. Jacques, Laura, illus. 2016. (SPA.). 32p. (J). (gr. k-3). pap. 9.95 *(978-1-62855-747-3(8))* Arbordale Publishing.
—Tornado Tamer, 1 vol. Jacques, Laura, illus. 2016. (ENG & SPA.). 32p. (J). (gr. k-3). 17.95 *(978-1-62855-733-6(8));* pap. 9.95 *(978-1-62855-740-4(0))* Arbordale Publishing.
Fifield, Lisa. Bears Make Rock Soup. Erdrich, Lise, illus. 2013. (ENG.). 32p. (J). pap. 9.95 *(978-0-89239-300-8(9),* Children's Book Press) Lee & Low Bks., Inc.
Figuerola, Maite. Las Estaciones del Ano. 2003. (Disney Collection). (SPA.). 32p. (J). 5.95 *(978-84-670-0300-0(6))* Espasa Calpe, S.A. ESP. Dist: Planeta Publishing Corp.
Finch, Mary. The Little Red Hen & the Ear of Wheat. 2011. (J). *(978-1-84686-576-3(X))* Barefoot Bks., Inc.
Fine, Anne. Jamie & Angus Together. Dale, Penny, illus. 2007. (ENG.). 112p. (J). (gr. -1-1). 15.99 *(978-0-7636-3374-5(7))* Candlewick Pr.
Finley, Thomas Murray. Alphapet City. 2012. (ENG.). 32p. pap. 9.99 *(978-1-4675-2587-9(1))* Independent Pub.
Finn, Isobel. The Very Lazy Ladybug. Tickle, Jack, illus. 2005. 16p. (J). bds. 6.95 *(978-1-58925-758-0(8))* Tiger Tales.
Finn, Isobel & Tickle, Jack. The Very Lazy Ladybug. 2003. (Illus.). (J). 16p. tchr. ed. 15.95 *(978-1-58925-714-6(6));* 32p. pap. 6.95 *(978-1-58925-379-7(5))* Tiger Tales.
Finnigan, Mary C. Our Family Trees. 2011. 28p. pap. 15.00 *(978-1-4634-1354-5(8))* AuthorHouse.
Fischer, Ellen. If an Armadillo Went to a Restaurant. Wood, Laura, illus. 2014. (ENG.). 32p. (J). (-2). 14.95 *(978-1-938063-39-8(2),* Mighty Media Kids) Mighty Media Pr.
—If an Elephant Went to School. Wood, Laura, illus. 2015. (ENG.). 32p. (J). (-2). 14.95 *(978-1-938063-61-9(9),* Mighty Media Kids) Mighty Media Pr.
Fischer, Scott M. Jump! Fischer, Scott M., illus. 2010. (ENG., Illus.). 32p. (J). (gr. -1-3). 15.99 *(978-1-4169-7884-8(4),* Simon & Schuster Bks. For Young Readers) Simon & Schuster Bks. For Young Readers.
Fisscher, Tiny. RUBY & the LION. 2008. (ENG.). 48p. (J). (gr. 1-7). 11.95 *(978-1-60136-014-4(2))* Audio Holdings, LLC.
Fitzgerald, Caroline. Animal Kingdom Goes to New York. 2011. 48p. pap. 18.46 *(978-1-4520-9966-8(9))* AuthorHouse.
Fitzgerald-Rodriguez, Mary. 20 Foxes. 2008. 30p. pap. 24.95 *(978-1-60672-282-4(4))* America Star Bks.
Fleischman, Paul. The Animal Hedge. Ibatoulline, Bagram, illus. 2008. (ENG.). 48p. (J). (gr. 1-4). pap. 8.99 *(978-0-7636-3842-9(0))* Candlewick Pr.
Fleming, Candace. Emma's Circus. Davenier, Christine, illus. 2017. (ENG.). 40p. (J). 17.99 *(978-0-374-39907-8(7),* 9780374399078, Farrar, Straus & Giroux (BYR)) Farrar, Straus & Giroux.
—Gator Gumbo: A Spicy-Hot Tale. Lambert, Sally Anne, illus. 2004. (ENG.). 32p. (J). (gr. -1-3). 18.99 *(978-0-374-38050-2(3),* 9780374380502, Farrar, Straus & Giroux (BYR)) Farrar, Straus & Giroux.
—Oh, No! Rohmann, Eric, illus. 2012. (ENG.). 40p. (J). (gr. -1-2). 17.99 *(978-0-375-84271-9(3),* Schwartz & Wade Bks.) Random Hse. Children's Bks.
—Who Invited You? Booth, George, illus. 2009. (ENG.). 36p. (J). (gr. -1-3). 10.99 *(978-1-4424-0219-5(9),* Atheneum Bks. for Young Readers) Simon & Schuster Children's Publishing.
Fleming, Denise. The Cow Who Clucked. 2007. (J). (gr. -1-1). 27.95 incl. audio *(978-0-8045-6951-4(7))* Spoken Arts, Inc.
—In the Small, Small Pond. Fleming, Denise, illus. 2007. (ENG., Illus.). 32p. (J). (gr. -1-k). pap. 27.99 *(978-0-8050-8117-6(8),* 9780805081176, Holt, Henry & Co. Bks. For Young Readers) Holt, Henry & Co.
—In the Tall, Tall, Grass. 2015. 32p. pap. 8.00 *(978-1-61003-609-2(3))* Center for the Collaborative Classroom.
—UnderGROUND. Fleming, Denise, illus. 2012. (ENG., Illus.). 40p. (J). (gr. -1-3). 17.99 *(978-1-4424-5882-6(8),* Beach Lane Bks.) Beach Lane Bks.
Fleming, Maria. Five Shiny Apples. Sexton, Brenda, illus. 2005. (Number Tales Ser.). (ENG.). 16p. (J). (gr. -1-1). pap. 2.99 *(978-0-439-69014-0(5))* Scholastic, Inc.
Fleming, Meg. I Heart You. Wright, Sarah Jane, illus. 2016. (ENG.). 40p. (J). (gr. -1-3). 17.99 *(978-1-4424-8895-3(6),* Beach Lane Bks.) Beach Lane Bks.
Fleming, Vicki & Dipietro, Kara. North Woods Numbers. 2010. 28p. pap. 13.99 *(978-1-4490-8420-2(6))* AuthorHouse.
Fletcher, Corina. Playbook Farm. Teckentrup, Britta, illus. 2012. (ENG.). 12p. (J). (gr. -1-2). 24.00 *(978-0-7636-6165-6(1),* Nosy Crow) Candlewick Pr.
—Up down Across. Marshall, Natalie, illus. 2015. (ENG.). 12p. (J). (— 1). bds. 8.95 *(978-1-4549-1562-1(5))* Sterling Publishing Co., Inc.
Flinn, Alex. Cloaked. 2011. (YA). 341p. lib. bdg. 17.89 *(978-0-06-087423-0(6));* (ENG.). 352p. (gr. 8-18). 16.99 *(978-0-06-087422-3(8))* HarperCollins Pubs. (HarperTeen).
Flintham, Thomas. Game over, Super Rabbit Boy! a Branches Book (Press Start! #1) 2016. (Press Start! Ser.: 1). (ENG.). 80p. (J). (gr. k-2). pap. 4.99 *(978-1-338-03471-4(5))* Scholastic, Inc.
Flintham, Thomas. Super Rabbit Boy Powers up! a Branches Book (Press Start! #2) 2017. (Press Start! Ser.: 2). (ENG.). 80p. (J). (gr. k-2). pap. 4.99 ***(978-1-338-03473-8(1))*** Scholastic, Inc.
Flor Ada, Alma. One More Friend. Fatus, Sophie, illus. 2007. 24p. (J). *(978-0-15-206278-1(5))* Harcourt Trade Pubs.
—The Unicorn of the West. 2007.Tr. of El Unicornio del Oeste. (ENG.). 32p. (J). (gr. -1-3). 11.99 *(978-1-4169-6843-6(1),* Simon & Schuster/Paula Wiseman Bks.) Simon & Schuster/Paula Wiseman Bks.
—Unicorn of the West (Spanish Edition) 2007. (ENG.). 32p. (J). (gr. -1-3). 11.99 *(978-1-4169-6844-3(X),* Simon & Schuster/Paula Wiseman Bks.) Simon & Schuster/Paula Wiseman Bks.
Flora, James, creator. The Day the Cow Sneezed. 2010. (ENG., Illus.). 48p. (J). (gr. -1-3). 16.95 *(978-1-59270-097-4(7))* Enchanted Lion Bks., LLC.
Florence Jahn Keller. Meet My Pets. 2009. 20p. pap. 10.49 *(978-1-4389-5710-4(6))* AuthorHouse.
Florian, Douglas. I Love My Hat, 0 vols. Keiser, Paige, illus. 2014. (ENG.). 24p. (J). (gr. -1-2). 16.99 *(978-1-4778-4780-0(4),* 9781477847800, Amazon Children's Publishing) Amazon Publishing.
Flowerpot Children's Press Staff, contrib. by. My Animal Buddies: With Duck, Pig, & Frog. 2015. (Illus.). (J). *(978-1-4351-6023-1(1))* Barnes & Noble, Inc.
Flynn, Caren. Exceptional Elvis. 2010. (Illus.). 24p. pap. 12.00 *(978-1-60844-481-6(3))* Dog Ear Publishing, LLC.
Flynn, Michael. Mutasia: The Wacky World of Figley Finch the Endless Caverns. 2012. (ENG.). pap. *(978-1-4675-1391-3(1))* Independent Pub.
Fogle, Llynda & González, Althea. A Friendship Place. 2005. (ENG & SPA., Illus.). (J). *(978-0-9760282-6-0(3))* RAPC - Sparkle & Shine Project.
Foley, Greg. Purple Little Bird. Foley, Greg, illus. 2011. (ENG., Illus.). 32p. (J). (gr. -1-2). 14.99 *(978-0-06-200828-2(5))* HarperCollins Pubs.
Foley, James M. Baxter Turns down His Buzz: A Story for Little Kids about ADHD. Ng-Benitez, Shirley, illus. 2016. 32p. (J). 15.95 *(978-1-4338-2268-1(7),* Magination Pr.) American Psychological Assn.
Folgueira, Rodrigo. Ribbit! Bernatene, Poly, illus. (ENG.). (J). 2016. 34p. (-k). bds. 8.99 *(978-0-553-53721-5(0))* 2013. 32p. (gr. -1-k). 15.99 *(978-0-307-98146-2(0))* Random Hse. Children's Bks. (Knopf Bks. for Young Readers).
Folsom, Michael & Elting, Mary. Q Is for Duck: An Alphabet Guessing Game. Kent, Jack & Kent, June K., illus. 2005. (ENG.). 64p. (J). (gr. -1-3). pap. 6.95 *(978-0-618-57412-4(3))* Houghton Mifflin Harcourt Publishing Co.
Fontenot, Mary Alice. Clovis Crawfish & Bertile's Bon Voyage, 1 vol. Blazek, Scott R., illus. 2008. (Clovis Crawfish Ser.). (ENG.). 32p. (J). (gr. k-3). 16.99 *(978-1-58980-541-5(0))* Pelican Publishing Co., Inc.
—Clovis Crawfish & Echo Gecko, 1 vol. Buckner, Julie Dupre, illus. 2003. (Clovis Crawfish Ser.). (ENG.). 32p. (J). (gr. k-3). 16.99 *(978-1-56554-708-7(X))* Pelican Publishing Co., Inc.
—Clovis Crawfish & His Friends, 1 vol. Graves, Keith, illus. 2009. (Clovis Crawfish Ser.). (ENG.). 32p. (J). (gr. k-3). 16.99 *(978-1-58980-762-4(6))* Pelican Publishing Co., Inc.
—Clovis Crawfish & Michelle Mantis, 1 vol. Blazek, Scott R., illus. 2008. (Clovis Crawfish Ser.). (ENG.). 32p. (J). (gr. k-3). 16.99 *(978-1-58980-540-8(2))* Pelican Publishing Co., Inc.
—Clovis Crawfish & Silvie Sulphur, 1 vol. Buckner, Julie Dupre, illus. 2004. (Clovis Crawfish Ser.). (ENG & FRE.). 32p. (J). (gr. k-3). 16.99 *(978-1-56554-864-0(7))* Pelican Publishing Co., Inc.
Fontenot, Mary Alice & Fontenot Landry, Julie. Clovis Crawfish & the Twin Sister, 1 vol. Butler, Julie Dupre & Buckner, Julie Dupre, illus. 2007. (Clovis Crawfish Ser.). (ENG.). 32p. (J). (gr. k-3). 16.99 *(978-1-58980-467-8(8))* Pelican Publishing Co., Inc.
Fontes, Justine. Crisis in Crittertown. 2014. (Cheddar's Tales Ser.). (ENG.). 176p. (J). (gr. 2-4). pap. 5.99 *(978-1-4380-0359-7(5))* Barron's Educational Series, Inc.
Forbes, Robert L. Beastly Feasts! A Mischievous Menagerie in Rhyme. Searle, Ronald, illus. 2007. (ENG.). 96p. (gr. 4-13). 19.95 *(978-1-58567-929-4(1),* 856929) Overlook Pr., The.
Ford, Carolyn. The Paper Bag. Diez-Luckie, Cathy, illus. 2005. (ENG.). 8p. (J). 5.75 *(978-1-57274-756-2(0),* 2494, Bks. for Young Learners) Owen, Richard C. Pubs., Inc.
Foreman, Michael. Hola, Mundo. 2004.Tr. of Hello, World. (SPA., Illus.). 28p. (J). 19.99 *(978-84-88342-41-6(1))* S.A. Kokinos ESP. Dist: Lectorum Pubns., Inc.
—Norman's Ark. Foreman, Michael, illus. 2006. (Tiger Tales Ser.). (Illus.). 24p. (J). (gr. -1-3). pap. 6.95 *(978-1-58925-401-5(5))* Tiger Tales.
Forest Trail. 2008. (Fold Out Pop-Ups Ser.). 6p. bds. *(978-1-4075-1301-0(X))* Parragon, Inc.
Forsythe, Matthew, illus. Please, Open This Book! 2015. (ENG.). 40p. (J). (gr. -1-3). 17.99 *(978-1-4424-5071-4(1),* Simon & Schuster/Paula Wiseman Bks.) Simon & Schuster/Paula Wiseman Bks.
Foster, Evelyn. Alan & the Animals. 2011. (Tadpoles Ser.). (ENG., Illus.). 24p. (J). (gr. k-2). *(978-0-7787-0573-4(0));* pap. *(978-0-7787-0584-0(6))* Crabtree Publishing Co.
Foster, Jennifer L. The Puppy with the White Paw. 2011. 28p. pap. 12.99 *(978-1-4567-3912-6(3))* AuthorHouse.
Foster, Kimberly. A Dolphin up a Tree! 2010. (Illus.). 30p. (J). 16.99 *(978-0-9664624-3-2(2))* Foster Branch Publishing.
Fox, Mem. Time for Bed: Lap-Sized Board Book. Dyer, Jane, illus. 2005. (ENG.). 28p. (J). (gr. k — 1). bds. 12.99

(978-0-15-205349-9(2)) Houghton Mifflin Harcourt Publishing Co.

Franco, Betsy. Pond Circle. Vitale, Stefano, illus. 2009. (ENG.). 32p. (J). (gr. -1-3). 17.99 (978-1-4169-4021-0(9), McElderry, Margaret K. Bks.) McElderry, Margaret K. Bks.

Franke, Kristina & Leberer, Sigrid. The Bunny Kindergarten. 2004. (Illus.). 32p. (J). 10.99 (978-1-59384-039-6(X)) Parklane Publishing.

Fraser, Mary Ann. Pet Shop Lullaby. Fraser, Mary Ann, illus. 2009. (ENG., Illus.). 32p. (J). (gr. -1-1). 16.95 (978-1-59078-618-5(1)) Boyds Mills Pr.

Fraser, W. A. The Outcasts. 2005. reprint ed. pap. 21.95 (978-1-4179-5533-6(3)) Kessinger Publishing, LLC.

Frazier, Craig. There Is a Monkey in My Drawers! 2003. (Illus.). 24p. (J). (gr. -1-k). 14.95 (978-1-932026-10-8(X)) Graphis, U.S., Inc.

Frederick, Susan. Miss Callie Lallie's Mouse Tales. Walter, J., illus. 2006. 48p. pap. 16.95 (978-1-4241-1431-3(4)) PublishAmerica, Inc.

Fredericks, Anthony D. Mountain Night Mountain Day. Spengler, Kenneth, illus. 2014. (ENG.). 32p. (J). 15.95 (978-1-933855-98-1(3), Rio Nuevo Pubs.) Rio Nuevo Pubs.

Free Wheelin' Coloring/Activity Book (English) 2005. (Illus.). (J). 2.99 (978-0-9770455-7-0(9)) Mighty Kids Media.

Freeberg, Eric, illus. Animal Stories. 2010. (Classic Starts(tm) Ser.). (ENG.). 160p. (J). (gr. 2-4). 6.95 (978-1-4027-6646-6(7)) Sterling Publishing Co., Inc.

Freedman, Claire, et al. Me & My Mommy: By My Side, Little Panda/Just for You!/Big Bear, Little Bear/the Most Precious Thing/Little Bear's Special Wish/My Mommy & Me. Tyger, Rory et al, illus. 2014. (ENG.). (J). (gr. -1). 11.99 (978-1-58925-449-7(X)) Tiger Tales.

Freeman, Don. Earl the Squirrel. Freeman, Don, illus. 2008. (Illus.). (J). (gr. -1-2). pap. 16.95 incl. audio (978-1-4301-0411-7(2)) Live Oak Media.

—Earl the Squirrel. Freeman, Don, illus. 2007. (ENG., Illus.). 48p. (J). (gr. -1-2). pap. 6.99 (978-0-14-240893-3(X), Puffin Books) Penguin Young Readers Group.

—Quiet! There's a Canary in the Library. 2009. (ENG.). 48p. (J). (gr. -1-k). pap. 7.99 (978-0-14-241452-1(2), Puffin Books) Penguin Young Readers Group.

Freeman, Tor. Olive & the Embarrassing Gift. Freeman, Tor, illus. 2014. (ENG., Illus.). 32p. (J). (gr. -1-3). 15.99 (978-0-7636-7406-9(0), Templar) Candlewick Pr.

Freisinger, Vickie. Reno Does Chores, 1 vol. 2009. 36p. pap. 24.95 (978-1-60813-027-6(4)) America Star Bks.

French, Jackie. Josephine Wants to Dance. Whatley, Bruce, illus. 2008. 32p. (J). pap. (978-0-207-20080-9(7)) HarperCollins Pubs. Australia.

French, Lisa S. A Planet Called Home: Eco-Pig's Animal Protection, 1 vol. Gott, Barry, illus. 2009. (Eco-Pig Ser.). (ENG.). 32p. (J). (gr. -1-2). 28.50 (978-1-60270-662-0(X)) ABDO Publishing Co.

Frey, Bob. Guide to Seldom Seen Animals. 2011. 28p. (gr. -1 — 1). pap. 12.95 (978-1-4634-0612-7(6)) AuthorHouse.

Friend, Alison. Freddy & Frito & the Clubhouse Rules. Friend, Alison, illus. 2015. (ENG., Illus.). 40p. (J). (gr. -1-3). 17.99 (978-0-06-228580-5(7)) HarperCollins Pubs.

Friend, R. Down on Friendly Acres Set 1: Books #1-4, 4. 2007. (Illus.). (J). (978-0-9743627-8-6(6)) Sunflower Seeds Pr.

Friester, Paul. Owl Howl. Goossens, Philippe, illus. 2014. (ENG.). 32p. (J). 15.95 (978-0-7358-4188-8(8)) North-South Bks., Inc.

Frisch, Aaron. The Lonely Pine. Delessert, Etienne, illus. 2011. (ENG.). 32p. (J). (gr. 1-3). 17.99 (978-1-56846-214-1(X), Creative Editions) Creative Co., The.

Froeb, Lori & Brown, Jo. Zoo! A Big Fold-Out Counting Book. 2007. (Big Fold-Out Flap Ser.). (ENG., Illus.). 10p. (J). (gr. -1-k). bds. 12.99 (978-0-7944-1361-3(7)) Reader's Digest Assn., Inc., The.

Froeb, Lori C. Butterphants & Eleflies. Rinaldo, Luana, illus. 2010. (Sliding Surprise Ser.). (ENG.). 10p. (J). bds. 7.99 (978-0-7944-1932-5(1)) Reader's Digest Assn., Inc., The.

—Noah & the Animals. Corke, Estelle, illus. 2015. (Open Door Book Ser.: 3). (ENG.). 16p. (J). (gr. -1 — 1). bds. 9.99 (978-0-7944-3342-0(1)) Studio Fun International.

Froese, Dorothy Cheever. Captain Rhino's Progress: An Allegory of the Workplace. 2003. (Illus.). 32p. pap. 9.00 (978-1-890437-86-2(7)) Western Reflections Publishing Co.

Frohlich, Anja. Animals in the Outhouse. Kiss, Gergely, illus. 2012. (ENG.). 28p. (J). (gr. k-3). 16.95 (978-1-61608-659-6(9), 608659, Sky Pony Pr.) Skyhorse Publishing Co., Inc.

Frost, Adam. Run! The Elephant Weighs a Ton! Chambers, Mark, illus. 2012. (ENG.). 128p. (J). (gr. -1-k). pap. 8.99 (978-1-4088-2707-9(7), 9781408827079, Bloomsbury USA Childrens) Bloomsbury Publishing USA.

Frrich, Lewandowski & Riccards, Michael. It's Christmas Again! Delisle, Kathryn H., illus. 2007. 32p. (J). 14.95 (978-1-929039-44-9(1)) Ambassador Bks., Inc.

Fry, Debbie, illus. Donkeywise & Otherwise: The Story of Daisy Doo & Dudley Duz. 2004. 44p. (J). (978-0-9759647-0-5(4), 1238040) Fry, Debbie.

Fuertes, Gloria. Cuentos de Humor: Un Pulpo en un Garaje. 2003. (SPA.). 128p. 15.16 (978-84-305-7987-7(7), SU5205) Susaeta Ediciones, S.A. ESP. Dist: Lectorum Pubns., Inc.

Fujikawa, Brian. The Adventures of Bibole, Ri: The CURSE of the WEREMOUSE. 2012. 52p. pap. 18.41 (978-1-4669-3547-1(2)) Trafford Publishing.

Furgang, Kathy. The Great Green Forest: Set Of 6. 2010. (Early Connections Ser.). (J). pap. 37.00 net. (978-1-4108-1373-2(8)) Benchmark Education Co.

Furman, A. L., ed. Wild Life Stories: Young Readers. Geer, Charles, illus. 2011. 192p. 42.95 (978-1-258-10201-2(3)) Literary Licensing, LLC.

Furman, Necah Stewart & Huff, Bailey. Lucy Swan's Circle. Clay, Joshua, illus. 2005. (Friends of Fairlane Woods Ser.). (ENG.). 40p. (J). (gr. -1-3). per. 16.99 (978-1-4134-8666-7(5)) Xlibris Corp.

Furrow, Eva & Napoli, Donna Jo. Take Your Time: A Tale of Harriet, the Galápagos Tortoise. Molk, Laurel, illus. 2017. (ENG.). 32p. (J). 16.99 (978-0-8050-9521-0(7), 9780805095210, Holt, Henry & Co. Bks. For Young Readers) Holt, Henry & Co.

The Furry Friends. 2005. (J). per. (978-0-9664783-2-7(0)) Jacqueline Beverly Hills.

Gaiman, Neil. Chu's First Day of School. Rex, Adam, illus. 2014. (ENG.). 32p. (J). (gr. -1-3). 17.99 (978-0-06-222397-5(6)) HarperCollins Pubs.

—Chu's First Day of School Board Book. Rex, Adam, illus. 2015. (ENG.). 36p. (J). (gr. -1 — 1). bds. 7.99 (978-0-06-237149-2(5), HarperFestival) HarperCollins Pubs.

—Odd & the Frost Giants. Riddell, Chris, illus. 2016. 128p. (J). (gr. 3-7). 19.99 (978-0-06-256795-6(0)) HarperCollins Pubs.

—Odd & the Frost Giants. Helquist, Brett, illus. 128p. (J). 2009. (ENG.). (gr. 3-18). 14.99 (978-0-06-167173-9(8)) 2008. lib. bdg. 15.89 (978-0-06-167175-3(4)) HarperCollins Pubs.

Galdone, Paul. Henny Penny. 2013. (Folk Tale Classics Ser.). (ENG., Illus.). 40p. (J). (gr. -1-3). 8.99 (978-0-547-90200-5(X)) Houghton Mifflin Harcourt Publishing Co.

—Rumpelstiltskin Big Book. 2015. (Paul Galdone Classics Ser.). (ENG., Illus.). 32p. (J). (gr. -1-3). 26.99 (978-0-544-55555-6(4), HMH Books For Young Readers) Houghton Mifflin Harcourt Publishing Co.

Gallo, Tina, adapted by. Kung Fu Road Trip. 2014. (Kung Fu Panda TV Ser.). (ENG., Illus.). 32p. (J). (gr. k-2). 16.99 (978-1-4814-0489-1(X), Simon Spotlight) Simon Spotlight.

Galvin, Laura. I Love My Sister. 2008. (ENG., Illus.). 16p. (J). (gr. -1-k). bds. 6.95 (978-1-59249-867-3(1)) Soundprints.

Galvin, Laura Gates. I Love My Brother. Oughton, Taylor, illus. 2008. (ENG.). 16p. (J). (gr. -1-k). bds. 6.95 (978-1-59249-866-6(3)) Soundprints.

—I Love My Daddy. 2011. (I Love My... Ser.). (ENG., Illus.). 16p. (J). (gr. -1-k). 6.95 (978-1-60727-346-2(2)) Soundprints.

—I Love My Sister. Oughton, Taylor et al, illus. 2011. (I Love My... Ser.). (ENG.). 16p. (gr. -1-k). 6.95 (978-1-60727-311-0(X)) Soundprints.

Gamble, Isobel. Quien Hay? 2003. (SPA.). 228p. (978-84-488-1080-1(5), BS30459) Beascoa, Ediciones S.A. ESP. Dist: Lectorum Pubns., Inc.

Gannett, Ruth Stiles. My Father's Dragon. Gannett, Ruth Chrisman, illus. 2014. (ENG.). 96p. (J). (gr. 1-4). pap. 5.99 (978-0-486-49283-4(4)) Dover Pubns., Inc.

Gansle, Sherry. Oops, a Curious Horse Big Book. Light, Carol, illus. 2003. 56p. (J). (978-0-9745803-6-4(8)) Little Big Tomes.

—Oops, a Curious Horse Little Book. Light, Carol, illus. 2003. 52p. (J). (978-0-9745803-7-1(6)) Little Big Tomes.

—Oops, a Curious Horse Story Book Reader. Light, Carol, illus. 2003. 58p. (J). (978-0-9745803-5-7(X)) Little Big Tomes.

Ganzer, Diane & St. Croix, Sammy. Adventures of a Kitten Named Raspberry & Other Tales. 2009. 176p. pap. 9.95 (978-1-935105-30-5(2)) Avid Readers Publishing Group.

—Llama Tails: Ricky's Adventure. Ganzer, Theresa, illus. 2008. 172p. pap. 9.99 (978-0-9801438-7-4(X)) Avid Readers Publishing Group.

Garcia, Nasario. The Talking Lizard: New Mexico's Magic & Mystery. Montoya, Jeremy, illus. 2014. (SPA & ENG.). (J). pap. (978-1-936744-36-7(8), Rio Grande Bks.) LPD Pr.

Garis, Howard R. Sammie & Susie Littletail. Wisa, Louis, illus. 2007. 120p. per. (978-1-4065-2770-4(X)) Dodo Pr.

—Uncle Wiggily & Old Mother Hubbard. 2008. 116p. per. 9.95 (978-1-60312-520-8(5)) Aegypan.

—Uncle Wiggily in the Woods. 2008. 132p. per. 11.95 (978-1-60312-521-5(3)) Aegypan.

—Uncle Wiggily's Travels. 2008. 132p. 24.95 (978-1-60664-906-0(X)); pap. 10.95 (978-1-60664-025-8(9)) Aegypan.

Garis, Howard Roger. Favorite Uncle Wiggily Animal Bedtime Stories. Kliros, Thea, illus. unabr. ed. 2011. (Dover Children's Thrift Classics Ser.). (ENG.). 64p. (J). (gr. 3-8). pap. 3.00 (978-0-486-40101-0(4)) Dover Pubns., Inc.

—Uncle Wiggily & the Littletails. Date not set. 192p. (J). 20.95 (978-0-8488-2279-8(X)) Amereon Ltd.

—Uncle Wiggily Bedtime Stories: In Easy-to-Read Type. Kliros, Thea, illus. unabr. ed. 2011. (Dover Children's Thrift Classics Ser.). (ENG.). 80p. (J). (gr. 3-8). pap. 2.50 (978-0-486-29372-1(6)) Dover Pubns., Inc.

—Uncle Wiggily's Adventures. 2005. 26.95 (978-1-4218-1468-1(4)); 164p. pap. 11.95 (978-1-4218-1568-8(0)) 1st World Publishing, Inc. (1st World Library - Literary Society).

Garland, Michael. Fish Had a Wish. Garland, Michael, illus. (I Like to Read(r) Ser.). (ENG., Illus.). 24p. (J). 2013. pap. 6.99 (978-0-8234-2757-4(9)) 2012. 14.95 (978-0-8234-2394-1(8)) Holiday Hse., Inc.

—Last Night at the Zoo. Garland, Michael, illus. 2003. (ENG., Illus.). 32p. (J). (gr. k-2). pap. 10.95 (978-1-59078-167-8(8)) Boyds Mills Pr.

—Lost Dog. 2015. (I Like to Read(r) Ser.). (ENG., Illus.). 24p. (J). (gr. -1-3). 14.95 (978-0-8234-3429-9(X)) Holiday Hse., Inc.

Garner, Albert. The Adventures of Dimi. 2013. (ENG.). 48p. (J). 24.95 (978-1-4787-1677-8(0)) Outskirts Pr., Inc.

Garr, Rebecca. Adventures of Baroness of the Arizona Desert. Davisson, Vanessa, illus. 2010. 60p. pap. 18.95 (978-1-60911-958-4(4), Eloquent Bks.) Strategic Book Publishing & Rights Agency (SBPRA).

Garrett, Cindy Crawford. Life's Lessons with the Silly Animals Out on the Ranch: What Is Wrong with Bob the Rooster? 2013. 24p. pap. 17.99 (978-1-4817-0574-5(1)) AuthorHouse.

Garson, Cindy. Welcome to Kristy's Farm, Book 2 (Black & White Version) 2007. 104p. pap. 14.00 (978-1-4303-0366-4(2)) Lulu Pr., Inc.

—Welcome to Kristy's Farm, Book 4. 2007. 104p. pap. 19.50 (978-1-4303-1000-6(6)) Lulu Pr., Inc.

Garton, Sam. Otter Goes to School. Garton, Sam, illus. 2016. (Illus.). 32p. (J). (gr. -1-3). 17.99 (978-0-06-235225-5(3)) HarperCollins Pubs.

Gassman, Julie. Crabby Pants, 1 vol. Watson, Richard, illus. 2012. (Little Boost Ser.). (ENG.). 32p. (gr. k-3). 7.95 (978-1-4048-7416-9(X), Little Boost) Picture Window Bks.

Gaston, Sharon D. Clean Your Own House & Misery Loves Company. 2009. 40p. pap. 18.50 (978-1-4389-7831-4(6)) AuthorHouse.

—Who's Laughing Now? & Don't Burn Your Bridge. 2009. 48p. pap. 19.50 (978-1-4389-7832-1(4)) AuthorHouse.

Gauthier, Lance C., text. The One-Eared Mouse of Pasture Hill. 2003. 55p. (J). per. 6.95 (978-1-884540-70-7(8)) Haley's.

Gay, Michel. El Cochecito. 2003. (SPA.). 68p. (978-84-8470-084-5(4)) Corimbo, Editorial S.L.

Gaylord, Laurel Porter. Quiero a Mi Mama Porque. Wolff, Ashley, illus. 2004.Tr. of I Love My Mommy Because. (SPA & ENG.). 22p. (J). (gr. -1 — 1). bds. 6.99 (978-0-525-47248-3(7), Dutton Books for Young Readers) Penguin Young Readers Group.

Gedovius, Juan. From the Vine. Gedovius, Juan, illus. (Illus.). 24p. (J). (gr. k-6). 14.95 (978-968-19-1053-2(2)) Santillana USA Publishing Co., Inc.

Geiger, Lorraine Lynch. A Wild & Woolly Night. Vargo, Sharon, illus. 2007. (J). (gr. -1-3). 15.95 (978-1-891795-25-1(2)) RGU Group, The.

Geist, Ken. Who's Who? Cole, Henry, illus. 2012. (ENG.). 28p. (J). (gr. -1 — 1). 16.99 (978-0-312-64437-6(X), 9780312644376) Feiwel & Friends.

George, Kallie. Fall. Graegin, Stephanie, illus. 2017. (Heartwood Hotel Ser.). (ENG.). 176p. (J). (gr. 2-5). 14.99 **(978-1-4847-3161-1(1))** Disney Pr.

—The Greatest Gift. 2017. (Heartwood Hotel Ser.: 2). (J). lib. bdg. 16.00 **(978-0-606-39967-8(4))** Turtleback Bks.

—Heartwood Hotel, Book 2 the Greatest Gift. Graegin, Stephanie, illus. 2017. (Heartwood Hotel Ser.). (ENG.). 176p. (J). (gr. 2-5). 14.99 **(978-1-4847-3234-2(0))**; pap. 5.99 **(978-1-4847-4639-4(2))** Hyperion Bks. for Children.

—The Lost Gift: A Christmas Story. Graegin, Stephanie, illus. 2016. (ENG.). 40p. (J). (gr. -1-3). 17.99 (978-0-553-52481-9(X), Schwartz & Wade Bks.) Random Hse. Children's Bks.

—The Missing Magic. Boiger, Alexandra, illus. 2017. (Magical Animal Adoption Agency Ser.). (ENG.). 128p. (J). (gr. 2-5). pap. 5.99 (978-1-4847-0147-8(X)) Hyperion Bks. for Children.

George, Lindsay Barrett. The Secret. George, Lindsay Barrett, illus. 2005. (Illus.). 32p. (J). 16.89 (978-0-06-029600-1(3)) HarperCollins Pubs.

Geraghty, Paul. Help Me! Geraghty, Paul, illus. 2011. (ENG., Illus.). 32p. (J). (gr. -1-k). pap. 8.99 (978-1-84939-027-9(4)) Andersen Pr. GBR. Dist: Independent Pubs. Group.

Gerrard, K. A. My Family Is a Zoo. Dodd, Emma, illus. 2016. (ENG.). 32p. (J). 16.99 (978-1-61963-851-8(7), 9781619638518, Bloomsbury USA Childrens) Bloomsbury Publishing USA.

Gershator, David. Where Did the Baby Go? Gershator, Phillis, illus. 2016. (J). pap. (978-1-934370-57-5(6)) Editorial Campana.

Gershator, Phillis. Who's in the Garden? McDonald, Jill, illus. 2010. (ENG.). 24p. (J). (gr. -1-k). 14.99 (978-1-84686-403-2(8)) Barefoot Bks., Inc.

Gershator, Phyllis. Who's in the Forest? McDonald, Jill, illus. 2010. (ENG.). 24p. (J). (gr. -1-k). bds. 14.99 (978-1-84686-476-6(3)) Barefoot Bks., Inc.

Gershenson, Harold P. Freddy Flamingo & the Kindertown Five. Mills, Christopher, illus. 2005. 27p. (J). (978-1-58987-070-3(0)) Kindermusik International.

—Noodles from Scratch. Mills, Christopher, illus. 2006. (J). (978-1-58987-007-9(7)) Kindermusik International.

Gerstein, Mordicai. The Night World. 2015. (ENG., Illus.). 40p. (J). (gr. -1-3). 18.00 (978-0-316-18822-7(0)) Little Brown & Co.

—The Sleeping Gypsy. Gerstein, Mordicai, illus. 2016. (ENG., Illus.). 32p. (J). 16.95 (978-0-8234-2142-8(2)) Holiday Hse., Inc.

Geste, Mal, et al. Zoo Room. Gelsthorpe, Loraine & Rex, Sue, eds. (Illus.). 32p. (J). pap. 14.95 (978-1-86368-339-5(9)) Fremantle Pr. AUS. Dist: Independent Pubs. Group.

Geyer, Clyde. The Awesome Adventures of Chuckie Chopper & Friends. 2012. 52p. pap. 15.95 (978-1-4575-0741-0(2)) Dog Ear Publishing, LLC.

Ghigna, Charles. Adeline Porcupine. East, Jacqueline, illus. 2015. (Tiny Tales Ser.). (ENG.). 64p. (gr. -1-2). lib. bdg. 23.99 (978-1-4795-6530-6(X)) Tiny Tales.

—Bobby Bear. East, Jacqueline, illus. 2015. (Tiny Tales Ser.). (ENG.). 64p. (gr. -1-2). lib. bdg. 23.99 (978-1-4795-6531-3(8)) Tiny Tales.

—Cuddle Bunny. East, Jacqueline, illus. 2015. (Tiny Tales Ser.). (ENG.). 64p. (gr. -1-2). lib. bdg. 23.99 (978-1-4795-6528-3(8)) Tiny Tales.

Ghosh, Premola, illus. Ten Timeless Tales. 2005. 38p. (J). (978-81-89013-35-6(1)) Zubaan.

Giachetti, Julia & Benchmark Education Co. Staff. A Tail for a Tail - Cherokee Trickster Tales. 2014. (Text Connections Ser.). (J). (gr. 5). (978-1-4900-1375-6(X)) Benchmark Education Co.

Giancamilli, Vanessa. Platypus Creek. Thivierge, Claude, illus. 2005. (Amazing Animal Adventures Ser.). (ENG.). 36p. (J). (gr. -1-2). 2.95 (978-1-59249-354-8(8), S7159); (gr. -1-2). 19.95 (978-1-59249-355-5(6), BC7109); (gr. -1-2). 9.95 (978-1-59249-357-9(2), PS7159); (gr. -1-2). 15.95 (978-1-59249-352-4(1), B7109); (gr. -1-2). pap. 6.95 (978-1-59249-353-1(X), S7109); (gr. 2-6). 8.95 (978-1-59249-356-2(4), SC7109) Soundprints.

Gibbons, Ted & Wilcox, S. Michael. Modern Fables. McCune, Mark, illus. 2010. (J). 14.99 (978-1-59955-307-8(4)) Cedar Fort, Inc./CFI Distribution.

Gibert, Bruno. A King Seen from the Sky. 2015. (ENG., Illus.). 32p. (J). 16.95 (978-1-60606-460-3(6), J. Paul Getty Museum) Getty Pubns.

Gibson, Ginger Foglesong. Tiptoe Joe. Rankin, Laura, illus. 2013. (ENG.). 32p. (J). (gr. -1-k). 17.99 (978-0-06-177203-0(8), Greenwillow Bks.) HarperCollins Pubs.

Gifford, Clive. Dead or Alive? Home, Sarah, illus. 2015. (ENG.). 48p. (J). (gr. 2-4). 14.99 (978-1-4052-6858-5(1)) Egmont Bks., Ltd. GBR. Dist: Independent Pubs. Group.

Giggle & grow with Plush. 2007. bds. 15.95 (978-1-58117-644-5(9), Intervisual/Piggy Toes) Bendon, Inc.

Gilbert, Diana. Guided by the Light. 2007. 48p. per. 16.95 (978-1-4241-7016-6(8)) America Star Bks.

Gilbert, Harry. Year of Sharing, Level 1. Oxford University Press Staff & Bassett, Jennifer, eds. 3rd ed. 2008. (ENG., Illus.). 64p. 10.00 (978-0-19-479077-2(0)) Oxford Univ. Pr., Inc.

Gilbert, Paul T. Bertram & His Funny Animals. Rousseff, Minnie H., illus. 2016. (ENG.). 140p. (J). 24.95 (978-0-7649-7372-7(X), POMEGRANATE KIDS) Pomegranate Communications, Inc.

Gilkey, Gail. No More Garbage. Gilkey, Gail, ed. Kittell DiOrio, Kathy, illus. 2003. 32p. (J). (gr. k-2). lib. bdg. 14.95 (978-0-9662983-4-5(9)) Windy Hill Pr.

Gillespie, Jane. G Is for Gecko: An Alphabet Adventure in Hawai'i. Robinson, Don, illus. 2013. (ENG.). 26p. (J). (gr. -1-1). 12.95 (978-1-933067-51-3(9)) Beachhouse Publishing, LLC.

Gilman, Grace. Dixie Wins the Race. 2012. (Dixie: I Can Read Ser.). (J). lib. bdg. 13.55 (978-0-606-26851-6(0), Turtleback) Turtleback Bks.

Ginsburg, Mirra. Mushroom in the Rain. Ginsburg, Mirra & Aruego, Jose, illus. 2010. (Rise & Shine Ser.). (ENG.). 32p. (C). (gr. -1-3). reprint ed. 11.95 (978-0-689-71441-2(6)) National Geographic School Publishing, Inc.

Giuliani, Alfred. Zootopia. Wu, Vivien, illus. 2016. (J). (978-1-4806-9720-1(6), Golden Bks.) Random Hse. Children's Bks.

Giulieri, Anne. In the Water, 1 vol. Hancock, Anna, illus. 2012. (Engage Literacy Magenta Ser.). (ENG.). 32p. (gr. k-2). pap. 5.99 (978-1-4296-8854-3(8), Engage Literacy) Capstone Press of Coughlan Cos.

Given, Cate. Cartwheeling. Hill-Peterson, Jodi, illus. 2006. (J). (978-0-9790057-1-8(X)) Paws In the Sand Publishing.

Glaeser, Patricia Heinz. A New Day for Foal. 2007. 40p. per. 24.95 (978-1-4241-8342-5(1)) America Star Bks.

Gleeson, Joseph M., illus. Just So Stories. 2013. 250p. pap. (978-1-909302-29-7(5)) Abela Publishing.

Glover, Dennis W. The Cat in the Woods. 2010. 20p. pap. 10.49 (978-1-4389-8492-5(8)) AuthorHouse.

Glynn, Gower. Stories Told in the Wigwam. 2006. pap. 24.95 (978-1-4254-9966-2(X)) Kessinger Publishing, LLC.

Gnoske, Alexandra. Loui Saves the Earth. 2010. 16p. 9.49 (978-1-4520-0034-3(4)) AuthorHouse.

Godsey, J. P. "Gus". How Scooter Gets His Tail Back. Del Russo, John William, Sr., illus. 2014. (ENG.). 46p. (gr. 2-6). pap. 9.95 (978-1-63047-003-6(1)) Morgan James Publishing.

Goedde, Kathy. Blogged Down. 2009. 28p. pap. 13.99 (978-1-4389-5055-6(1)) AuthorHouse.

Goembel, Ponder. Animal Fair, 0 vols. Goembel, Ponder, illus. 2010. (ENG., Illus.). 24p. (J). (gr. -1 — 1). 12.99 (978-0-7614-5642-1(2), 9780761456421, Amazon Children's Publishing) Amazon Publishing.

Golden Books. ABC Animals (Dora the Explorer) McGee, Warner, illus. 2013. (Color Plus Card Stock Ser.). (ENG.). 48p. (J). (gr. -1-2). pap. 3.99 (978-0-307-98218-6(1), Golden Bks.) Random Hse. Children's Bks.

—From Army Ants to Zebrafish: Animals That Hop, Fly & Swish! (Dr. Seuss/Cat in the Hat) Ruiz, Aristides, illus. 2013. (Deluxe Stickerific Ser.). (ENG.). 64p. (J). (gr. -1-2). pap. 5.99 (978-0-449-81432-1(7), Golden Bks.) Random Hse. Children's Bks.

—On the Farm (Bubble Guppies) Jackson, Mike, illus. 2012. (Super Color with Stickers Ser.). (ENG.). 96p. (J). (gr. -1-2). pap. 3.99 (978-0-307-93096-5(3), Golden Bks.) Random Hse. Children's Bks.

Golden Books Staff. Animal Tales. 2007. (Little Golden Book Treasury Ser.). (ENG., Illus.). 224p. (J). (gr. -1-2). 12.99 (978-0-375-84178-1(4), Golden Bks.) Random Hse. Children's Bks.

—Little Golden Book Favorites. Scarry, Richard & Golden Books Staff, illus. 2008. (Little Golden Book Favorites Ser.). (ENG.). 80p. (J). (gr. -1-2). 7.99 (978-0-375-84580-2(1), Golden Bks.) Random Hse. Children's Bks.

—Little Golden Book Favorites No. 1: The Poky Little Puppy/Scuffy the Tugboat/The Saggy Baggy Elephant. 2007. (Little Golden Book Favorites Ser.). (ENG., Illus.). 80p. (J). (gr. -1-2). 7.99 (978-0-375-84215-3(2), Golden Bks.) Random Hse. Children's Bks.

Goldie & the Fawn. 2005. (The Fawn Chapter Ser.). (J). 7.67 (978-1-58453-310-8(2)) Pioneer Valley Bks.

Goldsack, Gaby. Fire Engine. Lawson, Peter, illus. 2009. (Turn the Wheel Ser.). (ENG.). 10p. (J). (gr. -1-k). bds. 5.95 (978-0-7892-1022-7(3), Abbeville Kids) Abbeville Pr., Inc.

—Fishing Boat. Lawson, Peter, illus. 2009. (Turn the Wheel Ser.). (ENG.). 10p. (J). (gr. -1-k). bds. 5.95 (978-0-7892-1025-8(8), Abbeville Kids) Abbeville Pr., Inc.

Gomi, Taro. Everyone Poops. 2006. (ENG., Illus.). 28p. (J). (gr. -1). pap. 7.99 (978-1-929132-14-0(X)) Kane Miller.

—Mommy! Mommy! 2013. (ENG., Illus.). 22p. (J). (gr. -1 — 1). bds. 6.99 (978-1-4521-0834-6(X)) Chronicle Bks. LLC.

—My Friends. 2014. 40p. pap. 7.00 (978-1-61003-331-2(0)) Center for the Collaborative Classroom.

—My Friends/Mis Amigos. 2006. (ENG & SPA., Illus.). 40p. (J). (gr. -1-7). pap. 6.99 (978-0-8118-5204-3(0)) Chronicle Bks. LLC.

—Peekaboo! 2013. (ENG., Illus.). 16p. (J). (gr. -1 — 1). bds. 6.99 (978-1-4521-0835-3(8)) Chronicle Bks. LLC.

—Wiggle! 2013. (ENG., Illus.). 16p. (J). (gr. -1 — 1). bds. 6.99 (978-1-4521-0836-0(6)) Chronicle Bks. LLC.

Gondek, Heather. Who's in the Jungle? Lift-the-Flap 'n' Learn. Gilvan-Cartwright, Chris, illus. 2005. (Fun with Animals Ser.). 10p. (J). 9.95 (978-1-58117-075-7(0), Intervisual/Piggy Toes) Bendon, Inc.

Gooden, Sean Lawrence. The Mother of the Green Bear, 1 vol. 2009. (ENG.). 191p. pap. 24.95 (978-1-60749-815-5(4)) America Star Bks.

Goodwin, John. An Arkful of Animal Stories. Macnaughton, Tina, illus. 2008. 32p. (J). (gr. k-3). 13.95 (978-0-8198-0782-3(6)) Pauline Bks. & Media.

—Lion Book of Five-Minute Animal Stories. Bendall-Brunello, John, illus. 2009. (ENG.). 48p. (J). (gr. k-2). 16.99 (978-0-7459-6084-5(7)) Lion Hudson PLC GBR. Dist: Independent Pubs. Group.

Gorbachev, Valeri. Un Dia de lluvia. Gorbachev, Valeri, illus. 2007. (SPA., Illus.). 40p. (J). (gr. -1-3). pap. 8.95 (978-958-04-7074-8(X)) Norma S.A. COL. Dist: Distribuidora Norma, Inc.

—Pizza-Pie Snowman. 2016. (ENG., Illus.). 32p. (J). 16.95 (978-0-8234-3654-5(3)) Holiday Hse., Inc.

—Whose Hat Is It? Gorbachev, Valeri, illus. (My First I Can Read Ser.). (Illus.). 32p. (J). (gr. -1 — 1). 2005. (ENG.). pap. 3.99 (978-0-06-053436-3(2)) 2004. (ENG., 14.99 (978-0-06-053434-9(6)) 2004. lib. bdg. 15.89 (978-0-06-053435-6(4)) HarperCollins Pubs.

Gordon, Danielle. Garage Cat. 2012. (ENG.). pap. (978-1-4675-1344-9(X)) Independent Pub.

Gordon, David. Extremely Cute Animals Operating Heavy Machinery. Gordon, David, illus. 2016. (ENG., Illus.). 48p. (J). (gr. -1-3). 17.99 *(978-1-4169-2441-8(8),* Simon & Schuster Bks. For Young Readers) Simon & Schuster Bks. For Young Readers.

Goscinny, René. Nicholas Again. Bell, Anthea, tr. from FRE. Sempé, Jean-Jacques, illus. rev. ed. 2006. (ENG.). 120p. (gr. 8-17). 19.95 *(978-0-7148-4564-7(7))* Phaidon Pr., Inc.

—Nicholas on Vacation. Bell, Anthea, tr. from FRE. Sempé, Jean-Jacques, illus. rev. ed. 2006. (ENG.). 132p. (gr. 8-17). 19.95 *(978-0-7148-4678-1(3))* Phaidon Pr., Inc.

Goscinny, René, et al. Nicholas Again. Bell, Anthea, tr. from FRE. 2006. (ENG., Illus.). 120p. 19.95 *(978-0-7148-4491-6(8))* Phaidon Pr., Inc.

Gosline, Andrea Alban. Ten Little Wishes: A Baby Animal Counting Book. Bossi, Lisa Burnett, illus. 2007. 40p. (J). (gr. -1-k). 16.89 *(978-0-06-053411-0(7))* HarperCollins Pubs.

Goss, Matt. Bear Crimbo. 2010. (ENG., Illus.). 72p. (J). 17.95 *(978-0-9815381-3-6(4))* Hilton Publishing Co.

Graham, Bob. Tales from the Waterhole. Graham, Bob, illus. 2004. (ENG., Illus.). 64p. (J). (gr. -1-3). 16.99 *(978-0-7636-2324-1(5))* Candlewick Pr.

Graham, Oakley. 3 Go to London. 2016. (Learning Journeys Ser.). (ENG.). 24p. (J). (gr. -1-k). 14.99 *(978-1-78445-312-1(9))* Top That! Publishing PLC GBR. Dist: Independent Pubs. Group.

Grahame, Kenneth. The Gates of Dawn. Johnson, Joe, tr. Plessix, Michel, illus. 2003. (Wind in the Willows Ser.: Vol. 3). (ENG.). 32p. (gr. 4-7). pap. 15.95 *(978-1-56163-245-9(7))* NBM Publishing Co.

—Mr. Toad, Vol. 2. Johnson, Joe, tr. from FRE. 2003. (Wind in the Willows Ser.: Vol. 2). (ENG., Illus.). 32p. (gr. 4-7). 15.95 *(978-1-56163-218-3(X))* NBM Publishing Co.

—The Open Road. Iosa, Ann, illus. 2003. 32p. (J). *(978-0-7607-3215-1(9))* Barnes & Noble, Inc.

—Royal Raven Counter. 2003. (Illus.). 208p. (J). 159.50 *(978-0-590-70244-7(0))* Scholastic, Inc.

—El Viento en los Sauces.Tr. of Wind in the Willows. (SPA.). 192p. (J). l. 9.50 *(978-84-372-1882-3(9))*II. 9.50 *(978-84-372-1883-0(7))* Santillana USA Publishing Co., Inc.

—The Wind in the Willows. 224p. 2005. 27.95 *(978-1-4218-0646-4(0))* 2004. pap. 12.95 *(978-1-59540-046-8(X))* 1st World Publishing, Inc. (1st World Library - Literary Society).

—The Wind in the Willows. 2006. (ENG.). 168p. per. 13.95 *(978-1-59818-946-9(8))*; 24.95 *(978-1-59818-378-8(8))* Aegypan.

—The Wind in the Willows. Bransom, Paul, illus. 2013. 176p. pap. 35.00 *(978-1-927558-25-6(5))* Birch Tree Publishing.

—The Wind in the Willows. Roberts, David, illus. 2013. (ENG.). 256p. (J). (gr. 5). 24.99 *(978-0-7636-6526-5(6))* Candlewick Pr.

—The Wind in the Willows. Moore, Inga, illus. 184p. 2009. pap. 12.99 *(978-0-7606-4211-5(7))* 2003. (ENG.). (J). 21.99 *(978-0-7636-2242-8(7))* Candlewick Pr.

—The Wind in the Willows. Daily, Don, illus. 2014. (ENG.). 64p. (J). (gr. -1). 18.95 *(978-1-60433-478-4(9),* Applesauce Pr.) Cider Mill Pr. Bk. Pubs., LLC.

—The Wind in the Willows. 2005. 96p. per. 5.95 *(978-1-4209-2239-4(4))* Digireads.com Publishing.

—The Wind in the Willows. Benson, Patrick, illus. 2009. (ENG.). 304p. pap. 11.99 *(978-0-00-647926-0(X))* HarperCollins Pubs.

—The Wind in the Willows, 1 vol. Mullarkey, Lisa, illus. 2010. (Calico Illustrated Classics Ser.: No. 1). (ENG.). 112p. (J). (gr. 3-6). 27.07 *(978-1-60270-713-9(8))* Magic Wagon.

—The Wind in the Willows. 2013. 258p. pap. 12.99 *(978-1-60796-643-2(3))* Meirovich, Igal.

—The Wind in the Willows. Taso, Alex, illus. 2006. (ENG.). 240p. (J). (gr. 5-18). 5.95 *(978-0-451-53014-1(4),* Signet) Penguin Publishing Group.

—The Wind in the Willows. 2005. (ENG.). 240p. (gr. 2-5). 14.00 *(978-0-14-303909-9(1),* Penguin Classics) Penguin Publishing Group.

—The Wind in the Willows. 2013. (ENG., Illus.). 288p. (J). (gr. 4-7). pap. 10.99 *(978-0-09-957294-7(X))* Random Hse. GBR. Dist: Independent Pubs. Group.

—The Wind in the Willows. 2013. (Easy Reader Classics Ser.). (ENG., Illus.). 192p. (J). (gr. 1-3). pap. 9.95 *(978-1-4549-0590-5(5))* Sterling Publishing Co., Inc.

—The Wind in the Willows. Ingpen, Robert R., illus. 2012. (Sterling Illustrated Classics Ser.). (ENG.). 224p. (J). (gr. 2-8). 19.95 *(978-1-4027-8283-1(7))* Sterling Publishing Co., Inc.

—The Wind in the Willows. Hanft, Joshua, ed. (Great Illustrated Classics Ser.: Vol. 39). (Illus.). 240p. (J). (gr. 3-6). 9.95 *(978-0-86611-990-0(6))* Waldman Publishing Corp.

—The Wind in the Willows. Moore, Inga, illus. 2009. (Candlewick Illustrated Classics Ser.). (ENG.). 184p. (J). (gr. 5-12). pap. 14.99 *(978-0-7636-4211-2(8))* Candlewick Pr.

—The Wind in the Willows. Akib, Jamel, illus. 2007. (Classic Starts(tm) Ser.). (ENG.). 160p. (J). (gr. 2-4). 6.95 *(978-1-4027-3696-4(7))* Sterling Publishing Co., Inc.

—The Wind in the Willows. Shepard, Ernest H., illus. 2007. 259p. (J). (gr. 5-6). reprint ed. lib. bdg. 22.95 *(978-0-88411-877-0(0))* Amereon Ltd.

—The Wind in the Willows. l.t. ed. 2007. (ENG.). 174p. pap. 21.99 *(978-1-4264-6997-8(7))* Creative Media Partners, LLC.

—The Wind in the Willows. Kliros, Thea, illus. abr. ed. 2011. (Dover Children's Thrift Classics Ser.). (ENG.). 96p. (J). (gr. 3-8). pap. 4.00 *(978-0-486-28600-6(2))* Dover Pubns., Inc.

—The Wind in the Willows. Barnhart, Nancy, illus. 2004. reprint ed. pap. 33.95 *(978-1-4179-1206-3(5))* Kessinger Publishing, LLC.

—The Wind in the Willows. l.t. ed. 2005. (ENG.). 334p. 20.95 *(978-0-7862-7489-5(1))* Thorndike Pr.

—The Wind in the Willows. 3rd ed. 2008. (ENG., Illus.). 80p. 10.00 *(978-0-19-479137-3(8))* Oxford Univ. Pr., Inc.

Grahame, Kenneth & Lerer, Seth. The Wind in the Willows. Lerer, Seth, ed. annot. ed. 2009. (ENG., Illus.). 359p. 35.00 *(978-0-674-03447-1(3),* 11318, Belknap Pr.) Harvard Univ. Pr.

Grahame, Kenneth & Todd, Justin. The Wind in the Willows. 2013. (Calla Editions Ser.). (ENG., Illus.). 208p. (J). (gr. 3). 30.00 *(978-1-60660-044-3(3))* Dover Pubns., Inc.

Grandmother Littlewolf. Littlestar, 1 vol. Macpherson, Carol, illus. 2010. (ENG.). 19p. pap. 24.95 *(978-1-4489-8619-4(2))* America Star Bks.

Grandpa Bob. The Dirty Nose Series. 2008. 284p. pap. 16.99 *(978-0-557-02079-9(4))* Lulu Pr., Inc.

Grant, Carrie and David. Elephant's Birthday Bells: Jump up & Join In. Busby, Ailie, illus. 2013. 32p. (J). pap. 7.99 *(978-1-61067-181-1(3))* Kane Miller.

—Lion's Speedy Sauce: Jump up & Join In. Busby, Ailie, illus. 2013. 32p. (J). pap. 7.99 *(978-1-61067-180-4(5))* Kane Miller.

Grant, Jacob. Little Bird's Bad Word. 2015. (ENG., Illus.). 32p. (J). (gr. -1-2). 16.99 *(978-1-250-05149-3(5),* 9781250051493) Feiwel & Friends.

Grant, Robert. Jack in the Bush or A Summer on a Salmon River. 2005. pap. 33.95 *(978-1-4179-5573-2(2))* Kessinger Publishing, LLC.

Graphman, W. M. . Matthew. Chel & Riley Adventures: The Great Mountain Adventure. 2011. 80p. (gr. 4-6). pap. 9.99 *(978-1-4567-5592-8(7))* AuthorHouse.

Graves, Mary. The Adventures of Peanut George. 2007. 72p. per. 19.95 *(978-1-4241-8274-9(3))* America Star Bks.

Gravett, Emily, illus. Little Mouse's Big Book of Beasts. 2016. (ENG.). 32p. (J). (gr. -1-3). 17.99 *(978-1-4814-3929-9(4),* Simon & Schuster Bks. For Young Readers) Simon & Schuster Bks. For Young Readers.

Gray, Kes. Daisy & the Trouble with Giants. Sharratt, Nick & Parsons, Garry, illus. 2010. (Daisy Ser.: 10). (ENG.). 256p. (J). (gr. 2-4). pap. 11.99 *(978-1-86230-495-6(5),* Red Fox) Random House Children's Books GBR. Dist: Independent Pubs. Group.

—Frog on a Log? Field, Jim, illus. 2015. (ENG.). 32p. (J). (gr. -1-k). 16.99 *(978-0-545-68791-1(8),* Scholastic Pr.) Scholastic, Inc.

Gray, Rita. When the World Is Dreaming. Pak, Kenard, illus. 2016. (ENG.). 32p. (J). (gr. -1-3). 17.99 *(978-0-544-58262-0(4),* HMH Books For Young Readers) Houghton Mifflin Harcourt Publishing Co.

Gray, Susannah. Alligators Coming! Jones, Zach, illus. 2012. 20p. pap. 15.00 *(978-1-4575-1316-9(1))* Dog Ear Publishing, LLC.

Graziani, Maria. The Adventures of Valeria Veterinarian: Las Aventuras de Valeria Veterinaria, 1. Elejalde, Eliana, illus. l.t. ed. 2004. (SPA.). 23p. (J). 7.00 *(978-0-9762361-0-8(9))* Ed. Acespanish S.A.C.- Lima, Peru.

The Great Paua Mystery: Kyss Series. 2003. (J). mass mkt. *(978-1-932233-69-8(5))* Aurora Libris Corp.

Greathouse, Rebecca. Katie & Riley's Magical Adventures: Journey to the Amazon. 2006. 48p. pap. 16.95 *(978-1-4241-5341-1(7))* America Star Bks.

Greaves, Nick. When Bat Was a Bird: And Other Animal Tales from Africa. du Plessis, David, illus. 2005. (ENG.). 144p. per. 15.00 *(978-1-86872-998-2(2))* Penguin Random House Grupo Editorial ESP. Dist: Casemate Pubs. & Bk. Distributors, LLC.

Green, Alison. The Fox in the Dark. Allwright, Deborah, illus. (ENG.). 32p. (J). (gr. -1-1). 2012. pap. 7.95 *(978-1-58925-437-4(6))* 2010. 15.95 *(978-1-58925-091-8(5))* Tiger Tales.

Green, Judith. A Family Secret. Hammah, Aisha, illus. 2013. 32p. pap. *(978-0-9810759-7-6(5))* WTL International.

Green, Poppy. The Clover Curse. Bell, Jennifer A., illus. 2016. (Adventures of Sophie Mouse Ser.: 7). (ENG.). 128p. (J). (gr. k-4). 16.99 *(978-1-4814-5184-0(7),* Little Simon) Little Simon.

—The Emerald Berries. Bell, Jennifer A., illus. 2015. (Adventures of Sophie Mouse Ser.: 2). (ENG.). 128p. (J). (gr. k-4). pap. 5.99 *(978-1-4814-2835-4(7),* Little Simon) Little Simon.

—The Great Big Paw Print. Bell, Jennifer A., illus. 2016. (Adventures of Sophie Mouse Ser.: 9). (ENG.). 128p. (J). (gr. k-4). 16.99 *(978-1-4814-7149-7(X),* Little Simon) Little Simon.

—Looking for Winston. Bell, Jennifer A., illus. 2015. (Adventures of Sophie Mouse Ser.: 4). (ENG.). 128p. (J). (gr. k-4). pap. 5.99 *(978-1-4814-3003-6(3),* Little Simon) Little Simon.

—The Maple Festival. Bell, Jennifer A., illus. 2015. (Adventures of Sophie Mouse Ser.: 5). (ENG.). 128p. (J). (gr. k-4). pap. 5.99 *(978-1-4814-4196-4(5),* Little Simon) Little Simon.

—A New Friend. Bell, Jennifer A., illus. 2015. (Adventures of Sophie Mouse Ser.: 1). (ENG.). 128p. (J). (gr. k-4). pap. 5.99 *(978-1-4814-2832-3(2),* Little Simon) Little Simon.

—Winter's No Time to Sleep! Bell, Jennifer A., illus. 2015. (Adventures of Sophie Mouse Ser.: 6). (ENG.). 128p. (J). (gr. k-4). pap. 5.99 *(978-1-4814-4199-5(X),* Little Simon) Little Simon.

Green, Rico. Super Animals! 2016. (Illus.). 23p. (J). *(978-1-4806-9876-5(8))* Random Hse., Inc.

—Super Animals! 2016. (Step into Reading Level 2 Ser.). lib. bdg. 14.75 *(978-0-606-38487-2(1))* Turtleback Bks.

Green, Vyridian E. Ruby Red Finds a New Home. 2015. (ENG.). 44p. (J). (gr. 2-3). mass mkt. 13.95 *(978-1-78455-723-2(4),* c74571f1-0c9e-4fc5-ac85-cb7c36470ecb) Austin, Stan AUS. Dist: Bookmasters Distribution.

Greenberg, Nicki. The Naughtiest Reindeer Goes South. 2017. (Naughtiest Reindeer Ser.: 3). (ENG.). 32p. (J). (gr. -1-1). 12.99 ***(978-1-76029-311-6(3))*** Allen & Unwin AUS. Dist: Independent Pubs. Group.

Greenburg, J. C. In the Desert. Gerardi, Jan, illus. 2008. (Andrew Lost Ser.: 17). (ENG.). 96p. (J). (gr. 1-4). per. 3.99 *(978-0-375-84667-0(0),* Random Hse. Bks. for Young Readers) Random Hse. Children's Bks.

—With the Frogs. Gerardi, Jan, illus. 2008. (Andrew Lost Ser.: 18). (ENG.). 96p. (J). (gr. 1-4). 3.99 *(978-0-375-84668-7(9),* Random Hse. Bks. for Young Readers) Random Hse. Children's Bks.

Greene, Rhonda Gowler. Noah & the Mighty Ark, 1 vol. Spengler, Margaret L., illus. 2014. (ENG.). 32p. (J). 9.99 *(978-0-310-73217-4(4))* Zonderkidz.

—Santa's Stuck. Cole, Henry, illus. 2006. (ENG.). 32p. (J). (gr. -1-3). pap. 5.99 *(978-0-14-240686-1(4),* Puffin Books) Penguin Young Readers Group.

Greene, Stephanie. Moose's Big Idea, 0 vols. Mathieu, Joe, illus. 2010. (Moose & Hildy Ser.: 0). (ENG.). 64p. (J). (gr. 1-4). pap. 6.99 *(978-0-7614-5698-8(8),* 9780761456988, Amazon Children's Publishing) Amazon Publishing.

Greenwood, Grace. History of My Pets by Grace Greenwood [Pseud.], with Engravings from Designs by Billings. 2006. 128p. per. 16.99 *(978-1-4255-0870-8(7))* Michigan Publishing.

Greive, Bradley Trevor. Every Day Is Christmas. 2007. (ENG., Illus.). 120p. 9.99 *(978-0-7407-6860-6(3))* Andrews McMeel Publishing.

Grey, C. R. Animas, Book Two Flight of the King. 2016. (Animas Ser.). (ENG.). 320p. (J). (gr. 3-7). pap. 7.99 *(978-1-4231-8467-6(X))* Hyperion Bks. for Children.

Grey, Mini. Three by the Sea. 2011. (ENG.). 32p. (J). (gr. k-3). 17.99 *(978-0-375-86784-2(8),* Knopf Bks. for Young Readers) Random Hse. Children's Bks.

Grieser, Jeanne K. Touch & Feel Petting Zoo. Pedler, Caroline, illus. 2010. (ENG.). 20p. (J). (gr. k — 1). bds. 9.95 *(978-1-4027-6524-7(X))* Sterling Publishing Co., Inc.

Griffiths, Andy. The Big Fat Cow That Goes Kapow. Denton, Terry, illus. 2010. (ENG.). 144p. (J). (gr. -1-3). pap. 7.99 *(978-0-312-65301-9(8),* 9780312653019) Square Fish.

—The Cat on the Mat Is Flat. Denton, Terry, illus. 2009. (ENG.). 192p. (J). (gr. -1-3). pap. 7.99 *(978-0-312-53584-1(8),* 9780312535841) Square Fish.

Grimm, J. & W. Sleeping Beauty. Dusikova, Maja, illus. 2012. (ENG.). 32p. (J). (gr. -1-3). 17.95 *(978-0-7358-4087-4(3))* North-South Bks., Inc.

Grimm, Jacob, et al. Animal Fables, 4 bks., Set. Roederer, Charlotte, illus. 2007. (Abbeville Classic Fairy Tales Ser.). (ENG.). 112p. (J). (gr. 1-2). 19.95 *(978-0-7892-0951-1(9))* Abbeville Pr., Inc.

Grimsdell, Jeremy. Bushbaby Night. 2006. (ENG., Illus.). 32p. per. 17.95 *(978-1-77009-056-9(8))* Jacana Media ZAF. Dist: Independent Pubs. Group.

Grindley, Sally. Danger in the Dust. 2013. (ENG.). 128p. (YA). (gr. 3-6). pap. 10.99 *(978-1-4088-1946-3(5),* 9781408819463, Bloomsbury USA Childrens) Bloomsbury Publishing USA.

—Feathers in the Wind. 2012. (ENG.). 128p. (YA). (gr. 5-7). pap. 10.99 *(978-1-4088-1947-0(3),* 9781408819470) Bloomsbury Publishing USA.

Grindley, Sally, compiled by. Classic Animal Stories. 2008. (ENG., Illus.). 160p. (J). (gr. 1-5). 19.95 *(978-0-7534-6210-2(9),* 9780753462102, Kingfisher) Roaring Brook Pr.

Griner, Jack. Creature or Critter? Chase, Linda, illus. 2005. 107p. (J). per. 12.95 *(978-1-59879-064-1(1))* Lifevest Publishing, Inc.

Grooms, Molly. We Are Horses. 2005. 40p. bds. *(978-90-5843-814-0(7))* YoYo Bks.

Grosgebauer, Clare Ham. Snickerdoodle's Star-Spangled Fourth of July! Rissing, Karen, illus. 4th ed. 2005. 36p. (J). (gr. -1-3). 12.99 *(978-0-9741888-6-7(7))* Small Wonders Enterprises.

Grotholt, Yannick. Playing with Fire. 2016. (LEGO Legends of Chima Graphic Novels Ser.: 6). (J). lib. bdg. 18.40 *(978-0-606-38370-7(0))* Turtleback Bks.

Group/McGraw-Hill, Wright. Animal Mysteries, 6 vols. (Wildcats Ser.). 32p. (gr. 2-8). *(978-0-322-05859-0(7))* Wright Group/McGraw-Hill.

Gruber, Daveda. Red Barn & other Short Stories. 2010. 45p. pap. 19.50 *(978-0-557-41998-2(0))* Lulu Pr., Inc.

Guarino, Deborah. Is Your Mama a Llama? Kellogg, Steven, illus. 2010. (Rise & Shine Ser.). (ENG.). 32p. (C). (gr. -1-3). pap. 11.95 *(978-0-439-59842-2(7))* National Geographic School Publishing, Inc.

—Is Your Mama a Llama? Kellogg, Steven, illus. 2006. (ENG.). (J). (gr. -1-3). 18.95 incl. audio compact disk *(978-0-439-87594-3(3))*; 9.99 *(978-0-439-87588-2(9))* Scholastic, Inc.

Gugler, Laurel Dee. There's a Billy Goat in the Garden. Beaton, Clare, illus. 2003. 32p. (J). (gr. -1-2). 14.99 *(978-1-84148-089-3(4))* Barefoot Bks., Inc.

Guibert, Emmanuel. The Teeth of the Rabbit. 2016. (Ariol Ser.: 9). (J). lib. bdg. 24.50 *(978-0-606-39481-9(8))* Turtleback Bks.

Guih, Line Carol. Momo the Historian: The Powerful Ivorian Boy. 2011. 64p. pap. 19.95 *(978-1-4560-2705-6(0))* America Star Bks.

Guillain, Charlotte. Animal Fairy Tales, 1 vol. Beacon, Dawn, illus. (Animal Fairy Tales Ser.). (ENG.). 24p. 2014. (gr. 1-2). lib. bdg. 119.95 *(978-1-4109-6116-7(8))* 2013. (gr. -1-2). pap. 32.45 *(978-1-4109-5033-8(6))* 2013. (gr. -1-2). pap. 162.45 *(978-1-4109-5526-5(5))* 2013. (gr. -1-2). pap. 324.70 *(978-1-4109-5527-2(3))* 2013. (gr. -1-2). lib. bdg. 119.95 *(978-1-4109-5027-7(1))* Heinemann-Raintree. (NA-r).

—Animal Fairy Tales Big Book Collection. Beacon, Dawn, illus. 2013. (Animal Fairy Tales Ser.). (ENG.). 24p. (gr. -1-2). 130.00 *(978-1-4109-5045-1(X),* NA-r) Heinemann-Raintree.

Gupta, Jennifer. Silly Turtle! That's Not on the Menu! 2008. 28p. pap. 13.99 *(978-1-4343-9183-4(3))* AuthorHouse.

Gupta, Ranu. Campfires & Creepy Calls. (J). 2006. (ENG.). 44p. per. *(978-1-933449-42-5(X))* 2005. (Illus.). 26p. per. 16.95 *(978-0-9761289-1-5(8))* Nightengale Pr.

Gürth, Per-Henrik. Snowy Sports: Ready, Set, Play! Gürth, Per-Henrik, illus. 2009. (ENG., Illus.). 24p. (J). (gr. -1-2). 14.95 *(978-1-55337-367-4(7))* Kids Can Pr., Ltd. CAN. Dist: Hachette Bk. Group.

Gutierrez, Lorna. Hello, Mr. Moon. Watkins, Laura, illus. 2016. (J). ***(978-1-4351-6412-3(1))*** Barnes & Noble, Inc.

Gutman, Anne & Hallensleben, Georg. Daddy Cuddles. 2005. (ENG., Illus.). 14p. (J). (gr. -1 — 1). bds. 5.95 *(978-0-8118-4674-5(1))* Chronicle Bks. LLC.

—Daddy Dreams. 2017. (ENG., Illus.). 14p. (J). (gr. -1 — 1). bds. 5.99 *(978-1-4521-5823-5(1))* Chronicle Bks. LLC.

—Mommy Loves. 2005. (ENG., Illus.). 14p. (J). (gr. -1 — 1). bds. 5.99 *(978-0-8118-4616-5(4))* Chronicle Bks. LLC.

Hader, Berta and Elmer. The Big Snow & Other Stories: A Treasury of Caldecott Award Winning Tales. 2015. (ENG., Illus.). 160p. (J). (gr. 1-4). pap. 14.99 *(978-0-486-78163-1(1))* Dover Pubns., Inc.

Hadithi, Mwenye. Sleepy Cheetah. 2017. (African Animal Tales Ser.). (ENG., Illus.). 32p. (J). (gr. -1-k). pap. 7.99 *(978-1-4449-2620-0(9))* Hachette Children's Group GBR. Dist: Hachette Bk. Group.

Hadithi, Mwenye & Kennaway, Adrienne. Handsome Hog. 2010. (ENG., Illus.). 32p. (J). (gr. k-2). pap. 10.99 *(978-0-340-97035-5(9))* Hodder & Stoughton GBR. Dist: Hachette Bk. Group.

Hadley, Caroline. Woodside; or, Look, Listen & Learn. 2007. (ENG., Illus.). 80p. per. *(978-1-4065-1557-2(4))* Dodo Pr.

Haesche, Richard, Sr. The Bull of Death. 2007. (ENG.). 218p. (YA). 10.50 *(978-0-9798536-4-7(6))* Kreative X-Pressions Pubns.

—Ghost Wolf. 2007. (ENG.). 207p. (YA). 10.99 *(978-0-9798536-5-4(6))* Kreative X-Pressions Pubns.

Hague, Michael & Hague, Kathleen. Michael Hague's Treasury of Christmas Carols. 2011. (ENG., Illus.). 48p. (J). 9.95 *(978-1-4027-7812-4(0))* Sterling Publishing Co., Inc.

Hale, Bruce. From Russia with Lunch: A Chet Gecko Mystery. 2010. (Chet Gecko Ser.: 14). (ENG., Illus.). 128p. (J). (gr. 2-5). pap. 6.99 *(978-0-547-32882-9(6))* Houghton Mifflin Harcourt Publishing Co.

—Give My Regrets to Broadway. 2005. (Chet Gecko Mystery Ser.). (Illus.). 115p. (gr. 3-7). 16.00 *(978-0-7569-5247-1(6))* Perfection Learning Corp.

—The Hamster of the Baskervilles. 2003. (Chet Gecko Ser.: 5). (ENG., Illus.). 144p. (J). (gr. 2-5). pap. 6.99 *(978-0-15-202509-0(X))* Houghton Mifflin Harcourt Publishing Co.

—Hiss Me Deadly. Hale, Bruce, illus. 2009. (Chet Gecko Ser.: 13). (ENG., Illus.). 128p. (J). (gr. 2-5). pap. 5.99 *(978-0-15-206424-2(9))* Houghton Mifflin Harcourt Publishing Co.

—The Malted Falcon. 2007. (Chet Gecko Mystery Ser.). (Illus.). 107p. (J). (gr. 4-7). pap. 6.60 *(978-1-4189-5239-6(7))* Harcourt Trade Pubs.

—The Malted Falcon. 2008. (Chet Gecko Ser.: 7). (ENG., Illus.). 128p. (J). (gr. 2-5). pap. 5.99 *(978-0-15-216712-7(9))* Houghton Mifflin Harcourt Publishing Co.

—Murder, My Tweet. 2005. (Chet Gecko Mystery Ser.). (Illus.). 117p. (gr. 3-7). 16.00 *(978-0-7569-5248-8(4))* Perfection Learning Corp.

—The Possum Always Rings Twice. Hale, Bruce, illus. 2007. (Chet Gecko Ser.: 11). (ENG., Illus.). 128p. (J). (gr. 2-5). pap. 5.99 *(978-0-15-205233-1(X))* Houghton Mifflin Harcourt Publishing Co.

—This Gum for Hire. 2007. (Chet Gecko Mystery Ser.). (Illus.). 115p. (J). (gr. 4-7). pap. 6.60 *(978-1-4189-5216-7(8))* Houghton Mifflin Harcourt Supplemental Pubs.

—Trouble Is My Beeswax. 2004. (Chet Gecko Mystery Ser.). (Illus.). 111p. (gr. 3-7). 16.00 *(978-0-7569-3486-0(5))* Perfection Learning Corp.

—Trouble Is My Beeswax: A Chet Gecko Mystery. 2004. (Chet Gecko Ser.: 8). (ENG., Illus.). 144p. (J). (gr. 2-5). pap. 6.99 *(978-0-15-216724-0(2))* Houghton Mifflin Harcourt Publishing Co.

Hale, Rachael. Furry Friends. rev. ed. 2007. (Paw Pals Ser.). (ENG., Illus.). 20p. (J). (gr. -1 — 1). bds. 6.99 *(978-0-316-11319-9(0))* Little, Brown Bks. for Young Readers.

—Somebunny Loves You. 2009. (Paw Pals Ser.). (ENG., Illus.). 20p. (J). (gr. -1 — 1). bds. 6.99 *(978-0-316-11370-0(0))* Little, Brown Bks. for Young Readers.

Hale, Shannon. Fire & Ice. 2014. (Spirit Animals Ser.: 4). (ENG., Illus.). 192p. (J). (gr. 3-7). 16.99 *(978-0-545-59974-0(1))*; 12.99 *(978-0-545-52246-5(3))* Scholastic, Inc.

Hall, Dorothy. The Story of Little Granny Munklestump. 2012. 44p. pap. 32.70 *(978-1-4691-4754-3(8))* Xlibris Corp.

Hall, Kirsten. The Gold Leaf. Forsythe, Matthew, illus. 2017. (ENG.). 48p. (J). (gr. -1-3). 18.95 *(978-1-59270-214-5(7))* Enchanted Lion Bks., LLC.

—Slider's Pet: All about Nature. Luedecke, Bev, illus. 2004. (Beastieville Ser.). (J). 19.50 *(978-0-516-22898-3(6),* Children's Pr.) Scholastic Library Publishing.

Hall, Leanne. Iris & the Tiger. 2016. (ENG., Illus.). 240p. (J). (gr. 3-7). 8.99 *(978-1-925240-79-5(7))* Text Publishing Co. AUS. Dist: Consortium Bk. Sales & Distribution.

Hall, Shirley. A Fairy Tale. 2012. 20p. pap. 15.99 *(978-1-4685-5242-3(2))* AuthorHouse.

Hall, Susan, illus. Dora's Cousin Diego. 2011. (Dora & Diego Ser.). (ENG.). 24p. (J). pap. 3.99 *(978-1-4424-1399-3(9),* Simon Spotlight/Nickelodeon) Simon Spotlight/Nickelodeon.

Hallensleben, Georg & Gutman, Anne. Mommy Snuggles. 2017. (ENG., Illus.). 14p. (J). (gr. -1 — 1). bds. 5.99 *(978-1-4521-5822-8(3))* Chronicle Bks. LLC.

Hamilton, Tim. Is That a Cat? 2015. (ENG., Illus.). 32p. (J). (gr. -1-3). 16.95 *(978-0-8234-3384-1(6))* Holiday Hse., Inc.

Hammerslough, Jane. Langur Monkey's Day. Buelt, Laura, illus. 2005. (Wild Reading Adventures! Ser.). (ENG.). 36p. (J). (gr. -1-2). 2.95 *(978-1-59249-143-8(X),* S7156); 9.95 *(978-1-59249-144-5(8),* PS7156) Soundprints.

—Langur Monkey's Day. Buelt, Laura, tr. Buelt, Laura, illus. 2005. (Wild Reading Adventures! Ser.). (ENG.). 36p. (J). (gr. -1-2). 15.95 *(978-1-59249-141-4(3),* B7106); pap. 6.95 *(978-1-59249-142-1(1),* S7106) Soundprints.

—Langur Monkey's Day. Buelt, Laura, illus. 2005. (Wild Reading Adventures! Ser.). (ENG.). 32p. (J). (gr. -1-2). 19.95 *(978-1-59249-221-3(5),* BC7106); 8.95 *(978-1-59249-222-0(3),* SC7106) Soundprints.

Hammerslough, Jane & Smithsonian Institution Staff. Langur Monkey's Day. Buelt, Laura, illus. rev. ed. 2008. (ENG.). 24p. (J). (gr. -1-3). 4.99 *(978-1-59249-706-5(3),* Little Soundprints) Soundprints.

Hampstead, Tom. The Kingdom of the Two Great Houses. 2011. 86p. pap. 10.95 *(978-1-60911-895-2(2),* Strategic Bk. Publishing) Strategic Book Publishing & Rights Agency (SBPRA).

Hankins, Larry. Stickboy at the Fair. 2011. 32p. pap. 24.95 *(978-1-4512-2206-7(8))* America Star Bks.

Hannan, Peter. The Greatest Snowman in the World! Hannan, Peter, illus. 2010. (ENG., Illus.). 32p. (J). (gr. -1-3). 16.99 *(978-0-06-128480-9(7))* HarperCollins Pubs.

—Petlandia. Hannan, Peter, illus. 2015. (ENG., Illus.). 144p. (J). (gr. 2-5). 8.99 *(978-0-545-16211-1(4),* Scholastic Pr.) Scholastic, Inc.

Hansen, Doug, illus. California, the Magic Island. 2016. 45p. (J). *(978-1-59714-332-5(4))* Heyday.

Hansen, Paul. The Adventures of Gray Tail. 2011. 20p. 13.99 *(978-1-4567-2958-5(6))* AuthorHouse.

Hanson, Anders. Iguana Mama, 1 vol. 2007. (Critter Chronicles Ser.). (ENG., Illus.). 24p. (J). (gr. k-3). lib. bdg.

24.21 *(978-1-59928-444-6(8)*, SandCastle) ABDO Publishing Co.

Hanson, Thor. Bartholomew Quill: A Crow Learns to Tell Who's Who in the Animal World. Amim, Dana, illus. 2016. (ENG.). 32p. (J). (gr. -1-3). 17.99 *(978-1-63217-046-0(9)*, Little Bigfoot) Sasquatch Bks.

Hanson, Vic Jan Fegley. A Healing Child's Friend. 2009. 64p. pap. 21.99 *(978-1-4415-1358-8(2))* Xlibris Corp.

Hanton, Sophie, illus. Hugs: Tuck Each Baby into a Loving Hug. 2010. (ENG.). 12p. (J). (gr. -1 — 1). 9.99 *(978-1-60169-020-3(7))* Innovative Kids.

Hao, K. T. The Magic Book. Ferri, Giuliano, illus. 2008. (ENG.). 32p. (J). (gr. -1). 16.50 *(978-1-933327-44-0(8))*; 15.95 *(978-1-933327-43-3(X))* Purple Bear Bks., Inc.

Hapka, Catherine, pseud & Disney Book Group Staff. The Amulet & the Anthem. Disney Storybook Art Team, illus. 2013. (ENG.). 24p. (J). (gr. -1-k). pap. 4.99 *(978-1-4231-8023-4(2))* Disney Pr.

Hapka, Cathy, pseud & Disney Book Group Staff. Sofia Makes a Friend. Disney Storybook Artists Staff, illus. 2013. (World of Reading Ser.). (ENG.). 32p. (J). (gr. -1-k). pap. 3.99 *(978-1-4231-6408-1(3))* Disney Pr.

Hapka, Cathy, pseud, et al. The Royal Slumber Party. Disney Storybook Art Team, illus. 2013. (ENG.). 24p. (J). (gr. -1-k). pap. 3.99 *(978-1-4231-6410-4(5))* Disney Pr.

Happy Books. A Day at the Circus. 2012. (Day at ... Bks.). (ENG., Illus.). 8p. (J). bds. 7.99 *(978-0-7641-6531-3(3))* Barron's Educational Series, Inc.

A Hare, a Hound & Shy Mousey Brown. 2013. (J). *(978-1-4351-4729-4(4))* Barnes & Noble, Inc.

Harley, Bill. Bear's All-Night Party. Ferreira, Melissa, illus. 2005. (ENG.). 32p. (J). (gr. -1-2). 15.95 *(978-0-87483-572-4(0))* August Hse. Pubs., Inc.

—Sitting down to Eat. 2005. (ENG., Illus.). 32p. (J). (gr. -1-3). pap. 8.95 *(978-0-87483-603-5(4))* August Hse. Pubs., Inc.

Harlow, Patty Fayerweather. Rock with Rodney and, Party with Perky to Preserve Wildlife. 2006. (Illus.). 96p. (J). per. 16.95 *(978-1-60002-002-5(X)*, 3583) Mountain Valley Publishing, LLC.

Harper, Jamie. Miss Mingo & the Fire Drill. Harper, Jamie, illus. 2012. (ENG., Illus.). 40p. (J). (gr. -1-3). pap. 6.99 *(978-0-7636-6086-4(8))* Candlewick Pr.

—Miss Mingo Weathers the Storm. Harper, Jamie, illus. (ENG., Illus.). 40p. (J). (gr. -1-3). 2017. 6.99 ***(978-0-7636-9514-9(9))*** 2012. 15.99 *(978-0-7636-4931-9(7))* Candlewick Pr.

Harper, Jessica. A Place Called Kindergarten. Karas, G. Brian, illus. 2008. (ENG.). 32p. (J). (gr. -1-k). pap. 6.99 *(978-0-14-241174-2(4)*, Puffin Books) Penguin Young Readers Group.

Harper, Jo. I Could Eat You Up! Chorao, Kay, illus. 2007. (ENG.). 32p. (J). (gr. -1-3). 16.95 *(978-0-8234-1733-9(6))* Holiday Hse., Inc.

Harrah, Judith. Come Inside the Ark. Foster, Jack, illus. 2012. (J). pap. 17.99 *(978-1-937331-12-2(1))* ShadeTree Publishing, LLC.

Harrington, Janice N. The Chicken-Chasing Queen of Lamar County. Jackson, Shelley, illus. 2007. (ENG.). 40p. (J). (gr. -1-3). 17.99 *(978-0-374-31251-0(6)*, 9780374312510, Farrar, Straus & Giroux (BYR)) Farrar, Straus & Giroux.

Harris, Don. The Bluebird Story. 2013. 32p. pap. 21.99 *(978-1-4797-7949-9(0))* Xlibris Corp.

Harris, Joel Chandler. Nights with Uncle Remus. 2008. 288p. 29.95 *(978-1-60664-915-2(9))*; pap. 15.95 *(978-1-60664-035-7(6))* Aegypan.

—Told by Uncle Remus: New Stories of the. 2006. (Illus.). pap. 31.95 *(978-1-4254-9964-8(3))* Kessinger Publishing, LLC.

—Uncle Remus His Songs & His Sayings. 2017. (ENG., Illus.). (YA). (gr. 4-12). cd-rom *(978-1-892824-57-8(4))* AFCHRON.

Harris, Joel Chandler, et al. The Classic Tales of Brer Rabbit. Daily, Don, illus. 2008. (ENG.). 56p. (J). (gr. 1-17). 9.95 *(978-0-7624-3219-6(5))* Running Pr. Bk. Pubs.

Harris, Patricia. Rowdy Racket in the Jungle. 2017. (Jungle Fun Ser.). 24p. (gr. 4-6). pap. 8.25 ***(978-1-5383-2128-7(9)***, PowerKids Pr.) Rosen Publishing Group, Inc., The.

Harris, Robie H. Maybe a Bear Ate It! Emberley, Michael, illus. 2008. (ENG.). 40p. (J). (gr. -1-k). 16.99 *(978-0-439-92961-5(X)*, Orchard Bks.) Scholastic, Inc.

Harris, Stephen. Ballroom Bonanza: A Hidden Pictures ABC Book. Rycroft, Nina, illus. 2010. (ENG.). 40p. (J). (gr. k-2). 16.95 *(978-0-8109-8842-2(9)*, Abrams Bks. for Young Readers) Abrams, Inc.

Harris, Trudy. The Clock Struck One: A Time-Telling Tale. Hartman, Carrie, illus. 2009. (Math Is Fun! Ser.). (ENG.). 32p. (gr. k-2). 19.99 *(978-0-8225-9067-5(0)*, Millbrook Pr.) Lerner Publishing Group.

Harrison, David L. A Monster Is Coming! Wilhelm, Hans, illus. 2011. (Step into Reading Ser.). (ENG.). 32p. (J). (gr. -1-1). pap. 3.99 *(978-0-375-86677-7(9)*, Random Hse. Bks. for Young Readers) Random Hse. Children's Bks.

Harrison, Hannah E. Bernice Gets Carried Away. 2015. (ENG., Illus.). 32p. (J). (gr. -1-k). 16.99 *(978-0-8037-3916-1(8)*, Dial Bks) Penguin Young Readers Group.

Harrison, Marie P. Sir Jack Cat & Friends. 2007. 50p. pap. 16.95 *(978-1-4241-6577-3(6))* America Star Bks.

Harrison, Paula. The Lost Gold. 2013. (Rescue Princesses Ser.: 7). lib. bdg. 14.75 *(978-0-606-32374-1(0)*, Turtleback) Turtleback Bks.

—The Magic Rings. 2013. (Rescue Princesses Ser.: 6). lib. bdg. 14.75 *(978-0-606-32373-4(2)*, Turtleback) Turtleback Bks.

—The Moonlight Mystery. 2013. (Rescue Princesses Ser.: 3). lib. bdg. 14.75 *(978-0-606-31988-1(3)*, Turtleback) Turtleback Bks.

—The Stolen Crystals. 2013. (Rescue Princesses Ser.: 4). lib. bdg. 14.75 *(978-0-606-31989-8(1)*, Turtleback) Turtleback Bks.

Harrison, Sarah. A Day at a Zoo. 2009. (Time Goes By Ser.). (ENG.). 24p. (gr. k-3). pap. 6.95 *(978-1-58013-800-0(4)*, First Avenue Editions) Lerner Publishing Group.

Harry, Rebecca. Snow Bunny's Christmas Gift. 2015. (ENG., Illus.). 32p. (J). (gr. -1-3). 17.99 *(978-1-4998-0164-4(5))* Little Bee Books Inc.

—Snow Bunny's Christmas Wish. Harry, Rebecca, illus. 2013. (ENG., Illus.). 32p. (J). (gr. -1-3). 16.99 *(978-0-545-54103-9(4)*, Orchard Bks.) Scholastic, Inc.

Hart, Alison. Taking the Reins. Studios, Arcana, illus. 2010. (ENG.). 120p. (YA). (gr. 3-18). pap. 8.95 *(978-1-59369-760-0(0))* American Girl Publishing, Inc.

Hart, Penny. Our Forever Home Tails of the Cozy Red Barn. 2012. 102p. pap. 9.99 *(978-1-61286-096-1(6))* Avid Readers Publishing Group.

Hart, Sue. Tales of the Full Moon. Harvey, Chris, illus. 2006. (ENG.). 96p. (J). (gr. 2-4). pap. 16.95 *(978-1-55591-582-7(5)*, 800.992.2908) Fulcrum Publishing.

Harter, Debbie. The Animal Boogie: Blackstone, Stella, illus. 2005. 32p. (J). (gr. -1-1). 14.99 *(978-1-84148-094-7(0))* Barefoot Bks., Inc.

—The Animal Boogie. Harter, Debbie, illus. (Illus.). 32p. pap. 6.99 *(978-1-84148-996-4(4))*; 2005. (ENG., (J). (gr. -1-2). 6.99 *(978-1-905236-60-2(3))* Barefoot Bks., Inc.

—The Animal Boogie. 2005. (ENG., Illus.). 32p. (J). (gr. -1-2). 9.99 *(978-1-905236-22-0(0))* Barefoot Bks., Inc.

—Animal Boogie. Penner, Fred, illus. 2011. (ENG.). 32p. (J). (gr. -1-2). 9.99 *(978-1-84686-620-3(0))* Barefoot Bks., Inc.

—Cha-Cha-Cha en la Selva. Canetti, Yanitzia, tr. Harter, Debbie, illus. 2003.Tr. of Animal Boogie. (SPA., Illus.). 32p. (J). pap. 6.99 *(978-1-84148-265-1(X))* Barefoot Bks., Inc.

—Cha-Cha-Cha en la Selva. Harter, Debbie, illus. 2003. (SPA., Illus.). 32p. (J). (gr. -1-1). 9.99 *(978-1-84148-913-1(1))* Barefoot Bks., Inc.

—Walking Through the Jungle. Harter, Debbie, illus. 2004. (ENG & PAN., Illus.). 32p. (J). pap. *(978-1-85269-851-5(9))* Mantra Lingua.

Harter, Debbie, illus. Walking Through the Jungle. 2004. 30p. (J). *(978-1-85269-807-2(1))*; *(978-1-85269-811-9(X))*; *(978-1-85269-826-3(8))*; *(978-1-85269-831-7(4))*; *(978-1-85269-841-6(1))*; *(978-1-85269-846-1(2))*; *(978-1-85269-856-0(X))*; *(978-1-85269-861-4(6))*; *(978-1-85269-866-9(7))*; (ENG & SPA.). *(978-1-85269-871-3(3))*; *(978-1-85269-876-8(4))*; *(978-1-85269-881-2(0))*; *(978-1-85269-886-7(1))* Mantra Lingua.

Harter, Debbie, tr. & illus. Walking Through the Jungle: Duke Ecur Neper Xhungel. Harter, Debbie, illus. 2004. 30p. (J). *(978-1-85269-806-5(3))* Mantra Lingua.

—Walking Through the Jungle: Marchant a Travers la Jungle. Harter, Debbie, illus. 2004. (ENG & FRE.). 32p. (J). pap. *(978-1-85269-836-2(5))* Mantra Lingua.

Hartman, Bob & Poole, Susie. The Lion Storyteller Book of Animal Tales. 2003. (ENG., Illus.). 120p. (J). 19.99 *(978-0-7459-4581-1(3)*, Lion Books) Lion Hudson PLC GBR. Dist: Trafalgar Square Publishing.

Harvey, Keith. Tiberius & the Chocolate Cake. Kirk, Heather, illus. 2010. (Tiberius Tales Ser.). 24p. (J). (gr. -1-2). pap. 8.15 *(978-1-60754-836-2(4))*; lib. bdg. 22.60 *(978-1-60754-832-4(1))* Windmill Bks.

Hasan, K. A. Rufus' Big Scare. Primmasone, Bruce, illus. 2011. 48p. pap. 24.95 *(978-1-4626-0660-3(1))* America Star Bks.

Hasany, Syed M. Stop the Train, Monkey! 2013. 28p. pap. 16.09 *(978-1-4669-7792-1(2))* Trafford Publishing.

Hatke, Ben. Julia's House for Lost Creatures. Hatke, Ben, illus. 2014. (ENG., Illus.). 40p. (J). (gr. k-3). 17.99 *(978-1-59643-866-8(5)*, 9781596438668, First Second Bks.) Roaring Brook Pr.

Haughton, Chris. Goodnight Everyone. Haughton, Chris, illus. 2016. (ENG., Illus.). 32p. (J). (-k). 15.99 *(978-0-7636-9079-3(1))* Candlewick Pr.

—Little Owl Lost. Haughton, Chris, illus. 2010. (ENG., Illus.). 32p. (J). (gr. -1-k). 14.99 *(978-0-7636-5022-3(6))* Candlewick Pr.

Hauser, Dana. Imagination's Amazing Planet, 1 vol. 2009. 24p. pap. 24.95 *(978-1-60703-873-3(0))* America Star Bks.

Have You Seen a Javelina? Individual Title Six-Packs. (Literatura 2000 Ser.). (gr. 2-3). 33.00 *(978-0-7635-0201-0(4))* Rigby Education.

Hawkins, Al. April Is Born: Adventures of a New Quarter Horse Filly. Erickson, Terri, illus. l.t. ed. 2004. 24p. (J). pap. 9.50 *(978-0-9640056-5-5(4))* Arrowhead Publishing.

Hawkins, Colin. Mr. Wolf's Week. 2005. (ENG., Illus.). 12p. (J). pap. 8.99 *(978-1-4052-0708-9(6))* Egmont Bks., Ltd. GBR. Dist: Trafalgar Square Publishing.

—Mr Wolf's Week. 2004. (ENG., Illus.). 32p. (J). pap. 9.99 *(978-1-4052-0683-9(7))* Egmont Bks., Ltd. GBR. Dist: Trafalgar Square Publishing.

—What's the Time,Mr. Wolf? Mini Pop-Up. 2005. (Illus.). 14p. (J). bds. 8.99 *(978-1-4052-0707-2(8))* Egmont Bks., Ltd. GBR. Dist: Trafalgar Square Publishing.

Hawkins, Emily. Good Night, Little Bunny: A Changing-Picture Book. Butler, John, illus. 2011. (ENG.). 14p. (J). (gr. -1-2). 12.99 *(978-0-7636-5263-0(6)*, Templar) Candlewick Pr.

Haws, Ileen. Feet are Neat. 2008. 40p. pap. 18.50 *(978-1-4357-4437-0(3))* Lulu Pr., Inc.

Hayashi, Leslie Ann. Fables Beneath the Rainbow. Bishop, Kathleen Wong, illus. 2005. 32p. (J). 14.95 *(978-1-56647-741-3(7)*, 477417) Mutual Publishing LLC.

Hayes, Denis. Silly Animal Stories for Kids. 2014. 80p. pap. 36.26 *(978-1-4828-9436-3(X))* Partridge Pub.

Hayes, Geoffrey. The Mystery of the Riverboat Robber. 2016. (Step into Reading Ser.). (ENG., Illus.). 48p. (J). (gr. k-3). lib. bdg. 12.99 *(978-0-375-97470-0(9)*, Random Hse. Bks. for Young Readers) Random Hse. Children's Bks.

Hays, Anna Jane. The Pup Speaks Up. Petrone, Valeria, illus. 2003. (Step into Reading Ser.). 32p. (gr. -1-1). 14.00 *(978-0-7569-1696-1(8))* Perfection Learning Corp.

—The Pup Speaks Up. Petrone, Valeria, illus. 2003. (Step into Reading Ser.). (ENG.). 32p. (J). (gr. -1-1). pap. 3.99 *(978-0-375-81232-3(6)*, Random Hse. Bks. for Young Readers) Random Hse. Children's Bks.

Hays, Ethel. One, Two, Buckle My Shoe: an Alphabet & Counting Book. 2012. (Shape Bks.). (ENG., Illus.). 16p. (J). pap. 9.95 *(978-1-59583-624-3(1))* Laughing Elephant.

Hayward, Linda. It Takes Three. Koontz, Robin Michal, illus. 2003. (Silly Millies Ser.: 3). 32p. (J). (gr. 1-3). pap. 5.95 *(978-0-7613-1798-2(8))*; lib. bdg. 17.90 *(978-0-7613-2902-2(1)*, Millbrook Pr.) Lerner Publishing Group.

Heale, Jay. African Animal Tales. 2004. (Illus.). 96p. *(978-1-86872-704-9(1))* Penguin Random House South Africa.

Hedgman, Janis. Party in the Garden. 2009. (Illus.). 52p. pap. *(978-1-84748-514-4(6))* Athena Pr.

Heible, Bev. A Collection of Short Tails. 2012. 60p. 17.95 *(978-1-62709-686-7(8))*; pap. 17.95 *(978-1-62709-343-9(5))* America Star Bks.

Heide, Florence Parry. Tales for the Perfect Child. Ruzzier, Sergio, illus. 2017. (ENG.). 112p. (J). (gr. 1-5). 16.99 *(978-1-4814-6379-9(9))* Simon & Schuster Children's Publishing.

Heide, Florence Parry & Clief, Sylvia Van. That's What Friends Are For. Meade, Holly, illus. 2007. 30p. (gr. -1-3). 17.00 *(978-0-7569-8126-6(3))* Perfection Learning Corp.

Heim, Robert. The Squeaking Earl. 2009. 32p. pap. 16.50 *(978-1-60693-711-2(1)*, Strategic Bk. Publishing) Strategic Book Publishing & Rights Agency (SBPRA).

Heine, Helme. Abenteurer. pap. 14.95 *(978-3-257-25106-7(8))* Diogenes Verlag AG CHE. Dist: Distribooks, Inc.

Heinz, Brian J. A Coming of Winter in the Adirondacks. Healy, Maggie, illus. 2011. 32p. (J). 19.95 *(978-1-59531-038-5(X))* North Country Bks., Inc.

Helft, Claude. Dulces Suenos, Teddy! (SPA.). 28p. (J). *(978-84-488-0684-2(0))* Beascoa, Ediciones S.A. ESP. Dist: Lectorum Pubns., Inc.

Hello Goodbye, 6 Pack. (Literatura 2000 Ser.). (gr. k-1). 28.00 *(978-0-7635-0056-6(9))* Rigby Education.

Helquist, Brett. Grumpy Goat. Helquist, Brett, illus. 2013. (ENG., Illus.). 40p. (J). (gr. -1-3). 17.99 *(978-0-06-113953-6(X))* HarperCollins Pubs.

Henderson, Barbara. Down in Mr Brown's Garden. 2009. 40p. pap. 14.75 *(978-1-60860-703-7(8)*, Strategic Bk. Publishing) Strategic Book Publishing & Rights Agency (SBPRA).

Henderson, Kris. Animalmericks! Burt, Kelly, illus. 2009. 32p. pap. 14.99 *(978-1-4389-4333-6(4))* AuthorHouse.

Henkes, Kevin. A Good Day. Henkes, Kevin, illus. 2007. (ENG., Illus.). 32p. (J). (gr. -1-3). 16.99 *(978-0-06-114018-1(X)*, Greenwillow Bks.) HarperCollins Pubs.

—A Good Day Board Book. Henkes, Kevin, illus. 2010. (ENG., Illus.). 28p. (J). (gr. -1 — 1). bds. 7.99 *(978-0-06-185778-2(5)*, Greenwillow Bks.) HarperCollins Pubs.

Henry, Jed. Cheer up, Mouse! Henry, Jed, illus. 2013. (ENG., Illus.). 32p. (J). (gr. -1-3). 12.99 *(978-0-547-68107-8(0))* Houghton Mifflin Harcourt Publishing Co.

—Good Night, Mouse! Henry, Jed, illus. 2013. (ENG., Illus.). 32p. (J). (gr. -1-3). 16.99 *(978-0-547-98156-7(2))* Houghton Mifflin Harcourt Publishing Co.

Henry, Steve. Happy Cat. 2013. (I Like to Read(r) Ser.). (ENG., Illus.). 24p. (J). (gr. -1-3). 14.95 *(978-0-8234-2659-1(9))* Holiday Hse., Inc.

Hereford, L. F. Gerry the Grape. Skardarasy, Doreen L., illus. 2005. (J). pap. *(978-0-9728969-9-3(6))* Acorn Publishing.

Hergé. Tintin: Descubro Los Animales. 2004. (SPA.). 24p. 19.95 *(978-1-59497-065-8(3))* Public Square Bks.

Herlihy, Matt & Clarke, Nzingha, selected by. Sweet Fancy Moses: Book 2. 2005. per. *(978-0-9767048-0-5(3))* Arts and Minds Studio Inc.

Herman-O'Neal, Jackie. Moctezuma's Zoo: A Tale from an Enchanted City. 2013. 28p. pap. 24.95 *(978-1-62709-271-5(4))* America Star Bks.

Herriot, James. James Herriot's Treasury of Inspirational Stories for Children: Warm & Joyful Tales by the Author of All Creatures Great & Small. Brown, Ruth & Barrett, Peter, illus. 2005. (ENG.). 260p. (J). (gr. -1-3). 22.99 *(978-0-312-34972-1(6)*, 9780312349721, St. Martin's Griffin) St. Martin's Pr.

Hest, Amy. Little Chick. Jeram, Anita, illus. 2009. (ENG.). 56p. (J). (gr. -1-k). 17.99 *(978-0-7636-2890-1(5))* Candlewick Pr.

—You Can Do It, Sam. Jeram, Anita, illus. 2007. (Sam Bks.). (ENG.). 32p. (J). (gr. -1-k). pap. 4.99 *(978-0-7636-3688-3(6))* Candlewick Pr.

Heurtelou, Maude. Makso. Louissaint, Louis, illus. (CRP.). 24p. (J). (gr. k-2). pap. 8.50 *(978-1-58432-005-0(2))* Educa Vision Inc.

Heywood, Grandma Geny. Stegot: ... the Great. 2012. 44p. pap. 20.99 *(978-1-4685-5914-9(1))* AuthorHouse.

Hibbeler, Stephen Paul. A Wonderful, Magical World. 2006. 48p. pap. 16.95 *(978-1-4241-2631-6(2))* PublishAmerica, Inc.

Higgins, Heather. The Foal That Doesn't Have a Family. 2007. 24p. 13.95 *(978-1-4303-2336-5(1))* Lulu Pr., Inc.

Higgins, Ryan T. Be Quiet! Higgins, Ryan T., illus. 2017. (ENG., Illus.). 40p. (J). (gr. -1-k). 17.99 *(978-1-4847-3162-8(X))* Hyperion Bks. for Children.

—Hotel Bruce. Higgins, Ryan T., illus. 2016. (Mother Bruce Ser.). (ENG., Illus.). 48p. (J). (gr. -1-k). 17.99 *(978-1-4847-4362-1(8))* Hyperion Bks. for Children.

Higginson, Sheryl. Dilbert's Pets, 1 vol. 2010. 94p. pap. 19.95 *(978-1-4489-5757-6(5))* America Star Bks.

Hildahl, Esther J. Meadow Pnd. 2012. (ENG.). pap. *(978-1-4675-2452-0(2))* Independent Pub.

Hileman, Jane & Pitt, Marilyn. Home Alone. Bianchi, John, illus. 2010. (1G Potato Chip Bks.). (ENG.). 12p. (J). (gr. k-1). pap. 5.99 *(978-1-61541-407-9(X))* American Reading Co.

Hilgendorf, L. B. Orville Oak & Friends. Dow, S. B., illus. 2005. 26p. (gr. -1-1). bds. 11.95 *(978-1-58275-149-8(8))* Black Forest Pr.

Hill, Annemarie. Meaty Treats. 2012. 16p. pap. 15.41 *(978-1-4669-3118-3(3))* Trafford Publishing.

Hill, Eric. Spot Goes to the Park. Hill, Eric, illus. 2005. (Spot Ser.). (ENG., Illus.). 24p. (J). (gr. -1 — 1). bds. 7.99 *(978-0-399-24363-9(1)*, Warne) Penguin Young Readers Group.

—Spot's Halloween. Hill, Eric, illus. 2003. (Spot Ser.). (ENG., Illus.). 14p. (J). (gr. -1 — 1). bds. 5.99 *(978-0-399-24185-7(X)*, Warne) Penguin Young Readers Group.

—Where's Spot? Hill, Eric, illus. 2003. (Spot Ser.). (Illus.). (J). (gr. -1 — 1). (SPA & ENG.). 12p. bds. 7.99 *(978-0-399-24046-1(2)*, 53517281); (ENG., 24p. 7.99 *(978-0-14-250126-9(3))* Penguin Young Readers Group. (Warne).

—Where's Spot? Hill, Eric, illus. 2007. (Spot Ser.). (ENG., Illus.). 18.00 *(978-0-7569-7965-2(X))* Perfection Learning Corp.

—Where's Spot? 2003. (Spot Ser.). 18.40 *(978-1-4176-3889-5(3)*, Turtleback) Turtleback Bks.

Hill, Karen. Cat Tails. 2010. 24p. 14.99 *(978-1-4567-0049-2(9))* AuthorHouse.

Hill, Meggan. Nico & Lola: Kindness Shared Between a Boy & a Dog. Graunke, Susan M., illus. 2010. (ENG.). 40p. (J). (gr. -1-3). 16.99 *(978-0-06-199043-4(4))* HarperCollins Pubs.

Hill, Ros. Unexpected Tails. 2010. (ENG.). 32p. (J). (gr. -1-3). 15.95 *(978-1-59687-861-7(4)*, Milk & Cookies) ibooks, Inc.

Hill, Susan. Ruby Bakes a Cake. Moore, Margie, illus. 2004. (My First I Can Read Bks.). 32p. (J). (gr. k-3). lib. bdg. 16.89 *(978-0-06-008976-4(8))* HarperCollins Pubs.

—Ruby Bakes a Cake, 1 vol. Moore, Margie, illus. 2010. (I Can Read! / Ruby Raccoon Ser.). (ENG.). 32p. (J). pap. 3.99 *(978-0-310-72022-5(2))* Zonderkidz.

—Ruby's Perfect Day, 1 vol. Moore, Margie, illus. 2010. (I Can Read! / Ruby Raccoon Ser.). (ENG.). 32p. (J). pap. 3.99 *(978-0-310-72024-9(9))* Zonderkidz.

Hill, Susanna Leonard. Can't Sleep Without Sheep. Wohnoutka, Mike, illus. 2010. (ENG.). 40p. (J). (gr. -1-1). 16.99 *(978-0-8027-2066-5(8)*, 9780802720665, Bloomsbury USA Childrens) Bloomsbury Publishing USA.

Hillenbrand, Jane. What a Treasure! Hillenbrand, Will, illus. 2017. (ENG.). 24p. (J). (gr. -1-1). bds. 7.99 *(978-0-8234-3763-4(9))* Holiday Hse., Inc.

Hillerman, Tony. Buster Mesquite's Cowboy Band. 2006. (J). reprint ed. lib. bdg. 14.95 *(978-0-914001-12-6(4))* Sidewinder Publishing LLC.

Hillert, Margaret. The Purple Pussycat. Cosgrove, Kate, illus. 2016. (BeginningtoRead Ser.). (ENG.). 32p. (J). (gr. -1-2). pap. 11.94 *(978-1-60357-944-5(3))*; 21st ed. (gr. k-2). 22.60 *(978-1-59953-803-7(2))* Norwood Hse. Pr.

—Who Goes to School? Woodworth, Viki, illus. 2016. (BeginningtoRead Ser.). (ENG.). 32p. (J). (gr. -1-2). pap. 11.94 *(978-1-60357-949-0(4))*; (gr. k-2). 22.60 *(978-1-59953-808-2(3))* Norwood Hse. Pr.

Hilliard, Michael. Butter Bee Grows up Too Fast! 2010. 20p. pap. 12.49 *(978-1-4490-7300-8(X))* AuthorHouse.

Hillman, Iris H. Back Yard Critters: Things That Go Bump in the Night. 2010. 28p. 16.09 *(978-1-4269-4264-8(8))* Trafford Publishing.

Hills, Tad. R Is for Rocket: an ABC Book. 2015. (ENG., Illus.). 32p. (J). (gr. -1-2). 17.99 *(978-0-553-52228-0(0)*, Schwartz & Wade Bks.) Random Hse. Children's Bks.

Himmelman, John. Bunjitsu Bunny Jumps to the Moon. Himmelman, John, illus. 2016. (Bunjitsu Bunny Ser.). (ENG., Illus.). 128p. (J). 13.99 *(978-1-62779-732-0(7)*, 9781627797320, Holt, Henry & Co. Bks. For Young Readers) Holt, Henry & Co.

—Bunjitsu Bunny's Best Move. Himmelman, John, illus. 2015. (Bunjitsu Bunny Ser.: 2). (ENG., Illus.). 128p. (J). (gr. 1-3). 13.99 *(978-0-8050-9971-3(9)*, 9780805099713, Holt, Henry & Co. Bks. For Young Readers) Holt, Henry & Co.

—Tales of Bunjitsu Bunny. Himmelman, John, illus. 2014. (Bunjitsu Bunny Ser.: 1). (ENG., Illus.). 128p. (J). (gr. 1-3). 13.99 *(978-0-8050-9970-6(0)*, 9780805099706, Holt, Henry & Co. Bks. For Young Readers) Holt, Henry & Co.

Hinchcliffe, L. T. For the Love of Prudence Possum. 2008. 76p. pap. 15.50 *(978-1-60693-136-3(9)*, Eloquent Bks.) Strategic Book Publishing & Rights Agency (SBPRA).

Hincher, Theresa B. Baldy the Balloon. 2005. 16p. (J). (gr. -1). per. 13.95 *(978-0-933767-06-5(4))* Pex Publishing Co.

Hinkel, Patricia. Frog in My Bucket. 2012. 16p. pap. 15.99 *(978-1-4772-4815-7(3))* AuthorHouse.

Hix, Melvin. The Magic Speech Flower: Or Little Luke & His Animal Friends. 2007. (ENG.). 110p. pap. 18.99 *(978-1-4346-0790-4(9))*; 114p. pap. 19.99 *(978-1-4346-0797-3(6))* Creative Media Partners, LLC.

Ho, Jannie. The Great Matzoh Hunt. Ho, Jannie, illus. 2010. (ENG., Illus.). 12p. (J). (gr. -1-k). 6.99 *(978-0-8431-8969-8(X)*, Price Stern Sloan) Penguin Young Readers Group.

Hoban, Tana. I Wonder. 2003. (Green Light Readers Level 2 Ser.). (ENG., Illus.). 24p. (J). (gr. -1-3). pap. 3.95 *(978-0-15-204835-8(9))* Houghton Mifflin Harcourt Publishing Co.

—I Wonder. 2003. (Green Light Readers — Level 2 Ser.). (gr. k-3). lib. bdg. 13.50 *(978-0-613-64525-6(1)*, Turtleback) Turtleback Bks.

Hobbs-Wyatt, Debz, ed. Wild N Free. 2011. (Illus.). 150p. pap. *(978-0-9568939-4-9(5))* Paws n Claws Publishing.

Hoberman, Mary Ann. You Read to Me, I'll Read to You: Very Short Fables to Read Together. Emberley, Michael, illus. 2013. (You Read to Me, I'll Read to You Ser.). (ENG.). 32p. (J). (gr. -1-3). 7.00 *(978-0-316-21847-4(2))* Little, Brown Bks. for Young Readers.

Hobnob the Troll: Set B Individual Title Six-Packs. (Supersonic Phonics Ser.). (gr. k-3). 29.00 *(978-0-7635-0539-4(0))* Rigby Education.

Hobson, Mary Daniel & Rauh, Anna Isabel. The Wolf Who Ate the Sky. Hobson, Charles, illus. 2015. (J). *(978-1-59714-298-4(0))* Heyday.

Hocknell, Barbara. Gifts for God. 2007. (Illus.). 56p. per. *(978-1-84748-131-3(0))* Athena Pr.

Hodgkinson, Jo. The Talent Show. Hodgkinson, Jo, illus. 2011. (ENG., Illus.). 32p. (J). (gr. -1-3). 16.95 *(978-0-7613-7487-9(6))* Lerner Publishing Group.

Hodgkinson, Leigh. Limelight Larry. Hodgkinson, Leigh, illus. 2011. (ENG., Illus.). 32p. (J). *(978-1-58925-102-1(4))* Tiger Tales.

Hodgson, Mona Gansberg. Bedtime in the Southwest. Graef, Renee, illus. 2004. (ENG.). 32p. (J). (gr. -1-k). 14.95 *(978-0-87358-871-3(1))* Cooper Square Publishing Llc.

—Desert Critter Friends Set, 12 vols. (Desert Critter Friends Ser.). (J). 54.99 *(978-0-7586-0007-3(0))* Concordia Publishing Hse.

Hoeye, Michael. The Sands of Time. 2007. (ENG.). 288p. (J). (gr. 3-7). pap. 8.99 *(978-0-14-240983-1(9)*, Puffin Books) Penguin Young Readers Group.

—The Sands of Time: A Hermux Tantamoq AdventureTM. 2004. 288p. (J). (gr. 5-9). pap. 40.00 incl. audio *(978-1-4000-9016-7(4)*, Listening Library) Random Hse. Audio Publishing Group.

—Time Stops for No Mouse. 2007. (ENG.). 272p. (J). (gr. 3-7). 7.99 *(978-0-14-240984-8(7)*, Puffin Books) Penguin Young Readers Group.

—Time Stops for No Mouse. 2003. (Hermux Tantamoq Adventure Ser.). (Illus.). 250p. (J). (gr. 4-7). 18.40 *(978-0-613-62122-9(0)*, Turtleback) Turtleback Bks.

Hofmann-Maniyar, Ariane. Ice in the Jungle. Hofmann-Maniyar, Ariane, illus. 2015. (Child's Play Library).

A B

(ENG., Illus.). 32p. (J). (978-1-84643-731-1(8)) Child's Play International Ltd.

Holbrook, Florence. Why the Crocodile Has a Wide Mouth: And Other Nature Myths. 2004. (Dover Children's Classics Ser.). (ENG., Illus.). 128p. (gr. 3-5). pap. 5.95 (978-0-486-43649-4(7)) Dover Pubns., Inc.

Holden, Pam. Animal Art, 6 vols. Storey, Jim, illus. 2009. (Red Rocket Readers Ser.). (ENG.). 16p. (gr. 1-1). pap. (978-1-877419-73-7(7), Red Rocket Readers) Flying Start Bks.

—Greedy Gus the Pirate, 6 pack. Whimp, Pauline, illus. 2009. (Red Rocket Readers Ser.). (ENG.). 16p. (gr. 2-2). pap. (978-1-877363-74-0(X)) Flying Start Bks.

—Thirsty Baby Elephant. 2015. (ENG., Illus.). 16p. (-1). pap. (978-1-77654-076-1(X), Red Rocket Readers) Flying Start Bks.

Holloway, Jimmie Frances. Little Bit Finds His Kin or Does He? Hum! 2011. 24p. pap. 15.99 (978-1-4568-3919-2(5)) Xlibris Corp.

Holm, Jennifer L. & Holm, Matthew. Babymouse Goes for the Gold. Holm, Jennifer L. & Holm, Matthew, illus. 2016. (Babymouse Ser.: 20). (ENG., Illus.). 96p. (J). (gr. 2-5). pap. 6.99 (978-0-307-93163-4(3), Random Hse. Bks. for Young Readers) Random Hse. Children's Bks.

—Babymouse Tales from the Locker Presents Lights, Camera, Messy Whiskers. 2017. (Babymouse Tales from the Locker Ser.: 1). (ENG., Illus.). 208p. (J). (gr. 3-7). 13.99 (978-0-399-55438-4(6), Random Hse. Bks. for Young Readers) Random Hse. Children's Bks.

—Bad Babysitter. Holm, Jennifer L. & Holm, Matthew, illus. 2015. (Babymouse Ser.: 19). (ENG., Illus.). 96p. (J). (gr. 2-5). pap. 6.99 (978-0-307-93162-7(5), Random Hse. Bks. for Young Readers) Random Hse. Children's Bks.

—Burns Rubber. 2010. (Babymouse Ser.: 12). lib. bdg. 17.20 (978-0-606-07025-6(7), Turtleback) Turtleback Bks.

—Camp Babymouse. 2007. (Babymouse Ser.: 6). lib. bdg. 17.20 (978-1-4177-8070-9(3), Turtleback) Turtleback Bks.

—Captain Disaster. 2012. (Squish Ser.: 4). lib. bdg. 17.20 (978-0-606-26812-7(X), Turtleback) Turtleback Bks.

—Dragonslayer. Holm, Jennifer L. & Holm, Matthew, illus. 2009. (Babymouse Ser.: 11). (ENG., Illus.). 96p. (J). (gr. 2-5). pap. 6.99 (978-0-375-85712-6(5)); lib. bdg. 12.99 (978-0-375-95712-3(X)) Random Hse. Children's Bks. (Random Hse. Bks. for Young Readers).

—Mad Scientist. Holm, Jennifer L. & Holm, Matthew, illus. 2011. (Babymouse Ser.: No. 14). (ENG., Illus.). 96p. (J). (gr. 2-5). pap. 6.99 (978-0-375-86574-9(8)); lib. bdg. 12.99 (978-0-375-96574-6(2)) Random Hse. Children's Bks. (Random Hse. Bks. for Young Readers).

—The Musical. Holm, Jennifer L. & Holm, Matthew, illus. 2009. (Babymouse Ser.: 10). (ENG., Illus.). 96p. (J). (gr. 2-5). pap. 6.99 (978-0-375-84388-4(4)); lib. bdg. 12.99 (978-0-375-93791-0(9)) Random Hse. Children's Bks. (Random Hse. Bks. for Young Readers).

—Our Hero. 2005. (Babymouse Ser.: 2). (ENG., Illus.). 96p. (J). (gr. 2-5). pap. 6.99 (978-0-375-83230-7(0)); lib. bdg. 12.99 (978-0-375-93230-4(5)) Random Hse. Children's Bks. (Random Hse. Bks. for Young Readers).

—Queen of the World! 2005. (Babymouse Ser.: 1). (ENG., Illus.). 96p. (J). (gr. 2-5). pap. 6.99 (978-0-375-83229-1(7)); lib. bdg. 12.99 (978-0-375-93229-8(1)) Random Hse. Children's Bks. (Random Hse. Bks. for Young Readers).

—Super Amoeba. Holm, Jennifer L. & Holm, Matthew, illus. 2011. (Squish Ser.: No. 1). (ENG., Illus.). 96p. (J). (gr. 3-7). pap. 6.99 (978-0-375-84389-1(2)); lib. bdg. 12.99 (978-0-375-93783-5(8)) Random Hse. Children's Bks. (Random Hse. Bks. for Young Readers).

—A Very Babymouse Christmas. Holm, Jennifer L. & Holm, Matthew, illus. 2011. (Babymouse Ser.: 15). (ENG., Illus.). 96p. (J). (gr. 2-5). 12.99 (978-0-375-96779-5(6)); pap. 6.99 (978-0-375-86779-8(1)) Random Hse. Children's Bks. (Random Hse. Bks. for Young Readers).

Holt, Jenny. Who-O-o's Awake in the Desert. 2017. (ENG., Illus.). (J). (gr. -1-2). 12.95 **(978-1-941384-31-2(5))** Sunbelt Pubns., Inc.

Holtfreter, Nastja, illus. Push Puzzles: in the Woods. 2016. (ENG.). 10p. (J). (gr. -1 — 1). bds. 7.99 (978-1-4998-0349-5(4)) Little Bee Books Inc.

Holub, Joan. Shampoodle. Bowers, Tim, illus. 2009. (Step into Reading Ser.). (ENG.). 32p. (J). (gr. -1-1). pap. 3.99 (978-0-375-85576-4(9), Random Hse. Bks. for Young Readers) Random Hse. Children's Bks.

Holzwarth, Werner. I Wish I Were A... Jeschke, Stefanie, illus. 2013. (ENG.). 40p. (J). (gr. -1-k). 16.95 (978-1-62087-993-1(X), 620993, Sky Pony Pr.) Skyhorse Publishing Co., Inc.

Homer & Martín, Jean. Cuentos y Leyendas de la Ilíada. Campos, Paz, tr. 2nd ed. 2003. (Fábles & Legends Ser.). (SPA., Illus.). 116p. (J). 9.95 (978-84-239-6349-2(7)) Espasa Calpe, S.A. ESP. Dist: Planeta Publishing Corp.

Honey, Elizabeth. Hop up! Wriggle Over! 2017. (ENG., Illus.). 40p. (J). (gr. -1-3). 16.99 (978-0-544-79084-1(7), Clarion Bks.) Houghton Mifflin Harcourt Trade & Reference Pubs.

The Honey Tree, 6 Packs. (Literatura 2000 Ser.). (gr. 2-3). 33.00 (978-0-7635-0262-1(6)) Rigby Education.

Hong, Catherine Thao. The Adventures of Miss Turtle. Pipe, Jasper, illus. 2012. 24p. (J). pap. (978-0-9873790-0-9(3)) Icky Grass Books.

Honigsberg, Peter Jan. Armful of Memories. Morse, Tony, illus. 2004. 32p. 17.95 (978-1-57143-089-2(X)) RDR Bks.

Hood-Caddy, Karen. Howl. 2011. (Wild Place Adventure Ser.: 1). (ENG.). 256p. (J). (gr. 6-8). pap. 9.99 (978-1-926607-25-2(2)) Dundurn CAN. Dist: Ingram Publisher Services.

—The Truth about Brave. 2014. (Wild Place Adventure Ser.: 2). (ENG.). 224p. (J). pap. 12.99 (978-1-4597-1868-5(2), 9781459718685) Dundurn CAN. Dist: Ingram Publisher Services.

Hood, Karen Jean Matsko. Tanka Thoughts: A Collection of Poetry, bk. 11. Whispering Pine Press International, ed. Artistic Design Service Staff, illus. l.t. ed. 2014. (Hood Poetry Ser.). 224p. pap. 22.95 (978-1-59808-648-5(0)) Whispering Pine Pr. International, Inc.

Hood, Susan. Spike: The Mixed-Up Monster. Sweet, Melissa, illus. 2012. (ENG.). 40p. (J). (gr. -1-3). 16.99 (978-1-4424-0601-8(1), Simon & Schuster/Paula Wiseman Bks.) Simon & Schuster/Paula Wiseman Bks.

Hoover, Helen. Great Wolf & the Good Woodsman. Bowen, Betsy, illus. 2005. (Fesler-Lampert Minnesota Heritage Ser.). 40p. (J). (gr. -1-7). 14.95 (978-0-8166-4445-2(4)) Univ. of Minnesota Pr.

Hopgood, Sally. In the Forest: A Pull-The-Tab Book. Hinton, Stephanie, illus. 2014. (J). (978-1-4351-5689-0(7)) Barnes & Noble, Inc.

Hopkins, Lee Bennett. Mother Goose & Her Animal Friends. Fehlau, Dagmar et al, illus. 2005. (Lee Bennett Hopkins Mother Goose Ser.). (YA). (gr. -1-1). 76.50 (978-0-8215-0470-3(3)) Sadlier, William H. Inc.

Hopkins, William J. The Sandman: More Farm Stories (Yesterday's Classics) Williamson, Ada Clendenin, illus. 2009. 150p. pap. 8.95 (978-1-59915-301-8(7)) Yesterday's Classics.

Horácek, Petr. Suzy Goose & the Christmas Star: Midi Edition. Horácek, Petr, illus. 2010. (ENG., Illus.). 32p. (J). (gr. -1-2). 7.99 (978-0-7636-5000-1(5)) Candlewick Pr.

Horender, Philip M. Head West, Young Mouse: Transcontinental Railroad Traveler, 1 vol. Wolek, Guy, illus. 2013. (Maximilian P. Mouse, Time Traveler Ser.). (ENG.). 112p. (J). (gr. 3-6). lib. bdg. 27.07 (978-1-61641-959-2(8), Calico Chapter Bks) Magic Wagon.

—Patriotic Mouse: Boston Tea Party Participant, 1 vol. Wolek, Guy, illus. 2013. (Maximilian P. Mouse, Time Traveler Ser.). (ENG.). 112p. (J). (gr. 3-6). lib. bdg. 27.07 (978-1-61641-957-8(1), Calico Chapter Bks) Magic Wagon.

—Yankee Mouse: Gettysburg Address Observer, 1 vol. Wolek, Guy, illus. 2013. (Maximilian P. Mouse, Time Traveler Ser.). (ENG.). 112p. (J). (gr. 3-6). lib. bdg. 27.07 (978-1-61641-958-5(X), Calico Chapter Bks) Magic Wagon.

Horton, Michael. Original Animals. 2003. (J). per. 13.95 (978-0-943864-49-5(6)) Davenport, May Pubs.

Hossfeld, Harald. Rapacious Kings Sagacious Kids. 2010. 186p. pap. (978-3-8391-4994-2(0)) Books on Demand GmbH.

Housel, Debra. Charlotte's Web: An Instructional Guide for Literature. rev. ed. 2015. (Great Works). (ENG., Illus.). 72p. (gr. 3-5). pap. 9.99 (978-1-4807-6995-3(9)) Shell Educational Publishing.

Houseman, D. L. Harvey & His Friends Great Fishing Adventure. 2010. pap. 18.95 (978-0-578-05355-4(1)) Stuff on Paper.

Howard, Kate. The Duck Vinci Code & Other Tales. 2013. (ENG.). 112p. (J). (gr. 2-5). pap. 4.99 (978-0-545-49291-1(2)) Scholastic, Inc.

Howe, Deborah & Howe, James. A Rabbit-Tale of Mystery. unabr. ed. 2004. (Bunnicula Ser.). 98p. (J). (gr. 3-7). pap. 29.00 incl. audio (978-0-8072-8204-5(9), YYA139SP, Listening Library) Random Hse. Audio Publishing Group.

Howe, James. The Celery Stalks at Midnight. unabr. ed. 2004. (Bunnicula Ser.). 111p. (J). (gr. 3-7). pap. 29.00 incl. audio (978-0-8072-8357-8(6), YA173SP, Listening Library) Random Hse. Audio Publishing Group.

—Creepy-Crawly Birthday. Mack, Jeff, illus. (Bunnicula & Friends Ser.: 6). (ENG.). 48p. (J). (gr. 1-3). 2008. pap. 3.99 (978-0-689-85753-9(5)) 2007. 16.99 (978-0-689-85728-7(4)) Simon Spotlight. (Simon Spotlight).

—Nighty-Nightmare. unabr. ed. 2004. (Bunnicula Ser.). 128p. (J). (gr. 3-7). pap. 29.00 incl. audio (978-0-8072-8397-4(5), YA201SP, Listening Library) Random Hse. Audio Publishing Group.

Howell, Heather. Emanuele Goes to the Zoo. 2010. 20p. 10.49 (978-1-4490-4816-7(1)) AuthorHouse.

Howington, C. D. Aunt Cindy's House. 2011. 96p. pap. 19.95 (978-1-4626-1113-3(3)) America Star Bks.

Huang, Yu-Hsuan, illus. Baby Bear: Finger Puppet Book. 2016. (ENG.). 12p. (J). (gr. -1 — 1). bds. 6.99 (978-1-4521-4235-7(1)) Chronicle Bks. LLC.

Hubery, Julia. My Daddy. Elliot, Rebecca, illus. 2014. (J). (978-1-4351-5507-7(6)) Barnes & Noble, Inc.

Hubner, Franz. Moaning Morris. Kessler, Mario, illus. 2004. 32p. (J). pap. (978-81-87649-93-9(3)) Katha.

Hudson, Charlotte & Gormley, Greg. Monkey Words. 2003. (ENG., Illus.). 32p. (J). 19.99 (978-0-370-32636-8(9)) Random Hse. GBR. Dist: Independent Pubs. Group.

Hudson, Katy. Too Many Carrots. 2016. (ENG., Illus.). 32p. (gr. -1-1). 14.95 (978-1-62370-638-8(6)) Capstone Young Readers of Coughlan Cos.

Hughes, Dawn Marie. Oakley Farm Friends. 2006. 83p. pap. 16.95 (978-1-4241-2094-9(2)) PublishAmerica, Inc.

Hughes, Devon. Unnaturals: the Battle Begins. Richardson, Owen, illus. 2017. (Unnaturals Ser.: 1). 368p. (J). (gr. 3-7). pap. 6.99 (978-0-06-225755-0(2), Tegen, Katherine Bks) HarperCollins Pubs.

Hughes, Jennifer L. The Nature of Numbers. 2008. 23p. pap. 24.95 (978-1-60672-827-7(X)) America Star Bks.

Hughes, John H. B. Jiminy Tish - the Animal's Christmas. 2009. 61p. pap. 39.95 (978-1-4092-9279-1(7)) Lulu Pr., Inc.

Hughes, Laura. We're Going on an Egg Hunt. Hughes, Laura, illus. 2017. (ENG., Illus.). 24p. (J). 17.99 (978-1-68119-314-4(0), 9781681193144, Bloomsbury USA Childrens) Bloomsbury Publishing USA.

Hughes, Marghanita. Toffee at Home on the Farm. (Illus.). 20p. 13.95 (978-1-899827-50-3(1)) Scottish Children's Pr. GBR. Dist: Wilson & Assocs.

—Toffee Goes Camping. (Illus.). 20p. 13.95 (978-1-899827-51-0(X)) Scottish Children's Pr. GBR. Dist: Wilson & Assocs.

Hughes, Ted & Quarto Generic Staff. How the Whale Became: And Other Stories. Morris, Jackie, illus. 2012. (ENG.). 96p. (J). (gr. k-3). pap. 14.99 (978-1-84507-928-4(0), Frances Lincoln) Quarto Publishing Group UK GBR. Dist: Hachette Bk. Group.

Huguet, Andrea L. When God Turns off the Lights. 2008. 19p. pap. 24.95 (978-1-60672-922-9(5)) PublishAmerica, Inc.

Hulin, Pamela. Down under in Australia. Mendoza, Carlos, illus. 2007. 20p. per. 24.95 (978-1-4241-8929-8(2)) America Star Bks.

Huneck, Stephen. Sally in the Forest. 2014. (Sally Board Bks.). (ENG., Illus.). 20p. (J). (gr. -1 — 1). bds. 7.95 (978-1-4197-1226-5(8), Abrams Appleseed) Abrams, Inc.

Hunt, Bonnie. The Missing Chimp: A Grayson Twins Adventures, 1 vol. 2009. 100p. pap. 19.95 (978-1-60813-481-6(4)) America Star Bks.

Hunter, Anne. Cricket Song. 2016. (ENG., Illus.). 32p. (J). (gr. -1-3). 16.99 (978-0-544-58259-0(4), HMH Books For Young Readers) Houghton Mifflin Harcourt Publishing Co.

Hunter, Elizabeth. Home Oasis. 2009. (Illus.). 36p. pap. 15.49 (978-1-4389-6284-9(3)) AuthorHouse.

Hunter, Erin. Broken Pride. Richardson, Owen, illus. 2017. (Bravelands Ser.: 1). (ENG.). 336p. (J). (gr. 3-7). 16.99 (978-0-06-264202-8(2)) HarperCollins Pubs.

—Into the Wild. Stevenson, Dave, illus. 2004. (Warriors: the Prophecies Begin Ser.: 1). (ENG.). 288p. (J). (gr. 3-7). pap. 6.99 (978-0-06-052550-7(9)) HarperCollins Pubs.

—Into the Wild. 2003. (Warriors Ser.: Bk. 1). (Illus.). 304p. (J). pap. (978-0-00-714002-2(9), HarperCollins Children's Bks.) HarperCollins Pubs. Ltd.

—Middle Grade Series Launch. Richardson, Owen, illus. 2017. (Bravelands Ser.: 1). 336p. (J). (gr. 3-7). lib. bdg. 17.89 (978-0-06-264203-5(0)) HarperCollins Pubs.

Husar, Stephane. Cat & Mouse Meet the Animals! Mehee, Loic, illus. 2015. (Av2 Fiction Readalong 2016 Ser.). (ENG.). (J). lib. bdg. 34.28 (978-1-4896-3819-9(9), AV2 by Weigl) Weigl Pubs., Inc.

Huskins, Suzanne Hallier, illus. No Matter What! 2004. (J). (978-1-887905-93-0(6)) Parkway Pubs., Inc.

Hussey, Lorna. Little Lost Unicorn. 2009. (ENG., Illus.). 22p. (J). (gr. -1-2). 14.95 (978-1-4027-6861-3(3)) Sterling Publishing Co., Inc.

Hutchens, Calvin. The Adventures of Otis Possum. 2007. 52p. per. 16.95 (978-1-4241-7065-4(6)) America Star Bks.

Huxley, Aldous. The Crows of Pearblossom. (J). 15.95 (978-0-89190-167-9(1)) Amereon Ltd.

I Am a Bee: Individual Title, 6 Packs. (Sails Literacy Ser.). 16p. (gr. k-18). 27.00 (978-0-7635-4411-9(6)) Rigby Education.

I Can Say- Animals. 2005. (J). bds. (978-1-4194-0035-3(5)) Paradise Pr., Inc.

Ibbotson, Eva. Not Just a Witch. Hawkes, Kevin, illus. 2004. (ENG.). 192p. (J). (gr. 3-7). pap. 5.99 (978-0-14-240232-0(X), Puffin Books) Penguin Young Readers Group.

Ichikawa, Satomi. En Busca de Tesoros. (SPA., Illus.). 40p. (J). (gr. k-2). (978-84-95150-33-2(6), COR0428) Corimbo, Editorial S.L. ESP. Dist: Lectorum Pubns., Inc.

—En Busca De Tesoros. (SPA.). 40p. (978-84-95150-43-1(3)) Corimbo, Editorial S.L.

Ideals Publications Inc. Staff, ed. My Book of Wild Animals. 2008. (ENG.). 48p. (J). 10.99 (978-0-8249-5561-8(7), Ideal Pubns.) Worthy Publishing.

Ikegami, Aiko. Friends. Ikegami, Aiko, illus. 2016. (ENG., Illus.). 32p. (J). (gr. -1-3). 16.99 (978-0-8075-2550-0(2)) Whitman, Albert & Co.

Ikids Staff. Ibaby - Goodnight, Baby: Tuck All the Babies into Their Beds. Larranaga, Ana Martin, illus. 2006. (ENG.). 12p. (J). (gr. -1 — 1). 9.99 (978-1-58476-482-3(1), IKIDS) Innovative Kids.

—Old MacDonald's Farm. King, Travis, illus. 2010. (ENG.). 20p. (J). (gr. -1-k). 14.99 (978-1-60169-024-1(X)) Innovative Kids.

Ikpe, Ernest & Madge. African Stories about the Tortoise. 2011. 32p. pap. 17.00 (978-1-4634-2726-9(3)) AuthorHouse.

I'm Sorry! (Book of Manners... Ser.). 32p. (978-1-4054-9480-9(8)) Parragon, Inc.

The Imaginary Zoo. 2007. (J). 16.95 (978-0-9789880-0-5(0)) Wild About Learning, Inc.

In My Bed: Individual Title, 6 Packs. (Literatura 2000 Ser.). (gr. k-1). 28.00 (978-0-7635-0007-8(0)) Rigby Education.

In My Room: Individual Title Six-Packs. (Literatura 2000 Ser.). (gr. k-1). 28.00 (978-0-7635-0032-0(1)) Rigby Education.

Ingalls, Ann. Biggety Bat: Chow down, Biggety! Zenz, Aaron, illus. 2015. (Scholastic Reader, Level 1 Ser.). (ENG.). 32p. (J). (gr. -1-1). pap. 3.99 (978-0-545-66264-2(8)) Scholastic, Inc.

Ingraham, Corinne. The Peacock & the Wishing-Fairy & Other Stories. 2008. 192p. pap. 27.95 (978-1-4437-4409-6(3)) Thorndike Pr.

Inkpen, Mick. Bokobikes. 2006. (Blue Nose Island Ser.: Bk. 3). (Illus.). 34p. (J). (gr. -1). 11.95 (978-1-84456-240-4(9)) Hodder & Stoughton GBR. Dist: Trafalgar Square Publishing.

—Kipper's A to Z: An Alphabet Adventure. 2006. (Kipper Ser.). (Illus.). 54p. (gr. -1-2). 18.00 (978-0-7569-6557-0(8)) Perfection Learning Corp.

Interiano, Jeffrey. Critters of Forest City. 2006. pap. 10.00 (978-1-4257-1721-6(7)) Xlibris Corp.

Ipcar, Dahlov, illus. I Like Animals. 2014. (Dahlov Ipcar Collection). (ENG.). 40p. (J). (gr. -1-2). 17.95 (978-1-909263-25-3(7)) Flying Eye Bks. GBR. Dist: Consortium Bk. Sales & Distribution.

Irbinskas, Heather. Pauly the Adventurous Pallid Bat. Anthis, Brian, illus. Tuttle, Merlin D., photos by. 2003. 32p. (J). pap. 7.95 (978-1-58369-032-1(8)) Western National Parks Assn.

Irish, Rosario A. Lamy. 2012. 28p. pap. 13.54 (978-1-4669-6232-3(1)) Trafford Publishing.

Irvin-Marston, Hope. My Little Book of Whitetails. Magdalena-Brown, Maria, illus. 2004. 32p. (J). pap. 7.95 (978-0-89317-050-9(X), WW-050X, Windward Publishing) Finney Co., Inc.

Irwin, Bindi & Black, Jess. Bushfire! 2011. (Bindi's Wildlife Adventures Ser.: 3). (ENG.). 112p. (gr. 3-6). pap. 4.99 (978-1-4022-5520-5(9), Sourcebooks Jabberwocky) Sourcebooks, Inc.

—Rescue! Bindi Wildlife Adventures. 2011. (Bindi's Wildlife Adventures Ser.: 2). (ENG.). 112p. (gr. 3-6). pap. 4.99 (978-1-4022-5517-5(9), Sourcebooks Jabberwocky) Sourcebooks, Inc.

Is That Funny? 2004. (J). per. 15.95 (978-0-9741319-2-4(X)) 4N Publishing LLC.

Isaacs, Latricia. Mason & Baylee Learn to Count. 2011. 16p. (gr. -1). pap. 8.32 (978-1-4634-0442-0(5)) AuthorHouse.

Isadora, Rachel. Old Mikamba Had a Farm. Isadora, Rachel, illus. 2013. (ENG., Illus.). 40p. (J). (gr. -1-k). 17.99 (978-0-399-25740-7(3), Nancy Paulsen Books) Penguin Young Readers Group.

Ishida, Sanae. Chibi Samurai Wants a Pet: An Adventure with Little Kunoichi the Ninja Girl. 2017. (Little Kunoichi, the Ninja Girl Ser.). (ENG.). 32p. (J). (gr. -1-2). 16.99 **(978-1-63217-117-7(1)**, Little Bigfoot) Sasquatch Bks.

Island, Fiona. Wishbone's Magic Garden. 2006. (Illus.). 120p. pap. (978-1-84401-733-1(8)) Athena Pr.

Ismail, Yasmeen. Christmas for Greta & Gracie. Ismail, Yasmeen, illus. 2016. (ENG., Illus.). 32p. (J). (gr. -1-2). 15.99 (978-0-7636-8943-8(2), Nosy Crow) Candlewick Pr.

—Specs for Rex. 2015. (ENG., Illus.). 32p. (J). (gr. -1-3). 16.99 (978-1-61963-710-8(3), 9781619637108, Bloomsbury USA Childrens) Bloomsbury Publishing USA.

Isop, Laurie. How Do You Hug a Porcupine? Millward, Gwen, illus. 2011. (ENG.). 32p. (J). (gr. -1-1). 16.99 (978-1-4424-1291-0(7), Simon & Schuster Bks. For Young Readers) Simon & Schuster Bks. For Young Readers.

It Could Be Worse: Individual Title, 6 Packs. (gr. k-1). 23.00 (978-0-7635-8832-8(6)) Rigby Education.

Iwasa, Megumi. Yours Sincerely, Giraffe. Takabatake, Jun, illus. 2017. (Gecko Press Titles Ser.). (ENG.). 104p. (gr. k-3). 9.99 **(978-1-77657-114-7(2))** Gecko Pr. NZL. Dist: Lerner Publishing Group.

Jackson, Debra. Canines on Patrol: Special Lessons. 2009. (Illus.). 28p. pap. 12.49 (978-1-4343-8806-3(9)) AuthorHouse.

Jackson, Kathryn. The Animals' Merry Christmas. Scarry, Richard, illus. 2005. (ENG.). 72p. (J). (gr. -1-2). 15.99 (978-0-375-83341-0(2), Golden Bks.) Random Hse. Children's Bks.

—Richard Scarry's the Animals' Merry Christmas. Scarry, Richard, illus. 2016. (Little Golden Book Ser.). (ENG.). 24p. (J). (-k). 4.99 (978-1-101-93842-3(0), Golden Bks.) Random Hse. Children's Bks.

Jackson, Lyn D. The Perilous Journey Home. 2009. 200p. pap. 14.49 (978-1-4389-4651-1(1)) AuthorHouse.

Jackson, Maureen. You Count Too. 2012. 20p. pap. 17.99 (978-1-4772-1241-7(8)) AuthorHouse.

Jackson, Richard. All Ears, All Eyes. Tillotson, Katherine, illus. 2017. (ENG.). 40p. (J). (gr. -1-3). 17.99 (978-1-4814-1571-2(9)) Simon & Schuster Children's Publishing.

Jackson, Ruth Montgomery. A Bit of Magic with Wee Willie & Double Trouble. 2011. 76p. pap. 27.50 (978-1-4567-0050-8(2)) AuthorHouse.

Jackson, Spring. The Little Faucet That Never Stopped Dripping. 2012. 24p. pap. 17.99 (978-1-4685-4266-0(4)) AuthorHouse.

Jacobson, Leonard. In Search of the Light. 2011. 32p. 16.99 (978-1-890580-05-6(8)) Conscious Living Pubns.

Jacques, Brian. Doomwyte. 2010. (Redwall Ser.: 20). (ENG.). 368p. (J). (gr. 5). pap. 8.99 (978-0-441-01778-2(9), Ace Bks.) Penguin Publishing Group.

—Doomwyte. Elliot, David, illus. 2011. (Redwall Ser.). (ENG.). 384p. (J). (gr. 5-18). 8.99 (978-0-14-241853-6(6), Firebird) Penguin Young Readers Group.

—Eulalia! 2010. (Redwall Ser.). (ENG.). 400p. (J). (gr. 5-18). 8.99 (978-0-14-241495-8(6), Firebird) Penguin Young Readers Group.

—High Rhulain, 18 vols. Elliott, David, illus. 2007. (Redwall Ser.: 18). (ENG.). 336p. (J). (gr. 5-18). 7.99 (978-0-441-01436-1(4), Ace Bks.) Penguin Publishing Group.

—High Rhulain. Elliot, David, illus. 2008. (Redwall Ser.). (ENG.). 352p. (J). (gr. 5-18). 8.99 (978-0-14-240938-1(3), Firebird) Penguin Young Readers Group.

—High Rhulain. Elliot, David, illus. 2007. (Redwall Ser.). 320p. (gr. 3-7). 18.00 (978-0-7569-7763-4(0)) Perfection Learning Corp.

—High Rhulain. 2007. (Redwall Ser.: 18). 18.40 (978-1-4177-7458-6(4), Turtleback) Turtleback Bks.

—The Legend of Luke. 2005. (Redwall Ser.). (ENG., Illus.). 384p. (J). (gr. 5-7). pap. 8.99 (978-0-14-250109-2(3), Firebird) Penguin Young Readers Group.

—Lord Brocktree. Fangorn, illus. 2005. (Redwall Ser.). (ENG.). 384p. (J). (gr. 5-7). pap. 8.99 (978-0-14-250110-8(7), Firebird) Penguin Young Readers Group.

—Mariel of Redwall. Chalk, Gary, illus. 2003. (Redwall Ser.). (ENG.). 400p. (J). (gr. 5-5). pap. 9.99 (978-0-14-230239-2(2), Firebird) Penguin Young Readers Group.

—Mariel of Redwall. 2004. (Redwall Ser.). 1.00 (978-1-4175-6449-1(0)) Recorded Bks., Inc.

—Marlfox: A Tale from Redwall. 2005. (Redwall Ser.). (ENG.). 400p. (J). (gr. 5-5). reprint ed. 8.99 (978-0-14-250108-5(5), Firebird) Penguin Young Readers Group.

—Martin the Warrior. Chalk, Gary, illus. 2004. (Redwall Ser.). (ENG.). 384p. (J). (gr. 5-18). pap. 9.99 (978-0-14-240055-5(6), Firebird) Penguin Young Readers Group.

—Mattimeo. Chalk, Gary, illus. 2003. (Redwall Ser.). (ENG.). 448p. (J). (gr. 5-7). pap. 9.99 (978-0-14-230240-8(6), Firebird) Penguin Young Readers Group.

—Mattimeo. 2003. (Redwall Ser.). 1.00 (978-1-4175-5316-7(2)) Recorded Bks., Inc.

—Outcast of Redwall. 2006. (Redwall Ser.). 1.00 (978-1-4237-8693-1(9)) Recorded Bks., Inc.

—Rakkety Tam, 17 vols. 2005. (Redwall Ser.: 17). (ENG.). 384p. (J). (gr. 5-18). mass mkt. 8.99 (978-0-441-01318-0(X), Ace Bks.) Penguin Publishing Group.

—Rakkety Tam. 2004. (Redwall Ser.). 1.00 (978-1-4175-5517-8(3)) Recorded Bks., Inc.

—The Rogue Crew. 2012. (Redwall Ser.: 22). (ENG.). 368p. (J). (gr. 5). 8.99 (978-1-937007-48-5(0), Ace Bks.) Penguin Publishing Group.

—The Rogue Crew. Rubin, Sean, illus. 2011. (Redwall Ser.). (ENG.). 400p. (J). (gr. 5-18). 23.99 (978-0-399-25416-1(1), Philomel Bks.) Penguin Young Readers Group.

—The Rogue Crew. 2013. (Redwall Ser.: 22). lib. bdg. 20.85 (978-0-606-31702-3(3), Turtleback) Turtleback Bks.

—The Sable Quean, 21 vols. 2011. (Redwall Ser.: 21). (ENG.). 368p. (J). (gr. 5). 8.99 (978-0-441-01998-4(6), Ace Bks.) Penguin Publishing Group.

—The Sable Quean, 21 vols. Elliot, David, illus. 2010. (Redwall Ser.: 21). (ENG.). 448p. (J). (gr. 5-18). 23.99 (978-0-399-25164-1(2), Philomel Bks.) Penguin Young Readers Group.

—The Sable Quean. Elliot, David, illus. 2012. (Redwall Ser.: 21). lib. bdg. 19.65 (978-0-606-23646-1(5), Turtleback) Turtleback Bks.

—Salamandastron. Chalk, Gary, illus. 2003. (Redwall Ser.). (ENG.). 400p. (J). (gr. 5-3). pap. 9.99 (978-0-14-250152-8(2), Firebird) Penguin Young Readers Group.

—Taggerung. Standley, Peter & Chalk, Gary, illus. 2003. (Redwall Ser.). (ENG.). 448p. (J). (gr. 5-18). pap. 8.99 (978-0-14-250154-2(9), Firebird) Penguin Young Readers Group.
—Taggerung. 2003. (Redwall Ser.). 1.00 (978-1-4175-5326-6(X)) Recorded Bks., Inc.
—Triss. l.t. ed. 2004. (Redwall Ser.). 596p. (J). 23.95 (978-0-7862-6207-6(9)) Thorndike Pr.
Jaekel, Susan, illus. The Tortoise & the Hare: A Tale about Determination. 2006. (J). 6.99 (978-1-59939-015-4(9)) Cornerstone Pr.
Jalonen, Nicole. Magical Animal Army Adventures. 2012. 28p. pap. 15.99 (978-1-4691-7544-7(4)) Xlibris Corp.
James, Andrea. Adventures at Ja-Mar Farms: Pup-Pup, Padluck & PIG Take a Walk in the Wet Woods. 2005. 47p. pap. 24.95 (978-1-4137-3437-9(5)) PublishAmerica, Inc.
James, Catherine. The Sad Little House. Collier, Kevin Scott, illus. 2008. 24p. pap. 10.95 (978-1-935137-06-1(9)) 2006. 28p. (J). E-Book 9.95 incl. cd-rom (978-1-933090-18-4(9)) Guardian Angel Publishing, Inc.
James, Katy. My Favorite Summer Vacations. 2013. 12p. pap. 12.68 (978-1-4669-9690-8(0)) Trafford Publishing.
Jameson, Catherine. Zoe & the Fawn. Flett, Julie, illus. 2006. (ENG.). 32p. pap. 11.95 (978-1-894778-43-5(X)) Theytus Bks., Ltd. CAN. Dist: Univ. of Toronto Pr.
Jamiol, Paul. Bikers Are Animals: A Children's Book on Motorcycling. Habib, Linda, ed. 2009. 38p. pap. 14.95 (978-1-60844-232-4(2)) Dog Ear Publishing, LLC.
—Bikers Are Animals 4: Working & Riding. 2013. (Illus.). 38p. pap. 14.95 (978-1-4575-2323-6(X)) Dog Ear Publishing, LLC.
Janowski, Alice & Boyer, Colleen McKinnon. Dakota & the Magical Gardens. 2008. 28p. pap. 12.95 (978-1-59858-711-1(0)) Dog Ear Publishing, LLC.
Janssen, Ian. The Perils of Pierre Book 1, Gold Fever. 2013. 26p. pap. 12.99 (978-1-61160-594-5(6)) Whiskey Creek Restorations.
Jansson, Tove. Moominvalley Turns Jungle. 2012. (Moomin Ser.). (ENG., Illus.). 48p. (J). (gr. 4-7). pap. 9.95 (978-1-77046-097-3(7), 9781770460973) Drawn & Quarterly Pubns. CAN. Dist: Macmillan.
Januarius. James & the Pixie. Wigmore, Kitty, illus. 2015. (ENG.). 50p. (J). (gr. 3-4). 24.95 (978-1-78455-540-5(1), 5bd61eeb-94b8-41ac-94aa-57a16cb4eeda); pap. 13.95 (978-1-78455-538-2(X), 0a59afd6-d79f-4a96-b3d0-d19a1af0e939) Austin, Stan AUS. Dist: Bookmasters Distribution.
Janvier Gibeau, Claire. My Favorite Animal. 2009. 16p. pap. 8.49 (978-1-4490-4022-2(5)) AuthorHouse.
Jarkins, Sheila. Adv Marco Flamingo Under Sea. Jarkins, Sheila, illus. 2010. (ENG., Illus.). 32p. (J). (gr. -1-12). pap. 7.95 (978-1-934960-69-1(1), Raven Tree Pr.,Csi) Continental Sales, Inc.
Jay, Basil. The Adventures of Twig. 2011. (Illus.). 120p. pap. 32.90 (978-1-4567-8631-1(8)) AuthorHouse.
Jay, Em. Once. 2009. 28p. pap. 12.50 (978-1-4490-2662-2(1)) AuthorHouse.
Jayne, Mitch. Forest in the Wind. 2009. 146p. pap. 15.00 (978-1-882467-48-8(5)) Wildstone Media.
Jeffers, Oliver. The Great Paper Caper. Jeffers, Oliver, illus. 2009. (ENG., Illus.). 40p. (J). (gr. -1-k). 17.99 (978-0-399-25097-2(2), Philomel Bks.) Penguin Young Readers Group.
Jenkins, Gloria. Storm: The Peace Maker. 2006. (J). pap. 8.00 (978-0-8059-7116-3(5)) Dorrance Publishing Co., Inc.
Jennings, Linda. Animal Tales for Bedtime. Biro, Val, illus. 2013. (ENG.). 96p. (J). 16.50 (978-1-84135-932-8(7)) Award Pubns. Ltd. GBR. Dist: Parkwest Pubns., Inc.
Jennings, Patrick. We Can't All Be Rattlesnakes. 2011. (ENG.). 144p. (J). (gr. 3-7). pap. 5.99 (978-0-06-082117-3(5)) HarperCollins Pubs.
Jennings, Sharon. Franklin's Trading Cards. Jeffrey, Sean et al, illus. 2003. 32p. (J). (978-0-439-41816-4(X)) Scholastic, Inc.
Jennings, Sharon & Bourgeois, Paulette. Franklin's Trading Cards. Jeffrey, Sean et al, illus. 2004. (Franklin Ser.). 32p. (gr. 1-2). 13.95 (978-0-7569-4402-5(3)) Perfection Learning Corp.
Jensen, Derrick. Mischief in the Forest: A Yarn Yarn. McMillan, Stephanie, illus. 2010. (Flashpoint Press Ser.). (ENG.). 40p. (J). (gr. -1-k). pap. 14.95 (978-1-60486-081-8(2)) PM Pr.
Jensen, Ivan. Mary Rode to Bethlehem on Me. 2012. (ENG.). 45p. (J). pap. 17.95 (978-1-4327-9473-6(6)) Outskirts Pr., Inc.
Jensen, Jon. Adventures in the Desert. 2013. 32p. pap. 17.25 (978-1-4907-0918-5(5)) Trafford Publishing.
Jeram, Anita. Bunny My Honey. Jeram, Anita, illus. 2009. (ENG., Illus.). 22p. (J). (gr. k-k). bds. 7.99 (978-0-7636-4645-5(8)) Candlewick Pr.
Jeremy Fisher Rocks Out. 2015. (Illus.). (J). (978-1-4844-5560-9(6), Warne, Frederick Pubs.) Penguin Bks., Ltd.
JiSeung, Kook. Ouch! It Stings! JiSeung, Kook, illus. rev. ed. 2014. (MySELF Bookshelf Ser.). (ENG., Illus.). 32p. (J). (gr. k-2). pap. 11.94 (978-1-60357-653-6(3)); lib. bdg. 25.27 (978-1-59953-644-6(7)) Norwood Hse. Pr.
Joachimowski, Paula L. Swamp Band Lullaby. 2007. (J). per. 12.99 (978-1-59879-211-9(3)) Lifevest Publishing, Inc.
Johnson, Amy Crane. Cinnamon & the April Shower. Mommaerts, Robb, illus. 2009. (ENG.). 32p. (J). (gr. -1-3). 16.95 (978-1-934960-54-7(3), Raven Tree Pr.,Csi) Continental Sales, Inc.
Johnson, Christopher L. I Don't Have Crooked Legs. 2013. 130p. 28.99 (978-1-4497-8355-6(4)); pap. 11.99 (978-1-4497-8356-3(2)) Author Solutions, Inc. (WestBow Pr.).
Johnson, Jaime Gardner. The Ghost of Donley Farm, 1 vol. Klein, Laurie Allen, illus. 2015. (ENG.). 32p. (J). (gr. k-3). 17.95 (978-1-62855-451-9(7)); pap. 9.95 (978-1-62855-459-5(2)) Arbordale Publishing.
Johnson, Paul Brett. Fearless Jack. Johnson, Paul Brett, illus. 2007. (ENG., Illus.). 32p. (J). (gr. -1-3). 10.99 (978-1-4169-6833-7(4), Simon & Schuster/Paula Wiseman Bks.) Simon & Schuster/Paula Wiseman Bks.
Johnson, Pauletta Cox. Come under the Mushroom. 2004. 30p. (J). per. 7.95 (978-1-932496-23-9(8)) Penman Publishing, Inc.
Johnson, Rebecca. Outback Adventure. 2015. (Juliet, Nearly a Vet Ser.: 9). (ENG., Illus.). 96p. (J). (gr. 3-5). 8.99 (978-0-14-330871-3(8)) Penguin Books Australia AUS. Dist: Independent Pubs. Group.
Johnston, Tony. Desert Song, 1 vol. Young, Ed, illus. 2010. (ENG.). 32p. (J). (gr. 3-4). pap. 7.99 (978-1-57805-171-7(1)) Sierra Club Bks. for Children.
—Hanging Out. DiTerlizzi, Tony, illus. 2003. (Alien & Possum Ser.). 48p. (J). 11.65 (978-0-7569-1544-5(9)) Perfection Learning Corp.
—Winter Is Coming. LaMarche, Jim, illus. 2014. (ENG.). 40p. (J). (gr. -1-3). 17.99 (978-1-4424-7251-8(0), Simon & Schuster Bks. For Young Readers) Simon & Schuster Bks. For Young Readers.
Jolley, Dan. Shipwrecked on Mad Island, No. 11. Huddleston, Courtney, illus. 2009. (Twisted Journeys (r) Ser.: 11). (ENG.). 112p. (J). (gr. 4-7). 27.93 (978-0-8225-7911-3(1), Graphic Universe™) Lerner Publishing Group.
Jones, Allan. The Six Crowns: Fair Wind to Widdershins. Chalk, Gary, illus. 2011. (Six Crowns Ser.: 2). 176p. (J). (gr. 2-5). 15.99 (978-0-06-200626-4(6), Greenwillow Bks.) HarperCollins Pubs.
—The Six Crowns: the Ice Gate of Spyre. Chalk, Gary, illus. 2012. (Six Crowns Ser.: 4). 160p. (J). (gr. 3-7). 15.99 (978-0-06-200633-2(9), Greenwillow Bks.) HarperCollins Pubs.
—The Six Crowns: Trundle's Quest. Chalk, Gary, illus. 2011. (Six Crowns Ser.: 1). 176p. (J). (gr. 2-5). pap. 5.99 (978-0-06-200625-7(8), Greenwillow Bks.) HarperCollins Pubs.
Jones, Allan Frewin. Fire over Swallowhaven. Chalk, Gary, illus. 2012. (Six Crowns Ser.: 3). 160p. (J). (gr. 2-5). 15.99 (978-0-06-200629-5(0), Greenwillow Bks.) HarperCollins Pubs.
—Trundle's Quest. Chalk, Gary, illus. 2011. (Six Crowns Ser.: 1). 160p. (J). (gr. 2-5). 15.99 (978-0-06-200623-3(1), Greenwillow Bks.) HarperCollins Pubs.
Jones, C. B. Bog Hollow Boys. Green, Chris, illus. 2017. (Bog Hollow Boys Ser.). (ENG.). 72p. (gr. 4-5). 101.28 (978-1-4965-4063-8(8)) Stone Arch Bks.
Jones, Christianne C. Hello, Goodbye, & a Very Little Lie, 1 vol. Battuz, Christine, illus. 2012. (Little Boost Ser.). (ENG.). 32p. (gr. k-3). 7.95 (978-1-4048-7498-5(4), Little Boost) Picture Window Bks.
—The Messy One, 1 vol. Martinez-Neal, Juana, illus. 2012. (Little Boost Ser.). (ENG.). 32p. (gr. k-3). 7.95 (978-1-4048-7417-6(8), Little Boost) Picture Window Bks.
Jones, Christine A. & Schacker, Jennifer, eds. Feathers, Paws, Fins, & Claws: Fairy-Tale Beasts. 2015. (Series in Fairy-Tale Studies). (ENG., Illus.). 136p. (YA). 24.99 (978-0-8143-4069-1(5), 3842) Wayne State Univ. Pr.
Jones, Connie. On the Farm with Kaden & Moxie. 2010. 20p. 12.49 (978-1-4490-8047-1(2)) AuthorHouse.
Jones, Frankie. In the Wild. 2015. (What Can You Spot? Ser.). (ENG., Illus.). 18p. (J). (gr. -1 — 1). bds. 6.99 (978-1-4998-0055-5(X)) Little Bee Books Inc.
Jones, Janey Louise. Farrah the Shy Fawn. Poh, Jennie, illus. 2016. (Superfairies Ser.). (ENG.). 56p. (gr. k-3). lib. bdg. 23.99 (978-1-5158-0432-1(1)) Picture Window Bks.
—Sonny the Daring Squirrel. Poh, Jennie, illus. 2016. (Superfairies Ser.). (ENG.). 56p. (gr. k-3). lib. bdg. 23.99 (978-1-5158-0433-8(X)) Picture Window Bks.
—Superfairies: Adventures in Peaseblossom Woods. Poh, Jennie, illus. 2017. (ENG.). 192p. (gr. 1-3). pap. 6.95 (978-1-62370-819-1(2)) Capstone Young Readers of Coughlan Cos.
Jones, Rena. Pony Strings & Critter Things. Nielson, Ginger, illus. 2012. 28p. pap. 14.99 (978-0-9838018-0-1(0)) 4RV Publishing, LLC.
Jones, Sherryl. WELCOME to GOD's ACRE Room for No More Sherryl Jones. 2006. 24p. 15.01 (978-1-4116-8100-2(2)) Lulu Pr., Inc.
Jones, Steven E. Blue Eagle Meets Double Trouble. Jones, Steven E., Jr., illus. 2008. (Blue Eagle Ser.). (ENG.). 40p. (J). (gr. -1-2). 15.95 (978-0-9794655-0-5(8)) Blue Eagle Bks., Inc.
Jordan, Apple. Oh, Brother! Random House Disney Staff, illus. 2012. (Step into Reading Ser.). (ENG.). 32p. (J). (gr. -1-1). pap. 3.99 (978-0-7364-2887-3(9), RH/Disney) Random Hse. Children's Bks.
Jordan, Christina. I Wish I Were a Speedy Cheetah, 1 vol. Utomo, Gabhor, illus. 2011. (I Wish I Were ... Ser.). (ENG.). 24p. (J). (gr. k-3). 28.50 (978-1-61641-660-7(2)) Magic Wagon.
Jordan's Zoo: Individual Title, 6 packs. (gr. -1-2). 27.00 (978-0-7635-9456-5(3)) Rigby Education.
Joseph, Lila. The Boy Who Could Talk to Animals. 2008. 36p. pap. 18.95 (978-1-4327-2873-1(3)) Outskirts Pr., Inc.
Journey to see the King. 2006. (J). (978-0-9791168-0-3(5)) Lighthouse Bk. Publishing.
Juan, Ana. The Pet Shop Revolution. 2011. (J). pap. (978-0-545-12811-7(0), Levine, Arthur A. Bks.) Scholastic, Inc.
Judge, Lita. Good Morning to Me! Judge, Lita, illus. 2015. (ENG., Illus.). 40p. (J). (gr. -1-3). 17.99 (978-1-4814-0369-6(9)) Simon & Schuster Children's Publishing.
—Red Sled. Judge, Lita, illus. 2011. (ENG., Illus.). 40p. (J). (gr. -1-3). 17.99 (978-1-4424-2007-6(3), Atheneum Bks. for Young Readers) Simon & Schuster Children's Publishing.
Jumbo & Tempo, the Food Bandit. 2004. (J). per. 15.99 (978-0-9759122-1-8(6)) Golden Eagle Publishing Hse., Inc.
Jurassic News: Individual Title Six-Packs. (Bookweb Ser.). 32p. (gr. 6-18). 34.00 (978-0-7578-0891-3(3)) Rigby Education.
Kadohata, Cynthia. A Million Shades of Gray. 2010. (ENG., Illus.). 224p. (J). (gr. 5-9). 16.99 (978-1-4169-1883-7(3), Atheneum Bks. for Young Readers) Simon & Schuster Children's Publishing.
Kaiser, Amy L. If I Lived in the Jungle. 2012. 16p. pap. 12.68 (978-1-4669-3589-1(8)) Trafford Publishing.
Kamau, G. How Porcupine Got His Spines. 2004. (Illus.). 26p. pap. (978-9966-25-168-8(5)) Heinemann Kenya, Limited (East African Educational Publishers Ltd E.A.E.P.) KEN. Dist: Michigan State Univ. Pr.
—Why Beetles Roll Cowdung. 2004. 22p. pap. (978-9966-25-167-1(7)) Heinemann Kenya, Limited (East African Educational Publishers Ltd E.A.E.P.) KEN. Dist: Michigan State Univ. Pr.
Kangira, Jairos. Creatures Great & Small: A Collection of Short Stories. 2005. vi, 114p. (978-0-86922-786-2(6)) Mambo Pr.
Kankey, Andrew T. Penelope & Mrs Grace: A Swine Mystery. 2011. 80p. 17.95 (978-1-4575-0531-7(2)) Dog Ear Publishing, LLC.
Kaplan, Amy. A Well-Balanced Tale. 2010. 44p. 17.20 (978-0-557-50264-6(0)) Lulu Pr., Inc.
Karapetkova, Holly & Picou, Lin. Ouch! Stitches. Reese, Bob, illus. 2011. (ENG.). 24p. (gr. 1-2). pap. 8.95 (978-1-61236-023-2(8)) Rourke Educational Media.
Karas, G. Brian, illus. The Case of the Missing Monkey. 2004. (High-Rise Private Eyes Ser.: No. 1). (J). (gr. -1-2). pap. 31.95 incl. audio compact disk (978-1-59112-616-4(9)) Live Oak Media.
—The Case of the Puzzling Possum. 2004. (High-Rise Private Eyes Ser.: No. 3). (J). (gr. -1-2). pap. 31.95 incl. audio compact disk (978-1-59112-620-1(7)) Live Oak Media.
Karr, Lily. Easter Parade! Richards, Kirsten, illus. 2013. (ENG.). 24p. (J). (gr. -1-k). pap. 4.99 (978-0-545-45824-5(2), Cartwheel Bks.) Scholastic, Inc.
—Easter Parade! 2013. lib. bdg. 14.75 (978-0-606-31494-7(6), Turtleback) Turtleback Bks.
Kasza, Keiko. Badger's Fancy Meal. 2009. (ENG.). 32p. (J). (gr. -1-3). pap. 6.99 (978-0-14-241271-8(6), Puffin Books) Penguin Young Readers Group.
—El Estofado del Lobo. (Buenas Noches Ser.). (SPA.). (J). (978-958-04-1427-8(0), NR6443) Norma S.A.
—Silly Goose's Big Story. Kasza, Keiko, illus. 2012. (ENG., Illus.). 32p. (J). (gr. -1-k). 16.99 (978-0-399-25542-7(7), G.P. Putnam's Sons Books for Young Readers) Penguin Young Readers Group.
Kasza, Keiko & McPike, Elizabeth. Finders Keepers. Kasza, Keiko, illus. 2015. (ENG., Illus.). 32p. (J). (gr. -1-k). bds. 16.99 (978-0-399-16898-7(2), G.P. Putnam's Sons Books for Young Readers) Penguin Young Readers Group.
Kate Smith Designs, illus. Who's Playing on the Farm? 2011. (Magic Bath Bks.). (ENG.). 8p. (J). (gr. -1-3). 5.99 (978-1-4380-7179-4(5)) Barron's Educational Series, Inc.
—Who's Playing Outdoors? 2011. (Magic Bath Bks.). (ENG.). 8p. (J). (gr. -1-3). 5.99 (978-1-4380-7178-7(7)) Barron's Educational Series, Inc.
Katschke, Judy. The Imaginary Okapi (Disney Junior: the Lion Guard) Matta, Gabriella & Legramandi, Francesco, illus. 2017. (Little Golden Book Ser.). (ENG.). 24p. (J). (-k). 4.99 **(978-0-7364-3719-6(3)**, Golden/Disney) Random Hse. Children's Bks.
Katschke, Judy. Karate Kangaroos (Disney Junior: Doc Mcstuffins) Random House Disney Staff & Martinez, Heather, illus. 2016. (Little Golden Book Ser.). (ENG.). 24p. (J). (gr. -1-k). 4.99 (978-0-7364-3382-2(1), Golden/Disney) Random Hse. Children's Bks.
Katz, Karen. Vroom, Vroom, Trucks! Katz, Karen, illus. 2016. (ENG., Illus.). 14p. (J). (gr. -1 — 1). bds. 6.99 (978-1-4814-4209-1(0), Little Simon) Little Simon.
—Where Is Baby's Puppy? Katz, Karen, illus. 2011. (ENG., Illus.). 14p. (J). (gr. -1 — 1). bds. 6.99 (978-1-4169-8684-3(7), Little Simon) Little Simon.
—Zoom, Zoom, Baby! A Karen Katz Lift-The-Flap Book. Katz, Karen, illus. 2014. (ENG., Illus.). 14p. (J). (gr. -1 — 1). bds. 6.99 (978-1-4424-9314-8(3), Little Simon) Little Simon.
Kaufmann, Nancy. Bye, Bye! Spetter, Jung-Hee, illus. 2004. (ENG.). 32p. (J). (gr. -1-1). 14.95 (978-1-886910-95-9(2), Lemniscaat) Boyds Mills Pr.
Kawecki, Daniel. The Mad Moose. 2009. 32p. pap. 13.00 (978-1-60693-888-1(6), Eloquent Bks.) Strategic Book Publishing & Rights Agency (SBPRA).
Kay, Susan. Abby & Gabby Tales. 2009. 16p. pap. 9.99 (978-1-4389-6467-6(6)) AuthorHouse.
Kaylor, J. Garcia. Animal Magic Coloring Pages. 2012. (ENG.). pap. 11.99 (978-1-4675-2458-2(1)) Independent Pub.
Keeling, Evan. CrumbSnatchers. 2008. 60p. (J). per. 5.95 (978-0-9796902-4-2(2)) Silent Devil Productions.
Kehret, Peg. Race to Disaster. 2008. (ENG.). 128p. (J). (gr. 3-7). pap. 7.99 (978-1-4169-9108-3(5), Simon & Schuster/Paula Wiseman Bks.) Simon & Schuster/Paula Wiseman Bks.
Keller, Holly. Help! A Story of Friendship. Keller, Holly, illus. 2007. (ENG., Illus.). 40p. (J). (gr. -1-3). 16.99 (978-0-06-123913-7(5), Greenwillow Bks.) HarperCollins Pubs.
Kelly, David A. The Missing Marlin. Meyers, Mark, illus. 2014. (Ballpark Mysteries Ser.: Bk. 8). (ENG.). 112p. (J). (gr. 1-4). 4.99 (978-0-307-97782-3(X), Random Hse. Bks. for Young Readers) Random Hse. Children's Bks.
—The Missing Marlin. 2014. (Ballpark Mysteries Ser.: Bk. 8). lib. bdg. 14.75 (978-0-606-35565-0(0)) Turtleback Bks.
Kelly, Everett. Tiny Tom. 2007. 56p. (J). per. 15.95 (978-1-58939-983-9(8)) Virtualbookworm.com Publishing, Inc.
Kelly, Jacqueline & Grahame, Kenneth. Return to the Willows. Young, Clint, illus. 2012. (ENG.). 288p. (J). (gr. 3-7). 19.99 (978-0-8050-9413-8(X), 9780805094138, Holt, Henry & Co. Bks. For Young Readers) Holt, Henry & Co.
Kelly, L. J. R. Sometimes It's Storks. Hilts, Brothers, illus. 2017. (ENG.). 32p. (J). (-k). 16.99 (978-0-399-25682-0(2), G.P. Putnam's Sons Books for Young Readers) Penguin Young Readers Group.
Kelly, Mij. Lion's Lullaby. Clifton-Brown, Holly, illus. 2016. (ENG.). 32p. (J). (gr. -1 — 1). 16.99 (978-1-4847-2526-9(3)) Disney Pr.
Kendall, Diane & Marsh, Merle. Carousel Kids. York, Susanne, photos by. 2004. (Illus.). (J). (978-0-9762385-0-8(0)) Houston Zoo, Inc.
Kenna, Kara. Whose Ears? Nelson, Judy, illus. 2011. (Whose Whose Bks.). (ENG.). 10p. (gr. -1-k). bds. 9.99 (978-1-935498-52-0(5)) Just For Kids Pr., LLC.
—Whose Eyes? Nelson, Judy, illus. 2011. (Whose Whose Bks.). (ENG.). 10p. (gr. -1-k). bds. 9.99 (978-1-935498-51-3(7)) Just For Kids Pr., LLC.
—Whose Feet? Nelson, Judy, illus. 2011. (Whose Whose Bks.). (ENG.). 12p. (J). (gr. -1). bds. 9.99 (978-1-935498-53-7(3)) Just For Kids Pr., LLC.
—Whose Nose? Nelson, Judy A., illus. 2011. (Whose Whose Bks.). (ENG.). 10p. (gr. -1-k). bds. 9.99 (978-1-935498-54-4(1)) Just For Kids Pr., LLC.
Kennedy. Dabbling Doezee. 2014. (ENG., Illus.). (J). 16.95 (978-0-9915194-0-8(X)) Fabula.
Kennedy, Anne Vittur. The Farmer's Away! Baa! Neigh! Kennedy, Anne Vittur, illus. 2014. (ENG., Illus.). 32p. (J). (-k). 15.99 (978-0-7636-6679-8(3)) Candlewick Pr.
—One Big Turkey, 1 vol. 2016. (ENG., Illus.). 20p. (J). bds. 8.99 (978-0-7180-8711-1(9)) Nelson, Thomas Inc.
Kerr, Judith. Mog & the Granny. (Illus.). 32p. (J). pap. 9.99 (978-0-00-664592-4(5)) HarperCollins Pubs. Ltd. GBR. Dist: Trafalgar Square Publishing.
—Mog & the Vet. (ENG., Illus.). 34p. (J). 19.99 (978-0-00-198211-6(7)) HarperCollins Pubs. Ltd. GBR. Dist: Trafalgar Square Publishing.
Ketteman, Helen. Armadilly Chili. Terry, Will, illus. 2004. (ENG.). 32p. (J). (gr. k-3). pap. 7.99 (978-0-8075-0458-1(0)) Whitman, Albert & Co.
Keyser, Francois. Tiger Loses His Stripes. 2013. (ENG.). 24p. pap. 20.00 (978-1-4669-9203-0(4)) Trafford Publishing.
Keyworth, R. L. Gregory Giraffe's New Friends Adventure: Gregory Giraffe Is about to find some altogether different but new friends at his watering Hole. 2009. 20p. pap. 10.99 (978-1-4389-3284-2(7)) AuthorHouse.
Khan, Farheen. Ibrahim Khan & the Mystery of the Roaring Lion. 2010. (Ibrahim Khan Ser.). (ENG., Illus.). 56p. (J). (gr. 2-6). pap. 6.50 (978-0-86037-467-1(X)) Kube Publishing Ltd. GBR. Dist: Consortium Bk. Sales & Distribution.
Khanna, Balraj. Rajah: King of the Jungle. 2011. (ENG.). 112p. 16.95 (978-1-935677-03-1(9)) Mapin Publishing Pvt. Ltd IND. Dist: National Bk. Network.
Kheiriyeh, Rashin, illus. There Was an Old Lady Who Swallowed a Fly. 2014. (ENG.). 32p. (J). 17.95 (978-0-7358-4183-3(7)) North-South Bks., Inc.
Kherdian, David. Come Back, Moon. Hogrogian, Nonny, illus. 2013. (ENG.). 32p. (J). (gr. -1-3). 16.99 (978-1-4424-5887-1(9), Beach Lane Bks.) Beach Lane Bks.
Kiefer, Janet Kennedy. Curious Freckles. 2013. 56p. pap. (978-1-4602-2664-3(X)) FriesenPress.
Kieman, Tim. Liams Luck & Finnegans Fortune. 2009. (ENG.). 144p. pap. 10.95 (978-1-933916-48-4(6), Ferne Pr.) Nelson Publishing & Marketing.
Kiick, Lisa. Bailey & Friends. Stouch, Ryan, illus. 2008. 40p. pap. 14.95 (978-1-59858-743-2(9)) Dog Ear Publishing, LLC.
Kilgus, Walter C. Bess Takes a Ride. 2008. 36p. pap. 17.49 (978-1-4257-8807-0(6)) Xlibris Corp.
Kim, Cecil. Nicknames. Han, SooJin, illus. 2014. (MySELF Bookshelf Ser.). (ENG.). 32p. (J). (gr. k-2). pap. 11.94 (978-1-60357-699-4(1)); lib. bdg. 25.27 (978-1-59953-664-4(1)) Norwood Hse. Pr.
Kim, HoJeong. Kanga & Anger. Kim, SookKyeong, illus. rev. ed. 2014. (MySELF Bookshelf Ser.). (ENG.). 32p. (J). (gr. k-2). pap. 11.94 (978-1-60357-652-9(5)); lib. bdg. 25.27 (978-1-59953-643-9(9)) Norwood Hse. Pr.
Kim, JeongHo. Oh That Snow! Ok, SeoJeong, illus. 2014. (MySELF Bookshelf Ser.). (ENG.). 32p. (J). (gr. k-2). pap. 11.94 (978-1-60357-697-0(5)); lib. bdg. 25.27 (978-1-59953-662-0(5)) Norwood Hse. Pr.
King, Amy Sarig. Me & Marvin Gardens. 2017. (ENG.). 256p. (J). (gr. 3-7). 16.99 (978-0-545-87074-0(7), Levine, Arthur A. Bks.) Scholastic, Inc.
King, Terri. A Midwinter's Tail. 2008. 52p. pap. 16.95 (978-1-60703-800-9(5)) America Star Bks.
King, Thomas. Coyote Sings to the Moon. Wales, Johnny, illus. 2008. (ENG.). 36p. (J). pap. (978-1-55263-868-2(5)) Magma.
Kipling, Rudyard. A Collection of Rudyard Kipling's Just So Stories. Sís, Peter, illus. 2004. (ENG.). 128p. (J). (gr. k-12). 22.99 (978-0-7636-2629-7(5)) Candlewick Pr.
—How the Camel Got His Hump: The Graphic Novel, 1 vol. Rodriguez, Pedro, illus. 2012. (Graphic Spin Ser.). (ENG.). 40p. (gr. 1-3). pap. 5.95 (978-1-4342-3879-5(2)); lib. bdg. 23.99 (978-1-4342-3202-1(6)) Stone Arch Bks. (Graphic Revolve).
—How the Elephant Got His Trunk: The Graphic Novel, 1 vol. Rodriguez, Pedro, illus. 2012. (Graphic Spin Ser.). (ENG.). 40p. (gr. 1-3). pap. 5.95 (978-1-4342-3880-1(6)); lib. bdg. 23.99 (978-1-4342-3222-9(0)) Stone Arch Bks. (Graphic Revolve).
—How the Leopard Got His Spots, 1 vol. Lohstoeter, Lori, illus. 2005. (Rabbit Ears: A Classic Tale Ser.). (ENG.). 36p. (gr. 4-6). 25.65 (978-1-59679-344-6(9)) Spotlight.
—How the Leopard Got His Spots. Rodriguez, Pedro, illus. 2012. (Graphic Spin Ser.). (ENG.). 40p. (gr. 1-3). lib. bdg. 23.99 (978-1-4342-3223-6(9), Graphic Revolve) Stone Arch Bks.
—How the Leopard Got His Spots: The Graphic Novel, 1 vol. Rodriguez, Pedro, illus. 2012. (Graphic Spin Ser.). (ENG.). 40p. (gr. 1-3). pap. 5.95 (978-1-4342-3881-8(4), Graphic Revolve) Stone Arch Bks.
—How the Rhinoceros Got His Skin: The Graphic Novel, 1 vol. Rodriguez, Pedro, illus. 2012. (Graphic Spin Ser.). (ENG.). 40p. (gr. 1-3). pap. 5.95 (978-1-4342-3882-5(2), Graphic Revolve) Stone Arch Bks.
—How the Rhinoceros Got His Skin: The Graphic Novel, 1 vol. Rodriguez, Pedro, illus. 2012. (Graphic Spin Ser.). (ENG.). 40p. (gr. 1-3). lib. bdg. 23.99 (978-1-4342-3025-6(2), Graphic Revolve) Stone Arch Bks.
—The Jungle Book. Corvino, Lucy, illus. 2008. (Classic Starts(tm) Ser.). (ENG.). 160p. (J). (gr. 2-4). 6.95 (978-1-4027-4576-8(1)) Sterling Publishing Co., Inc.
—The Jungle Book. Rowe, John, ed. 2008. (Jungle Book Ser.: 1). (ENG.). 164p. pap. 8.95 (978-1-84232-943-6(X)) House of Stratus, Inc. GBR. Dist: Gardners Bks. Ltd.
—The Jungle Book: Rikki-Tikki-Tavi Moves In. Madsen, Jim, illus. 2008. (Easy Reader Classics Ser.). (ENG.). 32p. (gr. 4-7). lib. bdg. 24.21 (978-1-59961-336-9(0)) Spotlight.
—The Jungle Book: a Coloring Book. 2016. (ENG., Illus.). 96p. (J). (gr. k). pap. 12.99 (978-1-62686-702-4(X), Silver Dolphin Bks.) Readerlink Distribution Services, LLC.
—The Jungle Books. 2004. (Barnes & Noble Classics Ser.). (ENG., Illus.). 432p. pap. 7.95 (978-1-59308-109-6(X)) Barnes & Noble, Inc.
—The Jungle Books. 2013. (ENG.). 384p. (gr. 12). mass mkt. 5.95 (978-0-451-41918-7(9), Signet) Penguin Publishing Group.
—Just So Comics: Tales of the World's Wildest Beasts. Rodriguez, Pedro, illus. 2013. (Graphic Spin Ser.). (ENG.).

A
B

144p. (gr. 3-6). pap. 12.95 (978-1-4342-4880-0(1)) Stone Arch Bks.

—Just So Stories. Montefiore, Jan & Plotz, Judith, eds. 2011. (ENG., Illus.). 368p. (gr. 12). 9.00 (978-0-14-144240-2(9), Penguin Classics) Penguin Publishing Group.

—Just So Stories. Latimer, Àlex, illus. 2008. (ENG.). 224p. (J). (gr. 5-6). 5.99 (978-0-14-132162-2(8), Puffin Books) Penguin Young Readers Group.

—Just So Stories. Gleeson, J. M. & Bransom, Paul, illus. 2009. 208p. pap. 9.95 (978-1-59915-172-4(3)) Yesterday's Classics.

—Just So Stories Set: For Little Children. Date not set. (Illus.). 192p. (YA). (gr. 3-18). reprint ed. 7.95 (978-1-56852-137-4(5), Konecky & Konecky) Konecky, William S. Assocs., Inc.

—Just So Stories Set: For Little Children. Salter, Safaya, illus. 2003. (Chrysalis Childrens Classics Ser.). 125p. (YA). pap. (978-1-84365-036-2(3), Pavilion Children's Books) Pavilion Bks.

—El Libro de la Selva. 2003. (Timeless Classics Ser.).Tr. of Jungle Book. (SPA., Illus.). 176p. (J). (gr. 5-8). 12.95 (978-84-372-2230-1(3)) Altea, Ediciones, S.A. - Grupo Santillana ESP. Dist: Santillana USA Publishing Co., Inc.

—El Libro de la Selva.Tr. of Jungle Book. (SPA.). (J). 8.00 (978-958-04-7110-3(X)) Norma S.A. COL. Dist: Distribuidora Norma, Inc.

—Rikki-Tikki-Tavi & Toomai of the Elephants. 2008. (Unabridged Classics (in Audio) Ser.). (J). pap. 36.00 incl. audio compact disk (978-1-58472-431-5(5), In Audio) Sound Room Pubs., Inc.

Kipling, Rudyard & Busch, Jeffrey. The Jungle Books. (Classics Illustrated Ser.). (Illus.). 52p. (YA). pap. 4.95 (978-1-57209-022-4(7)) Classics International Entertainment, Inc.

Kipling, Rudyard & Landolf, Diane Wright. The Jungle Book. Rowe, John, illus. 2008. (Stepping Stone Book(TM) Ser.). (ENG.). 112p. (J). (gr. 1-4). per. 3.99 (978-0-375-84276-4(4), Random Hse. Bks. for Young Readers) Random Hse. Children's Bks.

Kipling, Rudyard & Pinkney, Jerry. Rikki-Tikki-Tavi. Pinkney, Jerry, illus. 2004. (ENG., Illus.). 48p. (J). (gr. -1-3). reprint ed. pap. 6.99 (978-0-06-058785-7(7)) HarperCollins Pubs.

Kipling, Rudyard & Solari, María J. El Libro de la Selva. Puerta, Carlos, tr. Puerta, Carlos, illus.Tr. of Jungle Book. (SPA.). 92p. (J). (gr. 5-8). pap. 12.95 (978-84-204-5766-6(3)) Santillana USA Publishing Co., Inc.

Kipling, Rudyard & Wolek, Guy. The Jungle Book, 1 vol. 2012. (Calico Illustrated Classics Ser.: No. 4). (ENG., Illus.). 112p. (J). (gr. 3-6). 27.07 (978-1-61641-616-4(5)) Magic Wagon.

Kirk, Daniel. The Thing about Spring. 2015. (ENG., Illus.). 32p. (J). (gr. -1-3). 16.95 (978-1-4197-1492-4(9), Abrams Bks. for Young Readers) Abrams, Inc.

Kirkpatrick, Teresa. Roscoe's Forest Adventures. 2008. 177p. pap. 24.95 (978-1-60672-328-9(6)) America Star Bks.

Kirkup, Mary. The Tales of Granny Grunt. 2008. 32p. pap. 12.99 (978-1-4389-1040-6(1)) AuthorHouse.

Kirkwood, Edith Brown. Animal Children: The Friends of the Forest & the Plain. Ross, M. T., illus. 2007. 100p. per. (978-1-4065-2907-4(9)) Dodo Pr.

Kirkwood, Neville A. Jungle Heroes. 2011. 138p. pap. 11.50 (978-1-60976-267-4(3), Eloquent Bks.) Strategic Book Publishing & Rights Agency (SBPRA).

Kirwan, Wednesday. Baby Loves to Boogie! Kirwan, Wednesday, illus. 2014. (ENG., Illus.). 30p. (J). (gr. -1 — 1). bds. 5.99 (978-1-4814-0383-2(4), Little Simon) Little Simon.

Kisseloff, Jeff & Wells, Rosemary. Ruby's Tea for Two. 2003. (Max & Ruby Ser.). (ENG.). 12p. (J). (gr. -1 — 1). bds. 6.99 (978-0-670-03652-3(8), Viking Books for Young Readers) Penguin Young Readers Group.

Kissock, Heather, ed. The Lion, the Bear, & the Fox: Is It Better to Cooperate or Compete? 2013. (AV2 Animated Storytime Ser.). (ENG., Illus.). 32p. (J). (gr. -1-3). 29.99 (978-1-62127-920-4(0), AV2 by Weigl) Weigl Pubs., Inc.

Klausmeier, Jesse. Open This Little Book. Lee, Suzy, illus. 2013. (ENG.). 40p. (J). (gr. -1-3). 16.99 (978-0-8118-6783-2(8)) Chronicle Bks. LLC.

Klein, Abby. Homework Hassles. McKinley, John, illus. 2004. (Ready, Freddy! Ser.: 3). (ENG.). 96p. (J). (gr. -1-3). 5.99 (978-0-439-55600-2(7), Blue Sky Pr., The) Scholastic, Inc.

Klein, Adria F. Circus Train, 1 vol. Cameron, Craig, illus. 2013. (Train Time Ser.). (ENG.). 32p. (gr. -1-1). pap. 5.95 (978-1-4342-4883-1(6)); lib. bdg. 22.65 (978-1-4342-4188-7(2)) Stone Arch Bks.

Kleven, Elisa. Sun Bread. 2004. (gr. k-3). 17.20 (978-0-613-83005-8(9), Turtleback) Turtleback Bks.

Kline, Trish. Super Hero: KA Reader 1. 2007. (Illus.). 32p. (J). per. 20.00 (978-0-9717234-2-9(7)) Ghost Hunter Productions.

Knapp, Rene & Berger, Marjorie B. The Little Lost Allygator. 2012. 44p. 24.95 (978-1-4626-9717-5(8)) America Star Bks.

—The Little Lost Allygator. Kurt D Williams and Jeff Baker, illus. 2012. 44p. pap. 24.95 (978-1-4626-8155-6(7)) America Star Bks.

Knight, Deborah Janet. A Puzzling Picnic. Hauvette, Marion, illus. 2010. 32p. pap. 13.00 (978-1-60860-963-5(4), Eloquent Bks.) Strategic Book Publishing & Rights Agency (SBPRA).

Knight-Mudie, Karen. Yarns from Yandilla. 2013. 344p. pap. (978-0-9875697-0-7(8)) Davey, Mary Stella.

Knight, P. B. The Secret Passage, 1 vol. 2009. 73p. pap. 14.95 (978-1-61546-421-0(2)) PublishAmerica, Inc.

Knisley, Eric. The Adventures of Furlington Mackelthwaite. 2005. 40p. pap. 19.95 (978-1-4116-4792-3(0)) Lulu Pr., Inc.

Knowles, Daniel S. Rodent. 2010. 718p. 34.99 (978-1-4535-2562-3(9)); pap. 23.99 (978-1-4535-2561-6(0)) Xlibris Corp.

Kobert, Michael Gilead & Donato, Dona. Who Goes with That Nose? The Wild Adventures of Juicy Coppertoes. Fuller, Laurie, illus. 2005. 40p. (J). per. 9.95 (978-0-9770700-0-8(X)) Giggling Gorilla Productions, LLC.

Koehler, Mary, illus. The Children are Happy Story CD with Animals from the Southwest. 2003. (J). cd-rom 5.00 (978-0-9744005-1-8(3)) In the Desert.

Koffsky, Ann D., illus. Shabbat Shalom, Hey! 2015. (J). (ENG.). 24p. (gr. -1-k). lib. bdg. 16.95 (978-1-4677-4917-6(6)); 6.99 (978-1-4677-6208-3(3)) Lerner Publishing Group. (Kar-Ben Publishing).

Kohara, Kazuno. Here Comes Jack Frost. Kohara, Kazuno, illus. 2011. (ENG., Illus.). 32p. (J). (gr. -1-1). pap. 7.99 (978-0-312-60446-2(7), 9780312604462) Square Fish.

—The Midnight Library. Kohara, Kazuno, illus. 2014. (ENG., Illus.). 32p. (J). (gr. -1-1). 16.99 (978-1-59643-985-6(8), 9781596439856) Roaring Brook Pr.

Kok, Gemma. Explore. 2008. 44p. pap. 18.50 (978-1-4092-2058-9(3)) Lulu Pr., Inc.

—Explore (Printed in black & White) 2008. 44p. pap. 8.00 (978-1-4092-2530-0(5)) Lulu Pr., Inc.

Kola, Pamela, ed. East African How Stories. 2003. (Illus.). 48p. pap. (978-9966-46-472-9(7)) Heinemann Kenya, Limited (East African Educational Publishers Ltd E.A.E.P.) KEN. Dist: Michigan State Univ. Pr.

—East African Why Stories. 2003. (Illus.). 48p. pap. (978-9966-46-448-4(4)) Heinemann Kenya, Limited (East African Educational Publishers Ltd E.A.E.P.) KEN. Dist: Michigan State Univ. Pr.

Konnikova, Svetlana. Grapette, the Runaway Who Rolled Away: A Timeless Tale of Love & Family: A Child Discovering the World. Smishliaev, Anatoli, illus. 2007. (Grapette's Adventures Ser.). (ENG.). 32p. (J). (gr. k-2). 15.95 (978-0-9791758-0-0(1)) Aurora Pubs., Inc.

Koontz, Robin. La Pequeña Lagartija, ¡el Cielo Se Está Cayendo! / Lizzie Little, the Sky Is Falling! 2012. (SPA & ENG.). 24p. (gr. 2-3). pap. 8.95 (978-1-61810-541-7(8)) Rourke Educational Media.

Koopmans, Loek. Frog, Bee & Snail Look for Snow, 1 vol. 2006. Orig. Title: Samen Op Zoek. (ENG., Illus.). 28p. (J). (gr. -1-3). 15.95 (978-0-86315-559-8(6)) Floris Bks. GBR. Dist: SteinerBooks, Inc.

Koorang, Mundara. The Little Platypus & the Fire Spirit. 2005. (ENG., Illus.). 32p. (gr. -1-k). pap. 22.45 (978-0-85575-494-5(X)) Aboriginal Studies Pr. AUS. Dist: Independent Pubs. Group.

Koppens, Judith. Good-Bye, Fish. van Lindenhuizen, Eline, illus. 2013. (Animal Square Ser.). (ENG.). 32p. (J). (gr. -1-k). 13.95 (978-1-60537-153-5(X)) Cobblestone Publishing Co.

—The Seesaw. van Lindenhuizen, Eline, illus. 2013. (Animal Square Ser.). (ENG.). 32p. (J). (gr. -1-k). 13.95 (978-1-60537-152-8(1)) Cobblestone Publishing Co.

Korda, Lerryn. Millions of Snow. Korda, Lerryn, illus. 2010. (Playtime with Little Nye Ser.). (ENG., Illus.). 32p. (J). (— 1). 8.99 (978-0-7636-4651-6(2)) Candlewick Pr.

—So Cozy. Korda, Lerryn, illus. 2015. (ENG., Illus.). 32p. (J). (— 1). 15.99 (978-0-7636-7373-4(0)) Candlewick Pr.

Korda, Lerryn & Korda, Lerryn. Rocket to the Moon. Korda, Lerryn & Korda, Lerryn, illus. 2010. (Playtime with Little Nye Ser.). (ENG., Illus.). 32p. (J). (— 1). 8.99 (978-0-7636-4652-3(0)) Candlewick Pr.

Korman, Gordon. Hideout. 2013. (Swindle Ser.: 5). lib. bdg. 17.20 (978-0-606-32405-2(4), Turtleback) Turtleback Bks.

—Slacker. 2017. (ENG.). 240p. (J). (gr. 3-7). pap. 6.99 **(978-0-545-82316-6(1)**, Scholastic Pr.) Scholastic, Inc.

Korman, Gordon. Zoobreak. 2010. (ENG.). 240p. (J). (gr. 3-7). pap. 6.99 (978-0-545-12500-0(6), Scholastic Paperbacks) Scholastic, Inc.

Korman, Susan. Continental Drift. 2012. (Ice Age Ser.). (ENG.). 144p. (J). (gr. 3-7). pap. 5.99 (978-0-06-210485-4(3), HarperFestival) HarperCollins Pubs.

Kormos, Lawrence. It Happened One Night in the Barn. Purdy, Joanne, illus. 2007. 24p. (978-1-55452-192-0(0)) Essence Publishing.

Krakower, Harold. Sugarland. 2008. 28p. pap. 12.50 (978-1-934925-12-6(8), Eloquent Bks.) Strategic Book Publishing & Rights Agency (SBPRA).

Krans, Kim. 123 Dream. 2016. (ENG., Illus.). 48p. (J). (gr. -1-2). 16.99 (978-0-553-53932-5(9), Random Hse. Bks. for Young Readers) Random Hse. Children's Bks.

Krebs, Laurie. We All Went on Safari: A Counting Journey Through Tanzania. Cairns, Julia, illus. 2010. (J). 18.10 (978-0-7569-9319-1(9)) Perfection Learning Corp.

—We're Roaming in the Rainforest. Wilson, Anne, illus. 2010. 40p. (J). (gr. k-5). (ENG.). 8.99 (978-1-84686-545-9(X)); (SPA.). pap. 8.99 (978-1-84686-551-0(4)) Barefoot Bks., Inc.

—We're Sailing to Galapagos: A Week in the Pacific. Restelli, Grazia, illus. 2007. (ENG.). 32p. (J). (gr. k-1). pap. 8.99 (978-1-84686-102-4(0)) Barefoot Bks., Inc.

Krensky, Stephen. Arthur & the 1,001 Dads. 2003. (Marc Brown Arthur Chapter Bks.). (Illus.). 57p. (J). (gr. 1-4). 11.90 (978-0-7569-1600-8(3)) Perfection Learning Corp.

—Noah's Bark. Girard, Roger, illus. 2010. (ENG.). 32p. (J). (gr. -1-2). lib. bdg. 16.95 (978-0-8225-7645-7(7)) Lerner Publishing Group.

Krensky, Stephen & Sarfatti, Esther. Arturo y la Carrera por la Lectura. 2004.Tr. of Arthur & the Race to Read. (SPA., Illus.). (J). pap. 4.95 (978-1-930332-60-7(2)) Lectorum Pubns., Inc.

Krider, Dave. Do Animals Go to Heaven?, 1 vol. 2009. 49p. pap. 16.95 (978-1-61546-049-6(7)) America Star Bks.

Krivinskas, Carol Italiano. Barnyard Babies to the Rescue. 2008. 20p. pap. 13.95 (978-1-4327-2183-1(6)) Outskirts Pr., Inc.

Kroll, Steven. Stuff! Reduce, Reuse, Recycle, 0 vols. Cox, Steve, illus. 2012. (ENG.). 32p. (J). (gr. -1-3). pap. 7.99 (978-0-7614-6237-8(6), 9780761462378, Amazon Children's Publishing) Amazon Publishing.

Kroll, Virginia. Equal Shmequal. O'Neill, Philomena, illus. 2005. (Math Adventures Ser.). (ENG.). 32p. (J). (gr. k-3). per. 7.95 (978-1-57091-892-6(9)) Charlesbridge Publishing, Inc.

—Mosquito, 1 vol. LePlatt, Betsy, illus. 2011. (ENG.). 32p. (J). (gr. k-3). 16.99 (978-1-58980-883-6(5)) Pelican Publishing Co., Inc.

Krulik, Nancy. Never Box with a Kangaroo #11. Braun, Sebastien, illus. 2016. (Magic Bone Ser.: 11). (ENG.). 128p. (J). (gr. 1-3). 4.99 (978-0-448-48876-9(0), Grosset & Dunlap) Penguin Young Readers Group.

Kuipers, Alice. Violet & Victor Write the Most Fabulous Fairy Tale. 2016. (ENG., Illus.). 40p. (J). (gr. -1-3). 17.00 (978-0-316-21202-1(4)) Little Brown & Co.

Kumin, Maxine. What Color Is Caesar? Friend, Alison, illus. 2010. (ENG.). 56p. (J). (gr. -1-k). 16.99 (978-0-7636-3432-2(8)) Candlewick Pr.

Kumon. What Does Baby See? 2008. (Illus.). 12p. (J). bds. (978-1-934618-27-1(6)) Begin Smart LLC.

Kuo, Julia. Everyone Eats. Kuo, Julia, illus. 2012. (ENG., Illus.). 22p. (J). (gr. -1). 9.95 (978-1-897476-74-1(4)) Simply Read Bks. CAN. Dist: Ingram Publisher Services.

Kureishy, Simala. Lore of Love Series: Bismi & the Secret of the Kohinoor. 2010. 60p. pap. 12.99 (978-1-4490-7340-4(9)) AuthorHouse.

Kurrus, Jeff. The Tale of Jacob Swift. Palmer, Rob, photos by. l.t. ed. 2014. (ENG., Illus.). 48p. 16.99 (978-0-9916389-1-8(3)) Forsberg, Michael Photography.

Kvasnosky, Laura McGee. Zelda & Ivy - Keeping Secrets. Kvasnosky, Laura McGee, illus. 2013. (Candlewick Sparks Ser.). (ENG., Illus.). 48p. (J). (gr. k-4). pap. 3.99 (978-0-7636-6636-1(X)) Candlewick Pr.

L. A. Goal Members, contrib. by. Disabled Fables: Aesop's Fables Retold & Illustrated by Artists with Developmental Disabilities, 1 vol. 2005. (ENG., Illus.). 32p. (J). (gr. 1-18). 19.95 (978-1-932065-97-8(0)) Star Bright Bks., Inc.

La Coccinella. Guess Who? 2014. (Look & See! Ser.). (ENG., Illus.). 24p. (J). (gr. -1 — 1). bds. 6.95 (978-1-4549-0852-4(1)) Sterling Publishing Co., Inc.

—Look at Me. 2015. (Peekaboo! Ser.). (ENG., Illus.). 26p. (J). (gr. -1-k). bds. 6.95 (978-1-4549-1584-3(6)) Sterling Publishing Co., Inc.

La Rue, Mabel Guinnip. A Letter to Popsey. Lenski, Lois, illus. 2011. 28p. pap. 35.95 (978-1-258-06342-9(5)) Literary Licensing, LLC.

Laden, Nina. Peek-A Zoo! 2014. (ENG., Illus.). 22p. (J). (gr. -1 — 1). bds. 6.99 (978-1-4521-1175-9(8)) Chronicle Bks. LLC.

—Who Loves You, Baby? 2007. (ENG., Illus.). 18p. (J). (gr. -1 — 1). bds. 6.95 (978-0-8118-5724-6(7)) Chronicle Bks. LLC.

Ladybird Five-Minute Stories. 2017. (ENG., Illus.). 108p. (J). (gr. k-4). 14.99 **(978-0-241-24242-1(8))** Penguin Bks., Ltd. GBR. Dist: Independent Pubs. Group.

Laird, Donivee M. Will Wai Kula & the Three Mongooses. Jossem, Carol, illus. 2003. 41p. (J). (gr. k-3). 9.95 (978-0-940350-24-3(6)) Barnaby Bks., Inc.

Lake Press Ltd. Baby Friends. 2016. (Little Grabbers Ser.). (ENG., Illus.). 6p. (J). (gr. -1 — 1). bds. 5.99 (978-0-7641-6833-8(9)) Barron's Educational Series, Inc.

Lakeshore Learning Materials Staff. Is Your Mama a Llama? Big Book Theme Packet. 2008. (J). pap. 44.50 (978-1-60666-043-0(8)) Lakeshore Learning Materials.

Lakin, Patricia. Max & Mo's Halloween Surprise. Floca, Brian, illus. 2008. (Max & Mo Ser.). (ENG.). 32p. (J). (gr. -1-1). pap. 3.99 (978-1-4169-2539-2(2), Simon Spotlight) Simon Spotlight.

Lallemand, Orianne. The Wolf Who Wanted to Travel the World. Thuillier, Eléonore, illus. 2013. (My Little Picture Book Ser.). (ENG.). 32p. (J). (gr. -1). pap. 6.95 (978-2-7338-2314-9(0)) Auzou, Philippe Editions FRA. Dist: Consortium Bk. Sales & Distribution.

Lambert, Shirley. Tales of Beaver Hollow: The Magic Flute, 1 vol. 2009. 31p. pap. 24.95 (978-1-60836-705-4(3)) America Star Bks.

Lambert, Susan Dodd. Clarence the Clam. Modugno, Tina, illus. 2013. 28p. pap. 6.95 (978-0-9883893-5-9(5)) Borgo Publishing.

Lammers, Elizabeth A. & McKinney, Dan. Pierre's Stupendous Birthday Bash. Epstein, Gabriela, illus. 2011. 48p. pap. 24.95 (978-1-4560-4294-3(7)) America Star Bks.

La'more, Sheila. Runt: The Omega Wolf. 2007. 48p. per. 16.95 (978-1-4241-8222-0(0)) PublishAmerica, Inc.

Landers, Ace. The Yoda Chronicles Trilogy. 2014. (Lego Star Wars Ser.). (ENG.). 96p. (J). (gr. -1-3). 7.99 (978-0-545-62901-0(2)) Scholastic, Inc.

Landry, Leo. Grin & Bear It. Landry, Leo, illus. (ENG., Illus.). 48p. (J). (gr. k-3). 2014. pap. 5.95 (978-1-57091-746-2(9)) 2011. 12.95 (978-1-57091-745-5(0)) Charlesbridge Publishing, Inc.

—What's up, Chuck? 2016. (ENG., Illus.). 48p. (J). (gr. k-3). lib. bdg. 12.95 (978-1-58089-698-6(7)) Charlesbridge Publishing, Inc.

Lane, Leonie. Fork Tongue Freimon. 2006. 164p. per. (978-1-84667-009-1(8)) Derwent Pr., The.

Lang, Andrew, ed. The Red Book of Animal Stories 1899. Ford, Henry J., illus. 2004. reprint ed. pap. 34.95 (978-1-4179-8249-3(7)) Kessinger Publishing, LLC.

Lannin, Ann. A Child from Nowhere. 2011. 128p. (gr. 2-4). 21.95 (978-1-4620-2346-2(0)); pap. 11.95 (978-1-4620-2347-9(9)) iUniverse, Inc.

LaRochelle, David. It's a Tiger! Tankard, Jeremy, illus. 2012. (ENG.). 36p. (J). (gr. -1-k). 16.99 (978-0-8118-6925-6(3)) Chronicle Bks. LLC.

Lasky, Kathryn. Star Wolf. 2013. (Wolves of the Beyond Ser.: 6). (ENG., Illus.). 256p. (J). (gr. 3-7). 16.99 (978-0-545-27962-8(3), Scholastic Pr.) Scholastic, Inc.

Latimer, Àlex. Lion vs Rabbit, 1 vol. Latimer, Àlex, illus. 2013. (ENG., Illus.). 32p. (J). (gr. -1-3). 15.95 (978-1-56145-709-0(4)) Peachtree Pubs.

Latimer, Alex. Lion vs. Rabbit, 1 vol. Latimer, Alex, illus. 2017. (ENG., Illus.). 32p. (J). (gr. -1-3). pap. 7.95 **(978-1-56145-898-1(8))** Peachtree Pubs.

Latimer, Àlex, illus. Penguin's Hidden Talent, 1 vol. 2012. (ENG.). 32p. (J). 15.95 (978-1-56145-629-1(2)) Peachtree Pubs.

Laughter, Jim. Strangers in the Stable. WillowRaven, Aidana, illus. 2011. 24p. pap. 13.99 (978-0-9832740-3-2(7)) 4RV Publishing, LLC.

Lawson, Jennifer. The Secret Tea Party at the Zoo. 2010. (Illus.). 34p. pap. 19.95 (978-0-557-13707-7(1)) Lulu Pr., Inc.

Lawson, Peter. Tractor. 2009. (Turn the Wheel Ser.). (ENG., Illus.). 10p. (J). (gr. -1-k). bds. 5.95 (978-0-7892-1023-4(1), Abbeville Kids) Abbeville Pr., Inc.

Lawson, Peter & Smith, Kathryn. Animal Ambulance. 2009. (Turn the Wheel Ser.). (ENG., Illus.). 10p. (J). (gr. -1-k). bds. 5.95 (978-0-7892-1026-5(6), Abbeville Kids) Abbeville Pr., Inc.

Lawson, Robert. Rabbit Hill. Lawson, Robert, illus. 2007. (Puffin Modern Classics Ser.). (ENG., Illus.). 128p. (J). (gr. 3-7). 6.99 (978-0-14-240796-7(8), Puffin Books) Penguin Young Readers Group.

Layden, Joseph Lyon. The Other Side of Yore. 2007. 156p. pap. 14.95 (978-1-60145-122-4(9)) Booklocker.com, Inc.

Lê, Minh. Let Me Finish! Roxas, Isabel, illus. 2016. (ENG.). 20p. (J). (gr. -1-k). 16.99 (978-1-4847-2173-5(X)) Disney Pr.

Leaf, Munro. Noodle. Bemelmans, Ludwig, illus. 2006. 56p. (J). 15.99 (978-0-590-04310-6(2), Levine, Arthur A. Bks.) Scholastic, Inc.

—The Story of Ferdinand. 2011. (ENG.). 72p. (J). (gr. -1-k). 21.00 (978-0-670-01323-4(4), Viking Books for Young Readers) Penguin Young Readers Group.

—The Story of Ferdinand. Lawson, Robert, illus. 2011. (ENG.). 32p. (J). (gr. -1-k). pap. 4.99 (978-0-448-45694-2(X), Grosset & Dunlap) Penguin Young Readers Group.

—The Story of Ferdinand. 2011. (gr. k-3). lib. bdg. 14.75 (978-0-613-30144-2(7), Turtleback) Turtleback Bks.

Leah. The Alligator Named Ally, 1 vol. 2009. 20p. pap. 24.95 (978-1-60749-726-4(3)) America Star Bks.

Lease, Janice. Manny the Marmot. 2008. 48p. pap. 19.95 (978-0-9800762-2-6(6)) Cinnamon Ridge Publishing.

Lechelt, Karen. What Do You Love about You? 2016. (ENG., Illus.). 32p. (J). 16.99 (978-1-68119-093-8(1), 9781681190938, Bloomsbury USA Childrens) Bloomsbury Publishing USA.

Lechner, John. Sticky Burr: Adventures in Burrwood Forest. Lechner, John, illus. 2008. (ENG., Illus.). 56p. (J). (gr. 1-4). pap. 7.99 (978-0-7636-3567-1(7)) Candlewick Pr.

LeCraw, Cynthia, retold by. The Tale of the Wonderful Tar Baby. 2007. (J). (978-0-9794203-2-0(6)) Southern Lion Bks.

LeCron, Helen Cowles. The Animal Etiquette Book of Rhymes. Day, Maurice, illus. 2014. (ENG.). 64p. (J). (gr. 1-5). pap. 4.99 (978-0-486-78234-8(4)) Dover Pubns., Inc.

Lee Follen, Eliza. Piccolissima. 2004. reprint ed. pap. 15.95 (978-1-4191-4149-2(X)); pap. 1.99 (978-1-4192-4149-9(4)) Kessinger Publishing, LLC.

Lee, Nancy. Hoover's Funny Little Kids. 2005. (J). spiral bd. 8.95 (978-0-9748087-8-9(4)) Journey Pubns., LLC.

Lee, Steven. TruthQuest: In the Beginning. 2009. 72p. (J). pap. 6.95 (978-1-4327-3473-2(3)) Outskirts Pr., Inc.

Leech, Richard W. Adventures of Button Broken Tail, Bk. II. 2011. 249p. (J). 29.99 (978-1-4535-5219-3(7)); pap. 19.99 (978-1-4535-5218-6(9)) Xlibris Corp.

Leedy, Loreen. Crazy Like a Fox. Leedy, Loreen, illus. 2009. (ENG., Illus.). 32p. (J). (gr. -1-3). 7.99 (978-0-8234-2248-7(8)) Holiday Hse., Inc.

Leese, Jennifer L. B. Two Spots Bakery. 2004. 41p. pap. 24.95 (978-1-4137-3207-8(0)) PublishAmerica, Inc.

Leeson, Christine. Molly & the Storm. Hansen, Gaby, illus. 2003. 32p. (J). (gr. k-2). tchr. ed. 15.95 (978-1-58925-027-7(3)) Tiger Tales.

Lefebvre, Gail. A Week at Snug Bend. 2009. 64p. pap. 19.50 (978-1-60693-627-6(1), Strategic Bk. Publishing) Strategic Book Publishing & Rights Agency (SBPRA).

Lehrhaupt, Adam. I Will Not Eat You. Magoon, Scott, illus. 2016. (ENG.). 40p. (J). (gr. -1-3). 17.99 (978-1-4814-2933-7(7), Simon & Schuster Bks. For Young Readers) Simon & Schuster Bks. For Young Readers.

Lehti, Kauko. Beautiful Animal Stories for Good Children. 2009. 44p. pap. 18.00 (978-1-60693-872-0(X), Strategic Bk. Publishing) Strategic Book Publishing & Rights Agency (SBPRA).

Leigh, C. J. The Ninjabread Man. Gall, Chris, illus. 2016. (ENG.). 40p. (J). (gr. -1-k). 16.99 (978-0-545-81430-0(8)) Scholastic, Inc.

Leland, Debbie. Daddy's Love. Rife, Ann Hollis, illus. 2006. (J). 15.95 (978-0-9667086-4-6(4)) Wildflower Run.

Lemay, Didi. A Winter Solstice Celebration. Campbell, Jacquie, illus. 2008. 56p. pap. 23.99 (978-1-4389-0998-1(5)) AuthorHouse.

Lemke, Donald B. The Amazing Mini-Mutts, 1 vol. Baltazar, Art, illus. 2012. (DC Super-Pets Ser.). (ENG.). 56p. (gr. 2-2). pap. 4.95 (978-1-4048-7218-9(3)); lib. bdg. 23.99 (978-1-4048-6488-7(1)) Picture Window Bks. (DC Super-Pets).

Lemonade Zoo Monkeys. 2006. (Illus.). 33p. (YA). 10.95 (978-0-9765321-2-5(3)) Taven Hill Studio.

LeMonde', Stephanie. The Misty Forest. 2007. (Illus.). 154p. (J). (gr. -1-3). 14.95 (978-1-934138-13-7(4)) Bouncing Ball Bks., Inc.

Lepage, Michaele L. I Wish I Had a Tail. Lovass-Nagy, Nicole, illus. 2008. 20p. pap. 12.49 (978-1-4343-4721-3(4)) AuthorHouse.

Lepp, Royden. Happy Birthday Barnabas, 1 vol. Lepp, Royden, illus. 2008. (I Can Read! / Barnabas Ser.). (ENG., Illus.). 32p. (J). (gr. -1-1). pap. 3.99 (978-0-310-71586-3(5)) Zonderkidz.

Lester, Alison. Noni the Pony Goes to the Beach. Lester, Alison, illus. 2015. (ENG., Illus.). 32p. (J). (gr. -1-3). 17.99 (978-1-4814-4625-9(8), Beach Lane Bks.) Beach Lane Bks.

Lester, Helen. All for Me & None for All. Munsinger, Lynn, illus. 2012. (ENG.). 32p. (J). (gr. -1-3). 16.99 (978-0-547-68834-3(2)) Houghton Mifflin Harcourt Publishing Co.

—Batter up Wombat. Munsinger, Lynn, illus. 2006. (ENG.). 32p. (J). (gr. k-3). 24.80 (978-1-4287-0160-1(5), Followbound) Follett School Solutions.

—It Wasn't My Fault. Munsinger, Lynn, illus. alt. ed. 2013. (Laugh-Along Lessons Ser.). (ENG.). 32p. (J). (gr. -1-3). 8.99 (978-0-544-00323-1(3)) Houghton Mifflin Harcourt Publishing Co.

—Tacky in Trouble. Munsinger, Lynn, illus. 2005. (Tacky the Penguin Ser.). (ENG.). 32p. (J). (gr. -1-3). 6.95 (978-0-618-38008-4(6)) Houghton Mifflin Harcourt Publishing Co.

Lester, Helen & Munsinger, Lynn. Laugh-Along Lessons 5-Minute Stories. 2015. (Laugh-Along Lessons Ser.). (ENG., Illus.). 256p. (J). (gr. -1-3). 12.99 (978-0-544-50392-2(9), HMH Books For Young Readers) Houghton Mifflin Harcourt Publishing Co.

LeTourneau, Marie, illus. Argyle Fox. 2017. (ENG.). 32p. (J). (gr. -1-2). 17.99 (978-1-939100-09-2(7)) Tanglewood Pr.

Lette, Lauren Britt. Kiwi's First Day of School. 2008. 32p. pap. 24.95 (978-1-60441-418-9(9)) America Star Bks.

Levandowski, Barbara. The Adventures of Muffin & Alexander: The Please & Thank You Tea Party. 2012. 36p. pap. 18.41 (978-1-4669-6246-0(1)) Trafford Publishing.

Levert, Mireille. Les Nuits de Rose. braille ed. 2004. (FRE.). (J). (gr. -1-k). spiral bd. (978-0-616-03073-8(8)) Canadian National Institute for the Blind/Institut National Canadien pour les Aveugles.

Levy, Janice. Diva Duck Dreams, 1 vol. Madden, Colleen M., illus. 2012. (Diva Duck Ser.). (ENG.). 32p. (J). (gr. -1-4). 28.50 (978-1-61641-886-1(9)) Magic Wagon.

—Diva Duck Goes to Hollywood, 1 vol. Madden, Colleen M., illus. 2012. (Diva Duck Ser.). (ENG.). 32p. (J). (gr. -1-4). 28.50 *(978-1-61641-887-8(7))* Magic Wagon.
—Diva Duck Travels the World, 1 vol. Madden, Colleen M., illus. 2012. (Diva Duck Ser.). (ENG.). 32p. (J). (gr. -1-4). 28.50 *(978-1-61641-888-5(5))* Magic Wagon.
—Flip-Flop & the Absolutely Awful New Baby, 1 vol. Madden, Colleen M., illus. 2011. (Flip-Flop Adventure Ser.). (ENG.). 32p. (J). (gr. k-3). 28.50 *(978-1-61641-651-5(3))* Magic Wagon.
—Flip-Flop & the BFFs, 1 vol. Madden, Colleen M., illus. 2011. (Flip-Flop Adventure Ser.). (ENG.). 32p. (J). (gr. k-3). 28.50 *(978-1-61641-652-2(1))* Magic Wagon.
—Flip-Flop & the Bully Frogs Gruff, 1 vol. Madden, Colleen M., illus. 2011. (Flip-Flop Adventure Ser.). (ENG.). 32p. (J). (gr. k-3). 28.50 *(978-1-61641-653-9(X))* Magic Wagon.
—School Rules for Diva Duck, 1 vol. Madden, Colleen M., illus. 2012. (Diva Duck Ser.). (ENG.). 32p. (J). (gr. -1-4). 28.50 *(978-1-61641-889-2(3))* Magic Wagon.
—Showtime for Flip-Flop, 1 vol. Madden, Colleen M., illus. 2011. (Flip-Flop Adventure Ser.). (ENG.). 32p. (J). (gr. k-3). 28.50 *(978-1-61641-654-6(8))* Magic Wagon.
Lewis, C. S. L' Armoire Magique. Orig. Title: The Lion, the Witch & the Wardrobe. (FRE.). 188p. pap. 21.95 *(978-2-07-054643-5(8))* Gallimard, Editions FRA. Dist: Distribooks, Inc.
—Le Neveu du Magicien. (FRE.). pap. 21.95 *(978-2-07-054642-8(X))* Gallimard, Editions FRA. Dist: Distribooks, Inc.
—Le Prince Caspian. (FRE.). pap. 21.95 *(978-2-07-054645-9(4))* Gallimard, Editions FRA. Dist: Distribooks, Inc.
Lewis, Cindy (Didas). Time to Head South with Cindy the Canadian Goose, 1 vol. 2010. 56p. pap. 16.95 *(978-1-4489-3879-7(1))* America Star Bks.
Lewis, Edwina. Who Jumps? Parker, Ant, illus. 2003. (Who... Ser.). 16p. (YA). *(978-1-85602-447-1(4)*, Pavilion Children's Books) Pavilion Bks.
—Who Plays? Parker, Ant, illus. 2003. (Who... Ser.). 16p. (J). *(978-1-85602-469-3(5)*, Pavilion Children's Books) Pavilion Bks.
—Who Swims? Parker, Ant, illus. 2003. (Who... Ser.). 16p. (YA). *(978-1-85602-448-8(2)*, Pavilion Children's Books) Pavilion Bks.
Lewis, J. Patrick. Earth & Me, Our Family Tree: Nature's Creatures. Canyon, Christopher, illus. 2004. (Sharing Nature with Children Book Ser.). 36p. (J). (gr. -1-5). 16.95 *(978-1-58469-031-3(3))*; pap. 7.95 *(978-1-58469-030-6(5))* Dawn Pubns.
—Tugg & Teeny. Denise, Christopher, illus. 2011. (I am a Reader Ser.). (ENG.). 40p. (J). (gr. k-2). pap. 3.99 *(978-1-58536-685-9(4))*;Bk. 1. lib. bdg. 9.95 *(978-1-58536-514-2(9))* Sleeping Bear Pr.
—What's Looking at You Kid? 2012. (ENG., Illus.). 32p. (J). (gr. k-5). 14.95 *(978-1-58536-793-1(1))* Sleeping Bear Pr.
Lewis, Lisa. Tsunaxen's Journey. 2013. (ENG.). 23p. (J). pap. 14.95 *(978-1-4787-1979-3(6))* Outskirts Pr., Inc.
Lewis, Siân. Josh in the Jungle. Roberts, Gill, illus. 2005. (ENG.). 32p. pap. 12.95 *(978-1-84323-462-3(9))* Beekman Bks., Inc.
Lewis, Wendy A. Cheetah, 1 vol. Ross, Graham, illus. 2007. (Orca Echoes Ser.). (ENG.). 64p. (J). (gr. 2-3). per. 6.95 *(978-1-55143-465-0(2))* Orca Bk. Pubs. USA.
Lewman, David. The Case of the Vanished Squirrel. Moore, Harry, illus. 2008. (SpongeBob SquarePants Ser.). (ENG.). 16p. (J). (gr. -1-3). pap. 5.99 *(978-1-4169-4939-8(9)*, Simon Spotlight/Nickelodeon) Simon Spotlight/Nickelodeon.
—Chuckle & Cringe: SpongeBob's Book of Embarrassing Stories. 2007. (SpongeBob SquarePants Ser.). (ENG., Illus.). 48p. (J). (gr. 2-5). pap. 3.99 *(978-1-4169-4746-2(9)*, Simon Spotlight/Nickelodeon) Simon Spotlight/Nickelodeon.
Liano, Dante, et al. The Honey Jar, 1 vol. Unger, David, tr. from SPA. Domi, illus. 2006. (ENG.). 56p. (J). (gr. 3). 18.95 *(978-0-88899-670-1(5))* Groundwood Bks. CAN. Dist: Publishers Group West (PGW).
Libby, Lori Ann. The Adventures of Henry Hamper & the Flying Fish. Lee, Tricia Ting, illus. 2010. 34p. pap. 13.95 *(978-1-60911-493-0(0)*, Eloquent Bks.) Strategic Book Publishing & Rights Agency (SBPRA).
Licata, Rosemarie & Reizer, Edwina. The Hare & the Hound. 2007. 17p. 14.95 *(978-1-4357-0439-8(8))* Lulu Pr., Inc.
Light, Carol. Chickensing Big Book. Light, Carol, illus. 2003. (Illus.). (J). *(978-0-9745803-2-6(5))* Little Big Tomes.
—Chickensing Little Book. Light, Carol, illus. 2003. (Illus.). 108p. (J). *(978-0-9745803-3-3(3))* Little Big Tomes.
—Chickensing Story Book Reader. Light, Carol, illus. 2003. (Illus.). 60p. (J). *(978-0-9745803-1-9(7))* Little Big Tomes.
Light, Carol, illus. Oops, a Curious Horse Story Telling Board. 2003. (J). *(978-0-9745803-4-0(1))* Little Big Tomes.
Lindenbaum, Pija. When Owen's Mom Breathed Fire. Dyssegaard, Elisabeth Kallick, tr. 2006. (Illus.). 32p. (J). (gr. -1-3). 16.00 *(978-91-29-66548-2(5))* R & S Bks. SWE. Dist: Macmillan.
Lindsay, Norman. The Magic Pudding. 2012. (Dover Children's Classics Ser.). (ENG., Illus.). 144p. (J). (gr. 3-8). per. 8.95 *(978-0-486-45281-4(6))* Dover Pubns., Inc.
—The Magic Pudding. deluxe ed. (Illus.). 180p. 20.00 *(978-0-207-18355-3(4))* HarperCollins Pubs.
—The Magic Pudding. 2004. reprint ed. pap. 1.99 *(978-1-4192-7119-9(9))*; pap. 15.95 *(978-1-4191-7119-2(4))* Kessinger Publishing, LLC.
—The Magic Pudding. Lindsay, Norman, illus. 2016. (ENG., Illus.). 184p. (J). (gr. 4-7). pap. 9.99 *(978-1-59017-994-9(3)*, NYRB Kids) New York Review of Bks., Inc., The.
—The Magic Pudding: The Adventures of Bunyip Bluegum. 2008. 208p. *(978-0-7322-8432-9(5))* HarperCollins Pubs. Australia.
Linenthal, Peter. Look at the Animals! 2006. (ENG., Illus.). 18p. (J). (gr. -1 — 1). bds. 6.99 *(978-0-525-47582-8(6)*, Dutton Books for Young Readers) Penguin Young Readers Group.
The Lion & the Hare: [an East African Folktale]. 2009. (On My Own Folklore Ser.). (gr. 3-5). pap. 6.95 *(978-1-58013-849-9(7)*, First Avenue Editions) Lerner Publishing Group.
The Lion, the Witch, & the Wardrobe: Response Journal. 2003. 44p. (YA). *(978-1-58049-975-0(9)*, RJ75) Prestwick Hse., Inc.
Lionni, Leo. Theodore & the Talking Mushroom. 2009. (ENG.). 32p. (J). (gr. -1-2). 16.99 *(978-0-375-84551-2(8)*, Knopf Bks. for Young Readers) Random Hse. Children's Bks.
Lipara, Laura. Gramma Shares Her Faith: Cain & Abel. 2006. per. 7.95 *(978-0-9791757-1-8(2))* Oak Manor Publishing, Inc.
Lisi, Branden. Count on the Farm. Lisi, Margaret, illus. 2006. (J). lib. bdg. 15.95 *(978-0-9771472-0-5(7))* Count On Learning.
Lithgow, John. The Carnival of the Animals. Kulikov, Boris, illus. 2004. (ENG.). 40p. (J). (gr. -1-3). 19.99 *(978-0-689-86721-7(2)*, Simon & Schuster Bks. For Young Readers) Simon & Schuster Bks. For Young Readers.
—Carnival of the Animals. Kulikov, Boris, illus. 2007. (ENG.). 40p. (J). (gr. -1-3). 7.99 *(978-0-689-87343-0(3)*, Simon & Schuster Bks. For Young Readers) Simon & Schuster Bks. For Young Readers.
—Marsupial Sue Presents the Runaway Pancake. Davis, Jack E., illus. 2008. (ENG.). 40p. (J). (gr. -1-3). 7.99 *(978-0-689-87848-0(6)*, Simon & Schuster Bks. For Young Readers) Simon & Schuster Bks. For Young Readers.
Lithgow, John & Davis, Jack E. Marsupial Sue Presents the Runaway Pancake. 2005. (ENG., Illus.). 40p. (J). (gr. -1-3). 19.99 *(978-0-689-87847-3(8)*, Simon & Schuster Bks. For Young Readers) Simon & Schuster Bks. For Young Readers.
The Little Animals of Oaxaca: Lap Book. (Pebble Soup Explorations Ser.). 16p. (gr. -1-18). 21.00 *(978-0-7578-1664-2(9))* Rigby Education.
The Little Animals of Oaxaca: Small Book. (Pebble Soup Explorations Ser.). 16p. (gr. -1-18). 5.00 *(978-0-7578-1704-5(1))* Rigby Education.
little bee books, little bee & Powell, Richard. If You See a Cow. Martin Larranaga, Ana, illus. 2015. (ENG.). 12p. (J). (gr. -1-k). 4.99 *(978-1-4998-0112-5(2))* Little Bee Books Inc.
Little Bee Books Staff. Who's Hiding? Baruzzi, Agnese, illus. 2015. (ENG.). 16p. (J). (gr. -1-1). 9.99 *(978-1-4998-0168-2(8))* Little Bee Books Inc.
Little Bunny. 2003. (Goodnight Mr. Moon Ser.). (Illus.). (J). bds. 2.98 *(978-0-7525-4741-1(0))* Parragon, Inc.
Little Engine- Animal Friends. 2005. (J). *(978-1-4194-0023-0(1))* Paradise Pr., Inc.
Little, Stephen R. The Home Tree. 2011. (Illus.). 24p. (gr. -1). pap. 14.99 *(978-1-4567-2572-3(6))* AuthorHouse.
Littlefield, Eireann. Maisie the Animal Minder: Maisie & Ben. Haynes, Penny, illus. 2012. 34p. pap. *(978-1-908128-35-5(6))* Spiderwize.
Litton, Jonathan. Peek-Through Forest. Nowowiejska, Kasia, illus. 2015. (Little Snappers Ser.). (ENG.). 12p. (J). (gr. -1-2). bds. 9.99 *(978-1-68010-508-7(6))* Tiger Tales.
—Snap: A Peek-Through Book of Shapes. Galloway, Fhiona, illus. 2014. (My Little World Ser.). (ENG.). 16p. (J). (gr. -1-k). bds. 7.99 *(978-1-58925-566-1(6))* Tiger Tales.
—Surprise: A Book of Christmas Shapes. Galloway, Fhiona, illus. 2014. (ENG.). 16p. (J). (gr. -1-k). bds. 7.99 *(978-1-58925-567-8(4))* Tiger Tales.
—Tall & Short: A Peek-Through Book of Opposites. Galloway, Fhiona, illus. 2014. (My Little World Ser.). (ENG.). 16p. (J). (gr. -1-k). bds. 7.99 *(978-1-58925-565-4(8))* Tiger Tales.
Liwska, Renata. Red Wagon. Liwska, Renata, illus. 2013. (ENG., Illus.). 32p. (J). (gr. -1 — 1). 6.99 *(978-0-399-16239-8(9)*, Philomel Bks.) Penguin Young Readers Group.
Lloyd, A. R. Kine. l.t. ed. 2005. (Ulverscroft Large Print Ser.). (Illus.). 384p. 32.50 *(978-1-84395-554-2(7))* Ulverscroft Large Print Bks. GBR. Dist: Ulverscroft Large Print Bks., Ltd.
Lloyd-Jones, Sally. Baby Wren & the Great Gift, 1 vol. Corace, Jen, illus. 2016. (ENG.). 32p. (J). 16.99 *(978-0-310-73389-8(8))* Zonderkidz.
—Old MacNoah Had an Ark. Newton, Jill, illus. 2008. (HarperBlessings Ser.). 32p. (J). (gr. -1-2). 17.89 *(978-0-06-055718-8(4))* HarperCollins Pubs.
—Time to Say Goodnight. Chapman, Jane, illus. 2006. (ENG.). 32p. (J). (gr. -1-2). 15.99 *(978-0-06-054328-0(0))* HarperCollins Pubs.
Lloyd, Stacy K. Friends & Letters. 2005. 36p. pap. 13.00 *(978-1-4116-0900-6(X))* Lulu Pr., Inc.
Lluch, Alex A. Zoo Clues Animal Alphabet: Learn with Me the ABCs. 2005. (ENG., Illus.). 52p. (J). (gr. -1-k). bds. 7.95 *(978-1-887169-49-3(0))* WS Publishing.
Lobel, Anita. Hello, Day! Lobel, Anita, illus. 2008. (ENG., Illus.). 40p. (J). (gr. -1 — 1). 16.99 *(978-0-06-078765-3(1)*, Greenwillow Bks.) HarperCollins Pubs.
Lobo, Cerdito, Pato y Oca (Wolf, Pig, Duck & Goose) (SPA.). 24p. (J). 4.95 *(978-84-246-1606-9(5))* La Galera, S.A. Editorial ESP. Dist: AIMS International Bks., Inc.
Lock, Brian. There's a Hippo in My Bathtub. 2007. (ENG.). 76p. per. 19.95 *(978-1-4241-7331-0(0))* America Star Bks.
Lodge, Alison & Lodge, Ali. Clever Chameleon. Lodge, Alison, illus. 2005. (Illus.). 24p. (J). 15.99 *(978-1-84148-347-4(8))* Barefoot Bks., Inc.
Loffredo, Edward. The Adventures of the First Buffarillo. 2013. 28p. pap. 13.95 *(978-1-4808-0195-0(X))* Archway Publishing.
Lofting, Hugh. The Story of Doctor Dolittle. 2005. 128p. pap. 10.95 *(978-1-4218-0147-6(7))*; 26.95 *(978-1-4218-0047-9(0))* 1st World Publishing, Inc. (1st World Library - Literary Society).
—The Story of Doctor Dolittle. 2005. 96p. per. 4.95 *(978-1-4209-2544-9(X))* Digireads.com Publishing.
—The Story of Doctor Dolittle. 2005. (Dover Children's Classics Ser.). (ENG., Illus.). 96p. (J). (gr. 3-7). pap. 3.99 *(978-0-486-43883-2(X))* Dover Pubns., Inc.
—The Story of Doctor Dolittle. 2016. (J). pap. *(978-1-5124-2606-9(7)*, First Avenue Editions) Lerner Publishing Group.
—The Story of Doctor Dolittle. unabr. ed. 2011. (Dover Children's Thrift Classics Ser.). (ENG., Illus.). 96p. (J). (gr. 3-8). reprint ed. pap. 4.00 *(978-0-486-29350-9(5))* Dover Pubns., Inc.
—The Story of Doctor Dolittle. 2004. reprint ed. pap. 15.95 *(978-1-4191-8383-6(4))*; pap. 1.99 *(978-1-4192-8383-3(9))* Kessinger Publishing, LLC.
—The Story of Doctor Dolittle: Animal Talk. Kanzler, John, illus. 2008. (Easy Reader Classics Ser.). (ENG.). 32p. (gr. 3-7). lib. bdg. 24.21 *(978-1-59961-338-3(7))* Spotlight.
—The Story of Doctor Dolittle, Original Version. Lofting, Hugh, illus. 2010. (ENG., Illus.). 204p. (J). pap. 25.95 *(978-4-87187-305-5(6))* Ishi Pr. International.
—The Voyages of Doctor Dolittle. 2005. 340p. pap. 14.95 *(978-1-4218-0148-3(5)*, 1st World Library - Literary Society) 1st World Publishing, Inc.
—The Voyages of Doctor Dolittle. 2003. (Signet Classics Ser.). (Illus.). 254p. 14.95 *(978-0-7569-1855-2(3))* Perfection Learning Corp.
—The Voyages of Doctor Dolittle. McKowen, Scott, illus. 2012. (Sterling Unabridged Classics Ser.). (ENG.). 256p. (J). (gr. 5). 9.95 *(978-1-4027-9721-7(4))* Sterling Publishing Co., Inc.
—The Voyages of Doctor Dolittle. Corvino, Lucy, illus. 2008. (Classic Starts(tm) Ser.). (ENG.). 160p. (J). (gr. 2-4). 6.95 *(978-1-4027-4574-4(5))* Sterling Publishing Co., Inc.
Logelin, Matthew & Jensen, Sara Bee. Be Glad Your Dad. Chapman, Jared, illus. 2016. (ENG.). 40p. (J). (gr. -1-3). 16.99 *(978-0-316-25438-0(X))* Little Brown & Co.
Logue, Mary. Sleep Like a Tiger. Zagarenski, Pamela, illus. 2012. (ENG.). 40p. (J). (gr. -1-3). 17.99 *(978-0-547-64102-7(8))* Houghton Mifflin Harcourt Publishing Co.
Lohlein, Henning. All Better! Bernd, Penners, illus. 2015. (ENG.). 16p. (J). bds. 12.99 *(978-1-61067-362-4(X))* Kane Miller.
Lombardi, Elizabeth L. Jonathan's Journey. 2012. (ENG.). (J). *(978-1-62148-014-3(3))* SteinerBooks, Inc.
Lonczak, Heather Suzanne. Mookey the Monkey Gets over Being Teased. Ramsey, Marcy Dunn, illus. 2006. 32p. (J). (gr. -1-3). 9.95 *(978-1-59147-480-7(9))*; 14.95 *(978-1-59147-479-1(5))* American Psychological Assn. (Magination Pr.).
London, C. Alexander. Moonlight Brigade. 2016. (Wild Ones Ser.: 2). (ENG.). 240p. (J). (gr. 3-7). 17.99 *(978-0-399-17100-0(2)*, Philomel Bks.) Penguin Young Readers Group.
London, C. Alexander & Mack, Jeff. The Wild Ones. 2015. (Wild Ones Ser.: 1). (ENG., Illus.). 256p. (J). (gr. 3-7). bds. 17.99 *(978-0-399-17099-7(5)*, Philomel Bks.) Penguin Young Readers Group.
London, Jack. The Call of the Wild. 2008. (Bring the Classics to Life Ser.). (Illus.). 72p. (gr. 2-12). pap., act. bk. ed. 10.95 *(978-0-931334-64-1(0)*, EDCTR-203B) EDCON Publishing Group.
—The Call of the Wild. Moser, Barry, illus. 2011. (ENG.). 144p. (J). (gr. 4-9). pap. 8.99 *(978-1-4424-3411-0(2)*, Simon & Schuster Bks. For Young Readers) Simon & Schuster Bks. For Young Readers.
—La Llamada de la Naturaleza. 2003. (Historias de Siempre Ser.).Tr. of Call of the Wild. (SPA., Illus.). 92p. (J). (gr. 5-8). pap. 10.95 *(978-84-204-5731-4(0))* Santillana USA Publishing Co., Inc.
London, Jonathan. Froggy Builds a Tree House. 2013. (Froggy Ser.). lib. bdg. 17.20 *(978-0-606-30518-1(1)*, Turtleback) Turtleback Bks.
—Froggy Goes to Camp. Remkiewicz, Frank, illus. 2010. (Froggy Ser.). (ENG.). 32p. (J). (gr. -1-k). pap. 6.99 *(978-0-14-241604-4(5)*, Puffin Books) Penguin Young Readers Group.
—Froggy Plays in the Band. Remkiewicz, Frank & Frank, Remkiewicz, illus. 2004. (Froggy Ser.). (ENG.). 32p. (J). (gr. -1-k). 6.99 *(978-0-14-240051-7(3)*, Puffin Books) Penguin Young Readers Group.
—Froggy Plays in the Band. Remkiewicz, Frank, illus. 2004. (Froggy Ser.). (J). (gr. -1-3). 13.65 *(978-0-7569-2955-8(5))* Perfection Learning Corp.
—Here Comes Doctor Hippo: A Little Hippo Story. Eduar, Gilles, illus. (Little Hippo Ser.). (ENG.). 32p. (J). (gr. -1-k). 2013. pap. 6.95 *(978-1-62091-595-0(2))* 2012. 15.95 *(978-1-59078-851-6(6))* Boyds Mills Pr.
Long, Ethan. Thank You! 2016. (Animal Sounds Ser.). (ENG., Illus.). 20p. (J). (gr. -1 — 1). bds. 7.95 *(978-1-4197-1364-4(7))* Abrams, Inc.
Long, Loren. Little Tree. Long, Loren, illus. 2015. (ENG., Illus.). 40p. (J). (gr. k-3). 17.99 *(978-0-399-16397-5(2)*, Philomel Bks.) Penguin Young Readers Group.
Long, Robert. Inside the Chrysanthemum: New Japanese Fables. 2007. 156p. pap. 53.30 *(978-1-4303-0543-9(6))* Lulu Pr., Inc.
Longenecker, Jeff & Longenecker, Brenda. The Adventures of Critterville: The Beginning of Critterville. 2011. 44p. 16.59 *(978-1-4520-7458-0(5))* AuthorHouse.
Longstreet, Barbara, et al. Woodsey School Kids Thanksgiving Feast. 2004. 28p. pap. 24.95 *(978-1-4137-1992-5(9))* PublishAmerica, Inc.
Look at the Animals: Individual Title, 6 Packs. (Sails Literacy Ser.). 16p. (gr. k-18). 27.00 *(978-0-7635-4423-2(X))* Rigby Education.
Lopez- Jackson, Lillian. Eight 8 Short Stories for Children. 2011. 104p. pap. 37.66 *(978-1-4634-4672-7(1))* AuthorHouse.
Lopez, Barbara J. Pepper's Wish. 2009. 32p. pap. 14.49 *(978-1-4389-4976-5(6))* AuthorHouse.
Lopshire, Robert. I Want to Be Somebody New! Lopshire, Robert, illus. 2009. (Beginner Books Ser.). (ENG., Illus.). 48p. (J). (gr. -1-2). 8.99 *(978-0-394-87616-0(4)*, Random Hse. Bks. for Young Readers) Random Hse. Children's Bks.
Lord, Cynthia. Merlin. McGuire, Erin, illus. 2015. (Shelter Pet Squad Ser.: 2). (ENG.). 128p. (J). (gr. 2-5). 16.99 *(978-0-545-63599-8(3))* Scholastic, Inc.
LOS MÚSICOS DE BREMEN. 2004. (Caballo Alado Clásicos-Al Galope Ser.). (SPA & ENG., Illus.). 24p. (J). (gr. k-2). 7.95 *(978-84-7864-783-5(X))* Combel Editorial, S.A. ESP. Dist: Independent Pubs. Group.
Lougheed, Cordelia. Tales of the Magpie. 2008. 36p. pap. 22.95 *(978-1-4327-2032-2(5))* Outskirts Pr., Inc.
Lougher, Jenny. Ted & His New Trousers. 2008. 24p. pap. *(978-1-905553-31-0(5))* BookPublishingWorld.
Lovejoy, Robert. The Golden Dog Book of Fairy Tales & Animal Stories. 2005. (ENG.). 140p. pap. 13.99 *(978-0-919614-66-6(3))* Dundurn CAN. Dist: Ingram Publisher Services.
Lovelace, Victoria. Animal Crackers & Alphabet Soup. 2014. (ENG.). 84p. pap. 19.95 *(978-1-4670-3532-3(7)*, b9230d6d-2918-4b50-9842-302a1082f149) AuthorHouse.
Low, J. H. The Visitor from Far Far Away. Low, J. H., illus. 2016. (ENG., Illus.). 32p. 10.00 *(978-981-4721-71-4(9))* Marshall Cavendish International (Asia) Private Ltd. SGP. Dist: National Bk. Network.
Lowell, Susan. Los Tres Pequenos Jabalies: The Three Little Javelinas. Harris, Jim, illus. 2004. (SPA, ENG & MUL.). 32p. (J). (gr. -1-3). 15.95 *(978-0-87358-661-0(1)*, NP611) Rowman & Littlefield Publishers, Inc.
Lu, Marie. The Evertree. 2015. (Spirit Animals Ser.: 7). (ENG., Illus.). 192p. (J). (gr. 3-7). 12.99 *(978-0-545-53521-2(2))* Scholastic, Inc.
Lubner, Susan. A Horse's Tale: A Colonial Williamsburg Adventure. Moore, Margie, illus. 2008. (ENG.). 32p. (J). (gr. -1-1). 17.95 *(978-0-8109-9490-4(9)*, Abrams Bks. for Young Readers) Abrams, Inc.
Lubratt, Mark. Buffy Meets the Zoonicorns. Weingartner, Sara, illus. 2015. 32p. (J). 16.95 *(978-1-59298-893-8(8))* Beaver's Pond Pr., Inc.
Lucado, Max. Itsy Bitsy Christmas: You're Never Too Little for His Love, 1 vol. 2013. (ENG., Illus.). 32p. (J). pap. 9.99 *(978-1-4003-2404-0(1))* Nelson, Thomas Inc.
Lucas, David. Peanut. Lucas, David, illus. 2008. (ENG., Illus.). 32p. (J). (gr. k-k). 15.99 *(978-0-7636-3925-9(7))* Candlewick Pr.
Lucas, Gareth, illus. Dig, Dig, Digger! 2017. (Gareth Lucas Noisy Bks.). (ENG.). 12p. (J). (gr. -1). bds. 14.99 *(978-1-62686-936-3(7)*, Silver Dolphin Bks.) Readerlink Distribution Services, LLC.
Lucas, Matthew. A Roar in the Pinelands. 2010. 308p. 28.95 *(978-1-4502-3193-0(4))*; pap. 18.95 *(978-1-4502-3191-6(8))* iUniverse, Inc.
Lucas, Ronne Kay. How the Cactus Got Its Thorns. 2013. 20p. pap. 24.95 *(978-1-4626-8915-6(9))* America Star Bks.
Lucero, Jaime. One Little Egg. Kennedy, Kelly, illus. 2005. (Number Tales Ser.). (ENG.). 16p. (J). (gr. -1-1). pap. 2.99 *(978-0-439-68997-7(X))* Scholastic, Inc.
Ludwig, Sabine. The Story of the Little Pig Who Couldn't Say No. Wilharm, Sabine, illus. 2013. (ENG.). 32p. (J). (gr. -1-1). 16.95 *(978-1-62087-684-8(1)*, 620684, Sky Pony Pr.) Skyhorse Publishing Co., Inc.
Lukkarinen, Ritva. Amy. Vainio, Pirkko, illus. 2009. (ENG.). 30p. (J). (gr. -1-k). 16.95 *(978-1-60537-058-3(4))* Cobblestone Publishing Co.
Lullaby Moon. 2003. (J). 14.99 *(978-0-89610-495-2(8))* Island Heritage Publishing.
Lumry, Amanda & Hurwitz, Laura. Adventures of Riley: Mission to Madagascar. McIntyre, Sarah, illus. 2005. 36p. (gr. 2-3). 15.95 *(978-0-9748411-2-0(9))* Eaglemont Pr.
Lund, Jillian. Have You Ever Seen a Jackalope? 2006. (Illus.). 26p. (J). 15.95 *(978-1-891795-11-4(2))* RGU Group, The.
Lundquist, Mary. Cat & Bunny. Lundquist, Mary, illus. 2015. (ENG., Illus.). 32p. (J). (gr. -1-3). 17.99 *(978-0-06-228780-9(X))* HarperCollins Pubs.
Lurie, Susan. Will You Be My Friend? Head, Murray, illus. 2016. (ENG.). 32p. (J). 16.99 *(978-1-250-04643-7(2)*, 9781250046437) Feiwel & Friends.
Lyle-Soffe, Shari. Nothing Stops Noah. Collier, Kevin Scott, illus. 2008. 24p. pap. 10.95 *(978-1-935137-19-1(0))* Guardian Angel Publishing, Inc.
Lynch, Chris. Prime Evil. 2010. (Cyberia Ser.: 3). (ENG.). 160p. (J). (gr. 3-7). 16.99 *(978-0-545-02795-3(0)*, Scholastic Pr.) Scholastic, Inc.
Lyon, George Ella. Sleepsong. Catalanotto, Peter, illus. 2008. (ENG.). 40p. (J). (gr. -1-k). 16.99 *(978-0-689-86973-0(8)*, Atheneum/Richard Jackson Bks.) Simon & Schuster Children's Publishing.
Lyons Stroud, Patricia. The Seven Keys to Adventure. 2007. 148p. 23.00 *(978-1-59048-252-0(2))* Long Riders' Guild Pr., The.
MacDonald, Margaret Read. Conejito: A Folktale from Panama. Valério, Geraldo, illus. 2015. (ENG.). 32p. (J). (gr. -1-3). pap. 8.95 *(978-1-939160-96-6(0))* August Hse. Pubs., Inc.
—Give up, Gecko!, 0 vols. Melmon, Deborah, illus. unabr. ed. 2013. (ENG.). 32p. (J). (gr. k-3). 16.99 *(978-1-4778-1635-6(6)*, 9781477816356, Amazon Children's Publishing) Amazon Publishing.
MacDonald, Margaret Read & Macdonald, Margaret. Farmyard Jamboree. 2012. *(978-1-84686-718-7(5))* Barefoot Bks., Ltd.
MacDonald, Suse. Alphabet Animals: A Slide-and-Peek Adventure. MacDonald, Suse, illus. 2008. (ENG., Illus.). 28p. (J). (gr. -1-k). 12.99 *(978-1-4169-5045-5(1)*, Little Simon) Little Simon.
—Shape by Shape. MacDonald, Suse, illus. 2009. (ENG., Illus.). 24p. (J). (gr. -1-3). 16.99 *(978-1-4169-7147-4(5)*, Little Simon) Little Simon.
MacHado, Ana Maria. Delantal Que el Viento Lleva. (SPA.). pap. 12.95 *(978-950-07-2220-9(8))* Editorial Sudamericana S.A. ARG. Dist: Distribooks, Inc.
—Pimienta en la Cebecita. (Torre de Papel Ser.). (SPA., Illus.). (J). 7.95 *(978-958-04-5049-8(8)*, NR3067) Norma S.A. COL. Dist: Distribuidora Norma, Inc., Lectorum Pubns., Inc.
MacHale, D. J. The Merchant of Death. 2007. (Pendragon Ser.: 1). (ENG.). 384p. (J). (gr. 5-9). 19.99 *(978-1-4169-3625-1(4)*, Aladdin) Simon & Schuster Children's Publishing.
MacIver, Juliette. Yak & Gnu. Chapman, Cat, illus. 2015. (ENG.). 32p. (J). (gr. -1-2). 14.99 *(978-0-7636-7561-5(X))* Candlewick Pr.
Mack, Dinah. Daddy, Look What I Can Do! 2013. (Look What I Can Do Ser.). (ENG.). 14p. (J). (— 1). bds. 10.95 *(978-1-60537-170-2(X))* Cobblestone Publishing Co.
—Mommy, Look What I Can Do! 2013. (Look What I Can Do Ser.). (ENG.). 14p. (J). (— 1). bds. 10.95 *(978-1-60537-169-6(6))* Cobblestone Publishing Co.
—Mommy, Where Are You? 2012. (ENG.). 14p. (J). (gr. k — 1). bds. 10.95 *(978-1-60537-130-6(0))* Cobblestone Publishing Co.
Mack, Jeff. Duck in the Fridge, 0 vols. 2014. (ENG.). 40p. (J). (gr. 1-3). 16.99 *(978-1-4778-4776-3(6)*, 9781477847763, Amazon Children's Publishing) Amazon Publishing.
—Mine. 2017. (ENG., Illus.). 40p. (J). 16.99 *(978-1-4521-5234-9(9))* Chronicle Bks. LLC.
Mack, Paulette. Cookout at Grandma's House: The Adventures of Mielle & Cheeky. 2006. (ENG., Illus.). 24p. per. 10.95 *(978-1-59800-998-9(2))* Outskirts Pr., Inc.

Mackall, Dandi Daley. Runaway. 2008. (Starlight Animal Rescue Ser.: 1). (ENG.). 224p. (J). (gr. 3-7). mass mkt. 5.99 (978-1-4143-1268-2(7), Tyndale Kids) Tyndale Hse. Pubs.

Mackay, J. A. Rockin' Roly Poly. 2005. (J). 9.95 (978-0-938423-14-0(2)) Eco Images.

MacLachlan, Patricia. The Moon's Almost Here. dePaola, Tomie, illus. 2016. (ENG.). 32p. (J). (gr. -1-3). 17.99 (978-1-4814-2062-4(3), McElderry, Margaret K. Bks.) McElderry, Margaret K. Bks.

MacLean, Kerry Lee. Moody Cow Learns Compassion. 2012. (ENG., Illus.). 32p. (J). (gr. -1-3). 16.95 (978-1-61429-033-9(4)) Wisdom Pubns.

Maclear, Kyo. Yak & Dove. Shapiro, Esmé, illus. 2017. (ENG.). 24p. (J). (gr. -1-3). 18.99 **(978-1-77049-494-7(4)**, Tundra Bks.) Tundra Bks. CAN. Dist: Penguin Random Hse. LLC.

MacLennan, Cathy. Spooky Spooky Spooky! 2009. (ENG., Illus.). 32p. (J). (gr. -1-1). 16.95 (978-1-906250-67-6(7)) Boxer Bks., Ltd. GBR. Dist: Sterling Publishing Co., Inc.

MacMillan, Ian C. Khala Maninge - the Little Elephant That Cried a Lot: An African Fable. MacMillan, Eric G., illus. 2nd ed. 2003. lib. bdg. 5.00 (978-0-9729698-0-2(2)) Maninge Mali.

Mad Dash. 2005. (J). 4.95 (978-1-59792-011-7(8)) F.A.S.T. Learning LLC.

Madden, Gloria. Grandmothers Bedtime Stories: Book 5. 2008. 144p. pap. 11.99 (978-1-4343-9515-3(4)) AuthorHouse.

Madou, Carol. When Pigs Can Fly! 2011. 40p. pap. 18.99 (978-1-4567-3534-0(9)) AuthorHouse.

Mae, Darcie. Sammy & Robert's Animal Adventures. 2008. 32p. pap. 24.95 (978-1-60703-987-7(7)) America Star Bks.

Magsamen, Sandra. Baa, Moo, I Love You! A Book of Animal Sounds. 2014. (I Love Learning Ser.). (ENG., Illus.). 14p. (J). (gr. -1 — 1). bds. 7.99 (978-0-316-13358-6(2)) Little, Brown Bks. for Young Readers.

—I'M Wild about You! Magsamen, Sandra, illus. 2016. (Heart-Felt Bks.). (ENG., Illus.). 10p. (J). (— 1). 7.99 (978-0-545-46839-8(6), Cartwheel Bks.) Scholastic, Inc.

—Peep, Peep, I Love You! 2012. (Padded Cloth Covers with Lift-The-Flaps Ser.). (ENG., Illus.). 10p. (J). (gr. -1-17). bds. 7.99 (978-0-316-07006-5(8)) Little, Brown Bks. for Young Readers.

Maguire, Gregory. Leaping Beauty: And Other Animal Fairy Tales. Demarest, Chris L., illus. 2006. (ENG.). 224p. (J). (gr. 3-7). reprint ed. pap. 7.99 (978-0-06-056419-3(9)) HarperCollins Pubs.

Mahmood, Kamaal Manzoor. Lost & Found. 2012. 24p. pap. 15.99 (978-1-4691-6009-2(9)) Xlibris Corp.

Mahy, Margaret. The Gargling Gorilla. Phillips, Mike, illus. 2007. (Collins Big Cat Ser.). (ENG.). 112p. (J). (gr. 3-4). pap. 8.99 (978-0-00-723089-1(3)) HarperCollins Pubs. Ltd. GBR. Dist: Independent Pubs. Group.

Malone, David P. The Adventures of Benny the Bunnyduck: Escape from Chindia. 2012. (ENG.). 45p. (J). pap. 23.95 (978-1-4327-9352-4(7)) Outskirts Pr., Inc.

Malone, Peter & Prokofiev, Sergei. Sergei Prokofiev's Peter & the Wolf: With a Fully-Orchestrated & Narrated CD. Malone, Peter, illus. 2004. (ENG., Illus.). 40p. (J). (gr. -1-2). 19.99 (978-0-375-82430-2(8), Knopf Bks. for Young Readers) Random Hse. Children's Bks.

Maloza, Herve. The Secret of Creation. 2011. 36p. 16.86 (978-1-4520-9878-4(6)) AuthorHouse.

Maltby, Ethel H. My Animal Story Book: A Treasury of Sunshine Stories for Children. Richardson, Frederick, illus. 2004. reprint ed. pap. 15.95 (978-1-4191-7300-4(6)) Kessinger Publishing, LLC.

Mamma Macs. Australian Animal Walkabout. 2013. 32p. pap. (978-0-9923379-0-2(9)) Serenity Press.

Maness, Branda Edwards. Animal Tales of Hawaii. 2011. 28p. pap. 12.15 (978-1-4634-3484-7(7)) AuthorHouse.

Mara, Nichole. So Many Feet. Vidal, Alexander & Santillanes, Alexander Vidal, illus. 2017. (ENG.). 34p. (J). (gr. -1 — 1). bds. 12.95 (978-1-4197-2318-6(9)) Abrams, Inc.

March, Julia. Power Up! 2015. (DK Reader Level 3 Ser.). lib. bdg. 13.55 (978-0-606-36691-5(1)) Turtleback Bks.

Marciano, John Bemelmans. Madeline & the Cats of Rome. 2008. (Madeline Ser.). (ENG.). 48p. (J). (gr. 1-3). 17.99 (978-0-670-06297-3(9), Viking Books for Young Readers) Penguin Young Readers Group.

Marcus, Ms. Elena N. Devon: The Wild Adventures of Devon & Friends. 2012. (ENG., Illus.). 74p. (gr. 1-6). pap. 18.00 (978-0-615-57545-2(5)) Elena Marcus Negoita.

Margulies, Julianna & Margulies, Paul. Three Magic Balloons. Shaffer, Grant, illus. 2016. (ENG.). 40p. (J). (gr. -1-2). 17.99 (978-1-101-93523-1(5), Random Hse. Bks. for Young Readers) Random Hse. Children's Bks.

Marie, E. The Porcupine Connection: The Story of a Young Girl's Journey from Tragedy to Healing, with the Help of Her Forest Friends. 2004. 48p. pap. 16.95 (978-1-4137-3480-5(4)) America Star Bks.

Marii, Danila. My Tree & Me: A Journey Beyond the Rainbow. 2013. 56p. pap. 23.99 (978-1-4525-8386-0(2), Balboa Pr.) Author Solutions, Inc.

Marino, Gianna. Following Papa's Song. 2014. (ENG., Illus.). 40p. (J). (gr. -1-k). 16.99 (978-0-670-01315-9(3), Viking Books for Young Readers) Penguin Young Readers Group.

Marion, L. K. Summer Holiday with Funny Bunny. 2012. 32p. pap. 17.25 (978-1-4669-6475-4(8)) Trafford Publishing.

Markes, Julie & Markes. Good Thing You're Not an Octopus! Smith, Maggie, illus. 2006. (ENG.). 40p. (J). (gr. -1-3). pap. 6.99 (978-0-06-443586-4(5)) HarperCollins Pubs.

Markle, Sandra. The Fledglings. 2003. (ENG.). 144p. (YA). (gr. 4-6). pap. 9.95 (978-1-56397-696-4(X)) Boyds Mills Pr.

—What If You Had an Animal Nose? McWilliam, Howard, illus. 2016. (ENG.). 32p. (J). (gr. -1-3). pap. 4.99 (978-0-545-85922-6(0)) Scholastic, Inc.

Markle, Sandra & Markle, William. Gone Forever: An Alphabet of Extinct Animals. Davalos, Felipe, illus. 2007. (ENG.). 40p. (J). (gr. 4-6). 14.99 (978-1-4169-6138-3(0), Simon & Schuster/Paula Wiseman Bks.) Simon & Schuster/Paula Wiseman Bks.

Marks, Darrell. Down on the Farm. 2013. 12p. pap. 15.99 (978-1-4817-0969-9(0)) AuthorHouse.

Marlow, Barb. Sweet Dreams! 2012. 28p. pap. 13.99 (978-1-4624-0430-8(8), Inspiring Voices) Author Solutions, Inc.

Marshall, James & Marshall, James. Wings: A Tale of Two Chickens. 2003. (ENG., Illus.). 32p. (J). (gr. -1-3). 6.95 (978-0-618-31659-5(0)) Houghton Mifflin Harcourt Publishing Co.

Marshall, Linda Elovitz. Shh... Shh... Shabbat. Golubeva, Evgenia, illus. 2016. (ENG.). 12p. (gr. -1 — 1). 5.99 (978-1-4677-5873-4(6)); 23.99 (978-1-4677-9615-6(8)) Lerner Publishing Group. (Kar-Ben Publishing).

Marshall, Natalie. My Turn to Learn Numbers. 2013. (My Turn to Learn Ser.). (ENG., Illus.). 12p. (J). (gr. -1 — 1). bds. 6.99 (978-0-316-25164-8(X)) Little, Brown Bks. for Young Readers.

—My Turn to Learn Opposites. 2013. (My Turn to Learn Ser.). (ENG.). 12p. (J). (gr. -1 — 1). bds. 6.99 (978-0-316-25165-5(8)) Little, Brown Bks. for Young Readers.

—My Turn to Learn Shapes. 2013. (My Turn to Learn Ser.). (ENG., Illus.). 12p. (J). (gr. -1 — 1). bds. 6.99 (978-0-316-25166-2(6)) Little, Brown Bks. for Young Readers.

Marsoli, Lisa Ann & Disney Book Group Staff. Welcome to Royal Prep, Level 1. Disney Storybook Art Team, illus. 2013. (World of Reading Ser.). (ENG.). 32p. (J). (gr. -1-k). pap. 3.99 (978-1-4231-6407-4(5)) Disney Pr.

Martin, Ann M. Everything for a Dog. 2011. (ENG.). 240p. (J). (gr. 4-7). pap. 7.99 (978-0-312-67484-7(8), 9780312674847) Square Fish.

Martin, Bill, Jr. Baby Bear, Baby Bear, What Do You See? Carle, Eric, illus. (Brown Bear & Friends Ser.). (ENG.). (J). (gr. -1-k). 2014. 28p. bds. 12.99 (978-0-8050-9949-2(2), 9780805099492) 2011. 40p. 8.99 (978-0-8050-9291-2(9), 9780805092912) 2009. 28p. bds. 7.99 (978-0-8050-8990-5(X), 9780805089905) 2007. 32p. 17.99 (978-0-8050-8336-1(7), 9780805083361) Holt, Henry & Co. (Holt, Henry & Co. Bks. For Young Readers).

—Baby Bear, Baby Bear, What Do You See? 10th Anniversary Edition with Audio CD. Carle, Eric, illus. 2016. (Brown Bear & Friends Ser.). (ENG.). 32p. (J). 19.99 (978-1-62779-731-3(9), 9781627797313, Holt, Henry & Co. Bks. For Young Readers) Holt, Henry & Co.

—Baby Bear, Baby Bear, What Do You See? Big Book. Carle, Eric, illus. 2011. (Brown Bear & Friends Ser.). (ENG.). 32p. (J). (gr. -1-k). pap. 27.99 (978-0-8050-9345-2(1), 9780805093452, Holt, Henry & Co. Bks. For Young Readers) Holt, Henry & Co.

—Brown Bear, Brown Bear, What Do You See? Carle, Eric, illus. (Brown Bear & Friends Ser.). (J). 2012. (ENG.). 28p. (gr. -1-k). bds. 12.99 (978-0-8050-9577-7(2), 9780805095777) 2010. (ENG.). 40p. (gr. -1-2). 8.99 (978-0-8050-9244-8(7), 9780805092448) 2007. 32p. pap. 7.95 (978-0-8050-8797-0(4)) 3rd anniv. ed. 2008. (ENG.). 32p. (gr. -1-k). pap. 27.95 (978-0-8050-8718-5(4), 9780805087185) 50th anniv. ed. 2016. (ENG.). 28p. bds. 9.99 (978-1-62779-722-1(X), 9781627797221) Holt, Henry & Co. (Holt, Henry & Co. Bks. For Young Readers).

—Brown Bear, Brown Bear, What Do You See? / Oso Pardo, Oso Pardo, ¿qué Ves Ahí? (Bilingual Board Book - Spanish Edition) Carle, Eric, illus. 2017. (ENG.). 28p. (J). bds. 9.99 **(978-1-250-15232-9(1)**, 9781250152329, Holt, Henry & Co. Bks. For Young Readers) Holt, Henry & Co.

—Oso Panda, Oso Panda, ¿Qué Ves Ahí? Mlawer, Teresa, tr. Carle, Eric, illus. 2008. (Brown Bear & Friends Ser.).Tr. of Brown Bear, Brown Bear, What Do You See? (SPA & ENG.). 32p. (J). (gr. -1-k). 17.95 (978-0-8050-8348-4(0), 9780805083484, Holt, Henry & Co. Bks. For Young Readers) Holt, Henry & Co.

—Oso Panda, Oso Panda, ¿Qué Ves Ahí? Mlawer, Teresa, tr. Carle, Eric, illus. 2009. (Brown Bear & Friends Ser.).Tr. of Brown Bear, Brown Bear, What Do You See? (SPA & ENG.). 26p. (J). (gr. -1-k). 9.99 (978-0-8050-8756-7(7), 9780805087567, Holt, Henry & Co. Bks. For Young Readers) Holt, Henry & Co.

—Panda Bear, Panda Bear, What Do You See? Carle, Eric, illus. (Brown Bear & Friends Ser.). (J). 2014. (ENG.). 28p. (gr. -1-k). bds. 12.99 (978-0-8050-9950-8(6), 9780805099508) 2011. (ENG.). 40p. (gr. -1-2). 8.99 (978-0-8050-9292-9(7), 9780805092929) 2007. 32p. 7.95 (978-0-8050-8799-4(0)) 2007. (ENG.). 32p. (gr. -1-k). pap. 27.99 (978-0-8050-8102-2(X), 9780805081022) 2006. (ENG.). 28p. (gr. -1-k). bds. 7.95 (978-0-8050-8078-0(3), 9780805080780) Holt, Henry & Co. (Holt, Henry & Co. Bks. For Young Readers).

—Panda Bear, Panda Bear, What Do You See?, 1 vol. Carle, Eric, illus. unabr. ed. 2011. (Brown Bear & Friends Ser.). (ENG.). (J). (gr. -1-k). 9.99 (978-1-4272-1254-2(6), 9781427212542) Macmillan Audio.

—Panda Bear, Panda Bear, What Do You See? Carle, Eric, illus. 2013. (Slide & Find Ser.). (ENG.). 22p. (J). (gr. -1 — 1). bds. 12.99 (978-0-312-51581-2(2), 9780312515812, Priddy Bks.) St. Martin's Pr.

—Panda Bear, Panda Bear, What Do You See? 10th Anniversary Edition. Carle, Eric, illus. 2013. (ENG.). 28p. (J). (gr. -1-k). 19.99 (978-0-8050-9778-8(3), 9780805097788, Holt, Henry & Co. Bks. For Young Readers) Holt, Henry & Co.

Martin, Bill, Jr., et al. Chicka Chicka Boom Boom. Ehlert, Lois, illus. 2008. (J). 13.99 (978-1-59319-935-7(X)) LeapFrog Enterprises, Inc.

Martin, Emily Winfield. Dream Animals: A Bedtime Journey. 2013. (ENG., Illus.). 32p. (J). (gr. -1-k). 17.99 (978-0-449-81080-4(1)); lib. bdg. 20.99 (978-0-375-97149-5(1)) Random Hse. Children's Bks. (Random Hse. Bks. for Young Readers).

—The Imaginaries. 2017. (J). lib. bdg. (978-0-375-97432-8(6)) Random Hse., Inc.

Martin, J. P. Uncle. Blake, Quentin, illus. 2017. (ENG.). 176p. (J). (gr. 4-7). pap. 9.99 **(978-1-68137-185-6(5)**, NYRB Kids) New York Review of Bks., Inc., The.

—Uncle. Blake, Quentin, illus. 2007. (New York Review Children's Collection). (ENG.). 176p. (J). (gr. 4-7). 17.95 (978-1-59017-239-1(6), NYR Children's Collection) New York Review of Bks., Inc., The.

—Uncle Cleans Up. Blake, Quentin, illus. 2008. (ENG.). 184p. (J). (gr. 4-7). 17.95 (978-1-59017-276-6(0), NYR Children's Collection) New York Review of Bks., Inc., The.

Martin, James E. The Chartreuse Mongoose: Another Grandpa Ed's Bedtime Storybook. 2008. 224p. pap. 18.49 (978-1-4343-6637-5(5)) AuthorHouse.

Martin, Lisa & Martin, Valerie. Anton & Cecil, Book 2: Cats on Track. Murphy, Kelly, illus. 2015. (Anton & Cecil Ser.: 2). (ENG.). 272p. (J). (gr. 3-7). 16.95 (978-1-61620-419-8(2)) Algonquin Bks. of Chapel Hill.

—Anton & Cecil, Book 3: Cats Aloft. Murphy, Kelly, illus. 2016. (Anton & Cecil Ser.: 3). (ENG.). 272p. (J). (gr. 3-7). 16.95 (978-1-61620-459-4(1)) Algonquin Bks. of Chapel Hill.

Martin, Ruth. The Little Moose. Boey, Stephanie, illus. 2008. (ENG.). 35p. (J). (978-1-55168-332-4(6)) Fenn, H. B. & Co., Ltd.

Martinez, Rene. The Journey of the Golden Sword. 2011. 64p. pap. 15.99 (978-1-4535-9187-1(7)) Xlibris Corp.

Martins, Isabel Minhós. My Neighbor Is a Dog. Herring, John, tr. from POR. Matoso, Madalena, illus. 2013. (ENG.). 32p. (J). (gr. -1-4). 16.95 (978-1-926973-68-5(2)) Owlkids Bks. Inc. CAN. Dist: Publishers Group West (PGW).

Masi, Sue. A Journey Through Fantasy Forest. 2012. 44p. pap. 21.99 (978-1-4691-4837-3(4)) Xlibris Corp.

Mason, Chad. Wake up, Bertha Bear! Wallace, Chad, illus. 2006. (ENG.). 32p. (J). (gr. -1-3). 15.95 (978-0-89272-655-4(5)) Down East Bks.

Massey, Jane, illus. Animales de la Granja. (Coloca y Siente). (SPA.). 10p. (J). (gr. k-2). bds. (978-968-5308-67-0(5), Silver Dolphin en Español) Advanced Marketing, S. de R. L. de C. V.

—Animales de la Selva. (Coloca y Siente). (SPA.). 10p. (J). (gr. k-2). bds. (978-968-5308-68-7(3), Silver Dolphin en Español) Advanced Marketing, S. de R. L. de C. V.

Massey, K. J. Everyday Things with Morgan. Bowser, Katya, illus. 2013. 24p. 19.99 (978-0-9910489-4-6(6)) NyreePr. Literary Group.

Masterson, Hoss. Animal All-Stars. 2017. (Animal All-Stars Ser.). (ENG.). 56p. (gr. 1-3). 101.28 (978-1-4965-4326-4(2)) Stone Arch Bks.

—Ball Hog. Alves, Josh, illus. 2017. (Animal All-Stars Ser.). (ENG.). 56p. (gr. 1-3). lib. bdg. 25.32 (978-1-4965-4308-0(4)) Stone Arch Bks.

—Soccer Sloth. Alves, Josh, illus. 2017. (Animal All-Stars Ser.). (ENG.). 56p. (gr. 1-3). lib. bdg. 25.32 (978-1-4965-4306-6(8)) Stone Arch Bks.

—Wild Receiver. Alves, Josh, illus. 2017. (Animal All-Stars Ser.). (ENG.). 56p. (gr. 1-3). lib. bdg. 25.32 (978-1-4965-4307-3(6)) Stone Arch Bks.

Mathy, Vincent, illus. Who's Hiding with Penguin? 2016. (ENG.). 10p. (J). (gr. -1 — 1). bds. 8.99 (978-1-4521-5661-3(1)) Chronicle Bks. LLC.

Mattsson, Jude. Angus Emu & Sara Mare. 2011. 20p. 11.99 (978-1-4567-3153-3(X)) AuthorHouse.

Maureen, Roffey, illus. A B C Animals Teach Me! 2014. (ENG.). 26p. (J). (gr. -1 — 1). bds. 5.99 (978-0-7944-3017-7(1)) Reader's Digest Assn., Inc., The.

Mawhinney, Art, illus. Dora & Diego to the Rescue! 2010. (Go, Diego, Go! Ser.). (ENG.). 48p. (J). pap. 5.99 (978-1-4424-0660-5(7), Simon Spotlight/Nickelodeon) Simon Spotlight/Nickelodeon.

—Look & Find Open Season. 2007. 32p. (J). (gr. -1-3). lib. bdg. 7.98 (978-1-4127-8889-2(7)) Publications International, Ltd.

Maxwell-Hyslop, Miranda. Fish Go Woof! 2005. (Illus.). 36p. (J). (978-0-340-87338-0(8)) Hodder & Stoughton.

May, Karen. Walk in the Woods. 2011. (Illus.). 26p. pap. (978-1-908147-75-2(X)) YouWriteOn.

Maybarduk, Linda. James the Dancing Dog. Johnson, Gillian, illus. 2004. (ENG.). 24p. (J). (gr. -1-2). 15.95 (978-0-88776-619-0(6), Tundra Bks.) Tundra Bks. CAN. Dist: Penguin Random Hse. LLC.

Mayer, Mercer. The Best Teacher Ever No. 6. Mayer, Mercer, illus. 2008. (Little Critter Ser.). (ENG., Illus.). 24p. (J). (gr. -1-2). pap. 3.99 (978-0-06-053960-3(7), HarperFestival) HarperCollins Pubs.

—The Fall Festival. Mayer, Mercer, illus. 2009. (My First I Can Read Ser.). (ENG., Illus.). 32p. (J). (gr. -1-3). pap. 3.99 (978-0-06-083551-4(6)) HarperCollins Pubs.

—The First Day of School No. 3. Mayer, Mercer, illus. 2009. (Little Critter Ser.). (ENG., Illus.). 20p. (J). (gr. -1-2). pap. 6.99 (978-0-06-053969-6(0), HarperFestival) HarperCollins Pubs.

—Going to the Sea Park. Mayer, Mercer, illus. 2009. (My First I Can Read Ser.). (ENG., Illus.). 32p. (J). (gr. -1-3). pap. 3.99 (978-0-06-083553-8(2)) HarperCollins Pubs.

—Grandma, Grandpa, & Me. Mayer, Mercer, illus. 2007. (Little Critter Ser.). (ENG., Illus.). 24p. (J). (gr. -1-2). pap. 3.99 (978-0-06-053951-1(8), HarperFestival) HarperCollins Pubs.

—Happy Mother's Day! Mayer, Mercer, illus. 2009. (Little Critter Ser.). (ENG., Illus.). 20p. (J). (gr. -1-2). pap. 6.99 (978-0-06-053970-2(4), HarperFestival) HarperCollins Pubs.

—Just a Little Sick. Mayer, Mercer, illus. 2009. (My First I Can Read Ser.). (ENG., Illus.). 32p. (J). (gr. -1-3). 16.99 (978-0-06-083556-9(7)); pap. 3.99 (978-0-06-083555-2(9)) HarperCollins Pubs.

—Just Saving My Money. Mayer, Mercer, illus. 2010. (My First I Can Read Ser.). (ENG., Illus.). 32p. (J). (gr. -1-3). pap. 3.99 (978-0-06-083557-6(5)) HarperCollins Pubs.

—Little Critter Collection. Mayer, Mercer, illus. 2012. (My First I Can Read Ser.). (ENG., Illus.). 96p. (J). (gr. -1 — 1). pap. 11.99 (978-0-06-207567-3(5)) HarperCollins Pubs.

—Little Critters, 1 vol. 2014. (ENG., Illus.). 24p. (J). bds. 9.99 (978-1-4003-2250-3(2)) Nelson, Thomas Inc.

—The Lost Dinosaur Bone. Mayer, Mercer, illus. 2007. (Little Critter Ser.). (ENG., Illus.). 24p. (J). (gr. -1-3). pap. 3.99 (978-0-06-053952-8(6), HarperFestival) HarperCollins Pubs.

—My Trip to the Hospital, No. 5. Mayer, Mercer, illus. 2005. (Little Critter Ser.). (ENG., Illus.). 24p. (J). (gr. -1-2). pap. 3.99 (978-0-06-053949-8(6), HarperFestival) HarperCollins Pubs.

—Play It Safe. 2004. (Mercer Mayer's Little Critter Ser.). (Illus.). 24p. (gr. -1-3). 14.45 (978-0-7569-3030-1(8)) Perfection Learning Corp.

McAdams, Susan. Shubert. McAdams, Caleb, illus. 2008. 16p. per. 24.95 (978-1-4241-9756-9(2)) America Star Bks.

McAnulty, Stacy. It's Not a Dinosaur! Boldt, Mike, illus. 2016. (Dino Files Ser.: 3). (ENG.). 128p. (J). (gr. 2-5). 9.99 (978-0-553-52197-9(7), Random Hse. Bks. for Young Readers) Random Hse. Children's Bks.

McBrayer, Cassidy. You Can, Toucan! You Can. 2008. 20p. pap. 15.95 (978-1-4327-1132-0(6)) Outskirts Pr., Inc.

McCabe, Lauren A. How Many Spots Have I Got? Foulke, Nancy, illus. 2005. (J). 16.00 (978-1-893516-02-1(4)) Our Child Pr.

McCanna, Tim. Barnyard Boogie! Black, Allison, illus. 2017. (ENG.). 24p. (gr. -1-k). 12.95 (978-1-4197-2346-9(4), Abrams Appleseed) Abrams, Inc.

McCarthy, Peggy & Rivers, Julia. Not for the Meek. 2013. (ENG.). 130p. (J). pap. 10.95 (978-1-4327-9157-5(5)) Outskirts Pr., Inc.

McCarty, Peter. Henry in Love. McCarty, Peter, illus. 2009. (ENG., Illus.). 48p. (J). (gr. -1-1). 16.99 (978-0-06-114288-8(3)) HarperCollins Pubs.

McCaughrean, Geraldine & Willey, Bee. Collins Big Cat - Think Again! 2005. (Collins Big Cat Ser.). (ENG.). 32p. (J). (gr. 1-3). pap. 7.99 (978-0-00-718643-3(6)) HarperCollins Pubs. Ltd. GBR. Dist: Independent Pubs. Group.

McClements, George. Dinosaur Woods: Can Seven Clever Critters Save Their Forest Home? McClements, George, illus. 2009. (ENG., Illus.). 40p. (J). (gr. -1-2). 16.99 (978-1-4169-8626-3(X), Beach Lane Bks.) Beach Lane Bks.

McClintock, Mike. A Fly Went By. Siebel, Fritz, illus. 2007. (Beginner Ser.). (ENG.). 68p. pap. (978-0-00-722482-1(6), HarperCollins Children's Bks.) HarperCollins Pubs. Ltd.

McCourt, Lisa. I Love You, Stinky Face. Moore, Cyd, illus. (ENG.). (J). 2009. (gr. -1-3). 18.95 (978-0-545-11944-3(8)) 2004. 16p. (gr. 3-7). bds. 6.99 (978-0-439-63572-1(1)) 2003. 32p. (gr. -1 — 1). pap. 6.99 (978-0-439-63469-4(5)) Scholastic, Inc.

McCracken, Harold. Pirate of the North. Tonk, Ernest, illus. 2011. 224p. 44.95 (978-1-258-09631-1(5)) Literary Licensing, LLC.

McCue, Lisa. The Animals' Advent. 2010. (ENG., Illus.). 14p. (J). (gr. k — 1). 5.99 (978-0-375-85815-4(6), Random Hse. Bks. for Young Readers) Random Hse. Children's Bks.

McCully, Emily Arnold. Late Nate in a Race. McCully, Emily Arnold, illus. 2013. (I Like to Read(r) Ser.). (ENG., Illus.). 24p. (J). (gr. -1-3). pap. 6.99 (978-0-8234-2755-0(2)) Holiday Hse., Inc.

McDiarmid, Gail S. & McGee, Marilyn S. Running for Home. Coffey, Durwood, illus. 2013. 76p. pap. 15.95 (978-0-9854677-0-8(3)) SunDog Enterprises.

McDonald, Jill. Over in the Meadow. McDonald, Jill & Reed, Susan, illus. 2011. (ENG.). 24p. (J). (gr. 1-4). 16.99 (978-1-84686-543-5(3)) Barefoot Bks., Inc.

McDonald, Jill, illus. Ghoulish Gang. 2008. (ENG.). 12p. (J). 9.95 (978-1-58117-782-4(8), Intervisual/Piggy Toes) Bendon, Inc.

McDonald, Lisa. The Adventures of Penelope the Tea Cup Pig. 2012. 36p. pap. 32.70 (978-1-4771-3182-4(5)) Xlibris Corp.

McElligott, Walter Lee. A Blessed Bethlehem Birth: As told by Abraham & Anna Mousenstern. Collier, Kevin Scott, illus. 2006. 28p. (J). E-Book 5.00 incl. cd-rom (978-1-933090-21-4(9)) Guardian Angel Publishing, Inc.

McElroy, Jean. Night-Night, Sleepyhead. Ramljak, Marijan, illus. 2010. (ENG.). 12p. (J). (gr. -1 — 1). 4.99 (978-1-4424-0902-6(9), Little Simon) Little Simon.

McGaa Tonemah, Paula & McGaa, Ed. The Animals Talk. 2009. 72p. (J). pap. (978-1-57579-373-3(3)) Pine Hill Pr.

McGee, Marni. Bear Can't Sleep! Julian, Sean, illus. 2015. (ENG.). 32p. (J). (gr. -1-3). 16.99 (978-1-58925-189-2(X)) Tiger Tales.

McGillicuddy, Barbara. Adventures in the Kingdom of Mim: Buddie Saves the Day. 2006. (J). per. 13.95 (978-0-9774513-7-1(2)) Changing Lives Publishing.

McGinnis, Mark W. Buddhist Animal Wisdom Stories. 2004. (ENG., Illus.). 112p. (J). (gr. -1-3). 19.95 (978-0-8348-0551-4(0), Weatherhill, Inc.) Shambhala Pubns., Inc.

McGowan, Jayme. One Bear Extraordinaire. 2015. (ENG., Illus.). 32p. (J). (gr. -1-3). 16.95 (978-1-4197-1654-6(9), Abrams Bks. for Young Readers) Abrams, Inc.

McGrath, Barbara Barbieri. Easter Counting. Tagel, Peggy, illus. 2017. (First Celebrations Ser.). (ENG.). 12p. (J). (— 1). bds. 6.99 (978-1-58089-535-4(2)) Charlesbridge Publishing, Inc.

McGrory, Anik, illus. The Christmas Fox. 2016. (ENG.). 32p. (J). (gr. -1-2). 16.99 (978-1-101-93500-2(6), Knopf Bks. for Young Readers) Random Hse. Children's Bks.

McIntyre, Sasha & Sinkner, Alice, adapted by. Franklin's Easter: A Sticker Activity Book. 2004. (Franklin Ser.). (ENG., Illus.). 16p. (J). (gr. k-3). 4.95 (978-1-55337-690-3(0)) Kids Can Pr., Ltd. CAN. Dist: Hachette Bk. Group.

McKay, Hilary. Lulu & the Duck in the Park. Lamont, Priscilla, illus. (Lulu Ser.: Book 1). (ENG.). (J). (gr. 1-5). 2012. 104p. 13.99 (978-0-8075-4808-0(1))Bk. 1. 2014. 112p. 4.99 (978-0-8075-4809-7(X)) Whitman, Albert & Co.

McKay, Sindy. We Both Read-My Day Big Book. Johnson, Meredith, illus. 2006. (We Both Read Ser.). 40p. (J). (gr. -1-4). pap. 29.95 (978-1-891327-93-3(3)) Treasure Bay, Inc.

McKee, David. Elmer & Grandpa Eldo. McKee, David, illus. 2016. (ENG., Illus.). 32p. (J). (gr. -1-3). 17.99 (978-1-5124-0569-9(8)) Lerner Publishing Group.

Mckee, David. Elmer & Super El. McKee, David, illus. 2012. (Andersen Press Picture Bks). (ENG.). 32p. (J). (gr. -1-3). 16.95 (978-0-7613-8989-7(X)) Lerner Publishing Group.

McKee, David. Elmer & the Flood. McKee, David, illus. 2015. (ENG., Illus.). 32p. (J). (gr. -1-3). 17.99 (978-1-4677-9314-8(0)); 17.99 (978-1-4677-9312-4(4)) Lerner Publishing Group.

—Elmer & the Lost Teddy. McKee, David, illus. 2004. (Elmer Bks.). (Illus.). 32p. (J). 9.99 (978-0-06-075243-9(2)) HarperCollins Pubs.

—Elmer & the Rainbow. McKee, David, illus. 2011. (Andersen Press Picture Bks). (ENG., Illus.). 32p. (J). (gr. -1-3). 16.95 (978-0-7613-7410-7(8)) Lerner Publishing Group.

McKendry, Sam. Imagine That! Samuel, Janet, illus. 2007. (ENG.). 12p. (gr. -1-k). 9.95 (978-1-58117-484-7(5), Intervisual/Piggy Toes) Bendon, Inc.

McKenna, Mark, et al, illus. Banana Tail. 2003. 32p. (J). 12.95 (978-0-9727681-3-9(0)) Active Media Publishing, LLC.

McKinna, Caelaach. Lion in the Living Room. Stone, A. R., illus. 2008. 24p. (J). pap. 14.99 (978-0-9797513-4-9(9)) 4RV Publishing, LLC.

McKissack, Patricia C. Where Crocodiles Have Wings. Barner, Bob, illus. 2005. (ENG.). 32p. (J). (gr. -1-3). 16.95 (978-0-8234-1748-3(4)) Holiday Hse., Inc.

McKittrick, Erin. My Coyote Nose & Ptarmigan Toes: An Almost-True Alaskan Adventure. Higman, Valisa, illus. 2016. (Paws IV Ser.). (ENG.). 32p. (J). (gr. -1-2). pap. 10.99 *(978-1-63217-031-6(0),* Little Bigfoot) Sasquatch Bks.
McLaughlin, Diane & Tully, Lisa. The WhizAnt Who Isn't Coloring & Activity Book. 2003. (Illus.). 32p. (J). cd-rom 15.95 *(978-0-9722249-1-8(2))* Bugeye Bks.
McMahon, Kara & Random House Disney Staff. Animal Alphabet: From Ape to Zebra. Moroney, Christopher, illus. 2005. (Sesame Street Start-to-Read Bks.). (ENG.). 20p. (J). (gr. k — 1). bds. 7.99 *(978-0-375-83228-4(9),* Random Hse. Bks. for Young Readers) Random Hse. Children's Bks.
McManis, Margaret. The Wild Texas Stampede!, 1 vol. Dupree, Bruce, illus. 2008. (ENG.). 32p. (J). (gr. 1-3). 16.99 *(978-1-58980-568-2(2))* Pelican Publishing Co., Inc.
McMasters, Anne. Anne's Stories for Children of All Ages. 2008. 24p. pap. 12.50 *(978-1-4343-9204-6(X))* AuthorHouse.
McMillian, Gordon. Scout. 2012. (ENG., Illus.). 40p. (J). 14.95 *(978-1-58536-797-9(4))* Sleeping Bear Pr.
McMullan, Kate. Bulldog's Big Day. Lemaître, Pascal, illus. 2011. (J). *(978-0-545-17156-4(3),* Orchard Bks.) Scholastic, Inc.
—Five Days till Summer. Alley, R. W., illus. 2014. (Pearl & Wagner Ser.: 5). (ENG.). 48p. (J). (gr. 1-3). pap. 3.99 *(978-0-448-48137-1(5),* Penguin Young Readers) Penguin Young Readers Group.
—One Funny Day. Alley, R. W., illus. 2012. (Pearl & Wagner Ser.: 1). (ENG.). 48p. (J). (gr. 1-3). pap. 3.99 *(978-0-448-45866-3(7),* Penguin Young Readers) Penguin Young Readers Group.
—Two Good Friends. Alley, R. W., illus. 2011. (Pearl & Wagner Ser.: 2). (ENG.). 48p. (J). (gr. 1-3). pap. 3.99 *(978-0-448-45690-4(7),* Penguin Young Readers) Penguin Young Readers Group.
McNamee, Kevin. If I Could Be Anything. Movshina, Marina, illus. 2009. 16p. pap. 9.95 *(978-1-61633-011-8(2))* Guardian Angel Publishing, Inc.
McNeal, Cari. What Would I Do If I Had a Zoo? Balogh, Jared, illus. 2012. 36p. 24.95 *(978-1-4560-4006-2(5))* America Star Bks.
McOmber, Rachel B., ed. Bags... Bags (Animals) rev. ed. (Illus.). (J). *(978-0-944991-97-8(1))* Swift Learning Resources.
MCP Staff. Goose Chase, Level 4, Bk. 20. (J). (gr. -1-3). 24.50 *(978-0-8136-2069-5(4))* Modern Curriculum Pr.
McPhail, David. Baby Pig Pig Talks. McPhail, David, illus. 2014. (ENG., Illus.). 14p. (J). (— 1). bds. 6.95 *(978-1-58089-597-2(2))* Charlesbridge Publishing, Inc.
McQuinn, Anna. Colm's Lambs. Young, Paul, illus. 2014. (ENG.). 32p. (J). pap. 13.95 *(978-1-84717-339-3(X))* O'Brien Pr., Ltd., The IRL. Dist: Dufour Editions, Inc.
McSween, Michele. Gordon & Li Li Learn Animals in Mandarin. Nam, Doan, illus. 2010. 32p. 9.99 *(978-0-9820881-2-8(4))* McWong Ink.
Mead, Purnima. Bibia Meets Gripper. 2013. 24p. pap. 12.45 *(978-1-4497-9751-5(2),* WestBow Pr.) Author Solutions, Inc.
Meadows, Daisy. Amelia Sparklepaw's Party Problem. 2016. (Magic Animal Friends Special Edition Ser.). (ENG.). 176p. (J). (gr. 2-5). pap. 6.99 *(978-0-545-94080-1(X),* Scholastic Pr.) Scholastic, Inc.
—Bella Tabbypaw I Trouble. 2015. (Magic Animal Friends Ser.: 4). lib. bdg. 14.75 *(978-0-606-37048-6(X))* Turtleback Bks.
—Chloe Slipperside's Secret. 2016. (Magic Animal Friends Ser.: 11). (ENG., Illus.). 112p. (J). (gr. 2-5). pap. 4.99 *(978-0-545-94078-8(8),* Scholastic Paperbacks) Scholastic, Inc.
—Ellie Featherbill All Alone. 2015. (Magic Animal Friends Ser.: 3). lib. bdg. 14.75 *(978-0-606-37047-9(1))* Turtleback Bks.
—Evie Scruffypup's Big Surprise. 2016. (Magic Animal Friends Ser.: 1). (ENG., Illus.). 112p. (J). (gr. 2-5). pap. 4.99 *(978-0-545-94077-1(X),* Scholastic Paperbacks) Scholastic, Inc.
—Evie Scruffypup's Surprise. 2016. (Magic Animal Friends Ser.: 10). lib. bdg. 14.75 *(978-0-606-38800-9(1))* Turtleback Bks.
—Grace Woollyhop's Musical Mystery. 2016. (Magic Animal Friends Ser.: 12). lib. bdg. 14.75 *(978-0-606-38802-3(8))* Turtleback Bks.
—Grace Woollyhop's Musical Mystery (Magic Animal Friends #12) 2016. (Magic Animal Friends Ser.: 12). (ENG., Illus.). 112p. (J). (gr. 2-5). pap. 4.99 *(978-0-545-94079-5(6),* Scholastic Paperbacks) Scholastic, Inc.
—Lucy Longwhiskers Gets Lost. 2015. (Magic Animal Friends Ser.: 1). lib. bdg. 14.75 *(978-0-606-37045-5(5))* Turtleback Bks.
—Molly Twinkletail Runs Away. 2015. (Magic Animal Friends Ser.: 2). lib. bdg. 14.75 *(978-0-606-37046-2(3))* Turtleback Bks.
—Olivia Nibblesqueak's Messy Mischief. 2016. (Magic Animal Friends Ser.: 9). (ENG., Illus.). 112p. (J). (gr. 2-5). pap. 4.99 *(978-0-545-94076-4(1),* Scholastic Paperbacks) Scholastic, Inc.
—Olivia Nibblesqueak's Messy Mischief. 2016. (Magic Animal Friends Ser.: 9). lib. bdg. 14.75 *(978-0-606-38804-7(4))* Turtleback Bks.
—Rosie Gigglepip's Lucky Escape. 2016. (Magic Animal Friends Ser.: 8). (ENG., Illus.). 112p. (J). (gr. 2-5). pap. 4.99 *(978-0-545-90747-7(0),* Scholastic Paperbacks) Scholastic, Inc.
—Ruby Fuzzybrush's Star Dance. 2016. (Magic Animal Friends Ser.: 7). (ENG., Illus.). 112p. (J). (gr. 2-5). pap. 4.99 *(978-0-545-90745-3(4),* Scholastic Paperbacks) Scholastic, Inc.
—Sophie Flufftail's Brave Plan. 2016. (Magic Animal Friends Ser.: 5). (ENG., Illus.). 112p. (J). (gr. 2-5). pap. 4.99 *(978-0-545-90741-5(1),* Scholastic Paperbacks) Scholastic, Inc.
Meadows, Daisy & Scott, Lisa Ann. Amelia Sparklepaw's Party Problem. 2016. (Magic Animal Friends Ser.). (ENG.). 176p. (J). (gr. 2-5). 17.20 *(978-0-606-39140-5(1))* Turtleback Bks.
Meadows, Michelle. Hibernation Station. Cyrus, Kurt, illus. 2010. (ENG.). 40p. (J). (gr. -1-3). 17.99 *(978-1-4169-3788-3(9),* Simon & Schuster Bks. For Young Readers) Simon & Schuster Bks. For Young Readers.
Medina, Juana. 1 Big Salad: A Delicious Counting Book. 2016. (ENG., Illus.). 32p. (J). (— 1). 17.99 *(978-1-101-99974-5(8),* Viking Books for Young Readers) Penguin Young Readers Group.
Medina, Sylvia M. & Ballock-Dixon, Saige J. Green Springs Junior. Eagle, Joy, illus. 2013. 36p. pap. 11.59 *(978-0-9836602-7-9(1))* Green Kids Club, Inc.
Meister, Cari. The Lucky Manatee, 1 vol. Harpster, Steve, illus. 2012. (Ocean Tales Ser.). (ENG.). 32p. (gr. 2-4). pap. 6.25 *(978-1-4342-4231-0(5))* Stone Arch Bks.
Mejuto, Eva. La Casa de la Mosca Fosca. Mora, Sergio, illus. 2017. (Libros para Soñar Ser.). (SPA.). 36p. (J). (gr. k-2). *(978-84-8464-143-8(0))* Kalandraka Ediciones Andalucía, S.L. ESP. Dist: Lectorum Pubns., Inc.
Melling, David. Hugless Douglas & the Big Sleepover. 2013. (ENG., Illus.). 32p. (J). *(978-1-58925-116-8(4))* Tiger Tales.
Melmed, Laura Krauss. I Love You As Much... Board Book & Picture Frame. 2003. (Illus.). 22p. (J). (gr. -1-2). 12.99 *(978-0-06-008659-6(9),* HarperFestival) HarperCollins Pubs.
—My Love Will Be with You. Sorensen, Henri, illus. 2009. (ENG.). 24p. (J). (gr. -1-2). 17.99 *(978-0-06-155260-1(7))* HarperCollins Pubs.
Meloy, Colin. Under Wildwood. Ellis, Carson, illus. (Wildwood Chronicles Ser.: 2). (ENG.). (J). (gr. 3). 2013. 592p. pap. 9.99 *(978-0-06-202473-2(6))* 2012. 576p. 17.99 *(978-0-06-202471-8(X))* HarperCollins Pubs.
—Wildwood. Ellis, Carson, illus. (Wildwood Chronicles Ser.: 1). (ENG.). (J). (gr. 3). 2012. 576p. pap. 9.99 *(978-0-06-202470-1(1))* 2011. 560p. 17.99 *(978-0-06-202468-8(X))* HarperCollins Pubs.
—Wildwood. Ellis, Carson, illus. 2012. (Wildwood Chronicles Ser.: 1). (J). lib. bdg. 20.85 *(978-0-606-26864-6(2),* Turtleback) Turtleback Bks.
—Wildwood Imperium: The Wildwood Chronicles, Book III. Ellis, Carson, illus. 2015. (Wildwood Chronicles Ser.: 3). (ENG.). 592p. (J). (gr. 3). pap. 9.99 *(978-0-06-202476-3(0))* HarperCollins Pubs.
Menard, Michele R. The Canopy House - Volume 1. 2013. 38p. pap. 13.50 *(978-0-9887969-7-3(X))* Four Menards, The.
—The Thanksgiving Ring. 2013. 56p. 24.95 *(978-0-9891734-8-3(8))* Four Menards, The.
Menifield, Gloria. What's the Matter, Mr. Giraffe? 2003. (Illus.). 32p. (J). per. 14.95 *(978-0-9716442-1-2(7))* Jackson Publishing.
Menix, Cinda. Tenbrook Farms. Menix, Cinda & McGuire, Bryan, illus. 2007. 67p. (J). (gr. 4-7). per. 23.99 *(978-1-59879-338-3(1))* Lifevest Publishing, Inc.
Meomi (Firm) Staff. The Octonauts & the Sea of Shade. 2007. (Octonauts Ser.). (ENG., Illus.). 36p. (J). (gr. k-2). 15.95 *(978-1-59702-010-7(9))* Immedium.
Meomi (Firm) Staff, contrib. by. The Octonauts & the Only Lonely Monster. 2006. (Octonauts Ser.). (ENG., Illus.). 36p. (J). (gr. -1-3). 15.95 *(978-1-59702-005-3(2))* Immedium.
Mercer, Rita C. Earl the Squatchem. 2007. 9.00 *(978-0-8059-8823-9(8))* Dorrance Publishing Co., Inc.
Merchant, Brenda C. Huga Huga Hippo. l.t. ed. 2010. (Illus.). 49p. (J). 26.00 *(978-0-9845023-0-1(0))* A-Gator Publishing.
Merlin, Christophe. Under the Hood. 2011. (ENG., Illus.). 14p. (J). (gr. -1-2). 14.99 *(978-0-7636-5535-8(X))* Candlewick Pr.
Merline, Sharlene. Sharlene & Her Animal Friends. Rongner, Bridget, ed. Murfield, Anna, illus. 2012. 106p. pap. 8.99 *(978-1-937165-09-3(4))* Orange Hat Publishing.
Merveille, David. Hello Mr. Hulot. 2013. (ENG., Illus.). 32p. (J). (gr. -1-3). 17.95 *(978-0-7358-4135-2(7))* North-South Bks., Inc.
Merz, Jennifer. Playground Day. 2007. 32p. 16.00 *(978-978-061-896-4(1),* Clarion Bks.) Houghton Mifflin Harcourt Trade & Reference Pubs.
Meschenmoser, Sebastian. Waiting for Winter. Meschenmoser, Sebastian, illus. 2015. (ENG., Illus.). 58p. (J). (gr. k-3). 10.99 *(978-1-61067-435-5(9))* Kane Miller.
Messner, Kate. Over & under the Snow. Neal, Christopher Silas, illus. 2014. (ENG.). 44p. (J). (gr. k-3). 7.99 *(978-1-4521-3646-2(7))* Chronicle Bks. LLC.
Metzger, Steve. Waiting for Santa. Edgson, Alison, illus. 2015. (ENG.). 32p. (J). (gr. 2-6). 16.99 *(978-1-58925-199-1(7))* Tiger Tales.
Meyer, C. The Very First Unicorn. 2013. 24p. pap. 24.95 *(978-1-63004-317-9(6))* America Star Bks.
Meyer, Diana. Samson's Great Adventure. 2009. 32p. pap. 10.50 *(978-1-60693-029-8(X),* Eloquent Bks.) Strategic Book Publishing & Rights Agency (SBPRA).
Meyrick, Rich. Jaspa's Journey: The Great Migration. 2015. (ENG., Illus.). 276p. (J). (gr. 4-6). pap. *(978-1-62815-313-2(X))* Speaking Volumes, LLC.
Miceli, Mary Anne. Confessor's Animal Wartime Blues. 2009. 56p. pap. 31.99 *(978-1-4415-2867-4(9))* Xlibris Corp.
Michel, Gay. UNA VEZ MAS. (SPA., Illus.). 32p. (J). 7.16 *(978-84-95150-32-5(8))* Corimbo, Editorial S.L. ESP. Dist: Lectorum Pubns., Inc.
Michels, Dia. Look What I See! Where Can I Be? With My Animal Friends. Bowles, Michael J. N. & Bowles, Michael J. N., photos by. 2007. (ENG., Illus.). 32p. (J). 9.95 *(978-1-930775-08-4(3))* Platypus Media, L.L.C.
Michels, Dia L. Look What I See! Where Can I Be? With My Animal Friends. Bowles, Michael J. N., photos by. l.t. ed. 2005. (Look What I See! Where Can I Be? Ser.: Vol. 3). (ENG., Illus.). 32p. (J). (gr. -1-12). 9.95 *(978-1-930775-07-7(5))* Platypus Media, L.L.C.
Middleton, Nancy. The Zookeeper's Christmas Eve. 2009. 36p. pap. 16.50 *(978-1-60693-302-2(7),* Eloquent Bks.) Strategic Book Publishing & Rights Agency (SBPRA).
Middleton, Patricia T. Given Strength. 2013. 24p. pap. 14.95 *(978-1-4787-1028-8(4))* Outskirts Pr., Inc.
Migy. And Away We Go! Migy, illus. 2014. (ENG., Illus.). 40p. (J). (gr. -1-1). 17.99 *(978-0-8050-9901-0(8),* 9780805099010, Holt, Henry & Co. Bks. For Young Readers) Holt, Henry & Co.
Mikaelsen, Ben. Touching Spirit Bear. 2005. (Spirit Bear Ser.: 1). (ENG.). 320p. (YA). (gr. 3-7). pap. 8.99 *(978-0-06-073400-8(0),* HarperTeen) HarperCollins Pubs.
—Touching Spirit Bear. unabr. ed. 2004. 256p. (J). (gr. 5-9). pap. 38.00 incl. audio *(978-0-8072-0788-8(8),* LYA 312 SP, Listening Library) Random Hse. Audio Publishing Group.
Milbourne, Anna. In the Castle. Davies, Benji, illus. 2006. (English Heritage Ser.). 24p. (J). (gr. -1-3). 9.99 *(978-0-7945-1243-9(7),* Usborne) EDC Publishing.
Miles, Brenda. Stickley Makes a Mistake! A Frog's Guide to Trying Again. Mack, Steve, illus. 2016. 32p. (J). *(978-1-4338-2264-3(4),* Magination Pr.) American Psychological Assn.
Miles, Ellen. Lucky. 2010. (Puppy Place Ser.: 15). (ENG.). 96p. (J). (gr. 2-5). 4.99 *(978-0-545-08347-8(8),* Scholastic Paperbacks) Scholastic, Inc.
Miller, Alex. Beyond the River, 1 vol. Miller, Caroline, illus. 2011. (ENG.). 64p. (J). 16.99 *(978-0-7643-3741-3(6),* 9780764337413, Schiffer Publishing Ltd) Schiffer Publishing, Ltd.
Miller Cormier, Susan. Life on the Farm. 2007. (Illus.). 28p. (J). pap. 12.78 *(978-1-4251-1913-3(1))* Trafford Publishing.
Miller, Edward. Recycling Day. Miller, Edward, illus. 2014. (ENG., Illus.). 32p. (J). (gr. -1-3). 16.95 *(978-0-8234-2419-1(7))* Holiday Hse., Inc.
Miller, Jay. Opal, Herby, & Squeaky. 2008. 44p. pap. 18.99 *(978-1-4389-1808-2(9))* AuthorHouse.
Miller, Jean. Curious Chucky. 2013. 32p. pap. 16.00 *(978-1-939615-05-3(4))* Perfect Bound Marketing.
Miller, Jennifer. Jennifer Miller's Run, Rasputin Run! Rasputin's Redemption (Book 3) 2007. (Illus.). 136p. per. 14.50 *(978-1-4251-1029-1(0))* Trafford Publishing.
Miller, Pat. Squirrel's New Year's Resolution. Ember, Kathi, illus. 2012. (J). 34.28 *(978-1-61913-135-4(8))* Weigl Pubs., Inc.
—Squirrel's New Year's Resolution. Ember, Kathi, illus. (ENG.). 32p. (J). (gr. k-2). 2017. pap. 7.99 **(978-0-8075-7592-5(5))** 2010. 16.99 *(978-0-8075-7591-8(7))* Whitman, Albert & Co.
Miller, S. L. Yellow Kitty, Life in the Garden. 2008. 316p. pap. 18.95 *(978-0-615-22038-3(X))* Polar Club Publishing.
Miller, Sharon Schwab. Good Morning Otis. 2012. 24p. pap. 15.99 *(978-1-4771-5942-2(8))* Xlibris Corp.
Miller, Victoria, illus. Dora & the Unicorn King. 2011. (Dora the Explorer Ser.). (ENG.). 24p. (J). pap. 3.99 *(978-1-4424-1312-2(3),* Simon Spotlight/Nickelodeon) Simon Spotlight/Nickelodeon.
Millett, Peter & Morden, Richard. It's a Jungle Out There. 2008. (Rigby Focus Forward: Level N Ser.). (Illus.). 24p. (J). (gr. -1-3). pap. *(978-1-4190-3838-9(9),* Rigby) Pearson Education Australia.
Milway, Alex. Pigsticks & Harold & the Tuptown Thief. Milway, Alex, illus. 2015. (ENG., Illus.). 80p. (J). (gr. k-4). 12.99 *(978-0-7636-7809-8(0))* Candlewick Pr.
Mindes, Erin. Missy Moo, Where Are You off to? Surfing Adventure. Harston, David, illus. 2011. (J). 14.95 *(978-0-9841558-8-0(0))* Tasty Minstrel Games.
Minne, Brigitte. The Best Bottom. Pottie, Marjolein, illus. 2006. (ENG.). 32p. (J). (gr. -1-3). pap. 5.95 *(978-1-59687-387-2(6))* IBks., Inc.
Minor, Wendell. My Farm Friends. Bodett, Tom, illus. 2012. 29.95 *(978-1-4301-1096-5(1))* Live Oak Media.
Minz-Kammer, Koda. Pinpot Tiger & the Lost Monkey. 2008. 54p. pap. 20.00 *(978-0-557-01646-4(0))* Lulu Pr., Inc.
Mirabella, Erin. Shawn Sheep the Soccer Star. Davis, Sarah, illus. 2008. (Barnsville Sports Squad Ser.). (ENG.). 32p. (J). (gr. k-3). 15.95 *(978-1-934030-16-5(3))* VeloPress.
Miranda, Twyla. Longfeather Ponds: A Chipmunk's Tale. 2006. 82p. pap. 16.95 *(978-1-4241-1785-7(2))* PublishAmerica, Inc.
Mitchell, Cynthia. A Big & Beastly Alphabet. 2006. pap. *(978-1-84401-716-4(8))* Athena Pr.
Mitchell, Lee Ann. Milo the Mighty Protector. 2010. 32p. pap. 12.99 *(978-1-4490-5447-2(1))* AuthorHouse.
Mitchell, Malinda. Spencer the Spring Chicken & Other Stories. Schandy, Rosita & Wooten, Neal, illus. 2007. 88p. pap. 23.95 *(978-0-9800675-0-7(2))* Mirror Publishing.
Mitchell, Melanie, illus. Good Morning. 2008. (ENG.). 10p. (J). bds. 5.95 *(978-1-58117-708-4(9),* Intervisual/Piggy Toes) Bendon, Inc.
—Good Morning, Good Night Bilingual: Buenos Dias! Buenas Noches! 2005. (ENG & SPA.). 12p. (J). 9.95 *(978-1-58117-389-5(X),* Intervisual/Piggy Toes) Bendon, Inc.
—Good Night. 2008. (ENG.). 6p. (J). bds. 5.95 *(978-1-58117-709-1(7),* Intervisual/Piggy Toes) Bendon, Inc.
—Wake up Little Ones. 2009. (ENG.). 12p. 10.95 *(978-1-58117-927-9(8),* Intervisual/Piggy Toes) Bendon, Inc.
Mitchell, Susan K. Kersplatypus, 1 vol. Rogers, Sherry, illus. 2008. (ENG.). 32p. (J). (gr. -1-2). 16.95 *(978-1-934359-07-5(6));* pap. 8.95 *(978-1-934359-23-5(8))* Arbordale Publishing.
Mitchell, Trish. Noah Pals: Noah & Friends Awesome Adventure. 2011. 56p. pap. 23.88 *(978-1-4520-0459-4(5))* AuthorHouse.
Mitton, Tony. All Afloat on Noah's Boat. Parker-Rees, Guy, illus. 2017. (ENG.). 32p. (J). (gr. -1-k). pap. 7.99 *(978-1-84616-242-8(4),* Orchard Bks.) Hachette Children's Group GBR. Dist: Hachette Bk. Group.
—Down by the Cool of the Pool (a StoryPlay Book) Parker-Rees, Guy, illus. 2017. (StoryPlay Ser.). (ENG.). 32p. (J). (gr. -1-k). 5.99 **(978-1-338-15841-0(4),** Cartwheel Bks.) Scholastic, Inc.
Mitton, Tony. Rainforest Adventure. 2015. (Amazing Animals Ser.). (ENG., Illus.). 24p. (J). (gr. -1-1). pap. 4.99 *(978-0-7534-7227-9(9),* 9780753472279, Kingfisher) Roaring Brook Pr.
Mitton, Tony & Parker, Ant. Rainforest Romp. 2009. (Amazing Animals Ser.). (ENG., Illus.). 24p. (J). (gr. -1-1). 9.99 *(978-0-7534-6298-0(2),* 9780753462980, Kingfisher) Roaring Brook Pr.
Miura, Taro. There, There. Miura, Taro, illus. 2016. (ENG., Illus.). 22p. (J). (— 1). bds. 8.99 *(978-0-7636-8785-4(5))* Candlewick Pr.
Miyakoshi, Akiko. The Tea Party in the Woods. Miyakoshi, Akiko, illus. 2015. (ENG., Illus.). 32p. (J). (gr. -1-2). 16.95 *(978-1-77138-107-9(8))* Kids Can Pr., Ltd. CAN. Dist: Hachette Bk. Group.
Mjolhus, Joy. Squirrel Babies & Friends. 2008. 16p. pap. 24.95 *(978-1-4241-8562-7(9))* America Star Bks.
Mmm Very Nice: Individual Title Six-Packs. (gr. k-1). 23.00 *(978-0-7635-8834-2(2))* Rigby Education.
Mock, Jean. The Amazing Animal ABC Book. Martin, Joyce, illus. 2005. (J). *(978-0-9767210-1-7(5))* JM2 Publishing Co.
—The Amazing Animal ABC Book (big Format) 2005. (J). *(978-0-9767210-0-0(7))* JM2 Publishing Co.
—The Amazing Animal ABC Book the Study Guide. Martin, Joyce, illus. 2005. *(978-0-9767210-2-4(3))* JM2 Publishing Co.
Moggie, Felix. Living with the Mach Factor: Four Paws. 2005. (Illus.). 336p. pap. *(978-1-84401-529-0(7))* Athena Pr.
Moghimi, Salmeh. The Adventures of Anoo & Pashmack. 2013. (ENG.). 44p. (J). 19.95 *(978-1-4525-5857-8(4),* Balboa Pr.) Author Solutions, Inc.
Mola, Astrid & Khakdan, Wahed. The Good-Night Kiss. 2004. (Illus.). 32p. (J). 10.99 *(978-1-59384-046-4(2))* Parklane Publishing.
Molchadsky, Yael. The Chameleon That Saved Noah's Ark. Bergman, Orit, illus. 2016. (ENG.). 32p. (J). (gr. k-3). 16.99 *(978-1-101-99676-8(5),* Nancy Paulsen Books) Penguin Young Readers Group.
Molina, Violet S. & Molina, Ruben. Animals Can Do Nothing. 2012. 20p. pap. 24.95 *(978-1-4626-7728-3(2))* America Star Bks.
Mon, Aunty. Braxton the Bull. 2010. 32p. pap. 13.00 *(978-1-60976-063-2(8),* Eloquent Bks.) Strategic Book Publishing & Rights Agency (SBPRA).
Moncure, Jane Belk. Away Went the Farmer's Hat: A Book about an Adventure. Regan, Dana, illus. 2013. (Magic Castle Readers Ser.). (ENG.). 32p. (J). (gr. -1-2). 25.64 *(978-1-62323-572-7(3),* 206309) Child's World, Inc., The.
—The Biggest Snowball of All: A Book about Sizes. Rooney, Ronnie, illus. 2013. (Magic Castle Readers Ser.). (ENG.). 32p. (J). (gr. -1-2). 25.64 *(978-1-62323-578-9(2),* 206315) Child's World, Inc., The.
—How Many Ways Can You Cut a Pie? A Book about Math. Rooney, Ronnie, illus. 2013. (Magic Castle Readers Ser.). (ENG.). 32p. (J). (gr. -1-2). 25.64 *(978-1-62323-579-6(0),* 206313) Child's World, Inc., The.
—Little Too-Tall: A Book about Friendship. DeSantis, Susan, illus. 2013. (Magic Castle Readers Ser.). (ENG.). 32p. (J). (gr. -1-2). 25.64 *(978-1-62323-568-0(5),* 206303) Child's World, Inc., The.
—Nanny Goat's Boat: A Book of Rhyming. Girouard, Patrick, illus. 2013. (Magic Castle Readers Ser.). (ENG.). 32p. (J). (gr. -1-2). 25.64 *(978-1-62323-567-3(7),* 206301) Child's World, Inc., The.
—One Tricky Monkey up on Top: A Counting Adventure. Rooney, Ronnie, illus. 2013. (Magic Castle Readers Ser.). (ENG.). 32p. (J). (gr. -1-2). 25.64 *(978-1-62323-581-9(2),* 206314) Child's World, Inc., The.
—A Pocketful of Pets: A Search-and-Count Adventure. Billin-Frye, Paige, illus. 2013. (Magic Castle Readers Ser.). (ENG.). 32p. (J). (gr. -1-2). 25.64 *(978-1-62323-584-0(7),* 206317) Child's World, Inc., The.
—Where Is Baby Bear? A Book about Animal Homes. Billin-Frye, Paige, illus. 2013. (Magic Castle Readers Ser.). (ENG.). 32p. (J). (gr. -1-2). 25.64 *(978-1-62323-585-7(5),* 206320) Child's World, Inc., The.
Moniz, Michael, illus. Wazzyjump. 2012. (ENG.). 44p. (J). (gr. -1-2). 16.95 *(978-1-897476-58-1(2))* Simply Read Bks. CAN. Dist: Ingram Publisher Services.
Monk, Carol & O'Connor, Ruth. The Walking Adventures of Ruthie & Coco. 2005. (Illus.). 29p. (J). pap. 12.95 *(978-1-56167-881-5(3))* American Literary Pr.
Monkman, Olga. Un Rey sin Corona. Sanchez, Javier G., illus. 2003. (SPA.). 39p. (J). (gr. k-3). pap. 7.95 *(978-950-511-368-2(4))* Santillana USA Publishing Co., Inc.
Monninger, Joseph. Whippoorwill. 2016. (ENG.). 288p. (YA). (gr. 7). pap. 9.99 *(978-0-544-81356-4(1),* HMH Books For Young Readers) Houghton Mifflin Harcourt Publishing Co.
Monroe, Chris. Bug on a Bike. Monroe, Chris, illus. 2014. (ENG., Illus.). 32p. (J). (gr. -1-2). 16.95 *(978-1-4677-2154-7(9),* Carolrhoda Bks.) Lerner Publishing Group.
—Monkey with a Tool Belt & the Maniac Muffins. Monroe, Chris, illus. 2016. (ENG., Illus.). 32p. (J). (gr. -1-2). 17.99 *(978-1-4677-2155-4(7),* Carolrhoda Bks.) Lerner Publishing Group.
Monroe, Chris. Monkey with a Tool Belt & the School Mystery. Monroe, Chris, illus. 2017. (ENG., Illus.). 32p. (gr. -1-2). 17.99 **(978-1-5124-3010-3(2),** Carolrhoda Bks.) Lerner Publishing Group.
Monroe, Colleen. A Wish to Be a Christmas Tree. Monroe, Michael Glenn, illus. 2005. (Holiday Ser.). (ENG.). 20p. (J). (gr. -1-1). bds. 8.99 *(978-1-58536-269-1(7),* 202284) Sleeping Bear Pr.
Montiel, Joaquin Londaiz, et al. Hormigosaurios/The Antosaurus. 2011. (SPA.). 72p. *(978-84-488-3164-6(0))* Penguin Random House Grupo Editorial.
Moody-Luther, Jacqueline. Panda Bear Cub. Nelson, Will, illus. 2006. (ENG.). 32p. (J). pap. 3.95 *(978-1-59249-585-6(0))* Soundprints.
Moon, Jo, illus. Old MacDonald Had a Farm. 2016. (Carousel Bks.). (ENG.). 10p. (J). (gr. -1 — 1). bds. 8.99 *(978-0-7641-6859-8(2))* Barron's Educational Series, Inc.
Mooney, Bel. Mr. Tubs Is Lost. 2006. (Blue Bananas Ser.). (ENG., Illus.). 48p. (J). (gr. -1-3). lib. bdg. *(978-0-7787-0858-2(6))* Crabtree Publishing Co.
Mooney, Ginger. Spirit Elk. 2009. 16p. pap. 9.99 *(978-1-4490-0447-7(4))* AuthorHouse.
Moore, Billy. Cracker's Mule. 2003. (ENG.). 256p. (J). pap. 12.95 *(978-1-58838-105-7(6),* NewSouth Bks.) NewSouth, Inc.
Moore, Inga. A House in the Woods. 2011. (ENG., Illus.). 48p. (J). (gr. -1-2). 16.99 *(978-0-7636-5277-7(6))* Candlewick Pr.
Moore, Jim. The All Animal Band. Hall, Norris, illus. l.t. ed. 2004. 36p. (J). 16.00 *(978-0-9752619-0-3(8))* Animal Band Productions, Inc., The.
Moore, Leslie. Guess What Ryan Saw at the Farm. 2008. 32p. pap. 19.50 *(978-1-4357-5024-1(1))* Lulu Pr., Inc.
Moore, Suzi. Whoops! Ayto, Russell, illus. 2016. (ENG.). 32p. (J). (gr. -1-2). 16.99 *(978-0-7636-8180-7(6),* Templar) Candlewick Pr.
Moore, Wendy Leptien. Eaglet & the River. 2011. 108p. 21.92 *(978-1-4269-5478-8(6));* pap. 11.92 *(978-1-4269-5477-1(8))* Trafford Publishing.
Moore, Yvonne. The Listening Gift. 2012. 24p. pap. 17.99 *(978-1-4772-9313-3(2))* AuthorHouse.
Mora, Pat. La Carrera del Sapo y el Venado, 1 vol. Domi, illus. 2004. (SPA.). 32p. (J). pap. 9.95 *(978-0-88899-650-3(0))* Groundwood Bks. CAN. Dist: Publishers Group West (PGW).
—The Song of Francis & the Animals. Frampton, David, illus. 2005. 32p. (J). (gr. -1-2). 16.00 *(978-0-8028-5253-3(X))* Eerdmans, William B. Publishing Co.

More about Animals Book Set 800940, 3 vols. 2005. (J). bds. *(978-1-59794-098-6(4))* Environments, Inc.

Moreau, Laurent. My Wild Family. 2015. (ENG., Illus.). 32p. (J). (gr. -1-k). 17.99 *(978-1-4521-4423-8(0))* Chronicle Bks. LLC.

Moree, Katie. Jesse's Peekaboo Safari. 2008. 20p. pap. 24.95 *(978-1-60672-473-6(8))* America Star Bks.

Moreton, Clara. Frank & Fanny: A Rural Story. 2007. (ENG.). 66p. per. 16.99 *(978-1-4346-2717-9(9))* Creative Media Partners, LLC.

Morgan, Kerry. Lickety Lick. 2012. 32p. pap. 16.49 *(978-1-4685-5510-3(3))* AuthorHouse.

Morgan, Michaela. Band of Friends. Price, Nick, illus. 2005. (ENG.). 24p. (J). lib. bdg. 23.65 *(978-1-59646-734-7(7))* Dingles & Co.

—Never Shake a Rattlesnake. Sharratt, Nick, illus. (ENG.). 32p. (J). (gr. -1-k). 2016. pap. 8.99 *(978-1-5098-1704-7(2))*1. 2012. pap. 8.99 *(978-0-330-51229-9(3))* Pan Macmillan GBR. Dist: Independent Pubs. Group.

—Tiger's Tales. Boon, Debbie, illus. 2005. (Collins Big Cat Ser.). (ENG.). 32p. (J). (gr. 1-3). pap. 7.99 *(978-0-00-718631-0(2))* HarperCollins Pubs. Ltd. GBR. Dist: Independent Pubs. Group.

Morgan, Michaela & Phillips, Mike. Tig in the Dumps: Lime. 2005. (Collins Big Cat Ser.). (ENG., Illus.). 32p. (J). (gr. 1-3). pap. 7.99 *(978-0-00-718636-5(3))* HarperCollins Pubs. Ltd. GBR. Dist: Independent Pubs. Group.

Morgan, Sally. Where is Galah? Morgan, Sally, illus. 2016. (ENG., Illus.). 24p. (J). (gr. -1-k). 17.99 *(978-1-921894-46-6(6))* Little Hare Bks. AUS. Dist: Independent Pubs. Group.

Morgaut, Philippe, tr. Le Cheval et Son Ecuyer. Baynes, Pauline, illus. 2005. (Chronicles of Narnia Ser.). (FRE.). 234p. (J). per. 21.95 *(978-2-07-054644-2(6))* Gallimard, Editions FRA. Dist: Distribooks, Inc.

Moriarty, Ros. Splosh for the Billabong. Balarinji, illus. 2015. (ENG.). 24p. (J). (— 1). 9.99 *(978-1-76011-212-7(7))* Allen & Unwin AUS. Dist: Independent Pubs. Group.

—Summer Rain. Balarinji, illus. 2016. (ENG.). 24p. (J). (gr. -1-k). 9.99 *(978-1-76011-211-0(9))* Allen & Unwin AUS. Dist: Independent Pubs. Group.

Morimoto, Diana. Max Makes a Visit. Wright, Sara Ann, illus. 2011. 28p. pap. 24.95 *(978-1-4512-4545-5(9))* America Star Bks.

Morningforest, Chris & Raymond, Rebecca. The Adventures of Nate & Naomi. 2006. 36p. (J). pap. 15.43 *(978-1-4116-9244-2(6))* Lulu Pr., Inc.

Moroni, Lisa. Watch Out for the Crocodile. 2014. (Illus.). 32p. (J). (gr. -1-3). 17.95 *(978-1-877579-89-9(0))* Gecko Pr. NZL. Dist: Lerner Publishing Group.

Morpurgo, Michael. The Nine Lives of Montezuma. 2004. (Illus.). 120p. (J). pap. 8.99 *(978-1-4052-0189-6(4))* Egmont Bks., Ltd. GBR. Dist: Trafalgar Square Publishing.

—Toro! Toro! Foreman, Michael, illus. 2007. (ENG.). 128p. (J). (gr. 4-7). pap. 8.99 *(978-0-00-710718-6(8),* HarperCollins Children's Bks.) HarperCollins Pubs. Ltd. GBR. Dist: HarperCollins Pubs.

Morpurgo, Michael, selected by. Greatest Animal Stories. 2017. (ENG.). 256p. (J). (gr. 2-7). 16.99 ***(978-1-4380-5003-4(8))*** Barron's Educational Series, Inc.

Morris, Jennifer E. The Sea Monster. 2014. (Scholastic Reader Level 1 Ser.). (Illus.). (J). lib. bdg. 13.55 *(978-0-606-36046-3(8))* Turtleback Bks.

Morrison, Kenny. Sevenlives & the Woof Pack. 2011. (Illus.). 104p. pap. 13.32 *(978-1-4567-8595-6(8))* AuthorHouse.

Morrissey, Tricia. My Mom Is a Dragon: And My Dad Is a Boar. 2005. (ENG., Illus.). 32p. (J). (gr. -1-3). 12.95 *(978-0-9715940-5-0(8))* ThingsAsian Pr.

Moseley, Tabitha. Pearl's Tales a Collection of Children's Stories. 2009. 92p. pap. 17.25 *(978-1-60860-670-2(8),* Strategic Bk. Publishing) Strategic Book Publishing & Rights Agency (SBPRA).

Moser, Lisa. Squirrel's World. Gorbachev, Valeri, illus. 2013. (Candlewick Sparks Ser.). (ENG.). 48p. (J). (gr. k-4). pap. 3.99 *(978-0-7636-6644-6(0))* Candlewick Pr.

Moses, Brian. Animal Pants! Boretzki, Anja, illus. 2012. (ENG.). 24p. (J). (gr. -1-k). pap. 8.99 *(978-0-230-73614-6(9))* Macmillan Pubs., Ltd. GBR. Dist: Independent Pubs. Group.

Mosier, Pamela. Elizabeth, the Eastern Gray Squirrel. 2008. 44p. pap. 18.95 *(978-1-4357-5407-2(7))* Lulu Pr., Inc.

Most, Bernard. The Cow That Went OINK. 2003. (ENG., Illus.). 40p. (J). (gr. -1 — 1). pap. 7.99 *(978-0-15-204763-4(8))* Houghton Mifflin Harcourt Publishing Co.

—La Vaca Que Decia Oink. Mlawer, Teresa, tr. from ENG.Tr. of Cow That Went Oink. (SPA., Illus.). (J). (gr. k-2). pap. 6.99 *(978-1-880507-66-7(8),* LC4889) Lectorum Pubns., Inc.

Motalebi, Majede. Wise Animals 2. 2012. 56p. pap. 24.99 *(978-1-4772-1622-4(7))* AuthorHouse.

Mother Goose & the Animal Friends: Take-Home Book. 2005. (Lee Bennett Hopkins Mother Goose Ser.). (YA). (gr. -1-1). 13.50 *(978-0-8215-0562-5(9))* Sadlier, William H. Inc.

Motto, Bernadine. The Adventures of Fluff the Bunny. 2007. 32p. per. 11.95 *(978-1-59800-908-8(7))* Outskirts Pr., Inc.

Moulton, Mark Kimball. One Enchanted Evening. Crouch, Karen Hillard, illus. 2003. 32p. (J). 14.95 *(978-0-8249-5480-2(7),* Ideal Pubns.) Worthy Publishing.

Mount, Jane. 26 Animals! 2009. 32p. pap. 17.98 *(978-0-557-17908-4(4))* Lulu Pr., Inc.

Mouser, Mary. Chigger: A Prairie Dog Tale. 2007. 152p. per. 24.95 *(978-1-4241-9791-0(0))* America Star Bks.

Move Like Us!, 6 Packs. (gr. k-1). 23.00 *(978-0-7635-9048-2(7))* Rigby Education.

Mueller, Kirk Jay. Harriet Can Carry It, 1 vol. Vonthron-Laver, Sarah, illus. 2014. (ENG.). 32p. (J). 16.99 *(978-1-59572-675-9(6))* Star Bright Bks., Inc.

Mueller, Richard. Zoonauts: The Secret of Animalville. Gosline, Sheldon, ed. Dal Chele, Egido Victor, illus. 2003. 210p. (J). 14.95 *(978-0-9719496-6-9(2))* Shangri-La Pubns.

Muldrow, Diane. How Do Giraffes Take Naps? Walker, David, illus. 2016. (Little Golden Book Ser.). (ENG.). 24p. (J). (gr. -1-k). 4.99 *(978-0-553-51333-2(8),* Golden Bks.) Random Hse. Children's Bks.

Mull, Brandon, et al. Tales of the Great Beasts. 2014. (Spirit Animals Ser.). (ENG., Illus.). 192p. (J). (gr. 4-7). 12.99 *(978-0-545-69516-9(3),* Scholastic Pr.) Scholastic, Inc.

Mullen, Robert. Where Do Your Animals Live. 2005. 35p. 11.03 *(978-1-4116-1670-7(7))* Lulu Pr., Inc.

Mullican, Norma Waldon & Zivney, Missy Mullican. A Collection of Squirrel Tales: Something to Crow About. 2009. 84p. pap. 10.99 *(978-1-60791-702-1(5))* Salem Author Services.

Mulryan, Doreen. Lucky Ducky. 2016. (ENG., Illus.). 32p. (J). (gr. k-2). 14.95 *(978-1-4197-1467-2(8),* Abrams Bks. for Young Readers) Abrams, Inc.

Munns, Skye. Who's at the Zoo. 2011. 24p. pap. 28.03 *(978-1-4568-5447-8(X))* Xlibris Corp.

Munter, June. Noah's Ark: The Animals Story. 2011. 20p. pap. 10.03 *(978-1-4634-4992-6(5))* AuthorHouse.

Murphy, Anne. Animal Island. 2009. 44p. pap. 16.99 *(978-1-4389-4263-6(X))* AuthorHouse.

Murphy, D. Cathy. Animals, Animals Everywhere. Burbridge, William J., illus. 2013. 16p. pap. 24.95 *(978-1-4626-2414-0(6))* America Star Bks.

Murphy, Mary. Are You My Mommy? Murphy, Mary, illus. 2015. (ENG., Illus.). 16p. (J). (gr. -1 — 1). bds. 6.99 *(978-0-7636-7372-7(2))* Candlewick Pr.

—Crocopotamus: Mix & Match the Wild Animals! 2016. (ENG., Illus.). 12p. (J). (— 1). bds. 8.99 *(978-0-7636-8102-9(4))* Candlewick Pr.

—Good Night Like This. Murphy, Mary, illus. 2016. (ENG., Illus.). 32p. (J). (gr. -1-k). 12.99 *(978-0-7636-7970-5(4))* Candlewick Pr.

—Panda Foo & the New Friend. Murphy, Mary, illus. 2007. (ENG., Illus.). 32p. (J). (gr. k-k). 15.99 *(978-0-7636-3405-6(0))* Candlewick Pr.

Murphy, Mary Elizabeth. I Kissed the Baby! Murphy, Mary Elizabeth, illus. 2004. (ENG., Illus.). 24p. (J). (— 1). bds. 6.99 *(978-0-7636-2443-9(8))* Candlewick Pr.

Murphy, Robert. The Pond. 2013. (ENG.). 288p. (gr. 7-12). 16.99 *(978-1-4683-0372-8(4),* 460372) Overlook Pr., The.

Murphy, Stephen & Zulli, Michael. The Puma Blues. 2015. (Dover Graphic Novels Ser.). (ENG., Illus.). 480p. 34.95 *(978-0-486-79813-4(5))* Dover Pubns., Inc.

Murphy, Stuart J. ¡Bien Hecho, Ajay! 2011. (I See I Learn Ser.).Tr. of Good Job, Ajay! (SPA., Illus.). 32p. (J). (-k). 14.95 *(978-1-58089-486-9(0));* pap. 6.95 *(978-1-58089-487-6(9))* Charlesbridge Publishing, Inc.

—Camille y Su Equipo. 2012. (I See I Learn Ser.). (SPA & ENG., Illus.). 32p. (J). (-k). 14.95 *(978-1-58089-490-6(9));* pap. 6.95 *(978-1-58089-491-3(7))* Charlesbridge Publishing, Inc.

—Camille's Team. 2011. (I See I Learn Ser.). (ENG., Illus.). 32p. (J). (gr. -1-k). 14.95 *(978-1-58089-458-6(5));* pap. 6.95 *(978-1-58089-459-3(3))* Charlesbridge Publishing, Inc.

—Emma Hace Amigos. 2011. (I See I Learn Ser.). (SPA & ENG., Illus.). 32p. (J). (-k). 14.95 *(978-1-58089-482-1(8));* pap. 6.95 *(978-1-58089-483-8(6))* Charlesbridge Publishing, Inc.

—En Busca de Freda. Mlawer, Teresa, tr. from ENG. Jones, Tim, illus. 2012. (I See I Learn Ser.). (SPA & ENG.). 32p. (J). (-k). 14.95 *(978-1-58089-494-4(1));* pap. 6.95 *(978-1-58089-495-1(X))* Charlesbridge Publishing, Inc.

—Freda Is Found. 2011. (I See I Learn Ser.). (ENG., Illus.). 32p. (J). (-k). 14.95 *(978-1-58089-462-3(3));* pap. 6.95 *(978-1-58089-463-0(1))* Charlesbridge Publishing, Inc.

—Freda Organiza una Merienda. 2011. (I See I Learn Ser.). (SPA & ENG., Illus.). 32p. (J). (-k). 14.95 *(978-1-58089-488-3(7));* pap. 6.95 *(978-1-58089-489-0(5))* Charlesbridge Publishing, Inc.

—Freda Says Please. Jones, Tim, illus. 2013. (I See I Learn Ser.). (ENG.). 32p. (J). (-k). pap. 6.95 *(978-1-58089-475-3(5))* Charlesbridge Publishing, Inc.

—Freda Says Please. Jones, Tim, illus. 2013. (I See I Learn Ser.). (ENG.). 32p. (J). (-k). lib. bdg. 14.95 *(978-1-58089-474-6(7))* Charlesbridge Publishing, Inc.

—Freda Stops a Bully. Jones, Tim, illus. 2012. (I See I Learn Ser.). (ENG.). 32p. (J). (-k). 14.95 *(978-1-58089-466-1(6));* pap. 6.95 *(978-1-58089-467-8(4))* Charlesbridge Publishing, Inc.

—Good Job, Ajay! 2010. (I See I Learn Ser.). (ENG., Illus.). 32p. (J). (gr. -1-k). pap. 6.95 *(978-1-58089-455-5(0))* Charlesbridge Publishing, Inc.

—Left, Right, Emma! 2012. (I See I Learn Ser.). (ENG., Illus.). 32p. (J). (-k). 14.95 *(978-1-58089-472-2(0));* pap. 6.95 *(978-1-58089-473-9(9))* Charlesbridge Publishing, Inc.

—Percy Gets Upset. 2011. (I See I Learn Ser.). (ENG., Illus.). 32p. (J). (gr. -1-k). 14.95 *(978-1-58089-460-9(7));* pap. 6.95 *(978-1-58089-461-6(5))* Charlesbridge Publishing, Inc.

—Percy Juega con Cuidado. 2011. (I See I Learn Ser.). (SPA & ENG., Illus.). 32p. (J). (-k). 14.95 *(978-1-58089-484-5(4));* pap. 6.95 *(978-1-58089-485-2(2))* Charlesbridge Publishing, Inc.

—Percy Listens Up. 2012. (I See I Learn Ser.). (ENG., Illus.). 32p. (J). (-k). 14.95 *(978-1-58089-468-5(2));* pap. 6.95 *(978-1-58089-469-2(0))* Charlesbridge Publishing, Inc.

—Percy Se Enoja. 2012. (I See I Learn Ser.). (SPA & ENG., Illus.). 32p. (J). (-k). 14.95 *(978-1-58089-492-0(5));* pap. 6.95 *(978-1-58089-493-7(3))* Charlesbridge Publishing, Inc.

Murray, Andrew. The Very Sleepy Sloth. Tickle, Jack, tr. Tickle, Jack, illus. 2003. 32p. (J). tchr. ed. 15.95 *(978-1-58925-033-8(8))* Tiger Tales.

Murray, Marjorie Dennis. Don't Wake up the Bear!, 0 vols. Wittmann, Patricia, illus. unabr. ed. 2006. (ENG.). 34p. (J). (gr. -1-2). per. 9.99 *(978-0-7614-5330-7(X),* 9780761453307, Amazon Children's Publishing) Amazon Publishing.

Murray, Tamsyn. Snug As a Bug. Abbot, Judi & Gavriaghi, Giuditta, illus. 2013. 30p. (J). *(978-1-4351-4731-7(6))* Barnes & Noble, Inc.

Murrell, Belinda. Lulu Bell's Fantastic Holiday Fun. 2016. (Lulu Bell Ser.). (ENG., Illus.). 384p. (J). (gr. 1-3). pap. 9.99 *(978-1-925324-37-2(0))* Random Hse. Australia AUS. Dist: Independent Pubs. Group.

—Lulu Bell's Amazing Animal Adventures. 2016. (Lulu Bell Ser.). (ENG., Illus.). 384p. (J). (gr. 1-3). pap. 9.99 *(978-1-925324-35-8(4))* Random Hse. Australia AUS. Dist: Independent Pubs. Group.

Musco, Rance K. The Legend of Sabor. 2009. 52p. pap. 22.50 *(978-1-4389-4573-6(6))* AuthorHouse.

Mwangi, Nyaruai. Argwings & the Lamplighters. 2008. 96p. (YA). pap. 13.95 *(978-0-9796476-8-0(1))* HM Bks.

My Big Book of Beginner Books about Me. 2011. (Beginner Books(R) Ser.). (ENG., Illus.). 208p. (J). (gr. -1-2). 16.99 *(978-0-307-93183-2(8),* Random Hse. Bks. for Young Readers) Random Hse. Children's Bks.

My First Book of Bedtime Stories. 2003. (J). 8.99 *(978-1-59384-013-6(6))* Parklane Publishing.

Myers, Walter Dean. Looking for the Easy Life. Harper, Lee, illus. 2011. (Looking at Other Countries Ser.). (ENG.). 40p. (J). (gr. -1-3). 16.99 *(978-0-06-054375-4(2))* HarperCollins Pubs.

Na, Il Sung. A Book of Sleep. 2011. (ENG.). 24p. (J). (gr. k — 1). bds. 6.99 *(978-0-375-86618-0(3),* Knopf Bks. for Young Readers) Random Hse. Children's Bks.

Na, Il Sung, illus. The Opposite Zoo. 2016. (ENG.). 24p. (J). (-k). 16.99 *(978-0-553-51127-7(0),* Knopf Bks. for Young Readers) Random Hse. Children's Bks.

Nagda, Ann Whitehead. Kevin Keeps Up. 2012. (ENG.). 96p. (J). 15.95 *(978-0-8234-2657-7(2))* Holiday Hse., Inc.

Nakawaki, Hatsue. Wait! Wait! Sakai, Komako, illus. 2013. (ENG.). 24p. (J). 14.95 *(978-1-59270-138-4(8))* Enchanted Lion Bks., LLC.

Namm, Diane. Pick a Pet. Suarez, Maribel, tr. Suarez, Maribel, illus. 2004. (My First Reader Ser.). (ENG.). 31p. (J). 18.50 *(978-0-516-24417-4(5),* Children's Pr.) Scholastic Library Publishing.

Nana B. & Brittany. Forest Friends of Maine: The Chipmunks Have an Argument. 2010. 16p. pap. 8.49 *(978-1-4490-0647-1(7))* AuthorHouse.

Napoli, Donna Jo. Storm. 2014. (ENG., Illus.). 368p. (YA). (gr. 9). 17.99 *(978-1-4814-0302-3(8),* Simon & Schuster/Paula Wiseman Bks.) Simon & Schuster/Paula Wiseman Bks.

Nat'l Children's Book & Literacy Alliance. The Exquisite Corpse Adventure. 2011. (ENG., Illus.). 288p. (J). (gr. 4-7). pap. 7.99 *(978-0-7636-5773-4(5))* Candlewick Pr.

Naylor, Phyllis Reynolds. Shiloh. 144p. (J). (Shiloh Ser.: No. 1). (gr. 4-7). pap. 4.99 *(978-0-8072-8330-1(4));*No. 1. 2004. (gr. 3-7). pap. 29.00 incl. audio *(978-0-8072-8329-5(0),* YA164SP) Random Hse. Audio Publishing Group. (Listening Library).

Neal, Michael. Bonnie's Rescue: A Courageous Critters« Series Book. 2009. 56p. pap. 8.95 *(978-1-4401-1237-9(1))* iUniverse, Inc.

Needham B.Ed, Louise. Flossie's Escape to Freedom. 2010. (Illus.). 44p. pap. 16.99 *(978-1-4490-9385-3(X))* AuthorHouse.

Neher, Anna-Luise. A Tale from the Trunk: No. 4 called Yum! Yum! 2009. 16p. pap. 7.31 *(978-1-4251-8701-9(3))* Trafford Publishing.

—A Tale from the Trunk No. 2: With Words! Words! Words! 2009. 56p. pap. 10.82 *(978-1-4251-8284-7(4))* Trafford Publishing.

Nelsen, Donald. Sam & Emma. Gorey, Edward, illus. 2016. (ENG.). 48p. 14.99 *(978-0-486-80590-0(5))* Dover Pubns., Inc.

Nelson, Gail M. & Nelson, Katie M. Go Eat, Pete. Nelson, Gail M., illus. 2013. (Illus.). 32p. pap. 9.99 *(978-1-936499-05-2(3))* Jewel Publishing LLC.

Nelson, Kadir. If You Plant a Seed. Nelson, Kadir, illus. 2015. (ENG., Illus.). 32p. (J). (gr. -1-3). 18.99 *(978-0-06-229889-8(5))* HarperCollins Pubs.

Nelson-Schmidt, Michelle. Bob Is a Unicorn. Nelson-Schmidt, Michelle, illus. 2014. (ENG., Illus.). 28p. (J). 14.99 *(978-1-61067-155-2(4))* Kane Miller.

Neno, Michael. The Children's Magical Adventure: 1 the Rescue. 2011. (Illus.). 48p. (gr. -1). pap. 19.59 *(978-1-4567-7887-3(0))* AuthorHouse.

Ness, Berthetta. Originals: Short Stories for Children. 2007. (YA). pap. *(978-1-57579-351-1(2))* Pine Hill Pr.

Nesselrode, Sandra. Princess Kelsie & Her Special Gifts. 2008. 28p. pap. 19.95 *(978-1-4327-1708-7(1))* Outskirts Pr., Inc.

Nettrour, Nelani. Imagynairs of Jemmidar. Nettrour, Autumn, illus. 2003. 78p. pap. 11.95 *(978-1-929381-99-9(9),* Third Millennium Publishing) Sci Fi-Arizona, Inc.

Newman, Lesléa. Where Is Bear? Gorbachev, Valeri, illus. 2006. (ENG.). 44p. (J). (gr. -1 — 1). pap. 6.99 *(978-0-15-205918-7(0))* Houghton Mifflin Harcourt Publishing Co.

Newton-Perry, Linda. Eye of the Beast. 2009. 62p. pap. 7.98 *(978-0-557-06333-8(7))* Lulu Pr., Inc.

—Lock Your Doors Country Folk. 2009. 62p. pap. 9.23 *(978-0-557-03913-5(4))* Lulu Pr., Inc.

Nguyen, Taohuu. Mighty Mite 2: Zoo Gone Wild. Nguyen, Taohuu, illus. 2007. (Illus.). (J). 14.95 *(978-0-9788469-2-3(3))* Amazing Factory, The.

Nichols, Travis. Fowl Play. 2015. (ENG., Illus.). 40p. (J). (gr. k-3). 14.99 *(978-1-4521-3182-5(1))* Chronicle Bks. LLC.

Nicholson, Doris. Michael & His Animals. 2007. 19.00 *(978-0-8059-8859-8(9))* Dorrance Publishing Co., Inc.

Nicholson, Lorna Schultz. Puckster Goes to the Olympics. Findley, Kelly, illus. 2013. (ENG.). 24p. (J). (gr. -1-3). pap. 6.99 *(978-1-77049-594-4(0),* Fenn-Tundra) Tundra Bks. CAN. Dist: Penguin Random Hse. LLC.

—Puckster's First Hockey Tryout. Findley, Kelly, illus. 2013. (ENG.). 24p. (J). (gr. -1-3). pap. 6.99 *(978-1-77049-596-8(7),* Fenn-Tundra) Tundra Bks. CAN. Dist: Penguin Random Hse. LLC.

Night Beast. 2005. (J). 4.95 *(978-1-59792-018-6(5))* F.A.S.T. Learning LLC.

Night of the Cougar. 2005. (J). 4.95 *(978-1-59792-014-8(2))* F.A.S.T. Learning LLC.

Night Visitor. 2005. (J). 4.95 *(978-1-59792-019-3(3))* F.A.S.T. Learning LLC.

Nighthawk, Tori. Don't Judge a Bird by Its Feathers. Nighthawk, Tori, illus. 2013. (ENG., Illus.). 60p. (J). (gr. -1-3). 17.99 *(978-0-9858811-9-1(4))* Stone, Anne Publishing.

Niland, Kilmeny. The Gingerbread Man. 2006. (Illus.). 16p. *(978-1-921049-49-1(9))* Little Hare Bks. AUS. Dist: HarperCollins Pubs. Australia.

Nimmo, Jenny. Pig on a Swing. Uff, Caroline, illus. 2003. (J). 16.99 *(978-0-340-85241-5(0))* Hodder & Stoughton GBR. Dist: Trafalgar Square Publishing.

Nirgad, Lia. A Kiss for Lily. Abulafia, Yossi, illus. 2006. (ENG.). 24p. (J). (gr. -1-1). 15.95 *(978-1-59692-163-4(3))* MacAdam/Cage Publishing, Inc.

Nite, Aluta. Folk Tales for Children's Enjoyment Book: Why & How Fables Number Two. 2011. 30p. pap. 16.95 *(978-1-4626-1033-4(1))* America Star Bks.

—Why & How Fables Number Three: Folk Tales for Children's Enjoyment Book 3. 2011. 40p. pap. 16.95 *(978-1-4626-2518-5(5))* America Star Bks.

Njenga, Wamoro P. Wow, What a Mama!! Webber, Penny, illus. 2012. 58p. pap. 13.70 *(978-0-9827461-2-7(1))* Prop-Abilities Inc.

Noble, Mariagorretti. The Animal Kingdom in Confusion. 2003. pap. 19.00 *(978-0-8059-5326-8(4))* Dorrance Publishing Co., Inc.

Noël, Alyson. La Cazadora de Almas. 2013. (Vintage Espanol Ser.). (SPA.). 464p. (YA). (gr. 7). pap. 10.95 *(978-0-345-80541-6(0),* Vintage Espanol) Knopf Doubleday Publishing Group.

Nolan, Allia Zobel. Animal Parade. Maddocks, Maria, illus. 2011. (ENG.). 10p. (J). (gr. -1 — 1). 12.99 *(978-0-547-55867-7(8))* Houghton Mifflin Harcourt Publishing Co.

Nolan, Tina. The Homeless Foal. Chernyshova, Anna, illus. 2017. (Animal Rescue Center Ser.). (ENG.). 112p. (J). (gr. 1-3). pap. 4.99 ***(978-1-58925-498-5(8))*** Tiger Tales.

Norfolk, Bobby & Norfolk, Sherry. Anansi & the Sky Kingdom. Hoffmire, Baird, illus. 2008. (Story Cove Ser.). (ENG.). 32p. (J). (gr. -1-3). pap. 4.95 *(978-0-87483-881-7(9))* August Hse. Pubs., Inc.

Norman, Kim. She'll Be Coming up the Mountain. Woodruff, Liza, illus. 2016. (ENG.). 32p. (J). (gr. -1). 14.95 *(978-1-4549-1610-9(9))* Sterling Publishing Co., Inc.

Norman, Kimberly. If It's Snowy & You Know It, Clap Your Paws! Woodruff, Liza, illus. 2013. (ENG.). 26p. (J). (gr. -1). 14.95 *(978-1-4549-0384-0(8))* Sterling Publishing Co., Inc.

—Ten on the Sled. Woodruff, Liza, illus. 2010. (ENG.). 26p. (J). (gr. -1). 14.95 *(978-1-4027-7076-0(6))* Sterling Publishing Co., Inc.

Norris, Eryl. Who's Who in the Woods? Mansfield, Andy, illus. 2015. (ENG.). 18p. (J). (gr. -1-1). 9.99 *(978-1-4998-0140-8(8))* Little Bee Books Inc.

North Bedford, Annie. The Jolly Barnyard. Gergely, Tibor, illus. 2004. (Little Golden Book Ser.). (ENG.). 24p. (J). (gr. -1-2). 4.99 *(978-0-375-82842-3(7),* Golden Bks.) Random Hse. Children's Bks.

North, Merry. All Gone. Woolf, Julia, illus. 2005. (J). *(978-1-57151-753-1(7))* Playhouse Publishing.

Northcutt, Allen. The Legend of Chris Moose: The Most Beautiful Moose in the World. 2012. (ENG.). 48p. (J). 17.95 *(978-1-938462-01-6(7))* Old Stone Pr.

Nosy Crow Staff. Can You Say It, Too? Growl! Growl! Braun, Sebastien, illus. 2014. (Can You Say It, Too? Ser.). (ENG.). 10p. (J). (— 1). bds. 8.99 *(978-0-7636-7396-3(X),* Nosy Crow) Candlewick Pr.

—Can You Say It, Too? Jingle! Jingle! Braun, Sebastien, illus. 2015. (Can You Say It, Too? Ser.). (ENG.). 10p. (J). (— 1). bds. 8.99 *(978-0-7636-8002-2(8),* Nosy Crow) Candlewick Pr.

—Can You Say It, Too? Quack! Quack! Braun, Sebastien, illus. 2015. (Can You Say It, Too? Ser.). (ENG.). 10p. (J). (— 1). bds. 8.99 *(978-0-7636-7589-9(X),* Nosy Crow) Candlewick Pr.

—Can You Say It, Too? Roar! Roar! Braun, Sebastien, illus. 2014. (Can You Say It, Too? Ser.). (ENG.). 10p. (J). (— 1). bds. 8.99 *(978-0-7636-7397-0(8),* Nosy Crow) Candlewick Pr.

—Get Out of My Bath! Teckentrup, Britta, illus. 2015. (ENG.). 24p. (J). (gr. -1-2). 15.99 *(978-0-7636-8006-0(0),* Nosy Crow) Candlewick Pr.

Numeroff, Laura Joffe. Dogs Don't Wear Sneakers. Mathieu, Joe, illus. 2014. 40p. pap. 8.00 *(978-1-61003-344-2(2))* Center for the Collaborative Classroom.

—What Aunts Do Best / What Uncles Do Best. Munsinger, Lynn, illus. 2004. (ENG.). 32p. (J). (gr. -1-3). 17.99 *(978-0-689-84825-4(0),* Simon & Schuster Bks. For Young Readers) Simon & Schuster Bks. For Young Readers.

Numeroff, Laura Joffe & Evans, Nate. The Jellybeans & the Big Dance. Munsinger, Lynn, illus. 2008. (ENG.). 32p. (J). (gr. -1-1). 17.95 *(978-0-8109-9352-5(X),* Abrams Bks. for Young Readers) Abrams, Inc.

—The Jellybeans Love to Dance. Munsinger, Lynn, illus. 2013. (ENG.). 24p. (J). (gr. -1 — 1). bds. 7.95 *(978-1-4197-0622-6(5),* Abrams Appleseed) Abrams, Inc.

Numeroff, Laura Joffe, et al. The Jellybeans & the Big Camp Kickoff. 2011. (ENG., Illus.). 32p. (J). (gr. k-2). 17.95 *(978-0-8109-9765-3(7),* Abrams Bks. for Young Readers) Abrams, Inc.

Nutkis, Phyllis. When the World Was Quiet. Argoff, Patti, illus. 2003. (J). pap. 10.95 *(978-1-929628-14-8(5))* Hachai Publishing.

Nwapa-Ibuaka, Njideka. Tales from Animal Kingdom. I.t. unabr. ed. 2003. (Illus.). (gr. 2-5). 30p. pap. 7.95 *(978-0-9661598-5-1(3));* 40p. pap. 7.95 *(978-0-9661598-4-4(5))* Ekwike Bks. & Publishing.

O'Brien, Melanie. Pat Them Gently. Runnells, Treesha, illus. 2006. (ENG.). 10p. (J). (gr. -1-3). bds. 8.95 *(978-1-58117-462-5(4),* Intervisual/Piggy Toes) Bendon, Inc.

Ocker, Christa Holder. A Crow Named Robin. 2006. (J). per. *(978-1-59872-712-8(5))* Instant Pub.

Odanaka, Barbara. A Crazy Day at the Critter Café. White, Lee, illus. 2009. (ENG.). 32p. (J). (gr. -1-3). 17.99 *(978-1-4169-3914-6(8),* McElderry, Margaret K. Bks.) McElderry, Margaret K. Bks.

Odgers, Darrel & Odgers, Sally. Cranky Paws. Dawson, Janine, illus. 2009. (Pet Vet Ser.: 1). 96p. (J). (gr. 2-6). pap. 4.99 *(978-1-935279-01-3(7))* Kane Miller.

O'Donnell, Liam. Pepper: A Snowy Search. Diefendorf, Cathy, illus. 2004. (Pet Tales Ser.). (ENG.). 32p. (J). (gr. -1-3). 4.95 *(978-1-59249-361-6(0),* 1B026) Soundprints.

—Pepper, a Snowy Search. Diefendorf, Cathy, illus. (Pet Tales Ser.). (ENG.). 32p. (J). (gr. -1-2). 2005. 2.95 *(978-1-59249-362-3(9),* 1B027) 2004. 9.95 *(978-1-59249-363-0(7),* 1B028) Soundprints.

Oelschlager, Vanita. Porcupette Finds a Family. Blanc, Mike, illus. 2010. (ENG.). 44p. (gr. -1-3). 15.95 *(978-0-9819714-7-6(4));* pap. 8.95 *(978-0-9819714-8-3(2))* VanitaBooks.

Oguneye, Kunle. Sikulu & Harambe by the Zambezi River: An African Vversion of the Good Samaritan Story. McCorkindale, Bruce & Youtsey, Scott, illus. 2008. 32p. (J). (gr. -1-5). 14.99 *(978-0-9777382-4-3(8))* Blue Brush Media.

Ohizep, Zolea. Rainbow's Ring. 2011. 24p. pap. 15.99 *(978-1-4567-5574-4(9))* AuthorHouse.

Ohmura, Tomoko. The Long, Long Line. 2013. (ENG., Illus.). 40p. (J). (gr. -1-2). 16.95 *(978-1-926973-92-0(5)*, Owlkids) Owlkids Bks. Inc. CAN. Dist: Publishers Group West (PGW).
Okamoto, Rod. Kingdom of Nu - TJ's Tale: TJ's Tale. Okamoto, Alan, illus. 2006. (J). per. 19.95 *(978-0-9764116-0-4(1))* Nutrishare Publishing.
Okrant, Mark. Judson's Island. 2006. per. 10.95 *(978-0-9791757-2-5(0))* Oak Manor Publishing, Inc.
Oldfield, Jenny. Crash. (Animal Alert Ser.: No. 6). (Illus.). 140p. (J). pap. 8.99 *(978-0-340-70869-9(7))* Hodder & Stoughton GBR. Dist: Trafalgar Square Publishing.
—Skin & Bone, Vol. 5. (Illus.). 138p. (J). pap. *(978-0-340-70878-1(6))* Hodder & Stoughton.
Oliver & Company. (Read-Along Ser.). (J). 7.99 incl. audio *(978-1-55723-024-9(2))* Walt Disney Records.
Oliver, Charles Folkes. Little Willy & the Party Animals. 2011. (Illus.). 20p. (gr. -1). pap. 14.99 *(978-1-4567-5138-8(7))* AuthorHouse.
Oliver, Ilanit. Are You My Daddy? Parker-Rees, Guy, illus. 2015. (ENG.). 16p. (J). (gr. -1-k). bds. 8.99 *(978-0-545-77558-8(2)*, Cartwheel Bks.) Scholastic, Inc.
Olsen, La Verne C. If A Peacock Follows You Home: Children's Stories by Grandma. 2007. 52p. pap. 15.99 *(978-1-4257-3087-1(6))* Xlibris Corp.
One Big Pair of Underwear. 2014. (ENG., Illus.). 40p. (J). (gr. -1-3). 17.99 *(978-1-4424-5336-4(2)*, Beach Lane Bks.) Beach Lane Bks.
O'Neill, Elizabeth. Alfred Visits Virginia. 2006. (Illus.). 24p. (J). (gr. -1-3). pap. 12.00 *(978-0-9771836-8-5(8))* Global Business Information Strategies, Inc.
Opal, Paola. Saffy. 2008. (ENG., Illus.). 24p. (J). (gr. -1 — 1). bds. 7.95 *(978-1-897476-02-4(7))* Simply Read Bks. CAN. Dist: Ingram Publisher Services.
Oppel, Kenneth. Darkwing. Thompson, Keith, illus. 2007. (Silverwing Ser.: 1). 432p. (J). (gr. 5-9). 17.99 *(978-0-06-085054-8(X))* HarperCollins Pubs.
Oram, Hiawyn. Counting Leopard's Spots & other Stories. Warnes, Tim, illus. 2005. 96p. (J). (gr. k-4). reprint ed. 17.00 *(978-0-7567-9252-7(5))* DIANE Publishing Co.
Orme, David. Lost Animals. Mongiovi, Jorge, illus. 2010. (Fact to Fiction Grafx Ser.). 36p. pap. 7.45 *(978-0-7891-7993-7(8))* Perfection Learning Corp.
—Strange Creatures. Lindblad, Stefan, illus. 2010. (Fact to Fiction Grafx Ser.). 36p. pap. 7.45 *(978-0-7891-7994-4(6))* Perfection Learning Corp.
Ormerod, Jan. The Animal Bop Won't Stop! Gardiner, Lindsey, illus. 2011. (J). *(978-1-4380-8419-0(6))* Barron's Educational Series, Inc.
—If You're Happy & You Know It! Gardiner, Lindsey, illus. 2003. 32p. (J). (gr. -1-3). 15.95 *(978-1-932065-07-7(5))*; pap. 5.95 *(978-1-932065-10-7(5))* Star Bright Bks., Inc.
Ormerod, Jan & Gardiner, Lindsey. Doing the Animal Bop. 2005. (ENG., Illus.). 32p. (J). (gr. -1-k). pap. 11.99 *(978-0-7641-7899-3(7))* Barron's Educational Series, Inc.
Ormerod, Jan, et al. Doing the Animal Bop. 2005. (Illus.). (J). *(978-0-7641-8299-0(4))* Barron's Educational Series, Inc.
Orr, Wendy. Discovered! A Beagle Called Bella. Castelao, Patricia, illus. 2013. (Rainbow Street Shelter Ser.: 6). (ENG.). 128p. (J). (gr. 2-5). 15.99 *(978-0-8050-9505-0(5)*, 9780805095050, Holt, Henry & Co. Bks. For Young Readers) Holt, Henry & Co.
Orth, Jack. Happy Days: Book 1. Sunshine, Mary Lou, illus. 2013. 50p. (J). pap. 9.95 *(978-1-61863-545-7(X))* Bookstand Publishing.
—Happy Days: Book 2. Sunshine, Mary Lou, illus. 2013. 50p. (J). pap. 9.95 *(978-1-61863-546-4(8))* Bookstand Publishing.
—Happy Days: Book 3. Sunshine, Mary Lou, illus. 2013. 50p. (J). pap. 9.95 *(978-1-61863-547-1(6))* Bookstand Publishing.
O'Ryan, Ellie, adapted by. Ice Age 2: The Meltdown: Geyser Blast! 2006. (I Can Read Bks.). (Illus.). 31p. (J). *(978-1-4156-5153-7(1))* HarperCollins Pubs.
—Ice Age 2: The Meltdown: Join the Pack! 2006. (I Can Read Bks.). (Illus.). 31p. (J). *(978-1-4156-5155-1(8))* HarperCollins Pubs.
Osborne, Mary Pope. Dingoes at Dinnertime. unabr. ed. 2004. (Magic Tree House Ser.: No. 20). 71p. (J). (gr. k-3). pap. 17.00 incl. audio *(978-0-8072-0929-5(5)*, S FTR 252 SP, Listening Library) Random Hse. Audio Publishing Group.
—Un Tigre Dientes de Sable en el Ocaso. 2004. (Casa del Arbol Ser.: 7).Tr. of Sunset of the Sabretooth. (SPA., Illus.). (J). pap. 5.99 *(978-1-930332-68-3(8))* Lectorum Pubns., Inc.
Osborne, Mary Pope, et al. Perros Salvajes a la Hora de la Cena. Murdocca, Sal, illus. 2008. (Casa del Arbol Ser.: 20).Tr. of Dingoes at Dinnertime. (SPA.). (J). (gr. 2-4). pap. 5.99 *(978-1-933032-50-4(2))* Lectorum Pubns., Inc.
Osburn, Jacquelyn. Willy, the Worried Worm. 2008. 24p. pap. 12.99 *(978-1-4343-8183-5(8))* AuthorHouse.
Osei-Agyemang, Andrew Nana. Before the Lion Became King. 2003. pap. 10.00 *(978-0-8059-6183-6(6))* Dorrance Publishing Co., Inc.
O'Shea, Pauleen. Buddy's Bedtime. Dohanish, Jason, illus. 2007. 32p. (J). 14.95 *(978-0-9778063-0-0(8))* Idlehour Entertainment.
Osorio, Rick. The Great Adventure of Sally Rock & the Cretaceous Chicken. 2006. 65p. pap. 16.95 *(978-1-4241-0971-5(X))* PublishAmerica, Inc.
Ostermeyer Photography. Frosty & Snowy's Arctic Adventures. 2011. (Illus.). 18.95 *(978-0-9794228-5-0(X))* Ostermeyer Photography.
Owens, Jim. New Allegory. 2006. (J). per. 12.00 *(978-0-9769132-4-5(0))* Capri Publishing.
Owl, Grey. The Adventures of Sajo & Her Beaver People. 2011. 164p. *(978-1-84902-465-5(0))* Benediction Classics.
—The Adventures of Sajo & Her Beaver People - with Original Bw Illustrations & a Glossary of Ojibway Indian Words. 2011. 164p. pap. *(978-1-84902-422-8(7))* Benediction Classics.
Owl's Forest Numbers. 2015. (Illus.). (J). *(978-1-58865-882-1(1))* Kidsbooks, LLC.
Oxenbury, Helen. It's My Birthday. Oxenbury, Helen, illus. 2010. (ENG., Illus.). 24p. (J). (gr. -1-k). bds. 8.99 *(978-0-7636-4970-8(8))* Candlewick Pr.
Pacovská, Kveta. Flying. Pacovská, Kveta, illus. 2005.Tr. of Turme. (Illus.). 39p. (J). reprint ed. 20.00 *(978-0-7567-8532-1(4))* DIANE Publishing Co.
Pagratis, Maggie & Pagratis, Illustrator Liliane, MaggieGrenier. Go Away Booboo! 2005. 29p. (J). 11.88 *(978-1-4116-3689-7(9))* Lulu Pr., Inc.
Paiba, Helen. Animal Stories for 5 Year Olds. 2017. (ENG., Illus.). 224p. (J). (gr. k-2). pap. 8.99 ***(978-1-5098-3877-6(5))*** Pan Macmillan GBR. Dist: Independent Pubs. Group.
—Animal Stories for 6 Year Olds. 2017. (ENG., Illus.). 240p. (J). (gr. k-2). pap. 8.99 ***(978-1-5098-3878-3(3))*** Pan Macmillan GBR. Dist: Independent Pubs. Group.
Paine, Albert Bigelow. The Hollow Tree & Deep Woods Book: Being a New Edition in One Volume of the Hollow Tree & in the Deep Woods with Several New Stories & Pictures Added. unabr. ed. 2012. (Illus.). 273p. 49.99 *(978-1-4622-9193-9(7))* Repressed Publishing LLC.
—The Hollow Tree & Deep Woods Book, Being a New Edition in One Volume of the Hollow Tree & in the Deep Woods with Several New Stories & Pictu. Condé, J. M., illus. 2012. 174p. *(978-1-78139-176-1(9))* Benediction Classics.
Palfreman-Bunker, Claire. Can Kittens Take a Catnap? Relf, Adam, illus. 2007. (J). pap. *(978-0-545-02595-9(8))* Scholastic, Inc.
Palmer, Barbara A., illus. A Clue Book for Boo-Boo. 2012. 32p. (J). *(978-0-9728228-3-1(6))* Palmer, Barbara A.
Palmer, W. G. Awaiting Whisperland: The Calling of Galahad Green. 2007. 340p. 29.95 *(978-0-595-68248-5(0))*; per. 19.95 *(978-0-595-43560-9(2))* iUniverse, Inc.
Panaitescu, Simona. The Unseen Paths of the Forest: 13 Tales about Love & Friendship. Moscal, Manuela, illus. 2012. (ENG.). 263p. pap. 14.95 *(978-1-4327-7908-5(7))* Outskirts Pr., Inc.
Pandey, Pooja. Little Monk's Buddha. 2015. (ENG.). 100p. pap. 14.95 *(978-81-8328-064-8(1))* SCB Distributors.
Panks, Kristin & Harpan, Gaile. The Ballad of Furrio the Cat. Reddy, Sneha, illus. 2008. 24p. pap. 12.95 *(978-0-9822540-4-2(0))* Peppertree Pr., The.
Pantoja, Stephen. The Amalaganimals: Eracism Sc. 2010. 33p. pap. 23.90 *(978-0-557-31722-6(3))* Lulu Pr., Inc.
Papa's Spaghetti: Individual Title Six-Packs. (Literatura 2000 Ser.). (gr. 1-2). 28.00 *(978-0-7635-0146-4(8))* Rigby Education.
Papineau, Lucie. Gontrand et le Croissant des Cavernes. 2004. (FRE., Illus.). (J). (gr. k-3). spiral bd. *(978-0-616-11145-1(2))* Canadian National Institute for the Blind/Institut National Canadien pour les Aveugles.
—Pas de Taches Pour une Girafe. 2004. (FRE., Illus.). (J). (gr. k-3). spiral bd. *(978-0-616-03075-2(4))* Canadian National Institute for the Blind/Institut National Canadien pour les Aveugles.
Paquet, Claudine, et al. Antonio, Plumero y Manchitas. 2006. (SPA., Illus.). 110p. (J). pap. *(978-958-30-2016-2(8))* Panamericana Editorial.
Paquette, Ammi-Joan. Bunny Bus. Withrow, Lesley Breen, illus. 2017. (ENG.). 32p. (J). 16.99 *(978-0-374-30225-2(1)*, 9780374302252, Farrar, Straus & Giroux (BYR)) Farrar, Straus & Giroux.
Parachini, Jodie. This Is a Serious Book. Rieley, Daniel, illus. 2016. 32p. (J). (gr. -1-3). 17.99 *(978-0-06-247052-2(3)*, Greenwillow Bks.) HarperCollins Pubs.
Paraskevas, Betty. Peter Pepper's Pet Spectacular. Paraskevas, Michael, illus. 2007. 32p. (J). (gr. 2-6). pap. 14.95 *(978-1-60095-257-9(7))* Carson-Dellosa Publishing, LLC.
Parent, Lauren A. Alphabet Kingdom. McGee, Mo, illus. 2009. (ENG.). 40p. (J). (gr. -1-1). pap. 8.95 *(978-1-55591-643-5(0))* Fulcrum Publishing.
Parenteau, Shirley. Bears on Chairs. Walker, David, illus. 2009. (ENG.). 32p. (J). (gr. -1-k). 15.99 *(978-0-7636-3588-6(X))* Candlewick Pr.
Parish, Herman. Amelia Bedelia Chapter Book #4: Amelia Bedelia Goes Wild! (Special Edition) 2014. (ENG.). 160p. (J). *(978-0-06-227058-0(3)*, Collins Design) HarperCollins Pubs.
—Amelia Bedelia Goes Wild! Avril, Lynne, illus. 2014. (Amelia Bedelia Ser.: No. 4). (ENG.). 160p. (J). (gr. 1-5). 15.99 *(978-0-06-209507-7(2)*, Greenwillow Bks.) HarperCollins Pubs.
—Goes Wild! Avril, Lynne, illus. 2014. (Amelia Bedelia Ser.: No. 4). (ENG.). 160p. (J). (gr. 1-5). pap. 5.99 *(978-0-06-209506-0(4)*, Greenwillow Bks.) HarperCollins Pubs.
Park, Linda Sue. Yaks Yak: Animal Word Pairs. Reinhardt, Jennifer Black, illus. 2016. (ENG.). 40p. (J). (gr. -1-3). 16.99 *(978-0-544-39101-7(2)*, Clarion Bks.) Houghton Mifflin Harcourt Trade & Reference Pubs.
Parker, Andy, illus. Mekanimals Clockwork Safari. 2004. 8p. (J). bds. 12.95 *(978-1-59223-145-4(4)*, Silver Dolphin Bks.) Readerlink Distribution Services, LLC.
Parker, Emma. Safari Adventure. 2010. (Illus.). pap. *(978-1-877561-29-0(0))* First Edition Ltd.
Parlato, Stephen. The World That Loved Books. rev. ed. 2008. (ENG., Illus.). 32p. (J). (gr. -1-3). 16.95 *(978-1-894965-98-9(1))* Simply Read Bks. CAN. Dist: Ingram Publisher Services.
Parr, Todd. Animals in Underwear ABC. 2013. (ENG., Illus.). 16p. (J). (gr. -1 — 1). bds. 7.99 *(978-0-316-20736-2(5))* Little, Brown Bks. for Young Readers.
—Otto Goes to the Beach. 2014. (Passport to Reading Level 1 Ser.). (ENG., Illus.). 32p. (J). (gr. -1-1). 3.99 *(978-0-316-24602-6(6))* Little, Brown Bks. for Young Readers.
Parrish, Edith E. It's Not Easy Being a Purple Goose. Odom, Kelly, illus. 2011. 44p. pap. 24.95 *(978-1-4626-4207-6(1))* America Star Bks.
—Sara the Purple Goose & Susan the Black Swan. 2010. 24p. pap. 17.99 *(978-1-4490-8879-8(1))* AuthorHouse.
Parrish, Emma. Little Owl Says Goodnight. 2016. (Slide-And-Seek Ser.). (ENG., Illus.). 10p. (J). (gr. -1-k). bds. 8.99 *(978-1-4998-0406-5(7))* Little Bee Books Inc.
Parrish, Fayrene. Pancho Saves the Day: Shipmates Learning Adventures Venture. Parrish, Fayrene, illus. 2010. (Illus.). 42p. (J). 15.95 *(978-0-9826717-8-8(X))* Parrish, Fayrene.
Parry, Jo. Under the Rainbow. 2009. (Wow! Bks.). (Illus.). (J). bds. 12.99 *(978-1-934650-04-2(8))* Just For Kids Pr., LLC.
Parsons, Leif. Only Fish Fall from the Sky. 2015. (ENG., Illus.). 32p. (J). (gr. -1-2). 17.95 *(978-1-57687-757-9(4)*, powerHouse Bks.) powerHouse Cultural Entertainment, Inc.
Pascal, Francine. Trabajo del Equipo. Orig. Title: Team Work. (SPA.). 120p. (J). 6.95 *(978-84-272-3797-1(9))* Molino, Editorial ESP. Dist: AIMS International Bks., Inc.
Patricelli, Leslie. Faster! Faster! Patricelli, Leslie, illus. 2013. (Leslie Patricelli Board Bks.). (ENG., Illus.). 30p. (J). (-k). bds. 6.99 *(978-0-7636-6222-6(4))* Candlewick Pr.
—Faster! Faster!/Mas Rapido! Mas Rapido! Patricelli, Leslie, illus. 2013. (Leslie Patricelli Board Bks.). (ENG., Illus.). 30p. (J). (-k). bds. 6.99 *(978-0-7636-6611-8(4))* Candlewick Pr.
—Tickle. Patricelli, Leslie, illus. 2014. (Leslie Patricelli Board Bks.). (ENG., Illus.). 26p. (J). (— 1). bds. 6.99 *(978-0-7636-6322-3(0))* Candlewick Pr.
Patrick, Rudolph. Mulligan's Rainbow. 2010. 24p. pap. 13.98 *(978-1-4490-4980-5(X))* AuthorHouse.
Patten, William. Animal & Nature Stories Vol. 8: The Junior Classics. 2004. reprint ed. pap. 1.99 *(978-1-4192-6805-2(8))* Kessinger Publishing, LLC.
Patterson, Shannon. The Princess & the Cheese. 2010. 43p. pap. 19.95 *(978-0-557-51615-5(3))* Lulu Pr., Inc.
Patterson, Teri Jo. Corky & Lizzie Go to the Circus. 2012. 108p. pap. 19.95 *(978-1-4626-9192-0(7))* America Star Bks.
Paul, Ann Whitford. Count on Culebra. Long, Ethan, illus. 2010. (ENG.). 40p. (J). (gr. -1-3). pap. 6.95 *(978-0-8234-2310-1(7))* Holiday Hse., Inc.
—Count on Culebra: Go from 1 to 10 in Spanish. Long, Ethan, illus. 2008. (ENG.). 40p. (J). (gr. -1-3). 16.95 *(978-0-8234-2124-4(4))* Holiday Hse., Inc.
—Fiesta Fiasco. Long, Ethan, illus. 2009. (ENG.). 32p. (J). (gr. -1-2). pap. 6.95 *(978-0-8234-2275-3(5))* Holiday Hse., Inc.
—Snail's Good Night. Litzinger, Rosanne, illus. 2008. (Holiday House Readers: Level 1 Ser.). (ENG.). 32p. (J). (gr. -1-3). 14.95 *(978-0-8234-1912-8(6))* Holiday Hse., Inc.
Paul, Ruth. Hedgehog's Magic Tricks. Paul, Ruth, illus. 2013. (ENG., Illus.). 32p. (J). (gr. -1-2). 12.99 *(978-0-7636-6385-8(9))* Candlewick Pr.
Paulding, Steve. The Wonderful Adventures of Bradley the Bat. Schmidt, Caleb & Schmidt, Carter, illus. 2013. 70p. pap. 18.95 *(978-0-615-74591-6(1))* Slow on the Draw Productions.
Paver, Michelle. Outcast. Taylor, Geoff, illus. 2009. (Chronicles of Ancient Darkness Ser.: 4). 352p. (J). (gr. 5). pap. 6.99 *(978-0-06-072836-6(1)*, Tegen, Katherine Bks) HarperCollins Pubs.
Payot Karpathakis, Emmanuelle. A Nova Casa Da Pixie. 2012. 32p. pap. *(978-1-909193-03-1(8))* Summertime Publishing.
—El Nuevo Hogar de Pixie. 2012. 32p. pap. *(978-1-909193-01-7(1))* Summertime Publishing.
—Pixie Déménage. 2012. 32p. pap. *(978-1-909193-00-0(3))* Summertime Publishing.
—Pixies Neue Heimat. 2012. 32p. pap. *(978-1-909193-02-4(X))* Summertime Publishing.
—Pixie's New Home. 2012. 32p. pap. *(978-1-904881-98-8(X))* Summertime Publishing.
Pearl, Paige. ARTLANTICA: the Secret Kingdom Beneath Galveston Island. 2008. 38p. 18.95 *(978-1-4357-0389-6(8))* Lulu Pr., Inc.
Pearson, Chris. Emma & Her Friends from Bluebell Wood. 2006. (ENG., Illus.). 76p. pap. *(978-1-84401-641-9(2))* Athena Pr.
Pearson, Tracey Campbell. Bob. Pearson, Tracey Campbell, illus. 2006. (ENG., Illus.). 32p. (J). (gr. -1-1). reprint ed. 8.99 *(978-0-374-40871-8(8)*, 9780374408718) Square Fish.
Peck, Jan. Way Far Away on a Wild Safari. Petrone, Valeria, illus. 2006. (ENG.). 32p. (J). (gr. -1-3). 17.99 *(978-1-4169-0072-6(1)*, Simon & Schuster Bks. For Young Readers) Simon & Schuster Bks. For Young Readers.
—Way Out West on My Little Pony, 1 vol. Leonhard, Herb, illus. 2010. (ENG.). 32p. (J). (gr. k-3). 16.99 *(978-1-58980-697-9(2))* Pelican Publishing Co., Inc.
—Way up High in a Tall Green Tree. Petrone, Valeria, illus. 2005. (ENG.). 32p. (J). (gr. -1-3). 18.99 *(978-1-4169-0071-9(3)*, Simon & Schuster Bks. For Young Readers) Simon & Schuster Bks. For Young Readers.
Peck, Steven L. The Rifts of Rime (Quickened Chronicles) 2012. pap. 14.99 *(978-1-59955-967-4(6))* Cedar Fort, Inc./CFI Distribution.
Peckham, Lori, ed. Guide's Greatest Animal Stories. 2006. 143p. (J). (gr. 5-9). per. 10.99 *(978-0-8280-1944-6(4))* Review & Herald Publishing Assn.
Peek, Megan. Friendly Furries: The Annual Animal County Hop-a-Thon , the un-Surprise Birthday , the New Soccer Friend , the School Play , the Cook-off Contest. 2007. 76p. per. 19.95 *(978-1-4241-6193-5(2))* America Star Bks.
Peek, Merle & Giblin, James Cross. Mary Wore Her Red Dress & Henry Wore His Green Sneakers, 1 vol. 2006. (Read along Book & CD Ser.). (ENG., Illus.). 32p. (J). (gr. k — 1). audio compact disk 10.99 *(978-0-618-75249-2(8))* Houghton Mifflin Harcourt Publishing Co.
Peeler, Penny. The Adventures of Spike & Sally. 2011. 52p. pap. 15.99 *(978-1-4568-9981-3(3))* Xlibris Corp.
Peet, Joy. Sophia's Flutterfly. 2008. 19p. pap. 24.95 *(978-1-60610-806-2(9))* America Star Bks.
Pellant, Terry. The Real Valentine's Story. 2004. 27p. (J). pap. 24.95 *(978-1-4137-2146-1(X))* PublishAmerica, Inc.
Pelosi, Vincent L. The Magical Underwater Kingdom of Balenarium. 2012. 200p. 46.72 *(978-1-4797-1951-8(X))*; pap. 28.03 *(978-1-4797-1950-1(1))* Xlibris Corp.
Penberthy, Stephen. The Adventures of Bird Dog & Friends. 2009. 24p. pap. 10.99 *(978-1-4269-0977-1(2))* Trafford Publishing.
Penn, Audrey. Un Beso en Mi Mano. Harper, Ruth E. & Leak, Nancy M., illus. 2006. (Kissing Hand Ser.). (SPA & ENG.). 32p. (J). (gr. -1-3). 16.95 *(978-1-933718-01-9(3))* Tanglewood Pr.
—Chester Raccoon & the Acorn Full of Memories. Gibson, Barbara L., illus. 2009. (Kissing Hand Ser.). (ENG.). 32p. (J). (gr. -1-3). 16.95 *(978-1-933718-29-3(3))* Tanglewood Pr.
—Chester Raccoon & the Almost Perfect Sleepover. Gibson, Barbara Leonard, illus. 2017. (Kissing Hand Ser.). (ENG.). 32p. (J). (gr. -1-3). 16.95 *(978-1-939100-11-5(9))* Tanglewood Pr.
—Feathers & Fur. Wyrick, Monica Dunsky, illus. 2006. (ENG.). 32p. (J). (gr. -1-3). pap. 7.99 *(978-0-9749303-8-1(5))* Tanglewood Pr.
—A Kiss Goodbye. Gibson, Barbara Leonard, illus. 2007. (Kissing Hand Ser.). (ENG.). 32p. (J). (gr. -1-3). 16.95 *(978-1-933718-04-0(8))* Tanglewood Pr.
—The Kissing Hand. Gibson, Barbara Leonard, illus. 2014. (Kissing Hand Ser.). (ENG.). 14p. (J). (-k). bds. 7.99 *(978-1-933718-77-4(3))* Tanglewood Pr.
—The Kissing Hand. Harper, Ruth E. & Leak, Nancy M., illus. 2007. (Kissing Hand Ser.). (ENG.). 32p. (J). (gr. -1-3). 28.95 *(978-1-933718-07-1(2))*; 12.95 *(978-1-933718-10-1(2))* Tanglewood Pr.
—A Pocket Full of Kisses. Gibson, Barbara Leonard, illus. 2004. (New Child & Family Press Titles Ser.). 32p. (gr. -1-1). 16.95 *(978-0-87868-894-4(3)*, 8943, Child & Family Pr.) Child Welfare League of America, Inc.
—A Pocket Full of Kisses. Gibson, Barbara Leonard, illus. 2006. (Kissing Hand Ser.). (ENG.). 32p. (J). (gr. -1-3). 16.95 *(978-1-933718-02-6(1))* Tanglewood Pr.
Penn, Audrey, et al, illus. The Kissing Hand. 2010. 23.05 *(978-0-7569-9299-6(0))* Natl Bk. Network.
Penn, Audrey & Cosgrove, Stephen. Sassafras. Harper, Ruth E. & James, Robin, illus. 2006. (ENG.). 32p. (J). (gr. -1-3). 16.95 *(978-1-933718-03-3(X))* Tanglewood Pr.
Penn, Audrey & Gibson, Barbara L. Chester Raccoon & the Big Bad Bully. 2008. (Kissing Hand Ser.). (ENG., Illus.). 32p. (J). (gr. -1-3). 16.95 *(978-1-933718-15-6(3))* Tanglewood Pr.
Penner, Lucille Recht. Bears on the Brain. Adams, Lynn, illus. 2003. (Science Solves It! Ser.). 32p. (J). pap. 5.95 *(978-1-57565-121-7(1))* Kane Press, Inc.
—Osos en la Mente. Adams, Lynn, illus. 2008. (Science Solves It! en Espanol Ser.). (SPA.). 32p. (J). (gr. -1-3). pap. 5.95 *(978-1-57565-261-0(7))* Kane Press, Inc.
Pepper, Dennis W. Stories of Little Joe Squirrel & Bob Rabbit. 2005. (Illus.). 62p. pap. *(978-1-84401-092-9(9))* Athena Pr.
Perkins, Larry B. Jake the Cow Hand. 2004. 27p. pap. 9.97 *(978-1-4116-1344-7(9))* Lulu Pr., Inc.
Perrin, Martine. Cock-a-Doodle Who? 2012. (ENG., Illus.). 40p. (J). (gr. -1-3). 12.99 *(978-0-8075-1107-7(2))* Whitman, Albert & Co.
—What Do You See? Perrin, Martine, illus. 2011. (ENG., Illus.). 16p. (J). (gr. -1-k). bds. 8.99 *(978-0-8075-6712-8(4))* Whitman, Albert & Co.
Persaud, Sandhya S. One Day. Ahmad, Maryam & Ramotar, Alexandra, illus. 2009. 12p. pap. 12.99 *(978-1-4389-4437-1(3))* AuthorHouse.
The Pet Parade: Individual Title Six-Packs. (Literatura 2000 Ser.). (gr. -1-1). 28.00 *(978-0-7635-0012-2(7))* Rigby Education.
Peter & the Wolf. 2004. (Illus.). (J). *(978-1-84458-040-8(7)*, Pavilion Children's Books) Pavilion Bks.
Peters, Andrew Fusek. Rabbit Cooks up a Cunning Plan! Robert, Bruno, illus. 2007. (Traditional Tales with a Twist Ser.). (ENG.). 32p. (J). (gr. 2-2). pap. *(978-1-84643-097-8(6))* Child's Play International Ltd.
Petersen, David. Snowy Valentine. Petersen, David, illus. 2011. (ENG., Illus.). 32p. (J). (gr. -1-3). 14.99 *(978-0-06-146378-5(7))* HarperCollins Pubs.
Petersen, Jean. Moose Shoes. Morrow, E., illus. 2007. 52p. per. 24.95 *(978-1-4241-8399-9(5))* America Star Bks.
Petreman, Gwen. A Weird Week. 2012. 20p. (-18). pap. 11.59 *(978-1-4669-5495-3(7))* Trafford Publishing.
Petty, Dev. I Don't Want to Be a Frog. Boldt, Mike, illus. 2015. (ENG.). 32p. (J). (gr. -1-2). lib. bdg. 19.99 *(978-0-375-97334-5(6)*, Doubleday Bks. for Young Readers) Random Hse. Children's Bks.
Petty, Dev. There's Nothing to Do! Boldt, Mike, illus. 2017. (ENG.). 32p. (J). (gr. -1-2). 16.99 ***(978-0-399-55803-0(9))***; lib. bdg. 19.99 ***(978-0-399-55804-7(7))*** Random Hse. Children's Bks. (Doubleday Bks. for Young Readers).
Phillips, Dee. Baby's Day. 2009. (Flip Flap Fun Bks.). (ENG.). 5p. (J). (gr. -1-k). bds. 5.95 *(978-1-84696-087-1(8)*, TickTock Books) Octopus Publishing Group GBR. Dist: Independent Pubs. Group.
Phillips, Ruby Ann. Pet Psychic. Isik, Semur, illus. 2015. (Krystal Ball Ser.). (ENG.). 112p. (gr. 2-3). lib. bdg. 25.32 *(978-1-4795-5875-9(3))* Picture Window Bks.
Pidgeon, Jean, illus. Brush Your Teeth, Please: A Pop-Up Book. 2013. (Pop-Up Book Ser.: 2). (ENG.). 12p. (J). (gr. -1-k). 14.99 *(978-0-7944-3040-5(6)*, Reader's Digest Children's Bks.) Studio Fun International.
Pierpont, James Lord. Jingle Bells. Siewert, Pauline, illus. 2015. (ENG.). 14p. (J). (— 1). 12.99 *(978-0-7636-8197-5(0))* Candlewick Pr.
Pierson, Clara Dillingham. Among the Farmyard People. Gordon, F. C., illus. 2008. 176p. pap. 8.95 *(978-1-59915-281-3(9))* Yesterday's Classics.
Piggy Toes Press, creator. Animals: Colors & Animals. 2011. (Crayola (Piggy Toes Press) Ser.). (Illus.). 6p. (J). (gr. -1-3). bds. 5.95 *(978-1-61524-286-3(4)*, Intervisual/Piggy Toes) Bendon, Inc.
—Color Party! 2007. (ENG., Illus.). 12p. (gr. -1-k). bds. 7.99 *(978-1-58117-585-1(X)*, Intervisual/Piggy Toes) Bendon, Inc.
—Giggle & Grow Baby's Body! 2007. (ENG., Illus.). 14p. (gr. -1-k). bds. 7.99 *(978-1-58117-586-8(8)*, Intervisual/Piggy Toes) Bendon, Inc.
Pignataro, Anna, illus. Agatha. 2015. (ENG.). 40p. (J). (gr. -1-3). 17.99 *(978-1-4998-0096-8(7))* Little Bee Books Inc.
Pilney, Dovie. Charlie the Cocky Rooster. 2010. 44p. pap. 18.49 *(978-1-4490-9806-3(1))* AuthorHouse.
—Charlie the Cocky Rooster: Another Adventure. 2008. 52p. pap. 20.95 *(978-1-4389-3517-1(X))* AuthorHouse.
—Charlie the Cocky Rooster: Leader of the Pack. 2011. 44p. (gr. -1). pap. 20.46 *(978-1-4567-4197-6(7))* AuthorHouse.
Pinder, Eric. If All the Animals Came Inside. Brown, Marc, illus. 2012. (ENG.). 40p. (J). (gr. -1-3). 17.99 *(978-0-316-09883-0(3))* Little Brown & Co.
Pinkney, Jerry, illus. Las Fabulas de Esopo. 2004.Tr. of Aesop's Fables. (SPA.). (J). pap. 10.99 *(978-84-316-7164-8(5))* Vicens-Vives, Editorial, S.A. ESP. Dist: Lectorum Pubns., Inc.
Piper, William Bowman. Giraffe of Montana, Volume 3. 2007. (Giraffe of Montana Ser.). (Illus.). 144p. (J). 19.95 *(978-0-9763359-6-2(4))* Little Pemberley Pr.
Pirc, Jerri J. Kate & Caboodle. Smith, Jane, illus. 2015. pap. *(978-0-473-32583-1(7))* Pirc, Jerri J.
Pirnot, Karen Hutchins. A Colorful Day. Klanot, Taryn Lane, illus. 2008. 28p. pap. 12.95 *(978-0-9814894-9-0(4))* Peppertree Pr., The.
Pirotta, Saviour. Aesop's Fables. Johnson, Richard, illus. 2007. (ENG.). 80p. (J). (gr. -1-3). pap. 9.99 *(978-0-7534-6133-4(1)*, 9780753461334, Kingfisher) Roaring Brook Pr.
Pitt, Marilyn & Hileman, Jane. My Babies. Bianchi, John, illus. 2010. (1G Potato Chip Bks.). (ENG.). 12p. (J). (gr. k-1). pap. 5.99 *(978-1-61541-065-1(1))* American Reading Co.

—Up Here. Bianchi, John, illus. 2010. (1G Potato Chip Bks.). (ENG.). 12p. (J). (gr. k-1). pap. 5.99 *(978-1-61541-015-6(5))* American Reading Co.

Pitt, Marilyn & Sánchez, Lucía M. Mis Bebés. Bianchi, John, illus. 2010. (1G Libros Papas Fritas Ser.).Tr. of My Babies. (SPA & ENG.). 12p. (J). (gr. k-1). pap. 6.99 *(978-1-61541-080-4(5))* American Reading Co.

Pitt, Sarah. Peek a Boo! Farm. 2009. (Little Peek a Boo Bks.). (Illus.). (J). bds. 9.99 *(978-1-934650-59-2(5))* Just For Kids Pr., LLC.

—Peek a Boo! Garden. 2009. (Little Peek a Boo Bks.). (Illus.). (J). bds. 9.99 *(978-1-934650-60-8(9))* Just For Kids Pr., LLC.

—Peek a Boo! Ocean. 2009. (Little Peek a Boo Bks.). (Illus.). (J). bds. 9.99 *(978-1-934650-58-5(7))* Just For Kids Pr., LLC.

Pixton, Amy, creator. Creepy Crawlies. 2006. (J). *(978-0-9779631-1-9(X))* TyBook.

Pixton, Kaaren. Jungle, Rumble! Hey Baby! Look at These Wild Animals! 2010. (Indestructibles Ser.). (ENG., Illus.). 12p. (J). (gr. k — 1). pap. 5.95 *(978-0-7611-5858-5(8)*, 15858) Workman Publishing Co., Inc.

—Plip, Plop, Pond! Hey Baby! Look at These Animals in the Pond! 2010. (Indestructibles Ser.). (ENG., Illus.). 12p. (J). (gr. k — 1). pap. 5.95 *(978-0-7611-5857-8(X)*, 15857) Workman Publishing Co., Inc.

Plonk, Michelle. Fritz, the Forgetful Frog. 2009. 40p. pap. 18.50 *(978-1-60860-123-3(4)*, Eloquent Bks.) Strategic Book Publishing & Rights Agency (SBPRA).

Plumb, Sally. A Pika's Tail: A Children's Story about Mountain Wildlife. Milligan, Sharlene, ed. Ormsby, Lawrence, illus. 2012. (ENG.). 40p. (J). (gr. -1-5). pap. 9.95 *(978-0-931895-25-8(1))* Grand Teton Assn.

Pochocki, Ethel. The Blessing of the Beasts. Moser, Barry, illus. 2014. (ENG.). 40p. (J). pap. 15.99 *(978-1-61261-582-0(1))* Paraclete Pr., Inc.

Pochocki, Ethel & Helms, Hal M. The Blessing of the Beasts. Moser, Barry, illus. 2007. (ENG.). 40p. (gr. -1-3). 18.95 *(978-1-55725-502-0(4))* Paraclete Pr., Inc.

Poehler, S. Applecheeks & the Pop E. Tree. 2012. 12p. pap. 15.99 *(978-1-4772-8180-2(0))* AuthorHouse.

Poet, Jonny. Waddling to the Pond. Luchsinger, Linda, illus. 2011. 40p. pap. 24.95 *(978-1-4560-4033-8(2))* America Star Bks.

Pokas, Dora. Muriel's Red Sweater. (J). 15.95 *(978-0-8118-3771-2(8))* Chronicle Bks. LLC.

Polak, Monique. No More Pranks, 1 vol. 2004. (Orca Soundings Ser.). (ENG.). 128p. (YA). (gr. 8-12). pap. 9.95 *(978-1-55143-315-8(X))* Orca Bk. Pubs. USA.

Pollock, Jim. A Whole Different Animal. Pollock, Mary Ellen, illus. 2007. 89p. (J). 17.00 net. *(978-0-9763675-2-9(1))* First Flight Bks.

Ponting, Susan. The Revenge of BB Wolf. 2011. 140p. (gr. -1). 28.98 *(978-1-4567-7528-5(6))*; (Illus.). pap. 17.23 *(978-1-4567-7011-2(X))* AuthorHouse.

Popper, Garry. High Noon in Didley Pidley. Forshaw, John, illus. 2004. (Bret the Vet Ser.). 40p. 7.00 *(978-1-84161-013-9(5))* Ravette Publishing, Ltd. GBR. Dist: Parkwest Pubns., Inc.

Porte, Barbara Ann. Beauty & the Serpent: Thirteen Tales of Unnatural Animals. Covey, Rosemary Feit, illus. 2008. (ENG.). 128p. (YA). (gr. 7). pap. 7.99 *(978-1-4169-7579-3(9)*, Simon & Schuster/Paula Wiseman Bks.) Simon & Schuster/Paula Wiseman Bks.

Porter, Annaliese & Bancroft, Bronwyn. The Outback. 2005. (Illus.). 28p. (J). *(978-1-875641-86-4(6))* Magabala Bks.

Porter-Gaylord, Laurel. I Love My Daddy Because... (Quiero a Mi Papa Porque...) Wolff, Ashley, illus. 2004. (ENG & SPA.). 22p. (J). (gr. -1 — 1). bds. 6.99 *(978-0-525-47251-3(7)*, Dutton Books for Young Readers) Penguin Young Readers Group.

—I Love My Mommy Because... Wolff, Ashley, illus. 2004. (ENG.). 22p. (J). (gr. -1 — 1). bds. 6.99 *(978-0-525-47247-6(9)*, Dutton Books for Young Readers) Penguin Young Readers Group.

Posner-Sanchez, Andrea. Follow That Hippo! (Disney Junior: the Lion Guard) Cortes, Mario & Colletti, Marco, illus. 2016. (Big Golden Book Ser.). (ENG.). 32p. (J). (-k). 9.99 *(978-0-7364-3391-4(0)*, Golden/Disney) Random Hse. Children's Bks.

—Toby the Cowsitter (Disney Junior: Sheriff Callie's Wild West) RH Disney Staff & Fruchter, Jason, illus. 2015. (Little Golden Book Ser.). (ENG.). 24p. (J). (-k). 4.99 *(978-0-7364-3299-3(X)*, Golden/Disney) Random Hse. Children's Bks.

—Wish upon a Star (Disney Princess) Random House Disney Staff, illus. 2013. (Pictureback(R) Ser.). (ENG.). 16p. (J). (gr. -1-2). pap. 4.99 *(978-0-7364-3046-3(6)*, RH/Disney) Random Hse. Children's Bks.

Potash, Mildred. Millie & Cupcake. 2013. (ENG.). 24p. (J). pap. 10.95 *(978-1-4787-0997-8(9))* Outskirts Pr., Inc.

Potter, Beatrix. Beatrix Potter Favorite Tales: The Tales of Peter Rabbit & Jemima Puddle-Duck. 2006. (Peter Rabbit Ser.). (ENG., Illus.). 64p. (J). (gr. -1-2). 10.99 *(978-0-7232-5879-7(1)*, Warne) Penguin Young Readers Group.

—The Great Big Treasury of Beatrix Potter. 2007. (ENG.). 104p. pap. 18.99 *(978-1-4264-3597-3(5))*; 114p. pap. 19.99 *(978-1-4264-3648-2(3))* Creative Media Partners, LLC.

—Peekaboo! 2009. (Peter Rabbit Naturally Better Ser.). (ENG.). 10p. (J). (gr. -1 — 1). bds. 6.99 *(978-0-7232-6350-0(7)*, Warne) Penguin Young Readers Group.

—The Tale of Peter Rabbit. 2009. (Peter Rabbit Naturally Better Ser.). (ENG.). 72p. (J). (gr. -1-2). 6.99 *(978-0-7232-6392-0(2)*, Warne) Penguin Young Readers Group.

—The Tale of Timmy Tiptoes. (Beatrix Potter Bookmark Board Book Ser.). (Illus.). 6p. (J). bds. 3.95 *(978-7-58989-204-0(6))* Thurman Hse., LLC.

—Tickle, Tickle, Peter! 2012. (Peter Rabbit Ser.). (ENG.). 10p. (J). (gr. -1-k). bds. 9.99 *(978-0-7232-6750-8(2)*, Warne) Penguin Young Readers Group.

—Where's Peter? 2011. (Peter Rabbit Ser.). (ENG.). 12p. (J). (gr. -1-k). bds. 10.99 *(978-0-7232-6636-5(0)*, Warne) Penguin Young Readers Group.

Potter, Beatrix, illus. The Tale of Peter Rabbit & Other Stories: The Beatrix Potter Collection. 2016. (J). pap. *(978-1-5124-2608-3(3)*, First Avenue Editions) Lerner Publishing Group.

Poulin, Andrée. The Best Time. Beha, Philippe, illus. 2009. (My First Stories Ser.). 24p. (J). (gr. -1-3). 22.60 *(978-1-60754-350-3(8))*; pap. 8.15 *(978-1-60754-351-0(6))* Windmill Bks.

Powell, Jillian. Let's Say Hello. Colnaghi, Stefania, illus. 2013. (Start Reading Ser.). (ENG.). 24p. (gr. k-1). pap. 7.95 *(978-1-4765-4111-2(6))* Capstone Press of Coughlan Cos.

Powell, Richard. Flap My Wings. Martin-Laranaga, Ana, illus. 2003. 10p. (J). 5.95 *(978-1-58925-690-3(5))* Tiger Tales.

—Lucy Lamb. Rhodes, Katie, illus. 2004. (Fuzzy Friends Ser.). 8p. (J). 7.95 *(978-1-58925-724-5(3))* Tiger Tales.

—Puppy's Tail. Davis, Carolina A., illus. 2003. (Animal Tails Ser.). 12p. (J). 3.95 *(978-1-58925-674-3(3))* Tiger Tales.

—Wag My Tail. Martin-Larranaga, Ana, illus. 2003. 10p. (J). 5.95 *(978-1-58925-691-0(3))* Tiger Tales.

—What's in the Box? Martin Larrañaga, Ana, illus. 2004. (Ana's Mini Movers Ser.). 12p. (J). 5.95 *(978-1-58925-742-9(1))* Tiger Tales.

—What's in the Egg? Martin Larrañaga, Ana, illus. 2004. (Ana's Mini Movers Ser.). 14p. (J). 5.95 *(978-1-58925-739-9(1))* Tiger Tales.

—Who Lives Here? Martin Larrañaga, Ana, illus. 2004. (Ana's Mini Movers Ser.). 14p. (J). 5.95 *(978-1-58925-741-2(3))* Tiger Tales.

—Whose Hat Is That? Martin Larrañaga, Ana, illus. 2004. (Ana's Mini Movers Ser.). 12p. (J). 5.95 *(978-1-58925-740-5(5))* Tiger Tales.

—Wiggle My Ears. Larranaga, Ana, illus. 2004. (Wrigglers Ser.). 8p. (J). bds. 5.95 *(978-1-58925-692-7(1))* Tiger Tales.

Powell-Tuck, Maudie. A Very Merry Christmas. Guile, Gill, illus. 2014. (ENG.). 22p. (J). (gr. -1-k). bds. 8.99 *(978-1-58925-560-9(7))* Tiger Tales.

Powelson, Jennifer. Rachel & Sammy Learn about Trees. 2012. (Illus.). 40p. pap. 15.00 *(978-1-61204-988-5(5)*, Strategic Bk. Publishing) Strategic Book Publishing & Rights Agency (SBPRA).

Power, Nicholas D. Paudie's Magical Adventures. 2009. 236p. 24.75 *(978-1-60693-534-7(8)*, Strategic Bk. Publishing) Strategic Book Publishing & Rights Agency (SBPRA).

Prager, Ellen. The Shark Rider. Caparo, Antonio Javier, illus. 2015. (Tristan Hunt & the Sea Guardians Ser.: 2). (ENG.). 326p. (J). (gr. 3-7). pap. 9.95 *(978-1-938063-51-0(1)*, Mighty Media Junior Readers) Mighty Media Pr.

Prasad, Sunayna. Alyssa's African Adventures. 2011. pap. 11.95 *(978-0-7414-6619-8(8))* Infinity Publishing.

Prasadam, Smriti. Hello, Animals! Bolam, Emily, illus. 2010. (Black & White Sparklers Ser.). (ENG.). 10p. (J). (gr. -1). bds. 6.99 *(978-1-58925-861-7(4))* Tiger Tales.

Prats, Joan de Déu. Un Topo en un Mar de Hierba. Caruncho, Isabel, illus. (SPA.). 31p. *(978-84-236-5040-8(5))* Edebé ESP. Dist: Lectorum Pubns., Inc.

Pratta, Barbara. The Weeping Willow Tree. 2011. 344p. 28.95 *(978-1-4634-0762-9(9))*; pap. 17.99 *(978-1-4634-0763-6(7))* AuthorHouse.

Pray, Linda. Characters in the Wild. 2011. 44p. pap. 16.95 *(978-1-4560-7904-8(2))* America Star Bks.

Preston-Gannon, Frann. How to Lose a Lemur. 2016. (ENG., Illus.). 30p. (J). (gr. -1 — 1). bds. 6.95 *(978-1-4549-2095-3(5))* Sterling Publishing Co., Inc.

—The Journey Home. 2016. (ENG., Illus.). 32p. (J). (gr. -1-3). 8.99 *(978-1-84365-209-0(9)*, Pavilion) Pavilion Bks. GBR. Dist: Independent Pubs. Group.

Preston, Helen M. Gra Gra's Stories. 2012. 72p. pap. 28.99 *(978-1-4772-9783-4(9))* AuthorHouse.

Previn, Alicia L. The Strange Disappearance of Walter Tortoise. Previn, Alicia L., illus. 2013. (Illus.). 36p. pap. 12.99 *(978-0-9847107-1-3(X))* Previn, Lovely Pubns.

Price, Mary Elizabeth. Wallbaby Bumblebees. 2004. (Illus.). 40p. (J). per. 15.75 *(978-0-9715402-2-4(5)*, 410-707-6686) Barnhardt & Ashe Publishing, Inc.

Price, Mathew. Polo Tiene Una Amiga. (SPA.). pap. 7.95 *(978-950-07-1980-3(0))* Editorial Sudamericana S.A. ARG. Dist: Distribooks, Inc.

Priddy, Roger. Alphaprints: Sweet Heart. 2015. (Alphaprints Ser.). (ENG., Illus.). 12p. (J). (gr. -1 — 1). bds. 7.99 *(978-0-312-51913-1(3)*, 9780312519131, Priddy Bks.) St. Martin's Pr.

—Baby Touch & Feel Baby Bunny. 2009. (Baby Touch & Feel Ser.). (ENG.). 12p. (J). (gr. -1 — 1). bds. 8.95 *(978-0-312-50606-3(6)*, 9780312506063, Priddy Bks.) St. Martin's Pr.

—Barnyard Fun! 2015. (Little Friends Ser.). (ENG., Illus.). 12p. (J). (gr. -1 — 1). bds. 8.99 *(978-0-312-51841-7(2)*, 9780312518417, Priddy Bks.) St. Martin's Pr.

—Charlie Champ Wins the Day. 2017. (Alphaprints Ser.). (ENG., Illus.). 32p. (J). 16.99 *(978-0-312-52177-6(4)*, 9780312521776, Priddy Bks.) St. Martin's Pr.

—Easter Surprise. 2011. (ENG., Illus.). (J). (gr. -1-k). bds. 9.99 *(978-0-312-51002-2(0)*, 9780312510022, Priddy Bks.) St. Martin's Pr.

—I Love You. 2015. (Mini Tab Ser.). (ENG.). 16p. (J). (gr. -1 — 1). bds. 5.99 *(978-0-312-51919-3(2)*, 9780312519193, Priddy Bks.) St. Martin's Pr.

—Little Friends: Big Adventure. 2015. (Little Friends Ser.). (ENG., Illus.). 12p. (J). (gr. -1 — 1). bds. 14.99 *(978-0-312-51869-1(2)*, 9780312518691, Priddy Bks.) St. Martin's Pr.

—My First Peekaboo: Where's My Home? 2015. (My First Peekaboo Ser.). (ENG., Illus.). 8p. (J). (gr. -1 — 1). bds. 8.99 *(978-0-312-51834-9(X)*, 9780312518349, Priddy Bks.) St. Martin's Pr.

—My First Peekaboo: Who Am I? 2015. (My First Peekaboo Ser.). (ENG., Illus.). 8p. (J). (gr. -1 — 1). bds. 8.99 *(978-0-312-51833-2(1)*, 9780312518332, Priddy Bks.) St. Martin's Pr.

—My First Peekaboo: Who's My Mom? 2015. (My First Peekaboo Ser.). (ENG., Illus.). 8p. (J). (gr. -1 — 1). bds. 8.99 *(978-0-312-51832-5(3)*, 9780312518325, Priddy Bks.) St. Martin's Pr.

—Noisy Peekaboo: Moo. 2016. (Noisy Peekaboo Ser.). (ENG.). 8p. (J). bds. 9.99 *(978-0-312-52062-5(X)*, 9780312520625, Priddy Bks.) St. Martin's Pr.

—Ten Barnyard Babies. 2009. (ENG.). 10p. (J). (gr. -1-k). bds. 15.99 *(978-0-312-50584-4(1)*, 9780312505844, Priddy Bks.) St. Martin's Pr.

Priddy, Roger & Crimi-Trent, Ellen. Making Friends. 2013. (Schoolies Ser.). (ENG., Illus.). 28p. (J). (gr. -1-1). 4.99 *(978-0-312-51610-9(X)*, 9780312516109, Priddy Bks.) St. Martin's Pr.

—My School Day. 2013. (Schoolies Ser.). (ENG., Illus.). 32p. (J). (gr. -1-1). 14.99 *(978-0-312-51607-9(X)*, 9780312516079, Priddy Bks.) St. Martin's Pr.

—School House. 2013. (Schoolies Ser.). (ENG., Illus.). 14p. (J). (gr. -1-1). 14.99 *(978-0-312-51613-0(4)*, 9780312516130, Priddy Bks.) St. Martin's Pr.

Prince, Cheryl. Belle's Wild Journey. 2012. 24p. pap. 24.95 *(978-1-4626-9794-6(1))* America Star Bks.

Printers, Caxton. Rufus & Friends. 2012. (ENG.). pap. *(978-1-4675-4751-2(4))*; pap. *(978-1-4675-4752-9(2))* Independent Pub.

Pritchard, Alicia Michele. Critter Pics. 2008. 53p. pap. 22.50 *(978-1-4357-1134-1(3))* Lulu Pr., Inc.

Prochovnic, Dawn Babb. A to Z Sign with Me: Sign Language for the Alphabet, 1 vol. Bauer, Stephanie, illus. 2012. (ENG.). 32p. 28.50 *(978-1-61641-835-9(4)*, Looking Glass Library) Magic Wagon.

—The Nest Where I Like to Rest: Sign Language for Animals, 1 vol. 2009. (Story Time with Signs & Rhymes Ser.). (ENG., Illus.). 32p. (gr. -1-3). 28.50 *(978-1-60270-670-5(0)*, Looking Glass Library) ABDO Publishing Co.

—Shape Detective: Sign Language for Shapes, 1 vol. Bauer, Stephanie, illus. 2012. (ENG.). 32p. 28.50 *(978-1-61641-840-3(0)*, Looking Glass Library) Magic Wagon.

Prokofiev, Sergei. Peter & the Wolf. Raschka, Chris, illus. 2008. (ENG.). 40p. (J). (gr. -1-2). 19.99 *(978-0-689-85652-5(0)*, Atheneum/Richard Jackson Bks.) Simon & Schuster Children's Publishing.

Pruitt, Lisa A. Savanna & the Magic Boots. 2011. 24p. (gr. 1-2). pap. 11.32 *(978-1-4634-0090-3(X))* AuthorHouse.

Pryce, Trevor. Amphibians' End. Greene, Sanford, illus. 2016. (Kulipari Ser.). (ENG.). 304p. (J). (gr. 3-7). pap. 8.95 *(978-1-4197-2194-6(1)*, Amulet Bks.) Abrams, Inc.

Pryce, Trevor & Naftali, Joel. Amphibians' End. 2015. (Kulipari Ser.). (ENG., Illus.). 304p. (J). (gr. 3-7). 15.95 *(978-1-4197-1648-5(4)*, Amulet Bks.) Abrams, Inc.

—The Rainbow Serpent. Greene, Sanford, illus. 2014. (Kulipari Ser.). (ENG.). 304p. (J). (gr. 3-7). 15.95 *(978-1-4197-1309-5(4)*, Amulet Bks.) Abrams, Inc.

Publications International Ltd. Staff, ed. Baby's Animals. 2010. 18p. (J). bds. 7.98 *(978-1-60553-962-1(7))* Publications International, Ltd.

—Classic Animal Tales. 2011. 96p. (J). bds. 10.98 *(978-1-4508-1481-2(6))* Publications International, Ltd.

—Disney Lion King - We Can Share. 2011. 12p. (J). bds. *(978-1-4508-1383-9(6))* Publications International, Ltd.

—Read to Me Grandma (Keepsake Story Collection) 2010. 96p. (J). 13.98 *(978-1-60553-792-4(6))* Publications International, Ltd.

—Record A Story: My Grandma Is Special. 2011. 20p. (J). bds. 19.99 *(978-1-4508-1352-5(6))* Phoenix International Publications, Inc.

—Record a Story: My Grandpa Is Special. 2011. 20p. (J). bds. 25.98 *(978-1-4508-1381-5(X))* Phoenix International Publications, Inc.

—Where in the World. 2010. 18p. (J). bds. 12.98 *(978-1-4127-4464-5(4)*, PIL Kids) Publications International, Ltd.

Pugliano-Martin, Carol. The Great Big Giant Turnip: Set Of 6. 2010. (Early Connections Ser.). (J). pap. 39.00 net. *(978-1-4108-1553-8(6))* Benchmark Education Co.

Pulchinski, Erin Elizabeth. Why, Oh, Why Does the Rain Fall from the Sky? 2013. 32p. pap. *(978-1-4602-1778-8(0))* FriesenPress.

Quaal, Jean. If Roosters Crow? 2009. 32p. pap. 14.95 *(978-1-4327-3671-2(X))* Outskirts Pr., Inc.

Quattlebaum, Mary. Jo MacDonald Saw a Pond. Bryant, Laura J., illus. 2013. (ENG.). 26p. (J). (gr. -1 — 1). bds. 7.95 *(978-1-58469-224-9(3))* Dawn Pubns.

Quayle, Susan. Mouse & the Storm. Muldoon, Melissa, illus. 2017. (ENG.). 56p. 15.95 *(978-1-84819-344-4(0)*, 9047, Singing Dragon) Kingsley, Jessica Pubs. GBR. Dist: Macmillan Distribution Ltd.

Quinton, Sasha, text. Tails. 2010. (Illus.). 10p. (J). *(978-1-936199-14-3(9))* Book Shop, Ltd., The.

Raab, Brigitte. Mama, I Can't Sleep. Olten, Manuela, illus. 2012. (ENG.). 32p. (J). (gr. -1-k). 16.95 *(978-1-61608-965-8(2)*, 608965, Sky Pony Pr.) Skyhorse Publishing Co., Inc.

Rabe, Tish. I Love the Nightlife! Ruiz, Aristides & Mathieu, Joe, illus. 2010. (Pictureback Ser.). (ENG.). 16p. (J). (gr. -1-2). pap. 3.99 *(978-0-375-86354-7(0)*, Random Hse. Bks. for Young Readers) Random Hse. Children's Bks.

—Spring into Summer! Mathieu, Joe & Ruiz, Aristides, illus. 2012. (Pictureback(R) Ser.). (ENG.). 32p. (J). (gr. -1-2). pap. 4.99 *(978-0-307-93057-6(2)*, Random Hse. Bks. for Young Readers) Random Hse. Children's Bks.

—Thump!/The Lost Egg (Cat in the Hat/Seuss) Ruiz, Aristides & Mathieu, Joe, illus. 2013. (Pictureback(R) Ser.). (ENG.). 32p. (J). (gr. -1-2). pap. 4.99 *(978-0-307-98063-2(4)*, Random Hse. Bks. for Young Readers) Random Hse. Children's Bks.

—What Cat Is That? All about Cats. Ruiz, Aristides & Mathieu, Joe, illus. 2013. (Cat in the Hat's Learning Library). (ENG.). 48p. (J). (gr. k-3). 9.99 *(978-0-375-86640-1(X)*, Random Hse. Bks. for Young Readers) Random Hse. Children's Bks.

Radosevich, Tina. The Binky Story. 2013. 20p. pap. 17.99 *(978-1-4817-0001-6(4))* AuthorHouse.

Rahman, Junam. Rudy the Rooster Loses His Voice. 2011. 28p. pap. 13.59 *(978-1-4520-0187-6(1))* AuthorHouse.

Raiku, Makoto. Animal Land 7. 2013. (Animal Land Ser.). (ENG., Illus.). 200p. (gr. 8-12). pap. 10.99 *(978-1-61262-249-1(6))* Kodansha America, Inc.

—Animal Land 8. 2013. (Animal Land Ser.). (ENG., Illus.). 208p. (gr. 8-12). pap. 10.99 *(978-1-61262-250-7(X))* Kodansha America, Inc.

Raines, Jennifer. Laughs for Porcupine, 1 vol. 2009. 18p. pap. 24.95 *(978-1-60836-784-9(3))* America Star Bks.

Raju, P. V. Ramaswami. Indian Fables. 2009. 178p. pap. 9.95 *(978-1-59915-374-2(2))* Yesterday's Classics.

Ralph, Donna J. Critter Chronicles: Stories of Critters in a Colorado Wildlife Rehabilitator's Life. 2007. 200p. per. 16.95 *(978-0-595-47858-3(1))* iUniverse, Inc.

Randall, Bob & McInerney, Kunyi June-Anne. Tracker Tjugingji. 2003. (ENG.). 36p. (J). pap. 22.95 incl. audio compact disk *(978-1-86465-030-3(3))* IAD Pr. AUS. Dist: Independent Pubs. Group.

Random House. Ice Team (Paw Patrol) Jackson, Mike, illus. 2015. (Glitter Picturebook Ser.). (ENG.). 16p. (J). (gr. -1-2). 5.99 *(978-0-553-52281-5(7)*, Random Hse. Bks. for Young Readers) Random Hse. Children's Bks.

Random House Disney Staff. Zootopia Junior Novelization (Disney Zootopia) Random House Disney Staff, illus. 2016. (Junior Novel Ser.). (ENG., Illus.). 128p. (J). (gr. 4-7). 5.99 *(978-0-7364-3394-5(5)*, RH/Disney) Random Hse. Children's Bks.

—Zootopia: the Official Handbook (Disney Zootopia) Random House Disney Staff, illus. 2016. (Official Guide Ser.). (ENG., Illus.). 64p. (J). (gr. 4-7). 7.99 *(978-0-7364-3395-2(3)*, RH/Disney) Random Hse. Children's Bks.

Random House Disney Staff & Green, Rico. Super Animals! Random House Disney Staff & Disney Storybook Art Team, illus. 2016. (Step into Reading Ser.). (ENG.). 24p. (J). (gr. -1-1). 4.99 *(978-0-7364-3454-6(2)*, RH/Disney) Random Hse. Children's Bks.

Random House Disney Staff & Knowles, Heather. Zootopia Little Golden Book (Disney Zootopia) Random House Disney Staff, illus. 2016. (Little Golden Book Ser.). (ENG., Illus.). 24p. (J). (gr. -1-k). 4.99 *(978-0-7364-3389-1(9)*, Golden/Disney) Random Hse. Children's Bks.

Random House Disney Staff & Scollon, Bill. The Big Case. Random House Disney Staff & Disney Storybook Art Team, illus. 2016. (Step into Reading Ser.). (ENG.). 32p. (J). (gr. -1-1). 4.99 *(978-0-7364-3456-0(9)*, RH/Disney) Random Hse. Children's Bks.

Random House Editors. Zootopia Junior Novelization. 2016. lib. bdg. 16.00 *(978-0-606-38491-9(X))* Turtleback Bks.

Rangel, Graciela. Anthony's Journey to God's Ark. 2007. 84p. pap. 8.95 *(978-1-59526-907-2(X)*, Llumina Christian Bks.) Aeon Publishing Inc.

Ranson, Erin. A Bright New Star: With Color-Changing Star Light. Crisp, Dan, illus. 2007. (Story Book Ser.). 16p. (J). (gr. -1-3). bds. *(978-1-84666-161-7(7)*, Tide Mill Pr.) Top That! Publishing PLC.

—Wild Animals. Green, Barry, illus. 2007. (Magnetic Story & Play Scene Ser.). (ENG.). 8p. (J). (gr. -1-1). 9.99 *(978-1-84666-093-1(9))* Top That! Publishing PLC GBR. Dist: Independent Pubs. Group.

Rao, Sirish. The Old Animals' Forest Band. Bai, Durga, illus. 2008. 40p. (J). (gr. -1-2). (ENG.). *(978-81-86211-45-8(4))*; *(978-81-86211-41-0(1))* Tara Publishing.

Rasheed, Winona. Smiles & Frowns Through Animal Town's Storybook. 2008. 55p. pap. 13.70 *(978-1-4357-4617-6(1))* Lulu Pr., Inc.

Rathmann, Peggy. Buenas Noches, Gorila. Mayobre, Maria Francisca, tr. from ENG. Rathmann, Peggy, illus. 2004. (SPA., Illus.). 36p. (gr. k). 12.99 *(978-980-257-265-6(9))* Ekare, Ediciones VEN. Dist: Lectorum Pubns., Inc.

—Buenas Noches, Gorila. Rathmann, Peggy, illus. 2004. (SPA & ENG., Illus.). 34p. (J). (gr. -1 — 1). bds. 7.99 *(978-0-399-24300-4(3)*, G.P. Putnam's Sons Books for Young Readers) Penguin Young Readers Group.

Ratzlaff, Aaron J. Quills. 2011. (ENG.). 40p. (J). pap. 13.99 *(978-0-8361-9509-5(4))* Herald Pr.

Rawlings, Marjorie Kinnan. The Secret River. Dillon, Leo & Dillon, Diane, illus. 2011. (ENG.). 56p. (J). (gr. -1-3). 19.99 *(978-1-4169-1179-1(0)*, Atheneum Bks. for Young Readers) Simon & Schuster Children's Publishing.

Rawlinson, Julia. Fletcher & the Snowflake Christmas. Beeke, Tiphanie, illus. 2010. (ENG.). 32p. (J). (gr. -1-2). 16.99 *(978-0-06-199033-5(7)*, Greenwillow Bks.) HarperCollins Pubs.

—Fletcher & the Springtime Blossoms. Beeke, Tiphanie, illus. 2009. (ENG.). 32p. (J). (gr. -1-2). 17.99 *(978-0-06-168855-3(X)*, Greenwillow Bks.) HarperCollins Pubs.

—Fletcher & the Springtime Blossoms. 2011. (J). (gr. -1-2). 29.95 *(978-0-545-32738-1(5))* Weston Woods Studios, Inc.

Ray, Mary Lyn. Go to Sleep, Little Farm. Neal, Christopher Silas, illus. (ENG.). (J). 2015. 38p. (— 1). bds. 8.99 *(978-0-544-57916-3(X))* 2014. 40p. (gr. -1-3). 16.99 *(978-0-544-15014-0(7))* Houghton Mifflin Harcourt Publishing Co. (HMH Books For Young Readers).

Raye, Rebekah. The Very Best Bed, 1 vol. Raye, Rebekah, illus. 2015. (Tilbury House Nature Book Ser.: 0). (ENG., Illus.). 36p. (gr. -1-3). pap. 8.95 *(978-0-88448-410-3(6)*, 884410) Tilbury Hse. Pubs.

Rayner, Catherine. Abigail. Rayner, Catherine, illus. 2013. (ENG., Illus.). 32p. (J). 14.99 *(978-1-58925-147-2(4))* Tiger Tales.

Rea, Lynn. Tug of War. 2006. (Neighborhood Readers Ser.). (ENG.). 16p. (gr. 1-3). pap. 6.50 *(978-1-4042-7272-9(0)*, Rosen Classroom) Rosen Publishing Group, Inc., The.

Reader's Digest Editors. Talking Puzzles Sounds on the Farm. 2009. (ENG., Illus.). 10p. (J). (gr. -1). bds. 15.99 *(978-0-7944-1821-2(X))* Reader's Digest Assn., Inc., The.

Reader's Digest Staff & Shepherd, Jodie. Guess Who Baby Animals. Ovresat, Laura, illus. 2011. (Guess Who Ser.). (ENG.). 10p. (J). (gr. -1-k). bds. 7.99 *(978-0-7944-2196-0(2))* Reader's Digest Assn., Inc., The.

Reasoner, Charles. Desert Tails. Nelson, Judy, illus. 2011. (Tail Spin Bks.). (ENG.). 14p. (J). (gr. -1). 9.99 *(978-1-934650-93-6(5))* Just For Kids Pr., LLC.

—Inside Old Mcdonald's Barn. Reasoner, Charles, illus. 2007. (Story Book Ser.). (Illus.). 12p. (J). (gr. k). bds. *(978-1-84666-287-4(7)*, Tide Mill Pr.) Top That! Publishing PLC.

Rebert, Brenda. Rooster Went A' Walkin' 2009. 28p. pap. 13.99 *(978-1-4389-3414-3(9))* AuthorHouse.

Rechlin, Ted. Changing of the Guard: The Yellowstone Chronicles. 2009. (Illus.). 38p. (J). pap. 22.95 *(978-1-4327-5008-4(9))* Outskirts Pr., Inc.

Redenius, John. Escaping the Yard, the Little Adventure of a Puppy Named Splinter. 2009. 88p. pap. 12.50 *(978-1-60693-985-7(8)*, Eloquent Bks.) Strategic Book Publishing & Rights Agency (SBPRA).

Redmond, E. S. Felicity Floo Visits the Zoo. Redmond, E. S., illus. 2010. (ENG., Illus.). 32p. (J). (-k). pap. 6.99 *(978-0-7636-4975-3(9))* Candlewick Pr.

Reed, J. Mac & Briggs-Greenberg, Ruthie. Sea of Echoes. 2015. (ENG., Illus.). 32p. (J). (gr. 3-7). 15.95 *(978-1-63076-107-3(9))* Taylor Trade Publishing.

Reed, Jennifer. That's Not Fair! Dufalla, Anita, illus. 2012. (ENG.). 24p. (gr. 1-2). pap. 8.95 *(978-1-61810-309-3(1))* Rourke Educational Media.

Rees-Jones, Paul. A Silly Animal World!, 1 vol. 2009. 37p. pap. 24.95 *(978-1-60836-729-0(0))* America Star Bks.

Reeve, Penny. God Made Something Beautiful. 2011. (Find the Animal Ser.). (ENG., Illus.). 16p. (J). pap. 4.99 *(978-1-85792-773-3(7),* fd1b69a1-49ce-42a0-ad98-005844a05b04) Christian Focus Pubns. GBR. Dist: Bookmasters Distribution.

—God Made Something Clever. 2011. (Find the Animal Ser.). (ENG., Illus.). 16p. (J). pap. 4.99 *(978-1-85792-772-6(9),* 35a2e541-8258-41d7-bf5e-37d06bf1ae40) Christian Focus Pubns. GBR. Dist: Bookmasters Distribution.

—God Made Something Strong. 2011. (Find the Animal Ser.). (ENG., Illus.). 16p. (J). pap. 4.99 *(978-1-85792-771-9(0),* d0f5e64a-af70-4238-9b31-eaaa8ac3bf4a) Christian Focus Pubns. GBR. Dist: Bookmasters Distribution.

Regan, Dian. The Dragon Stone, 0 vols. Curtis, Stacy, illus. 2013. (ENG.). 96p. (J). (gr. 2-4). pap. 9.99 *(978-1-4778-1632-5(1),* 9781477816325, Amazon Children's Publishing) Amazon Publishing.

—The Snow Blew Inn. Cushman, Doug, illus. 2011. (ENG.). 32p. (J). 16.95 *(978-0-8234-2351-4(4))* Holiday Hse., Inc.

Reibstein, Mark. Wabi Sabi. Young, Ed, illus. 2008. (ENG.). 40p. (J). (gr. -1-3). 18.99 *(978-0-316-11825-5(7))* Little Brown & Co.

—Wabi Sabi. 2009. (J). 1.25 *(978-1-4407-1925-7(X))*; 39.75 *(978-1-4407-1922-6(5))*; 37.75 *(978-1-4407-1920-2(9))*; 37.75 *(978-1-4407-1924-0(1))*; 192.75 *(978-1-4407-1919-6(5))*; 39.75 *(978-1-4407-1918-9(7))* Recorded Bks., Inc.

Reidy, Jean. Busy Builders, Busy Week! Timmers, Leo, illus. 2016. (ENG.). 32p. (J). 16.99 *(978-1-61963-556-2(9),* 9781619635562, Bloomsbury USA Childrens) Bloomsbury Publishing USA.

Reiffel, J. A., et al. Once upon an Antigmule: (... or, the Day Roseanna's Dreams Came True) 2012. 44p. pap. 21.99 *(978-1-4772-9618-9(2))* AuthorHouse.

Reilly, Carmel & Young, Karen. Anna Goes to the Zoo. 2008. (Rigby Focus Forward: Level D Ser.). (Illus.). 24p. (J). (gr. 4-7). pap. *(978-1-4190-3663-7(7),* Rigby) Pearson Education Australia.

Reilly, Pauline. Brolga. Rolland, Will, illus. (Picture Roo Bks.). 32p. (J). pap. *(978-0-86417-719-3(4),* Kangaroo Pr.) Simon & Schuster Australia.

Reimiller, Diane L. A Duck Named Quackers, 1 vol. Jastrzebski, Brandy, illus. 2009. 12p. pap. 24.95 *(978-1-60836-771-9(1))* America Star Bks.

Reintjes, Susan B. Through the Fairy Door. Sparling, Bren M., illus. 2012. 128p. (J). pap. 16.95 *(978-1-59715-085-9(1))* Chapel Hill Press, Inc.

Remenar, Kristen. Groundhog's Dilemma. Faulkner, Matt, illus. 2015. (ENG.). 32p. (J). (gr. -1-2). lib. bdg. 16.95 *(978-1-58089-600-9(6))* Charlesbridge Publishing, Inc.

Reminick, Gerald. Ollie Otter's Special Gift: A Story from Quiet Pond. Quintero, michelle, illus. 2013. 32p. (J). 10.00 *(978-1-889901-60-2(1),* Palo Alto Bks.) Glencannon Pr.

Remolina, Tere. Un Cambio de Piel. Martinez, Enrique, illus. (Barril Sin Fondo Ser.). (SPA.). (J). (gr. 3-5). pap. *(978-968-6465-20-4(0))* Casa de Estudios de Literatura y Talleres Artisticos Amaquemecan A.C. MEX. Dist: Lectorum Pubns., Inc.

Renert, Gerry. Nathan Saves Summer. Bradshaw, Carrie Anne, illus. 2010. (ENG.). 32p. (J). (gr. -1-3). 16.95 *(978-1-934960-76-9(4),* Raven Tree Pr.,Csi) Continental Sales, Inc.

—Nathan Saves Summer/Nathan Rescata el Verano. Bradshaw, Carrie Anne, illus. 2010. (ENG & SPA.). 32p. (J). (gr. -1-3). 16.95 *(978-1-934960-74-5(8),* Raven Tree Pr.,Csi) Continental Sales, Inc.

Resnick, Jacqueline. The Daring Escape of the Misfit Menagerie. 2013. (Misfit Menagerie Ser.: 1). (ENG.). 320p. (J). (gr. 3-7). pap. 7.99 *(978-1-59514-589-5(3),* Razorbill) Penguin Young Readers Group.

Rex, Michael. Truck Duck. Rex, Michael, illus. 2008. (ENG., Illus.). 26p. (J). (gr. -1 — -1). bds. 7.99 *(978-0-399-25092-7(1),* G.P. Putnam's Sons Books for Young Readers) Penguin Young Readers Group.

Rey, H. A. CG Puppies AMS Oversized Edition. 2005. (J). 12.99 *(978-0-618-56451-4(9))* Houghton Mifflin Harcourt Trade & Reference Pubs.

—Curious George at the Park. Meyer, Emily, ed. 2010. (Curious George Ser.). (ENG., Illus.). 10p. (J). (gr. -1 — 1). bds. 6.99 *(978-0-547-24300-9(6))* Houghton Mifflin Harcourt Publishing Co.

—My Curious Dreamer, Set. gif. ed. 2010. (Curious Baby Curious George Ser.). (ENG., Illus.). 10p. (J). (gr. k — 1). 14.99 *(978-0-547-24308-5(1))* Houghton Mifflin Harcourt Publishing Co.

—My Favorite Things. 2011. (Curious Baby Curious George Ser.). (ENG., Illus.). 14p. (J). (gr. -1 — 1). bds. 8.99 *(978-0-547-42893-2(6))* Houghton Mifflin Harcourt Publishing Co.

—A Treasury of Curious George (Coleccion de Oro Jorge el Curioso) 2011. (Curious George Ser.). (ENG & SPA., Illus.). 208p. (J). (gr. -1-3). 11.99 *(978-0-547-52310-1(6))* Houghton Mifflin Harcourt Publishing Co.

Rey, H. A. & Rey, Margret. Curious Baby My Growing World. 2011. (Curious Baby Curious George Ser.). (ENG., Illus.). 14p. (J). (gr. k — 1). bds. 9.99 *(978-0-547-27939-8(6))* Houghton Mifflin Harcourt Publishing Co.

—Curious George Feeds the Animals. 2005. (J). (gr. k-3). 9.95 *(978-0-618-55520-8(X))* Houghton Mifflin Harcourt Trade & Reference Pubs.

—The H. A. Rey Treasury of Stories. 2015. (Dover Children's Classics Ser.). (ENG., Illus.). 112p. (J). (gr. 2-4). pap. 14.99 *(978-0-486-78468-7(1))* Dover Pubns., Inc.

Reynolds, Aaron. Carnivores. Newman, Jeff & Santat, Dan, illus. 2013. (ENG.). 40p. (J). (gr. -1-3). 16.99 *(978-0-8118-6690-3(4))* Chronicle Bks. LLC.

RH Disney Staff. Brave Little Golden Book (Disney/Pixar Brave) RH Disney Staff, illus. 2012. (Little Golden Book Ser.). (ENG., Illus.). 24p. (J). (gr. k-k). 4.99 *(978-0-7364-2901-6(8),* Golden/Disney) Random Hse. Children's Bks.

—The Jungle Book. 2003. (Little Golden Book Ser.). (ENG., Illus.). 24p. (J). (gr. -1-k). 4.99 *(978-0-7364-2096-9(7),* Golden/Disney) Random Hse. Children's Bks.

—My Hero. RH Disney Staff, illus. 2008. (Step into Reading Ser.). (ENG., Illus.). 32p. (J). (gr. k-3). pap. 3.99 *(978-0-375-84812-4(6),* RH/Disney) Random Hse. Children's Bks.

RH Disney Staff & Trine, Greg. The Stinky Cheese Caper. RH Disney Staff & Loftis, Cory, illus. 2016. (Disney Chapters Ser.). (ENG.). 80p. (J). (gr. 1-4). 4.99 *(978-0-7364-3610-6(3),* RH/Disney) Random Hse. Children's Bks.

Rhijn, Patricia van & Álvarez, Rosanela. Cuentos de Animales Fantasticos para Ninos (Fantastic Animal Tales for Children) 2nd ed. (SPA., Illus.). 72p. (J). pap. 11.95 *(978-968-494-014-7(9),* NOR609) Centro de Informacion y Desarrollo de la Comunicacion y la Literatura MEX. Dist: Continental Bk. Co., Inc.

Rhodes, C. S. Bella Mouse at Mobberley Edge. 2010. (Illus.). 188p. pap. 14.49 *(978-1-4490-7338-1(7))* AuthorHouse.

Ricard, Anouk. Fore! Dascher, Helge, tr. from FRE. 2015. (Anna & Froga Ser.). (ENG., Illus.). 40p. (J). (gr. k-4). 14.95 *(978-1-77046-204-5(X),* 9781770462045) Drawn & Quarterly Pubns. CAN. Dist: Macmillan.

Ricci, Christine. Dora's Picnic. Hall, Susan, illus. 2003. (Ready-to-Read Ser.: Vol. 1). (ENG.). 24p. (J). pap. 3.99 *(978-0-689-85238-1(X),* Simon Spotlight/Nickelodeon) Simon Spotlight/Nickelodeon.

—Follow Those Feet! Hall, Susan, illus. 2003. (Dora the Explorer Ser.: Vol. 2). (ENG.). 24p. (J). pap. 3.99 *(978-0-689-85239-8(8),* Simon Spotlight/Nickelodeon) Simon Spotlight/Nickelodeon.

—Meet the Animals! Aikins, Dave, illus. 2006. (Dora the Explorer Ser.). (ENG.). 16p. (J). (gr. -1-k). 10.95 *(978-1-4169-1819-6(1),* Simon Spotlight/Nickelodeon) Simon Spotlight/Nickelodeon.

Rice, Dona Herwick. Paul Bunyan, 1 vol. 2009. (Building Fluency Through Reader's Theater Ser.). (ENG.). 24p. (J). (gr. 2-4). pap. 6.99 *(978-1-4333-0994-6(7))* Teacher Created Materials, Inc.

Rice, Joan W. The Winter Sleep: A Story of Hibernation. Slimp, Gwen H., illus. 2004. 48p. (J). (gr. k-3). *(978-0-9755573-0-3(0))* Coastal Publishing, LLC.

Rice, Myrtle Alley. Friends of Fur & Feather. 2005. reprint ed. pap. 20.95 *(978-1-4179-9023-8(6))* Kessinger Publishing, LLC.

Rich, Carol Bak. The Running Nose Book. Rich, Bobbie, illus. 2013. (ENG.). 41p. (J). pap. 9.95 *(978-1-4787-0062-3(9))* Outskirts Pr., Inc.

Richard, Lolita Louise. Walking with a B C Big Book Adventure. 2009. 60p. pap. 31.99 *(978-1-4415-3719-5(8))* Xlibris Corp.

Richards, Claire. Mai's Garden: Mickamoo's Rescue. 2011. (Illus.). 56p. (gr. -1). pap. 12.51 *(978-1-4567-7559-9(6))* AuthorHouse.

Richards, Lucy, illus. Animal Antics (with Header Card) 2004. (Cuddly Cuffs Ser.: No. 5). 10p. (J). tchr. ed. 5.95 *(978-1-58925-729-0(4))* Tiger Tales.

—Jumping Jungle (W/Hang Tag) 2004. (Cuddly Cuffs Ser.: No. 7). 12p. (J). tchr. ed. 5.95 *(978-1-58925-727-6(8))* Tiger Tales.

—Jumping Jungle (W/Header Card) 2004. (Cuddly Cuffs Ser.: 7). 6p. (J). tchr. ed. 5.95 *(978-1-58925-731-3(6))* Tiger Tales.

Richardson, Dick. The Oglin: A Hero's Journey Across Africa... Towards the Tomorrows. Feek, Cathy, illus. 2004. 417p. (J). 24.95 *(978-0-9759440-3-5(7))* Savanna Pr.

Richardson, Frederick. Great Children's Stories. 2016. (Calla Editions Ser.). (ENG.). 208p. (J). pap. 30.00 *(978-1-60660-085-6(0))* Dover Pubns., Inc.

Richardson, Levae. Skip & Marty. Richardson, Kayla, illus. 2007. 20p. per. 24.95 *(978-1-4241-8469-9(X))* America Star Bks.

Rickman, Jeanie Parker. The Rising Star Ball. Taylor, Jennifer, illus. 2006. 32p. per. 17.95 *(978-1-59858-201-7(1))* Dog Ear Publishing, LLC.

Riding, Gale. Milo Is Not So Different after All. 2009. 20p. pap. 12.49 *(978-1-4490-1976-1(5))* AuthorHouse.

Riegelman, Rianna & Accord Publishing Staff. Safari: A Build & Play Story. Chandler, Shannon, illus. 2012. (ENG.). 10p. (J). (gr. -1-1). bds. 15.99 *(978-1-4494-2191-5(1))* Andrews McMeel Publishing.

Rigby, Ed & Dooley, Angela. Mouse of the Match. 2009. 41p. pap. 10.50 *(978-1-4452-2692-7(8))* Lulu Pr., Inc.

Rigby Education Staff. Animal Advertisements. (Sails Literacy Ser.). (Illus.). 16p. (gr. 2-3). 27.00 *(978-0-7635-9944-7(1),* 699441C99) Rigby Education.

—Animals Say... (Sails Literacy Ser.). (Illus.). 16p. (gr. 2-3). 27.00 *(978-0-7635-9943-0(3),* 699433C99) Rigby Education.

—The Red Shoes. (Sails Literacy Ser.). (Illus.). 16p. (gr. 2-3). 27.00 *(978-0-7635-9945-4(X),* 699459C99) Rigby Education.

Riggs-Mayfield, Nellie. A Collection of Short Stories for Children. 2006. (J). per. 19.95 *(978-1-59872-640-4(4))* Instant Pub.

Rigo, L. & Caviezel, Giovanni, illus. Little Bunny. 2010. (Look at Me Bks.). (ENG.). 10p. (J). (gr. -1-k). bds. 7.99 *(978-0-7641-6322-7(1))* Barron's Educational Series, Inc.

—Little Puppy. 2010. (Look at Me Bks.). (ENG.). 10p. (J). (gr. -1-k). bds. 8.99 *(978-0-7641-6324-1(8))* Barron's Educational Series, Inc.

Riley, Judi. When I Am Quiet on Maui. 2008. 40p. 15.95 *(978-0-9740582-3-8(8))* Tiki Tales.

Riley's Bow-Wow Blast. 2006. (J). per. 12.95 *(978-0-9769058-0-6(9))* Boss Paws Publishing.

Rinck, Maranke. The Prince Child. Linden, Martijn van der, illus. 2004. (ENG & GER.). 32p. (J). 16.95 *(978-1-932425-15-4(2),* Lemniscaat) Boyds Mills Pr.

Rinck, Maranke & van der Linden, Martijn. I Feel a Foot. 2008. (ENG., Illus.). 32p. (J). (gr. -1-1). 16.95 *(978-1-59078-638-3(6),* Lemniscaat) Boyds Mills Pr.

Ringstad, Arnold. The Constellation Scorpius: The Story of the Scorpion. Morrow, J. T., illus. 2013. (Constellations Ser.). (ENG.). 32p. (J). (gr. 2-5). 29.93 *(978-1-62323-488-1(3),* 206251) Child's World, Inc., The.

Rinker, Sherri Duskey. Steam Train, Dream Train. Lichtenheld, Tom, illus. 2013. (ENG.). 40p. (J). (gr. -1-1). 16.99 *(978-1-4521-0920-6(6))* Chronicle Bks. LLC.

—Steam Train, Dream Train Colors. Lichtenheld, Tom, illus. 2016. (ENG.). 20p. (J). (gr. -1 — 1). bds. 7.99 *(978-1-4521-4915-8(1))* Chronicle Bks. LLC.

—Steam Train, Dream Train Counting. Lichtenheld, Tom, illus. 2016. (ENG.). 20p. (J). (gr. -1 — 1). bds. 7.99 *(978-1-4521-4914-1(3))* Chronicle Bks. LLC.

Riphagen, Loes, illus. Animals Home Alone. 2011. (ENG.). 32p. (J). (gr. -1-3). 15.95 *(978-1-934734-55-1(1))* Seven Footer Pr.

Ritchie, Joseph R. Baby Looney Tunes Visit a Haunted House. Halverson, Lydia, illus. 2005. (Baby Looney Tunes Ser.). 14p. (J). (gr. -1-3). bds. 9.95 *(978-0-8249-6609-6(0),* Ideal Pubns.) Worthy Publishing.

—Peter Cottontail's Busy Day. Halverson, Lydia, illus. (ENG.). (J). 2006. 26p. (gr. -1-k). 12.95 *(978-0-8249-6652-2(X))* 2005. 16p. bds. 9.95 *(978-0-8249-6571-6(X))* Worthy Publishing. (Ideal Pubns.).

—Peter Cottontail's Easter Egg Hunt. Thornburgh, Rebecca McKillip, illus. (J). 2012. 14p. bds. 6.99 *(978-0-8249-1880-4(0))* 2004. (ENG.). 12p. (gr. -1-k). bds. 9.95 *(978-0-8249-6522-8(1))* Worthy Publishing. (Ideal Pubns.).

—Peter Cottontail's Easter Surprise. Halverson, Lydia, illus. 2006. (ENG.). 18p. (J). (gr. -1-k). bds. 9.95 *(978-0-8249-6627-0(9),* Ideal Pubns.) Worthy Publishing.

—Peter Cottontaol's Easter Egg Hunt. Thornburgh, Rebecca, illus. 2006. (ENG.). 26p. (J). (gr. -1-k). 12.95 *(978-0-8249-6653-9(8),* Ideal Pubns.) Worthy Publishing.

—Where's Santa? Halverson, Lydia, illus. 2006. (ENG.). 14p. (J). (gr. -1-k). bds. 7.95 *(978-0-8249-6673-7(2),* Ideal Pubns.) Worthy Publishing.

Rivard, Erin. Agattu: The Alaskan Caribou. 2013. (J). pap. 9.95 *(978-1-59433-344-6(0))* Publication Consultants.

Rml. An Interesting Crew. 2012. 16p. (-18). pap. 15.99 *(978-1-4772-8699-9(3))* AuthorHouse.

Roberts, Daniel. The Good Night Book: A Book of Animal Sounds. 2009. 36p. pap. 16.99 *(978-1-4389-8278-6(X))* AuthorHouse.

Roberts, Pauline J. Girls Crying. 2007. 9.00 *(978-0-8059-8863-5(7))* Dorrance Publishing Co., Inc.

Roberts, Robin. Bedtime Bear's Big Surprise. 2011. 24p. pap. 14.99 *(978-1-4634-4498-3(2))* AuthorHouse.

Roberts, Scott A. The Rollicking Adventures of Tam O'Hare. Roberts, Scott A., illus. 2007. (ENG., Illus.). 228p. (J). (gr. 4-7). per. 16.95 *(978-1-60037-289-6(9))* Morgan James Publishing.

Roberts, Trina. The Lonley Little Birch. 2005. 9.00 *(978-0-8059-8053-0(9))* Dorrance Publishing Co., Inc.

Robertson, Betsey. Frisky's Forest Friends: Robin Rescue. 2009. 28p. pap. 12.49 *(978-1-4389-1906-5(9))* AuthorHouse.

Robertson, Donald. Mitford at the Fashion Zoo. 2015. (ENG., Illus.). 40p. (J). (gr. -1-2). 17.99 *(978-0-451-47542-8(9),* Viking Books for Young Readers) Penguin Young Readers Group.

—Mitford at the Hollywood Zoo. 2017. (ENG., Illus.). 40p. (J). (gr. -1-2). 17.99 *(978-0-451-47543-5(7),* Viking Books for Young Readers) Penguin Young Readers Group.

Robertson, J. Jean. Vote for Me! Mones, Marc, illus. 2012. (ENG.). 24p. (gr. 1-2). pap. 8.95 *(978-1-61810-316-1(4))* Rourke Educational Media.

Robertson, Jean. My Name Is Not... Dufalla, Anita, illus. 2012. (ENG.). 24p. (gr. 1-2). pap. 8.95 *(978-1-61810-320-8(2))* Rourke Educational Media.

Robertson, Kathy & Hooker, Jennifer. Jasmine & Chad Make New Friends. 2012. 28p. pap. 15.99 *(978-1-4797-1656-2(1))* Xlibris Corp.

Robertson, Susan, illus. Little Bunny. 2005. (Bedtime Babies Ser.). 8p. (J). (gr. -1). per., bds. 6.99 *(978-1-57755-503-2(1))* Flying Frog Publishing, Inc.

Robey, Katharine Crawford. Hare & the Big Green Lawn. MacDougall, Larry, illus. 2006. (ENG.). 32p. (J). (gr. -1-3). 15.95 *(978-0-87358-889-8(4))* Cooper Square Publishing Llc.

Robinson, Fiona. What Animals Really Like. 2011. (ENG., Illus.). 24p. (J). (gr. k-2). 15.95 *(978-0-8109-8976-4(X),* Abrams Bks. for Young Readers) Abrams, Inc.

—The 3-2-3 Detective Agency: The Disappearance of Dave Warthog. 2009. (ENG., Illus.). 80p. (J). (gr. 1-4). 18.95 *(978-0-8109-8489-9(X),* Amulet Bks.) Abrams, Inc.

Robinson, Michelle. And the Robot Went ... Ruzzier, Sergio, illus. 2017. (ENG.). 32p. (J). (gr. -1-3). 16.99 *(978-0-544-58652-9(2),* Clarion Bks.) Houghton Mifflin Harcourt Trade & Reference Pubs.

—There's a Lion in My Cornflakes. Field, Jim, illus. 2015. (ENG.). 32p. (J). (gr. -1-1). 16.99 *(978-0-8027-3836-3(2),* 9780802738363, Bloomsbury USA Childrens) Bloomsbury Publishing USA.

Robyck, Michael. Where Is Lauren's Cat, Chaulky? 2011. 28p. pap. 15.99 *(978-1-4568-8797-1(1))* Xlibris Corp.

Rock, Brian. The Deductive Detective, 1 vol. Rogers, Sherry, illus. 2013. (SPA.). 32p. (J). (gr. -1-2). pap. 9.95 *(978-1-62855-347-5(2))* Arbordale Publishing.

Rock, Brian & Rogers, Sherry. El Detective Deductivo, 1 vol. Rogers, Sherry, illus. 2013. (SPA., Illus.). 32p. (J). (gr. -1-2). 17.95 *(978-1-60718-708-0(6))* Arbordale Publishing.

Rockwell, Anne F. Katie Catz Makes a Splash. Meisel, Paul, illus. 2003. (Good Sports Ser.). 40p. (J). (gr. -1-1). 15.99 *(978-0-06-028441-1(2))* HarperCollins Pubs.

Rockwood, Roy. On a Torn-Away World. 2008. 136p. pap. 12.95 *(978-1-60664-174-3(3))* Aegypan.

Rodgers, Ilona. Nanny Musgrove & the New Baby. 2011. (ENG.). 36p. pap. 11.95 *(978-1-906768-68-3(4),* Stacey International) Stacey Publishing GBR. Dist: Casemate Pubs. & Bk. Distributors, LLC.

Rodrigues, Dulce. Once upon a Time ... a House: A Tale for Children & All Those Young at Heart. 2013. 60p. pap. 18.95 *(978-1-60976-766-2(7),* Strategic Bk. Publishing) Strategic Book Publishing & Rights Agency (SBPRA).

Rodriguez, Béatrice. The Chicken Thief. 2010. (Stories Without Words Ser.). Tr. of Voleur de Poule. (ENG., Illus.). 32p. (J). (gr. -1-2). 14.95 *(978-1-59270-092-9(6))* Enchanted Lion Bks., LLC.

Rodriguez, Béatrice, illus. Fox & Hen Together. 2011. (Stories Without Words Ser.). (ENG.). 32p. (J). (gr. -1-3). 14.95 *(978-1-59270-109-4(4))* Enchanted Lion Bks., LLC.

Rohmann, Eric. My Friend Rabbit. Rohmann, Eric, illus. 2011. (ENG., Illus.). 36p. (J). (gr. -1-3). bds. 7.99 *(978-1-59643-641-1(7),* 9781596436411) Roaring Brook Pr.

Roman, Celso. El Arbol de Los Tucanes. 2012. 44p. (J). (gr. 2-4). pap. 12.99 *(978-958-30-3662-0(5))* Panamericana Editorial COL. Dist: Lectorum Pubns., Inc.

Romay, Alexis. Diego Saves the Sloth! Mawhinney, Art, illus. 2007. (Go, Diego, Go! Ser.: 4). (ENG.). 24p. (J). (gr. -1-2). pap. 3.99 *(978-1-4169-3470-7(7),* Simon Spotlight/Nickelodeon) Simon Spotlight/Nickelodeon.

Roode, Daniel. Little Bea & the Snowy Day. Roode, Daniel, illus. 2011. (ENG., Illus.). 32p. (J). (gr. -1-k). 12.99 *(978-0-06-199395-4(6),* Greenwillow Bks.) HarperCollins Pubs.

Rookie Ready to Learn - Animals, 5 vols., Set. Incl. Great Bug Hunt. Dobkin, Bonnie. Dunnington, Tom, illus. 40p. lib. bdg. 25.00 *(978-0-531-26415-7(7))*; In My Backyard. Curry, Don L. O'Leary Brown, Erin, illus. 32p. lib. bdg. 25.00 *(978-0-531-26416-4(5))*; Lara Ladybug. Florie, Christine. Dalby, Danny Brooks, illus. 32p. lib. bdg. 25.00 *(978-0-531-26417-1(3))*; Luna the Wake-Up Cat. Simon, Charnan. Huang, Benrei, illus. 40p. lib. bdg. 25.00 *(978-0-531-26414-0(9))*; Old Mo. Hsu, Stacey W. Ritter, Adam, illus. 40p. lib. bdg. 25.00 *(978-0-531-26418-8(1))*; (J). (gr. -1-k). (Rookie Ready to Learn Ser.). 2011. Set lib. bdg. 115.00 *(978-0-531-27450-7(0),* Children's Pr.) Scholastic Library Publishing.

Rooks, Elizabeth. Rayne: Queen Water Supplier of the World. 2012. 32p. pap. 19.99 *(978-1-4772-2375-8(4))* AuthorHouse.

Rooney, M. A. Rudy the Rescue. 2005. 8p. 11.72 *(978-1-4116-6057-1(9))* Lulu Pr., Inc.

Root, Phyllis. Flip, Flap, Fly! A Book for Babies Everywhere. Walker, David, illus. 2011. (ENG.). 32p. (J). (gr. -1 — 1). bds. 6.99 *(978-0-7636-5325-5(X))* Candlewick Pr.

—One Duck Stuck: A Mucky Ducky Counting Book. Chapman, Jane, illus. 2008. (Candlewick Press Big Book Ser.). (ENG.). 40p. (J). (gr. k-k). pap. 24.99 *(978-0-7636-3817-7(X))* Candlewick Pr.

—One North Star: A Counting Book. Prange, Beckie & Bowen, Betsy, illus. 2016. (ENG.). 36p. (J). 16.95 *(978-0-8166-5063-7(2))* Univ. of Minnesota Pr.

—Snowy Sunday. Craig, Helen, illus. 2015. (ENG.). 24p. (J). (-k). 14.99 *(978-0-7636-3627-2(4))* Candlewick Pr.

Rorby, Ginny. Lost in the River of Grass. (Carolrhoda YA Ser.). (ENG.). 264p. (YA). (gr. 7-12). 2012. pap. 9.95 *(978-0-7613-8498-4(7))* 2011. 17.95 *(978-0-7613-5685-1(1))* Lerner Publishing Group. (Carolrhoda Lab™).

Rosa-Mendoza, Gladys. Animals at the Farm/Animales de la Granja. Wolff, Jason, illus. 2004. (English-Spanish Foundations Ser.). (SPA & ENG.). 20p. (J). (gr. -1). bds. 6.95 *(978-1-931398-13-8(5))* Me+Mi Publishing.

Rose, Caroline Starr. Over in the Wetlands: A Hurricane on the Bayou Story. Dunlavey, Rob, illus. 2015. (ENG.). 40p. (J). (gr. -1-3). 17.99 *(978-0-449-81016-3(X),* Schwartz & Wade Bks.) Random Hse. Children's Bks.

Rose, Tammy Marie. Munchkin. 2012. 24p. 24.95 *(978-1-4626-6095-7(9))* America Star Bks.

Rosen, Kymberlee S. Do You Have Better Manners Than the Monkeys at the Zoo? 2010. (Illus.). 32p. pap. 13.00 *(978-1-60911-179-3(6),* Eloquent Bks.) Strategic Book Publishing & Rights Agency (SBPRA).

Rosen, Michael. Barking for Bagels. Ross, Tony, illus. 2017. (ENG.). 96p. (J). (gr. 2-4). pap. 9.99 ***(978-1-78344-505-9(X))*** Andersen Pr. GBR. Dist: Independent Pubs. Group.

—Happy Harry's Cafe. Holland, Richard, illus. 2012. (ENG.). 32p. (J). (gr. -1-2). 16.99 *(978-0-7636-6239-4(9))* Candlewick Pr.

—Ronquidos! Langley, Jonathan, illus.Tr. of Snore! (SPA.). (J). (gr. 1-3). *(978-958-04-4646-0(6))* Norma S.A.

—Snore! Langley, Jonathan, illus. 2003. (ENG.). 32p. (J). (gr. -1-k). pap. 10.99 *(978-0-00-716031-0(3),* HarperCollins Children's Bks.) HarperCollins Pubs. Ltd. GBR. Dist: HarperCollins Pubs.

Rosen, Michael & Langley, Jonathan. Oww! 2004. (ENG., Illus.). 32p. (J). (gr. k-2). pap. 9.99 *(978-0-00-712443-5(0),* HarperCollins Children's Bks.) HarperCollins Pubs. Ltd. GBR. Dist: Independent Pubs. Group.

Rosenberg, Madelyn. Canary in the Coal Mine. 2013. (ENG., Illus.). 192p. (J). (gr. 2-7). 16.95 *(978-0-8234-2600-3(9))* Holiday Hse., Inc.

Rosenberg, Meira. Indiana Bamboo: A Novel. 2017. (J). pap. ***(978-1-60454-245-5(4),*** Iris Pr.) Iris Publishing Group, Inc., The.

Rosenthal, Amy Krouse. Duck! Rabbit! Lichtenheld, Tom, illus. (ENG.). 40p. (J). (gr. -1-k). 2014. bds. 7.99 *(978-1-4521-3733-9(1))* 2009. 16.99 *(978-0-8118-6865-5(6))* Chronicle Bks. LLC.

—Little Pea; Little Hoot; Little Oink, 3 vols., Set. Corace, Jen, illus. 2009. (ENG.). 80p. (J). (gr. -1 — 1). bds. 19.99 *(978-0-8118-7054-2(5))* Chronicle Bks. LLC.

Rosenthal, Betsy R. Porcupine's Picnic: Who Eats What? Capizzi, Giusi, illus. 2017. (ENG.). 32p. (gr. -1-2). 19.99 *(978-1-4677-9519-7(4),* Millbrook Pr.) Lerner Publishing Group.

Ross, Diana. The Little Red Engine & the Rocket. Wood, Leslie, illus. 2005. (Little Red Engine Ser.: 1). (ENG.). 32p. (J). (gr. k-2). pap. 8.99 *(978-0-233-00146-3(8))* Andre Deutsch GBR. Dist: Independent Pubs. Group.

Ross, Mandy. Animal Lullabies. Nagy, Krisztina Kallai, illus. 2007. (Poems for the Young Ser.). (ENG.). 32p. (J). incl. audio compact disk *(978-1-84643-052-7(6))* Child's Play International Ltd.

—Animal Lullabies. Kallai Nagy, Krisztina, illus. 2005. (Poems for the Young Ser.). (ENG.). 32p. (J). audio compact disk *(978-1-904550-93-8(2))* Child's Play International Ltd.

Ross, Thea. Molly Mole Loves to Garden. 2004. (Lift-the-Flap Surprise on Every Spread! Ser.). 12p. (J). 5.99 *(978-1-59384-044-0(6))* Parklane Publishing.

Rosseter, Patrick W. Grampa Pat's Little Animal Tales. 2005. 10.00 *(978-0-8059-9797-2(0))* Dorrance Publishing Co., Inc.

—Grampa Pat's Little Animal Tales. 2008. 88p. pap. 10.99 *(978-1-60647-466-2(9))* Salem Author Services.

Roth, Carol. Here Comes the Choo Choo! Cushman, Doug, illus. 2007. (J). (978-0-15-205582-0(7)) Harcourt Trade Pubs.
—The Little School Bus. Paparone, Pamela, illus. 2004. (ENG.). 32p. (J). (gr. k-1). pap. 7.95 (978-0-7358-1905-4(X)) North-South Bks., Inc.
—Will You Still Love Me? Howarth, Daniel, illus. 2011. (ENG.). 16p. (J). (gr. -1 — 1). bds. 7.99 (978-0-8075-9116-1(5)) Whitman, Albert & Co.
Roulaine, Katherine. Chang & Olan. 2011. 20p. pap. 24.95 (978-1-4560-8379-3(1)) America Star Bks.
Rouss, Sylvia. The Littlest Pair. Hannon, Holly, illus. 2005. 32p. (J). pap. 9.95 (978-1-930143-18-0(4), Devora Publishing) Simcha Media Group.
Rouss, Sylvia A. The Littlest Pair. Hannon, Holly, illus. 2005. 32p. (J). (gr. -1-1). 14.95 (978-1-930143-17-3(6), Devora Publishing) Simcha Media Group.
Rovetch, L. Bob. Frog Went A-Dancing. Berry, Holly, illus. 2006. (J). (978-1-58987-008-6(5)) Kindermusik International.
Rowe, John, ed. The Jungle Book. Alexander, Gregory, illus. 2003. (Chrysalis Childrens Classics Ser.). 159p. (YA). pap. (978-1-84365-038-6(X), Pavilion Children's Books) Pavilion Bks.
—The Jungle Book. 2007. (Illustrated Classics Ser.). (Illus.). 40p. (gr. 3-6). lib. bdg. 26.00 (978-0-8368-7663-5(6), Gareth Stevens Learning Library) Stevens, Gareth Publishing LLLP.
Rowe, Kysha D. What Creatures Teach Us, 1. 2005. (Illus.). 112p. (J). per. (978-0-9769339-0-8(X)) Rowe, Kysha.
Roy, Alene Adele. The Legend of Dragonfly Pond: Coloring Book. 2008. 56p. pap. 11.99 (978-1-4343-4628-5(5)) AuthorHouse.
Rozman, Jennifer Blue. With You Forever. 2011. 24p. pap. 11.95 (978-1-4520-9941-5(3)) AuthorHouse.
Ruben, Pamela J. Yenta the Chicken & Other Fowl Tales! Ruben, Anthony R., ed. 2004. (Illus.). 19p. (J). 12.95 (978-0-9764813-0-0(8)) Peppery Pr.
Ruben's Jungle. 2003.Tr. of Selva de Ruben. (SPA., Illus.). 26p. bds. 16.95 (978-0-9706953-1-4(4)) Globo Libros.
Rubin, Julian. The Orchid Grower. 2003. (J). 14.00 (978-1-894942-05-8(1)) Zumaya Pubns. LLC.
Rudd, Bill. Broken Circle: The Black-footed Ferrets. 2010. (Illus.). (J). 19.99 (978-1-60507-066-7(1)) Lunchbox Lessons.
Ruelle, Karen Gray. The Thanksgiving Beast Feast. (Holiday House Readers Ser.). (ENG., Illus.). 32p. (J). (gr. k-3). pap. 4.95 (978-0-8234-1802-2(2)) Holiday Hse., Inc.
—The Thanksgiving Beast Feast Level 2: A Holiday House Reader. Ruelle, Karen Gray, illus. (ENG., Illus.). 32p. (J). (gr. k-3). tchr. ed. 15.95 (978-0-8234-1511-3(2)) Holiday Hse., Inc.
Ruffenach, Jessie, ed. Baby Learns about Animals. Thomas, Peter, tr. from NAV. Blacksheep, Beverly, illus. 2004. (ENG & NAV.). 16p. (J). (gr. -1-12). 7.95 (978-1-893354-49-4(0)) Salina Bookshelf Inc.
Ruley, Rose. Quest for a Moose: An Alaska Tale of Searching for an Animal that Doesn't Exist — until it Is Found. 2004. (J). pap. 12.95 (978-1-59433-019-3(0)) Publication Consultants.
The Runaway Engine & Other Stories: Individual Title Six-Pack. (Story Steps Ser.). (gr. k-2). 48.00 (978-0-7635-9803-7(8)) Rigby Education.
Runels, Margie "B". Talon. 2009. 12p. pap. 8.49 (978-1-4490-3248-7(6)) AuthorHouse.
Rushing, John Alan. A. J. Puppy Learns to Swim. Fay, David, illus. 2009. 48p. (J). pap. (978-0-9776958-9-8(1)) CyPress Pubns.
Russell, Natalie. Hamish the Highland Cow. 2003. (J). 7.99 (978-1-58234-818-6(9)) Bloomsbury Publishing USA.
—Home Sweet Hamish. 2008. (Bloomsbury Paperbacks Ser.). (ENG., Illus.). 32p. (J). (gr. -1-2). pap. 10.95 (978-0-7475-8319-6(6)) Bloomsbury Publishing Plc GBR. Dist: Independent Pubs. Group.
Russo, Brian. Yoga Bunny. Russo, Brian, illus. 2016. (Illus.). 40p. (J). (gr. -1-3). 17.99 (978-0-06-242952-0(3)) HarperCollins Pubs.
Rutley, Erika L. Adventures in Pup-A-Dupping. 2012. 36p. pap. 24.95 (978-1-62709-710-9(4)) America Star Bks.
Ruzzier, Sergio. A Letter for Leo. 2014. (ENG., Illus.). 32p. (J). (gr. -1-3). 16.99 (978-0-544-22360-8(8)) Houghton Mifflin Harcourt Publishing Co.
Ryder, Joanne. Dance by the Light of the Moon. Francis, Guy, illus. 2006. (ENG.). 40p. (gr. -1-1). 15.99 (978-0-7868-1820-4(4)) Hyperion Pr.
Rylant, Cynthia. The Case of the Climbing Cat. Karas, G. Brian, illus. 2003. (High-Rise Private Eyes Ser.: No. 2). (J). (gr. k-3). 28.95 incl. audio compact disk (978-1-59112-611-9(8)) Live Oak Media.
—The Case of the Desperate Duck. Karas, G. Brian, illus. (I Can Read Level 2 Ser.: No. 8). 48p. (J). (gr. k-3). 2006. (ENG.). pap. 3.99 (978-0-06-053453-0(2), Greenwillow Bks.) 2005. 14.99 (978-0-06-053451-6(6)) 2005. lib. bdg. 15.89 (978-0-06-053452-3(4)) HarperCollins Pubs.
—The Case of the Desperate Duck, 4 bks., Set. 2007. (High-Rise Private Eyes Ser.: Bk. 8). (J). (gr. k-2). pap. 31.95 incl. audio compact disk (978-1-4301-0067-6(2)); pap. 29.95 incl. audio (978-1-4301-0065-2(6)) Live Oak Media.
—The Case of the Desperate Duck. Karas, G. Brian, illus. 2006. (High-Rise Private Eyes Ser.). 48p. (gr. -1-3). 14.00 (978-0-7569-6958-5(1)) Perfection Learning Corp.
—The Case of the Fidgety Fox. Karas, G. Brian, illus. unabr. ed. 2005. (High-Rise Private Eyes Ser.: No. 6). (J). (gr. k-4). 25.95 incl. audio (978-1-59519-405-3(3));Set. pap. 29.95 incl. audio (978-1-59519-406-0(1));Set. pap. 31.95 incl. audio compact disk (978-1-59519-410-7(X)) Live Oak Media.
—The Case of the Fidgety Fox. Karas, G. Brian, illus. 2004. (High-Rise Private Eyes Ser.). 58p. (J). (gr. 1-3). 11.65 (978-0-7569-3210-7(6)) Perfection Learning Corp.
—The Case of the Missing Monkey. Karas, G. Brian, illus. 2003. (High-Rise Private Eyes Ser.: No. 1). 28.95 incl. audio compact disk (978-1-59112-615-7(0)) Live Oak Media.
—The Case of the Puzzling Possum. Karas, G. Brian, illus. 2003. (High-Rise Private Eyes Ser.: No. 3). (J). (gr. k-3). 28.95 incl. audio compact disk (978-1-59112-619-5(3)) Live Oak Media.
—Gooseberry Park. Howard, Arthur, illus. 2007. (ENG.). 144p. (J). (gr. 2-5). pap. 6.99 (978-0-15-206159-3(2)) Houghton Mifflin Harcourt Publishing Co.
—Gooseberry Park & the Master Plan. Howard, Arthur, illus. 2015. (ENG.). 128p. (J). (gr. 3-7). 16.99 (978-1-4814-0449-5(0), Beach Lane Bks.) Beach Lane Bks.
—The High-Rise Private Eye: The\Case of the Troublesome Turtle. Karas, G. Brian, illus. 2003. (High-Rise Private Eyes Ser.: No. 4). (J). (gr. k-3). 25.95 incl. audio (978-1-59112-202-9(3)); 28.95 incl. audio compact disk (978-1-59112-623-2(1)); pap. 31.95 incl. audio compact disk (978-1-59112-624-9(X)); pap. 29.95 incl. audio (978-1-59112-203-6(1)) Live Oak Media.
—Life. Wenzel, Brendan, illus. 2017. (ENG.). 48p. (J). (gr. -1). 17.99 **(978-1-4814-5162-8(6)**, Beach Lane Bks.) Beach Lane Bks.
—The Octopus. McDaniels, Preston, illus. 2005. (Lighthouse Family Ser.: 5). (ENG.). 64p. (J). (gr. 1-5). 15.99 (978-0-689-86246-5(6), Simon & Schuster Bks. For Young Readers) Simon & Schuster Bks. For Young Readers.
—The Otter. McDaniels, Preston, illus. 2016. (Lighthouse Family Ser.: 6). (ENG.). 48p. (J). (gr. 1-5). 15.99 (978-1-4814-6045-3(5), Beach Lane Bks.) Beach Lane Bks.
—Poppleton in Winter. Teague, Mark, illus. 2008. 48p. (gr. -1-3). 14.00 (978-0-7569-8910-1(8)) Perfection Learning Corp.
—Poppleton Se Divierte. Teague, Mark, illus. 2006. (Poppleton Ser.). (SPA.). 48p. pap. 11.73 (978-0-15-356487-1(3)) Harcourt Children's Bks.
—The Sea Lion. McDaniels, Preston, illus. 2017. (Lighthouse Family Ser.: 7). (ENG.). 48p. (J). (gr. 1-5). 15.99 (978-1-4814-6025-5(0), Beach Lane Bks.) Beach Lane Bks.
—Thimbleberry Stories. Kneen, Maggie, illus. 2006. (ENG.). 64p. (J). (gr. -1-3). reprint ed. pap. 8.99 (978-0-15-205645-2(9)) Houghton Mifflin Harcourt Publishing Co.
—The Turtle. McDaniels, Preston, illus. 2006. (Lighthouse Family Ser.). 47p. (J). (gr. -1-3). 11.65 (978-0-7569-6611-9(6)) Perfection Learning Corp.
—The Turtle. McDaniels, Preston, illus. 2005. (Lighthouse Family Ser.: 4). (ENG.). 48p. (J). (gr. 1-5). 15.99 (978-0-689-86244-1(X), Simon & Schuster Bks. For Young Readers) Simon & Schuster Bks. For Young Readers.
—The Whale. McDaniels, Preston, illus. 2003. (Lighthouse Family Ser.: 2). (ENG.). 64p. (J). (gr. 1-5). 15.99 (978-0-689-84881-0(1), Simon & Schuster Bks. For Young Readers) Simon & Schuster Bks. For Young Readers.
Sabuda, Robert. Beauty & the Beast: A Pop-Up Adaptation of the Classic Tale. Sabuda, Robert, illus. 2010. (ENG., Illus.). 12p. (J). (gr. -1-2). 34.99 (978-1-4169-6079-9(1), Little Simon) Little Simon.
Sadar, Albin. Hamster Holmes: A Mystery Comes Knocking. Fabbretti, Valerio, illus. 2015. (Hamster Holmes Ser.: 1). (ENG.). 32p. (J). (gr. k-2). 16.99 (978-1-4814-2037-2(2), Simon Spotlight) Simon Spotlight.
—Hamster Holmes, Combing for Clues. Fabbretti, Valerio, illus. 2015. (Hamster Holmes Ser.: 2). (ENG.). 32p. (J). (gr. k-2). pap. 3.99 (978-1-4814-2039-6(9), Simon Spotlight) Simon Spotlight.
—Hamster Holmes, on the Right Track. Fabbretti, Valerio, illus. 2016. (Hamster Holmes Ser.). (ENG.). 32p. (J). (gr. k-2). pap. 3.99 (978-1-4814-2042-6(9), Simon Spotlight) Simon Spotlight.
—A Mystery Comes Knocking. Fabbretti, Valerio, illus. 2015. (Hamster Holmes Ser.: 1). (ENG.). 32p. (J). (gr. k-2). pap. 3.99 (978-1-4814-2036-5(4), Simon Spotlight) Simon Spotlight.
Sáenz, Benjamin Alire. Un Tiempo Perfecto para Sonar. Valencia, Esau Andrade, illus. 2008. (SPA & ENG.). 40p. (J). (gr. 1-4). 17.95 (978-1-933693-01-9(0)) Cinco Puntos Pr.
Sagar, Marie. Jimmy's Adventures: I'm Bored & Mr. Gray Bat. 2007. 20p. (J). 7.00 (978-0-8059-7494-2(6)) Dorrance Publishing Co., Inc.
Sagerman, Evan. Giraffe Rescue Company. Chou, Joey, illus. 2016. (J). (978-1-4424-1366-5(2)) Simon & Schuster Children's Publishing.
Sakmar-Sullivan, Eva M. Willie the Taxi Cat, 1 vol. 2013. (ENG., Illus.). 32p. (J). 16.99 (978-0-7643-4436-7(6), 9780764344367) Schiffer Publishing, Ltd.
Salley, Coleen. Epossumondas Plays Possum. Stevens, Janet, illus. 2009. (ENG.). 40p. (J). (gr. -1-3). 17.99 (978-0-15-206420-4(6)) Houghton Mifflin Harcourt Publishing Co.
Salten, Felix. A Forest World. Greenburger, Sanford Jerome & Milton, Paul R., trs. 2013. (Bambi's Classic Animal Tales Ser.). (ENG., Illus.). 288p. (J). (gr. 3-7). pap. 6.99 (978-1-4424-8637-9(6), Aladdin) Simon & Schuster Children's Publishing.
—A Forest World. Greenburger, Sanford Jerome & Milton, Paul R., trs. 2013. (Bambi's Classic Animal Tales Ser.). (ENG., Illus.). 288p. (J). (gr. 3-7). 16.99 (978-1-4424-8638-6(4), Simon & Schuster/Paula Wiseman Bks.) Simon & Schuster/Paula Wiseman Bks.
—Perri. Mussey, Barrows, tr. from GER. 2015. (Bambi's Classic Animal Tales Ser.). (ENG., Illus.). 256p. (J). (gr. 3-7). pap. 8.99 (978-1-4424-8760-4(7), Aladdin) Simon & Schuster Children's Publishing.
Saltzberg, Barney. Redbird: Friends Come in Different Sizes. 2015. (ENG., Illus.). 22p. (J). bds. 5.95 (978-0-7611-8190-3(3)) Workman Publishing Co., Inc.
Samos (Amos Amir). Nemo the Mole Rat: Stories from the Woodland. 2011. (Illus.). 52p. pap. 23.51 (978-1-4567-8187-3(1)) AuthorHouse.
Samoun, Abigail. How Hippo Says Hello! Watts, Sarah, illus. 2014. (Little Traveler Ser.). (ENG.). 22p. (J). (gr. -1-k). bds. 6.95 (978-1-4549-0820-3(3)) Sterling Publishing Co., Inc.
—How Penguin Says Please! Watts, Sarah, illus. 2015. (Little Traveler Ser.). (ENG & MUL.). 24p. (J). (gr. -1-k). bds. 6.95 (978-1-4549-1496-9(3)) Sterling Publishing Co., Inc.
—How Tiger Says Thank You! Watts, Sarah, illus. 2015. (Little Traveler Ser.). (ENG & MUL.). 22p. (J). (gr. -1-k). bds. 6.95 (978-1-4549-1497-6(1)) Sterling Publishing Co., Inc.
Sams, Carl R., II & Stoick, Jean. Find My Friends. 2006. (Illus.). 14p. (gr. -1-k). bds. 7.95 (978-0-9770108-5-1(6)) Sams, II, Carl R. Photography, Inc.
—Winter Friends. McDiarmid, Karen, ed. Sams, Carl R., II & Stoick, Jean, photos by. 2003. (ENG., Illus.). 14p. (J). bds. 7.95 (978-0-9671748-5-3(6)) Sams, II, Carl R. Photography, Inc.
Sams II, Carl R. A Magical Winter. 2016. (ENG., Illus.). (J). 19.95 (978-0-9827625-8-5(5)) Sams, II, Carl R. Photography, Inc.
Samuels, Linda Nissen. Cuando Elly Fue a la Reserva Ecologica. Samuels, Linda Nissen, illus. 2013. (Illus.). 40p. pap. (978-0-9511751-8-7(1)) Samuels, Linda Y.
—Elly e il Parco Degli Animali. Samuels, Linda Nissen, illus. 2013. (Illus.). 40p. pap. (978-0-9511751-7-0(3)) Samuels, Linda Y.
—When Elly Went to the Animal Park... Samuels, Linda Nissen, illus. 2013. (Illus.). 40p. pap. (978-0-9511751-5-6(7)) Samuels, Linda Y.
Samura, Juliet Tumoe. Animal Town: Fishing Trip. 2011. 28p. pap. 13.99 (978-1-4490-3981-3(2)) AuthorHouse.
Sanders, Cecilia. The Tale of the Perfect Whitetails. 2008. 36p. pap. 17.98 (978-1-4389-0644-7(7)) AuthorHouse.
Sanders, Jennifer. Tail Tales. 2005. 23p. 13.99 (978-1-4116-2914-1(0)) Lulu Pr., Inc.
Sandoval, Alex. Zack Goes to School. 2009. 20p. pap. 10.50 (978-1-4389-5537-7(5)) AuthorHouse.
Sandoval, Anthony J. Unusual Animals from A to Z. 2008. 30p. pap. 24.95 (978-1-60672-184-1(4)) America Star Bks.
Santa Takes A Vacation. 2005. (J). 5.95 (978-0-9769321-4-7(8)) Steingart, Nathan Publishing.
Santat, Dan & Willems, Mo. The Cookie Fiasco. Santat, Dan & Willems, Mo, illus. 2016. (Elephant & Piggie Like Reading! Ser.). (ENG., Illus.). 64p. (J). (gr. 1-3). 9.99 (978-1-4847-2636-5(7)) Hyperion Bks. for Children.
Santillo, LuAnn. Barnyard Buddies, 6 vols. Santillo, LuAnn, ed. 2003. (Half-Pint Kids Readers Ser.). (Illus.). 42p. (J). (gr. -1-1). pap. 6.95 (978-1-59256-063-9(6)) Half-Pint Kids, Inc.
—In the Meadow, 6 vols. Santillo, LuAnn, ed. 2003. (Half-Pint Kids Readers Ser.). (Illus.). 42p. (J). (gr. -1-1). pap. 6.95 (978-1-59256-105-6(5)) Half-Pint Kids, Inc.
Santini, Philip. Harvey's Adventures. Chambers, Z., illus. 2011. 44p. pap. 24.95 (978-1-4626-2078-4(7)) America Star Bks.
Santore, Charles. Aesop's Fables. 2012. (ENG., Illus.). 56p. (J). 14.95 (978-1-4027-8412-5(0)) Sterling Publishing Co., Inc.
Sareva, Ibrahim. West of Kilimanjaro 1: Book 1. 2010. 44p. pap. 16.99 (978-1-4520-3006-7(5)) AuthorHouse.
Sarfatti, Esther, tr. from ENG. Berto Da la Talla. 2006. (Libro de Capitulos de Arturo Ser.). (Illus.). 55p. (J). (gr. 6-8). per. 4.99 (978-1-930332-94-2(7)) Lectorum Pubns., Inc.
Sargent, Daina. Colors & the Number 10, 11 vols. Lenoir, Jane, illus. 2004. (Learn to Read Ser.: 11). 24p. (J). pap. 10.95 (978-1-59381-049-8(0)); per. 9.95 (978-1-59381-527-1(1)) Ozark Publishing.
—Colors & the Number 1/Los Colores y el Número 1, 11 vols. Lenoir, Jane, illus. 2004. (Learn to Read Ser.: 11). (SPA & ENG.). 24p. (J). pap. 10.95 (978-1-59381-129-7(2)) Ozark Publishing.
—Colors & the Number 2, 11 vols. Lenoir, Jane, illus. 2004. (Learn to Read Ser.: 11). 24p. (J). per. 10.95 (978-1-59381-529-5(8)) Ozark Publishing.
—Colors & the Number 2/Los Colores y el Número 2, 11 vols. Lenoir, Jane, illus. 2004. (Learn to Read Ser.: 11).Tr. of Los colores y el Nùmero 2. (SPA & ENG.). 24p. (J). pap. 10.95 (978-1-59381-131-0(4)); lib. bdg. 20.95 (978-1-59381-130-3(6)) Ozark Publishing.
—Colors & the Number 3, 11 vols. Lenoir, Jane, illus. 2004. (Learn to Read Ser.: 11). 24p. (J). pap. 10.95 (978-1-59381-530-1(1)); pap. 10.95 (978-1-59381-035-1(0)) Ozark Publishing.
—Colors & the Number 3/Los Colores y el Número 3, 11 vols. Lenoir, Jane, illus. 2004. (Learn to Read Ser.: 11).Tr. of Los colores y el el Nùmero 3. (SPA & ENG.). 24p. (J). pap. 10.95 (978-1-59381-133-4(0)); lib. bdg. 20.95 (978-1-59381-132-7(2)) Ozark Publishing.
—Colors & the Number 4, 11 vols. Lenoir, Jane, illus. 2004. (Learn to Read Ser.: 11). 24p. (J). per. 10.95 (978-1-59381-531-8(X)) Ozark Publishing.
—Colors & the Number 4/Los colores y el Número 4, 11 vols. Lenoir, Jane, illus. 2004. (Learn to Read Ser.: 11).Tr. of Los colores y el Número 4. (SPA & ENG.). 24p. (J). pap. 10.95 (978-1-59381-135-8(7)); lib. bdg. 20.95 (978-1-59381-134-1(9)) Ozark Publishing.
—Colors & the Number 5, 11 vols. Lenoir, Jane, illus. 2004. (Learn to Read Ser.: 11). 24p. (J). pap. 10.95 (978-1-59381-039-9(3)); per. 10.95 (978-1-59381-532-5(8)) Ozark Publishing.
—Colors & the Number 5/Los colores y el Número 5, 11 vols. Lenoir, Jane, illus. 2004. (Learn to Read Ser.: 11).Tr. of Los colores y el Número 5. (SPA & ENG.). 24p. (J). pap. 10.95 (978-1-59381-137-2(3)); lib. bdg. 20.95 (978-1-59381-136-5(5)) Ozark Publishing.
—Colors & the Number 6, 11 vols. Lenoir, Jane, illus. 2004. (Learn to Read Ser.: 11). 24p. (J). pap. 10.95 (978-1-59381-041-2(5)); per. 10.95 (978-1-59381-533-2(6)) Ozark Publishing.
—Colors & the Number 7, 11 vols. Lenoir, Jane, illus. 2004. (Learn to Read Ser.: 11). 24p. (J). pap. 10.95 (978-1-59381-043-6(1)); per. 10.95 (978-1-59381-534-9(4)) Ozark Publishing.
—Colors & the Number 7/Los Colores y el Número 7, 11 vols. Lenoir, Jane, illus. 2004. (Learn to Read Ser.: 11).Tr. of Los colores y el Número 7. (SPA & ENG.). 24p. (J). pap. 10.95 (978-1-59381-141-9(1)); lib. bdg. 20.95 (978-1-59381-140-2(3)) Ozark Publishing.
—Colors & the Number 8, 11 vols. Lenoir, Jane, illus. 2004. (Learn to Read Ser.: 11). 24p. (J). pap. 10.95 (978-1-59381-045-0(8)) Ozark Publishing.
—Colors & the Number 8/Los Colores y el Número 8, 11 vols. Lenoir, Jane, illus. 2004. (Learn to Read Ser.: 11).Tr. of Los colores y el Número 8. (SPA & ENG.). 24p. (J). pap. 10.95 (978-1-59381-143-3(8)); lib. bdg. 20.95 (978-1-59381-142-6(X)) Ozark Publishing.
—Colors & the Number 9, 11 vols. Lenoir, Jane, illus. 2004. (Learn to Read Ser.: 11). 24p. (J). pap. 10.95 (978-1-59381-047-4(4)) Ozark Publishing.
—Colors & the Number 9/Los Colores y el Número 9, 11 vols. Lenoir, Jane, illus. 2004. (Learn to Read Ser.: 11).Tr. of Los colores y el Número 9. (SPA & ENG.). 24p. (J). pap. 10.95 (978-1-59381-145-7(4)); lib. bdg. 20.95 (978-1-59381-144-0(6)) Ozark Publishing.
—Introduction to Colors & Niumbers, 11 vols. Lenoir, Jane, illus. 2005. (Learn to Read Ser.: 11). 24p. (J). pap. 10.95 (978-1-59381-051-1(2)) Ozark Publishing.
—Introduction to Colors & Numbers, 11 vols. Lenoir, Jane, illus. 2005. (Learn to Read Ser.: 11). 24p. (J). per. 10.95 (978-1-59381-528-8(X)) Ozark Publishing.
—Introduction to Colors & Numbers (BL) Introduccion a los colores y a los Numeros, 11 vols. Lenoir, Jane, illus. 2004. (Learn to Read Ser.: 11). (SPA & ENG.). 24p. (J). lib. bdg. 20.95 (978-1-59381-148-8(9)) Ozark Publishing.
Sargent, Pat. The Timber Wolf, 6 vols., Vol. 3. Lenoir, Jane, illus. 2003. (Barney the Bear Killer Ser.: Vol. 3). 123p. (J). pap. 10.95 (978-1-56763-968-1(2)); lib. bdg. 26.25 (978-1-56763-967-4(4)) Ozark Publishing.
Sargent, Pat L. The Cheetah, 6 vols., Vol. 6. Lenoir, Jane, illus. l.t. ed. 2004. (Barney the Bear Killer Ser.: No. 6). 146p. (YA). pap. 10.95 (978-1-56763-974-2(7)) Ozark Publishing.
Sarno, J. P. Little Paddle the Platypus & His First Day Outing Adventure. 2012. 136p. pap. 71.99 (978-1-4691-8746-4(9)) Xlibris Corp.
Sassi, Laura. Goodnight, Ark, 1 vol. Chapman, Jane, illus. 2014. (ENG.). 32p. (J). 16.99 (978-0-310-73784-1(2)) Zonderkidz.
Satterfield, Mary & Satterfield, Nathaniel. The Leaping Lady: A Tall Tale from Mary & Nathaniel Satterfield. 2011. (Illus.). 24p. (J). pap. 11.95 (978-1-58909-989-0(3)) Bookstand Publishing.
Sauer, Cat. Flip Flop & Hoot. Jankowski, Daniel, illus. l.t. ed. 2006. (Brown Bag Bedtime Bks.: 1). 35p. (J). (gr. -1-2). 16.95 incl. audio compact disk (978-0-9704460-6-0(3)) Writer's Ink. Studios, Inc.
Sauer, Tammi. I Love Cake! Starring Rabbit, Porcupine, & Moose. Rozelaar, Angie, illus. 2016. 40p. (J). (gr. -1-3). 17.99 (978-0-06-227894-4(0), Tegen, Katherine Bks) HarperCollins Pubs.
Saunders, Zina, illus. Say Please! A Book about Manners. 2006. (Backyardigans Ser.). (ENG.). 24p. (J). (gr. -1-2). pap. 3.99 (978-1-4169-1386-3(6), Simon Spotlight/Nickelodeon) Simon Spotlight/Nickelodeon.
Sava, Scott Christian. Animal Crackers. Holmes, Mike, illus. 2017. (Animal Crackers Ser.: 1). (ENG.). 96p. (J). 15.99 (978-1-62672-504-1(7), 9781626725041, First Second Bks.) Roaring Brook Pr.
Savage, Melissa. Lemons. 2017. (ENG.). 320p. (J). (gr. 3-7). 16.99 **(978-1-5247-0012-6(6))**; lib. bdg. 19.99 **(978-1-5247-0013-3(4))** Random Hse. Children's Bks. (Crown Books For Young Readers).
Sawyer-Aitch, Anne. Nalah & the Pink Tiger. Sawyer-Aitch, Anne, illus. 2013. (ENG., Illus.). 40p. pap. 13.95 (978-1-938063-00-8(7), Mighty Media Kids) Mighty Media Pr.
Sayre, April Pulley. If You're Hoppy. Urbanovic, Jackie, illus. 2011. (ENG.). 40p. (J). (gr. -1-k). 16.99 (978-0-06-156634-9(9), Greenwillow Bks.) HarperCollins Pubs.
Sazaklis, John. The Biggest Little Hero, 1 vol. Baltazar, Art, illus. 2012. (DC Super-Pets Ser.). (ENG.). 56p. (gr. 2-2). pap. 4.95 (978-1-4048-7664-4(2)); lib. bdg. 23.99 (978-1-4048-6490-0(3)) Picture Window Bks. (DC Super-Pets).
—Deep-Sea Duel, 1 vol. Baltazar, Art, illus. 2012. (DC Super-Pets Ser.). (ENG.). 56p. (gr. 2-2). pap. 4.95 (978-1-4048-7662-0(6)); lib. bdg. 23.99 (978-1-4048-6489-4(X)) Picture Window Bks. (DC Super-Pets).
—The Hopping Hero, 1 vol. Baltazar, Art, illus. 2011. (DC Super-Pets Ser.). (ENG.). 56p. (gr. 2-2). pap. 4.95 (978-1-4048-6843-4(7)); lib. bdg. 23.99 (978-1-4048-6477-1(6)) Picture Window Bks. (DC Super-Pets).
—Swamp Thing vs the Zombie Pets, 1 vol. Baltazar, Art, illus. 2012. (DC Super-Pets Ser.). (ENG.). 56p. (gr. 2-2). pap. 4.95 (978-1-4048-7667-5(7)); lib. bdg. 23.99 (978-1-4048-6491-7(1)) Picture Window Bks. (DC Super-Pets).
Scafuro, Lisa. Adventures at Cedar Hollow: Tigre Encounters the Great Horned Owl. 2005. (J). 18.00 (978-0-8059-6635-0(8)) Dorrance Publishing Co., Inc.
Scarry, Patricia. Richard Scarry's Just for Fun. Scarry, Richard, illus. 2016. (Little Golden Book Ser.). (ENG.). 24p. (J). (gr. -1-k). 4.99 (978-0-553-53662-1(1), Golden Bks.) Random Hse. Children's Bks.
Scarry, Richard. Best Lowly Worm Book Ever! 2014. (ENG., Illus.). 32p. (J). (gr. -1-2). 15.99 (978-0-385-38782-8(2), Random Hse. Bks. for Young Readers) Random Hse. Children's Bks.
—Cosas Que Nos Gustan.Tr. of Things We Love. (SPA., Illus.). (J). pap. 6.95 (978-950-04-1043-4(5)) Emecé Editores S.A. ARG. Dist: Planeta Publishing Corp.
—Egg in the Hole. Golden Books Staff, illus. 2011. (Shaped Board Book Ser.). (ENG.). 20p. (J). (gr. k — 1). bds. 8.99 (978-0-375-86291-5(9), Golden Bks.) Random Hse. Children's Bks.
—The Night Before the Night Before Christmas! Scarry, Richard, illus. 2014. (ENG., Illus.). 48p. (J). (gr. -1-2). 14.99 (978-0-385-38804-7(7), Golden Bks.) Random Hse. Children's Bks.
—Richard Scarry Mr. Paint Pig's ABC's. Random House Staff, illus. 2013. (ENG.). 12p. (J). (-k). bds. 5.99 (978-0-449-81902-9(7), Golden Bks.) Random Hse. Children's Bks.
—Richard Scarry's ABC Word Book. 2011. (ENG., Illus.). 60p. (J). (gr. -1-2). 12.95 (978-1-4027-7221-4(1)) Sterling Publishing Co., Inc.
—Richard Scarry's All the Colors of Busytown. 2013. (Richard Scarry's Concept Bks.). (ENG.). 18p. (J). (gr. -1 — 1). bds. 7.99 (978-0-7641-6601-3(8)) Barron's Educational Series, Inc.
—Richard Scarry's Best Busy Year Ever. 2011. (ENG., Illus.). 72p. (J). (gr. -1-2). 12.95 (978-1-4027-7219-1(X)) Sterling Publishing Co., Inc.
—Richard Scarry's Busytown on the Go! 2015. (ENG., Illus.). 18p. (J). (gr. -1-k). bds. 7.99 (978-0-7641-6776-8(6)) Barron's Educational Series, Inc.
—Richard Scarry's Funniest Storybook Ever! 2016. (ENG., Illus.). 64p. (J). (gr. -1-2). 15.99 (978-0-385-38297-7(9), Golden Bks.) Random Hse. Children's Bks.

—Richard Scarry's Good Morning, Busytown! 2015. (ENG., Illus.). 18p. (J). (gr. -1-k). bds. 7.99 *(978-0-7641-6777-5(4))* Barron's Educational Series, Inc.
—Richard Scarry's Great Big Schoolhouse. 2008. (ENG., Illus.). 72p. (J). (gr. -1-2). 14.95 *(978-1-4027-5820-1(0))* Sterling Publishing Co., Inc.
—Richard Scarry's Let's Count with Lowly. 2013. (Richard Scarry's Concept Bks.). (ENG.). 18p. (J). (gr. -1 — 1). bds. 7.99 *(978-0-7641-6600-6(X))* Barron's Educational Series, Inc.
—Richard Scarry's Mr. Fixit's Whacky Toolbox: Lift-The Flap Book. 2015. (ENG., Illus.). 10p. (J). (gr. -1 — 1). bds. 7.99 *(978-0-7641-6811-6(8))* Barron's Educational Series, Inc.
—Richard Scarry's Postman Pig & His Busy Neighbors. Scarry, Richard, illus. 2015. (Pictureback(R) Ser.). (ENG., Illus.). 32p. (J). (gr. -1-2). pap. 4.99 *(978-0-385-38419-3(X),* Random Hse. Bks. for Young Readers) Random Hse. Children's Bks.
—Richard Scarry's Smokey the Fireman. Scarry, Richard, illus. 2015. (Step into Reading Ser.). (ENG., Illus.). 32p. (J). (gr. -1-1). 12.99 *(978-0-375-97363-5(X),* Random Hse. Bks. for Young Readers) Random Hse. Children's Bks.
—Richard Scarry's the Adventures of Lowly Worm. 2010. (ENG., Illus.). 44p. (J). (gr. -1-2). 12.95 *(978-1-4027-7214-6(9))* Sterling Publishing Co., Inc.
—Richard Scarry's the Great Pie Robbery & Other Mysteries. 2008. (ENG., Illus.). 104p. (J). (gr. 1-3). 12.95 *(978-1-4027-5823-2(5))* Sterling Publishing Co., Inc.
—Richard Scarry's the Great Steamboat Mystery. 2014. (ENG., Illus.). 34p. (J). (gr. 1-2). 4.95 *(978-1-4549-1010-7(0))* Sterling Publishing Co., Inc.
—Richard Scarry's the Supermarket Mystery. 2014. (ENG., Illus.). 34p. (J). (gr. 1-2). 4.95 *(978-1-4549-1011-4(9))* Sterling Publishing Co., Inc.
—School Bus Box Set. 2014. (Illus.). (J). *(978-0-7641-6690-7(5))* Barron's Educational Series, Inc.
Scarry, Richard & Farber, Erica. Cake Soup. Scarry, Huck, illus. 2011. (Richard Scarry's Great Big Schoolhouse Ser.). (ENG.). 24p. (J). (gr. -1-k). pap. 3.95 *(978-1-4027-7317-4(X))* Sterling Publishing Co., Inc.
—Go, Huckle, Go! Scarry, Huck, illus. 2011. (Richard Scarry's Great Big Schoolhouse Ser.). (ENG.). 24p. (J). (gr. -1-k). pap. 3.95 *(978-1-4027-7316-7(1))* Sterling Publishing Co., Inc.
Scelsa, Greg & Debney, John. Friends Forever. Faulkner, Stacey, ed. Mahan, Benton, illus. 2006. (J). pap. 2.99 *(978-1-59198-322-4(3))* Creative Teaching Pr., Inc.
Schade, Susan. Simon's Dream. Buller, Jon, illus. 2009. (Fog Mound Ser.: 3). (ENG.). 208p. (J). (gr. 3-7). pap. 12.99 *(978-0-689-87689-9(0),* Aladdin) Simon & Schuster Children's Publishing.
—Travels of Thelonious. Buller, Jon, illus. 2007. (Fog Mound Ser.: 1). (ENG.). 224p. (J). (gr. 3-7). pap. 11.99 *(978-0-689-87685-1(8),* Aladdin) Simon & Schuster Children's Publishing.
Schade, Susan & Buller, Jon. Faradawn. 2008. (Fog Mound Ser.: 2). (ENG., Illus.). 208p. (J). (gr. 3-7). pap. 12.99 *(978-0-689-87687-5(4),* Aladdin) Simon & Schuster Children's Publishing.
Schaefer, Carole Lexa. Down in the Woods at Sleepytime. Cabban, Vanessa, illus. 2004. (ENG.). 24p. (J). (— 1). bds. 8.99 *(978-0-7636-2566-5(3))* Candlewick Pr.
Schaefer, Lola M. Please Pass the Manners! Mealtime Tips for Everyone. Lewis, Kellie, illus. 2009. (ENG.). 12p. (J). (gr. -1-1). 7.99 *(978-1-4169-4826-1(0),* Little Simon) Little Simon.
Scharer, Niko. Emily's House, 1 vol. Fitzgerald, Joanne, illus. 2010. (ENG.). 22p. (J). (gr. k — 1). bds. 7.95 *(978-0-88899-831-6(7))* Groundwood Bks. CAN. Dist: Publishers Group West (PGW).
Scher, Paula. The Brownstone. 2016. (ENG., Illus.). 32p. (J). (gr. -1-3). 17.95 *(978-1-61689-428-3(8))* Princeton Architectural Pr.
Schertle, Alice. Little Blue Truck. McElmurry, Jill, illus. 2010. (Little Blue Truck Ser.). (ENG.). 32p. (J). (gr. -1-3). 26.99 *(978-0-547-48248-4(5))* Houghton Mifflin Harcourt Publishing Co.
Schieber, Jennifer. Burt's Counting Stew. 2004. (Shared Connections Ser.). (J). pap., instr.'s gde. ed. 27.00 *(978-1-4108-1607-8(9))* Benchmark Education Co.
—Burt's Counting Stew: Small Book. 2004. (Shared Connections Ser.). (J). pap. *(978-1-4108-1631-3(1))* Benchmark Education Co.
—A contar con la sopa de Beto: Fiction-to-Fact Big Book. May, Gillie, illus. enl. ed. 2004. (SPA.). (J). pap. 26.00 *(978-1-4108-2361-8(X),* 2361X) Benchmark Education Co.
Schindel, John. Busy Kitties. Franzen, Sean, photos by. 2004. (Busy Book Ser.). (ENG., Illus.). 20p. (J). (— 1). bds. 6.99 *(978-1-58246-130-4(9),* Knopf Bks. for Young Readers) Random Hse. Children's Bks.
Schkolnik, Saul. Cuentos Ecologicos. Cardemil, Carmen, illus. 2nd ed. 2003. (la Orilla del Viento Ser.).Tr. of Ecological Tales. (SPA.). 56p. (J). (gr. 3-7). per. *(978-968-16-4757-5(2),* FC6400) Fondo de Cultura Economica MEX. Dist: Lectorum Pubns., Inc.
Schlaht, Kim. Ronnie's Rotten Recipes. Tijerina, Arnold G., III, ed. 2006. (Illus.). 70p. (J). (gr. -1). per. 18.95 *(978-0-9777688-1-3(3))* TICO Publishing.
Schlegl, Stacey Lynn. Little Frog. 2008. (J). per. 8.95 *(978-0-9801504-0-7(X))* Jan-Carol Publishing, INC.
Schlunke, Eva & Fitzgerald, Paul. Little Worm's Big Question, 1 vol. 2016. (ENG., Illus.). 36p. (J). (gr. -1-3). pap. 9.95 *(978-1-78026-261-1(2))* New Internationalist Pubns., Ltd. GBR. Dist: Consortium Bk. Sales & Distribution.
Schmatjen, Marc. My Giraffe Makes Me Laugh. 2010. 24p. 12.95 *(978-1-4520-0941-4(4))* AuthorHouse.
Schmidt, Hans-Christian. Are You Sleeping Little One. Lindgren, Laura, tr. from GER. Nemet, Andrea, illus. 2012. (ENG.). 18p. (J). (gr. k-k). bds. 6.95 *(978-0-7892-1120-0(3),* Abbeville Kids) Abbeville Pr., Inc.
Schmidt, Mollie. It Happened in Maine. Wood, Madeline, illus. 2013. (ENG.). 56p. (J). pap. 10.95 *(978-1-59713-137-7(7))* Goose River Pr.
Schneider, Rosemary. Bully Paws. 2011. 40p. pap. 18.46 *(978-1-4567-6294-0(X))* AuthorHouse.
Schoene, Kerstin & Gunetsreiner, Nina. Milo Is Not a Dog Today. 2015. (Illus.). 32p. (J). *(978-1-4896-3867-0(9))* Weigl Pubs., Inc.
—Milo Is Not a Dog Today. Schoene, Kerstin & Gunetsreiner, Nina, illus. 2014. (ENG., Illus.). 32p. (J). (gr. -1-3). 16.99 *(978-0-8075-4793-9(X))* Whitman, Albert & Co.
Schoenherr, Ian. Don't Spill the Beans! Schoenherr, Ian, illus. 2010. (Illus.). 32p. (J). (gr. -1 — 1). (ENG.). 16.99 *(978-0-06-172457-2(2));* lib. bdg. 17.89 *(978-0-06-172458-9(0))* HarperCollins Pubs. (Greenwillow Bks.).
Scholastic, Inc. Staff, contrib. by. Counting 1 To 20. 2014. (Rookie Toddler(r) Ser.). (ENG.). 12p. (J). bds. 6.95 *(978-0-531-20913-4(X))* Scholastic Library Publishing.
Schomp, Virginia. Brer Rabbit & the Goober Patch. 2013. (American Legends & Folktales 2 Ser.). (Illus.). 32p. (J). (gr. 6-9). pap. 10.58 *(978-1-62712-014-2(9))* Cavendish Square Publishing.
Schories, Pat. Pie for Chuck. 2015. (I Like to Read(r) Ser.). (ENG., Illus.). 24p. (J). (gr. -1-3). 14.95 *(978-0-8234-3392-6(7))* Holiday Hse., Inc.
Schories, Pat, illus. Biscuit Visits the Farm. 2012. (J). *(978-1-4351-4383-8(3),* HarperFestival) HarperCollins Pubs.
Schrader, Margaret. Green Knee-High Farm. Schrader, Kimberly, illus. 2009. 28p. pap. 12.95 *(978-1-60844-000-9(1))* Dog Ear Publishing, LLC.
Schrefer, Eliot. Fall of the Beasts, Bk. 1. 2015. (Spirit Animals: Fall of the Beasts Ser.: 1). (ENG.). 192p. (J). (gr. 3-7). 12.99 *(978-0-545-83000-3(1))* Scholastic, Inc.
—Rise & Fall. 2014. (Spirit Animals Ser.: 6). (ENG., Illus.). 192p. (J). (gr. 3-7). 12.99 *(978-0-545-52248-9(X))* Scholastic, Inc.
Schubert, Ingrid & Schubert, Dieter. Ophelia. 2009. (ENG.). 32p. (J). (gr. -1-1). 16.95 *(978-1-59078-659-8(9),* 9781590786598) Lemniscaat USA.
Schulz, Hal. Dak's Country Visit: The Painter & His Cat. 2011. 32p. pap. *(978-1-4269-6743-6(8))* Trafford Publishing (UK) Ltd.
Schwartz, Barry L. Adam's Animals. Doneva, Steliyana, illus. 2017. (J). ***(978-1-68115-530-2(3))*** Behrman Hse., Inc.
Schwartz, Corey Rosen & Gomez, Rebecca J. What about Moose? Yamaguchi, Keika, illus. 2015. (ENG.). 40p. (J). (gr. -1-3). 17.99 *(978-1-4814-0496-9(2),* Atheneum Bks. for Young Readers) Simon & Schuster Children's Publishing.
Schwartz, Tom. How Mother Nature Dealt with Creatures of the Earth. 2006. 157p. pap. 19.95 *(978-1-4137-7765-9(1))* America Star Bks.
—How Mother Nature Flowered the Fields. 2006. (Illus.). 120p. (J). per. 14.95 *(978-1-57545-102-2(6),* Reagent Pr. Echo) RP Media.
Schweizer, Chris. Tricky Coyote Tales. Thomas, Chad, illus. 2011. (Tricky Journeys Ser.: 1). (ENG.). (J). (gr. 2-4). pap. 39.62 *(978-0-7613-8625-4(4));*No. 1. 64p. pap. 6.95 *(978-0-7613-7859-4(6));*No. 1. 64p. lib. bdg. 27.93 *(978-0-7613-6601-0(6))* Lerner Publishing Group.
—Tricky Fox Tales. Paroline, Shelli & Paroline, Michelle, illus. 2011. (Tricky Journeys Ser.: 3). (ENG.). (J). (gr. 2-4). pap. 39.62 *(978-0-7613-8627-8(0))* Lerner Publishing Group.
—Tricky Fox Tales. Paroline, Shelli, illus. 2011. (Tricky Journeys Ser.: 3). (ENG.). 64p. (J). (gr. 2-4). pap. 6.95 *(978-0-7613-7861-7(8))* Lerner Publishing Group.
—Tricky Fox Tales, No. 3. Paroline, Shelli & Paroline, Michelle, illus. 2011. (Tricky Journeys Ser.: 3). (ENG.). 64p. (J). (gr. 2-4). lib. bdg. 27.93 *(978-0-7613-6605-8(9))* Lerner Publishing Group.
—Tricky Monkey Tales. Thomas, Chad, illus. 2011. (Tricky Journeys Ser.: 6). (ENG.). (J). (gr. 2-4). pap. 39.62 *(978-0-7613-8630-8(0));* 64p. pap. 6.95 *(978-0-7613-7860-0(X));*No. 6. 64p. lib. bdg. 27.93 *(978-0-7613-6611-9(3))* Lerner Publishing Group.
—Tricky Rabbit Tales. Giallongo, Zack, illus. 2011. (Tricky Journeys Ser.: 2). (ENG.). (J). (gr. 2-4). pap. 39.62 *(978-0-7613-8626-1(2));* 64p. pap. 6.95 *(978-0-7613-7862-4(6));*No. 2. 64p. lib. bdg. 27.93 *(978-0-7613-6607-2(5))* Lerner Publishing Group.
—Tricky Raven Tales. Witt, David, illus. 2011. (Tricky Journeys Ser.: 4). (ENG.). (J). (gr. 2-4). pap. 39.62 *(978-0-7613-8628-5(9));*No. 4. 64p. pap. 6.95 *(978-0-7613-7863-1(4));*No. 4. 64p. lib. bdg. 27.93 *(978-0-7613-6603-4(2))* Lerner Publishing Group.
—Tricky Spider Tales. Huddleston, Courtney, illus. 2011. (Tricky Journeys Ser.: 5). (ENG.). (J). (gr. 2-4). pap. 39.62 *(978-0-7613-8629-2(7));* 64p. pap. 6.95 *(978-0-7613-7864-8(2));*No. 5. 64p. lib. bdg. 27.93 *(978-0-7613-6609-6(1))* Lerner Publishing Group.
Scollon, Bill. The Big Case. 2016. (Step into Reading Level 3 Ser.). lib. bdg. 14.75 *(978-0-606-38488-9(X))* Turtleback Bks.
Scotford, Groenewald & Scotford, Tina. A Bush Buffet in the Land of Kachoo. 2014. (Land of Kachoo Ser.). (ENG.). 32p. (J). (gr. k-2). pap. 10.95 *(978-1-4314-0761-3(5))* Jacana Media ZAF. Dist: Independent Pubs. Group.
—The Mighty Elephant in the Land of Kachoo: The Land of Kachoo Series. Groenewald, Frans, illus. 2014. (Land of Kachoo Ser.). (ENG.). 32p. (J). (gr. k-2). pap. 10.95 *(978-1-4314-0759-0(3))* Jacana Media ZAF. Dist: Independent Pubs. Group.
Scotford, Tina. Saving the Rhino in the Land of Kachoo: The Land of Kachoo Series. Groenewald, Frans, illus. 2014. (Land of Kachoo Ser.). (ENG.). 32p. (J). (gr. k-2). pap. 10.95 *(978-1-4314-0760-6(7))* Jacana Media ZAF. Dist: Independent Pubs. Group.
Scott, Nathan Kumar. The Sacred Banana Leaf. 2008. (ENG., Illus.). 32p. (J). (gr. k-1). *(978-81-86211-28-1(4))* Tara Publishing.
Scotto, Michael. Just Flash. Gabriel, Evette et al, illus. 2009. (J). *(978-1-935193-50-0(3))* National Network of Digital Schls.
Scraper, Katherine. Garden Lunch. 2006. (Early Explorers Ser.). (J). pap. *(978-1-4108-6027-9(2))* Benchmark Education Co.
Scull, Paul E. The Animals Tell His Story. 2009. 20p. pap. 10.00 *(978-1-4251-8737-8(4))* Trafford Publishing.
Seabrook, Heather. Lego Chima - Heroes' Quest. 2014. (DK Reader Level 3 Ser.). lib. bdg. 13.55 *(978-0-606-35732-6(7))* Turtleback Bks.
Seder, Rufus Butler. ¡Al Galope! Un Libro de Scanimation. 2009. (Scanimation Ser.). (SPA., Illus.). 12p. (J). (gr. -1-3). 12.95 *(978-0-7611-5415-0(9),* 15415) Workman Publishing Co., Inc.
—Gallop! Cards: 8 Scanimation Gift Cards. 2008. (Scanimation Ser.). (ENG., Illus.). 18p. (J). (gr. -1-12). 16.00 *(978-0-7611-5239-2(3),* 15239) Workman Publishing Co., Inc.
—Waddle! 2009. (Scanimation Ser.). (ENG., Illus.). 12p. (gr. -1-2). 13.95 *(978-0-7611-5112-8(5),* 15112) Workman Publishing Co., Inc.
Segal, John. Carrot Soup. Segal, John, illus. 2006. (ENG., Illus.). 32p. (J). (gr. -1-3). 17.99 *(978-0-689-87702-5(1),* McElderry, Margaret K. Bks.) McElderry, Margaret K. Bks.
Segarra, Angelo M. Coca Finds a Shell. Segarra, Kirstie, ed. Segarra, Angelo M., illus. 2004. (Illus.). 24p. (J). 14.95 *(978-0-9752664-0-3(3))* Segarra, Angelo.
Seibold, J. Otto. Lost Sloth. 2013. (ENG., Illus.). 32p. 16.95 *(978-1-938073-35-9(5))* McSweeney's Publishing.
Seiss, Ellie & Random House Staff. Dora & the Unicorn King. 2013. (Dora the Explorer Step into Reading Ser.). lib. bdg. 13.55 *(978-0-606-32415-1(1),* Turtleback) Turtleback Bks.
Sellier, Marie. What the Rat Told Me. Louis, Catherine, illus. 2014. (ENG.). 32p. (J). (gr. k-3). 7.95 *(978-0-7358-4158-1(6))* North-South Bks., Inc.
Selous, Edmund. Tommy Smith's Animals. Ord, G. W., illus. 2009. 166p. pap. 9.95 *(978-1-59915-376-6(9))* Yesterday's Classics.
Seltzer, Eric. Bake, Mice, Bake! Rosenberg, Natascha, illus. 2012. (Penguin Young Readers, Level 1 Ser.). (ENG.). 32p. (J). (gr. k-1). mass mkt. 3.99 *(978-0-448-45763-5(6),* Penguin Young Readers) Penguin Young Readers Group.
—Bake, Mice, Bake! 2012. (Penguin Young Readers Level 1 Ser.). lib. bdg. 13.55 *(978-0-606-23625-6(2),* Turtleback) Turtleback Bks.
—Doodle Dog. Seltzer, Eric, illus. 2005. (Doodle Dog Ser.). (ENG., Illus.). 32p. (J). (gr. -1-1). pap. 3.99 *(978-0-689-85910-6(4),* Simon Spotlight) Simon Spotlight.
Seltzer, Eric & Hall, Kirsten. Dog on His Bus. Braun, Sebastien, illus. 2012. (Penguin Young Readers, Level 2 Ser.). (ENG.). 32p. (J). (gr. 1-2). pap. 3.99 *(978-0-448-45904-2(3),* Penguin Young Readers) Penguin Young Readers Group.
—Dog on His Bus. Braun, Sebastien, illus. 2012. (Penguin Young Readers Level 2 Ser.). lib. bdg. 13.55 *(978-0-606-25815-9(9),* Turtleback) Turtleback Bks.
Sensel, Joni. Bears Barge In. Bivins, Christopher, illus. 2003. 32p. (J). (gr. -1-18). 14.95 *(978-0-9701195-0-6(X))* Dream Factory Bks.
Serengeti Safari: Animal Adventures in Africa. 2010. 64p. pap. 6.00 *(978-81-7806-191-7(0))* Unicorn Bks. Pvt Ltd. IND. Dist: Mahal, Pustak Pubs., Booksellers & Order Suppliers.
Seton, Ernest Thompson. Johnny Bear. 2004. reprint ed. pap. 1.99 *(978-1-4192-2787-5(4));* pap. 15.95 *(978-1-4191-2787-8(X))* Kessinger Publishing, LLC.
—Wild Animals I Have Known. 2009. 116p. pap. 9.50 *(978-1-60459-623-6(6))* Wilder Pubns., Corp.
Settino, Erica. I Am Everything & Everything Is Me. 2011. 32p. pap. 19.95 *(978-1-4560-0275-6(9))* America Star Bks.
Seuling, Barbara. Robert Takes a Stand. Brewer, Paul, illus. 2004. (Robert Bks.). (ENG.). 120p. (J). 15.95 *(978-0-8126-2712-1(1))* Cricket Bks.
Seuss, Dr. All Aboard the Circus McGurkus. 2004. (Dr. Seuss Nursery Collection). (ENG., Illus.). 10p. (J). (— 1). bds. 7.99 *(978-0-375-83011-2(1),* Random Hse. Bks. for Young Readers) Random Hse. Children's Bks.
Sewell, Anna. Black Beauty. l.t. ed. 2010. (ENG.). 260p. pap. 22.95 *(978-1-4104-2390-0(5),* Kennebec Large Print) Cengage Gale.
Shaber, Mark. Animals & Stuff. LaGrange, Tiffany, illus. 2008. 32p. pap. 12.95 *(978-1-934246-10-8(7))* Peppertree Pr., The.
Shah, Idries. The Clever Boy & the Terrible, Dangerous Animal. Santiago, Rose Mary, illus. 2005. 32p. (J). (gr. -1 — 1). pap. 6.99 *(978-1-883536-51-0(0),* Hoopoe Bks.) I S H K.
—The Clever Boy & the Terrible, Dangerous Animal/el Muchachito Listo y el Terrible y Peligroso Animal. Wirkala, Rita, tr. Santiago, Rose Mary, illus. 2005. 32p. (J). (gr. -1-3). 18.00 *(978-1-883536-39-8(1));* pap., per. 6.95 *(978-1-883536-40-4(5))* I S H K. (Hoopoe Bks.).
Shannon, George. Lizard's Guest. Aruego, Jose & Dewey, Ariane, illus. 2003. 32p. (J). 16.89 *(978-0-06-009084-5(7))* HarperCollins Pubs.
—Turkey Tot. Mann, Jennifer K., illus. (ENG.). 32p. (J). (gr. -1-1). 2014. 6.99 *(978-0-8234-3175-5(4))* 2013. 16.95 *(978-0-8234-2379-8(4))* Holiday Hse., Inc.
—Wise Acres. Zemke, Deborah, illus. 2004. (ENG.). 40p. (J). (gr. -1-7). 15.95 *(978-1-59354-041-8(8),* Handprint Bks.) Chronicle Bks. LLC.
Sharp, Margery. The Rescuers. Williams, Garth, illus. 2016. (ENG.). 160p. (J). (gr. 4-7). pap. 9.99 *(978-1-68137-007-1(7),* NYRB Kids) New York Review of Bks., Inc., The.
Shaskan, Stephen. A Dog Is a Dog. 2011. (ENG., Illus.). 40p. (J). (gr. -1-1). 14.99 *(978-0-8118-7896-8(1))* Chronicle Bks. LLC.
Shaver, Susan M. Flying Cowboys. 2011. 32p. pap. 14.99 *(978-1-4567-9450-7(7))* AuthorHouse.
Shaw, Bill. If Baby Bucking Bulls Could Talk. Wells, Jack J., illus. 2010. 20p. 14.95 *(978-1-4269-3227-4(8))* Trafford Publishing.
Shaw, Dana Alton, III. My Friend Zundel. 2006. per. *(978-0-9791091-0-2(8))* Shaw, Dana.
Shaw, Stephanie. By the Light of the Moon. Harry, Rebecca, illus. 2016. (ENG.). 22p. (J). (gr. -1-k). bds. 8.99 *(978-1-58925-221-9(7))* Tiger Tales.
—Under the Sleepy Stars. Harry, Rebecca, illus. 2015. (ENG.). 22p. (J). (gr. -1-3). bds. 8.99 *(978-1-58925-204-2(7))* Tiger Tales.
Shea, Bob. Cheetah Can't Lose. Shea, Bob, illus. 2013. (ENG., Illus.). 40p. (J). (gr. -1-3). 17.99 *(978-0-06-173083-2(1))* HarperCollins Pubs.
Shea-Gass, Lucille. How Animals Sleep Vol. 1: In Africa. 2004. 48p. pap. 24.95 *(978-1-4137-2039-6(0))* PublishAmerica, Inc.
Shea, Therese. Bear Likes to Share. 2006. (Neighborhood Readers Ser.). (ENG.). 8p. (gr. -1-3). pap. 5.15 *(978-1-4042-5696-5(2),* Rosen Classroom) Rosen Publishing Group, Inc., The.
Shein, Daniel Erik. Aurora Spirit Bear of the North: Aurora. 2005. (ENG., Illus.). 32p. (J). pap. 9.99 *(978-0-9765358-1-2(5))* Ark Watch Holdings LLC.
Shepherd, Donna J. Bradybug. Grady, Kit, illus. 2010. 20p. pap. 10.95 *(978-1-61633-071-2(6))* Guardian Angel Publishing, Inc.
Sherry, Kevin. Meet the Bigfeet. 2014. (Yeti Files Ser.: 1). (ENG.). 128p. (J). (gr. 2-5). 8.99 *(978-0-545-55617-0(1),* Scholastic Pr.) Scholastic, Inc.
—Remy Sneakers vs. the Robo-Rats. Sherry, Kevin, illus. 2017. (Remy Sneakers Ser.: 1). (ENG., Illus.). 128p. (J). (gr. 2-5). 9.99 ***(978-1-338-03460-8(X),*** Scholastic Pr.) Scholastic, Inc.
Sherry, Kevin. Turtle Island. 2014. (ENG.). 40p. (J). (gr. -1-k). 16.99 *(978-0-8037-3391-6(7),* Dial Bks) Penguin Young Readers Group.
Sherwood, Lance. Grandpa Tales. 2012. 54p. pap. 14.95 *(978-0-615-72525-3(2))* Spitzer, Lance.
Shields, Carol Diggory. Wombat Walkabout. Blackall, Sophie, illus. 2009. (ENG.). 32p. (J). (gr. -1-k). 16.99 *(978-0-525-47865-2(5),* Dutton Books for Young Readers) Penguin Young Readers Group.
Shipman, Gary, illus. Pakkins' Land: Tavitah, 4. 2003. (Pakkins' Land: 4). 128p. pap. 16.95 *(978-0-9700241-4-5(2))* Pakkins Presents.
Shoshan, Beth. That's When I'm Happy. East, Jacqueline, illus. 2011. *(978-1-4351-3618-2(7))* Barnes & Noble, Inc.
The Show: Individual Title Six-Packs. (Sails Literacy Ser.). 16p. (gr. k-18). 27.00 *(978-0-7635-4413-3(2))* Rigby Education.
Shreeve, Elizabeth. Hector Afloat. Levy, Pamela R., illus. 2004. (Ready-For-Chapters Ser.: 3). (ENG.). 64p. (J). (gr. 1-4). pap. 6.99 *(978-0-689-86416-2(7),* Simon & Schuster/Paula Wiseman Bks.) Simon & Schuster/Paula Wiseman Bks.
Shue, Jenna. Animal Island. Herzog, Inge, illus. 2005. 27p. (J). (gr. -1-3). per. 14.95 *(978-1-4259-0039-7(9))* AuthorHouse.
Shulman, Mark. Foxy Fox. Chambers, Sally, illus. 2004. 8p. (J). bds. 6.95 *(978-1-58925-738-2(3))* Tiger Tales.
—Gorilla Garage, 0 vols. Nguyen, Vincent, illus. 2013. (ENG.). 42p. (J). (gr. -1-3). pap. 9.99 *(978-1-4778-1663-9(1),* 9781477816639, Amazon Children's Publishing) Amazon Publishing.
Shutt, Susan R. Four Seasons in the Spring House: Book 1. 2012. 16p. pap. 15.99 *(978-1-4772-7493-4(6))* AuthorHouse.
—Four Seasons in the Spring House: Book 1. 2013. 24p. pap. 9.99 *(978-0-9897588-0-2(X))* Omega Prime, LLC.
Siclari, Theresa. The Pond Behind Grandmother's House. 2007. 32p. per. 24.95 *(978-1-4137-8597-5(2))* America Star Bks.
Siebold, Kim, illus. ABC, Now You See Me. 2015. (ENG.). 14p. (J). (gr. -1-17). bds. 7.95 *(978-0-7624-5854-7(2),* Running Pr. Kids) Running Pr. Bk. Pubs.
Sierra, Judy. Make Way for Readers. Karas, G. Brian, illus. 2016. (ENG.). 32p. (J). (gr. -1-3). 17.99 *(978-1-4814-1851-5(3),* Simon & Schuster Bks. For Young Readers) Simon & Schuster Bks. For Young Readers.
—We Love Our School! A Read-Together Rebus Story. Davick, Linda, illus. 2011. (ENG.). 24p. (J). (gr. -1-2). 7.99 *(978-0-375-86728-6(7),* Knopf Bks. for Young Readers) Random Hse. Children's Bks.
Signor, Priscilla M. The Adventures of Hooch & Mile-A-Minute-Freebee. Buehrle, Jacquelyn, illus. 2011. 28p. pap. 24.95 *(978-1-4560-0936-6(2))* America Star Bks.
Silver Dolphin en Español Editors. Disney Animales Cine en Casa. 2003. (Cine en casa Disney Ser.). (SPA., Illus.). 46p. (J). *(978-970-718-112-0(5),* Silver Dolphin en Español) Advanced Marketing, S. de R. L. de C. V.
—Figuras Magicas: Disney Magical Magnets. 2005. (SPA., Illus.). 8p. (J). bds. *(978-970-718-242-4(3),* Silver Dolphin en Español) Advanced Marketing, S. de R. L. de C. V.
Silver Dolphin en Español Staff, creator. Musica en Casa Libro de Cuentos. 2007. (Illus.). 38p. (J). (gr. -1-3). incl. audio compact disk *(978-970-718-494-7(9),* Silver Dolphin en Español) Advanced Marketing, S. de R. L. de C. V.
Silverstein, Shel. A Giraffe & a Half. Silverstein, Shel, illus. 40th anniv. ed. 2014. (ENG., Illus.). 48p. (J). (gr. -1-3). 17.99 *(978-0-06-025655-5(9))* HarperCollins Pubs.
Silvestro, Annie. Bunny's Book Club. Mai-Wyss, Tatjana, illus. 2017. (ENG.). 40p. (J). (gr. -1-2). 17.99 *(978-0-553-53758-1(X),* Doubleday Bks. for Young Readers) Random Hse. Children's Bks.
Silvestro, Martha Jo. A to Z My Alphabet Zoo. 2010. 148p. pap. 33.75 *(978-1-60911-199-1(0),* Eloquent Bks.) Strategic Book Publishing & Rights Agency (SBPRA).
Silvey, Diane. Time of the Thunderbird. Mantha, John, illus. 2008. (ENG.). 88p. (J). (gr. 6-5). pap. 11.99 *(978-1-55002-792-1(1),* Sandcastle Bks.) Dundurn CAN. Dist: Ingram Publisher Services.
Simmons, Joy. I Can't Wait to Be on TV! 2013. (ENG., Illus.). 80p. pap. *(978-1-78306-103-7(0))* Troubador Publishing Ltd.
Simmons, Lynn Sheffield. Sugar Lump, the Orphan Calf, 1 vol. 2003. (ENG., Illus.). 50p. (J). (gr. k-5). 12.95 *(978-1-58980-216-2(0))* Pelican Publishing Co., Inc.
Simon, Romain, illus. Forest Animals. 2011. 90p. 38.95 *(978-1-258-10284-5(6))* Literary Licensing, LLC.
Simon Spotlight, creator. Dora & Diego's Adventures! 2007. (Dora the Explorer Ser.). (ENG., Illus.). 80p. (J). (gr. -1-2). 7.99 *(978-1-4169-3532-2(0),* Simon Spotlight/Nickelodeon) Simon Spotlight/Nickelodeon.
Simonson, Lona. Noodles by Mcnoodle. Herges, Connie, illus. 2008. 28p. pap. 24.95 *(978-1-60441-644-2(0))* America Star Bks.
Sims, Janice. Grandma's Basket. Storr, Nicola, illus. 2010. 28p. pap. *(978-1-904408-68-0(0))* Bank House Bks.
Sims, Lesley, ed. Illustrated Animal Stories. Mason, Conrad, illus. 2009. (Illustrated Stories Ser.). 352p. (YA). (gr. 3-18). 19.99 *(978-0-7945-2235-3(1),* Usborne) EDC Publishing.
Sims, Nat. Peekaboo Barn. Tabor, Nathan, illus. 2014. (Peekaboo Ser.). (ENG.). 20p. (J). (— 1). bds. 7.99 *(978-0-7636-7557-8(1),* Candlewick Entertainment) Candlewick Pr.
—¿Quién Está en el Granero? Tabor, Nathan, illus. 2017. (ENG & SPA.). 20p. (J). (— 1). bds. 7.99 *(978-0-7636-9315-2(4),* Candlewick Entertainment) Candlewick Pr.
Simson, Dana. Zooballie. 2003. (Sparkle Bks.). (J). bds. 10.95 *(978-1-74047-207-4(1))* Book Co. Publishing Pty, Ltd., The AUS. Dist: Penton Overseas, Inc.

Sina-Atanda, Moyin. The Phenomenal Four: Four on a Mission to Save the Animals. 2013. 52p. (gr. 4-6). pap. 10.03 (978-1-4669-7291-9(2)) Trafford Publishing.

Singer, Isaac Bashevis. Why Noah Chose the Dove. Shub, Elizabeth, tr. Carle, Eric, illus. 2013. (ENG.). 32p. (J). (gr. 2-4). 7.99 (978-1-250-02199-1(5), 9781250021991) Square Fish.

—Why Noah Chose the Dove. 2013. (J). lib. bdg. 18.40 (978-0-606-28425-7(7), Turtleback) Turtleback Bks.

Singleton, Linda Joy. Kelsey the Spy. 2016. (Curious Cat Spy Club Ser.: 3). (ENG.). 304p. (J). (gr. 3-7). pap. 9.99 (978-0-8075-1384-2(9)) Whitman, Albert & Co.

Sinnott, Bruce. A Special Place. 2005. (J). pap. 8.00 (978-0-8059-6678-7(1)) Dorrance Publishing Co., Inc.

Siomades, Lorianne. Cuckoo Can't Find You. Siomades, Lorianne, illus. 2003. (ENG., Illus.). 32p. (J). (gr. -1-18). 12.95 (978-1-56397-778-7(8)) Boyds Mills Pr.

Sirko, Teodora. Aesop's Fables. 2007. 36p. per. 17.95 (978-1-84753-698-3(0)) Lulu Pr., Inc.

Sís, Peter. Madlenka's Dog, 1 vol. (ENG., Illus.). 32p. 19.95 (978-0-88899-462-2(1)) Groundwood Bks. CAN. Dist: Publishers Group West (PGW).

Sisler, Celeste & Fox, Jennifer. Meet Fawn. 2015. (Passport to Reading Level 1 Ser.). (ENG., Illus.). 32p. (J). (gr. -1-3). pap. 3.99 (978-0-316-28350-2(9)) Little, Brown Bks. for Young Readers.

Skerwarski, N. D. Freddy Freckles: Friends, Flags, Facts & Fun. Wooten, Neal, illus. 2007. 52p. (J). pap. 16.99 (978-0-9800675-3-8(7)) Mirror Publishing.

Slate, Joseph. Miss Bindergarten Takes a Field Trip with Kindergarten. Wolff, Ashley, illus. 2004. (ENG.). 40p. (J). (gr. -1-k). pap. 6.99 (978-0-14-240139-2(0), Puffin Books) Penguin Young Readers Group.

Slater, Teddy. Four Fiddlers. Kennedy, Kelly, illus. 2005. (Number Tales Ser.). (ENG.). 16p. (J). (gr. -1-1). pap. 2.99 (978-0-439-69008-9(0)) Scholastic, Inc.

Slegers, Liesbet. Funny Tails. 2011. (Funny Board Bks.). (ENG.). 16p. (J). (gr. k — 1). bds. 9.95 (978-1-60537-090-3(8)) Cobblestone Publishing Co.

—Surprise! 2012. (ENG.). 12p. (J). (gr. k — 1). bds. 7.95 (978-1-60537-117-7(3)) Cobblestone Publishing Co.

Small, Lily. Daisy the Deer. 2017. (Fairy Animals of Misty Wood Ser.). (ENG., Illus.). 144p. (J). pap. 5.99 (978-1-62779-738-2(6), 9781627797382, Holt, Henry & Co. Bks. For Young Readers) Holt, Henry & Co.

—Hailey the Hedgehog. 2016. (Fairy Animals of Misty Wood Ser.). (ENG., Illus.). 144p. (J). pap. 5.99 (978-1-62779-735-1(1), 9781627797351, Holt, Henry & Co. Bks. For Young Readers) Holt, Henry & Co.

—Poppy the Pony. 2016. (Fairy Animals of Misty Wood Ser.). (ENG., Illus.). 144p. (J). pap. 5.99 (978-1-62779-734-4(3), 9781627797344, Holt, Henry & Co. Bks. For Young Readers) Holt, Henry & Co.

Smee, Nicola. Clip-Clop. 2006. (Illus.). 32p. (J). (978-1-905417-03-2(9)) Boxer Bks., Ltd.

—Jingle-Jingle. 2008. (ENG., Illus.). 32p. (J). (gr. -1-1). 14.95 (978-1-906250-08-9(1)) Boxer Bks., Ltd. GBR. Dist: Sterling Publishing Co,, Inc.

Smith, Clyde. The Bashful Bull of Buchanan County. 2012. 24p. pap. 24.95 (978-1-4626-8111-2(5)) America Star Bks.

Smith, E. Boyd. Noah's Ark: The Story of the Flood & After. 2011. (Dover Children's Classics Ser.). (ENG., Illus.). 112p. (gr. -1-5). pap. 15.00 (978-0-486-47745-9(2)) Dover Pubns., Inc.

Smith, Jeff. Rock Jaw: Master of the Eastern Border. Smith, Jeff & Hamaker, Steve, illus. 2007. (Bone Ser.: 5). (ENG.). 128p. (J). (gr. 4-7). pap. 12.99 (978-0-439-70636-0(X), Graphix) Scholastic, Inc.

—Rock Jaw: Master of the Eastern Border. Hamaker, Steve & Smith, Jeff, illus. 2007. (Bone Ser.: 5). (ENG.). 128p. (J). (gr. 4-7). 24.99 (978-0-439-70627-8(0), Graphix) Scholastic, Inc.

Smith, Jeff & Sniegoski, Tom. Tall Tales. Smith, Jeff, illus. 2010. (Bone Ser.). (ENG., Illus.). 128p. (J). (gr. 4-7). pap. 12.99 (978-0-545-14096-6(X), Graphix) Scholastic, Inc.

Smith, Jodene Lynn & Reid, Stephanie. Los Animales, 1 vol. rev. ed. 2010. (Early Childhood Themes Ser.). (SPA., Illus.). 16p. (J). (gr. -1-2). pap. 19.99 (978-1-4333-2119-1(X)); pap. 6.99 (978-1-4333-2118-4(1)) Shell Educational Publishing.

—Animals, 1 vol. 2010. (Early Childhood Themes Ser.). (ENG., Illus.). 16p. (J). (gr. -1-2). pap. 19.99 (978-1-4333-1480-3(0)); pap. 6.99 (978-1-4333-1479-7(7)) Shell Educational Publishing.

Smith, Jodene Lynn & Rice, Dona. Animal Homes, 1 vol. 2010. (Early Childhood Themes Ser.). (ENG., Illus.). 16p. (J). (gr. -1-2). pap. 6.99 (978-1-4333-1481-0(9)) Shell Educational Publishing.

Smith, Jodene Lynn & Rice, Dona Herweck. Animal Homes, 1 vol. 2010. (Early Childhood Themes Ser.). (ENG., Illus.). 16p. (J). (gr. -1-2). pap. 19.99 (978-1-4333-1482-7(7)) Shell Educational Publishing.

Smith, John D. H. The Whale Whisperers, 1 vol. Smith, Anne, illus. 2009. 17p. pap. 24.95 (978-1-60749-211-5(3)) America Star Bks.

Smith, Justine. Zak Zoo & the Baffled Burglar. Elsom, Clare, illus. 2013. (ENG.). 32p. (J). (gr. k-2). pap. 7.99 (978-1-4083-1342-8(1)) Hodder & Stoughton GBR. Dist: Hachette Bk. Group.

Smith, Kristie Lyn. Dottie & Dots See Animal Spots: Learning Braille with Dots & Dottie. 2007. 52p. per. 8.95 (978-0-595-47130-0(7)) iUniverse, Inc.

Smith, Lane. A Perfect Day. Smith, Lane, illus. 2017. (ENG., Illus.). 32p. (J). 17.99 (978-1-62672-536-2(5), 9781626725362) Roaring Brook Pr.

—There Is a Tribe of Kids. Smith, Lane, illus. 2016. (ENG., Illus.). 40p. (J). 18.99 (978-1-62672-056-5(8), 9781626720565) Roaring Brook Pr.

Smith, Laura R. & Fearis, J. S. Little Sir Echo. Faulkner, Stacey, ed. 2006. (J). pap. 2.99 (978-1-59198-318-7(5)) Creative Teaching Pr., Inc.

Smith, Laura Rountree. Snubby Nose & Tippy Toes. 2004. reprint ed. pap. 1.99 (978-1-4192-4792-7(1)); pap. 15.95 (978-1-4191-4792-0(7)) Kessinger Publishing, LLC.

Smith, Maggie Caldwell. Tommy Wilson, Junior Veterinarian: The Case of the Wounded Jack Rabbit. McHose, Jean, illus. 2005. 104p. (J). (gr. 3-6). pap. 7.95 (978-1-889159-14-0(X)) Magpie Pr., Pine Mountain Club, CA.

Smith, Naniloa. The Children are Happy CD with Animals from the Southwest. Smith, Naniloa, ed. 2004. (Illus.). (J). cd-rom 5.00 (978-0-9744005-2-5(1)) In the Desert.

Smith, Paul. The Little Lost Egg. Smith, Steven, illus. 2017. (ENG.). (gr. 1). pap. **(978-1-78222-500-3(5))** Paragon Publishing, Rothersthorpe.

Smith, Roland. Eruption. 2012. (Storm Runners Ser.: 3). (ENG.). 160p. (J). (gr. 3-7). 16.99 (978-0-545-08174-0(2), Scholastic Pr.) Scholastic, Inc.

—Storm Runners. (Storm Runners Ser.: Bk. 1). (ENG.). 160p. (J). (gr. 3-7). 2012. pap. 5.99 (978-0-545-08177-1(7), Scholastic Pr.) 2011. 16.99 (978-0-545-08175-7(0)) Scholastic, Inc.

—The Surge. 2011. (Storm Runners Ser.: 2). (J). (ENG.). 144p. (gr. 3-7). 16.99 (978-0-545-08179-5(3)); 133p. pap. (978-0-545-39462-8(7)) Scholastic, Inc. (Scholastic Pr.).

Smith, Sarah, illus. Where's My Mommy? 2009. (J). (978-0-7607-8404-4(3)) Barnes & Noble, Inc.

Smith, Sindy. Little Lucy Lou. Smith, Sindy, illus. 2012. (Illus.). 38p. 29.95 (978-1-4489-3350-1(1)) America Star Bks.

—Mr. Minko. Smith, Sindy, illus. 2012. (Illus.). 38p. 29.95 (978-1-4626-9863-9(8)) America Star Bks.

—The Tale of Pinky Wink Possum. 2013. 28p. 24.95 (978-1-63004-803-7(8)); pap. 24.95 (978-1-63004-388-9(5)) America Star Bks.

Smith, Timothy R. The Owls Don't Give a Hoot. 2007. (Buck Wilder's Adventure Ser.: 4). (Illus.). 80p. (J). (gr. -1-3). per. 5.95 (978-1-934133-11-8(6), Mackinac Island Press, Inc.) Charlesbridge Publishing, Inc.

Smithem, Beth. Cocoa Bean & Squirt. 2010. 68p. pap. 10.49 (978-1-4520-1929-1(0)) AuthorHouse.

—The Misadventures of Dust Bunny. 2009. 84p. pap. 10.49 (978-1-4389-4093-9(9)) AuthorHouse.

Smythe, I. H. Stories for Animals. 2011. 212p. 24.95 (978-1-4502-9666-3(1)); pap. 14.95 (978-1-4502-9625-0(4)) iUniverse, Inc.

Snappy Fun Slipcase. (Slipcase Ser.). (Illus.). (J). (gr. -1-k). (978-1-57584-678-1(0)) Studio Fun International.

Sniegoski, Tom & Smith, Jeff. Tall Tales. Smith, Jeff, illus. 2010. (Bone Ser.). (ENG., Illus.). 128p. (J). (gr. 4-7). 26.99 (978-0-545-14095-9(1), Graphix) Scholastic, Inc.

Snyder, Karen. Safari Smooches. LaGrange, Tiffany, illus. 2011. 24p. pap. 12.95 (978-1-936343-95-9(9)) Peppertree Pr., The.

Sockabasin, Allen & Raye, Rebekah. Thanks to the Animals, 1 vol. 2nd ed. 2014. (ENG., Illus.). 36p. (gr. 1-6). 17.95 (978-0-88448-414-1(9), 884414) Tilbury Hse. Pubs.

Soleim, Heather. God's Incredible Creatures: The Gift of Sharing. Greisen, Steve, ed. Hedgecock, Sean, illus. 2005. 24p. (J). bds. 14.95 (978-0-9707422-9-2(0)) Reel Productions, LLC.

Sollenne, Ava. Ava & Happy's Awesome Adventures. 2012. 32p. pap. 19.99 (978-1-4772-0538-9(1)) AuthorHouse.

Solomon, Carl, Sr. Do Animals Believe in God? 2004. 7p. (J). pap. 10.99 (978-1-4116-1312-6(0)) Lulu Pr., Inc.

Someday We'll Understand. 2006. (J). bds. 21.95 (978-0-9745191-1-1(1)) Lynn Tyner Mitchum & James Rogers.

Sommer, Carl. If Only I Were- James, Kennon, illus. 2014. (J). pap. (978-1-57537-954-8(6)) Advance Publishing, Inc.

—King of the Pond. 2003. (Another Sommer-Time Story Ser.). (Illus.). 48p. (J). (gr. k-4). lib. bdg. 23.95 incl. audio (978-1-57537-766-7(7)); (gr. 1-4). 16.95 incl. audio (978-1-57537-565-6(6)) Advance Publishing, Inc.

—King of the Pond. Budwine, Greg, illus. 2003. (Another Sommer-Time Story Ser.). (ENG.). 48p. (J). (gr. k-4). lib. bdg. 23.95 incl. audio compact disk (978-1-57537-716-2(0)); (gr. 1-4). 16.95 incl. audio compact disk (978-1-57537-516-8(8)) Advance Publishing, Inc.

—Noise! Noise! Noise! James, Kennon, illus. (J). 2014. pap. (978-1-57537-963-0(5)) 2003. (ENG.). 48p. 9.95 (978-1-57537-020-0(4)) 2003. (ENG.). 48p. lib. bdg. 16.95 (978-1-57537-069-9(7)) 2003. (ENG.). 48p. (gr. 1-4). 16.95 incl. audio compact disk (978-1-57537-519-9(2)) Advance Publishing, Inc.

—Noise! Noise! Noise! 2003. (Another Sommer-Time Story Ser.). (Illus.). 48p. (J). (gr. 1-4). 16.95 incl. audio (978-1-57537-568-7(0)) Advance Publishing, Inc.

—Noise! Noise! Noise! Read-along 2003. (Another Sommer-Time Story Ser.). (Illus.). 48p. (J). lib. bdg. 23.95 incl. audio (978-1-57537-769-8(1)) Advance Publishing, Inc.

—Noise! Noise! Noise!(Ruido! Ruido! Ruido!) James, Kennon, illus. 2009. (Another Sommer-Time Story Bilingual Ser.). (SPA & ENG.). 48p. (J). lib. bdg. 16.95 (978-1-57537-161-0(8)) Advance Publishing, Inc.

—The Sly Fox & the Chicks. 2003. (Another Sommer-Time Story Ser.). (Illus.). 48p. (J). (gr. 1-4). 16.95 incl. audio (978-1-57537-553-3(2)) Advance Publishing, Inc.

—The Sly Fox & the Chicks. James, Kennon, illus. 2003. (Another Sommer-Time Story Ser.). (ENG.). 48p. (J). 16.95 incl. audio compact disk (978-1-57537-504-5(4)) Advance Publishing, Inc.

—You Move You Lose. 2003. (Another Sommer-Time Story Ser.). (Illus.). 48p. (J). (gr. 1-4). 16.95 incl. audio (978-1-57537-554-0(0)) Advance Publishing, Inc.

—You Move You Lose. James, Kennon, illus. 2003. (Another Sommer-Time Story Ser.). (ENG.). 48p. (J). (gr. 1-4). 16.95 incl. audio compact disk (978-1-57537-505-2(2)) Advance Publishing, Inc.

Song & Juniper. 2006. (Song @ Juniper Ser.). (Illus.). 32p. (J). 17.95 (978-0-9771990-0-6(2)) Big Kid Bks.

Soto, Gary. Chato & the Party Animals. Guevara, Susan, illus. (Chato Ser.). 28.95 incl. audio compact disk (978-1-59112-920-2(6)); 25.95 incl. audio (978-1-59112-460-3(3)); pap. 39.95 incl. audio compact disk (978-1-59112-921-9(4)); pap. 37.95 incl. audio (978-1-59112-461-0(1)) Live Oak Media.

—Chato & the Party Animals. Guevara, Susan, illus. 2004. (Chato Ser.). (ENG.). 32p. (J). (gr. -1-3). reprint ed. pap. 7.99 (978-0-14-240032-6(7), Puffin Books) Penguin Young Readers Group.

—Chato & the Party Animals. Guevara, Susan, illus. 2004. (Chato Ser.). (gr. -1-3). 17.00 (978-0-7569-2921-3(0)) Perfection Learning Corp.

—Chato y los Amigos Pachangueros. Guevara, Susan, illus. 2004.Tr. of Chato & the Party Animals. (SPA & ENG.). 32p. (J). (gr. -1-3). reprint ed. pap. 7.99 (978-0-14-240033-3(5), Puffin Books) Penguin Young Readers Group.

Soule, Jean Conder. Never Tease a Weasel. Booth, George, illus. 2011. (ENG.). 40p. (J). (gr. -1-2). pap. 6.99 (978-0-375-87285-3(X), Dragonfly Bks.) Random Hse. Children's Bks.

Soundprints Staff. Smithsonian's Backyard Collection Micro 4 Book Set. 2007. (ENG.). 32p. 14.95 (978-1-59249-751-5(9)); 14.95 (978-1-59249-750-8(0)) Soundprints.

Souza, Sandy. Kirby & the Coyote. 2012. 20p. pap. 17.99 (978-1-4634-1928-8(7)) AuthorHouse.

Sowach, Rick. Critters, Flitters & Spitters: 24 Amazing Ohio Animal Tales. 2003. (J). 19.95 (978-0-9762412-3-2(4)) Sowash, Rick Publishing Co.

Sowash, Rick. Critters, Flitters & Spitters: 24 Amazing Ohio Animal Tales. 2003. (J). pap. 11.95 (978-0-9762412-2-5(6)) Sowash, Rick Publishing Co.

Spaeth, Heidi. Cici Finds a Home. 2009. 32p. pap. 16.99 (978-1-4490-3708-6(9)) AuthorHouse.

Spafford, Suzy. Helping-Out Day? Hooray! Spafford, Suzy, illus. 2003. (Tales from Duckport Ser.). (ENG., Illus.). 40p. (J). (gr. k-3). pap. 3.99 (978-0-439-38358-5(7)) Scholastic, Inc.

—Witzy's Fall Collection. 2010. (Illus.). (J). (978-1-4037-9599-1(1)) Creative Edge.

Spagnol, Estelle Billon. Little Benguin. Spagnol, Estelle Billon, illus. 2014. (ENG., Illus.). 32p. (J). (gr. -1-1). 16.95 (978-0-8234-2934-9(2)) Holiday Hse., Inc.

Spaht-Gill, Janie. Gator's Out, Said the Trout. Reese, Bob, illus. (J). (gr. k-2). 5.95 (978-0-89868-305-9(X)) ARO Publishing Co.

Spalding, Brenda M. Hayden's Garden. 2012. pap. 13.95 (978-0-7414-7961-7(3)) Infinity Publishing.

The Sparkling Beauty. 2006. Orig. Title: Televisual Book. (J). 18.99 (978-0-9779672-0-9(4)) Karsonkina, Tatiana.

Sparrow, Leilani. My First Day. Taylor, Dan, illus. 2015. (ENG.). 32p. (J). (gr. -1-k). 16.99 (978-1-4998-0111-8(4)) Little Bee Books Inc.

—My New Shoes. Taylor, Dan, illus. 2016. (ENG.). 32p. (J). (gr. -1-k). 16.99 (978-1-4998-0363-1(X)) Little Bee Books Inc.

Speed, Bryan W. Little Bent Cedar. Todd, Sheri, illus. 2007. (ENG.). 24p. (J). (gr. 2-4). per. (978-1-933255-38-5(2)) DNA Pr.

Spiewak, Chet. Vinney the Bug Man: The Journey Begins. 2007. (Illus.). 80p. (J). per. 9.95 (978-0-9785827-1-5(3)) CWS Studios, Inc.

Spinelli, Eileen. Buzz. Nguyen, Vincent, illus. 2010. (ENG.). 32p. (J). (gr. -1-3). 17.99 (978-1-4169-4925-1(9), Simon & Schuster Bks. For Young Readers) Simon & Schuster Bks. For Young Readers.

—Miss Fox's Class Earns a Field Trip. Kennedy, Anne, illus. 2012. (J). (978-1-61913-122-4(6)) Weigl Pubs., Inc.

—Miss Fox's Class Earns a Field Trip, 1 vol. Kennedy, Anne, illus. 2010. (Miss Fox's Class Ser.). (ENG.). 32p. (J). (gr. 1-3). 16.99 (978-0-8075-5169-1(4)) Whitman, Albert & Co.

—Miss Fox's Class Gets It Wrong. Kennedy, Anne, illus. 2012. (Miss Fox's Class Ser.). (ENG.). 32p. (J). (gr. -1-3). 16.99 (978-0-8075-5165-3(1)) Whitman, Albert & Co.

—Miss Fox's Class Goes Green. Kennedy, Anne, illus. 2012. (J). 34.28 (978-1-61913-123-1(4)) Weigl Pubs., Inc.

—Miss Fox's Class Goes Green. Kennedy, Anne, illus. 2011. (Miss Fox's Class Ser.). (ENG.). 32p. (J). (gr. 1-3). 6.99 (978-0-8075-5167-7(8)) Whitman, Albert & Co.

—Miss Fox's Class Shapes Up. Kennedy, Anne, illus. 2011. (ENG.). 32p. (J). (gr. 1-3). 16.99 (978-0-8075-5171-4(6)) Whitman, Albert & Co.

—Peace Week in Miss Fox's Class. Kennedy, Anne, illus. 2012. (J). (978-1-61913-155-2(2)) Weigl Pubs., Inc.

—When Christmas Came. Parmenter, Wayne, illus. 2006. (ENG.). 32p. (J). (gr. k-3). bds. 16.95 (978-0-8249-5507-6(2), Ideal Pubns.) Worthy Publishing.

Spohn, Kate. Turtle & Snake's Day at the Beach. Spohn, Kate, illus. 2004. (Puffin Easy-to-Read Ser.). (Illus.). 32p. (gr. k-3). 14.00 (978-0-7569-2826-1(5)) Perfection Learning Corp.

Sprout Street Neighbors: Five Stories. 2015. (Sprout Street Neighbors Ser.). (ENG., Illus.). 112p. (J). (gr. 1-4). 12.99 (978-0-385-75558-0(9), Knopf Bks. for Young Readers) Random Hse. Children's Bks.

Squier, Emma-Lindsay. On Autumn Trails & Adventures in Captivity. 2004. reprint ed. pap. 26.95 (978-1-4179-2651-0(1)) Kessinger Publishing, LLC.

Sretaw. Aussie Animal Friends. 2010. 36p. pap. 32.70 (978-1-4500-7415-5(4)) Xlibris Corp.

—Homonym Hunt. 2010. 24p. pap. 28.03 (978-1-4500-5228-3(2)) Xlibris Corp.

Srinivasan, Divya. Little Owl's Day. Srinivasan, Divya, illus. 2014. (ENG., Illus.). 32p. (J). (gr. -1-k). 16.99 (978-0-670-01650-1(0), Viking Books for Young Readers) Penguin Young Readers Group.

—Little Owl's Night. (ENG., 32p. (J). 2013. Illus.). (— 1). bds. 6.99 (978-0-670-01579-5(2)) 2011. (gr. -1-k). 16.99 (978-0-670-01295-4(5)) Penguin Young Readers Group. (Viking Books for Young Readers).

St. Aubyn, Douglas. Caribbean Fables. 2007. 72p. pap. (978-976-8054-72-2(7)) Paria Publishing Co., Ltd.

St. Jean, Alan. The Legend of OinkADoodleMoo. St. Jean, Alan, ed. Krock, Libby Carruth, illus. 2013. 32p. 19.95 (978-0-9777272-9-2(7)) Oren Village, LLC.

Stadler, John. Three Cheers for Hippo!, 1 vol. 2006. (ENG., Illus.). 32p. (J). (gr. -1-3). reprint ed. pap. 5.95 (978-1-59572-046-7(4)) Star Bright Bks., Inc.

Stanley, Mandy. Who Tickled Tilly? 2004. (Illus.). 32p. (J). (978-1-84458-047-7(4), Pavilion Children's Books) Pavilion Bks.

—Who Tickled Tilly? Stanley, Mandy, illus. 2011. (ENG., Illus.). 32p. (J). (gr. -1-k). pap. 7.99 (978-1-84365-192-5(0), Pavilion) Pavilion Bks. GBR. Dist: Independent Pubs. Group.

Stauffacher, Sue. Special Delivery! Lamont, Priscilla, illus. 2010. (Animal Rescue Team Ser.: No. 2). (ENG.). 176p. (J). (gr. 3-7). 12.99 (978-0-375-85848-2(2), Knopf Bks. for Young Readers) Random Hse. Children's Bks.

Staunton, Ted. Morgan Makes a Splash. Slavin, Bill, illus. 2004. (Formac First Novels Ser.: 28). (ENG.). 64p. (J). (gr. 1-5). 14.95 (978-0-88780-623-0(6), 9780887806230) Formac Publishing Co., Ltd. CAN. Dist: Casemate Pubs. & Bk. Distributors, LLC.

Stead, Philip C. Bear Has a Story to Tell. Stead, Erin E., illus. 2012. (ENG.). 32p. (J). (gr. -1-1). 16.99 (978-1-59643-745-6(6), 9781596437456) Roaring Brook Pr.

—Samson in the Snow. 2016. (ENG., Illus.). 40p. (J). 17.99 (978-1-62672-182-1(3), 9781626721821) Roaring Brook Pr.

Steig, William. Doctor de Soto. Steig, William, illus. 2010. (ENG., Illus.). 32p. (J). (gr. -1-3). pap. 7.99 (978-0-312-61189-7(7), 9780312611897) Square Fish.

Stein, David Ezra. The Nice Book. Stein, David Ezra, illus. 2013. (ENG., Illus.). 32p. (J). (gr. -1 — 1). bds. 6.99 (978-0-399-16534-4(7), Nancy Paulsen Books) Penguin Young Readers Group.

Steinkraus, Kyla. Los Problemas Del Intercambio. 2012. (SPA & ENG.). 24p. (gr. 2-3). pap. 8.95 (978-1-61810-543-1(4)) Rourke Educational Media.

—Table Wars! Dufalla, Anita, illus. 2012. (ENG.). 24p. (gr. 2-3). pap. 8.95 (978-1-61810-330-7(X)) Rourke Educational Media.

Steinkraus, Kyla & Moreta, Gladys. Stop Arguing! Reese, Bob, illus. 2011. (ENG.). 24p. (J). (gr. 2-3). pap. 8.95 (978-1-61236-036-2(X)) Rourke Educational Media.

Stephane, Nelly. Roland. François, André, illus. 2016. (ENG.). 36p. (J). (gr. -1-3). 17.95 (978-1-59270-204-6(X)) Enchanted Lion Bks., LLC.

Stephanie. The Beginning of Gerald. 2012. 28p. pap. 24.95 (978-1-62709-212-8(9)) America Star Bks.

Stephens, R. David. My Animal Friends, 1 vol. Shoemaker, Kathryn, illus. 2003. (ENG.). 32p. (J). (gr. k-3). pap. 6.95 (978-1-896580-74-6(2)) Tradewind Bks. CAN. Dist: Orca Bk. Pubs. USA.

Stephens, Sarah Hines. Super-Pets Showdown, 1 vol. Baltazar, Art, illus. 2012. (DC Super-Pets Ser.). (ENG.). 56p. (gr. 2-2). pap. 4.95 (978-1-4048-7216-5(7)); lib. bdg. 23.99 (978-1-4048-6486-3(5)) Picture Window Bks. (DC Super-Pets).

Stephenson, Midji. Whose Tail on the Trail at Grand Canyon. Spengler, Kenneth, illus. 2012. (J). (978-1-934656-55-6(0)) Grand Canyon Assn.

Steven, Kenneth. Fergus Finds a Friend, 1 vol. Crowe, Louise, illus. 2010. (ENG.). 32p. (J). (gr. -1-1). 11.95 (978-0-86315-778-3(5)) Floris Bks. GBR. Dist: SteinerBooks, Inc.

Stevens, Janet & Crummel, Susan Stevens. Jackalope. 2003. (ENG., Illus.). 56p. (J). (gr. -1-3). 17.00 (978-0-15-216736-3(6)) Houghton Mifflin Harcourt Publishing Co.

Stevenski, Linda. Chetty T Chipmunk's Journey to Aunt Ella's. 2010. 24p. (J). pap. 12.99 (978-1-4490-5448-9(X)) AuthorHouse.

Stevenson, James. Flying Feet: A Mud Flat Story. Stevenson, James, illus. 2004. (Illus.). 48p. (J). 15.99 (978-0-06-051975-9(4)) HarperCollins Pubs.

Steward, Margaret. Tamsi: The Errant Lamb. 2005. (YA). per. 9.95 (978-1-59094-094-5(6)) Jawbone Publishing Corp.

Stewart, Dianne. The Zebra's Stripes: And Other African Animal Tales. Pienaar, Kathy, illus. 2011. (ENG.). 144p. pap. 15.00 (978-1-86872-951-7(6)) Penguin Random House Grupo Editorial ESP. Dist: Casemate Pubs. & Bk. Distributors, LLC.

Stewart, Paul. Little Bit of Winter. Riddell, Chris, illus. 2013. (Rabbit & Hedgehog Ser.). (ENG.). 32p. (J). (gr. -1-k). pap. 12.99 (978-0-86264-998-2(6)) Andersen Pr. GBR. Dist: Independent Pubs. Group.

Stiefvater, Maggie & Pearce, Jackson. Pip Bartlett's Guide to Magical Creatures. 2015. (Pip Bartlett Ser.: 1). (ENG.). 192p. (J). (gr. 3-7). 16.99 (978-0-545-70926-2(1), Scholastic Pr.) Scholastic, Inc.

Stierle, Cynthia. Diego in the Dark: Being Brave at Night. Maher, Alex, illus. 2008. (Go, Diego, Go! Ser.). (ENG.). 16p. (J). (gr. -1-2). pap. 6.99 (978-1-4169-5935-9(1), Simon Spotlight/Nickelodeon) Simon Spotlight/Nickelodeon.

Stihler, Cherie B. Polar Polka: Counting Polar Bears in Alaska. Brooks, Erik, illus. 2008. (Paws IV Ser.). (ENG.). 32p. (J). (gr. -1-2). pap. 10.95 (978-1-57061-520-7(9), Little Bigfoot) Sasquatch Bks.

Stihler, Chérie B. The Sourdough Man: An Alaska Folktale. Lavallee, Barbara, illus. 2010. (Paws IV Ser.). (ENG.). 32p. (J). (gr. -1-2). pap. 10.99 (978-1-57061-594-8(2), Little Bigfoot) Sasquatch Bks.

Stileman, Kali. Roly Poly Egg. 2011. (ENG.). 26p. (J). (gr. -1-k). 12.95 (978-1-58925-852-5(5)) Tiger Tales.

—Snack Time for Confetti. 2013. (ENG., Illus.). 32p. (J). (gr. -1-1). 12.95 (978-1-58925-127-4(X)) Tiger Tales.

Stiles, Gannett Ruth. My Father's Dragon. 2014. (My Father's Dragon Ser.). (ENG.). 96p. (J). (gr. 4-7). 11.24 (978-1-63245-265-8(0)) Lectorum Pubns., Inc.

Stilton, Geronimo. Down & Out down Under. 2007. (Geronimo Stilton Ser.: 29). (ENG., Illus.). 128p. (J). (gr. 2-5). pap. 7.99 (978-0-439-84120-7(8), Scholastic Paperbacks) Scholastic, Inc.

—The Great Mouse Race. 2014. (Geronimo Stilton Cavemice Ser.: 5). (ENG., Illus.). 128p. (J). (gr. 2-5). pap. 7.99 (978-0-545-64654-3(5), Scholastic Paperbacks) Scholastic, Inc.

—I'm Too Fond of My Fur! Wolf, Matt, illus. 2004. (Geronimo Stilton Ser.: No. 4). 116p. (J). lib. bdg. 10.00 (978-1-4242-0698-8(7)) Fitzgerald Bks.

—The Way of the Samurai. 2012. (Geronimo Stilton Ser.: No. 49). (ENG.). 128p. (J). (gr. 2-5). pap. 7.99 (978-0-545-34101-1(9), Scholastic Paperbacks) Scholastic, Inc.

—The Way of the Samurai. 2012. (Geronimo Stilton Ser.: 49). lib. bdg. 18.40 (978-0-606-26094-7(3), Turtleback) Turtleback Bks.

Stilton, Thea. The Journey to Atlantis. 2012. (Thea Stilton Special Edition Ser.). (ENG.). 320p. (J). (gr. 2-5). 14.99 (978-0-545-44020-2(3), Scholastic Paperbacks) Scholastic, Inc.

Stine, Faye. The Magic Forest: The Magic of Childhood. 2009. 117p. (J). pap. 10.95 (978-1-4327-3617-0(5)) Outskirts Pr., Inc.

Stine, R. L. Creepy Creatures. Hernandez, Gabriel et al, illus. 2006. (Goosebumps Graphix Ser.: 1). (ENG.). 144p. (J). (gr. 3-7). pap. 9.99 (978-0-439-84125-2(9), Graphix) Scholastic, Inc.

—The Good, the Bad & the Very Slimy, 1 vol. Park, Trip, illus. 2011. (Rotten School Ser.: No. 3). (ENG.). 128p. (gr. 2-5). 24.21 *(978-1-59961-827-2(3))* Spotlight.
—Welcome to Camp Slither. 2009. (Goosebumps Horrorland Ser.: 9). (ENG.). 160p. (J). (gr. 3-7). 6.99 *(978-0-439-91877-0(4),* Scholastic Paperbacks) Scholastic, Inc.
—Werewolf of Fever Swamp. 2009. (Classic Goosebumps Ser.: 11). (ENG.). 160p. (J). (gr. 3-7). 6.99 *(978-0-545-15886-2(9),* Scholastic Paperbacks) Scholastic, Inc.
Stingley, Tanya. Jonas & the Pride of Fiona. 2008. pap. 9.00 *(978-0-8059-8685-3(5))* Dorrance Publishing Co., Inc.
Stockham, Jessica, illus. Visiting the Vet. 2011. (First Time Ser.). (ENG.). 24p. (J). (gr. 2-2). pap. *(978-1-84643-337-5(1))* Child's Play International Ltd.
Stockton, Frank Richard. Round-about Rambles in Lands of Fact & Fancy. 2006. pap. *(978-1-4068-3083-5(6))* Echo Library.
Stohner, Anu & Wilson, Henrike. Brave Charlotte. Wilson, Henrike, illus. 2005. (ENG., Illus.). 32p. (J). (gr. -1-3). 17.99 *(978-1-58234-690-8(9),* 9781582346908, Bloomsbury USA Childrens) Bloomsbury Publishing USA.
Stoick, Jean & Sams, Carl R., II, photos by. First Snow in the Woods. 2007. (ENG., Illus.). 49p. (J). (gr. -1-3). 19.95 *(978-0-9770108-6-8(4))* Sams, II, Carl R. Photography, Inc.
Stoick, Jean & Sams II, Carl R., photos by. Stranger in the Woods: Snowflake Edition. 2010. (ENG., Illus.). 48p. 21.95 *(978-0-9827625-0-9(X))* Sams, II, Carl R. Photography, Inc.
Stolberg, Tina. Little Shrew Caboose. O'Neill, Philomena, illus. 2009. (ENG.). 32p. (J). (gr. k-2). 16.95 *(978-0-9792035-7-2(0))* Pleasant St. Pr.
Stone, Jeff. Monkey. 2006. (Five Ancestors Ser.: Bk. 2). (ENG.). 208p. (J). (gr. 3-7). per. 6.99 *(978-0-375-83074-7(X),* Yearling) Random Hse. Children's Bks.
Stoop, Naoko. Red Knit Cap Girl & the Reading Tree. 2014. (ENG., Illus.). 40p. (J). (gr. -1-3). 17.00 *(978-0-316-22886-2(9))* Little, Brown Bks. for Young Readers.
Storey, Mike. Teddycats. 2016. (Teddycats Ser.: 1). (ENG.). 240p. (J). (gr. 3-7). 16.99 *(978-1-101-99883-0(0),* Razorbill) Penguin Young Readers Group.
Stortz, Diane. Adam Named the Animals from a to Z. Reed, Lisa, illus. 2012. (Roma Downey's Little Angels Ser.). 24p. (J). bds. 7.99 *(978-0-8249-5642-4(7),* Ideal Pubns.) Worthy Publishing.
Stossel, Sage. On the Loose in Boston. 2009. (Find the Animals Ser.). (ENG., Illus.). 36p. (J). (gr. k-3). 14.95 *(978-1-933212-92-0(6),* Commonwealth Editions) Applewood Bks.
—On the Loose in Washington, D. C. 2013. (ENG., Illus.). 28p. (J). (gr. -1-3). 14.95 *(978-1-938700-14-9(7),* Commonwealth Editions) Applewood Bks.
Stowe, Harriet Beecher. Queer Little Folks. 2006. pap. *(978-1-4065-1076-8(9))* Dodo Pr.
Strathie, Chae. Gorilla Loves Vanilla. O'Byrne, Nicola, illus. 2016. (ENG.). 32p. (J). (gr. -1-k). 11.99 *(978-0-7641-6853-6(3))* Barron's Educational Series, Inc.
Strauss, Kevin. Loon & Moon: And Other Animal Stories. Scheibe, Nancy, illus. 2005. 48p. (J). (gr. 4-6). per. 12.95 *(978-0-9766264-3-5(8))* Raven Productions, Inc.
Strelkoff, Tatiana. Jeremy & the Crow Nation. Martin, Bobi, ed. 2003. (Changer Ser.: Vol. 2). (Illus.). 128p. (Orig.). (J). (gr. 7-12). pap. 6.95 *(978-0-945522-04-1(5),* 2204-5) Rebecca Hse.
Stripland, Rubye Weldon. Lucy Bell, Queen of the Pasture Book Four. 2009. 94p. pap. 10.96 *(978-1-4357-4742-5(9))* Lulu Pr., Inc.
—Lucy Bell, Queen of the Pasture, Book Three. 2008. 90p. pap. 10.95 *(978-1-4357-3418-0(1))* Lulu Pr., Inc.
—Lucy Bell, Queen of the Pasture Book Two. 2008. 100p. pap. 10.95 *(978-1-4357-1895-1(X))* Lulu Pr., Inc.
Stroud-Peace, Glenda. Pearlie. Larkin, Paige A., illus. 2009. 48p. pap. 16.95 *(978-1-60844-033-7(8))* Dog Ear Publishing, LLC.
Stuart-Russell, C. Playtime with the Animals. 2007. 61p. pap. 19.95 *(978-1-4241-5473-9(1))* America Star Bks.
Studio Mouse Staff. Pooh & Roo. 2008. (ENG., Illus.). 36p. (J). (gr. -1). 7.99 *(978-1-59069-420-6(1))* Studio Mouse LLC.
—Pooh & Tigger. 2008. (ENG., Illus.). 36p. (J). (gr. -1). 7.99 *(978-1-59069-417-6(1))* Studio Mouse LLC.
Sturges, Philemon. How Do You Make a Baby Smile? Strevens-Marzo, Bridget, illus. 2007. 24p. (J). (gr. -1-k). lib. bdg. 17.89 *(978-0-06-076073-1(7))* HarperCollins Pubs.
Sturgill, Jean A. Bouncing Beaver Discovers God: A Drew's Animals Book. 2007. (ENG.). 30p. pap. 15.99 *(978-1-4196-7822-6(1))* CreateSpace Independent Publishing Platform.
Stutson, Caroline. Blue Corn Soup. Weidner, Teri, illus. 2017. (ENG.). 32p. (J). (gr. k-2). 16.99 ***(978-1-58536-967-6(5),*** 204325) Sleeping Bear Pr.
Style Guide Staff, illus. Kung Fu to the Rescue! 2014. (Kung Fu Panda TV Ser.). (ENG.). 96p. (J). (gr. 2-5). pap. 5.99 *(978-1-4814-0511-9(X),* Simon Spotlight) Simon Spotlight.
—Po's Secret Move. 2014. (Kung Fu Panda TV Ser.). (ENG.). 32p. (J). (gr. k-2). pap. 3.99 *(978-1-4424-9995-9(8),* Simon Spotlight) Simon Spotlight.
—Two to Kung Fu. 2014. (Kung Fu Panda TV Ser.). (ENG.). 96p. (J). (gr. 2-5). pap. 4.99 *(978-1-4424-9992-8(3),* Simon Spotlight) Simon Spotlight.
Style Guide, Style, illus. The Furry & the Furious. 2014. (Kung Fu Panda TV Ser.). (ENG.). 96p. (J). (gr. 2-5). pap. 4.99 *(978-1-4814-1703-7(7),* Simon Spotlight) Simon Spotlight.
Styles, Walker. The Big Bad Woof. Whitehouse, Ben, illus. 2017. (Rider Woofson Ser.: 8). (ENG.). 128p. (J). (gr. k-4). pap. 5.99 ***(978-1-4814-9188-4(1),*** Little Simon) Little Simon.
—The Case of the Missing Tiger's Eye. Whitehouse, Ben, illus. 2016. (Rider Woofson Ser.: 1). (ENG.). 128p. (J). (gr. k-4). 16.99 *(978-1-4814-5738-5(1),* Little Simon) Little Simon.
—Ghosts & Goblins & Ninja, Oh My! Whitehouse, Ben, illus. 2016. (Rider Woofson Ser.: 4). (ENG.). 128p. (J). (gr. k-4). pap. 5.99 *(978-1-4814-6306-5(3),* Little Simon) Little Simon.
—The Rival Detective. Whitehouse, Ben, illus. 2016. (Rider Woofson Ser.: 5). (ENG.). 128p. (J). (gr. k-4). pap. 5.99 *(978-1-4814-7107-7(4),* Little Simon) Little Simon.
—Something Smells Fishy. Whitehouse, Ben, illus. 2016. (Rider Woofson Ser.: 2). (ENG.). 128p. (J). (gr. k-4). 16.99 *(978-1-4814-5742-2(X),* Little Simon) Little Simon.
—Undercover in the Bow-Wow Club. Whitehouse, Ben, illus. 2016. (Rider Woofson Ser.: 3). (ENG.). 128p. (J). (gr. k-4). pap. 5.99 *(978-1-4814-6303-4(9),* Little Simon) Little Simon.
Sugg, Nan. Erin & Katrina. Huber, Becca & Pope, Lauren, illus. 2007. 32p. (J). 19.90 *(978-0-9788889-0-9(1))* Acorn Hill Pr.
Sugobono, Nahuel. Leyendas, Mitos, Cuentos y Otros Relatos Tobas. Huadi, illus. 2003. (SPA.). 86p. pap. 11.95 *(978-987-550-296-3(0))* Longseller S.A. ARG. Dist: Bilingual Pubns. Co., The.
Sullivan, Dana. Ozzie & the Art Contest. Sullivan, Dana, illus. 2013. (ENG., Illus.). 15.99 *(978-1-58536-820-4(2))* Sleeping Bear Pr.
Sullivan, Lori Lynn. Our Sunny Day Ride. 2011. 24p. (gr. 1-2). 10.95 *(978-1-4497-1467-3(6),* WestBow Pr.) Author Solutions, Inc.
SungJa, Cho. Bubbly & Grumpy. SukWon, Sa, illus. rev. ed. 2014. (MySELF Bookshelf Ser.). (ENG.). 32p. (J). (gr. k-2). pap. 11.94 *(978-1-60357-660-4(6))* Norwood Hse. Pr.
Surplice, Holly. Peek-a-Boo Bunny. Surplice, Holly, illus. 2014. (ENG., Illus.). 32p. (J). (gr. -1-3). 9.99 *(978-0-06-224265-5(2))* HarperCollins Pubs.
Sutherland, Paul H. Finding Utopia. Gibbons, Timothy M., illus. 2006. 44p. (J). (gr. k-7). 20.00 *(978-0-9661060-4-6(0))* Utopia Pr.
Sutherland, Tui T. Against the Tide. 2014. (Spirit Animals Ser.: 5). (ENG.). 192p. (J). (gr. 3-7). 16.99 *(978-0-545-59975-7(X));*Bk. 5. (Illus.). 12.99 *(978-0-545-52247-2(1))* Scholastic, Inc.
Sutton, Laurie S. Batman Battles the Penguin. Style Guide, illus. 2016. (Batman Unlimited Ser.). (ENG.). 64p. (J). (gr. k-4). 16.00 *(978-0-606-39248-8(3))* Turtleback Bks.
Suzuki, Mamoru. You Belong to Me. 2016. (ENG.). 32p. (J). (gr. -1-k). 12.99 *(978-1-940842-12-7(3))* Museyon.
Svendson, Elisabeth D. The Tale of Naughty Mac & Other Donkey Stories. (Illus.). 80p. (J). 17.95 *(978-1-873580-14-1(2))* Whittet Bks., Ltd. GBR. Dist: Diamond Farm Bk. Pubs.
Swain, Cynthia. Sorting at the Nature Center. 2006. (Early Explorers Ser.). (J). pap. *(978-1-4108-6039-2(6))* Benchmark Education Co.
Swain, Heather. All Kinds of Kisses. Henry, Steven, illus. 2016. (ENG.). 32p. (J). 16.99 *(978-1-250-06650-3(6),* 9781250066503) Feiwel & Friends.
Swann, Mary. A Fearsome Day. Swann, Mary, illus. 2007. (Illus.). 56p. (J). (gr. 1-3). 19.95 *(978-0-932616-87-6(9))* BrickHouse Bks., Inc.
Swanson, Bruce & Swanson, Bill. Gray Wolf's Search, 1 vol. Peterson, Gary, illus. 2007. (ENG.). 24p. (J). (gr. -1-2). 14.95 *(978-0-9779183-1-7(9),* 7th Generation) Book Publishing Co.
Swanson, Tina M. Silly Sierra & the Mysterious Mushroom. 2011. 28p. pap. 13.99 *(978-1-4634-3594-3(0))* AuthorHouse.
Swartz, Nancy Sohn. How Did the Animals Help God? Hall, Melanie, illus. 2004. (ENG.). 24p. (J). bds. 8.99 *(978-1-59473-044-3(X),* 9781594730443, Skylight Paths Publishing) LongHill Partners, Inc.
Swartz, Neva. Tommy the Timid Turtle. Steinbauer, Larry, illus. 2004. (ENG.). 24p. (J). 19.95 *(978-1-878044-75-4(3))* Mayhaven Publishing, Inc.
Sweeney, Monica & Yelvington, Lauren. Can You Yawn Like a Fawn? Watkins, Laura, illus. 2016. (ENG.). 32p. (J). 15.99 *(978-1-250-10416-8(5),* 9781250104168) St. Martin's Pr.
Sweeney, Tass. The Funny Friends & Faces of Henry P. Gruber. 2012. 32p. pap. 19.99 *(978-1-4772-9717-9(0))* AuthorHouse.
Sweet, George M. The Old Alligator & the Young Bird. 2011. 52p. pap. 19.39 *(978-1-4269-5357-6(7))* Trafford Publishing.
Swender, Jennifer & Jacobs, Paul DuBois. A Furry Fiasco. Laberis, Stephanie, illus. 2016. (Animal Inn Ser.: 1). (ENG.). 112p. (J). (gr. 2-5). pap. 5.99 *(978-1-4814-6223-5(7),* Aladdin) Simon & Schuster Children's Publishing.
Swenson, Jamie A. If You Were a Dog. Raschka, Chris, illus. 2014. (ENG.). 40p. (J). (gr. -1-1). 17.99 *(978-0-374-33530-4(3),* 9780374335304, Farrar, Straus & Giroux (BYR)) Farrar, Straus & Giroux.
Swickle, Dvora. The Legend of Santa Owl. 2012. 64p. pap. *(978-1-897512-65-4(1))* Saga Bks.
Swift, Julian. Merlin & His Teapot Eagles. 2012. 40p. pap. *(978-3-85040-802-8(7))* Chytra-Verlag Vindobona.
Switzer, Holly. Attitude of Gratitude. 2013. 32p. pap. *(978-1-4602-2463-2(9))* FriesenPress.
Sykes, Julie. Dora's Eggs. Chapman, Jane, illus. 2007. (Storytime Board Bks.). (J). (gr. -1-3). bds. 6.95 *(978-1-58925-801-3(0))* Tiger Tales.
Symes, Sally. Whose Toes Are Those? Sharratt, Nick, illus. 2012. (ENG.). 22p. (J). (gr. k-12). bds. 7.99 *(978-0-7636-6274-5(7))* Candlewick Pr.
—Yawn. Sharratt, Nick, illus. 2011. (ENG.). 24p. (J). (gr. -1-2). bds. 7.99 *(978-0-7636-5725-3(5))* Candlewick Pr.
Taback, Simms. Moo Baby Gift Set. 2007. 22.95 *(978-1-59354-630-4(0))* Handprint Bks.
Tabby, Abigail. Hokey Pokey Elmo. Brannon, Tom, illus. 2006. (Big Bird's Favorites Board Bks.). (ENG.). 24p. (J). (gr. k — 1). bds. 4.99 *(978-0-375-83507-0(5),* Random Hse. Bks. for Young Readers) Random Hse. Children's Bks.
Tafuri, Nancy. The Big Storm: A Very Soggy Counting Book. Tafuri, Nancy, illus. 2013. (Classic Board Bks.). (ENG., Illus.). 34p. (J). (gr. -1 — 1). bds. 7.99 *(978-1-4424-8179-4(X),* Little Simon) Little Simon.
—The Big Storm: A Very Soggy Counting Book. Tafuri, Nancy, illus. 2009. (ENG., Illus.). 32p. (J). (gr. -1-2). 18.99 *(978-1-4169-6795-8(8),* Simon & Schuster Bks. For Young Readers) Simon & Schuster Bks. For Young Readers.
—The Busy Little Squirrel. Tafuri, Nancy, illus. 2010. (Classic Board Bks.). (ENG., Illus.). 34p. (J). (gr. -1 — 1). bds. 7.99 *(978-1-4424-0721-3(2),* Little Simon) Little Simon.
—The Busy Little Squirrel. Tafuri, Nancy, illus. 2007. (ENG., Illus.). 32p. (J). (gr. -1-3). 17.99 *(978-0-689-87341-6(7),* Simon & Schuster Bks. For Young Readers) Simon & Schuster Bks. For Young Readers.
Talbot, Ethel. The Natural History Story Book. Noble, Edwin & Grieve, Walter G., illus. 2008. 336p. pap. 13.95 *(978-1-59915-295-0(9))* Yesterday's Classics.
Tallarico, Tony. How Fire Came to the Indians. 2005. (Classics Illustrated Junior Ser.). 32p. 5.99 *(978-1-894998-18-5(9))* Lake, Jack Productions, Inc. CAN. Dist: Hushion Hse. Publishing, Ltd.
Tama. Black Cow. 2012. 116p. pap. 14.95 *(978-1-4685-6680-2(6))* AuthorHouse.
Tankard, Jeremy. Boo Hoo Bird. Tankard, Jeremy, illus. 2009. (ENG., Illus.). 32p. (J). (gr. -1-k). 16.99 *(978-0-545-06570-2(4),* Scholastic Pr.) Scholastic, Inc.
—Grumpy Bird. 2016. (ENG.). 30p. (J). (— 1). bds. 6.99 *(978-0-545-87182-2(4),* Scholastic Pr.) Scholastic, Inc.
—Grumpy Bird. Tankard, Jeremy, illus. 2007. (ENG., Illus.). 32p. (J). (gr. -1-k). 16.99 *(978-0-439-85147-3(5),* Scholastic Pr.) Scholastic, Inc.
—Me Hungry! Tankard, Jeremy, illus. (ENG., Illus.). (J). 2010. 34p. (— 1). bds. 7.99 *(978-0-7636-4780-3(2))* 2008. 40p. (gr. -1-2). 15.99 *(978-0-7636-3360-8(7))* Candlewick Pr.
Tanner, Suzan. The Most Unusual Adventures of Black Shadow Smokey & the Blue Streak. 2003. 108p. 21.95 *(978-1-4140-0911-7(9))* AuthorHouse.
Taplin, Sam. Little Stories for Bedtime. Chiara, Francesca De, illus. 2010. (Bedtime Stories Ser.). 12p. (J). bds. 12.99 *(978-0-7945-2673-3(X),* Usborne) EDC Publishing.
—Sleepytime Stories. Chaira, Francesca di, illus. 2011. (Baby Board Books Ser.). 12p. (J). ring bd. 12.99 *(978-0-7945-3006-8(0),* Usborne) EDC Publishing.
Tarlow, Ellen. Mole Catches the Sky. Bogacki, Tomek, illus. 2014. (ENG.). (J). 16.99 *(978-1-59572-656-8(X))* Star Bright Bks., Inc.
—Pinwheel Days, 1 vol. Parker, Gretel, illus. 2007. (ENG.). 32p. (J). (gr. -1-3). pap. 6.95 *(978-1-59572-059-7(6))* Star Bright Bks., Inc.
Tarsy, Jean. Just Molly & Me & Nikki Make Three. LaGrange, Tiffany, illus. 2008. 36p. pap. 12.95 *(978-0-9820479-6-5(7))* Peppertree Pr., The.
Tashjian, Janet. My Life As a Book. Tashjian, Jake, illus. 2010. (My Life Ser.: 1). (ENG.). 224p. (J). (gr. 4-7). 17.99 *(978-0-8050-8903-5(9),* 9780805089035, Holt, Henry & Co. Bks. For Young Readers) Holt, Henry & Co.
—My Life As a Book. Tashjian, Jake, illus. 2011. (My Life Ser.: 1). (ENG.). 240p. (J). (gr. 4-7). pap. 7.99 *(978-0-312-67289-8(6),* 9780312672898) Square Fish.
Tavener, Carys. The Adventures of T. C & Friends. 2011. (Illus.). 132p. pap. 38.72 *(978-1-4567-7096-9(9))* AuthorHouse.
Taylor, Jacqui. Baobab Is Big: And Other Verses from Africa. 2005. (ENG., Illus.). 72p. 13.00 *(978-1-86872-946-3(X))* Penguin Random House Grupo Editorial ESP. Dist: Casemate Pubs. & Bk. Distributors, LLC.
Taylor, Je'. The Animal Dance. 2009. 32p. pap. 14.49 *(978-1-4490-2626-4(5))* AuthorHouse.
Taylor, Martin. The Lost Treasure of the Sunken City. Catling, Andy, illus. 2012. (J). *(978-1-4351-4330-2(2))* Barnes & Noble, Inc.
Taylor, Melissa Utz. Sneaky Snake. 2011. 24p. (gr. 1-2). pap. 14.99 *(978-1-4567-5518-8(8))* AuthorHouse.
Teague, Mark. The Sky Is Falling! 2015. (ENG., Illus.). 32p. (J). (gr. -1-k). 16.99 *(978-0-545-63217-1(X))* Scholastic, Inc.
Telchin, Eric. The Black & White Factory. Funck, Diego, illus. 2016. (ENG.). 40p. (J). (gr. -1-k). 17.99 *(978-1-4998-0277-1(3))* Little Bee Books Inc.
Temple, Valerie. Mud Witch Boy of Ghost Canyon. 2009. 113p. pap. 21.95 *(978-1-4327-1133-7(4));* pap. 10.95 *(978-1-4327-3103-8(3))* Outskirts Pr., Inc.
Tench, U. M. & Tench, D. A. Cramberry & Friends. l.t. ed. 2003. (Illus.). 31p. *(978-0-9686943-1-2(4))* Human Resources Projects.
Terada, Junzo. Animal Friends on Parade Puzzle. 2017. (ENG., Illus.). 12p. (J). (gr. -1-k). 14.99 ***(978-1-4521-5190-8(3))*** Chronicle Bks. LLC.
Terada, Junzo. Animal Friends: Swimming Hole Party! 2017. (ENG., Illus.). 10p. (J). bds. 9.99 *(978-1-4521-4983-7(6))* Chronicle Bks. LLC.
TerKeurst, Lysa. Win or Lose, I Love You! Sometimes You Learn, 1 vol. 2015. (ENG., Illus.). 32p. (J). 15.99 *(978-0-529-10400-7(8))* Nelson, Thomas Inc.
Terry, Michael. Rhinos Horns. 2003. (Illus.). (J). *(978-1-58234-796-7(4),* Bloomsbury USA Childrens) Bloomsbury Publishing USA.
Terry, Will, illus. The Frog with the Big Mouth, 1 vol. 2008. (ENG.). 32p. (J). (gr. k-3). 16.99 *(978-0-8075-2621-7(5))* Whitman, Albert & Co.
Testa, Susan L. Myra the House Cat & the Garbage Can Monster. 2011. 44p. pap. 24.95 *(978-1-4560-4887-7(2))* America Star Bks.
Texier, Ophélie & Guidoux, Valerie. Wild Animals. 2009. (Little Discoveries: Ser.). (ENG., Illus.). 6p. (J). (gr. -1-k). bds. 8.95 *(978-0-7892-1049-4(5),* Abbeville Kids) Abbeville Pr., Inc.
Thanet, Octave, pseud. The Rowdy. 2004. reprint ed. pap. 1.99 *(978-1-4192-8122-8(4));* pap. 15.95 *(978-1-4191-8122-1(X))* Kessinger Publishing, LLC.
Themerson, Franciszka & Themerson, Franciszka. My First Nursery Book. 2009. (ENG., Illus.). 72p. (J). (gr. k-2). 16.95 *(978-0-8109-7978-9(0),* Abrams Bks. for Young Readers) Abrams, Inc.
Thomas, Amy T. The Story of Rocco on Satterwhite Ridge: Spring Surprises. Lester, Roseanna, illus. 2009. 16p. pap. 8.49 *(978-1-4389-3142-5(5))* AuthorHouse.
Thomas, B. K. Logs. Thomas, B. K., illus. 2013. (Illus.). 36p. 24.95 *(978-1-4512-2170-1(3))* America Star Bks.
Thomas, Cameron. Shipwrecked on the Island of Skree. Krystoforski, Andrej, illus. 2004. (Jungle of Utt Ser.). 48p. (J). 16.95 *(978-0-921800-01-9(0))* MGT Developments, Ltd. CAN. Dist: Independent Pubs. Group.
—The Utt Jungle Airline: The Jungle of Utt. Krystoforski, Andrej, illus. 2004. (Jungle of Utt Ser.). 48p. (J). 16.95 *(978-0-921800-03-3(7))* MGT Developments, Ltd. CAN. Dist: Independent Pubs. Group.
Thomas, David, ed. Animal Stories: Young Readers. Osborne, Richard, illus. 2011. 190p. 42.95 *(978-1-258-10206-7(4))* Literary Licensing, LLC.
Thomas, Jan. A Birthday for Cow! 2008. (ENG., Illus.). 40p. (J). (gr. -1-3). 12.95 *(978-0-15-206072-5(3))* Houghton Mifflin Harcourt Publishing Co.
Thomas Nelson. Fit & Feel Moo. 2015. (ENG.). 12p. (gr. -1). bds. *(978-1-78393-438-6(7))* Make Believe Ideas.
—God Loves You Little One, 1 vol. 2016. (God's Little Ones Ser.). (ENG., Illus.). 12p. (J). (gr. -1). bds. 8.99 *(978-0-7180-8756-2(9))* Nelson, Thomas Inc.
—Oola the Owl Who Lost Her Hoot! 2016. (ENG.). 32p. (gr. -1-2). *(978-1-78598-763-2(1))* Make Believe Ideas.
Thomas, Rosemary. The Kiwi Kingdom. 2010. 154p. pap. 18.00 *(978-1-4349-0857-5(7))* Dorrance Publishing Co., Inc.
Thomas, Sara. McCoy & the Pond. 2013. 24p. pap. 24.95 *(978-1-62709-793-2(7))* America Star Bks.
Thomas, Wes. Down the Crawfish Hole, 1 vol. Thomas, Wes, illus. 2004. (ENG., Illus.). 32p. (J). (gr. k-3). 16.99 *(978-1-58980-163-9(6))* Pelican Publishing Co., Inc.
Thompson, Adria. Droves Cove. 2008. 72p. pap. 9.99 *(978-1-60477-653-9(6))* Salem Author Services.
Thompson, John. Daniel & the Amazing Tickling Keefro. 2011. (Illus.). 32p. pap. 14.73 *(978-1-4567-7630-5(4))* AuthorHouse.
Thompson, Kate. Midnight's Choice. unabr. ed. 2004. (Switchers Ser.: Vol. 2). 240p. (J). (gr. 5-9). pap. 38.00 incl. audio *(978-0-8072-8769-9(5),* Listening Library) Random Hse. Audio Publishing Group.
—Switchers. 220p. (J). (gr. 4-7). pap. 5.99 *(978-0-8072-1553-1(8));* 2004. (Switchers Ser.: Vol. 1). (gr. 5-9). pap. 38.00 incl. audio *(978-0-8072-8138-3(7),* YA115SP) Random Hse. Audio Publishing Group. (Listening Library).
Thompson, Lauren. One Starry Night. Bean, Jonathan, illus. (ENG.). 32p. (J). 2011. (gr. -1-3). lib. bdg. 17.99 *(978-0-689-82851-5(9))* 2003. 6.99 *(978-0-689-84215-3(5))* McElderry, Margaret K. Bks. (McElderry, Margaret K. Bks.).
Thornhill, Jan. Winter's Coming: A Story of Seasonal Change. Bisaillon, Josée, illus. 2014. (ENG.). 32p. (J). (gr. k-4). 16.95 *(978-1-77147-002-5(X),* Owlkids) Owlkids Bks. Inc. CAN. Dist: Publishers Group West (PGW).
Thorpe, Kiki. The Space Between. Christy, Jana & Random House Disney Staff, illus. 2013. (Never Girls Ser.: 2). (ENG.). 128p. (J). (gr. 1-4). 5.99 *(978-0-7364-2795-1(3),* RH/Disney) Random Hse. Children's Bks.
—The Space Between. Christy, Jana, illus. 2013. (Never Girls Ser.: 2). lib. bdg. 16.00 *(978-0-606-26974-2(6),* Turtleback) Turtleback Bks.
Thronson, Lloyd. Gomer the Goat & His New Home. 2011. 30p. pap. 16.95 *(978-1-4626-1590-2(2))* America Star Bks.
Tibo, Gilles. Au Boulot les Animaux. 2004. (FRE., Illus.). (J). (gr. -1-k). spiral bd. *(978-0-616-11146-8(0))* Canadian National Institute for the Blind/Institut National Canadien pour les Aveugles.
—Noches de Papel. (Barril Sin Fondo Ser.). (SPA.). (J). (gr. 3-5). pap. *(978-968-6465-32-7(4))* Casa de Estudios de Literatura y Talleres Artisticos Amaquemecan A.C. MEX. Dist: Lectorum Pubns., Inc.
—Les Quatre Saisons de Simon. 2006. (FRE., Illus.). 48p. (J). (gr. -1-3). 17.95 *(978-0-88776-794-4(X))* Tundra Bks. CAN. Dist: Penguin Random Hse. LLC.
Tickle, Jack. Look Out, Ladybug. 2013. (ENG., Illus.). 32p. (J). *(978-1-58925-128-1(8))* Tiger Tales.
Tidwell, Emmy. Superanimals. 2011. 42p. pap. 16.95 *(978-1-4626-4540-4(2))* America Star Bks.
Tiger Tales, ed. The Gingerbread Man. Latimer, Miriam, illus. 2016. (My First Fairy Tales Ser.). (ENG.). 32p. (J). (gr. -1-2). pap. 7.99 *(978-1-58925-477-0(5))* Tiger Tales.
—Ten Twinkly Stars. Julian, Russell, illus. 2016. (ENG.). 28p. (J). (gr. -1-k). mass mkt. 3.99 *(978-1-58925-475-6(9))* Tiger Tales.
Tiger Tales, ed. & compiled by. My Favorite Christmas Stories. Tiger Tales, compiled by. 2015. (ENG.). 128p. (J). (gr. -1-3). 12.99 *(978-1-68010-200-0(1))* Tiger Tales.
Tiger Tales Staff. Lift & See Animals. 2013. (My First Matching Book Ser.). (ENG.). 10p. bds. 7.99 *(978-1-58925-613-2(1))* Tiger Tales Pubns.
Tiger Tales Staff, creator. Animal Antics. 2004. (Cuddly Cuffs Ser.: No. 5). (Illus.). 10p. (J). (gr. -1-13). tchr. ed. 5.95 *(978-1-58925-725-2(1))* Tiger Tales.
—5 Minute Farm Tales. 2013. (ENG., Illus.). 292p. (J). (gr. -1-1). 14.95 *(978-1-58925-505-0(4))* Tiger Tales.
Tiitinen, Esko-Pekka. Drops of Life. 2012. (ENG., Illus.). 24p. (J). (gr. k-2). *(978-84-15241-31-7(3))* D P & G Military Pubs.
Tilby, Ginny. You Should, You Should. 2013. (ENG.). 32p. (J). (gr. k-3). 16.95 *(978-1-938301-70-4(6))* Familius LLC.
Tillman, Nancy. The Heaven of Animals. Tillman, Nancy, illus. 2014. (ENG., Illus.). 32p. (J). (gr. -1-3). 17.99 *(978-0-312-55369-2(2),* 9780312553692) Feiwel & Friends.
Tillman, Nancy & Metaxas, Eric. It's Time to Sleep, My Love. Tillman, Nancy, illus. (ENG., Illus.). (J). 2011. 34p. (— 1). bds. 7.99 *(978-0-312-67336-9(1),* 9780312673369) 2008. 32p. (gr. -1 — 1). 16.95 *(978-0-312-38371-8(1),* 9780312383718) Feiwel & Friends.
Tim, Fireball. Big Book of Wacky Rides! 2013. (ENG.). 32p. (J). (gr. -1). 17.95 *(978-1-933492-81-0(3))* Design Studio Pr.
Timmers, Leo. Gus's Garage. Timmers, Leo, illus. 2017. (ENG., Illus.). 32p. (gr. -1-k). 16.99 ***(978-1-77657-092-8(8));*** 9.99 ***(978-1-77657-094-2(4))*** Gecko Pr. NZL. Dist: Lerner Publishing Group.
Timmers, Leo. Who Is Driving? Timmers, Leo, illus. 2014. (ENG., Illus.). 30p. (J). (gr. -1-1). bds. 7.99 *(978-1-61963-169-4(5),* 9781619631694, Bloomsbury USA Childrens) Bloomsbury Publishing USA.
Timmis, Jeff. Arlo's Job Hunt. 2012. 36p. pap. 20.99 *(978-1-4772-7600-6(9))* AuthorHouse.
Tireman, Loyd. Baby Jack & Jumping Jack Rabbit. Douglass, Ralph, illus. 2015. (Mesaland Ser.). (ENG.). 48p. (J). 12.95 *(978-0-8263-5604-8(4))* Univ. of New Mexico Pr.
—Cocky. Douglass, Ralph, illus. 2015. (Mesaland Ser.). (ENG.). 48p. (J). 12.95 *(978-0-8263-5606-2(0))* Univ. of New Mexico Pr.
—Quills. Douglass, Ralph, illus. 2015. (Mesaland Ser.). (ENG.). 48p. (J). 12.95 *(978-0-8263-5609-3(5))* Univ. of New Mexico Pr.
—3 Toes. Douglass, Ralph, illus. 2015. (Mesaland Ser.). (ENG.). 48p. (J). 12.95 *(978-0-8263-5610-9(9))* Univ. of New Mexico Pr.
Todd, Traci N. Wiggle, Waggle, Loop-De-Loo! Barner, Bob, illus. 2006. (J). *(978-1-58987-009-3(3))* Kindermusik International.
Tokyopop and Art Impression Staff & Peymani, Christine. Skelanimals Vol. 1: It's a Wonderful Afterlife. 2011. (Illus.). 36p. 9.99 *(978-1-4278-3255-9(2))* TOKYOPOP, Inc.

Tolan, Stephanie S. Bartholomew's Blessing. Moore, Margie, illus. 2004. 32p. (J). (gr. -1-3). lib. bdg. 16.89 *(978-0-06-001198-7(X))* HarperCollins Pubs.

Tolman, Marije & Tolman, Ronald. The Island. 2012. (ENG., Illus.). 32p. (J). (gr. -1). 17.95 *(978-1-935954-19-4(9),* 9781935954194) Lemniscaat USA.

—The Tree House. 2010. (ENG., Illus.). 32p. (J). (gr. -1-1). 17.95 *(978-1-59078-806-6(0),* Lemniscaat) Boyds Mills Pr.

Toma, Al. Rainbow on the Tree of Life. 2005. (J). pap. 15.00 *(978-0-8059-6607-7(2))* Dorrance Publishing Co., Inc.

Tomlin, Chris & Barrett, Pat. Good Good Father, 1 vol. 2016. (ENG.). 32p. (J). 16.99 *(978-0-7180-8695-4(3))* Nelson, Thomas Inc.

Tomlinson, Jill. Three Favourite Animal Stories. Howard, Paul, illus. 2005. (ENG.). 304p. (J). (gr. k-2). 12.99 *(978-1-4052-2009-5(0))* Egmont Bks., Ltd. GBR. Dist: Independent Pubs. Group.

Toms, Kate. Funny Faces Cloth Book Jogger Dog. 2006. (Funny Faces (Make Believe Ideas) Ser.). (Illus.). 4p. (gr. -1). *(978-1-84610-289-9(8))* Make Believe Ideas.

Top That! Color Safari (large Version) Parry, Jo, illus. 2007. 10p. (J). (gr. -1). *(978-1-84666-554-7(X),* Tide Mill Pr.) Top That! Publishing PLC.

Top That!, creator. ABC Train. 2007. (Jigsaw Book Ser.). (Illus.). 18p. (J). (gr. -1-3). bds. *(978-1-84666-095-5(5))* Top That! Publishing PLC.

—Animals with Martha the Monkey. 2012. (Learn with Magnets Ser.). (ENG., Illus.). 10p. (gr. -1-k). *(978-1-84956-670-4(4))* Top That! Publishing PLC.

—123 Train. 2007. (Jigsaw Book Ser.). (Illus.). 18p. (J). (gr. -1-3). bds. *(978-1-84666-097-9(1))* Top That! Publishing PLC.

Torday, Piers. The Last Wild. (Last Wild Ser.: 1). (ENG.). (J). (gr. 3-7). 2015. 352p. 8.99 *(978-0-14-750965-9(3),* Puffin Books) 2014. (Illus.). 336p. 16.99 *(978-0-670-01554-2(7),* Viking Books for Young Readers) Penguin Young Readers Group.

Torrance-Matthews, Armer, et al. Miss Bertha, the Talking Tree: A Delightful Story of a Talking Tree. 2010. 36p. pap. 18.95 *(978-1-4269-2051-6(2))* Trafford Publishing.

Touchable Counting Books. 2005. (ENG.). (J). bds. 14.95 *(978-1-58117-284-3(2),* Intervisual/Piggy Toes) Bendon, Inc.

Toulon, Juliette Bellot. An Amazing Friendship. 2011. 24p. pap. 12.77 *(978-1-4634-0330-0(5))* AuthorHouse.

Touma, Patricia. Happy Times, the Adventures of Ish & Mish Vol. 1: Ish & Mish Go to the Circus. 2005. per. 7.00 *(978-1-58396-873-4(3))* Blue Unicorn Edition, LLC.

Townsend, Wendy. Blue Iguana. 2014. 188p. 18.95 *(978-1-60898-157-1(6))* namelos llc.

ToyBox Innovations, creator. Deep in the Jungle. abr. ed. 2006. (Disney's Read along Collection). (ENG.). (J). (gr. -1-3). pap. *(978-0-7634-2182-3(0))* Walt Disney Records.

ToyBox Innovations & Walt Disney Records Staff, creators. Disney's Lilo & Stitch: Read-along. 2006. (Disney's Read Along Ser.). (ENG., Illus.). 24p. (J). pap. *(978-0-7634-2173-1(1))* Walt Disney Records.

Tozier, Christopher. Olivia Brophie & the Pearl of Tagelus. 2012. (ENG.). 208p. (J). pap. 12.95 *(978-1-56164-519-0(2))* Pineapple Pr., Inc.

—Olivia Brophie & the Sky Island. 2014. (ENG.). 304p. (J). pap. 12.95 *(978-1-56164-680-7(6))* Pineapple Pr., Inc.

Trabert, John. Gnome Chronicles. 2007. 172p. pap. 4.99 *(978-1-4343-1950-0(4))* AuthorHouse.

Tracey, Alice. Animal Friends. 2012. 56p. 19.95 *(978-1-4626-6175-6(0))* America Star Bks.

Trasler, Janee. Mimi & Bear Make a Friend. Trasler, Janee, illus. 2017. (Mimi & Bear Ser.). (ENG., Illus.). 32p. (J). 16.99 *(978-0-374-30360-0(6),* 9780374303600, Farrar, Straus & Giroux (BYR)) Farrar, Straus & Giroux.

Travers, James A. Kitten & the Barn. 2008. 44p. pap. 24.95 *(978-1-4241-8771-3(0))* America Star Bks.

Trelogan, Stephanie. Mask Parade: Forest Animals. Armstrong, Katharine, illus. 2008. (ENG.). 14p. (J). (gr. -1). 12.95 *(978-1-58117-790-9(9),* Intervisual/Piggy Toes) Bendon, Inc.

Trimmer, Christian. Mimi & Shu in I'll Race You! Van der Paardt, Melissa, illus. 2015. (ENG.). 40p. (J). (gr. -1-3). 17.99 *(978-1-4814-2330-4(4))* Simon & Schuster Children's Publishing.

Tripp, Jenny. Pete & Fremont. Manders, John, illus. 2008. (ENG.). 192p. (J). (gr. 3-7). pap. 12.95 *(978-0-15-206238-5(6))* Houghton Mifflin Harcourt Publishing Co.

Trotter, Bob. Up the Wooden Hill: Bedtime Stories for Little Ones. Edgar, Barrie, illus. 2011. 98p. pap. 17.99 *(978-1-60976-139-4(1),* Eloquent Bks.) Strategic Book Publishing & Rights Agency (SBPRA).

Trout Fishing in America Staff & Jorisch, Stéphane, illus. Chicken Joe Forgets Something Important. 2011. (ENG.). 48p. (J). (gr. k-2). 16.95 *(978-2-923163-74-1(5))* La Montagne Secrete CAN. Dist: Independent Pubs. Group.

Trowbridge, Terri. Tulowly the Possum. McConkey, Barbara, illus. l.t. ed. 2005. 24p. (J). 9.95 *(978-0-9766418-0-3(1))* Sidewalk Publishing.

Tsavalas, Helena Macree. The Dazzling Beast. 2007. 56p. per. 10.00 *(978-1-4257-4295-9(5))* Xlibris Corp.

Tsinajinnie, Veronica. Johonaa'ei: Bringer of Dawn. Thomas, Peter A., tr. from NAV. Singer, Ryan, illus. 2007. (ENG & NAV.). 32p. (J). (gr. -1-3). 17.95 *(978-1-893354-54-8(7))* Salina Bookshelf Inc.

Tsong, Jing Jing & BeachHouse Publishing. Aloha Zoo. 2010. (ENG.). 16p. (J). (gr. -1-1). bds. 7.95 *(978-1-933067-32-2(2))* Beachhouse Publishing, LLC.

Tub Tales: The Farm. 2003. (Illus.). 10p. (J). 6.00 *(978-0-9713507-3-1(6),* 844) Panline U.S.A., Inc.

Tub Tales: The Jungle. 2003. (Illus.). 10p. (J). 6.00 *(978-0-9713507-2-4(8),* 843) Panline U.S.A., Inc.

Tukel, Onur. Rainstack!, 0 vols. 2013. (ENG.). 64p. (J). (gr. -1-3). 17.99 *(978-1-4778-1655-4(0),* 9781477816554, Amazon Children's Publishing) Amazon Publishing.

Tulip, Jenny, illus. Who's Hiding in the Jungle? A Mystery Touch-and-Feel Flap Book! 2008. 10p. (gr. -1-k). bds. 6.99 *(978-1-57755-784-5(0))* Flying Frog Publishing.

Tumbrello, Shannon. Freedom Forest. 2007. 17.00 *(978-0-8059-8880-2(7))* Dorrance Publishing Co., Inc.

Tupera, Tupera. Polar Bear's Underwear. 2015. (ENG., Illus.). 32p. (J). (gr. -1-k). 16.99 *(978-1-4521-4199-2(1))* Chronicle Bks. LLC.

Turcios, Omar. David, Fish & Penguins... 2012. (ENG., Illus.). 36p. (J). (gr. -1-k). *(978-84-15241-94-2(1))* D P & G Military Pubs.

—David, Peces, Pinguinos ... 2012. (SPA & ENG.). 36p. (J). (gr. -1-k). 14.95 *(978-84-15241-95-9(X))* Eastern National.

Turn-the-Wheel, 4 bks., Set. Incl. Animal Ambulance. Lawson, Peter & Smith, Kathryn. bds. 5.95 *(978-0-7892-1026-5(6));* Fire Engine. Goldsack, Gaby. Lawson, Peter, illus. bds. 5.95 *(978-0-7892-1022-7(3));* Fishing Boat. Goldsack, Gaby. Lawson, Peter, illus. bds. 5.95 *(978-0-7892-1025-8(8));* Tractor. Lawson, Peter. bds. 5.95 *(978-0-7892-1023-4(1));* 10p. (J). (gr. -1-k). (Turn the Wheel Ser.). (ENG., Illus.). 40p. 2009. Set bds. 22.95 *(978-0-7892-1027-2(4),* Abbeville Kids) Abbeville Pr., Inc.

Turner, Marie B. God Made the Animals. Romero, Naomi, illus. 2017. (J). 6.99 ***(978-1-5064-2185-8(7),*** Sparkhouse Family) Augsburg Fortress, Pubs.

Tuxford, Jenny & Brazier, Jenny. Fred Boggitt & the Great Garden Centre Plot. 2012. 128p. (gr. 2-4). pap. 15.18 *(978-1-4678-9703-7(5))* AuthorHouse.

Twiford, Jerod. Kisho. 2005. pap. 16.95 *(978-1-4241-0525-0(0))* PublishAmerica, Inc.

Twin Sisters(r) Staff. B-i-n-g-o. 2010. (J). (gr. k-1). 14.99 *(978-1-59922-630-9(8))* Twin Sisters IP, LLC.

—Five Little Skunks. 2010. (J). (gr. k-2). pap. 4.99 *(978-1-59922-509-8(3))* Twin Sisters IP, LLC.

Twin Sisters(r) Staff, et al, adapted by. B-i-n-g-o. 2010. (J). (gr. k-1). 14.99 *(978-1-59922-422-0(4))* Twin Sisters IP, LLC.

Twin Sisters(r) Staff & Thompson, Kim Mitzo. The Night-Night Song. 2011. (J). (gr. k-1). bds. 9.99 incl. audio compact disk *(978-1-59922-783-2(5))* Twin Sisters IP, LLC.

Twinem, Neecy. Baby Coyote Counts. 2004. (New Board Book Ser.).Tr. of Bebe Coyote cuenta. (ENG., Illus.). 12p. (J). (gr. -1-k). bds. 5.95 *(978-0-87358-852-2(5))* Cooper Square Publishing Llc.

—Baby Snake's Shapes. 2004. (New Board Book Ser.).Tr. of Las formas de Bebe Serpiente. (ENG, SPA & MUL., Illus.). 12p. (J). (gr. -1-k). 6.95 *(978-0-87358-866-9(5))* Cooper Square Publishing Llc.

Twitty, Mary F. Ashley Visits Urchin Village. 2008. 92p. pap. 51.99 *(978-1-4363-5578-0(8))* Xlibris Corp.

Tyler, Jenny. Animal Stories for Little Children. 2011. (Picture Books Ser.). 136p. (J). ring bd. 18.99 *(978-0-7945-2632-0(2),* Usborne) EDC Publishing.

Tyler, Jenny & Cartwright, S. Animal Hide-and-Seek. rev. ed. 2004. (Treasury of Farmyard Tales Ser.). 10p. (J). 15.95 *(978-0-7945-0513-4(9))* EDC Publishing.

U. S. National Geographic Society Staff. Anybody Home? 2008. (Mama Mirabelle Ser.). (ENG., Illus.). 24p. (J). (gr. -1-2). pap. 3.99 *(978-1-4263-0303-6(3));* lib. bdg. 11.90 *(978-1-4263-0304-3(1))* National Geographic Society. (National Geographic Children's Bks.).

—Get with the Beat! 2009. (Toot & Puddle Ser.). (ENG., Illus.). 24p. (J). (gr. -1-2). lib. bdg. 11.90 *(978-1-4263-0485-9(4),* National Geographic Children's Bks.) National Geographic Society.

—Get with the Beat. 2009. (Toot & Puddle Ser.). (ENG., Illus.). 24p. (J). (gr. -1-2). pap. 3.99 *(978-1-4263-0484-2(6),* National Geographic Children's Bks.) National Geographic Society.

—Hide & Seek. 2008. (Mama Mirabelle Ser.). (ENG., Illus.). 24p. (J). (gr. -1-2). pap. 3.99 *(978-1-4263-0305-0(X));* lib. bdg. 11.90 *(978-1-4263-0306-7(8))* National Geographic Society. (National Geographic Children's Bks.).

—How Does Your Garden Grow? 2009. (Toot & Puddle Ser.). (ENG., Illus.). 24p. (J). (gr. -1-2). pap. 3.99 *(978-1-4263-0482-8(X),* National Geographic Children's Bks.) National Geographic Society.

Ulerio, Michelle. Lily Finds Her Way Home. 2013. 24p. pap. 24.95 *(978-1-63000-956-4(3))* America Star Bks.

Umina, Lisa M. Milo with a Halo. 2nd ed. 2003. (Illus.). 28p. (YA). per. 9.99 *(978-0-9718350-1-6(2))* Halo Publishing International.

Uncle Markie. Piglettè & Bobo on Safari. 2003. (YA). ring bd. 9.95 *(978-1-933129-16-7(6))* Studio 403.

Underwood, Deborah. The Christmas Quiet Book. Liwska, Renata, illus. (ENG.). 32p. (J). (gr. -1-3). 2017. pap. 7.99 ***(978-1-328-74056-4(0),*** HMH Books For Young Readers) 2012. 12.99 *(978-0-547-55863-9(5))* Houghton Mifflin Harcourt Publishing Co.

—The Loud Book! Liwska, Renata, illus. 2011. (ENG.). 32p. (J). (gr. -1-3). 12.99 *(978-0-547-39008-6(4))* Houghton Mifflin Harcourt Publishing Co.

—The Quiet Book. Liwska, Renata, illus. (ENG.). 32p. (J). 2016. (gr. -1-3). pap. 6.99 *(978-0-544-80904-8(1),* HMH Books For Young Readers) 2013. (— 1). bds. 8.99 *(978-0-544-05667-1(1))* 2010. (gr. -1-3). 12.95 *(978-0-547-21567-9(3))* Houghton Mifflin Harcourt Publishing Co.

—The Quiet Book. 2016. lib. bdg. 17.20 *(978-0-606-38900-6(8))* Turtleback Bks.

Ungerer, Tomi. Crictor. (J). (gr. -1-3). pap. 12.95 incl. audio Weston Woods Studios, Inc.

Urban, Linda. Mouse Was Mad. Cole, Henry, illus. (ENG.). 40p. (J). (gr. -1-3). 2012. pap. 7.99 *(978-0-547-72750-9(X))* 2009. 16.99 *(978-0-15-205337-6(9))* Houghton Mifflin Harcourt Publishing Co.

Urbanovic, Jackie. Duck at the Door. Urbanovic, Jackie, illus. 2011. (Max the Duck Ser.: 1). (ENG., Illus.). 32p. (J). (gr. -1-2). pap. 6.99 *(978-0-06-121440-0(X))* HarperCollins Pubs.

—Duck Soup. Urbanovic, Jackie, illus. 2008. (Max the Duck Ser.: 2). (Illus.). 32p. (J). (gr. -1-2). (ENG.). 17.99 *(978-0-06-121441-7(8));* lib. bdg. 18.89 *(978-0-06-121442-4(6))* HarperCollins Pubs.

—Ducks in a Row. Urbanovic, Jackie & Mathieu, Joe, illus. 2011. (I Can Read Level 1 Ser.). (ENG.). 32p. (J). (gr. k-3). 16.99 *(978-0-06-186438-4(2));* pap. 3.99 *(978-0-06-186437-7(4))* HarperCollins Pubs.

—Happy Go Ducky. Urbanovic, Jackie & Mathieu, Joe, illus. 2012. (I Can Read Level 1 Ser.). (ENG.). 32p. (J). (gr. k-3). 16.99 *(978-0-06-186440-7(4));* pap. 3.99 *(978-0-06-186439-1(0))* HarperCollins Pubs.

—Sitting Duck. Urbanovic, Jackie, illus. 2010. (Illus.). 40p. (J). (gr. -1-2). (ENG.). 17.99 *(978-0-06-176583-4(X));* lib. bdg. 18.89 *(978-0-06-176584-1(8))* HarperCollins Pubs.

Ursu, Anne. The Shadow Thieves. Fortune, Eric, illus. 2007. (Cronus Chronicles Ser.: 1). (ENG.). 432p. (J). (gr. 3-7). pap. 8.99 *(978-1-4169-0588-2(X),* Atheneum Bks. for Young Readers) Simon & Schuster Children's Publishing.

Usera, Abe. The Pigs & Friends. 2012. 52p. pap. 21.99 *(978-1-4685-6152-4(9))* AuthorHouse.

Valério, Geraldo, illus. Go to Sleep, Gecko! A Balinese Folktale. 2015. (ENG.). 32p. (J). (gr. -1-3). pap. 8.95 *(978-1-939160-92-8(8))* August Hse. Pubs., Inc.

van de Vendel, Edward & van der Linden, Martijn. For You & No One Else. 2009. (ENG.). 32p. (J). (gr. -1-2). 16.95 *(978-1-59078-658-1(0),* Lemniscaat) Boyds Mills Pr.

Van Dusen, Chris. The Circus Ship. Van Dusen, Chris, illus. (ENG., Illus.). 40p. (J). (gr. -1-3). 2015. 6.99 *(978-0-7636-5592-1(9))* 2009. 16.99 *(978-0-7636-3090-4(X))* Candlewick Pr.

—The Circus Ship Big Book. 2011. (ENG., Illus.). 40p. (J). (gr. -1-3). pap. 24.99 *(978-0-7636-5593-8(7))* Candlewick Pr.

Van Fleet, Matthew. Alphabet. Skwarek, Skip, ed. Van Fleet, Matthew, illus. 2008. (ENG., Illus.). 20p. (J). (gr. -1-1). 19.99 *(978-1-4169-5565-8(8),* Simon & Schuster/Paula Wiseman Bks.) Simon & Schuster/Paula Wiseman Bks.

—Heads. Van Fleet, Matthew, illus. 2010. (ENG., Illus.). 18p. (J). (gr. -1-1). 19.99 *(978-1-4424-0379-6(9),* Simon & Schuster/Paula Wiseman Bks.) Simon & Schuster/Paula Wiseman Bks.

—Munch! Van Fleet, Matthew, illus. 2013. (ENG., Illus.). 14p. (J). (gr. -1-1). 9.99 *(978-1-4424-9425-1(5),* Simon & Schuster/Paula Wiseman Bks.) Simon & Schuster/Paula Wiseman Bks.

—Tails. 2017. (ENG., Illus.). 20p. (J). (— 1). 14.99 ***(978-1-328-88685-9(9),*** HMH Books For Young Readers) Houghton Mifflin Harcourt Publishing Co.

—Van Fleet Alphabet Heads: Alphabet; Heads. Van Fleet, Matthew, illus. 2013. (ENG., Illus.). 38p. (J). (gr. -1-2). 39.99 *(978-1-4424-8448-1(9),* Simon & Schuster/Paula Wiseman Bks.) Simon & Schuster/Paula Wiseman Bks.

—Van Fleet Sniff! Lick! Munch! Van Fleet, Matthew, illus. 2013. (ENG., Illus.). 42p. (J). (gr. -1-1). 29.99 *(978-1-4424-9509-8(X),* Simon & Schuster/Paula Wiseman Bks.) Simon & Schuster/Paula Wiseman Bks.

van Genechten, Guido. Big & Small. 2013. (Odd One Out Ser.). (ENG.). 18p. (J). (gr. -1-k). bds. 12.95 *(978-1-60537-149-8(1))* Cobblestone Publishing Co.

—The Big Potty Book. 2009. (ENG.). 20p. (J). (gr. k — 1). bds. 12.95 *(978-1-60537-031-6(2))* Cobblestone Publishing Co.

—Crinkle Animals - Garden. 2011. (Crinkle Animals Ser.). (ENG.). 8p. (J). (gr. k — 1). 9.95 *(978-1-60537-081-1(9))* Cobblestone Publishing Co.

—Guess Where? 2012. (Guess Along Ser.). (ENG.). 16p. (J). (gr. k — 1). 9.95 *(978-1-60537-115-3(7))* Cobblestone Publishing Co.

—Guess Who? van Genechten, Guido, illus. 2010. (ENG., Illus.). 28p. (J). (gr. k — 1). 8.95 *(978-1-60537-061-3(4))* Cobblestone Publishing Co.

—Look at That! Wild Animals. 2008. (Look at That! Ser.). (ENG., Illus.). 20p. (J). (gr. k — 1). bds. 6.95 *(978-1-60537-011-8(8))* Clavis Publishing.

—Mommies & Their Babies. 2012. (Black & White Ser.). (ENG.). 20p. (J). (gr. k — 1). bds. 9.95 *(978-1-60537-109-2(2))* Cobblestone Publishing Co.

—Moon Is Sad. 2010. (ENG.). 12p. (J). (gr. k — 1). bds. 8.95 *(978-1-60537-048-4(7))* Clavis Publishing.

van Genechten, Guido & Frippiat, Stéphanie. In, Out & All Around. 2013. (Odd One Out Ser.). (ENG.). 18p. (J). (gr. -1-k). bds. 12.95 *(978-1-60537-150-4(5))* Cobblestone Publishing Co.

Van Horn, William, et al. Walt Disney's Comics, Vol. 667. Clark, John, ed. 2006. (ENG., Illus.). 64p. pap. 6.95 *(978-1-888472-20-2(0),* 9781888472202) Gemstone Publishing, Inc.

Van Tassel, Mary A. Beach Ball's Return. DeBroech, Sarah, illus. 2011. 28p. pap. 24.95 *(978-1-4512-2124-4(X))* America Star Bks.

Vande Velde, Vivian. 8 Class Pets + 1 Squirrel ÷ 1 Dog = Chaos. Björkman, Steve, illus. (ENG.). 80p. (J). 2012. pap. 6.99 *(978-0-8234-2594-5(0))* 2011. 15.95 *(978-0-8234-2364-4(6))* Holiday Hse., Inc.

Vann, Robert Winter Owl. The Bull & the Peacock: And Other Animal Stories. 2003. (Illus.). 57p. (YA). 12.95 *(978-0-9741828-0-3(X))* GO-LA-NV Pr.

Vasquez, Paula. Not What It Seems, 1 vol. 2017. (ENG., Illus.). 40p. (J). 14.99 *(978-1-4236-4691-4(6))* Gibbs Smith, Publisher.

Vaughan, Marcia. The Treasure of Ghostwood Gully: A Southwest Mystery. Terry, Will, illus. 2004. (ENG.). 32p. (J). (gr. 1-3). 15.95 *(978-0-87358-858-4(4))* Cooper Square Publishing Llc.

Vázquez-Vigo, Carmen. La Fuerza de la Gacela. (Barco de Vapor). (SPA.). 64p. (J). (gr. 2-3). *(978-84-348-2040-1(4))* SM Ediciones.

Veldkamp, Tjibbe. Tom the Tamer. Hopman, Philip, illus. 2011. (ENG.). 32p. (J). (gr. -1). 16.95 *(978-1-935954-05-7(9),* 9781935954057) Lemniscaat USA.

Velthuijs, Max. Frog & the Stranger. 2014. (ENG., Illus.). 32p. (J). (-k). pap. 12.95 *(978-1-78344-143-3(7))* Andersen Pr. GBR. Dist: Independent Pubs. Group.

Velvin, Ellen. Rataplan. 2004. reprint ed. pap. 20.95 *(978-1-4191-4398-4(0));* pap. 1.99 *(978-1-4192-4398-1(5))* Kessinger Publishing, LLC.

—Rataplan, a Rogue Elephant & Other Stories. 2007. 96p. per. *(978-1-4068-1627-3(2))* Echo Library.

Venable, Colleen A. F. And Then There Were Gnomes. Yue, Stephanie, illus. 2010. (Guinea Pig, Pet Shop Private Eye Ser.: 2). (ENG.). 48p. (J). (gr. 2-5). pap. 6.95 *(978-0-7613-5480-2(8));* lib. bdg. 27.93 *(978-0-7613-4599-2(X))* Lerner Publishing Group.

—The Ferret's a Foot, 3 vols. Yue, Stephanie, illus. 2011. (Guinea Pig, Pet Shop Private Eye Ser.: 3). (ENG.). 48p. (J). (gr. 2-5). 27.93 *(978-0-7613-5223-5(6));* pap. 6.95 *(978-0-7613-5629-5(0))* Lerner Publishing Group.

—Fish You Were Here, No. 4. Yue, Stephanie, illus. 2011. (Guinea Pig, Pet Shop Private Eye Ser.: 4). (ENG.). 48p. (J). (gr. 2-5). pap. 6.95 *(978-0-7613-5630-1(4));* lib. bdg. 27.93 *(978-0-7613-5224-2(4))* Lerner Publishing Group.

—Going, Going, Dragon! 2013. 48p. pap. 14.95 *(978-1-4677-0973-6(5))* Lerner Publishing Group.

—Going, Going, Dragon! Yue, Stephanie, illus. 2013. (Guinea Pig, Pet Shop Private Eye Ser.: 6). (ENG.). 48p. (J). (gr. 2-5). pap. 6.95 *(978-1-4677-0726-8(0));* lib. bdg. 27.93 *(978-0-7613-6009-4(3))* Lerner Publishing Group.

—Going, Going, Dragon! Yue, Stephanie, illus. 2013. (Guinea Pig, Pet Shop Private Eye Ser.: 6). (ENG.). 46p. lib. bdg. 17.15 *(978-0-606-33994-0(9),* Turtleback) Turtleback Bks.

—Hamster & Cheese. Yue, Stephanie, illus. 2010. (Guinea Pig, Pet Shop Private Eye Ser.: 1). (ENG.). 48p. (J). (gr. 2-5). pap. 6.95 *(978-0-7613-5479-6(4));* lib. bdg. 27.93 *(978-0-7613-4598-5(1))* Lerner Publishing Group.

—Raining Cats & Detectives. Yue, Stephanie, illus. 2012. (Guinea Pig, Pet Shop Private Eye Ser.: 5). (ENG.). 48p. (J). (gr. 2-5). lib. bdg. 27.93 *(978-0-7613-6008-7(5))* Lerner Publishing Group.

Venable, Colleen Af. Mervin the Sloth Is about to Do the Best Thing in the World. Chan, Ruth, illus. 2016. 40p. (J). (gr. -1-3). 17.99 *(978-0-06-233847-1(1),* Greenwillow Bks.) HarperCollins Pubs.

Verburg, Bonnie. The Tree House That Jack Built. Teague, Mark, illus. 2014. (ENG.). 40p. (J). (gr. -1-k). 17.99 *(978-0-439-85338-5(9),* Orchard Bks.) Scholastic, Inc.

Verdick, Elizabeth. Peep Leap, 0 vols. Bendall-Brunello, John, illus. 2013. (ENG.). 32p. (J). (gr. -1-2). 16.99 *(978-1-4778-1640-0(2),* 9781477816400, Amazon Children's Publishing) Amazon Publishing.

Vere, Ed. Everyone's Noisy. 2003. (ENG., Illus.). 14p. (J). 8.99 *(978-0-333-78040-4(X))* Macmillan Pubs., Ltd. GBR. Dist: Trafalgar Square Publishing.

Verma, Monika. My Storyland Animals. 2008. 29p. pap. 24.95 *(978-1-60563-010-6(1))* America Star Bks.

Verne, Jules. The Field of Ice: Part II of the Adventures of Captain Hatteras. 2007. (ENG.). 154p. pap. 19.99 *(978-1-4264-3591-1(6));* 170p. pap. 21.99 *(978-1-4264-3642-0(4))* Creative Media Partners, LLC.

Vickers, Tamara. Mr. Green & the Animal Kingdom: (Imagine That!) You Draw the Picture! 2007. 228p. per. 24.95 *(978-1-4241-8256-5(5))* America Star Bks.

Vickery-Bharadwaj, Janice. Valentino & His Friends: It's Magic! 2012. 28p. pap. 12.99 *(978-1-4691-7709-0(9))* Xlibris Corp.

Villaloz, ChiChi & Etheridge, Katy. Do Dogs Vote? Villaloz, ChiChi & Etheridge, Katy, illus. 2008. (Illus.). 32p. (J). lib. bdg. 24.95 *(978-0-9722180-0-9(9))* Malamute Pr.

Virján, Emma J. What This Story Needs Is a Pig in a Wig. Virján, Emma J., illus. 2015. (Pig in a Wig Book Ser.). (ENG., Illus.). 40p. (J). (gr. -1-3). 9.99 *(978-0-06-232724-6(0))* HarperCollins Pubs.

Visconti, Guido. One Night in a Stable. Cimatoribus, Alessandra, illus. 2004. 32p. (J). 16.00 *(978-0-8028-5279-3(3))* Eerdmans, William B. Publishing Co.

—Wolf on a Leash. Vignoli, Daniella, illus. 2006. (Wolf on a Leash Ser.). 24p. (gr. k-3). lib. bdg. 24.00 *(978-0-8368-6261-4(9),* Gareth Stevens Learning Library) Stevens, Gareth Publishing LLLP.

Vitali, Daniela, illus. Play with My Animals ABCs. 2003. 16p. (J). bds. 5.99 *(978-1-931722-34-6(X),* Sixth Avenue Bks.) Grand Central Publishing.

Viva, Frank. A Trip to the Bottom of the World with Mouse. Viva, Frank, illus. 2012. (ENG., Illus.). 32p. (J). (gr. -1-k). 12.95 *(978-1-935179-19-1(5))* TOON Books / RAW Junior, LLC.

Viviani, Luisa. There Is Something Special Inside of Me. 2004. 25p. pap. 24.95 *(978-1-4137-2372-4(1))* PublishAmerica, Inc.

Voake, Charlotte. Tweedle Dee Dee. Voake, Charlotte, illus. 2008. (ENG., Illus.). 32p. (J). (gr. -1-2). 16.99 *(978-0-7636-3797-2(1))* Candlewick Pr.

Voake, Steve. Daisy Dawson & the Big Freeze. Meserve, Jessica, illus. 2011. (Daisy Dawson Ser.). (ENG.). 96p. (J). (gr. 1-4). pap. 5.99 *(978-0-7636-5627-0(5))* Candlewick Pr.

—Daisy Dawson & the Secret Pond. Meserve, Jessica, illus. 2010. (Daisy Dawson Ser.: 2). (ENG.). 96p. (J). (gr. 1-4). pap. 5.99 *(978-0-7636-4730-8(6))* Candlewick Pr.

—Daisy Dawson at the Beach. Meserve, Jessica, illus. (Daisy Dawson Ser.: 4). (ENG.). (J). (gr. 1-4). 2012. 96p. pap. 5.99 *(978-0-7636-5946-2(0))* 2011. 87p. 14.99 *(978-0-7636-5306-4(3))* Candlewick Pr.

—Daisy Dawson Is on Her Way! Meserve, Jessica, illus. 2009. (Daisy Dawson Ser.: 1). (ENG.). 112p. (J). (gr. 1-4). pap. 5.99 *(978-0-7636-4294-5(0))* Candlewick Pr.

—Daisy Dawson on the Farm. Meserve, Jessica, illus. 2012. (Daisy Dawson Ser.: 5). (ENG.). 96p. (J). (gr. 1-4). 14.99 *(978-0-7636-5882-3(0))* Candlewick Pr.

—Daisy Dawson on the Farm. Meserve, Jessica, illus. 2013. (Daisy Dawson Ser.). (ENG.). 96p. (J). (gr. 1-4). pap. 5.99 *(978-0-7636-6340-7(9))* Candlewick Pr.

Volpi, Sophia. White Fawn. 2004. 160p. 22.95 *(978-0-595-66708-6(2))* iUniverse, Inc.

Von Wielligh, G. R. Animal Tales, Vol. 1. Bankenaar, Dale, illus. 2012. (ENG.). 93p. pap. 12.00 *(978-1-86919-433-8(0))* Protea Boekhuis ZAF. Dist: Casemate Pubs. & Bk. Distributors, LLC.

—Animal Tales, Vol. 2. Bankenaar, Dale, illus. 2012. (ENG.). 93p. pap. 12.00 *(978-1-86919-504-5(3))* Protea Boekhuis ZAF. Dist: Casemate Pubs. & Bk. Distributors, LLC.

Voyer, Dorothy May. Henry Hedgehog's Holiday. 2012. (ENG.). (J). pap. *(978-1-4675-2084-3(5))* Independent Pub.

Wacker, Eileen. The Fujimini Adventure Series Box Set. 2013. (Fujimini Adventure Ser.). (ENG.). 128p. (J). (gr. 1-3). 29.99 *(978-1-4675-1747-8(X))* Oncekids.

Waddell, Martin. Farmer Duck. Oxenbury, Helen, illus. 2008. (Candlewick Storybook Animations Ser.). (ENG.). 40p. (J). (gr. -1-k). 14.99 *(978-0-7636-3512-1(X))* Candlewick Pr.

—Room for a Little One: A Christmas Tale. Cockcroft, Jason, illus. 2008. (ENG.). 26p. (J). (gr. -1-2). bds. 7.99 *(978-1-4169-6177-2(1),* Little Simon) Little Simon.

—Room for a Little One: A Christmas Tale. Cockcroft, Jason, illus. (ENG.). 32p. (J). (gr. -1-3). 2006. 11.99 *(978-1-4169-2518-7(X))* 2004. 18.99 *(978-0-689-86841-2(3))* McElderry, Margaret K. Bks. (McElderry, Margaret K. Bks.).

Wagele, Elizabeth. Finding the Birthday Cake: Helping Children Raise Their Self-Esteem. Wagele, Elizabeth, illus.

2007. (ENG., Illus.). 48p. (J). (gr. k-4). per. 8.95 *(978-0-88282-277-8(2))* New Horizon Pr. Pubs., Inc.
Walden, Libby. Finding First Animals & More! Galloway, Fhiona, illus. 2016. (My Little World Ser.). (ENG.). 12p. (J). (gr. -1-k). bds. 12.99 *(978-1-58925-229-5(2))* Tiger Tales.
Waldron, Kathleen Cook. Roundup at the Palace, 1 vol. Daniel, Alan & Daniel, Lea, illus. 2006. (ENG.). 32p. (J). (gr. -1). 17.95 *(978-0-88995-319-2(8))* Red Deer Pr. CAN. Dist: Ingram Publisher Services.
Waldron, Kevin. Mr. Peek & the Misunderstanding at the Zoo. Waldron, Kevin, illus. 2010. (ENG., Illus.). 48p. (J). (gr. k-12). 15.99 *(978-0-7636-4549-6(4),* Templar) Candlewick Pr.
A Walk at the Farm. 2005. (Gilbert the Pig Chapter Ser.). (ENG.). (J). pap. 7.67 *(978-1-58453-300-9(5))* Pioneer Valley Bks.
Walker, Mary. The Flower Tree. 2010. (Illus.). 50p. pap. 12.95 *(978-1-4327-3588-3(8))* Outskirts Pr., Inc.
Walker Styles Staff. Something Smells Fishy. Whitehouse, Ben, illus. 2016. (Rider Woofson Ser.: 2). (ENG.). 128p. (J). (gr. k-4). pap. 5.99 *(978-1-4814-5741-5(1),* Little Simon) Little Simon.
Wall, Dorothy. The Complete Adventures of Blinky Bill. 2011. (Illus.). 442p. *(978-1-84902-571-3(1))* Benediction Classics.
Wallace, Bill & Wallace, Carol. That Doggone Calf. 2009. (ENG.). 160p. (J). (gr. 3-7). 16.95 *(978-0-8234-2228-9(3))* Holiday Hse., Inc.
Wallace, Carol & Wallace, Bill. Bub, Snow, & the Burly Bear Scare. Gurney, John Steven, illus. 2003. (ENG.). 128p. (J). (gr. 3-7). pap. 7.99 *(978-0-7434-0640-6(0),* Aladdin) Simon & Schuster Children's Publishing.
Wallace, Dianne. Jungle in the Sky. 2012. (ENG.). 27p. (J). pap. 16.95 *(978-1-4327-4527-1(1))* Outskirts Pr., Inc.
Wallace, Suzanne. When I Was a Baby, What Did I Do? What Did I Do? 2012. 28p. pap. 21.99 *(978-1-4771-2144-3(7))* Xlibris Corp.
Wally the Walleye. 2004. (J). lib. bdg. *(978-0-9725485-3-3(X))* Waterfall Ridge.
Walsh, Ellen Stoll. Balancing Act. Walsh, Ellen Stoll, illus. 2010. (ENG., Illus.). 32p. (J). (gr. -1-3). 17.99 *(978-1-4424-0757-2(3),* Beach Lane Bks.) Beach Lane Bks.
Walsh, Sheila. Will, God's Mighty Warrior, 1 vol. Johnson, Meredith, illus. 2006. (Will, God's Mighty Warrior Ser.: 1). (ENG.). 32p. (gr. -1-3). 14.99 *(978-1-4003-0805-7(4))* Nelson, Thomas Inc.
Walter, Debbie. Introducing Russell. Walter, Debbie, illus. 2007. (Illus.). 68p. (J). per. 6.95 *(978-0-9766315-2-1(0))* Moose Run Productions.
Walters, Catherine. The Special Christmas Tree. Taylor-Kielty, Simon, illus. 2012. (J). *(978-1-4351-4315-9(9))* Barnes & Noble, Inc.
Walters, Eric. The Matatu, 1 vol. Campbell, Eva, illus. 2012. (ENG.). 32p. (J). (gr. -1-3). 19.95 *(978-1-55469-301-6(2))* Orca Bk. Pubs. USA.
Wan, Joyce. Are You My Mommy? 2014. (ENG.). 18p. (J). (gr. -1 — 1). bds. 6.99 *(978-0-545-54047-6(X),* Cartwheel Bks.) Scholastic, Inc.
—My Lucky Little Dragon. Wan, Joyce, illus. 2014. (ENG., Illus.). 14p. (J). (— 1). bds. 6.99 *(978-0-545-54046-9(1),* Cartwheel Bks.) Scholastic, Inc.
—Peek-A-Boo Farm. 2015. (ENG., Illus.). 14p. (J). (— 1). bds. 6.99 *(978-0-545-75045-5(8),* Cartwheel Bks.) Scholastic, Inc.
Wang, Dorthea Deprisco. Five Minutes until Bed. Vaux, Patricia, illus. 2012. (ENG.). 14p. (J). (-k). bds. 5.99 *(978-1-4494-2244-8(6))* Andrews McMeel Publishing.
Wang, Gabrielle. The Race for the Chinese Zodiac. Rippin, Sally & Abos, Regine, illus. 2013. (ENG.). 32p. (J). (gr. k-4). 14.99 *(978-0-7636-6778-8(1))* Candlewick Pr.
Wang, Margaret. I Love You, Every Little Bit. Butler, John, illus. 2006. (ENG.). 10p. (gr. -1-k). bds. 9.95 *(978-1-58117-482-3(9),* Intervisual/Piggy Toes) Bendon, Inc.
—Postcards from Kitty. Silver-Thompson, Pattie, illus. 2005. 12p. (J). (gr. -1-3). 9.95 *(978-1-58117-427-4(6),* Intervisual/Piggy Toes) Bendon, Inc.
Ward, Helen. Spots in a Box. Ward, Helen, illus. 2015. (ENG., Illus.). 40p. (J). (gr. -1-2). 16.99 *(978-0-7636-7597-4(0),* Templar) Candlewick Pr.
—The Town Mouse & the Country Mouse. Ward, Helen, illus. 2012. (ENG., Illus.). 48p. (J). (gr. -1-3). 16.99 *(978-0-7636-6098-7(1),* Templar) Candlewick Pr.
Ward, Jennifer. Because You Are My Baby. Long, Sylvia, illus. 2007. (ENG.). 32p. (J). (gr. -1-1). 15.95 *(978-0-87358-911-6(4))* Cooper Square Publishing Llc.
—The Little Creek. Scott, Julie, illus. 2005. 28p. (J). (gr. 3-7). pap. 7.95 *(978-1-58369-057-4(3))* Western National Parks Assn.
—The Seed & the Giant Saguaro. Rangner, Mike K., illus. 2003. (ENG.). 32p. (J). (gr. -1-3). 15.95 *(978-0-87358-845-4(2))* Cooper Square Publishing Llc.
—The Sunhat. Sisson, Stéphanie Roth, illus. 2013. (ENG.). (J). 15.95 *(978-1-933855-78-3(9),* Rio Nuevo Pubs.) Rio Nuevo Pubs.
Ward, Kris A. Tony's Day in the Park. 2008. 42p. pap. 24.95 *(978-1-60813-351-2(6))* America Star Bks.
Ward, Sarah. illus. Carry & Learn Opposites. 2016. (ENG.). 10p. (J). (— 1). bds. 7.99 *(978-0-545-79789-4(6),* Cartwheel Bks.) Scholastic, Inc.
Wargin, Kathy-jo. Minn from Minnesota. Holman, Karen Busch, illus. 2006. (Mitt Midwest Ser.: 2). (ENG.). 144p. (J). (gr. k-7). 14.95 *(978-1-58726-304-0(1),* Mitten Pr.) Ann Arbor Editions LLC.
—Mitt & Minn at the Wisconsin Cheese Jamboree. Holman, Karen Busch, illus. 2007. (Mitt Midwest Ser.: 3). (ENG.). 144p. (J). (gr. k-7). 14.95 *(978-1-58726-305-7(X),* Mitten Pr.) Ann Arbor Editions LLC.
Waring, Geoff. Oscar & the Frog: A Book about Growing. Waring, Geoff, illus. 2008. (Start with Science Ser.). (ENG., Illus.). 32p. (J). (gr. -1-3). pap. 6.99 *(978-0-7636-4030-9(1))* Candlewick Pr.
Warnes, Tim. Can't You Sleep, Dotty? Warnes, Tim, illus. 2003. (Illus.). 32p. (J). pap. 5.95 *(978-1-58925-376-6(0))* Tiger Tales.
—Daddy Hug. Chapman, Jane, illus. 2008. (ENG.). 32p. (J). (gr. -1-k). 17.99 *(978-0-06-058950-9(7))* HarperCollins Pubs.
—Happy Birthday, Dotty. Warnes, Tim, illus. 2003. (Illus.). 32p. (J). tchr. ed. 15.95 *(978-1-58925-026-0(5))* Tiger Tales.
Warrick, Karen Clemens. Who Needs That Nose? Neidigh, Sherry, tr. Neidigh, Sherry, illus. 2004. (ENG.). 32p. (J). (gr. -1-k). 15.95 *(978-1-55971-887-5(0))* Cooper Square Publishing Llc.
Washington, Donna L. Li'l Rabbit's Kwanzaa. Evans, Shane W., illus. 2010. (ENG.). 32p. (J). (gr. -1-2). 12.99 *(978-0-06-072816-8(7),* Tegen, Katherine Bks) HarperCollins Pubs.
Wassillie, Eliza, et al. Four Legged Adventures. Wassillie, Eliza et al, illus. 2006. (Adventure Story Collection Ser.). 28p. (J). (gr. 2-6). pap. 10.00 *(978-1-58084-250-1(X))* Lower Kuskokwim Schl. District.
Wassmann, Marilyn B. & Wassman, Paul A., illus. What the Wind Blew In: 6 Stories to Read with Children. 2010. 29p. (J). *(978-1-4535-6303-8(2))* Xlibris Corp.
Waterfield, Susan. Spunkie's Magical Garden. 2012. 32p. pap. 14.95 *(978-1-257-77576-7(6))* Lulu Pr., Inc.
Watt, Marg. Tales from Hallowed Hollow: Karma. Finn, Jenny, illus. 2012. 34p. (YA). pap. *(978-0-9872715-8-7(X))* Moonra Pubns.
Watts, Jeri. Kizzy Ann Stamps. 2012. (ENG., Illus.). 192p. (J). (gr. 4-7). 15.99 *(978-0-7636-5895-3(2))* Candlewick Pr.
Watts, Katherine. Tiger Tails. 2008. 76p. pap. 35.95 *(978-0-9556878-0-8(2))* Watts, Katherine GBR. Dist: Lulu Pr., Inc.
Wax, Wendy. Animal Family Christmas. 2007. (ENG.). 20p. (J). 14.95 *(978-1-58117-625-4(2),* Intervisual/Piggy Toes) Bendon, Inc.
—What Do You Say? Please & Thank You. Dillard, Sarah, illus. 2005. (J). *(978-1-58987-108-3(1))* Kindermusik International.
Wayne, Richard, ed. Poppin's Pumpkin Patch Parade. Carlson, Patrick, illus. 2016. (ENG.). 32p. (J). pap. 12.98 *(978-0-9801692-1-8(6))* Gemstone Literary.
Webb, Josh. Dudley's Muddley Day. Antonini, Gabriele, illus. 2011. (Red Bananas Ser.). (ENG.). 48p. (J). (gr. 1-3). pap. 5.99 *(978-1-4052-5948-4(5))* Egmont Bks., Ltd. GBR. Dist: Independent Pubs. Group.
Webber, Gail. Time of the Cats. 2013. 132p. 28.95 *(978-1-4582-1233-7(5),* Abbott Pr.) Author Solutions, Inc.
Wedekind, Annie & Haas, Jessie. Little Prince: The Story of a Shetland Pony. 2009. (Breyer Horse Collection: 2). (ENG.). 128p. (J). (gr. 4-7). pap. 5.99 *(978-0-312-59918-8(8),* 9780312599188) Feiwel & Friends.
Weeks, Sarah. Follow the Moon. Duranceau, Suzanne, illus. 2003. (ENG.). 32p. (J). (gr. -1-3). 17.99 *(978-0-06-055744-7(3))* HarperCollins Pubs.
—If I Were a Lion. Solomon, Heather M., illus. (ENG.). 40p. (J). (gr. -1-2). 2007. 7.99 *(978-1-4169-3837-8(0))* 2004. 17.99 *(978-0-689-84836-0(6))* Simon & Schuster Children's Publishing. (Atheneum Bks. for Young Readers).
Wehner, Adrienna. Elephants & Roses. 2003. (Illus.). (YA). (gr. 2-18). 22.00 *(978-0-9653866-3-0(5))* Wehner, Adrienna.
Weigl Publishers, creator. The Crow & the Raven: Why Should You Be Yourself? 2013. (AV2 Animated Storytime Ser.: Vol. 12). (ENG., Illus.). 32p. (J). (gr. -1-3). lib. bdg. 29.99 *(978-1-62127-916-7(2),* AV2 by Weigl) Weigl Pubs., Inc.
—The Goose & the Golden Egg: What Happens When You Are Greedy? 2013. (AV2 Animated Storytime Ser.: Vol. 14). (ENG., Illus.). 32p. (J). (gr. -1-3). lib. bdg. 29.99 *(978-1-62127-918-1(9),* AV2 by Weigl) Weigl Pubs., Inc.
—The Shoemaker & His Medicine: Why Should You Tell the Truth? 2013. (AV2 Animated Storytime Ser.: Vol. 18). (ENG., Illus.). 32p. (J). (gr. -1-3). lib. bdg. 29.99 *(978-1-62127-922-8(7),* AV2 by Weigl) Weigl Pubs., Inc.
—The Snake & His Tail: How Can You Support Your Team? 2013. (AV2 Animated Storytime Ser.: Vol. 19). (ENG., Illus.). 32p. (J). (gr. -1-3). lib. bdg. 29.99 *(978-1-62127-923-5(5),* AV2 by Weigl) Weigl Pubs., Inc.
—The Wild Donkey & the Tame Donkey: Why Should You Not Judge Others by Their Appearance? 2013. (AV2 Animated Storytime Ser.: Vol. 20). (ENG., Illus.). 32p. (J). (gr. -1-3). lib. bdg. 29.99 *(978-1-62127-924-2(3),* AV2 by Weigl) Weigl Pubs., Inc.
Weimer, Heidi R. Happy Birthday to You! 2007. (ENG., Illus.). 14p. (gr. -1-k). bds. 12.99 *(978-0-8249-6699-7(6),* Ideal Pubns.) Worthy Publishing.
—How Do I Kiss You? Sharp, Chris, illus. 2008. (ENG.). 18p. (J). (gr. -1-k). bds. 12.99 *(978-0-8249-1814-9(2),* Ideal Pubns.) Worthy Publishing.
Weiner, Marcella Bakur & Neimark, Jill. I Want Your Moo: A Story for Children about Self-Esteem. Adinolfi, JoAnn, illus. 2nd ed. 2009. 32p. (J). (gr. -1-3). 14.95 *(978-1-4338-0542-4(1));* pap. 9.95 *(978-1-4338-0552-3(9))* American Psychological Assn. (Magination Pr.).
Weinstone, David. All My Friends Are Fast Asleep. Le Huche, Magali, illus. 2017. (ENG.). 40p. (J). 17.99 ***(978-0-374-30535-2(8),*** 9780374305352, Farrar, Straus & Giroux (BYR)) Farrar, Straus & Giroux.
Weiss, Dylan. Sebastian's Tale: A Skunk Tales Trilogy Book. 2016. (J). *(978-1-943267-16-3(2))* Red Engine Pr.
Weiss, Ellen. Fruit Salad: A Touch-and-Learn Book. Bennett, Andy, illus. 2006. (PBS Kids Ser.). 8p. (J). (gr. -1-k). bds. 6.95 *(978-1-57791-314-6(0))* Brighter Minds Children's Publishing.
Weld, Larry. Counting with Silly Critters. 2008. 44p. pap. 19.49 *(978-1-4389-2074-0(1))* AuthorHouse.
Weller, Frances Ward. The Day the Animals Came: A Story of Saint Francis Day. Long, Loren, illus. 2006. 35p. (J). (gr. k-4). reprint ed. 17.00 *(978-1-4223-5396-7(6))* DIANE Publishing Co.
Welling, Peter J. Justin Potemkin & the 500-Mile Race, 1 vol. Welling, Peter J., illus. 2004. (ENG., Illus.). 32p. (J). (gr. k-3). 16.99 *(978-1-58980-149-3(0))* Pelican Publishing Co., Inc.
Wells, Robert E. & Wells, Robert. Hay Algo Mas Grande Que una Ballena Azul? 2003. (SPA., Illus.). 30p. (J). (gr. 1-3). 11.16 *(978-84-261-3030-3(5),* JV7302) Juventud, Editorial ESP. Dist: Lectorum Pubns., Inc.
—Hay Algo Mas Pequeno Que Una Musarana? 2003. (SPA., Illus.). 32p. (J). (gr. 1-3). 15.99 *(978-84-261-3031-0(3),* JV7997) Juventud, Editorial ESP. Dist: Lectorum Pubns., Inc.
Wells, Rosemary. Emily's First 100 Days of School. Wells, Rosemary, illus. 2005. (ENG., Illus.). 64p. (J). (gr. -1-1). pap. 9.99 *(978-0-7868-1354-4(7))* Hyperion Pr.
—Emily's First 100 Days of School. 2006. (Illus.). (J). (gr. -1-4). 18.95 *(978-0-439-84903-6(9),* WPCD654) Weston Woods Studios, Inc.
—Ivy Takes Care. LaMarche, Jim, illus. (ENG.). 208p. (J). (gr. 3-7). 2015. pap. 6.99 *(978-0-7636-7660-5(8))* 2013. 15.99 *(978-0-7636-5352-1(7))* Candlewick Pr.
—Stella's Starliner. Wells, Rosemary, illus. 2014. (ENG., Illus.). 32p. (J). (gr. -1-3). 15.99 *(978-0-7636-1495-9(5))* Candlewick Pr.
Wells, Shannon Nicole. Gold! A Tall Tale. 2009. (J). pap. 7.00 *(978-1-61623-111-8(4))* Independent Pub.
West, Judy. Do You Have My Purr? Warnes, Tim, illus. 2014. (My First Storybook Ser.). (ENG.). 32p. (J). (gr. -1-1). 6.99 *(978-1-58925-511-1(9))* Tiger Tales.
West, Robert. Escape from the Drooling Octopod!, 1 vol. 2008. (Star-Fighters of Murphy Street Ser.). (ENG., Illus.). 144p. (J). (gr. 4-7). pap. 6.99 *(978-0-310-71427-9(3))* Zonderkidz.
Weston Woods Staff, creator. Chato & the Party Animals. 2011. 38.75 *(978-0-439-84581-6(5))* 2011. 18.95 *(978-0-439-73984-9(5))* 2004. 29.95 *(978-1-55592-703-5(3))* Weston Woods Studios, Inc.
—Doctor de Soto. 2011. (SPA.). 38.75 *(978-0-439-78365-1(8));* 29.95 *(978-0-439-73624-4(2))* Weston Woods Studios, Inc.
—Emily's First 100 Days of School. 2011. 38.75 *(978-0-439-84892-3(X))* Weston Woods Studios, Inc.
—In the Small, Small Pond. 2011. 38.75 *(978-0-439-84578-6(5))* Weston Woods Studios, Inc.
—A Kiss for Little Bear. 2011. 29.95 *(978-0-439-73481-3(9));* 18.95 *(978-0-439-72735-8(9));* 38.75 *(978-0-439-72739-6(1))* Weston Woods Studios, Inc.
—May I Bring a Friend? 2011. 18.95 *(978-0-439-72783-9(9));* 29.95 *(978-0-439-73490-5(8));* 38.75 *(978-0-439-72836-2(3))* Weston Woods Studios, Inc.
—Possum Magic. 2011. 38.75 *(978-0-545-14784-2(0));* 18.95 *(978-0-545-08634-9(5))* Weston Woods Studios, Inc.
—A Story-A Story. 2011. 18.95 *(978-0-439-72891-1(6));* 29.95 *(978-0-439-73521-6(1))* Weston Woods Studios, Inc.
—A Story-Astory. 2011. 38.75 *(978-0-439-72892-8(4))* Weston Woods Studios, Inc.
—The Ugly Duckling. 2011. 29.95 *(978-0-439-72909-3(2))* Weston Woods Studios, Inc.
—Wings: A Tale of Two Chickens. 2011. 18.95 *(978-0-439-72920-8(3));* 38.75 *(978-0-439-72921-5(1))* Weston Woods Studios, Inc.
Wetherby, Mark. The Tales of Mossy Dell. 2009. (Illus.). 88p. pap. 10.49 *(978-1-4389-7726-3(3))* AuthorHouse.
Whatley, Bruce & Beatrice, Chris, illus. Aesop's Fables: A Pop-Up Book of Classic Tales. 2011. (ENG.). 14p. (J). (gr. -1-3). 27.99 *(978-1-4169-7146-7(7),* Little Simon) Little Simon.
What's Wrong with Gilbert. 2005. (Gilbert the Pig Chapter Ser.). (J). 7.67 *(978-1-58453-299-6(8))* Pioneer Valley Bks.
Wheatley, Sandra. Marmaduke the Mighty. 2010. (Illus.). 28p. (gr. -1). 13.99 *(978-1-4490-4290-5(2))* AuthorHouse.
Wheeler, J. D. Gummery & Lubber. 2008. 56p. pap. 16.95 *(978-1-60563-432-6(8))* America Star Bks.
Wheeler, Lisa. The Pet Project: Cute & Cuddly Vicious Verses. OHora, Zachariah, illus. 2013. (ENG.). 40p. (J). (gr. -1-3). 16.99 *(978-1-4169-7595-3(0),* Atheneum Bks. for Young Readers) Simon & Schuster Children's Publishing.
White, E. B. La Telarana de Carlota, 1 vol. Williams, Garth, illus. 2005. (SPA.). 224p. (J). (gr. 3-7). pap. 7.99 *(978-0-06-075740-3(X))* HarperCollins Pubs.
—The Telarana de Carlota (La Telarana de Carlota) Williams, Garth, illus. 2005. (Charlotte's Web Ser.). (SPA.). 224p. (J). 16.99 *(978-0-06-075739-7(6),* Rayo) HarperCollins Pubs.
White, E. B. & DiCamillo, Kate. Charlotte's Web: a Harper Classic. Williams, Garth, illus. 2017. (Harper Classic Ser.). 208p. (J). (gr. 3-7). 16.99 ***(978-0-06-265875-3(1))*** HarperCollins Pubs.
White, Kathryn. Snowshoe the Hare. Rivers, Ruth, illus. 2005. (Red Go Bananas Ser.). (ENG.). 48p. (J). (gr. 2-3). lib. bdg. *(978-0-7787-2677-7(0),* 1253648) Crabtree Publishing Co.
White, Kittie. The Magic Butterfly: And Other Tales. 2008. (ENG.). 52p. pap. 11.99 *(978-1-4196-9096-9(5))* CreateSpace Independent Publishing Platform.
White, Marsha. Bear's New Classes. White, Marsha, illus. (Illus.). 16p. (J). 10.95 *(978-1-58117-294-2(X),* Intervisual/Piggy Toes) Bendon, Inc.
Whittaker, Brian. Quest for the Kangoalaplatybat. 2010. 28p. pap. 17.99 *(978-1-4520-0844-8(2))* AuthorHouse.
Whitten, Mindy J. B. An Alpaca in My Pocket. 2011. 36p. (gr. 1-2). pap. 15.14 *(978-1-4567-2015-5(5))* AuthorHouse.
Who Hops? Who Hoots? Book Set 800945, 2 vols. 2005. (J). bds. *(978-1-59794-099-3(2))* Environments, Inc.
Who's Coming for a Ride? Individual Title, 6 packs. (Literatura 2000 Ser.). (gr. -1-1). 28.00 *(978-0-7635-0019-1(4))* Rigby Education.
Whose Egg Is This? Individual Title Six-Packs. (Story Steps Ser.). (gr. k-2). 32.00 *(978-0-7635-9607-1(8))* Rigby Education.
Whose Spots. 2005. (J). bds. 5.99 *(978-1-933200-05-7(7))* Family Bks. at Home.
Whybrow, Ian. Dear Little Wolf. Ross, Tony, illus. 2005. (Little Wolf Adventures Ser.). 64p. (gr. 3-6). pap., lib. bdg. 14.95 *(978-0-87614-902-7(6))* Lerner Publishing Group.
—Say Hello to the Snowy Animals! Eaves, Edward, illus. 2012. (J). *(978-0-7607-9675-7(0))* Barnes & Noble, Inc.
—That Naughty Meerkat! Parsons, Garry, illus. 2016. (ENG.). 32p. (J). 17.99 *(978-0-00-813945-2(8),* HarperCollins Children's Bks.) HarperCollins Pubs. Ltd. GBR. Dist: HarperCollins Pubs.
—The Tickle Book. Scheffler, Axel, illus. 2016. (ENG.). 12p. (J). (gr. -1-k). pap. 8.99 *(978-1-5098-0697-3(0))* Pan Macmillan GBR. Dist: Independent Pubs. Group.
Wicke, Ed. Wicked Tales. 2006. (ENG., Illus.). 156p. (J). per. 9.99 *(978-0-9677652-7-3(7),* BlacknBlue Pr. UK) Blacknblue Pr.
Widner, Jan. Then Came the Rains. 2013. 28p. pap. 16.95 *(978-1-4497-9456-9(4),* WestBow Pr.) Author Solutions, Inc.
Wiersum, Gale. The Animals' Christmas Eve. 2007. (Little Golden Book Ser.). (ENG., Illus.). 24p. (J). (gr. -1-k). 4.99 *(978-0-375-83923-8(2),* Golden Bks.) Random Hse. Children's Bks.
Wilcox, Leigh Attaway. All Better: A Touch-and-Heal Book. Wildish, Lee, illus. 2007. (ENG.). 12p. (gr. -1). 12.95 *(978-1-58117-591-2(4),* Intervisual/Piggy Toes) Bendon, Inc.
Wild, Margaret. Nighty Night!, 1 vol. Argent, Kerry, illus. 2014. (ENG.). 32p. (J). (gr. -1-1). 7.95 *(978-1-56145-812-7(0))* Peachtree Pubs.
Wilder, Laura Ingalls. Animal Adventures. 2017. (Little House Chapter Book Ser.: 3). (Illus.). 112p. (J). (gr. 1-5). pap. 4.99 *(978-0-06-237712-8(4))* HarperCollins Pubs.
Wildman, Dale. Do You Know the Way to Find an A? A Rhyming ABC Book. Sisung, Peter, illus. 2006. 24p. (J). per. 2.99 *(978-1-59958-002-9(0))* Journey Stone Creations, LLC.
Wildsmith, Brian. Animal Colors. Wildsmith, Brian, illus. 2004. (PER., Illus.). 16p. (J). bds. 4.99 *(978-1-932065-42-8(3))* Star Bright Bks., Inc.
—Jungle Party, 1 vol. Wildsmith, Brian, illus. 2006. (ENG., Illus.). 32p. (J). pap. 6.95 *(978-1-59572-053-5(7))* Star Bright Bks., Inc.
—Jungle Party, 1 vol. 2006. (ENG., Illus.). 32p. (J). (gr. -1-3). 17.95 *(978-1-59572-052-8(9))* Star Bright Bks., Inc.
—The Owl & the Woodpecker, 1 vol. Wildsmith, Brian, illus. 2006. (ENG., Illus.). 32p. (J). (gr. -1-3). 16.95 *(978-1-59572-043-6(X))* Star Bright Bks., Inc.
—Professor Noah's Spaceship, 1 vol. Wildsmith, Brian, illus. 2008. (ENG., Illus.). 32p. (J). 16.95 *(978-1-59572-124-2(X))* Star Bright Bks., Inc.
Wildsmith, Brian, illus. Brian Wildsmith's Animals to Count. 2004. (ARA.). 16p. (J). bds. 4.95 *(978-1-932065-45-9(8),* 718-784-9112) Star Bright Bks., Inc.
Wilhelm, Hans. Hello, Sun! Wilhelm, Hans, illus. 2005. (Illus.). 32p. (gr. k-2). 15.25 *(978-1-57505-348-6(9))* Lerner Publishing Group.
—A Hole in the Wall. Wilhelm, Hans, illus. 2016. (ENG., Illus.). 32p. (J). 16.95 *(978-0-8234-3535-7(0))* Holiday Hse., Inc.
Wilkinson, Lisa. Prickle Says I'm Sorry. McCord, Kathi, illus. 2015. (Faith That Sticks Bks.). (ENG.). 26p. (J). pap. 3.99 *(978-1-4964-0312-4(6))* Tyndale Hse. Pubs.
Willems, Mo. A Big Guy Took My Ball! Willems, Mo, illus. 2013. (Elephant & Piggie Ser.). (ENG., Illus.). 64p. (J). (gr. 1-3). 9.99 *(978-1-4231-7491-2(7))* Hyperion Bks. for Children.
—Cat the Cat Who Is That? Willems, Mo, illus. 2010. (Illus.). 32p. (J). (gr. -1-3). (ENG.). 10.99 *(978-0-06-172840-2(3));* lib. bdg. 14.89 *(978-0-06-172841-9(1))* HarperCollins Pubs.
—Let's Say Hi to Friends Who Fly! Willems, Mo, illus. 2010. (Illus.). 32p. (J). (gr. -1-3). (ENG.). 10.99 *(978-0-06-172842-6(X));* lib. bdg. 14.89 *(978-0-06-172846-4(2))* HarperCollins Pubs.
—My New Friend Is So Fun! Willems, Mo, illus. 2014. (Elephant & Piggie Ser.). (ENG., Illus.). 64p. (J). (gr. 1-3). 9.99 *(978-1-4231-7958-0(7))* Hyperion Bks. for Children.
—The Thank You Book. Willems, Mo, illus. 2016. (Elephant & Piggie Book Ser.). (ENG., Illus.). 64p. (J). (gr. 1-3). 9.99 *(978-1-4231-7828-6(9))* Hyperion Bks. for Children.
—Time to Sleep, Sheep the Sheep! Willems, Mo, illus. 2010. (Illus.). 32p. (J). (gr. -1-3). (ENG.). 10.99 *(978-0-06-172847-1(0));* lib. bdg. 14.89 *(978-0-06-172848-8(9))* HarperCollins Pubs.
—What's Your Sound, Hound the Hound? Willems, Mo, illus. 2010. (Illus.). 32p. (J). (gr. -1-3). lib. bdg. 14.89 *(978-0-06-172845-7(4))* HarperCollins Pubs.
—What's Your Sound Hound the Hound? Willems, Mo, illus. 2010. (ENG., Illus.). 32p. (J). (gr. -1-3). 10.99 *(978-0-06-172844-0(6))* HarperCollins Pubs.
—Who Sleeps, Cat the Cat? Willems, Mo, illus. 2014. (ENG., Illus.). 22p. (J). (gr. -1 — 1). bds. 6.99 *(978-0-06-230655-5(3))* HarperCollins Pubs.
Willems, Mo & Campoy, F. Isabel. ¡Un Tipo Grande Se Llevó Mi Pelota! Willems, Mo, illus. 2015. (Elephant & Piggie Book Ser.). (SPA., Illus.). 64p. (J). (gr. 1-3). 9.99 *(978-1-4847-2285-5(X))* Disney Publishing Worldwide.
William H. Sadlier Staff. Bye-bye, Katy, Vol. 3. 2005. (Emergent Library: Vol. 1). (gr. -1-1). 24.00 net. *(978-0-8215-8914-4(8))* Sadlier, William H. Inc.
Williamgoldenpen. Quacker's Bedtime Stories. 2006. 49p. pap. 16.95 *(978-1-4241-2236-3(8))* PublishAmerica, Inc.
—Quacker's Bedtime Stories... Continued. 2007. (ENG.). 68p. per. 19.95 *(978-1-4241-7448-5(1))* America Star Bks.
Williams, Alexandra & Williams, David, illus. Fairy Nyumbani. 2005. 24p. *(978-9966-956-41-5(7))* Jacaranda Designs Ltd.
Williams, Sam. I'm the Boss. Dufalla, Anita, illus. 2012. (ENG.). 24p. (gr. k-1). pap. 8.95 *(978-1-61810-297-3(4))* Rourke Educational Media.
—It's My Turn. Dufalla, Anita, illus. 2012. (ENG.). 24p. (gr. k-1). pap. 8.95 *(978-1-61810-296-6(6))* Rourke Educational Media.
Williams, Sue. I Went Walking. Vivas, Julie, illus. 2014. 32p. pap. 27.00 *(978-1-61003-230-8(6))* Center for the Collaborative Classroom.
—I Went Walking. Vivas, Julie, illus. 2004. (J). (gr. -1-2). audio compact disk 28.95 *(978-1-59112-720-8(3))* 2004. (J). (gr. -1-2). audio compact disk 28.95 *(978-1-59112-720-8(3))* 2003. pap. 39.95 incl. audio compact disk *(978-1-59112-721-5(1))* Live Oak Media.
Williams, Teresa Ann. Friends of Wildwood, 1 vol. 2009. 48p. pap. 16.95 *(978-1-4489-9419-9(5))* America Star Bks.
Williamson, Stafford. Puppy Goes to Lambergarten. 2005. 11p. 11.18 *(978-1-4116-3854-9(9))* Lulu Pr., Inc.
Willingham, Ellie. Wildwood. Willingham, Ellie, illus. 2007. (ENG., Illus.). 136p. (J). (gr. -1-3). per. 10.00 *(978-0-9792371-0-2(6))* Keene Publishing.
Willis, Jeanne. Be Gentle, Python! Birchall, Mark, illus. 2005. (Picture Bks.). 28p. (J). (gr. k-2). 7.95 *(978-1-57505-508-4(2))* Lerner Publishing Group.
—Be Quiet, Parrot! Birchall, Mark, illus. 2005. (Picture Bks.). 32p. (J). (gr. k-2). 7.25 *(978-1-57505-492-6(2))* Lerner Publishing Group.
—Boa's Bad Birthday. Ross, Tony, illus. 2014. (ENG.). 32p. (J). (gr. -1-3). 16.95 *(978-1-4677-3450-9(0))* Lerner Publishing Group.
—Daft Bat. Ross, Tony, illus. 2007. (ENG.). 32p. (J). (gr. k-2). 16.95 *(978-1-84270-476-9(1))* Transworld Publishers Ltd. GBR. Dist: Independent Pubs. Group.
—No Biting, Puma! Birchall, Mark, illus. 2005. (Picture Bks.). 28p. (J). (gr. k-2). 7.25 *(978-1-57505-509-1(0))* Lerner Publishing Group.
—Slug Needs a Hug! Ross, Tony, illus. 2015. (ENG.). 32p. (J). (gr. -1-3). 17.99 *(978-1-4677-9317-9(5));* 17.99 *(978-1-4677-9309-4(4))* Lerner Publishing Group.

—That's Not Funny! Reynolds, Adrian, illus. 2010. (Andersen Press Picture Bks). (ENG.). 32p. (J). (gr. -1-3). 16.95 (978-0-7613-6445-0(5)) Lerner Publishing Group.

Willis, Jeanne & Ross, Tony. Como Era Yo Cuando Era un Bebe? (Buenas Noches Ser.). (SPA., Illus.). (J). (gr. k-3). 8.95 (978-958-04-6031-2(0)) Norma S.A. COL. Dist: Distribuidora Norma, Inc., Lectorum Pubns., Inc.

Willson, Sarah. Class Confusion. Dress, Robert, illus. 2006. (SpongeBob SquarePants Ser.: 11). (ENG.). 24p. (J). (gr. -1-3). pap. 3.99 (978-1-4169-1239-2(8), Simon Spotlight/Nickelodeon) Simon Spotlight/Nickelodeon.

Wilsdon, Christina. A Wild Ride in Texas. Jaekel, Susan, illus. 2006. 26p. (J). 7.99 (978-1-59939-011-6(6)) Cornerstone Pr.

Wilson, Anna. Monkey Business, 1. unabr. ed. 2014. (ENG., Illus.). 256p. (J). (gr. 2-4). pap. 7.99 (978-0-330-50928-2(4)) Pan Macmillan GBR. Dist: Independent Pubs. Group.

Wilson, Hannah & Parrish, Emma. Hoppity Frog: A Hide-and-Seek Book. 2015. (Slide-And-Seek Ser.). (ENG., Illus.). 10p. (J). (gr. -1-k). 8.99 (978-1-4998-0030-2(4)) Little Bee Books Inc.

Wilson, Karma. Bear Feels Scared. Chapman, Jane, illus. 2011. (Bear Bks.). (ENG.). 34p. (J). (gr. -1 — 1). bds. 7.99 (978-1-4424-2755-6(8), Little Simon) Little Simon.

—Bear Feels Scared. Chapman, Jane, illus. 2008. (Bear Bks.). (ENG.). 40p. (J). (gr. -1-3). 17.99 (978-0-689-85986-1(4), McElderry, Margaret K. Bks.) McElderry, Margaret K. Bks.

—Bear Feels Sick. Chapman, Jane, illus. 2012. (Bear Bks.). (ENG.). 34p. (J). (gr. -1-2). bds. 7.99 (978-1-4424-4093-7(7), Little Simon) Little Simon.

—Bear Sees Colors. Chapman, Jane, illus. 2014. (Bear Bks.). (ENG.). 32p. (J). (gr. -1-2). 16.99 (978-1-4424-6536-7(0), McElderry, Margaret K. Bks.) McElderry, Margaret K. Bks.

—Bear Snores On. Chapman, Jane, illus. 2005. (Bear Bks.). (ENG.). 34p. (J). (gr. -1-k). bds. 7.99 (978-1-4169-0272-0(4), Little Simon) Little Simon.

—Bear Stays up for Christmas. Chapman, Jane, illus. 2004. (Bear Bks.). (ENG.). 40p. (J). (gr. -1-3). 17.99 (978-0-689-85278-7(9), McElderry, Margaret K. Bks.) McElderry, Margaret K. Bks.

—Bear Wants More. Chapman, Jane, illus. 2008. (Bear Bks.). (ENG.). 34p. (J). (gr. -1-2). bds. 7.99 (978-1-4169-4922-0(4), Little Simon) Little Simon.

—Bear's Loose Tooth. Chapman, Jane, illus. 2014. (Bear Bks.). (ENG.). 34p. (J). (gr. -1-k). bds. 7.99 (978-1-4424-8936-3(7), Little Simon) Little Simon.

—Bear's Loose Tooth. Chapman, Jane, illus. 2011. (Bear Bks.). (ENG.). 40p. (J). (gr. -1-3). 17.99 (978-1-4169-5855-0(X), McElderry, Margaret K. Bks.) McElderry, Margaret K. Bks.

—Bear's New Friend. Chapman, Jane, illus. 2006. (Bear Bks.). (ENG.). 40p. (J). (gr. -1-3). 17.99 (978-0-689-85984-7(8), McElderry, Margaret K. Bks.) McElderry, Margaret K. Bks.

—Big Bear, Small Mouse. Chapman, Jane, illus. 2016. (Bear Bks.). (ENG.). 32p. (J). (gr. -1-2). 16.99 (978-1-4814-5971-6(6), McElderry, Margaret K. Bks.) McElderry, Margaret K. Bks.

—Mama Always Comes Home. Dyer, Brooke, illus. 32p. (J). (gr. -1-1). 2007. (ENG.). pap. 6.99 (978-0-06-057507-6(7), Harper Trophy) 2005. 15.99 (978-0-06-057505-2(0)) HarperCollins Pubs.

—Trick or Treat, Calico! Erdogan, Buket, illus. 2014. (J). (978-1-4351-5610-4(2), Little Simon) Little Simon.

Wilson, Pauline. Animal & Other Antics. 2004. (Illus.). 56p. pap. (978-1-84401-313-5(8)) Athena Pr.

Wilson, Sarah. Love & Kisses. Sweet, Melissa, illus. 2014. (ENG.). 24p. (J). (— 1). bds. 6.99 (978-0-7636-7391-8(9)) Candlewick Pr.

Wind in the willows CD gift Book. 2006. (J). 9.99 (978-1-934004-02-9(2)) Byeway Bks.

Wineinger, Cherylann. Corgy & His Friends: A Trip to the Unknown. 2011. 24p. pap. 12.79 (978-1-4520-0349-8(1)) AuthorHouse.

Winnie the Pooh: Party in the Wood. 2011. 32p. pap. 4.99 (978-1-4231-5386-3(3)) Disney Pr.

Winskill, John. Jungle Friends. Disney Global Artists Staff & Random House Disney Staff, illus. 2003. (Step into Reading Ser.). (ENG.). 32p. (J). (gr. -1-1). pap. 3.99 (978-0-7364-2089-1(4), RH/Disney) Random Hse. Children's Bks.

Witte, Anna. El Loro Tico Tango. Witte, Anna, illus. 2011. (SPA., Illus.). 24p. (J). (gr. -1-1). 9.99 (978-1-84686-670-8(7)) Barefoot Bks., Inc.

—The Parrot Tico Tango. 2005. (ENG., Illus.). 24p. (J). (gr. -1-3). 6.99 (978-1-905236-11-4(5)) Barefoot Bks., Inc.

—The Parrot Tico Tango. Witte, Anna, illus. 2005. (Illus.). 24p. (J). (gr. k-3). 15.99 (978-1-84148-243-9(9)) Barefoot Bks., Inc.

Witte, Anna & Amador, Brian. The Parrot Tico Tango. Witte, Anna, illus. 2011. (ENG., Illus.). 24p. (J). (gr. -1-2). 9.99 (978-1-84686-669-2(3)) Barefoot Bks., Inc.

Wixom, Jason Kay & Wixom, Tedi Tuttle. Cock-a-Doodle-Doo, I Love You. Lancaster, Derek, illus. 2nd ed. 2003. (Ralph Rooster Ser.: Vol. 1). 16p. (J). (gr. -1-2). 6.95 (978-1-885227-05-8(1)) TNT Bks.

Wolf, Jackie. Night Night Sleep Tight. Garofoli, Viviana, illus. 2004. 10p. (J). (gr. -1-18). bds. 5.99 (978-1-57151-734-0(0)) Playhouse Publishing.

Wolf, Penny, et al. Bea's Almost Bad Day. Sweet Briar School, illus. 2011. 32p. (J). 8.00 (978-0-9802015-1-2(9)) Sweetbriar Crafts & Pubns.

Wolfe, Susan Markle. The Deer from Ponchatoula, 1 vol. Welch, Gracie, illus. 2009. 24p. pap. 24.95 (978-1-60813-519-6(5)) America Star Bks.

Wolff, Ashley. Baby Bear Counts One. Wolff, Ashley, illus. 2013. (Baby Bear Ser.). (ENG., Illus.). 40p. (J). (gr. -1-1). 16.99 (978-1-4424-4158-3(5), Beach Lane Bks.) Beach Lane Bks.

Wolos-Fonteno, Mary, et al. Tales with Tails: Animal Stories for Young People. Salaam, Kiini Ibura, ed. Wolos-Fonteno, Mary et al, illus. 2006. 168p. (YA). pap. 15.95 (978-0-940938-43-4(X), Pen & Rose Pr.) Harlin Jacque Pubns.

Wolverton, Barry. Neversink. Nielson, Sam, illus. (ENG.). (J). (gr. 3-7). 2013. 320p. pap. 6.99 (978-0-06-202793-1(X)) 2012. 304p. 16.99 (978-0-06-202791-7(3)) HarperCollins Pubs. (Waldon Pond Pr.).

—Neversink. Nielson, Sam, illus. 2012. xiii, 287p. (J). (978-0-06-202792-4(1)) Longman Publishing.

Won, Brian. Hooray for Books! 2017. (ENG., Illus.). 40p. (J). (gr. -1-3). 16.99 **(978-0-544-74802-6(6)**, HMH Books For Young Readers) Houghton Mifflin Harcourt Publishing Co.

—Hooray for Hat! 2014. (ENG., Illus.). 40p. (J). (gr. -1-3). 16.99 (978-0-544-15903-7(9), HMH Books For Young Readers) Houghton Mifflin Harcourt Publishing Co.

—Hooray for Hat! (Board Book) 2016. (ENG., Illus.). 32p. (J). (— 1). bds. 7.99 (978-0-544-78988-3(1), HMH Books For Young Readers) Houghton Mifflin Harcourt Publishing Co.

—Hooray for Today! 2016. (ENG., Illus.). 40p. (J). (gr. -1-3). 16.99 (978-0-544-74803-3(4), HMH Books For Young Readers) Houghton Mifflin Harcourt Publishing Co.

Wood, Audrey. The Full Moon at the Napping House. Wood, Don, illus. 2015. (ENG.). 32p. (J). (gr. -1-3). 17.99 (978-0-544-30832-9(8), HMH Books For Young Readers) Houghton Mifflin Harcourt Publishing Co.

—The Napping House. Wood, Don, illus. 2010. (ENG.). 34p. (J). (gr. k — 1). bds. 8.99 (978-0-547-48147-0(0)) Houghton Mifflin Harcourt Publishing Co.

—Silly Sally: Lap-Sized Board Book. 2007. (ENG., Illus.). 30p. (J). (gr. -1-3). bds. 11.99 (978-0-15-205902-6(4)) Houghton Mifflin Harcourt Publishing Co.

Wood, Douglas. When Mama Mirabelle Comes Home. Wagner, Andy, illus. 2007. (ENG.). 32p. (J). (gr. -1-2). 24.90 (978-1-4263-0195-7(2)); 16.95 (978-1-4263-0194-0(4)) National Geographic Society. (National Geographic Children's Bks.).

Wooden, John. Fiesta. Cornelison, Susan F., illus. 2007. (Coach John Wooden for Kids Ser.). 63p. (J). (gr. k-3). lib. bdg. 11.65 (978-0-7569-7791-7(6)); pap., per. 4.99 (978-0-7891-7187-0(2)) Perfection Learning Corp.

Woodside, Martin & Grahame, Kenneth. The Wind in the Willows. Akib, Jamel, illus. 2007. (Classic Starts Ser.). 152p. (J). (978-1-4287-4210-9(7)) Sterling Publishing Co., Inc.

Wrench, Peter. The Night of the Round Stable. Holland, Ruth, illus. 2012. 174p. pap. (978-1-908895-49-3(7)) FeedARead.com.

Wyatt, Cherokee. The Adventures of Margaret Mouse: Harvest Carnival. l.t. ed. 2006. (Illus.). 32p. (J). 6.95 (978-0-9761326-5-3(6)) www.margaretmouse.com publishing co.

—The Adventures of Margaret Mouse: The Magic Star. l.t. ed. 2006. (Illus.). 32p. (J). 6.95 (978-0-9761326-6-0(4)) www.margaretmouse.com publishing co.

Wyland Studios Staff, illus. Wyland's Spouty And Friends. 2004. 37p. 20.95 (978-1-884840-59-3(0)) Wyland Worldwide, LLC.

Yaccarino, Dan. Class Pet Squad: Journey to the Center of Town. 2016. (ENG., Illus.). 144p. (J). 13.99 (978-1-250-02462-6(5), 9781250024626) Feiwel & Friends.

—Journey to the Center of Town. 2017. (Class Pet Squad Ser.: 1). (J). lib. bdg. 17.20 **(978-0-606-39943-2(7))** Turtleback Bks.

Yaccarino, Dan. Morris Mole. Yaccarino, Dan, illus. 2017. (Illus.). 40p. (J). (gr. -1-3). 17.99 (978-0-06-241107-5(1)) HarperCollins Pubs.

Yarrow, Peter. Day Is Done. Sweet, Melissa, illus. 2009. (ENG.). 24p. (J). (gr. k-2). 16.95 (978-1-4027-4806-6(X)) Sterling Publishing Co., Inc.

Yates, Louise. Dog Loves Counting. 2013. (ENG.). 32p. (J). (gr. -1-3). 17.99 (978-0-449-81342-3(8), Knopf Bks. for Young Readers) Random Hse. Children's Bks.

—Dog Loves Drawing. 2012. (ENG.). 32p. (J). (gr. -1-3). 16.99 (978-0-375-87067-5(9), Knopf Bks. for Young Readers) Random Hse. Children's Bks.

Yee, Wong Herbert. Eek! There's a Mouse in the House, 1 vol. 2013. (ENG., Illus.). 24p. (J). (gr. -1-3). audio compact disk 10.99 (978-0-544-02282-9(3)) Houghton Mifflin Harcourt Publishing Co.

—Hamburger Heaven. 2005. (ENG., Illus.). 32p. (J). (gr. -1-3). reprint ed. 5.95 (978-0-618-54885-9(8)) Houghton Mifflin Harcourt Publishing Co.

—Tracks in the Snow. Yee, Wong Herbert, illus. 2007. (ENG., Illus.). 32p. (J). (gr. -1-1). per. 7.99 (978-0-312-37134-0(9), 9780312371340) Square Fish.

Yeh, Kat. The Friend Ship. Groenink, Chuck, illus. 2016. (ENG.). 32p. (J). (gr. -1-k). 16.99 (978-1-4847-0726-5(5)) Disney Pr.

Yenshu In: One Day, One Smile. 2003. 3.99 (978-0-915960-40-8(0)) Ebon Research Systems Publishing, LLC.

Yeoman, John. The Bear's Winter House. Blake, Quentin, illus. 2012. (J). (978-1-4351-4374-6(4)) Barnes & Noble, Inc.

—Mr. Nodd's Ark. Blake, Quentin, illus. 2016. (ENG.). 32p. (J). (-k). pap. 9.99 (978-1-78344-374-1(X)) Andersen Pr. GBR. Dist: Independent Pubs. Group.

Yepes, Rebecca. It Might Be A Crow. 2011. 12p. 8.95 (978-1-4567-1849-7(5)) AuthorHouse.

Ying, Jonathan. Lost & Found, What's That Sound? Ying, Victoria, illus. 2017. 32p. (J). (gr. -1-3). 14.99 (978-0-06-238068-5(0)) HarperCollins Pubs.

—Not Quite Black & White. Ying, Victoria, illus. 2016. 32p. (J). (gr. -1-3). 14.99 (978-0-06-238066-1(4)) HarperCollins Pubs.

Ying, Jonathan. Not Quite Black & White Board Book. Ying, Victoria, illus. 2017. 28p. (J). (gr. -1 — 1). bds. 7.99 **(978-0-06-238067-8(2)**, HarperFestival) HarperCollins Pubs.

Yoakem, Kevin. Wooly & Fuzzy. 2008. 24p. pap. 24.95 (978-1-60703-566-4(9)) America Star Bks.

Yokococo. Matilda & Hans. Yokococo, illus. 2013. (ENG., Illus.). 32p. (J). (gr. -1-2). 16.99 (978-0-7636-6434-3(0), Templar) Candlewick Pr.

Yolen, Jane. Trash Mountain. Monroe, Chris, illus. 2015. (J). 17.32 (978-1-4677-7170-2(8)); (ENG.). 184p. (gr. 3-6). 16.99 (978-1-4677-1234-7(5)) Lerner Publishing Group. (Carolrhoda Bks.).

Yolen, Jane & Stemple, Heidi E. Y. Sleep, Black Bear, Sleep. Dyer, Brooke, illus. 2007. 32p. (J). (gr. -1-1). (ENG.). 15.99 (978-0-06-081560-8(4)); lib. bdg. 16.89 (978-0-06-081561-5(2)) HarperCollins Pubs.

Yonezu, Yusuke, illus. We Love Each Other. 2013. (Yonezu Board Book Ser.). (ENG.). 28p. (J). (— 1). bds. 9.95 (978-988-8240-56-2(0)) Neugebauer, Michael (Publishing) Limited HKG. Dist: Independent Pubs. Group.

Yoon, Salina. Penguin's Big Adventure. 2015. (Penguin Ser.). (ENG., Illus.). 40p. (J). (gr. -1-1). 14.99 (978-0-8027-3828-8(1), 9780802738288, Bloomsbury USA Childrens) Bloomsbury Publishing USA.

Yoon, Salina, creator. Country Pals: A Sparkling Little Colors Book. 2005. (Sparkling Little Colors Book Ser.). (ENG., Illus.). 12p. (J). bds. 5.95 (978-1-58117-167-9(6), Intervisual/Piggy Toes) Bendon, Inc.

—Little Friends: A Sparkling Little Colors Book, 4 vols. 2005. (ENG., Illus.). 12p. (J). bds. 5.95 (978-1-58117-168-6(4), Intervisual/Piggy Toes) Bendon, Inc.

Yoon, Salina, illus. Pretend & Play: on the Farm. 2013. (Pretend & Play Ser.). (ENG.). 12p. (J). (gr. -1). bds. 12.95 (978-1-60710-635-7(3), Silver Dolphin Bks.) Readerlink Distribution Services, LLC.

York, M. J. How Many Spots Does a Leopard Have? An African Folktale. Zunon, Elizabeth, illus. 2012. (Folktales from Around the World Ser.). (ENG.). 24p. (J). (gr. k-3). 28.50 (978-1-61473-217-4(5), 204912) Child's World, Inc., The.

Yost-Filgate, Susan. The Treasure: A Rip Squeak Book. Filgate, Leonard, illus. 2005. (Rip Squeak Ser.). (ENG.). 32p. (J). (gr. -1-3). 16.95 (978-0-9747825-1-5(3), Raven Tree Pr.,Csi) Continental Sales, Inc.

Young, Annemarie. In the Garden. Redshaw, Louise, illus. 2013. (Start Reading Ser.). (ENG.). 24p. (gr. k-1). pap. 41.94 (978-1-4765-3220-2(6)); pap. 7.95 (978-1-4765-3192-2(7)) Capstone Press of Coughlan Cos.

Young, H. M. (Hal). The huskies & the christmas Fawn. 2007. 56p. pap. 9.95 (978-1-4357-0070-3(8)) Lulu Pr., Inc.

Young, Judy. The Missing Grizzly Cubs. 2016. (Wild World of Buck Bray Ser.). (ENG.). 240p. (J). (gr. 3-6). 16.99 (978-1-58536-970-6(5), 204107) Sleeping Bear Pr.

Young, Justin. A Most Vivid Day! 2010. (ENG., Illus.). 40p. (J). (gr. k-2). 16.95 (978-0-9785418-1-1(2)) Dream Character, Inc.

Young, Kimberly Rich. A Horse Is a Horse. 2008. 40p. pap. 24.95 (978-1-4241-9755-2(4)) America Star Bks.

Young, Rachel & Young, Jackie. The Tale of Squabbit. Lynch, Stephanie, illus. 2011. 42p. pap. 15.00 (978-1-60911-360-5(8), Eloquent Bks.) Strategic Book Publishing & Rights Agency (SBPRA).

Young, Rebecca & Accord Publishing Staff. Hop, Pop, & Play: A Mini Animotion Book. 2011. (ENG.). 12p. (J). 9.99 (978-1-4494-0177-1(5)) Andrews McMeel Publishing.

Younger, Mary. You're Not A Ladybird You've Got No Spots. 2011. (Illus.). 24p. 14.09 (978-1-4567-7082-2(9)) AuthorHouse.

Yu, Jennifer & Jenn, Lady. Texas Animal Ranch: Ricky's Secret Friends Picture Book Series, vols. 6, vol. 2. Yu, Jennifer & Jenn, Lady, illus. 2016. (Ricky's Secret Friends Picturebook Ser.: 6). (ENG & CHI., Illus.). (gr. 1-4). 29.95 (978-0-9787591-2-4(5)) Direct World Publishing.

Zabini, Eleni & Livanios, Eleni. Best Grandma in the World! Lütje, Susanne, illus. 2015. (ENG.). 16p. (J). bds. 7.95 (978-0-7358-4225-0(6)) North-South Bks., Inc.

—Best Grandpa in the World! Lütje, Susanne, illus. 2015. (ENG.). 16p. (J). bds. 7.95 (978-0-7358-4237-3(X)) North-South Bks., Inc.

Zalben, Jane Breskin. Saturday Night at the Beastro. Date not set. 32p. (J). (gr. 2-4). pap. 5.99 (978-0-06-443736-3(1)) HarperCollins Pubs.

—Saturday Night at the Beastro. Zalben, Jane Breskin, illus. 2004. (Illus.). 40p. (J). (gr. 2-4). lib. bdg. 16.89 (978-0-06-029228-7(8)) HarperCollins Pubs.

Zeeh, Shawn. Tucker Farm: Under the Big Top. 2012. 36p. pap. 21.99 (978-1-4771-2685-1(6)) Xlibris Corp.

Zenz, Aaron. The Hiccupotamus, 0 vols. 2009. (ENG.). 32p. (J). (gr. -1-2). 12.99 (978-0-7614-5622-3(8), 9780761456223, Amazon Children's Publishing) Amazon Publishing.

—I Love Ewe: An Ode to Animal Moms. Zenz, Aaron, illus. 2015. (ENG., Illus.). 22p. (J). (gr. -1-1). bds. 7.99 (978-1-61963-666-8(2), 9781619636668, Bloomsbury USA Childrens) Bloomsbury Publishing USA.

Zimmer, Elizabeth & Zimmer, Eric. The Turtle & the Deep Blue Sky. 2007. (ENG., Illus.). 32p. (J). (gr. -1-3). 12.95 (978-1-55591-597-1(3)) Fulcrum Publishing.

Zobel-Nolan, Allia. Animal Parade. Maddocks, Maria, illus. 2008. 10p. (J). (gr. -1). 12.95 (978-1-932915-63-1(X)) Sandvik Innovations, LLC.

Zoboli, Giovanna. The Big Book of Slumber. Mulazzani, Simona, illus. 2014. (ENG.). 26p. (J). 16.00 (978-0-8028-5439-1(7), Eerdmans Bks For Young Readers) Eerdmans, William B. Publishing Co.

Zoboli, Giovanna & Mathews, Leslie. I Wish I Had... Mulazzani, Simona, illus. 2013. (ENG.). 26p. (J). 16.00 (978-0-8028-5415-5(X), Eerdmans Bks For Young Readers) Eerdmans, William B. Publishing Co.

Zoboli, Giovanna & Watkinson, Laura. Animal Supermarket. Mulazzani, Simona, illus. 2015. (ENG.). 26p. (J). 16.00 (978-0-8028-5448-3(6), Eerdmans Bks For Young Readers) Eerdmans, William B. Publishing Co.

Zolan, Donald, illus. My Favorite Farm Animal Friends. 2010. (ENG.). 5p. (J). bds. 5.99 (978-0-7369-2663-8(1)) Harvest Hse. Pubs.

Zommer, Yuval. The Big Blue Thing on the Hill. Zommer, Yuval, illus. 2015. (ENG., Illus.). 32p. (J). (gr. -1-2). 16.99 (978-0-7636-7403-8(6), Templar) Candlewick Pr.

Zschock, Heather. Whoo's There? A Bedtime Shadow Book. Zschock, Martha Day, illus. 2005. (Activity Book Ser.). 16p. (J). (gr. -1-4). 12.99 (978-1-59359-904-1(8)) Peter Pauper Pr. Inc.

Zullo, Allan. Christmas Miracle Pets: Animals Who Saved the Day. 2012. 119p. (J). (978-0-545-38573-2(3)) Scholastic, Inc.

ANIMALS, FICTITIOUS

see Animals, Mythical

ANIMALS—FOLKLORE

Anderson, Holly Lynn. Unexplained Monsters & Cryptids. 2015. (J). (978-1-61900-071-1(7)) Eldorado Ink.

Artell, Mike. Three Little Cajun Pigs. Harris, Jim, illus. 2006. (ENG.). 32p. (J). (gr. k-3). 17.99 (978-0-8037-2815-8(8), Dial Bks) Penguin Young Readers Group.

Bruchac, Joseph. The Boy Who Lived with the Bears: And Other Iroquois Stories. Jacob, Murv, illus. 2003. (Storytime Ser.). 63p. (J). (gr. k-5). pap. 11.95 (978-0-930407-61-2(X)) Parabola Bks.

Buri & the Marrow. 2004. (J). (ENG & HIN.). (978-1-84444-668-1(9)); cd-rom (978-1-84444-454-0(6)) Mantra Lingua.

Christie, R. Gregory. Mousetropolis. 2015. (ENG., Illus.). 32p. (J). (gr. -1-3). 16.95 (978-0-8234-2319-4(0)) Holiday Hse., Inc.

Clynes, Kate. Goldilocks & the Three Bears. Daykin, Louise, illus. 32p. (J). 2004. (FRE & ENG.). pap. (978-1-84444-040-5(0)) 2004. (ENG & PAN.). pap. (978-1-84444-043-6(5)) 2004. (ENG & POR.). pap. (978-1-84444-044-3(3)) 2004. (ENG & URD.). pap. (978-1-84444-048-1(6)) 2004. (ENG & POL.). pap. (978-1-84444-051-1(6)) 2004. (ENG & HIN.). pap. (978-1-84444-059-7(1)) 2004. (ENG & ARA.). pap. (978-1-84444-036-8(2)) 2003. (BEN & ENG.). pap. (978-1-84444-037-5(0)) 2003. (CHI & ENG.). pap. (978-1-84444-038-2(9)) 2003. (RUS & ENG.). pap. (978-1-84444-052-8(4)) Mantra Lingua.

—Goldilocks & the Three Bears. Daykin, Louise, tr. Daykin, Louise, illus. 2003. (VIE & ENG.). 32p. (J). pap. 12.95 (978-1-84444-055-9(9)) Mantra Lingua GBR. Dist: Chinasprout, Inc.

Curlee, Lynn. Mythological Creatures: A Classical Bestiary. Curlee, Lynn, illus. 2008. (ENG., Illus.). 40p. (J). (gr. 3-7). 19.99 (978-1-4169-1453-2(6), Atheneum Bks. for Young Readers) Simon & Schuster Children's Publishing.

Daykin, Louise, illus. Goldilocks & the Three Bears. 2004. 32p. (J). (978-1-84444-054-2(0)); (ALB & ENG.). (978-1-84444-035-1(4)); (978-1-84444-039-9(7)); (GER & ENG.). (978-1-84444-041-2(9)); (978-1-84444-042-9(7)); (SOM & ENG.). (978-1-84444-045-0(1)); (ENG & SPA.). (978-1-84444-046-7(X)); (TUR & ENG.). (978-1-84444-047-4(8)); (CZE & ENG.). (978-1-84444-049-8(4)); (ITA & ENG.). (978-1-84444-050-4(8)); (SER & ENG.). (978-1-84444-053-5(2)) Mantra Lingua.

Daykin, Louise, tr. & illus. Goldilocks & the Three Bears. Daykin, Louise, illus. 2004. 31p. (J). (978-1-84444-057-3(5)) Mantra Lingua.

Dewey, Jennifer Owings. The Shaman & the Water Serpent. Yazzie, Benton, illus. 2007. (ENG.). 40p. (J). 19.95 (978-0-8263-4211-9(6)) Univ. of New Mexico Pr.

Halls, Kelly Milner, et al. Tales of the Cryptids: Mysterious Creatures That May or May Not Exist. 2006. (ENG., Illus.). 72p. (J). (gr. 5-12). 18.95 (978-1-58196-049-5(2), Darby Creek) Lerner Publishing Group.

Harris, Joel Chandler. The Story of Brer Rabbit & the Wonderful Tar Baby, 1 vol. Drescher, Henrik, illus. 2004. (Rabbit Ears-A Classic Tale Ser.). (ENG.). 40p. (gr. k-5). 25.65 (978-1-59197-761-2(4)) Spotlight.

Huang, Chungliang Al. The Chinese Book of Animal Powers. 2011. (ENG., Illus.). 32p. 19.95 (978-1-84819-066-5(2), 3161, Singing Dragon) Kingsley, Jessica Pubs. GBR. Dist: Macmillan Distribution Ltd.

Jorgensen, David, illus. The Three Little Pigs, 1 vol. 2005. (Rabbit Ears-A Classic Tale Set 2 Ser.). (ENG.). 28p. (gr. k-5). 25.65 (978-1-59197-755-1(X)) Spotlight.

Keating, Jess. What Makes a Monster? Discovering the World's Scariest Creatures. DeGrand, David, illus. 2017. (World of Weird Animals Ser.). (ENG.). 40p. (J). (gr. 1-4). 17.99 (978-0-553-51230-4(7), Knopf Bks. for Young Readers) Random Hse. Children's Bks.

Kessler, Brad & Harris, Joel Chandler. Brer Rabbit & Boss Lion, 1 vol. Mayer, Bill, illus. 2004. (Rabbit Ears-A Classic Tale Ser.). (ENG.). 40p. (gr. k-5). 25.65 (978-1-59197-760-5(6)) Spotlight.

Kimmel, Eric A. Brother Wolf, Sister Sparrow: Stories about Saints & Animals. Winch, John, illus. 2003. (ENG.). 64p. (J). (gr. 4-6). tchr. ed. 18.95 (978-0-8234-1724-7(7)) Holiday Hse., Inc.

Klepeis, Alicia. Animal Allstars: African Animals, Facts & Folklore. Bayer, Florian, illus. 2017. (ENG.). 64p. (J). (gr. 1-4). 24.95 **(978-3-89955-782-4(4))** Die Gestalten Verlag DEU. Dist: Penguin Random Hse. LLC.

Leedy, Loreen & Street, Pat. There's a Frog in My Throat! 440 Animal Sayings a Little Bird Told Me. Leedy, Loreen, illus. 2004. (ENG., Illus.). 48p. (J). (gr. k-3). reprint ed. pap. 8.99 (978-0-8234-1819-0(7)) Holiday Hse., Inc.

Lester, Julius. The Tales of Uncle Remus: The Adventures of Brer Rabbit. Pinkney, Jerry, illus. 2006. (Puffin Modern Classics Ser.). (ENG.). 160p. (J). (gr. 3-7). 7.99 (978-0-14-240720-2(8), Puffin Books) Penguin Young Readers Group.

MacDonald, Margaret Read. The Squeaky Door. DePalma, Mary Newell, illus. 2006. (ENG.). 40p. (J). (gr. -1-1). 16.99 (978-0-06-028373-5(4)) HarperCollins Pubs.

McGrath, Barbara Barbieri. The Little Gray Bunny. Kim, Violet, illus. 2013. (ENG.). 32p. (J). (gr. -1-2). 16.95 (978-1-58089-394-7(5)); pap. 7.95 (978-1-58089-395-4(3)) Charlesbridge Publishing, Inc.

McNab, Chris. Mythical Monsters: The Scariest Creatures from Legends, Books, & Movies. 2006. (Illus.). 95p. (J). (978-0-439-85479-5(2)) Scholastic, Inc.

Overwater, Georgien, illus. The Three Little Pigs. 2007. (Usborne First Reading: Level 3 Ser.). 48p. (J). 8.99 (978-0-7945-1598-0(3), Usborne) EDC Publishing.

Peters, Andrew & Fusek Peters, Andrew. Monkey's Clever Tale. Montgomery-Higham, Amanda, illus. 2003. (Traditional Tales with a Twist Ser.). (ENG.). 32p. (J). (gr. 2-3). (978-0-85953-051-4(5)) Child's Play International Ltd.

Polydoros, Lori. Top 10 Mythical Creatures, 1 vol. 2012. (Top 10 Unexplained Ser.). (ENG.). 32p. (gr. 1-2). 26.65 (978-1-4296-7640-3(X), Blazers) Capstone Press of Coughlan Cos.

Riggs, Kate. Magical Creatures. 2013. (Happily Ever After Ser.). (ENG., Illus.). 24p. (J). (gr. k-3). 25.65 (978-1-60818-242-8(8), Creative Education) Creative Co., The.

Schomp, Virginia & Harris, Joel Chandler. Brer Rabbit & the Number-Nine Shoes. 2013. (Illus.). 32p. (J). (gr. 6-9). 28.50 (978-1-60870-439-2(4)) Cavendish Square Publishing.

Sehgal, Kabir & Sehgal, Surishtha. A Bucket of Blessings. Tsong, Jing Jing, illus. 2014. (ENG.). 32p. (J). (gr. -1-3). 17.99 (978-1-4424-5870-3(4), Beach Lane Bks.) Beach Lane Bks.

Sherman, Patrice. Legendary Creatures. 2015. (Illus.). 64p. (978-1-61900-067-4(9)) Eldorado Ink.

Villaseñor, Victor. Frog & His Friends Save Humanity/la Rana y Sus Amigos Salvan ALA Humanidad. Ochoa, Edna, tr. Ramirez, Jose, illus. 2005. (ENG & SPA.). 32p. (J). (gr. -1). 16.95 *(978-1-55885-429-1(0)*, Piñata Books) Arte Publico Pr.

Yolen, Jane. Meow: Cat Stories from Around the World. Date not set. 40p. mass mkt. 6.99 *(978-0-06-440931-5(7))* HarperCollins Pubs.

Yomtov, Nelson. Tracking Sea Monsters, Bigfoot, & Other Legendary Beasts, 1 vol. 2010. (Unexplained Phenomena Ser.). (ENG.). 48p. (gr. 3-4). lib. bdg. 31.99 *(978-1-4296-4817-2(1))* Capstone Press of Coughlan Cos.

Young, Ed. Seven Blind Mice. Young, Ed, illus. 2007. (Illus.). pap. 14.95 incl. audio *(978-0-439-02784-7(5))*; (J). 24.95 incl. audio *(978-0-439-02782-3(9))* Scholastic, Inc.

—Seven Blind Mice. Young, Ed, illus. 2011. (Illus.). 18.95 *(978-0-439-02785-4(3))*; (J). 29.95 *(978-0-439-02783-0(7))* Weston Woods Studios, Inc.

ANIMALS, FOSSIL

see Fossils

ANIMALS, FRESH-WATER

see Freshwater Animals

ANIMALS—HABITATIONS

Abbott, Henry. Inside Anthills. 2015. (Inside Animal Homes Ser.). (ENG.). 24p. (J). (gr. 2-3). pap. 8.25 *(978-1-4994-0860-7(9)*, PowerKids Pr.) Rosen Publishing Group, Inc., The.

ABDO Publishing Company Staff & Salzmann, Mary Elizabeth. Animal Homes, 1 vol. 2012. (Animal Homes Ser.: 6). (ENG., Illus.). 24p. (J). (gr. k-3). lib. bdg. 145.26 *(978-1-61714-814-9(8)*, SandCastle) ABDO Publishing Co.

Aladjidi, Virginia. Animal Atlas. Ramsey, Cecelia, tr. from FRE. Tchoukriel, Emmanuelle, illus. 2016. (ENG.). 112p. (J). (gr. 5-8). 24.99 *(978-1-4926-4163-6(4)*, 9781492641636, Sourcebooks Jabberwocky) Sourcebooks, Inc.

Algarra, Alejandro & Bonilla, Rocio. Where Do Animals Live? 2016. (Curious Young Minds Ser.). (ENG., Illus.). 36p. (J). (gr. -1-2). pap. 7.99 *(978-1-4380-0894-3(5))* Barron's Educational Series, Inc.

Allen, Judy & Mendez, Simon. Flip the Flaps: Animal Homes. 2013. (Flip the Flaps Ser.). (ENG., Illus.). 32p. (J). (gr. -1-1). 6.99 *(978-0-7534-6950-7(2)*, 9780753469507, Kingfisher) Roaring Brook Pr.

Animal Invaders: Destroying Native Habitats. 2016. (Animal Invaders: Destroying Native Habitats Ser.). 00024p. (J). pap. 48.90 ***(978-1-4824-5844-2(6))*** Stevens, Gareth Publishing LLLP.

Aston, Dianna Hutts. A Nest Is Noisy. Long, Sylvia, illus. 2015. (ENG.). 40p. (J). (gr. k-3). 16.99 *(978-1-4521-2713-2(1))* Chronicle Bks. LLC.

—A Nest Is Noisy. Long, Sylvia, illus. 2017. (ENG.). 40p. (J). pap. 7.99 *(978-1-4521-6135-8(6))* Chronicle Bks. LLC.

AZ Books Staff. Find My Food & Home. Petrovskaya, Olga, ed. 2012. (Matching Game Ser.). (ENG.). 18p. (J). (gr. -1-k). spiral bd. 4.95 *(978-1-61889-010-8(7))* AZ Bks. LLC.

Bates, Matt. Inside Beehives. 2015. (Inside Animal Homes Ser.). (ENG.). 24p. (J). (gr. 2-3). 23.60 *(978-1-4994-0920-8(6)*, PowerKids Pr.) Rosen Publishing Group, Inc., The.

Benchmark Education Company, LLC Staff, compiled by. Habitats. 2006. (J). 148.00 *(978-1-4108-7029-2(4))* Benchmark Education Co.

Beullens-Maoui, Nathalie, ed. Animals Habitats: Armenian, 01 vols., 1. 2016. (Our Wonderful World Ser.). (ENG & SPA.). 8p. (J). pap. 9.35 *(978-1-5081-1209-9(6)*, Rosen Classroom) Rosen Publishing Group, Inc., The.

—Animals Habitats: Cantonese, 01 vols., 1. 2016. (Our Wonderful World Ser.). (ENG & SPA.). 8p. (J). pap. 9.35 *(978-1-5081-1221-1(5)*, Rosen Classroom) Rosen Publishing Group, Inc., The.

Blasco, Julio Antonio & Nassar, Daniel. Animal Architects: The Brilliant Builders of the Animal Kingdom. 2015. (ENG., Illus.). 32p. (J). (gr. 2-6). 15.95 *(978-1-78067-654-8(9))* King, Laurence Publishing GBR. Dist: Hachette Bk. Group.

Boldt, Claudia, illus. Animals at Home: Match 27 Animals to Their Homes. 2017. (Magma for Laurence King Ser.). (ENG.). 56p. (J). (gr. -1-k). bds. 14.99 ***(978-1-78627-027-6(7))*** King, Laurence Publishing GBR. Dist: Hachette Bk. Group.

Boothroyd, Jennifer. In a Tree. (First Step Nonfiction - Animal Homes Ser.). (ENG., Illus.). 8p. (gr. -1-1). 2015. 11.99 *(978-1-5124-1032-7(2))* 2006. pap. 4.95 *(978-0-8225-5663-3(4)*, Lerner Pubns.) Lerner Publishing Group.

Bradley, Timothy J. Animal Architects, 1 vol. 2nd rev. ed. 2012. (TIME for KIDS(r) Nonfiction Readers Ser.). (ENG., Illus.). 48p. (J). (gr. 4-4). pap. 9.99 *(978-1-4333-4822-8(5))* Teacher Created Materials, Inc.

—Wild Cities, 1 vol. 2nd rev. ed. 2012. (Nonfiction Readers Ser.). (ENG.). 48p. (J). (gr. 4-4). pap. 9.99 *(978-1-4333-4823-5(3))* Teacher Created Materials, Inc.

Breene, Robert G., III. A Widow Spider in Its Web. 2003. (Where Do Animals Live? Ser.). (J). *(978-1-58417-186-7(3))*; pap. *(978-1-58417-187-4(1))* Lake Street Pubs.

Brenner, Barbara. One Small Place in a Tree. Leonard, Tom, illus. 2004. (ENG.). 32p. (J). (gr. k-3). 17.99 *(978-0-688-17180-3(X))* HarperCollins Pubs.

Broom, Jenny. The Wonder Garden: Wander Through 5 Habitats to Discover 80 Amazing Animals. Williams, Kristjana S., illus. 2015. (ENG.). 48p. (J). 30.00 *(978-1-84780-647-5(3)*, Wide Eyed Editions) Quarto Publishing Group UK GBR. Dist: Littlehampton Bk Services, Ltd.

Carle, Eric. My Very First Book of Animal Homes. Carle, Eric, illus. 2007. (ENG., Illus.). 20p. (J). (gr. -1 — 1). bds. 5.99 *(978-0-399-24647-0(9)*, Philomel Bks.) Penguin Young Readers Group.

Cherrington, Janelle. Where Animals Live, 6 vols., Set. 2003. (Phonics Readers 1-36 Ser.). (ENG.). 8p. (gr. k-1). pap. 29.70 *(978-0-7368-3190-1(8)*, Phonics Readers) Capstone Press of Coughlan Cos.

Cobb, Allan B. Super Science Projects about Animals in Their Habitats. 2005. (Psyched for Science Ser.). (Illus.). 48p. (YA). (gr. 5-8). lib. bdg. 29.25 *(978-0-8239-3175-0(7)*, SCADHO) Rosen Publishing Group, Inc., The.

Corcorane, Ann. Animals Everywhere. 2011. (Wonder Readers Emergent Level Ser.). (ENG.). 16p. (gr. -1-1). pap. 35.94 *(978-1-4296-8070-7(9)*, Wonder Readers) Capstone Press of Coughlan Cos.

Crouthamel, Katherine. Animals & Their Habitats. 2009. (Real Life Readers Ser.). 8p. (gr. k-2). pap. 5.15 *(978-1-4042-7951-3(2)*, Rosen Classroom) Rosen Publishing Group, Inc., The.

Davies, Nicola. Who Lives Here? Boutavant, Marc, illus. 2012. (Flip the Flap & Find Out Ser.). (ENG.). 24p. (J). (gr. -1-2). 9.99 *(978-0-7636-6263-9(1))* Candlewick Pr.

Discovery Education: Habitats. 2013. (Discovery Education: Habitats Ser.). 32p. (J). (gr. 3-6). 176.75 *(978-1-4777-1549-9(5))*; pap. 420.00 *(978-1-4777-2702-7(7))*; pap. 70.00 *(978-1-4777-2701-0(9))* Rosen Publishing Group, Inc., The. (PowerKids Pr.).

Disney Book Group Staff. Wonderful World of Animals. 2012. (Wonderful World Of... Ser.). (ENG.). 64p. (J). (gr. 1-17). 8.99 *(978-1-4231-4940-8(8))* Disney Pr.

Donovan, Sandy. A Snake in Its Burrow. 2003. (Where Do Animals Live? Ser.). (J). pap. *(978-1-58417-193-5(6))*; lib. bdg. *(978-1-58417-192-8(8))* Lake Street Pubs.

Franchino, Vicky. Animal Architects. 2015. (ENG., Illus.). 48p. (J). lib. bdg. *(978-0-531-21547-0(4)*, Orchard Bks.) Scholastic, Inc.

Fredericks, Anthony D. Around One Log: Chipmunks, Spiders, & Creepy Insiders, 1 vol. DiRubbio, Jennifer, illus. 2011. 32p. (J). (gr. -1-5). (ENG.). 16.95 *(978-1-58469-137-2(9))*; pap. 8.95 *(978-1-58469-138-9(7))* Dawn Pubns.

Friesen, Helen Lepp. Needs in Nature. 2008. (Discovering & Exploring Science Ser.). (Illus.). 16p. (J). (gr. -1-3). lib. bdg. 12.95 *(978-0-7569-8424-3(6))* Perfection Learning Corp.

Ghiglieri, Carol. Tree Homes. 2007. (Illus.). 16p. (J). pap. *(978-0-545-00713-9(5))* Scholastic, Inc.

Graham-Barber, Lynda. The Animals' Winter Sleep. Willis, Nancy Carol, illus. 2008. (ENG.). 24p. (J). (gr. -1-k). pap. 7.95 *(978-0-9662761-6-9(7))* Birdsong Bks.

Habitats, 8 bks., Set. Incl. Coasts. Cumming, David. 1997. lib. bdg. 27.12 *(978-0-8172-4520-7(0))*; Forests. Ganeri, Anita. 1997. lib. bdg. 27.12 *(978-0-8172-4519-1(7))*; Grasslands. Waterlow, Julia. 1996. lib. bdg. 18.98 *(978-0-8172-4518-4(9))*; Islands. Waterlow, Julia. 1995. lib. bdg. 18.98 *(978-1-56847-387-1(7)*, AS387-7); Mountains. Cumming, David. 1999. lib. bdg. 18.98 *(978-0-8172-5239-7(8))*; Polar Regions. Bonner, Nigel. 1995. lib. bdg. 27.12 *(978-1-56847-386-4(9)*, AS386-9); Seas & Oceans. McLeish, Ewan. 1996. lib. bdg. 27.12 *(978-0-8172-4517-7(0))*; (Illus.). 48p. (YA). (gr. 4-9). Set lib. bdg. 151.84 *(978-0-7398-4112-9(2))* Heinemann-Raintree.

Halpern, Monica. Underground Towns, Treetops, & Other Animal Hiding Places. 2007. (Science Chapters Ser.). (ENG., Illus.). 48p. (J). (gr. 1-4). lib. bdg. 17.90 *(978-1-4263-0183-4(9)*, National Geographic Children's Bks.) National Geographic Society.

Ham, Catherine. Step Inside! A Look Inside Animal Homes. 2012. (ENG., Illus.). 32p. (J). (gr. -1-3). 14.95 *(978-0-9832014-2-7(0))* EarlyLight Bks., Inc.

—Step Inside! A Look inside Animal Homes. 2012. 14.95 *(978-1-60734-089-8(5))* Early Light Pr., LLC.

Hammersmith, Craig, et al. Habitats Around the World. 2011. (Habitats Around the World Ser.). (ENG.). 24p. (gr. k-1). pap. 166.80 *(978-1-4296-7158-3(0))*; pap. 27.80 *(978-1-4296-7157-6(2))* Capstone Press of Coughlan Cos. (Pebble Plus).

Hewitt, Sally. Hogares de Animales: Animal Homes. 2004. (Ladders Ser.). (SPA & ENG., Illus.). 32p. (J). (gr. -1-3). 12.95 *(978-1-58728-165-5(1))* Cooper Square Publishing Llc.

Hickman, Pamela. It's Moving Day! Valério, Geraldo, illus. (ENG.). 32p. (J). (gr. -1-2). 2012. pap. 8.95 *(978-1-55453-929-1(3))* 2008. 17.95 *(978-1-55453-074-8(1))* Kids Can Pr., Ltd. CAN. Dist: Hachette Bk. Group.

Holden, Pam. Look at My Home, 6 vols. East, Jacqueline, illus. 2009. (Red Rocket Readers Ser.). (ENG.). 16p. (gr. -1-1). pap. *(978-1-877363-04-7(9)*, Red Rocket Readers) Flying Start Bks.

Hopkins, Therese. Animal Dens. 2009. (Home Sweet Home Ser.). 24p. (J). (gr. k-2). pap. 8.25 *(978-1-4358-3072-1(5)*, PowerKids Pr.); 24p. (gr. 1-1). 42.50 *(978-1-61513-393-2(3)*, PowerKids Pr.); (J). (gr. k-2). lib. bdg. 22.60 *(978-1-4358-2698-4(1))* Rosen Publishing Group, Inc., The.

—Burrows. 2009. (Home Sweet Home Ser.). 24p. (J). (gr. k-2). pap. 8.25 *(978-1-4358-3071-4(7)*, PowerKids Pr.); 24p. (gr. 1-1). 42.50 *(978-1-61513-401-4(8)*, PowerKids Pr.); (J). (gr. k-2). lib. bdg. 22.60 *(978-1-4358-2697-7(3))* Rosen Publishing Group, Inc., The.

Houghton Mifflin Harcourt Publishing Company Staff & Nouvian, Judith. Homes. 2015. (Picture This Ser.). (ENG., Illus.). 42p. (J). (gr. -1-3). bds. 7.99 *(978-0-544-51263-4(4)*, HMH Books For Young Readers) Houghton Mifflin Harcourt Publishing Co.

Hughes, John. Animals of the Ice Age Gold Band. 2016. (Cambridge Reading Adventures Ser.). (ENG.). 24p. pap. 7.19 *(978-1-107-55162-6(5))* Cambridge Univ. Pr.

Kalman, Bobbie. Homes of Living Things. 2007. (Introducing Living Things Ser.). (ENG., Illus.). 24p. (J). (gr. 1-4). pap. *(978-0-7787-3252-5(5))* Crabtree Publishing Co.

—How & Why Do Animals Build Homes? 2014. (ENG., Illus.). 24p. (J). *(978-0-7787-0544-4(7))* Crabtree Publishing Co.

—Rapping about Animal Homes. 2012. (ENG., Illus.). 24p. (J). *(978-0-7787-2793-4(9))*; pap. *(978-0-7787-2800-9(5))* Crabtree Publishing Co.

—Seres Vivos de mi Jardín. 2008.Tr. of Homes of Living Things. (SPA.). 24p. (J). pap. *(978-0-7787-8690-0(0))* Crabtree Publishing Co.

—What Is It? 2011. (ENG., Illus.). 16p. (J). pap. *(978-0-7787-9572-8(1))*; lib. bdg. *(978-0-7787-9547-6(0))* Crabtree Publishing Co.

—Where Do Animals Live? 2010. (My World Ser.). (ENG., Illus.). 24p. (J). (gr. k-2). *(978-0-7787-9449-3(0))*; pap. *(978-0-7787-9493-6(8))* Crabtree Publishing Co.

Kaner, Etta. Have You Ever Seen a Stork Build a Log Cabin? Szuc, Jeff, illus. 2010. (Have You Ever Seen Ser.). (ENG.). 32p. (J). (gr. -1-2). 14.95 *(978-1-55453-336-7(8))* Kids Can Pr., Ltd. CAN. Dist: Hachette Bk. Group.

Kelly, Irene. Even an Octopus Needs a Home. 2011. (ENG., Illus.). 32p. (J). 16.95 *(978-0-8234-2235-7(6))* Holiday Hse., Inc.

Koontz, Robin Michal. Movers & Makers: How Animals Build & Use Tools to Survive. 2011. (Amazing Animal Skills Ser.). 48p. (gr. 4). 29.93 *(978-0-7614-4910-2(8))* Marshall Cavendish Corp.

Kubuitsile, Lauri. Animal Homes Pink a Band. 2016. (Cambridge Reading Adventures Ser.). (ENG., Illus.). 16p. pap. 6.56 *(978-1-316-60071-9(8))* Cambridge Univ. Pr.

Lawrence, Ellen. Building with Poop. 2017. (Scoop on Poop Ser.). (ENG.). (J). (gr. -1-3). lib. bdg. 17.95 ***(978-1-68402-247-2(9))*** Bearport Publishing Co., Inc.

Lehman, Julie. Kyle in His Compost Pile: The Story of a Red Wiggler. 2010. 28p. pap. 14.99 *(978-1-4490-9112-5(1))* AuthorHouse.

LernerClassroom Editors. First Step Nonfiction-Animal Homes Teaching Guide. 2009. pap. 7.95 *(978-0-8225-5672-5(3))* Lerner Publishing Group.

Lightning Bolt Books: Animal Close-Ups, 12 vols., Set. Incl. Let's Look at Armadillos. Jango-Cohen, Judith. (Illus.). (J). 2010. lib. bdg. 26.60 *(978-0-7613-3887-1(X)*, 1312736); Let's Look at Bats. Berman, Ruth. (Illus.). 2009. lib. bdg. 26.60 *(978-0-7613-3885-7(3))*; Let's Look at Brown Bears. Berman, Ruth. (Illus.). 2009. lib. bdg. 26.60 *(978-0-7613-3890-1(X))*; Let's Look at Earthworms. Dell'Oro, Suzanne Paul. (Illus.). (J). 2010. lib. bdg. 26.60 *(978-0-7613-5458-1(1)*, 1312737); Let's Look at Iguanas. Jango-Cohen, Judith. (Illus.). 2009. lib. bdg. 26.60 *(978-0-7613-3888-8(8))*; Let's Look at Monarch Butterflies. Waxman, Laura Hamilton. (Illus.). (J). 2010. lib. bdg. 25.26 *(978-0-7613-3886-4(1)*, 1312738); Let's Look at Pigeons. Piehl, Janet. (Illus.). 2009. lib. bdg. 26.60 *(978-0-8225-7897-0(2))*; Let's Look at Prairie Dogs. Zuchora-Walske, Christine. (J). 2009. lib. bdg. 25.26 *(978-0-7613-3891-8(8))*; Let's Look at Sea Otters. Levine, Michelle & Waxman, Laura. (Illus.). 2010. lib. bdg. 26.60 *(978-0-8225-7896-3(4))*; Let's Look at Sharks. Nelson, Kristin L. (Illus.). 2010. lib. bdg. 26.60 *(978-0-7613-3894-9(2))*; Let's Look at Sloths. Piehl, Janet. (Illus.). 2010. lib. bdg. 26.60 *(978-0-8225-7900-7(6))*; Let's Look at Snails. Levine, Michelle & Waxman, Laura. (Illus.). 2009. lib. bdg. 26.60 *(978-0-8225-7899-4(9))*; 32p. (gr. k-2). 2009. Set lib. bdg. 303.12 *(978-0-7613-3884-0(5)*, Lerner Pubns.) Lerner Publishing Group.

Lion, David C. Habitats, 6 bks., Set. Incl. Home in the Swamp. (Illus.). 24p. (J). (gr. 1-2). 2006. lib. bdg. 22.00 *(978-0-516-25349-7(2))*; (Scholastic News Nonfiction Readers Ser.). (Illus.). 2006. 114.00 o.p. *(978-0-516-25221-6(6)*, Children's Pr.) Scholastic Library Publishing.

Living in a Biome [Kaplan]. 2010. (Living in a Biome Ser.). 24p. pap. 41.70 *(978-1-4296-5968-0(8)*, Pebble Plus) Capstone Press of Coughlan Cos.

Lock, David. Animals at Home, Level 1. 2007. (DK Readers Ser.). (ENG., Illus.). 32p. (J). (gr. k-2). pap. 3.99 *(978-0-7566-3138-3(6)*, DK Children) Dorling Kindersley Publishing, Inc.

Lundgren, Julie K. Animal Habitats. 2011. (ENG., Illus.). 24p. (gr. 1-2). pap. 8.95 *(978-1-61741-934-8(6))* Rourke Educational Media.

MacDonald, Margaret. Animal Habitats. 2011. (Learn-Abouts: Level 10 Ser.). (Illus.). 16p. (J). pap. 7.95 *(978-1-59920-598-4(X))* Black Rabbit Bks.

Magic Wagon Staff & ABDO Publishing Company Staff. I Wish I Were ..., 1 vol. 2011. (I Wish I Were ... Ser.). (ENG., Illus.). 24p. 171.00 *(978-1-61641-655-3(6)*, Looking Glass Library) Magic Wagon.

Martin, Debbie. Animal Homes. Baker, Alan, illus. 2004. (Luxury Lift-the-Flap Ser.). 16p. (J). (gr. 1-18). 11.95 *(978-0-7945-0715-2(8)*, Usborne) EDC Publishing.

Maze, Stephanie, ed. Peaceful Moments in the Wild: Animals & Their Homes. 2006. (Moments in the Wild Ser.). (Illus.). 36p. (J). (gr. -1-1). pap. 8.00 *(978-0-9769542-1-7(4))* Moonstone Pr., LLC.

McKay, Sindy. Animals under Our Feet. Hunt, Judith, illus. 2007. 40p. (J). *(978-1-891327-97-1(6))*; pap. *(978-1-891327-98-8(4))* Treasure Bay, Inc.

—We Both Read-Animals under Our Feet. Hunt, Judith, illus. 2007. (We Both Read Ser.). 40p. (J). (gr. -1-3). pap. 4.99 *(978-1-60115-004-2(0))* Treasure Bay, Inc.

Mills, Nathan & Vasquez, Gloria. Animal Homes. 2012. (Rosen Readers Ser.). (ENG., Illus.). 24p. (J). (gr. 1-2). pap. 8.25 *(978-1-4488-8788-0(7)*, Rosen Classroom) Rosen Publishing Group, Inc., The.

Moignot, Daniel. Animals Underground. 2012. (ENG., Illus.). 36p. (J). (gr. -1-k). spiral bd. 12.99 *(978-1-85103-408-6(0))* Moonlight Publishing, Ltd. GBR. Dist: Independent Pubs. Group.

Muir, Suzanne. Animal Homes. 2007. (Steck-Vaughn BOLDPRINT Anthologies Ser.). (ENG., Illus.). 48p. (gr. 4-6). pap. 16.90 *(978-1-4190-4018-4(9))* Houghton Mifflin Harcourt Publishing Co.

Murphy, Julie. Whose Home Is This?, 1 vol. 2012. (Nature Starts Ser.). (ENG.). 32p. (gr. 1-2). pap. 8.10 *(978-1-4296-7855-1(0))*; pap. 47.70 *(978-1-4296-8300-5(7))*; lib. bdg. 27.32 *(978-1-4296-7555-0(1))* Capstone Press of Coughlan Cos. (Aplus Bks.).

National Geographic Kids Staff. Angry Birds Explore the World. 2014. (ENG., Illus.). 104p. (J). (gr. 3-7). lib. bdg. 18.90 *(978-1-4263-1987-7(8)*, National Geographic Children's Bks.) National Geographic Society.

National Wildlife Federation Staff & Bové, Jennifer. Ranger Rick Jr: Animal Bedtime. 2017. (Ranger Rick: Animal Fun for Young Children Ser.). (ENG., Illus.). 32p. (J). (gr. -1-1). pap. 5.99 *(978-1-63076-290-2(3))* Muddy Boots Pr.

Norris, Robert. Made in the Wild: Animal Builders. 2014. (ENG.). 24p. (gr. k-3). 28.50 *(978-1-62717-634-7(9))* Rourke Educational Media.

Patterson, Matt. Daylight Moonlight, 1 vol. 2013. (ENG., Illus.). 32p. (J). 16.99 *(978-0-7643-4282-0(7)*, 9780764342820) Schiffer Publishing, Ltd.

Pearson, Carrie A. & Wald, Christina. Un Fresco Cuento de Verano, 1 vol. Wald, Christina, illus. 2014.Tr. of Cool Summer Tail. (SPA & ENG., Illus.). 32p. (J). (gr. -1-3). pap. 9.95 *(978-1-62855-223-2(9))* Arbordale Publishing.

Pfeffer, Wendy. A Log's Life. Brickman, Robin, illus. 2007. (ENG.). 32p. (J). (gr. -1-3). 6.99 *(978-1-4169-3483-7(9)*, Aladdin) Simon & Schuster Children's Publishing.

Piper, Ross. Surviving in the World's Most Extreme Places. 2010. (Extreme! Ser.). (ENG.). 32p. (gr. 3-4). pap. 47.70 *(978-1-4296-5121-9(0)*, Fact Finders) Capstone Press of Coughlan Cos.

Press, Judy. Animal Habitats! Learning about North American Animals & Plants Through Art, Science & Creative Play. Day, Betsy, illus. (ENG.). 128p. (J). (gr. 3-7). 2008. per. 12.95 *(978-0-8249-6756-7(9))* 2005. 14.95 *(978-0-8249-6778-9(X))* Worthy Publishing. (Ideal Pubns.).

Raber, Angela. Doesn't Thatâ¿, 1 vol. 2010. 16p. 24.95 *(978-1-4489-4258-9(6))* PublishAmerica, Inc.

Rake, Jody Sullivan. Meerkats, Moles, & Voles: Animals of the Underground. 2015. (Underground Safari Ser.). (ENG., Illus.). 24p. (gr. 1-2). lib. bdg. 25.32 *(978-1-4914-5060-4(6))* Capstone Press of Coughlan Cos.

Rizzi, Kathleen. Who Lives Here?, 1 vol. 2013. (Photoflap Board Books Ser.). (ENG., Illus.). 16p. (J). bds. 5.99 *(978-1-59572-354-3(4))* Star Bright Bks., Inc.

Roemer, Heidi Bee. Whose Nest Is This? McLennan, Connie, illus. 2009. (ENG.). 32p. (J). (gr. -1-3). 16.95 *(978-1-58979-386-6(2))* Taylor Trade Publishing.

Rose, Emma. Animal Habitats, 6 vols., Set. 2004. (Phonics Readers Books 37-72 Ser.). (ENG.). 8p. (gr. k-1). pap. 35.70 *(978-0-7368-4071-2(0)*, Phonics Readers) Capstone Press of Coughlan Cos.

Rustad, Martha E. H. Baby Animals in Burrows. 2017. (Baby Animals & Their Homes Ser.). (ENG., Illus.). 24p. (gr. k-1). lib. bdg. 21.99 *(978-1-5157-3831-2(0))* Capstone Press of Coughlan Cos.

—Baby Animals in Dens. 2017. (Baby Animals & Their Homes Ser.). (ENG., Illus.). 24p. (gr. k-1). lib. bdg. 21.99 *(978-1-5157-3830-5(2))* Capstone Press of Coughlan Cos.

—Baby Animals in Nests. 2017. (Baby Animals & Their Homes Ser.). (ENG., Illus.). 24p. (gr. k-1). lib. bdg. 21.99 *(978-1-5157-3832-9(9))* Capstone Press of Coughlan Cos.

Salas, Laura Purdie. Do Turtles Sleep in Treetops? A Book about Animal Homes, 1 vol. Yesh, Jeff, illus. 2006. (Animals All Around Ser.). (ENG.). 24p. (gr. -1-2). lib. bdg. 26.65 *(978-1-4048-2232-0(1))* Picture Window Bks.

Singer, Marilyn. A Strange Place to Call Home: The World's Most Dangerous Habitats & the Animals That Call Them Home. Young, Ed, illus. 2015. (ENG.). 44p. (J). (gr. k-3). 7.99 *(978-1-4521-4125-1(8))* Chronicle Bks. LLC.

Smith, Natalie. Habitat Protection. 2008. (Saving Our World Ser.). 32p. (gr. 4-18). lib. bdg. 28.50 *(978-0-7614-3225-8(6)*, Benchmark Bks.) Marshall Cavendish Corp.

Stearns, Precious. Eye to Eye with Endangered Species, 10 vols., Set. Incl. Steller Sea Lions. (Illus.). 24p. (J). (gr. 3-6). 2009. lib. bdg. 27.07 *(978-1-60694-402-8(9))*; 2011. Set lib. bdg. 270.70 o.p. *(978-1-61590-960-5(5))* Rourke Educational Media.

Stetson, Emily. Create a Wildlife Habitat for Urban & Suburban Small Spaces. 2004. (ENG., Illus.). 128p. (J). pap. 12.95 *(978-0-8249-8665-0(2)*, Ideal Pubns.) Worthy Publishing.

Stradling, Jan. Nests & Shelters: Level H, 6 vols. (First Explorers Ser.). 24p. (gr. 1-2). 29.95 *(978-0-7699-1448-0(9))* Shortland Pubns. (U. S. A.) Inc.

Sundance/Newbridge LLC Staff. Where Do Animals Live? 2007. (Early Science Ser.). (gr. k-3). 18.95 *(978-1-4007-6251-4(0))*; pap. 6.10 *(978-1-4007-6247-7(2))* Sundance/Newbridge Educational Publishing.

Tagliaferro, Linda. Bears & Their Dens [Scholastic]. 2010. (Animal Homes Ser.). 24p. pap. 0.49 *(978-1-4296-5793-8(6)*, Pebble Plus) Capstone Press of Coughlan Cos.

Tatchell, Judy. Animal Homes. 2004. (Lift-the-Flap Ser.). (ENG., Illus.). 1p. (J). (gr. 1-18). pap. 8.95 *(978-0-7460-3315-9(X))* EDC Publishing.

Taylor, Saranne. Animal Homes. Chiacchiera, Moreno & Todd, Michelle, illus. 2014. (ENG.). 32p. (J). *(978-0-7787-1438-5(1))* Crabtree Publishing Co.

Things That Sting. 2015. (Things That Sting Ser.). (ENG.). 24p. (J). (gr. 2-3). pap., pap., pap. 293.40 *(978-1-4824-3498-9(9))* Stevens, Gareth Publishing LLLP.

Trussell-Cullen, Alan. Animal Groups, Vol. 4. 2014. (ENG.). 16p. spiral bd. 8.00 *(978-1-4085-0058-3(2))* Oxford Univ. Pr., Inc.

Webb, Barb. Helping Habitats. 2011. (ENG., Illus.). 24p. (gr. k-2). pap. 8.95 *(978-1-61741-972-0(9))* Rourke Educational Media.

Weber, Valerie J. Por qué Algunos Animales Tienen Caparazón. 2008. (Donde viven los animales (Where Animals Live) Ser.). (SPA., Illus.). 24p. (gr. 1-4). lib. bdg. 22.00 *(978-0-8368-8811-9(1)*, Weekly Reader Leveled Readers) Stevens, Gareth Publishing LLLP.

—Por qué algunos animales tienen caparazón (Why Animals Live in Shells) 2008. (Donde viven los animales (Where Animals Live) Ser.). (SPA.). 24p. (gr. 1-4). pap. 8.15 *(978-0-8368-8818-7(9)*, Weekly Reader Leveled Readers) Stevens, Gareth Publishing LLLP.

—Por Qué Algunos Animales Viven en Cuevas. 2008. (Donde viven los animales (Where Animals Live) Ser.). (SPA., Illus.). 24p. (J). (gr. 1-4). pap. 8.15 *(978-0-8368-8815-7(4)*, Weekly Reader Leveled Readers) Stevens, Gareth Publishing LLLP.

—Por Qué Algunos Animales Viven en Cuevas. 2008. (Donde viven los animales (Where Animals Live) Ser.). (SPA., Illus.). 24p. (J). (gr. 1-4). lib. bdg. 22.00 *(978-0-8368-8808-9(1)*, Weekly Reader Leveled Readers) Stevens, Gareth Publishing LLLP.

—Por Qué Algunos Animales Viven en Madrigueras. 2008. (Donde viven los animales (Where Animals Live) Ser.). (SPA., Illus.). 24p. (gr. 1-4). lib. bdg. 22.00 *(978-0-8368-8807-2(3)*, Weekly Reader Leveled Readers) Stevens, Gareth Publishing LLLP.

—Por qué algunos animales viven en madrigueras (Why Animals Live in Burrows) 2008. (Donde viven los animales (Where Animals Live) Ser.). (SPA.). 24p. (gr. 1-4). pap. 8.15 *(978-0-8368-8814-0(6)*, Weekly Reader Leveled Readers) Stevens, Gareth Publishing LLLP.

—Por Qué Algunos Animales Viven en Nidos. 2008. (Donde viven los animales (Where Animals Live) Ser.). (SPA.). 24p. (gr. 1-4). pap. 8.15 *(978-0-8368-8817-1(0)*, Weekly Reader Leveled Readers) Stevens, Gareth Publishing LLLP.

—Por Que Algunos Animales Viven en Nidos. 2008. (Donde viven los animales (Where Animals Live) Ser.). (SPA., Illus.). 24p. (gr. 1-4). lib. bdg. 22.00 *(978-0-8368-8810-2(3)*, Weekly Reader Leveled Readers) Stevens, Gareth Publishing LLLP.

—Why Animals Live in Burrows. 2008. (Where Animals Live Ser.). (Illus.). 24p. (gr. 1-4). lib. bdg. 22.00

(978-0-8368-8793-8(X), Weekly Reader Leveled Readers) Stevens, Gareth Publishing LLLP.

—Why Animals Live in Burrows. 2008. (Where Animals Live Ser.). (ENG & SPA.). 24p. (gr. 1-4). pap. 8.15 (978-0-8368-8800-3(6), Weekly Reader Leveled Readers) Stevens, Gareth Publishing LLLP.

—Why Animals Live in Caves. 2008. (Where Animals Live Ser.). 24p. (gr. 1-4). pap. 8.15 (978-0-8368-8801-0(4)); (Illus.). lib. bdg. 22.00 (978-0-8368-8794-5(8)) Stevens, Gareth Publishing LLLP. (Weekly Reader Leveled Readers).

—Why Animals Live in Nests. 2008. (Where Animals Live Ser.). (Illus.). 24p. (gr. 1-4). lib. bdg. 22.00 (978-0-8368-8796-9(4), Weekly Reader Leveled Readers) Stevens, Gareth Publishing LLLP.

—Why Animals Live in Nests. 2008. (Where Animals Live Ser.). 24p. (gr. 1-4). pap. 8.15 (978-0-8368-8803-4(0), Weekly Reader Leveled Readers) Stevens, Gareth Publishing LLLP.

—Why Animals Live in Shells. 2008. (Where Animals Live Ser.). (Illus.). 24p. (gr. 1-4). lib. bdg. 22.00 (978-0-8368-8797-6(2), Weekly Reader Leveled Readers) Stevens, Gareth Publishing LLLP.

Weber, Valerie J. & Weber, Valerie J. Why Animals Live in Shells. 2008. (Where Animals Live Ser.). (SPA.). 24p. (gr. 1-4). pap. 8.15 (978-0-8368-8804-1(9), Weekly Reader Leveled Readers) Stevens, Gareth Publishing LLLP.

Weitzman, Elizabeth. 10 Cosas Que Puedes Hacer para Proteger a Los Animales. 2017. (Rookie Star — Make a Difference (Spanish Translation) Ser.). (SPA.). 32p. (J). pap. 5.95 **(978-1-338-18778-6(3))**; lib. bdg. 25.00 **(978-0-531-22857-9(6))** Scholastic Library Publishing. (Children's Pr.).

Welvaert, Scott R. A Bear in Its Den. 2003. (Where Do Animals Live? Ser.). (J). (978-1-58417-184-3(7)); pap. (978-1-58417-185-0(5)) Lake Street Pubs.

Wilkins, John-Paul. What Can Live There?, 1 vol. 2014. (What Can Live There? Ser.). (ENG.). 24p. (gr. -1-1). 67.95 (978-1-4846-0579-0(9), Heinemann Read & Learn) Heinemann-Raintree.

Williams, Brenda. Home for a Tiger, Home for a Bear. Fowler, Rosamund, illus. (ENG.). 32p. (J). 2017. (gr. -1-1). 8.99 **(978-1-78285-343-5(X))** 2009. pap. 7.99 (978-1-84686-353-0(8)) Barefoot Bks., Inc.

Williams, Brenda & Fowler, Rosamund. Home for a Tiger, Home for a Bear. 2007. (ENG., Illus.). 32p. (J). (gr. k-3). 16.99 (978-1-905236-81-7(6)) Barefoot Bks., Inc.

Wolfe, Jane. Who Lives Here? Toy Box Staff, illus. 2013. (ENG.). 8p. bds. 6.99 (978-1-84322-651-2(0), Armadillo) Anness Publishing GBR. Dist: National Bk. Network.

Wood, Alix. Amazing Animal Homes. 2012. (Wow! Wildlife Ser.). (ENG., Illus.). 24p. (J). (gr. k-5). 22.60 (978-1-4488-8098-0(X)); pap. 8.25 (978-1-4488-8162-8(5)) Windmill Bks.

World Book, Inc Staff, contrib. by. Animal Homes. 2007. (J). (978-0-7166-7726-0(1)) World Bk., Inc.

ANIMALS—HABITS AND BEHAVIOR

Here are entered factual books whose aim is to describe and instruct. Fictional or legendary tales about animals are entered under Animals—Stories.

see also Animal Intelligence; Animals—Fiction; Animals—Migration; Nature Study; Tracking and Trailing

also names of animals with the subdivision Habits and Behavior, e.g. Birds—Habits and Behavior; etc.

ABDO Publishing Company Staff. Smartest Animals. 2014. (Smartest Animals Ser.: 6). (ENG.). 48p. (gr. 3-6). lib. bdg. 196.74 (978-1-62403-163-2(3)) ABDO Publishing Co.

Acampora, Courtney. Smithsonian First Discoveries: Big World. Riggs, Jenna, illus. 2016. (Smithsonian First Discoveries Ser.). (ENG.). 48p. (J). 16.95 (978-1-62686-483-2(7), Silver Dolphin Bks.) Readerlink Distribution Services, LLC.

Algarra, Alejandro. How Do Animals Use Their Five Senses? Bonilla, Rocio, illus. 2016. 35p. (J). **(978-1-5182-3150-6(0))** Barron's Educational Series, Inc.

Allman, Toney. Animal Life in Groups. 2009. (Animal Behavior Ser.). (Illus.). 136p. (gr. 5-8). lib. bdg. 32.95 (978-1-60413-142-0(X), Chelsea Hse.) Facts On File, Inc.

Allyn, Daisy. Animal Families. 2009. (Real Life Readers Ser.). 8p. (gr. k-1). pap. 5.15 (978-1-4042-7963-6(6), Rosen Classroom) Rosen Publishing Group, Inc., The.

Andrus, Aubre. Five-Minute True Stories: Animal BFFs. 2016. (ENG., Illus.). 160p. (J). (gr. -1-3). 12.99 (978-0-545-91419-2(1), Scholastic Nonfiction) Scholastic, Inc.

Animal Actions: Individual Title Six-Packs. (gr. k-1). 23.00 (978-0-7635-9047-5(9)) Rigby Education.

Animal Emotions. 2017. (Animal Emotions Ser.). 32p. (gr. 3-3). pap. 63.12 **(978-0-7660-8890-0(1))**; lib. bdg. 151.62 **(978-0-7660-8588-6(0))** Enslow Pubs., Inc.

Antle, Bhagavan. The Tiger Cubs & the Chimp: The True Story of How Anjana the Chimp Helped Raise Two Baby Tigers. Antle, Bhagavan, illus. Bland, Barry, photos by. 2013. (ENG., Illus.). 32p. (J). (gr. -1-3). 16.99 (978-0-8050-9319-3(2), 9780805093193, Holt, Henry & Co. Bks. For Young Readers) Holt, Henry & Co.

Armentrout, David & Armentrout, Patricia. Leaps & Bounds. 2008. (Illus.). 32p. (J). 28.50 (978-1-60472-304-5(1)) Rourke Educational Media.

Arnold, Caroline. Caroline Arnold's Habitats. Arnold, Caroline, illus. 2015. (Caroline Arnold's Habitats Ser.). (ENG., Illus.). 24p. (gr. 2-3). lib. bdg. 111.96 (978-1-4795-6235-0(1)) Picture Window Bks.

—A Day & Night in the Desert. Arnold, Caroline, illus. 2015. (Caroline Arnold's Habitats Ser.). (ENG., Illus.). 24p. (gr. 2-3). lib. bdg. 27.99 (978-1-4795-6072-1(3)) Picture Window Bks.

—A Day & Night in the Forest. Arnold, Caroline, illus. 2015. (Caroline Arnold's Habitats Ser.). (ENG., Illus.). 24p. (gr. 2-3). lib. bdg. 27.99 (978-1-4795-6075-2(8)) Picture Window Bks.

—A Day & Night in the Rain Forest. Arnold, Caroline, illus. 2015. (Caroline Arnold's Habitats Ser.). (ENG., Illus.). 24p. (gr. 2-3). lib. bdg. 27.99 (978-1-4795-6074-5(X)) Picture Window Bks.

—A Day & Night on the Prairie. Arnold, Caroline, illus. 2015. (Caroline Arnold's Habitats Ser.). (ENG., Illus.). 24p. (gr. 2-3). lib. bdg. 27.99 (978-1-4795-6073-8(1)) Picture Window Bks.

—A Wombat's World, 1 vol. Arnold, Caroline, illus. 2008. (Caroline Arnold's Animals Ser.). (ENG., Illus.). 24p. (gr. k-2). lib. bdg. 27.99 (978-1-4048-3986-1(0)) Picture Window Bks.

Arnold, Katya R. & Arnold, Katya. Elephants Can Paint Too! Arnold, Katya R. & Arnold, Katya, photos by. 2005. (ENG., Illus.). 40p. (J). (gr. -1-3). 18.99 (978-0-689-86985-3(1), Atheneum Bks. for Young Readers) Simon & Schuster Children's Publishing.

Aston, Dianna Hutts. A Nest Is Noisy. Long, Sylvia, illus. 2015. (ENG.). 40p. (J). (gr. k-3). 16.99 (978-1-4521-2713-2(1)) Chronicle Bks. LLC.

Austen, Amy. Look Out for the Dingo! 2015. (Surprisingly Scary! Ser.). (ENG., Illus.). 24p. (J). (gr. 2-3). pap. 8.25 (978-1-4994-0878-2(1), PowerKids Pr.) Rosen Publishing Group, Inc., The.

Awesome Animal Skills. 2015. (Awesome Animal Skills Ser.). (ENG.). 32p. (J). (gr. 4-4). pap., pap., pap. 360.00 (978-1-4994-8025-2(3), Windmill Bks.) Rosen Publishing Group, Inc., The.

Axelrod-Contrada, Joan. Pesky Critters! Squirrels, Raccoons, & Other Furry Invaders, 1 vol. 2013. (Nature's Invaders Ser.). (ENG.). 32p. (gr. 3-4). lib. bdg. 27.99 (978-1-4765-0141-3(6)) Capstone Press of Coughlan Cos.

AZ Books Staff. Find My Food & Home. Petrovskaya, Olga, ed. 2012. (Matching Game Ser.). (ENG.). 18p. (J). (gr. -1-k). spiral bd. 4.95 (978-1-61889-010-8(7)) AZ Bks. LLC.

—In the Forest. Ulasevich, Olga & Goncharik, Irina, eds. 2012. (Animal Sounds Ser.). (ENG.). 14p. (J). (gr. -1-k). bds. 7.95 (978-1-61889-126-6(X)) AZ Bks. LLC.

—In the Jungle. Efimova, Tatiana, ed. 2012. (Animal Sounds Ser.). (ENG.). 14p. (J). (gr. -1-k). bds. 7.95 (978-1-61889-125-9(1)) AZ Bks. LLC.

—In the Prairie & Desert. Efimova, Tatiana & Goncharik, Irina, eds. 2012. (Animal Sounds Ser.). (ENG.). 14p. (J). (gr. -1-k). bds. 7.95 (978-1-61889-128-0(6)) AZ Bks. LLC.

—In the Savanna. Ulasevich, Olga & Migits, Anna, eds. 2012. (Animal Sounds Ser.). (ENG.). 14p. (J). (-k). bds. 7.95 (978-1-61889-124-2(3)) AZ Bks. LLC.

—Polar Animals. Gorojan, Elena, ed. 2012. (My First Library). (ENG.). 12p. (J). (-k). bds. 8.95 (978-1-61889-122-8(7)) AZ Bks. LLC.

—What Do I Eat? Sisoj, Natalja, ed. 2012. (Peek-A-Boo Ser.). (ENG.). 10p. (J). (— 1). bds. 10.95 (978-1-61889-115-0(4)) AZ Bks. LLC.

Baillie, Marilyn. Whoosh! A Watery World of Wonderful Creatures, 0 vols. Mitchell, Susan & Owlkids Books Inc. Staff, illus. 2014. (ENG.). 32p. (J). (gr. -1-2). 16.95 (978-1-926973-98-2(4), Owlkids) Owlkids Bks. Inc. CAN. Dist: Publishers Group West (PGW).

Barner, Bob. Animal Baths. 2011. (ENG.). 32p. (J). (gr. -1-1). 15.99 (978-1-4521-0056-2(X)) Chronicle Bks. LLC.

Batten, Mary. Please Don't Wake the Animals: A Book about Sleep, 1 vol. Bond, Higgins, illus. 2008. (ENG.). 32p. (J). (gr. k-3). 16.95 (978-1-56145-393-1(5)) Peachtree Pubs.

Bearport Publishing Staff, contrib. by. They Don't Belong: Tracking Invasive Species. 2015. (They Don't Belong: Tracking Invasive Species Ser.: 5). (ENG.). 32p. (J). (gr. 2-7). lib. bdg. 133.00 (978-1-62724-826-6(9)) Bearport Publishing Co., Inc.

Behavior Matters. 2016. (Behavior Matters Ser.). 32p. (gr. 3-2). 163.50 (978-1-4994-8045-0(8)); pap. 60.00 (978-1-5081-9267-1(7)) Rosen Publishing Group, Inc., The. (Windmill Bks.).

Bekoff, Marc. Animals at Play: Rules of the Game. DiMotta, Michael J., illus. 2008. (Animals & Ethics Ser.). (ENG.). 32p. (J). (gr. 4-6). 17.95 (978-1-59213-551-6(X)) Temple Univ. Pr.

Benbow, Ann & Mably, Colin. Awesome Animal Science Projects. LaBaff, Tom, illus. 2009. (Real Life Science Experiments Ser.). 48p. (J). (gr. 2-5). lib. bdg. 25.27 (978-0-7660-3148-7(9)) Enslow Pubs., Inc.

Benchmark Education Company, LLC Staff, compiled by. Animal Behavior. 2006. (J). 265.00 (978-1-4108-7028-5(6)) Benchmark Education Co.

Berger, Melvin & Berger, Gilda. Dogs Bring Newspapers but Cats Bring Mice: And Other Fascinating Facts about Animal Behavior. 2004. (Illus.). 48p. (J). pap. (978-0-439-66433-2(0)) Scholastic, Inc.

—A Robin Grows Up. 2008. (Illus.). 32p. (J). (978-0-439-02525-6(7)) Scholastic, Inc.

Berkes, Marianne. Baby on Board: How Animals Carry Their Young, 1 vol. Morrison, Cathy, illus. 2016. (ENG.). 32p. (J). (gr. 8 — 1). 16.95 (978-1-58469-592-9(7)) Dawn Pubns.

Beullens-Maoui, Nathalie, ed. Animals Habitats: Filipino, 01 vols., 1. 2016. (Our Wonderful World Ser.). (ENG & SPA.). 8p. (J). pap. 9.35 (978-1-5081-1215-0(0), Rosen Classroom) Rosen Publishing Group, Inc., The.

—Animals Habitats: Hmong Green, 01 vols., 1. 2016. (Our Wonderful World Ser.). (ENG & SPA.). 8p. (J). pap. 9.35 (978-1-5081-1227-3(4), Rosen Classroom) Rosen Publishing Group, Inc., The.

—Animals Habitats: Hmong White, 01 vols., 1. 2016. (Our Wonderful World Ser.). (ENG & SPA.). 8p. (J). pap. 9.35 (978-1-5081-1233-4(9), Rosen Classroom) Rosen Publishing Group, Inc., The.

—Animals Habitats: Korean, 01 vols., 1. 2016. (Our Wonderful World Ser.). (ENG & SPA.). 8p. (J). pap. 9.35 (978-1-5081-1239-6(8), Rosen Classroom) Rosen Publishing Group, Inc., The.

—Animals Habitats: Russian, 01 vols., 1. 2016. (Our Wonderful World Ser.). (ENG & SPA.). 8p. (J). pap. 9.35 (978-1-5081-1245-7(2), Rosen Classroom) Rosen Publishing Group, Inc., The.

—Animals Habitats: Spanish, 01 vols., 1. 2016. (Our Wonderful World Ser.). (ENG & SPA.). 8p. (J). pap. 9.35 (978-1-5081-1251-8(7), Rosen Classroom) Rosen Publishing Group, Inc., The.

—Animals Habitats: Vietnamese, 01 vols., 1. 2016. (Our Wonderful World Ser.). (ENG & SPA.). 8p. (J). pap. 9.35 (978-1-5081-1257-0(6), Rosen Classroom) Rosen Publishing Group, Inc., The.

Bizarre Beast Battles. 2015. (Bizarre Beast Battles Ser.). (ENG.). 24p. (J). (gr. 2-3). pap., pap., pap. 48.90 (978-1-4824-3441-5(5)) Stevens, Gareth Publishing LLLP.

Bleiman, Andrew & Eastland, Chris. Snuggle up, ZooBorns! 2015. (ZooBorns Ser.). (J). (ENG., Illus.). 24p. (gr. -1-1). pap. 3.99 (978-1-4814-3100-2(5)); (978-1-4806-9333-3(2)) Simon Spotlight. (Simon Spotlight).

Blewett, Ashlee Brown. Horse Escape Artist! And More True Stories of Animals Behaving Badly. 2014. (NGK Chapters Ser.). (ENG.). 112p. (J). (gr. 2-5). pap. 5.99 (978-1-4263-1767-5(0), National Geographic Children's Bks.) National Geographic Society.

Blobaum, Cindy. Explore Predators & Prey! With 25 Great Projects. Aucoin, Matt, illus. 2016. (Explore Your World Ser.). (ENG.). 96p. (gr. 1-5). 19.95 (978-1-61930-456-7(2)) Open City Bks.

Bloom, Steve, et al. My Favourite Animal Families. 2010. (ENG., Illus.). 64p. (J). (gr. -1-k). 19.95 (978-0-500-54390-0(9), 554390) Thames & Hudson.

Bogue, Gary. There's a Skunk in My Backyard: The Big Stink. Todd, Chuck, illus. 2017. (J). **(978-1-59714-399-8(5))** Heyday.

Bozzo, Linda. When Dolphins Mourn. 2017. (Animal Emotions Ser.). 32p. (J). (gr. 3-3). lib. bdg. 25.27 **(978-0-7660-8615-9(1))** Enslow Pubs., Inc.

Bradley, Timothy. Animales Arquitectos. 2017. (TIME for Kids en Español - Level 4 Ser.). (SPA., Illus.). 48p. (gr. 4-4). lib. bdg. 31.99 (978-1-5157-5127-4(9)) Time for Kids Inc AUS. Dist: Capstone Pub.

—Ciudades Salvajes. 2017. (TIME for Kids en Español - Level 4 Ser.). (SPA., Illus.). 48p. (gr. 4-4). lib. bdg. 31.99 (978-1-5157-5128-1(7)) Time for Kids Inc AUS. Dist: Capstone Pub.

Bright, Michael. Behavior in Living Things, 1 vol. 2012. (Web of Life Ser.). (ENG.). 48p. (gr. 3-3). pap. 9.49 (978-1-4109-4432-0(8), Raintree Freestyle Express); (gr. 3-3). lib. bdg. 34.65 (978-1-4109-4425-2(5), Raintree Freestyle Express); (Illus.). (gr. 6-10). pap. 9.49 (978-1-4109-4405-4(0), Raintree Freestyle); (Illus.). (gr. 6-10). lib. bdg. 34.65 (978-1-4109-4398-9(4), Raintree Freestyle) Heinemann-Raintree.

British Museum of Natural History Staff, contrib. by. What Do Animals Eat Colouring Book. (Illus.). 8p. (J). (gr. -1-6). pap. 2.95 (978-0-565-00808-6(0)) Natural History Museum Pubns. GBR. Dist: Parkwest Pubns., Inc.

Brooklyn, Isabella. If You Were Raised by a Dinosaur. Levesque, Haude, illus. 2013. (ENG.). 80p. (J). (gr. 2-5). pap. 9.95 (978-1-62354-015-9(1)) Charlesbridge Publishing, Inc.

Brynie, Faith Hickman. Do Animals Work Together? 2010. (I Like Reading about Animals! Ser.). (Illus.). 32p. (J). (gr. k-3). 23.94 (978-0-7660-3328-3(7)); pap. 7.95 (978-0-7660-3749-6(5), Enslow Elementary) Enslow Pubs., Inc.

—How Do Animal Babies Live? 2010. (I Like Reading about Animals! Ser.). (Illus.). 32p. (J). pap. 7.95 (978-0-7660-3748-9(7), Enslow Elementary) Enslow Pubs., Inc.

—How Do Animals Keep Clean? 2010. (I Like Reading about Animals! Ser.). (Illus.). 32p. (J). (gr. k-3). 23.94 (978-0-7660-3330-6(9)); pap. 7.95 (978-0-7660-3750-2(9), Enslow Elementary) Enslow Pubs., Inc.

—How Do Animals Stay Safe? 2010. (I Like Reading about Animals! Ser.). (Illus.). 32p. (J). (gr. k-3). 23.94 (978-0-7660-3326-9(0)); pap. 7.95 (978-0-7660-3747-2(9), Enslow Elementary) Enslow Pubs., Inc.

Budayr, Valarie. The Fox Diaries: The Year the Foxes Came to Our Garden. 2011. (ENG., Illus.). 80p. (J). 14.95 (978-1-936426-18-8(8)) Audrey Pr.

Bull, Schuyler. Crocodile Crossing. Male, Alan, illus. 2005. (Amazing Animal Adventures Ser.). (ENG.). 36p. (J). (gr. -1-2). 15.95 (978-1-59249-051-6(4), B7104); (gr. -1-2). pap. 6.95 (978-1-59249-052-3(2), S7104); (gr. -1-2). 19.95 (978-1-59249-390-6(4), BC7104); (gr. 2-2). 8.95 (978-1-59249-391-3(2), SC7104) Soundprints.

Bullard, Lisa. Busy Animals: Learning about Animals in Autumn, 1 vol. Takvorian, Nadine, illus. 2010. (Autumn Ser.). (ENG.). 24p. (gr. 1-2). lib. bdg. 26.65 (978-1-4048-6014-8(2)) Picture Window Bks.

Burgess, Thornton W. The Burgess Animal Book for Children. 2005. 29.95 (978-1-4218-0996-0(6)); 304p. pap. 14.95 (978-1-59540-696-5(4)) 1st World Publishing, Inc. (1st World Library - Literary Society).

—The Burgess Animal Book for Children. 2009. 248p. 26.99 (978-1-60512-323-3(4)); (Illus.). pap. 13.99 (978-1-60512-423-0(0)) Akasha Publishing, LLC. (Akasha Classics).

—The Burgess Animal Book for Children. (J). 28.95 (978-0-8488-0716-0(2)) Amereon Ltd.

—The Burgess Animal Book for Children. Fuertes, Louis Agassiz, illus. 2008. 284p. (gr. 4-7). pap. (978-1-4099-2052-6(6)) Dodo Pr.

—The Burgess Animal Book for Children. 2004. (Dover Children's Classics Ser.). (ENG., Illus.). 288p. (gr. 1-5). pap. 9.99 (978-0-486-43745-3(0)) Dover Pubns., Inc.

—The Burgess Animal Book for Children. 2010. (Illus.). 130p. (gr. 4-7). pap. 19.99 (978-1-153-69658-6(4)); 146p. pap. 21.89 (978-1-152-50810-1(5)) General Bks. LLC.

—The Burgess Animal Book for Children. Fuertes, Louis Agassiz, illus. 2011. 478p. 52.95 (978-1-169-84273-1(9)) 2010. 478p. 42.36 (978-1-163-21392-6(6)) 2010. 478p. pap. 30.36 (978-1-162-64734-0(5)) 2004. 476p. (gr. 4-7). 52.95 (978-1-4326-2165-0(3)) Kessinger Publishing, LLC.

—The Burgess Animal Book for Children. 2004. reprint ed. pap. 1.99 (978-1-4192-5555-7(X)) Kessinger Publishing, LLC.

—The Burgess Animal Book for Children. Fuertes, Louis Agassiz, illus. 2004. reprint ed. pap. 37.95 (978-1-4179-2978-8(2)) Kessinger Publishing, LLC.

—The Burgess Animal Book for Children (Yesterday's Classics) Fuertes, Louis Agassiz, illus. 2006. (J). per. 13.95 (978-1-59915-171-7(5)) Yesterday's Classics.

Burgess, Thornton W. & Fuertes, Louis Agassiz. The Burgess Animal Book for Children. 2010. (ENG.). 484p. pap. 38.75 (978-1-171-73852-7(8)); 486p. pap. 38.75 (978-1-176-23716-2(0)) Creative Media Partners, LLC.

Burke, Johanna. A Kangaroo Mob. 2013. (Animal Groups Ser.). (Illus.). 24p. (J). (gr. 1-3). pap. 8.15 (978-1-4339-8200-2(5)); lib. bdg. 22.60 (978-1-4339-8199-9(8)) Stevens, Gareth Publishing LLLP.

Burroughs, John. Squirrels & Other Fur-Bearers (Yesterday's Classics) 2006. (Illus.). 144p. (J). per. 8.95 (978-1-59915-070-3(0)) Yesterday's Classics.

Burton, Margie, et al. Animals' Eyes & Ears. 2011. (Early Connections Ser.). (J). (978-1-61672-479-5(X)) Benchmark Education Co.

Butler, Nathalie. Bart Likes to Bark. 2017. (Learning with Stories Ser.). 24p. (gr. 4-6). pap. 8.25 **(978-1-5081-6241-4(7)**, PowerKids Pr.) Rosen Publishing Group, Inc., The.

Cain, Marie Mowery. Animals Say. 2013. (Big Books, Blue Ser.). (ENG & SPA., Illus.). 16p. pap. 33.00 (978-1-59246-008-3(9)) Big Books, by George!

Call of the Wild. 2016. (Call of the Wild Ser.). 32p. (gr. 3-3). pap. 63.48 (978-1-5026-2050-7(2)); lib. bdg. 171.00 (978-1-5026-1730-9(7)) Cavendish Square Publishing.

Canetti, Yanitzia. Acurrucarse: Ellos lo hacen bien nosotros Tambien. 2010. (SPA.). (J). pap. 5.99 (978-1-59835-228-3(8), BrickHouse Education) Cambridge BrickHouse, Inc.

—Agacharse: Ellos lo hacen bien nosotros Tambien. 2010. (J). pap. 5.99 (978-1-59835-230-6(X), BrickHouse Education) Cambridge BrickHouse, Inc.

—What They Can Do, We Can Too! Crouch. 2010. 24p. pap. 5.99 (978-1-59835-229-0(6), BrickHouse Education) Cambridge BrickHouse, Inc.

Cardenas, Ernesto A. Animal World. 2009. pap. 4.95 (978-1-60698-060-6(2)) Milo Educational Bks. & Resources.

Castaldo, Nancy F. Beastly Brains: Exploring How Animals Think, Talk, & Feel. 2017. (ENG., Illus.). 160p. (YA). (gr. 5-7). 16.99 (978-0-544-63335-3(0), HMH Books For Young Readers) Houghton Mifflin Harcourt Publishing Co.

Chung, Liz. Inside Rabbit Burrows. 2015. (Inside Animal Homes Ser.). (ENG., Illus.). 24p. (J). (gr. 2-3). pap. 8.25 (978-1-4994-0876-8(5), PowerKids Pr.) Rosen Publishing Group, Inc., The.

Clark, Willow. Dolphins: Life in the Pod. 2011. (Animal Families Ser.). 24p. (J). (ENG.). pap. 8.25 (978-1-4488-2610-0(1)); (Illus.). lib. bdg. 22.60 (978-1-4488-2512-7(1)) Rosen Publishing Group, Inc., The. (PowerKids Pr.).

—Gorillas: Life in the Troop. 2011. (Animal Families Ser.). 24p. (J). (ENG.). pap. 8.25 (978-1-4488-2614-8(4)); (Illus.). lib. bdg. 22.60 (978-1-4488-2514-1(8)) Rosen Publishing Group, Inc., The. (PowerKids Pr.).

—Lions: Leones: Life in the Pride: Vida en la Manada. 2011. (Animal Families / Familias de animales Ser.). (SPA & ENG., Illus.). 24p. lib. bdg. 22.60 (978-1-4488-3140-1(7), PowerKids Pr.) Rosen Publishing Group, Inc., The.

—Lions: Life in the Pride. 2011. (Animal Families Ser.). 24p. (J). (ENG.). pap. 8.25 (978-1-4488-2612-4(8)); (Illus.). lib. bdg. 22.60 (978-1-4488-2513-4(X)) Rosen Publishing Group, Inc., The. (PowerKids Pr.).

—Meerkats: Life in the Mob. 2011. (Animal Families Ser.). 24p. (J). (ENG.). pap. 8.25 (978-1-4488-2608-7(X)); (Illus.). lib. bdg. 22.60 (978-1-4488-2511-0(3)) Rosen Publishing Group, Inc., The. (PowerKids Pr.).

—Meerkats: Suricatas: Life in the Mob: Vida en la Colonia. 2011. (Animal Families / Familias de animales Ser.). (SPA & ENG., Illus.). 24p. lib. bdg. 22.60 (978-1-4488-3125-8(3), PowerKids Pr.) Rosen Publishing Group, Inc., The.

—Penguins: Life in the Colony. 2011. (Animal Families Ser.). 24p. (J). (ENG.). pap. 8.25 (978-1-4488-2606-3(3)); (Illus.). lib. bdg. 22.60 (978-1-4488-2510-3(5)) Rosen Publishing Group, Inc., The. (PowerKids Pr.).

—Penguins: Pingüinos: Life in the Colony: Vida en la Colonia. 2011. (Animal Families / Familias de animales Ser.). (SPA & ENG., Illus.). 24p. lib. bdg. 22.60 (978-1-4488-3124-1(5), PowerKids Pr.) Rosen Publishing Group, Inc., The.

—Wolves: Life in the Pack. 2011. (Animal Families Ser.). 24p. (J). (ENG.). pap. 8.25 (978-1-4488-2616-2(0)); (Illus.). lib. bdg. 22.60 (978-1-4488-2515-8(6)) Rosen Publishing Group, Inc., The. (PowerKids Pr.).

Clarke, Ginjer L. Fake Out! Animals That Play Tricks. Mueller, Pete, illus. 2007. (All Aboard Science Reader Ser.). 48p. (gr. 1-3). 14.00 (978-0-7569-8170-9(0)) Perfection Learning Corp.

—Far Out! Animals That Do Amazing Things. Mueller, Pete, illus. 2009. (Penguin Young Readers, Level 3 Ser.). (ENG.). 48p. (J). (gr. 1-3). mass mkt. 3.99 (978-0-448-44826-8(2), Penguin Young Readers) Penguin Young Readers Group.

—Gross Out! Animals That Do Disgusting Things. Mueller, Pete, illus. 2006. (Penguin Young Readers, Level 4 Ser.). (ENG.). 48p. (J). (gr. 3-4). mass mkt. 3.99 (978-0-448-44390-4(2), Penguin Young Readers) Penguin Young Readers Group.

—Gross Out! Animals That Do Disgusting Things. Mueller, Pete, illus. 2007. (All Aboard Science Reader Ser.). 46p. (gr. 1-3). 14.00 (978-0-7569-8172-3(7)) Perfection Learning Corp.

Clay, Kathryn. Animals in Spring. 2016. (Celebrate Spring Ser.). (ENG., Illus.). 24p. (gr. k-1). lib. bdg. 21.99 (978-1-4914-8302-2(4), Pebble Bks.) Capstone Press of Coughlan Cos.

Collard, Sneed B., III. Tough Terminators. 2004. (It's Nature! Ser.). (Illus.). 32p. (J). (gr. 3-6). pap. 7.95 (978-1-55971-633-8(9), Creative Publishing International) Quarto Publishing Group USA.

Confalone, Nick & Confalone, Chelsea. Ocean Monsters. 2013. (Penguin Young Readers, Level 4 Ser.). (ENG.). 48p. (J). (gr. 3-4). pap. 3.99 (978-0-448-46723-8(2), Penguin Young Readers) Penguin Young Readers Group.

Coupe, Robert. Predators & Prey: Battle for Survival. 2014. (Discovery Education: Animals Ser.). 32p. (J). (gr. 3-6). 26.25 (978-1-4777-6956-0(0)); pap. 10.00 (978-1-4777-6957-7(9)) Rosen Publishing Group, Inc., The. (PowerKids Pr.).

Crum, Anna-Maria. Animal Behaviorists: Set Of 6. 2011. (Navigators Ser.). (J). 44.00 net. (978-1-4108-0412-9(7)) Benchmark Education Co.

Cunning Creatures: Individual Title Six-Packs. (gr. k-1). 23.00 (978-0-7635-9032-1(0)) Rigby Education.

Cunningham, Kevin. Clownfish & Sea Anemones. 2016. (21st Century Junior Library: Better Together Ser.). (ENG., Illus.). 24p. (J). (gr. 2-5). 27.07 (978-1-63471-085-5(1), 208419) Cherry Lake Publishing.

—Egrets & Hippos. 2016. (21st Century Junior Library: Better Together Ser.). (ENG., Illus.). 24p. (J). (gr. 2-5). 27.07 (978-1-63471-081-7(9), 208403) Cherry Lake Publishing.

—Goby Fish & Pistol Shrimp. 2016. (21st Century Junior Library: Better Together Ser.). (ENG., Illus.). 24p. (J). (gr.

2-5). 27.07 (978-1-63471-084-8(3), 208415) Cherry Lake Publishing.

—Honeyguide Birds & Ratels. 2016. (21st Century Junior Library: Better Together Ser.). (ENG., Illus.). 24p. (J). (gr. 2-5). 27.07 (978-1-63471-086-2(X), 208423) Cherry Lake Publishing.

—Sea Turtles & Yellow Tang Fish. 2016. (21st Century Junior Library: Better Together Ser.). (ENG., Illus.). 24p. (J). (gr. 2-5). 27.07 (978-1-63471-088-6(6), 208431) Cherry Lake Publishing.

—Stick Insects & Ants. 2016. (21st Century Junior Library: Better Together Ser.). (ENG., Illus.). 24p. (J). (gr. 2-5). 27.07 (978-1-63471-087-9(8), 208427) Cherry Lake Publishing.

Cusick, Dawn. Animals That Make Me Say Look Out! (National Wildlife Federation) 2016. (ENG., Illus.). 80p. (J). (gr. 2-5). 14.95 (978-1-62354-080-7(1)) Charlesbridge Publishing, Inc.

—Get the Scoop on Animal Snot, Spit & Slime! From Snake Venom to Fish Slime, 251 Cool Facts about Mucus, Saliva & More! 2016. (Get the Scoop Ser.). (ENG.). 80p. (J). (gr. 3-7). 14.95 (978-1-63322-115-4(6), Moondance) Quarto Publishing Group USA.

Daly-Weir, Catherine. Whiskers. Leonard, Tom, illus. 2015. (Step into Reading Ser.). (ENG.). 32p. (J). (gr. -1-1). pap. 3.99 (978-0-307-26214-1(6), Random Hse. Bks. for Young Readers) Random Hse. Children's Bks.

Davies, Nicola. Deadly! The Truth about the Most Dangerous Creatures on Earth. Layton, Neal, illus. 2013. (Animal Science Ser.). (ENG.). 64p. (J). (gr. 3-7). 14.99 (978-0-7636-6231-8(3)) Candlewick Pr.

—Poop: A Natural History of the Unmentionable. Layton, Neal, illus. (Animal Science Ser.). (ENG.). 64p. (J). (gr. 3-7). 2011. pap. 7.99 (978-0-7636-4128-3(6)) 2007. 5.99 (978-0-7636-3544-2(8)) Candlewick Pr.

Davies, Valerie. Sounds of the Wild: Animals. Pledger, Maurice, illus. 2015. (Pledger Sounds Ser.). (ENG.). 16p. (J). (gr. k). 18.95 (978-1-62686-049-0(1), Silver Dolphin Bks.) Readerlink Distribution Services, LLC.

Dawson, Emily C. How Animals Find Water. 2010. (Our Animal World Ser.). 24p. (J). 25.65 (978-1-60753-011-4(2)) Amicus Publishing.

—How Animals Sleep. 2010. (Our Animal World Ser.). 24p. (J). 25.65 (978-1-60753-014-5(7)) Amicus Publishing.

De la Bédoyère, Camilla. I Love Baby Animals. 2014. (Illus.). 120p. (J). (978-1-4351-5532-9(7)) Barnes & Noble, Inc.

—I Love Hugs & Kisses. 2014. (Illus.). (J). (978-1-4351-5942-6(X)) Barnes & Noble, Inc.

—Splash. 2014. (Illus.). 48p. (J). pap. (978-0-545-83875-7(4)) Scholastic, Inc.

deMarin, Layne. Everybody Moves, 1 vol. 2011. (Wonder Readers Fluent Level Ser.). (ENG.). 32p. (gr. -1-2). pap. 5.99 (978-1-4296-7917-6(4), Wonder Readers) Capstone Press of Coughlan Cos.

Disney Book Group Staff. Wonderful World of Animals. 2012. (Wonderful World Of... Ser.). (ENG.). 64p. (J). (gr. 1-17). 8.99 (978-1-4231-4940-8(8)) Disney Pr.

Doherty, Gillian. 1001 Animales Que Buscar. 2004. (1001 Things to Spot Ser.).Tr. of 1001 Animals to Spot. (SPA., Illus.). (J). pap. 6.95 (978-0-7460-5081-1(X)) EDC Publishing.

Doran, Mark & Trius, Angie. Animal Doctors: Incredible Ways Animals Heal Themselves. Blasco, Julio Antonio, illus. 2016. (ENG.). 32p. (J). (gr. 2-6). 15.95 (978-1-78067-832-0(0)) King, Laurence Publishing GBR. Dist: Hachette Bk. Group.

Dorling Kindersley Publishing Staff. Animal Antics. 2014. (ENG., Illus.). 144p. (J). (gr. 2-5). pap. 9.99 (978-1-4654-2447-1(4), DK Children) Dorling Kindersley Publishing, Inc.

—Who Am I? Baby Animals. 2012. (ENG.). 28p. (J). (gr. -1 — 1). bds. 6.99 (978-0-7566-9018-2(8), DK Children) Dorling Kindersley Publishing, Inc.

Downer, Ann. The Animal Mating Game: The Wacky, Weird World of Sex in the Animal Kingdom. 2016. (ENG.). 104p. (YA). (gr. 7-12). 35.99 (978-1-4677-8571-6(7)); (Illus.). 53.32 (978-1-5124-1143-0(4)) Lerner Publishing Group. (Twenty-First Century Bks.).

Du Puy, William Atherton & Nelson, Edward William. Our Animal Friends & Foes. 2004. reprint ed. pap. 28.95 (978-1-4179-4364-7(5)) Kessinger Publishing, LLC.

Duehl, Kristine. Where Do I Live? Castronovo, Katy, illus. 2013. (Budding Biologist Ser.). (ENG.). 32p. (J). (gr. k-2). 9.99 (978-0-9855481-1-7(8)) Budding Biologist.

Dunne, Abbie. Animal Communication. 2016. (Life Science Ser.). (ENG., Illus.). 24p. (gr. k-1). lib. bdg. 26.65 (978-1-5157-0943-5(4), Pebble Plus) Capstone Press of Coughlan Cos.

—Animal Group Behaviors. 2016. (Life Science Ser.). (ENG., Illus.). 24p. (gr. k-1). lib. bdg. 26.65 (978-1-5157-0944-2(2), Pebble Plus) Capstone Press of Coughlan Cos.

Dussling, Jennifer. Deadly Poison Dart Frogs. 2016. (Gross-Out Defenses Ser.). (ENG.). 24p. (J). (gr. k-3). pap. 7.95 **(978-1-944998-42-4(X))** Bearport Publishing Co., Inc.

Eagan, Mary. Alexee's Animals from A-Z, 1 vol. King, Cheryl, illus. 2010. 30p. 24.95 (978-1-4489-3967-1(4)) PublishAmerica, Inc.

Echols, Jean C. Animal Defenses. Bevilacqua, Carol, illus. Hoyt, Richard, photos by. 2003. (Great Explorations in Math & Science Ser.). 40p. (Orig.). (J). reprint ed. pap., tchr. ed. 9.00 (978-0-924886-88-1(9), GEMS) Univ. of California, Berkeley, Lawrence Hall of Science.

Editors of Kingfisher. Who's That? Playing. 2013. (Who's That? Ser.). (ENG.). 14p. (J). (gr. -1-k). bds. 5.99 (978-0-7534-7071-8(3), 9780753470718, Kingfisher) Roaring Brook Pr.

Edwards, Roberta. Best Friends: The True Story of Owen & Mzee. Schwartz, Carol, illus. 2007. (All Aboard Science Reader Ser.). 32p. (gr. -1-3). 14.00 (978-0-7569-8167-9(0)) Perfection Learning Corp.

Ehren, Michael. They Sleep Too: An A-Zzz Animal Sleeping Patterns. l.t. ed. 2006. (Illus.). 32p. (J). lib. bdg. 18.95 (978-1-934190-06-7(3)) Ocean Front Bk. Publishing, Inc.

Ehren, Michael J. They Sleep Too: A to Zzzz Sleeping Patterns of Animals (and More) 2011. (Illus.). 32p. pap. 17.95 (978-1-4634-1466-5(8)) AuthorHouse.

Einspruch, Andrew. Migration: Animals on the Move. 2014. (Discovery Education: Animals Ser.). 32p. (J). (gr. 3-6). 26.25 (978-1-4777-6948-5(X)); pap. 10.00 (978-1-4777-6949-2(8)) Rosen Publishing Group, Inc., The. (PowerKids Pr.).

Endle, Kate. Who Hoo Are You? An Animals Book by Kate Endle. 2010. (ENG., Illus.). 10p. (J). (gr. k-k). bds. 10.99 (978-1-57061-647-1(7), Little Bigfoot) Sasquatch Bks.

Esbaum, Jill. Explore My World Nighttime. 2015. (Explore My World Ser.). (ENG.). 32p. (J). (gr. -1-2). pap. 4.99 (978-1-4263-2048-4(5), National Geographic Children's Bks.) National Geographic Society.

Eszterhas, Suzi, photos by. Elephant. 2014. (Eye on the Wild Ser.). (ENG., Illus.). 32p. (J). (gr. -1-2). 15.99 (978-1-84780-518-8(3), Frances Lincoln) Quarto Publishing Group UK GBR. Dist: Hachette Bk. Group.

Evans, Hubert R. Forest Friends: Stories of Animals, Fish, & Birds, West of the Rockies. 2012. 260p. 47.95 (978-1-258-23041-8(0)); pap. 32.95 (978-1-258-24397-5(0)) Literary Licensing, LLC.

Evans, Shira. Follow Me: Animal Parents & Babies. 2016. (ENG., Illus.). 48p. (J). (-k). pap. 4.99 (978-1-4263-2347-8(6), National Geographic Children's Bks.) National Geographic Society.

Fabulous Animal Families: Individual Title Six-Packs. (gr. k-1). 23.00 (978-0-7635-9034-5(7)) Rigby Education.

Fancy, Colin, et al. Dydy Crocodeilod Ddim yn Glanhau eu Dannedd. 2005. (WEL., Illus.). 32p. pap. (978-1-85596-660-4(3)) Dref Wen.

Farndon, John. Amazing Land Animals. Portolano, Cristina, illus. 2016. (Animal Bests Ser.). (ENG.). 32p. (J). (gr. 3-6). 26.65 (978-1-5124-0627-6(9)) Lerner Publishing Group.

—Marine Superstars. Portolano, Cristina, illus. 2016. (Animal Bests Ser.). (ENG.). 32p. (J). (gr. 3-6). lib. bdg. 26.65 (978-1-5124-0625-2(2)) Lerner Publishing Group.

Feeney, Kathy. Sharp Shooters. Underwood, Kay Povelite, illus. 2004. (It's Nature! Ser.). 32p. (J). (gr. 3-6). pap. 7.95 (978-1-55971-794-6(7), NorthWord Bks. for Young Readers) T&N Children's Publishing.

Feldman, Eve B. Animals Don't Wear Pajamas: A Book about Sleeping. 2004. (Illus.). 32p. (J). pap. 16.95 (978-0-9764957-0-3(8)) Saturn International.

Feldman, Thea. Safe & Sound Animal Defenses. 2007. (Illus.). 32p. (J). (978-0-545-02984-1(8)) Scholastic, Inc.

Felix, Rebecca. What Do Animals Do in Fall? 2013. (J). (978-1-61080-982-5(3)); (ENG.). 24p. 22.79 (978-1-61080-907-8(6), 202607); (ENG.). 24p. pap. 12.79 (978-1-61080-932-0(7), 202609) Cherry Lake Publishing.

Fenner, Matthew. A Pod of Dolphins. 2013. (Animal Groups Ser.). (Illus.). 24p. (J). (gr. 1-3). pap. 8.15 (978-1-4339-8215-6(3)); lib. bdg. 22.60 (978-1-4339-8214-9(5)) Stevens, Gareth Publishing LLLP.

Fiebelkorn, Ian. Staying Alive! How Animals Stay Safe. 2009. (Real Life Readers Ser.). 16p. (gr. 2-3). pap. 7.05 (978-1-4358-0041-0(9), Rosen Classroom) Rosen Publishing Group, Inc., The.

Fielding, Beth. Animal Colors: A Rainbow of Colors from Animals Around the World. (ENG.). 32p. (J). (gr. -1-3). 2010. pap. 8.95 (978-0-9832014-8-9(X)) 2009. 14.95 (978-0-9797455-4-6(3)) EarlyLight Bks., Inc.

Fleisher, Paul. Lake & Pond Food Webs. 2008. pap. 52.95 (978-0-8225-9352-2(1)) Lerner Publishing Group.

Fleming, Sally. Ferocious Fangs. Underwood, Kay Povelite, illus. 2004. (It's Nature! Ser.). 32p. (J). (gr. 3-6). pap. 7.95 (978-1-55971-587-4(1), NorthWord Bks. for Young Readers) T&N Children's Publishing.

Franchino, Vicky. Animal Architects. 2015. (ENG., Illus.). 48p. (J). lib. bdg. (978-0-531-21547-0(4), Orchard Bks.) Scholastic, Inc.

—Animal Brainiacs. 2015. (ENG., Illus.). 48p. (J). lib. bdg. (978-0-531-21543-2(1), Orchard Bks.) Scholastic, Inc.

Fredericks, Anthony D. Clever Camouflagers. 2004. (It's Nature! Ser.). (Illus.). 32p. (J). (gr. 3-6). pap. 7.95 (978-1-55971-751-9(3), Creative Publishing International) Quarto Publishing Group USA.

Fretland VanVoorst, Jenny. Animals in Spring. 2015. (Illus.). 24p. (J). lib. bdg. (978-1-62031-234-6(4), Bullfrog Bks.) Jump! Inc.

—Los Animales en la Primavera. 2015.Tr. of Animals in Spring. (SPA., Illus.). 24p. (J). lib. bdg. (978-1-62031-241-4(7), Bullfrog Bks.) Jump! Inc.

Fuge, Charles. Animal Babies Do the Strangest Things. 2016. (ENG., Illus.). 28p. (J). (gr. -1-k). 14.95 (978-1-63322-120-8(2), Moondance) Quarto Publishing Group USA.

Gagne, Tammy. Working Animals of the World. 2015. (All about Animals Ser.). (ENG.). 24p. (gr. 1-2). pap. 6.95 (978-1-4914-2238-0(6)) Capstone Press of Coughlan Cos.

Galvin, Laura Gates. Where Do I Live? 2010. (Explore & Grow Ser.). (ENG., Illus.). 16p. (J). (gr. -1). 6.95 (978-1-60727-156-7(7)) Soundprints.

Ganeri, Anita. I Wonder Why Camels Have Humps: And Other Questions about Animals. 2012. (I Wonder Why Ser.). (ENG., Illus.). (J). (gr. k-3). pap. 6.99 (978-0-7534-6701-5(1), 9780753467015, Kingfisher) Roaring Brook Pr.

—Orangutan. Incl. Anaconda. pap. 6.79 (978-1-4329-4123-9(2)); Capybara. (Illus.). pap. 6.79 (978-1-4329-4121-5(6)); Howler Monkey. pap. 6.79 (978-1-4329-4124-6(0)); Jaguar. (Illus.). pap. 6.79 (978-1-4329-4117-8(8)); Lemur. pap. 6.79 (978-1-4329-4122-2(4)); Macaw. pap. 6.79 (978-1-4329-4116-1(X)); pap. 6.79 (978-1-4329-4118-5(6)); Poison Dart Frog. pap. 6.79 (978-1-4329-4115-4(1)); (gr. k-2). (Day in the Life: Rain Forest Animals Ser.). (ENG.). 24p. 2010. Set pap. 54.32 (978-1-4329-4125-3(9), Heinemann Read & Learn) Heinemann-Raintree.

Gardner, Robert, et al. Ace Your Animal Science Project: Great Science Fair Ideas. 2009. (Ace Your Biology Science Project Ser.). (Illus.). 104p. (J). (gr. 5-9). lib. bdg. 33.27 (978-0-7660-3220-0(5)) Enslow Pubs., Inc.

George, Gale. Adaptation. 2016. (Spotlight on Ecology & Life Science Ser.). 00024p. (J). (gr. 4-6). pap. 10.00 (978-1-4994-2552-9(X), PowerKids Pr.) Rosen Publishing Group, Inc., The.

George, Isabel & Jones, Rob Lloyd. Animals at War. 2007. (Usborne Young Reading: Series Three Ser.). (Illus.). 64p. (J). (gr. 4-7). 8.99 (978-0-7945-1422-8(7), Usborne) EDC Publishing.

George, Lynn. Beavers: Dam Builders. 2010. (Animal Architects Ser.). (ENG.). 24p. (J). pap. 8.25 (978-1-4488-1357-5(3)); lib. bdg. 22.60 (978-1-4488-0698-0(4)) Rosen Publishing Group, Inc., The. (PowerKids Pr.).

Giogas, Valarie. In My Backyard. Zecca, Katherine, illus. 2007. (ENG.). 32p. (J). (gr. -1-3). pap. 8.95 (978-1-934359-17-4(3)) Arbordale Publishing.

Gleason, Katherine. The Social Lives of Animals: A Chapter Book. 2005. (True Tales Ser.). (ENG., Illus.). 48p. (J). (gr. 2-4). lib. bdg. 22.50 (978-0-516-25188-2(0), Children's Pr.) Scholastic Library Publishing.

Gleisner, Jenna Lee. What Do Animals Do in Spring? 2014. (21st Century Basic Skills Library: Let's Look at Spring Ser.). (ENG., Illus.). 24p. (J). (gr. k-3). 22.79 (978-1-62431-660-9(3), 203152) Cherry Lake Publishing.

Goldish, Meish. Disgusting Hagfish. 2008. (Gross-Out Defenses Ser.). (Illus.). 24p. (J). (gr. k-3). lib. bdg. 21.28 (978-1-59716-719-2(3), 1284313) Bearport Publishing Co., Inc.

Goldstein, Natalie. Animal Hunting & Feeding. 2009. (Animal Behavior Ser.). (Illus.). 128p. (gr. 5-8). lib. bdg. 32.95 (978-1-60413-143-7(8), Chelsea Hse.) Facts On File, Inc.

Goldsworthy, Steve. Behavior. 2016. (Illus.). 24p. (J). (978-1-5105-0915-3(1)) SmartBook Media, Inc.

Gould, Francesca & Haviland, David. Why Dogs Eat Poop: Gross but True Things You Never Knew about Animals. Coovert, J. P., illus. 2013. (ENG.). 176p. (J). (gr. 3-7). pap. 8.99 (978-0-399-16530-6(4), G.P. Putnam's Sons Books for Young Readers) Penguin Young Readers Group.

Gray, Leon. Amazing Animal Tool-Users & Tool-Makers. 2015. (Animal Scientists Ser.). (ENG., Illus.). 32p. (gr. 3-4). lib. bdg. 27.32 (978-1-4914-6984-2(6), Fact Finders) Capstone Press of Coughlan Cos.

Green, Ivah E. Animals under Your Feet. Reece, Maynard, illus. 2011. 140p. 40.95 (978-1-258-06244-6(5)) Literary Licensing, LLC.

Gregoire, Maryellen. Animales en el Bosque (Animals in the Forest) 2012. (Wonder Readers Spanish Emergent Ser.). (SPA.). 16p. (gr. -1-1). pap. 35.94 (978-1-62065-571-9(3)) Capstone Press of Coughlan Cos.

Gregory, Josh. Lemurs. 2016. (Nature's Children Ser.). (ENG., Illus.). 48p. (J). pap. 6.95 (978-0-531-21937-9(2), Children's Pr.) Scholastic Library Publishing.

—Rabbits. 2016. (Nature's Children Ser.). (ENG., Illus.). 48p. (J). pap. 6.95 (978-0-531-21934-8(8), Children's Pr.) Scholastic Library Publishing.

Guiberson, Brenda Z. Frog Song. Spirin, Gennady, illus. 2013. (ENG.). 40p. (J). (gr. -1-3). 17.99 (978-0-8050-9254-7(4), 9780805092547, Holt, Henry & Co. Bks. For Young Readers) Holt, Henry & Co.

Guillain, Charlotte. Extreme Animals. 2014. (Collins Big Cat Progress Ser.). (ENG., Illus.). 32p. (J). (gr. 4-5). pap. 7.99 (978-0-00-751928-6(1)) HarperCollins Pubs. Ltd. GBR. Dist: Independent Pubs. Group.

Gutman, Anne, et al. Besitos. 2003. (Collection Mira Mira Ser.). (SPA., Illus.). 16p. (J). (gr. -1-k). bds. 9.99 (978-84-261-3332-8(0)) Juventud, Editorial ESP. Dist: Lectorum Pubns., Inc.

—Los Colores. 2003. (Collection Mira Mira Ser.).Tr. of Colors. (SPA., Illus.). 16p. (J). (gr. -1-k). bds. 9.99 (978-84-261-3324-3(X)) Juventud, Editorial ESP. Dist: Lectorum Pubns., Inc.

—Ruidos. 2003. (Collection Mira Mira Ser.). (SPA., Illus.). 16p. (J). (gr. -1-k). bds. 9.99 (978-84-261-3330-4(4)) Juventud, Editorial ESP. Dist: Lectorum Pubns., Inc.

Haakonsen, Jens. Lynx Chase, Hares Dash. 2017. (Hunter & Hunted: Animal Survival Ser.). 24p. (J). (gr. 7-8). 23.60 **(978-1-5081-5664-2(6)**, PowerKids Pr.) Rosen Publishing Group, Inc., The.

Haddon, Jean. It's a Beautiful Day! Enright, Vicky, tr. Enright, Vicky, illus. 2005. (Silly Millies Level 2 Ser.). (ENG.). 32p. (J). (gr. 1-3). lib. bdg. 21.27 (978-0-7613-2834-6(3), Millbrook Pr.) Lerner Publishing Group.

Harris, Tim, ed. Lions. 2012. (Animal Families Ser.). (ENG., Illus.). 32p. (gr. 2-5). 31.35 (978-1-78121-004-8(7), Brown Bear Bks.) Windmill Bks. Ltd. GBR. Dist: Black Rabbit Bks.

Hatkoff, Craig, et al. Owen & Mzee: The True Story of a Remarkable Friendship. Greste, Peter, illus. 2006. (Owen & Mzee Ser.). (ENG.). 40p. (J). (gr. -1-3). 17.99 (978-0-439-82973-1(9), Scholastic Pr.) Scholastic, Inc.

Hawk, Fran. Count down to Fall, 1 vol. Neidigh, Sherry, illus. 2009. (ENG.). 32p. (J). (gr. -1-3). 16.95 (978-1-934359-94-5(7)) Arbordale Publishing.

Hendrix, Emilia. Seals & Pups. 2016. (Animal Family Ser.). (ENG., Illus.). 24p. (J). (gr. k-k). pap. 8.15 (978-1-4824-3787-4(2)) Stevens, Gareth Publishing LLLP.

—Tigers & Cubs. 2016. (Animal Family Ser.). (ENG.). 24p. (J). (gr. k-k). pap. 8.15 (978-1-4824-3791-1(0)) Stevens, Gareth Publishing LLLP.

Heos, Bridget. Do You Really Want to Meet a Camel? Fabbri, Daniele, illus. 2017. (Do You Really Want to Meet... Wild Animals? Ser.). (ENG.). 24p. (J). (gr. 1-3). pap. 8.99 (978-1-68152-116-9(4)) Amicus.

—Do You Really Want to Meet a Hippopotamus? Fabbri, Daniele, illus. 2017. (Do You Really Want to Meet... Wild Animals? Ser.). (ENG.). 24p. (J). (gr. 1-3). pap. 8.99 (978-1-68152-117-6(2)) Amicus.

—Do You Really Want to Meet a Wolf? Fabbri, Daniele, illus. 2017. (Do You Really Want to Meet... Wild Animals? Ser.). (ENG.). 24p. (J). (gr. 1-3). pap. 8.99 (978-1-68152-120-6(2)) Amicus.

Herriott, Charlotte. Boa Constrictor vs. Grizzly Bear. 2015. (Bizarre Beast Battles Ser.). (ENG., Illus.). 24p. (J). (gr. 2-3). pap. 8.15 (978-1-4824-2780-6(X)) Stevens, Gareth Publishing LLLP.

—Cheetah vs. Ostrich. 2015. (Bizarre Beast Battles Ser.). (ENG., Illus.). 24p. (J). (gr. 2-3). pap. 8.15 (978-1-4824-2784-4(2)) Stevens, Gareth Publishing LLLP.

—Rat vs. Cockroach. 2015. (Bizarre Beast Battles Ser.). (ENG.). 24p. (J). (gr. 2-3). pap. 8.15 (978-1-4824-2788-2(5)) Stevens, Gareth Publishing LLLP.

Hicks, Kelli L., et al. Learn about Animal Behavior. 2012. (Learn about Animal Behavior Ser.). (ENG.). 24p. (gr. 1-2). pap. 29.16 (978-1-4296-9314-1(2)); pap. 166.80 (978-1-4296-9315-8(0)) Capstone Press of Coughlan Cos. (First Facts).

Higgins, Nadia. Deadliest Adorable Animals. 2013. (ShockZone — Deadly & Dangerous Ser.). (ENG.). 32p. (gr. 5-8). lib. bdg. 26.60 (978-1-4677-0598-1(5), Lerner Pubns.) Lerner Publishing Group.

—Deadly Adorable Animals. 2013. (ShockZone — Deadly & Dangerous Ser.). (ENG., Illus.). 32p. (gr. 5-8). pap. 8.95 (978-1-4677-0888-3(7)) Lerner Publishing Group.

—Slimy Animals. Fretland VanVoorst, Jenny, ed. 2016. (Back off! Animal Defenses). 24p. (J). (gr. 2-5). lib. bdg. 25.65 (978-1-62031-306-0(5)) Jump! Inc.

—Stinky Animals. Fretland VanVoorst, Jenny, ed. 2016. (Back off! Animal Defenses). 24p. (J). (gr. 2-5). lib. bdg. 25.65 (978-1-62031-312-1(X), Pogo) Jump! Inc.

—Undercover Animals. Fretland VanVoorst, Jenny, ed. 2016. (Back off! Animal Defenses). 24p. (J). (gr. 2-5). lib. bdg. 25.65 (978-1-62031-307-7(3), Pogo) Jump! Inc.

Hile, Lori. Animal Survival. 2011. (Extreme Survival Ser.). (ENG.). 56p. (gr. 5-5). pap. 9.49 (978-1-4109-3980-7(4), Raintree Freestyle) Heinemann-Raintree.

Hirsch, Rebecca E. Gray Wolves: Howling Pack Mammals. 2015. (Comparing Animal Traits Ser.). (ENG., Illus.). 32p. (J). (gr. 2-4). lib. bdg. 26.65 (978-1-4677-5577-1(X), Lerner Pubns.) Lerner Publishing Group.

—Humpback Whales: Musical Migrating Mammals. 2015. (Comparing Animal Traits Ser.). (ENG., Illus.). 32p. (J). (gr. 2-4). lib. bdg. 26.65 (978-1-4677-5579-5(6), Lerner Pubns.) Lerner Publishing Group.

—Mountain Gorillas: Powerful Forest Mammals. 2015. (Comparing Animal Traits Ser.). (ENG.). 32p. (J). (gr. 2-4). lib. bdg. 26.65 (978-1-4677-5580-1(X), Lerner Pubns.) Lerner Publishing Group.

Hnatov, Catherine. Hip, Hop, 1 vol. 2010. (ENG., Illus.). 32p. (J). bds. 5.95 (978-1-59572-266-9(1)) Star Bright Bks., Inc.

Hoff, Mary. Fighting Back. 2003. (Illus.). 32p. (J). lib. bdg. (978-1-58341-266-4(2), Creative Education) Creative Co., The.

Holden, Pam. Animal Defences. (ENG., Illus.). 16p. pap. **(978-1-77654-135-5(9)**, Red Rocket Readers) Flying Start Bks.

Holland, Jennifer S. Unlikely Friendships for Kids: The Dog & the Piglet - And Four Other Stories of Animal Friendships. 2012. (Unlikely Friendships for Kids Ser.). (ENG., Illus.). 48p. (J). (gr. 2-12). 7.95 (978-0-7611-7012-9(X), 17012) Workman Publishing Co., Inc.

—Unlikely Friendships for Kids: The Monkey & the Dove - And 4 Other Stories of Animal Friendships. 2012. (Unlikely Friendships for Kids Ser.). (ENG., Illus.). 48p. (J). (gr. 2-12). 7.95 (978-0-7611-7011-2(1), 17011) Workman Publishing Co., Inc.

—Unlikely Friendships for Kids: the Leopard & the Cow: And Four Other Stories of Animal Friendships. 2012. (Unlikely Friendships for Kids Ser.). (ENG., Illus.). 48p. (J). (gr. 2-12). 7.95 (978-0-7611-7013-6(8), 17013) Workman Publishing Co., Inc.

Holland, Mary. The Beavers' Busy Year, 1 vol. Holland, Mary, photos by. 2014. (ENG., Illus.). 32p. (J). (gr. 1-4). pap. 9.95 (978-1-62855-213-3(1)) Arbordale Publishing.

Holmes, Parker. Pythons on the Hunt. 2017. (Searchlight Books (tm) — Predators Ser.). (ENG.). (J). (gr. 3-5). pap. 9.99 **(978-1-5124-5612-7(8))**; (Illus.). lib. bdg. 30.65 **(978-1-5124-3396-8(9))** Lerner Publishing Group.

Holt, Rinehart and Winston Staff. Holt Science & Technology Chapter 14: Life Science: Animals & Behavior. 5th ed. 2004. (Illus.). pap. 12.86 (978-0-03-030218-3(8)) Holt McDougal.

Holub, Joan. Why Do Horses Neigh? DiVito, Anna, illus. 2003. (Penguin Young Readers, Level 3 Ser.). (ENG.). 48p. (J). (gr. 1-3). pap. 3.99 (978-0-14-230119-7(1), Penguin Young Readers) Penguin Young Readers Group.

Horácek, Petr. Honk, Honk! Baa, Baa! Horácek, Petr, illus. 2014. (ENG., Illus.). 16p. (J). (— 1). bds. 7.99 (978-0-7636-6780-1(3)) Candlewick Pr.

Horowitz, Alexandra. Inside of a Dog: What Dogs See, Smell, & Know. Edgerton, Sean Vidal, illus. 2017. (ENG.). 272p. (J). (gr. 3-7). pap. 7.99 (978-1-4814-5094-2(8), Simon & Schuster Bks. For Young Readers) Simon & Schuster Bks. For Young Readers.

—Inside of a Dog: What Dogs See, Smell, & Know (Young Reader's Edition) Edgerton, Sean Vidal, illus. 2016. (ENG.). 256p. (J). (gr. 3-7). 16.99 (978-1-4814-5093-5(X), Simon & Schuster Bks. For Young Readers) Simon & Schuster Bks. For Young Readers.

Houran, Lori Haskins. Bloody Horned Lizards. 2008. (Gross-Out Defenses Ser.). (Illus.). 24p. (J). (gr. k-3). lib. bdg. 21.28 (978-1-59716-717-8(7), 1284315) Bearport Publishing Co., Inc.

Hunter & Hunted: Animal Survival. 2017. (Hunter & Hunted: Animal Survival Ser.). 24p. (gr. 7-8). 141.60 **(978-1-5081-5585-0(2))**; pap. 49.50 **(978-1-5081-5586-7(0))** Rosen Publishing Group, Inc., The. (PowerKids Pr.).

Jackson, Ellen. Tooling Around: Crafty Creatures & the Tools They Use. Benoit, Renne, illus. 2014. (ENG.). 32p. (J). (gr. -1-3). 17.95 (978-1-58089-564-4(6)) Charlesbridge Publishing, Inc.

Jackson, Tom. Animal Trackers. 2015. (Animal Trackers Ser.). (ENG.). 32p. (gr. 3-4). 136.60 (978-1-4914-7011-4(9), Fact Finders) Capstone Press of Coughlan Cos.

—Dangerous Dinosaurs. 2010. (Dangerous Animals Ser.). (ENG.). 32p. (J). (gr. 2-6). pap. 10.50 (978-1-4339-4038-5(8), Gareth Stevens Learning Library); (YA). (gr. 3-6). lib. bdg. 26.60 (978-1-4339-4037-8(X)) Stevens, Gareth Publishing LLLP.

Jacquet, Luc. March of the Penguins: The Official Children's Book. Maison, Jerome, photos by. 2005. (ENG., Illus.). 32p. (J). (gr. 2-12). lib. bdg. 22.90 (978-0-7922-6190-2(9), National Geographic Children's Bks.) National Geographic Society.

James, Emily. Do Monkeys Eat Marshmallows? A Question & Answer Book about Animal Diets. 2016. (Animals, Animals! Ser.). (ENG., Illus.). 32p. (gr. 1-2). lib. bdg. 27.32 (978-1-5157-2667-8(3), Aplus Bks.) Capstone Press of Coughlan Cos.

Jansen, Curt, et al. Badger & Her Babies. Date not set. (Wildlife Adventure Ser.: Vol. 2). (Orig.). (J). (gr. k-4). pap. (978-0-9614904-2-3(X)) Adventure Productions, Inc.

—Bobcat & Her Babies. Date not set. (Wildlife Adventure Ser.: Vol. 3). (Orig.). (J). (gr. k-4). pap. (978-0-9614904-3-0(8)) Adventure Productions, Inc.

Jenkins, Martin. The Emperor's Egg. Chapman, Jane, illus. 2008. (Read, Listen, & Wonder Ser.). (ENG.). 32p. (J). (gr. -1-3). pap. 8.99 (978-0-7636-3825-2(0)) Candlewick Pr.

Jenkins, Steve. Never Smile at a Monkey: And 17 Other Important Things to Remember. Jenkins, Steve, illus. 2009. (ENG., Illus.). 32p. (J). (gr. -1-3). 17.99 (978-0-618-96620-2(X)) Houghton Mifflin Harcourt Publishing Co.

Jenkins, Steve & Page, Robin. Animals Upside Down: A Pull, Pop, Lift & Learn Book! Jenkins, Steve, illus. 2013. (ENG., Illus.). 24p. (J). (gr. -1-3). 24.99 (978-0-547-34127-9(X)) Houghton Mifflin Harcourt Publishing Co.

—How to Swallow a Pig: Step-By-Step Advice from the Animal Kingdom. Jenkins, Steve, illus. 2015. (ENG., Illus.). 32p. (J). (gr. 1-4). 17.99 (978-0-544-31365-1(8), HMH Books For Young Readers) Houghton Mifflin Harcourt Publishing Co.

—Time for a Bath. Jenkins, Steve, illus. 2011. (ENG., Illus.). 24p. (J). (gr. -1-3). 12.99 (978-0-547-25037-3(1)) Houghton Mifflin Harcourt Publishing Co.

—Time to Eat. Jenkins, Steve, illus. 2011. (ENG., Illus.). 24p. (J). (gr. -1-3). 12.99 (978-0-547-25032-8(0)) Houghton Mifflin Harcourt Publishing Co.

—Time to Sleep. Jenkins, Steve, illus. 2011. (ENG., Illus.). 24p. (J). (gr. -1-3). 12.99 (978-0-547-25040-3(1)) Houghton Mifflin Harcourt Publishing Co.

Johnson, Jinny. Animal Tracks & Signs: Track over 400 Animals from Big Cats to Backyard Birds. 2008. (ENG., Illus.). 192p. (J). (gr. 5-9). 24.95 (978-1-4263-0253-4(3)); lib. bdg. 32.90 (978-1-4263-0254-1(1)) National Geographic Society. (National Geographic Children's Bks.).

—Caribou. 2014. (North American Mammals Ser.). 24p. (gr. 2-5). 28.50 (978-1-62588-033-8(2)) Black Rabbit Bks.

—Clash of the Dinos: Watch Dinosaurs Do Battle! 2014. (ENG., Illus.). 64p. (J). (gr. 3-6). pap. 9.95 (978-1-77085-458-1(4), 9781770854581) Firefly Bks., Ltd.

Julia Barnes. Puppies, Vol. 12. 2016. (Understanding & Caring for Your Pet Ser.: Vol. 12). (ENG., Illus.). 128p. (J). (gr. 5-8). 25.95 (978-1-4222-3702-1(8)) Mason Crest.

Kalman, Bobbie. Animals That Live in Social Groups. 2016. (ENG., Illus.). 32p. (J). lib. bdg. (978-0-7787-2787-3(4)) Crabtree Publishing Co.

—A Bath. 2010. (My World Ser.). (ENG.). 16p. (J). (gr. k-3). (978-0-7787-9496-7(2)); pap. (978-0-7787-9521-6(7)) Crabtree Publishing Co.

—Can It Fly? 2010. (My World Ser.). (ENG.). 16p. (J). (gr. k-3). (978-0-7787-9502-5(0)); pap. (978-0-7787-9527-8(6)) Crabtree Publishing Co.

—¿Como Encuentran Alimento los Animales? 2007. (Ciencia de los Seres Vivos Ser.). (SPA., Illus.). 32p. (J). (gr. 4-7). pap. (978-0-7787-8814-0(8)) Crabtree Publishing Co.

—¿Cómo Se Esconden los Animales? 2010. (SPA., Illus.). 24p. (J). pap. (978-0-7787-8592-7(0)); lib. bdg. (978-0-7787-8566-8(1)) Crabtree Publishing Co.

—Familias de Animales. 2008.Tr. of Animal Families. (SPA.). 24p. (J). pap. (978-0-7787-8685-6(4)) Crabtree Publishing Co.

—Hip-Hop Dancers. 2010. (My World Ser.). (ENG., Illus.). 16p. (J). (gr. k-2). (978-0-7787-9431-8(8)); pap. (978-0-7787-9475-2(X)) Crabtree Publishing Co.

—How & What Do Animals Learn? 2015. (ENG., Illus.). 24p. (J). (978-0-7787-1462-0(4)) Crabtree Publishing Co.

—How & Why Do Animals Move? 2014. (ENG., Illus.). 24p. (J). (978-0-7787-0554-3(4)) Crabtree Publishing Co.

—How Do Animals Hide? 2010. (My World Ser.). (ENG., Illus.). 24p. (J). (gr. k-2). (978-0-7787-9447-9(4)); pap. (978-0-7787-9491-2(1)) Crabtree Publishing Co.

—I Can Write a Book Called If I Could Talk to Animals... 2012. (ENG.). 32p. (J). (978-0-7787-7994-0(7)); pap. (978-0-7787-8003-8(1)) Crabtree Publishing Co.

—L'Alimentation des Animaux. 2009. (FRE., Illus.). 32p. (J). pap. 9.95 (978-2-89579-249-9(6)) Bayard Canada Livres CAN. Dist: Crabtree Publishing Co.

—¿Qué Hacen Estos Animales? 2009. (SPA.). 24p. (J). (978-0-7787-8702-0(8)); pap. (978-0-7787-8741-9(9)) Crabtree Publishing Co.

—Rapping about What Animals Eat. 2012. (ENG., Illus.). 24p. (J). (978-0-7787-2798-9(X)); pap. (978-0-7787-2805-4(6)) Crabtree Publishing Co.

—Symbiosis: How Different Animals Relate. 2016. (ENG., Illus.). 32p. (J). lib. bdg. (978-0-7787-2785-9(8)) Crabtree Publishing Co.

—What Are These Animals Doing? 2008. (Looking at Nature Ser.). (ENG., Illus.). 24p. (J). (gr. -1-2). pap. (978-0-7787-3344-7(0)); lib. bdg. (978-0-7787-3324-9(6)) Crabtree Publishing Co.

—What Senses Do Animals Have? 2009. (Big Science Ideas Ser.). (ENG., Illus.). 32p. (J). (gr. 1-4). pap. (978-0-7787-3305-8(X)) Crabtree Publishing Co.

Kaner, Etta. Animal Groups: How Animals Live Together. Stephens, Pat, illus. 2004. (Animal Behavior Ser.). (ENG.). 40p. (J). (gr. 4-6). 7.95 (978-1-55337-338-4(3)) Kids Can Pr., Ltd. CAN. Dist: Hachette Bk. Group.

—Animals, Do Too! How They Behave Just Like You. Faucher, Marilyn, illus. 2017. (ENG.). 32p. (J). (gr. -1-2). 16.95 (978-1-77138-569-5(3)) Kids Can Pr., Ltd. CAN. Dist: Hachette Bk. Group.

—Friend or Foe: The Whole Truth about Animals That People Love to Hate. Anderson, David, illus. 2015. (ENG.). 48p. (J). (gr. 3-7). 16.95 (978-1-77147-064-3(X), Owlkids) Owlkids Bks. Inc. CAN. Dist: Publishers Group West (PGW).

—Have You Ever Seen an Octopus with a Broom? Szuc, Jeff, illus. 2009. (Have You Ever Seen Ser.). (ENG.). 32p. (J). (gr. -1-2). 14.95 (978-1-55453-247-6(7)) Kids Can Pr., Ltd. CAN. Dist: Hachette Bk. Group.

Kaplan, Osman. Giants of the World. Kalender, Oznur, illus. 2008. (Amazing Animals Ser.). (ENG.). 56p. (J). (gr. 2-4). 9.95 (978-1-59784-139-9(0)) Tughra Bks.

—Wonders of the Land. Kalender, Oznur, illus. 2008. (Amazing Animals Ser.). (ENG.). 56p. (J). (gr. -1-3). 9.95 (978-1-59784-145-0(5)) Tughra Bks.

Kemp, Steve. Who Pooped in the Park? Great Smoky Mountains National Park. Rath, Robert, illus. 2005. 48p. (J). pap. 11.95 (978-1-56037-321-6(0)) Farcountry Pr.

Killer Animals. 2010. (Killer Animals Ser.). (ENG.). 32p. (gr. 1-2). lib. bdg. 106.60 (978-1-4296-4420-4(6), Blazers) Capstone Press of Coughlan Cos.

Kingfisher Editors. Who's That? Jumping. 2013. (Who's That? Ser.). (ENG., Illus.). 14p. (J). (gr. -1-k). bds. 5.99 (978-0-7534-6971-2(5), 9780753469712, Kingfisher) Roaring Brook Pr.

—Who's That? Roaring. 2013. (Who's That? Ser.). (ENG., Illus.). 14p. (J). (gr. -1-k). bds. 5.99 (978-0-7534-6970-5(7), 9780753469705, Kingfisher) Roaring Brook Pr.

Klepeis, Alicia. Nocturnal & Diurnal Animals Explained. 2016. (Distinctions in Nature Ser.). 32p. (J). pap. 10.58 (978-1-5026-2173-3(8)) Cavendish Square Publishing.

Klepeis, Alicia Z. Nature's Undead: Snapping Rattlesnakes, Frozen Frogs, & Other Animals That Seem to Rise from the Grave. 2016. (Real-Life Zombies Ser.). (ENG., Illus.). 32p. (gr. 3-4). lib. bdg. 27.99 (978-1-5157-2481-0(6), Edge Bks.) Capstone Press of Coughlan Cos.

Knowlton, Laurie Lazzaro. Hide & Seek. 2005. (J). (978-1-933248-09-7(2)) World Quest Learning.

Koenig, Jenaya. Jumping Animals! Relate Addition & Subtraction to Length. 2014. (Math Masters: Measurement & Data Ser.). (Illus.). 24p. (J). (gr. 2-3). 23.60 (978-1-4777-6439-8(9), Rosen Classroom) Rosen Publishing Group, Inc., The.

Kosara, Tori. Hibernation. 2012. (Scholastic Reader Level 2 Ser.). (ENG.). 32p. (J). (gr. -1-3). pap. 3.99 (978-0-545-36582-6(1), Scholastic Paperbacks) Scholastic, Inc.

Kuskowski, Alex. A Flock of Sheep: Animal Groups on the Farm, 1 vol. 2012. (Animal Groups Ser.). (ENG.). 24p. (J). (gr. k-3). lib. bdg. 24.21 (978-1-61783-538-4(2), SandCastle) ABDO Publishing Co.

—A Gaggle of Geese: Animal Groups on Lakes & Rivers, 1 vol. 2012. (Animal Groups Ser.). (ENG.). 24p. (J). (gr. k-3). lib. bdg. 24.21 (978-1-61783-540-7(4), SandCastle) ABDO Publishing Co.

—A Herd of Deer: Animal Groups in the Forest, 1 vol. 2012. (Animal Groups Ser.). (ENG.). 24p. (J). (gr. k-3). lib. bdg. 24.21 (978-1-61783-539-1(0), SandCastle) ABDO Publishing Co.

—A School of Fish: Animal Groups in the Ocean, 1 vol. 2012. (Animal Groups Ser.). (ENG.). 24p. (J). (gr. k-3). lib. bdg. 24.21 (978-1-61783-541-4(2), SandCastle) ABDO Publishing Co.

—A Streak of Tigers: Animal Groups in the Jungle, 1 vol. 2012. (Animal Groups Ser.). (ENG.). 24p. (J). (gr. k-3). lib. bdg. 24.21 (978-1-61783-542-1(0), SandCastle) ABDO Publishing Co.

—A Zeal of Zebras: Animal Groups on an African Safari, 1 vol. 2012. (Animal Groups Ser.). (ENG.). 24p. (J). (gr. k-3). lib. bdg. 24.21 (978-1-61783-543-8(9), SandCastle) ABDO Publishing Co.

La Coccinella. Look & See: What Do I Eat? 2008. (Look & See! Ser.). (ENG., Illus.). 26p. (J). (gr. -1-1). bds. 6.95 (978-1-4027-5827-0(8)) Sterling Publishing Co., Inc.

Labella, Susan. How Animals Migrate. 2007. (On the Move: Animal Migration Ser.). (Illus.). 24p. (gr. 1-4). pap. 8.15 (978-0-8368-8421-0(3)); lib. bdg. 22.00 (978-0-8368-8416-6(7)) Stevens, Gareth Publishing LLLP. (Weekly Reader Leveled Readers).

Lake, G. G. Woodland Wildlife. 2016. (Woodland Wildlife Ser.). (ENG.). 24p. (gr. k-1). 159.90 (978-1-5157-0851-3(9), Pebble Plus) Capstone Press of Coughlan Cos.

Landstrom, Lee Ann & Shragg, Karen. Nature's Yucky! 2: The Desert Southwest. Rogge, Rachel, illus. 2007. (Nature's Yucky Ser.). 48p. (J). (gr. k-7). pap. 12.00 (978-0-87842-529-7(2)) Mountain Pr. Publishing Co., Inc.

Landstrom, Lee Ann & Shragg, Karen I. Nature's Yucky! 3: The Eastern United States. Rogge, Rachel, illus. 2013. 48p. (J). pap. 12.00 (978-0-87842-601-0(9)) Mountain Pr. Publishing Co., Inc.

Lang, Diane. Daytime Nighttime, All Through the Year, 1 vol. Gabriel, Andrea, illus. 2017. (ENG.). 32p. (J). (gr. -1-3). 16.95 **(978-1-58469-606-3(0))**; pap. 8.95 **(978-1-58469-607-0(9))** Dawn Pubns.

Larson, Kirsten W. Super Powers in Nature. 2015. (Freaky Nature Ser.). (ENG., Illus.). 32p. (J). (gr. 2-4). 19.95 (978-1-60753-781-6(8)) Amicus Publishing.

—Zombies in Nature. 2015. (Freaky Nature Ser.). (ENG., Illus.). 32p. (J). (gr. 2-4). 19.95 (978-1-60753-783-0(4)) Amicus Publishing.

Lay, Kathryn. Extreme Senses: Animals with Unusual Senses for Hunting Prey. Wald, Christina, illus. 2012. pap. 28.50 (978-1-61478-860-7(X)) ABDO Publishing Co.

—Extreme Senses: Animals with Unusual Senses for Hunting Prey, 1 vol. Wald, Christina, illus. 2012. (Sensing Their Prey Ser.). (ENG.). 32p. (J). (gr. -1-4). lib. bdg. 28.50 (978-1-61641-865-6(6), Looking Glass Library) Magic Wagon.

—Hearing Their Prey: Animals with an Amazing Sense of Hearing, 1 vol. Wald, Christina, illus. 2012. (Sensing Their Prey Ser.). (ENG.). 32p. (J). (gr. -1-4). lib. bdg. 28.50 (978-1-61641-866-3(4), Looking Glass Library) Magic Wagon.

—Seeing Their Prey: Animals with an Amazing Sense of Sight, 1 vol. Wald, Christina, illus. 2012. (Sensing Their Prey Ser.). (ENG.). 32p. (J). (gr. -1-4). lib. bdg. 28.50 (978-1-61641-867-0(2), Looking Glass Library) Magic Wagon.

—Smelling Their Prey: Animals with an Amazing Sense of Smell, 1 vol. Wald, Christina, illus. 2012. (Sensing Their Prey Ser.). (ENG.). 32p. (J). (gr. -1-4). lib. bdg. 28.50 (978-1-61641-868-7(0), Looking Glass Library) Magic Wagon.

—Tasting Their Prey: Animals with an Amazing Sense of Taste, 1 vol. Wald, Christina, illus. 2012. (Sensing Their Prey Ser.). (ENG.). 32p. (J). (gr. -1-4). lib. bdg. 28.50 (978-1-61641-869-4(9), Looking Glass Library) Magic Wagon.

—Touching Their Prey: Animals with an Amazing Sense of Touch, 1 vol. Wald, Christina, illus. 2012. (Sensing Their Prey Ser.). (ENG.). 32p. (J). (gr. -1-4). lib. bdg. 28.50 (978-1-61641-870-0(2), Looking Glass Library) Magic Wagon.

Leigh, Autumn. A Penguin Colony. 2013. (Animal Groups Ser.). (Illus.). 24p. (J). (gr. 1-3). pap. 8.15 (978-1-4339-8210-1(2)); lib. bdg. 22.60 (978-1-4339-8209-5(9)) Stevens, Gareth Publishing LLLP.

Lindeen, Mary. Animal Defenses. 2017. (BeginningtoRead Ser.). (ENG.). 32p. (J). (-2). 22.60 **(978-1-59953-877-8(6))**; pap. 11.94 **(978-1-68404-096-4(5))** Norwood Hse. Pr.

—Animal Mothers & Fathers. 2017. (BeginningtoRead Ser.). (ENG.). 32p. (J). (-2). 22.60 **(978-1-59953-879-2(2))**; pap. 11.94 **(978-1-68404-098-8(1))** Norwood Hse. Pr.

Lindeen, Mary. Dancing Bees & Other Amazing Communicators. 2017. (Searchlight Books (tm) — Animal Superpowers Ser.). (ENG.). 40p. (J). (gr. 3-5). 16.99 **(978-1-5124-3657-0(7)**, Lerner Pubns.); 46.65 **(978-1-5124-2821-6(3)**, Lerner Pubns.); 46.65 **(978-1-5124-3656-3(9)**, Lerner Pubns.); (Illus.). 30.65 (978-1-5124-2545-1(1)) Lerner Publishing Group.

Lock, Deborah. Wild Baby Animals. 2016. (Illus.). 48p. (J). (978-1-5182-1132-4(1)) Dorling Kindersley Publishing, Inc.

Loh-Hagan, Virginia. Top 10 - Cheats. 2017. (Wild Wicked Wonderful Ser.). (ENG., Illus.). 32p. (J). (gr. 4-8). 29.93 (978-1-63472-142-4(X), 209140, 45th Parallel Press) Cherry Lake Publishing.

—Top 10 - Dads. 2016. (Wild Wicked Wonderful Ser.). (ENG., Illus.). 32p. (J). (gr. 4-8). 29.93 (978-1-63471-098-5(3), 208503, 45th Parallel Press) Cherry Lake Publishing.

—Top 10 - Defenders. 2016. (Wild Wicked Wonderful Ser.). (ENG., Illus.). 32p. (J). (gr. 4-8). 29.93 (978-1-63471-100-5(9), 208511, 45th Parallel Press) Cherry Lake Publishing.

—Top 10 - Moms. 2016. (Wild Wicked Wonderful Ser.). (ENG., Illus.). 32p. (J). (gr. 4-8). 29.93 (978-1-63471-097-8(5), 208499, 45th Parallel Press) Cherry Lake Publishing.

—Top 10 - Partnerships. 2017. (Wild Wicked Wonderful Ser.). (ENG., Illus.). 32p. (J). (gr. 4-8). 29.93 (978-1-63472-139-4(X), 209128, 45th Parallel Press) Cherry Lake Publishing.

Long, William. Secrets of the Woods. 2007. 148p. 19.99 (978-1-59986-710-6(9)) Filiquarian Publishing, LLC.

Low, William & Cobalt Illustrations Studio Staff. Daytime Nighttime. Low, William & Cobalt Illustrations Studio Staff, illus. (ENG., Illus.). (J). (gr. -1-3). 2015. 28p. bds. 7.99 (978-1-62779-172-4(8), 9781627791724) 2014. 40p. 16.99 (978-0-8050-9751-1(1), 9780805097511) Holt, Henry & Co. (Holt, Henry & Co. Bks. For Young Readers).

Lowery, Lawrence F. What Can an Animal Do? Pfloog, Jan, illus. 2012. (I Wonder Why Ser.). (ENG.). 32p. (J). (gr. k-3). pap. 11.95 (978-1-936959-45-7(3)) National Science Teachers Assn.

Lunde, Darrin P. Whose Poop Is That? Oseid, Kelsey, illus. 2017. (ENG.). 32p. (J). (gr. -1-2). lib. bdg. 16.99 (978-1-57091-798-1(1)) Charlesbridge Publishing, Inc.

Marciniak, Kristin. Astonishing Animals. 2018. (ENG.). 32p. (gr. 3-6). 31.35 **(978-1-63235-417-4(9))** Pr. Room Editions LLC.

Markle, Sandra. A Mother's Journey. Marks, Alan, illus. 2006. (gr. 4-7). 16.95 (978-0-7569-6967-7(0)) Perfection Learning Corp.

Marquardt, Meg. Polar Bears on the Hunt. 2017. (Searchlight Books (tm) — Predators Ser.). (ENG.). (J). (gr. 3-5). pap. 9.99 **(978-1-5124-5611-0(X))**; (Illus.). lib. bdg. 30.65 **(978-1-5124-3397-5(7))** Lerner Publishing Group.

—Wolves on the Hunt. 2017. (Searchlight Books (tm) — Predators Ser.). (ENG.). (J). (gr. 3-5). pap. 9.99 **(978-1-5124-5614-1(4))**; (Illus.). lib. bdg. 30.65 **(978-1-5124-3399-9(3))** Lerner Publishing Group.

Martel, Sara & Cramb, Sara Lynn. If You Are a Kaka, You Eat Doo Doo: And Other Poop Tales from Nature, 1 vol. 2016. (Tilbury House Nature Book Ser.: 0). (ENG., Illus.). 36p. (gr. 1-6). 17.95 (978-0-88448-488-2(2), 884488) Tilbury Hse. Pubs.

Mary Holland. The Beavers' Busy Year, 1 vol. 2014. (ENG., Illus.). 32p. (J). (gr. 1-4). 17.95 (978-1-62855-204-1(2)) Arbordale Publishing.

Massey, Kay. Where Do Animals Hide? Canals, Sonia, illus. 2009. (Little Green Footprints Ser.). 12p. (J). (gr. -1-k). bds. 11.40 (978-1-60754-696-2(5)) Windmill Bks.

Mayo, Margaret. Roar! Ayliffe, Alex, illus. 2007. (Carolrhoda Picture Bks.). 32p. (J). (gr. -1-3). 15.95 (978-0-7613-9473-0(7), Carolrhoda Bks.) Lerner Publishing Group.

Maze, Stephanie. Momentos Tiernos en el Reino Animal: Los Animales y Sus Bebes. (Coleccion Momentos en el Reino Animal). (SPA., Illus.). (J). (gr. k-3). 15.00 (978-0-9707768-2-2(9), MST31405) Moonstone Pr., LLC.

Maze, Stephanie, ed. Amusing Moments in the Wild: Animals & Their Friends. 2006. (Moments in the Wild Ser.). (Illus.). 36p. (J). (gr. -1-k). pap. 8.00 (978-0-9769542-4-8(9)) Moonstone Pr., LLC.

—Momentos Divertidos en el Reino Animal: Los Animales y Sus Amigos. 2006. (Momentos en el reino Animal Ser.). (SPA., Illus.). 28p. (J). (gr. -1-k). pap. 8.00 (978-0-9769542-6-2(5)) Moonstone Pr., LLC.

McAneney, Caitlin. How Elephants & Other Animals Hear the Earth. 2015. (Superior Animal Senses Ser.). (ENG., Illus.). 24p. (J). (gr. 3-4). pap. 8.25 (978-1-4994-0991-8(5), PowerKids Pr.) Rosen Publishing Group, Inc., The.

Mebane, Jeanie, et al. Learn about Animal Behavior. 2012. (Learn about Animal Behavior Ser.). (ENG.). 24p. (gr. 1-2). lib. bdg. 75.96 (978-1-4296-9154-3(9), First Facts) Capstone Press of Coughlan Cos.

Meister, Cari. Armored Animals. Fretland VanVoorst, Jenny, ed. 2016. (Back off! Animal Defenses). 24p. (J). (gr. 2-5). lib. bdg. 25.65 (978-1-62031-308-4(1), Pogo) Jump! Inc.

—Electric Animals. Fretland VanVoorst, Jenny, ed. 2016. (Back off! Animal Defenses). 24p. (J). (gr. 2-5). lib. bdg. 25.65 (978-1-62031-309-1(X), Pogo) Jump! Inc.

—Horned Animals. Fretland VanVoorst, Jenny, ed. 2016. (Back off! Animal Defenses). 24p. (J). (gr. 2-5). lib. bdg. 25.65 (978-1-62031-310-7(3), Pogo) Jump! Inc.

Messner, Kate. Over & under the Snow. Neal, Christopher Silas, illus. 2011. (ENG.). 44p. (J). (gr. -1-3). 17.99 (978-0-8118-6784-9(6)) Chronicle Bks. LLC.

Miller, Connie Colwell. Disgusting Animals. 2016. (That's Disgusting! Ser.). (ENG.). 32p. pap. 7.95 (978-1-5157-6275-1(0), Blazers) Capstone Press of Coughlan Cos.

Minor, Wendell & Airgood, Ellen. Daylight Starlight Wildlife. Minor, Wendell, illus. 2015. (ENG., Illus.). 32p. (J). (gr. -1-k). 17.99 (978-0-399-24662-3(2), Nancy Paulsen Books) Penguin Young Readers Group.

Mitchell, Susan K. Animal Chemical Combat: Poisons, Smells, & Slime. 2008. (Amazing Animal Defenses Ser.). (Illus.). 48p. (J). (gr. 5-9). lib. bdg. 25.27 (978-0-7660-3294-1(9)) Enslow Pubs., Inc.

—Animals with Wicked Weapons: Stingers, Barbs, & Quills. 2008. (Amazing Animal Defenses Ser.). (Illus.). 48p. (J). (gr. 5-9). lib. bdg. 25.27 (978-0-7660-3292-7(2)) Enslow Pubs., Inc.

Moore Niver, Heather. When Monkeys Laugh. 2017. (Animal Emotions Ser.). 32p. (J). (gr. 3-3). pap. 10.52 **(978-0-7660-8861-0(8))** Enslow Pubs., Inc.

Moore, Philip. When Is This A Home? 2014. (Little Books of Answers: Level a Ser.). (Illus.). 16p. (gr. k-2). pap. 7.95 (978-1-927136-07-2(5)) Three Crows Media NZL. Dist: RiverStream Publishing.

Muldrow, Diane. How Do Lions Say I Love You? Walker, David, illus. 2013. (Little Golden Book Ser.). (ENG.). 24p. (J). (-k). 4.99 (978-0-449-81256-3(1), Golden Bks.) Random Hse. Children's Bks.

Murray, Julie. Disgusting Animals, 1 vol. 2010. (That's Wild!: A Look at Animals Ser.). (ENG.). 32p. (J). (gr. 2-5). 28.50 (978-1-60453-977-6(1)) ABDO Publishing Co.

Nagelhout, Ryan. How Pigeons & Other Animals Sense Magnetic Fields. 2015. (Superior Animal Senses Ser.). (ENG., Illus.). 24p. (J). (gr. 3-4). pap. 8.25 (978-1-4994-0992-5(3), PowerKids Pr.) Rosen Publishing Group, Inc., The.

Nascimbeni, Barbara. Animals & Their Families. Zimic, Lesley, tr. from FRE. Nascimbeni, Barbara, illus. 2012. (ENG., Illus.). 72p. (J). (gr. -1-2). 17.95 (978-1-926973-32-6(1)) Owlkids Bks. Inc. CAN. Dist: Publishers Group West (PGW).

National Geographic Kids. National Geographic Kids Thank You Cards. 2017. (ENG., Illus.). 32p. (J). (gr. 1-4). pap. 9.99 (978-1-4263-2769-8(2), National Geographic Children's Bks.) National Geographic Society.

National Geographic Kids Staff. Animal Friendship! Collection: Amazing Stories of Animal Friends & the Humans That Love Them. 2015. (NGK Chapters Ser.). (ENG.). 336p. (J). (gr. 2-5). pap. 14.99 (978-1-4263-2022-4(1), National Geographic Children's Bks.) National Geographic Society.

—Funny Animals! Collection: Amazing Stories of Hilarious Animals & Surprising Talents. 2015. (NGK Chapters Ser.). (ENG., Illus.). 336p. (J). (gr. 2-5). pap. 14.99 (978-1-4263-2024-8(8), National Geographic Children's Bks.) National Geographic Society.

National Geographic Kids Staff & Donohue, Moira Rose. Kangaroo to the Rescue! And More True Stories of Amazing Animal Heroes. 2015. (NGK Chapters Ser.). (ENG.). 112p. (J). (gr. 2-5). pap. 5.99 (978-1-4263-1913-6(4)); lib. bdg. 14.90 (978-1-4263-1915-0(0)) National Geographic Society. (National Geographic Children's Bks.).

National Wildlife Federation Staff. My First Book of Animal Hugs & Kisses. 2016. (ENG., Illus.). 22p. (J). (— 1). bds. 6.95 (978-1-62354-061-6(5)) Charlesbridge Publishing, Inc.

National Wildlife Federation Staff & Bové, Jennifer. Ranger Rick Jr: Animal Bedtime. 2017. (Ranger Rick: Animal Fun for Young Children Ser.). (ENG., Illus.). 32p. (J). (gr. -1-1). pap. 5.99 (978-1-63076-290-2(3)) Muddy Boots Pr.

Newman, Aline Alexander. Ape Escapes! And More Stories of Animals Behaving Badly. 2012. (NGK Chapters Ser.). (ENG., Illus.). 112p. (J). (gr. 2-5). lib. bdg. 14.90 (978-1-4263-0955-7(4), National Geographic Children's Bks.) National Geographic Society.

Newman, Patricia. Surviving Animal Attacks. 2014. (Shockzone: True Survival Stories Ser.). (ENG., Illus.). 32p. (gr. 5-8). lib. bdg. 26.60 (978-1-4677-1435-8(6), Lerner Pubns.) Lerner Publishing Group.

Nichols, Catherine. Prickly Porcupines. 2008. (Gross-Out Defenses Ser.). (Illus.). 24p. (J). (gr. k-3). lib. bdg. 21.28 (978-1-59716-721-5(5), 1284311) Bearport Publishing Co., Inc.

Nol, Sally. Watch Where You Go!Tr. of Attention Ou Tu Vas! (FRE., Illus.). (J). pap. 5.99 (978-0-590-24231-8(8)) Scholastic, Inc.

O'Connell, Caitlin. Bridge to the Wild: Behind the Scenes at the Zoo. Rodwell, Timothy, photos by. 2016. (ENG., Illus.). 208p. (J). (gr. 5-7). 18.99 (978-0-544-27739-7(2), HMH Books For Young Readers) Houghton Mifflin Harcourt Publishing Co.

Odd Adaptations. 2017. (Odd Adaptations Ser.). 32p. (gr. 3-4). pap. 63.00 **(978-1-5382-0488-7(6))**; lib. bdg. 159.60 **(978-1-5382-0474-0(6))** Stevens, Gareth Publishing LLLP.

Ornelas, Lourdes. So Can I. 2013. 32p. 25.99 (978-1-4808-0189-9(5)); pap. 16.99 (978-1-4808-0187-5(9)) Archway Publishing.

Orr, Nicole. Backyard Jungle Safari Foxes. 2015. (ENG., Illus.). 32p. (J). 26.50 (978-1-62469-098-3(X)) Purple Toad Publishing, Inc.

O'Shaughnessy, Ruth. Bats after Dark. 2015. (Animals of the Night Ser.). (ENG.). 32p. (J). (gr. 3-4). pap. 10.52 (978-0-7660-6750-9(5)); (Illus.). 25.27 (978-0-7660-6752-3(1)) Enslow Pubs., Inc.

—Big Cats after Dark. 2015. (Animals of the Night Ser.). (ENG.). 32p. (J). (gr. 3-4). pap. 10.52 (978-0-7660-7044-8(1)); (Illus.). 25.27 (978-0-7660-7046-2(8)) Enslow Pubs., Inc.

—Crocodiles & Alligators after Dark. 2015. (Animals of the Night Ser.). (ENG.). 32p. (J). (gr. 3-4). pap. 10.52 (978-0-7660-6754-7(8)); (Illus.). 25.27 (978-0-7660-6756-1(4)) Enslow Pubs., Inc.

—Owls after Dark. 2015. (Animals of the Night Ser.). (ENG.). 32p. (J). (gr. 3-4). pap. 10.52 (978-0-7660-6758-5(0)); (Illus.). 25.27 (978-0-7660-6760-8(2)) Enslow Pubs., Inc.

—Raccoons after Dark. 2015. (Animals of the Night Ser.). (ENG.). 32p. (J). (gr. 3-4). pap. 10.52 (978-0-7660-6762-2(9)); (Illus.). 25.27 (978-0-7660-6764-6(5)) Enslow Pubs., Inc.

—Snakes after Dark. 2015. (Animals of the Night Ser.). (ENG.). 32p. (J). (gr. 3-4). pap. 10.52 (978-0-7660-6766-0(1)); (Illus.). 25.27 (978-0-7660-6768-4(8)) Enslow Pubs., Inc.

Oxlade, Chris. Be a Tracker. Sassin, Eva, illus. 2015. (Go Wild Ser.). (ENG.). 32p. (J). (gr. 3-6). pap. 7.99 (978-1-4677-7650-9(5), Lerner Pubns.) Lerner Publishing Group.

Packard, Mary. Talented Animals. 2003. (True Tales Ser.). (ENG., Illus.). 48p. (J). 22.50 (978-0-516-22911-9(7), Children's Pr.) Scholastic Library Publishing.

Page, Robin & Jenkins, Steve. How to Clean a Hippopotamus: A Look at Unusual Animal Partnerships. Jenkins, Steve, illus. 2013. (ENG., Illus.). 32p. (J). (gr. 1-4). pap. 7.99 *(978-0-547-99484-0(2))* Houghton Mifflin Harcourt Publishing Co.

Parker, Steve. Animal Life. 2010. (Science Library). 40p. (J). (gr. 3-18). lib. bdg. 19.95 *(978-1-4222-1547-0(4))* Mason Crest.

—Survival & Change. (Life Processes Ser.). 32p. pap. 7.50 *(978-1-4034-4076-1(X))* Heinemann-Raintree.

Patterson, Caroline. Who Pooped in the Zoo? San Diego Zoo: Exploring the Weirdest, Wackiest, Grossest & Most Surprising Facts about Zoo Poo. Rath, Robert, illus. 2007. (Farcountry Explorer Bks.). 41p. (J). (gr. 3-7). pap. 14.95 *(978-1-56037-421-3(7))* Farcountry Pr.

Pattison, Darcy. Desert Baths, 1 vol. Rietz, Kathleen, illus. 2012. (SPA & ENG.). 32p. (J). (gr. -1-3). 17.95 *(978-1-60718-525-3(3))*; pap. 9.95 *(978-1-60718-534-5(2))* Arbordale Publishing.

Payne, Jan, et al. Rabbits Eat Their Own Poop: And Other Facts about Animals. 2016. (True or False? Ser.). (Illus.). 48p. (J). (gr. 3-3). pap. 11.70 *(978-0-7660-7728-7(4))* Enslow Pubs., Inc.

Perish, Patrick. Disgusting Animals. 2014. (Totally Disgusting Ser.). (ENG.). 24p. (J). (gr. 3-7). 25.95 *(978-1-62617-127-5(0)*, Epic Bks.) Bellwether Media.

Perritano, John. The Most Disgusting Animals on the Planet, 1 vol. 2012. (Disgusting Stuff Ser.). (ENG., Illus.). 48p. (gr. 3-4). lib. bdg. 31.99 *(978-1-4296-7535-2(7))* Capstone Press of Coughlan Cos.

Peters, Gregory N. Real Animal Heroes, 1 vol. 2014. (Real World Adventures Ser.). (ENG.). 48p. (gr. 4-12). 31.99 *(978-1-4765-8532-1(6))* Capstone Press of Coughlan Cos.

Peterson, Megan Cooley, et al. Super Trivia Collection. 2012. (Super Trivia Collection). (ENG.). 32p. (gr. 3-4). lib. bdg. 83.97 *(978-1-4296-8190-2(X)*, Edge Bks.) Capstone Press of Coughlan Cos.

Phillips, Dee. I Want to Know about Dinosaurs. 2012. (I Want to Know about (New Forest Press) Ser.). (ENG., Illus.). 32p. (gr. 2-5). lib. bdg. 28.50 *(978-1-84898-527-8(4))* Black Rabbit Bks.

—Kangaroo Rat's Burrow. 2015. (Illus.). 24p. (J). lib. bdg. *(978-1-62724-310-0(0))* Bearport Publishing Co., Inc.

—Wombat's Burrow. 2014. (Science Slam: the Hole Truth Ser.). 24p. (J). (gr. -1-3). lib. bdg. 23.93 *(978-1-62724-091-8(8))* Bearport Publishing Co., Inc.

Polydoros, Lori. Strange but True Animals, 1 vol. 2010. (Strange but True Ser.). (ENG.). 32p. (gr. 1-2). lib. bdg. 26.65 *(978-1-4296-4551-5(2)*, Blazers) Capstone Press of Coughlan Cos.

Pratt, Sabina Carlin. Range Land Animal Tales: Nature's School on the High Desert of Oregon. 2011. 56p. 36.95 *(978-1-258-08228-4(4))* Literary Licensing, LLC.

Pryor, Kimberley Jane. Amazing Armor. 2009. (Animal Attack & Defense Ser.). 32p. (gr. 3). 28.50 *(978-0-7614-4424-4(6))* Marshall Cavendish Corp.

—Clever Camouflage. 2009. (Animal Attack & Defense Ser.). 32p. (gr. 3). 28.50 *(978-0-7614-4420-6(3))* Marshall Cavendish GBR. Dist: Marshall Cavendish Corp.

—Mimicry & Relationships. 2009. (Animal Attack & Defense Ser.). 32p. (gr. 3). 28.50 *(978-0-7614-4421-3(1))* Marshall Cavendish Corp.

—Warning Colors. 2009. (Animal Attack & Defense Ser.). 32p. (gr. 3). 28.50 *(978-0-7614-4419-0(X))* Marshall Cavendish Corp.

Pryor, Kimberley Jane & National Geographic Learning Staff. Tricky Behavior. 2010. (ENG.). 32p. (C). (gr. 3). 51.95 *(978-0-7614-4425-1(4))* National Geographic School Publishing, Inc.

Publications International Ltd. Staff, ed. The World of Eric Carle(tm) Hear Bear Roar. 2014. 24p. (J). bds. 16.98 *(978-1-4508-7477-9(0)*, 1450874770) Phoenix International Publications, Inc.

Publishers, Chelsea House, creator. Animal Behavior Set, 6-Volumes. 2009. (Animal Behavior Ser.). (gr. 5-8). 197.70 *(978-1-60413-652-4(9)*, Chelsea Hse.) Facts On File, Inc.

Quattlebaum, Mary. Together Forever! True Stories of Amazing Animal Friendships! 2016. (NGK Chapters Ser.). (ENG., Illus.). 112p. (J). (gr. 2-5). pap. 5.99 *(978-1-4263-2464-2(2))*; lib. bdg. 15.90 *(978-1-4263-2465-9(0))* National Geographic Society. (National Geographic Children's Bks.).

Rabe, Tish. Hello, My Baby (Dr. Seuss/Cat in the Hat) Mathieu, Joe & Ruiz, Aristides, illus. 2013. (Nifty Lift-And-Look Ser.). (ENG.). 12p. (J). (— 1). bds. 5.99 *(978-0-449-81434-5(3)*, Random Hse. Bks. for Young Readers) Random Hse. Children's Bks.

—High? Low? Where Did It Go? All about Animal Camouflage. Ruiz, Aristides & Mathieu, Joe, illus. 2016. (Cat in the Hat's Learning Library). (ENG.). 48p. (J). (gr. k-3). 9.99 *(978-0-449-81496-3(3)*, Random Hse. Bks. for Young Readers) Random Hse. Children's Bks.

—King Cecil the Sea Horse (Dr. Seuss/Cat in the Hat) Moroney, Christopher, illus. 2013. (Little Golden Book Ser.). (ENG.). 24p. (J). (-k). 3.99 *(978-0-449-81010-1(0)*, Golden Bks.) Random Hse. Children's Bks.

Racanelli, Marie. Animal Mimics. 2010. (Crazy Nature Ser.). 24p. (J). (gr. 1-5). lib. bdg., E-Book 42.50 *(978-1-4488-0150-3(8))* Rosen Publishing Group, Inc., The.

—Camouflaged Creatures. 2010. (Crazy Nature Ser.). 24p. (J). (gr. 1-5). lib. bdg., E-Book 42.50 *(978-1-4488-0152-7(4))* Rosen Publishing Group, Inc., The.

Rake, Jody. Animal Training at SeaWorld, Busch Gardens, & Discovery Cove: Behind the Scenes. 2003. (Seaworld Education Ser.). (Illus.). 68p. per. 7.99 *(978-1-893698-09-3(2)*, B01, SeaWorld Education Dept.) SeaWorld, Inc.

Rake, Jody Sullivan. Disgusting Creature Diets. 2015. (Disgusting Creature Diets Ser.). (ENG.). 32p. (gr. 1-2). lib. bdg. 106.60 *(978-1-4914-2551-0(2)*, Blazers) Capstone Press of Coughlan Cos.

—Garbage Gorgers of the Animal World. 2015. (Disgusting Creature Diets Ser.). (ENG., Illus.). 32p. (gr. 1-2). 26.65 *(978-1-4914-1999-1(7))* Capstone Press of Coughlan Cos.

—Gross Me Out. 2012. (Gross Me Out Ser.). (ENG.). 24p. (gr. 1-2). pap. 21.87 *(978-1-4296-8380-7(5))*; pap. 166.80 *(978-1-4296-8381-4(3))*; lib. bdg. 101.28 *(978-1-4296-8148-3(9))* Capstone Press of Coughlan Cos. (First Facts).

—Poop & Puke Eaters of the Animal World. 2015. (Disgusting Creature Diets Ser.). (ENG., Illus.). 32p. (gr. 1-2). 26.65 *(978-1-4914-2000-3(6))* Capstone Press of Coughlan Cos.

—Why Vampire Bats Suck Blood & Other Gross Facts about Animals, 1 vol. 2012. (Gross Me Out Ser.). (ENG.). 24p. (gr. 1-2). pap. 7.29 *(978-1-4296-7957-2(3))*; pap. 41.70 *(978-1-4296-8379-1(1))*; lib. bdg. 25.32 *(978-1-4296-7611-3(6))* Capstone Press of Coughlan Cos. (First Facts).

Reade, Clara. El Olfato / Smell, 1 vol., 1. De La Vega, Eida, ed. 2014. (Tus Cinco Sentidos y Tu Sexto Sentido / Your Five Senses & Your Sixth Sense Ser.). (SPA & BYN.). 24p. (J). (gr. k-2). 23.60 *(978-1-4777-3277-9(2)*, PowerKids Pr.) Rosen Publishing Group, Inc., The.

—Smell, 1 vol., 1. 2014. (Your Five Senses & Your Sixth Sense Ser.). (ENG.). 24p. (J). (gr. k-2). 23.60 *(978-1-4777-2857-4(0)*, PowerKids Pr.) Rosen Publishing Group, Inc., The.

Reher, Matt. Some Animals Play Tricks. 2015. (1B Zoology Magazine Ser.). (ENG., Illus.). 20p. (J). pap. 5.99 *(978-1-63437-218-3(2))* American Reading Co.

Rice, Dona. Please Don't Feed the Animals. 2015. (Building Fluency Through Reader's Theater Ser.). (ENG., Illus.). 32p. (gr. 3-3). pap. 7.99 *(978-1-4938-1288-2(2))* Teacher Created Materials, Inc.

Riehecky, Janet. Slime, Poop, & Other Wacky Animal Defenses. 2012. (Animal Weapons & Defenses Ser.). (ENG.). 32p. (gr. 1-2). pap. 47.70 *(978-1-4296-8501-6(8)*, Blazers) Capstone Press of Coughlan Cos.

Riehecky, Janet & Rake, Jody Sullivan. Animal Weapons & Defenses. 2012. (Animal Weapons & Defenses Ser.). (ENG.). 32p. (gr. 1-2). pap. 286.20 *(978-1-4296-8506-1(9))*; pap. 47.70 *(978-1-4296-8505-4(0))*; lib. bdg. 159.90 *(978-1-4296-6510-0(6))* Capstone Press of Coughlan Cos. (Blazers).

Ringstad, Arnold. True Stories of Animal Tricks & Talents. 2014. (True Animal Stories Ser.). (ENG.). 24p. (J). (gr. 1-4). 28.50 *(978-1-62687-360-5(7)*, 207200) Child's World, Inc., The.

Ripley Entertainment Staff, contrib. by. Animal Antics. 2010. (Ripley's Believe It or Not Ser.). 36p. (YA). (gr. 3-18). lib. bdg. 19.95 *(978-1-4222-1535-7(0))* Mason Crest.

—Extraordinary Animals. 2010. (Ripley's Believe It or Not Ser.). 36p. (YA). (gr. 3-18). lib. bdg. 19.95 *(978-1-4222-1533-3(4))* Mason Crest.

Rissman, Rebecca. Night Safari, 1 vol. 2014. (Night Safari Ser.). (ENG.). 24p. (gr. k-2). 116.60 *(978-1-4846-0314-7(1)*, Heinemann Read & Learn) Heinemann-Raintree.

Robson, Gary D. Who Pooped in the Cascades? Scat & Tracks for Kids. Rath, Robert, illus. 2013. 48p. (J). pap. 11.95 *(978-1-56037-362-9(8))* Farcountry Pr.

—Who Pooped in the Park? Scat & Tracks for Kids. Rath, Robert, illus. 2008. 48p. (J). (gr. 3-7). pap. 9.95 *(978-1-56037-403-9(9))* Farcountry Pr.

—Who Pooped in the Park? Rocky Mountain National Park: Scats & Tracks for Kids. Clark, Elijah Brady, illus. 2005. 48p. (J). (gr. -1-5). per. 11.95 *(978-1-56037-320-9(2))* Farcountry Pr.

—Who Pooped in the Park? Yosemite National Park. Clark, Elijah Brady, illus. 2005. 80p. (J). pap. 11.95 *(978-1-56037-318-6(0))* Farcountry Pr.

Rodriguez, Ana Maria. The Secret of the Bird's Smart Brain... & More! 2017. (Animal Secrets Revealed! Ser.). 48p. (J). (gr. 4-4). pap. 11.70 ***(978-0-7660-8852-8(9))***; lib. bdg. 27.93 ***(978-0-7660-8623-4(2))*** Enslow Pubs., Inc.

—The Secret of the Scorpion-Eating Meerkats... & More! 2017. (Animal Secrets Revealed! Ser.). 48p. (J). (gr. 4-4). lib. bdg. 27.93 ***(978-0-7660-8627-2(5))*** Enslow Pubs., Inc.

—The Secret of the Scuba Diving Spider... & More! 2017. (Animal Secrets Revealed! Ser.). 48p. (J). (gr. 4-4). lib. bdg. 27.93 ***(978-0-7660-8629-6(1))*** Enslow Pubs., Inc.

—The Secret of the Squiggly Green Bombers... & More! 2017. (Animal Secrets Revealed! Ser.). 48p. (gr. 4-4). lib. bdg. 27.93 ***(978-0-7660-8631-9(3))*** Enslow Pubs., Inc.

—The Shocking Secret of the Electric Eel... & More! 2017. (Animal Secrets Revealed! Ser.). 48p. (J). (gr. 4-4). lib. bdg. 27.93 ***(978-0-7660-8726-2(3))*** Enslow Pubs., Inc.

Roop, Peter & Roop, Connie. Animal Families. 2012. (Illus.). 31p. (J). pap. *(978-0-545-38556-5(3))* Scholastic, Inc.

Rose, Elizabeth. Animal Adaptions for Survival. 2009. (Life Science Library). 24p. (gr. 3-4). 42.50 *(978-1-60853-999-4(7)*, PowerKids Pr.) Rosen Publishing Group, Inc., The.

Rose, Simon. Family Groups. 2016. (Illus.). 24p. (J). *(978-1-5105-0921-4(6))* SmartBook Media, Inc.

—Family Groups. 2015. (Illus.). 24p. (J). *(978-1-4896-3667-6(6))* Weigl Pubs., Inc.

—Resource Conservation. 2015. (Illus.). 24p. (J). *(978-1-4896-3683-6(8))* Weigl Pubs., Inc.

Rosen Publishing Staff. Scatalog: A Kid's Field Guide to Animal Poop: Set 2, 1 vol. 2015. (Scatalog: a Kid's Field Guide to Animal Poop Ser.). (ENG.). 24p. (J). 141.60 *(978-1-4777-5438-2(5)*, Windmill Bks.) Rosen Publishing Group, Inc., The.

Royston, Angela. Adapted to Survive, 1 vol. 2014. (Adapted to Survive Ser.). (ENG.). 32p. (gr. 1-3). lib. bdg. 179.94 *(978-1-4109-6152-5(4)*, Read Me!) Heinemann-Raintree.

—Adapted to Survive: Animals That Dig, 1 vol. 2014. (Adapted to Survive Ser.). (ENG., Illus.). 32p. (gr. 1-3). lib. bdg. 29.99 *(978-1-4109-6146-4(X)*, Read Me!) Heinemann-Raintree.

—Adapted to Survive: Animals That Hide, 1 vol. 2014. (Adapted to Survive Ser.). (ENG.). 32p. (gr. 1-3). lib. bdg. 29.99 *(978-1-4109-6149-5(4)*, Read Me!) Heinemann-Raintree.

—Adapted to Survive: Animals That Hunt, 1 vol. 2014. (Adapted to Survive Ser.). (ENG., Illus.). 32p. (gr. 1-3). lib. bdg. 29.99 *(978-1-4109-6151-8(6)*, Read Me!) Heinemann-Raintree.

—Adapted to Survive: Animals That Run, 1 vol. 2014. (Adapted to Survive Ser.). (ENG., Illus.). 32p. (gr. 1-3). lib. bdg. 29.99 *(978-1-4109-6150-1(8)*, Read Me!) Heinemann-Raintree.

Roza, Greg. Poke! The Sea Urchin & Other Animals with Spikes. 2011. (Armed & Dangerous Ser.). (Illus.). 24p. (J). pap. 8.25 *(978-1-4488-2688-9(8)*, PowerKids Pr.); (YA). (gr. 1-4). lib. bdg. 22.60 *(978-1-4488-2552-3(0))* Rosen Publishing Group, Inc., The.

—Tasmanian Devil vs. Hyena. 2015. (Bizarre Beast Battles Ser.). (ENG.). 24p. (J). (gr. 2-3). 22.60 *(978-1-4824-2798-1(2))* Stevens, Gareth Publishing LLLP.

Rustad, Martha E. H. Animales en Invierno/Animals in Winter, 1 vol. 2012. (Todo Sobre el Invierno/All about Winter Ser.). (SPA, ENG & MUL.). 24p. (gr. k-1). lib. bdg. 26.65 *(978-1-4296-8239-8(6))* Capstone Press of Coughlan Cos.

—Animals in Fall: Preparing for Winter. Enright, Amanda, illus. 2011. (Fall's Here! Ser.). pap. 39.62 *(978-0-7613-8643-8(2)*, Millbrook Pr.); (ENG.). 24p. (J). lib. bdg. 23.93 *(978-0-7613-5066-8(7))*; (ENG.). 24p. pap. 6.95 *(978-0-7613-8506-6(1)*, Millbrook Pr.) Lerner Publishing Group.

—Do Chicks Ask for Snacks? Noticing Animal Behaviors. Morandin, Mike, illus. 2015. (ENG.). 24p. (J). (gr. k-2). 25.32 *(978-1-4677-8558-7(X))* Lerner Publishing Group.

—Do Trees Get Hungry? Noticing Plant & Animal Traits. Moran, Mike, illus. 2015. (ENG.). 24p. (gr. k-2). lib. bdg. 25.32 *(978-1-4677-8559-4(8)*, Millbrook Pr.) Lerner Publishing Group.

Ruurs, Margriet. Amazing Animals: The Remarkable Things That Creatures Do. Hancock, W. Allan, illus. 2011. (ENG.). 34p. (J). (gr. 1-4). 17.95 *(978-0-88776-973-3(X)*, Tundra Bks.) Tundra Bks. CAN. Dist: Penguin Random Hse. LLC.

Sabatino, Michael. T. Rex vs. Crocodile. 2015. (Bizarre Beast Battles Ser.). (ENG., Illus.). 24p. (J). (gr. 2-3). lib. bdg. 22.60 *(978-1-4824-2802-5(4))* Stevens, Gareth Publishing LLLP.

Salaka, Michael. Animals in Hiding. 2017. (Animals in My World Ser.). 24p. (J). (gr. 4-6). pap. 8.25 ***(978-1-5383-2148-5(3)***, PowerKids Pr.) Rosen Publishing Group, Inc., The.

Schaefer, Lola M. Run for Your Life! Predators & Prey on the African Savanna. Meisel, Paul, illus. 2016. (ENG.). 32p. (J). 16.95 *(978-0-8234-3555-5(5))* Holiday Hse., Inc.

Schubert, Ingrid & Schubert, Dieter. Like People. 2008. (ENG., Illus.). 32p. (J). (gr. -1-3). 16.95 *(978-1-59078-576-8(2)*, 9781590785768) Lemniscaat USA.

Schuh, Mari. Animals in Fall. 2013. (ENG., Illus.). 24p. (J). lib. bdg. 25.65 *(978-1-62031-056-4(2))* Jump! Inc.

Schuh, Mari C. I Notice Animals in Fall. 2016. (First Step Nonfiction — Observing Fall Ser.). (ENG., Illus.). 24p. (J). (gr. k-2). 23.99 *(978-1-5124-0792-1(5))* Lerner Publishing Group.

Scott, Keith. The Bear Man. Hill, Steve, illus. 2010. 32p. (J). pap. 5.95 *(978-0-88839-655-6(4))* Hancock Hse. Pubs.

Seton, Ernest Thompson. Wild Animal Ways. 2009. 232p. pap. 11.95 *(978-1-59915-335-3(1))* Yesterday's Classics.

Shea, Betty. Animals of the Desert: Adapting to Survive. 2009. (Look at Life Science Ser.). 24p. (gr. 3-3). 42.50 *(978-1-61511-213-5(8)*, PowerKids Pr.) Rosen Publishing Group, Inc., The.

Shea, Therese. How Dolphins & Other Animals Use Sonar. 2015. (Superior Animal Senses Ser.). (ENG., Illus.). 24p. (J). (gr. 3-4). pap. 8.25 *(978-1-4994-0988-6(5)*, PowerKids Pr.) Rosen Publishing Group, Inc., The.

Sheehy, Shawn. Welcome to the Neighborwood. Sheehy, Shawn, illus. 2015. (ENG., Illus.). 18p. (J). (gr. -1-3). 29.99 *(978-0-7636-6594-4(0))* Candlewick Pr.

Silverstein, Alvin, et al. Dung Beetles, Slugs, Leeches, & More: The Yucky Animal Book. Kelley, Gerald, illus. 2010. (Yucky Science Ser.). 48p. (J). (gr. 5-9). 25.27 *(978-0-7660-3317-7(1))* Enslow Pubs., Inc.

Simons, Lisa M. B. Amazing Animal Stunts. 2015. (Wild Stunts Ser.). (ENG., Illus.). 32p. (gr. 3-4). lib. bdg. 27.99 *(978-1-4914-4253-1(0))* Capstone Press of Coughlan Cos.

Slade, Suzanne. What Do You Know about Animal Adaptations? 2009. (20 Questions: Science Ser.). 24p. (gr. 2-3). 42.50 *(978-1-60854-961-0(5)*, PowerKids Pr.) Rosen Publishing Group, Inc., The.

Spilsbury, Louise. Kill or Die: Extreme Life Cycles. 2015. (Extreme Biology Ser.). (ENG., Illus.). 48p. (J). (gr. 4-4). lib. bdg. 31.95 *(978-1-4824-2246-7(8))* Stevens, Gareth Publishing LLLP.

—Octopus Set. Incl. Dolphin. pap. 6.79 *(978-1-4329-4006-5(6))*; Jellyfish. pap. 6.79 *(978-1-4329-4007-2(4))*; Octopus. pap. 6.79 *(978-1-4329-4011-9(2))*; Sea Turtle. pap. 6.79 *(978-1-4329-4008-9(2))*; Seal. pap. 6.79 *(978-1-4329-4009-6(0))*; Shark. pap. 6.79 *(978-1-4329-4010-2(4))*; (gr. k-2). (Day in the Life: Sea Animals Ser.). (ENG.). 24p. 2010. Set pap. 40.74 *(978-1-4329-4012-6(0)*, Heinemann Read & Learn) Heinemann-Raintree.

—Survival of the Fittest: Extreme Adaptations. 2015. (Extreme Biology Ser.). (ENG., Illus.). 48p. (J). (gr. 4-4). lib. bdg. 31.95 *(978-1-4824-2250-4(6))* Stevens, Gareth Publishing LLLP.

Spilsbury, Louise & Spilsbury, Richard. Chimpanzee Troops. 2013. (Animal Armies Ser.). (ENG., Illus.). 32p. (J). (gr. k-5). pap. 10.00 *(978-1-4777-0328-1(4))*; lib. bdg. 25.25 *(978-1-4777-0303-8(9))* Rosen Publishing Group, Inc., The. (PowerKids Pr.).

Spilsbury, Richard. Adaptation & Survival. 2013. (Life Science Stories Ser.). (Illus.). 32p. (J). (gr. 3-5). pap. 10.50 *(978-1-4339-8700-7(7))*; lib. bdg. 26.60 *(978-1-4339-8699-4(X))* Stevens, Gareth Publishing LLLP.

—Animal Homes & Hangouts. 2017. (Engineered by Nature Ser.). (ENG., Illus.). 32p. (J). (gr. 3-8). lib. bdg. 25.95 *(978-1-62617-586-0(1)*, Pilot Bks.) Bellwether Media.

—Animal Traps & Lairs. 2017. (Engineered by Nature Ser.). (ENG., Illus.). 32p. (J). (gr. 3-8). lib. bdg. 25.95 *(978-1-62617-587-7(X)*, Pilot Bks.) Bellwether Media.

Spilsbury, Richard & Spilsbury, Louise. Ant Colonies. 2013. (Animal Armies Ser.). (ENG., Illus.). 32p. (J). (gr. k-5). pap. 10.00 *(978-1-4777-0326-7(8))*; lib. bdg. 25.25 *(978-1-4777-0302-1(0))* Rosen Publishing Group, Inc., The. (PowerKids Pr.).

—Dolphin & Whale Pods. 2013. (Animal Armies Ser.). (ENG., Illus.). 32p. (J). (gr. k-5). pap. 10.00 *(978-1-4777-0332-8(2))*; lib. bdg. 25.25 *(978-1-4777-0305-2(5))* Rosen Publishing Group, Inc., The. (PowerKids Pr.).

—Wolf Packs. 2013. (Animal Armies Ser.). (ENG., Illus.). 32p. (J). (gr. k-5). pap. 10.00 *(978-1-4777-0336-6(5))*; lib. bdg. 25.25 *(978-1-4777-0307-6(1))* Rosen Publishing Group, Inc., The. (PowerKids Pr.).

Spilsbury, Richard & Spilsbury, Richard. Deadly Predators. 2017. (Engineered by Nature Ser.). (ENG., Illus.). 32p. (J). (gr. 3-8). lib. bdg. 25.95 *(978-1-62617-589-1(6)*, Pilot Bks.) Bellwether Media.

St. James, Cassidy. Teaming Up: Animal Partners. 2014. (ENG.). 24p. (gr. k-3). 28.50 *(978-1-62717-631-6(4))* Rourke Educational Media.

Star Bright Books. Families (Spanish/English), 1 vol. Fiol, Maria A., tr. 2009. (Babies Everywhere Ser.). (ENG & SPA., Illus.). 32p. (J). (gr. -1). bds. 6.95 *(978-1-59572-201-0(7))* Star Bright Bks., Inc.

Stefoff, Rebecca. How Animals Feel. 2013. 80p. (J). (gr. 6-9). 34.21 *(978-1-60870-511-5(0))*; pap. 17.64 *(978-1-62712-022-7(X))* Cavendish Square Publishing.

—How Animals Play. 2013. 80p. (J). (gr. 6-9). 34.21 *(978-1-60870-512-2(9))*; pap. 17.64 *(978-1-62712-023-4(8))* Cavendish Square Publishing.

Sterling Publishing Co., Inc. Oink, Moo, Meow. 2012. (Say & Play Ser.). (ENG., Illus.). 28p. (J). (gr. k — 1). bds. 4.95 *(978-1-4027-9889-4(X))* Sterling Publishing Co., Inc.

Stewart, Melissa. Beneath the Sun, 1 vol. Bergum, Constance R., illus. 2014. (ENG.). 32p. (J). (gr. -1-3). 16.95 *(978-1-56145-733-5(7))* Peachtree Pubs.

—Summertime Sleep. Chen, Jordan, illus. 2017. (J). lib. bdg. *(978-1-58089-716-7(9))* Charlesbridge Publishing, Inc.

—When Rain Falls, 1 vol. Bergum, Constance R., illus. 2008. (ENG.). 32p. (J). (gr. k-3). 16.95 *(978-1-56145-438-9(9))* Peachtree Pubs.

Stockdale, Susan. Carry Me! Animal Babies on the Move, 1 vol. Stockdale, Susan, illus. (ENG., Illus.). 32p. (J). (gr. k-1). 2008. pap. 7.95 *(978-1-56145-449-5(4))* 2005. 15.95 *(978-1-56145-328-3(5))* Peachtree Pubs.

Stockland, Patricia M. Strange Dances & Long Flights: A Book about Animal Behavior. Ouren, Todd, illus. 2005. (Animal Wise Ser.). (ENG.). 24p. (J). (gr. k-2). 26.65 *(978-1-4048-0936-9(8))* Picture Window Bks.

Stout, Frankie. Nature's Nastiest Biters. 2009. (Extreme Animals Ser.). 24p. (gr. 2-3). 42.50 *(978-1-61512-380-3(6)*, PowerKids Pr.) Rosen Publishing Group, Inc., The.

—Nature's Slowest Animals. 2008. (Extreme Animals Ser.). (Illus.). 24p. (J). (gr. 3-7). lib. bdg. 22.60 *(978-1-4042-4160-2(4)*, PowerKids Pr.) Rosen Publishing Group, Inc., The.

Sundance/Newbridge LLC Staff. Predators & Prey. 2007. (Early Science Ser.). (gr. k-3). 18.95 *(978-1-4007-6540-9(4))*; pap. 6.10 *(978-1-4007-6536-2(6))* Sundance/Newbridge Educational Publishing.

Superior Animal Senses. 2015. (Superior Animal Senses Ser.). (ENG.). 24p. (J). (gr. 3-4). pap., pap., pap. 297.00 *(978-1-4994-1317-5(3)*, PowerKids Pr.) Rosen Publishing Group, Inc., The.

Surprisingly Scary! 2015. (Surprisingly Scary! Ser.). (ENG.). 24p. (J). (gr. 2-3). pap., pap., pap. 297.00 *(978-1-4994-1319-9(X)*, PowerKids Pr.) Rosen Publishing Group, Inc., The.

Swanson, Jennifer A. How Have Animals Evolved & Adapted? 2015. (Let's Find Out! Animal Life Ser.). (ENG., Illus.). 32p. (J). (gr. 2-3). 23.45 *(978-1-62275-996-5(6)*, Britannica Educational Publishing) Rosen Publishing Group, Inc., The.

Swimow, Linda. What's New at the Zoo? A PhotoPhOnics (c)Reader. 2009. 32p. pap. 12.99 *(978-1-4490-2218-1(9))* AuthorHouse.

Tagliaferro, Linda. Bears & Their Cubs [Scholastic]. 2011. (Animal Offspring Ser.). 24p. pap. 0.50 *(978-1-4296-6294-9(8)*, Pebble Plus) Capstone Press of Coughlan Cos.

—Bears & Their Dens [Scholastic]. 2010. (Animal Homes Ser.). 24p. pap. 0.49 *(978-1-4296-5793-8(6)*, Pebble Plus) Capstone Press of Coughlan Cos.

—Rabbits & Their Burrows [Scholastic]. 2010. (Animal Homes Ser.). 24p. pap. 0.49 *(978-1-4296-5796-9(0)*, Pebble Plus) Capstone Press of Coughlan Cos.

Tarakson, Stella. Lethal Animals. 2017. (Gross & Frightening Animal Facts Ser.: Vol. 6). (ENG.). (YA). (gr. 5-8). 20.95 ***(978-1-4222-3927-8(6))*** Mason Crest.

—Scary Animals. 2017. (Gross & Frightening Animal Facts Ser.: Vol. 6). (ENG.). (YA). (gr. 5-8). 20.95 ***(978-1-4222-3928-5(4))*** Mason Crest.

Tatham, Betty. How Animals Play. 2004. (Watts Library). (ENG., Illus.). 64p. (J). (gr. 5-7). pap. 8.95 *(978-0-531-16236-1(2))*; 25.50 *(978-0-531-12173-3(9))* Scholastic Library Publishing. (Watts, Franklin).

Taylor, Barbara. Stinky Skunks & Other Animal Adaptations. 2014. (ENG.). 32p. (J). *(978-0-7787-1420-0(9))* Crabtree Publishing Co.

Taylor, Saranne. Animal Homes. Chiacchiera, Moreno & Todd, Michelle, illus. 2014. (ENG.). 32p. (J). *(978-0-7787-1438-5(1))* Crabtree Publishing Co.

Tekiela, Stan. Critter Litter. 2016. (ENG., Illus.). 26p. (J). (-k). 12.95 *(978-1-59193-590-2(3))* Adventure Pubns.

—Critter Litter Southwest, 1 vol. 2016. (ENG., Illus.). 26p. (J). (-k). 12.95 *(978-1-59193-586-5(5))* Adventure Pubns.

—Snouts & Sniffers, 1 vol. 2013. (Adventure Boardbook Ser.). (ENG.). 22p. (J). (gr. -1-k). bds. 6.95 *(978-1-59193-426-4(5))* Adventure Pubns.

Thimmesh, Catherine. Friends: True Stories of Extraordinary Animal Friendships. 2011. (ENG., Illus.). 32p. (J). (gr. -1-3). 16.99 *(978-0-547-39010-9(6))* Houghton Mifflin Harcourt Publishing Co.

Things That Sting. 2015. (Things That Sting Ser.). (ENG.). 24p. (J). (gr. 2-3). 135.60 *(978-1-4824-1645-9(X))* Stevens, Gareth Publishing LLLP.

Thomas, Isabel. Animal Strength & Combat Sports. 2016. (Animalympics Ser.). (ENG.). 32p. (gr. 1-3). lib. bdg. 29.99 *(978-1-4109-8091-5(X)*, Read Me!) Heinemann-Raintree.

—City Safari, 1 vol. 2014. (City Safari Ser.). (ENG.). 24p. (gr. 1-1). lib. bdg. 139.92 *(978-1-4329-8812-8(3)*, Heinemann Read & Learn) Heinemann-Raintree.

—Fox: City Safari, 1 vol. 2014. (City Safari Ser.). (ENG., Illus.). 24p. (gr. 1-1). lib. bdg. 23.32 *(978-1-4329-8808-1(5)*, Heinemann Read & Learn) Heinemann-Raintree.

—Raccoon: City Safari, 1 vol. 2014. (City Safari Ser.). (ENG., Illus.). 24p. (gr. 1-1). lib. bdg. 23.32 *(978-1-4329-8811-1(5)*, Heinemann Read & Learn) Heinemann-Raintree.

—Seagull: City Safari, 1 vol. 2014. (City Safari Ser.). (ENG., Illus.). 24p. (gr. 1-1). lib. bdg. 23.32 *(978-1-4329-8810-4(7)*, Heinemann Read & Learn) Heinemann-Raintree.

—Squirrel: City Safari, 1 vol. 2014. (City Safari Ser.). (ENG., Illus.). 24p. (gr. 1-1). lib. bdg. 23.32 (978-1-4329-8809-8(3), Heinemann Read & Learn) Heinemann-Raintree.

Tiger Tales Staff, ed. Animals Go. Emily, Bolam, illus. 2010. (Touch, Look, & Learn! Ser.). (ENG.). 10p. (J). (gr. -1). bds. 5.95 (978-1-58925-854-9(1)) Tiger Tales.

Time Living Wonders: The Marvels & Mysteries of Life on Earth. 2009. (Time Inc. Home Entertainment Library-Bound Titles Ser.). (ENG.). 128p. (gr. 5-12). 39.93 (978-0-7613-4229-8(X), Twenty-First Century Bks.) Lerner Publishing Group.

Tjernagel, Kelsi Turner. Animals That Live in Groups. 2012. (Learn about Animal Behavior Ser.). (ENG.). 24p. (gr. 1-2). pap. 41.70 (978-1-4296-9309-7(6), First Facts); (Illus.). pap. 7.29 (978-1-4296-9308-0(8)); (Illus.). lib. bdg. 25.32 (978-1-4296-8413-2(5)) Capstone Press of Coughlan Cos.

Toft, Barbara. The Complete Guide to Animals. 2015. (Illus.). 144p. (J). (978-1-4351-6160-3(2)) Barnes & Noble, Inc.

Tomecek, Stephen M. & West, Krista. Animal Courtship. 2009. (Animal Behavior Ser.). (Illus.). 128p. (gr. 5-8). lib. bdg. 32.95 (978-1-60413-090-4(3), Chelsea Hse.) Facts On File, Inc.

Townsend, John. Amazing Animal Senses, 1 vol. 2012. (Animal Superpowers Ser.). (ENG.). 32p. (gr. 1-3). lib. bdg. 29.99 (978-1-4109-4747-5(5), Read Me!) Heinemann-Raintree.

—Amazing Animal Survivors, 1 vol. 2012. (Animal Superpowers Ser.). (ENG.). 32p. (gr. 1-3). pap. 8.29 (978-1-4109-4755-0(6), Read Me!) Heinemann-Raintree.

Trussell-Cullen, Alan. Animal Disguises, Vol. 17. 2014. (ENG.). 16p. spiral bd. 8.00 (978-1-4085-0071-2(X)) Oxford Univ. Pr., Inc.

—Animal Groups, Vol. 4. 2014. (ENG.). 16p. spiral bd. 8.00 (978-1-4085-0058-3(2)) Oxford Univ. Pr., Inc.

Turner, Pamela S. Crow Smarts: Inside the Brain of the World's Brightest Bird. Comins, Andy, photos by. 2016. (Scientists in the Field Ser.). (ENG., Illus.). 80p. (J). (gr. 5-7). 18.99 (978-0-544-41619-2(8), HMH Books For Young Readers) Houghton Mifflin Harcourt Publishing Co.

Turner, Sarah Elizabeth. Ribbon's Way, 1 vol. 2013. (ENG., Illus.). 40p. (J). (gr. -1-3). 9.95 (978-1-55039-200-5(X)) Sono Nis Pr. CAN. Dist: Orca Bk. Pubs. USA.

Ultimate Animal Defenses. 2016. (Ultimate Animal Defenses Ser.). 24p. (gr. 3-2). pap. 48.90 (978-1-4824-4514-5(X)); lib. bdg. 135.60 (978-1-4824-4439-1(9)) Stevens, Gareth Publishing LLLP.

Underwood, Deborah. Creature Camouflage, 1 vol., Set. Incl. Hiding in Deserts. pap. 8.29 (978-1-4329-4030-0(9)); Hiding in Grasslands. pap. 8.29 (978-1-4329-4033-1(3)); Hiding in Mountains. pap. 8.29 (978-1-4329-4032-4(5)); Hiding in Oceans. (Illus.). pap. 8.29 (978-1-4329-4029-4(5)); Hiding in Rain Forests. pap. 8.29 (978-1-4329-4035-5(X)); Hiding in the Polar Regions. (Illus.). pap. 8.29 (978-1-4329-4036-2(8)); Hiding in Wetlands. (Illus.). pap. 8.29 (978-1-4329-4034-8(1)); (gr. 1-3). (Creature Camouflage Ser.). (ENG.). 32p. 2010. Set pap. 58.03 (978-1-4329-4037-9(6), Heinemann First Library) Heinemann-Raintree.

Vaughn, Marcia. I Howl, I Growl: Southwest Animal Antics. Powell, Polly, illus. 2003. (ENG.). 26p. (J). (gr. -1-k). bds. 7.95 (978-0-87358-835-5(5)) Cooper Square Publishing Llc.

Ventura, Marne. How to Survive an Animal Attack. 2015. (Survival Guides). (ENG.). 24p. (J). (gr. 2-5). 27.07 (978-1-60973-163-2(8), 208794) Child's World, Inc., The.

Vescia, Monique. What Is Animal Behavior? 2015. (Let's Find Out! Animal Life Ser.). (ENG., Illus.). 32p. (J). (gr. 2-3). 23.45 (978-1-62275-991-0(5), Britannica Educational Publishing) Rosen Publishing Group, Inc., The.

Von Kessel, Carola. Understanding Horses with Caddie. Guhe, Irmtraud, illus. 2004. (ENG.). 32p. (J). (gr. 4). 13.95 (978-3-86127-948-8(7)) Cadmos Verlag GmbH DEU. Dist: Independent Pubs. Group.

WalkerTheo. FEEDING TIME: THE FEEDING HABITS OF ANIMALS HIGH BEGINNING BOOK WITH ONLINE ACCESS. 2014. (ENG., Illus.). 24p. (J). pap. 9.50 (978-1-107-67867-5(6)) Cambridge Univ. Pr.

Wallace, Karen, et al. It Takes Two. 2010. (Rise & Shine Ser.). (ENG., Illus.). 32p. (J). (gr. k-3). pap. 17.95 (978-0-531-15325-3(8)) National Geographic School Publishing, Inc.

We Both Read Bilingual Edition-We All Sleep/Todos Dormimos. 2014. (Illus.). 44p. (J). pap. 4.99 (978-1-60115-054-7(7)) Treasure Bay, Inc.

Weill, Cynthia. Animal Talk: Mexican Folk Art Animal Sounds in English & Spanish. 2016. (First Concepts in Mexican Folk Art Ser.). (ENG & SPA., Illus.). 32p. (J). (gr. -1-2). 14.95 (978-1-941026-32-8(X)) Cinco Puntos Pr.

Wilsdon, Christina. Animal Defenses. 2009. (Animal Behavior Ser.). (Illus.). 136p. (gr. 5-8). lib. bdg. 32.95 (978-1-60413-089-8(X), Chelsea Hse.) Facts On File, Inc.

Wilson, Emily. Inside Beaver Lodges. 2015. (Inside Animal Homes Ser.). (ENG.). 24p. (J). (gr. 2-3). pap. 8.25 (978-1-4994-0872-0(2), PowerKids Pr.) Rosen Publishing Group, Inc., The.

Winer, Yvonne. Frogs Sing Songs. Oliver, Tony, illus. 2003. 32p. (J). pap. 6.95 (978-1-57091-549-9(0)); (gr. -1-4). 16.95 (978-1-57091-548-2(2)) Charlesbridge Publishing, Inc.

Winkelman, Barbara Gaines. Puffer's Surprise. Petruccio, Steven James, illus. 2003. (Smithsonian Oceanic Collection). (ENG.). 32p. (J). (gr. -1-3). 9.95 (978-1-59249-038-7(7), PB4074) Soundprints.

Woelfle, Gretchen. Animal Families, Animal Friends. Hynes, Robert, illus. 2005. (ENG.). 32p. (J). (gr. k-3). 15.95 (978-1-55971-901-8(X)) Cooper Square Publishing Llc.

Woodward, John. Swarms. 2005. (Planet's Most Extreme Ser.). (J). 23.70 (978-1-4103-0394-3(2)); 9.95 (978-1-4103-0436-0(1)) Cengage Gale. (Blackbirch Pr., Inc.).

Woog, Adam. SCRATCHbot. 2010. (Great Idea Ser.). 48p. (J). (gr. 4-6). lib. bdg. 26.60 (978-1-59953-380-3(4)) Norwood Hse. Pr.

World Book, Inc Staff, contrib. by. Animal Behavior. 2014. (Illus.). 32p. (J). (978-0-7166-2821-7(X)) World Bk., Inc.

—Seasonal Forests. 2012. (J). (978-0-7166-0444-0(2)) World Bk., Inc.

Yardi, Robin. ¡Ellos Ya Saben! Instintos de Los Animales, 1 vol. Klein, Laurie Allen, illus. 2015. (SPA & ENG.). 32p. (J). (gr. k-3). pap. 9.95 (978-1-62855-644-5(7)) Arbordale Publishing.

—They Just Know: Animal Instincts, 1 vol. Klein, Laurie Allen, illus. 2015. (ENG.). 32p. (J). (gr. k-3). 17.95 (978-1-62855-634-6(X)) Arbordale Publishing.

Zayarny, Jack. Camouflage. 2016. (Illus.). 24p. (J). (978-1-5105-0918-4(6)) SmartBook Media, Inc.

Zolotow, Charlotte. Sleepy Book. Date not set. (ENG.). 40p. (J). (gr. -1-3). pap. 5.99 (978-0-06-443737-0(X)) HarperCollins Pubs.

Zubek, Adeline. Foxes in the Dark. 2012. (Creatures of the Night Ser.). (Illus.). 24p. (J). (gr. 1-3). pap. 8.15 (978-1-4339-6370-4(1)); lib. bdg. 22.60 (978-1-4339-6368-1(X)) Stevens, Gareth Publishing LLLP.

Zuckerman, Andrew, photos by. Creature Sounds. 2014. (ENG., Illus.). 20p. (J). (gr. -1 — 1). bds. 7.99 (978-1-4521-1722-5(5)) Chronicle Bks. LLC.

Zullo, Allan. Bad Pets Save Christmas! 2012. 139p. (J). pap. (978-0-545-61229-6(2)) Scholastic, Inc.

1000 Strange but True Animal Facts. 2014. (Illus.). 223p. pap. (978-1-4723-4646-9(7)) Parragon Bk. Service Ltd.

ANIMALS—HABITS AND BEHAVIOR—FICTION

Alexander, John. The Adventures of Thunder & Avalanche: Laws of Nature. Alexander, John, illus. 2013. (Illus.). 46p. 18.99 (978-0-9887625-0-3(1)) Mountain Thunder Publishing.

Aliki. Quiet in the Garden. Aliki, illus. 2009. (ENG., Illus.). 32p. (J). (gr. -1-2). 17.99 (978-0-06-155207-6(0), Greenwillow Bks.) HarperCollins Pubs.

Arndt, Michael. Cat Says Meow & Other Animalopoeia. 2014. (ENG., Illus.). 36p. (J). (gr. -1-k). 12.99 (978-1-4521-1234-3(7)) Chronicle Bks. LLC.

Arnold, Marsha Diane. Baby Animals Take a Bath. Tildes, Phyllis Limbacher, illus. 2017. (ENG.). 10p. (J). (— 1). bds. 6.99 (978-1-58089-538-5(7)) Charlesbridge Publishing, Inc.

AZ Books Staff. Babbling Pond. Tulup, Natalia, ed. 2012. (How We Speak Ser.). (ENG.). 12p. (J). (gr. -1-k). bds. 10.95 (978-1-61889-097-9(2)) AZ Bks. LLC.

—Our Cozy Forest. Zayceva, Irina, ed. 2012. (Hook-And-Loop-Pictures Ser.). (ENG.). 8p. (J). (-k). bds. 11.95 (978-1-61889-157-0(X)) AZ Bks. LLC.

Bauer, Marion Dane. Why Do Kittens Purr? Cole, Henry, illus. 2007. (ENG.). 32p. (J). (gr. -1-2). 9.99 (978-1-4169-6850-4(4), Aladdin) Simon & Schuster Children's Publishing.

Beitler, Stacey Ann. Willy Goes to the Farm. 2009. 30p. pap. 14.50 (978-1-60860-474-6(8), Eloquent Bks.) Strategic Book Publishing & Rights Agency (SBPRA).

Benchmark Education Company, LLC Staff, compiled by. Habitats: Theme Set. 2006. (J). 237.00 (978-1-4108-7105-3(3)) Benchmark Education Co.

Berkes, Marianne. Anybody Home?, 1 vol. Dickinson, Rebecca, illus. 2013. (ENG.). 32p. (J). (gr. -1-3). 17.95 (978-1-60718-618-2(7), 9781607186182); pap. 9.95 (978-1-60718-630-4(6)) Arbordale Publishing.

Bester, Maryanne. Three Friends & a Taxi. Bester, Shayle, illus. 2007. (Cool Nguni Ser.: 1). (ENG.). 24p. (J). (gr. k-2). 12.00 (978-1-77009-265-5(X)) Jacana Media ZAF. Dist: Independent Pubs. Group.

Bonnell, Kris. Who Can Wiggle? 2006. (J). pap. 5.95 (978-1-933727-42-4(X)) Reading Reading Bks., LLC.

BrickHouse Education & Colón, Priscilla. Wild ABC's. 2009. 40p. (J). 8.99 (978-1-59835-116-3(8)) Cambridge BrickHouse, Inc.

Bringsvaerd, Tor Age. When Two Are Angry at Each Other. Vetleseter, Tonje, tr. from NOR. Soli, Tina, illus. 2008. 32p. (J). (gr. -1-1). 14.95 (978-0-9790347-8-7(7)) Mackenzie Smiles, LLC.

Bryson, Theresa. Farm Work. 2011. (Early Connections Ser.). (J). (978-1-61672-351-4(3)) Benchmark Education Co.

Buckley, Richard. The Greedy Python. Carle, Eric, illus. 2009. (World of Eric Carle Ser.). (ENG.). 24p. (J). (gr. -1-k). bds. 7.99 (978-1-4169-8290-6(6), Little Simon) Little Simon.

Canetti, Yanitzia. ABeCedario Salvaje. 2009. (SPA.). 40p. (J). (gr. -1-3). pap. 7.99 (978-1-59835-117-0(6)) Cambridge BrickHouse, Inc.

Carle, Eric. The Very Quiet Cricket. Carle, Eric, illus. 2014. (Penguin Young Readers, Level 3 Ser.). (ENG., Illus.). 32p. (J). (gr. 1-3). pap. 3.99 (978-0-448-48138-8(3), Penguin Young Readers) Penguin Young Readers Group.

Chou, Yih-fen. The Potty Story. Chen, Zhiyuan, illus. 2011. (J). (978-0-9845523-8-2(3)) Heryin Publishing Corp.

Crow, Nosy. Can You Say It, Too? Woof! Woof! Braun, Sebastien, illus. 2014. (Can You Say It, Too? Ser.). (ENG.). 10p. (J). (— 1). bds. 8.99 (978-0-7636-6605-7(X), Nosy Crow) Candlewick Pr.

Derrick, David G., Jr. Animals Don't, So I Won't! 2012. (ENG., Illus.). 36p. (J). (gr. -1-3). 15.95 (978-1-59702-029-9(X)) Immedium.

Dharma Publishing Staff. The King Who Understood Animals: A Story about Using Knowledge Wisely. 2nd ed. 2013. (ENG.). 36p. (gr. -1-7). pap. 8.95 (978-0-89800-520-2(5)) Dharma Publishing.

Donaldson, Julia. What the Ladybug Heard. Monks, Lydia, illus. 2010. (ENG.). 32p. (J). (gr. -1-1). 18.99 (978-0-8050-9028-4(2), 9780805090284, Holt, Henry & Co. Bks. For Young Readers) Holt, Henry & Co.

Dowson, Nick. Tracks of a Panda: Read & Wonder. Rong, Yu, illus. 2010. (Read & Wonder Ser.). (ENG.). 32p. (J). (gr. -1-3). pap. 6.99 (978-0-7636-4737-7(3)) Candlewick Pr.

Eze-Offornezie, Ngozika. An Invitation from the Fairy. 2008. 64p. pap. 23.49 (978-1-4343-9784-3(X)) AuthorHouse.

Fleming, Candace. Seven Hungry Babies. Yelchin, Eugene, illus. 2010. (ENG.). 40p. (J). (gr. -1-2). 16.99 (978-1-4169-5402-6(3), Atheneum Bks. for Young Readers) Simon & Schuster Children's Publishing.

Gabriel, Andrea. Wandering Woolly, 1 vol. 2015. (ENG., Illus.). 32p. (J). (gr. 1-4). 17.95 (978-1-62855-558-5(0)) Arbordale Publishing.

George, Lindsay Barrett & George, Lindsay B. In the Garden: Who's Been Here? George, Lindsay Barrett, illus. 2006. (ENG., Illus.). 48p. (J). (gr. -1-3). 17.99 (978-0-06-078762-2(7), Greenwillow Bks.) HarperCollins Pubs.

Gilland, Gary P. The Turtle Train Troop. 2011. 24p. pap. 24.95 (978-1-4626-3210-7(6)) America Star Bks.

Gillingham, Sara & Chronicle Books Staff. In My Flower. Siminovich, Lorena, illus. 2009. (ENG.). 12p. (J). (gr. -1 — 1). bds. 8.99 (978-0-8118-7339-0(0)) Chronicle Bks. LLC.

—In My Meadow. Siminovich, Lorena, illus. 2009. (ENG.). 12p. (J). (gr. -1 — 1). bds. 8.99 (978-0-8118-7338-3(2)) Chronicle Bks. LLC.

Giogas, Valarie. In My Backyard, 1 vol. Zecca, Katherine, illus. 2007. (ENG.). 32p. (J). (gr. -1-3). 15.95 (978-0-9777423-1-8(8)) Arbordale Publishing.

Goodman, Susan E. Unseen Rainbows, Silent Songs: The World of Animal Senses. Duncan, Beverly, illus. 2008. (ENG.). 40p. (J). (gr. 4-6). 12.99 (978-1-4169-7575-5(6), Aladdin) Simon & Schuster Children's Publishing.

Grogan, John. Snow Dog Marley. Cowdrey, Richard, illus. 2010. (I Can Read Level 2 Ser.). (ENG.). 32p. (J). (gr. k-3). 16.99 (978-0-06-185393-7(3)); pap. 3.99 (978-0-06-185392-0(5)) HarperCollins Pubs.

Harcourt School Publishers Staff. Looking Back, Unit 5. 3rd ed. 2003. (Horizons Ser.). (Illus.). (gr. 1). pap. 166.70 (978-0-15-340224-1(5)) Harcourt Schl. Pubs.

Harris, Annabel. Look Out, it's the First of October! 2010. (Illus.). 48p. pap. 12.10 (978-1-4520-9819-7(0)) AuthorHouse.

Harris, Jane Ellen. Room for One More. Cole, Al, illus. 2007. 24p. (J). (gr. -1-3). pap. 11.98 (978-0-9800733-0-0(8), LSP) LSP Digital, LLC.

Harvey, Gwendolyn Fowlkes. The Backyard Plum Tree. 2009. (J). pap. (978-1-61623-481-2(4)) Independent Pub.

Helquist, Brett. Bedtime for Bear. Helquist, Brett, illus. 2010. (ENG., Illus.). 32p. (J). (gr. -1-2). 16.99 (978-0-06-050205-8(3)) HarperCollins Pubs.

Hnatov, Catherine. Yum, Yum, 1 vol. 2011. (ENG., Illus.). 32p. (J). (gr. -1). bds. 5.95 (978-1-59572-275-1(0)) Star Bright Bks., Inc.

Hosta, Dar. I Love the Night. Hosta, Dar, illus. l.t. ed. 2003. (Illus.). 32p. (J). (gr. k-3). 16.95 (978-0-9721967-0-3(6)) Brown Dog Bks.

Imbody, Amy E. & Imbody, Amy. Snug as a Bug, 1 vol. Gordon, Mike, illus. 2008. (I Can Read! Ser.). (ENG.). 32p. (J). (gr. -1-1). pap. 3.99 (978-0-310-71575-7(X)) Zonderkidz.

Johnson, Amy Crane. A Home for Pearl Squirrel. Mommaerts, Robb, illus. 2009. (ENG.). 32p. (J). (gr. -1-3). 16.95 (978-1-934960-58-5(6), Raven Tree Pr.,Csi) Continental Sales, Inc.

—Lewis Cardinal's First Winter. Mommaerts, Robb, illus. 2009. (ENG.). 32p. (J). (gr. 4-7). 16.95 (978-1-934960-60-8(8), Raven Tree Pr.,Csi) Continental Sales, Inc.

Jones, Andrea. The Spitting Twins. Kulka, Joe, illus. 2004. 32p. (J). (978-1-58394-095-2(2), Frog Ltd.) North Atlantic Bks.

Joosse, Barbara M. & Lisberg, Anneke. Better Together: A Book of Family. Schorr, Jared, illus. 2017. (ENG.). 22p. (J). (gr. -1-k). bds. 14.95 **(978-1-4197-2538-8(6)**, Abrams Appleseed) Abrams, Inc.

La Coccinella. Look & See: What Sound Do You Make? 2014. (Look & See! Ser.). (ENG., Illus.). 24p. (J). (gr. -1 — 1). bds. 6.95 (978-1-4549-0642-1(1)) Sterling Publishing Co., Inc.

Lansky, Bruce. Monkey See, Monkey Do at the Zoo. Wummer, Amy, illus. 2010. 10p. (J). bds. 6.99 (978-1-4169-9317-9(7)) Meadowbrook Pr.

Lewis, Edwina. Who Eats? Parker, Ant, illus. 2003. (Who... Ser.). 16p. (YA). (978-1-85602-470-9(9), Pavilion Children's Books) Pavilion Bks.

Litton, Jonathan. Roar: A Big-Mouthed Book of Sounds! Galloway, Fhiona, illus. 2014. (ENG.). 16p. (J). bds. 7.99 (978-1-58925-593-7(3)) Tiger Tales.

Long, Ethan. Hi! 2015. (Animal Sounds Ser.). (ENG., Illus.). 20p. (J). (gr. -1 — 1). bds. 7.95 (978-1-4197-1365-1(5)) Abrams, Inc.

Louie, Mary. Amazing Amand. 2009. 16p. pap. 13.49 (978-1-4389-7903-8(7)) AuthorHouse.

Love, Maryann Cusimano. Sleep, Baby, Sleep. van Lieshout, Maria, illus. 2013. (ENG.). 30p. (J). (gr. -1-k). bds. 6.99 (978-0-399-16144-5(9), Philomel Bks.) Penguin Young Readers Group.

Luke, Melinda. El Perro Verde; the Green Dog. 2008. pap. 34.95 (978-1-58013-770-6(9)) Kane Press, Inc.

Malone, Jean M. Dexter the Very Good Goat, 1 vol. Min Lin, Jia, illus. 2016. (ENG.). 32p. (J). 14.99 (978-0-7643-5051-1(X), 9780764350511) Schiffer Publishing, Ltd.

Martin, Bill, Jr. Polar Bear, Polar Bear, What Do You Hear? Carle, Eric, illus. 2010. (My First Reader Ser.). (ENG.). 40p. (J). (gr. -1-2). 8.99 (978-0-8050-9245-5(5), 9780805092455, Holt, Henry & Co. Bks. For Young Readers) Holt, Henry & Co.

Martin, Bill, Jr. & Sampson, Michael R. Listen to Our World. Sweet, Melissa, illus. 2016. (ENG.). 40p. (J). (gr. -1-3). 17.99 (978-1-4424-5472-9(5), Simon & Schuster Bks. For Young Readers) Simon & Schuster Bks. For Young Readers.

Milbourne, Anna. Peek Inside Animal Homes. Dimitri, Simona, illus. 2014. (Peek Inside Board Bks.). (ENG.). 14p. (gr. -1). bds. 11.99 (978-0-7945-2549-1(0), Usborne) EDC Publishing.

Miller, Pat. Substitute Groundhog. Ember, Kathi, illus. 2012. (J). (978-1-61913-133-0(1)) Weigl Pubs., Inc.

—Substitute Groundhog, 1 vol. Ember, Kathi, illus. 2010. (ENG.). 32p. (J). (gr. k-3). pap. 6.99 (978-0-8075-7644-1(1)) Whitman, Albert & Co.

Mitchell, Melanie, illus. Good Morning, Good Night! 2007. (Touch & Feel Ser.). 13p. 15.95 (978-1-58117-572-1(8), Intervisual/Piggy Toes) Bendon, Inc.

Murphy, Mary. Say Hello Like This. Murphy, Mary, illus. 2014. (ENG., Illus.). 32p. (J). (-k). 12.99 (978-0-7636-6951-5(2)) Candlewick Pr.

Na, Il Sung. A Book of Sleep. 2011. (ENG.). 24p. (J). (gr. k — 1). bds. 6.99 (978-0-375-86618-0(3), Knopf Bks. for Young Readers) Random Hse. Children's Bks.

Paul, Ann Whitford. If Animals Kissed Good Night. Walker, David, illus. 2014. (ENG.). 34p. (J). (gr. -1-1). bds. 7.99 (978-0-374-30021-0(6), 9780374300210, Farrar, Straus & Giroux (BYR)) Farrar, Straus & Giroux.

Popova, Natalya. The Guinea Pig Story. 2008. 54p. pap. 24.50 (978-1-4092-1336-9(6)) Lulu Pr., Inc.

Priddy, Roger. My First Peekaboo: Who Says Roar? 2015. (My First Peekaboo Ser.). (ENG., Illus.). 8p. (J). (gr. -1 — 1). bds. 8.99 (978-0-312-51836-3(6), 9780312518363, Priddy Bks.) St. Martin's Pr.

Ritchie, Joseph R. Peter Cottontail's Busy Day. Halverson, Lydia, illus. 2009. 14p. (J). (gr. -1-k). bds. 6.99 (978-0-8249-1842-2(8), Ideal Pubns.) Worthy Publishing.

Roberts, Chalres G. D. Children of the Wild. l.t. ed. 2007. (ENG.). 176p. pap. 21.99 (978-1-4264-9254-9(5)) Creative Media Partners, LLC.

Runion, Laura K. Sleepy Faces in Sleeping Places. 2012. 28p. pap. 16.10 (978-1-4669-4020-8(4)) Trafford Publishing.

Sapp, Karen. Who Is Sleeping? 2009. (Rookie Preschool-NEW Ser.). (ENG.). 24p. (J). pap. 6.95 (978-0-531-24586-6(1)); (gr. -1). lib. bdg. 23.00 (978-0-531-24411-1(3)) Scholastic Library Publishing. (Children's Pr.).

Schneider, Josh. Everybody Sleeps (but Not Fred) 2015. (ENG., Illus.). 32p. (J). (gr. -1-3). 16.99 (978-0-544-33924-8(X)) Houghton Mifflin Harcourt Publishing Co.

Shadrick, Crystal Star. My Name Was Fear. Stone, Karen, ed. Marie, Berri, illus. 2013. 60p. pap. 12.95 (978-1-935186-41-0(8)) Waldenhouse Pubs., Inc.

Shapiro, Arnold. Mice Squeak, We Speak. 2014. 16.00 (978-1-63419-673-4(2)) Perfection Learning Corp.

Siminovich, Lorena, illus. You Are My Baby: Woodland. 2014. (ENG.). 10p. (J). (gr. -1 — 1). bds. 8.99 (978-1-4521-3431-4(6)) Chronicle Bks. LLC.

Slegers, Liesbet. Move! 2012. (ENG.). 12p. (J). (gr. k — 1). bds. 7.95 (978-1-60537-118-4(1)) Cobblestone Publishing Co.

Spafford, Suzy. Helping-Out Day? Hooray! Spafford, Suzy, illus. 2003. (Tales from Duckport Ser.). (ENG., Illus.). 40p. (J). (gr. k-3). pap. 3.99 (978-0-439-38358-5(7)) Scholastic, Inc.

Stower, Adam. Naughty Kitty! Stower, Adam, illus. 2014. (ENG., Illus.). 40p. (J). (gr. -1-k). 16.99 (978-0-545-57604-8(0), Orchard Bks.) Scholastic, Inc.

Truman, Dennay H. The Happy Endings. 2007. 65p. per. 8.95 (978-1-59824-435-9(3)) E-BookTime LLC.

Zolotow, Charlotte. Sleepy Book. Bobri, Vladimir, illus. 2016. (ENG.). 36p. (J). 20.00 (978-1-85124-457-7(3)) Bodleian Library GBR. Dist: Chicago Distribution Ctr.

Zullo, Allan. Bad Pets: On the Loose! 2012. 125p. (J). pap. (978-0-545-46041-5(7)) Scholastic, Inc.

ANIMALS—HIBERNATION

Alinsky, Shelby. Sleep, Bear! (1 Hardcover/1 CD) 2017. (National Geographic Kids Ser.). (ENG.). (J). 29.95 **(978-1-4301-2649-2(3))** Live Oak Media.

—Sleep, Bear! (1 Paperback/1 CD) 2017. (National Geographic Kids Ser.). (ENG.). (J). pap. 19.95 **(978-1-4301-2648-5(5))** Live Oak Media.

—Sleep, Bear! (4 Paperbacks/1 CD), 4 vols. 2017. (National Geographic Kids Ser.). (ENG.). (J). pap., pap. 31.95 **(978-1-4301-2650-8(7))** Live Oak Media.

Crossingham, John & Kalman, Bobbie. Qué Es la Hibernación? 2005. (Serie la Ciencia de los Seres Vivos Ser.). (FRE & SPA., Illus.). 32p. (J). (gr. 3-4). lib. bdg. (978-0-7787-8758-7(3)) Crabtree Publishing Co.

—¿Qué Es la Hibernación? 2005. (Ciencia de los Seres Vivos Ser.). (SPA., Illus.). 32p. (J). (gr. 7-12). pap. (978-0-7787-8804-1(0)) Crabtree Publishing Co.

Duden, Jane. Why Do Bears Sleep All Winter? [Chicago]: A Book about Hibernation. 2010. (Why in the World? Ser.). (ENG.). 24p. pap. 6.95 (978-1-4296-5183-7(0), First Facts) Capstone Press of Coughlan Cos.

Hickman, Pamela. Animals Hibernating: How Animals Survive Extreme Conditions. Stephens, Pat, illus. 2005. (Animal Behavior Ser.). (ENG.). 40p. (J). (gr. 2-6). 6.95 (978-1-55337-663-7(3)) Kids Can Pr., Ltd. CAN. Dist: Hachette Bk. Group.

Higginson, Mel. Hibernation. 2006. (Nature's Cycles Discovery Library). (Illus.). 24p. (J). (gr. 3-7). lib. bdg. 22.79 (978-1-60044-177-6(7)) Rourke Educational Media.

Lindeen, Mary. Frozen Frogs & Other Amazing Hibernators. 2017. (Searchlight Books (tm) — Animal Superpowers Ser.). (ENG.). 40p. (J). (gr. 3-5). 16.99 **(978-1-5124-3663-1(1)**, Lerner Pubns.); 46.65 **(978-1-5124-2820-9(5)**, Lerner Pubns.); 46.65 **(978-1-5124-3662-4(3)**, Lerner Pubns.); (Illus.). 30.65 (978-1-5124-2547-5(8)) Lerner Publishing Group.

Lundgren, Julie K. What Do Critters Do in the Winter? 2011. (ENG., Illus.). 24p. (gr. 2-3). pap. 8.95 (978-1-61741-948-5(6)) Rourke Educational Media.

Markovics, Joyce L. Little Brown Bats. 2015. (Illus.). 24p. (J). lib. bdg. (978-1-62724-315-5(1)) Bearport Publishing Co., Inc.

Martin, David. Why Do Animals Hibernate? 2012. (InfoMax Readers Ser.). (ENG., Illus.). 24p. (J). (gr. 1-2). pap. 8.25 (978-1-4488-8995-2(2), Rosen Classroom) Rosen Publishing Group, Inc., The.

McDowell, Pamela. Hibernation. 2016. (Illus.). 24p. (J). (978-1-5105-0945-0(3)) SmartBook Media, Inc.

—Hibernation. 2015. (Illus.). 24p. (J). (978-1-4896-3675-1(7)) Weigl Pubs., Inc.

Mebane, Jeanie. Animal Hibernation, 1 vol. 2012. (Learn about Animal Behavior Ser.). (ENG.). 24p. (gr. 1-2). pap. 7.29 (978-1-4296-9310-3(X)); pap. 41.70 (978-1-4296-9311-0(8), First Facts); lib. bdg. 25.32 (978-1-4296-8266-4(3)) Capstone Press of Coughlan Cos.

Mills, Nathan & Wilson, Emily. Good Night, Bears: Learning about Hibernation. 2012. (Rosen Readers Ser.). (ENG., Illus.). 24p. (J). (gr. 1-2). pap. 8.25 (978-1-4488-8776-7(3), Rosen Classroom) Rosen Publishing Group, Inc., The.

Nelson, Robin. Hibernación. 2012. (Mi Primer Paso Al Mundo Real - Descubriendo Los Ciclos de la Naturaleza (First Step Nonfiction - Discovering Nature's Cycles) Ser.).Tr. of Hibernation. (Illus.). 24p. (gr. k-2). (ENG & SPA.). pap. 6.95 (978-0-7613-9351-1(X)); (SPA., lib. bdg. 23.93 (978-0-7613-9336-8(6)) Lerner Publishing Group. (Ediciones Lerner).

—Hibernation. 2010. pap. 33.92 (978-0-7613-6914-1(7)); (ENG.). 24p. pap. 6.95 (978-0-7613-5681-3(9)); (ENG., Illus.). 24p. (J). lib. bdg. 23.93 (978-0-7613-4579-4(5)) Lerner Publishing Group.

Plourde, Lynn. Baby Bear's Not Hibernating, Vol. Weidner, Teri, illus. 2016. (ENG.). 40p. (J). 16.95 (978-1-60893-622-9(8)) Down East Bks.

Salas, Laura Purdie. Do Polar Bears Snooze in Hollow Trees? A Book about Animal Hibernation. Ouren, Todd, illus. 2006. (Animals All Around Ser.). (ENG.). 24p. (gr. -1-2). lib. bdg. 26.65 (978-1-4048-2231-3(3)) Picture Window Bks.

Troupe, Thomas Kingsley. What's with the Long Naps, Bears? Learning about Hibernation with the Garbage Gang. Toye,

Derek, illus. 2015. (Garbage Gang's Super Science Questions Ser.). (ENG.). 24p. (gr. k-2). lib. bdg. 26.65 *(978-1-4795-7056-0(7))* Picture Window Bks.

Ulinski, Michael. Why Do Animals Hibernate? 2013. (Nature's Super Secrets Ser.). (Illus.). 24p. (gr. 1-3). 22.60 *(978-1-4339-8175-3(0))*; pap. 8.15 *(978-1-4339-8176-0(9))* Stevens, Gareth Publishing LLLP.

ANIMALS, IMAGINARY

see Animals, Mythical

ANIMALS—INFANCY

Acampora, Courtney & DiPerna, Kaitlyn. Read with Me! Pre, Level 1. 2016. (Smithsonian Readers Ser.). (ENG., Illus.). 200p. (J). (gr. -1). 14.95 *(978-1-62686-571-6(X)*, Silver Dolphin Bks.) Readerlink Distribution Services, LLC.

Ackland, Nick. In the Jungle. McDonald, Jake, illus. 2017. (Who's Hiding? Bks.). (ENG.). 10p. (J). (gr. -1 — 1). bds. 7.99 *(978-0-7641-6876-5(2))* Barron's Educational Series, Inc.

All about Baby Zoo Animals. 2015. (All about Baby Zoo Animals Ser.). (ENG.). 24p. (J). (gr. -1-1). pap., pap., pap. 336.60 *(978-0-7660-6690-8(8))* Enslow Pubs., Inc.

Andrews McMeel Publishing, LLC Staff. Zoo Babies. 2015. (ENG.). 12p. (J). bds. 5.99 *(978-1-4494-6058-7(5))* Andrews McMeel Publishing.

Arlon, Penelope. Mirame Crecer. 2013. (Scholastic Explora Tu Mundo Ser.). (SPA.). 32p. (J). (gr. -1-3). 7.99 *(978-0-545-49084-9(7)*, Scholastic en Espanol) Scholastic, Inc.

—Puppies & Kittens. 2013. (Scholastic Discover More Ser.). (ENG., Illus.). 32p. (J). (gr. -1-3). 7.99 *(978-0-545-49566-0(0)*, Scholastic Reference) Scholastic, Inc.

Arlon, Penny & Arlon, Penelope. See Me Grow. 2012. (Scholastic Discover More Ser.). (ENG., Illus.). 32p. (J). (gr. k-1). 7.99 *(978-0-545-34513-2(8)*, Scholastic Reference) Scholastic, Inc.

Austen, Elizabeth. Baby Animals, 1 vol. rev. ed. 2014. (Science Readers: Content & Literacy Ser.). (ENG., Illus.). 24p. (gr. k-k). pap. 22.96 *(978-1-4938-1131-1(2))*; pap. 8.99 *(978-1-4807-4521-6(9))* Teacher Created Materials, Inc.

AZ Books Staff. Where's My Baby? Sisoj, Natalja, ed. 2012. (Peek-A-Boo Ser.). (ENG.). 10p. (J). (— 1). bds. 10.95 *(978-1-61889-117-4(0))* AZ Bks. LLC.

Baby Animals. 2005. (Illus.). (J). per. 4.99 *(978-1-933581-19-4(0))* Byeway Bks.

Baby Animals. (Illus.). 24p. (J). 1.99 *(978-1-59445-022-8(6))* Dogs in Hats Children's Publishing Co.

Baby Animals. (Sticker Shapes Ser.). Date not set. (Illus.). 16p. (J). 2.98 *(978-0-7525-8137-8(6))* Date not set. (Illus.). 16p. (J). 5.98 *(978-0-7525-7696-1(8))* Date not set. (Illus.). 16p. (J). 2.98 *(978-0-7525-9760-7(4))* 2008. 96p. *(978-1-4075-1770-4(8))* 2003. 32p. (J). 3.98 *(978-0-7525-8893-3(1))* Parragon, Inc.

Baby Animals. 2006. 16p. (J). pap. 1.99 *(978-0-7847-1387-7(1)*, 22125) Standard Publishing.

Baby Australian Animals, 1 vol., Set. Incl. It's a Baby Australian Fur Seal! Hengel, Katherine. lib. bdg. 24.21 *(978-1-60453-574-7(1))*; It's a Baby Flying Fox! Hengel, Katherine. lib. bdg. 24.21 *(978-1-60453-575-4(X))*; It's a Baby Kangaroo! Doudna, Kelly. lib. bdg. 24.21 *(978-1-60453-576-1(8))*; It's a Baby Koala! Hengel, Katherine. lib. bdg. 24.21 *(978-1-60453-577-8(6))*; It's a Baby Spiny Anteater! Hengel, Katherine. lib. bdg. 24.21 *(978-1-60453-578-5(4))*; It's a Baby Tasmanian Devil! Hengel, Katherine. lib. bdg. 24.21 *(978-1-60453-579-2(2))*; (J). (gr. k-3). (Baby Australian Animals Ser.: 6). (ENG., Illus.). 24p. 2010. Set lib. bdg. 145.26 *(978-1-60453-573-0(3)*, SandCastle) ABDO Publishing Co.

Baggott, Stella. Baby's Very First Little Book of Baby Animals. 2012. (Baby's Very First Board Book Ser.). 10p. (J). ring bd. 6.99 *(978-0-7945-3217-8(9)*, Usborne) EDC Publishing.

Barnes, J. Chicks & Chickens: Learning the CH Sound. 2009. (PowerPhonics Ser.). 24p. (gr. 1-1). 39.90 *(978-1-60851-438-0(2)*, PowerKids Pr.) Rosen Publishing Group, Inc., The.

Barnes, L. Cats & Kittens: Learning the Hard C & K Sound. 2009. (PowerPhonics Ser.). 24p. (gr. 1-1). 39.90 *(978-1-60851-437-3(4)*, PowerKids Pr.) Rosen Publishing Group, Inc., The.

Bell, Samantha S. Meet a Baby Giraffe. 2015. (ENG., Illus.). 32p. (J). (gr. k-2). 26.65 *(978-1-4677-7975-3(X)*, Lerner Pubns.) Lerner Publishing Group.

Berger, Melvin. Bebés de Animales Polares: Polar Animal Babies. 2006. (SPA & ENG., Illus.). (J). *(978-0-439-87986-6(8))* Scholastic, Inc.

Berger, Melvin & Berger, Gilda. Baby Animals. 2008. (Scholastic True or False Ser.: 1). (ENG., Illus.). 48p. (J). (gr. 2-5). pap. 4.99 *(978-0-545-00391-9(1)*, Scholastic Reference) Scholastic, Inc.

Berkes, Marianne. Baby on Board: How Animals Carry Their Young, 1 vol. Morrison, Cathy, illus. 2016. (ENG.). 32p. (J). (gr. 8 — 1). 16.95 *(978-1-58469-592-9(7))* Dawn Pubns.

Bicknell, Joanna. Cuddle Buddy: Baby Animals. 2006. 10p. (gr. -1). *(978-1-84610-093-2(3))* Make Believe Ideas.

Bleiman, Andrew & Eastland, Chris. ABC ZooBorns! 2013. (ZooBorns Ser.). (ENG., Illus.). 40p. (J). (gr. -1 — 1). bds. 7.99 *(978-1-4424-7376-8(2)*, Little Simon) Little Simon.

—Hello, Mommy ZooBorns! 2013. (ZooBorns Ser.). (ENG., Illus.). 24p. (J). (gr. -1-1). 16.99 *(978-1-4424-4382-2(0))*; pap. 3.99 *(978-1-4424-4383-9(9))* Simon Spotlight. (Simon Spotlight).

—I Love You, ZooBorns! 2012. (ZooBorns Ser.). (ENG., Illus.). 24p. (J). (gr. -1-1). 15.99 *(978-1-4424-4379-2(0))*; pap. 3.99 *(978-1-4424-4380-8(4))* Simon Spotlight. (Simon Spotlight).

—Nighty Night, ZooBorns. 2013. (ZooBorns Ser.). (ENG., Illus.). 24p. (J). (gr. -1-1). 16.99 *(978-1-4424-4385-3(5))*; pap. 3.99 *(978-1-4424-4386-0(3))* Simon Spotlight. (Simon Spotlight).

—ZooBorns! Zoo Babies from Around the World. 2010. (ZooBorns Ser.). (ENG.). 40p. (J). (gr. -1-1). 12.99 *(978-1-4424-1272-9(0)*, Beach Lane Bks.) Beach Lane Bks.

—ZooBorns! Zoo Babies from Around the World. 2012. (ZooBorns Ser.). (ENG.). 40p. (J). (gr. -1 — 1). bds. 7.99 *(978-1-4424-4329-7(4)*, Little Simon) Little Simon.

Bloomsbury USA. Carry & Play: Spring Friends. 2016. (ENG., Illus.). 10p. (J). (— 1). bds. 6.99 *(978-1-61963-828-0(2)*, 9781619638280, Bloomsbury Activity Bks.) Bloomsbury Publishing USA.

Borgert-Spaniol, Megan. Baby Foxes. 2015. (Super Cute! Ser.). (ENG., Illus.). 24p. (J). (gr. k-3). lib. bdg. 25.95 *(978-1-62617-215-9(3)*, Blastoff! Readers) Bellwether Media.

—Baby Giraffes. 2015. (Super Cute! Ser.). (ENG., Illus.). 24p. (J). (gr. k-3). 25.95 *(978-1-62617-216-6(1)*, Blastoff! Readers) Bellwether Media.

—Baby Hedgehogs. 2015. (Super Cute! Ser.). (ENG., Illus.). 24p. (J). (gr. k-3). lib. bdg. 25.95 *(978-1-62617-217-3(X)*, Blastoff! Readers) Bellwether Media.

—Baby Koalas. 2015. (Super Cute! Ser.). (ENG., Illus.). 24p. (J). (gr. k-3). lib. bdg. 25.95 *(978-1-62617-219-7(6)*, Blastoff! Readers) Bellwether Media.

—Baby Raccoons. 2017. (Super Cute! Ser.). (ENG., Illus.). 24p. (J). (gr. k-3). lib. bdg. 25.95 *(978-1-62617-545-7(4)*, Blastoff! Readers) Bellwether Media.

—Baby Rhinos. 2017. (Super Cute! Ser.). (ENG., Illus.). 24p. (J). (gr. k-3). lib. bdg. 25.95 *(978-1-62617-546-4(2)*, Blastoff! Readers) Bellwether Media.

—Baby Squirrels. 2015. (Super Cute! Ser.). (ENG., Illus.). 24p. (J). (gr. k-3). lib. bdg. 25.95 *(978-1-62617-220-3(X)*, Blastoff! Readers) Bellwether Media.

—Baby Zebras. 2017. (Super Cute! Ser.). (ENG., Illus.). 24p. (J). (gr. k-3). lib. bdg. 25.95 *(978-1-62617-548-8(9)*, Blastoff! Readers) Bellwether Media.

Bové, Jennifer. Meet Ranger Rick Jr: Busy Moms. 2016. (Ranger Rick: Animal Fun for Young Children Ser.). (ENG., Illus.). 32p. (J). (gr. -1-1). pap. 5.99 *(978-1-63076-212-4(1))* Taylor Trade Publishing.

Brannon, Cecelia H. Baby Whales at the Zoo. 2016. (All about Baby Zoo Animals Ser.). 24p. (J). (gr. 1-k). 22.60 *(978-0-7660-7563-4(X))* Enslow Pubs., Inc.

Bredeson, Carmen. Baby Animals of Lakes & Ponds. 2011. (Nature's Baby Animals Ser.). (Illus.). 24p. (J). (gr. k-18). pap. 7.95 *(978-1-59845-224-2(X)*, Enslow Elementary); (gr. 1-3). lib. bdg. 22.60 *(978-0-7660-3563-8(8))* Enslow Pubs., Inc.

—Baby Animals of the Desert. (Nature's Baby Animals Ser.). (Illus.). 24p. (J). 2012. (gr. k-18). pap. 7.95 *(978-1-59845-404-8(8)*, Enslow Elementary) 2008. (gr. 1-3). lib. bdg. 22.60 *(978-0-7660-3007-7(5))* Enslow Pubs., Inc.

—Baby Animals of the Frozen Tundra. (Nature's Baby Animals Ser.). (Illus.). 24p. (J). 2012. (gr. k-18). pap. 7.95 *(978-1-59845-405-5(6)*, Enslow Elementary) 2009. (gr. 1-3). lib. bdg. 22.60 *(978-0-7660-3002-2(4))* Enslow Pubs., Inc.

—Baby Animals of the Grasslands. (Nature's Baby Animals Ser.). (Illus.). 24p. (J). 2012. (gr. k-18). pap. 7.95 *(978-1-59845-406-2(4)*, Enslow Elementary) 2008. (gr. 1-3). lib. bdg. 22.60 *(978-0-7660-3006-0(7))* Enslow Pubs., Inc.

—Baby Animals of the Mountains. 2011. (Nature's Baby Animals Ser.). (Illus.). 24p. (J). (gr. k-18). pap. 7.95 *(978-1-59845-225-9(8)*, Enslow Elementary); (gr. 1-3). lib. bdg. 22.60 *(978-0-7660-3562-1(X))* Enslow Pubs., Inc.

—Baby Animals of the Ocean. 2012. (Nature's Baby Animals Ser.). (Illus.). 24p. (J). (gr. k-18). pap. 7.95 *(978-1-59845-407-9(2)*, Enslow Elementary) Enslow Pubs., Inc.

—Baby Animals of the Seashore. 2011. (Nature's Baby Animals Ser.). (Illus.). 24p. (J). (gr. k-18). pap. 7.95 *(978-1-59845-226-6(6)*, Enslow Elementary); (gr. 1-3). lib. bdg. 22.60 *(978-0-7660-3565-2(4))* Enslow Pubs., Inc.

—Baby Animals of the Tropical Rain Forest. 2012. (Nature's Baby Animals Ser.). (Illus.). 24p. (J). (gr. k-18). pap. 7.95 *(978-1-59845-408-6(0)*, Enslow Elementary) Enslow Pubs., Inc.

—Baby Animals of the Wetlands. 2011. (Nature's Baby Animals Ser.). (Illus.). 24p. (J). (gr. k-18). pap. 7.95 *(978-1-59845-227-3(4)*, Enslow Elementary); (gr. 1-3). lib. bdg. 22.60 *(978-0-7660-3564-5(6))* Enslow Pubs., Inc.

—Baby Animals of the Woodland Forest. 2012. (Nature's Baby Animals Ser.). (Illus.). 24p. (J). (gr. k-18). pap. 7.95 *(978-1-59845-409-3(9)*, Enslow Elementary) Enslow Pubs., Inc.

—Baby Animals of the World. 2011. (Nature's Baby Animals Ser.). (Illus.). 112p. (J). (gr. k-18). pap. 11.99 *(978-1-59845-218-1(5)*, Enslow Elementary) Enslow Pubs., Inc.

Bruning, Matt. Baby Animal Picture Puzzles, 1 vol. 2009. (Look, Look Again Ser.). (ENG.). 32p. (gr. 1-2). lib. bdg. 27.32 *(978-1-4296-3288-1(7)*, Aplus Bks.) Capstone Press of Coughlan Cos.

Brynie, Faith Hickman. How Do Animal Babies Live? 2010. (I Like Reading about Animals! Ser.). (Illus.). 32p. (J). (gr. k-3). 23.94 *(978-0-7660-3327-6(9))*; pap. 7.95 *(978-0-7660-3748-9(7)*, Enslow Elementary) Enslow Pubs., Inc.

Cain, Marie Mowery. Baby Animals. 2013. (Big Books, Blue Ser.). (ENG & SPA., Illus.). 16p. pap. 33.00 *(978-1-59246-001-4(1))* Big Books, by George!

Camm, Sue, illus. Baby Animals. 2004. 24p. (J). bds. 6.99 *(978-1-85854-728-2(8))* Brimax Books Ltd. GBR. Dist: Byeway Bks.

Cardenas, Ernesto A. Baby, Mom, & Dad. 2009. 19.95 *(978-1-60698-002-6(5))*; pap. 3.95 *(978-1-60698-000-2(9))* Milo Educational Bks. & Resources.

Carlton Publishing Group. Animal Babies. 2017. (Cool & Calm Coloring for Kids Ser.). (ENG.). 48p. (J). (gr. 2-6). pap. 6.99 *(978-1-4380-1031-1(1))* Barron's Educational Series, Inc.

Cartwright, Stephen. Animal Babies. 2004. (Usborne Farmyard Tales Ser.). (ENG., Illus.). 1p. (J). (gr. -1-k). bds. 4.95 *(978-0-7460-4105-5(5))* EDC Publishing.

Chambers, Jo. Caring for Wild Animals. 2007. (Trackers-Math Ser.). (gr. 2-5). pap. 5.00 *(978-1-59055-933-8(9))* Pacific Learning, Inc.

Chang, Flora, illus. Look at Me! 2016. (ENG.). 10p. (J). bds. 7.99 *(978-1-62686-762-8(3)*, Silver Dolphin Bks.) Readerlink Distribution Services, LLC.

Ciencin, Scott & Carrano, Matthew T. Growing up Dino. 2006. (Illus.). 32p. (J). pap. *(978-0-439-83874-0(6))* Scholastic, Inc.

Clarke, Ginjer L. Baby Elephant. Cuddy, Robin & Wummer, Amy, illus. 2009. (Penguin Young Readers, Level 3 Ser.). (ENG.). 48p. (J). (gr. 1-3). mass mkt. 3.99 *(978-0-448-44825-1(4)*, Penguin Young Readers) Penguin Young Readers Group.

—Baby Meerkats. Cuddy, Robbin, illus. 2010. (Penguin Young Readers, Level 3 Ser.). (ENG.). 48p. (J). (gr. 1-3). mass mkt. 3.99 *(978-0-448-45106-0(9)*, Penguin Young Readers) Penguin Young Readers Group.

Cuidando a los animales: Keeping Baby Animals Safe. 2005. (Take-Home Bks.). (SPA.). (YA). (gr. -1-3). 15.75 *(978-0-8215-1206-7(4))* Sadlier, William H. Inc.

Currie, Robin. Baby Bible Animals. 2003. (Baby Bible Ser.). (Illus.). 48p. (J). bds. 12.99 *(978-0-7814-3865-0(9)*, 0781438659) Cook, David C.

Curtis, Jennifer Keats. Kali's Story: An Orphaned Polar Bear Rescue, 1 vol. Gomes, John, photos by. 2014. (ENG., Illus.). 32p. (J). (gr. 1-4). 17.95 *(978-1-62855-208-9(5))* Arbordale Publishing.

—The Lucky Litter: Wolf Pups Rescued from Wildfire, 1 vol. Gomes, John, illus. 2015. (ENG.). 32p. (J). (gr. 2-5). 17.95 *(978-1-62855-718-3(4))* Arbordale Publishing.

Dale, Jay. Baby Farm Animals, 1 vol. 2012. (Engage Literacy Blue Ser.). (ENG.). 32p. (gr. k-2). pap. 5.99 *(978-1-4296-8990-8(0)*, Engage Literacy) Capstone Press of Coughlan Cos.

Dalmatian Press Staff. Pop & Touch Baby Animals. 2008. (ENG.). 12p. (J). 10.95 *(978-1-58117-674-2(0)*, Intervisual/Piggy Toes) Bendon, Inc.

Dalton, Kippy. Babies. 2016. (Spring Forward Ser.). (J). (gr. 1). *(978-1-4900-6017-0(0))* Benchmark Education Co.

De la Bédoyère, Camilla. I Love Baby Animals. 2014. (Illus.). 120p. (J). *(978-1-4351-5532-9(7))* Barnes & Noble, Inc.

de Lambilly-Bresson, Elisabeth. Baby Animals. 2007. (Animal Show & Tell Ser.). (Illus.). 16p. (gr. -1-3). lib. bdg. 19.00 *(978-0-8368-7835-6(3)*, Gareth Stevens Learning Library) Stevens, Gareth Publishing LLLP.

—Crias de Animales. 2007. (Los animales nos cuentan su vida (Animal Show & Tell) Ser.). (SPA., Illus.). 16p. (gr. -1-3). lib. bdg. 19.00 *(978-0-8368-8109-7(5)*, Gareth Stevens Learning Library) Stevens, Gareth Publishing LLLP.

Delano, Marfe Ferguson. Explore My World Baby Animals. 2015. (Explore My World Ser.). (ENG., Illus.). 32p. (J). (gr. -1-2). pap. 4.99 *(978-1-4263-2046-0(9)*, National Geographic Children's Bks.) National Geographic Society.

deMarin, Layne. Oh Baby! 2011. (Wonder Readers Fluent Level Ser.). (ENG.). (gr. -1-2). 16p. pap. 35.94 *(978-1-4296-8134-6(9))*; 32p. pap. 5.99 *(978-1-4296-7940-4(9))* Capstone Press of Coughlan Cos. (Wonder Readers).

Deneux, Xavier. Baby Animals. 2016. (ENG., Illus.). 16p. (J). (gr. -1 — 1). bds. 14.99 *(978-1-4521-4519-8(9))* Chronicle Bks. LLC.

Dickens, Lydia. The Little Donkey Nico / el Burrito Nico. 2012. 32p. pap. 19.99 *(978-1-4772-7026-4(4))* AuthorHouse.

Dorling Kindersley Publishing Staff. Baby Animal Friends. 2016. (ENG., Illus.). 14p. (J). (— 1). bds. 5.99 *(978-1-4654-5072-2(6)*, DK Children) Dorling Kindersley Publishing, Inc.

—Baby Animals. (My First Bks.). (ENG.). (J). 2017. 36p. (— 1). bds. 5.99 *(978-1-4654-5678-6(3))* 2013. 14p. (gr. -1 — 1). bds. 7.99 *(978-1-4654-1427-4(4))* 2011. 12p. (gr. -1-k). bds. 6.99 *(978-0-7566-8991-9(0))* 2009. 14p. (gr. -1 — 1). bds. 5.99 *(978-0-7566-4301-0(5))* Dorling Kindersley Publishing, Inc. (DK Children).

—Fluffy Animals. 2012. (Baby Touch & Feel Ser.). (ENG.). 14p. (J). (gr. -1 — 1). bds. 5.99 *(978-0-7566-9786-0(7)*, DK Children) Dorling Kindersley Publishing, Inc.

—Follow the Trail: Baby Animals. 2016. (Follow the Trail Ser.). (ENG., Illus.). 14p. (J). (-k). bds. 9.99 *(978-1-4654-4514-8(5)*, DK Children) Dorling Kindersley Publishing, Inc.

—Follow the Trail: Baby Dinosaurs. 2017. (Follow the Trail Ser.). (ENG., Illus.). 14p. (J). (— 1). bds. 9.99 *(978-1-4654-5669-4(4)*, DK Children) Dorling Kindersley Publishing, Inc.

—My First Animals. 2015. (My First Bks.). (ENG.). 36p. (J). (gr. -1 — 1). bds. 5.99 *(978-1-4654-2901-8(8)*, DK Children) Dorling Kindersley Publishing, Inc.

—Playtime Peekaboo! 2005. (ENG., Illus.). 12p. (J). (gr. -1-k). bds. 6.99 *(978-0-7566-1144-6(X)*, DK Children) Dorling Kindersley Publishing, Inc.

—Really Feely: Baby Animals. 2017. (ENG., Illus.). 12p. (J). (— 1). bds. 6.99 *(978-1-4654-5697-7(X)*, DK Children) Dorling Kindersley Publishing, Inc.

—Squeaky Baby Bath: Baby Animals: Baby Animals. 2014. (ENG.). 14p. (J). (gr. -1 — 1). 6.99 *(978-1-4654-2461-7(X)*, DK Children) Dorling Kindersley Publishing, Inc.

—Ultimate Sticker Book: Baby Animals. 2016. (ENG.). 32p. (J). (gr. k-4). pap. 6.99 *(978-1-4654-4717-3(2)*, DK Children) Dorling Kindersley Publishing, Inc.

—Who Am I? Baby Animals. 2012. (ENG.). 28p. (J). (gr. -1 — 1). bds. 6.99 *(978-0-7566-9018-2(8)*, DK Children) Dorling Kindersley Publishing, Inc.

Doudna, Kelly. It's a Baby African Elephant!, 1 vol. 2009. (Baby African Animals Ser.). (ENG., Illus.). 24p. (J). (gr. k-3). lib. bdg. 24.21 *(978-1-60453-149-7(5)*, SandCastle) ABDO Publishing Co.

—It's a Baby Baboon!, 1 vol. 2009. (Baby African Animals Ser.). (ENG., Illus.). 24p. (J). (gr. k-3). lib. bdg. 24.21 *(978-1-60453-150-3(9)*, SandCastle) ABDO Publishing Co.

—It's a Baby Beaver!, 1 vol. 2008. (Baby Mammals Ser.). (ENG., Illus.). 24p. (J). (gr. k-3). lib. bdg. 24.21 *(978-1-60453-022-3(7))* ABDO Publishing Co.

—It's a Baby Giraffe!, 1 vol. 2009. (Baby African Animals Ser.). (ENG., Illus.). 24p. (J). (gr. k-3). lib. bdg. 24.21 *(978-1-60453-154-1(1)*, SandCastle) ABDO Publishing Co.

—It's a Baby Gray Wolf!, 1 vol. 2008. (Baby Mammals Ser.). (ENG., Illus.). 24p. (J). (gr. k-3). lib. bdg. 24.21 *(978-1-60453-024-7(3))* ABDO Publishing Co.

—It's a Baby Hippopotamus!, 1 vol. 2009. (Baby African Animals Ser.). (ENG., Illus.). 24p. (J). (gr. k-3). lib. bdg. 24.21 *(978-1-60453-155-8(X)*, SandCastle) ABDO Publishing Co.

—It's a Baby Kangaroo!, 1 vol. 2010. (Baby Australian Animals Ser.). (ENG., Illus.). 24p. (J). (gr. k-3). lib. bdg. 24.21 *(978-1-60453-576-1(8)*, SandCastle) ABDO Publishing Co.

—It's a Baby Lion!, 1 vol. 2009. (Baby African Animals Ser.). (ENG., Illus.). 24p. (J). (gr. k-3). lib. bdg. 24.21 *(978-1-60453-156-5(8)*, SandCastle) ABDO Publishing Co.

—It's a Baby Lynx!, 1 vol. 2008. (Baby Mammals Ser.). (ENG., Illus.). 24p. (J). (gr. k-3). lib. bdg. 24.21 *(978-1-60453-025-4(1))* ABDO Publishing Co.

—It's a Baby Meerkat!, 1 vol. 2009. (Baby African Animals Ser.). (ENG., Illus.). 24p. (J). (gr. k-3). lib. bdg. 24.21 *(978-1-60453-157-2(6)*, SandCastle) ABDO Publishing Co.

—It's a Baby Moose!, 1 vol. 2008. (Baby Mammals Ser.). (ENG., Illus.). 24p. (J). (gr. k-3). lib. bdg. 24.21 *(978-1-60453-026-1(X))* ABDO Publishing Co.

—It's a Baby Mustang!, 1 vol. 2008. (Baby Mammals Ser.). (ENG., Illus.). 24p. (J). (gr. k-3). lib. bdg. 24.21 *(978-1-60453-027-8(8))* ABDO Publishing Co.

—It's a Baby Opossum!, 1 vol. 2008. (Baby Mammals Ser.). (ENG., Illus.). 24p. (J). (gr. k-3). lib. bdg. 24.21 *(978-1-60453-028-5(6))* ABDO Publishing Co.

—It's a Baby Prairie Dog!, 1 vol. 2008. (Baby Mammals Ser.). (ENG., Illus.). 24p. (J). (gr. k-3). lib. bdg. 24.21 *(978-1-60453-029-2(4))* ABDO Publishing Co.

—It's a Baby Raccoon!, 1 vol. 2008. (Baby Mammals Ser.). (ENG., Illus.). 24p. (J). (gr. k-3). lib. bdg. 24.21 *(978-1-60453-030-8(8))* ABDO Publishing Co.

—It's a Baby Red Fox!, 1 vol. 2008. (Baby Mammals Ser.). (ENG., Illus.). 24p. (J). (gr. k-3). lib. bdg. 24.21 *(978-1-60453-031-5(6))* ABDO Publishing Co.

—It's a Baby Rhinoceros!, 1 vol. 2009. (Baby African Animals Ser.). (ENG., Illus.). 24p. (J). (gr. k-3). lib. bdg. 24.21 *(978-1-60453-158-9(4)*, SandCastle) ABDO Publishing Co.

—It's a Baby Skunk!, 1 vol. 2008. (Baby Mammals Ser.). (ENG., Illus.). 24p. (J). (gr. k-3). lib. bdg. 24.21 *(978-1-60453-032-2(4))* ABDO Publishing Co.

—It's a Baby White-Tailed Deer!, 1 vol. 2008. (Baby Mammals Ser.). (ENG., Illus.). 24p. (J). (gr. k-3). lib. bdg. 24.21 *(978-1-60453-033-9(2))* ABDO Publishing Co.

—It's a Baby Wildebeest!, 1 vol. 2009. (Baby African Animals Ser.). (ENG., Illus.). 24p. (J). (gr. k-3). lib. bdg. 24.21 *(978-1-60453-159-6(2)*, SandCastle) ABDO Publishing Co.

—It's a Baby Zebra!, 1 vol. 2009. (Baby African Animals Ser.). (ENG., Illus.). 24p. (J). (gr. k-3). lib. bdg. 24.21 *(978-1-60453-160-2(6)*, SandCastle) ABDO Publishing Co.

Dowley, Tim. Bible Animals, 1 vol. 2016. (Activity Fun Ser.). (ENG.). 64p. (J). pap. 4.99 *(978-1-78128-256-4(0)*, Candle Bks.) Lion Hudson PLC GBR. Dist: Kregel Pubns.

Dromgoole, Glenn. What Puppies Teach Us: Life's Lessons Learned from Our Little Friends. 2003. (Illus.). 32p. tchr. ed. 12.95 *(978-1-57223-684-4(1)*, 6841) Willow Creek Pr., Inc.

Duopress Labs Staff. Hello, Baby Animals: A High-Contrast Book. 2016. (ENG., Illus.). 20p. (J). (— 1). bds. 7.95 *(978-1-938093-68-5(2))* Duo Pr. LLC.

Eason, Sarah. Drawing Baby Animals. 2013. (Learn to Draw Ser.). 32p. (J). (gr. 2-5). pap. 10.50 *(978-1-4339-9525-5(5))*; lib. bdg. 26.60 *(978-1-4339-9524-8(7))* Stevens, Gareth Publishing LLLP.

—Drawing Baby Animals. Santillan, Jorge, illus. 2013. (Learn to Draw Ser.). 32p. (J). (gr. 2-5). pap. 63.00 *(978-1-4339-9526-2(3))* Stevens, Gareth Publishing LLLP.

Easton, Marilyn. Big & Little. 2011. (Illus.). 62p. (J). pap. *(978-0-545-38782-8(5))* Scholastic, Inc.

Eggs & Baby Birds, 6 vols. (Sunshinetm Science Ser.). 24p. (gr. 1-2). 37.50 *(978-0-7802-1392-0(0))*; 41.95 *(978-0-7802-1391-3(2))* Wright Group/McGraw-Hill.

Elora, Grace. Foals. 2011. (Cute & Cuddly: Baby Animals Ser.). (Illus.). 24p. (gr. k-2). 69.20 *(978-1-4339-6150-2(4))* Stevens, Gareth Publishing LLLP.

—Piglets. 2011. (Cute & Cuddly: Baby Animals Ser.). (Illus.). 24p. (gr. k-2). 69.20 *(978-1-4339-6152-6(0))* Stevens, Gareth Publishing LLLP.

—Puppies. 2011. (Cute & Cuddly: Baby Animals Ser.). (Illus.). 24p. (gr. k-2). 69.20 *(978-1-4339-6153-3(9))* Stevens, Gareth Publishing LLLP.

Eszterhas, Suzi, photos by. Elephant. 2014. (Eye on the Wild Ser.). (ENG., Illus.). 32p. (J). (gr. -1-2). 15.99 *(978-1-84780-518-8(3)*, Frances Lincoln) Quarto Publishing Group UK GBR. Dist: Hachette Bk. Group.

Evans, Shira. Follow Me: Animal Parents & Babies. 2016. (ENG., Illus.). 48p. (J). (-k). pap. 4.99 *(978-1-4263-2347-8(6)*, National Geographic Children's Bks.) National Geographic Society.

Feely, Jenny. Looking after Baby Animals. 2004. (Illus.). (J). *(978-0-7608-7879-8(X))* Sundance/Newbridge Educational Publishing.

Feldman, Thea. Katya's Busy Morning. 2006. (Illus.). (J). *(978-0-696-23292-3(8))* Meredith Bks.

Figueras, Emmanuelle. My Encyclopedia of Baby Animals. 2016. (My Encyclopedia Ser.). (ENG., Illus.). 128p. (J). lib. bdg. 34.00 *(978-0-531-22471-7(6)*, Children's Pr.) Scholastic Library Publishing.

Fiol, Maria A., tr. Las Familias, 1 vol. 2010. (Bebes Por Dondequiera Ser.).Tr. of Families. (SPA., Illus.). 32p. (J). bds. 6.95 *(978-1-59572-224-9(6))* Star Bright Bks., Inc.

Florian, Douglas. Once I Was a Pollywog. Bakos, Barbara, illus. 2016. (Animals Play Ser.). (ENG.). 18p. (J). (gr. -1-1). bds. 6.99 *(978-1-4998-0141-5(6))* Little Bee Books Inc.

Frost, Helen. Wake Up! Lieder, Rick, illus. 2017. (ENG.). 32p. (J). (gr. -1-2). 15.99 *(978-0-7636-8149-4(0))* Candlewick Pr.

Fuge, Charles. Animal Babies Do the Strangest Things. 2016. (ENG., Illus.). 28p. (J). (gr. -1-k). 14.95 *(978-1-63322-120-8(2)*, Moondance) Quarto Publishing Group USA.

Fujikawa, Gyo. Baby Animals. Fujikawa, Gyo, illus. 2008. (ENG., Illus.). 24p. (J). (gr. -1-2). bds. 5.95 *(978-1-4027-5701-3(8))* Sterling Publishing Co., Inc.

Galbraith, Kathryn O. Where Is Baby?, 1 vol. Butler, John, illus. 2013. (ENG.). 32p. (J). (gr. -1-1). 16.95 *(978-1-56145-707-6(8))* Peachtree Pubs.

Galbraith, Kathryn Osebold. Traveling Babies. Dippold, Jane, illus. 2006. (Animal Babies Ser.). (ENG.). 32p. (J). (gr. -1-k). 16.95 *(978-1-55971-939-1(7))* Cooper Square Publishing Llc.

Gamble, Adam & Jasper, Mark. Good Night Baby Animals. Chan, Suwin, illus. 2016. (Good Night Our World Ser.). (ENG.). 20p. (J). (— 1). bds. 9.95 *(978-1-60219-499-1(8))* Good Night Bks.

Giogas, Valarie. In My Backyard. Zecca, Katherine, illus. 2007. (ENG.). 32p. (J). (gr. -1-3). pap. 8.95 *(978-1-934359-17-4(3))* Arbordale Publishing.

Gregoire, Maryellen. A Tiger Cub. 2012. (Wonder Readers Emergent Level Ser.). (ENG.). 8p. (gr. -1-1). pap. 35.94 *(978-1-4296-9198-7(0)*, Wonder Readers) Capstone Press of Coughlan Cos.

Grossman, Rena. Families, 1 vol. 2009. (Babies Everywhere Ser.). (ENG.). 32p. (J). (gr. -1). bds. 6.95 *(978-1-59572-176-1(2))* Star Bright Bks., Inc.

AB

Gunzi, Christiane. Fluffy Babies. 2006. (Feels Real Bks.). (ENG., Illus.). 10p. (J). (gr. -1). bds. 6.99 (978-0-7641-5948-0(8)) Barron's Educational Series, Inc.

Hall, Margaret. Ducks & Their Ducklings [Scholastic]. 2011. (Animal Offspring Ser.). 24p. pap. 0.50 (978-1-4296-6295-6(6), Pebble Plus) Capstone Press of Coughlan Cos.

—Tigers & Their Cubs. 2007. (Animal Offspring Ser.). (ENG.). 24p. (gr. k-1). pap. 41.70 (978-1-4296-0565-6(0), Pebble Plus) Capstone Press of Coughlan Cos.

Hamsa, Bobbie. Animal Babies. Dunnington, Tom, illus. 2011. (Rookie Ready to Learn Ser.). 40p. (J). (gr. -1-k). (ENG.). pap. 5.95 (978-0-531-26800-1(4)); lib. bdg. 23.00 (978-0-531-25640-4(5)) Scholastic Library Publishing. (Children's Pr.).

Harpster, Steve. Baby Animals. 2014. (Pencil, Paper, Draw!(r) Ser.). (ENG., Illus.). 64p. (J). (gr. k-3). pap. 6.95 (978-1-4549-1149-4(2)) Sterling Publishing Co., Inc.

Hegarty, Patricia. Noisy Baby Animals. 2016. (My First Ser.). (ENG.). 12p. (J). (gr. -1-k). bds. 12.99 (978-1-58925-231-8(4)) Tiger Tales.

Helman, Andrea. Northwest Animal Babies. Wolfe, Art, photos by. 2006. (ENG., Illus.). 32p. (J). (gr. -1-2). pap. 10.99 (978-1-57061-462-0(8), Little Bigfoot) Sasquatch Bks.

Heos, Bridget. What to Expect When You're Expecting Hatchlings: A Guide for Crocodilian Parents (and Curious Kids) Jorisch, Stéphane, illus. 2012. (Expecting Animal Babies Ser.). (ENG.). 32p. (gr. 2-5). lib. bdg. 25.26 (978-0-7613-5860-2(9)) Lerner Publishing Group.

Heritage House Group Staff, ed. More Baby Wild Animals, 1 vol. 2016. (Kids' Own Nature Book Ser.). (ENG., Illus.). 48p. (J). (gr. k-1). pap. 6.95 **(978-1-77203-138-6(0))** Heritage Hse. CAN. Dist: Orca Bk. Pubs. USA.

Heritage House, Inc. Staff, ed. Baby Barnyard Animals, 1 vol. 2016. (Kids' Own Nature Book Ser.). (ENG., Illus.). 48p. (J). (gr. k-1). pap. 6.95 **(978-1-77203-145-4(3))** Heritage Hse. CAN. Dist: Orca Bk. Pubs. USA.

Hewett, Joan. A Flamingo Chick Grows Up. Hewett, Richard, photos by. (Baby Animals Ser.). (Illus.). 32p. 2005. (gr. k-3). lib. bdg. 21.27 (978-1-57505-164-2(8)) 2003. (J). (gr. -1-2). pap. 6.95 (978-0-8225-0090-2(6), Lerner Pubns.) Lerner Publishing Group.

—A Kangaroo Joey Grows Up. Hewett, Richard, photos by. 2005. (Baby Animals Ser.). (Illus.). 32p. (J). (gr. k-3). lib. bdg. 21.27 (978-1-57505-165-9(6)) Lerner Publishing Group.

Hewett, Richard, illus. & photos by. A Giraffe Calf Grows Up. Hewett, Richard, photos by. Hewett, Joan, photos by. 2004. (Baby Animals Ser.). 32p. (J). (gr. -1-2). pap. 6.95 (978-1-57505-630-2(5)); (gr. k-3). lib. bdg. 21.27 (978-1-57505-197-0(4)) Lerner Publishing Group.

—A Koala Joey Grows Up. Hewett, Richard, photos by. Hewett, Joan, photos by. 2004. (Baby Animals Ser.). 32p. (J). (gr. k-3). lib. bdg. 21.27 (978-1-57505-198-7(2)) Lerner Publishing Group.

—A Monkey Baby Grows Up. Hewett, Richard, photos by. Hewett, Joan, photos by. 2004. (Baby Animals Ser.). 32p. (J). (gr. k-3). lib. bdg. 21.27 (978-1-57505-199-4(0)) Lerner Publishing Group.

—A Penguin Chick Grows Up. Hewett, Richard, photos by. Hewett, Joan, photos by. 2004. (Baby Animals Ser.). 32p. (J). (gr. k-3). lib. bdg. 21.27 (978-1-57505-200-7(8)) Lerner Publishing Group.

Hickman, Pamela. Animals & Their Young: How Animals Produce & Care for Their Babies. Stephens, Pat, illus. 2003. (Animal Behavior Ser.). (ENG.). 40p. (J). (gr. 2-6). 5.95 (978-1-55337-062-8(7)) Kids Can Pr., Ltd. CAN. Dist: Hachette Bk. Group.

Hieronymus, Carol Fegley. Blackie & Her Kittens: A True Story. 2011. 28p. pap. 13.99 (978-1-4567-4768-8(1)) AuthorHouse.

Hinkler Books, ed. Baby Animals. 2012. (Busy Blocks Ser.). 12p. (J). 5.99 (978-1-74308-888-3(4)) Hinkler Bks. Pty, Ltd. AUS. Dist: Ideals Pubns.

Hoffman, Pam. Sadie Dog. 2007. (Illus.). 40p. (J). per. 14.95 (978-0-9798230-0-8(5)) G.P. Hoffman Publishing.

Holmes, Thom & Holmes, Laurie. Baby Dinosaurs: Eggs, Nests, & Recent Discoveries. Skrepnick, Michael William, illus. 2003. (Dinosaur Library). 104p. (J). (gr. 6-12). lib. bdg. 26.60 (978-0-7660-2074-0(6)) Enslow Pubs., Inc.

Howell, Theresa, ed. Baby Animals of the Southwest. 2007. (ENG., Illus.). 24p. (J). (gr. -1 — 1). bds. 6.95 (978-0-87358-924-6(6)) Cooper Square Publishing Llc.

Husar, Lisa & Husar, Mike. Grand Canyon Babies. 2011. 26p. 8.95 (978-1-56037-507-4(8)) Farcountry Pr.

Innovative Kids Staff. Baby Animals. 2009. (ENG., Illus.). 20p. (J). (gr. -1-1). 6.99 (978-1-58476-809-8(6)) Innovative Kids.

James, Emily. Do Cows Have Kittens? A Question & Answer Book about Animal Babies. 2016. (Animals, Animals! Ser.). (ENG., Illus.). 32p. (gr. 1-2). lib. bdg. 27.32 (978-1-5157-2665-4(7), Aplus Bks.) Capstone Press of Coughlan Cos.

Jansen, Curt, et al. Badger & Her Babies. Date not set. (Wildlife Adventure Ser.: Vol. 2). (Orig.). (J). (gr. k-4). pap. (978-0-9614904-2-3(X)) Adventure Productions, Inc.

—Bobcat & Her Babies. Date not set. (Wildlife Adventure Ser.: Vol. 3). (Orig.). (J). (gr. k-4). pap. (978-0-9614904-3-0(8)) Adventure Productions, Inc.

Jenkins, Steve & Page, Robin. My First Day: What Animals Do on Day One. Jenkins, Steve, illus. 2013. (ENG., Illus.). 32p. (J). (gr. -1-3). 17.99 (978-0-547-73851-2(X)) Houghton Mifflin Harcourt Publishing Co.

Johnson, Jinny. Puppy. 2014. (My New Pet Ser.). 24p. (gr. k-3). lib. bdg. 28.50 (978-1-62588-027-7(8)) Black Rabbit Bks.

Judge, Lita. Born in the Wild: Baby Mammals & Their Parents. Judge, Lita, illus. 2014. (ENG., Illus.). 48p. (J). (gr. k-3). 18.99 (978-1-59643-925-2(4), 9781596439252) Roaring Brook Pr.

Kalman, Bobbie. Animal Mothers. 2011. (ENG.). 16p. (J). (978-0-7787-9555-1(1)); pap. (978-0-7787-9580-3(2)) Crabtree Publishing Co.

—Baby Animal Names. 2010. (ENG., Illus.). 16p. (J). (gr. k-2). (978-0-7787-9421-9(0)); pap. (978-0-7787-9465-3(2)) Crabtree Publishing Co.

—Baby Animal Names: Nombres de Animales Bebé. 2010. (SPA, ENG & MUL.). 16p. (J). pap. (978-0-7787-8266-7(2)); lib. bdg. (978-0-7787-8273-5(5)) Crabtree Publishing Co.

—Baby Animals in Cities. 2013. (ENG., Illus.). 24p. (J). (978-0-7787-1017-2(3)); pap. (978-0-7787-1029-5(7)) Crabtree Publishing Co.

—Baby Animals in Desert Habitats. 2011. (Habitats of Baby Animals Ser.). (ENG.). 24p. (J). (gr. k-3). (978-0-7787-7725-0(1)); pap. (978-0-7787-7738-0(3)) Crabtree Publishing Co.

—Baby Animals in Forest Habitats. 2011. (Habitats of Baby Animals Ser.). (ENG.). 24p. (J). (gr. k-3). (978-0-7787-7726-7(X)); pap. (978-0-7787-7739-7(1)) Crabtree Publishing Co.

—Baby Animals in Grassland Habitats. 2011. (Habitats of Baby Animals Ser.). (ENG.). 24p. (J). (gr. k-3). (978-0-7787-7727-4(8)); pap. (978-0-7787-7740-3(5)) Crabtree Publishing Co.

—Baby Animals in Land Habitats. 2011. (ENG.). 24p. (J). pap. (978-0-7787-7744-1(8)); (978-0-7787-7731-1(6)) Crabtree Publishing Co.

—Baby Animals in Mountain Habitats. 2011. (Habitats of Baby Animals Ser.). (ENG., Illus.). 24p. (J). (gr. k-3). (978-0-7787-7728-1(6)); pap. (978-0-7787-7741-0(3)) Crabtree Publishing Co.

—Baby Animals in Ocean Habitats. 2011. (Habitats of Baby Animals Ser.). (ENG.). 24p. (J). (gr. k-3). (978-0-7787-7729-8(4)); pap. (978-0-7787-7742-7(1)) Crabtree Publishing Co.

—Baby Animals in Rainforest Habitats. 2011. (ENG.). 24p. (J). pap. (978-0-7787-7745-8(6)) Crabtree Publishing Co.

—Baby Animals in Savanna Habitats. 2011. (ENG.). 24p. (J). pap. (978-0-7787-7746-5(4)); (978-0-7787-7733-5(2)) Crabtree Publishing Co.

—Baby Animals in Wetland Habitats. 2011. (Habitats of Baby Animals Ser.). (ENG.). 24p. (J). (gr. k-3). (978-0-7787-7730-4(8)); pap. (978-0-7787-7743-4(X)) Crabtree Publishing Co.

—Baby Animals on Islands. 2013. (ENG., Illus.). 24p. (J). (978-0-7787-1016-5(5)); pap. (978-0-7787-1027-1(0)) Crabtree Publishing Co.

—Baby Apes. 2008. (It's Fun to Learn about Baby Animals Ser.). (ENG., Illus.). 24p. (J). (gr. 3-7). pap. (978-0-7787-3967-8(8)) Crabtree Publishing Co.

—Baby Elephants. 2010. (ENG.). 24p. (J). (978-0-7787-3959-3(7)); pap. (978-0-7787-3978-4(3)) Crabtree Publishing Co.

—Baby Foxes. 2010. (ENG., Illus.). 24p. (J). (978-0-7787-3960-9(0)); pap. (978-0-7787-3979-1(1)) Crabtree Publishing Co.

—Baby Giraffes. 2010. (ENG., Illus.). 24p. (J). (978-0-7787-3961-6(9)); pap. (978-0-7787-3980-7(5)) Crabtree Publishing Co.

—Baby Raccoons. 2010. (ENG., Illus.). 24p. (J). (978-0-7787-3963-0(5)); pap. (978-0-7787-3982-1(1)) Crabtree Publishing Co.

—Endangered Baby Animals. 2012. (ENG., Illus.). 24p. (J). (978-0-7787-4076-6(5)); pap. (978-0-7787-4081-0(1)) Crabtree Publishing Co.

—How Do Baby Animals Learn? 2012. (ENG., Illus.). 24p. (J). (978-0-7787-4077-3(3)); pap. (978-0-7787-4082-7(X)) Crabtree Publishing Co.

—Nombres de Animales Bebé. 2010. (SPA.). 16p. (J). pap. (978-0-7787-8581-1(5)); lib. bdg. (978-0-7787-8555-2(6)) Crabtree Publishing Co.

—What Is Hatching? 2010. (My World Ser.). (ENG.). 16p. (J). (gr. k-3). (978-0-7787-9509-4(8)); pap. (978-0-7787-9534-6(9)) Crabtree Publishing Co.

Katirgis, Jane. Baby Backyard Animals. 2010. (All about Baby Animals Ser.). (Illus.). 24p. (J). pap. 7.95 (978-1-59845-158-0(8)); lib. bdg. 22.60 (978-0-7660-3795-3(9)) Enslow Pubs., Inc. (Enslow Elementary).

—Baby Farm Animals. 2010. (All about Baby Animals Ser.). (Illus.). 24p. (J). pap. 7.95 (978-1-59845-157-3(X)); lib. bdg. 22.60 (978-0-7660-3794-6(0)) Enslow Pubs., Inc. (Enslow Elementary).

—Baby Forest Animals. 2010. (All about Baby Animals Ser.). (Illus.). 24p. (J). pap. 7.95 (978-1-59845-161-0(8)); lib. bdg. 22.60 (978-0-7660-3798-4(3)) Enslow Pubs., Inc. (Enslow Elementary).

—Baby Grassland Animals. 2010. (All about Baby Animals Ser.). (Illus.). 24p. (J). pap. 7.95 (978-1-59845-156-6(1)); lib. bdg. 22.60 (978-0-7660-3793-9(2)) Enslow Pubs., Inc. (Enslow Elementary).

—Baby Snow Animals. 2010. (All about Baby Animals Ser.). (Illus.). 24p. (J). pap. 7.95 (978-1-59845-160-3(X)); lib. bdg. 22.60 (978-0-7660-3797-7(5)) Enslow Pubs., Inc. (Enslow Elementary).

—Baby Zoo Animals. 2010. (All about Baby Animals Ser.). (Illus.). 24p. (J). 22.60 (978-0-7660-3796-0(7)); pap. 7.95 (978-1-59845-159-7(6)) Enslow Pubs., Inc. (Enslow Elementary).

Kavanaugh, Missy & Gurman, Sarah, texts. Babies. 2009. (Illus.). (J). (978-1-4351-1778-5(6)) Barnes & Noble, Inc.

Keating, Brian. Amazing Animal Adventures Around the World. 2004. (Illus.). 48p. pap. (978-1-894856-12-6(0)) Fifth Hse. Pubs.

Keiser, Cody. Baby Animals. 2012. (InfoMax Readers Ser.). (ENG., Illus.). 16 pp.p. (J). (gr. k-1). pap. 7.00 (978-1-4488-8923-5(5), Rosen Classroom) Rosen Publishing Group, Inc., The.

Kimmelman, Leslie. The Three Bully Goats. Terry, Will, illus. 2012. (J). (978-1-61913-136-1(6)) Weigl Pubs., Inc.

Kingfisher Editors. Animal Babies in Rain Forests. 2007. (Animal Babies Ser.). (ENG., Illus.). 28p. (J). (gr. -1-k). bds. 6.99 (978-0-7534-6060-3(2), 9780753460603, Kingfisher) Roaring Brook Pr.

—Baby Animals - In the Sea. 2012. (Baby Animals Ser.). (ENG., Illus.). 14p. (J). (gr. -1-k). bds. 5.99 (978-0-7534-6689-6(9), 9780753466896, Kingfisher) Roaring Brook Pr.

—Baby Animals in the Forest. 2011. (Baby Animals Ser.). (ENG., Illus.). 14p. (J). (gr. -1-k). bds. 5.99 (978-0-7534-6566-0(3), 9780753465660, Kingfisher) Roaring Brook Pr.

—Baby Animals in the Jungle. 2011. (Baby Animals Ser.). (ENG., Illus.). 14p. (J). (gr. -1-k). bds. 5.99 (978-0-7534-6491-5(8), 9780753464915, Kingfisher) Roaring Brook Pr.

—In Grasslands. 2011. (Baby Animals Ser.). (ENG., Illus.). 14p. (J). (gr. -1-k). bds. 5.99 (978-0-7534-6492-2(6), 9780753464922, Kingfisher) Roaring Brook Pr.

Kingfisher Editors, ed. Animal Babies Around the House. 2005. (Animal Babies Ser.). (ENG., Illus.). 24p. (J). (gr. -1-k). bds. 6.99 (978-0-7534-5840-2(3), 9780753458402, Kingfisher) Roaring Brook Pr.

Kingfisher Publications, Inc. Staff, creator. Animal Babies in Ponds & Rivers. 2007. (Animal Babies Ser.). (ENG., Illus.). 24p. (J). (gr. -1-k). bds. 6.99 (978-0-7534-6059-7(9), 9780753460597, Kingfisher) Roaring Brook Pr.

—Animal Babies on Mountains. 2005. (Animal Babies Ser.). (ENG., Illus.). 24p. (J). (gr. -1-k). bds. 6.99 (978-0-7534-5839-6(X), 9780753458396, Kingfisher) Roaring Brook Pr.

Kingfisher Publications, Inc. Staff, ed. Animal Babies in Towns & Cities. 2005. (Animal Babies Ser.). (ENG., Illus.). 8p. (J). (gr. -1-k). bds. 6.99 (978-0-7534-5841-9(1), 9780753458419, Kingfisher) Roaring Brook Pr.

Krauskopf, Sharma. Moose Family Close Up. Holdsworth, Henry, photos by. 2007. (Illus.). 28p. per. (978-0-9543367-4-5(7)) Scottish Radiance Pubns.

Kunhardt, Katharine. Let's Count the Puppies. 2004. (Illus.). 32p. (J). (gr. -1-1). 13.89 (978-0-06-054337-2(X)) HarperCollins Pubs.

Kuskowski, Alex. Foals, 1 vol. 2013. (Baby Animals Set 1 Ser.). (ENG.). 24p. (J). (gr. k-3). lib. bdg. 24.21 (978-1-61783-837-8(3), SandCastle) ABDO Publishing Co.

Leaf, Christina. Baby Elephants. 2015. (Super Cute! Ser.). (ENG., Illus.). 24p. (J). (gr. k-3). lib. bdg. 25.95 (978-1-62617-169-5(6)) Bellwether Media.

—Baby Gorillas. 2015. (Super Cute! Ser.). (ENG., Illus.). 24p. (J). (gr. k-3). lib. bdg. 25.95 (978-1-62617-170-1(X), Blastoff! Readers) Bellwether Media.

—Baby Lions. 2014. (Super Cute! Ser.). (ENG., Illus.). 24p. (J). (gr. k-3). lib. bdg. 25.95 (978-1-60014-974-0(X), Blastoff! Readers) Bellwether Media.

—Baby Orangutans. 2015. (Super Cute! Ser.). (ENG., Illus.). 24p. (J). (gr. k-3). lib. bdg. 25.95 (978-1-62617-171-8(8), Blastoff! Readers) Bellwether Media.

—Baby Pigs. 2014. (Super Cute! Ser.). (ENG., Illus.). 24p. (J). (gr. k-3). lib. bdg. 25.95 (978-1-60014-975-7(8), Blastoff! Readers) Bellwether Media.

—Baby Sea Otters. 2014. (Super Cute! Ser.). (ENG., Illus.). 24p. (J). (gr. k-3). lib. bdg. 25.95 (978-1-60014-976-4(6), Blastoff! Readers) Bellwether Media.

—Baby Seals. 2014. (Super Cute! Ser.). (ENG., Illus.). 24p. (J). (gr. k-3). lib. bdg. 25.95 (978-1-60014-977-1(4), Blastoff! Readers) Bellwether Media.

—Baby Sheep. 2014. (Super Cute! Ser.). (ENG., Illus.). 24p. (J). (gr. k-3). lib. bdg. 25.95 (978-1-60014-978-8(2), Blastoff! Readers) Bellwether Media.

—Baby Tigers. 2015. (Super Cute! Ser.). (ENG., Illus.). 24p. (J). (gr. k-3). lib. bdg. 25.95 (978-1-62617-173-2(4), Blastoff! Readers) Bellwether Media.

Leeson, Tom and Pat, et al, photos by. Cascade Babies. 2013. (Illus.). 26p. (J). 8.95 (978-1-56037-330-8(X)) Farcountry Pr.

Little & Large Sticker Activity - Baby Animals. 2006. (J). 3.99 (978-1-933581-29-3(8)) Byeway Bks.

Little & Large Sticker Activity Baby Animals. 2008. 24p. pap. (978-1-84810-055-8(8)) Miles Kelly Publishing, Ltd.

little bee books, little bee. Animal Babies. Max & Sid, Max &, illus. 2015. (Tiny Touch Ser.). (ENG.). 12p. (J). (gr. -1 — 1). bds. 4.99 (978-1-4998-0058-6(4)) Little Bee Books Inc.

Litton, Jonathan. Baby Animals Sticker Activities. Isherwood, Matthew, illus. 2014. (My First Sticker Activity Book Ser.). (ENG.). 96p. (J). (gr. -1-3). pap. 9.99 (978-1-58925-302-5(7)) Tiger Tales.

Llewellyn, Claire. How Animals Grow. 2006. (I Know That, Growth & Change Set Ser.). (Illus.). 24p. (J). lib. bdg. 22.80 (978-1-59771-022-0(9)) Sea-To-Sea Pubns.

Lock, Deborah. Wild Baby Animals. 2016. (Illus.). 48p. (J). (978-1-5182-1132-4(1)) Dorling Kindersley Publishing, Inc.

Lomp, Stephan, illus. Indestructibles: Baby Animals. 2017. (Indestructibles Ser.). (ENG.). 12p. (J). pap. 5.95 (978-0-7611-9308-1(1)) Workman Publishing Co., Inc.

Love, Pamela. A Moose's Morning. Sochor, Lesia, illus. 2007. (ENG.). 32p. (J). (gr. -1-3). 15.95 (978-0-89272-733-9(0)) Down East Bks.

Lundgren, Julie K. Who Do I Look Like? A Book about Animal Babies. 2011. (ENG., Illus.). 24p. (gr. k-1). pap. 8.95 (978-1-61741-921-8(4)) Rourke Educational Media.

Machell, Dawn, illus. Super Sticker Activity: Baby Animals. 2016. (ENG.). 32p. (J). (gr. -1). 5.99 (978-1-62686-648-5(1), Silver Dolphin Bks.) Readerlink Distribution Services, LLC.

Mack, Dinah & van Gageldonk, Mack. Vicks, the Polar Bear Cub. 2013. (ENG.). 32p. (J). (gr. -1-k). 15.95 (978-1-60537-154-2(8)) Cobblestone Publishing Co.

MacKinnon, Catherine-Anne. Animals Baby Flashcards. MacKinnon, Catherine-Anne, illus. 2007. (Baby Flashcards Ser.). (Illus.). 16p. (J). (gr. -1-k). 9.99 (978-0-7945-1498-3(7), Usborne) EDC Publishing.

Magsamen, Sandra. I Love Hugs & Kisses. 2016. (Heart-Felt Bks.). (ENG.). 12p. (J). (gr. -1-k). 7.99 (978-0-545-92796-3(X), Cartwheel Bks.) Scholastic, Inc.

Main, Katy. Baby Animals of the North. 2015. (ENG., Illus.). 36p. (J). (gr. k-3). pap. 9.99 (978-1-941821-51-0(0), Alaska Northwest Bks.) Graphic Arts Ctr. Publishing Co.

Make Believe Ideas, creator. Lift Stick & Learn Baby Animals. 2006. (Lift Stick & Learn Ser.). (Illus.). 12p. (J). (gr. -1-k). pap. (978-1-84610-280-6(4)) Make Believe Ideas.

—Touch & Learn Baby Animals Casebound. 2007. per. (978-1-84610-508-1(0)) Make Believe Ideas.

Markle, Sandra. Snow School. Marks, Alan, illus. 2013. (ENG.). 32p. (J). (gr. -1-3). lib. bdg. 16.95 (978-1-58089-410-4(0)) Charlesbridge Publishing, Inc.

—Wolves. (Animal Predators Ser.). (ENG.). (gr. 3-6). 2005. 39p. pap. 7.95 (978-1-57505-748-4(4)) 2004. (Illus.). 40p. lib. bdg. 26.60 (978-1-57505-732-3(8)) Lerner Publishing Group.

Maze, Stephanie, ed. Tender Moments in the Wild: Animals & Their Babies. 2006. (Moments in the Wild Ser.). (Illus.). 36p. (J). (gr. -1-k). pap. 8.00 (978-0-9769542-0-0(6)) Moonstone Pr., LLC.

McCurry, Kristen. City Babies. 2007. (Animal Babies Ser.). (ENG., Illus.). 22p. (J). (gr. -1 — 1). bds. 5.95 (978-1-55971-981-0(8)) Cooper Square Publishing Llc.

Michaels, Chris. Animal Babies. 2010. (Sight Word Readers Ser.). (J). 3.49 (978-1-60719-628-0(X)) Newmark Learning LLC.

Michels, Dia L. If My Mom Were A Platypus- Hebrew Language Edition. Barthelmes, Andrew, illus. 2006. Orig. Title: #1488;#1501; #1488;#1502;#1497; #1492;#1497;#1514;#1492; #1508;#1500;#1496;#1497;#1508;#1493;#1505;. 64p. (J). 29.95 (978-0-9678020-9-1(1)) Science, Naturally!

—If My Mom Were a Platypus- Hebrew Language Edition. Barthelmes, Andrew, illus. 2006. Orig. Title: #1488;#1501; #1488;#1502;#1497; #1492;#1497;#1514;#1492; #1508;#1500;#1496;#1497;#1508;#1493;#1505;. (HEB.). 64p. (J). 19.95 (978-0-9678020-8-4(3)) Science, Naturally!

Miles, Ellen. Kitty Corner: Guide to Kittens. 2013. (Kitty Corner Ser.). lib. bdg. 16.00 (978-0-606-31502-9(0), Turtleback) Turtleback Bks.

Mills, Nathan & Morrison, Chloe. Animals & Their Babies. 2012. (Rosen Readers Ser.). (ENG., Illus.). 16p. (J). (gr. k-1). pap. 7.00 (978-1-4488-8704-0(6), Rosen Classroom) Rosen Publishing Group, Inc., The.

Mitchell, Melanie S. Ducks. 2005. (First Step Nonfiction Ser.). (Illus.). 24p. (gr. k-2). lib. bdg. 17.27 (978-0-8225-4602-3(7)) Lerner Publishing Group.

—Rabbits. (First Step Nonfiction Ser.). (Illus.). (gr. k-2). 2005. 24p. lib. bdg. 17.27 (978-0-8225-4604-7(3)) 2003. 23p. (J). pap. 5.95 (978-0-8225-4605-4(1), Lerner Pubns.) Lerner Publishing Group.

—Snakes. (First Step Nonfiction Ser.). (Illus.). (gr. k-2). 2005. 24p. lib. bdg. 17.27 (978-0-8225-4606-1(X)) 2003. 23p. (J). pap. 5.95 (978-0-8225-4607-8(8), Lerner Pubns.) Lerner Publishing Group.

Moldovo, Eustacia. Baby Elephants at the Zoo. 2015. (J). (978-0-7660-6613-7(4)) Enslow Pubs., Inc.

—Baby Giraffes at the Zoo. 2015. (All about Baby Zoo Animals Ser.). (ENG., Illus.). 24p. (J). (gr. -1-1). 22.60 (978-0-7660-7084-4(0)); pap. 9.35 (978-0-7660-7081-3(6)) Enslow Pubs., Inc.

—Baby Lions at the Zoo. 2015. (J). (978-0-7660-6609-0(6)) Enslow Pubs., Inc.

—Baby Monkeys at the Zoo. 2015. (J). (978-0-7660-6597-0(9)); (ENG., Illus.). 24p. (gr. -1-1). pap. 9.35 (978-0-7660-7073-8(5)) Enslow Pubs., Inc.

—Baby Pandas at the Zoo. 2015. (All about Baby Zoo Animals Ser.). (ENG., Illus.). 24p. (J). (gr. -1-1). 22.60 (978-0-7660-7079-0(4)) Enslow Pubs., Inc.

—Baby Zebras at the Zoo. 2015. (J). (978-0-7660-6617-5(7)) Enslow Pubs., Inc.

Murphy, Chuck. Animal Babies A to Z. 2007. (ENG.). 8p. (J). bds. 16.95 (978-1-58117-652-0(X), Intervisual/Piggy Toes) Bendon, Inc.

Murphy, Julie. Whose Baby Is This? 2012. (Nature Starts Ser.). (ENG.). 32p. (gr. 1-2). pap. 47.70 (978-1-4296-8298-5(1), Aplus Bks.) Capstone Press of Coughlan Cos.

Nagda, Ann Whitehead & Bickel, Cindy. Polar Bear Math: Learning about Fractions from Klondike & Snow. 2007. (ENG., Illus.). 32p. (J). (gr. -1-3). per. 8.99 (978-0-312-37749-6(5), 9780312377496) Square Fish.

National Geographic Kids. National Geographic Readers: Let's Play. 2017. (Readers Ser.). (ENG.). 96p. (J). (-k). lib. bdg. 17.90 (978-1-4263-2792-6(7), National Geographic Children's Bks.) National Geographic Society.

National Geographic Kids Staff. Baby Animal Pop! With 5 Incredible, Life-Size Fold-Outs. 2011. (ENG., Illus.). 20p. (J). (gr. -1-k). 14.95 (978-1-4263-0765-2(9), National Geographic Children's Bks.) National Geographic Society.

—Baby Animals. 2014. (Look & Learn Ser.). (ENG.). 24p. (J). (-k). bds. 6.99 (978-1-4263-1482-7(5), National Geographic Children's Bks.) National Geographic Society.

National Wildlife Federation Staff. My First Book of Baby Animals (National Wildlife Federation) 2014. (ENG., Illus.). 22p. (J). (— 1). bds. 6.95 (978-1-62354-028-9(3)) Charlesbridge Publishing, Inc.

Nault, Jennifer. Project Polar Bear. Kissock, Heather & Marshall, Diana, eds. 2003. (Zoo Life Ser.). (Illus.). 24p. (J). pap. 8.95 (978-1-59036-060-6(5)) Weigl Pubs., Inc.

Nelson, Robin. From Egg to Chicken. 2003. (Start to Finish Ser.). (ENG., Illus.). 24p. (gr. k-3). lib. bdg. 19.93 (978-0-8225-4662-7(0)) Lerner Publishing Group.

—From Foal to Horse. 2003. (Start to Finish Ser.). (ENG., Illus.). 24p. (gr. k-3). lib. bdg. 19.93 (978-0-8225-0941-7(5)) Lerner Publishing Group.

Nicholson, Sue. Animal Babies in Deserts. 2006. (Animal Babies Ser.). (ENG., Illus.). 10p. (J). (gr. -1-k). bds. 6.99 (978-0-7534-5942-3(6), 9780753459423, Kingfisher) Roaring Brook Pr.

Norma Staff, ed. Animales Bebe. 2005. 14p. (978-958-04-8067-9(2)) Norma S.A.

NorthWord Books for Young Readers Editors, contrib. by. Polar Babies. 2003. (Animal Babies Ser.). (ENG., Illus.). 22p. (J). (gr. -1 — 1). bds. 5.95 (978-1-55971-875-2(7)) Cooper Square Publishing Llc.

—Prairie Babies. 2003. (Animal Babies Ser.). (ENG., Illus.). 22p. (J). (gr. -1 — 1). bds. 6.95 (978-1-55971-873-8(0)) Cooper Square Publishing Llc.

Olson, Bethany. Baby Cats. 2013. (Super Cute! Ser.). (ENG., Illus.). 24p. (J). (gr. k-3). lib. bdg. 25.95 (978-1-60014-923-8(5), Blastoff! Readers) Bellwether Media.

—Baby Deer. 2013. (Super Cute! Ser.). (ENG., Illus.). 24p. (J). (gr. k-3). lib. bdg. 25.95 (978-1-60014-925-2(1), Blastoff! Readers) Bellwether Media.

—Baby Horses. 2013. (Super Cute! Ser.). (ENG., Illus.). 24p. (J). (gr. k-3). lib. bdg. 25.95 (978-1-60014-928-3(6), Blastoff! Readers) Bellwether Media.

—Baby Pandas. 2013. (Super Cute! Ser.). (ENG., Illus.). 24p. (J). (gr. k-3). lib. bdg. 25.95 (978-1-60014-930-6(8), Blastoff! Readers) Bellwether Media.

—Baby Rabbits. 2013. (Super Cute! Ser.). (ENG., Illus.). 24p. (J). (gr. k-3). lib. bdg. 25.95 (978-1-60014-932-0(4), Blastoff! Readers) Bellwether Media.

—Baby Wolves. 2013. (Super Cute! Ser.). (ENG., Illus.). 24p. (J). (gr. k-3). lib. bdg. 25.95 (978-1-60014-934-4(0), Blastoff! Readers) Bellwether Media.

Owen, Ruth. Arctic Fox Pups. 2011. (Wild Baby Animals Ser.). 24p. (J). (gr. k-3). lib. bdg. 19.96 (978-1-61772-156-4(5)); lib. bdg., E-Book 39.93 (978-1-61772-238-7(3)) Bearport Publishing Co., Inc.

—Lion Cubs. 2011. (Wild Baby Animals Ser.). 24p. (J). (gr. k-3). lib. bdg. 19.96 (978-1-61772-159-5(X)) Bearport Publishing Co., Inc.

—Raccoon Cubs. 2011. (Wild Baby Animals Ser.). 24p. (J). (gr. k-3). lib. bdg. 19.96 (978-1-61772-154-0(9)) Bearport Publishing Co., Inc.

—Wild Baby Animals, 8 vols., Set. Incl. Arctic Fox Pups. lib. bdg., E-Book 39.93 (978-1-61772-238-7(3)); Beaver Kits. lib. bdg., E-Book 39.93 (978-1-61772-239-4(1)); Lion Cubs. lib. bdg., E-Book 39.93 (978-1-61772-240-0(5)); Polar Bear Cubs. lib. bdg., E-Book 39.93 (978-1-61772-241-7(3)); Raccoon Cubs. lib. bdg., E-Book 39.93 (978-1-61772-242-4(1)); Skunk Kits. lib. bdg., E-Book 39.93 (978-1-61772-243-1(X)); Squirrel Kits. lib. bdg., E-Book 39.93 (978-1-61772-244-8(8)); Tiger Cubs. lib. bdg., E-Book 39.93 (978-1-61772-245-5(6)); 24p. (J). (gr. k-3). 2011. Set lib. bdg., E-Book 319.47 (978-1-61772-237-0(5)) Bearport Publishing Co., Inc.

Owings, Lisa. Meet a Baby Hippo. 2015. (ENG., Illus.). 32p. (J). (gr. k-2). 26.65 (978-1-4677-8115-2(0), Lerner Pubns.) Lerner Publishing Group.

—Meet a Baby Zebra. 2015. (ENG., Illus.). 32p. (J). (gr. k-2). 26.65 (978-1-4677-8114-5(2)) Lerner Publishing Group.

Packham, Chris. Amazing Animal Babies. Cockcroft, Jason, illus. 2017. (ENG.). 32p. (J). (gr. -1). 14.95 (978-1-4549-2337-4(7)) Sterling Publishing Co., Inc.

Page, Nick & Page, Claire. Funny Faces: Baby Animals. 2006. (Funny Faces Ser.). (Illus.). 10p. (gr. -1-k). per., bds. (978-1-84610-118-2(2)) Make Believe Ideas.

Parker, Steve. Baby Animals. Jackson, Ian, illus. 2010. (I Love Animals Ser.). (ENG.). 24p. (J). (gr. 1-5). pap. 8.15 (978-1-61533-231-1(6)); lib. bdg. 22.60 (978-1-61533-225-0(1)) Windmill Bks.

—Wild Animals. 2010. (Science Library). 40p. (J). (gr. 3-18). lib. bdg. 19.95 (978-1-4222-1556-2(3)) Mason Crest.

Patrick, Valerie. Safari Animal Babies. 2011. 44p. pap. 24.95 (978-1-4626-1364-9(0)) PublishAmerica, Inc.

Penner, Lucille Recht. Dinosaur Babies. Barrett, Peter, illus. 2015. 32p. pap. 5.00 (978-1-61003-602-3(6)) Center for the Collaborative Classroom.

Picthall, Chez. Baby Animals. 2015. (ENG., Illus.). 10p. (J). 7.99 (978-1-906572-07-5(0)) Award Pubns. Ltd. GBR. Dist: Parkwest Pubns., Inc.

Pingry, Patricia A. Baby Giraffe. 2003. (San Diego Zoo Animal Library: Vol. 4). (ENG., Illus.). 26p. (J). bds. 6.95 (978-0-8249-6529-7(9), Ideal Pubns.) Worthy Publishing.

—Baby Hippopotamus. Sharp, Chris, illus. 2004. 26p. (J). bds. 6.95 (978-0-8249-6554-9(X), Ideal Pubns.) Worthy Publishing.

—Baby Koala. 2003. (San Diego Zoo Animal Library: Vol. 3). (ENG., Illus.). 24p. (J). bds. 6.95 (978-0-8249-6528-0(0), Ideal Pubns.) Worthy Publishing.

—Baby Zebra. Sharp, Chris, illus. 2004. (San Diego Zoo Animal Library: Vol. 6). (ENG.). 26p. (J). bds. 6.95 (978-0-8249-6556-3(6), Ideal Pubns.) Worthy Publishing.

Pingry, Patricia A. & Sharp, Chris. Baby Chimpanzee. 2003. (San Diego Zoo Animal Library: Vol. 2). (ENG., Illus.). 24p. (J). bds. 6.95 (978-0-8249-6530-3(2), Ideal Pubns.) Worthy Publishing.

—Baby Tiger. 2003. (San Diego Zoo Animal Library). (ENG., Illus.). 24p. (J). bds. 6.95 (978-0-8249-6527-3(2), Ideal Pubns.) Worthy Publishing.

Pinnington, Andrea. Animal Babies. 2012. (Scholastic Discover More Ser.). (ENG.). 32p. (J). (gr. -1-3). 7.99 (978-0-545-36568-0(6), Scholastic Reference) Scholastic, Inc.

Pinnington, Andrea & Gordon-Harris, Tory. Animal Babies. 2012. (Illus.). 32p. (J). lib. bdg. (978-0-531-22950-7(5)) Scholastic, Inc.

Posada, Mia. Adivina Qué Está Creciendo Dentro de Este Huevo. Translations.com Staff, tr. from ENG. Posada, Mia, illus. 2008. (SPA., Illus.). 32p. (J). (gr. k-3). 16.95 (978-0-7613-3906-9(X)) Lerner Publishing Group.

—Guess What Is Growing Inside This Egg. Posada, Mia, illus. 2007. (ENG., Illus.). 32p. (J). (gr. k-3). 15.95 (978-0-8225-6192-7(1), Millbrook Pr.) Lerner Publishing Group.

Priddy, Roger. Baby Animals. 2006. (Bright Baby Touch & Feel Ser.). (ENG., Illus.). 10p. (J). (gr. -1 — 1). bds. 4.95 (978-0-312-49858-0(6), 9780312498580, Priddy Bks.) St. Martin's Pr.

—A Is for Animal. 2013. (ABC Bks.). (ENG.). 24p. (J). (gr. -1 — 1). bds. 12.99 (978-0-312-51637-6(1), 9780312516376, Priddy Bks.) St. Martin's Pr.

Publications International Ltd. Staff, ed. Baby Animals (Listen & Learn Sound Book) 2011. 19p. (J). bds. 11.98 (978-1-4508-1440-9(9)) Phoenix International Publications, Inc.

Rabe, Tish. Hello, My Baby (Dr. Seuss/Cat in the Hat) Mathieu, Joe & Ruiz, Aristides, illus. 2013. (Nifty Lift-And-Look Ser.). (ENG.). 12p. (J). (— 1). bds. 5.99 (978-0-449-81434-5(3), Random Hse. Bks. for Young Readers) Random Hse. Children's Bks.

Rappoport, Bernice. Baby Animals. Cassels, Jean, illus. 2004. (Treasure Tree Ser.). 32p. (J). (978-0-7166-1615-3(7)) World Bk., Inc.

Raymos, Rick. Born in the Wild: Baby Animals. 2014. (ENG.). 24p. (gr. k-3). 28.50 (978-1-62717-637-8(3)) Rourke Educational Media.

Reasoner, Charles. Ooink! 2009. (Lift & Learn Ser.). (Illus.). 10p. (J). (gr. -1-k). 10.99 (978-1-934650-12-7(9)) Just For Kids Pr., LLC.

Redford, Margorie & Rice, Courtney. God's Baby Animals. Marlin, Kathryn, illus. 2014. (Happy Day Ser.). (ENG.). 16p. (J). pap. 2.49 (978-1-4143-9418-3(7)) Tyndale Hse. Pubs.

Regan, Lisa. How to Draw Baby Animals. Roberts, Steve, illus. 2008. (How to Draw Ser.). 47p. (J). (gr. 4-7). (978-1-84810-066-4(3)) Miles Kelly Publishing, Ltd.

Reher, Matt. Blue Whale Babies. 2015. (2G Marine Life Ser.). (ENG., Illus.). 24p. (J). pap. 5.99 (978-1-63437-084-4(8)) American Reading Co.

Rennert, Violette. Little Lions. 2005. (Born to Be Wild Ser.). (Illus.). 24p. (gr. k-3). lib. bdg. 23.00 (978-0-8368-4737-6(7), Gareth Stevens Learning Library) Stevens, Gareth Publishing LLLP.

Rice, Dona. Raising Babies: What Animal Parents Do, 1 vol. rev. ed. 2014. (Science Readers: Content & Literacy Ser.). (ENG., Illus.). 24p. (gr. 1-1). pap. 22.96 (978-1-4938-1148-9(7)) Teacher Created Materials, Inc.

—What Animal Parents Do, 1 vol. rev. ed. 2014. (Science Readers: Content & Literacy Ser.). (ENG., Illus.). 24p. (gr. 1-1). pap. 8.99 (978-1-4807-4561-2(8)) Teacher Created Materials, Inc.

Rice, Dona Herweck. Animal Mothers & Babies, 1 vol. 2nd rev. ed. 2013. (Nonfiction Readers Ser.). (ENG., Illus.). 12p. (J). (gr. 1-1). pap. 15.96 (978-1-4807-1018-4(0)) Shell Educational Publishing.

—Animal Mothers & Babies, 1 vol. 2nd rev. ed. 2011. (Nonfiction Readers Ser.). (ENG.). 12p. (J). (gr. 1-1). pap. 4.99 (978-1-4333-3579-2(4)) Teacher Created Materials, Inc.

—Madres Animales y Sus Crías, 1 vol. 2nd rev. ed. 2011. (Nonfiction Readers Ser.). (SPA., Illus.). 12p. (J). (gr. 1-1). pap. 4.99 (978-1-4333-4418-3(1)) Teacher Created Materials, Inc.

Ring, Susan. Polar Bear Babies. McCue, Lisa, illus. 2016. (Step into Reading Ser.). (ENG.). 32p. (J). (gr. -1-1). 3.99 (978-0-399-54954-0(4), Random Hse. Bks. for Young Readers) Random Hse. Children's Bks.

—Project Elephant. Kissock, Heather & Marshall, Diana, eds. 2003. (Zoo Life Ser.). 24p. (J). pap. 8.95 (978-1-59036-056-9(7)) Weigl Pubs., Inc.

—Project Hippopotamus. Kissock, Heather & Marshall, Diana, eds. 2003. (Zoo Life Ser.). (Illus.). 24p. (J). pap. 8.95 (978-1-59036-057-6(5)) Weigl Pubs., Inc.

—Project Hippopotamus. 2003. (Zoo Babies Ser.). (Illus.). 24p. (J). (gr. 2-4). lib. bdg. 24.45 (978-1-59036-013-2(3)) Weigl Pubs., Inc.

—Project Orangutan. Marshall, Diana & Nault, Jennifer, eds. 2003. (Zoo Life Ser.). (Illus.). 24p. (J). pap. 8.95 (978-1-59036-058-3(3)) Weigl Pubs., Inc.

—Project Otter. Kissock, Heather & Marshall, Diana, eds. 2003. (Zoo Life Ser.). (Illus.). 24p. (J). pap. 8.95 (978-1-59036-059-0(1)) Weigl Pubs., Inc.

—Project Tiger. Marshall, Diana & Nault, Jennifer, eds. 2003. (Zoo Life Ser.). (Illus.). 24p. (J). pap. 8.95 (978-1-59036-061-3(3)) Weigl Pubs., Inc.

Rizzi, Kathleen. Are You My Baby?, 1 vol. 2012. (ENG., Illus.). 32p. (J). bds. 5.95 (978-1-59572-259-1(9)) Star Bright Bks., Inc.

—Are You My Baby? (Hmong/English), 1 vol. 2012. (HMN & ENG., Illus.). 24p. (J). 5.95 (978-1-59572-361-1(7)) Star Bright Bks., Inc.

—Are You My Baby? (Portuguese/English), 1 vol. 2012. (POR & ENG., Illus.). 24p. (J). 5.95 (978-1-59572-362-8(5)) Star Bright Bks., Inc.

—Are You My Baby? (Spanish/English), 1 vol. 2012. (SPA & ENG., Illus.). 32p. (J). bds. 5.95 (978-1-59572-348-2(X)) Star Bright Bks., Inc.

Royston, Angela. Rabbit. 2004. (J). lib. bdg. 27.10 (978-1-59389-160-2(1)) Chrysalis Education.

Rustad, Martha E. H. Baby Animals & Their Homes. 2017. (Baby Animals & Their Homes Ser.). (ENG.). 24p. (gr. k-1). 87.96 (978-1-5157-3849-7(3), Pebble Bks.) Capstone Press of Coughlan Cos.

—Baby Animals in Burrows. 2017. (Baby Animals & Their Homes Ser.). (ENG., Illus.). 24p. (gr. k-1). lib. bdg. 21.99 (978-1-5157-3831-2(0)) Capstone Press of Coughlan Cos.

—Baby Animals in Dens. 2017. (Baby Animals & Their Homes Ser.). (ENG., Illus.). 24p. (gr. k-1). lib. bdg. 21.99 (978-1-5157-3830-5(2)) Capstone Press of Coughlan Cos.

—Baby Animals in Nests. 2017. (Baby Animals & Their Homes Ser.). (ENG., Illus.). 24p. (gr. k-1). lib. bdg. 21.99 (978-1-5157-3832-9(9)) Capstone Press of Coughlan Cos.

—A Baby Polar Bear Story. 2011. (Baby Animals Ser.). (ENG.). 24p. (gr. k-1). pap. 41.70 (978-1-4296-7099-9(1), Pebble Plus) Capstone Press of Coughlan Cos.

—A Baby Sea Otter Story. 2011. (Baby Animals Ser.). (ENG.). 24p. (gr. k-1). pap. 41.70 (978-1-4296-7101-9(7), Pebble Plus) Capstone Press of Coughlan Cos.

—A Baby Seal Story. 2011. (Baby Animals Ser.). (ENG.). 24p. (gr. k-1). pap. 41.70 (978-1-4296-7102-6(5), Pebble Plus) Capstone Press of Coughlan Cos.

Rustad, Martha E. H. & Wittrock, Jeni. Animales Bebé. Strictly Spanish, LLC., tr. 2012. (Animales Bebé/Baby Animals Ser.).Tr. of Baby Animals. (MUL.). 24p. (gr. k-1). lib. bdg. 53.30 (978-1-4296-9223-6(5)) Capstone Press of Coughlan Cos.

Ruurs, Margriet. Wild Babies. Kiss, Andrew, illus. 2003. (ENG.). 32p. (J). (gr. -1-3). 14.95 (978-0-88776-627-5(7), Tundra Bks.) Tundra Bks. CAN. Dist: Penguin Random Hse. LLC.

SAMI Staff. Look, Baby! 2009. (ENG., Illus.). 20p. (J). (— 1). 9.95 (978-1-934706-26-8(4)) Blue Apple Bks.

Schindel, John. Busy Doggies. Sparks, Beverly, photos by. 2003. (Busy Book Ser.). (ENG., Illus.). 20p. (J). (— 1). bds. 6.99 (978-1-58246-090-1(6), Knopf Bks. for Young Readers) Random Hse. Children's Bks.

Schmidt, Dennis & Schmidt, Esther. Baby Wild Animals. 2007. (Illus.). 48p. pap. (978-1-55153-254-7(9)) Altitude Publishing Canada Ltd.

—Baby Wild Animals, 1 vol. 2nd ed. 2015. (ENG., Illus.). 48p. (J). (gr. -1-1). pap. 6.95 (978-1-77203-090-7(2)) Heritage Hse. CAN. Dist: Orca Bk. Pubs. USA.

Scholastic, Inc. Staff. Touch & Feel Baby Animals. 2015. (Scholastic Early Learners Ser.). (ENG.). 14p. (J). (— 1). bds. 6.99 (978-0-545-90319-6(X), Cartwheel Bks.) Scholastic, Inc.

Scholastic, Inc. Staff, contrib. by. Animal Babies. (Pictureback Ser.). (J). Random Hse. Children's Bks.

—Baby Animals. 2013. (Rookie Toddler(r) Ser.). (ENG.). 12p. (J). bds. 6.95 (978-0-531-21577-7(6), Children's Pr.) Scholastic Library Publishing.

—Baby Animals at the Zoo. 2013. (ENG.). 12p. (J). bds. 6.95 (978-0-531-27251-0(6)) Scholastic Library Publishing.

—Baby Animals on the Farm. 2013. (ENG.). 12p. (J). bds. 6.95 (978-0-531-27252-7(4)) Scholastic Library Publishing.

—Bedtime for Rainforest Babies. 2016. (Rookie Toddler(tm) Ser.). (ENG.). 12p. (J). bds. 6.95 (978-0-531-22697-1(2), Children's Pr.) Scholastic Library Publishing.

Schrier, Allyson Valentine. How Many Baby Animals? 2008. (Discovering & Exploring Science Ser.). (Illus.). 16p. (J). (gr. -1-3). lib. bdg. 12.95 (978-0-7569-8436-6(X)) Perfection Learning Corp.

Schuetz, Kari. Baby Bears. 2013. (Super Cute! Ser.). (ENG., Illus.). 24p. (J). (gr. k-3). lib. bdg. 25.95 (978-1-60014-922-1(7), Blastoff! Readers) Bellwether Media.

—Baby Cows. 2013. (Super Cute! Ser.). (ENG., Illus.). 24p. (J). (gr. k-3). lib. bdg. 25.95 (978-1-60014-924-5(3), Blastoff! Readers) Bellwether Media.

—Baby Dogs. (Illus.). 24p. (J). 2014. (978-0-531-22279-9(9)) 2013. (ENG., lib. bdg. 25.95 (978-1-60014-926-9(X), Blastoff! Readers) Bellwether Media.

—Baby Goats. 2013. (Super Cute! Ser.). (ENG., Illus.). 24p. (J). (gr. k-3). lib. bdg. 25.95 (978-1-60014-927-6(8), Blastoff! Readers) Bellwether Media.

—Baby Monkeys. 2013. (Super Cute! Ser.). (ENG., Illus.). 24p. (J). (gr. k-3). lib. bdg. 25.95 (978-1-60014-929-0(4), Blastoff! Readers) Bellwether Media.

—Baby Penguins. 2013. (Super Cute! Ser.). (ENG., Illus.). 24p. (J). (gr. k-3). lib. bdg. 25.95 (978-1-60014-931-3(6), Blastoff! Readers) Bellwether Media.

—Baby Sloths. 2013. (Super Cute! Ser.). (ENG., Illus.). 24p. (J). (gr. k-3). lib. bdg. 25.95 (978-1-60014-933-7(2), Blastoff! Readers) Bellwether Media.

Scott, Johnathan & Scott, Angela. Big Cat Babies. Scott, Jonathan, illus. 2005. (Collins Big Cat Ser.). (ENG.). 48p. (J). (gr. k-1). pap. 6.99 (978-0-00-718594-8(4)) HarperCollins Pubs. Ltd. GBR. Dist: Independent Pubs. Group.

Shattil, Wendy, et al, photos by. Sierra Babies. 2013. (Illus.). 26p. (J). 8.95 (978-1-56037-557-9(4)) Farcountry Pr.

Shields, Amy. National Geographic Readers: Saving Animal Babies. 2013. (Readers Ser.). (ENG., Illus.). 32p. (J). (gr. k-3). lib. bdg. 13.90 (978-1-4263-1041-6(2), National Geographic Children's Bks.) National Geographic Society.

—Saving Animal Babies. 2013. (Readers Ser.). (ENG., Illus.). 32p. (J). (gr. k-3). pap. 3.99 (978-1-4263-1040-9(4), National Geographic Children's Bks.) National Geographic Society.

Sidman, Joyce & Swan, Susan. Just Us Two: Poems about Dads. 2003. (Single Titles Ser.: Vol. 3). 32p. pap. 7.95 (978-0-7613-1833-0(X), Millbrook Pr.) Lerner Publishing Group.

Silver Dolphin Staff, ed. Peek-A-Boo Sliders: Baby Animals. Choux, Nathalie, illus. 2016. (Peek-A-Boo Sliders Ser.). (ENG.). 10p. (J). bds. 8.99 (978-1-62686-731-4(3), Silver Dolphin Bks.) Readerlink Distribution Services, LLC.

Siminovich, Lorena, illus. You Are My Baby: Pets. 2014. (ENG.). 10p. (J). (gr. -1 — 1). bds. 8.99 (978-1-4521-3430-7(8)) Chronicle Bks. LLC.

Sjonger, Rebecca & Kalman, Bobbie. Los Cachorros. Crabtree, Marc, photos by. 2006. (Cuidado de las Mascotas Ser.). (SPA., Illus.). 32p. (J). (gr. 3-7). pap. (978-0-7787-8477-7(0)) Crabtree Publishing Co.

—Puppies. 2003. (Pet Care Ser.). (ENG., Illus.). 32p. (J). lib. bdg. (978-0-7787-1751-5(8)) Crabtree Publishing Co.

Slade, Suzanne. The Great Divide, 1 vol. Hunter, Erin E., illus. 2012. (Basic Math Operations Ser.). (ENG.). 32p. (J). (gr. -1-4). 17.95 (978-1-60718-521-5(0)); pap. 9.95 (978-1-60718-530-7(X)) Arbordale Publishing.

Small World Creations. Baby Animals. 2016. (Crinkle Cloth Bks.). (ENG.). 8p. (J). (gr. -1 — 1). 9.99 (978-1-4380-7751-2(3)) Barron's Educational Series, Inc.

Smith, Alastair. Baby Animals. 2004. (Lift-the-Flap Learners Ser.). (SPA & ENG., Illus.). 1p. (J). (gr. 1-18). pap. 8.95 (978-0-7945-0133-4(8), Usborne) EDC Publishing.

—Baby Animals Lift-the-Flap. Butler, John, illus. 2005. 16p. (J). (gr. 1-18). 11.95 (978-0-7945-0966-8(5), Usborne) EDC Publishing.

Smith, Carrie. Baby Animals: Lap Book. 2009. (My First Reader's Theater Set B Ser.). (J). 28.00 (978-1-4108-8536-4(4)) Benchmark Education Co.

Soltaire, Delores. Baby Animals Are Born. 2016. (We Love Spring! Ser.). 00024p. (J). pap. 8.15 (978-1-4824-5468-0(8)) Stevens, Gareth Publishing LLLP.

Soundprints Staff. Elephant & Mommy. 2011. (Let's Go to the Zoo! Ser.). (ENG., Illus.). 16p. (gr. -1). 5.95 (978-1-60727-452-0(3)) Soundprints.

Stanek, Linda. Beco's Big Year: A Baby Elephant Turns One. 2010. 48p. (J). (gr. 3-7). pap. 8.95 (978-0-9841554-3-9(0)); lib. bdg. 18.95 (978-0-9841554-2-2(2)) Columbus Zoo & Aquarium, The.

Star Bright Books. Families (Portuguese/English), 1 vol. Icibaci, Neusa, tr. 2009. (Babies Everywhere Ser.). (ENG & POR., Illus.). 20p. (J). (gr. -1). 6.95 (978-1-59572-202-7(5)) Star Bright Bks., Inc.

—Families (Spanish/English), 1 vol. Fiol, Maria A., tr. 2009. (Babies Everywhere Ser.). (ENG & SPA., Illus.). 32p. (J). (gr. -1). bds. 6.95 (978-1-59572-201-0(7)) Star Bright Bks., Inc.

Star Bright Books, creator. Families (Vietnamese/English), 1 vol. 2010. (Babies Everywhere Ser.). (VIE & ENG., Illus.). 20p. (J). 6.95 (978-1-59572-215-7(7)) Star Bright Bks., Inc.

Sterling Children's Staff. My Mommy's the Bestest. 2016. (ENG., Illus.). 22p. (J). (— 1). bds. 6.95 (978-1-4549-1876-9(4)) Sterling Publishing Co., Inc.

Sterling Publishing Co., Inc. Baby Animals. 2012. (Say & Play Ser.). (ENG., Illus.). 28p. (J). (gr. k — 1). bds. 4.95 (978-1-4027-9890-0(3)) Sterling Publishing Co., Inc.

—Bebes Animales(Bebes Animales) 2013. (Say & Play Ser.). (ENG & SPA., Illus.). 28p. (J). (— 1). bds. 4.95 (978-1-4549-1037-4(2)) Sterling Publishing Co., Inc.

Stowe, Debbie. Baby Animals. 2009. (Illus.). 160p. (J). (978-1-4351-1819-5(7)) Metro Bks.

Stradling, Jan. Animal Babies: Level H, 6 vols. (First Explorers Ser.). 24p. (gr. 1-2). 29.95 (978-0-7699-1443-5(8)) Shortland Pubns. (U. S. A.) Inc.

Surry, Emma, illus. Animal Babies, 4 vols. 2015. (ENG.). 48p. (J). (gr. -1 — 1). bds. 14.99 (978-1-4380-7588-4(X)) Barron's Educational Series, Inc.

Taylor, Barbara. Slimy Spawn & Other Gruesome Life Cycles. 2014. (ENG., Illus.). 32p. (J). (978-0-7787-1402-6(0)) Crabtree Publishing Co.

Teora Staff. Baby Animals. 2007. 18p. pap. 5.95 (978-1-59496-427-5(0)) Teora USA LLC.

Tiger Tales, ed. & compiled by. Baby Animals. Tiger Tales, compiled by. 2014. (My First Lift & Learn Ser.). (ENG.). 10p. (J). (gr. -1 — 1). bds. 7.99 (978-1-58925-624-8(7)) Tiger Tales.

Tildes, Phyllis Limbacher. Baby Animals Day & Night. Tildes, Phyllis Limbacher, illus. 2016. (ENG., Illus.). 10p. (J). (— 1). bds. 6.95 (978-1-58089-609-2(X)) Charlesbridge Publishing, Inc.

—Baby Animals Spots & Stripes. Tildes, Phyllis Limbacher, illus. 2015. (ENG., Illus.). 10p. (J). (— 1). bds. 6.95 (978-1-58089-608-5(1)) Charlesbridge Publishing, Inc.

Tuxworth, Nicola. Baby Animals. 2015. (ENG., Illus.). 20p. (J). (gr. -1-12). bds. 6.99 (978-1-86147-357-8(5), Armadillo) Anness Publishing GBR. Dist: National Bk. Network.

Twine, Alice. Baby Animals, 6 vols., Set 2. 2008. (J). (gr. k-3). lib. bdg. 127.50 (978-1-4042-4243-2(0)) Rosen Publishing Group, Inc., The.

—Baby Animals/Bebe Animales, 6 vols., Set 1. 2008. (ENG & SPA.). (J). (gr. k-3). lib. bdg. 127.50 (978-1-4042-7650-5(5), Editorial Buenas Letras) Rosen Publishing Group, Inc., The.

—Baby Elephants. 2009. (Baby Animals Ser.). 24p. (gr. 1-1). 42.50 (978-1-61511-486-3(6), PowerKids Pr.) Rosen Publishing Group, Inc., The.

—Bears. 2009. (Baby Animals Ser.). 24p. (gr. 1-1). 42.50 (978-1-61511-487-0(4), PowerKids Pr.) Rosen Publishing Group, Inc., The.

—Bears/Osos. 2009. (Baby Animals/Animales bebé Ser.). (ENG & SPA.). 24p. (gr. 1-1). 42.50 (978-1-61511-498-6(X), Editorial Buenas Letras) Rosen Publishing Group, Inc., The.

—Bears/Osos. Obregon, Jose Maria, tr. 2007. (Baby Animals / Animales Bebé Ser.). (ENG & SPA., Illus.). 24p. (J). (gr. -1-3). lib. bdg. 22.60 (978-1-4042-7634-5(3), Editorial Buenas Letras) Rosen Publishing Group, Inc., The.

—Cats of the Wild/Gatos Salvajes. Obregon, Jose Maria, tr. 2007. (Baby Animals / Animales Bebé Ser.). (ENG & SPA., Illus.). 24p. (J). (gr. -1-3). lib. bdg. 22.60 (978-1-4042-7631-4(9), Editorial Buenas Letras) Rosen Publishing Group, Inc., The.

—Ducks/Patos. Obregon, Jose Maria, tr. 2007. (Baby Animals / Animales Bebé Ser.). (ENG & SPA., Illus.). 24p. (J). (gr. -1-3). lib. bdg. 22.60 (978-1-4042-7633-8(5), Editorial Buenas Letras) Rosen Publishing Group, Inc., The.

—Elephants/Elefantes Bebé. 2009. (Baby Animals/Animales bebé Ser.). (ENG & SPA.). 24p. (gr. 1-1). 42.50 (978-1-61511-501-3(3), Editorial Buenas Letras) Rosen Publishing Group, Inc., The.

—Horses/Caballos. 2009. (Baby Animals/Animales bebé Ser.). (SPA.). 24p. (gr. 1-1). 42.50 (978-1-61511-502-0(1), Editorial Buenas Letras) Rosen Publishing Group, Inc., The.

—Monkeys. 2007. (Baby Animals Ser.: Vol. 4). (Illus.). 24p. (J). (gr. -1-3). lib. bdg. 22.60 (978-1-4042-3775-9(5)) Rosen Publishing Group, Inc., The.

—Monkeys/Monos. Obregon, Jose Maria, tr. 2007. (Baby Animals / Animales Bebé Ser.). (ENG & SPA., Illus.). 24p. (J). (gr. -1-3). lib. bdg. 22.60 (978-1-4042-7635-2(1), Editorial Buenas Letras) Rosen Publishing Group, Inc., The.

—Seals. (Baby Animals Ser.). 24p. 2009. (gr. 1-1). 42.50 (978-1-61511-496-2(3), PowerKids Pr.) 2007. (Illus.). (J). (gr. 3-7). lib. bdg. 22.60 (978-1-4042-3773-5(9)) Rosen Publishing Group, Inc., The.

—Seals/Focas. 2009. (Baby Animals/Animales bebé Ser.). (ENG & SPA.). 24p. (gr. 1-1). 42.50 (978-1-61511-508-2(0), Editorial Buenas Letras) Rosen Publishing Group, Inc., The.

—Seals/Focas. Obregon, Jose Maria, tr. 2007. (Baby Animals / Animales Bebé Ser.). (ENG & SPA., Illus.). 24p. (J). (gr. -1-3). lib. bdg. 22.60 (978-1-4042-7632-1(7), Editorial Buenas Letras) Rosen Publishing Group, Inc., The.

Vanasse, Deb. Alaska Animal Babies. Jecan, Gavriel, photos by. 2005. (Paws IV Ser.). (ENG., Illus.). 32p. (J). (gr. -1-2). pap. 10.99 (978-1-57061-433-0(4), Little Bigfoot) Sasquatch Bks.

Veitch, Catherine. Animal Babies. 2013. (Animal Babies Ser.). (ENG.). 24p. (gr. -1-1). pap. 35.94 (978-1-4329-8422-9(5)); pap. 215.64 (978-1-4329-8429-8(2)); lib. bdg. 135.90 (978-1-4329-7497-8(1)) Heinemann-Raintree. (Acorn).

—Fish Babies, 1 vol. 2013. (Animal Babies Ser.). (ENG.). 24p. (gr. -1-1). 22.65 (978-1-4329-7493-0(9)); pap. 6.95 (978-1-4329-8418-2(7)); pap. 35.94 (978-1-4329-8425-0(X)) Heinemann-Raintree. (Acorn).

Vize, Dania. Lift, Stick & Learn Baby Animals. 2006. (Illus.). 24p. (J). (gr. -1-k). pap. (978-1-84610-032-1(1)) Make Believe Ideas.

Walker, Niki & Kalman, Bobbie. Kittens. 2014. 32p. pap. 9.00 (978-1-61003-354-1(X)) Center for the Collaborative Classroom.

—Kittens. 2003. (Pet Care Ser.). (ENG., Illus.). 32p. (J). pap. (978-0-7787-1782-9(8)) Crabtree Publishing Co.

Walker, Rob. Baby Animals. 2009. (Chunkie Hunkies Ser.). (ENG.). 18p. (J). (gr. -1). bds. 4.99 (978-0-7641-6212-1(8)) Barron's Educational Series, Inc.

Wallace, Karen. Bears in the Forest: Read & Wonder. Firth, Barbara, illus. 2009. (Read & Wonder Ser.). (ENG.). 32p. (J). (gr. -1-3). pap. 6.99 (978-0-7636-4522-9(2)) Candlewick Pr.

—DK Readers L2: Wild Baby Animals. 2016. (DK Readers Ser.). (ENG., Illus.). 48p. (J). (gr. k-2). 14.99 (978-1-4654-4598-8(6), DK Children) Dorling Kindersley Publishing, Inc.

Watt, Fiona. Animals. Wells, Rachel, illus. 2006. 10p. (J). (gr. -1-k). bds. 9.99 (978-0-7945-1227-9(5), Usborne) EDC Publishing.

Watts, Barrie. Mouse. 2004. (Illus.). 32p. (J). (gr. -1-17). lib. bdg. 24.25 (978-1-58340-231-3(4)) Black Rabbit Bks.

Wildlife Education, Ltd. Staff. Animal Babies 1. 2003. (Zoobooks Ser.). (Illus.). 24p. (J). (gr. k-6). reprint ed. 15.95 (978-1-932396-07-2(1)) Wildlife Education, Ltd.

Williams, Garth. Baby Animals. Williams, Garth, illus. 2004. (Little Golden Book Ser.). (ENG., Illus.). 24p. (J). (gr. -1-2). 4.99 (978-0-375-82933-8(4), Golden Bks.) Random Hse. Children's Bks.

—Baby Farm Animals. 2016. (Little Golden Board Book Ser.). (ENG., Illus.). 26p. (J). (gr. -1-k). bds. 7.99 (978-0-553-53632-4(X), Golden Bks.) Random Hse. Children's Bks.

Wilson, Hannah. Flip the Flaps: Baby Animals. Palin, Nicki, illus. 2012. (Flip the Flaps Ser.). (ENG.). 32p. (J). (gr. -1-1). 6.99 (978-0-7534-6849-4(2), 9780753468494, Kingfisher) Roaring Brook Pr.

Wittrock, Jeni. A Baby Rabbit Story. 2011. (Baby Animals Ser.). (ENG.). 24p. (gr. k-1). pap. 41.70 (978-1-4296-7100-2(9), Pebble Plus) Capstone Press of Coughlan Cos.

The Wonder of Baby Animals. 2013. (Illus.). 47p. (J). (978-1-61628-789-4(6)) Fog City Pr.

World Book, Inc Staff, contrib. by. Animal Babies. 2010. (J). (978-0-7166-7736-9(9)) World Bk., Inc.

Young, Mary. We Like to Nurse Too. Parker, Zac, illus. 2015. (ENG.). 32p. (J). (gr. -1). pap. 9.95 (978-1-890772-98-7(4)) Hohm Pr.

Young, Mary & Parker, Zac. Tambian a Nosotros Nos Gusta Amamantar: We Like to Nurse Too. 2009. (ENG & SPA.). 32p. (J). pap. 10.95 *(978-1-890772-99-4(2))* Hohm Pr.
Zuckerman, Andrew, photos by. Creature Baby Animals. 2014. (ENG., Illus.). 20p. (J). (gr. -1 — -1). bds. 7.99 *(978-1-4521-1721-8(7))* Chronicle Bks. LLC.

ANIMALS—INFANCY—FICTION

Adams, Diane. Love Is. Keane, Claire, illus. 2017. (ENG.). 32p. (J). 15.99 *(978-1-4521-3997-5(0))* Chronicle Bks. LLC.
Adams, Pam. Tiger. 2005. (ENG., Illus.). 12p. (J). (gr. -1-k). bds. *(978-1-904550-28-0(2))* Child's Play International Ltd.
Alderton, Sylvia. A Real Name for Puppy. McCartney, Michael David, illus. 2006. (J). *(978-1-930566-58-3(1)*, WestWind Pr.) Scott, D.& F. Publishing, Inc.
Allen, Jonathan. I'm Not Reading! 2013. (Baby Owl Ser.). (ENG., Illus.). 32p. (J). (gr. -1-k). 16.95 *(978-1-907967-44-3(3))* Boxer Bks., Ltd. GBR. Dist: Sterling Publishing Co., Inc.
Andreae, Giles. Love Is a Handful of Honey. Cabban, Vanessa, illus. 2004. 32p. (J). (gr. -1-k). 5.95 *(978-1-58925-353-7(1))*; tchr. ed. 15.95 *(978-1-58925-003-1(6))* Tiger Tales.
Appelt, Kathi. Mogie: The Heart of the House. Rosenthal, Marc, illus. 2014. (ENG.). 40p. (J). (gr. -1-3). 17.99 *(978-1-4424-8054-4(8)*, Atheneum Bks. for Young Readers) Simon & Schuster Children's Publishing.
Applegate, Katherine. Never Race a Runaway Pumpkin. Biggs, Brian, illus. 2009. (Roscoe Riley Rules Ser.: 7). (ENG.). 96p. (J). (gr. 1-5). 15.99 *(978-0-06-178372-2(2))*; pap. 4.99 *(978-0-06-178370-8(6))* HarperCollins Pubs.
—Never Race a Runaway Pumpkin. 2009. (Roscoe Riley Rules Ser.: 7). (J). lib. bdg. 14.75 *(978-0-606-06090-5(1)*, Turtleback) Turtleback Bks.
Arnold, Marsha Diane. Baby Animals Take a Bath. Tildes, Phyllis Limbacher, illus. 2017. (ENG.). 10p. (J). (— 1). bds. 6.99 *(978-1-58089-538-5(7))* Charlesbridge Publishing, Inc.
—Baby Animals Take a Nap. Tildes, Phyllis Limbacher, illus. 2017. (ENG.). 10p. (J). (— 1). bds. 6.99 *(978-1-58089-539-2(5))* Charlesbridge Publishing, Inc.
Arnosky, Jim. Babies in the Bayou. Arnosky, Jim, illus. 2010. (ENG., Illus.). 32p. (J). (gr. -1-k). pap. 6.99 *(978-0-14-241463-7(8)*, Puffin Books) Penguin Young Readers Group.
Austin, Heather. Boatyard Ducklings. Austin, Heather, illus. 2008. (ENG., Illus.). 32p. (J). (gr. -1-3). 15.95 *(978-0-89272-663-9(6))* Down East Bks.
Averbeck, Jim. Except If. Averbeck, Jim, illus. 2011. (ENG., Illus.). 40p. (J). (gr. -1-1). 12.99 *(978-1-4169-9544-9(7)*, Atheneum Bks. for Young Readers) Simon & Schuster Children's Publishing.
Baby Farm Animals Chunky Photo Book. 2006. (J). bds. 3.99 *(978-1-934004-00-5(6))* Byeway Bks.
Baby Pets: Chunky photo Book. 2006. (J). bds. 3.99 *(978-1-934004-01-2(4))* Byeway Bks.
Baglio, Ben M. Dalmatian in the Daisies. Baum, Ann & Lasher, Mary Ann, illus. 2007. 154p. (J). *(978-0-439-87120-4(4))* Scholastic, Inc.
Bajaj, Varsha. This Is Our Baby, Born Today. Wheeler, Eliza, illus. 2016. (ENG.). 32p. (J). (-k). 16.99 *(978-0-399-16684-6(X)*, Nancy Paulsen Books) Penguin Young Readers Group.
Barad, Alexis. Puppy Love. East, Jacqueline, illus. 2013. (J). *(978-0-545-47733-8(6))* Scholastic, Inc.
Bardhan-Quallen, Sudipta. Chicks Run Wild. Jenkins, Ward, illus. 2011. (ENG.). 32p. (J). (gr. -1-1). 15.99 *(978-1-4424-0673-5(9)*, Simon & Schuster Bks. For Young Readers) Simon & Schuster Bks. For Young Readers.
—Quackenstein Hatches a Family. Jones, Brian T., illus. 2010. (ENG.). 32p. (J). (gr. k-2). 15.95 *(978-0-8109-8973-3(5)*, Abrams Bks. for Young Readers) Abrams, Inc.
Barriman, Lydia. The Runaway Puppy: A Mystery with Probability. Grutzik, Becky, illus. 2010. (Manga Math Mysteries Ser.: 8). (ENG.). 48p. (gr. 3-5). 29.27 *(978-0-7613-4910-5(3))* Lerner Publishing Group.
—Thr Runaway Puppy: A Mystery with Probability. Grutzik, Becky, illus. 2011. (Manga Math Mysteries Ser.: 8). (ENG.). 46p. (gr. 3-5). pap. 6.95 *(978-0-7613-8137-2(6)*, Graphic Universe™) Lerner Publishing Group.
—#8 the Runaway Puppy: A Mystery with Probability. Grutzik, Becky, illus. 2011. (Manga Math Mysteries Set II Ser.). pap. 39.62 *(978-0-7613-8365-9(4)*, Graphic Universe™) Lerner Publishing Group.
Bateman, Teresa. The Christmas Pups. Kanzler, John, illus. 2012. (J). *(978-1-61913-112-5(9))* Weigl Pubs., Inc.
Bauer, Marion Dane. Little Cat's Luck. Bell, Jennifer A., illus. 2016. (ENG.). 224p. (J). (gr. 3-7). 17.99 *(978-1-4814-2488-2(2)*, Simon & Schuster Bks. For Young Readers) Simon & Schuster Bks. For Young Readers.
Bechtold, Lisze. Buster the Very Shy Dog Finds a Kitten. 2015. (Green Light Readers Level 3 Ser.). (ENG., Illus.). 32p. (J). (gr. 1-4). 12.99 *(978-0-544-33604-9(6))*; pap. 3.99 *(978-0-544-33605-6(4))* Houghton Mifflin Harcourt Publishing Co. (HMH Books For Young Readers).
Beckhorn, Susan Williams. Moose Eggs: Or, Why Moose Has Flat Antlers. Stevens, Helen, illus. 2007. (ENG.). 32p. (J). (gr. -1-3). 15.95 *(978-0-89272-689-9(X))* Down East Bks.
Bedford, David. Mole's Babies. Beardshaw, Rosalind, illus. 2012. (ENG.). 32p. (J). *(978-1-58925-108-3(3))*; pap. *(978-1-58925-435-0(X))* Tiger Tales.
Bentley, Sue. Picture Perfect #13. Swan, Angela & Farley, Andrew, illus. 2014. (Magic Kitten Ser.: 13). (ENG.). 128p. (J). (gr. 1-3). 4.99 *(978-0-448-46796-2(8)*, Grosset & Dunlap) Penguin Young Readers Group.
Berenstain, Jan & Berenstain, Mike. Kitten Rescue, 1 vol. 2011. (I Can Read! / Berenstain Bears / Good Deed Scouts / Living Lights Ser.). (ENG.). 32p. (J). (gr. -1-2). pap. 3.99 *(978-0-310-72097-3(4))* Zonderkidz.
Bergstein, Rita M. Your Own Big Bed. Hartung, Susan Kathleen, illus. 2008. (ENG.). 36p. (J). (gr. -1-k). 15.99 *(978-0-670-06079-5(8)*, Viking Books for Young Readers) Penguin Young Readers Group.
Berkes, Marianne. Over in Australia: Amazing Animals down Under, 1 vol. Dubin, Jill, illus. 2011. (ENG.). 32p. (J). (gr. -1-3). 16.95 *(978-1-58469-135-8(2))*; pap. 8.95 *(978-1-58469-136-5(0))* Dawn Pubns.
—Over in the Arctic: Where the Cold Winds Blow, 1 vol. Dubin, Jill, illus. 2008. (ENG.). 32p. (J). (gr. -1-2). 16.95 *(978-1-58469-109-9(3))*; pap. 8.95 *(978-1-58469-110-5(7))* Dawn Pubns.
—Over in the Forest: Come & Take a Peek, 1 vol. Dubin, Jill, illus. 2012. (ENG.). 32p. (J). 16.95 *(978-1-58469-162-4(X))*; pap. 8.95 *(978-1-58469-163-1(8))* Dawn Pubns.
—Over on a Mountain: Somewhere in the World, 1 vol. Dubin, Jill, illus. 2015. (ENG.). 32p. (J). (gr. -1-3). 16.95 *(978-1-58469-518-9(8))* Dawn Pubns.
Berkes, Marianne Collins. Over on the Farm. Morrison, Cathy, illus. 2016. (ENG.). 32p. (J). (gr. -1-2). 16.95 *(978-1-58469-548-6(X))* Dawn Pubns.
Birney, Betty G. Humphrey's Playful Puppy Problem. Burris, Priscilla, illus. 2014. (Humphrey's Tiny Tales Ser.: 2). (ENG.). 96p. (J). (gr. k-3). pap. 4.99 *(978-0-14-751484-4(3)*, Puffin Books) Penguin Young Readers Group.
Blackstone, Stella. Alligator Alphabet. Bauer, Stephanie, illus. 2007. (ENG.). 32p. (J). (gr. -1-k). 8.99 *(978-1-84686-073-7(3))* Barefoot Bks., Inc.
—Who Are You, Baby Kangaroo? Beaton, Clare, illus. 2004. 32p. (J). 14.99 *(978-1-84148-217-0(X))* Barefoot Bks., Inc.
—Who Are You Baby Kangaroo? Beaton, Clare, illus. 2011. (ENG.). 32p. (J). (gr. -1-2). pap. 6.99 *(978-1-84686-190-1(X))* Barefoot Bks., Inc.
Blair, Karen. Baby Animal Farm. Blair, Karen, illus. 2014. (ENG., Illus.). 16p. (J). (— 1). bds. 6.99 *(978-0-7636-7069-6(3))* Candlewick Pr.
Blomgren, Jennifer. Where Do I Sleep? A Pacific Northwest Lullaby. Gabriel, Andrea, illus. 2008. (ENG.). 20p. (J). (gr. k-k). pap. 10.99 *(978-1-57061-593-1(4)*, Little Bigfoot) Sasquatch Bks.
Boelts, Maribeth. Pupunzel. 2016. (Step into Reading Ser.). (ENG., Illus.). 48p. (J). (gr. k-3). lib. bdg. 12.99 *(978-1-101-93447-0(6)*, Random Hse. Bks. for Young Readers) Random Hse. Children's Bks.
—Sleeping Bootsie. Cantor, Patricia, illus. 2011. (Step into Reading Ser.). (ENG.). 48p. (J). (gr. k-3). pap. 3.99 *(978-0-375-86678-4(7)*, Random Hse. Bks. for Young Readers) Random Hse. Children's Bks.
Bonnell, Kris. Mother Animals. 2007. (J). pap. 5.95 *(978-1-933727-49-3(7))* Reading Reading Bks., LLC.
Bonnet, Rosalinde. Daddy Honk Honk! Bonnet, Rosalinde, illus. 2017. (ENG., Illus.). 32p. (J). (-k). 16.99 *(978-0-399-18676-9(X)*, Dial Bks) Penguin Young Readers Group.
A Book of Babies. (ENG.). 24p. (J). (— 1). 2015. bds. 6.99 *(978-0-553-50779-9(6))* 2014. 15.99 *(978-0-385-75290-9(3))* Random Hse. Children's Bks. (Knopf Bks. for Young Readers).
Bourguignon, Laurence. Heart in the Pocket. D'heur, Valérie, illus. 2008. 26p. (J). (gr. -1-3). 16.50 *(978-0-8028-5343-1(9))* Eerdmans, William B. Publishing Co.
Bowman, Crystal. Thank You, God, for This Day. Fletcher, Rusty, illus. 2014. (Happy Day Ser.). (ENG.). 16p. (J). pap. 2.49 *(978-1-4143-9486-2(1))* Tyndale Hse. Pubs.
Bramsen, Carin. Hey, Duck! 2013. (ENG., Illus.). 40p. (J). (gr. -1-2). 17.99 *(978-0-375-86990-7(5)*, Random Hse. Bks. for Young Readers) Random Hse. Children's Bks.
Brett, Jan. Annie & the Wild Animals. 2012. (ENG., Illus.). 32p. (J). (gr. -1-3). audio compact disk 10.99 *(978-0-547-85082-5(4))* Houghton Mifflin Harcourt Publishing Co.
—Annie & the Wild Animals. Brett, Jan, illus. 2012. (ENG., Illus.). 32p. (J). (gr. -1-k). 17.99 *(978-0-399-16104-9(X)*, G.P. Putnam's Sons Books for Young Readers) Penguin Young Readers Group.
—Annie & the Wild Animals Send-A-Story. 2011. (Send a Story Ser.). (ENG., Illus.). 32p. (J). (gr. -1-3). pap. 4.99 *(978-0-547-56692-4(1))* Houghton Mifflin Harcourt Publishing Co.
Brown, Jo. Hoppity Skip Little Chick. 2005. (Illus.). 32p. (J). 15.95 *(978-1-58925-045-1(1))* Tiger Tales.
Brown, Ruby. Cuddles for Mommy. Macnaughton, Tina, illus. 2016. (ENG.). 32p. (J). (gr. -1-3). 16.99 *(978-1-4998-0203-0(X))* Little Bee Books Inc.
Brown, Ruth. Gracie, the Lighthouse Cat. Brown, Ruth, illus. 2011. (Andersen Press Picture Bks). (ENG., Illus.). 32p. (J). (gr. -1-3). 16.95 *(978-0-7613-7454-1(X))* Lerner Publishing Group.
Browne, Anthony. Little Beauty. Browne, Anthony, illus. 2010. (ENG., Illus.). 32p. (J). (gr. -1-2). pap. 6.99 *(978-0-7636-4967-8(8))* Candlewick Pr.
—Little Beauty. 2010. lib. bdg. 17.20 *(978-0-606-14714-9(4)*, Turtleback) Turtleback Bks.
Bunting, Eve. The Baby Shower. Love, Judy, illus. 2007. (ENG.). 28p. (J). (gr. -1-2). 15.95 *(978-1-58089-139-4(X))* Charlesbridge Publishing, Inc.
Butler, John. Bedtime in the Jungle. Butler, John, illus. 2009. (Illus.). 32p. (J). (gr. -1-1). 16.95 *(978-1-56145-486-0(9))* Peachtree Pubs.
—Hush, Little Ones. Butler, John, illus. 2003. (Illus.). 24p. (J). (gr. k-k). bds. 6.95 *(978-1-56145-297-2(1))* Peachtree Pubs.
Buzzeo, Toni. My Bibi Always Remembers. Wohnoutka, Mike, illus. 2014. (ENG.). 32p. (J). (gr. -1-k). 16.99 *(978-1-4231-8385-3(1))* Hyperion Bks. for Children.
—Stay Close to Mama. Wohnoutka, Mike, illus. 2012. (ENG.). 32p. (J). (gr. -1-k). 15.99 *(978-1-4231-3482-4(6))* Hyperion Pr.
Campbell, Rod. Baby's Fluffy Friends. 2003. (ENG., Illus.). 12p. (J). bds. 8.99 *(978-0-333-74126-9(9))* Macmillan Pubs., Ltd. GBR. Dist: Trafalgar Square Publishing.
Caniac, Nina. Baby Pets Play! Caniac, Nina, illus. 2012. (ENG., Illus.). 10p. (J). (gr. -1). 12.95 *(978-2-7338-2153-4(9))* Auzou, Philippe Editions FRA. Dist: Consortium Bk. Sales & Distribution.
Capucilli, Alyssa Satin. Biscuit & the Little Pup. Schories, Pat, illus. 2007. (My First I Can Read Ser.). (ENG.). 32p. (J). (gr. -1 — 1). 16.99 *(978-0-06-074170-9(8))* HarperCollins Pubs.
—Biscuit Feeds the Pets. Schories, Pat, illus. 2016. (My First I Can Read Ser.). 32p. (J). (gr. -1-3). pap. 3.99 *(978-0-06-223696-8(2))* HarperCollins Pubs.
—Biscuit Goes Camping. Schories, Pat, illus. 2015. (My First I Can Read Ser.). (ENG.). 32p. (J). (gr. -1-3). pap. 3.99 *(978-0-06-223693-7(8))* HarperCollins Pubs.
—Biscuit in the Garden. 2013. (Biscuit: My First I Can Read! Ser.). (J). lib. bdg. 13.55 *(978-0-606-27157-8(0)*, Turtleback) Turtleback Bks.
—Biscuit Meets the Class Pet. Schories, Pat, illus. 2009. (My First I Can Read Ser.). (ENG.). 32p. (J). (gr. -1-3). 16.99 *(978-0-06-117747-7(4))*; pap. 3.99 *(978-0-06-117749-1(0))* HarperCollins Pubs.
—Biscuit Meets the Class Pet. 2009. (Biscuit: My First I Can Read! Ser.). (J). lib. bdg. 13.55 *(978-0-606-06960-1(7)*, Turtleback) Turtleback Bks.
—Biscuit's 123. Schories, Pat & Berlin, Rose Mary, illus. 2012. (Biscuit Ser.). (ENG.). 16p. (J). (gr. -1-1). pap. 6.99 *(978-0-06-162523-7(X)*, HarperFestival) HarperCollins Pubs.
Carrick, Carol. Mothers Are Like That. Carrick, Paul, illus. 2007. (ENG.). 32p. (J). (gr. k — 1). 5.95 *(978-0-618-75241-6(2))* Houghton Mifflin Harcourt Publishing Co.
Casteel, Seth. Puppy Pool Party! An Underwater Dogs Adventure. 2016. (ENG., Illus.). 40p. (J). (gr. -1-3). 16.99 *(978-0-316-37633-4(7))* Little Brown & Co.
Catalanotto, Peter. Kitten Red, Yellow, Blue. Catalanotto, Peter, illus. 2005. (ENG., Illus.). 32p. (J). (gr. -1-k). 18.99 *(978-0-689-86562-6(7)*, Atheneum/Richard Jackson Bks.) Simon & Schuster Children's Publishing.
Chaconas, Dori. Looking for Easter. Moore, Margie, illus. 2012. (J). 34.28 *(978-1-61913-120-0(X))* Weigl Pubs., Inc.
Chall, Marsha Wilson. One Pup's Up. Cole, Henry, illus. 2010. (ENG.). 32p. (J). (gr. -1 — 1). 16.99 *(978-1-4169-7960-9(3)*, McElderry, Margaret K. Bks.) McElderry, Margaret K. Bks.
Chapman, Linda. Twilight Magic. Kronheimer, Ann, illus. 2008. 149p. (J). pap. *(978-0-545-03160-8(5))* Scholastic, Inc.
Children's Press, contrib. by. The Three Little Kittens Get Dressed. 2009. (Rookie Preschool-NEW Ser.). (ENG.). 24p. (J). pap. 6.95 *(978-0-531-24579-8(9)*, Children's Pr.) Scholastic Library Publishing.
Chin, Oliver. The Year of the Tiger: Tales from the Chinese Zodiac. Roth, Justin, illus. 2010. (Tales from the Chinese Zodiac Ser.). (ENG.). 36p. (J). (gr. -1-3). 15.95 *(978-1-59702-020-6(6))* Immedium.
Christian, Cheryl. Where's the Kitten? (Haitian Creole/English), 1 vol. Dwight, Laura, photos by. 2005. (Photoflaps Ser.). (HAT & ENG., Illus.). 12p. (J). (gr. -1). 5.95 *(978-1-59572-028-3(6))* Star Bright Bks., Inc.
—Where's the Puppy? (Haitian Creole/English), 1 vol. Dwight, Laura, photos by. 2005. (Photoflaps Ser.). (HAT & ENG., Illus.). 12p. (J). (gr. -1). 5.95 *(978-1-59572-029-0(4))* Star Bright Bks., Inc.
Chrustowski, Rick. My Little Fox. Chrustowski, Rick, illus. 2017. (ENG., Illus.). 40p. (J). (gr. -1-k). 17.99 ***(978-1-4814-6961-6(4)**, Beach Lane Bks.)* Beach Lane Bks.
Churchman, Jennifer & Churchman, John. Brave Little Finn. 2016. (Sweet Pea & Friends Ser.). (ENG., Illus.). 40p. (J). (gr. -1-3). 17.99 *(978-0-316-27359-6(7))* Little, Brown Bks. for Young Readers.
Clark, Leslie Ann. Peepsqueak! Clark, Leslie Ann, illus. 2012. (ENG., Illus.). 32p. (J). (gr. -1-k). 12.99 *(978-0-06-207801-8(1))* HarperCollins Pubs.
—Peepsqueak Wants a Friend! Clark, Leslie Ann, illus. 2013. (ENG., Illus.). 32p. (J). (gr. -1-3). 15.99 *(978-0-06-207804-9(6))* HarperCollins Pubs.
Cole, Henry. Trudy. Cole, Henry, illus. 2009. (ENG., Illus.). 32p. (J). (gr. -1-3). 17.99 *(978-0-06-154267-1(9)*, Greenwillow Bks.) HarperCollins Pubs.
Collicott, Sharleen. Mildred & Sam. Collicott, Sharleen, illus. (I Can Read Bks.). (Illus.). (J). 2008. 64p. (gr. -1-2). lib. bdg. 17.89 *(978-0-06-058115-2(8)*, Geringer, Laura Book) 2004. (ENG., 48p. (gr. k-3). pap. 3.99 *(978-0-06-000200-8(X))* 2003. 48p. (gr. -1-18). 15.99 *(978-0-06-026681-3(3))* HarperCollins Pubs.
Conrad, Liz, illus. Little Chick. 2009. (My Sparkling Springtime Friends Ser.). (ENG.). 10p. (J). bds. 3.95 *(978-1-58117-866-1(2)*, Intervisual/Piggy Toes) Bendon, Inc.
Coons, Susan Anderson. Lighthouse Mouse Meets Simon the Cat. Sanne, Don, illus. 2012. 52p. pap. 10.03 *(978-1-4669-1223-6(5))* Trafford Publishing.
Cordell, Ryan & Cordell, Evie. Two Girls Want a Puppy. Lam, Maple, illus. 2015. (ENG.). 32p. (J). (gr. -1-3). 17.99 *(978-0-06-229261-2(7))* HarperCollins Pubs.
Corgliano, K. L. Millie & Me Fourth Grade Field Day. 2012. 44p. pap. 13.99 *(978-0-615-56735-8(5))* K.L.Corgliano.
Costello, Emily. Realm of the Panther: A Story of South Florida's Forests. 2005. (Habitat Ser.). (ENG., Illus.). 32p. (J). (gr. 1-4). 19.95 *(978-1-56899-849-7(X))* Soundprints.
—Realm of the Panther: A Story of South Florida's Forests. Siegrist, Wes, illus. 2005. (Habitat Ser.). (ENG.). 32p. (J). (gr. 1-4). 15.95 *(978-1-56899-847-3(3))*; pap. 6.95 *(978-1-56899-848-0(1))* Soundprints.
Cote, Nancy, illus. Watch the Birdie! 2016. (ENG.). 32p. (J). (gr. -1-k). 16.99 *(978-1-63450-202-3(7)*, Sky Pony Pr.) Skyhorse Publishing Co., Inc.
Coven, Wanda. Heidi Heckelbeck & the Magic Puppy. Burris, Priscilla, illus. 2017. (Heidi Heckelbeck Ser.: 20). (ENG.). 128p. (J). (gr. k-4). pap. 5.99 ***(978-1-4814-9521-9(6)**, Little Simon)* Little Simon.
Cowell, Cressida. What Shall We Do with the Boo Hoo Baby? Godon, Ingrid, illus. 2004. (J). (ALB & ENG.). 25p. *(978-1-85269-790-7(3))*; 25p. *(978-1-85269-679-5(6))*; (VIE & ENG.). 25p. *(978-1-85269-276-6(6))*; 25p. *(978-1-85269-274-2(X))*; (TUR & ENG.). 25p. *(978-1-85269-273-5(1))*; (CZE & ENG.). 25p. *(978-1-85269-794-5(6))*; 25p. *(978-1-85269-795-2(4))*; (SER & ENG.). 25p. *(978-1-85269-862-1(4))*; (POR & ENG.). 25p. *(978-1-85269-254-4(5))*; 25p. *(978-1-85269-255-1(3))*; (ITA & ENG.). 25p. *(978-1-85269-256-8(1))*; (SOM & ENG.). 25p. *(978-1-85269-270-4(7))*; (ENG & SPA.). 25p. *(978-1-85269-271-1(5))*; 25p. *(978-1-85269-272-8(3))*; (GER & ENG.). 25p. *(978-1-85269-799-0(7))*; (ENG & ARA.). 32p. pap. *(978-1-85269-791-4(1))*; (FRE & ENG.). 32p. pap. *(978-1-85269-796-9(2))*; (ENG & CHI.). 32p. pap. *(978-1-85269-793-8(8))*; (ENG & BEN.). 32p. pap. *(978-1-85269-792-1(X))*; (ENG & PAN.). 32p. pap. *(978-1-85269-258-2(8))*; (POL & ENG.). 32p. pap. *(978-1-85269-683-2(4))* Mantra Lingua.
Cowen-Fletcher, Jane. Hello, Puppy! Cowen-Fletcher, Jane, illus. 2010. (ENG., Illus.). 32p. (J). (gr. -1-k). 12.99 *(978-0-7636-4303-4(3))* Candlewick Pr.
Coxon, Michele. Kitten's Adventure (Portuguese/English), 1 vol. 2006. (POR, ABK, ACE & ENG., Illus.). 12p. (J). (gr. -1-k). pap. 6.00 *(978-1-59572-047-4(2))* Star Bright Bks., Inc.
—Kitten's Adventure (Spanish/English), 1 vol. Coxon, Michele, illus. 2006. (SPA., Illus.). 32p. (J). (gr. -1-k). pap. 5.95 *(978-1-59572-048-1(0))* Star Bright Bks., Inc.
Cronin, Doreen. Click, Clack, Peep! Lewin, Betsy, illus. 2015. (Click, Clack Book Ser.). (ENG.). 40p. (J). (gr. -1-3). 17.99 *(978-1-4814-2411-0(4))* Simon & Schuster Children's Publishing.
—Smick! Medina, Juana, illus. 2015. (ENG.). 34p. (J). (gr. -1-k). 16.99 *(978-0-670-78578-0(4)*, Viking Books for Young Readers) Penguin Young Readers Group.
Cyrus, Kurt. Shake a Leg, Egg! Cyrus, Kurt, illus. 2017. (ENG., Illus.). 32p. (J). (gr. -1-3). 17.99 *(978-1-4814-5848-1(5)*, Beach Lane Bks.) Beach Lane Bks.
Daddo, Andrew. Goodnight, Me. Quay, Emma, illus. 2007. (ENG.). 32p. (J). (gr. -1-k). 14.99 *(978-1-59990-153-4(6)*, 9781599901534, Bloomsbury USA Childrens) Bloomsbury Publishing USA.
Dahl, Michael. Nap Time for Kitty, 1 vol. Vidal, Oriol, illus. 2011. (Hello Genius Ser.). (ENG.). 20p. (gr. 1-2). bds. 7.99 *(978-1-4048-5216-7(6))* Picture Window Bks.
—Snack Time for Cow, 1 vol. Vidal, Oriol, illus. 2011. (Hello Genius Ser.). (ENG.). 20p. (gr. 1-2). bds. 7.99 *(978-1-4048-6496-2(2))* Picture Window Bks.
—Story Time for Lamb, 1 vol. Vidal, Oriol, illus. 2011. (Hello Genius Ser.). (ENG.). 20p. (gr. 1-2). bds. 7.99 *(978-1-4048-6495-5(4))* Picture Window Bks.
Dale, Jenny. Snowy the Surprise Puppy. Hellard, Susan, illus. 2005. 60p. (J). pap. *(978-0-439-79124-3(3))* Scholastic, Inc.
Dalmatian Press Staff. Mommy, Is That You? 2008. (ENG.). 5p. bds. 4.95 *(978-1-58117-714-5(3)*, Intervisual/Piggy Toes) Bendon, Inc.
Dannenbring, Cheryl. My Puppy Gave to Me, 1 vol. Kremsner, Cynthia, illus. 2014. (ENG.). 32p. (J). (gr. k-3). 16.99 *(978-1-4556-1943-6(4))* Pelican Publishing Co., Inc.
Davis, Dana A. Teala & Tony's Adventure to Baby Land. 2008. 16p. pap. 24.95 *(978-1-4241-4459-4(0))* America Star Bks.
Day, Alexandra. Carl & the Sick Puppy. 2012. (My Readers Ser.). (ENG., Illus.). 32p. (J). (gr. -1-1). 15.99 *(978-1-250-00152-8(9)*, 9781250001528); pap. 4.99 *(978-1-250-00153-5(6)*, 9781250001535) Square Fish.
—Carl & the Sick Puppy. 2012. (My Readers: Level 1 Ser.). (J). lib. bdg. 13.55 *(978-0-606-26121-0(4)*, Turtleback) Turtleback Bks.
Deal-Trainor, Carol. Marilee: A Manatee's First Journey to the Springs. 2008. 48p. pap. 16.95 *(978-1-60563-660-3(6))* America Star Bks.
Depken, Kristen L. & Schurr, Cathleen. The Shy Little Kitten. DiCicco, Sue, illus. 2015. (Step into Reading Ser.). (ENG.). 32p. (J). (gr. -1-1). 12.99 *(978-0-375-97377-2(X)*, Random Hse. Bks. for Young Readers) Random Hse. Children's Bks.
Deprisco Wang, Dorothea. I Love You Little One. Eriksen, Tone, illus. 2007. (Story Book Ser.). 10p. (J). (gr. -1). bds. *(978-1-84666-173-0(0)*, Tide Mill Pr.) Top That! Publishing PLC.
—My Baby. Gevry, Christine, illus. 2007. (Story Book Ser.). 10p. (J). (gr. -1). *(978-1-84666-263-8(X)*, Tide Mill Pr.) Top That! Publishing PLC.
DeStefano, Anthony. The Puppy That No One Wanted. Cowdrey, Richard, illus. 2015. (ENG.). 32p. 14.99 *(978-1-61636-928-6(0)*, Servant Bks.) Franciscan Media.
Diaz, Katacha. Wild Horse Country. Casale, Paul, illus. (Wild Reading Adventures! Ser.). (ENG.). (J). 2005. 32p. (gr. -1-2). 8.95 *(978-1-59249-220-6(7)*, SC7105) 2005. 36p. (gr. -1-2). 15.95 *(978-1-59249-137-7(5)*, B7105) 2005. 36p. (gr. -1-2). pap. 6.95 *(978-1-59249-138-4(3)*, S7105) 2005. 32p. (gr. -1-3). 19.95 *(978-1-59249-219-0(3)*, BC7105) 2003. 36p. (gr. 2-2). pap. 2.95 *(978-1-59249-139-1(1)*, S7155) Soundprints.
Diaz, Katacha & Bosson, Jo-Ellen. Wild Horse Country. Casale, Paul, illus. 2005. (Wild Reading Adventures! Ser.). (ENG.). 36p. (J). (gr. -1-2). 9.95 *(978-1-59249-140-7(5)*, PS7155) Soundprints.
Dicmas, Courtney. WILD! Mealtime/¡QUÉ LOCURA! a la Hora de Comer. Dicmas, Courtney, illus. 2016. (Wild!/¡quÉ Locura! Ser.: 4). (ENG & SPA., Illus.). 14p. (J). bds. *(978-1-84643-905-6(1))* Child's Play International Ltd.
—WILD! Playtime/¡QUÉ LOCURA! a la Hora de Jugar. Dicmas, Courtney, illus. 2016. (Wild!/¡quÉ Locura! Ser.: 4). (ENG & SPA., Illus.). 14p. (J). bds. *(978-1-84643-906-3(X))* Child's Play International Ltd.
Disney Publishing Staff & Studiomouse Staff. Panda Cub Explores. 2011. (ENG.). 20p. (J). *(978-1-59069-944-7(0))* Studio Mouse LLC.
Dodd, Emma. When You Were Born. Dodd, Emma, illus. 2015. (Emma Dodd's Love You Bks.). (ENG., Illus.). 24p. (J). (-k). 12.99 *(978-0-7636-7405-2(2)*, Templar) Candlewick Pr.
Dolan, Penny. The Lovely Duckling. 2014. (ENG., Illus.). 32p. (J). *(978-0-7787-0445-4(9))*; pap. *(978-0-7787-0480-5(7))* Crabtree Publishing Co.
Dorman, Clive & Dorman, Helen. Okomi Wakes up Early, Vol. 6. Hutchings, Tony, illus. 2004. (Sharing Nature with Children Book Ser.). 24p. (J). pap. 4.95 *(978-1-58469-056-6(9))* Dawn Pubns.
—Okomi Wanders Too Far, Vol. 8. Hutchings, Tony, illus. 2004. (Sharing Nature with Children Book Ser.). 24p. (J). pap. 4.95 *(978-1-58469-058-0(5))* Dawn Pubns.
Dorman, Helen & Dorman, Clive. Okomi & the Tickling Game, Vol. 2. Hutchings, Tony, illus. 2004. (Sharing Nature with Children Book Ser.: 2). 24p. (J). pap. 4.95 *(978-1-58469-046-7(1))* Dawn Pubns.
—Okomi Climbs a Tree, Vol. 4. Hutchings, Tony, illus. 2004. (Sharing Nature with Children Book Ser.: 4). 24p. (J). pap. 4.95 *(978-1-58469-045-0(3))* Dawn Pubns.
—Okomi Plays in the Leaves, Vol. 3. Hutchings, Tony, illus. 2004. (Sharing Nature with Children Book Ser.: 3). 24p. (J). pap. 4.95 *(978-1-58469-047-4(X))* Dawn Pubns.
—Okomi, the New Baby. Hutchings, Tony, illus. 2004. (Sharing Nature with Children Book Ser.: 1). 24p. (J). pap. 4.95 *(978-1-58469-044-3(5))* Dawn Pubns.
Dower, Laura. Sunny & the Secret Passage. 2013. (Palace Puppies Ser.: 4). (J). lib. bdg. 14.75 *(978-0-606-35108-9(6)*, Turtleback) Turtleback Bks.
Downer, Ann. Shark Baby, 1 vol. Bersani, Shennen, illus. 2013. (SPA & ENG.). 32p. (J). (gr. -1-3). 17.95 *(978-1-60718-622-9(5))*; pap. 9.95 *(978-1-62855-351-2(0))*; pap. 9.95 *(978-1-60718-634-2(9))* Arbordale Publishing.

—Tiburoncito, 1 vol. Bersani, Shennen, illus. 2013. (SPA.). 32p. (J). (gr. -1-3). 17.95 *(978-1-60718-709-7(4))* Arbordale Publishing.

Downing, Sue. Cheep, Cheep! Baby Animal Sounds. 2016. (ENG., Illus.). 10p. (J). bds. 7.99 *(978-1-61963-833-4(9)*, 9781619638334, Bloomsbury USA Childrens) Bloomsbury Publishing USA.

—Look, Look! Baby Animal Friends. 2016. (ENG., Illus.). 10p. (J). bds. 7.99 *(978-1-61963-832-7(0)*, 9781619638327, Bloomsbury USA Childrens) Bloomsbury Publishing USA.

Dowson, Nick. Tigress. Chapman, Jane, illus. 2008. (Read, Listen, & Wonder Ser.). (ENG.). 32p. (J). (gr. -1-3). pap. 8.99 *(978-0-7636-3872-6(2))* Candlewick Pr.

—Tigress, Pack. Chapman, Jane, illus. 2008. (Read, Listen, & Wonder Ser.). (ENG.). 32p. (J). (gr. -1-3). pap. 9.99 *(978-0-7636-4189-4(8))* Candlewick Pr.

—Tigress: Read & Wonder. Chapman, Jane, illus. 2007. (Read & Wonder Ser.). (ENG.). 32p. (J). (gr. -1-3). pap. 6.99 *(978-0-7636-3314-1(3))* Candlewick Pr.

—Tracks of a Panda. Rong, Yu, illus. 2007. (ENG.). 32p. (J). (gr. k-3). 16.99 *(978-0-7636-3146-8(9))* Candlewick Pr.

—Tracks of a Panda: Read & Wonder. Rong, Yu, illus. 2010. (Read & Wonder Ser.). (ENG.). 32p. (J). (gr. -1-3). pap. 6.99 *(978-0-7636-4737-7(3))* Candlewick Pr.

Doyle, Malachy. Horse. Rinaldi, Angelo, illus. 2008. (ENG.). 32p. (J). (gr. k-4). 17.99 *(978-1-4169-2467-8(1)*, McElderry, Margaret K. Bks.) McElderry, Margaret K. Bks.

Duey, Kathleen. Korow: A Baby Chimpanzee's Story. Gurin, Lara, illus. 2008. (My Animal Family Ser.). (ENG.). 32p. (J). (gr. -1-3). 12.99 *(978-0-8249-1816-3(9)*, Ideal Pubns.) Worthy Publishing.

—Leo: A Baby Lion's Story. Gurin, Lara, illus. 2008. (My Animal Family Ser.). 32p. (J). (gr. -1-3). 12.99 *(978-0-8249-1817-0(7)*, Ideal Pubns.) Worthy Publishing.

Dunrea, Olivier. Gus. 2015. (Gossie & Friends Ser.). (ENG., Illus.). 32p. (J). (— 1). 9.99 *(978-0-547-86761-8(1)*, HMH Books For Young Readers) Houghton Mifflin Harcourt Publishing Co.

Dussling, Jennifer. Picky Peggy. Adams, Lynn, tr. Adams, Lynn, illus. 2004. (Science Solves It! Ser.). 32p. (J). pap. 5.95 *(978-1-57565-138-5(6))* Kane Press, Inc.

Dwire, Joyann. What Kind of Cow Are You? Being Content with How God Made You. Dickson, Bill, illus. 2006. 24p. (J). per. 2.99 *(978-1-59958-006-7(3))* Journey Stone Creations, LLC.

Dyckman, Ame. Wolfie the Bunny. OHora, Zachariah, illus. 2015. (ENG.). 40p. (J). (gr. -1-1). 17.99 *(978-0-316-22614-1(9))* Little, Brown Bks. for Young Readers.

Eastman, P. D. Are You My Mother?/¿Eres Tú Mi Mamá? 2016. (ENG & SPA., Illus.). 72p. (J). (gr. 1-4). 16.99 *(978-0-553-53990-5(6)*, Random Hse. Bks. for Young Readers) Random Hse. Children's Bks.

—¿Eres Tú Mi Mamá? (Are You My Mother?) 2016. (Beginner Books(R) Ser.). (ENG & SPA., Illus.). 72p. (J). (gr. 1-4). 9.99 *(978-0-553-53989-9(2)*, Random Hse. Bks. for Young Readers) Random Hse. Children's Bks.

Edgar, Amy. The Muddy Puppy (Scholastic Reader, Level 2: Pet Charms #1) Tejido, Jomike, illus. 2017. (Scholastic Reader, Level 2 Ser.: 1). (ENG.). 32p. (J). (gr. k-2). pap. 5.99 *(978-1-338-04589-5(X))* Scholastic, Inc.

Edwards, Karl Newsom. I Got a New Friend. 2017. (ENG., Illus.). 32p. (J). (gr. -1-3). 16.99 *(978-0-399-55700-2(8)*, Knopf Bks. for Young Readers) Random Hse. Children's Bks.

Elsohn Ross, Michael. Mama's Milk. Wolff, Ashley, illus. 2007. (ENG.). 32p. (J). (gr. -1-2). 12.95 *(978-1-58246-181-6(3)*, Tricycle Pr.) Random Hse. Children's Bks.

—Mama's Milk / Mamá Me Alimenta. Wolff, Ashley, illus. 2016. (ENG & SPA.). 24p. (J). (-k). bds. 7.99 *(978-0-553-53874-8(8)*, Tricycle Pr.) Random Hse. Children's Bks.

Emma Treehouse Ltd. My Babies. Davis, Caroline, illus. 2007. (Easy Flaps Ser.). 10p. (J). (gr. -1). bds. 6.95 *(978-1-58925-822-8(3))* Tiger Tales.

Equipo Staff. Este No es Mi Conejito. 2004.Tr. of That's Not My Bunny. (SPA., Illus.). 12p. (J). (gr. -1). 7.95 *(978-0-7460-4512-1(3))* EDC Publishing.

Esbaum, Jill. Tom's Tweet. Stone, Kyle M. & Santat, Dan, illus. 2011. (ENG.). 32p. (J). (gr. -1-2). 16.99 *(978-0-375-85171-1(2)*, Knopf Bks. for Young Readers) Random Hse. Children's Bks.

Falwell, Cathryn. Pond Babies, 1 vol. Falwell, Cathryn, illus. 2011. (ENG., Illus.). 32p. (gr. -1-k). 15.95 *(978-0-89272-920-3(1))* Down East Bks.

Faulconer, Maria. A Mom for Umande. Hartung, Susan Kathleen, illus. 2014. (ENG.). 32p. (J). (gr. -1-3). 16.99 *(978-0-8037-3762-4(9)*, Dial Bks) Penguin Young Readers Group.

Feiffer, Kate. Which Puppy? Feiffer, Kate & Feiffer, Jules, illus. 2009. (ENG.). 32p. (J). (gr. -1-3). 16.99 *(978-1-4169-9147-2(6)*, Simon & Schuster/Paula Wiseman Bks.) Simon & Schuster/Paula Wiseman Bks.

Fernandes, Eugenie. Kitten's Spring. Fernandes, Eugenie, illus. 2010. (ENG., Illus.). 24p. (J). (gr. -1 — 1). 14.95 *(978-1-55453-340-4(6))* Kids Can Pr., Ltd. CAN. Dist: Hachette Bk. Group.

Ferry, Beth. Land Shark. Mantle, Ben, illus. 2015. (ENG.). 36p. (J). (gr. -1-k). 16.99 *(978-1-4521-2458-2(2))* Chronicle Bks. LLC.

Fisch, Sarah. The Little Flower Seed. Roper, Robert, illus. 2007. (J). pap. *(978-0-439-90899-3(X))* Scholastic, Inc.

Fleming, Candace. Seven Hungry Babies. Yelchin, Eugene, illus. 2010. (ENG.). 40p. (J). (gr. -1-2). 16.99 *(978-1-4169-5402-6(3)*, Atheneum Bks. for Young Readers) Simon & Schuster Children's Publishing.

Fleming, Denise. Sleepy, Oh So Sleepy. Fleming, Denise, illus. 2010. (ENG., Illus.). 32p. (J). (gr. -1-k). 16.99 *(978-0-8050-8126-8(7)*, 9780805081268, Holt, Henry & Co. Bks. For Young Readers) Holt, Henry & Co.

Flor Ada, Alma. Celebrate Kwanzaa with Boots & Her Kittens. Docampo, Valeria, illus. 2007. (Cuentos para Celebrar / Stories to Celebrate Ser.). 30p. (gr. k-6). per. 11.95 *(978-1-59820-135-2(2))* Santillana USA Publishing Co., Inc.

Ford, Bernette G. Princess Puppy. Williams, Sam, illus. 2013. (J). *(978-0-545-53967-8(6)*, Cartwheel Bks.) Scholastic, Inc.

Foreman, Michael. Cat & Dog. Foreman, Michael, illus. 2014. (ENG., Illus.). 32p. (J). (gr. -1-3). 16.95 *(978-1-4677-5124-7(3))* Lerner Publishing Group.

Fox, Mem. Hello Baby! Jenkins, Steve, illus. 2009. (ENG.). 32p. (J). (gr. -1-k). 17.99 *(978-1-4169-8513-6(1)*, Beach Lane Bks.) Beach Lane Bks.

—Nellie Belle. Austin, Mike, illus. 2015. (ENG.). 32p. (J). (gr. -1-3). 17.99 *(978-1-4169-9005-5(4)*, Beach Lane Bks.) Beach Lane Bks.

Fraggalosch, Audrey. Let's Explore, Moose! Forest, Crista, illus. 2005. (ENG.). 32p. (J). (gr. -1-1). pap. 3.95 *(978-1-59249-151-3(0)*, S2017) Soundprints.

—Trails above the Tree Line: A Story of a Rocky Mountain Meadow. Bond, Higgins, illus. 2005. (Soundprints' Wild Habitats Ser.). (ENG.). (J). (gr. 1-4). 36p. 15.95 *(978-1-56899-941-8(0)*, B7021); 32p. pap. 6.95 *(978-1-56899-942-5(9)*, S7021) Soundprints.

Freedman, Claire. Where Snowflakes Fall. Macnaughton, Tina, illus. 2012. 24p. (J). *(978-1-4351-4321-0(3))* Barnes & Noble, Inc.

Friedman, Laurie. Ruby Valentine & the Sweet Surprise. Avril, Lynne, illus. 2014. (ENG.). 32p. (J). (gr. k-3). 16.95 *(978-0-7613-8873-9(7)*, Carolrhoda Bks.) Lerner Publishing Group.

Friedman, Mel, et al. Un Castillo para Gatitos. Adams, Lynn, illus. 2008. (SPA.). (J). *(978-1-57565-275-7(7))* Kane Press, Inc.

Galbraith, Kathryn O. Sparky & Tidbit. Kelley, Gerald, illus. 2015. (Ready-To-Reads Ser.). (ENG.). 40p. (J). (gr. 1-3). pap. 3.99 *(978-1-4814-0424-2(5)*, Simon Spotlight) Simon Spotlight.

Galvin, Laura. Baby Dolphin's Busy Day. 2008. (Smithsonian Baby Animals Ser.). (ENG., Illus.). 16p. (gr. -1-k). 13.95 *(978-1-59249-792-8(6))* Soundprints.

—Baby Duck Gets Lost. 2008. (Smithsonian Baby Animals Ser.). (ENG., Illus.). 16p. (gr. -1-k). 13.95 *(978-1-59249-789-8(6))* Soundprints.

—Baby Koala & Mommy. 2008. (Smithsonian Baby Animals Ser.). (ENG., Illus.). 16p. (gr. -1-k). 13.95 *(978-1-59249-791-1(8))* Soundprints.

—Baby Pig Time to Play. 2008. (Smithsonian Baby Animals Ser.). (ENG., Illus.). 16p. (gr. -1-k). 13.95 *(978-1-59249-788-1(8))* Soundprints.

—I Love My Mommy. 2009. (I Love My... Ser.). (ENG., Illus.). 16p. (J). 12.95 *(978-1-59249-801-7(9))* Soundprints.

Galvin, Laura, told to. I Love My Mommy. 2007. (ENG., Illus.). 16p. (J). (gr. -1-k). bds. 6.95 *(978-1-59249-730-0(6))* Soundprints.

Galvin, Laura G. & Galvin, Laura. I Love My Mommy (with Download) 2011. (ENG.). 16p. (J). *(978-1-60727-345-5(4))* Soundprints.

Galvin, Laura Gates. Baby Dolphin's Busy Day. 2007. (Baby Animals Ser.). (ENG., Illus.). 16p. (gr. -1-k). 6.95 *(978-1-59249-745-4(4))* Soundprints.

—Baby Dolphins Busy Day. 2011. (Baby Animals (Soundprints) Ser.). (ENG., Illus.). 16p. (gr. -1-k). 15.95 *(978-1-60727-329-5(2))* Soundprints.

—Baby Polar Bear Learns to Swim. 2008. (Smithsonian Baby Animals Ser.). (ENG., Illus.). 16p. (gr. -1-k). 13.95 *(978-1-59249-786-7(1))* Soundprints.

Galvin, Laura Gates & Odierno, Lisa. Puppy Explores. 2008. (ENG.). 16p. (J). (gr. -1-k). 6.95 *(978-1-59249-863-5(9))* Soundprints.

Gehrmann, Katja, illus. Goose the Bear. 2014. (ENG.). 40p. (J). (gr. -1-3). 16.95 *(978-1-62636-384-7(6)*, Sky Pony Pr.) Skyhorse Publishing Co., Inc.

George, Kallie. The Enchanted Egg. Boiger, Alexandra, illus. 2015. (Magical Animal Adoption Agency Ser.). (ENG.). 138p. (J). (gr. 3-7). 14.99 *(978-1-4231-8383-9(5))* Disney Pr.

—The Enchanted Egg. Boiger, Alexandra, illus. 2016. (Magical Animal Adoption Agency Ser.). (ENG.). 160p. (J). (gr. 2-5). pap. 5.99 *(978-1-4847-0146-1(1))* Hyperion Bks. for Children.

Gerver, Jane E. Good Night. Flint, Gillian, illus. 2015. (ENG.). 14p. (J). (— 1). bds. 4.99 *(978-1-62979-415-0(5)*, Highlights) Boyds Mills Pr.

Geyer, Kim. Go to Sleep, Monty! Geyer, Kim, illus. 2015. (ENG., Illus.). 32p. (J). (gr. -1-3). 17.99 *(978-1-4677-9311-7(6))* Lerner Publishing Group.

Gilman, Grace. Dixie. McConnell, Sarah, illus. 2011. (I Can Read Level 1 Ser.). (ENG.). 32p. (J). (gr. -1-3). 16.99 *(978-0-06-171914-1(5))*; pap. 3.99 *(978-0-06-171913-4(7))* HarperCollins Pubs.

Giogas, Valarie. In My Backyard, 1 vol. Zecca, Katherine, illus. 2007. (ENG.). 32p. (J). (gr. -1-3). 15.95 *(978-0-9777423-1-8(8))* Arbordale Publishing.

Glover, Darryl. The Pirate Kitty. Austin, Britta, ed. Kosir, Ana, illus. 2008. 24p. (J). 16.95 *(978-0-9821387-0-0(9))* MagicStar Inc.

Grogan, John. Marley & the Kittens. Cowdrey, Richard, illus. 2010. (Marley Ser.). 40p. (J). (gr. -1-3). (ENG.). 17.99 *(978-0-06-171486-3(0))*; lib. bdg. 18.89 *(978-0-06-171487-0(9))* HarperCollins Pubs.

—Trick or Treat, Marley! Cowdrey, Richard, illus. (Marley Ser.). (ENG.). 40p. (J). (gr. -1-3). 2013. 9.99 *(978-0-06-211368-9(2))* 2011. 17.99 *(978-0-06-185755-3(6))* HarperCollins Pubs.

Gudeon, Adam. Peep & Zeep. 2017. (I Like to Read(r) Ser.). (ENG.). 24p. (J). (gr. -1-3). 14.95 *(978-0-8234-3674-3(8))* Holiday Hse., Inc.

—Peeper & Zeep. 2017. (I Like to Read(r) Ser.). (ENG.). 24p. (J). (gr. -1-3). 6.99 *(978-0-8234-3779-5(5))* Holiday Hse., Inc.

Guest, Elissa Haden. Bella's Rules. Halpin, Abigail, illus. 2013. (ENG.). 32p. (J). (gr. -1-k). 16.99 *(978-0-8037-3393-0(3)*, Dial Bks) Penguin Young Readers Group.

Guion, Melissa. Baby Penguins Everywhere! Guion, Melissa, illus. (ENG., Illus.). (J). (gr. -1-k). 2013. 28p. bds. 6.99 *(978-0-399-16516-0(9))* 2012. 32p. 16.99 *(978-0-399-25535-9(4))* Penguin Young Readers Group. (Philomel Bks.).

—Baby Penguins Love Their Mama. Guion, Melissa, illus. 2014. (ENG., Illus.). 32p. (J). (gr. -1-k). 16.99 *(978-0-399-16365-4(4)*, Philomel Bks.) Penguin Young Readers Group.

Hacohen, Dean. Tuck Me In! Scharschmidt, Sherry, illus. 2010. (ENG.). 40p. (J). (gr. -1 — 1). 9.99 *(978-0-7636-4728-5(4))* Candlewick Pr.

Hacohen, Dean & Scharschmidt, Sherry. Tuck Me In! 2010. (Illus.). (J). *(978-0-7636-5363-7(2))* Candlewick Pr.

Halfmann, Janet. Canada Goose at Cattail Lane. Stegos, Daniel J., illus. 2011. (Smithsonian's Backyard Ser.). (ENG.). 32p. (J). (gr. -1-3). 19.95 *(978-1-60727-632-6(1))*; pap. 8.95 *(978-1-60727-633-3(X))* Soundprints.

—Little Black Ant on Park Street. Rietz, Kathleen, illus. 2009. (ENG.). 32p. 19.95 *(978-1-60727-005-8(6))*; 10.95 *(978-1-60727-008-9(0))*; 9.95 *(978-1-60727-006-5(4))*; (J). pap. 6.95 *(978-1-60727-003-4(X))* Soundprints.

Hallensleben, Georg & Gutman, Anne. Mommy Snuggles. 2017. (ENG., Illus.). 14p. (J). (gr. -1 — 1). bds. 5.99 *(978-1-4521-5822-8(3))* Chronicle Bks. LLC.

Harimann, Sierra. Diploma Day. 2011. (Illus.). 30p. (J). pap. *(978-0-545-28143-0(1))* Scholastic, Inc.

—Water Pups. 2013. (Illus.). 30p. (J). *(978-0-545-47235-7(0))* Scholastic, Inc.

Harvey, Sarah N. Puppies on Board, 1 vol. Cowles, Rose, illus. 2005. (ENG.). 32p. (J). (gr. -1-3). 17.95 *(978-1-55143-390-5(7))* Orca Bk. Pubs. USA.

Hashmi-Alikhan, Saira. Snuggly Baby. 2007. 24p. per. 10.95 *(978-1-4327-0777-4(9))* Outskirts Pr., Inc.

Hayes, Karel. Snowflake Comes to Stay. 2010. (ENG.). 32p. (J). (gr. -1-3). 16.95 *(978-0-89272-850-3(7))* Down East Bks.

Henderson, Kathy. Tabby Cat's Secret. 2003. (Illus.). 36p. pap. *(978-0-7112-1883-3(8))* ReiseArt Buchhandlung GmbH.

Henderson, Sara. Howie Finds a Hug, 1 vol. Zenz, Aaron, illus. 2008. (I Can Read! / Howie Ser.). (ENG.). 32p. (J). (gr. -1-3). pap. 3.99 *(978-0-310-71607-5(1))* Zonderkidz.

—Howie's Tea Party, 1 vol. Zenz, Aaron, illus. 2008. (I Can Read! / Howie Ser.). (ENG.). 32p. (J). (gr. -1-3). pap. 3.99 *(978-0-310-71605-1(5))* Zonderkidz.

Henderson, Sara & Zenz, Aaron. Howie Goes Shopping(Fido Va de Compras), 1 vol. Henderson, Sara & Zenz, Aaron, illus. 2009. (I Can Read! / Howie Series / ¡Yo Sé Leer! / Serie: Fido Ser.). (ENG., Illus.). 32p. (J). pap. 3.99 *(978-0-310-71874-1(0))* Zonderkidz.

—Howie Wants to Play, 1 vol. Henderson, Sara & Zenz, Aaron, illus. 2009. (I Can Read! / Howie Series / ¡Yo Sé Leer! / Serie: Fido Ser.). (ENG., Illus.). 32p. (J). pap. 3.99 *(978-0-310-71875-8(9))* Zonderkidz.

Henkes, Kevin. Egg. Henkes, Kevin, illus. 2017. (Illus.). 40p. (J). (gr. -1-3). 17.99 *(978-0-06-240872-3(0)*, Greenwillow Bks.) HarperCollins Pubs.

—Kitten's First Full Moon. Henkes, Kevin, illus. 2004. (ENG., Illus.). 40p. (J). (gr. -1-3). 17.99 *(978-0-06-058828-1(4)*, Greenwillow Bks.) HarperCollins Pubs.

—Little White Rabbit. Henkes, Kevin, illus. 2011. (Illus.). 40p. (J). (gr. -1-3). (ENG.). 16.99 *(978-0-06-200642-4(8))*; 17.89 *(978-0-06-200643-1(6))* HarperCollins Pubs. (Greenwillow Bks.).

—Little White Rabbit Board Book. Henkes, Kevin, illus. 2014. (ENG., Illus.). 34p. (J). (gr. -1-3). bds. 7.99 *(978-0-06-231409-3(2)*, Greenwillow Bks.) HarperCollins Pubs.

—La Primera Luna Llena de Gatita, 1 vol. Henkes, Kevin, illus. 2006. Orig. Title: Kitten's First Full Moon. (SPA., Illus.). 40p. (J). (gr. -1-2). 17.99 *(978-0-06-087223-6(3))* HarperCollins Pubs.

Higgins, Ryan T. Mother Bruce. Higgins, Ryan T., illus. 2015. (Mother Bruce Ser.). (ENG., Illus.). 48p. (J). (gr. -1-k). 17.99 *(978-1-4847-3088-1(7))* Disney Pr.

Higginson, Hadley. Keeker & the Pony Camp Catastrophe, Bk. 5. Perrett, Lisa, illus. 2007. (Keeker & the Sneaky Pony Ser.: KEEK). (ENG.). 56p. (J). (gr. k-3). per. 4.99 *(978-0-8118-5597-6(X))* Chronicle Bks. LLC.

—Keeker & the Springtime Surprise. Perrett, Lisa, illus. 2007. (Keeker & the Sneaky Pony Ser.: KEEK). (ENG.). 58p. (J). (gr. k-3). per. 4.99 *(978-0-8118-5599-0(6))* Chronicle Bks. LLC.

Hill, Eric. Spot Goes to the Farm. 2003. (Spot Ser.). (gr. -1-2). lib. bdg. 18.40 *(978-0-613-86708-5(4)*, Turtleback) Turtleback Bks.

Hillert, Margaret. The Baby Bunny. Bond, Denny, illus. 2016. (BeginningtoRead Ser.). (ENG.). 32p. (J). (gr. k-2). 22.60 *(978-1-59953-793-1(1))* Norwood Hse. Pr.

—The Little Runaway. Dumm, Brian, illus. 2016. (BeginningtoRead Ser.). (ENG.). 32p. (J). (gr. k-2). 22.60 *(978-1-59953-801-3(6))* Norwood Hse. Pr.

Hillert, Margaret. Who Feels Happy, Dear Dragon? Pullan, Jack, illus. 2017. (BeginningtoRead Ser.). (ENG.). 32p. (J). (-2). 22.60 **(978-1-59953-824-2(5))**; pap. 11.94 **(978-1-68404-002-5(7))** Norwood Hse. Pr.

Hills, Jodi. Hope-So. Bjornson, Barbara, illus. 2004. (ENG.). 36p. (J). 16.95 *(978-0-9726504-2-7(3))* TRISTAN Publishing, Inc.

Himmelman, John. Katie & the Puppy Next Door. Himmelman, John, illus. 2013. (ENG., Illus.). 32p. (J). (gr. -1-1). 16.99 *(978-0-8050-9484-8(9)*, 9780805094848, Holt, Henry & Co. Bks. For Young Readers) Holt, Henry & Co.

—Katie Loves the Kittens. Himmelman, John, illus. 2008. (ENG., Illus.). 32p. (J). (gr. -1-3). 18.99 *(978-0-8050-8682-9(X)*, 9780805086829, Holt, Henry & Co. Bks. For Young Readers) Holt, Henry & Co.

Hodgkins, Fran. If You Were My Baby: A Wildlife Lullaby. Bryant, Laura J., illus. (Simply Nature Book Ser.). (J). (gr. -1 — 1). 2007. 26p. bds. 7.95 *(978-1-58469-090-0(9))* 2005. 32p. pap. 8.95 *(978-1-58469-075-7(5))* 2005. (ENG.). 32p. 16.95 *(978-1-58469-074-0(7))* Dawn Pubns.

Holt, Sharon. Did My Mother Do That? Lovelock, Brian, illus. 2010. (ENG.). 32p. (J). (gr. -1-2). 15.99 *(978-0-7636-4685-1(7))* Candlewick Pr.

Holub, Joan. Itty Bitty Kitty. Burks, James, illus. 2015. (ENG.). 32p. (J). (gr. -1-3). 17.99 *(978-0-06-232219-7(2))* HarperCollins Pubs.

Horning, Sandra. Chicks! Goodell, Jon, illus. 2013. (Step into Reading Ser.). (ENG.). 32p. (J). (gr. -1-1). pap. 3.99 *(978-0-307-93221-1(4))*; lib. bdg. 12.99 *(978-0-375-97117-4(3))* Random Hse. Children's Bks. (Random Hse. Bks. for Young Readers).

Houran, Lori Haskins. I Will Keep You Safe & Sound. Brown, Petra, illus. 2013. (J). *(978-0-545-19752-6(X)*, Scholastic Pr.) Scholastic, Inc.

—Next to You: A Book of Adorableness. Hanson, Sydney, illus. 2016. (ENG.). 32p. (J). (gr. -1-3). 16.99 *(978-0-8075-5600-9(9))* Whitman, Albert & Co.

Howatt, Sandra J. Sleepyheads. Wan, Joyce, illus. 2014. (ENG.). 32p. (J). (gr. -1-3). 17.99 *(978-1-4424-2266-7(1)*, Beach Lane Bks.) Beach Lane Bks.

Howland, Leila. Nantucket Summer [Nantucket Blue & Nantucket Red Bind-Up]. 2017. (Nantucket Blue Ser.). (ENG.). 608p. (YA). (gr. 9-17). pap. 11.99 *(978-1-368-00212-7(9))* Hyperion Bks. for Children.

Huang, Yu-Hsuan, illus. Baby Bunny: Finger Puppet Book. 2017. (ENG.). 12p. (J). bds. 6.99 *(978-1-4521-5609-5(3))* Chronicle Bks. LLC.

—Baby Chipmunk: Finger Puppet Book. 2017. (ENG.). 12p. (J). (gr. -1 — 1). bds. 6.99 *(978-1-4521-5612-5(3))* Chronicle Bks. LLC.

—Baby Elephant: Finger Puppet Book. 2016. (ENG.). 12p. (J). (gr. -1 — 1). 6.99 *(978-1-4521-4237-1(8))* Chronicle Bks. LLC.

—Baby Fish: Finger Puppet Book. 2017. (ENG.). 12p. (J). bds. 6.99 *(978-1-4521-5610-1(7))* Chronicle Bks. LLC.

—Baby Giraffe: Finger Puppet Book. 2017. (ENG.). 12p. (J). (gr. -1 — 1). bds. 6.99 *(978-1-4521-5611-8(5))* Chronicle Bks. LLC.

—Baby Reindeer. 2016. (ENG.). 12p. (J). (gr. -1 — 1). 6.99 *(978-1-4521-4661-4(6))* Chronicle Bks. LLC.

—Baby Tiger: Finger Puppet Book. 2016. (ENG.). 12p. (J). (gr. -1 — 1). bds. 6.99 *(978-1-4521-4236-4(X))* Chronicle Bks. LLC.

Hughes, Susan. Bijou. 2017. (Puppy Pals Ser.: 4). (ENG.). 112p. (J). (gr. 2-5). pap. 5.99 *(978-1-4926-3403-4(4)*, 9781492634034, Sourcebooks Jabberwocky) Sourcebooks, Inc.

—Murphy. 2016. (Puppy Pals Ser.: 3). (ENG.). 128p. (J). (gr. 2-5). pap. 5.99 *(978-1-4926-3400-3(X)*, 9781492634003, Sourcebooks Jabberwocky) Sourcebooks, Inc.

—Riley. 2016. (Puppy Pals Ser.: 2). (ENG.). 128p. (J). (gr. 2-5). pap. 5.99 *(978-1-4926-3397-6(6)*, 9781492633976, Sourcebooks Jabberwocky) Sourcebooks, Inc.

Hulst, W. G. van de & Hulst, Willem G. van de, illus. The Black Kitten. 2014. (J). *(978-1-928136-07-1(9))* Inheritance Pubns.

—Herbie, the Runaway Duck. 2014. (J). *(978-1-928136-19-4(2))* Inheritance Pubns.

—Kittens, Kittens Everywhere. 2014. (J). *(978-1-928136-20-0(6))* Inheritance Pubns.

Hung, Yating. Where Is Mama? A Pop-Up Story. 2013. (ENG., Illus.). 24p. (J). (gr. -1-k). 19.95 *(978-1-4197-0718-6(3)*, Abrams Appleseed) Abrams, Inc.

Hutchins, Pat. Where, Oh Where, Is Rosie's Chick? 2016. (ENG., Illus.). 32p. (J). (gr. -1-3). 17.99 *(978-1-4814-6071-2(4)*, Simon & Schuster Bks. For Young Readers) Simon & Schuster Bks. For Young Readers.

Idle, Molly. Flora & the Chicks. 2017. (ENG., Illus.). 20p. (J). bds. 9.99 *(978-1-4521-4657-7(8))* Chronicle Bks. LLC.

Image Books Staff. Little Chick: Finger Puppet Book. Put, Klaartje van der, illus. 2015. (ENG.). 12p. (J). (gr. -1 — 1). bds. 6.99 *(978-1-4521-2917-4(7))* Chronicle Bks. LLC.

Jackson, Ellen. Beastly Babies. Wenzel, Brendan, illus. 2015. (ENG.). 32p. (J). (gr. -1-3). 17.99 *(978-1-4424-0834-0(0)*, Beach Lane Bks.) Beach Lane Bks.

Jackson, Leona Novy. The Littlest Christmas Kitten. Dupre, Kelly, illus. 2005. 32p. (J). 16.00 *(978-0-930643-18-8(6)*, 1250560) Images Unlimited Publishing.

Jacobson, Jennifer Richard. Andy Shane Is Not in Love. Carter, Abby, illus. 2009. (Andy Shane Ser.: 4). (ENG.). 64p. (J). (gr. k-3). 4.99 *(978-0-7636-4403-1(X))* Candlewick Pr.

James, Simon. George Flies South. 2011. (ENG., Illus.). 40p. (J). (gr. -1-2). 16.99 *(978-0-7636-5724-6(7))* Candlewick Pr.

Janovitz, Marilyn. We Love School (¡Nos Encanta la Escuela!) Janovitz, Marilyn, illus. 2009. (ENG & SPA., Illus.). 32p. (J). (gr. -1-k). 7.95 *(978-0-7358-2246-7(8))* North-South Bks., Inc.

Johansson, Cecilia, illus. Just Like Mommy. 2006. (ENG.). 16p. (J). (gr. -1 — 1). bds. 7.99 *(978-1-4169-1218-7(5)*, Little Simon) Little Simon.

Joosse, Barbara M. Higgledy-Piggledy Chicks. Chrustowski, Rick, illus. 2010. 40p. (J). (gr. -1-k). (ENG.). 16.99 *(978-0-06-075042-8(1))*; lib. bdg. 17.89 *(978-0-06-075043-5(X))* HarperCollins Pubs. (Greenwillow Bks.).

Judge, Lita. Red Hat. Judge, Lita, illus. 2013. (ENG., Illus.). 40p. (J). (gr. -1-k). 16.99 *(978-1-4424-4232-0(8)*, Atheneum Bks. for Young Readers) Simon & Schuster Children's Publishing.

Kantner, Seth. Pup & Pokey. Hill, Beth, illus. 2014. 48p. pap. 14.95 *(978-1-60223-241-9(5))* Univ. of Alaska Pr.

Kats, Jewel. Prince Preemie: A Tale of a Tiny Puppy Who Arrives Early. Lenart, Claudia, illus. 2016. (J). pap. **(978-1-61599-306-2(1))** Loving Healing Pr., Inc.

Kaufman, Seufert. Wee Wilhelmina & Her Magic Marbles. 2012. (ENG.). pap. *(978-1-4675-4364-4(0))* Independent Pub.

Kerby, Johanna. Little Pink Pup. Kerby, Johanna, photos by. 2010. (ENG., Illus.). 32p. (J). (gr. -1-k). 16.99 *(978-0-399-25435-2(8)*, G.P. Putnam's Sons Books for Young Readers) Penguin Young Readers Group.

Kimmelman, Leslie. The Three Bully Goats. Terry, Will, illus. 2012. (J). *(978-1-61913-136-1(6))* Weigl Pubs., Inc.

—The Three Bully Goats. Terry, Will, illus. 2011. (ENG.). 32p. (J). (gr. -1-3). 16.99 *(978-0-8075-7900-8(9))* Whitman, Albert & Co.

King-smith, Dick. Funny Frank. Eastwood, John, illus. 2003. (ENG.). 112p. (J). (gr. 1-4). 5.99 *(978-0-440-41880-1(1)*, Yearling) Random Hse. Children's Bks.

Klimo, Kate. The Dragon in the Sock Drawer. Shroades, John, illus. 2009. (Dragon Keepers Ser.). (ENG.). 192p. (J). (gr. 3-7). 6.99 *(978-0-375-85588-7(2)*, Yearling) Random Hse. Children's Bks.

Knudsen, Michelle. Argus. Wesson, Andrea, illus. 2011. (ENG.). 32p. (J). (gr. -1-3). 15.99 *(978-0-7636-3790-3(4))* Candlewick Pr.

Kosara, Victoria. Graduation Party. Durk, Jim, illus. 2010. (J). pap. *(978-0-545-23400-9(X))* Scholastic, Inc.

Kreloff, Elliot, illus. My Little Baby. 2010. 12p. (J). bds. *(978-1-60906-008-4(3))* Begin Smart LLC.

Laden, Nina. Grow Up! 2003. (ENG., Illus.). 26p. (J). (gr. -1-7). bds. 6.99 *(978-0-8118-3761-3(0))* Chronicle Bks. LLC.

Langeland, Deirdre. Be Careful, Kangaroo! Ordaz, Frank, illus. 2005. (Soundprints' Read-and-Discover Ser.). (ENG.). 48p.

(J). (gr. -1-1). 12.95 (978-1-59249-146-9(4), PS2010) Soundprints.

—Be Careful, Kangaroo!, Level 1. 2005. (ENG., Illus.). 32p. (J). (gr. -1-1). pap. 3.95 (978-1-59249-145-2(6), S2010) Soundprints.

Lawrence, John. This Little Chick. Lawrence, John, illus. 2013. (ENG., Illus.). 32p. (J). (gr. -1-k). 4.99 (978-0-7636-6350-6(6)) Candlewick Pr.

Le Gall, Frank. Freedom! Balthazar, Flore, illus. 2012. (Miss Annie Ser.). 48p. (J). (gr. 2-4). pap. 39.62 (978-0-7613-9281-1(5)); (ENG.). lib. bdg. 29.27 (978-0-7613-7884-6(7)) Lerner Publishing Group. (Graphic Universe™).

—Miss Annie. Balthazar, Flore, illus. 2012. (Miss Annie Ser.). 48p. (J). (gr. 2-4). lib. bdg. 58.54 (978-0-7613-8902-6(4), Graphic Universe™) Lerner Publishing Group.

—Miss Annie: 6Pack Set. Balthazar, Flore, illus. 2012. (Miss Annie Ser.). 48p. (J). (gr. 2-4). pap. 79.23 (978-0-7613-9284-2(X), Graphic Universe™) Lerner Publishing Group.

—Miss Annie: Single Copy Set. Balthazar, Flore, illus. 2012. (Miss Annie Ser.). 48p. (J). (gr. 2-4). pap. 13.21 (978-0-7613-9283-5(1), Graphic Universe™) Lerner Publishing Group.

—Rooftop Cat. Balthazar, Flore, illus. 2012. (Miss Annie Ser.). 48p. (J). (gr. 2-4). pap. 39.62 (978-0-7613-9282-8(3)); (ENG.). lib. bdg. 29.27 (978-0-7613-7885-3(5)) Lerner Publishing Group. (Graphic Universe™).

Lee, Quinlan B. Beach Day. Haefele, Steve, illus. 2006. (J). (978-0-439-81618-2(1)) Scholastic, Inc.

Lewis, Gill. Murphy & the Great Surf Rescue. Horne, Sarah, illus. 2017. (Puppy Academy Ser.). (ENG.). 128p. (J). 16.99 (978-1-62779-800-6(5), 9781627798006, Holt, Henry & Co. Bks. For Young Readers) Holt, Henry & Co.

—Pip & the Paw of Friendship. Horne, Sarah, illus. 2017. (Puppy Academy Ser.). (ENG.). 128p. (J). pap. 5.99 (978-1-250-09285-4(X), 9781250092854, Holt, Henry & Co. Bks. For Young Readers) Holt, Henry & Co.

—Scout & the Sausage Thief. Horne, Sarah, illus. 2016. (Puppy Academy Ser.). (ENG.). 128p. (J). 16.99 (978-1-62779-794-8(7), 9781627797948, Holt, Henry & Co. Bks. For Young Readers) Holt, Henry & Co.

—Star on Stormy Mountain. Horne, Sarah, illus. 2016. (Puppy Academy Ser.). (ENG.). 128p. (J). 16.99 (978-1-62779-796-2(3), 9781627797962, Holt, Henry & Co. Bks. For Young Readers) Holt, Henry & Co.

Lewison, Wendy Cheyette. The Prince & the Potty. Motoyama, Keiko, illus. 2006. (ENG.). 40p. (J). (gr. -1-3). 16.99 (978-0-689-87808-4(7), Simon & Schuster Bks. For Young Readers) Simon & Schuster Bks. For Young Readers.

Little Bee Books Staff & Brook-Piper, Holly. Animal Homes. Max and Sid Staff, illus. 2015. (Tiny Touch Ser.). (ENG.). 12p. (J). (gr. -1 — 1). bds. 4.99 (978-1-4998-0023-4(1)) Little Bee Books Inc.

Little Kitten. 2003. (Goodnight Mr. Moon Ser.). (Illus.). (J). bds. 2.98 (978-0-7525-4743-5(7)) Parragon, Inc.

Little Puppy. 2003. (Goodnight Mr. Moon Ser.). (Illus.). (J). bds. 2.98 (978-0-7525-4742-8(9)) Parragon, Inc.

Litton, Jonathan. I Love My Daddy. Galloway, Fhiona, illus. 2016. (My Little World Ser.). (ENG.). 16p. (J). (gr. -1-k). bds. 7.99 (978-1-58925-217-2(9)) Tiger Tales.

—I Love My Mommy. Galloway, Fhiona, illus. 2016. (My Little World Ser.). (ENG.). 16p. (J). (gr. -1-k). bds. 7.99 (978-1-58925-216-5(0)) Tiger Tales.

Lloyd-Jones, Sally. Bunny's First Spring, 1 vol. McPhail, David, illus. 2015. (ENG.). 32p. (J). 16.99 (978-0-310-73386-7(3)) Zonderkidz.

London, Jonathan. Honey Paw & Lightfoot. Van Zyle, Jon, illus. 2014. (ENG.). 32p. (J). 16.99 (978-1-941821-10-7(3), Alaska Northwest Bks.) Graphic Arts Ctr. Publishing Co.

—Little Lost Tiger, 0 vols. Spirin, Ilya, illus. 2012. (ENG.). 32p. (J). (gr. k-3). 17.99 (978-0-7614-6130-2(2), 9780761461302, Amazon Children's Publishing) Amazon Publishing.

—Little Penguin: The Emperor of Antarctica, 0 vols. Olson, Julie, illus. 2011. (ENG.). 36p. (J). (gr. -1-3). 17.99 (978-0-7614-5954-5(5), 9780761459545, Amazon Children's Publishing) Amazon Publishing.

—Little Puffin's First Flight. Van Zyle, Jon, illus. 2016. (ENG.). 32p. (J). (gr. -1-3). 10.99 (978-0-88240-924-5(7), Alaska Northwest Bks.) Graphic Arts Ctr. Publishing Co.

—Little Swan, 0 vols. Rodanas, Kristina, illus. 2009. (ENG.). 32p. (J). (gr. -1-3). 17.99 (978-0-7614-5523-3(X), 9780761455233, Amazon Children's Publishing) Amazon Publishing.

—The Seasons of Little Wolf. Van Zyle, Jon, illus. 2014. (ENG.). 32p. (J). 16.99 (978-1-941821-06-0(5), West Winds Pr.) Graphic Arts Ctr. Publishing Co.

Long, Loren. Otis & the Puppy. Long, Loren, illus. (Otis Ser.: 3). (ENG., Illus.). (J). (gr. -1-k). 2014. 38p. bds. 8.99 (978-0-399-17196-3(7)) 2013. 40p. 17.99 (978-0-399-25469-7(2)) Penguin Young Readers Group. (Philomel Bks.).

Losey, Tori. The Ducks of Congress Park. Liguori, Kathy, illus. 2004. 36p. (J). (978-0-925168-97-9(1)) North Country Bks., Inc.

Lowrey, Janette Sebring. The Poky Little Puppy. Tenggren, Gustaf, illus. 2007. (Little Golden Book Ser.). (ENG.). 26p. (J). (gr. k — 1). bds. 4.99 (978-0-375-83925-2(9), Golden Bks.) Random Hse. Children's Bks.

Lucy Lamb. 2006. (J). per. 3.99 (978-1-934004-16-6(2)) Byeway Bks.

Lujan, Jorge. Trunk to Trunklet. Sadat, Madana, illus. 2016. (ENG.). 32p. (J). (gr. -1-2). 16.95 (978-1-59270-194-0(9)) Enchanted Lion Bks., LLC.

Luther, Jacqueline & Lind, Alan. Black Bear Cub. Trachock, Cathy, illus. 2006. (ENG.). 32p. (J). pap. 3.95 (978-1-59249-587-0(7)) Soundprints.

MacLachlan, Patricia & Charest, Emily MacLachlan. I Didn't Do It. Schneider, Katy, illus. 2010. (ENG.). 32p. (J). (gr. -1-3). 16.99 (978-0-06-135833-3(9), Tegen, Katherine Bks) HarperCollins Pubs.

Magoon, Scott. Breathe. Magoon, Scott, illus. 2014. (ENG., Illus.). 40p. (J). (gr. -1-3). 17.99 (978-1-4424-1258-3(5), Simon & Schuster/Paula Wiseman Bks.) Simon & Schuster/Paula Wiseman Bks.

Magsamen, Sandra. I Ruff You (Made with Love) Magsamen, Sandra, illus. 2016. (ENG., Illus.). 12p. (J). (gr. -1-k). bds. 7.99 (978-1-338-11082-1(9), Cartwheel Bks.) Scholastic, Inc.

Marr, Melissa & Airgood, Ellen. Bunny Roo, I Love You. White, Teagan, illus. 2015. (ENG.). 32p. (J). (gr. -1 — 1). 16.99 (978-0-399-16742-3(0), Nancy Paulsen Books) Penguin Young Readers Group.

Marsh, Laura F. Big Enough. 2009. (Mama Mirabelle Ser.). (ENG., Illus.). 24p. (J). (gr. -1-2). lib. bdg. 11.90 (978-1-4263-0433-0(1), National Geographic Children's Bks.) National Geographic Society.

—What's in a Tail? 2009. (Mama Mirabelle Ser.). (ENG., Illus.). 24p. (J). (gr. -1-2). lib. bdg. 11.90 (978-1-4263-0431-6(5), National Geographic Children's Bks.) National Geographic Society.

Marshall, Linda Elovitz. The Passover Lamb. Mai-Wyss, Tatjana, illus. 2013. (ENG.). 32p. (J). (gr. 1-4). 17.99 (978-0-307-93177-1(3), Random Hse. Bks. for Young Readers) Random Hse. Children's Bks.

Matison, Jimbo. I'm Going to Catch My Tail! 2014. (ENG., Illus.). 40p. (J). (gr. k-2). 14.95 (978-1-4197-1382-8(5), Abrams Bks. for Young Readers) Abrams, Inc.

McAnulty, Stacy. It's Not a Dinosaur! Boldt, Mike, illus. 2016. (Dino Files Ser.: 3). (ENG.). 128p. (J). (gr. 2-5). 9.99 (978-0-553-52197-9(7), Random Hse. Bks. for Young Readers) Random Hse. Children's Bks.

—A Mysterious Egg. Boldt, Mike, illus. (Dino Files Ser.: 1). (ENG.). 128p. (J). (gr. 2-5). 2017. 4.99 **(978-1-5247-0150-5(5))** 2016. 9.99 (978-0-553-52191-7(8)) Random Hse. Children's Bks. (Random Hse. Bks. for Young Readers).

—Too Big to Hide. Boldt, Mike, illus. (Dino Files Ser.: 2). (ENG.). 128p. (J). (gr. 2-5). 2017. 4.99 **(978-1-5247-0151-2(3))** 2016. 9.99 (978-0-553-52194-8(2)) Random Hse. Children's Bks. (Random Hse. Bks. for Young Readers).

McClure, Nikki. How to Be a Cat. 2013. (ENG., Illus.). 40p. (J). (gr. -1-k). 16.95 (978-1-4197-0528-1(8), Abrams Bks. for Young Readers) Abrams, Inc.

McCully, Emily Arnold. Little Ducks Go. McCully, Emily Arnold, illus. (I Like to Read(r) Ser.). (ENG., Illus.). 24p. (J). (gr. -1-2). 2015. 6.99 (978-0-8234-3300-1(5)) 2014. 14.95 (978-0-8234-2941-7(5)) Holiday Hse., Inc.

McGee, Warner, illus. Diego's Egyptian Expedition. 2009. (Go, Diego, Go! Ser.). (ENG.). 24p. (J). pap. 3.99 (978-1-4169-6870-2(9), Simon Spotlight/Nickelodeon) Simon Spotlight/Nickelodeon.

McLean, Linda. The Adventures of Simba the Frisky Feline. Faschi, Silvia, illus. 2012. (J). 14.95 (978-1-937406-24-0(5)) Mascot Bks., Inc.

McManis, Margaret. Olé! Cinco de Mayo!, 1 vol. Harrington, David, illus. 2013. (ENG.). 32p. (J). (gr. k-3). 16.99 (978-1-4556-1754-8(7)) Pelican Publishing Co., Inc.

McPike, Elizabeth. Little Bitty Friends. Barton, Patrice, illus. 2016. (ENG.). 32p. (J). (— 1). 16.99 (978-0-399-17255-7(6), G.P. Putnam's Sons Books for Young Readers) Penguin Young Readers Group.

Meade, Holly. If I Never Forever Endeavor. Meade, Holly, illus. 2011. (ENG., Illus.). 32p. (J). (gr. -1-3). 16.99 (978-0-7636-4071-2(9)) Candlewick Pr.

Meadows, Daisy. Katie the Kitten Fairy. Ripper, Georgie, illus. 2008. (J). (Pet Fairies Ser.: 1). (ENG.). 80p. (gr. -1-3). pap. 4.99 (978-0-545-02816-5(7), Scholastic Paperbacks); 65p. pap. (978-0-545-13320-3(3)) Scholastic, Inc.

—Katie the Kitten Fairy. Ripper, Georgie, illus. 2008. (Rainbow Magic — the Pet Fairies Ser.). 65p. (gr. 1-4). lib. bdg. 14.75 (978-1-4178-2999-6(0), Turtleback) Turtleback Bks.

—Mara the Meerkat Fairy: A Rainbow Magic Book. 2015. (Baby Animal Rescue Fairies Ser.: 3). (ENG.). 80p. (J). (gr. 2-5). pap. 4.99 (978-0-545-70850-0(8), Scholastic Paperbacks) Scholastic, Inc.

Miles, Ellen. Chewy & Chica. 2010. 132p. (J). pap. (978-0-545-22697-4(X)) Scholastic, Inc.

Miller, Sibley. A Horse's Best Friend. Chang, Tara Larsen & Gershman, Jo, illus. 2011. (Wind Dancers Ser.: 9). (ENG.). 80p. (J). (gr. 1-4). pap. 6.99 (978-0-312-60542-1(0), 9780312605421) Feiwel & Friends.

Moore, Eva. Lucky Ducklings. Carpenter, Nancy, illus. 2013. (ENG.). 32p. (J). (gr. k-2). 16.99 (978-0-439-44861-1(1), Orchard Bks.) Scholastic, Inc.

Mora, Pat. Here, Kitty, Kitty! (Ven, Gatita, Ven!) Suarez, Maribel, illus. 2008. (My Family: Mi Familia Ser.). (SPA & ENG.). 24p. (J). (gr. 4-7). lib. bdg. 15.89 (978-0-06-085045-6(0), Rayo) HarperCollins Pubs.

—Here Kitty Kitty!/Ven Gatita Ven! Suarez, Maribel, illus. 2008. (My Family: Mi Familia Ser.). (SPA & ENG.). 24p. (J). (gr. -1-1). 14.99 (978-0-06-085044-9(2), Rayo) HarperCollins Pubs.

Morgan, Mary. Pip Sits. 2017. (I Like to Read(r) Ser.). (ENG.). 24p. (J). (gr. -1-3). 6.99 (978-0-8234-3778-8(7)); (Illus.). 14.95 (978-0-8234-3676-7(4)) Holiday Hse., Inc.

Mucklow, Hope. Rojo the Baby Red Panda at the Zoo: An Allegory about Self-Worth Through a Red Panda & Giant Panda Comparison. 2014. (ENG., Illus.). 32p. (J). (gr. -1-3). 14.95 (978-1-62086-593-4(9)) Mascot Bks., Inc.

Murphy, Mary. Utterly Lovely One. 2012. (ENG., Illus.). 32p. (J). (gr. -1-k). 16.99 (978-0-7636-5267-8(9)) Candlewick Pr.

Murphy, Patricia. Mama, Look! Diaz, David, illus. 2017. (ENG.). 40p. (J). (gr. -1-k). 17.99 (978-1-4998-0080-7(0)) Little Bee Books Inc.

Murray, Alison. One Two That's My Shoe! Murray, Alison, illus. 2012. (ENG., Illus.). 32p. (J). (gr. -1-1). 16.99 (978-1-4231-4329-1(9)) Hyperion Pr.

My Little Library of Baby Animals. 2008. (Pocket Libraries Ser.). 5p. bds. (978-1-4075-3191-5(3)) Parragon, Inc.

Nicklaus, Terry. Schweppe. 2012. 24p. pap. 15.99 (978-1-4771-4565-4(6)) Xlibris Corp.

Nolan, Lucy & Nolan. Jack Quack, 1 vol. Wesson, Andrea, illus. 2003. (ENG.). 32p. (J). (gr. k-3). pap. 5.95 (978-0-7614-5153-2(6)) Marshall Cavendish Corp.

Numeroff, Laura Joffe. What Puppies Do Best. Munsinger, Lynn, illus. 2011. (ENG.). 32p. (J). (gr. -1-2). 14.99 (978-0-8118-6601-9(7)) Chronicle Bks. LLC.

Nussbaum, Ben. Toko the Hippo. Wenzel, Gregory, illus. 2006. (ENG.). 36p. (J). 8.95 (978-1-59249-580-1(X)); 14.99 (978-1-59249-577-1(X)); pap. 6.95 (978-1-59249-578-8(8)); pap. 2.95 (978-1-59249-579-5(6)) Soundprints.

Nyeu, Tao. Bunny Days. Nyeu, Tao, illus. 2010. (ENG., Illus.). 48p. (J). (gr. -1-k). 16.99 (978-0-8037-3330-5(5), Dial Bks) Penguin Young Readers Group.

Oates, Joyce Carol. Naughty Cherie! Graham, Mark, illus. 2008. 32p. (J). (gr. -1-3). lib. bdg. 17.89 (978-0-06-074359-8(X)) HarperCollins Pubs.

Odiemo, Lisa. Kitten & Her Sister. 2009. (ENG.). 16p. (J). 6.95 (978-1-60727-000-3(5)) Soundprints.

Ogata, Michael, illus. New Friend for Nai'a. 2009. (J). (978-1-56647-912-7(6)) Mutual Publishing LLC.

O'Hair, Margaret. My Pup, 0 vols. Lyon, Tammie, illus. 2010. (ENG.). 24p. (J). (gr. -1-2). bds. 7.99 (978-0-7614-5644-5(9), 9780761456445, Amazon Children's Publishing) Amazon Publishing.

Opal, Paola. Ollie. 2010. (ENG., Illus.). 24p. (J). (gr. -1 — 1). bds. 7.95 (978-1-897476-12-3(4)) Simply Read Bks. CAN. Dist: Ingram Publisher Services.

Ormerod, Jan. The Baby Swap. Joyner, Andrew, illus. 2015. (ENG.). 32p. (J). (gr. -1-1). 16.99 (978-1-4814-1914-7(5), Little Simon) Little Simon.

Orr, Wendy. Abandoned! - A Lion Called Kiki. Castelao, Patricia, illus. 2012. (Rainbow Street Shelter Ser.: 4). (ENG.). 128p. (J). (gr. 2-5). 15.99 (978-0-8050-9501-2(2), 9780805095012, Holt, Henry & Co. Bks. For Young Readers) Holt, Henry & Co.

O'Ryan, Ray. The Prehistoric Planet. Jack, Colin, illus. 2013. (Galaxy Zack Ser.: 3). (ENG.). 128p. (J). (gr. k-4). 16.99 (978-1-4424-6716-3(9)); pap. 5.99 (978-1-4424-6715-6(0)) Little Simon. (Little Simon).

—The Prehistoric Planet. 2013. (Galaxy Zack Ser.: 3). lib. bdg. 16.00 (978-0-606-32461-8(5), Turtleback) Turtleback Bks.

Page, Gail. How to Be a Good Cat. 2011. (ENG., Illus.). 32p. (J). 16.99 (978-1-59990-474-0(8), 9781599904740, Bloomsbury USA Childrens) Bloomsbury Publishing USA.

—How to Be a Good Cat. Page, Gail, illus. 2011. (ENG., Illus.). 32p. (J). (gr. -1-1). 17.89 (978-1-59990-475-7(6), 9781599904757, Bloomsbury USA Childrens) Bloomsbury Publishing USA.

Partis, Joanne. Stripe. Partis, Joanne, illus. (Carolrhoda Picture Books Ser.). (Illus.). 32p. (J). 2004. pap. 6.95 (978-1-57505-667-8(4)) 2003. (gr. -1-3). 14.95 (978-1-57505-450-6(7)) Lerner Publishing Group.

Patterson, Ellie. Baby Bear & the Big, Wide World. Kolanovic, Dubravka, illus. 2013. (J). (978-1-4351-4929-8(7)) Barnes & Noble, Inc.

Peschke, Marci. Spelling Queen, 1 vol. Mourning, Tuesday, illus. 2012. (Kylie Jean Ser.). (ENG.). 112p. (gr. 2-3). pap. 5.95 (978-1-4048-7212-7(4)); lib. bdg. 22.65 (978-1-4048-6801-4(1)) Picture Window Bks. (Kylie Jean).

Pfeffer, Wendy. Mallard Duck at Meadow View Pond. Oughton, Taylor, illus. (Smithsonian's Backyard Ser.). (ENG.). 32p. (J). (gr. -1-2). 2005. pap. 4.95 (978-1-56899-957-9(7), B5071) 2003. 8.95 (978-1-59249-063-9(8), SC5021) Soundprints.

—Mallard Duck at Mountain View Pond. Oughton, Taylor, illus. 2005. (Smithsonian's Backyard Ser.). (ENG.). 32p. (J). (gr. -1-2). 15.95 (978-1-56899-956-2(9), B5021) Soundprints.

Phinn, Gervase. Who Am I? Phinn, Gervase, illus. 2012. (Andersen Press Picture Bks). (ENG., Illus.). 32p. (J). (gr. -1-3). 16.95 (978-0-7613-8996-5(2)) Lerner Publishing Group.

Pledger, Maurice, illus. Daisy Duckling's Adventure. 2014. (ENG.). 16p. (J). (gr. -1). bds. 10.95 (978-1-62686-015-5(7), Silver Dolphin Bks.) Readerlink Distribution Services, LLC.

Porter-Gaylord, Laurel. I Love My Daddy Because... Wolff, Ashley, illus. 2004. (ENG.). 20p. (J). (gr. -1 — 1). bds. 6.99 (978-0-525-47250-6(9), Dutton Books for Young Readers) Penguin Young Readers Group.

Poskitt, Kjartan & Hargis, Wes. Agatha Parrot & the Thirteenth Chicken. 2017. (Agatha Parrot Ser.). (ENG., Illus.). 160p. (J). (gr. 2-5). 16.99 (978-0-544-50909-2(9)) Houghton Mifflin Harcourt Publishing Co.

Powell, Richard. Kitty's Tail. Davis, Caroline, illus. 2003. (Animal Tails Ser.). 10p. (J). 3.95 (978-1-58925-673-6(5)) Tiger Tales.

Pryor, Bonnie. Greenbrook Farm. 2013. (ENG.). 36p. (J). (gr. -1-3). 14.99 (978-1-4424-8873-1(5), Atheneum Bks. for Young Readers) Simon & Schuster Children's Publishing.

Publications International Ltd. Staff. My 1St Libraries Disney Baby Animals. 2011. 12p. 12.98 (978-1-4508-1571-0(5)) Phoenix International Publications, Inc.

Publications International Ltd. Staff, ed. Wonder Pets: Save the Baby Kitten. 2008. (J). bds. 10.98 (978-1-4127-9198-4(7)) Publications International, Ltd.

Puppy Love. 2014. (Flirt Ser.). (ENG., Illus.). 240p. (YA). (gr. 7). pap. 10.99 (978-1-4424-8412-2(8), Simon Pulse) Simon Pulse.

Raum, Elizabeth. The Christmas Star. Johnson, Meredith, illus. (ENG.). (J). (gr. -1-k). 2008. 32p. per. 3.99 (978-0-8249-5567-0(6)) 2005. 28p. bds. 7.95 (978-0-8249-6620-1(1)) Worthy Publishing. (Ideal Pubns.).

Reasoner, Charles. Farm Babies. Devaney, Adam, illus. 2009. (Baby Animal Board Bks.). 12p. (J). (gr. -1-k). bds. 7.99 (978-1-934650-52-3(8)) Just For Kids Pr., LLC.

—Jungle Babies. Devaney, Adam & Doherty, Paula, illus. 2009. (Baby Animal Board Bks.). 12p. (J). (gr. -1-k). bds. 7.99 (978-1-934650-50-9(1)) Just For Kids Pr., LLC.

Reasoner, Charles, illus. Peep! Peep! 2015. (J). (978-1-4795-5943-5(1)) Picture Window Bks.

—Puppy Love. 2015. (J). (978-1-4795-5946-6(6)) Picture Window Bks.

Rey, H. A. Farm Babies. 2017. (ENG., Illus.). 24p. (J). (gr. -1-3). 8.99 (978-0-544-94907-2(2), HMH Books For Young Readers) Houghton Mifflin Harcourt Publishing Co.

Reyes, Gabrielle. Dolphin Tale 2: The Junior Novel. 2014. (Dolphin Tale 2 Ser.). (ENG.). 144p. (J). (gr. 2-5). pap. 5.99 (978-0-545-68174-2(X)) Scholastic, Inc.

—Dolphin Tale 2: Movie Reader. 2014. (Dolphin Tale 2 Ser.). (ENG.). 32p. (J). (gr. -1-3). pap. 3.99 (978-0-545-68175-9(8)) Scholastic, Inc.

Rigo, L. Little Kitten. 2012. (Look at Me Bks.). (ENG., Illus.). 10p. (J). bds. 7.99 (978-0-7641-6523-8(2)) Barron's Educational Series, Inc.

—Little Lion. 2012. (Look at Me Bks.). (ENG., Illus.). 10p. (J). bds. 7.99 (978-0-7641-6525-2(9)) Barron's Educational Series, Inc.

Rissi, Anica Mrose. Anna, Banana, & the Little Lost Kitten. Park, Meg, illus. 2017. (Anna, Banana Ser.: 5). (ENG.). 144p. (J). (gr. 1-5). 16.99 **(978-1-4814-8669-9(1)**, Simon & Schuster Bks. For Young Readers) Simon & Schuster Bks. For Young Readers.

Robertson, Susan, illus. Little Puppy. 2005. (Bedtime Babies Ser.). 8p. (J). (gr. -1). per., bds. 6.99 (978-1-57755-501-8(5)) Flying Frog Publishing, Inc.

Rosoff, Meg. Moose Baby. Ercolini, David, illus. 2017. (J). **(978-0-399-16664-8(5)**, Putnam Juvenile) Penguin Publishing Group.

Ross, Michael Elsohn. Mama Me Alimenta. Wolff, Ashley, illus. 2008.Tr. of Mama's Milk. (ENG & SPA.). 32p. (J). (gr. -1-2). pap. 6.99 (978-1-58246-245-5(3), Tricycle Pr.) Random Hse. Children's Bks.

Roy, Ronald. Calendar Mysteries #12: December Dog. Gurney, John Steven, illus. 2014. (Calendar Mysteries Ser.: 12). (ENG.). 80p. (J). (gr. 1-4). 4.99 (978-0-385-37168-1(3), Random Hse. Bks. for Young Readers) Random Hse. Children's Bks.

—December Dog. 2014. (Calendar Mysteries Ser.: 12). lib. bdg. 14.75 (978-0-606-36019-7(0)) Turtleback Bks.

Rylant, Cynthia. Annie & Snowball & the Cozy Nest. Stevenson, Suçie, illus. (Annie & Snowball Ser.: 5). (ENG.). 40p. (J). (gr. k-2). 2010. pap. 3.99 (978-1-4169-3947-4(4)) 2009. 16.99 (978-1-4169-3943-6(1)) Simon Spotlight. (Simon Spotlight).

—Puppy Mudge Has a Snack. Mones, Isidre, illus. 2005. (Puppy Mudge Ser.). (gr. -1-k). 14.00 (978-0-7569-5764-3(8)) Perfection Learning Corp.

—Puppy Mudge Has a Snack. Mones, Isidre, illus. 2003. (Puppy Mudge Ser.). (ENG.). 32p. (J). (gr. -1-k). 16.99 (978-0-689-83981-8(2), Simon Spotlight) Simon Spotlight.

—The Sea Lion. McDaniels, Preston, illus. 2017. (Lighthouse Family Ser.: 7). (ENG.). 48p. (J). (gr. 1-5). 15.99 (978-1-4814-6025-5(0), Beach Lane Bks.) Beach Lane Bks.

Sáenz, Benjamin Alire. La Perrita Que le Encantaban las Tortillas. Garcia, Geronimo, illus. 2009. (Little Diego Book Ser.).Tr. of Dog Who Loved Tortillas. (SPA & ENG.). 40p. (J). (gr. 1-4). 17.95 (978-1-933693-54-5(1)) Cinco Puntos Pr.

Salten, Felix. Bambi's First Day. van Frankenhuyzen, Gijsbert, illus. 2008. (ENG.). 32p. (J). (gr. k-6). 15.95 (978-1-58536-422-0(3)) Sleeping Bear Pr.

Schaefer, Lola M. Follow Me, Mittens. Hartung, Susan Kathleen, illus. 2008. (My First I Can Read Ser.). (ENG.). 32p. (J). (gr. -1 — 1). pap. 3.99 (978-0-06-054667-0(0)) HarperCollins Pubs.

—Happy Halloween, Mittens. Hartung, Susan Kathleen, illus. 2010. (My First I Can Read Ser.). (ENG.). 32p. (J). (gr. -1-3). 16.99 (978-0-06-170222-8(6)); pap. 3.99 (978-0-06-170221-1(8)) HarperCollins Pubs.

—Mittens. Hartung, Susan Kathleen, illus. 2007. (My First I Can Read Ser.). (ENG.). 32p. (J). (gr. -1-3). pap. 3.99 (978-0-06-054661-8(1)) HarperCollins Pubs.

—Mittens. Hartung, Susan Kathleen, illus. 2007. (I Can Read Bks.). 25p. (gr. -1-k). 14.00 (978-0-7569-8104-4(2)) Perfection Learning Corp.

—Mittens. 2007. (My First I Can Read Ser.). (J). lib. bdg. 13.55 (978-1-4178-1001-7(7), Turtleback) Turtleback Bks.

—Mittens at School. 2012. (My First I Can Read Ser.). (J). lib. bdg. 13.55 (978-0-606-26292-7(X), Turtleback) Turtleback Bks.

—Mittens, Where Is Max? Hartung, Susan Kathleen, illus. 2011. (My First I Can Read Ser.). (ENG.). 32p. (J). (gr. -1 — 1). 16.99 (978-0-06-170227-3(7)); pap. 3.99 (978-0-06-170226-6(9)) HarperCollins Pubs.

—What's That, Mittens? Hartung, Susan Kathleen, illus. 2009. (My First I Can Read Ser.). (ENG.). 32p. (J). (gr. -1 — 1). pap. 3.99 (978-0-06-054664-9(6)) HarperCollins Pubs.

Scholastic Library Publishing. The Three Little Kittens Get Dressed. 2009. (Rookie Preschool Ser.). 24p. (J). (gr. -1). lib. bdg. 23.00 (978-0-531-24404-3(0), Children's Pr.) Scholastic Library Publishing.

Schories, Pat, illus. Biscuit Visits the Farm. 2012. (J). (978-1-4351-4383-8(3), HarperFestival) HarperCollins Pubs.

Schories, Pat & Capucilli, Alyssa Satin. Biscuit & the Little Pup. Schories, Pat, illus. 2007. (My First I Can Read Ser.). (ENG., Illus.). 32p. (J). (gr. -1 — 1). pap. 3.99 (978-0-06-074172-3(4)) HarperCollins Pubs.

Schwartz, Anna L. Okie the Wonder Dog. Dumm, Brian Caleb, illus. 2016. 62p. (J). pap. (978-1-63293-111-5(7)) Sunstone Pr.

Schwartz, Betty Ann & Seresin, Lynn. Run, Run Piglet. Ng, Neiko, illus. 2015. (Follow-Along Book Ser.). (ENG.). 10p. (J). (gr. -1 — 1). bds. 9.99 (978-1-4521-2467-4(1)) Chronicle Bks. LLC.

Seresin, Lynn & Schwartz, Betty Ann. Hop, Hop Bunny. Ng, Neiko, illus. 2015. (Follow-Along Book Ser.). (ENG.). 10p. (J). (gr. -1 — 1). bds. 9.99 (978-1-4521-2464-3(7)) Chronicle Bks. LLC.

Shaw, Ellie. Together Again. 2012. 24p. pap. 24.95 (978-1-4626-6427-6(X)) America Star Bks.

Shaw, Stephanie. Bedtime in the Meadow. Watkins, Laura, illus. 2013. (ENG.). 20p. (gr. -1). bds. 8.95 (978-1-58925-628-6(X)) Tiger Tales.

—A Cookie for Santa. Robert, Bruno, illus. 2014. (ENG.). 32p. (J). (gr. 1-4). 15.99 (978-1-58536-883-9(0), 203675) Sleeping Bear Pr.

Sheneman, Drew. Nope. 2017. (ENG., Illus.). 40p. (J). (-k). 17.99 (978-1-101-99731-4(1), Viking Books for Young Readers) Penguin Young Readers Group.

Sherrow, Victoria. Bottlenose Dolphin. Wertheim, Anne, illus. 2012. (ENG.). 24p. (J). pap. 3.95 (978-1-60727-724-8(7)) Soundprints.

Shoulders, Michael. Say Daddy! Weidner, Teri, illus. (ENG.). (J). 2013. 26p. (gr. -1-k). 8.99 (978-1-58536-863-1(6), 202383) 2008. 32p. (gr. k-6). 15.95 (978-1-58536-354-4(5)) Sleeping Bear Pr.

Sias, Ryan. Sniff! Sniff! 2015. (ENG., Illus.). 32p. (J). (gr. -1-2). 14.95 (978-1-4197-1490-0(2)) Abrams, Inc.

Sierra, Judy. Wild about You! Brown, Marc, illus. 2012. (ENG.). 40p. (J). (gr. -1-3). 17.99 (978-0-307-93178-8(1), Knopf Bks. for Young Readers) Random Hse. Children's Bks.

Silverman, Erica. Cowgirl Kate & Cocoa. Lewin, Betsy, illus. 2007. (Cowgirl Kate & Cocoa Ser.). (gr. 1-4). 15.95 (978-0-7569-8043-6(7)) Perfection Learning Corp.

—Cowgirl Kate & Cocoa: Spring Babies. Lewin, Betsy, illus. 2011. (Cowgirl Kate & Cocoa Ser.: 6). (ENG.). 40p. (J). (gr.

1-4). pap. 5.99 *(978-0-547-56685-6(9))* Houghton Mifflin Harcourt Publishing Co.

Siminovich, Lorena, illus. You Are My Baby - Farm. 2013. (ENG.). 10p. (J). (gr. -1 — 1). bds. 8.99 *(978-1-4521-0643-4(6))* Chronicle Bks. LLC.

—You Are My Baby - Safari. 2013. (ENG.). 10p. (J). (gr. -1 — 1). bds. 8.99 *(978-1-4521-0642-7(8))* Chronicle Bks. LLC.

—You Are My Baby: Garden. 2014. (ENG.). 10p. (J). (gr. -1 — 1). bds. 8.99 *(978-1-4521-2649-4(6))* Chronicle Bks. LLC.

—You Are My Baby: Meadow. 2015. (ENG.). 10p. (J). (gr. -1 — 1). bds. 8.99 *(978-1-4521-4011-7(1))* Chronicle Bks. LLC.

—You Are My Baby: Ocean. 2014. (ENG.). 10p. (J). (gr. -1 — 1). bds. 8.99 *(978-1-4521-2650-0(X))* Chronicle Bks. LLC.

Small, Lily. Kylie the Kitten. 2017. (Fairy Animals of Misty Wood Ser.). (ENG., Illus.). 144p. (J). pap. 5.99 ***(978-1-250-12698-6(3)***, 9781250126986, Holt, Henry & Co. Bks. For Young Readers) Holt, Henry & Co.

—Paddy the Puppy. 2015. (Fairy Animals of Misty Wood Ser.: 3). (ENG., Illus.). 144p. (J). (gr. k-3). pap. 5.99 *(978-1-62779-143-4(4)*, 9781627791434, Holt, Henry & Co. Bks. For Young Readers) Holt, Henry & Co.

Small, Lily. Penelope the Pony. 2017. (Fairy Animals of Misty Wood Ser.). (ENG., Illus.). 144p. (J). pap. 5.99 ***(978-1-250-12700-6(9)***, 9781250127006, Holt, Henry & Co. Bks. For Young Readers) Holt, Henry & Co.

Smallman, Steve. The Lamb Who Came for Dinner. Dreidemy, Joëlle, illus. 2007. 32p. (J). (gr. -1-2). 15.95 *(978-1-58925-067-3(2))* Tiger Tales.

Smith, Stephanie. Snowshoe Hare's Family. Hynes, Robert, illus. 2nd ed. 2007. (Soundprints' Read-and-Discover Ser.). (ENG.). (J). (gr. 1-3). 32p. 12.95 *(978-1-931465-44-1(4)*, PS2053); 48p. pap. 3.95 *(978-1-931465-15-1(0)*, S2003) Soundprints.

Smith, Stephanie & Smith, Stephanie A. Gray Wolf Pup's Adventure. Hynes, Robert, illus. 2nd ed. 2003. (ENG.). 32p. (J). (gr. 1-3). 12.95 *(978-1-931465-43-4(6)*, PS2077) Soundprints.

Soundprints. Panda Cub in the Bamboo Forest: Wilderness Adventures. 2012. (ENG.). 32p. (J). pap. 3.95 *(978-1-60727-872-6(3))* Soundprints.

—Polar Bear Cub & Mommy: Wilderness Adventures. 2012. (ENG.). 32p. (J). pap. 3.95 *(978-1-60727-871-9(5))* Soundprints.

Spinelli, Eileen. Hero Cat, 0 vols. Stammen, Jo Ellen McAllister, illus. 2011. (ENG.). 32p. (J). (gr. -1-3). pap. 9.99 *(978-0-7614-5837-1(9)*, 9780761458371, Amazon Children's Publishing) Amazon Publishing.

Springer, Susan Woodward. Seldovia Sam & the Sea Otter Rescue. Meissner, Amy, illus. 2003. (Misadventures of Seldovia Sam Ser.: Vol. 2). (ENG.). 64p. (J). (gr. 1-4). pap. 6.95 *(978-0-88240-571-1(3))* Graphic Arts Ctr. Publishing Co.

Springett, Martin. Kate & Pippin: An Unlikely Love Story. Springett, Isobel, photos by. 2012. (My Readers Ser.). (ENG., Illus.). 32p. (J). (gr. -1-3). 16.99 *(978-0-8050-9487-9(3)*, 9780805094879, Holt, Henry & Co. Bks. For Young Readers) Holt, Henry & Co.

Stasinska, Marta. In the Forest. Fratczak-Rodak, Monika, illus. 2015. (Mommy & Me Bath Bks.). (ENG.). 6p. (J). (gr. -1 — 1). 4.99 *(978-1-4380-7590-7(1))* Barron's Educational Series, Inc.

Steers, Billy. Lift-The-Flap Tab: Tractor Mac: Friends on the Farm. 2015. (Lift-The-Flap Tab Bks.). (ENG., Illus.). 16p. (J). (gr. -1-k). bds. 8.99 *(978-0-374-30168-2(9)*, 9780374301682) Square Fish.

Stein, David Ezra. Pouch! Stein, David Ezra, illus. 2010. (Rise & Shine Ser.). (ENG., Illus.). 32p. (C). (gr. -1-k). 25.95 *(978-0-399-25051-4(4))* National Geographic School Publishing, Inc.

—Pouch! Stein, David Ezra, illus. 2012. (ENG., Illus.). 32p. (J). (gr. -1 — 1). bds. 7.99 *(978-0-399-25738-4(1)*, Nancy Paulsen Books) Penguin Young Readers Group.

Summers, Terry. Peter Wanted a Pet. Kai, illus. 2012. 26p. 24.95 *(978-1-4626-6120-6(3))* America Star Bks.

Swinburne, Stephen R. Safe in a Storm. Bell, Jennifer, illus. 2016. (J). *(978-0-545-66987-0(1))*; (ENG.). 32p. (gr. -1-k). 10.99 *(978-0-545-86792-4(4))* Scholastic, Inc.

Tafuri, Nancy. Five Little Chicks. Tafuri, Nancy, illus. 2011. (Classic Board Bks.). (ENG., Illus.). 34p. (J). (gr. -1 — 1). bds. 7.99 *(978-1-4424-0722-0(0)*, Little Simon) Little Simon.

—Five Little Chicks. Tafuri, Nancy, illus. 2006. (ENG., Illus.). 32p. (J). (gr. -1-3). 16.99 *(978-0-689-87342-3(5)*, Simon & Schuster Bks. For Young Readers) Simon & Schuster Bks. For Young Readers.

Tangerine Designs Ltd. Casey Chick. 2015. (Little Loves Rattle Bks.). (ENG.). 8p. (J). (gr. -1 — 1). 7.99 *(978-1-4380-7563-1(4))* Barron's Educational Series, Inc.

—Katie Kitten. 2015. (Little Loves Rattle Bks.). (ENG.). 8p. (J). (gr. -1 — 1). 7.99 *(978-1-4380-7564-8(2))* Barron's Educational Series, Inc.

—Lucy Lamb. 2015. (Little Loves Rattle Bks.). (ENG.). 8p. (J). (gr. -1 — 1). 7.99 *(978-1-4380-7565-5(0))* Barron's Educational Series, Inc.

Taplin, Sam. Baby Animals. 2014. (Usborne Flap Book Ser.). (ENG., Illus.). 10p. (J). (gr. -1). bds. 7.99 *(978-0-7945-2105-9(3)*, Usborne) EDC Publishing.

Tetlow, Karin. Harry the Carousel Horse. Guze, Tessa, illus. 2012. 32p. pap. 15.96 *(978-0-615-55671-0(X))* Juping Horse Pr.

Texier, Ophélie. Baby Animals. 2009. (Little Discoveries: Ser.). (ENG., Illus.). 6p. (J). (gr. -1-k). bds. 8.95 *(978-0-7892-0984-9(5)*, Abbeville Kids) Abbeville Pr., Inc.

Thomas Nelson. Touch & Sparkle Baby Animals. 2016. (ENG.). 12p. (gr. -1). bds. *(978-1-78598-132-6(3))* Make Believe Ideas.

Thompson, Lauren. Cuaquito (Little Quack) Anderson, Derek, illus. 2010. (SPA.). 34p. (J). (gr. -1-1). bds. 7.99 *(978-1-4169-9894-5(2)*, Libros Para Ninos) Libros Para Ninos.

—Little Bunny. Butler, John, illus. 2013. (ENG.). 30p. (J). (gr. -1-k). bds. 5.99 *(978-1-4424-5851-2(8)*, Little Simon) Little Simon.

—Little Chick. Butler, John, illus. 2014. (ENG.). 30p. (J). (gr. -1-k). bds. 5.99 *(978-1-4424-9311-7(9)*, Little Simon) Little Simon.

—Little Chick. Butler, John, illus. 2014. (J). *(978-1-4351-5351-6(0)*, Simon & Schuster Bks. For Young Readers) Simon & Schuster Bks. For Young Readers.

—Little Lamb. Butler, John, illus. 2014. (J). *(978-1-4351-5352-3(9)*, Simon & Schuster Bks. For Young Readers) Simon & Schuster Bks. For Young Readers.

—Little Quack. Anderson, Derek, illus. 2005. (Classic Board Bks.). (ENG.). 32p. (J). (gr. -1-k). bds. 7.99 *(978-0-689-87645-5(9)*, Little Simon) Little Simon.

—Little Quack's Bath Book. Anderson, Derek, illus. 2006. (ENG.). 8p. (J). (gr. -1 — 1). 8.99 *(978-1-4169-0803-6(X)*, Little Simon) Little Simon.

—Wee Little Bunny. Butler, John, illus. 2010. (Wee Little Ser.). (ENG.). 32p. (J). (gr. -1-1). 14.99 *(978-1-4169-7937-1(9)*, Simon & Schuster Bks. For Young Readers) Simon & Schuster Bks. For Young Readers.

—Wee Little Chick. Butler, John, illus. 2008. (Wee Little Ser.). (ENG.). 32p. (J). (gr. -1-1). 15.99 *(978-1-4169-3468-4(5)*, Simon & Schuster Bks. For Young Readers) Simon & Schuster Bks. For Young Readers.

—Wee Little Lamb. Butler, John, illus. 2009. (Wee Little Ser.). (ENG.). 32p. (J). (gr. -1-3). 16.99 *(978-1-4169-3469-1(3)*, Simon & Schuster Bks. For Young Readers) Simon & Schuster Bks. For Young Readers.

Thompson, Lauren & Anderson, Derek. Little Quack. 2003. (ENG., Illus.). 32p. (J). (gr. -1-3). 17.99 *(978-0-689-84723-3(8)*, Simon & Schuster Bks. For Young Readers) Simon & Schuster Bks. For Young Readers.

Thomson, Sarah L. Cub's Big World. Cepeda, Joe, illus. 2013. (ENG.). 32p. (J). (gr. -1-3). 16.99 *(978-0-544-05739-5(2))* Houghton Mifflin Harcourt Publishing Co.

Tiger Tales, ed. Hello Baby! Ward, Sarah, illus. 2016. (To Baby with Love Ser.). (ENG.). 10p. (J). (gr. -1 — 1). bds. 9.99 *(978-1-58925-210-3(1))* Tiger Tales.

—Peekaboo Baby! Ward, Sarah, illus. 2016. (To Baby with Love Ser.). (ENG.). 10p. (J). (gr. -1 — 1). bds. 9.99 *(978-1-58925-212-7(8))* Tiger Tales.

Tiger Tales, Tiger, ed. Peekaboo Baby Animals. Frost, Maddie, illus. 2017. (Slide & Seek Ser.). (ENG.). 12p. (J). (gr. -1-1). bds. 7.99 ***(978-1-68010-514-8(0))*** Tiger Tales.

Tilert, Heather R. Ming-Ming Saves the Day: Follow the Reader Level 1. 2008. (Wonder Pets! Ser.). (ENG.). 24p. (J). 24.99 *(978-1-4169-6459-9(2)*, Simon Scribbles) Simon Scribbles.

Townsend, Michael. Cute & Cuter. 2013. (ENG., Illus.). 40p. (J). (gr. k-3). lib. bdg. 18.99 *(978-0-375-95718-5(9)*, Knopf Bks. for Young Readers) Random Hse. Children's Bks.

Twinem, Neecy. Baby Coyote Counts. 2004. (New Board Book Ser.).Tr. of Bebe Coyote cuenta. (ENG., Illus.). 12p. (J). (gr. -1-k). bds. 5.95 *(978-0-87358-852-2(5))* Cooper Square Publishing Llc.

—Baby Snake's Shapes. 2004. (New Board Book Ser.).Tr. of Las formas de Bebe Serpiente. (ENG., Illus.). 12p. (J). (gr. -1-k). 5.95 *(978-0-87358-850-8(9))* Cooper Square Publishing Llc.

Vail, Rachel. Piggy Bunny. Tankard, Jeremy, illus. 2012. (ENG.). 32p. (J). (gr. -1-1). 14.99 *(978-0-312-64988-3(6)*, 9780312649883) Feiwel & Friends.

van Genechten, Guido. The Big Baby Book. 2011. (ENG.). 22p. (J). (gr. k — 1). bds. 12.95 *(978-1-60537-079-8(7))* Cobblestone Publishing Co.

—Daddies & Their Babies. 2012. (Black & White Ser.). (ENG.). 20p. (J). (gr. k — 1). bds. 9.95 *(978-1-60537-110-8(6))* Cobblestone Publishing Co.

Vere, Ed. Max at Night. 2016. (Max Ser.: 2). (ENG.). 32p. (J). (-2). 16.99 *(978-1-4926-3296-2(1)*, 9781492632962, Sourcebooks Jabberwocky) Sourcebooks, Inc.

Waddell, Martin. Owl Babies Book & Toy Gift Set. Benson, Patrick, illus. 2016. (ENG.). (J). (-k). bds. 15.99 *(978-0-7636-8898-1(3))* Candlewick Pr.

Wallace, Nancy Elizabeth. Recycle Every Day!, 0 vols. Wallace, Nancy Elizabeth, illus. 2006. (ENG., Illus.). 41p. (J). (gr. -1-3). pap. 9.99 *(978-0-7614-5290-4(7)*, 9780761452904, Amazon Children's Publishing) Amazon Publishing.

Wang, Margaret. I Love You, Every Little Bit. Butler, John, illus. 2006. (ENG.). 10p. (gr. -1-k). bds. 9.95 *(978-1-58117-482-3(9)*, Intervisual/Piggy Toes) Bendon, Inc.

Ward, Jennifer. Way up in the Arctic. Spengler, Kenneth J., illus. 2007. (SPA & ENG.). 32p. (J). (gr. -1-3). 15.95 *(978-0-87358-928-4(9))* Cooper Square Publishing Llc.

Waring, Geoff. Oscar & the Bird: A Book about Electricity. Waring, Geoff, illus. 2011. (Start with Science Ser.). (ENG., Illus.). 32p. (J). (gr. -1-3). pap. 6.99 *(978-0-7636-5302-6(0))* Candlewick Pr.

—Oscar & the Cricket: A Book about Moving & Rolling. Waring, Geoff, illus. 2009. (Start with Science Ser.). (ENG., Illus.). 32p. (J). (gr. -1-3). pap. 6.99 *(978-0-7636-4512-0(5))* Candlewick Pr.

—Oscar & the Snail: A Book about Things That We Use. Waring, Geoff, illus. (Start with Science Ser.). (ENG., Illus.). 32p. (J). (gr. -1-3). 2011. pap. 6.99 *(978-0-7636-5303-3(9))* 2009. 14.99 *(978-0-7636-4039-2(5))* Candlewick Pr.

Watson, Jane Werner. Walt Disney's the Lucky Puppy (Disney Classic: the Lucky Puppy) Walt Disney Studio et al, illus. 2017. (Little Golden Book Ser.). (ENG.). 24p. (J). (-k). 4.99 ***(978-0-7364-3686-1(3)***, Golden/Disney) Random Hse. Children's Bks.

Watts, Frances. Kisses for Daddy. Legge, David, illus. 2008. 24p. (J). bds. *(978-1-921272-56-1(2))* Little Hare Bks. AUS. Dist: HarperCollins Pubs. Australia.

—Kisses for Daddy. Legge, David, illus. 2010. (ENG.). 26p. (J). (gr. -1-k). bds. 7.99 *(978-1-4169-8721-5(5)*, Little Simon) Little Simon.

Weston Woods Staff, creator. Kitten's First Full Moon. 2011. 29.95 *(978-0-545-37422-4(7))* Weston Woods Studios, Inc.

Where's My Mommy? 2015. (J). *(978-1-4351-5982-2(9))* Barnes & Noble, Inc.

Wiggin, Kate Douglas. The Bird's Christmas Carol. 2008. 88p. (gr. 4-7). pap. 8.95 *(978-1-60664-191-0(3))* Aegypan.

Wildsmith, Brian. The Little Wood Duck, 1 vol. 2007. (ENG., Illus.). 32p. (J). (gr. -1-3). 16.95 *(978-1-59572-042-9(1))* Star Bright Bks., Inc.

—The Little Wood Duck, 1 vol. Wildsmith, Brian, illus. 2006. (ENG., Illus.). 32p. (J). pap. 6.95 *(978-1-59572-049-8(9))* Star Bright Bks., Inc.

Willis, Jeanne. Fly, Chick, Fly! Ross, Tony, illus. 2012. (Andersen Press Picture Bks). (ENG.). 32p. (J). (gr. -1-3). 16.95 *(978-1-4677-0314-7(1))* Lerner Publishing Group.

—Upside down Babies. Reynolds, Adrian, illus. 2014. (ENG.). 32p. (J). (gr. -1-3). 16.95 *(978-1-4677-3424-0(1))* Lerner Publishing Group.

Wilson, Karma. What's in the Egg, Little Pip? Chapman, Jane, illus. 2010. (ENG.). 40p. (J). (gr. -1-3). 17.99 *(978-1-4169-4204-7(1)*, McElderry, Margaret K. Bks.) McElderry, Margaret K. Bks.

—Where Is Home, Little Pip? Chapman, Jane, illus. 2008. (ENG.). 40p. (J). (gr. -1-3). 17.99 *(978-0-689-85983-0(X)*, McElderry, Margaret K. Bks.) McElderry, Margaret K. Bks.

Winnick, Karen B. Good Night, Baby Animals: You've Had a Busy Day. Watkins, Laura, illus. 2017. (ENG.). 64p. (J). 17.99 *(978-0-8050-9883-9(6)*, 9780805098839, Holt, Henry & Co. Bks. For Young Readers) Holt, Henry & Co.

Wissman, Celeste Farris. When I Teach My Monkey How to Dance. 2012. 24p. pap. 17.99 *(978-1-4772-6035-7(8))* AuthorHouse.

Wolff, Ashley. The Baby Chicks Are Singing: Sing along in English & Spanish! Wolff, Ashley, illus. 2005. (ENG., Illus.). 22p. (J). (gr. -1 — 1). bds. 7.99 *(978-0-316-06732-4(6))* Little, Brown Bks. for Young Readers.

Young, Jeanna Stolle & Johnson, Jacqueline Kinney. Princess Grace & the Little Lost Kitten, 1 vol. Aranda, Omar, illus. 2011. (Princess Parables Ser.). (ENG.). 32p. (J). (gr. -1-2). 14.99 *(978-0-310-71640-2(3))* Zonderkidz.

Young, Norene. Cathy, the Castaway Cat. Woodyard, Sandy Lilly, illus. 2012. 34p. 24.95 *(978-1-4626-6111-4(4))* America Star Bks.

Yuly, Toni. Night Owl. Yuly, Toni, illus. 2015. (ENG., Illus.). 40p. (J). (— 1). 15.99 *(978-1-250-05457-9(5)*, 9781250054579) Feiwel & Friends.

Zalme, Ron, illus. Sunny Day Tales. 2009. (J). *(978-1-59078-735-9(8))* Highlights for Children.

Zoehfeld, Kathleen Weidner. Seal Pup Grows Up: The Story of a Harbor Seal. Bonforte, Lisa, illus. 2011. (Smithsonian Oceanic Collection Ser.). (ENG.). 32p. (J). (gr. -1-3). 19.95 *(978-1-60727-663-0(1))* Soundprints.

ANIMALS—LANGUAGE

see Animal Communication

ANIMALS—LEGENDS

see Animals—Folklore

ANIMALS, MARINE

see Marine Animals

ANIMALS—MIGRATION

see also names of animals with the subdivision Migration, e.g. Birds—Migration

Ariel, A. D. How Do Animals Move? 2016. (Spring Forward Ser.). (J). (gr. 1). *(978-1-4900-2238-3(4))* Benchmark Education Co.

Berkes, Marianne. Going Home: The Mystery of Animal Migration, 1 vol. DiRubbio, Jennifer, illus. 2010. 32p. (J). (gr. -1-5). (ENG.). 16.95 *(978-1-58469-126-6(3))*; pap. 8.95 *(978-1-58469-127-3(1))* Dawn Pubns.

Best, B. J. Geese. 2016. (Migrating Animals Ser.). 24p. (J). lib. bdg. 24.21 *(978-1-5026-2100-9(2))* Cavendish Square Publishing.

Booth, Jack. The 10 Most Amazing Migrations. 2008. (J). 14.99 *(978-1-55448-522-2(3))* Scholastic Library Publishing.

Braun, Eric. Curious Pearl Observes Migration: 4D an Augmented Reality Science Experience. Dehennin, Stephanie, illus. 2017. (Curious Pearl, Science Girl 4D Ser.). (ENG.). 24p. (gr. k-2). lib. bdg. 20.65 ***(978-1-5158-1344-6(4))*** Picture Window Bks.

Brynie, Faith Hickman. Do Animals Migrate? 2010. (I Like Reading about Animals! Ser.). (Illus.). 32p. (J). 23.94 *(978-0-7660-3325-2(2))*; pap. 7.95 *(978-0-7660-3746-5(0)*, Enslow Elementary) Enslow Pubs., Inc.

Carmichael, L. E. Locust Migration. 2012. (Animal Migrations Ser.). (ENG., Illus.). 32p. (J). (gr. 2-5). lib. bdg. 29.93 *(978-1-60973-623-1(0)*, 201200) Child's World, Inc., The.

Carney, Elizabeth. Great Migrations: Whales, Wildebeests, Butterflies, Elephants, & Other Amazing Animals on the Move. 2010. (Illus.). (J). (ENG.). 48p. (gr. 3-7). 27.90 *(978-1-4263-0701-0(2)*, National Geographic Children's Bks.); 45p. *(978-1-4263-0811-6(6))* National Geographic Society.

Carney, Elizabeth & National Geographic Kids Staff. Great Migrations: Whales, Wildebeests, Butterflies, Elephants, & Other Amazing Animals on the Move. 2010. (ENG., Illus.). 48p. (J). (gr. 3-7). 17.95 *(978-1-4263-0700-3(4)*, National Geographic Children's Bks.) National Geographic Society.

Catt, Thessaly. Migrating with the Caribou. 2011. (Animal Journeys Ser.). (Illus.). 24p. (YA). (gr. 1-4). 22.60 *(978-1-4488-2541-7(5))* Rosen Publishing Group, Inc., The.

Cohn, Scotti. Avanzando ... de Aquí para Allá 1 vol. Migraciones Masivas. Detwiler, Susan, illus. 2013. (SPA.). 32p. (J). (gr. -1-4). 17.95 *(978-1-60718-712-7(4)*, 9781607187127) Arbordale Publishing.

—On the Move: Mass Migrations, 1 vol. Detwiler, Susan, illus. 2013. (SPA.). 32p. (J). (gr. -1-4). pap. 9.95 *(978-1-62855-350-5(2))* Arbordale Publishing.

Cooper, Sharon Katz. Extraordinary Migrations. Leonard, Tom et al, illus. 2015. (Extraordinary Migrations Ser.). (ENG.). 24p. (gr. 2-3). lib. bdg. 106.60 *(978-1-4795-6247-3(5))* Picture Window Bks.

—When Butterflies Cross the Sky: The Monarch Butterfly Migration. Brunet, Joshua S., illus. 2015. (Extraordinary Migrations Ser.). (ENG.). 24p. (gr. 2-3). pap. 8.95 *(978-1-4795-6100-1(2))*; lib. bdg. 26.65 *(978-1-4795-6076-9(6))* Picture Window Bks.

—When Crabs Cross the Sand: The Christmas Island Crab Migration. Wald, Christina, illus. 2015. (Extraordinary Migrations Ser.). (ENG.). 24p. (gr. 2-3). lib. bdg. 26.65 *(978-1-4795-6077-6(4))* Picture Window Bks.

—When Penguins Cross the Ice: The Emperor Penguin Migration. Leonard, Tom, illus. 2015. (Extraordinary Migrations Ser.). (ENG.). 24p. (gr. 2-3). lib. bdg. 26.65 *(978-1-4795-6078-3(2))* Picture Window Bks.

—When Whales Cross the Sea: The Gray Whale Migration. Leonard, Tom, illus. 2015. (Extraordinary Migrations Ser.). (ENG.). 24p. (gr. 2-3). lib. bdg. 26.65 *(978-1-4795-6079-0(0))* Picture Window Bks.

Cosson, M. J. Golden Eagles: A Solo Journey. 2016. (Illus.). 32p. (J). *(978-1-4896-4515-9(2))* Weigl Pubs., Inc.

—Salmon: A Journey Home. 2016. (Illus.). 32p. (J). *(978-1-4896-4523-4(3))* Weigl Pubs., Inc.

Crossingham, John & Kalman, Bobbie. ¿Qué Es la Migración? 2007. (Ciencia de los Seres Vivos Ser.). (SPA., Illus.). 32p. (J). (gr. 3-7). lib. bdg. *(978-0-7787-8769-3(9))* Crabtree Publishing Co.

—¿Que Es la Migracion? 2007. (Ciencia de los Seres Vivos Ser.). (SPA., Illus.). 32p. (J). (gr. 3-7). pap. *(978-0-7787-8815-7(6))* Crabtree Publishing Co.

De La Bedoyere, Camilla. Animal Migrations. 2017. (Epic! Ser.). (ENG., Illus.). 32p. (J). (gr. 4-6). pap. 11.99 *(978-0-7502-9730-1(1)*, Wayland) Hachette Children's Group GBR. Dist: Hachette Bk. Group.

Einspruch, Andrew. Migration: Animals on the Move. 2014. (Discovery Education: Animals Ser.). 32p. (J). (gr. 3-6). 26.25 *(978-1-4777-6948-5(X))*; pap. 10.00 *(978-1-4777-6949-2(8))* Rosen Publishing Group, Inc., The. (PowerKids Pr.).

Feldman, Thea. Animales Migratorios: Por Tierra. 2007. (En marcha: Migraciones animales (Spanish- on the Move: Animal Migration) Ser.). (SPA.). 24p. (gr. 1-4). pap. 8.15 *(978-0-8368-8433-3(7)*, Weekly Reader Leveled Readers) Stevens, Gareth Publishing LLLP.

Franchino, Vicky. Animal Migrations. 2015. (ENG., Illus.). 48p. (J). lib. bdg. *(978-0-531-21545-6(8)*, Orchard Bks.) Scholastic, Inc.

Hegarty, Patricia. Animal Journeys. Courtney-Tickle, Jessica, illus. 2017. (360 Degrees Ser.). (ENG.). 76p. (J). (gr. 3-12). 12.99 ***(978-1-944530-04-4(5)***, 360 Degrees) Tiger Tales.

High Tide for Horseshoe Crabs. 2015. (ENG., Illus.). 40p. (J). (gr. -1-2). lib. bdg. 16.95 *(978-1-58089-604-7(9))* Charlesbridge Publishing, Inc.

Hirsch, Rebecca E. Caribou: A Tundra Journey. 2016. (Illus.). 32p. (J). *(978-1-4896-4513-5(6))* Weigl Pubs., Inc.

—Green Sea Turtles: A Nesting Journey. 2016. (Illus.). 32p. (J). *(978-1-4896-4517-3(9))* Weigl Pubs., Inc.

—Monarch Butterflies: A Generational Journey. 2016. (Illus.). 32p. (J). *(978-1-4896-4521-0(7))* Weigl Pubs., Inc.

Hirsch, Rebecca E. Thousand-Mile Fliers & Other Amazing Migrators. 2017. (Searchlight Books (tm) — Animal Superpowers Ser.). (ENG.). 40p. (J). (gr. 3-5). 16.99 ***(978-1-5124-3666-2(6)***, Lerner Pubns.); 46.65 ***(978-1-5124-2822-3(1)***, Lerner Pubns.); 46.65 ***(978-1-5124-3665-5(8)***, Lerner Pubns.); (Illus.). 30.65 *(978-1-5124-2546-8(X))* Lerner Publishing Group.

Hogenkamp, S. They Crawl! Learning the CR Sound. 2009. (PowerPhonics Ser.). 24p. (gr. 1-1). 39.90 *(978-1-60851-474-8(9)*, PowerKids Pr.) Rosen Publishing Group, Inc., The.

Hughes, Mónica. Migration. 2016. (Nature's Patterns Ser.). (ENG.). 32p. (gr. 1-3). pap. 8.29 *(978-1-4846-3636-7(8)*, Heinemann First Library) Heinemann-Raintree.

Johnson, Rebecca L. & National Geographic Learning Staff. Tracking Animal Migrators. 2007. (Reading Expeditions Ser.). (ENG., Illus.). 32p. (J). pap. 17.95 *(978-0-7922-8449-9(6))* CENGAGE Learning.

Kalman, Bobbie. Why Do Animals Migrate? 2009. (Big Science Ideas Ser.). (ENG., Illus.). 32p. (J). (gr. 1-4). pap. *(978-0-7787-3303-4(3))*; (gr. 2-4). *(978-0-7787-3283-9(5))* Crabtree Publishing Co.

Kaner, Etta. Animals Migrating: How, When, Where & Why Animals Migrate. Stephens, Pat, illus. 2005. (Animal Behavior Ser.). (ENG.). 40p. (J). (gr. 2-6). 6.95 *(978-1-55337-548-7(3))* Kids Can Pr., Ltd. CAN. Dist: Hachette Bk. Group.

Kant, Tanya. The Migration of a Whale. Bergin, Mark, illus. 2008. (Amaze Ser.). (ENG.). 32p. (J). (gr. k-3). 27.00 *(978-0-531-24049-6(5))*; pap. 8.95 *(978-0-531-23803-5(2))* Scholastic Library Publishing. (Children's Pr.).

Kopp, Megan. Migration. 2016. (Illus.). 24p. (J). *(978-1-5105-0930-6(5))* SmartBook Media, Inc.

—Migration. 2015. (Illus.). 24p. (J). *(978-1-4896-3679-9(X))* Weigl Pubs., Inc.

Labella, Susan. Animales Migratorios: En el Agua. 2007. (En marcha: Migraciones animales (Spanish- on the Move: Animal Migration) Ser.). (SPA., Illus.). 24p. (gr. 1-4). pap. 8.15 *(978-0-8368-8431-9(0)*, Weekly Reader Leveled Readers) Stevens, Gareth Publishing LLLP.

—How Animals Migrate. 2007. (On the Move: Animal Migration Ser.). (Illus.). 24p. (gr. 1-4). pap. 8.15 *(978-0-8368-8421-0(3))*; lib. bdg. 22.00 *(978-0-8368-8416-6(7))* Stevens, Gareth Publishing LLLP. (Weekly Reader Leveled Readers).

LaBella, Susan & Labella, Susan. Cómo Migran los Animales. 2007. (En marcha: Migraciones animales (Spanish- on the Move: Animal Migration) Ser.). (SPA.). 24p. (gr. 1-4). pap. 8.15 *(978-0-8368-8434-0(5)*, Weekly Reader Leveled Readers) Stevens, Gareth Publishing LLLP.

Lindsey, Marta. Little Gray's Great Migration, 1 vol. Gabriel, Andrea, illus. 2015. (ENG.). 32p. (J). (gr. k-3). 17.95 *(978-1-62855-452-6(5))* Arbordale Publishing.

Marsh, Laura. Amazing Animal Journeys. 2010. (Readers Ser.). (ENG., Illus.). 48p. (J). (gr. 2-4). pap. 3.99 *(978-1-4263-0741-6(1)*, National Geographic Children's Bks.) National Geographic Society.

—Great Migrations - Amazing Animal Journeys. 2010. (Readers Ser.). (ENG., Illus.). 48p. (J). (gr. 2-4). 13.90 *(978-1-4263-0742-3(X)*, National Geographic Children's Bks.) National Geographic Society.

—Great Migrations - Elephants. 2010. (Readers Ser.). (ENG., Illus.). 48p. (J). (gr. 2-4). 13.90 *(978-1-4263-0744-7(6))*; pap. 3.99 *(978-1-4263-0743-0(8))* National Geographic Society. (National Geographic Children's Bks.).

—Great Migrations Whales. 2010. (Readers Ser.). (ENG., Illus.). 48p. (J). (gr. 2-4). pap. 3.99 *(978-1-4263-0745-4(4)*, National Geographic Children's Bks.) National Geographic Society.

—Whales. 2010. (Readers Ser.). (ENG., Illus.). 48p. (J). (gr. 2-4). 13.90 *(978-1-4263-0746-1(2)*, National Geographic Children's Bks.) National Geographic Society.

Martins, Isabel Minhós. Coming & Going. Carvalho, Bernardo, illus. 2014. (ENG.). 48p. (J). (gr. -1-3). 16.95 *(978-1-84976-161-1(2))* Tate Publishing, Ltd. GBR. Dist: Abrams, Inc.

McDowell, Pamela. Flight. 2016. (Illus.). 24p. (J). *(978-1-5105-0924-5(0))* SmartBook Media, Inc.

Mebane, Jeanie. Animal Migration. 2012. (Learn about Animal Behavior Ser.). (ENG.). 24p. (gr. 1-2). pap. 41.70 (978-1-4296-9307-3(X), First Facts); pap. 7.29 (978-1-4296-9306-6(1)) Capstone Press of Coughlan Cos.

Migrating Animals. 2016. (Migrating Animals Ser.). 24p. (J). lib. bdg. 145.26 (978-1-5026-2400-0(1)) Cavendish Square Publishing.

Migrating with the Caribou. 2011. (Animal Journeys Ser.). (Illus.). 24p. (J). pap. 8.25 (978-1-4488-2666-7(7), PowerKids Pr.) Rosen Publishing Group, Inc., The.

Miller, Debbie S. A Caribou Journey. 2010. (ENG., Illus.). 32p. (J). pap. 9.95 (978-1-60223-096-5(X)) Univ. of Alaska Pr.

Nelson, Robin. Migración. 2012. (Mi Primer Paso Al Mundo Real - Descubriendo Los Ciclos de la Naturaleza (First Step Nonfiction - Discovering Nature's Cycles) Ser.).Tr. of Migration. (Illus.). 24p. (gr. k-2). (ENG & SPA.). pap. 6.95 (978-0-7613-9354-2(4)); (SPA., lib. bdg. 23.93 (978-0-7613-9338-2(2)) Lerner Publishing Group. (Ediciones Lerner).

—Migration. 2010. pap. 33.92 (978-0-7613-6915-8(5)); (ENG.). 24p. pap. 6.95 (978-0-7613-5682-0(7)); (ENG., Illus.). 24p. lib. bdg. 23.93 (978-0-7613-4580-0(9)) Lerner Publishing Group.

Norris, Robert. On the Move: Animal Migration. 2014. (ENG.). 24p. (gr. k-3). 28.50 (978-1-62717-633-0(0)) Rourke Educational Media.

O'Sullivan, Joanne. Migration Nation: Animals on the Go from Coast to Coast. 2015. (ENG., Illus.). 96p. (J). (gr. 3-7). 15.95 (978-1-62354-050-0(X)) Charlesbridge Publishing, Inc.

Schueller, Gretel H. & Schueller, Sheila K. Animal Migration. 2009. (Animal Behavior Ser.). (Illus.). 120p. (gr. 5-8). lib. bdg. 32.95 (978-1-60413-127-7(6), Chelsea Hse.) Facts On File, Inc.

Schuh, Mari C. I Notice Animals in Fall. 2016. (First Step Nonfiction — Observing Fall Ser.). (ENG., Illus.). 24p. (J). (gr. k-2). 23.99 (978-1-5124-0792-1(5)) Lerner Publishing Group.

Schweppe, Deirdre. Migrating Animals: Use Place Value Understanding & Properties of Operations to Add & Subtract. 2014. (Math Masters: Number & Operations in Base Ten Ser.). 24p. (J). (gr. 2-3). 23.60 (978-1-4777-6434-3(8)); (ENG.). pap. 8.25 (978-1-4777-4751-3(6)) Rosen Publishing Group, Inc., The. (Rosen Classroom).

Shea, Therese. What Is Animal Migration? 2015. (Let's Find Out! Animal Life Ser.). (ENG., Illus.). 32p. (J). (gr. 2-3). 23.45 (978-1-68048-010-8(3), Britannica Educational Publishing) Rosen Publishing Group, Inc., The.

Shetterly, Susan Hand. Swimming Home. Raye, Rebekah, illus. 2014. (Tilbury House Nature Book Ser.: 0). (ENG.). 32p. (gr. 1-6). 16.95 (978-0-88448-354-0(1), 884354) Tilbury Hse. Pubs.

Strauss, Holden. Animal Migration. 2016. (Spotlight on Ecology & Life Science Ser.). 00024p. (J). (gr. 4-6). pap. 10.00 (978-1-4994-2579-6(1), PowerKids Pr.) Rosen Publishing Group, Inc., The.

Thornhill, Jan. Is This Panama? A Migration Story. Kim, Soyeon & Owlkids Books Inc. Staff, illus. 2013. (ENG.). 40p. (J). (gr. k-4). 16.95 (978-1-926973-88-3(7), Owlkids) Owlkids Bks. Inc. CAN. Dist: Publishers Group West (PGW).

Trussell-Cullen, Alan. Animal Travellers, Vol. 82. 2014. (ENG.). 24p. spiral bd. 9.00 (978-1-4085-0137-5(6)) Oxford Univ. Pr., Inc.

Wood, Alix. Amazing Animal Journeys. 2012. (Wow! Wildlife Ser.). (ENG., Illus.). 24p. (J). (gr. k-5). 22.60 (978-1-4488-8099-7(8)); pap. 8.25 (978-1-4488-8163-5(3)) Windmill Bks.

Zuravicky, Orli. The Galloping Book. 2009. (Let's Get Moving Ser.). 24p. (gr. k-k). 42.50 (978-1-61514-226-2(6), PowerKids Pr.) Rosen Publishing Group, Inc., The.

—The Galloping Book / Trotar. 2009. (Let's Get Moving / Diviértete en movimiento Ser.). (ENG & SPA.). 24p. (gr. k-1). 42.50 (978-1-61514-232-3(0), Editorial Buenas Letras) Rosen Publishing Group, Inc., The.

ANIMALS, MYTHICAL

see also names of mythical animals, e.g. Dragons, Unicorn, etc.

ABDO Publishing Company Staff. Creatures of Legend. 2014. (Creatures of Legend Ser.: 6). (ENG.). 48p. (gr. 3-6). lib. bdg. 196.74 (978-1-62403-149-6(8)) ABDO Publishing Co.

Ames, Lee J. & Mitchell, Andrew. Draw 50 Magical Creatures: The Step-By-Step Way to Draw Unicorns, Elves, Cherubs, Trolls, & Many More. 2013. (ENG., Illus.). 64p. pap. 9.99 (978-0-8230-8610-8(0), Watson-Guptill) Potter/TenSpeed/Harmony.

Barr, Steve. Draw Crazy Creatures. 2013. (Kids DIY Ser.). (ENG.). 64p. (J). pap. 12.99 (978-1-4403-2220-4(1), Impact) F&W Media, Inc.

Baynes, Pauline. Questionable Creatures: A Bestiary. Baynes, Pauline, illus. 2006. (ENG., Illus.). 48p. (J). (gr. 5-18). 18.00 (978-0-8028-5284-7(X)) Eerdmans, William B. Publishing Co.

BeaverSimon. FANTASTIC CREATURES: MONSTERS, MERMAIDS, AND WILD MEN BEGINNING BOOK WITH ONLINE ACCESS. 2014. (ENG.). 24p. (J). pap. 9.50 (978-1-107-69637-2(2)) Cambridge Univ. Pr.

Bechtold, Phyliss. Seymour Bluffs & the Legend of the Piasa Bird. 2007. 26p. 9.95 (978-0-9728532-8-6(6)) New Horizons Christian Ctr.

Bechtold, Phyllis. Seymour Bluffs Activities Coloring Book. 2006. 32p. spiral bd. 5.95 (978-0-9728538-3-5(9)) Amica Publishing.

Becker, Helaine. Monster Science: Could Monsters Survive (and Thrive!) in the Real World? McAndrew, Phil, illus. 2016. (ENG.). 96p. (J). (gr. 3-7). 18.95 (978-1-77138-054-6(3)) Kids Can Pr., Ltd. CAN. Dist: Hachette Bk. Group.

Bergin, Mark. Magical Creatures & Mythical Beasts. 2009. (How to Draw Ser.). (Illus.). 32p. (J). (ENG.). (gr. 4-6). pap. 11.75 (978-1-4358-2647-2(7)); lib. bdg. 26.50 (978-1-4358-2518-5(7)) Rosen Publishing Group, Inc., The. (PowerKids Pr.).

Berry, Bob & Destefano, Merrie. How to Draw Magical, Monstrous & Mythological Creatures: Discover the Magic of Drawing More Than 20 Legendary Folklore, Fantasy, & Horror Characters. 2011. (Walter Foster Studio Ser.). (ENG., Illus.). 128p. (J). (gr. 5-11). pap. 16.95 (978-1-60058-228-8(1), 1600582281) Quarto Publishing Group USA.

Boyce, Natalie Pope & Osborne, Mary Pope. Dragons & Mythical Creatures. Molinari, Carlo, illus. 2016. (Magic Tree House - Fact Tracker Ser.: 35). (ENG.). 128p. (J). (gr. 2-5). 6.99 (978-1-101-93636-8(3), Random Hse. Bks. for Young Readers) Random Hse. Children's Bks.

Bradley, Timothy. The Science of Monsters (Grade 6) 2016. (TIME for KIDS(r) Nonfiction Readers Ser.). (Illus.). 64p. (J). (gr. 6-6). 10.99 (978-1-4938-3607-9(2)) Teacher Created Materials, Inc.

Castellano, Peter. Chupacabras. 2016. (Monsters! Ser.). (ENG., Illus.). 32p. (J). (gr. 1-2). pap. 10.50 (978-1-4824-4082-9(2)) Stevens, Gareth Publishing LLLP.

Cerato, Mattia & Sexton, Brenda. Easy-to-Draw Mythical Creatures. Cerato, Mattia & Sexton, Brenda, illus. 2011. (You Can Draw Ser.). (ENG., Illus.). 48p. (gr. 1-2). pap. 5.19 (978-1-4048-7059-8(8)) Picture Window Bks.

Cox, Barbara & Forbes, Scott. Spooky Spirits & Creepy Creatures, Vol. 1. 2014. (Creepy Chronicles Ser.). (ENG., Illus.). 32p. (J). (gr. 5-6). 26.60 (978-1-4824-0243-8(2)) Stevens, Gareth Publishing LLLP.

Curran, Bob. Frankenstein & Other Man-Made Monsters. 2013. (Haunted: Ghosts & the Paranormal Ser.). (Illus.). 208p. (YA). (gr. 7-12). 37.25 (978-1-4777-0679-4(8)) Rosen Publishing Group, Inc., The.

Eason, Sarah. Drawing Fairies, Mermaids, & Unicorns. Santillan, Jorge, illus. 2013. (Learn to Draw Ser.). 32p. (J). (gr. 2-5). pap. 63.00 (978-1-4339-9538-5(7)); pap. 10.50 (978-1-4339-9537-8(9)) Stevens, Gareth Publishing LLLP.

Edwards, Katie. Myths & Monsters: Secrets Revealed. Mendez, Simon, illus. 2004. 29p. (J). pap. 6.95 (978-1-57091-582-6(2)) Charlesbridge Publishing, Inc.

Gale Editor & Redmond, Shirley Raye, eds. Golem. 2011. (Monsters Ser.). (Illus.). 48p. (YA). (gr. 7-12). lib. bdg. 30.45 (978-0-7377-5866-5(X)) Cengage Gale.

Galeano, Eduardo. MITOS: DE MEMORIA DEL FUEGO. (SPA.). 80p. 14.95 (978-84-667-1709-0(9)) Suma de Letras, S.L. ESP. Dist: Distribooks, Inc.

Ganeri, Anita & West, David. Creatures of Myths & Legends. 2012. (J). 70.50 (978-1-4488-5235-2(8)); pap. 11.75 (978-1-4488-5234-5(X)); lib. bdg. 26.50 (978-1-4488-5198-0(X)) Rosen Publishing Group, Inc., The. (PowerKids Pr.).

Godfrey, Linda S. Lake & Sea Monsters. 2008. (Mysteries, Legends, & Unexplained Phenomena Ser.). (Illus.). 128p. (YA). (gr. 7-12). 29.95 (978-0-7910-9393-1(X)) Facts On File, Inc.

—Mythical Creatures. 2009. (Mysteries, Legends, & Unexplained Phenomena Ser.). (Illus.). 160p. (YA). (gr. 7-12). 29.95 (978-0-7910-9394-8(8)) Facts On File, Inc.

Hamilton, John. Unicorns & Other Magical Creatures, 1 vol. 2004. (Fantasy & Folklore Ser.). (ENG., Illus.). 32p. (gr. 4-8). 27.07 (978-1-59197-715-5(0), Abdo & Daughters) ABDO Publishing Co.

Hinds, Kathryn. Sphinxes & Centaurs. 2013. (Creatures of Fantasy Ser.). 64p. (J). (gr. 4-8). pap. 15.28 (978-1-62712-054-8(8)) Cavendish Square Publishing.

Holland, Simon. A Miscellany of Magical Beasts. Wyatt, David et al, illus. 2016. (ENG.). 48p. (J). 17.99 (978-1-68119-430-1(9), 9781681194301, Bloomsbury USA Childrens) Bloomsbury Publishing USA.

Hunter, Llyn. A Little Book of Magical Beings. Hunter, Llyn, illus. 2008. (Illus.). 32p. (J). 7.95 (978-0-9776419-1-8(0)) Bobcat Publishing.

Hunter, Nick. Does the Yeti Exist? 2016. (Top Secret! Ser.). (ENG., Illus.). 48p. (gr. 4-6). lib. bdg. 33.32 (978-1-4109-8161-5(4)) Heinemann-Raintree.

Johnson, Sandi. 5 - Dorp the Scottish Dragon: In the Bermuda Triangle, bk. 5. Brundige, Britt & Durant, Sybrina, eds. Praker, Jon, illus. 2014. 5. (ENG.). 30p. (J). (gr. -1-6). pap. 12.99 (978-1-929063-62-8(8), 161) Moons & Stars Publishing For Children.

Knudsen, Shannon. Fantastical Creatures & Magical Beasts. 2009. (Fantasy Chronicles Ser.). (ENG., Illus.). 48p. (gr. 4-7). lib. bdg. 27.93 (978-0-8225-9987-6(2)) Lerner Publishing Group.

—Mermaids & Mermen. 2009. (Fantasy Chronicles Ser.). (ENG.). 48p. (gr. 4-7). lib. bdg. 27.93 (978-0-8225-9981-4(3)) Lerner Publishing Group.

Krensky, Stephen. Creatures from the Deep. 2008. pap. 52.95 (978-0-8225-9871-8(X)) 2007. (ENG., Illus.). 48p. (gr. 4-7). lib. bdg. 26.60 (978-0-8225-6761-5(X), Lerner Pubns.) Lerner Publishing Group.

Levin, Freddie. 1-2-3 Draw Mythical Creatures: A Step-by-Step Guide. Levin, Freddie, illus. 2014. Orig. Title: 2003. (Illus.). 64p. (J). pap. (978-0-939217-06-9(6)) Peel Productions, Inc.

Loh-Hagan, Virginia. Dragons: Magic, Myth, & Mystery. 2016. (Magic, Myth, & Mystery Ser.). (ENG., Illus.). 32p. (J). (gr. 4-8). 29.93 (978-1-63471-113-5(0), 208563, 45th Parallel Press) Cherry Lake Publishing.

—Kraken. 2017. (Magic, Myth, & Mystery Ser.). (ENG., Illus.). 32p. (J). (gr. 4-8). 29.93 (978-1-63472-148-6(9), 209164, 45th Parallel Press) Cherry Lake Publishing.

—Unicorns: Magic, Myth, & Mystery. 2016. (Magic, Myth, & Mystery Ser.). (ENG., Illus.). 32p. (J). (gr. 4-8). 29.93 (978-1-63471-115-9(7), 208571, 45th Parallel Press) Cherry Lake Publishing.

—Werewolves: Magic, Myth, & Mystery. 2016. (Magic, Myth, & Mystery Ser.). (ENG., Illus.). 32p. (J). (gr. 4-8). 29.93 (978-1-63471-110-4(6), 208551, 45th Parallel Press) Cherry Lake Publishing.

Macdonald, Fiona. Murderous Mythical Creatures. 2010. (Top 10 Worst Ser.). (Illus.). 32p. (J). (gr. 3-6). (ENG.). pap. 10.50 (978-1-4339-4083-5(3)); lib. bdg. 26.60 (978-1-4339-4082-8(5)) Stevens, Gareth Publishing LLLP. (Gareth Stevens Learning Library).

Marsico, Katie. Beastly Monsters: From Dragons to Griffins. 2017. (Monster Mania Ser.). (ENG.). 32p. (J). (gr. 2-5). 12.99 **(978-1-5124-3818-5(9)**, Lerner Pubns.); 39.99 **(978-1-5124-3819-2(7)**, Lerner Pubns.); 39.99 **(978-1-5124-2814-8(0)**, Lerner Pubns.); (Illus.). 26.65 (978-1-5124-2592-5(3)) Lerner Publishing Group.

—Undead Monsters: From Mummies to Zombies. 2017. (Monster Mania Ser.). (ENG.). 32p. (J). (gr. 2-5). 12.99 **(978-1-5124-3830-7(8)**, Lerner Pubns.); 39.99 **(978-1-5124-3831-4(6)**, Lerner Pubns.); 39.99 **(978-1-5124-2818-6(3)**, Lerner Pubns.); (Illus.). 26.65 (978-1-5124-2594-9(X)) Lerner Publishing Group.

McNab, Chris. Mythical Monsters: The Scariest Creatures from Legends, Books, & Movies. 2006. (Illus.). 95p. (J). (978-0-439-85479-5(2)) Scholastic, Inc.

Mokele-Mbembe: Fact or Fiction? 2010. (Creature Scene Investigation: the Science of Cryptozoology Ser.). (ENG., Illus.). 104p. (gr. 5-8). 32.95 (978-0-7910-9781-6(1), Chelsea Hse.) Facts On File, Inc.

Mortensen, Lori. Leprechauns. 2007. (Mysterious Encounters Ser.). (ENG., Illus.). 48p. (J). (gr. 3-5). 29.00 (978-0-7377-3663-2(1), Kidhaven) Cengage Gale.

Nagle, Jeanne. Investigating the Abominable Snowman & Other Legendary Beasts, 1 vol. 2015. (ENG.). 48p. (J). 25.85 (978-1-62275-853-1(6), Britannica Educational Publishing) Rosen Publishing Group, Inc., The.

Ogburn, Jacqueline K. A Dignity of Dragons. Ceccoli, Nicoletta, illus. 2010. (ENG.). 32p. (J). (gr. -1-3). 17.00 (978-0-618-86254-2(4)) Houghton Mifflin Harcourt Publishing Co.

Omoth, Tyler. Handbook to Bigfoot, Nessie, & Other Unexplained Creatures. 2016. (Paranormal Handbooks Ser.). (ENG., Illus.). 32p. (gr. 3-4). lib. bdg. 27.99 (978-1-5157-1311-1(3), Edge Bks.) Capstone Press of Coughlan Cos.

Onn, Aidan. A Field Guide to Monsters & Mythical Beings. Hodgson, Rob, illus. 2017. (Magma for Laurence King Ser.). (ENG.). 56p. (J). (gr. 1-4). 17.99 **(978-1-78627-067-2(6))** King, Laurence Publishing GBR. Dist: Hachette Bk. Group.

Osborne, Mary Pope & Boyce, Natalie Pope. Sea Monsters: A Nonfiction Companion to Dark Day in the Deep Sea. Murdocca, Sal, illus. 2008. (Magic Tree House Research Guides: No. 17). 121p. (J). (gr. 1-5). 12.65 (978-0-7569-8809-8(8)) Perfection Learning Corp.

Owen, Ruth. Half-Human Monsters & Other Fiends. 2013. (Not near Normal: the Paranormal Ser.). 32p. (J). (gr. 3-8). lib. bdg. 26.60 (978-1-61772-725-2(3)) Bearport Publishing Co., Inc.

Peebles, Alice. Demons & Dragons. Chilvers, Nigel, illus. 2015. (Mythical Beasts Ser.). (ENG.). 32p. (J). (gr. 3-6). pap. 7.99 (978-1-4677-7651-6(3), Lerner Pubns.) Lerner Publishing Group.

—Giants & Trolls. Chilvers, Nigel, illus. 2015. (Mythical Beasts Ser.). (ENG.). 32p. (J). (gr. 3-6). 26.65 (978-1-4677-6340-0(3), Lerner Pubns.) Lerner Publishing Group.

—Mighty Mutants. Chilvers, Nigel, illus. 2015. (Mythical Beasts Ser.). (ENG.). 32p. (J). (gr. 3-6). lib. bdg. 26.65 (978-1-4677-6343-1(8)) Lerner Publishing Group.

Peterson, Megan Cooley. Super Scary Monsters. 2016. (Super Scary Stuff Ser.). (ENG., Illus.). 24p. (gr. 1-2). lib. bdg. 25.32 (978-1-5157-0277-1(4)) Capstone Press of Coughlan Cos.

Polydoros, Lori. Top 10 Mythical Creatures, 1 vol. 2012. (Top 10 Unexplained Ser.). (ENG.). 32p. (gr. 1-2). 26.65 (978-1-4296-7640-3(X), Blazers) Capstone Press of Coughlan Cos.

Reading Friends Staff. Dragon Books. (J). (978-0-8136-3751-8(1)) Modern Curriculum Pr.

Riggs, Kate. Magical Creatures. 2013. (Happily Ever After Ser.). (ENG., Illus.). 24p. (J). (gr. k-3). 25.65 (978-1-60818-242-8(8), Creative Education) Creative Co., The.

Rowe, Brooke. What Creature Are You Most Like? 2015. (Illus.). 32p. (J). (978-1-63470-038-2(4)) Cherry Lake Publishing.

—What Monster Are You Most Like? 2016. (Illus.). 32p. (J). (978-1-63470-511-0(4)) Cherry Lake Publishing.

Russo, Monica. Mythical Animals Dot-to-Dot. 2003. (Illus.). 64p. (J). (gr. 5-7). pap. 5.95 (978-0-8069-9716-2(8)) Sterling Publishing Co., Inc.

Santillan, Jorge & Eason, Sarah. Drawing Fairies, Mermaids, & Unicorns. 2013. (Learn to Draw Ser.). (ENG., Illus.). 32p. (J). (gr. 2-5). lib. bdg. 26.60 (978-1-4339-9536-1(0)) Stevens, Gareth Publishing LLLP.

Sautter, A. J. Discover Dragons, Giants, & Other Deadly Fantasy Monsters. 2017. (All about Fantasy Creatures Ser.). (ENG.). 32p. (gr. 1-2). lib. bdg. 26.65 **(978-1-5157-6839-5(2)**, Blazers) Capstone Press of Coughlan Cos.

—Discover Gnomes, Halflings, & Other Wondrous Fantasy Beings. 2017. (All about Fantasy Creatures Ser.). (ENG.). 32p. (gr. 1-2). lib. bdg. 26.65 **(978-1-5157-6838-8(4)**, Blazers) Capstone Press of Coughlan Cos.

—Discover Harpies, Minotaurs, & Other Mythical Fantasy Beasts. 2017. (All about Fantasy Creatures Ser.). (ENG.). 32p. (gr. 1-2). lib. bdg. 26.65 **(978-1-5157-6836-4(8)**, Blazers) Capstone Press of Coughlan Cos.

—Discover Orcs, Boggarts, & Other Nasty Fantasy Creatures. 2017. (All about Fantasy Creatures Ser.). (ENG.). 32p. (gr. 1-2). lib. bdg. 26.65 **(978-1-5157-6837-1(6)**, Blazers) Capstone Press of Coughlan Cos.

—Fantasy Field Guides, 1 vol. McGrath, Tom & Juta, Jason, illus. 2014. (Fantasy Field Guides). (ENG.). 32p. (gr. 3-4). 111.96 (978-1-4914-0705-9(0), Edge Bks.) Capstone Press of Coughlan Cos.

—A Field Guide to Goblins, Gremlins, & Other Wicked Creatures, 1 vol. Ashcroft, Colin Michael et al, illus. 2014. (Fantasy Field Guides). (ENG.). 32p. (gr. 3-4). lib. bdg. 27.99 (978-1-4914-0689-2(5)) Capstone Press of Coughlan Cos.

—A Field Guide to Griffins, Unicorns, & Other Mythical Beasts, 1 vol. Juta, Jason, illus. 2014. (Fantasy Field Guides). (ENG.). 32p. (gr. 3-4). lib. bdg. 27.99 (978-1-4914-0690-8(9)) Capstone Press of Coughlan Cos.

Schach, David. Sea Monsters. 2011. (Unexplained Ser.). (ENG., Illus.). 24p. (J). (gr. 3-7). lib. bdg. 25.95 (978-1-60014-644-2(9), Torque Bks.) Bellwether Media.

Shea, Therese. Real-Life Monsters? 2015. (History's Mysteries Ser.). (ENG., Illus.). 32p. (J). (gr. 4-5). pap. 10.50 (978-1-4824-2094-4(5)) Stevens, Gareth Publishing LLLP.

Sherman, Patrice. Legendary Creatures. 2015. (Illus.). 64p. (978-1-61900-067-4(9)) Eldorado Ink.

Torpie, Kate. Magical Creatures. Shroades, John, illus. 2007. (ENG.). 24p. (J). (gr. 2-7). 19.99 (978-1-58476-619-3(0), IKIDS) Innovative Kids.

Townsend, John. Strange Creatures. 2010. (Amazing Mysteries Ser.). (YA). (gr. 3-6). 28.50 (978-1-59920-365-2(0)) Black Rabbit Bks.

Troupe, Thomas Kingsley. The Legend of the Werewolf, 1 vol. Ice, D. C., illus. 2010. (Legend Has It Ser.). (ENG.). 32p. (gr. 2-4). lib. bdg. 27.32 (978-1-4048-6033-9(9)) Picture Window Bks.

Turner, Tracy. Beasts & Monsters. 2015. (Head-To-Head Ser.). (ENG., Illus.). 24p. (gr. 3-8). 28.50 (978-1-62588-153-3(3)) Black Rabbit Bks.

Valentino, Serena. How to Be a Werewolf: The Claws-On Guide for the Modern Lycanthrope. 2011. (ENG., Illus.). 144p. (YA). (gr. 7-18). 14.99 (978-0-7636-5387-3(X)) Candlewick Pr.

Vaughn, Royce, illus. Seymour Bluffs & the Legend of the Piasa Bird. 2006. 24p. (J). pap. 9.95 (978-0-9728538-2-8(0)) Amica Publishing.

Whiting, Jim. Scary Monsters. 2010. (Really Scary Stuff Ser.). (ENG.). 24p. (gr. 1-2). lib. bdg. 25.32 (978-1-4296-3968-2(7), First Facts) Capstone Press of Coughlan Cos.

Whitmore, Andrew. How to Build a Monster. 2007. 96p. (J). (978-1-4207-0727-4(2)) Sundance/Newbridge Educational Publishing.

Winterbottom, Julie. Frightlopedia: An Encyclopeidia of Everything Scary, Creepy, & Spine-Chilling, from Arachnids to Zombies. 2016. lib. bdg. 20.80 (978-0-606-39014-9(6)) Turtleback Bks.

Yasuda, Anita. Dragon, the Phoenix, & the Beautiful Pearl: A Chinese Dragon Spirit Myth. 2014. (Short Tales Chinese Myths Ser.). 32p. (J). (gr. 3-6). lib. bdg. 24.21 (978-1-62402-030-8(5), Short Tales) Magic Wagon.

Yo-Kai Watch. Seek & Find. 2016. (ENG., Illus.). 24p. (J). (gr. 1-4). 8.99 (978-0-316-39621-9(4)) Little, Brown Bks. for Young Readers.

Yomtov, Nelson. Tracking Sea Monsters, Bigfoot, & Other Legendary Beasts, 1 vol. 2010. (Unexplained Phenomena Ser.). (ENG.). 48p. (gr. 3-4). lib. bdg. 31.99 (978-1-4296-4817-2(1)) Capstone Press of Coughlan Cos.

Young, Judy. The Hidden Bestiary of Marvelous, Mysterious, & (Maybe Even) Magical Creatures. Filippucci, Laura Francesca, illus. 2009. (ENG.). 32p. (J). (gr. 1-4). 16.95 (978-1-58536-433-6(9), 1299753) Sleeping Bear Pr.

Zombie Animals: Parasites Take Control! 2015. (Zombie Animals: Parasites Take Control! Ser.). (ENG.). 24p. (J). (gr. 2-3). pap., pap., pap. 48.90 (978-1-4824-3501-6(2)) Stevens, Gareth Publishing LLLP.

ANIMALS, MYTHICAL—FICTION

Abbott, Ellen Jensen. Watersmeet, 0 vols. 2012. (Watersmeet Ser.: 1). (ENG.). 352p. (YA). (gr. 7-11). pap. 8.99 (978-0-7614-5992-7(8), 9780761459927, Amazon Children's Publishing) Amazon Publishing.

ABDO Publishing Company Staff. Monster Hunters, 1 vol. 2014. (Monster Hunters Ser.: 4). (ENG.). 80p. (J). (gr. 8-12). lib. bdg. 108.28 (978-1-62402-043-8(7), Calico Chapter Bks) Magic Wagon.

Addison, Angelee. Nanny & the Noomies. 2011. (Illus.). 52p. pap. 22.56 (978-1-4567-8916-9(3)) AuthorHouse.

Almond, David. Mouse Bird Snake Wolf. Mckean, Dave, illus. 2013. (ENG.). 80p. (J). (gr. 2-5). 17.99 (978-0-7636-5912-7(6)) Candlewick Pr.

Alvarez, Jennifer Lynn. Landfall. 2016. (Guardian Herd Ser.: 3). (Illus.). 352p. (J). (gr. 3-7). 16.99 (978-0-06-228612-3(9)) HarperCollins Pubs.

—Landfall. 2016. (Guardian Herd Ser.: 3). (J). lib. bdg. 17.20 **(978-0-606-40049-7(4))** Turtleback Bks.

—Starfire. (Guardian Herd Ser.: 1). (ENG., Illus.). (J). (gr. 3-7). 2015. 320p. pap. 6.99 (978-0-06-228607-9(2)) 2014. 272p. 16.99 (978-0-06-228606-2(4)) HarperCollins Pubs.

—Starfire. 2015. (Guardian Herd Ser.: 1). (J). lib. bdg. 17.20 (978-0-606-36951-0(1)) Turtleback Bks.

—Stormbound. McClellan, David, illus. 2015. (Guardian Herd Ser.: 2). (ENG.). 320p. (J). (gr. 3-7). 16.99 (978-0-06-228609-3(9)) HarperCollins Pubs.

Anders, Lou. Nightborn. 2015. (Thrones & Bones Ser.). (ENG.). 368p. (J). (gr. 3-7). 16.99 (978-0-385-39036-1(X), Crown Books For Young Readers) Random Hse. Children's Bks.

Anders, Lou. Skyborn. (Thrones & Bones Ser.: 3). (ENG., Illus.). (J). (gr. 3-7). 2017. 400p. 7.99 **(978-0-385-39043-9(2)**, Yearling) 2016. 384p. 16.99 (978-0-385-39040-8(8), Crown Books For Young Readers) Random Hse. Children's Bks.

Anderson, Al. Adventures with Bingo Borden. Agora Publications Staff, tr. Kurzyca, Krystyna Emilia, illus. 2010. 77p. (J). pap. 9.50 (978-1-887250-46-7(8)) Agora Pubns., Inc.

Anderson, Jodi Lynn. My Diary from the Edge of the World. 2015. (ENG., Illus.). 432p. (J). (gr. 3-7). 16.99 (978-1-4424-8387-3(3), Aladdin) Simon & Schuster Children's Publishing.

—My Diary from the Edge of the World. 2017. (ENG., Illus.). 448p. (J). (gr. 3-7). pap. 7.99 (978-1-4424-8388-0(1), Simon & Schuster/Paula Wiseman Bks.) Simon & Schuster/Paula Wiseman Bks.

Baker, E. D. Fairy Lies. (ENG., (YA). 2013. Illus.). 272p. (gr. 1-8). pap. 7.99 (978-1-61963-035-2(4), 9781619630352) 2012. 256p. (gr. 5-8). 16.99 (978-1-59990-550-1(7), 9781599905501) Bloomsbury Publishing USA. (Bloomsbury USA Childrens).

—The Flying Horse. Manuzak, Lisa, illus. 2017. (ENG.). 128p. (J). pap. 5.99 (978-1-68119-141-6(5), 9781681191416, Bloomsbury USA Childrens) Bloomsbury Publishing USA.

—Maggie & the Flying Horse. Manuzak, Lisa, illus. 2017. (ENG.). 128p. (J). 16.99 (978-1-68119-312-0(4), 9781681193120, Bloomsbury USA Childrens) Bloomsbury Publishing USA.

—Maggie & the Flying Pigs. 2017. (ENG., Illus.). 128p. (J). 16.99 **(978-1-68119-489-9(9)**, 9781681194899, Bloomsbury USA Childrens) Bloomsbury Publishing USA.

—Magic Animal Rescue 4: Maggie & the Flying Pigs. 2017. (ENG., Illus.). 128p. (J). pap. 5.99 **(978-1-68119-485-1(6)**, 9781681194851, Bloomsbury USA Childrens) Bloomsbury Publishing USA.

Baker, E. D. The Wish Fish. Manuzak, Lisa, illus. 2017. (ENG.). 128p. (J). pap. 5.99 (978-1-68119-143-0(1), 9781681191430, Bloomsbury USA Childrens) Bloomsbury Publishing USA.

Banks, Anna. Of Triton. 2013. (Syrena Legacy Ser.: 2). (ENG.). 256p. (YA). (gr. 8-12). 17.99 (978-1-250-00333-1(4), 9781250003331) Feiwel & Friends.

Barchers, Suzanne. Bunyip in the Moon: A Tale from Australia. Clarke, Peter, illus. 2015. (Tales of Honor Ser.). (ENG.). 32p.

(gr. 1-3). lib. bdg. 26.60 *(978-1-939656-77-3(X))* Red Chair Pr.

Bently, Peter. King Jack & the Dragon Board Book. Oxenbury, Helen, illus. 2013. (ENG.). 14p. (J). (gr. -1 — 1). bds. 7.99 *(978-0-8037-3987-1(7),* Dial Bks) Penguin Young Readers Group.

Blue, Sebastien. Liquid Diamond. 2013. 176p. *(978-1-4602-3345-0(X))* FriesenPress.

Blume, Lesley M. M. The Wondrous Journals of Dr. Wendell Wellington Wiggins. Foote, David, illus. 2013. (ENG.). 256p. (J). (gr. 3-7). pap. 7.99 *(978-0-375-87218-1(3),* Knopf Bks. for Young Readers) Random Hse. Children's Bks.

Boylan, Jennifer Finney. Falcon Quinn & the Black Mirror. Dorman, Brandon, illus. (Falcon Quinn Ser.: 1). (ENG.). (J). (gr. 5-9). 2011. 512p. pap. 7.99 *(978-0-06-172834-1(9))* 2010. 496p. 16.99 *(978-0-06-172832-7(2))* HarperCollins Pubs. (Tegen, Katherine Bks).

—Falcon Quinn & the Crimson Vapor. 2011. (Falcon Quinn Ser.: 2). (ENG.). 384p. (J). (gr. 5-9). 16.99 *(978-0-06-172835-8(7),* Tegen, Katherine Bks) HarperCollins Pubs.

Brockway, Stephanie. Mystic Phyles: Beasts. Masiello, Ralph, illus. 2011. (ENG.). 144p. (J). (gr. 4-7). 15.95 *(978-1-57091-718-9(3))* Charlesbridge Publishing, Inc.

Burgess, Thornton W. Happy Jack. 2006. pap. 34.99 *(978-1-4219-7082-0(1))* IndyPublish.com.

Campbell, Roy. Song of the Jackalope. Bosworth, David, illus. 2nd ed. 2006. 140p. (YA). pap. 12.95 *(978-1-933538-04-4(X))* Bridgeway Bks.

Carman, Patrick. Floozombies! Sheesley, Brian, illus. 2016. (Fizzopolis Ser.: 2). 176p. (J). (gr. 3-7). 12.99 *(978-0-06-239392-0(8),* Tegen, Katherine Bks) HarperCollins Pubs.

Chan, Marty. Barnabas Bigfoot: a Hairy Tangle. 2012. (ENG.). 104p. (gr. 4-6). 9.95 *(978-1-927068-05-2(3))* Thistledown Pr., Ltd. CAN. Dist: Univ. of Toronto Pr.

Coats, Lucy. Centaur School. 2016. (Beasts of Olympus Ser.: 5). lib. bdg. 17.20 *(978-0-606-38410-0(3))* Turtleback Bks.

—Centaur School #5. Bean, Brett, illus. 2016. (Beasts of Olympus Ser.: 5). (ENG.). 144p. (J). (gr. 2-4). 6.99 *(978-1-101-99505-1(X),* Grosset & Dunlap) Penguin Young Readers Group.

—Dragon Healer. Bean, Brett, illus. 2015. 136p. (J). ***(978-1-4806-8442-3(2),*** Grosset & Dunlap) Penguin Publishing Group.

—Dragon Healer. 2015. (Beasts of Olympus Ser.: 4). lib. bdg. 16.00 *(978-0-606-38409-4(X))* Turtleback Bks.

—Dragon Healer #4. Bean, Brett, illus. 2015. (Beasts of Olympus Ser.: 4). (ENG.). 144p. (J). (gr. 2-4). 5.99 *(978-0-448-46196-0(X),* Grosset & Dunlap) Penguin Young Readers Group.

—Hound of Hades #2. Bean, Brett, illus. 2015. (Beasts of Olympus Ser.: 2). (ENG.). 144p. (J). (gr. 2-4). 6.99 *(978-0-448-46194-6(3),* Grosset & Dunlap) Penguin Young Readers Group.

—Steeds of the Gods #3. Bean, Brett, illus. 2015. (Beasts of Olympus Ser.: 3). (ENG.). 144p. (J). (gr. 2-4). 6.99 *(978-0-448-46195-3(1),* Grosset & Dunlap) Penguin Young Readers Group.

Collins, Ross. Medusa Jones. 2008. (J). *(978-0-439-90101-7(4),* Levine, Arthur A. Bks.) Scholastic, Inc.

Cook, Alison Reeger. The Scholar, the Sphinx & the Shades of Nyx. 2013. (Scholar & the Sphinx Ser.: 1). (ENG.). 296p. (YA). pap. *(978-1-908483-87-4(3))* Knox Robinson Pubs.

Cossantelli, Veronica. The Extincts. Muradov, Roman, illus. 2016. (ENG.). 240p. (J). 16.99 *(978-1-62779-403-9(4),* 9781627794039, Holt, Henry & Co. Bks. For Young Readers) Holt, Henry & Co.

Coville, Bruce. Diary of a Mad Brownie. 2015. (Enchanted Files Ser.). (ENG., Illus.). 256p. (J). (gr. 3-7). lib. bdg. 19.99 *(978-0-385-39248-8(6),* Random Hse. Bks. for Young Readers) Random Hse. Children's Bks.

Coville, Katherine. Ivy. 2017. (ENG.). 144p. (J). (gr. 2-5). lib. bdg. 19.99 *(978-0-553-53976-9(0),* Knopf Bks. for Young Readers) Random Hse. Children's Bks.

Cummings, Lindsay. The Fires of Calderon. 2014. (Balance Keepers Ser.: 1). (ENG.). 352p. (J). (gr. 3-7). 16.99 *(978-0-06-227518-9(6),* Tegen, Katherine Bks) HarperCollins Pubs.

—The Pillars of Ponderay. 2015. (Balance Keepers Ser.: 2). (ENG.). 384p. (J). (gr. 3-7). 16.99 *(978-0-06-227521-9(6),* Tegen, Katherine Bks) HarperCollins Pubs.

Darlison, Aleesah. Ellabeth's Test. Brailsford, Jill, illus. 2016. (Unicorn Riders Ser.). (ENG.). 112p. (gr. 3-5). lib. bdg. 22.65 *(978-1-4795-6547-4(4))* Picture Window Bks.

—Ellabeth's Test Cancelled. Brailsford, Jill, illus. 2017. (Unicorn Riders Ser.). (ENG.). 112p. (gr. 3-5). pap. 5.95 *(978-1-4795-6555-9(5))* Picture Window Bks.

Davies, Anna. Wrecked. 2012. (ENG., Illus.). 336p. (YA). (gr. 9). 16.99 *(978-1-4424-3278-9(0),* Simon & Schuster Bks. For Young Readers) Simon & Schuster Bks. For Young Readers.

Don, Lari. First Aid for Fairies & Other Fabled Beasts. 2008. (ENG.). 224p. (J). pap. *(978-0-86315-636-6(3))* Floris Bks.

Dorset, Skylar. The Boy with the Hidden Name. 2014. (Otherworld Ser.: 2). (ENG.). 320p. (YA). (gr. 7-12). pap. 9.99 *(978-1-4022-9256-9(2),* 9781402292569) Sourcebooks, Inc.

Duncalf, Joanne. The Zookeeper's Menagerie. 2007. pap. 15.95 *(978-0-9797232-1-6(3))* Twelve Star Pr.

Eaton, Deborah J. My Wild Woolly. Karas, G. Brian, illus. 2005. (Green Light Readers Level 2 Ser.). (gr. k-2). 13.95 *(978-0-7569-5445-1(2))* Perfection Learning Corp.

Ecton, Emily. Project Jackalope. 2012. (ENG., Illus.). 256p. (J). (gr. 3-7). 15.99 *(978-1-4521-0155-2(8))* Chronicle Bks. LLC.

Edwards, Wallace. Unnatural Selections, 1 vol. 2014. (ENG., Illus.). 32p. (J). (gr. -1-3). 19.95 *(978-1-4598-0555-2(0))* Orca Bk. Pubs. USA.

Favorite, Deborah. The Tush People. Arinsberg, Norman, illus. (J). 11.95 *(978-0-9722514-0-2(5))* Tush People, The.

Finnish, V. K. The Society's Traitor. Oshida, Tim, illus. 2012. (The Discoveries of Arthur Grey ser.: 1). (ENG.). 298p. (J). (gr. 4-8). 27.99 *(978-0-9852202-0-4(1))* Panama Hat Publishing, Ltd.

Freeman, R. Gregory. A Carpenter's Tale: The Mystery of Kidron Valley. 2006. (Illus.). 34p. per. 10.95 *(978-1-60002-118-3(2),* 3901) Mountain Valley Publishing, LLC.

Friedman, Aimee. Sea Change. 2010. (ENG.). 320p. (J). (gr. 7). 8.99 *(978-0-439-92230-2(5))* Scholastic, Inc.

Funaro, Gregory. Alistair Grim's Odditorium. 2015. (Alistair Grim Ser.). (ENG.). (J). (gr. 3-7). 448p. pap. 7.99 *(978-1-4847-0899-6(7));* (Illus.). 432p. 16.99 *(978-1-4847-0006-8(6))* Hyperion Bks. for Children.

—Alistair Grim's Odditorium. 2015. (J). lib. bdg. 18.40 *(978-0-606-37399-9(3))* Turtleback Bks.

Funke, Cornelia. Dragon Rider. 2011.Tr. of Drachenreiter. (ENG.). 560p. (J). (gr. 2-5). pap. 9.99 *(978-0-545-31648-4(0),* Chicken Hse., The) Scholastic, Inc.

Gaiman, NEil. Unnatural Creatures: Stories Selected by Neil Gaiman. 2013. (ENG., Illus.). 480p. (YA). (gr. 8). 17.99 *(978-0-06-223629-6(6));* pap. 9.99 *(978-0-06-223630-2(X))* HarperCollins Pubs.

—Unnatural Creatures: Stories Selected by Neil Gaiman. 2013. (YA). lib. bdg. 20.85 *(978-0-606-31804-4(6),* Turtleback) Turtleback Bks.

Gall, Chris. Dinotrux. Gall, Chris, illus. 2009. (Dinotrux Ser.: 1). (ENG., Illus.). 32p. (gr. -1-3). 16.99 *(978-0-316-02777-9(4))* Little Brown & Co.

—Dinotrux. 2012. (J). lib. bdg. 17.20 *(978-0-606-26144-9(3),* Turtleback) Turtleback Bks.

Gallicano, Todd Calgi. Guardians of the Gryphon's Claw. 2017. (Sam London Adventure Ser.: 1). (ENG.). 384p. (J). (gr. 5). 16.99 ***(978-1-5247-1365-2(1));*** lib. bdg. 19.99 ***(978-1-5247-1366-9(X))*** Random Hse. Children's Bks. (Delacorte Bks. for Young Readers).

George, Kallie. Clover's Luck. 2015. (Magical Animal Adoption Agency Ser.: 1). (J). lib. bdg. 16.00 *(978-0-606-37504-7(X))* Turtleback Bks.

—The Enchanted Egg. Boiger, Alexandra, illus. 2016. (Magical Animal Adoption Agency Ser.). (ENG.). 160p. (J). (gr. 2-5). pap. 5.99 *(978-1-4847-0146-1(1))* Hyperion Bks. for Children.

—The Magical Animal Adoption Agency - Clover's Luck. Boiger, Alexandra, illus. 2015. (Magical Animal Adoption Agency Ser.). (ENG.). 138p. (J). (gr. 2-5). 14.99 *(978-1-4231-8382-2(7))* Hyperion Bks. for Children.

Gilbert, Paul. Bertram & His Fabulous Animals. Rousseff, Minnie & Maynard, Barbara, illus. 2016. 152p. (J). 24.95 *(978-0-7649-7539-4(0),* POMEGRANATE KIDS) Pomegranate Communications, Inc.

Golding, Julia. The Chimera's Curse, 0 vols. 2010. (Companions Quartet Ser.: 4). (ENG.). 320p. (J). (gr. 4-7). pap. 9.99 *(978-0-7614-5726-8(7),* 9780761457268, Amazon Children's Publishing) Amazon Publishing.

—The Gorgon's Gaze, 0 vols., Bk. 2. 2010. (Companions Quartet Ser.: 2). (ENG.). 320p. (J). (gr. 4-7). pap. 9.99 *(978-0-7614-5653-7(8),* 9780761456537, Amazon Children's Publishing) Amazon Publishing.

—Mines of the Minotaur, 0 vols., Bk. 3. unabr. ed. 2010. (Companions Quartet Ser.: 3). (ENG.). 288p. (gr. 5-9). pap. 9.99 *(978-0-7614-5796-1(8),* 9780761457961, Amazon Children's Publishing) Amazon Publishing.

—Secret of the Sirens, 0 vols. 2009. (Companions Quartet Ser.: 1). (ENG.). 368p. (J). (gr. 4-7). pap. 9.99 *(978-0-7614-5617-9(1),* 9780761456179, Amazon Children's Publishing) Amazon Publishing.

Goodhart, Pippa. Nature Detectives, 1 vol. Mason, Sue, illus. 2013. (Start Reading Ser.). (ENG.). 24p. (gr. k-1). pap. 7.95 *(978-1-4765-4121-1(3))* Capstone Press of Coughlan Cos.

Hand, Cynthia, et al. My Lady Jane. 512p. (YA). (gr. 8). 2017. pap. 9.99 *(978-0-06-239176-6(3))* 2016. 17.99 *(978-0-06-239174-2(7))* HarperCollins Pubs. (HarperTeen).

Hartman, Moreta. The Adventures of the Rocky Mountain Tea Twerps. Mantzke, Jurgen, illus. 2003. 56p. 18.95 *(978-0-9743937-0-4(3))* Hallelujah Acres Publishing.

Harvey, Tom. The Gnome Home. 2012. 72p. pap. 23.29 *(978-1-4669-3542-6(1))* Trafford Publishing.

Headley, Maria Dahvana. Aerie. 2016. (Magonia Ser.: 2). 320p. (YA). (gr. 8). 17.99 *(978-0-06-232055-1(6))* HarperCollins Pubs.

—Magonia. (Magonia Ser.: 1). (YA). (gr. 8). 2016. 336p. pap. 9.99 *(978-0-06-232053-7(X))* 2015. (ENG.). 320p. 17.99 *(978-0-06-232052-0(1),* HarperTeen) HarperCollins Pubs.

Hegarty, Shane. The Legends Begin. de la Rue, James, illus. 2015. (Darkmouth Ser.: 1). (ENG.). 416p. (J). (gr. 3-7). 16.99 *(978-0-06-231125-2(5))* HarperCollins Pubs.

Howard, Kate. The Misadventures of Jibanyan, Bk. 1. 2016. (Yo-Kai Watch Ser.: 1). (ENG.). 64p. (J). (gr. 2-5). pap. 4.99 *(978-1-338-05462-0(7))* Scholastic, Inc.

Ihara, Shigekatsu. Pokémon Vol. 8: Diamond & Pearl Adventure! Ihara, Shigekatsu, illus. 2010. (ENG., Illus.). 192p. (J). pap. 9.99 *(978-1-4215-3671-2(4))* Viz Media.

—Pokémon: Diamond & Pearl Adventure!, Vol. 6. Ihara, Shigekatsu, illus. 2010. (ENG., Illus.). 192p. (J). pap. 9.99 *(978-1-4215-3170-0(4))* Viz Media.

—Pokémon: Diamond & Pearl Adventure!, Vol. 7. Ihara, Shigekatsu, illus. 2010. (ENG., Illus.). 192p. (J). pap. 9.99 *(978-1-4215-3491-6(6))* Viz Media.

Johnson, Alaya. The Goblin King. Gandy, Meg, illus. 2009. (Twisted Journeys (r) Ser.: 10). (ENG.). 112p. (J). (gr. 4-7). pap. 7.95 *(978-0-8225-9259-4(2))* Lerner Publishing Group.

Johnson, Alaya Dawn. The Goblin King, No. 10. Gandy, Meg & Olson, Meagan, illus. 2009. (Twisted Journeys (r) Ser.: 10). (ENG.). 112p. (J). (gr. 4-7). 27.93 *(978-0-8225-9253-2(3),* Graphic Universe™) Lerner Publishing Group.

Johnson, Jane. The Secret Country. Stower, Adam, illus. 2007. (Eidolon Chronicles Ser.: 1). (ENG.). 336p. (J). (gr. 3-7). per. 15.99 *(978-1-4169-3815-6(X),* Simon & Schuster Bks. For Young Readers) Simon & Schuster Bks. For Young Readers.

Jordan, Devin. The Dragon's Pearl. Di Bartolo, Jim, illus. 2010. (ENG.). 352p. (YA). (gr. 5-9). pap. 8.99 *(978-1-4169-6411-7(8),* Simon & Schuster Bks. For Young Readers) Simon & Schuster Bks. For Young Readers.

Jules, Jacqueline. Noah & the Ziz. Kahn, Katherine Janus, illus. 2005. (ENG.). 32p. (J). (gr. -1-2). per. 10.95 *(978-1-58013-121-6(2),* Kar-Ben Publishing) Lerner Publishing Group.

—The Princess & the Ziz. Kahn, Katherine Janus, illus. 2008. 32p. (J). (gr. -1-3). lib. bdg. 17.95 *(978-0-8225-7377-7(6));* (ENG.). pap. 7.95 *(978-0-8225-7382-1(2))* Lerner Publishing Group. (Kar-Ben Publishing).

—The Ziz & the Hanukkah Miracle. Kahn, Katherine Janus, illus. 2006. (ENG.). 32p. (J). (gr. -1-2). per. 9.95 *(978-1-58013-164-3(6),* Kar-Ben Publishing) Lerner Publishing Group.

Jules, Jacqueline & Hechtkopf, Jacqueline. Noah & the Ziz. Kahn, Katherine Janus, illus. 2005. (ENG.). 32p. (J). (gr. -1-2). 9.95 *(978-0-929371-01-6(1),* Kar-Ben Publishing) Lerner Publishing Group.

—The Ziz & the Hanukkah Miracle. Kahn, Katherine Janus, illus. 2006. (ENG.). 32p. (J). (gr. -1-2). lib. bdg. 17.95 *(978-1-58013-160-5(3),* Kar-Ben Publishing) Lerner Publishing Group.

Katschke, Judy. Shrek the Third: King for a Day, Ogre for Life. 2007. (Shrek the Third Ser.). (Illus.). 64p. (J). (gr. 2-5). 4.99 *(978-0-06-122864-3(8),* Harper Entertainment) HarperCollins Pubs.

Keltie, Helen. The Mysterious Lake: Otriana. 2013. 68p. pap. 8.99 *(978-1-4525-0949-5(2),* Balboa Pr.) Author Solutions, Inc.

Kilpatrick, Irene. Foofa's Happy Book. 2012. (Yo Gabba Gabba! Ser.). (ENG.). 12p. (J). (gr. -1-1). bds. 5.99 *(978-1-4424-5444-6(X),* Simon Spotlight) Simon Spotlight.

Konishi, Noriyuki. Yo-kai Watch, Vol. 1. 2015. (ENG., Illus.). 192p. (J). pap. 9.99 *(978-1-4215-8251-1(1))* Viz Media.

—Yo-kai Watch, Vol. 2. 2015. (ENG., Illus.). 192p. (J). pap. 9.99 *(978-1-4215-8252-8(X))* Viz Media.

Kraegel, Kenneth. King Arthur's Very Great Grandson. Kraegel, Kenneth, illus. 2012. (ENG., Illus.). 40p. (J). (gr. k-3). 16.99 *(978-0-7636-5311-8(X))* Candlewick Pr.

Kusaka, Hidenori. Pokémon Adventures Vol. 3: Black & White. Yamamoto, Satoshi, illus. 2014. (ENG.). 208p. (J). pap. 9.99 *(978-1-4215-6178-3(6))* Viz Media.

—Pokémon Black & White, Vol. 15. Yamamoto, Satoshi, illus. 2014. (ENG.). 80p. (J). pap. 4.99 *(978-1-4215-6767-9(9))* Viz Media.

LaFevers, R. L. The Basilisk's Lair. Murphy, Kelly, illus. 2011. (Nathanial Fludd, Beastologist Ser.: 2). (ENG.). 160p. (J). (gr. 1-4). pap. 6.99 *(978-0-547-54957-6(1))* Houghton Mifflin Harcourt Publishing Co.

—Flight of the Phoenix Bk. 1. Murphy, Kelly, illus. 2010. (Nathaniel Fludd, Beastologist Ser.: 1). (ENG.). 144p. (J). (gr. 1-4). pap. 5.99 *(978-0-547-40845-3(5))* Houghton Mifflin Harcourt Publishing Co.

—The Wyverns' Treasure. 2012. (Nathaniel Fludd, Beastologist Ser.: 3). lib. bdg. 16.00 *(978-0-606-24516-6(2),* Turtleback) Turtleback Bks.

Lao, Samantha. The Scared Panda. 2009. 20p. pap. 10.49 *(978-1-4389-9226-6(2))* AuthorHouse.

Lindner, Brooke. Dance with Brobee! 2012. (Yo Gabba Gabba! Ser.). (ENG.). 12p. (J). (gr. -1-1). bds. 5.99 *(978-1-4424-5445-3(8),* Simon Spotlight) Simon Spotlight.

Lindsay, Fitzroy A. Two Aliens Looking in My Window. 2012. 36p. pap. 20.99 *(978-1-4772-5333-5(5))* AuthorHouse.

Malatesta, Resa. Jewel & Chin Chin's Adventure. 2013. 20p. pap. 10.95 *(978-1-4525-7610-7(6),* Balboa Pr.) Author Solutions, Inc.

Malik, Katherine. Giselle's Magical World, 1 vol. 2009. 150p. pap. 24.95 *(978-1-4489-1902-4(9))* America Star Bks.

Martin, Emily Winfield. Day Dreamers: A Journey of Imagination. (ENG., Illus.). 32p. (J). 2016. (— 1). bds. 8.99 *(978-1-101-93522-4(7))* 2014. (gr. -1-2). 17.99 *(978-0-385-37670-9(7))* 2014. (gr. -1-2). lib. bdg. 20.99 *(978-0-375-97326-0(5))* Random Hse. Children's Bks. (Random Hse. Bks. for Young Readers).

McKinley, Robin & Dickinson, Peter. Fire: Tales of Elemental Spirits. 2010. (ENG.). 304p. (gr. 12). 15.00 *(978-0-441-01919-9(6),* Ace Bks.) Penguin Publishing Group.

—Fire: Tales of Elemental Spirits. 2011. (ENG.). 320p. (YA). (gr. 7-18). 9.99 *(978-0-14-241945-8(1),* Firebird) Penguin Young Readers Group.

McQuerry, Maureen Doyle. Time Out of Time. 2015. (Time Out of Time Ser.). (ENG., Illus.). 368p. (J). (gr. 5-9). 16.95 *(978-1-4197-1494-8(5),* Amulet Bks.) Abrams, Inc.

—Time Out of Time: Book One: Beyond the Door. 2015. (Time Out of Time Ser.). (ENG., Illus.). 400p. (J). (gr. 5-9). pap. 7.95 *(978-1-4197-1493-1(7),* Amulet Bks.) Abrams, Inc.

—Time Out of Time: Book Two: the Telling Stone. 2016. (ENG., Illus.). 376p. (J). (gr. 3-7). pap. 8.95 *(978-1-4197-1916-5(5),* Amulet Bks.) Abrams, Inc.

—Time Out of Time Bk. 1: Beyond the Door. 2014. (Time Out of Time Ser.). (ENG., Illus.). 384p. (J). (gr. 3-7). 16.95 *(978-1-4197-1016-2(8),* Amulet Bks.) Abrams, Inc.

Meyer, Kai. The Glass Word. Crawford, Elizabeth D., tr. from GER. 2008. (ENG.). 288p. (YA). (gr. 7). (Dark Reflections Trilogy Ser.: 3). pap. 9.99 *(978-0-689-87792-6(7));* (Dark Reflections Trilogy: Bk. 3). 16.99 *(978-0-689-87791-9(9))* McElderry, Margaret K. Bks. (McElderry, Margaret K. Bks.).

Meyer, Maggie. Big Foot Adventures down Under: Book One in the Series 'Spirits Alive' 2013. 244p. (gr. 1-1). 46.72 *(978-1-4797-4547-0(2));* pap. 28.03 *(978-1-4797-4546-3(4))* Xlibris Corp.

Molinari, Laurice E. Pillars of Fire, 1 vol. 2016. (Ether Novel Ser.). (ENG.). 368p. (J). pap. 8.99 *(978-0-310-73562-5(9))* Zonderkidz.

Molinari, Laurice Elehwany. The Ether: Vero Rising, 1 vol. 2014. (Ether Novel Ser.). (ENG.). 368p. (J). pap. 8.99 *(978-0-310-73561-8(0))* Zonderkidz.

—Pillars of Fire, 1 vol. 2015. (Ether Novel Ser.). (ENG.). 368p. (J). 16.99 *(978-0-310-73556-4(4))* Zonderkidz.

Mull, Brandon. Rise of the Evening Star. Dorman, Brandon, illus. 2008. (Fablehaven Ser.: 2). (ENG.). 480p. (J). (gr. 3-8). pap. 7.99 *(978-1-4169-5770-6(7),* Aladdin) Simon & Schuster Children's Publishing.

Nelson, Peter. Creature Keepers & the Hijacked Hydro-Hide. Rao, Rohitash, illus. 2014. (Creature Keepers Ser.: 1). (ENG.). 384p. (J). (gr. 3-7). 12.99 *(978-0-06-223643-2(1))* HarperCollins Pubs.

—Creature Keepers & the Swindled Soil-Soles. Rao, Rohitash, illus. 2015. (Creature Keepers Ser.: 2). (ENG.). 384p. (J). (gr. 3-7). 12.99 *(978-0-06-223645-6(8))* HarperCollins Pubs.

Oppel, Kenneth. Skybreaker. 2007. (Illus.). 560p. (YA). (gr. 8). per. 9.99 *(978-0-06-053229-1(7))* HarperCollins Pubs.

Orion, Cody. Do You Believe? 2008. 24p. pap. 12.99 *(978-1-4363-2434-2(3))* Xlibris Corp.

Ormondroyd, Edward. David & the Phoenix. 2009. 76p. (gr. 4-7). pap. 4.75 *(978-1-60459-691-5(0))* Wilder Pubns., Corp.

Oshida, Tim, illus. The Society's Traitor. 2nd ed. 2015. (The Discoveries of Arthur Grey ser.: 1). (ENG.). 304p. (J). (gr. 4-8). 27.99 *(978-1-943317-00-4(3))* Panama Hat Publishing, Ltd.

Park, Jennifer. The Shadows We Know by Heart. 2017. (ENG., Illus.). 304p. (YA). (gr. 7). 17.99 *(978-1-4814-6351-5(9),* Simon Pulse) Simon Pulse.

Patey, Nicola. Aspireland & the story of George. 2010. 101p. pap. 16.95 *(978-1-4457-2458-4(8))* Lulu Pr., Inc.

Pearce, Jackson & Stiefvater, Maggie. Pip Bartlett's Guide to Magical Creatures. 2016. (Pip Bartlett Ser.: 1). (ENG.). 192p. (J). (gr. 3-7). 9.99 *(978-1-338-08815-1(7))* Scholastic, Inc.

Pearl, Alexa. The #1: Big Secret. Sordo, Paco, illus. 2017. (Tales of Sasha Ser.: 1). (ENG.). 112p. (J). (gr. 1-3). pap. 5.99 *(978-1-4998-0389-1(3))* Little Bee Books Inc.

—#2: Journey Beyond the Trees. Sordo, Paco, illus. 2017. (Tales of Sasha Ser.: 2). (ENG.). 112p. (J). (gr. 1-3). pap. 5.99 *(978-1-4998-0391-4(5))* Little Bee Books Inc.

Quinn, Jordan. The Pegasus Quest. McPhillips, Robert, illus. 2016. (Kingdom of Wrenly Ser.: 10). (ENG.). 128p. (J). (gr. k-4). pap. 5.99 *(978-1-4814-5870-2(1),* Little Simon) Little Simon.

Rabe, Tish. Look for the Lorax. 2012. (Step into Reading Level 1 Ser.). lib. bdg. 13.55 *(978-0-606-23720-8(8),* Turtleback) Turtleback Bks.

Rabe, Tish & Seuss, Dr. Look for the Lorax. Ruiz, Aristides et al, illus. 2012. (Step into Reading Ser.). (ENG.). 32p. (J). (gr. -1-1). pap. 3.99 *(978-0-375-86999-0(9),* Random Hse. Bks. for Young Readers) Random Hse. Children's Bks.

Riordan, Rick. The Battle of the Labyrinth, Bk. 4. (Percy Jackson & the Olympians Ser.). (ENG.). (J). (gr. 5-9). 2009. 400p. pap. 7.99 *(978-1-4231-0149-9(9))* 2008. 384p. 17.99 *(978-1-4231-0146-8(4))* Hyperion Pr.

—The Battle of the Labyrinth. 2011. 9.68 *(978-0-7848-3442-8(3),* Everbind) Marco Bk. Co.

—The Battle of the Labyrinth. l.t. ed. 2008. (Percy Jackson & the Olympians Ser.: Bk. 4). (ENG.). 462p. (J). (gr. 4-7). 23.95 *(978-1-4104-1018-4(8))* Thorndike Pr.

—The Battle of the Labyrinth. 2009. (Percy Jackson & the Olympians Ser.: 4). (J). lib. bdg. 18.40 *(978-0-606-02158-6(2),* Turtleback) Turtleback Bks.

—The Demigod Files. James, Steve, illus. 2009. (ENG.). 160p. (J). (gr. 5-6). 12.99 *(978-1-4231-2166-4(X))* Hyperion Pr.

—The Last Olympian, Bk. 5. (Percy Jackson & the Olympians Ser.). (ENG.). (J). (gr. 5-9). 2011. 432p. pap. 7.99 *(978-1-4231-0150-5(2))* 5th ed. 2009. 400p. 17.99 *(978-1-4231-0147-5(2))* Hyperion Pr.

—Percy Jackson & the Olympians, Set. 2010. (ENG.). 1744p. (J). (gr. 5-17). 89.99 *(978-1-4231-4189-1(X))* Hyperion Pr.

—Percy Jackson & the Olympians. l.t. ed. 2009. (Percy Jackson & the Olympians Ser.). (ENG.). 485p. (YA). 23.95 *(978-1-4104-1678-0(X))* Thorndike Pr.

—Percy Jackson & the Olympians. 2011. (Percy Jackson & the Olympians Ser.: 5). (J). lib. bdg. 18.40 *(978-0-606-10567-5(0),* Turtleback) Turtleback Bks.

—The Titan's Curse, Bk. 3. rev. ed. 2007. (Percy Jackson & the Olympians Ser.: Bk. 3). (ENG.). 320p. (J). (gr. 5-9). 17.99 *(978-1-4231-0145-1(6))* Disney Publishing Worldwide.

—The Titan's Curse. 2008. (Percy Jackson & the Olympians Ser.: No. 3). 312p. (J). lib. bdg. 20.00 *(978-1-4242-4710-3(1))* Fitzgerald Bks.

—The Titan's Curse, Bk. 3. 2008. (Percy Jackson & the Olympians Ser.). (ENG.). 352p. (J). (gr. 5-9). pap. 7.99 *(978-1-4231-0148-2(0))* Hyperion Pr.

—The Titan's Curse. 2011. 9.68 *(978-0-7848-3441-1(5),* Everbind) Marco Bk. Co.

—The Titan's Curse. l.t. rev. ed. 2007. (Percy Jackson & the Olympians Ser.: 3). (ENG.). 402p. (gr. 5-9). 23.95 *(978-0-7862-9701-6(8))* Thorndike Pr.

Riordan, Rick & Venditti, Robert. The Titan's Curse. Futaki, Attila & Guilhaumond, Gregory, illus. 2013. (Percy Jackson & the Olympians Ser.). (ENG.). 128p. (J). (gr. 5-9). pap. 14.99 *(978-1-4231-4551-6(8))* Hyperion Pr.

—The Titan's Curse. 2013. (Percy Jackson & the Olympians Graphic Novels Ser.: 3). (J). lib. bdg. 26.95 *(978-0-606-32286-7(8),* Turtleback) Turtleback Bks.

Ritter, William. Jackaby. (Jackaby Ser.: 1). (ENG.). 304p. (YA). (gr. 9-12). 2015. pap. 9.95 *(978-1-61620-546-1(6))* 2014. 16.95 *(978-1-61620-353-5(6),* 73353) Algonquin Bks. of Chapel Hill.

Robinson, Gary. Supranormal. 2015. (ENG.). 128p. (J). pap. *(978-1-939053-12-1(9))* Book Publishing Co.

Rowling, J. K. Fantastic Beasts & Where to Find Them. 2017. (Harry Potter Ser.). (ENG.). 128p. (J). (gr. 3). 12.99 *(978-1-338-13231-1(8))* Scholastic, Inc.

Rusu, Meredith. Yo-Kai Watch. Scholastic, illus. 2016. (Yo-Kai Watch Ser.). (ENG.). 32p. (J). (gr. -1-3). pap. 3.99 *(978-1-338-05444-6(9))* Scholastic, Inc.

Saddleback Educational Publishing Staff, ed. Creature, 1 vol. 2013. (Heights Ser.). (ENG.). 51p. (gr. 5-8). 7.95 *(978-1-62250-050-5(4))* Saddleback Educational Publishing, Inc.

Savage, J. Scott. Evil Twins. Holgate, Doug, illus. 2014. (Case File 13 Ser.: 3). (ENG.). 272p. (J). (gr. 3-7). 14.99 *(978-0-06-213337-3(3))* HarperCollins Pubs.

Selfors, Suzanne. The Lonely Lake Monster. Santat, Dan, illus. 2014. (Imaginary Veterinary Ser.: 2). (ENG.). 240p. (J). (gr. 2-7). pap. 7.99 *(978-0-316-22561-8(4))* Little, Brown Bks. for Young Readers.

—The Sasquatch Escape. Santat, Dan, illus. 2014. (Imaginary Veterinary Ser.: 1). (ENG.). 240p. (J). (gr. 2-7). pap. 7.99 *(978-0-316-22569-4(X))* Little, Brown Bks. for Young Readers.

Seuss, Dr. If I Ran the Zoo. 2014. (Classic Seuss Ser.). (ENG., Illus.). 64p. (J). (gr. k-4). 17.99 *(978-0-385-37905-2(6),* Random Hse. Bks. for Young Readers) Random Hse. Children's Bks.

Shi, Charleston. The Quest of the Phoenix: Book Two, Storm of the Kraken. 2010. 180p. pap. 14.95 *(978-1-60844-352-9(3))* Dog Ear Publishing, LLC.

Smith, Roland. Mutation. (ENG.). 352p. (J). (gr. 3-7). 2016. (Cryptid Hunters Ser.: 4). pap. 6.99 *(978-0-545-08181-8(5))* 2014. 16.99 *(978-0-545-08180-1(7))* Scholastic, Inc. (Scholastic Pr.).

St. John, Lauren. The White Giraffe. 2008. (ENG., Illus.). 208p. (J). (gr. 2-5). 7.99 *(978-0-14-241152-0(3),* Puffin Books) Penguin Young Readers Group.

Steps To Literacy Staff, compiled by. Percy Jackson & the Olympians Series: Variety Pack (5 Titles, 1 Each) 2010. (J). pap. 39.95 *(978-1-60923-745-5(5))* Steps To Literacy, LLC.

Sutherland, Tui T. & Sutherland, Kari. Dragon on Trial. 2015. (Menagerie Ser.: 2). (ENG.). 320p. (J). (gr. 3-7). pap. 6.99 *(978-0-06-085145-3(7))* HarperCollins Pubs.

Sutherland, Tui T. & Sutherland, Kari H. The Menagerie. (Menagerie Ser.: 3). (J). (gr. 3-7). 2016. 368p. pap. 6.99 *(978-0-06-078069-2(X))* 2015. (ENG.). 368p. 16.99 *(978-0-06-078067-8(3))* 2013. (ENG., Illus.). 288p. 16.99 *(978-0-06-078064-7(9))* HarperCollins Pubs.

Thompson, Kate. The Last of the High Kings. 2008. 323p. (YA). (gr. 7-18). lib. bdg. 17.89 *(978-0-06-117596-1(X),* HarperTeen) HarperCollins Pubs.

Townsend, Charlene. The Trap & the Trip. 2013. 90p. pap. 8.99 *(978-1-4808-0219-3(0))* Archway Publishing.

Trent, Tiffany. The Unnaturalists. (ENG., (YA). (gr. 7). 2013. Illus.). 336p. pap. 9.99 *(978-1-4424-2207-0(6))* 2012. 320p. 16.99 *(978-1-4424-2206-3(8))* Simon & Schuster Bks. For Young Readers. (Simon & Schuster Bks. For Young Readers).

Ursu, Anne. The Immortal Fire. Swaab, Neil, illus. 2010. (Cronus Chronicles Ser.: 3). (ENG.). 528p. (J). (gr. 3-7). pap. 7.99 *(978-1-4169-0592-9(8),* Atheneum Bks. for Young Readers) Simon & Schuster Children's Publishing.

—The Shadow Thieves. Fortune, Eric, illus. 2006. (Cronus Chronicles Ser.: 1). (ENG.). 432p. (J). (gr. 3-7). 17.99 *(978-1-4169-0587-5(1),* Atheneum Bks. for Young Readers) Simon & Schuster Children's Publishing.

—The Siren Song. Fortune, Eric, illus. (Cronus Chronicles Ser.: 2). (ENG.). (J). (gr. 3-7). 2008. 464p. pap. 7.99 *(978-1-4169-0590-5(1))* 2007. 448p. 19.99 *(978-1-4169-0589-9(8))* Simon & Schuster Children's Publishing. (Atheneum Bks. for Young Readers).

Varian, H. K. The Emerald Mask. 2016. (Hidden World of Changers Ser.: 2). (ENG., Illus.). 176p. (J). (gr. 3-7). pap. 6.99 *(978-1-4814-6619-6(4),* Simon Spotlight) Simon Spotlight.

Venditti, Robert & Riordan, Rick. The Titan's Curse. Futaki, Attila & Guilhaumond, Gregory, illus. 2013. (Percy Jackson & the Olympians Ser.). (ENG.). 128p. (J). (gr. 5-9). 19.99 *(978-1-4231-4530-1(5))* Disney Pr.

Vernon, Ursula. Revenge of the Horned Bunnies, No. 6. 6th ed. 2012. (Dragonbreath Ser.: 6). (ENG.). 208p. (J). (gr. 3-7). 12.99 *(978-0-8037-3677-1(0),* Dial Bks) Penguin Young Readers Group.

von Rosenberg, Byron. Dale the Uniclyde: An adventure in Friendship. Parrott, Heather, illus. 2007. 22p. (J). 11.95 *(978-0-9759858-6-1(8))* Red Mountain Creations.

Wakefield, S. A. The Selected Adventures of Bottersnikes & Gumbles. Digby, Desmond, illus. 2017. 224p. 6.99 *(978-1-4607-5192-3(2))* HarperCollins Pubs. Australia AUS. Dist: HarperCollins Pubs.

West, Tracey. Race to Danger (Pokémon: Chapter Book) 2017. (Pokémon Ser.). (ENG.). 96p. (J). (gr. 2-5). pap. 4.99 ***(978-1-338-17585-1(8))*** Scholastic, Inc.

West, Tracey, adapted by. Phantom Unmasked. 2006. (Illus.). 62p. (J). pap. *(978-0-439-80000-6(5))* Scholastic, Inc.

Westerfeld, Scott. Behemoth. Thompson, Keith, illus. (Leviathan Trilogy Ser.). (ENG.). (YA). (gr. 7). 2011. 512p. pap. 12.99 *(978-1-4169-7176-4(9))* 2010. 496p. 18.99 *(978-1-4169-7175-7(0))* Simon Pulse. (Simon Pulse).

—Behemoth. Thompson, Keith, illus. l.t. ed. 2010. (Leviathan Trilogy: Bk. 2). (ENG.). 540p. 23.99 *(978-1-4104-3066-3(9))* Thorndike Pr.

—Behemoth. 2011. (Leviathan Ser.: 2). lib. bdg. 24.50 *(978-0-606-22407-9(6),* Turtleback) Turtleback Bks.

—Leviathan: Leviathan; Behemoth; Goliath. Thompson, Keith, illus. 2012. (Leviathan Trilogy Ser.). (ENG.). 1552p. (YA). (gr. 7). pap. 37.99 *(978-1-4424-8377-4(6),* Simon Pulse) Simon Pulse.

Weston, Robert Paul. The Creature Department. Framestore, illus. 2014. (Creature Department Ser.: 1). (ENG.). 352p. (J). (gr. 3-7). pap. 8.99 *(978-1-59514-684-7(9),* Razorbill) Penguin Young Readers Group.

Weston, Robert Paul & Loftin, Nikki. Gobbled by Ghorks. Framestore, illus. 2015. (Creature Department Ser.: 2). (ENG.). 240p. (J). (gr. 3-7). 8.99 *(978-1-59514-751-6(9),* Razorbill) Penguin Young Readers Group.

Whittle, J. Robert & Sandilands, Joyce. Leprechaun Magic. Galego, Ane M., illus. 2004. 64p. (J). *(978-0-9685061-2-7(7))* Whitlands Publishing, Ltd.

Williams, Tad & Beale, Deborah. The Dragons of Ordinary Farm. Swearingen, Greg, illus. 2009. (ENG.). 416p. (J). (gr. 4-7). 16.99 *(978-0-06-154345-6(4))* HarperCollins Pubs.

Yolen, Jane & Stemple, Adam. The Last Changeling. 2014. (Seelie Wars Ser.). (ENG.). 304p. (J). (gr. 3-7). 16.99 *(978-0-670-01435-4(4),* Viking Books for Young Readers) Penguin Young Readers Group.

ANIMALS—PHOTOGRAPHY

see Photography of Animals

ANIMALS—PICTORIAL WORKS

Aladjidi, Virginia. Animal Atlas. Ramsey, Cecelia, tr. from FRE. Tchoukriel, Emmanuelle, illus. 2016. (ENG.). 112p. (J). (gr. 5-8). 24.99 *(978-1-4926-4163-6(4),* 9781492641636, Sourcebooks Jabberwocky) Sourcebooks, Inc.

Animal Friends. Date not set. 88p. (J). 7.98 *(978-0-7525-9845-1(7))* Parragon, Inc.

Animal Wise, 6 vols. 2005. (Animal Wise Ser.). (ENG.). 24p. (gr. k-2). 79.95 *(978-1-4048-0990-1(2))* Picture Window Bks.

Anness Publishing Ltd. Let's Look & See: Canadian Animals. 2014. (ENG., Illus.). 24p. (J). (gr. -1-k). bds. 6.99 *(978-1-86147-377-6(X),* Armadillo) Anness Publishing GBR. Dist: National Bk. Network.

Antonelli, Gina. Who Is Ollie? Antonelli, Gina, illus. 2006. (Illus.). 31p. (J). (gr. -1-3). per. 10.99 *(978-1-883573-07-2(6))* Blue Forge Pr.

Armadillo, Jeffrey. My First Animals: Over 200 Animals to Name & Learn About. Lewis, Jan, illus. 2015. (ENG.). 48p. bds. 9.99 *(978-1-86147-652-4(3),* Armadillo) Anness Publishing GBR. Dist: National Bk. Network.

Award, Anna. My First Animals. 2012. (ENG., Illus.). 10p. (J). bds. 9.95 *(978-1-84135-556-6(9))*; bds. 6.50 *(978-1-84135-555-9(0))* Award Pubns. Ltd. GBR. Dist: Parkwest Pubns., Inc.

Baggott, Stella. Baby's Very First Little Book of Baby Animals. 2012. (Baby's Very First Board Book Ser.). 10p. (J). ring bd. 6.99 *(978-0-7945-3217-8(9),* Usborne) EDC Publishing.

Barlow, Amanda. Animals. 2004. (Baby Board Bks.). (ENG., Illus.). 1p. (J). (gr. -1-18). bds. 4.95 *(978-0-7460-4102-4(0))* EDC Publishing.

Bartholomew, Linda & Bartholomew, Al. Adventures in the Tropics. Bartholomew, Linda & Bartholomew, Al, photos by. 2005. (Illus.). 76p. (J). 15.00 *(978-0-9764802-1-1(2))* Solutions for Human Services, LLC.

—The Rain Forest Book for Kids. Bartholomew, Linda & Bartholomew, Al, photos by. 2005. (Illus.). 32p. (J). 9.00 *(978-0-9764802-0-4(4))* Solutions for Human Services, LLC.

Barwood, Lee. Klassic Koalas: Ancient Aboriginal Tales in New Retellings, BW Edition. 2007. (ENG., Illus.). 24p. (J). pap. 14.99 *(978-0-9764698-6-5(3))* Koala Jo Publishing.

Baylis, Aless. ABC Spanish: Take a Fun Journey Through the Alphabet & Learn Some Spanish! 2017. (Little Concepts Ser.). (ENG, EST & SPA., Illus.). 36p. (J). (gr. -1-1). 12.95 *(978-1-63322-283-0(7),* Walter Foster) Quarto Publishing Group USA.

Bayrock, Fiona. Bubble Homes & Fish Farts. Conahan, Carolyn Digby, illus. 2009. (ENG.). 48p. (J). (gr. 1-4). pap. 7.95 *(978-1-57091-670-0(5))* Charlesbridge Publishing, Inc.

Bedford, David. Tails. Worthington, Leonie, illus. 2008. (ENG.). 16p. (J). (gr. k-k). 5.95 *(978-1-921272-37-0(6))* Little Hare Bks. AUS. Dist: Independent Pubs. Group.

Bedford, David & Worthington, Leonie. Mums. 2007. (Illus.). 16p. *(978-1-921049-78-1(2))* Little Hare Bks. AUS. Dist: HarperCollins Pubs. Australia.

Bergeron, Alain M., et al. Les Rhinocéros. 2010. (FRE., Illus.). 64p. (J). pap. 8.95 *(978-2-89435-500-8(9))* Quintin Pubs./Editions Michel Quintin CAN. Dist: Crabtree Publishing Co.

Bicknell, Joanna. My First BK of Animals. 2010. 16p. (J). bds. 8.99 *(978-1-84879-361-3(8))* Make Believe Ideas GBR. Dist: Nelson, Thomas Inc.

Bloom, Steve, et al. My Favourite Animal Families. 2010. (ENG., Illus.). 64p. (J). (gr. -1-k). 19.95 *(978-0-500-54390-0(9),* 554390) Thames & Hudson.

Bové, Jennifer. Meet Ranger Rick Jr: Busy Moms. 2016. (Ranger Rick: Animal Fun for Young Children Ser.). (ENG., Illus.). 32p. (J). (gr. -1-1). pap. 5.99 *(978-1-63076-212-4(1))* Taylor Trade Publishing.

Branzei, Sylvia. Animal Grossology: The Science of Creatures Gross & Disgusting. Keely, Jack, illus. 2004. (Grossology Ser.). (ENG.). 80p. (J). (gr. 3-7). reprint ed. mass mkt. 9.99 *(978-0-8431-1011-1(2),* Price Stern Sloan) Penguin Young Readers Group.

Brooks, David, illus. Animals. 2005. (My First Book Ser.). 9p. (J). (gr. -1-1). bds. 3.95 *(978-1-933050-09-6(8))* Sweetwater Pr.

Burkhard, Balthasar. Click, Said the Camera. 2006. (Illus.). 42p. pap. 30.00 *(978-3-907044-56-8(8))* Lars Muller Pubs. CHE. Dist: Springer.

Charbonnel-Bojman, Severine. My Picture Book of Animals. 2012. (ENG., Illus.). 256p. (J). (gr. -1-k). 9.95 *(978-1-77085-112-2(7),* 9781770851122) Firefly Bks., Ltd.

Clissold, Caroline. Wild Animals. 2007. (Trackers-Math Ser.). (gr. 2-5). pap. 5.00 *(978-1-59055-916-1(9))* Pacific Learning, Inc.

Cocoretto, illus. In the Snow. 2016. (Peekaboo! Ser.: 4). (ENG.). 12p. (J). bds. *(978-1-84643-865-3(9))* Child's Play International Ltd.

Cook, Gladys Emerson. Zoo Animals. 2011. 54p. 36.95 *(978-1-258-10530-3(6))* Literary Licensing, LLC.

Davis, Caroline. Bugs. Davis, Caroline, illus. 2010. (ENG., Illus.). 20p. (J). bds. *(978-1-4083-0784-7(7),* Orchard Bks.) Hachette Children's Group GBR. Dist: Hachette Bk. Group.

Diaw, Boris. Hoops to Hippos! True Stories of a Basketball Star on Safari! 2015. (NGK Chapters Ser.). (ENG., Illus.). 112p. (J). (gr. 2-5). pap. 5.99 *(978-1-4263-2052-1(3),* National Geographic Children's Bks.) National Geographic Society.

Dicmas, Courtney. Colours. Dicmas, Courtney, illus. 2017. (Wild! Concepts Ser.: 4). (ENG., Illus.). 14p. (J). bds. ***(978-1-84643-995-7(7))*** Child's Play International Ltd.

—Numbers. Dicmas, Courtney, illus. 2017. (Wild! Concepts Ser.: 4). (ENG., Illus.). 14p. (J). bds. ***(978-1-84643-993-3(0))*** Child's Play International Ltd.

—Opposites. Dicmas, Courtney, illus. 2017. (Wild! Concepts Ser.: 4). (ENG., Illus.). 14p. (J). bds. ***(978-1-84643-997-1(3))*** Child's Play International Ltd.

—Shapes. Dicmas, Courtney, illus. 2017. (Wild! Concepts Ser.: 4). (ENG., Illus.). 14p. (J). bds. ***(978-1-84643-994-0(9))*** Child's Play International Ltd.

Doak, Angela K. Atlantic Animal ABCs, 1 vol. 2017. (ENG., Illus.). 26p. (J). (gr. -1-k). bds. 14.95 ***(978-1-77108-463-5(4))*** Nimbus Publishing, Ltd. CAN. Dist: Orca Bk. Pubs. USA.

Dorling Kindersley Publishing Staff. Animal Colors. 2012. (Touch & Feel Ser.). (ENG.). 12p. (J). (gr. -1-k). bds. 6.99 *(978-1-4654-0164-9(4),* DK Children) Dorling Kindersley Publishing, Inc.

—My First Baby Animals: Let's Find Our Favorites! 2011. (Tab Board Bks.). (ENG.). 28p. (J). (gr. -1 — 1). bds. 9.99 *(978-0-7566-8988-9(0),* DK Children) Dorling Kindersley Publishing, Inc.

—Wildlife of the World. 2015. (ENG., Illus.). 480p. 50.00 *(978-1-4654-3804-1(1),* DK) Dorling Kindersley Publishing, Inc.

Dubuc, Marianne. Animal Masquerade. Dubuc, Marianne, illus. 2012. (ENG., Illus.). 120p. (J). (gr. -1-2). 16.95 *(978-1-55453-782-2(7))* Kids Can Pr., Ltd. CAN. Dist: Hachette Bk. Group.

Familius Staff & Miles, David. Slide-N-Seek: Earth. 2017. (ENG., Illus.). 10p. (J). 15.95 *(978-1-944822-45-3(3))* Familius LLC.

Farmyard Friends. (Magnets on the Move Ser.). 8p. (J). bds. *(978-2-7643-0147-0(2))* Phidal Publishing, Inc./Editions Phidal, Inc.

Farnsworth, Lauren. Clever Babies Love Art - Wild Animals. 2016. (Clever Babies Love Art Ser.). (ENG., Illus.). 14p. (J). (— 1). bds. 7.99 *(978-1-78055-397-9(8))* O'Mara, Michael Bks., Ltd. GBR. Dist: Independent Pubs. Group.

Fiedler, Heidi. Fur & Feathers: A Close-Up Photographic Look Inside Your World. 2016. (Up Close Ser.). (ENG., Illus.). 64p. (J). (gr. 1-3). 14.95 *(978-1-63322-167-3(9),* Walter Foster Jr) Quarto Publishing Group USA.

Flintham, Thomas. Animal Numbers. Flintham, Thomas, illus. 2016. (ENG., Illus.). 24p. (J). (gr. -1 — 1). bds. 7.99 *(978-1-4814-6937-1(1),* Little Simon) Little Simon.

Flying Frog Publishing, ed. Safari Animals. 2012. (Drawing in Color Ser.). 96p. (J). 12.99 *(978-1-60745-376-5(2))* Flying Frog Publishing, Inc.

Ganeri, Anita. The Animal Atlas. 2006. (Atlas Ser.). (Illus.). 32p. (J). 10.95 *(978-0-8437-0918-6(9),* 709189) Langenscheidt Publishing Group.

Gibeau, Claire Janvier. Active Alphabet. 2009. 16p. pap. 8.49 *(978-1-4490-3828-1(X))* AuthorHouse.

Groves, Julia, illus. Animal Babies in the Meadow! 2016. (Animal Babies Ser.: 4). (ENG.). 14p. (J). bds. *(978-1-84643-879-0(9))* Child's Play International Ltd.

—Animal Babies in the River! 2016. (Animal Babies Ser.: 4). (ENG.). 14p. (J). bds. *(978-1-84643-880-6(2))* Child's Play International Ltd.

—Animal Babies on the Mountain! 2016. (Animal Babies Ser.: 4). (ENG.). 14p. (J). bds. *(978-1-84643-881-3(0))* Child's Play International Ltd.

Haas, Robert B. African Critters. 2008. (ENG., Illus.). 96p. (J). (gr. 1-4). lib. bdg. 26.90 *(978-1-4263-0318-0(1),* National Geographic Children's Bks.) National Geographic Society.

Haas, Robert B. & National Geographic Kids Staff. African Critters. 2008. (ENG., Illus.). 96p. (J). (gr. 1-4). 17.95 *(978-1-4263-0317-3(3),* National Geographic Children's Bks.) National Geographic Society.

Hale, Rachael. Furry Friends. rev. ed. 2007. (Paw Pals Ser.). (ENG., Illus.). 20p. (J). (gr. -1 — 1). bds. 6.99 *(978-0-316-11319-9(0))* Little, Brown Bks. for Young Readers.

Halls, Kelly Milner. Tiger in Trouble! And More True Stories of Amazing Animal Rescues. 2012. (NGK Chapters Ser.). (ENG.). 112p. (J). (gr. 2-5). lib. bdg. 14.90 *(978-1-4263-1079-9(X),* National Geographic Children's Bks.) National Geographic Society.

Halls, Kelly Milner & National Geographic Kids Staff. Tiger in Trouble! And More True Stories of Amazing Animal Rescues. 2012. (NGK Chapters Ser.). (ENG.). 112p. (J). (gr. 2-5). pap. 5.99 *(978-1-4263-1078-2(1),* National Geographic Children's Bks.) National Geographic Society.

Harper, Charley. ABC's. 2013. (ENG., Illus.). 62p. (J). 16.95 *(978-1-62326-003-3(5))* AMMO Bks., LLC.

Harrison, Paul. Animal Fun. 2011. (Window on the World Ser.). (Illus.). 32p. *(978-1-84089-661-9(2))* Zero to Ten, Ltd.

Helman, Andrea. O Is for Orca. Wolfe, Art, photos by. 2016. (ENG., Illus.). 20p. (J). (— 1). bds. 9.99 *(978-1-63217-033-0(7),* Little Bigfoot) Sasquatch Bks.

—1, 2, 3 Moose. Wolfe, Art, photos by. 2016. (ENG., Illus.). 20p. (J). (— 1). bds. 9.99 *(978-1-63217-032-3(9),* Little Bigfoot) Sasquatch Bks.

Hess, Paul. Safari Animals. Hess, Paul, illus. 2009. (Animal Verse Ser.). (ENG., Illus.). 24p. (J). (gr. -1-k). pap. *(978-1-84089-562-9(4))* Zero to Ten, Ltd.

Hicks, R. Animals in Art. 2006. (Children's Art Ser. from the National Gallery of Victoria Ser.). (ENG., Illus.). 28p. (J). (gr. -1-12). pap. 9.95 *(978-0-7241-0236-5(1))* National Gallery of Victoria AUS. Dist: National Bk. Network.

Houghton Mifflin Harcourt Publishing Company Staff & Nouvian, Judith. Homes. 2015. (Picture This Ser.). (ENG., Illus.). 42p. (J). (gr. -1-3). bds. 7.99 *(978-0-544-51263-4(4),* HMH Books For Young Readers) Houghton Mifflin Harcourt Publishing Co.

Hynes, Margaret. Picture This! Animals: Amazing Information-Right Before Your Eyes! 2014. (Picture This Ser.). (ENG., Illus.). 64p. (J). (gr. 3-8). 12.99 *(978-0-7534-6887-6(5),* 9780753468876, Kingfisher) Roaring Brook Pr.

Ikids Staff. Farm Faces: A Book of Masks. Larranaga, Ana Martin, illus. 2006. (ENG.). 12p. (J). (gr. -1 — 1). bds. 6.99 *(978-1-58476-471-7(6),* IKIDS) Innovative Kids.

Irving Ed.D., Harry R. Un Image-Word D'Enfants et Livre Simple de Phrase: Version Francaise Catégories Primaires. 2010. 192p. pap. 51.53 *(978-1-4251-6396-9(3))* Trafford Publishing.

James, Soloman & Salt, Allan. Little Book of Animals. 2010. (OJI & ENG., Illus.). 43p. *(978-0-9745168-6-8(4))* Cotsen Occasional Pr.

Jerome, Kate B. The Wise Animal Handbook Maryland. 2017. (Arcadia Kids Ser.). (ENG., Illus.). 32p. (J). 16.99 ***(978-0-7385-2824-3(2))*** Arcadia Publishing.

—The Wise Animal Handbook Michigan. 2017. (Arcadia Kids Ser.). (ENG., Illus.). 32p. (J). 16.99 ***(978-0-7385-2826-7(9))*** Arcadia Publishing.

—The Wise Animal Handbook Minnesota. 2017. (Arcadia Kids Ser.). (ENG., Illus.). 32p. (J). 16.99 ***(978-0-7385-2827-4(7))*** Arcadia Publishing.

—The Wise Animal Handbook Missouri. 2017. (Arcadia Kids Ser.). (ENG., Illus.). 32p. (J). 16.99 ***(978-0-7385-2828-1(5))*** Arcadia Publishing.

—The Wise Animal Handbook Montana. 2017. (Arcadia Kids Ser.). (ENG., Illus.). 32p. (J). 16.99 ***(978-0-7385-2829-8(3))*** Arcadia Publishing.

—The Wise Animal Handbook Nevada. 2017. (Arcadia Kids Ser.). (ENG., Illus.). 32p. (J). 16.99 ***(978-0-7385-2831-1(5))*** Arcadia Publishing.

—The Wise Animal Handbook New Jersey. 2017. (Arcadia Kids Ser.). (ENG., Illus.). 32p. (J). 16.99 ***(978-0-7385-2832-8(3))*** Arcadia Publishing.

—The Wise Animal Handbook New Mexico. 2017. (Arcadia Kids Ser.). (ENG., Illus.). 32p. (J). 16.99 ***(978-0-7385-2833-5(1))*** Arcadia Publishing.

—The Wise Animal Handbook NorCal. 2017. (Arcadia Kids Ser.). (ENG., Illus.). 32p. (J). 16.99 ***(978-0-7385-2836-6(6))*** Arcadia Publishing.

—The Wise Animal Handbook North Carolina. 2017. (Arcadia Kids Ser.). (ENG., Illus.). 32p. (J). 16.99 ***(978-0-7385-2835-9(8))*** Arcadia Publishing.

—The Wise Animal Handbook Ohio. 2017. (Arcadia Kids Ser.). (ENG., Illus.). 32p. (J). 16.99 ***(978-0-7385-2837-3(4))*** Arcadia Publishing.

—The Wise Animal Handbook Oklahoma. 2017. (Arcadia Kids Ser.). (ENG., Illus.). 32p. (J). 16.99 ***(978-0-7385-2838-0(2))*** Arcadia Publishing.

—The Wise Animal Handbook Oregon. 2017. (Arcadia Kids Ser.). (ENG., Illus.). 32p. (J). 16.99 ***(978-0-7385-2839-7(0))*** Arcadia Publishing.

—The Wise Animal Handbook Pennsylvania. 2017. (Arcadia Kids Ser.). (ENG., Illus.). 32p. (J). 16.99 ***(978-0-7385-2840-3(4))*** Arcadia Publishing.

—The Wise Animal Handbook Socal. 2017. (Arcadia Kids Ser.). (ENG., Illus.). 32p. (J). 16.99 ***(978-0-7385-2843-4(9))*** Arcadia Publishing.

—The Wise Animal Handbook South Carolina. 2017. (Arcadia Kids Ser.). (ENG., Illus.). 32p. (J). 16.99 ***(978-0-7385-2841-0(2))*** Arcadia Publishing.

—The Wise Animal Handbook South Dakota. 2017. (Arcadia Kids Ser.). (ENG., Illus.). 32p. (J). 16.99 ***(978-0-7385-2842-7(0))*** Arcadia Publishing.

—The Wise Animal Handbook Tennessee. 2017. (Arcadia Kids Ser.). (ENG., Illus.). 32p. (J). 16.99 ***(978-0-7385-2844-1(7))*** Arcadia Publishing.

—The Wise Animal Handbook Texas. 2017. (Arcadia Kids Ser.). (ENG., Illus.). 32p. (J). 16.99 ***(978-0-7385-2845-8(5))*** Arcadia Publishing.

—The Wise Animal Handbook Utah. 2017. (Arcadia Kids Ser.). (ENG., Illus.). 32p. (J). 16.99 ***(978-0-7385-2846-5(3))*** Arcadia Publishing.

—The Wise Animal Handbook Virginia. 2017. (Arcadia Kids Ser.). (ENG., Illus.). 32p. (J). 16.99 ***(978-0-7385-2847-2(1))*** Arcadia Publishing.

—The Wise Animal Handbook Washington. 2017. (Arcadia Kids Ser.). (ENG., Illus.). 32p. (J). 16.99 ***(978-0-7385-2848-9(X))*** Arcadia Publishing.

—The Wise Animal Handbook Wisconsin. 2017. (Arcadia Kids Ser.). (ENG., Illus.). 32p. (J). 16.99 ***(978-0-7385-2849-6(8))*** Arcadia Publishing.

Kainen, Dan & Kaufmann, Carol. Safari: A Photicular Book. 2012. (Photicular Ser.). (ENG., Illus.). 32p. 25.95 *(978-0-7611-6380-0(8),* 16380) Workman Publishing Co., Inc.

Kalman, Bobbie. Les Dragons de Komodo. 2010. (Petit Monde Vivant Ser.). (FRE., Illus.). 32p. (J). pap. 9.95 *(978-2-89579-315-1(8))* Bayard Canada Livres CAN. Dist: Crabtree Publishing Co.

—Les Grenouilles et Autres Amphibiens. 2010. (Petit Monde Vivant Ser.). (FRE., Illus.). 32p. (J). pap. 9.95 *(978-2-89579-319-9(0))* Bayard Canada Livres CAN. Dist: Crabtree Publishing Co.

Kalman, Bobbie & Dyer, Hadley. Les Léopards. 2010. (Petit Monde Vivant Ser.). (FRE., Illus.). 32p. (J). pap. 9.95 *(978-2-89579-316-8(6))* Bayard Canada Livres CAN. Dist: Crabtree Publishing Co.

Kalman, Bobbie & Johnson, Robin. Les Koalas et Autres Marsupiaux. 2010. (Petit Monde Vivant Ser.). (FRE., Illus.). 32p. (J). pap. 9.95 *(978-2-89579-320-5(4))* Bayard Canada Livres CAN. Dist: Crabtree Publishing Co.

Katirgis, Jane. Baby Forest Animals. 2010. (All about Baby Animals Ser.). (Illus.). 24p. (J). lib. bdg. 22.60 *(978-0-7660-3798-4(3),* Enslow Elementary) Enslow Pubs., Inc.

Killen, Nicola. Animal Opposites. 2014. (Nicola Killen Animals Ser.). (ENG., Illus.). 10p. (J). (— 1). bds. 9.99 *(978-1-4052-6286-6(9))* Egmont Bks., Ltd. GBR. Dist: Independent Pubs. Group.

Killer Animals. 2010. (Killer Animals Ser.). (ENG.). 32p. (gr. 1-2). lib. bdg. 106.60 *(978-1-4296-4420-4(6),* Blazers) Capstone Press of Coughlan Cos.

Könnecke, Ole. The Big Book of Animals of the World. Könnecke, Ole, illus. 2015. (ENG., Illus.). 20p. (J). (gr. -1-k). bds. 14.99 *(978-1-77657-012-6(X))* Gecko Pr. NZL. Dist: Lerner Publishing Group.

Kuchler, B. L. That's Life. 2003. (ENG., Illus.). 112p. (J). tchr. ed. 14.95 *(978-1-57223-709-4(0),* 7090) Willow Creek Pr., Inc.

Kuchler, Bonnie Louise, compiled by. Just Kids: Pictures, Poems & Other Silly Animal Stuff Just for Kids! 2003. (ENG., Illus.). 32p. tchr. ed. 12.95 *(978-1-57223-598-4(5),* 5985) Willow Creek Pr., Inc.

Lessem, Don. National Geographic Kids Ultimate Dinopedia: The Most Complete Dinosaur Reference Ever. Tempesta, Franco, illus. 2010. (ENG.). 272p. (J). (gr. 2-5). 24.95 *(978-1-4263-0164-3(2))*; lib. bdg. 34.90 *(978-1-4263-0165-0(0))* National Geographic Society. (National Geographic Children's Bks.).

Letherland, Lucy. Atlas of Animal Adventures. 2016. (Atlas Of Ser.). (ENG.). 96p. (J). (gr. 1-4). 30.00 *(978-1-84780-841-7(7),* Wide Eyed Editions) Quarto Publishing Group UK GBR. Dist: Hachette Bk. Group.

Lewis, Jan, illus. Animals: Turn the Wheels Find the Pictures. 2016. (ENG.). 10p. bds. 14.99 *(978-1-86147-713-2(9),* Armadillo) Anness Publishing GBR. Dist: National Bk. Network.

—Ask Me about Animals: Lift the Flaps & Find the Answers! 2016. (ENG.). 14p. (J). (gr. -1-12). 10.99 *(978-1-86147-774-3(0),* Armadillo) Anness Publishing GBR. Dist: National Bk. Network.

—My First Animals. 2014. (ENG.). 24p. (J). (gr. -1-k). bds. 6.99 *(978-1-86147-373-8(7),* Armadillo) Anness Publishing GBR. Dist: National Bk. Network.

Litchfield & Allman. Los Animales (Animals) 2004. (First Words Board Bks.). (SPA., Illus.). 12p. (J). 4.95 *(978-0-7460-4519-0(0))* EDC Publishing.

Ljungkvist, Laura. Search & Spot: Animals! 2015. (Search & Spot Book Ser.). (ENG., Illus.). 40p. (J). (gr. -1-3). 16.99 *(978-0-544-54005-7(0),* HMH Books For Young Readers) Houghton Mifflin Harcourt Publishing Co.

Llewellyn, Claire. It's Fun to Learn about Animals: A Busy Picture Book Full of Fabulous Facts & Things to Do! 2016. (ENG., Illus.). 32p. 9.99 *(978-1-86147-701-9(5),* Armadillo) Anness Publishing GBR. Dist: National Bk. Network.

Make Believe Ideas, Ltd. Touch & Learn - God's Animals. 2007. (Illus.). 12p. (J). (gr. -1). bds. 6.97 *(978-1-59145-555-4(3))* Nelson, Thomas Inc.

Martin, John David. My Little Wild Animal Book. 2011. (Illus.). 24p. (J). (gr. -1). pap. 1.75 *(978-0-7399-2427-3(3))* Rod & Staff Pubs., Inc.

Maskell, Hazel. Animal Picture Atlas. Edwards, Linda, illus. 2008. (Atlases Ser.). 48p. (J). 12.99 *(978-0-7945-2083-0(9),* Usborne) EDC Publishing.

Maze, Stephanie, ed. Momentos de Paz en el Reino Animal: Los Animales y Sus Hogares. 2006. (Moments in the Wild Ser.). (SPA., Illus.). 36p. (J). (gr. -1-k). pap. 8.00 *(978-0-9769542-3-1(0))* Moonstone Pr., LLC.

—Momentos Tiernos en el Reino Animal: Los Animales y Sus Bebes. 2006. (Moments in the Wild Ser.). (SPA., Illus.). 36p. (J). (gr. -1-k). pap. 8.00 (978-0-9769542-2-4(2)) Moonstone Pr., LLC.

National Geographic Staff. Nat Geo Wild Animal Atlas: Earth's Astonishing Animals & Where They Live. 2010. (ENG., Illus.). 64p. (J). (gr. k-4). 18.95 (978-1-4263-0699-0(7), National Geographic Children's Bks.) National Geographic Society.

National Wildlife Federation Staff. My First Book of Funny Animals. 2015. (ENG., Illus.). 22p. (J). (— 1). bds. 6.95 (978-1-62354-051-7(8)) Charlesbridge Publishing, Inc.

Ogwang, Evelynn. My Alphabet Safari. 2012. 60p. pap. 21.99 (978-1-4567-5621-5(4)) AuthorHouse.

O'Toole, Janet & Anness Publishing Staff. Animals: Lift the Flaps to Find Out about Animals! Adams, Ben, illus. 2013. (ENG.). 16p. bds. 6.99 (978-1-84322-793-9(2), Armadillo) Anness Publishing GBR. Dist: National Bk. Network.

Pattullo, Alice. An Animal ABC. 2017. (ENG., Illus.). 64p. (J). (gr. -1-1). 17.99 **(978-1-84365-313-4(3)**, Pavilion) Pavilion Bks. GBR. Dist: Independent Pubs. Group.

Picthall, Chez. Baby Sees Boxed Set: Shapes. 2015. (ENG.). 32p. (J). 20.00 (978-1-905503-49-0(0)) Award Pubns. Ltd. GBR. Dist: Parkwest Pubns., Inc.

—First Library. 2015. (ENG., Illus.). 32p. (J). 15.00 (978-1-907604-93-5(6)) Award Pubns. Ltd. GBR. Dist: Parkwest Pubns., Inc.

—Zoo Animals. 2015. (ENG., Illus.). 10p. (J). 7.99 (978-1-906572-06-8(2)) Award Pubns. Ltd. GBR. Dist: Parkwest Pubns., Inc.

Picthall, Chez & Award, Anna. A Very First Book. 2015. (ENG., Illus.). 10p. (J). 9.99 (978-1-907604-42-3(1)) Award Pubns. Ltd. GBR. Dist: Parkwest Pubns., Inc.

Pomaska, Anna. My First Mandalas - Animals. 2010. (Dover Coloring Bks.). (ENG., Illus.). 32p. (J). (gr. -1-2). pap. 3.99 (978-0-486-47558-5(1)) Dover Pubns., Inc.

Post, Lee. Alaska! Big & Small: A big book of Alaskan Animals from itsy-bitsy to Gigantic. Post, Lee, illus. 2007. (Illus.). 32p. per. 9.95 (978-1-934443-94-1(8)) ExpandingBooks.com.

Priddy Books Staff & Priddy, Roger. My Big Animal Book. 2011. (ENG.). 14p. (J). bds. (978-0-312-51365-8(8), Priddy Bks.) St. Martin's Pr.

Priddy, Roger. Baby Shaker Teethers Animals. 2012. (ENG., Illus.). 22p. (J). (gr. -1 — 1). bds. 5.99 (978-0-312-51465-5(4), 9780312514655, Priddy Bks.) St. Martin's Pr.

Publications International Ltd. Staff, ed. Animals. 2010. 120p. (J). 18.98 (978-1-60553-155-7(3), PIL Kids) Publications International, Ltd.

—Baby's ABC. 2010. 18p. (J). bds. 7.98 (978-1-60553-961-4(9)) Publications International, Ltd.

—Baby's First Year Animals Memory Keeper. 2010. 48p. spiral bd. 15.98 (978-1-60553-834-1(5)) Phoenix International Publications, Inc.

Publishing, Sterling. Daddy & Me. 2008. (Illus.). 12p. (J). bds. (978-1-934618-44-8(6)) Begin Smart LLC.

Ragel-Dial, Tasha. Say What?, a Photo Book of Inspirational Bible Verses for Kids - Featuring the Photography of Tasha Ragel-Dial. Ragel-Dial, Tasha, photos by. 2013. (Illus.). 24p. 22.95 (978-1-61493-215-4(8)) Peppertree Pr., The.

Rinaldo, Luana & Prasadam-halls, Smriti. Who Am I? This Is My Mouth. 2012. (ENG., Illus.). 12p. (J). (gr. -1-k). 7.99 (978-1-4083-1509-5(2)) Hodder & Stoughton GBR. Dist: Hachette Bk. Group.

—Who Am I? This Is My Tail. 2012. (ENG., Illus.). 12p. (J). (gr. -1-k). 7.99 (978-1-4083-1510-1(6)) Hodder & Stoughton GBR. Dist: Hachette Bk. Group.

Rivoal, Marine. Are You a Monkey? A Tale of Animal Charades. Gartner, Maya, ed. 2017. (ENG., Illus.). 40p. (gr. -1-k). 16.95 **(978-0-7148-7417-3(5))** Phaidon Pr., Inc.

Robinson, Gary D. Who Pooped in the Park: Glacier. 2004. (Illus.). 48p. (J). pap. 11.95 (978-1-56037-279-0(6)) Farcountry Pr.

Robson, Gary D. Who Pooped in Park: Grand Teton. 2004. (Illus.). 48p. (J). pap. 11.95 (978-1-56037-280-6(X)) Farcountry Pr.

Rutherford, Peter, illus. Giant Fun-to-Find Puzzles Busy Animals: Search for Pictures in Eight Exciting Scenes. 2015. (ENG.). 24p. pap. 6.99 (978-1-86147-460-5(1), Armadillo) Anness Publishing GBR. Dist: National Bk. Network.

Ruurs, Margriet. In My Backyard. Broda, Ron, illus. 2007. (ENG.). 32p. (J). (gr. -1-3). 18.95 (978-0-88776-775-3(3), Tundra Bks.) Tundra Bks. CAN. Dist: Penguin Random Hse. LLC.

—Wild Babies. Kiss, Andrew, illus. 2003. (ENG.). 32p. (J). (gr. -1-3). 14.95 (978-0-88776-627-5(7), Tundra Bks.) Tundra Bks. CAN. Dist: Penguin Random Hse. LLC.

Sajnani, Surya. Can You Find Me? Sajnani, Surya, illus. 2017. (Animosaic Ser.). (ENG., Illus.). 20p. (J). (gr. -1 — 1). bds. 12.95 **(978-1-68297-146-8(5)**, Words & Pictures) Quarto Publishing Group UK GBR. Dist: Hachette Bk. Group.

Salariya, David & Williams, Mark. Animal Atlas. 2014. (Where on Earth? Ser.). (ENG., Illus.). 16p. (J). (gr. -1). bds. 8.95 (978-1-905638-43-7(4), Scribblers) Book Hse. GBR. Dist: Sterling Publishing Co., Inc.

Schaefer, Lola M. Lifetime: The Amazing Numbers in Animal Lives. Neal, Christopher Silas, illus. 2013. (ENG.). 40p. (J). (gr. -1-3). 17.99 (978-1-4521-0714-1(9)) Chronicle Bks. LLC.

Schmidt, Dennis & Schmidt, Esther. Baby Wild Animals, 1 vol. 2nd ed. 2015. (ENG., Illus.). 48p. (J). (gr. -1-1). pap. 6.95 **(978-1-77203-090-7(2))** Heritage Hse. CAN. Dist: Orca Bk. Pubs. USA.

Schwartz, David M. Animal Noses. Kuhn, Dwight, photos by. (Plants & Animals Ser.). (Illus.). 16p. (J). (gr. 1-3). pap. 2.99 (978-1-57471-321-3(3), 3030) Creative Teaching Pr., Inc.

Schwartz, David M. & Schy, Yael. Where in the Wild? Camouflaged Creatures Concealed... & Revealed. Kuhn, Dwight, photos by. 2011. (ENG., Illus.). 44p. (J). (gr. -1-2). pap. 8.99 (978-1-58246-399-5(9), Tricycle Pr.) Random Hse. Children's Bks.

Seder, Rufus Butler. Gallop! 2007. (Scanimation Ser.). (ENG., Illus.). 12p. (gr. -1-12). 13.95 (978-0-7611-4763-3(2), 14763) Workman Publishing Co., Inc.

Sherwin, Frank. Guide to God's Animals. 2015. (ENG.). 120p. (J). (gr. 4-7). 16.99 (978-0-7369-6542-2(4)) Harvest Hse. Pubs.

Sherwin, Frank J. Guide to Animals. 2013. (Illus.). 117p. (J). (978-1-935587-36-1(6)) Institute for Creation Research.

Siwanowicz, Igor. Animals up Close: Zoom in on the World's Most Incredible Creatures. 2014. (Illus.). 96p. (J). (978-1-4351-5620-3(X)) Barnes & Noble, Inc.

Storey Publishing Staff. Eye See You. Balmuth, Deborah L. & Guare, Sarah, eds. 2006. (ENG., Illus.). 64p. (J). (gr. 2-8). pap. 9.95 (978-1-58017-848-8(0), 67848) Storey Publishing, LLC.

Stout, William. William Stout - Animal Sketches from Around the World. 2003. (Illus.). 54p. (YA). per. 15.00 (978-0-9712716-8-5(2)) Stout, William Inc.

—William Stout - Tribute to Ray Harryhausen. 2003. (Illus.). 70p. (YA). per. 20.00 (978-0-9712716-9-2(0)) Stout, William Inc.

Stowe, Debbie. Baby Animals. 2009. (Illus.). 160p. (J). (978-1-4351-1819-5(7)) Metro Bks.

Tai, Elise See. Wild Animal Alphabet. 2014. (Lumpy Bumpy Ser.). (ENG., Illus.). 10p. (J). (gr. -1 — 1). 5.99 (978-0-7641-6709-6(X)) Barron's Educational Series, Inc.

Thompson, Richard & Thompson, Ofa. Ko 'Eku Tohi 'oe Fanga Manu. Slutz, Stephani, illus. l.t. ed. 2004. (TON.). 16p. (J). (gr. -1-18). 5.00 (978-0-9678979-2-9(0)) Friendly Isles Pr.

Thurlby, Paul. Paul Thurlby's Wildlife. Thurlby, Paul, illus. 2013. (ENG., Illus.). 32p. (J). (gr. k-4). 17.99 (978-0-7636-6563-0(0), Templar) Candlewick Pr.

Tiere der Nacht. (GER.). (978-3-411-09261-1(0)) Bibliographisches Institut & F. A. Brockhaus AG DEU. Dist: i. b. d., Ltd.

Toft, Kim Michelle. The World That We Want. 2005. (Illus.). 32p. (J). (gr. -1 — 1). pap. 6.95 (978-1-58089-115-8(2)); bds. 16.95 (978-1-58089-114-1(4)) Charlesbridge Publishing, Inc.

Top That. Let's Stencil Animals. 2008. (978-1-84666-651-3(1)) Top That! Publishing PLC.

TUXWORTH NICOLA. Animals. 2014. (ENG., Illus.). 20p. (J). (gr. -1-k). bds. 6.99 (978-1-84322-859-2(9), Armadillo) Anness Publishing GBR. Dist: National Bk. Network.

U. S. National Geographic Society Staff. Nat Geo Wild Animal Atlas: Earth's Astonishing Animals & Where They Live. 2010. (ENG., Illus.). 64p. (J). (gr. k-4). lib. bdg. 27.90 (978-1-4263-0727-0(6), National Geographic Children's Bks.) National Geographic Society.

Valério, Geraldo, illus. Moose, Goose, Animals on the Loose! A Canadian Wildlife ABC. 2016. (ENG.). 40p. (J). (gr. -1-1). 16.95 (978-1-77147-174-9(3), Owlkids) Owlkids Bks. Inc. CAN. Dist: Publishers Group West (PGW).

Vander Klipp, Michael. God Made Animals, 1 vol. 2008. (God Made... Ser.). 14p. (J). bds. 3.99 (978-0-8254-3911-7(6)) Kregel Pubns.

Walters, Eric. An African Alphabet, 1 vol. Todd, Sue, illus. 2017. (ENG.). 28p. (J). (gr. -1-k). bds. 9.95 (978-1-4598-1070-9(8)) Orca Bk. Pubs. USA.

Watt, Fiona. Baby's Very First Little Touchy-Feely Play Book. 2012. (Baby's Very First Board Book Ser.). 10p. (J). ring bd. 11.99 (978-0-7945-3166-9(0), Usborne) EDC Publishing.

Watts, Gillian. Creatures Close Up. Martin, Philippe, photos by. 2016. (ENG., Illus.). 64p. (J). (gr. 3-7). pap. 9.95 (978-1-77085-782-7(6), 9781770857827) Firefly Bks., Ltd.

White, Teagan. Adventures with Barefoot Critters. (ENG., Illus.). (J). 2017. 30p. (— 1). bds. 7.99 (978-1-101-91913-2(2)) 2014. 32p. (gr. -1-3). 16.99 (978-1-77049-624-8(6)) Tundra Bks. CAN. (Tundra Bks.). Dist: Penguin Random Hse. LLC.

Wild Animals Sticker Activity Book. (My Sticker Activity Ser.). (Illus.). 12p. (J). (978-1-4054-1183-7(X)) Parragon, Inc.

Wildsmith, Brian. Animal Colors, 1 vol. 2009. (BEN & ENG., Illus.). 16p. (J). bds. 4.99 (978-1-59572-135-8(5)) Star Bright Bks., Inc.

—Animal Colors, 1 vol. wintranslation.com, tr. 2009. (ARA & ENG., Illus.). 16p. (J). bds. 4.99 (978-1-59572-168-6(1)) Star Bright Bks., Inc.

—Brian Wildsmith's Opposites, 1 vol. 2009. (ENG., Illus.). 32p. (J). bds. 4.99 (978-1-59572-139-6(8)) Star Bright Bks., Inc.

Williams, Brenda. Home for a Tiger, Home for a Bear. Fowler, Rosamund, illus. (ENG.). 32p. (J). 2017. (gr. -1-1). 8.99 **(978-1-78285-343-5(X))** 2009. pap. 7.99 (978-1-84686-353-0(8)) Barefoot Bks., Inc.

Williams, Rachel & Hawkins, Emily. Atlas of Animal Adventures: Natural Wonders, Exciting Experiences & Fun Festivities from the Four Corners of the Globe. Letherland, Lucy, illus. 2016. (Atlas Of Ser.). (ENG.). 96p. (J). 30.00 (978-1-84780-792-2(5), Wide Eyed Editions) Quarto Publishing Group UK GBR. Dist: Littlehampton Bk Services, Ltd.

Wilson, Anne, illus. My First Box of Books: 1 2 3 Colours Animals, 3 vols. 2016. (ENG.). 72p. (J). (gr. -1-2). bds. 9.99 (978-1-86147-416-2(4), Armadillo) Anness Publishing GBR. Dist: National Bk. Network.

Wolfe, Jane. Who Says Moo? Toy Box Staff, illus. 2013. (ENG.). 8p. bds. 6.99 (978-1-84322-679-6(0), Armadillo) Anness Publishing GBR. Dist: National Bk. Network.

—Who's Hiding? Toy Box Staff, illus. 2013. (ENG.). 8p. bds. 6.99 (978-1-84322-657-4(X), Armadillo) Anness Publishing GBR. Dist: National Bk. Network.

The Wonder of Baby Animals. 2013. (Illus.). 47p. (J). (978-1-61628-789-4(6)) Fog City Pr.

Worthington, Leonie & Bedford, David. Bums. 2004. (ENG., Illus.). 16p. (J). (gr. -1-k). 10.95 (978-1-877003-71-4(9)) Little Hare Bks. AUS. Dist: Independent Pubs. Group.

Wynne Pechter, Lesley. Alligator, Bear, Crab: A Baby's ABC, 1 vol. 2017. (ENG., Illus.). 28p. (J). (gr. -1-k). 6.95 (978-1-4598-1507-0(6)) Orca Bk. Pubs. USA.

ANIMALS—POETRY

Abel, Simone, illus. Cuddly Critters: Animal Nursery Rhymes, 1 vol. 2007. (Mother Goose Rhymes Ser.). (ENG.). 32p. (gr. -1-2). lib. bdg. 25.99 (978-1-4048-2344-0(1), 1265749, Nonfiction Picture Bks.) Picture Window Bks.

Alarcón, Francisco X. Animal Poems of the Iguazú: Animalario del Iguazú. Gonzalez, Maya Christina, illus. 2013. (ENG & SPA.). 32p. (J). pap. 9.95 (978-0-89239-299-5(1), Children's Book Press) Lee & Low Bks., Inc.

Alexander, Kwame. Animal Ark: Celebrating our Wild World in Poetry & Pictures. Sartore, Joel, photos by. 2017. (ENG., Illus.). 48p. (J). (gr. -1-3). lib. bdg. 25.90 (978-1-4263-2768-1(4), National Geographic Children's Bks.) National Geographic Society.

Alexander, Kwame & Sartore, Joel. Animal Ark: Celebrating our Wild World in Poetry & Pictures. 2017. (ENG., Illus.). 48p. (J). (gr. -1-3). 15.99 (978-1-4263-2767-4(6), National Geographic Children's Bks.) National Geographic Society.

Andreae, Giles. ABC Animal Jamboree. Wojtowycz, David, illus. 2010. (ENG.). 32p. (J). (gr. -1-2). 16.95 (978-1-58925-092-5(3)) Tiger Tales.

—Bustle in the Bushes. Wojtowycz, David, illus. 2012. (ENG.). 32p. (J). (978-1-58925-109-0(1)) Tiger Tales.

—Commotion in Ocean. Wojtowycz, David, illus. 2011. (ENG.). 24p. (J). bds. 9.95 (978-1-58925-863-1(0)) Tiger Tales.

Bagert, Brod. Giant Children. Arnold, Tedd, illus. 2005. (ENG.). 32p. (J). (gr. -1-3). pap. 6.99 (978-0-14-240192-7(7), Puffin Books) Penguin Young Readers Group.

Beaton, Clare. Clare Beaton's Farmyard Rhymes. Beaton, Clare, illus. 2012. (ENG., Illus.). 14p. (J). (gr. -1-k). 6.99 (978-1-84686-736-1(3)) Barefoot Bks., Inc.

Belloc, Hilaire. More Beasts for Worse Children. B. T. B., illus. 2008. 48p. pap. (978-1-4099-1329-0(5)) Dodo Pr.

Beynette, Kathy Dezarn. When I Am Not Myself. 2014. (ENG., Illus.). 48p. (J). 14.95 (978-0-7649-6673-6(1)) Pomegranate Communications, Inc.

—When Your Porcupine Feels Prickly. 2012. 48p. 14.95 (978-0-7649-6318-6(X)) Pomegranate Communications, Inc.

Blanchard, Eliza. A Child's Book of Animal Poems & Blessings. 2010. (ENG.). 32p. (J). 12.00 (978-1-55896-558-4(0), Skinner Hse. Bks.) Unitarian Universalist Assn.

Bolocan, D. Stephie Learns about Animals: Funny Rhymes for Children about Toys & Animals. 2010. (Illus.). 56p. pap. 21.99 (978-1-4490-9045-6(1)) AuthorHouse.

Bond, Felicia. Tumble Bumble. braille ed. 2004. (Illus.). (J). (gr. 1). spiral bd., bds. (978-0-616-03081-3(9)) Canadian National Institute for the Blind/Institut National Canadien pour les Aveugles.

Brown, Margaret Wise. Where Have You Been? Dillon, Leo & Dillon, Diane, illus. 2004. 32p. (J). (gr. -1-1). lib. bdg. 16.89 (978-0-06-028379-7(3)) HarperCollins Pubs.

Bulion, Leslie. At the Sea Floor Café: Odd Ocean Critter Poems, 1 vol. Evans, Leslie, illus. 2011. (ENG.). 48p. (J). (gr. 3-7). 14.95 (978-1-56145-565-2(2)) Peachtree Pubs.

Canetti, Yanitzia. Quien me mira Asi? ¿quien Me Mira Así? 2010. (SPA.). 24p. (J). pap. 8.99 (978-1-59835-127-9(3)) Cambridge BrickHouse, Inc.

Cordova, Soledad. Poemas de Perros y Gatos. Graullera, Fabiola, illus. 2003. (SPA.). 21p. (J). (gr. 3-5). pap. 7.95 (978-968-19-0987-1(9)) Santillana USA Publishing Co., Inc.

Cotner, June, ed. Bless the Beasts: Children's Prayers & Poems about Animals. Waldherr, Kris, illus. 2006. 63p. (J). (gr. 4-8). reprint ed. 13.00 (978-0-7567-9952-6(X)) DIANE Publishing Co.

Cowle, Ken. Harold Can't Stand to Be Alone. Dorland, Andrew, illus. 2006. 24p. per. (978-0-9781338-3-2(8)) Soul Asylum Poetry.

Cox, Kenyon & Edwards, Wallace. Mixed Beasts. Edwards, Wallace, illus. 2013. (ENG., Illus.). 32p. (J). (gr. 1-6). pap. 9.95 (978-1-77138-035-5(7)) Kids Can Pr., Ltd. CAN. Dist: Hachette Bk. Group.

Cricket Books Staff. Ladybug, Ladybug: And Other Favorite Poems. 2007. (ENG., Illus.). 40p. (J). (gr. k-k). 17.95 (978-0-8126-7936-6(9)) Cricket Bks.

Crozier, Lorna. So Many Babies, 1 vol. Watson, Laura, illus. 2015. (ENG.). 24p. (J). (gr. -1-k). bds. 9.95 (978-1-4598-0831-7(2)) Orca Bk. Pubs. USA.

Curtiss, A. B. Dragons Guard the Zoo. 2010. (ENG.). 320p. (J). (gr. 4-7). 24.95 (978-0-932529-69-5(0)) Oldcastle Publishing.

Daniel, Danielle. Sometimes I Feel Like a Fox, 1 vol. 2015. (ENG., Illus.). 40p. (J). (gr. -1-2). 16.95 (978-1-55498-750-4(4)) Groundwood Bks. CAN. Dist: Publishers Group West (PGW).

Dean, Jan & Stevens, Roger. The Penguin in Lost Property. unabr. ed. 2014. (ENG., Illus.). 96p. (J). pap. 8.99 (978-1-4472-4858-3(9)) Pan Macmillan GBR. Dist: Independent Pubs. Group.

Dyan, Penelope. Animal Rescue, Book 1, Seals, Sea Lions & Elephant Seals, Oh My! Weigand, John D., photos by. 2008. (Illus.). 60p. pap. 15.95 (978-1-935118-21-3(8)) Bellissima Publishing, LLC.

—Endangered — the Peninsular Bighorn Sheep. Weigand, John D., photos by. 2010. (Illus.). 44p. pap. 11.95 (978-1-935630-10-4(5)) Bellissima Publishing, LLC.

Elliott, David. In the Sea. 2014. lib. bdg. 17.20 (978-0-606-35168-3(X)) Turtleback Bks.

—In the Wild. Meade, Holly, illus. 2013. (ENG.). 32p. (J). (gr. -1-3). pap. 6.99 (978-0-7636-6337-7(9)) Candlewick Pr.

Evans, Michael, illus. Over in the Meadow. 2004. (Classic Books with Holes 8x8 Ser.). (ENG.). 16p. (J). pap. (978-0-85953-692-9(0)) Child's Play International Ltd.

Evans, Michael, Jr., illus. Over in the Meadow. 2007. (Classic Books with Holes 8x8 Ser.). (ENG.). 16p. (J). (gr. -1-1). pap. (978-1-84643-136-4(0)) Child's Play International Ltd.

Ewing, Susan. Lucky Hares & Itchy Bears: And Other Alaskan Animals. Blessing, Marlene, ed. Zerbetz, Evon, illus. 2012. (ENG.). 32p. (J). 16.95 (978-0-9858506-0-9(4)) Octopoda Pr.

Forbes, Robert. Let's Have a Bite! A Banquet of Beastly Rhymes. Searle, Ronald, illus. 2010. (ENG.). 96p. (gr. 4-13). 19.95 (978-1-59020-409-2(3), 902409) Overlook Pr., The.

Forbes, Robert L. Beast Friends Forever. Searle, Ronald, illus. 2013. (ENG.). 80p. (J). (gr. 4-13). 19.95 (978-1-59020-808-3(0), 902808) Overlook Pr., The.

Foster, John & Williams, Brenda. Animal Poems & Family Poems. 2008. (Illus.). 24p. (J). lib. bdg. 23.65 (978-1-59646-586-2(7)) Dingles & Co.

Foster, John & Williams, Brenda, selected by. Animal Poems & Family Poems. 2008. (Illus.). 32p. (J). pap. 10.95 (978-1-59646-587-9(5)) Dingles & Co.

George, Kristine O'Connell. Fold Me a Poem. Stringer, Lauren, illus. 2005. (ENG.). 56p. (J). (gr. 1-4). 17.99 (978-0-15-202501-4(4)) Houghton Mifflin Harcourt Publishing Co.

Goldberg Eds, Gail C. Animals A-Z: Poems for Early Readers. 2013. 56p. pap. 24.99 (978-1-4817-1255-2(1)) AuthorHouse.

Gottfried, Maya. Our Farm: By the Animals of Farm Sanctuary. Zakanitch, Robert Rahway, illus. 2010. (ENG.). 40p. (J). (gr. k-3). 17.99 (978-0-375-86118-5(1), Knopf Bks. for Young Readers) Random Hse. Children's Bks.

Grimsley, Barbara J. A to Z of Animal Poetry for Children. 2012. 36p. pap. (978-1-4669-1738-5(5)) Trafford Publishing (UK) Ltd.

Hall, Shirley. Monkey Monkey. 2012. 24p. pap. 14.99 (978-1-4772-9064-4(8)) AuthorHouse.

Harley, Avis. African Acrostics: A Word in Edgeways. Noyes, Deborah, photos by. 2012. (ENG., Illus.). 40p. (J). (gr. 3-7). pap. 7.99 (978-0-7636-5818-2(9)) Candlewick Pr.

—African Acrostics: A Word in Edgeways. Noyes, Deborah, illus. Noyes, Deborah, photos by. 2012. lib. bdg. 18.40 (978-0-606-23808-3(5), Turtleback) Turtleback Bks.

Harris, Tony. There's a Wombat in My Bed. 2nd rev. ed. 2012. (Illus.). 32p. (J). (978-1-875763-00-9(7)) ThinkSoft.

Harter, Penny. The Beastie Book: An Alphabestiary. Miller, Alexandra, illus. 2009. (ENG.). 56p. (J). 21.95 (978-1-934860-05-2(0)) Shenanigan Bks.

Hauth, Katherine B. What's for Dinner? Quirky, Squirmy Poems from the Animal World. Clark, David, illus. 2011. (ENG.). 48p. (J). (gr. 2-5). pap. 8.95 (978-1-57091-472-0(9)) Charlesbridge Publishing, Inc.

Hazen, Barbara Shook. The Please & Thank You Book. Choillat, Emilie, illus. 2009. (Little Golden Book Ser.). (ENG.). 24p. (J). (gr. -1-2). 4.99 (978-0-375-84758-5(8), Golden Bks.) Random Hse. Children's Bks.

Held, George. Neighbors: The Yard Critters Book 1. Kim, Joung Un, illus. 2011. (ENG.). 32p. 20.00 (978-0-916754-25-9(1)) Filsinger & Co., Ltd.

Hess, Paul. Polar Animals. Hess, Paul, illus. 2009. (Animal Verse Ser.). (ENG., Illus.). 24p. (J). (gr. -1-k). pap. (978-1-84089-561-2(6)) Zero to Ten, Ltd.

Hopkins, Lee Bennett. A Pet for Me. Manning, Jane, illus. 2003. (I Can Read Bks.). (ENG.). 48p. (J). (gr. k-3). 15.99 (978-0-06-029111-2(7)) HarperCollins Pubs.

Hughes, David Pierce. One Sea. 2006. (Illus.). 48p. (J). pap. 7.99 (978-1-905470-20-4(7)) SeaSquirt Pubns. GBR. Dist: Basic Distribution, Inc.

Jones, Tim. Wild Critters. Walker, Tom, photos by. 2nd ed. 2007. (ENG., Illus.). 48p. (gr. -1-6). 9.95 (978-0-9790470-2-2(1)) Epicenter Pr., Inc.

Jubb, Mike. The Ghost of My Pussycat's Bottom. 2006. (ENG.). 96p. per. (978-1-904529-23-1(2), Back to Front) Solidus.

Kuskin, Karla. Roar & More. 2004. (ENG., Illus.). 48p. (J). (gr. -1-3). 11.95 (978-1-59078-249-1(6)) Boyds Mills Pr.

Lacome, Julie. Walking Through the Jungle Big Book. Lacome, Julie, illus. 2004. (Big Books! Ser.). (ENG., Illus.). 32p. (J). (gr. k-k). pap. 24.99 (978-0-7636-2471-2(3)) Candlewick Pr.

Lang, Diane. Vulture Verses: Love Poems for the Unloved. Gallegos, Lauren, illus. 2015. (ENG.). 32p. (J). (gr. -1-2). pap. 9.95 (978-1-938849-64-0(7)) Prospect Park Bks., LLC.

Laskin, Pamela, et al. Animal Crackers & Their Friends, 1 vol. 2009. 102p. pap. 19.95 (978-1-61582-038-2(8)) America Star Bks.

Lear, Edward. The Owl & the Pussycat. Jorisch, Stéphane, illus. 2007. (Visions in Poetry Ser.). (ENG.). 48p. (J). (gr. 5-9). pap. 9.95 (978-1-55453-232-2(9)) Kids Can Pr., Ltd. CAN. Dist: Hachette Bk. Group.

—The Owl & the Pussycat. Jorisch, Stéphane, illus. 2007. (Visions in Poetry Ser.). (ENG.). 48p. (J). (gr. 5-9). 17.95 (978-1-55337-828-0(8)) Kids Can Pr., Ltd. CAN. Dist: Hachette Bk. Group.

—The Owl & the Pussycat: And Other Nonsense. Ingpen, Robert R., illus. 2012. (ENG.). 192p. (J). (gr. 2-4). 14.99 (978-0-9571483-0-7(5)) Palazzo Editions, Ltd. GBR. Dist: Independent Pubs. Group.

Lee, Patty. Wild Animals: What Is That I Ask? Lee, Jack, illus. 2013. 30p. pap. 14.00 (978-1-4349-3518-2(3), RoseDog Bks.) Dorrance Publishing Co., Inc.

Lewis, J. Patrick. Swan Song. Wormell, Chris, illus. 2005. 32p. (J). reprint ed. 17.00 (978-0-7567-8662-5(2)) DIANE Publishing Co.

Lewis, J. Patrick & Nesbitt, Kenn. Bigfoot Is Missing! MinaLima, illus. 2015. (ENG.). 40p. (J). (gr. 2-5). 17.99 (978-1-4521-1895-6(7)) Chronicle Bks. LLC.

McDonald, Jill. Over in the Meadow. (J). 2012. (ENG., Illus.). 24p. (gr. -1-2). 9.99 (978-1-84686-747-7(9)) 2011. (978-1-84686-542-8(5)) Barefoot Bks., Inc.

Mendon Center Elementary School (Pittsford, N.Y.) Staff, contrib. by. Rejoice! Poetry Celebrating Life in the Amazon Rainforest. 2009. (Illus.). 31p. pap. (978-0-545-21330-1(4)) Scholastic, Inc.

Meyer, Eileen R. Sweet Dreams, Wild Animals! A Story of Sleep, 1 vol. Caple, Laurie A., illus. 2015. (ENG.). 32p. (J). pap. (978-0-87842-637-9(X)) Mountain Pr. Publishing Co., Inc.

Michelson, Richard. Animals That Ought to Be: Poems about Imaginary Pets. Baskin, Leonard, illus. 2011. (ENG.). 32p. (J). (gr. k-3). 16.99 (978-1-4424-3409-7(0), Simon & Schuster Bks. For Young Readers) Simon & Schuster Bks. For Young Readers.

Nash, Myrna Lee. Spinman, Katydid & Bump: A Spider Vane Collection. Johnson, Sharon, illus. 2003. 48p. (YA). (gr. 4-10). 11.95 (978-0-9724549-0-2(X)) Chapter & Verse Pr.

Norris, Mike. Mommy Goose: Rhymes from the Mountains. Adkins, Minnie, illus. 2015. (ENG.). 48p. 19.95 (978-0-8131-6614-8(4)) Univ. Pr. of Kentucky.

Paschkis, Julie. Flutter & Hum / Aleteo y Zumbido: Animal Poems / Poemas de Animales. Paschkis, Julie, illus. 2015. (ENG & SPA., Illus.). 32p. (J). (gr. -1-3). 17.99 (978-1-62779-103-8(5), 9781627791038, Holt, Henry & Co. Bks. For Young Readers) Holt, Henry & Co.

Pearson, Susan. Who Swallowed Harold? And Other Poems about Pets, 0 vols. Slonim, David, illus. 2013. (ENG.). 32p. (J). (gr. k-4). pap. 9.99 (978-1-4778-1595-3(3), 9781477815953, Amazon Children's Publishing) Amazon Publishing.

Polisar, Barry Louis. Curious Creatures: Animal Poems. Clark, David, illus. 2010. (Rainbow Morning Music Picture Bks.). (ENG.). 32p. (J). (gr. 2-4). 14.95 (978-0-938663-52-2(6)) Rainbow Morning Music Alternatives.

Porter, Matthew. Monkey World. 2008. (ENG., Illus.). 32p. (J). (gr. -1-3). 16.95 (978-1-894965-95-8(7)) Simply Read Bks. CAN. Dist: Ingram Publisher Services.

Prelutsky, Jack. The Carnival of the Animals. GrandPré, Mary, illus. 2010. (Book & CD Ser.). (ENG.). 40p. (J). (gr. k-3).

19.99 (978-0-375-86458-2(X), Knopf Bks. for Young Readers) Random Hse. Children's Bks.

—In Aunt Giraffe's Green Garden. Mathers, Petra, illus. 2007. 64p. (J). (gr. -1-3). lib. bdg. 18.89 (978-0-06-623869-2(2)) HarperCollins Pubs.

Priddy, Roger. Pop-Up Little Lamb. 2013. (ENG., Illus.). 10p. (J). (gr. -1-k). 9.99 (978-0-312-51584-3(7), 9780312515843, Priddy Bks.) St. Martin's Pr.

Robbins, Karen. Care for Our World. Ball, Alexandra, illus. 2012. (ENG.). 36p. (J). (gr. -1-3). 16.95 (978-1-935414-61-2(5)) Compendium, Inc., Publishing & Communications.

Ross, Mandy. Animal Exercises: Poems to Keep Fit. Rešcek, Sanja, illus. 2006. (Poems for the Young Ser.). (ENG.). 32p. (J). (gr. 2-2). pap. (978-1-84643-044-2(5)) Child's Play International Ltd.

Ruddell, Deborah. Who Said Coo? Luebs, Robin, illus. 2010. (ENG.). 40p. (J). (gr. -1-2). 17.99 (978-1-4169-8510-5(7), Beach Lane Bks.) Beach Lane Bks.

Sidman, Joyce. Dark Emperor & Other Poems of the Night. Allen, Rick, illus. 2010. (ENG.). 32p. (J). (gr. 1-4). 16.99 (978-0-547-15228-8(0)) Houghton Mifflin Harcourt Publishing Co.

—Song of the Water Boatman & Other Pond Poems. Prange, Beckie, illus. 2005. (ENG.). 32p. (J). (gr. -1-3). 17.99 (978-0-618-13547-9(2)) Houghton Mifflin Harcourt Publishing Co.

Sidman, Joyce & Swan, Susan. Just Us Two: Poems about Dads. 2003. (Single Titles Ser.: Vol. 3). 32p. pap. 7.95 (978-0-7613-1833-0(X), Millbrook Pr.) Lerner Publishing Group.

Silverstein, Shel. Runny Babbit: A Billy Sook. Silverstein, Shel, illus. (ENG., Illus.). 96p. (J). (gr. -1-3). 2015. 18.99 (978-0-06-025653-1(2)) 2006. 22.99 (978-0-06-113047-2(8)) HarperCollins Pubs.

Silverstein, Shel. Runny Babbit Returns. Silverstein, Shel, illus. 2017. (Illus.). 96p. (J). (gr. -1-3). 19.99 **(978-0-06-247939-6(3))**; lib. bdg. 20.89 **(978-0-06-247985-3(7))** HarperCollins Pubs.

Skene, Pat. What a Hippopota-Mess!, 1 vol. Ross, Graham, illus. 2006. (Orca Echoes Ser.). (ENG.). 64p. (J). (gr. 2-3). per. 4.99 (978-1-55143-402-5(4)) Orca Bk. Pubs. USA.

Smythe, I. H. Poetry for Animals. 2011. 152p. 22.95 (978-1-4620-0201-6(3)) iUniverse, Inc.

Squillace, Elisa, illus. Down in the Jungle. 2013. (Classic Books with Holes 8x8 with CD Ser.). (ENG.). 16p. (J). (gr. -1). pap. incl. audio compact disk (978-1-84643-623-9(0)) Child's Play International Ltd.

Swinburne, Stephen R. Ocean Soup. Peterson, Mary, illus. alt. ed. 2010. (Rise & Shine Ser.). (ENG.). 32p. (C). (gr. k-3). pap. 13.95 (978-1-58089-201-8(9)) National Geographic School Publishing, Inc.

Swindle, James L. If I Had a Purple Horse: Poems Mostly for Fun. 2007. (Illus.). 32p. (J). 5.99 (978-0-9801020-0-0(6)) 2Giggles.

Thomson, Sarah L. Around the Neighborhood: A Counting Lullaby, 0 vols. Christy, Jana, illus. 2012. (ENG.). 32p. (J). (gr. -1-3). 16.99 (978-0-7614-6164-7(7), 9780761461647, Amazon Children's Publishing) Amazon Publishing.

Thornhill, Jan. Over in the Meadow. Thornhill, Jan, illus. rev. ed. 2012. (ENG., Illus.). 32p. (J). (gr. -1-1). pap. 7.95 (978-1-926973-06-7(2), Owlkids) Owlkids Bks. Inc. CAN. Dist: Publishers Group West (PGW).

Trombley, Carl L. Animals, Questions, & One Big Tale. 2010. (Illus.). 52p. pap. 17.00 (978-1-60860-716-7(X), Strategic Bk. Publishing) Strategic Book Publishing & Rights Agency (SBPRA).

Tugeau, Jeremy, illus. Animal Tales from Mother Goose, 1 vol. 2011. (Mother Goose Nursery Rhymes Ser.). (ENG.). 32p. (gr. -1-2). 28.50 (978-1-61641-142-8(2), Looking Glass Library) ABDO Publishing Co.

Van Wassenhove, Sue. The Seldom-Ever-Shady Glades. 2008. (ENG., Illus.). 32p. (J). (gr. 3-7). 17.95 (978-1-59078-352-8(2), Wordsong) Boyds Mills Pr.

Webster, Dennis & Cunningham, Kim Webster. Absolutely Wild. 2008. (ENG., Illus.). 32p. (J). 17.95 (978-1-56792-375-9(5)) Godine, David R. Pub.

Weidner, Teri, illus. Sleep, Baby, Sleep. 2009. 20p. (J). (gr. -1-k). 8.95 (978-1-58925-843-3(6)) Tiger Tales.

Wilson, Karma. Bear Hugs: Romantically Ridiculous Animal Rhymes. Watts, Suzanne, illus. (ENG.). (J). (gr. -1-1). 2009. 64p. 9.99 (978-1-4169-9427-5(0)) 2007. 32p. 7.99 (978-1-4169-4958-9(5)) McElderry, Margaret K. Bks. (McElderry, Margaret K. Bks.).

Worth, Valerie. Animal Poems. Jenkins, Steve, illus. 2007. (ENG.). 48p. (J). (gr. -1-3). 18.99 (978-0-374-38057-1(0), 9780374380571, Farrar, Straus & Giroux (BYR)) Farrar, Straus & Giroux.

—Pug: And Other Animal Poems. Jenkins, Steve, illus. 2013. (ENG.). 40p. (J). (gr. -1-1). 16.99 (978-0-374-35024-6(8), 9780374350246, Farrar, Straus & Giroux (BYR)) Farrar, Straus & Giroux.

Yolen, Jane. Count Me a Rhyme: Animal Poems by the Numbers. Stemple, Jason, photos by. 2014. (ENG., Illus.). 32p. (J). (gr. 1-5). pap. 6.95 (978-1-62091-733-6(5), Wordsong) Boyds Mills Pr.

—Count Me a Rhyme: Animal Poems by the Numbers. Stemple, Jason, illus. Stemple, Jason, photos by. 2006. (ENG.). 32p. (J). (gr. 5-7). 18.95 (978-1-59078-345-0(X), Wordsong) Boyds Mills Pr.

Yoon, JooHee, illus. Beastly Verse. 2015. (ENG.). 48p. (J). (gr. -1-3). 18.95 (978-1-59270-166-7(3)) Enchanted Lion Bks., LLC.

Young, Gary. More Than Two: Under the Sea. 2014. (ENG., Illus.). 80p. (J). (gr. 2-3). 9.99 (978-1-74257-539-1(0)) New Holland Pubs. Pty, Ltd. AUS. Dist: Midpoint Trade Bks., Inc.

ANIMALS, PREHISTORIC

see Fossils

ANIMALS—PROTECTION

see Animals—Treatment

ANIMALS—PSYCHOLOGY

see Animal Psychology

ANIMALS, SEA

see Marine Animals

ANIMALS—SONGS AND MUSIC

Anderson, Airlie, illus. Cows in the Kitchen. 2013. (Classic Books with Holes 8x8 with CD Ser.). (ENG.). 16p. (J). (gr. -1). pap. incl. audio compact disk (978-1-84643-625-3(7)) Child's Play International Ltd.

Gobo. Animal Songs. 2007. (Baby Sing & Play Ser.). (Illus.). 8p. (J). (gr. -1-k). audio compact disk 12.95 (978-1-932915-43-3(5)) Sandvik Innovations, LLC.

Graham, Carolyn. Clifford's Big Ideas. 2005. (Illus.). 32p. (J). (978-0-439-64561-4(1)); (978-0-439-64552-2(2)) Scholastic, Inc.

Merrill, Bob & Trapani, Iza. How Much Is That Doggie in the Window? 2004. (ENG., Illus.). 32p. (J). (gr. k-k). pap. 7.95 (978-1-58089-030-4(X)) Charlesbridge Publishing, Inc.

Music Sales. The Animal Songbook. 2009. (ENG.). 112p. (J). 9.95 (978-1-84772-578-3(3), AM993817) Wise Pubns. GBR. Dist: Music Sales Corp.

Quattlebaum, Mary. Jo MacDonald Had a Garden. Bryant, Laura J., illus. 2013. (ENG.). 26p. (J). (gr. -1 — 1). bds. 7.95 (978-1-58469-225-6(1)) Dawn Pubns.

—Jo MacDonald Saw a Pond. Bryant, Laura J., illus. 2011. 32p. (J). 16.95 (978-1-58469-150-1(6)); (ENG.). pap. 8.95 (978-1-58469-151-8(4)) Dawn Pubns.

Schnetzler, Pattie. Earth Day Birthday. Wallace, Chad, illus. 2004. (Sharing Nature with Children Book Ser.). 32p. (J). 8.95 (978-1-58469-054-2(2)); 16.95 (978-1-58469-053-5(4)) Dawn Pubns.

Staines, Bill. All God's Critters. Nelson, Kadir, illus. 2009. (ENG.). 36p. (J). (gr. k-3). 16.99 (978-0-689-86959-4(2), Simon & Schuster Bks. For Young Readers) Simon & Schuster Bks. For Young Readers.

Thompson, Kim Mitzo & Hilderbrand, Karen Mitzo. Farm Animals. 2010. 12p. (J). (gr. k-2). bds. 8.99 (978-1-59922-572-2(7)) Twin Sisters IP, LLC.

—Wild Animals. 2010. 12p. (J). (gr. k-2). bds. 8.99 (978-1-59922-571-5(9)) Twin Sisters IP, LLC.

Twelsiek, Monika, ed. Animals: 30 Easy Piano Pieces for Children. 2009. (ENG.). 48p. pap. 12.99 (978-3-7957-5874-5(2), 3795758742) Schott Music Corp.

ANIMALS—TRAINING

see also names of animals with the subdivision Training, e.g., Dogs—Training; Horses—Training; etc.

Cohn, Jessica. ¡Trabajo Salvaje! Entrenadores de Animales. 2016. (TIME for Kids en Español - Level 5 Ser.). (SPA & ENG.). 64p. (gr. 5-5). lib. bdg. 31.99 (978-1-5157-2945-7(1)) Time for Kids Inc AUS. Dist: Capstone Pub.

Cohn, Jessica & Kuligowski, Stephanie. Wild Work! Animal Trainers, 1 vol. 2nd rev. ed. 2013. (Nonfiction Readers Ser.). (ENG.). 64p. (J). (gr. 5-5). pap. 10.99 (978-1-4333-4942-3(6)) Teacher Created Materials, Inc.

French, Karen. Dr. Frenchy's Pet Training from a to Z: A Fun, Colorful, Stimulating Alphabet Pattern Book. 2003. (J). per. 9.95 (978-1-888125-07-8(1)) Publication Consultants.

Gray, Susan H. Animals Helping to Detect Diseases. 2015. (ENG.). 48p. (J). pap. 6.95 (978-0-531-21288-2(2), Orchard Bks.) Scholastic Library Publishing.

Guillain, Charlotte. Animals, 1 vol. 2012. (Jobs If You Like... Ser.). (ENG.). 32p. (gr. 1-3). pap. 8.29 (978-1-4329-6814-4(9)); lib. bdg. 27.32 (978-1-4329-6803-8(3)) Heinemann-Raintree. (Heinemann First Library).

Koehler, Susan & National Geographic Learning Staff. Animal Trainer. 2010. (Rise & Shine Ser.). (ENG., Illus.). 32p. (C). (gr. 4-8). pap. 14.95 (978-1-60694-559-9(9)) National Geographic School Publishing, Inc.

Kuligowski, Stephanie. Wild Work! Animal Trainers, 1 vol. 2nd rev. ed. 2013. (Nonfiction Readers Ser.). (ENG., Illus.). 64p. (J). (gr. 5-5). pap. 31.96 (978-1-4333-7441-8(2)) Teacher Created Materials, Inc.

Lewin, Ted & Lewin, Betsy. Balarama: A Royal Elephant. Lewin, Ted & Lewin, Betsy, illus. 2009. (Adventures Around the World Ser.). (ENG., Illus.). 56p. (J). (gr. 1-6). 19.95 (978-1-60060-265-8(7)) Lee & Low Bks., Inc.

Loh-Hagan, Virginia. Big Animal Trainer. 2016. (Odd Jobs Ser.). (ENG., Illus.). 32p. (J). (gr. 4-8). 29.93 (978-1-63471-093-0(2), 208483, 45th Parallel Press) Cherry Lake Publishing.

Perish, Patrick. Animal Trainer. 2015. (Dangerous Jobs Ser.). (ENG., Illus.). 24p. (J). (gr. 3-7). lib. bdg. 25.95 (978-1-62617-196-1(3), Torque Bks.) Bellwether Media.

Raatma, Lucia. Animals Helping at Home. 2015. (ENG., Illus.). 48p. (J). pap. 6.95 (978-0-531-21285-1(8), Orchard Bks.) Scholastic Library Publishing.

Rake, Jody. Animal Training at SeaWorld, Busch Gardens, & Discovery Cove: Behind the Scenes. 2003. (Seaworld Education Ser.). (Illus.). 68p. per. 7.99 (978-1-893698-09-3(2), B01, SeaWorld Education Dept.) SeaWorld, Inc.

Simons, Lisa M. B. Amazing Animal Stunts. 2015. (Wild Stunts Ser.). (ENG., Illus.). 32p. (gr. 3-4). lib. bdg. 27.99 (978-1-4914-4253-1(0)) Capstone Press of Coughlan Cos.

Squire, Ann O. Animals Helping at Work. 2015. (ENG.). 48p. (J). pap. 6.95 (978-0-531-20535-8(5), Orchard Bks.) Scholastic Library Publishing..

Trueit, Trudi Strain. Animal Trainer. 2014. 64p. pap. 34.21 (978-1-62712-461-4(6)) Cavendish Square Publishing.

—Animal Trainer. 2013. (J). (978-0-7614-8075-4(7)) Marshall Cavendish Corp.

Wood, Alix. Animal Handler, 1 vol., 1. 2014. (World's Coolest Jobs Ser.). (ENG.). 32p. (J). (gr. 3-6). 26.25 (978-1-4777-6007-9(5), PowerKids Pr.) Rosen Publishing Group, Inc., The.

ANIMALS—TREATMENT

Abramovitz, Melissa. Thinking Critically: Animal Rights. 2017. (ENG.). 80p. (YA). (gr. 5-12). **(978-1-68282-263-0(X))** ReferencePoint Pr., Inc.

Adkins, Linda. The Dog Who Couldn't Wag His Tail: A True Story about a Stray Who Made a Difference. Dilworth, Kristopher & Rhodes, Sean C., eds. 2003. (J). 13.95 (978-0-9718632-0-0(2)) Keep Me Company Publishing Co.

Animal Control Offices. 2014. (Animal Rescue Ser.). (Illus.). 32p. (J). (gr. 3-6). lib. bdg. 26.25 (978-1-4777-7019-1(4), PowerKids Pr.) Rosen Publishing Group, Inc., The.

Animal Rescue. 2014. (Animal Rescue Ser.). 32p. (J). (gr. 3-6). 105.00 (978-1-4777-7077-1(1), PowerKids Pr.) Rosen Publishing Group, Inc., The.

Applegate, Katherine. Ivan: the Remarkable True Story of the Shopping Mall Gorilla. Karas, G. Brian, illus. 2014. (ENG.). 40p. (J). (gr. -1-3). 17.99 (978-0-544-25230-1(6), Clarion Bks.) Houghton Mifflin Harcourt Publishing Co.

Barghoorn, Linda. Temple Grandin: Pioneer for Animal Rights & Autism Awareness. 2016. (Remarkable Lives Revealed Ser.). (ENG., Illus.). 32p. (J). (gr. 2-5). (978-0-7787-2688-3(6)) Crabtree Publishing Co.

Bass, Sheila M. Because You Cared. 2005. (J). per. (978-0-9766366-0-1(3)) Bass, Sheila.

Bedell, J. M. So, You Want to Work with Animals? Discover Fantastic Ways to Work with Animals, from Veterinary Science to Aquatic Biology. 2017. (Be What You Want Ser.). (ENG., Illus.). 256p. (J). (gr. 3-7). 19.99 (978-1-58270-596-5(8)) Aladdin/Beyond Words.

Berlatsky, Noah. Animal Rights. Greenhaven Press Staff, ed. 2015. (Current Controversies Ser.). (ENG.). 224p. (gr. 10-12). lib. bdg. 46.40 (978-0-7377-7207-4(7), Greenhaven Pr., Inc.) Cengage Gale.

Biniok, Janice. Adopting a Pet. 2011. (J). 34.95 (978-1-932904-73-4(5)) Eldorado Ink.

Bowman, Chris. Animal Control Officer. 2014. (Dangerous Jobs Ser.). (ENG., Illus.). 24p. (J). (gr. 3-7). lib. bdg. 25.95 (978-1-62617-109-1(2), Torque Bks.) Bellwether Media.

Byers, Ann. Internship & Volunteer Opportunities for People Who Love Animals. 2012. (Foot in the Door Ser.). (ENG., Illus.). 80p. (YA). (gr. 7-12). lib. bdg. 33.25 (978-1-4488-8293-9(1)) Rosen Publishing Group, Inc., The.

Clendening, John. Animal Shelters. 2014. (Animal Rescue Ser.). 32p. (J). (gr. 3-6). 26.25 (978-1-4777-7011-5(9), PowerKids Pr.) Rosen Publishing Group, Inc., The.

Cohn, Jessica. Hand to Paw - Protecting Animals, 1 vol. 2nd rev. ed. 2012. (TIME for KIDS(r) Nonfiction Readers Ser.). (ENG.). 48p. (J). (gr. 4-4). pap. 9.99 (978-1-4333-4867-9(5)) Teacher Created Materials, Inc.

—Una Mano a la Pata: Protegiendo Los Animales. 2017. (TIME for Kids en Español - Level 4 Ser.). (SPA., Illus.). 48p. (gr. 4-4). lib. bdg. 31.99 (978-1-5157-5148-9(1)) Time for Kids Inc AUS. Dist: Capstone Pub.

Coster, Patience. Animal Rights. 2012. (Both Sides of the Story Ser.). (ENG., Illus.). 48p. (J). (gr. 5-8). lib. bdg. 29.25 (978-1-4488-7184-1(0), Rosen Reference) Rosen Publishing Group, Inc., The.

Curtis, Jennifer Keats. Animal Helpers: Sanctuaries, 1 vol. 2013. (ENG.). 32p. (J). (gr. 2-5). pap. 9.95 (978-1-60718-623-6(3), 9781607186236); (Illus.). 17.95 (978-1-60718-611-3(X)) Arbordale Publishing.

Dike, Diane. Gracie Comes Home: The Adventures of Gracie & Diane. Grasso, Craig A. & Grasso, Samantha A., illus. 2007. (J). 14.95 (978-1-932738-45-2(2)) Western Reflections Publishing Co.

Engdahl, Sylvia. Animal Welfare. 2010. (Issues on Trial Ser.). (Illus.). 240p. (J). 42.15 (978-0-7377-4737-9(4), Greenhaven Pr., Inc.) Cengage Gale.

Ewing, Susan M. Working with Animals. 2018. (ENG.). 32p. (gr. 3-6). **(978-1-63235-452-5(7)**, 12-Story Library) Pr. Room Editions LLC.

Fisanick, Christina. Animal Welfare. 2011. (Global Viewpoints Ser.). 160p. 40.45 (978-0-7377-5187-1(8)); (ENG.). 224p. pap. 31.70 (978-0-7377-5188-8(6)) Cengage Gale. (Greenhaven Pr., Inc.).

Friedman, Lauri S. Animal Rights. 2010. (Introducing Issues with Opposing Viewpoints Ser.). (ENG.). 144p. 36.95 (978-0-7377-4937-3(7), Greenhaven Pr., Inc.) Cengage Gale.

Furstinger, Nancy. Mercy: The Incredible Story of Henry Bergh, Founder of the ASPCA & Friend to Animals. Desjardins, Vincent, illus. 2016. (ENG.). 192p. (J). (gr. 5-7). 16.99 (978-0-544-65031-2(X), HMH Books For Young Readers) Houghton Mifflin Harcourt Publishing Co.

Furstinger, Nancy & Pipe, Sheryl L. Kids Making a Difference for Animals. 2009. (ASPCA Kids Ser.: 4). (ENG., Illus.). 108p. 12.99 (978-0-470-41086-8(8), Howell Bk. Hse.) Wiley, John & Sons, Inc.

Gleason, Carrie & Rodger, Ellen. Animal Rights Activist. 2009. (Get Involved! Ser.). (ENG.). 32p. (J). (gr. 3-6). (978-0-7787-4693-5(3)); pap. (978-0-7787-4705-5(0)) Crabtree Publishing Co.

Goldish, Meish. Animal Control Officers to the Rescue. 2013. (Work of Heroes: First Responders in Action Ser.). 32p. (J). (gr. 1-6). lib. bdg. 25.27 (978-1-61772-747-4(4)) Bearport Publishing Co., Inc.

Hargreaves, Susan. Animal Hero Kids: Voices for the Voiceless. 2014. (Illus.). 284p. (J). pap. 27.95 (978-0-615-99522-9(5)) Animal Hero Kids.

Hartman, Eve & Meshbesher, Wendy. Do Scientists Care about Animal Welfare?, 1 vol. 2012. (Sci-Hi: Science Issues Ser.). (ENG., Illus.). 48p. (gr. 4-4). lib. bdg. 33.32 (978-1-4109-4462-7(X), Sci-Hi) Heinemann-Raintree.

Heneghan, Judith. At the Dog Rescue Centre. 2016. (Helping Out Ser.). (ENG., Illus.). 24p. (J). (gr. 2-4). pap. 10.99 (978-0-7502-9432-4(9), Wayland) Hachette Children's Group GBR. Dist: Hachette Bk. Group.

Hicks, Kelli. Animal Sanctuaries. 2015. (ENG.). 24p. (gr. 1-4). 28.50 (978-1-63430-066-7(1)) Rourke Educational Media.

Jackson, Emma. A Home for Dixie: The True Story of a Rescued Puppy. Carey, Bob, illus. 2010. (ENG.). 40p. (J). (gr. -1-3). pap. 6.99 (978-0-06-144964-2(4), Collins) HarperCollins Pubs.

Kallgren, Beverly H. A Duck Named Goose. 2004. (Illus.). 48p. (J). per. 10.00 (978-1-930648-90-6(1)) Goose River Pr.

King, Corinne & Fenton, Corinne. Queenie: One Elephant's Story. Gouldthorpe, Peter, illus. 2013. (ENG.). 24p. (J). (gr. k-3). 16.99 (978-0-7636-6375-9(1)) Candlewick Pr.

Laidlaw, Rob. Cat Champions: Caring for Our Feline Friends. (ENG., Illus.). 64p. (J). (gr. 3-7). 2015. pap. 11.95 (978-1-927485-54-5(1)) 2014. 15.95 (978-1-927485-31-6(2)) Pajama Pr. CAN. Dist: Ingram Publisher Services.

—No Shelter Here: Making the World a Kinder Place for Dogs. (ENG., Illus.). 64p. (J). (gr. 3-7). 2013. pap. 11.95 (978-0-9869495-2-4(3)) 2012. 15.95 (978-0-9869495-5-5(8)) Pajama Pr. CAN. Dist: Ingram Publisher Services.

Leduc-Lenmark, MaryAlice. Meet Mister Muttley. Speas, Joann, illus. 2004. 25p. (J). 16.95 (978-0-9760733-0-7(7)) Heartstrings Publishing.

Lishak, Antony. Animal Welfare. 2007. (What's That Got to Do with Me?/Watts Ser.). (Illus.). 32p. (YA). (gr. 4-7). lib. bdg. 28.50 (978-1-59920-034-7(1)) Black Rabbit Bks.

Marsico, Katie. Horse Rescue. 2013. 48p. (J). (gr. 4-8). 29.93 (978-1-60870-836-9(5)); pap. 12.93 (978-1-62712-086-9(6)) Cavendish Square Publishing.

—The Humane Society. 2016. (Community Connections: How Do They Help? Ser.). (ENG., Illus.). 24p. (J). (gr. 2-5). 27.07 (978-1-63471-050-3(9), 208280) Cherry Lake Publishing.

Mickelson, Trina. Free-Range Farming. 2016. (Growing Green Ser.). (ENG., Illus.). 64p. (J). (gr. 6-8). lib. bdg. 34.65 (978-1-4677-9389-6(2)); 51.99 (978-1-4677-9710-8(3), Lerner Pubns.) Lerner Publishing Group.

Miller, Debra A. The Rights of Animals. 2008. (Current Controversies Ser.). (ENG., Illus.). 176-240p. (YA). (gr. 10-12). 28.45 (978-0-7377-4147-6(3)); pap. 40.95 (978-0-7377-4146-9(5)) Cengage Gale. (Greenhaven Pr., Inc.).

Miller-Schroeder, Patricia. The ASPCA. 2003. (International Organizations Ser.). (Illus.). 32p. (J). (gr. 4-7). lib. bdg. 26.00 (978-1-59036-024-8(9)) Weigl Pubs., Inc.

Montgomery, Sy & Grandin, Temple. Temple Grandin: How the Girl Who Loved Cows Embraced Autism & Changed the World. 2012. (ENG., Illus.). 160p. (J). (gr. 5-7). 18.99 (978-0-547-44315-7(3)) Houghton Mifflin Harcourt Publishing Co.

Newkirk, Ingrid. 50 Awesome Ways Kids Can Help Animals: Fun & Easy Ways to Be a Kind Kid. 2006. (ENG., Illus.). 304p. (gr. 8-17). per. 20.99 (978-0-446-69828-3(8)) Grand Central Publishing.

Parker, Vic. Let's Think about Animal Rights, 1 vol. 2014. (Let's Think About Ser.). (ENG., Illus.). 48p. (gr. 3-6). 33.32 (978-1-4846-0291-1(9)); pap. 8.99 (978-1-4846-0296-6(X)) Heinemann-Raintree. (Heinemann InfoSearch).

Parker, Victoria. Helping Animals, 1 vol. 2012. (I Can Make a Difference Ser.). (ENG., Illus.). 32p. (gr. 1-3). pap. 8.29 (978-1-4329-5948-7(4)); lib. bdg. 27.32 (978-1-4329-5943-2(3)) Heinemann-Raintree. (Heinemann First Library).

Perdew, Laura. Animal Rights Movement, 1 vol. 2013. (Essential Library of Social Change Ser.). (ENG.). 112p. (J). (gr. 6-12). lib. bdg. 35.64 (978-1-61783-884-2(5), Essential Library) ABDO Publishing Co.

Person, Stephen. Saving Animals after Tornadoes. 2012. (Rescuing Animals from Disasters Ser.). 32p. (J). (gr. 2-7). lib. bdg. 25.27 (978-1-61772-458-9(0)) Bearport Publishing Co., Inc.

Povey, Karen D. Animal Rights. 2008. (Hot Topics Ser.). (ENG., Illus.). 128p. (gr. 7-10). lib. bdg. 39.40 (978-1-4205-0079-0(1), LML02109-242083, Lucent Bks.) Cengage Gale.

Rich, Mari. Big-Animal Vets!, Vol. 10. 2015. (Scientists in Action Ser.). (Illus.). 48p. (J). (gr. 5). 20.95 (978-1-4222-3419-8(3)) Mason Crest.

Ritchey, Kate & Bader, Bonnie. Lion, Tiger, & Bear, Level 4. 2015. (Penguin Young Readers, Level 4 Ser.). (ENG., Illus.). 48p. (J). (gr. 3-4). pap. 3.99 (978-0-448-48336-8(X), Penguin Young Readers) Penguin Young Readers Group.

Roth, Ruby. V Is for Vegan: The ABCs of Being Kind. Roth, Ruby, illus. 2013. (ENG., Illus.). 32p. (J). (gr. -1-2). 12.95 (978-1-58394-649-7(7)) North Atlantic Bks.

Stories from Black Dog Ranch: Dog Tales about Hope & Second Chances. 2008. (Illus.). 64p. 18.00 (978-0-9817830-0-0(7)) BRIO Pr.

Suen, Anastasia. Asociación para la prevención de la crueldad de los animales, ASPCA (the Association for the Prevention of Cruelty to Animals) 2009. (Organizaciones de ayuda (Helping Organizations) Ser.). (SPA.). 24p. (gr. 2-2). 42.50 (978-1-60851-143-3(X), Editorial Buenas Letras) Rosen Publishing Group, Inc., The.

—The Association for the Prevention of Cruelty to Animals. 2009. (Helping Organizations Ser.). 24p. (gr. 2-2). 42.50 (978-1-61513-260-7(0), PowerKids Pr.) Rosen Publishing Group, Inc., The.

Taylor, Patty. Critical World Issues: Animal Rights, Vol. 16. 2016. (Critical World Issues Ser.: Vol. 16). (ENG., Illus.). 112p. (J). (gr. 7-12). 25.95 (978-1-4222-3647-5(1)) Mason Crest.

Ward, Eva D. Calvin C. Waxwing. York, Deborah Ward, illus. l.t. ed. 2006. 34p. (J). per. 14.00 (978-0-9776514-5-0(2)) Beech River Bks.

Yount, Lisa. Animal Rights. 2nd rev. ed. 2007. (Library in a Book). (Illus.). 320p. (C). (gr. 9-18). 45.00 (978-0-8160-7130-2(6)) Facts On File, Inc.

ANIMALS—TREATMENT—FICTION

Anderson, Laurie Halse. Fight for Life. 2007. (Vet Volunteers Ser.: 1). (ENG.). 160p. (J). (gr. 3-7). 6.99 (978-0-14-240862-9(X), Puffin Books) Penguin Young Readers Group.

—Trapped. 2009. (Vet Volunteers Ser.: 8). (ENG.). 144p. (J). (gr. 3-7). 6.99 (978-0-14-241223-7(6), Puffin Books) Penguin Young Readers Group.

Applegate, Katherine. The One & Only Ivan. Castelao, Patricia, illus. (Harper Classic Ser.). (J). (gr. 3-7). 2017. 336p. 16.99 (978-0-06-264194-6(8)) 2015. (ENG.). 352p. 24.99 (978-0-06-242524-9(2)) 2015. (ENG.). 272p. pap. 7.99 (978-0-06-199227-8(5)) 2012. (ENG.). 305p. 17.99 (978-0-06-199225-4(9)) HarperCollins Pubs.

—The One & Only Ivan. Castelao, Patricia, illus. 2015. (ENG.). (J). (gr. 3-7). lib. bdg. 18.60 **(978-1-62765-963-5(3))** Perfection Learning Corp.

—The One & Only Ivan. Castelao, Patricia, illus. 2015. (J). lib. bdg. 18.40 (978-0-606-35481-3(6)) Turtleback Bks.

Backman, Laura. Lemon the Duck. l.t. ed. 2012. 64p. (J). pap. (978-1-4596-3450-3(0)) ReadHowYouWant.com, Ltd.

Banks, Lynne Reid. Tiger, Tiger. 2007. (ENG.). 208p. (YA). (gr. 7-11). mass mkt. 6.99 (978-0-440-42044-6(X), Laurel Leaf) Random Hse. Children's Bks.

Brezenoff, Steve. The Seals That Wouldn't Swim, 1 vol. Calo, Marcos, illus. 2011. (Field Trip Mysteries Ser.). (ENG.). 88p. (gr. 2-3). pap. 6.10 (978-1-4342-3428-5(2)); lib. bdg. 25.32 (978-1-4342-3225-0(5)) Stone Arch Bks.

Casanova, Mary. Stealing Thunder. 2014. (Fesler-Lampert Minnesota Heritage Ser.). (ENG.). 144p. pap. 9.95 (978-0-8166-9210-1(6)) Univ. of Minnesota Pr.

Culverwell, C. Ellen. The Horse Lady. 2009. (J). pap. *(978-0-88092-723-9(2))*; lib. bdg. *(978-0-88092-722-2(4))* Royal Fireworks Publishing Co.

DiCamillo, Kate. Francine Poulet Meets the Ghost Raccoon. Van Dusen, Chris, illus. 2015. (Tales from Deckawoo Drive Ser.: Vol. 2). (ENG.). 112p. (J). (gr. 1-4). 12.99 *(978-0-7636-6886-0(9))* Candlewick Pr.

—The Tiger Rising. (ENG.). (J). (gr. 5). 2015. 144p. pap. 6.99 *(978-0-7636-8087-9(7))* 2011. (Illus.). 128p. 15.99 *(978-0-7636-5270-8(9))* Candlewick Pr.

—The Tiger Rising. Sheban, Chris, illus. 2006. 144p. (J). (gr. 5). pap. 5.99 *(978-0-7636-2916-8(2))* Candlewick Pr.

—The Tiger Rising. aut. ed. 2011. (ENG., Illus.). 128p. (J). (gr. 5). 50.00 *(978-0-7636-5383-5(7))* Candlewick Pr.

—The Tiger Rising. unabr. ed. 2004. (Middle Grade Cassette Librariestm Ser.). 128p. (J). (gr. 5-9). pap. 29.00 incl. audio *(978-0-8072-0998-1(8))*, S YA 285 SP, Listening Library) Random Hse. Audio Publishing Group.

Dickinson, Peter. Eva. 2005. 220p. (YA). (gr. 7-12). 21.50 *(978-0-8446-7274-8(2)*, 3589) Smith, Peter Pub., Inc.

Ely, Kosa. The Peaceable Forest: India's Tale of Kindness to Animals. Johansson, Anna, illus. 2012. (ENG.). 32p. (gr. k). 16.99 *(978-1-60887-115-5(0))* Mandala Publishing.

Fleming, Bryn. Cassie & Jasper to the Rescue. 2014. (Range Riders Ser.). (ENG.). 128p. (YA). (gr. 3-7). 23.99 *(978-1-941821-04-6(9))*; pap. 9.99 *(978-0-88240-992-4(1))* Graphic Arts Ctr. Publishing Co. (West Winds Pr.).

Hopkinson, Deborah. A Bandit's Tale: The Muddled Misadventures of a Pickpocket. 2016. (ENG.). 304p. (J). (gr. 3-7). lib. bdg. 19.99 *(978-0-385-75500-9(7)*, Knopf Bks. for Young Readers) Random Hse. Children's Bks.

Kehret, Peg. Ghost Dog Secrets. 2011. (ENG.). 192p. (J). (gr. 5-18). 6.99 *(978-0-14-241964-9(8)*, Puffin Books) Penguin Young Readers Group.

Kelly, Lynne. Chained. 1 vol. 2012. (ENG.). 256p. (J). (gr. 5-9). 17.99 *(978-0-374-31237-4(0)*, 9780374312374, Farrar, Straus & Giroux (BYR)) Farrar, Straus & Giroux.

Korman, Gordon. Hideout. 2013. (Swindle Ser.: 5). (ENG.). 256p. (J). (gr. 3-7). 16.99 *(978-0-545-44866-6(2)*, Scholastic Pr.) Scholastic, Inc.

Lang, Andrew. The Hut in the Forest: A Tale about Being Kind to Animals. Johnson, Meredith, illus. 2006. (J). *(978-1-59939-083-3(3)*, Reader's Digest Young Families, Inc.) Studio Fun International.

Lee, Gia. Hurricane Hound. Davis, Jason, illus. 2011. 40p. pap. 24.95 *(978-1-4560-9743-1(1))* America Star Bks.

Lewis, Gill. Moon Bear. Gottardo, Alessandro, illus. 2015. (ENG.). 384p. (J). (gr. 3-7). 16.99 *(978-1-4814-0094-7(0))* Simon & Schuster Children's Publishing.

Libster, Bernard. The Bonsai Bear. Cheung, Aries, illus. 2006. 31p. (J). (gr. k-4). reprint ed. 16.00 *(978-1-4223-5857-3(7))* DIANE Publishing Co.

McGovern, Ann. Little Wolf. 2011. 48p. (gr. 2-4). pap. 8.95 *(978-1-4620-2711-8(3))* iUniverse, Inc.

Messner, Kate. Marty McGuire Has Too Many Pets! Floca, Brian, illus. 2015. (Marty Mcguire Ser.). (ENG.). 176p. (J). (gr. -1-3). pap. 5.99 *(978-0-545-53560-1(3)*, Scholastic Pr.) Scholastic, Inc.

Monninger, Joseph. Whippoorwill. 2015. (ENG.). 288p. (YA). (gr. 7). 17.99 *(978-0-544-53123-9(X)*, HMH Books For Young Readers) Houghton Mifflin Harcourt Publishing Co.

Nanette. Tootie the Green Kitten. 2004. (Life on Granny's Farm Ser.). (J). 12.95 *(978-0-9741269-7-5(7))* St. Bernard Publishing, LLC.

Neri, Greg. Grand Theft Horse: A Graphic Novel. Wilkin, Corban, illus. 2016. (YA). *(978-1-4677-9463-3(5)*, Graphic Universe™) Lerner Publishing Group.

Patton, Roni. An Opossum Dilemma: Crossing the Streets at Night. 2010. 24p. pap. 14.93 *(978-1-4269-3242-7(1))* Trafford Publishing.

Rex, Michael. Furious George Goes Bananas: A Primate Parody. Rex, Michael, illus. 2010. (ENG., Illus.). 32p. (J). (gr. k-3). 15.99 *(978-0-399-25433-8(1)*, G.P. Putnam's Sons Books for Young Readers) Penguin Young Readers Group.

Ricci, Christine. Animal Adventure. Aikins, Dave et al, illus. 2007. (Little Life Lessons Ser.). (J). pap. *(978-1-4127-8922-6(2))* Publications International, Ltd.

Sandford, John, pseud & Cook, Michele. Uncaged. (Singular Menace Ser.: Bk. 1). (ENG.). 416p. (gr. 9). 2015. (YA). pap. 10.99 *(978-0-385-75305-0(5)*, Ember) 2014. (J). 18.99 *(978-0-385-75306-7(3)*, Knopf Bks. for Young Readers) 2014. (YA). lib. bdg. 21.99 *(978-0-385-75307-4(1)*, Knopf Bks. for Young Readers) Random Hse. Children's Bks.

Schrefer, Eliot. Rescued. 2016. (ENG.). 272p. (J). (gr. 7). 18.99 *(978-0-545-65503-3(X)*, Scholastic Pr.) Scholastic, Inc.

Sewell, Anna. Black Beauty. unabr. ed. 2004. (Chrysalis Childrens Classics Ser.). (Illus.). 190p. (YA). pap. *(978-1-84365-062-1(2)*, Pavilion Children's Books) Pavilion Bks.

—Black Beauty. 2013. (ENG.). 320p. (J). (gr. 4-7). pap. 10.99 *(978-0-09-957293-0(1))* Random Hse. GBR. Dist: Independent Pubs. Group.

Singleton, Linda Joy. The Curious Cat Spy Club. 2015. (Curious Cat Spy Club Ser.: 1). (ENG.). 256p. (J). (gr. 3-7). 14.99 *(978-0-8075-1376-7(8))* Whitman, Albert & Co.

Stratton-Porter, Gene. The Strike at Shane's. 2006. 92p. per. *(978-1-4067-9583-7(6)*, Pierides Pr.) Read Bks.

Subramaniam, Manasi. Dancing Bear. Gwangjo & Park, Jung-a, illus. 2013. (ENG.). 32p. (J). (gr. k). pap. 9.95 *(978-81-8190-200-9(9))* Karadi Tales Co. Pvt. Ltd. IND. Dist: Consortium Bk. Sales & Distribution.

White, Ellen Emerson. Webster: Tale of an Outlaw. 2015. (ENG., Illus.). 256p. (J). (gr. 3-7). 17.99 *(978-1-4814-2201-7(4)*, Aladdin) Simon & Schuster Children's Publishing.

Willocks, Tim. Doglands. 2012. (ENG.). 324p. (YA). (gr. 7). pap. 9.99 *(978-0-375-85818-5(0)*, Ember) Random Hse. Children's Bks.

ANIMALS, USEFUL AND HARMFUL

see Zoology, Economic

ANIMALS—WAR USE

Bausum, Ann. Stubby the War Dog: The True Story of World War I's Bravest Dog. 2014. (ENG., Illus.). 80p. (J). (gr. 5). 17.99 *(978-1-4263-1486-5(8)*, National Geographic Children's Bks.) National Geographic Society.

Gagne, Tammy. Military Dogs. 1 vol. 2013. (Dogs on the Job Ser.). (ENG.). 32p. (gr. 3-4). 27.99 *(978-1-4765-0130-7(0)*, Edge Bks.) Capstone Press of Coughlan Cos.

Grayson, Robert. Military. 2010. (Working Animals Ser.). 64p. (gr. 5-18). 28.50 *(978-1-60870-164-3(6))* Marshall Cavendish Corp.

Green, Sara. Military Dogs. 2013. (Dogs to the Rescue! Ser.). (ENG., Illus.). 24p. (J). (gr. 3-8). lib. bdg. 25.95 *(978-1-60014-956-6(1)*, Pilot Bks.) Bellwether Media.

Greenwood, Mark. The Donkey of Gallipoli: A True Story of Courage in World War I. Lessac, Frané, illus. 2008. (ENG.). 32p. (J). (gr. 1-4). 16.99 *(978-0-7636-3913-6(3))* Candlewick Pr.

Long, David. Jet the Rescue Dog: And Other Extraordinary Stories of Animals in Wartime. Bailey, Peter, illus. 2016. (ENG.). 240p. (gr. 3-6). 8.95 *(978-0-571-30493-6(1))* Faber & Faber, Inc.

Mooney, Carla. Remarkable Military Animals. 1 vol. 2014. (Ready for Military Action Ser.). (ENG., Illus.). 48p. (J). (gr. 3-6). lib. bdg. 32.79 *(978-1-62403-655-2(4))* ABDO Publishing Co.

Murray, Julie. Military Animals. 1 vol. 2009. (Going to Work:Animal Edition Ser.). (ENG., Illus.). 32p. (J). (gr. 2-5). 27.07 *(978-1-60453-562-4(8))* ABDO Publishing Co.

Orr, Tamra B. Animals Helping to Keep the Peace. 2015. (ENG., Illus.). 48p. (J). pap. 6.95 *(978-0-531-21287-5(4)*, Orchard Bks.) Scholastic Library Publishing.

Squire, Ann O. Animals Helping at Work. 2015. (ENG.). 48p. (J). pap. 6.95 *(978-0-531-20535-8(5)*, Orchard Bks.) Scholastic Library Publishing.

ANIMALS AND CIVILIZATION

Burt, Jonathan. Rat. 2nd ed. 2006. (Animal Ser.). (ENG., Illus.). 192p. per. 19.95 *(978-1-86189-224-9(1))* Reaktion Bks., Ltd. GBR. Dist: Chicago Distribution Ctr.

MacLeod, Elizabeth. Galloping Through History: Incredible True Horse Stories. 2015. (ENG., Illus.). 88p. (J). (gr. 4-7). pap. 14.95 *(978-1-55451-699-5(4)*, 9781554516995) Annick Pr., Ltd. CAN. Dist: Publishers Group West (PGW).

Moberg, Julia. Animal Heroes: The Wolves, Camels, Elephants, Dogs, Cats, Horses, Penguins, Dolphins, & Other Remarkable Animals That Proved They Are Man's Best Friend. Albrecht Studios, Jeff, illus. 2017. (ENG.). 96p. (J). (gr. 2-7). 14.95 *(978-1-63322-159-8(8)*, Moondance) Quarto Publishing Group USA.

—Historical Animals. Jeff Albrecht Studios Staff, illus. 2015. (ENG.). 96p. (J). (gr. 3-7). 15.95 *(978-1-62354-048-7(8))* Charlesbridge Publishing, Inc.

Stott, Rebecca. Oyster. 2004. (Animal Ser.). (ENG., Illus.). 240p. pap. 19.95 *(978-1-86189-221-8(7))* Reaktion Bks., Ltd. GBR. Dist: Chicago Distribution Ctr.

ANIMALS IN ART

see also Animal Painting and Illustration

Ames, Lee J. Draw 50 Animals. 2012. (Draw 50 Ser.). lib. bdg. 20.85 *(978-0-606-26426-6(4)*, Turtleback) Turtleback Bks.

—Draw 50 Animals: The Step-by-Step Way to Draw Elephants, Tigers, Dogs, Fish, Birds, & Many More... 2012. (ENG., Illus.). 64p. pap. 9.99 *(978-0-8230-8578-1(3)*, Watson-Guptill) Potter/TenSpeed/Harmony.

—Draw 50 Baby Animals. 2012. (Draw 50 Ser.). lib. bdg. 20.85 *(978-0-606-26427-3(2)*, Turtleback) Turtleback Bks.

—Draw 50 Cats. 2012. (Draw 50 Ser.). lib. bdg. 20.85 *(978-0-606-26440-2(X)*, Turtleback) Turtleback Bks.

—Draw 50 Dinosaurs & Other Prehistoric Animals. 2012. (Draw 50 Ser.). lib. bdg. 20.85 *(978-0-606-26441-9(8)*, Turtleback) Turtleback Bks.

—Draw 50 Dinosaurs & Other Prehistoric Animals: The Step-by-Step Way to Draw Tyrannosauruses, Wooly Mammoths, & Many More... 2012. (ENG., Illus.). 64p. pap. 9.99 *(978-0-8230-8574-3(0)*, Watson-Guptill) Potter/TenSpeed/Harmony.

—Draw 50 Dogs. 2012. (Draw 50 Ser.). lib. bdg. 20.85 *(978-0-606-26433-4(7)*, Turtleback) Turtleback Bks.

—Draw 50 Endangered Animals. 2013. (Draw 50 Ser.). (Illus.). (J). lib. bdg. 20.85 *(978-0-606-26506-5(6)*, Turtleback) Turtleback Bks.

—Draw 50 Horses. 2012. (Draw 50 Ser.). lib. bdg. 20.85 *(978-0-606-26430-3(2)*, Turtleback) Turtleback Bks.

—Draw 50 Horses: The Step-by-Step Way to Draw Broncos, Arabians, Thoroughbreds, Dancers, Prancers, & Many More... 2012. (ENG., Illus.). 64p. pap. 9.99 *(978-0-8230-8581-1(3)*, Watson-Guptill) Potter/TenSpeed/Harmony.

—Draw 50 Monsters: The Step-by-Step Way to Draw Creeps, Superheroes, Demons, Dragons, Nerds, Ghouls, Giants, Vampires, Zombies, & Other Scary Creatures. 2012. (ENG., Illus.). 64p. pap. 9.99 *(978-0-8230-8584-2(8)*, Watson-Guptill) Potter/TenSpeed/Harmony.

—Draw 50 Sharks, Whales, & Other Sea Creatures. 2012. (Draw 50 Ser.). lib. bdg. 20.85 *(978-0-606-26429-7(9)*, Turtleback) Turtleback Bks.

Ames, Lee J. & Burns, Ray. Draw 50 Creepy Crawlies. 2013. (Draw 50 Ser.). (Illus.). (J). lib. bdg. 20.85 *(978-0-606-26512-6(0)*, Turtleback) Turtleback Bks.

Ames, Lee J. & Zak, Murray. Draw 50 Baby Animals: The Step-by-Step Way to Draw Kittens, Lambs, Chicks, & Other Adorable Offspring. 2012. (ENG., Illus.). 64p. pap. 9.99 *(978-0-8230-8573-6(2)*, Watson-Guptill) Potter/TenSpeed/Harmony.

Antram, David. Drawing Manga Pets. 2015. (Art Class: the Art of Drawing Manga Ser.). (ENG., Illus.). 32p. (gr. 2-6). 31.35 *(978-1-62588-353-7(6))* Black Rabbit Bks.

—How to Draw Pets. 2012. (Illus.). 32p. (J). 70.50 *(978-1-4488-4523-1(8))*; pap. 11.75 *(978-1-4488-4517-0(3))*; lib. bdg. 26.50 *(978-1-4488-4511-8(4))* Rosen Publishing Group, Inc., The. (PowerKids Pr.).

Azzità, Emanuele. Origami Land & Sea Animals. 2017. (Exciting Origami Ser.). 48p. (J). (gr. 3-3). lib. bdg. 27.93 ***(978-0-7660-8718-7(2))*** Enslow Pubs., Inc.

Balart, Maïté. Farm Animals. 2016. (Drawing with Your Hand Ser.). (ENG., Illus.). 48p. (J). (gr. -1-1). pap. 9.95 *(978-1-63322-174-1(1)*, Walter Foster Jr) Quarto Publishing Group USA.

—Wild Animals. 2016. (Drawing with Your Hand Ser.). (ENG., Illus.). 48p. (J). (gr. -1-1). pap. 9.95 *(978-1-63322-175-8(X)*, Walter Foster Jr) Quarto Publishing Group USA.

Baumbusch, Brigitte. Animals in Art. 2005. (What Makes a Masterpiece? Ser.). (Illus.). 32p. (gr. 1-4). lib. bdg. 23.00 *(978-0-8368-4442-9(4)*, Gareth Stevens Learning Library) Stevens, Gareth Publishing LLLP.

Beaumont, Steve. Drawing Diplodocus & Other Plant-Eating Dinosaurs. 2010. (Drawing Dinosaurs Ser.). (Illus.). 32p. (J). pap. 11.75 *(978-1-4488-0424-5(8))*; (gr. 2-5). lib. bdg. 26.50 *(978-1-61531-902-2(6))* Rosen Publishing Group, Inc., The.

—Drawing Giganotosaurus & Other Giant Dinosaurs. 2010. (Drawing Dinosaurs Ser.). (Illus.). 32p. (J). pap. 11.75 *(978-1-4488-0430-6(2))*; (gr. 2-5). lib. bdg. 26.50 *(978-1-61531-905-3(0))* Rosen Publishing Group, Inc., The.

—Drawing Plesiosaurus & Other Ocean Dinosaurs. 2010. (Drawing Dinosaurs Ser.). (Illus.). 32p. (J). pap. 11.75 *(978-1-4488-0426-9(4))*; (gr. 2-5). lib. bdg. 26.50 *(978-1-61531-903-9(4))* Rosen Publishing Group, Inc., The.

—Drawing Pteranodon & Other Flying Reptiles. 2010. (Drawing Dinosaurs Ser.). (Illus.). 32p. (J). pap. 11.75 *(978-1-4488-0428-3(0))*; (gr. 2-5). lib. bdg. 26.50 *(978-1-61531-904-6(2))* Rosen Publishing Group, Inc., The.

—Drawing T. Rex & Other Meat-Eating Dinosaurs. 2010. (Drawing Dinosaurs Ser.). (Illus.). 32p. (J). pap. 11.75 *(978-1-4488-0434-4(5))*; (gr. 2-5). lib. bdg. 26.50 *(978-1-61531-907-7(7))* Rosen Publishing Group, Inc., The.

—Drawing Triceratops & Other Armored Dinosaurs. 2010. (Drawing Dinosaurs Ser.). (Illus.). 32p. (J). pap. 11.75 *(978-1-4488-0432-0(9))*; (gr. 2-5). lib. bdg. 26.50 *(978-1-61531-906-0(9))* Rosen Publishing Group, Inc., The.

Beery, Barbara. Mermaid Cookbook. 1 vol. Shultz, Kirsten, photos by. 2008. (ENG., Illus.). 64p. (J). (gr. 1). spiral bd. 14.99 *(978-1-4236-0417-4(2))* Gibbs Smith, Publisher.

Bergin, Mark. Dinosaurs & Other Prehistoric Creatures. 2009. (How to Draw Ser.). (Illus.). 32p. (J). lib. bdg. 26.50 *(978-1-4358-2517-8(9)*, PowerKids Pr.) Rosen Publishing Group, Inc., The.

—Draw Cats & Kittens. Mark Bergin, illus. 2017. (Step-By-Step Ser.). 32p. (gr. 3-8). 31.35 ***(978-1-911242-21-5(0))*** Book Hse. GBR. Dist: Black Rabbit Bks.

—How to Draw Dinosaurs & Other Prehistoric Creatures. 2009. (How to Draw Ser.). (Illus.). 32p. (gr. 4-6). pap. 11.75 *(978-1-4358-2646-5(9)*, Rosen Classroom) Rosen Publishing Group, Inc., The.

—It's Fun to Draw Farm Animals. 2012. (It's Fun to Draw Ser.). (ENG., Illus.). 32p. (J). (gr. -1-3). pap. 5.95 *(978-1-61608-669-5(6)*, 608669, Sky Pony Pr.) Skyhorse Publishing Co., Inc.

—It's Fun to Draw Pets. 2014. (ENG., Illus.). 32p. (J). (gr. -1-3). 5.95 *(978-1-62636-385-4(4)*, Sky Pony Pr.) Skyhorse Publishing Co., Inc.

—It's Fun to Draw Safari Animals. 2011. (It's Fun to Draw Ser.). (ENG., Illus.). 32p. (J). (gr. -1-3). pap. 5.95 *(978-1-61608-477-6(4)*, 608477, Sky Pony Pr.) Skyhorse Publishing Co., Inc.

—Mammoths & Other Prehistoric Animals. 2012. (How to Draw Ser.). (ENG.). 32p. (J). (gr. 4-6). pap. 11.75 *(978-1-4488-6471-3(2))*; lib. bdg. 26.50 *(978-1-4488-6462-1(3))* Rosen Publishing Group, Inc., The. (PowerKids Pr.).

—Pets. 2012. (It's Fun to Draw Ser.). (Illus.). 32p. (J). (gr. k-3). lib. bdg. 26.50 *(978-1-61533-597-8(8))* Windmill Bks.

—Safari Animals. 2011. (It's Fun to Draw Ser.). (ENG., Illus.). 32p. (J). (gr. k-3). lib. bdg. 26.50 *(978-1-61533-348-6(7))* Windmill Bks.

—Sea Creatures. 2012. (It's Fun to Draw Ser.). (Illus.). 32p. (J). (gr. k-3). lib. bdg. 26.50 *(978-1-61533-598-5(6))* Windmill Bks.

Bergin, Mark, illus. It's Fun to Draw Ponies & Horses. 2015. (It's Fun to Draw Ser.). (ENG.). 32p. (J). (gr. -1-3). 5.99 *(978-1-63220-415-8(0)*, Sky Pony Pr.) Skyhorse Publishing Co., Inc.

Bird, Benjamin. Animal Doodles with Scooby-Doo! Neely, Scott, illus. 2017. (Scooby-Doodles! Ser.). (ENG.). 32p. (J). (gr. 3-6). lib. bdg. 27.99 *(978-1-5157-3405-5(6))* Capstone Press of Coughlan Cos.

Bolte, Mari. Draw Amazing Animal Mash-Ups. 2017. (Drawing Mash-Ups Ser.). (ENG.). 32p. (gr. 3-4). lib. bdg. 27.99 ***(978-1-5157-6936-1(4)**, Edge Bks.)* Capstone Press of Coughlan Cos.

Bolte, Mari. Drawing Pets: A Step-By-Step Sketchpad. 1 vol. Makuc, Lucy & Dynamo Limited Staff, illus. 2014. (My First Sketchpads Ser.). (ENG.). 48p. (gr. 1-2). pap. 5.95 *(978-1-4914-0290-0(3)*, First Facts) Capstone Press of Coughlan Cos.

Bontinck, Helga. Animal Favorites. 2006. (Simple Steps to Drawing Ser.). (Illus.). 24p. (gr. k-3). lib. bdg. 23.00 *(978-0-8368-6311-6(9)*, Gareth Stevens Learning Library) Stevens, Gareth Publishing LLLP.

—At the Seashore. 2006. (Simple Steps to Drawing Ser.). (Illus.). 24p. (gr. k-3). lib. bdg. 23.00 *(978-0-8368-6313-0(5)*, Gareth Stevens Learning Library) Stevens, Gareth Publishing LLLP.

Brecke, Nicole & Stockland, Patricia M. Dinosaurs & Other Prehistoric Creatures You Can Draw. Brecke, Nicole, illus. 2010. (Ready, Set, Draw! Ser.). (ENG., Illus.). 32p. (gr. 2-4). lib. bdg. 25.26 *(978-0-7613-4169-7(2)*, Millbrook Pr.) Lerner Publishing Group.

—Dogs You Can Draw. Brecke, Nicole, illus. 2009. (Ready, Set, Draw! Ser.). (ENG., Illus.). 32p. (gr. 2-4). lib. bdg. 25.26 *(978-0-7613-4159-8(5)*, Millbrook Pr.) Lerner Publishing Group.

—Extinct & Endangered Animals You Can Draw. Brecke, Nicole, illus. 2010. (Ready, Set, Draw! Ser.). (ENG., Illus.). 32p. (gr. 2-4). lib. bdg. 25.26 *(978-0-7613-4165-9(X)*, Millbrook Pr.) Lerner Publishing Group.

—Sea Creatures You Can Draw. Brecke, Nicole, illus. 2010. (Ready, Set, Draw! Ser.). (ENG., Illus.). 32p. (gr. 2-4). lib. bdg. 25.26 *(978-0-7613-4168-0(4)*, Millbrook Pr.) Lerner Publishing Group.

Brodman, Larisa. Pom-Pom Pets. Magruder, Trula, ed. 2006. (ENG., Illus.). 48p. (J). (gr. -1-3). 17.95 *(978-1-59369-151-6(3)*, American Girl) American Girl Publishing, Inc.

Brooks, Susie. Animals: Enjoy Great Art - Then Create Your Own! 2013. (Get into Art Ser.). (ENG., Illus.). 32p. (J). (gr. 2-9). 14.99 *(978-0-7534-7058-9(6)*, 9780753470589, Kingfisher) Roaring Brook Pr.

—Get into Art Animals: Enjoy Great Art — Then Create Your Own! 2015. (Get into Art Ser.). (ENG., Illus.). 32p. (J). (gr. 2-9). 8.99 *(978-0-7534-7217-0(1)*, 9780753472170, Kingfisher) Roaring Brook Pr.

Budnick, Madeleine. Animal Amigos! Artsy Creatures in English y Espanol. 2013. (ArteKids Ser.). (ENG & SPA., Illus.). 16p. (J). (-k). bds. 7.95 *(978-1-59534-152-5(8))* Trinity Univ. Pr.

Campbell, Kathy. Let's Draw a Bear with Squares. 2009. (Let's Draw with Shapes Ser.). 24p. (gr. k-k). 42.50 *(978-1-61514-202-6(9)*, PowerKids Pr.) Rosen Publishing Group, Inc., The.

—Let's Draw a Bear with Squares / Vamos a dibujar un oso usando Cuadrados. 2009. (Let's Draw with Shapes / Vamos a dibujar con figuras Ser.). (ENG & SPA.). 24p. (gr. k-1). 42.50 *(978-1-61514-220-0(7)*, Editorial Buenas Letras) Rosen Publishing Group, Inc., The.

Carle, Eric. What's Your Favorite Animal? Carle, Eric, illus. (ENG., Illus.). (J). (gr. -1-1). 2015. 30p. bds. 8.99 *(978-1-62779-303-2(8)*, 9781627793032) 2014. 40p. 17.99 *(978-0-8050-9641-5(8)*, 9780805096415) Holt, Henry & Co. (Holt, Henry & Co. Bks. For Young Readers).

Carroll, Colleen. Dogs. 2008. (How Artists See Jr.: Ser.). (ENG., Illus.). 18p. (J). (gr. -1-k). bds. 7.95 *(978-0-7892-0972-6(1)*, Abbeville Kids) Abbeville Pr., Inc.

—The Elements Set 1: Animals - People - Families - Play - Feelings - Weather. 6 vols. 2008. (How Artists See Ser.). (ENG., Illus.). 288p. (J). (gr. k-7). 65.00 *(978-0-7892-0962-7(4))* Abbeville Pr., Inc.

—Horses. 2008. (How Artists See Jr.: Ser.). (ENG., Illus.). 18p. (J). (gr. -1-k). bds. 7.95 *(978-0-7892-0975-7(6)*, Abbeville Kids) Abbeville Pr., Inc.

—How Artists See Set 1: Animals - People - Feelings - Weather. 4 vols. 2008. (How Artists See Ser.). (ENG., Illus.). 192p. (J). (gr. k-7). 45.00 *(978-0-7892-0964-1(0))* Abbeville Pr., Inc.

Chambers, Ailin. Animals. 2014. (Ready, Set, Draw! Ser.). (Illus.). 32p. (J). (gr. 2-5). 26.60 *(978-1-4824-0907-9(0))* Stevens, Gareth Publishing LLLP.

Claridge, Marit. How to Draw Dinosaurs & Prehistoric Life. Tatchell, Judy, ed. Biro, Val, illus. 2006. (Young Artist Ser.). 32p. (J). (gr. 4-7). pap. 5.99 *(978-0-7945-1372-6(7)*, Usborne) EDC Publishing.

Cleyet-Merle, Laurence, illus. Animal Stencil Book. 2006. (Stencil Bks.). 14p. (J). (gr. -1-3). bds. 12.99 *(978-0-7945-1140-1(6)*, Usborne) EDC Publishing.

Colich, Abby. Drawing Amazing Animals. Calle, Juan & Howard, Colin, illus. 2015. (Drawing Amazing Animals Ser.). (ENG.). 32p. (gr. 3-4). lib. bdg. 111.96 *(978-1-4914-2559-6(8)*, Snap Bks.) Capstone Press of Coughlan Cos.

—Drawing Fascinating Animals. Howard, Colin, illus. 2015. (Drawing Amazing Animals Ser.). (ENG.). 32p. (gr. 3-4). 27.99 *(978-1-4914-2133-8(9)*, Snap Bks.) Capstone Press of Coughlan Cos.

—Drawing Ocean Animals. Calle, Juan, illus. 2015. (Drawing Amazing Animals Ser.). (ENG.). 32p. (gr. 3-4). 27.99 *(978-1-4914-2131-4(2)*, Snap Bks.) Capstone Press of Coughlan Cos.

—Drawing Wild Animals. Juta, Jason, illus. 2015. (Drawing Amazing Animals Ser.). (ENG.). 32p. (gr. 3-4). 27.99 *(978-1-4914-2132-1(0)*, Snap Bks.) Capstone Press of Coughlan Cos.

—Drawing Your Pets. Azzalin, Stefano, illus. 2015. (Drawing Amazing Animals Ser.). (ENG.). 32p. (gr. 3-4). 27.99 *(978-1-4914-2134-5(7)*, Snap Bks.) Capstone Press of Coughlan Cos.

—The Ultimate Girls' Guide to Drawing: Puppies, Polar Bears, & Other Adorable Animals. Howard, Colin, illus. 2015. (ENG.). 144p. (gr. 3-4). pap. 14.95 *(978-1-62370-229-8(1))* Capstone Young Readers of Coughlan Cos.

Cook, Trevor & Miles, Lisa. Drawing Pets & Farm Animals. 2011. (Drawing Is Fun Ser.). (Illus.). 32p. (J). (gr. 1-3). pap. 10.50 *(978-1-4339-5071-1(5)*, Gareth Stevens Learning Library); lib. bdg. 26.60 *(978-1-4339-5026-1(X))* Stevens, Gareth Publishing LLLP.

—Drawing Wild Animals. 2011. (Drawing Is Fun Ser.). (Illus.). 32p. (J). (gr. 1-3). pap. 10.50 *(978-1-4339-5079-7(0)*, Gareth Stevens Learning Library); lib. bdg. 26.60 *(978-1-4339-5032-2(4))* Stevens, Gareth Publishing LLLP.

Cotton, Katie. Counting Lions: Portraits from the Wild. Walton, Stephen, illus. 2015. (ENG.). 40p. (J). (gr. k-12). 22.00 *(978-0-7636-8207-1(1))* Candlewick Pr.

Creative Team at Walter Foster Publishing Staff. I Love Dogs! Pup-Tacular Stickers, Trivia, Step-by-Step Drawing Projects, & More for the Dog Lover in You! Fisher, Diana, illus. 2011. (I Love Activity Bks.). (ENG.). 112p. (J). (gr. 1-3). pap., act. bk. ed. 9.95 *(978-1-60058-225-7(7)*, 1600582257) Quarto Publishing Group USA.

Cuddy, Robbin. All about Drawing Farm & Forest Animals: Learn to Draw More Than 40 Barnyard Animals & Wildlife Critters Step by Step. 2013. (All about Drawing Ser.). (ENG., Illus.). 80p. (J). (gr. 1-3). pap. 9.95 *(978-1-60058-361-2(X)*, 160058361X) Quarto Publishing Group USA.

—Learn to Draw Cats & Kittens: Step-By-Step Instructions for More Than 25 Favorite Feline Friends. 2015. (Learn to Draw Ser.). (ENG., Illus.). 64p. (J). (gr. 1-3). pap. 8.95 *(978-1-60058-480-0(2)*, Walter Foster Jr) Quarto Publishing Group USA.

—Learn to Draw Dinosaurs: Step-By-step Instructions for More Than 25 Prehistoric Creatures. 2015. (Learn to Draw Ser.). (ENG., Illus.). 64p. (J). (gr. 1-3). pap. 8.95 *(978-1-63322-030-0(3)*, Walter Foster Jr) Quarto Publishing Group USA.

—Learn to Draw Exotic Animals: Step-By-step Instructions for More Than 25 Unusual Animals. 2016. (Learn to Draw Ser.). (ENG., Illus.). 64p. (J). (gr. 1-3). pap. 8.95 *(978-1-63322-065-2(6)*, Walter Foster Jr) Quarto Publishing Group USA.

—Learn to Draw Forest Animals: Step-By-step Instructions for More Than 25 Woodland Creatures. 2015. (Learn to Draw Ser.). (ENG., Illus.). 64p. (J). (gr. 1-3). pap. 8.95 *(978-1-60058-482-4(9))* Quarto Publishing Group USA.

—Learn to Draw Safari Animals: Step-By-step Instructions for More Than 25 Exotic Animals. 2015. (Learn to Draw Ser.). (ENG., Illus.). 64p. (J). (gr. 1-3). pap. 8.95 *(978-1-60058-481-7(0)*, Walter Foster Jr) Quarto Publishing Group USA.

—Learn to Draw Zoo Animals: Step-By-step Instructions for More Than 25 Zoo Animals. 2016. (Learn to Draw Ser.).

(ENG., Illus.). 64p. (J). (gr. 1-3). pap. 8.95 (978-1-63322-103-1(2)) Quarto Publishing Group USA.

—Polar Animals: Draw More Than 25 Favorite Arctic & Antarctic Wildlife Critters. 2014. (Learn to Draw Ser.). (ENG., Illus.). 64p. (J). (gr. 1-3). pap. 8.95 (978-1-60058-386-5(5), 1600583865) Quarto Publishing Group USA.

Cuddy, Robbin, illus. Learn to Draw Dogs & Puppies: Step-By-Step Instructions for More Than 25 Different Breeds. 2015. (Learn to Draw: Expanded Edition Ser.). (ENG.). 64p. (gr. k-5). 33.27 (978-1-939581-52-5(4)) Quarto Publishing Group USA.

—Learn to Draw Forest Animals & Wildlife: Step-by-Step Instructions for 25 Different Woodland Animals. 2012. (Learn to Draw Ser.). (ENG.). 40p. (J). (gr. 1-3). pap. 4.95 (978-1-60058-308-7(3), 1600583083) Quarto Publishing Group USA.

—Learn to Draw Pets: Step-By-Step Instructions for More Than 25 Cute & Cuddly Animals. 2015. (Learn to Draw: Expanded Edition Ser.). (ENG.). 64p. (J). (gr. k-5). 33.27 (978-1-939581-53-2(2)) Quarto Publishing Group USA.

—Learn to Draw Polar Animals: Draw More Than 25 Favorite Arctic & Antarctic Wildlife Critters. 2015. (Learn to Draw: Expanded Edition Ser.). (ENG.). 64p. (J). (gr. k-5). 33.27 (978-1-939581-51-8(6)) Quarto Publishing Group USA.

—Learn to Draw Rainforest & Jungle Animals: Step-by-Step Drawing Instructions for 25 Exotic Creatures. 2013. (Learn to Draw Ser.). (ENG.). 40p. (J). (gr. 1-3). pap. 4.95 (978-1-60058-309-4(1), 1600583091) Quarto Publishing Group USA.

—Learn to Draw Sea Creatures. 2015. (Learn to Draw: Expanded Edition Ser.). (ENG.). 64p. (J). (gr. k-5). 33.27 (978-1-939581-54-9(0)) Quarto Publishing Group USA.

Cuddy, Robin. Learn to Draw Horses & Ponies: Step-by-Step Instructions for More Than 25 Different Breeds. 2014. (Learn to Draw Ser.). (ENG., Illus.). 64p. (J). (gr. 1-3). pap. 8.95 (978-1-60058-446-6(2)) Quarto Publishing Group USA.

—Learn to Draw Pets: Step-By-step Instructions for More Than 25 Cute & Cuddly Animals. 2014. (Learn to Draw Ser.). (ENG., Illus.). 64p. (J). (gr. 1-3). pap. 8.95 (978-1-60058-444-2(6)) Quarto Publishing Group USA.

—Learn to Draw Sea Creatures: Step-by-Step Instructions for More Than 25 Ocean Animals. 2014. (Learn to Draw Ser.). (ENG., Illus.). 64p. (J). (gr. 1-3). pap. 8.95 (978-1-60058-445-9(4)) Quarto Publishing Group USA.

Curto, Rosa M. Fun & Easy Drawing at Sea. 2013. (Fun & Easy Drawing Ser.). 36p. (J). lib. bdg. 23.94 (978-0-7660-6039-5(X)); pap. 7.95 (978-0-7660-6040-1(3)) Enslow Pubs., Inc. (Enslow Elementary).

—Fun & Easy Drawing on the Farm. 2013. (Fun & Easy Drawing Ser.). 36p. (J). lib. bdg. 23.94 (978-0-7660-6037-1(3)); pap. 7.95 (978-0-7660-6038-8(1)) Enslow Pubs., Inc. (Enslow Elementary).

Dicker, Katie. You Can Draw Cats! Saunders, Mike, illus. 2013. (Draw Your Pet! Ser.). 32p. (gr. 3-5). 26.60 (978-1-4339-8727-4(9)); pap. 10.50 (978-1-4339-8728-1(7)) Stevens, Gareth Publishing LLLP. (Gareth Stevens Learning Library).

—You Can Draw Exotic Pets! Saunders, Mike, illus. 2013. (Draw Your Pet! Ser.). 32p. (gr. 3-5). 26.60 (978-1-4339-8735-9(X)); pap. 10.50 (978-1-4339-8736-6(8)) Stevens, Gareth Publishing LLLP. (Gareth Stevens Learning Library).

—You Can Draw Fish! Saunders, Mike, illus. 2013. (Draw Your Pet! Ser.). 32p. (gr. 3-5). 26.60 (978-1-4339-8739-7(2)); pap. 10.50 (978-1-4339-8740-3(6)) Stevens, Gareth Publishing LLLP. (Gareth Stevens Learning Library).

—You Can Draw Horses! Saunders, Mike, illus. 2013. (Draw Your Pet! Ser.). 32p. (gr. 3-5). 26.60 (978-1-4339-8743-4(0)); pap. 10.50 (978-1-4339-8744-1(9)) Stevens, Gareth Publishing LLLP. (Gareth Stevens Learning Library).

Dickler, Katie. You Can Draw Dogs! Saunders, Mike, illus. 2013. (Draw Your Pet! Ser.). 32p. (J). (gr. 3-5). pap. 10.50 (978-1-4339-8732-8(5)); lib. bdg. 26.60 (978-1-4339-8731-1(7)) Stevens, Gareth Publishing LLLP.

Dompierre, Judith. I See Pigs Everywhere. 2012. 32p. pap. 25.00 (978-1-4626-9333-7(4)) America Star Bks.

DreamWorks Animation LLC Staff. Learn to Draw DreamWorks Animation's Kung Fu Panda. Vance, Joe, illus. 2017. (Learn to Draw Favorite Characters: Expanded Edition Ser.). (ENG.). 64p. (J). (gr. 3-5). 33.32 (978-1-942875-21-5(5)) Quarto Publishing Group USA.

DuBosque, D. C., illus. Draw Animals: Ocean - Rainforest - Desert - Grassland. 2015. 321p. (J). pap. (978-1-943158-00-3(2), Blackbirch Pr., Inc.) Peel Productions, Inc.

Dudziuk, Kasia. Let's Draw Pets & Farm Animals. 2016. (Let's Draw Step by Step Ser.). 00032p. (J). (gr. 1-2). pap. 11.75 (978-1-4994-8179-2(9), Windmill Bks.) Rosen Publishing Group, Inc., The.

—Let's Draw Wild Animals. 2016. (Let's Draw Step by Step Ser.). 00032p. (J). (gr. 1-2). pap. 11.75 (978-1-4994-8188-4(8), Windmill Bks.) Rosen Publishing Group, Inc., The.

Eason, Sarah. Drawing Baby Animals. 2013. (Learn to Draw Ser.). 32p. (J). (gr. 2-5). pap. 10.50 (978-1-4339-9525-5(5)); lib. bdg. 26.60 (978-1-4339-9524-8(7)) Stevens, Gareth Publishing LLLP.

—Drawing Baby Animals. Santillan, Jorge, illus. 2013. (Learn to Draw Ser.). 32p. (J). (gr. 2-5). pap. 63.00 (978-1-4339-9526-2(3)) Stevens, Gareth Publishing LLLP.

—Drawing Dinosaurs. Santillan, Jorge, illus. 2013. (Learn to Draw Ser.). 32p. (J). (gr. 2-5). pap. 63.00 (978-1-4339-9530-9(1)); pap. 10.50 (978-1-4339-9529-3(8)) Stevens, Gareth Publishing LLLP.

—Drawing Fairies, Mermaids, & Unicorns. Santillan, Jorge, illus. 2013. (Learn to Draw Ser.). 32p. (J). (gr. 2-5). pap. 63.00 (978-1-4339-9538-5(7)); pap. 10.50 (978-1-4339-9537-8(9)) Stevens, Gareth Publishing LLLP.

Escandell, Victor. A Wonderful World of Animals: Doodle Art Book. 2014. (ENG., Illus.). 164p. (J). (gr. -1). 14.95 (978-84-92810-72-7(6), Promopress) Promotora de prensa internacional S.A ESP. Dist: Consortium Bk. Sales & Distribution.

Falken, Linda & The Metropolitan Museum of Art, The Metropolitan. Puzzling Cats. 2015. (ENG., Illus.). 16p. (J). (gr. -1-1). 16.95 (978-1-4197-1363-7(9), Abrams Bks. for Young Readers) Abrams, Inc.

—Puzzling Dogs. 2015. (ENG., Illus.). 16p. (J). (gr. -1-1). 16.95 (978-1-4197-1362-0(0), Abrams Bks. for Young Readers) Abrams, Inc.

Farrell, Russell & Creative Team at Walter Foster Publishing Staff. I Love Horses! Giddy-Up Great Stickers, Trivia, Step-by-Step Drawing Projects, & More for the Horse Lover in You! Fisher, Diana, illus. 2011. (I Love Activity Bks.). (ENG.). 112p. (J). (gr. 1-3). pap. 9.95 (978-1-60058-226-4(5), 1600582265) Quarto Publishing Group USA.

Farrell, Russell & Fisher, Diana, illus. All about Drawing Sea Creatures & Animals. 2010. (All about Drawing Ser.). 80p. (J). 34.25 (978-1-936309-08-5(4)) Quarto Publishing Group USA.

Farrell, Russell & Mueller, Peter. All about Horses & Pets. 2010. (All about Drawing Ser.). 80p. (J). 34.25 (978-1-936309-06-1(8)) Quarto Publishing Group USA.

Fisher, Diana, illus. Watch Me Draw Favorite Pets. 2012. 24p. (J). (978-1-936309-77-1(7)) Quarto Publishing Group USA.

—Watch Me Draw the Zoo. 2013. (Watch Me Draw Ser.). 24p. (J). (gr. -1-2). 25.65 (978-1-936309-90-0(4)) Quarto Publishing Group USA.

Fisher, Diana & Shelly, Jeff, illus. All about Dinosaurs & Reptiles. 2010. (All about Drawing Ser.). 80p. (J). 34.25 (978-1-936309-07-8(6)) Quarto Publishing Group USA.

Franklin, Carolyn. How to Draw Big Cats. 2009. (How to Draw Ser.). (Illus.). 32p. (gr. 4-6). pap. 11.75 (978-1-4358-2645-8(0), Rosen Classroom) Rosen Publishing Group, Inc., The.

Gabriel, Faith K. Nifty Thrifty Animal Crafts. Ponte, June, illus. 2007. (Nifty Thrifty Crafts for Kids Ser.). 32p. (J). (gr. 3-4). lib. bdg. 23.94 (978-0-7660-2779-4(1), Enslow Elementary) Enslow Pubs., Inc.

Garbot, Dave. Furry & Feathered Friends. 2015. (Cartooning for Kids Ser.). (ENG., Illus.). 64p. (J). (gr. k-5). 33.32 (978-1-939581-49-5(4)) Quarto Publishing Group USA.

Getha, Patricia, et al. Art of Drawing & Painting Horses: Capture the Majesty of Horses & Ponies in Pencil, Oil, Acrylic, Watercolor & Pastel. 2011. (Collector's Ser.). (ENG., Illus.). 144p. pap. 19.95 (978-1-60058-237-0(0), 1600582370) Quarto Publishing Group USA.

—The Art of Drawing Animals: Discover all the techniques you need to know to draw amazingly lifelike Animals. 2008. (Collector's Ser.). (ENG., Illus.). 144p. pap. 19.95 (978-1-60058-130-4(7), 1600581307) Quarto Publishing Group USA.

Gibson, Ray. I Can Draw Animals Kid Kit. 2007. (Kid Kits Ser.). (Illus.). 32p. (J). (gr. -1). pap. 7.99 (978-1-60130-018-8(2), Usborne) EDC Publishing.

Gilbert, Elizabeth T., illus. Watch Me Draw Tiggerific Tales. 2013. (Watch Me Draw Ser.). 24p. (gr. -1-2). 25.65 (978-1-936309-87-0(4)) Quarto Publishing Group USA.

Gilbert, Elizabeth T., et al. DIY Dog Portraits. Barnes, Jessica L., illus. 2016. (DIY Ser.). (ENG.). 128p. (J). (gr. 3-8). 34.65 (978-1-942875-13-0(4), Walter Foster Jr) Quarto Publishing Group USA.

Gowen, Fiona, illus. How to Draw Amazing Animals & Incredible Insects. 2015. (How to Draw Ser.). (ENG.). 32p. (J). (gr. 2-6). pap. 4.99 (978-1-4380-0583-6(0)) Barron's Educational Series, Inc.

Gray, Peter. Animals. (Drawing Manga Ser.). 32p. 2009. (gr. 4-4). 50.50 (978-1-61512-196-0(X)) 2006. (Illus.). (YA). (gr. 3-6). lib. bdg. 26.50 (978-1-4042-3329-4(6)) Rosen Publishing Group, Inc., The.

—How to Draw Cats & Dogs & Other Pets. 2013. (How to Draw Animals Ser.). 32p. (J). (gr. 3-6). 26.50 (978-1-4777-1300-6(X)); pap. 11.75 (978-1-4777-1411-9(1)); pap. 70.50 (978-1-4777-1412-6(X)) Rosen Publishing Group, Inc., The. (PowerKids Pr.).

—How to Draw Tigers & Other Big Cats. 2013. (How to Draw Animals Ser.). 32p. (J). (gr. 3-6). 26.50 (978-1-4777-1304-4(2)); pap. 70.50 (978-1-4777-1420-1(0)); pap. 11.75 (978-1-4777-1419-5(7)) Rosen Publishing Group, Inc., The. (PowerKids Pr.).

Green, Barry & Lambert, Nat. How to Draw 101 Dinosaurs. Green, Dan, illus. 2013. (ENG.). 48p. (J). (gr. k-2). pap. 4.99 (978-1-78244-612-5(5)) Top That! Publishing PLC GBR. Dist: Independent Pubs. Group.

Hall, Susan T., illus. Watch Me Draw Diego's Animal Adventures. 2013. (Watch Me Draw Ser.). 24p. (J). (gr. -1-2). 25.65 (978-1-936309-88-7(2)) Quarto Publishing Group USA.

Hankin, Rosie. Cut & Paste Farm Animals. 2007. (Cut, Paste, & Create Ser.). (Illus.). 32p. (gr. k-3). lib. bdg. 26.00 (978-0-8368-7719-9(5), Gareth Stevens Learning Library) Stevens, Gareth Publishing LLLP.

—Cut & Paste Sea Creatures. 2007. (Cut, Paste, & Create Ser.). (Illus.). 32p. (gr. k-3). lib. bdg. 26.00 (978-0-8368-7720-5(9), Gareth Stevens Learning Library) Stevens, Gareth Publishing LLLP.

Harbo, Christopher L. Easy Animal Origami, 1 vol. 2010. (Easy Origami Ser.). (ENG.). 24p. (gr. 1-2). lib. bdg. 25.32 (978-1-4296-5384-8(1), First Facts) Capstone Press of Coughlan Cos.

Hardyman, Roby. Origami Fun: Pets. 2017. (Origami Fun Ser.). (ENG., Illus.). 24p. (YA). (gr. 3-7). lib. bdg. 25.95 **(978-1-62617-714-7(7)**, Express Bks.) Bellwether Media.

Hardyman, Robyn. Origami Fun: Jungle Animals. 2017. (Origami Fun Ser.). (ENG., Illus.). 24p. (YA). (gr. 3-7). lib. bdg. 25.95 **(978-1-62617-712-3(0)**, Express Bks.) Bellwether Media.

—Origami Fun: Ocean Animals. 2017. (Origami Fun Ser.). (ENG., Illus.). 24p. (YA). (gr. 3-7). 25.95 **(978-1-62617-713-0(9)**, Express Bks.) Bellwether Media.

Harpster, Steve. Pencil, Paper, Draw! - Animals. 2014. (Pencil, Paper, Draw!(r) Ser.). (ENG., Illus.). 64p. (J). (gr. k-3). pap. 6.95 (978-1-4549-1148-7(4)) Sterling Publishing Co., Inc.

—Pencil, Paper, Draw! - Dogs. 2014. (Pencil, Paper, Draw!(r) Ser.). (ENG., Illus.). 64p. (J). (gr. k-3). pap. 6.95 (978-1-4549-1152-4(2)) Sterling Publishing Co., Inc.

—Pencil, Paper, Draw!(r) - Horses. 2014. (Pencil, Paper, Draw!(r) Ser.). (ENG., Illus.). 64p. (J). (gr. k-3). pap. 6.95 (978-1-4549-1155-5(7)) Sterling Publishing Co., Inc.

Hart, Christopher. Drawing Animals Shape by Shape: Create Cartoon Animals with Circles, Squares, Rectangles & Triangles. 2015. (Drawing Shape by Shape Ser.). (ENG., Illus.). 176p. (J). (gr. -1). pap. 14.95 (978-1-936096-95-4(1), Hart, Chris Bks.) Sixth&Spring Bks.

—Kids Draw Animals. 2003. (Kids Draw Ser.). (ENG., Illus.). 64p. (J). (gr. 2-4). pap. 11.95 (978-0-8230-2631-9(0), Watson-Guptill) Potter/TenSpeed/Harmony.

—You Can Draw Cartoon Animals: A Simple Step-by-Step Drawing Guide! 2009. (ENG., Illus.). 120p. (J). (gr. 1-3). pap., instr.'s gde. ed. 12.95 (978-1-60058-611-8(2), 1600586112) Quarto Publishing Group USA.

—Young Artists Draw Animals. 2012. (ENG., Illus.). 144p. pap. 14.99 (978-0-8230-0718-9(9), Watson-Guptill) Potter/TenSpeed/Harmony.

Hayn, Carter. Drawing Werewolves. 2013. (Drawing Monsters Step-By-Step Ser.). (ENG., Illus.). 24p. (gr. 3-6). 26.50 (978-1-61533-692-0(3)); pap. 12.85 (978-1-61533-704-0(0)) Windmill Bks.

Heller, D. M. Let's Make a Lion with Everyday Materials. 2009. (Let's Do Arts & Crafts Ser.). 24p. (gr. 2-2). 42.50 (978-1-61514-199-9(5), PowerKids Pr.) Rosen Publishing Group, Inc., The.

—Let's Make a Monkey with Everyday Materials. 2009. (Let's Do Arts & Crafts Ser.). 24p. (gr. 2-2). 42.50 (978-1-61514-200-2(2), PowerKids Pr.) Rosen Publishing Group, Inc., The.

Hodge, Susie. Animals. Roberts, Steve, illus. 2010. (Let's Draw Ser.). (ENG.). 32p. (gr. 3-5). 22.60 (978-1-61533-269-4(3)); pap. 10.55 (978-1-61533-270-0(7)) Windmill Bks.

—How to Draw Animals. Roberts, Steve, illus. 2008. (How to Draw Ser.). 47p. (J). (gr. 4-7). (978-1-84810-005-3(1)) Miles Kelly Publishing, Ltd.

Hosley, Maria. Cats, 1 vol. 2007. (First Drawings Ser.). (ENG., Illus.). 24p. (gr. -1-3). 25.65 (978-1-59679-801-4(7), Buddy Bks.) ABDO Publishing Co.

—Dogs, 1 vol. 2007. (First Drawings Ser.). (ENG., Illus.). 24p. (gr. -1-3). 25.65 (978-1-59679-803-8(3), Buddy Bks.) ABDO Publishing Co.

How to Draw Animals. 2013. (How to Draw Animals Ser.). 32p. (J). (gr. 3-6). 159.00 (978-1-4777-1545-1(2)); pap. 423.00 (978-1-4777-2729-4(9)); pap. 70.50 (978-1-4777-2728-7(0)) Rosen Publishing Group, Inc., The. (PowerKids Pr.).

Huff, Abby. Draw Your Own Animal Zendoodles. Scudamore, Angelika et al, illus. 2017. (Draw Your Own Zendoodles Ser.). (ENG.). 48p. (gr. 4-5). lib. bdg. 31.32 (978-1-5157-4840-3(5)) Capstone Press of Coughlan Cos.

Jantner, Janos, illus. Drawing Mythological Monsters. 2013. (How to Draw Monsters Ser.). (ENG.). 32p. (J). (gr. 3-6). pap. 11.75 (978-1-4777-0340-3(3), PowerKids Pr.) Rosen Publishing Group, Inc., The.

—Drawing Unexplained-Mystery Monsters. 2013. (How to Draw Monsters Ser.). (ENG.). 32p. (J). (gr. 3-6). pap. 11.75 (978-1-4777-0346-5(2)); lib. bdg. 26.50 (978-1-4777-0312-0(8)) Rosen Publishing Group, Inc., The. (PowerKids Pr.).

Jeffus, Sharon2006, as told by. Artsy Animals: Learn to Read. 2006. (Illus.). 70p. (J). 19.95 (978-0-9715970-9-9(X)) Visual Manna.

Jones, Richard & Santillan, Jorge. Manga Animals. 2012. (Learn to Draw Manga Ser.). (ENG., Illus.). 32p. (J). (gr. 4-6). pap. 11.75 (978-1-4488-7943-4(4)); lib. bdg. 26.50 (978-1-4488-7872-7(1)) Rosen Publishing Group, Inc., The. (PowerKids Pr.).

—Manga Dinosaurs. 2012. (Learn to Draw Manga Ser.). (ENG., Illus.). 32p. (J). (gr. 4-6). pap. 11.75 (978-1-4488-7944-1(2)); lib. bdg. 26.50 (978-1-4488-7873-4(X)) Rosen Publishing Group, Inc., The. (PowerKids Pr.).

—Manga Dragons. 2012. (Learn to Draw Manga Ser.). (ENG., Illus.). 32p. (J). (gr. 4-6). pap. 11.75 (978-1-4488-7945-8(0)); lib. bdg. 26.50 (978-1-4488-7874-1(8)) Rosen Publishing Group, Inc., The. (PowerKids Pr.).

Kranking, Kathy. In the Spotlight: Animal Superstars. 2007. (Illus.). 32p. (J). pap. (978-0-439-02576-8(1)) Scholastic, Inc.

La Coccinella. Animals at Play. 2015. (Play & Draw Ser.). (ENG., Illus.). 22p. (J). (gr. k-3). spiral bd. 9.95 (978-1-4549-1556-0(0)) Sterling Publishing Co., Inc.

Labaff, Stephanie. Draw Animals in 4 Easy Steps: Then Write a Story. LaBaff, Tom, illus. 2012. (Drawing in 4 Easy Steps Ser.). 48p. (J). (gr. 3-18). pap. 8.95 (978-1-4644-0013-1(X), Enslow Elementary) Enslow Pubs., Inc.

Lee, Justin. How to Draw African Animals. 2009. (Kid's Guide to Drawing Ser.). 24p. (gr. 3-3). 47.90 (978-1-61511-008-7(9), PowerKids Pr.) Rosen Publishing Group, Inc., The.

—How to Draw Animals of the Rain Forest. 2009. (Kid's Guide to Drawing Ser.). 24p. (gr. 3-3). 47.90 (978-1-61511-010-0(0), PowerKids Pr.) Rosen Publishing Group, Inc., The.

Legendre, Philippe. I Can Draw! Dinosaurs, Dragons & Prehistoric Creatures. 2015. (I Can Draw Ser.). (ENG., Illus.). 48p. (J). (gr. -1-3). 30.65 (978-1-939581-60-0(5)) Quarto Publishing Group USA.

Let's Make a Monkey with Everyday Materials. 2006. (Let's Do Arts & Crafts Ser.). (Illus.). 24p. (J). (gr. 3-7). lib. bdg. 22.60 (978-1-4042-3061-3(0)) Rosen Publishing Group, Inc., The.

Levin, Freddie. 1-2-3 Draw Ocean Life. 2014. 64p. pap. 9.00 (978-1-61003-323-7(X)) Center for the Collaborative Classroom.

Levin, Freddie & Gordon, Freddie. 1-2-3 Draw Baby Animals. Levin, Freddie, illus. 2006. (ENG., Illus.). 64p. (J). pap. 8.99 (978-0-939217-45-8(7)) Peel Productions, Inc.

Levy, Barbara Soloff. How to Draw Dogs. 2011. (Dover How to Draw Ser.). (ENG.). 64p. (J). (gr. k-5). pap. 4.99 (978-0-486-47201-0(9)) Dover Pubns., Inc.

Levy, Barbara Soloff & Drawing Staff. ART START Animals: How to Draw with Simple Shapes. 2010. (Dover How to Draw Ser.). (ENG., Illus.). 64p. (J). (gr. k-3). pap. 4.99 (978-0-486-47677-3(4)) Dover Pubns., Inc.

Lim, Annalees. Farmyard Animal Crafts, 01 vols., 1. 2016. (Creating Creature Crafts Ser.). (ENG., Illus.). 24p. (J). pap. 10.60 (978-1-5081-9105-6(0), 1397690, Windmill Bks.) Rosen Publishing Group, Inc., The.

—Pet Crafts, 01 vols., 1. 2016. (Creating Creature Crafts Ser.). (ENG., Illus.). 24p. (J). pap. 10.60 (978-1-5081-9109-4(3), 1397691, Windmill Bks.) Rosen Publishing Group, Inc., The.

—Sea Animal Crafts, 01 vols., 1. 2016. (Creating Creature Crafts Ser.). (ENG., Illus.). 24p. (J). pap. 10.60 (978-1-5081-9113-1(1), 1397692, Windmill Bks.) Rosen Publishing Group, Inc., The.

—Wild Animal Crafts, 01 vols., 1. 2016. (Creating Creature Crafts Ser.). (ENG., Illus.). 24p. (J). pap. 10.60 (978-1-5081-9117-9(4), Windmill Bks.) Rosen Publishing Group, Inc., The.

Littlefield, Cindy A. Pop-Out & Paint Dogs & Cats. 2014. (ENG., Illus.). 48p. (J). (gr. 3-8). pap. 12.95 (978-1-61212-140-6(3), 622140) Storey Publishing, LLC.

Masiello, Ralph. Ralph Masiello's Farm Drawing Book. Masiello, Ralph, illus. 2012. (Illus.). (J). (ENG.). 32p. (gr. k-3). 16.95 (978-1-57091-537-6(7)); (ENG., 32p. (gr. k-3). pap. 7.95 (978-1-57091-538-3(5)); (gr. 1-4). pap. 16.95 (978-1-60734-082-9(8)) Charlesbridge Publishing, Inc.

—Ralph Masiello's Ocean Drawing Book. Masiello, Ralph, illus. 2006. (Ralph Masiello's Drawing Bks.). (ENG., Illus.). 32p. (J). (gr. k-3). pap. 7.95 (978-1-57091-530-7(X), 1258410) Charlesbridge Publishing, Inc.

McCurry, Kristen. How to Draw Amazing Animals, 1 vol. Meschini, Leonardo, illus. 2013. (Smithsonian Drawing Bks.). (ENG.). 64p. (gr. 3-4). pap. 7.19 (978-1-62065-726-3(0)); pap. 41.70 (978-1-62065-727-0(9)) Capstone Press of Coughlan Cos.

—How to Draw Incredible Ocean Animals, 1 vol. Osterhold, Jared, illus. 2013. (Smithsonian Drawing Bks.). (ENG.). 64p. (gr. 3-4). pap. 7.19 (978-1-62065-728-7(7)); pap. 41.70 (978-1-62065-729-4(5)); lib. bdg. 33.99 (978-1-4296-9940-2(X)) Capstone Press of Coughlan Cos.

McGill, Jordan. Amazing Animals. 2011. (J). (978-1-61690-985-7(4)) Weigl Pubs., Inc.

—Backyard Animals. 2011. (J). (978-1-61690-987-1(0)) Weigl Pubs., Inc.

McGill, Jordan, ed. Amazing Animals. 2011. (J). (gr. 3-5). pap. 13.95 (978-1-61690-862-1(9), AV2 by Weigl); (Illus.). 32p. 28.55 (978-1-61690-856-0(4)) Weigl Pubs., Inc.

—Backyard Animals. 2011. (J). (gr. 3-5). pap. 13.95 (978-1-61690-863-8(7), AV2 by Weigl); (Illus.). 32p. 28.55 (978-1-61690-857-7(2)) Weigl Pubs., Inc.

—Pets. 2011. (J). (gr. 3-5). pap. 13.95 (978-1-61690-861-4(0), AV2 by Weigl); (Illus.). 32p. 28.55 (978-1-61690-855-3(6)) Weigl Pubs., Inc.

Merberg, Julie & Bober, Suzanne. Animals in Art: Art from the Start. 2011. (ENG.). 22p. (J). (gr. -1). bds. 6.99 (978-1-935703-15-0(3)) Downtown Bookworks.

Morris, Ting & Morris, Neil. Animals. Levy, Ruth, illus. 2006. (Sticky Fingers Ser.). 32p. (J). lib. bdg. 28.50 (978-1-59771-025-1(3)) Sea-To-Sea Pubns.

Mosqueda, Olga T. & Tucker, Marianne, illus. Learn to Draw Plus Disney Winnie the Pooh. 2012. (J). (978-1-936309-68-9(8)) Quarto Publishing Group USA.

Murray, Julie. Acting Animals, 1 vol. 2009. (Going to Work:Animal Edition Ser.). (ENG., Illus.). 32p. (J). (gr. 2-5). 27.07 (978-1-60453-560-0(1)) ABDO Publishing Co.

Muschinske, Emily, illus. Fingerprint Critters: Turning Your Prints into Fun Art. 2006. 48p. (J). pap. (978-0-439-81338-9(7)) Scholastic, Inc.

Nishida, Masaki. Drawing Manga Animals. (How to Draw Manga Ser.). 24p. 2009. (gr. 3-3). 47.90 (978-1-61513-437-3(9), PowerKids Pr.) 2007. (Illus.). (J). (gr. 4-7). lib. bdg. 25.25 (978-1-4042-3846-6(8)) Rosen Publishing Group, Inc., The.

—Drawing Manga Dinosaurs. 2009. (How to Draw Manga Ser.). 24p. (gr. 3-3). 47.90 (978-1-61513-438-0(7), PowerKids Pr.) Rosen Publishing Group, Inc., The.

Nuytten, Bobbie. Fingerprint Animals. Nuytten, Bobbie, illus. 2016. (Fun with Fingerprints Ser.). (ENG., Illus.). 24p. (gr. k-1). lib. bdg. 26.65 (978-1-4795-8687-5(0)) Picture Window Bks.

Osle, Janessa. Animals Around the World. Legendre, Philippe, illus. 2015. (I Can Draw Ser.). (ENG.). 48p. (J). (gr. -1-3). 30.65 (978-1-939581-56-3(7)) Quarto Publishing Group USA.

—Favorite Pets. Legendre, Philippe, illus. 2015. (I Can Draw Ser.). (ENG.). 48p. (J). (gr. -1-3). 30.65 (978-1-939581-55-6(9)) Quarto Publishing Group USA.

—Sea Creatures & Other Favorite Animals. Legendre, Philippe, illus. 2015. (I Can Draw Ser.). (ENG.). 48p. (J). (gr. -1-3). 30.65 (978-1-939581-57-0(5)) Quarto Publishing Group USA.

Owen, Ruth. Desert Animals. 2014. (Origami Safari Ser.). (Illus.). 32p. (J). (gr. 3-6). pap. 11.75 (978-1-4777-9242-1(2)) Windmill Bks.

—Grassland Animals. 2014. (Origami Safari Ser.). (Illus.). 32p. (J). (gr. 3-6). lib. bdg. 27.50 (978-1-4777-9253-7(8)) Windmill Bks.

—Jungle Animals. 2014. (Origami Safari Ser.). (Illus.). 32p. (J). (gr. 3-6). lib. bdg. 27.50 (978-1-4777-9238-4(4)) Windmill Bks.

—Mountain Animals. 2014. (Origami Safari Ser.). (Illus.). 32p. (J). (gr. 3-6). lib. bdg. 27.50 (978-1-4777-9257-5(0)) Windmill Bks.

—Ocean Animals. 2014. (Origami Safari Ser.). (Illus.). 32p. (J). (gr. 3-6). lib. bdg. 27.50 (978-1-4777-9249-0(X)) Windmill Bks.

—Polar Animals. 2014. (Origami Safari Ser.). (Illus.). 32p. (J). (gr. 3-6). lib. bdg. 27.50 (978-1-4777-9245-2(7)) Windmill Bks.

Peter Pauper Press, Inc., creator. Learn to Draw... Animals! Easy Step-By-Step Drawing Guide. 2014. (ENG., Illus.). 48p. (J). 5.99 (978-1-4413-0270-0(0), 9781441302700) Peter Pauper Pr. Inc.

Piatti, Celestino. Celestino Piatti's Animal ABC. 2015. (ENG., Illus.). 40p. (J). 17.95 (978-0-7358-4206-9(X)) North-South Bks., Inc.

Porter, Steve. Mythical Beasts. 2014. (You Can Draw It! Ser.). (ENG., Illus.). 24p. (J). (gr. 3-8). lib. bdg. 25.95 (978-1-62617-098-8(3), Express Bks.) Bellwether Media.

Radtke, Becky J. Draw It! Animals. 2013. (ENG.). 80p. (J). (gr. 3-8). pap. 3.99 (978-0-486-49955-0(3)) Dover Pubns., Inc.

—Draw It! Sea Life. 2013. (ENG.). 80p. (J). (gr. 3-8). pap. 3.99 (978-0-486-49958-1(8)) Dover Pubns., Inc.

Randolph, Joanne. Let's Draw a Dinosaur with Shapes. 2009. (Let's Draw with Shapes Ser.). 24p. (gr. k-k). 42.50 (978-1-61514-205-7(3), PowerKids Pr.) Rosen Publishing Group, Inc., The.

—Let's Draw a Dinosaur with Shapes/Vamos a dibujar un dinasaurio usando Figuras. 2009. (Let's Draw with Shapes / Vamos a dibujar con figuras Ser.). (ENG & SPA.). 24p. (gr.

k-1). 42.50 *(978-1-61514-215-6(0),* Editorial Buenas Letras) Rosen Publishing Group, Inc., The.

—Let's Draw a Horse with Rectangles. 2009. (Let's Draw with Shapes Ser.). 24p. (gr. k-k). 42.50 *(978-1-61514-209-5(6),* PowerKids Pr.) Rosen Publishing Group, Inc., The.

—Let's Draw a Horse with Rectangles / Vamos a dibujar un caballo usando Rectángulos. 2009. (Let's Draw with Shapes / Vamos a dibujar con figuras Ser.). (ENG & SPA.). 24p. (gr. k-1). 42.50 *(978-1-61514-224-8(X),* Editorial Buenas Letras) Rosen Publishing Group, Inc., The.

Robinson, Nick. Origami Adventures: Animals. Quigley, Sebastian, illus. 2014. (Origami Adventures Ser.). (ENG.). 76p. (J). (gr. 1). spiral bd. 15.95 *(978-1-60710-763-7(5),* Silver Dolphin Bks.) Readerlink Distribution Services, LLC.

Rosier, Maggie. Dinosaurs. 2013. (You Can Draw It! Ser.). (ENG., Illus.). 24p. (J). (gr. 3-8). lib. bdg. 25.95 *(978-1-60014-899-6(9),* Express Bks.) Bellwether Media.

Santa Maria, Christa, des. Zoo Animal Crafts, 01 vols., 1. 2016. (Creating Creature Crafts Ser.). (ENG., Illus.). 24p. (J). pap. 10.60 *(978-1-5081-9121-6(2),* 1397694, Windmill Bks.) Rosen Publishing Group, Inc., The.

Santillan, Jorge & Eason, Sarah. Drawing Dinosaurs. 2013. (Learn to Draw Ser.). (ENG., Illus.). 32p. (J). (gr. 2-5). lib. bdg. 26.60 *(978-1-4339-9528-6(X))* Stevens, Gareth Publishing LLLP.

—Drawing Fairies, Mermaids, & Unicorns. 2013. (Learn to Draw Ser.). (ENG., Illus.). 32p. (J). (gr. 2-5). lib. bdg. 26.60 *(978-1-4339-9536-1(0))* Stevens, Gareth Publishing LLLP.

Sautter, A. J. How to Draw Griffins, Unicorns, & Other Mythical Beasts. Howard, Colin et al, illus. 2016. (Drawing Fantasy Creatures Ser.). (ENG.). 32p. (gr. 3-4). lib. bdg. 27.99 *(978-1-4914-8025-0(4),* Edge Bks.) Capstone Press of Coughlan Cos.

Scrace, Carolyn. Drawing Animals. 2016. (Art Works). 32p. (gr. 2-6). 31.35 *(978-1-62588-343-8(9),* Smart Apple Media) Black Rabbit Bks.

—Drawing Dinosaurs & Other Prehistoric Animals. 2016. (Art Works). 32p. (gr. 2-6). 31.35 *(978-1-62588-344-5(7),* Smart Apple Media) Black Rabbit Bks.

—Portraits & Animals. 2015. (How to Art Doodle Ser.). (Illus.). 24p. (gr. 3-6). 28.50 *(978-1-909645-49-3(4))* Book Hse. GBR. Dist: Black Rabbit Bks.

Seal, Daisy, selected by. Cute Animals: Color by Numbers. 2016. (Hobbies & Craft Ser.). (ENG., Illus.). 128p. pap. 15.99 *(978-1-78664-043-7(0),* 9781786640437) Flame Tree Publishing GBR. Dist: Bookmasters Distribution.

Sexton, Brenda. You Can Draw Pets, 1 vol. Sexton, Brenda, illus. 2010. (You Can Draw Ser.). (ENG., Illus.). 24p. (gr. 1-2). lib. bdg. 26.65 *(978-1-4048-6277-7(3))* Picture Window Bks.

Sexton, Brenda & Ho, Jannie. Easy-To-Draw Animals: A Step-By-Step Drawing Book. Sexton, Brenda & Ho, Jannie, illus. 2014. (You Can Draw Ser.). (ENG., Illus.). 64p. (gr. 1-2). pap. 6.95 *(978-1-4795-5511-6(8))* Picture Window Bks.

Silvani, James. Draw-A-Saurus: Everything You Need to Know to Draw Your Favorite Dinosaurs. 2014. (ENG., Illus.). 160p. (gr. 2-5). pap. 18.99 *(978-0-385-34580-4(1),* Watson-Guptill) Potter/TenSpeed/Harmony.

Silver Dolphin en Español Editors. Libro de actividades con plantillas: Disney Animales: Animals Stencil. 2007. (Illus.). 10p. (J). bds. *(978-970-718-435-0(3),* Silver Dolphin en Español) Advanced Marketing, S. de R. L. de C. V.

—Serie Aprendizaje: Let's Draw with Pixar. 2006. (SPA., Illus.). 22p. (J). bds. 16.95 *(978-970-718-320-9(9))* Readerlink Distribution Services, LLC.

Smith, Lucy. How to Draw Horses. Chapman, Chris et al, illus. 2006. (Young Artist Ser.). 32p. (J). (gr. 4-7). pap. 5.99 *(978-0-7945-1368-9(9),* Usborne); pap. 13.99 *(978-1-58086-969-0(6))* EDC Publishing.

Stanley, Robert E., Sr. Northwest Native Arts: Creative Colors 1, 2 vols. 2003. (Northwest Native Arts Ser.). (Illus.). 32p. (J). (gr. 3-18). pap. 6.95 *(978-0-88839-532-0(9))* Hancock Hse. Pubs.

—Northwest Native Arts: Creative Colors 2, 2 vols., Vol. 3. 2003. (North West Native Arts Ser.). (Illus.). 24p. (J). pap. 5.95 *(978-0-88839-533-7(7))* Hancock Hse. Pubs.

Tallarico, Tony & Drawing Staff. Quick Draw Animals. 2011. (Dover How to Draw Ser.). (ENG., Illus.). 64p. (J). (gr. 3-8). pap. 4.99 *(978-0-486-48118-0(2))* Dover Pubns., Inc.

Thomas, Isabel. Hip Hamster Projects. 2015. (Pet Projects Ser.). (ENG., Illus.). 32p. (gr. 3-5). 27.99 *(978-1-4109-8067-0(7),* Snap Bks.) Capstone Press of Coughlan Cos.

Usborne Books Staff, creator. How to Draw Horses Kid Kit. rev. ed. 2006. (Kid Kits Ser.). (Illus.). 32p. (J). (gr. 4). pap. 13.99 *(978-1-58086-970-6(X))* EDC Publishing.

Walter Foster Creative Team. Dogs & Puppies: Step-by-Step Insructions for 25 Different Breeds. Fisher, Diana, illus. 2011. (Learn to Draw Ser.). 32p. (J). (gr. 1-4). 28.50 *(978-1-936309-18-4(1))* Quarto Publishing Group USA.

—Learn to Draw Exotic Animals: Step-By-Step Instructions for More Than 25 Unusual Animals. Cuddy, Robbin, illus. 2016. (Learn to Draw: Expanded Edition Ser.). (ENG.). 64p. (J). (gr. 3-5). 33.32 *(978-1-939581-97-6(4),* Walter Foster Jr) Quarto Publishing Group USA.

—Learn to Draw Zoo Animals: Step-By-Step Instructions for More Than 25 Popular Animals. Cuddy, Robbin, illus. 2016. (Learn to Draw: Expanded Edition Ser.). (ENG.). 64p. (J). (gr. 3-5). lib. bdg. 33.32 *(978-1-939581-99-0(0),* Walter Foster Jr) Quarto Publishing Group USA.

—Pets: Step-by-Step Insructions for 23 Favorite Animals. Mueller, Peter, illus. 2011. (Learn to Draw Ser.). 32p. (J). (gr. 1-4). 28.50 *(978-1-936309-17-7(3))* Quarto Publishing Group USA.

—Sea Creatures: Step-by-Step Insructions for 25 Ocean Animals. Farrell, Russell, illus. 2011. (Learn to Draw Ser.). 32p. (J). (gr. 1-4). 28.50 *(978-1-936309-19-1(X))* Quarto Publishing Group USA.

Walter Foster Creative Team & Legendre, Philippe. Animals Around the World: Learn to Draw More Than 25 Exotic Animals Step by Step! 2014. (I Can Draw Ser.). (ENG., Illus.). 48p. (J). (gr. -1-3). pap. 6.95 *(978-1-60058-438-1(1))* Quarto Publishing Group USA.

Walter Foster Creative Team Staff & Legendre, Philippe. Favorite Pets: Learn to Draw More Than 25 Furry Friends & Cute Companions Step by Step. 2014. (I Can Draw Ser.). (ENG., Illus.). 48p. (J). (gr. -1-3). pap. 6.95 *(978-1-60058-437-4(3))* Quarto Publishing Group USA.

—Sea Creatures & Other Favorite Animals: Learn to Draw More Than 25 Land & Sea Animals Step by Step! 2014. (I Can Draw Ser.). (ENG., Illus.). 48p. (J). (gr. -1-3). pap. 6.95 *(978-1-63470-058-X(X))* Quarto Publishing Group USA.

Watt, Fiona. Animal Fun. 2008. (Preschool Activities Ser.). 23p. (J). spiral bd. 12.99 *(978-0-7945-2049-6(9),* Usborne) EDC Publishing.

—Farm Fun. 2008. (Preschool Activities Ser.). 23p. (J). spiral bd. 12.99 *(978-0-7945-2080-9(4),* Usborne) EDC Publishing.

Weill, Cynthia. Animal Talk. 2017. (First Concepts in Mexican Folk Art Ser.). (ENG.). 32p. (J). (— 1). bds. 9.95 *(978-1-941026-69-4(9))* Cinco Puntos Pr.

—Animal Talk: Mexican Folk Art Animal Sounds in English & Spanish. 2016. (First Concepts in Mexican Folk Art Ser.). (ENG & SPA., Illus.). 32p. (J). (gr. -1-2). 14.95 *(978-1-941026-32-8(X))* Cinco Puntos Pr.

Wild Animals. Date not set. (Illus.). 16p. (J). 5.98 *(978-0-7525-7699-2(2));* 2.98 *(978-0-7525-9763-8(9))* Parragon, Inc.

Winterberg, Jenna. Dolphins, Whales, Fish & More. Fisher, Diana, illus. 2015. (J). *(978-1-939581-34-1(6))* Quarto Publishing Group USA.

Young, Rae. The Ultimate Guide to Drawing Horses, 1 vol. Q2AMedia Services Private Ltd Staff, illus. 2013. (Drawing Horses Ser.). (ENG.). 144p. (gr. 3-4). pap. 14.95 *(978-1-4765-3992-8(8),* Snap Bks.) Capstone Press of Coughlan Cos.

Yuan, Margaret Speaker. Beatrix Potter. 2005. (Who Wrote That? Ser.). (Illus.). 120p. (gr. 6-12). lib. bdg. 35.00 *(978-0-7910-8655-1(0),* Chelsea Hse.) Facts On File, Inc.

Zuffi, Stefano. The Cat in Art. Jones, Simon, tr. 2007. (ENG., Illus.). 360p. (gr. 8-17). 40.00 *(978-0-8109-9328-0(7))* Abrams, Inc.

ANIMATED CARTOONS

see Animated Films

ANIMATED FILMS

Allahverdi, Artin. My Good Friend Walt Disney. 2009. 68p. pap. 11.99 *(978-1-4490-4627-9(4))* AuthorHouse.

Allen, John. Anime & Manga. 2014. (Discovering Art). (ENG., Illus.). 80p. (J). lib. bdg. *(978-1-60152-696-0(2))* ReferencePoint Pr., Inc.

Animation. 2010. (What Can I Do Now? Ser.). 224p. (gr. 6-12). 32.95 *(978-0-8160-8077-9(1),* Ferguson Publishing Co.) Facts On File, Inc.

Apodaca, Blanca. All in a Day's Work: Animator, 1 vol. 2nd rev. ed. 2013. (TIME for KIDS(r) Nonfiction Readers Ser.). (ENG.). 64p. (J). (gr. 5-5). pap. 10.99 *(978-1-4333-4907-2(8))* Teacher Created Materials, Inc.

Bellen-Berthézène, Cyndie. Flipping Out! How to Draw Flip Animation. Steck, Jim, illus. 2005. 48p. (J). *(978-0-439-81335-8(2))* Scholastic, Inc.

Bliss, John. Art That Moves: Animation Around the World. 2011. (Illus.). 32p. (J). *(978-1-4062-1712-4(3))* Heinemann-Raintree.

Bodden, Valerie. The Story of Disney. 2011. (ENG., Illus.). 48p. (J). (gr. 5-17). pap. *(978-1-897563-01-4(9))* Saunders Bk. Co.

Buckley, A. M. Pixar: The Company & Its Founders, 1 vol. 2011. (Technology Pioneers Set 1 Ser.). (ENG., Illus.). 112p. (J). (gr. 6-12). lib. bdg. 35.64 *(978-1-61714-810-1(5))* ABDO Publishing Co.

Careers in Focus: Animation. 2010. (Careers in Focus Ser.). (Illus.). 208p. (J). (gr. 6-12). 32.95 *(978-0-8160-8015-1(1),* Ferguson Publishing Co.) Facts On File, Inc.

Ford, Carin T. Walt Disney: Meet the Cartoonist. 2003. (Meeting Famous People Ser.). (Illus.). 32p. (J). (gr. 1-4). lib. bdg. 23.94 *(978-0-7660-1857-0(1))* Enslow Pubs., Inc.

Gilbert, Sara. Built for Success: the Story of Pixar. 2015. (Built for Success Ser.). (ENG.). 48p. (J). (gr. 5-8). pap. 12.00 *(978-0-89812-983-0(4),* Creative Paperbacks) Creative Co., The.

—The Story of Pixar. 2014. (Illus.). 48p. (J). *(978-1-60818-396-8(3),* Creative Education) Creative Co., The.

Gregory, Josh. Animation. 2014. (ENG., Illus.). 64p. (J). 30.00 *(978-0-531-20613-3(0))* Scholastic Library Publishing.

Hahn, Don. The Alchemy of Animation: Making an Animated Film in the Modern Age. 3rd ed. 2008. (Disney Editions Deluxe (Film) Ser.). (ENG., Illus.). 144p. (YA). (gr. 5-9). pap. 19.99 *(978-1-4231-0476-6(5),* Disney Editions) Disney Pr.

Hamalaine, Karina. Animation. 2017. (True Book — Behind the Scenes Ser.). (ENG.). 48p. (J). pap. 7.95 ***(978-0-531-24147-9(5))***; lib. bdg. 31.00 ***(978-0-531-23504-1(1))*** Scholastic Library Publishing. (Children's Pr.).

Herweck, Diana, et al. Un día de Trabajo: Animado. 2016. (TIME for Kids en Español - Level 5 Ser.). (SPA.). 64p. (gr. 5-5). lib. bdg. 31.99 *(978-1-5157-2950-1(8))* Time for Kids Inc AUS. Dist: Capstone Pub.

Horn, Geoffrey M. Movie Animation. 2006. (Making Movies Ser.). (Illus.). 32p. (gr. 5-8). lib. bdg. 26.00 *(978-0-8368-6837-1(4))* Stevens, Gareth Publishing LLLP.

Jackson, Aurelia. Disney's Pixar(r): How Steve Jobs Changed Hollywood. 2014. (Wizards of Technology Ser.: 10). 64p. (J). (gr. 7-18). 23.95 *(978-1-4222-3180-7(1))* Mason Crest.

Kallen, Stuart. Animation. 2014. (Discovering Art). (ENG., Illus.). 80p. (J). lib. bdg. *(978-1-60152-664-9(4))* ReferencePoint Pr., Inc.

Lenburg, Jeff. Genndy Tartakovsky. 2012. (Legends of Animation Ser.). (Illus.). 120p. (gr. 6-12). 34.95 *(978-1-60413-842-9(4),* Chelsea Hse.) Facts On File, Inc.

—Hayao Miyazaki. 2012. (Legends of Animation Ser.). (Illus.). 120p. (gr. 6-12). 34.95 *(978-1-60413-841-2(6),* Chelsea Hse.) Facts On File, Inc.

—John Lasseter. 2012. (Legends of Animation Ser.). (Illus.). 136p. (gr. 6-12). 34.95 *(978-1-60413-840-5(8),* Chelsea Hse.) Facts On File, Inc.

—Tex Avery. 2011. (Legends of Animation Ser.). (Illus.). 128p. (J). (gr. 6-12). 34.95 *(978-1-60413-835-1(1),* Chelsea Hse.) Facts On File, Inc.

—Walter Lantz. 2012. (Legends of Animation Ser.). (Illus.). 136p. (gr. 6-12). 34.95 *(978-1-60413-839-9(4),* Chelsea Hse.) Facts On File, Inc.

Lenburg, Jeff & Kurtz, Bob. Career Opportunities in Animation. 2011. (Career Opportunities Ser.). 320p. (C). (gr. 9). pap. 18.95 *(978-0-8160-8183-7(2),* Checkmark Bks.); 2nd rev. ed. 49.50 *(978-0-8160-8182-0(4),* Ferguson Publishing Co.) Facts On File, Inc.

Loh-Hagan, Virginia. Sound Effects Artist. 2015. (Illus.). 32p. (J). pap. 14.21 *(978-1-63470-056-6(2))* Cherry Lake Publishing.

Marcovitz, Hal. Anime. 2007. (Eye on Art Ser.). (ENG., Illus.). 104p. (J). (gr. 3-7). lib. bdg. 34.80 *(978-1-59018-995-5(7),* Lucent Bks.) Cengage Gale.

Mullins, Matt. Multimedia Artist & Animator. 2010. (21st Century Skills Library: Cool Careers Ser.). (ENG.). 32p. (gr. 4-8). lib. bdg. 28.50 *(978-1-60279-942-4(3),* 200629) Cherry Lake Publishing.

Norwich, Grace. I Am #11: Walt Disney. 2014. (I Am Ser.: 11). (ENG.). 128p. (J). (gr. 2-5). pap. 5.99 *(978-0-545-62918-8(7),* Scholastic Paperbacks) Scholastic, Inc.

Quan-D'Eramo, Sandra. The 10 Most Amazing Animated Movies. 2007. (J). 14.99 *(978-1-55448-513-0(4))* Scholastic Library Publishing.

Rauf, Don & Vescia, Monique. Cartoon Animator. 2008. (Virtual Apprentice Ser.). (Illus.). 64p. (gr. 4-9). 29.95 *(978-0-8160-6760-2(0),* Ferguson Publishing Co.) Facts On File, Inc.

—Virtual Apprentice: Cartoon Animator. 2009. (Virtual Apprentice Ser.). 64p. (gr. 4-9). pap. 9.95 *(978-0-8160-7892-9(0),* Checkmark Bks.) Facts On File, Inc.

Spence, Kelly. Get into Claymation. 2017. (Get-Into-It Guides). (ENG., Illus.). 32p. (J). (gr. 3-6). pap. ***(978-0-7787-3404-8(8))*** Crabtree Publishing Co.

Trueit, Trudi Strain. Animation. 2008. (21st Century Skills Innovation Library: Innovation in Entertainment Ser.). (ENG., Illus.). 32p. (gr. 4-8). lib. bdg. 28.50 *(978-1-60279-219-7(4),* 200150) Cherry Lake Publishing.

ANIMORPHS (FICTITIOUS CHARACTERS)—FICTION

Applegate, K. A., pseud. Animorphs #7: the Stranger. 2012. (Animorphs Ser.: 7). (ENG.). 176p. (J). (gr. 3-7). pap. 6.99 *(978-0-545-42414-1(3),* Scholastic Paperbacks) Scholastic, Inc.

—The Message. 2011. (Animorphs Ser.: 4). (ENG.). 192p. (J). (gr. 3-7). pap. 6.99 *(978-0-545-29156-9(9),* Scholastic Paperbacks) Scholastic, Inc.

ANNE OF GREEN GABLES (FICTITIOUS CHARACTER)—FICTION

see Shirley, Anne (Fictitious Character)—Fiction

ANNING, MARY, 1799-1847

Barnham, Kay. Mary Anning. 2017. (History VIPs Ser.). (ENG., Illus.). 32p. (J). (gr. 2-4). pap. 11.99 *(978-0-7502-9914-5(2),* Wayland) Hachette Children's Group GBR. Dist: Hachette Bk. Group.

Collins Big Cat Staff. Fossil Hunter, Bd. 17. 2017. (ENG., Illus.). 56p. (J). pap. 8.95 ***(978-0-00-820893-6(X))*** HarperCollins Pubs. Ltd. GBR. Dist: Independent Pubs. Group.

Goodhue, Thomas W. Curious Bones: Mary Anning & the Birth of Paleontology. 2004. (Profiles in Science Ser.). (Illus.). 112p. (YA). (gr. 6-12). lib. bdg. 23.95 *(978-1-883846-93-0(5),* First Biographies) Reynolds, Morgan Inc.

Pearson, Debora. Mary Anning: the Girl Who Cracked Open the World (Paperback) Copyright 2016. 2015. (ENG.). (gr. k-6). pap. 6.97 *(978-0-328-83292-7(8),* Scott Foresman) Addison Wesley Schl.

Snedden, Robert. Mary Anning: Fossil Hunter. 2015. (Superheroes of Science Ser.). (ENG., Illus.). 48p. (J). (gr. 6-6). pap. 14.05 *(978-1-4824-3145-2(9))* Stevens, Gareth Publishing LLLP.

Walker, Sally M. Mary Anning: Fossil Hunter. Saroff, Phyllis V., illus. 2007. (On My Own Biographies Ser.). 48p. (J). (gr. 2-5). per. 6.95 *(978-1-57505-457-5(4),* First Avenue Editions) Lerner Publishing Group.

ANNIVERSARIES

see Holidays

ANNULMENT OF MARRIAGE

see Divorce

ANOREXIA NERVOSA

see Eating Disorders

ANSWERS TO QUESTIONS

see Questions and Answers

ANT

see Ants

ANTARCTIC REGIONS

see Antarctica

ANTARCTICA

see also Scientific Expeditions; South Pole

Aloian, Molly & Kalman, Bobbie. The Antarctic Habitat. 2006. (Introducing Habitats Ser.). (ENG., Illus.). 32p. (J). (gr. -1-3). pap. *(978-0-7787-2984-6(2));* lib. bdg. *(978-0-7787-2956-3(7))* Crabtree Publishing Co.

—El Hábitat de la Antárdia. 2007. (Introduction a Los Habitats Ser.). (SPA & ENG., Illus.). 32p. (J). (gr. k-3). lib. bdg. *(978-0-7787-8332-9(4))* Crabtree Publishing Co.

—El Habitat de la Antardia. rev. ed. 2007. (Introduction a Los Habitats Ser.). (SPA & ENG., Illus.). 32p. (J). (gr. k-3). pap. *(978-0-7787-8356-5(1))* Crabtree Publishing Co.

—El Hábitat de la Antártida. 2007. (Libro de Bobbie Kalman Ser.). (SPA., Illus.). 32p. (J). *(978-1-4287-3159-2(8))* Crabtree Publishing Co.

Antarctica (30), Vol. 30. (Early Intervention Levels Ser.). 5.31 *(978-0-7362-0652-5(3))* CENGAGE Learning.

Arctic & Antarctic Habitats. 2013. (Discovery Education: Habitats Ser.). 32p. (J). (gr. 3-6). pap. 60.00 *(978-1-4777-1482-9(0),* PowerKids Pr.) Rosen Publishing Group, Inc., The.

Aspen-Baxter, Linda. Antarctica. (J). 2016. pap. ***(978-1-4896-5741-1(X))*** 2012. *(978-1-61913-449-2(7))* 2012. pap. *(978-1-61913-450-8(0))* 2005. (Illus.). 32p. (gr. 4-6). lib. bdg. 26.00 *(978-1-59036-317-1(5))* Weigl Pubs., Inc.

Bailey, Diane. Arctic Culture: The People of the Ice. 2017. (Exploring the Polar Regions Today Ser.: Vol. 8). (ENG.). (YA). (gr. 7-12). 23.95 ***(978-1-4222-3866-0(0))*** Mason Crest.

Baker, Stuart. In the Antarctic. 2009. (Climate Change Ser.). 32p. (gr. 4). 28.50 *(978-0-7614-4438-1(6))* Marshall Cavendish GBR. Dist: Marshall Cavendish Corp.

Blake, Kevin. Lost in the Antarctic. 2014. (Stranded! Ser.). (ENG.). 32p. (J). (gr. 2-7). lib. bdg. 26.60 *(978-1-62724-289-9(9))* Bearport Publishing Co., Inc.

Bledsoe, Lucy Jane. How to Survive in Antarctica. 2006. (ENG., Illus.). 96p. (J). (gr. 5-9). 17.95 *(978-0-8234-1890-9(1))* Holiday Hse., Inc.

Bluthenthal, Todd. The South Pole. 2017. (Where on Earth? Mapping Parts of the World Ser.). 24p. (J). (gr. 1-2). pap. 8.15 ***(978-1-4824-6433-7(0))***; pap. 48.90 ***(978-1-4824-6434-4(9))*** Stevens, Gareth Publishing LLLP.

Brasch, Nicolas. Ernest Shackleton's Antarctic Expedition. 2013. (Discovery Education: Sensational True Stories Ser.). (ENG., Illus.). 32p. (J). (gr. 3-6). pap. 10.00 *(978-1-4777-0111-9(7));* lib. bdg. 25.25 *(978-1-4777-0063-1(3))* Rosen Publishing Group, Inc., The. (PowerKids Pr.).

Britton, Arthur K. Life at a Polar Research Station. 2013. (Extreme Jobs in Extreme Places Ser.). (Illus.). 32p. (J). (gr. 3-6). pap. 10.50 *(978-1-4339-8483-9(0))* Stevens, Gareth Publishing LLLP.

Buckley, James, Jr. Who Was Ernest Shackleton? Hergenrother, Max, illus. 2013. (Who Was? Ser.). (ENG.). 112p. (J). (gr. 3-7). 5.99 *(978-0-448-47931-6(1),* Grosset & Dunlap) Penguin Young Readers Group.

Buckley, James. Who Was Ernest Shackleton? 2013. (Who Was... ? Ser.). lib. bdg. 16.00 *(978-0-606-34162-2(5),* Turtleback) Turtleback Bks.

Burleigh, Robert. Black Whiteness: Admiral Byrd Alone in the Antarctic. Krudop, Walter Lyon, illus. 2011. (ENG.). 40p. (J). (gr. 2-5). pap. 19.99 *(978-1-4424-5334-0(6),* Atheneum Bks. for Young Readers) Simon & Schuster Children's Publishing.

Chambers, Mary & Meinking, Mary. Who Counts the Penguins? Working in Antarctica. 2010. (Wild Work Ser.). (ENG.). 32p. (gr. 1-2). 29.99 *(978-1-4109-3855-8(7),* Read Me!) Heinemann-Raintree.

Currie, Stephen. Antarctica. 2003. (Exploration & Discovery Ser.). (ENG., Illus.). 112p. (J). (gr. 7-10). 30.85 *(978-1-59018-495-0(5),* Lucent Bks.) Cengage Gale.

Darian-Smith, Kate. Australia, Antarctica, & the Pacific. 2005. (Continents of the World Ser.). 64p. (gr. 5-12). pap. 14.05 *(978-0-8368-5919-5(7));* (Illus.). lib. bdg. 34.00 *(978-0-8368-5912-6(X))* Stevens, Gareth Publishing LLLP. (Gareth Stevens Secondary Library).

Davis, Linda. Sir Ernest Shackleton. 2009. (Great Explorers Ser.). (Illus.). 144p. (gr. 6-12). 30.00 *(978-1-60413-421-6(6),* Chelsea Hse.) Facts On File, Inc.

Dickmann, Nancy. The South Pole, 1 vol. 2012. (Explorer Tales Ser.). (ENG.). 32p. (gr. 1-3). 29.99 *(978-1-4109-4785-7(8));* pap. 8.29 *(978-1-4109-4792-5(0))* Heinemann-Raintree. (Read Me!).

Discovering Antarctica. 2005. (Discovering Antarctica Ser.). (Illus.). 32p. (gr. 4-6). 112.00 *(978-0-7910-7057-4(3))* Facts On File, Inc.

Donaldson, Madeline. Antarctica. 2005. (Pull Ahead Bks.). (Illus.). 32p. (gr. k-3). (J). lib. bdg. 22.60 *(978-0-8225-4724-2(4));* (ENG., pap. 7.95 *(978-0-8225-2490-8(2),* Lerner Pubns.) Lerner Publishing Group.

Dorling Kindersley Publishing Staff. DK Adventures: Antarctic Expedition. 2015. (DK Adventures Ser.). (ENG., Illus.). 128p. (J). (gr. 3-7). 16.99 *(978-1-4654-3862-1(9),* DK Children) Dorling Kindersley Publishing, Inc.

Dowdeswell, Evelyn, et al. Scott of the Antarctic. 2012. (ENG., Illus.). 32p. (gr. 1-3). 26.65 *(978-1-4329-6890-8(4));* pap. 6.49 *(978-1-4329-6891-5(2))* Heinemann-Raintree. (Heinemann First Library).

Dumbleton, Mike. Meet Douglas Mawson. Green, Snip, illus. 2015. (Meet... Ser.). (ENG.). 36p. (J). (gr. k-3). 14.99 *(978-0-85798-196-7(X))* Random Hse. Australia AUS. Dist: Independent Pubs. Group.

Dunphy, Madeleine. Here Is Antarctica. Leonard, Tom, illus. 2008. (Web of Life Ser.). (ENG.). 32p. (J). (gr. -1-3). 16.95 *(978-0-9777539-4-9(8))* Web of Life Children's Bks.

Feldman, Thea & Steele, Philip. Arctic & Antarctic. 2013. (Kingfisher Readers Ser.). (ENG., Illus.). 32p. (J). (gr. k-3). 12.99 *(978-0-7534-7092-3(6),* 9780753470923); pap. 3.99 *(978-0-7534-7093-0(4),* 9780753470930) Roaring Brook Pr. (Kingfisher).

Friedman, Mel. Antarctica. (True Book(tm), A — Continents Ser.). (ENG., 48p. (J). 2008. Illus.). 32p. (gr. 2-5). 31.00 *(978-0-531-16864-6(6))* 2009. pap. 6.95 *(978-0-531-21826-6(0),* Children's Pr.) Scholastic Library Publishing.

Ganeri, Anita. Endurance: Shackleton's Incredible Antarctic Expedition. 2016. (ENG., Illus.). 48p. (J). (gr. 4-6). pap. 12.99 *(978-0-7502-9709-7(3),* Wayland) Hachette Children's Group GBR. Dist: Hachette Bk. Group.

—Introducing Antarctica, 1 vol. 2013. (Introducing Continents Ser.). (ENG.). 32p. (gr. 1-3). 27.32 *(978-1-4329-8040-5(8));* pap. 8.95 *(978-1-4329-8048-1(3))* Heinemann-Raintree. (Heinemann First Library).

Gigliotti, Jim. Antarctica & the Arctic: Facts, Figures, & Stories. 2017. (Exploring the Polar Regions Today Ser.: Vol. 8). (ENG.). (YA). (gr. 7-12). 23.95 ***(978-1-4222-3865-3(2))*** Mason Crest.

Goldsworthy, Steve. Antarctica. 2014. (J). *(978-1-4896-0938-0(5))* Weigl Pubs., Inc.

Gonzales, Doreen. The Stormy Southern Ocean. 2013. (Our Earth's Oceans Ser.). 48p. (J). (gr. 3-4). pap. 8.95 *(978-1-4644-0149-7(7),* Enslow Elementary); 25.27 *(978-0-7660-4091-5(7))* Enslow Pubs., Inc.

Graham, Amy. Discovering Antarctica's Land, People, & Wildlife: A MyReportLinks. com Book. 2004. (Continents of the World Ser.). (Illus.). 48p. (J). lib. bdg. 26.60 *(978-0-7660-5205-5(2),* MyReportLinks.com Bks.) Enslow Pubs., Inc.

Green, Jen. You Wouldn't Want to Be a Polar Explorer! (Revised Edition) Antram, David, illus. 2017. (You Wouldn't Want to... Adventurers & Explorers Ser.). (ENG.). 40p. (J). pap. 9.95 *(978-0-531-23154-8(2),* Children's Pr.) Scholastic Library Publishing.

Grill, William, illus. Shackleton's Journey. 2014. (ENG.). 80p. (J). (gr. -1-2). 24.00 *(978-1-909263-10-9(9))* Flying Eye Bks. GBR. Dist: Consortium Bk. Sales & Distribution.

Grochowicz, Joanna. Into the White: Scott's Antarctic Odyssey. 2017. (ENG.). 288p. (J). (gr. 5-9). pap. 12.99 ***(978-1-76029-365-9(2))*** Allen & Unwin AUS. Dist: Independent Pubs. Group.

Hanel, Rachael. Can You Survive Antarctica? An Interactive Survival Adventure, 1 vol. 2011. (You Choose: Survival Ser.).

AB

(ENG.). 112p. (gr. 3-4). pap. 6.95 (978-1-4296-7345-7(1)); pap. 41.70 (978-1-4296-7346-4(X)); lib. bdg. 31.99 (978-1-4296-6589-6(0)) Capstone Press of Coughlan Cos. (You Choose Bks.).

Heller, Esther Susan. Menorah under the Sea. Ginsburg, David, photos by. 2009. (Hanukkah Ser.). (Illus.). 32p. (J). (gr. k-2). 17.95 (978-0-8225-7386-9(5), Kar-Ben Publishing) Lerner Publishing Group.

—Menorah under the Sea. 2009. (Hanukkah Ser.). (ENG.). 32p. (J). (gr. k-3). pap. 7.95 (978-0-8225-7390-6(3), Kar-Ben Publishing) Lerner Publishing Group.

Hinds, Maurene J. Antarctica, 1 vol. 2013. (Continents Ser.). (ENG., Illus.). 48p. (J). (gr. 3-6). lib. bdg. 32.79 (978-1-61783-929-0(9)) ABDO Publishing Co.

—Antarctica Paperback. 2013. (Continents Ser.). (ENG., Illus.). 48p. (J). pap. 15.64 (978-1-61783-994-8(9), Core Library) ABDO Publishing Co.

Hirsch, Rebecca E. & Cottle, John. Antarctica. 2012. (ENG.). 32p. (J). lib. bdg. 23.00 (978-0-531-28976-1(1)); (gr. -1-1). pap. 5.95 (978-0-531-29276-1(2)) Scholastic Library Publishing.

Hoena, Blake A. & Hoena, B. A. Shackleton & the Lost Antarctic Expedition, 1 vol. Hoover, Dave et al, illus. 2006. (Disasters in History Ser.). (ENG.). 32p. (gr. 3-4). 30.65 (978-0-7368-5482-5(7), Graphic Library) Capstone Press of Coughlan Cos.

Hovanec, Erin M. An Online Visit to Antarctica. 2009. (Internet Field Trips Ser.). 24p. (gr. 3-3). 45.00 (978-1-61513-602-5(9), PowerKids Pr.) Rosen Publishing Group, Inc., The.

Kalman, Bobbie & Aloian, Molly. Polar Oceans. 2003. (Living Ocean Ser.). (ENG., Illus.). 32p. (J). (gr. 2-9). lib. bdg. (978-0-7787-1297-8(4)) Crabtree Publishing Co.

Kalman, Bobbie & Sjonger, Rebecca. Explora la Antártida. 2007. (Explora Los Continentes Ser.). (SPA., Illus.). 32p. (J). (gr. 4-7). pap. (978-0-7787-8296-4(4)) Crabtree Publishing Co.

—Explore Antarctica. rev. ed. 2007. (Explore the Continents Ser.). (ENG., Illus.). 32p. (J). (gr. -1-3). pap. (978-0-7787-3085-9(9)) Crabtree Publishing Co.

Karner, Julie. Roald Amundsen: The Conquest of the South Pole. 2006. (In the Footsteps of Explorers Ser.). (ENG., Illus.). 32p. (J). (gr. 3-7). lib. bdg. (978-0-7787-2432-2(8)) Crabtree Publishing Co.

Kirkwood, Roger. Antarctica. 2008. (ENG.). 48p. 14.95 (978-1-921073-36-6(5)) New Holland Pubs. Pty, Ltd. AUS. Dist: Midpoint Trade Bks., Inc.

Kostyal, K. M. Trial by Ice: A Photobiography of Sir Ernest Shackleton. 2006. (Illus.). 64p. pap. 7.99 (978-0-15-356619-6(1)) Houghton Mifflin Harcourt School Pubs.

Latham, Irene. When the Sun Shines on Antarctica: And Other Poems about the Frozen Continent. Wadham, Anna, illus. 2016. (ENG.). 32p. (gr. 3-6). (J). 19.99 (978-1-4677-5216-9(9)); 30.65 (978-1-4677-9729-0(4), Millbrook Pr.) Lerner Publishing Group.

Latta, Sara L. Ice Scientist: Careers in the Frozen Antarctic. 2009. (Wild Science Careers Ser.). (Illus.). 128p. (J). (gr. 5-9). lib. bdg. 33.27 (978-0-7660-3048-0(2)) Enslow Pubs., Inc.

L'Heureux, J. J. Good Day Book. 2006. spiral bd. (978-0-9785892-0-2(3)) BrainStream.

Llanas, Sheila Griffin. Who Reached the South Pole First? (Race for History Ser.). (ENG.). 32p. (gr. 3-4). 2011. pap. 47.70 (978-1-4296-6413-4(4)) 2010. lib. bdg. 27.32 (978-1-4296-3344-4(1)) Capstone Press of Coughlan Cos. (Fact Finders).

Mahoney, Emily. Antarctic Researchers, 01 vols., 1. 2016. (Out of the Lab: Extreme Jobs in Science Ser.). (ENG., Illus.). 32p. (J). pap. 10.00 (978-1-5081-4505-9(9), PowerKids Pr.) Rosen Publishing Group, Inc., The.

Mapping Antarctica. 2013. (Mapping the World Ser.). 24p. (J). (gr. 2-5). pap. 48.90 (978-1-4339-9096-0(2)) Stevens, Gareth Publishing LLLP.

Mara, Wil. Antarctica. 2017. (Enchantment of the World(tm) Ser.). (ENG.). 144p. (J). lib. bdg. 40.00 (978-0-531-22082-5(6), Children's Pr.) Scholastic Library Publishing.

Marsico, Katie. The Hottest & the Coldest. 2015. (True Book(tm), a — Extreme Places Ser.). (ENG., Illus.). 48p. (J). lib. bdg. 31.00 (978-0-531-21844-0(9), Children's Pr.) Scholastic Library Publishing.

Mason, Theodore. The South Pole Ponies. 2007. 232p. (gr. 7). per. 18.00 (978-1-59048-251-3(4)) Long Riders' Guild Pr., The.

Matsen, Bradford. An Extreme Dive under the Antarctic Ice. 2003. (Incredible Deep-Sea Adventures Ser.). (Illus.). 48p. (J). lib. bdg. 25.27 (978-0-7660-2190-7(4)) Enslow Pubs., Inc.

Mattern, Joanne. Antarctica: World's Biggest Glacier. 2009. (Nature's Greatest Hits Ser.). 24p. (gr. 2-2). 42.50 (978-1-61514-838-7(8), PowerKids Pr.) Rosen Publishing Group, Inc., The.

—Antartida: El glaciar más grande del mundo (Antarctica: World's Biggest Glacier) 2009. (Maravillas naturales (Natures Greatest Hits) Ser.). 24p. (gr. 2-2). 42.50 (978-1-61514-360-3(2), Editorial Buenas Letras) Rosen Publishing Group, Inc., The.

McAllan, Kate. Arctic & Antarctic Habitats. 2013. (Discovery Education: Habitats Ser.). 32p. (J). (gr. 3-6). 25.25 (978-1-4777-1323-5(9)); pap. 10.00 (978-1-4777-1481-2(2)) Rosen Publishing Group, Inc., The. (PowerKids Pr.).

McNeil, Niki, et al. Antarctica. 2007. (In the Hands of a Child: Project Pack Continent Study Ser.). (Illus.). 82p. spiral bd. 21.00 (978-1-60308-057-6(0)) In the Hands of a Child.

Miller, Sara Swan. Emperor Penguins of the Antarctic. 2009. (Brrr! Polar Animals Ser.). (Illus.). 24p. (J). (gr. k-5). pap. 8.25 (978-1-4358-3146-9(2), 1291788, PowerKids Pr.); 24p. (gr. 2-3). 42.50 (978-1-61511-748-2(2), PowerKids Pr.); (YA). (gr. k-3). lib. bdg. 22.60 (978-1-4358-2742-4(2)) Rosen Publishing Group, Inc., The.

—Seals of the Antarctic. 2009. (Brrr! Polar Animals Ser.). 24p. (Illus.). (J). (gr. k-5). pap. 8.25 (978-1-4358-3149-0(7)); (gr. 2-3). 42.50 (978-1-61511-754-3(7)) Rosen Publishing Group, Inc., The. (PowerKids Pr.).

Nelson, John. Polar Ice Caps in Danger: Expedition to Antarctica. 2008. (Jr. Graphic Environmental Dangers Ser.). (ENG.). 24p. (J). 47.90 (978-1-61532-097-4(0), PowerKids Pr.) Rosen Publishing Group, Inc., The.

Oachs, Emily Rose. Antarctica. (Antarctica Ser.). 24p. (J). (gr. k-3). 2017. pap. 6.99 **(978-1-61891-255-8(0))** 2016. (ENG., Illus.). lib. bdg. 25.95 (978-1-62617-324-8(9)) Bellwether Media. (Blastoff! Readers).

Oachs, Emily Rose. Southern Ocean. 2016. (Discover the Oceans Ser.). (ENG., Illus.). 24p. (J). (gr. k-3). lib. bdg. 25.95 (978-1-62617-334-7(6), Blastoff! Readers) Bellwether Media.

Osborne, Mary Pope & Boyce, Natalie Pope. Penguins & Antarctica: A Nonfiction Companion to Eve of the Emperor Penguin. Murdocca, Sal, illus. 2008. (Magic Tree House - Fact Tracker Ser.: 18). (ENG.). 128p. (J). (gr. 2-5). 6.99 (978-0-375-84664-9(6), Random Hse. Bks. for Young Readers) Random Hse. Children's Bks.

Petersen, Christine. Learning about Antarctica. 2015. (ENG., Illus.). 40p. (J). (gr. 3-5). pap. 9.99 (978-1-4677-8345-3(5)) Lerner Publishing Group.

Prokos, Anna. Ice Queen: Exploring Icebergs & Glaciers. Tablason, Jamie, illus. 2017. (Imagine That! Ser.). (ENG.). 32p. (J). (gr. 2-4). lib. bdg. 26.65 (978-1-63440-149-4(2)); 39.99 **(978-1-63440-161-6(1))** Red Chair Pr.

Rae, Rowena. Southern Ocean. 2016. (J). (978-1-4896-4741-2(4)) Weigl Pubs., Inc.

Riddle, John. Robert F. Scott: British Explorer of the South Pole. 2013. (People of Importance Ser.: 21). (Illus.). 32p. (J). (gr. 4-18). 19.95 (978-1-4222-2855-5(X)) Mason Crest.

Rockett, Paul. Mapping Australia & Oceania, & Antarctica. 2016. (Illus.). 32p. (J). (978-0-7787-2614-2(2)) Crabtree Publishing Co.

Roumanis, Alexis. Antarctica. 2014. (Illus.). 24p. (J). (978-1-4896-3026-1(0)) Weigl Pubs., Inc.

Roza, Greg. Mapping Antarctica. 2013. 24p. (J). (gr. 2-5). 22.60 (978-1-4339-9094-6(6)); pap. 8.15 (978-1-4339-9095-3(4)) Stevens, Gareth Publishing LLLP.

Sanford, Candace. Captain Nathaniel Brown Palmer. Scala, Susan, illus. 2007. 96p. (YA). pap. 14.95 (978-0-9773725-9-1(6)) Flat Hammock Pr.

Sayre, April Pulley. Hooray for Antarctica! 2003. 32p. (J). (gr. 2-5). pap. 7.95 (978-0-7613-1992-4(1)); (Our Amazing Continents Ser.: 4). (Illus.). lib. bdg. 21.90 (978-0-7613-2152-1(7)) Lerner Publishing Group. (Millbrook Pr.).

Scott, Jonathan & Scott, Angela. Antarctica: Land of the Penguins. 2005. (Collins Big Cat Ser.). (ENG., Illus.). 32p. (J). (gr. 1-3). pap. 7.99 (978-0-00-718640-2(1)) HarperCollins Pubs. Ltd. GBR. Dist: Independent Pubs. Group.

Seiple, Samantha. Byrd & Igloo: A Polar Adventure. 2013. (ENG.). 192p. (J). (gr. 3-7). 18.99 (978-0-545-56276-8(7), Scholastic Pr.) Scholastic, Inc.

Sisk, Maeve T. Mount Terror. 2014. (Scariest Places on Earth Ser.). 24p. (J). (gr. 2-5). 22.60 (978-1-4824-1156-0(3)) Stevens, Gareth Publishing LLLP.

Sjonger, Rebecca. L'Antarctique. 2012. (FRE.). 32p. (J). pap. 9.95 (978-2-89579-456-1(1)) Bayard Canada CAN. Dist: Crabtree Publishing Co.

Smith, Michael. Shackleton - the Boss: The Remarkable Adventures of Ernest Shackleton. Brady, Annie, illus. 2nd rev. ed. 2010. (ENG.). 128p. (J). pap. 15.95 (978-1-905172-27-6(3)) Collins Pr., The IRL. Dist: Dufour Editions, Inc.

Spilsbury, Louise & Spilsbury, Richard. At the Poles. 2016. (Science on Patrol Ser.). 00048p. (J). pap. 14.05 **(978-1-4824-5968-5(X))** Stevens, Gareth Publishing LLLP.

Tulloch, Coral. Antarctica: The Heart of the World. 2006. (ENG., Illus.). 48p. (J). (gr. 3-7). 17.95 (978-1-59270-054-7(3)) Enchanted Lion Bks., LLC.

Tylers, Michael. Predators of South America & Antarctica. 2015. (J). lib. bdg. (978-1-62713-550-4(2)) Cavendish Square Publishing.

Vierow, Wendy. Antarctica. (Atlas of the Seven Continents Ser.). 24p. (gr. 3-3). 2009. 42.50 (978-1-61511-477-1(7), PowerKids Pr.) 2004. (Illus.). (YA). lib. bdg. 22.60 (978-0-8239-6688-2(7)) Rosen Publishing Group, Inc., The.

Walker, Sally M. Frozen Secrets: Antarctica Revealed. 2010. (Exceptional Social Studies Titles for Intermediate Grades). (ENG.). 104p. (gr. 4-8). lib. bdg. 20.95 (978-1-58013-607-5(9)) Lerner Publishing Group.

Waxman, Malcolm & Porter, Malcolm. Atlas of South America & Antarctica. 2009. (Atlases of the World Ser.). (Illus.). 48p. (YA). (gr. 5-8). 29.25 (978-1-4358-8459-5(0), Rosen Reference) Rosen Publishing Group, Inc., The.

World Book, Inc Staff, contrib. by. Icy Worlds. 2011. (J). (978-0-7166-1788-4(9)) World Bk., Inc.

Wynne, Patricia J. & MacPhee, Ross. Race to the South Pole Coloring Book. 2010. (Dover History Coloring Book Ser.). (ENG.). 32p. (gr. 3-8). pap. 3.99 (978-0-486-47668-1(5)) Dover Pubns., Inc.

ANTARCTICA—FICTION

Antarctica: The Last Frontier. 2005. (J). audio, cd-rom 24.95 (978-0-9771381-9-7(4)) Williams, Geoffrey T.

Bailey, Ella, illus. One Day in Antarctica. 2016. (One Day on Our Blue Planet Ser.). (ENG.). 32p. (J). (gr. -1-2). 16.95 (978-1-909263-67-3(2)) Flying Eye Bks. GBR. Dist: Consortium Bk. Sales & Distribution.

Barell, John. Surviving Erebus: An Antarctic Adventure Onboard Her Majesty's Ships Erebus & Terror. 2008. (YA). pap. (978-0-88092-703-1(8)); lib. bdg. (978-0-88092-702-4(X)) Royal Fireworks Publishing Co.

Bart, Kathleen. Town Teddy & Country Bear Go Global. Bart, Kathleen, illus. 2011. (Illus.). (J). (gr. k-3). 16.95 (978-1-932485-60-8(0)) Reverie Publishing Co.

Bowen, Carl & Fuentes, Benny. Phantom Sun, 1 vol. Tortosa, Wilson, illus. 2014. (Shadow Squadron Ser.). (ENG.). 112p. (gr. 4-8). 26.65 (978-1-4342-6399-5(1)) Stone Arch Bks.

Creek, Silent. All the Ice of Afric. 2009. 160p. 22.95 (978-1-4401-2118-0(4)) iUniverse, Inc.

Edquist, Patrick. Zombie Penguins of the Antarctic. 2011. 40p. pap. 16.99 (978-1-4567-6291-9(5)) AuthorHouse.

Goldfrap, John Henry. The Boy Aviators' Polar Dash: Or Facing Death in the Antarctic. 2007. (ENG.). 180p. pap. 19.99 (978-1-4264-5072-3(9)); 200p. pap. 21.99 (978-1-4264-5373-1(6)) Creative Media Partners, LLC.

Greenberg, Nicki. The Naughtiest Reindeer Goes South. 2017. (Naughtiest Reindeer Ser.: 3). (ENG.). 32p. (J). (gr. -1-1). 12.99 **(978-1-76029-311-6(3))** Allen & Unwin AUS. Dist: Independent Pubs. Group.

Helget, Nicole. Wonder at the Edge of the World. 2017. (ENG., Illus.). 400p. (J). (gr. 3-7). pap. 7.99 (978-0-316-24508-1(9)) Little, Brown Bks. for Young Readers.

Hendry, Frances. Atlantis. l.t. ed. 2007. 228p. per. (978-1-905665-20-4(2)) Pollinger In Print.

Hooper, Meredith. Tom Crean's Rabbit: A True Story from Scott's Last Voyage. Kitchen, Bert, illus. 2005. (ENG.). 32p. (J). (gr. -1-3). pap. 9.99 (978-1-84507-393-0(2), Frances Lincoln) Quarto Publishing Group UK GBR. Dist: Hachette Bk. Group.

Kurtz, Chris. The Adventures of a South Pole Pig: A Novel of Snow & Courage. (ENG., Illus.). 288p. (J). (gr. 5-7). 2015. pap. 7.99 (978-0-544-54070-5(0), HMH Books For Young Readers) 2013. 16.99 (978-0-547-63455-5(2)) Houghton Mifflin Harcourt Publishing Co.

Lawrence, Iain. The Winter Pony. 2012. (ENG., Illus.). 256p. (J). (gr. 4-7). 7.99 (978-0-440-23972-7(9), Yearling) Random Hse. Children's Bks.

Leicht, Martin & Neal, Isla. A Stranger Thing. 2013. (Ever-Expanding Universe Ser.: 2). (ENG., Illus.). 288p. (YA). (gr. 9). 17.99 (978-1-4424-2963-5(1), Simon & Schuster Bks. For Young Readers) Simon & Schuster Bks. For Young Readers.

L'Engle, Madeleine. Troubling a Star. 2008. (Austin Family Ser.: 5). (ENG.). 336p. (J). (gr. 6-12). pap. 10.99 (978-0-312-37934-6(X), 9780312379346) Square Fish.

Lester, Alison. Sophie Scott Goes South. 2013. (ENG., Illus.). 40p. (J). (gr. 1-4). 17.99 (978-0-544-08895-5(6)) Houghton Mifflin Harcourt Publishing Co.

London, Jonathan. Little Penguin: The Emperor of Antarctica, 0 vols. Olson, Julie, illus. 2011. (ENG.). 36p. (J). (gr. -1-3). 17.99 (978-0-7614-5954-5(5), 9780761459545, Amazon Children's Publishing) Amazon Publishing.

Lumry, Amanda & Hurwitz, Laura. South Pole Penguins. 2007. (Adventures of Riley Ser.). (Illus.). 36p. (J). (gr. -1-3). 15.95 (978-0-9748411-5-1(3)); lib. bdg. 18.95 (978-0-9748411-8-2(8)) Eaglemont Pr.

McCaughrean, Geraldine. The White Darkness. (YA). 2008. (ENG.). 400p. (gr. 8). pap. 9.99 (978-0-06-089037-7(1)) 2007. 373p. (gr. 7-12). 18.89 (978-0-06-089036-0(3)) HarperCollins Pubs. (HarperTeen).

McFarlane, Susannah. Hot & Cold: EJ12 Girl Hero. 2015. 126p. (J). pap. (978-1-61067-381-5(6)) Kane Miller.

Mitcham Davis, Zipporah. The Fox & Emily's Long Migration. 2008. 28p. pap. 13.99 (978-1-4389-0326-2(X)) AuthorHouse.

Nye, Bill & Mone, Gregory. Jack & the Geniuses: At the Bottom of the World. Iluzada, Nicholas, illus. 2017. (ENG.). 256p. (J). (gr. 3-7). 13.95 (978-1-4197-2303-2(0), Amulet Bks.) Abrams, Inc.

Osborne, Mary Pope. Eve of the Emperor Penguin. Murdocca, Sal, illus. (Magic Tree House Merlin Mission Ser.: No. 12). (ENG.). (J). (gr. 2-5). 2009. 144p. 5.99 (978-0-375-83734-0(5)) 2008. 128p. 11.99 (978-0-375-83733-3(7)) Random Hse. Children's Bks. (Random Hse. Bks. for Young Readers).

Patterson, James. The Final Warning. 2008. (Maximum Ride Ser.: 4). (ENG.). 304p. (YA). (gr. 5-17). pap. 10.00 (978-0-316-00287-5(9), Jimmy Patterson) Little Brown & Co.

—The Final Warning. l.t. ed. 2009. (Maximum Ride Ser.: No. 4). 420p. (YA). 23.95 (978-1-4104-1626-1(7)) Thorndike Pr.

Ripley's Believe It or Not Editors & Ripley's Believe It Or Not! Staff. Sub-Zero Survival. 2010. (Rbi Ser.: 6). (ENG.). 128p. (J). pap. 4.99 (978-1-893951-57-0(X)) Ripley Entertainment, Inc.

Rockwood, Roy. Under the Ocean to the South Pole. 2007. 120p. per. (978-1-4068-3972-2(8)) Echo Library.

—Under the Ocean to the South Pole. 2009. 152p. 24.95 (978-1-60664-626-7(5)); pap. 12.95 (978-1-60664-365-5(7)) Rodgers, Alan Bks.

—Under the Ocean to the South Pole or the Strange Cruise of the Submarine Wonder. 2007. 180p. 95.99 (978-1-4280-7589-4(5)); per. 89.99 (978-1-4280-7588-7(7)) IndyPublish.com.

Sansone, V. K. Pandora's Incredible Journey. 2009. 32p. pap. 8.98 (978-0-557-07374-0(X)) Lulu Pr., Inc.

Viva, Frank. A Trip to the Bottom of the World with Mouse. Viva, Frank, illus. 2012. (ENG., Illus.). 32p. (J). (gr. -1-k). 12.95 (978-1-935179-19-1(5)) TOON Books / RAW Junior, LLC.

Wilson, Karma. Where Is Home, Little Pip? Chapman, Jane, illus. 2008. (ENG.). 40p. (J). (gr. -1-3). 17.99 (978-0-689-85983-0(X), McElderry, Margaret K. Bks.) McElderry, Margaret K. Bks.

Yomtov, Nelson. Trapped in Antarctica! Nickolas Flux & the Shackleton Expedition. Simmons, Mark, illus. 2015. (Nickolas Flux History Chronicles Ser.). (ENG.). 32p. (gr. 3-4). lib. bdg. 30.65 (978-1-4914-2069-0(3), Graphic Library) Capstone Press of Coughlan Cos.

Young, Louise. Penguin Comes Home. Elmore, Larry, illus. 2005. (Soundprints' Amazing Animal Adventures! Ser.). (ENG.). 32p. (J). (gr. -1-2). 9.95 (978-1-59249-329-6(7), PS7158) Soundprints.

Young, Louise O. Penguin Comes Home. Elmore, Larry, illus. (Amazing Animal Adventures Ser.). (ENG.). 36p. (J). (gr. -1-2). 2005. 2.95 (978-1-59249-325-8(4), S7158) 2005. 15.95 (978-1-59249-324-1(6), B7108) 2004. pap. 6.95 (978-1-59249-326-5(2), S7108) Soundprints.

Zucker, Jonny. Mission 5: Subzero. Woodman, Ned, illus. 2013. (Max Flash Ser.: 5). (ENG.). 144p. (gr. 2-5). pap. 7.95 (978-1-4677-1481-5(X)); lib. bdg. 27.93 (978-1-4677-1212-5(4)) Lerner Publishing Group. (Darby Creek).

—Mission 6: Short Circuit. Woodman, Ned, illus. 2013. (Max Flash Ser.: 6). (ENG.). 144p. (gr. 2-5). pap. 7.95 (978-1-4677-1480-8(1)); lib. bdg. 27.93 (978-1-4677-1211-8(6)) Lerner Publishing Group. (Darby Creek).

ANTEATERS

Anteaters. 2014. (ENG.). 48p. (J). lib. bdg. 28.00 (978-0-531-20667-6(X)) Scholastic Library Publishing.

Borgert-Spaniol, Megan. Anteaters. 2012. (Animal Safari Ser.). (ENG., Illus.). 24p. (J). (gr. k-3). lib. bdg. 25.95 (978-1-60014-714-2(3), Blastoff! Readers) Bellwether Media.

Calhoun, Kelly. Sneaky Snouts: Giant Anteater. 2015. (Guess What Ser.). (ENG., Illus.). 24p. (J). (gr. k-2). pap. 12.79 (978-1-63362-710-9(1), 206701) Cherry Lake Publishing.

Gillespie, Katie. Giant Anteater. 2016. (J). **(978-1-4896-5378-9(3))** Weigl Pubs., Inc.

Markovics, Joyce L. Mi Nariz Es Larga y Peluda. 2015. (Pistas de Animales Ser.). (SPA., Illus.). 24p. (J). (gr. -1-3). lib. bdg. 23.93 (978-1-62724-583-8(9)) Bearport Publishing Co., Inc.

Rafferty, John P., ed. Rats, Bats, & Xenarthrans. 2011. (Britannica Guide to Predators & Prey Ser.). (Illus.). 256p. (YA). 103.40 (978-1-61530-456-1(8)) Rosen Publishing Group, Inc., The.

Rebman, Renee C. Anteaters. 2006. (Animals Animals Ser.). (Illus.). 48p. (J). (gr. 3-7). lib. bdg. 29.93 (978-0-7614-2234-1(X), Benchmark Bks.) Marshall Cavendish Corp.

Schuh, Mari. Anteaters. 2015. (J). lib. bdg. 25.65 (978-1-62031-172-1(0), Bullfrog Bks.) Jump! Inc.

Seiple, Samantha & Seiple, Todd. Giant Anteaters. 2008. (Early Bird Nature Bks.). (ENG., Illus.). 48p. (gr. 2-5). lib. bdg. 26.60 (978-0-8225-7887-1(5)) Lerner Publishing Group.

ANTEATERS—FICTION

Anfousse, Ginette. Mon Ami Pichou. 2004. (FRE.). (J). (gr. -1-1). spiral bd. (978-0-616-01824-8(X)) Canadian National Institute for the Blind/Institut National Canadien pour les Aveugles.

Dalmatian Press Staff. The Icky Sticky Anteater. 2008. (ENG.). 8p. bds. 4.95 (978-1-58117-711-4(9), Intervisual/Piggy Toes) Bendon, Inc.

De Luca, Daniela. Josh the Anteater. 2008. (It's a Wildlife, Buddy! Ser.). (ENG., Illus.). 30p. (J). (gr. -1-1). 12.95 (978-88-6098-090-8(9)) McRae Bks. Srl ITA. Dist: Independent Pubs. Group.

deRubertis, Barbara. Alexander Anteater's Amazing Act. Alley, R. W., illus. 2010. (Animal Antics A to Z Ser.). 32p. (J). (ENG.). (gr. -1-3). pap. 7.95 (978-1-57565-300-6(1)); (gr. k-1). lib. bdg. 22.60 (978-1-57565-304-4(4)) Kane Press, Inc.

deRubertis, Barbara & DeRubertis, Barbara. Alexander Anteater's Amazing Act. Alley, R. W., illus. 2012. (Animal Antics A to Z Ser.). 32p. (J). (gr. 2 — 1). cd-rom 7.95 (978-1-57565-394-5(X)) Kane Press, Inc.

Desmet, Sara. Scared Silly. Desmet, Sara, illus. 2006. (Illus.). 32p. (J). (gr. -1-3). 15.95 (978-1-60108-009-7(3)) Red Cygnet Pr.

Emerson, Carl. Nosy Arnie the Anteater, 1 vol. Trover, Zachary, illus. 2007. (Animal Underdogs Ser.). (ENG.). 32p. (gr. -1-4). 28.50 (978-1-60270-016-1(8), Looking Glass Library) ABDO Publishing Co.

Wilson, Veronica B. Aswald's ABC Adventure. 2008. 28p. pap. 24.95 (978-1-60441-691-6(2)) America Star Bks.

ANTELOPES

Carr, Aaron. Arabian Oryx. 2014. (Illus.). 24p. (J). (978-1-62127-280-9(X)) Weigl Pubs., Inc.

Cooper, Ross Gordon. Common Antelope in Africa, 1 vol. 2010. 22p. pap. 24.95 (978-1-4489-5552-7(1)) PublishAmerica, Inc.

Doudna, Kelly. It's a Baby Wildebeest!, 1 vol. 2009. (Baby African Animals Ser.). (ENG., Illus.). 24p. (J). (gr. k-3). lib. bdg. 24.21 (978-1-60453-159-6(2), SandCastle) ABDO Publishing Co.

Ganeri, Anita. Arabian Oryx, 1 vol. 2011. (Day in the Life: Desert Animals Ser.). (ENG., Illus.). 24p. (gr. k-2). lib. bdg. 23.32 (978-1-4329-4769-9(9), Heinemann Read & Learn) Heinemann-Raintree.

Gates, Margo. Antelopes. 2013. (Animal Safari Ser.). (ENG., Illus.). 24p. (J). (gr. k-3). lib. bdg. 25.95 (978-1-60014-907-8(3), Blastoff! Readers) Bellwether Media.

Gibbs, Maddie. Antelope. 2011. (Safari Animals Ser.). (ENG.). 24p. (J). pap. 8.25 (978-1-4488-2602-5(0)); lib. bdg. 22.60 (978-1-4488-2507-3(5)) Rosen Publishing Group, Inc., The. (PowerKids Pr.).

—Antelope / Antílopes. 2011. (Safari Animals / Animales de Safari Ser.). (ENG & SPA., Illus.). 24p. (J). (gr. -1-2). 22.60 (978-1-4488-3122-7(9)) Rosen Publishing Group, Inc., The.

Gish, Melissa. Antelopes. 2013. (Illus.). 46p. (J). 35.65 (978-1-60818-284-8(3), Creative Education) Creative Co., The.

—Living Wild: Antelopes. 2014. (Living Wild Ser.). (ENG., Illus.). 48p. (J). (gr. 4-7). pap. 12.00 (978-0-89812-837-6(4), Creative Paperbacks) Creative Co., The.

Jackson, Tom. Pronghorns. 2008. (Illus.). 52p. (J). (978-0-7172-6279-3(0)) Grolier, Ltd.

Riggs, Kate. Antelopes. 2016. (Amazing Animals Ser.). (Illus.). 24p. (J). (ENG.). (gr. 1-3). pap. 8.99 (978-1-62832-214-9(4), Creative Paperbacks); 28.50 (978-1-60818-608-2(3), Creative Education) Creative Co., The.

ANTHONY, SUSAN B. (SUSAN BROWNELL), 1820-1906

Archer, Jules. The Feminist Revolution: A Story of the Three Most Inspiring & Empowering Women in American History: Susan B. Anthony, Margaret Sanger, & Betty Friedan. rev. ed. 2015. (Jules Archer History for Young Readers Ser.). (ENG., Illus.). 200p. (J). (gr. 6). 16.99 (978-1-63220-603-9(X), Sky Pony Pr.) Skyhorse Publishing Co., Inc.

Auch, Allison. Women Who Dared & Mujeres que se Atrevieron: 6 English, 6 Spanish Adaptations. 2011. (ENG & SPA.). (J). 97.00 net. (978-1-4108-5692-0(5)) Benchmark Education Co.

Bohannon, Lisa Frederkisen. Failure Is Impossible: The Story of Susan B. Anthony. 2004. (Feminist Voices Ser.). (Illus.). 112p. (YA). (gr. 6-12). 23.95 (978-1-883846-77-0(3), First Biographies) Reynolds, Morgan Inc.

Boothroyd, Jennifer. Susan B. Anthony: A Life of Fairness. 2006. (Pull Ahead Bks.). 32p. (Illus.). (J). (gr. 3-7). lib. bdg. 22.60 (978-0-8225-3479-2(7), Lerner Pubns.); (ENG.). (gr. k-3). pap. 7.95 (978-0-8225-5699-2(5)) Lerner Publishing Group.

—Susan B. Anthony: Una Vida de Igualdad. Translations.com Staff, tr. 2006. (Libros para Avanzar-Biografias (Pull Ahead Books-Biographies) Ser.). (ENG & SPA., Illus.). 32p. (gr. k-3). lib. bdg. 22.60 (978-0-8225-6234-4(0)) Lerner Publishing Group.

—Susan B. Anthony: Una vida de igualdad (A Life of Fairness) 2006. (Libros para Avanzar-Biografias (Pull Ahead Books-Biographies Ser.). (Illus.). 32p. (J). (gr. 3-7). per. 6.95 (978-0-8225-6558-1(7), Ediciones Lerner) Lerner Publishing Group.

Connors, Kathleen. The Life of Susan B. Anthony, Vol. 1. 2014. (Famous Lives Ser.). (ENG.). 24p. (J). (gr. 1-2). 22.60 *(978-1-4824-0425-8(7))* Stevens, Gareth Publishing LLLP.
Edison, Erin. Susan B. Anthony. 2013. (Great Women in History Ser.). (ENG.). 24p. (gr. k-1). pap. 35.70 *(978-1-62065-866-6(6))*; pap. 6.29 *(978-1-62065-865-9(8))*; (Illus.). lib. bdg. 21.99 *(978-1-62065-075-2(4))* Capstone Press of Coughlan Cos. (Pebble Bks.).
Frey, Wendy. Citizen Heroes. 2007. (Illus.). 68p. (J). *(978-1-4105-0887-4(0))*; *(978-1-4105-0888-1(9))* Johnston, Don Inc.
Fry, Erin. The Power of Friendship. 2005. (Illus.). 16p. (J). pap. *(978-0-7367-2920-8(8))* Zaner-Bloser, Inc.
Gehret, Jeanne. Susan B. Anthony: And Justice for All. 2003. (ENG., Illus.). 120p. (J). (gr. 4-18). 14.95 *(978-0-9625136-9-5(5))*; pap. 6.95 *(978-0-9625136-8-8(7))* Verbal Images Pr.
Ghiglieri, Carol. Easy Reader Biographies: Susan B. Anthony: Fighter for Women's Rights. 2007. (ENG.). 16p. pap. 2.99 *(978-0-439-77413-0(6))*, Teaching Resources) Scholastic, Inc.
Goddu, Krystyna Poray. What's Your Story, Susan B. Anthony? 2016. (Cub Reporter Meets Famous Americans Ser.). (ENG.). 32p. (J). (gr. k-3). 26.65 *(978-1-4677-8785-7(X))*, Lerner Pubns.) Lerner Publishing Group.
Herweck, Dona. Susan B. Anthony, 1 vol. 2nd rev. ed. 2014. (TIME for KIDS(r) Nonfiction Readers Ser.). (ENG., Illus.). 28p. (J). (gr. 2-2). pap. 23.96 *(978-1-4807-1063-4(6))* Shell Educational Publishing.
—Susan B. Anthony, 1 vol. 2nd rev. ed. 2011. (Nonfiction Readers Ser.). (ENG.). 28p. (J). (gr. 2-2). pap. 6.99 *(978-1-4333-3642-3(1))* Teacher Created Materials, Inc.
Hopkinson, Deborah. Susan B. Anthony: Fighter for Women's Rights. Bates, Amy, illus. 2005. 32p. (J). lib. bdg. 15.00 *(978-1-4242-1563-8(3))* Fitzgerald Bks.
—Susan B. Anthony: Fighter for Women's Rights. Bates, Amy June, illus. 2005. (Ready-To-read SOFA Ser.). (ENG.). 32p. (J). (gr. 1-3). pap. 3.99 *(978-0-689-86909-9(6))*, Simon Spotlight) Simon Spotlight.
Isecke, Harriet. Susan B. Anthony & Elizabeth Cady Stanton: Early Suffragists, 1 vol. 2011. (Primary Source Readers Ser.). (ENG., Illus.). 32p. (J). (gr. 4-4). pap. 8.99 *(978-1-4333-1506-0(8))* Teacher Created Materials, Inc.
Kendall, Martha E. Failure Is Impossible! The History of American Women's Rights. 3rd ed. 2005. (People's History Ser.). (Illus.). 96p. (gr. 6-12). lib. bdg. 26.60 *(978-0-8225-1744-3(2))* Lerner Publishing Group.
—Susan B. Anthony: Fighter for Women's Voting Rights. 2015. (Legendary American Biographies Ser.). 96p. (J). (gr. 6-12). 27.94 *(978-0-7660-6500-0(6))*; pap. 10.95 *(978-0-7660-6501-7(4))* Enslow Pubs., Inc.
Litwin, Laura Baskes. Susan. B. Anthony: Social Reformer & Feminist. 2016. (Heroes of the Women's Suffrage Movement Ser.). (Illus.). 128p. (J). (gr. 6-6). 37.27 *(978-0-7660-7888-8(4))* Enslow Pubs., Inc.
Malaspina, Ann. Heart on Fire: Susan B. Anthony Votes for President. James, Steven, illus. 2012. (ENG.). 32p. (J). (gr. 1-3). 16.99 *(978-0-8075-3188-4(X))* Whitman, Albert & Co.
Mattern, Joanne. Elizabeth Cady Stanton & Susan B. Anthony: Fighting Together for Women's Rights. (Women Who Shaped History Ser.). 24p. 2009. (gr. 2-3). 42.50 *(978-1-60854-818-7(X))* 2003. (Illus.). (J). lib. bdg. 22.60 *(978-0-8239-6503-8(1))* Rosen Publishing Group, Inc., The. (PowerKids Pr.).
McPherson, Stephanie Sammartino. Susan B. Anthony. 2006. (History Maker Bios Ser.). (Illus.). 48p. (J). (gr. 3-7). lib. bdg. 26.60 *(978-0-8225-5938-2(2))*, Lerner Pubns.) Lerner Publishing Group.
Orr, Tamra B. The Life & Times of Susan B. Anthony. 2006. (Profiles in American History Ser.). (Illus.). 48p. (J). (gr. 3-7). lib. bdg. 29.95 *(978-1-58415-445-7(4))* Mitchell Lane Pubs., Inc.
Penn, Barbra. Susan B. Anthony: Pioneering Leader of the Women's Rights Movement. 2015. (Britannica Beginner Bios Ser.). (ENG.). 32p. (J). (gr. 2-3). 46.90 *(978-1-62275-953-8(2))*, Britannica Educational Publishing) Rosen Publishing Group, Inc., The.
Penne, Barbra. Susan B. Anthony: Pioneering Leader of the Women's Rights Movement. 2015. (Britannica Beginner Bios Ser.). (ENG.). 32p. (J). 23.45 *(978-1-62275-951-4(6))*, Britannica Educational Publishing) Rosen Publishing Group, Inc., The.
Pollack, Pamela D. & Belviso, Meg. Who Was Susan B. Anthony? Lacey, Mike & Harrison, Nancy, illus. 2014. (Who Was? Ser.). (ENG.). 112p. (J). (gr. 3-7). 5.99 *(978-0-448-47963-7(X))*, Grosset & Dunlap) Penguin Young Readers Group.
—Who Was Susan B. Anthony? 2014. (Who Was... ? Ser.). (Illus.). 105p. (J). lib. bdg. 16.00 *(978-0-606-36172-9(3))* Turtleback Bks.
Slade, Suzanne. Friends for Freedom: The Story of Susan B. Anthony & Frederick Douglass. Tadgell, Nicole, illus. 2014. (ENG.). 40p. (J). (gr. 1-4). 16.95 *(978-1-58089-568-2(9))* Charlesbridge Publishing, Inc.
—Friends for Freedom: The Story of Susan B. Anthony & Frederick Douglass. 2014. (Illus.). 39p. *(978-1-60734-651-7(6))* Charlesbridge Publishing, Inc.
Todd, Anne M. Susan B. Anthony: Activist. 2009. (Women of Achievement Ser.). (Illus.). 128p. (gr. 6-12). 35.00 *(978-1-60413-087-4(3))*, Chelsea Hse.) Facts On File, Inc.
Wallner, Alexandra. Susan B. Anthony. Wallner, Alexandra, illus. 2012. (ENG., Illus.). 32p. (J). 16.95 *(978-0-8234-1953-1(3))* Holiday Hse., Inc.
Weidt, Maryann N. Fighting for Equal Rights: A Story about Susan B. Anthony. Sartor, Amanda, tr. Sartor, Amanda, illus. 2003. (Creative Minds Biographies Ser.). (ENG.). 64p. (gr. 4-8). pap. 8.95 *(978-1-57505-609-8(7))* Lerner Publishing Group.

ANTHROPOGEOGRAPHY

see Human Geography

ANTHROPOLOGY

see also Anthropometry; Archaeology; Assimilation (Sociology); Civilization; Ethnology; Human Beings; Human Geography; Human Skin Color; Language and Languages; Social Change also names of races and tribes

Adams, Bradley J. Forensic Anthropology. 2006. (Inside Forensic Science Ser.). (Illus.). 103p. (J). (gr. 9-12). 32.95 *(978-0-7910-9198-2(8))* Facts On File, Inc.
Barnett, Annette. Myth, Magic, & Mystery: An Introduction to Anthropology for Kids in the 21st Century. 2004. 41p. per. 17.30 *(978-1-4116-0598-5(5))* Lulu Pr., Inc.
—One World, Many People: Anthropology Made Fun for Kids. Barnett, Isa, illus. 2006. 80p. (J). pap. 19.95 *(978-0-9787138-0-5(X))* Young Scholars Pr.
Croce, Nicholas. Anthropology: The Study of Humankind, 01 vols., 1. 2016. (Britannica Guide to the Social Sciences Ser.). (ENG.). 128p. (J). 35.25 *(978-1-62275-540-0(5))*, Britannica Educational Publishing) Rosen Publishing Group, Inc., The.
Discovering Cultures - Group 2, 6 vols. 2003. 288p. (YA). (gr. 2-18). lib. bdg. 158.86 *(978-0-7614-1514-5(9))* Marshall Cavendish Corp.
Doudna, Kelly. Boys & Girls Around the World: Set of 6, 1 vol. 2004. (Around the World Ser.: 6). (ENG., Illus.). 24p. (J). (gr. k-3). lib. bdg. 145.26 *(978-1-59197-563-2(8))*, SandCastle) ABDO Publishing Co.
Duffy, Beth. Anthropology for Children. 2007. (Illus.). 105p. spiral bd. *(978-0-9778602-5-8(6))* Newport Valley Pr.
Eggleton, Jill. Treasures. 2007. (Connectors Ser.). (gr. 2-5). pap. *(978-1-877453-17-5(X))* Global Education Systems Ltd.
Facchini, Fiorenzo. A Day with Homo Erectus: Life 400,000 Years Ago. Baldanzi, Alessandro, illus. 2003. (Early Humans Ser.). 48p. (gr. 6-18). lib. bdg. 23.90 *(978-0-7613-2766-0(5))*, Twenty-First Century Bks.) Lerner Publishing Group.
Hopping, Lorraine Jean. Bone Detective: The Story of Forensic Anthropologist Diane France. 2006. (ENG., Illus.). 128p. (gr. 7-9). per. 19.95 *(978-0-309-09550-1(6))*, Joseph Henry Pr.) National Academies Pr.
Museo de Antropologia (Para Colorear) 2003. (SPA.). 4.48 *(978-968-855-273-5(9))* Suromex, Ediciones, S.A. MEX. Dist: Giron Bks.
Shea, Therese. Anthropologists at Work. 2017. (Scientists at Work Ser.). 32p. (J). (gr. 6-8). 24.45 ***(978-1-68048-743-5(4))***; pap. 12.90 ***(978-1-68048-741-1(8))*** Rosen Publishing Group, Inc., The. (Britannica Educational Publishing).
Shone, Rob. Corpses & Skeletons: The Science of Forensic Anthropology. 2009. (Graphic Forensic Science Ser.). (ENG.). 48p. (YA). (gr. 5-5). 58.50 *(978-1-61512-944-7(8))*, Rosen Reference) Rosen Publishing Group, Inc., The.
—Corpses & Skeletons: The Science of Forensic Anthropology. Spender, Nick, illus. 2008. (Graphic Forensic Science Ser.). (ENG.). 48p. (gr. 5-8). per. 14.05 *(978-1-4042-1441-5(0))*; (YA). lib. bdg. 31.95 *(978-1-4042-1440-8(2))* Rosen Publishing Group, Inc., The.
Townsend, John. Bone Dectectives. 2008. (Crabtree Contact Ser.). (ENG., Illus.). 32p. (J). (gr. 3-7). lib. bdg. *(978-0-7787-3806-0(X))* Crabtree Publishing Co.
Walker, Sally M. Written in Bone: Buried Lives of Jamestown & Colonial Maryland. 2009. (Exceptional Social Studies Titles for Intermediate Grades). (ENG., Illus.). 144p. (J). (gr. 5-8). lib. bdg. 22.95 *(978-0-8225-7135-3(8))* Lerner Publishing Group.

ANTHROPOLOGY—DICTIONARIES

Cultures of the World, 6 bks., Group 9. 2nd rev. ed. Incl. Cuba. Sheehan, Sean & Jermyn, Leslie. lib. bdg. 42.79 *(978-0-7614-1965-5(9))*; Dominican Republic. Foley, Erin & Jermyn, Leslie. lib. bdg. 42.79 *(978-0-7614-1966-2(7))*; Haiti. Ngcheong-Lum, Roseline & Jermyn, Leslie. lib. bdg. 42.79 *(978-0-7614-1968-6(3))*; Nicaragua. Kott, Jennifer & Streiffert, Kristi. lib. bdg. 42.79 *(978-0-7614-1969-3(1))*; Puerto Rico. Levy, Patricia & Bahrawi, Nazry. lib. bdg. 42.79 *(978-0-7614-1970-9(5))*; Salvador. Foley, Erin & Hapipi, Rafiz. lib. bdg. 42.79 *(978-0-7614-1967-9(5))*; (Illus.). 144p. (gr. 6-10). (Cultures of the World 9 Ser.). 2005. 256.74 *(978-0-7614-1964-8(0))*, Benchmark Bks.) Marshall Cavendish Corp.
Cultures of the World, 6 vols., Set. 2003. 864p. (gr. 5-18). 222.43 *(978-0-7614-1496-4(7))* 2nd ed. 222.43 *(978-0-7614-1472-8(X))* Marshall Cavendish Corp. (Marshall Cavendish Reference Bks.).

ANTHROPOMETRY

Birmingham, Maria. Biometrics: Your Body & the Science of Security. Turner, Ian, illus. 2017. (ENG.). 48p. (J). (gr. 6-6). 16.95 ***(978-1-77147-193-0(X))*** Owlkids Bks. Inc. CAN. Dist: Publishers Group West (PGW).
Bradley, Timothy. Strange but True: Tiny Creatures, 1 vol. 2nd rev. ed. 2013. (Nonfiction Readers Ser.). (ENG., Illus.). 48p. (J). (gr. 4-4). pap. 29.96 *(978-1-4807-1114-3(4))* Shell Educational Publishing.

ANTIBIOTICS

see also names of specific antibiotics, e.g. Penicillin; etc.

Adams, Jonathan S. Antibiotics. 2017. ***(978-1-5026-2873-2(2))*** Cavendish Square Publishing.
Emmeluth, Donald. Antibiotics. 2011. (Understanding Drugs Ser.). (YA). (gr. 9-12). 34.95 *(978-1-60413-531-2(X))* Facts On File, Inc.
Gagne, Tammy. Battling Against Drug-Resistant Bacteria. 2017. (Science Frontiers Ser.). (ENG., Illus.). 32p. (J). (gr. 3-6). 21.95 *(978-1-63235-373-3(3))* Pr. Room Editions LLC.
Gagne, Tammy & Mangor, Jodie. Battling Against Drug-Resistant Bacteria. 2016. (Science Frontiers Ser.). (ENG., Illus.). 32p. (J). pap. 9.95 *(978-1-63235-390-0(3))* Pr. Room Editions LLC.
Goldsmith, Connie. Superbugs Strike Back: When Antibiotics Fail. 2007. (Discovery! Ser.). (ENG., Illus.). 112p. (gr. 6-12). lib. bdg. 31.93 *(978-0-8225-6607-6(9))* Lerner Publishing Group.
Klosterman, Lorrie. Drug-Resistant Diseases & Superbugs. 2009. (Health Alert 6 Ser.). 64p. (gr. 4). 32.79 *(978-0-7614-3981-3(1))* Marshall Cavendish GBR. Dist: Marshall Cavendish Corp.
Kovacs, Vic. Antibiotics. 2016. (Miracles of Medicine Ser.). 00048p. (J). pap. 14.05 ***(978-1-4824-6163-3(3))*** Stevens, Gareth Publishing LLLP.
Lew, Kristi. Antibiotics. 2013. (Illus.). 64p. (YA). (gr. 6-9). 34.21 *(978-1-60870-465-1(3))*; pap. 15.28 *(978-1-62712-008-1(4))* Cavendish Square Publishing.
Orr, Tamra B. Antibiotics. 2016. (True Book(tm), a — Greatest Discoveries & Discoverers Ser.). (ENG., Illus.). 48p. (J). lib. bdg. 31.00 *(978-0-531-21860-0(0))*, Children's Pr.) Scholastic Library Publishing.
Rooney, Anne. You Wouldn't Want to Live Without Antibiotics. Antram, David, illus. 2014. (You Wouldn't Want to Live Without... Ser.). (ENG.). 32p. (J). lib. bdg. 29.00 *(978-0-531-21218-9(1))*, Watts, Franklin) Scholastic Library Publishing.
Sherman, Josepha. The War Against Germs. (Germs: the Library of Disease-Causing Organisms Ser.). 48p. 2009. (gr. 5-5). 53.00 *(978-1-61512-718-4(6))* 2004. (Illus.). (gr. 7-12). lib. bdg. 29.25 *(978-0-8239-4495-8(6))* Rosen Publishing Group, Inc., The.
Williams, Mary E. Antibiotics. Greenhaven Press Editors, ed. 2014. (Introducing Issues with Opposing Viewpoints Ser.). (ENG., Illus.). 144p. (gr. 7-10). lib. bdg. 42.00 *(978-0-7377-6919-7(X))*, Greenhaven Pr., Inc.) Cengage Gale.
Zuchora-Walske, Christine. Antibiotics, 1 vol. 2013. (Medical Marvels Ser.). (ENG.). 112p. (J). (gr. 6-12). lib. bdg. 35.64 *(978-1-61783-901-6(9))*, Essential Library) ABDO Publishing Co.

ANTI-COMMUNIST MOVEMENTS

Giblin, James Cross. The Rise & Fall of Senator Joe McCarthy. 2009. (ENG., Illus.). 304p. (YA). (gr. 7-18). 22.00 *(978-0-618-61058-7(8))* Houghton Mifflin Harcourt Publishing Co.
Hillstrom, Kevin. McCarthyism & the Communist Threat. 2011. (Defining Moments Ser.). 266p. 55.00 *(978-0-7808-1184-3(4))* Omnigraphics, Inc.
Hudak, Heather C. McCarthyism & the Red Scare. 2017. 48p. (J). ***(978-0-7787-3939-5(2))*** Crabtree Publishing Co.
Immell, Myra. The McCarthy Era. Gale Editors, ed. 2011. (Perspectives on Modern World History Ser.). (ENG.). 224p. (gr. 12-12). lib. bdg. 47.80 *(978-0-7377-5260-1(2))*, Greenhaven Pr., Inc.) Cengage Gale.
Sahgal, Lara & Axelrod, Toby. Hans & Sophie Scholl, 01 vols., 1. 2016. (Holocaust Ser.). (ENG., Illus.). 112p. (J). 35.60 *(978-1-4994-6244-9(1))*, Rosen Young Adult) Rosen Publishing Group, Inc., The.
Storrs, Landon & Storrs, Landon R. Y. The Second Red Scare & the Unmaking of the New Deal Left. 2012. (Politics & Society in Modern America Ser.). (ENG., Illus.). 424p. (C). 47.95 *(978-0-691-15396-4(5))* Princeton Univ. Pr.
Tracy, Kathleen. The McCarthy Era. 2008. (Monumental Milestones Ser.). (Illus.). 48p. (YA). (gr. 4-7). lib. bdg. 29.95 *(978-1-58415-694-9(5))* Mitchell Lane Pubs., Inc.
Zeinert, Karen. McCarthyism & the Communist Scare in United States History. 2015. (In United States History Ser.). 96p. (J). (gr. 5-12). 27.94 *(978-0-7660-6345-7(3))*; pap. 10.95 *(978-0-7660-6346-4(1))* Enslow Pubs., Inc.

ANTIPATHIES

see Prejudices

ANTIQUES

see also Art Objects; Collectors and Collecting

Faulkner, Nicholas. A Visual History of the World's Enduring Mysteries. 2016. (Visual History of the World Ser.). 00096p. (J). (gr. 8-8). 37.10 *(978-1-4994-6578-5(5))* Rosen Publishing Group, Inc., The.
Schiffer, Nancy N. Rhinestones! A Collector's Handbook & Price Guide, 1 vol. 4th rev. ed. 2003. (ENG., Illus.). 160p. (gr. 10-13). pap. 16.95 *(978-0-7643-1751-4(2))*, 9780764317514) Schiffer Publishing, Ltd.
Shone, Rob. Ancient Treasures. 2009. (Graphic Discoveries Ser.). (ENG.). 48p. (YA). (gr. 5-5). 58.50 *(978-1-61512-923-2(5))*, Rosen Reference) Rosen Publishing Group, Inc., The.
Soriano, Joan & Malizia, Diana. A Visual History of Archaeological Discoveries Around the World. 2016. (Visual History of the World Ser.). 00096p. (J). (gr. 8-8). 37.10 *(978-1-4994-6576-1(9))* Rosen Publishing Group, Inc., The.
Wolfe, Mike & Sprengelmeyer, Lily. Kid Pickers: How to Turn Junk into Treasure. Right, Mike, illus. 2013. (ENG.). 128p. (J). (gr. 2-7). 19.99 *(978-1-250-00848-0(4))*, 9781250008480); pap. 14.99 *(978-1-250-01930-1(3))*, 9781250019301) Feiwel & Friends.

ANTIQUITIES

see Archaeology; Bible—Antiquities; Classical Antiquities; Human Beings—Origin; Indians of North America—Antiquities; Prehistoric Peoples

see names of countries, cities, etc. with the subdivision Antiquities, e.g. United States—Antiquities; etc

ANTIQUITIES, BIBLICAL

see Bible—Antiquities

ANTIQUITIES, CLASSICAL

see Classical Antiquities

ANTIQUITY OF MAN

see Human Beings—Origin

ANTI-REFORMATION

see Reformation

ANTISEMITISM

see also Jews—Persecutions

Berlatsky, Noah. Anti-Semitism. Greenhaven Press Editors, ed. 2014. (Opposing Viewpoints Ser.). (ENG., Illus.). 224p. (gr. 7-10). lib. bdg. 48.80 *(978-0-7377-6947-0(5))*, Greenhaven Pr., Inc.) Cengage Gale.
—Anti-Semitism. Greenhaven Press Editors & Gale Editors, eds. 2014. (Opposing Viewpoints Ser.). (ENG., Illus.). 224p. (gr. 7-12). pap. 33.80 *(978-0-7377-6948-7(3))*, Greenhaven Pr., Inc.) Cengage Gale.
Byers, Ann. Anti-Semitism & the Final Solution: The Holocaust Overview. 2014. (Remembering the Holocaust Ser.). 96p. (J). (gr. 6-12). pap. 10.95 *(978-0-7660-6193-4(0))* Enslow Pubs., Inc.
—Remembering the Holocaust: Anti-Semitism & the "Final Solution": The Holocaust Overview. 2014. (Remembering the Holocaust Ser.). (Illus.). 96p. (J). (gr. 6-12). 27.94 *(978-0-7660-6192-7(2))* Enslow Pubs., Inc.
Gottfried, Ted. Nazi Germany: The Face of Tyranny. Alcorn, Stephen, illus. (Holocaust History Ser.). 112p. (YA). (gr. 7-12). 22.95 *(978-1-58013-203-9(0))*, Kar-Ben Publishing) Lerner Publishing Group.
Heitkamp, Kristina Lyn. Confronting Anti-Semitism. 2017. (J). ***(978-1-5081-7742-5(2))***, Rosen Young Adult) Rosen Publishing Group, Inc., The.
Mara, Wil. Kristallnacht: Nazi Persecution of the Jews in Europe. 2009. (Perspectives on Ser.). 112p. (gr. 7). 39.93 *(978-0-7614-4026-0(7))* Marshall Cavendish Corp.
Palmer, Bill. Gallup Guides for Youth Facing Persistent Prejudice. 2012. (Gallup Guides for Youth Facing Persistent Prejudice Ser.). 64p. (J). (gr. 7-8). 22.95 *(978-1-4222-2466-3(X))* Mason Crest.
Ramen, Fred. Hermann Goering: Hitler's Second in Command. 2005. (Holocaust Biographies Ser.). (Illus.). 112p. (YA). (gr. 7-12). lib. bdg. 34.60 *(978-0-8239-3307-5(5))*, HBGORI) Rosen Publishing Group, Inc., The.
—Hermann Goring: Hitler's Second-in-Command. 2009. (Holocaust Biographies Ser.). 112p. (gr. 7-12). 63.90 *(978-1-61513-387-1(9))* Rosen Publishing Group, Inc., The.
Roscoe, Kelly & Roberts, Jeremy. Joseph Goebbels, 01 vols., 1. 2016. (Holocaust Ser.). (ENG., Illus.). 112p. (J). 35.60 *(978-1-5081-7049-5(5))*, Rosen Young Adult) Rosen Publishing Group, Inc., The.
Shoup, Kate. Nazi Propaganda: Jews in Hitler's Germany. 2016. (Public Persecutions Ser.). 128p. (J). 45.64 *(978-1-5026-2321-8(8))* Cavendish Square Publishing.

ANTISEMITISM—FICTION

Griffis, Molly Levite. Simon Says. 2004. vi, 263p. (J). 22.95 *(978-1-57168-836-1(6))*; pap. *(978-1-57168-847-7(1))* Eakin Pr. (Eakin Pr.).
Laurel Carter, Anne. The Shepherd's Granddaughter. 2013. 236p. pap. *(978-1-4596-6490-6(6))* ReadHowYouWant.com, Ltd.
mendelsohn, martha. Bromley Girls. 2015. (ENG.). 192p. (YA). pap. 14.95 *(978-0-89672-922-3(2))* Texas Tech Univ. Pr.
Poulsen, David A. Numbers. 2008. (ENG.). 232p. (YA). (gr. 6-18). *(978-1-55470-095-0(7))* Me to We.
Shapiro, David L. Sara's Journey. 2005. (ENG.). 224p. (gr. 7-12). per. 16.95 *(978-0-8276-0776-7(8))* Jewish Pubn. Society.
Tunis, John Roberts. Keystone Kids. 2006. (Odyssey/Harcourt Young Classic Ser.). 239p. (J). (gr. 3). 13.65 *(978-0-7569-7102-1(0))* Perfection Learning Corp.
Vernick, Shirley Reva. The Blood Lie. 2011. (ENG.). 144p. (J). (gr. 7). 15.95 *(978-1-933693-84-2(3))* Cinco Puntos Pr.
Wiseman, Eva. Puppet. 2012. (ENG., Illus.). 248p. (YA). (gr. 5). pap. 9.95 *(978-1-77049-296-7(8))*, Tundra Bks.) Tundra Bks. CAN. Dist: Penguin Random Hse. LLC.

ANTISLAVERY

see Slavery

ANTS

Abbott, Henry. Inside Anthills. 2015. (Inside Animal Homes Ser.). (ENG.). 24p. (J). (gr. 2-3). pap. 8.25 *(978-1-4994-0860-7(9))*, PowerKids Pr.) Rosen Publishing Group, Inc., The.
All about Ants, 6 vols. (Book2WebTM Ser.). (gr. 4-8). 36.50 *(978-0-322-02977-4(5))* Wright Group/McGraw-Hill.
Allen, Judy. Are You an Ant? Humphries, Tudor, illus. 2004. (Backyard Bks.). (ENG.). 32p. (J). (gr. k-3). pap. 6.99 *(978-0-7534-5803-7(9))*, 9780753458037, Kingfisher) Roaring Brook Pr.
Amstutz, Lisa J. Ants. 2016. (Little Critters Ser.). (ENG., Illus.). 24p. (gr. k-1). lib. bdg. 21.99 *(978-1-5157-1936-6(7))*, Pebble Bks.) Capstone Press of Coughlan Cos.
Ang, Karen. Inside the Ants' Nest. 2013. (Science Slam: Snug As a Bug-Where Bugs Live Ser.). 24p. (J). (gr. -1-3). lib. bdg. 23.93 *(978-1-61772-902-7(7))* Bearport Publishing Co., Inc.
Ants, 6 vols. (Sunshinetm Science Ser.). 24p. (gr. 1-2). 36.95 *(978-0-7802-0538-3(3))*; 31.50 *(978-0-7802-0287-0(2))* Wright Group/McGraw-Hill.
Ants: Level K, 6 vols. (Wonder Worldtm Ser.). 16p. 34.95 *(978-0-7802-1193-3(6))* Wright Group/McGraw-Hill.
Ants, Ants, Ants, 6 vols. (Sunshinetm Science Ser.). 24p. (gr. 1-2). 31.50 *(978-0-7802-0286-3(4))*; 36.95 *(978-0-7802-0537-6(5))* Wright Group/McGraw-Hill.
Ants Aren't Antisocial: Individual Title Six-Packs. (Action Packs Ser.). 104p. (gr. 3-5). 44.00 *(978-0-7635-2986-4(9))* Rigby Education.
Ants Sets: 1 Each of 3 Student Books. (Sunshinetm Science Ser.). (gr. 1-2). 17.95 *(978-0-7802-0267-2(8))* Wright Group/McGraw-Hill.
Aronin, Miriam. The Ant's Nest: A Huge Underground City. 2016. (Spectacular Animal Towns Ser.). (ENG.). 32p. (J). (gr. 2-7). pap. 8.95 *(978-1-944998-58-5(6))* Bearport Publishing Co., Inc.
—The Ant's Nest: A Huge, Underground City. 2009. (Spectacular Animal Towns Ser.). (Illus.). 32p. (J). (gr. 2-7). lib. bdg. 25.27 *(978-1-59716-868-7(8))* Bearport Publishing Co., Inc.
Ashley, Susan. Ants. (Incredible World of Insects Ser.). (Illus.). 24p. 2011. (J). (gr. 1-3). pap. 8.15 *(978-1-4339-4572-4(X))* 2011. (J). (gr. 1-3). lib. bdg. 22.60 *(978-1-4339-4571-7(1))* 2004. (gr. k-3). pap. 8.15 *(978-0-8368-4057-5(7))*, Weekly Reader Leveled Readers) 2004. (gr. k-3). lib. bdg. 22.00 *(978-0-8368-4050-6(X))*, Weekly Reader Leveled Readers) Stevens, Gareth Publishing LLLP.
Baer, Jasper. Hormiguitas Pequeitas / Itty Bitty Ants, Vol. 1. 2014. (Animales Pequeñitos / Itty Bitty Animals Ser.). (SPA & BYN.). 24p. (J). (gr. k-2). 22.60 *(978-1-4339-9901-7(3))* Stevens, Gareth Publishing LLLP.
—Itty Bitty Ants, Vol. 1. 2014. (Itty Bitty Animals Ser.). (Illus.). 24p. (J). (gr. k-k). (ENG.). pap. 8.15 *(978-1-4339-9876-8(9))*; 22.60 *(978-1-4339-9874-4(2))* Stevens, Gareth Publishing LLLP.
Barner, Bob. Ants Rule: The Long & Short of It. 2017. (ENG.). 32p. (J). (gr. -1-3). 16.95 *(978-0-8234-3660-6(8))*; ***(978-0-8234-3790-0(6))*** Holiday Hse., Inc.
Beer, Amy-Jane. Ants. 2008. (Nature's Children Ser.). (Illus.). 52p. (J). *(978-0-7172-6216-8(2))* Grolier, Ltd.
Berger, Melvin & Berger, Gilda. Ants. 2011. (Illus.). 16p. (J). pap. *(978-0-545-24449-7(8))* Scholastic, Inc.
Black, Nessa. Ants. 2017. (Spot Creepy Crawlies Ser.). (ENG.). 16p. (gr. k-3). 17.95 ***(978-1-68151-104-7(5))*** Amicus Publishing.
Bodden, Valerie. Ants. 2013. (Illus.). 24p. (J). 25.65 *(978-1-60818-230-5(4))*, Creative Education) Creative Co., The.
—Creepy Creatures: Ants. 2013. (Creepy Creatures Ser.). (ENG., Illus.). 24p. (J). (gr. 1-3). pap. 8.99 *(978-0-89812-793-5(9))*, Creative Paperbacks) Creative Co., The.
Bronson, Wilfrid S., illus. The Wonder World of Ants. 2009. 96p. (J). pap. 19.95 *(978-0-86534-691-8(7))* Sunstone Pr.

A
B

Canetti, Yanitzia. Canta y Cuenta Las Hormigas. 2010. (J). *(978-1-59835-150-7(8))* Cambridge BrickHouse, Inc.
—1-2-3 Do, Re, Mi Ants. 2010. (J). *(978-1-59835-154-5(0))* Cambridge BrickHouse, Inc.
Chapman, J. An Ant: Learning the Short A Sound. 2009. (PowerPhonics Ser.). 24p. (gr. 1-1). 39.90 *(978-1-60851-432-8(3),* PowerKids Pr.) Rosen Publishing Group, Inc., The.
Claybourne, Anna. A Colony of Ants: And Other Insect Groups, 1 vol. 2012. (Animals in Groups Ser.). (ENG.). 48p. (gr. 4-6). pap. 9.95 *(978-1-4329-6487-0(9));* lib. bdg. 33.32 *(978-1-4329-6480-1(1))* Heinemann-Raintree. (Heinemann InfoSearch).
Cooper, Jason. Ants. 2005. (ENG., Illus.). 24p. (gr. k-2). pap. 8.95 *(978-1-59515-738-6(7))* Rourke Educational Media.
—Hormigas. 2005. (SPA.). 24p. (gr. k-2). pap. 7.95 *(978-1-59515-694-5(1))* Rourke Educational Media.
Crevola, Carmend & Vineis, Mark. Thinking about Ants. 2010. (ENG., Illus.). 32p. (C). (gr. -1-3). pap. 10.95 *(978-1-57255-209-8(3))* National Geographic School Publishing, Inc.
Cunningham, Kevin. Stick Insects & Ants. 2016. (21st Century Junior Library: Better Together Ser.). (ENG., Illus.). 24p. (J). (gr. 2-5). 27.07 *(978-1-63471-087-9(8),* 208427) Cherry Lake Publishing.
de Nijs, Erika. An Ant's Colony. 2016. (Animal Builders Ser.). 24p. (J). pap. 8.22 *(978-1-5026-2075-0(8))* Cavendish Square Publishing.
Demuth, Patricia Brennan. Those Amazing Ants. Schindler, S. D., illus. 2012. (ENG.). 32p. (J). (gr. -1-3). pap. 16.99 *(978-1-4424-5932-8(8),* Simon & Schuster Bks. For Young Readers) Simon & Schuster Bks. For Young Readers.
Dyer, Hadley & Kalman, Bobbie. Les Fourmis. Briere, Marie-Josee, tr. from ENG. rev. ed. 2007. (Petit Monde Vivant Ser.). (FRE., Illus.). 32p. (J). (gr. 1-7). pap. 9.95 *(978-2-89579-125-6(2))* Bayard Canada Livres CAN. Dist: Crabtree Publishing Co.
—The Life Cycle of an Ant. 2005. (Life Cycle Ser.). (ENG., Illus.). 32p. (J). (gr. 1-7). pap. *(978-0-7787-0700-4(8));* lib. bdg. *(978-0-7787-0670-0(2))* Crabtree Publishing Co.
Enslow, Brian. Counting Ants 1-2-3. 2011. (All about Counting Bugs 1-2-3 Ser.). (Illus.). 24p. (J). (gr. -1-18). pap. 7.95 *(978-1-59845-249-5(5),* Enslow Elementary); (gr. k-3). lib. bdg. 22.60 *(978-0-7660-3919-3(6))* Enslow Pubs., Inc.
Falchetta, Drew. Ant Builders. 2015. (1B Bugs Ser.). (ENG., Illus.). 28p. (J). pap. 5.99 *(978-1-63437-117-9(8))* American Reading Co.
Fowler, Allan & National Geographic Learning Staff. Inside an Ant Colony. 2010. (Rise & Shine Ser.). (ENG., Illus.). 32p. (C). (gr. 1-2). per. 7.95 *(978-0-516-26365-6(X))* National Geographic School Publishing, Inc.
Gallagher, Debbie. Ants. 2011. (Mighty Minibeasts Ser.). 32p. (gr. 2). 28.50 *(978-1-60870-542-9(0))* Marshall Cavendish Corp.
Gillespie, Katie. Ants. 2017. (Illus.). 24p. (J). ***(978-1-4896-4495-4(4))*** Weigl Pubs., Inc.
Goldish, Meish. Red Imported Fire Ants: Attacking Everything. 2015. (They Don't Belong: Tracking Invasive Species Ser.). (ENG., Illus.). 32p. (J). (gr. 2-7). lib. bdg. 26.60 *(978-1-62724-831-0(5))* Bearport Publishing Co., Inc.
Gomel, Luc. Face-to-Face with the Ant: Energetic Worker. Amann, Remy & Stoffel, Dominique, photos by. 2004. (Face to Face Ser.). (Illus.). 28p. (J). (gr. -1-2). 9.95 *(978-1-57091-451-5(6))* Charlesbridge Publishing, Inc.
Green, Emily K. Ants. 2006. (World of Insects Ser.). (ENG., Illus.). 24p. (J). (gr. k-3). lib. bdg. 25.95 *(978-1-60014-008-2(4))* Bellwether Media.
Gregory, Josh. Ants. 2016. (Nature's Children Ser.). (ENG., Illus.). 48p. (J). pap. 6.95 *(978-0-531-21932-4(1),* Children's Pr.) Scholastic Library Publishing.
Hall, Margaret. Ants [Scholastic]. 2010. (Bugs, Bugs, Bugs! Ser.). 24p. pap. 0.52 *(978-1-4296-5051-9(6),* Pebble Plus) Capstone Press of Coughlan Cos.
Hamilton, S. L. Ants. 2014. (Xtreme Insects Ser.). (ENG.). 32p. (gr. 3-9). lib. bdg. 27.07 *(978-1-62403-686-6(4),* Abdo & Daughters) ABDO Publishing Co.
Hansen, Grace. Ants, 1 vol. 2014. (Insects Ser.). (ENG.). 24p. (J). (gr. 4-8). lib. bdg. 28.50 *(978-1-62970-036-6(3))* ABDO Publishing Co.
Hansen, Grace, et al. Hormigas. 2015. (Insectos Ser.). (SPA., Illus.). 24p. (gr. k-1). pap. 7.95 *(978-1-4966-0475-0(X))* Capstone Classroom.
Harrod-Eagles, Cynthia. Fantastic Ants. 2008. (Science Vocabulary Readers Ser.). (Illus.). 24p. (J). *(978-0-545-00737-5(2))* Scholastic, Inc.
Hayward, Tim, et al. Ant's Diary: A Year in My Life. 2016. (ENG., Illus.). 32p. 9.99 *(978-1-86147-657-9(4),* Armadillo) Anness Publishing GBR. Dist: National Bk. Network.
Heather C Hudak. Ants. 2008. (World of Wonder Ser.). (Illus.). 24p. (J). (gr. k-3). pap. 8.95 *(978-1-59036-863-3(0))* Weigl Pubs., Inc.
Heather C Hudak & Hudak, Heather C. Ants. 2008. (World of Wonder Ser.). (Illus.). 24p. (J). (gr. k-3). lib. bdg. 24.45 *(978-1-59036-862-6(2))* Weigl Pubs., Inc.
Heos, Bridget. Ants. Clark, David, illus. 2017. (Just Like Us! Ser.). (ENG.). 32p. (J). (gr. -1-3). 14.99 *(978-0-544-57043-6(X),* HMH Books For Young Readers) Houghton Mifflin Harcourt Publishing Co.
Hipp, Andrew. Gardening Ants. (Really Wild Life of Animals Ser.). 24p. 2009. (gr. 3-4). 42.50 *(978-1-60854-191-1(6))* 2003. (Illus.). (J). lib. bdg. 22.60 *(978-0-8239-6243-3(1))* Rosen Publishing Group, Inc., The. (PowerKids Pr.).
How Ants Live, 6 vols. (Sunshinetm Science Ser.). 24p. (gr. 1-2). 36.95 *(978-0-7802-0539-0(1));* 31.50 *(978-0-7802-0288-7(0))* Wright Group/McGraw-Hill.
Johnson, Jinny. An Ant. Sanzi, Desiderio, illus. 2015. (J). pap. *(978-1-68152-073-5(7))* Amicus Publishing.
—What's It Like to Be... Ant? Sanzi, Desiderio, illus. 2011. (What's It Like to Be... ? Ser.). 24p. (J). (gr. -1-k). 25.65 *(978-1-60753-183-8(6))* Amicus Publishing.
Kenney, Karen Latchana. March with the Ants, 1 vol. Hedicker, Lisa, illus. 2010. (Bug's World Ser.). (ENG.). 32p. 28.50 *(978-1-60270-788-7(X),* Looking Glass Library- Nonfiction) Magic Wagon.
Lockwood, Sophie. Ants. 2007. (World of Insects Ser.). (ENG., Illus.). 40p. (J). (gr. 3-6). 31.36 *(978-1-59296-817-6(1),* 200970) Child's World, Inc., The.
Markle, Sandra. Army Ants. (Animal Scavengers Ser.). (Illus.). (J). (gr. 3-7). 2006. 39p. pap. 7.95 *(978-0-8225-3472-3(X),* First Avenue Editions) 2005. (ENG.). 40p. lib. bdg. 25.26 *(978-0-8225-3196-8(8),* Lerner Pubns.) Lerner Publishing Group.
—Las Hormigas Legionaria; Army Ants. 2008. pap. 46.95 *(978-0-8225-9288-4(6))* Lerner Publishing Group.
—Las Hormigas Legionarias. 2007. (Animales carroñeros (Animal Scavengers) Ser.). (SPA., Illus.). 39p. (J). (gr. -1-3). lib. bdg. 25.26 *(978-0-8225-7730-0(5),* Ediciones Lerner) Lerner Publishing Group.
—Las Hormigas Legionarias. Translations.com Staff, tr. 2007. (Animales carroñeros (Animal Scavengers) Ser.). (SPA., Illus.). 40p. (gr. 3-6). per. 7.95 *(978-0-8225-7734-8(8))* Lerner Publishing Group.
Marwood, Diane. The Ant & the Grasshopper. 2012. (ENG., Illus.). 24p. (J). *(978-0-7787-7889-9(4));* pap. *(978-0-7787-7901-8(7))* Crabtree Publishing Co.
Micucci, Charles. The Life & Times of the Ant. 2006. (ENG., Illus.). 32p. (J). (gr. -1-3). reprint ed. pap. 6.95 *(978-0-618-68949-1(4))* Houghton Mifflin Harcourt Publishing Co.
Miller, David. Ant. 2017. (Up Close & Scary Ser.). (Illus.). 32p. (gr. 2-5). 31.35 ***(978-1-911242-03-1(2))*** Book Hse. GBR. Dist: Black Rabbit Bks.
Morgan, Sally. Ants: Animal Lives Series. 2008. (J). lib. bdg. 18.95 *(978-1-59566-534-8(X))* QEB Publishing Inc.
Morris, Neil & Morris, Ting. Ant. 2003. (Illus.). 32p. (J). lib. bdg. 27.10 *(978-1-58340-376-1(0))* Black Rabbit Bks.
Murray, Julie. Ants, 1 vol. 2010. (Big Buddy Bks.). (ENG.). 32p. (J). (gr. 2-5). 28.50 *(978-1-61613-481-5(X))* ABDO Publishing Co.
Murray, Laura K. Ants. 2015. (Illus.). 24p. (J). *(978-1-60818-579-5(6),* Creative Education) Creative Co., The.
—Ants: Seedlings. 2016. (Seedlings Ser.). (ENG.). 24p. (J). (gr. k-2). pap. 7.99 *(978-1-62832-184-5(9),* Creative Paperbacks) Creative Co., The.
Nagle, Frances. Zombie Ants. 2015. (Zombie Animals: Parasites Take Control! Ser.). (ENG.). 24p. (J). (gr. 2-3). pap. 8.15 *(978-1-4824-2828-5(8))* Stevens, Gareth Publishing LLLP.
National Geographic Editors. Creepy Crawly Collection. 2012. lib. bdg. 18.40 *(978-0-606-26822-6(7),* Turtleback) Turtleback Bks.
Nelson, Kristin L. Busy Ants. 2004. (Pull Ahead Bks.). 32p. (J). (gr. k-2). (ENG.). pap. 6.95 *(978-0-8225-9885-5(X));* (Illus.). lib. bdg. 22.60 *(978-0-8225-3775-5(3))* Lerner Publishing Group.
Nirgiotis, Nicholas. Killer Ants. Stevenson, Emma, illus. 2009. (ENG.). 32p. (J). (gr. 1-5). 17.95 *(978-0-8234-2034-6(5))* Holiday Hse., Inc.
Pearson, Scott. Red Fire Ants. 2017. (Invasive Species Takeover Ser.). (ENG., Illus.). 32p. (J). (gr. 3-7). 31.35 ***(978-1-68072-014-3(7),*** Bolt) Black Rabbit Bks.
Perish, Patrick. Ants. 2017. (Insects up Close Ser.). (ENG., Illus.). 24p. (J). (gr. k-3). lib. bdg. 25.95 ***(978-1-62617-657-7(4),*** Blastoff! Readers) Bellwether Media.
Petrie, Kristin. Ants, 1 vol. 2009. (Bugs! Ser.). (ENG.). 32p. (gr. 3-6). 27.07 *(978-1-60453-062-9(6),* Checkerboard Library) ABDO Publishing Co.
Ponka, Katherine. Carpenter Ants. 2014. (Animals of Mass Destruction Ser.). 32p. (J). (gr. 2-5). 25.25 *(978-1-4824-1024-2(9))* Stevens, Gareth Publishing LLLP.
Rissman, Rebecca. Ants, 1 vol. 2012. (Creepy Critters Ser.). (ENG.). 24p. (gr. -1-k). pap. 9.95 *(978-1-4109-4814-4(5))* Heinemann-Raintree.
Rodriguez, Ana Maria & Rodriguez, Ana Maria. Secret of the Plant-Killing Ants ... & More! 2008. (Animal Secrets Revealed! Ser.). (Illus.). 48p. (J). (gr. 5-9). lib. bdg. 25.27 *(978-0-7660-2953-8(0))* Enslow Pubs., Inc.
Roza, Greg. Inside an Ant Colony. 2009. (Real Life Readers Ser.). 16p. (gr. 2-3). pap. 7.05 *(978-1-4358-0224-7(1),* Rosen Classroom) Rosen Publishing Group, Inc., The.
Rustad, Martha E. H. Ants & Aphids Work Together. 2011. (Animals Working Together Ser.). (ENG.). 24p. (gr. k-1). pap. 41.70 *(978-1-4296-6366-3(9),* Pebble Plus) Capstone Press of Coughlan Cos.
Schuetz, Kari. Fire Ants. 2015. (Creepy Crawlies Ser.). (ENG., Illus.). 24p. (J). (gr. k-3). lib. bdg. 25.95 *(978-1-62617-222-7(6),* Blastoff! Readers) Bellwether Media.
Schuh, Mari. Ants. 2013. (ENG., Illus.). 24p. (J). lib. bdg. 25.65 *(978-1-62031-050-2(3))* Jump! Inc.
Simon, Seymour. Deadly Ants. Downey, William, illus. 2012. (Dover Children's Science Bks.). (ENG.). 64p. (J). (gr. 3-5). pap. 5.99 *(978-0-486-48468-6(8))* Dover Pubns., Inc.
Slade, Suzanne. Ants. (Under the Microscope: Backyard Bugs Ser.). 24p. 2009. (gr. 2-3). 42.50 *(978-1-60854-611-4(X),* PowerKids Pr.) 2007. (Illus.). (J). (gr. -1-3). lib. bdg. 22.60 *(978-1-4042-3823-7(9))* Rosen Publishing Group, Inc., The.
Somervill, Barbara. Fire Ant. 2009. (21st Century Skills Library: Animal Invaders Ser.). (ENG.). 32p. (gr. 4-8). lib. bdg. 28.50 *(978-1-60279-328-6(X),* 200224) Cherry Lake Publishing.
Spilsbury, Richard & Spilsbury, Louise. Ant Colonies. 2013. (Animal Armies Ser.). (ENG., Illus.). 32p. (J). (gr. k-5). pap. 10.00 *(978-1-4777-0326-7(8));* lib. bdg. 25.25 *(978-1-4777-0302-1(0))* Rosen Publishing Group, Inc., The. (PowerKids Pr.).
Squire, Ann O. Ants. 2003. (True Bks.). (ENG., Illus.). 48p. (J). 25.00 *(978-0-516-22659-0(2),* Children's Pr.) Scholastic Library Publishing.
Steffora, Tracey. Animal Math: Adding, Taking Away, & Skip Counting, 1 vol. 2014. (Animal Math Ser.). (ENG.). 32p. (gr. -1-1). 29.99 *(978-1-4846-0061-0(4),* NA-h) Heinemann-Raintree.
Stewart, Melissa. Ants. 2010. (Readers Ser.). (ENG., Illus.). 32p. (J). (gr. -1-1). 13.90 *(978-1-4263-0609-9(1));* pap. 3.99 *(978-1-4263-0608-2(3))* National Geographic Society. (National Geographic Children's Bks.).
Sundance/Newbridge LLC Staff. The World of Ants. 2007. (Early Science Ser.). (gr. k-3). 18.95 *(978-1-4007-6621-5(4));* pap. 6.10 *(978-1-4007-6617-8(6))* Sundance/Newbridge Educational Publishing.
Sweet, Melissa. Ants (1 Hardcover/1 CD) 2016. (National Geographic Readers: Pre-Reader Ser.). (ENG.). (J). *(978-1-4301-2115-2(7))* Live Oak Media.
—Ants (1 Paperback/1 CD) 2016. (National Geographic Readers: Pre-Reader Ser.). (ENG.). (J). pap. *(978-1-4301-2114-5(9))* Live Oak Media.
Tabletop Zoo: Ants. 2003. 43.95 *(978-0-673-57978-2(6))* Celebration Pr.
Taylor, Trace. Ants. 2008. (2G Bugs Ser.). (ENG.). 12p. (J). (gr. k-2). pap. 5.99 *(978-1-59301-854-2(1))* American Reading Co.
Taylor, Trace & Sanchez, Lucia M. Hormigas (Ants) 2011. (poder de 100 - Bichos Ser.). (SPA.). 12p. pap. 33.92 *(978-1-61541-289-1(1))* American Reading Co.
Troupe, Thomas Kingsley. Do Ants Get Lost? Learning about Animal Communication with the Garbage Gang, 1 vol. Toye, Derek, illus. 2014. (Garbage Gang's Super Science Questions Ser.). (ENG.). 24p. (gr. k-2). lib. bdg. 26.65 *(978-1-4795-5478-2(2))* Picture Window Bks.
Trueit, Trudi Strain. Ants. 2013. 32p. (J). (gr. 6-9). 28.50 *(978-1-60870-240-4(5));* pap. 10.58 *(978-1-62712-026-5(2))* Cavendish Square Publishing.
—Ants. 2009. (Benchmark Rebus Ser.). 24p. (gr. k-1). 15.95 *(978-0-7614-3961-5(7))* Marshall Cavendish Corp.
Twist, Clint. The Life Cycle of Army Ants. 2013. (Creepy Crawlies Ser.). 32p. (gr. 3-6). *(978-1-84898-517-9(7),* TickTock Books) Octopus Publishing Group.
Waldendorf, Kurt. How Strong Is an Ant? 2017. (Comparison Fun Ser.). (ENG.). 24p. (J). (gr. -1-2). lib. bdg. 27.07 *(978-1-5038-1681-7(8),* 211516) Child's World, Inc., The.
Washington, Joi. The Ant. 2011. (Power 50 - Predator Bugs Ser.). 32p. (J). (gr. k-2). pap. 7.95 *(978-1-61541-391-1(X))* American Reading Co.
—Ants. 2011. (Predator Bugs Ser.). 16p. pap. 39.62 *(978-1-61541-360-7(X))* American Reading Co.
Washington, Joi & Byerly, Robbie. Ants. Byerly, Robbie, illus. 2010. (1-3Y Bugs Ser.). (ENG., Illus.). 16p. (J). (gr. k-2). pap. 5.99 *(978-1-61541-359-1(6))* American Reading Co.
Washington, Joi, et al. Hormigas: Ants. 2011. (2Y Bichos Depredadores Ser.). (SPA., Illus.). 16p. (J). (gr. k-2). pap. 6.99 *(978-1-61541-361-4(8))* American Reading Co.
West, William. All about Ants. (Real Readers - Upper Emergent Ser.). (ENG., Illus.). 12p. (gr. 1-2). 2008. pap. 5.90 *(978-0-8239-8120-5(7))* 2006. 33.50 *(978-1-4042-6213-3(X))* Rosen Publishing Group, Inc., The.
Whiting, Sue. All about Ants. 2006. (Science Chapters Ser.). (ENG., Illus.). 40p. (J). (gr. 1-4). lib. bdg. 17.90 *(978-0-7922-5948-0(3),* National Geographic Children's Bks.) National Geographic Society.
William H. Sadlier Staff. Alexander Ant Cools Off. 2005. (Early Library). (gr. k-2). 24.00 net. *(978-0-8215-8950-2(4))* Sadlier, William H. Inc.
Wimmer, Teresa. Ants. 2006. (My First Look at: Insects Ser.). (Illus.). 24p. (J). lib. bdg. 15.95 *(978-1-58341-453-8(3),* Creative Education) Creative Co., The.
Woodward, John. Ant. 2010. (Garden Minibeasts up Close Ser.). 32p. (gr. 2-4). 30.00 *(978-1-60413-896-2(3),* Chelsea Clubhouse) Facts On File, Inc.

ANTS—FICTION

Aesop. The Ant & the Grasshopper. 2012. (J). 29.99 *(978-1-61913-106-4(4))* Weigl Pubs., Inc.
—The Grasshopper & the Ant: A Tale about Planning. Hockerman, Dennis, illus. 2006. (J). *(978-1-59939-082-6(5),* Reader's Digest Young Families, Inc.) Studio Fun International.
Allen, Teresa R. The Tale of the Teeny, Tiny Black Ant: Helping Children Learn Persistence. Seroya, Tea, illus. 2011. (Let's Talk Ser.). (ENG.). 48p. (J). (gr. -1-2). pap. 9.95 *(978-0-88282-351-5(5))* New Horizon Pr. Pubs., Inc.
Ammerman, Michelle. Amos's Beautiful Day. 2005. 12p. 6.99 *(978-1-4116-3819-8(0))* Lulu Pr., Inc.
Anderson, Jane. Inspector Insector. 2005. (J). pap. *(978-1-4108-4196-4(0))* Benchmark Education Co.
The Ant & the Grasshopper: Individual Title Six-Packs. (Story Steps Ser.). (gr. k-2). 32.00 *(978-0-7635-9846-4(1))* Rigby Education.
The Ant & the Grasshopper: Small Book. (Pebble Soup Explorations Ser.). 16p. (gr. -1-18). 5.00 *(978-0-7635-7049-1(4))* Rigby Education.
Anthony, Ross. Please Don't Step on the Ants. Anthony, Ross, illus. 2006. (ENG, CHI, SPA & JPN., Illus.). (J). per. *(978-0-9727894-4-8(8))* Arizona Blueberry Studios.
Ariel, A. D. The Ant & the Butterfly. 2016. (Spring Forward Ser.). (J). (gr. 1). *(978-1-4900-2239-0(2))* Benchmark Education Co.
Avi. A Beginning, a Muddle, & an End: The Right Way to Write Writing. Tusa, Tricia, illus. 2008. (ENG.). 176p. (J). (gr. 2-5). 14.95 *(978-0-15-205555-4(X))* Houghton Mifflin Harcourt Publishing Co.
—The End of the Beginning: Being the Adventures of a Small Snail (and an Even Smaller Ant) Tusa, Tricia, illus. 2008. (ENG.). 144p. (J). (gr. 2-5). pap. 6.95 *(978-0-15-205532-5(0))* Houghton Mifflin Harcourt Publishing Co.
Ayozie, Ben-EL. Ants Everywhere. 2011. 20p. 11.49 *(978-1-4520-3431-7(1))* AuthorHouse.
Bahz, Kahanni. Ants? in My Pants? An Animated Tale. Fraser, Kevin, illus. 2005. 72p. (J). (gr. k-4). reprint ed. 22.00 *(978-0-7567-8705-9(X))* DIANE Publishing Co.
Bailer, Darice, et al. El Saltamontes y Las Hormigas. Bassa, illus. 2007. (SPA & ENG.). 28p. (J). *(978-0-545-02965-0(1))* Scholastic, Inc.
Baker, Keith. Just How Long Can a Long String Be? 2009. (J). pap. *(978-0-545-08662-2(0),* Levine, Arthur A. Bks.) Scholastic, Inc.
Banner, Angela. Ant & Bee. 2014. (Ant & Bee Ser.: 1). (ENG., Illus.). 112p. (Orig.). (J). (gr. -1-k). 7.99 *(978-1-4052-6671-0(6))* Egmont Bks., Ltd. GBR. Dist: Independent Pubs. Group.
—Ant & Bee & Kind Dog. 2014. (Ant & Bee Ser.). (ENG., Illus.). 112p. (J). (gr. -1-k). 7.99 *(978-1-4052-7075-5(6))* Egmont Bks., Ltd. GBR. Dist: Independent Pubs. Group.
—Ant & Bee & the ABC. 2014. (Ant & Bee Ser.). (ENG., Illus.). 96p. (J). (gr. -1-k). 7.99 *(978-1-4052-7074-8(8))* Egmont Bks., Ltd. GBR. Dist: Independent Pubs. Group.
—Ant & Bee & the Doctor. 2014. (Ant & Bee Ser.). (ENG., Illus.). 88p. (J). (gr. -1-k). 7.99 *(978-1-4052-7073-1(X))* Egmont Bks., Ltd. GBR. Dist: Independent Pubs. Group.
—Ant & Bee & the Rainbow. 2014. (Ant & Bee Ser.). (ENG., Illus.). 96p. (J). (gr. -1-k). 7.99 *(978-1-4052-6674-1(0))* Egmont Bks., Ltd. GBR. Dist: Independent Pubs. Group.
—Ant & Bee Count 123. 2015. (Ant & Bee Ser.). (ENG., Illus.). 96p. (J). (gr. -1-k). 7.99 *(978-1-4052-7513-2(8))* Egmont Bks., Ltd. GBR. Dist: Independent Pubs. Group.
—Ant & Bee Go Shopping. 2015. (Ant & Bee Ser.). (ENG., Illus.). 84p. (J). (gr. -1-k). 7.99 *(978-1-4052-7514-9(6))* Egmont Bks., Ltd. GBR. Dist: Independent Pubs. Group.
—Ant & Bee Time. 2015. (Ant & Bee Ser.). (ENG., Illus.). 96p. (J). (gr. -1-k). 7.99 *(978-1-4052-7516-3(2))* Egmont Bks., Ltd. GBR. Dist: Independent Pubs. Group.
—Around the World with Ant & Bee. 2014. (Ant & Bee Ser.). (ENG., Illus.). 96p. (J). (gr. -1-k). 7.99 *(978-1-4052-6676-5(7))* Egmont Bks., Ltd. GBR. Dist: Independent Pubs. Group.
—Happy Birthday with Ant & Bee. 2014. (Ant & Bee Ser.). (ENG., Illus.). 96p. (J). (gr. -1-k). 7.99 *(978-1-4052-6675-8(9))* Egmont Bks., Ltd. GBR. Dist: Independent Pubs. Group.
—More & More Ant & Bee. 2014. (Ant & Bee Ser.: 3). (ENG., Illus.). 112p. (J). (gr. -1-k). 7.99 *(978-1-4052-6673-4(2))* Egmont Bks., Ltd. GBR. Dist: Independent Pubs. Group.
—More Ant & Bee. 2014. (Ant & Bee Ser.: 2). (ENG., Illus.). 112p. (J). (gr. -1-k). 7.99 *(978-1-4052-6672-7(4))* Egmont Bks., Ltd. GBR. Dist: Independent Pubs. Group.
Bapiraju Gandham. The Wizard of Ants. 2010. 88p. pap. 33.48 *(978-1-4269-1940-4(9))* Trafford Publishing.
Beatty, Susi. Angie the Ant & the Bumblebee Tree. 2006. (Illus.). 30p. (J). 19.95 *(978-0-9773653-0-2(1))* Susi B. Marketing, Inc.
Bishop, Clive. Trophy Trouble. 2009. 74p. pap. 9.99 *(978-1-60860-547-7(7),* Strategic Bk. Publishing) Strategic Book Publishing & Rights Agency (SBPRA).
Blackwell, Nancy. Andy the Ant in Precious Cargo. Ettinger, Charles, illus. 2011. 40p. pap. 14.99 *(978-1-937129-03-3(9))* Faithful Life Pubs.
Bolander, Sharon Miller. I Wish That I Could Fly. 2011. 36p. pap. 24.95 *(978-1-4560-8058-7(X))* America Star Bks.
Bradley, Timothy J. Infestation. Bradley, Timothy J., illus. 2013. (ENG., Illus.). 192p. (J). (gr. 3-7). pap. 5.99 *(978-0-545-45904-4(4),* Scholastic Paperbacks) Scholastic, Inc.
Bray, Pamela. Elephant & Ant. 2012. 36p. 24.95 *(978-1-4626-5986-9(1))* America Star Bks.
Britton, Vicky Lynn. Can You Play Today? 2013. 24p. pap. 24.95 *(978-1-4626-9149-4(8))* America Star Bks.
Brouwer, Sigmund. Bug's Eye View: Annie Ant, Don't Cry! 2004. (Bug's-Eye View Bks.). (ENG., Illus.). 18p. (J). pap. 4.99 *(978-0-8499-7757-2(6))* Nelson, Thomas Inc.
—Daddy Ant, You Never Listen. 2004. (Bug's-Eye View Bks.). (ENG., Illus.). 18p. (J). pap. 4.99 *(978-0-8499-7755-8(X))* Nelson, Thomas Inc.
—Mommy Ant, Eat Your Vegetables. 2004. (Bug's-Eye View Bks.). (ENG., Illus.). 18p. (J). pap. 4.99 *(978-0-8499-7756-5(8))* Nelson, Thomas Inc.
Burris, Priscilla. The Ants Go Marching: Count-and-Sing. Burris, Priscilla, illus. 2016. (ENG., Illus.). 16p. (J). (— 1). bds. 6.99 *(978-0-545-82504-7(0),* Cartwheel Bks.) Scholastic, Inc.
Calabrese, Paul. The Good Bug Book ... (and Other Cool Creatures) 2012. 24p. pap. 15.99 *(978-1-4797-4131-1(0))* Xlibris Corp.
Cannon, Janell. Crickwing. 2005. (Illus.). (gr. 1-4). 17.00 *(978-0-7569-5051-4(1))* Perfection Learning Corp.
CHARLES, A. M. A. N. & 1st World Publishing. Dad & Me Go to School. 2006. 24p. per. 9.95 *(978-1-4218-9924-4(8))* 1st World Publishing, Inc.
Ciocon-Heller, Vicky. Paquita-Gamita's Wiggling? 2012. 48p. pap. 10.00 *(978-1-4349-1232-9(9))* Dorrance Publishing Co., Inc.
Clark, Wendy S. The Troubles with Bubbles. 2010. 32p. pap. 13.00 *(978-1-60911-658-3(5),* Eloquent Bks.) Strategic Book Publishing & Rights Agency (SBPRA).
Coccia, Mina. Mother Nature & Mz Bee. 2012. 36p. pap. 14.95 *(978-1-4575-0709-0(9))* Dog Ear Publishing, LLC.
Cooper, Ann Goode. Zebordee Goes to the Races. Jessee, Diana, illus. 2005. 32p. (J). (gr. -1-3). *(978-1-933251-01-1(8))* Parkway Pubs., Inc.
Crisp, Dan, illus. The Ants Go Marching! (Classic Books with Holes 8x8 with CD Ser.). (ENG.). 16p. (J). 2013. (gr. -1). pap. incl. audio compact disk *(978-1-84643-622-2(2))* 2009. (gr. -1-1). *(978-1-84643-207-1(3))* 2009. pap. incl. audio compact disk *(978-1-84643-256-9(1))* Child's Play International Ltd.
Cummings, Troy. Whack of the P-Rex. 2014. (Notebook of Doom Ser.: 5). (ENG.). 96p. (J). (gr. 1-3). pap. 4.99 *(978-0-545-69895-5(2))* Scholastic, Inc.
Dalton, Nicola. The Adventurers - the Mystery of the Magical Crystal. 2011. 108p. (gr. -1). 21.23 *(978-1-4520-6661-5(2));* pap. 10.99 *(978-1-4520-6660-8(4))* AuthorHouse.
Danley, Jerry J. Billy Black Ant's Exciting Adventures. Hilley, Thomas, illus. 2012. 56p. pap. 12.99 *(978-0-9885180-5-6(8))* Mindstir Media.
Depner, Stefan. Aunt Francy the Ant Book II. 2009. (J). pap. *(978-1-61584-724-2(3))* Independent Pub.
Dickey, Eric Wayne. Alex the Ant Goes to the Beach. Paccia, Abbey, illus. 2014. (ENG.). 32p. (J). (gr. k-2). 17.99 *(978-1-940052-08-3(4))* Craigmore Creations.
Dietrich, David. Revenge of the Lucky Thirteen. 2004. (Illus.). 76p. pap. *(978-1-84401-288-6(3))* Athena Pr.
Duguay, Kathleen. Andy Finds a Home. 2012. 24p. pap. 28.03 *(978-1-4691-7390-0(5))* Xlibris Corp.
Edwards, Antonio. Script the Strong Ant. 2011. 32p. pap. 15.99 *(978-1-4634-2201-1(6))* AuthorHouse.
Edwards, Pamela Duncan. The Wacky Wedding: A Book of Alphabet Antics. 2005. 32p. (J). pap. *(978-0-7868-1172-4(2))* Hyperion Bks. for Children.
Emberley, Rebecca. The Ant & the Grasshopper. Emberley, Ed, illus. 2012. (ENG.). 28p. (J). (gr. -1-2). 18.99 *(978-1-59643-493-6(7),* 9781596434936) Roaring Brook Pr.
Emberley, Rebecca & Emberley, Ed. The Ant & the Grasshopper. 2013. 29.95 incl. audio compact disk *(978-0-545-57140-1(5))* Weston Woods Studios, Inc.
Eyckerman, Merel, illus. The Ant & the Grasshopper. 2013. (Usborne First Reading: Level 1 Ser.). (ENG.). 32p. (J). (gr. -1-3). 6.99 *(978-0-7945-2257-5(2),* Usborne) EDC Publishing.

Flor Ada, Alma. One More Friend. Fatus, Sophie, illus. 2007. 24p. (J). *(978-0-15-206278-1(5))* Harcourt Trade Pubs.

Frontiera, Deborah K. New South Dairy Colony 50. 2nd ed. 2004. (Chronicles of Henry Roach-Dairier: Bk. 2). 247p. (YA). (gr. 5-18). per. 15.95 *(978-0-9753410-2-5(2))* Jade Enterprises.

—To Build a Tunnel. 2nd ed. 2004. (Chronicles of Henry Roach-Dairier: Bk. 1). 218p. (YA). (gr. 5-18). per. 15.95 *(978-0-9753410-1-8(4))* Jade Enterprises.

Glennon, Michelle. My Big Green Teacher: Please Turn off the Lights. Glennon, Michelle, illus. 2008. (ENG., Illus.). 32p. (J). 19.95 *(978-0-9796625-3-9(2))* GDG Publishing.

Gokhale, Ruby. Emma & Kelly. 2011. 20p. pap. 11.99 *(978-1-4567-5288-0(X))* AuthorHouse.

Gray, Deanne. Ante: Strangers. 2011. 24p. pap. 12.79 *(978-1-4634-1967-7(8))* AuthorHouse.

Gray, Luli. Ant & Grasshopper. Ferri, Giuliano, illus. 2011. (ENG.). 32p. (J). (gr. -1-2). 17.99 *(978-1-4169-5140-7(7),* McElderry, Margaret K. Bks.) McElderry, Margaret K. Bks.

Greenburg, Dan. Secrets of Dripping Fang: Attack of the Giant Octopus. Fischer, Scott M., illus. 2009. (Secrets of Dripping Fang Ser.). (ENG.). 160p. 25.65 *(978-1-59961-537-0(1))* Spotlight.

—Secrets of Dripping Fang: Fall of the House of Mandible. Fischer, Scott M., illus. 2009. (Secrets of Dripping Fang Ser.). (ENG.). 160p. 25.65 *(978-1-59961-535-6(5))* Spotlight.

—Secrets of Dripping Fang: Please Don't Eat the Children: Book 7: Book 7. Fischer, Scott M., illus. 2009. (Secrets of Dripping Fang Ser.). (ENG.). 160p. 25.65 *(978-1-59961-538-7(X))* Spotlight.

—Secrets of Dripping Fang: The Onts. Fischer, Scott M., illus. 2009. (Secrets of Dripping Fang Ser.). (ENG.). 144p. 25.65 *(978-1-59961-532-5(0))* Spotlight.

—Secrets of Dripping Fang: The Shluffmuffin Boy Is History. Fischer, Scott M., illus. 2009. (Secrets of Dripping Fang Ser.). (ENG.). 176p. 25.65 *(978-1-59961-536-3(3))* Spotlight.

—Secrets of Dripping Fang: Treachery & Betrayal at Jolly Days. Fischer, Scott M., illus. 2009. (Secrets of Dripping Fang Ser.). (ENG.). 144p. 25.65 *(978-1-59961-533-2(9))* Spotlight.

—Secrets of Dripping Fang: When Bad Snakes Attack Good Children. Fischer, Scott M., illus. 2009. (Secrets of Dripping Fang Ser.). (ENG.). 144p. 25.65 *(978-1-59961-539-4(8))* Spotlight.

—Secrets of Dripping Fang, Book Seven: Please Don't Eat the Children. Fischer, Scott M., illus. 2007. (Secrets of Dripping Fang Ser.: Bk. 7). (ENG.). 160p. (J). (gr. 2-5). 11.95 *(978-0-15-206047-3(2))* Houghton Mifflin Harcourt Publishing Co.

Groves. Ant Eggs, Bk. 2. Date not set. (Illus.). 16p. (J). pap. 129.15 *(978-0-582-18793-1(1))* Addison-Wesley Longman, Ltd. GBR. Dist: Trans-Atlantic Pubns., Inc.

Halfmann, Janet. Little Black Ant on Park Street. Rietz, Kathleen, illus. 2009. (ENG.). 32p. 10.95 *(978-1-60727-008-9(0));* 9.95 *(978-1-60727-006-5(4));* 19.95 *(978-1-60727-005-8(6));* (J). pap. 6.95 *(978-1-60727-003-4(X))* Soundprints.

Hall, Michael. It's an Orange Aardvark! Hall, Michael, illus. 2014. (ENG., Illus.). 40p. (J). (gr. -1-3). 17.99 *(978-0-06-225206-7(2),* Greenwillow Bks.) HarperCollins Pubs.

Hanson, Anders. Ant King, 1 vol. Haberstroh, Anne, illus. 2007. (Critter Chronicles Ser.). (ENG.). 24p. (J). (gr. k-3). lib. bdg. 24.21 *(978-1-59928-430-9(8),* SandCastle) ABDO Publishing Co.

Harris, Nelson. Andrew of the Antimites. 2006. 83p. pap. 16.95 *(978-1-4241-3429-8(3))* PublishAmerica, Inc.

Hart, Kim. Beatrice & Raymond: A Universal MessagesTM Book. 2012. 32p. pap. 16.99 *(978-1-4772-4951-2(6))* AuthorHouse.

Hart, Teresa. The Ant & the Alligator. 2007. 84p. per. 19.95 *(978-1-4241-7182-8(2))* America Star Bks.

—The Ant & the Lost Spider, 1 vol. 2009. 76p. pap. 19.95 *(978-1-60749-296-2(2))* America Star Bks.

Hofmeister, Alan, et al. Ben the Ant. (Reading for All Learners Ser.). (Illus.). (J). pap. *(978-1-56861-123-5(4))* Swift Learning Resources.

Holub, Joan. Big Heart! A Valentine's Day Tale. Terry, Will, illus. 2007. (Ant Hill Ser.). (ENG.). 24p. (J). (gr. -1-k). lib. bdg. 13.89 *(978-1-4169-2562-0(7),* Simon & Schuster/Paula Wiseman Bks.) Simon & Schuster/Paula Wiseman Bks.

—Big Heart! A Valentine's Day Tale. Terry, Will, illus. 2007. (Ant Hill Ser.). (ENG.). 24p. (J). (gr. -1-k). pap. 3.99 *(978-1-4169-0957-6(5),* Simon Spotlight) Simon Spotlight.

—Good Luck! A St. Patrick's Day Story. Terry, Will, illus. 2007. (Ant Hill Ser.). (ENG.). 24p. (J). (gr. -1-k). lib. bdg. 11.89 *(978-1-4169-2560-6(0),* Aladdin Library) Simon & Schuster Children's Publishing.

—Good Luck! A St. Patrick's Day Story. Terry, Will, illus. 2007. (Ant Hill Ser.). (ENG.). 24p. (J). (gr. -1-k). pap. 3.99 *(978-1-4169-0955-2(9),* Simon Spotlight) Simon Spotlight.

—Scaredy-Pants! A Halloween Story. Terry, Will, illus. 2007. (Ant Hill Ser.). (ENG.). 24p. (J). (gr. -1-k). pap. 3.99 *(978-1-4169-0956-9(7),* Simon Spotlight/Nickelodeon) Simon Spotlight/Nickelodeon.

—Spring Is Here! A Story about Seeds. Terry, Will, illus. 2008. (Ant Hill Ser.). (ENG.). 24p. (J). (gr. -1-k). lib. bdg. 13.89 *(978-1-4169-5132-2(6),* Simon & Schuster/Paula Wiseman Bks.) Simon & Schuster/Paula Wiseman Bks.

—Spring Is Here! A Story about Seeds. Terry, Will, illus. 2008. (Ant Hill Ser.). (ENG.). 24p. (J). (gr. -1-k). pap. 3.99 *(978-1-4169-5131-5(8),* Simon Spotlight) Simon Spotlight.

Hoose, Phillip & Hoose, Hannah. Oye, Hormiguita. Tilley, Debbie, illus. 2004.Tr. of Hey Little Ant! (SPA.). 32p. (J). (gr. -1-2). pap. 7.99 *(978-1-58246-089-5(2),* Tricycle Pr.) Random Hse. Children's Bks.

La Hormiga y el Saltamontes: Lap Book. (Pebble Soup Exploraciones Ser.). (SPA.). 16p. (gr. -1-18). 21.00 *(978-0-7578-1682-6(7))* Rigby Education.

La hormiga y el Saltamontes: Small Book. (Pebble Soup Exploraciones Ser.). (SPA.). 16p. (gr. -1-18). 5.00 *(978-0-7578-1722-9(X))* Rigby Education.

Horwill, Alice. Arnold Ant. 2015. (ENG., Illus.). 53p. (J). (gr. 1-2). pap. 18.95 *(978-1-78455-113-1(9),* b7429fa0-861a-48af-92ed-ebb2c8e85511) Austin, Stan AUS. Dist: Bookmasters Distribution.

House, Brandy. Adam Ant, 1 vol. 2009. 18p. pap. 19.95 *(978-1-4489-1940-6(1))* PublishAmerica, Inc.

Houseal, Phil, et al. Sam Has Ants. 2013. 30p. pap. 12.95 *(978-0-9832564-2-7(X))* Full House Productions.

Ives, Bob. The Three Ants & Mother Bird. Deskov, Vladimir, ed. Fairy, Meg, illus. 2004. 40p. (J). *(978-1-920832-06-3(8))* Four Heads Publishing Group Pty, Ltd.

Jackowski, Rosemarie. Busy Ants under Red Bricks. 2011. 24p. pap. 11.69 *(978-1-4634-1716-1(0))* AuthorHouse.

Jackson, Jasmine. Robert's Really Restless. 2011. 24p. pap. 15.99 *(978-1-4568-5343-3(0))* Xlibris Corp.

James, Anne. !Ataque de las Hormigas! Ramirez, Alma B., tr. from ENG. Lewis, Anthony, illus. 2008. (Science Solves It! en Espanol Ser.). (SPA.). 32p. (J). (gr. -1-3). pap. 5.95 *(978-1-57565-278-8(1))* Kane Press, Inc.

—¡ataque de Las Hormigas! (Ant Attack!) 2009. (SPA.). pap. 34.95 *(978-0-7613-4802-3(6))* Lerner Publishing Group.

Jarman, Julia. Ants in Your Pants! Parker-Rees, Guy, illus. 2011. (ENG.). 32p. (J). (gr. -1-k). pap. 10.99 *(978-1-4083-0525-6(9))* Hodder & Stoughton GBR. Dist: Hachette Bk. Group.

Joseph, Patricia L. A Look At. 2009. 20p. pap. 12.50 *(978-1-4490-2421-5(1))* AuthorHouse.

Katschke, Judy & Nickle, John. The Ant Bully: Movie Novel. 2006. (Illus.). 88p. (J). *(978-1-4156-8331-6(X))* Scholastic, Inc.

Kelly, Cheryl. Adam the Adventurous Ant. 2011. 24p. pap. 15.99 *(978-1-4568-6366-1(5))* Xlibris Corp.

Krishnaswami, Uma. The Ants Have a Picnic. 2006. (Early Explorers Ser.). (J). pap. *(978-1-4108-6115-3(5))* Benchmark Education Co.

The Little Ant. (Early Intervention Levels Ser.). 47.88 *(978-0-7362-1103-1(9))* CENGAGE Learning.

Malcolm, James. Anthology: Ants Odyssey. 2012. 176p. pap. 19.99 *(978-1-4771-2183-2(8))* Xlibris Corp.

—Anthology 1: Ants Odyssey. 2012. 174p. (gr. 1-1). 29.99 *(978-1-4771-2184-9(6))* Xlibris Corp.

Mandla. Garden Green Hills: And Finally Ants Run the Village. 2013. 102p. pap. 15.99 *(978-1-4797-1482-7(8))* Xlibris Corp.

Marquis, Melanie. Bugbug & the Ants. 2013. 44p. pap. 12.99 *(978-1-60820-841-8(9))* MLR Pr., LLC.

Martin, David Lozell. All for Pie, Pie for All. Gorbachev, Valeri, illus. 2008. (ENG.). 32p. (J). (gr. -1-2). pap. 6.99 *(978-0-7636-3891-7(9))* Candlewick Pr.

Marvel & Wyatt, Chris. Marvel's Ant-Man: the Junior Novel. 2015. (ENG.). 144p. (J). (gr. 3-7). pap. 6.99 *(978-0-316-25674-2(9))* Little, Brown Bks. for Young Readers.

Marvel Staff & Palacios, Tomas. Marvel's Ant-Man: Reader. 2015. (Passport to Reading Level 2 Ser.). (ENG., Illus.). 32p. (J). (gr. -1-3). pap. 3.99 *(978-0-316-25671-1(4))* Little, Brown Bks. for Young Readers.

Massey, W. A. Joey an Ant's Story. 2008. 20p. pap. 24.95 *(978-1-60441-910-8(5))* America Star Bks.

McClure, Brian D. The Ants. Plumlee, Buddy, illus. 2009. (Brian D. Mcclure Childrens Book Collection). 57p. (J). (gr. -1-3). 16.95 *(978-1-933426-10-5(1))* Universal Flag Publishing.

McDonald, Megan. Ant & Honey Bee: A Pair of Friends at Halloween. Karas, G. Brian, illus. 2013. (Candlewick Sparks Ser.). (ENG.). 48p. (J). (gr. k-4). pap. 3.99 *(978-0-7636-6864-8(8))* Candlewick Pr.

—Ant & Honey Bee: A Pair of Friends in Winter. Karas, G. Brian, illus. (Candlewick Sparks Ser.). (ENG.). 64p. (J). (gr. k-4). 2014. pap. 3.99 *(978-0-7636-6862-4(1))* 2013. 14.99 *(978-0-7636-5712-3(3))* Candlewick Pr.

McElligott, Matthew. The Lion's Share. McElligott, Matthew, illus. 2012. (ENG., Illus.). 40p. (J). (gr. k-8). pap. 8.99 *(978-0-8027-2360-4(8),* 9780802723604, Bloomsbury USA Childrens) Bloomsbury Publishing USA.

—The Lion's Share: A Tale of Halving Cake & Eating It, Too. McElligott, Matthew, illus. 2009. (ENG., Illus.). 32p. (J). (gr. k-3). 16.99 *(978-0-8027-9768-1(7),* 9780802797681, Bloomsbury USA Childrens) Bloomsbury Publishing USA.

McGough, Wallace D. The Adventures of Walter Ant Bk. I: The Unknown. 56p. (J). pap. 9.95 *(978-0-9645180-0-1(7))* Family Value Publishing.

McLaughlin, Diane & Tully, Lisa. The WhizAnt Who Isn't Coloring & Activity Book. 2003. (Illus.). 32p. (J). cd-rom 15.95 *(978-0-9722249-1-8(2))* Bugeye Bks.

Menconi, James Pasqual. Queen Mariella & the Fable of the Peony. 2011. 24p. (gr. -1). pap. 13.50 *(978-1-4567-3934-8(4))* AuthorHouse.

Michie, Brandon J. Andie the Ant: Animal Lessons. 2012. 16p. pap. 14.97 *(978-1-4670-2585-0(2))* AuthorHouse.

Mihalko, Ross, et al. Ant & the Grasshopper (Musical) 2012. (J). 8.95 *(978-0-573-70112-2(1))* French, Samuel Inc.

Miller, Roger Carlton. The Ant & the Grasshopper l.t. ed. 2003. Orig. Title: Same. (Illus.). 14p. *(978-0-9712104-2-4(X))* Texas Woman's Univ. Pr.

Mills, Claudia. The Trouble with Ants. Kath, Katie, illus. (Nora Notebooks Ser.: 1). (ENG.). 176p. (J). (gr. 2-5). 2016. 6.99 *(978-0-385-39163-4(3),* Yearling) 2015. lib. bdg. 17.99 *(978-0-385-39162-7(5),* Knopf Bks. for Young Readers) Random Hse. Children's Bks.

Miyares, Daniel. Bring Me a Rock! Miyares, Daniel, illus. 2016. (ENG., Illus.). 40p. (J). (gr. -1-3). 17.99 *(978-1-4814-4602-0(9),* Simon & Schuster Bks. For Young Readers) Simon & Schuster Bks. For Young Readers.

Moeller mé illuminé, Jo, illus. La Hormiguita ¿ A Folktale about the Perseverant Little Ant. 2005. (SPA.). (J). *(978-0-9644678-4-2(4))* Bilingual Pubns.

Montiel, Joaquin Londaiz, et al. Hormigosaurios/The Antosaurus. 2011. (SPA.). 72p. *(978-84-488-3164-6(0))* Penguin Random House Grupo Editorial.

Mora, Pat. Una Cesta de Cumpleanos para Tia Abuela. Lang, Cecily, illus. (SPA.). (J). (gr. k-2). pap. 3.16 net. *(978-0-395-78817-2(X),* HMS088) Houghton Mifflin Harcourt Publishing Co.

Moran, Alex. What Day Is It? (¿Qué Día es Hoy?) Campoy, F. Isabel & Flor Ada, Alma, trs. Moreton, Daniel, illus. 2008. (Green Light Readers Level 1 Ser.). (ENG & SPA.). 28p. (J). (gr. -1-3). pap. 3.95 *(978-0-15-206281-1(5))* Houghton Mifflin Harcourt Publishing Co.

Moran, Alex & Trimble, Patti. What Day Is It? Moreton, Daniel, illus. 2003. (Green Light Readers Level 1 Ser.). (ENG.). 24p. (J). (gr. -1-3). pap. 3.95 *(978-0-15-204846-4(4))* Houghton Mifflin Harcourt Publishing Co.

Navarro-Talavera, Carmen. The Ant Lucy & the Hurricane. 2009. 48p. pap. 17.49 *(978-1-4389-7788-1(3))* AuthorHouse.

—La Hormiguita Lucy y el Huracán. 2009. 48p. pap. 17.49 *(978-1-4389-7787-4(5))* AuthorHouse.

Nguyen, Llustrated By Luan. Story of an Ant: Ant & an Elephant. 2008. 36p. pap. 16.99 *(978-1-4389-1534-0(9))* AuthorHouse.

O'Nan, Gerald D. The Adventures of Andy Ant: Lawn Mower on the Loose. McGary, Norman, illus. 2014. (ENG.). 28p. (gr. -1-4). pap. 9.95 *(978-1-61448-673-2(5))* Morgan James Publishing.

O'Nan, Lawrence W. & O'Nan, Gerald D. The Adventures of Andy Ant: The Swimming Hole Disaster. McGary, Norman, illus. 2014. (ENG.). 34p. (gr. -1-4). pap. 9.95 *(978-1-61448-799-9(5))* Morgan James Publishing.

Orshoski, Paul & Max, Dave. We Both Read-The Ant & the Pancake. 2015. (ENG., Illus.). 44p. (J). (gr. k-1). pap. 4.99 *(978-1-60115-272-5(8))* Treasure Bay, Inc.

Palacios, Tomas. I Am Ant-Man. 2015. (Illus.). 32p. *(978-0-316-26255-2(2))* Little Brown & Co.

La Paloma y la Hormiga. (SPA.). pap. 5.95 incl. audio compact disk *(978-88-8148-801-8(9))* EMC/Paradigm Publishing.

Park, Wan-Seo. 7 Nyeon Donganui Jam. 2015. (KOR., Illus.). 40p. (J). *(978-89-7288-768-3(4))* Jag-ga Jeongsin Publishing Co.

Parker, Emma. Sebastian the Ant. 2010. (Illus.). pap. *(978-1-877561-14-6(2))* First Edition Ltd.

Peirs, Adam. Hopper's Helpful Day. 2012. 24p. pap. 14.99 *(978-1-105-25383-6(X))* Lulu Pr., Inc.

Penina, M. The Ant & the Wheat Kernel: For Young Readers. Kaufman, Yaki, illus. 2012. 24p. 19.75 net. *(978-1-60046-090-6(9))* Yofi Bk. Publishing, Inc.

Perugini, Donna. Do Angels Go Camping? 2010. 32p. (Orig.). pap. 9.99 *(978-0-88144-536-7(3))* Yorkshire Publishing Group.

Phillips, Gina & Martin, Stuart. Ants & Caterpillars. 2003. (Busy Bugs Ser.). 12p. (J). bds. 14.95 *(978-1-74047-240-1(3))* Book Co. Publishing Pty, Ltd., The AUS. Dist: Penton Overseas, Inc.

Phillips, Noell G. The Ants That Were & Wish They Are, 1 vol. 2009. 96p. pap. 19.95 *(978-1-60813-952-1(2))* America Star Bks.

Philpot, Lorna & Philpot, Graham. Find Anthony Ant. 2006. (Illus.). 24p. (J). (gr. -1-1). 12.95 *(978-1-905417-10-0(1))* Boxer Bks., Ltd. GBR. Dist: Sterling Publishing Co., Inc.

Pichard, Alexandra. Pen Pals. Pichard, Alexandra, illus. 2017. (ENG., Illus.). 48p. (J). (gr. -1-2). 17.99 *(978-1-4814-7247-0(X),* Simon & Schuster/Paula Wiseman Bks.) Simon & Schuster/Paula Wiseman Bks.

Pinkney, Jerry. The Grasshopper & the Ants. 2015. (ENG., Illus.). 40p. (J). (gr. -1-3). 18.00 *(978-0-316-40081-7(5))* Little, Brown Bks. for Young Readers.

Poe. Breve Ant de Ctos Policiales. (SPA.). pap. 11.95 *(978-950-07-1006-0(4))* Editorial Sudamericana S.A. ARG. Dist: Distribooks, Inc.

Powell, Glenda. Cassie & Mr. Ant. Mitchell, Hazel, illus. 2008. 30p. (J). (gr. -1-3). per. 7.95 *(978-0-9779445-6-9(5))* Zoe Life Publishing.

Prignano, Barbara. Angelo: The Underappreciated Ant. 2012. 28p. pap. 12.95 *(978-1-61897-177-7(8),* Strategic Bk. Publishing) Strategic Book Publishing & Rights Agency (SBPRA).

Prince, Joshua. I Saw an Ant on the Railroad Track. Pamintuan, Macky, illus. 2006. (ENG.). 24p. (J). (gr. -1-k). 14.95 *(978-1-4027-2183-0(8),* 1252268) Sterling Publishing Co., Inc.

Pritchard, Gabby. Lost! Blue Band. Stuart, Jon, illus. 2016. (Cambridge Reading Adventures Ser.). (ENG.). 16p. pap. 6.56 *(978-1-316-60078-8(5))* Cambridge Univ. Pr.

Punter, Russell. Underpants for Ants. Blunt, Fred, illus. 2014. (Usborne Phonics Readers Ser.). (ENG.). (J). (gr. -1-3). pap. 6.99 *(978-0-7945-3396-0(5),* Usborne) EDC Publishing.

Quackenbush, Robert. Henry's Awful Mistake. Quackenbush, Robert, illus. rev. deluxe ed. 2005. (Illus.). 40p. (J). (gr. k-2). reprint ed. 12.95 *(978-0-9712757-0-6(X))* Quackenbush, Robert Studios.

Ramos, Doreen. The Brave Ant. 2011. 28p. pap. 15.99 *(978-1-4568-9876-2(0))* Xlibris Corp.

Razilov, Evelyn. The Little Ant & the Apple Tree. 2013. 24p. pap. 12.56 *(978-1-4669-7729-7(9))* Trafford Publishing.

Read, Kit. Alexis Ant Marooned in Afric. 2012. 152p. *(978-1-4602-0314-9(3));* pap. *(978-1-4602-0313-2(5))* FriesenPress.

Rector, Lori. Adventures of A. 2013. (ENG.). 21p. (J). pap. 12.95 *(978-1-4787-1005-9(5))* Outskirts Pr., Inc.

Reid, Nakeil W. & Reid, Neil W. The Adventure of Avery the Ant: Experience the Next Children?ÇÖS Classic. 2011. 49p. pap. 14.95 *(978-1-4327-6597-2(3))* Outskirts Pr., Inc.

Rice, Dona Herwick & Housel, Debra. The Grasshopper & the Ants, 1 vol. 2008. (Building Fluency Through Reader's Theater Ser.). (ENG., Illus.). 24p. (J). (gr. 1-3). pap. 6.99 *(978-1-4333-0292-3(6))* Teacher Created Materials, Inc.

Rosenblatt, Joe. Tommy Fry & the Ant Colony, 1 vol. 2003. (ENG., Illus.). 30p. pap. *(978-0-88753-054-8(0))* Black Moss Pr. CAN. Dist: LitDistCo.

Rouss, Sylvia. Holiday for Ari Ant. 2016. (Illus.). 24p. (J). pap. *(978-965-229-664-1(3))* Gefen Bks.

Rouss, Sylvia A. A Holiday for Ari Ant. Kahn, Katherine, illus. 2016. (J). *(978-1-68115-507-4(9))* Behrman Hse., Inc.

Sanborn, Perry F. Little Ant A, 1 vol. Wright, Spencer, illus. 2010. 20p. pap. 24.95 *(978-1-4489-6159-7(9))* PublishAmerica, Inc.

Santillo, LuAnn. The Seeds. Santillo, LuAnn, ed. 2003. (Half-Pint Kids Readers Ser.). (Illus.). 7p. (J). (gr. -1-1). pap. 1.00 *(978-1-59256-109-4(8))* Half-Pint Kids, Inc.

The Secret Song & Other Stories: Individual Title Six-Pack. (Story Steps Ser.). (gr. k-2). 48.00 *(978-0-7635-9808-2(9))* Rigby Education.

Shaw, Dawn. Anthony's First Ant March. 2008. 36p. pap. 24.95 *(978-1-60672-992-2(6))* America Star Bks.

Shekunov, Vladimir. Nature & Us: Whether Ants Can Think. 2011. 24p. pap. 14.00 *(978-1-4520-5863-4(6))* AuthorHouse.

Shores, Lloyd. The Adventures of Mr. Ant. 2013. 28p. pap. 13.95 *(978-1-4497-9747-8(4),* WestBow Pr.) Author Solutions, Inc.

Smith, Timothy R. The Ants Dig to China. 2007. (Buck Wilder's Adventure Ser.: 3). (Illus.). 96p. (J). (gr. -1-3). per. *(978-1-934133-07-1(8),* Mackinac Island Press, Inc.) Charlesbridge Publishing, Inc.

Sommer, Carl. The Ant & the Grasshopper. Noé, Ignacio, illus. 2016. (ENG.). 32p. (J). (gr. k-4). lib. bdg. 16.95 *(978-1-57537-925-8(2),* Another Sommer-Time Story) Advance Publishing, Inc.

—No Longer a Dilly Dally, 1 bk. 2003. (Another Sommer-Time Story Ser.). (Illus.). 48p. (J). 16.95 incl. audio *(978-1-57537-550-2(8))* Advance Publishing, Inc.

—No Longer a Dilly Dally, 11 vols. James, Kennon, illus. 2003. (Another Sommer-Time Story Ser.). (ENG.). 48p. (J). (gr. 1-4). 16.95 incl. audio compact disk *(978-1-57537-501-4(X))* Advance Publishing, Inc.

Sparkes, Ali. Ant Attack. Collins, Ross, illus. 2013. (S. W. I. T. C. H. Ser.: 4). (ENG.). 104p. (J). (gr. 2-5). pap. 7.95 *(978-1-4677-0713-8(9),* Darby Creek) Lerner Publishing Group.

—Ant Attack. Collins, Ross, illus. 2013. (S. W. I. T. C. H. Ser.: 4). (ENG.). 104p. (J). (gr. 2-5). lib. bdg. 27.93 *(978-0-7613-9202-6(5))* Lerner Publishing Group.

Spin & Match - Kings, Cookies, & Quakers: The Cookie Man, New Clothes for the King, the Ugly Baby Duck. 2006. (ENG.). 66p. (J). 9.99 *(978-1-59204-203-6(1))* Learning Wrap-Ups, Inc.

Stevens, A. P. The Volcano: The Adventures of Antboy & Mr Cricket. Finn, N. K., ed. Deskcube, illus. 2008. (ENG.). 29p. pap. 9.95 *(978-0-9798886-0-1(3))* Mugsy and Sugar Pressed.

Stockland, Patricia M. Anthill Home Repair, 1 vol. Haugen, Ryan, illus. 2008. (Safari Friends Ser.). (ENG.). 32p. (gr. -1-3). 28.50 *(978-1-60270-082-6(6),* Looking Glass Library) ABDO Publishing Co.

Stone, Forrest. The Ant & Grasshopper Show. 2006. (J). pap. *(978-1-4108-6183-2(X))* Benchmark Education Co.

Tahir "Z", Zarghuna. The Lazy Froggies. 2012. 28p. (-18). pap. 19.99 *(978-1-4772-8907-5(0))* AuthorHouse.

Trimble, Patti. What Day Is It? Moreton, Daniel, illus. 2003. (Green Light Readers — Level 1 Ser.). (gr. -1-3). lib. bdg. 13.50 *(978-0-613-66388-5(8),* Turtleback) Turtleback Bks.

Trimble, Patti & Moran, Alex. Lost! Moreton, Daniel, illus. 2003. (Green Light Readers Level 1 Ser.). (ENG.). 24p. (J). (gr. -1-3). pap. 3.95 *(978-0-15-204864-8(2))* Houghton Mifflin Harcourt Publishing Co.

—Lost! Moreton, Daniel, illus. 2003. (Green Light Readers — Level 1 Ser.). (gr. -1-3). lib. bdg. 13.50 *(978-0-613-64539-3(1),* Turtleback) Turtleback Bks.

Van Laan, Nancy. Nit-Pickin' Booth, George, illus. 2008. (ENG.). 32p. (J). (gr. -1-3). 15.99 *(978-0-689-83898-9(0),* Atheneum Bks. for Young Readers) Simon & Schuster Children's Publishing.

Vantrease, Norma. Ants in My Pants. Cox, Steve, illus. 2004. (Rookie Readers Ser.). 31p. (J). 12.60 *(978-0-7569-4280-9(2))* Perfection Learning Corp.

—Ants in My Pants. Cox, Steve, illus. 2004. (Rookie Reader Skill Set Ser.). (ENG.). 32p. (J). (gr. k-2). pap. 4.95 *(978-0-516-25839-3(7),* Children's Pr.) Scholastic Library Publishing.

Wagner, Sandra Glahn. The Ants Have Dyed. Wagner, Sandra Glahn, illus. 2013. (Illus.). 20p. pap. 12.95 *(978-1-61493-171-3(2))* Peppertree Pr., The.

Waldrep, Susan. Papa Ant's Picnic. 2008. 24p. 15.00 *(978-1-4357-1129-7(7))* Lulu Pr., Inc.

Walter, Jackie. The Ants & the Grasshopper. 2017. (Must Know Stories: Level 1 Ser.). (ENG., Illus.). 32p. (J). (gr. k-2). 4.99 ***(978-1-4451-4454-2(9),*** Franklin Watts) Hachette Children's Group GBR. Dist: Hachette Bk. Group.

Watier, Matt. Ants. 32p. 12.95 *(978-1-58330-736-6(2))* Feldheim Pubs.

Watkins, Samuel R. Ant-Bee Kingdom. 2011. 12p. (gr. -1). pap. 12.68 *(978-1-4269-5272-2(4))* Trafford Publishing.

Watson, Regal. The Ant That Can't, 1. l.t. ed. 2005. (Illus.). 50p. (J). per. 10.95 *(978-0-9763686-0-1(9))* Rapha Publishing.

Weatherwalk, Wendy. Ants Don't Eat That. 2011. 16p. pap. 8.32 *(978-1-4634-1848-9(5))* AuthorHouse.

Wells, Rosemary. Max's ABC. 2008. (Max & Ruby Ser.). (ENG.). 32p. (J). (gr. -1-k). pap. 6.99 *(978-0-14-241172-8(8),* Puffin Books) Penguin Young Readers Group.

—Max's ABC. 2008. (Max & Ruby Ser.). (Illus.). 26p. (gr. -1-k). 17.00 *(978-0-7569-8924-8(8))* Perfection Learning Corp.

Wheatonnovember. The Little Hermit Ant. 2011. 28p. pap. 24.95 *(978-1-4626-3805-5(8))* America Star Bks.

White, Mark. The Ant & the Grasshopper: A Retelling of Aesop's Fable, 1 vol. Pérez, Sara Rojo, illus. 2011. (My First Classic Story Ser.). (ENG.). 24p. (gr. k-3). pap. 7.10 *(978-1-4048-7363-6(5),* My First Classic Story) Picture Window Bks.

White, Mark & Aesop Enterprise Inc. Staff. The Ant & the Grasshopper: A Retelling of Aesop's Fable, 1 vol. Pérez, Sara Rojo, illus. 2011. (My First Classic Story Ser.). (ENG.). 24p. (gr. k-3). lib. bdg. 22.65 *(978-1-4048-6505-1(5),* My First Classic Story) Picture Window Bks.

Williams, Greg. Albert the Ant. 2011. 36p. pap. 19.00 *(978-1-60746-326-9(1))* FastPrncl, Inc.

Wrecks, Billy. Ant-Man. Spaziante, Patrick, illus. 2016. (Little Golden Book Ser.). (ENG.). 24p. (J). (-k). 4.99 *(978-0-399-55097-3(6),* Golden Bks.) Random Hse. Children's Bks.

ANTS—POETRY

Martin, Tamara & Quebodeaux, Vernice. The Flea & the Ant. 2009. (J). pap. *(978-0-9789446-9-8(0))* Little Red Tree Publishing LLC.

Rosenblatt, Danielle. The Ant in the Cellar. Kirk, Jacqueline, illus. 2008. (J). per. 16.95 *(978-0-9801555-5-6(X))* Argus Enterprises International, Inc.

ANXIETY

see also Fear; Separation Anxiety

Adams, Christine A. Worry, Worry Go Away. Alley, R. W., illus. 2012. 32p. (J). pap. 7.95 *(978-0-87029-471-6(7))* Abbey Pr.

Bellisario, Gina. Keep Calm! My Stress-Busting Tips. Kurilla, Renee, illus. 2014. (Cloverleaf Books — My Healthy Habits Ser.). (ENG.). 24p. (gr. k-2). lib. bdg. 23.93 *(978-1-4677-1354-2(6),* Millbrook Pr.) Lerner Publishing Group.

Brinkerhoff, Shirley. Drug Therapy & Anxiety Disorders. (Encyclopedia of Psychiatric Drugs & Their Disorders Ser.). (Illus.). (YA). 2004. 128p. lib. bdg. 24.95 *(978-1-59084-561-5(7))* 2003. 124p. (gr. 7). pap. 14.95 *(978-1-4222-0385-9(9))* Mason Crest.

Buron, Kari D. & Buron, Kari Dunn. When My Worries Get Too Big! A Relaxation Book for Children Who Live with Anxiety. 2006. (Illus.). 124p. pap. 16.95 *(978-1-931282-92-5(7))* Autism Asperger Publishing Co.

Collins-Donnelly, Kate. Starving the Anxiety Gremlin: A Cognitive Behavioural Therapy Workbook on Anxiety Management for Young People. 2013. (Gremlin & Thief CBT Workbooks Ser.). (ENG., Illus.). 168p. (C). pap. 19.95 *(978-1-84905-341-9(3)*, 1990) Kingsley, Jessica Pubs. GBR. Dist: Macmillan Distribution Ltd.

Etingoff, Kim. Fear & Anxiety. Croft, Cindy, ed. 2014. (Causes & Effects of Emotions Ser.: 13). 64p. (J). (gr. 7-18). 23.95 *(978-1-4222-3073-2(2))* Mason Crest.

Freeland, Claire A.B. & Toner, Jacqueline B. What to Do When You Feel Too Shy: A Kid's Guide to Overcoming Social Anxiety. McDonnell, Janet, illus. 2016. 80p. (J). pap. *(978-1-4338-2276-6(8)*, Magination Pr.) American Psychological Assn.

Giacobello, John. Everything You Need to Know about Anxiety & Panic Attacks. 2005. (Need to Know Library). (Illus.). 64p. (YA). (gr. 7-12). lib. bdg. 31.95 *(978-0-8239-3219-1(2)*, NTANPA) Rosen Publishing Group, Inc., The.

Hovanec, Erin M. Everything You Need to Know about Phobias. 2005. (Need to Know Library). (Illus.). 64p. (YA). (gr. 7-12). lib. bdg. 31.95 *(978-0-8239-3226-9(5)*, NTPHOB) Rosen Publishing Group, Inc., The.

Huebner, Dawn. What to Do When You Worry Too Much: A Kid's Guide to Overcoming Anxiety. Candace, Bonnie & Ellen, illus. 2005. ("What to Do" Workbooks for Kids). 80p. (J). (gr. 1-7). per. 15.95 *(978-1-59147-314-5(4)*, Magination Pr.) American Psychological Assn.

Hyman, Bruce M. & Pedrick, Cherry. Anxiety Disorders. 2006. (Twenty-First Century Medical Library). (ENG.). 96p. (gr. 6-12). lib. bdg. 33.26 *(978-0-7613-2827-8(0))* Lerner Publishing Group.

Kissen, Debra, et al. The Panic Workbook for Teens: Breaking the Cycle of Fear, Worry, & Panic Attacks. 2015. (ENG., Illus.). 176p. (YA). (gr. 5-12). pap. 17.95 *(978-1-62625-221-9(1)*, 1392504) New Harbinger Pubns.

Levin, Judith. Anxiety & Panic Attacks. 2009. (Teen Mental Health Ser.). 48p. (gr. 5-6). 53.00 *(978-1-60853-294-0(1))* Rosen Publishing Group, Inc., The.

Lite, Lori. Affirmation Weaver: A Believe in Yourself Story, Designed to Help Children Boost Self-Esteem While Decreasing Stress & Anxiety (Indigo Dreams) 2008. (Illus.). 35p. (J). 14.95 *(978-0-9787781-5-6(4))* Stress Free Pubs.

—Affirmation Weaver: A Believe in Yourself Story Designed to Help Children Increase Self-Esteem While Decreasing Stress & Anxiety. 2nd ed. 2011. 24p. pap. 14.95 *(978-0-9836256-9-8(7))* Stress Free Pubs.

—Angry Octopus: An Anger Management Story Introducing Active Progressive Muscular Relaxation & Deep Breathing. 2011. (Illus.). 30p. (gr. -1-3). pap. 14.95 *(978-0-9836256-8-1(9))* Stress Free Pubs.

—A Boy & a Turtle: A Relaxation Story Teaching Young Children Visualization Techniques to Increase Creativity While Lowering Stress & Anxiety Lev. 3rd ed. 2012.Tr. of niño y una Tortuga. (ENG.). 16p. (J). pap. 12.95 *(978-1-937985-13-4(X))* Stress Free Pubs.

—Bubble Riding: A Relaxation Story Designed to Teach Children Visualization Techniques to Increase Creativity While Lowering Stress & Anxiety. 2012.Tr. of Montando Burbujas. (ENG.). (J). pap. 14.95 *(978-1-937985-03-5(2))* Stress Free Pubs.

—Buenas Noches Oruga: Una Historia para la Relajación Que Ayuda a Los Niños a Controlar la Ira y el Estrés para Que Se Queden Dormidos Sosegadamente. 2012.Tr. of Goodnight Caterpillar. (SPA., Illus.). 16p. (J). pap. 12.95 *(978-1-937985-16-5(4))* Stress Free Pubs.

—Caleta de la Nutria Marina: Un Cuento para la Ansiedad Infantil, Enseña la Relajación, la Respiración Profunda para Reducir la Ansiedad, el Estrés y la Ira, a la Vez Que Fomenta el Sueño Sosegado. 2011.Tr. of Sea Otter Cove. (SPA., Illus.). 28p. (J). pap. 14.95 *(978-1-937985-11-0(3))* Stress Free Pubs.

—The Goodnight Caterpillar: A Children's Relaxation Story to Improve Sleep, Manage Stress, Anxiety, Anger. 3rd abr. ed. 2011.Tr. of Buenas Noches, Oruga. (ENG.). 18p. (J). pap. 12.95 *(978-1-937985-00-4(8))* Stress Free Pubs.

—Montando Burbujas: Un Cuento con Ejercicios de Relajación para Niños, Diseñada para Enseñar a Los Niños Técnicas de Visualización para Aumentar la Creatividad Mientras Disminuyen Sus Niveles de Ansiedad y de Estrés. 2012.Tr. of Bubble Riding. (SPA., Illus.). 32p. (J). pap. 14.95 *(978-1-937985-12-7(1))* Stress Free Pubs.

—El Niño y la Tortuga: Un Cuento para Promover la Relajación. 2012.Tr. of Boy & a Turtle. (SPA., Illus.). 16p. (J). pap. 12.95 *(978-1-937985-17-2(2))* Stress Free Pubs.

—El Pulpo Enojado: Un Cuento Sobre Cómo Controlar la Ira Que Enseña la Relajación Muscular Activa y Progresiva, y la Respiración: un Cuento Sobre Cómo Controlar la Ira Que Enseña la Relajación Muscular Activa y Progresiva, y la Respiración. 2012.Tr. of Angry Octopus. (SPA., Illus.). 30p. (J). pap. 14.95 *(978-1-937985-01-1(6))* Stress Free Pubs.

—Sea Otter Cove: A Relaxation Story, Introducing Deep Breathing to Decrease Anxiety, Stress & Anger While Promoting Peaceful Sleep. 2nd ed. 2012.Tr. of Caleta de la Nutria Marina. (SPA & ENG., Illus.). 24p. (J). 14.95 *(978-1-937985-08-0(3))* Stress Free Pubs.

—Tejedor de Afirmaciones: Un Cuento Que Aumenta la Autoestima en Los Niños, Creer en Ellos Mismos, Mientras Que Reducen Su Estrés y Su Ansiedad. 2012.Tr. of Affirmation Weaver. (SPA., Illus.). 24p. (J). pap. 14.95 *(978-1-937985-02-8(4))* Stress Free Pubs.

MacGregor, Lucy. Everything You Need to Know about Social Anxiety. 2009. (Need to Know Library). 64p. (gr. 5-5). 58.50 *(978-1-60854-087-7(1))* Rosen Publishing Group, Inc., The.

Mandel, Joey. Anxiety: Deal with It Before It Ties You up in Knots. Heeley, Ted, illus. 2014. (Lorimer Deal with It Ser.). (ENG.). 32p. (YA). (gr. 4-6). pap. 12.95 *(978-1-4594-0709-1(1)*, 9781459407091) Lorimer, James & Co., Ltd., Pubs. CAN. Dist: Casemate Pubs. & Bk. Distributors, LLC.

Moehn, Heather. Coping with Social Anxiety. (Coping Ser.). 192p. (gr. 7-12). 2009. 63.90 *(978-1-61512-012-3(2))* 2005. (Illus.). (YA). lib. bdg. 34.60 *(978-0-8239-3363-1(6))* Rosen Publishing Group, Inc., The.

Moss, Wendy. School Made Easier: A Kid's Guide to Study Strategies & Anxiety-Busting Tools. 2014. (Illus.). vii, 128p. pap. *(978-1-4338-1336-8(X)*, Magination Pr.) American Psychological Assn.

O'Connor, Frances. Frequently Asked Questions about Academic Anxiety. 2007. (FAQ: Teen Life Ser.). (Illus.). 64p. (YA). (gr. 7-12). lib. bdg. 31.95 *(978-1-4042-1937-3(4))* Rosen Publishing Group, Inc., The.

Peters, Daniel B., et al. The Warrior Workbook: A Guide for Conquering Your Worry Monster. 2017. (Illus.). vii, 96p. (J). pap. 16.95 *(978-1-935067-44-3(3))* Great Potential Pr., Inc.

Poole, Hilary W. Catastrophes. 2017. (J). ***(978-1-4222-3721-2(4))*** Mason Crest.

—Family Fears. 2017. (J). ***(978-1-4222-3725-0(7))*** Mason Crest.

—Nighttime Fears. 2017. (J). ***(978-1-4222-3727-4(3))*** Mason Crest.

—Separation Anxiety. 2017. (J). ***(978-1-4222-3730-4(3))*** Mason Crest.

—Symptoms & Treatments of Anxiety Disorders. 2017. (J). ***(978-1-4222-3732-8(X))*** Mason Crest.

Poole, Hilary W. & Walters, Anne S. Medical Fears. 2017. (J). ***(978-1-4222-3726-7(5))*** Mason Crest.

Ross, Allison J. Everything You Need to Know about Social Anxiety. 2005. (Need to Know Library). (Illus.). 64p. (YA). (gr. 7-12). 31.95 *(978-0-8239-3324-2(5))* Rosen Publishing Group, Inc., The.

Shannon, Jennifer. The Anxiety Survival Guide for Teens: CBT Skills to Overcome Fear, Worry, & Panic. Shannon, Doug, illus. 2015. (Instant Help Solutions Ser.). (ENG.). 256p. (YA). (gr. 5-12). pap. 17.95 *(978-1-62625-243-1(2))* New Harbinger Pubns.

Shuman, Carol. Jenny Is Scared! When Sad Things Happen in the World. Pillo, Cary, tr. Pillo, Cary, illus. 2003. 32p. (J). (gr. k-3). pap. 9.95 *(978-1-59147-003-8(X))*; 14.95 *(978-1-59147-002-1(1))* American Psychological Assn. (Magination Pr.).

Smith, Paula. Phobias & Other Anxiety Disorders. 2013. (Illus.). 48p. (J). pap. *(978-0-7787-0862-9(4))* Crabtree Publishing Co.

Spalding, Maddie & Marquardt, Meg. 12 Tips for Managing Stress & Anxiety. 2016. (Healthy Living Ser.). (ENG., Illus.). 32p. (J). pap. 9.95 *(978-1-63235-384-9(9))* Pr. Room Editions LLC.

Sunderland, Margot & Hancock, Nicky. Helping Children with Fear: A Guidebook, 2 vols. Armstrong, Nicky, tr. 2012. (Helping Children with Feelings Ser.). (ENG., Illus.). 140p. (C). pap. 34.95 *(978-0-86388-464-1(4)*, Y329801, Routledge) Taylor & Francis Group GBR. Dist: Taylor & Francis Group.

Swigget, Chelsea. Rae: My True Story of Fear, Anxiety, & Social Phobia. 2010. (Louder Than Words Ser.). (ENG.). 168p. (YA). (gr. 7-12). pap. 7.95 *(978-0-7573-1527-5(5)*, HCI Teens) Health Communications, Inc.

Tool Kits for Kids LLC Staff, creator. Outsmart Your Worry - Tool Kit for Kids: Elementary School Edition. 2008. (Illus.). 23p. (J). 39.95 *(978-0-9819483-0-0(8))* Tool Kits For Kids LLC.

—Outsmart Your Worry - Tool Kit for Kids: High School / Middle School Edition. 2008. (Illus.). (J). 39.95 *(978-0-9819483-1-7(6))* Tool Kits For Kids LLC.

Van Duyne, Sara. Stress & Anxiety-Related Disorders. 2003. (Diseases & People Ser.). (Illus.). 112p. (J). lib. bdg. 26.60 *(978-0-7660-1900-3(4))* Enslow Pubs., Inc.

Way, Jennifer & Van Duyne, Sara. What You Can Do about Stress & Anxiety. 2015. (Contemporary Diseases & Disorders Ser.). (ENG., Illus.). 128p. (J). (gr. 7-7). 37.27 *(978-0-7660-7042-4(5))* Enslow Pubs., Inc.

Way, Jennifer L. & Monroe, Judy. Are You Afraid? 2015. (Got Issues? Ser.). (ENG.). 128p. (J). (gr. 7-7). 37.27 *(978-0-7660-6977-0(X))* Enslow Pubs., Inc.

Wells, Polly. Freaking Out: Real-Life Stories about Anxiety. Mitchell, Peter, illus. 2013. (ENG.). 136p. (YA). (gr. 7-12). 22.95 *(978-1-55451-545-5(9)*, 9781554515455); pap. 12.95 *(978-1-55451-544-8(0)*, 9781554515448) Annick Pr., Ltd. CAN. Dist: Publishers Group West (PGW).

Willard, Christopher. The Mindfulness for Teen Anxiety: A Workbook for Overcoming Anxiety at Home, at School, & Everywhere Else. 2014. (ENG.). 168p. (YA). (gr. 5-12). pap. 16.95 *(978-1-60882-910-1(3))* New Harbinger Pubns.

Willetts, Lucy & Waite, Polly. Can I Tell You about Anxiety? A Guide for Friends, Family & Professionals. Tay, Kaiyee, illus. 2014. (Can I Tell You About... ? Ser.). (ENG.). 56p. pap. 14.95 *(978-1-84905-527-7(0)*, 5439) Kingsley, Jessica Pubs. GBR. Dist: Macmillan Distribution Ltd.

Wyborny, Sheila. Anxiety Disorders. 2008. (Diseases & Disorders Ser.). (ENG., Illus.). 128p. (gr. 7-10). lib. bdg. 39.90 *(978-1-4205-0071-4(6)*, LML02109-242075, Lucent Bks.) Cengage Gale.

Zelinger, Laurie & Zelinger, Jordan. Please Explain Anxiety to Me! Simple Biology & Solutions for Children & Parents. Sabella, Elisa, illus. 2010. 38p. 32.95 *(978-1-61599-051-1(8))*; 40p. pap. 21.95 *(978-1-61599-029-0(1))* Loving Healing Pr., Inc.

Zelinger, Laurie E. & Zelinger, Jordan. Please Explain "Anxiety" to Me! Simple Biology & Solutions for Children & Parents. Sabella, Elisa, illus. 2014. (J). pap. 15.95 *(978-1-61599-216-4(2))* Loving Healing Pr., Inc.

APARTHEID

Here are entered works on the political, economic and social policies of the government of South Africa designed to keep racial groups in South Africa and Namibia separated.

Baptiste, Tracey. Nelson Mandela: Nobel Peace Prize-Winning Champion for Hope & Harmony. 2015. (Britannica Beginner Bios Ser.). (ENG.). 32p. (J). (gr. 2-3). 46.90 *(978-1-62275-943-9(5)*, Britannica Educational Publishing) Rosen Publishing Group, Inc., The.

—Nelson Mandela: Nobel Peace Prize-Winning Warrior for Hope & Harmony. 2015. (Britannica Beginner Bios Ser.). (ENG., Illus.). 32p. (J). 23.45 *(978-1-62275-941-5(9)*, Britannica Educational Publishing) Rosen Publishing Group, Inc., The.

Chalk, Frank. South Africa: Never Again! Greenhaven Press Editors & Gale Editors, eds. 2014. (Genocide & Persecution Ser.). (ENG., Illus.). 240p. (gr. 10-12). lib. bdg. 42.00 *(978-0-7377-6894-7(0)*, Greenhaven Pr., Inc.) Cengage Gale.

Clark, Domini. South Africa: The People. 3rd rev. ed. 2008. (Lands, Peoples, & Cultures Ser.). (ENG., Illus.). 32p. (J). (gr. 3-9). pap. *(978-0-7787-9659-6(0))* Crabtree Publishing Co.

—South Africa - The People. 3rd rev. ed. 2008. (Lands, Peoples, & Cultures Ser.). (ENG., Illus.). 32p. (J). (gr. 3-9). lib. bdg. *(978-0-7787-9291-8(9))* Crabtree Publishing Co.

Cruden, Alex & Bryfonski, Dedria. The End of Apartheid. 2009. (Perspectives on Modern World History Ser.). (Illus.). 224p. (YA). (gr. 10-12). 42.45 *(978-0-7377-4557-3(6)*, Greenhaven Pr., Inc.) Cengage Gale.

The End of Apartheid in South Africa. 2010. (Milestones in World History Ser.). (Illus.). 120p. (C). (gr. 9-18). 35.00 *(978-1-60413-409-4(7)*, Chelsea Hse.) Facts On File, Inc.

Koosman, Melissa. The Fall of Apartheid in South Africa. 2009. (Monumental Milestones Ser.). 48p. (YA). (gr. 4-7). lib. bdg. 29.95 *(978-1-58415-736-6(4))* Mitchell Lane Pubs., Inc.

Magoon, Kekla. Nelson Mandela: A Leader for Freedom, 1 vol. 2008. (Essential Lives Set 2 Ser.). (ENG., Illus.). 112p. (J). (gr. 6-12). lib. bdg. 35.64 *(978-1-60453-038-4(3))* ABDO Publishing Co.

Malaspina, Ann. Nelson Mandela: Fighting to Dismantle Apartheid. 2017. (Rebels with a Cause Ser.). 128p. (YA). (gr. 8-8). lib. bdg. 37.27 ***(978-0-7660-8517-6(1))*** Enslow Pubs., Inc.

World Book, Inc Staff, contrib. by. South Africa's Anti-Apartheid Movement. 2010. (Illus.). 62p. (J). *(978-0-7166-1507-1(X))* World Bk., Inc.

APARTMENT HOUSES

see also Housing

Landau, Jennifer. Smart Strategies for Sharing, Subletting, & Renting an Apartment. 2014. (Financial Security & Life Success for Teens Ser.). (Illus.). 80p. (J). (gr. 7-12). pap. 14.15 *(978-1-4777-7632-2(X))* Rosen Publishing Group, Inc., The.

APARTMENT HOUSES—FICTION

Alter, Anna. Sprout Street Neighbors - A New Arrival. 2016. (Sprout Street Neighbors Ser.). (ENG., Illus.). 128p. (J). (gr. 1-4). 12.99 *(978-0-385-75562-7(7)*, Knopf Bks. for Young Readers) Random Hse. Children's Bks.

—Sprout Street Neighbors: a New Arrival. 2017. (Sprout Street Neighbors Ser.: 2). (ENG.). 128p. (J). (gr. 1-4). pap. 6.99 ***(978-0-385-75564-1(3)***, Yearling) Random Hse. Children's Bks.

—Sprout Street Neighbors: Bon Voyage. 2017. (Sprout Street Neighbors Ser.: 3). (ENG., Illus.). 96p. (J). (gr. 1-4). pap. 6.99 ***(978-1-5247-0053-9(3)***, Yearling) Random Hse. Children's Bks.

Arnold, Tedd. No Jumping on the Bed! 25th anniv. ed. 2012. (ENG., Illus.). 32p. (J). (gr. -1-1). 16.99 *(978-0-8037-3563-7(4)*, Dial Bks) Penguin Young Readers Group.

Ashford, Jeron. Winter Candle. Schuett, Stacey, illus. 2014. (ENG.). 28p. (J). (gr. -1-6). 16.95 *(978-1-939547-10-1(5))* Creston Bks.

Atwood, Megan. The Haunting of Apartment 101. 2012. (Paranormalists Ser.: 1). (ENG.). 112p. (YA). (gr. 6-12). pap. 7.95 *(978-0-8225-9077-4(8)*, Darby Creek) Lerner Publishing Group.

Barnett, Mac. Noisy Night. Biggs, Brian, illus. 2017. (ENG.). 32p. (J). 16.99 *(978-1-59643-967-2(X)*, 9781596439672) Roaring Brook Pr.

Chambers, Mark, illus. Zach & Lucy & the Museum of Natural Wonders. 2016. (Zach & Lucy Ser.). (ENG.). 40p. (J). (gr. 1-3). pap. 3.99 *(978-1-4814-3935-0(9)*, Simon Spotlight) Simon Spotlight.

—Zach & Lucy & the Yoga Zoo. 2016. (Zach & Lucy Ser.). (ENG.). 40p. (J). (gr. 1-3). pap. 3.99 *(978-1-4814-3938-1(3)*, Simon Spotlight) Simon Spotlight.

Cole, Brock. The Money We'll Save. Cole, Brock, illus. 2011. (ENG., Illus.). 40p. (J). (gr. -1-3). 16.99 *(978-0-374-35011-6(6)*, 9780374350116, Farrar, Straus & Giroux (BYR)) Farrar, Straus & Giroux.

Collesano, Melissa J. Pheobe Mckeeby's Garden Apartment. 2011. 44p. pap. 21.99 *(978-1-4628-5506-3(7))* Xlibris Corp.

Darryl the Doorman: Individual Title, 6 Packs. (gr. -1-2). 27.00 *(978-0-7635-9444-2(X))* Rigby Education.

DiCerto, Jospeh J. The Wall People: In Search of a Home. 2014. (Illus.). 128p. (J). pap. 14.00 *(978-0-87842-633-1(7))* Mountain Pr. Publishing Co., Inc.

Ellen, Raskin. The Westing Game. 2014. (Puffin Modern Classics Ser.). (ENG.). 192p. (J). (gr. 5-12). 12.24 *(978-1-63245-142-2(5))* Lectorum Pubns., Inc.

Feasey, Steve. Wereling. 2010. (Wereling Ser.: 1). (ENG.). 288p. (YA). (gr. 7-18). pap. 9.99 *(978-0-312-59612-5(X)*, 9780312596125) Feiwel & Friends.

Frank, Lucy. Just Ask Iris. 2003. (ENG., Illus.). 224p. (J). (gr. 5-9). pap. 10.99 *(978-0-689-84454-6(9)*, Atheneum Bks. for Young Readers) Simon & Schuster Children's Publishing.

Fudge, Keith. The Rainy Day Discovery. 2006. (J). per. 11.95 *(978-1-889743-37-0(2))* Robbie Dean Pr.

Gonzalez, Rigoberto & González, Rigoberto. Soledad Sigh-Sighs. Ibarra, Rosa, illus. 2014.Tr. of Soledad Suspiros. (ENG & SPA.). 32p. (J). pap. 8.95 *(978-0-89239-309-1(2)*, Children's Book Press) Lee & Low Bks., Inc.

Good Night, City Lights: Individual Title Six-Packs. (gr. -1-2). 27.00 *(978-0-7635-9451-0(2))* Rigby Education.

Greene, Janice. The White Room, 1 vol. unabr. ed. 2010. (Q Reads Ser.). (ENG.). 32p. (YA). (gr. 9-12). pap. 6.95 *(978-1-61651-197-5(4))* Saddleback Educational Publishing, Inc.

Greenwald, Lisa. Sweet Treats & Secret Crushes. (ENG.). (YA). (gr. 3-7). 2011. 320p. pap. 7.95 *(978-1-4197-0029-3(4))* 2010. 304p. 16.95 *(978-0-8109-8990-0(5))* Abrams, Inc. (Amulet Bks.).

Harrison, Dorothy. A Better Tomorrow? 2003. 128p. pap. 13.95 *(978-0-595-28429-0(9)*, Backinprint.com) iUniverse, Inc.

Henry, Steve. Happy Cat. 2013. (I Like to Read(r) Ser.). (ENG., Illus.). 24p. (J). (gr. -1-3). 14.95 *(978-0-8234-2659-1(9))* Holiday Hse., Inc.

Hyde, Catherine Ryan. Jumpstart the World. 2011. (ENG.). 192p. (YA). (gr. 9). pap. 7.99 *(978-0-375-86626-5(4)*, Ember) Random Hse. Children's Bks.

The Lil Dudes. 2006. (YA). per. *(978-1-59872-308-3(1))* Instant Pub.

Martin, Ann M. Ten Rules for Living with My Sister. 2011. (ENG.). 240p. (J). (gr. 4-7). 16.99 *(978-0-312-36766-4(X)*, 9780312367664) Feiwel & Friends.

Naylor, Phyllis Reynolds. Cuckoo Feathers, 0 vols. Ramsey, Marcy, illus. 2009. (Simply Sarah Ser.: 0). (ENG.). 96p. (J). (gr. 2-5). pap. 6.99 *(978-0-7614-5541-7(8)*, 9780761455417, Amazon Children's Publishing) Amazon Publishing.

Night, P. J. Home, Sweet Haunt. 2013. (You're Invited to a Creepover Ser.: 15). (ENG., Illus.). 160p. (J). (gr. 3-7). pap. 6.99 *(978-1-4424-7240-2(5)*, Simon Spotlight) Simon Spotlight.

Pennypacker, Sara. Clementine. Frazee, Marla, illus. (ENG.). (J). 2008. 160p. (gr. 2-5). pap. 5.99 *(978-0-7868-3883-7(3))* 2006. 144p. (gr. 1-3). 14.99 *(978-0-7868-3882-0(5))* Hyperion Pr.

Potter, Ellen. Olivia Kidney. Aguilar, Carmen, tr. 2006. (SPA., Illus.). 159p. (J). (gr. 3-7). per. 16.99 *(978-84-7871-408-7(1))* RBA Libros, S.A. ESP. Dist: Lectorum Pubns., Inc.

—Olivia Kidney. Reynolds, Peter, illus. 2004. (ENG.). 176p. (J). (gr. 3-7). reprint ed. 6.99 *(978-0-14-240234-4(6)*, Puffin Books) Penguin Young Readers Group.

—Otis Dooda: Strange but True. Heatley, David, illus. 2013. (Otis Dooda Ser.: 1). (ENG.). 240p. (J). (gr. 2-5). 13.99 *(978-1-250-01176-3(0)*, 9781250011763) Feiwel & Friends.

—Otis Dooda: Downright Dangerous. Heatley, David, illus. 2014. (Otis Dooda Ser.: 2). (ENG.). 240p. (J). (gr. 2-5). 13.99 *(978-1-250-01177-0(9)*, 9781250011770) Feiwel & Friends.

Raskin, Ellen. The Westing Game. 2003. 182p. (J). lib. bdg. 15.00 *(978-1-4242-2271-1(0))* Fitzgerald Bks.

Ritz, Karen. Windows with Birds. 2010. (ENG., Illus.). 32p. (J). (gr. k-2). 16.95 *(978-1-59078-656-7(4))* Boyds Mills Pr.

Roberts, Willo Davis. The Pet-Sitting Peril. 2016. (ENG., Illus.). 256p. (J). (gr. 3-7). pap. 7.99 *(978-1-4814-7492-4(8)*, Aladdin) Simon & Schuster Children's Publishing.

Rylant, Cynthia. The Case of the Sleepy Sloth. Karas, G. Brian, illus. unabr. ed. 2005. (High-Rise Private Eyes Ser.: No. 5). (J). (gr. k-4). 28.95 incl. audio compact disk *(978-1-59519-417-6(7))*; 29.95 incl. audio *(978-1-59519-413-8(4))*;Set. pap. 31.95 incl. audio compact disk *(978-1-59519-418-3(5))*;Set. pap. 29.95 incl. audio *(978-1-59519-414-5(2))* Live Oak Media.

Scher, Paula. The Brownstone. 2016. (ENG., Illus.). 32p. (J). (gr. -1-3). 17.95 *(978-1-61689-428-3(8))* Princeton Architectural Pr.

Schwab, Victoria. The Archived. 2014. (Archived Ser.). (ENG., Illus.). 352p. (YA). (gr. 7-12). pap. 9.99 *(978-1-4231-7108-9(X))* Hyperion Bks. for Children.

Sprout Street Neighbors: Five Stories. 2015. (Sprout Street Neighbors Ser.). (ENG., Illus.). 112p. (J). (gr. 1-4). 12.99 *(978-0-385-75558-0(9)*, Knopf Bks. for Young Readers) Random Hse. Children's Bks.

Stadler, John. The Cats of Mrs. Calamari, 1 vol. 2011. (ENG., Illus.). 32p. (J). pap. 6.95 *(978-1-59572-257-7(2))* Star Bright Bks., Inc.

Stead, Rebecca. Liar & Spy. (ENG.). (J). (gr. 3-7). 2013. 208p. 7.99 *(978-0-375-85087-5(2)*, Yearling) 2012. 192p. 15.99 *(978-0-385-73743-2(2)*, Lamb, Wendy Bks.) Random Hse. Children's Bks.

Strange, Jason. 23 Crow's Perch, 1 vol. Evergreen, Nelson & Kendall, Bradford, illus. 2012. (Jason Strange Ser.). (ENG.). 72p. (gr. 2-3). pap. 6.25 *(978-1-4342-3885-6(7))*; lib. bdg. 25.32 *(978-1-4342-3297-7(2))* Stone Arch Bks.

Tiddle, Deanna Hessedal. Apartment Horse & Friends. 2003. 62p. (J). pap. 9.95 *(978-0-7414-1724-4(3))* Infinity Publishing.

Trachtenberg, Stanley. The Elevator Man. Cox, Paul, illus. 2009. 34p. (J). (gr. -1-3). 18.00 *(978-0-8028-5315-8(3))* Eerdmans, William B. Publishing Co.

Trees, Annie Mae. The Old Apartment Building: A Tale from the Trees. 2012. 24p. 24.95 *(978-1-4626-6093-3(2))* America Star Bks.

Troupe, Thomas Kingsley. Furry & Flo, 1 vol. (Furry & Flo Ser.). (ENG.). 128p. (gr. 2-3). 2014. 101.28 *(978-1-4342-6400-8(9))* 2013. 50.64 *(978-1-4342-6348-3(7))* Stone Arch Bks.

Vujadinovic, Nenad. Ronny. Fur, Emil, illus. 2007. (POL & ENG.). 32p. (J). pap. 12.95 *(978-1-60195-105-2(1))* International Step by Step Assn.

Wiebe, Trina. Lizards Don't Wear Lip Gloss. Sarrazin, Marisol, illus. 2004. (Abby & Tess Pet-Sitters Ser.). 91p. 15.95 *(978-0-7569-3425-5(7))* Perfection Learning Corp.

APES

see also Chimpanzees; Gorilla; Orangutans

Barker, David. Top 50 Reasons to Care about Great Apes: Animals in Peril. 2010. (Top 50 Reasons to Care about Endangered Animals Ser.). (Illus.). 104p. (J). (gr. 5-9). 33.27 *(978-0-7660-3456-3(9))* Enslow Pubs., Inc.

Chambers, Catherine E. Ape Adventures, Level 3. 2013. (DK Readers Ser.). (ENG.). 48p. (J). (gr. 2-4). pap. 3.99 *(978-1-4654-0239-4(X)*, DK Children) Dorling Kindersley Publishing, Inc.

De la Bédoyère, Camilla. Monkeys & Apes. 2014. (Animal Q & A Ser.). (Illus.). 24p. (J). (gr. k-3). lib. bdg. 23.60 *(978-1-4777-9190-5(6))* Windmill Bks.

Dennard, Deborah. Apes & Monkeys. McGee, John F., illus. 2003. (Our Wild World Ser.). (ENG.). 192p. (J). (gr. 2-5). 16.95 *(978-1-55971-863-9(3))* Cooper Square Publishing Llc.

Ellis, Carol. Apes. 2010. (Endangered! 2 Ser.). 48p. (gr. 3). lib. bdg. 29.93 *(978-0-7614-4046-8(1))* Marshall Cavendish Corp.

Goecke, Michael P. Giant Ape, 1 vol. 2003. (Prehistoric Animals Ser.). (ENG.). 24p. (gr. k-4). 25.65 *(978-1-57765-967-9(8)*, Buddy Bks.) ABDO Publishing Co.

Great Apes. 2006. (Zootles Ser.). (J). 4.95 *(978-1-932396-19-5(5))* Wildlife Education, Ltd.

Green, John. Monkeys & Apes Coloring Book. 2013. (Dover Nature Coloring Book Ser.). (ENG., Illus.). 48p. (J). (gr. 3-12). pap. 4.99 *(978-0-486-25798-3(3))* Dover Pubns., Inc.

Hardyman, Robyn. Apes & Monkeys. 2008. (World of Animals Ser.). 32p. (gr. 2-5). 31.35 *(978-1-933834-37-5(4))* Brown Bear Bks.

Herrington, Lisa M. Monkeys & Apes. 2015. (Rookie Read-About(tm) Science: What's the Difference? Ser.). (ENG., Illus.). 32p. (J). lib. bdg. 25.00 (978-0-531-21486-2(9), Children's Pr.) Scholastic Library Publishing.

James, Adele. Adding with Apes. 2011. (Animal Math Ser.). 24p. (J). (gr. 1-3). pap. 8.15 (978-1-4339-5656-0(X)); lib. bdg. 22.60 (978-1-4339-5654-6(3)) Stevens, Gareth Publishing LLLP.

Jenkins, Martin. Ape. White, Vicky, illus. (ENG.). 48p. (J). (gr. -1-2). 2010. pap. 7.99 (978-0-7636-4974-6(0)) 2007. 16.99 (978-0-7636-3471-1(9)) Candlewick Pr.

Kalman, Bobbie. Baby Apes. 2008. (It's Fun to Learn about Baby Animals Ser.). (ENG., Illus.). 24p. (J). (gr. 3-7). pap. (978-0-7787-3967-8(8)) Crabtree Publishing Co.

Keller, Susanna. Meet the Ape. 2010. (At the Zoo Ser.). 24p. (J). (ENG.). pap. 8.25 (978-1-4358-9734-2(X)); (Illus.). (gr. -1-1). lib. bdg. 22.60 (978-1-4358-9311-5(5)) Rosen Publishing Group, Inc., The. (PowerKids Pr.).

Kralovansky, Susan. Monkey or Ape?, 1 vol. 2014. (This or That? Ser.). (ENG.). 24p. (gr. 5-10). lib. bdg. 25.65 (978-1-62403-287-5(7), Super SandCastle) ABDO Publishing Co.

Laman, Tim, et al. Face to Face with Orangutans. 2009. (Face to Face with Animals Ser.). (ENG., Illus.). 32p. (J). (gr. 2-5). 16.95 (978-1-4263-0464-4(1), National Geographic Children's Bks.) National Geographic Society.

Macheske, Felicia. Swinging Smarties: Orangutan. 2017. (Guess What Ser.). (ENG., Illus.). 24p. (J). (gr. k-2). lib. bdg. 28.50 (978-1-63472-171-4(3), 209256) Cherry Lake Publishing.

Mattern, Joanne. Orangutans, 1 vol. 2010. (Asian Animals Ser.). (ENG.). 24p. (gr. k-1). pap. 7.29 (978-1-4296-4848-6(1)); pap. 41.70 (978-1-4296-5097-7(4)) Capstone Press of Coughlan Cos. (Pebble Plus).

Murray, Julie. Gibbons, 1 vol. 2013. (Asian Animals Ser.). (ENG.). 32p. (J). (gr. 2-5). lib. bdg. 28.50 (978-1-61783-554-4(4), Big Buddy Bks.) ABDO Publishing Co.

Newman, Aline Alexander. Ape Escapes! And More True Stories of Animals Behaving Badly. 2012. (NGK Chapters Ser.). (ENG., Illus.). 112p. (J). (gr. 2-5). pap. 5.99 (978-1-4263-0936-6(8), National Geographic Children's Bks.) National Geographic Society.

Owen, Ruth. Amazing Apes. 2012. (Eye to Eye with Animals Ser.). (ENG., Illus.). 32p. (J). (gr. k-5). 25.25 (978-1-4488-8067-6(X)); pap. 10.00 (978-1-4488-8103-1(X)) Windmill Bks.

Pelusey, Michael & Pelusey, Jane. Apes & Monkeys. 2008. (Zoo Animals Ser.). 32p. (gr. 2-3). lib. bdg. 18.56 (978-0-7614-3144-2(6), Benchmark Bks.) Marshall Cavendish Corp.

Rabe, Tish. Can You See a Chimpanzee? All about Primates. Ruiz, Aristides & Mathieu, Joe, illus. 2014. (Cat in the Hat's Learning Library). (ENG.). 48p. (J). (gr. k-3). lib. bdg. 13.99 (978-0-375-97074-0(6), Random Hse. Bks. for Young Readers) Random Hse. Children's Bks.

Redmond, Ian. Gorilas. Anderson, Peter & Brighting, Geoff, illus. 2003. (SPA.). 64p. 14.95 (978-84-372-2323-0(7)) Altea, Ediciones, S.A. - Grupo Santillana ESP. Dist: Santillana USA Publishing Co., Inc.

Redwood, Adelaide. Apes & Babies. 2017. (Animal Family Ser.). 24p. (gr. k-k). pap. 8.15 **(978-1-4824-6365-1(2))** Stevens, Gareth Publishing LLLP.

Wildlife Education, compiled by. Great Apes. 2005. (Zootles Ser.). (Illus.). 23p. (J). lib. bdg. 10.95 (978-1-932396-08-9(X)) Wildlife Education, Ltd.

World Book, Inc. Staff, contrib. by. Gorillas & Other Apes. 2005. (World Book's Animals of the World Ser.). (Illus.). 64p. (J). (978-0-7166-1263-6(1)) World Bk., Inc.

APES—FICTION

Axt, Katie & Byerly, Robbie. Bigfoots Have Big Toes. 2016. (1B Fiction Ser.). (ENG., Illus.). 24p. (J). pap. 5.99 **(978-1-63437-577-1(7))** American Reading Co.

Buehner, Caralyn & Buehner, Mark. The Escape of Marvin the Ape. 2010. (Illus.). 16.10 (978-0-7569-9295-8(8)) Penguin Publishing Group.

Carlson, Dale. The Human Apes. Carlson, Al & Nicklaus, Carol, illus. 2nd ed. 2005. (ENG.). 155p. (gr. 8-12). reprint ed. pap. 14.95 (978-1-884158-31-5(5)) Team Kreskin Productions, LLC.

Dharma Publishing Staff. A Wise Ape Teaches Kindness: A Story about the Power of Positive Actions. 2nd ed. 2013. (ENG.). 36p. (gr. -1-7). pap. 8.95 (978-0-89800-519-6(1)) Dharma Publishing.

Engle, Margarita. Orangutanka. Kurilla, Renee, illus. 2015. (ENG.). 40p. (J). (gr. -1-3). 17.99 (978-0-8050-9839-6(9), 9780805098396, Holt, Henry & Co. Bks. For Young Readers) Holt, Henry & Co.

Greco, Francesca. Cyril the Mandrill, 1 vol. 2004. (ENG., Illus.). 32p. (J). (gr. -1 — 1). 16.95 (978-1-932065-92-3(X)) Star Bright Bks., Inc.

Hobbs, Leigh. Mr Badger & the Missing Ape. l.t. ed. 2012. 120p. (J). pap. (978-1-4596-3344-5(5)) ReadHowYouWant.com, Ltd.

King Sr., Billy. The Story. 2010. 73p. pap. 11.95 (978-0-557-25606-8(2)) Lulu Pr., Inc.

Lucas, David. Peanut. Lucas, David, illus. 2008. (ENG., Illus.). 32p. (J). (gr. k-k). 15.99 (978-0-7636-3925-9(7)) Candlewick Pr.

McMullan, Kate. A Wedding for Wiglaf?, 1 vol. Basso, Bill, illus. 2007. (Dragon Slayers' Academy Ser.: No. 4). (ENG.). 109p. (gr. 4-7). 24.21 (978-1-59961-380-2(8)) Spotlight.

Moncure, Jane Belk. Apes Find Shapes: A Book about Recognizing Shapes. Ronney, Ronnie, illus. 2013. (Magic Castle Readers Ser.). (ENG.). 32p. (J). (gr. -1-2). 25.64 (978-1-62323-577-2(4), 206312) Child's World, Inc., The.

Rex, Michael. Furious George Goes Bananas: A Primate Parody. Rex, Michael, illus. 2010. (ENG., Illus.). 32p. (J). (gr. k-3). 15.99 (978-0-399-25433-8(1), G.P. Putnam's Sons Books for Young Readers) Penguin Young Readers Group.

Rey, H. A. A Treasury of Curious George. 2017. (Curious George Ser.). (ENG., Illus.). 208p. (J). (gr. -1-3). 11.99 **(978-1-328-90514-7(4)**, HMH Books For Young Readers) Houghton Mifflin Harcourt Publishing Co.

Sampson, Brent. One Wacky Wasp: The Perfect Children's Book for Kids Ages 3-6 Who Are Learning to Read. 2010. 24p. (J). 14.95 (978-1-4327-6217-9(6)); pap. 9.95 (978-1-4327-0465-0(6)) Outskirts Pr., Inc.

San Souci, Robert D. & Burroughs, Edgar Rice. Tarzan. McCurdy, Michael, illus. 2004. 31p. (J). (gr. k-4). reprint ed. 16.00 (978-0-7567-7576-6(0)) DIANE Publishing Co.

Schrefer, Eliot. Endangered. 2014. (ENG.). 288p. (J). (gr. 7). pap. 9.99 (978-0-545-16577-8(6), Scholastic Paperbacks) Scholastic, Inc.

Sturm, James. Ape & Armadillo Take over the World: Toon Level 340. 2016. (ENG., Illus.). 40p. (J). (gr. k-4). 12.95 (978-1-943145-09-6(1)) TOON Books / RAW Junior, LLC.

APICULTURE

see Bees

APOLLO PROJECT

see Project Apollo (U.S.)

APOSTLES

Aquilina, Michael, III. St. Jude: A Friend in Hard Times. Neely, Keith, illus. 2004. 76p. (J). 14.95 (978-0-8198-7075-9(7), 332-371) Pauline Bks. & Media.

Jones, Rufus Matthew. St. Paul the Hero. 2007. (J). pap. (978-1-59731-350-6(5)) Perennis, Sophia.

MacDonald, Mindy. Jesus & the 12 Dudes Who Did. 2004. (GodCounts Ser.). (ENG.). 24p. bds. 14.99 (978-1-59052-383-4(0), Multnomah Bks.) Crown Publishing Group.

Sanders, Nancy I. Apostle Paul, 1 vol. 2014. (Get to Know Ser.). (ENG.). 128p. (J). pap. 7.99 (978-0-310-74473-3(3)) Zonderkidz.

Self, David. Saint Paul. Cockcroft, Jason, illus. 2009. (ENG.). 48p. (J). (gr. 2-7). 14.95 (978-0-7459-6097-5(9)) Lion Hudson PLC GBR. Dist: Independent Pubs. Group.

Selucky, Oldrich. Adventures of Saint Paul. Trouve, Marianne Lorraine, tr. from CZE. Krejcova, Zdenka, illus. 2008. Orig. Title: Pavel, dobrudruh Viry. 96p. (J). (gr. 1-3). pap. (978-0-8198-0786-1(9)) Pauline Bks. & Media.

Skipworth, Kelly. Twelve Ordinary Men. 2009. (Illus.). 16p. (J). (gr. k-4). pap. 2.49 (978-0-7586-1611-1(2)) Concordia Publishing Hse.

Wallis, Mary Alice & Lindstrom, C. G. Prophets & Apostles. 2008. (LDS Puzzle Pals Ser.). 122p. pap. 14.99 (978-1-59955-126-5(8), Cedar Fort, Inc.) Cedar Fort, Inc./CFI Distribution.

Zondervan Staff. Jesus & His Friends, 1 vol. Pulley, Kelly, illus. 2009. (I Can Read! / the Beginner's Bible / ¡Yo Sé Leer! Ser.). (SPA & ENG.). 32p. (J). pap. 3.99 (978-0-310-71889-5(9)) Zonderkidz.

APPALACHIAN MOUNTAINS

Aloian, Molly. The Appalachians. 2011. (ENG., Illus.). 48p. (J). pap. (978-0-7787-7568-3(2)); (gr. 4-7). lib. bdg. (978-0-7787-7561-4(5)) Crabtree Publishing Co.

Bennett, Doraine. Appalachian Plateau. 2011. (Illus.). 32p. (J). (978-1-935884-09-5(3)); pap. (978-1-935884-14-9(X)) State Standards Publishing, LLC.

Flowers, Pam & Farnsworth, Bill. Ellie's Long Walk: The True Story of Two Friends on the Appalachian Trail. 2012. (ENG., Illus.). 32p. (J). (gr. -1-3). pap. 11.99 (978-0-88240-885-9(2), West Winds Pr.) Graphic Arts Ctr. Publishing Co.

Herrin, Roberta Teague. Appalachian Children's Literature: An Annotated Bibliography. 2009. (Contributions to Southern Appalachian Studies: 26). (ENG., Illus.). 355p. pap. 75.00 (978-0-7864-1040-8(X)) McFarland & Co., Inc. Pubs.

Maynard, Charles W. The Appalachians. (Great Mountain Ranges of the World Ser.). 24p. (gr. 3-3). 2009. 42.50 (978-1-61513-169-3(8), PowerKids Pr.) 2004. (Illus.). (YA). lib. bdg. 22.60 (978-0-8239-6695-0(X)) Rosen Publishing Group, Inc., The.

APPALACHIAN MOUNTAINS—FICTION

Bowling, Joyce E. & Sester, Richard. A Path of Stitches, 1 vol. 2010. 22p. pap. 24.95 (978-1-4489-6426-0(1)) PublishAmerica, Inc.

Bradfield, Carl. Tecumseh's Trail: The Appalachian Trail, Then & Now. (Illus.). 137p. (Orig.). (YA). (gr. 8-12). pap. (978-0-9632319-3-2(6)) ASDA Publishing, Inc.

Bryan, Jennifer Liu & Kendle, Hazel Cole. Cole Family Christmas. Julich, Jenniffer, illus. 2008. 80p. (J). (gr. 4-7). 17.95 (978-0-9816265-0-5(5)) Next Chapter Pr.

Davis, Donald. The Pig Who Went Home on Sunday: An Appalachian Folktale. Mazzucco, Jennifer, illus. 2007. (ENG.). 40p. (J). (gr. -1-3). 8.95 (978-0-87483-851-0(7)) August Hse. Pubs., Inc.

Doolittle, Sara. Lillie's Smile. Locke, Margo, illus. 2011. 32p. (J). pap. 18.99 (978-0-9827611-6-8(3), Catch the Spirit of Appalachia) Ammons Communications, Ltd.

Ebel, Julia Taylor. The Picture Man. Canter, Idalia, illus. 2009. (ENG.). 32p. (J). 16.95 (978-1-933251-63-9(8)) Parkway Pubs., Inc.

Ernst, Kathleen. Midnight in Lonesome Hollow: A Kit Mystery. 2007. (American Girl Mysteries Ser.). (ENG., Illus.). 192p. (gr. 4-7). 10.95 (978-1-59369-161-5(0), American Girl) American Girl Publishing, Inc.

—Midnight in Lonesome Hollow: A Kit Mystery. Tibbles, Jean-Paul, illus. 2007. (ENG.). 192p. (gr. 4-7). pap. 6.95 (978-1-59369-160-8(2), American Girl) American Girl Publishing, Inc.

Henson, Heather. That Book Woman. Small, David, illus. 2008. (ENG.). 40p. (J). (gr. -1-3). 17.99 (978-1-4169-0812-8(9), Atheneum Bks. for Young Readers) Simon & Schuster Children's Publishing.

—That Book Woman. Small, David, illus. 2011. (J). (gr. 2-4). 29.95 (978-0-545-23715-4(7)) Weston Woods Studios, Inc.

Johnson, Paul Brett, illus. & adapted by. Jack Outwits the Giants. Johnson, Paul Brett, adapted by. 2008. (ENG.). 36p. (J). (gr. -1-3). 11.99 (978-1-4169-7861-9(5), Simon & Schuster/Paula Wiseman Bks.) Simon & Schuster/Paula Wiseman Bks.

Kelley, Jane. Nature Girl. 2011. (ENG., Illus.). 256p. (J). (gr. 3-7). pap. 6.99 (978-0-375-85635-8(8), Yearling) Random Hse. Children's Bks.

Levitt, Steve. Journey to the MountainA Roots Tale. 2007. 144p. pap. 19.95 (978-1-84728-086-2(2)) Lulu Pr., Inc.

Mills, Lauren A. Minna's Patchwork Coat. 2015. (ENG., Illus.). 288p. (J). (gr. 3-7). 17.00 (978-0-316-40621-5(X)) Little Brown & Co.

Naylor, Phyllis Reynolds. Sang Spell. 224p. (YA). (gr. 5-18). pap. 4.99 (978-0-8072-8294-6(4), Listening Library) Random Hse. Audio Publishing Group.

Nolan, Han. When We Were Saints. 2005. (ENG.). 312p. (YA). (gr. 7-12). pap. 15.95 (978-0-15-205322-2(0)) Houghton Mifflin Harcourt Publishing Co.

Pace, Dianne. Odel's Diner. 2007. (J). per. 12.95 (978-0-89315-419-6(9)) Lambert Bk. Hse., Inc.

Ruff, Zeata P. The Gumdrop Tree. Ruff, Zeata P. & Ruff, Jim, illus. 2013. 34p. 16.95 (978-1-937449-25-4(4)) YAV.

Wood, D. K. Nightmare at Indian Cave. 2006. pap. 10.00 (978-1-4257-1640-0(7)) Xlibris Corp.

APPALACHIAN MOUNTAINS—SOCIAL LIFE AND CUSTOMS

Hall, Francie. Appalachian Christmas ABCs. Oehm, Kent, illus. 2010. (ENG.). 53p. (J). 16.95 (978-1-57072-328-5(1)) Overmountain Pr.

Pack, Linda Hager. A Is for Appalachia: The Alphabet Book of Appalachian Heritage. Banks, Pat, illus. 2009. (ENG.). 44p. 16.95 (978-0-8131-2556-5(1)) Univ. Pr. of Kentucky.

APPARATUS, SCIENTIFIC

see Scientific Apparatus and Instruments

APPARITIONS

see also Ghosts

Bolte, Mari. Encountering Ghosts: Eyewitness Accounts, 1 vol. Kako, Franco, illus. 2014. (Eyewitness to the Unexplained Ser.). (ENG.). 32p. (gr. 3-4). 30.65 (978-1-4914-0245-0(8), Graphic Library) Capstone Press of Coughlan Cos.

Owings, Lisa. Ghost Ships. 2015. (Unexplained Mysteries Ser.). (ENG., Illus.). 24p. (J). (gr. 3-7). lib. bdg. 25.95 (978-1-62617-202-9(1), Epic Bks.) Bellwether Media.

Serrano, Francisco. La Virgen de Guadalupe. Dávalos, Felipe, illus.Tr. of Virgin of Guadalupe. (SPA.). (J). (gr. 2-4). 18.00 (978-968-494-070-3(X)) Centro de Informacion y Desarrollo de la Comunicacion y la Literatura MEX. Dist: Lectorum Pubns., Inc.

APPETIZERS

Cornell, Kari. Awesome Snacks & Appetizers. Cohen, Brie, photos by. 2013. (You're the Chef Ser.). (ENG., Illus.). 32p. (gr. 3-5). lib. bdg. 26.60 (978-0-7613-6642-3(3), Millbrook Pr.) Lerner Publishing Group.

APPLE

see Apples

APPLE COMPUTERS

Blumenthal, Karen. Steve Jobs: The Man Who Thought Different. 2012. (ENG., Illus.). 320p. (YA). (gr. 7-12). 17.99 (978-1-250-01557-0(X), 9781250015570) Feiwel & Friends.

—Steve Jobs: The Man Who Thought Different. 2012. (ENG., Illus.). 320p. (YA). (gr. 7-12). pap. 10.99 (978-1-250-01445-0(X), 9781250014450) Square Fish.

Brackett, Virginia. Steve Jobs: Computer Genius of Apple. 2003. (Internet Biographies Ser.). (Illus.). 48p. (J). (gr. 4-10). lib. bdg. 23.93 (978-0-7660-1970-6(5)) Enslow Pubs., Inc.

Brennan, Patricia. Who Is Bill Gates? 2013. (Who Is... ? Ser.). lib. bdg. 16.00 (978-0-606-30038-4(4), Turtleback) Turtleback Bks.

Corrigan, Jim. Steve Jobs. 2008. (Business Leaders Ser.). 128p. (YA). (gr. 7-12). lib. bdg. 27.95 (978-1-59935-076-9(9)) Reynolds, Morgan Inc.

Gilbert, Sara. The Story of Apple. 2011. (Built for Success Ser.). (Illus.). 46p. (J). (gr. 5-9). 34.25 (978-1-60818-061-5(1)) Creative Co., The.

—The Story of Apple - Built for Success. 2012. (Built for Success Ser.). (ENG.). 48p. (J). (gr. 4-7). pap. 12.00 (978-0-89812-659-4(2), Creative Paperbacks) Creative Co., The.

Gillam, Scott. Steve Jobs: Apple & iPod Wizard, 1 vol. 2008. (Essential Lives Set 2 Ser.). (ENG., Illus.). 112p. (J). (gr. 6-12). lib. bdg. 35.64 (978-1-60453-037-7(5)) ABDO Publishing Co.

—Steve Jobs: Apple ICon, 1 vol. 2012. (Essential Lives Set 2 Ser.). (ENG.). 112p. (J). (gr. 6-12). lib. bdg. 35.64 (978-1-60453-997-4(6), Essential Library) ABDO Publishing Co.

Goldsworthy, Steve. Steve Jobs. 2011. (J). (gr. 4-6). pap. 12.95 (978-1-61690-675-7(8), AV2 by Weigl); (Illus.). 24p. (YA). (gr. 3-6). 27.13 (978-1-61690-670-2(7)) Weigl Pubs., Inc.

Green, Sara. Apple. (Apple Ser.). 24p. (J). (gr. 3-8). 2017. pap. 7.99 **(978-1-61891-251-0(8))** 2015. (ENG., Illus.). lib. bdg. 25.95 (978-1-62617-286-9(2)) Bellwether Media. (Pilot Bks.).

Gregory, Josh. Steve Jobs. 2013. (True Book(tm), A — Biographies Ser.). (ENG., Illus.). (J). 48p. lib. bdg. 31.00 (978-0-531-21907-2(0)); 64p. pap. 8.95 (978-0-531-21964-5(X)); 48p. pap. 6.95 (978-0-531-23878-3(4)); 64p. lib. bdg. 30.00 (978-0-531-23606-2(4)) Scholastic Library Publishing.

Hunter, Nick. Steve Jobs, 1 vol. 2012. (Titans of Business Ser.). (ENG.). 48p. (gr. 4-6). pap. 8.99 (978-1-4329-6435-1(6)); lib. bdg. 32.00 (978-1-4329-6428-3(3)) Heinemann-Raintree. (NA-h).

Imbimbo, Anthony. Steve Jobs: The Brilliant Mind Behind Apple. 2009. (Life Portraits Ser.). (Illus.). 112p. (YA). (gr. 7-12). lib. bdg. 36.00 (978-1-4339-0060-0(2)) Stevens, Gareth Publishing LLLP.

Klein, Adria F. Steve Jobs. 2009. pap. 13.25 (978-1-60559-071-4(1)) Hameray Publishing Group, Inc.

La Bella, Laura. Steve Jobs & Steve Wozniak, 01 vols., 1. 2016. (Tech Pioneers Ser.). (ENG.). 112p. (J). 35.60 (978-1-4994-6286-9(7), Rosen Young Adult) Rosen Publishing Group, Inc., The.

Lakin, Patricia. Steve Jobs: Thinking Differently. 2012. (ENG.). 192p. (J). (gr. 3-7). pap. 7.99 (978-1-4424-5393-7(1), Aladdin) Simon & Schuster Children's Publishing.

—Steve Jobs: Thinking Differently. 2012. (ENG.). 192p. (J). (gr. 3-7). 17.99 (978-1-4424-5394-4(X), Simon & Schuster/Paula Wiseman Bks.) Simon & Schuster/Paula Wiseman Bks.

Lemke, Donald B. Steve Jobs, Steve Wozniak, & the Personal Computer, 1 vol. Smith, Tod G. & Milgrom, Al, illus. 2006. (Inventions & Discovery Ser.). (ENG.). 32p. (gr. 3-4). 30.65 (978-0-7368-6488-6(1), Graphic Library) Capstone Press of Coughlan Cos.

—Steve Jobs, Steve Wozniak, & the Personal Computer, 1 vol. Milgrom, Al & Smith, Tod G., illus. 2006. (Inventions & Discovery Ser.). (ENG.). 32p. (gr. 3-4). pap. 8.10 (978-0-7368-9650-4(3)); pap. 47.70 (978-0-7368-9762-4(3)) Capstone Press of Coughlan Cos. (Graphic Library).

Lusted, Marcia Amidon. Apple: The Company & Its Visionary Founder, Steve Jobs, 1 vol. 2012. (Technology Pioneers Set 2 Ser.). (ENG., Illus.). 112p. (J). (gr. 6-12). lib. bdg. 35.64 (978-1-61783-331-1(2), Essential Library) ABDO Publishing Co.

Lusted, Marcia Amidon & National Geographic Learning Staff. Apple: The Company & Its Visionary Founder, Steve Jobs. 2013. (ENG.). 112p. (C). pap. 14.95 (978-1-60453-998-1(4)) National Geographic School Publishing, Inc.

Mattern, Joanne. Steve Jobs. 2013. (Rookie Biographies(r) Ser.). (ENG.). 32p. (J). pap. 5.95 (978-0-531-24705-1(8), Children's Pr.); lib. bdg. 23.00 (978-0-531-24739-6(2)) Scholastic Library Publishing.

Perritano, John. Apple. 2017. (J). **(978-1-5105-2358-6(8))** SmartBook Media, Inc.

Pollack, Pam, et al. Who Was Steve Jobs? Harrison, Nancy et al, illus. 2012. (Who Was? Ser.). (ENG.). 112p. (J). (gr. 3-7). pap. 5.99 (978-0-448-46211-0(7), Grosset & Dunlap) Penguin Young Readers Group.

Pollack, Pamela & Belviso, Meg. Who Was Steve Jobs? 2012. (Who Was... ? Ser.). lib. bdg. 16.00 (978-0-606-26649-9(6), Turtleback) Turtleback Bks.

Shea, Therese. Steve Jobs & Apple. 2012. (Internet Biographies Ser.). (ENG., Illus.). 128p. (YA). (gr. 7-12). lib. bdg. 34.60 (978-1-4488-6910-7(2)) Rosen Publishing Group, Inc., The.

Sheen, Barbara. Steve Jobs. 2009. (People in the News Ser.). (ENG., Illus.). 128p. (YA). (gr. 7-12). 33.95 (978-1-4205-0160-5(7)) Cengage Gale.

Steve Jobs & Apple. 2011. (Graphic Nonfiction Biographies Ser.). (ENG.). 48p. (YA). (gr. 5-8). (978-1-4488-5546-9(2)); pap. (978-1-4488-5645-9(0)) Rosen Publishing Group, Inc., The. (Rosen Reference).

Venezia, Mike. Steve Jobs & Steve Wozniak: Geek Heroes Who Put the Personal in Computers. 2010. (Getting to Know the World's Greatest Inventors & Scientists Ser.). 32p. (J). pap. 6.95 (978-0-531-22351-2(5), Children's Pr.) Scholastic Library Publishing.

Ventura, Marne & Feynman, Drew. The Creators of the iPhone. Glass, Simon, illus. 2017. (Awesome Minds Ser.). (ENG.). 56p. (J). (gr. 1-5). 14.99 (978-1-938093-77-7(1), Duo Pr. Llc (US)) Duo Pr. LLC.

Washburne, Sophie & Sheen, Barbara. Steve Jobs: Computer Visionary. 2017. (People in the News Ser.). 104p. (J). (gr. 7-7). lib. bdg. 39.40 **(978-1-5345-6031-4(9)**, Lucent Pr.) Greenhaven Publishing LLC.

APPLES

Ackelsberg, Amy. A Day at the Apple Orchard. Thomas, Laura, illus. 2013. (Strawberry Shortcake Ser.). (ENG.). 24p. (J). (gr. -1-k). 4.99 (978-0-448-46752-8(6), Grosset & Dunlap) Penguin Young Readers Group.

Blair, Eric. Johnny Appleseed, 1 vol. Muehlenhardt, Amy Bailey, illus. 2011. (My First Classic Story Ser.).Tr. of Johnny Appleseed. (ENG.). 32p. (gr. k-3). pap. 7.10 (978-1-4048-7367-4(8), My First Classic Story) Picture Window Bks.

Bluemel Oldfield, Dawn. Apple. 2015. (See It Grow Ser.). (ENG., Illus.). 24p. (J). (gr. -1-3). lib. bdg. 23.93 (978-1-62724-839-6(0)) Bearport Publishing Co., Inc.

Bodden, Valerie. Apple. 2014. (Illus.). 32p. (J). (978-1-60818-404-0(8), Creative Education) Creative Co., The.

—Grow with Me: Apple. 2015. (Grow with Me Ser.). (ENG.). 32p. (J). (gr. 3-5). pap. 9.99 (978-0-89812-990-8(7), Creative Paperbacks) Creative Co., The.

Brannon, Cecelia H. Apples. 2017. (All about Food Crops Ser.). 24p. (gr. k-1). lib. bdg. 22.60 **(978-0-7660-8575-6(9))** Enslow Pubs., Inc.

Brown, Carron. Secrets of the Apple Tree. Nassner, Alyssa, illus. 2014. (ENG.). 36p. (J). 12.99 (978-1-61067-243-6(7)) Kane Miller.

Bulla, Clyde Robert. A Tree Is a Plant. Schuett, Stacey, illus. 2016. (Let's-Read-And-Find-Out Science 1 Ser.). 40p. (J). (gr. -1-3). pap. 6.99 (978-0-06-238210-8(1)) HarperCollins Pubs.

Chernesky, Felicia Sanzari. From Apple Trees to Cider, Please! Patton, Julia, illus. 2015. (ENG.). 32p. (J). (gr. -1-3). 16.99 (978-0-8075-6513-1(X)) Whitman, Albert & Co.

Clark, Rosalyn. A Visit to the Orchard. 2017. (Bumba Books (tm) — Places We Go Ser.). (ENG., Illus.). 24p. (J). (gr. -1-1). 25.32 **(978-1-5124-3375-3(6))** Lerner Publishing Group.

Clifton, Gillian. The Life Cycle of an Apple Tree: Over & over Again. 2017. (Computer Science for the Real World Ser.). 16p. (gr. 7-8). pap. 7.95 **(978-1-5383-5243-4(5)**, Rosen Classroom) Rosen Publishing Group, Inc., The.

Codell, Esmé Raji. Seed by Seed: The Legend & Legacy of John Appleseed Anniversary. Perkins, Lynne Rae, illus. 2012. 32p. (J). (gr. -1-3). 17.89 (978-0-06-145516-2(4), Greenwillow Bks.) HarperCollins Pubs.

—Seed by Seed: The Legend & Legacy of John Appleseed Chapman. Perkins, Lynne Rae, illus. 2012. (ENG.). 32p. (J). (gr. -1-3). 16.99 (978-0-06-145515-5(6), Greenwillow Bks.) HarperCollins Pubs.

Dickmann, Nancy. An Apple's Life, 1 vol. 2010. (Watch It Grow Ser.). (ENG., Illus.). 24p. (gr. -1-1). pap. 6.29 (978-1-4329-4150-5(X), Acorn) Heinemann-Raintree.

—La Vida de la Manzana, 1 vol. 2011. (¡Mira Cómo Crece! Ser.). (Illus.). 24p. (gr. -1-1). (SPA & ENG.). 22.65 (978-1-4329-5274-7(9)); (ENG & SPA.). pap. 6.29 (978-1-4329-5286-0(2)) Heinemann-Raintree. (Bellota).

Dunn, Mary R. An Apple Tree's Life Cycle. 2017. (Explore Life Cycles Ser.). (ENG.). 24p. (gr. k-1). lib. bdg. 26.65 **(978-1-5157-7055-8(9)**, Pebble Plus) Capstone Press of Coughlan Cos.

Esbaum, Jill. Apples for Everyone. 2009. (Picture the Seasons Ser.). (Illus.). 16p. (J). (ENG.). (gr. -1-3). pap. 5.95 (978-1-4263-0523-8(0), National Geographic Children's Bks.); (978-0-329-74348-2(1)) National Geographic Society.

Farmer, Jacqueline. Apples. Tildes, Phyllis Limbacher, illus. 2007. (ENG.). 32p. (J). (gr. k-3). 6.95 (978-1-57091-695-3(0)) Charlesbridge Publishing, Inc.

Felix, Rebecca. We Harvest Apples in Fall. 2013. (Illus.). 24p. (J). (978-1-61080-980-1(7)); (ENG., 22.79 (978-1-61080-905-4(X), 202599); (ENG., pap. 12.79 (978-1-61080-930-6(0), 202601) Cherry Lake Publishing.

Franck, Irene M. & Brownstone, David M. Riches of the Earth, 16 vols. 2003. (Illus.). 32p. (J). 289.00 (978-0-7172-5730-0(4), Grolier) Scholastic Library Publishing.

Gleisner, Jenna Lee. Apple Harvest. 2017. (Welcome, Fall! Ser.). (ENG.). 24p. (J). (gr. -1-2). lib. bdg. 27.07 *(978-1-5038-1660-2(5),* 211496) Child's World, Inc., The.

Gregoire, Maryellen. Apple Trees. 2011. (Wonder Readers Emergent Level Ser.). (ENG.). (gr. -1-1). 8p. pap. 35.94 *(978-1-4296-8219-0(1));* 32p. pap. 5.99 *(978-1-4296-7839-1(9))* Capstone Press of Coughlan Cos. (Wonder Readers).

Griswold, Cliff. Let's Go Apple Picking! 2015. (Fun in Fall Ser.). (ENG.). 24p. (J). (gr. k-k). lib. bdg. 22.60 *(978-1-4824-1780-7(4))* Stevens, Gareth Publishing LLLP.

Heos, Bridget. So You Want to Grow a Pie? Fabbri, Daniele, illus. 2015. (Grow Your Food Ser.). (ENG.). 24p. (gr. 1-3). 19.95 *(978-1-60753-739-7(7))* Amicus Publishing.

Hoffman, Mary Ann. Watch Apple Trees Grow. 2011. (Watch Plants Grow! Ser.). 24p. (gr. k-2). 69.20 *(978-1-4339-6154-0(7))* Stevens, Gareth Publishing LLLP.

—Watch Apple Trees Grow / ¡Mira cómo crece el Manzano! 2011. (Watch Plants Grow! / ¡Mira cómo crecen las plantas! Ser.). (ENG & SPA., Illus.). 24p. (J). (gr. -1-2). 22.60 *(978-1-4339-4820-6(6))* Stevens, Gareth Publishing LLLP.

Hubbell, Will, illus. Apples Here! 2015. 32p. (J). *(978-1-4896-3846-5(6))* Weigl Pubs., Inc.

Knudsen, Shannon. Seed, Sprout, Fruit: An Apple Tree Life Cycle, 1 vol. Smith, Simon, illus. 2011. (First Graphics: Nature Cycles Ser.). (ENG.). 24p. (gr. 1-2). pap. 6.29 *(978-1-4296-6230-7(1));* pap. 35.70 *(978-1-4296-6399-1(5))* Capstone Press of Coughlan Cos.

Koontz, Robin. Apples, Apples Everywhere! Learning about Apple Harvests, 1 vol. Takvorian, Nadine, illus. 2010. (Autumn Ser.). (ENG.). 24p. (gr. 1-2). pap. 8.95 *(978-1-4048-6388-0(5))* Picture Window Bks.

Lindeen, Mary. I Eat Apples in Fall. 2016. (First Step Nonfiction — Observing Fall Ser.). (ENG., Illus.). 24p. (J). (gr. k-2). 23.99 *(978-1-5124-0793-8(3))* Lerner Publishing Group.

Llewellyn, Claire. Apples. 2005. (Illus.). 24p. (YA). (gr. 1-18). lib. bdg. 22.80 *(978-1-932889-39-0(6))* Sea-To-Sea Pubns.

—Tree. Mendez, Simon, tr. Mendez, Simon, illus. 2004. (Starting Life Ser.). (ENG.). 24p. (J). (gr. k-3). 16.95 *(978-1-55971-879-0(X))* Cooper Square Publishing Llc.

Lundgren, Julie K. Apple Trees & the Seasons. 2011. (ENG., Illus.). 24p. (gr. k-1). pap. 8.95 *(978-1-61741-924-9(9))* Rourke Educational Media.

Mattern, Joanne. Cómo crecen los Manzanos. 2006. (How Plants Grow/ Como crecen las plantas Ser.). (ENG & SPA., Illus.). 24p. (gr. k-3). lib. bdg. 22.00 *(978-0-8368-6460-1(3),* Weekly Reader Leveled Readers) Stevens, Gareth Publishing LLLP.

Mayo, Gretchen Will. Applesauce. 2004. (Weekly Reader Early Learning Library). (Illus.). 24p. (gr. 1-4). pap. 8.15 *(978-0-8368-4071-1(2));* lib. bdg. 21.00 *(978-0-8368-4064-3(X))* Stevens, Gareth Publishing LLLP. (Weekly Reader Leveled Readers).

McNamara, Margaret. Apple ABC. Parker, Jake, illus. 2012. (J). *(978-0-439-72809-6(6))* Scholastic, Inc.

Meachen Rau, Dana. Applesauce. 2008. (What's Cooking? Ser.). 24p. (gr. k-1). lib. bdg. 15.95 *(978-0-7614-2894-7(1),* Benchmark Bks.) Marshall Cavendish Corp.

Murray, Julie. Apples, 1 vol. 2007. (Life Cycles Ser.). (ENG.). 24p. (gr. 4-7). 25.65 *(978-1-59928-701-0(3),* Buddy Bks.) ABDO Publishing Co.

Naslund, Gorel Kristina & Digman, Kristina. Our Apple Tree. Digman, Kristina, illus. 2006. (ENG., Illus.). 32p. (J). (gr. -1-3). pap. 8.99 *(978-1-59643-191-1(1),* 9781596431911) Square Fish.

Nelson, Robin. Apple Trees. 2009. pap. 34.95 *(978-0-7613-4114-7(5));* (ENG.). 24p. 23.93 *(978-0-7613-4071-3(8),* Lerner Pubns.) Lerner Publishing Group.

Owen, Ruth. Fruit! Life on an Apple Farm. 2012. (Food from Farmers Ser.). (Illus.). 32p. (J). (gr. k-3). pap. 11.75 *(978-1-61533-538-1(2));* lib. bdg. 26.50 *(978-1-61533-530-5(7))* Windmill Bks.

Pascoe, Elaine. The Ecosystem of an Apple Tree. (Library of Small Ecosystems Ser.). 24p. 2009. (gr. 3-4). 47.90 *(978-1-60853-860-7(5))* 2003. (Illus.). (J). lib. bdg. 25.25 *(978-0-8239-6304-1(7))* Rosen Publishing Group, Inc., The. (PowerKids Pr.).

Peters, Elisa. It's an Apple Tree! 2009. (Everyday Wonders Ser.). 24p. (gr. 1-1). 42.50 *(978-1-61512-325-4(3));* (Illus.). (J). lib. bdg. 22.60 *(978-1-4042-4457-3(3))* Rosen Publishing Group, Inc., The. (PowerKids Pr.).

—It's an Apple Tree! Es un Manzano! 2009. (Everyday Wonders / Maravillas de Todos Los días Ser.). (SPA & ENG., Illus.). 24p. (J). lib. bdg. 22.60 *(978-1-4358-2522-2(5),* PowerKids Pr.) Rosen Publishing Group, Inc., The.

—It's an Apple Tree! / ¡Es un Manzano! 2009. (Everyday Wonders / Maravillas de todos los días Ser.). (ENG & SPA.). 24p. (gr. 1-1). 42.50 *(978-1-61512-331-5(8),* Editorial Buenas Letras) Rosen Publishing Group, Inc., The.

Rajczak, Kristen. Watch Apple Trees Grow. 2011. (Watch Plants Grow! Ser.). (Illus.). 24p. (J). (gr. k-2). pap. 8.15 *(978-1-4339-4817-6(6));* lib. bdg. 22.60 *(978-1-4339-4816-9(8))* Stevens, Gareth Publishing LLLP.

Robbins, Ken. Apples. Robbins, Ken, photos by. 2013. (ENG., Illus.). 32p. (J). (gr. 1-4). pap. 16.99 *(978-1-4814-0165-4(3),* Atheneum Bks. for Young Readers) Simon & Schuster Children's Publishing.

Royston, Angela. La Manzana, 1 vol. 2010. (Ciclo de Vida Ser.). (SPA & ENG.). 32p. (gr. 1-3). 27.32 *(978-1-4329-4364-6(2))* Heinemann-Raintree.

Rustad, Martha E. H. Fall Apples: Crisp & Juicy. Enright, Amanda, illus. 2011. (Fall's Here! Ser.). pap. 39.62 *(978-0-7613-8644-5(0),* Millbrook Pr.); (ENG.). 24p. pap. 6.95 *(978-0-7613-8507-3(X),* Millbrook Pr.); (ENG.). 24p. lib. bdg. 23.93 *(978-0-7613-5064-4(0))* Lerner Publishing Group.

Saunders-Smith, Gail. Apple Trees. 2016. (Plants: Life Cycles Ser.). (ENG.). 24p. (gr. k-1). pap. 6.29 *(978-1-5157-4232-6(6),* Pebble Bks.) Capstone Press of Coughlan Cos.

Schuh, Mari. Apples Grow on a Tree, 1 vol. 2011. (How Fruits & Vegetables Grow Ser.). (ENG., 24p. (gr. k-1). Illus.). pap. 6.29 *(978-1-4296-6181-2(X));* pap. 35.70 *(978-1-4296-6182-9(8))* Capstone Press of Coughlan Cos. (Pebble Bks.).

—Apples in Fall. 2013. (ENG., Illus.). 24p. (J). lib. bdg. 25.65 *(978-1-62031-057-1(0))* Jump! Inc.

Sévigny, Eric, illus. Caillou Goes Apple Picking. 2014. (Clubhouse Ser.). (ENG.). 24p. (J). (gr. -1 — 1). pap. 3.99 *(978-2-89718-145-1(1))* Caillouet, Gerry.

Shores, Erika L. Apples. 2015. (Celebrate Fall Ser.). (ENG., Illus.). 24p. (gr. k-1). lib. bdg. 21.99 *(978-1-4914-6001-6(6),* Pebble Bks.) Capstone Press of Coughlan Cos.

Slovacek, Joe. The Apple Chase. 2010. 24p. 14.95 *(978-1-4490-8289-5(0))* AuthorHouse.

Snyder, Inez. Apples. 2004. (Harvesttime Ser.). (ENG.). 24p. (J). 19.00 *(978-0-516-27595-6(X),* Children's Pr.) Scholastic Library Publishing.

Sundance/Newbridge LLC Staff. An Apple a Day. 2007. (Early Science Ser.). (gr. k-3). 18.95 *(978-1-4007-6359-7(2));* pap. 6.10 *(978-1-4007-6355-9(X))* Sundance/Newbridge Educational Publishing.

Taus-Bolstad, Stacy. From Shoot to Apple. (Start to Finish, Second Series: Nature's Cycles Ser.). 24p. (gr. k-3). 2012. (ENG.). pap. 39.62 *(978-0-7613-9295-8(5))* 2012. (ENG.). pap. 6.95 *(978-0-7613-8576-9(2))* 2012. (ENG., Illus.). lib. bdg. 23.93 *(978-0-7613-7734-4(4))* 2003. (Illus.). (J). 18.60 *(978-0-8225-0719-2(6),* Lerner Pubns.) Lerner Publishing Group.

Thomson, Ruth. The Life Cycle of an Apple. 2009. (Learning about Life Cycles Ser.). 24p. (J). (ENG.). (gr. k-5). pap. 8.25 *(978-1-4358-2886-5(0),* PowerKids Pr.); (gr. 2-5). lib. bdg. 22.60 *(978-1-4358-2836-0(4))* Rosen Publishing Group, Inc., The.

Trosper, Chad. Apples in a Pail. 2011. 28p. pap. 12.50 *(978-0-557-25147-6(8))* Lulu Pr., Inc.

Tuminelly, Nancy. Let's Cook with Apples! Delicious & Fun Apple Dishes Kids Can Make, 1 vol. 2012. (Super Simple Recipes Ser.). (ENG.). 32p. (J). (gr. k-4). lib. bdg. 27.07 *(978-1-61783-418-9(1),* Super SandCastle) ABDO Publishing Co.

Ziefert, Harriet. One Red Apple. Gudeon, Karla, illus. 2009. 36p. (J). 15.99 *(978-1-934706-46-6(9))* Blue Apple Bks.

APPLESEED, JOHNNY, 1774-1845

Adil, Janeen. Johnny Appleseed. 2003. (Folk Heroes Ser.). (Illus.). 24p. (J). lib. bdg. 24.45 *(978-1-59036-075-0(3))* Weigl Pubs., Inc.

Benjamin, Margaret. Johnny Appleseed. 2014. (Illus.). 31p. (J). pap. *(978-1-62712-278-8(8))* Cavendish Square Publishing.

Blair, Eric. Johnny Appleseed, 1 vol. Muehlenhardt, Amy Bailey, illus. 2011. (My First Classic Story Ser.).Tr. of Johnny Appleseed. (ENG.). 32p. (gr. k-3). pap. 7.10 *(978-1-4048-7367-4(8),* My First Classic Story) Picture Window Bks.

—Johnny Appleseed, 1 vol. Robledo, Sol, tr. Muehlenhardt, Amy Bailey, illus. 2006. (Read-It! Readers en Español: Cuentos Exagerados Ser.).Tr. of Johnny Appleseed. (SPA.). 32p. (gr. k-3). 21.32 *(978-1-4048-1655-8(0),* Easy Readers) Picture Window Bks.

Braun, Eric & Meister, Cari. American Folk Legends, 1 vol. 2014. (American Folk Legends Ser.). (ENG.). 32p. (gr. k-2). 109.28 *(978-1-4795-5531-4(2))* Picture Window Bks.

Burkes-Larrañaga, Dustin, illus. Johnny Appleseed Plants Trees Across the Land, 1 vol. 2014. (American Folk Legends Ser.). (ENG.). 32p. (gr. k-2). lib. bdg. 27.32 *(978-1-4795-5428-7(6))* Picture Window Bks.

Codell, Esmé Raji. Seed by Seed: The Legend & Legacy of John Appleseed Anniversary. Perkins, Lynne Rae, illus. 2012. 32p. (J). (gr. -1-3). 17.89 *(978-0-06-145516-2(4),* Greenwillow Bks.) HarperCollins Pubs.

—Seed by Seed: The Legend & Legacy of John Appleseed Chapman. Perkins, Lynne Rae, illus. 2012. (ENG.). 32p. (J). (gr. -1-3). 16.99 *(978-0-06-145515-5(6),* Greenwillow Bks.) HarperCollins Pubs.

Ditchfield, Christin. Johnny Appleseed. 2003. (Rookie Biographies Ser.). (ENG.). 32p. (J). (gr. 1-2). pap. 4.95 *(978-0-516-27816-2(9),* Children's Pr.) Scholastic Library Publishing.

Feinstein, Stephen. Read about Johnny Appleseed. 2006. (I Like Biographies! Ser.). (Illus.). 24p. (J). (gr. 1-3). lib. bdg. 22.60 *(978-0-7660-2599-8(3),* Enslow Elementary) Enslow Pubs., Inc.

Fischer, Jeff, illus. Johnny Appleseed. 2006. (Famous Fables Ser.). (J). 6.99 *(978-1-59939-028-4(0))* Cornerstone Pr.

Johnston, Marianne. Johnny Appleseed. 2009. (American Legends Ser.). 24p. (gr. 3-3). 42.50 *(978-1-61511-383-5(5),* PowerKids Pr.) Rosen Publishing Group, Inc., The.

Kunstler, James Howard. Johnny Appleseed. Olson, Stan, illus. 2005. (Rabbit Ears-A Classic Tale Ser.). 36p. (J). (gr. k-5). 25.65 *(978-1-59197-765-0(7))* Spotlight.

Kurtz, Jane. Johnny Appleseed. Haverfield, Mary, illus. 2004. (Ready-To-Reads Ser.). (ENG.). 32p. (J). (gr. -1-1). pap. 3.99 *(978-0-689-85958-8(9),* Simon Spotlight) Simon Spotlight.

Miller, Dean & Talbot, Jeffrey. Johnny Appleseed. 2014. (Illus.). 32p. (J). 28.50 *(978-1-62712-277-1(X))* Cavendish Square Publishing.

Saviola, Ava. The Story of Johnny Appleseed. 2009. (Real Life Readers Ser.). 12p. (gr. 1-2). pap. 5.90 *(978-1-4042-7927-8(X),* Rosen Classroom) Rosen Publishing Group, Inc., The.

Smith, Andrea P. Johnny Appleseed. 2012. (Illus.). 24p. (J). 63.60 *(978-1-4488-5225-3(0));* pap. 10.60 *(978-1-4488-5224-6(2));* lib. bdg. 25.25 *(978-1-4488-5193-5(9))* Rosen Publishing Group, Inc., The. (PowerKids Pr.).

Snyder, Geraldine Ann. Johnny Appleseed: Musical. 2003. (Illus.). 41p. (YA). pap. 6.95 *(978-1-58342-127-7(0),* J04) Dramatic Publishing Co.

Swain, Gwenyth. Johnny Appleseed. Porter, Janice Lee, illus. 2003. (On My Own Biographies Ser.). 48p. (J). (gr. 1-3). pap. 6.95 *(978-1-57505-534-3(1))* Lerner Publishing Group.

Sweeney, Alyse. Easy Reader Biographies: Johnny Appleseed: An American Who Made a Difference. 2007. (ENG.). 16p. pap. 2.99 *(978-0-439-77414-7(4),* Teaching Resources) Scholastic, Inc.

Winters, Kay. John Appleseed: A Trail of Trees. Pullen, Zachary, illus. 2007. (J). *(978-1-4263-0101-8(4))* National Geographic Society.

Worth, Richard. Johnny Appleseed: Select Good Seeds & Plant Them in Good Ground. 2010. (Americans—the Spirit of a Nation Ser.). (Illus.). 128p. (J). lib. bdg. 33.27 *(978-0-7660-3352-8(X))* Enslow Pubs., Inc.

Yolen, Jane. Johnny Appleseed: The Legend & the Truth. Burke, Jim, illus. (ENG.). 32p. (J). (gr. 1-4). 2011. pap. 6.99 *(978-0-06-059137-3(4))* 2008. 16.99 *(978-0-06-059135-9(8))* HarperCollins Pubs.

Zarzycki, Daryl Davis. Johnny Appleseed. 2007. (What's So Great About... ? Ser.). (Illus.). 32p. (YA). (gr. 2-4). lib. bdg. 25.70 *(978-1-58415-483-9(7))* Mitchell Lane Pubs., Inc.

APPLESEED, JOHNNY, 1774-1845—FICTION

Brown, Gregory. Johnny Appleseed: An American Tall Tale. 2006. (J). pap. *(978-1-4108-7157-2(6))* Benchmark Education Co.

Capstone Press Staff. The Legend of Johnny Appleseed. Lamoreaux, Michelle, illus. 2010. (Graphic Spin Ser.). (ENG.). 40p. (gr. 1-3). lib. bdg. 25.32 *(978-1-4342-1895-7(3),* Graphic Revolve) Stone Arch Bks.

Christopher, Matt. Johnny Long Legs. 2005. (Sports Classics II Ser.). 117p. (J). lib. bdg. 15.00 *(978-1-59054-760-1(8))* Fitzgerald Bks.

Stone Arch Books Staff. The Legend of Johnny Appleseed. Lamoreaux, M. A. & Lamoreaux, Michelle, illus. 2010. (Graphic Spin Ser.). (ENG.). 40p. (gr. 1-3). pap. 5.95 *(978-1-4342-2266-4(7),* Graphic Revolve) Stone Arch Bks.

Suen, Anastasia. Johnny Appleseed. Myer, Ed, illus. 2012. (ENG.). 24p. (gr. k-1). pap. 8.95 *(978-1-61810-301-7(6))* Rourke Educational Media.

Weston Woods Staff, creator. Johnny Appleseed. 2011. 38.75 *(978-0-439-72733-4(2));* 18.95 *(978-0-439-72731-0(6))* Weston Woods Studios, Inc.

APPLIANCES, ELECTRIC

see Household Appliances, Electric

APPLIED PSYCHOLOGY

see Psychology, Applied

APPLIED SCIENCE

see Technology

APPRAISAL OF BOOKS

see Books and Reading; Criticism; Literature—History and Criticism

APPRECIATION OF ART

see Art Appreciation

APPRECIATION OF MUSIC

see Music Appreciation

APPRENTICES—FICTION

Alger, Horatio. Bound to Rise: Or: up the Ladder. 2007. (ENG.). 172p. per. 19.99 *(978-1-4346-5059-7(6));* 188p. per. 21.99 *(978-1-4346-5060-3(X))* Creative Media Partners, LLC.

Alloway, Kit. Dreamfire. 2015. (Dream Walker Trilogy Ser.: 1). (ENG.). 368p. (YA). (gr. 8-12). 18.99 *(978-1-250-06366-3(3),* 9781250063663, St. Martin's Griffin) St. Martin's Pr.

Axelrod, Amy & Axelrod, David. The Bullet Catch. 2015. (ENG.). 320p. (J). (gr. 5-9). 17.95 *(978-0-8234-2858-8(3))* Holiday Hse., Inc.

Banks, Kate. The Magician's Apprentice. Sís, Peter, illus. 2012. (ENG.). 224p. (J). (gr. 5-9). 16.99 *(978-0-374-34716-1(6),* 9780374347161, Farrar, Straus & Giroux (BYR)) Farrar, Straus & Giroux.

Beaty, Erin. The Traitor's Kiss. 2017. (Traitor's Trilogy Ser.: 1). (ENG.). 352p. (YA). 18.99 *(978-1-250-11794-6(1),* 9781250117946) Imprint IND. Dist: Macmillan.

Black, Kat. A Templar's Apprentice. 2009. (Book of Tormod Ser.: 1). (ENG.). 288p. (J). (gr. 7-18). 17.99 *(978-0-545-05654-0(3))* Scholastic, Inc.

—A Templar's Gifts. 2011. (Book of Tormod Ser.: 2). (ENG.). 272p. (J). (gr. 7-7). 17.99 *(978-0-545-05675-5(6),* Scholastic Pr.) Scholastic, Inc.

Blackwood, Gary. Curiosity. 2015. (ENG.). 336p. (J). (gr. 4-7). 8.99 *(978-0-14-242448-3(X),* Puffin Books) Penguin Young Readers Group.

—Shakespeare's Spy. 2005. 281p. (gr. 5-9). 17.00 *(978-0-7569-5216-7(6))* Perfection Learning Corp.

Blackwood, Gary L. Shakespeare's Spy. 2005. (ENG.). 288p. (J). (gr. 3-7). 6.99 *(978-0-14-240311-2(3),* Puffin Books) Penguin Young Readers Group.

Cowley, Marjorie. The Golden Bull. 2012. (ENG.). 216p. (J). (gr. 4-7). pap. 8.95 *(978-1-58089-182-0(9))* Charlesbridge Publishing, Inc.

Cox, R. The Lonely Wizard Named Wizzy: The Apprentice. 2009. 16p. pap. 8.49 *(978-1-4490-2236-5(7))* AuthorHouse.

Cremer, Andrea. Rift. 2013. (Nightshade Ser.). (ENG.). 480p. (YA). (gr. 9). pap. 9.99 *(978-0-14-242493-3(5),* Speak) Penguin Young Readers Group.

DeFelice, Cynthia C. The Apprenticeship of Lucas Whitaker. 2007. (ENG.). 160p. (J). (gr. 5-9). per. 9.99 *(978-0-374-40014-9(8),* 9780374400149) Square Fish.

Delaney, Joseph. Attack of the Fiend. Arrasmith, Patrick, illus. 2009. (Last Apprentice Ser.: 4). (ENG.). 576p. (YA). (gr. 8-18). pap. 9.99 *(978-0-06-089129-9(7),* Greenwillow Bks.) HarperCollins Pubs.

—Clash of the Demons. Arrasmith, Patrick, illus. (Last Apprentice Ser.: 6). (YA). (gr. 8). 2009. 416p. lib. bdg. 18.89 *(978-0-06-134463-3(X))* 2009. (ENG.). 416p. 17.99 *(978-0-06-134462-6(1))*Bk. 6. 2010. (ENG.). 432p. pap. 9.99 *(978-0-06-134464-0(8))* HarperCollins Pubs. (Greenwillow Bks.).

—Curse of the Bane. Arrasmith, Patrick, illus. (Last Apprentice Ser.: 2). (YA). (gr. 8-9). 2007. (ENG.). 496p. pap. 9.99 *(978-0-06-076623-8(9))* 2006. (ENG.). 480p. 17.99 *(978-0-06-076621-4(2))*Bk. 2. 2006. 480p. lib. bdg. 19.89 *(978-0-06-076622-1(0))* HarperCollins Pubs. (Greenwillow Bks.).

—Fury of the Seventh Son, Bk. 13. Arrasmith, Patrick, illus. 2014. (Last Apprentice Ser.: 13). (ENG.). 480p. (YA). (gr. 8). 17.99 *(978-0-06-219231-8(0),* Greenwillow Bks.) HarperCollins Pubs.

—Grimalkin the Witch Assassin Bk. 9, Bk. 9. Arrasmith, Patrick, illus. 2012. (Last Apprentice Ser.: 9). (ENG.). 400p. (YA). (gr. 8). 17.99 *(978-0-06-208207-7(8),* Greenwillow Bks.) HarperCollins Pubs.

—The Last Apprentice Bk. 8: Rage of the Fallen. Arrasmith, Patrick, illus. 2012. (Last Apprentice Ser.: 8). (ENG.). 416p. (YA). (gr. 8). pap. 9.99 *(978-0-06-202758-0(1),* Greenwillow Bks.) HarperCollins Pubs.

—The Last Apprentice - Revenge of the Witch, Bk. 1. Arrasmith, Patrick, illus. 2006. (Last Apprentice Ser.: 1). (ENG.). 384p. (YA). (gr. 8). reprint ed. pap. 9.99 *(978-0-06-076620-7(4),* Greenwillow Bks.) HarperCollins Pubs.

—A New Darkness. 2014. (ENG.). 352p. (YA). (gr. 8). 17.99 *(978-0-06-233453-4(0),* Greenwillow Bks.) HarperCollins Pubs.

—Night of the Soul Stealer, Bk. 3. 2008. (Last Apprentice Ser.: 3). (ENG.). 528p. (YA). (gr. 8-18). pap. 9.99 *(978-0-06-076626-9(3),* Greenwillow Bks.) HarperCollins Pubs.

—Night of the Soul Stealer Bk. 3. Arrasmith, Patrick, illus. 2007. (Last Apprentice Ser.: 3). (ENG.). 512p. (YA). (gr. 8-9). 17.99 *(978-0-06-076624-5(7),* Greenwillow Bks.) HarperCollins Pubs.

—Rage of the Fallen, Bk. 8. Arrasmith, Patrick, illus. 2011. (Last Apprentice Ser.: 8). (ENG.). 416p. (YA). (gr. 8-18). 17.99 *(978-0-06-202756-6(5),* Greenwillow Bks.) HarperCollins Pubs.

—Revenge of the Witch, Bk. 1. Arrasmith, Patrick, illus. 2005. (Last Apprentice Ser.: 1). (ENG.). 368p. (YA). (gr. 8). 17.99 *(978-0-06-076618-4(2),* Greenwillow Bks.) HarperCollins Pubs.

—Rise of the Huntress, Bk. 7. Arrasmith, Patrick, illus. 2010. (Last Apprentice Ser.: 7). (ENG.). 448p. (YA). (gr. 8-18). 17.99 *(978-0-06-171510-5(7),* Greenwillow Bks.) HarperCollins Pubs.

—Rise of the Huntress Bk. 7, Bk. 7. Arrasmith, Patrick, illus. 2011. (Last Apprentice Ser.: 7). (ENG.). 464p. (YA). (gr. 8). pap. 9.99 *(978-0-06-171512-9(3),* Greenwillow Bks.) HarperCollins Pubs.

—Slither, Bk. 11. 2014. (Last Apprentice Ser.). (ENG.). 432p. (YA). (gr. 8). pap. 9.99 *(978-0-06-219235-6(3),* Greenwillow Bks.) HarperCollins Pubs.

—The Spook's Bestiary: The Guide to Creatures of the Dark. Heller, Julek, illus. 2011. (Last Apprentice Short Fiction Ser.: 3). (ENG.). 240p. (YA). (gr. 8). 16.99 *(978-0-06-208114-8(4),* Greenwillow Bks.) HarperCollins Pubs.

—Wrath of the Bloodeye. (Last Apprentice Ser.: 5). (ENG.). (YA). (gr. 8-18). 2009. 544p. pap. 9.99 *(978-0-06-134461-9(3))*Bk. 5. 2008. 528p. 17.99 *(978-0-06-134459-6(1))* HarperCollins Pubs. (Greenwillow Bks.).

Dixon, Heather. Illusionarium. 2015. (ENG.). 368p. (YA). (gr. 8). 17.99 *(978-0-06-200105-4(1),* Greenwillow Bks.) HarperCollins Pubs.

Duble, Kathleen Benner. Madame Tussaud's Apprentice: An Untold Story of Love in the French Revolution. 2014. (ENG.). 224p. (YA). 17.99 *(978-1-4405-8116-8(9),* Simon Pulse) Simon Pulse.

Flanagan, John. Erak's Ransom, Bk. 7. (Ranger's Apprentice Ser.: 7). (ENG.). (J). (gr. 5-18). 2011. 416p. 8.99 *(978-0-14-241525-2(1),* Puffin Books) 2010. 384p. 18.99 *(978-0-399-25205-1(3),* Philomel Bks.) Penguin Young Readers Group.

—The Lost Stories. (Ranger's Apprentice Ser.: 11). (ENG.). (J). (gr. 5). 2013. 464p. pap. 8.99 *(978-0-14-242195-6(2),* Puffin Books) 2011. (Illus.). 432p. 18.99 *(978-0-399-25618-9(0),* Philomel Bks.) Penguin Young Readers Group.

—The Lost Stories. 2013. (Ranger's Apprentice Ser.: 11). lib. bdg. 19.65 *(978-0-606-31700-9(7),* Turtleback) Turtleback Bks.

—The Royal Ranger. 2013. (Ranger's Apprentice Ser.: 12). (ENG.). 464p. (J). (gr. 5). 18.99 *(978-0-399-16360-9(3),* Philomel Bks.) Penguin Publishing Group.

—The Royal Ranger. 2014. (Ranger's Apprentice Ser.: 12). (ENG.). 480p. (J). (gr. 5). pap. 8.99 *(978-0-14-242731-6(4),* Puffin Books) Penguin Young Readers Group.

—The Royal Ranger. 2014. (Ranger's Apprentice Ser.: 12). lib. bdg. 19.65 *(978-0-606-36604-5(0))* Turtleback Bks.

Flanagan, John A. The Tournament at Gorlan. 2016. (Ranger's Apprentice the Early Years Ser.: 1). lib. bdg. 19.65 *(978-0-606-39332-4(3))* Turtleback Bks.

Forde, Patricia. The List. 2017. (ENG.). 368p. (J). (gr. 5-8). 16.99 *(978-1-4926-4796-6(9),* 9781492647966, Sourcebooks Jabberwocky) Sourcebooks, Inc.

Forward, Toby. Doubleborn: A Dragonborn Novel. 2016. (Dragonborn Ser.: 3). (ENG.). 352p. (J). pap. 8.99 *(978-1-61963-921-8(1),* 9781619639218, Bloomsbury USA Childrens) Bloomsbury Publishing USA.

—Dragonborn. (Dragonborn Ser.: 1). (ENG.). (YA). (gr. 3-6). 2013. 368p. pap. 8.99 *(978-1-59990-983-7(9),* 9781599909837) 2012. 352p. 16.99 *(978-1-59990-724-6(0),* 9781599907246) Bloomsbury Publishing USA. (Bloomsbury USA Childrens).

—Fireborn. 2015. (Dragonborn Ser.: 2). (ENG.). 448p. (YA). (gr. 5-8). pap. 8.99 *(978-1-61963-439-8(2),* 9781619634398, Bloomsbury USA Childrens) Bloomsbury Publishing USA.

—Starborn: A Dragonborn Novel. (Dragonborn Ser.). (ENG.). 448p. (J). 2017. pap. 9.99 *(978-1-68119-277-2(2),* 9781681192772) 2016. 16.99 *(978-1-61963-842-6(8),* 9781619638426) Bloomsbury Publishing USA. (Bloomsbury USA Childrens).

Funaro, Gregory. Alistair Grim's Odd Aquaticum. 2016. (Alistair Grim Ser.). (ENG.). 448p. (J). (gr. 3-7). pap. 7.99 *(978-1-4847-0900-9(4))* Hyperion Bks. for Children.

—Alistair Grim's Odd Aquaticum. 2016. (Alistair Grim Ser.). (ENG., Illus.). 448p. (J). (gr. 3-7). 16.99 *(978-1-4847-0007-5(4))* Hyperion Pr.

—Alistair Grim's Odditorium. 2015. (Alistair Grim Ser.). (ENG.). (J). (gr. 3-7). 448p. pap. 7.99 *(978-1-4847-0899-6(7));* (Illus.). 432p. 16.99 *(978-1-4847-0006-8(6))* Hyperion Bks. for Children.

—Alistair Grim's Odditorium. 2015. (J). lib. bdg. 18.40 *(978-0-606-37399-9(3))* Turtleback Bks.

Gayton, Sam. Lilliput, 1 vol. Ratterree, Alice, illus. 256p. (J). (gr. 3-6). 2017. (ENG.). pap. 8.95 ***(978-1-68263-006-8(4))*** 2016. (SPA & ENG.). 16.95 *(978-1-56145-806-6(6))* Peachtree Pubs.

Goodman, Alison. Eon: Dragoneye Reborn. 2010. (ENG.). 576p. (YA). (gr. 7-18). 10.99 *(978-0-14-241711-9(4),* Firebird) Penguin Young Readers Group.

—Eon: Dragoneye Reborn. 2010. (Eon Ser.: 1). lib. bdg. 22.10 *(978-0-606-23647-8(3),* Turtleback) Turtleback Bks.

Grant, Michael. Messenger of Fear. 2014. (Messenger of Fear Ser.: 1). (ENG.). 272p. (YA). (gr. 9). 17.99 *(978-0-06-220740-1(7),* Tegen, Katherine Bks) HarperCollins Pubs.

—The Tattooed Heart. (Messenger of Fear Ser.: 2). (YA). (gr. 9). 2016. 416p. pap. 9.99 *(978-0-06-220744-9(X),* Tegen,

Katherine Bks) 2015. (ENG.). 400p. 17.99 (978-0-06-220743-2(1)) HarperCollins Pubs.

Higgins, F. E. The Black Book of Secrets. 2010. (ENG.). 304p. (J). (gr. 4-7). pap. 9.99 (978-0-312-62905-2(2), 9780312629052) Square Fish.

Jinks, Catherine. How to Catch a Bogle. Watts, Sarah, illus. 2014. (How to Catch a Bogle Ser.: 1). (ENG.). 336p. (J). (gr. 5-7). pap. 7.99 (978-0-544-33627-8(5), HMH Books For Young Readers) Houghton Mifflin Harcourt Publishing Co.

—The Last Bogler. (How to Catch a Bogle Ser.: 3). (ENG.). 336p. (J). (gr. 5-7). 2017. pap. 7.99 (978-0-544-81309-0(X)) 2016. (Illus.). 16.99 (978-0-544-08696-8(1)) Houghton Mifflin Harcourt Publishing Co. (HMH Books For Young Readers).

—A Plague of Bogles. 2015. (How to Catch a Bogle Ser.: 2). (ENG.). 336p. (J). (gr. 5-7). pap. 6.99 (978-0-544-54067-5(0)); (Illus.). 16.99 (978-0-544-08747-7(X)) Houghton Mifflin Harcourt Publishing Co. (HMH Books For Young Readers).

Karchut, Darby. Griffin Rising. 2011. 176p. (YA). pap. 15.95 (978-1-60619-210-8(8)) Twilight Times Bks.

Koller, Jackie French. The Wizard's Apprentice. Guay, Rebecca, illus. 2003. (ENG.). 192p. (J). (gr. 3-7). pap. 9.99 (978-0-689-85592-4(3), Aladdin) Simon & Schuster Children's Publishing.

Levine, Gail Carson. The Lost Kingdom of Bamarre. 2017. 400p. (J). (gr. 3-7). 16.99 (978-0-06-207466-9(0)) HarperCollins Pubs.

—A Tale of Two Castles. Call, Greg, illus. (ENG.). (J). (gr. 3-7). 2012. 352p. pap. 6.99 (978-0-06-122967-1(9)) 2011. 336p. 16.99 (978-0-06-122965-7(2)) HarperCollins Pubs.

Magaziner, Lauren. The Only Thing Worse Than Witches. 2014. (ENG.). 272p. (J). (gr. 3-7). 16.99 (978-0-8037-3918-5(4), Dial Bks) Penguin Young Readers Group.

Matharu, Taran. The Novice. 2015. (Summoner Trilogy: Bk. 1). (ENG.). 384p. (YA). (gr. 7). 18.99 (978-1-250-06712-8(X), 9781250067128) Feiwel & Friends.

—The Novice. Barcellona, Christine, ed. 2016. (Summoner Trilogy Ser.: Bk. 1). (ENG.). 384p. (YA). pap. 10.99 (978-1-250-08005-9(3), 9781250080059) Square Fish.

—The Novice. 2016. (Summoner Trilogy: Bk. 1). (ENG.). (YA). (gr. 7-12). lib. bdg. 22.10 **(978-0-606-39884-8(8))** Turtleback Bks.

McCombie, Karen. Candy Girl. 2012. (Stoke Books Titles Ser.). 64p. (J). (gr. 5-8). pap. 45.32 (978-0-7613-9215-6(7)) Stoke Bks.

Methods, Bryan. The Shanghai Incident. 2017. (Master Diplexito & Mr. Scant Ser.). (ENG.). 264p. (J). (gr. 5-8). 17.99 **(978-1-5124-0580-4(9)**, Carolrhoda Bks.) Lerner Publishing Group.

Methods, Bryan. The Thief's Apprentice. 2016. (Master Diplexito & Mr. Scant Ser.: 1). (ENG.). 272p. (gr. 5-8). (J). 17.99 (978-1-5124-0579-8(5)); 35.99 (978-1-5124-0891-1(3)) Lerner Publishing Group. (Carolrhoda Bks.).

Meyer, Kai. Dark Reflections: The Water Mirror - The Stone Light; the Glass Word. Crawford, Elizabeth D., tr. from GER. 2010. (Dark Reflections Trilogy Ser.). (ENG.). 896p. (YA). (gr. 7). pap. 9.99 (978-1-4424-0938-5(X), McElderry, Margaret K. Bks.) McElderry, Margaret K. Bks.

Moriarty, Chris. The Inquisitor's Apprentice. Geyer, Mark Edward, illus. (ENG.). 352p. (J). (gr. 5-7). 2013. pap. 7.99 (978-0-547-85084-9(0)) 2011. 16.99 (978-0-547-58135-4(1)) Houghton Mifflin Harcourt Publishing Co.

—The Watcher in the Shadows. Geyer, Mark Edward, illus. (ENG.). 336p. (J). (gr. 5-7). 2014. pap. 7.99 (978-0-544-22776-7(X), HMH Books For Young Readers) 2013. 16.99 (978-0-547-46632-3(3)) Houghton Mifflin Harcourt Publishing Co.

Morrisette, Sharon. Toads & Tessellations. O'Neill, Philomena, illus. 2012. (ENG.). 32p. (J). (gr. 2-5). 16.95 (978-1-58089-354-1(6)); pap. 7.95 (978-1-58089-355-8(4)) Charlesbridge Publishing, Inc.

Nathan, Sarah & Disney Book Group Staff. Sofia the First Sofia's Magic Lesson. 2014. (ENG.). 32p. (J). (gr. -1-k). pap. 3.99 (978-1-4231-9854-3(9)) Disney Pr.

Oliver, Jana. The Demon Trapper's Daughter. 2011. (Demon Trappers Ser.: 1). (ENG.). 368p. (YA). (gr. 7-18). pap. 9.99 (978-0-312-61478-2(0), 9780312614782, St. Martin's Griffin) St. Martin's Pr.

Prineas, Sarah. Found. Caparo, Antonio Javier, illus. 2011. (Magic Thief Ser.: 3). (ENG.). 384p. (J). (gr. 5). pap. 7.99 (978-0-06-137595-8(0)) HarperCollins Pubs.

—Lost. Caparo, Antonio Javier, illus. 2009. (Magic Thief Ser.: 2). (ENG.). 400p. (J). (gr. 5-18). 17.99 (978-0-06-137589-7(6)) HarperCollins Pubs.

—Lost. 2009. (Magic Thief Ser.: 2). (J). 88.75 (978-1-4407-3133-4(0)); 130.75 (978-1-4407-3129-7(2)); (SPA.). 265.75 (978-1-4407-3124-2(1)); 112.75 (978-1-4407-3123-5(3)); 1.25 (978-1-4407-3131-0(4)); 110.75 (978-1-4407-3125-9(X)); 132.75 (978-1-4407-3127-3(6)) Recorded Bks., Inc.

—The Magic Thief. Caparo, Antonio Javier, illus. (Magic Thief Ser.: 1). (ENG.). (J). (gr. 5). 2009. 448p. pap. 7.99 (978-0-06-137590-3(X)) 2008. 432p. 16.99 (978-0-06-137587-3(X)) HarperCollins Pubs.

—The Magic Thief - Found. Caparo, Antonio Javier, illus. 2010. (Magic Thief Ser.: 3). (ENG.). 368p. (J). (gr. 5-18). 16.99 (978-0-06-137593-4(4)) HarperCollins Pubs.

—The Magic Thief - Lost. Caparo, Antonio Javier, illus. 2010. (Magic Thief Ser.: 2). (ENG.). 416p. (J). (gr. 5). pap. 7.99 (978-0-06-137592-7(6)) HarperCollins Pubs.

—The Magic Thief: Home. Caparo, Antonio Javier, illus. 2014. (Magic Thief Ser.: 4). (ENG.). 416p. (J). (gr. 3-7). 17.99 (978-0-06-220954-2(X)) HarperCollins Pubs.

Reeve, Philip. No Such Thing As Dragons. 2010. (ENG.). 192p. (J). (gr. 3-7). 16.99 (978-0-545-22224-2(9), Scholastic Pr.) Scholastic, Inc.

Regan, Dian. Cam's Quest: The Continuing Story of Princess Nevermore & the Wizard's Apprentice. 2007. (Junior Library Guild Selection Ser.). 334p. (J). (gr. 4-8). 17.95 (978-1-58196-056-3(5), Darby Creek) Lerner Publishing Group.

Sage, Angie. Darke. Zug, Mark, illus. (Septimus Heap Ser.: 6). 656p. (J). (gr. 4). 2012. (ENG.). pap. 7.99 (978-0-06-124244-1(6)) 2011. lib. bdg. 18.89 (978-0-06-124243-4(8))Bk. 6. 2011. (ENG.). 17.99 (978-0-06-124242-7(X)) HarperCollins Pubs. (Tegen, Katherine Bks).

—Darke. (Septimus Heap Ser.: 6). (J). 1.25 (978-1-4498-6226-8(8)); 131.75 (978-1-4498-6218-3(7)); 297.75 (978-1-4498-6217-6(9)); 2013. 92.75 (978-1-4498-6225-1(X)); 2011. 131.75 (978-1-4498-6222-0(5)); 2011. 133.75 (978-1-4498-6220-6(9)) Recorded Bks., Inc.

—Darke. Zug, Mark, illus. 2012. (Septimus Heap Ser.: 6). (J). lib. bdg. 18.40 (978-0-606-26264-4(4), Turtleback) Turtleback Bks.

—Physik. Zug, Mark, illus. (Septimus Heap Ser.: 3). (ENG.). (J). (gr. 4-7). 2007. 560p. 17.99 (978-0-06-057737-7(1))Bk. 3. 2008. 576p. pap. 7.99 (978-0-06-057739-1(8)) HarperCollins Pubs. (Tegen, Katherine Bks).

—Physik, 11 vols. 2007. (Septimus Heap Ser.: 3). (J). 133.75 (978-1-4281-4580-1(X)); 113.75 (978-1-4281-4576-4(1)); (SPA.). 131.75 (978-1-4281-4582-5(6)); 1.25 (978-1-4281-4573-3(7)); 277.75 (978-1-4281-4577-1(X)); 111.75 (978-1-4281-4578-8(8)) Recorded Bks., Inc.

—Physik. 2008. (Septimus Heap Ser.: 3). (J). lib. bdg. 18.40 (978-1-4178-1565-4(5), Turtleback) Turtleback Bks.

—Queste. Zug, Mark, illus. 2009. (Septimus Heap Ser.: 4). (ENG.). 624p. (J). (gr. 4). pap. 7.99 (978-0-06-088209-9(3), Tegen, Katherine Bks) HarperCollins Pubs.

—Queste. Zug, Mark, illus. 2009. (Septimus Heap Ser.: 4). 596p. (J). lib. bdg. 18.40 (978-0-606-02607-9(X), Turtleback) Turtleback Bks.

—Sandrider. 2015. (World of Septimus Heap Ser.: 2). (ENG., Illus.). 480p. (J). (gr. 3-7). 17.99 (978-0-06-227248-5(9), Tegen, Katherine Bks) HarperCollins Pubs.

—Syren. Zug, Mark, illus. (Septimus Heap Ser.: 5). (J). (gr. 4). 2011. (ENG.). 656p. pap. 7.99 (978-0-06-088212-9(3)) 2009. 640p. lib. bdg. 18.89 (978-0-06-088211-2(5)) 2009. (ENG.). 640p. 17.99 (978-0-06-088210-5(7)) HarperCollins Pubs. (Tegen, Katherine Bks).

Sands, Kevin. The Blackthorn Key. (Blackthorn Key Ser.: 1). (ENG., Illus.). (J). (gr. 5-9). 2016. 400p. pap. 7.99 (978-1-4814-4652-5(5)) 2015. 384p. 18.99 (978-1-4814-4651-8(7)) Simon & Schuster Children's Publishing. (Aladdin).

—The Blackthorn Key. 2016. lib. bdg. 18.40 (978-0-606-38966-2(0)) Turtleback Bks.

Sands, Kevin. Mark of the Plague. (Blackthorn Key Ser.: 2). (ENG.). (J). (gr. 5-9). 2017. 560p. pap. 7.99 **(978-1-4814-4675-4(4))** 2016. (Illus.). 544p. 17.99 (978-1-4814-4674-7(6)) Simon & Schuster Children's Publishing. (Aladdin).

Selfors, Suzanne. The Fairy Swarm. Santat, Dan, illus. 2016. (Imaginary Veterinary Ser.: 6). (ENG.). 240p. (J). (gr. 2-7). pap. 7.99 (978-0-316-28692-3(3)) Little, Brown Bks. for Young Readers.

—The Lonely Lake Monster. Santat, Dan, illus. 2014. (Imaginary Veterinary Ser.: 2). (ENG.). 240p. (J). (gr. 2-7). pap. 7.99 (978-0-316-22561-8(4)) Little, Brown Bks. for Young Readers.

—The Order of the Unicorn. Santat, Dan, illus. 2014. 197p. (J). (978-0-316-32339-0(X)) Little Brown & Co.

—The Order of the Unicorn: The Imaginary Veterinary. Santat, Dan, illus. 2014. (Imaginary Veterinary Ser.: 4). (ENG.). 208p. (J). (gr. 2-7). 16.00 (978-0-316-36406-5(1)) Little, Brown Bks. for Young Readers.

Shaw, Stephanie. Schnitzel: A Cautionary Tale for Lazy Louts. Barry, Kevin, illus. 2016. (ENG.). 32p. (J). (gr. k-3). 16.99 (978-1-58536-957-7(8), 204104) Sleeping Bear Pr.

Skelton, Matthew. Endymion Spring. 2008. (ENG.). 416p. (YA). (gr. 7). pap. 9.99 (978-0-385-73456-1(5), Delacorte Bks. for Young Readers) Random Hse. Children's Bks.

Smith, Sherri L. The Toymaker's Apprentice. 2015. (ENG., Illus.). 400p. (J). (gr. 5). 16.99 (978-0-399-25295-2(9), G.P. Putnam's Sons Books for Young Readers) Penguin Young Readers Group.

Snicket, Lemony, pseud. File Under - 13 Suspicious Incidents. Seth, illus. 2014. (ENG.). 272p. (J). (gr. 3-17). 12.00 (978-0-316-28403-5(3)) Little, Brown Bks. for Young Readers.

—Shouldn't You Be in School? Seth, illus. (All the Wrong Questions Ser.: 3). (ENG.). (J). (gr. 3-17). 2015. 352p. pap. 7.99 (978-0-316-38060-7(1)) 2014. 336p. 16.00 (978-0-316-12306-8(4)) 2014. 352p. 18.00 (978-0-316-40968-1(5)) Little, Brown Bks. for Young Readers.

—Who Could That Be at This Hour? Seth, illus. (All the Wrong Questions Ser.: 1). (ENG.). (J). (gr. 3-17). 2014. 288p. pap. 7.99 (978-0-316-33547-8(9)) 2012. 272p. 15.99 (978-0-316-12308-2(0)) Little, Brown Bks. for Young Readers.

—Why Is This Night Different from All Other Nights? Seth, illus. 2015. (ENG.). 304p. (J). (gr. 3-17). 16.00 (978-0-316-12304-4(8)) Little, Brown Bks. for Young Readers.

Snicket, Lemony, pseud & Seth. Who Could That Be at This Hour? 2012. (978-0-316-24771-9(5)) Little Brown & Co.

Stroud, Jonathan. The Amulet of Samarkand, Bk. 1. 2003. (Bartimaeus Novel Ser.). (ENG., Illus.). 464p. (J). (gr. 5-9). 17.99 (978-0-7868-1859-4(X)) Disney Publishing Worldwide.

—Bartimaeus, 3 vols., Set. 2010. (ENG.). 1552p. (J). (gr. 5-6). pap. 24.99 (978-1-4231-3682-8(9)) Disney Pr.

—The Golem's Eye, Bk. 2. 2nd rev. ed. 2006. (Bartimaeus Novel Ser.). (ENG.). 592p. (J). (gr. 5-9). reprint ed. per. 8.99 (978-0-7868-3654-3(7)) Disney Publishing Worldwide.

Thompson, Paul B. The Brightworking, Bk. 1. 2012. (Brightstone Saga Ser.). (Illus.). 160p. (J). (gr. 5-18). 18.95 (978-0-7660-3950-6(1)) Enslow Pubs., Inc.

—The Brightworking: Book I of the Brightstone Saga. 2013. (Brightstone Saga Ser.). 160p. (J). (gr. 5-12). pap. 10.95 (978-1-4644-0169-5(1)) Enslow Pubs., Inc.

Toby Forward Staff. Doubleborn. 2015. (Dragonborn Ser.: 3). (ENG.). 336p. (YA). (gr. 5-8). 16.99 (978-1-61963-528-9(3), 9781619635289, Bloomsbury USA Childrens) Bloomsbury Publishing USA.

—Fireborn. 2013. (Dragonborn Ser.: 2). (ENG.). 432p. (YA). (gr. 5-6). 16.99 (978-1-59990-889-2(1), 9781599908892, Bloomsbury USA Childrens) Bloomsbury Publishing USA.

Ursu, Anne. The Real Boy. McGuire, Erin, illus. 2015. (ENG.). 352p. (J). (gr. 3-7). pap. 6.99 (978-0-06-201508-2(7), Waldon Pond Pr.) HarperCollins Pubs.

Walsh, Ann. The Doctor's Apprentice: A Barkerville Mystery. 2007. (Barkerville Mystery Ser.: 2). (ENG.). 160p. (J). pap. 9.99 (978-1-55002-633-7(X), Sandcastle Bks.) Dundurn CAN. Dist: Ingram Publisher Services.

Westwood, Chris. Graveyard Shift. (Hauntings Ser.: bk.1). (ENG.). 304p. (J). (gr. 3-7). 2014. pap. 6.99 (978-0-545-39920-3(3)) 2012. 17.99 (978-0-545-39919-7(X)) Scholastic, Inc. (Scholastic Pr.).

Wexler, Django. The Mad Apprentice. Jansson, Alexander, illus. 2015. (Forbidden Library). (ENG.). 352p. (J). (gr. 5). 16.99 (978-0-8037-3976-5(1), Kathy Dawson Books) Penguin Young Readers Group.

Wilson, N. D. The Dragon's Tooth. (Ashtown Burials Ser.: Bk. 1). (ENG.). 496p. (J). (gr. 3-7). 2012. 8.99 (978-0-375-86396-7(6), Yearling) 2011. 16.99 (978-0-375-86439-1(3), Random Hse. Bks. for Young Readers) Random Hse. Children's Bks.

—The Drowned Vault. 2013. (Ashtown Burials Ser.: Bk. 2). (ENG.). 464p. (J). (gr. 3-7). 8.99 (978-0-375-86397-4(4), Yearling) Random Hse. Children's Bks.

Yancey, Rick. The Curse of the Wendigo. 2011. (Monstrumologist Ser.: 2). (ENG.). 464p. (YA). (gr. 9). pap. 12.99 (978-1-4169-8451-1(8), Simon & Schuster Bks. For Young Readers) Simon & Schuster Bks. For Young Readers.

—The Final Descent. 2013. (Monstrumologist Ser.: 4). (ENG., Illus.). 320p. (YA). (gr. 9). 18.99 (978-1-4424-5153-7(X), Simon & Schuster Bks. For Young Readers) Simon & Schuster Bks. For Young Readers.

—The Isle of Blood. 2011. (Monstrumologist Ser.: 3). (ENG., Illus.). 560p. (YA). (gr. 9). 18.99 (978-1-4169-8452-8(6), Simon & Schuster Bks. For Young Readers) Simon & Schuster Bks. For Young Readers.

—The Monstrumologist. (Monstrumologist Ser.: 1). (ENG.). (YA). (gr. 9). 2010. 464p. pap. 11.99 (978-1-4169-8449-8(6)) 2009. 448p. 21.99 (978-1-4169-8448-1(8)) Simon & Schuster Bks. For Young Readers. (Simon & Schuster Bks. For Young Readers).

Yolen, Jane & Stemple, Adam. The Last Changeling. 2014. (Seelie Wars Ser.). (ENG.). 304p. (J). (gr. 3-7). 16.99 (978-0-670-01435-4(4), Viking Books for Young Readers) Penguin Young Readers Group.

APRIL FOOLS' DAY

Jones, Theodore. April Fools' Day: What a Joke! 2016. (History of Our Holidays Ser.). (ENG., Illus.). 24p. (J). (gr. 1-2). pap. 8.15 (978-1-4824-3882-6(8)) Stevens, Gareth Publishing LLLP.

Kroll, Steven & Bassett, Jeni. Poisson d'Avril. (FRE.). (J). pap. 6.99 (978-0-590-73953-5(0)) Scholastic, Inc.

LaRoche, Amelia. April Fool's Day Jokes to Tickle Your Funny Bone. 2013. (Funnier Bone Jokes Ser.). 48p. (J). (gr. 3-4). lib. bdg. 22.60 (978-0-7660-4122-6(0)) Enslow Pubs., Inc.

Schiller, Melissa. April Fool's Day. 2003. (Rookie Read-About Holidays Ser.). (ENG., Illus.). 32p. (J). (gr. 1-2). pap. 5.95 (978-0-516-27942-8(4), Children's Pr.) Scholastic Library Publishing.

Williams, Colleen Madonna Flood. My Adventure on April Fool's Day. 2009. (ENG.). 44p. (J). 8.99 (978-1-59092-544-7(0)) Blue Forge Pr.

APRIL FOOLS' DAY—FICTION

Baratz-Logsted, Lauren. Jackie's Jokes. 2009. (Sisters Eight Ser.: 4). (ENG., Illus.). 128p. (J). (gr. 1-4). pap. 5.99 (978-0-547-05328-8(2)) Houghton Mifflin Harcourt Publishing Co.

Bateman, Teresa. April Foolishness. Westcott, Nadine Bernard, illus. 2004. (ENG.). 32p. (J). (gr. k-3). 6.99 (978-0-8075-0405-5(X)) Whitman, Albert & Co.

deGroat, Diane. April Fool! Watch Out at School! deGroat, Diane, illus. 2009. (Gilbert Ser.). (Illus.). 32p. (J). (gr. -1-3). (ENG.). 17.99 (978-0-06-143042-8(0)); lib. bdg. 18.89 (978-0-06-143043-5(9)) HarperCollins Pubs.

Jones, Christianne C. Morning Mystery, 1 vol. Simard, Remy, illus. 2010. (My First Graphic Novel Ser.). (ENG.). 32p. (gr. k-2). lib. bdg. 24.65 (978-1-4342-1890-2(2), My First Graphic Novel) Stone Arch Bks.

Katschke, Judy, et al. April Fools' Rules. 2004. (ENG., Illus.). 112p. (978-0-00-714460-0(1), HarperCollins Children's Bks.) HarperCollins Pubs. Ltd.

Kvasnosky, Laura McGee. Keeping Secrets. Kvasnosky, Laura McGee, illus. 2009. (Zelda & Ivy Ser.). (ENG., Illus.). 48p. (J). (gr. k-4). 15.99 (978-0-7636-4179-5(0)) Candlewick Pr.

—Zelda & Ivy - Keeping Secrets. Kvasnosky, Laura McGee, illus. 2013. (Candlewick Sparks Ser.). (ENG., Illus.). 48p. (J). (gr. k-4). pap. 3.99 (978-0-7636-6636-1(X)) Candlewick Pr.

McMullan, Kate. One Funny Day. Alley, R. W., illus. 2012. (Pearl & Wagner Ser.: 1). (ENG.). 48p. (J). (gr. 1-3). pap. 3.99 (978-0-448-45866-3(7), Penguin Young Readers) Penguin Young Readers Group.

Meadows, Daisy. Rainbow Magic Special Edition: Addison the April Fool's Day Fairy. 2014. (Rainbow Magic Special Edition Ser.). (ENG.). 176p. (J). (gr. 2-5). pap. 6.99 (978-0-545-60538-0(5), Scholastic Paperbacks) Scholastic, Inc.

Pascal, Francine. Bromas de Primavera. Orig. Title: April Fool. (SPA.). 120p. (J). 6.95 (978-84-272-3798-8(7)) Molino, Editorial ESP. Dist: AIMS International Bks., Inc.

Sateren, Shelley Swanson. Max & Zoe: Too Many Tricks, 1 vol. Sullivan, Mary, illus. 2013. (Max & Zoe Ser.). (ENG.). 32p. (gr. k-2). pap. 5.19 (978-1-4795-2327-6(5), Max & Zoe) Picture Window Bks.

—Too Many Tricks. Sullivan, Mary, illus. 2013. (Max & Zoe Ser.). (ENG.). 32p. (gr. k-2). lib. bdg. 21.32 (978-1-4048-7197-7(7), Max & Zoe) Picture Window Bks.

Scanlon, Rachel. Operation Reverse April Fools' 2008. 56p. pap. 16.95 (978-1-60441-649-7(1)) America Star Bks.

Thaler, Mike. April Fools' Day from the Black Lagoon. Lee, Jared, illus. 2008. (J). (978-0-545-01767-1(X)) Scholastic, Inc.

—April Fools' Day from the Black Lagoon, 1 vol. Lee, Jared, illus. 2012. (Black Lagoon Adventures Ser.: No. 2). (ENG.). 64p. (J). (gr. 2-5). 24.21 (978-1-59961-959-0(8)) Spotlight.

Welling, Peter J. Michael le Soufflé & the April Fool, 1 vol. Welling, Peter J., illus. 2003. (ENG., Illus.). 32p. (J). (gr. k-3). 16.99 (978-1-58980-105-9(9)) Pelican Publishing Co., Inc.

Wright, Maureen. Barnyard Fun, 0 vols. De Tagyos, Paul Ratz, illus. 2013. (ENG.). 24p. (J). (gr. -1-3). 16.99 (978-1-4778-1643-1(7), 9781477816431, Amazon Children's Publishing) Amazon Publishing.

AQUARIUMS

see also Fish Culture; Goldfish

Anderson, Lynne. The Aquarium Adds Up. 2011. (Early Connections Ser.). (J). (978-1-61672-599-0(0)) Benchmark Education Co.

The Aquarium, 6 vols., Pack. (Kinderstarters Ser.). 8p. (gr. -1-1). 21.00 (978-0-7635-8706-2(0)) Rigby Education.

Arnold, Tedd. Sharks. Arnold, Tedd, illus. 2013. (Fly Guy Ser.). (ENG., Illus.). 32p. (J). (gr. -1-3). pap. 3.99 (978-0-545-50771-4(5), Scholastic Reference) Scholastic, Inc.

Bakowski, Barbara. What Happens at an Aquarium? 2009. (Where People Work Ser.). 24p. (gr. -1-3). (J). lib. bdg. 22.00 (978-1-4339-0074-7(2)); (SPA & ENG.). pap. 8.15 (978-1-4339-0146-1(3)); pap. 8.15 (978-1-4339-0138-6(2)) Stevens, Gareth Publishing LLLP. (Weekly Reader Leveled Readers).

—What Happens at an Aquarium?/¿Qué Pasa en un Acuario? 2009. (Where People Work/Dónde Trabaja la Gente? Ser.). (SPA & ENG.). 24p. (J). (gr. -1-3). lib. bdg. 22.00 (978-1-4339-0082-2(3), Weekly Reader Leveled Readers) Stevens, Gareth Publishing LLLP.

Beylon, Cathy. At the Aquarium. 2003. (Dover Coloring Bks.). (ENG., Illus.). 32p. (J). (gr. -1-2). pap. 3.99 (978-0-486-42371-5(9)) Dover Pubns., Inc.

—At the Aquarium/en el Acuario: Bilingual Coloring Book. Gongora, Oscar, tr. 2011. (Dover Children's Bilingual Coloring Book Ser.). (ENG & SPA., Illus.). 32p. (J). (gr. k-6). pap. 3.99 (978-0-486-47813-5(0)) Dover Pubns., Inc.

Bodden, Valerie. Fish. 2009. (My First Look at: Pets Ser.). (J). (gr. 1-5). 24.25 (978-1-58341-722-5(2), Creative Education) Creative Co., The.

Curtis, Jennifer Keats. Animal Helpers: Aquariums, 1 vol. 2014. (Animal Helpers Ser.). (ENG., Illus.). 32p. (J). (gr. 2-5). pap. 9.95 (978-1-62855-212-6(3)) Arbordale Publishing.

—Animal Helpers Aquariums: Aquariums, 1 vol. 2014. (Animal Helpers Ser.). (ENG., Illus.). 32p. (J). (gr. 2-5). 17.95 (978-1-62855-203-4(4)) Arbordale Publishing.

—Ayudantes de Animales: Acuarios, 1 vol. 2014.Tr. of Animal Helpers: Aquariums. (SPA.). 32p. (J). (gr. 2-5). pap. 9.95 (978-1-62855-221-8(2)) Arbordale Publishing.

Danby, Nicholai. My Aquarium. 2013. (Rosen Readers Ser.). (ENG.). 24p. (J). (gr. 2-3). pap. 49.50 (978-1-4777-2252-7(1)); pap. 8.25 (978-1-4777-2251-0(3)) Rosen Publishing Group, Inc., The. (Rosen Classroom).

Giulieri, Anne. The Aquarium, 1 vol. 2012. (Engage Literacy Yellow Ser.). (ENG.). 32p. (gr. k-2). pap. 5.99 (978-1-4296-8970-0(6), Engage Literacy) Capstone Press of Coughlan Cos.

—My Rock Pool, 1 vol. Meldrum, Ned, photos by. 2012. (Engage Literacy Green Ser.). (ENG., Illus.). 32p. (gr. k-2). pap. 5.99 (978-1-4296-9013-3(5), Engage Literacy) Capstone Press of Coughlan Cos.

Glaser, Rebecca. Fish Swim. 2017. (Amicus Ink Board Bks.). (ENG., Illus.). 14p. (J). (gr. -1 — 1). bds. 7.99 **(978-1-68152-198-5(9))** Amicus.

Gorman, Jacqueline Laks. The Aquarium. 2005. (I Like to Visit Ser.). (Illus.). 24p. (gr. k-3). pap. 8.15 (978-0-8368-4458-0(0)); lib. bdg. 22.00 (978-0-8368-4451-1(3)) Stevens, Gareth Publishing LLLP. (Weekly Reader Leveled Readers).

—The Aquarium (El Acuario) Acosta, Tatiana & Gutiérrez, Guillermo, trs. 2005. (I Like to Visit/Me Gusta Visitar Ser.). (ENG & SPA., Illus.). 24p. (gr. k-3). lib. bdg. 22.00 (978-0-8368-4595-2(1), Weekly Reader Leveled Readers) Stevens, Gareth Publishing LLLP.

—The Aquarium/el Acuario. 2005. (I Like to Visit/ Me gusta visitar Ser.). (ENG & SPA., Illus.). 24p. (gr. k-3). pap. 8.15 (978-0-8368-4602-7(8), Weekly Reader Leveled Readers) Stevens, Gareth Publishing LLLP.

Hamilton, Lynn. Caring for Your Fish. 2005. (Caring for Your Pet Ser.). (Illus.). 32p. (J). (gr. 4-7). lib. bdg. 26.00 (978-1-59036-035-4(4)) Weigl Pubs., Inc.

Jeffrey, Laura S. Fish: How to Choose & Care for a Fish. 2004. (American Humane Pet Care Library). (Illus.). 48p. (J). lib. bdg. 25.27 (978-0-7660-2517-2(9)) Enslow Pubs., Inc.

Jepson, Lance. Aquarium, Vol. 12. 2016. (Understanding & Caring for Your Pet Ser.: Vol. 12). (ENG., Illus.). 128p. (J). (gr. 5-8). 25.95 (978-1-4222-3692-5(7)) Mason Crest.

Jerome, Kate Boehm. Science at the Aquarium. 2006. (Reading Expeditions Ser.). (ENG., Illus.). 24p. (J). pap. 14.95 (978-0-7922-8625-7(1)) CENGAGE Learning.

Kawa, Katie. My First Trip to the Aquarium. 2012. (My First Adventures Ser.). (Illus.). 24p. (gr. k-2). 69.20 (978-1-4339-8047-3(9)); (J). pap. 8.15 (978-1-4339-7301-7(4)); (J). lib. bdg. 22.60 (978-1-4339-7300-0(6)) Stevens, Gareth Publishing LLLP.

—My First Trip to the Aquarium: Mi Primera Visita Al Acuario. 2012. (My First Adventures / Mis primeras aventuras Ser.). (SPA & ENG., Illus.). 24p. (J). (gr. k-2). lib. bdg. 22.60 (978-1-4339-7372-7(3)) Stevens, Gareth Publishing LLLP.

Komiya, Teruyuki. Life-Size Aquarium. Miyakoshi, Junko, tr. from JPN. Matsuhashi, Toshimitsu, photos by. 2010. (ENG., Illus.). 48p. (gr. -1-2). 18.95 (978-1-934734-59-9(4)) Seven Footer Pr.

Larson, Jennifer S. Guppies. 2008. (J). lib. bdg. 25.26 (978-0-8225-7902-1(2), Lerner Pubns.) Lerner Publishing Group.

Lindeen, Mary. A Visit to the Aquarium. 2015. (BeginningtoRead Ser.). (ENG.). 32p. (J). (gr. k-2). pap. 11.94 (978-1-60357-754-0(8)); (Illus.). lib. bdg. 22.60 (978-1-59953-694-1(3)) Norwood Hse. Pr.

McReynolds, Stacy. San Antonio Zoo. 2003. (Great Zoos of the United States Ser.). (Illus.). 24p. (J). lib. bdg. 22.60 (978-0-8239-6319-5(5), PowerKids Pr.) Rosen Publishing Group, Inc., The.

Meister, Cari. El Acuario. 2016. (Los Primeros Viajes Escolares (First Field Trips)).Tr. of Aquarium. (SPA.). 24p. (J). (gr. k-2). lib. bdg. 25.65 (978-1-62031-326-8(X), Bullfrog Bks.) Jump! Inc.

—Aquarium. Fretland VanVoorst, Jenny, ed. 2016. (First Field Trips). 24p. (J). (gr. k-2). lib. bdg. 25.65 (978-1-62031-292-6(1), Bullfrog Bks.) Jump! Inc.

Mercurio, Jodi. Life in an Aquarium. 2013. (InfoMax Readers Ser.). (ENG.). 24p. (J). (gr. 2-3). pap. 8.25

(978-1-4777-2410-1(9)); pap. 49.50 (978-1-4777-2411-8(7)) Rosen Publishing Group, Inc., The. (Rosen Classroom).

Ripley's Believe It Or Not! Staff & Ripley's Believe It Or Not! Editors. Ripley's Aquarium of Canada. 2014. (ENG.). 64p. pap. 16.95 (978-1-60991-107-2(5)) Ripley Entertainment, Inc.

Salzmann, Mary Elizabeth. Flashy Fish, 1 vol. Craig, Diane, ed. 2007. (Perfect Pets Ser.). (ENG., Illus.). 24p. (J). (gr. k-3). lib. bdg. 24.21 (978-1-59928-747-8(1), SandCastle) ABDO Publishing Co.

Schuetz, Kari. Caring for Your Fish. 2010. (Pet Care Library). (ENG., Illus.). 24p. (J). (gr. 2-5). lib. bdg. 25.95 (978-1-60014-467-7(5), Blastoff! Readers) Bellwether Media.

Silverstein, Alvin, et al. Fabulous Fish. 2003. (What a Pet! Ser.). (ENG., Illus.). 48p. (gr. 3-6). lib. bdg. 23.93 (978-0-7613-2514-7(X), Millbrook Pr.) Lerner Publishing Group.

Williams, Colleen Madonna Flood. My Adventure at the Sea Life Park. 2009. (ENG.). 44p. (J). 8.99 (978-1-59092-578-2(5)) Blue Forge Pr.

Wood, Selina. Fish. 2008. (Owning a Pet Ser.). (Illus.). 32p. (YA). (gr. 2-5). lib. bdg. 28.50 (978-1-59771-057-2(1)) Sea-To-Sea Pubns.

AQUATIC ANIMALS

see also Freshwater Animals; Marine Animals

Baillie, Marilyn. Whoosh! A Watery World of Wonderful Creatures, 0 vols. Mitchell, Susan & Owlkids Books Inc. Staff, illus. 2014. (ENG.). 32p. (J). (gr. -1-2). 16.95 (978-1-926973-98-2(4), Owlkids) Owlkids Bks. Inc. CAN. Dist: Publishers Group West (PGW).

Baker, Charles F., ed. Water Animals. 2005. (ENG., Illus.). 32p. (J). (gr. 1-5). 17.95 (978-0-8126-7927-4(X)) Cobblestone Publishing Co.

Barraclough, Susan. Sharks & Other Creatures of the Deep. 2007. (Illus.). 192p. (J). (978-0-7607-9143-1(0)) Barnes & Noble, Inc.

Boothroyd, Jennifer. In the Water. (First Step Nonfiction - Animal Homes Ser.). (ENG., Illus.). 8p. (gr. -1-1). 2015. 11.99 (978-1-5124-1033-4(0)) 2006. pap. 4.95 (978-0-8225-5664-0(2), Lerner Pubns.) Lerner Publishing Group.

Britannica Learning Library Staff. Creatures of the Waters. 2003. (Illus.). 64p. 14.95 (978-1-59339-045-7(9)) Encyclopaedia Britannica, Inc.

Cheshire, Gerard. Scary Creatures of the River. Francis, John et al, illus. 2009. (Scary Creatures Ser.). (ENG.). 32p. (J). (gr. 2-4). 27.00 (978-0-531-21823-5(6), Watts, Franklin); pap. 8.95 (978-0-531-22228-7(4), Children's Pr.) Scholastic Library Publishing.

Crewe, Sabrina. In the Ocean. 2010. (Under the Microscope Ser.). 32p. (gr. 2-4). 30.00 (978-1-60413-827-6(0), Chelsea Clubhouse) Facts On File, Inc.

Curtis, Jennifer Keats. Animal Helpers: Aquariums, 1 vol. 2014. (Animal Helpers Ser.). (ENG., Illus.). 32p. (J). (gr. 2-5). pap. 9.95 (978-1-62855-212-6(3)) Arbordale Publishing.

—Animal Helpers Aquariums: Aquariums, 1 vol. 2014. (Animal Helpers Ser.). (ENG., Illus.). 32p. (J). (gr. 2-5). 17.95 (978-1-62855-203-4(4)) Arbordale Publishing.

Darling, F. Fraser. The Seasons & the Fisherman: A Book for Children. Tunnicliffe, C. F., illus. 2011. (ENG.). 84p. pap. 22.99 (978-0-521-17594-4(1)) Cambridge Univ. Pr.

Dayton, Connor. Wetland Animals. 2009. (American Habitats Ser.). 24p. (gr. 2-3). 42.50 (978-1-61511-363-7(0), PowerKids Pr.) Rosen Publishing Group, Inc., The.

Kalman, Bobbie. Baby Animals in Water Habitats. 2011. (ENG.). 24p. (J). pap. (978-0-7787-7747-2(2)); (978-0-7787-7734-2(0)) Crabtree Publishing Co.

Lewis, J. Patrick. My Home in the Water. 2017. (Rookie Poetry(tm) — Animal Homes Ser.). (ENG., Illus.). 24p. (J). lib. bdg. 25.00 (978-0-531-22874-6(6), Children's Pr.) Scholastic Library Publishing.

Lourie, Peter. The Manatee Scientists: Saving Vulnerable Species. 2011. (Scientists in the Field Ser.). (ENG., Illus.). 80p. (J). (gr. 5-7). 18.99 (978-0-547-15254-7(X)) Houghton Mifflin Harcourt Publishing Co.

Marais, Vivian. Life in a Swamp: A Wetlands Habitat. 2009. (Real Life Readers Ser.). 24p. (gr. 3-4). pap. 8.25 (978-1-4358-0141-7(5), Rosen Classroom) Rosen Publishing Group, Inc., The.

Marais, Vivien. Life in a Swamp: A Wetlands Habitat. 2009. (Look at Life Science Ser.). (J). lib. bdg. 22.60 (978-1-4358-2972-5(7), PowerKids Pr.) Rosen Publishing Group, Inc., The.

May, Suellen. Invasive Aquatic & Wetland Animals. 2006. (Invasive Species Ser.). (Illus.). 100p. (J). (gr. 6-12). 30.00 (978-0-7910-9129-6(5), Chelsea Hse.) Facts On File, Inc.

Newland, Sonya. Wetland Animals. 2011. (Saving Wildlife Ser.). 32p. (gr. 4-7). lib. bdg. 31.35 (978-1-59920-661-5(7)) Black Rabbit Bks.

Olsen, Alana. Look Out for the Blue-Ringed Octopus! 2015. (Surprisingly Scary! Ser.). (ENG., Illus.). 24p. (J). (gr. 2-3). pap. 8.25 (978-1-4994-0877-5(3), PowerKids Pr.) Rosen Publishing Group, Inc., The.

Radley, Gail. Waterways. Sherlock, Jean, illus. 2003. (Vanishing from Ser.). 32p. (J). (gr. 3-5). 6.95 (978-1-57505-569-5(4)) Lerner Publishing Group.

Rake, Matthew. Creatures of the Deep. Mendez, Simon, illus. 2015. (Real-Life Monsters Ser.). (ENG.). 32p. (J). (gr. 3-6). 26.65 (978-1-4677-6360-8(8)) Lerner Publishing Group.

Rosenberg, Pam. Yikes! Icky, Sticky, Gross Stuff Underwater. Ramos, Beatriz Helena, illus. 2007. (Icky, Sticky, Gross-Out Bks.). (ENG.). 24p. (J). (gr. 3-6). 27.07 (978-1-59296-901-2(1), 200358) Child's World, Inc., The.

Stevens, Dave. Weirdly Wonderful a to Z: Exotic, Aquatic Creatures from the West Coast of British Columbia, Canada. Stevens, Dave, illus. 2016. (ENG., Illus.). 32p. (J). (978-0-9950594-0-5(3)) Treewind Publishing.

Ugly Creatures under Water. 2013. (Earth's Grossest Animals Ser.). 32p. (J). (gr. k-5). pap. 60.00 (978-1-61533-784-2(9), PowerKids Pr.) Rosen Publishing Group, Inc., The.

Ward, Brian R. Tunas. 2009. (Illus.). 52p. (J). (978-0-7172-8076-6(4)) Grolier, Ltd.

Wood, Alix. Ugly Creatures under Water. 2013. (Earth's Grossest Animals Ser.). 32p. (J). (gr. k-5). 25.25 (978-1-61533-733-0(4)); pap. 10.00 (978-1-61533-783-5(0)) Rosen Publishing Group, Inc., The. (PowerKids Pr.).

World Book, Inc Staff, contrib. by. Rivers, Lakes, & Wetlands. 2012. (J). (978-0-7166-0442-6(6)) World Bk., Inc.

AQUATIC PLANTS

see also Freshwater Plants; Marine Plants

Lawrence, Ellen. Water Plants. 2015. (Plant-Ology Ser.). (ENG., Illus.). 24p. (J). (gr. -1-3). lib. bdg. 23.93 (978-1-62724-865-5(X)) Bearport Publishing Co., Inc.

Marais, Vivian. Life in a Swamp: A Wetlands Habitat. 2009. (Real Life Readers Ser.). 24p. (gr. 3-4). pap. 8.25 (978-1-4358-0141-7(5), Rosen Classroom) Rosen Publishing Group, Inc., The.

Marais, Vivien. Life in a Swamp: A Wetlands Habitat. 2009. (Look at Life Science Ser.). (J). lib. bdg. 22.60 (978-1-4358-2972-5(7), PowerKids Pr.) Rosen Publishing Group, Inc., The.

Nugent, Samantha. Water Plants. 2016. (Illus.). 24p. (J). (978-1-5105-1413-3(9)) SmartBook Media, Inc.

Rushworth, Gary. The Life Cycle of Water Plants: Set Of 6. 2011. (Navigators Ser.). (J). pap. 44.00 net. (978-1-4108-6225-9(9)) Benchmark Education Co.

AQUATIC SPORTS

see also Boats and Boating; Canoes and Canoeing; Diving; Fishing; Rowing; Sailing; Skin Diving; Swimming; Yachts and Yachting

Bailey, Diane. Water Sports, Vol. 10. 2016. (Great Outdoors! Ser.). (Illus.). 48p. (J). (gr. 5). 20.95 (978-1-4222-3575-1(0)) Mason Crest.

Blomquist, Christopher. Wakeboarding in the X Games. 2009. (Kid's Guide to the X Games Ser.). 24p. (gr. 3-3). 42.50 (978-1-61511-212-8(X), PowerKids Pr.) Rosen Publishing Group, Inc., The.

Butler, Erin K. Extreme Water Sports. 2017. (Sports to the Extreme Ser.). (ENG.). 32p. (gr. 3-4). lib. bdg. 27.99 **(978-1-5157-7862-2(2)**, Edge Bks.) Capstone Press of Coughlan Cos.

Child's World Staff & Kelley, K. C. Weird Water Sports. 2011. (Weird Sports Ser.). (ENG., Illus.). 24p. (J). (gr. 2-5). lib. bdg. 28.50 (978-1-60954-380-8(7), 201058) Child's World, Inc., The.

David, Jack. Kiteboarding. 2008. (Action Sports Ser.). (ENG., Illus.). 24p. (J). (gr. 3-7). lib. bdg. 25.95 (978-1-60014-197-3(8)) Bellwether Media.

Eck, Kristin. Wakeboarding: Check It Out. 2009. (Extreme Sports Ser.). 24p. (gr. 1-1). 42.50 (978-1-61512-460-2(8), PowerKids Pr.) Rosen Publishing Group, Inc., The.

Endres, Hollie. Wakeboarding. 2007. (Action Sports Ser.). (ENG., Illus.). 24p. (J). (gr. 3-7). lib. bdg. 25.95 (978-1-60014-129-4(3)) Bellwether Media.

Gigliotti, Jim. Water Sports, 1 vol. 2011. (Extreme Sports Ser.). (ENG., Illus.). 32p. (gr. 1-2). 29.99 (978-1-4109-4219-7(8), Read Me!) Heinemann-Raintree.

Hamilton, S. L. Aqua Sports. 2015. (Illus.). 32p. (J). 27.07 (978-1-62403-749-8(6), 1391351) ABDO Publishing Co.

—Wakeboarding. 2015. (Illus.). 32p. (J). 27.07 (978-1-62403-753-5(4), 1391384) ABDO Publishing Co.

Lanser, Amanda. The Science Behind Swimming, Diving, & Other Water Sports. 2016. (Illus.). 32p. (J). (978-1-4914-8169-1(2)) Capstone Press of Coughlan Cos.

Luke, Andrew. Water Sports. 2017. (Illus.). 48p. (J). **(978-1-4222-3704-5(4))** Mason Crest.

McFee, Shane. Whitewater Rafting. 2009. (Living on the Edge Ser.). 24p. (gr. 2-3). 42.50 (978-1-61514-303-0(3), PowerKids Pr.) Rosen Publishing Group, Inc., The.

Orr, Tamara B. Extreme Wakeboarding. 2013. (Sports on the Edge 2 Ser.). (Illus.). 48p. (J). (gr. 4-8). pap. 12.93 (978-1-62712-134-7(X)) Cavendish Square Publishing.

Orr, Tamra B. Extreme Wakeboarding. 2013. (Illus.). 48p. (J). (gr. 4-8). 29.93 (978-1-60870-224-4(3)) Cavendish Square Publishing.

Page, Jason. Rowing, Sailing, & Other Sports on the Water. 2008. (Olympic Sports Ser.). (ENG., Illus.). 32p. (J). (gr. 3-7). pap. (978-0-7787-4034-6(X)); lib. bdg. (978-0-7787-4017-9(X)) Crabtree Publishing Co.

Peterson, Christine. The Science Behind Swimming, Diving, & Other Water Sports. 2016. (Science of the Summer Olympics Ser.). (ENG.). 32p. (gr. 3-4). pap. 7.95 (978-1-4914-8161-5(7)); (Illus.). lib. bdg. 27.99 (978-1-4914-8157-8(9)) Capstone Press of Coughlan Cos. (Edge Bks.).

Savage, Jeff. Dallas Friday. 2007. (Amazing Athletes Ser.). (ENG.). 32p. (gr. 2-5). 25.26 (978-0-8225-6595-6(1)); pap. 7.95 (978-0-8225-6599-4(4), First Avenue Editions) Lerner Publishing Group.

Wood, Alix. Wacky in the Water. 2014. (Wacky World of Sports Ser.). (Illus.). 32p. (J). (gr. 3-6). pap. 63.00 (978-1-4824-1240-6(3)) Stevens, Gareth Publishing LLLP.

Woods, Bob. Water Sports. 2003. (Extreme Sports Ser.). (Illus.). 24p. (gr. 2-5). lib. bdg. 23.00 (978-0-8368-3727-8(4), Gareth Stevens Learning Library) Stevens, Gareth Publishing LLLP.

Zahensky, Kenneth & Egan, Tracie. An Insider's Guide to Water Polo, 1 vol. 2015. (ENG.). 48p. (YA). 30.25 (978-1-4777-8085-5(8), Rosen Reference) Rosen Publishing Group, Inc., The.

AQUATIC SPORTS—FICTION

Jones, Penri. Dan Leuad Llyn. 2005. (WEL.). 196p. pap. (978-0-86243-028-3(3)) Y Lolfa.

McEwan, Jamie. Whitewater Scrubs. Margeson, John, illus. 2005. (ENG.). 80p. (J). (gr. 2-4). 14.99 (978-1-58196-038-9(7), Darby Creek) Lerner Publishing Group.

Strasser, Todd. Take Off. 2004. (ENG.). 320p. (YA). (gr. 9). mass mkt. 5.99 (978-0-689-87029-3(9), Simon Pulse) Simon Pulse.

AQUATIC SPORTS—SAFETY MEASURES

Knowlton, MaryLee. Safety Around Water. 2008. (Staying Safe Ser.). (ENG.). 32p. (J). (gr. -1-3). lib. bdg. (978-0-7787-4315-6(2)) Crabtree Publishing Co.

Lindeen, Mary & Kesselring, Susan. Being Safe around Water. McGeehan, Dan & Moore, David, Jr., illus. 2011. (Be Safe Ser.). (ENG.). 24p. (J). (gr. k-3). lib. bdg. 27.07 (978-1-60954-298-6(3), 200078) Child's World, Inc., The.

Pendziwol, Jean E. A Treasure at Sea for Dragon & Me: Water Safety for Kids (and Dragons) Gourbault, Martine, illus. 2006. (ENG.). 32p. (J). (gr. -1-2). 7.95 (978-1-55337-880-8(6)) Kids Can Pr., Ltd. CAN. Dist: Hachette Bk. Group.

Rau, Dana Meachen. Water Safety: Seguridad en el Agua. 2009. (Bookworms — Bilingual Editions: Safe Kids/Ninos Seguros Ser.). (SPA & ENG.). 32p. (gr. k-2). lib. bdg. 15.95 (978-0-7614-4779-5(2)) Marshall Cavendish GBR. Dist: Marshall Cavendish Corp.

Rau, Dana Meachen & Meachen Rau, Dana. Water Safety: Seguridad en el Agua. 2009. (Bookworms: Safe Kids Ser.). (SPA & ENG.). 32p. (gr. k-2). 15.95 (978-0-7614-4088-8(7)) Marshall Cavendish Corp.

ARAB COUNTRIES

Abboud, Tony. Al Kindi: The Father of Arab Philosophy. 2009. (Great Muslim Philosophers & Scientists of the Middle Ages Ser.). 112p. (gr. 6-6). 66.50 (978-1-61513-176-1(0), Rosen Reference) Rosen Publishing Group, Inc., The.

Anderson, Marilyn D. Arab Americans. 2006. (World Almanac Library of American Immigration). (Illus.). 48p. (gr. 5-12). lib. bdg. 31.00 (978-0-8368-7307-8(6), Gareth Stevens Secondary Library) Stevens, Gareth Publishing LLLP.

Bakarat, Ibtisam. Balcony on the Moon: Growing up in Palestine. 2016. (ENG.). 240p. (J). 17.99 (978-0-374-30251-1(0), 9780374302511, Farrar, Straus & Giroux (BYR)) Farrar, Straus & Giroux.

Burnett, Betty. The Attack on the USS Cole in Yemen on October 12 2000. 2009. (Terrorist Attacks Ser.). 64p. (gr. 5-5). 58.50 (978-1-60853-311-4(5)) Rosen Publishing Group, Inc., The.

Cohn, Jessica. The Medieval Islamic World, 1 vol. 2012. (Primary Source Readers Ser.). (ENG.). 32p. (J). (gr. 5-5). pap. 8.99 (978-1-4333-5003-0(3)) Teacher Created Materials, Inc.

Eugster, Rachel & Lassieur, Allison. Trade & Commerce in the Early Islamic World. 2012. (Life in the Early Islamic World Ser.). (ENG., Illus.). 48p. (J). pap. (978-0-7787-2179-6(5)) Crabtree Publishing Co.

Eugster, Rachel & Whiting, Jim. The Role of Religion in the Early Islamic World. 2012. (Life in the Early Islamic World Ser.). (ENG., Illus.). 48p. (J). pap. (978-0-7787-2176-5(0)) Crabtree Publishing Co.

Jeffrey, Gary. Lawrence of Arabia & the Middle East & Africa. 2013. (ENG., Illus.). 48p. (J). (978-0-7787-0912-1(4)); pap. (978-0-7787-0918-3(3)) Crabtree Publishing Co.

Losleben, Elizabeth. The Bedouin of the Middle East. 2005. (First Peoples Ser.). (Illus.). 48p. (gr. 4-8). lib. bdg. 23.95 (978-0-8225-0663-8(7)) Lerner Publishing Group.

Marcovitz, Hal. Yemen. (Major Muslim Nations Ser.). (Illus.). 120p. (J). 2010. (gr. 7-18). 25.95 (978-1-4222-1396-4(X)) 2008. pap. 14.95 (978-1-4222-1426-8(5)) Mason Crest.

Marín-Guzman, Roberto & Zéraoui, Zidane. Arab Immigration in Mexico in the Nineteenth & Twentieth Centuries: Assimilation & Arab Heritage. 2003. (Illus.). 208p. per. 18.95 (978-0-9636882-2-4(7)) Augustine Pr.

McCoy, Lisa. Qatar. 2010. (Major Muslim Nations Ser.). (Illus.). 111p. (YA). (gr. 5-18). lib. bdg. 25.95 (978-1-4222-1398-8(6)) Mason Crest.

Orr, Tamra. Qatar. 2007. (Cultures of the World Ser.). 144p. (gr. 6). lib. bdg. 42.79 (978-0-7614-2566-3(7), Benchmark Bks.) Marshall Cavendish Corp.

Ramen, Fred. Albucasis (Abu al-Qasim Al-Zahrawi) Renowned Muslim Surgeon of the Tenth Century. 2009. (Great Muslim Philosophers & Scientists of the Middle Ages Ser.). 112p. (gr. 6-6). 66.50 (978-1-61513-178-5(7), Rosen Reference) Rosen Publishing Group, Inc., The.

Robson, David. Israeli-Palestinian Conflict. 2010. (World History Ser.). (Illus.). 128p. (J). 34.95 (978-1-4205-0239-8(5), Lucent Bks.) Cengage Gale.

Romanek, Trudee. Science, Medicine, & Math in the Early Islamic World. 2012. (Life in the Early Islamic World Ser.). (ENG., Illus.). 48p. (J). pap. (978-0-7787-2177-2(9)) Crabtree Publishing Co.

Romano, Amy. A Historical Atlas of the United Arab Emirates. 2009. (Historical Atlases of South Asia, Central Asia, & the Middle East Ser.). 64p. (gr. 6-6). 61.20 (978-1-61513-330-7(5)) Rosen Publishing Group, Inc., The.

—A Historical Atlas of Yemen. 2009. (Historical Atlases of South Asia, Central Asia, & the Middle East Ser.). 64p. (gr. 6-6). 61.20 (978-1-61513-331-4(3)) Rosen Publishing Group, Inc., The.

Royston, Angela. Hoping for Peace in the Middle East. 2012. (Peace Pen Pals Ser.). (Illus.). 48p. (J). (gr. 6-8). 31.95 (978-1-4339-7743-5(5)); pap. 14.05 (978-1-4339-7744-2(3)) Stevens, Gareth Publishing LLLP.

Samuels, Charlie. Timeline of the Muslim World. 2010. (History Highlights: A Gareth Stevens Timeline Ser.). (Illus.). 48p. (gr. 6-8). (J). pap. 14.05 (978-1-4339-3490-2(6)); (YA). lib. bdg. 31.95 (978-1-4339-3489-6(2)) Stevens, Gareth Publishing LLLP. (Gareth Stevens Secondary Library).

Toffolo, Cris E. The Arab League. 2008. (Global Organizations Ser.). (Illus.). 144p. (YA). (gr. 7-12). 35.00 (978-0-7910-9565-2(7)) Facts On File, Inc.

Wolny, Philip. Muslims Around the World Today. 2009. (Understanding Islam Ser.). 64p. (gr. 6-6). 58.50 (978-1-60854-626-8(8)) Rosen Publishing Group, Inc., The.

ARAB-ISRAEL WAR, 1967

see Israel-Arab War, 1967

ARAB-JEWISH RELATIONS

see Jewish-Arab Relations

ARABIA

see Arabian Peninsula

ARABIAN PENINSULA

Cohn, Jessica. The Medieval Islamic World, 1 vol. 2012. (Primary Source Readers Ser.). (ENG.). 32p. (J). (gr. 5-5). pap. 8.99 (978-1-4333-5003-0(3)) Teacher Created Materials, Inc.

Cooke, Tim. The Exploration of Arabia & Asia. 2013. (Explorers Discovering the World Ser.). (Illus.). 48p. (gr. 4-6). 31.95 (978-1-4339-8615-4(9)); pap. 14.05 (978-1-4339-8616-1(7)) Stevens, Gareth Publishing LLLP. (Gareth Stevens Learning Library).

Hestler, Anna & Spilling, Jo-Ann. Yemen. 2nd rev. ed. 2009. (Cultures of the World 18 Ser.). 144p. (gr. 6). 42.79 (978-0-7614-4850-1(0)) Marshall Cavendish GBR. Dist: Marshall Cavendish Corp.

Johnson, Julia & Styles, Emily. A Is for Arabia. 2012. (ENG., Illus.). 32p. (gr. -1-3). pap. 8.50 (978-1-900988-93-3(3), Stacey International) Stacey Publishing GBR. Dist: Casemate Pubs. & Bk. Distributors, LLC.

ARABIAN PENINSULA—FICTION

Clynes, Kate. Ali Baba. Anstey, David, illus. 2005. (SWA & ENG.). 32p. (J). pap. (978-1-84444-429-8(5)) Mantra Lingua.

Croall, Marie P. Ali Baba: Fooling the Forty Thieves: an Arabian Tale. 2008. (Graphic Myths & Legends Ser.). (Illus.). 48p. (J). (gr. 3-7). lib. bdg. 26.60 (978-0-8225-7525-2(6), Graphic Universe™) Lerner Publishing Group.

Gallego Garcia, Laura & Bellm, Dan. The Legend of the Wandering King. 2005. (J). (978-0-439-58557-6(0), Levine, Arthur A. Bks.) Scholastic, Inc.

Johnson, Julia, ed. Arabian Star. Climent, Henry, illus. 2009. (ENG.). 52p. 11.99 (978-1-905299-84-3(2), Stacey International) Stacey Publishing GBR. Dist: Casemate Pubs. & Bk. Distributors, LLC.

Mydin, Liza. The Three Village Boys of Al Haidar: The First Adventure. 2012. 20p. pap. 16.00 (978-1-4669-2792-6(5)) Trafford Publishing.

ARABIC ART

see Islamic Art

ARABIC LANGUAGE

Adly, Muhammad S. Let's Count in Arabic, Bk. 1. 24p. (978-1-894264-46-4(0)) Al-Attique Pubs., Inc.

Affaya, Colett & Affaya, Otman. Arkam, Numero & Numbers, 1 vol. Affaya, Colette, illus. 2009. 16p. pap. 24.95 (978-1-60749-929-9(0)) America Star Bks.

Al-Mouhawaka, Kira. Learn to Read Arabic. (ARA & ENG., Illus.). 68p. (J). (gr. -1-5). pap., wbk. ed. 6.95 (978-0-86685-769-7(9)) International Bk. Ctr., Inc.

—Learn to Read Arabic: Drills. (ARA & ENG., Illus.). 68p. (J). (gr. -1-5). pap. 6.95 (978-0-86685-770-3(2)) International Bk. Ctr., Inc.

—Learn to Read Arabic: Exercise Book. (ARA & ENG., Illus.). 68p. (J). (gr. -1-5). pap. 7.95 (978-0-86685-407-8(X)) International Bk. Ctr., Inc.

Amery, Heather. First Thousand Words in Arabic. Cartwright, Stephen, illus. 2004. (First Thousand Words Ser.). (ENG.). 64p. (J). 12.99 (978-0-7945-0030-6(7), Usborne) EDC Publishing.

Berlitz Kids Staff, contrib. by. 1000 Arabic Words. 2011. (1000 Words Ser.). (ARA & ENG., Illus.). 64p. pap. 11.99 (978-981-268-576-6(6)) APA Publications Services SGP. Dist: Ingram Publisher Services.

Corbeil, Jean-Claude, et al. Milet Bilingual Visual Dictionary: English-Arabic. 2005. (ENG & ARA., Illus.). 232p. (gr. 1-3). 29.95 (978-1-84059-256-6(7)) Milet Publishing.

Elias, Joseph. Dictionary for Children: Arabic-Arabic. (ARA., Illus.). 378p. (J). 18.95 (978-0-86685-754-3(0)) International Bk. Ctr., Inc.

Haxhia, Miranda. The Doll's Nose. Kohrer, Ursula, illus. 2014. (ARA.). (J). **(978-0-9856237-4-6(8))** East West Discovery Pr.

Kalz, Jill. My First Arabic Phrases, 1 vol. TransPerfect Translations Staff, tr. Fabbri, Daniele, illus. 2012. (Speak Another Language! Ser.). (ARA & ENG.). 32p. (gr. 1-3). lib. bdg. 26.65 (978-1-4048-7517-3(4)) Picture Window Bks.

Kudela, Katy R. My First Book of Arabic Words, 1 vol. Translations.com Staff, tr. (Bilingual Picture Dictionaries Ser.). 32p. (gr. 1-2). 2011. (ENG, ARA & MUL., Illus.). pap. 8.10 (978-1-4296-6161-4(5)) 2011. (MUL.). pap. 47.70 (978-1-4296-6162-1(3)) 2010. (MUL & ENG.). lib. bdg. 27.32 (978-1-4296-5266-7(7)) Capstone Press of Coughlan Cos. (Aplus Bks.).

Milet Publishing Staff. Animals - My First Bilingual Book. 2011. (My First Bilingual Book Ser.). (ENG., Illus.). 24p. (J). (gr. k — 1). bds. 7.99 (978-1-84059-608-3(2)) Milet Publishing.

—Bilingual Visual Dictionary. 2011. (Milet Multimedia Ser.). (ENG & ARA., Illus.). 1p. (J). (gr. k-2). cd-rom 19.95 (978-1-84059-580-2(9)) Milet Publishing.

—Colors. 2011. (My First Bilingual Book Ser.). (ENG.). 24p. (J). (gr. k — 1). bds. 8.99 (978-1-84059-597-0(3)) Milet Publishing.

—Fruit - My First Bilingual Book. 2011. (My First Bilingual Book Ser.). (ENG., Illus.). 24p. (J). (gr. k — 1). bds. 7.99 (978-1-84059-624-3(4)) Milet Publishing.

—Home (English-Arabic) 2011. (My First Bilingual Book Ser.). (ENG., Illus.). 24p. (J). (gr. k — 1). bds. 7.99 (978-1-84059-640-3(6)) Milet Publishing.

—Music. 2012. (My First Bilingual Book Ser.). (ENG & ARA., Illus.). 24p. (J). (gr. k — 1). bds. 7.99 (978-1-84059-716-5(X)) Milet Publishing.

—My Bilingual Book-Hearing (English-Arabic) 2014. (My Bilingual Book Ser.). (ENG & ARA., Illus.). 28p. (J). (gr. -1-k). 9.95 (978-1-84059-772-1(0)) Milet Publishing.

—My Bilingual Book-Smell (English-Arabic) 2014. (My Bilingual Book Ser.). (ENG & ARA., Illus.). 28p. (J). (gr. -1-k). 9.95 (978-1-84059-804-9(2)) Milet Publishing.

—My Bilingual Book-Taste (English-Arabic) 2014. (My Bilingual Book Ser.). (ENG & ARA., Illus.). 28p. (J). (gr. -1-k). 9.95 (978-1-84059-820-9(4)) Milet Publishing.

—My Bilingual Book-Touch (English-Arabic) 2014. (My Bilingual Book Ser.). (ENG & ARA., Illus.). 28p. (J). (gr. -1-k). 9.95 (978-1-84059-836-0(0)) Milet Publishing.

—My First Bilingual Book - Opposites. 2012. (My First Bilingual Book Ser.). (ENG & ARA., Illus.). 24p. (J). (gr. k — 1). bds. 7.99 (978-1-84059-732-5(1)) Milet Publishing.

—My First Bilingual Book-Jobs. 2012. (My First Bilingual Book Ser.). (ENG & ARA., Illus.). 24p. (J). (gr. k — 1). bds. 7.99 (978-1-84059-700-4(3)) Milet Publishing.

—My First Bilingual Book-Vegetables (English-Arabic) 2011. (My First Bilingual Book Ser.). (ENG., Illus.). 24p. (J). (gr. k — 1). bds. 8.99 (978-1-84059-656-4(2)) Milet Publishing.

—Sight - English-Arabic. 2014. (My Bilingual Book Ser.). (ENG & ARA., Illus.). 28p. (J). (gr. -1-k). 9.95 (978-1-84059-788-2(7)) Milet Publishing.

—Sports. 2012. (My First Bilingual Book Ser.). (ENG & ARA., Illus.). 24p. (J). (gr. k — 1). bds. 7.99 (978-1-84059-748-6(8)) Milet Publishing.

Morris, Neil. First Arabic Words. Melling, David, illus. 2009. (First Words Ser.). (ARA & ENG.). 48p. (YA). (gr. 3-18). pap. 12.95 (978-0-19-911135-0(9)) Oxford Univ. Pr., Inc.

Parnell, Declan. Amr Speaks Arabic, 01 vols., 1. 2016. (Rosen REAL Readers: Social Studies Nonfiction / Fiction: Family, Community, & the World Ser.). (ENG.). 12p. (J). pap. 6.33 (978-1-5081-1812-1(4), Rosen Classroom) Rosen Publishing Group, Inc., The.

The Phoenicians. (Butterfly Bks.). (J). (gr. 4-8). 9.95 *(978-0-86685-705-5(2)*, LDL60E) International Bk. Ctr., Inc.

Siddiqa, Juma, illus. My Arabic Words Book. 2007. (ARA & ENG.). 30p. (J). (gr. -1-6). 18.00 *(978-1-879402-33-1(5))* Tahrike Tarsile Quran, Inc.

Speak Arabic: Arabic Script Version. 144p. (YA). pap. 180.00 incl. audio, VHS *(978-0-88432-519-2(9)*, SAR202) Pavilion Pubs.

Speak Arabic: Transliterated Version. 160p. (YA). pap. 180.00 incl. audio, VHS *(978-0-88432-518-5(0)*, SAR201) Pavilion Pubs.

Tommalieh, Fakhri & Hujeer, Majeda. 1st Grade Learning Arabic Language Step - by - Step Approach Workbook Part 2,Third Edition: Learn Arabic Language. Al-Ghussinu, Wa'ad Diab, illus. 2012. (ARA.). 104p. pap. 21.99 *(978-0-9853772-0-5(8))* Dar Asadeeq Publishing & Distribution, Inc.

Turhan, Sedat. New Bilingual Visual Dictionary (English-Arabic) 2nd ed. 2017. (New Bilingual Visual Dictionary Ser.). (ENG & ARA., Illus.). 144p. (J). (gr. k-2). 19.95 ***(978-1-78508-881-0(5))*** Milet Publishing.

ARABS

see also Bedouins

Brexel, Bernadette. Yasser Arafat. 2009. (Middle East Leaders Ser.). 112p. (gr. 5-8). 66.50 *(978-1-61514-649-9(0)*, Rosen Reference) Rosen Publishing Group, Inc., The.

Carew-Miller, Anna. The Palestinians. 2010. (Major Muslim Nations Ser.). 135p. (YA). (gr. 5-18). lib. bdg. 25.95 *(978-1-4222-1389-6(7))* Mason Crest.

Moreno, Barry. The Arab Americans. 2007. (Major American Immigration Ser.). (YA). pap. 9.95 *(978-1-4222-0671-3(8))* Mason Crest.

Moreno, Barry & Temple, Bob. The Arab Americans. 2010. (Major American Immigration Ser.). (Illus.). 64p. (YA). (gr. 9-12). 22.95 *(978-1-4222-0604-1(1))* Mason Crest.

Rosaler, Maxine. Hamas: (Rev) Palestinian Terrorists. 2005. (Inside the World's Most Infamous Terrorist Organizations Ser.). (Illus.). 64p. (J). (gr. -1-7). lib. bdg. 31.95 *(978-1-4042-0634-2(5))* Rosen Publishing Group, Inc., The.

Woog, Adam. The Palestinian National Authority. 2nd rev. ed. 2008. (Creation of the Modern Middle East Ser.). (Illus.). 136p. (gr. 6-12). 35.00 *(978-1-60413-020-1(2)*, Chelsea Hse.) Facts On File, Inc.

ARABS—FICTION

Blanchard, Anne & Cerisier, Emmanuel. Arab Science & Invention in the Golden Age. Brent, R. M., tr. from FRE. 2009. (ENG., Illus.). 80p. (J). (gr. 3). 19.95 *(978-1-59270-080-6(2))* Enchanted Lion Bks., LLC.

Croall, Marie. Sinbad: Sailing into Peril. Hilinski, Clint, illus. 2007. (Graphic Myths & Legends Ser.). (ENG.). 48p. (gr. 4-8). lib. bdg. 27.93 *(978-0-8225-6375-4(4))* Lerner Publishing Group.

Croall, Marie P. Sinbad: Sailing into Peril. Hilinski, Clint, illus. 2008. (Graphic Myths & Legends Ser.). (ENG.). 48p. (gr. 4-8). pap. 8.95 *(978-0-8225-8516-9(2))* Lerner Publishing Group.

Fairy Tale- Aladdin. 2005. (J). bds. *(978-1-4194-0037-7(1))* Paradise Pr., Inc.

Fein, Eric. The Fisherman & the Genie, 1 vol. Garcia, Eduardo, illus. 2010. (Classic Fiction Ser.). (ENG.). 72p. (gr. 2-3). 27.99 *(978-1-4342-2134-6(2))*; pap. 7.15 *(978-1-4342-2777-5(4))* Stone Arch Bks. (Graphic Revolve).

Khan, Rukhsana. Big Red Lollipop. Blackall, Sophie, illus. 2010. (ENG.). 40p. (J). (gr. -1-3). 16.99 *(978-0-670-06287-4(1)*, Viking Books for Young Readers) Penguin Young Readers Group.

Malaspina, Ann. Feraj & the Magic Lute: An Arabian Folktale. Peluso, Martina, illus. 2013. (Folktales from Around the World Ser.). (ENG.). 24p. (J). (gr. k-3). 28.50 *(978-1-62323-613-7(4)*, 206380) Child's World, Inc., The.

Martinez, Jessica. The Vow. 2013. (ENG.). 432p. (YA). (gr. 9). 17.99 *(978-1-4424-5864-2(X)*, Simon Pulse) Simon Pulse.

Pike, Christopher, pseud. The Secret of Ka. 2011. (ENG.). 416p. (YA). (gr. 7). pap. 8.99 *(978-0-547-57729-6(X))* Houghton Mifflin Harcourt Publishing Co.

Powell, Martin. The Seven Voyages of Sinbad, 1 vol. Pérez, Daniel et al, illus. 2010. (Classic Fiction Ser.). (ENG.). 72p. (gr. 2-3). 27.99 *(978-1-4342-1987-9(9)*, Graphic Revolve) Stone Arch Bks.

—The Seven Voyages of Sinbad. Pérez, Daniel et al, illus. 2010. (Classic Fiction Ser.). (ENG.). 72p. (gr. 2-3). pap. 7.15 *(978-1-4342-2775-1(8)*, Graphic Revolve) Stone Arch Bks.

Samira's Eid. 2004. (ENG & KUR.). (J). *(978-1-84444-667-4(0))* Mantra Lingua.

Siks, Geraldine B. Ali Baba & the Forty Thieves. (Illus.). (YA). (gr. 6-12). 6.00 *(978-0-87602-103-3(8))* Family Plays.

Tarnowska, Wafa'. The Arabian Nights. Henaff, Carole, illus. 2010. (ENG.). 128p. (J). (gr. 3-18). 24.99 *(978-1-84686-122-2(5))* Barefoot Bks., Inc.

—The Arabian Nights Chapter. Hénaff, Carole, illus. 2011. (ENG.). 160p. (J). (gr. 4-6). pap. 12.99 *(978-1-84686-568-8(9))* Barefoot Bks., Inc.

ARABS—HISTORY

Dennis, Yvonne Wakim & Addasi, Maha. A Kid's Guide to Arab American History. 2013. (Kid's Guide Ser.). (ENG., Illus.). 224p. (J). (gr. 2-4). pap. 16.95 *(978-1-61374-017-0(4))* Chicago Review Pr., Inc.

January, Brendan. The Arab Conquests of the Middle East. 2009. (Pivotal Moments in History Ser.). (ENG.). 160p. (gr. 9-12). 38.60 *(978-0-8225-8744-6(0))* Lerner Publishing Group.

Marschner, Janice. California's Arab Americans. 2003. (Illus.). 160p. lib. bdg. 18.95 *(978-0-9677069-7-9(1))* Coleman Ranch Pr.

Schur, Joan Brodsky. The Arabs. 2004. (gr. 10-12). 22.45 *(978-0-7377-2149-2(9)*, Greenhaven Pr., Inc.) Cengage Gale.

ARABUS FAMILY (FICTITIOUS CHARACTER)—FICTION

Hurt, Avery. Arab Nationalism & Zionism. 2017. (J). ***(978-1-5026-2720-9(5))*** Cavendish Square Publishing.

ARBOR DAY

Gleisner, Jenna Lee. We Celebrate Arbor Day in Spring. 2014. (21st Century Basic Skills Library: Let's Look at Spring Ser.). (ENG., Illus.). 24p. (J). (gr. k-3). 22.79 *(978-1-62431-656-2(5)*, 203136) Cherry Lake Publishing.

Peppas, Lynn. Arbor Day. 2012. (ENG.). 32p. (J). *(978-0-7787-4085-8(4))*; pap. *(978-0-7787-4090-2(0))* Crabtree Publishing Co.

ARBOR DAY—FICTION

Galbraith, Kathryn O. Arbor Day Square, 1 vol. Moore, Cyd, illus. 2016. (ENG.). 32p. (J). (gr. -1-3). pap. 7.95 *(978-1-56145-922-3(4))* Peachtree Pubs.

Galbraith, Kathryn Osebold. Arbor Day Square, 1 vol. Moore, Cyd, illus. 2010. (ENG.). 32p. (J). (gr. -1-3). 16.95 *(978-1-56145-517-1(2))* Peachtree Pubs.

ARCHAEOLOGISTS

Aksomitis, Gerard. Solving the Mysteries of the Past. 2008. (Science Solves It Ser.). (ENG., Illus.). 32p. (J). (gr. 3-7). lib. bdg. *(978-0-7787-4171-8(0))* Crabtree Publishing Co.

Capek, Michael. Unsolved Archaeological Mysteries. 2015. (Unsolved Mystery Files Ser.). (ENG., Illus.). 32p. (gr. 3-4). pap. 7.95 *(978-1-4914-4338-5(3))* Capstone Press of Coughlan Cos.

Cline, Eric H. & Rubalcaba, Jill. Digging for Troy: From Homer to Hisarlik. Brannen, Sarah S., illus. 2011. (ENG.). 80p. (J). (gr. 4-7). 17.95 *(978-1-58089-326-8(0))*; pap. 9.95 *(978-1-58089-327-5(9))* Charlesbridge Publishing, Inc.

Harasymiw, Mark J. Be an Archaeologist. 2014. (Be a Scientist! Ser.). (Illus.). 32p. (J). (gr. 3-6). pap. 63.00 *(978-1-4824-1198-0(9))* Stevens, Gareth Publishing LLLP.

Kerns, Ann. Troy. 2008. (Unearthing Ancient Worlds Ser.). (ENG.). 80p. (gr. 5-8). lib. bdg. 30.60 *(978-0-8225-7582-5(5))* Lerner Publishing Group.

Macdonald, Fiona. Amazing Archaeologists: True Stories of Astounding Archaeological Discoveries, 1 vol. 2014. (Ultimate Adventurers Ser.). (ENG.). 48p. (gr. 6-6). lib. bdg. 29.99 *(978-1-4109-5419-0(6))* Heinemann-Raintree.

Owen, Ruth. Paleontologists & Archaeologists. 2013. (Out of the Lab: Extreme Jobs in Science Ser.). 32p. (J). (gr. 3-6). 25.25 *(978-1-4777-1290-0(9))*; pap. 10.00 *(978-1-4777-1380-8(8))*; pap. 60.00 *(978-1-4777-1387-7(5))* Rosen Publishing Group, Inc., The. (PowerKids Pr.).

Peterson, Judy Monroe. Digging up History: Archaeologists. 2009. (Extreme Scientists Ser.). 24p. (gr. 2-3). 42.50 *(978-1-61512-450-3(0)*, PowerKids Pr.); (Illus.). (YA). lib. bdg. 22.60 *(978-1-4042-4523-5(5))* Rosen Publishing Group, Inc., The.

Rubalcaba, Jill & Robertshaw, Peter. Every Bone Tells a Story: Hominin Discoveries, Deductions, & Debates. 2010. (ENG., Illus.). 192p. (J). (gr. 5-8). 18.95 *(978-1-58089-164-6(0))* Charlesbridge Publishing, Inc.

Schlitz, Laura Amy. The Hero Schliemann: The Dreamer Who Dug up Troy. Byrd, Robert, illus. 2006. (ENG.). 80p. (J). (gr. 4-7). lib. bdg. 17.99 *(978-0-7636-2283-1(4))* Candlewick Pr.

Thomas, William David & Nations, Susan. Archaeologist. 2009. (Cool Careers: on the Go Ser.). 32p. (gr. 5-8). pap. 10.50 *(978-1-4339-0164-5(1))*; (YA). lib. bdg. 26.00 *(978-1-4339-0000-6(9))* Stevens, Gareth Publishing LLLP.

Thompson, Clifford. Archaeologists!, Vol. 10. 2015. (Scientists in Action Ser.). (Illus.). 48p. (J). (gr. 5). lib. bdg. 20.95 *(978-1-4222-3417-4(7))* Mason Crest.

Venezia, Mike. Mary Leakey - Archaeologist Who Really Dug Her Work. Venezia, Mike, illus. 2009. (Getting to Know the World's Greatest Inventors & Scientists Ser.). (ENG., Illus.). 32p. (J). (gr. 2-5). 28.00 *(978-0-531-23727-4(3))* Scholastic Library Publishing.

ARCHAEOLOGY

see also Art, Primitive; Bible—Antiquities; Christian Art and Symbolism; Classical Antiquities; Cliff Dwellers and Cliff Dwellings; Ethnology; Excavations (Archaeology); Extinct Cities; Funeral Rites and Ceremonies; Gems; Heraldry; Indians of North America—Antiquities; Mounds and Mound Builders; Mummies; Numismatics; Pottery; Prehistoric Peoples; Pyramids; Stone Age; Temples; Weapons

also subdivision Antiquities under names of countries, cities, etc.

ABDO Publishing Company Staff. Digging up the Past. 2014. (Digging up the Past Ser.: 8). (ENG.). 112p. (J). (gr. 6-12). lib. bdg. 285.12 *(978-1-62403-230-1(3)*, Essential Library) ABDO Publishing Co.

Anderson, Dale. How Do We Know the Nature of Humankind. 2005. (Great Scientific Questions & the Scientists Who Answered Them Ser.). (Illus.). 112p. (J). (gr. 7-12). lib. bdg. 34.60 *(978-1-4042-0077-7(0))* Rosen Publishing Group, Inc., The.

Archeology. 2010. (Careers in Focus Ser.). (Illus.). 224p. (gr. 6-12). 32.95 *(978-0-8160-8022-9(4)*, Ferguson Publishing Co.) Facts On File, Inc.

Askomitis, Gerard & Aksomitis, Gerard. Solving the Mysteries of the Past. 2008. (Science Solves It Ser.). (ENG., Illus.). 32p. (J). (gr. 3-7). pap. *(978-0-7787-4178-7(8))* Crabtree Publishing Co.

Bacchin, Matteo & Signore, Marco. A Jurassic Mystery: Archaeopteryx. Shore, Marguerite, tr. from ITA. 2008. (Dinosaurs: Ser.). (ENG., Illus.). 61p. (J). (gr. 4-6). 18.95 *(978-0-7892-1016-6(9)*, Abbeville Kids) Abbeville Pr., Inc.

Bailey, Linda. Adventures in the Ice Age. Slavin, Bill, illus. 2004. (Good Times Travel Agency Ser.). (ENG.). 48p. (J). (gr. 3-7). 8.95 *(978-1-55337-504-3(1))* Kids Can Pr., Ltd. CAN. Dist: Hachette Bk. Group.

Barber, Nicola. Tomb Explorers, 1 vol. 2013. (Treasure Hunters Ser.). (ENG.). 48p. (gr. 5-8). pap. 9.25 *(978-1-4109-4962-2(1))*; lib. bdg. 29.99 *(978-1-4109-4955-4(9))* Heinemann-Raintree.

Biskup, Agnieszka. Graphic Expeditions. Stewart, Roger, illus. 2016. (Graphic Expeditions Ser.). (ENG.). 32p. (gr. 3-4). lib. bdg. 245.20 *(978-1-5157-4023-0(4)*, Graphic Library) Capstone Press of Coughlan Cos.

Bow, James. Hidden Worlds. 2013. (ENG., Illus.). 32p. (J). *(978-0-7787-1124-7(2))*; pap. *(978-0-7787-1128-5(5))* Crabtree Publishing Co.

Burnham, Brad. Qumran Caves: Hiding Place for the Dead Sea Scrolls. 2009. (Famous Caves of the World Ser.). 24p. (gr. 3-4). 42.50 *(978-1-61512-499-2(3)*, PowerKids Pr.) Rosen Publishing Group, Inc., The.

Capek, Michael. Unsolved Archaeological Mysteries. 2015. (Unsolved Mystery Files Ser.). (ENG., Illus.). 32p. (gr. 3-4). pap. 7.95 *(978-1-4914-4338-5(3))* Capstone Press of Coughlan Cos.

Cassells, E. Steve. Tracing the Past: Archaeology along the Rocky Mountain Expansion Loop Pipeline, 1. 2003. (Illus.). 40p. 6.95 *(978-0-9743137-0-2(X))* Alpine Archaeological Consultants, Inc.

Croy, Anita. Exploring the Past. 2010. (Invisible Worlds Ser.). 48p. (gr. 4). 28.50 *(978-0-7614-4194-6(8))* Marshall Cavendish GBR. Dist: Marshall Cavendish Corp.

De Winter, James. Discovering Lost Cities & Pirate Gold. 2010. (Extreme! Ser.). (ENG.). 32p. (gr. 3-4). pap. 47.70 *(978-1-4296-5112-7(1)*, Fact Finders) Capstone Press of Coughlan Cos.

Dicker, Katie. Mysterious Places. 2015. (Mystery! Ser.). (Illus.). 24p. (gr. 3-6). 28.50 *(978-1-62588-204-2(1))* Black Rabbit Bks.

Dig This! How Archaeologists Uncover Our Past. 2003. (Illus.). 96p. (J). 17.95 *(978-1-58013-078-3(X)*, Kar-Ben Publishing) Lerner Publishing Group.

Digging into History, 6 bks., Set. Incl. Solving the Mysteries of Ancient Rome. Hanbury-Murphy, Trudy. lib. bdg. 29.93 *(978-0-7614-3101-5(2))*; Solving the Mysteries of Aztec Cities. Croy, Anita. lib. bdg. 29.93 *(978-0-7614-3102-2(0))*; Solving the Mysteries of Machu Picchu. Croy, Anita. lib. bdg. 29.93 *(978-0-7614-3103-9(9))*; Solving the Mysteries of Pompeii. Samuel, Charlie. lib. bdg. 29.93 *(978-0-7614-3105-3(5))*; Solving the Mysteries of Stonehenge. Gray, Leon. lib. bdg. 29.93 *(978-0-7614-3110-7(1))*; Solving the Mysteries of the Pyramids. MacDonald, Fiona. lib. bdg. 29.93 *(978-0-7614-3106-0(3))*; 32p. (gr. 4-18). (Digging into History Ser.). 2008. Set lib. bdg. 179.58 *(978-0-7614-3100-8(4)*, Benchmark Bks.) Marshall Cavendish Corp.

Down, David. Archaeology Book. 2009. 96p. (YA). 16.99 *(978-0-89051-573-0(5))* Master Bks.

Farndon, John. Archeology. 2010. (Unpredictable Nature Ser.). (Illus.). 48p. (J). (gr. 3-18). lib. bdg. 19.95 *(978-1-4222-1994-2(1))* Mason Crest.

Faulkner, Nicholas. A Visual History of the World's Enduring Mysteries. 2016. (Visual History of the World Ser.). 00096p. (J). (gr. 8-8). 37.10 *(978-1-4994-6578-5(5))* Rosen Publishing Group, Inc., The.

Fay, Gail, et al. Archaeological Mysteries, 1 vol. 2014. (Archaeological Mysteries Ser.). (ENG.). 32p. (gr. 3-4). 111.96 *(978-1-4765-9920-5(3)*, Edge Bks.) Capstone Press of Coughlan Cos.

Forensic Archaeology. 2011. (Crime Scene Investigations Ser.). 128p. lib. bdg. 33.45 *(978-1-4205-0548-1(3)*, Lucent Bks.) Cengage Gale.

Ganeri, Anita & West, David. The Curse of King Tut's Tomb & Other Ancient Discoveries. 2011. (Incredible True Adventures Ser.). (ENG.). 48p. (YA). (gr. 5-8). pap. 11.75 *(978-1-4488-6661-8(8))*; lib. bdg. 29.25 *(978-1-4488-6657-1(X))* Rosen Publishing Group, Inc., The.

Gordon, Nick. The Bone Chapel. 2013. (Scariest Places on Earth Ser.). (ENG., Illus.). 24p. (J). (gr. 3-7). lib. bdg. 25.95 *(978-1-60014-946-7(4)*, Torque Bks.) Bellwether Media.

Hanson, Anders. Archaeologist's Tools, 1 vol. 2011. (Professional Tools Ser.). (ENG., Illus.). 24p. (J). (gr. 3-5). lib. bdg. 25.65 *(978-1-61613-577-5(8)*, Super SandCastle) ABDO Publishing Co.

Harrison, Micah. Perimeters of Ancient Buildings: Recognize Perimeter. 2014. (Rosen Common Core Math Readers Ser.). (ENG.). 24p. (J). (gr. 3-4). pap. 8.25 *(978-1-4777-4888-6(1)*, Rosen Classroom) Rosen Publishing Group, Inc., The.

Hibbert, Adam. World Wonders. 2010. (Unpredictable Nature Ser.). 48p. (J). (gr. 3-18). lib. bdg. 19.95 *(978-1-4222-2008-5(7))* Mason Crest.

Huey, Lois Miner. American Archaeology Uncovers the Earliest English Colonies. 2009. (American Archaeology Ser.). 64p. (gr. 5-6). 31.36 *(978-0-7614-4264-6(2))* Marshall Cavendish Corp.

—American Archeology Uncovers the Dutch Colonies. 2009. (American Archaeology Ser.). 64p. (gr. 5-6). 31.36 *(978-0-7614-4263-9(4))* Marshall Cavendish Corp.

Huey, Lois Miner. Children of the Past: Archaeology & the Lives of Kids. 2017. (Nonfiction — Grades 4-8 Ser.). (ENG.). 56p. (J). (gr. 4-8). 16.99 ***(978-1-5124-3878-9(2))***; 47.99 ***(978-1-5124-2843-8(4))***; 47.99 ***(978-1-5124-3879-6(0))***; (Illus.). 31.99 *(978-1-5124-1316-8(X))* Lerner Publishing Group. (Millbrook Pr.).

Hunter, Nick. Ancient Treasures, 1 vol. 2013. (Treasure Hunters Ser.). (ENG., Illus.). 48p. (gr. 5-8). pap. 9.25 *(978-1-4109-4957-8(5))*; lib. bdg. 29.99 *(978-1-4109-4950-9(8))* Heinemann-Raintree.

Kerrigan, Juliet. Underwater Treasure. 2016. (ENG.). 32p. (J). (gr. 2-3). pap. 8.95 *(978-0-00-816384-6(7))* HarperCollins Pubs. Ltd. GBR. Dist: Independent Pubs. Group.

LaFevers, R. L. Theodosia & the Staff of Osiris. Tanaka, Yoko, illus. 2009. (ENG.). 400p. (J). (gr. 2-5). pap. 7.99 *(978-0-547-24819-6(9))* Houghton Mifflin Harcourt Publishing Co.

Lange, Sarah, et al, eds. Contextualising Grave Inventories in the Ancient near East: Proceedings of a Workshop at the London 7th ICAANE in April 2010 & an International Symposium in Tubingen in November 2010, Both Organised by the Tubingen Post-Graduate School 'Symbols of the Dead' 2014. (Qatna-Studien. Supplementa Ser.: 3). (ENG., Illus.). 312p. (C). 125.00 *(978-3-447-10237-7(3))* Harrassowitz DEU. Dist: ISD.

Malam, John. Gladiator's Grave. 2011. (History Detectives Ser.). (ENG.). 32p. (J). (gr. 4-7). spiral bd. 9.95 *(978-1-84898-188-1(0)*, TickTock Books) Octopus Publishing Group GBR. Dist: Independent Pubs. Group.

—Settlements: Discover Stone, Bronze & Iron Age Britain. 2016. (Prehistoric Adventures Ser.). (ENG., Illus.). 32p. (J). (gr. 2-4). 17.99 *(978-0-7502-9592-5(9)*, Wayland) Hachette Children's Group GBR. Dist: Hachette Bk. Group.

Malam, John. Stone Circles: Discover Stone, Bronze & Iron Age Britain. 2017. (Prehistoric Adventures Ser.). (ENG., Illus.). 32p. (J). (gr. 4-6). pap. 12.99 ***(978-1-5263-0159-8(8)***, Wayland) Hachette Children's Group GBR. Dist: Hachette Bk. Group.

Manis, Shirley & Manis, Shirley. In a Scoop of Dirt: How Digging a Pond Changed North America's Prehistory. l.t. ed. 2011. (ENG., Illus.). 38p. pap. 17.95 *(978-0-9839286-0-7(6))* Manis, Shirley.

Millard, Anne. A Street Through Time. Noon, Steve, illus. 2012. (ENG.). 48p. (J). (gr. 5-12). 17.99 *(978-0-7566-9792-1(1)*, DK Children) Dorling Kindersley Publishing, Inc.

Mitchell, Mark. Raising la Belle. Mitchell, Mark, illus. (Professor Wigglestix & the Weather Ser.). (Illus.). 112p. 10.95 *(978-1-57168-703-6(3))* Eakin Pr.

Moore, Shannon Baker. King Tut's Tomb, 1 vol. 2014. (Digging up the Past Ser.). (ENG.). 112p. (J). (gr. 6-12). lib. bdg. 35.64 *(978-1-62403-233-2(8)*, Essential Library) ABDO Publishing Co.

Newton, Afton Lisette. The Mystery of the Sabotaged Dig. 2004. 100p. (J). per. 4.99 *(978-0-9762326-0-5(X))* ACTNew Bks.

Niver, Heather Moore. Archaeology: Excavating Our Past. 2014. (Study of Science Ser.). 160p. (YA). (gr. 7-12). 35.25 *(978-1-62275-403-8(4))* Rosen Publishing Group, Inc., The.

O'Shei, Tim, et al. Archaeological Mysteries, 1 vol. 2014. (Archaeological Mysteries Ser.). (ENG.). 32p. (gr. 3-4). pap. 31.80 *(978-1-4765-9933-5(5)*, Edge Bks.) Capstone Press of Coughlan Cos.

Owen, Ruth. Paleontologists & Archaeologists. 2013. (Out of the Lab: Extreme Jobs in Science Ser.). 32p. (J). (gr. 3-6). 25.25 *(978-1-4777-1290-0(9))*; pap. 60.00 *(978-1-4777-1387-7(5))*; pap. 10.00 *(978-1-4777-1380-8(8))* Rosen Publishing Group, Inc., The. (PowerKids Pr.).

Rau, Dana Meachen. Pyramid. 2007. (J). pap. 6.99 *(978-0-7614-3302-6(3))* Marshall Cavendish Corp.

Rubalcaba, Jill & Robertshaw, Peter. Every Bone Tells a Story: Hominin Discoveries, Deductions, & Debates. 2010. (ENG., Illus.). 192p. (J). (gr. 5-8). 18.95 *(978-1-58089-164-6(0))* Charlesbridge Publishing, Inc.

Shea, Therese. Crypts & Tombs. 2014. (Digging up the Dead Ser.). 32p. (J). (gr. 4-6). pap. 63.00 *(978-1-4824-1225-3(X))* Stevens, Gareth Publishing LLLP.

Shone, Rob. Ancient Treasures. Spender, Nick, illus. 2008. (Graphic Nonfiction Ser.). (ENG.). 48p. (gr. 3-8). pap. 14.05 *(978-1-4042-9593-3(3))*; (YA). (gr. 5-9). lib. bdg. 31.95 *(978-1-4042-1089-9(X))* Rosen Publishing Group, Inc., The.

Soriano, Joan & Malizia, Diana. A Visual History of Archaeological Discoveries Around the World. 2016. (Visual History of the World Ser.). 00096p. (J). (gr. 8-8). 37.10 *(978-1-4994-6576-1(9))* Rosen Publishing Group, Inc., The.

Spence, Kelly & Burns, Kylie. Be an Artifact Detective. 2017. (Be a Document Detective Ser.). (ENG., Illus.). 24p. (J). ***(978-0-7787-3039-2(5))*** Crabtree Publishing Co.

Steele, Kathryn. Stones & Bones: Archaeology in Action. 2013. (Discovery Education: Ancient Civilizations Ser.). (ENG., Illus.). 32p. (J). (gr. 3-6). pap. 10.00 *(978-1-4777-0091-4(9))*; lib. bdg. 25.25 *(978-1-4777-0053-2(6))* Rosen Publishing Group, Inc., The. (PowerKids Pr.).

Thomas, William David & Nations, Susan. Archaeologist. 2009. (Cool Careers: on the Go Ser.). 32p. (gr. 5-8). pap. 10.50 *(978-1-4339-0164-5(1))*; (YA). lib. bdg. 26.00 *(978-1-4339-0000-6(9))* Stevens, Gareth Publishing LLLP.

Thompson, Gare. Civil War Battleship: The Monitor. Day, Larry, illus. 2003. (Penguin Young Readers, Level 4 Ser.). (ENG.). 48p. (J). (gr. 3-4). mass mkt. 3.99 *(978-0-448-43245-8(5)*, Penguin Young Readers) Penguin Young Readers Group.

ticktock Media, Ltd. The Ultimate Guide to Dinosaurs. 2009. (ENG.). 128p. (J). (gr. 4-7). pap. 12.95 *(978-1-84696-988-1(3)*, TickTock Books) Octopus Publishing Group GBR. Dist: Independent Pubs. Group.

Walker, Kathryn. Mysteries of the Ancients. 2009. (Unsolved! Ser.). (ENG., Illus.). 32p. (J). (gr. 3-5). pap. *(978-0-7787-4160-2(5))*; (gr. 4-6). lib. bdg. *(978-0-7787-4147-3(8))* Crabtree Publishing Co.

Weaver, Anne H. Children of Time: Evolution & the Human Story. Celeskey, Matt, illus. 2012. (ENG.). 192p. (J). 19.95 *(978-0-8263-4442-7(9))* Univ. of New Mexico Pr.

Weil, Ann. The World's Most Amazing Lost Cities, 1 vol. 2011. (Landmark Top Tens Ser.). (ENG.). 32p. (gr. 3-5). pap. 8.29 *(978-1-4109-4250-0(3))*; 30.65 *(978-1-4109-4239-5(2))* Heinemann-Raintree. (Raintree Perspectives).

Weitzman, Elizabeth. Mysteries of Stonehenge. 2017. (Ancient Mysteries Ser.). (ENG.). 32p. (J). (gr. 3-6). 27.99 *(978-1-5124-4016-4(7))* Lerner Publishing Group.

Wilcox, Charlotte. Mummies, Bones & Body Parts. 2003. (Photo Bks.). (Illus.). 64p. (J). (gr. 3-6). 7.95 *(978-1-57505-486-5(8))* Lerner Publishing Group.

Winter, James de. Discovering Lost Cities & Pirate Gold, 1 vol. 2010. (Extreme Adventures! Ser.). (ENG.). 32p. (gr. 3-4). lib. bdg. 27.32 *(978-1-4296-4566-9(0)*, Fact Finders) Capstone Press of Coughlan Cos.

Wolny, Philip. Investigating Atlantis & Other Lost Cities, 1 vol. 2015. (ENG.). 48p. (J). 25.85 *(978-1-62275-857-9(9)*, Britannica Educational Publishing) Rosen Publishing Group, Inc., The.

Woods, Michael & Woods, Mary B. Ancient Construction Technology: From Pyramids to Fortresses. 2011. (Technology in Ancient Cultures Ser.). (ENG., Illus.). 96p. (J). (gr. 6-12). lib. bdg. 31.93 *(978-0-7613-6527-3(3))* Lerner Publishing Group.

Woolf, Alex. The Impact of Technology in History & Archaeology. 2015. (Impact of Technology Ser.). (ENG., Illus.). 56p. (gr. 6-9). pap. 9.49 *(978-1-4846-2642-9(7))* Heinemann-Raintree.

ARCHAEOLOGY, BIBLICAL

see Bible—Antiquities

ARCHAEOLOGY, CLASSICAL

see Classical Antiquities

ARCHAEOLOGY—FICTION

Abbott, Tony. Wade & the Scorpion's Claw. 2014. (Copernicus Archives Ser.: 1). (ENG.). 224p. (J). (gr. 3-7). pap. 3.99 *(978-0-06-231472-7(6)*, Tegen, Katherine Bks) HarperCollins Pubs.

Collins, Terry & Schulz, Barbara. Escape from Pompeii: An Isabel Soto Archaeology Adventure, 1 vol. 2010. (Graphic Expeditions Ser.). (ENG., Illus.). 32p. (gr. 3-4). pap. 8.10 *(978-1-4296-5634-4(4)*, Graphic Library) Capstone Press of Coughlan Cos.

Collins, Terry, et al. Escape from Pompeii: An Isabel Soto Archaeology Adventure, 1 vol. 2010. (Graphic Expeditions Ser.). (ENG., Illus.). 32p. (gr. 3-4). lib. bdg. 30.65 *(978-1-4296-4771-7(X)*, Graphic Library) Capstone Press of Coughlan Cos.

Gardner, Graham. The Santa Beacon. LeBlanc, Nancy, illus. 2012. 40p. (J). 19.95 *(978-0-9859358-0-1(4),* Belle Isle Bks.) Brandylane Pubs., Inc.

Gordon, Roderick. Closer, 12 vols. (Tunnels Ser.: 4). (J). 121.75 *(978-1-4498-2159-3(6));* 1.25 *(978-1-4498-2165-4(0));* 296.75 *(978-1-4498-2158-6(8));* 2011. 134.75 *(978-1-4498-2161-6(8));* 2011. 132.75 *(978-1-4498-2163-0(4))* Recorded Bks., Inc.

—Deeper, 15 vols. 2009. (J). 134.75 *(978-1-4361-3721-8(7));* 128.75 *(978-1-4361-3717-1(9));* 132.75 *(978-1-4361-3723-2(3));* 126.75 *(978-1-4361-3719-5(5));* 301.75 *(978-1-4361-3718-8(7));* 1.25 *(978-1-4361-3714-0(4))* Recorded Bks., Inc.

—Spiral, 9 vols. 2012. (Tunnels Ser.: 5). (J). 296.75 *(978-1-4618-4515-7(7));* 132.75 *(978-1-4618-4519-5(X));* 134.75 *(978-1-4618-4517-1(3));* 121.75 *(978-1-4618-4516-4(5))* Recorded Bks., Inc.

Gordon, Roderick & Williams, Brian. The Tunnels. 2009. (Tunnels Ser.: 1). (ENG.). 496p. (J). (gr. 3-7). pap. 8.99 *(978-0-545-07881-8(4),* Scholastic Paperbacks) Scholastic, Inc.

Gordon, Roderick & Williams, Brian James. Terminal. 2013. (J). *(978-0-545-47963-9(0))* Scholastic, Inc.

Hapka, Catherine, pseud & Rey, H. A. Curious George's Dinosaur Discovery. Hines, Anna Grossnickle, illus. 2006. (Curious George Ser.). (ENG.). 24p. (J). (gr. -1-3). pap. 4.99 *(978-0-618-66377-4(0))* Houghton Mifflin Harcourt Publishing Co.

Herr, Melody & Darnell, Regna. Edward Sapir: Linguist, Anthropologist, Humanist. 2010. (ENG., Illus.). 520p. pap. 35.00 *(978-0-8032-2437-7(0))* Univ. of Nebraska Pr.

Hobbs, Will & Hobbs, William. Wild Man Island. 2003. (ENG.). 192p. (J). (gr. 5-18). pap. 5.99 *(978-0-380-73310-1(2))* HarperCollins Pubs.

Hoeye, Michael. The Sands of Time. 2007. (ENG.). 288p. (J). (gr. 3-7). pap. 8.99 *(978-0-14-240963-1(9),* Puffin Books) Penguin Young Readers Group.

—The Sands of Time: A Hermux Tantamoq AdventureTM. 2004. 288p. (J). (gr. 5-9). pap. 40.00 incl. audio *(978-1-4000-9016-7(4),* Listening Library) Random Hse. Audio Publishing Group.

Johnson, Maureen. Girl at Sea. 2008. (ENG., Illus.). 336p. (YA). (gr. 8-12). pap. 8.99 *(978-0-06-054146-0(6),* HarperTeen) HarperCollins Pubs.

Jones, Allan Frewin. Legend of the Anaconda King. 2006. 186p. (J). pap. *(978-0-439-85670-6(1))* Scholastic, Inc.

Koops, Sheena. Voice of the Valley, 1 vol. 2006. (ENG.). 224p. (YA). (gr. 8-12). per. 8.95 *(978-1-55143-514-5(4))* Orca Bk. Pubs. USA.

Levine, Anna. Jodie's Hanukkah Dig. Topaz, Ksenia, illus. 2008. (Hanukkah Ser.). (ENG.). 32p. (J). (gr. k-3). 17.95 *(978-0-8225-7391-3(1));* pap. 7.95 *(978-0-8225-7402-6(0))* Lerner Publishing Group. (Kar-Ben Publishing).

—Jodie's Shabbat Surprise. Topaz, Ksenia, illus. 2015. (J). (gr. k-3). (ENG.). 32p. lib. bdg. 17.95 *(978-1-4677-3465-3(9));* 6.99 *(978-1-4677-6204-5(0))* Lerner Publishing Group. (Kar-Ben Publishing).

Mahle, Melissa & Dennis, Kathryn. Lost in Petra. 2012. (Anatolia Steppe Mysteries: 1). (ENG., Illus.). 246p. (J). pap. 10.99 *(978-0-9852273-0-2(3))* SpyGirls Pr.

Marsh, Carole. The Mystery of the Ancient Pyramid: Cairo, Egypt. 2006. (Around the World in 80 Mysteries Ser.). (Illus.). 128p. (J). lib. bdg. 18.99 *(978-0-635-07006-7(5),* Marsh, Carole Mysteries) Gallopade International.

McMurchy-Barber, Gina. Reading the Bones. 2008. (Peggy Henderson Adventure Ser.: 1). (ENG.). 152p. (J). (gr. 6). pap. 11.99 *(978-1-55002-732-7(8),* Sandcastle Bks.) Dundurn CAN. Dist: Ingram Publisher Services.

Messner, Kate. Hide & Seek. 2013. (ENG., Illus.). 256p. (J). (gr. 3-7). 16.99 *(978-0-545-41975-8(1),* Scholastic Pr.) Scholastic, Inc.

Moore, Elizabeth & Couvillon, Alice. Ancient Mounds of Watson Brake: Oldest Earthworks in North America, 1 vol. Anderson, Rick, illus. 2010. (ENG.). 32p. (J). (gr. k-3). 16.99 *(978-1-58980-656-6(5))* Pelican Publishing Co., Inc.

Mull, Brandon. Keys to the Demon Prison. 2010. (Fablehaven Ser.: 5). (ENG., Illus.). 600p. (J). (gr. 3). 21.99 *(978-1-60641-238-1(8),* Shadow Mountain) Shadow Mountain Publishing.

O'Neill, Katrina. Key of the Mayan Kingdom. 2007. (Illus.). 52p. (J). pap. *(978-1-4207-0717-5(5))* Sundance/Newbridge Educational Publishing.

—Protecting the Sunken City. 2007. (Illus.). 52p. (J). pap. *(978-1-4207-0724-3(8))* Sundance/Newbridge Educational Publishing.

—The Red Rain of Easter Island. 2007. (Illus.). 52p. (J). pap. *(978-1-4207-0723-6(X))* Sundance/Newbridge Educational Publishing.

O'Neill, Katrina & Thompson, Lisa. Hunting down the Grail. 2007. (Illus.). 52p. (J). pap. *(978-1-4207-0722-9(1))* Sundance/Newbridge Educational Publishing.

—Missing among the Pyramids. 2007. (Illus.). 56p. (J). pap. *(978-1-4207-0720-5(5))* Sundance/Newbridge Educational Publishing.

Pennypacker, Sara & Brown, Jeff. The Great Egyptian Grave Robbery. Pamintuan, Macky, illus. 2009. (Flat Stanley's Worldwide Adventures Ser.: 2). (ENG.). 96p. (J). (gr. 2-5). pap. 4.99 *(978-0-06-142992-7(9))* HarperCollins Pubs.

—The Great Egyptian Grave Robbery No. 2. Pamintuan, Macky, illus. 2009. (Flat Stanley's Worldwide Adventures Ser.: 2). (ENG.). 96p. (J). (gr. 2-5). 15.99 *(978-0-06-142993-4(7))* HarperCollins Pubs.

Peterson, Will. The Gathering. 2010. (Triskellion Ser.: 3). (ENG., Illus.). 384p. (YA). (gr. 9-18). 16.99 *(978-0-7636-4847-3(7))* Candlewick Pr.

Pike, Christopher, pseud. The Sacred Veil. 2013. (Thirst Ser.: 5). (ENG., Illus.). 512p. (YA). (gr. 7). pap. 12.99 *(978-1-4424-6731-6(2),* Simon Pulse) Simon Pulse.

Poulsen, David A. No Time Like the Past. 3rd rev. ed. 2007. (Salt & Pepper Chronicles). (ENG., Illus.). 160p. (J). (gr. 4-7). 6.95 *(978-1-55263-807-1(3))* Leaf Storm Pr.

Roberts, Ken. Thumb & the Bad Guys, 1 vol. Franson, Leanne, illus. 2011. (ENG.). 120p. (J). (gr. 1-5). pap. 7.95 *(978-0-88899-917-7(8))* Groundwood Bks. CAN. Dist: Publishers Group West (PGW).

—Thumb & the Bad Guys. 2013. 104p. pap. *(978-1-4596-6491-3(4))* ReadHowYouWant.com, Ltd.

Rollins, James. Jake Ransom & the Howling Sphinx. (Jake Ransom Ser.: 2). (ENG.). 384p. (J). (gr. 5). 2012. pap. 7.99 *(978-0-06-147384-5(7))* 2011. 16.99 *(978-0-06-147382-1(0))* HarperCollins Pubs.

—Jake Ransom & the Skull King's Shadow. 2010. (Jake Ransom Ser.: 1). (ENG.). 432p. (J). (gr. 5). pap. 7.99 *(978-0-06-147381-4(2))* HarperCollins Pubs.

Roy, Pat & Roy, Sandy. Jonathan Park: a New Beginning. 2013. (Jonathan Park Adventure Fiction Ser.: Vol. 2). (ENG.). 145p. (J). (gr. 4-7). pap. 10.00 *(978-1-937460-60-0(6))* Vision Forum, Inc., The.

Russell, Elaine. Martin Mcmillan & the Lost Inca City. Cornell du Houx, Emily M. D., illus. 2005. 128p. (gr. 5-18). pap. 10.00 *(978-1-882190-86-7(6))* Polar Bear & Co.

Service, Pamela F. Alien Expedition. Gorman, Mike, illus. 2009. (Alien Agent Ser.: 3). (ENG.). 160p. (J). (gr. 4-6). 16.95 *(978-0-8225-8870-2(6),* Carolrhoda Bks.) Lerner Publishing Group.

Simonds, Kevin. The Tomb of Father Time. 2011. 178p. pap. 24.95 *(978-1-4626-2739-4(0))* America Star Bks.

Thompson, Lisa. Quest for El Dorado. 2007. (Illus.). 48p. (J). pap. *(978-1-4207-0721-2(3))* Sundance/Newbridge Educational Publishing.

—Search for the Lost Cavern. 2007. (Illus.). 56p. (J). pap. *(978-1-4207-0718-2(3))* Sundance/Newbridge Educational Publishing.

—The Wreck of the Atocha. 2007. (Illus.). 52p. (J). pap. *(978-1-4207-0719-9(1))* Sundance/Newbridge Educational Publishing.

Trout, Richard. Eclipse of the Jaguar, 1 vol. 2011. (ENG., Illus.). 224p. (YA). (gr. 8-12). 16.99 *(978-1-58980-872-0(X))* Pelican Publishing Co., Inc.

ARCHAEOLOGY—HISTORY

Barber, Nicola. Lost Cities. 1 vol. 2013. (Treasure Hunters Ser.). (ENG., Illus.). 48p. (gr. 5-8). pap. 9.25 *(978-1-4109-4959-2(1));* lib. bdg. 29.99 *(978-1-4109-4952-3(4))* Heinemann-Raintree.

Linde, Barbara M. & Benchmark Education Co. Staff. Mysteries Set in Stone. 2014. (Text Connections Ser.). (J). (gr. 6). *(978-1-4900-1531-6(0))* Benchmark Education Co.

Morrison, Yvonne. Carved in Stone: Clues about Cultures. 2008. (Illus.). 36p. (J). pap. *(978-0-531-15462-5(9))* Children's Pr., Ltd.

Parker, S. M. The Rattled Bones. 2017. (ENG., Illus.). 384p. (YA). (gr. 9). 17.99 ***(978-1-4814-8204-2(1),*** Simon Pulse) Simon Pulse.

ARCHAEOLOGY—VOCATIONAL GUIDANCE

Bedell, J. M. So, You Want to Work with the Ancient & Recent Dead? Unearthing Careers from Paleontology to Forensic Science. 2015. (Be What You Want Ser.). (ENG., Illus.). 256p. (J). (gr. 3-7). pap. 11.99 *(978-1-58270-545-3(3))* Aladdin/Beyond Words.

ARCHEOLOGY

see Archaeology

ARCHERY

DiLorenzo, Michael A. Bows, Does & Bucks! An Introduction to Archery Deer Hunting. Julich, Jenniffer, illus. 2010. 88p. (J). 19.95 *(978-0-9777210-2-3(7))* Running Moose Publications.

Klein, Adam G. Archery, 1 vol. 2008. (Outdoor Adventure! Ser.). (ENG.). 32p. (gr. k-6). 27.07 *(978-1-59928-955-7(5),* Checkerboard Library) ABDO Publishing Co.

Rowe, Ruth & Anderson, Alan. Simple Maintenance for Archery: Easy Things You Can Do to Maintain Your Equipment, 1. 2003. (Illus.). 96p. spiral bd. 11.99 *(978-0-9715298-1-6(7))* Quintessential Corp.

ARCHIMEDES

Bendick, Jeanne. Archimedes & the Door of Science: Immortals of Science. 2011. 154p. (gr. 5-8). 41.95 *(978-1-258-01488-9(2))* Literary Licensing, LLC.

Boothroyd, Jennifer. What Floats? What Sinks? 2010. pap. 45.32 *(978-0-7613-6933-2(3))* Lerner Publishing Group.

—What Floats? What Sinks? A Look at Density. 2010. (Lightning Bolt Books (tm) — Exploring Physical Science Ser.). (ENG., Illus.). 32p. (gr. k-2). lib. bdg. 26.60 *(978-0-7613-5433-8(6))* Lerner Publishing Group.

Famighetti, Robert, et al. Why Do Ships Float? 2009. (Science in the Real World Ser.). (Illus.). 32p. (gr. 4-6). 28.00 *(978-1-60413-466-7(6),* Chelsea Clubhouse) Facts On File, Inc.

Gow, Mary. Archimedes: Genius Mathematician. 2015. (Genius Scientists & Their Genius Ideas Ser.). 96p. (J). (gr. 5-12). 27.94 *(978-0-7660-6530-7(8));* pap. 10.95 *(978-0-7660-6531-4(6))* Enslow Pubs., Inc.

—Archimedes: Mathematical Genius of the Ancient World. 2005. (Great Minds of Science Ser.). (Illus.). 128p. (J). (gr. 4-10). lib. bdg. 27.94 *(978-0-7660-2502-8(0))* Enslow Pubs., Inc.

Hasan, Heather. Archimedes: The Father of Mathematics. (Library of Greek Philosophers Ser.). 112p. 2009. (gr. 6-6). 66.50 *(978-1-60853-657-3(2),* Rosen Reference) 2005. (Illus.). (YA). (gr. 5-9). lib. bdg. 34.60 *(978-1-4042-0774-5(0))* Rosen Publishing Group, Inc., The.

Hightower, Paul. The Greatest Mathematician: Archimedes & His Eureka! Moment. 2009. (Great Minds of Ancient Science & Math Ser.). (Illus.). 128p. (J). (gr. 4-7). lib. bdg. 33.27 *(978-0-7660-3408-2(9))* Enslow Pubs., Inc.

Jones, Viola & Hasan, Heather. Archimedes: Innovative Mathematician, Engineer, & Inventor. 2015. (Greatest Greek Philosophers Ser.). (ENG., Illus.). 112p. (J). (gr. 7-8). 35.60 *(978-1-4994-6124-4(0),* Rosen Young Adult) Rosen Publishing Group, Inc., The.

Keating, Susan. Archimedes: Ancient Greek Mathematician. 2013. (People of Importance Ser.: 21). (Illus.). 32p. (J). (gr. 4-18). 19.95 *(978-1-4222-2841-8(X))* Mason Crest.

Keating, Susan K. Archimedes: Ancient Greek Mathematician. 2004. (Great Names Ser.). (Illus.). 32p. (J). (gr. 3-18). lib. bdg. 19.95 *(978-1-59084-152-5(2))* Mason Crest.

Zannos, Susan. The Life & Times of Archimedes. 2004. (Biography from Ancient Civilizations Ser.). (Illus.). 48p. (J). (gr. 4-8). lib. bdg. 29.95 *(978-1-58415-242-2(7))* Mitchell Lane Pubs., Inc.

ARCHITECTS

Bell, Samantha. Architect. 2015. (21st Century Skills Library: Cool STEAM Careers Ser.). (ENG., Illus.). 32p. (J). (gr. 4-7). 29.93 *(978-1-63362-554-9(0),* 206400) Cherry Lake Publishing.

Bennett, Doraine. Frank Lloyd Wright: Little World Biographies. 2013. (ENG.). 24p. (gr. k-3). pap. 8.95 *(978-1-61810-290-4(7))* Rourke Educational Media.

Bodden, Valerie & Gehry, Frank O. Frank Gehry. 2008. (Xtraordinary Artists Ser.). 48p. (J). (gr. 4-7). lib. bdg. 22.95 *(978-1-58341-662-4(5),* Creative Education) Creative Co., The.

Chandler, Alton. A Salute to African American Architects: Learning Activities. Chapman, Loring F., ed. Still, Wayne A., illus. 24p. (Orig.). (J). (gr. 3-8). pap. 1.75 *(978-1-877804-16-8(9))* Chandler/White Publishing Co.

Cohn, Jessica. Architect. 2009. (Cool Careers: Cutting Edge Ser.). (ENG.). 32p. (J). (gr. 5-8). pap. 10.50 *(978-1-4339-2153-7(7));* lib. bdg. 26.00 *(978-1-4339-1954-1(0))* Stevens, Gareth Publishing LLLP.

Dacquino, V. T. I. M. Pei. 2011. (Early Connections Ser.). (J). *(978-1-61672-552-5(4))* Benchmark Education Co.

Dunlap, Julie & Olmsted, Frederick Law. Parks for the People: The Life of Frederick Law Olmsted. 2011. (ENG., Illus.). 112p. (J). (gr. 4-7). pap. 12.95 *(978-1-55591-470-7(5))* Fulcrum Publishing.

Fandel, Jennifer. Frank Lloyd Wright. (Illus.). (J). 2016. 80p. *(978-1-60818-718-8(7))* 2005. 48p. (gr. 5-9). lib. bdg. 21.95 *(978-1-58341-378-4(2))* Creative Co., The. (Creative Education).

Going, K. L. The Shape of the World: A Portrait of Frank Lloyd Wright. Stringer, Lauren, illus. 2017. (ENG.). 40p. (J). (gr. k-5). 17.99 ***(978-1-4424-7821-3(7))*** Beach Lane Bks.

Harvey, Jeanne Walker. Maya Lin: Artist-Architect of Light & Lines. Phumiruk, Dow, illus. 2017. (ENG.). 32p. (J). 17.99 *(978-1-250-11249-1(4),* 9781250112491, Holt, Henry & Co. Bks. For Young Readers) Holt, Henry & Co.

Heine, Florian. 13 Architects Children Should Know. 2014. (ENG., Illus.). 48p. (J). (gr. 3-7). 14.95 *(978-3-7913-7184-9(3))* Prestel Verlag GmbH & Co KG. DEU. Dist: Penguin Random Hse. LLC.

Hunt, Jilly & Collins UK Staff. Great Architects. 2016. (ENG.). 32p. (J). (gr. 2-3). pap. 8.95 *(978-0-00-816378-5(2))* HarperCollins Pubs. Ltd. GBR. Dist: Independent Pubs. Group.

Labrecque, Ellen & dePaola, Tomie. Who Was Frank Lloyd Wright? Copeland, Gregory & Harrison, Nancy, illus. 2015. (Who Was? Ser.). (ENG.). 112p. (J). (gr. 3-7). 5.99 *(978-0-448-48313-9(0),* Grosset & Dunlap) Penguin Young Readers Group.

Lashnits, Tom. Maya Lin. 2007. (Asian Americans of Achievement Ser.). (Illus.). 128p. (J). (gr. 7-12). lib. bdg. 35.00 *(978-0-7910-9268-2(2))* Facts On File, Inc.

Lazo, Caroline Evensen. Frank Gehry. 2005. (Biography Ser.). (Illus.). 112p. (J). (gr. 4-7). pap. 7.95 *(978-0-8225-3388-7(X))* Lerner Publishing Group.

Lewis, Anna M. Women of Steel & Stone: 22 Inspirational Architects, Engineers, & Landscape Designers. 2014. (Women of Action Ser.). (ENG., Illus.). 272p. (YA). (gr. 7). 19.95 *(978-1-61374-508-3(7))* Chicago Review Pr., Inc.

Manatt, Kathleen. Architects. 2007. (21st Century Skills Library: Cool Science Careers Ser.). (ENG.). 32p. (gr. 4-8). pap. 14.21 *(978-1-60279-078-0(7),* 200639) Cherry Lake Publishing.

Manatt, Kathleen G. Architects. 2007. (21st Century Skills Library: Cool Science Careers Ser.). (ENG., Illus.). 32p. (gr. 4-8). lib. bdg. 28.50 *(978-1-60279-052-0(3),* 200011) Cherry Lake Publishing.

Martin, Carme & Herrero, Teresa. Gaudí. 2010. (Me Llamo... Ser.). (SPA., Illus.). 63p. (J). pap. *(978-84-342-3337-9(1))* Parramon Ediciones S.A.

Mayo, Gretchen Will. Frank Lloyd Wright. 2004. (Trailblazers of the Modern World Ser.). (Illus.). 48p. (gr. 5-12). pap. 14.05 *(978-0-8368-5261-5(3));* lib. bdg. 31.00 *(978-0-8368-5101-4(3))* Stevens, Gareth Publishing LLLP. (Gareth Stevens Secondary Library).

Michelson, Richard. Twice as Good: The story of William Powell & Clearview, the only golf course designed, built, & owned by an African-American. 2012. (ENG., Illus.). 32p. (J). (gr. 1-4). 16.95 *(978-1-58536-466-4(5),* 202308) Sleeping Bear Pr.

Nardo, Don, ed. Frank Lloyd Wright. 2012. (Eye on Art Ser.). (ENG., Illus.). 128p. (J). (gr. 7-10). lib. bdg. 34.80 *(978-1-4205-0813-0(X),* Lucent Bks.) Cengage Gale.

Prestel Staff. Antoni Gaudí: Create Your Own City. 2013. (ENG., Illus.). 16p. (J). (gr. 1-4). pap. 9.95 *(978-3-7913-7148-1(7))* Prestel Verlag GmbH & Co KG. DEU. Dist: Penguin Random Hse. LLC.

Riggs, Kate & Fandel, Jennifer. Frank Lloyd Wright. 2017. (Odysseys in Artistry Ser.). (ENG., Illus.). 80p. (J). (gr. 7-11). pap. 14.99 *(978-1-62832-314-6(0),* Creative Paperbacks) Creative Co., The.

Rodriguez, Rachel Victoria. Building on Nature: The Life of Antoni Gaudí. Paschkis, Julie, illus. 2009. (ENG.). 32p. (J). (gr. k-3). 19.99 *(978-0-8050-8745-1(1),* 9780805087451, Holt, Henry & Co. Bks. For Young Readers) Holt, Henry & Co.

Rubalcaba, Jill & Pei, I.M. I. M. Pei: Architect of Time, Place, & Purpose, 0 vols. 2011. (ENG., Illus.). 128p. (J). (gr. 7-9). 23.99 *(978-0-7614-5973-6(1),* 9780761459736, Amazon Children's Publishing) Amazon Publishing.

Sheen, Barbara. Careers in Architecture & Construction. 2016. (ENG.). 80p. (J). (gr. 5-12). 38.60 *(978-1-60152-806-3(X))* ReferencePoint Pr., Inc.

Slavicek, Louise Chipley. I. M. Pei. 2009. (Asian Americans of Achievement Ser.). (Illus.). 120p. (YA). (gr. 7-12). 35.00 *(978-1-60413-567-1(0))* Facts On File, Inc.

Thorne-Thomsen, Kathleen. Frank Lloyd Wright for Kids: His Life & Ideas. 2nd ed. 2014. (For Kids Ser.). (ENG., Illus.). 144p. (J). (gr. 4). pap. 16.95 *(978-1-61374-474-1(9))* Chicago Review Pr., Inc.

What Does a Construction Worker Do? 2006. (What Does a Community Helper Do? Ser.). (Illus.). 24p. (J). (gr. -1-3). lib. bdg. 21.26 *(978-0-7660-2326-0(5),* Enslow Elementary) Enslow Pubs., Inc.

Winegarten, Debra L. Katherine Stinson: The Flying Schoolgirl. 2004. (Illus.). 133p. (gr. 4-7). 26.95 *(978-1-57168-459-2(X))* Eakin Pr.

Winter, Jeanette. The World Is Not a Rectangle: A Portrait of Architect Zaha Hadid. Winter, Jeanette, illus. 2017. (ENG., Illus.). 56p. (J). (gr. k-5). 17.99 ***(978-1-4814-4669-3(X),*** Beach Lane Bks.) Beach Lane Bks.

Yomtov, Nel. Transportation Planner. 2013. (21st Century Skills Library: Cool STEM Careers Ser.). (ENG.). 32p. (J). (gr. 4-8). 28.50 *(978-1-62431-008-9(7),* 202483); pap. 14.21 *(978-1-62431-032-4(X),* 202485) Cherry Lake Publishing.

Zaunders, Bo. The Great Bridge-Building Contest. Munro, Roxie, illus. 2006. 30p. (J). (gr. 4-8). reprint ed. 17.00 *(978-1-4223-5239-7(0))* DIANE Publishing Co.

ARCHITECTS—FICTION

Eldarova, Sofia. Builder Mouse. 2016. (ENG., Illus.). 32p. (J). (gr. -1-3). 16.99 *(978-0-544-35766-2(3),* Clarion Bks.) Houghton Mifflin Harcourt Trade & Reference Pubs.

Skinner, Tina. Christopher Wren Avian Architect, 1 vol. LouLou, illus. 2008. (ENG.). 32p. (J). 15.99 *(978-0-7643-3169-5(8),* 9780764331695) Schiffer Publishing, Ltd.

Viva, Frank. Young Frank, Architect. 2013. (ENG., Illus.). 40p. (gr. -1-2). 16.95 *(978-0-87070-893-0(7))* Abrams, Inc.

Woodruff, Elvira. Fearless. 2011. (ENG.). 240p. (J). (gr. 3-7). pap. 6.99 *(978-0-439-67704-2(1),* Scholastic Pr.) Scholastic, Inc.

ARCHITECTURAL DRAWING

Ames, Lee J. Draw 50 Buildings & Other Structures. 2013. (Draw 50 Ser.). (Illus.). (J). lib. bdg. 20.85 *(978-0-606-26511-9(2),* Turtleback) Turtleback Bks.

Chronicle Books Staff. Draw Bridge: A Draw-Your-Own Adventure. Walsh, Sarah, illus. 2017. (ENG.). 96p. (J). (gr. 1-17). pap. 14.99 ***(978-1-4521-6097-9(X))*** Chronicle Bks. LLC.

Masters, Nancy Robinson. How Did They Build That? Water Park. 2011. (Community Connections: How Did They Build That? Ser.). (ENG.). 24p. (gr. 2-5). lib. bdg. 25.64 *(978-1-60279-983-7(0),* 200956) Cherry Lake Publishing.

ARCHITECTURAL ENGINEERING

see Building

ARCHITECTURAL PERSPECTIVE

see Perspective

ARCHITECTURE

see also Building; Castles; Cathedrals; Church Architecture; Monuments; Palaces; Skyscrapers; Synagogues; Temples; Theaters

also headings beginning with the word Architectural

Anderson, Rane. On the Job: Contractors: Perimeter & Area (Grade 3) 2017. (Mathematics Readers Ser.). (Illus.). 32p. (J). (gr. 3-3). pap. 8.99 ***(978-1-4807-5811-7(6))*** Teacher Created Materials, Inc.

Arbogast, Joan Marie. Buildings in Disguise: Architecture That Looks Like Animals, Food, & Other Things. 2010. (ENG.). 48p. (J). (gr. 2-4). pap. 12.95 *(978-1-59078-824-0(9),* Calkins Creek) Boyds Mills Pr.

Armstrong, Simon. Cool Architecture: 50 Fantastic Facts for Kids of All Ages. 2015. (ENG., Illus.). 112p. (J). (gr. 5). 14.99 *(978-1-909396-79-1(6),* Pavilion) Pavilion Bks. GBR. Dist: Independent Pubs. Group.

Art & Architecture. 2010. (Experimenting with Everyday Science Ser.). (Illus.). 176p. (J). (gr. 6-12). 35.00 *(978-1-60413-168-0(3),* Chelsea Hse.) Facts On File, Inc.

Banting, Erinn. Empire State Building. 2013. (J). *(978-1-62127-462-9(4));* pap. *(978-1-62127-468-1(3))* Weigl Pubs., Inc.

Beasant, Pam. How to Draw Buildings. Tatchell, Judy, ed. Ashman, Iain, illus. 2006. (Young Artist Ser.). 32p. (J). (gr. 4-7). pap. 5.99 *(978-0-7945-1371-9(9),* Usborne) EDC Publishing.

Beaty, Andrea. Iggy Peck's Big Project Book for Amazing Architects. Roberts, David, illus. 2017. (ENG.). 96p. (J). (gr. k-2). pap. 14.99 ***(978-1-4197-1892-2(4),*** Abrams Bks. for Young Readers) Abrams, Inc.

Beck, Barbara. The Future Architect's Handbook, 1 vol. 2014. (ENG., Illus.). 48p. (J). (gr. 8-12). 16.99 *(978-0-7643-4676-7(8),* 9780764346767) Schiffer Publishing, Ltd.

—The Future Architect's Tool Kit, 1 vol. 2016. (ENG.). 48p. (J). 29.99 *(978-0-7643-5193-8(1),* 9780764351938) Schiffer Publishing, Ltd.

Bigger, Better, Bolder! Individual Title Six-Packs. (Bookweb Ser.). 32p. (gr. 6-18). 34.00 *(978-0-7578-0910-1(3))* Rigby Education.

Bullard, Lisa. The Gateway Arch. 2009. (Lightning Bolt Books (tm) — Famous Places Ser.). (ENG.). 32p. (gr. k-2). 26.60 *(978-0-8225-9406-2(4),* Lerner Pubns.) Lerner Publishing Group.

Byers, Ann. Jobs As Green Builders & Planners. 2010. (Green Careers Ser.). (Illus.). 80p. (YA). (gr. 7-12). lib. bdg. 33.25 *(978-1-4358-3566-5(2))* Rosen Publishing Group, Inc., The.

Campbell, Ellen Langas. Raising the Roof, 3 bks., No. 2. 2005. (Girls Know How Ser.: No. 2 - Construction). (ENG., Illus.). 128p. (J). pap. 4.95 *(978-0-9743604-1-6(4),* GIRLS KNOW HOW) NouSoma Communications, Inc.

Campodonica, Carol A. How to Build a California Mission: Santa Barbara, 20 vols. Wardup, Shirley et al, eds. Sousa, Jay, photos by. Date not set. (How to Build a California Mission Ser.). (Illus.). (J). (gr. 4-5). pap. *(978-0-9648488-3-2(X))* Buzzard Pr. International.

—How to Build a California Mission: Santa Cruz, 20 vols. Weber, Francis J. et al, eds. Anderson, Bill, illus. Anderson, Jay, photos by. Date not set. (How to Build a California Mission Ser.). (J). (gr. 4-5). pap. *(978-0-9648488-5-6(6))* Buzzard Pr. International.

Chanko, Pamela. Totally Wacky Roadside Attractions. 2017. (Rookie Amazing America(tm) Ser.). (ENG., Illus.). 32p. (J). pap. 5.95 *(978-0-531-22592-9(5),* Children's Pr.) Scholastic Library Publishing.

Clements, Gillian. Indus Valley City. 2009. (Building History Ser.). (Illus.). 32p. (J). (gr. 3-5). lib. bdg. 27.10 *(978-1-59771-144-9(6))* Sea-To-Sea Pubns.

Coleman, Miriam. Earth-Friendly Buildings. 2011. (How to Be Earth Friendly Ser.). (Illus.). 32p. (J). pap. 10.00 *(978-1-4488-2765-7(5),* PowerKids Pr.); (YA). (gr. 3-6). lib. bdg. 25.25 *(978-1-4488-2588-2(1))* Rosen Publishing Group, Inc., The.

Community Connections: How Did They Build That?, 12 vols., Set. Incl. How Did They Build That? Airport. Mullins, Matt. 2009. lib. bdg. 25.64 *(978-1-60279-486-3(3),* 200253); How Did They Build That? Bridge. Franchino, Vicky. 2009. lib. bdg. 25.64 *(978-1-60279-483-2(9),* 200254); How Did They Build That? Dam. Mullins, Matt. 2009. lib. bdg. 25.64

(978-1-60279-488-7(X), 200255); How Did They Build That? House. Masters, Nancy Robinson. 2011. lib. bdg. 25.64 (978-1-60279-982-0(2), 200954); How Did They Build That? Lighthouse. Orr, Tamra B. 2011. lib. bdg. 25.64 (978-1-61080-114-0(8), 201122); How Did They Build That? Road. Nittinger, Sharon. 2009. lib. bdg. 25.64 (978-1-60279-482-5(0), 200256); How Did They Build That? School. Mullins, Matt. 2009. lib. bdg. 25.64 (978-1-60279-487-0(1), 200257); How Did They Build That? Skyscraper. Franchino, Vicky. 2009. lib. bdg. 25.64 (978-1-60279-485-6(5), 200258); How Did They Build That? Stadium. Mullins, Matt. 2009. lib. bdg. 25.64 (978-1-60279-489-4(8), 200259); How Did They Build That? Tunnel. Franchino, Vicky. 2009. lib. bdg. 25.64 (978-1-60279-484-9(7), 200260); How Did They Build That? Water Park. Masters, Nancy Robinson. 2011. lib. bdg. 25.64 (978-1-60279-983-7(0), 200956); How Did They Build That? Zoo. Orr, Tamra. 2011. lib. bdg. 25.64 (978-1-61080-113-3(X), 201120); 24p. (gr. 2-5). 2011. Set lib. bdg. 307.68 (978-1-61080-151-5(2)) Cherry Lake Publishing.

Construction TCG. 3rd rev. ed. 2004. 56p. pap. (978-0-86657-512-6(X)) Lab-Volt Systems, Inc.

Cooper, Jason. Man Made Wonders, Set. (Illus.). (J). (gr. k-4). lib. bdg. (978-0-86592-626-4(3)) Rourke Enterprises, Inc.

Cormand, Bernat. Barcelona, Tell Us about Gaudí. Kliczkowski, H., ed. Rifa, Fina, illus. 80p. (978-84-89439-29-0(X)) A. Asppan, S.L. Distribuidora Internacional de Libros y Revistas.

Crabtree, Marc. Meet My Neighbor, the Builder. 2009. (Meet my Neighbor Ser.). (ENG., Illus.). 24p. (J). (gr. k-2). pap. (978-0-7787-4580-8(5)) Crabtree Publishing Co.

Croy, Anita. Solving the Mysteries of Machu Picchu. 2008. (Digging into History Ser.). 32p. (gr. 4-18). lib. bdg. 29.93 (978-0-7614-3103-9(9), Benchmark Bks.) Marshall Cavendish Corp.

Crum, Anna-Maria. Math to Build on & Matemáticas para Construir: 6 English, 6 Spanish Adaptations. 2011. (ENG & SPA.). (J). 97.00 net. (978-1-4108-5696-8(8)) Benchmark Education Co.

da Vignola, Giacomo Barozzi. Canon of the Five Orders of Architecture. Leeke, John, tr. from ITA. 2012. (Dover Architecture Ser.). (ENG., Illus.). 108p. pap. 12.95 (978-0-486-47262-1(0)) Dover Pubns., Inc.

Dacquino, V. T. I. M. Pei. 2011. (Early Connections Ser.). (J). (978-1-61672-552-5(4)) Benchmark Education Co.

Delafosse, Claude & Valat, Pierre-Marie. Let's Look at Building Sites by Night. Valat, Pierre-Marie, illus. 2007. (ENG., Illus.). 38p. (J). (gr. k-3). pap. 11.99 (978-1-85103-368-3(8)) Moonlight Publishing, Ltd. GBR. Dist: Independent Pubs. Group.

Delafosse, Claude, et al. Let's Look at Life below the City. 2012. (ENG., Illus.). 38p. (J). (gr. k-3). pap. 11.99 (978-1-85103-313-3(0)) Moonlight Publishing, Ltd. GBR. Dist: Independent Pubs. Group.

D'Hooghe, Alexander & MIT Center for Advanced Urbanism Staff. Infrastructure Monument. 2016. (ENG., Illus.). 160p. pap. 29.95 (978-1-61689-420-7(2)) Princeton Architectural Pr.

Dillon, Patrick. The Story of Buildings: From the Pyramids to the Sydney Opera House & Beyond. Biesty, Stephen, illus. 2014. (ENG.). 96p. (J). (gr. 4-7). 19.99 (978-0-7636-6990-4(3)) Candlewick Pr.

Duffey, Gary. Windows. 2012. 16p. pap. 7.95 (978-1-4582-0512-4(6), Abbott Pr.) Author Solutions, Inc.

DuTemple, Lesley A. The Taj Mahal. 2003. (Great Building Feats Ser.). (ENG., Illus.). 96p. (gr. 5-9). 27.93 (978-0-8225-4694-8(9)) Lerner Publishing Group.

Ennett, Jonathan. Town Underground. 2016. (Cambridge Reading Adventures Ser.). (ENG.). 24p. pap. 7.19 (978-1-316-50333-1(X)) Cambridge Univ. Pr.

Enz, Tammy. Under the Lights: Exploring the Secrets of a Sports Stadium, 1 vol. 2010. (Hidden Worlds Ser.). (ENG.). 32p. (gr. 1-2). lib. bdg. 26.65 (978-1-4296-3376-5(X), Blazers) Capstone Press of Coughlan Cos.

Farrell, Courtney. Construir Casas Verdes. 2012. (SPA & ENG.). 48p. (gr. 4-8). pap. 10.95 (978-1-61810-468-7(3)) Rourke Educational Media.

Ferreira, Rute Nieto & Alessandra, Amandine. The Big Letter Hunt: London: An Architectural a-Z Around the City. 2016. (ENG., Illus.). 64p. pap. 14.95 (978-1-84994-366-6(4), Batsford) Pavilion Bks. GBR. Dist: Sterling Publishing Co., Inc.

Fisanick, Christina. Ecoarchitecture. 2008. (Opposing Viewpoints Ser.). (ENG., Illus.). 234p. (YA). (gr. 5-18). 29.45 (978-0-7377-3997-8(5), LML02109-239961); pap. 42.95 (978-0-7377-3996-1(7), LML02109-239953) Cengage Gale. (Greenhaven Pr., Inc.).

Flood Williams, Colleen Madonna. Mexican Art & Architecture. 2009. (Mexico: Beautiful Land, Diverse People Ser.). (Illus.). 64p. (YA). (gr. 7-12). 21.95 (978-1-4222-0656-0(4)) Mason Crest.

Foran, Jill. Buildings. 2004. (American Symbols Ser.). (Illus.). 24p. (J). (gr. 4-7). per. 8.95 (978-1-59036-175-7(X)); (gr. 1-3). lib. bdg. 24.45 (978-1-59036-132-0(6)) Weigl Pubs., Inc.

Friend, Robyn C. & Cohen, Judith Love. A Clean City: The Green Construction Story. 2008. (Illus.). 44p. (J). pap. 7.00 (978-1-880599-84-6(8)) Cascade Pass, Inc.

Friend, Robyn C. & cohen, Judith Love. A Clean City: The Green Construction Story. 2008. (Illus.). 44p. (J). 13.95 (978-1-880599-85-3(6)) Cascade Pass, Inc.

Garbe, Suzanne. Secrets of Machu Picchu: Lost City of the Incas, 1 vol. 2014. (Archaeological Mysteries Ser.). (ENG.). 32p. (gr. 3-4). lib. bdg. 27.99 (978-1-4765-9919-9(X)) Capstone Press of Coughlan Cos.

Gibson, Brylee. Wonders of the World Megastructures. 2007. (Connectors Ser.). (gr. 2-5). pap. (978-1-877453-20-5(X)) Global Education Systems Ltd.

Goldsworthy, Kaite. St. Paul's Cathedral. 2014. (J). (978-1-4896-1154-3(1)) Weigl Pubs., Inc.

Gonzales, Doreen. Seven Wonders of the Modern World: A MyReportLinks. com Book. 2005. (Seven Wonders of the World Ser.). (Illus.). 48p. (J). lib. bdg. 25.26 (978-0-7660-5292-5(3), MyReportLinks.com Bks.) Enslow Pubs., Inc.

—What Are the 7 Wonders of the Modern World? 2013. (What Are the Seven Wonders of the World? Ser.). 48p. (J). (gr. 4-10). pap. 8.95 (978-1-4644-0231-9(0)); 25.27 (978-0-7660-4152-3(2)) Enslow Pubs., Inc.

Gordon, Sherri Mabry & Library. Green & Clean Energy: What You Can Do. 2010. (Green Issues in Focus Ser.). (Illus.). 128p. (J). (gr. 7-12). lib. bdg. 33.27 (978-0-7660-3348-1(1)) Enslow Pubs., Inc.

Graham, Ian. Amazing Stadiums. 2010. (Superstructures Ser.). 32p. (YA). (gr. 4-7). lib. bdg. 28.50 (978-1-60753-131-9(3)) Amicus Publishing.

—Amazing Stadiums. 2012. (What's in My Food Ser.). 32p. (gr. 1-4). lib. bdg. 27.10 (978-1-59920-418-5(5)) Black Rabbit Bks.

—Great Building Designs 1900-Today. 2015. (Iconic Designs Ser.). (ENG., Illus.). 48p. (gr. 4-6). 33.32 (978-1-4846-2619-1(2)) Heinemann-Raintree.

—Megastructures: Tallest, Longest, Biggest, Deepest. 2012. (ENG., Illus.). 128p. (J). (gr. 2-4). 19.95 (978-1-77085-111-5(9), 9781770851115) Firefly Bks., Ltd.

Guillain, Charlotte. Es Rígido o Se Dobla, 1 vol. 2010. (Las Propiedades de Los Materiales Ser.). (SPA., Illus.). 24p. (gr. -1-1). pap. 6.29 (978-1-4329-4252-6(2), Bellota) Heinemann-Raintree.

—Es Rigido O Se Dobla. 2010. (Las Propiedades de Los Materiales Ser.).Tr. of Stiff or Bendable. (SPA., Illus.). 24p. (gr. -1-1). 22.65 (978-1-4329-4244-1(1), Bellota) Heinemann-Raintree.

Gunderson, Jessica. Gothic Art. 2008. (Movements in Art Ser.). 48p. (YA). (gr. 5-9). 22.95 (978-1-58341-610-5(2)) Creative Co., The.

—Gothic Art: Movements in Art. 2015. (Illus.). 80p. (J). (978-1-60818-532-0(X), Creative Education) Creative Co., The.

Gurney, Stella & Tailfeather, Speck Lee. Architecture According to Pigeons. 2013. (ENG.). 64p. 19.95 (978-0-7148-6389-4(0)); (Illus.). 19.95 (978-0-7148-6353-5(X)) Phaidon Pr., Inc.

Hamilton, Robert. Encyclopedia of Amazing Places: Discover Famous Wonders of the World. 2012. (Illus.). 224p. (J). (978-1-4351-4347-0(7)) Barnes & Noble, Inc.

Hanson, Anders & Mann, Elissa. Cool Structures: Creative Activities That Make Math & Science Fun for Kids!, 1 vol. 2013. (Cool Art with Math & Science Ser.). (ENG.). 32p. (J). (gr. 3-6). lib. bdg. 28.50 (978-1-61783-825-5(X), Checkerboard Library) ABDO Publishing Co.

Harrison, Micah. Perimeters of Ancient Buildings: Recognize Perimeter. 2014. (Rosen Common Core Math Readers Ser.). (ENG.). 24p. (J). (gr. 3-4). pap. 8.25 (978-1-4777-4888-6(1), Rosen Classroom) Rosen Publishing Group, Inc., The.

Heine, Florian. 13 Architects Children Should Know. 2014. (ENG., Illus.). 48p. (J). (gr. 3-7). 14.95 (978-3-7913-7184-9(3)) Prestel Verlag GmbH & Co KG. DEU. Dist: Penguin Random Hse. LLC.

Hibbert, Adam. World Wonders. 2010. (Unpredictable Nature Ser.). 48p. (J). (gr. 3-18). lib. bdg. 19.95 (978-1-4222-2008-5(7)) Mason Crest.

Hill, Isabel T. Urban Animals, 1 vol. Hill, Isabel T., photos by. 2009. (ENG., Illus.). 32p. (J). (gr. 2-7). 17.95 (978-1-59572-209-6(2)); pap. 7.95 (978-1-59572-210-2(6)) Star Bright Bks., Inc.

Hilliam, David. Castles & Cathedrals. 2004. (Library of the Middle Ages Ser.). (Illus.). 64p. (YA). (gr. 5-9). lib. bdg. 31.95 (978-0-8239-3990-9(1)) Rosen Publishing Group, Inc., The.

—Castles & Cathedrals: The Great Buildings of Medieval Times. 2009. (Library of the Middle Ages Ser.). 64p. (gr. 5-8). 58.50 (978-1-60853-896-6(6), Rosen Reference) Rosen Publishing Group, Inc., The.

Hobeika, Noelia, tr. The Illustrated Atlas of Architecture & Marvelous Monuments. Verhille, Alexandre & Tavernier, Sarah, illus. 2016. (ENG.). 48p. (J). (gr. 3-7). 27.95 (978-3-89955-775-6(1)) Die Gestalten Verlag DEU. Dist: Penguin Random Hse. LLC.

Hollihan-Elliot, Sheila. Art & Architecture of China. Wang, Jianwei, ed. 2012. (China: the Emerging Superpower Ser.). 120p. (J). (gr. 7). 24.95 (978-1-4222-2155-6(5)) Mason Crest.

—Chinese Art & Architecture. 2011. (J). pap. (978-1-4222-2166-2(0)) Mason Crest.

Howse, Jennifer. The Great Synagogue of Budapest. 2014. (Illus.). 24p. (J). (978-1-4896-2611-0(5)) Weigl Pubs., Inc.

—Palace of Versailles. 2015. (J). (978-1-4896-3400-9(2)) Weigl Pubs., Inc.

Isaacson, Philip M. Round Buildings, Square Buildings, & Buildings That Wiggle Like a Fish. 2016. (ENG., Illus.). 128p. (YA). (gr. 7). pap. 15.99 (978-1-101-93320-6(8), Ember) Random Hse. Children's Bks.

Kaner, Etta. Earth-Friendly Buildings, Bridges & More: The Eco-Journal of Corry Lapont. MacEachern, Stephen, illus. 2012. (ENG.). 64p. (J). (gr. 3-7). 18.95 (978-1-55453-570-5(0)) Kids Can Pr., Ltd. CAN. Dist: Hachette Bk. Group.

Kaur, Ramandeep. The Bird's Nest. 2015. (How Did They Build That? Ser.). (ENG., Illus.). 32p. (gr. 3-8). 27.99 (978-1-62920-560-1(5)) Scobre Pr. Corp.

Kenney, Karen Latchana. The Lincoln Memorial, 1 vol. Hunt, Judith A., illus. 2011. (Our Nation's Pride Set 2 Ser.). (ENG.). 32p. (J). (gr. 1-4). 28.50 (978-1-61641-151-0(1)) Magic Wagon.

—The White House, 1 vol. Hunt, Judith A., illus. 2011. (Our Nation's Pride Set 2 Ser.). (ENG.). 32p. (J). (gr. 1-4). 28.50 (978-1-61641-154-1(6)) Magic Wagon.

Kenney, Sean. Cool City. Kenney, Sean, illus. 2011. (ENG., Illus.). 32p. (J). (gr. -1-3). 12.99 (978-0-8050-8762-8(1), 9780805087628, Holt, Henry & Co. Bks. For Young Readers) Holt, Henry & Co.

Kerns, Ann. Seven Wonders of Architecture. 2010. (Seven Wonders Ser.). (YA). (gr. 5-9). lib. bdg. 33.26 (978-0-7613-4236-6(2)) Twenty First Century Bks.

Kissock, Heather. Taj Mahal. 2011. (J). (978-1-61690-436-4(4)) Weigl Pubs., Inc.

Kissock, Heather, ed. Taj Mahal. 2011. (J). (gr. 4-6). pap. 12.95 (978-1-61690-769-3(X), AV2 by Weigl); (Illus.). 24p. (gr. 2-5). 27.13 (978-1-61690-765-5(7)) Weigl Pubs., Inc.

Krpan, Cathy Marks. The 10 Most Phenomenal Modern Buildings. 2008. 14.99 (978-1-55448-496-6(0)) Scholastic Library Publishing.

Die Kunst des Bauens.Tr. of Art of Building. (GER., Illus.). (YA). 31.95 (978-3-411-09101-0(0), MY9101E) Bibliographisches Institut & F. A. Brockhaus AG DEU. Dist: Continental Bk. Co., Inc.

Kuntz, Lynn. The Roman Colosseum. 2004. (Great Structures in History Ser.). (ENG., Illus.). 48p. (J). (gr. 4-7). 27.50 (978-0-7377-1561-3(8), Greenhaven Pr., Inc.) Cengage Gale.

Laidlaw, Jill. Cities. 2010. (Sustaining Our Environment Ser.). 48p. (J). lib. bdg. 35.65 (978-1-60753-135-7(6)) Amicus Publishing.

Lassieur, Allison. Building the Empire State Building: An Interactive Engineering Adventure, 1 vol. 2014. (You Choose: Engineering Marvels Ser.). (ENG.). 112p. (gr. 3-4). 31.99 (978-1-4914-0400-3(0), You Choose Bks.) Capstone Press of Coughlan Cos.

Laxton, Laura. The Budding Builder. 2012. (Budding Ser.). (ENG., Illus.). 72p. pap. 9.95 (978-0-87659-381-3(3), Gryphon House Inc) Gryphon Hse., Inc.

Leardi, Jeanette. Making Cities Green. 2009. (Going Green Ser.). (Illus.). 32p. (YA). (gr. 3-6). lib. bdg. 25.27 (978-1-59716-961-5(7)) Bearport Publishing Co., Inc.

LernerClassroom Editors. First Step Nonfiction-Community Buildings Teaching Guide. 2009. pap. 7.95 (978-0-8225-9063-7(8)) Lerner Publishing Group.

Levy, Janey. The Architecture of Frank Lloyd Wright: Understanding the Concepts of Parallel & Perpendicular. (PowerMath Ser.). 32p. 2009. (ENG., Illus.). (gr. 5-6). pap. 10.00 (978-1-4042-5144-1(8), PowerKids Pr.) 2009. (gr. 4-5). 47.90 (978-1-60851-418-2(8), PowerKids Pr.) 2005. (Illus.). (YA). (gr. 5-9). lib. bdg. 25.25 (978-1-4042-2940-2(X)) Rosen Publishing Group, Inc., The.

Look Inside [Capstone Sole Source]. 2010. (Look Inside Ser.). 24p. lib. bdg. 143.94 (978-1-4296-5869-0(X), Pebble Plus) Capstone Press of Coughlan Cos.

Luxbacher, Irene. 123 I Can Build! Luxbacher, Irene, illus. 2009. (Starting Art Ser.). (ENG., Illus.). 24p. (J). (gr. -1-2). pap. 6.95 (978-1-55453-316-9(3)) Kids Can Pr., Ltd. CAN. Dist: Hachette Bk. Group.

Mabry-Gordon, Sherri. Out of Gas: Using up Fossil Fuels. 2016. (End of Life As We Know It Ser.). (ENG.). 128p. (J). (gr. 7-8). lib. bdg. 37.27 (978-0-7660-7306-7(8)) Enslow Pubs., Inc.

Macaulay, David. Building Big. Macaulay, David, illus. 2006. (Illus.). 192p. reprint ed. 30.00 (978-1-4223-5328-8(1)) DIANE Publishing Co.

—Building Big. 2004. (ENG., Illus.). 192p. (YA). (gr. 5-18). reprint ed. pap. 15.99 (978-0-618-46527-9(8)) Houghton Mifflin Harcourt Publishing Co.

—Building Big, 5 cass.; set. 2004. (Building Big Ser.). (gr. 4-18). pap., act. bk. ed. 69.95 incl. VHS (978-1-57807-544-7(0), WG965) WGBH Boston Video.

—Built to Last. 2010. (ENG., Illus.). 272p. (J). (gr. 5-7). 24.99 (978-0-547-34240-5(3)) Houghton Mifflin Harcourt Publishing Co.

—Cathedral: The Story of Its Construction. rev. ed. 2013. (ENG., Illus.). 80p. (J). (gr. 5-7). 19.99 (978-0-544-10000-8(X)) Houghton Mifflin Harcourt Publishing Co.

Mann, Elizabeth. Empire State Building: When New York Reached for the Skies. Witschonke, Alan, illus. Hine, Lewis, photos by. (Wonders of the World Book Ser.). (ENG.). 48p. (J). (gr. 4-8). 2006. pap. 12.95 (978-1-931414-08-1(4), 9781931414081) 2003. 19.95 (978-1-931414-06-7(8), 9781931414067) Mikaya Pr.

Manning, Jack. Pueblos, 1 vol. 2014. (American Indian Homes Ser.). (ENG.). 24p. (gr. 1-2). lib. bdg. 25.32 (978-1-4914-0315-0(2)) Capstone Press of Coughlan Cos.

Mason, Adrienne. Build It! Structures, Systems & You. Dávila, Claudia, illus. 2006. (Primary Physical Science Ser.). (ENG.). 32p. (J). (gr. -1-2). 7.95 (978-1-55337-836-5(9)) Kids Can Pr., Ltd. CAN. Dist: Hachette Bk. Group.

Mattern, Joanne. Built to Last. 2011. (ENG., Illus.). 48p. (gr. 4-6). pap. 10.95 (978-1-61741-989-8(3)) Rourke Educational Media.

Matthews, Sheelagh. The Sydney Opera House. 2008. (Structural Wonders Ser.). (Illus.). 32p. (J). (gr. 4-6). pap. 9.95 (978-1-59036-937-1(8)); lib. bdg. 26.00 (978-1-59036-936-4(X)) Weigl Pubs., Inc.

Meister, Cari. Totally Amazing Facts about Stuff We've Built. 2017. (Mind Benders Ser.). (ENG.). 112p. (gr. 1-3). lib. bdg. 23.32 (978-1-5157-4753-6(0)) Capstone Press of Coughlan Cos.

Monsman, Stacy. Engineering Marvels: Stand-Out Skyscrapers: Area (Grade 3) 2017. (Mathematics Readers Ser.). (Illus.). 32p. (gr. 3-3). pap. 8.99 **(978-1-4807-5810-0(8))** Teacher Created Materials, Inc.

Mooney, Carla. Stadiums & Coliseums. 2015. (ENG.). 48p. (gr. 3-6). 35.64 (978-1-63430-417-7(9)) Rourke Educational Media.

Moskal, Greg. Modern Buildings: Identifying Bilateral & Rotational Symmetry & Transformations. (PowerMath Ser.). 32p. 2009. (Illus.). (gr. 4-5). pap. 10.00 (978-0-8239-8902-7(X)) 2009. (gr. 4-5). 47.90 (978-1-60851-397-0(1)) 2004. (Illus.). (J). lib. bdg. 25.25 (978-0-8239-8989-8(5)) Rosen Publishing Group, Inc., The. (PowerKids Pr.).

Nanji, Shenaaz. Notre Dame. 2014. (J). (978-1-4896-1146-8(0)) Weigl Pubs., Inc.

Nardo, Don. Ancient Roman Art & Architecture. 2011. (Eye on Art Ser.). (ENG.). 128p. (gr. 7-10). lib. bdg. 39.40 (978-1-4205-0714-0(1), Lucent Bks.) Cengage Gale.

—Architecture. 2007. (Eye on Art Ser.). (ENG., Illus.). 112p. (J). (gr. 3-7). lib. bdg. 34.80 (978-1-4205-0003-5(1), Lucent Bks.) Cengage Gale.

Nardo, Don, ed. Medieval European Art & Architecture. 2012. (Eye on Art Ser.). (Illus.). 128p. (J). (gr. 7-10). lib. bdg. 34.80 (978-1-4205-0715-7(X), Lucent Bks.) Cengage Gale.

Nelson, Robin. Del Cemento Al Puente (From Cement to Bridge) 2006. (De Principio a Fin (Start to Finish) Ser.). (Illus.). 24p. (J). (gr. 4-7). per. 5.95 (978-0-8225-6630-4(3), Ediciones Lerner) Lerner Publishing Group.

Owen, Ruth. Building Green Places: Careers in Planning, Designing, & Building. 2009. (Green-Collar Careers Ser.). (ENG., Illus.). 64p. (J). (gr. 5-8). pap. (978-0-7787-4863-2(4)); lib. bdg. (978-0-7787-4852-6(9)) Crabtree Publishing Co.

Pascal, Janet & dePaola, Tomie. Where Is the Empire State Building? Groff, David, illus. 2015. (Where Is? Ser.). (ENG.). 112p. (J). (gr. 3-7). 5.99 (978-0-448-48426-6(9), Grosset & Dunlap) Penguin Young Readers Group.

Pease, Pamela. Design Dossier. 2011. (Design Dossiers Ser.). (ENG., Illus.). 96p. (J). (gr. 4-7). 24.00 (978-0-9777905-4-8(1)); 24.00 (978-0-9777905-3-1(3)) Paintbox Pr.

Pettiford, Rebecca. Stadiums. 2015. (Illus.). 24p. (J). lib. bdg. 25.65 (978-1-62031-214-8(X)) Jump! Inc.

Phillips, Cynthia & Priwer, Shana. Ancient Monuments. 2009. (ENG., Illus.). 115p. (C). (gr. 6-18). lib. bdg. 158.00 (978-0-7656-8123-2(4), Y181320) Routledge.

—Bridges & Spans, 5 bks., Set. Incl. Ancient Monuments. 115p. lib. bdg. 158.00 (978-0-7656-8123-2(4), Y181320); 112p. lib. bdg. 158.00 (978-0-7656-8120-1(X), Y181468); Dams & Waterways. 112p. lib. bdg. 158.00 (978-0-7656-8122-5(6), Y181910); Modern Wonders. 112p. lib. bdg. 158.00 (978-0-7656-8124-9(2), Y182653); Skyscrapers & High Rises. 115p. lib. bdg. 158.00 (978-0-7656-8121-8(8), Y183566); (C). (gr. 6-18). (ENG., Illus.). 112p. 2009. Set lib. bdg. 158.00 (978-0-7656-8119-5(6), Y182339) Routledge.

—Modern Wonders. 2009. (ENG., Illus.). 112p. (C). (gr. 6-18). lib. bdg. 158.00 (978-0-7656-8124-9(2), Y182653) Routledge.

Potter, Tony, prod. Plantation Home Model. 2005. 3p. (J). pap. 19.95 (978-1-58980-274-2(8)) Pelican Publishing Co., Inc.

Reeves, Diane Lindsey. Architecture & Construction. 2017. (Bright Futures Press: World of Work Ser.). (ENG., Illus.). 32p. (J). (gr. 4-7). lib. bdg. 29.93 (978-1-63472-623-8(5), 209526) Cherry Lake Publishing.

Richards, Jon & Simkins, Ed. Record-Breaking Building Feats. 2015. (Infographic Top 10s Ser.). (ENG.). 32p. (J). (gr. 4-6). 26.65 (978-1-4677-8594-5(6)) Lerner Publishing Group.

Richardson, Gillian. Machu Picchu. 2008. (J). 9.95 (978-1-59036-943-2(2)); (Illus.). 32p. (gr. 4-6). lib. bdg. 26.00 (978-1-59036-942-5(4)) Weigl Pubs., Inc.

Richardson, Gillian & Kissock, Heather. Machu Picchu. 2012. (J). 27.13 (978-1-61913-250-4(8)); pap. 12.95 (978-1-61913-256-6(7)) Weigl Pubs., Inc.

Rose, Simon. Sheikh Zayed Al Nahyan Grand Mosque. 2014. (Illus.). 24p. (J). (978-1-4896-2612-7(3)) Weigl Pubs., Inc.

Rosen, Michael J. & Kassoy, Ben. Crazy Buildings. 2013. 32p. pap. 26.60 (978-1-4677-1705-2(3)) Lerner Publishing Group.

—Crazy Buildings. Jones, Doug, illus. 2013. (No Way! Ser.). (ENG.). 32p. (gr. 3-5). lib. bdg. 26.60 (978-0-7613-8986-6(5), Millbrook Pr.) Lerner Publishing Group.

Ruffin, Frances E. The Gateway Arch. 2006. (Places in American History Ser.). (Illus.). 24p. (gr. 1-4). pap. 8.15 (978-0-8368-6416-8(6)); lib. bdg. 22.00 (978-0-8368-6409-0(3)) Stevens, Gareth Publishing LLLP. (Weekly Reader Leveled Readers).

Rustad, Martha. Can We Ring the Liberty Bell? Poling, Kyle, illus. 2014. (Cloverleaf Books — Our American Symbols Ser.). 24p. (J). (gr. k-2). lib. bdg. 23.93 (978-1-4677-2137-0(9), Millbrook Pr.) Lerner Publishing Group.

Sheen, Barbara. Careers in Architecture & Construction. 2016. (ENG.). 80p. (J). (gr. 5-12). 38.60 (978-1-60152-806-3(X)) ReferencePoint Pr., Inc.

Silate, Jennifer. The Liberty Bell. 2009. (Primary Sources of American Symbols Ser.). 24p. (gr. 3-3). 42.50 (978-1-60851-509-7(5), PowerKids Pr.) Rosen Publishing Group, Inc., The.

Simonds, Lucy. The Sky Is the Limit. 2007. (Trackers-Math Ser.). (gr. 2-5). pap. 5.00 (978-1-59055-922-2(3)) Pacific Learning, Inc.

Sims, Lesley. El Gran Libro de Los Castillos - Internet Linked. Groebner, Dominic, illus. 2004. (Titles in Spanish Ser.). (SPA.). 104p. (J). pap. 14.95 (978-0-7460-5089-7(5), Usborne) EDC Publishing.

Sirvaitis, Karen. Seven Wonders of Green Building Technology. 2010. (Seven Wonders Ser.). 80p. (J). (gr. 5-9). lib. bdg. 33.26 (978-0-7613-4242-7(7)) Twenty First Century Bks.

Slade, Suzanne. The House That George Built. Bond, Rebecca, illus. 2012. (ENG.). 32p. (J). (gr. 1-4). 16.95 (978-1-58089-262-9(0)) Charlesbridge Publishing, Inc.

Smith, A. G. Cut & Assemble an Early American Seaport, Vol. 181. 2017. (ENG.). 48p. (J). (gr. 2-8). pap. 12.95 (978-0-486-24754-0(6)) Dover Pubns., Inc.

Thomas, Mark. Discoverer Enterprise: La Plataforma de Perforacion Mas Grande Del Mundo. 2004. (Estructuras extraordinarias (Record-Breaking Structures) Ser.). (SPA & ENG., Illus.). 24p. (J). (gr. 1-4). lib. bdg. 22.60 (978-0-8239-6864-0(2)) Rosen Publishing Group, Inc., The.

—Maracana: El Estadio de Futbol Mas Grande del Mundo. 2004. (Estructuras extraordinarias (Record-Breaking Structures) Ser.). (SPA & ENG., Illus.). 24p. (J). (gr. 3-6). lib. bdg. 22.60 (978-0-8239-6863-3(4), Editorial Buenas Letras) Rosen Publishing Group, Inc., The.

—La Represa de Itaipu: La Represa Mas Grande Del Mundo. 2004. (Estructuras extraordinarias (Record-Breaking Structures) Ser.). (SPA & ENG., Illus.). 24p. (J). (gr. 3-6). lib. bdg. 22.60 (978-0-8239-6865-7(0), Editorial Buenas Letras) Rosen Publishing Group, Inc., The.

Viereckskonstruktionen. (Duden-Schuelerhilfen Ser.). (GER.). 112p. (YA). (gr. 7-8). (978-3-411-06181-5(2)) Bibliographisches Institut & F. A. Brockhaus AG DEU. Dist: International Bk. Import Service, Inc.

von Daniken, Erich. The Mysterious Master Builders of the Stone Age, 01 vols., 1. 2016. (Ancient Secrets & Alien Gods Ser.). (ENG.). 224p. (YA). 38.25 (978-1-5081-7102-7(5), Rosen Young Adult) Rosen Publishing Group, Inc., The.

Wallach, Paul Ross. Chief Architect 9.5 tutorials Workbook. 2004. 77p. spiral bd. 24.95 (978-0-9740796-4-6(2)) Technology Education Concepts Inc.

Weber, Matt. California's Missions: From A to Z. 2010. (ENG.). 60p. (J). (gr. 2-4). 12.95 (978-0-9841931-9-6(7)) 121 Pubns.

Webster, Christine. Taj Mahal. 2007. (Structural Wonders Ser.). (Illus.). 32p. (J). (gr. 4-7). lib. bdg. 26.00 (978-1-59036-729-2(4)); per. 9.95 (978-1-59036-730-8(8)) Weigl Pubs., Inc.

Weitzman, Elizabeth. Guarding the Super Bowl Stadium. 2016. (Highly Guarded Places Ser.). (ENG.). 24p. (J). (gr.

2-5). 28.50 (978-1-5038-0814-0(9), 210650) Child's World, Inc., The.

Winnick, Nick. Build Green. 2010. (Being Green Ser.). (Illus.). 32p. (YA). (gr. 3-6). lib. bdg. 27.13 (978-1-61690-088-5(1)); (J). (gr. 4-6). pap. 12.95 (978-1-61690-089-2(X)) Weigl Pubs., Inc.

Winter, Jeanette. The World Is Not a Rectangle: A Portrait of Architect Zaha Hadid. Winter, Jeanette, illus. 2017. (ENG., Illus.). 56p. (J). (gr. k-5). 17.99 **(978-1-4814-4669-3(X)**, Beach Lane Bks.) Beach Lane Bks.

Wolny, Philip. Getting a Job in the Construction Industry. 2016. (Job Basics: Getting the Job You Need Ser.). 80p. (J). (gr. 8-8). 35.75 (978-1-4777-8564-5(7)) Rosen Publishing Group, Inc., The.

Woods, Michael & Woods, Mary B. Seven Wonders of Ancient Africa. 2008. (Seven Wonders Ser.). (ENG., Illus.). 80p. (gr. 5-8). lib. bdg. 33.26 (978-0-8225-7571-9(X)) Lerner Publishing Group.

—Seven Wonders of the Ancient Middle East. 2008. (Seven Wonders Ser.). (ENG., Illus.). 80p. (gr. 5-8). lib. bdg. 33.26 (978-0-8225-7573-3(6)) Lerner Publishing Group.

Woolf, Alex, et al. Design & Engineering for STEM. 2013. (Design & Engineering for STEM Ser.). (ENG.). 56p. (gr. 6-8). lib. bdg. 103.95 (978-1-4329-7033-8(X)) Heinemann-Raintree.

World Book, Inc Staff, contrib. by. Architecture & Engineering. 2009. (J). (978-0-7166-0386-3(1)) World Bk., Inc.

—Green Buildings. 2008. (J). (978-0-7166-1404-3(9)) World Bk., Inc.

Yancey, Diane. Ancient Greek Art & Architecture. Nardo, Don, ed. 2011. (Eye on Art Ser.). (ENG., Illus.). 128p. (J). (gr. 7-10). lib. bdg. 39.40 (978-1-4205-0685-3(4), Lucent Bks.) Cengage Gale.

Yomtov, Nel. From Termite Den to Office Building. 2014. (21st Century Skills Innovation Library: Innovations from Nature Ser.). (ENG., Illus.). 32p. (J). (gr. 4-8). 28.50 (978-1-62431-755-2(3), 203288) Cherry Lake Publishing.

Zeiger, Jennifer. Restoring Structures. 2015. (Explorer Library: Science Explorer Ser.). (ENG., Illus.). 32p. (J). (gr. 4-8). lib. bdg. 29.93 (978-1-63362-388-0(2), 206972) Cherry Lake Publishing.

ARCHITECTURE, DOMESTIC

see also Apartment Houses; Houses

Bailey, Gerry. Adventure Homes. Dreidemy, Joëlle et al, illus. 2013. (ENG.). 32p. (J). (978-0-7787-0287-0(1)); pap. (978-0-7787-0291-7(X)) Crabtree Publishing Co.

—Storybook Homes. Radford, Karen & Dreidemy, Joëlle, illus. 2013. (ENG.). 32p. (J). (978-0-7787-0288-7(X)); pap. (978-0-7787-0298-6(7)) Crabtree Publishing Co.

—Working Homes. Dreidemy, Joëlle et al, illus. 2013. (ENG.). 32p. (J). (978-0-7787-0290-0(1)) Crabtree Publishing Co.

Barber, Nicola. City Homes. 2007. (Homes Around the World Ser.). (ENG., Illus.). 32p. (J). (gr. 3-7). pap. (978-0-7787-3554-0(0)) Crabtree Publishing Co.

Bass, Hester Thompson & Thompson-Bass, Hester. So Many Houses. Arzoumanian, Alik, illus. 2006. (Rookie Reader Skill Set Ser.). (ENG.). 32p. (J). (gr. k-2). pap. 4.95 (978-0-516-24999-5(1)) Scholastic Library Publishing.

Beco, Alice. Cool Careers Without College for People Who Love Houses & Apartments. 2017. (Cool Careers Without College Ser.). 112p. (gr. 12-12). 38.45 **(978-1-5081-7538-4(1)**, Rosen Young Adult) Rosen Publishing Group, Inc., The.

Bode, Achim, et al. Where We Live. 2005. (GER., Illus.). 27p. (J). (gr. 4-8). reprint ed. pap. 17.00 (978-0-7567-9381-4(5)) DIANE Publishing Co.

Bowden, Rob. Building Homes for Tomorrow. 2010. (Development Without Damage Ser.). (YA). (gr. 5-9). 34.25 (978-1-59920-252-5(2)) Black Rabbit Bks.

Bullard, Lisa. My Home, Your Home. 2015. (Cloverleaf Books (tm) — Alike & Different Ser.). (ENG., Illus.). 24p. (J). (gr. k-2). lib. bdg. 23.99 (978-1-4677-4904-6(4), Millbrook Pr.) Lerner Publishing Group.

Champion, Neil. Making Shelter. 2010. (Survive Alive Ser.). 32p. (YA). (gr. 3-6). 28.50 (978-1-60753-041-1(4)) Amicus Publishing.

Champion, Neil & Ganeri, Anita. Making Shelter. 2011. (How the World Makes Music Ser.). 32p. (gr. 4-7). lib. bdg. 31.35 (978-1-59920-477-2(0)) Black Rabbit Bks.

Cornille, Didier. Who Built That? Modern Houses: An Introduction to Modern Houses & Their Architects. 2014. (Who Built That? Ser.). (ENG., Illus.). 84p. (J). (gr. 2-7). 16.95 (978-1-61689-263-0(3)) Princeton Architectural Pr.

Deneux, Xavier. Homes. 2016. (ENG., Illus.). 16p. (J). (gr. -1 — 1). bds. 14.99 (978-1-4521-4518-1(0)) Chronicle Bks. LLC.

Ghigna, Charles. Get Out. Stay Out! Thomas, Glenn, illus. 2017. (Fire Safety Ser.). (ENG.). 24p. (gr. k-2). 33.99 **(978-1-68410-029-3(1))** Cantata Learning.

—Plan & Prepare! Thomas, Glenn, illus. 2017. (Fire Safety Ser.). (ENG.). 24p. (gr. k-2). 33.99 **(978-1-68410-045-3(3))** Cantata Learning.

Glenn, Patricia Brown. Under Every Roof: A Kid's Style & Field Guide to the Architecture of American Houses. 2009. (ENG.). 112p. (J). (gr. 5-12). pap. 35.00 (978-0-470-59359-2(8), Wiley) Wiley, John & Sons, Inc.

Gregory, Helen. All about Homes, 1 vol. 2011. (Wonder Readers Early Level Ser.). (ENG.). 32p. (gr. -1-1). pap. 5.99 (978-1-4296-7794-3(5), Wonder Readers) Capstone Press of Coughlan Cos.

Guin, Valerie. Where We Live. 2005. (One World (Smart Apple Media) Ser.). (Illus.). 30p. (J). (gr. 3-6). lib. bdg. 27.10 (978-1-58340-698-4(0)) Black Rabbit Bks.

Harrison, Paul. Ancient Roman Homes. 2010. (Ancient Communities: Roman Life Ser.). 32p. (J). (ENG.). pap. 10.60 (978-1-61532-313-5(9)); (Illus.). (gr. 3-6). lib. bdg. 26.50 (978-1-61532-305-0(8)) Rosen Publishing Group, Inc., The. (PowerKids Pr.).

Hayden, Kate. Amazing Buildings. 2003. (DK Reader Level 2 Ser.). (gr. k-3). lib. bdg. 13.55 (978-0-613-62431-2(9), Turtleback) Turtleback Bks.

Hayden, Kate & Lock, Deborah. Amazing Buildings, Vol. 2. 2003. (DK Readers Ser.). (ENG., Illus.). 32p. (J). (gr. 1-3). pap. 3.99 (978-0-7894-9220-3(2), DK Children) Dorling Kindersley Publishing, Inc.

Haywood, John. Home, Family & Everyday Life Through the Ages: Compare the Food, Homes & Daily Lives of Ancient People from All the Major Civilizations. 2008. (ENG., Illus.). 64p. (J). (gr. 4-7). pap. 12.99 (978-1-84476-602-4(0)) Anness Publishing GBR. Dist: National Bk. Network.

Jovinelly, Joann. The Crafts & Culture of a Medieval Manor. 2009. (Crafts & Cultures of the Middle Ages Ser.). 48p. (gr. 5-5). 58.50 (978-1-61512-053-6(X), Rosen Reference) Rosen Publishing Group, Inc., The.

Kalman, Bobbie. This Is My Home. 2010. (My World Ser.). (ENG., Illus.). 16p. (J). (gr. k-2). (978-0-7787-9433-2(4)); pap. (978-0-7787-9477-6(6)) Crabtree Publishing Co.

—A Visual Dictionary of Victorian Life. 2010. (Crabtree Visual Dictionaries Ser.). (ENG.). 32p. (J). (gr. 1-7). lib. bdg. (978-0-7787-3507-6(9)) Crabtree Publishing Co.

Kurchinski, Catherine Celli. Hurray for the Yoder Barn! 2004. (Illus.). 23p. (J). (978-0-9761744-0-0(5)) Moon Pie Pr.

Labrecque, Ellen. Green General Contractor. 2016. (21st Century Skills Library: Cool Vocational Careers Ser.). (ENG., Illus.). 32p. (J). (gr. 4-7). 29.93 (978-1-63471-063-3(0), 208331) Cherry Lake Publishing.

Lewis, Clare. Homes Around the World, 1 vol. 2014. (Around the World Ser.). (ENG., Illus.). 24p. (gr. -1-1). 22.65 (978-1-4846-0369-7(9)); pap. 5.99 (978-1-4846-0376-5(1)) Heinemann-Raintree. (Acorn).

Lindeen, Mary. Where People Live. 2011. (Wonder Readers Fluent Level Ser.). (ENG.). 16p. (gr. -1-2). pap. 35.94 (978-1-4296-8207-7(8), Wonder Readers) Capstone Press of Coughlan Cos.

Lock, Deborah, et al. Homes Around the World. 2009. (DK Readers Ser.). (ENG.). 32p. (J). (gr. k-2). 3.99 (978-0-7566-4522-9(0), DK Children) Dorling Kindersley Publishing, Inc.

Manning, Jack. American Indian Homes, 1 vol. 2014. (American Indian Homes Ser.). (ENG.). 24p. (gr. 1-2). 101.28 (978-1-4914-0326-6(8), First Facts) Capstone Press of Coughlan Cos.

Masters, Nancy Robinson. How Did They Build That? House. 2011. (Community Connections: How Did They Build That? Ser.). (ENG.). 24p. (gr. 2-5). lib. bdg. 25.64 (978-1-60279-982-0(2), 200954) Cherry Lake Publishing.

McDowell, Tina. At Home Around the World. 2003. (Rosen Real Readers: Upper Emergent Ser.). (ENG., Illus.). 12p. (gr. 1-2). pap. 5.90 (978-0-8239-6363-8(2)) Rosen Publishing Group, Inc., The.

Nelson, Robin. Homes. 2004. (First Step Nonfiction - Basic Human Needs Ser.). (ENG., Illus.). 8p. (gr. -1-1). pap. 4.95 (978-0-8225-3930-8(6), Lerner Pubns.) Lerner Publishing Group.

Nishiyama, Akira & Komatsu, Eiko, illus. Wonderful Houses Around the World. Komatsu, Yoshio, photos by. 2004. (ENG.). 48p. (J). pap. 12.95 (978-0-936070-34-6(X)) Shelter Pubns., Inc.

Northcott, Richard. Where People Live, Level 4. 2010. (ENG., Illus.). 36p. 4.81 (978-0-19-440110-4(3)) Oxford Univ. Pr., Inc.

Onyefulu, Ifeoma. Home. 2013. (ENG., Illus.). 32p. (J). (gr. -1-k). 17.99 (978-1-84780-266-8(4), Frances Lincoln) Quarto Publishing Group UK GBR. Dist: Hachette Bk. Group.

Oxlade, Chris. Homes, 1 vol. 2012. (Science Behind Ser.). (ENG.). 32p. (gr. 3-3). pap. 8.29 (978-1-4109-4499-3(9)); lib. bdg. 30.65 (978-1-4109-4488-7(3)) Heinemann-Raintree. (Raintree Perspectives).

Rau, Dana Meachen. Igloo. 2007. (J). pap. 6.99 (978-0-7614-3299-9(X)) Marshall Cavendish Corp.

Raum, Elizabeth. The Scoop on Clothes, Homes, & Daily Life in Colonial America. 2011. (Life in the American Colonies Ser.). (ENG.). 32p. (gr. 3-4). pap. 47.70 (978-1-4296-7214-6(5), Fact Finders) Capstone Press of Coughlan Cos.

Rice, Dona Herweck. Casas Alrededor Del Mundo, 1 vol. 2nd rev. ed. 2012. (Nonfiction Readers Ser.).Tr. of Homes Around the World. (SPA., Illus.). 20p. (J). (gr. 1-1). pap. 4.99 (978-1-4333-4431-2(9)) Teacher Created Materials, Inc.

—Homes Around the World, 1 vol. 2nd rev. ed. 2011. (Nonfiction Readers Ser.). (ENG.). 20p. (J). (gr. 1-1). pap. 4.99 (978-1-4333-3598-3(0)) Teacher Created Materials, Inc.

Ring, Susan. Places We Live. 2005. (Yellow Umbrella Fluent Level Ser.). (ENG.). 16p. (gr. k-1). pap. 35.70 (978-0-7368-5316-3(2), Yellow Umbrella Bks.) Capstone Press of Coughlan Cos.

Rosa-Mendoza, Gladys. My House/Mi Casa. Borlasca, Hector, illus. 2006. (# 1 Bilingual Board Book Ser.). (ENG & SPA.). 20p. (J). (gr. -1-k). bds. 6.95 (978-1-931398-18-3(6)) Me+Mi Publishing.

Royston, Angela. Homes That Move. 2011. (Big Picture: Homes Ser.). (ENG.). 24p. (gr. 1-2). pap. 41.70 (978-1-4296-6729-6(X), First Facts) Capstone Press of Coughlan Cos.

Sargent, Brian. Life on the Edge. 2014. (ENG.). 28p. (J). pap. 9.50 (978-1-107-63028-4(2)) Cambridge Univ. Pr.

Schmauss, Judy Kentor. Just the Right Home. Harrald-Pilz, Marilee, illus. 2006. (Reader's Clubhouse Level 2 Reader Ser.). (ENG.). 24p. (J). (gr. 1-4). pap. 3.99 (978-0-7641-3299-5(7)) Barron's Educational Series, Inc.

Skinner, Tina. Log & Timber Frame Homes, 1 vol. 2003. (ENG., Illus.). 224p. (gr. 10-13). 44.95 (978-0-7643-1754-5(7), 9780764317545) Schiffer Publishing, Ltd.

Smith, Alastair, ed. Homes & Houses Then & Now. 2004. (Then & Now Flip Flaps Ser.). (SPA & ENG., Illus.). 1p. (J). (gr. 2-18). pap. 7.95 (978-0-7460-3100-1(9)) EDC Publishing.

Smith, Sian. Homes in the Past, 1 vol. 2013. (Where We Live Ser.). (ENG.). 24p. (gr. -1-1). 22.65 (978-1-4329-8068-9(8)); pap. 6.95 (978-1-4329-8073-3(4)) Heinemann-Raintree. (Acorn).

—Homes That Move, 1 vol. 2013. (Where We Live Ser.). (ENG.). 24p. (gr. -1-1). pap. 6.95 (978-1-4329-8072-6(6), Acorn) Heinemann-Raintree.

Spilsbury, Louise & Spilsbury, Richard. Houses & Homes. 2013. (Start-Up Connections Ser.). (ENG., Illus.). 32p. (J). pap. 12.99 (978-0-237-54372-3(9)) Evans Brothers, Ltd. GBR. Dist: Independent Pubs. Group.

Staniford, Linda. A Place to Live. 2015. (Wants vs Needs Ser.). (ENG., Illus.). 24p. (gr. k-2). 23.32 (978-1-4846-0942-2(5), Heinemann Read & Learn) Heinemann-Raintree.

Tate, Nikki & Tate-Stratton, Dani. Take Shelter: At Home Around the World, 1 vol. 2014. (Orca Footprints Ser.). (ENG., Illus.). 48p. (J). (gr. 3-7). 19.95 (978-1-4598-0742-6(1)) Orca Bk. Pubs. USA.

Taylor, Saranne. Green Homes. Chiacchiera, Moreno & Todd, Michelle, illus. 2014. (ENG.). 32p. (J). (978-0-7787-1452-1(7)) Crabtree Publishing Co.

Thomas, Isabel & Collins UK Staff. How to Build a House. 2016. (ENG.). 56p. (J). (gr. 4-5). pap. 9.95 (978-0-00-816394-5(4)) HarperCollins Pubs. Ltd. GBR. Dist: Independent Pubs. Group.

ARCHITECTURE, ECCLESIASTICAL

see Church Architecture

ARCHITECTURE—EGYPT

Meachen Rau, Dana. Pyramid. 2006. (Bookworms Ser.). (Illus.). 32p. (gr. k-2). lib. bdg. 15.95 (978-0-7614-2275-4(7), Benchmark Bks.) Marshall Cavendish Corp.

ARCHITECTURE—FICTION

Ansley, Frank & Wheeler, Lisa. Who's Afraid of Granny Wolf? Ansley, Frank, tr. 2004. (Fitch & Chip Ser.: 3). (ENG., Illus.). 48p. (J). (gr. 1-3). 16.99 (978-0-689-84952-7(4), Simon Spotlight) Simon Spotlight.

Armstrong, Cara. Moxie: The Dachshund of Fallingwater. 2010. (ENG.). 32p. (J). 19.95 (978-1-933979-70-0(4), 10cb4a3a-e256-4798-b1d9-ce1ed88e1459) Bright Sky Pr.

Barnett, Mac, et al. The Clock Without a Face. Teplin, Scott & Rex, Adam, illus. 2010. (ENG.). 30p. (gr. 2-18). bds. 19.95 (978-1-934781-71-5(1)) McSweeney's Publishing.

Chen, Justina. Return to Me. 2013. (ENG.). 352p. (YA). (gr. 7-17). 17.99 (978-0-316-10255-1(5)) Little Brown & Co.

Colello, Nicholas. Architecture Alphabet. 2010. 61p. pap. 10.95 (978-0-557-40226-7(3)) Lulu Pr., Inc.

Cousins, Lucy. Where Does Maisy Live? Cousins, Lucy, illus. 2010. (Maisy Ser.). (ENG., Illus.). 12p. (J). (-k). bds. 5.99 (978-0-7636-4668-4(7)) Candlewick Pr.

Daley, Michael J. Pinch & Dash & the Terrible Couch. Yezerski, Thomas F., illus. 2013. (ENG.). 48p. (J). (gr. k-3). 12.95 (978-1-58089-379-4(1)); pap. 5.95 (978-1-58089-380-0(5)) Charlesbridge Publishing, Inc.

Jenkins, Donna. When I Grow up, I Want to Be a Builder. 2010. 16p. pap. 10.49 (978-1-4490-6072-5(2)) AuthorHouse.

Kleven, Elisa. Welcome Home, Mouse. Kleven, Elisa, illus. 2010. (ENG., Illus.). 32p. (J). (gr. -1-2). 15.99 (978-1-58246-277-6(1), Tricycle Pr.) Random Hse. Children's Bks.

Konigsburg, E. L. The Second Mrs. Gioconda. 2005. (ENG.). 160p. (YA). (gr. 7). pap. 9.99 (978-1-4169-0342-0(9), Atheneum Bks. for Young Readers) Simon & Schuster Children's Publishing.

Laden, Nina. Roberto: the Insect Architect. 2016. (ENG., Illus.). 40p. (J). (gr. k-3). 7.99 (978-1-4521-5646-0(8)) Chronicle Bks. LLC.

Lecher, Doris. A New House for Charlie. 2014. (ENG., Illus.). 28p. (J). (gr. -1-k). 16.95 (978-1-62873-814-8(6), Sky Pony Pr.) Skyhorse Publishing Co., Inc.

Malone, Marianne. The Sixty-Eight Rooms. Triplett, Gina & Call, Greg, illus. 2011. (Sixty-Eight Rooms Adventures Ser.). (ENG.). 288p. (J). (gr. 3-7). pap. 6.99 (978-0-375-85711-9(7), Yearling) Random Hse. Children's Bks.

McCoy, Mimi, pseud. The Dead End. 2010. 174p. (J). (978-0-545-25838-8(3)) Scholastic, Inc.

Raghbeer, Anjali. A Jar of Sound: Bhil Art. Kundu, Kunal, illus. 2012. (Art Tales from India Ser.). (ENG.). 24p. 14.95 (978-81-8328-188-1(5)) Wisdom Tree IND. Dist: SCB Distributors.

Sharon, Callen. This Is the Tower That Frank Built, 1 vol. 2013. (Fiction Readers Ser.). (ENG., Illus.). 24p. (J). (gr. 2-2). pap. 6.99 (978-1-4333-5535-6(3)) Shell Educational Publishing.

Stine, R. L. The Curse of the Mummy's Tomb. 2009. (Goosebumps Ser.: 6). lib. bdg. 17.20 (978-0-606-00243-1(X), Turtleback) Turtleback Bks.

Valentine, Sally. The Ghost of the Charlotte Lighthouse. 2006. (J). (978-1-59531-013-2(4)) North Country Bks., Inc.

Wells, Rosemary, et al. My Havana: Memories of a Cuban Boyhood. Ferguson, Peter, illus. 2010. (ENG.). 72p. (J). (gr. 2-5). 17.99 (978-0-7636-4305-8(X)) Candlewick Pr.

ARCHITECTURE—HISTORY

Arnold, Caroline & Comora, Madeleine. Taj Mahal. Bhushan, Rahul, illus. 2007. (ENG.). 32p. (J). (gr. k-12). lib. bdg. 17.95 (978-0-7613-2609-0(X), Millbrook Pr.) Lerner Publishing Group.

Bussagli, Marco. Understanding Architecture, 2 vols. Bettinelli, Sara & Galleschi, M. Lucrezia, eds. Frost, Catherine, tr. from ITA. 2004. (ENG., Illus.). 384p. lib. bdg. 158.00 (978-0-7656-8071-6(8), 0765680718) Routledge.

Dellaccio, Tanya. The Art of Architecture. 2017. (J). **(978-1-5345-6095-6(5))** Greenhaven Publishing LLC.

Dhillon, Natasha C. The History of Western Architecture. 2015. (Britannica Guide to the Visual & Performing Arts Ser.). (ENG., Illus.). 128p. (J). (gr. 9-10). 45.00 (978-1-68048-088-7(X), Britannica Educational Publishing) Rosen Publishing Group, Inc., The.

Dhillon, Natasha C., ed. The History of Western Architecture. 2015. (Britannica Guide to the Visual & Performing Arts Ser.). (ENG.). 128p. (YA). (gr. 9-10). 90.00 (978-1-68048-089-4(8), Britannica Educational Publishing) Rosen Publishing Group, Inc., The.

DuTemple, Lesley A. The Colosseum. 2003. (Great Building Feats Ser.). (ENG., Illus.). 96p. (gr. 5-9). 27.93 (978-0-8225-4693-1(0)) Lerner Publishing Group.

Henzel, Cynthia Kennedy. Taj Mahal, 1 vol. 2011. (Troubled Treasures: World Heritage Sites Ser.). (ENG., Illus.). 32p. (J). (gr. 3-6). 27.07 (978-1-61613-568-3(9)) ABDO Publishing Co.

Hoggard, Brian. Crusader Castles: Christian Fortresses in the Middle East. (Library of the Middle Ages Ser.). 64p. (gr. 5-8). 2009. 58.50 (978-1-60853-897-3(4), Rosen Reference) 2004. (Illus.). (YA). lib. bdg. 31.95 (978-0-8239-4212-1(0)) Rosen Publishing Group, Inc., The.

Langley, Andrew. Every Building Has a History, 1 vol. 2014. (Everything Has a History Ser.). (ENG., Illus.). 64p. (gr. 7-8). pap. 10.95 (978-1-4329-9588-1(X)); lib. bdg. 35.99 (978-1-4329-9583-6(9)) Heinemann-Raintree.

Macaulay, David. City: A Story of Roman Planning & Construction. 2012. 21.00 (978-1-61383-577-7(9)) Perfection Learning Corp.

—Mosque. 2008. (ENG., Illus.). 96p. (YA). (gr. 4-7). pap. 9.95 (978-0-547-01547-7(X)) Houghton Mifflin Harcourt Publishing Co.

Paxmann, Christine. From Mud Huts to Skyscrapers. Ibelings, Anne, illus. 2012. (ENG.). 64p. (J). (gr. 3-7). 19.95 (978-3-7913-7113-9(4)) Prestel Verlag GmbH & Co KG. DEU. Dist: Penguin Random Hse. LLC.

Simply Wright: A Journey into the Ideas of Frank Lloyd Wright's Architecture. 2004. (J). spiral bd. 17.95 (978-0-9677348-3-5(5)) Castleconal Pr.

World Book, Inc. Staff, contrib. by. Adobe Shelters to Steel Skyscrapers: A Timeline of Building. 2016. (J). (978-0-7166-3540-6(2)) World Bk., Inc.

ARCHITECTURE, NAVAL

see Shipbuilding

ARCHITECTURE, RURAL

see Architecture, Domestic

ARCHITECTURE—VOCATIONAL GUIDANCE

Bell, Samantha. Architect. 2015. (21st Century Skills Library: Cool STEAM Careers Ser.). (ENG., Illus.). 32p. (J). (gr. 4-7). 29.93 (978-1-63362-554-9(0), 206400) Cherry Lake Publishing.

Cohn, Jessica. Architect. 2009. (Cool Careers: Cutting Edge Ser.). (ENG.). 32p. (J). (gr. 5-8). pap. 10.50 (978-1-4339-2153-7(7)); lib. bdg. 26.00 (978-1-4339-1954-1(0)) Stevens, Gareth Publishing LLLP.

—On the Job in Construction. Scheuer, Lauren, illus. 2016. (Core Content Social Studies — on the Job Ser.). (ENG.). 32p. (J). (gr. 2-5). lib. bdg. 26.65 (978-1-63440-109-8(3)) Red Chair Pr.

Ferguson, creator. Architecture & Building. 2007. (Careers in Focus Ser.). (Illus.). 192p. (gr. 6-12). 32.95 (978-0-8160-6569-1(1), Ferguson Publishing Co.) Facts On File, Inc.

Harmon, Daniel E. Careers in Roofing & Flooring, 01 vols., 1. 2016. (Essential Careers Ser.). (ENG.). 80p. (J). 34.25 (978-1-4994-6213-5(1), Rosen Young Adult) Rosen Publishing Group, Inc., The.

Leavitt, Amie Jane. The Vo-Tech Track to Success in Architecture & Construction. 2014. (Learning a Trade, Preparing for a Career Ser.). (Illus.). 80p. (J). (gr. 7-12). 34.25 (978-1-4777-7726-8(1)) Rosen Publishing Group, Inc., The.

Manatt, Kathleen. Architects. 2007. (21st Century Skills Library: Cool Science Careers Ser.). (ENG.). 32p. (gr. 4-8). pap. 14.21 (978-1-60279-078-0(7), 200639) Cherry Lake Publishing.

Manatt, Kathleen G. Architects. 2007. (21st Century Skills Library: Cool Science Careers Ser.). (ENG., Illus.). 32p. (gr. 4-8). lib. bdg. 28.50 (978-1-60279-052-0(3), 200011) Cherry Lake Publishing.

Niver, Heather Moore. Careers in Construction. 2013. (Essential Careers Ser.). (ENG., Illus.). 80p. (YA). (gr. 7-12). lib. bdg. 33.25 (978-1-4488-9476-5(X), Rosen Classroom) Rosen Publishing Group, Inc., The.

ARCTIC EXPEDITIONS

see Arctic Regions

ARCTIC REGIONS

see also North Pole; Northwest Passage; Scientific Expeditions

Aloian, Molly & Kalman, Bobbie. The Arctic Habitat. 2006. (Introducing Habitats Ser.). (ENG., Illus.). 32p. (J). (gr. -1-3). pap. (978-0-7787-2981-5(8)) Crabtree Publishing Co.

—El Habitat del Arctico. 2007. (Introduccion A los Habitats Ser.). (SPA & ENG., Illus.). 32p. (J). (gr. k-3). lib. bdg. (978-0-7787-8330-5(8)) Crabtree Publishing Co.

—El Habitat del Artico. rev. ed. 2007. (Introduction a Los Habitats Ser.). (SPA & ENG., Illus.). 32p. (J). (gr. k-3). pap. (978-0-7787-8354-1(5)) Crabtree Publishing Co.

Anema, Durlynn. Louise Arner Boyd: Arctic Explorer. 2004. (Women Adventurers Ser.). (Illus.). 112p. (gr. 5-18). 21.95 (978-1-883846-42-8(0)) Reynolds, Morgan Inc.

Arctic & Antarctic Habitats. 2013. (Discovery Education: Habitats Ser.). 32p. (J). (gr. 3-6). pap. 60.00 (978-1-4777-1482-9(0), PowerKids Pr.) Rosen Publishing Group, Inc., The.

Awa, Simon, et al. Uumajut Vol. 2: Learn More about Arctic Wildlife!, 1 vol., Vol. 2. Otak, Leah, tr. Caron, Romi, illus. 2011. (ENG.). 32p. (J). (gr. 1-3). pap. 9.95 (978-1-926569-22-2(9)) Inhabit Media Inc. CAN. Dist: Independent Pubs. Group.

Awa, Solomon. Igluvigaliurniq Qamusiurnirlu: How to Build an Iglu & a Qamutiik, 1 vol. Breithaupt, Andrew, illus. 2013. (ENG.). 32p. (J). (gr. 3-6). 9.95 (978-1-927095-31-7(X)) Inhabit Media Inc. CAN. Dist: Independent Pubs. Group.

Bailey, Diane. Arctic Culture: The People of the Ice. 2017. (Exploring the Polar Regions Today Ser.: Vol. 8). (ENG.). (YA). (gr. 7-12). 23.95 **(978-1-4222-3866-0(0))** Mason Crest.

Bailey, Gerry. Alone in the Arctic. 2014. (ENG., Illus.). 32p. (J). (978-0-7787-0428-7(9)) Crabtree Publishing Co.

Baker, Stuart. In the Arctic. 2009. (Climate Change Ser.). 32p. (gr. 4). 28.50 (978-0-7614-4437-4(8)) Marshall Cavendish GBR. Dist: Marshall Cavendish Corp.

Brelsfoard, Sam. Life Inside the Arctic Circle. 2005. (Illus.). 24p. (J). (978-0-328-13638-4(7), Scott Foresman) Addison-Wesley Educational Pubs., Inc.

Brooks, Sheldon. Life in the Arctic. (Life in Extreme Environments Ser.). 64p. (gr. 5-8). 2009. 53.00 (978-1-61514-270-5(3)) 2004. (Illus.). lib. bdg. 31.95 (978-0-8239-3984-8(7)) Rosen Publishing Group, Inc., The. (Rosen Reference).

Built for Cold: Arctic Animals, 6 vols., Set. Incl. Arctic Wolf: The High Arctic. DeLallo, Laura. lib. bdg. 25.27 (978-1-61772-132-8(8)); Caribou: And Reindeer, Too. Markovics, Joyce L. lib. bdg. 25.27 (978-1-61772-130-4(1)); Polar Bear: Shrinking Ice. Person, Stephen. lib. bdg. 25.27 (978-1-61772-129-8(8)); Sled Dog: Powerful Miracle. Person, Stephen. lib. bdg. 25.27 (978-1-61772-134-2(4)); Walrus: Tusk, Tusk. Person, Stephen. lib. bdg. 25.27 (978-1-61772-133-5(6)); Wolverine: Super Strong. Markovics, Joyce L. lib. bdg. 25.27 (978-1-61772-131-1(X)); (YA). (gr. 1-4). 32p. 2011. Set lib. bdg. 151.62 (978-1-61772-128-1(X)) Bearport Publishing Co., Inc.

Centore, Michael. Oil & Gas in the Arctic. 2017. (Exploring the Polar Regions Today Ser.: Vol. 8). (ENG.). (YA). (gr. 7-12). 23.95 **(978-1-4222-3869-1(5))** Mason Crest.

Chapman, Simon. At the North Pole. 2005. (Illus.). 115p. (J). lib. bdg. 20.00 (978-1-4242-0629-2(4)) Fitzgerald Bks.

Christopher, Neil. Arctic Giants, 1 vol. Widermann, Eva, illus. 2010. (ENG.). 128p. (J). (gr. 3). 24.95 (978-1-926569-09-3(1)) Inhabit Media Inc. CAN. Dist: Independent Pubs. Group.

Christopher, Nick. Arctic Wolves of the Tundra. 2017. (J). **(978-1-5345-2215-2(8)**, KidHaven Publishing) Greenhaven Publishing LLC.

Clarke, Penny. The Arctic. 2008. (Scary Creatures Ser.). (ENG., Illus.). 32p. (J). (gr. 2-4). 27.00 (978-0-531-20449-8(9), Children's Pr.) Scholastic Library Publishing.

—Scary Creatures of the Arctic. 2008. (Scary Creatures Ser.). (ENG., Illus.). 32p. (J). (gr. 2-4). pap. 8.95 (978-0-531-21008-6(1), Watts, Franklin) Scholastic Library Publishing.

Cocoretto, illus. In the Snow. 2016. (Peekaboo! Ser.: 4). (ENG.). 12p. (J). bds. (978-1-84643-865-3(9)) Child's Play International Ltd.

DeLallo, Laura. Arctic Wolf: The High Arctic. 2011. (Built for Cold Ser.). 32p. (YA). (gr. 1-4). lib. bdg. 25.27 (978-1-61772-132-8(8)); (J). (gr. 4-5). lib. bdg., E-Book 49.22 (978-1-61772-219-6(7)) Bearport Publishing Co., Inc.

Doak, Robin S. Arctic Peoples, 1 vol. 2011. (First Nations of North America Ser.). (ENG.). 48p. (gr. 3-3). pap. 9.95 (978-1-4329-4956-3(X), Heinemann InfoSearch) Heinemann-Raintree.

Dowson, Nick. North: The Amazing Story of Arctic Migration. Benson, Patrick, illus. 2013. (ENG.). 56p. (J). (gr. 2-5). 7.99 (978-0-7636-6663-7(7)) Candlewick Pr.

Dunn, Joeming W. Reaching the North Pole, 1 vol. Espinosa, Rod, illus. 2008. (Graphic History Ser.). (ENG.). 32p. 28.50 (978-1-60270-185-4(7), Graphic Planet- Nonfiction) ABDO Publishing Co.

Emily Rose Townsend. Arctic Foxes [Scholastic]. 2009. (Polar Animals Ser.). 24p. (gr. k-1). pap. 0.34 (978-1-4296-4227-9(0), Pebble Bks.) Capstone Press of Coughlan Cos.

Feldman, Thea & Steele, Philip. Arctic & Antarctic. 2013. (Kingfisher Readers Ser.). (ENG., Illus.). 32p. (J). (gr. k-3). 12.99 (978-0-7534-7092-3(6), 9780753470923); pap. 3.99 (978-0-7534-7093-0(4), 9780753470930) Roaring Brook Pr. (Kingfisher).

Flaherty, William, et al. Narwhal, 1 vol. Lim, Hwei & McLeod, Kagan, illus. 2016. (Animals Illustrated Ser.). (ENG.). 24p. (J). (gr. -1-k). 15.95 (978-1-77227-080-8(6)) Inhabit Media Inc. CAN. Dist: Independent Pubs. Group.

Flowers, Pam. Big-Enough Anna. Farnsworth, Bill, illus. 2003. (ENG.). 32p. (J). (gr. -1-18). 15.95 (978-0-88240-577-3(2)) Graphic Arts Ctr. Publishing Co.

—Big-Enough Anna. Farnsworth, Bill, tr. Farnsworth, Bill, illus. 2003. (ENG.). 32p. (J). pap. 10.99 (978-0-88240-580-3(2)) Graphic Arts Ctr. Publishing Co.

Foran, Jill. Search for the Northwest Passage. 2004. (Great Journeys Ser.). (Illus.). 32p. (J). lib. bdg. 26.00 (978-1-59036-205-1(5)) Weigl Pubs., Inc.

—The Search for the Northwest Passage. 2005. (Great Journeys Ser.). (Illus.). 32p. (J). (gr. -1-3). per. 9.95 (978-1-59036-259-4(4)) Weigl Pubs., Inc.

Franchino, Vicky. Antarctic Tundra. 2016. (Community Connections: Getting to Know Our Planet Ser.). (ENG., Illus.). 24p. (J). (gr. 2-5). 27.07 (978-1-63470-514-1(9), 207787) Cherry Lake Publishing.

—Arctic Foxes. 2013. (ENG.). 48p. (J). 28.00 (978-0-531-23354-2(5)); pap. 6.95 (978-0-531-25152-2(7)) Scholastic Library Publishing.

Gigliotti, Jim. Antarctica & the Arctic: Facts, Figures, & Stories. 2017. (Exploring the Polar Regions Today Ser.: Vol. 8). (ENG.). (YA). (gr. 7-12). 23.95 **(978-1-4222-3865-3(2))** Mason Crest.

Goldsmith, Ros. Who Lives near the North Pole? 2014. (Little Books of Answers: Level e Ser.). (Illus.). 16p. (gr. k-2). pap. 7.95 (978-1-927136-45-4(8)) Three Crows Media NZL. Dist: RiverStream Publishing.

Gonzales, Doreen. The Frigid Arctic Ocean. 2013. (Our Earth's Oceans Ser.). 48p. (J). (gr. 3-4). pap. 8.95 (978-1-4644-0148-0(9), Enslow Elementary); 25.27 (978-0-7660-4087-8(9)) Enslow Pubs., Inc.

Gustaitis, Joseph Alan. Arctic Trucker. 2010. (Benchmark Rockets: Dirty & Dangerous Jobs Ser.). 32p. (J). (gr. 3-6). 28.50 (978-1-60870-169-8(7)) Marshall Cavendish Corp.

Hainnu, Rebecca & Ziegler, Anna. A Walk on the Tundra, 1 vol. Leng, Qin, illus. 2011. (ENG.). 40p. (J). (gr. 1-3). 13.95 (978-1-926569-43-7(1)) Inhabit Media Inc. CAN. Dist: Independent Pubs. Group.

Halfmann, Janet. Narwhal: The Unicorn of the Sea. Petruccio, Steven James, illus. 2008. (ENG.). 32p. (J). (gr. -1-2). 19.95 (978-1-59249-872-7(8)) Soundprints.

—Narwhal: Unicorn of the Sea. Petruccio, Steven James, illus. 2008. (ENG.). 32p. (J). (gr. -1-2). 16.95 (978-1-59249-868-0(X)); 4.95 (978-1-59249-869-7(8)); pap. 6.95 (978-1-59249-870-3(1)); pap. 9.95 (978-1-59249-871-0(X)) Soundprints.

Harrison, Ted. A Northern Alphabet. (ABC Our Country Ser.). (ENG., Illus.). (J). 2017. 28p. (— 1). bds. 8.99 (978-1-101-91896-8(9)) 2009. 32p. (gr. 1-4). pap. 7.99 (978-0-88776-960-3(8)) Tundra Bks. CAN. (Tundra Bks.). Dist: Penguin Random Hse. LLC.

Haslam, Andrew. Arctic Peoples. 2004. (Make It Work! History Ser.). (Illus.). 64p. (J). (gr. 3-6). pap. 7.95 (978-1-58728-304-8(2), Two-Can Publishing) T&N Children's Publishing.

Hopkinson, Deborah. Keep On! The Story of Matthew Henson, Co-Discoverer of the North Pole, 1 vol. Alcorn, Stephen, illus. 2009. (ENG.). 36p. (J). (gr. 1-5). 17.95 (978-1-56145-473-0(7)) Peachtree Pubs.

Hyde, Natalie. Expedition to the Arctic. 2013. (ENG., Illus.). 48p. (J). (978-0-7787-1169-8(2)); pap. (978-0-7787-1177-3(3)) Crabtree Publishing Co.

Isaacs, Sally. Helen Thayer's Arctic Adventure: A Woman & a Dog Walk to the North Pole. Sasheva, Iva, illus. 2016. (Encounter: Narrative Nonfiction Picture Bks.). (ENG.). 32p. (gr. 4-5). lib. bdg. 28.65 (978-1-4914-8044-1(0)) Encounter Bks.

Isaacs, Sally Senzell. Helen Thayer's Arctic Adventure: A Woman & a Dog Walk to the North Pole. Sasheva, Iva, illus. 2017. (Encounter: Narrative Nonfiction Picture Bks.). (ENG.). 32p. (gr. 4-5). pap. 7.95 (978-1-4914-8045-8(9)) Capstone Press of Coughlan Cos.

Jackie, Glassman. Amazing Arctic Animals, Vol. 2. 2014. (Penguin Young Readers, L3 Ser.). (ENG.). 48p. (J). (gr. 2-12). 8.24 (978-1-63245-253-5(7)) Lectorum Pubns., Inc.

Jenson-Elliott, Cindy. Arctic Communities Past & Present, 1 vol. 2014. (Who Lived Here? Ser.). (ENG.). 24p. (gr. 1-2). pap. 7.95 (978-1-4765-5142-5(1)); lib. bdg. 25.32 (978-1-4765-4060-3(8)) Capstone Press of Coughlan Cos. (First Facts).

Kallen, Stuart A. Native Peoples of the Arctic. 2016. (North American Indian Nations Ser.). (ENG., Illus.). 48p. (J). (gr. 3-5). 33.32 (978-1-4677-7937-1(7)) Lerner Publishing Group.

—Native Peoples of the Subarctic. 2016. (North American Indian Nations Ser.). (ENG., Illus.). 48p. (J). (gr. 3-5). 33.32 (978-1-4677-7938-8(5)) Lerner Publishing Group.

Kalman, Bobbie & Aloian, Molly. Polar Oceans. 2003. (Living Ocean Ser.). (ENG., Illus.). 32p. (J). (gr. 2-9). lib. bdg. (978-0-7787-1297-8(4)) Crabtree Publishing Co.

Kalman, Bobbie & Sjonger, Rebecca. Life in the Far North. 2003. (Native Nations of North America Ser.). (ENG., Illus.). 32p. (J). (gr. 5). pap. (978-0-7787-0469-0(6)); lib. bdg. (978-0-7787-0377-8(0)) Crabtree Publishing Co.

Kavanagh, James. My First Arctic Nature. Leung, Raymond, illus. 2011. (Nature Activity Book Ser.). (ENG.). 32p. (J). (gr. 2-4). act. bk. ed. 6.95 (978-1-58355-586-6(2)) Western National Parks Assn.

Knudsen, Anders. Sir John Franklin: The Search for the Northwest Passage. 2007. (In the Footsteps of Explorers Ser.). (ENG., Illus.). 32p. (J). (gr. 4-7). lib. bdg. (978-0-7787-2420-9(4)); pap. (978-0-7787-2456-8(5)) Crabtree Publishing Co.

Kras, Sara Louise. The Hunted: Polar Prey. 2014. 64p. (J). 15.95 (978-1-62285-080-8(7)) Enslow Pubs., Inc.

Labrecque, Ellen. Arctic Tundra, 1 vol. 2014. (Earth's Last Frontiers Ser.). (ENG.). 32p. (gr. 1-3). lib. bdg. 29.99 (978-1-4109-6177-8(X), Read Me!) Heinemann-Raintree.

Leeson, Cole. Arctic. 2003. (Wild America Habitats Ser.). (Illus.). 24p. (J). 21.20 (978-1-56711-798-1(8), Blackbirch Pr., Inc.) Cengage Gale.

Levy, Janey. Discovering the Arctic Tundra. 2007. (World Habitats Ser.). (Illus.). 32p. (YA). (gr. 3-6). lib. bdg. 25.25 (978-1-4042-3787-2(9)) Rosen Publishing Group, Inc., The.

Lewis, J. Patrick. My Home on the Ice. 2017. (Rookie Poetry(tm) — Animal Homes Ser.). (ENG., Illus.). 24p. (J). lib. bdg. 25.00 (978-0-531-22872-2(X), Children's Pr.) Scholastic Library Publishing.

Loughran, Donna. Living in the Tundra. 2004. (Rookie Read-About Geography Ser.). (ENG., Illus.). 32p. (J). (gr. 1-2). pap. 5.95 (978-0-516-27331-0(0), Children's Pr.) Scholastic Library Publishing.

Love, Ann & Drake, Jane. The Kids Book of the Far North. Bouchard, Jocelyne, illus. 2009. (Kids Book Of Ser.). (ENG.). 48p. (J). (gr. 3-7). 14.95 (978-1-55453-258-2(2)) Kids Can Pr., Ltd. CAN. Dist: Hachette Bk. Group.

Lynch, Wayne. The Arctic. Lynch, Wayne, photos by. 2007. (Our Wild World Ser.). (ENG., Illus.). 64p. (J). (gr. 3-7). pap. 8.95 (978-1-55971-961-2(3)) Cooper Square Publishing Llc.

—Arctic A to Z. 2009. (ENG., Illus.). 32p. (J). (gr. 1-5). 19.95 (978-1-55407-579-9(3), 9781554075799); pap. 7.95 (978-1-55407-578-2(5), 9781554075782) Firefly Bks., Ltd.

Lynette, Rachel. Who Lives on the Icy, Cold Tundra? 2010. (Exploring Habitats Ser.). (ENG.). 24p. (J). pap. 8.25 (978-1-4488-1279-0(8)); lib. bdg. 22.60 (978-1-4488-0675-1(5)) Rosen Publishing Group, Inc., The. (PowerKids Pr.).

Martin, Jacqueline Briggs. The Lamp, the Ice, & the Boat Called Fish: Based on a True Story. Krommes, Beth, illus. 2005. (ENG.). 48p. (J). (gr. -1-3). 7.99 (978-0-618-54895-8(5)) Houghton Mifflin Harcourt Publishing Co.

Mattern, Joanne. Will Steger, 1 vol. 2014. (Conservationists Ser.). (ENG., Illus.). 32p. (gr. 3-6). lib. bdg. 27.07 (978-1-62403-096-3(3), Checkerboard Library) ABDO Publishing Co.

McAllan, Kate. Arctic & Antarctic Habitats. 2013. (Discovery Education: Habitats Ser.). 32p. (J). (gr. 3-6). 25.25 (978-1-4777-1323-5(9)); pap. 10.00 (978-1-4777-1481-2(2)) Rosen Publishing Group, Inc., The. (PowerKids Pr.).

Miller, Debbie S. Arctic Lights, Arctic Nights. Van Zyle, Jon, illus. 2007. (ENG.). 32p. (J). (gr. k-4). pap. 8.99 (978-0-8027-9636-3(2), 9780802796363, Bloomsbury USA Childrens) Bloomsbury Publishing USA.

Miller, Sara Swan. Polar Bears of the Arctic. 2009. (Brrr! Polar Animals Ser.). (Illus.). 24p. (J). (gr. k-5). pap. 8.25 (978-1-4358-3145-2(4), PowerKids Pr.); 24p. (gr. 2-3). 42.50 (978-1-61511-751-2(2), PowerKids Pr.); (J). (gr. k-3). lib. bdg. 22.60 (978-1-4358-2741-7(4)) Rosen Publishing Group, Inc., The.

—Whales of the Arctic. 2009. (Brrr! Polar Animals Ser.). (Illus.). 24p. (J). (gr. k-5). pap. 8.25 (978-1-4358-3147-6(0), 1291789, PowerKids Pr.) Rosen Publishing Group, Inc., The.

Montgomery, Richard. Pechuck. 2005. reprint ed. pap. 31.95 (978-1-4179-9755-8(9)) Kessinger Publishing, LLC.

Newhouse, Maxwell. Counting on Snow. 2010. (ENG., Illus.). 24p. (J). (gr. k-k). 14.99 (978-0-88776-985-6(3), Tundra Bks.) Tundra Bks. CAN. Dist: Penguin Random Hse. LLC.

Nugent, Samantha. Arctic Ocean. 2016. (J). (978-1-4896-4733-7(3)) Weigl Pubs., Inc.

Oachs, Emily Rose. Arctic Ocean. 2016. (Discover the Oceans Ser.). (ENG., Illus.). 24p. (J). (gr. k-3). lib. bdg. 25.95 (978-1-62617-330-9(3), Blastoff! Readers) Bellwether Media.

O'Brien, Cynthia. Explore with John Franklin. 2015. (Travel with the Great Explorers Ser.). (ENG., Illus.). 32p. (J). (gr. 3-6). (978-0-7787-1703-4(8)) Crabtree Publishing Co.

Osborne, Mary Pope & Boyce, Natalie Pope. Polar Bears & the Arctic: A Nonfiction Companion to Polar Bears Past Bedtime. Murdocca, Sal, illus. 2007. (Magic Tree House - Fact Tracker Ser.: 16). (ENG.). 128p. (J). (gr. 2-5). 6.99 (978-0-375-83222-2(X), Random Hse. Bks. for Young Readers) Random Hse. Children's Bks.

Ottina, Laura. In the Arctic. Ranchetti, Sebastiano, illus. 2009. (Learn with Animals Ser.). (ENG.). 24p. (J). (gr. -1-2). pap. 8.15 (978-1-4339-2088-2(3)); lib. bdg. 22.00 (978-1-4339-1911-4(7)) Stevens, Gareth Publishing LLLP. (Weekly Reader Leveled Readers).

Patkau, Karen. Who Needs an Iceberg? 2012. (Ecosystem Ser.). (ENG., Illus.). 32p. (J). (gr. 2-5). 17.95 (978-0-88776-993-1(4), Tundra Bks.) Tundra Bks. CAN. Dist: Penguin Random Hse. LLC.

Pelletier, Mia. Avati: Discovering Arctic Ecology, 1 vol. Otterstätter, Sara, illus. 2013. (ENG.). 46p. (J). (gr. 2-5). 14.95 (978-1-927095-13-3(1)) Inhabit Media Inc. CAN. Dist: Independent Pubs. Group.

Pettiford, Rebecca. Arctic Food Chains. 2016. (Who Eats What?). 24p. (J). (gr. 2-5). lib. bdg. 25.65 (978-1-62031-300-8(6), Pogo) Jump! Inc.

Phillips, Dee. Collared Lemming. 2015. (Arctic Animals: Life Outside the Igloo Ser.). (ENG.). 24p. (J). (gr. -1-3). lib. bdg. 23.93 (978-1-62724-528-9(6)) Bearport Publishing Co., Inc.

—Polar Bear. 2015. (Arctic Animals: Life Outside the Igloo Ser.). (ENG.). 24p. (J). (gr. -1-3). lib. bdg. 23.93 (978-1-62724-526-5(X)) Bearport Publishing Co., Inc.

Rodger, Ellen. Arctic Research Journal. 2017. (Illus.). 32p. (J). **(978-0-7787-3468-0(4))**; pap. **(978-0-7787-3493-2(5))** Crabtree Publishing Co.

Rogers, Stan. Northwest Passage, 1 vol. James, Matt, illus. 2013. (ENG.). 56p. (J). (gr. k). 24.95 (978-1-55498-153-3(0)) Groundwood Bks. CAN. Dist: Publishers Group West (PGW).

Roza, Greg. An Arctic Ecosystem. 2009. (Real Life Readers Ser.). 32p. (gr. 4-5). pap. 10.00 (978-1-4358-0149-3(0), Rosen Classroom); 47.90 (978-1-60853-033-5(7), PowerKids Pr.) Rosen Publishing Group, Inc., The.

Rustad, Martha E. H. Animal Camouflage in the Snow [Scholastic]. 2010. (Hidden in Nature Ser.). pap. 0.52 (978-1-4296-5049-6(4), Pebble Plus) Capstone Press of Coughlan Cos.

Schwartz, Simon. First Man: The Voyages of Matthew Henson. Watkinson, Laura, tr. from GER. 2015. (ENG., Illus.). 160p. (J). (gr. 8-12). 31.99 (978-1-4677-5842-0(6), Graphic Universe™) Lerner Publishing Group.

Shields, Mary & Grace, Susan. What's a Shrew to You? Van Zyle, Jon, illus. 2008. (J). (978-0-9618348-7-6(0)) Pyrola Publishing.

Sisk, Maeve T. Arctic Foxes. 2010. (Animals That Live in the Tundra Ser.). (ENG.). 24p. (J). (gr. -1-3). 22.60 (978-1-4339-3887-0(1)); pap. 8.15 (978-1-4339-3888-7(X)) Stevens, Gareth Publishing LLLP.

—Arctic Wolves. 2010. (Animals That Live in the Tundra Ser.). (ENG.). 24p. (J). (gr. -1-3). pap. 8.15 (978-1-4339-3894-8(4)); lib. bdg. 22.60 (978-1-4339-3893-1(6)) Stevens, Gareth Publishing LLLP.

Spilsbury, Louise. Polar Bear. 2013. (Top of the Food Chain Ser.). 32p. (J). (gr. k-5). 25.25 (978-1-61533-739-2(3)); pap. 10.00 (978-1-61533-795-8(4)) Windmill Bks.

—Polar Bear: Killer King of the Arctic. 2013. (Top of the Food Chain Ser.). 32p. (J). (gr. k-5). pap. 60.00 (978-1-61533-796-5(2)) Windmill Bks.

Spilsbury, Louise & Spilsbury, Richard. Arctic Ocean. 2015. (Oceans of the World Ser.). (ENG., Illus.). 32p. (gr. 1-3). 27.32 (978-1-4846-0774-9(0), Heinemann First Library) Heinemann-Raintree.

Stamper, Judith. Polar Bear Patrol. Haefele, Steve, illus. 2010. (Magic School Bus Science Chapter Bks.). (KOR.). 106p. (J). (978-89-491-5321-6(1)) Biryongso Publishing Co.

Sturm, Matthew & Sturm, M. Apun: The Arctic Snow. 2nd ed. 2009. (ENG., Illus.). 44p. (J). pap. 12.95 (978-1-60223-069-9(2)) Univ. of Alaska Pr.

Tarbox, A. D. An Arctic Tundra Food Chain. 2008. (Nature's Bounty Ser.). (Illus.). 43p. (YA). (gr. 5-8). lib. bdg. 22.95 (978-1-58341-596-2(3), Creative Education) Creative Co., The.

—An Arctic Tundra Food Chain: Nature's Bounty. 2nd ed. 2015. (Illus.). 80p. (J). (978-1-60818-538-2(9), Creative Education) Creative Co., The.

—An Arctic Tundra Food Chain: Odysseys in Nature. 2016. (Odysseys in Nature Ser.). (ENG.). 80p. (J). (gr. 7-10). pap. 14.99 (978-1-62832-139-5(3), Creative Paperbacks) Creative Co., The.

Thomson, Sarah L. Where Do Polar Bears Live? Chin, Jason, illus. 2009. (Let's-Read-And-Find-Out Science 2 Ser.). (ENG.). 40p. (J). (gr. k-4). 16.99 (978-0-06-157518-1(6)); pap. 5.99 (978-0-06-157517-4(8)) HarperCollins Pubs. (Collins).

Traveling Wild. 2014. (Traveling Wild Ser.). 32p. (J). (gr. 3-6). pap. 42.00 (978-1-4824-1588-9(7)) Stevens, Gareth Publishing LLLP.

Warrick, Karen Clemens. The Perilous Search for the Fabled Northwest Passage in American History. 2004. (In American History Ser.). (Illus.). 128p. (J). lib. bdg. 26.60 (978-0-7660-2148-8(3)) Enslow Pubs., Inc.

Wells, Robert E. Polar Bear, Why Is Your World Melting? Wells, Robert E., illus. 2008. (Wells of Knowledge Science Ser.). (ENG., Illus.). 32p. (J). (gr. 2-3). pap. 7.99 (978-0-8075-6599-5(7)) Whitman, Albert & Co.

Wojahn, Rebecca Hogue & Wojahn, Donald. A Tundra Food Chain: A Who-Eats-What Adventure in the Arctic. 2009. (Follow That Food Chain Ser.). (ENG.). 64p. (gr. 3-5). 30.60 (978-0-8225-7500-9(0)) Lerner Publishing Group.

Woolf, Alex. Expedition to the Arctic. 2014. (Traveling Wild Ser.). 32p. (J). (gr. 3-6). pap. 63.00 (978-1-4824-1250-5(0)) Stevens, Gareth Publishing LLLP.

World Book, Inc Staff, contrib. by. Icy Worlds. 2011. (J). (978-0-7166-1788-4(9)) World Bk., Inc.

—Peoples of the Arctic & Subarctic. 2009. (J). (978-0-7166-2132-4(0)) World Bk., Inc.

Worth, Bonnie. Ice Is Nice! All about the North & South Poles. Ruiz, Aristides & Mathieu, Joe, illus. 2010. (Cat in the Hat's Learning Library). (ENG.). 48p. (J). (gr. -1-3). 9.99 (978-0-375-82885-0(0), Random Hse. Bks. for Young Readers) Random Hse. Children's Bks.

Wulffson, Don L. The Upside-Down Voyage. Lyall, Dennis, illus. 2005. (J). (978-1-59336-334-5(6)); pap. (978-1-59336-335-2(4)) Mondo Publishing.

Zondervan Staff. Polar Pals, 1 vol. 2011. (I Can Read! / Made by God Ser.). (ENG.). 32p. (J). pap. 3.99 (978-0-310-72188-8(1)) Zonderkidz.

ARCTIC REGIONS—FICTION

Arctic. 2003. (J). per. (978-1-57657-885-8(2)) Paradise Pr., Inc.

Ballantyne, R. M. The Walrus Hunters. 2007. 268p. per. (978-1-4065-2066-8(7)) Dodo Pr.

—The Walrus Hunters. 2004. reprint ed. pap. 26.95 (978-1-4191-8706-3(6)); pap. 1.99 (978-1-4192-8706-0(0)) Kessinger Publishing, LLC.

—The Walrus Hunters. 2009. 212p. 26.95 (978-1-60664-594-9(3)); pap. 14.95 (978-1-60664-323-5(1)) Rodgers, Alan Bks.

Ballantyne, Robert Michael. The Walrus Hunters: A Romance of the Realms of Ice. 2007. 258p. pap. 21.99 (978-1-4346-3699-7(2)); (ENG.). 286p. pap. 23.99 (978-1-4346-3747-5(6)) Creative Media Partners, LLC.

Bania, Michael. Kumak's River: A Tall Tale from the Far North. 2012. (ENG., Illus.). 32p. (J). (gr. -1-2). pap. 9.99 (978-0-88240-887-3(9), Alaska Northwest Bks.) Graphic Arts Ctr. Publishing Co.

Barton, Bob. Trouble on the Voyage. 2010. (ENG., Illus.). 240p. (J). (gr. 4-7). pap. 10.95 (978-1-926607-10-8(4), Napoleon & Co.) Dundurn CAN. Dist: Ingram Publisher Services.

Berkes, Marianne. Over in the Arctic: Where the Cold Winds Blow, 1 vol. Dubin, Jill, illus. 2008. (ENG.). 32p. (J). (gr. -1-2). 16.95 (978-1-58469-109-9(3)); pap. 8.95 (978-1-58469-110-5(7)) Dawn Pubns.

Biddulph, Rob. Blown Away. Biddulph, Rob, illus. 2015. (ENG., Illus.). 40p. (J). (gr. -1-3). 17.99 (978-0-06-236724-2(2)) HarperCollins Pubs.

Brett, Jan. Home for Christmas. Brett, Jan, illus. 2011. (ENG., Illus.). 32p. (J). (gr. -1-k). 17.99 (978-0-399-25653-0(9), G.P. Putnam's Sons Books for Young Readers) Penguin Young Readers Group.

Brière-Haquet, Alice. ONE Very Big Bear. Philipponneau, Olivier & Enjary, Raphaële, illus. 2016. (ENG.). 32p. (J). (gr. -1-k). 14.95 (978-1-4197-2117-5(8), Abrams Appleseed) Abrams, Inc.

Burgess, Thornton W. The Christmas Reindeer. Chase, Rhoda, illus. 2013. (Dover Children's Classics Ser.). (ENG.). 160p. (J). (gr. k-3). pap. 5.99 (978-0-486-49153-0(6)) Dover Pubns., Inc.

Carson, Marlene R. & Carson, John E. Ramblin' Rose: The Secret in the Arctic Ice. 2008. 136p. pap. 8.99 (978-0-9800034-0-6(7)) BBM Bks.

Clarke, Christie. Star Spirit. 2013. 118p. pap. (978-0-9917348-2-5(3)) RedemptionHse. Publishing.

Crawford, Ken. Cappy, the Arctic Tern. 2016. (Illus.). 64p. (J). pap. (978-0-8163-6108-3(8)) Pacific Pr. Publishing Assn.

Currie, Robin. Tuktuk: Tundra Tale, 1 vol. Saroff, Phyllis, illus. 2016. (ENG & SPA.). 32p. (J). (gr. k-3). 17.95 (978-1-62855-879-1(2)) Arbordale Publishing.

—Tuktuk: Un Cuento Sobre la Tundra. Saroff, Phyllis, illus. 2016. (SPA.). 32p. (J). (gr. k-3). pap. 9.95 (978-1-62855-881-4(4)) Arbordale Publishing.

Delsol, Wendy. Frost. (ENG., Illus.). (YA). (gr. 7). 2012. 384p. pap. 8.99 (978-0-7636-6249-3(6)) 2011. 376p. 15.99 (978-0-7636-5386-6(1)) Candlewick Pr.

d'Lacey, Chris. The Fire Eternal. 2008. (Last Dragon Chronicles Ser.: 4). (ENG.). 512p. (J). (gr. 3-7). 17.99 (978-0-545-05163-7(0), Orchard Bks.) Scholastic, Inc.

—The Fire Eternal. 2010. (Last Dragon Chronicles Ser.: 4). lib. bdg. 19.65 (978-0-606-12558-1(2), Turtleback) Turtleback Bks.

—Fire Star. 2008. (Last Dragon Chronicles Ser.: 3). (ENG.). 560p. (J). (gr. 3-7). 8.99 (978-0-439-90185-7(5), Orchard Bks.) Scholastic, Inc.

—Icefire. 2007. (Last Dragon Chronicles Ser.: 2). (ENG.). 432p. (J). (gr. 3-7). pap. 8.99 (978-0-439-67246-7(5), Orchard Bks.) Scholastic, Inc.

Doupe, Pauline Wood. My Arctic Circle of Friends. Fawcett, Vicki, illus. Belair, Brenda Brousseau, photos by. 2009. 24p. pap. 16.98 (978-1-4251-8097-3(3)) Trafford Publishing.

Dunphy, Madeleine. Here Is the Arctic Winter. Robinson, Alan James, illus. 2007. (Web of Life Ser.). (ENG.). 32p. (J). (gr. -1-3). 16.95 (978-0-9777539-1-8(3)); pap. 9.95 (978-0-9777539-0-1(5)) Web of Life Children's Bks.

Durst, Sarah Beth. Ice. (ENG.). (YA). (gr. 7). 2010. 336p. pap. 8.99 (978-1-4169-8644-7(8)) 2009. 320p. 16.99 (978-1-4169-8643-0(X)) McElderry, Margaret K. Bks. (McElderry, Margaret K. Bks.).

Dwyer, Mindy. Sweet Dreams, Polar Bear. 2004. (ENG., Illus.). 32p. (J). 15.95 (978-0-88240-554-4(3)); pap. 8.99 (978-0-88240-555-1(1)) Graphic Arts Ctr. Publishing Co.

Earhart, Kristin. Arctic Freeze. 2015. (Race the Wild Ser.: 3). (ENG.). 144p. (J). (gr. 2-5). pap. 4.99 (978-0-545-77355-3(5), Scholastic Paperbacks) Scholastic, Inc.

Emerson, Kevin. The Far Dawn. 2014. (Atlanteans Ser.: 3). (ENG.). 368p. (YA). (gr. 8). pap. 9.99 (978-0-06-206286-4(7), Tegen, Katherine Bks) HarperCollins Pubs.

Evert, Lori. The Christmas Wish. Breiehagen, Per, illus. Breiehagen, Per, photos by. 2013. (ENG.). 48p. (J). (gr. -1-2). 17.99 (978-0-449-81681-3(8), Random Hse. Bks. for Young Readers) Random Hse. Children's Bks.

—The Christmas Wish. Breiehagen, Per, illus. Breiehagen, Per, photos by. 2013. (J). (978-0-449-81942-5(6)) Random Hse., Inc.

—The Reindeer Wish. Breiehagen, Per, illus. Breiehagen, Per, photos by. 2015. (ENG.). 48p. (J). (gr. -1-2). 20.99 (978-0-375-97335-2(4), Random Hse. Bks. for Young Readers) Random Hse. Children's Bks.

Ewashen, Julie. Life in the Arctic with Nina & Nikita. 2013. 56p. pap. (978-1-4602-2727-5(1)) FriesenPress.

Foresman, Timothy. The Last Little Polar Bear: A Global Change Adventure Story. Laura Lee, Cundiff, illus. 2007. 60p. (J). per. 19.95 (978-0-9776906-2-6(8)) Blueline Publishing.

French, Jackie. My Pa the Polar Bear. 2015. (Wacky Families Ser.: 08). 128p. 5.99 (978-0-207-20078-6(5)) HarperCollins Pubs. Australia AUS. Dist: HarperCollins Pubs.

Frisch, Aaron. The Lonely Pine. Delessert, Etienne, illus. 2011. (ENG.). 32p. (J). (gr. 1-3). 17.99 (978-1-56846-214-1(X), Creative Editions) Creative Co., The.

Furlong, C. T. Arctic6Adventures: 6Pack Set. 2012. (Arctic6 Adventure Ser.). 192p. (YA). (gr. 4-6). pap. 136.63 (978-0-7613-9213-2(0)) Lerner Publishing Group.

—Arctic6Adventures: Single Copy Set. 2012. (Arctic6 Adventure Ser.). 192p. (YA). (gr. 4-6). pap. 22.77 (978-0-7613-9212-5(2)) Lerner Publishing Group.

George, Jean Craighead. Ice Whale. Hendrix, John, illus. 2015. (ENG.). 224p. (J). (gr. 4-7). 7.99 (978-0-14-242741-5(1), Puffin Books) Penguin Young Readers Group.

—The Last Polar Bear. Minor, Wendell, illus. (ENG.). 32p. (J). (gr. -1-2). 2014. pap. 6.99 (978-0-06-124069-0(9)) 2009. 16.99 (978-0-06-124067-6(2)) HarperCollins Pubs.

Halfman, Janet. Polar Bear Horizon. Chesterman, Adrian, illus. 2006. (Smithsonian Oceanic Collection). (ENG.). 32p. (J). 19.95 (978-1-59249-568-9(0)); (gr. -1-3). 9.95 (978-1-59249-570-2(2)) Soundprints.

Halfmann, Janet. Polar Bear Horizon. Chesterman, Adrian, illus. 2006. (Smithsonian Oceanic Collection). (ENG.). 32p. (J). 8.95 (978-1-59249-569-6(9)); 4.95 (978-1-59249-567-2(2)); (gr. -1-3). 15.95 (978-1-59249-565-8(6)); (gr. -1-3). mass mkt. 6.95 (978-1-59249-566-5(4)) Soundprints.

Halfmann, Janet & Smithsonian Institution Staff. El horizonte del Oso Polar: Polar Bear Horizon. 2008. (MUL.). 16p. 14.95 (978-1-59249-852-9(3)) Soundprints.

Hatton, Libby. Pete Puffin's Wild Ride Cruising Alaska's Currents. Hatton, Libby, illus. 2008. (Illus.). (J). pap. 16.95 (978-0-930931-92-6(0)) Alaska Geographic Assn.

Hautala, Beth. Waiting for Unicorns. 2015. (ENG.). 256p. (J). (gr. 5). 16.99 (978-0-525-42631-8(0), Philomel Bks.) Penguin Young Readers Group.

Heder, Thyra. The Bear Report. 2015. (ENG., Illus.). 48p. (J). (gr. -1-3). 17.95 (978-1-4197-0783-4(3), Abrams Bks. for Young Readers) Abrams, Inc.

Heinz, Brian J. Kayuktuk: An Arctic Quest. Van Zyle, Jon, illus. 2004. (J). pap. 6.95 (978-0-936335-09-4(2)); 14.95 (978-0-936335-08-7(4)) Ballyhoo BookWorks, Inc.

Hergé. The Shooting Star. 2012. (Adventures of Tintin: Young Readers Edition Ser.). (ENG., Illus.). 96p. (J). (gr. 3-7). pap. 8.99 (978-0-316-19875-2(7)) Little, Brown Bks. for Young Readers.

Hopgood, Sally & Graham, Oakley. Arctic Wonders. Wood, Hannah, illus. 2012. (Sparkling Slide Nature Bks.). (ENG.). 12p. (J). (gr. -1-k). 9.99 (978-1-84956-675-9(5)) Top That! Publishing PLC GBR. Dist: Independent Pubs. Group.

Hunt, Elizabeth Singer. The Fight for the Frozen Land, Bk.12. Williamson, Brian, illus. 2009. (Secret Agent Jack Stalwart Ser.: 12). (ENG.). 128p. (J). (gr. 1-4). pap. 5.99 (978-1-60286-099-5(8), Weinstein Bks.) Perseus Bks. Group.

Immi's Gift, 1 vol. 2014. (ENG., Illus.). 32p. (J). (gr. -1-3). 7.95 (978-1-56145-813-4(9)) Peachtree Pubs.

Jalonen, Riitta. Tundra Mouse Mountain. Ledgard, J. M., tr. from FIN. Louhi, Kristiina, illus. 2006. (Picture books from around the World Seri Ser.). (ENG.). 56p. (J). (gr. k-2). 20.95 (978-1-905341-05-4(9)) WingedChariot Pr. GBR. Dist: Independent Pubs. Group.

Kirkpatrick, Katherine. Between Two Worlds. (ENG.). 304p. (YA). (gr. 9). 2015. pap. 9.99 (978-0-375-87221-1(3), Ember) 2014. 16.99 (978-0-385-74047-0(6), Lamb, Wendy Bks.) Random Hse. Children's Bks.

Kras, Sara Louise. The Hunted: Polar Prey. 2014. 64p. (J). (gr. 3-4). pap. 9.95 (978-1-62285-081-5(5)) Enslow Pubs., Inc.

Landers, Ace. Arctic Blast. White, Dave, illus. 2012. 32p. (J). (978-0-545-33455-6(1)) Scholastic, Inc.

Lemke, Donald. The Penguin's Arctic Adventure. Roberts, Jeremy, illus. 2014. (ENG.). 24p. (J). (gr. -1-3). pap. 3.99 (978-0-06-221000-5(9), HarperFestival) HarperCollins Pubs.

Lincoln, Hazel. Little Snow Bear, 1 vol. Lincoln, Hazel, illus. 2004. (ENG., Illus.). 32p. (J). pap. 17.95 (978-0-86315-454-6(9)) Floris Bks. GBR. Dist: SteinerBooks, Inc.

Littlewood, Karin. Immi's Gift, 1 vol. Littlewood, Karin, illus. 2010. (ENG., Illus.). 32p. (J). (gr. -1-3). 15.95 (978-1-56145-545-4(8)) Peachtree Pubs.

Mason, Jane B., et al. Ice & Flame, 1 vol. 2011. (Flash Ser.). (ENG., Illus.). 56p. (gr. 2-3). pap. 4.95 (978-1-4342-3416-2(9)); lib. bdg. 26.65 (978-1-4342-2630-3(1)) Stone Arch Bks. (DC Super Heroes).

Mathy, Vincent, illus. Who's Hiding with Penguin? 2016. (ENG.). 10p. (J). (gr. -1 — 1). bds. 8.99 (978-1-4521-5661-3(1)) Chronicle Bks. LLC.

Mawhinney, Art, illus. Diego's Arctic Rescue. 2009. (Go, Diego, Go! Ser.). (ENG.). 24p. (J). (gr. -1-2). pap. 3.99 (978-1-4169-8504-4(2), Simon Spotlight/Nickelodeon) Simon Spotlight/Nickelodeon.

Norman, Kim. She'll Be Coming up the Mountain. Woodruff, Liza, illus. 2016. (ENG.). 32p. (J). (gr. -1). 14.95 (978-1-4549-1610-9(9)) Sterling Publishing Co., Inc.

Ostermeyer Phoitography. Frosty & Snowy's Arctic Adventures. 2011. (Illus.). 18.95 (978-0-9794228-5-0(X)) Ostermeyer Photography.

Patterson, Ellie. Baby Bear & the Big, Wide World. Kolanovic, Dubravka, illus. 2013. (J). (978-1-4351-4929-8(7)) Barnes & Noble, Inc.

Pollock, J. A. Titus & Otis & the Arctic Adventure. 2009. 151p. pap. 12.00 (978-0-557-03427-7(2)) Lulu Pr., Inc.

Pullman, Philip. Once upon a Time in the North. 2008. (His Dark Materials Ser.). (ENG., Illus.). 112p. (978-0-385-61432-0(2)) Fickling, David Bks.

Reeve, Philip. Pugs of the Frozen North. McIntyre, Sarah, illus. 2016. (Not-So-Impossible Tale Ser.). (ENG.). 224p. (J). (gr. 2-5). 12.99 (978-0-385-38796-5(2), Random Hse. Bks. for Young Readers) Random Hse. Children's Bks.

Riel, Jørn, et al. The Snowstorm. Cann, Helen, illus. 2012. (ENG.). 128p. (J). (gr. 4-6). pap. 9.99 (978-1-84686-797-2(5)) Barefoot Bks., Inc.

Roy Rockwood. Through the Air to the North Pole: Or the Wonderful Cruise of the Electric Monarch. l.t. ed. 2007. 78p. pap. 21.99 (978-1-4264-8207-6(8)) Creative Media Partners, LLC.

Sandrey, Alexander & Sellers, Carolyn. Cold Weather Bro's Arctic Adventure. 2012. 36p. 17.95 (978-1-4575-1701-3(9)) Dog Ear Publishing, LLC.

Sansone, V. K. A Daunting Quest for Quincy & Quigley. 2009. 32p. pap. 8.98 (978-0-557-03594-6(5)) Lulu Pr., Inc.

Sís, Peter. A Small Tall Tale from the Far Far North. (Illus.). (J). pap. 7.95 (978-0-88899-431-8(1)) Groundwood Bks. CAN. Dist: Publishers Group West (PGW).

Smith, Danna. Arctic White. White, Lee, illus. 2016. (ENG.). 32p. (J). (gr. -1-3). 17.99 (978-1-62779-104-5(3), 9781627791045, Holt, Henry & Co. Bks. For Young Readers) Holt, Henry & Co.

Snell, Roy J. Little White Fox & His Arctic Friends. 2008. 108p. 22.95 (978-1-60664-935-0(3)); 104p. pap. 9.95 (978-1-60664-055-5(0)) Aegypan.

—Lost in the Air. 2007. (ENG.). 132p. pap. 18.99 (978-1-4264-4244-5(0)) 2006. 148p. pap. 19.99 (978-1-4264-4308-4(0)) Creative Media Partners, LLC.

—Lost in the Air. 2004. reprint ed. pap. 1.99 (978-1-4192-3128-5(6)); pap. 20.95 (978-1-4191-3128-8(1)) Kessinger Publishing, LLC.

—Lost in the Air. 2011. 112p. 23.95 (978-1-4638-9934-9(3)); pap. 9.95 (978-1-60664-429-4(7)) Rodgers, Alan Bks.

Stables, Gordon. The Cruise of the Snowbird - a Story of Arctic Adventure. 2011. 382p. pap. 30.95 (978-1-4474-2398-0(4)) Research Pr.

Stamper, Judith B. Polar Bear Patrol. Haefele, Steve, illus. 2003. (Magic School Bus Science Chapter Bks.). 91p. (J). (gr. 2-5). 12.65 (978-0-7569-1577-3(5)) Perfection Learning Corp.

Stefansson, Vilhjalmur & Irwin, Violet. The Shaman's Revenge: Based on the Arctic Diaries of Vilhjalmur Stefansson. Grier, Geoffrey, illus. 2011. 306p. 48.95 (978-1-258-05790-9(5)) Literary Licensing, LLC.

Stephenson, Sasha. Iceling. 2016. (ENG.). 272p. (YA). (gr. 7). 17.99 (978-1-59514-769-1(1), Razorbill) Penguin Young Readers Group.

Stratton, Bart. Arctic Mall Adventure. Riddle, Scott, illus. 2010. 28p. pap. 15.95 (978-1-60844-558-5(5)) Dog Ear Publishing, LLC.

Sundell, Joanne. Arctic Shadow. 2015. (Watch Eyes Trilogy Ser.: 2). (ENG.). 278p. (YA). 25.95 (978-1-4328-3008-3(2), Five Star Trade) Cengage Gale.

Taylor, Theodore & Taylor, Theodore. Ice Drift. 2006. (ENG., Illus.). 240p. (J). (gr. 2-5). pap. 7.99 (978-0-15-205550-9(9)) Houghton Mifflin Harcourt Publishing Co.

Thompson, Kate. Switchers. 220p. (J). (gr. 4-7). pap. 5.99 (978-0-8072-1553-1(8)); 2004. (Switchers Ser.: Vol. 1). (gr. 5-9). pap. 38.00 incl. audio (978-0-8072-8138-3(7), YA115SP) Random Hse. Audio Publishing Group. (Listening Library).

Verne, Jules. The Field of Ice: Part II of the Adventures of Captain Hatteras. 2007. (ENG.). 154p. pap. 19.99 (978-1-4264-3591-1(6)); 170p. pap. 21.99 (978-1-4264-3642-0(4)) Creative Media Partners, LLC.

Walters, Eric. The Pole. 2008. (ENG.). 256p. (J). (gr. 3-7). 7.99 (978-0-14-331248-2(0), Penguin Global) Penguin Publishing Group.

Ward, Jennifer. Way up in the Arctic. Spengler, Kenneth J., illus. 2007. (SPA & ENG.). 32p. (J). (gr. -1-3). 15.95 (978-0-87358-928-4(9)) Cooper Square Publishing Llc.

Westerfeld, Scott. Horizon. 2017. (Horizon Ser.: 1). (ENG.). 256p. (J). (gr. 4-7). 16.99 **(978-1-338-19658-0(8))** Scholastic, Inc.

White, Kathryn. Snowshoe the Hare. Rivers, Ruth, illus. 2005. (Red Go Bananas Ser.). (ENG.). 48p. (J). (gr. 2-3). lib. bdg. (978-0-7787-2677-7(0), 1253648) Crabtree Publishing Co.

Whybrow, Ian. Say Hello to the Snowy Animals! Eaves, Edward, illus. 2012. (J). (978-0-7607-9675-7(0)) Barnes & Noble, Inc.

Whyman, Matt. Icecore: A Carl Hobbes Thriller. 2007. (ENG.). 320p. (YA). (gr. 7-18). 16.99 (978-1-4169-4907-7(0), Atheneum Bks. for Young Readers) Simon & Schuster Children's Publishing.

—Icecore: A Thriller. 2009. (ENG.). 320p. (YA). (gr. 7). pap. 14.99 (978-1-4169-8960-8(9), Atheneum Bks. for Young Readers) Simon & Schuster Children's Publishing.

Wolverton, Barry. Neversink. Nielson, Sam, illus. (ENG.). (J). (gr. 3-7). 2013. 320p. pap. 6.99 (978-0-06-202793-1(X)) 2012. 304p. 16.99 (978-0-06-202791-7(3)) HarperCollins Pubs. (Waldon Pond Pr.).

—Neversink. Nielson, Sam, illus. 2012. xiii, 287p. (J). (978-0-06-202792-4(1)) Longman Publishing.

ARDENNES, BATTLE OF THE, 1944-1945

Atkinson, Rick. The Battle of the Bulge. 2015. (ENG., Illus.). 256p. (J). (gr. 3-7). 19.99 (978-1-62779-113-7(2), 9781627791137, Holt, Henry & Co. Bks. For Young Readers) Holt, Henry & Co.

McNeese, Tim. Battle of the Bulge. 2003. (Great Battles Through the Ages Ser.). (Illus.). 112p. (gr. 6-12). 30.00 (978-0-7910-7435-0(8), Chelsea Hse.) Facts On File, Inc.

Sears, Stephen W. The Battle of the Bulge. 2005. 160p. pap. 9.95 (978-0-7434-9333-8(8)) ibooks, Inc.

Vansant, Wayne. The Battle of the Bulge: A Graphic History of Allied Victory in the Ardennes 1944-1945. Vansant, Wayne, illus. 2015. (Graphic Histories Ser.). (ENG., Illus.). 104p. (J). (gr. 8-12). 34.65 (978-1-939581-75-4(3)) Quarto Publishing Group USA.

ARGENTINA

Burshtein, Karen. Lionel Messi: Soccer's Top Scorer. 2015. (Living Legends of Sports Ser.). (ENG.). 48p. (J). (gr. 5-6). pap. 14.05 (978-1-68048-130-3(4), Britannica Educational Publishing) Rosen Publishing Group, Inc., The.

Crooker, Richard A. Argentina. 2003. (Modern World Nations Ser.). (Illus.). 150p. (gr. 6-12). 35.00 (978-0-7910-7480-0(3), Chelsea Hse.) Facts On File, Inc.

Dell'Oro, Suzanne Paul. Argentina. 2008. (Country Explorers Ser.). (J). (gr. 2-5). 27.93 (978-0-8225-9413-0(7)) Lerner Publishing Group.

Ejaz, Khadija. Lionel Messi. 2013. (ENG.). 32p. (gr. 4-8). lib. bdg. 25.70 (978-1-61228-467-5(1)) Mitchell Lane Pubs., Inc.

Ernesto Che Guevara. 2010. (Great Hispanic Heritage Ser.). (Illus.). 128p. (gr. 6-12). 35.00 (978-1-60413-732-3(0), Chelsea Hse.) Facts On File, Inc.

Eva Peron. 2010. (Great Hispanic Heritage Ser.). (Illus.). 104p. (gr. 6-12). 35.00 (978-1-60413-729-3(0), Chelsea Hse.) Facts On File, Inc.

Favor, Lesli J. Eva Perón. 2010. (Leading Women Ser.). 96p. (gr. 6). 39.93 (978-0-7614-4962-1(0)) Marshall Cavendish Corp.

Furstinger, Nancy. Buenos Aires, 1 vol. 2005. (Cities Set 1 Ser.). (ENG., Illus.). 32p. (gr. k-6). 27.07 (978-1-59197-855-8(6), Checkerboard Library) ABDO Publishing Co.

Gatto, Kimberly. Lionel Messi: A Soccer Star Who Cares. 2013. (Sports Stars Who Care Ser.). 48p. (J). 25.27 (978-0-7660-4299-5(5)); (gr. 3-4). pap. 8.95 (978-1-4644-0543-3(3), Enslow Elementary) Enslow Pubs., Inc.

Holiday, Jane. Exploring Argentina with the Five Themes of Geography. 2009. (Library of the Western Hemisphere Ser.). 24p. (gr. 4-4). 42.50 (978-1-60853-921-5(0), PowerKids Pr.) Rosen Publishing Group, Inc., The.

Jökulsson, Illugi. Messi. 2nd ed. 2015. (ENG., Illus.). 64p. (J). (gr. 1). 13.95 (978-0-7892-1225-2(0), Abbeville Kids) Abbeville Pr., Inc.

Kalman, Bobbie. Spotlight on Argentina. 2013. (ENG.). 32p. (J). (978-0-7787-0863-6(2)); (Illus.). pap. (978-0-7787-0867-4(5)) Crabtree Publishing Co.

Kaplan, Leslie C. A Primary Source Guide to Argentina. (Countries of the World). 24p. 2009. (gr. 2-3). 42.50 (978-1-61512-024-6(6)) 2005. (Illus.). (J). (gr. k-5). lib. bdg. 22.60 (978-1-4042-2749-1(0)) Rosen Publishing Group, Inc., The. (PowerKids Pr.).

Link, Theodore. Argentina: A Primary Source Cultural Guide. 2009. (Primary Sources of World Cultures Ser.). 128p. (gr. 4-5). 79.90 (978-1-60851-916-3(3)) Rosen Publishing Group, Inc., The.

Link, Theodore & McCarthy, Rose. Argentina: A Primary Source Cultural Guide. 2004. (Primary Sources of World Cultures Ser.). (Illus.). 128p. (YA). (gr. 5-9). lib. bdg. 37.25 (978-0-8239-3997-8(9)) Rosen Publishing Group, Inc., The.

Logothetis, Paul. Lionel Messi: Soccer Sensation, 1 vol. 2016. (ENG., Illus.). 32p. (J). (978-1-62403-839-6(5), SportsZone) ABDO Publishing Co.

Maerov, Jeff. Boca Buddies. Can't We Just Say Goodnight? 2012. 40p. pap. 11.99 (978-0-578-11402-6(X)) Maerov, Jeffrey.

Marabini, Sergio. Juan D. Perón. 2004. (Protagonistas Ser.). (SPA.). (YA). (978-987-1129-46-1(7)) Grupo Visor E.A.S.A.

Morganelli, Adrianna. Cultural Traditions in Argentina. 2016. (ENG., Illus.). 32p. (J). lib. bdg. (978-0-7787-8086-1(4)) Crabtree Publishing Co.

Morreale, Marie. Lionel Messi. 2016. (Real Bios Ser.). (ENG.). 48p. (J). lib. bdg. 29.00 (978-0-531-22379-6(5), Children's Pr.) Scholastic Library Publishing.

Murray, Julie. Argentina, 1 vol. 2014. (Explore the Countries Set 2 Ser.). (ENG.). 40p. (gr. 7-11). lib. bdg. 29.93 (978-1-62403-341-4(5), Big Buddy Bks.) ABDO Publishing Co.

Obregón, José María. Argentina. 2009. (Great National Soccer Teams / Grandes selecciones del fútbol mundial Ser.). (SPA & ENG.). 24p. pap. 8.25 (978-1-4358-2495-9(4), PowerKids Pr.) Rosen Publishing Group, Inc., The.

—Argentina. Benson, Megan, tr. from SPA. 2009. (Great National Soccer Teams / Grandes Selecciones Del Fútbol Mundial Ser.). (SPA & ENG., Illus.). 24p. (J). (gr. 2-5). lib. bdg. 22.60 (978-1-4042-8088-5(X), PowerKids Pr.) Rosen Publishing Group, Inc., The.

—Lionel Messi. 2009. (World Soccer Stars / Estrellas del fútbol mundial Ser.). (ENG & SPA.). 24p. (gr. 2-2). 42.50 (978-1-60854-848-4(1)); (SPA & ENG.). (J). lib. bdg. 22.60 (978-1-4358-2729-5(5)) Rosen Publishing Group, Inc., The. (Editorial Buenas Letras).

Pohl, Kathleen. Descubramos Argentina. 2008. (Descubramos países del mundo (Looking at Countries) Ser.). (SPA.). 32p. (gr. 1-5). pap. 10.50 (978-0-8368-8786-0(7)); (Illus.). lib. bdg. 26.00 (978-0-8368-8779-2(4)) Stevens, Gareth Publishing LLLP. (Gareth Stevens Learning Library).

—Looking at Argentina. 2008. (Looking at Countries Ser.). 32p. (gr. 1-5). pap. 10.50 (978-0-8368-8772-3(7)); (Illus.). lib. bdg. 26.00 (978-0-8368-8765-5(4)) Stevens, Gareth Publishing LLLP. (Gareth Stevens Learning Library).

Schuetz, Kari. Argentina. 2011. (Exploring Countries Ser.). (ENG., Illus.). 32p. (YA). (gr. 3-7). lib. bdg. 26.95 (978-1-60014-616-9(3), Blastoff! Readers) Bellwether Media.

Shields, Charles J. Argentina. (South America Today Ser.). 64p. (gr. 4-7). 2009. (Illus.). (J). 21.95 (978-1-4222-0631-7(9)) 2007. (YA). pap. 9.95 (978-1-4222-0698-0(X)) Mason Crest.

—Argentina, Vol. 13. Henderson, James D., ed. 2015. (Discovering South America: History, Politics, & Culture Ser.). (Illus.). 64p. (J). (gr. 7). lib. bdg. 22.95 (978-1-4222-3294-1(8)) Mason Crest.

Sosa, Carlos. Lionel Messi. 2012. (Superstars of Soccer ENGLISH Ser.). (ENG., Illus.). 32p. (J). (gr. 4-7). lib. bdg. 19.95 (978-1-4222-2659-9(X)) Mason Crest.

Streissguth, Thomas & Streissguth, Tom. Argentina in Pictures. 2nd ed. 2003. (Visual Geography Ser.). (Illus.). 80p. (J). (gr. 5-12). 27.93 (978-0-8225-0372-9(7)) Lerner Publishing Group.

Torres, John Albert. Soccer Star Lionel Messi. 2014. (Goal! Latin Stars of Soccer Ser.). 48p. 14.95 (978-1-62285-221-5(4)) Enslow Pubs., Inc.

Wiseman, Blaine. Argentina. 2014. (J). (978-1-4896-3050-6(3)) Weigl Pubs., Inc.

Wittekind, Erika. Argentina, 1 vol. 2011. (Countries of the World Set 1 Ser.). (ENG., Illus.). 144p. (J). (gr. 6-12). lib. bdg. 37.07 (978-1-61783-105-8(0)) ABDO Publishing Co.

ARGENTINA—FICTION

Ahrens, Mario. Tapiz Argentino. 2004. Orig. Title: Argentine Tapestry. (SPA.). 167p. per. 20.00 (978-0-9744675-1-1(0)) Pampa Publishing.

Alcántara, Ricardo. La Ronda de Cada Dia. 2003. (SPA., Illus.). 176p. (978-84-236-3872-7(3), ED1602) Edebé ESP. Dist: Lectorum Pubns., Inc.

Barron, T. A. Ghost Hands. Low, William, illus. 2011. (ENG.). 40p. (J). (gr. k-3). 18.99 (978-0-399-25083-5(2), Philomel Bks.) Penguin Young Readers Group.

Conway, Celeste. When You Open Your Eyes. 2012. (ENG.). 320p. (YA). (gr. 9). 16.99 (978-1-4424-4229-0(8)); pap. 9.99 (978-1-4424-3031-0(1)) Simon Pulse. (Simon Pulse).

Egea, Marcelo. Sobe, the Cat That Thinks He's a Dog. 2012. 24p. pap. 15.99 (978-1-4691-5925-6(2)) Xlibris Corp.

Eisele, Barbara. Curious Cozy. 2011. 48p. pap. 9.99 (978-1-4567-1746-9(4)) AuthorHouse.

Henty, George Alfred. On the Pampas: Or the Young Settlers. 2007. (ENG.). 228p. per. 20.99 (978-1-4346-4675-0(0)); 250p. per. 22.99 (978-1-4346-4676-7(9)) Creative Media Partners, LLC.

Kaltovich, Edith Rusconi. The Adventures of Juan, the Fox: Argentine Tales & Fables. 2010. 64p. pap. 26.49 (978-1-4490-8778-4(7)) AuthorHouse.

Littman, Sarah Darer. Life, After. 2010. (ENG.). 288p. (J). (gr. 7-18). 17.99 (978-0-545-15144-3(9), Scholastic Pr.) Scholastic, Inc.

Pechero-Loewen, Mariella. I Want to Know How You Found Me. 2004. 39p. pap. 24.95 (978-1-4137-2955-9(X)) PublishAmerica, Inc.

Smith, Roland. Jack's Run. 2007. (ENG.). 256p. (J). (gr. 5-17). pap. 6.99 (978-1-4231-0407-0(2)) Hyperion Pr.

Steele, Michael A. At Large. 2013. (Tony Hawk: Live2Skate Ser.). (ENG.). 72p. (gr. 3-4). pap. 35.70 (978-1-4342-6267-7(7), Tony Hawk's 900 Revolution) Stone Arch Bks.

—At Large, 1 vol. Cano, Fernando, illus. 2013. (Tony Hawk: Live2Skate Ser.). (ENG.). 72p. (gr. 4-5). lib. bdg. 25.32 (978-1-4342-4087-3(8)) Stone Arch Bks.

Steele, Michael Anthony. At Large, 1 vol. Cano, Fernando, illus. 2013. (Tony Hawk: Live2Skate Ser.). (ENG.). 72p. (gr. 4-5). pap. 5.95 (978-1-4342-6189-2(1)) Stone Arch Bks.

Vidali, Valerio & Uman, Jennifer. Jemmy Button. Vidali, Valerio & Uman, Jennifer, illus. 2013. (ENG., Illus.). 48p. (J). (gr. k-12). 16.99 (978-0-7636-6487-9(1), Templar) Candlewick Pr.

Whelan, Gloria. The Disappeared. 2010. (ENG.). 144p. (YA). (gr. 7-18). 6.99 (978-0-14-241540-5(5), Speak) Penguin Young Readers Group.

ARGENTINE REPUBLIC

see Argentina

ARGONAUTS

Colum, Padraic. The Golden Fleece: And the Heroes Who Lived Before Achilles. Pogány, Willy, illus. 2004. 316p. (J). (gr. 5). 17.60 (978-0-7569-4048-5(6)) Perfection Learning Corp.

Phillipps, Francis, illus. Jason & the Golden Fleece: A Greek Legend. 2004. (ENG.). 24p. (J). (gr. 3-3). pap. 6.47 net. (978-0-7685-2126-9(2), Dominie Elementary) Pearson Schl.

ARGUMENTATION

see Debates and Debating; Logic

ARISTOCRACY (SOCIAL CLASS)

Schomp, Virginia. Victoria & Her Court. 2010. (Life in Victorian England Ser.). 80p. (gr. 6). 34.21 (978-1-60870-028-8(3)) Marshall Cavendish Corp.

ARISTOTLE

Anderson, Margaret J. & Stephenson, Karen F. Aristotle: Genius Philosopher & Scientist. 2015. (Genius Scientists & Their Genius Ideas Ser.). 96p. (J). (gr. 5-12). 27.94 (978-0-7660-6535-2(9)); pap. 10.95 (978-0-7660-6536-9(7)) Enslow Pubs., Inc.

—Aristotle: Philosopher & Scientist. 2004. (Great Minds of Science Ser.). (Illus.). 112p. (J). lib. bdg. 27.94 (978-0-7660-2096-2(7)) Enslow Pubs., Inc.

Downey, Glanville. Aristotle, Dean of Early Science. 2011. 158p. 41.95 (978-1-258-02165-8(X)) Literary Licensing, LLC.

Gow, Mary. The Great Thinker: Aristotle & the Foundations of Science. 2010. (Great Minds of Ancient Science & Math Ser.). 128p. (J). (gr. 4-7). 33.27 (978-0-7660-3121-0(7)) Enslow Pubs., Inc.

Isle, Mick. Aristotle: Pioneering Philosopher & Founder of the Lyceum. 2009. (Library of Greek Philosophers Ser.). 112p. (gr. 6-6). 66.50 (978-1-60853-658-0(0), Rosen Reference) Rosen Publishing Group, Inc., The.

Roscoe, Kelly & Isle, Mick. Aristotle: The Father of Logic. 2015. (Greatest Greek Philosophers Ser.). (ENG.). 112p. (J). (gr. 7-8). 35.60 (978-1-4994-6126-8(7), Rosen Young Adult) Rosen Publishing Group, Inc., The.

Whiting, Jim. The Life & Times of Aristotle. 2006. (Biography from Ancient Civilizations Ser.). (Illus.). 48p. (J). (gr. 3-7). lib. bdg. 29.95 (978-1-58415-508-9(6)) Mitchell Lane Pubs., Inc.

ARITHMETIC

Aboff, Marcie. If You Were an Even Number [LTD Commodities]. Dillard, Sarah, illus. 2010. (Math Fun Ser.). 24p. pap. 3.50 (978-1-4048-6259-3(5), Nonfiction Picture Bks.) Picture Window Bks.

—If You Were an Even Number [Scholastic]. Dillard, Sarah, illus. 2010. (Math Fun Ser.). 24p. pap. 0.47 (978-1-4048-6547-1(0), Nonfiction Picture Bks.) Picture Window Bks.

—If You Were an Odd Number [LTD Commodities]. Dillard, Sarah, illus. 2010. (Math Fun Ser.). 24p. pap. 3.50 (978-1-4048-6260-9(9), Nonfiction Picture Bks.) Picture Window Bks.

—If You Were an Odd Number [Scholastic]. Dillard, Sarah, illus. 2010. (Math Fun Ser.). 24p. pap. 0.47 (978-1-4048-6546-4(2), Nonfiction Picture Bks.) Picture Window Bks.

Adams, Colleen. Magic Squares: Learning the Inverse Relationships Between Addition & Subtraction. (Math for the REAL World Ser.). 16p. 2009. (gr. 2-3). pap. 7.05 (978-0-8239-8907-2(0), Rosen Classroom) 2006. (Illus.). (J). (gr. 3-7). lib. bdg. 18.75 (978-1-4042-3335-5(0), PowerKids Pr.) Rosen Publishing Group, Inc., The.

Adamson, Thomas K. and Heather. 2, 4, Skip Count Some More. 2012. (Fun with Numbers Ser.). (ENG.). 32p. (gr. 1-2). pap. 47.70 (978-1-4296-8303-6(1), Aplus Bks.) Capstone Press of Coughlan Cos.

Adding & Subtracting. 2003. (Gold Star Workbooks Ser.). (Illus.). 32p. (J). 2.98 (978-1-4054-1188-2(0)); 2.98 (978-1-4054-1189-9(9)) Parragon, Inc.

Adding & Subtracting Activity Book. 2017. (Math Sticker Activity Books* Ser.). (ENG.). (J). pap. 9.99 **(978-0-7945-3870-5(3)**, Usborne) EDC Publishing.

Adler, David A. Money Math: Addition & Subtraction. Miller, Edward, illus. 2017. (ENG.). 32p. (J). 17.95 **(978-0-8234-3698-9(5))** Holiday Hse., Inc.

Ainsworth, Kimberly. Hootenanny! A Festive Counting Book. Brown, Jo, illus. 2011. (ENG.). 32p. (J). (gr. -1-k). 12.99 (978-1-4424-2273-5(4), Little Simon) Little Simon.

Alaina, Maria. Adding Animals, 1 vol. 2011. (Wonder Readers Early Level Ser.). (ENG.). (gr. -1-1). 32p. pap. 5.99 (978-1-4296-7832-2(1)); 16p. pap. 35.94 (978-1-4296-8064-6(4)) Capstone Press of Coughlan Cos. (Wonder Readers).

—Counting Money, 1 vol. 2013. (Wonder Readers Next Steps: Math Ser.). (ENG.). 20p. (gr. -1-1). 22.65 (978-1-4765-2366-8(5), Wonder Readers) Capstone Press of Coughlan Cos.

—You Can Count!, 1 vol. 2011. (Wonder Readers Early Level Ser.). (ENG.). 32p. (gr. -1-1). pap. 5.99 *(978-1-4296-7831-5(3)*, Wonder Readers) Capstone Press of Coughlan Cos.

Alaskan Iditarod Adventure: Represent & Solve Problems Involving Multiplication. 2014. (Rosen Common Core Math Readers Ser.). (ENG., Illus.). 24p. (J). (gr. 3-4). pap. 8.25 *(978-1-4777-4962-3(4)*, PowerKids Pr.) Rosen Publishing Group, Inc., The.

Allyn, Daisy. Which Has More? 2012. (InfoMax Readers Ser.). (ENG., Illus.). 16 pp.p. (J). (gr. k-1). pap. 7.00 *(978-1-4488-8884-9(0)*, Rosen Classroom) Rosen Publishing Group, Inc., The.

Alpha Omega Publishing Staff. Mathematics, 2 bks., Set. 2004. (Illus.). pap. 59.95 *(978-0-7403-0313-5(9)*, JKC120, Horizons) Alpha Omega Pubns., Inc.

Anderson, Jill. Adding with Sebastian Pig & Friends at the Circus. Amy Huntington, illus. 2013. (Math Fun with Sebastian Pig & Friends! Ser.). 32p. (J). (gr. k-3). pap. 7.95 *(978-0-7660-5973-3(1)*, Enslow Elementary) Enslow Pubs., Inc.

—Adding with Sebastian Pig & Friends at the Circus. Huntington, Amy, illus. 2009. (Math Fun with Sebastian Pig & Friends! Ser.). 32p. (J). (gr. k-3). lib. bdg. 23.94 *(978-0-7660-3360-3(0))* Enslow Pubs., Inc.

—Subtracting with Sebastian Pig & Friends on a Camping Trip. 2013. (Math Fun with Sebastian Pig & Friends! Ser.). (Illus.). 32p. (J). (gr. k-3). pap. 7.95 *(978-0-7660-5984-9(7)*, Enslow Elementary) Enslow Pubs., Inc.

—Subtracting with Sebastian Pig & Friends on a Camping Trip. Huntington, Amy, illus. 2009. (Math Fun with Sebastian Pig & Friends! Ser.). 32p. (J). (gr. k-3). lib. bdg. 23.94 *(978-0-7660-3361-0(9))* Enslow Pubs., Inc.

Arias, Lisa. Dive into Division: Estimation & Partial Quotients. 2014. (ENG.). 32p. (gr. 3-6). 32.79 *(978-1-62717-715-3(9))* Rourke Educational Media.

—Multiplication Master: Divisibility Rules. 2014. (ENG.). 32p. (gr. 3-6). 32.79 *(978-1-62717-710-8(8))* Rourke Educational Media.

—Positive & Negative Numbers, Oh My! Number Lines. 2014. (ENG.). 32p. (gr. 3-6). 32.79 *(978-1-62717-719-1(1))* Rourke Educational Media.

Armadillo Publishing Staff. Times Table - 1 to 20: Includes Instant Answer Number Matrix Chart. 2015. (ENG.). 24p. pap. 6.99 *(978-1-86147-473-5(3)*, Armadillo) Anness Publishing GBR. Dist: National Bk. Network.

Arvoy, Marsha & Nardi, Dorianne. Percentage. 2010. (ENG., Illus.). 24p. (J). *(978-0-7787-5246-2(1))*; pap. *(978-0-7787-5293-6(3))* Crabtree Publishing Co.

Atwood, Megan. Sparrows Singing: Discovering Addition & Subtraction, 1 vol. Holm, Sharon, illus. 2012. (Count the Critters Ser.). (ENG.). 24p. (J). (gr. k-3). 27.07 *(978-1-61641-856-4(7))* Magic Wagon.

Austen, Mary. I Can Add! Understanding Addition. 2013. (InfoMax Math Readers Ser.). (ENG.). 16p. (J). (gr. k-1). pap. 42.00 *(978-1-4777-1989-3(X))*; pap. 7.00 *(978-1-4777-1988-6(1))* Rosen Publishing Group, Inc., The. (Rosen Classroom).

Austin, Judi. How Many Cookies? Learning to Subtract 1 from One-Digit Numbers. 2009. (Math for the Real World: Early Emergent Ser.). (ENG., Illus.). 8p. (gr. k-1). pap. 5.15 *(978-0-8239-8886-0(4))* Rosen Publishing Group, Inc., The.

Ayers, Amy. Adding & Subtracting in Math Club. Andersen, Gregg, photos by. 2007. (Math in Our World Ser.). (Illus.). 24p. (gr. 1-2). lib. bdg. 22.00 *(978-0-8368-8470-8(1)*, Weekly Reader Leveled Readers) Stevens, Gareth Publishing LLLP.

Back to Basics: Multiplication. (Math Ser.). (J). incl. audio NewSound, LLC.

Back to Basics: Subtraction. (Math Ser.). (J). incl. audio NewSound, LLC.

Baker, Maryann. My Mom Is a Carpenter: Relate Addition & Subtraction to Length. 2014. (Rosen Common Core Math Readers Ser.). (ENG.). 24p. (J). (gr. 2-3). pap. 8.25 *(978-1-4777-4813-8(X)*, Rosen Classroom) Rosen Publishing Group, Inc., The.

Baranski, Diane. Summer Fun: Work with Addition & Subtraction Equations. 2013. (InfoMax Math Readers Ser.). (ENG.). 24p. (J). (gr. 1-2). pap. 49.50 *(978-1-4777-2128-5(2))*; (Illus.). pap. 8.25 *(978-1-4777-2127-8(4))* Rosen Publishing Group, Inc., The. (Rosen Classroom).

Barker, Lori. How Do They Make That? rev. ed. 2012. (Mathematics Readers Ser.). (ENG.). 32p. (J). (gr. 6-6). pap. 8.99 *(978-1-4333-3453-5(4))* Teacher Created Materials, Inc.

—Watch It Grow. rev. ed. 2012. (Mathematics Readers Ser.). (ENG.). 32p. (J). (gr. 6-6). pap. 8.99 *(978-1-4333-3454-2(2))* Teacher Created Materials, Inc.

—What Did I Eat? rev. ed. 2012. (Mathematics Readers Ser.). (ENG.). 32p. (J). (gr. 6-6). pap. 8.99 *(978-1-4333-3452-8(6))* Teacher Created Materials, Inc.

Baron, Jessica. Trading Baseball Cards: Learning the Symbols +, -, And = 2009. (Math for the REAL World Ser.). 12p. (gr. 1-2). pap. 5.90 *(978-0-8239-8865-5(1)*, Rosen Classroom) Rosen Publishing Group, Inc., The.

Batterson, Jason. Beast Academy Guide 3B. Owen, Erich, illus. 2012. 104p. (J). pap. 15.00 *(978-1-934124-42-0(7))* AoPS Inc.

Baxter, Nicola. I Can Learn Times Tables: With Magnetic Numbers to Use Again & Again! Elliott, Rebecca, illus. 2013. (ENG.). 16p. (J). (gr. -1-7). bds. 17.99 *(978-1-84322-986-5(2)*, Armadillo) Anness Publishing GBR. Dist: National Bk. Network.

Becker, Ann. Multiplication. 2009. (ENG., Illus.). 24p. (J). lib. bdg. *(978-0-7787-4348-4(9)*, 1302751); pap. *(978-0-7787-4366-8(7)*, 1302751) Crabtree Publishing Co.

Bellefontaine, Kim. Canada 123. Gürth, Per-Henrik, illus. 2011. (ENG.). 24p. (J). (gr. -1-1). 7.95 *(978-1-55453-659-7(6))* Kids Can Pr., Ltd. CAN. Dist: Hachette Bk. Group.

Benchmark Education Company, LLC Staff, compiled by. Adding & Subtracting: Theme Set. 2006. (J). 343.00 *(978-1-4108-7073-5(1))* Benchmark Education Co.

—Addition & Subtraction. 2006. (J). 118.00 *(978-1-4108-7052-0(9))* Benchmark Education Co.

—Comparing Numbers: Theme Set. 2006. (J). 109.00 *(978-1-4108-7093-3(6))* Benchmark Education Co.

Beshears, Linda Gills. Times Tables Made Fun & Easy. Theresa Speight, L.L.C. Staff, ed. 2008. (Illus.). 197p. (YA). per. 28.00 *(978-0-9795007-8-7(8))* Complete in Christ Ministries, Inc.

Biesanz, Thomas. EZ Times Table: An easy visual way to learn multiplication & division by playing with patterns & making friends with Numbers. Marsh, Jakob, illus. 2nd rev. ed. 2008. (ENG.). 80p. (J). per. 12.95 *(978-0-9799636-1-2(3))* Growth-Ink.

Biesanz, Thomas/John. Ez times Table: An easy, visual way to learn multiplication & division by playing with patterns, & making friends with Numbers. 2008. (Illus.). 60p. (J). 12.95 *(978-0-9799636-0-5(5))* Growth-Ink.

Blackmon, Clarissa. Join the Club! Foundations for Multiplication. 2014. (Rosen Common Core Math Readers Ser.). 24p. (J). (gr. 2-3). (ENG.). pap. 49.50 *(978-1-4777-4643-1(9))*; (Illus.). 23.60 *(978-1-4777-6425-1(9))* Rosen Publishing Group, Inc., The. (Rosen Classroom).

Blackwood, Melissa, et al. Maths - Problem Solving & Reasoning Age 7-9. 2015. (Letts Wild about Learning Ser.). (ENG.). 48p. (J). (gr. 2-4). pap. 8.95 *(978-0-84419-788-0(3))* HarperCollins Pubs. Ltd. GBR. Dist: Independent Pubs. Group.

Blood, Danielle. Multiplication: 22 Motivating Manipulatives That Help Kids Learn the Times Table. 2004. (Fun-Flap Facts Ser.). (ENG.). 32p. pap. 8.99 *(978-0-439-36544-4(9)*, Teaching Resources) Scholastic, Inc.

Bochenski, Cristina. Emma Has One More. 2012. (InfoMax Readers Ser.). (ENG., Illus.). 16 pp.p. (J). (gr. k-1). pap. 7.00 *(978-1-4488-8890-0(5)*, Rosen Classroom) Rosen Publishing Group, Inc., The.

Boothroyd, Jennifer. Skip Counting. 2007. (First Step Nonfiction - Early Math Ser.). (ENG.). 8p. (gr. -1-1). pap. 4.95 *(978-0-8225-6828-5(4))* Lerner Publishing Group.

Brinker, Spencer. Counting to Add with Baron Von Madd. 2015. (Spooky Math Ser.). (ENG., Illus.). 32p. (J). (gr. -1-3). lib. bdg. 26.60 *(978-1-62724-867-9(6))* Bearport Publishing Co., Inc.

—More or Less & a Vampire's Guess. 2015. (Illus.). 32p. (J). lib. bdg. *(978-1-62724-330-8(5))* Bearport Publishing Co., Inc.

—Zombie Take Away. 2015. (Spooky Math Ser.). (ENG., Illus.). 32p. (J). (gr. -1-3). lib. bdg. 26.60 *(978-1-62724-868-6(4))* Bearport Publishing Co., Inc.

Bristow, Michael. Backyard Bugs: Understand & Apply Properties of Operations. 2013. (InfoMax Math Readers Ser.). (ENG.). 24p. (J). (gr. 1-2). pap. 49.50 *(978-1-4777-2119-3(3))*; pap. 8.25 *(978-1-4777-2118-6(5))* Rosen Publishing Group, Inc., The. (Rosen Classroom).

Brocket, Jane. 1 Cookie, 2 Chairs, 3 Pears: Numbers Everywhere. Brocket, Jane, photos by. 2013. (Jane Brocket's Clever Concepts Ser.). (ENG., Illus.). 32p. (gr. -1-2). lib. bdg. 26.60 *(978-1-4677-0232-4(3)*, Millbrook Pr.) Lerner Publishing Group.

Brooks, Felicity & Litchfield, Jo. First Numbers. Allman, Howard, photos by. 2006. (Usborne First Numbers Ser.). (Illus.). 48p. (J). (gr. -1). pap. 8.99 *(978-0-7945-0746-6(8)*, Usborne) EDC Publishing.

Brunner-Jass, Renata. The Science Olympiad: Proportions & Ratios. 2013. (IMath Ser.). (Illus.). 48p. (J). (gr. 5-6). pap. 11.94 *(978-1-60357-515-7(4))* Norwood Hse. Pr.

Brunner-Jass, Renata & Loughran, Donna. The Science Olympiad: Proportions & Ratios. 2013. (IMath Ser.). (Illus.). 48p. (J). (gr. 5-6). lib. bdg. 23.94 *(978-1-59953-576-0(9))* Norwood Hse. Pr.

Buchanan, Heather. Logan's Landscaping: Foundations for Multiplication. 2014. (Rosen Common Core Math Readers Ser.). 24p. (J). (gr. 2-3). (ENG.). pap. 49.50 *(978-1-4777-4649-3(8))*; (Illus.). 23.60 *(978-1-4777-6400-8(3))*; (ENG., Illus.). pap. 8.25 *(978-1-4777-4648-6(X))* Rosen Publishing Group, Inc., The. (Rosen Classroom).

Burganti, Darien. Fun at the Dojo: Use Place Value Understanding & Properties of Operations to Add. 2014. (Math Masters: Number & Operations in Base Ten Ser.). 24p. (J). (gr. 2-3). 23.60 *(978-1-4777-6433-6(X))*; (ENG.). pap. 8.25 *(978-1-4777-4717-9(6))* Rosen Publishing Group, Inc., The. (Rosen Classroom).

Burnett, Calvin & Irons, Calvin. The Fun Machines: A Book about Addition & Subtraction. 2012. (J). *(978-1-921959-31-8(2))* Origo Education.

Burnett, James. Our Sister's Surprise: A Book about Missing-Addend Subtraction. 2012. (J). *(978-1-921959-28-8(2))* Origo Education.

Burnett, James & Irons, Calvin. The Pirates' Gold: A Book about Division (sharing) 2012. (J). *(978-1-921959-29-5(0))* Origo Education.

Burstein, John. Doblar: Estrellas Del Circo. 2006. (Monstruos Matematicos Ser.). (SPA., Illus.). 24p. (J). (gr. k-4). lib. bdg. 21.00 *(978-0-8368-6669-8(X)*, Weekly Reader Leveled Readers) Stevens, Gareth Publishing LLLP.

—Hacer Decenas: Grupos de Gollyluvas. 2006. (Monstruos Matematicos Ser.). (SPA., Illus.). 24p. (J). (gr. k-4). lib. bdg. 21.00 *(978-0-8368-6672-8(X)*, Weekly Reader Leveled Readers) Stevens, Gareth Publishing LLLP.

—Making Tens: Groups of Gollywomples. Destiny Images Staff, illus. 2003. (Math Monsters Ser.). 24p. (J). (gr. k-4). lib. bdg. 21.00 *(978-0-8368-3812-1(2)*, Weekly Reader Leveled Readers) Stevens, Gareth Publishing LLLP.

Bussell, Linda. Multiplicar para Planear una Fiesta. 2008. (Matemáticas en Nuestro Mundo - Nivel 3 (Math in Our World - Level 3) Ser.). (SPA.). 24p. (gr. 2-5). (J). lib. bdg. 22.00 *(978-0-8368-9293-2(3))*; pap. 8.15 *(978-0-8368-9392-2(1))* Stevens, Gareth Publishing LLLP. (Weekly Reader Leveled Readers).

—Multiply to Make Party Plans. 2008. (Math in Our World - Level 3 Ser.). 24p. (gr. 2-5). (J). lib. bdg. 22.00 *(978-0-8368-9285-7(2))*; pap. 8.15 *(978-0-8368-9384-7(0))* Stevens, Gareth Publishing LLLP. (Weekly Reader Leveled Readers).

—Using Division at Sports Camp. 2008. (Math in Our World Ser.). (Illus.). 24p. (J). (gr. 2-5). pap. 8.15 *(978-0-8368-9387-8(5))*; lib. bdg. 22.00 *(978-0-8368-9288-8(7))* Stevens, Gareth Publishing LLLP. (Weekly Reader Leveled Readers).

—Using Division Facts in the Garden. 2008. (Math in Our World - Level 3 Ser.). (Illus.). 24p. (J). (gr. 2-5). pap. 8.15 *(978-0-8368-9385-4(9))*; lib. bdg. 22.00 *(978-0-8368-9286-4(0))* Stevens, Gareth Publishing LLLP. (Weekly Reader Leveled Readers).

Byrd, Josiah. Makayla's Birthday Money! Work with Money. 2014. (Math Masters: Measurement & Data Ser.). 24p. (J). (gr. 2-3). 23.60 *(978-1-4777-6407-7(0))*; (ENG.). pap. 8.25 *(978-1-4777-4822-0(9))* Rosen Publishing Group, Inc., The. (Rosen Classroom).

Campbell, Kenneth. Great Leaps Oral Calculations Addition Mixed Facts. 2006. spiral bd. 25.00 *(978-1-59347-628-1(0))* Diarmuid Inc.

Canavan, Thomas. Computation Skills: 50 Math Super Puzzles. 2011. (Math Standards Workout Ser.). (ENG., Illus.). 48p. (YA). (gr. 5-8). pap. 11.75 *(978-1-4488-6680-9(4)*, Rosen Reference); lib. bdg. 29.25 *(978-1-4488-6673-1(1))* Rosen Publishing Group, Inc., The.

—Mental Math: 50 Math Super Puzzles. 2011. (Math Standards Workout Ser.). (ENG., Illus.). 48p. (YA). (gr. 5-9). lib. bdg. 29.25 *(978-1-4488-6677-9(4))* Rosen Publishing Group, Inc., The.

Caron, Lucille & St. Jacques, Philip M. Multiplication & Division Smarts! 2011. (Math Smarts! Ser.). (Illus.). 64p. (J). (gr. 5-18). pap. 8.95 *(978-1-59845-320-1(3))* Enslow Pubs., Inc.

Caron, Lucille, et al. Multiplication & Division Smarts! 2011. (Math Smarts! Ser.). (Illus.). 64p. (J). (gr. 5-18). lib. bdg. 29.27 *(978-0-7660-3937-7(4))* Enslow Pubs., Inc.

Carroll, Danielle. The Great Divide, 6 vols., Set. 2005. (Yellow Umbrella Fluent Level Ser.). (ENG., Illus.). 16p. (gr. k-1). pap. 35.70 *(978-0-7368-5327-9(8)*, Yellow Umbrella Bks.) Capstone Press of Coughlan Cos.

—Is It Odd or Even? 2005. (Yellow Umbrella Fluent Level Ser.). (ENG., Illus.). 16p. (gr. k-1). pap. 35.70 *(978-0-7368-5321-7(9)*, Yellow Umbrella Bks.) Capstone Press of Coughlan Cos.

Carson-Dellosa Publishing Staff. Add & Subtract, Grade 1. 2010. (Home Workbooks Ser.). (ENG.). 64p. (gr. 1-1). pap. 4.49 *(978-1-60418-792-2(1))* Carson-Dellosa Publishing, LLC.

—Add & Subtract, Grade 2. 2010. (Home Workbooks Ser.). (ENG.). 64p. (gr. 2-2). pap. 4.49 *(978-1-60418-797-7(2))* Carson-Dellosa Publishing, LLC.

—Addition 0 to 12. 2006. (ENG., Illus.). 54p. (gr. 1-3). 2.99 *(978-0-7696-7711-8(8)*, Brighter Child) Carson-Dellosa Publishing, LLC.

—Division 0 to 12. 2006. (ENG., Illus.). 54p. (gr. 3-5). 2.99 *(978-0-7696-7723-1(1)*, Brighter Child) Carson-Dellosa Publishing, LLC.

—Multiplication 0 to 12. 2006. (ENG., Illus.). 54p. (gr. 3-5). 2.99 *(978-0-7696-7743-9(6)*, Brighter Child) Carson-Dellosa Publishing, LLC.

—Multiplication, Grade 3. 2010. (Home Workbooks Ser.). (ENG.). 64p. (gr. 3-3). pap. 4.49 *(978-1-60418-802-8(2))* Carson-Dellosa Publishing, LLC.

—Subtraction 0 to 12. 2006. (ENG., Illus.). 54p. (gr. 1-3). 2.99 *(978-0-7696-7721-7(5)*, Brighter Child) Carson-Dellosa Publishing, LLC.

Cartogna, Eileen. Fun at the Fair: Learning Subtraction Facts To 10. 2009. (Math for the REAL World Ser.). 12p. (gr. 1-2). pap. 5.90 *(978-0-8239-8846-4(5)*, Rosen Classroom) Rosen Publishing Group, Inc., The.

Chilek, Laurie. Counting at the Zoo: Learning to Add 1 to One-Digit Numbers. 2009. (Math for the Real World Ser.). (ENG., Illus.). 8p. (gr. k-1). pap. 5.15 *(978-0-8239-8909-6(7))* Rosen Publishing Group, Inc., The.

Chrismer, Melanie. Multiply This! 2005. (Rookie Read-About Math Ser.). (ENG., Illus.). 32p. (J). (gr. 1-2). lib. bdg. 20.50 *(978-0-516-25264-3(X)*, Children's Pr.) Scholastic Library Publishing.

Cipriano, Jeri S. Arithmetricks. 2004. (Illus.). 160p. pap. 14.95 *(978-0-673-58896-8(3))* Good Year Bks.

—Arithmetricks: More Than 100 Amazing Math Tricks. 2nd ed. 2006. (Illus.). 156p. per. 17.95 *(978-1-59647-112-2(3))* Good Year Bks.

Clay, Jonathan. At the Basketball Game. 2013. (Core Math Skills: Operations & Algebraic Thinking Ser.). 24p. (J). (gr. 1-2). 22.60 *(978-1-4777-2234-3(3))*; (ENG.). pap. 8.25 *(978-1-4777-2088-2(X))* Rosen Publishing Group, Inc., The. (Rosen Classroom).

—At the Basketball Game: Work with Addition & Subtraction Equations. 2013. (Rosen Math Readers Ser.). (ENG.). 24p. (J). (gr. 1-2). pap. 49.50 *(978-1-4777-2089-9(8)*, Rosen Classroom) Rosen Publishing Group, Inc., The.

Cleary, Brian P. The Action of Subtraction. Gable, Brian, illus. 2006. (Math Is CATegorical (r) Ser.). (ENG.). 32p. (J). (gr. k-3). lib. bdg. 16.95 *(978-0-7613-9461-7(3)*, Millbrook Pr.) Lerner Publishing Group.

—The Mission of Addition. Gable, Brian, illus. 2005. (Math Is CATegorical (r) Ser.). (ENG.). 32p. (gr. k-3). lib. bdg. 16.95 *(978-1-57505-859-7(6)*, Millbrook Pr.) Lerner Publishing Group.

Clemson, Wendy & Clemson, David. Zookeeper for a Day. 2007. (Math Adventures Ser.). (Illus.). 32p. (gr. 1-4). pap. 10.50 *(978-0-8368-8142-4(7))*; lib. bdg. 26.00 *(978-0-8368-7843-1(4))* Stevens, Gareth Publishing LLLP. (Gareth Stevens Learning Library).

Clissold, Caroline. Let's Go. 2007. (Trackers-Math Ser.). (gr. 2-5). pap. 5.00 *(978-1-59055-915-4(0))* Pacific Learning, Inc.

Coan, Sharon. Mi Fiesta de Cumpleaños (My Birthday Party) 2016. (TIME for KIDS(r) Nonfiction Readers Ser.). (SPA., Illus.). 12p. (J). (gr. k-k). 4.99 *(978-1-4938-2972-9(6))* Teacher Created Materials, Inc.

—My Birthday Party. 2015. (TIME for KIDS(r) Nonfiction Readers Ser.). (ENG., Illus.). 12p. (gr. k-k). 4.99 *(978-1-4938-2063-4(X))* Teacher Created Materials, Inc.

Cohen, Leslie. I've Got 5 Dollars! Understanding Addition & Subtraction. 2013. (Rosen Math Readers Ser.). (ENG.). 16p. (J). (gr. k-1). pap. 42.00 *(978-1-4777-1669-4(6))*; (Illus.). pap. 7.00 *(978-1-4777-1668-7(8))* Rosen Publishing Group, Inc., The. (Rosen Classroom).

Collins Easy Learning & Greaves, Simon. Times Tables Workbook, Ages 7-11. 2015. (Collins Easy Learning Ser.). (ENG.). 32p. (J). (gr. 2-6). pap. 6.95 *(978-0-00-813441-9(3))* HarperCollins Pubs. Ltd. GBR. Dist: Independent Pubs. Group.

Collins Easy Learning, Collins Easy. Addition & Subtraction Quick Quizzes Ages 5-7. 2017. (Collins Easy Learning KS1 Ser.). (ENG., Illus.). 32p. (J). (gr. k-2). pap. 6.99 ***(978-0-00-821247-6(3))*** HarperCollins Pubs. Ltd. GBR. Dist: Independent Pubs. Group.

—Addition & Subtraction Quick Quizzes Ages 7-9. 2017. (Collins Easy Learning KS2 Ser.). (ENG., Illus.). 32p. (J). (gr. 2-4). pap. 6.99 *(978-0-00-821256-8(2))* HarperCollins Pubs. Ltd. GBR. Dist: Independent Pubs. Group.

—Multiplication & Division Bumper Book Ages 7-9. 2017. (Collins Easy Learning KS2 Ser.). (ENG.). 64p. (J). (gr. 2-4). pap. 9.99 ***(978-0-00-821242-1(2))*** HarperCollins Pubs. Ltd. GBR. Dist: Independent Pubs. Group.

Collins Easy Learning, Collins Easy. Times Tables Quick Quizzes Ages 5-7. 2017. (Collins Easy Learning KS1 Ser.). (ENG., Illus.). 32p. (J). (gr. k-3). pap. 6.95 *(978-0-00-821249-0(X))* HarperCollins Pubs. Ltd. GBR. Dist: Independent Pubs. Group.

Collins Easy Learning Staff & Clarke, Peter. Addition & Subtraction, Ages 5-7. 2015. (Collins Easy Learning Ser.). (ENG.). 32p. (J). (gr. k-2). pap., wbk. ed. 6.95 *(978-0-00-813429-7(4))* HarperCollins Pubs. Ltd. GBR. Dist: Independent Pubs. Group.

—Addition & Subtraction Ages 5-7. 2015. (Collins Easy Learning Ser.). (ENG.). 32p. (J). (gr. k-2). pap. 6.95 *(978-0-00-813428-0(6))* HarperCollins Pubs. Ltd. GBR. Dist: Independent Pubs. Group.

—Addition & Subtraction, Ages 7-9. 2015. (Collins Easy Learning Ser.). (ENG.). 32p. (J). (gr. 2-4). pap. 6.95 *(978-0-00-813421-1(9))* HarperCollins Pubs. Ltd. GBR. Dist: Independent Pubs. Group.

—Mental Maths Ages 5-7. 2015. (Collins Easy Learning Ser.). (ENG.). 32p. (J). (gr. 1-2). pap. 6.95 *(978-0-00-813433-4(2))* HarperCollins Pubs. Ltd. GBR. Dist: Independent Pubs. Group.

—Multiplication & Division, Ages 5-7. 2015. (Collins Easy Learning Ser.). (ENG.). 32p. (J). (gr. 1-2). pap. 6.95 *(978-0-00-813434-1(0))* HarperCollins Pubs. Ltd. GBR. Dist: Independent Pubs. Group.

—Multiplication & Division, Ages 7-9. 2015. (Collins Easy Learning Ser.). (ENG.). 32p. (J). (gr. 2-4). pap. 6.95 *(978-0-00-813426-6(X))* HarperCollins Pubs. Ltd. GBR. Dist: Independent Pubs. Group.

Collins Easy Learning Staff & Greaves, Simon. Times Tables Ages 5-7. 2015. (Collins Easy Learning Ser.). (ENG.). 32p. (J). (gr. k-2). pap. 6.95 *(978-0-00-813438-9(3))* HarperCollins Pubs. Ltd. GBR. Dist: Independent Pubs. Group.

—Times Tables, Ages 7-11. 2015. (Collins Easy Learning Ser.). (ENG.). 32p. (J). (gr. 2-6). pap. 6.95 *(978-0-00-813440-2(5))* HarperCollins Pubs. Ltd. GBR. Dist: Independent Pubs. Group.

Collins, Kathleen. Our New Fish Tank: Learning to Estimate & Round Numbers to the Nearest Ones, Tens, & Hundreds Places. 2009. (PowerMath: Beginning Ser.). 16p. (gr. 2-2). 37.50 *(978-1-60851-375-8(0)*, PowerKids Pr.) Rosen Publishing Group, Inc., The.

—Our New Fish Tank: Learning to Estimate to the Nearest Ones, Tens, & Hundreds Places. 2006. (Rosen Publishing Group's Reading Room Collection). (Illus.). 16p. lib. bdg. 18.75 *(978-1-4042-3338-6(5)*, PowerKids Pr.) Rosen Publishing Group, Inc., The.

Colson, Rob. Super Sums: Addition, Subtraction, Multiplication, & Division. 2017. (Math Everywhere Ser.). (ENG.). 32p. (J). pap. 8.95 ***(978-0-531-23320-7(0))***; lib. bdg. 27.00 ***(978-0-531-22884-5(3))*** Scholastic Library Publishing. (Children's Pr.).

—Your Number's Up: Digits, Number Lines, Negative & Positive Numbers. 2017. (Math Everywhere Ser.). (ENG.). 32p. (J). pap. 8.95 ***(978-0-531-23322-1(7))***; lib. bdg. 27.00 ***(978-0-531-22886-9(X))*** Scholastic Library Publishing. (Children's Pr.).

Connors, Bill. Aiden's Aquarium Adventure: Add Within 20. 2013. (InfoMax Math Readers Ser.). (ENG.). 24p. (J). (gr. 1-2). pap. 49.50 *(978-1-4777-2155-1(X))*; (Illus.). pap. 8.25 *(978-1-4777-2154-4(1))* Rosen Publishing Group, Inc., The. (Rosen Classroom).

Corcorane, Ann. Animals Everywhere, 1 vol. 2011. (Wonder Readers Emergent Level Ser.). (ENG.). 32p. (gr. -1-1). pap. 5.99 *(978-1-4296-7861-2(5)*, Wonder Readers) Capstone Press of Coughlan Cos.

—Subtracting. 2011. (Wonder Readers Emergent Level Ser.). (ENG.). (gr. -1-1). 16p. pap. 35.94 *(978-1-4296-8163-6(2))*; 32p. pap. 5.99 *(978-1-4296-7873-5(9))* Capstone Press of Coughlan Cos. (Wonder Readers).

—A Zoo Full of Birds, 1 vol. 2011. (Wonder Readers Emergent Level Ser.). (ENG.). (gr. -1-1). 32p. pap. 5.99 *(978-1-4296-7857-5(7))*; 16p. pap. 35.94 *(978-1-4296-8063-9(6))* Capstone Press of Coughlan Cos. (Wonder Readers).

Corporate Contributor Staff & West, David. Dinosaur Numbers. 2012. (ENG.). 24p. (J). *(978-0-7787-7455-6(4))*; pap. *(978-0-7787-7460-0(0))* Crabtree Publishing Co.

Dahl, Michael. Eggs & Legs: Counting by Twos, 1 vol. Ouren, Todd, illus. 2005. (Know Your Numbers Ser.). (ENG.). 24p. (gr. -1-2). 26.65 *(978-1-4048-0945-1(7))* Picture Window Bks.

Dapice, Carmine. Lets Rhyme with Time. 2013. 38p. pap. 13.95 *(978-1-4497-8822-3(X)*, WestBow Pr.) Author Solutions, Inc.

Deanthony, Dylan. Show a Soldier You Care! Understand the Relationship Between Multiplication & Division, 1 vol. 2015. (InfoMax Common Core Math Readers Ser.). (ENG.). 24p. (J). pap. 8.25 *(978-1-4777-4696-7(X)*, Rosen Classroom) Rosen Publishing Group, Inc., The.

Deen, Marilyn. Divided By, 1 vol. (Wonder Readers: Mathematics Ser.). (ENG.). (gr. -1-2). 2012. 20p. lib. bdg. 22.65 *(978-1-4296-9606-7(0))* 2011. 16p. pap. 35.94 *(978-1-4296-8083-7(0))* 2011. 32p. pap. 5.99 *(978-1-4296-7914-5(X))* Capstone Press of Coughlan Cos. (Wonder Readers).

—Odd & Even, 1 vol. 2012. (Wonder Readers: Mathematics Ser.). (ENG.). 20p. (gr. -1-2). lib. bdg. 22.65 *(978-1-4296-9608-1(7)*, Wonder Readers) Capstone Press of Coughlan Cos.

—Odd or Even. 2011. (Wonder Readers Fluent Level Ser.). (ENG.). 32p. (gr. -1-2). pap. 5.99 *(978-1-4296-7933-6(6)*, Wonder Readers) Capstone Press of Coughlan Cos.

DeGroat, Harry De W. & Firman, Sidney G. The Iroquois Arithmetics for School & Life Book: Grades Five & Six. 2005.

A
B

reprint ed. pap. 31.95 *(978-1-4179-3343-3(7))* Kessinger Publishing, LLC.

—The Iroquois Arithmetics for School & Life Book: Grades Seven & Eight. 2005. reprint ed. pap. 33.95 *(978-1-4191-7680-7(3))* Kessinger Publishing, LLC.

Diedrick, Noah. Submarines: Use Place Value Understanding & Properties of Operations to Perform Multi-Digit Arithmetic. 2014. (Rosen Common Core Math Readers Ser.). (ENG.). 24p. (J). (gr. 3-4). pap. 8.25 *(978-1-4777-4936-4(5),* PowerKids Pr.) Rosen Publishing Group, Inc., The.

DiPiero, Josh. Tickets for the Talent Show: Use Place Value Understanding & Properties of Operations to Add & Subtract. 2014. (Math Masters: Number & Operations in Base Ten Ser.). (Illus.). 24p. (J). (gr. 2-3). 23.60 *(978-1-4777-6432-9(1));* (ENG., pap. 8.25 *(978-1-4777-4706-3(0))* Rosen Publishing Group, Inc., The. (Rosen Classroom).

Division. 2003. (Sabio y Prudente Ser.). (SPA., Illus.). 64p. (J). 4.99 *(978-0-8254-0912-7(8))* Kregel Pubns.

Division Mastery w/Audio CD: Kit with Book, Wrap-up & CD. 2004. (ENG.). (J). 19.99 *(978-0-943343-98-3(4))* Learning Wrap-Ups, Inc.

Dolphin, Colleen. Ice Hockey by the Numbers, 1 vol. 2010. (Team Sports by the Numbers Ser.). (ENG.). 24p. (J). (gr. k-3). lib. bdg. 24.21 *(978-1-60453-770-3(1),* SandCastle) ABDO Publishing Co.

—Soccer by the Numbers, 1 vol. 2010. (Team Sports by the Numbers Ser.). (ENG.). 24p. (J). (gr. k-3). lib. bdg. 24.21 *(978-1-60453-771-0(X),* SandCastle) ABDO Publishing Co.

—Volleyball by the Numbers, 1 vol. 2010. (Team Sports by the Numbers Ser.). (ENG.). 24p. (J). (gr. k-3). lib. bdg. 24.21 *(978-1-60453-772-7(8),* SandCastle) ABDO Publishing Co.

Dorling Kindersley Publishing Staff. Adding & Subtracting. 2016. (Skills for Starting School Ser.). (ENG., Illus.). 40p. (J). (gr. -1-k). pap. 6.99 *(978-1-4654-5128-6(5),* DK Children) Dorling Kindersley Publishing, Inc.

—Turn to Learn Multiplication. 2016. (ENG., Illus.). 18p. (J). (gr. k-3). 14.99 *(978-1-4654-5187-3(0),* DK Children) Dorling Kindersley Publishing, Inc.

—10 Minutes a Day: Multiplication, Third Grade. 2013. (ENG., Illus.). 80p. (J). (gr. 2-4). pap. 9.99 *(978-1-4654-1712-1(5),* DK Children) Dorling Kindersley Publishing, Inc.

Dowdy, Penny & Becker, Ann. Subtraction. 2009. (ENG.). 24p. (J). lib. bdg. *(978-0-7787-4350-7(0))* Crabtree Publishing Co.

Education.com. Number Roundup: A Workbook of Place Values & Number Strategies. 2015. (ENG.). 128p. (J). (gr. 2-2). pap. 7.99 *(978-0-486-80264-0(7))* Dover Pubns., Inc.

Endres, Hollie J. Fair Share. 2005. (Yellow Umbrella Fluent Level Ser.). (ENG., Illus.). 16p. (gr. k-1). pap. 35.70 *(978-0-7368-5318-7(9),* Yellow Umbrella Bks.) Capstone Press of Coughlan Cos.

—How Much Money? 2005. (Yellow Umbrella Fluent Level Ser.). (ENG.). 16p. (gr. k-1). pap. 35.70 *(978-0-7368-5325-5(1),* Yellow Umbrella Bks.) Capstone Press of Coughlan Cos.

Enslow, Brian. Counting Ants 1-2-3. 2011. (All about Counting Bugs 1-2-3 Ser.). (Illus.). 24p. (J). (gr. k-3). lib. bdg. 22.60 *(978-0-7660-3919-3(6))* Enslow Pubs., Inc.

—Counting Butterflies 1-2-3. 2011. (All about Counting Bugs 1-2-3 Ser.). (Illus.). 24p. (J). (gr. k-3). lib. bdg. 22.60 *(978-0-7660-3921-6(8))* Enslow Pubs., Inc.

Ericson, Emma. I Collect Bugs! Understanding Addition. 2013. (InfoMax Math Readers Ser.). (ENG.). 16p. (J). (gr. k-1). pap. 42.00 *(978-1-4777-2007-3(3));* (Illus.). pap. 7.00 *(978-1-4777-2006-6(5))* Rosen Publishing Group, Inc., The. (Rosen Classroom).

Evans, Renee Call & Perucca, Nancy Call. Multiplication Camp. Perucca, Nancy Call, illus. 2004. (Illus.). (J). pap. 29.95 *(978-0-9748074-0-9(0))* Nancy's Artworks.

Faulkner, Keith. Flip-Flap Math: Flip the Fipas to Check Your Answers! Irish, Martin, illus. 2005. 12 p.p. (J). *(978-0-439-78578-5(2))* Scholastic, Inc.

—Maths Machine: A Fun New Way to Do Maths! Tyger, Rory, illus. 2004. (J). *(978-0-439-72174-5(1))* Scholastic, Inc.

Faulkner, Keith & Holmes, Stephen. Animal ? Math. Faulkner, Keith & Holmes, Stephen, illus. 2003. (Illus.). (J). *(978-0-439-62755-9(9))* Scholastic, Inc.

Figorito, Marcus. Let's Play Basketball! Learning Addition Facts to 10. 2009. (Math for the REAL World Ser.). 12p. (gr. 1-2). pap. 5.90 *(978-0-8239-8866-2(X),* Rosen Classroom) Rosen Publishing Group, Inc., The.

Finifrock, Jacob E. & Pierson, Melinda. Multiplicity: Lesson Planning Guide. 2004. 85p. spiral bd. 21.95 *(978-1-930731-18-9(3))* DAC Educational Pubns.

First, Rachel. Add It Up! Fun with Addition, 1 vol. 2016. (Math Beginnings Ser.). (ENG., Illus.). 24p. (J). (gr. k-3). 24.21 *(978-1-62403-932-4(4))* ABDO Publishing Co.

—Count It! Fun with Counting & Comparing, 1 vol. 2016. (Math Beginnings Ser.). (ENG., Illus.). 24p. (J). (gr. k-3). 24.21 *(978-1-62403-933-1(2))* ABDO Publishing Co.

—Subtract It! Fun with Subtraction, 1 vol. 2016. (Math Beginnings Ser.). (ENG., Illus.). 24p. (J). (gr. k-3). 24.21 *(978-1-62403-935-5(9))* ABDO Publishing Co.

Fitzgerald, Lee. My Birthday Surprise: Understanding Subtraction. 2013. (InfoMax Math Readers Ser.). (ENG.). 16p. (J). (gr. k-1). pap. 42.00 *(978-1-4777-1980-0(6));* pap. 7.00 *(978-1-4777-1979-4(2))* Rosen Publishing Group, Inc., The. (Rosen Classroom).

Flash Kids Editors, ed. Number Activities: Grade Pre-K-K (Flash Skills) 2010. (Flash Skills Ser.). (ENG.). 64p. (J). pap. 3.95 *(978-1-4114-3468-4(4),* Spark Publishing Group) Sterling Publishing Co., Inc.

—Number Dot-to-Dot, Grade Pre-K-K. 2010. (Flash Skills Ser.). (ENG.). 64p. (J). pap. 3.95 *(978-1-4114-3461-5(7),* Spark Publishing Group) Sterling Publishing Co., Inc.

Flip Flash Addition. 2004. (Flip Flash Pads Ser.). 64p. (J). act. bk. ed. 6.99 *(978-1-85997-585-5(2))* Byeway Bks.

Flip Flash Subtraction. 2004. (Flip Flash Pads Ser.). 64p. (J). act. bk. ed. 6.99 *(978-1-85997-586-2(0))* Byeway Bks.

Fontes, Justine. Cheerios Count to 100. Croll, Carolyn, illus. 2005. (J). *(978-0-439-70341-3(7))* Scholastic, Inc.

Fosnot, Catherine Twomey. Bunk Beds & Apple Boxes: Early Number Sense. 2008. (ENG.). 80p. (gr. k-1). pap. 31.25 *(978-0-325-01006-9(4),* E01006, Firsthand) Heinemann.

Fosnot, Catherine Twomey & Dolk, Maarten. Multiplication & Division Minilessons, Grades 3-5. 2005. (Young Mathematicians at Work Ser.). (ENG.). (J). (gr. 3-5). cd-rom 39.38 *(978-0-325-00775-5(6),* E00775) Heinemann.

Francis, Eugenia. Ensene a Su Hijo: Las Tablas de Multiplicar (Written in Spanish) 2007. 169p. pap. 14.95 *(978-0-7414-3998-7(0))* Infinity Publishing.

Francis, Isabelle. New York City: Yesterday & Today: Understand Properties of Multiplication, 1 vol. 2015. (InfoMax Common Core Math Readers Ser.). (ENG.). 24p. (J). pap. 8.25 *(978-1-4777-4699-8(4),* Rosen Classroom) Rosen Publishing Group, Inc., The.

Freeman, Marcia S. More Ice Cream: Words for Math Comparisons. 2007. (Illus.). 24p. (J). pap. 7.95 *(978-1-60044-685-6(X));* (gr. 3-7). lib. bdg. 22.79 *(978-1-60044-641-2(8))* Rourke Educational Media.

Freese, Joan. Diversion con Dobles en la Granja. 2008. (Matemáticas en Nuestro Mundo - Nivel 2 (Math in Our World - Level 2) Ser.). (SPA., Illus.). 24p. (gr. 1-4). lib. bdg. 22.00 *(978-0-8368-9020-4(5),* Weekly Reader Leveled Readers) Stevens, Gareth Publishing LLLP.

—Diversión con Dobles en la Granja. 2008. (Las matemáticas en nuestro mundo - Nivel 2 (Math in Our World - Level 2) Ser.). (SPA.). 24p. (gr. 1-4). pap. 8.15 *(978-0-8368-9029-7(9),* Weekly Reader Leveled Readers) Stevens, Gareth Publishing LLLP.

—Doubles Fun on the Farm. 2008. (Math in Our World - Level 2 Ser.). 24p. (gr. 1-4). pap. 8.15 *(978-0-8368-9011-2(6));* (Illus.). lib. bdg. 22.00 *(978-0-8368-9002-0(7))* Stevens, Gareth Publishing LLLP. (Weekly Reader Leveled Readers).

—Using Math to Make Party Plans. 2008. (Math in Our World - Level 2 Ser.). 24p. (gr. 1-4). pap. 8.15 *(978-0-8368-9012-9(4),* Weekly Reader Leveled Readers) Stevens, Gareth Publishing LLLP.

—Using Math to Make Party Plans. Andersen, Gregg, photos by. 2008. (Math in Our World: Level 2 Ser.). (Illus.). 24p. (gr. 1-4). lib. bdg. 22.00 *(978-0-8368-9003-7(5));* lib. bdg. 22.00 *(978-0-8368-9003-7(5))* Stevens, Gareth Publishing LLLP. (Weekly Reader Leveled Readers).

—Vamos A Planear una Fiesta Con Matematicas. Andersen, Gregg, photos by. 2008. (Matemáticas en Nuestro Mundo - Nivel 2 (Math in Our World - Level 2) Ser.). (SPA., Illus.). 24p. (gr. 1-4). lib. bdg. 22.00 *(978-0-8368-9021-1(3),* Weekly Reader Leveled Readers) Stevens, Gareth Publishing LLLP.

—Vamos a Planear una Fiesta con Matemáticas. 2008. (Las matemáticas en nuestro mundo - Nivel 2 (Math in Our World - Level 2) Ser.). (SPA.). 24p. (gr. 1-4). pap. 8.15 *(978-0-8368-9030-3(2),* Weekly Reader Leveled Readers) Stevens, Gareth Publishing LLLP.

Gabel, Frank. Sam's Summer Job: Relate Area to Multiplication & to Addition, 1 vol. 2015. (InfoMax Common Core Math Readers Ser.). (ENG.). 24p. (J). pap. 8.25 *(978-1-4777-4588-5(2),* Rosen Classroom) Rosen Publishing Group, Inc., The.

Gant, Robert, illus. My Big Box of Addition & Subtraction. gif. ed. 2005. 64p. (J). cd-rom 24.95 *(978-1-57791-196-8(2))* Brighter Minds Children's Publishing.

Ghigna, Charles. Addition. Saburi, Misa, illus. 2017. (Winter Math Ser.). (ENG.). 24p. (gr. k-2). 33.99 ***(978-1-68410-007-1(0))*** Cantata Learning.

Girard, Robert. The American Flag: Learning to Identify Two-Digit Numbers up to 50. 2009. (Math for the REAL World Ser.). 12p. (gr. 1-2). pap. 5.90 *(978-0-8239-8888-4(0),* Rosen Classroom) Rosen Publishing Group, Inc., The.

Glenn, Suki & Carpenter, Susan. Patterns in Arithmetic: Parent/Teacher Guide & Student Workbook: Book 1. Minns, Karen M. C., illus. 2004. 305p. (YA). spiral bd. 45.00 *(978-0-9729248-2-5(5))* Pattern Pr.

—Patterns in Arithmetic: Student Workbook: Book 1, 2 vols. 2004. (Illus.). 150p. (YA). ring bd., wbk. ed. 15.00 *(978-0-9729248-1-8(7))* Pattern Pr.

—Patterns in Arithmetic 2: Student Workbook: Book 2. Minns, Karen Marie Christa, illus. 2005. (ENG.). 269p. (gr. 2-18). spiral bd. *(978-0-9729248-5-6(X))* Pattern Pr.

—Patterns in Arithmetic Bk. 2: Student Workbook. 2005. (Illus.). 278p. (J). (gr. 2-18). ring bd., wbk. ed. 22.00 *(978-0-9729248-4-9(1))* Pattern Pr.

Goldwater, Mitchell. Molly Goes to the Farmer's Market: Use Place Value & Properties of Operations to Add. 2013. (InfoMax Math Readers Ser.). (ENG., Illus.). 24p. (J). (gr. 1-2). pap. 8.25 *(978-1-4777-2166-7(5),* Rosen Classroom) Rosen Publishing Group, Inc., The.

Great Leaps Oral Calculations - Easel. 2006. 10.00 *(978-1-59347-632-8(9))* Diarmuid Inc.

Great Leaps Oral Calculations addition & Subtraction. 2006. (J). (gr. 1-4). spiral bd. 49.50 net. *(978-1-59347-626-7(4))* Diarmuid Inc.

Great Leaps Oral Calculations Division. 2006. spiral bd. 20.00 *(978-1-59347-631-1(0))* Diarmuid Inc.

Great Leaps Oral Calculations Multiplication. 2006. spiral bd. 20.00 *(978-1-59347-630-4(2))* Diarmuid Inc.

Great Leaps Oral Calculations Multiplication & Division. 2006. (J). (gr. 3-7). spiral bd. 49.50 net. *(978-1-59347-627-4(2))* Diarmuid Inc.

Great Leaps Oral Calculations Package: Addition, Subtraction, Mutiplication & Division. 2006. (J). (gr. 1). spiral bd. 72.60 net. *(978-1-59347-625-0(6))* Diarmuid Inc.

Great Leaps Oral Calculations Subtraction. 2006. spiral bd. 20.00 *(978-1-59347-629-8(9))* Diarmuid Inc.

Greathouse, Lisa. The Bakery. rev. ed. 2011. (Mathematics Readers Ser.). (ENG.). 32p. (J). (gr. k-k). pap. 8.99 *(978-1-4333-3435-1(6))* Teacher Created Materials, Inc.

—Count Me In! What's for Lunch?, 1 vol. 2nd rev. ed. 2014. (TIME for KIDS(r) Nonfiction Readers Ser.). (ENG., Illus.). 28p. (J). (gr. 2-2). pap. 23.96 *(978-1-4807-1060-3(1))* Shell Educational Publishing.

—Fun in the Sun. rev. ed. 2011. (Mathematics Readers Ser.). (ENG.). 32p. (J). (gr. k-k). pap. 8.99 *(978-1-4333-3433-7(X))* Teacher Created Materials, Inc.

—The Snack Shop. rev. ed. 2011. (Mathematics Readers Ser.). (ENG.). 32p. (J). (gr. k-k). pap. 8.99 *(978-1-4333-3434-4(8))* Teacher Created Materials, Inc.

Greenwald, Susan. Five Times Five Is Not Ten: Make Multiplication Easy. 2008. 168p. (J). per. 16.95 *(978-0-9777323-1-9(2))* Longevity Publishing, LLC.

Grundrechenarten 1. (Duden-Schuelerhilfen Ser.). (GER.). 96p. (J). *(978-3-411-02636-4(7))* Bibliographisches Institut & F. A. Brockhaus AG DEU. Dist: International Bk. Import Service, Inc.

Grundrechenarten 2. (Duden-Schuelerhilfen Ser.). (GER.). 96p. (J). (gr. 3-4). *(978-3-411-04561-7(2))* Bibliographisches Institut & F. A. Brockhaus AG DEU. Dist: International Bk. Import Service, Inc.

Guzman, Jaime. I've Got 10! Understanding Addition. 2013. (InfoMax Math Readers Ser.). (ENG.). 16p. (J). (gr. k-1). pap. 42.00 *(978-1-4777-1932-9(6));* (Illus.). pap. 7.00 *(978-1-4777-1931-2(8))* Rosen Publishing Group, Inc., The. (Rosen Classroom).

Haeick, Reese. Marlon's Trip to the Marina: Multiply Within 100, 1 vol. 2015. (InfoMax Common Core Math Readers Ser.). (ENG.). 24p. (J). pap. 8.25 *(978-1-4777-4693-6(5),* Rosen Classroom) Rosen Publishing Group, Inc., The.

Hague, Jane. A Very Busy Week: Stories from Tilly's Number Town. 2012. (ENG., Illus.). 36p. pap. *(978-0-9806737-3-9(9))* 123 Number Fun Pty, Ltd.

Halloran, Corey. Our Neighborhood Food Drive. 2013. (Core Math Skills: Numbers & Operations in Base 10 Ser.). 24p. (J). (gr. 1-2). 22.60 *(978-1-4777-2221-3(1),* Rosen Classroom) Rosen Publishing Group, Inc., The.

—Our Neighborhood Food Drive: Extend the Counting Sequence. 2013. (Rosen Math Readers Ser.). (ENG.). 24p. (J). (gr. 1-2). pap. 49.50 *(978-1-4777-2068-4(5));* (Illus.). pap. 8.25 *(978-1-4777-2067-7(7))* Rosen Publishing Group, Inc., The. (Rosen Classroom).

Handley, Bill. Speed Math for Kids: The Fast, Fun Way to Do Basic Calculations. 2007. (ENG., Illus.). 256p. (gr. 4-7). per. 14.95 *(978-0-7879-8863-0(4),* Jossey-Bass) Wiley, John & Sons, Inc.

Harcourt, Lalie & Wortzman, Rickie. Red Riding Hood's Math Adventure. Mazille, Capucine, illus. 2006. 19p. (J). (gr. k-4). reprint ed. 15.00 *(978-0-7567-9957-1(0))* DIANE Publishing Co.

Harper, Scott. Morgan's Birthday Surprise: Understanding Subtraction. 2013. (Rosen Math Readers Ser.). (ENG.). 16p. (J). (gr. k-1). pap. 42.00 *(978-1-4777-1594-9(0));* (Illus.). pap. 7.00 *(978-1-4777-1593-2(2))* Rosen Publishing Group, Inc., The. (Rosen Classroom).

Hayn, Carter. Subtracting with Shapes. 2015. (Rosen REAL Readers: STEM & STEAM Collection). (ENG.). 8p. pap. 5.46 *(978-1-4994-9680-2(X),* Rosen Classroom) Rosen Publishing Group, Inc., The.

Head, Vivian. Times Tables. 2013. (ENG., Illus.). 14p. (J). (gr. 1-5). 9.99 *(978-1-84322-936-0(6),* Armadillo) Anness Publishing GBR. Dist: National Bk. Network.

Hesse, Leah. Colin Counts To 50. 2012. (InfoMax Readers Ser.). (ENG., Illus.). 16 pp.p. (J). (gr. k-1). pap. 7.00 *(978-1-4488-8953-2(7),* Rosen Classroom) Rosen Publishing Group, Inc., The.

The History of New York City: Understand Properties of Multiplication. 2014. (Rosen Common Core Math Readers Ser.). (ENG., Illus.). 24p. (J). (gr. 3-4). pap. 8.25 *(978-1-4777-4958-6(6),* PowerKids Pr.) Rosen Publishing Group, Inc., The.

Hoban, Malcolm. Yolanda's Yard Sale. 2013. (Core Math Skills: Operations & Algebraic Thinking Ser.). 24p. (J). (gr. 1-2). 22.60 *(978-1-4777-2211-4(4),* Rosen Classroom) Rosen Publishing Group, Inc., The.

—Yolanda's Yard Sale: Add & Subtract Within 20. 2013. (Rosen Math Readers Ser.). (ENG.). 24p. (J). (gr. 1-2). pap. 8.25 *(978-1-4777-2064-6(2));* pap. 49.50 *(978-1-4777-2065-3(0))* Rosen Publishing Group, Inc., The. (Rosen Classroom).

Hoena, Blake. Monster Party: A Song about Drawing with Numbers. Palin, Tim, illus. 2017. (Sing & Draw! Ser.). (ENG.). 24p. (gr. 1-3). 33.99 ***(978-1-68410-041-5(0))*** Cantata Learning.

Hollis, Matthew. Jada Makes Jewelry: Use Place Value Understanding & Properties of Operations to Add & Subtract. 2014. (Math Masters: Number & Operations in Base Ten Ser.). 24p. (J). (gr. 2-3). 23.60 *(978-1-4777-6402-2(X));* (ENG.). pap. 8.25 *(978-1-4777-4742-1(7))* Rosen Publishing Group, Inc., The. (Rosen Classroom).

HOP LLC Staff. Hooked on Math - Division. 2005. (J). (gr. 3-5). 64.99 *(978-1-931020-52-7(3))* HOP, LLC.

—Hooked on Math - Multiplication. 2005. (J). (gr. 2-4). 64.99 *(978-1-931020-51-0(5))* HOP, LLC.

I'm Learning to Add. 2004. (Flash Card + Music CD Learning Kits Ser.). (Illus.). 20p. 18.99 *(978-1-894677-62-2(5))* Kidzup Productions.

James, Adele. Adding with Apes. 2011. (Animal Math Ser.). 24p. (J). (gr. 1-3). pap. 8.15 *(978-1-4339-5656-0(X));* lib. bdg. 22.60 *(978-1-4339-5654-6(3))* Stevens, Gareth Publishing LLLP.

James, Dawn. Neighborhood Math. 2015. (J). *(978-1-62713-447-7(6))* Cavendish Square Publishing.

—Playground Math. 2015. (Math Around Us Ser.). (ENG.). 24p. (J). (gr. 1-1). pap. 24.21 *(978-1-5026-0152-0(4))* Cavendish Square Publishing.

—Store Math. 2015. (Math Around Us Ser.). (ENG.). 24p. (J). (gr. 1-1). pap. 8.22 *(978-1-5026-0165-0(6))* Cavendish Square Publishing.

Jaworowicz, Grace. Chelsea's Cheerleading Squad: Add Within 20. 2014. (Rosen Common Core Math Readers Ser.). (ENG.). 24p. (J). (gr. 2-3). pap. 8.25 *(978-1-4777-4636-3(6),* Rosen Classroom) Rosen Publishing Group, Inc., The.

Jordan, Ashley. Gabriella's Butterfly Garden. 2013. (Core Math Skills: Operations & Algebraic Thinking Ser.). 24p. (J). (gr. 1-2). 22.60 *(978-1-4777-2209-1(2));* (ENG.). pap. 8.25 *(978-1-4777-2025-7(1))* Rosen Publishing Group, Inc., The. (Rosen Classroom).

—Gabriella's Butterfly Garden: Understand & Apply Properties of Operations. 2013. (Rosen Math Readers Ser.). (ENG.). 24p. (J). (gr. 1-2). pap. 49.50 *(978-1-4777-2026-4(X),* Rosen Classroom) Rosen Publishing Group, Inc., The.

Kaminski, Mary. Raising Reptiles: Divide Within 100. 2014. (Rosen Common Core Math Readers Ser.). (ENG., Illus.). 24p. (J). (gr. 3-4). pap. 8.25 *(978-1-4777-4949-4(7),* PowerKids Pr.) Rosen Publishing Group, Inc., The.

Katz, Karen. Baby's Numbers. Katz, Karen, illus. 2010. (ENG., Illus.). 14p. (J). (gr. -1 — 1). bds. 5.99 *(978-1-4424-0827-2(8),* Little Simon) Little Simon.

Kawa, Katie. Claire's Clothing Drive: Represent & Solve Problems Involving Subtraction. 2014. (Rosen Common Core Math Readers Ser.). 24p. (J). (gr. 2-3). (ENG.). pap. 49.50 *(978-1-4777-4634-9(X));* (Illus.). 23.60 *(978-1-4777-6399-5(6))* Rosen Publishing Group, Inc., The. (Rosen Classroom).

—Oliver's Orchard: Perform Multi-Digit Arithmetic, 1 vol. 2015. (InfoMax Common Core Math Readers Ser.). (ENG.). 24p. (J). pap. 8.25 *(978-1-4777-4624-0(2),* Rosen Classroom) Rosen Publishing Group, Inc., The.

Kidzup Productions Staff. I'm Learning to Multiply. 2004. 54p. (J). (gr. 1-3). audio compact disk 18.99 *(978-1-894677-65-3(X))* Kidzup Productions.

Kiernan, Denise. Multiplication & Division: Familiar & Flexible Games with Dozens of Variations That Help Struggling Learners Practice & Really Master Multiplication & Division Facts. 2007. (Math Games to Master Basic Skills Ser.). (ENG., Illus.). 48p. pap. 10.99 *(978-0-439-51773-7(7),* Teaching Resources) Scholastic, Inc.

Kirk, Heather, illus. My First Picture Numbers. 2012. (ENG.). 24p. (J). 9.95 *(978-1-84135-795-9(2))* Award Pubns. Ltd. GBR. Dist: Parkwest Pubns., Inc.

Kompelein, Tracy. I Can Add, It's Not So Bad!, 1 vol. 2007. (Math Made Fun Ser.). (ENG., Illus.). 24p. (J). (gr. k-3). lib. bdg. 24.21 *(978-1-59928-513-9(4),* SandCastle) ABDO Publishing Co.

—I Can Subtract, It's Not an Act!, 1 vol. 2007. (Math Made Fun Ser.). (ENG., Illus.). 24p. (J). (gr. k-3). lib. bdg. 24.21 *(978-1-59928-523-8(1),* SandCastle) ABDO Publishing Co.

—Skip Count by 2, Now Can You?, 1 vol. 2007. (Math Made Fun Ser.). (ENG., Illus.). 24p. (J). (gr. k-3). lib. bdg. 24.21 *(978-1-59928-545-0(2),* SandCastle) ABDO Publishing Co.

—Skip Count by 5, Its No Jive!, 1 vol. 2007. (Math Made Fun Ser.). (ENG., Illus.). 24p. (J). (gr. k-3). lib. bdg. 24.21 *(978-1-59928-543-6(6),* SandCastle) ABDO Publishing Co.

Kompelien, Tracy. I Can Divide, I Need No Guide!, 1 vol. 2007. (Math Made Fun Ser.). (ENG., Illus.). 24p. (J). (gr. k-3). lib. bdg. 24.21 *(978-1-59928-515-3(0),* SandCastle) ABDO Publishing Co.

—I Can Multiply, It's Not a Lie!, 1 vol. 2007. (Math Made Fun Ser.). (ENG., Illus.). 24p. (J). (gr. k-3). lib. bdg. 24.21 *(978-1-59928-521-4(5),* SandCastle) ABDO Publishing Co.

—I Know about Money, It Is So Funny!, 1 vol. 2007. (Math Made Fun Ser.). (ENG., Illus.). 24p. (J). (gr. k-3). lib. bdg. 24.21 *(978-1-59928-527-6(4),* SandCastle) ABDO Publishing Co.

—Skip Count by 10, Lets Do It Again!, 1 vol. 2007. (Math Made Fun Ser.). (ENG., Illus.). 24p. (J). (gr. k-3). lib. bdg. 24.21 *(978-1-59928-541-2(X),* SandCastle) ABDO Publishing Co.

Krech, Bob & Novelli, Joan. Multiplication & Division: Engaging Story Problems for Students to Read, Fill-In, Solve, & Sharpen Their Math Skills. 2009. (50 Fill-in Math Word Problems Ser.). (ENG.). 64p. (gr. 4-6). pap. 11.99 *(978-0-545-07485-8(1),* Teaching Resources) Scholastic, Inc.

Krech, Bob, et al. Addition & Subtraction: Mini-Lessons, Games, & Activities to Review & Reinforce Essential Math Concepts & Skills. 2008. (Reteaching Math Ser.). (ENG.). 96p. pap. 14.99 *(978-0-439-52964-8(6),* Teaching Resources) Scholastic, Inc.

Kumon Publishing, creator. My Book of Simple Addition. 2005. (Illus.). 80p. per. 7.95 *(978-1-933241-00-5(4))* Kumon Publishing North America, Inc.

—My Book of Simple Subtraction, 20 vols. 2005. (Kumon Workbooks Ser.). (ENG., Illus.). 80p. (J). (gr. -1-3). per. 7.95 *(978-1-933241-06-7(3))* Kumon Publishing North America, Inc.

—My Book of Subtraction, 20 vols. 2005. (Kumon Workbooks Ser.). (ENG., Illus.). 82p. (J). (gr. -1-3). per. 6.95 *(978-1-933241-07-4(1))* Kumon Publishing North America, Inc.

Kumon Publishing North America, ed. Grow to Know Subtraction. 2016. (Illus.). 64p. (J). pap. 4.99 *(978-1-941082-47-8(5))* Kumon Publishing North America, Inc.

Lacey, Saskia. Spectacular Sports: World's Toughest Races: Understanding Fractions (Grade 3) 2017. (Mathematics Readers Ser.). (Illus.). 32p. (gr. 3-3). 8.99 ***(978-1-4807-5802-5(7))*** Teacher Created Materials, Inc.

Lalley, Kristine. How Many Legs? Learning to Multiply Using Repeated Addition. (Rosen Publishing Group's Reading Room Collection). 16p. 2006. (Illus.). (J). (gr. 3-7). lib. bdg. 18.75 *(978-1-4042-3336-2(9),* PowerKids Pr.) 2004. (ENG.). (gr. 2-3). 37.95 *(978-0-8239-7638-6(6))* Rosen Publishing Group, Inc., The.

—How Many Legs? Learning to Multiply Using Repeated Action. 2009. (Math for the REAL World Ser.). 16p. (gr. 2-3). pap. 7.05 *(978-0-8239-8929-4(1),* Rosen Classroom) Rosen Publishing Group, Inc., The.

LaRochelle, David. 1+1=5: And Other Unlikely Additions. Sexton, Brenda, illus. 2010. (ENG.). 32p. (J). (gr. k). 14.95 *(978-1-4027-5995-6(9))* Sterling Publishing Co., Inc.

Lawler, Janet. Ocean Counting. Skerry, Brian, photos by. 2013. (ENG., Illus.). 32p. (J). (-k). 16.95 *(978-1-4263-1116-1(8));* lib. bdg. 25.90 *(978-1-4263-1117-8(6))* National Geographic Society. (National Geographic Children's Bks.).

Letts, Amelia. What Happens at an Orchard? Perform Multi-Digit Arithmetic. 2014. (Rosen Common Core Math Readers Ser.). (ENG., Illus.). 24p. (J). (gr. 3-4). pap. 8.25 *(978-1-4777-4933-3(0),* PowerKids Pr.) Rosen Publishing Group, Inc., The.

Levy, Janey. At Sea on a Viking Ship: Solving Problems of Length & Weight Using the Four Math Operations. (PowerMath Ser.). (ENG., 24p. (gr. 3-4). 2009. Illus.). pap. 8.25 *(978-0-8239-8922-5(4),* PowerKids Pr.) 2004. 43.95 *(978-0-8239-7642-3(4))* Rosen Publishing Group, Inc., The.

—Recipes for a Medieval Feast: Medieval Feast: Working Flexibly with Fractions. 2009. (PowerMath: Advanced Proficiency Plus Ser.). 32p. (gr. 5-5). 47.90 *(978-1-60851-364-2(5),* PowerKids Pr.) Rosen Publishing Group, Inc., The.

—Recipes for a Medieval Feast: Working Flexibly with Fractions. (Math for the Real World Ser.). (Illus.). 32p. 2009. (ENG.). (gr. 6-7). pap. 10.00 *(978-1-4042-6061-0(7))* 2006. (YA). (gr. 5-9). lib. bdg. 25.25 *(978-1-4042-3354-6(7))* Rosen Publishing Group, Inc., The.

Lewis, J. Patrick. Arithme-Tickle: An Even Number of Odd Riddle-Rhymes. Remkiewicz, Frank, illus. 2007. (ENG.). 32p. (J). (gr. 1-4). pap. 7.99 *(978-0-15-205848-7(6))* Houghton Mifflin Harcourt Publishing Co.

Lin, Amy. The Book Sale: Represent & Solve Subtraction Problems. 2013. (InfoMax Math Readers Ser.). (ENG.). 24p. (J). (gr. 1-2). pap. 49.50 *(978-1-4777-2146-9(0))*; pap. 8.25 *(978-1-4777-2145-2(2))* Rosen Publishing Group, Inc., The. (Rosen Classroom).

Linde, Barbara. Climates of the World: Identifying & Comparing Mean, Median, & Mode. 2009. (PowerMath: Proficiency Plus Ser.). 32p. (gr. 4-5). 47.90 *(978-1-60851-407-6(2),* PowerKids Pr.) Rosen Publishing Group, Inc., The.

—Managing Your Money: Understanding Math Operations Involving Decimals & Integers. 2009. (PowerMath: Advanced Proficiency Plus Ser.). 32p. (gr. 5-5). 47.90 *(978-1-60851-361-1(0),* PowerKids Pr.) Rosen Publishing Group, Inc., The.

Linde, Barbara M. Climates of the World: Identifying & Comparing Mean, Median, & Mode. 2005. (Math for the REAL World Ser.). 32p. 47.50 *(978-1-4042-5219-6(3),* Rosen Classroom) Rosen Publishing Group, Inc., The.

—The Price of a Pioneer Journey: Adding & Subtracting Two-Digit Dollar Amounts. (Math for the REAL World Ser.). 16p. 2009. (gr. 2-3). pap. 7.05 *(978-0-8239-8906-5(2),* Rosen Classroom) 2009. (gr. 2-2). 37.50 *(978-1-60851-376-5(9),* PowerKids Pr.) 2006. (Illus.). (J). (gr. 3-7). lib. bdg. 18.75 *(978-1-4042-3337-9(7),* PowerKids Pr.) Rosen Publishing Group, Inc., The.

—Traveling Around the United States: Learning to Add 2 Three-Digit Numbers Without Regrouping. 2009. (Math for the REAL World Ser.). 16p. (gr. 2-3). pap. 7.05 *(978-0-8239-8899-0(6),* Rosen Classroom) Rosen Publishing Group, Inc., The.

—Working at the Farmer's Market: Solving Money Problems Involving the Four Math Operations. 2009. (PowerMath Ser.). (Illus.). 24p. (gr. 3-4). pap. 8.25 *(978-0-8239-8920-1(8),* PowerKids Pr.) Rosen Publishing Group, Inc., The.

Llewellyn, Claire. It's Fun to Learn about Sums: A Busy Picture Book Full of Fabulous Facts & Things to Do! 2016. (ENG., Illus.). 32p. (J). (gr. -1-12). 9.99 *(978-1-86147-762-0(7),* Armadillo) Anness Publishing GBR. Dist: National Bk. Network.

Lluch, Alex A. Let's Leap Ahead - Numbers Play & Learn! 2013. (ENG.). 126p. (J). (gr. -1). pap. 7.95 *(978-1-61351-070-4(5))* WS Publishing.

Lockerd, Jodi. Nocturnal Animals: Represent & Solve Problems Involving Multiplication. 2014. (Rosen Common Core Math Readers Ser.). (ENG.). 24p. (J). (gr. 3-4). pap. 49.50 *(978-1-4777-4969-2(1),* Rosen Classroom) Rosen Publishing Group, Inc., The.

Lopez, Daniela. Maria Makes 10: Understanding Addition. 2013. (Rosen Math Readers Ser.). (ENG.). 16p. (J). (gr. k-1). pap. 42.00 *(978-1-4777-1642-7(4))*; (Illus.). pap. 7.00 *(978-1-4777-1641-0(6))* Rosen Publishing Group, Inc., The. (Rosen Classroom).

Loren, Josephina. Cody Helps at the Race: Subtract Within 20. 2014. (Math Masters: Operations & Algebraic Thinking Ser.). (Illus.). 24p. (J). (gr. 2-3). 23.60 *(978-1-4777-6424-4(0),* Rosen Classroom) Rosen Publishing Group, Inc., The.

Loughran, Donna. Picnic Fun: Hot Dog Operations. 2013. (IMath Ser.). (Illus.). 24p. (J). (gr. k-2). lib. bdg. 21.27 *(978-1-59953-548-7(3))* Norwood Hse. Pr.

Loughran, Donna & Brunner-Jass, Renata. The Garden Club: Operations with Fractions. 2013. (IMath Ser.). (Illus.). 48p. (J). (gr. 5-6). pap. 11.94 *(978-1-60357-509-6(X))*; lib. bdg. 23.94 *(978-1-59953-570-8(X))* Norwood Hse. Pr.

—Hidden Ducks: Describing & Interpreting Data. 2013. (IMath Ser.). (Illus.). 48p. (J). (gr. 5-6). lib. bdg. 23.94 *(978-1-59953-572-2(6))* Norwood Hse. Pr.

—Save Now, Buy Later: Finding Unit Prices. 2013. (IMath Ser.). (Illus.). 48p. (J). (gr. 5-6). pap. 11.94 *(978-1-60357-508-9(1))*; lib. bdg. 23.94 *(978-1-59953-569-2(6))* Norwood Hse. Pr.

—Stir It Up: Mixing Decimals. 2013. (IMath Ser.). (Illus.). 48p. (J). (gr. 5-6). pap. 11.94 *(978-1-60357-507-2(3))*; lib. bdg. 23.94 *(978-1-59953-568-5(8))* Norwood Hse. Pr.

Mahaney, Ian F. The Math of Baseball. 2011. (J). 49.50 *(978-1-4488-2693-3(4),* PowerKids Pr.); pap. 8.25 *(978-1-4488-2692-6(6),* PowerKids Pr.); (gr. 2-5). lib. bdg. 22.60 *(978-1-4488-2554-7(7))* Rosen Publishing Group, Inc., The.

—The Math of Football. 2011. (J). 49.50 *(978-1-4488-2691-9(8),* PowerKids Pr.); (J). pap. 8.25 *(978-1-4488-2690-2(X),* PowerKids Pr.); (YA). (gr. 2-5). lib. bdg. 22.60 *(978-1-4488-2553-0(9))* Rosen Publishing Group, Inc., The.

—The Math of Hockey. 2011. (J). 49.50 *(978-1-4488-2699-5(3),* PowerKids Pr.); pap. 8.25 *(978-1-4488-2698-8(5),* PowerKids Pr.); (gr. 2-5). lib. bdg. 22.60 *(978-1-4488-2556-1(3))* Rosen Publishing Group, Inc., The.

—The Math of Soccer. 2011. (J). 49.50 *(978-1-4488-2701-5(9),* PowerKids Pr.); pap. 8.25 *(978-1-4488-2700-8(0),* PowerKids Pr.); (gr. 2-5). lib. bdg. 22.60 *(978-1-4488-2557-8(1))* Rosen Publishing Group, Inc., The.

Marsico, Katie. Football. 2008. (21st Century Skills Library: Real World Math Ser.). (ENG., Illus.). 32p. (gr. 4-8). lib. bdg. 28.50 *(978-1-60279-247-0(X),* 200198) Cherry Lake Publishing.

—Speed Skating. 2008. (21st Century Skills Library: Real World Math Ser.). (ENG.). 32p. (gr. 4-8). lib. bdg. 28.50 *(978-1-60279-250-0(X),* 200128) Cherry Lake Publishing.

—Tennis. 2008. (21st Century Skills Library: Real World Math Ser.). (ENG., Illus.). 32p. (gr. 4-8). lib. bdg. 28.50 *(978-1-60279-248-7(8),* 200127) Cherry Lake Publishing.

Marsico, Katie, et al. Running. 2008. (21st Century Skills Library: Real World Math Ser.). (ENG., Illus.). 32p. (gr. 4-8). lib. bdg. 28.50 *(978-1-60279-249-4(6),* 200032) Cherry Lake Publishing.

Marzollo, Jean. Help Me Learn Addition. Philips, Chad, photos by. 2013. (ENG., Illus.). 32p. (J). pap. 6.99 *(978-0-8234-2759-8(5))* Holiday Hse., Inc.

—Help Me Learn Subtraction. Philips, Chad, photos by. 2013. (ENG., Illus.). 32p. (J). (gr. -1-3). pap. 6.99 *(978-0-8234-2822-9(2))* Holiday Hse., Inc.

—Help Me Learn Subtraction. Phillips, Chad, illus. Phillips, Chad, photos by. 2012. (ENG.). 32p. (J). (gr. -1-3). 15.95 *(978-0-8234-2401-6(4))* Holiday Hse., Inc.

Math Art Gr. 1-2 Spanish Version. 2007. (J). per. *(978-1-58232-164-6(7))* ECS Learning Systems, Inc.

Math Art Gr. 2-3 Spanish Version. 2007. (J). per. *(978-1-58232-165-3(5))* ECS Learning Systems, Inc.

Mattern, Joanne. At the Football Game. 2006. (Rosen Publishing Group's Reading Room Collection). (Illus.). 16p. (J). (gr. 3-7). lib. bdg. 18.75 *(978-1-4042-3339-3(3),* PowerKids Pr.) Rosen Publishing Group, Inc., The.

—At the Football Game: Learning the Symbols , And = 2009. (PowerMath: Beginning Ser.). 16p. (gr. 2-2). 37.50 *(978-1-60851-372-7(6),* PowerKids Pr.) Rosen Publishing Group, Inc., The.

—I Use Math at the Game. 2005. (I Use Math Ser.). (Illus.). 24p. (gr. k-3). pap. 8.15 *(978-0-8368-4862-5(4))*; lib. bdg. 22.00 *(978-0-8368-4855-7(1))* Stevens, Gareth Publishing LLLP. (Weekly Reader Leveled Readers).

—I Use Math at the Store. 2005. (I Use Math Ser.). (Illus.). 24p. (gr. k-3). pap. 8.15 *(978-0-8368-4863-2(2))*; lib. bdg. 22.00 *(978-0-8368-4856-4(X))* Stevens, Gareth Publishing LLLP. (Weekly Reader Leveled Readers).

—I Use Math in the Kitchen. 2005. (I Use Math Ser.). (Illus.). 24p. (gr. k-3). pap. 8.15 *(978-0-8368-4864-9(0))*; lib. bdg. 22.00 *(978-0-8368-4857-1(8))* Stevens, Gareth Publishing LLLP. (Weekly Reader Leveled Readers).

—I Use Math in the Workshop. 2005. (I Use Math Ser.). (Illus.). 24p. (gr. k-3). pap. 8.15 *(978-0-8368-4865-6(9))*; lib. bdg. 22.00 *(978-0-8368-4858-8(6))* Stevens, Gareth Publishing LLLP. (Weekly Reader Leveled Readers).

—I Use Math on a Trip. 2005. (I Use Math Ser.). (Illus.). 24p. (gr. k-3). pap. 8.15 *(978-0-8368-4866-3(7))*; lib. bdg. 22.00 *(978-0-8368-4859-5(4))* Stevens, Gareth Publishing LLLP. (Weekly Reader Leveled Readers).

—Make It 100! 2011. (ENG., Illus.). 24p. (gr. -1-1). pap. 8.95 *(978-1-61741-967-6(2))* Rourke Educational Media.

Mattern, Joanne, et al. I Use Math at the Store (USO las Matematicas en la Tienda) 2005. (I Use Math/ Uso las matematicas Ser.). (ENG & SPA., Illus.). 24p. (gr. k-3). lib. bdg. 22.00 *(978-0-8368-6001-6(2),* Weekly Reader Leveled Readers) Stevens, Gareth Publishing LLLP.

—I Use Math in the Kitchen (USO las Matematicas en la Cocina) 2005. (I Use Math/ Uso las matematicas Ser.). (ENG & SPA., Illus.). 24p. (gr. k-3). lib. bdg. 22.00 *(978-0-8368-6002-3(0),* Weekly Reader Leveled Readers) Stevens, Gareth Publishing LLLP.

Matzke, Ann. Who's Right, Addition or Multiplication? 2011. (ENG., Illus.). 24p. (gr. -1-1). pap. 8.95 *(978-1-61741-965-2(6))* Rourke Educational Media.

McAneney, Caitlin. North American Birds: Represent & Solve Problems Involving Multiplication. 2014. (Rosen Common Core Math Readers Ser.). (ENG.). 24p. (J). (gr. 3-4). pap. 49.50 *(978-1-4777-4972-2(1),* Rosen Classroom) Rosen Publishing Group, Inc., The.

McCurry, Kristen. Counting. Banks, Timothy, illus. 2013. (Wizard of Oz Ser.). (ENG.). 24p. (gr. 1-2). 27.99 *(978-1-4765-3766-5(6))* Capstone Press of Coughlan Cos.

McGrath, Barbara Barbieri. The M & M's(r) Brand Addition Book. 2004. (Illus.). 24p. (J). 16.95 *(978-0-88106-348-6(7))*; pap. 6.95 *(978-0-88106-349-3(5))* Charlesbridge Publishing, Inc.

—The M&M's(r) Brand Subtraction Book. 2005. (Illus.). 32p. (J). 16.95 *(978-1-57091-358-7(7))*; pap. 6.95 *(978-1-57091-359-4(5))* Charlesbridge Publishing, Inc.

—Teddy Bear Addition. Nihoff, Tim, illus. 2014. (McGrath Math Ser.). (ENG.). 32p. (J). (gr. -1-3). pap. 7.95 *(978-1-58089-425-8(9))* Charlesbridge Publishing, Inc.

—Teddy Bear Subtraction. Nihoff, Tim, illus. (McGrath Math Ser.). (J). 2016. (ENG.). 32p. (gr. -1-3). pap. 7.95 *(978-1-58089-427-2(5))* 2016. (ENG.). 32p. (gr. -1-3). lib. bdg. 17.95 *(978-1-58089-426-5(7))* 2014. *(978-1-60734-652-4(4))* Charlesbridge Publishing, Inc.

Midthun, Joseph. Addition. Hiti, Samuel, illus. 2013. (Building Blocks of Mathematics Ser.). 32p. (J). pap. 169.00 *(978-0-7166-1432-6(4))* World Bk., Inc.

—Division. Hiti, Samuel, illus. 2013. (Building Blocks of Mathematics Ser.). 32p. pap. 169.00 *(978-0-7166-1433-3(2))* World Bk., Inc.

—Multiplication. Hiti, Samuel, illus. 2013. (Building Blocks of Mathematics Ser.). 32p. (J). pap. 169.00 *(978-0-7166-1437-1(5))* World Bk., Inc.

Midthun, Joseph & Hiti, Samuel. Addition. 2013. (Illus.). 32p. (J). *(978-0-7166-1431-9(6))* World Bk., Inc.

—Division. 2013. (Illus.). 32p. pap. *(978-0-7166-1474-6(X))* World Bk., Inc.

Midthun, Joseph & Samuel, Hiti. Multiplication. 2013. (Illus.). 32p. (J). pap. *(978-0-7166-1476-0(6))* World Bk., Inc.

Milah, Nick. A Trip to the Aquarium: Add Within 20. 2013. (Rosen Math Readers Ser.). (ENG.). 24p. (J). (gr. 1-2). pap. 49.50 *(978-1-4777-2062-2(6))*; (Illus.). pap. 8.25 *(978-1-4777-2061-5(8))* Rosen Publishing Group, Inc., The. (Rosen Classroom).

Minden, Cecilia. Baseball. 2008. (21st Century Skills Library: Real World Math Ser.). (ENG., Illus.). 32p. (gr. 4-8). lib. bdg. 28.50 *(978-1-60279-243-2(7),* 200194) Cherry Lake Publishing.

—Gardening by the Numbers. 2007. (21st Century Skills Library: Real World Math Ser.). (ENG., Illus.). 32p. (gr. 4-8). lib. bdg. 28.50 *(978-1-60279-008-7(6),* 200064) Cherry Lake Publishing.

—Lunch by the Numbers. 2007. (21st Century Skills Library: Real World Math Ser.). (ENG., Illus.). 32p. (gr. 4-8). lib. bdg. 28.50 *(978-1-60279-012-4(4),* 200066) Cherry Lake Publishing.

—Restaurants by the Numbers. 2007. (21st Century Skills Library: Real World Math Ser.). (ENG.). 32p. (gr. 4-8). lib. bdg. 28.50 *(978-1-60279-009-4(4),* 200067) Cherry Lake Publishing.

—Soccer. 2008. (21st Century Skills Library: Real World Math Ser.). (ENG., Illus.). 32p. (gr. 4-8). lib. bdg. 28.50 *(978-1-60279-244-9(5),* 200195) Cherry Lake Publishing.

—Swimming. 2008. (21st Century Skills Library: Real World Math Ser.). (ENG., Illus.). 32p. (gr. 4-8). lib. bdg. 28.50 *(978-1-60279-246-3(1),* 200197) Cherry Lake Publishing.

Mitchell, Cindi. Connect-the-Dot Math: 35 Reproducible Dot-to-Dot Activities That Help Kids Practice Multi-Digit Addition & Subtraction & Basic Multiplication & Division Facts. 2009. (ENG.). 80p. pap. 12.99 *(978-0-439-44993-9(6),* Teaching Resources) Scholastic, Inc.

Montague-Smith, Ann. Adding, 8 vols. 2005. (QEB Math Club Ser.). (Illus.). 24p. (J). (gr. k-1). lib. bdg. 15.95 *(978-1-59566-096-1(8))* QEB Publishing Inc.

—Adding & Subtracting Book Two, 8 vols. 2005. (QEB Math Club Ser.). (Illus.). 24p. (J). (gr. k-1). lib. bdg. 15.95 *(978-1-59566-116-6(6))* QEB Publishing Inc.

—Multiplying, 8 vols. 2005. (QEB Start Math Ser.). (Illus.). 24p. (J). (gr. k-1). lib. bdg. 15.95 *(978-1-59566-114-2(X))* QEB Publishing Inc.

Montessori ADvantage, des. Addition Wokbook. 2005. (J). pap. *(978-0-9766453-0-6(0))* Montessori Advantage.

Moore, Kimberly. Arithmetic Village Presents King David Divide. Moore, Kimberly, illus. 2nd ed. 2012. (Illus.). 24p. pap. *(978-0-9845731-9-6(4))* Roxby Media Ltd.

—Arithmetic Village Presents Linus Minus. Moore, Kimberly, illus. 2nd ed. 2012. (Illus.). 24p. pap. *(978-0-9845731-7-2(8))* Roxby Media Ltd.

—Arithmetic Village Presents Tina Times. Moore, Kimberly, illus. 2nd ed. 2012. (Illus.). 24p. pap. *(978-0-9845731-8-9(6))* Roxby Media Ltd.

Moore, Kimberly & Moore, Kimberly. Arithmetic Village Presents Arithmetic Village. 2nd ed. 2012. 24p. pap. *(978-0-9845731-5-8(1))* Roxby Media Ltd.

Moore, Kimberly Ann. Arithmetic Village Presents Polly Plus. Moore, Kimberly Ann, illus. 2nd ed. 2012. (Illus.). 24p. pap. *(978-0-9845731-6-5(X))* Roxby Media Ltd.

Moraghan, Stephanie. Harry's Magic Tables: Learn Your Times Tables in as Little as a Week! 2012. (ENG., Illus.). 64p. (J). pap. 12.95 *(978-0-7171-5106-6(9))* M.H. Gill & Co. U. C. IRL. Dist: Dufour Editions, Inc.

Mr. R.'s Math Poems. 2003. spiral bd. 20.00 *(978-0-9702641-1-4(9))* MATHSTORY.COM.

Multiplication Dot-to-Dot (Gr. 3-4) 2003. (J). *(978-1-58232-107-3(8))* ECS Learning Systems, Inc.

Multiplication Facts (Gr. 3-4) 2003. (J). *(978-1-58232-086-1(1))* ECS Learning Systems, Inc.

Multiplication Mastery W/CD: Multiplication Mastery with Audio CD. 2004. (ENG.). (J). 19.99 *(978-0-943343-00-6(3))* Learning Wrap-Ups, Inc.

Multiplication Rap & Hip Hop. 2004. pap. 12.99 *(978-1-57583-269-2(0))* Twin Sisters IP, LLC.

Multiplication Skills (Gr. 3-5) 2003. (J). *(978-1-58232-087-8(X))* ECS Learning Systems, Inc.

Murphy, Patricia J. Adding Puppies & Kittens. 2007. (Puppy & Kitten Math Ser.). (Illus.). 32p. (J). (gr. 1-2). lib. bdg. 23.94 *(978-0-7660-2726-8(0),* Enslow Elementary) Enslow Pubs., Inc.

—Counting Puppies & Kittens. 2007. (Puppy & Kitten Math Ser.). (Illus.). 32p. (J). (gr. 1-2). lib. bdg. 23.94 *(978-0-7660-2724-4(4),* Enslow Elementary) Enslow Pubs., Inc.

—Subtracting Puppies & Kittens. 2007. (Puppy & Kitten Math Ser.). (Illus.). 32p. (J). (gr. 1-2). lib. bdg. 23.94 *(978-0-7660-2725-1(2),* Enslow Elementary) Enslow Pubs., Inc.

Murphy, Stuart J. Leaping Lizards. Adinolfi, JoAnn, illus. 2005. (MathStart 1 Ser.). (ENG.). 40p. (J). (gr. -1). pap. 5.99 *(978-0-06-000132-2(1))* HarperCollins Pubs.

—Leaping Lizards. Adinolfi, JoAnn, illus. 2005. (MathStart Level 1 Ser.). 33p. (J). (gr. -1-3). lib. bdg. 16.00 *(978-1-4176-7758-0(9),* Turtleback) Turtleback Bks.

—Less Than Zero. Remkiewicz, Frank, illus. 2003. (MathStart 3 Ser.: Vol. 49). (ENG.). 40p. (J). (gr. 2-18). pap. 5.99 *(978-0-06-000126-1(7))* HarperCollins Pubs.

—Less Than Zero. 2003. (MathStart Level 3 Ser.). (J). (gr. k-3). lib. bdg. 16.00 *(978-0-613-68443-9(5),* Turtleback) Turtleback Bks.

—More or Less. Wenzel, David T., illus. 2005. (MathStart 2 Ser.). (ENG.). 40p. (J). (gr. 1-18). pap. 5.99 *(978-0-06-053167-6(3))* HarperCollins Pubs.

—More or Less. Wenzel, David T., illus. 2005. (Mathstart Ser.). 33p. (gr. 1-4). 16.00 *(978-0-7569-5225-9(5))* Perfection Learning Corp.

Murphy, Stuart J. & Andriani, Renee. Mall Mania. 2006. (Mathstart Ser.). (Illus.). 33p. (gr. 1-4). 16.00 *(978-0-7569-6666-9(3))* Perfection Learning Corp.

Murray, Aaron R. Counting in the Desert 1-2-3. 2012. (All about Counting in the Biomes Ser.). (Illus.). 24p. (J). pap. 7.95 *(978-1-4644-0061-2(X))* Enslow Pubs., Inc.

—Counting in the Rain Forest 1-2-3. 2012. (All about Counting in the Biomes Ser.). (Illus.). (J). 24p. pap. 7.95 *(978-1-4644-0063-6(6))*; 23p. E-Book *(978-1-4645-0970-4(0))* Enslow Pubs., Inc.

—Counting in the Tundra 1-2-3. 2012. (All about Counting in the Biomes Ser.). (Illus.). (J). 24p. pap. 7.95 *(978-1-4644-0064-3(4))*; 23p. E-Book *(978-1-4645-0971-1(9))* Enslow Pubs., Inc.

Murray, Stuart A. P. Score with Basketball Math. 2013. (Score with Sports Math Ser.). 48p. (J). lib. bdg. 25.27 *(978-0-7660-4178-3(6),* Enslow Elementary) Enslow Pubs., Inc.

—Score with Football Math. 2013. (Score with Sports Math Ser.). 48p. (J). lib. bdg. 25.27 *(978-0-7660-4173-8(5),* Enslow Elementary) Enslow Pubs., Inc.

My Book of Addition. 2005. (Illus.). 80p. (J). per. 6.95 *(978-1-933241-01-2(2))* Kumon Publishing North America, Inc.

Nagda, Ann Whitehead. Cheetah Math: Learning about Division from Baby Cheetahs. rev. ed. 2007. (ENG., Illus.). 32p. (J). (gr. 2-5). 18.99 *(978-0-8050-7645-5(X),* 9780805076455, Holt, Henry & Co. Bks. For Young Readers) Holt, Henry & Co.

Nations, Susan & Weekly Reader Editorial Staff. I Know Same & Different (Igual y Diferente) 2006. (I'm Ready for Math/YA Puedo Aprender Matematicas Ser.). (ENG & SPA., Illus.). 16p. (gr. -1-2). lib. bdg. 19.00 *(978-0-8368-6486-1(7),* Weekly Reader Leveled Readers) Stevens, Gareth Publishing LLLP.

O'Donnell, Kayla. What Do Carpenters Do? Relate Addition & Subtraction to Length, 1 vol. 2015. (InfoMax Common Core Math Readers Ser.). (ENG.). 24p. (J). pap. 8.25 *(978-1-4777-4765-0(6),* Rosen Classroom) Rosen Publishing Group, Inc., The.

O'Donnell, Kerri. The California Gold Rush: Multiplying & Dividing Using Three- & Four-Digit Numbers. (PowerMath Ser.). (Illus.). 32p. (gr. 5-6). 2009. (ENG.). pap. 10.00 *(978-1-4042-5131-1(6),* PowerKids Pr.) 2005. (YA). lib. bdg. 25.25 *(978-1-4042-2934-1(5))* Rosen Publishing Group, Inc., The.

—Explorers in North America: Solving Addition & Subtraction Problems Using Timelines. 2009. (PowerMath Ser.). (ENG., Illus.). 32p. (gr. 4-5). pap. 10.00 *(978-0-8239-8898-3(8),* PowerKids Pr.) Rosen Publishing Group, Inc., The.

Oliver, Alison & HarperCollins Publishers Ltd. Staff. Addition & Subtraction Age 6-7. 2013. (Letts Monster Practice Ser.). (ENG., Illus.). 16p. (J). (gr. 1-2). pap. 6.99 *(978-1-84419-752-1(2))* HarperCollins Pubs. Ltd. GBR. Dist: Independent Pubs. Group.

Oliver, Alison & Letts Monster Practice Staff. Addition & Subtraction Age 5-6. 2013. (Letts Monster Practice Ser.). (ENG., Illus.). 16p. (J). (gr. k-1). pap. 6.99 *(978-1-84419-751-4(4))* HarperCollins Pubs. Ltd. GBR. Dist: Independent Pubs. Group.

Onish, Liane B. Solve-the-Riddle Math Practice: 50+ Reproducible Activity Sheets That Help Students Master Key Math Skills - And Solve Rib - Tickling Riddles. 2009. (ENG.). 64p. pap. 11.99 *(978-0-545-10102-8(6),* Teaching Resources) Scholastic, Inc.

Osborne, Amy, ed. Multables, Inc. McGee, Thomas, illus. 3p. (J). (gr. 2-5). 13.99 *(978-0-9645004-0-2(X))* Multables, Inc.

Overdeck, Laura. Fun Excuse to Stay up Late. Paillot, Jim, illus. 2013. (Bedtime Math Ser.). (ENG.). 96p. (J). (gr. -1-2). 15.99 *(978-1-250-03585-1(6),* 9781250035851) Feiwel & Friends.

—This Time It's Personal. Paillot, Jim, illus. 2014. (Bedtime Math Ser.). (ENG.). 96p. (J). (gr. -1-2). 15.99 *(978-1-250-04096-1(5),* 9781250040961) Feiwel & Friends.

Pallotta, Jerry. The Addition Book. Bolster, Rob, illus. 2006. 32p. (J). *(978-0-439-89637-5(1))* Scholastic, Inc.

—The Subtraction Book. Bolster, Rob, illus. 2007. 32p. (J). *(978-0-439-89638-2(X))* Scholastic, Inc.

Park, Margaret. Now for My Next Number! Songs for Multiplying Fun. Esterman, Sophia, illus. 2007. 48p. (J). (gr. -1-3). 16.95 *(978-0-915556-38-0(3))* Great River Bks.

Paz, Naomi. At the Hardware Store. 2013. (Core Math Skills: Numbers & Operations in Base 10 Ser.). 24p. (J). (gr. 1-2). 22.60 *(978-1-4777-2224-4(6))*; (ENG.). pap. 8.25 *(978-1-4777-2091-2(X))* Rosen Publishing Group, Inc., The. (Rosen Classroom).

—At the Hardware Store: Understand Place Value. 2013. (Rosen Math Readers Ser.). (ENG.). 24p. (J). (gr. 1-2). pap. 49.50 *(978-1-4777-2092-9(8),* Rosen Classroom) Rosen Publishing Group, Inc., The.

Penn, M. W. It's Addition! 2011. (Pebble Math Ser.). (ENG.). 24p. (gr. k-1). pap. 35.70 *(978-1-4296-7072-2(X))*; lib. bdg. 21.99 *(978-1-4296-6038-9(4))* Capstone Press of Coughlan Cos. (Pebble Bks.).

—It's Subtraction! 2011. (Pebble Math Ser.). (ENG.). 24p. (gr. k-1). pap. 35.70 *(978-1-4296-7074-6(6))*; lib. bdg. 21.99 *(978-1-4296-6039-6(2))* Capstone Press of Coughlan Cos. (Pebble Bks.).

—2 Lines. Firos, Daphne, illus. 2011. (ENG.). 32p. (J). pap. 11.95 *(978-0-9840425-0-0(4))* MathWord Pr., LLC.

Peppas, Lynn & Becker, Ann. Division. 2009. (ENG., Illus.). 24p. (J). lib. bdg. *(978-0-7787-4346-0(2,* 1302749); pap. *(978-0-7787-4364-4(0,* 1302749) Crabtree Publishing Co.

Peppas, Lynn & Challen, Paul. Addition. 2009. (My Path to Math Ser.). (ENG.). 24p. (J). (gr. k-1). pap. *(978-0-7787-4363-7(2))* Crabtree Publishing Co.

Perritano, John. Football Numbers: Graphing Numbers. 2013. (IMath Ser.). (Illus.). 32p. (J). (gr. 3-4). pap. 11.94 *(978-1-60357-505-8(7))* Norwood Hse. Pr.

—Mummies in the Library: Divide the Pages. 2013. (IMath Ser.). (ENG., Illus.). 32p. (J). (gr. 3-4). lib. bdg. 22.60 *(978-1-59953-558-6(0))* Norwood Hse. Pr.

Pesce, Dom. At the Kennel: Understanding Addition. 2013. (InfoMax Math Readers Ser.). (ENG.). 16p. (J). (gr. k-1). pap. 42.00 *(978-1-4777-2016-5(2))*; (Illus.). pap. 7.00 *(978-1-4777-2015-8(4))* Rosen Publishing Group, Inc., The. (Rosen Classroom).

Peterson's. The Vaughn Cube(Tm) for Multiplication. 2nd ed. 2017. (ENG.). pap. 29.95 *(978-0-7689-4177-7(6))* Peterson's.

Pezzimenti, Grace. The Pizza Party: Learning Basic Problem-Solving Skills. 2009. (Math for the REAL World Ser.). 12p. (gr. 1-2). pap. 5.90 *(978-0-8239-8914-0(3),* Rosen Classroom) Rosen Publishing Group, Inc., The.

Phillipe, Monica. Danielle's Dance Class: Foundations for Multiplication. 2014. (Rosen Common Core Math Readers Ser.). 24p. (J). (gr. 2-3). (ENG.). pap. 49.50 *(978-1-4777-4646-2(3))*; (Illus.). 23.60 *(978-1-4777-6426-8(7))* Rosen Publishing Group, Inc., The. (Rosen Classroom).

Piddock, Claire. Regrouping. 2010. (ENG.). 24p. (J). *(978-0-7787-6785-5(X))* Crabtree Publishing Co.

Pioch, Melissa. Amazing Animals: Wild Whales: Addition & Subtraction (Grade 3) 2017. (Mathematics Readers Ser.). (Illus.). 32p. (J). (gr. 3-3). pap. 8.99 ***(978-1-4807-5795-0(0))*** Teacher Created Materials, Inc.

Pluckrose, Henry. How Many Are There? 2006. (Let's Explore, Maths Set Ser.). (Illus.). 32p. (J). (gr. -1-3). lib. bdg. 27.10 *(978-1-59771-037-4(7))* Sea-To-Sea Pubns.

Pomerleau, Annie. At the Arcade: Understand Place Value. 2014. (Rosen Common Core Math Readers Ser.). 24p. (J). (gr. 2-3). (ENG.). pap. 49.50 *(978-1-4777-4661-5(7))*; (Illus.). 23.60 *(978-1-4777-6430-5(5))* Rosen Publishing Group, Inc., The. (Rosen Classroom).

Potter, Beatrix. Peter Rabbit 1 2 3. 2013. (Peter Rabbit Ser.). (ENG., Illus.). 24p. (J). (gr. -1-k). bds. 6.99 *(978-0-7232-6867-3(3),* Warne) Penguin Young Readers Group.

Powell, Elizabeth. Math at the Game. 2016. (Math Is Everywhere! Ser.). 00024p. (J). pap. 8.15 *(978-1-4824-5482-6(3))* Stevens, Gareth Publishing LLLP.

—Math at the Zoo. 2016. (Math Is Everywhere! Ser.). 00024p. (J). pap. 8.15 *(978-1-4824-5500-7(5))* Stevens, Gareth Publishing LLLP.

Practice Pals Bilingual Practice Book: Addition & Subtraction. 2006. (ENG & FRE., Illus.). 16p. (J). (gr. k-2). spiral bd. *(978-1-930355-52-1(1))* Bright of America.

Practice Power Bilingual Practice Book: Addition. 2003. (Illus.). 16p. (J). (gr. k-2). spiral bd. *(978-1-930355-47-7(5))* Bright of America.

Practice Power Bilingual Practice Book: Subtraction. 2003. (Illus.). 16p. (J). (gr. k-2). spiral bd. *(978-1-930355-48-4(3))* Bright of America.

Prior, Jennifer Overend & Prior, Jennifer. Addition & Subtraction: 14 Reproducible Games That Help Struggling Learners Practice & Really Master Basic Addition & Subtraction Skills. 2007. (Math Games to Master Basic Skills Ser.). (ENG., Illus.). 48p. pap. 10.99 *(978-0-439-55415-2(2),* Teaching Resources) Scholastic, Inc.

Pulse- Fun with Addition & Subtraction. 2006. cd-rom 4.99 *(978-1-60245-036-3(6))* GDL Multimedia, LLC.

Pulse- Fun with Multiplication & Division. 2006. cd-rom 4.99 *(978-1-60245-038-7(2))* GDL Multimedia, LLC.

QEB Maths Club National Book Stores Edition: Adding. 2006. (J). per. *(978-1-59566-287-3(1))* QEB Publishing Inc.

QEB Maths Club National Book Stores Edition: Adding & Subtracting. 2006. (J). per. *(978-1-59566-285-9(5))* QEB Publishing Inc.

QEB Maths Club National Book Stores Edition: Adding & Subtracting Book 2. 2006. (J). per. *(978-1-59566-289-7(8))* QEB Publishing Inc.

QEB Maths Club National Book Stores Edition: Dividing. 2006. (J). per. *(978-1-59566-292-7(8))* QEB Publishing Inc.

QEB Maths Club National Book Stores Edition: Multiplying. 2006. (J). per. *(978-1-59566-291-0(X))* QEB Publishing Inc.

QEB Maths Club National Book Stores Edition: Subtracting. 2006. (J). per. *(978-1-59566-288-0(X))* QEB Publishing Inc.

QEB Start Math Book National Book Stores Edition: Numbers - Book 1. 2006. (J). per. *(978-1-59566-272-9(3))* QEB Publishing Inc.

Rauen, Amy. Adding & Subtracting at the Lake. 2008. (Getting Started with Math Ser.). 16p. (gr. -1-2). pap. 5.30 *(978-0-8368-8988-8(6),* Weekly Reader Leveled Readers) Stevens, Gareth Publishing LLLP.

—Adding & Subtracting at the Lake. Walter, Lorin, illus. 2008. (Getting Started with Math Ser.). 16p. (gr. -1-2). lib. bdg. 19.00 *(978-0-8368-8983-3(5),* Weekly Reader Leveled Readers) Stevens, Gareth Publishing LLLP.

—Using Math at the Class Party. McKinley, Kay, photos by. 2007. (Math in Our World Ser.). (Illus.). 24p. (gr. 1-2). lib. bdg. 22.00 *(978-0-8368-8475-3(2),* Weekly Reader Leveled Readers) Stevens, Gareth Publishing LLLP.

—Vamos a Sumar y Restar en el Lago. Walter, Lorin, illus. 2008. (Matemáticas para Empezar (Getting Started with Math) Ser.). (SPA.). 16p. (gr. -1-2). lib. bdg. 19.00 *(978-0-8368-8993-2(2),* Weekly Reader Leveled Readers) Stevens, Gareth Publishing LLLP.

Rauen, Amy & Ayers, Amy. Sumando y Restando en el Club de Matematicas. 2007. (Las matimaticas en nuestro mundo (Spanish- Math in Our World) Ser.). (SPA.). 24p. (gr. 1-2). pap. 8.15 *(978-0-8368-8497-5(3),* Weekly Reader Leveled Readers) Stevens, Gareth Publishing LLLP.

—Sumando y Restando en el Club de Matematicas. Andersen, Gregg, photos by. 2007. (Matimáticas en Nuestro Mundo (Math in Our World) Ser.). (SPA., Illus.). 24p. (gr. 1-2). lib. bdg. 22.00 *(978-0-8368-8488-3(4),* Weekly Reader Leveled Readers) Stevens, Gareth Publishing LLLP.

—Usamos Matemáticas en la Fiesta Del Salón. 2007. (Las matimaticas en nuestro mundo (Spanish- Math in Our World) Ser.). (SPA.). 24p. (gr. 1-2). pap. 8.15 *(978-0-8368-8502-6(3),* Weekly Reader Leveled Readers) Stevens, Gareth Publishing LLLP.

—Usamos Matematicas en la Fiesta del Salon. McKinley, Kay, photos by. 2007. (Matimáticas en Nuestro Mundo (Math in Our World) Ser.). (SPA., Illus.). 24p. (gr. 1-2). lib. bdg. 22.00 *(978-0-8368-8493-7(0),* Weekly Reader Leveled Readers) Stevens, Gareth Publishing LLLP.

Reeves, Pamela. Numbers All in a Row. LaGrange, Tiffany, illus. 2008. 24p. pap. 12.95 *(978-0-9820479-5-8(9))* Peppertree Pr., The.

Reich, Kass. Hamsters Holding Hands, 1 vol. 2012. (ENG., Illus.). 24p. (J). (gr. -1-k). bds. 9.95 *(978-1-4598-0123-3(7))* Orca Bk. Pubs. USA.

Rhodes, Immacula A. Addition & Subtraction: 10 Ready-to-Go Games That Motivate Children to Practice & Strengthen Essential Math Skills-Independently! 2010. (File-Folder Games in Color Ser.). (ENG.). 144p. (gr. k-2). pap. 19.99 *(978-0-545-22609-7(0),* Teaching Resources) Scholastic, Inc.

Rice, Dona. Use Math: Compare It. 2015. (TIME for KIDS(r) Nonfiction Readers Ser.). (ENG., Illus.). 12p. (gr. k-k). 4.99 *(978-1-4938-2143-3(1))* Teacher Created Materials, Inc.

—Use Your Math Mind: Group It. 2015. (TIME for KIDS(r) Nonfiction Readers Ser.). (ENG., Illus.). 12p. (gr. k-k). 4.99 *(978-1-4938-2144-0(X))* Teacher Created Materials, Inc.

Rice, Dona Herweck. USA Las Matematicas (Use Math - Compare It) 2016. (TIME for KIDS(r) Nonfiction Readers Ser.). (SPA.). 12p. (J). (gr. k-k). 4.99 *(978-1-4938-3024-4(4))* Teacher Created Materials, Inc.

Richert, Catherine. Animal Rescue: Represent & Solve Problems Involving Addition. 2014. (Math Masters: Operations & Algebraic Thinking Ser.). (Illus.). 24p. (J). (gr. 2-3). 23.60 *(978-1-4777-6398-8(8),* Rosen Classroom) Rosen Publishing Group, Inc., The.

Robinson, C. L. MATH1on1 Add & Subtract Fractions. 2006. (YA). per. 9.99 *(978-0-9786767-2-8(6))* Robinson, Consuelo.

—MATH1on1 Multiply & Divide Fractions. 2006. (YA). per. 9.99 *(978-0-9786767-3-5(4))* Robinson, Consuelo.

Rock 'N Learn, creator. Addition & Subtraction Rap. 2010. (Rock 'n Learn Ser.). (J). pap. 12.99 incl. audio compact disk *(978-1-878489-18-0(6))* Rock 'N Learn, Inc.

Rosado, Tom. On the Elevator: Add & Subtract Within 20. 2013. (InfoMax Math Readers Ser.). (ENG.). 24p. (J). (gr. 1-2). pap. 49.50 *(978-1-4777-2125-4(8));* (Illus.). pap. 8.25 *(978-1-4777-2124-7(X))* Rosen Publishing Group, Inc., The. (Rosen Classroom).

Rosario, Miguel. Backyard Math. 2015. (J). lib. bdg. *(978-1-62713-439-2(5))* Cavendish Square Publishing.

—Car Math. 2015. (J). lib. bdg. *(978-1-62713-442-2(5))* Cavendish Square Publishing.

Rosenberg, Pam. Is It Still a Number? 2006. (Rookie Read-About Math Ser.). (ENG., Illus.). 32p. (J). (gr. 1-2). lib. bdg. 20.50 *(978-0-516-25443-2(X))* Scholastic Library Publishing.

Roy, Jennifer Rozines & Roy, Gregory. Addition in the Forest. 2007. (J). pap. 6.99 *(978-0-7614-3404-7(6))* 2005. (Illus.). 32p. (gr. 2-7). lib. bdg. 29.93 *(978-0-7614-2000-2(2),* Benchmark Bks.) Marshall Cavendish Corp.

—Division with Toys. 2006. (Math All Around Ser.). (Illus.). 32p. (gr. 2-7). lib. bdg. 29.93 *(978-0-7614-2269-3(2),* Benchmark Bks.) Marshall Cavendish Corp.

—Money at the Store. 2007. (J). pap. 6.99 *(978-0-7614-3385-9(6))* Marshall Cavendish Corp.

—Multiplication on the Farm. (Math All Around Ser.). (Illus.). 2007. 31p. (J). (gr. -1-3). pap. 6.99 *(978-0-7614-3386-6(4))* 2006. 32p. (gr. 2-7). lib. bdg. 29.93 *(978-0-7614-2268-6(4))* Marshall Cavendish Corp. (Benchmark Bks.).

—Numbers on the Street. 2005. (Math All Around Ser.). (Illus.). 32p. (gr. 2-7). lib. bdg. 29.93 *(978-0-7614-2002-6(9),* Benchmark Bks.) Marshall Cavendish Corp.

—Subtraction at School. 2007. (J). pap. 6.99 *(978-0-7614-3409-2(7))* 2005. (Illus.). 32p. (gr. 2-7). lib. bdg. 29.93 *(978-0-7614-2003-3(7),* Benchmark Bks.) Marshall Cavendish Corp.

Ruffin, Frances E. Creating a City Park: Dividing Three-digit Numbers by One-digit Numbers Without Remainders. 2009. (PowerMath: Intermediate Ser.). 24p. (gr. 3-4). 45.00 *(978-1-60851-380-2(7),* PowerKids Pr.) Rosen Publishing Group, Inc., The.

Russell, Gloria. Taylor's Talent Show: Use Place Value Understanding & Properties of Operations to Add & Subtract, 1 vol. 2015. (InfoMax Common Core Math Readers Ser.). (ENG.). 24p. (J). pap. 8.25 *(978-1-4777-4810-7(5),* Rosen Classroom) Rosen Publishing Group, Inc., The.

Rustad, Martha E. H. One More Bug: An Insect Addition Book. 2016. (1, 2, 3 Count with Me Ser.). (ENG., Illus.). 24p. (J). (gr. k-3). lib. bdg. 20.95 *(978-1-60753-923-0(3))* Amicus Publishing.

Salzmann, Mary Elizabeth. Football by the Numbers, 1 vol. 2010. (Team Sports by the Numbers Ser.). (ENG.). 24p. (J). (gr. k-3). lib. bdg. 24.21 *(978-1-60453-769-7(8),* SandCastle) ABDO Publishing Co.

Sargent, Brian. Pen Pals Compare. (Rookie Read-About Math Ser.). (ENG., Illus.). 32p. (J). (gr. 1-2). 2006. per. 5.95 *(978-0-516-25363-3(8))* 2005. lib. bdg. 20.50 *(978-0-516-25262-9(3))* Scholastic Library Publishing. (Children's Pr.).

—Slumber Party Problem Solving. 2006. (Rookie Read-About Math Ser.). (ENG., Illus.). 32p. (J). (gr. 1-2). lib. bdg. 20.50 *(978-0-516-24962-9(2),* Children's Pr.) Scholastic Library Publishing.

Saviola, Joseph A. The Tour de France: Solving Addition Problems Involving Renaming. 2009. (PowerMath Ser.). (ENG., Illus.). 24p. (gr. 3-4). pap. 8.25 *(978-0-8239-8851-8(1),* PowerKids Pr.) Rosen Publishing Group, Inc., The.

—The Tour de France: Solving Addition Problems Using Regrouping. (PowerMath: Intermediate Ser.). 24p. 2009. (gr. 3-4). 45.00 *(978-1-60851-386-4(6))* 2004. (Illus.). (J). lib. bdg. 22.50 *(978-0-8239-8963-8(1))* Rosen Publishing Group, Inc., The. (PowerKids Pr.).

Scholastic, Inc. Staff, contrib. by. More or Less. 2015. (Rookie Toddler(r) Ser.). (ENG.). 12p. (J). bds. 6.95 *(978-0-531-20571-6(1))* Scholastic Library Publishing.

School Zone Publishing Company Staff. Addition & Subraction 1-2. deluxe ed. 2005. (ENG.). 64p. (J). (gr. 1-2). pap., wbk. ed. 3.79 *(978-1-58947-323-2(X))* School Zone Publishing Co.

—Addition & Subtraction 2. (Illus.). (J). 19.99 incl. audio compact disk *(978-0-88743-950-6(0))* School Zone Publishing Co.

—Addition & Subtraction Grade 1-2 A Wipe-off Book: Hours of Reusable Fun. rev. ed. 2005. (ENG.). 26p. (J). (gr. k-1). pap. 3.79 *(978-1-58947-784-1(7))* School Zone Publishing Co.

—Bilingual Multiplication & Division 3-4. 2007. (ENG.). 64p. (J). (gr. 3-4). pap. 3.99 *(978-1-58947-963-0(7))* School Zone Publishing Co.

—Multiplication: Hours of Reusable Fun! rev. ed. 2005. (ENG.). 26p. (J). (gr. 3-4). pap. 3.79 *(978-1-58947-785-8(5))* School Zone Publishing Co.

—Multiplication Facts. 2007. (ENG.). 64p. (J). (gr. 3-4). pap. 2.69 *(978-1-58947-965-4(3))* School Zone Publishing Co.

—Numbers 1-12. (Illus.). (J). 19.99 incl. audio compact disk *(978-0-88743-949-0(7))* School Zone Publishing Co.

School Zone Staff. Addition. rev. ed. 2004. (ENG.). 55p. (J). 2.79 *(978-1-58947-984-5(X))* School Zone Publishing Co.

—Bilingual Multiplication 0-12. rev. ed. 2004. (ENG.). 56p. (J). 2.99 *(978-1-58947-986-9(6))* School Zone Publishing Co.

—Division. rev. ed. 2004. (ENG.). 56p. (J). 2.79 *(978-1-58947-987-6(4))* School Zone Publishing Co.

—Math War Addition & Subtraction. 2004. (ENG.). 56p. (J). 2.79 *(978-1-58947-993-7(9))* School Zone Publishing Co.

—Math War Multiplication. 2004. (ENG.). 56p. (J). 2.79 *(978-1-58947-994-4(7))* School Zone Publishing Co.

—Subtraction. rev. ed. 2004. (ENG.). (J). 2.79 *(978-1-58947-985-2(8))* School Zone Publishing Co.

School Zone Staff, ed. Multiplication & Division 3-4. deluxe ed. 2004. (Activity Zone Workbook Ser.). (ENG.). 64p. (J). (gr. 3-4). pap. 3.99 *(978-1-58947-329-4(9),* 02215) School Zone Publishing Co.

Schrier, Allyson Valentine. How Many in All? 2008. (Discovering & Exploring Science Ser.). (Illus.). 16p. (J). (gr. -1-3). lib. bdg. 12.95 *(978-0-7569-8423-6(8))* Perfection Learning Corp.

Schuh, Mari C. The Crayola Counting Book. 2017. (Crayola (r) Concepts Ser.). (ENG.). 24p. (J). (gr. -1-3). 26.65 ***(978-1-5124-3288-6(1))*** Lerner Publishing Group.

Schwartz, David M. How Much Is a Million? Kellogg, Steven, illus. 20th anniv. ed. 2004. (Reading Rainbow Bks.). (ENG.). 40p. (J). (gr. -1-3). pap. 7.99 *(978-0-688-09933-6(5))* HarperCollins Pubs.

—How Much Is a Million? 2004. (J). (gr. k-3). 18.40 *(978-0-8085-7914-4(2),* Turtleback) Turtleback Bks.

Schwartz, Richard Evan. The Gallery of the Infinite. 2016. (Illus.). 187p. (J). pap. 29.00 *(978-1-4704-2557-9(2))* American Mathematical Society.

Schweppe, Deirdre. Migrating Animals: Use Place Value Understanding & Properties of Operations to Add & Subtract. 2014. (Math Masters: Number & Operations in Base Ten Ser.). 24p. (J). (gr. 2-3). 23.60 *(978-1-4777-6434-3(8));* (ENG.). pap. 8.25 *(978-1-4777-4751-3(6))* Rosen Publishing Group, Inc., The. (Rosen Classroom).

Sciarrino, Stephanie. Multiplication at the Marina: Multiply Within 100. 2014. (Rosen Common Core Math Readers Ser.). (ENG.). 24p. (J). (gr. 3-4). pap. 49.50 *(978-1-4777-4951-7(9),* Rosen Classroom) Rosen Publishing Group, Inc., The.

Sebe, Masayuki. 100 Hungry Monkeys!, 0 vols. Sebe, Masayuki, illus. 2014. (ENG., Illus.). 32p. (J). (gr. -1-2). 16.95 *(978-1-77138-045-4(4))* Kids Can Pr., Ltd. CAN. Dist: Hachette Bk. Group.

Sellers, Charles. Subtracting with Seals. 2011. (Animal Math Ser.). 24p. (J). (gr. 1-3). pap. 8.15 *(978-1-4339-5672-0(1));* lib. bdg. 22.60 *(978-1-4339-5670-6(5))* Stevens, Gareth Publishing LLLP.

Shah, Kieran. Math by the Ocean. 2016. (Math Is Everywhere! Ser.). 00024p. (J). pap. 8.15 *(978-1-4824-5508-3(0))* Stevens, Gareth Publishing LLLP.

—Math in the Garden. 2016. (Math Is Everywhere! Ser.). 00024p. (J). pap. 8.15 *(978-1-4824-5441-3(6))* Stevens, Gareth Publishing LLLP.

—Math in the Kitchen. 2016. (Math Is Everywhere! Ser.). 00024p. (J). pap. 8.15 *(978-1-4824-5447-5(5))* Stevens, Gareth Publishing LLLP.

Shaskan, Trisha Speed. If You Were a Minus Sign, 1 vol. Carabelli, Francesca, illus. 2008. (Math Fun Ser.). (ENG.). 24p. (gr. 2-4). pap. 7.95 *(978-1-4048-4788-0(X))* Picture Window Bks.

—If You Were a Plus Sign, 1 vol. Carabelli, Francesca, illus. 2008. (Math Fun Ser.). (ENG.). 24p. (gr. 2-4). pap. 7.95 *(978-1-4048-4785-9(5))* Picture Window Bks.

Simons, Rae. Sports Math. 2013. (Math 24/7 Ser.: 10). 48p. (J). (gr. 5-18). 19.95 *(978-1-4222-2909-5(2))* Mason Crest.

Simpson, Jeff. Addition, Subtraction & Place Value Student Edition: Count, Notice & Remember Math Intervention Volume I, AS. Simpson, Marilyn, ed. 2007. (Count, Notice & Remember Ser.: Volume I, AS). ring bd. 50.00 *(978-1-888976-41-0(1))* Mastery Learning Systems.

—The Best Stuff for Multiplying & Dividing, Student Edition: Count, Notice & Remember Math Intervention MD-1. Simpson, Marilyn, ed. 2nd ed. 2006. (Count, Notice, & Remember Ser.: 14). stu. ed., ring bd. *(978-1-888976-38-0(1),* 530S) Mastery Learning Systems.

Simpson, Jeffrey L. Core Processes of Mathematics, Student Edition: Count, Notice & Remember Math Intervention, Volume 4. Simpson, Marilyn Bohlen, ed. 2007. ring bd. 59.95 *(978-1-888976-53-3(5))* Mastery Learning Systems.

—Fractions & Decimals, Student Edition: Count, Notice & Remember Math Intervention, Volume 2. Simpson, Marilyn Bohlen, ed. 2007. stu. ed., ring bd. 69.95 *(978-1-888976-47-2(0))* Mastery Learning Systems.

—Functions & Equations, Student Edition: Count, Notice & Remember Math Intervention, Volume 5. Simpson, Marilyn Bohlen, ed. 2007. ring bd. 59.95 *(978-1-888976-56-4(X))* Mastery Learning Systems.

Slade, Suzanne. The Great Divide, 1 vol. Hunter, Erin E., illus. 2012. (Basic Math Operations Ser.). (ENG.). 32p. (J). (gr. -1-4). 17.95 *(978-1-60718-521-5(0));* pap. 9.95 *(978-1-60718-530-7(X))* Arbordale Publishing.

—Multiply on the Fly, 1 vol. Hunter, Erin E., illus. 2011. (ENG.). 32p. (J). (gr. -1-4). 16.95 *(978-1-60718-128-6(2));* pap. 8.95 *(978-1-60718-138-5(X))* Arbordale Publishing.

Slade, Suzanne & Waites, Joan. What's New at the Zoo? An Animal Adding Adventure, 1 vol. 2009. (Basic Math Operations Ser.). (ENG., Illus.). 32p. (J). (gr. -1-3). 16.95 *(978-1-934359-93-8(9));* pap. 8.95 *(978-1-60718-038-8(3),* 9781607180388) Arbordale Publishing.

Somerville, Louisa. Times Tables, Ages 6-7. Tulip, Jenny, illus. 2016. (ENG.). 32p. pap. 6.99 *(978-1-86147-688-3(4),* Armadillo) Anness Publishing GBR. Dist: National Bk. Network.

Steck-Vaughn Staff. Early Math: 2 Digit Addition & Subtraction, 10 Pack. 2005. pap. 29.95 *(978-1-4190-0356-1(9))* Steck-Vaughn.

—Early Math: 2 Digit Subtraction with Regrouping. 2005. pap. 2.99 *(978-1-4190-0335-6(6));* pap. 29.95 *(978-1-4190-0359-2(3))* Steck-Vaughn.

—Early Math: 3 Digit Addition & Subtraction with Regrouping. 2005. pap. 2.99 *(978-1-4190-0336-3(4));* pap. 29.95 *(978-1-4190-0360-8(7))* Steck-Vaughn.

—Early Math: Addition. 2005. (gr. k-5). pap. 2.99 *(978-1-4190-0323-3(2));* (gr. 6-10). pap. 2.99 *(978-1-4190-0324-0(0));* (gr. 6-10). pap. 29.95 *(978-1-4190-0348-6(8))* Steck-Vaughn.

—Early Math: Fractions I. 2005. pap. 2.99 *(978-1-4190-0330-1(5))* Steck-Vaughn.

—Early Math: Fractions II. 2005. pap. 2.99 *(978-1-4190-0340-0(2))* Steck-Vaughn.

—Early Math: Place Value. 2005. (J). (gr. 1). pap. 2.99 *(978-1-4190-0322-6(4))* Steck-Vaughn.

—Early Math: Place Value 1, 10 Pack. 2005. (gr. 1). pap. 29.95 *(978-1-4190-0346-2(1))* Steck-Vaughn.

—Early Math: Place Value II. 2005. pap. 2.99 *(978-1-4190-0334-9(8))* Steck-Vaughn.

—Early Math: Subtraction. 2005. (gr. 1-10). pap. 2.99 *(978-1-4190-0325-7(9))* Steck-Vaughn.

—Early Math 10-pack: Place Value II. 2005. pap. 29.95 *(978-1-4190-0358-5(5))* Steck-Vaughn.

—Early Math 10-pack: Subtraction. 2005. (gr. 1-10). pap. 29.95 *(978-1-4190-0349-3(6))* Steck-Vaughn.

—Focus on Math Level C: Addition & Subtraction. 2005. pap. 2.99 *(978-1-4190-0265-6(1))* Harcourt Schl. Pubs.

—Focus on Math Level C: Multiplication & Division. 2005. pap. 2.99 *(978-1-4190-0266-3(X))* Harcourt Schl. Pubs.

—Focus on Math Level C 10-pack: Addition & Subtractions. 2005. pap. 29.95 *(978-1-4190-0289-2(9))* Harcourt Schl. Pubs.

—Focus on Math Level C 10-pack: Multiplication & Division. 2005. pap. 29.95 *(978-1-4190-0290-8(2))* Harcourt Schl. Pubs.

—Focus on Math Level E 10-pack: Ratio Percent. 2005. pap. 29.95 *(978-1-4190-0306-6(2))* Harcourt Schl. Pubs.

—Focus on Math Level F: Ration Percent. 2005. pap. 2.99 *(978-1-4190-0287-8(2))* Harcourt Schl. Pubs.

—Focus on Math Level F 10-pack: Ratio Percent. 2005. pap. 29.95 *(978-1-4190-0311-0(9))* Harcourt Schl. Pubs.

Steck-Vaughn Staff, ed. Early Math: Addition. 2005. (gr. k-5). pap. 29.95 *(978-1-4190-0347-9(X))* Steck-Vaughn.

Steffora, Tracey. Adding with Ants, 1 vol. 2013. (Animal Math Ser.). (ENG.). 24p. (gr. -1-1). 22.65 *(978-1-4329-7558-6(7));* pap. 6.95 *(978-1-4329-7565-4(X))* Heinemann-Raintree. (NA-h).

—Taking Away with Tigers, 1 vol. 2013. (Animal Math Ser.). (ENG.). 24p. (gr. -1-1). 22.65 *(978-1-4329-7563-0(3));* pap. 6.95 *(978-1-4329-7570-8(6))* Heinemann-Raintree. (NA-h).

—Using Addition at Home, 1 vol. 2011. (Math Around Us Ser.). (ENG.). 24p. (gr. -1-1). pap. 6.29 *(978-1-4329-4932-7(2),* Acorn) Heinemann-Raintree.

—Using Subtraction at the Park, 1 vol. 2011. (Math Around Us Ser.). (ENG.). 24p. (gr. -1-1). 22.65 *(978-1-4329-4925-9(X));* pap. 6.29 *(978-1-4329-4933-4(0))* Heinemann-Raintree. (Acorn).

Sterling, Kristin. Addition. 2008. pap. 22.95 *(978-0-8225-9359-1(9))* Lerner Publishing Group.

—Subtraction. 2008. pap. 22.95 *(978-0-8225-9363-8(7))* Lerner Publishing Group.

Sterling Publishing Co., Inc. Numbers/Numeros. 2013. (Say & Play Ser.). (ENG & SPA., Illus.). 28p. (J). (— 1). bds. 4.95 *(978-1-4549-1040-4(2))* Sterling Publishing Co., Inc.

Stills, Caroline. Mice Mischief: Math Facts in Action. Rossell, Judith, illus. 2014. (ENG.). 24p. (J). (gr. -1-1). 16.95 *(978-0-8234-2947-9(4))* Holiday Hse., Inc.

Strazzabosco, John. Aircraft Carriers, Supplies for a City at Sea: Multiplying Multidigit Numbers with Regrouping. (PowerMath Ser.). (Illus.). 32p. 2009. (gr. 4-5). pap. 10.00 *(978-0-8239-8919-5(4),* PowerKids Pr.) 2004. (YA). (gr. 5-9). lib. bdg. 25.25 *(978-0-8239-8995-9(X))* Rosen Publishing Group, Inc., The.

—Extreme Temperatures: Learning about Positive & Negative Numbers. 2004. (Math for the REAL World Ser.). (ENG.). 32p. (gr. 4-5). 47.50 *(978-0-8239-7649-2(1))* Rosen Publishing Group, Inc., The.

Subtraction. 2004. (Help with Homework Ser.). 32p. (J). (gr. k-2). wbk. ed. 3.99 *(978-1-904586-25-8(2))* Byeway Bks.

Subtraction. (Substitute Teaching Ser.). (J). 2.50 *(978-0-931993-14-5(8),* GP-014) Garlic Pr.

Subtraction Mastery w/Audio CD: Kit with Book, Wrap-up & CD. 2004. (ENG.). (J). 19.99 *(978-0-943343-99-0(2))* Learning Wrap-Ups, Inc.

Sullivan, Courtney. Reptiles at the Zoo: Divide Within 100, 1 vol. 2015. (InfoMax Common Core Math Readers Ser.). (ENG.). 24p. (J). pap. 8.25 *(978-1-4777-4690-5(0),* Rosen Classroom) Rosen Publishing Group, Inc., The.

Swazinski, Ed. At the Carnival: Understand & Apply Properties of Operations. 2013. (Rosen Math Readers Ser.). 24p. (J). (gr. 1-2). (ENG.). pap. 49.50 *(978-1-4777-2059-2(6),* Rosen Classroom); lib. bdg. 22.60 *(978-1-4777-2210-7(6),* PowerKids Pr.); (ENG., Illus.). pap. 8.25 *(978-1-4777-2058-5(8),* Rosen Classroom) Rosen Publishing Group, Inc., The.

Swenson, Julie. High-Speed Trains: Use Place Value Understanding & Properties of Operations to Add & Subtract. 2014. (Rosen Common Core Math Readers Ser.). (ENG.). 24p. (J). (gr. 2-3). pap. 8.25 *(978-1-4777-4759-4(1),* Rosen Classroom) Rosen Publishing Group, Inc., The.

Tang, Greg. Math Potatoes: Mind-Stretching Brain Food. Briggs, Harry, illus. 2005. (Math Potatoes Ser.). (ENG.). 40p. (J). (gr. 2-5). 18.99 *(978-0-439-44390-6(3),* Scholastic Pr.) Scholastic, Inc.

Teddy Bear Addition. 2004. (Help with Homework Ser.). 32p. (J). (gr. k-2). wbk. ed. 3.99 *(978-1-904586-23-4(6))* Byeway Bks.

Thanner, Eric. Leaping Lengths! Relate Addition & Subtraction to Length, 1 vol. 2015. (InfoMax Common Core Math Readers Ser.). (ENG.). 24p. (J). pap. 8.25 *(978-1-4777-4760-5(5),* Rosen Classroom) Rosen Publishing Group, Inc., The.

Thompson, Kim Mitzo & Hilderbrand, Karen Mitzo. Multiplication Rap. 2008. (Playaway Children Ser.). (J). 44.99 *(978-1-59922-324-7(4))* Findaway World, LLC.

Thompson, Kim Mitzo & Hilderbrand, Karen Mitzo, adapted by. Multiplication. 2011. (J). (gr. k-1). wbk. ed. 4.99 incl. audio compact disk *(978-1-59922-145-8(4))* Twin Sisters IP, LLC.

Times Tables. 2004. (Help with Homework Ser.). 32p. (J). (gr. 1-4). wbk. ed. 3.99 *(978-1-904586-28-9(7))* Byeway Bks.

Torres, Zoe. At the Block Sale: Add & Subtract Within 20. 2013. (InfoMax Math Readers Ser.). (ENG.). 24p. (J). (gr. 1-2). pap. 49.50 *(978-1-4777-2158-2(4));* (Illus.). pap. 8.25 *(978-1-4777-2157-5(6))* Rosen Publishing Group, Inc., The. (Rosen Classroom).

Tourville, Amanda Doering. Penguin Pairs: Counting By 2s, 1 vol. Holm, Sharon Lane, illus. 2008. (Count the Critters Ser.). (ENG.). 24p. (J). (gr. k-3). 27.07 *(978-1-60270-265-3(9))* Magic Wagon.

—Prairie Dogs Perching: Counting By 3s, 1 vol. Holm, Sharon Lane, illus. 2008. (Count the Critters Ser.). (ENG.). 24p. (J). (gr. k-3). 27.07 *(978-1-60270-266-0(7))* Magic Wagon.

Trembley, Becky A. Nimbus Numbers. 2013. 28p. pap. 14.95 *(978-1-4575-1955-0(0))* Dog Ear Publishing, LLC.

Tripp, Natalie. We Care! Making Care Packages: Understand the Relationship Between Multiplication & Division. 2014. (Rosen Common Core Math Readers Ser.). (ENG., Illus.). 24p. (J). (gr. 3-4). pap. 8.25 *(978-1-4777-4955-5(1),* PowerKids Pr.) Rosen Publishing Group, Inc., The.

Trumbauer, Lisa. Double the Animals. 2005. (Yellow Umbrella Fluent Level Ser.). (ENG., Illus.). 16p. (gr. k-1). pap. 35.70 *(978-0-7368-5320-0(0),* Yellow Umbrella Bks.) Capstone Press of Coughlan Cos.

Tulip, Jenny. My First Book of Numbers. 2004. (Early Learning Ser.). (Illus.). 18p. (J). bds. 5.99 *(978-1-85854-216-4(2))* Brimax Books Ltd. GBR. Dist: Byeway Bks.

Twin Sisters(r) Staff. Multiplication Workbook & Music CD. 2009. pap. 12.99 incl. audio compact disk *(978-1-57583-894-6(X))* Twin Sisters IP, LLC.

Twin Sisters(r) Staff & Hilderbrand, Karen Mitzo, adapted by. Subtraction. 2011. (J). (gr. k-1). wbk. ed. 4.99 incl. audio compact disk *(978-1-59922-144-1(6))* Twin Sisters IP, LLC.

Vail, Grace. Dolphin Doubles. 2013. (Animal Math Ser.). 24p. (J). (gr. 1-3). 22.60 *(978-1-4339-9306-0(6));* pap. 8.15 *(978-1-4339-9303-9(1));* pap. 48.90 *(978-1-4339-9304-6(X))* Stevens, Gareth Publishing LLLP.

Visto, Joy. How Much Is Infinity? 2015. (Illus.). 48p. (J). *(978-1-60818-572-6(9),* Creative Education) Creative Co., The.

—How Much Is Infinity? Making Math Work. 2016. (Making Math Work Ser.). (ENG.). 48p. (J). (gr. 5-9). pap. 12.00 *(978-1-62832-173-9(3)*, Creative Paperbacks) Creative Co., The.

Walsh, Kieran. Animal Math. 2005. (Math & My World Ser.). (Illus.). 48p. (J). (gr. 4-6). lib. bdg. 20.95 *(978-1-59515-491-0(4))* Rourke Educational Media.

—Construction Math. 2005. (Math & My World Ser.). (Illus.). 48p. (J). (gr. 4-6). lib. bdg. 20.95 *(978-1-59515-492-7(2))* Rourke Educational Media.

—Space Math. 2005. (Math & My World Ser.). (Illus.). 48p. (J). (gr. 4-6). lib. bdg. 20.95 *(978-1-59515-494-1(9))* Rourke Educational Media.

—Sports Math. 2005. (Math & My World Ser.). (Illus.). 48p. (J). (gr. 4-6). lib. bdg. 20.95 *(978-1-59515-495-8(7))* Rourke Educational Media.

Ward, Ian. The Magic of the Matrix: Making Arithmetic Practice Fun. 2007. (ENG.). 46p. (J). pap. 16.00 *(978-1-899618-77-4(5))* Parkwest Pubns., Inc.

Watt, Fiona. The Usborne Color by Numbers Book. Harrison, Erica, illus. 2014. (ENG.). (J). pap. 5.99 *(978-0-7945-3251-2(9)*, Usborne) EDC Publishing.

Watt, Fiona & Wells, Rachel. Starting Times Tables. 2004. (Usborne Sticker Math Ser.). (ENG., Illus.). 1p. (J). (gr. k-1). pap., act. bk. ed. 6.95 *(978-0-7460-3735-5(X))* EDC Publishing.

Weakland, Mark. Scooby-Doo! a Subtraction Mystery: The Case of the Disappearing Doughnuts, 1 vol. Gross, Scott, illus. 2014. (Solve It with Scooby-Doo!: Math Ser.). (ENG.). 24p. (gr. k-2). lib. bdg. 27.99 *(978-1-4914-1540-5(1))* Capstone Press of Coughlan Cos.

—Scooby-Doo! an Addition Mystery: The Case of the Angry Adder, 1 vol. Gross, Scott, illus. 2014. (Solve It with Scooby-Doo!: Math Ser.). (ENG.). 24p. (gr. k-2). lib. bdg. 27.99 *(978-1-4914-1539-9(8))* Capstone Press of Coughlan Cos.

Weatherall, Donald M. & Quinn. Addition & Subtraction Learning Module. pap. *(978-0-89290-131-9(4))* S V E & Churchill Media.

Webster, Belinda. Magic Times Tables. 2013. (ENG., Illus.). 128p. (J). 9.95 *(978-1-84837-922-0(6))* Arcturus Publishing GBR. Dist: Bookmasters Distribution.

Weekly Reader Editorial Staff. I Know Same & Different. 2006. (I'm Ready for Math Ser.). (Illus.). 16p. (gr. -1-2). pap. 5.30 *(978-0-8368-6481-6(6)*, Weekly Reader Leveled Readers) Stevens, Gareth Publishing LLLP.

—I Know Same & Different. 2006. (I'm Ready for Math Ser.). (Illus.). 16p. (gr. -1-2). lib. bdg. 19.00 *(978-0-8368-6476-2(X)*, Weekly Reader Leveled Readers) Stevens, Gareth Publishing LLLP.

Weekly Reader Editorial Staff, contrib. by. I Know Same & Different (Igual y Diferente) 2006. (I'm Ready for Math/ Ya puedo aprender matematicas Ser.). (ENG & SPA., Illus.). 16p. (gr. -1-2). pap. 5.30 *(978-0-8368-6491-5(3)*, Weekly Reader Leveled Readers) Stevens, Gareth Publishing LLLP.

Weizen, Jon. I Know Numbers. 2016. (What I Know Ser.). 00024p. (J). pap. 8.15 *(978-1-4824-5464-2(5))* Stevens, Gareth Publishing LLLP.

Wen, Dref. Fy Llyfr Rhifau Cyntaf. 2005.Tr. of My First Numbers. (WEL., Illus.). 34p. *(978-1-85596-672-7(7))* Dref Wen.

Wesolowski, Janice. A Day at the Beach: Represent & Solve Addition Problems. 2013. (Rosen Math Readers Ser.). (ENG.). 24p. (J). (gr. 1-2). pap. 49.50 *(978-1-4777-2020-2(0))*; pap. 8.25 *(978-1-4777-2019-6(7))* Rosen Publishing Group, Inc., The. (Rosen Classroom).

Williams, Zachary. Cleaning up the Park: Learning to Count by Fives. 2004. (Math Big Bookstm Ser.). (ENG.). 12p. (gr. 1-2). 33.50 *(978-0-8239-7633-1(5))* Rosen Publishing Group, Inc., The.

Williams, Zella & Wingard-Nelson, Rebecca. Word Problems Using Multiplication & Division. 2016. (Mastering Math Word Problems Ser.). 48p. (J). pap. 11.70 *(978-0-7660-8264-9(4))* Enslow Pubs., Inc.

Wingard-Nelson, Rebecca. Addition & Subtraction. 2012. (Ace Your Math Test Ser.). (Illus.). 104p. (J). (gr. 5-18). lib. bdg. 33.27 *(978-0-7660-3778-6(9))* Enslow Pubs., Inc.

—Addition & Subtraction: Ace Your Math Test. 2012. (Ace Your Math Test Ser.). (Illus.). 104p. (J). (gr. 5-18). pap. 10.95 *(978-1-4644-0005-6(9))* Enslow Pubs., Inc.

—Animal Word Problems Starring Addition & Subtraction. LaBaff, Tom, illus. 2009. (Math Word Problems Solved Ser.). 48p. (J). (gr. 2-5). lib. bdg. 25.27 *(978-0-7660-2917-0(4))* Enslow Pubs., Inc.

—Big Truck & Car Word Problems Starring Multiplication & Division. 2009. (Math Word Problems Solved Ser.). (Illus.). 48p. (J). (gr. 2-5). lib. bdg. 25.27 *(978-0-7660-2918-7(2))* Enslow Pubs., Inc.

—Division & Multiplication: It's Easy. 2014. (Easy Genius Math Ser.). 64p. (J). (gr. 4-18). lib. bdg. 29.27 *(978-0-7660-4287-2(1))* Enslow Pubs., Inc.

—Division Made Easy. LaBaff, Tom, illus. 2005. (Making Math Easy Ser.). 48p. (J). (gr. 2-4). lib. bdg. 25.27 *(978-0-7660-2511-0(X)*, Enslow Elementary) Enslow Pubs., Inc.

—I Can Add Bills & Coins. 2009. (I Like Money Math! Ser.). (Illus.). 24p. (J). pap. 7.95 *(978-0-7660-3657-4(X)*, Enslow Elementary); (gr. 1-3). lib. bdg. 22.60 *(978-0-7660-3143-2(8))* Enslow Pubs., Inc.

—I Can Subtract Bills & Coins. 2009. (I Like Money Math! Ser.). (Illus.). 24p. (J). pap. 7.95 *(978-0-7660-3661-1(8)*, Enslow Elementary); (gr. 1-3). lib. bdg. 22.60 *(978-0-7660-3144-9(6))* Enslow Pubs., Inc.

—Multiplication & Division. 2012. (Ace Your Math Test Ser.). (Illus.). 104p. (J). (gr. 5-18). 33.27 *(978-0-7660-3779-3(7))* Enslow Pubs., Inc.

—Multiplication & Division: Ace Your Math Test. 2012. (Ace Your Math Test Ser.). (Illus.). 104p. (J). (gr. 5-18). pap. 10.95 *(978-1-4644-0006-3(7))* Enslow Pubs., Inc.

—Multiplication & Division Word Problems: No Problem! 2010. (Math Busters Word Problems Ser.). 64p. (J). 29.27 *(978-0-7660-3370-2(8))* Enslow Pubs., Inc.

—Multiplication Made Easy. LaBaff, Tom, illus. 2005. (Making Math Easy Ser.). 48p. (J). (gr. 2-4). lib. bdg. 25.27 *(978-0-7660-2510-3(1)*, Enslow Elementary) Enslow Pubs., Inc.

—Percents & Ratios. 2012. (Ace Your Math Test Ser.). (Illus.). 104p. (J). (gr. 5-18). 33.27 *(978-0-7660-3781-6(9))* Enslow Pubs., Inc.

—Ratios & Percents: It's Easy. 2014. (Easy Genius Math Ser.). 64p. (J). (gr. 4-18). lib. bdg. 29.27 *(978-0-7660-4289-6(8))* Enslow Pubs., Inc.

—Ready for Addition. 2014. (Ready for Math Ser.). (Illus.). 48p. (J). (gr. 3-18). 25.27 *(978-0-7660-4245-2(6))* Enslow Pubs., Inc.

—Ready for Addition. LaBaff, Tom, illus. 2014. (Ready for Math Ser.). 48p. (J). pap. 8.95 *(978-1-4644-0433-7(X)*, Enslow Elementary) Enslow Pubs., Inc.

—Ready for Division. LaBaff, Tom, illus. 2014. (Ready for Math Ser.). 48p. (J). (gr. 3-18). lib. bdg. 25.27 *(978-0-7660-4249-0(9)*, Enslow Elementary) Enslow Pubs., Inc.

—Ready for Multiplication. LaBaff, Tom, illus. 2014. (Ready for Math Ser.). 48p. (J). pap. 8.95 *(978-1-4644-0439-9(9)*, Enslow Elementary); (gr. 3-18). 25.27 *(978-0-7660-4248-3(0))* Enslow Pubs., Inc.

—Ready for Subtraction. LaBaff, Tom, illus. 2014. (Ready for Math Ser.). 48p. (J). (gr. 3-18). lib. bdg. 25.27 *(978-0-7660-4246-9(4)*, Enslow Elementary) Enslow Pubs., Inc.

—Sports Word Problems Starring Decimals & Percents. 2009. (Math Word Problems Solved Ser.). (Illus.). 48p. (J). (gr. 2-5). lib. bdg. 25.27 *(978-0-7660-2920-0(4))* Enslow Pubs., Inc.

—Subtraction & Addition. 2008. (Math Busters Ser.). (Illus.). 64p. (J). (gr. 5-18). lib. bdg. 29.27 *(978-0-7660-2875-3(5))* Enslow Pubs., Inc.

—Subtraction & Addition: It's Easy. 2014. (Easy Genius Math Ser.). 64p. (J). pap. 8.95 *(978-1-4644-0531-0(X))*; (gr. 4-18). 29.27 *(978-0-7660-4291-9(X))* Enslow Pubs., Inc.

—Subtraction Made Easy. LaBaff, Tom, illus. 2005. (Making Math Easy Ser.). 48p. (J). (gr. 2-4). lib. bdg. 25.27 *(978-0-7660-2509-7(8)*, Enslow Elementary) Enslow Pubs., Inc.

World Book, Inc Staff, contrib. by. Fun with Numbers. 2011. (J). *(978-0-7166-0228-6(8))* World Bk., Inc.

—Subtraction. 2013. (Illus.). 32p. (J). pap. *(978-0-7166-1478-4(2))* World Bk., Inc.

Worth, Bonnie. One Cent, Two Cents, Old Cent, New Cent: All about Money. Ruiz, Aristides & Mathieu, Joseph, illus. 2008. (Cat in the Hat's Learning Library). (ENG.). 48p. (J). (gr. -1-3). 9.99 *(978-0-375-82881-2(8)*, Random Hse. Bks. for Young Readers) Random Hse. Children's Bks.

Young, Owen. Our Camping Trip: Subtract Within 20. 2013. (InfoMax Math Readers Ser.). (ENG.). 24p. (J). (gr. 1-2). pap. 49.50 *(978-1-4777-2187-2(8))*; (Illus.). pap. 8.25 *(978-1-4777-2186-5(X))* Rosen Publishing Group, Inc., The. (Rosen Classroom).

Zacharies, Mae. The Farmer's Market: Use Place Value & Properties of Operations to Add. 2013. (Rosen Math Readers Ser.). (ENG.). 24p. (J). (gr. 1-2). pap. 49.50 *(978-1-4777-2074-5(X))*; (Illus.). pap. 8.25 *(978-1-4777-2073-8(1))* Rosen Publishing Group, Inc., The. (Rosen Classroom).

Zuravicky, Orli. Amazing Animals: Multiplying Multidigit Numbers by a One-Digit Number with Regrouping. 2009. (PowerMath Ser.). (Illus.). 24p. (gr. 3-4). pap. 8.25 *(978-0-8239-8861-7(9)*, PowerKids Pr.) Rosen Publishing Group, Inc., The.

ARITHMETIC—FICTION

Aber, Linda Williams. Quien Tiene Manchas; Who's Got Spots? 2008. pap. 34.95 *(978-1-58013-759-1(8))* Kane Press, Inc.

Adams, Jennifer. Pride & Prejudice: A Counting Primer, 1 vol. Oliver, Alison, illus. 2011. (ENG.). 22p. (J). (gr. k-1). bds. 9.99 *(978-1-4236-2202-4(2))* Gibbs Smith, Publisher.

Amani, Ahmad. Math City. 2011. (Illus.). 24p. 13.14 *(978-1-4567-7375-5(5))* AuthorHouse.

Arena, Jen. One Hundred Snowmen, 0 vols. Gilpin, Stephen, illus. 2013. (ENG.). 24p. (J). (gr. k-3). 14.99 *(978-1-4778-4703-9(0)*, 9781477847039, Amazon Children's Publishing) Amazon Publishing.

Armstrong, Gregory D. Count with Buddy Coloring Book. 2013. 24p. pap. 12.99 *(978-0-9895026-5-8(1))* Armstrong, Greg.

Awdry, W. Thomas' 123 Book. Courtney, Richard, illus. 2013. (Pictureback(R) Ser.). (ENG.). 24p. (J). (gr. -1-2). pap. 3.99 *(978-0-307-98203-2(3)*, Random Hse. Bks. for Young Readers) Random Hse. Children's Bks.

—Thomas' 123 Book. 2013. (Thomas & Friends 8X8 Ser.). lib. bdg. 13.55 *(978-0-606-26991-9(6)*, Turtleback) Turtleback Bks.

Banks, Kate. Max's Math. Kulikov, Boris, illus. 2015. (Max's Words Ser.: 4). (ENG.). 40p. (J). (gr. -1-3). 17.99 *(978-0-374-34875-5(8)*, 9780374348755, Farrar, Straus & Giroux (BYR)) Farrar, Straus & Giroux.

Barton, Byron. My Bus. Barton, Byron, illus. 2014. (ENG., Illus.). 40p. (J). (gr. -1-3). 16.99 *(978-0-06-228736-6(2)*, Greenwillow Bks.) HarperCollins Pubs.

Beaton, Clare & Blackstone, Stella. Un Alce, Veinte Ratones. Beaton, Clare, illus. 2006.Tr. of One Moose, Twenty Mice. (ENG., Illus.). 32p. (J). (gr. -1-k). bds. 6.99 *(978-1-84686-019-5(9))* Barefoot Bks., Inc.

Birtha, Becky. Lucky Beans. Tadgell, Nicole, illus. 2012. (J). 34.28 *(978-1-61913-129-3(3))* Weigl Pubs., Inc.

—Lucky Beans. Tadgell, Nicole, illus. 2010. (ENG.). 32p. (J). (gr. 2-3). 16.99 *(978-0-8075-4782-3(4))* Whitman, Albert & Co.

Blackstone, Stella & Harter, Debbie. Oso en un Cuadrado. 2013. (SPA & ENG., Illus.). 24p. (J). 7.99 *(978-1-78285-030-4(9))* Barefoot Bks., Inc.

Bruce, Sheila. Todos Ganan! Billin-Frye, Paige, illus. 2006. (Math Matters en Espanol Ser.). (SPA.). 32p. (J). (gr. -1-3). pap. 5.95 *(978-1-57565-162-0(9))* Kane Press, Inc.

Cabrera, Jane. The 12 Days of Christmas. 2013. (ENG., Illus.). 32p. (J). (gr. -1-k). 16.95 *(978-0-8234-2870-0(2))* Holiday Hse., Inc.

Calvert, Pam. Multiplying Menace: The Revenge of Rumpelstiltskin. Geehan, Wayne, illus. 2006. (Math Adventures Ser.). (ENG.). 32p. (J). (gr. 2-5). per. 7.95 *(978-1-57091-890-2(2))* Charlesbridge Publishing, Inc.

—The Multiplying Menace Divides! Geehan, Wayne, illus. 2011. (ENG.). 32p. (J). (gr. 2-5). pap. 7.95 *(978-1-57091-782-0(5))* Charlesbridge Publishing, Inc.

Cave, Kathryn & Riddell, Chris. Counting Sheep: A Bedtime Adventure! Riddell, Chris, illus. 2014. (ENG., Illus.). 32p. (J). (gr. -1-2). pap. 8.99 *(978-1-84780-480-8(2)*, Frances Lincoln) Quarto Publishing Group UK GBR. Dist: Hachette Bk. Group.

Charlesworth, Liza. Three Bouncing Balls. Jones, Doug, illus. 2005. (Number Tales Ser.). (ENG.). 16p. (J). (gr. -1-1). pap. 2.99 *(978-0-439-68999-1(6))* Scholastic, Inc.

—Two Bunny Slippers. Jones, Doug, illus. 2005. (Number Tales Ser.). (ENG.). 16p. (J). (gr. -1-1). pap. 2.99 *(978-0-439-68998-4(8))* Scholastic, Inc.

—Zero Spots. Jones, Doug, illus. 2005. (Number Tales Ser.). (ENG.). 16p. (J). (gr. -1-1). pap. 2.99 *(978-0-439-69022-5(6))* Scholastic, Inc.

Charlesworth, Liza & Scholastic, Inc. Staff. The Happy Hippos. Mahoney, Daniel J., illus. 2005. (Number Tales Ser.). (ENG.). 16p. (J). (gr. -1-1). pap. 2.99 *(978-0-439-69023-2(4))* Scholastic, Inc.

—Monkey's Missing Bananas. Sexton, Brenda, illus. 2005. (Number Tales Ser.). (ENG.). 16p. (J). (gr. -1-1). pap. 2.99 *(978-0-439-69032-4(3))* Scholastic, Inc.

—Ten Fingers Can! Kennedy, Anne, illus. 2005. (Number Tales Ser.). (ENG.). 16p. (J). (gr. -1-1). pap. 2.99 *(978-0-439-69021-8(8))* Scholastic, Inc.

—100 Wacky Wishes. Kennedy, Kelly, illus. 2005. (Number Tales Ser.). (ENG.). 16p. (J). (gr. -1-1). pap. 2.99 *(978-0-439-69030-0(7))* Scholastic, Inc.

Corbett, Robyn. Kokoye Kiko Yo: Kiko's Coconuts. 2013. (ENG.). 44p. (J). pap. 18.95 *(978-1-4787-1533-7(2))* Outskirts Pr., Inc.

Dalmatian Press Staff. Maggie Can Count. 2008. (ENG.). 5p. (J). bds. 4.95 *(978-1-58117-728-2(3)*, Intervisual/Piggy Toes) Bendon, Inc.

Davies, Jacqueline. The Lemonade War. (Lemonade War Ser.: 1). (ENG.). 192p. (J). (gr. 2-5). 2009. pap. 7.99 *(978-0-547-23765-7(0))* 2007. (Illus.). 16.99 *(978-0-618-75043-6(6))* Houghton Mifflin Harcourt Publishing Co.

Davis, Darren. Atlas 123S for Superheroes. 2006. (ENG.). 16p. (J). (gr. -1-12). bds. 5.99 *(978-1-59559-117-3(6))* Left Field,Angel Gate.

deRubertis, Barbara. Una Coleccion para Kate (A Collection for Kate) Fiammenghi, Gioia, illus. 2007. (Math Matters Ser.). (SPA.). 29p. (J). (gr. -1-3). pap. 5.95 *(978-1-57565-240-5(4))* Kane Press, Inc.

Dussling, Jennifer. Lo Justo Es Justo; Fair Is Fair. 2008. pap. 34.95 *(978-1-58013-785-0(7))* Kane Press, Inc.

Eissler, Trevor. 4,962,571. Chung, Ruth, illus. 2011. (ENG.). 32p. (J). 20.00 *(978-0-9835558-0-3(X))* June Bks., LLC.

Fisher, Doris & Sneed, Dani. Un día Non, 1 vol. Lee, Karen, illus. 2006. (SPA.). 32p. (J). (gr. -1-3). 17.95 *(978-1-60718-694-6(2))* Arbordale Publishing.

—Mi día Par, 1 vol. Lee, Karen, illus. 2007. (SPA & ENG.). 32p. (J). (gr. -1-3). 17.95 *(978-1-60718-692-2(6))* Arbordale Publishing.

—My Even Day, 1 vol. Lee, Karen, illus. 2007. (Basic Math Numbers Ser.). (ENG.). 32p. (J). (gr. -1-3). pap. 8.95 *(978-1-934359-22-8(X))* Arbordale Publishing.

—One Odd Day, 1 vol., Vol. 1. Lee, Karen, illus. 2006. (Basic Math Numbers Ser.). (ENG.). 32p. (J). (gr. -1-3). pap. 8.95 *(978-1-934359-33-4(5))* Arbordale Publishing.

Fleming, Denise. Shout! Shout It Out! Fleming, Denise, illus. 2011. (ENG., Illus.). 40p. (J). (gr. -1-1). 16.99 *(978-0-8050-9237-0(4)*, 9780805092370, Holt, Henry & Co. Bks. For Young Readers) Holt, Henry & Co.

Fleming, Maria & Scholastic Canada Ltd. Staff. 30 Mice Are Very Nice. Borlasca, Hector, illus. 2005. (Number Tales Ser.). (ENG.). 16p. (J). (gr. -1-1). pap. 2.99 *(978-0-439-69026-3(9))* Scholastic, Inc.

Fromental, Jean-Luc. 365 Penguins. Jolivet, Joëlle, illus. 2006. (ENG.). 48p. (J). (gr. -1-3). 19.95 *(978-0-8109-4460-2(X)*, Abrams Bks. for Young Readers) Abrams, Inc.

Galan, Alvaro. Billy Bully. Simpson, Steve, illus. 2009. (ENG.). 32p. (J). (gr. -1-3). pap. 3.99 *(978-0-545-11012-9(2))* Scholastic, Inc.

Garton, Michael. Countdown by the Sea. 2012. (ENG.). 20p. (J). bds. *(978-1-60727-701-9(8))* Soundprints.

Giganti, Paul. How Many Blue Birds Flew Away? A Counting Book with a Difference. Crews, Donald, illus. 2005. 32p. (J). lib. bdg. 16.89 *(978-0-06-000763-8(X))* HarperCollins Pubs.

Hanton, Sophie. Numbers in the Jungle. 2009. (Mag-NUT-Tics! Ser.). (Illus.). (J). bds. 9.99 *(978-1-934650-76-9(5))* Just For Kids Pr., LLC.

Henry, Isabelle. The Hundred-Penny Rub. 2008. 36p. pap. 16.99 *(978-1-4343-4912-5(8))* AuthorHouse.

Holm, Jennifer L. & Holm, Matthew. Dragonslayer. Holm, Jennifer L. & Holm, Matthew, illus. 2009. (Babymouse Ser.: 11). (ENG., Illus.). 96p. (J). (gr. 2-5). lib. bdg. 12.99 *(978-0-375-95712-3(X)*, Random Hse. Bks. for Young Readers) Random Hse. Children's Bks.

Houran, Lori Haskins. A Thousand Theos: Doubling. Pilz, M. H., illus. 2015. (Math Matters(r) Ser.). (ENG.). 32p. (gr. 1-3). 11.99 *(978-1-57565-804-9(6))* Kane Press, Inc.

Hughes, Jennifer L. The Nature of Numbers. 2008. 23p. pap. 24.95 *(978-1-60672-827-7(X))* America Star Bks.

Johnson, Jay, illus. Ten Little Pumpkins. 2012. (J). *(978-0-545-46862-6(0))* Scholastic, Inc.

Karr, Lily. Five Bouncing Bunnies. Rogers, Jacqueline, illus. 2013. (ENG.). 10p. (J). (gr. -1 — 1). bds. 6.99 *(978-0-545-45825-2(0)*, Cartwheel Bks.) Scholastic, Inc.

Kass, Daniele L., ed. The City Trail: A Skip-Counting Tale. 2010. 40p. pap. 18.49 *(978-1-4520-1219-3(9))* AuthorHouse.

Katz, Karen. Ten Tiny Babies. Katz, Karen, illus. 2008. (ENG., Illus.). 32p. (J). (gr. -1-k). 17.99 *(978-1-4169-3546-9(0)*, McElderry, Margaret K. Bks.) McElderry, Margaret K. Bks.

Kids Can Press Staff. Math Stories - Addition. 2003. (Kids Can Learn with Franklin Ser.). (ENG., Illus.). 32p. (J). (gr. 1-3). 3.95 *(978-1-55337-593-7(9))* Kids Can Pr., Ltd. CAN. Dist: Hachette Bk. Group.

Kiely, Orla. Numbers. Kiely, Orla, illus. 2012. (ENG., Illus.). 20p. (J). (gr. -1 — 1). bds. 12.99 *(978-0-8050-9492-3(X)*, 9780805094923, Holt, Henry & Co. Bks. For Young Readers) Holt, Henry & Co.

Law, Felicia & Way, Steve. The Mystery of Nine: Number Place & Value in Action. Spoor, Mike & Mostyn, David, illus. 2010. (Mandrill Mountain Math Mysteries Ser.). 32p. (J). (gr. 2-6). 22.60 *(978-1-60754-819-5(4))*; pap. 10.55 *(978-1-60754-824-9(0))* Windmill Bks.

Lazar, Tara. 7 Ate 9. MacDonald, Ross, illus. 2017. (ENG.). 32p. (J). (gr. -1-k). 17.99 ***(978-1-4847-1779-0(1))*** Hyperion Bks. for Children.

Lostorto, Eric. Rounding Rescue, a Rounding Numbers Story. Cotton, Sue Lynn, illus. 2013. 16p. pap. 11.95 *(978-1-61493-217-8(4))* Peppertree Pr., The.

Lubar, David. Numbed! 2014. (ENG., Illus.). 144p. (J). (gr. 2-5). pap. 6.95 *(978-1-4677-1596-6(4)*, Millbrook Pr.) Lerner Publishing Group.

Lucero, Jaime. One Little Egg. Kennedy, Kelly, illus. 2005. (Number Tales Ser.). (ENG.). 16p. (J). (gr. -1-1). pap. 2.99 *(978-0-439-68997-7(X))* Scholastic, Inc.

Maltby, Robert I. My Money Got Gobbled, 1 vol. 2010. 36p. 24.95 *(978-1-4489-6407-9(5))* PublishAmerica, Inc.

Manos, John. The Mail Comes to Main Street. 2006. (Early Explorers Ser.). (J). pap. *(978-1-4108-6118-4(X))* Benchmark Education Co.

Mariconda, Barbara. Sort It Out!, 1 vol. Rogers, Sherry, illus. 2008. (ENG.). 32p. (J). (gr. k-4). 16.95 *(978-1-934359-11-2(4))*; pap. 8.95 *(978-1-934359-32-7(7))* Arbordale Publishing.

McGranaghan, John. Saturn for My Birthday, 1 vol. Edelson, Wendy, illus. 2008. (ENG.). 32p. (J). (gr. 1-4). 16.95 *(978-1-934359-13-6(0))*; pap. 8.95 *(978-1-934359-27-3(0))* Arbordale Publishing.

McNamara, Margaret & Thompson, Kay. Eloise Has a Lesson. Mitter, Kathryn, illus. 2005. (Eloise Ser.). (ENG.). 32p. (J). (gr. -1-1). pap. 3.99 *(978-0-689-87367-6(0)*, Simon Spotlight) Simon Spotlight.

Melcher, Mary, illus. Puppies Count. 2010. (J). *(978-1-58865-596-7(2))* Kidsbooks, LLC.

Mills, Claudia. 7 X 9 = Trouble! Karas, G. Brian, illus. 2004. 103p. (J). (gr. 2-5). 13.60 *(978-0-7569-3397-5(8))* Perfection Learning Corp.

Moncure, Jane Belk. The Magic Moon Machine: A Counting Adventure. Rooney, Ronnie, illus. 2013. (Magic Castle Readers Ser.). (ENG.). 32p. (J). (gr. -1-2). 25.64 *(978-1-62323-580-2(4)*, 206316) Child's World, Inc., The.

—One Tricky Monkey up on Top: A Counting Adventure. Rooney, Ronnie, illus. 2013. (Magic Castle Readers Ser.). (ENG.). 32p. (J). (gr. -1-2). 25.64 *(978-1-62323-581-9(2)*, 206314) Child's World, Inc., The.

Penn, Mw. Sidney the Silly Who Only Eats 6. Tommer, Sarah, illus. 2013. 36p. pap. 13.95 *(978-0-9840425-7-9(1))* MathWord Pr., LLC.

Penner, Lucille Recht. Apaguen las Luces! Smath, Jerry, illus. 2007. (Math Matters (Kane Press Spanish) Ser.). 32p. (J). (gr. -1-3). pap. 5.95 *(978-1-57565-241-2(2))* Kane Press, Inc.

—A Limpiar el Campamento; Clean Sweep Campers. 2008. pap. 34.95 *(978-1-58013-758-4(X))* Kane Press, Inc.

Reasoner, Charles. Numbers under the Sea. Pitt, Sarah, illus. 2009. (3D Board Bks.). 12p. (J). (gr. -1-k). bds. 9.99 *(978-1-934650-37-0(4))* Just For Kids Pr., LLC.

Rosenthal, Amy Krouse. This Plus That: Life's Little Equations. Corace, Jen, illus. 2011. (ENG.). 40p. (J). (gr. -1-3). 14.99 *(978-0-06-172655-2(9))* HarperCollins Pubs.

Sadler, Marilyn & Comstock, Eric. Charlie Piechart & the Case of the Missing Pizza Slice. Comstock, Eric, illus. 2015. (Charlie Piechart Ser.). (ENG., Illus.). 40p. (J). (gr. -1-3). 17.99 *(978-0-06-237054-9(5)*, Tegen, Katherine Bks) HarperCollins Pubs.

Schwartz, Corey Rosen. Twinderella, a Fractioned Fairy Tale. Marcero, Deborah, illus. 2017. (ENG.). 32p. (J). (gr. -1-3). 17.99 ***(978-0-399-17633-3(0)***, G.P. Putnam's Sons Books for Young Readers) Penguin Young Readers Group.

Scieszka, Jon. Math Curse. 2004. (Illus.). (J). (gr. k-4). spiral bd. *(978-0-616-01778-4(2))* Canadian National Institute for the Blind/Institut National Canadien pour les Aveugles.

Seven, John & Christy, Jana. Happy Punks 1 2 3: A Counting Story. 2013. (ENG., Illus.). 32p. (gr. -1). bds. 15.95 *(978-1-933149-67-7(1))* Manic D Pr.

Skinner, Daphne. Henry Lleva la Cuenta; Henry Keeps Score. 2008. pap. 34.95 *(978-1-58013-757-7(1))* Kane Press, Inc.

Slater, David Michael. Seven Ate Nine, 1 vol. Trover, Zachary, illus. 2007. (Missy Swiss & More Ser.). (ENG.). 32p. (gr. -1-4). 28.50 *(978-1-60270-012-3(5)*, Looking Glass Library) ABDO Publishing Co.

Sneed, Dani & Fisher, Doris. My Half Day, 1 vol. Lee, Karen, illus. 2008. (Basic Math Numbers Ser.). (ENG.). 32p. (J). (gr. -1-3). 16.95 *(978-1-934359-14-3(9))*; pap. 8.95 *(978-1-934359-29-7(7))* Arbordale Publishing.

Stamper, Judith Bauer. Breakfast at Danny's Diner: A Book about Multiplication. Demarest, Chris L., illus. 2003. (All Aboard Math Reader Ser.). 48p. (J). (gr. 2-4). 11.65 *(978-0-7569-1695-4(X))* Perfection Learning Corp.

Stein, Renea. The Wise Old Owl & Those Tricky Times Tables. 2008. 36p. pap. 24.95 *(978-1-60474-228-2(3))* America Star Bks.

Texier, Ophélie & Baumann, Anne-Sophie. Numbers. 2009. (Little Discoveries: Ser.). (ENG., Illus.). 6p. (J). (gr. -1-k). bds. 8.95 *(978-0-7892-0983-2(7)*, Abbeville Kids) Abbeville Pr., Inc.

Top That Publishing Staff, ed. In My Little Blue Bed. Henley, Claire, illus. 2007. 11p. (J). (gr. -1-k). bds. *(978-1-84666-280-5(X)*, Tide Mill Pr.) Top That! Publishing PLC.

—In My Little Pink Bed: A Counting Book. Henley, Claire, illus. 2007. (In My Bed Book Ser.). 11p. (J). (gr. -1-k). bds. *(978-1-84666-285-0(0)*, Tide Mill Pr.) Top That! Publishing PLC.

Troutt, Susan. The Math Problem. 2012. 120p. (gr. 4-6). pap. 14.95 *(978-1-4772-6521-5(X))* AuthorHouse.

V. Nine & a Half Dozen, 1 vol. Swope, Brenda, illus. 2010. 24p. 24.95 *(978-1-4489-2596-4(7))* PublishAmerica, Inc.

123. 2004. (Illus.). (J). *(978-1-59060-333-8(8))* Waldman Publishing Corp.

ARITHMETIC—STUDY AND TEACHING

see also Counting Books

Engelbrite, Eve. Arithmability: Addition & Subtraction of Whole Numbers: Dyscalculia Workbook. 2003. 68p. spiral bd. 19.95 *(978-1-931203-07-4(5))* Inspired Idea.

Evan-Moor Educational Publishers, creator. At-Home Tutor Math, Grade 2. 2014. (ENG., Illus.). 89p. (J). (gr. 2). pap. 9.99 *(978-1-61368-982-0(9))* Evan-Moor Educational Pubs.

Flash Kids Editors, Flash Kids, ed. Subtraction Cards. 2015. (Write-On Wipe-off Learning Cards Ser.). (ENG., Illus.). 40p. (J). (gr. 1-2). 8.95 (978-1-4114-7114-6(8), Spark Publishing Group) Sterling Publishing Co., Inc.

Long, Ethan. The Wing Wing Brothers Math Spectacular! 2013. (ENG.). 32p. (J). (gr. -1-1). pap. 6.99 (978-0-8234-2918-9(0)) Holiday Hse., Inc.

Major, Sarah. Right-Brained Addition & Subtraction: A Forget Memorization Book. Major, Sarah, illus. 2013. (ENG., Illus.). 182p. (J). pap. 28.95 (978-1-936981-54-0(8)) Child1st Pubns., LLC.

—Right-Brained Place Value: A Forget Memorization Book. Major, Sarah, illus. 2013. (Illus.). 224p. (J). pap. 29.95 (978-1-936981-55-7(6)) Child1st Pubns., LLC.

Mercer, Susan. Pathway to Pre-Algebra Proficiency. 2008. 76p. per. 14.95 (978-1-4327-1719-3(7)) Outskirts Pr., Inc.

Saunders, Nicholas & Faber, Laurie. The Times Table Rap. 2004. (J). audio compact disk 15.00 (978-0-9761132-0-1(1)) Blue Lion Productions, Ltd.

Sundance/Newbridge LLC Staff. The Fact Families. 2004. (Reading PowerWorks Ser.). (gr. 1-3). 37.50 (978-0-7608-9305-0(5)); pap. 6.10 (978-0-7608-9306-7(3)) Sundance/Newbridge Educational Publishing.

ARIZONA

Andres, Dennis Michael. The Insider's Guide to Sedona. Lindahl, Larry, photos by. 2003. (Illus.). 222p. per. 16.95 (978-0-9721202-1-0(1), 825-694) Meta Adventures Publishing & DIA Publishing.

Bauer, Marion Dane. Celebrating Arizona: 50 States to Celebrate. Canga, C. B., illus. 2013. (Green Light Readers Level 3 Ser.). (ENG.). 40p. (J). (gr. 1-4). 12.99 (978-0-544-04387-9(1)); pap. 3.99 (978-0-544-04419-7(3)) Houghton Mifflin Harcourt Publishing Co.

Becker, Michelle Aki. Arizona. Risco, Eida del, tr. from ENG. Ancona, George, photos by. 2004. (Rookie Readers Spanish Ser.). (SPA., Illus.). 32p. (J). 19.50 (978-0-516-25106-6(6), Watts, Franklin) Scholastic Library Publishing.

Brezina, Corona. Arizona: Past & Present. 2010. (United States: Past & Present Ser.). (ENG., Illus.). 48p. (J). pap. 11.75 (978-1-4358-8483-0(3)); lib. bdg. 29.25 (978-1-4358-3516-0(6)) Rosen Publishing Group, Inc., The. (Rosen Reference).

Brown, Jonatha A. Arizona. 2006. (Portraits of the States Ser.). (Illus.). 32p. (gr. 2-6). pap. 10.50 (978-0-8368-4679-9(6)); lib. bdg. 26.00 (978-0-8368-4660-7(5)) Stevens, Gareth Publishing LLLP. (Gareth Stevens Learning Library).

Brown, Vanessa. Arizona. (Bilingual Library of the United States of America Ser.). 32p. 2009. (gr. 2-2). 47.90 (978-1-60853-343-5(3), Editorial Buenas Letras) 2005. (ENG & SPA., Illus.). (J). (gr. 3-6). lib. bdg. 25.25 (978-1-4042-3067-5(X)) Rosen Publishing Group, Inc., The.

Craats, Rennay. Arizona: The Grand Canyon State. 2016. (J). (978-1-5105-0653-4(5)) SmartBook Media, Inc.

—Arizona: The Grand Canyon State. 2016. (J). (978-1-4896-4821-1(6)) Weigl Pubs., Inc.

Ellis, Paula. Arizona Activity Book, 1 vol. Nitzsche, Shane, illus. 2012. (Color & Learn Ser.). (ENG.). 64p. (J). (gr. 2-3). pap. 5.95 (978-1-59193-288-8(2)) Adventure Pubns.

Filbin, Dan. Arizona. (J). 2012. lib. bdg. 25.26 (978-0-7613-4521-3(3), Lerner Pubns.) 2nd exp. rev. ed. 2003. (Illus.). 84p. (gr. 3-6). pap. 6.95 (978-0-8225-4133-2(5)) Lerner Publishing Group.

Gowan, Barbara. Desert Digits: An Arizona Number Book. Toddy, Irving, illus. 2006. (Count Your Way Across the U. S. A. Ser.). (ENG.). 40p. (J). (gr. -1-3). 17.95 (978-1-58536-162-5(3)) Sleeping Bear Pr.

Kirchner, Jason. Arizona. 2016. (States Ser.). (ENG., Illus.). 32p. (gr. 3-4). lib. bdg. 27.32 (978-1-5157-0389-1(4)) Next Page Pr., The.

Labairon, Cassandra Sharri. Arizona. 2008. (This Land Called America Ser.). 32p. (YA). (gr. 3-6). 22.95 (978-1-58341-628-0(5)) Creative Co., The.

Marsh, Carole. Arizona Current Events Projects: 30 Cool, Activities, Crafts, Experiments & More for Kids to Do to Learn about Your State! 2003. (Arizona Experience Ser.). 32p. (gr. k-5). pap. 5.95 (978-0-635-02022-2(X), Marsh, Carole Bks.) Gallopade International.

—Arizona Geography Projects: 30 Cool, Activities, Crafts, Experiments & More for Kids to Do to Learn about Your State! 2003. (Arizona Experience Ser.). 32p. (gr. k-5). pap. 5.95 (978-0-635-01822-9(5), Marsh, Carole Bks.) Gallopade International.

—Arizona Government Projects: 30 Cool, Activities, Crafts, Experiments & More for Kids to Do to Learn about Your State! 2003. (Arizona Experience Ser.). 32p. (gr. k-5). pap. 5.95 (978-0-635-01922-6(1), Marsh, Carole Bks.) Gallopade International.

—Arizona People Projects: 30 Cool, Activities, Crafts, Experiments & More for Kids to Do to Learn about Your State! 2003. (Arizona Experience Ser.). 32p. (gr. k-5). pap. 5.95 (978-0-635-01972-1(8), Marsh, Carole Bks.) Gallopade International.

—Arizona Symbols & Facts Projects: 30 Cool, Activities, Crafts, Experiments & More for Kids to Do to Learn about Your State! 2003. (Arizona Experience Ser.). 32p. (gr. k-5). pap. 5.95 (978-0-635-01871-7(3), Marsh, Carole Bks.) Gallopade International.

McDaniel, Melissa & Mead, Wendy. Arizona. 2nd rev. ed. 2008. (Celebrate the States Ser.). 144p. (gr. 6-18). lib. bdg. 42.79 (978-0-7614-3398-9(8), Benchmark Bks.) Marshall Cavendish Corp.

McHugh, Erin. Arizona. Schrier, Alfred, illus. 2007. (ENG.). 48p. (J). (gr. -1-17). 9.95 (978-1-57912-701-5(0), 81701, Black Dog & Leventhal Pubs. Inc.) Hachette Bks.

Murray, Julie. Arizona, 1 vol. 2006. (Buddy Book Ser.). (ENG., Illus.). 32p. (J). (gr. 2-5). 27.07 (978-1-59197-662-2(6)) ABDO Publishing Co.

Nicole, Taylor. Schooled on Fat: What Teens Tell Us about Gender, Body Image, & Obesity. 2015. (ENG.). 204p. (C). 144.00 (978-1-138-92420-8(2), Y202719) Routledge.

Ollhoff, Jim. Arizona, 1 vol. 2009. (United States Ser.). (ENG., Illus.). 48p. (YA). (gr. 2-5). 27.07 (978-1-60453-638-6(1)) ABDO Publishing Co.

Quasha, Jennifer. How to Draw Arizona's Sights & Symbols. 2009. (Kid's Guide to Drawing America Ser.). 32p. (gr. k-k). 50.50 (978-1-61511-045-2(3), PowerKids Pr.) Rosen Publishing Group, Inc., The.

Somervill, Barbara A. Arizona (Revised Edition) 2014. (America the Beautiful, Third Ser. (Revised Edition) Ser.). (ENG.). 144p. (J). lib. bdg. 40.00 (978-0-531-28275-5(9)) Scholastic Library Publishing.

Taylor, Nicole. Schooled on Fat: What Teens Tell Us about Gender, Body Image, & Obesity. 2015. (ENG.). 204p. (C). pap. 39.95 (978-1-138-92421-5(0), Y202720) Routledge.

Wyner, Zach. Phoenix Suns. 2014. (On the Hardwood Ser.). (gr. 3-8). pap. 8.95 (978-1-61570-921-2(5)) Scobre Pr. Corp.

ARIZONA—FICTION

Alarid, Carilyn & Markel, Marilyn, illus. Runs Like the Wind Stops in Her Tracks: Mimbres Children Learn about Trustworthiness. 2016. (J). pap. (978-1-63293-099-6(4)) Sunstone Pr.

Allen, J. Kent. Embritt Waters & the Mark of the Rattlesnake. 2006. 229p. (J). pap. 14.95 (978-0-7414-2769-4(9)) Infinity Publishing.

Allred, Sylvester. Rascal, the Tassel-Eared Squirrel. Iverson, Diane, illus. 2007. (ENG.). 64p. 16.95 (978-0-938216-88-9(0)) Grand Canyon Assn.

Amato, Carol J. The Lost Treasure of the Golden Sun. 2005. 172p. (J). (978-0-9713756-3-5(1)) Stargazer Publishing Co.

Authords, D. K. Being Alone. 2013. 120p. pap. 19.95 (978-1-63000-114-8(7)) America Star Bks.

Avalos, Cecilia O. El Sombrero de Luis Lucero. 2003. (SPA.). pap. 15.96 net. (978-0-7608-2262-3(X), SW3166) Sundance/Newbridge Educational Publishing.

Avrech, Robert J. The Hebrew Kid & the Apache Maiden. 2006. (Illus.). 220p. (J). (gr. 4-7). per. 11.95 (978-0-9754382-2-0(0)) Seraphic Pr.

Bily, Ro. My Red Island in the Sky. 2012. 530p. 34.95 (978-1-4626-6645-4(0)); pap. 34.95 (978-1-4626-6971-4(9)) America Star Bks.

Broach, Elise. Missing on Superstition Mountain. Caparó, Antonio Javier, illus. 2011. (Superstition Mountain Mysteries Ser.: 1). (ENG.). 272p. (J). (gr. 3-7). 15.99 (978-0-8050-9047-5(9), 9780805090475, Holt, Henry & Co. Bks. For Young Readers) Holt, Henry & Co.

—Revenge of Superstition Mountain. Ivanov, Aleksey & Ivanov, Olga, illus. 2014. (Superstition Mountain Mysteries Ser.: 3). (ENG.). 304p. (J). (gr. 3-7). 16.99 (978-0-8050-8909-7(8), 9780805089097, Holt, Henry & Co. Bks. For Young Readers) Holt, Henry & Co.

—Revenge of Superstition Mountain. Ivanov, Olga & Ivanov, Aleksey, illus. 2015. (Superstition Mountain Mysteries Ser.: 3). (ENG.). 320p. (J). (gr. 3-7). pap. 8.99 (978-1-250-05686-3(1), 9781250056863) Square Fish.

—Treasure on Superstition Mountain. Caparó, Antonio Javier, illus. 2013. (Superstition Mountain Mysteries Ser.: 2). (ENG.). 288p. (J). (gr. 3-7). 15.99 (978-0-8050-7763-6(4), 9780805077636, Holt, Henry & Co. Bks. For Young Readers) Holt, Henry & Co.

Clapp. Eloy the Elk & His Desert Friends. Clapp, ed. Drotar, illus. 2009. (J). pap. 9.95 (978-0-9825181-0-6(2)) Arizona Elk Society.

Coffey, Ethel. How Meg Changed Her Mind. Schweitzer-Johnson, Betty, illus. 2014. (ENG.). 32p. pap. 11.95 (978-1-4525-8377-8(3), Balboa Pr.) Author Solutions, Inc.

Collins, Bert McLemore. Excitement at Double B Acres. 2009. 52p. pap. 22.49 (978-1-4389-8447-6(2)) AuthorHouse.

Conkling, Winifred. Sylvia & Aki. (ENG.). 160p. (J). 2013. (gr. 4-7). 6.99 (978-1-58246-345-2(X), Yearling) 2011. (Illus.). (gr. 3-7). 16.99 (978-1-58246-337-7(9), Tricycle Pr.) Random Hse. Children's Bks.

Cook, Beatrice. A Journey with the Spider & Snake to Arizona. Campis, Adrian, Jr., illus. 2007. (J). 14.95 (978-0-9795867-0-5(4)) Travel America Bks.

Cottrell-Bentley, Lisa M. Wright on Time: Minnesota. Bauerle, Tanja, illus. 2012. 126p. pap. 12.99 (978-1-937848-02-6(7)) Do Life Right, Inc.

Flood, Nancy Bo. Soldier Sister, Fly Home. Begay, Shonto, illus. 2016. (ENG.). 176p. (YA). (gr. 5). lib. bdg. 16.95 (978-1-58089-702-0(9)) Charlesbridge Publishing, Inc.

Franciosi, Pete. Dusty Wants A Kitty. 2011. 23p. 14.95 (978-1-4327-7596-4(0)) Outskirts Pr., Inc.

Gamble, Adam. Good Night Arizona. Veno, Joe & Hansen, Red, illus. 2008. (Good Night Our World Ser.). (ENG.). 20p. (J). (gr. k — 1). bds. 9.95 (978-1-60219-000-9(3)) Good Night Bks.

Garr, Rebecca. Adventures of Baroness of the Arizona Desert. Davisson, Vanessa, illus. 2010. 60p. pap. 18.95 (978-1-60911-958-4(4), Eloquent Bks.) Strategic Book Publishing & Rights Agency (SBPRA).

Giacomucci, Carol. A New Home. 2006. 23p. pap. 10.95 (978-0-7414-3498-2(9)) Infinity Publishing.

Glazer, Maryann. The Adventures of Teddy Bark-Lee: Teddy Comes Home. 2009. 28p. pap. 13.99 (978-1-4389-4569-9(8)) AuthorHouse.

Golio, Janet & Golio, Mike. Present from the Past. 2nd ed. 2009. (ENG.). 120p. (YA). pap. 14.99 (978-1-59092-145-6(3)) Blue Forge Pr.

—Puzzle from the Past. 2nd ed. 2009. (ENG.). 120p. (YA). pap. 14.99 (978-1-59092-146-3(1)) Blue Forge Pr.

Grace & the Guiltless. 2014. (Wanted Ser.). (ENG.). 272p. 16.95 (978-1-63079-001-1(X)) Switch Pr.

Grant, Katy. Hide & Seek, 1 vol. (ENG.). 240p. (J). 2012. pap. 7.95 (978-1-56145-669-7(1)) 2010. (gr. 3-7). 15.95 (978-1-56145-542-3(3)) Peachtree Pubs.

Gutman, Dan. The Homework Machine. 2014. (ENG.). 176p. (J). (gr. 3-7). 11.24 (978-1-63245-274-0(X)) Lectorum Pubns., Inc.

—The Homework Machine. 2006. (ENG., Illus.). 160p. (J). (gr. 3-7). 17.99 (978-0-689-87678-3(5), Simon & Schuster Bks. For Young Readers) Simon & Schuster Bks. For Young Readers.

Hamilton, Elizabeth L. Lost on Superstition Mountain. 2004. (Character Mystery Ser.: No. 3). (Illus.). 144p. (J). per. 9.95 (978-0-9754629-5-9(4), Character-in-Action) Quiet Impact, Inc.

Hancock, H. Irving. The Young Engineers in Arizona. rev. ed. 2006. 216p. 27.95 (978-1-4218-1751-4(9)); pap. 12.95 (978-1-4218-1851-1(5)) 1st World Publishing, Inc. (1st World Library - Literary Society).

—The Young Engineers in Arizona. 2007. 180p. per. (978-1-4065-1992-1(8)) Dodo Pr.

—The Young Engineers in Arizona. 2004. reprint ed. pap. 21.95 (978-1-4191-8913-5(1)) Kessinger Publishing, LLC.

—The Young Engineers in Arizona, or Laying Tracks on the Man-Killer Quicksand. 2004. reprint ed. pap. 1.99 (978-1-4192-8913-2(6)) Kessinger Publishing, LLC.

Harvey, Gwen. Esperanza Means Hope. Porfirio, Guy, illus. 2010. (J). (978-0-910037-51-8(5)); pap. (978-0-910037-52-5(3)) Arizona Historical Society.

Hayes, Joe. Ghost Fever (Mal de Fantasma) 2006. (ENG & SPA., Illus.). 90p. (J). (gr. 4-6). pap. 8.95 (978-1-933693-03-3(7)) Cinco Puntos Pr.

—Ghost Fever (Mal de Fantasma) Pennypacker, Mona, illus. 2004. (ENG & SPA.). 80p. (J). (gr. 4-6). 14.95 (978-0-938317-83-8(0)) Cinco Puntos Pr.

Hays, Summer. Mrs. Gambel the Quirky Quail. 2013. (ENG.). 32p. (J). (gr. k-2). 16.95 (978-1-57197-517-1(9), Ivy House Publishing Group) Pentland Pr., Inc.

Hollingsworth, Suzi. Birding with Bobbie. 2011. 23p. (J). pap. 15.95 (978-1-4327-6422-7(5)) Outskirts Pr., Inc.

Hopkins, Suzette. Little Wolf's Christmas. Taylor, Jill, illus. 2004. (Little Wolf & Friends Ser.). 19p. (J). 12.95 (978-1-932133-72-1(0)) Writers' Collective, The.

Howey, Paul M. Freckles: The Mystery of the Little White Dog in the Desert. Zabriskie, Judy Mehn, illus. 2003. 72p. (gr. 2-5). lib. bdg. 14.95 (978-0-9677292-1-3(1)) AZTexts Publishing, Inc.

Hubbard, L. Ron, contrib. by. The Toughest Ranger: Literature Guide for Teachers & Librarians, Based on Common Core ELA Standards for Classrooms 6-9. 2013. (Stories from the Golden Age Ser.). (ENG.). 35p. (gr. 6-9). pap., tchr. ed. 14.95 (978-1-61986-220-3(4)) Galaxy Pr., LLC.

Jacobs, Lily. The Littlest Bunny in Arizona: An Easter Adventure. 2015. (ENG.). 32p. (J). (-3). 9.99 (978-1-4926-1024-3(0), Sourcebooks Jabberwocky) Sourcebooks, Inc.

James, Eric. A Halloween Scare in Arizona. Le Ray, Marina, illus. 2015. (ENG.). 32p. (J). (-5). 9.99 (978-1-4926-2362-5(8), 9781492623625, Sourcebooks Jabberwocky) Sourcebooks, Inc.

—Santa's Sleigh Is on Its Way to Arizona: A Christmas Adventure. Dunn, Robert, illus. 2016. (ENG.). 32p. (J). (-2). 12.99 (978-1-4926-4316-6(5), 9781492643166, Sourcebooks Jabberwocky) Sourcebooks, Inc.

Jenkins, Jerry B. & Fabry, Chris. Canyon Echoes. 2005. (Red Rock Mysteries Ser.: 8). (ENG.). 234p. (YA). pap. 6.99 (978-1-4143-0147-1(2), Tyndale Kids) Tyndale Hse. Pubs.

Jerry, Spinelli. Stargirl. 2014. (ENG.). 208p. (YA). 11.24 (978-1-63245-152-1(2)) Lectorum Pubns., Inc.

Johnson, Erin. Her Cold Revenge. 2015. (Wanted Ser.). (ENG.). 272p. 16.95 (978-1-63079-007-3(9)) Switch Pr.

Johnson, Kristin F. Black Blizzard. 2017. (Day of Disaster Ser.). (ENG.). 112p. (gr. 6-12). (J). 26.65 (978-1-5124-2774-5(8)); (YA). 12.99 **(978-1-5124-3507-8(4)**, Darby Creek); (YA). 39.99 **(978-1-5124-2781-3(0)**, Darby Creek); (YA). 39.99 **(978-1-5124-3506-1(6)**, Darby Creek) Lerner Publishing Group.

Johnson, Tim. Lost Dutchman in Cochise County? Incidents & Coincidences. 2003. (Illus.). 52p. 19.95 (978-0-9742351-0-3(5)) MCM Prime, Inc.

Kadohata, Cynthia. Weedflower. (ENG.). 272p. (J). (gr. 5-9). 2009. pap. 7.99 (978-1-4169-7566-3(7)) 2006. (Illus.). 19.99 (978-0-689-86574-9(0)) Simon & Schuster Children's Publishing. (Atheneum Bks. for Young Readers).

King, A. S. Everybody Sees the Ants. 2011. (ENG.). 288p. (YA). (gr. 10-17). 18.00 (978-0-316-12928-2(3)) Little Brown & Co.

—Everybody Sees the Ants. 2012. (ENG.). 320p. (YA). (gr. 10-17). pap. 10.00 (978-0-316-12927-5(5)) Little, Brown Bks. for Young Readers.

Kloepfer, John. Nothing Left to Ooze. DeGrand, David, illus. 2014. (Zombie Chasers Ser.: 5). (ENG.). 224p. (J). (gr. 3-7). 16.99 (978-0-06-223098-0(0)) HarperCollins Pubs.

—Undead Ahead. Wolfhard, Steve, illus. 2011. (Zombie Chasers Ser.: 2). (ENG.). 224p. (J). (gr. 3-7). pap. 6.99 (978-0-06-185308-1(9)); 16.99 (978-0-06-185307-4(0)) HarperCollins Pubs.

—The Zombie Chasers #7: World Zombination. DeGrand, David, illus. 2015. (Zombie Chasers Ser.: 7). (ENG.). 240p. (J). (gr. 3-7). 16.99 (978-0-06-229027-4(4)) HarperCollins Pubs.

Koertge, Ronald. The Arizona Kid. 2005. (ENG.). 304p. (YA). (gr. 9-18). pap. 6.99 (978-0-7636-2695-2(3)) Candlewick Pr.

Kostro, Ed. Mystery of Madera Canyon. 2004. 108p. (gr. -1-7). per. 11.95 (978-1-59113-622-4(9)) Booklocker.com, Inc.

Leveen, Tom. Hellworld. 2017. (ENG., Illus.). 304p. (YA). (gr. 9). 17.99 (978-1-4814-6633-2(X), Simon Pulse) Simon Pulse.

Lewis, Floyd. The Foundered Mule. 2006. (YA). 9.95 (978-0-9788283-2-5(1)) Acacia Publishing, Inc.

The Little Saguaro. 2007. (YA). pap. 15.95 (978-1-886679-37-5(1)) Arizona Sonora Desert Museum Pr.

Ludwig, Elisa. Pretty Crooked. 2012. (Pretty Crooked Trilogy Ser.: 1). (ENG.). 368p. (YA). (gr. 8). 17.99 (978-0-06-206606-0(4), Tegen, Katherine Bks) HarperCollins Pubs.

MacColl, Michaela & Nichols, Rosemary. Rory's Promise. 2014. (Hidden Histories Ser.). (ENG.). 288p. (J). (gr. 4-7). 16.95 (978-1-62091-623-0(1), Calkins Creek) Boyds Mills Pr.

Marsh, Carole. The Mystery of the Haunted Ghost Town. 2009. (Real Kids, Real Places Ser.). 144p. (J). 18.99 (978-0-635-07044-9(8), Marsh, Carole Mysteries) Gallopade International.

Matthews. Death in the Desert. (Thumbprint Mysteries Ser.). 32.86 (978-0-8092-0416-8(9)) McGraw-Hill/Contemporary.

Mayaprua, Alejandro Taish. Nantu & Auju: How the Moon & the Potoo Bird Came to Be. Youth of the Achuar Tribe of Ecuador, illus. 2005. (J). 15.95 (978-0-9745477-0-1(0)) Arutam Pr.

Mcallister, Herb West. Doo West to Toadstool. 2011. 44p. pap. 21.99 (978-1-4628-5530-8(X)) Xlibris Corp.

McIntosh, Kenneth. Poison & Peril: Forensic Toxicology. 2009. (J). pap. 24.95 (978-1-4222-1453-4(2)) Mason Crest.

—Poison & Peril: Forensic Toxicology, 4 vols. Miller, Justin, illus. 2007. (Crime Scene Club Ser.). 144p. (YA). (gr. 9-12). lib. bdg. 24.95 (978-1-4222-0250-0(X)) Mason Crest.

—The Trickster's Image: Forensic Art. 2009. (J). pap. 24.95 (978-1-4222-1452-7(4)) 2007. (Illus.). 144p. (YA). (gr. 8-12). pap. 9.95 (978-1-4222-0873-1(7)) Mason Crest.

—The Trickster's Image: Forensic Art, 3 vols. Miller, Justin, illus. 2007. (Crime Scene Club Ser.). 144p. (YA). (gr. 9-12). lib. bdg. 24.95 (978-1-4222-0249-4(6)) Mason Crest.

Medina, Sylvia M. & Ballock-Dixon, Saige J. Desert Mirage. Eagle, Joy, illus. 2012. 32p. pap. 11.59 (978-0-9836602-6-2(3)) Green Kids Club, Inc.

Morrison, Kevin. Frank Is a Chihuahua. De La Cruz, Erin Harris, illus. 2007. 32p. (J). (gr. 1-4). (978-1-929039-43-2(3)) Ambassador Bks., Inc.

Murrow, Marjorie. The Surprise in Grandma's Eyes. 2009. (Illus.). 16p. pap. 10.98 (978-1-4389-8104-8(X)) AuthorHouse.

Narayan, Natasha. The Shaman's Secret. 2011. (Kit Salter Adventures Ser.). (ENG., Illus.). 272p. (J). (gr. 4-6). pap. 8.99 (978-1-84916-555-6(6)) Quercus GBR. Dist: Hachette Bk. Group.

Neil Wallace, Sandra. Muckers. 2013. (ENG.). 288p. (YA). (gr. 7). 16.99 (978-0-375-86754-5(6), Knopf Bks. for Young Readers) Random Hse. Children's Bks.

O'Neill, Elizabeth. Alfred Visits Arizona. 2006. (Illus.). 24p. pap. 12.00 (978-0-9790240-0-9(5)) Global Business Information Strategies, Inc.

Peschke, Marci. Dead Man's Map, 1 vol. Smith, Tod G., illus. 2008. (Vortex Bks.). (ENG.). 112p. (gr. 2-3). pap. 7.19 (978-1-59889-921-4(X), 1271328, Vortex Bks.) Stone Arch Bks.

Pintozzi, Nick. Bentley & the Great Fire. Pintozzi, Nick et al, illus. 2004. 16.95 (978-0-9749465-2-8(4)) BentDaiSha, LLC.

Riley, Vicki. Squirt's Adventures: Episode 1. 2010. 48p. pap. 16.50 (978-1-60911-627-9(5), Eloquent Bks.) Strategic Book Publishing & Rights Agency (SBPRA).

Roy, Lillian Elizabeth. Girl Scouts in Arizona & New Mexico. Lehman, A. C., illus. 2011. 250p. 46.95 (978-1-258-05940-8(1)) Literary Licensing, LLC.

Sanders, Jeane F. Ramón. 2008. 100p. pap. 19.95 (978-1-60610-768-3(2)) America Star Bks.

Sargent, Dave & Sargent, Pat. Buttons: (Muddy Dun) Have Courage, Vol. 9. Lenoir, Jane, illus. 2003. (Saddle up Ser.: Vol. 9). 42p. (J). pap. 10.95 (978-1-56763-688-8(8)); lib. bdg. 23.60 (978-1-56763-687-1(X)) Ozark Publishing.

Shanks, Cindy. Emilia Camina la Vereda de Borregos. 2009. 48p. pap. 19.95 (978-1-4490-2388-1(6)) AuthorHouse.

—Emily Walks the Sheep Trail. 2009. 48p. pap. 19.95 (978-1-4490-2208-2(1)) AuthorHouse.

Silvano, Wendi. Love Is All Around Arizona. Czernichowska, Joanna, illus. 2016. (ENG.). 32p. (J). (-6). 12.99 (978-1-4926-2903-0(0), Sourcebooks Jabberwocky) Sourcebooks, Inc.

Simonds, Kevin. The Tomb of Father Time. 2011. 178p. pap. 24.95 (978-1-4626-2739-4(0)) America Star Bks.

Skurzynski, Gloria & Ferguson, Alane. Over the Edge. 2008. (Mysteries in Our National Park Ser.). (ENG., Illus.). 160p. (J). (gr. 3-7). per. 4.99 (978-1-4263-0177-3(4), National Geographic Children's Bks.) National Geographic Society.

Smallman, Steve. Santa Is Coming to Tucson. Dunn, Robert, illus. 2013. (ENG.). 32p. (J). (-3). 9.99 (978-1-4022-8976-7(6), Sourcebooks Jabberwocky) Sourcebooks, Inc.

Spinelli, Jerry. Stargirl. 2003. (EMC Masterpiece Series Access Editions). xiv, 199p. (YA). 12.99 (978-0-8219-2504-1(0), 35378) EMC/Paradigm Publishing.

—Stargirl. unabr. ed. 2004. 192p. (J). (gr. 7-18). pap. 40.00 incl. audio (978-0-8072-0855-7(8), LYA 323 SP, Listening Library) Random Hse. Audio Publishing Group.

—Stargirl. 2004. (ENG.). 208p. (YA). (gr. 7). mass mkt. 7.99 (978-0-440-41677-7(9), Laurel Leaf) Random Hse. Children's Bks.

Stephenson, Midji. Whose Tail on the Trail at Grand Canyon. Spengler, Kenneth, illus. 2012. (J). (978-1-934656-55-6(0)) Grand Canyon Assn.

Stewart, Jennifer J. The Twelve Days of Christmas in Arizona. Avril, Lynne, illus. 2010. (Twelve Days of Christmas in America Ser.). (ENG.). 40p. (J). (gr. k). 12.95 (978-1-4027-7036-4(7)) Sterling Publishing Co., Inc.

Stilton, Geronimo. Flight of the Red Bandit. 2014. (ENG., Illus.). 128p. (J). (gr. 2-5). pap. 7.99 (978-0-545-55630-9(9), Scholastic Paperbacks) Scholastic, Inc.

—Flight of the Red Bandit. 2014. (Geronimo Stilton Ser.: 56). lib. bdg. 18.40 (978-0-606-35195-9(7)) Turtleback Bks.

Stoneskipper. 2005. (J). per. 19.95 (978-0-9743789-0-9(9)) Freeverse Enterprises Inc.

Summy, Barrie. I So Don't Do Spooky. 2010. (ENG.). 304p. (J). (gr. 3-7). 7.99 (978-0-385-73605-3(3), Yearling) Random Hse. Children's Bks.

Tarore, Martha. The Runaway Bubble. 2011. (ENG.). 35p. (J). pap. 16.95 (978-1-4327-5898-1(5)) Outskirts Pr., Inc.

Tribolet, Leslie L. Danny's Tale: Adventures of an Arabian Horse in his Own Words. 2010. (Illus.). 112p. 24.95 (978-1-4490-6065-7(X)); pap. 14.95 (978-1-4490-6064-0(1)) AuthorHouse.

Wallace, Rich. Double-Crossed at Cactus Flats: An Up2 U Western Adventure, 1 vol. Mitchell, Hazel, illus. 2013. (Up2U Adventures Ser.). (ENG.). 80p. (J). (gr. 2-5). lib. bdg. 27.07 (978-1-61641-966-0(0), Calico Chapter Bks) Magic Wagon.

Walser, Jo. Chasing the Rising Moon. 2012. 452p. pap. 14.95 (978-1-935807-04-9(8)) Stansbury Publishing.

Watt, Cliff. Jenny Brown & the Search for Eusebio's Star. 2008. 77p. pap. 19.95 (978-1-60672-169-8(0)) America Star Bks.

Whipple, Natalie. Transparent. 2013. (ENG.). 368p. (YA). (gr. 8). pap. 9.99 (978-0-06-212016-8(6), HarperTeen) HarperCollins Pubs.

White, Jan. Mystery of Mingus Mountain. 2012. (ENG., Illus.). 138p. (YA). (gr. 7-13). pap. 9.99 (978-0-89824-370-3(X)) Royal Fireworks Publishing Co.

Wittman, Kathy A. Raina's Vision Quest, 1 vol. 2010. 78p. pap. 19.95 (978-1-61582-656-8(4)) America Star Bks.

Wofford, Delaney. For Courage. 2010. 229p. pap. 17.98 (978-0-557-17045-6(1)) Lulu Pr., Inc.

Wood, Elizabeth Lamb. There Go the Apaches. 2005. pap. 26.95 (978-1-4191-5979-4(8)) Kessinger Publishing, LLC.

Zambarano, Richard, illus. Wilbur & Wilma's Colorful Campus Tour - University of Arizona A-Z. 2004. (J). 9.99 (978-1-933069-02-9(3)) Odd Duck Ink, Inc.

ARIZONA—HISTORY

Alagna, Magdalena. Wyatt Earp: Lawman of the American West. (Primary Sources of Famous People in American History Ser.). 32p. 2009. (gr. 2-3). 47.90 *(978-1-60851-747-3(0))* 2004. (ENG., Illus.). (gr. 4-8). pap. 10.00 *(978-0-8239-4195-7(7))* 2004. (Illus.). (J). (gr. 3-7). 22.50 *(978-0-8239-4123-0(X)*, Rosen Reference) Rosen Publishing Group, Inc., The.

—Wyatt Earp: Lawman of the American West / Sheriff del oeste Americano. 2009. (Famous People in American History/Grandes personajes en la historia de los Estados Unidos Ser.). (ENG & SPA.). 32p. (gr. 2-3). 47.90 *(978-1-61512-558-6(2)*, Editorial Buenas Letras) Rosen Publishing Group, Inc., The.

—Wyatt Earp: Sheriff del oeste americano (Wyatt Earp: Lawman of the American West) 2009. (Grandes personajes en la historia de los Estados Unidos (Famous People in American History) Ser.). (SPA.). 32p. (gr. 2-3). 47.90 *(978-1-61512-811-2(5)*, Editorial Buenas Letras) Rosen Publishing Group, Inc., The.

The Arizona Constitution. 4th ed. 2003. (YA). pap., wbk. ed. 7.00 *(978-0-9740200-0-6(1))* Academic Solutions, Inc.

The Arizona Story Program Kit: All program components for the Arizona Story, 1 vol. 2009. (gr. 4-4). 149.95 *(978-1-4236-0713-7(9))* Gibbs Smith, Publisher.

Becker, Michelle Aki. Arizona. 2005. (Rookie Espanol: Geografia Ser.). (SPA., Illus.). 32p. (J). (gr. k-2). pap. 5.95 *(978-0-516-25512-5(6)*, Children's Pr.) Scholastic Library Publishing.

Craats, Rennay. Arizona. 2011. (Illus.). 48p. (YA). (gr. 3-6). 29.99 *(978-1-61690-775-4(4))* Weigl Pubs., Inc.

Derzipilski, Kathleen & Hudson, Amanda. Arizona. 2nd rev. ed. 2011. (It's My State! 2 Ser.). 80p. (gr. 3). 31.36 *(978-1-60870-521-4(8))* Marshall Cavendish GBR. Dist: Marshall Cavendish Corp.

Durrett, Deanne. Arizona. 2003. (Seeds of a Nation Ser.). (Illus.). 48p. (J). (gr. 3-5). 23.70 *(978-0-7377-1537-8(5)*, Kidhaven) Cengage Gale.

Durrie, Karen. Arizona: The Grand Canyon State. 2012. (J). 27.13 *(978-1-61913-325-9(3))* Weigl Pubs., Inc.

Goodman, Michael E. Wyatt Earp. 2005. (Legends of the West Ser.). (Illus.). 48p. (J). (gr. 5-9). lib. bdg. 21.95 *(978-1-58341-339-5(1)*, Creative Education) Creative Co., The.

Gowan, Barbara. Little Arizona. 2012. (My Little State Ser.). (ENG., Illus.). 20p. (J). (gr. k-3). 9.95 *(978-1-58536-208-0(5))* Sleeping Bear Pr.

Hall, Carol S. & Hansen, T. J. This Is Arizona. (Illus.). 298p. (J). (gr. 1-6). pap. 49.95 *(978-1-56861-061-0(0))* Swift Learning Resources.

Hernandez, Daniel. They Call Me a Hero: A Memoir of My Youth. 2014. (ENG., Illus.). 240p. (YA). (gr. 7). pap. 9.99 *(978-1-4424-6235-9(3)*, Simon & Schuster Bks. For Young Readers) Simon & Schuster Bks. For Young Readers.

Hirsch, Rebecca E. What's Great about Arizona? 2015. (Our Great States Ser.). (ENG., Illus.). 32p. (J). (gr. 2-5). pap. 7.95 *(978-1-4677-6086-7(2))*; lib. bdg. 26.60 *(978-1-4677-3862-0(X))* Lerner Publishing Group. (Lerner Pubns.).

Hook, Sue Vander & Kamisar, Yale. Miranda v. Arizona: An Individual's Rights When under Arrest, 1 vol. 2012. (Landmark Supreme Court Cases Ser.). (ENG., Illus.). 160p. (J). (gr. 6-12). 37.07 *(978-1-61783-474-5(2))* ABDO Publishing Co.

Houser, Aimee. Tragedy in Tucson: The Arizona Shooting Rampage, 1 vol. 2012. (Essential Events Set 8 Ser.). (ENG.). 112p. (J). (gr. 6-12). lib. bdg. 35.64 *(978-1-61783-312-0(6))* ABDO Publishing Co.

Jastrzembski, Joseph C. The Apache Wars: The Final Resistance. 2007. (Landmark Events in Native American History Ser.). (Illus.). 133p. (YA). (gr. 9-12). pap. 35.00 *(978-0-7910-9343-6(3))* Facts On File, Inc.

Jerome, Kate B. Lucky to Live in Arizona. 2017. (Arcadia Kids Ser.). (ENG., Illus.). 32p. (J). 16.99 ***(978-0-7385-2779-6(3))*** Arcadia Publishing.

Larson, Kirsten W. The West: Arizona, California, Nevada. 2015. (Let's Explore the States Ser.). (Illus.). 64p. (J). (gr. 5). 23.95 *(978-1-4222-3337-5(5))* Mason Crest.

Lyon, Robin. The Spanish Missions of Arizona. 2010. (True Book(tm), a — Spanish Missions Ser.). 48p. (J). (gr. 2-5). 31.00 *(978-0-531-20576-1(2))*; (ENG.). pap. 6.95 *(978-0-531-21239-4(4))* Scholastic Library Publishing.

Marsh, Carole. Arizona History Projects: 30 Cool, Activities, Crafts, Experiments & More for Kids to Do to Learn about Your State! 2003. (Arizona Experience Ser.). 32p. (gr. k-5). pap. 5.95 *(978-0-635-01772-7(5)*, Marsh, Carole Bks.) Gallopade International.

—Exploring Arizona Through Project-Based Learning. 2016. (Arizona Experience Ser.). (ENG.). (J). pap. 9.99 *(978-0-635-12327-5(4))* Gallopade International.

—I'm Reading about Arizona. 2014. (Arizona Experience Ser.). (ENG., Illus.). (J). pap., pap. 8.99 *(978-0-635-11279-8(5))* Gallopade International.

—I'm Reading about the Grand Canyon. 2016. (I'm Reading about Mount Rushmore Ser.). (ENG., Illus.). (J). lib. bdg. 24.99 *(978-0-635-12179-0(4))* Gallopade International.

Ruffner, Melissa. Whatever Happened to Baby Harry: The True Story of the First Child Born to an Officer's Family at Camp Apache, Arizona Territory. Summerhayes, Roger, photos by. 2003. (Illus.). 19p. (YA). pap. 12.95 *(978-0-9673171-1-3(8))* Primrose Pr.

Silverman, Steve. The Story of the Phoenix Suns. 2010. (NBA — A History of Hoops Ser.). 48p. (YA). (gr. 5-18). 23.95 *(978-1-58341-958-8(6)*, Creative Education) Creative Co., The.

Somervill, Barbara A. Arizona. 2011. (America the Beautiful, Third Ser.). 144p. (J). pap. 12.95 *(978-0-531-22916-3(5)*, Children's Pr.) Scholastic Library Publishing.

Standard, Carole K. Arizona. 2009. (From Sea to Shining Sea, Second Ser.). (ENG.). 80p. (J). pap. 7.95 *(978-0-531-21125-0(8)*, Children's Pr.) Scholastic Library Publishing.

Tieck, Sarah. Arizona, 1 vol. 2012. (Explore the United States Ser.). (ENG.). 32p. (J). (gr. 2-5). lib. bdg. 28.50 *(978-1-61783-341-0(X)*, Big Buddy Bks.) ABDO Publishing Co.

Tucker, Regina E. The Legend of the Lost Dutchman's Gold Mine. 2004. (J). (gr. 3-7). 250.00 *(978-0-9754261-2-8(5))*; 96p. (gr. 3-7). spiral bd. 15.00 *(978-0-9754261-1-1(7))*; 2nd l.t. ed. (Tales of the Old West Ser.: 1). (Illus.). 88p. per. 15.00 *(978-0-9754261-0-4(9))* Sol de Oro Pubns.

Urban, William. Wyatt Earp: The O. K. Corral & the Law of the American West. 2009. (Library of American Lives & Times Ser.). 112p. (gr. 5-5). 69.20 *(978-1-60853-512-5(6))* Rosen Publishing Group, Inc., The.

—Wyatt Earp: The OK Corral & the Law of the American West. 2005. (Library of American Lives & Times). (Illus.). 112p. (YA). (gr. 4-8). lib. bdg. 34.60 *(978-0-8239-5740-8(3))* Rosen Publishing Group, Inc., The.

Waldman, Scott. Gunfight at the O. K. Corral: Wyatt Earp Upholds the Law. 2009. (Great Moments in American History Ser.). 32p. (gr. 3-3). 47.90 *(978-1-61513-143-3(4))* Rosen Publishing Group, Inc., The.

Waring, Kerry Jones, et al. Arizona. 2015. (It's My State! (r) Ser.). (ENG., Illus.). 80p. (J). (gr. 4-4). 34.21 *(978-1-62712-476-8(4))* Cavendish Square Publishing.

Watson, Marilyn Myrick. Rose Mofford: State Greats Arizona. 2007. (Acacia Biographies Ser.). (Illus.). 28p. (J). (gr. 3-7). lib. bdg. 16.95 *(978-0-9788283-5-6(6))*; (gr. 4-7). per. 6.95 *(978-0-9790826-1-0(7))* Acacia Publishing, Inc.

ARIZONA DIAMONDBACKS (BASEBALL TEAM)

Gilbert, Sara. The Story of the Arizona Diamondbacks. 2007. (Baseball Ser.). (gr. 4-7). (YA). 34.25 *(978-1-60818-031-8(X))*; (Illus.). 48p. (J). lib. bdg. 32.80 *(978-1-58341-478-1(9)*, Creative Education) Creative Co., The.

Sandler, Michael. Randy Johnson & the Arizona Diamondbacks: 2001 World Series. 2008. (World Series Superstars). (Illus.). 24p. (J). (gr. 1-4). lib. bdg. 22.61 *(978-1-59716-638-6(3))* Bearport Publishing Co., Inc.

Stewart, Mark. The Arizona Diamondbacks. 2012. (Team Spirit Ser.). 48p. (J). (gr. 3-6). 29.27 *(978-1-59953-472-5(X))* Norwood Hse. Pr.

Tricchinelli, Rob. Arizona Diamondbacks, 1 vol. (Inside MLB Ser.). (ENG., Illus.). 48p. (gr. 3-6). 2011. (YA). lib. bdg. 32.79 *(978-1-61714-034-1(1))* 2014. (J). lib. bdg. 32.79 *(978-1-62403-460-2(8)*, SportsZone) ABDO Publishing Co.

ARKANSAS

Altman, Linda Jacobs, et al. Arkansas. 2nd rev. ed. 2008. (Celebrate the States Ser.). 144p. (gr. 6-18). lib. bdg. 42.79 *(978-0-7614-3001-8(6)*, Benchmark Bks.) Marshall Cavendish Corp.

Bailer, Darice. What's Great about Arkansas? 2014. (Our Great States Ser.). (Illus.). 32p. (J). (gr. 2-5). lib. bdg. 26.60 *(978-1-4677-3345-8(8)*, Lerner Pubns.) Lerner Publishing Group.

Brown, Vanessa. Arkansas. 2009. (Bilingual Library of the United States of America Ser.). 32p. (gr. 2-2). 47.90 *(978-1-60853-344-2(1)*, Editorial Buenas Letras) Rosen Publishing Group, Inc., The.

—Arkansas. Brusca, Maria Cristina, tr. 2005. (Bilingual Library of the United States of America Ser.: Set 1). (ENG & SPA., Illus.). 32p. (J). (gr. 3-6). lib. bdg. 25.25 *(978-1-4042-3068-2(8))* Rosen Publishing Group, Inc., The.

Di Piazza, Domenica. Arkansas. 2012. (J). lib. bdg. 25.26 *(978-0-7613-4522-0(1)*, Lerner Pubns.) Lerner Publishing Group.

Kavanaugh, Dorothy. Central Mississippi River Basin: Arkansas, Iowa, Missouri, Vol. 19. 2015. (Let's Explore the States Ser.). (Illus.). 64p. (J). (gr. 5). lib. bdg. 23.95 *(978-1-4222-3321-4(9))* Mason Crest.

King, David C. Arkansas. 2007. (It's My State! Ser.). (Illus.). 80p. (J). (gr. 3-7). lib. bdg. 21.95 *(978-0-7614-2215-0(3))* Marshall Cavendish GBR. Dist: Marshall Cavendish Corp.

Kjelle, Marylou Morano. Arkansas: A MyReportLinks. Com Book. 2003. (States Ser.). (Illus.). 48p. (J). lib. bdg. 25.26 *(978-0-7660-5152-2(8)*, MyReportLinks.com Bks.) Enslow Pubs., Inc.

Lantier, Patricia. Arkansas. 2006. (Portraits of the States Ser.). (Illus.). 32p. (gr. 2-6). pap. 10.50 *(978-0-8368-4680-5(X)*, Gareth Stevens Learning Library) Stevens, Gareth Publishing LLLP.

Lantier-Sampon, Patricia. Arkansas. 2006. (Portraits of the States Ser.). (Illus.). 32p. (gr. 2-6). lib. bdg. 26.00 *(978-0-8368-4661-4(3)*, Gareth Stevens Learning Library) Stevens, Gareth Publishing LLLP.

Lucas, Eileen. The Little Rock Nine Stand up for Their Rights. Gustavson, Adam, illus. 2011. 48p. pap. 9.95 *(978-0-7613-7118-2(4))*; pap. 56.72 *(978-0-7613-7634-7(8))* Lerner Publishing Group.

Marsh, Carole. Arkansas Current Events Projects: 30 Cool, Activities, Crafts, Experiments & More for Kids to Do to Learn about Your State! 2003. (Arkansas Experience Ser.). 32p. (gr. k-8). pap. 5.95 *(978-0-635-02023-9(8)*, Marsh, Carole Bks.) Gallopade International.

—Arkansas Geography Projects: 30 Cool, Activities, Crafts, Experiments & More for Kids to Do to Learn about Your State! 2003. (Arkansas Experience Ser.). 32p. (gr. k-5). pap. 5.95 *(978-0-635-01823-6(3)*, Marsh, Carole Bks.) Gallopade International.

—Arkansas Government Projects: 30 Cool, Activities, Crafts, Experiments & More for Kids to Do to Learn about Your State! 2003. (Arkansas Experience Ser.). 32p. (gr. k-5). pap. 5.95 *(978-0-635-01923-3(X)*, Marsh, Carole Bks.) Gallopade International.

—Arkansas Jeopardy! Answers & Questions about Our State! 2004. (Illus.). 32p. (J). (gr. 3-8). pap. 7.95 *(978-0-7933-9792-1(8))* Gallopade International.

—Arkansas "Jography" A Fun Run Thru Our State! 2004. (Carole Marsh Arkansas Bks.). (Illus.). 32p. (J). (gr. 3-8). pap. 7.95 *(978-0-7933-9821-8(5))* Gallopade International.

—Arkansas People Projects: 30 Cool, Activities, Crafts, Experiments & More for Kids to Do to Learn about Your State! 2003. (Arkansas Experience Ser.). 32p. (gr. k-5). pap. 5.95 *(978-0-635-01973-8(6)*, Marsh, Carole Bks.) Gallopade International.

—Arkansas Symbols & Facts Projects: 30 Cool, Activities, Crafts, Experiments & More for Kids to Do to Learn about Your State! 2003. (Arkansas Experience Ser.). 32p. (gr. k-5). pap. 5.95 *(978-0-635-01872-4(1)*, Marsh, Carole Bks.) Gallopade International.

—The Cool Arkansas Coloring Book. 2004. (Carole Marsh Arkansas Bks.). (Illus.). 32p. (J). (gr. k-2). pap. 3.95 *(978-0-7933-9850-8(9))* Gallopade International.

Murray, Julie. Arkansas, 1 vol. 2006. (Buddy Book Ser.). (ENG., Illus.). 32p. (gr. k-4). 27.07 *(978-1-59197-663-9(4)*, Buddy Bks.) ABDO Publishing Co.

Pezzi, Bryan. Arkansas: The Natural State. 2016. (J). *(978-1-5105-0656-5(X))* SmartBook Media, Inc.

—Arkansas: The Natural State. 2016. (J). *(978-1-4896-4824-2(0))* Weigl Pubs., Inc.

Prentzas, G. S. Arkansas (Revised Edition) 2014. (America the Beautiful, Third Ser. (Revised Edition) Ser.). (ENG.). 144p. (J). lib. bdg. 40.00 *(978-0-531-28276-2(7))* Scholastic Library Publishing.

Quasha, Jennifer. How to Draw Arkansas's Sights & Symbols. 2009. (Kid's Guide to Drawing America Ser.). 32p. (gr. k-k). 50.50 *(978-1-61511-046-9(1)*, PowerKids Pr.) Rosen Publishing Group, Inc., The.

Shofner, Shawndra. Arkansas. 2008. (This Land Called America Ser.). 32p. (YA). (gr. 3-6). 22.95 *(978-1-58341-629-7(3))* Creative Co., The.

Shoulders, Michael. N Is for Natural State: An Arkansas Alphabet. Anderson, Rick, illus. 2003. (Discover America State by State Ser.). (ENG.). 40p. (J). (gr. k-6). 17.95 *(978-1-58536-067-3(8))* Sleeping Bear Pr.

—Natural Numbers: An Arkansas Number Book. Anderson, Rick, illus. 2008. (Count Your Way Across the U. S. A. Ser.). (ENG.). 40p. (J). 17.95 *(978-1-58536-172-4(0))* Sleeping Bear Pr.

Smith, Rich. Arkansas, 1 vol. 2009. (United States Ser.). (ENG., Illus.). 48p. (YA). (gr. 2-5). 27.07 *(978-1-60453-639-3(X))* ABDO Publishing Co.

ARKANSAS—FICTION

Bennett, W. J., Jr. Sydney & Garrett's Great Arkansas Adventury. 2005. (J). pap. *(978-0-9794044-6-7(0))* Archeological Assessments, Inc.

—Vivianna Becomes an Arkansan. 2005. (J). pap. *(978-0-9794044-7-4(9))* Archeological Assessments, Inc.

Chesne, Sabrina. Lillie's Treasures/Los tesoros de Lili. Capasso, Diana, tr. Patagonia School, illus. 2004. (ENG & SPA.). 32p. per. 15.00 *(978-0-9630310-9-9(0))* Will Hall Bks.

Dragonwagon, Crescent & Zindel, Paul. To Take a Dare. 2016. (ENG.). (YA). (gr. 7-12). pap. 9.99 *(978-1-63168-028-1(5))* Graymalkin Media.

Draper, Sharon M. Fire from the Rock. 2014. (ENG.). 240p. (YA). (gr. 7-12). 12.24 *(978-1-63245-286-3(3))* Lectorum Pubns., Inc.

—Fire from the Rock. 2008. (ENG.). 240p. (YA). (gr. 7-18). 7.99 *(978-0-14-241199-5(X)*, Speak) Penguin Young Readers Group.

Fickey, Brenda. Beckoning Shadows, 1 vol. 2009. (ENG.). 179p. pap. 24.95 *(978-1-61546-330-5(5))* America Star Bks.

—Echoing Silence. 2008. 123p. pap. 19.95 *(978-1-60563-816-4(1))* America Star Bks.

—Whispering Darkness. 2007. (ENG.). 136p. per. 24.95 *(978-1-4241-6932-0(1))* America Star Bks.

Fields, Jan. Hunt the Ozark Howler, 1 vol. Brundage, Scott, illus. 2016. (ENG.). 80p. (J). lib. bdg. *(978-1-62402-152-7(2))* Magic Wagon.

Finch, Donna. Brandy & the Rapids, 1 vol. Plante, Beth, illus. 2009. 36p. pap. 24.95 *(978-1-60749-150-7(8))* America Star Bks.

Greene, Bette. I've Already Forgotten Your Name, Philip Hall! Jenkins, Leonard, illus. 2004. 176p. (J). (gr. 5-18). 15.99 *(978-0-06-051835-6(9))* HarperCollins Pubs.

—Summer of My German Soldier. 2006. (Puffin Modern Classics Ser.). (ENG.). 240p. (J). (gr. 5-18). 7.99 *(978-0-14-240651-9(1)*, Puffin Books) Penguin Young Readers Group.

Hansen, Susan. The Flying Quilt. 2011. pap. 9.95 *(978-0-7414-6469-9(1))* Infinity Publishing.

Haze, Armand. Beautiful Blossom. 2012. 322p. 29.95 *(978-1-4626-7056-7(3))* America Star Bks.

Hilmo, Tess. With a Name Like Love. 2013. (ENG.). 272p. (J). (gr. 5-9). pap. 10.99 *(978-1-250-02733-7(0)*, 9781250027337) Square Fish.

Jacobs, Lily. The Littlest Bunny in Arkansas: An Easter Adventure. 2015. (ENG.). 32p. (J). (-3). 9.99 *(978-1-4926-1027-4(5)*, Sourcebooks Jabberwocky) Sourcebooks, Inc.

—The Littlest Bunny in Bentonville: An Easter Adventure. 2015. (ENG.). 32p. (J). (-3). 9.99 *(978-1-4926-1030-4(5)*, Sourcebooks Jabberwocky) Sourcebooks, Inc.

Jaimet, Kate. Edge of Flight, 1 vol. 2012. (Orca Sports Ser.). (ENG.). 160p. (YA). (gr. 6-10). pap. 9.95 *(978-1-4598-0160-8(1))* Orca Bk. Pubs. USA.

James, Eric. A Halloween Scare in Arkansas. Le Ray, Marina, illus. 2015. (ENG.). 32p. (J). (-5). 9.99 *(978-1-4926-2363-2(6)*, 9781492623632, Sourcebooks Jabberwocky) Sourcebooks, Inc.

—A Halloween Scare in Bentonville. Le Ray, Marina, illus. 2015. (ENG.). 32p. (J). (-5). 9.99 *(978-1-4926-2364-9(4)*, 9781492623649, Sourcebooks Jabberwocky) Sourcebooks, Inc.

—Santa's Sleigh Is on Its Way to Arkansas: A Christmas Adventure. Dunn, Robert, illus. 2016. (ENG.). 32p. (J). (-2). 12.99 *(978-1-4926-4317-3(3)*, 9781492643173, Sourcebooks Jabberwocky) Sourcebooks, Inc.

Levine, Kristin. The Lions of Little Rock. 2012. (ENG.). 304p. (J). (gr. 5-18). 16.99 *(978-0-399-25644-8(X)*, G.P. Putnam's Sons Books for Young Readers) Penguin Young Readers Group.

Linker, Julie. Disenchanted Princess. 2007. (ENG.). 240p. (YA). (gr. 9-18). pap. 11.99 *(978-1-4169-3472-1(3)*, Simon Pulse) Simon Pulse.

Loye, Scott. Moon Ring. 2011. 160p. (gr. 10-12). 22.95 *(978-1-4502-9682-3(3))*; pap. 12.95 *(978-1-4502-9680-9(7))* iUniverse, Inc.

Manley, Candace. Skeeter's Dream. 2010. (ENG.). 192p. (J). (gr. 7-18). pap. 14.95 *(978-0-9785634-8-6(4))* La Frontera Publishing.

Mason, Richard. The Red Scarf: A Country Boy's Christmas Story. 2011. (ENG.). 155p. (J). (gr. 3-7). pap. 11.95 *(978-0-87483-954-8(8))* August Hse. Pubs., Inc.

McBrier, Page. The Chicken & the Worm. Peterson, Rick, illus. 2008. 36p. (J). *(978-0-9798439-2-1(8))* Heifer Project International.

Medearis, Mary. Big Doc's Girl. 2006. (Buried Treasure Ser.). (ENG.). 140p. (J). (gr. -1-7). pap. 11.95 *(978-0-935304-87-9(8))* August Hse. Pubs., Inc.

Mitchell, Stan R. Oskar & Myer at the Lake. 2013. 24p. pap. 24.95 *(978-1-63000-414-9(6))* America Star Bks.

Parkhurst, Liz S. Under One Flag: A Year at Rohwer. Clifton, Tom, illus. 2006. (ENG.). 32p. (J). (gr. 3-7). 16.95 *(978-0-87483-759-9(6)*, 1241971) August Hse. Pubs., Inc.

Sandage, Charley. ALL AROUND ARKANSAS Big Book. 2005. (Illus.). (J). pap. *(978-0-9794044-2-9(8))* Archeological Assessments, Inc.

—ALL AROUND ARKANSAS student Edition. 2005. (Illus.). (J). pap. *(978-0-9638956-5-3(6))* Archeological Assessments, Inc.

—Big Bear's Arkansas ABCs. Przybylek, Leslie, illus. 2004. 56p. (J). (gr. k-2). pap. 14.95 *(978-0-9638956-9-1(9))* Archeological Assessments, Inc.

—Big Bear's Arkansas ABCs Big Book. 2005. (Illus.). (J). pap. *(978-0-9794044-1-2(X))* Archeological Assessments, Inc.

—"I Can Tell You Stories, If You Gather Near"... The Big Bear of Arkansas. Daniel, R. F., illus. 2004. 46p. (J). (gr. k-2). pap. 14.95 *(978-0-9638956-7-7(2))* Archeological Assessments, Inc.

—I can tell you stories, if you gather round Big Book. 2005. (Illus.). (J). pap. *(978-0-9794044-3-6(6))* Archeological Assessments, Inc.

—Where did we come from, Grandpa? Big Book. 2005. (Illus.). (J). pap. *(978-0-9794044-5-0(2))* Archeological Assessments, Inc.

—Where did we come from, Grandpa? student Edition. 2005. (Illus.). (J). pap. *(978-0-9794044-4-3(4))* Archeological Assessments, Inc.

Sargent, Daina. Arkansas: Dream Big. Lenoir, Jane, illus. l.t. ed. 2004. (Double Trouble Ser.). 48p. (J). pap. 10.95 *(978-1-59381-123-5(3))*; lib. bdg. *(978-1-59381-122-8(5))* Ozark Publishing.

Scattergood, Augusta. Making Friends with Billy Wong. 2016. (ENG.). 224p. (J). (gr. 3-7). 16.99 *(978-0-545-92425-2(1)*, Scholastic Pr.) Scholastic, Inc.

Silvano, Wendi. Love Is All Around Arkansas. Czernichowska, Joanna, illus. 2016. (ENG.). 32p. (J). (-6). 12.99 *(978-1-4926-2904-7(9)*, Sourcebooks Jabberwocky) Sourcebooks, Inc.

Sisco, Joann Ellen. Bonnie from Blue Mountain: 1. 2012. 88p. pap. 13.95 *(978-1-4772-7070-7(1))* AuthorHouse.

Smallman, Steve. Santa Is Coming to Arkansas. Dunn, Robert, illus. 2013. (ENG.). 32p. (J). (-3). 9.99 *(978-1-4022-9066-4(7)*, Sourcebooks Jabberwocky) Sourcebooks, Inc.

—Santa Is Coming to Bentonville. Dunn, Robert, illus. 2013. (ENG.). 32p. (J). (-3). 9.99 *(978-1-4022-9109-8(4)*, Sourcebooks Jabberwocky) Sourcebooks, Inc.

Solano, Carolyn. Tree Top Angels. 2010. 56p. (gr. 4-6). pap. 8.95 *(978-1-4502-2276-1(5))* iUniverse, Inc.

Summer of the Secret Squadron. 2005. Orig. Title: Return of the Secret Squadron. (YA). kivar 14.95 *(978-0-9765750-0-9(0))* Ball, Michael.

Viguie, Debbie & Holder, Nancy. Unleashed. 2012. (Wolf Spring Chronicles Ser.). (ENG.). 400p. (YA). (gr. 7). pap. 9.99 *(978-0-385-74099-9(9)*, Ember) Random Hse. Children's Bks.

Whaley, John Corey. Where Things Come Back. (ENG., Illus.). (YA). (gr. 9). 2012. 256p. pap. 11.99 *(978-1-4424-1334-4(4))* 2011. 240p. 16.99 *(978-1-4424-1333-7(6))* Simon & Schuster Children's Publishing. (Atheneum Bks. for Young Readers).

Wiles, Patricia. My Mom's a Mortician. 2016. (ENG.). 132p. (J). pap. *(978-1-5040-2943-8(7))* Open Road Integrated Media, Inc.

Woody, Velma B. Branscum. Bandits, Bears & Backaches: A Collection of Short Stories Based on Arkansas History. 2004. (ENG.). 78p. per. 15.00 *(978-0-9708574-2-2(X))* Butler Ctr. for Arkansas Studies.

Wright, Lloyd. More Stories for Gramp's Little Friends. 2004. 180p. (J). 23.95 *(978-0-595-66836-6(4))* iUniverse, Inc.

ARKANSAS—HISTORY

Aretha, David. The Story of the Little Rock Nine & School Desegregation in Photographs. 2014. (Story of the Civil Rights Movement in Photographs Ser.). 48p. (J). lib. bdg. 25.27 *(978-0-7660-4235-3(9))* Enslow Pubs., Inc.

Bailer, Darice. What's Great about Arkansas? 2014. (Our Great States Ser.). (ENG., Illus.). 32p. (gr. 2-5). pap. 7.95 *(978-1-4677-4532-1(4))* Lerner Publishing Group.

Coleman, Miriam. Arkansas: The Natural State. 2010. (Our Amazing States Ser.). (ENG.). 24p. (J). pap. 8.25 *(978-1-4488-0742-0(5))*; lib. bdg. 22.60 *(978-1-4488-0655-3(0))* Rosen Publishing Group, Inc., The. (PowerKids Pr.).

Durrie, Karen. Arkansas: The Natural State. 2012. (J). *(978-1-61913-327-3(X))*; pap. *(978-1-61913-328-0(8))* Weigl Pubs., Inc.

Hopper, Shay E., et al. An Arkansas History for Young People. 4th ed. 2008. (ENG., Illus.). xxxiv, 490p. (J). pap. 25.00 *(978-1-55728-846-2(1))*; 525p. 39.95 *(978-1-55728-845-5(3))* Univ. of Arkansas Pr.

Jerome, Kate B. Lucky to Live in Arkansas. 2017. (Arcadia Kids Ser.). (ENG., Illus.). 32p. (J). 16.99 ***(978-0-7385-2766-6(1))*** Arcadia Publishing.

King, David C. Arkansas. 2014. (J). lib. bdg. *(978-1-62712-238-2(9))* Cavendish Square Publishing.

King, David C. & Bass, Elissa. Arkansas. 2016. (ENG., Illus.). 80p. (J). 34.21 *(978-1-62713-232-9(5))* Cavendish Square Publishing.

Kirchner, Jason. Arkansas. 2016. (States Ser.). (ENG., Illus.). 32p. (gr. 3-4). lib. bdg. 27.32 *(978-1-5157-0390-7(8))* Next Page Pr., The.

Levy, Janey. Arkansas: Past & Present. 2010. (United States: Past & Present Ser.). (ENG.). 48p. (YA). pap. 11.75 *(978-1-4358-9504-1(5))*; lib. bdg. 29.25 *(978-1-4358-9476-1(6))* Rosen Publishing Group, Inc., The. (Rosen Reference).

Lucas, Eileen. Cracking the Wall: The Struggles of the Little Rock Nine. Anthony, Mark, illus. 2007. pap. 39.95 incl. audio compact disk *(978-0-8225-6743-5(9))*; pap. 37.95 incl. audio *(978-1-59519-939-3(X))* Live Oak Media.

Macaulay, Ellen. Arkansas. 2009. (From Sea to Shining Sea, Second Ser.). (ENG.). 80p. (J). pap. 7.95

(978-0-531-21126-7(6), Children's Pr.) Scholastic Library Publishing.
Marsh, Carole. Arkansas History Projects: 30 Cool, Activities, Crafts, Experiments & More for Kids to Do to Learn about Your State! 2003. (Arkansas Experience Ser.). 32p. (gr. k-5). pap. 5.95 (978-0-635-01773-4(3), Marsh, Carole Bks.) Gallopade International.
—Exploring Arkansas Through Project-Based Learning. 2016. (Arkansas Experience Ser.). (ENG.). (J). pap. 9.99 (978-0-635-12328-2(2)) Gallopade International.
—I'm Reading about Arkansas. 2014. (Arkansas Experience Ser.). (ENG., Illus.). (J). pap., pap. 8.99 (978-0-635-11280-4(9)) Gallopade International.
Pezzi, Bryan. Arkansas. 2011. (Guide to American States Ser.). (Illus.). 48p. (YA). (gr. 3-6). 29.99 (978-1-61690-776-1(2)); (J). (978-1-61690-451-7(8)) Weigl Pubs., Inc.
Poe, Marshall. Little Rock Nine. Purvis, Leland & Lindner, Ellen, illus. 2008. (Turning Points Ser.). (ENG.). 128p. (J). (gr. 3-7). pap. 7.99 (978-1-4169-5066-0(4), Simon & Schuster/Paula Wiseman Bks.) Simon & Schuster/Paula Wiseman Bks.
Publications International Ltd. Staff. Yesterday & Todayfootball University of Arkansas. 2009. 144p. 24.95 (978-1-4127-7516-8(7)) Publications International, Ltd.
Teske, Steven. Natural State Notables: Twenty-One Famous People from Arkansas. 2012. (ENG., Illus.). 65p. (YA). pap. 9.95 (978-1-935106-52-4(X)) Butler Ctr. for Arkansas Studies.
Tieck, Sarah. Arkansas, 1 vol. 2012. (Explore the United States Ser.). (ENG.). 32p. (J). (gr. 2-5). 28.50 (978-1-61783-342-7(8)) ABDO Publishing Co.

ARMADA, 1588

Guy, John. Elizabeth: The Forgotten Years. 2004. (Illus.). 32p. (J). (gr. 4-7). pap. 5.95 (978-1-86007-029-7(9), TickTock Books) Octopus Publishing Group GBR. Dist: Independent Pubs. Group.
Malam, John. You Wouldn't Want to Sail in the Spanish Armada! An Invasion You'd Rather Not Launch. Antram, David, illus. 2006. (You Wouldn't Want to Ser.). (ENG.). 32p. (J). (gr. 2-5). 29.00 (978-0-531-14974-4(9)); pap. 9.95 (978-0-531-16999-5(5), Watts, Franklin) Scholastic Library Publishing.
Ross, Stewart. Sink the Armada! Sir Francis Drake & the Spanish Armada of 1588. Shields, Susan, illus. 62p. (J). pap. (978-0-237-51959-9(3)) Evans Brothers, Ltd.

ARMADA, 1588—FICTION

Vogel, Sean. Celtic Run. 2012. 159p. (978-0-9850814-0-9(6)) MB Publishing, LLC.

ARMADILLOS

Armadillos. 2013. (Awesome Armored Animals Ser.). 24p. (J). (gr. k-5). pap. 49.50 (978-1-4777-0967-2(3), PowerKids Pr.) Rosen Publishing Group, Inc., The.
Baxter, Bethany. Armadillos. 2013. (Awesome Armored Animals Ser.). 24p. (J). (gr. k-5). 22.60 (978-1-4777-0797-5(2)); pap. 8.25 (978-1-4777-0966-5(5)) Rosen Publishing Group, Inc., The. (PowerKids Pr.).
Borgert-Spaniol, Megan. Nine-Banded Armadillos. 2015. (North American Animals Ser.). (ENG., Illus.). 24p. (J). (gr. k-3). lib. bdg. 25.95 (978-1-62617-261-6(7), Blastoff! Readers) Bellwether Media.
Carr, Aaron. Armadillos. 2014. (J). (978-1-4896-2930-2(0)) Weigl Pubs., Inc.
Davin, Rose. Armadillos. 2017. (Meet Desert Animals Ser.). (ENG., Illus.). 24p. (gr. k-1). lib. bdg. 26.65 (978-1-5157-4602-7(X), Pebble Plus) Capstone Press of Coughlan Cos.
Gish, Melissa. Armadillos. (Living Wild Ser.). (Illus.). (J). 2017. (ENG.). 48p. (gr. 4-7). pap. 12.00 (978-1-62832-299-6(3), Creative Paperbacks) 2016. 46p. (978-1-60818-703-4(9), Creative Education) Creative Co., The.
Goecke, Michael P. Giant Armadillo, 1 vol. 2003. (Prehistoric Animals Set II Ser.). (ENG.). 24p. (gr. k-4). 25.65 (978-1-57765-974-7(0), Buddy Bks.) ABDO Publishing Co.
Jango-Cohen, Judith. Armadillos. 2003. (Animals Animals Ser.). (Illus.). 48p. (YA). (gr. 3-6). lib. bdg. 29.93 (978-0-7614-1617-3(X)) Marshall Cavendish Corp.
—Let's Look at Armadillos. 2010. pap. 45.32 (978-0-7613-6981-3(3)); (ENG., Illus.). 32p. (J). pap. 7.95 (978-0-7613-6038-4(7), 1312736); (ENG., Illus.). 32p. (J). lib. bdg. 26.60 (978-0-7613-3887-1(X), 1312736, Lerner Pubns.) Lerner Publishing Group.
Llanas, Sheila Griffin. Armadillos, 1 vol. 2013. (Animal Icons Ser.). (ENG.). 32p. (J). (gr. 3-6). lib. bdg. 27.07 (978-1-61783-567-4(6), Checkerboard Library) ABDO Publishing Co.
Markovics, Joyce. Mi Cuerpo Es Duro y Gris (Armadillo) 2016. (Pistas de Animales 2 Ser.). (SPA.). 24p. (J). (gr. -1-3). 17.95 (978-1-944102-81-4(7)) Bearport Publishing Co., Inc.
Markovics, Joyce L. My Body Is Tough & Gray. 2016. (Zoo Clues 2 Ser.). (ENG.). 24p. (J). (gr. -1-3). lib. bdg. 17.95 (978-1-944102-63-0(9)) Bearport Publishing Co., Inc.
Mckerley, Jennifer. Amazing Armadillos. Mirocha, Paul, illus. 2009. (Step into Reading Ser.). (ENG.). 48p. (J). (gr. k-3). pap. 3.99 (978-0-375-84352-5(3), Random Hse. Bks. for Young Readers) Random Hse. Children's Bks.
Phillips, Dee. Armadillo's Burrow. 2013. (Science Slam: the Hole Truth! Underground Animal Life Ser.). 24p. (J). (gr. -1-3). lib. bdg. 23.93 (978-1-61772-746-7(6)) Bearport Publishing Co., Inc.
Potts, Steve. Armadillos, 1 vol. 2012. (North American Animals Ser.). (ENG.). 24p. (gr. k-1). pap. 7.29 (978-1-4296-7921-3(2)); pap. 41.70 (978-1-4296-8358-6(9)); lib. bdg. 26.65 (978-1-4296-7704-2(X)) Capstone Press of Coughlan Cos. (Pebble Plus).
Rafferty, John P., ed. Rats, Bats, & Xenarthrans. 2011. (Britannica Guide to Predators & Prey Ser.). (Illus.). 256p. (YA). 103.40 (978-1-61530-456-1(8)) Rosen Publishing Group, Inc., The.
Robb, Jackie & Stringle, Berny. The Story of Armadillo. Duncan, Karen & Stringle, Sam, illus. 2003. (Bang on the Door Ser.). 32p. (YA). pap. (978-1-85602-337-5(0), Pavilion Children's Books) Pavilion Bks.
Schuetz, Kari. Armadillos. 2011. (Backyard Wildlife Ser.). (ENG., Illus.). 24p. (J). (gr. k-3). lib. bdg. 25.95 (978-1-60014-594-0(9), Blastoff! Readers) Bellwether Media.
Sebastian, Emily. Armadillos. 2012. (Illus.). 24p. (J). 49.50 (978-1-4488-5053-2(3), PowerKids Pr.); pap. 8.25 (978-1-4488-5052-5(5), PowerKids Pr.); lib. bdg. 22.60 (978-1-4488-4951-2(9)) Rosen Publishing Group, Inc., The.
Soundprints Staff, ed. Backyard Collection: Daddy Longlegs, Owl, Armadillo & Ladybug Books, 4 microbks., No. III. (Smithsonian's Backyard Ser.). (Illus.). 128p. (J). (gr. -1-2). 18.95 (978-1-56899-634-9(9)) Soundprints.
Swinburne, Stephen R. & Hiscock, Bruce. Armadillo Trail: The Northward Journey of the Armadillo. Hiscock, Bruce, illus. 2009. (ENG., Illus.). 32p. (J). (gr. 2-4). 16.95 (978-1-59078-463-1(4)) Boyds Mills Pr.
Wittrock, Jeni. Ancient Armadillos. 2015. (Ice Age Animals Ser.). (ENG.). 24p. (J). (gr. k-1). pap. 6.95 (978-1-4914-2322-6(6), Pebble Plus) Capstone Press of Coughlan Cos.

ARMAMENTS

see Military Weapons

ARMED FORCES

see Armies; Soldiers
see names of countries and international organizations with the subdivision Armed Forces, e.g. U. S.—Armed Forces; etc.

ARMED FORCES—VOCATIONAL GUIDANCE

Ferry, Monica. Search & Rescue Specialist & Careers in FEMA. 2006. (Homeland Security & Counterterrorism Careers Ser.). (Illus.). 128p. (J). (gr. 5-9). lib. bdg. 33.27 (978-0-7660-2650-6(7)) Enslow Pubs., Inc.
Military Jobs. 2015. (Military Jobs Ser.). (ENG.). 48p. (YA). (gr. 8-8). 156.80 (978-1-5026-0308-1(X)) Cavendish Square Publishing.
Stillwell, Alexander. Green Berets: What It Takes to Join the Elite. 2015. lib. bdg. (978-1-62713-461-3(1)) Cavendish Square Publishing.

ARMENIA (REPUBLIC)

De Capua, Sarah. Armenia in Pictures. 2008. (Visual Geography Ser.). (YA). (gr. 7-12). lib. bdg. 31.93 (978-0-8225-8576-3(6)) Twenty First Century Bks.
Dhilawala, Sakina & Nevins, Debbie. Armenia. 2017. (J). **(978-1-5026-2740-7(X))** Cavendish Square Publishing.

ARMENIA (REPUBLIC)—FICTION

Cretan, Gladys Yessayan. Road Map to Wholeness. Jefferson, Robert Louis, illus. 145.00 (978-0-687-02526-8(5)) Abingdon Pr.
Weston Woods Staff, creator. One Fine Day. 2011. 29.95 (978-0-545-23362-0(3)); 38.75 (978-0-545-23364-4(X)); 18.95 (978-0-545-23363-7(1)) Weston Woods Studios, Inc.

ARMENIANS

Freedman, Jeri. The Armenian Genocide. 2009. (Genocide in Modern Times Ser.). 64p. (gr. 6-6). 58.50 (978-1-61512-676-7(7)) Rosen Publishing Group, Inc., The.
Norsigian Rowles, Helen. Armenian History: A Journey for Children. 2009. 36p. pap. 17.99 (978-1-4389-4113-4(7)) AuthorHouse.

ARMIES

see also Disarmament; Draft; Military Art and Science; Soldiers; War
also names of countries with the subhead Army (e.g. United States—Army; etc.); and headings beginning with the word Military

Alpert, Barbara. Military Robots, 1 vol. 2012. (Military Machines Ser.). (ENG.). 24p. (gr. k-1). lib. bdg. 26.65 (978-1-4296-7573-4(X), Pebble Plus) Capstone Press of Coughlan Cos.
Bolitho, Mark. Fold Your Own Origami Army. 2013. 32p. (J). (gr. 3-6). 26.50 (978-1-4777-1317-4(4)); pap. 11.75 (978-1-4777-1465-2(0)) Rosen Publishing Group, Inc., The. (PowerKids Pr.).
Brush, Jim. Armed Services. 2011. (Action Force Ser.). 32p. (YA). (gr. 4-7). pap. 28.50 (978-1-59771-291-0(4)) Sea-To-Sea Pubns.
Entin, Cindy. Los Marines. Boldman, Craig, illus. 2014. (ENG & SPA.). 10p. (J). bds. 5.99 (978-1-60433-458-6(4), Applesauce Pr.) Cider Mill Pr. Bk. Pubs., LLC.
Fold Your Own Origami Army. 2013. (Origami Army Ser.). 32p. (J). (gr. 3-6). pap. 70.50 (978-1-4777-1466-9(9), PowerKids Pr.) Rosen Publishing Group, Inc., The.
Fowler, Will. Counterterrorism in West Africa: The Most Dangerous SAS Assault. 2011. (Most Daring Raids in History Ser.). (Illus.). 64p. (YA). (gr. 7-12). lib. bdg. 31.95 (978-1-4488-1871-6(0)) Rosen Publishing Group, Inc., The.
Haerens, Margaret. Veterans. 2010. (Opposing Viewpoints Ser.). (ENG.). 240p. pap. 29.45 (978-0-7377-4995-3(4)); (gr. 10-12). 46.45 (978-0-7377-4994-6(6)) Cengage Gale. (Greenhaven Pr., Inc.).
Otfinoski, Steven. World War II Infantrymen: An Interactive History Adventure. 2013. (You Choose: World War II Ser.). (ENG.). 112p. (gr. 3-4). pap. 41.70 (978-1-62065-717-1(1), You Choose Bks.) Capstone Press of Coughlan Cos.
Park, Louise. The Pharaohs' Armies. 2009. (Ancient & Medieval People Ser.). 32p. (gr. 5). 28.50 (978-0-7614-4451-0(3)) Marshall Cavendish Corp.
Sofer, Barbara. Keeping Israel Safe: Serving the Israel Defense Forces. 2008. (Israel Ser.). (ENG., Illus.). 56p. (J). (gr. 3-7). lib. bdg. 16.95 (978-0-8225-7221-3(4), Kar-Ben Publishing) Lerner Publishing Group.
Soriano, Joan & Malizia, Diana, eds. A Visual History of Soldiers & Armies Around the World. 2016. (Visual History of the World Ser.). 00096p. (YA). (gr. 8-8). 37.10 (978-1-4994-6592-1(0), Rosen Young Adult) Rosen Publishing Group, Inc., The.
Walsh, David. British Redcoats. 2011. (History's Greatest Warriors Ser.). (ENG., Illus.). 24p. (J). (gr. 3-7). lib. bdg. 25.95 (978-1-60014-627-5(9), Torque Bks.) Bellwether Media.

ARMOR

Bergin, Mark. Warfare in the Ancient World. 2015. (Warriors Ser.). (Illus.). 48p. (gr. 4-7). 37.10 (978-1-62588-355-1(2)) Black Rabbit Bks.
Biskup, Agnieszka. Batsuits & Capes: The Science Behind Batman's Body Armor, 1 vol. 2014. (Batman Science Ser.). (ENG.). 32p. (gr. 3-4). 27.32 (978-1-4765-3942-3(1), DC Super Heroes) Stone Arch Bks.
Clarke, Catriona. Armor. McKenna, Terry, illus. 2007. (Usborne Beginners Ser.). 32p. (J). (gr. -1-3). 4.99 (978-0-7945-1578-2(9), Usborne) EDC Publishing.
Dorling Kindersley Publishing Staff. Arms & Armor. 2011. (DK Eyewitness Bks.). (ENG.). 72p. (J). (gr. 3-7). 19.99 (978-0-7566-8686-4(5)); 16.99 (978-0-7566-7319-2(4)) Dorling Kindersley Publishing, Inc. (DK Children).
—Castles & Knights. 2014. (Eye Wonder Ser.). (ENG.). 56p. (J). (gr. k-4). 10.99 (978-1-4654-1562-2(9), DK Children) Dorling Kindersley Publishing, Inc.
Firth, Rachel. Knights & Armor. Gaudenzi, Giacinto & Montgomery, Lee, illus. 2006. 95p. (J). (gr. 4-7). 17.99 (978-0-7945-1279-8(8), Usborne) EDC Publishing.
Lusted, Marcia Amidon. Ninja Science: Camouflage, Weapons, & Stealthy Attacks. 2016. (Warrior Science Ser.). (ENG., Illus.). 32p. (gr. 3-4). lib. bdg. 27.99 (978-1-4914-8115-8(3), Edge Bks.) Capstone Press of Coughlan Cos.
Matthews, Rupert. Arms & Armor. 2013. (Illus.). 48p. (J). (978-1-4351-5085-0(6)) Barnes & Noble, Inc.
Shirley, Rebekah Joy. I Want to Be a Knight. 2011. (Let's Play Dress up Ser.). (ENG., Illus.). 24p. (J). (gr. k-3). lib. bdg. 25.25 (978-1-61533-354-7(1)) Windmill Bks.
Tango Books Staff. Armour. Moulder, Bob, illus. 2011. (3-Dimensional Exploration Bks.). (ENG.). 20p. (J). (gr. -1-2). 22.95 (978-1-85707-664-6(8)) Tango Bks. GBR. Dist: Independent Pubs. Group.

ARMORED CARS (TANKS)

see Tanks (Military Science)

ARMS, COATS OF

see Heraldry

ARMS AND ARMOR

see Armor; Weapons

ARMS CONTROL

see Disarmament

ARMSTRONG, ANNIE, 1850-1938

Vogel, Cara Lynn. The Lottie & Annie Upside-down Book. Adkins, Loretta B., illus. 2003. 16p. (J). 8.99 (978-1-56309-627-3(7)) Woman's Missionary Union.

ARMSTRONG, LANCE, 1971-

Bankston, John. Lance Armstrong. 2004. (Blue Banner Biography Ser.). (Illus.). 32p. (J). lib. bdg. 25.70 (978-1-58415-334-4(2)) Mitchell Lane Pubs., Inc.
Benson, Michael. Lance Armstrong, Cyclist. 2003. (Ferguson Career Biographies Ser.). (Illus.). 144p. (gr. 6-12). 25.00 (978-0-8160-5479-4(7), Ferguson Publishing Co.) Facts On File, Inc.
Brocker, Susan. Sports Legends & Leyendas del Deporte: 6 English, 6 Spanish Adaptations. 2011. (ENG & SPA.). (J). 89.00 net. (978-1-4108-5678-4(X)) Benchmark Education Co.
Christopher, Matt. On the Bike with... Lance Armstrong. 2003. (Matt Christopher Sports Ser.). (Illus.). 116p. (J). (gr. 4-7). 12.65 (978-0-7569-1607-7(0)) Perfection Learning Corp.
Doeden, Matt. Lance Armstrong. 2006. (Sports Heroes & Legends Ser.). (ENG., Illus.). 120p. (gr. 5-12). lib. bdg. 30.60 (978-0-8225-5959-7(5)) Lerner Publishing Group.
Donovan, Sandra. Lance Armstrong. 2nd rev. ed. 2006. (Amazing Athletes Ser.). (Illus.). 32p. (YA). (gr. 2-5). lib. bdg. 22.60 (978-0-8225-6052-4(6)) Lerner Publishing Group.
Donovan, Sandy. Lance Armstrong. (Amazing Athletes Ser.). (Illus.). 32p. 2005. (J). (gr. 3-4). lib. bdg. 23.93 (978-0-8225-3691-8(9)) 2004. (J). (gr. 2-5). per. 5.95 (978-0-8225-2039-9(7)) 2007. (ENG., (gr. 2-5). pap. 7.95 (978-0-8225-8748-4(3), First Avenue Editions) Lerner Publishing Group.
Ellwood, Nancy. Lance Armstrong: With a Discussion of Determination. 2004. (Values in Action Ser.). (J). (978-1-59203-073-6(4)) Learning Challenge, Inc.
Gutman, Bill. Lance Armstrong: A Biography. 2009. (ENG.). 192p. (YA). (gr. 7). pap. 9.99 (978-1-4169-9845-7(4), Simon Pulse) Simon Pulse.
Hicks, Peter. Lance Armstrong - Racing Hero. 2011. (Famous Lives Ser.). (Illus.). 32p. (YA). (gr. 3-6). lib. bdg. 26.50 (978-1-4488-3289-7(6)) Rosen Publishing Group, Inc., The.
Hill, Christine M. Lance Armstrong: Cycling, Surviving, Inspiring Hope. 2007. (People to Know Today Ser.). (Illus.). 128p. (J). (gr. 6). lib. bdg. 33.27 (978-0-7660-2694-0(9)) Enslow Pubs., Inc.
Jones, Brenn. Learning about Resilience from the Life of Lance Armstrong. 2009. (Character Building Book Ser.). 24p. (gr. 2-3). 42.50 (978-1-60854-967-2(4), PowerKids Pr.) Rosen Publishing Group, Inc., The.
Kramer, Barbara. Lance Armstrong: Determined to Beat the Odds. 2005. (Awesome Values in Famous Lives Ser.). (Illus.). 48p. (J). (gr. 4-7). lib. bdg. 25.27 (978-0-7660-2377-2(X), Enslow Elementary) Enslow Pubs., Inc.
Lance Armstrong. 2004. (J). 31.36 (978-0-7614-1761-3(3)) Marshall Cavendish Corp.
Sandler, Michael. Cycling: Lance Armstrong's Impossible Ride. 2006. (Upsets & Comebacks Ser.). (Illus.). 32p. (J). (gr. 3-6). lib. bdg. 25.27 (978-1-59716-167-1(5)) Bearport Publishing Co., Inc.
Sillett, Helen. Whatever It Takes: The Lance Armstrong Story. 2007. (Overcoming the Odds Sports Biographies Ser.). pap. 9.95 (978-1-4105-0869-0(2)) Johnston, Don Inc.
Young, Ian. Lance Armstrong: Champion for Life! 2004. (High Five Reading - Purple Ser.). (ENG., Illus.). 64p. (gr. 3-4). per. 9.00 (978-0-7368-3850-4(3), High Five Reading (RBL)) Capstone Press of Coughlan Cos.
—Lance Armstrong Set: Champion for Life!, 6 vols. 2004. (High Five Reading - Purple Ser.). (ENG.). 64p. (gr. 3-4). pap. 54.00 (978-0-7368-3868-9(6), High Five Reading (RBL)) Capstone Press of Coughlan Cos.

ARMSTRONG, LOUIS, 1900-1971

Cline-Ransome, Lesa. Just a Lucky So & So: The Story of Louis Armstrong. Ransome, James E., illus. 2016. (ENG.). 32p. (J). 16.95 (978-0-8234-3428-2(1)) Holiday Hse., Inc.
Collins, Terry. Louis Armstrong: Jazz Legend, 1 vol. Pope, Richie, illus. 2012. (American Graphic Ser.). (ENG.). 32p. (gr. 3-4). pap. 8.10 (978-1-4296-9336-3(3)); pap. 47.70 (978-1-4296-9337-0(1)); lib. bdg. 30.65 (978-1-4296-8622-8(7)) Capstone Press of Coughlan Cos. (Graphic Library).
Elish, Dan. Louis Armstrong & the Jazz Age. 2005. (Cornerstones of Freedom Ser.). (ENG., Illus.). 48p. (YA). (gr. 4-7). 26.00 (978-0-516-23629-2(6)) Scholastic Library Publishing.
Foley, Colin. Who Was Louis Armstrong? 2013. (Rosen Readers Ser.). (ENG.). 24p. (J). (gr. 2-3). pap. 49.50 (978-1-4777-2279-4(3)); pap. 8.25 (978-1-4777-2278-7(5)) Rosen Publishing Group, Inc., The. (Rosen Classroom).
Holland, Gini & O'Hern, Kerri. Louis Armstrong. Spay, Anthony & Campbell, Alex, illus. 2007. (Biografías Gráficas (Graphic Biographies) Ser.). (SPA.). 32p. (gr. 5-8). lib. bdg. 27.00 (978-0-8368-7878-3(7)) Stevens, Gareth Publishing LLLP.
January, Brendan. Louis Armstrong. 2004. (Great Names Ser.). (Illus.). 32p. (J). (gr. 3-18). lib. bdg. 19.95 (978-1-59084-135-8(2)) Mason Crest.
Josephson, Judith Pinkerton. Louis Armstrong. 2008. (History Maker Biographies Ser.). (Illus.). 47p. (J). (gr. 3-7). lib. bdg. 26.60 (978-0-8225-7169-8(2), Lerner Pubns.); pap. 52.95 (978-0-8225-9392-8(0)) Lerner Publishing Group.
Kimmel, Eric A. A Horn for Louis. Bernardin, James, illus. 2006. (Stepping Stone Book Ser.). (ENG.). 96p. (J). (gr. 2-5). per. 4.99 (978-0-375-84005-0(2), Random Hse. Bks. for Young Readers) Random Hse. Children's Bks.
McDonough, Yona Zeldis. Who Was Louis Armstrong? O'Brien, John A. & Harrison, Nancy, illus. 2004. (Who Was? Ser.). (ENG.). 112p. (J). (gr. 3-7). pap. 5.99 (978-0-448-43368-4(0), Grosset & Dunlap) Penguin Young Readers Group.
McKissack, Patricia C. & McKissack, Fredrick L. Louis Armstrong: King of Jazz. 2013. (Famous African Americans Ser.). (Illus.). 24p. (J). (gr. k-18). 22.60 (978-0-7660-4106-6(9)); pap. 7.95 (978-1-4644-0200-5(0)) Enslow Pubs., Inc. (Enslow Elementary).
Mellark, Kat. Louis Armstrong: American Musician. 2013. (InfoMax Readers Ser.). (ENG.). 24p. (J). (gr. 2-3). pap. 49.50 (978-1-4777-2429-3(X)); (Illus.). pap. 8.25 (978-1-4777-2428-6(1)) Rosen Publishing Group, Inc., The. (Rosen Classroom).
O'Hern, Kerri & Holland, Gini. Louis Armstrong. Spay, Anthony & Campbell, Alex, illus. 2007. (Biografías Gráficas (Graphic Biographies) Ser.). (SPA.). 32p. (gr. 5-8). pap. 10.50 (978-0-8368-7885-1(X)) Stevens, Gareth Publishing LLLP.
Old, Wendie C. The Life of Louis Armstrong: King of Jazz. 2014. (Legendary African Americans Ser.). (Illus.). 96p. (J). (gr. 6-12). 27.94 (978-0-7660-6142-2(6)) Enslow Pubs., Inc.
Orr, Tamra. Louis Armstrong. 2012. (J). lib. bdg. 29.95 (978-1-61228-264-0(4)) Mitchell Lane Pubs., Inc.
Partridge, Kenneth. Louis Armstrong. 2nd rev. ed. 2011. (Black Americans of Achievement Legacy Edition Ser.). 120p. (YA). (gr. 6-12). 35.00 (978-1-60413-833-7(5)) Facts On File, Inc.
Schuman, Michael A. Louis Armstrong: Jazz Is Played from the Heart. 2007. (African-American Biography Library). (Illus.). 128p. (J). (gr. 6-12). lib. bdg. 33.27 (978-0-7660-2700-8(7)) Enslow Pubs., Inc.
Weinstein, Muriel Harris. Play, Louis, Play! The True Story of a Boy & His Horn. Morrison, Frank, illus. (ENG.). 112p. (J). (gr. 2-4). 2013. pap. 5.99 (978-1-59990-994-3(4), 9781599909943) 2010. 15.99 (978-1-59990-375-0(X), 9781599903750) Bloomsbury Publishing USA. (Bloomsbury USA Childrens).

ARMY

see Armies; Military Art and Science

ARMY SCHOOLS

see Military Education

ARMY VEHICLES

see Vehicles, Military

ARNOLD, BENEDICT, 1741-1801

Burgan, Michael. Benedict Arnold: American Hero & Traitor, 1 vol. Beatty, Terry, illus. 2007. (Graphic Biographies Ser.). (ENG.). 32p. (gr. 3-4). per. 8.10 (978-0-7368-7906-4(4), Graphic Library) Capstone Press of Coughlan Cos.
Gunderson, Jessica. Benedict Arnold: Battlefield Hero or Selfish Traitor?, 1 vol. 2013. (Perspectives on History Ser.). (ENG.). 32p. (gr. 3-4). 27.32 (978-1-4765-0243-4(9)); pap. 7.95 (978-1-4765-3407-7(1)) Capstone Press of Coughlan Cos. (Fact Finders).
Powell, Walter L. Benedict Arnold: Revolutionary War Hero & Traitor. (Library of American Lives & Timestm Ser.). 112p. (Illus.). (J). (gr. 4-8). lib. bdg. 31.95 (978-1-4042-6627-8(5)); 2009. (gr. 5-5). 69.20 (978-1-60853-471-5(5)) Rosen Publishing Group, Inc., The.
Powell, Walter Louis. Benedict Arnold: Revolutionary War Hero & Traitor. 2005. (Library of American Lives & Times). (Illus.). 112p. (YA). (gr. 4-7). lib. bdg. 34.60 (978-0-8239-6627-1(5)) Rosen Publishing Group, Inc., The.
Sheinkin, Steve. The Notorious Benedict Arnold: A True Story of Adventure, Heroism & Treachery. 2010. (ENG., Illus.). 352p. (YA). (gr. 6-9). 19.99 (978-1-59643-486-8(4), 9781596434868) Roaring Brook Pr.
—The Notorious Benedict Arnold: A True Story of Adventure, Heroism & Treachery. 2013. (ENG., Illus.). 368p. (YA). (gr. 6-9). pap. 9.99 (978-1-250-02460-2(9), 9781250024602) Square Fish.
—The Notorious Benedict Arnold: A True Story of Adventure, Heroism & Treachery. 2013. (YA). lib. bdg. 20.85 (978-0-606-28487-5(7), Turtleback) Turtleback Bks.

ARNOLD, BENEDICT, 1741-1801—FICTION

Rinaldi, Ann. Finishing Becca: A Story about Peggy Shippen & Benedict Arnold. 2004. (Great Episodes Ser.). (ENG.). 384p. (YA). (gr. 7-8). pap. 17.95 (978-0-15-205079-5(5)) Houghton Mifflin Harcourt Publishing Co.

ART

see also African Americans in Art; Anatomy, Artistic; Animals in Art; Archaeology; Architecture; Art—Forgeries; Art Objects; Christian Art and Symbolism; Collage; Collectors and Collecting; Commercial Art; Composition (Art); Design, Decorative; Drawing; Folk Art; Gems; Graphic Arts; Illustration of Books; Painting; Photography, Artistic; Pictures; Portraits; Sculpture; Symbolism

ABDO Publishing Company Staff. Super Simple Cultural Art Set 2. 2014. (Super Simple Cultural Art Set 2 Ser.: 6). (ENG.). 32p. (gr. 5-10). lib. bdg. 162.42 (978-1-62403-277-6(X), Super SandCastle) ABDO Publishing Co.
Ajmera, Maya & Ivanko, John D. To Be an Artist. 2004. (ENG., Illus.). 32p. (J). (gr. -1-3). 16.95 (978-1-57091-503-1(2)) Charlesbridge Publishing, Inc.

Albright, Tawnya, et al, illus. Puppetry Clip Art Book & CD. rev. ed. 2003. 44p. (YA). 25.00 *(978-1-58302-229-0(5))* One Way St., Inc.

Andelin, Darline. Easy String Art for All Seasons. 70p. (J). (gr. 1-6). pap. 7.95 *(978-1-56861-047-4(5))* Swift Learning Resources.

Angelou, Maya. My Painted House, My Friendly Chicken, & Me. Courtney-Clarke, Margaret, illus. 2003. (ENG.). 48p. (J). (gr. -1-2). pap. 7.99 *(978-0-375-82567-5(3),* Crown Books For Young Readers) Random Hse. Children's Bks.

Apodaca, Bianca & Serwich, Michael. Detrás de Lienzo: La Vida de un Artista. 2017. (TIME for Kids en Español - Level 4 Ser.). (SPA.). 48p. (gr. 4-4). lib. bdg. 31.99 *(978-1-5157-5131-1(7))* Time for Kids Inc AUS. Dist: Capstone Pub.

Apodaca, Blanca. Behind the Canvas: An Artist's Life, 1 vol. 2nd rev. ed. 2013. (Nonfiction Readers Ser.). (ENG., Illus.). 48p. (J). (gr. 4-4). pap. 29.96 *(978-1-4807-1102-0(0))* Shell Educational Publishing.

Appleby, Alex. Puedo Ser un Artista / I Can Be an Artist. 2014. (Cuando Sea Grande / When I Grow Up Ser.). (SPA.). 24p. (J). (gr. k-2). 22.60 *(978-1-4824-0861-4(9))* Stevens, Gareth Publishing LLLP.

Die Arbeit des Bildhausers.Tr. of Sculptor's Work. (GER., Illus.). (YA). 31.95 *(978-3-411-09081-5(2),* MY9081E) Bibliographisches Institut & F. A. Brockhaus AG DEU. Dist: Continental Bk. Co., Inc.

Arte. (SPA.). (J). 29.00 *(978-958-04-5746-6(8))* Norma S.A. COL. Dist: Distribuidora Norma, Inc.

Awesome Arts. 2014. (Ripleys Believe It or Not! Download the Weird Ser.: 8). 36p. (J). (gr. 4-18). lib. bdg. 20.95 *(978-1-4222-3148-7(8))* Mason Crest.

Bank Street College of Education. The Prado: Family Fold-Out Guide. 2006. (ENG., Illus.). 8p. pap. 9.95 *(978-1-85759-369-3(3))* Scala, Editions FRA. Dist: Antique Collectors' Club.

Baumbusch, Brigitte. Clothing in Art. 2005. (What Makes a Masterpiece? Ser.). (Illus.). 32p. (gr. 1-4). lib. bdg. 23.00 *(978-0-8368-4780-2(6),* Gareth Stevens Learning Library) Stevens, Gareth Publishing LLLP.

—Faces in Art. 2004. (What Makes a Masterpiece? Ser.). (Illus.). 32p. (gr. 1-4). lib. bdg. 23.00 *(978-0-8368-4378-1(9),* Gareth Stevens Learning Library) Stevens, Gareth Publishing LLLP.

—Figures in Art. 2004. (What Makes a Masterpiece? Ser.). (Illus.). 32p. (gr. 1-4). lib. bdg. 23.00 *(978-0-8368-4379-8(7),* Gareth Stevens Learning Library) Stevens, Gareth Publishing LLLP.

—Food in Art. 2004. (What Makes a Masterpiece? Ser.). (Illus.). 32p. (gr. 1-4). lib. bdg. 23.00 *(978-0-8368-4380-4(0),* Gareth Stevens Learning Library) Stevens, Gareth Publishing LLLP.

—Houses in Art. 2004. (What Makes a Masterpiece? Ser.). (Illus.). 32p. (gr. 1-4). lib. bdg. 23.00 *(978-0-8368-4381-1(9),* Gareth Stevens Learning Library) Stevens, Gareth Publishing LLLP.

—The Sky in Art. 2005. (What Makes a Masterpiece? Ser.). (Illus.). 32p. (gr. 1-4). lib. bdg. 23.00 *(978-0-8368-4783-3(0),* Gareth Stevens Learning Library) Stevens, Gareth Publishing LLLP.

Bayles, Jennifer L. An Adventure in Looking & Listening: Exploring Masterworks at the Albright-Knox Art Gallery. Barnett, Janet, illus. 2003. (J). *(978-1-887457-01-9(1))* Buffalo Fine Arts/Albright-Knox Art Gallery.

Be a Plant Scientist: Level L, 6 vols. (Take-Twostm Ser.). 16p. 36.95 *(978-0-322-03403-7(5))* Wright Group/McGraw-Hill.

Beaumont, Steve. How to Draw Magical Kings & Queens. 2007. (Drawing Fantasy Art Ser.: Vol. 2). (Illus.). 32p. (J). (gr. 4-7). lib. bdg. 26.50 *(978-1-4042-3860-2(3))* Rosen Publishing Group, Inc., The.

—How to Draw Orcs, Elves, & Dwarves. 2007. (Drawing Fantasy Art Ser.: Vol. 2). (Illus.). 32p. (J). (gr. 4-7). lib. bdg. 26.50 *(978-1-4042-3859-6(X))* Rosen Publishing Group, Inc., The.

—How to Draw Warriors. 2007. (Drawing Fantasy Art Ser.: Vol. 2). (Illus.). 32p. (J). (gr. 4-7). lib. bdg. 26.50 *(978-1-4042-3858-9(1))* Rosen Publishing Group, Inc., The.

Beery, Barbara. Fairies Cookbook, 1 vol. 2007. (ENG., Illus.). 64p. (J). (gr. 4-7). 14.99 *(978-1-4236-0290-3(0))* Gibbs Smith, Publisher.

Benduhn, Tea. What Is Color? 2009. (Get Art Smart Ser.). (ENG., Illus.). 24p. (J). (gr. k-3). pap. *(978-0-7787-5137-3(6));* lib. bdg. *(978-0-7787-5123-6(6))* Crabtree Publishing Co.

Beylon, Cathy. Firefighters Tattoos. 2008. (Dover Tattoos Ser.). (ENG., Illus.). 2p. (J). (gr. 1-4). pap. 1.99 *(978-0-486-46659-0(0))* Dover Pubns., Inc.

Bober, Suzanne & Merberg, Julie. How Is Mona Lisa Feeling? 2010. (ENG.). 22p. (J). bds. 6.99 *(978-1-935703-02-0(1))* Downtown Bookworks.

Bone, Emily. Art Deco Patterns to Color. 2013. (ENG., Illus.). 32p. (J). 5.99 *(978-0-7945-3209-3(8),* Usborne) EDC Publishing.

Branin, Larissa. Great Artists of the World. 2017. (Art Collections: Vol. 7). (ENG., Illus.). (YA). (gr. 9-12). 26.95 ***(978-1-4222-3934-6(9))*** Mason Crest.

Brett, Tyler & Romano, Tony. False Creek. 2010. (ENG., Illus.). 22p. bds. 9.95 *(978-1-897476-66-6(3))* Simply Read Bks. CAN. Dist: Ingram Publisher Services.

Brooks, Susie. People: Discover Great Art & Create Your Own! 2013. (Get into Art Ser.). (ENG., Illus.). 32p. (J). (gr. 2-9). 14.99 *(978-0-7534-7059-6(4),* 9780753470596, Kingfisher) Roaring Brook Pr.

Brown Reference Group PLC. Encyclopedia of Art for Young People, 8 vols., Set. Kwint, Marius, ed. 2008. (Encyclopedia of Art for Young People Ser.). 768p. (gr. 6-12). 280.00 *(978-0-7910-9477-8(4),* Chelsea Hse.) Facts On File, Inc.

Brush & Paint. 2003. (Gateways to the Sun Ser.). 32p. (J). (gr. 1-2). pap. 11.95 *(978-1-58105-575-7(7))* Santillana USA Publishing Co., Inc.

Buckley, A. M. Arts, 1 vol. 2011. (Inside the Industry Ser.). (ENG., Illus.). 112p. (J). (gr. 6-12). lib. bdg. 35.64 *(978-1-61714-797-5(4),* Essential Library) ABDO Publishing Co.

Budnick, Madeleine. Black & Blanco! Engaging Art in English y Español. 2013. (ArteKids Ser.). (ENG & SPA., Illus.). 16p. (J). (-k). bds. 7.95 *(978-1-59534-154-9(4))* Trinity Univ. Pr.

But Is It Art? 2015. (But Is It Art? Ser.). (ENG.). 32p. (J). (gr. 4-5). 159.60 *(978-1-4824-2297-9(2))* Stevens, Gareth Publishing LLLP.

Butterfield, Moira. Art & Culture. 2017. (Discover the Anglo-Saxons Ser.). (ENG., Illus.). 32p. (J). (gr. 4-6). pap. 11.99 *(978-1-4451-3343-0(1),* Franklin Watts) Hachette Children's Group GBR. Dist: Hachette Bk. Group.

Canetti, Yanitzia. Rhyming Tongue-Twisters Art. 2010. pap. 6.99 *(978-1-59835-261-0(X),* BrickHouse Education) Cambridge BrickHouse, Inc.

—Trabalenguas Artisticos. 2010. (J). pap. 6.99 *(978-1-59835-260-3(1))* Cambridge BrickHouse, Inc.

Carroll, Colleen. How Artists See Jr. Boxed Set. 2009. (How Artists See Jr.: Ser.). (ENG., Illus.). 72p. (J). (-k). 28.95 *(978-0-7892-1050-0(9),* Abbeville Kids) Abbeville Pr., Inc.

Carver Middle School & compiled by: Voices from the Middle: Stepping into the Real World. Carver Middle School, compiled by. 2004. 224p. (YA). per. 9.99 *(978-0-9749811-3-0(3),* Sonship Pr.) 21st Century Pr.

Chapman, D. Artist Cards: Level 1. 2003. (Adventures in Art Ser.). (Illus.). (gr. 1-18). pap. 22.95 *(978-0-87192-369-1(6))* Davis Pubns., Inc.

—Artist Cards: Level 2. 2003. (Adventures in Art Ser.). (Illus.). (gr. 2-18). pap. 22.95 *(978-0-87192-370-7(X))* Davis Pubns., Inc.

—Artist Cards: Level 5. 2003. (Adventures in Art Ser.). (Illus.). (gr. 5-18). pap. 22.95 *(978-0-87192-373-8(4))* Davis Pubns., Inc.

Chapman, Laura H. Big Book Bk. 1: Level One, Vol. 1. (Illus.). 70p. (gr. 1-18). 334.95 *(978-0-87192-263-2(0))* Davis Pubns., Inc.

Civardi, Anne. Action! Movement in Art. 2005. (Artventures Ser.). (Illus.). 32p. (YA). (gr. 3-6). lib. bdg. 27.10 *(978-1-58340-625-0(5),* 1247312) Black Rabbit Bks.

Como Usted Vea: Fernando Botero. 2005. (Coleccion Los Grandes Para Los Mas Pequenos Ser.). (SPA.). (J). pap. 8.95 *(978-968-7381-37-4(X))* Tecolote, Ediciones, S.A. de C.V. MEX. Dist: Iaconi, Mariuccia Bk. Imports.

Conway, Agnes Ethel & Conway, William Martin. The Book of Art for Young People. 2007. (ENG.). 126p. pap. 18.99 *(978-1-4346-4973-7(3));* 138p. pap. 19.99 *(978-1-4346-4974-4(1))* Creative Media Partners, LLC.

Cook, Trevor & Miles, Lisa. Drawing Fantasy Figures. 2011. (Drawing Is Fun Ser.). (Illus.). 32p. (J). (gr. 1-3). pap. 10.50 *(978-1-4339-5065-0(0),* Gareth Stevens Learning Library); lib. bdg. 26.60 *(978-1-4339-5022-3(7))* Stevens, Gareth Publishing LLLP.

—Drawing Vehicles. 2011. (Drawing Is Fun Ser.). (Illus.). 32p. (J). (gr. 1-3). pap. 10.50 *(978-1-4339-5077-3(4),* Gareth Stevens Learning Library); lib. bdg. 26.60 *(978-1-4339-5030-8(8))* Stevens, Gareth Publishing LLLP.

Cooper, Rhonda. Masterpieces of Chinese Art. 2017. (Art Collections: Vol. 7). (ENG., Illus.). (YA). (gr. 9-12). 26.95 ***(978-1-4222-3936-0(5))*** Mason Crest.

Courtauld, Sarah & Davies, Kate. Impressionists Sticker Book. Chiang, Shirley, illus. 2011. (Art Ser.). 32p. (J). pap. 9.99 *(978-0-7945-2961-1(5),* Usborne) EDC Publishing.

Courtauld, Sarah & Dickens, Rosie. Art Coloring Book with Stickers. 2012. (Art Coloring Book with Stickers Ser.). 32p. (J). pap. 8.99 *(978-0-7945-2976-5(3),* Usborne) EDC Publishing.

Creating Fantasy Art. 2017. (Creating Fantasy Art Ser.). 48p. (gr. 12-12). 127.00 ***(978-1-4994-6659-1(5))***; pap. 47.00 ***(978-1-5081-7597-1(7))*** Rosen Publishing Group, Inc., The. (Rosen Young Adult).

Crismon, Joy. Start with Art. 339p. (J). (gr. 1-7). pap. 59.95 *(978-1-56861-046-7(7))* Swift Learning Resources.

De Duve, Catherine. Hello Matisse: Get to Know Matisse Through Stories, Games & Draw-It-Yourself Fun. 2006. 32p. per. 9.95 *(978-1-59960-002-4(1))* Birdcage Pr.

De Long, Ron, et al. Dream-Makers Mathematics: Art & Mathematics. De Long, Ron et al, eds. 2007. (Illus.). 104p. spiral bd. 9.99 *(978-0-86696-327-5(8))* Binney & Smith, Inc.

DeLong, Ron, ed. Dream-Makers: Visual Art & Literacy 2003. (Illus.). 48p. 6.00 *(978-0-86696-315-2(4))* Binney & Smith, Inc.

Demilly, Christian. Pop Art. 2007. (Illus.). 31p. (YA). (gr. 8-18). 14.95 *(978-3-7913-3894-1(3))* Prestel Publishing.

DePietro, Frank. Latino Arts in the United States. Limón, José E., ed. 2012. (Hispanic Americans: Major Minority Ser.). (Illus.). 64p. (J). (gr. 4). 22.95 *(978-1-4222-2324-6(8))* Mason Crest.

—Spain Arrives in the Americas. 2012. (Illus.). 64p. (J). pap. *(978-1-4222-2341-3(8))* Mason Crest.

Deuchars, Marion. Let's Make Some Great Art. 2011. (ENG., Illus.). 224p. (J). (gr. 3-7). pap. 19.95 *(978-1-85669-786-6(X))* King, Laurence Publishing GBR. Dist: Hachette Bk. Group.

Dickens, Rosie. Introduction to Modern Art - Internet Linked. 2005. (Introduction to Art Ser.). 96p. (J). 19.95 *(978-0-7945-0923-1(1),* Usborne) EDC Publishing.

—My First Art Sticker Book. Ballesteros, Carles, illus. 2013. (Art Ser.). 23p. (J). pap. 8.99 *(978-0-7945-3202-4(0),* Usborne) EDC Publishing.

—My Very First Art Coloring Book with Stickers. 2012. (Art Ser.). 24p. (J). pap. 5.99 *(978-0-7945-3273-4(X),* Usborne) EDC Publishing.

Dickens, Rosie & Courtauld, Sarah. My Very First Art Book. Gordan, Gus, illus. 2011. (Art Ser.). 48p. (J). pap. 12.99 *(978-0-7945-3018-1(4),* Usborne) EDC Publishing.

Dickens, Rosie, et al. The Usborne Book of Art. 2005. (ENG., Illus.). 196p. *(978-0-7460-7006-2(3))* Usborne Publishing, Ltd.

Dickins, Rosie. Usborne the Children's Book of Art: Internet Linked. Armstrong, Carrie, ed. Mayer, Uwe, illus. 2006. 64p. (J). (gr. 5-9). 14.99 *(978-0-7945-1223-1(2),* Usborne) EDC Publishing.

Domeniconi, David. M Is for Masterpiece: An Art Alphabet. Bullas, Will, illus. rev. ed. 2006. (Art & Culture Ser.). (ENG.). 48p. (J). (gr. -1-3). 17.95 *(978-1-58536-276-9(X))* Sleeping Bear Pr.

Dorling Kindersley Publishing Staff. All about Everything. 2014. (ENG., Illus.). 304p. (J). (gr. 4-7). pap. 12.99 *(978-1-4654-1746-6(X),* DK Children) Dorling Kindersley Publishing, Inc.

—The Arts: a Visual Encyclopedia. 2017. (ENG.). 304p. (J). (gr. 3-7). pap. 19.99 ***(978-1-4654-6178-0(7),*** DK Children) Dorling Kindersley Publishing, Inc.

Dorling Kindersley Publishing Staff. Children's Book of Art: An Introduction to the World's Most Amazing. 2009. (ENG.). 144p. (J). (gr. 2-5). 24.99 *(978-0-7566-5511-2(0),* DK Children) Dorling Kindersley Publishing, Inc.

Dover. Knux — Knuckle Tattoos. 2015. (ENG.). 2p. (J). (gr. 1-4). pap. 1.99 *(978-0-486-79390-0(7))* Dover Pubns., Inc.

—Knux - Knuckle Tattoos. 2015. (Dover Little Activity Bks.). (ENG.). 2p. (J). (gr. 1-4). pap. 1.99 *(978-0-486-79388-7(5))* Dover Pubns., Inc.

Dunn, Mary. My Adventure at an Artist's Studio: Where You Create the Story. 2006. (My Adventure Ser.). 44p. (J). (gr. -1-3). pap. 8.99 *(978-1-59092-290-3(5))* Blue Forge Pr.

Durrie, Karen. The Arts. 2011. (Illus.). 24p. (J). *(978-1-61690-593-4(X));* (ENG., lib. bdg. 27.13 *(978-1-61690-948-2(X),* AV2 by Weigl) Weigl Pubs., Inc.

Encyclopaedia Britannica, Inc. Staff, compiled by. Arts. 2003. (Illus.). 64p. 14.95 *(978-1-59339-035-8(1))* Encyclopaedia Britannica, Inc.

Express Yourself! Scholastic Edition. 2005. 7.95 *(978-0-8230-2492-6(X))* Watson-Guptill Pubns., Inc.

Facts on File, Inc. Staff. Art. 2011. (Discovering Careers Ser.). (Illus.). 122p. (gr. 4-9). 24.95 *(978-0-8160-8055-7(0),* Ferguson Publishing Co.) Facts On File, Inc.

Finger, Brad. 13 Art Movements Children Should Know. 2014. (ENG., Illus.). 48p. (J). (gr. 3-7). 14.95 *(978-3-7913-7158-0(4))* Prestel Verlag GmbH & Co KG. DEU. Dist: Penguin Random Hse. LLC.

—13 Modern Artists Children Should Know. 2010. (ENG., Illus.). 48p. (J). (gr. 3-7). 14.95 *(978-3-7913-7015-6(4))* Prestel Verlag GmbH & Co KG. DEU. Dist: Penguin Random Hse. LLC.

Fitzgerald, Stephanie. What Is Texture? 2009. (Get Art Smart Ser.). (ENG., Illus.). 24p. (J). (gr. k-3). pap. *(978-0-7787-5141-0(4))* Crabtree Publishing Co.

Fitzpatrick, Anne. The Baroque Period. 2005. (Movements in Art Ser.). (Illus.). 48p. (YA). (gr. 5-9). lib. bdg. 21.95 *(978-1-58341-346-3(4))* Creative Co., The.

—The Baroque Period: Movements in Art. 2015. (Illus.). 80p. (J). *(978-1-60818-530-6(3),* Creative Education) Creative Co., The.

—The Baroque Period: Odysseys in Art. 2016. (Odysseys in Art Ser.). (ENG.). 80p. (J). (gr. 7-10). pap. 14.99 *(978-1-62832-131-9(8),* Creative Paperbacks) Creative Co., The.

—Late Modernism: Odysseys in Art. 2016. (Odysseys in Art Ser.). (ENG.). 80p. (J). (gr. 7-10). pap. 14.99 *(978-1-62832-135-7(0),* Creative Paperbacks) Creative Co., The.

Fleming, Christine. Art As Science. 2007. (Shockwave: Science in Practice Ser.). 36p. (J). lib. bdg. 6.95 *(978-0-531-15461-8(0),* Children's Pr.) Scholastic Library Publishing.

Flood Williams, Colleen Madonna. Mexican Art & Architecture. 2009. (Mexico: Beautiful Land, Diverse People Ser.). (Illus.). 64p. (YA). (gr. 7-12). 21.95 *(978-1-4222-0656-0(4))* Mason Crest.

Fraser, Fil. Alberta's Camelot Vol. 1: Culture & the Arts in the Lougheed Years, 1 vol. rev. ed. 2003. (ENG., Illus.). 240p. (gr. 4). pap. 21.95 *(978-1-55105-393-6(4),* 1551053934) Lone Pine Publishing USA.

Friedland, Katy & Shoemaker, Maria K. Art Museum Opposites. 2010. (ENG., Illus.). 44p. (J). (gr. -1-3). 16.95 *(978-1-4399-0523-4(1))* Temple Univ. Pr.

—A Is for Art Museum. 2008. (ENG., Illus.). 64p. (J). (gr. -1-k). 18.95 *(978-1-59213-963-7(9))* Temple Univ. Pr.

Friedland, Katy & Shoemaker, Maria K. A Is for Art Museum. 2008. (Illus.). (J). *(978-0-87633-203-0(3))* Philadelphia Museum of Art.

—Art Museum Opposites. 2010. (Illus.). *(978-0-87633-222-1(X))* Philadelphia Museum of Art.

Furey, Hester. Body Piercing & Tattoos. 2015. (Issues That Concern You Ser.). (ENG., Illus.). 144p. (gr. 7-10). 42.00 *(978-0-7377-7238-8(7),* Greenhaven Pr., Inc.) Cengage Gale.

Gale, Riana, et al. Artistic Expressions of a Child. 2010. 32p. pap. 15.50 *(978-1-4520-8154-0(9))* AuthorHouse.

Gates Galvin, Laura. Alphabet of Art. Tabbutt, Steven, illus. 2011. (ENG.). 40p. (J). 9.95 *(978-1-60727-196-3(6))* Soundprints.

Gogerly, Liz. Graffiti Culture. 2012. (On the Radar: Street Style Ser.). (ENG.). 32p. (gr. 4-8). lib. bdg. 26.60 *(978-0-7613-7767-2(0),* Lerner Pubns.) Lerner Publishing Group.

Gowing, Lawrence, ed. Facts on File Encyclopedia of Art & Artists Set. 2005. 1840p. (C). (gr. 9). 585.00 *(978-0-8160-6378-9(8))* Facts On File, Inc.

Greenwell, Jessica. My First Coloring Book. 2011. (First Sticker Coloring Book Ser.). 46p. (J). pap. 10.99 *(978-0-7945-2964-2(X),* Usborne) EDC Publishing.

Groenendyk, Doretta. I'm Drawing a Story, 1 vol. 2016. (ENG.). 32p. (J). (gr. -1-3). pap. 12.95 *(978-1-927502-50-1(0))* Acorn Pr., The CAN. Dist: Orca Bk. Pubs. USA.

Gunderson, Jessica. Gothic Art. 2008. (Movements in Art Ser.). 48p. (YA). (gr. 5-9). 22.95 *(978-1-58341-610-5(2))* Creative Co., The.

—Gothic Art: Movements in Art. 2015. (Illus.). 80p. (J). *(978-1-60818-532-0(X),* Creative Education) Creative Co., The.

—Gothic Art: Odysseys in Art. 2016. (Odysseys in Art Ser.). (ENG.). 80p. (J). (gr. 7-10). pap. 14.99 *(978-1-62832-133-3(4),* Creative Paperbacks) Creative Co., The.

—Impressionism: Movements in Art. 2015. (Illus.). 80p. (J). *(978-1-60818-533-7(8),* Creative Education) Creative Co., The.

—Realism. 2008. (Movements in Art Ser.). (Illus.). 48p. (YA). (gr. 5-9). 22.95 *(978-1-58341-612-9(9))* Creative Co., The.

—Realism: Odysseys in Art. 2016. (Odysseys in Art Ser.). (ENG.). 80p. (J). (gr. 7-10). pap. 14.99 *(978-1-62832-136-4(9),* Creative Paperbacks) Creative Co., The.

—Romanticism. 2008. (Movements in Art Ser.). 48p. (YA). (gr. 5-9). 22.95 *(978-1-58341-613-6(7))* Creative Co., The.

—Romanticism: Movements in Art. 2015. (Illus.). 80p. (J). *(978-1-60818-537-5(0),* Creative Education) Creative Co., The.

—Romanticism: Odysseys in Art. 2016. (Odysseys in Art Ser.). (ENG.). 80p. (J). (gr. 7-10). pap. 14.99 *(978-1-62832-138-8(5),* Creative Paperbacks) Creative Co., The.

Hamilton, Tracy Brown. For People Who Love the Arts. 2016. (Cool Careers Without College Ser.). 00104p. (J). (gr. 7-7). 38.45 *(978-1-5081-7288-8(9))* Rosen Publishing Group, Inc., The.

Harcourt School Publishers Staff. Art. 3rd ed. 2003. (Harcourt School Publishers Art Everywhere Ser.). (ENG.). 104p. (gr. 3-3). pap., tchr. ed. 44.55 *(978-0-15-339498-0(6));* (Illus.). 96p. (gr. 2-2). pap., tchr. ed. 44.55 *(978-0-15-339497-3(8))* Harcourt Schl. Pubs.

—Art Big Book. 4th ed. 2004. (Illus.). (gr. 3). 207.80 *(978-0-15-343688-8(3));* (gr. 4). 207.80 *(978-0-15-343689-5(1));* (gr. 5). 207.80 *(978-0-15-343690-1(5))* Harcourt Schl. Pubs.

—Art Everywhere: Artist's Workshop Activities. 3rd ed. 2003. (SPA & ENG., Illus.). pap. 15.60 *(978-0-15-339899-5(X));* pap. 15.60 *(978-0-15-339901-5(5));* pap. 15.60 *(978-0-15-339900-8(7));* 64p. (gr. 4-4). pap. 17.20 *(978-0-15-339902-2(3));* 64p. (gr. 5-5). pap. 17.20 *(978-0-15-339903-9(1))* Harcourt Schl. Pubs.

—Art, Grade 1. 4th ed. 2004. pap., tchr. ed. 97.10 *(978-0-15-342012-2(X))* Harcourt Schl. Pubs.

—Art, Grade 1: Teacher Resource Book. 3rd ed. 2003. (Harcourt School Publishers Art Everywhere Ser.). (ENG., Illus.). 96p. (gr. 1-1). pap., tchr. ed. 44.55 *(978-0-15-339496-6(X))* Harcourt Schl. Pubs.

—Art, Grade 2. 4th ed. 2004. pap., tchr. ed. 97.10 *(978-0-15-342013-9(8))* Harcourt Schl. Pubs.

—Art, Grade 3. 4th ed. 2004. pap., tchr. ed. 97.10 *(978-0-15-342014-6(6))* Harcourt Schl. Pubs.

—Art, Grade 4. 4th ed. 2004. pap., tchr. ed. 97.10 *(978-0-15-342015-3(4))* Harcourt Schl. Pubs.

—Art, Grade 4: Teacher Resource Book. 3rd ed. 2003. (Harcourt School Publishers Art Everywhere Ser.). (ENG., Illus.). 96p. (gr. 4-4). pap., tchr. ed. 44.55 *(978-0-15-339499-7(4))* Harcourt Schl. Pubs.

—Art, Grade 5. 4th ed. 2004. pap., tchr. ed. 97.10 *(978-0-15-342016-0(2))* Harcourt Schl. Pubs.

—Big Book Art 2006 - Grade 1. 3rd ed. 2003. (Illus.). pap. 207.80 *(978-0-15-339507-9(9))* Harcourt Schl. Pubs.

—Big Book Art 2006 - Grade 2. 3rd ed. 2003. (Illus.). pap. 207.80 *(978-0-15-339508-6(7))* Harcourt Schl. Pubs.

—Harcourt School Publishers Art Everywhere. 3rd ed. 2003. (Harcourt School Publishers Art Everywhere Ser.). (ENG.). 96p. (gr. 5-5). pap. 44.55 *(978-0-15-339501-7(X))* Harcourt Schl. Pubs.

Haring, Keith, et al. Art for Baby: High-Contrast Images by Eleven Contemporary Artists to Explore with Your Child. 2009. (ENG., Illus.). 12p. (J). (gr. -1 — 1). bds. 21.99 *(978-0-7636-4424-6(2),* Templar) Candlewick Pr.

Harris, John & Lorenz, Catherine. Discovering Art Kids. 2009. (ENG., Illus.). 24p. (gr. -1). 4.95 *(978-0-89236-952-2(3))* Oxford Univ. Pr., Inc.

Haruch, Tony. Kurtal Explores Australian Aboriginal Art. 2007. (ENG.). 32p. (J). 15.95 *(978-1-56290-533-0(3))* Crystal Productions.

Heine, Florian. 13 Art Inventions Children Should Know. 2011. (ENG., Illus.). 48p. (J). (gr. 3-7). 14.95 *(978-3-7913-7060-6(X))* Prestel Verlag GmbH & Co KG. DEU. Dist: Penguin Random Hse. LLC.

Hensley, Laura. Art for All: What Is Public Art? 2010. (Culture in Action Ser.). (ENG.). 32p. (gr. 3-6). 30.65 *(978-1-4109-3923-4(5),* NA-r) Heinemann-Raintree.

Herrera, Nicholas. High Riders, Saints & Death Cars: A Life Saved by Art, 1 vol. Denne, John, photos by. 2011. (ENG., Illus.). 56p. (J). (gr. 4-18). 24.95 *(978-0-88899-854-5(6))* Groundwood Bks. CAN. Dist: Publishers Group West (PGW).

Hodge, Susie, et al. Why Is Art Full of Naked People? 2016. (ENG., Illus.). 96p. (J). (gr. 3-7). 19.95 *(978-0-500-65080-6(2),* 565080) Thames & Hudson.

Hollihan-Elliot, Sheila. Art & Architecture of China. Wang, Jianwei, ed. 2012. (China: the Emerging Superpower Ser.). 120p. (J). (gr. 7). 24.95 *(978-1-4222-2155-6(5))* Mason Crest.

—Chinese Art & Architecture. 2011. (J). pap. *(978-1-4222-2166-2(0))* Mason Crest.

Hook, Dianne J., creator. Schooltime Borders: Creative Borders for Classroom & Home. 2005. (Illus.). 64p. pap. 22.99 incl. cd-rom *(978-1-59441-187-8(5),* DJ-604006, DJ Inkers) Carson-Dellosa Publishing, LLC.

Howard Ed.D., Tequila E. Earth Day. 2012. 32p. pap. 17.25 *(978-1-4669-2081-1(5))* Trafford Publishing.

Huff, Abby. Draw Your Own Lettering & Decorative Zendoodles. Grover, James et al, illus. 2017. (Draw Your Own Zendoodles Ser.). (ENG.). 48p. (gr. 4-5). lib. bdg. 31.32 *(978-1-5157-4841-0(3))* Capstone Press of Coughlan Cos.

Hulsbosch, Marianne, et al. Art & Me: Cambridge Senior Visual Arts (Stage 6) Pack. 2nd ed. 2014. (ENG.). pap. *(978-1-107-43444-8(0))* Cambridge Univ. Pr.

Inside the Industry, 8 vols., Set. Incl. Arts. Buckley, A. M. lib. bdg. 35.64 *(978-1-61714-797-5(4));* Engineering. Hamon, Susan E. lib. bdg. 35.64 *(978-1-61714-798-2(2));* Entertainment. Lusted, Marcia Amidon. lib. bdg. 35.64 *(978-1-61714-799-9(0));* Fashion. Freese, Susan M. lib. bdg. 35.64 *(978-1-61714-800-2(8));* Green Jobs. Farrell, Courtney. lib. bdg. 35.64 *(978-1-61714-801-9(6));* Medicine. Reece, Richard. lib. bdg. 35.64 *(978-1-61714-802-6(4));* Publishing. Townsend, Beth. lib. bdg. 35.64 *(978-1-61714-803-3(2));* Sports. Howell, Brian. lib. bdg. 35.64 *(978-1-61714-804-0(0));* (J). (gr. 6-12). (Inside the Industry Ser.: 8). (ENG., Illus.). 112p. 2011. Set lib. bdg. 285.12 *(978-1-61714-796-8(6),* Essential Library) ABDO Publishing Co.

It's All About Baby. 2004. (J). mass mkt. *(978-0-9728472-3-0(5))* Signator Publishing Group Inc.

Jacobs, Frank & Bursill, Henry. Hand Shadow Fun. 2015. (ENG., Illus.). 64p. (J). (gr. 3-7). pap. 1.99 *(978-0-486-79674-1(4))* Dover Pubns., Inc.

Kim, H. Y. Michelle. Art Play-Ground A-1: A Complete & Self-Contained Curriculum for Art Education. 2005. (Art Play-Ground Ser.). (Illus.). 42p. spiral bd., wbk. ed. 12.95 *(978-89-91302-05-1(X))* Michelle's A & E KOR. Dist: APG Sales & Distribution Services.

—Art Play-Ground A-2: A Complete & Self-Contained Curriculum for Art Education. 2005. (Art Play-Ground Ser.). (Illus.). 42p. spiral bd., wbk. ed. 12.95 *(978-89-91302-06-8(8))* Michelle's A & E KOR. Dist: APG Sales & Distribution Services.

—Art Play-Ground A-3: A Complete & Self-Contained Curriculum for Art Education. 2005. (Art Play-Ground Ser.). (Illus.). 42p. spiral bd., wbk. ed. 12.95 *(978-89-91302-07-5(6))* Michelle's A & E KOR. Dist: APG Sales & Distribution Services.

—Art Play-Ground B-1: A Complete & Self-Contained Curriculum for Art Education. 2005. 42p. spiral bd., wbk. ed. 12.95 *(978-89-91302-02-0(5))* Michelle's A & E KOR. Dist: APG Sales & Distribution Services.

—Art Play-Ground C-1: A Complete & Self-Contained Curriculum for Art Education. 2005. (Art Play-Ground Ser.). (Illus.). 42p. spiral bd. 12.95 *(978-89-91302-08-2(4))* Michelle's A & E KOR. Dist: APG Sales & Distribution Services.

—Art Play-Ground C-2: A Complete & Self-Contained Curriculum for Art Education. 2005. (Art Play-Ground Ser.). (Illus.). 42p. spiral bd., wbk. ed. 12.95 *(978-89-91302-09-9(2))* Michelle's A & E KOR. Dist: APG Sales & Distribution Services.

—Art Play-Ground C-3: A Complete & Self-Contained Curriculum for Art Education. 2005. (Art Play-Ground Ser.). (Illus.). 42p. spiral bd. 12.95 *(978-89-91302-10-5(6))* Michelle's A & E KOR. Dist: APG Sales & Distribution Services.

—Art Play-Ground E-1: A Complete & Self-Contained Curriculum for Art Education. 2005. (Art Play-Ground Ser.). (Illus.). 42p. spiral bd. 12.95 *(978-89-91302-11-2(4))* Michelle's A & E KOR. Dist: APG Sales & Distribution Services.

—Art Play-Ground E-2: A Complete & Self-Contained Curriculum for Art Education. 2005. (Art Play-Ground Ser.). (Illus.). 42p. spiral bd. 12.95 *(978-89-91302-12-9(2))* Michelle's A & E KOR. Dist: APG Sales & Distribution Services.

—Art Play-Ground E-3: A Complete & Self-Contained Curriculum for Art Education. 2005. (Art Play-Ground Ser.). (Illus.). 42p. spiral bd., wbk. ed. 12.95 *(978-89-91302-13-6(0))* Michelle's A & E KOR. Dist: APG Sales & Distribution Services.

—Art Play-Ground F-1: A Complete & Self-Contained Curriculum for Art Education. 2005. (Art Play-Ground Ser.). (Illus.). 42p. spiral bd. 12.95 *(978-89-954869-1-7(0))* Michelle's A & E KOR. Dist: APG Sales & Distribution Services.

—Art Play-Ground F-2: A Complete & Self-Contained Curriculum for Art Education. 2005. (Art Play-Ground Ser.). (Illus.). 42p. spiral bd., wbk. ed. 12.95 *(978-89-954869-2-4(9))* Michelle's A & E KOR. Dist: APG Sales & Distribution Services.

—Art Play-Ground F-3: A Complete & Self-Contained Curriculum for Art Education. 2005. (Art Play-Ground Ser.). (Illus.). 42p. spiral bd. 12.95 *(978-89-954869-3-1(7))* Michelle's A & E KOR. Dist: APG Sales & Distribution Services.

Kim, Michelle. Art Play-Ground B-2. 2005. 42p. pap., wbk. ed. 12.95 *(978-89-91302-03-7(3))* Michelle's A & E KOR. Dist: APG Sales & Distribution Services.

—Art Play-Ground B-3. 2005. 42p. pap. 12.95 *(978-89-91302-04-4(1))* Michelle's A & E KOR. Dist: APG Sales & Distribution Services.

—Art Play-Ground D-1. 2005. 42p. pap., wbk. ed. 12.95 *(978-89-954869-4-8(5))* Michelle's A & E KOR. Dist: APG Sales & Distribution Services.

—Art Play-Ground D-2. 2005. 42p. pap. 12.95 *(978-89-91302-00-6(9))* Michelle's A & E KOR. Dist: APG Sales & Distribution Services.

—Art Play-Ground D-3. 2005. 42p. pap. 12.95 *(978-89-91302-01-3(7))* Michelle's A & E KOR. Dist: APG Sales & Distribution Services.

Kishimoto, Masashi. Uzumaki Naruto: Illustrations. 2015. (ENG., Illus.). 104p. pap. 19.99 *(978-1-4215-8439-3(5))* Viz Media.

Klein, Jacky & Klein, Suzy, texts. What Is Contemporary Art? a Guide for Kids. 2012. (ENG., Illus.). 64p. 22.95 *(978-0-87070-809-1(0))* Museum of Modern Art.

Knight, Ernie C. Bean Heads, Another Batch. 2003. (Illus.). 58p. per. 16.99 *(978-1-932338-06-5(3))* Lifevest Publishing, Inc.

Kohl, MaryAnn F. & Potter, Jean. Storybook Art: Hands-On Art for Children in the Styles of 100 Great Picture Book Illustrators. Davis, Katheryn & Van Slyke, Rebecca, illus. 2003. (Bright Ideas for Learning Ser.: 7). (ENG.). 144p. (J). (gr. -1-6). pap. 18.95 *(978-0-935607-03-1(X))* Bright Ring Publishing, Inc.

Kohl, MaryAnn F. & Solga, Kim. Great American Artists for Kids: Hands-On Art Experiences in the Styles of Great American Masters. 2008. (Bright Ideas for Learning Ser.: 8). (ENG., Illus.). 144p. (J). (gr. -1-4). pap. 18.95 *(978-0-935607-00-0(5))* Bright Ring Publishing, Inc.

Kohl, MaryAnn F. & Zaborowski, Barbara. Action ART: Hands-On Active Art Adventures. 2015. (Bright Ideas for Learning (TM) Ser.: 9). (ENG., Illus.). 144p. (J). (gr. -1-7). pap. 21.95 *(978-0-935607-34-5(X))* Chicago Review Pr., Inc.

Korn, Irene. Great Masterpieces of the World. 2017. (Art Collections: Vol. 7). (ENG., Illus.). (YA). (gr. 9-12). 26.95 ***(978-1-4222-3935-3(7))*** Mason Crest.

Kramer, Ann. Egyptian Myth: A Treasury of Legends, Art, & History. 2007. (Myth Ser.). (Illus.). 96p. (J). (gr. 4-7). pap. 7.99 *(978-0-7858-2347-6(6))*, Chartwell) Book Sales, Inc.

—Egyptian Myth: A Treasury of Legends, Art, & History. 2007. (ENG., Illus.). 96p. (C). (gr. 6-18). lib. bdg. 158.00 *(978-0-7656-8105-8(6)*, Y182128) Routledge.

Kubit, Glenna. Art Is .... Elements & Principles If Design. 2013. (ENG., Illus.). 32p. (J). 14.95 *(978-1-56290-705-1(0))* Crystal Productions.

Kunst: Fotografie, Grafik, Neue Medien, Architektur, Malerei, Skulptur, Techniken. (Duden-Schuelerduden Ser.). (YA). *(978-3-411-05942-3(7))* Bibliographisches Institut & F. A. Brockhaus AG DEU. Dist: International Bk. Import Service, Inc.

Kuskowski, Alex. Super Simple Australian Art: Fun & Easy Art from Around the World, 1 vol. 2014. (Super Simple Cultural Art Set 2 Ser.). (ENG.). 32p. (gr. 5-10). lib. bdg. 27.07 *(978-1-62403-278-3(8)*, Super SandCastle) ABDO Publishing Co.

—Super Simple Indian Art: Fun & Easy Art from Around the World, 1 vol. 2014. (Super Simple Cultural Art Set 2 Ser.). (ENG.). 32p. (gr. 5-10). lib. bdg. 27.07 *(978-1-62403-280-6(X)*, Super SandCastle) ABDO Publishing Co.

Laxton, Laura, ed. The Budding Artist. 2012. (Budding Ser.). (ENG., Illus.). 72p. pap. 9.95 *(978-0-87659-384-4(8)*, Gryphon House Inc) Gryphon Hse., Inc.

Linser, Joseph Michael & Hopkins, Eva. Dawn: Behind the Scenes. 2011. (Illus.). 128p. (YA). pap. 14.99 *(978-1-60706-357-5(3))* Image Comics.

Loh-Hagan, Virginia. Art Show. 2016. (Illus.). 32p. (J). *(978-1-63470-494-6(0))* Cherry Lake Publishing.

Loonin, Meryl. Public Art. Greenhaven Press Editors, ed. 2014. (Eye on Art Ser.). (ENG., Illus.). 128p. (gr. 7-10). lib. bdg. 39.40 *(978-1-4205-0917-5(9)*, Lucent Bks.) Cengage Gale.

Luo, Keyi, illus. Colorful Childhood. 2004. (CHI.). (J). pap. 27.50 *(978-1-932002-47-8(2)*, Cozy Publishing Hse.) Cozy Graphics Corp.

MacDonald, Fiona. Design. 2004. (Culture Encyclopedia Ser.). (Illus.). 40p. (YA). (gr. 5-18). lib. bdg. 19.95 *(978-1-59084-476-2(9))* Mason Crest.

Mack, Steve. Cutting & Pasting. Flash Kids Editors, ed. 2012. (Flash Kids Preschool Activity Bks.). (ENG., Illus.). 80p. (J). pap. 5.95 *(978-1-4114-5807-9(9)*, Spark Publishing Group) Sterling Publishing Co., Inc.

—Tracing. Flash Kids Editors, ed. 2012. (Flash Kids Preschool Activity Bks.). (ENG., Illus.). 80p. (J). pap. 5.95 *(978-1-4114-5811-6(7)*, Spark Publishing Group) Sterling Publishing Co., Inc.

Maderna, Victoria. Glow-In-the-Dark Tattoos Owls. 2015. (Dover Little Activity Bks.). (ENG.). 2p. (J). (gr. 1-4). 1.50 *(978-0-486-80323-4(6))* Dover Pubns., Inc.

Magruder, Trula & American Girl Editors, eds. Design by Me Wings: Fancy Art & Fun Display Ideas! Ingham, Julie, illus. 2011. (ENG.). 32p. (J). spiral bd. 14.95 *(978-1-59369-897-3(6))* American Girl Publishing, Inc.

Make Believe Ideas. Cookie Catcher Art. 2015. (ENG.). 80p. (J). pap. 9.99 *(978-1-78235-991-3(5))* Make Believe Ideas GBR. Dist: Nelson, Thomas Inc.

Marcovitz, Hal. Art Conservation. 2006. (Eye on Art Ser.). (ENG., Illus.). 104p. (J). (gr. 3-7). lib. bdg. 34.80 *(978-1-59018-964-1(7)*, Lucent Bks.) Cengage Gale.

—Surrealism. 2007. (Eye on Art Ser.). (ENG., Illus.). 104p. (J). (gr. 3-7). lib. bdg. 34.80 *(978-1-4205-0005-9(8)*, Lucent Bks.) Cengage Gale.

Markowitz-Meredith, Susan. What Is Line? 2009. (Get Art Smart Ser.). (ENG., Illus.). 24p. (J). (gr. k-3). pap. *(978-0-7787-5136-6(8))*; lib. bdg. *(978-0-7787-5122-9(8))* Crabtree Publishing Co.

—What Is Space? 2009. (Get Art Smart Ser.). (ENG., Illus.). 24p. (J). (gr. k-3). pap. *(978-0-7787-5140-3(6))*; lib. bdg. *(978-0-7787-5126-7(0))* Crabtree Publishing Co.

Mason, Antony. Art. 2004. (Culture Encyclopedia Ser.). (Illus.). 40p. (YA). (gr. 5-18). lib. bdg. 19.95 *(978-1-59084-475-5(0))* Mason Crest.

—El Arte Impresionista: En Los Tiempos de Renoir. 2005. (Arte Alrededor del Mundo Ser.). (Illus.). 48p. (J). (gr. 4-7). pap. 9.95 *(978-85-7416-229-4(9))* Callis Editora Ltda BRA. Dist: Independent Pubs. Group.

—El Arte Moderno: En los Tiempos de Picasso. 2005. (Arte Alrededor del Mundo Ser.). (Illus.). 48p. (J). (gr. 4-7). pap. 9.95 *(978-85-7416-240-9(X))* Callis Editora Ltda BRA. Dist: Independent Pubs. Group.

—El arte Renacentista: En los tiempos de Miguel Angel. 2005. (Arte Alrededor del Mundo Ser.). 48p. (J). pap. 9.95 *(978-85-7416-228-7(0))* Callis Editora Ltda BRA. Dist: Independent Pubs. Group.

Mattison, Mary Lee. You be the Artist. 2007. (Illus.). 38p. (J). pap. 12.99 net. *(978-0-9799090-0-9(7))* Merrimack Bk. Works.

Mazurkiewicz, Jessica. SPARK - Mandalas Coloring Book. 2015. (ENG., Illus.). 64p. (J). (gr. 1-4). pap. 5.99 *(978-0-486-80214-5(0))* Dover Pubns., Inc.

McAneney, Caitlin. Quadrilaterals in Art: Reason with Shapes & Their Attributes. 2014. (Rosen Common Core Math Readers Ser.). (ENG.). 24p. (J). (gr. 3-4). pap. 8.25 *(978-1-4777-4878-7(4)*, PowerKids Pr.) Rosen Publishing Group, Inc., The.

McGraw-Hill Staff. Exploring Art. 3rd ed. 2004. (Exploring Art Ser.). (ENG., Illus.). 368p. (gr. 6-8). stu. ed. 105.92 *(978-0-07-846514-7(1)*, 0078465141) McGraw-Hill Education.

Merberg, Julie & Bober, Suzanne. Green Squares & More Colors & Shapes: Art from the Start. 2013. (ENG.). 22p. (J). bds. 6.99 *(978-1-935703-14-3(5))* Downtown Bookworks.

Metropolitan Museum of Art Staff. Nyc ABC. 2011. (ENG., Illus.). 60p. (J). (gr. -1-3). 15.95 *(978-0-8478-3701-4(7)*, Skira) Rizzoli International Pubns., Inc.

Michele, Tracey. African Art. 2011. (Learn-Abouts Ser.). (Illus.). 16p. (J). pap. 7.95 *(978-1-59920-637-0(4))* Black Rabbit Bks.

Micklethwait, Lucy. I Spy Shapes in Art. 2004. (ENG., Illus.). 40p. (J). (gr. -1-3). 19.99 *(978-0-06-073193-9(1)*, Greenwillow Bks.) HarperCollins Pubs.

Miller, Heather. The 10 Most Provocative 20th Century Artworks. 2007. (J). 14.99 *(978-1-55448-483-6(9))* Scholastic Library Publishing.

Miller, Reagan & Richardson, Hazel. Arts & Culture in the Ancient World. 2011. (ENG., Illus.). 32p. (J). *(978-0-7787-1732-4(1))* Crabtree Publishing Co.

—Arts & Culture in the Ancient World. Crabtree Publishing Co. Staff, ed. 2011. (Life in the Ancient World Ser.: No. 1). (ENG., Illus.). 32p. (J). (gr. 5-8). pap. *(978-0-7787-1739-3(9))* Crabtree Publishing Co.

Mini Artist: Set 2. 2015. (Mini Artist Ser.). (ENG.). 24p. (J). (gr. 1-2). pap., pap., pap. 254.40 *(978-1-4777-5681-2(7)*, Windmill Bks.) Rosen Publishing Group, Inc., The.

Minnerly, Denise Bennett. Painting the Town. 2009. (ENG.). 32p. (J). 15.95 *(978-1-56290-616-0(X))* Crystal Productions.

Minond, Edgardo. Drac, Tell Us about Modernism. (SPA.). 80p. *(978-84-96137-13-4(9))* A. Asppan, S.L. Distribuidora Internacional de Libros y Revistas.

Mitchell Lane Publishers Inc. Staff. Art Profiles for Kids, 11 vols., Set. 2010. (J). (gr. 4-8). lib. bdg. 329.45 *(978-1-58415-747-2(X))* Mitchell Lane Pubs., Inc.

Mittler, et al. Introducing Art. 2nd ed. 2004. (Introducing Art (6th Grade) Ser.). (ENG.). 368p. (gr. 6-8). stu. ed. 105.84 *(978-0-07-846499-7(4)*, 0078464994) McGraw-Hill Education.

—Understanding Art. 3rd ed. 2004. (Understanding Art Ser.). (ENG.). 400p. (gr. 6-8). stu. ed. 99.96 *(978-0-07-846529-1(X)*, 007846529X) McGraw-Hill Higher Education.

Moore, Cyd. Diary of a Michigan Kid. 2010. (State Journal Ser.). (ENG.). 128p. (J). (gr. 4-8). pap. 9.95 *(978-1-58536-523-4(8)*, 202211) Sleeping Bear Pr.

Munro, Roxie. Masterpiece Mix. 2017. (ENG., Illus.). 32p. (J). 16.95 ***(978-0-8234-3699-6(3))*** Holiday Hse., Inc.

Murray, Carol. ABC Art Riddles. Levin, Freddie, illus. 2005. (ABC Riddles Ser.). 32p. (J). (gr. -1-3). 13.95 *(978-0-939217-58-8(9))* Peel Productions, Inc.

National Gallery of Australia Staff. Parole Grande per Persone Piccole: Big Words for Little People. 2003. (Illus.). 56p. pap. 12.95 *(978-0-642-54207-6(4))* National Gallery of Australia AUS. Dist: Univ. of Washington Pr.

Nelson, Andy. The Impressionists Coloring Book. Nelson, Andy, illus. 2nd ed. 2004. (Illus.). 96p. (Orig.). (J). (gr. 1-6). pap. 8.95 *(978-0-929636-26-9(0))* Syren Bk. Co.

Nemmers, Lee. Monsters: An Art Activity Book for Creative Kids of All Ages. Zschock, Martha Day, illus. 2013. (Scratch & Sketch Ser.). (ENG.). 64p. (J). (gr. k). spiral bd. 12.99 *(978-1-4413-1154-2(8))* Peter Pauper Pr. Inc.

Nestler, David, illus. The Art of Dave Nestler. 2003. 48p. (YA). (gr. 12-18). pap. *(978-0-86562-065-0(2))* Anabas Marketing, Ltd.

Nicholson, Sue. World Art, 6 vols. (QEB Learn Art Ser.). (Illus.). 32p. (J). 2005. per. 8.95 *(978-1-59566-124-1(7))* 2004. lib. bdg. 18.95 *(978-1-59566-049-7(6))* QEB Publishing Inc.

—World Art: Unique Projects from Cultures Around the Globe. 2006. (Art Smart Ser.). (ENG., Illus.). 32p. (J). (gr. 2-5). pap. 9.95 *(978-1-58728-536-3(3)*, 1253683) Cooper Square Publishing Llc.

Nicholson, Sue & Robins, Deri. The Great Big Art Activity Book. 2008. (Illus.). 240p. (J). *(978-1-84538-618-4(3))* New Burlington Bks.

Noble, Marty. Mexican Folk Art Tattoos. 2008. (Dover Tattoos Ser.). (ENG., Illus.). 2p. (gr. 1). pap. 1.99 *(978-0-486-46760-3(0))* Dover Pubns., Inc.

—Paisley Designs Coloring Book. 2008. (Dover Design Coloring Bks.). (ENG., Illus.). 32p. (gr. 3-8). 3.99 *(978-0-486-45642-3(0))* Dover Pubns., Inc.

Nolan, Mary. Totem Poles & Masks: Art of Northwest Coast Tribes. 2013. (Rosen Readers Ser.). (ENG.). 24p. (J). (gr. 3-4). pap. 8.25 *(978-1-4777-2611-2(X))*; pap. 49.50 *(978-1-4777-2612-9(8))* Rosen Publishing Group, Inc., The. (Rosen Classroom).

O'Brien, Gregory. Welcome to the South Seas: Contemporary New Zealand Art for Young People. 2005. (ENG., Illus.). 96p. 24.95 *(978-1-86940-328-7(2))* Auckland Univ. Pr. NZL. Dist: Independent Pubs. Group.

Ohlig, Rudolf & Hogen, Hildegard. Kunst und Kultur, 6 Bands, Set. (Bibliothek Ser.). (GER., Illus.). *(978-3-7653-6700-7(1))* Brockhaus, F. A., GmbH DEU. Dist: International Bk. Import Service, Inc.

O'Reilly, Wenda. Art Ditto. 2007. 24.95 *(978-1-889613-56-7(8))* Birdcage Pr.

—Go Fish for Art. 2004. 238.80 *(978-1-889613-53-6(3))* Birdcage Pr.

Parsonage, Betty. Butterfly Wings. 2003. (Illus.). 50p. 12.95 *(978-1-59094-013-6(X)*, 159094013X) Jawbone Publishing Corp.

Pease, Pamela. Design Dossier. 2009. (Design Dossiers Ser.). (ENG., Illus.). 78p. (J). (gr. 4). 24.00 *(978-0-9777905-0-0(9))* Paintbox Pr.

Pereira, Diego Jourdan. Thumbs up! Thumbbuddies Tattoos. 2015. (ENG., Illus.). 2p. (J). (gr. 1-4). pap. 1.99 *(978-0-486-80236-7(1))* Dover Pubns., Inc.

—Thumbs up! Thumbwrestler Tattoos. 2015. (ENG., Illus.). 2p. (J). (gr. 1-4). pap. 1.99 *(978-0-486-80235-0(3))* Dover Pubns., Inc.

Phaidon Press Editors & Renshaw, Amanda. The Art Book for Children. Ace, Jane & Kloet, Chris, eds. 2006. (SPA.). (gr. 8-17). 19.95 *(978-0-7148-9863-6(5))* Phaidon Pr., Inc.

Pirnot, Dr Karen Hutchins & Pirnot, Karen Hutchins. The Colors of Myself. Klanot, Sameon Clay, illus. 2010. 20p. pap. 12.95 *(978-1-936051-96-0(6))* Peppertree Pr., The.

Pitamic, Maja & Laidlaw, Jill. Modern Art Adventures: 36 Creative, Hands-On Projects Inspired by Artists from Monet to Banksy. 2015. (Art Adventures Ser.). (ENG., Illus.). 160p. (J). (gr. 1). pap. 19.95 *(978-1-61373-177-2(9))* Chicago Review Pr., Inc.

Pleasant, Jalal & Pleasant, David. Pleasant Signs. 2011. (ENG., Illus.). 21p. (YA). 45.00 *(978-1-61061-045-2(8))* ePub Bud.

Publications International Ltd. Staff, ed. Baby Faces 6 Book Pack. 2011. (J). bds. 5.98 *(978-1-4508-1888-9(9))* Publications International, Ltd.

QEB Learn Art National Book Stores Edition: Special Effects. 2006. (J). per. *(978-1-59566-282-8(0))* QEB Publishing Inc.

QEB Learn Art National Book Stores Edition: World Art. 2006. (J). per. *(978-1-59566-284-2(7))* QEB Publishing Inc.

Raczka, Bob. Action Figures: Paintings of Fun, Daring, & Adventure. 2009. (Bob Raczka's Art Adventures Ser.). (ENG.). 32p. (gr. -1-3). 25.26 *(978-0-7613-4140-6(4)*, Millbrook Pr.) Lerner Publishing Group.

—Art Classroom Library. 2008. pap. 106.95 *(978-1-58013-929-8(9))* Lerner Publishing Group.

—Name That Style: All about Isms in Art. 2008. (Bob Raczka's Art Adventures Ser.). (ENG., Illus.). 32p. (gr. 3-12). 25.26 *(978-0-8225-7586-3(8)*, Millbrook Pr.) Lerner Publishing Group.

Raimondo, Joyce. Make It Pop! Activities & Adventures in Pop Art. 2006. (Art Explorers Ser.). (ENG., Illus.). 48p. (J). (gr. k-4). 13.99 *(978-0-8230-2507-7(1)*, Watson-Guptill) Potter/TenSpeed/Harmony.

Renshaw, Amanda & Phaidon Press Editors. The Art Book for Children, Bk. 2. rev. ed. 2007. (ENG., Illus.). 80p. (gr. 8-17). 19.95 *(978-0-7148-4706-1(2))* Phaidon Pr., Inc.

Revenson, Jody. J. K. Rowling's Wizarding World: the Dark Arts: a Movie Scrapbook. 2017. (J. K. Rowling's Wizarding World Ser.). (ENG.). 48p. (J). (gr. 5). 19.99 ***(978-0-7636-9591-0(2))*** Candlewick Pr.

Reynolds, Virginia. Fine Art Scratch & Sketch: A Cool Art Activity Book for Budding Fine Artists of All Ages. 2005. (Activity Journal Ser.). (Illus.). (J). 12.99 *(978-0-88088-596-6(3))* Peter Pauper Pr. Inc.

Rhatigan, Joe. Hey Diddle Diddle. O'Kif, Alejandro, illus. 2017. (Classic Nursery Rhymes Retold Ser.). (ENG.). 32p. (J). (gr. -1-k). 12.95 *(978-1-63322-161-1(X)*, Moondance) Quarto Publishing Group USA.

Riggs, Kate. What Is Cubism? 2016. (Illus.). 24p. (J). *(978-1-60818-624-2(5)*, Creative Education) Creative Co., The.

—What Is Gothic Art? 2016. (Artworld Ser.). 24p. (J). (ENG.). (gr. 2-4). pap. 9.99 *(978-1-62832-223-1(3)*, Creative Paperbacks); (Illus.). *(978-1-60818-625-9(3)*, Creative Education) Creative Co., The.

—What Is Realism? 2016. (Artworld Ser.). (ENG.). 24p. (J). (gr. 2-4). pap. 9.99 *(978-1-62832-226-2(8)*, Creative Paperbacks) Creative Co., The.

—What Is Romanticism? 2016. (Artworld Ser.). (ENG.). 24p. (J). (gr. 2-4). pap. 9.99 *(978-1-62832-227-9(6)*, Creative Paperbacks) Creative Co., The.

Ripley Publishing Staff, contrib. by. Extraordinary Art. 2013. (Illus.). 36p. (J). pap. *(978-1-4222-2795-4(2))* Mason Crest.

—Unbelievable Art. 2013. (Ripley's Believe It or Not! Enter If You Dare Ser.). (Illus.). 36p. (J). (gr. 4-18). pap. 9.95 *(978-1-4222-2800-5(2))* Mason Crest.

Ripley's Believe It or Not Editors. The Remarkable Revealed: Curious Creations. 2009. (Ripley's Remarkable & Unexpected Ser.). 36p. (J). (gr. 3-18). pap. 8.95 *(978-1-4222-2051-1(6))* Mason Crest.

Ripley's Believe It Or Not! Staff. Extraordinary Art. 2013. (Ripley's Believe It or Not! Strikingly True Ser.: 8). 36p. (J). (gr. 4-18). 19.95 *(978-1-4222-2778-7(2))* Mason Crest.

—Seeing Is Believing. 2012. (Ripley's Disbelief & Shock Ser.). 36p. (J). (gr. 3-4). 19.95 *(978-1-4222-2561-5(5))* Mason Crest.

—Unbelievable Art. 2013. (Ripley's Believe It or Not! Enter If You Dare Ser.: 8). 36p. (J). (gr. 4-18). 19.95 *(978-1-4222-2783-1(9))* Mason Crest.

Robins, Deri. Special Effects. 2004. (QEB Learn Art Ser.). (Illus.). 32p. (J). lib. bdg. 27.10 *(978-1-59566-047-3(X))* QEB Publishing Inc.

—Stencils & Prints. 2006. (Art Smart Ser.). (ENG., Illus.). 32p. (J). (gr. 2-5). pap. 9.95 *(978-1-58728-544-8(4))* Cooper Square Publishing Llc.

Robinson, Shannon. Cubism. 2005. (Movements in Art Ser.). (Illus.). 48p. (YA). (gr. 5-9). lib. bdg. 21.95 *(978-1-58341-347-0(2))* Creative Co., The.

—Cubism: Odysseys in Art. 2016. (Odysseys in Art Ser.). (ENG.). 80p. (J). (gr. 7-10). pap. 14.99 *(978-1-62832-132-6(6)*, Creative Paperbacks) Creative Co., The.

Rodgers, Catherine. DIY Nail Art: Easy, Step-By-Step Instructions for 75 Creative Nail Art Designs. 2016. (ENG.). 64p. (J). (gr. 4-7). 9.99 *(978-1-76012-597-4(0))* Hardie Grant Egmont Pty, Ltd. AUS. Dist: Independent Pubs. Group.

—Totally Cool Nails: 50 Fun & Easy Nail Art Designs for Kids. 2014. (ENG., Illus.). 144p. pap. 15.99 *(978-1-4405-7241-8(0))* Adams Media Corp.

Ross, Kathy. Fairy World Crafts. In Den Bosch, Nicole, illus. 2008. (Girl Crafts Ser.). (ENG.). 48p. (gr. 2-5). per. 7.95 *(978-0-8225-9024-8(7)*, First Avenue Editions) Lerner Publishing Group.

Rubin, Susan Goldman & Magritte, Rene. Magritte's Imagination. 2009. (ENG., Illus.). 24p. (J). (gr. -1 — 1). bds. 7.99 *(978-0-8118-6583-8(5))* Chronicle Bks. LLC.

Ruth, Annie. I Can Read. Ruth, Annie, illus. l.t. ed. 2005. (Illus.). 32p. (J). (gr. -1-3). pap. 10.00 *(978-0-9656306-7-2(6))* Ruth, A. Creations.

Saltzberg, Barney. Beautiful Oops! 2010. (ENG., Illus.). 28p. (J). (gr. -1-2). 15.95 *(978-0-7611-5728-1(X)*, 15728) Workman Publishing Co., Inc.

Schwake, Susan. Art Lab for Kids: 52 Creative Adventures in Drawing, Painting, Printmaking, Paper, & Mixed Media - For Budding Artists of All Ages. Schwake, Rainer, photos by. 2012. (Lab Ser.). (ENG., Illus.). 144p. pap. 22.99 *(978-1-59253-765-5(0)*, 1592537650, Quarry Bks.) Quarto Publishing Group USA.

—Susan Schwake's Kids Art: Art Camp. Schwake, Rainer, photos by. 2015. (ENG., Illus.). 144p. (J). pap. 16.95 *(978-0-9912935-6-8(8))* Two Little Birds Bks.

Scratch & Sparkle Spiro Art. 2015. (ENG.). 50p. (J). *(978-1-78393-704-2(1))* Make Believe Ideas.

Seddon, Wayne & Seddon, Leigh. Scribbles: Using your eyes to see with your Mind. 2008. 44p. pap. 20.00 *(978-1-59858-559-9(2))* Dog Ear Publishing, LLC.

Shaffer, Christy. Glow-In-the-Dark Tattoos Snowflakes. 2015. (Dover Little Activity Bks.). (ENG.). 2p. (J). (gr. 1-4). 1.50 *(978-0-486-80358-6(9))* Dover Pubns., Inc.

Shapiro, J. H. Magic Trash. Brantley-Newton, Vanessa, illus. 2015. (ENG.). 32p. (J). (gr. k-3). pap. 7.95 *(978-1-58089-386-2(4))* Charlesbridge Publishing, Inc.

Shyam, Bhajju, illus. The London Jungle Book. 2nd ed. 2014. (ENG.). 48p. 19.95 *(978-81-923171-2-0(9))* Tara Books Agency IND. Dist: Publishers Group West (PGW).

Smith, Lucy. How to Draw Horses. Chapman, Chris et al, illus. rev. ed. 2006. (Kid Kits Ser.). 32p. (J). (gr. 4). pap. 13.99 *(978-1-58086-969-0(6))* EDC Publishing.

Sokol, Dawn DeVries. Kennel Club, 1 vol. 2017. (ENG., Illus.). 22p. (J). bds. 9.99 *(978-1-4236-4702-7(5))* Gibbs Smith, Publisher.

Solotareff, Gregoire. Nieve. 2003. (SPA.). 86p. 21.99 *(978-84-8470-039-5(9))* Corimbo, Editorial S.L. ESP. Dist: Lectorum Pubns., Inc.

Spiro Art. 2015. (ENG.). 80p. (J). pap. *(978-1-78393-834-6(X))* Make Believe Ideas.

Stanley, Mandy. Arty Friends: Early Learning Through Art. 2016. (Arty Mouse Sticker Doodles Ser.). (ENG.). 24p. (J). (gr. -1-2). pap. 6.99 *(978-1-78445-864-5(3))* Top That! Publishing PLC GBR. Dist: Independent Pubs. Group.

—Arty World. 2017. (Arty Mouse Sticker Doodles Ser.). (ENG., Illus.). 24p. (J). (gr. -1-2). pap. 6.99 *(978-1-78445-857-7(0))*

Top That! Publishing PLC GBR. Dist: Independent Pubs. Group.

Stawicki, Matt. How to Draw & Paint Fantasy Combat: A Step-By-Step Guide to Epic Combat Scenes. 2014. (ENG.). 128p. pap. 21.99 *(978-1-4380-0346-7(3))* Barron's Educational Series, Inc.

Stephens, Pamela Geiger. Dropping in on Picasso. McNeill, Jim, illus. 2004. 32p. (J). 15.95 *(978-1-56290-325-1(X))* Crystal Productions.

Sterling Children's, Sterling. Super Scratch Art Pads: Mythical Creatures. 2017. (ENG., Illus.). 30p. (J). (gr. 1). pap. 12.95 ***(978-1-4549-2504-0(3))*** Sterling Publishing Co., Inc.

—Super Scratch Art Pads: Nature. 2017. (ENG., Illus.). 30p. (J). (gr. 1). pap. 12.95 ***(978-1-4549-2506-4(X))*** Sterling Publishing Co., Inc.

Stich, Bill. Let's Make Art! 2012. (InfoMax Readers Ser.). (ENG., Illus.). 16 pp.p. (J). (gr. k-1). pap. 7.00 *(978-1-4488-8926-6(X),* Rosen Classroom) Rosen Publishing Group, Inc., The.

Sun, Ming-Ju & Creative Haven Staff. Creative Haven Art Nouveau Fashions Coloring Book. 2013. (Adult Coloring Ser.). (ENG., Illus.). 64p. (gr. 3). pap. 5.99 *(978-0-486-49211-7(7))* Dover Pubns., Inc.

Sutherland, Adam. Street Art. 2012. (On the Radar: Street Style Ser.). (ENG.). 32p. (gr. 4-8). lib. bdg. 26.60 *(978-0-7613-7768-9(9),* Lerner Pubns.) Lerner Publishing Group.

Syrewicz, Connor. The Arts: Dance, Music, Theater, & Fine Art. 2013. (Earning $50,000 - $100,000 with a High School Diploma or Less Ser.: 14). 64p. (J). (gr. 7-18). 22.95 *(978-1-4222-2888-3(6))* Mason Crest.

Tauber, Sabine. Hieronymus Bosch: Sticker Book. 2015. (ENG.). 16p. (J). (gr. 1-4). pap. 9.95 *(978-3-7913-7241-9(6))* Prestel Verlag GmbH & Co KG. DEU. Dist: Penguin Random Hse. LLC.

Teckentrup, Britta. Find the Line. 2016. (Find the Shape Ser.). (ENG., Illus.). 24p. (J). (— 1). bds. 6.95 *(978-1-4549-1760-1(1))* Sterling Publishing Co., Inc.

The Mailbox Books Staff. Totally for Twos: Art Age 2. 2010. (Illus.). 128p. (J). 18.95 *(978-1-56234-934-9(1),* Mailbox Bks., The) Education Ctr., Inc.

Thomas, Isabel. Cool Cat Projects. 2015. (Pet Projects Ser.). (ENG., Illus.). 32p. (gr. 3-5). 27.99 *(978-1-4109-8064-9(2),* Snap Bks.) Capstone Press of Coughlan Cos.

Thomas Nelson. Art Book Neon Art. 2017. (ENG.). (J). (gr. 1-7). pap. ***(978-1-78598-962-9(6))*** Make Believe Ideas.

—Art Books Best Friends Art. 2016. (ENG.). 80p. (J). (gr. 1-5). spiral bd. *(978-1-78598-351-1(2))* Make Believe Ideas.

—Emily's Room: Monogram Art. 2015. (ENG.). (J). *(978-1-78393-885-8(4))* Make Believe Ideas.

—Emily's Room: Silhouette Art. 2015. (ENG.). (J). *(978-1-78393-881-0(1))* Make Believe Ideas.

Thomsen, Ruth. Ghastly & Gruesome. 2004. (Illus.). (J). lib. bdg. 16.95 *(978-1-931983-70-9(4))* Chrysalis Education.

—Myths & Legends. 2004. (Illus.). lib. bdg. 16.95 *(978-1-931983-68-6(2))* Chrysalis Education.

Thomson, Ruth. The Art Creativity Book. 2012. (Creativity Bks.). (ENG.). 80p. (J). (gr. 1-6). pap. 12.99 *(978-1-4380-0126-5(6))* Barron's Educational Series, Inc.

—Celebrations. 2005. (First Look at Art Ser.). (Illus.). 32p. (gr. 4-6). 23.00 *(978-0-7910-8315-4(2),* Chelsea Hse.) Facts On File, Inc.

—Creatures. 2003. (First Look at Art Ser.). (Illus.). 32p. (gr. 4-6). 23.00 *(978-0-7910-7945-4(7),* Chelsea Hse.) Facts On File, Inc.

—Families: Relationships in Art. 2005. (Artventures Ser.). (Illus.). 32p. (YA). (gr. 3-6). lib. bdg. 27.10 *(978-1-58340-627-4(1))* Black Rabbit Bks.

—A First Look At. 2005. (First Look at Art Ser.). 32p. (gr. 4-6). 184.00 *(978-0-7910-8461-8(2),* Chelsea Hse.) Facts On File, Inc.

—Journeys. 2005. (First Look at Art Ser.). (Illus.). 32p. (gr. 4-6). 23.00 *(978-0-7910-8317-8(9),* Chelsea Hse.) Facts On File, Inc.

—Weather. 2005. (First Look at Art Ser.). (Illus.). 32p. (gr. 4-6). 23.00 *(978-0-7910-8318-5(7),* Chelsea Hse.) Facts On File, Inc.

TickTock Books Ltd. The Cold Book. 2012. 48p. 9.95 *(978-1-84898-360-1(3),* TickTock Books) Octopus Publishing Group GBR. Dist: Independent Pubs. Group.

Tidey, John & Tidey, Jackie. Arts & Culture. 2008. (China Ser.). 32p. (gr. 4-18). lib. bdg. 18.56 *(978-0-7614-3154-1(3),* Benchmark Bks.) Marshall Cavendish Corp.

Top That Publishing Staff, ed. Celtic Double Cross. 2004. (Wicked Tattoos Ser.). (Illus.). 16p. (J). pap. *(978-1-84510-113-8(8))* Top That! Publishing PLC.

Triggs, Teal. The School of Art. Frost, Daniel, illus. 2015. (School Of Ser.). (ENG.). 96p. (J). (gr. 2-5). 19.99 *(978-1-84780-700-7(3),* Wide Eyed Editions) Quarto Publishing Group UK GBR. Dist: Hachette Bk. Group.

Tullet, Hervé. The Big Book of Art. 2013. (ENG., Illus.). 86p. 27.95 *(978-0-7148-6349-8(1))* Phaidon Pr., Inc.

—Doodle Cook. Barbour, Susan, tr. from FRE. 2011. (ENG., Illus.). 48p. pap. 14.95 *(978-0-7148-6070-1(0))* Phaidon Pr., Inc.

—The Game of Mix-Up Art. 2011. (ENG.). 14p. (gr. -1 — 1). 12.95 *(978-0-7148-6188-3(X))* Phaidon Pr., Inc.

Two-Can Publishing Ltd, creator. Hearts & Stars. 2007. (Art-Baby Ser.). (ENG., Illus.). 10p. (J). (gr. -1 — 1). bds. 5.95 *(978-1-58728-595-0(9))* Cooper Square Publishing Llc.

—Spots & Dots. 2007. (Art-Baby.Ser.). (ENG., Illus.). 10p. (J). (gr. -1 — 1). bds. 6.95 *(978-1-58728-594-3(0))* Cooper Square Publishing Llc.

Ultimate Comic Art. 2017. (Ultimate Comic Art Ser.). 32p. (gr. 7-8). 165.00 ***(978-1-4994-3404-0(9))***; pap. 70.50 ***(978-1-5081-5588-1(7))*** Rosen Publishing Group, Inc., The. (PowerKids Pr.).

Uschan, Michael V. Graffiti. 2010. (Eye on Art Ser.). (ENG.). 128p. 34.80 *(978-1-4205-0324-1(3),* Lucent Bks.) Cengage Gale.

Wall, Matthew. So You Want to Learn: Juggling. Wall, Matthew, illus. 2017. (Illus.). 30p. (J). pap. 11.99 ***(978-1-941429-57-0(2))*** Handersen Publishing.

—So You Want to Learn: Juggling. 2017. (Illus.). 30p. (J). 17.99 ***(978-1-941429-59-4(9))*** Handersen Publishing.

Walter Foster Creative Team Staff, et al. The Big Book of Art - Draw! Paint! Create! An Adventurous Journey into the Wild & Wonderful World of Art! 2015. (Big Book Ser.). (ENG.). 128p. (J). (gr. k-3). pap. 14.95 *(978-1-60058-434-3(9))* Quarto Publishing Group USA.

Watt, Fiona. Art Projects. Miller, Antonia et al, illus. Allman, Howard, photos by. 2005. 96p. (J). (gr. 5-9). 7.99 *(978-0-7945-1111-1(2),* Usborne) EDC Publishing.

—Art Projects. 2004. (Art Ideas Ser.). 96p. (J). lib. bdg. 26.95 *(978-1-58086-638-5(7),* Usborne) EDC Publishing.

—Art Projects. Miller, Antonia & Figg, Non, illus. Allman, Howard, photos by. 2003. (Art Ideas Ser.). (ENG.). 96p. (J). (gr. 5-9). 18.95 *(978-0-7945-0657-5(7),* Usborne) EDC Publishing.

—Mini Art Ideas. Barlow, Amanda, illus. 2004. 96p. (J). 7.95 *(978-0-7945-0842-5(1),* Usborne) EDC Publishing.

Wenzel, Angela. 13 Paintings Children Should Know. 2009. (ENG., Illus.). 48p. (J). (gr. 3-7). 14.95 *(978-3-7913-4323-5(8))* Prestel Verlag GmbH & Co KG. DEU. Dist: Penguin Random Hse. LLC.

Whitely, Heather. Line. 2006. (Children's Art Ser. from the National Gallery of Victoria Ser.). (ENG., Illus.). 28p. (J). (gr. -1-3). pap. 9.95 *(978-0-7241-0238-9(8))* National Gallery of Victoria AUS. Dist: National Bk. Network.

Wickham, Geoffrey. Rapid Perspective. (YA). (gr. 10-18). 9.95 *(978-0-85458-050-7(6))*; pap. 7.95 *(978-0-85458-051-4(4))* Transatlantic Arts, Inc.

Wilkinson, Philip. Chinese Myth: A Treasury of Legends, Art, & History. 2007. (Myth Ser.). (Illus.). 96p. (J). (gr. 4-7). pap. 7.99 *(978-0-7858-2348-3(4),* Chartwell) Book Sales, Inc.

—Chinese Myth: A Treasury of Legends, Art, & History. 2007. (ENG., Illus.). 96p. (C). (gr. 6-18). lib. bdg. 158.00 *(978-0-7656-8103-4(X),* Y181705) Routledge.

Wistow, David, et al. Meet the Group of Seven. 2005. (Snapshots: Images of People & Places in History Ser.). (ENG., Illus.). 48p. (J). (gr. 3-7). 9.95 *(978-1-55074-694-5(4))* Kids Can Pr., Ltd. CAN. Dist: Hachette Bk. Group.

Wood, Alix. Body Art. 2015. (But Is It Art? Ser.). (ENG.). 32p. (J). (gr. 4-5). lib. bdg. 26.60 *(978-1-4824-2277-1(8))* Stevens, Gareth Publishing LLLP.

—Cubist Art. 2016. (Create It! Ser.). 32p. (gr. 5-4). pap. 10.50 *(978-1-4824-5039-2(9))* Stevens, Gareth Publishing LLLP.

—Impressionist Art. 2016. (Create It! Ser.). 32p. (gr. 5-4). pap. 10.50 *(978-1-4824-5028-6(3))* Stevens, Gareth Publishing LLLP.

—Pop Art. 2016. (Create It! Ser.). 32p. (gr. 5-4). lib. bdg. 26.60 *(978-1-4824-5026-2(7))* Stevens, Gareth Publishing LLLP.

—Surrealist Art. 2016. (Create It! Ser.). 32p. (gr. 5-4). pap. 10.50 *(978-1-4824-5021-7(6))* Stevens, Gareth Publishing LLLP.

World Art, 6 bks. 2005. (QEB Learn Art Ser.). (Illus.). 32p. (J). per. 8.95 *(978-1-59566-128-9(X))* QEB Publishing Inc.

World Book, Inc Staff, contrib. by. The Arts. 2009. (J). *(978-0-7166-0383-2(7))* World Bk., Inc.

—Fun with Painting & Sculpture. 2011. (J). *(978-0-7166-0226-2(1))* World Bk., Inc.

Xie, Feng, ed. Works by Young Artists. Xie, Feng, . 2010. (Illus.). 150p. (YA). 47.00 *(978-0-9778403-1-1(X))* East West Hse.

Yale, Dallas. Searching for Shapes in Art: Reason with Shapes & Their Attributes, 1 vol. 2015. (InfoMax Common Core Math Readers Ser.). (ENG.). 24p. (J). pap. 8.25 *(978-1-4777-4579-3(3),* Rosen Classroom) Rosen Publishing Group, Inc., The.

Yamamoto, Satoshi. Pokémon Adventures 20th Anniversary Illustration Book: The Art of Pokémon Adventures. 2017. (Pokemon Ser.: 1). (ENG., Illus.). 168p. pap. 24.99 ***(978-1-4215-9451-4(X))*** Viz Media.

Yenawine, Philip. Places. 2006. (Illus.). 22p. (J). (gr. 4-8). reprint ed. 15.00 *(978-1-4223-5407-0(5))* DIANE Publishing Co.

Yoon, Salina, illus. At the Beach Mad Art. 2009. (Mad Art Ser.). (ENG.). 12p. (J). (gr. -1-k). 6.99 *(978-0-8431-3527-5(1),* Price Stern Sloan) Penguin Young Readers Group.

Zagon, Laurie. Art for Healing: A Beginner's Workshop, 1. 2003. 34p. (J). spiral bd. *(978-0-9748462-0-0(1))* Art & Creativity For Healing, Inc.

Zschock, Martha Day. Super Sand Art. 2006. (Activity Book Ser.). (Illus.). 56p. (J). (gr. 1). 12.99 *(978-1-59359-934-8(X))* Peter Pauper Pr. Inc.

ART, ABSTRACT

Bocchino, Serena. What Am I? the Story of an Abstract Painting. Bocchino, Serena, illus. l.t. ed. 2005. (Illus.). 32p. (J). per. 19.95 *(978-0-9767674-0-4(6))* Serena Bocchino/In His Perfect Time Collection.

Hamernik, Cathy. What Do You See? 2008. 24p. pap. 16.50 *(978-1-60693-388-6(4),* Strategic Bk. Publishing) Strategic Book Publishing & Rights Agency (SBPRA).

Johnson, Stephen T. A Is for Art: An Abstract Alphabet. Johnson, Stephen T., illus. 2008. (ENG., Illus.). 40p. (J). (gr. k-4). 18.99 *(978-0-689-86301-1(2),* Simon & Schuster/Paula Wiseman Bks.) Simon & Schuster/Paula Wiseman Bks.

Lacey, Saskia. Art & Culture: Abstract Art: Lines, Rays, & Angles (Grade 4) 2017. (Mathematics Readers Ser.). (Illus.). 32p. (J). (gr. 4-4). pap. 8.99 ***(978-1-4258-5563-5(6))*** Teacher Created Materials, Inc.

Wood, Alix. Abstract Art. 2016. (Create It! Ser.). 32p. (gr. 5-4). pap. 10.50 *(978-1-4824-5043-9(7))* Stevens, Gareth Publishing LLLP.

ART, AFRICAN AMERICAN

see African American Art

ART, AMERICAN

Fallon, Michael. How to Analyze the Works of Georgia O'Keeffe, 1 vol. 2010. (Essential Critiques Set 1 Ser.). (ENG.). 112p. (J). (gr. 6-12). lib. bdg. 35.64 *(978-1-61613-535-5(2),* Essential Library) ABDO Publishing Co.

Finger, Bradley. 13 American Artists Children Should Know. 2010. (ENG., Illus.). 48p. (J). (gr. 3-7). 14.95 *(978-3-7913-7036-1(7))* Prestel Verlag GmbH & Co KG. DEU. Dist: Penguin Random Hse. LLC.

Fitzpatrick, Anne. Late Modernism. 2005. (Movements in Art Ser.). (Illus.). 48p. (YA). (gr. 5-9). lib. bdg. 21.95 *(978-1-58341-348-7(0))* Creative Co., The.

—Late Modernism: Movements in Art. 2015. (Illus.). 80p. (J). *(978-1-60818-534-4(6),* Creative Education) Creative Co., The.

Geis Conti, Patricia. Andy Warhol. 2010. (¡Mira Qué Artista! Ser.). (SPA.). 18p. (J). (gr. 2-4). 21.95 *(978-84-9825-485-3(X))* Combel Editorial, S.A. ESP. Dist: Independent Pubs. Group.

Harris, Lois. Charlie Russell: Tale-Telling Cowboy Artist, 1 vol. 2010. (ENG., Illus.). 32p. (J). (gr. k-3). 16.99 *(978-1-58980-758-7(8))* Pelican Publishing Co., Inc.

Haskins, James. The Harlem Renaissance. 2004. (J). pap. 10.95 *(978-0-940975-95-8(5),* Sankofa Bks.) Just Us Bks., Inc.

Kissock, Heather & McGill, Jordan. Tigua. 2010. (American Indian Art & Culture Ser.). 24p. (J). (gr. 3-6). lib. bdg. 25.70 *(978-1-60596-982-4(6))* Weigl Pubs., Inc.

—Tigua: American Indian Art & Culture. 2010. pap. 9.95 *(978-1-60596-983-1(4))* Weigl Pubs., Inc.

Kügler, Tina & Kügler, Carson. In Mary's Garden. Kügler, Tina & Kügler, Carson, illus. 2015. (ENG., Illus.). 32p. (J). (gr. 1-4). 17.99 *(978-0-544-27220-0(X),* HMH Books For Young Readers) Houghton Mifflin Harcourt Publishing Co.

Mason, Antony. El Arte Contemporaneo: En los Tiempos de Warhol. 2005. (Arte Alrededor del Mundo Ser.). (Illus.). 48p. pap. 9.95 *(978-85-7416-241-6(8))* Callis Editora Ltda BRA. Dist: Independent Pubs. Group.

McLean, Linda. Heidelberg Project: A Street of Dreams. 2007. (ENG.). 32p. pap. 13.95 *(978-1-933916-06-4(0))* Nelson Publishing & Marketing.

Merrill, Yvonne Y. America Vol. 2: Art Activities about Colonial America, African-Americans, & Southeast Indians. 2006. (Hands-on Ser.). (ENG., Illus.). 71p. (J). (gr. k-9). pap. 20.00 *(978-0-9778797-0-0(4))* KK.

O'Reilly, Wenda. American Art Ditto. 2006. 24.95 *(978-1-889613-84-0(3))* Birdcage Pr.

Osofsky, Randy & Charlesbridge Publishing Staff. Art in Early America. 2003. (Come Look with Me Ser.). (ENG.). 32p. (J). (gr. k-3). 16.95 *(978-1-890674-12-0(5))* Charlesbridge Publishing, Inc.

Pearlman, Debra. Where Is Jasper Johns? 2006. (Adventures in Art (Prestel) Ser.). (Illus.). 30p. (J). 14.95 *(978-3-7913-3711-1(4))* Prestel Publishing.

Prestel Publishing. Roy Lichtenstein: Coloring Book. 2013. (ENG., Illus.). 32p. (J). (gr. 1-4). pap. 8.95 *(978-3-7913-7146-7(0))* Prestel Verlag GmbH & Co KG. DEU. Dist: Penguin Random Hse. LLC.

Puck & Pohlen, Jerome. Doodle Texas: Create Imagine Draw Your Way Through the Lone Star State. Lemay, Violet, illus. 2013. (ENG.). 120p. (J). (gr. k-5). pap. 12.95 *(978-1-938093-05-0(4))* Duo Pr. LLC.

Raczka, Bob. The Art of Freedom: How Artists See America. 2008. (Bob Raczka's Art Adventures Ser.). (ENG., Illus.). 32p. (gr. -1-2). lib. bdg. 25.26 *(978-0-8225-7508-5(6),* Millbrook Pr.) Lerner Publishing Group.

—The Art of Freedom: How Artists See America. 2010. (Rise & Shine Ser.). (ENG., Illus.). 32p. (C). (gr. -1-2). pap. 16.95 *(978-1-58013-881-9(0))* National Geographic School Publishing, Inc.

Roche, Judith, ed. The Bottom of Heaven: Artwork & Poetry of the Remann Hall Women's Project. 2003. (J). per. 19.95 *(978-0-9726649-0-5(4))* Museum of Glass.

Thomas, Dina M. & Thomas, Andy, eds. The Artful Journey: The Artwork of Andy Thomas. Thomas, Tria M., photos by. l.t. ed. 2003. (Illus.). 122p. 50.00 *(978-0-9742285-0-1(8))* Maze Creek Studio.

ART—ANALYSIS, INTERPRETATION, APPRECIATION

see Art—Study and Teaching; Art Appreciation

ART, ANCIENT

see also Art, Primitive; Classical Antiquities

Hodge, Susie. Prehistoric Art. 2003. (Art in History Ser.). (Illus.). 32p. (J). (gr. 5-7). per. 6.95 *(978-1-4034-4021-1(2))* Heinemann-Raintree.

Kaplan, Leslie C. Art & Religion in Ancient Egypt. 2004. (Primary Sources of Ancient Civilizations Ser.). (ENG.). 24p. (gr. 4-8). pap. 8.25 *(978-0-8239-8932-4(1),* PowerKids Pr.) Rosen Publishing Group, Inc., The.

ART, APPLIED

see Art Industries and Trade

ART, ARAB

see Islamic Art

ART, ASIAN

Burnham, Brad. Caves of the Thousand Buddhas: Treasure House of Chinese Art. 2009. (Famous Caves of the World Ser.). 24p. (gr. 3-4). 42.50 *(978-1-61512-496-1(9),* PowerKids Pr.) Rosen Publishing Group, Inc., The.

DiCicco, Sue. Adventures in Asian Art: Discovering Art Treasure, Celebrating Cultures. 2nd ed. 2017. (ENG., Illus.). 48p. (J). (gr. k-3). 15.95 *(978-0-8048-4730-8(4))* Tuttle Publishing.

Kerrigan, Michael, et al. Exploring the Life, Myth, & Art of the Ancient near East. 2016. (Civilizations of the World Ser.). (ENG.). 144p. (J). (gr. 8-8). lib. bdg. 45.10 *(978-1-4994-6397-2(9))* Rosen Publishing Group, Inc., The.

Lane, Kimberly & Charlesbridge Publishing Staff. Asian Art. 2008. (Come Look with Me Ser.). (ENG., Illus.). 32p. (J). (gr. k-3). 15.95 *(978-1-890674-19-9(2))* Charlesbridge Publishing, Inc.

Mis, Melody S. How to Draw China's Sights & Symbols. 2004. (Kid's Guide to Drawing the Countries of the World Ser.). (Illus.). 48p. (J). lib. bdg. 29.25 *(978-0-8239-6664-6(X),* PowerKids Pr.) Rosen Publishing Group, Inc., The.

Ram-Prasad, Chakravarthi. Exploring the Life, Myth, & Art of India. 2009. (Civilizations of the World Ser.). (YA). (gr. 7-12). lib. bdg. 42.60 *(978-1-4358-5615-8(5))* Rosen Publishing Group, Inc., The.

ART, CHRISTIAN

see Christian Art and Symbolism

ART, CLASSICAL

see Art, Greek; Art, Roman

ART, COMMERCIAL

see Commercial Art

ART—COMPOSITION

see Composition (Art)

ART—CRITICISM

see Art Criticism

ART, DECORATIVE

Here are entered general works on the decoration and use of artistic objects. Works limited to the external ornamentation of objects are entered under Design, Decorative.

see also Calligraphy; Decoration and Ornament; Design, Decorative; Enamel and Enameling; Furniture; Illustration of Books; Mosaics; Needlework; Pottery

Chapman, D. Artist Cards: Level 3. 2003. (Adventures in Art Ser.). (Illus.). (gr. 3-18). pap. 22.95 *(978-0-87192-371-4(8))* Davis Pubns., Inc.

—Artist Cards: Level 4. 2003. (Adventures in Art Ser.). (Illus.). (gr. 4-18). pap. 22.95 *(978-0-87192-372-1(6))* Davis Pubns., Inc.

Harow, Penny. Festival of Lights: A Delightful Collection of Handmade Chanukiot. 2008. (ENG., Illus.). 160p. (J). *(978-965-524-009-2(6))* Urim Pubns.

Hutchinson, Alberta & Creative Haven Staff. Square Mandalas. 2012. (Adult Coloring Ser.). (ENG., Illus.). 64p. (J). (gr. 3). pap. 5.99 *(978-0-486-49094-6(7))* Dover Pubns., Inc.

Kiser, Penny & Bell, Margie, eds. Paris Moderne: Art Deco Works from the Musee d'Art Moderne de la Ville de Paris. 2004. 170p. 34.95 *(978-0-9662859-4-9(8))* International Arts & Artists.

Kuskowski, Alex. Super Simple Mexican Art: Fun & Easy Art from Around the World, 1 vol. 2012. (ENG.). 32p. 27.07 *(978-1-61783-213-0(8),* Super SandCastle) ABDO Publishing Co.

Modern Publishing Staff. When I Grow Up: Giant Wall Art Flash Cards. 2007. (Illus.). (J). (gr. -1-k). bds. 12.99 *(978-0-7666-2700-0(4))* Modern Publishing.

Noble, Marty, et al. Mosaic Masterpieces. 2012. (Adult Coloring Ser.). (ENG., Illus.). 64p. (gr. 3). pap. 5.99 *(978-0-486-49748-8(8))* Dover Pubns., Inc.

Rau, Dana Meachen. Carving Pumpkins. 2012. (How-To Library). (ENG.). 32p. (gr. 3-6). 28.50 *(978-1-61080-470-7(8),* 202080); pap. 14.21 *(978-1-61080-644-2(1),* 202254) Cherry Lake Publishing.

ART, ECCLESIASTICAL

see Christian Art and Symbolism

ART—EDUCATION

see Art—Study and Teaching

ART—FICTION

Anholt, Laurence. Degas y la Pequena Bailarina: Un Cuento Sobre Edgar Degas. 2003.Tr. of Degas & the Little Dancer. (SPA., Illus.). 29p. (J). (gr. 2-4). 18.99 *(978-84-88061-36-2(6))* Serres, Ediciones, S. L. ESP. Dist: Lectorum Pubns., Inc.

Avignone, June. A Peek into the Secret Little Ones of Turtle Back Island. My Wolf Dog, illus. 2004. 40p. (J). pap. *(978-0-9654628-2-2(X))* Mill Street Forward, The.

Bardhan-Quallen, Sudipta. Purrmaids #2: the Catfish Club. 2017. (Purrmaids Ser.: 2). (ENG.). 96p. (J). (gr. 1-4). lib. bdg. 12.99 ***(978-1-5247-0165-9(3))***; (Illus.). 4.99 ***(978-1-5247-0164-2(5))*** Random Hse. Children's Bks. (Random Hse. Bks. for Young Readers).

Barnes, Hannah. Rainbow Colored Skin a Father-Son Tattoo Tale. 2013. 28p. pap. 12.99 *(978-1-300-77380-1(4))* Lulu Pr., Inc.

Barrowman, John & Barrowman, Carole E. Book of Beasts. 2016. (Hollow Earth Ser.). (ENG.). 336p. (J). (gr. 3-7). pap. 7.99 *(978-1-4814-4231-2(7),* Simon & Schuster/Paula Wiseman Bks.) Simon & Schuster/Paula Wiseman Bks.

Bersson, Robert & Shoup, Dolores. Stripes & Stars. Bersson, Robert & Trobaugh, Scott, illus. l.t. ed. 2003. 40p. (J). (gr. 1-4). per. 16.95 *(978-0-9740585-0-4(5))* Legacy Group Productions, LLC.

Bober, Suzanne & Merberg, Julie. Mama, Baby, & Other First Words. 2010. (ENG.). 22p. (J). bds. 6.99 *(978-1-935703-03-7(X))* Downtown Bookworks.

Boyce, Frank Cottrell. Framed. 2006. 306p. (J). (gr. 3-7). lib. bdg. 17.89 *(978-0-06-073403-9(5))* HarperCollins Pubs.

—Framed, 1. Lenton, Steven, illus. 2nd ed. 2008. (ENG.). 336p. 17.95 *(978-0-330-45292-2(4),* Macmillan) Pan Macmillan GBR. Dist: Trans-Atlantic Pubns., Inc.

Brennan-Nelson, Denise & Brennan, Rosemarie. Willow. Moore, Cyd, illus. 2008. (ENG.). 32p. (J). (gr. k-6). 16.95 *(978-1-58536-342-1(1))* Sleeping Bear Pr.

Brezenoff, Steve. The Case of the Counterfeit Painting. Weber, Lisa K., illus. 2016. (Museum Mysteries Ser.). (ENG.). 128p. (gr. 2-3). pap. 6.95 *(978-1-4965-2522-2(1))*; lib. bdg. 26.65 *(978-1-4965-2518-5(3))* Stone Arch Bks. (Museum Mysteries).

Brown, Monica & Dominguez, Adriana. Maya's Blanket, 1 vol. Diaz, David, illus. 2015. (SPA & ENG.). 32p. (J). 17.95 *(978-0-89239-292-6(4))* Lee & Low Bks., Inc.

Brown, Tiffany M. Gallery Eleven Twenty-Two. Sefcik, Wendy, illus. 2013. 30p. 17.99 *(978-0-9854423-0-9(1))*; pap. 9.99 *(978-0-9854423-1-6(X))* Brewster Moon.

Browne, Anthony & Bartholin, Hanne. Frida & Bear Play the Shape Game! 2016. (ENG.). 32p. (J). (gr. -1-2). 15.99 *(978-0-7636-7837-1(6))* Candlewick Pr.

Bruna, Dick. Miffy the Artist. (ENG., Illus.). (J). (gr. -1-k). 2016. 12p. bds. 14.50 *(978-1-84976-395-0(X))* 2009. 32p. 11.95 *(978-1-85437-823-1(6))* Tate Publishing, Ltd. GBR. Dist: Abrams, Inc.

Bursztynski, Susan. The Sea's Secret. Power, Margaret, illus. 2004. iv, 36p. (J). pap. *(978-0-7608-6737-2(2))* Sundance/Newbridge Educational Publishing.

Butcher, Kristin. El Plan de Zee, 1 vol. 2008. (Spanish Soundings Ser.).Tr. of Zee's Way. (SPA.). 112p. (YA). (gr. 8-12). pap. 9.95 *(978-1-55469-057-2(9))* Orca Bk. Pubs. USA.

Calandrelli, Emily. Ada Lace Sees Red. Kurilla, Renée, illus. 2017. (Ada Lace Adventure Ser.: 2). (ENG.). 144p. (J). (gr. 1-5). 16.99 ***(978-1-4814-8602-6(0))***; pap. 6.99 ***(978-1-4814-8601-9(2))*** Simon & Schuster Bks. For Young Readers. (Simon & Schuster Bks. For Young Readers).

Camossa, Silvia. Elecciones Que Brillan. Moreno, Camila, illus. 2004. 64p. pap. 8.95 *(978-85-7416-193-8(4))* Callis Editora Ltda BRA. Dist: Independent Pubs. Group.

Childs, Tera Lynn. Ten Things Sloane Hates about Tru. 2015. (ENG., Illus.). 240p. (J). pap. 14.99 *(978-1-943892-44-0(X))* Entangled Publishing, LLC.

Colman, Michelle Sinclair. Artsy Babies Wear Paint. Dion, Nathalie, illus. 2011. (Urban Babies Wear Black Book Ser.).

A
B

(ENG.). 20p. (J). (gr. k — 1). bds. 6.99 (978-1-58246-371-1(9), Tricycle Pr.) Random Hse. Children's Bks.

Corlett, Mary Lee. Belle: The Amazing, Astonishingly Magical Journey of an Artfully Painted Lady. Saroff, Phyllis, illus. 12th ed. 2011. (ENG.). 52p. (J). (gr. 3-4). pap. 25.00 (978-1-59373-084-0(5)) Bunker Hill Publishing, Inc.

—Belle's Wild Ride: The Artful Adventure of a Butterfly & a Cabbie. Cayless, Sophie, illus. 2015. (ENG.). 32p. (J). (gr. 3-7). 17.95 (978-1-907804-51-9(X)) Giles, D. Ltd. GBR. Dist: Consortium Bk. Sales & Distribution.

Crompton, Laurie Boyle. Love & Vandalism. 2017. (ENG.). 336p. (YA). (gr. 8-12). pap. 10.99 (978-1-4926-3605-2(3), 9781492636052) Sourcebooks, Inc.

Culbertson, Jan E. The Legend of the Lost Tiki. 2006. 95p. (YA). pap. 13.95 (978-1-58909-315-7(1)) Bookstand Publishing.

Dallas, Sandra. The Quilt Walk. 2013. (ENG.). 216p. (J). (gr. 4-7). pap. 9.95 (978-1-58536-799-3(0), 202373) Sleeping Bear Pr.

Daly, Cathleen. Emily's Blue Period. Brown, Lisa, illus. 2014. (ENG.). 56p. (J). (gr. -1-2). 17.99 (978-1-59643-469-1(4), 9781596434691) Roaring Brook Pr.

DiMartino, Michael Dante. Rebel Genius. 2016. (Rebel Geniuses Ser.). (ENG., Illus.). 384p. (J). 16.99 (978-1-62672-336-8(2), 9781626723368) Roaring Brook Pr.

Disney Publishing Staff. An Arts & Crafts Day, 15 vols. 2003. (It's Fun to Learn Ser.). (Illus.). 32p. (J). (gr. -1-3). 3.99 (978-1-57973-130-4(9)) Advance Pubs. LLC.

Dream Catchers - Evaluation Guide: Evaluation Guide. 2006. (J). (978-1-55942-403-5(6)) Witcher Productions.

Dubois, Marie. The Village Children, an Introduction to the Art of Painting Children & Their Stories. 2009. (FRE & ENG., Illus.). 120p. pap. 36.99 (978-1-4343-7847-7(0)) AuthorHouse.

Ehlert, Lois. Hands: Growing up to Be an Artist. 2004. (ENG., Illus.). 48p. (J). (gr. -1-3). 16.99 (978-0-15-205107-5(4)) Houghton Mifflin Harcourt Publishing Co.

Elmore, Wanda M. & Elmore, Wardon O. Mr. Fix, Design It, Carry It with You, My Dadee & Me. 2011. 30p. pap. 9.00 (978-1-4349-8601-6(2), RoseDog Bks.) Dorrance Publishing Co., Inc.

Emerson, Carl. Monster Boy's Art Project, 1 vol. Levin, Lon, illus. 2010. (Monster Boy Set 2 Ser.). (ENG.). 32p. (J). (gr. k-3). 28.50 (978-1-60270-780-1(4)) ABDO Publishing Co.

Falwell, Cathryn. Butterflies for Kiri, 1 vol. 2003. (ENG., Illus.). 32p. (J). pap. 9.95 (978-1-60060-342-6(4)) Lee & Low Bks., Inc.

Finotti, M. C. Paintbrushes & Arrows. 2016. 113p. (J). **(978-1-56164-968-6(6))** Pineapple Pr., Inc.

Finotti, M. C. Paintbrushes & Arrows: A Story of St. Augustine. 2016. (ENG.). 112p. (J). pap. 9.95 (978-1-56164-963-1(5)) Pineapple Pr., Inc.

Fisher, Daniel, ed. 638 Potential Paper Cuts: 638 Pages of Stories by Sixth-Grade Students of Berkshire Middle School. 2008. (ENG.). 638p. pap. 11.00 (978-1-4196-9572-8(X)) CreateSpace Independent Publishing Platform.

Fitzgerald, Laura Marx. The Gallery. 2016. (ENG.). 336p. (J). (gr. 5-7). 16.99 (978-0-525-42865-7(8), Dial Bks) Penguin Young Readers Group.

—Under the Egg. (ENG.). 256p. (J). (gr. 3-7). 2015. 7.99 (978-0-14-242765-1(9), Puffin Books) 2014. 16.99 (978-0-8037-4001-3(8), Dial Bks) Penguin Young Readers Group.

Fletcher, Alison. Lucy & Lila. Lyles, Christopher, illus. 2016. (ENG.). 32p. (J). (gr. -1-3). 16.99 (978-1-4998-0156-9(4)) Little Bee Books Inc.

Foglia, Auttem. The Big Picture. 2010. 48p. pap. 10.59 (978-1-4520-6681-3(7)) AuthorHouse.

Fox, Mem. The Straight Line Wonder. (978-1-57255-567-9(X)) Mondo Publishing.

Fulton-Vengco, Aletha. Felicidad & Her Pen Pal Kamar. 2009. 33p. 13.90 (978-0-578-02728-9(3)) Vengco, Aletha Fulton.

Gardner, Whitney. You're Welcome, Universe. 2017. (ENG., Illus.). 304p. (YA). (gr. 7). 17.99 (978-0-399-55141-3(7), Knopf Bks. for Young Readers) Random Hse. Children's Bks.

Garmon, Larry Mike. The Calamari Code: an Agatha Pixie Mystery. 2007. 244p. pap. 15.49 (978-0-615-15267-7(8)) Zu Bks.

Gerstein, Mordicai. The Sleeping Gypsy. Gerstein, Mordicai, illus. 2016. (ENG., Illus.). 32p. (J). 16.95 (978-0-8234-2142-8(2)) Holiday Hse., Inc.

Getsinger, Mary. A Dream Come True. 2009. 20p. pap. 9.50 (978-1-4251-8885-6(0)) Trafford Publishing.

Goldin, David. Meet Me at the Art Museum: A Whimsical Look Behind the Scenes. 2012. (ENG., Illus.). 40p. (J). (gr. k-2). 19.95 (978-1-4197-0187-0(8), Abrams Bks. for Young Readers) Abrams, Inc.

Gordon, Amy. Return to Gill Park. 2006. (ENG., Illus.). 240p. (J). (gr. 4-7). 16.95 (978-0-8234-1998-2(3)) Holiday Hse., Inc.

Graziano, Alexandra Marie. The Colors of Rayne. 2012. 140p. pap. 19.99 (978-1-4771-0791-1(6)) Xlibris Corp.

Greenacres, Levi. Mommy's New Tattoo: A Bedtime Story for People, 1 vol. 2013. (ENG., Illus.). 32p. 16.99 (978-0-7643-4389-6(0), 9780764343896) Schiffer Publishing, Ltd.

Hays, Tommy. What I Came to Tell You. 2014. (ENG., Illus.). 304p. (J). (gr. 5). pap. 8.99 (978-1-60684-545-5(4), Carolrhoda Bks.) Lerner Publishing Group.

Hergé. Tintín: Descubro Los Números. 2004. (SPA., Illus.). 48p. 19.95 (978-1-59497-067-2(X)) Public Square Bks.

Hicks, Deron R. The Van Gogh Deception. 2017. (ENG.). 320p. (J). (gr. 5-7). 16.99 (978-0-544-75927-5(3), HMH Books For Young Readers) Houghton Mifflin Harcourt Publishing Co.

Huelin, Jodi. Alvin & the Big Art Show. 2013. (I Can Read! Level 2 Ser.). (J). lib. bdg. 13.55 (978-0-606-35040-2(3), Turtleback) Turtleback Bks.

—Alvin & the Chipmunks: Alvin & the Big Art Show. Artful Doodlers Limited Staff, illus. 2013. (I Can Read Level 2 Ser.). (ENG.). 32p. (J). (gr. -1-3). pap. 3.99 (978-0-06-225225-8(9), HarperFestival) HarperCollins Pubs.

Hughes-Odgers, Kyle. One Thousand Trees. 2017. (ENG.). 32p. (J). (gr. -1-3). 14.99 **(978-1-925164-72-5(1))** Fremantle Pr. AUS. Dist: Independent Pubs. Group.

Jacobson, Rick. The Mona Lisa Caper. Jacobson, Rick & Fernandez, Laura, illus. 2005. (ENG.). 24p. (J). (gr. k-3). 16.99 (978-0-88776-726-5(5), Tundra Bks.) Tundra Bks. CAN. Dist: Penguin Random Hse. LLC.

Jafa, Manorama. My Mother Taught Me Origami (English) 2013. (ENG.). 16p. pap. 4.95 (978-93-5036-109-2(4)) Ratna, Sagar Pvt. Ltd. IND. Dist: Midpoint Trade Bks., Inc.

Karr, Kathleen. The Seventh Knot, 1 vol. 2003. (ENG., Illus.). 300p. (J). 15.95 (978-0-7614-5135-8(8)) Marshall Cavendish Corp.

—The 7th Knot, 1 vol. 2007. (ENG., Illus.). 192p. (J). (gr. 5-9). pap. 5.99 (978-0-7614-5368-0(7)) Marshall Cavendish Corp.

Kephart, Beth. Nothing but Ghosts. 2009. (ENG.). 288p. (J). (gr. 8-18). 17.99 (978-0-06-166796-1(X), HarperTeen) HarperCollins Pubs.

Key, Pamela Marie. Kitty Fantastic in Monroe's Art Adventure. 2006. (Illus.). 40p. (J). (gr. -1-3). per. 17.95 (978-0-9771971-1-8(5)) Brass Frog Bookworks.

Khan, Nicholai. Nicho the Tiger - Create Your World. 2011. (Illus.). 28p. (J). 14.95 (978-0-9820801-2-2(3)) Nicho The Tiger LLC.

Klausner, Julie. Art Girls Are Easy. 2013. (ENG.). 240p. (YA). (gr. 10-17). pap. 18.99 (978-0-316-24362-9(0), Poppy) Little, Brown Bks. for Young Readers.

Konigsburg, E. L. The Mysterious Edge of the Heroic World. 2007. (ENG., Illus.). 256p. (J). (gr. 4-8). 16.99 (978-1-4169-4972-5(0), Atheneum Bks. for Young Readers) Simon & Schuster Children's Publishing.

Krosoczka, Jarrett J. Lunch Lady & the Field Trip Fiasco. 2011. (Lunch Lady Ser.). (ENG.). 96p. (J). (gr. 3-7). pap. 6.99 (978-0-375-86730-9(9), Knopf Bks. for Young Readers) Random Hse. Children's Bks.

Lam, Fiona Tinwei. Rainbow Rocket. 2013. (ENG., Illus.). 32p. 19.95 (978-0-88982-282-5(4)) Oolichan Bks. CAN. Dist: Univ. of Toronto Pr.

LaRochelle, David. Arlo's ARTrageous Adventure! Includes 50 Flaps to Flip. 2013. (ENG., Illus.). 28p. (J). (gr. -1-3). 14.95 (978-1-4027-9226-7(3)) Sterling Publishing Co., Inc.

Leavitt, Martine. Heck Superhero!, 1 vol. 2005. (ENG.). 144p. pap. 12.95 (978-0-88995-333-8(3)) Red Deer Pr. CAN. Dist: Ingram Publisher Services.

—Heck, Superhero. 2003. (ENG.). 172p. (J). (gr. 4-7). 16.95 (978-1-886910-94-2(4), Lemniscaat) Boyds Mills Pr.

Lee, Quinlan B. A Christmas Tree for Me: A New Holiday Tradition for Your Family. Basaluzzo, Constanza, illus. 2013. (ENG.). 32p. (J). (gr. -1-2). 14.99 (978-0-7944-3018-4(X)) Reader's Digest Assn., Inc., The.

Light, John. Dotty. 2005. (Illus.). 28p. (978-1-897968-26-0(4)) Photon Pr.

Light, Kelly. Louise Loves Art. Light, Kelly, illus. 2014. (ENG., Illus.). 40p. (J). (gr. -1-3). 17.99 (978-0-06-224817-6(0)) HarperCollins Pubs.

Lionni, Leo. Nicolas, Where Have You Been? 2010. (ENG., Illus.). 32p. (J). (gr. -1-2). pap. 6.99 (978-0-375-85549-8(1), Dragonfly Bks.) Random Hse. Children's Bks.

Lodding, Linda Ravin. Painting Pepette. Fletcher, Claire, illus. 2016. (ENG.). 40p. (J). (gr. -1-3). 17.99 (978-1-4998-0136-1(X)) Little Bee Books Inc.

Lowenstein, Sallie Claire. Waiting for Eugene. 2006. (Illus.). 201p. (J). (978-1-4156-6166-6(9)) Book Wholesalers, Inc.

Malone, Marianne. Stealing Magic. Call, Greg, illus. (Sixty-Eight Rooms Adventures Ser.). (ENG.). (J). (gr. 3-7). 2013. 272p. pap. 6.99 (978-0-375-86790-3(2), Yearling) 2012. 256p. 16.99 (978-0-375-86819-1(4), Random Hse. Bks. for Young Readers) Random Hse. Children's Bks.

Mayhew, James. Katie & the Bathers. 2016. (Katie Ser.). (ENG., Illus.). 32p. (J). (gr. k-17). pap. 9.99 (978-1-4083-3189-7(6), Orchard Bks.) Hachette Children's Group GBR. Dist: Hachette Bk. Group.

—Katie & the Spanish Princess. Mayhew, James, illus. 2007. (ENG., Illus.). 32p. (J). (gr. -1-k). pap. 10.99 (978-1-84616-248-0(3)) Hodder & Stoughton GBR. Dist: Hachette Bk. Group.

—Katie's Picture Show. Mayhew, James, illus. 2014. (ENG., Illus.). 32p. (J). (gr. -1-k). 16.99 (978-1-4083-3605-2(7)) Hodder & Stoughton GBR. Dist: Hachette Bk. Group.

McHeffey, Adam. Rudy & Claude Splash into Art, 0 vols. 2014. (ENG., Illus.). 32p. (J). (gr. -1-2). 16.99 (978-1-4778-4777-0(4), 9781477847770, Amazon Children's Publishing) Amazon Publishing.

McKissack, Patricia C. Stitchin' & Pullin' A Gee's Bend Quilt. Cabrera, Cozbi A., illus. 2016. (ENG.). 48p. (J). (gr. k-4). 8.99 (978-0-399-54950-2(1), Dragonfly Bks.) Random Hse. Children's Bks.

McOmber, Rachel B., ed. String Art Vol. 1: For All Seasons. rev. ed. (Illus.). (J). (978-0-944991-95-4(5)) Swift Learning Resources.

—String Art Vol. 2: For All Seasons. rev. ed. (Illus.). (J). (978-0-944991-96-1(3)) Swift Learning Resources.

Mejias, John & Mejias, John, illus. The Hungry Brothers. 2009. (ENG.). 32p. (J). (gr. -1-2). 15.95 (978-0-9798841-1-5(X)) 4N Publishing LLC.

Menchin, Scott. Grandma in Blue with Red Hat. Bliss, Harry, illus. 2015. (ENG.). 32p. (J). (gr. -1-3). 16.95 (978-1-4197-1484-9(8), Abrams Bks. for Young Readers) Abrams, Inc.

Merberg, Julie & Bober, Suzanne. Mini Masters: 4 Board Books Inside! Degas, Matisse, Monet, Van Gogh, 4 vols. 2006. (Mini Masters Ser.: MINI). (ENG., Illus.). (J). (gr. -1 — 1). bds. 19.99 (978-0-8118-5518-1(X)) Chronicle Bks. LLC.

Metz, Melinda. S. M. A. R. T. S. & the Invisible Robot. McKenzie, Heath, illus. 2015. (S. M. A. R. T. S. Ser.). (ENG.). 128p. (gr. 3-6). 22.65 (978-1-4965-0463-0(1)) S.M.A.R.T.S. Learning System.

Millen, C. M. The Ink Garden of Brother Theophane. Wisnewski, Andrea, illus. 2010. (ENG.). 32p. (J). (gr. k-3). 17.95 (978-1-58089-179-0(9)) Charlesbridge Publishing, Inc.

Mona, Larkins. Pablo's Art Adventures: Exploring the Studio. Mona, Larkins, illus. 2004. (Illus.). 27p. (J). 14.99 (978-0-9740841-3-8(1)) K&B Products.

Mondalto, Diane. Have You Ever Wished. 2009. 32p. pap. 12.99 (978-1-4389-4865-2(4)) AuthorHouse.

Montanari, Eva. Chasing Degas. 2009. (ENG., Illus.). 32p. (J). (gr. k-2). 18.95 (978-0-8109-3878-6(2), Abrams Bks. for Young Readers) Abrams, Inc.

Mullarkey, Lisa. The Artsy Fartsy Auction: Book 8, 1 vol. Harris, Phyllis, illus. 2012. (Katharine the Almost Great Ser.). (ENG.). 80p. (J). (gr. 1-4). 27.07 (978-1-61641-829-8(X)) Magic Wagon.

Mullarkey, Lisa & Mullarkey, John. Monet Changes Mediums, 1 vol. Bernard, Courtney, illus. 2015. (ENG.). 128p. (J). (978-1-62402-089-6(5)) Magic Wagon.

Neff, Henry H. The Hound of Rowan. 2008. (Tapestry Ser.: 1). (ENG., Illus.). 448p. (J). (gr. 3-7). 7.99 (978-0-375-83895-8(3), Yearling) Random Hse. Children's Bks.

O'Connor, Jane. Fancy Nancy at the Museum. Enik, Ted & Glasser, Robin Preiss, illus. 2008. (I Can Read Level 1 Ser.). (ENG.). 32p. (J). (gr. -1-3). 16.99 (978-0-06-123608-2(X)); pap. 3.99 (978-0-06-123607-5(1)) HarperCollins Pubs.

O'Connor, Jane & Harper Collins / LeapFrog. Fancy Nancy at the Museum. Glasser, Robin Preiss, illus. 2008. (Fancy Nancy Ser.). (J). 13.99 (978-1-59319-940-1(6)) LeapFrog Enterprises, Inc.

Oliver, Lin. Beware! Shadows in the Night. Kallis, Samantha, illus. 2016. (Fantastic Frame Ser.: 3). (ENG.). 128p. (J). (gr. 2-4). 11.99 (978-0-448-48091-6(3), Grosset & Dunlap) Penguin Young Readers Group.

—Danger! Tiger Crossing. 2016. (Illus.). 115p. (J). pap. (978-0-448-48086-2(7), Grosset & Dunlap) Penguin Young Readers Group.

—Splat! Another Messy Sunday 2. 2016. (Fantastic Frame Ser.: 2). (ENG., Illus.). 128p. (J). (gr. 2-4). 11.99 (978-0-448-48089-3(1), Grosset & Dunlap) Penguin Young Readers Group.

O'Neal, Shaquille. Little Shaq. Taylor, Theodore, III, illus. 2016. (ENG.). 80p. (J). 9.99 (978-1-61963-844-0(4), 9781619638440, Bloomsbury USA Childrens) Bloomsbury Publishing USA.

O'Toole-Freel, Judy. Aardvark, Aardvark, How Do You Do!, 1 vol. 2008. (ENG.). 31p. 24.95 (978-1-4241-6618-3(7)) America Star Bks.

Parish, Herman. Amelia Bedelia's Masterpiece. Sweat, Lynn, illus. (I Can Read Level 2 Ser.). (ENG.). 64p. (J). (gr. k-3). 2008. pap. 3.99 (978-0-06-084357-1(8)) 2007. 16.99 (978-0-06-084355-7(1)) HarperCollins Pubs. (Greenwillow Bks.).

Paulsen, Gary. Paintings from the Cave: Three Novellas. (ENG.). (YA). (gr. 7-7). 2012. 174p. pap. 8.99 (978-0-553-49466-2(X), Ember) 2011. 176p. 15.99 (978-0-385-74684-7(9), Lamb, Wendy Bks.) Random Hse. Children's Bks.

Payne, Sandy. Find Your Magic. Goodpaster, Nancy, illus. 2013. 50p. pap. 12.95 (978-1-937508-16-6(1)) Bearhead Publishing, LLC.

Pearsall, Shelley. The Seventh Most Important Thing. 2015. (ENG., Illus.). 288p. (J). (gr. 5). 16.99 (978-0-553-49728-1(6), Knopf Bks. for Young Readers) Random Hse. Children's Bks.

Pedrow, Debra A. Aunt Debra & My Favorite Things Poster. Karper, Deborah, ed. Reynolds, Sarah, illus. 2003. 40p. (J). 15.95 (978-1-928681-09-0(3)) Gladstone Publishing.

Picasso, Pablo. Birds & Other Animals with Pablo Picasso. 2017. (First Concepts with Fine Artists Ser.). (ENG.). 30p. (J). (gr. -1 — 1). bds. 9.95 **(978-0-7148-7418-0(3))** Phaidon Pr., Inc.

Potter, Noel Gyro. Writing a Wrong, 1 vol. Cannon, Joseph, illus. 2010. (Adventures of Marshall & Art Set 2 Ser.). (ENG.). 32p. (gr. -1-4). 28.50 (978-1-60270-739-9(1), Looking Glass Library) ABDO Publishing Co.

Rabley, Stephen. Marcel & the Mona Lisa. 2nd ed. 2009. (ENG., Illus.). 20p. pap. 11.99 (978-1-4058-6955-3(0)) Pearson Education.

Reynolds, Peter H. The Dot. Reynolds, Peter H., illus. 2003. (Creatrilogy Ser.). (ENG., Illus.). 32p. (J). (gr. k-12). 15.00 (978-0-7636-1961-9(2), 53509533) Candlewick Pr.

—El Punto. 2003. (SPA., Illus.). 32p. (J). (gr. k-2). 18.50 (978-84-8488-110-0(5)) Serres, Ediciones, S. L. ESP. Dist: Lectorum Pubns., Inc.

Richard Scott Morris. Irving the Duck in the Tortoise Shell Suit. 2009. 36p. pap. 20.00 (978-1-4389-5356-4(9)) AuthorHouse.

Richards, Chuck. Catch That Cat! A Chase up & down & Through M.C. Escher's Art. 2016. (J). (978-0-553-53562-4(5)) Bantam Doubleday Dell Large Print Group, Inc.

Rudge, Glen. The Sun Rose & the Wind Blue. 2009. 16p. pap. 12.95 (978-1-4389-5735-7(1)) AuthorHouse.

Rumford, James. Silent Music: A Story of Baghdad. Rumford, James, illus. 2008. (ENG., Illus.). 32p. (J). (gr. -1-3). 18.99 (978-1-59643-276-5(4), 9781596432765) Roaring Brook Pr.

Runholt, Susan. The Mystery of the Third Lucretia. 2009. (Kari & Lucas Mystery Ser.). (ENG.). 304p. (J). (gr. 5-18). pap. 6.99 (978-0-14-241338-8(0), Puffin Books) Penguin Young Readers Group.

Saltzberg, Barney. My Book of Beautiful Oops! A Scribble It, Smear It, Fold It, Tear It Journal for Young Artists. 2017. (ENG., Illus.). 52p. (J). (gr. -1-1). 15.95 (978-0-7611-8950-3(5)) Workman Publishing Co., Inc.

Sandell, Lisa Ann. A Map of the Known World. (ENG.). 288p. (J). (gr. 7-7). 2011. pap. 8.99 (978-0-545-06971-7(8)) 2009. 16.99 (978-0-545-06970-0(X)) Scholastic, Inc. (Scholastic Pr.).

Sateren, Shelley Swanson. Max & Zoe: the Very Best Art Project, 1 vol. Sullivan, Mary, illus. 2013. (Max & Zoe Ser.). (ENG.). 32p. (gr. k-2). pap. 5.19 (978-1-4795-2329-0(1), Max & Zoe) Picture Window Bks.

Say, Allen. Emma's Rug. 2003. (ENG., Illus.). 32p. (J). pap. 7.99 (978-0-618-33523-7(4)) Houghton Mifflin Harcourt Publishing Co.

Scanlon, Liz Garton. Think Big. Newton, Vanessa & Magnette, Paul, illus. 2012. (ENG.). 32p. (J). (gr. -1-6). 16.99 (978-1-59990-611-9(2), 9781599906119, Bloomsbury USA Childrens) Bloomsbury Publishing USA.

Seltzer, Eric. Doodle Dog. Seltzer, Eric, illus. 2005. (Doodle Dog Ser.). (ENG., Illus.). 32p. (J). (gr. -1-1). pap. 3.99 (978-0-689-85910-6(4), Simon Spotlight) Simon Spotlight.

Sherman, Linda. Art Fair for Grandma. 2007. (Illus.). 28p. (J). per. 10.00 (978-0-615-16017-7(4)) Sherman, Linda.

Solotareff, Gregoire & Le Saux, Alain - Solotareff. Pequeno Museo. 2003. (SPA.). 275p. (978-84-95150-78-3(6)) Corimbo, Editorial S.L.

Sorrells, W. A. Nairobi Nightmare. Bancroft, Tom & Corley, Rob, illus. 2007. 144p. (J). (978-0-9792912-1-0(6)) KidsGive, LLC.

Spanyol, Jessica. Clive & His Art. Spanyol, Jessica, illus. 2016. (All about Clive Ser.: 4). (ENG., Illus.). 14p. (J). bds. (978-1-84643-883-7(7)) Child's Play International Ltd.

Spinelli, Eileen. La Obra de Sofia. Dyer, Jane, illus. 2004. (SPA.). 32p. (J). 16.99 (978-84-8488-052-3(4)) Serres, Ediciones, S. L. ESP. Dist: Lectorum Pubns., Inc.

Stilton, Geronimo. The Mona Mousa Code. Wolf, Matt, illus. 2005. (Geronimo Stilton Ser.: No. 15). 113p. (J). lib. bdg. 10.00 (978-1-4242-0284-3(1)) Fitzgerald Bks.

Strom, Maria Diaz. Rainbow Joe & Me. 2004. (J). (gr. k-3). spiral bd. (978-0-616-03097-4(5)) Canadian National Institute for the Blind/Institut National Canadien pour les Aveugles.

Suen, Anastasia. Scissors, Paper & Sharing, 1 vol. Ebbeler, Jeffrey, illus. 2007. (Main Street School - Kids with Character Ser.). (ENG.). 32p. (gr. -1-4). 28.50 (978-1-60270-032-1(X), Looking Glass Library) ABDO Publishing Co.

Tagged. 2015. (ENG.). 288p. (YA). (gr. 7). lib. bdg. 16.95 (978-1-58089-583-5(2)) Charlesbridge Publishing, Inc.

Thaler, Mike. The Art Teacher from the Black Lagoon, 1 vol. Lee, Jared, illus. 2012. (Black Lagoon Set 2 Ser.: No. 2). (ENG.). 32p. (J). (gr. 1-4). lib. bdg. 24.21 (978-1-59961-952-1(0)) Spotlight.

Tildes, Phyllis Limbacher. The Magic Babushka. Tildes, Phyllis Limbacher, illus. 2009. (ENG., Illus.). 32p. (J). (gr. k-3). pap. 7.95 (978-1-58089-225-4(6)) Charlesbridge Publishing, Inc.

Torres, J. Checkers & Dot at the Zoo. Lum, J., illus. 2012. (Checkers & Dot Ser.). (ENG.). 16p. (J). (gr. k — 1). bds. 7.95 (978-1-77049-442-8(1), Tundra Bks.) Tundra Bks. CAN. Dist: Penguin Random Hse. LLC.

Trice, Linda. Kenya's Art. Mitchell, Hazel, illus. 2016. (ENG.). 32p. (J). (gr. -1-3). 16.95 (978-1-57091-848-3(1)) Charlesbridge Publishing, Inc.

Van Draanen, Wendelin. Sammy Keyes & the Art of Deception. 2008. (Sammy Keyes Ser.: Bk. 8). (J). 64.99 (978-1-60640-640-3(X)) Findaway World, LLC.

—Sammy Keyes & the Art of Deception. 2005. (Sammy Keyes Ser.). (Illus.). 272p. (J). (gr. 4-7). 14.15 (978-0-7569-5069-9(4)) Perfection Learning Corp.

Vincent, Harris T. & Brewer, Mary. When Grandmother Was A Little Girl. 2010. 40p. 23.99 (978-1-4520-7728-4(2)) AuthorHouse.

Wahl, Jan. The Art Collector. Bonnet, Rosalinde, illus. 2011. (ENG.). 32p. (J). (gr. k-3). 15.95 (978-1-58089-270-4(1)) Charlesbridge Publishing, Inc.

Watt, Mélanie. Augustine. Watt, Mélanie, illus. 2008. (ENG., Illus.). 32p. (J). (gr. -1-2). pap. 7.95 (978-1-55453-268-1(X)) Kids Can Pr., Ltd. CAN. Dist: Hachette Bk. Group.

Webb, Mack Henry, Jr. Little Bianca. Tuck, Beverly, illus. 2006. 52p. (J). per. 15.95 (978-0-9779576-0-6(8)) Pilinut Pr., Inc.

Wells, Marcia. Mystery in Mayan Mexico. 2016. (Eddie Red Undercover Ser.: 2). lib. bdg. 18.40 (978-0-606-39664-6(0)) Turtleback Bks.

Whitney, Daisy. Starry Nights. (ENG.). (YA). (gr. 7). 2014. 304p. pap. 9.99 (978-1-61963-436-7(8), 9781619634367) 2013. 288p. 17.99 (978-1-61963-133-5(4), 9781619631335) Bloomsbury Publishing USA. (Bloomsbury USA Childrens).

Wolfgang, Jane. Art Today. 2013. (ENG., Illus.). 32p. (J). 14.95 (978-1-56290-706-8(9)) Crystal Productions.

Young, Jessica. Finley Flowers Collection. Secheret, Jessica, illus. 2016. (Finley Flowers Ser.). (ENG.). 256p. (gr. 2-3). 9.99 (978-1-4795-9850-2(X), Finley Flowers) Picture Window Bks.

ART—FORGERIES

Jefferson, E. Louis. The Little Tadpole-A Story of Friendship: Companion Coloring Book. 2012. 48p. pap. 7.00 (978-1-105-61123-0(X)) Lulu.com GBR. Dist: Lulu Pr., Inc.

Kutschbach, Doris. Art Detective: Spot the Difference! 2013. (ENG., Illus.). 48p. (J). (gr. 3-7). 14.95 (978-3-7913-7104-7(5)) Prestel Verlag GmbH & Co KG. DEU. Dist: Penguin Random Hse. LLC.

Sheppard, Bonnie. The 10 Greatest Art Forgers. 2007. (J). 14.99 (978-1-55448-473-7(1)) Scholastic Library Publishing.

ART—GALLERIES AND MUSEUMS

see Art Galleries, Commercial; Art Museums

ART, GRAPHIC

see Graphic Arts

ART, GREEK

Bingham, Jane. Classical Myth: A Treasury of Greek & Roman Legends, Art, & History. 2007. (Myth Ser.). (Illus.). 96p. (J). (gr. 4-7). pap. 7.99 (978-0-7858-2350-6(6)) Book Sales, Inc.

—Classical Myth: A Treasury of Greek & Roman Legends, Art, & History. 2007. (ENG., Illus.). 96p. (C). (gr. 6-18). lib. bdg. 140.00 (978-0-7656-8104-1(8), Y181755) Routledge.

Blanco Freijeiro, Antonio. Arte Griego. (SPA.). 96p. (J). (978-84-207-3730-0(5)) Grupo Anaya, S.A.

Yancey, Diane. Ancient Greek Art & Architecture. Nardo, Don, ed. 2011. (Eye on Art Ser.). (ENG., Illus.). 128p. (J). (gr. 7-10). lib. bdg. 39.40 (978-1-4205-0685-3(4), Lucent Bks.) Cengage Gale.

ART—HISTORY

Armstrong, Simon. Cool Art: 50 Fantastic Facts for Kids of All Ages. 2014. (ENG., Illus.). 112p. (J). (gr. 5). 14.99 (978-1-909396-42-5(7)) Pavilion Bks. GBR. Dist: Independent Pubs. Group.

Barbe-Gall, Françoise. How to Talk to Children about Art. 2005. (ENG., Illus.). 208p. (J). (gr. k-12). pap. 18.95 (978-1-55652-580-3(X)) Chicago Review Pr., Inc.

Brommer, Gerald. Discovering Art History 4th Edition SE. 4th ed. 2007. (Illus.). 638p. (J). stu. ed. (978-0-87192-719-4(5)) Davis Pubns., Inc.

Carroll, Colleen. How Artists See Heroes: Myth, History, War, Everyday. 2003. (How Artists See Ser.). (ENG., Illus.). 48p. (J). (gr. k-7). 12.95 (978-0-7892-0773-9(7)) Abbeville Pr., Inc.

Chapman, D. Vocabulary Cards. 2003. (Adventures in Art Ser.). 1. (J). (gr. 1-18). 22.95 (978-0-87192-349-3(1))2. (J). (gr. 2-18). 22.95 (978-0-87192-350-9(5))3. (gr. 3-18). 22.95 (978-0-87192-351-6(3))4. (gr. 4-18). 22.95 (978-0-87192-352-3(1))5. (gr. 5-18). 22.95 (978-0-87192-353-0(X))6. (J). (gr. 6-18). 22.95 (978-0-87192-354-7(8)) Davis Pubns., Inc.

Copmbined, Slide. Discovering Art History. (978-0-87192-311-0(4)) Davis Pubns., Inc.

Dickins, Rosie. Art Treasury. Butler, Nicola, illus. 2007. (Art Treasury Ser.). 94p. (J). 19.99 *(978-0-7945-1452-5(9),* Usborne) EDC Publishing.

—Introduction to Art - Internet Linked. Chisholm, Jane, ed. 2004. (Introduction to Art Ser.). (ENG.). 144p. (J). 19.95 *(978-0-7945-0661-2(5),* Usborne) EDC Publishing.

—The Usborne First Book of Art. Hopman, Philip, illus. 2008. (Usborne First Book Ser.). 62p. (J). (gr. -1-3). 18.99 *(978-0-7945-2035-9(9),* Usborne) EDC Publishing.

Dickins, Rosie, et al. The Usborne Introduction to Art: In Association with the National Gallery, London. 2005. (Illus.). 144p. (J). *(978-0-439-79202-8(9))* Scholastic, Inc.

Dixon, Kathryn. The Little Girl's Little Book of Art. 2014. (ENG., Illus.). 128p. 24.95 *(978-1-62732-013-9(X),* Bellagio Pr.) Taj Bks. International LLC.

Hodge, Susie. The Children's Interactive Story of Art. 2016. (ENG., Illus.). 96p. (J). (gr. 3). 19.95 *(978-1-78312-130-4(0))* Carlton Kids GBR. Dist: Sterling Publishing Co., Inc.

Kalman, Maira. Ah-Ha to Zig-Zag: 31 Objects from Cooper Hewitt, Smithsonian Design Museum. 2014. (ENG., Illus.). 48p. (J). (gr. k — 1). 17.95 *(978-0-8478-4377-0(7),* Skira) Rizzoli International Pubns., Inc.

Kunstgeschichte I: Von den Anfaengen bis zum 18. Jahrhundert. 2nd ed. (Duden Abiturhilfen Ser.). (GER.). 112p. (YA). (gr. 12-13). *(978-3-411-04142-8(0))* Bibliographisches Institut & F. A. Brockhaus AG DEU. Dist: International Bk. Import Service, Inc.

Kunstgeschichte II: 19. und 20. Jahrhundert. 2nd ed. (Duden Abiturhilfen Ser.). (GER.). 112p. (YA). (gr. 12-13). *(978-3-411-04192-3(7))* Bibliographisches Institut & F. A. Brockhaus AG DEU. Dist: International Bk. Import Service, Inc.

Marchioro, Narcisa. 13 Art Materials Children Should Know. 2017. (Children Should Know Ser.). (ENG., Illus.). 48p. (J). (gr. 3-7). 14.95 ***(978-3-7913-7260-0(2))*** Prestel Verlag GmbH & Co KG. DEU. Dist: Penguin Random Hse. LLC.

Mines, Cynthia J. Cubism. 2006. (Eye on Art Ser.). (ENG.). 128p. (gr. 3-7). lib. bdg. 39.40 *(978-1-59018-961-0(2),* Lucent Bks.) Cengage Gale.

Nardo, Don. Arts & Literature in Ancient Mesopotamia. 2008. (Lucent Library of Historical Eras Ser.). (ENG., Illus.). 104p. (YA). (gr. 7-12). lib. bdg. 37.45 *(978-1-4205-0099-8(6),* LML02109-244222) Cengage Gale.

Nichols, Catherine. Color Yourself Smart: Masterpieces of Art. Bright, Joe, illus. 2013. (Color Yourself Smart Ser.). (ENG.). 128p. 19.95 *(978-1-60710-572-5(1),* Thunder Bay Pr.) Readerlink Distribution Services, LLC.

Parker, Graham. 1, 2, 3 the Art of Counting. 2006. (Children's Art Ser. from the National Gallery of Victoria Ser.). (ENG., Illus.). 24p. (J). (gr. -1 — 1). pap. 9.95 *(978-0-7241-0234-1(5))* National Gallery of Victoria AUS. Dist: National Bk. Network.

Perdew, Laura. History of Art, 1 vol. 2014. (Essential Library of Cultural History Ser.). (ENG.). 112p. (J). (gr. 6-12). lib. bdg. 35.64 *(978-1-62403-551-7(5),* Essential Library) ABDO Publishing Co.

Phaidon Press Editors & Renshaw, Amanda. The Art Book for Children. Ace, Jane & Kloet, Chris, eds. 2006. (SPA.). (gr. 8-17). 19.95 *(978-0-7148-9863-6(5))* Phaidon Pr., Inc.

Ramirez, Juan Antonio. Arte Prehistorico y Primitivo. (SPA.). 96p. (YA). *(978-84-207-3190-2(0))* Grupo Anaya, S.A.

Renshaw, Amanda. The Art Book for Children. Kloet, Chris & Ace, Jane, eds. rev. ed. 2005. (ENG., Illus.). 80p. (gr. 8-17). 19.95 *(978-0-7148-4530-2(2))* Phaidon Pr. Ltd. GBR. Dist: Hachette Bk. Group.

Richards, Mary. Splat! The Most Exciting Artists of All Time. 2016. (ENG., Illus.). 96p. (J). (gr. 4-6). 19.95 *(978-0-500-65065-3(9),* 565065) Thames & Hudson.

Vadeboncoeur, Jim, Jr., prod. Black & White Images: 2004. 2004. (Illus.). 112p. per. 20.00 *(978-0-9724697-1-5(0))* Vadeboncoeur, Jim.

Von Sperber, Annabelle, illus. Where Is the Artist? From Cave Paintings to Modern Art: a Look & Find Book. 2015. (ENG.). 32p. (J). (gr. 3-7). 19.95 *(978-3-7913-7233-4(5))* Prestel Verlag GmbH & Co KG. DEU. Dist: Penguin Random Hse. LLC.

Wenzel, Angela. The Mad, Mad, Mad World of Salvador Dali. 2003. (Adventures in Art Ser.). (Illus.). 30p. 14.95 *(978-3-7913-2944-4(8))* Prestel Publishing.

West, David & Parker, Steve. A Brief Illustrated History of Art. 2017. (Brief Illustrated History Ser.). (ENG.). 32p. (gr. 3-5). lib. bdg. 27.32 *(978-1-5157-2523-7(5),* Fact Finders) Capstone Press of Coughlan Cos.

ART, INDIAN

see Indians of North America—Art

ART, ISLAMIC

see Islamic Art

ART, JAPANESE

Antram, David. How to Draw Manga Warriors. 2010. (How to Draw Ser.). (Illus.). 32p. (YA). (gr. 6-18). pap. 11.75 *(978-1-4488-1609-5(2));* lib. bdg. 26.50 *(978-1-4488-1581-4(9))* Rosen Publishing Group, Inc., The. (PowerKids Pr.).

Campos, Leo. Creating Manga Comics, 1 vol. 2015. (ENG., Illus.). 32p. (J). lib. bdg. 27.50 *(978-1-4777-5926-4(3),* PowerKids Pr.) Rosen Publishing Group, Inc., The.

Orr, Tamra. Manga Artists. 2008. (Extreme Careers Ser.). (Illus.). 64p. (YA). (gr. 5-9). lib. bdg. 31.95 *(978-1-4042-1854-3(8))* Rosen Publishing Group, Inc., The.

Sibbett, Ed, Jr., et al. Japanese Prints. 2012. (Adult Coloring Ser.). (ENG., Illus.). 64p. (gr. 3). pap. 5.99 *(978-0-486-49136-3(6))* Dover Pubns., Inc.

Sun, Ming-Ju. Creative Haven Japanese Kimono Designs Coloring Book. 2013. (Adult Coloring Ser.). (ENG., Illus.). 64p. (gr. 3). pap. 5.99 *(978-0-486-49344-2(X))* Dover Pubns., Inc.

ART, MEDIEVAL

Allan, Tony, et al. Exploring the Life, Myth, & Art of the Medieval World. 2016. (Civilizations of the World Ser.). (ENG.). 144p. (J). (gr. 8-8). lib. bdg. 45.10 *(978-1-4994-6395-8(2))* Rosen Publishing Group, Inc., The.

Cels, Marc. Arts & Literature in the Middle Ages. 2004. (Medieval World Ser.). (ENG., Illus.). 32p. (J). pap. *(978-0-7787-1387-6(3))* Crabtree Publishing Co.

Nardo, Don, ed. Medieval European Art & Architecture. 2012. (Eye on Art Ser.). (Illus.). 128p. (J). (gr. 7-10). lib. bdg. 34.80 *(978-1-4205-0715-7(X),* Lucent Bks.) Cengage Gale.

O'Brien, Cynthia. Your Guide to the Arts in the Middle Ages. 2017. (Destination: Middle Ages Ser.). (ENG., Illus.). 32p. (J). ***(978-0-7787-2995-2(8))***; pap. ***(978-0-7787-3002-6(6))*** Crabtree Publishing Co.

ART, MOHAMMEDAN

see Islamic Art

ART, MOORISH

see Islamic Art

ART—MUSEUMS

see Art Museums

ART, NONOBJECTIVE

see Art, Abstract

ART, ORIENTAL

see Art, Asian

ART, PRIMITIVE

see also Cave Paintings; Folk Art; Indians of North America—Art

also names of countries, cities, etc. with the subdivision Antiquities, e.g. United States—Antiquities; etc.

Burnham, Brad. Cave of Lascaux: The Cave of Prehistoric Wall Paintings. 2009. (Famous Caves of the World Ser.). 24p. (gr. 3-4). 42.50 *(978-1-61512-495-4(0),* PowerKids Pr.) Rosen Publishing Group, Inc., The.

Hodge, Susie. Prehistoric Art. 2003. (Art in History Ser.). (Illus.). 32p. (J). (gr. 5-7). per. 6.95 *(978-1-4034-4021-1(2))* Heinemann-Raintree.

Lauber, Patricia. Painters of the Caves. 2005. (Reader's Workshop Ser.). (ENG., Illus.). 48p. (C). pap. 21.95 *(978-0-7362-2807-7(1))* CENGAGE Learning.

Lewis, Richard. Cave: An Evocation of the Beginnings of Art. Crawford, Elizabeth, illus. Hirose, George, photos by. 2003. 56p. pap. 14.00 *(978-1-929299-03-4(6))* Touchstone Ctr. Pubns.

Stephens, Pam. Dropping in on Rousseau. 2003. (ENG., Illus.). 32p. (J). 15.95 *(978-1-56290-303-9(9))* Crystal Productions.

ART, RENAISSANCE

Blanch, Gregory & Stathis, Roberta. Renaissance Artists Who Inspired the World. 2003. (Explore the Ages Ser.). (Illus.). 79p. 17.00 *(978-1-55501-593-0(X))* Ballard & Tighe Pubs.

Corrain, Lucia. The Art of the Renaissance. 2008. (Art Masters Ser.). 64p. (YA). (gr. 6-18). lib. bdg. 24.95 net. *(978-1-934545-04-1(X))* Oliver Pr., Inc.

Fitzpatrick, Anne. The Renaissance. 2005. (Movements in Art Ser.). (Illus.). 48p. (YA). (gr. 5-9). lib. bdg. 21.95 *(978-1-58341-349-4(9))* Creative Co., The.

—The Renaissance: Movements in Art. 2015. (Illus.). 80p. (J). *(978-1-60818-536-8(2),* Creative Education) Creative Co., The.

—The Renaissance: Odysseys in Art. 2016. (Odysseys in Art Ser.). (ENG.). 80p. (J). (gr. 7-10). pap. 14.99 *(978-1-62832-137-1(7),* Creative Paperbacks) Creative Co., The.

Geiger Stephens, Pamela. Dropping in on Renaissance Artists. McNeill, Jim, illus. 2010. 32p. (J). 15.95 *(978-1-56290-658-0(5))* Crystal Productions.

Kallen, Stuart A. Renaissance Art. 2008. (Eye on Art Ser.). (ENG., Illus.). 128p. (YA). (gr. 7-10). lib. bdg. 34.80 *(978-1-4205-0047-9(3),* LML02109-240035) Cengage Gale.

Kuiper, Kathleen, ed. The 100 Most Influential Painters & Sculptors of the Renaissance. 2009. (Britannica Guide to the World's Most Influential People Ser.). (Illus.). 376p. (YA). (gr. 9-12). lib. bdg. 53.00 *(978-1-61530-004-4(X))* Rosen Publishing Group, Inc., The.

Kuligowski, Stephanie. Leonardo Da Vinci: Renaissance Artist & Inventor, 1 vol. 2012. (Primary Source Readers Ser.). (ENG.). 32p. (J). (gr. 4-4). pap. 8.99 *(978-1-4333-5008-5(4))* Teacher Created Materials, Inc.

Meyer, Eric Christopher. Art in the Renaissance: Set Of 6. 2010. (Navigators Ser.). (J). 50.00 net. *(978-1-4108-6265-5(8))* Benchmark Education Co.

Quill, Charlie. Michelangelo: His Life & Art. 2009. (Reading Room Collection 2 Ser.). 24p. (gr. 3-4). 42.50 *(978-1-60851-980-4(5),* PowerKids Pr.) Rosen Publishing Group, Inc., The.

ART, ROMAN

Allan, Tony. Exploring the Life, Myth, & Art of Ancient Rome. 2011. (Civilizations of the World Ser.). (YA). (gr. 7-12). lib. bdg. 42.60 *(978-1-4488-4831-7(8))* Rosen Publishing Group, Inc., The.

Bingham, Jane. Classical Myth: A Treasury of Greek & Roman Legends, Art, & History. 2007. (Myth Ser.). (Illus.). 96p. (J). (gr. 4-7). pap. 7.99 *(978-0-7858-2350-6(6))* Book Sales, Inc.

—Classical Myth: A Treasury of Greek & Roman Legends, Art, & History. 2007. (ENG., Illus.). 96p. (C). (gr. 6-18). lib. bdg. 140.00 *(978-0-7656-8104-1(8),* Y181755) Routledge.

Gedacht, Daniel C. Art & Religion in Ancient Rome. (Primary Sources of Ancient Civilizations Ser.). 24p. 2009. (gr. 3-3). 42.50 *(978-1-60851-555-4(9))* 2004. (ENG., Illus.). (gr. 4-8). pap. 8.25 *(978-0-8239-8944-7(5))* 2004. (Illus.). (J). lib. bdg. 19.95 *(978-0-8239-6776-6(X))* Rosen Publishing Group, Inc., The. (PowerKids Pr.).

Nardo, Don. Ancient Roman Art & Architecture. 2011. (Eye on Art Ser.). (ENG.). 128p. (gr. 7-10). lib. bdg. 39.40 *(978-1-4205-0714-0(1),* Lucent Bks.) Cengage Gale.

ART—STUDY AND TEACHING

Art & Architecture. 2010. (Experimenting with Everyday Science Ser.). (Illus.). 176p. (J). (gr. 6-12). 35.00 *(978-1-60413-168-0(3),* Chelsea Hse.) Facts On File, Inc.

Cherrington, Joan. Color Theory for the Young Artist. 2009. pap. 24.95 *(978-1-61584-124-0(5))* Independent Pub.

Schmutz, Janine, et al, texts. What Is Art? 27 Questions 27 Answers. 2013. (ENG., Illus.). 216p. pap. 30.00 *(978-3-7757-3527-8(5))* Hatje Cantz Verlag GmbH & Co KG DEU. Dist: D.A.P./Distributed Art Pubs.

Vry, Silke. 13 Art Illusions Children Should Know. 2012. (ENG., Illus.). 48p. (J). (gr. 3-7). 14.95 *(978-3-7913-7110-8(X))* Prestel Verlag GmbH & Co KG. DEU. Dist: Penguin Random Hse. LLC.

Yenawine, Philip. Places, 1 vol. 3rd ed. 2006. (ENG., Illus.). 24p. (J). (gr. -1-3). 14.95 *(978-0-87070-173-3(8))* D.A.P./Distributed Art Pubs.

ART—TECHNIQUE

Armstrong, Reed & Armstrong, Roxlana. Art 4 for Young Catholics. 2013. pap. 12.00 *(978-1-60704-109-2(X))* Seton Pr.

Armstrong, Simon. Cool Art: 50 Fantastic Facts for Kids of All Ages. 2014. (ENG., Illus.). 112p. (J). (gr. 5). 14.99 *(978-1-909396-42-5(7))* Pavilion Bks. GBR. Dist: Independent Pubs. Group.

Beal, Denice. Easy Art. 2008. 68p. pap. 25.49 *(978-1-4389-3774-8(1))* AuthorHouse.

Booth, Scott, illus. How to Draw Superheroes & Super Villains. 2003. 64p. (J). *(978-0-439-55133-5(1))* Scholastic, Inc.

Brommer, Gerald F. Illustrated Elements of Art & Principles of Design: Full Color Reproductions, Descriptions of Each Concept, Hands-On Activities. 2010. 72p. (J). spiral bd. 19.95 *(978-1-56290-665-8(8))* Crystal Productions.

Brooks, Susie. Get into Art People: Enjoy Great Art — Then Create Your Own! 2015. (Get into Art Ser.). (ENG., Illus.). 32p. (J). (gr. 2-9). 8.99 *(978-0-7534-7218-7(X),* 9780753472187, Kingfisher) Roaring Brook Pr.

—Get into Art Places: Discover Great Art & Create Your Own! 2014. (Get into Art Ser.). (ENG., Illus.). 32p. (J). (gr. 2-9). 14.99 *(978-0-7534-7182-1(5),* 9780753471821, Kingfisher) Roaring Brook Pr.

—Get into Art Telling Stories: Enjoy Great Art — Then Create Your Own! 2015. (Get into Art Ser.). (ENG., Illus.). 32p. (J). (gr. 2-9). 14.99 *(978-0-7534-7183-8(3),* 9780753471838, Kingfisher) Roaring Brook Pr.

Campos, Leo. Creating Manga Comics, 1 vol. 2015. (ENG., Illus.). 32p. (J). lib. bdg. 27.50 *(978-1-4777-5926-4(3),* PowerKids Pr.) Rosen Publishing Group, Inc., The.

Chambers, Jo. Art Gallery. 2007. (Trackers-Math Ser.). (gr. 2-5). pap. 5.00 *(978-1-59055-927-7(4))* Pacific Learning, Inc.

Cheverton, Edward. Meet the Circus. 2016. (ENG., Illus.). 32p. (J). (gr. 1-4). pap. 9.95 *(978-1-84976-366-0(6))* Tate Publishing, Ltd. GBR. Dist: Abrams, Inc.

Create It! 2016. (Create It! Ser.). 32p. (gr. 5-4). pap. 63.00 *(978-1-4824-5313-3(4));* lib. bdg. 159.60 *(978-1-4824-4972-3(2))* Stevens, Gareth Publishing LLLP.

De Long, Ron, et al. Dream-Makers Principles of Art & Design: Art & Design. De Long, Ron et al, eds. 2007. (Illus.). 104p. spiral bd. 9.99 *(978-0-86696-329-9(4))* Binney & Smith, Inc.

Deuchars, Marion. Draw Paint Print Like the Great Artists. 2014. (ENG., Illus.). 224p. (J). (gr. 3-7). pap. 19.95 *(978-1-78067-281-6(0))* King, Laurence Publishing GBR. Dist: Hachette Bk. Group.

Diana, Carla. LEO the Maker Prince: Journeys in 3D Printing. 2013. (ENG., Illus.). 64p. pap. 14.99 *(978-1-4571-8314-0(5),* 9781457183140) O'Reilly Media, Inc.

Disney Storybook Artists Staff, ed. Celebrated Characters Collection: Including Your Disney/Pixar Favorites! 2009. (Licensed Learn to Draw Ser.). (ENG.). 144p. (J). (gr. 1-3). pap. 19.95 *(978-1-60058-144-1(7),* 1600581447) Quarto Publishing Group USA.

Distance-It with Space/Build-It with Form. 2005. (J). spiral bd. 45.00 *(978-0-9755413-9-5(0))* ArtAnswer.

Dyer, Janice. Get into Mixed Media. 2017. (Get-Into-It Guides). (ENG.). 32p. (J). (gr. 3-6). ***(978-0-7787-3402-4(1))***; (Illus.). pap. ***(978-0-7787-3406-2(4))*** Crabtree Publishing Co.

Emert, Phyllis Raybin. Art in Glass. 2007. (Eye on Art Ser.). (ENG., Illus.). 128p. (gr. 7-10). lib. bdg. 39.40 *(978-1-59018-983-2(3),* LML02109-230147, Lucent Bks.) Cengage Gale.

Flugge, Klaus. Letters to Klaus. 2013. (ENG., Illus.). 96p. (J). (gr. k). pap. 12.99 *(978-1-84939-750-6(3))* Andersen Pr. GBR. Dist: Independent Pubs. Group.

Flying Frog Publishing, ed. Gigantic Paper Planes. 2012. 48p. (J). 14.99 *(978-1-934967-81-2(5))* Flying Frog Publishing, Inc.

—Gigantic Sky Cruising Paper Planes. 2012. 48p. (J). 14.99 *(978-1-60745-073-3(9))* Flying Frog Publishing, Inc.

Gerner, Jochen. ARTastic! 200+ Art Smart Activities. 2007. (FRE & ENG., Illus.). 208p. (J). (gr. k-3). 14.95 *(978-2-89579-140-9(6))* Owlkids Bks. Inc. CAN. Dist: Publishers Group West (PGW).

Gilbert, Elizabeth T., et al. DIY Dog Portraits. Barnes, Jessica L., illus. 2016. (DIY Ser.). (ENG.). 128p. (J). (gr. 3-8). 34.65 *(978-1-942875-13-0(4),* Walter Foster Jr) Quarto Publishing Group USA.

Golightly, Holly. Witches n Whatnot. Golightly, Holly, . 2004. (Illus.). 48p. (YA). per. 9.99 *(978-0-9745367-6-7(8))* BroadSword Comics/ Jim Balent Studios.

Hachette Children's Group. Art. 2017. (Mad About Ser.). (ENG., Illus.). 32p. (J). (gr. 4-6). pap. 11.99 *(978-0-7502-9453-9(1),* Wayland) Hachette Children's Group GBR. Dist: Hachette Bk. Group.

Hart, Christopher. Kids Draw Animals. 2003. (Kids Draw Ser.). (ENG., Illus.). 64p. (J). (gr. 2-4). pap. 11.95 *(978-0-8230-2631-9(0),* Watson-Guptill) Potter/TenSpeed/Harmony.

Henry, Sandi. Making Amazing Art! 40 Activities Using the 7 Elements of Art Design. Cole, Sarah, illus. (ENG.). 128p. (J). (gr. 3-7). 2008. pap. 12.99 *(978-0-8249-6795-6(X))* 2007. 16.99 *(978-0-8249-6794-9(1))* Worthy Publishing. (Ideal Pubns.).

—Using Color in Your Art! Chossing Colors for Impact & Pizzazz. Rakitin, Sarah, illus. 2005. (Williamson Kids Can! Ser.). 128p. (J). (gr. 3-7). 14.95 *(978-0-8249-6772-7(0),* Ideal Pubns.) Worthy Publishing.

Hodge, Anthony. Collage. 2006. (SPA.). 32p. *(978-958-30-1835-0(X))* Panamericana Editorial.

Jeffus, Sharon. Art Adventures in Narnia. 2006. (Illus.). 58p. (J). 17.95 *(978-0-9715970-7-5(3))* Visual Manna.

Jones, William. Arte de la Manipulacion.Tr. of Art of Manipulation. (SPA.). 9.98 *(978-968-403-964-3(6))* Selector, S.A. de C.V. MEX. Dist: AIMS International Bks., Inc.

Kallen, Stuart A. The Artist's Tools. 2006. (Eye on Art Ser.). (Illus.). 104p. (J). (gr. 4-7). lib. bdg. 33.45 *(978-1-59018-957-3(4),* Lucent Bks.) Cengage Gale.

Loop, et al. Think & Make Like an Artist. 2017. (ENG., Illus.). 80p. (gr. 3-8). pap. 19.95 ***(978-0-500-65098-1(5)***, 565098) Thames & Hudson.

Luxbacher, Irene. The Jumbo Book of Art. Luxbacher, Irene, illus. 2003. (Jumbo Bks.). (ENG., Illus.). 208p. (J). (gr. 3-7). 14.95 *(978-1-55074-762-1(2))* Kids Can Pr., Ltd. CAN. Dist: Hachette Bk. Group.

—The Jumbo Book of Outdoor Art. Luxbacher, Irene, illus. 2006. (Jumbo Bks.). (ENG., Illus.). 144p. (J). (gr. 3-7). 16.95 *(978-1-55337-680-4(3))* Kids Can Pr., Ltd. CAN. Dist: Hachette Bk. Group.

Martin, Courtney Autumn, et al, illus. Life in Color: A Coloring Book of Teenage Confusion, Creativity, & Discovery. 2016. (ENG.). 96p. (gr. 9-11). pap. 12.95 *(978-1-63079-059-2(1))* Switch Pr.

McCully, Jennifer. ARTrageous! 2016. (DIY Ser.). (ENG., Illus.). 128p. (J). (gr. 3-8). 34.65 *(978-1-942875-10-9(X),* Walter Foster Jr) Quarto Publishing Group USA.

Miller, Ron. Digital Art: Painting with Pixels. 2008. (Exceptional Social Studies Titles for Upper Grades). (ENG., Illus.). 120p. (gr. 7-12). lib. bdg. 31.93 *(978-0-8225-7516-0(7))* Lerner Publishing Group.

Mis, Melody S. How to Draw Brazil's Sights & Symbols. 2004. (Kid's Guide to Drawing the Countries of the World Ser.). (Illus.). 48p. (J). lib. bdg. 29.25 *(978-0-8239-6667-7(4),* PowerKids Pr.) Rosen Publishing Group, Inc., The.

—How to Draw Poland's Sights & Symbols. 2004. (Kid's Guide to Drawing the Countries of the World Ser.). (Illus.). 48p. (J). lib. bdg. 29.25 *(978-0-8239-6669-1(0),* PowerKids Pr.) Rosen Publishing Group, Inc., The.

—How to Draw Russia's Sights & Symbols. 2004. (Kid's Guide to Drawing the Countries of the World Ser.). (Illus.). 48p. (J). lib. bdg. 29.25 *(978-0-8239-6666-0(6),* PowerKids Pr.) Rosen Publishing Group, Inc., The.

—How to Draw South Africa's Sights & Symbols. 2004. (Kid's Guide to Drawing the Countries of the World Ser.). (Illus.). 48p. (J). lib. bdg. 29.25 *(978-0-8239-6665-3(8),* PowerKids Pr.) Rosen Publishing Group, Inc., The.

Nicholson, Sue. World Art. rev. ed. 2005. (Learn Art Ser.). (Illus.). 32p. (J). pap. *(978-1-84538-130-1(0),* QED Publishing) Quarto Publishing Group UK.

Nishida, Masaki. Drawing Manga Martial Arts Figures. 2009. (How to Draw Manga Ser.). 24p. (gr. 3-3). 47.90 *(978-1-61513-440-3(9),* PowerKids Pr.) Rosen Publishing Group, Inc., The.

Parrish, Fayrene. Pancho Saves the Day: Shipmates Learning Adventures Venture. Parrish, Fayrene, illus. 2010. (Illus.). 42p. (J). 15.95 *(978-0-9826717-8-8(4))* Parrish, Fayrene.

Peot, Margaret. Inkblot: Drip, Splat, & Squish Your Way to Creativity. Peot, Margaret, illus. 2011. (ENG., Illus.). 56p. (J). (gr. 6-18). 19.95 *(978-1-59078-720-5(X))* Boyds Mills Pr.

Philippe Chabot, Jean & Sorbier, Frédéric. El Impresionismo. 2003. (Coleccion Mundo Maravilloso). (SPA., Illus.). (J). (gr. 3-5). 13.56 *(978-84-348-6570-9(X))* SM Ediciones ESP. Dist: Lectorum Pubns., Inc.

Piven, Hanoch. Let's Make Faces. Piven, Hanoch, illus. 2013. (ENG., Illus.). 40p. (J). (gr. -1-3). 16.99 *(978-1-4169-1532-4(X))* Simon & Schuster Children's Publishing.

Pohlen, Jerome. Doodle America: Create. Imagine. Doodle Your Way from Sea to Shining Sea. Lemay, Violet, illus. 2013. (Doodle Bks.). (ENG.). 180p. (J). (gr. k-2). pap. 12.95 *(978-1-938093-14-2(3))* Duo Pr. LLC.

Puck. Yummy Food Doodles: Perfect for Restaurants, Picnics, Parties, School, & Doodling on the Road! Lemay, Violet, illus. 2013. (Doodle Bks.). (ENG.). 120p. (J). (gr. k-3). pap. 12.95 *(978-1-938093-15-9(1))* Duo Pr. LLC.

Randolph, Joanne. Let's Draw a Bird with Shapes. Muschinske, Emily, illus. 2005. (Let's Draw with Shapes Ser.). 24p. (J). (gr. k-1). lib. bdg. 22.60 *(978-1-4042-2792-7(X),* PowerKids Pr.) Rosen Publishing Group, Inc., The.

Riggs, Kate. What Is Cubism? 2016. (Artworld Ser.). (ENG.). 24p. (J). (gr. 2-4). pap. 9.99 *(978-1-62832-222-4(5),* Creative Paperbacks) Creative Co., The.

Robins, Deri. Special Effects. 2005. (Learn Art Ser.). (Illus.). 32p. (J). (ENG.). pap. *(978-1-84538-280-3(3));* pap. *(978-1-84538-128-8(9))* Quarto Publishing Group UK. (QED Publishing).

—Stencils & Prints. 2004. (QEB Learn Art Ser.). (Illus.). 32p. (J). lib. bdg. 18.95 *(978-1-59566-048-0(8),* 1236548) QEB Publishing Inc.

Ros, Jordina & Estadella, Pere. Fun Crafts with 2D & 3D Figures. 2006. (Arts & Crafts Fun Ser.). (Illus.). 48p. (J). (gr. 3-4). lib. bdg. 25.27 *(978-0-7660-2652-0(3),* Enslow Elementary) Enslow Pubs., Inc.

—Fun Crafts with Colors. 2006. (Arts & Crafts Fun Ser.). (Illus.). 48p. (J). (gr. 3-7). lib. bdg. 25.27 *(978-0-7660-2655-1(8),* Enslow Elementary) Enslow Pubs., Inc.

—Fun Crafts with Dots & Lines. 2006. (Arts & Crafts Fun Ser.). (Illus.). 48p. (J). (gr. 3-7). lib. bdg. 25.27 *(978-0-7660-2656-8(6),* Enslow Elementary) Enslow Pubs., Inc.

—Fun Crafts with Shapes. 2006. (Arts & Crafts Fun Ser.). (Illus.). 48p. (J). (gr. 3-7). lib. bdg. 25.27 *(978-0-7660-2657-5(4),* Enslow Elementary) Enslow Pubs., Inc.

—Fun Crafts with Sizes & Spaces. 2006. (Arts & Crafts Fun Ser.). (Illus.). 48p. (J). (gr. 3-4). lib. bdg. 25.27 *(978-0-7660-2653-7(1),* Enslow Elementary) Enslow Pubs., Inc.

—Fun Crafts with Textures. 2006. (Arts & Crafts Fun Ser.). (Illus.). 48p. (J). (gr. 3-4). lib. bdg. 25.27 *(978-0-7660-2654-4(X),* Enslow Elementary) Enslow Pubs., Inc.

Schwake, Susan. Art for All Seasons. 2014. (Kids Art Ser.). (ENG., Illus.). 144p. (J). pap. 24.95 *(978-0-9912935-9-9(2))* Two Little Birds Bks.

—3D Art Lab for Kids: 32 Hands-On Adventures in Sculpture & Mixed Media - Including Fun Projects Using Clay, Plaster, Cardboard, Paper, Fiber Beads & More! Schwake, Rainer, photos by. 2013. (Lab Ser.). (ENG., Illus.). 144p. pap. 24.99 *(978-1-59253-815-7(0),* 1592538150, Quarry Books) Quarto Publishing Group USA.

Scrace, Carolyn. Printing & Other Amazing Techiques. 2015. (How to Art Doodle Ser.). (Illus.). 24p. (gr. 3-6). 28.50 *(978-1-909645-51-6(6))* Book Hse. GBR. Dist: Black Rabbit Bks.

—Printing & Other Amazing Techniques. 2015. (ENG., Illus.). 24p. (J). pap. 8.95 *(978-1-910184-38-7(1))* RiverStream Publishing.

Stegenga, Wil. Spectacular Star Designs. 2009. (Dover Design Coloring Bks.). (ENG., Illus.). 32p. (gr. 3-5). pap. 3.99 (978-0-486-46993-5(X)) Dover Pubns., Inc.
Tatchell, Judy. Pocket Artist. 2004. (Young Artist Ser.). (Illus.). 288p. (J). (gr. 2-18). 8.95 (978-0-7945-0100-6(1), Usborne) EDC Publishing.
Tecco, Betsy Dru. How to Draw France's Sights & Symbols. 2004. (Kid's Guide to Drawing the Countries of the World Ser.). (Illus.). 48p. (J). lib. bdg. 29.25 (978-0-8239-6683-7(6), PowerKids Pr.) Rosen Publishing Group, Inc., The.
—How to Draw Germany's Sights & Symbols. 2004. (Kid's Guide to Drawing the Countries of the World Ser.). (Illus.). 48p. (J). lib. bdg. 29.25 (978-0-8239-6685-1(2), PowerKids Pr.) Rosen Publishing Group, Inc., The.
—How to Draw Italy's Sights & Symbols. 2004. (Kid's Guide to Drawing the Countries of the World Ser.). (Illus.). 48p. (J). lib. bdg. 29.25 (978-0-8239-6686-8(0), PowerKids Pr.) Rosen Publishing Group, Inc., The.
—How to Draw Japan's Sights & Symbols. 2004. (Kid's Guide to Drawing the Countries of the World Ser.). 48p. (J). lib. bdg. 29.25 (978-0-8239-6681-3(X), PowerKids Pr.) Rosen Publishing Group, Inc., The.
—How to Draw the United Kingdom's Sights & Symbols. 2004. (Kid's Guide to Drawing the Countries of the World Ser.). (Illus.). 48p. (J). lib. bdg. 29.25 (978-0-8239-6684-4(4), PowerKids Pr.) Rosen Publishing Group, Inc., The.
Top That Publishing Staff, ed. Cartoon Sculpture. 2005. (Illus.). 48p. (978-1-84510-305-7(X)) Top That! Publishing PLC.
Turnbull, Stephanie. Art Skills. 2012. (Super Skills Ser.). (Illus.). 32p. (gr. 3-6). lib. bdg. 31.35 (978-1-59920-798-8(2)) Black Rabbit Bks.
—An Artist. 2016. (How to Be... Ser.). 24p. (gr. 2-6). 28.50 (978-1-62588-365-0(X), Smart Apple Media) Black Rabbit Bks.
van der Meer, Ron & Whitford, Frank. The Interactive Art Book. 2013. (ENG., Illus.). 14p. (J). (gr. k). 27.99 (978-1-60887-183-4(5)) Insight Editions.
Visca, Curt & Visca, Kelley. How to Draw Cartoon Holiday Symbols. 2004. (Kid's Guide to Drawing Ser.). (Illus.). 24p. (YA). (gr. 2-5). lib. bdg. 25.25 (978-0-8239-6726-1(3)) Rosen Publishing Group, Inc., The.
Watt, F. Art Ideas Pack. 2004. (Activity Kits Ser.). (ENG., Illus.). 1p. (J). act. bk. ed. 16.95 (978-0-7945-0119-8(2), Usborne) EDC Publishing.
—Art Skills. 2004. (Art Ideas Ser.). (Illus.). 96p. (J). (gr. 5-18). lib. bdg. 26.95 (978-1-58086-497-8(X)) EDC Publishing.
Watt, Fiona. Art Ideas Drawing Pack: Internet-Linked. 2004. (Activity Kits Ser.). (ENG.). 32p. (J). pap., act. bk. ed. 16.95 (978-0-7945-0539-4(2)) EDC Publishing.
—Art Skills. 2005. (Illus.). 96p. (J). (gr. 4-7). 7.95 (978-0-7945-1110-4(4), Usborne) EDC Publishing.
—Art Skills. Miller, Antonia, illus. 2004. (Art Ideas Ser.). (ENG.). 96p. (J). pap. 18.95 (978-0-7945-0351-2(9)) EDC Publishing.
—Complete Book of Art Ideas. rev. ed. 2011. (Art Ser.). 288p. (J). pap. 19.99 (978-0-7945-2642-9(X), Usborne) EDC Publishing.
—The Usborne Book of Art Ideas. Barlow, Amanda, illus. rev. ed. 2006. (Art Ideas Ser.). 96p. (J). pap. 14.99 (978-0-7945-0893-7(6), Usborne) EDC Publishing.
—The Usborne Complete Book of Art Ideas. Miller, Antonia et al, illus. 2006. (Art Ideas Ser.). 288p. (J). pap. 19.99 (978-0-7945-1439-6(1), Usborne) EDC Publishing.
Wenzel, Angela. 13 Art Techniques Children Should Know. 2013. (ENG., Illus.). 48p. (J). (gr. 3-7). 14.95 (978-3-7913-7136-8(3)) Prestel Verlag GmbH & Co KG. DEU. Dist: Penguin Random Hse. LLC.
Wheeler, Annie. Painting on a Canvas: Art Adventures for Kids, 1 vol. Dixon, Debra Spina & Spina Dixon, Debra, illus. 2006. (ENG.). 64p. (J). (gr. 3-7). pap. 9.95 (978-1-58685-839-1(4)) Gibbs Smith, Publisher.
Witty One Restickable Art Frames. 2003. per. (978-1-932435-02-3(6)) Cardinal Brands, Inc.
Wolfe, Gillian & Quarto Generic Staff. Look! Really Smart Art. 2013. (Look! Ser.). (ENG., Illus.). 48p. (J). (gr. 3-6). pap. 9.99 (978-1-84780-414-3(4), Frances Lincoln) Quarto Publishing Group UK GBR. Dist: Hachette Bk. Group.
Wood, Alix. Expressionist Art. 2016. (Create It! Ser.). 32p. (gr. 5-4). pap. 10.50 (978-1-4824-5035-4(6)) Stevens, Gareth Publishing LLLP.
Zalme, Ron, illus. How to Draw Nintendo Greatest Heroes & Villains. 2007. (978-0-439-91324-9(1)) Scholastic, Inc.

ART—VOCATIONAL GUIDANCE

Childress, Kim. Find Your Future in Art. 2016. (Bright Futures Press: Find Your Future in STEAM Ser.). (ENG., Illus.). 32p. (J). (gr. 4-6). 29.93 (978-1-63471-901-8(8), 208925) Cherry Lake Publishing.
Clark, Richard & Fehl, Pamela. Career Opportunities in the Visual Arts. 2006. (Career Opportunities Ser.). 320p. (gr. 8-12). per. 18.95 (978-0-8160-5928-7(4), Checkmark Bks.) Facts On File, Inc.
Craig, Joe. The Vo-Tech Track to Success in Manufacturing, Mechanics, & Automotive Care. 2014. (Learning a Trade, Preparing for a Career Ser.). (Illus.). 80p. (J). (gr. 7-12). 34.25 (978-1-4777-7734-3(2)) Rosen Publishing Group, Inc., The.
Facts on File, Inc. Staff, contrib. by. Top Careers for Art Graduates. 2004. (Top Careers Ser.). (Illus.). 368p. (gr. 9). pap. 14.95 (978-0-8160-5565-4(3), Checkmark Bks.) Facts On File, Inc.
Ferguson. Art. 2nd rev. ed. 2008. (Careers in Focus Ser.). 204p. (gr. 6-12). 32.95 (978-0-8160-7283-5(3), Ferguson Publishing Co.) Facts On File, Inc.
Ferguson Publishing Staff, creator. Art. 2007. (What Can I Do Now? Ser.). 176p. (YA). (gr. 7-12). 32.95 (978-0-8160-6025-2(8)) Facts On File, Inc.
Guillain, Charlotte. Art, 1 vol. 2012. (Jobs If You Like... Ser.). (ENG.). 32p. (gr. 1-3). pap. 8.29 (978-1-4329-6815-1(7)); lib. bdg. 27.32 (978-1-4329-6804-5(1)) Heinemann-Raintree. (Heinemann First Library).
—Get Drawing!, 1 vol. 2014. (Dream It, Do It! Ser.). (ENG.). 32p. (gr. 1-3). lib. bdg. 29.99 (978-1-4109-6262-1(8), Read Me!) Heinemann-Raintree.
Hagler, Gina. Money-Making Opportunities for Teens Who Are Artistic. 2013. (Make Money Now! Ser.). (Illus.). 80p. (YA). (gr. 7-12). lib. bdg. 33.25 (978-1-4488-9387-4(9)) Rosen Publishing Group, Inc., The.
Kallen, Stuart A. Careers If You Like the Arts. 2016. (ENG.). 80p. (J). (gr. 5-12). lib. bdg. (978-1-68282-008-7(4)) ReferencePoint Pr., Inc.
Marlowe, Christie. Cosmetologist. 2014. (Illus.). 64p. (J). (978-1-4222-2886-9(X)) Mason Crest.
Orr, Tamra. Manga Artists. 2008. (Extreme Careers Ser.). (Illus.). 64p. (YA). (gr. 5-9). lib. bdg. 31.95 (978-1-4042-1854-3(8)) Rosen Publishing Group, Inc., The.
Reeves, Diane Lindsey. Career Ideas for Teens in the Arts & Communications. 2006. (Career Ideas for Teens Ser.). (Illus.). 176p. (gr. 8-12). per. 16.95 (978-0-8160-6918-7(2), Checkmark Bks.) Facts On File, Inc.
Rooney, Anne. Creative & Media Careers. 2010. (In the Workplace Ser.). 48p. (J). lib. bdg. 34.25 (978-1-60753-090-9(2)) Amicus Publishing.
Rooney, Anne & Savery, Annabel. Creative & Media Careers. 2011. (Been There! Ser.). 32p. (J). (gr. 3-6). lib. bdg. 28.50 (978-1-59920-470-3(3)) Black Rabbit Bks.

ART ANATOMY

see Anatomy, Artistic

ART AND MYTHOLOGY

Beaumont, Steve. Drawing Griffins & Other Winged Wonders. 2011. (Drawing Legendary Monsters Ser.). (Illus.). 32p. (J). (gr. 3-6). lib. bdg. 26.50 (978-1-4488-3253-8(5), PowerKids Pr.) Rosen Publishing Group, Inc., The.
—Drawing the Minotaur & Other Demihumans. 2011. (Drawing Legendary Monsters Ser.). 32p. (J). (ENG.). pap. 11.75 (978-1-4488-3259-0(4)); (Illus.). (gr. 3-6). lib. bdg. 26.50 (978-1-4488-3250-7(0)) Rosen Publishing Group, Inc., The. (PowerKids Pr.).
—Drawing Unicorns & Other Mythical Beasts. 2011. (Drawing Legendary Monsters Ser.). 32p. (J). (ENG.). pap. 11.75 (978-1-4488-3261-3(6)); (Illus.). (gr. 3-6). lib. bdg. 26.50 (978-1-4488-3251-4(9)) Rosen Publishing Group, Inc., The. (PowerKids Pr.).
Bergin, Mark. Magical Creatures & Mythical Beasts. 2009. (How to Draw Ser.). (Illus.). 32p. (J). (ENG.). (gr. 4-6). pap. 11.75 (978-1-4358-2647-2(7)); lib. bdg. 26.50 (978-1-4358-2518-5(7)) Rosen Publishing Group, Inc., The. (PowerKids Pr.).
Levin, Freddie. 1-2-3 Draw Mythical Creatures: A Step-by-Step Guide. Levin, Freddie, illus. 2014. Orig. Title: 2003. (Illus.). 64p. (J). pap. (978-0-939217-06-9(6)) Peel Productions, Inc.
Sautter, Aaron. The Young Artist's Guide to Drawing Fantasy Creatures. Bustamante, Martin et al, illus. 2016. (Drawing Fantasy Creatures Ser.). (ENG.). 112p. (gr. 3-4). pap. 9.95 (978-1-4914-8670-2(8)) Capstone Young Readers of Coughlan Cos.
Spilsbury, Richard. Stories Behind the Art - Sculpture. 2017. (Stories in Art Ser.). (ENG., Illus.). 32p. (J). (gr. 4-6). pap. 11.99 (978-0-7502-9486-7(8), Wayland) Hachette Children's Group GBR. Dist: Hachette Bk. Group.

ART APPRECIATION

see also Art—Study and Teaching; Art Criticism; Painting; Pictures

Armstrong, Simon. Cool Art: 50 Fantastic Facts for Kids of All Ages. 2014. (ENG., Illus.). 112p. (J). (gr. 5). 14.99 (978-1-909396-42-5(7)) Pavilion Bks. GBR. Dist: Independent Pubs. Group.
Barbe-Gall, Françoise. How to Talk to Children about Art. 2005. (ENG., Illus.). 208p. (J). (gr. k-12). pap. 18.95 (978-1-55652-580-3(X)) Chicago Review Pr., Inc.
Bayles, Jennifer L. An Adventure in Looking & Listening: Exploring Masterworks at the Albright-Knox Art Gallery. Barnett, Janet, illus. 2003. (J). (978-1-887457-01-9(1)) Buffalo Fine Arts/Albright-Knox Art Gallery.
Blake, Quentin. Cuentame un Cuadro. 2005.Tr. of Tell Me a Picture. (SPA., Illus.). 128p. (J). (gr. 3-5). pap. 25.99 (978-84-8488-218-3(7)) Serres, Ediciones, S. L. ESP. Dist: Lectorum Pubns., Inc.
—Tell Me a Picture. Blake, Quentin, illus. 2003. (Single Titles Ser.). (Illus.). 128p. lib. bdg. 29.90 (978-0-7613-2748-6(7), Millbrook Pr.) Lerner Publishing Group.
—Tell Me a Picture. 2003. (Illus.). 128p. (gr. 3-18). pap. 17.95 (978-0-7613-1893-4(3), Millbrook Pr.) Lerner Publishing Group.
Brommer, Gerald. Discovering Art History 4th Edition SE. 4th ed. 2007. (Illus.). 638p. (J). stu. ed. (978-0-87192-719-4(5)) Davis Pubns., Inc.
Carroll, Colleen. Dogs. 2008. (How Artists See Jr.: Ser.). (ENG., Illus.). 18p. (J). (gr. -1-k). bds. 7.95 (978-0-7892-0972-6(1), Abbeville Kids) Abbeville Pr., Inc.
—The Elements Set 1: Animals - People - Families - Play - Feelings - Weather, 6 vols. 2008. (How Artists See Ser.). (ENG., Illus.). 288p. (J). (gr. k-7). 65.00 (978-0-7892-0962-7(4)) Abbeville Pr., Inc.
—Horses. 2008. (How Artists See Jr.: Ser.). (ENG., Illus.). 18p. (J). (gr. -1-k). bds. 7.95 (978-0-7892-0975-7(6), Abbeville Kids) Abbeville Pr., Inc.
—How Artists See Set 1: Animals - People - Feelings - Weather, 4 vols. 2008. (How Artists See Ser.). (ENG., Illus.). 192p. (J). (gr. k-7). 45.00 (978-0-7892-0964-1(0)) Abbeville Pr., Inc.
—How Artists See Set 2: Work; Heroes; Cities; Elements; America; Artists, 6 vols. 2008. (How Artists See Ser.). (ENG., Illus.). 192p. (J). (gr. 3-4). 65.00 (978-0-7892-0963-4(2)) Abbeville Pr., Inc.
—How Artists See Heroes, Artists, Cities, Elements, 4 vols. 2008. (How Artists See Ser.). (ENG., Illus.). 192p. (J). (gr. k-7). 45.00 (978-0-7892-0966-5(7)) Abbeville Pr., Inc.
—How Artists See Work/Play/Families/America Set 2, 4 vols., Set. 2008. (How Artists See Ser.). (ENG., Illus.). 192p. (J). (gr. k-7). 45.00 (978-0-7892-0965-8(9)) Abbeville Pr., Inc.
Copmbined, Slide. Discovering Art History. (978-0-87192-311-0(4)) Davis Pubns., Inc.
Cormack, Malcolm & Twiggs, Ruth. Tigers & Sails & ABC Tales. 2006. (ENG., Illus.). 64p. (gr. 17). 14.95 (978-0-917046-65-0(X)) University of Virginia Pr.
Cressy, Judith. Can You Find It, Too? Search & Discover More Than 150 Details in 20 Works of Art. 2004. (Illus.). 40p. (J). 15.95 (978-1-58839-053-0(5)) Metropolitan Museum of Art, The.
Dickens, Rosie. The Children's Book of Art: Internet Linked. 2005. (Illus.). 64p. (J). (978-0-439-88981-0(2)) Scholastic, Inc.
Dickins, Rosie, et al. The Usborne Introduction to Art: In Association with the National Gallery, London. 2005. (Illus.). 144p. (J). (978-0-439-79202-8(9)) Scholastic, Inc.
—The Usborne Introduction to Modern Art. 2006. (Illus.). 96p. (J). (978-0-439-89532-3(4)) Scholastic, Inc.
Dixon, Kathryn. The Little Girl's Little Book of Art. 2014. (ENG., Illus.). 128p. 24.95 (978-1-62732-013-9(X), Bellagio Pr.) Taj Bks. International LLC.
Evans, Brooke DiGiovanni. Are You an Art Sleuth? Look, Discover, Learn! 2016. (ENG.). 104p. (J). (gr. -1-2). 17.99 (978-1-63159-131-0(2), Rockport Publishers) Quarto Publishing Group USA.
Falken, Linda & The Metropolitan Museum of Art, The Metropolitan. Puzzling Cats. 2015. (ENG., Illus.). 16p. (J). (gr. -1-1). 16.95 (978-1-4197-1363-7(9), Abrams Bks. for Young Readers) Abrams, Inc.
Fallon, Michael. How to Analyze the Works of Andy Warhol, 1 vol. 2010. (Essential Critiques Set 1 Ser.). (ENG., Illus.). 112p. (J). (gr. 6-12). lib. bdg. 35.64 (978-1-61613-534-8(4), Essential Library) ABDO Publishing Co.
—How to Analyze the Works of Georgia O'Keeffe, 1 vol. 2010. (Essential Critiques Set 1 Ser.). (ENG.). 112p. (J). (gr. 6-12). lib. bdg. 35.64 (978-1-61613-535-5(2), Essential Library) ABDO Publishing Co.
Gittings, Clare. What Are You Looking At? Band 14. 2007. (Collins Big Cat Ser.). (ENG., Illus.). 48p. (J). (gr. 3-4). pap. 8.99 (978-0-00-723091-4(5)) HarperCollins Pubs. Ltd. GBR. Dist: Independent Pubs. Group.
Gray, Amy & Holland, Lucy E. Myths, Angels, & Masquerades: Exploring European Art. 2017. (ENG., Illus.). 104p. 18.95 (978-0-692-39101-3(0)) Marquand Bks., Inc.
Hensley, Laura. How to Read a Work of Art, 1 vol. 2010. (Culture in Action Ser.). (ENG.). 32p. (gr. 3-6). 30.65 (978-1-4109-3925-8(1), NA-r) Heinemann-Raintree.
Lach, Will. Master-Pieces. 2016. (ENG.). 28p. (J). (-3). 15.95 (978-0-7892-1274-0(9), Abbeville Kids) Abbeville Pr., Inc.
Lane, Kimberly & Charlesbridge Publishing Staff. Asian Art. 2008. (Come Look with Me Ser.). (ENG., Illus.). 32p. (J). (gr. k-3). 15.95 (978-1-890674-19-9(2)) Charlesbridge Publishing, Inc.
Le Tord, Bijou. A Bird or Two: A Story about Henri Matisse. Le Tord, Bijou, illus. 2004. (Illus.). 32p. (gr. 2-7). 18.00 (978-0-8028-5184-0(3)) Eerdmans, William B. Publishing Co.
Mason, Antony. El Arte Contemporaneo: En los Tiempos de Warhol. 2005. (Arte Alrededor del Mundo Ser.). (Illus.). 48p. pap. 9.95 (978-85-7416-241-6(8)) Callis Editora Ltda BRA. Dist: Independent Pubs. Group.
—El Arte Moderno: En los Tiempos de Picasso. 2005. (Arte Alrededor del Mundo Ser.). (Illus.). 48p. (J). (gr. 4-7). pap. 9.95 (978-85-7416-240-9(X)) Callis Editora Ltda BRA. Dist: Independent Pubs. Group.
Merberg, Julie & Bober, Suzanne. Dancing with Degas. 2003. (Mini Masters Ser.: MINI). (ENG., Illus.). 22p. (J). (gr. -1-7). bds. 6.99 (978-0-8118-4047-7(6)) Chronicle Bks. LLC.
—A Picnic with Monet. 2003. (Mini Masters Ser.: MINI). (ENG., Illus.). 22p. (J). (gr. -1-7). bds. 6.99 (978-0-8118-4046-0(8)) Chronicle Bks. LLC.
Micklethwait, Lucy. I Spy Shapes in Art. 2004. (ENG., Illus.). 40p. (J). (gr. -1-3). 19.99 (978-0-06-073193-9(1), Greenwillow Bks.) HarperCollins Pubs.
Minnerly, Denise Bennett, illus. Molly Meets Mona & Friends: A Magical Day in the Museum. 2004. (ENG.). 40p. (J). 17.95 (978-1-56290-324-4(1)) Crystal Productions.
Murphy, Patricia J. Creative Minds. 2005. (Real Deal Ser.). (Illus.). 32p. (J). (978-0-7608-9637-2(2)) Sundance/Newbridge Educational Publishing.
National Gallery of Art. An Eye for Art: Focusing on Great Artists & Their Work. 2013. (ENG., Illus.). 180p. (J). (gr. 4-7). pap. 19.95 (978-1-61374-897-8(3)) Chicago Review Pr., Inc.
Nilson, Anna. Art Shark: Collect Great Art, Auction It, Hide It, Steal It! 2006. (Illus.). (J). (gr. 2). 24.95 (978-1-889613-88-8(6)) Birdcage Pr.
Osofsky, Randy & Charlesbridge Publishing Staff. Art in Early America. 2003. (Come Look with Me Ser.). (ENG.). 32p. (J). (gr. k-3). 16.95 (978-1-890674-12-0(5)) Charlesbridge Publishing, Inc.
Peel, Yana. Faces for Baby: An Art for Baby Book. 2013. (ENG., Illus.). 12p. (J). (gr. k — 1). bds. 21.99 (978-0-7636-6433-6(2), Templar) Candlewick Pr.
Phaidon Press Editors & Renshaw, Amanda. The Art Book for Children. Ace, Jane & Kloet, Chris, eds. 2006. (SPA.). (gr. 8-17). 19.95 (978-0-7148-9863-6(5)) Phaidon Pr., Inc.
Pitamic, Maja & Laidlaw, Jill A. Fine Art Adventures: Over 35 Fun & Creative Art Projects Inspired by Classic Masterpieces from Around the World. 2017. (Art Adventures Ser.). (ENG.). 144p. (J). (gr. 1). pap. 19.99 **(978-0-912777-04-7(4))** Chicago Review Pr., Inc.
Raczka, Bob. Art Is... 2003. (Bob Raczka's Art Adventures Ser.). (ENG., Illus.). 32p. (gr. k-12). pap. 9.95 (978-0-7613-1832-3(1), First Avenue Editions) Lerner Publishing Group.
—More Than Meets the Eye: Seeing Art with All Five Senses. 2003. (Bob Raczka's Art Adventures Ser.). (ENG., Illus.). 32p. (gr. k-12). pap. 9.95 (978-0-7613-1994-8(8), First Avenue Editions) Lerner Publishing Group.
—Name That Style: All about Isms in Art. 2009. (Bob Raczka's Art Adventures Ser.). (ENG.). 32p. (gr. 3-12). pap. 9.95 (978-1-58013-824-6(1), First Avenue Editions) Lerner Publishing Group.
—Unlikely Pairs: Fun with Famous Works of Art. 2005. (Bob Raczka's Art Adventures Ser.). (ENG., Illus.). 32p. (gr. k-12). pap. 9.95 (978-0-7613-2378-5(3), First Avenue Editions); lib. bdg. 25.26 (978-0-7613-2936-7(6)) Lerner Publishing Group.
—Where in the World? Around the Globe in 13 Works of Art. 2007. (Bob Raczka's Art Adventures Ser.). (Illus.). 31p. (J). (gr. -1-3). lib. bdg. 23.93 (978-0-8225-6371-6(1), Millbrook Pr.) Lerner Publishing Group.
—Where in the World? Around the Globe in Thirteen Works of Art. 2008. (Bob Raczka's Art Adventures Ser.). (ENG., Illus.). 32p. (gr. 3-12). per. 9.95 (978-0-8225-6372-3(X), First Avenue Editions) Lerner Publishing Group.
Raimondo, Joyce. Imagine That! Activities & Adventures in Surrealism. 2004. (Art Explorers Ser.). (ENG., Illus.). 48p. (J). (gr. k-4). 13.99 (978-0-8230-2502-2(0), Watson-Guptill) Potter/TenSpeed/Harmony.
Renshaw, Amanda. The Art Book for Children. Kloet, Chris & Ace, Jane, eds. rev. ed. 2005. (ENG., Illus.). 80p. (gr. 8-17). 19.95 (978-0-7148-4530-2(2)) Phaidon Pr. Ltd. GBR. Dist: Hachette Bk. Group.
Renshaw, Amanda & Phaidon Press Editors. The Art Book for Children, Bk. 2. 2007. (ENG., Illus.). 80p. (gr. 3-18). 19.95 (978-0-7148-4705-4(4)) Phaidon Pr., Inc.
Richardson, R. Sarah & Charlesbridge Publishing Staff. The Artist at Work. 2003. (Come Look with Me Ser.). (ENG.). 32p. (J). (gr. k-3). 16.95 (978-1-890674-09-0(5)) Charlesbridge Publishing, Inc.
Sabbeth, Carol. Frida Kahlo & Diego Rivera: Their Lives & Ideas, 24 Activities. 2005. (For Kids Ser.). (ENG., Illus.). 160p. (J). (gr. 4). pap. 17.95 (978-1-55652-569-8(9), 1241061) Chicago Review Pr., Inc.
Stephens, Pamela Geiger. Dropping in on Matisse. McNeill, Jim, illus. 2004. 32p. (J). 15.95 (978-1-56290-322-0(5)) Crystal Productions.
Thomson, Ruth. Families. 2003. (First Look at Art Ser.). (Illus.). 32p. (gr. 4-6). 23.00 (978-0-7910-7946-1(5), Chelsea Hse.) Facts On File, Inc.
—Places. 2003. (First Look at Art Ser.). (Illus.). 32p. (gr. 4-6). 23.00 (978-0-7910-7947-8(3), Chelsea Hse.) Facts On File, Inc.
Venezia, Mike. Diego Velázquez. Venezia, Mike, illus. 2004. (Getting to Know the World's Greatest Artists Ser.). (ENG., Illus.). 32p. (J). (gr. 3-4). pap. 6.95 (978-0-516-26980-1(1), Children's Pr.) Scholastic Library Publishing.
—Eugene Delacroix. Venezia, Mike, illus. 2003. (Getting to Know World Artists Ser.). (ENG., Illus.). 32p. (J). 28.00 (978-0-516-22576-0(6), Children's Pr.) Scholastic Library Publishing.
Wolfe, Gillian & Quarto Generic Staff. Look! Really Smart Art. 2013. (Look! Ser.). (ENG., Illus.). 48p. (J). (gr. 3-6). pap. 9.99 (978-1-84780-414-3(4), Frances Lincoln) Quarto Publishing Group UK GBR. Dist: Hachette Bk. Group.
Wright, Jessica Noelani. Exploring Modern Art. 2003. (Come Look with Me Ser.). (ENG.). 32p. (J). (gr. k-3). 16.95 (978-1-890674-10-6(9)) Charlesbridge Publishing, Inc.
Yenawine, Philip. People, 1 vol. 3rd ed. 2006. (ENG., Illus.). 24p. (gr. 13-18). 14.95 (978-0-87070-174-0(6)) D.A.P./Distributed Art Pubs.
—Places. 2006. (Illus.). 22p. (J). (gr. 4-8). reprint ed. 15.00 (978-1-4223-5407-0(5)) DIANE Publishing Co.
—Stories, 1 vol. 2nd ed. 2006. (ENG., Illus.). 24p. (J). (gr. -1-3). 14.95 (978-0-87070-178-8(9)) D.A.P./Distributed Art Pubs.

ART APPRECIATION—FICTION

Verde, Susan. The Museum. Reynolds, Peter H., illus. 2013. (ENG.). 32p. (J). (gr. k-2). 16.95 (978-1-4197-0594-6(6), Abrams Bks. for Young Readers) Abrams, Inc.
Wallace, Nancy Elizabeth & Friedlaender, Linda. Look! Look! Look! at Sculpture, 0 vols. 2012. (ENG.). 40p. (J). (gr. k-3). 17.99 (978-0-7614-6132-6(9), 9780761461326, Amazon Children's Publishing) Amazon Publishing.

ART CRITICISM

see also Art Appreciation

Fallon, Michael. How to Analyze the Works of Andy Warhol, 1 vol. 2010. (Essential Critiques Set 1 Ser.). (ENG., Illus.). 112p. (J). (gr. 6-12). lib. bdg. 35.64 (978-1-61613-534-8(4), Essential Library) ABDO Publishing Co.
—How to Analyze the Works of Georgia O'Keeffe, 1 vol. 2010. (Essential Critiques Set 1 Ser.). (ENG.). 112p. (J). (gr. 6-12). lib. bdg. 35.64 (978-1-61613-535-5(2), Essential Library) ABDO Publishing Co.
Geis Conti, Patricia. Andy Warhol. 2010. (¡Mira Qué Artista! Ser.). (SPA.). 18p. (J). (gr. 2-4). 21.95 (978-84-9825-485-3(X)) Combel Editorial, S.A. ESP. Dist: Independent Pubs. Group.
Giraudon, David, illus. Our Living Earth: A Story of People, Ecology, & Preservation. Arthus-Bertrand, Yann, photos by. 2008. (ENG.). 160p. (J). (gr. 3-7). 24.95 (978-0-8109-7132-5(1), Abrams Bks. for Young Readers) Abrams, Inc.
Holzhey, Magdalena. Frida Kahlo: The Artist in the Blue House. 2003. (Adventures in Art Ser.). (Illus.). 30p. (J). (gr. 5-18). 14.95 (978-3-7913-2863-8(8)) Prestel Publishing.
—Frida Kahlo: The Artist in the Blue House. 2015. (ENG., Illus.). 32p. (J). (gr. 3-7). pap. 9.95 (978-3-7913-7229-7(7)) Prestel Verlag GmbH & Co KG. DEU. Dist: Penguin Random Hse. LLC.
Isaacson, Philip M. A Short Walk Around the Pyramids & Through the World of Art. 2015. (ENG.). 128p. (YA). (gr. 7). pap. 15.99 (978-0-553-53550-1(1), Ember) Random Hse. Children's Bks.
Jacobson, Rick. Picasso: Soul on Fire. Jacobson, Rick & Fernandez, Laura, illus. 2011. (ENG.). 32p. (J). (gr. 5-18). pap. 8.95 (978-1-77049-263-9(1), Tundra Bks.) Tundra Bks. CAN. Dist: Penguin Random Hse. LLC.
Langmuir, Erika & Thomson, Ruth. Looking at Paintings: An Introduction to Fine Art for Young People. 2004. (ENG., Illus.). 160p. (J). (gr. 3-4). 14.95 (978-1-59373-008-6(X)) Bunker Hill Publishing, Inc.
Randolph, Joanne. Let's Draw a Dinosaur with Shapes. Muschinske, Emily, illus. 2005. (Let's Draw with Shapes Ser.). 24p. (J). (gr. k-1). lib. bdg. 22.60 (978-1-4042-2793-4(8), PowerKids Pr.) Rosen Publishing Group, Inc., The.
—Let's Draw a Fire Truck with Shapes. Muschinske, Emily, illus. 2005. (Let's Draw with Shapes Ser.). 24p. (J). (gr. k-1). lib. bdg. 22.60 (978-1-4042-2794-1(6), PowerKids Pr.) Rosen Publishing Group, Inc., The.
—Let's Draw a Truck with Shapes. Muschinske, Emily, illus. 2005. (Let's Draw with Shapes Ser.). 24p. (J). (gr. k-1). lib. bdg. 22.60 (978-1-4042-2796-5(2), PowerKids Pr.) Rosen Publishing Group, Inc., The.
Seurat, Georges Pierre. Make a Masterpiece — Seurat's a Sunday Afternoon on the Island of la Grande Jatte. 2014. (Dover Little Activity Bks.). (ENG.). 4p. (J). (gr. k-3). pap. 1.99 (978-0-486-78951-4(9)) Dover Pubns., Inc.
Wenzel, Angela. The Mad, Mad, Mad World of Salvador Dalí. 2003. (Adventures in Art Ser.). (Illus.). 30p. 14.95 (978-3-7913-2944-4(8)) Prestel Publishing.

ART EDUCATION

see Art—Study and Teaching

ART FORGERIES

see Art—Forgeries

ART GALLERIES, COMMERCIAL

Hill, Z. B. Art Festivals & Galleries: The Art of Selling Art. 2014. (Art Today! Ser.: 10). 64p. (J). (gr. 7-18). 23.95 *(978-1-4222-3169-2(0))* Mason Crest.

ART IN ADVERTISING

see Commercial Art

ART INDUSTRIES AND TRADE

see also Commercial Art; Folk Art

also special industries, trades, etc., e.g. Glass painting and staining; Leather Work

Guillain, Charlotte. Building Things, 1 vol. 2012. (Jobs If You Like... Ser.). (ENG.). 32p. (gr. 1-3). pap. 8.29 *(978-1-4329-6816-8(5),* Heinemann First Library) Heinemann-Raintree.

MacConnel, Kim. A Collection of Applied Design. 2004. (Illus.). (YA). 5.00 *(978-0-9744804-6-6(0),* Athenaeum Music & Arts Library) Library Assn. of La Jolla.

Trowbridge, J. T. Lawrence's Adventures among the Ice-Cutters, Glass-Makers, Coal-Miners, Iron-Men, & Ship-Builders by J T Trowbridge. 2006. 256p. per. 23.99 *(978-1-4255-2277-3(7))* Michigan Publishing.

ART MUSEUMS

see also Art Galleries, Commercial

Avery, Emmajane. The Wallace Collection Children's Art Book. 2009. (Wallace Collection). (Illus.). 48p. pap. 20.00 *(978-0-900785-90-0(X))* Holberton, Paul Publishing GBR. Dist: Casemate Pubs. & Bk. Distributors, LLC.

Blake, Quentin. Cuentame un Cuadro. 2005.Tr. of Tell Me a Picture. (SPA., Illus.). 128p. (J). (gr. 3-5). pap. 25.99 *(978-84-8488-218-3(7))* Serres, Ediciones, S. L. ESP. Dist: Lectorum Pubns., Inc.

—Tell Me a Picture. Blake, Quentin, illus. 2003. (Single Titles Ser.). (Illus.). 128p. lib. bdg. 29.90 *(978-0-7613-2748-6(7),* Millbrook Pr.) Lerner Publishing Group.

—Tell Me a Picture. 2003. (Illus.). 128p. (gr. 3-18). pap. 17.95 *(978-0-7613-1893-4(3),* Millbrook Pr.) Lerner Publishing Group.

Diemer, Lauren. The Guggenheim Museum. 2014. (Illus.). 24p. (J). *(978-1-4896-3240-1(9))* Weigl Pubs., Inc.

Gregory, Joy. The Metropolitan Museum of Art. 2014. (Illus.). 24p. (J). *(978-1-4896-1194-9(0))* Weigl Pubs., Inc.

Harris, John & Lorenz, Catherine. Cats. 2009. (ENG., Illus.). 24p. (gr. -1). 4.95 *(978-0-89236-951-5(5))* Oxford Univ. Pr., Inc.

Howse, Jennifer. The Louvre. 2014. (J). *(978-1-4896-1190-1(8))* Weigl Pubs., Inc.

—The State Hermitage Museum. 2014. (Illus.). 24p. (J). *(978-1-4896-3244-9(1))* Weigl Pubs., Inc.

Meister, Cari. Art Museum. Fretland VanVoorst, Jenny, ed. 2016. (First Field Trips). 24p. (J). (gr. k-2). lib. bdg. 25.65 *(978-1-62031-293-3(X),* Bullfrog Bks.) Jump! Inc.

—El Museo de Arte. 2016. (Los Primeros Viajes Escolares (First Field Trips)).Tr. of Art Museum. (SPA.). 24p. (J). (gr. k-2). lib. bdg. 25.65 *(978-1-62031-331-2(6),* Bullfrog Bks.) Jump! Inc.

Minnerly, Denise Bennett, illus. Molly Meets Mona & Friends: A Magical Day in the Museum. 2004. (ENG.). 40p. (J). 17.95 *(978-1-56290-324-4(1))* Crystal Productions.

Myers, Jenna. The J. Paul Getty Museum. 2014. (J). *(978-1-4896-3256-2(5))* Weigl Pubs., Inc.

Robertson, Charles & Broun, Elizabeth. American Louvre: A History of the Renwick Gallery Building. 2015. (ENG., Illus.). 108p. pap. 24.95 *(978-1-907804-81-6(1))* Giles, D. Ltd. GBR. Dist: Consortium Bk. Sales & Distribution.

Schmutz, Janine, et al, texts. What Is Art? 27 Questions 27 Answers. 2013. (ENG., Illus.). 216p. pap. 30.00 *(978-3-7757-3527-8(5))* Hatje Cantz Verlag GmbH & Co KG DEU. Dist: D.A.P./Distributed Art Pubs.

Walker, Sylvia. The Art Museum: A Sticker Story Coloring Book. 2011. (Dover Coloring Bks.). (ENG.). 32p. (J). (gr. 1-5). pap. 5.99 *(978-0-486-48039-8(9))* Dover Pubns., Inc.

ART OBJECTS

see also classes of art objects, e.g. Furniture; pottery; etc.

Conklin, Wendy. Moctezuma: Aztec Ruler, 1 vol. 2007. (Primary Source Readers Ser.). (ENG.). 32p. (J). (gr. 4-4). pap. 8.99 *(978-0-7439-0457-5(5))* Shell Educational Publishing.

ART OBJECTS, FORGERY OF

see Art—Forgeries

ART SCHOOLS

see Art—Study and Teaching

ARTESIAN WELLS

see Wells

ARTHRITIS

Bjorklund, Ruth. Arthritis. 2009. (Health Alert 6 Ser.). 64p. (gr. 4). 32.79 *(978-0-7614-3984-4(6))* Marshall Cavendish Corp.

Fall, G. Everything You Need to Know about Juvenile Arthritis. 2009. (Need to Know Library). 64p. (gr. 5-5). 58.50 *(978-1-60854-074-7(X))* Rosen Publishing Group, Inc., The.

Fall, Guy. Everything You Need to Know about Juvenile Arthritis. 2005. (Need to Know Library). (Illus.). 64p. (YA). (gr. 4-6). lib. bdg. 31.95 *(978-0-8239-3614-4(7))* Rosen Publishing Group, Inc., The.

ARTHRITIS—FICTION

Antesberger, Barbara. My Grandma's Hands Are Special, 1 vol. 2009. 19p. pap. 24.95 *(978-1-61582-730-5(7))* America Star Bks.

ARTHROPODA

see also Centipedes; Crabs; Insects; Lobsters; Millipedes; Scorpions; Spiders

Bonotaux, Gilles. Dirty Rotten Bugs? Arthropods Unite to Tell Their Side of the Story. Bonotaux, Gilles, illus. 2007. (ENG., Illus.). 48p. (J). (gr. 3-6). 14.95 *(978-1-58728-593-6(2),* 1267604) Cooper Square Publishing Llc.

Boothroyd, Jennifer. Shells. 2011. (First Step Nonfiction / Body Coverings Ser.). pap. 33.92 *(978-0-7613-8610-0(6))* Lerner Publishing Group.

Dover. Dover Digital Design Source #6: Spiders, Insects & Crustaceans. 2010. (Dover Electronic Clip Art Ser.). (ENG., Illus.). 128p. pap. 19.95 *(978-0-486-99070-5(2))* Dover Pubns., Inc.

Gingold, Janet. My Adventure with Arthropods: Advanced My Adventure. 2007. 44p. (J). pap. 8.99 *(978-1-59092-447-1(9))* Blue Forge Pr.

Gray, Susan H. Experiment with Bugs. 2010. (Explorer Junior Library: Science Explorer Junior Ser.). (ENG.). 32p. (gr. 3-6). lib. bdg. 28.50 *(978-1-60279-842-7(7),* 200550) Cherry Lake Publishing.

Harrison, Paul. Micro Bugs. 2007. (Up Close Ser.). (Illus.). 24p. (J). (gr. 3-7). lib. bdg. 25.25 *(978-1-4042-3760-5(7),* PowerKids Pr.) Rosen Publishing Group, Inc., The.

Hemstock, Annie Wendt. Horseshoe Crabs, 1 vol. 2015. (ENG., Illus.). 24p. (J). lib. bdg. 23.60 *(978-1-4777-5822-9(4),* PowerKids Pr.) Rosen Publishing Group, Inc., The.

Huggins-Cooper, Lynn. Beastly Bugs. 2006. (Killer Nature! Ser.). (Illus.). 32p. (J). (gr. 3-5). lib. bdg. 28.50 *(978-1-58340-936-7(X))* Black Rabbit Bks.

Lewis, Clare. Bug Body Parts. 2015. (J). *(978-1-4846-2555-2(2))* Heinemann-Raintree.

Markle, Sandra. Mites: Master Sneaks. 2012. (Arachnid World Ser.). (ENG.). 48p. (gr. 4-8). lib. bdg. 29.27 *(978-0-7613-5046-0(2))* Lerner Publishing Group.

Morgan, Emily. Next Time You See a Pill Bug. 2013. (Next Time You See Ser.). (ENG., Illus.). 32p. (J). (gr. k-5). pap. 12.95 *(978-1-936959-17-4(8))* National Science Teachers Assn.

Murphy, Julie. Arachnids. 2010. (Weird, Wild, & Wonderful Ser.). (Illus.). 24p. (J). (gr. 2-5). lib. bdg. 22.00 *(978-1-4339-3570-1(8),* Gareth Stevens Learning Library) Stevens, Gareth Publishing LLLP.

Nelson, Robin. Speedy Centipedes. 2016. (First Step Nonfiction — Backyard Critters Ser.). (ENG., Illus.). 24p. (J). (gr. k-2). 23.99 *(978-1-5124-0885-0(9))* Lerner Publishing Group.

Oberhauser, Karen, ed. Monarchs & More: 3-6 Curriculum Guide. 2007. spiral bd. 25.00 *(978-0-9800653-1-2(3))* Monarchs in the Classroom.

—Monarchs & More: K-2 Curriculum Guide. 2007. spiral bd. 25.00 *(978-0-9800653-0-5(5))* Monarchs in the Classroom.

—Monarchs & More: Middle School Curriculum Guide. 2007. spiral bd. 25.00 *(978-0-9800653-2-9(1))* Monarchs in the Classroom.

O'Neill, Amanda. I Wonder Why Spiders Spin Webs: And Other Questions about Creepy Crawlies. 2011. (I Wonder Why Ser.). (ENG., Illus.). 32p. (J). (gr. k-3). pap. 6.99 *(978-0-7534-6524-0(8),* 9780753465240, Kingfisher) Roaring Brook Pr.

Rake, Matthew. Creepy, Crawly Creatures. Mendez, Simon, illus. 2015. (Real-Life Monsters Ser.). (ENG.). 32p. (J). (gr. 3-6). lib. bdg. 26.65 *(978-1-4677-6362-2(4))* Lerner Publishing Group.

Riggs, Kate. That's Creepy! Dogi, Fiammetta, illus. 2013. (ENG.). 14p. (J). (gr. -1-k). bds. 7.99 *(978-1-56846-236-3(0),* Creative Editions) Creative Co., The.

Shea, Nicole. Creepy Bugs. 2012. (Nature's Creepiest Creatures Ser.). (ENG.). 24p. (J). (gr. 2-5). pap. 8.15 *(978-1-4339-6491-6(0));* lib. bdg. 22.60 *(978-1-4339-6489-3(9))* Stevens, Gareth Publishing LLLP. (Gareth Stevens Learning Library).

Smith, Molly. Roly-Poly Pillbugs. 2009. (No Backbone! Ser.). (Illus.). 24p. (J). (gr. k-3). lib. bdg. 21.28 *(978-1-59716-754-3(1))* Bearport Publishing Co., Inc.

Smithyman, Kathryn & Kalman, Bobbie. Les Arthropodes. 2004. (Petit Monde Vivant Ser.). (FRE., Illus.). 32p. (J). pap. 9.95 *(978-2-89579-026-6(4))* Bayard Canada Livres CAN. Dist: Crabtree Publishing Co.

Stefoff, Rebecca. The Arachnid Class. 2008. (Family Trees Ser.). 96p. (YA). (gr. 6-18). lib. bdg. 34.21 *(978-0-7614-3075-9(X),* Benchmark Bks.) Marshall Cavendish Corp.

Stevens, Danielle. Minibeasts. 2013. (World of Wonder Ser.). (Illus.). 32p. (gr. 1-3). 31.35 ***(978-1-905087-09-9(8))*** Book Hse. GBR. Dist: Black Rabbit Bks.

Stewart, Melissa. Creepy, Crawly Jokes about Spiders & Other Bugs: Laugh & Learn about Science. Kelley, Gerald, illus. 2012. (Super Silly Science Jokes Ser.). 48p. (J). (gr. 3-4). 25.27 *(978-0-7660-3966-7(8),* Enslow Elementary) Enslow Pubs., Inc.

Turner, Matt. Tiny Creepy Crawlers. Calle, Santiago, illus. 2017. (Crazy Creepy Crawlers Ser.). (ENG.). 32p. (J). (gr. 3-6). 26.65 *(978-1-5124-1555-1(3));* 7.99 ***(978-1-5124-3606-8(2));*** 39.99 ***(978-1-5124-2715-8(2));*** 39.99 ***(978-1-5124-3605-1(4))*** Lerner Publishing Group.

Veitch, Catherine. Bug Babies, 1 vol. 2013. (Animal Babies Ser.). (ENG.). 24p. (gr. -1-1). 22.65 *(978-1-4329-7495-4(5));* pap. 6.95 *(978-1-4329-8420-5(9));* pap. 35.94 *(978-1-4329-8427-4(6))* Heinemann-Raintree. (Acorn).

Visca, Kelly. How to Draw Cartoon Crustaceans. 2009. (Kid's Guide to Drawing Ser.). 24p. (gr. 3-3). 47.90 *(978-1-61511-013-1(5),* PowerKids Pr.) Rosen Publishing Group, Inc., The.

ARTHROPODA—FICTION

Durant, Alan. That's Not Right! McEwen, Katharine, illus. 2004. (Flying Foxes Ser.). 48p. (J). (gr. k-2). 13.10 *(978-0-7569-3057-8(X))* Perfection Learning Corp.

Korell, Jennifer. A Day at the Beach with Shrimp & Friends. 2013. 20p. pap. 24.95 *(978-1-63000-677-8(7))* America Star Bks.

Nickel, Scott. Curse of the Red Scorpion, 1 vol. Harpster, Steve, illus. 2006. (Graphic Sparks Ser.). (ENG.). 40p. (gr. 1-3). 23.99 *(978-1-59889-034-1(4),* Graphic Sparks) Stone Arch Bks.

Ogle, Bonnie. Arthur the Arthropod. 2012. 28p. pap. 15.99 *(978-1-4771-1424-7(6))* Xlibris Corp.

ARTHUR (FICTITIOUS CHARACTER: BROWN)—FICTION

Brown, Marc. Arthur & the Bad-Luck Brain, Bk. 30. 2003. (ENG., Illus.). 64p. (J). (gr. 1-4). pap. 4.25 *(978-0-316-12377-8(3))* Little, Brown Bks. for Young Readers.

—Arthur & the Big Snow. Brown, Marc, illus. 2005. (ENG., Illus.). 24p. (J). (gr. -1-1). per. 3.99 *(978-0-316-05770-7(3))* Little, Brown Bks. for Young Readers.

—Arthur & the Comet Crisis. 2005. (Arthur Chapter Bks.: No. 27). (Illus.). 54p. (J). lib. bdg. 15.00 *(978-1-59054-719-9(5))* Fitzgerald Bks.

—Arthur & the Double Dare. 2005. (Arthur Chapter Bks.: Bk. 25). (Illus.). 56p. (J). lib. bdg. 15.00 *(978-1-59054-722-9(5))* Fitzgerald Bks.

—Arthur & the Lost Diary. 2005. (Arthur Chapter Bks.: Bk. 9). (Illus.). 55p. (J). lib. bdg. 15.00 *(978-1-59054-723-6(3))* Fitzgerald Bks.

—Arthur & the Lost Diary. (Arthur Chapter Bks.: Bk. 9). 55p. (J). (gr. 3-6). pap. 3.95 *(978-0-8072-1305-6(5),* Listening Library) Random Hse. Audio Publishing Group.

—Arthur & the Mystery of the Stolen Bike. 2012. (ENG., Illus.). 64p. (J). (gr. 1-4). pap. 4.99 *(978-0-316-13363-0(9))* Little, Brown Bks. for Young Readers.

—Arthur & the Nerves of Steal. 2005. (Arthur Chapter Bks.: Bk. 32). (Illus.). 53p. (J). lib. bdg. 15.00 *(978-1-59054-724-3(1))* Fitzgerald Bks.

—Arthur & the Nerves of Steal. 32nd ed. 2004. (ENG., Illus.). 64p. (J). (gr. 1-4). pap. 4.25 *(978-0-316-12618-2(7),* Tingley, Megan Bks.) Little, Brown Bks. for Young Readers.

—Arthur & the No-Brainer. 2005. (Arthur Chapter Bks.: Bk. 26). (Illus.). 55p. (J). lib. bdg. 15.00 *(978-1-59054-725-0(X))* Fitzgerald Bks.

—Arthur & the Poetry Contest. 2005. (Arthur Chapter Bks.: No. 18). (Illus.). 60p. (J). lib. bdg. 15.00 *(978-1-59054-727-4(6))* Fitzgerald Bks.

—Arthur & the Popularity Test. 2005. (Arthur Chapter Bks.: Bk. 12). (Illus.). 58p. (J). lib. bdg. 15.00 *(978-1-59054-728-1(4))* Fitzgerald Bks.

—Arthur & the Popularity Test. (Arthur Chapter Bks.: Bk. 12). 58p. (J). (gr. 3-6). pap. 3.95 *(978-0-8072-1308-7(X));* 2004. (gr. 2-4). pap. 17.00 incl. audio *(978-0-8072-0413-9(7),* FTR204SP) Random Hse. Audio Publishing Group. (Listening Library).

—Arthur & the School Pet. 2005. (Step into Reading Sticker Bks.). (Illus.). 24p. 14.00 *(978-0-7569-5571-7(8))* Perfection Learning Corp.

—Arthur & the School Pet. 2003. (Step into Reading Ser.). (ENG., Illus.). 24p. (J). (gr. k-3). pap. 3.99 *(978-0-375-81001-5(3),* Random Hse. Bks. for Young Readers) Random Hse. Children's Bks.

—Arthur & the School Pet. 2003. (Arthur Step into Reading Ser.). (gr. -1-2). lib. bdg. 13.55 *(978-0-613-57492-1(3),* Turtleback) Turtleback Bks.

—Arthur & the True Francine. (Arthur Adventure Ser.). (J). (gr. k-3). 7.98 incl. audio NewSound, LLC.

—Arthur & the World Record. 33rd ed. 2005. (ENG., Illus.). 64p. (J). (gr. 1-4). pap. 4.25 *(978-0-316-12681-6(0))* Little, Brown Bks. for Young Readers.

—Arthur Helps Out. 2005. (ENG., Illus.). 24p. (J). (gr. -1-1). pap. 3.99 *(978-0-316-05772-1(X))* Little, Brown Bks. for Young Readers.

—Arthur Locked in the Library! 2012. (ENG., Illus.). 64p. (J). (gr. 1-4). pap. 5.99 *(978-0-316-13362-3(0))* Little, Brown Bks. for Young Readers.

—Arthur Loses His Marbles. 31st ed. 2004. (ENG., Illus.). 64p. (J). (gr. 1-4). pap. 4.25 *(978-0-316-12557-4(1))* Little, Brown Bks. for Young Readers.

—Arthur Lost & Found. 2004. (Arthur Adventure Ser.). (J). (gr. k-3). spiral bd. *(978-0-616-11102-4(9))* Canadian National Institute for the Blind/Institut National Canadien pour les Aveugles.

—Arthur Plays the Blues. 2005. (Arthur Chapter Bks.: Bk. 29). (Illus.). 53p. (J). lib. bdg. 15.00 *(978-1-59054-732-8(2))* Fitzgerald Bks.

—Arthur Plays the Blues. 29th ed. 2003. (ENG., Illus.). 64p. (J). (gr. 1-4). pap. 4.25 *(978-0-316-12314-3(5))* Little, Brown Bks. for Young Readers.

—Arthur Rocks with Binky. (Arthur Chapter Bks.: Bk. 11). 61p. (J). (gr. 3-6). pap. 3.95 *(978-0-8072-1307-0(1));* Vol. 11. 2004. (gr. 2-4). pap. 17.00 incl. audio *(978-0-8072-0410-8(2),* FTR203SP) Random Hse. Audio Publishing Group. (Listening Library).

—Arthur Turns Green. 2014. (ENG.). 32p. (J). (gr. 1-4). 7.00 *(978-0-316-12923-7(2))* Little Brown & Co.

—Arthur Turns Green. 2014. (Arthur Adventures Ser.). (J). lib. bdg. 17.20 *(978-0-606-34069-4(6),* Turtleback) Turtleback Bks.

—Arthur Writes a Story. 2004. (Arthur Adventure Ser.). (J). (gr. k-3). spiral bd. *(978-0-616-01604-6(2));* spiral bd. *(978-0-616-01605-3(0))* Canadian National Institute for the Blind/Institut National Canadien pour les Aveugles.

—Arthur Writes a Story. 2003. (Arthur Adventure Ser.). (Illus.). 14.95 *(978-1-59319-021-7(2))* LeapFrog Enterprises, Inc.

—Arthur's Birthday Surprise. 2004. (ENG., Illus.). 24p. (J). (gr. -1-1). pap. 3.99 *(978-0-316-73379-3(2))* Little, Brown Bks. for Young Readers.

—Arthur's Classroom Fib. 2007. (Arthur Step into Reading Ser.). lib. bdg. 13.55 *(978-1-4177-7281-0(6),* Turtleback) Turtleback Bks.

—Arthur's Family Vacation. 2004. (Arthur Adventure Ser.). (J). (gr. k-3). spiral bd. *(978-0-616-01601-5(8));* spiral bd. *(978-0-616-01602-2(6))* Canadian National Institute for the Blind/Institut National Canadien pour les Aveugles.

—Arthur's Heart Mix-Up. 2004. (ENG., Illus.). 24p. (J). (gr. -1-1). pap. 3.99 *(978-0-316-73381-6(4))* Little, Brown Bks. for Young Readers.

—Arthur's Jelly Beans. 2004. (ENG., Illus.). 24p. (J). (gr. -1-1). pap. 3.99 *(978-0-316-73382-3(2))* Little, Brown Bks. for Young Readers.

—Arthur's Mystery Babysitter. Brown, Marc, illus. 2004. (ENG., Illus.). 24p. (J). (gr. -1-1). pap. 3.99 *(978-0-316-73394-6(6),* Tingley, Megan Bks.) Little, Brown Bks. for Young Readers.

—Arthur's New Puppy. (Arthur Adventure Ser.). (J). (gr. k-3). 7.98 incl. audio NewSound, LLC.

—Arthur's off to School. 2004. (ENG., Illus.). 24p. (J). (gr. -1-1). pap. 3.99 *(978-0-316-73378-6(4))* Little, Brown Bks. for Young Readers.

—Arthur's Perfect Christmas. 2004. (ENG., Illus.). 40p. (J). (gr. -1-1). pap. 6.99 *(978-0-316-00130-4(9),* Tingley, Megan Bks.) Little, Brown Bks. for Young Readers.

—Arthur's Pet Business. Brown, Marc, illus. rev. ed. 2007. (ENG., Illus.). 32p. (J). (gr. -1-3). pap. 10.99 *(978-0-316-11863-7(X))* Little, Brown Bks. for Young Readers.

—Arthur's Teacher Trouble. 2004. (Arthur Adventure Ser.). (J). (gr. k-3). spiral bd. *(978-0-616-00406-7(0));* spiral bd. *(978-0-616-01603-9(4))* Canadian National Institute for the Blind/Institut National Canadien pour les Aveugles.

—Arthur's Tree House. 2007. (ENG., Illus.). 24p. (J). (gr. -1-1). pap. 3.99 *(978-0-316-05776-9(2))* Little, Brown Bks. for Young Readers.

—Arthur's Underwear. 2004. (Arthur Adventure Ser.). (Illus.). (J). (gr. k-3). spiral bd. *(978-0-616-14563-0(2));* spiral bd. *(978-0-616-14564-7(0))* Canadian National Institute for the Blind/Institut National Canadien pour les Aveugles.

—Buster's Dino Dilemma. (Arthur Chapter Bks.: Bk. 7). 58p. (J). (gr. 3-6). pap. 3.95 *(978-0-8072-1303-2(9),* Listening Library) Random Hse. Audio Publishing Group.

—Francine, Believe It or Not. 2005. (Arthur Chapter Bks.: Bk. 14). (Illus.). 58p. (J). lib. bdg. 15.00 *(978-1-59054-741-0(1))* Fitzgerald Bks.

—King Arthur. 2005. (Arthur Chapter Bks.: Bk. 13). (Illus.). 58p. (J). lib. bdg. 15.00 *(978-1-59054-742-7(X))* Fitzgerald Bks.

—King Arthur. unabr. ed. 2004. (Arthur Chapter Bks.: Bk. 13). 58p. (J). (gr. 2-4). pap. 17.00 incl. audio *(978-0-8072-0344-6(0),* Listening Library) Random Hse. Audio Publishing Group.

—Marc Brown Arthur: King Arthur; Francine, Believe it or Not; Arthur & the Cootie-Catcher; (Arthur Chapter Bks.: No. 5). 58p. (J). (gr. 3-6). pap. 3.95 *(978-0-8072-1299-8(7),* Listening Library) Random Hse. Audio Publishing Group.

—Marc Brown's Arthur: Arthur & the Crunch Cereal Contest; Arthur Accused!; Locked in the Library. (Arthur Chapter Bks.: No. 2). 58p. (J). (gr. 3-6). pap. 3.95 *(978-0-8072-1296-7(2),* Listening Library) Random Hse. Audio Publishing Group.

—Marc Brown's Arthur: Arthur & the Scare-Your-Pants-off Club; Arthur Makes the Team. (Arthur Chapter Bks.: No. 1). (J). (gr. 3-6). 12.78 incl. audio NewSound, LLC.

—Marc Brown's Arthur: Arthur & the Scare-Your-Pants-off Club; Arthur Makes the Team. (Arthur Chapter Bks.: No. 1). 58p. (J). (gr. 3-6). pap. 3.95 *(978-0-8072-1295-0(4),* Listening Library) Random Hse. Audio Publishing Group.

—Marc Brown's Arthur: Buster's Dino Dilemma; The Mystery of the Stolen Bike; Arthur & the Lost Diary. (Arthur Chapter Bks.: No. 3). 61p. (J). (gr. 3-6). pap. 3.95 *(978-0-8072-1297-4(0));* pap. 3.95 *(978-0-8072-1298-1(9))* Random Hse. Audio Publishing Group. (Listening Library).

—The Mystery of the Stolen Bike. (Arthur Chapter Bks.: Bk. 8). 59p. (J). (gr. 3-6). pap. 3.95 *(978-0-8072-1304-9(7),* Listening Library) Random Hse. Audio Publishing Group.

—La Visita del Senor Rataquemada. Sarfatti, Esther, tr. from ENG. 2003.Tr. of Arthur's Teacher Moves In. (SPA.). (J). (gr. k-2). pap. 6.95 *(978-1-930332-41-6(6))* Lectorum Pubns., Inc.

—Who's in Love with Arthur? (Arthur Chapter Bks.: Bk. 10). 57p. (J). (gr. 3-6). pap. 3.95 *(978-0-8072-1306-3(3),* Listening Library) Random Hse. Audio Publishing Group.

Brown, Marc & Sarfatti, Esther. Arturo y la Navidad. 2004. (SPA.). (J). pap. 6.95 *(978-1-930332-48-5(3))* Lectorum Pubns., Inc.

Krensky, Stephen. Locked in the Library! (Arthur Chapter Bks.: Bk. 6). 58p. (J). (gr. 3-6). pap. 3.95 *(978-0-8072-1300-1(4),* Listening Library) Random Hse. Audio Publishing Group.

Krensky, Stephen, text. Arthur Makes the Team. 2005. (Arthur Chapter Bks.: Bk. 3). (Illus.). (J). lib. bdg. 15.00 *(978-1-59054-731-1(4))* Fitzgerald Bks.

ARTHUR, KING

see also Grail

Cutler, U. Waldo. Stories of King Arthur & His Knights. 2011. 160p. 24.95 *(978-1-4638-9661-4(1))* Rodgers, Alan Bks.

Ganeri, Anita. King Arthur's Tale. 2011. (ENG.). 24p. (J). pap. *(978-0-7787-7872-1(X));* (gr. 3-6). *(978-0-7787-7850-9(9))* Crabtree Publishing Co.

Gilbert, Henry. King Arthur's Knights: The Tales Retold for Boys & Girls. 2004. reprint ed. pap. 27.95 *(978-1-4191-2865-3(5));* pap. 1.99 *(978-1-4192-2865-0(X))* Kessinger Publishing, LLC.

Harkins, Susan & Harkins, William H. The Life & Times of King Arthur: The Evolution of the Legend. 2006. (Biography from Ancient Civilizations Ser.). (Illus.). 48p. (J). (gr. 3-7). lib. bdg. 29.95 *(978-1-58415-513-3(2))* Mitchell Lane Pubs., Inc.

Hunter, Nick. Did King Arthur Really Exist? 2016. (Top Secret! Ser.). (ENG., Illus.). 48p. (gr. 4-6). lib. bdg. 33.32 *(978-1-4109-8160-8(6))* Heinemann-Raintree.

Korn, David M. Young King Arthur in Brooklyn. 2003. 210p. (YA). (gr. 6-10). pap. 9.95 *(978-0-9723382-0-2(9))* Jester Bks.

Lace, William W. King Arthur. 2008. (Mysterious & Unknown Ser.). (Illus.). 104p. (YA). (gr. 3-7). lib. bdg. *(978-1-60152-033-3(6))* ReferencePoint Pr., Inc.

Lang, Andrew. The Book of Romance. 2004. reprint ed. pap. 34.95 *(978-0-7661-8836-5(1))* Kessinger Publishing, LLC.

Lang, Andrew, ed. The Book of Romance. Ford, H. J., illus. 2004. reprint ed. pap. 34.95 *(978-1-4179-1718-1(0))* Kessinger Publishing, LLC.

Limke, Jeff. El Rey Arturo: La Espada Excalibur Desenvainada; King Arthur: Excalibur Unsheathed. 2008. pap. 52.95 *(978-0-8225-9636-3(9))* Lerner Publishing Group.

Mersey, Daniel. King Arthur, 1 vol. 2015. (ENG., Illus.). 80p. (J). 35.60 *(978-1-4777-8135-7(8),* Rosen Young Adult) Rosen Publishing Group, Inc., The.

Pyle, Howard. The Story of the Champions of the Round Table. 2004. reprint ed. pap. 28.95 *(978-1-4191-8405-5(9));* pap. 1.99 *(978-1-4192-8405-2(3))* Kessinger Publishing, LLC.

Radford, Maude L. King Arthur & His Knights. 2008. 128p. 23.95 *(978-1-60664-799-8(7));* pap. 11.95 *(978-1-60664-171-2(9))* Aegypan.

Roberts, Jeremy. King Arthur. 2005. (How History Is Invented Ser.). (Illus.). 112p. (J). (gr. 6-12). lib. bdg. 23.93 *(978-0-8225-4891-1(7))* Lerner Publishing Group.

Spong, Clive, illus. King Arthur & the Magic Sword: An English Legend. 2004. (ENG.). 24p. (J). (gr. 3-3). pap. 6.47 net. *(978-0-7685-2123-8(8),* Dominie Elementary) Pearson Schl.

Thompson, Frank. King Arthur. 2004. (ENG., Illus.). 304p. mass mkt. 6.50 *(978-0-7868-9083-5(5))* Hyperion Pr.

Wolfson, Evelyn. Mythology of King Arthur & His Knights. 2014. (Mythology, Myths, & Legends Ser.). (Illus.). 96p. (J). (gr. 6-12). 27.94 *(978-0-7660-6182-8(5))* Enslow Pubs., Inc.

World Book, Inc Staff, contrib. by. The Legend of King Arthur. 2014. (J). *(978-0-7166-2664-0(0))* World Bk., Inc.

ARTHUR, KING—FICTION

Anderson, M. T. Yvain: The Knight of the Lion. Offermann, Andrea, illus. 2017. (ENG.). 144p. (J). (gr. 7). 19.99 *(978-0-7636-5939-4(8))* Candlewick Pr.

Bowler, Michael J. Children of the Knight [Library Edition]. 2013. 344p. pap. 17.99 *(978-1-62380-925-6(8),* Harmony Ink Pr.) Dreamspinner Pr.

A
B

Brooks, Felicity. Tales of King Arthur. 2004. (Paperback Classics Ser.). 144p. (J). lib. bdg. 12.95 (978-1-58086-433-6(3)) EDC Publishing.

Los Caballeros del Rey Arturo. (SPA., Illus.). (YA). 14.95 (978-84-7281-107-2(7), AF1107) Auriga, Ediciones S.A. ESP. Dist: Continental Bk. Co., Inc.

Cabot, Meg. Avalon High. 2007. (Avalon High Coronation Ser.: Bk. 1). (ENG.). 320p. (YA). (gr. 8-12). pap. 8.99 (978-0-06-075588-1(1), HarperTeen) HarperCollins Pubs.

—Homecoming. Coronado, Jinky, illus. 2008. (Avalon High Coronation Ser.: Bk. 2). (ENG.). 192p. (YA). (gr. 8-18). pap. 9.99 (978-0-06-117709-5(1)) HarperCollins Pubs.

—The Merlin Prophecy. (Avalon High Coronation Ser.: Bk. 1). 304p. (YA). 2006. (ENG.). (gr. 7-12). 16.99 (978-0-06-075586-7(5)) 2005. (gr. 8-12). lib. bdg. 17.89 (978-0-06-075587-4(3), HarperTeen) HarperCollins Pubs.

—The Merlin Prophecy. Coronado, Jinky, illus. 2007. (Avalon High Coronation Ser.: Bk. 1). 128p. pap. 7.99 (978-1-4278-0106-7(1)) TOKYOPOP, Inc.

Castle, Amber. Chloe the Storm Sister. Hall, Mary, illus. 2013. (ENG.). 160p. (J). (gr. 2-4). pap. 7.99 (978-0-85707-254-2(4), Simon & Schuster Children's) Simon & Schuster, Ltd. GBR. Dist: Simon & Schuster, Inc.

Clement-Davies, David. The Telling Pool. Huebsch, Rand, illus. 2007. (ENG.). 382p. (YA). (gr. 7-17). per. 8.95 (978-0-8109-9257-3(4)) Abrams, Inc.

—The Telling Pool. 2005. (ENG., Illus.). 376p. (J). (gr. 7-17). 19.95 (978-0-8109-5758-9(2), Abrams Bks. for Young Readers) Abrams, Inc.

—The Telling Pool. 2006. 1.00 (978-1-4237-6417-5(X)) Recorded Bks., Inc.

Crossley-Holland, Kevin. At the Crossing-Places. 2004. (Arthur Trilogy). (Illus.). 394p. (YA). (gr. 7-12). 15.65 (978-0-7569-3182-7(7)) Perfection Learning Corp.

—Crossing to Paradise. 2008. (J). pap. (978-0-545-05868-1(6), Levine, Arthur A. Bks.) Scholastic, Inc.

Cuillain, Adam. Zak's King Arthur Adventure. 2014. (ENG., Illus.). 32p. (J). (978-0-7787-1315-9(6)) Crabtree Publishing Co.

Darden, Amy. Yesterday Once Again: Guenevere's Quest. 2003. (J). pap. 11.00 (978-0-8059-9238-0(3), RoseDog Bks.) Dorrance Publishing Co., Inc.

Davie, Jan. Arthur's Amulet. 2004. 86p. pap. (978-1-84401-228-2(X)) Athena Pr.

Dennis, Peter, illus. The Adventures of King Arthur. 2003. (Young Reading Ser.). 64p. (J). (gr. k-7). pap. 5.99 (978-0-7945-0447-2(7), Usborne) EDC Publishing.

—The Adventures of King Arthur. 2003. (Usborne Young Reading: Series Two Ser.). 64p. (J). (gr. k-7). 8.99 (978-0-7945-1871-4(0), Usborne) EDC Publishing.

Duey, Kathleen. Arthur. Epstein, Eugene, illus. Gould, Robert, photos by. 2004. (Time Soldiers Ser.: Bk. 4). (ENG.). 48p. (J). (gr. k-2). 15.95 (978-1-929945-05-4(1)) Big Guy Bks., Inc.

—Arthur. Gould, Robert, photos by. 2006. (Time Soldiers Ser.). (ENG., Illus.). 96p. (gr. -1-4). 24.21 (978-1-59961-224-9(0)) Spotlight.

Gale, Eric Kahn. The Wizard's Dog. 2017. (ENG., Illus.). 288p. (J). (gr. 3-7). 16.99 (978-0-553-53736-9(9), Crown Books For Young Readers) Random Hse. Children's Bks.

Gilman, Laura Anne. The Camelot Spell. 2006. (Grail Quest Ser.: No. 1). 291p. (J). (gr. 5-9). 10.99 (978-0-06-077279-6(4)) HarperCollins Pubs.

Green, Norman, illus. Knights of the Round Table. 2005. (Reader's Workshop Ser.). (ENG.). 112p. (C). pap. 19.95 (978-0-7362-2786-5(5)) CENGAGE Learning.

Guerra, Elisa Puricelli. Merlin's Island, 1 vol. Pernigotti, Chiara, tr. from ITA. Bernstein, Gabo León, illus. 2014. (Minerva Mint Ser.). (ENG.). 160p. (gr. 2-4). pap. 7.99 (978-1-4342-6514-2(5)) Capstone Young Readers of Coughlan Cos.

—Merlin's Island, 1 vol. Pernigotti, Chiara, tr. from ITA. Bernstein, Gabo León, illus. 2014. (Minerva Mint Ser.). (ENG.). 160p. (gr. 2-4). 25.32 (978-1-4342-6511-1(0)) Stone Arch Bks.

Hodges, Margaret & Malory, Sir Thomas. Merlin & the Making of the King. Hyman, Trina Schart, tr. Hyman, Trina Schart, illus. 2004. (ENG.). 40p. (J). (gr. 4-6). tchr. ed. 16.95 (978-0-8234-1647-9(X)) Holiday Hse., Inc.

Hoffman, Mary. The Sword in the Stone. Ginevra, Dante, illus. 2014. (Collins Big Cat Progress Ser.). (ENG.). 32p. (J). (gr. 4-5). pap. 7.99 (978-0-00-751935-4(4)) HarperCollins Pubs. Ltd. GBR. Dist: Independent Pubs. Group.

—Women of Camelot: Queens & Enchantresses at the Court of King Arthur. Balit, Christina, illus. 2006. 69p. (YA). (gr. 5-9). 20.00 (978-1-4223-5260-1(9)) DIANE Publishing Co.

Ioan, Elwyn & Gruffudd, Garmon. Arthur A'r Cleddyf. 2005. (WEL., Illus.). 16p. pap. (978-0-86243-378-9(9)) Y Lolfa.

Johnson-Shelton, Nils. The Dragon King. 2013. (Otherworld Chronicles Ser.: 3). (ENG.). 352p. (J). (gr. 3-7). 16.99 (978-0-06-207097-5(5)) HarperCollins Pubs.

—The Invisible Tower. 2012. (J). 335p. 9.99 (978-0-06-213192-8(3)); (Otherworld Chronicles Ser.: 1). (ENG.). 352p. (gr. 5). 16.99 (978-0-06-207086-9(X)) HarperCollins Pubs.

—Otherworld Chronicles #2: the Seven Swords. 2013. (Otherworld Chronicles Ser.: 2). (ENG.). 384p. (J). (gr. 3-7). pap. 6.99 (978-0-06-207095-1(9)) HarperCollins Pubs.

—The Seven Swords. 2013. (Otherworld Chronicles Ser.: 2). (ENG.). 368p. (J). (gr. 3-7). 16.99 (978-0-06-207094-4(0)) HarperCollins Pubs.

Ladybird Books Staff & Dunkerley, Desmond. King Arthur. 2016. (Ladybird Classics Ser.). (ENG., Illus.). 72p. (J). (gr. k-3). 11.99 (978-0-7232-9560-0(3)) Penguin Bks., Ltd. GBR. Dist: Independent Pubs. Group.

Leighton-Porter, Wendy. The Shadow of Camelot. 2013. 262p. pap. (978-1-909411-06-7(X)) Mauve Square Publishing.

Leung, Julie. Mice of the Round Table #1: a Tail of Camelot. Carr, Lindsey, illus. 2017. (Mice of the Round Table Ser.: 1). 320p. (J). (gr. 3-7). pap. 6.99 **(978-0-06-240400-8(8))** HarperCollins Pubs.

Limke, Jeff. Arthur & Lancelot: The Fight for Camelot. Yeates, Thomas, illus. 2008. (Graphic Myths & Legends Ser.). (ENG.). 48p. (gr. 4-8). pap. 8.95 (978-0-8225-8513-8(8)) Lerner Publishing Group.

—Arthur & Lancelot: The Fight for Camelot - An English Legend. Yeates, Thomas, illus. 2007. (Graphic Myths & Legends Ser.). (ENG.). 48p. (J). (gr. 4-8). lib. bdg. 27.93 (978-0-8225-6296-2(0), Graphic Universe™) Lerner Publishing Group.

—Arthur & Lancelot: The Fight for Camelot [an English Legend]. Yeates, Thomas, illus. 2015. (Graphic Myths & Legends Ser.). (ENG.). 48p. (gr. 4-8). 21.32 (978-1-4677-5979-3(1), Lerner Digital) Lerner Publishing Group.

—King Arthur: Excalibur Unsheathed. Yeates, Thomas, illus. 2007. (Graphic Myths & Legends Ser.). (ENG.). 48p. (gr. 4-8). per. 8.95 (978-0-8225-6483-6(1)) Lerner Publishing Group.

—El Rey Arturo: La Espada Excalibur Desenvainada: Una Leyenda Inglesa. Translations.com Staff, tr. from ENG. Yeates, Thomas, illus. 2007. (Mitos y leyendas en viñetas (Graphic Myths & Legends) Ser.).Tr. of King Arthur - Excalibur Unsheathed [An English Legend. (SPA.). 48p. (gr. 4-8). per. 8.95 (978-0-8225-7968-7(5)) Lerner Publishing Group.

Masson, Sophie, ed. The Road to Camelot: Tales of the Young Merlin, Arthur, Lancelot & More. 2010. (ENG.). 282p. (J). (gr. 7). 9.99 (978-1-86471-948-2(6)) Random Hse. Australia AUS. Dist: Independent Pubs. Group.

Matthews, John. The Chronicles of Arthur: Sword of Fire & Ice. Collins, Mike, illus. 2009. (ENG.). 128p. (J). (gr. 3-7). 21.99 (978-1-4169-8683-6(9), Simon & Schuster/Paula Wiseman Bks.) Simon & Schuster/Paula Wiseman Bks.

Matthews, John & Matthe, John. Arthur of Albion. Tatamikau, Pavel, illus. 2008. (ENG.). 96p. (J). (gr. 3-6). 24.99 (978-1-84686-049-2(0)) Barefoot Bks., Inc.

Matthews, Rodney, illus. Tales of King Arthur. rev. ed. 2007. (Usborne Classics Retold Ser.). 139p. (J). (gr. 4-7). per. 4.99 (978-0-7945-1483-9(9), Usborne) EDC Publishing.

Mayhew, James. The Magic Sword. 2016. (Early Reader Ser.). (ENG., Illus.). 64p. (J). (gr. k-2). pap. 6.99 (978-1-4440-1573-7(7), Orion Children's Bks.) Hachette Children's Group GBR. Dist: Hachette Bk. Group.

McCusker, Paul. Out of Time, 1 vol. 2009. (Time Thriller Trilogy Ser.: Bk. 2). (ENG., Illus.). 240p. (YA). (gr. 8-11). pap. 9.99 (978-0-310-71437-8(0)) Zondervan.

Meister, Cari. King Arthur & the Sword in the Stone, 1 vol. Erkocak, Sahin, illus. 2008. (Read-It! Readers: Legends Ser.). (ENG.). 32p. (gr. k-3). 21.32 (978-1-4048-4837-5(1), Easy Readers) Picture Window Bks.

Milbourne, Anna. Stories of Knights & Castles. Doherty, Gillian, ed. Marks, Alan, illus. 2007. (Stories for Young Children Ser.). 96p. (J). 16.99 (978-0-7945-1466-2(9), Usborne) EDC Publishing.

Morris, Gerald. The Adventures of Sir Givret the Short. Renier, Aaron, illus. 2009. (Knights' Tales Ser.: 2). (ENG.). 112p. (J). (gr. 1-4). pap. 8.95 (978-0-547-24818-9(0)) Houghton Mifflin Harcourt Publishing Co.

—Parsifal's Page. 2008. (Squire's Tales Ser.: 4). (ENG.). 240p. (J). (gr. 5-7). pap. 7.99 (978-0-547-01434-0(1)) Houghton Mifflin Harcourt Publishing Co.

Namm, Diane. King Arthur & His Knights. Calo, Marcos, illus. 2014. (Silver Penny Stories Ser.). (ENG.). 48p. (J). (gr. -1-1). 4.95 (978-1-4027-8432-3(5)) Sterling Publishing Co., Inc.

Pyle, Howard. King Arthur & the Knights of the Round Table, 1 vol. Mullarkey, Lisa, illus. 2010. (Calico Illustrated Classics Ser.: No. 1). (ENG.). 112p. (YA). (gr. 3-6). 27.07 (978-1-60270-707-8(3)) Magic Wagon.

—The Story of King Arthur & His Knights. Pyle, Howard, illus. 2006. (ENG., Illus.). 416p. (gr. 12-18). 6.95 (978-0-451-53024-0(1), Signet) Penguin Publishing Group.

—The Story of King Arthur & His Knights. McKowen, Scott, illus. 2005. (Sterling Unabridged Classics Ser.). (ENG.). 320p. (J). (gr. 5-9). 14.95 (978-1-4027-2503-6(5), 1252056) Sterling Publishing Co., Inc.

—The Story of Sir Lancelot & His Companions. 2004. reprint ed. pap. 27.95 (978-1-4179-5609-8(7)) Kessinger Publishing, LLC.

Randall, Daniel & Randall, Ronne. Tales of King Arthur: Ten Legendary Stories of the Knights of the Round Table. Howells, Graham, illus. 2013. (ENG.). 80p. pap. 9.99 (978-1-84322-922-3(6)) Anness Publishing GBR. Dist: National Bk. Network.

Reeve, Philip. Here Lies Arthur. 2008. (ENG.). 352p. (J). (gr. 7-18). 17.99 (978-0-545-09334-7(1), Scholastic Pr.) Scholastic, Inc.

—Here Lies Arthur. 2010. lib. bdg. 19.65 (978-0-606-10557-6(3), Turtleback) Turtleback Bks.

Richards, C. E., illus. King Arthur. 2010. (Classic Fiction Ser.). 72p. 4.75 (978-1-4342-2603-7(4), Graphic Revolve) Stone Arch Bks.

Rowley, Melissa. The Falcon Shield. 2009. (J). 6.99 (978-1-60641-103-2(9)) Deseret Bk. Co.

Rowley, M'lin. Knights of Right, BK 4: The Fiery Gloves. 2010. 80p. (J). pap. 6.99 (978-1-60641-241-1(8), Shadow Mountain) Shadow Mountain Publishing.

—The Silver Coat. 2009. (Knights of Right Ser.: Bk. 2). 71p. (J). (gr. 1-5). pap. 6.99 (978-1-60641-104-9(7), Shadow Mountain) Shadow Mountain Publishing.

Rowleym'Lin. Knights of Right, BK 3: The Warrior's Guard. 2010. 80p. (J). pap. 6.99 (978-1-60641-240-4(X), Shadow Mountain) Shadow Mountain Publishing.

Roytman, Arkady. The Adventures of King Arthur Coloring Book. 2013. (ENG., Illus.). 32p. (J). (gr. 3-12). pap. 3.99 (978-0-486-49829-4(8)) Dover Pubns., Inc.

Salerni, Dianne K. The Eighth Day. McClellan, David, illus. (Eighth Day Ser.: 1). (ENG.). (J). (gr. 3-7). 2015. 336p. pap. 6.99 (978-0-06-227216-4(0)) 2014. 320p. 16.99 (978-0-06-227215-7(2)) HarperCollins Pubs.

—The Inquisitor's Mark. 2015. (Eighth Day Ser.: 2). (ENG.). (J). (gr. 3-7). 368p. pap. 6.99 (978-0-06-227219-5(5)); 352p. 16.99 (978-0-06-227218-8(7)) HarperCollins Pubs.

Sanderson, Jeannette. The Sword in Stone: A King Arthur Legend. 2006. (J). pap. (978-1-4108-6179-5(1)) Benchmark Education Co.

Saxena, Shalini. The Legend of King Arthur. 2015. (Famous Legends Ser.). (ENG., Illus.). 32p. (J). (gr. 2-3). 25.25 (978-1-4824-2738-7(9)) Stevens, Gareth Publishing LLLP.

Spinner, Stephanie. Damosel: In Which the Lady of the Lake Renders a Frank & Often Startling Account of Her Wondrous Life & Times. 2010. (ENG.). 208p. (YA). (gr. 7). pap. 8.99 (978-0-553-49511-9(9), Knopf Bks. for Young Readers) Random Hse. Children's Bks.

—The Magic of Merlin. Sokolova, Valerie, illus. 2004. (Stepping Stones: A Chapter Book: Fantasy Ser.). 42p. (J). 11.65 (978-0-7569-0905-5(8)) Perfection Learning Corp.

Thomas, Gwyn. King Arthur. Jones, Margaret, illus. 2006. (ENG.). 144p. (J). pap. 21.95 (978-0-86243-798-5(9)) Y Lolfa GBR. Dist: Dufour Editions, Inc.

Treskillard, Robert. Merlin's Nightmare, 1 vol. 2014. (Merlin Spiral Ser.). (ENG.). 432p. (YA). pap. 12.99 (978-0-310-73509-0(2)) Blink.

Twain, Mark, pseud. A Connecticut Yankee in King Arthur's Court. 2008. (Bring the Classics to Life Ser.). (ENG., Illus.). 72p. (gr. 3-12). pap., act. bk. ed. 10.95 (978-1-55576-357-2(X), EDCTR-309B) EDCON Publishing Group.

Uletilovuic, Patricia. Merlin's Return. 2004. (YA). lib. bdg. 5.50 (978-1-59431-135-2(8)) Write Words, Inc.

Vande Velde, Vivian & Bash, Barbara. The Book of Mordred. 2007. (ENG.). 352p. (YA). (gr. 7-12). pap. 8.99 (978-0-618-80916-5(3)) Houghton Mifflin Harcourt Publishing Co.

Wallace, Karen & Chapman, Neil. Arthur the King. 2009. (Hopscotch Adventures Ser.). (Illus.). 31p. (J). (gr. 1). lib. bdg. 25.65 (978-1-59771-173-9(X)) Sea-To-Sea Pubns.

—The Round Table. 2009. (Hopscotch Adventures Ser.). (Illus.). 31p. (J). (gr. 1). lib. bdg. 25.65 (978-1-59771-175-3(6)) Sea-To-Sea Pubns.

Williams, David Morgan. Dragonrise. 2006. (ENG.). 96p. (J). pap. 11.95 (978-0-86243-637-7(0)) Y Lolfa GBR. Dist: Dufour Editions, Inc.

Yolen, Jane. Sword of the Rightful King: A Novel of King Arthur. 2004. (ENG., Illus.). 384p. (YA). (gr. 7-12). reprint ed. pap. 7.99 (978-0-15-202533-5(2)) Houghton Mifflin Harcourt Publishing Co.

ARTHURIAN ROMANCES

see Arthur, King

ARTIFICIAL FLOWERS

Carreiro, Jen. Felt Flowers: 7 Fabulous Flowers to Make & Share. 2015. (ENG., Illus.). 32p. 9.95 (978-1-63186-349-3(5), 9781631863493) Taunton Pr., Inc.

Dickerson, Jennifer. Mini Flower Loom Crafts: 18 Super Simple Projects. 2015. (ENG., Illus.). 32p. 9.95 (978-1-63186-483-4(1), 9781631864834) Taunton Pr., Inc.

Fontichiaro, Kristin. Hacking Fashion: Fleece. 2015. (21st Century Skills Innovation Library: Makers As Innovators Ser.). (ENG., Illus.). 32p. (J). (gr. 4-8). pap. 14.21 (978-1-63362-404-7(8), 206925) Cherry Lake Publishing.

ARTIFICIAL INTELLIGENCE

Allen, John. What Is the Future of Artificial Intelligence? 2016. (ENG.). 80p. (J). (gr. 5-12). (978-1-68282-060-5(2)) ReferencePoint Pr., Inc.

Cunningham, Anne C., ed. Artificial Intelligence & the Technological Singularity. 2017. (Opposing Viewpoints Ser.). 224p. (YA). (gr. 10-12). pap. 33.80 **(978-1-5345-0029-7(4))**; lib. bdg. 48.80 **(978-1-5345-0027-3(8))** Greenhaven Publishing LLC. (Greenhaven Publishing).

Fritz, Sandy. Robotics & Artificial Intelligence. 2003. (Hot Science Ser.). (J). lib. bdg. 28.50 (978-1-58340-364-8(7)) Black Rabbit Bks.

Greenberger, Robert. Careers in Artificial Intelligence. (Cutting-Edge Careers Ser.). 64p. (gr. 7-7). 2009. 55.90 (978-1-61512-098-7(X)) 2006. (Illus.). (YA). lib. bdg. 31.95 (978-1-4042-0953-4(0)) Rosen Publishing Group, Inc., The.

Harris, Michael C. Artificial Intelligence. 2010. (Cool Science Ser.). 48p. (J). (gr. 3-6). 28.50 (978-1-60870-076-9(3)) Marshall Cavendish GBR. Dist: Marshall Cavendish Corp.

Karam, P. Andrew. Artificial Intelligence. 2012. (Science Foundations Ser.). (Illus.). 109p. (gr. 6-12). 35.00 (978-1-61753-027-2(1), Chelsea Hse.) Facts On File, Inc.

McPherson, Stephanie Sammartino. Artificial Intelligence: Building Smarter Machines. 2017. (ENG.). 104p. (YA). (gr. 8-12). 35.99 **(978-1-5124-1826-2(9)**, Twenty-First Century Bks.) Lerner Publishing Group.

Sherman, Jill. Zoom in on Caregiving Robots. 2017. (J). **(978-0-7660-9229-7(1))** Enslow Pubs., Inc.

Winter, Max. Powering up a Career in Artificial Intelligence. 2015. (Preparing for Tomorrow's Careers Ser.). (ENG., Illus.). 80p. (J). (gr. 7-8). 34.25 (978-1-4994-6089-6(9), Rosen Young Adult) Rosen Publishing Group, Inc., The.

ARTIFICIAL SATELLITES

see also Meteorological Satellites; Space Stations; Space Vehicles

Asimov, Isaac & Hantula, Richard. Exploring Outer Space. 2005. (Isaac Asimov's 21st Century Library of the Universe). (Illus.). 32p. (gr. 2-6). lib. bdg. 26.00 (978-0-8368-3981-4(1), Gareth Stevens Learning Library) Stevens, Gareth Publishing LLLP.

Baker, David. Satellites. 2008. (Exploring Space Ser.). (Illus.). 32p. (J). (gr. 4-6). lib. bdg. 26.00 (978-1-59036-777-3(4)) Weigl Pubs., Inc.

Baker, David & Kissock, Heather. Satellites. (J). 2016. **(978-1-4896-5830-2(0)**, AV2 by Weigl) 2008. (Illus.). 32p. (gr. 4-6). pap. 9.95 (978-1-59036-778-0(2)) Weigl Pubs., Inc.

Chester, Michael & Kramer, Saunders B. Discoverer: The Story of A Satellite. 2011. 50p. 35.95 (978-1-258-01875-7(6)) Literary Licensing, LLC.

Cobb, Allan. Weather Observation Satellites. 2003. 68p. pap. 29.25 (978-1-4358-3643-3(X)) Rosen Publishing Group, Inc., The.

Elish, Dan. Satellites. 2006. (Kaleidoscope Space Ser.). (Illus.). 48p. (gr. 3-7). lib. bdg. 20.95 (978-0-7614-2098-9(3), Benchmark Bks.) Marshall Cavendish Corp.

Feldman, Heather. Sputnik: The First Satellite. 2003. (Space Firsts Ser.). (Illus.). 24p. (J). lib. bdg. 22.60 (978-0-8239-6244-0(X), PowerKids Pr.) Rosen Publishing Group, Inc., The.

Goldberg, Jan. Earth Imaging Satellites. (Library of Satellites Ser.). 64p. (gr. 5-8). 2009. 58.50 (978-1-60853-832-4(X)) 2003. (Illus.). (YA). lib. bdg. 31.95 (978-0-8239-3853-7(0)) Rosen Publishing Group, Inc., The. (Rosen Reference).

Gross, Miriam. All about Satellites. 2009. (Blast Off! Ser.). 24p. (gr. 2-3). 42.50 (978-1-61511-620-1(6), PowerKids Pr.) Rosen Publishing Group, Inc., The.

Gross, Miriam J. All about Satellites. 2009. (Blast Off! Ser.). (Illus.). 24p. (J). (gr. 2-5). pap. 8.25 (978-1-4358-3134-6(9)); lib. bdg. 22.60 (978-1-4358-2736-3(8)) Rosen Publishing Group, Inc., The. (PowerKids Pr.).

Hansen, Jim & Burns, John. How to Draw Superheroes. 2007. (Rosen Middle School Ser.: Vol. 4). (Illus.). 32p. (J). (gr. 4-7). lib. bdg. 25.25 (978-1-4042-3855-8(7)) Rosen Publishing Group, Inc., The.

Helbrough, Emma. A Day in the Life of a Pirate. Firenze, Inklink, illus. 2007. (Day in the Life Ser.: Vol. 4). 32p. (J). (gr. 3-7). lib. bdg. 25.25 (978-1-4042-3853-4(0)) Rosen Publishing Group, Inc., The.

Johnson, Jordan. Sputnik & the Space Race. 2017. (J). **(978-1-5026-2732-2(9))** Cavendish Square Publishing.

Johnson, Rebecca L. Satellites. 2005. (Cool Science Ser.). (ENG., Illus.). 48p. (gr. 4-8). lib. bdg. 27.93 (978-0-8225-2908-8(4), Lerner Pubns.) Lerner Publishing Group.

Kupperberg, Paul. Spy Satellites. 2009. (Library of Satellites Ser.). 64p. (gr. 5-8). 58.50 (978-1-60853-833-1(8), Rosen Reference) Rosen Publishing Group, Inc., The.

Labrecque, Ellen. Yvonne Brill & Satellite Propulsion. 2017. (21st Century Junior Library: Women Innovators Ser.). (ENG., Illus.). 24p. (J). (gr. 2-5). lib. bdg. 27.07 (978-1-63472-184-4(5), 209308) Cherry Lake Publishing.

Leigh, Autumn. A Trip Through Our Solar System. 2009. (Reading Room Collection 1 Ser.). 16p. (gr. 2-3). 37.50 (978-1-60851-940-8(6), PowerKids Pr.) Rosen Publishing Group, Inc., The.

Miller, Ron. Satellites. 2007. (Space Innovations Ser.). (ENG., Illus.). 112p. (gr. 6-8). lib. bdg. 31.93 (978-0-8225-7154-4(4)) Lerner Publishing Group.

Morey, Allan. Earth Satellites. 2017. (Space Tech Ser.). (ENG., Illus.). 24p. (J). (gr. 3-7). lib. bdg. 25.95 **(978-1-62617-699-7(X)**, Epic Bks.) Bellwether Media.

Nelson, Robin. The Night Sky. 2010. pap. 33.92 (978-0-7613-6917-2(1)) Lerner Publishing Group.

O'Donnell, Kerri. Moons of Our Solar System. 2009. (Science Scope Ser.). 32p. (gr. 5-5). 47.90 (978-1-60853-055-7(8), PowerKids Pr.) Rosen Publishing Group, Inc., The.

Owen, Ruth. Satellites, 1 vol. 2015. (Objects in Space Ser.). (ENG., Illus.). 32p. (J). 26.25 (978-1-4777-5856-4(9), PowerKids Pr.) Rosen Publishing Group, Inc., The.

Parker, Steve. Satellites. West, David, illus. 2015. (Story of Space Ser.). (ENG.). 32p. (J). (gr. 3-6). 31.35 (978-1-62588-079-6(0)) Black Rabbit Bks.

Rice, Earle. Rockets & Satellites: Surveillance from Space. 2016. (Military Engineering in Action Ser.). (Illus.). 48p. (J). (gr. 6-5). pap. 11.70 (978-0-7660-7529-0(X)) Enslow Pubs., Inc.

Rudy, Lisa Jo. Eyes in the Sky: Satellite Spies Are Watching You! 2007. (24/7: Science Behind the Scenes Ser.). (ENG., Illus.). 64p. (J). (gr. 8-12). pap. 7.95 (978-0-531-18732-6(2), Watts, Franklin) Scholastic Library Publishing.

Squishy, Fishy Robot Explorers: Meet NASA Inventor Mason Peck & His Team's. 2017. (J). **(978-0-7166-6156-6(X))** World Bk., Inc.

A True Book & Trade - Dr. Mae Jemison & 100 Year Starship & Trade. 2013. (True Book™—Dr. Mae Jemison & 100 Year Starship™ Ser.). (J). 116.00 (978-0-531-25339-7(2), Children's Pr.) Scholastic Library Publishing.

Wolny, Philip. Weapons Satellites. (Library of Satellites Ser.). 64p. (gr. 5-8). 2009. 58.50 (978-1-60853-834-8(6)) 2003. (Illus.). (YA). lib. bdg. 31.95 (978-0-8239-3855-1(7)) Rosen Publishing Group, Inc., The. (Rosen Reference).

Zappa, Marcia. Rockets & Satellites, 1 vol. 2011. (Universe Set 2 Ser.). (ENG., Illus.). 32p. (gr. 3-5). 27.07 (978-1-61714-691-6(9), Buddy Bks.) ABDO Publishing Co.

ARTIFICIAL SATELLITES IN TELECOMMUNICATION

Byers, Ann. Communication Satellites. 2003. (Library of Satellites Ser.). (Illus.). 64p. (YA). (gr. 5-8). lib. bdg. 31.95 (978-0-8239-3851-3(4), Rosen Reference) Rosen Publishing Group, Inc., The.

—Communications Satellites. 2009. (Library of Satellites Ser.). 64p. (gr. 5-8). 58.50 (978-1-60853-831-7(1), Rosen Reference) Rosen Publishing Group, Inc., The.

Gray, Leon. Global Positioning System: Who's Tracking You? 2013. (Ask the Experts Ser.). (Illus.). 48p. (J). (gr. 6-8). 31.95 (978-1-4339-8639-0(6)); pap. 14.05 (978-1-4339-8640-6(X)) Stevens, Gareth Publishing LLLP. (Gareth Stevens Secondary Library).

Whiting, Jim. John R. Pierce: Pioneer in Satellite Communication. 2003. (Unlocking the Secrets of Science Ser.). (Illus.). 56p. (J). (gr. 4-10). lib. bdg. 25.70 (978-1-58415-205-7(2)) Mitchell Lane Pubs., Inc.

ARTIFICIAL WEATHER CONTROL

see Weather Control

ARTILLERY

see also Ordnance

Adams, Simon. Artillery. 2009. (War Machines Ser.). (YA). (gr. 5-9). 28.50 (978-1-59920-226-6(3)) Black Rabbit Bks.

Hamilton, John. Paladins. 2011. (Military Vehicles Ser.). (Illus.). 32p. (YA). (gr. 4-7). 27.07 (978-1-61783-077-8(1)) ABDO Publishing Co.

Oxlade, Chris. Inside Tanks & Heavy Artillery. Viana, Tatio, illus. 2017. (Inside Military Machines Ser.). (ENG.). (J). (gr. 3-6). lib. bdg. 26.65 **(978-1-5124-3226-8(1))** Lerner Publishing Group.

ARTISTIC ANATOMY

see Anatomy, Artistic

ARTISTIC PHOTOGRAPHY

see Photography, Artistic

ARTISTS

see also Architects; Art—Vocational Guidance; Painters; Sculptors; Women Artists

Adler, David A. & Adler, Michael S. A Picture Book of Harry Houdini. Matt, Collins, illus. 2010. (ENG.). 32p. (J). (gr. -1-3). pap. 7.99 (978-0-8234-2302-6(6)) Holiday Hse., Inc.

Ajmera, Maya & Ivanko, John D. To Be an Artist. 2005. (ENG., Illus.). 32p. (J). (gr. -1-3). per. 7.95 (978-1-57091-576-5(8)) Charlesbridge Publishing, Inc.

Amidon Lusted, Marcia. Career Building Through Using Multimedia Art & Animation Tools. 2013. (Digital Career Building Ser.). 64p. (YA). (gr. 7-12). 31.95 (978-1-4777-1725-7(0)); pap. 12.95 (978-1-4777-1743-1(9)) Rosen Publishing Group, Inc., The.

Anderson, Kirsten. Who Was Andy Warhol? 2014. (Who Was... ? Ser.). (Illus.). 105p. (J). lib. bdg. 14.75 *(978-0-606-36183-5(9))* Turtleback Bks.

Apodaca, Bianca & Serwich, Michael. Detrás de Lienzo: La Vida de un Artista. 2017. (TIME for Kids en Español - Level 4 Ser.). (SPA.). 48p. (gr. 4-4). lib. bdg. 31.99 *(978-1-5157-5131-1(7))* Time for Kids Inc AUS. Dist: Capstone Pub.

Apodaca, Bianca. Behind the Canvas: An Artist's Life, 1 vol. 2nd rev. ed. 2013. (Nonfiction Readers Ser.). (ENG., Illus.). 48p. (J). (gr. 4-4). pap. 29.96 *(978-1-4807-1102-0(0))* Shell Educational Publishing.

—Behind the Canvas: An Artist's Life, 1 vol. 2nd rev. ed. 2012. (TIME for KIDS(r) Nonfiction Readers Ser.). (ENG.). 48p. (J). (gr. 4-4). pap. 9.99 *(978-1-4333-4826-6(8))* Teacher Created Materials, Inc.

Appleby, Alex. I Can Be an Artist. 2014. (When I Grow Up Ser.). 24p. (J). (gr. k-2). 22.60 *(978-1-4824-0751-8(5))* Stevens, Gareth Publishing LLLP.

—Puedo Ser un Artista / I Can Be an Artist. 2014. (Cuando Sea Grande / When I Grow Up Ser.). (SPA.). 24p. (J). (gr. k-2). 22.60 *(978-1-4824-0861-4(9))* Stevens, Gareth Publishing LLLP.

Art Profiles for Kids, 6 vols., Set. Incl. Canaletto. Rice, Earle, Jr. lib. bdg. 29.95 *(978-1-58415-561-4(2))*; Claude Monet. Whiting, Jim. lib. bdg. 29.95 *(978-1-58415-563-8(9))*; Michelangelo. Whiting, Jim. lib. bdg. 29.95 *(978-1-58415-562-1(0))*; Paul Cezanne. Tracy, Kathleen. lib. bdg. 29.95 *(978-1-58415-565-2(5))*; Pierre-Auguste Renoir. Somervill, Barbara A. lib. bdg. 29.95 *(978-1-58415-566-9(3))*; Vincent Van Gogh. Whiting, Jim. lib. bdg. 29.95 *(978-1-58415-564-5(7))*; 48p. (YA). (gr. 4-7). (Art Profiles for Kids Ser.). (Illus.). 2007. 179.70 *(978-1-58415-567-6(1))* Mitchell Lane Pubs., Inc.

Artists of the Harlem Renaissance. 2016. (Artists of the Harlem Renaissance Ser.). (ENG.). 128p. (YA). (gr. 9-9). lib. bdg. 365.12 *(978-1-5026-1092-8(2))* Cavendish Square Publishing.

Artists Through the Ages: Set 3. 2015. (Artists Through the Ages Ser.). (ENG.). 32p. (J). (gr. 2-3). pap., pap., pap. 360.00 *(978-1-4994-8021-4(0)*, Windmill Bks.) Rosen Publishing Group, Inc., The.

Aston, Paul, tr. Coloring Book: Wassily Kandinsky. Kutschbach, Doris, illus. 2006. (ENG.). 32p. (J). (gr. 1-4). 8.95 *(978-3-7913-3712-8(2))* Prestel Verlag GmbH & Co KG. DEU. Dist: Penguin Random Hse. LLC.

Bankston, John. Diego Rivera. 2003. (Latinos in American History Ser.). (Illus.). 56p. (J). (gr. 4-8). lib. bdg. 29.95 *(978-1-58415-208-8(7))* Mitchell Lane Pubs., Inc.

Bingham, Hettie. Banksy: Art Breaks the Rules. 2017. (ENG., Illus.). 48p. (J). (gr. 4-6). 14.99 ***(978-0-7502-9976-3(2)***, Wayland) Hachette Children's Group GBR. Dist: Hachette Bk. Group.

Björk, Christina. Linnea in Monet's Garden. Sandin, Joan, tr. Anderson, Lena, illus. 2012. (ENG.). 48p. (J). (-3). 16.99 *(978-1-4022-7729-0(6)*, Sourcebooks Jabberwocky) Sourcebooks, Inc.

Blohm, Craig E. Great Cartoonists. 2016. (ENG.). 80p. (J). (gr. 5-12). *(978-1-60152-996-1(1))* ReferencePoint Pr., Inc.

Branin, Larissa. Great Artists of the World. 2017. (Art Collections: Vol. 7). (ENG., Illus.). (YA). (gr. 9-12). 26.95 ***(978-1-4222-3934-6(9))*** Mason Crest.

Britannica Learning Library Staff. Artists Around the World. 2003. (Illus.). 64p. 14.95 *(978-1-59339-036-5(X))* Encyclopaedia Britannica, Inc.

Brocklehurst, Ruth, et al. Famous Artists. 2012. (Art Ser.). 95p. (J). ring bd. 16.99 *(978-0-7945-3123-2(7)*, Usborne) EDC Publishing.

Bryson, Theresa. On Stage. 2011. (Early Connections Ser.). (J). *(978-1-61672-238-8(X))* Benchmark Education Co.

Burleigh, Robert. Into the Woods: John James Audubon Lives His Dream. Minor, Wendell, illus. 2011. (ENG.). 40p. (J). (gr. 1-4). pap. 19.99 *(978-1-4424-5337-1(0)*, Atheneum Bks. for Young Readers) Simon & Schuster Children's Publishing.

—Toulouse-Lautrec: The Moulin Rouge & the City of Light. 2006. (Illus.). 32p. (J). (gr. 4-8). 18.00 *(978-1-4223-5493-3(8))* DIANE Publishing Co.

Burnett, Craig. Jeff Wall. 2006. (ENG., Illus.). 128p. (gr. 8-17). pap. 24.95 *(978-1-85437-611-4(X))* Tate Publishing, Ltd. GBR. Dist: Hachette Bk. Group.

Career Building Through Using Multimedia Art & Animation Tools. 2013. (Digital Career Building Ser.). 64p. (YA). (gr. 7-12). pap. 77.70 *(978-1-4777-1745-5(5))* Rosen Publishing Group, Inc., The.

Cernak, Linda. Vincent Van Gogh. Morrow, J. T., illus. 2014. (World's Greatest Artists Ser.). (ENG.). 24p. (J). (gr. 2-5). 28.50 *(978-1-62687-355-1(0)*, 207195) Child's World, Inc., The.

Charleyboy, Lisa & Leatherdale, Mary Beth. Dreaming in Indian: Contemporary Native American Voices. 2016. (ENG., Illus.). 128p. (J). (gr. 6). pap. 12.95 *(978-1-55451-686-5(2))* Annick Pr., Ltd. CAN. Dist: Publishers Group West (PGW).

Ciovacco, Justine. Leonardo Da Vinci, 1 vol. 2015. (ENG., Illus.). 32p. (J). 23.45 *(978-1-62275-677-3(0)*, Britannica Educational Publishing) Rosen Publishing Group, Inc., The.

Civardi, A. First Experiences. 2004. (ENG.). 1p. (J). 19.95 *(978-0-7460-2254-2(9)*, Usborne) EDC Publishing.

Colich, Abby. Grace Lin, 1 vol. Byers, Michael, illus. 2013. (Your Favorite Authors Ser.). (ENG.). 24p. (gr. 1-2). 25.32 *(978-1-4765-3158-8(7))*; pap. 7.95 *(978-1-4765-3445-9(4))* Capstone Press of Coughlan Cos. (First Facts).

Cook, Diane. Michelangelo: Renaissance Artist. 2013. (People of Importance Ser.: 21). (Illus.). 32p. (J). (gr. 4-18). 19.95 *(978-1-4222-2851-7(7))* Mason Crest.

—Paul Gauguin: 18th Century French Painter. 2004. (Great Names Ser.). (Illus.). 32p. (J). (gr. 3-18). lib. bdg. 19.95 *(978-1-59084-153-2(0))* Mason Crest.

—Paul Gauguin: 18th Century French Painter. 2013. (People of Importance Ser.: 21). (Illus.). 32p. (J). (gr. 4-18). 19.95 *(978-1-4222-2854-8(1))* Mason Crest.

Corbett, Sean. Andy Warhol. 2016. (J). *(978-1-4896-4617-0(5))* Weigl Pubs., Inc.

Crabtree, Marc. Meet My Neighbor, the Taekwondo Master. 2009. (Meet my Neighbor Ser.). (ENG., Illus.). 24p. (J). (gr. k-2). lib. bdg. *(978-0-7787-4572-3(4))* Crabtree Publishing Co.

Davies, Carolyn. Josef Herman in Wales. 2004. (ENG., Illus.). 32p. pap. 15.95 *(978-1-85902-999-2(X))* Beekman Bks., Inc.

De Mille, Agnes. Dance to the Piper. 2015. (ENG., Illus.). 368p. pap. 17.95 *(978-1-59017-908-6(0)*, NYRB Classics) New York Review of Bks., Inc., The.

Delessert, Etienne. Night Circus. Delessert, Etienne, illus. 2015. (ENG., Illus.). 32p. (J). (gr. 2-4). 19.99 *(978-1-56846-277-6(8)*, Creative Editions) Creative Co., The.

Deutsch, Stacia & Cohon, Rhody. Carlos Mencia. 2009. (Sharing the American Dream Ser.). 64p. (YA). (gr. 7-12). 22.95 *(978-1-4222-0578-5(9))* Mason Crest.

Dickens, Rosie. The Children's Book of Art: Internet Linked. 2005. (Illus.). 64p. (J). *(978-0-439-88981-0(2))* Scholastic, Inc.

Dickins, Rosie. The Usborne First Book of Art. Hopman, Philip, illus. 2008. (Usborne First Book Ser.). 62p. (J). (gr. -1-3). 18.99 *(978-0-7945-2035-9(9)*, Usborne) EDC Publishing.

Duignan, Brian, ed. The Britannica Guide to the World's Most Influential People (Print/eBook Combo Set), 8 vols., Set. Incl. 100 Most Influential Philosophers of All Time. 368p. (YA). (gr. 9-12). 2009. E-Book 106.00 *(978-1-61530-072-3(4))*; (Britannica Guide to the World's Most Influential People Ser.). 384p. 2009. Set E-Book 848.00 *(978-1-61530-165-2(8))* Rosen Publishing Group, Inc., The.

Edgers, Geoff. Who Is Stan Lee? 2014. (Who Is... ? Ser.). lib. bdg. 16.00 *(978-0-606-36175-0(8))* Turtleback Bks.

Emert, Phyllis, ed. Michelangelo. 2012. (Eye on Art Ser.). (ENG., Illus.). 128p. (gr. 7-10). lib. bdg. 39.40 *(978-1-4205-0696-9(X)*, Lucent Bks.) Cengage Gale.

Eric Carle Museum of Picture Book Art Staff. Artist to Artist: 23 Major Illustrators Talk to Children about Their Art. Gauch, Patricia Lee et al, eds. Carle, Eric et al, illus. 2007. (ENG.). 114p. (J). (gr. k-3). 30.00 *(978-0-399-24600-5(2)*, Philomel Bks.) Penguin Young Readers Group.

Falconer, Shelley & White, Shawna. Stones, Bones & Stitches: Storytelling Through Inuit Art. 2007. (Lord Museum Book Ser.). (ENG., Illus.). 48p. (J). (gr. k-12). 22.95 *(978-0-88776-854-5(7)*, Tundra Bks.) Tundra Bks. CAN. Dist: Penguin Random Hse. LLC.

Fandel, Jennifer. Pablo Picasso. 2016. (Illus.). 80p. (J). *(978-1-60818-720-1(9)*, Creative Education) Creative Co., The.

Ferrara, Cos. Mary Cassatt: The Life & Art of a Genteel Rebel. 2004. (Girls Explore, Reach for the Stars Ser.). (Illus.). 101p. (J). 20.00 *(978-0-9749456-3-7(3)*, Girls Explore) Girls Explore LLC.

Finger, Brad. 13 Modern Artists Children Should Know. 2010. (ENG., Illus.). 48p. (J). (gr. 3-7). 14.95 *(978-3-7913-7015-6(4))* Prestel Verlag GmbH & Co KG. DEU. Dist: Penguin Random Hse. LLC.

Finger, Bradley. 13 American Artists Children Should Know. 2010. (ENG., Illus.). 48p. (J). (gr. 3-7). 14.95 *(978-3-7913-7036-1(7))* Prestel Verlag GmbH & Co KG. DEU. Dist: Penguin Random Hse. LLC.

Flath, Camden. Media in the 21st Century: Artists, Animators, & Graphic Designers. 2010. (New Careers for the 21st Century Ser.). 64p. (YA). (gr. 7-18). lib. bdg. 22.95 *(978-1-4222-1816-7(3))* Mason Crest.

Fleischman, Sid. Escape! The Story of the Great Houdini. 2006. (Illus.). (J). (ENG.). 224p. (gr. 3-7). 19.99 *(978-0-06-085094-4(9)*, Greenwillow Bks.); 210p. (gr. 4-8). lib. bdg. 19.89 *(978-0-06-085095-1(7))* HarperCollins Pubs.

Flor Ada, Alma & Campoy, F. Isabel. Brocha y Pincel. (Literature Collection of Puertas Al Sol Ser.).Tr. of Brush & Paint. (SPA.). 32p. (J). (gr. k-6). pap. 13.95 *(978-1-59437-705-1(7))* Santillana USA Publishing Co., Inc.

—Caballete. (Literature Collection of Puertas Al Sol Ser.). (SPA.). 32p. (J). (gr. k-6). pap. 13.95 *(978-1-59437-708-2(1))* Santillana USA Publishing Co., Inc.

—Lienzo y Papel. (Literature Collection of Puertas Al Sol Ser.). (SPA.). 32p. (J). (gr. k-6). pap. 13.95 *(978-1-59437-711-2(1))* Santillana USA Publishing Co., Inc.

Flor Ada, Alma & Campoy, F. Isabel, contrib. by. Azul y Verde. (Literature Collection of Puertas Al Sol Ser.).Tr. of Blue & Green. (SPA.). 32p. (J). (gr. k-6). pap. 13.95 *(978-1-59437-702-0(2))* Santillana USA Publishing Co., Inc.

Frey, Lisa A. The Story of Monet & Renoir. Frey, Lisa A. & Darroch, Jane, eds. Darroch, Jane & Riley, Scott, illus. 2004. (Color & Learn Book Ser.). 32p. (gr. k-4). pap. 12.99 *(978-0-9707110-1-4(8))* Starshell Pr., Ltd.

Frith, Margaret. Frida Kahlo: The Artist Who Painted Herself. dePaola, Tomie, illus. 2003. (Smart about Art Ser.). (ENG.). 32p. (J). (gr. k-4). 5.99 *(978-0-448-42677-8(3)*, Grosset & Dunlap) Penguin Young Readers Group.

Furgang, Adam. Famous Immigrant Artists. 2017. (J). ***(978-0-7660-9245-7(3))*** Enslow Pubs., Inc.

Gale, Riana, et al. Artistic Expressions of a Child. 2010. 32p. pap. 15.50 *(978-1-4520-8154-0(9))* AuthorHouse.

Gerlings, Charlotte. Great Artists. 2012. (Great People in History Ser.). (ENG., Illus.). 128p. (YA). (gr. 8-12). 34.60 *(978-1-4777-0401-1(9))* Rosen Publishing Group, Inc., The.

Getting to Know the World's Greatest Artists. 2014. (Getting to Know the World's Greatest Artists Ser.). (J). lib. bdg. 87.00 *(978-0-531-24353-4(2))* Scholastic Library Publishing.

Goldberg, Dana, ed. On My Block: Stories & Paintings by Fifteen Artists. 2007. (ENG., Illus.). 32p. (J). (gr. k-4). 16.95 *(978-0-89239-220-9(7))* Lee & Low Bks., Inc.

Gowing, Lawrence, ed. Facts on File Encyclopedia of Art & Artists Set. 2005. 1840p. (C). (gr. 9). 585.00 *(978-0-8160-6378-9(8))* Facts On File, Inc.

Grahame-Smith, Deborah. Dr. Seuss. 2014. (Spotlight on Children's Authors Ser.). 48p. (J). (gr. 4-6). lib. bdg. 29.93 *(978-1-62712-846-9(8))* Cavendish Square Publishing.

Great Artists. 2014. (Great Artists Ser.). 32p. (J). (gr. 3-6). pap. 63.00 *(978-1-4824-1569-8(0))*; (gr. 4-6). 159.60 *(978-1-4824-1178-2(4))* Stevens, Gareth Publishing LLLP.

Greek, Joe. A Career in Computer Graphics & Design, 1 vol. 2015. (ENG., Illus.). 80p. (J). 34.25 *(978-1-4777-7888-3(8)*, Rosen Young Adult) Rosen Publishing Group, Inc., The.

Greenberger, Robert. Will Eisner. 2009. (Library of Graphic Novelists Ser.). 112p. (gr. 7-12). 63.90 *(978-1-60853-656-6(4))* Rosen Publishing Group, Inc., The.

Guerrero, Ernesto, tr. from ENG. Family Stories (Cuentos Familiares) Castro, Maria Elena et al, illus. 2006. (ENG & SPA.). 27p. 15.95 *(978-0-9716580-7-3(2))* Lectura Bks.

Hall, M. C. Leonardo Da Vinci, 1 vol. 2007. (Essential Lives Set 1 Ser.). (ENG., Illus.). 112p. (J). (gr. 6-12). lib. bdg. 35.64 *(978-1-59928-844-4(3))* ABDO Publishing Co.

Hamilton, Sue L. Forensic Artist: Solving the Case with a Face, 1 vol. 2008. (Crime Scene Investigation Ser.). (ENG.). 32p. (gr. 4-8). 27.07 *(978-1-59928-989-2(X)*, Abdo & Daughters) ABDO Publishing Co.

Harper, Charley, illus. Charley Harper's Tree of Life. 2013. (ENG.). (J). 7.95 *(978-0-7649-6514-2(X))* Pomegranate Communications, Inc.

Harris, Godfrey, et al. The Life & Contributions of Leonardo Da Vinci. 2006. 58p. (J). pap. *(978-0-935047-60-8(3))* Americas Group, The.

Harris, Lois V. Mary Cassatt: Impressionist Painter, 1 vol. Cassatt, Mary, illus. 2007. (ENG.). 32p. (J). (gr. k-3). 16.99 *(978-1-58980-452-4(X))* Pelican Publishing Co., Inc.

Hodge, Susie. Artists & Their Pets: True Stories of Famous Artists & Their Animal Friends. Lemay, Violet, illus. 2017. (ENG.). 192p. (J). (gr. 2-5). 14.95 ***(978-1-946064-01-1(7))*** Duo Pr. LLC.

Hodge, Susie. The Children's Interactive Story of Art. 2016. (ENG., Illus.). 96p. (J). (gr. 3). 19.95 *(978-1-78312-130-4(0))* Carlton Kids GBR. Dist: Sterling Publishing Co., Inc.

Howard, Annabel. The Life & Art of Wassily Kandinsky. Simpson, Adam, illus. 2016. (Lives of Great Artists Ser.). 00080p. (J). (gr. 8-8). 35.75 *(978-1-4994-6582-2(3)*, Rosen Young Adult) Rosen Publishing Group, Inc., The.

Hyde, Margaret E., ed. Impressionists for Kids. 2004. (Great Art for Kids Ser.). (Illus.). (J). 12p. pap. 8.95 *(978-1-58980-203-2(9))*; 2nd ed. (ENG., 14p. (gr. -1-k). bds. 8.95 *(978-1-58980-265-0(9))* Pelican Publishing Co., Inc.

Hyman, Trina Schart. Self-Portrait: Trina Schart Hyman. (ENG.). 100p. 12.95 *(978-0-201-09308-7(1))* HarperCollins Pubs.

Ingram, Catherine. The Life & Art of Andy Warhol. Rae, Andrew, illus. 2016. (Lives of Great Artists Ser.). 00080p. (J). (gr. 8-8). 35.75 *(978-1-4994-6585-3(8)*, Rosen Young Adult) Rosen Publishing Group, Inc., The.

—The Life & Art of Salvador Dali. Rae, Andrew, illus. 2016. (Lives of Great Artists Ser.). 00080p. (J). (gr. 8-8). 35.75 *(978-1-4994-6580-8(7))* Rosen Publishing Group, Inc., The.

January, Brendan. Leonardo Da Vinci. 2004. (Great Names Ser.). (Illus.). 32p. (J). (gr. 3-18). lib. bdg. 19.95 *(978-1-59084-134-1(4))* Mason Crest.

johns, Michael-Anne. Today's Coolest Stars. 2008. (Star Scene Ser.). (Illus.). 48p. (J). pap. *(978-0-545-05106-4(1))* Scholastic, Inc.

Kallen, Stuart A. Matt Groening the Simpsons: The Simpsons. 2015. (ENG., Illus.). 80p. (YA). lib. bdg. *(978-1-60152-784-4(5))* ReferencePoint Pr., Inc.

Kelley, True. Who Was Pablo Picasso? Kelley, True & Harrison, Nancy, illus. 2009. (Who Was? Ser.). (ENG.). 112p. (J). (gr. 3-7). pap. 5.99 *(978-0-448-44987-6(0)*, Grosset & Dunlap) Penguin Young Readers Group.

Kinney, Patrick & dePaola, Tomie. Who Is Jeff Kinney? Hinderliter, John, illus. 2015. (Who Was? Ser.). (ENG.). 112p. (J). (gr. 3-7). 5.99 *(978-0-448-48677-2(6)*, Grosset & Dunlap) Penguin Young Readers Group.

Klein, Adam G. Pablo Picasso, 1 vol. 2007. (Great Artists Set 2 Ser.). (ENG., Illus.). 32p. (gr. -1-3). 27.07 *(978-1-59679-733-8(9)*, Checkerboard Library) ABDO Publishing Co.

—Rembrandt, 1 vol. 2007. (Great Artists Set 2 Ser.). (ENG., Illus.). 32p. (gr. -1-3). 27.07 *(978-1-59679-735-2(5)*, Checkerboard Library) ABDO Publishing Co.

—Salvador Dali, 1 vol. 2007. (Great Artists Set 2 Ser.). (ENG., Illus.). 32p. (gr. -1-3). 27.07 *(978-1-59679-728-4(2)*, Checkerboard Library) ABDO Publishing Co.

Klein, Rebecca. Jimmy Fallon, 01 vols., 1. 2016. (Giants of Comedy Ser.). (ENG., Illus.). 112p. (J). 35.60 *(978-1-4994-6254-8(9)*, Rosen Young Adult) Rosen Publishing Group, Inc., The.

Koestler-Grack, Rachel A. Leonardo Da Vinci: Artist, Inventor, & Renaissance Man. 2005. (Makers of the Middle Ages & Renaissance Ser.). (Illus.). 152p. (gr. 5-8). lib. bdg. 32.95 *(978-0-7910-8626-1(7)*, Chelsea Hse.) Facts On File, Inc.

Kohl, MaryAnn F. & Solga, Kim. Great American Artists for Kids: Hands-On Art Experiences in the Styles of Great American Masters. 2008. (Bright Ideas for Learning Ser.: 8). (ENG., Illus.). 144p. (J). (gr. -1-4). pap. 18.95 *(978-0-935607-00-0(5))* Bright Ring Publishing, Inc.

Kraske, Robert. Harry Houdini. 2015. 72p. pap. 7.00 *(978-1-61003-493-7(7))* Center for the Collaborative Classroom.

Krull, Kathleen. Lives of the Artists: Masterpieces, Messes (and What the Neighbors Thought) Hewitt, Kathryn, illus. (Lives Of ... Ser.). (ENG.). 96p. (J). (gr. 5-7). 2014. pap. 8.99 *(978-0-544-25223-3(3)*, HMH Books For Young Readers) 2011. pap. 12.99 *(978-0-547-51991-3(5))* Houghton Mifflin Harcourt Publishing Co.

Kudlinski, Kathleen. Dr. Seuss: Young Author & Artist. Henderson, Meryl, illus. 2005. 184p. (J). lib. bdg. 18.46 *(978-1-4242-2201-8(X))* Fitzgerald Bks.

Lacey, Saskia & Wallace, Elise. Jurassic Classics: the Prehistoric Masters of Art: Discover Art History with a Prehistoric Twist! 2016. (Jurassic Classics Ser.). (ENG., Illus.). 40p. (J). (gr. 2-6). 14.95 *(978-1-63322-180-2(6)*, Walter Foster Jr) Quarto Publishing Group USA.

Landmann, Bimba. I Am Marc Chagall. Landmann, Bimba, illus. 2006. (Eerdmans Books for Young Readers). (ENG., Illus.). 34p. (J). (gr. 2). 18.00 *(978-0-8028-5305-9(6)*, Eerdmans Bks For Young Readers) Eerdmans, William B. Publishing Co.

Lappe, S. M. Street Painting: A Guide for Young Artists. 2011. 36p. pap. 13.95 *(978-1-60976-963-5(5)*, Strategic Bk. Publishing) Strategic Book Publishing & Rights Agency (SBPRA).

Levithan, David. What We Remember, What We Forget: The Best Young Writers & Artists in America. Levithan, David, ed. 2012. (ENG.). 304p. (J). (gr. 7-7). pap. 10.99 *(978-0-545-39714-8(6)*, PUSH) Scholastic, Inc.

The Lives of Great Artists. 2016. (Lives of Great Artists Ser.). 00080p. (YA). (gr. 8-8). 214.50 *(978-1-4994-6562-4(9)*, Rosen Young Adult) Rosen Publishing Group, Inc., The.

Lives of the Artists, 4 bks. Incl. Michelangelo. Connolly, Sean & Michelangelo Buonarroti. pap. 14.05 *(978-0-8368-5605-7(8))*; Pablo Picasso. Hodge, Susie & Picasso, P. pap. 14.05 *(978-0-8368-5606-4(6))*; Vincent van Gogh. Bassil, Andrea & van Gogh, Vincent. pap. 14.05 *(978-0-8368-5607-1(4))*; 48p. (gr. 5-12)., Gareth Stevens Secondary Library (Illus.). 2004. Set pap. 47.80 o.p. *(978-0-8368-5603-3(1))*; Set lib. bdg. 117.06 o.p. *(978-0-8368-5598-2(1))* Stevens, Gareth Publishing LLLP. (World Almanac Library).

Llanas, Sheila Griffin. Hip-Hop Stars [Scholastic]. 2010. (Hip-Hop World Ser.). 48p. pap. 1.00 *(978-1-4296-5980-2(7))* Capstone Press of Coughlan Cos.

Lomberg, Michelle. Pablo Picasso. 2016. (J). *(978-1-4896-4625-5(6))* Weigl Pubs., Inc.

Marcovitz, Hal. Maurice Sendak. 2006. (Who Wrote That? Ser.). (Illus.). 136p. (gr. 6-12). lib. bdg. 35.00 *(978-0-7910-8796-1(4)*, Chelsea Hse.) Facts On File, Inc.

Mason, Antony. El Arte Impresionista: En Los Tiempos de Renoir. 2005. (Arte Alrededor del Mundo Ser.). (Illus.). 48p. (J). (gr. 4-7). pap. 9.95 *(978-85-7416-229-4(9))* Callis Editora Ltda BRA. Dist: Independent Pubs. Group.

Mason, Helen. Makeup Artist. 2014. (Creative Careers Ser.). 48p. (J). (gr. 4-8). pap. 84.30 *(978-1-4824-1303-8(5))* Stevens, Gareth Publishing LLLP.

Mattern, Joanne. Andy Warhol, 1 vol. 2005. (Great Artists Set 1 Ser.). (ENG., Illus.). 32p. (gr. k-6). 27.07 *(978-1-59197-850-3(5)*, Checkerboard Library) ABDO Publishing Co.

—Leonardo Da Vinci, 1 vol. 2005. (Great Artists Set 1 Ser.). (ENG., Illus.). 32p. (gr. k-6). 27.07 *(978-1-59197-842-8(4)*, Checkerboard Library) ABDO Publishing Co.

—Marc Chagall, 1 vol. 2005. (Great Artists Set 1 Ser.). (ENG., Illus.). 32p. (gr. k-6). 27.07 *(978-1-59197-841-1(6)*, Checkerboard Library) ABDO Publishing Co.

—Mary Cassatt, 1 vol. 2005. (Great Artists Set 1 Ser.). (ENG., Illus.). 32p. (gr. k-6). 27.07 *(978-1-59197-840-4(8)*, Checkerboard Library) ABDO Publishing Co.

—Michelangelo, 1 vol. 2005. (Great Artists Set 1 Ser.). (ENG., Illus.). 32p. (gr. k-6). 27.07 *(978-1-59197-845-9(9)*, Checkerboard Library) ABDO Publishing Co.

McGehee, Claudia. My Wilderness. 2017. (ENG.). 32p. (J). (gr. k-4). 10.99 *(978-1-57061-951-9(4)*, Little Bigfoot) Sasquatch Bks.

McNeese, Tim. Michelangelo: Painter, Sculptor & Architect. 2005. (Makers of the Middle Ages & Renaissance Ser.). (Illus.). 160p. (gr. 5-8). lib. bdg. 32.95 *(978-0-7910-8627-8(5)*, Chelsea Hse.) Facts On File, Inc.

—Salvador Dali. 2006. (Great Hispanic Heritage Ser.). (Illus.). 112p. (gr. 6-12). lib. bdg. 35.00 *(978-0-7910-8837-1(5)*, Chelsea Hse.) Facts On File, Inc.

Miller, Eileen Rudisill. Doodle Design & Draw Dream Bridal Fashions. 2017. (Dover Doodle Bks.). (ENG.). 64p. (J). (gr. 3-6). pap. 5.99 *(978-0-486-81273-1(1))* Dover Pubns., Inc.

Mini Artist. 2014. (Mini Artist Ser.). 24p. (J). (gr. k-3). 105.00 *(978-1-4777-9131-8(0))* Windmill Bks.

Morreale, Marie. What's in the Stars? 2008. (Illus.). 48p. (J). pap. *(978-0-545-00184-7(6))* Scholastic, Inc.

Morrissey, Simon. Richard Wilson. 2006. (ENG., Illus.). 128p. (gr. 8-17). pap. 27.50 *(978-1-85437-570-4(9))* Tate Publishing, Ltd. GBR. Dist: Hachette Bk. Group.

Mullins, Matt. Multimedia Artist & Animator. 2010. (21st Century Skills Library: Cool Careers Ser.). (ENG.). 32p. (gr. 4-8). lib. bdg. 28.50 *(978-1-60279-942-4(3)*, 200629) Cherry Lake Publishing.

Nichols, Catherine. Leonardo Da Vinci. 2006. (Primary Source Library of Famous Artists Ser.). (Illus.). 32p. (J). (gr. -1-3). lib. bdg. 23.95 *(978-1-4042-2762-0(8)*, PowerKids Pr.) Rosen Publishing Group, Inc., The.

—Michelangelo Buonarroti. 2006. (Primary Source Library of Famous Artists Ser.). (Illus.). 32p. (J). (gr. 3-7). lib. bdg. 23.95 *(978-1-4042-2763-7(6)*, PowerKids Pr.) Rosen Publishing Group, Inc., The.

—Pablo Picasso. (Primary Source Library of Famous Artists Ser.). 32p. (gr. 3-4). 2009. 42.50 *(978-1-60854-103-4(7))* 2006. (Illus.). (J). lib. bdg. 23.95 *(978-1-4042-2764-4(4))* Rosen Publishing Group, Inc., The. (PowerKids Pr.).

—Vincent Van Gogh. 2006. (Primary Source Library of Famous Artists Ser.). (Illus.). 32p. (J). (gr. 3-7). lib. bdg. 23.95 *(978-1-4042-2766-8(0)*, PowerKids Pr.) Rosen Publishing Group, Inc., The.

Novesky, Amy. Cloth Lullaby: The Woven Life of Louise Bourgeois. Arsenault, Isabelle, illus. 2016. (ENG.). 40p. (J). (gr. k-2). 18.95 *(978-1-4197-1881-6(9)*, Abrams Bks. for Young Readers) Abrams, Inc.

Ollhoff, Jim. Masters & Heroes, 1 vol. 2008. (World of Martial Arts Ser.). (ENG.). 32p. (gr. 4-8). 27.07 *(978-1-59928-981-6(4)*, Abdo & Daughters) ABDO Publishing Co.

Osborne, Mary Pope & Boyce, Natalie Pope. Leonardo Da Vinci: A Nonfiction Companion to Monday with a Mad Genius. 2009. (Magic Tree House Fact Tracker Ser.: 19). lib. bdg. 16.00 *(978-0-606-01834-0(4)*, Turtleback) Turtleback Bks.

Paredes, Julio. Eugéne Delacroix. 2005. (SPA.). 132p. (YA). *(978-958-30-1358-4(7))* Panamericana Editorial.

Paris, David. Fantastic Kids: Young Artists (Level 4) 2017. (Exploring Reading Ser.). (Illus.). 32p. (gr. 4-4). 9.99 ***(978-1-4258-4982-5(2))*** Teacher Created Materials, Inc.

Parker, Marjorie Blain & Matisse, Henri. Colorful Dreamer: The Story of Artist Henri Matisse. Berry, Holly, illus. 2012. (ENG.). 32p. (J). (gr. -1-k). 16.99 *(978-0-8037-3758-7(0)*, Dial Bks) Penguin Young Readers Group.

Pascal, Janet. Who Was Maurice Sendak? 2013. (Who Was... ? Ser.). lib. bdg. 16.00 *(978-0-606-26962-9(2)*, Turtleback) Turtleback Bks.

Paulding, Barbara. Water Magic. Steckler, Kerren Barbas, illus. 2009. (Young Artist Ser.). 24p. (J). (gr. -1). 15.99 *(978-1-59359-842-6(4))* Peter Pauper Pr. Inc.

Penguin Young Readers. The Tale of Beatrix Potter. 2016. (Penguin Young Readers, Level 4 Ser.). (ENG.). 48p. (J). (gr. 1-3). pap. 3.99 *(978-0-241-24937-6(6)*, Penguin Young Readers) Penguin Young Readers Group.

Penrose, Antony & Picasso, Pablo. The Boy Who Bit Picasso. 2011. (ENG., Illus.). 48p. (J). (gr. k-2). 17.95 *(978-0-8109-9728-8(2)*, Abrams Bks. for Young Readers) Abrams, Inc.

Plain, Nancy. Frederic Remington: Artist of the American West. 2003. (Historical American Biographies Ser.). (Illus.). 160p.

A
B

(J). (gr. 6-12). lib. bdg. 27.94 *(978-0-7660-1975-1(6))* Enslow Pubs., Inc.

The Primary Source Library of Famous Artists. (Illus.). (J). (gr. 3-5). 127.50 *(978-1-4042-3302-7(4))* Rosen Publishing Group, Inc., The.

Raczka, Bob. Here's Looking at Me: How Artists See Themselves. (Illus.). 32p. (J). 2008. (gr. 4-7). per. 9.95 *(978-0-8225-7305-0(9)*, First Avenue Editions) 2006. (gr. k-12). 23.93 *(978-0-7613-3404-0(1)*, Millbrook Pr.) Lerner Publishing Group.

Razcka, Bob. Here's Looking at Me: How Artists See Themselves. 2006. (Illus.). 32p. (J). (gr. 4-7). 17.60 *(978-0-7569-8145-7(X))* Perfection Learning Corp.

Reed, Jennifer. Leonardo da Vinci: Genius of Art & Science. 2005. (Great Minds of Science Ser.). (Illus.). 128p. (J). lib. bdg. 27.94 *(978-0-7660-2500-4(4))* Enslow Pubs., Inc.

Reynolds, Toby. Mini Artist: Set 2. 2015. (Mini Artist Ser.). (ENG.). 24p. (J). 105.00 *(978-1-4777-5660-7(4)*, Windmill Bks.) Rosen Publishing Group, Inc., The.

Richardson, Adele. Michelangelo. (Illus.). (J). 2016. 80p. *(978-1-60818-719-5(5))* 2005. 48p. (gr. 5-9). lib. bdg. 21.95 *(978-1-58341-379-1(0))* Creative Co., The. (Creative Education).

Richardson, R. Sarah & Charlesbridge Publishing Staff. The Artist at Work. 2003. (Come Look with Me Ser.). (ENG.). 32p. (J). (gr. k-3). 16.95 *(978-1-890674-09-0(5))* Charlesbridge Publishing, Inc.

Rinaldo, Denise. Leonardo Da Vinci: With a Discussion of Imagination. 2003. (Values in Action Ser.). (J). *(978-1-59203-066-8(1))* Learning Challenge, Inc.

Roberts, Russell. Rembrandt. 2008. (Art Profiles for Kids Ser.). (Illus.). 48p. (YA). (gr. 4-7). lib. bdg. 29.95 *(978-1-58415-710-6(0))* Mitchell Lane Pubs., Inc.

Roddam, George. The Life & Art of Paul Gauguin. Harasymowicz, Slawa, illus. 2016. (Lives of Great Artists Ser.). 00080p. (J). (gr. 8-8). 35.75 *(978-1-4994-6581-5(5)*, Rosen Young Adult) Rosen Publishing Group, Inc., The.

—The Life & Art of Vincent Van Gogh. Harasymowicz, Sawa, illus. 2016. (Lives of Great Artists Ser.). 00080p. (J). (gr. 8-8). 35.75 *(978-1-4994-6583-9(1))* Rosen Publishing Group, Inc., The.

Roeder, Annette. Leonardo Da Vinci: Coloring Book. 2011. (ENG.). 32p. (J). (gr. 1-4). pap. 8.95 *(978-3-7913-7065-1(0))* Prestel Verlag GmbH & Co KG. DEU. Dist: Penguin Random Hse. LLC.

Rollyson, Carl. Pablo Picasso: A Biography for Beginners. 2009. 88p. pap. 9.95 *(978-1-4401-3247-6(X))* iUniverse, Inc.

Rosen Publishing Staff. Artists Through the Ages: Set 2, 1 vol. 2015. (Artists Through the Ages Ser.). (ENG.). 32p. (J). 157.50 *(978-1-4777-5413-9(X)*, Windmill Bks.) Rosen Publishing Group, Inc., The.

Rosenstock, Barb. The Noisy Paint Box: The Colors & Sounds of Kandinsky's Abstract Art. GrandPré, Mary, illus. 2014. (ENG.). 40p. (J). (gr. -1-3). 17.99 *(978-0-307-97848-6(6)*, Knopf Bks. for Young Readers) Random Hse. Children's Bks.

Rubin, Susan Goldman. Everyone Paints! The Lives & Art of the Wyeth Family. 2014. (ENG.). 105p. (J). (gr. 3-7). 16.99 *(978-0-8118-6984-3(9))* Chronicle Bks. LLC.

Rulers, Scholars, & Artists of the Renaissance, 6 bk. set. 2005. (YA). (gr. 5-8). lib. bdg. 191.70 *(978-1-4042-0370-9(2))* Rosen Publishing Group, Inc., The.

Saddleback Educational Publishing Staff, ed. Houdini, 1 vol. unabr. ed. 2008. (Graphic Biographies Ser.). (ENG., Illus.). 25p. (YA). (gr. 9-12). pap. 7.95 *(978-1-59905-224-3(5))* Saddleback Educational Publishing, Inc.

Samanci, Özge. Dare to Disappoint: Growing up in Turkey. 2015. (ENG., Illus.). 200p. (YA). (gr. 9). pap. 16.99 *(978-0-374-31698-3(8)*, 9780374316983, Farrar, Straus & Giroux (BYR)) Farrar, Straus & Giroux.

Saxena, Shalini, ed. Top 101 Artists, 1 vol., 1. 2014. (People You Should Know Ser.). (ENG.). 160p. (YA). (gr. 7-12). 35.25 *(978-1-62275-129-7(9))* Rosen Publishing Group, Inc., The.

Say, Allen. Drawing from Memory. 2011. *(978-0-545-17687-3(5)*, Scholastic Pr.) Scholastic, Inc.

—Drawing from Memory. Say, Allen, illus. 2011. (ENG., Illus.). 64p. (J). (gr. 5-18). 18.99 *(978-0-545-17686-6(7)*, Scholastic Pr.) Scholastic, Inc.

Scarry, Richard. Scarry Busy Week - Four in One Bind-Up. 2013. (Busy Kids Ser.). 384p. (gr. -1-2). 12.95 *(978-1-62588-922-5(4))* Black Rabbit Bks.

Sheen, Barbara, ed. Paul Cezanne. 2012. (Eye on Art Ser.). (ENG., Illus.). 128p. (J). (gr. 7-10). lib. bdg. 34.80 *(978-1-4205-0858-1(X)*, Lucent Bks.) Cengage Gale.

Smith, Elwood. How to Draw with Your Funny Bone. Smith, Elwood, illus. 2015. (ENG., Illus.). 40p. (J). (gr. 1-3). 17.99 *(978-1-56846-243-1(3)*, Creative Editions) Creative Co., The.

Spence, David. The Impressionists: Monet, Cezanne, Renoir, Degas. 2010. (ENG.). 128p. (J). (gr. 4-7). pap. 12.95 *(978-1-84696-217-2(X)*, TickTock Books) Octopus Publishing Group GBR. Dist: Independent Pubs. Group.

Stabler, David & Horner, Doogie. Kid Artists. 2016. (Kid Legends Ser.: 3). (ENG., Illus.). 208p. (J). (gr. 4-7). 13.95 *(978-1-59474-896-7(9))* Quirk Bks.

Stair, Nancy L. Michelle Yeoh. 2009. (Martial Arts Masters Ser.). 112p. (gr. 5-5). 63.90 *(978-1-61514-375-7(0))* Rosen Publishing Group, Inc., The.

Stanley, Diane. Michelangelo. Stanley, Diane, illus. 2003. (ENG., Illus.). 48p. (J). (gr. 2-18). pap. 6.99 *(978-0-06-052113-4(9))* HarperCollins Pubs.

Stephens, Pamela Geiger. Dropping in on Andy Warhol. McNeill, Jim, illus. 2006. (J). 15.95 *(978-1-56290-433-3(7))* Crystal Productions.

Surrey, Ellen. 50 Creative Women from the Mid 20th Century. 2016. (ENG., Illus.). 116p. 29.95 *(978-1-62326-082-8(5))* AMMO Bks., LLC.

Sutcliffe, Jane & Walt Disney Company Staff. Walt Disney. 2009. (History Maker Biographies Ser.). (gr. 3-6). 26.60 *(978-1-58013-704-1(0)*, Lerner Pubns.) Lerner Publishing Group.

Sutherland, Adam. Potty Painters, Writers & Other Barmy Artists. 2017. (Barmy Biogs Ser.). (ENG., Illus.). 96p. (J). (gr. 4-6). pap. 7.99 ***(978-0-7502-8378-6(5)***, Wayland) Hachette Children's Group GBR. Dist: Hachette Bk. Group.

Sutoski, Jennifer. Barbara Reid. 2015. (Canadian Biographies Ser.). (ENG., Illus.). 24p. (gr. k-1). lib. bdg. 26.65 *(978-1-4914-7838-7(1)*, Pebble Plus) Capstone Press of Coughlan Cos.

Tan, Shaun. The Bird King: An Artist's Notebook. 2013. (ENG.). 128p. (J). (gr. 7-9). 19.99 *(978-0-545-46513-7(3)*, Levine, Arthur A. Bks.) Scholastic, Inc.

Taylor, Charlotte. Get to Know Andy Warhol. 2016. (Famous Artists Ser.). (ENG., Illus.). 48p. (J). (gr. 3-4). 27.93 *(978-0-7660-7218-3(5))* Enslow Pubs., Inc.

—Get to Know Willem de Kooning. 2016. (Famous Artists Ser.). (ENG.). 48p. (J). (gr. 3-4). 27.93 *(978-0-7660-7242-8(8))* Enslow Pubs., Inc.

Thomas, Dina M. & Thomas, Andy, eds. The Artful Journey: The Artwork of Andy Thomas. Thomas, Tria M., photos by. l.t. ed. 2003. (Illus.). 122p. 50.00 *(978-0-9742285-0-1(8))* Maze Creek Studio.

Venezia, Mike. Diego Velázquez. Venezia, Mike, illus. 2004. (Getting to Know the World's Greatest Artists Ser.). (ENG., Illus.). 32p. (J). (gr. 3-4). pap. 6.95 *(978-0-516-26980-1(1)*, Children's Pr.) Scholastic Library Publishing.

—Leonardo Davinci. Venezia, Mike, illus. rev. ed. 2015. (Getting to Know the World's Greatest Artists Ser.). (ENG., Illus.). 40p. (J). pap. 7.95 *(978-0-531-21289-9(0))* Scholastic Library Publishing.

—Winslow Homer. Venezia, Mike, illus. 2004. (Getting... Know Artists Ser.). (ENG., Illus.). 32p. (J). (gr. 3-4). pap. 6.95 *(978-0-516-26979-5(8)*, Children's Pr.) Scholastic Library Publishing.

Venezia, Mike & Magritte, Rene. René Magritte. Venezia, Mike, illus. 2003. (Getting to Know the World's Greatest Artists Ser.). (ENG., Illus.). 32p. (J). (gr. 3-4). pap. 6.95 *(978-0-516-27814-8(2)*, Children's Pr.) Scholastic Library Publishing.

Waldman, Neil. Out of the Shadows: An Artist's Journey. 2006. (ENG., Illus.). 148p. (J). (gr. 5). 21.95 *(978-1-59078-411-2(1))* Boyds Mills Pr.

Warhola, James. Uncle Andy's. Warhola, James, illus. 2005. (ENG., Illus.). 32p. (J). (gr. k-3). reprint ed. pap. 5.99 *(978-0-14-240347-1(4)*, Puffin Books) Penguin Young Readers Group.

Welton, Jude. Marc Chagall. 2003. (Artists in Their Time Ser.). (ENG., Illus.). 48p. (J). 24.00 *(978-0-531-12235-8(2))*; (gr. 5-7). pap. 6.95 *(978-0-531-16645-1(7))* Scholastic Library Publishing. (Watts, Franklin).

Wenzel, Angela. 13 Art Techniques Children Should Know. 2013. (ENG., Illus.). 48p. (J). (gr. 3-7). 14.95 *(978-3-7913-7136-8(3))* Prestel Verlag GmbH & Co KG. DEU. Dist: Penguin Random Hse. LLC.

Wheeler, Jill C. Chris Van Allsburg, 1 vol. 2005. (Children's Illustrators Set 1 Ser.). (ENG.). 24p. (gr. k-6). 25.65 *(978-1-59197-721-6(5)*, Checkerboard Library) ABDO Publishing Co.

—Garth Williams, 1 vol. 2005. (Children's Illustrators Set 1 Ser.). (ENG., Illus.). 24p. (gr. k-6). 25.65 *(978-1-59197-723-0(1)*, Checkerboard Library) ABDO Publishing Co.

—Robert Mccloskey, 1 vol. 2005. (Children's Illustrators Set 1 Ser.). (ENG., Illus.). 24p. (gr. k-6). 25.65 *(978-1-59197-719-3(3)*, Checkerboard Library) ABDO Publishing Co.

—William Steig, 1 vol. 2005. (Children's Illustrators Set 1 Ser.). (ENG., Illus.). 24p. (gr. k-6). 25.65 *(978-1-59197-720-9(7)*, Checkerboard Library) ABDO Publishing Co.

Whitehead, Kathy. Art from Her Heart: Folk Artist Clementine Hunter. Evans, Shane W., illus. 2008. (ENG.). 32p. (J). (gr. 1-3). 16.99 *(978-0-399-24219-9(8)*, G.P. Putnam's Sons Books for Young Readers) Penguin Young Readers Group.

Whiting, Jim. Edvard Munch. 2008. (Art Profiles for Kids Ser.). (Illus.). 48p. (YA). (gr. 4-7). lib. bdg. 29.95 *(978-1-58415-712-0(7))* Mitchell Lane Pubs., Inc.

Willett, Edward & Warhol, Andy. Andy Warhol: "Everyone Will Be Famous for 15 Minutes" 2010. (American Rebels Ser.). 160p. (YA). (gr. 7-12). 35.94 *(978-0-7660-3385-6(6))* Enslow Pubs., Inc.

Wood, Alix. Anthony Van Dyck, 1 vol. 2015. (ENG., Illus.). 32p. (J). pap. 10.00 *(978-1-4777-5398-9(2)*, Windmill Bks.) Rosen Publishing Group, Inc., The.

—Artists Through the Ages: Set 2, 1 vol. 2015. (Artists Through the Ages Ser.). (ENG.). 32p. (J). 60.00 *(978-1-4994-8022-1(9)*, Windmill Bks.) Rosen Publishing Group, Inc., The.

—Artists Through the Ages: Set 3. 2015. (Artists Through the Ages Ser.). (ENG.). 32p. (J). 157.50 *(978-1-4777-5661-4(2)*, Windmill Bks.) Rosen Publishing Group, Inc., The.

—Edgar Degas, 1 vol. 2015. (ENG., Illus.). 32p. (J). lib. bdg. 26.25 *(978-1-4777-5409-2(1)*, Windmill Bks.) Rosen Publishing Group, Inc., The.

—Paul Gauguin, 1 vol. 2015. (ENG., Illus.). 32p. (J). lib. bdg. 26.25 *(978-1-4777-5405-4(9)*, Windmill Bks.) Rosen Publishing Group, Inc., The.

Young, Ed. The House Baba Built: An Artist's Childhood in China. 2011. (ENG.). 48p. (J). (gr. -1-3). 17.99 *(978-0-316-07628-9(7))* Little, Brown Bks. for Young Readers.

Yuan, Margaret Speaker. Beatrix Potter. 2005. (Who Wrote That? Ser.). (Illus.). 120p. (gr. 6-12). lib. bdg. 35.00 *(978-0-7910-8655-1(0)*, Chelsea Hse.) Facts On File, Inc.

Zannos, Susan. Samuel Morse & the Telegraph. 2004. (Uncharted, Unexplored, & Unexplained Ser.). (Illus.). 48p. (J). (gr. 4-8). lib. bdg. 29.95 *(978-1-58415-269-9(9))* Mitchell Lane Pubs., Inc.

ARTISTS, AFRICAN AMERICAN

see African American Artists

ARTISTS, AMERICAN

Adler, David A. & Adler, Michael S. A Picture Book of Harry Houdini. Collins, Matt, illus. 2009. (ENG.). 32p. (J). (gr. -1-3). 17.95 *(978-0-8234-2059-9(0))* Holiday Hse., Inc.

Anderson, Kirsten. Who Was Andy Warhol? Salamunic, Tim et al, illus. 2014. (Who Was? Ser.). (ENG.). 112p. (J). (gr. 3-7). 5.99 *(978-0-448-48242-2(8)*, Grosset & Dunlap) Penguin Young Readers Group.

Bankston, John. Alicia Keys. 2004. (Blue Banner Biography Ser.). (Illus.). 32p. (J). lib. bdg. 25.70 *(978-1-58415-327-6(X))* Mitchell Lane Pubs., Inc.

Bass, Hester. The Secret World of Walter Anderson. Lewis, E. B., illus. 2014. (Candlewick Biographies Ser.). (ENG.). 48p. (J). (gr. 3-7). 14.99 *(978-0-7636-7116-7(9))* Candlewick Pr.

Bass, Hester & Anderson, Walter Inglis. The Secret World of Walter Anderson. Lewis, E. B., illus. 2009. (ENG.). 48p. (J). (gr. 1-4). 17.99 *(978-0-7636-3583-1(9))* Candlewick Pr.

Benson, Kathleen. Draw What You See: The Life & Art of Benny Andrews. Andrews, Benny, illus. 2015. (ENG.). 32p. (J). (gr. -1-3). 17.99 *(978-0-544-10487-7(0)*, Clarion Bks.) Houghton Mifflin Harcourt Trade & Reference Pubs.

Biskup, Agnieszka. Houdini: The Life of the Great Escape Artist, 1 vol. Kinsella, Pat, illus. 2011. (American Graphic Ser.). (ENG.). 32p. (gr. 3-4). pap. 8.10 *(978-1-4296-6268-0(9))*; pap. 47.70 *(978-1-4296-6435-6(5))* Capstone Press of Coughlan Cos. (Graphic Library).

Carlson, Cheryl. Dr. Seuss [Scholastic]. 2011. (First Biographies - Writers, Artists, & Athletes Ser.). 24p. pap. 0.50 *(978-1-4296-6317-5(0)*, Pebble Bks.) Capstone Press of Coughlan Cos.

Carlson, Laurie M. Harry Houdini for Kids: His Life & Adventures with 21 Magic Tricks & Illusions. 2009. (For Kids Ser.). (ENG., Illus.). 144p. (J). (gr. 4-7). pap. 18.95 *(978-1-55652-782-1(9))* Chicago Review Pr., Inc.

Cefrey, Holly. Justin Timberlake. 2009. (Contemporary Musicians & Their Music Ser.). (Illus.). 48p. (gr. 7-12). pap. 11.75 *(978-1-4358-5123-8(4)*, Rosen Classroom) Rosen Publishing Group, Inc., The.

Christie, R. Gregory. It Jes' Happened: When Bill Traylor Started to Draw, 1 vol. Tate, Don, illus. 2012. (ENG.). 1p. (J). 17.95 *(978-1-60060-260-3(6))* Lee & Low Bks., Inc.

Close, Chuck & Mouly, Françoise. Chuck Close: Face Book. 2012. (ENG., Illus.). 64p. (J). (gr. 3-7). 19.95 *(978-1-4197-0163-4(0)*, Abrams Bks. for Young Readers) Abrams, Inc.

Colich, Abby. Mo Willems, 1 vol. Byers, Michael, illus. 2013. (Your Favorite Authors Ser.). (ENG.). 24p. (gr. 1-2). 25.32 *(978-1-4765-3157-1(9))*; pap. 7.95 *(978-1-4765-3444-2(6))* Capstone Press of Coughlan Cos. (First Facts).

Davis, Lynn. Samuel Morse, 1 vol. 2016. (ENG., Illus.). 24p. (J). *(978-1-62403-725-2(9))* ABDO Publishing Co.

dePaola, Tomie. For the Duration: The War Years, 8 vols. dePaola, Tomie, illus. 2009. (26 Fairmount Avenue Book Ser.: 8). (ENG., Illus.). 80p. (J). (gr. 2-5). 17.99 *(978-0-399-25209-9(6)*, G.P. Putnam's Sons Books for Young Readers) Penguin Young Readers Group.

Deutsch, Stacia & Cohon, Rhody. Samuel L. Jackson. 2007. (Sharing the American Dream Ser.). 64p. (YA). (gr. 7-18). pap. 9.95 *(978-1-4222-0750-5(1))* Mason Crest.

Foa, Emma. Edward Hopper. 2003. (Artists in Their Time Ser.). (ENG., Illus.). 48p. (J). 24.00 *(978-0-531-12240-2(9))*; (gr. 5-7). pap. 6.95 *(978-0-531-16641-3(4))* Scholastic Library Publishing. (Watts, Franklin).

Foxley Leach, Deba. Grant Wood: The Artist in the Hayloft. 2005. (Adventures in Art Ser.). (Illus.). 29p. 14.95 *(978-3-7913-3401-1(8))* Prestel Publishing.

Gitlin, Martin. Stan Lee: Comic Book Superhero, 1 vol. 2009. (Essential Lives Set 4 Ser.). (ENG., Illus.). 112p. (J). (gr. 6-12). lib. bdg. 35.64 *(978-1-60453-702-4(7))* ABDO Publishing Co.

Greenberg, Jan & Jordan, Sandra. Andy Warhol, Prince of Pop. 2007. (Illus.). 208p. 17.00 *(978-0-7569-7952-2(8))* Perfection Learning Corp.

—Andy Warhol, Prince of Pop. 2007. (ENG., Illus.). 232p. (YA). (gr. 7-7). mass mkt. 7.99 *(978-0-385-73275-8(9)*, Laurel Leaf) Random Hse. Children's Bks.

—The Mad Potter: George E. Ohr, Eccentric Genius. 2013. (ENG., Illus.). 56p. (J). (gr. 2-6). 17.99 *(978-1-59643-810-1(X)*, 9781596438101) Roaring Brook Pr.

Greenberger, Robert. Christina Aguilera. 2008. (Contemporary Musicians & Their Music Ser.). (Illus.). 48p. (J). lib. bdg. 29.25 *(978-1-4042-1816-1(5))* Rosen Publishing Group, Inc., The.

Guillain, Charlotte. Dr. Seuss, 1 vol. 2012. (Author Biographies Ser.). (ENG.). 24p. (gr. 1-2). 23.32 *(978-1-4329-5959-3(X))*; pap. 6.79 *(978-1-4329-5965-4(4))* Heinemann-Raintree. (Heinemann Read & Learn).

—Maurice Sendak, 1 vol. 2012. (Author Biographies Ser.). (ENG.). 24p. (gr. 1-2). pap. 6.79 *(978-1-4329-5967-8(0)*, Heinemann Read & Learn) Heinemann-Raintree.

Hamilton, Sue L. Stan Lee, 1 vol. 2006. (Comic Book Creators Ser.). (ENG.). 32p. (YA). (gr. 3-6). 27.07 *(978-1-59928-301-2(8))* ABDO Publishing Co.

Haring, Kay. Keith Haring: The Boy Who Just Kept Drawing. Neubecker, Robert, illus. 2017. (ENG.). 40p. (J). (gr. k-3). 16.99 *(978-0-525-42819-0(4)*, Dial Bks) Penguin Young Readers Group.

Harvey, Jeanne Walker. Maya Lin: Artist-Architect of Light & Lines. Phumiruk, Dow, illus. 2017. (ENG.). 32p. (J). 17.99 *(978-1-250-11249-1(4)*, 9781250112491, Holt, Henry & Co. Bks. For Young Readers) Holt, Henry & Co.

Herkert, Barbara. Mary Cassatt: Extraordinary Impressionist Painter. Swiatkowska, Gabi, illus. 2015. (ENG.). 32p. (J). (gr. -1-3). 17.99 *(978-1-62779-016-1(0)*, 9781627790161, Holt, Henry & Co. Bks. For Young Readers) Holt, Henry & Co.

Herrera, Nicholas. High Riders, Saints & Death Cars: A Life Saved by Art, 1 vol. Denne, John, photos by. 2011. (ENG., Illus.). 56p. (J). (gr. 4-18). 24.95 *(978-0-88899-854-5(6))* Groundwood Bks. CAN. Dist: Publishers Group West (PGW).

Hillstrom, Laurie Collier. Kelly Clarkson. 2007. (People in the News Ser.). (ENG., Illus.). 104p. (YA). (gr. 7-12). lib. bdg. 33.95 *(978-1-4205-0013-4(9))* Cengage Gale.

Klimo, Kate. Dr. Seuss: The Great Doodler. Johnson, Steve & Fancher, Lou, illus. 2016. (Step into Reading Ser.). (ENG.). 48p. (J). (gr. k-3). 12.99 *(978-1-101-93551-4(0)*, Random Hse. Bks. for Young Readers) Random Hse. Children's Bks.

—Dr. Seuss: the Great Doodler. 2016. (Step into Reading Ser.). (ENG., Illus.). 48p. (J). (gr. k-3). lib. bdg. 15.99 *(978-0-375-97376-5(1)*, Random Hse. Bks. for Young Readers) Random Hse. Children's Bks.

Koerner, Henry. The Early Works of Henry Koerner 1945-1957. 2004. (Illus.). 96p. (YA). (gr. 13-18). pap. 35.00 *(978-0-9703425-5-3(1))* Frick Art & Historical Ctr.,The.

Landowne, Youme. Mali under the Night Sky: A Lao Story of Home. 2010. (ENG., Illus.). 40p. (J). (gr. k-4). 17.95 *(978-1-933693-68-2(1))* Cinco Puntos Pr.

Lenburg, Jeff. Genndy Tartakovsky. 2012. (Legends of Animation Ser.). (Illus.). 120p. (gr. 6-12). 34.95 *(978-1-60413-842-9(4)*, Chelsea Hse.) Facts On File, Inc.

—Walter Lantz. 2012. (Legends of Animation Ser.). (Illus.). 136p. (gr. 6-12). 34.95 *(978-1-60413-839-9(4)*, Chelsea Hse.) Facts On File, Inc.

Llanas, Sheila Griffin. Brian Selznick, 1 vol. 2012. (Children's Illustrators Set 2 Ser.). (ENG.). 24p. 25.65 *(978-1-61783-248-2(0)*, Checkerboard Library) ABDO Publishing Co.

—Jerry Pinkney, 1 vol. 2012. (Children's Illustrators Set 2 Ser.). (ENG.). 24p. 25.65 *(978-1-61783-247-5(2)*, Checkerboard Library) ABDO Publishing Co.

—Marla Frazee, 1 vol. 2012. (Children's Illustrators Set 2 Ser.). (ENG.). 24p. 25.65 *(978-1-61783-246-8(4)*, Checkerboard Library) ABDO Publishing Co.

—Tony Diterlizzi, 1 vol. 2012. (Children's Illustrators Set 2 Ser.). (ENG.). 24p. 25.65 *(978-1-61783-245-1(6)*, Checkerboard Library) ABDO Publishing Co.

Lyons, Deborah. Edward Hopper: Summer at the Seaside. 2003. (Adventures in Art Ser.). (Illus.). 30p. (gr. 5-18). 14.95 *(978-3-7913-2737-2(2))* Prestel Publishing.

Manger, Barbara & Smith, Janine. Mary Nohl: A Lifetime in Art. 2013. (Badger Biographies Ser.). (ENG., Illus.). 128p. (J). pap. 12.95 *(978-0-87020-577-4(3))* Wisconsin Historical Society.

Mason, Antony. El Arte Contemporaneo: En los Tiempos de Warhol. 2005. (Arte Alrededor del Mundo Ser.). (Illus.). 48p. pap. 9.95 *(978-85-7416-241-6(8))* Callis Editora Ltda BRA. Dist: Independent Pubs. Group.

McGehee, Claudia. My Wilderness: An Alaskan Adventure. 2015. (ENG., Illus.). 32p. (J). (gr. k-4). 16.99 *(978-1-57061-950-2(6)*, Little Bigfoot) Sasquatch Bks.

McMullan, James. Leaving China: An Artist Paints His World War II Childhood. 2014. (ENG., Illus.). 128p. (YA). (gr. 7-12). 19.95 *(978-1-61620-255-2(6)*, 73255) Algonquin Bks. of Chapel Hill.

Miller, Raymond H. Stan Lee: Creator of Spider-Man. 2006. (Inventors & Creators Ser.). (Illus.). 48p. (J). (gr. 4-8). lib. bdg. 26.20 *(978-0-7377-3447-8(7)*, Greenhaven Pr., Inc.) Cengage Gale.

Morrow, Paula. Mo Willems, 1 vol. 2015. (ENG.). 32p. (J). 23.45 *(978-1-62275-685-8(1)*, Britannica Educational Publishing) Rosen Publishing Group, Inc., The.

National Geographic Learning. Huong's Journey. 2009. (Inside the USA Ser.). (ENG., Illus.). 16p. (C). pap. 13.95 *(978-0-7362-7059-5(0))* CENGAGE Learning.

Neysters, Silvia & Soll-Tauchert, Sabine. Andy Warhol: Paintings for Children. 2004. (Adventures in Art Ser.). (Illus.). 30p. (J). 14.95 *(978-3-7913-3063-1(2))* Prestel Publishing.

Nobleman, Marc Tyler. Boys of Steel: Creators of Superman. 2013. lib. bdg. 18.40 *(978-0-606-31931-7(X)*, Turtleback) Turtleback Bks.

O'Rourke, Davey. American Artists Help Keep America Beautiful. 2017. (Text Connections Guided Close Reading Ser.). (J). (gr. 2). *(978-1-4900-1840-9(9))* Benchmark Education Co.

Powers, J. L. Colors of the Wind: The Story of Blind Artist & Champion Runner George Mendoza. Mendoza, George, illus. 2014. (J). 18.95 *(978-1-930900-73-8(2))* Purple Hse. Pr.

Ray, Deborah Kogan. Wanda Gág: The Girl Who Lived to Draw. 2008. (ENG., Illus.). 40p. (J). (gr. 1-3). 16.99 *(978-0-670-06292-8(8)*, Viking Books for Young Readers) Penguin Young Readers Group.

Reich, Susanna. Painting the Wild Frontier: The Art & Adventures of George Catlin. 2008. (ENG., Illus.). 176p. (J). (gr. 5-7). 22.00 *(978-0-618-71470-4(7))* Houghton Mifflin Harcourt Publishing Co.

Rubin, Susan Goldman. Roy's House. 2016. (ENG., Illus.). 40p. (J). (gr. -1-k). 15.99 *(978-1-4521-1185-8(5))* Chronicle Bks. LLC.

—Whaam! The Art & Life of Roy Lichtenstein. 2008. (ENG., Illus.). 48p. (J). (gr. 3-7). 21.95 *(978-0-8109-9492-8(5)*, Abrams Bks. for Young Readers) Abrams, Inc.

Say, Allen. The Inker's Shadow. 2015. (ENG.). 80p. (J). (gr. 7). 19.99 *(978-0-545-43776-9(8)*, Scholastic Pr.) Scholastic, Inc.

Schuetz, Kari. Charles Schulz. 2015. (Children's Storytellers Ser.). (ENG., Illus.). 24p. (J). (gr. 2-5). lib. bdg. 25.95 *(978-1-62617-264-7(1)*, Blastoff! Readers) Bellwether Media.

Stalcup, Ann & Politi, Leo. Leo Politi: Artist of the Angels. 2004. (gr. 4). 24.95 *(978-1-893110-38-0(9))* Silver Moon Pr.

Steptoe, Javaka. Radiant Child: The Story of Young Artist Jean-Michel Basquiat. 2016. (ENG., Illus.). 40p. (J). (gr. -1-3). 17.99 *(978-0-316-21388-2(8))* Little Brown & Co.

Stone, Tanya Lee. Sandy's Circus: A Story about Alexander Calder. Kulikov, Boris, illus. 2008. (ENG.). 40p. (J). (gr. 1-3). 16.99 *(978-0-670-06268-3(5)*, Viking Books for Young Readers) Penguin Young Readers Group.

Swain, Cynthia, et al. Charles R. Knight Was an Amazing Artist in Many Ways. 2017. (Text Connections Guided Close Reading Ser.). (J). (gr. 2). *(978-1-4900-1844-7(1))* Benchmark Education Co.

Taylor, Charlotte. Get to Know Andy Warhol. 2016. (Famous Artists Ser.). (ENG.). 48p. (J). (gr. 3-4). pap. 11.70 *(978-0-7660-7216-9(9))* Enslow Pubs., Inc.

—Get to Know Edward Hopper. 2016. (Famous Artists Ser.). (ENG.). 48p. (J). (gr. 3-4). pap. 11.70 *(978-0-7660-7220-6(7))*; (Illus.). 27.93 *(978-0-7660-7222-0(3))* Enslow Pubs., Inc.

—Get to Know John Singer Sargent. 2016. (Famous Artists Ser.). (ENG.). 48p. (J). (gr. 3-4). pap. 11.70 *(978-0-7660-7227-5(4))* Enslow Pubs., Inc.

—Get to Know Mary Cassatt. 2016. (Famous Artists Ser.). (ENG.). 48p. (J). (gr. 3-4). pap. 11.70 *(978-0-7660-7232-9(0))* Enslow Pubs., Inc.

—Get to Know Norman Rockwell. 2016. (Famous Artists Ser.). (ENG.). 48p. (J). (gr. 3-4). pap. 11.70 *(978-0-7660-7236-7(3))* Enslow Pubs., Inc.

—Get to Know Willem de Kooning. 2016. (Famous Artists Ser.). (ENG.). 48p. (J). (gr. 3-4). pap. 11.70 *(978-0-7660-7240-4(1))* Enslow Pubs., Inc.

Venezia, Mike. Faith Ringgold. Venezia, Mike, illus. (Getting to Know the World's Greatest Artists Ser.). (ENG., Illus.). 32p. (J). (gr. 3-4). 2008. pap. 6.95 *(978-0-531-14757-3(6))* 2007. 28.00 *(978-0-531-18526-1(5))* Scholastic Library Publishing. (Children's Pr.).

—Frederic Remington. Venezia, Mike, illus. 2003. (Getting to Know the World's Greatest Artists Ser.). (ENG., Illus.). 32p. (J). (gr. 3-4). pap. 6.95 *(978-0-516-27812-4(6)*, Children's Pr.) Scholastic Library Publishing.

—James McNeill Whistler. Venezia, Mike, illus. 2003. (Getting to Know World Artists Ser.). (ENG., Illus.). 32p. (J). 28.00 *(978-0-516-22578-4(2)*, Children's Pr.) Scholastic Library Publishing.

Waxman, Laura Hamilton. Dr. Seuss. 2010. (History Maker Biographies Ser.). (ENG.). 48p. (gr. 3-6). lib. bdg. 27.93 *(978-0-7613-5206-8(6)*, Lerner Pubns.) Lerner Publishing Group.

Wheeler, Jill C. David Wiesner, 1 vol. 2005. (Children's Illustrators Set 1 Ser.). (ENG.). 24p. (gr. k-6). 25.65 *(978-1-59197-722-3(3)*, Checkerboard Library) ABDO Publishing Co.

Williams, Jack S. Craftsmen & Craftswomen of the California Mission Frontier. 2009. (People of the California Missions Ser.). 64p. (gr. 4-4). 58.50 *(978-1-60851-156-3(1)*, PowerKids Pr.) Rosen Publishing Group, Inc., The.

Winter, Jeanette. Mr. Cornell's Dream Boxes. Winter, Jeanette, illus. 2014. (ENG., Illus.). 40p. (J). (gr. -1-3). 17.99 *(978-1-4424-9900-3(1)*, Beach Lane Bks.) Beach Lane Bks.

—My Name Is Georgia. 2003. (ENG., Illus.). 48p. (J). (gr. -1-3). pap. 7.99 *(978-0-15-204597-5(X))* Houghton Mifflin Harcourt Publishing Co.

Wood, Alix. Georgia O'Keeffe. 2015. (Artists Through the Ages Ser.). (ENG., Illus.). 32p. (J). (gr. 2-3). 26.25 *(978-1-4777-5440-5(7)*, 1391981, Windmill Bks.) Rosen Publishing Group, Inc., The.

Woog, Adam. John Lasseter: Pixar Animator. 2008. (Innovators Ser.). (ENG., Illus.). 48p. (J). (gr. 4-8). lib. bdg. 29.95 *(978-0-7377-4080-6(9)*, LML02109-242875, Kidhaven) Cengage Gale.

Zaczek, Iain. Mary Cassatt. 2014. (Great Artists Ser.). 32p. (J). (gr. 3-6). pap. 10.50 *(978-1-4824-1219-2(5))* Stevens, Gareth Publishing LLLP.

ARTISTS, BRITISH

Bankston, John. Randolph J. Caldecott & the Story of the Caldecott Medal. 2003. (Great Achiever Awards Ser.). (Illus.). 48p. (J). (gr. 4-8). lib. bdg. 29.95 *(978-1-58415-200-2(1))* Mitchell Lane Pubs., Inc.

Fabiny, Sarah. Who Was Beatrix Potter? Lacey, Mike, illus. 2015. 105p. (J). *(978-1-4806-8934-3(3)*, Grosset & Dunlap) Penguin Publishing Group.

Family Stories: Ten Stories. 2005. (SPA & ENG., Illus.). 27p. (J). pap. *(978-0-9716580-8-0(0))* Lectura Bks.

Guillain, Charlotte. Beatrix Potter, 1 vol. 2012. (Author Biographies Ser.). (ENG., Illus.). 24p. (gr. 1-2). 23.32 *(978-1-4329-5960-9(3))*; pap. 6.79 *(978-1-4329-5966-1(2))* Heinemann-Raintree. (Heinemann Read & Learn).

Hegel, Claudette. Randolph Caldecott: An Illustrated Life. 2004. (Avisson Young Adult Ser.). (Illus.). 176p. (J). lib. bdg. 27.50 *(978-1-888105-60-5(7))* Avisson Pr., Inc.

Hurtig, Jennifer. Beatrix Potter. 2008. (My Favorite Writer Ser.). (Illus.). 32p. (YA). (gr. 5-18). pap. 9.95 *(978-1-59036-923-4(8))*; lib. bdg. 26.00 *(978-1-59036-922-7(X))* Weigl Pubs., Inc.

McPhail, David. Beatrix Potter & Her Paint Box. McPhail, David, illus. 2015. (ENG., Illus.). 40p. (J). (gr. -1-3). 17.99 *(978-0-8050-9170-0(X)*, 9780805091700, Holt, Henry & Co. Bks. For Young Readers) Holt, Henry & Co.

ARTISTS, DUTCH

Bassil, Andrea & van Gogh, Vincent. Vincent Van Gogh. 2004. (Lives of the Artists Ser.). (Illus.). 48p. (gr. 5-12). lib. bdg. 31.00 *(978-0-8368-5602-6(3)*, Gareth Stevens Secondary Library) Stevens, Gareth Publishing LLLP.

—Vincent van Gogh. 2004. (Lives of the Artists Ser.). (Illus.). 48p. (gr. 5-12). pap. 14.05 *(978-0-8368-5607-1(4)*, Gareth Stevens Secondary Library) Stevens, Gareth Publishing LLLP.

Crispino, Enrica. Van Gogh. 2008. (Art Masters Ser.). 64p. (YA). (gr. 6-18). lib. bdg. 24.95 net. *(978-1-934545-05-8(8))* Oliver Pr., Inc.

Mis, Melody S. Rembrandt. 2009. (Meet the Artist Ser.). 24p. (gr. 2-3). 42.50 *(978-1-61514-632-1(6)*, PowerKids Pr.) Rosen Publishing Group, Inc., The.

Pescio, Claudio. Rembrandt. 2008. (Art Masters Ser.). 64p. (YA). (gr. 6-18). lib. bdg. 24.95 net. *(978-1-934545-02-7(3))* Oliver Pr., Inc.

ARTISTS—FICTION

Adam, Paul. Escape from Shadow Island. 2010. (ENG.). 304p. (J). (gr. 5-18). 16.99 *(978-0-06-186323-3(8)*, Waldon Pond Pr.) HarperCollins Pubs.

Agee, Jon. The Incredible Painting of Felix Clousseau. 2015. 32p. pap. 8.00 *(978-1-61003-620-7(4))* Center for the Collaborative Classroom.

Alfaro Sifontes, Manuel Guillermo. Alboroto en un Lugar Remoto. 2005. (Illus.). 32p. (J). *(978-1-58018-052-8(3))* Cambridge BrickHouse, Inc.

Alphin, Elaine Marie. Simon Says. 2005. (ENG.). 264p. (YA). (gr. 9-12). pap. 14.95 *(978-0-15-204678-1(X))* Houghton Mifflin Harcourt Publishing Co.

Anholt, Laurence. The Magical Garden of Claude Monet. 2003. (ENG., Illus.). 32p. (J). 16.99 *(978-0-7641-5574-1(1))* Barron's Educational Series, Inc.

—Matisse: the King of Color. 2007. (Anholt's Artists Books for Children Ser.). (ENG., Illus.). 32p. (J). (gr. 1-3). 16.99 *(978-0-7641-6047-9(8))* Barron's Educational Series, Inc.

—Picasso & the Girl with a Ponytail. 2007. (Anholt's Artists Books for Children Ser.). (ENG., Illus.). 32p. (J). (gr. -1-3). pap. 8.99 *(978-0-7641-3853-9(7))* Barron's Educational Series, Inc.

—Van Gogh & the Sunflowers. 2007. (Anholt's Artists Books for Children Ser.). (ENG., Illus.). 32p. (J). (gr. -1-3). *(978-0-7641-3854-6(5))* Barron's Educational Series, Inc.

Anjelais, M. Breaking Butterflies. 2014. (ENG.). 272p. (J). (gr. 9). 17.99 *(978-0-545-66766-1(6)*, Chicken Hse., The) Scholastic, Inc.

Arcos, Carrie. Crazy Messy Beautiful. 2017. (ENG.). 320p. (YA). (gr. 7). 17.99 *(978-0-399-17553-4(9)*, Philomel Bks.) Penguin Young Readers Group.

Ardizzone, Edward. Sarah & Simon & No Red Paint. Ardizzone, Edward, illus. 2011. (Illus.). 48p. (J). 17.95 *(978-1-56792-410-7(7))* Godine, David R. Pub.

Barshaw, Ruth McNally. New Kid in School. Barshaw, Ruth McNally, illus. 2013. (Ellie Mcdoodle Diaries). (ENG., Illus.). 192p. (YA). (gr. 3-6). 12.99 *(978-1-61963-174-8(1)*, 9781619631748, Bloomsbury USA Childrens) Bloomsbury Publishing USA.

Bauer, Michael Gerard. The Running Man. 2008. 304p. (YA). (gr. 9-18). lib. bdg. 17.89 *(978-0-06-145509-4(1)*, HarperTeen) HarperCollins Pubs.

—The Running Man. 2004. 280p. (YA). pap. *(978-1-86291-575-6(X)*, Omnibus Bks.) Scholastic Australia.

Beaty, Andrea. Artist Ted. Lemaître, Pascal, illus. 2012. (ENG.). 32p. (J). (gr. -1-3). 17.99 *(978-1-4169-5374-6(4)*, McElderry, Margaret K. Bks.) McElderry, Margaret K. Bks.

Bennett, Jenn. The Anatomical Shape of a Heart. 2015. (ENG.). 304p. (YA). (gr. 7). 17.99 *(978-1-250-06645-9(X)*, 9781250066459) Feiwel & Friends.

Bick, Ilsa J. Draw the Dark. (Carolrhoda YA Ser.). (ENG.). 344p. (YA). (gr. 9-12). 2011. pap. 9.95 *(978-0-7613-8131-0(7))* 2010. 16.95 *(978-0-7613-5686-8(X))* Lerner Publishing Group. (Carolrhoda Lab™).

Bingham, Kelly. Formerly Shark Girl. (ENG.). 352p. (YA). (gr. 7). 2015. pap. 8.99 *(978-0-7636-7673-5(X))* 2013. 16.99 *(978-0-7636-5362-0(4))* Candlewick Pr.

—Shark Girl. (ENG., Illus.). 288p. (YA). (gr. 7). 2010. pap. 8.99 *(978-0-7636-4627-1(X))* 2007. 16.99 *(978-0-7636-3207-6(4))* Candlewick Pr.

Bird, Michael. Vincent's Starry Night & Other Stories: A Children's History of Art. Evans, Kate, illus. 2016. (ENG.). 336p. (J). (gr. 4-8). 29.95 *(978-1-78067-615-9(8))* King, Laurence Publishing GBR. Dist: Hachette Bk. Group.

Bolognese, Don. The Warhorse. Bolognese, Don, illus. 2010. (ENG., Illus.). 176p. (J). (gr. 5-9). pap. 9.99 *(978-1-4424-2942-0(9)*, Simon & Schuster Bks. For Young Readers) Simon & Schuster Bks. For Young Readers.

Britto, Romero. Where Is Friendship Bear? Britto, Romero, illus. 2010. (ENG., Illus.). 16p. (J). (gr. -1-k). 12.99 *(978-1-4169-9623-1(0)*, Little Simon) Little Simon.

Broach, Elise. Masterpiece. 2010. 18.00 *(978-1-60686-888-1(8))* Perfection Learning Corp.

—Masterpiece. Murphy, Kelly, illus. 2010. (ENG.). 320p. (J). (gr. 4-7). pap. 7.99 *(978-0-312-60870-5(5)*, 9780312608705) Square Fish.

—Masterpiece. 2010. (J). lib. bdg. 18.40 *(978-0-606-14604-3(0)*, Turtleback) Turtleback Bks.

Browning, Diane. Signed, Abiah Rose. Browning, Diane, illus. 2010. (ENG., Illus.). 32p. (J). (gr. -1-2). 15.99 *(978-1-58246-311-7(5)*, Tricycle Pr.) Random Hse. Children's Bks.

Bryant, Jen. Georgia's Bones. Andersen, Bethanne, illus. 2005. (ENG.). 32p. (J). 17.00 *(978-0-8028-5217-5(3))* Eerdmans, William B. Publishing Co.

—Pieces of Georgia. 2007. (ENG., Illus.). 176p. (J). (gr. 5-9). per. 6.99 *(978-0-440-42055-2(5)*, Yearling) Random Hse. Children's Bks.

Burns, Suzanne. The Moon Painters. 2003. 192p. 14.00 *(978-1-894942-36-2(1))* Zumaya Pubns. LLC.

Cagan, Kayla. Piper Perish. 2017. (ENG., Illus.). 416p. (YA). 17.99 *(978-1-4521-5583-8(6))* Chronicle Bks. LLC.

Capatti, Bérénice. Klimt & His Cat. Monaco, Octavia, illus. 2004. (ENG.). 40p. (J). 20.00 *(978-0-8028-5282-3(3))* Eerdmans, William B. Publishing Co.

Carle, Eric. The Artist Who Painted a Blue Horse. Carle, Eric, illus. (ENG., Illus.). (J). (gr. -1 — 1). 2013. 22p. bds. 7.99 *(978-0-399-16402-6(2))* 2011. 32p. 17.99 *(978-0-399-25713-1(6))* Penguin Young Readers Group. (Philomel Bks.).

Castillo, Gary D. Quesadilla Moon. 2007. 100p. (J). (gr. 3-7). per. 9.95 *(978-1-55885-433-8(9)*, Piñata Books) Arte Publico Pr.

Catalanotto, Peter. Emily's Art. Catalanotto, Peter, illus. 2006. (ENG., Illus.). 32p. (J). (gr. k-3). 7.99 *(978-1-4169-2688-7(7)*, Atheneum Bks. for Young Readers) Simon & Schuster Children's Publishing.

Chibbaro, Julie. Into the Dangerous World. Sovak, Jean-Marc Superville, illus. 2015. (ENG.). 352p. (YA). (gr. 9-12). 17.99 *(978-0-8037-3910-9(9)*, Viking Books for Young Readers) Penguin Publishing Group.

Childress, Robert. Who Ever Heard of a Horse in the House? Childress, Nancy, ed. 2005. (ENG., Illus.). 80p. per. *(978-1-933002-00-2(X))* PublishingWorks.

Chur, R. G. Crescent Bay. 2012. 92p. 21.38 *(978-1-4669-2984-5(7))*; pap. 11.38 *(978-1-4669-2982-1(0))* Trafford Publishing.

Coatsworth, Elizabeth. The Cat Who Went to Heaven. 2011. 7.64 *(978-0-7848-3455-8(5)*, Everbind) Marco Bk. Co.

Cole, Henry. A Nest for Celeste: A Story about Art, Inspiration, & the Meaning of Home. Cole, Henry, illus. (Nest for Celeste Ser.: 1). (ENG., Illus.). 352p. (J). (gr. 3-7). 2012. pap. 6.99 *(978-0-06-170412-3(1))* 2010. 16.99 *(978-0-06-170410-9(5))* HarperCollins Pubs. (Tegen, Katherine Bks).

Comora, Madeleine. Rembrandt & Titus: Artist & Son. Locker, Thomas, illus. 2005. (ENG.). 32p. (J). (gr. 3-5). 17.95 *(978-1-55591-490-5(X))* Fulcrum Publishing.

Cornwell, Autumn. Carpe Diem. 2009. (ENG.). 368p. (YA). (gr. 7-12). pap. 12.99 *(978-0-312-56129-1(6)*, 9780312561291) Square Fish.

Cox, Greg. Riese: Kingdom Falling. 2013. (ENG., Illus.). 288p. (YA). (gr. 7). pap. 9.99 *(978-1-4424-2970-3(4)*, Simon & Schuster Bks. For Young Readers) Simon & Schuster Bks. For Young Readers.

Cronn-Mills, Kirstin. Original Fake. Johnson, E. Eero, illus. 2016. (ENG.). 352p. (YA). (gr. 7). 17.99 *(978-0-399-17326-4(9)*, G.P. Putnam's Sons Books for Young Readers) Penguin Young Readers Group.

Crowley, Cath. Graffiti Moon. 2012. (ENG.). 272p. (YA). (gr. 9). pap. 8.99 *(978-0-375-87195-5(0)*, Ember); 16.99 *(978-0-375-86953-2(0)*, Knopf Bks. for Young Readers) Random Hse. Children's Bks.

Crummel, Susan Stevens. City Dog, Country Dog, 0 vols. Donohue, Dorothy, illus. 2010. (ENG.). 42p. (J). (gr. k-4). pap. 9.99 *(978-0-7614-5538-7(8)*, 9780761455387, Amazon Children's Publishing) Amazon Publishing.

Cullen, Lyn. I Am Rembrandt's Daughter. 2011. 8.88 *(978-0-7848-3491-6(1)*, Everbind) Marco Bk. Co.

De la Cruz, Melissa. Angels on Sunset Boulevard. 2008. (Angels on Sunset Boulevard Ser.: Bk. 1). (ENG.). 240p. (YA). (gr. 9-18). pap. 8.99 *(978-1-4169-3991-7(1)*, Simon & Schuster Bks. For Young Readers) Simon & Schuster Bks. For Young Readers.

de Trevino, Elizabeth Borton. I, Juan de Pareja. 3rd ed. pap. 3.95 *(978-0-13-800129-2(4))* Prentice Hall (Schl. Div.).

—I, Juan de Pareja. 2008. (ENG.). 192p. (YA). (gr. 7-12). pap. 7.99 *(978-0-312-38005-2(4)*, 9780312380052) Square Fish.

—I, Juan de Pareja. l.t. ed. 2005. 244p. 20.95 *(978-0-7862-7666-0(5))* Thorndike Pr.

Demi & Demi Staff. The Boy Who Painted Dragons. Demi & Demi Staff, illus. 2007. (ENG., Illus.). 52p. (J). (gr. 2-5). 21.99 *(978-1-4169-2469-2(8)*, McElderry, Margaret K. Bks.) McElderry, Margaret K. Bks.

Dines, Carol. The Queen's Soprano. 2007. (ENG., Illus.). 336p. (YA). (gr. 9). pap. 18.95 *(978-0-15-206102-9(9))* Houghton Mifflin Harcourt Publishing Co.

Disney Book Group Staff & Heddle, Jennifer. World of Reading Star Wars Rebels. 2015. (World of Reading Ser.). (ENG.). 32p. (J). (gr. 1-3). pap. 3.99 *(978-1-4847-0491-2(6)*, Disney Lucasfilm Press) Disney Publishing Worldwide.

Dolson, Carol Bland. Hattie & the Higgledy-Piggledy Hedge. Rabon, Elaine Hearn, illus. 2012. (ENG.). 32p. (J). 18.95 *(978-0-9827614-4-1(9)*, 9780982761441) Moose Hill Bks., Inc.

Dunlap Cather, Katherine. Boyhood Stories of Famous Men. 2013. 292p. pap. *(978-3-95507-921-5(X))* DOGMA. in Europäischer Hochschulverlag GmbH & Co. KG.

Eareckson Tada, Joni. I'll Be with You Always. Nelson, Craig, illus. 2004. 32p. (gr. 8-12). 14.99 *(978-1-58134-000-6(1))* Crossway.

Ehlert, Lois. Hands: Growing up to Be an Artist. 2004. (ENG., Illus.). 48p. (J). (gr. -1-3). 16.99 *(978-0-15-205107-5(4))* Houghton Mifflin Harcourt Publishing Co.

Everson, Chance. Discoveries: Tales of the Mandrasaurs, Volume the Third. Geary, Steve, illus. 2004. cd-rom 9.95 *(978-0-9760303-2-4(2))* R.A.R.E. TALES.

Farrey, Brian. With or Without You. 2011. (ENG., Illus.). 368p. (YA). (gr. 11-18). pap. 8.99 *(978-1-4424-0699-5(2)*, Simon Pulse) Simon Pulse.

Franco, Betsy. Metamorphosis: Junior Year. Franco, Tom & Franco, Betsy, illus. 2009. (ENG.). 128p. (YA). (gr. 9-18). 16.99 *(978-0-7636-3765-1(3))* Candlewick Pr.

Freely, Jessica. All the Colors of Love. 2016. (ENG., Illus.). (YA). (gr. 9-12). 24.99 ***(978-1-63477-932-6(0)***, Harmony Ink Pr.) Dreamspinner Pr.

Friedlander, Mark P., Jr. Innovators in Action! Leonardo Da Vinci Gets a Do-Over. Sakprayoonpong, Worachet Boon, illus. 2014. (Innovators in Action Ser.: 1). (ENG.). 208p. (J). (gr. 5-9). pap. 12.95 *(978-0-9678020-6-0(7))* Science, Naturally!

Friedman, Samantha, et al. Matisse's Garden. 2014. (ENG., Illus.). 48p. (J). (gr. -1-3). 19.95 *(978-0-87070-910-4(0))* Museum of Modern Art.

Friesen, Jonathan. Both of Me, 1 vol. 2016. (ENG.). 256p. (J). pap. 9.99 *(978-0-310-73187-0(9))* Blink.

Froeb, Lori. I Am Picasso. Melman, Debra, illus. 2015. (Rescue Readers Ser.: 4). (ENG.). 32p. (J). (gr. 1-2). lib. bdg. 16.99 *(978-0-7944-3515-8(7))* Reader's Digest Assn., Inc., The.

Froeb, Lori C. ASPCA Rescue Readers - I Am Picasso! Melman, Debra, illus. 2015. (Rescue Readers Ser.). (ENG.). 32p. (J). (gr. k-2). pap. 3.99 *(978-0-7944-3514-1(9)*, Reader's Digest Children's Bks.) Studio Fun International.

Fulton-Vengco, Aletha. Felicidad's Sidewalk Art. 2009. 36p. 14.80 *(978-0-578-00890-5(4))* Vengco, Aletha Fulton.

Garza, Xavier. Rooster Joe & the Bully / el Gallo Joe y el Abusón. 2016. (ENG & SPA.). 128p. (J). (gr. 5-8). pap. 9.95 *(978-1-55885-835-0(0)*, Piñata Books) Arte Publico Pr.

Gerstein, Mordicai. The Sleeping Gypsy. Gerstein, Mordicai, illus. 2016. (ENG., Illus.). 32p. (J). 16.95 *(978-0-8234-2142-8(2))* Holiday Hse., Inc.

Giff, Patricia Reilly. Pictures of Hollis Woods. 2014. (ENG.). 176p. (J). (gr. 3-7). 11.24 *(978-1-63245-318-1(5))* Lectorum Pubns., Inc.

—Pictures of Hollis Woods. 2004. (ENG.). 176p. (J). (gr. 3-7). 7.99 *(978-0-440-41578-7(0)*, Yearling) Random Hse. Children's Bks.

Ginesin, Lucia. Prince Jack, the Little Artist. Ginesin, Zack, illus. 2009. 28p. pap. 11.99 *(978-1-59858-983-2(0))* Dog Ear Publishing, LLC.

Gingras, Charlotte. Pieces of Me. Ouriou, Susan, tr. from FRE. 2009. (ENG.). 144p. (J). (gr. 7-9). 17.95 *(978-1-55453-242-1(6))* Kids Can Pr., Ltd. CAN. Dist: Hachette Bk. Group.

Graham, Sabrina Depina. Breanna. 2008. 24p. pap. 21.99 *(978-1-4363-0900-4(X))* Xlibris Corp.

Griffin, Adele. The Unfinished Life of Addison Stone: A Novel. 2016. (ENG., Illus.). 256p. (YA). (gr. 9). pap. 11.99 *(978-1-61695-596-0(1)*, Soho Teen) Soho Pr., Inc.

Gulledge, Laura Lee. Page by Paige. 2011. (ENG., Illus.). 192p. (YA). (gr. 7-17). 18.95 *(978-0-8109-9721-9(5))*; pap. 9.95 *(978-0-8109-9722-6(3))* Abrams, Inc. (Amulet Bks.).

Haas, Jessie. Saige Paints the Sky. Davis, Sarah, illus. 2012. (American Girl Today Ser.: Bk. 2). lib. bdg. 17.15 *(978-0-606-31569-2(1)*, Turtleback) Turtleback Bks.

Harvey, Jeanne Walker. My Hands Sing the Blues: Romare Bearden's Childhood Journey, 0 vols. Zunon, Elizabeth, illus. 2011. (ENG.). 40p. (J). (gr. k-3). 17.99 *(978-0-7614-5810-4(7)*, 9780761458104, Amazon Children's Publishing) Amazon Publishing.

Hazen, Lynn E. The Amazing Trail of Seymour Snail. Cushman, Doug, illus. 2009. (ENG.). 64p. (J). (gr. 1-4). 16.99 *(978-0-8050-8698-0(6)*, 9780805086980, Holt, Henry & Co. Bks. For Young Readers) Holt, Henry & Co.

Hearn, Julie. Ivy. (ENG.). (YA). (gr. 7). 2009. 384p. pap. 9.99 *(978-1-4169-2507-1(4))* 2008. 368p. 17.99 *(978-1-4169-2506-4(6))* Simon & Schuster Children's Publishing. (Atheneum Bks. for Young Readers).

Heasley, Gwendolyn. A Long Way from You. 2012. (Where I Belong Ser.: 2). (ENG.). 336p. (YA). (gr. 8). pap. 8.99 *(978-0-06-197885-2(X)*, HarperTeen) HarperCollins Pubs.

Henry, Marguerite. Benjamin West & His Cat Grimalkin. Dennis, Wesley, illus. 2014. (ENG.). 160p. (J). (gr. 3-7). pap. 7.99 *(978-1-4814-0394-8(X)*, Aladdin) Simon & Schuster Children's Publishing.

—The Marguerite Henry Complete Collection: Benjamin West & His Cat Grimalkin; Black Gold; Born to Trot; Brighty; Brown Sunshine; Cinnabar; Gaudenzia; Justin Morgan; King of the Wind; Misty of Chincoteague; Misty's Twilight; Mustang; Sea Star; Stormy; San Domingo; White Stallion of Lipizza. 2014. (ENG., Illus.). 3056p. (J). (gr. 3-7). pap. 99.99 *(978-1-4814-2299-4(5)*, Simon & Schuster/Paula Wiseman Bks.) Simon & Schuster/Paula Wiseman Bks.

Hershenhorn, Esther. Fancy That. Lloyd, Megan, illus. 2003. (ENG.). 32p. (J). (gr. k-3). tchr. ed. 16.95 *(978-0-8234-1605-9(4))* Holiday Hse., Inc.

Hicks, Barbara Jean & Disney Book Group Staff. A Sister More Like Me. Disney Storybook Artists Staff et al, illus. 2013. (ENG.). 32p. (J). (gr. 1-3). 15.99 *(978-1-4231-7014-3(8))* Disney Pr.

Hillyer, Brenda L. Mystery in the Marsh. 2008. 48p. pap. 16.95 *(978-1-60703-784-2(X))* America Star Bks.

Hubbard, Kirsten. Wanderlove. (ENG.). 352p. (YA). (gr. 9). 2013. pap. 9.99 *(978-0-385-73938-2(9)*, Ember) 2012. 17.99 *(978-0-385-73937-5(0)*, Delacorte Bks. for Young Readers) Random Hse. Children's Bks.

Hurd, Thacher & Hurd. Art Dog. Hurd, Thacher, illus. 2004. (ENG., Illus.). 32p. (J). (gr. -1-3). 18.99 *(978-0-06-024424-8(0))* HarperCollins Pubs.

I, Juan de Pareja. 3rd ed. (J). pap., stu. ed. *(978-0-13-667452-8(6))* Prentice Hall (Schl. Div.).

Jackson, Everett E. Kimme Meets Squirrelly D. 2008. 28p. pap. 16.95 *(978-1-4389-0971-4(3))* AuthorHouse.

Johnson, Alaya Dawn. The Summer Prince. 2014. (ENG.). 304p. (J). (gr. 9). pap. 9.99 *(978-0-545-41780-8(5)*, Levine, Arthur A. Bks.) Scholastic, Inc.

Johnson, Maureen. Girl at Sea. 2008. (ENG., Illus.). 336p. (YA). (gr. 8-12). pap. 8.99 *(978-0-06-054146-0(6)*, HarperTeen) HarperCollins Pubs.

—13 Little Blue Envelopes. (13 Little Blue Envelopes Ser.: 1). (ENG., Illus.). (YA). (gr. 8-18). 2005. 336p. 17.99 *(978-0-06-054141-5(5))* 2010. 368p. reprint ed. pap. 9.99 *(978-0-06-054143-9(1))* HarperCollins Pubs. (HarperTeen).

—13 Little Blue Envelopes. 2007. 317p. 20.00 *(978-0-7569-7830-3(0))* Perfection Learning Corp.

Juby, Susan & Wells, Rosemary. The Truth Commission. 2015. (ENG., Illus.). 320p. (YA). (gr. 9). bds. 18.99 *(978-0-451-46877-2(5)*, Viking Books for Young Readers) Penguin Young Readers Group.

Kahler, A. R. Echoes of Memory. 2017. (Ravenborn Ser.: 2). (ENG., Illus.). 336p. (YA). (gr. 9). 17.99 *(978-1-4814-3260-3(5)*, Simon Pulse) Simon Pulse.

—Shades of Darkness. 2016. (Ravenborn Ser.: 1). (ENG., Illus.). 304p. (YA). (gr. 9). 17.99 *(978-1-4814-3257-3(5)*, Simon Pulse) Simon Pulse.

Kamata, Suzanne. Gadget Girl: The Art of Being Invisible. 2013. (ENG., Illus.). 256p. (YA). pap. 14.95 *(978-1-936846-38-2(1))* GemmaMedia.

Karcz, Lauren. The Gallery of Unfinished Girls. 2017. 352p. (YA). (gr. 8). 17.99 *(978-0-06-246777-5(8)*, HarperTeen) HarperCollins Pubs.

Kidd, Ronald. The Year of the Bomb. 2009. (ENG.). 208p. (YA). (gr. 7-18). 16.99 *(978-1-4169-5892-5(4)*, Simon & Schuster Bks. For Young Readers) Simon & Schuster Bks. For Young Readers.

Kinkade, Thomas. Katherine's Story. 2004. (Girls of Lighthouse Lane Ser.). 176p. (J). (gr. 5-18). 13.89 *(978-0-06-054342-6(6))* HarperCollins Pubs.

Kinkade, Thomas & Tamar, Erika. Rose's Story. 2004. (Girls of Lighthouse Lane Ser.: No. 2). (Illus.). 192p. (J). (gr. 5-18). 12.99 *(978-0-06-054344-0(2))* HarperCollins Pubs.

Koja, Kathe. Buddha Boy. 2004. (ENG.). 128p. (YA). (gr. 7-11). reprint ed. 6.99 *(978-0-14-240209-2(5)*, Speak) Penguin Young Readers Group.

—Buddha Boy. 2004. 117p. (gr. 3-7). 16.00 *(978-0-7569-3117-9(7))* Perfection Learning Corp.

Krosoczka, Jarrett J. Lunch Lady & the Picture Day Peril. 2012. (Lunch Lady Ser.: 8). lib. bdg. 17.20 *(978-0-606-26811-0(1)*, Turtleback) Turtleback Bks.

Krull, Kathleen & Brewer, Paul. Fartiste. Kulikov, Boris, illus. 2008. (ENG.). 40p. (J). (gr. -1-3). 17.99 *(978-1-4169-2828-7(6)*, Simon & Schuster Bks. For Young Readers) Simon & Schuster Bks. For Young Readers.

LaChanze. Little Diva. Pinkney, Brian, illus. 2010. (ENG.). 32p. (J). (gr. -1-3). 16.99 *(978-0-312-37010-7(5)*, 9780312370107) Feiwel & Friends.

LaCour, Nina. The Disenchantments. (ENG.). (YA). (gr. 9). 2013. 336p. pap. 10.99 *(978-0-14-242391-2(2)*, Speak) 2012. 320p. 16.99 *(978-0-525-42219-8(6)*, Dutton Books for Young Readers) Penguin Young Readers Group.

Landry, Leo. What's up, Chuck? 2016. (ENG., Illus.). 48p. (J). (gr. k-3). lib. bdg. 12.95 *(978-1-58089-698-6(7))* Charlesbridge Publishing, Inc.

Leavey, Peggy Dymond. Trouble at Turtle Narrows. 2008. (ENG.). 144p. (J). (gr. 4-18). pap. 9.95 *(978-1-894917-71-1(5)*, Napoleon & Co.) Dundurn CAN. Dist: Ingram Publisher Services.

Lee, Sharon. Max. 2012. (Illus.). 24p. pap. 19.82 *(978-1-4772-3133-3(1))* AuthorHouse.

Léger, Diane Carmel. Emily Carr's Attic, 1 vol. Léger, Michael, illus. 2008. (ENG.). 32p. (J). (gr. -1-3). pap. 9.95 *(978-1-55143-958-7(1))* Orca Bk. Pubs. USA.

Lester, Julius. When Dad Killed Mom. 2003. (YA). (gr. 7-12). mass mkt. 6.95 *(978-0-15-524698-0(4)*, Silver Whistle) Harcourt Trade Pubs.

—When Dad Killed Mom. 2003. (ENG.). 216p. (YA). (gr. 7-12). pap. 13.95 *(978-0-15-204698-9(4))* Houghton Mifflin Harcourt Publishing Co.

Leveen, Tom. Zero. 2013. (ENG.). 320p. (YA). (gr. 9). pap. 9.99 *(978-0-375-87337-9(6)*, Ember) Random Hse. Children's Bks.

Levy, Janice. Showtime for Flip-Flop, 1 vol. Madden, Colleen M., illus. 2011. (Flip-Flop Adventure Ser.). (ENG.). 32p. (J). (gr. k-3). 28.50 *(978-1-61641-654-6(8))* Magic Wagon.

Lichtenheld, Tom. Bridget's Beret. Lichtenheld, Tom, illus. 2010. (ENG., Illus.). 40p. (J). (gr. -1-2). 16.99 *(978-0-8050-8775-8(3)*, 9780805087758, Holt, Henry & Co. Bks. For Young Readers) Holt, Henry & Co.

Linn, Laurent. Draw the Line. Linn, Laurent, illus. 2016. (ENG., Illus.). 528p. (YA). (gr. 7). 17.99 *(978-1-4814-5280-9(0)*, McElderry, Margaret K. Bks.) McElderry, Margaret K. Bks.

Lithgow, John. Micawber. Payne, C. F., illus. 2005. (ENG.). 40p. (J). (gr. -1-3). reprint ed. 8.99 *(978-0-689-83542-1(6)*, Simon & Schuster Bks. For Young Readers) Simon & Schuster Bks. For Young Readers.

Lockhart, E. Fly on the Wall: How One Girl Saw Everything. 2007. (ENG., Illus.). 192p. (YA). (gr. 7-12). pap. 8.99

(978-0-385-73282-6(1), Delacorte Pr) Random House Publishing Group.

Lodding, Linda Ravin. Painting Pepette. Fletcher, Claire, illus. 2016. (ENG.). 40p. (J). (gr. -1-3). 17.99 *(978-1-4998-0136-1(X))* Little Bee Books Inc.

Lois, Lowry. Gathering Blue. 2012. (Giver Quartet Ser.: 2). (ENG.). 256p. (YA). (gr. 7). 17.99 *(978-0-547-99568-7(7))* Houghton Mifflin Harcourt Publishing Co.

—Gathering Blue. unabr. ed. 2004. (Middle Grade Cassette Librariestm Ser.). 224p. (J). (gr. 5-9). pap. 38.00 incl. audio *(978-0-8072-0989-9(9),* S YA 250 SP, Listening Library) Random Hse. Audio Publishing Group.

—Gathering Blue. 2013. (Giver Quartet Ser.: 2). lib. bdg. 20.85 *(978-0-606-31673-6(6),* Turtleback) Turtleback Bks.

Look, Lenore. Brush of the Gods. So, Meilo, illus. 2013. (ENG.). 40p. (J). (gr. -1-3). 17.99 *(978-0-375-87001-9(6),* Schwartz & Wade Bks.) Random Hse. Children's Bks.

Lyons, Stefanie. Dating Down. 2015. (ENG., Illus.). 312p. (YA). pap. 9.99 *(978-0-7387-4337-0(2),* Flux) North Star Editions.

MacLachlan, Patricia & MacLachlan, Emily. Painting the Wind. Schneider, Katy, illus. 2006. (Joanna Cotler Bks.). (ENG.). 40p. (J). (gr. -1-3). reprint ed. pap. 7.99 *(978-0-06-443825-4(2))* HarperCollins Pubs.

Manning, Sarra. Guitar Girl. 2005. 217p. (gr. 9-12). 17.00 *(978-0-7569-5702-5(8))* Perfection Learning Corp.

Markun, Patricia M. The Little Painter of Sabana Grande. Casilla, Robert, illus. 2014. (ENG.). 32p. (J). (gr. -1-3). 13.99 *(978-1-4814-4458-3(1),* Simon & Schuster Bks. For Young Readers) Simon & Schuster Bks. For Young Readers.

Maysonet, Melody. A Work of Art. 2015. (ENG.). 240p. (YA). 17.99 *(978-1-4405-8254-7(8),* Simon Pulse) Simon Pulse.

Mazzio, Joann. Leaving Eldorado. 2014. (ENG.). 176p. (YA). (gr. 7). pap. 10.99 *(978-0-544-33613-1(5),* HMH Books For Young Readers) Houghton Mifflin Harcourt Publishing Co.

McBroom, Danielle Loiselle. A Painted Dream. 2008. 20p. pap. 24.95 *(978-1-60441-694-7(7))* America Star Bks.

McNamara, Margaret. Dad Goes to School. Gordon, Mike, illus. 2007. (Robin Hill School Ser.). (ENG.). 32p. (J). (gr. -1-1). pap. 3.99 *(978-1-4169-1541-6(9),* Simon Spotlight) Simon Spotlight.

Merberg, Julie & Bober, Suzanne. Sharing with Renoir. 2005. (Mini Masters Ser.: MINI). (ENG., Illus.). 22p. (J). (gr. -1 — 1). bds. 6.99 *(978-0-8118-4757-5(8))* Chronicle Bks. LLC.

—Sunday with Seurat. 2005. (Mini Masters Ser.: MINI). (ENG., Illus.). 16p. (J). (gr. -1 — 1). bds. 6.95 *(978-0-8118-4758-2(6))* Chronicle Bks. LLC.

Montanari, Eva. Chasing Degas. 2009. (ENG., Illus.). 32p. (J). (gr. k-2). 18.95 *(978-0-8109-3878-6(2),* Abrams Bks. for Young Readers) Abrams, Inc.

Mullarkey, Lisa. Trail Ride Troubles, 1 vol. 2014. (Storm Cliff Stables Ser.). (ENG.). 112p. (J). (gr. 7-11). lib. bdg. 27.07 *(978-1-62402-052-0(6),* Calico Chapter Bks) Magic Wagon.

Murray, Victoria Christopher. Aaliyah. 2009. (Divas Ser.). (ENG.). 208p. pap. 14.99 *(978-1-4165-6351-8(2),* Gallery Bks.) Gallery Bks.

Nancy Mann Israel. The Juggler & His Wife. 2009. 24p. pap. 12.95 *(978-1-4389-5334-2(8))* AuthorHouse.

Nelson, Jandy. I'll Give You the Sun. 2015. (CHI.). 384p. (YA). (gr. 9). pap. *(978-986-359-180-1(7))* Ecus Publishing Hse.

—I'll Give You the Sun. 2014. (ENG.). 384p. (YA). (gr. 9). 17.99 *(978-0-8037-3496-8(4),* Dial Bks) Penguin Publishing Group.

—I'll Give You the Sun. 2015. (ENG.). 400p. (YA). (gr. 9-12). pap. 10.99 *(978-0-14-242576-3(1),* Speak) Penguin Young Readers Group.

—I'll Give You the Sun. 2015. (ENG.). 400p. (YA). (gr. 9). 21.30 *(978-1-68065-512-4(4))* Perfection Learning Corp.

—I'll Give You the Sun. 2015. lib. bdg. 22.10 *(978-0-606-37572-6(4))* Turtleback Bks.

Nesbit, Sara E. Mary Wants to Be an Artist. 2009. 28p. pap. 12.49 *(978-1-4490-2609-7(5))* AuthorHouse.

Newbery, Linda. Andie's Moon. 2009. (Historical House Ser.). 208p. (YA). (gr. 5-18). pap. 5.99 *(978-0-7945-2333-6(1),* Usborne) EDC Publishing.

Nichols, Amy K. Now That You're Here. (Duplexity Ser.). (ENG.). (YA). (gr. 7). 2016. 608p. pap. 12.99 *(978-0-385-75396-8(9),* Ember) 2014. 304p. 16.99 *(978-0-385-75389-0(6),* Knopf Bks. for Young Readers) Random Hse. Children's Bks.

Nicholson, Simon. The Magician's Fire. (Young Houdini Ser.: 1). (ENG.). (J). 2015. 272p. (gr. 4-7). pap. 7.99 *(978-1-4926-0949-0(8))* 2014. (Illus.). 240p. (gr. 5-8). 15.99 *(978-1-4926-0332-0(5),* 9781492603320, Sourcebooks Jabberwocky) Sourcebooks, Inc.

Noble, Trinka Hakes. The Orange Shoes. Ettinger, Doris, illus. rev. ed. 2007. (ENG.). 40p. (J). (gr. k-6). 16.95 *(978-1-58536-277-6(8))* Sleeping Bear Pr.

Nolan, Han. Send Me down a Miracle. 2003. (ENG.). 276p. (YA). (gr. 7-12). pap. 15.95 *(978-0-15-204680-4(1))* Houghton Mifflin Harcourt Publishing Co.

Novesky, Amy. Me, Frida. Diaz, David, illus. (ENG.). 32p. (J). (gr. k-2). 2015. 9.95 *(978-1-4197-1516-7(X))* 2010. 18.99 *(978-0-8109-8969-6(7))* Abrams, Inc. (Abrams Bks. for Young Readers).

O'Connor, Jane. Aspiring Artist. Glasser, Robin Preiss, illus. 2011. (Fancy Nancy Ser.). (ENG.). 32p. (J). (gr. -1-2). 12.99 *(978-0-06-191526-0(2))* HarperCollins Pubs.

Olson, Norah. Twisted Fate. 2015. (ENG.). 272p. (YA). (gr. 8). 17.99 *(978-0-06-227204-1(7))* HarperCollins Pubs.

Patron, Kristine Mary. An Artist? That's Me! 2013. 20p. (J). pap. 6.95 *(978-1-4327-8377-8(7))* Outskirts Pr., Inc.

Patterson, Valerie O. The Other Side of Blue. 2011. (ENG.). 240p. (YA). (gr. 7). pap. 13.99 *(978-0-547-55215-6(7))* Houghton Mifflin Harcourt Publishing Co.

Peacock, Shane. The Artist & Me. Casson, Sophie, illus. 2016. (ENG.). 40p. (J). (gr. k-4). 16.95 *(978-1-77147-138-1(7),* Owlkids) Owlkids Bks. Inc. CAN. Dist: Publishers Group West (PGW).

Pearce, Jackson. As You Wish. (ENG.). 304p. (YA). (gr. 8). 2010. pap. 8.99 *(978-0-06-166154-9(6))* 2009. 16.99 *(978-0-06-166152-5(X))* HarperCollins Pubs. (HarperTeen).

Pearsall, Shelley. The Seventh Most Important Thing. 2015. (ENG., Illus.). 288p. (J). (gr. 5). 16.99 *(978-0-553-49728-1(6),* Knopf Bks. for Young Readers) Random Hse. Children's Bks.

Pelley, Kathleen T. The Sandal Artist, 1 vol. Sprague, Lois, illus. 2012. (ENG.). 32p. (J). (gr. k-3). 16.99 *(978-1-58980-910-9(6))* Pelican Publishing Co., Inc.

Phillips, Linda Vigen. Crazy. 2014. (ENG.). 320p. (YA). pap. 9.00 *(978-0-8028-5437-7(0),* Eerdmans Bks For Young Readers) Eerdmans, William B. Publishing Co.

Philpot, Chelsey. Even in Paradise. (YA). (gr. 8). 2016. 384p. pap. 9.99 *(978-0-06-229370-1(2))* 2014. (ENG.). 368p. 17.99 *(978-0-06-229369-5(9))* HarperCollins Pubs.

Place, Francois. The Old Man Mad about Drawing: A Tale of Hokusai. Rodarmor, William, tr. from FRE. 2004. (ENG., Illus.). 112p. (J). 19.95 *(978-1-56792-260-8(0))* Godine, David R. Pub.

Place, John. The Good Artist. Trimmer, Tony, illus. 2007. (ENG.). 36p. *(978-1-85345-424-0(9))* Crusade for World Revival.

Ploss, Skip. If Picasso Were a Fish. Ploss, Skip, illus. 2006. (Illus.). 40p. (gr. k-2). 15.99 *(978-1-4116-9220-6(9))* Lulu Pr., Inc.

Polacco, Patricia. The Art of Miss Chew. Polacco, Patricia, illus. 2012. (ENG., Illus.). 40p. (J). (gr. k-3). 17.99 *(978-0-399-25703-2(9),* G.P. Putnam's Sons Books for Young Readers) Penguin Young Readers Group.

Prendergast, Gabrielle. Audacious, 1 vol. 2015. (ENG.). 336p. (YA). (gr. 8-12). pap. 12.95 *(978-1-4598-0264-3(0))* Orca Bk. Pubs. USA.

Rainfield, Cheryl. Scars. 2011. 8.67 *(978-0-7848-3439-8(3),* Everbind) Marco Bk. Co.

Ricci, Dorothy. Through Goya's Eyes: The World of the Spanish Painter & His Friend & Mentor, Gaspar Jovellanos. 2008. (YA). pap. *(978-0-88092-763-5(1));* lib. bdg. *(978-0-88092-762-8(3))* Royal Fireworks Publishing Co.

Robbins, Trina. A Match Made in Heaven. Ota, Yuko & Studio, Xian Nu, illus. 2013. (My Boyfriend Is a Monster Ser.: 8). (ENG.). 128p. (YA). (gr. 7-12). pap. 9.95 *(978-1-4677-0732-9(5),* Graphic Universe™) Lerner Publishing Group.

—A Match Made in Heaven. Xian Nu Studio Staff, illus. 2013. (My Boyfriend Is a Monster Ser.: 8). (ENG.). 128p. (YA). (gr. 7-12). lib. bdg. 29.27 *(978-0-7613-6857-1(4),* Graphic Universe™) Lerner Publishing Group.

Robert, Bulla Clyde. The Chalk Box Kid. 10th rev. ed. 2014. (Stepping Stone Book Ser.). (ENG.). 64p. (J). (gr. 12-12). 8.24 *(978-1-63245-220-7(0))* Lectorum Pubns., Inc.

Robinson, Fiona. Whale Shines: An Artistic Tale. 2013. (ENG., Illus.). 32p. (J). (gr. k-2). 18.95 *(978-1-4197-0848-0(1),* Abrams Bks. for Young Readers) Abrams, Inc.

Rose, Lisa. Shmulik Paints the Town. Echeverri, Catalina, illus. 2016. (ENG.). 32p. (J). (gr. -1-3). 17.99 *(978-1-4677-5239-8(8),* Kar-Ben Publishing) Lerner Publishing Group.

Russell, Rachel Renée. Tales from a Not-So-Fabulous Life. Russell, Rachel Renée, illus. 2009. (Dork Diaries: 1). (ENG., Illus.). 304p. (J). (gr. 4-8). 13.99 *(978-1-4169-8006-3(7),* Aladdin) Simon & Schuster Children's Publishing.

—Tales from a Not-So-Fabulous Life. 2009. (Dork Diaries: 1). lib. bdg. 25.75 *(978-0-606-32419-9(4),* Turtleback) Turtleback Bks.

—Tales from a Not-So-Smart Miss Know-It-All. Russell, Rachel Renée, illus. 2012. (Dork Diaries: 5). (ENG., Illus.). 368p. (J). (gr. 4-8). 13.99 *(978-1-4424-4961-9(6),* Aladdin) Simon & Schuster Children's Publishing.

Ryan, Hope. The Geek & His Artist. 2016. (ENG., Illus.). (J). 29.99 ***(978-1-63477-965-4(7),*** Harmony Ink Pr.) Dreamspinner Pr.

Ryan, Pam Muñoz. El Soñador. Sís, Peter, illus. 2010. (SPA.). 368p. (J). (gr. 3-7). pap. 8.99 *(978-0-545-17600-2(X),* Scholastic en Espanol) Scholastic, Inc.

Sandler, Steve. My Uncle Rob. Cunningham, Rob, illus. 2008. 32p. (J). pap. 12.95 *(978-0-9715721-5-7(1))* Washington Pubs.

Say, Allen. The Favorite Daughter. 2013. (J). pap. *(978-0-545-17663-7(8),* Levine, Arthur A. Bks.) Scholastic, Inc.

—The Favorite Daughter. Say, Allen, illus. 2013. (ENG., Illus.). 32p. (J). (gr. -1-3). 17.99 *(978-0-545-17662-0(X),* Levine, Arthur A. Bks.) Scholastic, Inc.

—The Ink-Keeper's Apprentice. 2006. 149p. (YA). 14.60 *(978-0-7569-6811-3(9))* Perfection Learning Corp.

—The Sign Painter. 2013. (ENG., Illus.). 32p. (J). (gr. -1-3). pap. 6.99 *(978-0-544-10514-0(1))* Houghton Mifflin Harcourt Publishing Co.

Schindler, Holly. A Blue So Dark. 2010. (ENG.). 288p. (YA). (gr. 9-18). pap. 11.99 *(978-0-7387-1926-9(9),* Flux) North Star Editions.

Scott, Elaine. The Spanish Web: An Encounter with Picasso. 2004. (Art Encounters Ser.). (J). 15.95 *(978-0-8230-0410-2(4));* pap. 6.99 *(978-0-8230-0413-3(9))* Watson-Guptill Pubns., Inc.

Seidler, Tor. A Rat's Tale. Marcellino, Fred, illus. 2008. (ENG.). 192p. (J). (gr. 3-7). pap. 11.99 *(978-0-374-40031-6(8),* 9780374400316, Farrar, Straus & Giroux (BYR)) Farrar, Straus & Giroux.

Sierra, Judy. Ballyhoo Bay. Anderson, Derek, illus. 2009. (ENG.). 40p. (J). (gr. -1-3). 16.99 *(978-1-4169-5888-8(6),* Simon & Schuster/Paula Wiseman Bks.) Simon & Schuster/Paula Wiseman Bks.

Smith, Brian. The Intrepid EscapeGoat: Curse of the Buddha's Tooth. Conkling, Jon & DeVito, Michael A., eds. 2012. (ENG., Illus.). 96p. pap. 12.95 *(978-0-9832161-3-1(4),* 9780983216131) Th3rd World Studios.

Sones, Sonya. What My Girlfriend Doesn't Know. 2011. 9.68 *(978-0-7848-3389-6(3),* Everbind) Marco Bk. Co.

—What My Girlfriend Doesn't Know. 2013. (ENG., Illus.). 320p. (YA). (gr. 7). pap. 9.99 *(978-1-4424-9384-1(4),* Simon & Schuster Bks. For Young Readers) Simon & Schuster Bks. For Young Readers.

Strauss, Victoria. Color Song, 0 vols. 2014. (Passion Blue Novel Ser.: 2). (ENG.). 344p. (J). (gr. 7-9). pap. 9.99 *(978-1-4778-2504-4(5),* 9781477825044, Skyscape) Amazon Publishing.

Tagged. 2015. (ENG.). 288p. (YA). (gr. 7). lib. bdg. 16.95 *(978-1-58089-583-5(2))* Charlesbridge Publishing, Inc.

Taylor, Laini. Daughter of Smoke & Bone. 2011. (ENG.). 432p. (YA). (gr. 10-17). 20.00 *(978-0-316-13402-6(3))* Little Brown & Co.

—Daughter of Smoke & Bone. 2012. (ENG.). (YA). (gr. 10-17). 448p. pap. 12.99 *(978-0-316-13399-9(X));* 624p. pap. 28.99 *(978-0-316-22435-2(9))* Little, Brown Bks. for Young Readers.

—Daughter of Smoke & Bone. 2012. (Daughter of Smoke & Bone Ser.: 1). (YA). lib. bdg. 24.50 *(978-0-606-26704-5(2),* Turtleback) Turtleback Bks.

—Days of Blood & Starlight. 2012. (ENG., (YA). (gr. 10-17). Illus.). 528p. 18.99 *(978-0-316-13397-5(3));* 688p. 39.99 *(978-0-316-22433-8(2))* Little, Brown Bks. for Young Readers.

Towbin, Meredith. Straightjacket. 2013. (ENG.). 272p. pap. 12.99 *(978-1-939194-70-1(9))* Etopia Pr.

Tullson, Diane. Zero. 2006. (ENG.). 185p. (J). (gr. 7-18). per. *(978-1-55041-950-4(1))* Fitzhenry & Whiteside, Ltd.

Van Draanen, Wendelin. Sammy Keyes & the Art of Deception. 2008. (Sammy Keyes Ser.: Bk. 8). (J). 64.99 *(978-1-60640-640-3(X))* Findaway World, LLC.

—Sammy Keyes & the Art of Deception. 2005. (Sammy Keyes Ser.). (Illus.). 272p. (J). (gr. 4-7). 14.15 *(978-0-7569-5069-9(4))* Perfection Learning Corp.

Van Dyne, Edith. Aunt Jane's Nieces at Work. 2005. 204p. pap. 12.95 *(978-1-4218-1523-7(0),* 1st World Library - Literary Society) 1st World Publishing, Inc.

Vanderwerf, Rob. The Craftsman. 2006. 32p. per. 12.99 *(978-1-59919-010-5(9))* Elim Publishing.

Velasquez, Eric. Grandma's Gift. Velasquez, Eric, illus. 2013. (ENG., Illus.). 32p. (J). (gr. k-1). pap. 9.99 *(978-0-8027-3536-2(3),* 9780802735362, Bloomsbury USA Childrens) Bloomsbury Publishing USA.

Vivian, Siobhan. Same Difference. 2014. (ENG.). 304p. (J). pap. 9.99 *(978-0-545-75802-4(5))* Scholastic, Inc.

Wade, Rebecca. The Theft & the Miracle. 2007. 351p. (J). (gr. 4-7). lib. bdg. 17.89 *(978-0-06-077495-0(9))* HarperCollins Pubs.

Waldman, Neil. Starry Night. 2010. (ENG.). 32p. (J). pap. 11.95 *(978-1-59078-780-9(3))* Boyds Mills Pr.

Waldman, Neil & Boyds Mills Press Staff. The Starry Night. 2007. (ENG., Illus.). 32p. (C). (gr. -1-2). 26.95 *(978-1-56397-736-7(2))* National Geographic School Publishing, Inc.

Webb, Mack Henry, Jr. Little Bianca. Tuck, Beverly, illus. 2006. 52p. (J). per. 15.95 *(978-0-9779576-0-6(8))* Pilinut Pr., Inc.

Wiesner, David. Art & Max. 2012. (CHI.). 37p. (J). *(978-7-5434-9586-9(4))* Hebei Jiaoyu Chubanshe.

—Art & Max. 2010. (ENG., Illus.). 40p. (J). (gr. -1-3). 17.99 *(978-0-618-75663-6(9),* Clarion Bks.) Houghton Mifflin Harcourt Trade & Reference Pubs.

Wiggins, Thalia. Greg & the Mural, 1 vol. Tate, Don, illus. 2012. (Making Choices: the Mcnair Cousins Ser.). (ENG.). 64p. 27.07 *(978-1-61641-631-7(9),* Calico Chapter Bks) Magic Wagon.

Winch, John. Run, Hare, Run. 2007. (Illus.). 40p. pap. *(978-1-921049-55-2(3))* Little Hare Bks. AUS. Dist: HarperCollins Pubs. Australia.

Wong, Joyce Lee. Seeing Emily. 2005. (ENG., Illus.). 288p. (J). (gr. 7-11). 16.95 *(978-0-8109-5757-2(4),* Abrams Bks. for Young Readers) Abrams, Inc.

Worm, Piet. Three Little Horses. 2007. (Illus.). 61p. (J). (gr. -1-3). 18.95 *(978-1-930900-36-3(8))* Purple Hse. Pr.

Wright, Bil. Putting Makeup on the Fat Boy. (ENG., 240p. (YA). (gr. 7). 2012. Illus.). pap. 9.99 *(978-1-4169-4004-3(9))* 2011. 16.99 *(978-1-4169-3996-2(2))* Simon & Schuster Bks. For Young Readers. (Simon & Schuster Bks. For Young Readers).

Wu, Mike. Ellie. Wu, Mike, illus. 2015. (ENG., Illus.). 40p. (J). (gr. -1-k). 16.99 *(978-1-4847-1239-9(0))* Disney Publishing Worldwide.

Wyatt, Melissa. Funny How Things Change. 2009. (ENG.). 208p. (YA). (gr. 9-13). 26.99 *(978-0-374-30233-7(2),* Farrar, Straus & Giroux (BYR)) Farrar, Straus & Giroux.

Wynne-Jones, Tim. The Uninvited. 2009. (ENG., Illus.). 368p. (YA). (gr. 9). 16.99 *(978-0-7636-3984-6(2))* Candlewick Pr.

Wynne, Rhys. The Magic Pencil, 1 vol. 2009. 13p. pap. 24.95 *(978-1-60749-089-0(7))* America Star Bks.

Yep, Laurence & Ryder, Joanne. A Dragon's Guide to the Care & Feeding of Humans. GrandPré, Mary, illus. 2015. (Dragon's Guide Ser.). (ENG.). 160p. (J). (gr. 3-7). 15.99 *(978-0-385-39228-0(1),* Crown Books For Young Readers) Random Hse. Children's Bks.

Young, Janet Ruth. My Beautiful Failure. (ENG., Illus.). 320p. (YA). (gr. 7). 2013. pap. 9.99 *(978-1-4424-8269-2(9))* 2012. 16.99 *(978-1-4169-5489-7(9))* Simon & Schuster Children's Publishing. (Atheneum Bks. for Young Readers).

Zalben, Jane Breskin. Mousterpiece. Zalben, Jane Breskin, illus. 2012. (ENG., Illus.). 36p. (J). (gr. -1-2). 16.99 *(978-1-59643-549-0(6),* 9781596435490) Roaring Brook Pr.

ARTISTS, GERMAN

Wing, Natasha. An Eye for Color: The Story of Josef Albers. Breckenreid, Julia, illus. 2009. (ENG.). 40p. (J). (gr. 1-4). 18.99 *(978-0-8050-8072-8(4),* 9780805080728, Holt, Henry & Co. Bks. For Young Readers) Holt, Henry & Co.

ARTISTS, ITALIAN

Bailey, Gerry & Foster, Karen. Leonardo's Pallete. Radford, Karen & Noyes, Leighton, illus. 2008. (Stories of Great People Ser.). (ENG.). 40p. (J). (gr. 3-8). lib. bdg. *(978-0-7787-3687-5(3))* Crabtree Publishing Co.

Blanch, Gregory & Stathis, Roberta. Renaissance Artists Who Inspired the World. 2003. (Explore the Ages Ser.). (Illus.). 79p. 17.00 *(978-1-55501-593-0(X))* Ballard & Tighe Pubs.

Brasch, Nicholas. Leonardo Da Vinci. 2013. (Discovery Education: Discoveries & Inventions Ser.). 32p. (J). (gr. 3-6). 25.25 *(978-1-4777-1330-3(1),* PowerKids Pr.) Rosen Publishing Group, Inc., The.

—Leonardo Da Vinci: The Greatest Inventor. 2013. (Discovery Education: Discoveries & Inventions Ser.). 32p. (J). (gr. 3-6). pap. 60.00 *(978-1-4777-1503-1(7),* PowerKids Pr.) Rosen Publishing Group, Inc., The.

Brasch, Nicolas. Leonardo Da Vinci: The Greatest Inventor. 2013. (Discovery Education: Discoveries & Inventions Ser.). (ENG., Illus.). 32p. (J). (gr. 3-6). pap. 10.00 *(978-1-4777-1502-4(9),* PowerKids Pr.) Rosen Publishing Group, Inc., The.

Carr, Simonetta. Michelangelo for Kids: His Life & Ideas, with 21 Activities. 2016. (For Kids Ser.). (ENG., Illus.). 144p. (J). (gr. 4). pap. 18.99 *(978-1-61373-193-2(0))* Chicago Review Pr., Inc.

Conklin, Wendy. 16th Century Superstar: Da Vinci. 2017. (TIME for KIDS(r) Nonfiction Readers Ser.). (Illus.). 32p. (J). (gr. 7-7). pap. 8.99 *(978-1-4938-3630-7(7))* Teacher Created Materials, Inc.

Connolly, Sean & Michelangelo Buonarroti. Michelangelo. 2004. (Lives of the Artists Ser.). (Illus.). 48p. (gr. 5-12). pap. 14.05 *(978-0-8368-5605-7(8));* lib. bdg. 31.00 *(978-0-8368-5600-2(7))* Stevens, Gareth Publishing LLLP. (Gareth Stevens Secondary Library).

Di Cagno, Gabriella. Michelangelo. 2008. (Art Masters Ser.). 64p. (YA). (gr. 6-18). lib. bdg. 24.95 net. *(978-1-934545-01-0(5))* Oliver Pr., Inc.

Edwards, Roberta. Who Was Leonardo da Vinci? Kelley, True, illus. 2005. (Who Was... ? Ser.). 106p. (J). (gr. 2-6). 12.65 *(978-0-7569-6971-4(9))* Perfection Learning Corp.

Geiger Stephens, Pamela. Dropping in on Renaissance Artists. McNeill, Jim, illus. 2010. 32p. (J). 15.95 *(978-1-56290-658-0(5))* Crystal Productions.

Howse, Jennifer. Michelangelo. 2016. (Illus.). 32p. (J). *(978-1-4896-4623-1(X))* Weigl Pubs., Inc.

Kalz, Jill. The Mona Lisa. 2004. (What in the World? Ser.). (Illus.). 48p. 19.95 *(978-1-58341-272-5(7),* Creative Education) Creative Co., The.

Kennon, Caroline. Leonardo Da Vinci in His Own Words. 2016. (Eyewitness to History Ser.). (ENG.). 32p. (J). (gr. 4-5). pap. 10.50 *(978-1-4824-4074-4(1))* Stevens, Gareth Publishing LLLP.

Malam, John. Leonardo Da Vinci: El Genio Que Definio el Renacimiento. P. López, Wendy, tr. from ENG. 2007. (Altea Biografías Ser.).Tr. of Leonardo da Vinci. (SPA., Illus.). 64p. (J). (gr. -1-3). 17.99 *(978-84-372-2467-1(5))* Altea, Ediciones, S.A. - Grupo Santillana ESP. Dist: Santillana USA Publishing Co., Inc.

Nardo, Don, ed. Leonardo da Vinci. 2012. (Eye on Art Ser.). (ENG., Illus.). 128p. (J). (gr. 7-10). lib. bdg. 34.80 *(978-1-4205-0735-5(4),* Lucent Bks.) Cengage Gale.

Nichols, Catherine. Leonardo da Vinci. 2009. (Primary Source Library of Famous Artists Ser.). 32p. (gr. 3-4). 42.50 *(978-1-60854-101-0(0),* PowerKids Pr.) Rosen Publishing Group, Inc., The.

—Michelangelo Buonarroti. 2009. (Primary Source Library of Famous Artists Ser.). 32p. (gr. 3-4). 42.50 *(978-1-60854-102-7(9),* PowerKids Pr.) Rosen Publishing Group, Inc., The.

Novelli, Luca. Leonardo Da Vinci & the Pen That Drew the Future. 2017. (Flashes of Genius Ser.). (ENG.). 112p. (J). (gr. 3). pap. 9.99 ***(978-1-61373-869-6(2))*** Chicago Review Pr., Inc.

Osborne, Mary Pope & Boyce, Natalie Pope. Leonardo Da Vinci: A Nonfiction Companion to Monday with a Mad Genius. Murdocca, Sal, illus. 2009. (Magic Tree House - Fact Tracker Ser.: 19). (ENG.). 128p. (J). (gr. 2-5). 6.99 *(978-0-375-84665-6(4),* Random Hse. Bks. for Young Readers) Random Hse. Children's Bks.

Phillips, John & National Geographic Kids Staff. Leonardo Da Vinci: The Genius Who Defined the Renaissance. 2008. (National Geographic World History Biographies Ser.). (ENG., Illus.). 64p. (J). (gr. 3-7). pap. 7.99 *(978-1-4263-0248-0(7),* National Geographic Children's Bks.) National Geographic Society.

Quill, Charlie. Michelangelo: His Life & Art. 2009. (Reading Room Collection 2 Ser.). 24p. (gr. 3-4). 42.50 *(978-1-60851-980-4(5),* PowerKids Pr.) Rosen Publishing Group, Inc., The.

Rice, Earle, Jr. Canaletto. 2007. (Art Profiles for Kids Ser.). (Illus.). 48p. (YA). (gr. 4-7). lib. bdg. 29.95 *(978-1-58415-561-4(2))* Mitchell Lane Pubs., Inc.

Rockett, Paul. Leonardo Da Vinci, 01 vols., 1. 2016. (Inspiring Artists Ser.). (ENG.). 48p. (J). 30.25 *(978-1-5081-7054-9(1),* Rosen Young Adult) Rosen Publishing Group, Inc., The.

Romeo, Francesca. Leonardo Da Vinci. 2008. (Art Masters Ser.). 64p. (YA). (gr. 6-18). lib. bdg. 24.95 net. *(978-1-934545-00-3(7))* Oliver Pr., Inc.

Strom, Laura Layton. Leonardo Da Vinci. 2007. (Shockwave: Life Stories Ser.). (ENG., Illus.). 36p. (J). (gr. 3-5). 25.00 *(978-0-531-17771-6(8),* Children's Pr.) Scholastic Library Publishing.

Tracy, Kathleen. Leonardo Da Vinci. 2008. (Art Profiles for Kids Ser.). (Illus.). 48p. (YA). (gr. 4-7). lib. bdg. 29.95 *(978-1-58415-711-3(9))* Mitchell Lane Pubs., Inc.

Whiting, Jim. Michelangelo. 2007. (Art Profiles for Kids Ser.). (Illus.). 48p. (YA). (gr. 4-7). lib. bdg. 29.95 *(978-1-58415-562-1(0))* Mitchell Lane Pubs., Inc.

Wood, Alix. Leonardo Da Vinci. 2013. (Artists Through the Ages Ser.). (ENG., Illus.). 32p. (J). (gr. 3-6). pap. 10.00 *(978-1-61533-629-6(X));* lib. bdg. 25.25 *(978-1-61533-621-0(4))* Windmill Bks.

ARTISTS, JAPANESE

Kishimoto, Masashi. Naruto Illustration Book. Kishimoto, Masashi, illus. 2010. (ENG., Illus.). 100p. pap. 19.99 *(978-1-4215-3869-3(5))* Viz Media.

Lenburg, Jeff. Hayao Miyazaki. 2012. (Legends of Animation Ser.). (Illus.). 120p. (gr. 6-12). 34.95 *(978-1-60413-841-2(6),* Chelsea Hse.) Facts On File, Inc.

Say, Allen. The Inker's Shadow. 2015. (ENG.). 80p. (J). (gr. 7). 19.99 *(978-0-545-43776-9(8),* Scholastic Pr.) Scholastic, Inc.

ARTISTS, MEXICAN

Alvarez, Mateo. Frida Kahlo: Famous Mexican Artist. 2015. (Exceptional Latinos Ser.). (ENG.). 24p. (J). (gr. 3-4). pap. 9.35 *(978-0-7660-6714-1(9))* Enslow Pubs., Inc.

Flood Williams, Colleen Madonna. Mexican Art & Architecture. 2009. (Mexico: Beautiful Land, Diverse People Ser.). (Illus.). 64p. (YA). (gr. 7-12). 21.95 *(978-1-4222-0656-0(4))* Mason Crest.

Foard, Sheila Wood. Diego Rivera. 2nd rev. ed. 2010. (Great Hispanic Heritage Ser.). (Illus.). 120p. (gr. 6-12). 35.00 *(978-1-60413-845-0(9),* Chelsea Hse.) Facts On File, Inc.

Holzhey, Magdalena. Frida Kahlo: The Artist in the Blue House. 2003. (Adventures in Art Ser.). (Illus.). 30p. (J). (gr. 5-18). 14.95 *(978-3-7913-2863-8(8))* Prestel Publishing.

Jauregui, Diego. Libros de Arte para Ninos: Diego Rivera.Tr. of Art Books for Children: Diego Rivera. (SPA., Illus.). 73p. (YA). (gr. 5-8). pap. *(978-968-494-026-0(2))* Centro de Informacion y Desarrollo de la Comunicacion y la Literatura.

Kent, Deborah. Frida Kahlo: An Artist Celebrates Life. 2004. (Proud Heritage: the Hispanic Library). (ENG., Illus.). 40p. (J). (gr. 3-6). 29.93 *(978-1-59296-167-2(3),* 200008) Child's World, Inc., The.

Laidlaw, Jill A. Frida Kahlo. 2003. (Artists in Their Time Ser.). (ENG., Illus.). 48p. (J). (gr. 5-7). pap. 6.95

(978-0-531-16642-0(2), Watts, Franklin) Scholastic Library Publishing.

Muro, Claudia Burr. Yo Miro, Miro Todo el Tiempo: Basada en Pinturas y Textos de Rufino Tamayo. 2005. (Coleccion Los Grandes Para Los Mas Pequenos Ser.). (SPA., Illus.). 35p. (J). (gr. 3-5). pap. 8.95 (978-968-7381-28-2(0)) Tecolote, Ediciones, S.A. de C.V. MEX. Dist: Iaconi, Mariuccia Bk. Imports.

Sabbeth, Carol. Frida Kahlo & Diego Rivera: Their Lives & Ideas, 24 Activities. 2005. (For Kids Ser.). (ENG., Illus.). 160p. (J). (gr. 4). pap. 17.95 (978-1-55652-569-8(9), 1241061) Chicago Review Pr., Inc.

Tonatiuh, Duncan. Funny Bones: Posada & His Day of the Dead Calaveras. 2015. (ENG., Illus.). 40p. (J). (gr. 1-5). 18.95 (978-1-4197-1647-8(6), Abrams Bks. for Young Readers) Abrams, Inc.

Venezia, Mike. Diego Rivera. Venezia, Mike, illus. 2015. (Getting to Know the World's Greatest Artists Ser.). (ENG., Illus.). 40p. (J). lib. bdg. 29.00 (978-0-531-21261-5(0), Children's Pr.) Scholastic Library Publishing.

Weill, Cynthia. Opuestos: Mexican Folk Art Opposites in English & Spanish. 2009. (First Concepts in Mexican Folk Art Ser.). (SPA & ENG., Illus.). 32p. (J). (gr. -1-1). 14.95 (978-1-933693-56-9(8)) Cinco Puntos Pr.

ARTISTS, NEGRO

see African American Artists

ARTISTS, SPANISH

Ross, Michael Elsohn. Salvador Dali & the Surrealists: Their Lives & Ideas, 21 Activities. 2003. (For Kids Ser.). (ENG., Illus.). 144p. (J). (gr. 5-18). pap. 17.95 (978-1-55652-479-0(X)) Chicago Review Pr., Inc.

Warhola, James & WARHOLA, JAMES. Mi Tío Andy. 2004. (SPA., Illus.). 32p. (J). (gr. 2-3). 18.99 (978-84-8488-131-5(8)) Serres, Ediciones, S. L. ESP. Dist: Lectorum Pubns., Inc.

Wood, Alix. Francisco Goya. 2013. (Artists Through the Ages Ser.). (ENG., Illus.). 32p. (J). (gr. 3-6). pap. 10.00 (978-1-61533-635-7(4)); lib. bdg. 25.25 (978-1-61533-624-1(9)) Windmill Bks.

ARTISTS' MATERIALS

Campbell, Trenton, ed. Drawing: Materials, Technique, Styles, & Practice. 2016. (Britannica's Practical Guide to the Arts Ser.). 128p. (J). (gr. 10-10). lib. bdg. 36.25 (978-1-68048-371-0(4)) Rosen Publishing Group, Inc., The.

Cunningham, Kevin. Pencils. 2008. (21st Century Skills Library: Global Products Ser.). (ENG.). 32p. (gr. 4-8). lib. bdg. 28.50 (978-1-60279-122-0(8), 200104) Cherry Lake Publishing.

dePaola, Tomie. What a Year. dePaola, Tomie, illus. 2003. (26 Fairmount Avenue Bks.). (Illus.). 72p. (gr. 2-5). 16.00 (978-0-7569-1546-9(5)) Perfection Learning Corp.

Green, Sara. Crayola. 2017. (Crayola Ser.). 24p. (J). (gr. 3-8). pap. 7.99 **(978-1-61891-252-7(6)**, Pilot Bks.) Bellwether Media.

Gregoire, Maryellen. Contar Crayones (Counting Crayons) 2012. (Wonder Readers Spanish Emergent Ser.). (SPA.). 8p. (gr. -1-1). pap. 35.94 (978-1-62065-569-6(1)) Capstone Press of Coughlan Cos.

—Counting Crayons, 1 vol. 2012. (Wonder Readers Emergent Level Ser.). (ENG.). (gr. -1-1). 32p. pap. 5.99 (978-1-4296-9188-8(3)); 8p. pap. 35.94 (978-1-4296-9197-0(2)) Capstone Press of Coughlan Cos. (Wonder Readers).

Guidone, Lisa M. What Happens at a Crayon Factory? ¿Qué Pasa en una Fábrica de Crayones? 2008. (Where People Work/Dónde Trabaja la Gente? Ser.). (SPA.). 24p. (gr. -1-3). pap. 8.15 (978-0-8368-9378-6(6), Weekly Reader Leveled Readers) Stevens, Gareth Publishing LLLP.

—What Happens at a Crayon Factory?/¿Qué Pasa en una Fábrica de Crayones? 2008. (Where People Work/Dónde Trabaja la Gente? Ser.). (ENG & SPA.). 24p. (J). (gr. -1-3). lib. bdg. 22.00 (978-0-8368-9279-6(8), Weekly Reader Leveled Readers) Stevens, Gareth Publishing LLLP.

Hannah, Sue. Crafty Concoctions: 101 Craft Supply Recipes. 2003. (Illus.). xi, 140p. (J). 7.95 (978-0-88166-462-1(6)) Meadowbrook Pr.

Kuhtz, Cleo, ed. Sculpture: Materials, Technique, Styles, & Practice. 2016. (Britannica's Practical Guide to the Arts Ser.). 128p. (J). (gr. 10-10). lib. bdg. 36.25 (978-1-68048-375-8(7)) Rosen Publishing Group, Inc., The.

Marchioro, Narcisa. 13 Art Materials Children Should Know. 2017. (Children Should Know Ser.). (ENG., Illus.). 48p. (J). (gr. 3-7). 14.95 **(978-3-7913-7260-0(2))** Prestel Verlag GmbH & Co KG. DEU. Dist: Penguin Random Hse. LLC.

McGuinness, Denis E., ed. Painting: Materials, Technique, Styles, & Practice. 2016. (Britannica's Practical Guide to the Arts Ser.). 128p. (J). (gr. 10-10). lib. bdg. 36.25 (978-1-68048-373-4(0)) Rosen Publishing Group, Inc., The.

McKinley, Herald. Turning Wax into Crayons. 2014. (Step-By-Step Transformations Ser.). 24p. (J). (gr. k-2). lib. bdg. 24.21 (978-1-62712-366-2(0)) Cavendish Square Publishing.

Meachen Rau, Dana. Artists. 2007. (Tools We Use Ser.). (Illus.). 32p. (gr. k-2). lib. bdg. 15.95 (978-0-7614-2655-4(8), Benchmark Bks.) Marshall Cavendish Corp.

—Artists/Los Artistas. 2007. (Tools We Use/Instrumentos de Trabajo Ser.). (SPA & ENG., Illus.). 32p. (gr. k-2). lib. bdg. 15.95 (978-0-7614-2820-6(8), Benchmark Bks.) Marshall Cavendish Corp.

—Los Artistas. 2007. (Instrumentos de Trabajo Ser.). (SPA & ENG., Illus.). 32p. (gr. k-2). lib. bdg. 15.95 (978-0-7614-2796-4(1), Benchmark Bks.) Marshall Cavendish Corp.

—Tools We Use, 6 vols., Set. Incl. Artists. 32p. (gr. k-2). lib. bdg. 15.95 (978-0-7614-2655-4(8)); Builders. 31p. (J). (gr. -1-3). lib. bdg. 22.79 (978-0-7614-2656-1(6)); Chefs. 32p. (gr. k-2). lib. bdg. 15.95 (978-0-7614-2657-8(4)); Doctors. 32p. (gr. k-2). lib. bdg. 15.95 (978-0-7614-2659-2(0)); EMTs. 32p. (gr. k-2). lib. bdg. 15.95 (978-0-7614-2660-8(4)); Librarians. 32p. (gr. k-2). lib. bdg. 15.95 (978-0-7614-2662-2(0)); (Illus.). 2007. 136.71 (978-0-7614-2654-7(X), Benchmark Bks.) Marshall Cavendish Corp.

Murray, Julie. Wax to Crayon, 1 vol. 2006. (Beginning to End Set 1 - 8 Titles Ser.). (ENG., Illus.). 24p. (gr. k-4). 25.65 (978-1-59679-915-8(3), Buddy Bks.) ABDO Publishing Co.

Nelson, Robin. From Wax to Crayon. 2013. (Start to Finish, Second Series: Everyday Products Ser.). (ENG., Illus.). 24p. (gr. k-3). pap. 6.95 (978-1-4677-0798-5(8)); lib. bdg. 23.93 (978-0-7613-9183-8(5), Lerner Pubns.) Lerner Publishing Group.

Rau, Dana Meachen. Artists. 2007. (J). pap. 6.99 (978-0-7614-3288-3(4)) Marshall Cavendish Corp.

Ryall, Jeanette. Junk Art. 2012. (Awesome Art Ser.). (ENG., Illus.). 32p. (J). (gr. 3-6). 26.50 (978-1-4488-8087-4(4)); pap. 11.75 (978-1-4488-8140-6(4)) Windmill Bks.

ARTS, GRAPHIC

see Graphic Arts

ARTS, USEFUL

see Technology

ARTS AND CRAFTS

see Handicraft

ASHE, ARTHUR, 1943-1993

Donohue, Moira Rose & Scott, Clarke C. Arthur R. Ashe, Jr. 2012. (Illus.). 32p. (J). (978-1-935884-58-3(1)); pap. (978-1-935884-64-4(6)) State Standards Publishing, LLC.

Fry, Erin. Arthur Ashe Against the Odds. 2005. (Voices Reading Ser.). (Illus.). 16p. (J). (978-0-7367-2915-4(1)) Zaner-Bloser, Inc.

Hubbard, Crystal & Belford, Kevin. Game, Set, Match, Champion Arthur Ashe. (ENG., Illus.). 48p. (J). (gr. 2-5). 2016. pap. 11.95 **(978-1-62014-316-2(X))** 2010. 19.95 (978-1-60060-366-2(1)) Lee & Low Bks., Inc.

Mantell, Paul. Arthur Ashe: Young Tennis Champion. Henderson, Meryl, illus. 2006. (Childhood of Famous Americans Ser.). 213p. (J). 13.65 (978-0-7569-6387-3(7)) Perfection Learning Corp.

—Arthur Ashe: Young Tennis Champion. Henderson, Meryl, illus. 2006. (Childhood of Famous Americans Ser.). (ENG.). 224p. (J). (gr. 3-7). pap. 10.99 (978-0-689-87346-1(8), Simon & Schuster/Paula Wiseman Bks.) Simon & Schuster/Paula Wiseman Bks.

McDougall, Chros. Arthur Ashe: Tennis Great & Civil Rights Leader, 1 vol. 2011. (Legendary Athletes Ser.). (ENG., Illus.). 112p. (YA). (gr. 7-12). 34.22 (978-1-61714-753-1(2)) ABDO Publishing Co.

ASIA

see also Southeast Asia

Aretha, David. Discovering Asia's Land, People, & Wildlife: A MyReportLinks.com Book. 2004. (Continents of the World Ser.). (Illus.). 48p. (J). lib. bdg. 26.60 (978-0-7660-5183-6(8), MyReportLinks.com Bks.) Enslow Pubs., Inc.

AZ Books Staff. Ancient Asia. Kazimirova, Karina & Snezhana, Ivinskaya, eds. 2012. (Mysteries of History Ser.). (ENG.). 18p. (J). (gr. 1-3). bds. 17.95 (978-1-61889-091-7(3)) AZ Bks. LLC.

Benchmark Education Co., LLC. The Geography of Asia & Australia. 2014. (PRIME Ser.). (J). (gr. 6-8). pap. (978-1-4509-9504-7(7)) Benchmark Education Co.

Benhart, John & Pomeroy, George. South Asia. Gritzner, Charles F., ed. 2005. (Modern World Cultures Ser.). (Illus.). 128p. (gr. 6-12). lib. bdg. 30.00 (978-0-7910-8147-1(8), Chelsea Hse.) Facts On File, Inc.

Bryan, Antonia D. The United Arab Emirates. 2009. (True Book(tm), A— Countries Ser.). (ENG., Illus.). 48p. (J). (gr. 2-5). 31.00 (978-0-531-16888-2(3)) Scholastic Library Publishing.

Clark, Willow. Asian Dolphins & Other Marine Mammals. 2012. (Animals of Asia Ser.). (ENG., Illus.). 24p. (J). (gr. 1-5). 22.60 (978-1-4488-7419-4(X)); pap. 8.25 (978-1-4488-7492-7(0)) Rosen Publishing Group, Inc., The. (PowerKids Pr.).

Cooper, Robert & Yong, Jui Lin. Bhutan. 2nd rev. ed. 2010. (Cultures of the World 22 Ser.). 144p. (gr. 6). 42.79 (978-1-60870-453-8(X)) Marshall Cavendish Corp.

CultureGrams 2005 World Edition - Asia & Oceania. 2004. (YA). per. 39.99 (978-1-931694-92-6(3)) ProQuest LLC.

Dalby, Elizabeth, et al. Introduction to Asia. 2006. (Illus.). 96p. (J). (978-0-439-88982-7(0)) Scholastic, Inc.

Encyclopaedia Britannica, Inc. Staff, compiled by. My First Britannica: Asia, Australia, & New Zealand. 2008. (gr. 7-12). (978-1-59339-407-3(1)) Encyclopaedia Britannica, Inc.

Encyclopaedia Britannica Publishers, Inc. Staff. Views of Asia & Australia. 2003. (Britannica Learning Library). (Illus.). 14.95 (978-1-59339-010-5(6)) Encyclopaedia Britannica, Inc.

Glencoe McGraw-Hill Staff, creator. Exploring Our World - Eastern Hemisphere: People, Places, & Cultures. 2nd ed. 2007. (WORLD & ITS PEOPLE EASTERN Ser.). (ENG., Illus.). 766p. (gr. 6-8). lib. bdg., stu. ed. 98.00 (978-0-07-874578-2(0), 0078745780) McGraw-Hill Education.

Hovanec, Erin M. An Online Visit to Asia. 2009. (Internet Field Trips Ser.). 24p. (gr. 3-3). 45.00 (978-1-61513-603-2(7), PowerKids Pr.) Rosen Publishing Group, Inc., The.

Hunkins, Boehm Armstrong & McGraw-Hill Education Editors. Exploring Our World: People, Places, & Cultures. 2007. (WORLD & ITS PEOPLE EASTERN Ser.). (ENG., Illus.). 95p. (gr. 6-9). pap. 6.48 (978-0-07-877743-1(7), 0078777437) McGraw-Hill Higher Education.

Kalman, Bobbie & Sjonger, Rebecca. Explore Asia. rev. ed. 2007. (Explore the Continents Ser.). (ENG., Illus.). 32p. (J). (gr. 1-5). pap. (978-0-7787-3086-6(7)) Crabtree Publishing Co.

Knowlton, Mary Lee. Turkmenistan. 2005. (Cultures of the World Ser.). (Illus.). 144p. (gr. 6-10). lib. bdg. 42.79 (978-0-7614-2014-9(2), Benchmark Bks.) Marshall Cavendish Corp.

Mason, Paul & Cavendish, Marshall. The Indian Subcontinent. 2008. (Global Hotspots Ser.). 32p. (gr. 5-18). lib. bdg. 18.56 (978-0-7614-3178-7(0), Benchmark Bks.) Marshall Cavendish Corp.

Mattern, Joanne. Asia: El Continente Mas Grande del Mundo. 2004. (Maravillas Naturales (Natures Greatest Hits) Ser.). (SPA.). 24p. (J). (gr. 2-4). lib. bdg. 22.60 (978-0-8239-6875-6(8)) Rosen Publishing Group, Inc., The.

—Asia: El continente más grande del mundo (Asia: World's Largest Continent) 2009. (Maravillas naturales (Natures Greatest Hits) Ser.). 24p. (gr. 2-2). 42.50 (978-1-61514-361-0(0), Editorial Buenas Letras) Rosen Publishing Group, Inc., The.

—Asia: World's Largest Continent. 2009. (Nature's Greatest Hits Ser.). 24p. (gr. 2-2). 42.50 (978-1-61514-839-4(6), PowerKids Pr.) Rosen Publishing Group, Inc., The.

McGraw-Hill Education Editors. Exploring Our World: People, Places, & Cultures - Eastern Hemisphere. 2007. (WORLD & ITS PEOPLE EASTERN Ser.). (ENG., Illus.). 192p. (gr. 6-8). per. 23.20 (978-0-07-878166-7(3), 0078781663) McGraw-Hill Education.

McGraw-Hill Staff. Exploring Our World, Eastern Hemisphere, Interactive Tutor Self Assessment. 2007. (WORLD & ITS PEOPLE EASTERN Ser.). (ENG.). (gr. 6-8). cd-rom 104.00 (978-0-07-879098-0(0), 0078790980) McGraw-Hill Education.

McNeil, Niki, et al. Asia. 2007. (In the Hands of a Child: Project Pack Continent Study Ser.). (Illus.). 97p. spiral bd. 22.00 (978-1-60308-065-1(1)) In the Hands of a Child.

Murray, Julie. Tigers, 1 vol. 2013. (Asian Animals Ser.). (ENG.). 32p. (J). (gr. 2-5). lib. bdg. 28.50 (978-1-61783-558-2(7), Big Buddy Bks.) ABDO Publishing Co.

Oachs, Emily Rose. Asia. 2016. (Discover the Continents Ser.). (ENG., Illus.). 24p. (J). (gr. k-3). lib. bdg. 25.95 (978-1-62617-325-5(7), Blastoff! Readers) Bellwether Media.

O'Dea, Colleen. Tajikistan. 2007. (Growth & Influence of Islam in the Nations of Asia & Central Asia Ser.). (Illus.). 120p. (YA). (gr. 4-7). lib. bdg. 25.95 (978-1-59084-885-2(3)) Mason Crest.

Sayre, April Pulley. Greeting, Asia! The Ultimate Guide to America's 4 Regional Styles of 'Cue. 2003. (Illus.). 32p. lib. bdg. 21.90 (978-0-7613-2124-8(1), Millbrook Pr.) Lerner Publishing Group.

—Greetings, Asia! 2003. 32p. (J). (gr. 2-5). pap. 7.95 (978-0-7613-1991-7(3), Millbrook Pr.) Lerner Publishing Group.

Schaefer, A. R. Spotlight on Asia, 1 vol. 2010. (Spotlight on the Continents Ser.). (ENG.). 24p. (gr. 1-2). lib. bdg. 25.32 (978-1-4296-6623-7(4), First Facts) Capstone Press of Coughlan Cos.

Striveildi, Cheryl. Asia. 2003. (Continents Ser.). (ENG.). 32p. (J). (gr. k-4). lib. bdg. 27.07 (978-1-57765-960-0(0), Buddy Bks.) ABDO Publishing Co.

Vierow, Wendy. Asia. 2009. (Atlas of the Seven Continents Ser.). 24p. (gr. 3-3). 42.50 (978-1-61511-478-8(5), PowerKids Pr.) Rosen Publishing Group, Inc., The.

Waters, Bella. Uzbekistan in Pictures. 2006. (Visual Geography Series, Second Ser.). (ENG., Illus.). 80p. (gr. 5-12). lib. bdg. 31.93 (978-0-8225-2673-5(5)) Lerner Publishing Group.

Wojahn, Rebecca Hogue & Wojahn, Donald. A Mangrove Forest Food Chain: A Who-Eats-What Adventure in Asia. 2009. (Follow That Food Chain Ser.). (ENG.). 64p. (gr. 3-5). 30.60 (978-0-8225-7615-0(5)) Lerner Publishing Group.

Woods, Michael & Woods, Mary B. Seven Natural Wonders of Asia & the Middle East. 2009. (Seven Wonders Ser.). (ENG., Illus.). 80p. (gr. 5-8). 33.26 (978-0-8225-9073-6(5)) Lerner Publishing Group.

Yespolov, Johnson & Kalna-Dubinyuk, Arynova. Extension in Kazakhstan & the Experience of the Us: Lessons from a Working National Model. 2012. 154p. 29.99 (978-1-4771-4694-1(6)) Xlibris Corp.

ASIA, CENTRAL

Harmon, Daniel E. Kyrgyzstan. 2006. (Growth & Influence of Islam in the Nations of Asia & Central Asia Ser.). (Illus.). 120p. (YA). (gr. -1-7). lib. bdg. 25.95 (978-1-59084-883-8(7)) Mason Crest.

King, David C. Kyrgyzstan. 2005. (Cultures of the World Ser.). (Illus.). 144p. (gr. 6-10). lib. bdg. 42.79 (978-0-7614-2013-2(4)) Marshall Cavendish Corp.

Mondschein, Ken. South & Central Asia, Vol. 10. 2016. (Social Progress & Sustainability Ser.). (Illus.). 80p. (J). (gr. 7). 24.95 (978-1-4222-3500-3(9)) Mason Crest.

Pavlovic, Zoran. Kazakhstan. 2003. (Modern World Nations Ser.). (Illus.). 150p. (gr. 6-12). 35.00 (978-0-7910-7231-8(2), Chelsea Hse.) Facts On File, Inc.

ASIA, CENTRAL—FICTION

Yep, Laurence. City of Death. 2013. (City Trilogy Ser.: 3). (ENG.). 384p. (J). (gr. 3-7). 17.99 (978-0-7653-1926-5(8), 9780765319265, Starscape) Doherty, Tom Assocs., LLC.

ASIA—DESCRIPTION AND TRAVEL

Bowden, Rob. Asia. 2005. (Continents of the World Ser.). (Illus.). 64p. (gr. 5-12). pap. 14.05 (978-0-8368-5918-8(9)); lib. bdg. 34.00 (978-0-8368-5911-9(1)) Stevens, Gareth Publishing LLLP. (Gareth Stevens Secondary Library).

Cooke, Tim. Explore with Marco Polo. 2014. (ENG., Illus.). 32p. (J). (978-0-7787-1428-6(4)) Crabtree Publishing Co.

Crompton, Samuel Willard. Marco Polo: Epic Traveler Throughout Asia. 2017. (Spotlight on Explorers & Colonization Ser.). 48p. (gr. 10-11). 70.50 **(978-1-5081-7504-9(7)**, Rosen Young Adult) Rosen Publishing Group, Inc., The.

DiPiazza, Francesca Davis. Kuwait in Pictures. 2nd ed. 2007. (Visual Geography Series, Second Ser.). (ENG., Illus.). 80p. (gr. 5-12). lib. bdg. 31.93 (978-0-8225-6589-5(7)) Lerner Publishing Group.

—Yemen in Pictures. 2007. (Visual Geography (Lerner) Ser.). (Illus.). 80p. (YA). (gr. 7-12). lib. bdg. 31.93 (978-0-8225-7149-0(8)) Twenty First Century Bks.

Doeden, Matt. Laos in Pictures. 2007. (Visual Geography Series, Second Ser.). (ENG., Illus.). 80p. (gr. 5-12). 31.93 (978-0-8225-6590-1(0)) Lerner Publishing Group.

Donaldson, Madeline. Asia. 2005. (Pull Ahead Bks.). (Illus.). 32p. (gr. k-3). (J). lib. bdg. 22.60 (978-0-8225-4721-1(X)); (ENG., pap. 7.95 (978-0-8225-2491-5(0), Lerner Pubns.) Lerner Publishing Group.

Feeney, Kathy. Marco Polo: Explorer of China. 2004. (Explorers! Ser.). (Illus.). 48p. (J). lib. bdg. 23.93 (978-0-7660-2145-7(9)) Enslow Pubs., Inc.

Hare, Eric B. Jungle Heroes & Other Stories. 2005. (Illus.). 106p. (J). 9.99 (978-0-8163-2063-9(2)) Pacific Pr. Publishing Assn.

Holub, Joan. Who Was Marco Polo? O'brien, John et al, illus. 2007. (Who Was? Ser.). (ENG.). 112p. (J). (gr. 3-7). pap. 5.99 (978-0-448-44540-3(9), Grosset & Dunlap) Penguin Young Readers Group.

—Who Was Marco Polo? O'brien, John, illus. 2007. (Who Was...? Ser.). 105p. (gr. 4-7). 15.00 (978-0-7569-8165-5(4)) Perfection Learning Corp.

Linde, Barbara M. Mapping Asia. 2013. 24p. (J). (gr. 2-5). 22.60 (978-1-4339-9099-1(7)); pap. 48.90 (978-1-4339-9101-1(2)); pap. 8.15 (978-1-4339-9100-4(4)) Stevens, Gareth Publishing LLLP.

Lonely Planet Publications Staff. Asia: Everything You Ever Wanted to Know, 1 vol. 2013. (Lonely Planet Kids Ser.). (ENG., Illus.). 96p. (J). pap. 12.99 (978-1-74321-910-2(5), 4624) Lonely Planet Pubns.

McNeese, Tim. Marco Polo & the Realm of Kublai Khan. Goetzmann, William H., ed. 2005. (Explorers of New Lands Ser.). (Illus.). 100p. (gr. 5-8). lib. bdg. 30.00 (978-0-7910-8612-4(7)) Facts On File, Inc.

Morley, Jacqueline. You Wouldn't Want to Explore with Marco Polo! A Really Long Trip You'd Rather Not Take. Antram, David, illus. 2009. (You Wouldn't Want to Ser.). (ENG.). 32p. (J). (gr. 3-12). 29.00 (978-0-531-21327-8(7)); pap. 9.95 (978-0-531-20518-1(5)) Scholastic Library Publishing.

Porterfield, Jason. Marco Polo. 2016. (Silk Road's Greatest Travelers Ser.). 112p. (gr. 6-6). 37.10 (978-1-5081-7152-2(1)) Rosen Publishing Group, Inc., The.

Smalley, Roger. The Adventures of Marco Polo, 1 vol. Carter, Greg & Bascle, Brian, illus. 2005. (Graphic History Ser.). (ENG.). 32p. (gr. 3-4). 30.65 (978-0-7368-3830-6(9), Graphic Library) Capstone Press of Coughlan Cos.

Tabilio, Marco & Schwandt, Kerstin. Marco Polo: The Silk Road. Tabilio, Marco, illus. 2017. (ENG., Illus.). 208p. (J). (gr. 9-12). 29.32 (978-1-5124-1182-9(5), Graphic Universe™) Lerner Publishing Group.

Vierow, Wendy. Asia. 2004. (Atlas of the Seven Continents Ser.). (Illus.). 24p. (YA). (gr. 3-6). lib. bdg. 22.60 (978-0-8239-6689-9(5)) Rosen Publishing Group, Inc., The.

Waters, Bella. Kazakhstan in Pictures. 2007. (Visual Geography Series, Second Ser.). (ENG., Illus.). 80p. (gr. 5-12). 31.93 (978-0-8225-6588-8(9)) Lerner Publishing Group.

Worth, Richard. The Great Empire of China & Marco Polo in World History. 2003. (In World History Ser.). (Illus.). 112p. (J). lib. bdg. 26.60 (978-0-7660-1939-3(X)) Enslow Pubs., Inc.

ASIA—FICTION

Bird, Helen. Fighting Back. 2005. (Shades Ser.). 64p. (J). pap. (978-0-237-52845-4(2)) Evans Brothers, Ltd.

Bowen, Carl & Fuentes, Benny. White Needle, 1 vol. Tortosa, Wilson, illus. 2014. (Shadow Squadron Ser.). (ENG.). 112p. (gr. 4-8). 26.65 (978-1-4342-6398-8(3)) Stone Arch Bks.

Cage, Elizabeth. If Looks Could Kill. 2013. (Spy Girls Ser.: 6). (ENG., Illus.). 192p. (YA). (gr. 7). pap. 13.99 (978-1-4814-2085-3(2), Simon Pulse) Simon Pulse.

Cohn, Diana. Crane Boy. 2015. (ENG., Illus.). 40p. (J). (gr. 2-5). 17.95 (978-1-941026-16-8(8)) Cinco Puntos Pr.

Culpepper, R. B. W. Ellena & the Magic Lamp. 2011. 182p. pap. 24.95 (978-1-4626-2830-8(3)) America Star Bks.

Dahi, Khetam. The Mulberry Tree. 2013. 100p. (gr. -1). pap. 11.65 (978-1-4669-8313-7(2)) Trafford Publishing.

Fine, Sarah. Of Metal & Wishes. 2015. (ENG., Illus.). 352p. (YA). (gr. 9). pap. 11.99 (978-1-4424-8359-0(8), McElderry, Margaret K. Bks.) McElderry, Margaret K. Bks.

Gilligan, Shannon. Cup of Death. Nugent, Suzanne, illus. 2006. (Choose Your Own Adventure Ser.). 144p. (J). (gr. 4-8). per. 6.99 (978-1-933390-70-3(0)) Chooseco LLC.

Guerrera, Debra. The Adventures of Baby Caterpillar & His Traveling Butterfly Family. 2011. 28p. pap. 15.99 (978-1-4628-9982-1(X)) Xlibris Corp.

Han, Xuemei. Brave Little Mongolian Sisters. Han, Xuemei, illus. 2007. (Illus.). (J). pap. 12.99 (978-0-9763168-7-9(0)) DigitalKu.

—The Radish & the Girl with Long Hair. Han, Xuemei, illus. 2008. (Illus.). (J). per. (978-0-9763168-6-2(2)) DigitalKu.

Jensen, Kathryn. Splash! 2012. 194p. 29.95 (978-1-4489-6574-8(8)) America Star Bks.

Kadohata, Cynthia. A Million Shades of Gray. 2010. (ENG., Illus.). 224p. (J). (gr. 5-9). 16.99 (978-1-4169-1883-7(3), Atheneum Bks. for Young Readers) Simon & Schuster Children's Publishing.

Lyons, Kay, et al. Asian Children's Favorite Stories: A Treasury of Folktales from China, Japan, Korea, India, the Philippines, Thailand, Indonesia & Malaysia. Yee, Patrick, illus. 2006. (ENG.). 112p. (J). (gr. k-8). 24.95 (978-0-8048-3669-2(8)) Tuttle Publishing.

Malaspina, Ann. Yasmin's Hammer. Chayka, Doug, illus. 2010. (ENG.). 40p. (J). (gr. k-6). 18.95 (978-1-60060-359-4(9)) Lee & Low Bks., Inc.

Malone, David P. The Adventures of Benny the Bunnyduck: Escape from Chindia. 2012. (ENG.). 45p. (J). pap. 23.95 (978-1-4327-9352-4(7)) Outskirts Pr., Inc.

Manivong, Laura. Escaping the Tiger. 2010. (ENG.). 224p. (J). (gr. 5-18). 15.99 (978-0-06-166177-8(5)) HarperCollins Pubs.

Masson, J. Moussaieff. The Cat Who Came in from the Cold: A Fable. 2004. 107p. (978-0-345-47867-2(3), Ballantine Bks.) Random House Publishing Group.

Merchant, Brenda C. Huga Huga Hippo. l.t. ed. 2010. (Illus.). 49p. (J). 26.00 (978-0-9845023-0-1(0)) A-Gator Publishing.

Montgomery, R. A. The Abominable Snowman Peguy, Laurence, illus. 2006. (Choose Your Own Adventure Ser.). 144p. (J). (gr. 4-8). per. 6.99 (978-1-933390-01-7(8), CHCL01) Chooseco LLC.

—Return to Haunted House. 2010. (Illus.). 80p. (J). pap. 7.99 (978-1-933390-40-6(9)) Chooseco LLC.

Perkins, Mitali. Rickshaw Girl. Hogan, Jamie, illus. 2007. (ENG.). 96p. (J). (gr. 2-5). 14.95 (978-1-58089-308-4(2)) Charlesbridge Publishing, Inc.

—Tiger Boy. Hogan, Jamie, illus. 2015. (ENG.). 144p. (J). (gr. 2-5). lib. bdg. 14.95 (978-1-58089-660-3(X)) Charlesbridge Publishing, Inc.

Powell, Kelley. The Merit Birds. 2015. (ENG.). 240p. (YA). pap. 14.99 (978-1-4597-2931-5(5)) Dundurn CAN. Dist: Ingram Publisher Services.

Renier Nash, Oliver. The Primate Puzzle: A tale of two friends & the missing long-nosed Monkeys. 2009. 272p. pap. 15.49 (978-1-4490-3099-5(8)) AuthorHouse.

Sher, Steven. Where the Shouting Began. 2008. (J). (978-1-932727-08-1(6)) Montemayor Pr.

Windover, Liz. Blood Island. Utomo, Gabhor, illus. 2014. (ENG.). 144p. (J). mass mkt. 6.99 (978-1-937133-46-7(X)) Chooseco LLC.

ASIA—HISTORY

Abazov, Rafis. Tajikistan. 2005. (Cultures of the World Ser.). (Illus.). 144p. (gr. 6-10). lib. bdg. 42.79 (978-0-7614-2012-5(6)) Marshall Cavendish Corp.

Abdo Publishing. Asian Animals, 1 vol. 2013. (Asian Animals Ser.: 6). (ENG.). 32p. (J). (gr. 2-5). lib. bdg. 171.00 *(978-1-61783-552-0(8)*, Big Buddy Bks.) ABDO Publishing Co.

Aspen-Baxter, Linda. Asia. (J). 2016. ***(978-1-4896-5734-3(7))*** 2012. *(978-1-61913-445-4(4))* 2012. pap. *(978-1-61913-446-1(2))* 2005. (Illus.). 32p. (gr. 4-6). lib. bdg. 26.00 *(978-1-59036-318-8(3))* Weigl Pubs., Inc.

Baldwin, Douglas. The War in Afghanistan. 2011. 48p. (J). (gr. 8-10). *(978-1-55388-721-8(2))*; pap. *(978-1-55388-725-6(5))* Weigl Educational Pubs. Ltd.

Bauer, Susan Wise & Weiss, Jim. Early Modern Times Vol. 3: From Elizabeth the First to the Forty-Niners. 2nd unabr. ed. 2008. (Story of the World Ser.: 0). (ENG.). 1p. cd-rom 49.95 *(978-1-933339-17-7(9)*, 333917) Well-Trained Mind Pr.

Blackwell, Amy Hackney. East Asia & the Pacific, Vol. 10. 2016. (Social Progress & Sustainability Ser.). (Illus.). 80p. (J). (gr. 7). 24.95 *(978-1-4222-3494-5(0))* Mason Crest.

Blashfield, Jean F. Yemen, 1 vol. 2011. (Countries Around the World Ser.). (ENG.). 48p. (gr. 3-6). pap. 9.95 *(978-1-4329-5243-3(9))*; 33.32 *(978-1-4329-5218-1(8))* Heinemann-Raintree. (NA-h).

Campbell, Rusty & Porter, Malcolm. Atlas of Asia. 2009. (Atlases of the World Ser.). (Illus.). 48p. (YA). (gr. 5-8). 29.25 *(978-1-4358-8455-7(8)*, Rosen Reference) Rosen Publishing Group, Inc., The.

Ceceri, Kathy. The Silk Road: Explore the World's Most Famous Trade Route with 20 Projects. Ceceri, Kathy, illus. 2011. (Build It Yourself Ser.). (ENG., Illus.). 128p. (J). (gr. 3-7). pap. 15.95 *(978-1-934670-62-0(6))* Open City Bks.

Cooke, Tim. The Exploration of Arabia & Asia. 2013. (Explorers Discovering the World Ser.). (Illus.). 48p. (gr. 4-6). 31.95 *(978-1-4339-8615-4(9))*; pap. 14.05 *(978-1-4339-8616-1(7))* Stevens, Gareth Publishing LLLP. (Gareth Stevens Learning Library).

Cooper, R., et al. Bahrain. 2nd rev. ed. 2010. (Cultures of the World 21 Ser.). 144p. (gr. 6). lib. bdg. 42.79 *(978-1-60870-213-8(8))* Marshall Cavendish Corp.

Corrigan, Jim. Kazakhstan. 2006. (Growth & Influence of Islam in the Nations of Asia & Central Asia Ser.). (Illus.). 128p. (YA). (gr. -1-7). lib. bdg. 25.95 *(978-1-59084-882-1(9))* Mason Crest.

Cunningham, Kevin. The Bubonic Plague, 1 vol. 2011. (Essential Events Set 6 Ser.). (ENG., Illus.). 112p. (J). (gr. 6-12). lib. bdg. 35.64 *(978-1-61714-762-3(1))* ABDO Publishing Co.

Dawson, Patricia A. Asia Through the Ages: Early History to European Colonialism. 2015. (Exploring the Ancient & Medieval Worlds Ser.). (ENG., Illus.). 160p. (J). (gr. 8-8). lib. bdg. 45.64 *(978-1-5026-0683-9(6))* Cavendish Square Publishing.

Dillon, Doug. A Brief Political & Geographic History of Asia: Where Are... Saigon, Kampuchea, & Burma. 2007. (Places in Time Ser.). (Illus.). 112p. (YA). (gr. 5-9). lib. bdg. 37.10 *(978-1-58415-623-9(6))* Mitchell Lane Pubs., Inc.

Dupré, Judith. The Magic Passport. 2011. (Navigators Ser.). (J). pap. *(978-1-61672-965-3(1))* Benchmark Education Co.

Elizabeth Anne Biddle. A Girl Called Nothing: A Tale of Cambodia. 2010. 124p. pap. 13.95 *(978-1-4502-2017-0(7))* iUniverse, Inc.

Encyclopaedia Britannica, Inc. Staff, compiled by. Views of Asia & Australia. 2003. (Illus.). 64p. 14.95 *(978-1-59339-041-9(6))* Encyclopaedia Britannica, Inc.

Everything You Need to Teach Asia. 2005. (YA). ring bd. 149.95 *(978-1-933558-01-1(6))* InspirEd Educators.

Foreign Policy Research Institute Staff, ed. The Growth & Influence of Islam in the Nations of Asia & Central Asia, 17 vols., Set. 2006. (Illus.). 112,128p. (YA). lib. bdg. 441.15 *(978-1-59084-832-6(2))* Mason Crest.

Freedman, Russell. Angel Island: Gateway to Gold Mountain. 2014. (ENG., Illus.). 96p. (J). (gr. 5-7). 17.99 *(978-0-547-90378-1(2))* Houghton Mifflin Harcourt Publishing Co.

Ganeri, Anita. Introducing Asia, 1 vol. 2013. (Introducing Continents Ser.). (ENG.). 32p. (gr. 1-3). 27.32 *(978-1-4329-8039-9(4))*; pap. 8.95 *(978-1-4329-8047-4(5))* Heinemann-Raintree. (Heinemann First Library).

Glascodine, Carolyn, ed. Access Asia: Primary Teaching & Learning Units. Mo, Xiangyi, illus. 2003. 192p. pap. 35.95 *(978-1-86366-345-8(2))* Education Services Australia Ltd. AUS. Dist: Cheng & Tsui Co.

Group/McGraw-Hill, Wright. Amazing Asia, 6 vols. (Book2WebTM Ser.). (gr. 4-8). 36.50 *(978-0-322-04437-1(5))* Wright Group/McGraw-Hill.

Habeeb, William Mark. Turkmenistan. 2006. (Growth & Influence of Islam in the Nations of Asia & Central Asia Ser.). (Illus.). 128p. (YA). lib. bdg. 25.95 *(978-1-59084-886-9(1))* Mason Crest.

Hall, Derek. Asia. 2008. (Facts at Your Fingertips Ser.). (Illus.). 64p. (YA). (gr. 7-12). lib. bdg. 34.25 *(978-1-933834-11-5(0))* Brown Bear Bks.

Hart, Joyce. Kim Jong Il: Leader of North Korea. 2007. (Newsmakers Ser.). (Illus.). 112p. (YA). (gr. 7-12). lib. bdg. 34.60 *(978-1-4042-1901-4(3))* Rosen Publishing Group, Inc., The.

Heing, Bridey. Trade Routes to India. 2017. (J). ***(978-1-5026-2694-3(2))*** Cavendish Square Publishing.

Himsl, Sharon M. Events That Changed the World - 1940-1960. 2003. (EVENTS THAT CHANGED the WRLD Ser.). (ENG., Illus.). lib. bdg. 38.45 *(978-0-7377-1756-3(4))* Cengage Gale.

Hinds, Kathryn. Huns. 2009. (Barbarians! Ser.). 80p. (gr. 6). 35.64 *(978-0-7614-4066-6(6))* Marshall Cavendish GBR. Dist: Marshall Cavendish Corp.

Hirsch, Rebecca E. & Cybriwsky, Roman A. Asia. 2012. (Rookie Read-About(tm) Geography — Continents Ser.). (ENG.). 32p. (J). lib. bdg. 25.00 *(978-0-531-28977-8(X))*; pap. 5.95 *(978-0-531-29277-8(0))* Scholastic Library Publishing.

Influential Asians. 2016. (Influential Asians Ser.). 128p. (gr. 7-6). lib. bdg. 223.62 *(978-0-7660-7506-1(0))* Enslow Pubs., Inc.

Kalman, Bobbie & Sjonger, Rebecca. Explora Asia. 2007. (Explora Los Continentes Ser.). (SPA., Illus.). 32p. (J). (gr. 1-5). pap. *(978-0-7787-8297-1(2))* Crabtree Publishing Co.

Kennedy, Mike & Stewart, Mark. Soccer in Asia. 2011. (Smart about Soccer Ser.). 24p. (J). (gr. k-3). lib. bdg. 22.60 *(978-1-59953-448-0(7))* Norwood Hse. Pr.

Kenoyer, Jonathan M. & Heuston, Kimberley Burton. The Ancient South Asian World. 2006. (World in Ancient Times Ser.). 32.95 *(978-0-19-522243-2(1))* Oxford Univ. Pr., Inc.

Khan, Aisha. A Historical Atlas of Kyrgyzstan. 2004. (Historical Atlases of South Asia, Central Asia, & the Middle East Ser.). (Illus.). 64p. (gr. 7-12). lib. bdg. 31.95 *(978-0-8239-4499-6(9))* Rosen Publishing Group, Inc., The.

King, David C. Azerbaijan. 2005. (Cultures of the World Ser.). (Illus.). 144p. (gr. 6-10). lib. bdg. 42.79 *(978-0-7614-2011-8(8))* Marshall Cavendish Corp.

Knowlton, Mary Lee. Uzbekistan. 2005. (Cultures of the World Ser.). (Illus.). 144p. (gr. 6-10). lib. bdg. 42.79 *(978-0-7614-2016-3(9))* Marshall Cavendish Corp.

Kummer, Patricia K. Asia. 2014. (J). *(978-0-7614-8090-7(0))* Marshall Cavendish Corp.

—The Changing Climate of Asia. 2014. 48p. pap. 12.93 *(978-1-62712-443-0(8))* Cavendish Square Publishing.

Madison, Amelia. Predators of Asia & Australia. 2015. (J). lib. bdg. *(978-1-62713-556-6(1))* Cavendish Square Publishing.

Matray, James Irving. Korea Divided: The Thirty-Eighth Parallel & the Demilitarized Zone. 2004. (Arbitrary Borders Ser.). (Illus.). 120p. (C). (gr. 9-13). 35.00 *(978-0-7910-7829-7(9))*, Chelsea Hse.) Facts On File, Inc.

McCoy, Lisa. Bahrain. 2010. (Major Muslim Nations Ser.). (Illus.). 112p. (J). (gr. 5-18). lib. bdg. 25.95 *(978-1-4222-1397-1(8))* Mason Crest.

Miller, Jennifer. South Korea. 2010. (Country Explorers Ser.). (ENG.). 48p. (gr. 2-4). pap. 9.95 *(978-0-7613-5561-8(8))* Lerner Publishing Group.

Miller, Jennifer A. South Korea. 2010. (Country Explorers Ser.). (ENG.). 48p. (gr. 2-4). lib. bdg. 29.27 *(978-1-58013-605-1(2))* Lerner Publishing Group.

Mondschein, Ken. South & Central Asia, Vol. 10. 2016. (Social Progress & Sustainability Ser.). (Illus.). 80p. (J). (gr. 7). 24.95 *(978-1-4222-3500-3(9))* Mason Crest.

Murray, Julie. Gibbons, 1 vol. 2013. (Asian Animals Ser.). (ENG.). 32p. (J). (gr. 2-5). lib. bdg. 28.50 *(978-1-61783-554-4(4)*, Big Buddy Bks.) ABDO Publishing Co.

—Komodo Dragons, 1 vol. 2013. (Asian Animals Ser.). (ENG.). 32p. (J). (gr. 2-5). lib. bdg. 28.50 *(978-1-61783-555-1(2)*, Big Buddy Bks.) ABDO Publishing Co.

Oachs, Emily Rose. Asia. 2017. (Asia Ser.). 24p. (J). (gr. k-3). pap. 6.99 ***(978-1-61891-256-5(9)***, Blastoff! Readers) Bellwether Media.

Onsgard, Bethany. Asia, 1 vol. 2013. (Continents Ser.). (ENG.). 48p. (J). (gr. 3-6). lib. bdg. 32.79 *(978-1-61783-930-6(2))* ABDO Publishing Co.

Pang, Guek Cheng. Kazakhstan. 2nd rev. ed. 2010. (Cultures of the World 22 Ser.). 144p. (gr. 6). 42.79 *(978-1-60870-455-2(6))* Marshall Cavendish GBR. Dist: Marshall Cavendish Corp.

Piddock, Charles. Kazakhstan. 2006. (Nations in the News Ser.). (Illus.). 48p. (gr. 5-12). lib. bdg. 31.00 *(978-0-8368-6708-4(4)*, Gareth Stevens Secondary Library) Stevens, Gareth Publishing LLLP.

Randolph, Joanne. Number Crunch Your Way Around Asia. 2015. (Math Exploration: Using Math to Learn about the Continents Ser.). (ENG., Illus.). 32p. (J). (gr. 3-4). pap. 10.00 *(978-1-4994-1236-9(3)*, PowerKids Pr.) Rosen Publishing Group, Inc., The.

Rice, Earle. The Life & Times of Attila the Hun. 2009. (Biography from Ancient Civilizations Ser.). 48p. (J). (gr. 4-8). 29.95 *(978-1-58415-741-0(0))* Mitchell Lane Pubs., Inc.

Rockett, Paul. Mapping Asia. 2016. (Illus.). 32p. (J). *(978-0-7787-2613-5(4))* Crabtree Publishing Co.

Roumanis, Alexis. Exploring Continents: Asia. 2015. 24p. pap. 12.95 *(978-1-4896-3033-9(3))* Weigl Pubs., Inc.

Sexton, Colleen & Simmons, Walter. Thailand. 2010. (Exploring Countries Ser.). (ENG., Illus.). 32p. (J). (gr. 3-7). lib. bdg. 26.95 *(978-1-60014-491-2(8)*, Blastoff! Readers) Bellwether Media.

The Silk Road's Greatest Travelers. 2016. (Silk Road's Greatest Travelers Ser.). 112p. (gr. 6-6). 148.40 *(978-1-4777-8548-5(5)*, Rosen Young Adult) Rosen Publishing Group, Inc., The.

Sjonger, Rebecca. L'Asie. 2012. (FRE.). 32p. (J). pap. 9.95 *(978-2-89579-457-8(X))* Bayard Canada CAN. Dist: Crabtree Publishing Co.

Sonneborn, Liz. Yemen. 2016. (Enchantment of the World Ser.). (ENG., Illus.). 144p. (J). lib. bdg. 40.00 *(978-0-531-23299-6(9)*, Children's Pr.) Scholastic Library Publishing.

Sonnier, Suzanne. Shinto, Spirits, & Shrines: Religion in Japan. 2007. (Lucent Library of Historical Eras:Twentieth-Century Japan Ser.). (ENG., Illus.). 96p. (J). (gr. 4-7). lib. bdg. 34.80 *(978-1-4205-0029-5(5)*, Lucent Bks.) Cengage Gale.

Spencer, Linda. The War at Home: Japan During World War II. 2007. (Lucent Library of Historical Eras:Twentieth-Century Japan Ser.). (ENG., Illus.). 96p. (J). (gr. 3-7). lib. bdg. 34.80 *(978-1-4205-0027-1(9)*, Lucent Bks.) Cengage Gale.

Spilsbury, Richard & Spilsbury, Louise. Animals in Danger in Asia, 1 vol. 2013. (Animals in Danger Ser.). (ENG.). 32p. (gr. 1-3). 27.32 *(978-1-4329-7673-6(7))*; pap. 8.95 *(978-1-4329-7680-4(X))* Heinemann-Raintree. (Heinemann First Library).

Wang, Andrea. Learning about Asia. 2015. (ENG., Illus.). 40p. (J). (gr. 3-5). 29.32 *(978-1-4677-8014-8(6))* Lerner Publishing Group.

Wells, Donald. The Silk Road. 2004. (Great Journeys Ser.). (Illus.). 32p. (J). lib. bdg. 26.00 *(978-1-59036-207-5(1))* Weigl Pubs., Inc.

Williams, Brian. Daily Life in the Indus Valley Civilization. 2015. (Daily Life in Ancient Civilizations Ser.). (ENG., Illus.). 48p. (gr. 3-6). pap. 8.99 *(978-1-4846-2582-8(X))* Heinemann-Raintree.

Yasuda, Anita. Asia. 2014. (J). *(978-1-4896-0942-7(3))* Weigl Pubs., Inc.

ASIA, SOUTHEASTERN

see Southeast Asia

ASIAN AMERICANS

Abrams, Dennis. Maxine Hong Kingston. 2009. (Asian Americans of Achievement Ser.). (Illus.). 128p. (YA). (gr. 7-12). 35.00 *(978-1-60413-568-8(9))* Facts On File, Inc.

Asian-American Writers. 2010. (Multicultural Voices Ser.). (Illus.). 146p. (gr. 6-12). 35.00 *(978-1-60413-313-4(9)*, Chelsea Hse.) Facts On File, Inc.

Asian Americans of Achievement Set, 16-Volumes. 2009. (Asian Americans of Achievement Ser.). (gr. 6-12). 560.00 *(978-0-7910-9917-9(2)*, Chelsea Hse.) Facts On File, Inc.

Barr, Linda. Long Road to Freedom: Journey of the Hmong. 2004. (High Five Reading - Purple Ser.). (ENG., Illus.). 64p. (gr. 3-4). per. 9.00 *(978-0-7368-3852-8(X)*, High Five Reading (RBL)) Capstone Press of Coughlan Cos.

Bryan, Nichol. Filipino Americans, 1 vol. 2004. (One Nation Set 1 Ser.). (ENG.). 32p. (gr. k-6). 27.07 *(978-1-57765-988-4(0)*, Checkerboard Library) ABDO Publishing Co.

—Indian Americans, 1 vol. 2004. (One Nation Set 1 Ser.). (ENG.). 32p. (gr. k-6). 27.07 *(978-1-57765-984-6(8)*, Checkerboard Library) ABDO Publishing Co.

Corrigan, Jim. Filipino Immigration. 2005. (Changing Face of North America Ser.). (Illus.). 112p. (YA). lib. bdg. 24.95 *(978-1-59084-684-1(2))* Mason Crest.

Darraj, Susan Muaddi. Amy Tan. 2007. (Asian Americans of Achievement Ser.). 112p. (YA). (gr. 7-12). lib. bdg. 35.00 *(978-0-7910-9269-9(0))* Facts On File, Inc.

Exceptional Asians. 2016. (Exceptional Asians Ser.). 24p. (gr. 3-2). pap. 56.10 *(978-0-7660-7968-7(6))*; lib. bdg. 135.60 *(978-0-7660-7492-7(7))* Enslow Pubs., Inc.

Girod, Christina M. Indian Americans. 2003. (Immigrants in America Ser.). (ENG., Illus.). 112p. (J). 30.85 *(978-1-59018-270-3(7)*, Lucent Bks.) Cengage Gale.

Hansen-Krening, Nancy, et al, eds. Kaleidoscope: A Multicultural Booklist for Grades K-8. 4th ed. 2003. (NCTE Bibliography Ser.). (Illus.). 118p. (J). pap. 30.95 *(978-0-8141-2539-7(5)*, 25395) National Council of Teachers of English.

Hill, Z. B. Gallup Guides for Youth Facing Persistent Prejudice. 2012. (Gallup Guides for Youth Facing Persistent Prejudice Ser.). 64p. (J). (gr. 7-8). 22.95 *(978-1-4222-2463-2(5))* Mason Crest.

Kingston, Anna. Respecting the Contributions of Asian Americans. 2012. (Stop Bullying Now! Ser.). (ENG., Illus.). 24p. (J). (gr. 3-6). pap. 8.25 *(978-1-4488-7520-7(X))*; lib. bdg. 22.60 *(978-1-4488-7447-7(5))* Rosen Publishing Group, Inc., The.

Knight, Margy Burns. Who Belongs Here? An American Story, 1 vol. O'Brien, Anne Sibley, illus. 2nd ed. 2003. (SPA & ENG.). 40p. (gr. 2-6). 8.95 *(978-0-88448-169-0(7)*, 884169) Tilbury Hse. Pubs.

Knight, Margy Burns, et al. Who Belongs Here? An American Story. 2nd ed. 2004. (Illus.). 40p. (gr. 3-8). 16.95 *(978-0-88448-110-2(7))* Tilbury Hse. Pubs.

Louie, Ai-Ling. Vera Wang Queen of Fashion; Amazing Chinese American: Biographies of Amazing Asian Americans. 2007. (Biographies of Amazing Asian Americans Ser.). (ENG., Illus.). 48p. (J). pap. 12.99 *(978-0-9787465-3-7(8))* Dragoneagle Pr.

Marvis, Barbara J. Famous People of Asian Ancestry, 5 vols. Incl. Vol. IV. Contemporary American Success Stories: Famous People of Asian Ancestry. (Illus.). 1994. pap. 10.95 *(978-1-883845-09-4(2))*; Vol. I. 1993. pap. 10.95 *(978-1-883845-06-3(8))*; Vol. II. 1993. pap. 10.95 *(978-1-883845-07-0(6))*; Vol. III. (Illus.). 1993. pap. 10.95 *(978-1-883845-08-7(4))*; Vol. V. (Illus.). 1994. pap. 10.95 *(978-1-883845-11-7(4))*; 96p. (YA). (gr. 5-18). (Contemporary American Success Stories Ser.). (Illus.). Set pap. 54.75 *(978-1-883845-13-1(0))* Mitchell Lane Pubs., Inc.

Media Projects, Inc., Staff. Almanac of Asian American History, 2 vols., Vol. 1. 2004. (Illus.). 144p. (C). (gr. 6-8). stu. ed. 97.00 *(978-0-313-32602-8(9)*, MS2602, Greenwood) ABC-CLIO, LLC.

Moore, Dave, compiled by. A Free People: Tracing Our Hmong Roots. 2nd ed. 2003. (ENG., Illus.). 144p. (J). per. 19.95 *(978-1-888194-42-5(1))* Master Communications, Inc.

Mussari, Mark. Amy Tan. 2010. (Today's Writers & Their Works). 128p. (gr. 7-18). 42.79 *(978-0-7614-4127-4(1))* Marshall Cavendish Corp.

O'Keefe, Sherry. From China to America: The Story of Amy Tan. 2011. (World Writers Ser.). 112p. (gr. 7-18). lib. bdg. 28.95 *(978-1-59935-138-4(2))* Reynolds, Morgan Inc.

Orr, Tamra. Brenda Song. 2009. (Robbie Reader Ser.). (Illus.). 32p. (YA). (gr. 2-5). lib. bdg. 25.70 *(978-1-58415-753-3(4))* Mitchell Lane Pubs., Inc.

Petrillo, Valerie. Asian American History: More Than 70 Activities. 2007. (Kid's Guide Ser.). (ENG., Illus.). 256p. (J). (gr. 2-4). pap. 16.95 *(978-1-55652-634-3(2))* Chicago Review Pr., Inc.

Rawson, Katherine. Brenda Song. (J). 2010. pap. 9.40 *(978-1-4358-3406-4(2))* 2009. (Illus.). 24p. lib. bdg. 22.60 *(978-1-4042-8136-3(3))* Rosen Publishing Group, Inc., The. (PowerKids Pr.).

Sirvaitis, Karen. The Asian Pacific American Experience. 2010. (USA TODAY Cultural Mosaic Ser.). 80p. (YA). (gr. 6-8). lib. bdg. 33.26 *(978-0-7613-4089-8(0))* Lerner Publishing Group.

Sterngass, Jon. Filipino Americans. 2007. (New Immigrants Ser.). (Illus.). 144p. (gr. 6-12). lib. bdg. 30.00 *(978-0-7910-8791-6(3)*, Chelsea Hse.) Facts On File, Inc.

Worth, Richard. Vera Wang: Fashion Designer. 2016. (Influential Asians Ser.). 128p. (J). (gr. 7-6). 37.27 *(978-0-7660-7903-8(1))* Enslow Pubs., Inc.

Yoder, Carolyn. Filipino Americans. 2003. (We Are America Ser.). (Illus.). 32p. (J). (gr. 2-4). lib. bdg. *(978-1-4034-0164-9(0))* Heinemann-Raintree.

ASIAN AMERICANS—FICTION

Asai, Carrie. The Book of the Pearl. Verhoye, Annabelle & Alarcao, Renato, illus. 2003. (Samurai Girl Ser.: 3). (ENG.). 240p. (YA). (gr. 11). pap. 6.99 *(978-0-689-86432-2(9)*, Simon Pulse) Simon Pulse.

—The Book of the Sword. Verhoye, Annabelle, illus. 2003. (Samurai Girl Ser.: 1). (ENG.). 224p. (YA). (gr. 11). pap. 11.99 *(978-0-689-85948-9(1)*, Simon Pulse) Simon Pulse.

Asai, Carrie & Gray, Mitchel. The Book of the Wind. Verhoye, Annabelle & Alarcão, Renato, illus. 2003. (Samurai Girl Ser.: 4). (ENG.). 224p. (YA). (gr. 11). pap. 6.99 *(978-0-689-86433-9(7)*, Simon Pulse) Simon Pulse.

Budhos, Marina. Watched. 2016. (ENG.). 272p. (YA). (gr. 7). 17.99 *(978-0-553-53418-4(1)*, Lamb, Wendy Bks.) Random Hse. Children's Bks.

Farizan, Sara. Tell Me Again How a Crush Should Feel. 2014. (ENG.). 304p. (YA). (gr. 9-12). 16.95 *(978-1-61620-284-2(X)*, 73284) Algonquin Bks. of Chapel Hill.

Glock-Cooper, Allison. Changers Book Three: Kim. 2016. (Changers Ser.). (ENG.). 240p. (J). (gr. 6). pap. 11.95 *(978-1-61775-489-0(7)*, Black Sheep) Akashic Bks.

Menon, Sandhya. When Dimple Met Rishi. 2017. (ENG., Illus.). 384p. (YA). (gr. 7). 17.99 ***(978-1-4814-7868-7(0)***, Simon Pulse) Simon Pulse.

Nazemian, Abdi. The Authentics. 2017. 288p. (YA). (gr. 8). 17.99 *(978-0-06-248646-2(2))* HarperCollins Pubs.

O'Brien, Anne Sibley. I'm New Here. O'Brien, Anne Sibley, illus. 2015. (ENG., Illus.). 32p. (J). (gr. k-3). lib. bdg. 16.95 *(978-1-58089-612-2(X))* Charlesbridge Publishing, Inc.

Sonnenblick, Jordan. Zen & the Art of Faking It. 2007. (ENG.). 272p. (J). (gr. 7-12). 16.99 *(978-0-439-83707-1(3)*, Scholastic Pr.) Scholastic, Inc.

Sullivan, Deirdre. Ming Goes to School. Löfdahl, Maja, illus. 2016. (ENG.). 32p. (J). (gr. -1-k). 16.99 *(978-1-5107-0050-5(1)*, Sky Pony Pr.) Skyhorse Publishing Co., Inc.

ASIANS—UNITED STATES

see also Asian Americans

Kingston, Anna. Respecting the Contributions of Asian Americans. 2012. (Stop Bullying Now! Ser.). (ENG., Illus.). 24p. (J). (gr. 3-6). pap. 8.25 *(978-1-4488-7520-7(X))*; lib. bdg. 22.60 *(978-1-4488-7447-7(5))* Rosen Publishing Group, Inc., The.

ASIMOV, ISAAC, 1920-1992

Boerst, William J. Isaac Asimov: Writer of the Future. 2004. (World Writers Ser.). (Illus.). 112p. (YA). (gr. 6-12). 23.95 *(978-1-883846-32-9(3)*, First Biographies) Reynolds, Morgan Inc.

Hoppa, Jocelyn. Isaac Asimov: Science Fiction Trailblazer. 2009. (Authors Teens Love Ser.). (Illus.). 104p. (J). (gr. 6). lib. bdg. 33.27 *(978-0-7660-2961-3(1))* Enslow Pubs., Inc.

Wolny, Philip. Isaac Asimov. 2014. (Great Science Writers Ser.). (Illus.). 112p. (J). (gr. 7-12). 35.60 *(978-1-4777-7689-6(3))* Rosen Publishing Group, Inc., The.

ASSASSINATION

see also names of persons and groups of persons with the subdivision Assassination, e.g. Presidents—United States—Assassination

Cunningham, Anne C. Critical Perspectives on Government-Sponsored Assassinations. 2017. (Analyzing the Issues Ser.). 208p. (gr. 8-8). lib. bdg. 47.93 ***(978-0-7660-8483-4(3))*** Enslow Pubs., Inc.

Kingsbury, Robert. The Assassination of James A. Garfield. 2003. (Library of Political Assassinations Ser.). (Illus.). 64p. (YA). (gr. 7-12). lib. bdg. 31.95 *(978-0-8239-3540-6(X))* Rosen Publishing Group, Inc., The.

MacLeod, Elizabeth. Royal Murder: The Deadly Intrigue of Ten Sovereigns. 2008. (ENG., Illus.). 128p. (J). (gr. 5-7). 24.95 *(978-1-55451-128-0(3)*, 9781554511280); pap. 14.95 *(978-1-55451-127-3(5)*, 9781554511273) Annick Pr., Ltd. CAN. Dist: Publishers Group West (PGW).

Swanson, James L. Chasing Lincoln's Killer: The Search for John Wilkes Booth. 2009. (ENG., Illus.). 208p. (J). (gr. 7-18). 16.99 *(978-0-439-90354-7(8)*, Scholastic Pr.) Scholastic, Inc.

ASSEMBLY, RIGHT OF

see also Freedom of Speech

Smith, Rich. First Amendment: The Right of Expression, 1 vol. 2007. (Bill of Rights Ser.). (ENG.). 32p. (gr. 3-7). 27.07 *(978-1-59928-914-4(8)*, Abdo & Daughters) ABDO Publishing Co.

Wittmann, Kelly. Freedom of Assembly. 2016. (Our Basic Freedoms Ser.). 00048p. (J). pap. 14.05 ***(978-1-4824-6104-6(8))*** Stevens, Gareth Publishing LLLP.

ASSERTIVENESS (PSYCHOLOGY)

Berry, Joy. Winning Skills You Can Work It! an Anthology of Six Books. Bartholomew, illus. 2010. (Winning Skills Ser.). (ENG.). 304p. (J). (gr. 5-7). pap. 9.95 *(978-1-60577-604-0(1))* Berry, Joy Enterprises.

Burstein, John. Speak Up! Communicating Confidently. 2010. (ENG., Illus.). 32p. (J). pap. *(978-0-7787-4813-7(8)*, 1317441) Crabtree Publishing Co.

—Speak up! Communicating Confidently. 2010. (ENG., Illus.). 32p. (J). lib. bdg. *(978-0-7787-4797-0(2)*, 1317441) Crabtree Publishing Co.

Fixman, Jennifer. Make a Difference with Miss Jenny. 2009. 64p. 19.99 *(978-1-930979-14-7(2))* Edutunes.

Laouénan, Christine. Stand Up! How to Stay True to Yourself. Moloney, Kate, ed. Bertrand, Cécile, illus. 2012. (ENG.). 80p. (YA). (gr. 5-9). pap. 12.95 *(978-1-4197-0198-6(3)*, Amulet Bks.) Abrams, Inc.

Palmer, Pat. The Mouse, the Monster & Me: Assertiveness for Young People. Shondeck, Betty, illus. rev. ed. 2010. 100p. (J). pap. 12.99 *(978-0-9622834-3-7(6))* Uplift Pr.

Roberts, Emily. Express Yourself: A Teen Girl's Guide to Speaking up & Being Who You Are. 2015. (Instant Help Solutions Ser.). (ENG.). 232p. (YA). (gr. 6-12). pap. 17.95 *(978-1-62625-148-9(7))* New Harbinger Pubns.

Schab, Lisa M. Cool, Calm, & Confident: A Workbook to Help Kids Learn Assertiveness Skills. 2009. (Instant Help Ser.). (ENG.). 184p. (J). (gr. k-5). pap. 18.95 *(978-1-57224-630-0(8)*, Instant Help Books) New Harbinger Pubns.

ASSERTIVENESS (PSYCHOLOGY)—FICTION

Asher, Sandy. Too Many Frogs! Graves, Keith, illus. 2005. (ENG.). 32p. (J). (gr. -1-k). 16.99 *(978-0-399-23978-6(2)*, Philomel Bks.) Penguin Young Readers Group.

Calonita, Jen. Sleepaway Girls. 2010. (ENG.). 320p. (J). (gr. 7-17). pap. 18.99 *(978-0-316-01718-3(3)*, Poppy) Little, Brown Bks. for Young Readers.

Ellis, Deborah. Mud City. 2013. 156p. pap. *(978-1-4596-6445-6(0))* ReadHowYouWant.com, Ltd.

Hartt-Sussman, Heather. Noni Says No. Côté, Geneviève, illus. 2011. (ENG.). 24p. (J). (gr. -1-2). 17.95 *(978-1-77049-233-2(X)*, Tundra Bks.) Tundra Bks. CAN. Dist: Penguin Random Hse. LLC.

Hearn, Julie. Ivy. (ENG.). (YA). (gr. 7). 2009. 384p. pap. 9.99 *(978-1-4169-2507-1(4))* 2008. 368p. 17.99

(978-1-4169-2506-4(6)) Simon & Schuster Children's Publishing. (Atheneum Bks. for Young Readers).
Hrdlitschka, Shelley. Sister Wife, 1 vol. 2008. (ENG.). 280p. (YA). (gr. 7-12). pap. 12.95 (978-1-55143-927-3(1)) Orca Bk. Pubs. USA.
Ludwig, Sabine. The Story of the Little Pig Who Couldn't Say No. Wilharm, Sabine, illus. 2013. (ENG.). 32p. (J). (gr. -1-1). 16.95 (978-1-62087-684-8(1), 620684, Sky Pony Pr.) Skyhorse Publishing Co., Inc.
MacRae, Tom. The Opposite, 1 vol. Odriozola, Elena, illus. 2006. (ENG.). 32p. (J). (gr. k-3). 15.95 (978-1-56145-371-9(4)) Peachtree Pubs.
Moss, Peggy. Say Something, 1 vol. Lyon, Lea, illus. 2004. (ENG.). 32p. (gr. 2-7). 16.95 (978-0-88448-261-1(8), 884261) Tilbury Hse. Pubs.
Myracle, Lauren. The Infinite Moment of Us. (ENG.). 336p. (YA). (gr. 9-17). 2014. pap. 8.95 (978-1-4197-1358-3(2)) 2013. 18.95 (978-1-4197-0793-3(0)) Abrams, Inc. (Amulet Bks.).
Stranaghan, Crystal J. Then It Rained. Espadaler, Rosa, illus. 2007. 24p. (J). (978-0-9784047-8-9(5)) Pays et Terroirs.
Wells, Rosemary. Felix Stands Tall. Wells, Rosemary, illus. 2015. (ENG., Illus.). 32p. (J). (gr. k-3). 14.99 (978-0-7636-6111-3(2)) Candlewick Pr.
Winthrop, Elizabeth. Squashed in the Middle. Cummins, Pat, illus. 2008. (J). (gr. k-4). 25.95 incl. audio (978-1-4301-0440-7(6)); 28.95 incl. audio compact disk (978-1-4301-0443-8(0)) Live Oak Media.

ASSIMILATION (SOCIOLOGY)

see also Emigration and Immigration; Ethnic Relations; Minorities

Cohen, Marina. Changing Cultural Landscapes: How Are People & Their Communities Affected by Migration & Settlement? 2010. (Investigating Human Migration & Settlement Ser.). (ENG., Illus.). 48p. (J). (gr. 5-8). (978-0-7787-5178-6(3)); pap. (978-0-7787-5193-9(7)) Crabtree Publishing Co.
Wachtel, Alan. Southeast Asian Americans. 2009. (New Americans Ser.). 80p. (gr. 5-8). 35.64 (978-0-7614-4312-4(6)) Marshall Cavendish Corp.

ASSIMILATION (SOCIOLOGY)—FICTION

Krishnaswami, Uma. Chachaji's Cup. Sitaraman, Soumya, illus. 2013. (ENG.). 32p. (J). (gr. 1-18). 16.95 (978-0-89239-178-3(2)) Lee & Low Bks., Inc.
O'Brien, Anne Sibley. I'm New Here. O'Brien, Anne Sibley, illus. 2015. (ENG., Illus.). 32p. (J). (gr. k-3). lib. bdg. 16.95 (978-1-58089-612-2(X)) Charlesbridge Publishing, Inc.
Scott, Mary Ann. New Girl, 1 vol. 2003. (ENG.). 208p. (YA). (978-1-55041-725-8(8)) Fitzhenry & Whiteside, Ltd.

ASSISI (ITALY)

Gray, Tricia. The Wondrous Adventures of St. Francis of Assisi. rev. ed. 2003. (Illus.). 164p. (J). pap. 14.95 (978-0-86716-480-0(8)) Franciscan Media.
Streit, Jakob. Brother Francis: The Life of Francis of Assisi. Kuettel, Nina, tr. from GER. 2013. (ENG., Illus.). 56p. (J). pap. 10.00 (978-1-936367-40-5(8)) Waldorf Publications.
Trouve, Marianne Lorraine. Saint Clare of Assisi: A Light for the World. Peterson, Mary Joseph, illus. 2009. (J). pap. 7.95 (978-0-8198-7122-0(2)) Pauline Bks. & Media.

ASSISI (ITALY)—FICTION

Campbell, Jeffrey. St. Francis & the Christmas Miracle of Greccio. Bianco, Francesca, illus. 2014. (ENG.). 28p. (J). 14.95 (978-0-9796766-3-5(0), Tau Publishing) Vesuvius Pr. Inc.

ASSISTANCE TO UNDERDEVELOPED AREAS

see Economic Assistance

ASSISTED SUICIDE

see also Euthanasia

Engdahl, Sylvia. Assisted Suicide. 2008. (Current Controversies Ser.). (ENG., Illus.). 176-240p. (gr. 10-12). 27.50 (978-0-7377-4133-9(3)); pap. 39.70 (978-0-7377-4132-2(5)) Cengage Gale. (Greenhaven Pr., Inc.).
Ferguson, John E. & Ferguson, John E., Jr. The Right to Die. 2007. (Point/Counterpoint Ser.). (Illus.). 109p. (YA). (gr. 9-12). lib. bdg. 35.00 (978-0-7910-9287-3(9)) Facts On File, Inc.
Forman, Lillian. Assisted Suicide, 1 vol. 2008. (Essential Viewpoints Set 2 Ser.). (ENG., Illus.). 112p. (J). (gr. 6-12). lib. bdg. 35.64 (978-1-60453-056-8(1)) ABDO Publishing Co.
Medina, Loreta M., ed. Euthanasia. 2004. (History of Issues Ser.). (ENG.). 235p. (YA). (gr. 10-13). lib. bdg. 42.15 (978-0-7377-2005-1(0), Greenhaven Pr., Inc.) Cengage Gale.
Ondrey, James H. Physician-Assisted Suicide. 2006. (At Issue Ser.). (ENG., Illus.). 128p. (gr. 10-12). 39.40 (978-0-7377-3245-0(8)); pap. 27.80 (978-0-7377-3246-7(6), Greenhaven Pr., Inc.) Cengage Gale.
Stefoff, Rebecca. The Right to Die. 2008. (Open for Debate Ser.). 128p. (gr. 7-18). lib. bdg. 42.79 (978-0-7614-2948-7(4), Benchmark Bks.) Marshall Cavendish Corp.
Thompson, Tamara. The Right to Die. Gale, G., ed. 2014. (At Issue Ser.). (ENG.). 128p. (gr. 10-12). lib. bdg. 39.40 (978-0-7377-6850-3(9), Greenhaven Pr., Inc.) Cengage Gale.
Yount, Lisa. Right to Die & Euthanasia. 2nd rev. ed. 2007. (Library in a Book). (Illus.). 320p. (C). (gr. 9-18). 45.00 (978-0-8160-6275-1(7)) Facts On File, Inc.

ASSYRIA

Matthews, Rupert. Assyrian Soldier! An Ancient Army You'd Rather Not Join. Antram, David, illus. 2007. (You Wouldn't Want to... Ser.). (ENG.). 32p. (J). (gr. 2-5). 29.00 (978-0-531-18727-2(6)) Scholastic Library Publishing.
Tracy, Kathleen. Ancient Assyria. 2012. (Explore Ancient Worlds Ser.). 48p. (J). (gr. 3-6). lib. bdg. 29.95 (978-1-61228-282-4(2)) Mitchell Lane Pubs., Inc.

ASSYRIA—FICTION

Bower, Tamara. How the Amazon Queen Fought the Prince of Egypt. Bower, Tamara, illus. 2014. (ENG., Illus.). 36p. (J). (gr. 2-6). 16.99 (978-1-4814-2526-1(9), Atheneum Bks. for Young Readers) Simon & Schuster Children's Publishing.

ASTERIX (FICTITIOUS CHARACTER)—FICTION

Ferri, Jean-Yves. Asterix & the Missing Scroll. Conrad, Didier, illus. 2015. (ENG.). 48p. (J). (gr. 4-6). 17.99 (978-1-5101-0045-9(8), Asterix) Hachette Children's Group GBR. Dist: Hachette Bk. Group.
—Asterix & the Picts. Conrad, Didier, illus. 2013. (ENG.). 48p. (J). (gr. 4-7). 17.99 (978-1-4440-1167-8(7), Orion) Orion Publishing Group, Ltd. GBR. Dist: Hachette Bk. Group.
Ferri, Jean-Yves, et al. Asterix & the Missing Scroll. Conrad, Didier, illus. 2016. (Asterix Ser.). (ENG.). 48p. (J). (gr. 2-4). pap. 12.99 (978-1-5101-0046-6(6), Orion Children's Bks.) Hachette Children's Group GBR. Dist: Hachette Bk. Group.
—Asterix & the Picts. Conrad, Didier, illus. 2014. (ENG.). 48p. (J). (gr. 4-6). pap. 12.99 (978-1-4440-1169-2(3), Orion) Orion Publishing Group, Ltd. GBR. Dist: Hachette Bk. Group.
Goscinny, René. Asterix & Caesar's Gift. Uderzo, Albert, illus. 2004. (ENG.). 48p. pap. 12.99 (978-0-7528-6646-8(X), Orion) Orion Publishing Group, Ltd. GBR. Dist: Hachette Bk. Group.
—Asterix & Cleopatra. Uderzo, Albert, illus. 2004. (ENG.). 48p. 17.99 (978-0-7528-6606-2(0), Orion) Orion Publishing Group, Ltd. GBR. Dist: Hachette Bk. Group.
—Asterix & Obelix's Birthday. Uderzo, Albert, illus. 2010. (ENG.). 56p. (J). (gr. 4-6). pap. 12.99 (978-1-4440-0095-5(0), Orion) Orion Publishing Group, Ltd. GBR. Dist: Hachette Bk. Group.
—Asterix & the Banquet. Uderzo, Albert, illus. 2004. (ENG.). 48p. 17.99 (978-0-7528-6608-6(7), Orion) Orion Publishing Group, Ltd. GBR. Dist: Hachette Bk. Group.
—Asterix & the Cauldron. Uderzo, Albert, illus. 2004. (ENG.). 48p. 17.99 (978-0-7528-6628-4(1), Orion) Orion Publishing Group, Ltd. GBR. Dist: Hachette Bk. Group.
—Asterix & the Golden Sickle. Uderzo, Albert, illus. 2004. (ENG.). 48p. 17.99 (978-0-7528-6612-3(5)); pap. 12.99 (978-0-7528-6613-0(3)) Orion Publishing Group, Ltd. GBR. (Orion). Dist: Hachette Bk. Group.
—Asterix & the Goths. Uderzo, Albert, illus. 2004. (ENG.). 48p. 17.99 (978-0-7528-6614-7(1), Orion) Orion Publishing Group, Ltd. GBR. Dist: Hachette Bk. Group.
—Asterix & the Normans. (Illus.). (J). pap. 9.95 (978-0-02-497290-3(8)) International Language Centre.
—Asterix & the Roman Agent. Uderzo, Albert, illus. 2004. (ENG.). 48p. 17.99 (978-0-7528-6632-1(X), Orion) Orion Publishing Group, Ltd. GBR. Dist: Hachette Bk. Group.
—Asterix & the Vikings: The Book of the Film. Uderzo, Albert, illus. 2007. (ENG.). 72p. pap. 12.99 (978-0-7528-8876-7(5), Orion) Orion Publishing Group, Ltd. GBR. Dist: Hachette Bk. Group.
—Asterix aux Jeux Olympiques. (FRE.). (J). pap. 21.95 (978-2-01-210144-9(5)) Hachette Groupe Livre FRA. Dist: Distribooks, Inc.
—Asterix en Hispanie. (FRE.). (J). pap. 21.95 (978-2-01-210146-3(1)) Hachette Groupe Livre FRA. Dist: Distribooks, Inc.
—Asterix et Cleopatre. (FRE.). (J). pap. 21.95 (978-2-01-210138-8(0)); (Illus.). 21.95 (978-2-01-210111-1(9)) Hachette Groupe Livre FRA. Dist: Distribooks, Inc.
—Asterix et les Normaands. (FRE.). (J). pap. 21.95 (978-2-01-210141-8(0)) Hachette Groupe Livre FRA. Dist: Distribooks, Inc.
—Asterix in Belgium. Uderzo, Albert, illus. 2005. (ENG.). 48p. 17.99 (978-0-7528-6649-9(4)); pap. 12.99 (978-0-7528-6650-5(8)) Orion Publishing Group, Ltd. GBR. (Orion). Dist: Hachette Bk. Group.
—Asterix in Britain. Uderzo, Albert, illus. 2004. (ENG.). 48p. 17.99 (978-0-7528-6618-5(4), Orion) Orion Publishing Group, Ltd. GBR. Dist: Hachette Bk. Group.
—Asterix in Spain. Uderzo, Albert, illus. 2004. (ENG.). 48p. 17.99 (978-0-7528-6630-7(3), Orion) Orion Publishing Group, Ltd. GBR. Dist: Hachette Bk. Group.
—Asterix in Switzerland. Uderzo, Albert, illus. 2004. (ENG.). 48p. 17.99 (978-0-7528-6634-5(6), Orion) Orion Publishing Group, Ltd. GBR. Dist: Hachette Bk. Group.
—Asterix le Gaulois. 2005. audio compact disk 45.00 (978-0-320-06624-5(X)) French & European Pubns., Inc.
—Asterix le Gaulois. (FRE.). (J). pap. 21.95 (978-2-01-210133-3(X)) Hachette Groupe Livre FRA. Dist: Distribooks, Inc.
—Asterix Omnibus 11: Asterix & the Actress; Asterix & the Class Act; Asterix & the Falling Sky. Uderzo, Albert, illus. 2011. (ENG.). 168p. (J). (gr. 4-6). pap. 22.99 (978-1-4440-0426-7(3), Orion) Orion Publishing Group, Ltd. GBR. Dist: Hachette Bk. Group.
—Asterix Omnibus 2: Asterix the Gladiator; Asterix & the Banquet; Asterix & Cleopatra. Uderzo, Albert, illus. 2011. (ENG.). 156p. (J). (gr. 4-6). pap. 22.99 (978-1-4440-0424-3(7), Orion) Orion Publishing Group, Ltd. GBR. Dist: Hachette Bk. Group.
—Asterix Omnibus 3: Asterix & the Big Fight; Asterix in Britain; Asterix & the Normans. Uderzo, Albert, illus. (ENG.). 156p. (J). (gr. 4-7). 2012. pap. 22.99 (978-1-4440-0475-5(1)) 2011. 29.99 (978-1-4440-0427-4(1)) Orion Publishing Group, Ltd. GBR. (Orion). Dist: Hachette Bk. Group.
—Asterix Omnibus 4: Asterix the Legionary; Asterix & the Chieftain's Shield; Asterix at the Olympic Games. Uderzo, Albert, illus. 2012. (ENG.). 152p. (J). (gr. 4-6). pap. 22.99 (978-1-4440-0487-8(5), Orion) Orion Publishing Group, Ltd. GBR. Dist: Hachette Bk. Group.
—Asterix Omnibus 6: Asterix in Switzerland; the Mansion of the Gods; Asterix & the Laurel Wreath. Uderzo, Albert, illus. 2013. (ENG.). 156p. (J). (gr. 4-7). pap. 22.99 (978-1-4440-0491-5(3), Orion) Orion Publishing Group, Ltd. GBR. Dist: Hachette Bk. Group.
—Asterix Omnibus 7: Asterix & the Soothsayer - Asterix in Corsica - And Asterix & Caesar's Gift. Uderzo, Albert, illus. 2013. (ENG.). 156p. (J). (gr. 4-7). 29.99 (978-1-4440-0835-7(8), Orion) Orion Publishing Group, Ltd. GBR. Dist: Hachette Bk. Group.
—Asterix Omnibus 8: Asterix & the Great Crossing; Obelix & Co; Asterix in Belgium. Uderzo, Albert, illus. 2014. (ENG.). 156p. (J). (gr. 4-6). pap. 22.99 (978-1-4440-0838-8(2), Orion) Orion Publishing Group, Ltd. GBR. Dist: Hachette Bk. Group.
—Asterix on the Warpath: Pop-Up. 2015. (ENG., Illus.). 14p. (J). (gr. 4-6). 35.00 (978-1-5101-0042-8(3), Asterix) Hachette Children's Group GBR. Dist: Hachette Bk. Group.
—Asterix the Legionary. Uderzo, Albert, illus. 2004. (ENG.). 48p. 17.99 (978-0-7528-6620-8(6), Orion) Orion Publishing Group, Ltd. GBR. Dist: Hachette Bk. Group.
—The Gaul. Uderzo, Albert, illus. 2004. (ENG.). 48p. 17.99 (978-0-7528-6604-8(4), Orion) Orion Publishing Group, Ltd. GBR. Dist: Hachette Bk. Group.
—How Obelix Fell into the Magic Potion: When He Was a Little Boy. Uderzo, Albert, illus. 2010. (ENG.). 32p. (YA). (gr. 7-17). pap. 12.99 (978-1-4440-0094-8(2), Orion) Orion Publishing Group, Ltd. GBR. Dist: Hachette Bk. Group.
—Omnibus 1: Asterix the Gaul; Asterix & the Golden Sickle; Asterix & the Goths. Uderzo, Albert, illus. 2011. (ENG.). 152p. (J). (gr. 4-6). pap. 22.99 (978-1-4440-0423-6(9), Orion) Orion Publishing Group, Ltd. GBR. Dist: Hachette Bk. Group.
—Omnibus 5: Asterix & the Cauldron; Asterix in Spain; Asterix & the Roman Agent. Uderzo, Albert, illus. 2013. (ENG.). 156p. (J). (gr. 4-6). pap. 22.99 (978-1-4440-0490-8(5), Orion) Orion Publishing Group, Ltd. GBR. Dist: Hachette Bk. Group.
—Omnibus 8: Asterix & the Great Crossing; Obelix & Co.; & Asterix in Belgium. Uderzo, Albert, illus. 2013. (ENG.). 152p. (J). (gr. 4-6). 29.99 (978-1-4440-0837-1(4), Orion) Orion Publishing Group, Ltd. GBR. Dist: Hachette Bk. Group.
—Where's Asterix? Uderzo, Albert, illus. 2012. (ENG.). 32p. (J). (gr. 4-6). pap. 9.99 (978-1-4440-0554-7(5), Orion) Orion Publishing Group, Ltd. GBR. Dist: Hachette Bk. Group.
Goscinny, René & Uderzo, Albert. Asterix & Caesar's Gift. 2004. (ENG., Illus.). 48p. 17.99 (978-0-7528-6645-1(1), Orion) Orion Publishing Group, Ltd. GBR. Dist: Hachette Bk. Group.
—Asterix & Cleopatra. Uderzo, Albert, illus. 2004. (ENG., Illus.). 48p. pap. 12.99 (978-0-7528-6607-9(9), Orion) Orion Publishing Group, Ltd. GBR. Dist: Hachette Bk. Group.
—Asterix & Obelix's Birthday: The Golden Book. 2009. (ENG., Illus.). 56p. 17.99 (978-1-4440-0027-6(6), Orion) Orion Publishing Group, Ltd. GBR. Dist: Hachette Bk. Group.
—Asterix & the Banquet. Uderzo, Albert, illus. 2004. (ENG., Illus.). 48p. pap. 12.99 (978-0-7528-6609-3(5), Orion) Orion Publishing Group, Ltd. GBR. Dist: Hachette Bk. Group.
—Asterix & the Big Fight. 2004. (ENG., Illus.). 48p. 17.99 (978-0-7528-6616-1(8), Orion) Orion Publishing Group, Ltd. GBR. Dist: Hachette Bk. Group.
—Asterix & the Big Fight. Uderzo, Albert, illus. 2004. (ENG., Illus.). 48p. pap. 12.99 (978-0-7528-6617-8(6), Orion) Orion Publishing Group, Ltd. GBR. Dist: Hachette Bk. Group.
—Asterix & the Cauldron. Uderzo, Albert, illus. 2004. (ENG., Illus.). 48p. pap. 12.99 (978-0-7528-6629-1(X), Orion) Orion Publishing Group, Ltd. GBR. Dist: Hachette Bk. Group.
—Asterix & the Chieftain's Shield. Uderzo, Albert, illus. 2004. (ENG., Illus.). 48p. pap. 12.99 (978-0-7528-6625-3(7), Orion) Orion Publishing Group, Ltd. GBR. Dist: Hachette Bk. Group.
—Asterix & the Chieftan's Shield. 2004. (ENG., Illus.). 48p. 17.99 (978-0-7528-6624-6(9), Orion) Orion Publishing Group, Ltd. GBR. Dist: Hachette Bk. Group.
—Asterix & the Goths. Uderzo, Albert, illus. 2004. (ENG., Illus.). 48p. pap. 12.99 (978-0-7528-6615-4(X), Orion) Orion Publishing Group, Ltd. GBR. Dist: Hachette Bk. Group.
—Asterix & the Great Crossing. 2004. (ENG., Illus.). 48p. 17.99 (978-0-7528-6647-5(8)); pap. 12.99 (978-0-7528-6648-2(6)) Orion Publishing Group, Ltd. GBR. (Orion). Dist: Hachette Bk. Group.
—Asterix & the Laurel Wreath. Uderzo, Albert, illus. 2004. (ENG., Illus.). 48p. 17.99 (978-0-7528-6636-9(2)); pap. 12.99 (978-0-7528-6637-6(0)) Orion Publishing Group, Ltd. GBR. (Orion). Dist: Hachette Bk. Group.
—Asterix & the Normans. Uderzo, Albert, illus. 2004. (ENG., Illus.). 48p. 17.99 (978-0-7528-6622-2(2)); pap. 12.99 (978-0-7528-6623-9(0)) Orion Publishing Group, Ltd. GBR. (Orion). Dist: Hachette Bk. Group.
—Asterix & the Roman Agent. Uderzo, Albert, illus. 2004. (ENG., Illus.). 48p. pap. 12.99 (978-0-7528-6633-8(8), Orion) Orion Publishing Group, Ltd. GBR. Dist: Hachette Bk. Group.
—Asterix & the Soothsayer. Uderzo, Albert, illus. 2004. (ENG., Illus.). 48p. 17.99 (978-0-7528-6641-3(9)); pap. 12.99 (978-0-7528-6642-0(7)) Orion Publishing Group, Ltd. GBR. (Orion). Dist: Hachette Bk. Group.
—Asterix at the Olympic Games. Uderzo, Albert, illus. 2004. (ENG., Illus.). 48p. 17.99 (978-0-7528-6626-0(5), Orion) Orion Publishing Group, Ltd. GBR. Dist: Hachette Bk. Group.
—Asterix Chez les Helvetes. (FRE.). (J). pap. 21.95 (978-2-01-210016-9(3)) Hachette Groupe Livre FRA. Dist: Distribooks, Inc.
—Asterix en Corse. (FRE.). 21.95 (978-2-01-210020-6(1)) Hachette Groupe Livre FRA. Dist: Distribooks, Inc.
—Asterix en Hispanie. (FRE.). 21.95 (978-2-01-210014-5(7)) Hachette Groupe Livre FRA. Dist: Distribooks, Inc.
—Asterix et le Bombe. (FRE.). 21.95 (978-2-01-210008-4(2)) Hachette Groupe Livre FRA. Dist: Distribooks, Inc.
—Asterix French. 21.95 (978-2-01-210022-0(8)); 21.95 (978-2-01-210009-1(0)) Hachette Groupe Livre FRA. Dist: Distribooks, Inc.
—Asterix in Britain. Uderzo, Albert, illus. 2004. (ENG., Illus.). 48p. pap. 12.99 (978-0-7528-6619-2(2), Orion) Orion Publishing Group, Ltd. GBR. Dist: Hachette Bk. Group.
—Asterix in Corsica. Uderzo, Albert, illus. 2004. (ENG., Illus.). 48p. 17.99 (978-0-7528-6643-7(5), Orion) Orion Publishing Group, Ltd. GBR. Dist: Hachette Bk. Group.
—Asterix in Spain. Uderzo, Albert, illus. 2004. (ENG., Illus.). 48p. pap. 12.99 (978-0-7528-6631-4(1), Orion) Orion Publishing Group, Ltd. GBR. Dist: Hachette Bk. Group.
—Asterix in Switzerland. Uderzo, Albert, illus. 2004. (ENG., Illus.). 48p. pap. 12.99 (978-0-7528-6635-2(4), Orion) Orion Publishing Group, Ltd. GBR. Dist: Hachette Bk. Group.
—Asterix Omnibus 10: Asterix & the Magic Carpet; Asterix & the Secret Weapon; Asterix & Obelix All at Sea. 2011. (ENG., Illus.). 156p. (J). (gr. 4-6). pap. 22.99 (978-1-4440-0425-0(5), Orion) Orion Publishing Group, Ltd. GBR. Dist: Hachette Bk. Group.
—Asterix Omnibus 5: Includes Asterix & the Cauldron, Asterix in Spain, & Asterix & the Roman Agent. 2012. (ENG., Illus.). 152p. (J). (gr. 4-6). 29.99 (978-1-4440-0488-5(3), Orion) Orion Publishing Group, Ltd. GBR. Dist: Hachette Bk. Group.
—Asterix the Gladiator. Uderzo, Albert, illus. 2004. (ENG., Illus.). 48p. 17.99 (978-0-7528-6610-9(9)); pap. 12.99 (978-0-7528-6611-6(7)) Orion Publishing Group, Ltd. GBR. (Orion). Dist: Hachette Bk. Group.
—Asterix the Legionary. Uderzo, Albert, illus. 2004. (ENG., Illus.). 48p. pap. 12.99 (978-0-7528-6621-5(4), Orion) Orion Publishing Group, Ltd. GBR. Dist: Hachette Bk. Group.
—The Gaul. Uderzo, Albert, illus. 2004. (ENG., Illus.). 48p. pap. 12.99 (978-0-7528-6605-5(2), Orion) Orion Publishing Group, Ltd. GBR. Dist: Hachette Bk. Group.
—How Obelix Fell into the Magic Potion: When He Was a Little Boy. 2009. (ENG., Illus.). 32p. 17.99 (978-1-4440-0026-9(8), Orion) Orion Publishing Group, Ltd. GBR. Dist: Hachette Bk. Group.
—The Mansions of the Gods. Uderzo, Albert, illus. 2004. (ENG., Illus.). 48p. 17.99 (978-0-7528-6638-3(9), Orion) Orion Publishing Group, Ltd. GBR. Dist: Hachette Bk. Group.
—Obelix & Co. 2005. (ENG., Illus.). 48p. 17.99 (978-0-7528-6651-2(6), Orion) Orion Publishing Group, Ltd. GBR. Dist: Hachette Bk. Group.
—Omnibus 9: Asterix & the Great Divide; Asterix & the Black Gold; Asterix & Son. 2015. (Asterix Ser.). (ENG., Illus.). 152p. (J). (gr. 4-6). pap. 22.99 (978-1-4440-0966-8(4), Asterix) Hachette Children's Group GBR. Dist: Hachette Bk. Group.
Goscinny, René & Uderzo, M. Asterix el Galo. (SPA., Illus.). (J). (gr. 7-10). 24.95 (978-0-8288-4933-3(1)) French & European Pubns., Inc.
—Streit um Asterix. (GER., Illus.). (J). 24.95 (978-0-8288-4906-7(4)) French & European Pubns., Inc.
Uderzo, Albert. ASTÉRIX EN HISPANIA. 2009. (SPA., Illus.). 48p. 19.95 (978-84-345-6732-0(6)) Grupo Anaya, S.A. ESP. Dist: Baker & Taylor Bks.
Uderzo, Albert & Goscinny, René. Asterix & the Falling Sky. Bell, Anthea & Hockridge, Derek, trs. from FRE. Uderzo, Albert, illus. (ENG., Illus.). 48p. 2006. pap. 12.99 (978-0-7528-7548-4(5)) 2005. 17.99 (978-0-7528-7301-5(6)) Orion Publishing Group, Ltd. GBR. (Orion). Dist: Hachette Bk. Group.
—Asterix at the Olympic Games. Uderzo, Albert, illus. 2004. (ENG., Illus.). 48p. pap. 12.99 (978-0-7528-6627-7(3), Orion) Orion Publishing Group, Ltd. GBR. Dist: Hachette Bk. Group.
—Asterix Omnibus 4: Includes Asterix the Legionary #10, Asterix & the Chieftain's Shield #11, & Asterix at the Olympic Games #12. 2011. (ENG., Illus.). 144p. (J). (gr. 4-6). 29.99 (978-1-4440-0428-1(X), Orion) Orion Publishing Group, Ltd. GBR. Dist: Hachette Bk. Group.

ASTHMA

Asthma in Action. 2005. (Book Treks Ser.). (J). (gr. 3-18). stu. ed. 34.95 (978-0-673-62843-5(4)) Celebration Pr.
Ballard, Carol. What Is an Asthma Attack? Respiration, 1 vol. 2011. (Inside My Body Ser.). (ENG.). 32p. (gr. 3-5). 30.65 (978-1-4109-4012-4(8), NA-r) Heinemann-Raintree.
Berger, William E. Living with Asthma. 2008. (Teen's Guides). 192p. (gr. 6-12). per. 14.95 (978-0-8160-7560-7(3), Checkmark Bks.) Facts On File, Inc.
—Teen's Guide to Living with Asthma. 2007. (Teen's Guides). 192p. (gr. 6-12). 34.95 (978-0-8160-6483-0(0)) Facts On File, Inc.
Chilman-Blair, Kim & Taddeo, John. "What's up with Max?" Medikidz Explain Asthma. 2010. (Superheroes on a Medical Mission Ser.). (Illus.). 40p. (YA). (gr. 5-8). lib. bdg. 29.25 (978-1-4358-3534-4(4), Rosen Reference) Rosen Publishing Group, Inc., The.
DeLand, M. Maitland. The Great Katie Kate Offers Answers about Asthma. 2014. (ENG., Illus.). 32p. (J). 14.95 (978-1-62634-053-4(6), Greenleaf Book Group Pr.) Greenleaf Book Group.
Ford, Jean. Allergies & Asthma. Bridgemohan, Carolyn & Forman, Sara, eds. 2013. (Young Adult's Guide to the Science of Health Ser.: 15). 128p. (J). (gr. 7-18). 24.95 (978-1-4222-2804-3(5)) Mason Crest.
—Breathe Easy! A Teen's Guide to Allergies & Asthma. 2006. (Science of Health Ser.). (Illus.). 128p. (YA). 24.95 (978-1-59084-842-5(X)) Mason Crest.
Kittinger, Jo S., et al. Un Aliento de Esperanza. Galey, Chuck, illus. 2013. (SPA.). (J). (978-1-61438-868-5(7)) American Bar Assn.
Lahey, Cindy. Nose Medicine. 2011. 20p. pap. 24.95 (978-1-4626-1885-9(5)) America Star Bks.
Landau, Elaine. Asthma. 2008. (Head-to-Toe Health Ser.). 32p. (gr. 2-7). lib. bdg. 28.50 (978-0-7614-2845-9(3), Benchmark Bks.) Marshall Cavendish Corp.
Levene, Anna. My Friend Has Asthma. 2003. (Illus.). (J). (gr. 3-5). lib. bdg. 16.95 (978-1-932333-25-1(8)) Chrysalis Education.
Levine, Michelle. Asthma. 2015. (Living With... Ser.). (Illus.). 32p. (J). lib. bdg. 28.50 (978-1-60753-478-5(9)) Amicus Publishing.
Marcovitz, Hal. Asthma. 2010. (Compact Research Ser.). 96p. (YA). (gr. 7-12). lib. bdg. 25.95 (978-1-60152-104-0(9)) ReferencePoint Pr., Inc.
Moore-Malinos, Jennifer & Moore-Mallinos, Jennifer. I Have Asthma. Curto, Rosa M. & Curto, Rosa Maria, illus. 2007. (What Do You Know about? Bks.). (ENG.). 36p. (J). (gr. -1-2). pap. 7.99 (978-0-7641-3785-3(9)) Barron's Educational Series, Inc.
Murphy, Wendy. Asthma. 2011. (USA TODAY Health Reports: Diseases & Disorders Ser.). (ENG.). 128p. (gr. 6-12). 34.60 (978-0-7613-5457-4(3)) Lerner Publishing Group.
Paquette, Penny Hutchins. Asthma: The Ultimate Teen Guide. 2006. (It Happened to Me Ser.: 5). (ENG., Illus.). 184p. (gr. 8-12). per. 20.00 (978-0-8108-5759-9(6)) Scarecrow Pr., Inc.
Parker, Vic. I Know Someone with Asthma, 1 vol. 2011. (Understanding Health Issues Ser.). (ENG.). 32p. (gr. 1-3). 27.32 (978-1-4329-4556-5(4), Heinemann First Library) Heinemann-Raintree.
Powell, Jillian. Asthma. 2008. (Feeling Sick? Ser.). (Illus.). 23p. (J). (gr. 2-4). lib. bdg. (978-1-84234-472-9(2)) Cherrytree Pubns., Inc.
Robbins, Lynette. How to Deal with Asthma. 2009. (Kids' Health Ser.). 24p. (ENG.). (J). pap. 8.25 (978-1-4358-3418-7(6), PowerKids Pr.); (Illus.). (YA). (gr. 2-5). lib. bdg. 22.60 (978-1-4042-8141-7(X)) Rosen Publishing Group, Inc., The.

Royston, Angela. Asthma. 2009. (How's Your Health? Ser.). (J). (gr. 1-4). 28.50 (978-1-59920-219-8(0)) Black Rabbit Bks.

—Explaining Asthma. 2009. (Explaining... Ser.). 48p. (gr. 7-12). 37.10 (978-1-59920-315-7(4)) Black Rabbit Bks.

Sheen, Barbara. Asthma. 2011. (Diseases & Disorders Ser.). 128p. 34.95 (978-1-4205-0591-7(2), Lucent Bks.) Cengage Gale.

Silverstein, Alvin, et al. The Asthma Update. 2006. (Disease Update Ser.). (Illus.). 128p. (J). (gr. 5-9). lib. bdg. 33.27 (978-0-7660-2482-3(2)) Enslow Pubs., Inc.

Silverstein, Virginia. Handy Health Guide to Asthma. 2013. (Handy Health Guides). 48p. (J). (gr. 5-12). pap. 8.95 (978-1-4644-0481-8(X)) Enslow Pubs., Inc.

Silverstein, Virginia B. & Nunn, Laura Silverstein. Handy Health Guide to Asthma. 2013. (Handy Health Guides). 48p. (J). (gr. 5-18). 25.27 (978-0-7660-4269-8(3)) Enslow Pubs., Inc.

Smith, Terry L. Asthma. 2009. (Genes & Disease Ser.). (Illus.). 128p. (YA). (gr. 7-12). 35.00 (978-0-7910-9663-5(7)) Facts On File, Inc.

Squire, Ann O. Asthma. 2015. (ENG., Illus.). 48p. (J). lib. bdg. (978-0-531-21471-8(0), Orchard Bks.) Scholastic, Inc.

ASTHMA—FICTION

Cupala, Holly. Don't Breathe a Word. 2012. (ENG.). 320p. (YA). (gr. 9). pap. 8.99 (978-0-06-176669-5(0), HarperTeen) HarperCollins Pubs.

DeLand, M. Maitland. The Great Katie Kate Offers Answers about Asthma. 2011. (Illus.). 32p. 14.95 (978-1-60832-074-5(X)) Greenleaf Book Group.

Diggle, David Mark. Frederick: Thinking Makes Breathing Easy. Diggle, Daniel James, illus. 2011. 24p. (J). pap. (978-0-9871657-8-7(X)) Diggle de Doo Productions Pty, Ltd.

Gosselin, Kim. Sportsercise: A School Story about Exercise-Induced Asthma. Ravanelli, Terry, illus. 2nd ed. 2004. (Children's Asthma Ser.). (J). per. 9.95 (978-1-891383-25-0(6)) JayJo Bks., LLC.

Hurwitz, Johanna. Mighty Monty: More First-Grade Adventures. McGrory, Anik, illus. 2010. (Monty Ser.). (ENG.). 112p. (J). (gr. 1-4). pap. 5.99 (978-0-7636-4786-5(1)) Candlewick Pr.

Hurwitz, Johanna & McCrory, Anik. Mostly Monty. McGrory, Anik, illus. 2008. (Monty Ser.: 1). (ENG.). 96p. (J). (gr. 1-4). pap. 5.99 (978-0-7636-4062-0(X)) Candlewick Pr.

Latter, Kym & Stroud, Cassie. The Trouble with Bear Hugs: A Story about Asthma. 2012. (Illus.). 32p. (J). pap. (978-0-9873747-0-7(2)) Latter, Kym.

Leota, Kealaulaokamamo. Zhaka. 2008. (ENG & HAW., Illus.). (J). lib. bdg. (978-0-9773495-9-3(4)) Na Kamalei Koolauloa Early Education Program.

London, Jonathan. The Lion Who Had Asthma. Westcott, Nadine Bernard, illus. 2012. (J). (978-1-61913-119-4(6)) Weigl Pubs., Inc.

McCormick, Shawn R. Zoey & the Zones: A Story for Children with Asthma. 2003. per. 8.95 (978-0-9718120-8-6(X)) HealthSprings, LLC.

Mceowen, Mari R. Maggie Braves the Waves with Asthma. 2012. 16p. pap. 9.99 (978-0-9853650-2-8(1)) Mindstir Media.

McNish, Cliff. Breathe: A Ghost Story. (Exceptional Reading & Language Arts Titles for Intermediate Grades Ser.). (ENG.). 264p. (J). (gr. 4-8). 2009. pap. 6.95 (978-0-7613-4962-4(6), First Avenue Editions) 2006. lib. bdg. 15.95 (978-0-8225-6443-0(2), Carolrhoda Bks.) Lerner Publishing Group.

Muirhead, Maria. My Asthma Book. 2007. 72p. (J). (gr. 1-2). per. 11.95 (978-0-595-42925-7(4)) iUniverse, Inc.

Spring, Debbie. Breathing Soccer, 1 vol. 2008. (ENG.). 208p. (J). (gr. 4-8). pap. 10.95 (978-1-897235-42-3(9)) Thistledown Pr., Ltd. CAN. Dist: Univ. of Toronto Pr.

Walden, Pamela Charlene. Puff Bear Goes to the Hospital. 2013. 44p. pap. 9.99 (978-1-62839-470-2(6)) Salem Author Services.

Yee, Lisa. Bobby the Brave (Sometimes) Santat, Dan, illus. 2012. (ENG.). 160p. (J). (gr. 2-5). pap. 5.99 (978-0-545-05595-6(4), Levine, Arthur A. Bks.) Scholastic, Inc.

ASTOR, JOHN JACOB, 1763-1848

Parker, Lewis K. John Jacob Astor & the Fur Trade. (American Tycoons Ser.). 24p. 2009. (gr. 3-3). 42.50 (978-1-61511-393-4(2)) 2003. (Illus.). (J). lib. bdg. 22.60 (978-0-8239-6447-5(7)) Rosen Publishing Group, Inc., The. (PowerKids Pr.).

ASTROLOGY

see also Occultism

Beyerl, Paul V. The Symbols & Magick of Tarot. 2005. (Illus.). xvi, 212p. pap. (978-0-9655687-4-6(1)) Hermit's Grove, The.

Faulkner, Danny. Universe by Design. 2004. (Illus.). 160p. (YA). pap. 13.99 (978-0-89051-415-3(1), 303-029) New Leaf Pub. Group.

Hamanaka, Sheila. Space. 2005. (J). (978-0-7868-0144-2(1)); (978-0-7868-2117-4(5)) Hyperion Pr.

Huang, Chungliang Al. The Chinese Book of Animal Powers. 2011. (ENG., Illus.). 32p. 19.95 (978-1-84819-066-5(2), 3161, Singing Dragon) Kingsley, Jessica Pubs. GBR. Dist: Macmillan Distribution Ltd.

Morningstar, Sally. La Sabiduria de la Luna. (SPA.). 64p. (J). 12.00 (978-84-342-3018-7(6)) Parramon Ediciones S.A. ESP. Dist: Distribuidora Norma, Inc.

Olson, Elsie. Astrological Signs: Facts, Trivia, & Quizzes. 2017. (Mind Games Ser.). (ENG., Illus.). 32p. (J). (gr. 2-5). 27.99 **(978-1-5124-3415-6(9)**, Lerner Pubns.) Lerner Publishing Group.

Place, Robert M. Astrology & Divination. 2008. (Mysteries, Legends, & Unexplained Phenomena Ser.). (Illus.). 136p. (YA). (gr. 7-12). lib. bdg. 29.95 (978-0-7910-9385-6(9)) Facts On File, Inc.

Pluto Project Staff & Semkiw, Walter. Astrology for Regular People. Milner, Fran & Brewer, Trish, illus. 2007. (For Regular People Ser.). (ENG.). 198p. pap. 24.95 (978-0-9662982-7-7(6)) Pluto Project.

Roberts, Russell. The Life & Times of Nostradamus. 2007. (Biography from Ancient Civilizations Ser.). (Illus.). 48p. (J). (gr. 4-8). lib. bdg. 29.95 (978-1-58415-544-7(2)) Mitchell Lane Pubs., Inc.

Stefoff, Rebecca. Astrology & Astronomy. 2014. 48p. pap. 29.93 (978-1-62712-506-2(X)) Cavendish Square Publishing.

—Astrology or Astronomy: Is Your Fate in the Stars? 2013. (J). (978-0-7614-8144-7(3)) Marshall Cavendish.

Storm, Rayne. In the Night Sky: The Astrological Zodiac for Children, 1 vol. 2014. (ENG., Illus.). 88p. (J). pap. 16.99 (978-0-7643-4503-6(6), 9780764345036) Schiffer Publishing, Ltd.

Swainson, Esme. The Adventures of Rex & Zendah in the Zodiac. 2011. 136p. 40.95 (978-1-258-04279-0(7)) Literary Licensing, LLC.

Takken, Sylvia, illus. Aquarius: January 21-February 19. 2014. (Zodiac Sign Bks.). (ENG.). 12p. (J). (gr. -1 — 1). bds. 3.99 (978-0-7641-6676-1(X)) Barron's Educational Series, Inc.

—Aries: March 21-April 20. 2014. (Zodiac Sign Bks.). (ENG.). 12p. (J). (gr. -1 — 1). bds. 3.99 (978-0-7641-6678-5(6)) Barron's Educational Series, Inc.

—Cancer. 2014. (Zodiac Sign Bks.). (ENG.). 12p. (J). (gr. -1 — 1). bds. 3.99 (978-0-7641-6681-5(6)) Barron's Educational Series, Inc.

—Capricorn: December 22-January 20. 2014. (Zodiac Sign Bks.). (ENG.). 12p. (J). (gr. -1 — 1). bds. 3.99 (978-0-7641-6675-4(1)) Barron's Educational Series, Inc.

—Gemini: May 22-June 21. 2014. (Zodiac Sign Bks.). (ENG.). 12p. (J). (gr. -1 — 1). bds. 3.99 (978-0-7641-6679-2(4)) Barron's Educational Series, Inc.

—Leo: July 23-August 23. 2014. (Zodiac Sign Bks.). (ENG.). 12p. (J). (gr. -1 — 1). bds. 3.99 (978-0-7641-6682-2(4)) Barron's Educational Series, Inc.

—Libra: September 24-October 23. 2014. (Zodiac Sign Bks.). (ENG.). 12p. (J). (gr. -1 — 1). bds. 3.99 (978-0-7641-6684-6(0)) Barron's Educational Series, Inc.

—Pisces: February 20-March 20. 2014. (Zodiac Sign Bks.). (ENG.). 12p. (J). (gr. -1 — 1). bds. 3.99 (978-0-7641-6677-8(8)) Barron's Educational Series, Inc.

—Sagittarius: November 23-December 21. 2014. (Zodiac Sign Bks.). (ENG.). 12p. (J). (gr. -1 — 1). bds. 3.99 (978-0-7641-6686-0(7)) Barron's Educational Series, Inc.

—Scorpio: October 24-November 22. 2014. (Zodiac Sign Bks.). (ENG.). 12p. (J). (gr. -1 — 1). bds. 3.99 (978-0-7641-6685-3(9)) Barron's Educational Series, Inc.

—Taurus: April 21-May 21. 2014. (Zodiac Sign Bks.). (ENG.). 12p. (J). (gr. -1 — 1). bds. 3.99 (978-0-7641-6680-8(8)) Barron's Educational Series, Inc.

—Virgo: August 24-September 23. 2014. (Zodiac Sign Bks.). (ENG.). 12p. (J). (gr. -1 — 1). bds. 3.99 (978-0-7641-6683-9(2)) Barron's Educational Series, Inc.

Tang, Sanmu. Chinese Zodiac Animals. Jingwen, Zhu, tr. 2011. (ENG., Illus.). 56p. (J). (gr. 4-6). pap. 8.95 (978-1-60220-977-0(4)) BetterLink Pr., Inc.

Wand, Kelly. Astrology. 2006. (Fact or Fiction Ser.). (ENG., Illus.). 134p. (J). (gr. 4-7). lib. bdg. 36.55 (978-0-7377-3506-2(6), Greenhaven Pr., Inc.) Cengage Gale.

Yasuda, Anita. Jade Emperor: A Chinese Zodiac Myth. 2014. (Short Tales Chinese Myths Ser.). 32p. (J). (gr. 3-6). lib. bdg. 24.21 (978-1-62402-031-5(3), Short Tales) Magic Wagon.

Zenkel, Suzanne Siegel. Fashion Astrology. Bigda, Diane, illus. 2005. (Charming Petites Ser.). 80p. 4.95 (978-0-88088-842-4(3)) Peter Pauper Pr. Inc.

ASTRONAUTICS

Here are entered general works on the scientific, technological, and engineering disciplines needed for the exploration of outer space. Works on the physics and technical details of locomotion beyond earth's atmosphere are entered under Space Flight.

see also Artificial Satellites; Interplanetary Voyages; Manned Space Flight; Outer Space; Rocketry; Space Flight; Space Flight to the Moon; Space Sciences; Space Stations; Space Vehicles

Aldrin, Buzz. Look to the Stars. Minor, Wendell, illus. 2009. (ENG.). 40p. (J). (gr. 1-3). 17.99 (978-0-399-24721-7(1), G.P. Putnam's Sons Books for Young Readers) Penguin Young Readers Group.

Anderson, Michael, ed. Pioneers in Astronomy & Space Exploration. 2012. (Inventors & Innovators Ser.). (ENG., Illus.). 112p. (gr. 7-12). (J). 32.90 (978-1-61530-695-4(1)); (YA). 65.80 (978-1-61530-786-9(9)) Rosen Publishing Group, Inc., The.

Angelo, Joseph A., Jr. Human Spaceflight. 2007. (Frontiers in Space Ser.). (Illus.). 272p. (C). (gr. 9-10). 45.00 (978-0-8160-5775-7(3)) Facts On File, Inc.

—Robot Spacecraft. 2006. (Frontiers in Space Ser.). (Illus.). 320p. (C). (gr. 9). 45.00 (978-0-8160-5773-3(7)) Facts On File, Inc.

Asimov, Isaac & Hantula, Richard. Global Space Programs: Past & Present. 2005. (Isaac Asimov's 21st Century Library of the Universe). (Illus.). 32p. (gr. 2-6). lib. bdg. 26.00 (978-0-8368-3982-1(X), Gareth Stevens Learning Library) Stevens, Gareth Publishing LLLP.

Bailey, Gerry. Space Challenge. 2011. (Planet SOS Ser.). (Illus.). 48p. (J). (gr. 3-6). pap. 14.05 (978-1-4339-4983-8(0), Gareth Stevens Learning Library) Stevens, Gareth Publishing LLLP.

Baker, David. Satellites. 2008. (Exploring Space Ser.). (Illus.). 32p. (J). (gr. 4-6). lib. bdg. 26.00 (978-1-59036-777-3(4)) Weigl Pubs., Inc.

Baker, David & Kissock, Heather. Satellites. 2008. (Exploring Space Ser.). (Illus.). 32p. (J). (gr. 4-6). pap. 9.95 (978-1-59036-778-0(2)) Weigl Pubs., Inc.

Barchers, Suzanne I. Revolution in Space. 2009. (It Works! Ser.). 32p. (gr. 3). 28.50 (978-0-7614-4377-3(0)) Marshall Cavendish Corp.

Benoit, Peter. The Space Race. 2012. (Cornerstones of Freedom, Third Ser.). (ENG.). 64p. (J). pap. 8.95 (978-0-531-28165-9(5)); (gr. 4-6). lib. bdg. 30.00 (978-0-531-23065-7(1)) Scholastic Library Publishing. (Children's Pr.).

Berne, Emma Carlson. Totally Wacky Facts about Space. 2015. (Mind Benders Ser.). (ENG., Illus.). 240p. (gr. 1-3). pap. 7.95 (978-1-4914-6526-4(3)) Capstone Press of Coughlan Cos.

Bortz, Fred. Seven Wonders of Space Technology. 2011. (Seven Wonders Ser.). (ENG., Illus.). 80p. (gr. 5-8). 33.26 (978-0-7613-5453-6(0)) Lerner Publishing Group.

Braun, Eric. If I Were an Astronaut, 1 vol. Harmer, Sharon, illus. 2009. (Dream Big! Ser.). (ENG.). 24p. (gr. k-3). lib. bdg. 26.65 (978-1-4048-5534-2(3)); pap. 8.95 (978-1-4048-5710-0(9)) Picture Window Bks.

Bredeson, Carmen. What Do Astronauts Do? 2008. (I Like Space! Ser.). (Illus.). 32p. (J). (gr. 3-7). lib. bdg. 23.94 (978-0-7660-2942-2(5), Enslow Elementary) Enslow Pubs., Inc.

Clarke, Penny. The Story of the Exploration of Space. Antram, David et al, illus. 2013. 64p. (J). (978-1-4351-5030-0(9)) Barnes & Noble, Inc.

Cole, Michael D. The Columbia Space Shuttle Disaster: From First Liftoff to Tragic Final Flight. 2003. (Countdown to Space Ser.). (Illus.). 48p. (J). lib. bdg. 25.27 (978-0-7660-2295-9(1)) Enslow Pubs., Inc.

Collison, Cathy & Campbell, Janis. G Is for Galaxy: An Out of This World Alphabet. Stacy, Alan, illus. rev. ed. 2006. (Science Ser.). (ENG.). 40p. (J). (gr. k-5). pap. 7.95 (978-1-58536-335-3(9)) Sleeping Bear Pr.

Countdown to Space, 40 bks. , Set. (Illus.). (YA). (gr. 4-10). lib. bdg. 758.00 (978-0-89490-562-9(7)) Enslow Pubs., Inc.

Crompton, Samuel Willard. Sputnik/Explorer I: The Race to Conquer Space. 2007. (Milestones in American History Ser.). (Illus.). 106p. (YA). (gr. 7-12). lib. bdg. 35.00 (978-0-7910-9357-3(3)) Facts On File, Inc.

Culp, Jennifer. Neil DeGrasse Tyson. 2014. (Great Science Writers Ser.). (Illus.). 112p. (J). (gr. 7-12). 35.60 (978-1-4777-7691-9(5)) Rosen Publishing Group, Inc., The.

Dakers, Diane. Chris Hadfield: Inspiring New Generations to Explore Space. 2015. (Crabtree Groundbreaker Biographies Ser.). (ENG., Illus.). 112p. (J). (gr. 5-8). (978-0-7787-2558-9(8)) Crabtree Publishing Co.

Daynes, Katie. Living in Space. Fox, Christyan & Pang, Alex, illus. 2003. (Usborne Beginners Ser.). 32p. (J). (gr. 1). lib. bdg. 12.99 (978-1-58086-930-0(0), Usborne) EDC Publishing.

Daynes, Katie & Wray, Zoe. Life in Space. Fox, Christyan & Pang, Alex, illus. 2008. (Usborne Beginners Ser.). 32p. (J). (978-0-545-06963-2(7)) Scholastic, Inc.

DiPrimio, Peter. Neil Degrasse Tyson. 2015. (ENG., Illus.). 32p. (J). 26.50 (978-1-62469-090-7(4)) Purple Toad Publishing, Inc.

Down, Heather, text. Postcards from Space: The Chris Hadfield Story. 2014. (Illus.). 48p. (978-1-894813-68-6(5)) Wintertickle Pr.

Dugan, Christine. La Exploración Del Espacio. 2017. (TIME for Kids en Español - Level 3 Ser.). (SPA.). 32p. (gr. 3-3). lib. bdg. 31.99 **(978-1-5157-5181-6(3))** Time for Kids Inc AUS. Dist: Capstone Pub.

Dunn, Joe. Moon Landing, 1 vol. Espinosa, Rod et al, illus. 2007. (Graphic History Ser.). (ENG.). 32p. (gr. 3-6). 28.50 (978-1-60270-078-9(8), Graphic Planet- Nonfiction) ABDO Publishing Co.

Dunn, Joeming & Dunn, Ben. Albert II: The 1st Monkey in Space, 1 vol. 2011. (Famous Firsts: Animals Making History Ser.). (ENG., Illus.). 32p. (YA). (gr. 3-6). 28.50 (978-1-61641-637-9(8)) Magic Wagon.

—Laika: The 1st Dog in Space, 1 vol. 2011. (Famous Firsts: Animals Making History Ser.). (ENG., Illus.). 32p. (YA). (gr. 3-6). 28.50 (978-1-61641-641-6(6)) Magic Wagon.

Elish, Dan. NASA. 2006. (Kaleidoscope Space Ser.). (Illus.). 48p. (gr. 3-7). lib. bdg. 20.95 (978-0-7614-2046-0(0), Benchmark Bks.) Marshall Cavendish Corp.

Encyclopaedia Britannica, Inc. Staff, compiled by. Space Exploration. 2008. 49.95 (978-1-59339-689-3(9)) Encyclopaedia Britannica, Inc.

Engdahl, Sylvia. Challenger Disaster. Greenhaven Press Editors, ed. 2013. (Perspectives on Modern World History Ser.). (ENG., Illus.). 224p. (gr. 10-12). lib. bdg. 47.80 (978-0-7377-6365-2(5), Greenhaven Pr., Inc.) Cengage Gale.

Exploring Space, Revised Edition. 2nd rev. ed. 2009. (Discovery & Exploration Ser.). (Illus.). 120p. (gr. 5-8). 35.00 (978-1-60413-188-8(8), Chelsea Hse.) Facts On File, Inc.

Eyewitness - Space Exploration. 2014. (DK Eyewitness Bks.). (ENG., Illus.). 72p. (J). (gr. 3-7). lib. bdg. 19.99 (978-1-4654-2621-5(3), DK Children) Dorling Kindersley Publishing, Inc.

Famighetti, Robert, et al. How Does a Spacecraft Reach the Moon? 2009. (Science in the Real World Ser.). (Illus.). 32p. (gr. 4-6). 28.00 (978-1-60413-470-4(4), Chelsea Clubhouse) Facts On File, Inc.

Felix, Rebecca. 12 Things to Know about Space Exploration. 2015. (ENG., Illus.). 32p. (J). (978-1-63235-032-9(7)) Pr. Room Editions LLC.

Ferrie, Chris. Rocket Science for Babies. 2017. (Baby University Ser.: 0). (ENG., Illus.). 24p. (J). bds. 9.99 **(978-1-4926-5625-8(9)**, Sourcebooks Jabberwocky) Sourcebooks, Inc.

Fradin, Dennis Brindell. The First Lunar Landing. 2009. (Turning Points in U. S. History Ser.). 48p. (gr. 3-18). 31.36 (978-0-7614-4256-1(1)) Marshall Cavendish Corp.

Franklin, Kent. Exploring Earth & Space Systems. 2006. 96p. pap. 9.95 (978-1-4116-3469-5(1)) Lulu Pr., Inc.

Furgang, Kathy. Rocket Science & Spacecraft Fundamentals. 2017. (From Earth to the Stars Ser.). 48p. (gr. 10-12). pap. 14.05 **(978-1-68048-673-5(X)**, Britannica Educational Publishing) Rosen Publishing Group, Inc., The.

Galvin, Laura Gates. Alphabet of Space. Bond, Higgins, illus. (ENG.). 40p. 2009. 9.95 (978-1-59249-990-8(2)) 2007. (J). (gr. -1-k). 15.95 (978-1-59249-656-3(3)) Soundprints.

Gibson, Karen Bush. Women in Space: 23 Stories of First Flights, Scientific Missions, & Gravity-Breaking Adventures. 2014. (Women of Action Ser.). (ENG., Illus.). 240p. (YA). (gr. 7). 19.95 (978-1-61374-844-2(2)) Chicago Review Pr., Inc.

Gifford, Clive. Astronomy, Astronauts, & Space Exploration. 2015. (Watch This Space! Ser.). (ENG., Illus.). 32p. (J). (gr. 3-7). lib. bdg. (978-0-7787-2021-8(7)) Crabtree Publishing Co.

Goldsworthy, Steve. Famous Explorers. 2011. (J). (gr. 4-6). pap. 13.95 (978-1-61690-636-8(7), AV2 by Weigl); (Illus.). 32p. (YA). (gr. 2-5). 28.55 (978-1-61690-632-0(4)) Weigl Pubs., Inc.

Goldsworthy, Steve. Space Explorers. 2017. (J). **(978-1-4896-5815-9(7)**, AV2 by Weigl) Weigl Pubs., Inc.

Gonzalez, Lissette. Astronauts in Action. (Dangerous Jobs Ser.). 24p. 2009. (gr. 2-3). 42.50 (978-1-61512-132-8(3), PowerKids Pr.) 2007. (Illus.). (J). (gr. 3-7). lib. bdg. 22.60 (978-1-4042-3776-6(3)) Rosen Publishing Group, Inc., The.

Gross, Miriam. All about Astronauts. 2009. (Blast Off! Ser.). 24p. (gr. 2-5). (Illus.). (J). pap. 8.25 (978-1-4358-3137-7(3)); 42.50 (978-1-61511-614-0(1)) Rosen Publishing Group, Inc., The. (PowerKids Pr.).

—All about Space Missions. 2009. (Blast Off! Ser.). 24p. (gr. 2-3). 42.50 (978-1-61511-623-2(0), PowerKids Pr.) Rosen Publishing Group, Inc., The.

Gross, Miriam J. All about Astronauts. 2009. (Blast Off! Ser.). 24p. (J). (gr. 2-5). lib. bdg. 22.60 (978-1-4358-2739-4(2), PowerKids Pr.) Rosen Publishing Group, Inc., The.

—All about Space Missions. 2009. (Blast Off! Ser.). 24p. (J). (gr. 2-5). (ENG.). pap. 8.25 (978-1-4358-3138-4(1)); lib. bdg. 22.60 (978-1-4358-2740-0(6)) Rosen Publishing Group, Inc., The. (PowerKids Pr.).

Grove, Tim & National Air and Space Museum, National Air. Milestones of Flight: From Hot-Air Balloons to SpaceShipOne. 2016. (ENG., Illus.). 112p. (J). (gr. 5-9). 21.95 (978-1-4197-2003-1(1), Abrams Bks. for Young Readers) Abrams, Inc.

Hamilton, S. L. Robots & Rovers. 2011. (Xtreme Space Ser.). (Illus.). 32p. (gr. 3-9). 27.07 (978-1-61714-738-8(9), A&D Xtreme) ABDO Publishing Co.

Hansen, Ole Steen. Space Flight. 2003. (Story of Flight Ser.). (ENG., Illus.). 32p. (J). (gr. 2-9). lib. bdg. (978-0-7787-1207-7(9)) Crabtree Publishing Co.

Harris, Joseph. Space Exploration: The Impact of Science & Technology. 2009. (Pros & Cons Ser.). (ENG.). 64p. (YA). (gr. 5-9). lib. bdg. 35.00 (978-1-4339-1989-3(3)) Stevens, Gareth Publishing LLLP.

Hartman, Eve & Meshbesher, Wendy. Mission to Mars, 1 vol. 2011. (Science Missions Ser.). (ENG.). 56p. (gr. 3-3). 34.65 (978-1-4109-3989-0(8), Raintree Freestyle Express) Heinemann-Raintree.

Hense, Mary, et al. How Astronauts Use Math. 2009. (Math in the Real World Ser.). 32p. (gr. 4-6). 28.00 (978-1-60413-610-4(3), Chelsea Clubhouse) Facts On File, Inc.

Hermsen, Sarah. Space Exploration Library Cumulative Index. 2004. (Space Exploration Reference Library). (ENG.). 42p. (J). lib. bdg. 5.00 (978-0-7876-9214-8(X), UXL) Cengage Gale.

Hofer, Charles. Spacecraft. (World's Fastest Machines Ser.). 24p. 2009. (gr. 2-3). 42.50 (978-1-60854-855-2(4)) 2008. (Illus.). lib. bdg. 22.60 (978-1-4042-4178-7(7)) Rosen Publishing Group, Inc., The. (PowerKids Pr.).

Holcroft, John & Candlewick Press Staff. Space Exploration: Panorama Pops. Holcroft, John, illus. 2015. (ENG., Illus.). 30p. (J). (gr. k-4). 8.99 (978-0-7636-7699-5(3)) Candlewick Pr.

Jedicke, Peter. Great Moments in Space Exploration. 2007. (Scientific American Ser.). (Illus.). 72p. (YA). (gr. 5-9). lib. bdg. 30.00 (978-0-7910-9046-6(9)) Facts On File, Inc.

Jefferis, David & Irvine, Mat. Flight into Orbit. 2007. (Humans in Space Ser.). (ENG., Illus.). 32p. (J). (gr. 3-7). lib. bdg. (978-0-7787-3101-6(4)); pap. (978-0-7787-3115-3(4)) Crabtree Publishing Co.

—Race into Space. 2007. (Humans in Space Ser.). (ENG., Illus.). 32p. (J). (gr. 3-7). lib. bdg. (978-0-7787-3102-3(2)); pap. (978-0-7787-3116-0(2)) Crabtree Publishing Co.

Jeffrey, Gary. Incredible Space Missions. 2009. (Graphic Discoveries Ser.). (ENG.). 48p. (YA). (gr. 5-5). 58.50 (978-1-61512-929-4(4), Rosen Reference) Rosen Publishing Group, Inc., The.

—Incredible Space Missions. Lacey, Mike, illus. 2008. (Graphic Discoveries Ser.). (ENG.). 48p. (J). (gr. 5-9). lib. bdg. 31.95 (978-1-4042-1090-5(3)) Rosen Publishing Group, Inc., The.

—Incredible Space Missions: By Gary Jeffrey: Illustrated by Mike Lacey. Lacey, Mike, illus. 2008. (Graphic Nonfiction Ser.). (ENG.). 48p. (gr. 3-8). pap. 14.05 (978-1-4042-9595-7(X)) Rosen Publishing Group, Inc., The.

Jones, Tom. Ask the Astronaut: A Galaxy of Astonishing Answers to Your Questions on Spaceflight. 2016. (ENG., Illus.). 224p. (YA). (gr. 5-12). pap. 12.95 (978-1-58834-537-0(8), Smithsonian Bks.) Smithsonian Institution Scholarly Pr.

Karner, Julie. Space Disaster & Meteorite Alert! 2005. (Disaster Alert! Ser.). (ENG., Illus.). 32p. (J). (gr. 4-7). lib. bdg. (978-0-7787-1583-2(3)) Crabtree Publishing Co.

Kerrod, Robin. Dawn of the Space Age. 2004. (History of Space Exploration Ser.). (Illus.). 48p. (gr. 5-12). lib. bdg. 31.00 (978-0-8368-5705-4(4), Gareth Stevens Secondary Library) Stevens, Gareth Publishing LLLP.

Khan, Hena & Dyson, Marianne J. The Space Explorer's Guide to Out-Of-This-World Science. 2004. (Space University Ser.). (Illus.). 48p. (J). (978-0-439-55747-4(X)) Scholastic, Inc.

Kopp, Megan. Space Tech. 2017. (Illus.). 32p. (J). **(978-0-7787-3602-8(4))** Crabtree Publishing Co.

Kuhn, Betsy. The Race for Space: The United States & the Soviet Union Compete for the New Frontier. 2006. (People's History Ser.). (ENG., Illus.). 112p. (gr. 5-12). lib. bdg. 33.26 (978-0-8225-5984-9(6)) Lerner Publishing Group.

Lakin, Patricia. The Stellar Story of Space Travel. Burroughs, Scott, illus. 2016. (History of Fun Stuff Ser.). (ENG.). 48p. (J). (gr. 1-3). pap. 3.99 (978-1-4814-5623-4(7), Simon Spotlight) Simon Spotlight.

Lassieur, Allison. The Race to the Moon: An Interactive History Adventure, 1 vol. 2014. (You Choose: History Ser.). (ENG.). 112p. (gr. 3-4). 31.99 (978-1-4765-4185-3(X), You Choose Bks.) Capstone Press of Coughlan Cos.

Linde, Barbara M. Rocket Scientists, 01 vols., 1. 2016. (Out of the Lab: Extreme Jobs in Science Ser.). (ENG., Illus.). 32p. (J). pap. 10.00 (978-1-4994-1855-2(8), PowerKids Pr.) Rosen Publishing Group, Inc., The.

Mason, Roger. Space Race - Space Busters. 2004. pap. 48.30 (978-1-4109-0294-8(3)) Harcourt Schl. Pubs.

Mattern, Joanne. Astronautas. 2004. (Trabajo en Grupo (Working Together) Ser.). (SPA & ENG., Illus.). 24p. (J). (gr. 1-4). lib. bdg. 22.60 (978-0-8239-6842-8(1)) Rosen Publishing Group, Inc., The.

McAneney, Caitie. Mujeres en la Exploracion Del Espacio (Women in Space) 2015. (Ellas Abrieron Camino (Women Groundbreakers) Ser.). (ENG & SPA.). 32p. (J). (gr. 4-5). 26.25 (978-1-4994-0551-4(0), PowerKids Pr.) Rosen Publishing Group, Inc., The.

McCarthy, Meghan. Astronaut Handbook. 2008. (ENG., Illus.). 40p. (J). (gr. -1-2). 16.99 *(978-0-375-84459-1(7)*, Knopf Bks. for Young Readers) Random Hse. Children's Bks.

McConnell, William S., ed. Living Through the Space Race. 2006. (Living Through the Cold War Ser.). (ENG., Illus.). 135p. (J). (gr. 10-12). lib. bdg. 35.75 *(978-0-7377-2134-8(0)*, Greenhaven Pr., Inc.) Cengage Gale.

McGowen, Tom. Space Race: The Mission, the Men, the Moon. 2008. (America's Living History Ser.). (Illus.). 128p. (J). (gr. 5-9). lib. bdg. 33.27 *(978-0-7660-2910-1(7))* Enslow Pubs., Inc.

Miller, Gary. The Outer Limits: The Future of Space Exploration. 2009. (Current Science Ser.). (ENG.). 48p. (gr. 4-7). (YA). lib. bdg. 31.00 *(978-1-4339-2242-8(8))*; (J). pap. 8.95 *(978-1-4339-2246-6(0)*, Gareth Stevens Learning Library) Stevens, Gareth Publishing LLLP.

Miller, Ron. Space Exploration. 2007. (Space Innovations Ser.). (ENG., Illus.). 112p. (gr. 6-8). lib. bdg. 31.93 *(978-0-8225-7155-1(2))* Lerner Publishing Group.

Mitchell, Don. Liftoff: A Photobiography of John Glenn. 2006. (Photobiographies Ser.). (ENG., Illus.). 64p. (J). (gr. 5-7). 17.95 *(978-0-7922-5899-5(1))*; lib. bdg. 27.90 *(978-0-7922-5900-8(9))* National Geographic Society. (National Geographic Children's Bks.).

Moore, Gareth. Space Puzzles. 2016. (Brain Game Treasure Hunts Ser.). (ENG., Illus.). 32p. (J). (gr. 3-6). 26.65 *(978-1-5124-0624-5(4))* Lerner Publishing Group.

Morris, Neil. What Does Space Exploration Do for Us?, 1 vol. 2011. (Earth, Space, & Beyond Ser.). (ENG.). 48p. (gr. 3-3). pap. 9.49 *(978-1-4109-4183-1(3)*, Raintree Freestyle Express); (gr. 3-3). 34.65 *(978-1-4109-4177-0(9)*, Raintree Freestyle Express); (gr. 6-6). 34.65 *(978-1-4109-4159-6(0)*, Raintree Freestyle) Heinemann-Raintree.

Morris, Ting & Morris, Neil. Space. Turvey, Raymond, illus. 2006. (Sticky Fingers Ser.). 32p. (J). lib. bdg. 27.10 *(978-1-59771-032-9(6))* Sea-To-Sea Pubns.

Moskal, Greg. The History of Space Exploration: Sequencing Events Chronologically on a Timeline. 2009. (PowerMath Ser.). (ENG., Illus.). 24p. (gr. 3-4). pap. 8.25 *(978-0-8239-8850-1(3)*, PowerKids Pr.) Rosen Publishing Group, Inc., The.

Murphy, Patricia J. Explorando el Espacio con una Astronauta/Exploring Space with an Astronaut. 2008. (I Like Science! Bilingual Ser.). (ENG & SPA., Illus.). 24p. (J). (gr. 1-3). lib. bdg. 22.60 *(978-0-7660-2977-4(8)*, Enslow Elementary) Enslow Pubs., Inc.

—Exploring Space with an Astronaut. 2004. (I Like Science! Ser.). (Illus.). 24p. (J). lib. bdg. 22.60 *(978-0-7660-2268-3(4))* Enslow Pubs., Inc.

Nagelhout, Ryan. Astronauts, 01 vols., 1. 2016. (Out of the Lab: Extreme Jobs in Science Ser.). (ENG., Illus.). 32p. (J). pap. 10.00 *(978-1-5081-4509-7(1)*, PowerKids Pr.) Rosen Publishing Group, Inc., The.

Nardo, Don. Destined for Space: Our Story of Exploration, 1 vol. 2012. (Smithsonian Ser.). (ENG.). 64p. (gr. 4-5). pap. 8.95 *(978-1-4296-8024-0(5))*; pap. 53.70 *(978-1-4296-8524-5(7))* Capstone Press of Coughlan Cos.

Nelson, Maria. Life on the International Space Station. 2013. (Extreme Jobs in Extreme Places Ser.). (Illus.). 32p. (gr. 3-6). 26.60 *(978-1-4339-8507-2(1))*; pap. 10.50 *(978-1-4339-8508-9(X))* Stevens, Gareth Publishing LLLP. (Gareth Stevens Learning Library).

Nicolson, Cynthia. Discover Space. Slavin, Bill, illus. 2005. 32p. (J). lib. bdg. 15.38 *(978-1-4242-1193-7(X))* Fitzgerald Bks.

Ohlin, Nancy. The Space Race. Simo, Roger, illus. 2017. (Blast Back! Ser.). (ENG.). 112p. (J). (gr. 2-5). pap. 5.99 ***(978-1-4998-0452-2(0))*** Little Bee Books Inc.

Outer Space. Date not set. (Illus.). 12p. (J). 3.98 *(978-1-4054-0498-3(1))* Parragon, Inc.

Oxlade, Chris. Why Why Why... Do Astronauts Float in Space? 2010. (Why Why Why Ser.). 32p. (J). (gr. 1-3). lib. bdg. 18.95 *(978-1-4222-1578-4(4))* Mason Crest.

Paris, Stephanie. Siglo Xxii: El Futuro Del Espacio. 2016. (TIME for Kids en Español - Level 5 Ser.). (SPA.). 64p. (gr. 5-5). lib. bdg. 31.99 *(978-1-5157-2936-5(2))* Time for Kids Inc AUS. Dist: Capstone Pub.

Parker, Steve. In Space. 2010. (J). 28.50 *(978-1-59920-285-3(9))* Black Rabbit Bks.

—In Space. 2011. (Future Transport Ser.). (Illus.). 32p. (J). (gr. 4). 28.50 *(978-1-60870-778-2(4))* Marshall Cavendish GBR. Dist: Marshall Cavendish Corp.

Parks, Peggy J. Space Research. 2010. (Inside Science Ser.). (Illus.). 96p. (J). (gr. 7-12). 26.95 *(978-1-60152-111-8(1)*, 1316146) ReferencePoint Pr., Inc.

Peterson, Judy Monroe. Exploring Space: Astronauts & Astronomers. 2009. (Extreme Scientists Ser.). 24p. (gr. 2-3). 42.50 *(978-1-61512-451-0(9)*, PowerKids Pr.) Rosen Publishing Group, Inc., The.

Rauf, Don & Vescia, Monique. Choose Your Own Career Adventure at NASA. 2016. (Bright Futures Press: Choose Your Own Career Adventure Ser.). (ENG., Illus.). 32p. (J). (gr. 4-6). 29.93 *(978-1-63471-913-1(1)*, 208973) Cherry Lake Publishing.

Red Bird Press Staff. Amazing Spaceships. 2004. (Build Your Own Ser.). 20p. (J). pap. 5.95 *(978-1-902626-70-3(2))* Red Bird Publishing GBR. Dist: Weatherhill, Inc.

Robertson, Ann E. The Militarization of Space. 2011. (Global Issues Ser.). 408p. (C). (gr. 9). 45.00 *(978-0-8160-7873-8(4))* Facts On File, Inc.

Rooney, Anne. Space Record Breakers. 2014. (ENG., Illus.). 128p. (J). (gr. 3). pap. 14.95 *(978-1-78312-072-7(X))* Carlton Bks., Ltd. GBR. Dist: Sterling Publishing Co., Inc.

Royston, Angela. Astronauts Working in Space. 2010. (Big Picture: People & Culture Ser.). (ENG.). 24p. (gr. 1-2). pap. 41.70 *(978-1-4296-5819-5(3)*, First Facts) Capstone Press of Coughlan Cos.

Rusch, Elizabeth. The Mighty Mars Rovers: The Incredible Adventures of Spirit & Opportunity. (Scientists in the Field Ser.). (ENG., Illus.). 80p. (J). (gr. 5-7). 2017. pap. 9.99 *(978-0-544-93246-3(3)*, HMH Books For Young Readers) 2012. 18.99 *(978-0-547-47881-4(X))* Houghton Mifflin Harcourt Publishing Co.

—The Mighty Mars Rovers: The Incredible Adventures of Spirit & Opportunity. 2017. (Scientists in the Field Ser.). (ENG.). (J). (gr. 5-7). lib. bdg. 20.85 ***(978-0-606-39812-1(0))*** Turtleback Bks.

Rustad, Martha E. H. NASA, 1 vol. 2012. (Exploring Space Ser.). (ENG.). 24p. (gr. k-1). lib. bdg. 26.65 *(978-1-4296-7581-9(0)*, Pebble Plus) Capstone Press of Coughlan Cos.

Saari, Peggy. Primary Sources - Space Exploration. 2004. (Space Exploration Reference Library). (ENG., Illus.). 203p. (J). lib. bdg. 106.00 *(978-0-7876-9213-1(1)*, UXL) Cengage Gale.

Salzmann, Mary Elizabeth. Astronauts, 1 vol. 2015. (ENG., Illus.). 24p. (J). 17.95 *(978-1-62403-742-9(9))* ABDO Publishing Co.

Schmermund, Elizabeth. Telescopes, Probes, Spacecraft, & the Future of Space Exploration. 2016. (Space Systems Ser.). 112p. (J). lib. bdg. 42.79 *(978-1-5026-2293-8(9))* Cavendish Square Publishing.

Shirley, Rebekah Joy. I Want to Be an Astronaut. 2011. (Let's Play Dress up Ser.). (ENG., Illus.). 24p. (J). (gr. k-3). pap. 10.60 *(978-1-61533-397-4(5))*; lib. bdg. 25.25 *(978-1-61533-359-2(2))* Windmill Bks.

Silverman, Buffy. Mars Missions: A Space Discovery Guide. 2017. (Space Discovery Guides). (ENG.). 48p. (J). (gr. 4-6). 16.99 ***(978-1-5124-3809-3(X)***, Lerner Pubns.); 47.99 ***(978-1-5124-2795-0(0)***, Lerner Pubns.); 47.99 ***(978-1-5124-3810-9(3)***, Lerner Pubns.); (Illus.). 31.99 *(978-1-5124-2585-7(0))* Lerner Publishing Group.

Simon, Seymour. Space Travelers. 2004. (See More Readers Ser.). (Illus.). (gr. 2-4). 13.95 *(978-0-7569-4335-6(3))* Perfection Learning Corp.

Siy, Alexandra. Cars on Mars: Roving the Red Planet. 2011. (ENG., Illus.). 64p. (J). (gr. 3-7). pap. 9.95 *(978-1-57091-463-8(X))* Charlesbridge Publishing, Inc.

Smibert, Angie. Amazing Feats of Aerospace Engineering, 1 vol. 2014. (Great Achievements in Engineering Ser.). (ENG.). 112p. (J). (gr. 6-12). lib. bdg. 35.64 *(978-1-62403-425-1(X)*, Essential Library) ABDO Publishing Co.

Smithsonian Institution Staff, contrib. by. Destined for Space: Our Story of Exploration, 1 vol. 2012. (Smithsonian Ser.). (ENG.). 64p. (gr. 4-5). lib. bdg. 34.65 *(978-1-4296-7540-6(3))* Capstone Press of Coughlan Cos.

Space Exploration. 2014. (DK Eyewitness Bks.). (ENG., Illus.). 72p. (J). (gr. 3-7). pap. 9.99 *(978-1-4654-2616-1(7)*, DK Children) Dorling Kindersley Publishing, Inc.

Space Exploration: Science Technology Engineering. 2014. (Calling All Innovators: a Career for You Ser.). (ENG.). 64p. (J). lib. bdg. 32.00 *(978-0-531-20615-7(7))* Scholastic Library Publishing.

Sparrow, Giles & John, Judith. Shuttles & Space Missions. 2016. (Discoveries in Space Science Ser.). (ENG., Illus.). 80p. (YA). (gr. 9-9). lib. bdg. 35.64 *(978-1-5026-1016-4(7)*, 1398739) Cavendish Square Publishing.

Tagliaferro, Linda. Who Walks in Space? Working in Space. 2010. (Wild Work Ser.). (ENG.). 32p. (gr. 1-2). 29.99 *(978-1-4109-3849-7(2)*, Read Me!) Heinemann-Raintree.

Trotman, Felicity. Exploration of Space. 2010. (History of Exploration Ser.). 48p. 32.80 *(978-1-84898-302-1(6))* Black Rabbit Bks.

Waxman, Laura Hamilton. Exploring the International Space Station. 2011. (Searchlight Books Whats Amazing about Space Ser.). (ENG., Illus.). (gr. 3-5). pap. 51.01 *(978-0-7613-8416-8(2))*; 40p. pap. 8.95 *(978-0-7613-7879-2(0))*; 40p. lib. bdg. 27.93 *(978-0-7613-5443-7(3))* Lerner Publishing Group.

West, David. Ten of the Best Adventures in Space. 2015. (Ten of the Best: Stories of Exploration & Adventure Ser.). (ENG., Illus.). 24p. (J). (gr. 3-6). *(978-0-7787-1836-9(0))* Crabtree Publishing Co.

Willett, Edward. Careers in Outer Space: New Business Opportunities. 2009. (Career Resource Library). 192p. (gr. 7-12). 63.90 *(978-1-60853-401-2(4))* Rosen Publishing Group, Inc., The.

Wimmer, Teresa. National Aeronautics & Space Administration. (Agents of Government Ser.). 48p. 2016. (ENG.). (J). (gr. 5-9). pap. 12.00 *(978-1-62832-148-7(2)*, Creative Paperbacks) 2015. (Illus.). (YA). *(978-1-60818-547-4(8)*, Creative Education) Creative Co., The.

Wittrock, Jeni. Laika the Space Dog: First Hero in Outer Space, 1 vol. Toth, Shannon, illus. 2014. (Animal Heroes Ser.). (ENG.). 32p. (gr. k-2). 28.65 *(978-1-4795-5463-8(4))* Picture Window Bks.

Wittrock, Jeni, et al. Animal Heroes, 1 vol. 2014. (Animal Heroes Ser.). (ENG.). 32p. (gr. k-2). 114.60 *(978-1-4795-5555-0(X))* Picture Window Bks.

Woods, Michael & Woods, Mary B. Space Disasters. 2008. (Disasters up Close Ser.). (ENG., Illus.). 64p. (gr. 4-8). lib. bdg. 27.93 *(978-0-8225-6775-2(X)*, Lerner Pubns.) Lerner Publishing Group.

Wooster, Patricia. An Illustrated Timeline of Space Exploration, 1 vol. Doty, Eldon, illus. 2011. (Visual Timelines in History Ser.). (ENG.). 32p. (gr. 3-4). lib. bdg. 28.65 *(978-1-4048-6660-7(4))* Picture Window Bks.

Zappa, Marcia. NASA, 1 vol. 2011. (Universe Set 2 Ser.). (ENG., Illus.). 32p. (gr. 3-5). 27.07 *(978-1-61714-690-9(0)*, Buddy Bks.) ABDO Publishing Co.

—Space Exploration, 1 vol. 2011. (Universe Set 2 Ser.). (ENG., Illus.). 32p. (gr. 3-5). 27.07 *(978-1-61714-692-3(7)*, Buddy Bks.) ABDO Publishing Co.

Zobel, Derek. NASA. 2010. (Exploring Space Ser.). (ENG., Illus.). 24p. (J). (gr. k-3). lib. bdg. 25.95 *(978-1-60014-293-2(1)*, Blastoff! Readers) Bellwether Media.

ASTRONAUTICS—BIOGRAPHY

Alagna, Magdalena. Mae Jemison: The First African American Woman in Space. 2004. (Women Hall of Famers in Mathematics & Science Ser.). (Illus.). 112p. (gr. 5-8). lib. bdg. 34.60 *(978-0-8239-3878-0(6)*, Rosen Reference) Rosen Publishing Group, Inc., The.

Aldrin, Buzz. Reaching for the Moon. Minor, Wendell, illus. (ENG.). 40p. (J). (gr. 1-4). 2008. 6.99 *(978-0-06-055447-7(9)*, Collins) 2005. 17.99 *(978-0-06-055445-3(2))* HarperCollins Pubs.

—Reaching for the Moon. Minor, Wendell, illus. unabr. ed. 2005. (Picture Book Readalong Ser.). (gr. k-4). 28.95 incl. audio compact disk *(978-1-59519-582-1(3))* Live Oak Media.

Benge, Janet & Benge, Geoff. Christian Heroes Then & Now - Alan Shepard: Higher & Faster. 2007. (Heroes of History Ser.). 229p. (J). (gr. 3-7). per. *(978-1-932096-41-5(8))* Emerald Bks.

Burleigh, Robert. Look Up! Henrietta Leavitt, Pioneering Woman Astronomer. Colón, Raúl, illus. 2013. (ENG.). 32p. (J). (gr. -1-3). 16.99 *(978-1-4169-5819-2(3)*, Simon & Schuster Bks. For Young Readers) Simon & Schuster/Paula Wiseman Bks.

Edwards, Roberta. Who Was Neil Armstrong? Harrison, Nancy & Marchesi, Stephen, illus. 2008. (Who Was? Ser.). (ENG.). 112p. (J). (gr. 3-7). pap. 5.99 *(978-0-448-44907-4(2)*, Grosset & Dunlap) Penguin Young Readers Group.

Gueldenpfennig, Sonia. Spectacular Women in Space, 1 vol. 2005. (Women's Hall of Fame Ser.). (ENG., Illus.). 112p. (J). (gr. 4-8). pap. 10.95 *(978-1-896764-88-7(6))* Second Story Pr. CAN. Dist: Orca Bk. Pubs. USA.

Holden, Henry M. Pioneering Astronaut Sally Ride: A MyReportLinks. com Book. 2004. (Space Flight Adventures & Disasters Ser.). (Illus.). 48p. (J). lib. bdg. 26.60 *(978-0-7660-5169-0(2)*, MyReportLinks.com Bks.) Enslow Pubs., Inc.

Indovino, Shaina Carmel. Women in Space. 2013. (J). *(978-1-4222-2923-1(8))* Mason Crest.

—Women in Space. Lee-Karlon, Ann, ed. 2013. (Major Women in Science Ser.: 10). 64p. (J). (gr. 7-18). 22.95 *(978-1-4222-2931-6(9))* Mason Crest.

Latham, Donna. Ellen Ochoa: Reach for the Stars! 2005. (Defining Moments Ser.). (Illus.). 32p. (J). (gr. 2-5). lib. bdg. 25.27 *(978-1-59716-076-6(8))* Bearport Publishing Co., Inc.

Padmanabhan, Anil. Kalpana Chawla: A Life. 2003. (Illus.). xi, 94p. pap. *(978-0-14-333586-3(3)*, Puffin) Penguin Publishing Group.

Peak, Doris-Jean. Wernher Von Braun: Alabama's Rocket Scientist. 2009. (Alabama Roots Biography Ser.). (Illus.). 112p. (J). *(978-1-59421-044-0(6))* Seacoast Publishing, Inc.

Smithsonian Institution Staff, creator. Astronauts & Other Space Heroes. 2007. (For Your Information Ser.). (Illus.). 80p. (J). (gr. 3-7). 16.99 *(978-0-06-089945-5(X))* Smithsonian Institution Pr.

Stine, Megan. Who Was Sally Ride? 2013. (Who Was... ? Ser.). lib. bdg. 16.00 *(978-0-606-31683-5(3)*, Turtleback) Turtleback Bks.

Stone, Tanya Lee. Ilan Ramon: Israel's First Astronaut. 2003. 48p. pap. 7.95 *(978-0-7613-2376-1(7))*; lib. bdg. 23.90 *(978-0-7613-2888-9(2))* Lerner Publishing Group. (Twenty-First Century Bks.).

Thiel, Kristin. Mae C. Jemison: First African American Woman in Space. 2017. (J). ***(978-1-5026-2751-3(5))*** Cavendish Square Publishing.

Ventura, Marne. Astrophysicist & Space Advocate Neil Degrasse Tyson. 2014. (STEM Trailblazer Bios Ser.). (ENG., Illus.). 32p. (gr. 2-5). lib. bdg. 26.60 *(978-1-4677-2461-6(0)*, Lerner Pubns.) Lerner Publishing Group.

Wukovits, John F. Ellen Ochoa, First Female Hispanic Astronaut. 2006. (Twentieth Century's Most Influential Hispanics Ser.). (ENG., Illus.). 104p. (YA). (gr. 7-12). lib. bdg. 34.80 *(978-1-59018-976-4(0)*, 1256844) Cengage Gale.

ASTRONAUTICS—DICTIONARIES

Dowswell, Paul. First Encyclopedia of Space. 2004. (First Encyclopedia Ser.). (SPA & ENG., Illus.). (J). (gr. 3-18). 1p. pap. 9.99 *(978-0-7945-0035-1(8)*, Usborne); 64p. lib. bdg. 17.95 *(978-1-58086-357-5(4))* EDC Publishing.

Nagel, Rob. Space Exploration - Almanac, 2 vols. 2004. (Space Exploration Reference Library). (ENG., Illus.). 400p. lib. bdg. 191.00 *(978-0-7876-9209-4(3)*, UXL) Cengage Gale.

ASTRONAUTICS—VOCATIONAL GUIDANCE

Ferguson, creator. Space Exploration. 2007. (Careers in Focus Ser.). (Illus.). 192p. (gr. 6-12). 32.95 *(978-0-8160-6570-7(5)*, Ferguson Publishing Co.) Facts On File, Inc.

Halls, Kelly Milner. Astronaut. 2009. (21st Century Skills Library: Cool Science Careers Ser.). (ENG.). 32p. (gr. 4-8). lib. bdg. 28.50 *(978-1-60279-502-0(9)*, 200308) Cherry Lake Publishing.

Hutson, Matt. Totally Amazing Careers in Aerospace. 2006. (J). 7.80 *(978-1-933798-03-5(3))* Sally Ride Science.

Peterson, Judy Monroe. Exploring Space: Astronauts & Astronomers. 2009. (Extreme Scientists Ser.). (Illus.). 24p. (YA). (gr. 2-5). lib. bdg. 22.60 *(978-1-4042-4528-0(6))* Rosen Publishing Group, Inc., The.

Sparrow, Giles. Astronauts. 2006. (Secrets of the Universe Ser.). (Illus.). 48p. (gr. 6-12). pap. 14.05 *(978-0-8368-7282-8(7))*; lib. bdg. 31.00 *(978-0-8368-7275-0(4))* Stevens, Gareth Publishing LLLP. (Gareth Stevens Secondary Library).

Tieck, Sarah. Astronauts, 1 vol. 2011. (Extreme Jobs Ser.). (ENG., Illus.). 32p. (J). (gr. 2-5). 28.50 *(978-1-61783-024-2(0))* ABDO Publishing Co.

West, David. Astronauts. Robins, Jim, illus. 2008. (Graphic Careers Ser.). 48p. (gr. 5-8). per. 14.05 *(978-1-4042-1462-0(3))*; (YA). lib. bdg. 31.95 *(978-1-4042-1461-3(5))* Rosen Publishing Group, Inc., The.

Willett, Edward. Careers in Outer Space: New Business Opportunities. 2005. (Career Resource Library). (Illus.). 192p. (YA). (gr. 7-12). lib. bdg. 34.60 *(978-0-8239-3358-7(X))* Rosen Publishing Group, Inc., The.

ASTRONAUTS

Alagna, Magdalena. Mae Jemison: The First African American Woman in Space. 2009. (Women Hall of Famers in Mathematics & Science Ser.). 112p. (gr. 5-8). 63.90 *(978-1-60854-813-2(9)*, Rosen Reference) Rosen Publishing Group, Inc., The.

Aldrin, Buzz. Look to the Stars. Minor, Wendell, illus. 2009. (ENG.). 40p. (J). (gr. 1-3). 17.99 *(978-0-399-24721-7(1)*, G.P. Putnam's Sons Books for Young Readers) Penguin Young Readers Group.

—Reaching for the Moon. Minor, Wendell, illus. (ENG.). 40p. (J). (gr. 1-4). 2008. 6.99 *(978-0-06-055447-7(9)*, Collins) 2005. 17.99 *(978-0-06-055445-3(2))* HarperCollins Pubs.

—Reaching for the Moon. Minor, Wendell, illus. unabr. ed. 2005. (Picture Book Readalong Ser.). (gr. k-4). 28.95 incl. audio compact disk *(978-1-59519-582-1(3))* Live Oak Media.

Anderson, AnnMarie. When I Grow up - Sally Ride. Kelley, Gerald, illus. 2015. (Scholastic Reader Level 3 Ser.). (ENG.). 32p. (J). (gr. 1-2). pap. 3.99 *(978-0-545-60983-8(6)*, Scholastic Paperbacks) Scholastic, Inc.

Appleby, Alex. I Can Be an Astronaut. 2014. (When I Grow Up Ser.). 24p. (J). (gr. k-2). 22.60 *(978-1-4824-0754-9(X))* Stevens, Gareth Publishing LLLP.

—Puedo Ser un Astronauta / I Can Be an Astronaut. 2014. (Cuando Sea Grande / When I Grow Up Ser.). (SPA.). 24p. (J). (gr. k-2). 22.60 *(978-1-4824-0863-8(5))* Stevens, Gareth Publishing LLLP.

Ashley, Michele. Where Is This Astronaut? 2014. (Little Books of Answers: Level a Ser.). (Illus.). 16p. (gr. k-2). pap. 7.95 *(978-1-927136-06-5(7))* Three Crows Media NZL. Dist: RiverStream Publishing.

Astronauts. (Awesome Adventures Ser.). 16p. (J). *(978-2-7643-0119-7(7))* Phidal Publishing, Inc./Editions Phidal, Inc.

Astronauts: Level K, 6 vols. (Wonder Worldtm Ser.). 16p. 34.95 *(978-0-7802-4595-2(4))* Wright Group/McGraw-Hill.

Bailey, Gerry & Foster, Karen. Armstrong's Moon Rock. Radford, Karen & Noyes, Leighton, illus. 2008. (Stories of Great People Ser.). (ENG.). 40p. (J). (gr. 3-8). lib. bdg. *(978-0-7787-3684-4(9))*; (gr. 5-8). pap. *(978-0-7787-3706-3(3))* Crabtree Publishing Co.

Baker, David. Living in Space. 2008. (Exploring Space Ser.). (Illus.). 32p. (J). (gr. 4-6). lib. bdg. 26.00 *(978-1-59036-769-8(3))* Weigl Pubs., Inc.

Baker, David & Kissock, Heather. Living in Space. 2008. (Exploring Space Ser.). (Illus.). 32p. (J). (gr. 4-6). pap. 9.95 *(978-1-59036-770-4(7))* Weigl Pubs., Inc.

Barghoorn, Linda. Mae Jemison: Trailblazing Astronaut, Doctor, & Teacher. 2016. (Remarkable Lives Revealed Ser.). (ENG., Illus.). 32p. (J). (gr. 2-5). *(978-0-7787-2693-7(2))* Crabtree Publishing Co.

Berne, Emma Carlson. Totally Wacky Facts about Exploring Space. 2015. (Mind Benders Ser.). (ENG., Illus.). 112p. (gr. 1-3). lib. bdg. 23.32 *(978-1-4914-6524-0(7))* Capstone Press of Coughlan Cos.

—Totally Wacky Facts about Space. 2015. (Mind Benders Ser.). (ENG., Illus.). 240p. (gr. 1-3). pap. 7.95 *(978-1-4914-6526-4(3))* Capstone Press of Coughlan Cos.

Bindi, Paulo. Sally Ride: The Sky's the Limit. 2013. (InfoMax Readers Ser.). (ENG.). 24p. (J). (gr. 2-3). pap. 49.50 *(978-1-4777-2452-1(4))*; (Illus.). pap. 8.25 *(978-1-4777-2451-4(6))* Rosen Publishing Group, Inc., The. (Rosen Classroom).

Biskup, Agnieszka. Amazing Story of Space Travel. Pop Art Properties Staff, illus. 2013. (STEM Adventures Ser.). (ENG.). 32p. (gr. 3-4). 30.65 *(978-1-4765-0124-6(6)*, Graphic Library) Capstone Press of Coughlan Cos.

Braun, Eric. If I Were an Astronaut, 1 vol. Harmer, Sharon, illus. 2009. (Dream Big! Ser.). (ENG.). 24p. (gr. k-3). lib. bdg. 26.65 *(978-1-4048-5534-2(3))*; pap. 8.95 *(978-1-4048-5710-0(9))* Picture Window Bks.

Bredeson, Carmen. What Do Astronauts Do? 2008. (I Like Space! Ser.). (Illus.). 32p. (J). (gr. 3-7). lib. bdg. 23.94 *(978-0-7660-2942-2(5)*, Enslow Elementary) Enslow Pubs., Inc.

Bredeson, Carmen & Dyson, Marianne. Astronauts Explore the Galaxy. 2015. (Launch into Space! Ser.). (ENG.). 32p. (J). (gr. 3-4). pap. 10.52 *(978-0-7660-6813-1(7))* Enslow Pubs., Inc.

Bredeson, Carmen, et al. Astronauts Explore the Galaxy. 2015. (Launch into Space! Ser.). (ENG., Illus.). 32p. (J). (gr. 3-4). 25.27 *(978-0-7660-6815-5(3))* Enslow Pubs., Inc.

Brown, Carron. Space Station. Johnson, Bee, illus. 2016. (ENG.). 36p. (J). 12.99 *(978-1-61067-411-9(1))* Kane Miller.

Brown, Jonatha A. Neil Armstrong. 2005. (People We Should Know Ser.). 24p. (gr. 1-4). (SPA.). pap. 8.15 *(978-0-8368-4765-9(2))*; (Illus.). pap. 8.15 *(978-0-8368-4751-2(2))*; (SPA., Illus.). lib. bdg. 22.00 *(978-0-8368-4758-1(X))*; (Illus.). lib. bdg. 22.00 *(978-0-8368-4744-4(X))* Stevens, Gareth Publishing LLLP. (Weekly Reader Leveled Readers).

Buckley, Annie. Ellen Ochoa. 2007. (21st Century Skills Library: Life Skills Biographies Ser.). (ENG., Illus.). 48p. (gr. 4-8). lib. bdg. 31.36 *(978-1-60279-075-9(2)*, 200041) Cherry Lake Publishing.

Buckley, James, Jr., et al. Space Heroes, Level 3: Amazing Astronauts. 2003. (DK Readers Ser.: Level. 2). (ENG., Illus.). 48p. (J). (gr. 2-4). pap. 3.99 *(978-0-7894-9896-0(0)*, DK Children) Dorling Kindersley Publishing, Inc.

Calkhoven, Laurie. Mae Jemison. Dong, Monique, illus. 2016. (You Should Meet Ser.). (ENG.). 48p. (J). (gr. 1-3). pap. 3.99 *(978-1-4814-7649-2(1)*, Simon Spotlight) Simon Spotlight.

Caper, William. The Challenger Space Shuttle Explosion. 2016. (Code Red Ser.). (ENG.). 32p. (J). (gr. 2-7). pap. 8.95 *(978-1-944998-73-8(X))* Bearport Publishing Co., Inc.

Casil, Amy Sterling. Buzz Aldrin: The Pilot of the First Moon Landing. 2009. (Library of Astronaut Biographies Ser.). 112p. (gr. 5-8). 63.90 *(978-1-60853-519-4(3)*, Rosen Reference) Rosen Publishing Group, Inc., The.

Chambers, Catherine. Neil Armstrong, 1 vol. 2014. (Science Biographies Ser.). (ENG.). 32p. (gr. 2-4). lib. bdg. 30.65 *(978-1-4109-6237-9(7)*, Raintree Perspectives) Heinemann-Raintree.

Clay, Kathryn. Astronaut in Training. 2017. (Little Astronauts Ser.). (ENG., Illus.). 32p. (gr. 1-2). lib. bdg. 27.99 *(978-1-5157-3660-8(1))* Capstone Press of Coughlan Cos.

—Little Astronauts. 2017. (Little Astronauts Ser.). (ENG.). 32p. (gr. 1-2). 111.96 *(978-1-5157-3666-0(0))* Capstone Press of Coughlan Cos.

Clemson, Wendy & Clemson, David. Rocket to the Moon. 2007. (Math Adventures Ser.). (Illus.). 32p. (gr. 1-4). (SPA.). pap. 10.50 *(978-0-8368-8140-0(0))*; lib. bdg. 26.00 *(978-0-8368-7841-7(8))* Stevens, Gareth Publishing LLLP. (Gareth Stevens Learning Library).

Colins, Luke. Mae Jemison, 1 vol. 2014. (Great African-Americans Ser.). (ENG.). 24p. (gr. k-1). lib. bdg. 21.99 *(978-1-4765-3954-6(5)*, Pebble Bks.) Capstone Press of Coughlan Cos.

Collard, Sneed B., III. John Glenn: Hooked on Flying. 2008. (American Heroes Ser.). (Illus.). 48p. (J). (gr. 3-18). lib. bdg. 29.93 *(978-0-7614-3066-7(0)*, Benchmark Bks.) Marshall Cavendish Corp.

Dakers, Diane. Chris Hadfield: Inspiring New Generations to Explore Space. 2015. (Crabtree Groundbreaker Biographies Ser.). (ENG., Illus.). 112p. (J). (gr. 5-8). *(978-0-7787-2558-9(8))* Crabtree Publishing Co.

Deutsch, Stacia & Cohon, Rhody. John B. Herrington. (Sharing the American Dream Ser.). 64p. (YA). (gr. 7-12). 2009. 22.95 *(978-1-4222-0579-2(7))* 2007. pap. 9.95 *(978-1-4222-0747-5(1))* Mason Crest.

Dixon-Engel, Tara & Jackson, Mike. Neil Armstrong: One Giant Leap for Mankind. 2008. (Sterling Biographies(r) Ser.). (ENG., Illus.). 128p. (J). (gr. 5). pap. 5.95 *(978-1-4027-4496-9(X))* Sterling Publishing Co., Inc.

Donaldson, Chelsea. Chris Hadfield, 1 vol. 2014. (Canadian Biographies Ser.). (ENG.). 24p. (gr. k-1). 26.65 *(978-1-4914-1957-1(1),* Pebble Plus) Capstone Press of Coughlan Cos.

Down, Heather. Cartes Postales de L'Espace: L'Histoire de Chris Hadfield. Garon, Pierre, tr. 2013. 34p. pap. *(978-1-894813-69-3(3))* Wintertickle Pr.

Down, Heather, text. Postcards from Space: The Chris Hadfield Story. 2014. (Illus.). 48p. *(978-1-894813-68-6(5))* Wintertickle Pr.

Dugan, Christine. Living in Space, 1 vol. 2nd rev. ed. 2012. (Nonfiction Readers Ser.). (ENG.). 32p. (J). (gr. 3-3). pap. 8.99 *(978-1-4333-3675-1(8))* Teacher Created Materials, Inc.

Edison, Erin. Sally Ride, 1 vol. 2014. (Great Women in History Ser.). (ENG.). 24p. (gr. k-1). lib. bdg. 21.99 *(978-1-4765-4215-7(5),* Pebble Bks.) Capstone Press of Coughlan Cos.

Ertle-Rickard, Stephen. Astronaut. 2008. (321 Go! Ser.). (ENG., Illus.). 36p. pap. *(978-1-84167-781-1(7))* Ransom Publishing Ltd.

Feinstein, Stephen. Read about Neil Armstrong. 2005. (I Like Biographies! Ser.). (Illus.). 24p. (J). lib. bdg. 22.60 *(978-0-7660-2593-6(4),* Enslow Elementary) Enslow Pubs., Inc.

Feldman, Heather. Valentina Tereshkova: The First Woman in Space. (Space Firsts Ser.). 24p. 2009. (gr. 3-4). 42.50 *(978-1-60853-114-1(7))* 2003. (Illus.). (J). lib. bdg. 22.60 *(978-0-8239-6246-4(6))* Rosen Publishing Group, Inc., The. (PowerKids Pr.).

—Yuri Gagarin: The First Man in Space. 2003. (Space Firsts Ser.). (Illus.). 24p. (J). lib. bdg. 22.60 *(978-0-8239-6245-7(8),* PowerKids Pr.) Rosen Publishing Group, Inc., The.

Furgang, Adam. Human Spaceflight. 2017. (From Earth to the Stars Ser.). 48p. (gr. 10-12). pap. 14.05 ***(978-1-68048-669-8(1),*** Britannica Educational Publishing) Rosen Publishing Group, Inc., The.

Garcia, Juan. Neil Armstrong: First Man on the Moon. 2013. (InfoMax Readers Ser.). (ENG.). 24p. (J). (gr. 3-4). pap. 49.50 *(978-1-4777-2641-9(1));* (Illus.). pap. 8.25 *(978-1-4777-2640-2(3))* Rosen Publishing Group, Inc., The. (Rosen Classroom).

Gibson, Karen Bush. Women in Space: 23 Stories of First Flights, Scientific Missions, & Gravity-Breaking Adventures. 2014. (Women of Action Ser.). (ENG., Illus.). 240p. (YA). (gr. 7). 19.95 *(978-1-61374-844-2(2))* Chicago Review Pr., Inc.

Gifford, Clive. Astronomy, Astronauts, & Space Exploration. 2015. (Watch This Space! Ser.). (ENG., Illus.). 32p. (J). (gr. 3-7). lib. bdg. *(978-0-7787-2021-8(7))* Crabtree Publishing Co.

Goldberg, Jan. James Lovell: The Rescue of Apollo 13. (Library of Astronaut Biographies Ser.). 112p. (gr. 5-8). 2009. 63.90 *(978-1-60853-522-4(3))* 2004. (Illus.). lib. bdg. 34.60 *(978-0-8239-4459-0(X))* Rosen Publishing Group, Inc., The. (Rosen Reference).

Goldstein, Margaret J. Astronauts: A Space Discovery Guide. 2017. (Space Discovery Guides). (ENG.). 48p. (J). (gr. 4-6). 16.99 ***(978-1-5124-3800-0(6),*** Lerner Pubns.); 47.99 ***(978-1-5124-3801-7(4),*** Lerner Pubns.); 47.99 ***(978-1-5124-2793-6(4),*** Lerner Pubns.); (Illus.). 31.99 *(978-1-5124-2588-8(5))* Lerner Publishing Group.

Goldsworthy, Steve. Famous Explorers. 2011. (J). (gr. 4-6). pap. 13.95 *(978-1-61690-636-8(7),* AV2 by Weigl); (Illus.). 32p. (YA). (gr. 2-5). 28.55 *(978-1-61690-632-0(4))* Weigl Pubs., Inc.

Goldsworthy, Steve. Space Explorers. 2017. (J). ***(978-1-4896-5815-9(7),*** AV2 by Weigl) Weigl Pubs., Inc.

Gomez, Rebecca. Sally Ride, 1 vol. 2003. (First Biographies Ser.). (ENG., Illus.). 32p. (gr. k-4). 27.07 *(978-1-57765-948-8(1),* Buddy Bks.) ABDO Publishing Co.

Gonzalez, Lissette. Astronauts in Action. (Dangerous Jobs Ser.). 24p. 2009. (gr. 2-3). 42.50 *(978-1-61512-132-8(3),* PowerKids Pr.) 2007. (Illus.). (J). (gr. 3-7). lib. bdg. 22.60 *(978-1-4042-3776-6(3))* Rosen Publishing Group, Inc., The.

Goodman, Susan E. Ultimate Field Trip #5: Blasting off to Space Academy. Doolittle, Michael J., illus. 2011. (ENG.). 48p. (J). (gr. 3-7). pap. 19.99 *(978-1-4424-4345-7(6),* Atheneum Bks. for Young Readers) Simon & Schuster Children's Publishing.

Greenberger, Robert. Gus Grissom: The Tragedy of Apollo 1. 2009. (Library of Astronaut Biographies Ser.). 112p. (gr. 5-8). 63.90 *(978-1-60853-521-7(5),* Rosen Reference) Rosen Publishing Group, Inc., The.

Gross, Miriam. All about Astronauts. 2009. (Blast Off! Ser.). 24p. (gr. 2-5). (Illus.). (J). pap. 8.25 *(978-1-4358-3137-7(3));* 42.50 *(978-1-61511-614-0(1))* Rosen Publishing Group, Inc., The. (PowerKids Pr.).

Gross, Miriam J. All about Astronauts. 2009. (Blast Off! Ser.). 24p. (J). (gr. 2-5). lib. bdg. 22.60 *(978-1-4358-2739-4(2),* PowerKids Pr.) Rosen Publishing Group, Inc., The.

Gueldenpfennig, Sonia. Women in Space Who Changed the World. 2011. (Great Women of Achievement Ser.). (ENG., Illus.). 112p. (YA). (gr. 5-8). lib. bdg. 34.60 *(978-1-4488-5998-6(0),* Rosen Reference) Rosen Publishing Group, Inc., The.

Guzmán, Lila & Guzmán, Rick. Ellen Ochoa: First Latina Astronaut. 2006. (Famous Latinos Ser.). (Illus.). 32p. (J). (gr. 4-7). lib. bdg. 23.94 *(978-0-7660-2642-1(6),* Enslow Elementary) Enslow Pubs., Inc.

—Ellen Ochoa: La Primera Astronauta Latina. (Latinos Famosos Ser.). 32p. 2014. (gr. 2). pap. 7.95 *(978-0-7660-6086-9(1))* 2007. (SPA., Illus.). (J). (gr. 3-7). lib. bdg. 23.94 *(978-0-7660-2677-3(9),* Enslow Elementary) Enslow Pubs., Inc.

Hamilton, S. L. Astronaut. 2015. 32p. pap. 27.07 *(978-1-62403-756-6(9))* ABDO Publishing Co.

—Astronaut Firsts. 2011. (Xtreme Space Ser.). (Illus.). 32p. (gr. 3-9). 27.07 *(978-1-61714-736-4(2),* A&D Xtreme) ABDO Publishing Co.

Hayden, Kate. Astronaut: Living in Space. 2013. (DK Reader Level 2 Ser.). (gr. k-3). lib. bdg. 13.55 *(978-0-613-24252-3(1),* Turtleback) Turtleback Bks.

Holden, Henry M. Pioneering Astronaut Sally Ride: A MyReportLinks.com Book. 2004. (Space Flight Adventures & Disasters Ser.). (Illus.). 48p. (J). lib. bdg. 26.60 *(978-0-7660-5169-0(2),* MyReportLinks.com Bks.) Enslow Pubs., Inc.

—Trailblazing Astronaut John Glenn: A MyReportLinks.com Book. 2004. (Space Flight Adventures & Disasters Ser.). (Illus.). 48p. (J). lib. bdg. 26.60 *(978-0-7660-5166-9(8),* MyReportLinks.com Bks.) Enslow Pubs., Inc.

Hord, Colleen. Joe Acaba. 2013. (ENG., Illus.). 24p. (gr. k-3). pap. 8.95 *(978-1-61810-284-3(2))* Rourke Educational Media.

Houran, Lori Haskins. A Trip into Space: An Adventure to the International Space Station. Marquez, Francisca, illus. 2014. (ENG.). 24p. (J). (gr. -1-3). 15.99 *(978-0-8075-8091-2(0))* Whitman, Albert & Co.

Hubbard, Ben. Neil Armstrong & Getting to the Moon. 2015. (Adventures in Space Ser.). (ENG., Illus.). 48p. (gr. 4-6). 33.32 *(978-1-4846-2515-6(3))* Heinemann-Raintree.

—Yuri Gagarin & the Race to Space. 2015. (Adventures in Space Ser.). (ENG., Illus.). 48p. (gr. 4-6). 33.32 *(978-1-4846-2514-9(5))* Heinemann-Raintree.

Hunter, Nick. Christopher Columbus & Neil Armstrong. 2015. (Comparing People from the Past Ser.). (ENG., Illus.). 32p. (gr. 3-3). pap. 6.49 *(978-1-4846-0920-0(4),* Heinemann First Library) Heinemann-Raintree.

I'm Going to be the Best Astronaut Ever! 2008. (I'm Going to be Storybooks... Ser.). 32p. *(978-1-4075-1705-6(8))* Parragon, Inc.

Indovino, Shaina Carmel. Women in Space. 2013. (J). *(978-1-4222-2923-1(8))* Mason Crest.

—Women in Space. Lee-Karlon, Ann, ed. 2013. (Major Women in Science Ser.: 10). 64p. (J). (gr. 7-18). 22.95 *(978-1-4222-2931-6(9))* Mason Crest.

Jaffe, Elizabeth Dana. Ellen Ochoa. (Rookie Biographies Ser.). (Illus.). 2005. (ENG.). 32p. (J). (gr. 1-2). pap. 4.95 *(978-0-516-25827-0(3))* 2004. 31p. 20.50 *(978-0-516-21721-5(6))* Scholastic Library Publishing. (Children's Pr.).

Jenkins, Martin. Exploring Space: from Galileo to the Mars Rover & Beyond. Biesty, Stephen, illus. 2017. (ENG.). 64p. (J). (gr. 3-7). 17.99 *(978-0-7636-8931-5(9))* Candlewick Pr.

Jones, Tom. Ask the Astronaut: A Galaxy of Astonishing Answers to Your Questions on Spaceflight. 2016. (ENG., Illus.). 224p. (YA). (gr. 5-12). pap. 12.95 *(978-1-58834-537-0(8),* Smithsonian Bks.) Smithsonian Institution Scholarly Pr.

Joyce, Jeffrey. Who Was Neil Armstrong? 2013. (Rosen Readers Ser.). (ENG.). 24p. (J). (gr. 3-4). pap. 49.50 *(978-1-4777-2584-9(9));* pap. 8.25 *(978-1-4777-2582-5(2))* Rosen Publishing Group, Inc., The. (Rosen Classroom).

Juarez, Christine. Ellen Ochoa. 2016. (Great Hispanic & Latino Americans Ser.). (ENG.). 24p. (gr. k-1). lib. bdg. 21.99 *(978-1-5157-1888-8(3),* Pebble Bks.) Capstone Press of Coughlan Cos.

—John Danny Olivas. 2016. (Great Hispanic & Latino Americans Ser.). (ENG.). 24p. (gr. k-1). lib. bdg. 21.99 *(978-1-5157-1890-1(5),* Pebble Bks.) Capstone Press of Coughlan Cos.

Karner, Julie. Space Disaster & Meteorite Alert! 2005. (Disaster Alert! Ser.). (ENG., Illus.). 32p. (J). (gr. 4-7). pap. *(978-0-7787-1615-0(5))* Crabtree Publishing Co.

Keedle, Jayne. Ellen Ochoa. 2009. (People We Should Know Ser.). 32p. (gr. 3-5). (J). lib. bdg. 31.00 *(978-1-4339-0019-8(X));* pap. 10.50 *(978-1-4339-0159-1(5))* Stevens, Gareth Publishing LLLP. (Gareth Stevens Learning Library).

Kelley, K. C. Astronauts!, Vol. 10. 2015. (Scientists in Action Ser.). (Illus.). 48p. (J). (gr. 5). 20.95 *(978-1-4222-3418-1(5))* Mason Crest.

Koestler-Grack, Rachel A. Neil Armstrong. 2009. (People We Should Know Ser.). 48p. (J). (gr. 3-5). pap. 10.50 *(978-1-4339-2147-6(2));* lib. bdg. 31.00 *(978-1-4339-1948-0(6))* Stevens, Gareth Publishing LLLP. (Gareth Stevens Learning Library).

Kramer, Barbara. Neil Armstrong: Meet the Famous Astronaut. 2003. (Meeting Famous People Ser.). (Illus.). 32p. (J). lib. bdg. 22.60 *(978-0-7660-2007-8(X))* Enslow Pubs., Inc.

Kupperberg, Paul. John Glenn: The First American in Orbit & His Return to Space. 2009. (Library of Astronaut Biographies Ser.). 112p. (gr. 5-8). 63.90 *(978-1-60853-523-1(1),* Rosen Reference) Rosen Publishing Group, Inc., The.

Langley, Andrew. Chris Hadfield & Living on the International Space Station. 2015. (Adventures in Space Ser.). (ENG., Illus.). 48p. (gr. 4-6). 33.32 *(978-1-4846-2517-0(X))* Heinemann-Raintree.

—Sally Ride & the Shuttle Missions. 2015. (Adventures in Space Ser.). (ENG., Illus.). 48p. (gr. 4-6). 33.32 *(978-1-4846-2516-3(1))* Heinemann-Raintree.

Levin, Amy. Astronauts, 6 vols., Set. 2003. (Phonics Readers 1-36 Ser.). (ENG.). 8p. (gr. k-1). pap. 29.70 *(978-0-7368-3197-0(5),* Phonics Readers) Capstone Press of Coughlan Cos.

Littlejohn, Randy. Life in Outer Space. (Life in Extreme Environments Ser.). 64p. (gr. 5-8). 2009. 53.00 *(978-1-61514-269-9(X))* 2004. (Illus.). lib. bdg. 31.95 *(978-0-8239-3989-3(8))* Rosen Publishing Group, Inc., The. (Rosen Reference).

Lock, Deborah & Hayden, Kate. Astronaut Living in Space, Level 2. 2013. (DK Readers Ser.). (ENG.). 32p. (J). (gr. 1-4). pap. 3.99 *(978-1-4654-0241-7(1),* DK Children) Dorling Kindersley Publishing, Inc.

Marsh, Carole. Ellen Ochoa: First Hispanic American Woman in Space: First Hispanic American Woman in Space. 2003. 12p. (gr. k-4). 2.95 *(978-0-635-02138-0(2))* Gallopade International.

Mattern, Joanne. Astronautas. 2004. (Trabajo en Grupo (Working Together) Ser.). (SPA & ENG., Illus.). 24p. (J). (gr. 1-4). lib. bdg. 22.60 *(978-0-8239-6842-8(1))* Rosen Publishing Group, Inc., The.

—Astronautas (Astronauts) 2009. (Trabajo en grupo (Working Together) Ser.). 24p. (gr. 1-2). 42.50 *(978-1-60854-574-2(1),* Editorial Buenas Letras) Rosen Publishing Group, Inc., The.

—Astronauts. 2009. (Working Together Ser.). 24p. (gr. 1-2). 42.50 *(978-1-60854-828-6(7),* PowerKids Pr.) Rosen Publishing Group, Inc., The.

—Sally Ride: Astronaut. 2005. (Ferguson Career Biographies Ser.). (Illus.). 122p. (gr. 6-12). 25.00 *(978-0-8160-5892-1(X),* Ferguson Publishing Co.) Facts On File, Inc.

Maxwell, Scott & Chambers, Catherine. Mars Rover Driver. 2013. (Coolest Jobs on the Planet Ser.). (ENG., Illus.). 48p. (gr. 5-8). 32.65 *(978-1-4109-5483-1(8));* pap. 8.99 *(978-1-4109-5488-6(9))* Heinemann-Raintree.

McAneney, Caitlin. Women in Space. 2015. (Women Groundbreakers Ser.). (ENG., Illus.). 32p. (J). (gr. 4-5). pap. 10.00 *(978-1-4994-1048-8(4),* PowerKids Pr.) Rosen Publishing Group, Inc., The.

McCarthy, Meghan. Astronaut Handbook. 2017. (ENG., Illus.). 40p. (J). (gr. -1-2). 7.99 *(978-0-399-55546-6(3),* Dragonfly Bks.) Random Hse. Children's Bks.

McPherson, Stephanie Sammartino. The First Men on the Moon. 2009. (History Maker Biographies Ser.). (ENG.). 48p. (gr. 3-6). 27.93 *(978-0-7613-4949-5(9),* Lerner Pubns.) Lerner Publishing Group.

Meachen Rau, Dana. Neil Armstrong. 2014. (Rookie Biographies(r) Ser.). (ENG.). 32p. (J). lib. bdg. 23.00 *(978-0-531-21063-5(4))* Scholastic Library Publishing.

Meachen-Rau, Dana. Neil Armstrong. 2003. (Rookie Biographies Ser.). (ENG., Illus.). 32p. (J). (gr. 1-2). lib. bdg. 20.50 *(978-0-516-22592-0(8),* Children's Pr.) Scholastic Library Publishing.

Melvin, Leland & Caulkhoven, Laurie. Chasing Space Young Readers' Edition. 2017. (Illus.). 240p. (J). (gr. 3-7). 17.99 *(978-0-06-266592-8(8),* Amistad) HarperCollins Pubs.

Mitchell, Don. Liftoff: A Photobiography of John Glenn. 2006. (Photobiographies Ser.). (ENG., Illus.). 64p. (J). (gr. 5-7). 17.95 *(978-0-7922-5899-5(1));* lib. bdg. 27.90 *(978-0-7922-5900-8(9))* National Geographic Society. (National Geographic Children's Bks.).

Mitchell, Edgar & Mahoney, Ellen. Earthrise: My Adventures As an Apollo 14 Astronaut. 2014. (ENG., Illus.). 192p. (YA). (gr. 7). 19.95 *(978-1-61374-901-2(5))* Chicago Review Pr., Inc.

Moore, Philip. When Did American Astronauts Explore Space? 2014. (Little Books of Answers: Level C Ser.). (Illus.). 16p. (gr. k-2). pap. 7.95 *(978-1-927136-26-3(1))* Three Crows Media NZL. Dist: RiverStream Publishing.

Morris, Neil. What Does Space Exploration Do for Us?, 1 vol. 2011. (Earth, Space, & Beyond Ser.). (ENG.). 48p. (gr. 6-6). pap. 9.49 *(978-1-4109-4165-7(5),* Raintree Freestyle) Heinemann-Raintree.

—Who Traveled to the Moon?, 1 vol. 2014. (Primary Source Detectives Ser.). (ENG.). 64p. (gr. 7-8). lib. bdg. 35.99 *(978-1-4329-9605-5(3))* Heinemann-Raintree.

Murphy, Patricia J. Explorando el Espacio con una Astronauta/Exploring Space with an Astronaut. 2008. (I Like Science! Bilingual Ser.). (ENG & SPA., Illus.). 24p. (J). (gr. 1-3). lib. bdg. 22.60 *(978-0-7660-2977-4(8),* Enslow Elementary) Enslow Pubs., Inc.

Murphy, Sage. Sally Ride: Female Astronaut. 2013. (Rosen Readers Ser.). (ENG.). 24p. (J). (gr. 2-3). pap. 49.50 *(978-1-4777-2307-4(2));* pap. 8.25 *(978-1-4777-2306-7(4))* Rosen Publishing Group, Inc., The. (Rosen Classroom).

Naden, Corinne J. & Blue, Rose. Mae Jeminson: Out of This World. 2003. (Gateway Biography Ser.: 4). (Illus.). 48p. lib. bdg. 23.90 *(978-0-7613-2570-3(0),* Millbrook Pr.) Lerner Publishing Group.

Nagelhout, Ryan. Astronauts, 01 vols., 1. 2016. (Out of the Lab: Extreme Jobs in Science Ser.). (ENG., Illus.). 32p. (J). pap. 10.00 *(978-1-5081-4509-7(1),* PowerKids Pr.) Rosen Publishing Group, Inc., The.

—Neil Armstrong in His Own Words. 2016. (Eyewitness to History Ser.). (ENG., Illus.). 32p. (J). (gr. 4-5). pap. 10.50 *(978-1-4824-4078-2(4))* Stevens, Gareth Publishing LLLP.

Nettleton, Pamela Hill. Sally Ride: Astronaut, Scientist, Teacher. Yesh, Jeff & Nichols, Garry, illus. 2003. (Biographies Ser.). (ENG.). 24p. (gr. k-3). 26.65 *(978-1-4048-0189-9(8))* Picture Window Bks.

O'Brien, Eileen & Denne, Ben. Space. 2004. (Discovery Program Ser.). (SPA., Illus.). 48p. (J). pap. 8.95 *(978-0-7945-0126-6(5),* Usborne); lib. bdg. 16.95 *(978-1-58086-388-9(4))* EDC Publishing.

Ollhoff, Jim. Neil Armstrong. 2013. (Great Explorers Ser.). 32p. (J). (gr. 5-9). lib. bdg. 27.07 *(978-1-61783-963-4(9),* Abdo & Daughters) ABDO Publishing Co.

Orr, Tamra. Alan Shepard: The First American in Space. (Library of Astronaut Biographies Ser.). 112p. (gr. 5-8). 2009. 63.90 *(978-1-60853-518-7(5))* 2004. (Illus.). (J). lib. bdg. 34.60 *(978-0-8239-4455-2(7))* Rosen Publishing Group, Inc., The. (Rosen Reference).

O'Shaughnessy, Tam. Sally Ride: A Photobiography of America's Pioneering Woman in Space. 2015. (ENG., Illus.). 160p. (J). (gr. 5-8). 19.99 *(978-1-59643-994-8(7),* 9781596439948) Roaring Brook Pr.

Paige, Joy. Ellen Ochoa: The First Hispanic Woman in Space. (Library of Astronaut Biographies Ser.). 112p. (gr. 5-8). 2009. 63.90 *(978-1-60853-520-0(7))* 2004. (Illus.). lib. bdg. 34.60 *(978-0-8239-4457-6(3))* Rosen Publishing Group, Inc., The. (Rosen Reference).

Parker, Steve. Race to the Moon. West, David, illus. 2015. (Story of Space Ser.). (ENG.). 32p. (J). (gr. 3-6). 31.35 *(978-1-62588-078-9(2))* Black Rabbit Bks.

—Space Pioneers. West, David, illus. 2015. (Story of Space Ser.). (ENG.). 32p. (J). (gr. 3-6). 31.35 *(978-1-62588-080-2(4),* 1389452) Black Rabbit Bks.

Peterson, Judy Monroe. Exploring Space: Astronauts & Astronomers. 2009. (Extreme Scientists Ser.). 24p. (gr. 2-3). 42.50 *(978-1-61512-451-0(9),* PowerKids Pr.); (Illus.). (YA). lib. bdg. 22.60 *(978-1-4042-4528-0(6))* Rosen Publishing Group, Inc., The.

Portman, Michael. Why Do Astronauts Wear Spacesuits? 2013. 32p. (J). (gr. 2-5). 25.25 *(978-1-4339-9238-4(8));* pap. 63.00 *(978-1-4339-9240-7(X));* pap. 10.50 *(978-1-4339-9239-1(6))* Stevens, Gareth Publishing LLLP.

PRESS, Celebration. Ellen Ochoa: Reaching for the Stars. 2003. (ENG.). (J). (gr. 2-5). pap., stu. ed. 34.95 *(978-0-673-62081-1(6),* Celebration Pr.) Pearson Schl.

Putnam, Jeff. Explorers of the Sky. 2004. (ZB Reads Trio Books). (Illus.). 74p. (gr. 4-6). pap. 5.00 *(978-0-7367-1796-0(X))* Zaner-Bloser, Inc.

Pye, Michael & Dalley, Kirsten, eds. Ancient Secret Societies & Lost Knowledge, 01 vols., 1. 2016. (Ancient Secrets & Alien Gods Ser.). (ENG.). 224p. (YA). 38.25 *(978-1-5081-7100-3(9),* Rosen Young Adult) Rosen Publishing Group, Inc., The.

Reid, Struan. Astronauts Sticker Book IR. 2015. (Sticker Dressing Ser.). (ENG.). 24+10p. (J). (gr. k-5). pap. 8.99 *(978-0-7945-3511-7(9),* Usborne) EDC Publishing.

Rice, Dona Herweck & Rice, Dona. ¡Locos por Insectos y Arañas!, 1 vol. 2nd rev. ed. 2012. (Nonfiction Readers Ser.).Tr. of Going Buggy. (SPA.). 20p. (J). (gr. 1-1). pap. 4.99 *(978-1-4333-4424-4(6))* Teacher Created Materials, Inc.

Rice, William. Despegar Hacia el Campamento Espacial. 2017. (TIME for Kids en Español - Level 3 Ser.). (SPA.). 32p. (gr. 3-3). lib. bdg. 31.99 ***(978-1-5157-5180-9(5))*** Time for Kids Inc AUS. Dist: Capstone Pub.

Rice, William B. & Wolfe, Hillary. Blast off to Space Camp, 1 vol. 2nd rev. ed. 2012. (Nonfiction Readers Ser.). (ENG.). 32p. (J). (gr. 3-3). pap. 8.99 *(978-1-4333-3673-7(1))* Teacher Created Materials, Inc.

Rich, Mari. Space, Vol. 10. Gilmore, Malinda & Pouson, Mel, eds. 2016. (Black Achievement in Science Ser.). (Illus.). 64p. (J). (gr. 7). 23.95 *(978-1-4222-3563-8(7))* Mason Crest.

Riddolls, Tom. Sally Ride: The First American Woman in Space. 2010. (Crabtree Groundbreaker Biographies Ser.). (ENG., Illus.). 112p. (J). pap. *(978-0-7787-2550-3(2));* (gr. 5-8). lib. bdg. *(978-0-7787-2541-1(3))* Crabtree Publishing Co.

Ross, Jerry L. & Gunderson, Susan G. Becoming a Spacewalker: My Journey to the Stars. 2014. (ENG., Illus.). 40p. (J). 16.95 *(978-1-55753-693-8(7),* e5b8fc3c-8198-4711-bb0a-bd7f87ffa1b0) Purdue Univ. Pr.

Saari, Peggy. Biography, Space Exploration. 2004. (Space Exploration Reference Library). (ENG.). 288p. (J). lib. bdg. 106.00 *(978-0-7876-9212-4(3),* UXL) Cengage Gale.

Sally Ride: Life on a Mission. 2014. (Real-Life Story Ser.). (ENG., Illus.). 160p. (J). (gr. 3-7). 18.99 *(978-1-4424-8854-0(9),* Aladdin) Simon & Schuster Children's Publishing.

Salzmann, Mary Elizabeth. Astronauts, 1 vol. 2015. (ENG., Illus.). 24p. (J). 17.95 *(978-1-62403-742-9(9))* ABDO Publishing Co.

Schraff, Anne E. Ellen Ochoa: Astronaut & Inventor. 2009. (Latino Biography Library). (Illus.). 128p. (J). (gr. 6-18). lib. bdg. 33.27 *(978-0-7660-3163-0(2))* Enslow Pubs., Inc.

Schwartz, Heather E. Astronaut Ellen Ochoa. 2017. (STEM Trailblazer Bios Ser.). (ENG.). 32p. (J). (gr. 2-5). pap. 8.99 ***(978-1-5124-5627-1(6));*** (Illus.). 26.65 ***(978-1-5124-3449-1(3),*** Lerner Pubns.) Lerner Publishing Group.

Seddon, Rhea, et al. Rise to the Challenge: Memoir of an Astronaut. 2014. (Text Connections Ser.). (J). (gr. 3). *(978-1-4509-9663-1(9))* Benchmark Education Co.

Sexton, Colleen. Astronauts. 2010. (Exploring Space Ser.). (ENG., Illus.). 24p. (J). (gr. k-3). lib. bdg. 25.95 *(978-1-60014-284-0(2),* Blastoff! Readers) Bellwether Media.

Shepherd, Jodie. Mae Jemison. 2015. (Rookie Biographies(r) Ser.). (ENG., Illus.). 32p. (J). pap. 5.95 *(978-0-531-20997-4(0))* Scholastic Library Publishing.

Sofer, Barbara. Ilan Ramon: Israel's Space Hero. 2003. (Illus.). 64p. (J). (gr. 3-6). 16.95 *(978-1-58013-115-5(8));* pap. 6.95 *(978-1-58013-116-2(6))* Lerner Publishing Group. (Kar-Ben Publishing).

Sparrow, Giles. Astronauts. 2006. (Secrets of the Universe Ser.). (Illus.). 48p. (gr. 6-12). pap. 14.05 *(978-0-8368-7282-8(7));* lib. bdg. 31.00 *(978-0-8368-7275-0(4))* Stevens, Gareth Publishing LLLP. (Gareth Stevens Secondary Library).

—Space Exploration. 2011. (Exploring Space: Space Travel Guides). 32p. (gr. 3-6). lib. bdg. 31.35 *(978-1-59920-665-3(X))* Black Rabbit Bks.

Sparrow, Giles & John, Judith. Exploring Space. 2016. (Discoveries in Space Science Ser.). (ENG., Illus.). 80p. (YA). (gr. 9-9). lib. bdg. 35.64 *(978-1-5026-1012-6(4),* 1398704) Cavendish Square Publishing.

Speregen, Debra Newberger. Ilan Ramon: Jewish Star. 2004. (ENG., Illus.). 120p. (J). pap. 13.00 *(978-0-8276-0769-5(5))* Jewish Pubn. Society.

Stine, Megan. Who Was Sally Ride? 2013. (Who Was? Ser.). (ENG.). 112p. (J). (gr. 3-7). pap. 5.99 *(978-0-448-46687-3(2),* Grosset & Dunlap) Penguin Young Readers Group.

Stone, Tanya Lee. Almost Astronauts: 13 Women Who Dared to Dream. 2009. (ENG., Illus.). 144p. (J). (gr. 5). 24.99 *(978-0-7636-3611-1(6));* pap. 17.99 *(978-0-7636-4502-1(8))* Candlewick Pr.

—Ilan Ramon: Israel's First Astronaut. 48p. (J). (gr. 4-7). 17.95 *(978-1-58013-204-6(9),* Kar-Ben Publishing) Lerner Publishing Group.

Stowell, Louie. Astronaut's Handbook IR. 2015. (Handbooks Ser.). (ENG.). 128p. (J). (gr. k-5). pap. 9.99 *(978-0-7945-3497-4(X),* Usborne) EDC Publishing.

Streissguth, Tom. John Glenn. 2004. (Just the Facts Biographies Ser.). (ENG., Illus.). 112p. (J). (gr. 5-12). lib. bdg. 27.93 *(978-0-8225-2274-4(8))* Lerner Publishing Group.

Tagliaferro, Linda. Who Walks in Space? Working in Space. 2010. (Wild Work Ser.). (ENG.). 32p. (gr. 1-2). 29.99 *(978-1-4109-3849-7(2),* Read Me!) Heinemann-Raintree.

Taylor, Charlotte & Feinstein, Stephen. Mae Jemison: First African-American Woman in Space. 2015. (Exceptional African Americans Ser.). (ENG.). 24p. (J). (gr. 3-4). 22.60 *(978-0-7660-6664-9(9));* pap. 9.35 *(978-0-7660-6662-5(2))* Enslow Pubs., Inc.

Tieck, Sarah. Astronauts, 1 vol. 2011. (Extreme Jobs Ser.). (ENG., Illus.). 32p. (J). (gr. 2-5). 28.50 *(978-1-61783-024-2(0))* ABDO Publishing Co.

Van Vleet, Carmella & Sullivan, Kathy. To the Stars! The First American Woman to Walk in Space. Wong, Nicole, illus. 2016. (ENG.). 40p. (J). (gr. k-3). lib. bdg. 16.95 *(978-1-58089-644-3(8))* Charlesbridge Publishing, Inc.

Visca, Curt. How to Draw Cartoon Spacecraft & Astronauts in Action. 2009. (Kid's Guide to Drawing Ser.). 24p. (gr. 3-3). 47.90 *(978-1-61511-019-3(4),* PowerKids Pr.) Rosen Publishing Group, Inc., The.

Visca, Curt & Visca, Kelley. How to Draw Cartoon Spacecraft & Astronauts in Action. 2004. (Kid's Guide to Drawing Ser.). (Illus.). 24p. (J). lib. bdg. 25.25 *(978-0-8239-6729-2(8),* PowerKids Pr.) Rosen Publishing Group, Inc., The.

Wearing, Judy. Roberta Bondar: Canada's First Woman in Space. 2010. (Crabtree Groundbreaker Biographies Ser.). (ENG., Illus.). 112p. (J). (gr. 5-8). lib. bdg. *(978-0-7787-2540-4(5))* Crabtree Publishing Co.

Weber, Rebecca. Ellen Ochoa. 2011. (Early Connections Ser.). (J). *(978-1-61672-550-1(8))* Benchmark Education Co.

West, David. Astronauts. 2009. (Graphic Careers Ser.). (ENG.). 48p. (YA). (gr. 5-5). 58.50 *(978-1-61512-877-8(8),* Rosen Reference) Rosen Publishing Group, Inc., The.

—Astronauts. Robins, Jim, illus. 2008. (Graphic Careers Ser.). 48p. (gr. 5-8). per. 14.05 *(978-1-4042-1462-0(3));* (YA). lib. bdg. 31.95 *(978-1-4042-1461-3(5))* Rosen Publishing Group, Inc., The.

—Lots of Things You Want to Know about Astronauts ...and Some You Don't! 2015. (Lots of Things You Want to Know About Ser.). (Illus.). 24p. (J). 28.50 *(978-1-62588-088-8(X))* Black Rabbit Bks.

—Ten of the Best Adventures in Space. 2015. (Ten of the Best: Stories of Exploration & Adventure Ser.). (ENG., Illus.). 24p. (J). (gr. 3-6). *(978-0-7787-1836-9(0))* Crabtree Publishing Co.

Wheeler, Jill C. Mae Jemison: Awesome Astronaut, 1 vol. 2012. (Women in Science Ser.). (ENG., Illus.). 32p. (J). (gr. 3-6). lib. bdg. 27.07 *(978-1-61783-447-9(5),* Checkerboard Library) ABDO Publishing Co.

Wolfe, Hillary & Rice, William B. Blast off to Space Camp, 1 vol. 2nd rev. ed. 2014. (TIME for KIDS(r) Nonfiction Readers Ser.). (ENG., Illus.). 32p. (J). (gr. 3-3). pap. 25.96 *(978-1-4807-1082-5(2))* Shell Educational Publishing.

Yasuda, Anita. Neil Armstrong. 2013. (J). *(978-1-62127-304-2(0));* pap. *(978-1-62127-310-3(5))* Weigl Pubs., Inc.

Zelon, Helen. The Mercury 6 Mission: The First American Astronaut to Orbit Earth. 2009. (Space Missions Ser.). 24p. (gr. 3-4). 42.50 *(978-1-60853-120-2(1),* PowerKids Pr.) Rosen Publishing Group, Inc., The.

Zemlicka, Shannon. Neil Armstrong. 2003. (History Maker Bios Ser.). (Illus.). 48p. (J). (gr. 2-4). 26.60 *(978-0-8225-0395-8(6),* Lerner Pubns.) Lerner Publishing Group.

ASTRONAUTS—CLOTHING

Owen, Ruth. Space Survival Guide. 2010. (ENG., Illus.). 32p. (J). pap. *(978-0-7787-7553-9(4));* lib. bdg. *(978-0-7787-7531-7(3))* Crabtree Publishing Co.

ASTRONAUTS—FICTION

Agee, Jon. Life on Mars. 2017. (ENG., Illus.). 32p. (J). (gr. -1-3). 17.99 *(978-0-399-53852-0(6),* Dial Bks) Penguin Young Readers Group.

Agnew, Kate. Space Saver. Castle, Frances, illus. 2014. (Blue Bananas Ser.). (ENG.). 48p. (J). (gr. k-2). pap. 5.99 *(978-1-4052-5677-3(X))* Egmont Bks., Ltd. GBR. Dist: Independent Pubs. Group.

Barrett, Judi. Cloudy with a Chance of Meatballs 3: Planet of the Pies. Mones, Isidre, illus. 2013. (ENG.). 32p. (J). (gr. -1-3). 17.99 *(978-1-4424-9027-7(6),* Atheneum Bks. for Young Readers) Simon & Schuster Children's Publishing.

Barth, Kathleen E. The Amazing Adventures of Quigley D Pigley & His Friends. 2009. 16p. pap. 8.49 *(978-1-4389-8322-6(0))* AuthorHouse.

—The Amazing Adventures of Quigley D Pigley & His Friends: How to Become an Astronaut. 2009. 16p. pap. 8.49 *(978-1-4389-8606-7(8))* AuthorHouse.

Bean, Raymond. The Curse of Mars. 2016. (Out of This World Ser.). (ENG., Illus.). 112p. (gr. 2-5). lib. bdg. 32.65 *(978-1-4965-3615-0(0))* Out of this World GBR. Dist: Capstone Pub.

Bloomsbury USA. Lift & Look: in Space. 2016. (ENG., Illus.). 12p. (J). (— 1). bds. 8.99 *(978-1-61963-826-6(6),* 9781619638266, Bloomsbury Activity Bks.) Bloomsbury Publishing USA.

Boné, Thomas H., illus. The Teacher Who Would Not Retire Discovers a New Planet. 2009. (J). 17.95 *(978-0-9792918-3-8(6))* Blue Marlin Pubns.

Borgenicht, David & Khan, Hena. Mars: You Decide How to Survive! Labat, Yancey, illus. 2011. (Worst Case Scenario Ser.: WORS). (ENG.). 208p. (J). (gr. 4-7). 12.99 *(978-0-8118-7124-2(X))* Chronicle Bks. LLC.

Brett, Jan. Hedgie Blasts Off! Brett, Jan, illus. 2006. (ENG., Illus.). 32p. (J). (gr. -1-3). 17.99 *(978-0-399-24621-0(5),* G.P. Putnam's Sons Books for Young Readers) Penguin Young Readers Group.

Bright, J. E. Cyborg Superman. Levins, Tim, illus. 2013. (Man of Steel Ser.). (ENG.). 88p. (gr. 2-3). pap. 5.95 *(978-1-4342-4219-8(6))* Stone Arch Bks.

—Cyborg Superman, 1 vol. Levins, Tim & DC Comics Staff, illus. 2013. (Man of Steel Ser.). (ENG.). 88p. (gr. 2-3). 26.65 *(978-1-4342-4089-7(4))* Stone Arch Bks.

Brockington, Drew. CatStronauts: Mission Moon. 2017. (CatStronauts Ser.: 1). (ENG., Illus.). 160p. (J). (gr. 1-5). 16.99 *(978-0-316-30747-5(5));* pap. 7.99 *(978-0-316-30745-1(9))* Little Brown & Co.

—CatStronauts: Race to Mars. 2017. (CatStronauts Ser.: 2). (ENG.). 184p. (J). (gr. 1-5). 16.99 *(978-0-316-30748-2(3))* Little, Brown Bks. for Young Readers.

Brown, Jennifer. Life on Mars. 2014. (ENG.). 240p. (YA). (gr. 3-6). 16.99 *(978-1-61963-252-3(7),* 9781619632523, Bloomsbury USA Childrens) Bloomsbury Publishing USA.

Brown, Ruby. I Want to Be ... an Astronaut. Coburn, Alisa, illus. 2016. (ENG.). 22p. (J). bds. 8.99 *(978-1-61067-406-5(5))* Kane Miller.

Brunson, Emma. Survivor Spirit Book: Megan's Ark. 2010. 204p. pap. 13.50 *(978-1-60911-834-1(0),* Eloquent Bks.) Strategic Book Publishing & Rights Agency (SBPRA).

Caviezel, Giovanni. Astronaut. Mesturini, C., illus. 2012. (Little People Shape Bks.). (ENG.). 10p. (J). (gr. k-2). bds. 8.99 *(978-0-7641-6573-3(9))* Barron's Educational Series, Inc.

Chad, Jon. Leo Geo & the Cosmic Crisis. Chad, Jon, illus. 2013. (ENG., Illus.). 40p. (J). (gr. 2-6). 16.99 *(978-1-59643-822-4(3),* 9781596438224) Roaring Brook Pr.

Courtenay, L. A. Space Penguins Cosmic Crash! Davies, James, illus. 2015. (Space Penguins Ser.). (ENG.). 112p. (gr. 2-3). lib. bdg. 22.65 *(978-1-4342-9785-3(3))* Stone Arch Bks.

—Space Penguins Galaxy Race! Davies, James, illus. 2015. (Space Penguins Ser.). (ENG.). 112p. (gr. 2-3). lib. bdg. 22.65 *(978-1-4342-9783-9(7))* Stone Arch Bks.

—Space Penguins Meteor Madness! Davies, James, illus. 2015. (Space Penguins Ser.). (ENG.). 112p. (gr. 2-3). lib. bdg. 22.65 *(978-1-4342-9782-2(9))* Stone Arch Bks.

—Space Penguins Star Attack! Davies, James, illus. 2015. (Space Penguins Ser.). (ENG.). 112p. (gr. 2-3). lib. bdg. 22.65 *(978-1-4342-9784-6(5))* Stone Arch Bks.

Dean, James. Pete the Cat: Out of This World. Dean, James, illus. 2017. (Pete the Cat Ser.). (Illus.). 24p. (J). (gr. -1-3). pap. 4.99 *(978-0-06-240443-5(1),* HarperFestival) HarperCollins Pubs.

Draper, Sharon M. The Space Mission Adventure. Watson, Jesse Joshua, illus. 2012. (Clubhouse Mysteries Ser.: 4). (ENG.). 112p. (J). (gr. 3-7). 15.99 *(978-1-4424-4225-2(5));* pap. 5.99 *(978-1-4424-4226-9(3))* Simon & Schuster Children's Publishing. (Aladdin).

Dusek, Cheryl. Maybe One Day: What Do You Want to Be? 2009. 36p. pap. 16.99 *(978-1-4389-6689-2(X))* AuthorHouse.

Espluga, Maria. I Am an Astronaut. 2009. (I Am A... (Alphabet Soup) Ser.). (Illus.). 24p. (J). (gr. k-1). pap. 8.15 *(978-1-60754-246-9(3));* lib. bdg. 22.60 *(978-1-60754-245-2(5))* Windmill Bks.

—I, Astronaut: Yo, Astronauta. 2009. (SPA & ENG.). 28p. (J). 13.95 *(978-1-931398-56-5(9))* Me+Mi Publishing.

Fay, Nicole. Andy & Armadillo Are Astronauts. 2008. 20p. pap. 10.49 *(978-1-4389-1057-4(6))* AuthorHouse.

Ferris, Margaret Ann. Bart the Batronaut. Gove, Frank Stanley, illus. 2011. (ENG.). 32p. (J). pap. *(978-0-9832819-8-6(X))* BookCrafters.

Frederick, Heather Vogel. Once upon a Toad. (ENG., Illus.). (J). (gr. 5-9). 2013. 288p. pap. 6.99 *(978-1-4169-8479-5(8))* 2012. 272p. 16.99 *(978-1-4169-8478-8(X))* Simon & Schuster Bks. For Young Readers. (Simon & Schuster Bks. For Young Readers).

Fritz, Julie. My Mother Is an Astronaut. 2008. 16p. pap. 10.50 *(978-1-4343-7551-3(X))* AuthorHouse.

Ganz-Schmitt, Sue. Planet Kindergarten. Prigmore, Shane, illus. 2016. (ENG.). 36p. (J). (gr. -1-k). 7.99 *(978-1-4521-5644-6(1))* Chronicle Bks. LLC.

—Planet Kindergarten: 100 Days in Orbit. Prigmore, Shane, illus. 2016. (ENG.). 36p. (J). (gr. -1-k). 16.99 *(978-1-4521-3776-6(5))* Chronicle Bks. LLC.

Graves, Robin. Space Diaries: The Saga of Robby, Boy Astronaut. 2005. pap. 6.95 *(978-1-57646-915-6(8))* Quiet Vision Publishing.

Hadfield, Chris. The Darkest Dark. Fan, Eric et al, illus. 2016. (ENG.). 48p. (J). (gr. -1-3). 17.99 *(978-0-316-39472-7(6))* Little, Brown Bks. for Young Readers.

Harstad, Johan. 172 Hours on the Moon. 2013. (ENG.). 384p. (J). (gr. 8-17). pap. 10.99 *(978-0-316-18289-8(3))* Little, Brown Bks. for Young Readers.

Harstad, Johan & Chace, Tara. 172 Hours on the Moon. 2012. (ENG.). 368p. (gr. 7-17). 17.99 *(978-0-316-18288-1(5))* Little Brown & Co.

Hawking, Lucy & Hawking, Stephen W. George's Cosmic Treasure Hunt. Parsons, Garry, illus. 2011. (George's Secret Key Ser.). (ENG.). 352p. (J). (gr. 3-7). pap. 11.99 *(978-1-4424-2175-2(4),* Simon & Schuster Bks. For Young Readers) Simon & Schuster Bks. For Young Readers.

Hoena, Blake A. The Black Hole Report, 1 vol. Harpster, Steve, illus. 2014. (Eek & Ack Early Chapter Bks.). (ENG.). 32p. (gr. k-2). lib. bdg. 22.65 *(978-1-4342-6409-1(2))* Stone Arch Bks.

Jansen, Karen. The Coming of an Astronaut. 2009. 68p. pap. 9.99 *(978-1-60911-076-5(5),* Eloquent Bks.) Strategic Book Publishing & Rights Agency (SBPRA).

Kelly, Mark. Mousetronaut: Based on a (Partially) True Story. Payne, C. F., illus. 2012. (ENG.). 40p. (J). (gr. -1-3). 17.99 *(978-1-4424-5824-6(0),* Simon & Schuster/Paula Wiseman Bks.) Simon & Schuster/Paula Wiseman Bks.

—Mousetronaut Goes to Mars. Payne, C. F., illus. 2013. (ENG.). 40p. (J). (gr. -1-3). 16.99 *(978-1-4424-8426-9(8),* Simon & Schuster/Paula Wiseman Bks.) Simon & Schuster/Paula Wiseman Bks.

Krulik, Nancy. How Do You Pee in Space? 2014. (George Brown, Class Clown Ser.: 13). lib. bdg. 14.75 *(978-0-606-36163-7(4))* Turtleback Bks.

Landers, Melissa. Starfall. 2017. (Starflight Ser.). (ENG.). 368p. (YA). (gr. 9-17). 17.99 *(978-1-4847-5025-4(X))* Hyperion Bks. for Children.

Lawson, Janet. The Alberts & Me. 2009. (J). *(978-0-15-205327-7(1))* Harcourt Trade Pubs.

Marsalis, Dustin S. The Alligator Astronauts Go to the Zipper Zoo. 2013. 36p. pap. 15.99 *(978-1-4624-0678-4(5),* Inspiring Voices) Author Solutions, Inc.

Potter, Anne & DeNize, Anne. The Recycled Window. 2010. 70p. pap. 13.50 *(978-1-4461-2821-3(0))* Lulu Pr., Inc.

Rider, Cynthia. The Spaceship. Aguilar, Sandra, illus. 2013. (Start Reading Ser.). (ENG.). 24p. (gr. k-1). pap. 7.95 *(978-1-4765-4137-2(X))* Capstone Press of Coughlan Cos.

Rockwell, Carey. On the Trail of Space Pirates. 2007. 140p. 24.95 *(978-1-60312-781-3(X))* Aegypan.

—Sabotage in Space. 2007. (ENG.). 162p. pap. 19.99 *(978-1-4264-9345-4(2));* 184p. pap. 21.99 *(978-1-4264-9726-1(1))* Creative Media Partners, LLC.

Rockwell, Carey & Ley, Willy. Treachery in Outer Space: A Tom Corbett Space Cadet Adventure. Glanzman, Louis, illus. 2011. 220p. 44.95 *(978-1-258-09685-4(4))* Literary Licensing, LLC.

Roman, Dave. Zero Gravity. Roman, Dave, illus. 2011. (Astronaut Academy Ser.: 1). (ENG., Illus.). 192p. (J). (gr. 5-9). 17.99 *(978-1-59643-756-2(1),* 9781596437562); pap. 9.99 *(978-1-59643-620-6(4),* 9781596436206) Roaring Brook Pr. (First Second Bks.).

Rouss, Sylvia A. Reach for the Stars. 2005. (Illus.). 40p. (J). (gr. 3-7). 16.95 *(978-1-930143-82-1(6));* pap. 9.95 *(978-1-930143-83-8(4))* Simcha Media Group. (Devora Publishing).

Sleep Tight Spaceboy. 2003. (Spaceboy Set 1 Ser.). (J). 7.33 *(978-1-932570-02-1(0))* Pioneer Valley Bks.

Spaceboy Finds a Friend. 2003. (Spaceboy Set 1 Ser.). (J). 7.33 *(978-1-932570-01-4(2))* Pioneer Valley Bks.

Spaceboy Plays Hide & Seek. 2003. (Spaceboy Set 1 Ser.). (J). 7.33 *(978-1-932570-05-2(5))* Pioneer Valley Bks.

Spaceboy Set 1. 2003. (J). *(978-1-932570-00-7(4))* Pioneer Valley Bks.

Spence, Kenlyn Foster. Astronaut Noodle on Planet Velocity. 2005. (Illus.). 31p. (J). 14.95 *(978-0-9768760-1-4(9))* BelleBks., Inc.

Stefano, Tony. Tommy & the Dream MacHine — What a Trip! a Boy, a Soda MacHine & a Voyage to Save the Planet. 2012. 138p. pap. 11.95 *(978-1-61897-489-1(0),* Strategic Bk. Publishing) Strategic Book Publishing & Rights Agency (SBPRA).

Strungis, Elaine. Sammi & Danny Learn about Jupiter. 2012. 32p. pap. 14.50 *(978-1-4669-5411-3(6))* Trafford Publishing.

—Sammi & Danny Learn about Mercury. 2012. 28p. pap. 13.55 *(978-1-4669-5413-7(2))* Trafford Publishing.

—Sammi & Danny Learn about the Earth. 2012. 32p. pap. 14.50 *(978-1-4669-3731-4(9))* Trafford Publishing.

—Sammi & Danny Learn about Uranus. 2012. 32p. pap. 14.50 *(978-1-4669-6297-2(6))* Trafford Publishing.

—Sammi & Danny Learn about Venus. 2012. 32p. pap. 14.50 *(978-1-4669-3733-8(5))* Trafford Publishing.

Swank-Gattuso, Jill. Gabrielle Rae: Who Do You Want to Be Today? 2012. 32p. pap. 17.50 *(978-1-4685-4101-4(3))* AuthorHouse.

Westover, Alli. My Daddy Works at NASA. 2005. (J). 15.95 *(978-1-888237-59-7(7))* Baxter Pr.

Williams, Allen. Claude the Backward-Jumping Bullfrog: Space Shuttle Commander. 2009. 32p. pap. 17.99 *(978-1-4490-0479-8(2))* AuthorHouse.

ASTRONOMERS

Anderson, Dale. Maria Mitchell. 2003. (Women in Science Ser.). (Illus.). 112p. (gr. 6-12). 30.00 *(978-0-7910-7249-3(5),* Chelsea Hse.) Facts On File, Inc.

Anderson, Michael, ed. Pioneers in Astronomy & Space Exploration. 2012. (Inventors & Innovators Ser.). (ENG., Illus.). 112p. (gr. 7-12). (J). 32.90 *(978-1-61530-695-4(1));* (YA). 65.80 *(978-1-61530-786-9(9))* Rosen Publishing Group, Inc., The.

Andronik, Catherine M. Copernicus: Founder of Modern Astronomy. 2009. (Great Minds of Science Ser.). (Illus.). 128p. (J). (gr. 5). lib. bdg. 33.27 *(978-0-7660-3013-8(X))* Enslow Pubs., Inc.

—Copernicus: Genius of Modern Astronomy. 2015. (Genius Scientists & Their Genius Ideas Ser.). 96p. (J). (gr. 5-12). 27.94 *(978-0-7660-6550-5(2));* pap. 10.95 *(978-0-7660-6551-2(0))* Enslow Pubs., Inc.

Astronomers. 2013. (Out of the Lab: Extreme Jobs in Science Ser.). 32p. (J). (gr. 3-6). pap. 60.00 *(978-1-4777-1379-2(4),* PowerKids Pr.) Rosen Publishing Group, Inc., The.

Bailey, Gerry & Foster, Karen. Galileo's Telescope. Noyes, Leighton & Radford, Karen, illus. 2008. (Stories of Great People Ser.). (ENG.). 40p. (J). (gr. 3-7). pap. *(978-0-7787-3716-2(0))* Crabtree Publishing Co.

Boekhoff, P. M. Galileo. 2003. (Inventors & Creators Ser.). (Illus.). 48p. (J). 23.70 *(978-0-7377-1891-1(9),* Greenhaven Pr., Inc.) Cengage Gale.

Boerst, William J. Johannes Kepler: Discovering the Laws of Celestial Motion. 2004. (Profiles in Science Ser.). (Illus.). 144p. (YA). (gr. 6-12). lib. bdg. 26.95 *(978-1-883846-98-5(6),* First Biographies) Reynolds, Morgan Inc.

—Nicholas Copernicus & the Founding of Modern Astronomy. 2004. (Profiles in Science Ser.). (Illus.). 144p. (YA). (gr. 6-12). lib. bdg. 26.95 *(978-1-883846-99-2(4),* First Biographies) Reynolds, Morgan Inc.

—Tycho Brahe: Mapping the Heavens. 2004. (Profiles in Science Ser.). (Illus.). 144p. (YA). (gr. 6-12). 26.95 *(978-1-883846-97-8(8),* First Biographies) Reynolds, Morgan Inc.

Boothroyd, Jennifer. Galileo Galilei: A Life of Curiosity. 2007. (Pull Ahead Bks.). (Illus.). 32p. (J). (gr. 3-7). lib. bdg. 22.60 *(978-0-8225-6460-7(2),* Lerner Pubns.) Lerner Publishing Group.

Borisovna, Gabrielle. Carl Sagan. 2014. (Great Science Writers Ser.). (Illus.). 112p. (J). (gr. 7-12). 35.60 *(978-1-4777-7681-0(8))* Rosen Publishing Group, Inc., The.

Bortz, Fred. The Big Bang Theory: Edwin Hubble & the Origins of the Universe. 2013. (Revolutionary Discoveries of Scientific Pioneers Ser.). (Illus.). 80p. (J). (gr. 7-12). 33.25 *(978-1-4777-1803-2(6))* Rosen Publishing Group, Inc., The.

—Johannes Kepler & the Three Laws of Planetary Motion. 2013. (Revolutionary Discoveries of Scientific Pioneers Ser.). 80p. (YA). (gr. 7-12). 33.25 *(978-1-4777-1805-6(2))* Rosen Publishing Group, Inc., The.

—The Sun-Centered Universe & Nicolaus Copernicus. 2013. (Revolutionary Discoveries of Scientific Pioneers Ser.). 80p. (YA). (gr. 7-12). 33.25 *(978-1-4777-1801-8(X))* Rosen Publishing Group, Inc., The.

Brezina, Corona. Galileo Galilei. 2017. (Leaders of the Scientific Revolution Ser.). 112p. (J). (gr. 12-13). 37.10 ***(978-1-5081-7468-4(7),*** Rosen Young Adult) Rosen Publishing Group, Inc., The.

Burleigh, Robert. Look Up! Henrietta Leavitt, Pioneering Woman Astronomer. Colón, Raúl, illus. 2013. (ENG.). 32p. (J). (gr. -1-3). 16.99 *(978-1-4169-5819-2(3),* Simon & Schuster Bks. For Young Readers) Simon & Schuster/Paula Wiseman Bks.

Butts, Ellen R. & Schwartz, Joyce R. Carl Sagan. 2005. (Biography Ser.). (Illus.). 112p. (gr. 6-12). lib. bdg. 27.93 *(978-0-8225-4986-4(7))* Lerner Publishing Group.

Butzer, Anna. Maria Mitchell, 1 vol. 2014. (Great Women in History Ser.). (ENG.). 24p. (gr. k-1). pap. 6.29 *(978-1-4914-0542-0(2),* Pebble Bks.) Capstone Press of Coughlan Cos.

Christensen, Bonnie. I, Galileo. 2012. (ENG., Illus.). 40p. (J). (gr. 3-7). 17.99 *(978-0-375-86753-8(8));* 20.99 *(978-0-375-96753-5(2))* Random Hse. Children's Bks. (Knopf Bks. for Young Readers).

Colson, Mary. Albert Einstein & Sir Arthur Eddington. 2014. (Dynamic Duos of Science Ser.). 48p. (YA). (gr. 5-8). pap. 84.30 *(978-1-4824-1276-5(4))* Stevens, Gareth Publishing LLLP.

Datnow, Claire L. Edwin Hubble: Discoverer of Galaxies. rev. ed. 2007. (Great Minds of Science Ser.). (Illus.). 128p. (J). (gr. 4-10). lib. bdg. 33.27 *(978-0-7660-2791-6(0))* Enslow Pubs., Inc.

—Edwin Hubble: Genius Discoverer of Galaxies. 2015. (Genius Scientists & Their Genius Ideas Ser.). 96p. (J). (gr. 5-12). 27.94 *(978-0-7660-6555-0(3));* pap. 10.95 *(978-0-7660-6556-7(1))* Enslow Pubs., Inc.

De Almeida, Guilherme, et al. Galileo Galilei. 2010. (Me Llamo... Ser.). (SPA., Illus.). 63p. (J). pap. *(978-84-342-3617-2(6))* Parramon Ediciones S.A.

Demuth, Patricia Brennan. Who Was Galileo? 2015. (Who Was... ? Ser.). lib. bdg. 16.00 *(978-0-606-36594-9(X))* Turtleback Bks.

Demuth, Patricia Brennan & dePaola, Tomie. Who Was Galileo? O'brien, John & Harrison, Nancy, illus. 2015. (Who Was? Ser.). (ENG.). 112p. (J). (gr. 3-7). 5.99 *(978-0-448-47985-9(0),* Grosset & Dunlap) Penguin Young Readers Group.

Don Nardo. The Trial of Galileo. 2003. (Famous Trials Ser.). (ENG., Illus.). 112p. (J). 29.95 *(978-1-59018-423-3(8))* Cengage Gale.

Fradin, Dennis Brindell. Nicolaus Copernicus: The Earth Is a Planet. von Buhler, Cynthia, tr. von Buhler, Cynthia, illus. 2003. 32p. (J). (gr. 2-6). 15.95 *(978-1-59336-006-1(1));* pap. *(978-1-59336-007-8(X))* Mondo Publishing.

Gerber, Carole. Annie Jump Cannon, Astronomer, 1 vol. Wald, Christina, illus. 2011. (ENG.). 32p. (J). (gr. 1-5). 16.99 *(978-1-58980-911-6(4))* Pelican Publishing Co., Inc.

Gernadnik, Mary. How Do We Know the Age of the Universe? 2009. (Great Scientific Questions & the Scientists Who Answered Them Ser.). 112p. (gr. 7-12). 63.90 *(978-1-61513-197-6(3))* Rosen Publishing Group, Inc., The.

Ghez, Andrea Mia & Cohen, Judith Love. You Can Be A Woman Astronomer. Katz, David Arthur, illus. i.t. ed. 40p. (J). 2006. pap. 12.95 incl. DVD *(978-1-880599-77-8(5))* 2005. 17.95 incl. DVD *(978-1-880599-78-5(3))* Cascade Pass, Inc.

Goldsworthy, Steve. Famous Explorers. 2011. (J). (gr. 4-6). pap. 13.95 *(978-1-61690-636-8(7),* AV2 by Weigl); (Illus.). 32p. (YA). (gr. 2-5). 28.55 *(978-1-61690-632-0(4))* Weigl Pubs., Inc.

Goldsworthy, Steve. Space Explorers. 2017. (J). ***(978-1-4896-5815-9(7),*** AV2 by Weigl) Weigl Pubs., Inc.

Gordon, Fernando. Anders Celsius, 1 vol. 2016. (ENG., Illus.). 24p. (J). *(978-1-68078-153-3(7))* ABDO Publishing Co.

Gormley, Beatrice. Maria Mitchell: The Soul of an Astronomer. 2004. (Illus.). 166p. (J). pap. 12.00 *(978-0-8028-5264-9(5))* Eerdmans, William B. Publishing Co.

Gow, Mary. Johannes Kepler: Discovering the Laws of Planetary Motion. 2003. (Great Minds of Science Ser.). (Illus.). 128p. (J). lib. bdg. 27.94 *(978-0-7660-2098-6(3))* Enslow Pubs., Inc.

—Measuring the Earth: Eratosthenes & His Celestial Geometry. 2009. (Great Minds of Ancient Science & Math Ser.). (Illus.). 128p. (J). (gr. 4-7). lib. bdg. 33.27 *(978-0-7660-3120-3(9))* Enslow Pubs., Inc.

Greathouse, Lisa E. Astronomers Through Time, 1 vol. 2007. (Science Readers Ser.). (ENG.). 32p. (J). (gr. 4-4). pap. 8.99 *(978-0-7439-0562-6(8))* Shell Educational Publishing.

Greve, Tom. Astronomers. 2015. (ENG.). 48p. (J). (gr. 3-6). 35.64 *(978-1-63430-413-9(6))* Rourke Educational Media.

Hall, Derek. Chemistry, Earth, & Space Sciences. 2010. (Facts at Your Fingertips Ser.). (YA). (gr. 7-12). 35.65 *(978-1-933834-47-4(1))* Brown Bear Books.

Harmon, Daniel E. Johannes Kepler. 2017. (Leaders of the Scientific Revolution Ser.). 112p. (gr. 12-13). 37.10 ***(978-1-5081-7472-1(5),*** Rosen Young Adult) Rosen Publishing Group, Inc., The.

Hartman, Eve & Meshbesher, Wendy. The Scientists Behind Space, 1 vol. 2011. (Sci-Hi: Scientists Ser.). (ENG.). 48p. (gr. 4-4). 33.32 *(978-1-4109-4049-0(7));* pap. 9.95 *(978-1-4109-4056-8(X))* Heinemann-Raintree. (Sci-Hi).

Hasan, Heather. Kepler & the Laws of Planetary Motion. (Primary Sources of Revolutionary Scientific Discoveries & Theories Ser.). 64p. 2009. (gr. 5-5). 58.50 *(978-1-60851-845-6(0))* 2004. (Illus.). (J). lib. bdg. 31.95 *(978-1-4042-0308-2(7))* Rosen Publishing Group, Inc., The.

Hightower, Paul. Galileo: Astronomer & Physicist. rev. ed. 2008. (Great Minds of Science Ser.). (Illus.). 128p. (J). (gr. k-5). lib. bdg. 33.27 *(978-0-7660-3008-4(3))* Enslow Pubs., Inc.

Hightower, Paul W. Galileo: Genius Astronomer. 2015. (Genius Scientists & Their Genius Ideas Ser.). 96p. (J). (gr. 5-12). 27.94 *(978-0-7660-6560-4(X));* pap. 10.95 *(978-0-7660-6561-1(8))* Enslow Pubs., Inc.

Hilliam, Rachel. Galileo Galilei: Father of Modern Science. (Rulers, Scholars, & Artists of the Renaissance Ser.). 112p. 2009. (gr. 5-8). 66.50 *(978-1-60852-941-4(X),* Rosen Reference) 2004. (Illus.). (J). lib. bdg. 34.60 *(978-1-4042-0314-3(1))* Rosen Publishing Group, Inc., The.

Ingram, Scott. Nicolaus Copernicus: Father of Modern Astronomy. 2004. (Illus.). 64p. (J). 26.20 *(978-1-56711-489-8(X),* Blackbirch Pr., Inc.) Cengage Gale.

Kupperberg, Paul. Hubble & the Big Bang. (Primary Sources of Revolutionary Scientific Discoveries & Theories Ser.). 64p. 2009. (gr. 5-5). 58.50 *(978-1-60851-844-9(2))* 2004. (Illus.). (J). lib. bdg. 31.95 *(978-1-4042-0307-5(9))* Rosen Publishing Group, Inc., The.

Lee, David. A Day at Work with an Astronomer, 01 vols., 1. 2016. (Super STEM Careers Ser.). (ENG., Illus.). 24p. (J). pap. 8.25 *(978-1-5081-4419-9(2),* PowerKids Pr.) Rosen Publishing Group, Inc., The.

Lim, Bridget & Brezina, Corona. Al-Khwarizmi. 2016. (Physicians, Scientists, & Mathematicians of the Islamic World Ser.). 112p. (J). (gr. 6-6). 37.10 *(978-1-5081-7144-7(0))* Rosen Publishing Group, Inc., The.

Lin, Yoming S. Galileo & the Telescope. 2012. (Eureka! Ser.). (Illus.). 24p. (J). (gr. 3-6). lib. bdg. 22.60 *(978-1-4488-5030-3(4))* Rosen Publishing Group, Inc., The.

Litwin, Laura Baskes. The Life of Benjamin Banneker: Astronomer & Mathematician. 2014. (Legendary African Americans Ser.). (Illus.). 96p. (J). (gr. 6-12). 27.94 *(978-0-7660-6112-5(4))* Enslow Pubs., Inc.

Loria, Laura. Astronomers at Work. 2017. (Scientists at Work Ser.). 32p. (gr. 6-8). pap. 12.90 ***(978-1-68048-745-9(0),*** Britannica Educational Publishing) Rosen Publishing Group, Inc., The.

Marsh, Carole. Benjamin Banneker. 2003. 12p. (gr. k-4). 2.95 *(978-0-635-02129-8(3))* Gallopade International.

Martin, Isabel. Benjamin Banneker, 1 vol. 2014. (Great African-Americans Ser.). (ENG.). 24p. (gr. k-1). pap. 5.95 *(978-1-4914-0506-2(6),* Pebble Bks.) Capstone Press of Coughlan Cos.

Matejovsky, Char. Shadow on the Moon: A Child's Guide to the Discovery of the Universe. Ream, Robaire, illus. 2014. (J). *(978-1-59815-151-0(7))* Polebridge Pr.

McCombs, Kevin. Caroline Herschel: Astronomer & Cataloger of the Sky. 2016. (Women in Science Ser.). 128p. (YA). lib.

bdg. 45.64 *(978-1-5026-2317-1(X))* Cavendish Square Publishing.

McCully, Emily Arnold. Caroline's Comets: A True Story. 2017. (ENG.). 40p. (J). (gr. -1-3). 16.95 *(978-0-8234-3664-4(0))* Holiday Hse., Inc.

McCutcheon, Scott & McCutcheon, Bobbi. Space & Astronomy: The People Behind the Science. 2005. (Pioneers in Science Ser.). (Illus.). 192p. (gr. 6-12). 29.95 *(978-0-8160-5467-1(3))* Facts On File, Inc.

Morris, Neil. Astronomers. (Illus.). 48p. (YA). (gr. 5-18). lib. bdg. 29.95 *(978-1-932333-78-7(9))* Chrysalis Education.

O'Donnell, Kerri. Galileo: Man of Science. 2009. (Reading Room Collection 2 Ser.). 24p. (gr. 3-4). 42.50 *(978-1-60851-964-4(3),* PowerKids Pr.) Rosen Publishing Group, Inc., The.

Owen, Ruth. Astronomers. 2013. (Out of the Lab: Extreme Jobs in Science Ser.). 32p. (J). (gr. 3-6). 25.25 *(978-1-4777-1289-4(5));* pap. 10.00 *(978-1-4777-1378-5(6))* Rosen Publishing Group, Inc., The. (PowerKids Pr.).

Panchyk, Richard. Galileo for Kids: His Life & Ideas, 25 Activities. 2005. (For Kids Ser.). (ENG., Illus.). 184p. (J). (gr. 4). pap. 18.95 *(978-1-55652-566-7(4))* Chicago Review Pr., Inc.

Peterson, Judy Monroe. Exploring Space: Astronauts & Astronomers. 2009. (Extreme Scientists Ser.). 24p. (gr. 2-3). 42.50 *(978-1-61512-451-0(9),* PowerKids Pr.); (Illus.). (YA). lib. bdg. 22.60 *(978-1-4042-4528-0(6))* Rosen Publishing Group, Inc., The.

Ridley, Sarah. Galileo Galilei. 2017. (Super Scientists Ser.). (ENG., Illus.). 24p. (J). (gr. 1-3). pap. 9.99 ***(978-1-4451-5358-2(0),*** Franklin Watts) Hachette Children's Group GBR. Dist: Hachette Bk. Group.

—Nicolaus Copernicus. 2017. (Super Scientists Ser.). (ENG., Illus.). 24p. (J). (gr. 1-3). pap. 9.99 ***(978-1-4451-5356-8(4),*** Franklin Watts) Hachette Children's Group GBR. Dist: Hachette Bk. Group.

Robinson, Ella May. Stars in Her Heart. 2005. 127p. per. 10.95 *(978-1-57258-318-4(5))* TEACH Services, Inc.

Romero, Libby. Comets. 2006. (J). pap. *(978-1-4108-6505-2(3))* Benchmark Education Co.

Ruiz, Jaime Alejandro Rodriguez. Johannes Kepler -Del otro lado está Dios. 2005. (SPA.). 124p. (YA). *(978-958-30-1647-9(0))* Panamericana Editorial.

Rusch, Elizabeth & Francis, Guy. The Planet Hunter: The Story Behind What Happened to Pluto. 2007. (ENG., Illus.). 32p. (J). (gr. -1-3). 15.95 *(978-0-87358-926-0(2))* Cooper Square Publishing Llc.

Sakolsky, Josh. Copernicus & Modern Astronomy. (Primary Sources of Revolutionary Scientific Discoveries & Theories Ser.). 64p. 2009. (gr. 5-5). 58.50 *(978-1-60851-840-1(X))* 2004. (Illus.). (J). lib. bdg. 31.95 *(978-1-4042-0305-1(2))* Rosen Publishing Group, Inc., The.

Science Readers Staff & Jankowski, Connie. From Hubble to Hubble: Astromers & Outer Space, 1 vol. 2007. (Science Readers Ser.). (ENG., Illus.). 32p. (J). (gr. 3-3). pap. 8.99 *(978-0-7439-0564-0(4))* Shell Educational Publishing.

Shaffer, Jody Jensen. Benjamin Banneker: Self-Made Man. 2016. (Primary Source Readers Ser.). (Illus.). 32p. (J). (gr. 4-5). pap. 8.99 *(978-1-4938-3082-4(1))* Teacher Created Materials, Inc.

Shea, Nicole. Be an Astronomer. 2014. (Be a Scientist! Ser.). 32p. (J). (gr. 3-6). pap. 63.00 *(978-1-4824-1199-7(7))* Stevens, Gareth Publishing LLLP.

Sisson, Stephanie Roth. Star Stuff: Carl Sagan & the Mysteries of the Cosmos. Sisson, Stephanie Roth, illus. 2014. (ENG., Illus.). 42p. (J). (gr. -1-3). 17.99 *(978-1-59643-960-3(2),* 9781596439603) Roaring Brook Pr.

Steele, Philip. Galileo: The Genius Who Faced the Inquisition. 2005. (National Geographic World History Biographies Ser.). (ENG., Illus.). 64p. (J). (gr. 3-7). 17.95 *(978-0-7922-3656-6(4));* lib. bdg. 27.90 *(978-0-7922-3657-3(2))* National Geographic Society. (National Geographic Children's Bks.).

Turiel, Isaac. How Do We Know the Size of the Solar System? 2009. (Great Scientific Questions & the Scientists Who Answered Them Ser.). 112p. (gr. 7-12). 63.90 *(978-1-61513-206-5(6))* Rosen Publishing Group, Inc., The.

Wadsworth, Ginger. Benjamin Banneker: Pioneering Scientist. Orback, Craig, illus. 2003. (On My Own Biography Ser.). (ENG.). 48p. (gr. 2-4). 25.26 *(978-0-87614-916-4(6))* Lerner Publishing Group.

—Benjamin Banneker: Pioneering Scientist. Orback, Craig, illus. 2006. (On My Own Biographies Ser.). 47p. (gr. 2-5). 17.00 *(978-0-7569-6705-5(8))* Perfection Learning Corp.

Wagner, Heather Lehr. Benjamin Banneker. 2010. (Leaders of the Colonial Era Ser.). 104p. (gr. 5-8). 35.00 *(978-1-60413-744-6(4),* Chelsea Hse.) Facts On File, Inc.

Welch, Catherine A. Benjamin Banneker. 2008. (History Maker Biographies Ser.). (Illus.). 48p. (J). (gr. 3-7). lib. bdg. 26.60 *(978-0-8225-7167-4(6),* Lerner Pubns.); pap. 52.95 *(978-0-8225-9386-7(6))* Lerner Publishing Group.

Yount, Lisa. Edward Pickering & His Women Computers. 2012. (Trailblazers in Science & Technology Ser.). 150p. (gr. 6-12). 35.00 *(978-1-60413-664-7(2),* Chelsea Hse.) Facts On File, Inc.

ASTRONOMICAL INSTRUMENTS

see also Telescopes

Angelo, Joseph A., Jr. Spacecraft for Astronomy. 2006. (Frontiers in Space Ser.). (Illus.). 304p. (C). (gr. 9). 45.00 *(978-0-8160-5774-0(5))* Facts On File, Inc.

Gregersen, Erik. Astronomical Observations: Astronomy & the Study of Deep Space. 2009. (Explorer's Guide to the Universe Ser.). (ENG.). 216p. (YA). 80.00 *(978-1-61530-077-8(5))* Rosen Publishing Group, Inc., The.

World Book, Inc Staff, contrib. by. Observatories in Space. 2010. (J). *(978-0-7166-9554-7(5))* World Bk., Inc.

ASTRONOMICAL OBSERVATORIES

Angelo, Joseph A., Jr. Spacecraft for Astronomy. 2006. (Frontiers in Space Ser.). (Illus.). 304p. (C). (gr. 9). 45.00 *(978-0-8160-5774-0(5))* Facts On File, Inc.

Astronomers. 2013. (Out of the Lab: Extreme Jobs in Science Ser.). 32p. (J). (gr. 3-6). pap. 60.00 *(978-1-4777-1379-2(4),* PowerKids Pr.) Rosen Publishing Group, Inc., The.

Gardner, Robert & Conklin, Joshua. A Kid's Book of Experiments with Stars. 2016. (Surprising Science Experiments Ser.). (ENG., Illus.). 48p. (J). (gr. 4-4). lib. bdg. 27.93 *(978-0-7660-7270-1(3))* Enslow Pubs., Inc.

Owen, Ruth. Astronomers. 2013. (Out of the Lab: Extreme Jobs in Science Ser.). 32p. (J). (gr. 3-6). 25.25 *(978-1-4777-1289-4(5));* pap. 10.00 *(978-1-4777-1378-5(6))* Rosen Publishing Group, Inc., The. (PowerKids Pr.).

World Book, Inc Staff, contrib. by. Observatories in Space. 2010. (J). *(978-0-7166-9554-7(5))* World Bk., Inc.

—Observatories on Earth. 2010. (J). *(978-0-7166-9553-0(7))* World Bk., Inc.

Yomtov, Nel. Observatory Director. 2015. (21st Century Skills Library: Cool STEAM Careers Ser.). (ENG., Illus.). 32p. (J). (gr. 4-7). 29.93 *(978-1-63362-008-7(5),* 205944) Cherry Lake Publishing.

Zobel, Derek. The Hubble Telescope. 2010. (Exploring Space Ser.). (ENG., Illus.). 24p. (J). (gr. k-3). lib. bdg. 25.95 *(978-1-60014-296-3(6),* Blastoff! Readers) Bellwether Media.

ASTRONOMICAL PHYSICS

see Astrophysics

ASTRONOMICAL SPECTROSCOPY

see Astrophysics

ASTRONOMY

see also Almanacs; Astrology; Astrophysics; Life on Other Planets; Meteorites; Meteors; Moon; Outer Space; Planets; Quasars; Radio Astronomy; Seasons; Solar System; Space Sciences; Stars; Sun; Tides

Aguilar, David A. Alien Worlds: Your Guide to Extraterrestrial Life. 2013. (ENG.). 80p. (J). (gr. 3-7). lib. bdg. 25.90 *(978-1-4263-1111-6(7));* (Illus.). 16.95 *(978-1-4263-1110-9(9))* National Geographic Society. (National Geographic Children's Bks.).

—Cosmic Catastrophes. 2016. (Smithsonian Ser.). (ENG., Illus.). 80p. (J). (gr. 3-7). 18.99 *(978-0-451-47684-5(0),* Viking Books for Young Readers) Penguin Young Readers Group.

—Space Encyclopedia: A Tour of Our Solar System & Beyond. Aguilar, David A., illus. 2013. (ENG., Illus.). 192p. (J). (gr. 5). 24.95 *(978-1-4263-0948-9(1));* lib. bdg. 38.90 *(978-1-4263-1560-2(0))* National Geographic Society. (National Geographic Children's Bks.).

—Super Stars: The Biggest, Hottest, Brightest, & Most Explosive Stars in the Milky Way. 2010. (ENG., Illus.). 48p. (J). (gr. 2-4). 16.95 *(978-1-4263-0601-3(6));* 25.90 *(978-1-4263-0602-0(4))* National Geographic Society. (National Geographic Children's Bks.).

Albrecht, Oliver, et al. Build Your Own Galaxy: The Big Unofficial Lego Builder's Book. 2013. (ENG., Illus.). 400p. pap. 29.99 *(978-3-86852-777-3(X))* Heel Verlag GmbH DEU. Dist: National Bk. Network.

Alex, Joanne DeFilipp. I Wonder What's Out There: A Vision of the Universe for Primary Classes. 2003. (Illus.). 64p. (J). spiral bd. *(978-0-939195-32-9(1))* Parent Child Pr., Inc.

Ally, Daisy. Solar Eclipses. 2009. (Science Scope Ser.). 32p. (gr. 5-5). 47.90 *(978-1-60853-057-1(4),* PowerKids Pr.) Rosen Publishing Group, Inc., The.

Ameet Studio Staff. Epic Space Adventures. Ameet Studio Staff, illus. 2016. (Lego Star Wars Ser.). (ENG., Illus.). 32p. (J). (gr. 1-3). pap. 8.99 *(978-0-545-91727-8(1))* Scholastic, Inc.

Arlon, Penelope & Arlon, Penny. Planets. 2012. (Scholastic Discover More Ser.). (ENG., Illus.). 80p. (J). (gr. 2-5). 12.99 *(978-0-545-33028-2(9),* Scholastic Reference) Scholastic, Inc.

Arnold, Tedd. Space. Arnold, Tedd, illus. 2013. (ENG., Illus.). 32p. (J). (gr. -1-3). pap. 3.99 *(978-0-545-56492-2(1),* Scholastic Reference) Scholastic, Inc.

Artell, Mike. Starry Skies: Questions, Facts, & Riddles about the Universe. 2007. (Illus.). 96p. (J). (gr. 4-7). per. 14.95 *(978-1-59647-022-4(4))* Good Year Bks.

Asimov, Isaac. Astronomy Today: Past & Present. 2005. (Isaac Asimov's 21st Century Library of the Universe). (Illus.). 32p. (gr. 2-6). lib. bdg. 26.00 *(978-0-8368-3980-7(3),* Gareth Stevens Learning Library) Stevens, Gareth Publishing LLLP.

Asimov, Isaac & Hantula, Richard. Astronomy Projects. 2005. (Isaac Asimov's 21st Century Library of the Universe). (Illus.). 32p. (gr. 2-6). lib. bdg. 26.00 *(978-0-8368-3979-1(X),* Gareth Stevens Learning Library) Stevens, Gareth Publishing LLLP.

—Black Holes, Pulsars, & Quasars. 2005. (Isaac Asimov's 21st Century Library of the Universe). (Illus.). 32p. (gr. 2-6). lib. bdg. 26.00 *(978-0-8368-3965-4(X),* Gareth Stevens Learning Library) Stevens, Gareth Publishing LLLP.

—Legends, Folklore, & Outer Space. 2005. (Isaac Asimov's 21st Century Library of the Universe). (Illus.). 32p. (gr. 2-6). lib. bdg. 26.00 *(978-0-8368-3951-7(X),* Gareth Stevens Learning Library) Stevens, Gareth Publishing LLLP.

—The Milky Way & Other Galaxies. 2005. (Isaac Asimov's 21st Century Library of the Universe). (Illus.). 32p. (gr. 2-6). lib. bdg. 26.00 *(978-0-8368-3968-5(4),* Gareth Stevens Learning Library) Stevens, Gareth Publishing LLLP.

—A Stargazer's Guide. 2005. (Isaac Asimov's 21st Century Library of the Universe). (Illus.). 32p. (gr. 2-6). lib. bdg. 26.00 *(978-0-8368-3953-1(6),* Gareth Stevens Learning Library) Stevens, Gareth Publishing LLLP.

Astronaut Adventure, Vol. 2. (Early Intervention Levels Ser.). 3.55 *(978-0-7362-0099-8(1))* CENGAGE Learning.

Astronomers. 2013. (Out of the Lab: Extreme Jobs in Science Ser.). 32p. (J). (gr. 3-6). pap. 60.00 *(978-1-4777-1379-2(4),* PowerKids Pr.) Rosen Publishing Group, Inc., The.

Baggett, Denise. Smithsonian Discover: Space. 2014. (Smithsonian Discover Ser.). (ENG., Illus.). 64p. (J). (gr. 2). spiral bd. 16.95 *(978-1-62686-161-9(7),* Silver Dolphin Bks.) Readerlink Distribution Services, LLC.

Baines, Becky. Every Planet Has a Place. 2008. (ZigZag Ser.). (ENG., Illus.). 32p. (J). (gr. k-3). 14.95 *(978-1-4263-0313-5(0));* lib. bdg. 19.90 *(978-1-4263-0314-2(9))* National Geographic Society. (National Geographic Children's Bks.).

Ball, Robert Stawell. Star-Land: Being Talks with Young People about the Wonders of the Heavens. 2010. (Cambridge Library Collection - Astronomy Ser.). (ENG., Illus.). 396p. pap. 45.99 *(978-1-108-01417-5(8))* Cambridge Univ. Pr.

Barr, Catherine & Williams, Steve. The Story of Space: A First Book about Our Universe. Husband, Amy, illus. 2017. (ENG.). 40p. (J). (gr. k-3). 18.99 ***(978-1-78603-003-0(9),*** Frances Lincoln Children's Bks.) Quarto Publishing Group UK GBR. Dist: Hachette Bk. Group.

Basher, Simon & Green, Dan. Astronomy: Out of This World! Basher, Simon, illus. 2009. (Basher Science Ser.). (ENG., Illus.). 128p. (J). (gr. 5-9). pap. 8.99 *(978-0-7534-6290-4(7),* 9780753462904, Kingfisher) Roaring Brook Pr.

Beauregard, Lynda. The Great Space Case: A Mystery about Astronomy. Helmer, Der-Shing, illus. 2013. (Summer Camp Science Mysteries Ser.: 7). (ENG.). 48p. (gr. 3-6). pap. 6.95 *(978-1-4677-0735-0(X));* lib. bdg. 29.27 *(978-1-4677-0169-3(6))* Lerner Publishing Group. (Graphic Universe™).

Becklake, Sue & Parker, Steve. Astronomy. 2013. (Illus.). 48p. (J). *(978-1-4351-5086-7(4))* Barnes & Noble, Inc.

Bell, Trudy E. Comets, Meteors, Asteroids, & the Outer Reaches. 2003. (New Solar System Ser.). (J). lib. bdg. 28.50 *(978-1-58340-289-4(6))* Black Rabbit Bks.

—Earth's Journey Through Space. 2007. (Scientific American Ser.). (Illus.). 80p. (YA). (gr. 5-9). lib. bdg. 30.00 *(978-0-7910-9050-3(7))* Facts On File, Inc.

Bellisario, Gina. To the Stars! Moran, Mike, illus. 2017. (Cloverleaf Books (tm) — Space Adventures Ser.). (ENG.). 24p. (J). (gr. k-2). 25.32 *(978-1-5124-2537-6(0));* 6.99 ***(978-1-5124-3897-0(9));*** 38.65 ***(978-1-5124-3896-3(0));*** 38.65 ***(978-1-5124-2834-6(5))*** Lerner Publishing Group. (Millbrook Pr.).

Benchmark Education Company, LLC Staff, compiled by. Earth & Space. 2005. spiral bd. 110.00 *(978-1-4108-3873-5(0))* Benchmark Education Co.

—Earth & Space: Theme Set. 2006. (J). 239.00 *(978-1-4108-7120-6(7));* 237.00 *(978-1-4108-7106-0(1))* Benchmark Education Co.

Bendick, Jeanne. Archimedes & the Door of Science: Immortals of Science. 2011. 154p. (gr. 5-8). 41.95 *(978-1-258-01488-9(2))* Literary Licensing, LLC.

Berger, Melvin & Berger, Gilda. Planets. 2010. (Scholastic True or False Ser.: 9). (ENG.). 48p. (J). (gr. 2-5). pap. 4.99 *(978-0-545-20204-6(3),* Scholastic Paperbacks) Scholastic, Inc.

Between the Lions - Early Literacy Kit - Shooting Stars, 1 cass., 1 bk. 2005. (Between the Lions Ser.). 36p. (J). VHS 29.95 *(978-1-59375-285-9(7),* WG38633) WGBH Boston Video.

Bhathal, Ragbir & Bhathal, Jenny. Australian Backyard Astronomy. 2006. (Illus.). 132p. (J). pap. *(978-0-642-27632-2(3))* National Library of Australia.

Birch, Robin. Space Series, 6 vols., Set. 2005. (Space Ser.). (Illus.). 32p. (gr. 2-4). 69.00 *(978-0-7910-7053-6(0),* Chelsea Hse.) Facts On File, Inc.

Blast Off!, 6 Pack. (gr. k-1). 23.00 *(978-0-7635-9078-9(9))* Rigby Education.

Blast Off!, 6 vols., Set. Incl. All about Astronauts. Gross, Miriam J. lib. bdg. 22.60 *(978-1-4358-2739-4(2));* All about Rockets. Gross, Miriam. lib. bdg. 22.60 *(978-1-4358-2735-6(X));* All about Satellites. Gross, Miriam J. (Illus.). lib. bdg. 22.60 *(978-1-4358-2736-3(8));* All about Space Missions. Gross, Miriam J. lib. bdg. 22.60 *(978-1-4358-2740-0(6));* All about Space Shuttles. Gross, Miriam J. lib. bdg. 22.60 *(978-1-4358-2738-7(4));* All about Space Stations. Gross, Miriam. lib. bdg. 22.60 *(978-1-4358-2737-0(6));* 24p. (J). (gr. 2-5). 2009. Set lib. bdg. 127.50 *(978-1-4358-2781-3(3),* PowerKids Pr.) Rosen Publishing Group, Inc., The.

Boerst, William J. Johannes Kepler: Discovering the Laws of Celestial Motion. 2004. (Profiles in Science Ser.). (Illus.). 144p. (YA). (gr. 6-12). lib. bdg. 26.95 *(978-1-883846-98-5(6),* First Biographies) Reynolds, Morgan Inc.

Bone, Emily. My Very First Space Book IR (was Book of Space) 2015. (My Very First Bks.). (ENG.). 30p. (J). 11.99 *(978-0-7945-1734-2(X),* Usborne) EDC Publishing.

Bone, Emily & Maskell, Hazel. Astronomy & Space Sticker Book IR. 2013. (Astronomy & Space Sticker Book Ser.). 32p. (J). pap. 9.99 *(978-0-7945-3359-5(0),* Usborne) EDC Publishing.

Bortolotti, Dan. Exploring Saturn. 2003. (ENG., Illus.). 64p. (J). (gr. 4-8). pap. 9.95 *(978-1-55297-765-1(X),* 9781552977651) Firefly Bks., Ltd.

Bortz, Fred. Johannes Kepler & the Three Laws of Planetary Motion. 2013. (Revolutionary Discoveries of Scientific Pioneers Ser.). 80p. (YA). (gr. 7-12). 33.25 *(978-1-4777-1805-6(2))* Rosen Publishing Group, Inc., The.

Bourgeois, Paulette. Le Soleil. Slavin, Bill, illus.Tr. of Destination Univers: Le Soleil. (FRE.). 40p. (J). pap. 8.99 *(978-0-590-16019-3(2))* Scholastic, Inc.

Bourgeois, Paulette & Slavin, Bill. Starting with Space: The Moon.Tr. of Destination Univers: La Lune. (FRE., Illus.). 40p. (J). pap. 8.99 *(978-0-590-16020-9(6))* Scholastic, Inc.

Bow, James. Space Mysteries Revealed. 2010. (ENG., Illus.). 32p. (J). pap. *(978-0-7787-7431-0(7));* (gr. 4-7). lib. bdg. *(978-0-7787-7416-7(3))* Crabtree Publishing Co.

Brake, Mark. Really, Really Big Questions about Space & Time. Choksi, Nishant, illus. 2012. (Really Really Big Questions Ser.). (ENG.). 64p. (J). (gr. 4-7). pap. 8.99 *(978-0-7534-6747-3(X),* 9780753467473, Kingfisher) Roaring Brook Pr.

Bredeson, Carmen. Weird but True Space Facts. 2011. (Weird but True Science Ser.). (Illus.). 24p. (J). (gr. k-18). pap. 7.95 *(978-1-59845-371-3(8),* Enslow Elementary); (gr. 5-9). lib. bdg. 22.60 *(978-0-7660-3863-9(7))* Enslow Pubs., Inc.

Bredeson, Carmen & Dyson, Marianne. Exploring the Stars. 2015. (Launch into Space! Ser.). (ENG.). 32p. (J). (gr. 3-4). pap. 10.52 *(978-0-7660-6829-2(3))* Enslow Pubs., Inc.

Bredeson, Carmen, et al. Exploring the Stars. 2015. (Launch into Space! Ser.). (ENG., Illus.). 32p. (J). (gr. 3-4). 25.27 *(978-0-7660-6831-5(5))* Enslow Pubs., Inc.

Britannica, Learning Library. Exploring Space. 2003. (Illus.). 64p. 14.95 *(978-1-59339-031-0(9))* Encyclopaedia Britannica, Inc.

Bryant, Ray, illus. The Book of Space. 2013. (Questions Ser.). (ENG.). 64p. (J). (gr. k-3). 7.99 *(978-0-7534-7099-2(3),* 9780753470992, Kingfisher) Roaring Brook Pr.

Bulletpoints Astronomy. 2005. (Illus.). (J). per. 4.99 *(978-1-933581-00-2(X),* Byeway) Byeway Bks.

Bullock, Linda. Looking Through a Telescope. 2004. (Rookie Read-About Science Ser.). (ENG., Illus.). 32p. (J). (gr. 1-2). pap. 4.95 *(978-0-516-27906-0(8),* Children's Pr.) Scholastic Library Publishing.

Burnie, David, et al. Animal Kingdom: A Thrilling Adventure with Nature's Creatures. 2016. (ENG., Illus.). 80p. (J). 15.99 *(978-0-7534-7278-1(3),* 9780753472781, Kingfisher) Roaring Brook Pr.

Burton, Margie, et al. Looking into Space. 2011. (Early Connections Ser.). (J). *(978-1-61672-499-3(4))* Benchmark Education Co.

Butterfield, Moira & Jacobs, Pat. Space. 2016. (Know It All Ser.). (ENG., Illus.). 32p. (J). (gr. 5-5). pap. 10.58 *(978-1-5026-0882-6(0),* 1398906) Cavendish Square Publishing.

Canavan, Thomas. Why Are Black Holes Black? Questions & Answers about Space. 2013. (Science F. A. Q. Ser.). 32p. (gr. 3-6). 31.35 *(978-1-78212-395-8(4))* Arcturus Publishing GBR. Dist: Black Rabbit Bks.

Capstone Press Editors. The Story of Orion: A Roman Constellation Myth, 1 vol. Guerlais, Gérald, illus. 2012. (Night Sky Stories Ser.). (ENG.). 24p. (gr. 2-3). lib. bdg. 26.65 *(978-1-4048-7377-3(5))* Picture Window Bks.

Carson, Jana. We Both Read Bilingual Edition-About Space/Acerca Del Espacio. 2011. (SPA., Illus.). 44p. (J). pap. 4.99 *(978-1-60115-052-3(0))* Treasure Bay, Inc.

Carson, Mary Kay. Exploring the Solar System: A History with 22 Activities. rev. ed. 2008. (For Kids Ser.). (ENG., Illus.). 176p. (J). (gr. 4-7). pap. 19.99 *(978-1-55652-715-9(2))* Chicago Review Pr., Inc.

Castaldo, Nancy F. Leap into Space: Exploring the Universe & Your Place in It. McRae, Patrick, illus. 2008. (ENG.). 128p. (J). (gr. 3-7). 16.99 *(978-0-8249-6815-1(8));* pap. 12.99 *(978-0-8249-6816-8(6))* Worthy Publishing. (Ideal Pubns.).

Channing, Margot. Stars & Planets. 2014. (Closer Look At... Ser.). (Illus.). 32p. (gr. 3-6). 31.35 *(978-1-905087-08-2(X),* 1374553) Book Hse. GBR. Dist: Black Rabbit Bks.

Chiger, Arielle & Houk Maley, Adrienne. 20 Fun Facts about Asteroids & Comets. 2014. (Fun Fact File: Space! Ser.). 32p. (J). (gr. 2-5). 25.25 *(978-1-4824-0791-4(4))* Stevens, Gareth Publishing LLLP.

Cole, Joanna. Lost in the Solar System. Degen, Bruce, illus. 2010. (Magic School Bus Ser.). (ENG.). (J). (gr. -1-3). 18.95 *(978-0-545-22337-9(7))* Scholastic, Inc.

Cole, Michael D. Eye on the Universe: The Incredible Hubble Space Telescope. 2012. (American Space Missions — Astronauts, Exploration, & Discovery Ser.). (Illus.). 48p. (J). (gr. 5-18). 25.27 *(978-0-7660-4077-9(1))* Enslow Pubs., Inc.

Collison, Cathy & Campbell, Janis. G Is for Galaxy: An Out of This World Alphabet. Stacy, Alan, illus. (World/Country Alphabet Ser.). (ENG.). 40p. (J). (gr. k-5). 2005. 16.95 *(978-1-58536-255-4(7))* 2006. pap. 7.95 *(978-1-58536-335-3(9))* Sleeping Bear Pr.

The Constellation Collection. 2015. (Constellation Collection). (ENG.). 24p. (J). (gr. 3-3). pap., pap., pap. 297.00 *(978-1-4994-1321-2(1),* PowerKids Pr.) Rosen Publishing Group, Inc., The.

Contemporary Discourse in the Field of Astronomy, 6 bks., Set. 2006. (YA). lib. bdg. 183.60 *(978-1-4042-0628-1(0))* Rosen Publishing Group, Inc., The.

Cross, Matthew & Croft, Malcolm. Cool Astronomy: 50 Fantastic Facts for Kids of All Ages. 2014. (ENG., Illus.). 112p. (J). (gr. 5). 14.99 *(978-1-909396-41-8(9))* Pavilion Bks. GBR. Dist: Independent Pubs. Group.

Dakota, Heather. Space. Myers, Lawrence E., illus. 2008. 64p. (J). pap. *(978-0-545-08503-8(9))* Scholastic, Inc.

Davis, Kenneth C. Don't Know Much about Space. unabr. ed. 2004. (Don't Know Much about Ser.). 144p. (J). (gr. 4-7). pap. 29.00 incl. audio *(978-0-8072-0661-4(X),* Listening Library) Random Hse. Audio Publishing Group.

Daynes, Katie & Wray, Zoe. Life in Space. Fox, Christyan & Pang, Alex, illus. 2008. (Usborne Beginners Ser.). 32p. (J). *(978-0-545-06963-2(7))* Scholastic, Inc.

DeCristofano, Carolyn Cinami. A Black Hole Is Not a Hole. Carroll, Michael, illus. 2012. (ENG.). 80p. (J). (gr. 4-7). 18.95 *(978-1-57091-783-7(3))* Charlesbridge Publishing, Inc.

Dell, Pamela. Mapping the Sky. 2010. (Mapping Our World Ser.). 32p. (gr. 4). 28.50 *(978-1-60870-119-3(0))* Marshall Cavendish GBR. Dist: Marshall Cavendish Corp.

Diagram Group Staff. Space & Astronomy: An Illustrated Guide to Science. 2006. (Science Visual Resources Ser.). (Illus.). 208p. (gr. 6-12). 49.50 *(978-0-8160-6168-6(8))* Facts On File, Inc.

Discovery. Discovery Spaceopedia: The Complete Guide to Everything Space. 2015. (ENG., Illus.). 192p. (J). (gr. 1-17). pap. 19.95 *(978-1-61893-407-9(4))* Time Inc. Bks.

Dorling Kindersley Publishing Staff. DK Eyewitness Books: Universe: Universe. 2015. (DK Eyewitness Bks.). (ENG., Illus.). 72p. (J). (gr. 3-7). 19.99 *(978-1-4654-3362-6(7),* DK Children) Dorling Kindersley Publishing, Inc.

—Eyewitness - Universe. 2015. (DK Eyewitness Bks.). (ENG.). 72p. (J). (gr. 3-7). pap. 9.99 *(978-1-4654-3187-5(X),* DK Children) Dorling Kindersley Publishing, Inc.

—Eyewitness Explorer: Night Sky Detective: Night Sky Detective. 2015. (ENG., Illus.). 72p. (J). (gr. 3-7). pap. 9.99 *(978-1-4654-3501-9(8),* DK Children) Dorling Kindersley Publishing, Inc.

—First Space Encyclopedia. 2016. (ENG., Illus.). 136p. (J). (gr. 1-4). 16.99 *(978-1-4654-4343-4(6),* DK Children) Dorling Kindersley Publishing, Inc.

—Pocket Genius: Space. 2016. (Pocket Genius Ser.). (ENG., Illus.). 160p. (J). (gr. 3-7). pap. 4.99 *(978-1-4654-4593-3(5),* DK Children) Dorling Kindersley Publishing, Inc.

—Space: A Visual Encyclopedia. 2010. (Visual Encyclopedia Ser.). (ENG.). 256p. (J). (gr. 2-5). 24.99 *(978-0-7566-6277-6(X),* DK Children) Dorling Kindersley Publishing, Inc.

—Space Visual Encyclopedia. 2016. (ENG., Illus.). 208p. (J). (gr. 4-7). 16.99 *(978-1-4654-5472-0(1),* DK Children) Dorling Kindersley Publishing, Inc.

—Sticker Encyclopedia Space. 2009. (ENG.). 96p. (J). (gr. k-2). pap. 12.99 *(978-0-7566-5839-7(X),* DK Children) Dorling Kindersley Publishing, Inc.

Dorling Kindersley Publishing Staff & Cruddas, Sarah. Did You Know? Space. 2017. (ENG.). 144p. (J). (gr. 1-3). 21.99 ***(978-1-4654-6186-5(8),*** DK Children) Dorling Kindersley Publishing, Inc.

Dorling Kindersley Publishing Staff & Lippincott, Kristen. Eyewitness Books - Astronomy. 2013. (DK Eyewitness Bks.). (ENG.). 72p. (J). (gr. 3-7). 16.99 *(978-1-4654-0895-2(9),* DK Children) Dorling Kindersley Publishing, Inc.

Dowswell, Paul. Mi Primera Enciclopedia del Espacio. rev. ed. 2004. (Bible Tales Readers Ser.).Tr. of First Encyclopedia of

Space. (SPA.). 16p. (J). lib. bdg. 17.95 (978-1-58086-495-4(3)) EDC Publishing.

Doyle, Bill. The Space Explorer's Guide to the Universe. Labat, Yancey C., illus. 2003. (Space University Ser.). 48p. (J). (978-0-439-55739-9(9)) Scholastic, Inc.

Driscoll, Michael. A Child's Introduction to the Night Sky: The Story of the Stars, Planets & Constellations - And How You Can Find Them in the Sky. Hamilton, Meredith, illus. 2004. (ENG.). 96p. (J). (gr. 3-7). tchr. ed. 19.99 (978-1-57912-366-6(X), 81366, Black Dog & Leventhal Pubs. Inc.) Hachette Bks.

Dusek, Jiri & Pisala, Jan. Space Atlas. Tuma, Tomas, illus. 2014. (ENG.). 34p. (J). (gr. 1-3). 16.95 (978-1-4549-1237-8(5)) Sterling Publishing Co., Inc.

Dybvik, Tina. Space Cowboy Caleb & the Night Sky Round-Up: Learning about the Night Sky, 1 vol. Record, Adam, illus. 2013. (Take It Outside Ser.). (ENG.). 24p. (gr. k-2). pap. 8.95 (978-1-4795-1938-5(3)); lib. bdg. 27.32 (978-1-4048-8317-8(7)) Picture Window Bks.

Dyer, Alan. Space. 2007. (Insiders Ser.). (ENG., Illus.). 64p. (J). (gr. 3-7). 17.99 (978-1-4169-3860-6(5), Simon & Schuster Bks. For Young Readers) Simon & Schuster Bks. For Young Readers.

Editors of TIME For Kids Magazine. Space. 2014. (TIME for Kids X-WHY-Z Ser.). (ENG., Illus.). 96p. (J). (gr. -1-1). 14.95 (978-1-61893-126-9(1)) Time Inc. Bks.

Elish, Dan. Galaxies. 2006. (Kaleidoscope Space Ser.). (Illus.). 48p. (gr. 3-7). 20.95 (978-0-7614-2047-7(9), Benchmark Bks.) Marshall Cavendish Corp.

Farndon, John. What Do We Know about Stars & Galaxies?, 1 vol. 2011. (Earth, Space, & Beyond Ser.). (ENG.). 48p. (gr. 6-6). pap. 9.49 (978-1-4109-4168-8(X)); 34.65 (978-1-4109-4162-6(0)) Heinemann-Raintree. (Raintree Freestyle).

Faulkner, Danny R. The New Astronomy Book. 2014. (Illus.). 96p. (J). (978-0-89051-834-2(3)) Master Bks.

Faust, Daniel R. Collision Course: Asteroids & Earth. 2008. (Jr. Graphic Environmental Dangers Ser.). (ENG., Illus.). 24p. (J). (gr. 3-6). lib. bdg. 25.25 (978-1-4042-4228-9(7)) Rosen Publishing Group, Inc., The.

Fea, Kenneth Hugh. Astronomy & Beginning Astrophysics. 2012. 212p. 44.95 (978-1-258-25076-8(4)); pap. 29.95 (978-1-258-25543-5(X)) Literary Licensing, LLC.

Finton, Nancy. Explore the Solar System! 2010. (Illus.). 29p. (J). (978-0-545-28884-2(3)) Scholastic, Inc.

Firestone, Mary. Astrobiologist. 2005. (Weird Careers in Science Ser.). (Illus.). 64p. (gr. 5-8). lib. bdg. 25.00 (978-0-7910-8971-2(1), Chelsea Hse.) Facts On File, Inc.

Firth, Rachel. Astronomy - Internet Linked. rev. ed. 2008. (Discovery Nature Ser.). 48p. (J). 8.99 (978-0-7945-2423-4(0), Usborne) EDC Publishing.

Flight Science. 2004. (Formula Fun Ser.). (Illus.). 48p. (J). (978-1-84229-589-2(6)) Top That! Publishing PLC.

Fontany, Elena. Other Worlds Than This. 2005. reprint ed. pap. 19.95 (978-1-4179-9707-7(9)) Kessinger Publishing, LLC.

Ford, Adam. Stars: A Family Guide to the Night Sky. 2016. (Discover Together Guides). (ENG., Illus.). 48p. 16.95 (978-1-61180-283-2(0), Roost Books) Shambhala Pubns., Inc.

Forest, Christopher. The Kids' Guide to the Constellations, 1 vol. 2011. (Kids' Guides). (ENG.). 32p. (gr. 3-4). lib. bdg. 27.99 (978-1-4296-6007-5(4), Edge Bks.) Capstone Press of Coughlan Cos.

Fried, Ellen. Stars & Galaxies. 2007. (Reading Expeditions Ser.). (ENG., Illus.). 32p. (J). pap. 17.95 (978-0-7922-4574-2(1)) CENGAGE Learning.

Galat, Joan Marie. Black Holes & Supernovas, 1 vol. 2011. (Solar System & Beyond Ser.). (ENG.). 32p. (gr. 3-4). pap. 8.10 (978-1-4296-7225-2(0)); pap. 47.70 (978-1-4296-7226-9(9)); lib. bdg. 27.32 (978-1-4296-6004-4(X)) Capstone Press of Coughlan Cos. (Fact Finders).

Galaxies. 2015. (J). (978-1-60818-482-8(X), Creative Education) Creative Co., The.

Galaxies & the Universe. 2006. (World Book's Solar System & Space Exploration Library). 63p. (J). (978-0-7166-9508-0(1)) World Bk., Inc.

The Galaxy. (gr. 2-5). 331.95 (978-0-7368-8978-0(7)) Red Brick Learning.

The Galaxy Guides. 2015. (Galaxy Guides). (ENG.). 32p. (J). (gr. 4-4). pap., pap., pap. 360.00 (978-1-4994-1323-6(8), PowerKids Pr.) Rosen Publishing Group, Inc., The.

Gardner, Robert. Astronomy Experiments in Your Own Observatory. 2015. (Design, Build, Experiment Ser.). (ENG., Illus.). 128p. (J). (gr. 7-7). lib. bdg. 37.27 (978-0-7660-6951-0(6)) Enslow Pubs., Inc.

—Astronomy Projects with an Observatory You Can Build. 2007. (Build-A-Lab! Science Experiments Ser.). (Illus.). 128p. (J). (gr. 3-7). lib. bdg. 33.27 (978-0-7660-2808-1(9)) Enslow Pubs., Inc.

Gardner, Robert & Conklin, Joshua. A Kid's Book of Experiments with Stars. 2016. (Surprising Science Experiments Ser.). (ENG., Illus.). 48p. (J). (gr. 4-4). lib. bdg. 27.93 (978-0-7660-7270-1(3)) Enslow Pubs., Inc.

Gareth Stevens Publishing Staff, contrib. by. The Universe. 2003. (Discovery Channel School Science Ser.). (Illus.). 32p. (gr. 4-8). lib. bdg. 26.00 (978-0-8368-3374-4(0), Gareth Stevens Learning Library) Stevens, Gareth Publishing LLLP.

Garlick, Mark A. Atlas of the Universe. 2008. (Insiders Ser.). (ENG., Illus.). 128p. (J). (gr. 4-9). 24.99 (978-1-4169-5558-0(5), Simon & Schuster Bks. For Young Readers) Simon & Schuster Bks. For Young Readers.

Gendell, Megan & Connolly, Rachel. Lost in Space: Everything You Wanted to Know about Planets, Stars, Galaxies, & Beyond. 2007. (Illus.). 32p. (J). pap. (978-0-545-04455-4(3)) Scholastic, Inc.

Gendell, Megan & O'Dea, Tierney. Shoot for the Stars: Everything You Wanted to Know about Astronomy, Stars, & Constellations. 2008. (Illus.). 32p. (J). (978-0-545-04458-5(8)) Scholastic, Inc.

Gendell, Megan & Sweitzer, James. Spinning 'round the Sun: Everything You Wanted to Know about the Solar System & Everything in It. 2008. (Illus.). 32p. (J). pap. (978-0-545-04459-2(6)) Scholastic, Inc.

George, Michael. Stars: Beacons in the Sky. 2003. (LifeViews Ser.). (Illus.). 32p. (J). lib. bdg. (978-1-58341-250-3(6), Creative Education) Creative Co., The.

Gibbons, Gail. Galaxies, Galaxies! Gibbons, Gail, illus. 2006. (ENG., Illus.). 32p. (J). (gr. 3-7). 17.95 (978-0-8234-2002-5(7)) Holiday Hse., Inc.

Gifford, Clive. Out of This World: All the Cool Stuff about Space You Want to Knkow. 2012. (ENG.). 144p. (YA). (gr. 4-6). 9.99 (978-1-60652-519-7(0)) Reader's Digest Assn., Inc., The.

—Out of This World: All the Cool Stuff about Space You Want to Know. Pinder, Andrew, illus. 2012. (J). (978-1-60652-571-5(9)) Reader's Digest Assn., Inc., The.

Goldsmith, Mike. The Kingfisher Space Encyclopedia. 2017. (Kingfisher Encyclopedias Ser.). (ENG.). 160p. (J). pap. 13.99 (978-0-7534-7353-5(4), 9780753473535, Kingfisher) Roaring Brook Pr.

—Space. 2010. (Ripley Twists Ser.). 48p. (J). (gr. 3-18). lib. bdg. 19.95 (978-1-4222-1833-4(3)) Mason Crest.

—Stars & Planets. 2011. (Navigators Ser.). (ENG., Illus.). 48p. (J). (gr. 4-7). pap. 8.99 (978-0-7534-6682-7(1), 9780753466827, Kingfisher) Roaring Brook Pr.

Goldsworthy, Steve. Constellations. 2016. (J). **(978-1-4896-5809-8(2)**, AV2 by Weigl) 2011. (Illus.). 32p. (YA). (gr. 2-5). 28.55 (978-1-61690-633-7(2)) Weigl Pubs., Inc.

Gottlieb. Earth & Beyond. 2004. (Wonders of Science Ser.). (ENG.). 176p. (gr. 7-12). pap., tchr. ed. 27.70 (978-0-7398-9187-2(1)) Houghton Mifflin Harcourt Publishing Co.

Graham, Ian. Galaxies & Stars. 2015. (Space Ser.). (Illus.). 24p. (gr. 3-6). lib. bdg. 28.50 (978-1-62588-208-0(4)) Black Rabbit Bks.

Graham, Ian & Jones, Geriant. H. Exploring Science: Space an Amazing Fact File & Hands-On Project Book. 2015. (ENG., Illus.). 64p. (J). (gr. -1-6). 12.99 (978-1-86147-386-8(9), Armadillo) Anness Publishing GBR. Dist: National Bk. Network.

Grant, Donald. Atlas of Space. 2012. (ENG., Illus.). 36p. (J). (gr. -1-k). 14.99 (978-1-85103-407-9(2)) Moonlight Publishing, Ltd. GBR. Dist: Independent Pubs. Group.

Graun, Ken. Our Constellations & Their Stars. 2004. (Twenty-First Century Astronomy Ser.: 3). (Illus.). 36p. (J). 15.95 (978-1-928771-09-8(2)) Ken Pr.

Greathouse, Lisa E. Astronomers Through Time, 1 vol. 2007. (Science Readers Ser.). (ENG.). 32p. (J). (gr. 4-4). pap. 8.99 (978-0-7439-0562-6(8)) Shell Educational Publishing.

Gregersen, Erik. Astronomical Observations: Astronomy & the Study of Deep Space. 2009. (Explorer's Guide to the Universe Ser.). (ENG.). 216p. (YA). 80.00 (978-1-61530-077-8(5)) Rosen Publishing Group, Inc., The.

Grego, Peter. My Little Book of Space. 2014. (Illus.). 64p. (J). (978-1-4351-5530-5(0)) Barnes & Noble, Inc.

Gregoire, Maryellen. Things in Space, 1 vol. 2011. (Wonder Readers Emergent Level Ser.). (ENG.). (gr. -1-1). 32p. pap. 5.99 (978-1-4296-7848-3(8)); 8p. pap. 35.94 (978-1-4296-8235-0(3)) Capstone Press of Coughlan Cos. (Wonder Readers).

Grice, Noreen. The Little Moon Phase Book. Gendler, Robert, photos by. 2005. (Illus.). 12p. (J). spiral bd. 23.95 (978-0-9773285-0-5(3)) Ozone Publishing, Corp.

Griffin, Ingrid. The Story of Cassiopeia. 2015. (Stories in the Stars Ser.). (ENG., Illus.). 24p. (J). (gr. 1-2). pap. 8.15 (978-1-4824-2661-8(7)) Stevens, Gareth Publishing LLLP.

—The Story of Hercules. 2015. (Stories in the Stars Ser.). (ENG., Illus.). 24p. (J). (gr. 1-2). pap. 8.15 (978-1-4824-2669-4(2)) Stevens, Gareth Publishing LLLP.

—The Story of the Great Bear. 2015. (Stories in the Stars Ser.). (ENG., Illus.). 24p. (J). (gr. 1-2). pap. 8.15 (978-1-4824-2665-6(X)) Stevens, Gareth Publishing LLLP.

Hamilton, S. L. Sky Watch. 2011. (Xtreme Space Ser.). (Illus.). 32p. (gr. 3-9). 27.07 (978-1-61714-739-5(7), A&D Xtreme) ABDO Publishing Co.

Hansen, Rosanna. Mysteries in Space: Exploration & Discovery. 2005. (True Tales Ser.). (ENG., Illus.). 48p. (J). (gr. 2-4). 22.50 (978-0-516-25185-1(6), Children's Pr.) Scholastic Library Publishing.

—Seven Wonders of the Sun & Other Stars. 2011. (Seven Wonders Ser.). (ENG.). 80p. (gr. 5-8). 33.26 (978-0-7613-5450-5(6)) Lerner Publishing Group.

Hanson, Anders & Mann, Elissa. Cool String Art: Creative Activities That Make Math & Science Fun for Kids!, 1 vol. 2013. (Cool Art with Math & Science Ser.). (ENG.). 32p. (J). (gr. 3-6). lib. bdg. 28.50 (978-1-61783-824-8(1), Checkerboard Library) ABDO Publishing Co.

Harcourt School Publishers Staff. How the Sky Got Its Starr. 3rd ed. 2004. (Trophies Reading Program Ser.). (Illus.). (gr. k). pap. 11.50 (978-0-15-340895-3(2)) Harcourt Schl. Pubs.

Harris, Nicholas. The Glow in the Dark Book of Space: The Book You Can Read in the Dark! Sebastian Quigley, Sebastian, illus. 2013. (ENG.). 32p. (J). (gr. -1-2). 17.99 (978-1-84780-417-4(9), Frances Lincoln) Quarto Publishing Group UK GBR. Dist: Hachette Bk. Group.

Harrison, Lorraine. Pisces. 2015. (Constellation Collection). (ENG., Illus.). 24p. (J). (gr. 3-3). pap. 8.25 (978-1-4994-0935-2(4), PowerKids Pr.) Rosen Publishing Group, Inc., The.

Harrod-Eagles, Cynthia. Stars & Constellations. 2007. (Illus.). 16p. (J). (978-0-545-00734-4(8)) Scholastic, Inc.

Hasan, Heather, ed. How Mathematical Models, Computer Simulations, & Exploration Can Be Used to Study the Universe: An Anthology of Current Thought. 2009. (Contemporary Discourse in the Field of Astronomy Ser.). 240p. (gr. 10-10). 63.90 (978-1-61511-904-2(3)) Rosen Publishing Group, Inc., The.

Hayden, Kate, et al. Starry Sky. 2006. (DK Readers Ser.). (ENG., Illus.). 32p. (J). (gr. 1-3). pap. 3.99 (978-0-7566-1959-6(9), DK Children) Dorling Kindersley Publishing, Inc.

Hayes, Susan. Read It Build It Space. Abbott, Simon, illus. 2015. (Read It Build It Ser.). (ENG.). 16p. (J). (gr. -1-1). 15.99 (978-1-4052-7165-3(5)) Egmont Bks., Ltd. GBR. Dist: Independent Pubs. Group.

Henry, Jonathan. The Astronomy Book. 2006. (Wonders of Creation Ser.). 51p. pap., stu. ed. 3.99 (978-1-893345-61-4(0)) Answers in Genesis Ministries.

Higgins, Nadia. The Solar System Through Infographics. Waananen, Lisa, illus. 2013. (Super Science Infographics Ser.). (ENG.). 32p. (gr. 3-5). pap. 8.95 (978-1-4677-1594-2(8)); lib. bdg. 26.60 (978-1-4677-1289-7(2), Lerner Pubns.) Lerner Publishing Group.

Hodgkins, Fran. The Secret Galaxy, 1 vol. Taylor, Mike, photos by. 2014. (Tilbury House Nature Book Ser.: 0). (ENG., Illus.). 32p. (gr. 1-6). 17.95 (978-0-88448-391-5(6), 884391) Tilbury Hse. Pubs.

Hollar, Sherman. Astronomy: Understanding the Universe. 2011. (Illus.). 96p. (J). lib. bdg. 31.70 (978-1-61530-520-9(3)) Rosen Publishing Group, Inc., The.

Holt, Laurence. Stikky Night Skies. 2003. (ENG., Illus.). 240p. (YA). pap. 12.00 (978-1-56858-253-5(6)) Avalon Publishing Group.

Holt, Rinehart and Winston Staff. Astronomy, Vol. J. 3rd ed. 2003. (Holt Science & Technology Ser.). (SPA.). 18.60 (978-0-03-069319-9(5)) Holt McDougal.

Howard, Fran. Asteroids, Comets, & Meteoroids, 1 vol. 2008. (Universe Ser.). (ENG.). 32p. (gr. k-4). 27.07 (978-1-59928-925-0(3), Buddy Bks.) ABDO Publishing Co.

Hudson, Rachel. Objects in the Sky. 2012. (Exploring Earth & Space Ser.). (ENG., Illus.). 24p. (J). (gr. 1-3). 22.60 (978-1-4488-8578-7(7), PowerKids Pr.) Rosen Publishing Group, Inc., The.

Hughes, Catherine D. National Geographic Little Kids First Big Book of Space. Aguilar, David A., illus. 2012. (National Geographic Little Kids First Big Bks.). (ENG.). 128p. (J). (gr. -1-3). 14.95 (978-1-4263-1014-0(5)); lib. bdg. 23.90 (978-1-4263-1015-7(3)) National Geographic Society. (National Geographic Children's Bks.).

Hunter, Nick. Eclipses, 1 vol. 2013. (Night Sky: & Other Amazing Sights in Space Ser.). (ENG.). 32p. (gr. 1-3). 27.32 (978-1-4329-7515-9(3)); pap. 8.95 (978-1-4329-7520-3(X)) Heinemann-Raintree. (Heinemann First Library).

—The Night Sky: & Other Amazing Sights. 2013. (Night Sky: & Other Amazing Sights in Space Ser.). (ENG.). 32p. (gr. 1-3). pap. 31.96 (978-1-4329-7523-4(4)); lib. bdg. 109.28 (978-1-4329-7518-0(8)) Heinemann-Raintree. (Heinemann First Library).

—Space, 1 vol. 2012. (Explorer Tales Ser.). (ENG.). 32p. (gr. 1-3). 29.99 (978-1-4109-4782-6(3), Read Me!) Heinemann-Raintree.

Hutmacher, Kimberly. The Night Sky. 2012. (ENG.). 24p. (gr. 3-4). pap. 8.95 (978-1-61810-225-6(7)) Rourke Educational Media.

Jackson, Ellen. Mysterious Universe: Supernovae, Dark Energy, & Black Holes. Bishop, Nic, illus. Bishop, Nic, photos by. 2008. (Scientists in the Field Ser.). (ENG.). 64p. (J). (gr. 5-7). 18.00 (978-0-618-56325-8(3)) Houghton Mifflin Harcourt Publishing Co.

—Mysterious Universe: Supernovae, Dark Energy, & Black Holes. Bishop, Nic, photos by. 2011. (Scientists in the Field Ser.). (ENG., Illus.). 64p. (J). (gr. 5-7). pap. 9.99 (978-0-547-51992-0(3)) Houghton Mifflin Harcourt Publishing Co.

Jacobs, Heidi Hayes & LeVasseur, Michal L. World Studies: Medieval Times to Today: With Text Purchase, Add StudentEXPRESS. (Illus.). 96p. cd-rom 1.25 (978-0-13-166975-8(3)) Prentice Hall (Schl. Div.).

James, Lincoln. Solar Eclipses. 2009. (Real Life Readers Ser.). (J). (ENG., Illus.). 32p. (gr. 5-6). pap. 10.00 (978-1-4358-0191-2(1), 1291696); lib. bdg. 25.25 (978-1-4358-2998-5(0)); (Illus.). 32p. 60.00 (978-1-4358-0192-9(X), 1291696) Rosen Publishing Group, Inc., The. (PowerKids Pr.).

Jasper, Mark & Gamble, Adam. Good Night Galaxy. Kelly, Cooper, illus. 2012. (Good Night Our World Ser.). (ENG.). 20p. (J). (gr. k — 1). bds. 9.95 (978-1-60219-065-8(8)) Good Night Bks.

Jefferis, David. Galaxies: Immense Star Islands. 2008. (Exploring our Solar System Ser.). (ENG., Illus.). 32p. (J). (gr. 4-9). pap. (978-0-7787-3740-7(3)) Crabtree Publishing Co.

—Star Spotters: Telescopes & Observatories. 2008. (Exploring Our Solar System Ser.). (ENG., Illus.). 32p. (J). (gr. 4-9). pap. (978-0-7787-3742-1(X)) Crabtree Publishing Co.

Jerome, Kate Boehm & National Geographic Learning Staff. Exploring Space. 2006. (Nonfiction Reading & Writing Workshops Ser.). (ENG., Illus.). 32p. (J). pap. 17.95 (978-0-7922-8870-1(X)) CENGAGE Learning.

Kamberg, Mary-Lane. Stephen Hawking. 2014. (Great Science Writers Ser.). (Illus.). 112p. (J). (gr. 7-12). 35.60 (978-1-4777-7683-4(4)) Rosen Publishing Group, Inc., The.

Kawa, Katie. Freaky Space Stories. 2015. (Freaky True Science Ser.). (ENG., Illus.). 32p. (J). (gr. 4-5). 26.60 (978-1-4824-2958-9(6)) Stevens, Gareth Publishing LLLP.

Kazlow, Samuel, ed. Astronomy: Understanding Celestial Bodies. 2014. (Study of Science Ser.). 160p. (YA). (gr. 7-12). 35.25 (978-1-62275-406-9(9)) Rosen Publishing Group, Inc., The.

Kerrod, Robin. Find Out about Astronomy. 2013. (ENG., Illus.). 64p. (J). (gr. 2-7). 9.99 (978-1-84322-868-4(8)) Anness Publishing GBR. Dist: National Bk. Network.

Khan, Hena. The Space Explorer's Guide to Earth's Neighborhood. 2003. (Space University Ser.). (Illus.). 48p. (J). (978-0-439-55741-2(0)) Scholastic, Inc.

Khan, Sarah. Night Sky Sticker Book. Clarke, Phillip, ed. 2007. (Usborne Sticker Bks.). (Illus.). 24p. (J). (gr. -1-3). pap. 8.99 (978-0-7945-1563-8(0), Usborne) EDC Publishing.

Kim, F. S. Constellations. 2010. (True Book Ser.). (ENG.). 48p. (J). (gr. 3-5). pap. 6.95 (978-0-531-22802-9(9), Children's Pr.) Scholastic Library Publishing.

Kochanoff, Peggy. Be a Night Detective: Solving the Mysteries of Twilight, Dusk, & Nightfall, 1 vol. 2017. (ENG., Illus.). 56p. (J). (gr. -1-3). pap. 14.95 **(978-1-77108-464-2(2))** Nimbus Publishing, Ltd. CAN. Dist: Orca Bk. Pubs. USA.

Koellhoffer, Tara, ed. Space & Astronomy. 2006. (Science News for Kids Ser.). (Illus.). 136p. (gr. 4-6). lib. bdg. 30.00 (978-0-7910-9125-8(2), Chelsea Clubhouse) Facts On File, Inc.

Kopp, Megan. The Milky Way & Other Galaxies, 1 vol. 2011. (Solar System & Beyond Ser.). (ENG.). 32p. (gr. 3-4). pap. 8.10 (978-1-4296-7227-6(7)); pap. 47.70 (978-1-4296-7228-3(5)) Capstone Press of Coughlan Cos. (Fact Finders).

Koupelis, Theo. In Quest of the Stars & Galaxies. rev. ed. 2010. (ENG.). 457p. (J). pap. 149.95 (978-0-7637-6630-6(5)) Jones & Bartlett Learning, LLC.

Kulavis, Allyson. Space-Tacular! 2012. (Science with Stuff Ser.: 2). (ENG.). 48p. (J). (gr. 1). 11.99 (978-1-935703-48-8(X)) Downtown Bookworks.

Lacey, Saskia. Art & Culture: The Stories of Constellations: Shapes (Grade 3) 2017. (Mathematics Readers Ser.). (Illus.). 32p. (gr. 3-3). 8.99 **(978-1-4807-5812-4(4))** Teacher Created Materials, Inc.

LaFontaine, Bruce. Constellations of the Night Sky. 2003. (Dover Nature Coloring Book Ser.). (ENG., Illus.). 48p. (J). (gr. 3-8). pap. 4.99 (978-0-486-42648-8(3)) Dover Pubns., Inc.

Las Galaxias. (SPA.). (J). 10.00 (978-84-342-1815-4(1)) Parramon Ediciones S.A. ESP. Dist: Distribuidora Norma, Inc.

Latham, Donna. Space: Surviving in Zero-G. 2005. (X-treme Places Ser.). (Illus.). 32p. (YA). (gr. 2-5). lib. bdg. 25.27 (978-1-59716-090-2(3)) Bearport Publishing Co., Inc.

Latta, Sara L. Black Holes: The Weird Science of the Most Mysterious Objects in the Universe. 2017. (ENG.). (YA). (gr. 8-12). 35.99 (978-1-5124-1568-1(5), Twenty-First Century Bks.) Lerner Publishing Group.

Lawrence, Richard. Our Universe. 2004. (Illus.). vi, 134p. (gr. 1-6). pap. 18.00 (978-0-9725365-4-7(X)) Boarding House Publishing.

Levy, Joel. The Universe Explained, 1 vol., 1. 2014. (Guide for Curious Minds Ser.). (ENG.). 136p. (YA). (gr. 7-12). 38.25 (978-1-4777-2958-8(5)) Rosen Publishing Group, Inc., The.

The Library of the Nine Planets, 9 Bks, Set. 2004. (J). 238.50 (978-1-4042-0346-4(X)) Rosen Publishing Group, Inc., The.

little bee books, little bee. Listopia: Space. 2016. (ENG., Illus.). 208p. (J). (gr. 2-4). pap. 9.99 (978-1-4998-0280-1(3)) Little Bee Books Inc.

Lord, Pia. The Night the Moon Went Out. Thompson, Karin, illus. 2011. 28p. pap. 24.95 (978-1-4626-0010-6(7)) America Star Bks.

Loria, Laura. Astronomers at Work. 2017. (Scientists at Work Ser.). 32p. (gr. 6-8). pap. 12.90 **(978-1-68048-745-9(0)**, Britannica Educational Publishing) Rosen Publishing Group, Inc., The.

Loria, Laura. What Is a Constellation? 2014. (Let's Find Out! Ser.). 32p. (J). (gr. 3-6). 23.45 (978-1-62275-476-2(X)) Rosen Publishing Group, Inc., The.

Love, Ann & Drake, Jane. The Kids Book of the Night Sky. Collins, Heather, tr. Collins, Heather, illus. 2004. (Family Fun Ser.). (ENG.). 144p. (J). (gr. 3-7). pap. 16.95 (978-1-55337-128-1(3)) Kids Can Pr., Ltd. CAN. Dist: Hachette Bk. Group.

Lucas, Debra. Our Moon. 2005. (Yellow Umbrella Fluent Level Ser.). (ENG., Illus.). 16p. (gr. k-1). pap. 35.70 (978-0-7368-5296-8(4), Yellow Umbrella Bks.) Capstone Press of Coughlan Cos.

Lunis, Natalie. Watching the Night Sky. Date not set. (Thinking Like a Scientist Ser.). (Illus.). 20p. (J). pap. 16.95 (978-1-58273-079-0(2)) Sundance/Newbridge Educational Publishing.

Mack, Gail. The Stars. 2009. (Space!). 64p. (gr. 5-18). lib. bdg. 32.79 (978-0-7614-4250-9(2)) Marshall Cavendish Corp.

The Magic School Bus: Lost in the Solar System. 2011. (J). audio compact disk 9.99 (978-0-545-22880-0(8)) Scholastic, Inc.

Maloof, Torrey. Looking Up!, 1 vol. (Science Readers: Content & Literacy Ser.). (ENG., Illus.). 24p. (gr. 1-1). 2015. (J). 22.96 (978-1-4938-1159-5(2)) 2014. pap. 8.99 (978-1-4807-4572-8(3)) Teacher Created Materials, Inc.

Marchesi, Stephen, illus. Glow-In-The-Dark Constellations. 2006. (J). (978-1-59412-171-5(0)) Mud Puddle, Inc.

Marsh, Laura. National Geographic Readers: Night Sky. 2017. (Readers Ser.). (ENG.). 32p. (J). (gr. k-3). pap. 3.99 **(978-1-4263-2815-2(X)**, National Geographic Children's Bks.) National Geographic Society.

Martin, Ruth. Little Explorers: Outer Space. Sanders, Allan, illus. 2016. (Little Explorers Ser.). (ENG.). 18p. (J). (gr. -1-3). 9.99 (978-1-4998-0250-4(1)) Little Bee Books Inc.

Mason, Jennifer. The Space Race. 2017. (Great Race: Fight to the Finish Ser.). 48p. (gr. 4-5). pap. 84.30 **(978-1-5382-0808-3(3))** Stevens, Gareth Publishing LLLP.

Massey, Steve. Space, Stars & Planets. 2009. (Young Reed Ser.). (ENG.). 1p. (J). 14.95 (978-1-921073-06-9(3)) New Holland Pubs. Pty, Ltd. AUS. Dist: Tuttle Publishing.

May, Brian, et al. Exploring the Mysteries of the Universe. 2016. (STEM Guide to the Universe Ser.). (ENG.). 200p. (J). (gr. 9-9). lib. bdg. 46.10 (978-1-4994-6407-8(X)) Rosen Publishing Group, Inc., The.

McAuliffe, Bill. Galaxies. 2012. (Mysteries of the Universe Ser.). (Illus.). 48p. (J). (gr. 5-12). 23.95 (978-1-60818-188-9(X), Creative Education) Creative Co., The.

—Mysteries of the Universe: Galaxies. 2013. (Mysteries of the Universe Ser.). (ENG., Illus.). 48p. (J). (gr. 4-7). pap. 12.00 (978-0-89812-913-7(3), Creative Paperbacks) Creative Co., The.

McGill, Jordan. Space Science Fair Projects. 2011. (J). (gr. 3-5). pap. 12.95 (978-1-61690-657-3(X), AV2 by Weigl); (Illus.). 24p. 27.13 (978-1-61690-653-5(7)) Weigl Pubs., Inc.

McMahon, Michael. Why Do Stars Twinkle? 2010. (Solving Science Mysteries Ser.). (Illus.). 24p. (J). pap. 8.25 (978-1-61531-921-3(2), PowerKids Pr.); (YA). (gr. 3-6). lib. bdg. 22.60 (978-1-61531-895-7(X)) Rosen Publishing Group, Inc., The.

McNeil, Niki, et al. HOCPP 1081 Galaxies. 2006. spiral bd. 16.50 (978-1-60308-081-1(3)) In the Hands of a Child.

—HOCPP 1088 Advanced Astronomy. 2006. spiral bd. 26.50 (978-1-60308-088-0(0)) In the Hands of a Child.

Menges, Jeff A. Glow-in-the-Dark Night Sky. 2006. (Dover Little Activity Books Stickers Ser.). (ENG., Illus.). 2p. (J). (gr. 1-4). 1.99 (978-0-486-44915-9(7)) Dover Pubns., Inc.

Miles, Lisa. Astronomy & Space. 2010. (Complete Bks). 96p. (J). pap. 14.99 (978-0-7945-2626-9(8), Usborne) EDC Publishing.

Miles, Lisa & Smith, Alastair. Astronomy & Space. 2003. (Complete Bks.). (ENG., Illus.). 1p. (YA). (gr. 3-18). pap. 14.95 (978-0-7460-3104-9(1)) EDC Publishing.

Miller, Derek L. Earth, Sun, & Moon: Cyclic Patterns of Lunar Phases, Eclipses, & the Seasons. 2016. (Space Systems Ser.). 112p. (J). 42.79 (978-1-5026-2291-4(2)) Cavendish Square Publishing.

Miller, Ron. Recentering the Universe: The Radical Theories of Copernicus, Kepler, Galileo, & Newton. 2013. 88p. pap. 31.93 (978-1-4677-1662-8(6)) Lerner Publishing Group.

Mills, Nathan & Hudson, Rachel. Objects in the Sky. 2012. (Rosen Readers Ser.). (ENG., Illus.). 24p. (J). (gr. 1-2). pap. 8.25 (978-1-4488-8848-1(4), Rosen Classroom) Rosen Publishing Group, Inc., The.

Mitchell, Chris. How Do Astronauts Wee in Space? Pinder, Andrew, illus. 2016. (Dr Dino's Learnatorium Ser.). (ENG.). 192p. (J). (gr. 4-7). pap. 8.99 (978-1-78418-653-1(8)) Blake, John Publishing, Ltd. GBR. Dist: Independent Pubs. Group.

Mitton, Jacqueline. Once upon a Starry Night: A Book of Constellations. Balit, Christina, illus. 2009. (ENG.). 32p. (J). (gr. 1-4). pap. 8.95 (978-1-4263-0391-3(2), National Geographic Children's Bks.) National Geographic Society.

—Zoo in the Sky. 2014. 17.95 (978-1-63419-754-0(2)) Perfection Learning Corp.

—Zoo in the Sky: A Book of Animal Constellations. Balit, Christina, illus. 2006. (ENG.). 32p. (J). (gr. 1-4). pap. 7.95 (978-0-7922-5935-0(1), National Geographic Children's Bks.) National Geographic Society.

Mitton, Jacqueline & Balit, Christina. Once upon a Starry Night: A Book of Constellations. 2004. (ENG., Illus.). 32p. (J). (gr. 1-4). 16.95 (978-0-7922-6332-6(4), National Geographic Children's Bks.) National Geographic Society.

Moon, Walt K. Let's Explore the Stars. 2017. (Bumba Books (tm) — a First Look at Space Ser.). (ENG.). 24p. (J). (gr. -1-1). 25.32 **(978-1-5124-3347-0(0))** Lerner Publishing Group.

Moore Niver, Heather. Viaje a Través de la Vía láctea (a Trip Through the Milky Way) 2015. (Maravillosos Viajes a Través de la Ciencia (Fantastic Science Journeys) Ser.). (SPA., Illus.). 32p. (J). (gr. 2-3). 25.25 (978-1-4824-2024-1(4), 1384038) Stevens, Gareth Publishing LLLP.

Moore, Patrick. First Book of Stars. 2010. (ENG., Illus.). 96p. pap. 22.95 (978-1-84868-291-7(3)) Amberley Publishing GBR. Dist: Independent Pubs. Group.

Moore, Patrick & Lawrence, Pete. Exploring the Mysteries of Astronomy. 2016. (STEM Guide to the Universe Ser.). (ENG.). 192p. (YA). (gr. 9-9). lib. bdg. 46.10 (978-1-4994-6411-5(8)) Rosen Publishing Group, Inc., The.

Morgan, Elizabeth. Gemini. 2015. (Constellation Collection). (ENG., Illus.). 24p. (J). (gr. 3-3). pap. 8.25 (978-1-4994-0932-1(X), PowerKids Pr.) Rosen Publishing Group, Inc., The.

Morrison, Jessica. Eclipses. 2011. (J). (gr. 4-6). pap. 13.95 (978-1-61690-635-1(9), AV2 by Weigl); (Illus.). 32p. (YA). (gr. 2-5). 28.55 (978-1-61690-631-3(6)) Weigl Pubs., Inc.

Morrison, Jessica & Goldsworthy, Steve. Eclipses. 2016. (J). **(978-1-4896-5812-8(2)**, AV2 by Weigl) Weigl Pubs., Inc.

Moser, Richard. The Examined Universe. 2004. per. 24.00 (978-0-9746865-0-9(6)) MEC Publishing.

Murphy, Glenn. Space: The Whole Whizz-Bang Story. 2014. (Science Sorted Ser.). (ENG., Illus.). 192p. (J). (gr. 2-4). pap. 7.99 (978-1-4472-2623-9(2)) Pan Macmillan GBR. Dist: Independent Pubs. Group.

Nardo, Don. Hubble Deep Field: How a Photo Revolutionized Our Understanding of the Universe. 2017. (Captured Science History Ser.). (ENG.). 64p. (gr. 5-7). lib. bdg. 34.65 **(978-0-7565-5643-3(0)**, CPB Grades 4-8) Compass Point Bks.

National Geographic Kids Staff. National Geographic Kids Super Space Sticker Activity Book: Over 1,000 Stickers! 2014. (ENG., Illus.). 56p. (J). (gr. -1-3). pap. 6.99 (978-1-4263-1556-5(2), National Geographic Children's Bks.) National Geographic Society.

Nichols, Michelle. Astronomy Lab for Kids: 52 Family Friendly Activities. 2016. (Lab Ser.). (ENG., Illus.). 144p. (J). (gr. 1-17). pap. 24.99 (978-1-63159-134-1(7), Quarry Bks.) Quarto Publishing Group USA.

Night Sky Spotter's Guide - Internet Linked. rev. ed. 2006. 64p. (J). pap. 5.99 (978-0-7945-1301-6(8), Usborne) EDC Publishing.

O'DellKathryn. THE SCIENCE OF DARKNESS LOW INTERMEDIATE BOOK WITH ONLINE ACCESS. 2014. (ENG., Illus.). 28p. (J). pap. 9.50 (978-1-107-65493-8(9)) Cambridge Univ. Pr.

Outer Space. Date not set. (Illus.). 12p. (J). 3.98 (978-1-4054-0498-3(1)) Parragon, Inc.

Owen, Ruth. Astronomers. 2013. (Out of the Lab: Extreme Jobs in Science Ser.). 32p. (J). (gr. 3-6). 25.25 (978-1-4777-1289-4(5)); pap. 10.00 (978-1-4777-1378-5(6)) Rosen Publishing Group, Inc., The. (PowerKids Pr.).

—Galaxies. 2012. (Explore Outer Space Ser.). (ENG., Illus.). 32p. (J). (gr. 3-6). pap. 10.00 (978-1-4488-8116-1(1)); lib. bdg. 25.25 (978-1-4488-8074-4(2)) Windmill Bks.

—Nebulae. 2012. (Explore Outer Space Ser.). (ENG., Illus.). 32p. (J). (gr. 3-6). pap. 10.00 (978-1-4488-8117-8(X)); lib. bdg. 25.25 (978-1-4488-8075-1(0)) Windmill Bks.

—Probes, 1 vol. 2015. (Objects in Space Ser.). (ENG.). 32p. (J). pap. 10.00 (978-1-4777-5846-5(1), PowerKids Pr.) Rosen Publishing Group, Inc., The.

—Solar & Lunar Eclipses. 2012. (Explore Outer Space Ser.). (ENG., Illus.). 32p. (J). (gr. 3-6). pap. 10.00 (978-1-4488-8118-5(8)); lib. bdg. 25.25 (978-1-4488-8077-5(7)) Rosen Publishing Group, Inc., The. (PowerKids Pr.).

—Space Garbage, 1 vol. 2015. (Objects in Space Ser.). (ENG.). 32p. (J). pap. 10.00 (978-1-4777-5863-2(1), PowerKids Pr.) Rosen Publishing Group, Inc., The.

Oxlade, Chris. Why Why Why... Do Astronauts Float in Space? 2010. (Why Why Why Ser.). 32p. (J). (gr. 1-3). lib. bdg. 18.95 (978-1-4222-1578-4(4)) Mason Crest.

Paris, Stephanie. Siglo Xxi: Misterios Del Espacio Sideral. 2016. (TIME for Kids en Español - Level 5 Ser.). (SPA.). 64p. (gr. 5-5). lib. bdg. 31.99 (978-1-5157-2937-2(0)) Time for Kids Inc AUS. Dist: Capstone Pub.

Parker. Space Mysteries - Space Busters. 2004. (YA). pap. 48.30 (978-1-4109-0293-1(5)) Harcourt Schl. Pubs.

Parker, Katie. Black Holes. 2009. (Big Ideas in Science Ser.). 48p. (gr. 5). 31.36 (978-0-7614-4392-6(4)) Marshall Cavendish GBR. Dist: Marshall Cavendish Corp.

Pasachoff, Jay M. Peterson First Guide to Astronomy. 2nd ed. 2014. (Peterson First Guide Ser.). (ENG., Illus.). 128p. pap. 7.95 (978-0-544-16562-5(4)) Houghton Mifflin Harcourt Publishing Co.

Peters, Elisa. Outer Space. 2012. (PowerKids Readers: the Universe Ser.). (ENG., Illus.). 24p. (J). (gr. k-2). 22.60 (978-1-4488-7390-6(8)); pap. 8.25 (978-1-4488-7469-9(6)) Rosen Publishing Group, Inc., The. (PowerKids Pr.).

—Outer Space: El Espacio Exterior. 2012. (PowerKids Readers: the Universe / el universo Ser.). (SPA & ENG., Illus.). 24p. (J). (gr. k-2). lib. bdg. 22.60 (978-1-4488-7826-0(8), PowerKids Pr.) Rosen Publishing Group, Inc., The.

Peters, Stephanie True. Orion. 2009. (Library of Constellations Ser.). 24p. (gr. 3-4). 45.00 (978-1-60853-575-0(4), PowerKids Pr.) Rosen Publishing Group, Inc., The.

—Pisces. 2009. (Library of Constellations Ser.). 24p. (gr. 3-4). 45.00 (978-1-60853-576-7(2), PowerKids Pr.) Rosen Publishing Group, Inc., The.

Peterson, Judy Monroe. Exploring Space: Astronauts & Astronomers. 2009. (Extreme Scientists Ser.). 24p. (gr. 2-3). 42.50 (978-1-61512-451-0(9), PowerKids Pr.) Rosen Publishing Group, Inc., The.

Pfeffer, Wendy. A New Beginning: Celebrating the Spring Equinox. Bleck, Linda, illus. 2016. (ENG.). 40p. (J). (gr. 1-4). pap. 8.99 (978-1-101-99771-0(0), Puffin Books) Penguin Young Readers Group.

Phelan, Glen. Earth in Space. 2007. (Language, Literacy, & Vocabulary - Reading Expeditions Ser.). (ENG., Illus.). 36p. (J). pap. 18.95 (978-0-7922-5428-7(7)) CENGAGE Learning.

—Earth, Sun, Moon. 2007. (Reading Expeditions Ser.). (ENG., Illus.). 32p. (J). pap. 17.95 (978-0-7922-4573-5(3)) CENGAGE Learning.

Phelan, Glen & National Geographic Learning Staff. Stars. 2007. (Language, Literacy, & Vocabulary - Reading Expeditions Ser.). (ENG., Illus.). 36p. (J). pap. 18.95 (978-0-7922-5433-1(3)) CENGAGE Learning.

Picray, Michael E. The Sun with Code. 2012. (Sky Science Ser.). (ENG., Illus.). 24p. (J). (gr. 3-7). pap. 12.95 (978-1-61913-544-4(2), AV2 by Weigl) Weigl Pubs., Inc.

Poolos, Christine. What Is an Object in the Sky? 2014. (Let's Find Out! Ser.). 32p. (J). (gr. 3-6). 23.45 (978-1-62275-471-7(9)) Rosen Publishing Group, Inc., The.

Portman, Michael. Could We Live on Other Planets? 2013. 32p. (J). (gr. 2-5). 25.25 (978-1-4339-9213-1(2)); pap. 10.50 (978-1-4339-9214-8(0)); pap. 63.00 (978-1-4339-9215-5(9)) Stevens, Gareth Publishing LLLP.

—What Is an Eclipse? 2013. 32p. (J). (gr. 2-5). 25.25 (978-1-4339-9233-9(7)); pap. 10.50 (978-1-4339-9234-6(5)) Stevens, Gareth Publishing LLLP.

Proctor, Mary. Stories of Starland. 2006. pap. 22.95 (978-1-4286-0644-9(0)) Kessinger Publishing, LLC.

Purslow, Frances. Constellations. 2006. (Science Matters Ser.). (Illus.). 24p. (J). (gr. 3-7). lib. bdg. 24.45 (978-1-59036-410-9(4)); pap. 8.95 (978-1-59036-416-1(3)) Weigl Pubs., Inc.

Que Vemos en el Cielo, 6 vols. (Explorers. Exploradores Nonfiction Sets Ser.). (SPA.). 32p. (gr. 3-6). 44.95 (978-0-7699-0631-7(1)) Shortland Pubns. (U. S. A.) Inc.

Rao, Joe. Looking Up! The Science of Stargazing. Borgions, Mark, illus. 2017. (Science of Fun Stuff Ser.). (ENG.). 48p. (J). (gr. 1-3). pap. 3.99 (978-1-4814-7917-2(2), Simon Spotlight) Simon Spotlight.

Regan, Lisa. A Cool Kid's Field Guide to Space. Bull, Peter, illus. 2009. (Cool Kid's Field Guide Ser.). 26p. (J). (gr. 1-3). spiral bd. 6.99 (978-0-8416-7142-3(7)) Hammond World Atlas Corp.

Reilly, Carmel. Comets, Asteroids, & Meteoroids. 2011. (Sky Watching Ser.). 32p. (gr. 2-4). 28.50 (978-1-60870-579-5(X)) Marshall Cavendish GBR. Dist: Marshall Cavendish Corp.

—The Moon. 2011. (Sky Watching Ser.). 32p. (gr. 2-4). 28.50 (978-1-60870-581-8(1)) Marshall Cavendish Corp.

—The Planets. 2011. (Sky Watching Ser.). 32p. (gr. 2-4). 28.50 (978-1-60870-582-5(X)) Marshall Cavendish Corp.

—The Stars. 2011. (Sky Watching Ser.). 32p. (gr. 2-4). 28.50 (978-1-60870-583-2(8)) Marshall Cavendish GBR. Dist: Marshall Cavendish Corp.

—The Sun. 2011. (Sky Watching Ser.). 32p. (gr. 2-4). 28.50 (978-1-60870-584-9(6)) Marshall Cavendish GBR. Dist: Marshall Cavendish Corp.

Rice, Dona Herweck. Into Space, 1 vol. 2012. (Early Childhood Themes Ser.). (ENG.). 16p. (J). (gr. -1-2). pap. 19.99 (978-1-4333-3470-2(4)); pap. 6.99 (978-1-4333-3469-6(0)) Teacher Created Materials, Inc.

Richards, Charles. What Is a Space Probe? 2012. (InfoMax Readers Ser.). (ENG., Illus.). 24p. (J). (gr. 1-2). pap. 8.25 (978-1-4488-9082-8(9), Rosen Classroom) Rosen Publishing Group, Inc., The.

Ridpath, Ian. Facts on File Stars & Planets Atlas: New Edition. 3rd rev. ed. 2005. (Facts on File Atlas Ser.). 96p. (gr. 4-6). 18.95 (978-0-8160-6294-2(3), Checkmark Bks.) Facts On File, Inc.

Riggs, Kate. Across the Universe: Galaxies. 2015. (Across the Universe Ser.). (ENG.). 24p. (J). (gr. 1-3). pap. 9.99 (978-1-62832-082-4(6), Creative Paperbacks) Creative Co., The.

Riley, Peter & Lorimer, Lawrence. The Solar System. 2013. (Jigsaw Journey Ser.). (ENG., Illus.). 48p. (J). (gr. k). 15.95 (978-1-60710-949-5(2), Silver Dolphin Bks.) Readerlink Distribution Services, LLC.

Riley, Peter D. Space. 2011. (Real Scientist Investigates Ser.). (Illus.). 32p. (J). (gr. 3-5). lib. bdg. 28.50 (978-1-59771-284-2(1)) Sea-To-Sea Pubns.

Ripley's Inc. Staff. Zoom! Graziano, John, illus. 2012. (Ripley's Shout Outs Ser.: 2). (ENG.). 96p. (J). (gr. 2-5). pap. 4.99 (978-0-545-38076-8(6)) Scholastic, Inc.

Robinson, Ella May. Stars in Her Heart. 2005. 127p. per. 10.95 (978-1-57258-318-4(5)) TEACH Services, Inc.

Rockett, Paul. 70 Thousand Million, Million, Million Stars in Space. Ruffle, Mark, illus. 2015. (Big Countdown Ser.). (ENG.). 32p. (gr. 3-5). 29.99 (978-1-4109-6875-3(8), Raintree Perspectives) Heinemann-Raintree.

Roesser, Blanche. The Story of Leo the Lion. 2015. (Stories in the Stars Ser.). (ENG., Illus.). 24p. (J). (gr. 1-2). pap. 8.15 (978-1-4824-2673-1(0)) Stevens, Gareth Publishing LLLP.

Roland, James. Black Holes: A Space Discovery Guide. 2017. (Space Discovery Guides). (ENG.). 48p. (J). (gr. 4-6). 16.99 **(978-1-5124-3803-1(0)**, Lerner Pubns.); 47.99 **(978-1-5124-3805-5(7)**, Lerner Pubns.); 47.99 **(978-1-5124-2794-3(2)**, Lerner Pubns.); (Illus.). 31.99 (978-1-5124-2586-4(9)) Lerner Publishing Group.

Rose, Simon. Andromeda: The Myth & Science. 2015. (Illus.). 24p. (J). (978-1-5105-0012-9(X)); (978-1-5105-0265-9(3)) SmartBook Media, Inc.

—Cygnus the Swan: The Myth & Science. 2015. (Illus.). 24p. (J). (978-1-5105-0014-3(6)); pap. (978-1-5105-0266-6(1)) SmartBook Media, Inc.

—Cygnus the Swan: The Myth & Science. 2015. (J). (978-1-4896-3320-0(0)) Weigl Pubs., Inc.

—Hercules: The Myth & Science. 2015. (Illus.). 24p. (J). (978-1-5105-0016-7(2)); pap. (978-1-5105-0267-3(X)) SmartBook Media, Inc.

—Orion: The Myth & Science. 2015. (Illus.). 24p. (J). (978-1-5105-0018-1(9)); pap. (978-1-5105-0268-0(8)) SmartBook Media, Inc.

—Orion: The Myth & Science. 2015. (J). (978-1-4896-3328-6(6)) Weigl Pubs., Inc.

—Pegasus: The Myth & Science. 2015. (J). (978-1-5105-0020-4(0)); pap. (978-1-5105-0269-7(6)) SmartBook Media, Inc.

—Pegasus: The Myth & Science. 2015. (J). (978-1-4896-3332-3(4)) Weigl Pubs., Inc.

—Ursa Major: The Myth & Science. 2015. (Illus.). 24p. (J). (978-1-5105-0022-8(7)); pap. (978-1-5105-0270-3(X)) SmartBook Media, Inc.

—Ursa Major: The Myth & Science. 2015. (J). (978-1-4896-3336-1(7)) Weigl Pubs., Inc.

Roza, Greg. What Is a Black Hole? 2013. 32p. (J). (gr. 2-5). 25.25 (978-1-4339-9228-5(0)); pap. 10.50 (978-1-4339-9229-2(9)) Stevens, Gareth Publishing LLLP.

Running Press Staff. Posters to Color: Space. 2016. (ENG., Illus.). 24p. (J). (gr. -1-17). pap. 9.95 (978-0-7624-5997-1(2), Running Pr. Kids) Running Pr. Bk. Pubs.

Rustad, Martha E. Space. 2016. (Space Ser.). (ENG.). 24p. (gr. k-1). 87.96 (978-1-4914-8337-4(7), Pebble Bks.) Capstone Press of Coughlan Cos.

Rustad, Martha E. H. Black Holes, 1 vol. 2012. (Exploring Space Ser.). (ENG.). 24p. (gr. k-1). pap. 7.29 (978-1-4296-7891-9(7)); pap. 41.70 (978-1-4296-8326-5(0)); lib. bdg. 26.65 (978-1-4296-7584-0(5)) Capstone Press of Coughlan Cos. (Pebble Plus).

—Constellations, 1 vol. 2012. (Exploring Space Ser.). (ENG.). 24p. (gr. k-1). lib. bdg. 26.65 (978-1-4296-7582-6(9), Pebble Plus) Capstone Press of Coughlan Cos.

—En el Espacio. 2012. (En el Espacio/Out in Space Ser.). (MUL.). 24p. (gr. k-1). pap. 23.80 (978-1-4296-8558-0(1)); pap. 142.80 (978-1-4296-8559-7(X)) Capstone Press of Coughlan Cos.

—The Milky Way, 1 vol. 2012. (Exploring Space Ser.). (ENG., Illus.). 24p. (gr. k-1). lib. bdg. 26.65 (978-1-4296-7583-3(7), Pebble Plus) Capstone Press of Coughlan Cos.

—Space, 1 vol. 2013. (Little Scientist Ser.). (ENG., Illus.). 32p. (gr. 1-2). 6.95 (978-1-4765-3545-6(0)); 27.99 (978-1-4765-0251-9(X)); pap. 6.95 (978-1-4765-3551-7(5)) Capstone Press of Coughlan Cos.

Sabatino, Michael. How Long Will the Sun Last? 2013. 32p. (J). (gr. 2-5). 25.25 (978-1-4339-9223-0(X)); pap. 10.50 (978-1-4339-9224-7(8)); pap. 63.00 (978-1-4339-9225-4(6)) Stevens, Gareth Publishing LLLP.

—20 Fun Facts about Galaxies. 2014. (Fun Fact File: Space! Ser.). 32p. (J). (gr. 2-5). 25.25 (978-1-4824-0996-3(8)) Stevens, Gareth Publishing LLLP.

Sakolsky, Josh. Copernicus & Modern Astronomy. 2009. (Primary Sources of Revolutionary Scientific Discoveries & Theories Ser.). 64p. (gr. 5-5). 58.50 (978-1-60851-840-1(X)) Rosen Publishing Group, Inc., The.

Salzano, Tammi J. Destination, Space. 2006. (Illus.). 30p. (J). (978-0-439-88736-6(4)) Scholastic, Inc.

—Night Sky. Myers, Lawrence E., illus. 2009. 48p. (J). pap. (978-0-545-13832-1(9)) Scholastic, Inc.

Scagell, Robin & Dorling Kindersley Publishing Staff. Night Sky Atlas. rev. ed. 2007. (ENG., Illus.). 48p. (J). (gr. 5-12). 22.99 (978-0-7566-2839-0(3), DK Children) Dorling Kindersley Publishing, Inc.

Schaaf, Fred. Seeing the Sky: 100 Projects, Activities & Explorations in Astronomy. Myers, Doug, illus. 2012. (Dover Children's Science Bks.). (ENG.). 224p. (C). (gr. 8). pap. 14.95 (978-0-486-48888-2(8)) Dover Pubns., Inc.

Schatz, Dennis & Fraknoi, Andrew. Solar Science: Exploring Sunspots, Seasons, Eclipses, & More. 2015. (ENG., Illus.). 360p. (J). pap. 39.95 (978-1-941316-07-8(7)) National Science Teachers Assn.

Schmermund, Elizabeth. New Frontiers in Astronomy. 2016. (Great Discoveries in Science Ser.). (Illus.). 128p. (J). (gr. 9-9). 45.64 (978-1-5026-1959-4(8)) Cavendish Square Publishing.

Schneider, Howard. Ultimate Explorer Field Guide: Night Sky: Find Adventure! Go Outside! Have Fun! Be a Backyard Stargazer! 2016. (ENG., Illus.). 160p. (J). (gr. 3-7). pap. 12.99 (978-1-4263-2546-5(0), National Geographic Children's Bks.) National Geographic Society.

Schoeller, Jen. Biggest, Baddest Book of Space, 1 vol. 2014. (Biggest, Baddest Books Set 2 Ser.). (ENG.). 24p. (gr. k-4). 25.65 (978-1-62403-518-0(3)) ABDO Publishing Co.

Scientific American Staff. Mysteries of the Milky Way. 2009. (Scientific American Cutting-Edge Science Ser.). 136p. (gr. 9-9). 63.90 (978-1-60853-079-3(5)) Rosen Publishing Group, Inc., The.

Seuling, Barbara. Earth Is Like a Giant Magnet: And Other Freaky Facts about Planets, Oceans, & Volcanoes. Skeens, Matthew, illus. (Freaky Facts Ser.). 40p. 2010. pap. 0.50 (978-1-4048-6202-9(1)) 2008. (gr. 3-5). pap. 3.00 (978-1-4048-5289-1(1)) Picture Window Bks. (Nonfiction Picture Bks.).

Shereda, Laura. Spectacular Space Trivia. 2013. (Ultimate Trivia Challenge Ser.). 32p. (J). (gr. 2-5). pap. 63.00 (978-1-4339-8298-9(6)); (Illus.). pap. 10.50 (978-1-4339-8297-2(8)); (Illus.). lib. bdg. 25.25 (978-1-4339-8296-5(X)) Stevens, Gareth Publishing LLLP.

Sherman, Jill. Exploring Eclipses. 2017. (Discover the Night Sky Ser.). (ENG.). 32p. (gr. 3-4). lib. bdg. 27.32 **(978-1-5157-8736-5(2)**, Fact Finders) Capstone Press of Coughlan Cos.

Sherman, Suzanne. The Milky Way: A River of Stars. 2015. (Science Readers: Content & Literacy Ser.). (Illus.). 32p. (J). (gr. 5-5). pap. 8.99 (978-1-4807-4727-2(0)) Teacher Created Materials, Inc.

Silverman, Buffy. Exploring Dangers in Space: Asteroids, Space Junk, & More. 2011. (Searchlight Books Whats Amazing about Space Ser.). (ENG., Illus.). (gr. 3-5). pap. 51.01 (978-0-7613-8414-4(6)); 40p. pap. 8.95 (978-0-7613-7882-2(0)) Lerner Publishing Group.

Silverstein, Alvin, et al. The Universe. (Science Concepts Ser.). (ENG., 2003. Illus.). 64p. (gr. 5-9). lib. bdg. 26.60 (978-0-7613-2255-9(8), Twenty-First Century Bks.) 2009. 112p. (gr. 6-8). 31.93 (978-0-7613-3937-3(X)) Lerner Publishing Group.

Simon, Seymour. Destination: Space. 2004. (ENG.). 32p. (J). pap. 6.99 (978-0-06-059681-1(3), Harper Trophy) HarperCollins Pubs.

—Destination - Space. 2006. (ENG., Illus.). 32p. (J). (gr. k-4). pap. 6.99 (978-0-06-087723-1(5), Collins) HarperCollins Pubs.

—Destination Space. 2006. (Illus.). 32p. (gr. k-4). 17.00 (978-0-7569-6746-8(5)) Perfection Learning Corp.

Smibert, Angie. Space Myths, Busted! 2017. (Science Myths, Busted! Ser.). (ENG., Illus.). 32p. (J). (gr. 3-6). 21.95 (978-1-63235-305-4(9)) Pr. Room Editions LLC.

Smith, A. Book of Astronomy & Space. 2004. (Complete Bks.). (SPA., Illus.). 96p. (J). lib. bdg. 22.95 (978-1-58086-385-8(X)) EDC Publishing.

Smith, David J. If: A Mind-Bending New Way of Looking at Big Ideas & Numbers. Adams, Steve, illus. 2014. (ENG.). 40p. (J). (gr. 3-7). 18.95 (978-1-894786-34-8(3)) Kids Can Pr., Ltd. CAN. Dist: Hachette Bk. Group.

Smith, Ian. What's in the Sky? 2004. (QEB Start Writing Ser.). (Illus.). 24p. (J). lib. bdg. 15.95 (978-1-59566-019-0(4)) QEB Publishing Inc.

Snedden, Robert. Exploring Space. 2016. (Sci-Hi: Earth & Space Science Ser.). (ENG.). 48p. (gr. 4-4). pap. 8.99 (978-1-4109-8522-4(9), Sci-Hi) Heinemann-Raintree.

—How Do Scientists Explore Space?, 1 vol. 2011. (Earth, Space, & Beyond Ser.). (ENG.). 48p. (gr. 6-6). pap. 9.49 (978-1-4109-4164-0(7), Raintree Freestyle); (gr. 3-3). 34.65 (978-1-4109-4176-3(0), Raintree Freestyle Express); (gr. 6-6). 34.65 (978-1-4109-4158-9(2), Raintree Freestyle) Heinemann-Raintree.

The Solar System & Beyond. 2011. (Solar System & Beyond Ser.). (ENG.). 32p. (gr. 3-4). pap. 79.50 (978-1-4296-7231-3(5)); pap. 477.00 (978-1-4296-7232-0(3)); lib. bdg. 191.24 (978-1-4296-6496-7(7)) Capstone Press of Coughlan Cos. (Fact Finders).

Solway, Andrew. The Universe. 2010. (CC: 21st Century Science Ser.). 112p. (gr. 6-12). 42.80 (978-1-933834-76-4(5)) Brown Bear Bks.

Space, Stars, & Planets (Gr. 3-4) 2003. (J). (978-1-58232-074-8(8)) ECS Learning Systems, Inc.

Sparrow, Giles. Night Sky. 2012. (J). lib. bdg. (978-0-531-22958-3(0)); (ENG.). 112p. (gr. 3-7). 15.99 (978-0-545-38374-5(9), Scholastic Reference) Scholastic, Inc.

—Observing the Universe. 2006. (Secrets of the Universe Ser.). (Illus.). 48p. (gr. 6-12). pap. 14.05 (978-0-8368-7284-2(3)); lib. bdg. 31.00 (978-0-8368-7277-4(0)) Stevens, Gareth Publishing LLLP. (Gareth Stevens Secondary Library).

Sparrow, Giles & John, Judith. How the Universe Works. 2016. (Discoveries in Space Science Ser.). (ENG., Illus.). 80p. (YA). (gr. 9-9). lib. bdg. 35.64 (978-1-5026-1014-0(0)) Cavendish Square Publishing.

Spilsbury, Louise. Projects with Space. 2014. (Make & Learn Ser.). (Illus.). 32p. (J). (gr. 3-6). lib. bdg. 27.50 (978-1-4777-7177-8(8), PowerKids Pr.) Rosen Publishing Group, Inc., The.

Stanley, Joseph. The Big Dipper. 2015. (Constellation Collection). (ENG., Illus.). 24p. (J). (gr. 3-3). pap. 8.25 (978-1-4994-0937-6(0), PowerKids Pr.) Rosen Publishing Group, Inc., The.

—The Little Dipper. 2015. (Constellation Collection). (ENG., Illus.). 24p. (J). (gr. 3-3). pap. 8.25 (978-1-4994-0939-0(7), PowerKids Pr.) Rosen Publishing Group, Inc., The.

Steele, Philip. Galileo: The Genius Who Faced the Inquisition. 2005. (National Geographic World History Biographies Ser.). (ENG., Illus.). 64p. (J). (gr. 3-7). 17.95 (978-0-7922-3656-6(4)); lib. bdg. 27.90 (978-0-7922-3657-3(2)) National Geographic Society. (National Geographic Children's Bks.).

Stefoff, Rebecca. Astrology & Astronomy. 2014. 48p. pap. 29.93 (978-1-62712-506-2(X)) Cavendish Square Publishing.

—Astrology or Astronomy: Is Your Fate in the Stars? 2013. (J). (978-0-7614-8144-7(3)) Marshall Cavendish.

Stephens, Catherine. Volcanoes. 2007. (Language, Literacy, & Vocabulary - Reading Expeditions Ser.). (ENG., Illus.). 36p. (J). pap. 18.95 (978-0-7922-5434-8(1)) CENGAGE Learning.

Storm, Dunlop. Atlas of the Night Sky. Tirion, Wil & Rukl, Antonin, illus. 2005. (Smithsonian Institution Ser.). 224p. 29.95 (978-0-06-081891-3(3)) HarperCollins Pubs.

Stott, Carole. Eye Wonder: Space. 2016. (Eye Wonder Ser.). (ENG., Illus.). 56p. (J). (gr. k-4). 10.99 (978-1-4654-1856-2(3), DK Children) Dorling Kindersley Publishing, Inc.

—I Wonder Why Stars Twinkle. 2011. (I Wonder Why Ser.). (ENG., Illus.). 32p. (J). (gr. k-3). pap. 6.99 (978-0-7534-6520-2(5), 9780753465202, Kingfisher) Roaring Brook Pr.

—Mission: Space: Explore the Galaxy. 2016. (Illus.). 128p. (J). (978-1-4654-5376-1(8)) Dorling Kindersley Publishing, Inc.

—Stars & Planets. Bull, Peter, illus. 2013. (Explorers Ser.). (ENG.). 32p. (J). (gr. 2-5). 6.99 (978-0-7534-7063-3(2), 9780753470633, Kingfisher) Roaring Brook Pr.

Stowell, Louie. Story of Astronomy & Space: Internet-Referenced. Allen, Peter, illus. 2009. (Science Stories Ser.). 104p. (YA). (gr. 3-18). pap. 10.99 (978-0-7945-2139-4(8), Usborne) EDC Publishing.

Stuart, Colin. Why Space Matters to Me. 2015. (ENG., Illus.). 48p. (J). (gr. 2-4). 12.99 (978-1-60684-589-9(6), Millbrook Pr.) Lerner Publishing Group.

Sundance/Newbridge LLC Staff. Out in Space. 2007. (Early Science Ser.). (gr. k-3). 18.95 (978-1-4007-6422-8(X)); pap.

6.10 *(978-1-4007-6418-1(1))* Sundance/Newbridge Educational Publishing.
Teacher Created Resources Staff. Space Guides - Discovering the Universe: A Galaxy of Mind-Expanding Information! 2008. (ENG., Illus.). 32p. (gr. 4-13). pap. 7.99 *(978-1-4206-8268-7(7))* Teacher Created Resources, Inc.
Than, Ker. Black Holes. (True Book Ser.). (ENG., 48p. (J). 2010. Illus.). pap. 6.95 *(978-0-531-22801-2(0))* 2009. (gr. 2-5). 29.00 *(978-0-531-16894-3(8))* Scholastic Library Publishing.
Thomas, Isabel. Stars & Galaxies, 1 vol. 2012. (Astronaut Travel Guides). (ENG.). 48p. (gr. 3-6). lib. bdg. 32.65 *(978-1-4109-4573-0(1),* NA-r) Heinemann-Raintree.
Trammel, Howard K. Galaxies. (True Book(tm), A — Space Ser.). (ENG.). 48p. (J). 2009. (gr. 2-5). 31.00 *(978-0-531-16896-7(4))* 2010. pap. 6.95 *(978-0-531-22803-6(7),* Children's Pr.) Scholastic Library Publishing.
Trueba, Jose Luis. Descubre... La Tierra y el Cosmos. Cortes, Osvaldo, illus. 2004. (Ser. Descubre). (SPA.). 96p. (J). (gr. 3-5). pap. 18.95 *(978-970-29-0509-7(5))* Santillana USA Publishing Co., Inc.
Van Order, Bill. The Wondrous Sky. 2006. (Illus.). 24p. (J). per. 10.95 *(978-1-59879-187-7(7))* Lifevest Publishing, Inc.
VanCleave, Janice. More of Janice VanCleave's Wild, Wacky, & Weird Astronomy Experiments. 2016. (Janice VanCleave's Wild, Wacky, & Weird Science Experiments Ser.). 00064p. (J). (gr. 5-5). pap. 12.95 *(978-1-4994-6537-2(8),* Rosen Young Adult) Rosen Publishing Group, Inc., The.
—Step-by-Step Science Experiments in Astronomy. 2012. (Janice VanCleave's First-Place Science Fair Projects Ser.). (ENG., Illus.). 80p. (J). (gr. 5-8). 33.25 *(978-1-4488-6978-7(1));* pap. 14.15 *(978-1-4488-8461-2(6))* Rosen Publishing Group, Inc., The. (Rosen Reference).
VanCleave, Janice Pratt. Even More of Janice VanCleave's Wild, Wacky, & Weird Astronomy Experiments. 2017. (Janice VanCleave's Wild, Wacky, & Weird Science Experiments Ser.). 64p. (gr. 10-10). 77.70 ***(978-1-4994-6678-2(1),*** Rosen Central) Rosen Publishing Group, Inc., The.
—Janice VanCleave's Wild, Wacky, & Weird Astronomy Experiments. 2016. (Janice VanCleave's Wild, Wacky, & Weird Science Experiments Ser.). (ENG., Illus.). 64p. (J). (gr. 5-5). pap. 12.95 *(978-1-4777-8961-2(8),* Rosen Reference) Rosen Publishing Group, Inc., The.
VanCleave, Janice Pratt. Many More of Janice VanCleave's Wild, Wacky, & Weird Astronomy Experiments. 2017. (J). ***(978-1-4994-3941-0(5));*** pap. ***(978-1-4994-3939-7(3))*** Rosen Publishing Group, Inc., The.
Venezia, Mike. Stephen Hawking: Cosmologist Who Gets a Big Bang Out of the Universe. Venezia, Mike, illus. 2009. (Getting to Know the World's Greatest Inventors & Scientists Ser.). (ENG., Illus.). 32p. (J). (gr. 3-4). pap. 6.95 *(978-0-531-21337-7(4),* Children's Pr.); (gr. 2-5). 28.00 *(978-0-531-23728-1(1))* Scholastic Library Publishing.
Vogt, Gregory. Is There Life on Other Planets? And Other Questions about Space. 2010. (Is That a Fact? Ser.). 40p. (YA). (gr. 3-6). lib. bdg. 26.60 *(978-0-8225-9082-8(4))* Lerner Publishing Group.
—The Milky Way. 2010. (Early Bird Astronomy Ser.). (ENG.). 48p. (gr. 2-5). lib. bdg. 26.60 *(978-0-7613-3875-8(6));* (Illus.). pap. 8.95 *(978-0-7613-4989-1(8),* 1306460, Lerner Pubns.) Lerner Publishing Group.
Wadsworth, Pamela. Golwg Gyntaf Ar Amser a Gofod. 2005. (WEL., Illus.). 24p. pap. *(978-1-85596-248-4(9))* Dref Wen.
Walliman, Dominic. Professor Astro Cat's Frontiers of Space. Newman, Ben, illus. 2013. (ENG.). 64p. (J). (gr. 2-6). 24.00 *(978-1-909263-07-9(9))* Flying Eye Bks. GBR. Dist: Consortium Bk. Sales & Distribution.
Ward, D. J. Seven Wonders of Space Phenomena. 2011. (Seven Wonders Ser.). (ENG.). 80p. (gr. 5-8). 33.26 *(978-0-7613-5452-9(2))* Lerner Publishing Group.
Warner, Gertrude Chandler. Star Stories for Little Folks. 2006. pap. 12.95 *(978-1-59605-906-1(0),* Cosimo Classics) Cosimo, Inc.
Watt, Fiona. Space Sticker Book. 2015. (Sticker Activity Bks.). (ENG.). 24+10p. (J). (gr. k-5). pap. 8.99 *(978-0-7945-3496-7(1),* Usborne) EDC Publishing.
Waxman, Laura Hamilton. Exploring Black Holes. 2011. (Searchlight Books Whats Amazing about Space Ser.). (ENG., Illus.). (gr. 3-5). pap. 51.01 *(978-0-7613-8413-7(8));* 40p. pap. 8.95 *(978-0-7613-7877-8(4));* 40p. lib. bdg. 27.93 *(978-0-7613-5442-0(5))* Lerner Publishing Group.
Way, Steve & Bailey, Gerry. Space. 2008. (Simply Science Ser.). (Illus.). 32p. (YA). (gr. 3-6). lib. bdg. 26.00 *(978-0-8368-9232-1(1))* Stevens, Gareth Publishing LLLP.
What Is a Black Hole? 2013. (Space Mysteries Ser.). 32p. (J). (gr. 2-5). pap. 63.00 *(978-1-4339-9230-8(2))* Stevens, Gareth Publishing LLLP.
What Is an Eclipse? 2013. (Space Mysteries Ser.). 32p. (J). (gr. 2-5). pap. 63.00 *(978-1-4339-9235-3(3))* Stevens, Gareth Publishing LLLP.
Where Are the Stars During the Day? (Discovery Readers Ser.). 48p. (J). pap. 3.95 *(978-0-8249-5319-5(3),* Ideal Pubns.) Worthy Publishing.
Whiting, Jim. Black Holes. 2012. (Mysteries of the Universe Ser.). (Illus.). 48p. (J). (gr. 5-12). 23.95 *(978-1-60818-186-5(3),* Creative Education) Creative Co., The.
—Mass & Matter. 2012. (Mysteries of the Universe Ser.). (Illus.). 48p. (J). (gr. 5-12). 23.95 *(978-1-60818-191-9(X),* Creative Education) Creative Co., The.
—Mysteries of the Universe: Black Holes. 2013. (Mysteries of the Universe Ser.). (ENG., Illus.). 48p. (J). (gr. 4-7). pap. 12.00 *(978-0-89812-911-3(7),* Creative Paperbacks) Creative Co., The.
—Mysteries of the Universe: Mass & Matter. 2013. (Mysteries of the Universe Ser.). (ENG., Illus.). 48p. (J). (gr. 4-7). pap. 12.00 *(978-0-89812-916-8(8),* Creative Paperbacks) Creative Co., The.
Willett, Edward. Space. 2009. (Science Q & A Ser.). (Illus.). 48p. (YA). (gr. 5-8). pap. 10.95 *(978-1-60596-073-9(X));* lib. bdg. 29.05 *(978-1-60596-072-2(1))* Weigl Pubs., Inc.
—What Is the Milky Way? 2014. (Let's Find Out! Ser.). 32p. (J). (gr. 3-6). 23.45 *(978-1-62275-481-6(6));* pap. 77.40 *(978-1-62275-484-7(0));* pap. 12.90 *(978-1-62275-483-0(2))* Rosen Publishing Group, Inc., The.
Williams, Zella. Experiments about Planet Earth. (Do-It-Yourself Science Ser.). 24p. (gr. 2-3). 2009. 47.90 *(978-1-61512-185-4(4),* PowerKids Pr.) 2007. (Illus.). (J). lib. bdg. 25.25 *(978-1-4042-3662-2(7))* Rosen Publishing Group, Inc., The.
Wingard-Nelson, Rebecca. Space Word Problems Starring Ratios & Proportions: Math Word Problems Solved. 2009. (Math Word Problems Solved Ser.). (Illus.). 48p. (J). (gr. 2-5). lib. bdg. 25.27 *(978-0-7660-2921-7(2))* Enslow Pubs., Inc.
Wollard, Kathy. El Porque de las Cosas. (SPA.). 224p. *(978-84-95456-69-4(9),* 87419) Ediciones Oniro S.A.
Wolny, Philip. Discovering Dark Matter, 1 vol. 2015. (ENG.). 112p. (J). 35.60 *(978-1-4777-8004-6(1),* Rosen Young Adult) Rosen Publishing Group, Inc., The.
Workman Publishing Company Staff. Space. 2014. (Eyelike Stickers Ser.). (ENG.). 12p. (J). pap. 6.95 *(978-0-7611-7965-8(8),* 17965) Workman Publishing Co., Inc.
World Book, contrib. by. Galaxies & the Universe. 2nd ed. 2006. (World Book's Solar System & Space Exploration Library). (Illus.). 64p. (J). *(978-0-7166-9513-4(8))* World Bk., Inc.
World Book, Inc Staff, contrib. by. Earth & Space. 2008. (J). *(978-0-7166-3017-3(6))* World Bk., Inc.
—Galaxies. 2010. (J). *(978-0-7166-9549-3(9))* World Bk., Inc.
—Galaxies & the Universe. 2010. (J). *(978-0-7166-9542-4(1))* World Bk., Inc.
—Learning about the Sun, Moon, Planets, & Stars. 2011. (J). *(978-0-7166-0232-3(6))* World Bk., Inc.
—The Milky Way. 2010. (J). *(978-0-7166-9550-9(2))* World Bk., Inc.
World Book, Inc. Staff, contrib. by. Stargazing to Space Travel: A Timeline of Space Exploration. 2016. (J). *(978-0-7166-3545-1(3))* World Bk.-Childcraft International.
Wright, Russell G. Asteroid! Investigations in Astronomy. (Event-Based Science Ser.). 32p. (gr. 5-9). pap., tchr.'s training gde. ed. 25.95 incl. VHS *(978-0-201-49446-4(9))* Seymour, Dale Pubns.
Yasuda, Anita. Astronomy: Cool Women in Space. 2015. (Girls in Science Ser.). (ENG., Illus.). 112p. (gr. 3-7). 19.95 *(978-1-61930-326-3(4))* Open City Bks.
Young-Brown, Fiona. The Universe to Scale: Similarities & Differences in Objects in Our Solar System. 2016. (Space Systems Ser.). 112p. (YA). 42.79 *(978-1-5026-2289-1(0))* Cavendish Square Publishing.
Young, Karen Romano. Space Junk: The Dangers of Polluting Earth's Orbit. 2016. (ENG., Illus.). 64p. (YA). (gr. 7-12). 50.65 *(978-1-4677-8806-9(6),* Twenty-First Century Bks.) Lerner Publishing Group.
Zappa, Marcia. Black Holes, 1 vol. 2011. (Universe Set 2 Ser.). (ENG., Illus.). 32p. (gr. 3-5). 27.07 *(978-1-61714-686-2(2),* Buddy Bks.) ABDO Publishing Co.
—Eclipses, 1 vol. 2011. (Universe Set 2 Ser.). (ENG., Illus.). 32p. (gr. 3-5). 27.07 *(978-1-61714-688-6(9),* Buddy Bks.) ABDO Publishing Co.
—Galaxies, 1 vol. 2011. (Universe Set 2 Ser.). (ENG., Illus.). 32p. (gr. 3-5). 27.07 *(978-1-61714-689-3(7),* Buddy Bks.) ABDO Publishing Co.
Zimmerman, W. Our Colorful Moon: Beautiful Images to Energize & Delight. 2007. 40p. per. 18.27 *(978-1-934840-04-7(1))* Nimble Bks. LLC.
Zimmerman, W. Frederick. Cool Science Images for Curious Kids #1: Our Splendid Sun. 2007. (Illus.). 36p. (J). per. *(978-0-9799205-0-9(7))* Nimble Bks. LLC.
Zuchora-Walske, Christine. Key Discoveries in Earth & Space Science. 2015. (Science Discovery Timelines Ser.). (ENG., Illus.). 48p. (J). (gr. 6-8). lib. bdg. 30.65 *(978-1-4677-5787-4(X),* Lerner Pubns.) Lerner Publishing Group.
—We're the Center of the Universe! Science's Biggest Mistakes about Astronomy & Physics. 2014. (Science Gets It Wrong Ser.). (Illus.). 32p. (gr. 4-6). pap. 7.95 *(978-1-4677-4552-9(9));* (ENG.). lib. bdg. 26.60 *(978-1-4677-3663-3(5),* Lerner Pubns.) Lerner Publishing Group.

ASTRONOMY, ANCIENT

Asimov, Isaac & Hantula, Richard. Astronomy in Ancient Times: Past & Present. 2005. (Isaac Asimov's 21st Century Library of the Universe). (Illus.). 32p. (gr. 2-6). lib. bdg. 26.00 *(978-0-8368-3978-4(1),* Gareth Stevens Learning Library) Stevens, Gareth Publishing LLLP.

ASTRONOMY—DICTIONARIES

Anderson, Amy & Anderson, Brian. Space Dictionary for Kids: The Everything Guide for Kids Who Love Space. 2016. (ENG., Illus.). 200p. (J). (gr. 4-7). 13.95 *(978-1-61821-515-4(9),* 9781618215154) Prufrock Pr.
World Book, Inc Staff, contrib. by. Encyclopedia of Space. 2013. (J). *(978-0-7166-7523-5(4))* World Bk., Inc.

ASTRONOMY—HISTORY

Anderson, Michael, ed. Pioneers in Astronomy & Space Exploration. 2012. (Inventors & Innovators Ser.). (ENG., Illus.). 112p. (gr. 7-12). (J). 32.90 *(978-1-61530-695-4(1));* (YA). 65.80 *(978-1-61530-786-9(9))* Rosen Publishing Group, Inc., The.
Andronik, Catherine M. Copernicus: Genius of Modern Astronomy. 2015. (Genius Scientists & Their Genius Ideas Ser.). 96p. (J). (gr. 5-12). 27.94 *(978-0-7660-6550-5(2));* pap. 10.95 *(978-0-7660-6551-2(0))* Enslow Pubs., Inc.
Atkinson, Mary. The Earth Is Flat! 2007. (Shockwave: Science in Practice Ser.). (ENG., Illus.). 36p. (J). (gr. 3-5). 25.00 *(978-0-531-17580-4(4),* Children's Pr.) Scholastic Library Publishing.
Carson, Mary Kay. Beyond the Solar System: Exploring Galaxies, Black Holes, Alien Planets, & More; a History with 21 Activities. 2013. (For Kids Ser.). (ENG., Illus.). 144p. (J). (gr. 4). pap. 18.95 *(978-1-61374-544-1(3))* Chicago Review Pr., Inc.
Datnow, Claire L. Edwin Hubble: Genius Discoverer of Galaxies. 2015. (Genius Scientists & Their Genius Ideas Ser.). 96p. (J). (gr. 5-12). 27.94 *(978-0-7660-6555-0(3))* Enslow Pubs., Inc.
Green, Jen. The Sun & Our Solar System. 2017. (Great Scientific Theories Ser.). (ENG.). 32p. (J). (gr. 4-6). lib. bdg. 30.65 ***(978-1-4109-8730-3(2),*** Raintree Perspectives) Heinemann-Raintree.
Hall, Derek. Chemistry, Earth, & Space Sciences. 2010. (Facts at Your Fingertips Ser.). (YA). (gr. 7-12). 35.65 *(978-1-933834-47-4(1))* Brown Bear Books.
Harmon, Daniel E. The Early Days of Space Exploration. 2017. (From Earth to the Stars Ser.). 48p. (gr. 10-12). pap. 14.05 ***(978-1-68048-665-0(9),*** Britannica Educational Publishing) Rosen Publishing Group, Inc., The.
Hartman, Eve & Meshbesher, Wendy. The Scientists Behind Space, 1 vol. 2011. (Sci-Hi: Scientists Ser.). (ENG.). 48p. (gr. 4-4). 33.32 *(978-1-4109-4049-0(7));* pap. 9.95 *(978-1-4109-4056-8(X))* Heinemann-Raintree. (Sci-Hi).
Keranen, Rachel. The Composition of the Universe: The Evolution of Stars & Galaxies. 2016. (Space Systems Ser.). 112p. (J). 42.79 *(978-1-5026-2285-3(8))* Cavendish Square Publishing.
Matejovsky, Char. Shadow on the Moon: A Child's Guide to the Discovery of the Universe. Ream, Robaire, illus. 2014. (J). *(978-1-59815-151-0(7))* Polebridge Pr.
McCutcheon, Scott & McCutcheon, Bobbi. Space & Astronomy: The People Behind the Science. 2005. (Pioneers in Science Ser.). (Illus.). 192p. (gr. 6-12). 29.95 *(978-0-8160-5467-1(3))* Facts On File, Inc.
Miller, Ron. Recentering the Universe: The Radical Theories of Copernicus, Kepler, & Galileo. 2013. (YA). lib. bdg. *(978-0-7613-5885-5(4))* Twenty First Century Bks.
Rose, Simon. Andromeda: The Myth & Science. 2015. (J). *(978-1-4896-3316-3(2))* Weigl Pubs., Inc.
—Hercules: The Myth & Science. 2015. (J). *(978-1-4896-3324-8(3))* Weigl Pubs., Inc.
Sakolsky, Josh. Copernicus & Modern Astronomy. 2004. (Primary Sources of Revolutionary Scientific Discoveries & Theories Ser.). (Illus.). 64p. (J). lib. bdg. 31.95 *(978-1-4042-0305-1(2))* Rosen Publishing Group, Inc., The.
Science Readers Staff & Jankowski, Connie. From Hubble to Hubble: Astromers & Outer Space, 1 vol. 2007. (Science Readers Ser.). (ENG., Illus.). 32p. (J). (gr. 3-3). pap. 8.99 *(978-0-7439-0564-0(4))* Shell Educational Publishing.
Stefoff, Rebecca. Earth or Sun: Which One Is in the Center? 2013. (J). *(978-0-7614-8147-8(8))* Marshall Cavendish.
—Flat Earth & Round Earth. 2014. 48p. pap. 29.93 *(978-1-62712-512-3(4))* Cavendish Square Publishing.
Whiting, Jim. Galileo. 2007. (What's So Great About... ? Ser.). (Illus.). 32p. (YA). (gr. 2-4). lib. bdg. 25.70 *(978-1-58415-575-1(2))* Mitchell Lane Pubs., Inc.
World Book, Inc Staff, contrib. by. Astronomy. 2009. (J). *(978-0-7166-0387-0(X))* World Bk., Inc.
Zuchora-Walske, Christine. Key Discoveries in Earth & Space Science. 2015. (Science Discovery Timelines Ser.). (ENG., Illus.). 48p. (J). (gr. 6-8). pap. 8.99 *(978-1-4677-6157-4(5),* Lerner Pubns.) Lerner Publishing Group.

ASTRONOMY—VOCATIONAL GUIDANCE

Ghez, Andrea Mia & Cohen, Judith Love. You Can Be A Woman Astronomer. Katz, David Arthur, illus. I.t. ed. 40p. (J). 2006. pap. 12.95 incl. DVD *(978-1-880599-77-8(5))* 2005. 17.95 incl. DVD *(978-1-880599-78-5(3))* Cascade Pass, Inc.
Lee, David. A Day at Work with an Astronomer, 01 vols., 1. 2016. (Super STEM Careers Ser.). (ENG., Illus.). 24p. (J). pap. 8.25 *(978-1-5081-4419-9(2),* PowerKids Pr.) Rosen Publishing Group, Inc., The.
Peterson, Judy Monroe. Exploring Space: Astronauts & Astronomers. 2009. (Extreme Scientists Ser.). (Illus.). 24p. (YA). (gr. 2-5). lib. bdg. 22.60 *(978-1-4042-4528-0(6))* Rosen Publishing Group, Inc., The.
Yomtov, Nel. Observatory Director. 2015. (21st Century Skills Library: Cool STEAM Careers Ser.). (ENG., Illus.). 32p. (J). (gr. 4-7). 29.93 *(978-1-63362-008-7(5),* 205944) Cherry Lake Publishing.

ASTROPHYSICS

Hunter, Nick. Northern Lights, 1 vol. 2013. (Night Sky: & Other Amazing Sights in Space Ser.). (ENG.). 32p. (gr. 1-3). 27.32 *(978-1-4329-7516-6(1));* pap. 8.95 *(978-1-4329-7521-0(8))* Heinemann-Raintree. (Heinemann First Library).
Kalz, Jill. Northern Lights. 2004. (Natural Wonders of the World Ser.). (Illus.). 32p. (J). lib. bdg. 18.95 *(978-1-58341-326-5(X),* Creative Education) Creative Co., The.
Riley, Peter D. Space. 2011. (Real Scientist Investigates Ser.). (Illus.). 32p. (J). (gr. 3-5). lib. bdg. 28.50 *(978-1-59771-284-2(1))* Sea-To-Sea Pubns.
Silverman, Buffy. Exploring Dangers in Space: Asteroids, Space Junk, & More. 2011. (Searchlight Books Whats Amazing about Space Ser.). (ENG., Illus.). 40p. (gr. 3-5). lib. bdg. 27.93 *(978-0-7613-5446-8(8))* Lerner Publishing Group.
World Book, Inc Staff, contrib. by. The Universe — A Cosmic Tour. 2010. (J). *(978-0-7166-9545-5(6))* World Bk., Inc.

ASWAN HIGH DAM (EGYPT)

Parks, Peggy J. Aswan High Dam. (Building World Landmarks Ser.). (J). 2004. 26.19 *(978-1-4103-0204-5(0))* 2003. (Illus.). 48p. 24.95 *(978-1-56711-329-7(X))* Cengage Gale. (Blackbirch Pr., Inc.).

ATHENS (GREECE)

De Medeiros, James. Parthenon. 2007. (Structural Wonders Ser.). (Illus.). 32p. (J). (gr. 4-7). lib. bdg. 26.00 *(978-1-59036-727-8(8));* per. 9.95 *(978-1-59036-728-5(6))* Weigl Pubs., Inc.
Dyan, Penelope. The Squeaky Wheel Gets to Greece —-A Kid's Guide to Athens, Greece. Weigand, John D., photos by. 2011. (Illus.). 36p. pap. 11.95 *(978-1-935630-58-6(X))* Bellissima Publishing, LLC.
Kotapish, Dawn. Daily Life in Ancient & Modern Athens. Moulder, Bob, illus. 2005. (Cities Through Time Ser.). 64p. (gr. 5-12). 25.26 *(978-0-8225-3216-3(6))* Lerner Publishing Group.
Leavitt, Amie Jane. Ancient Athens. 2012. (Explore Ancient Worlds Ser.). 48p. (J). (gr. 3-6). lib. bdg. 29.95 *(978-1-61228-275-6(X))* Mitchell Lane Pubs., Inc.
Leoni, Cristiana. In Pericles' Athens with Socrates. Cappon, Manuela, illus. 2008. (Come See My City Ser.). 48p. (gr. 4-8). lib. bdg. 28.50 *(978-0-7614-4326-1(6),* Benchmark Bks.) Marshall Cavendish Corp.
Naden, Corinne J. & Blue, Rose. Ancient Greeks & the Parthenon. 2003. (J). *(978-1-58417-314-4(9));* pap. *(978-1-58417-315-1(7))* Lake Street Pubs.
Nardo, Don. Pericles: Great Leader of Ancient Athens. 2006. (Rulers of the Ancient World Ser.). (Illus.). 160p. (YA). (gr. 6-12). lib. bdg. 29.27 *(978-0-7660-2561-5(6))* Enslow Pubs., Inc.

ATHENS (GREECE)—FICTION

Chappas, Bess. Kiki & the Red Shoes. Branam, Sandy, illus. 2007. (J). 17.99 *(978-1-60131-012-5(9))* Big Tent Bks.
De Michel. What's an Egg Got to Do with It? A Dozen Adventures with God for Grades 4-6. 2007. 108p. pap. 19.95 *(978-1-4241-8994-6(2))* America Star Bks.
Holub, Joan & Williams, Suzanne. Athena the Proud. 2014. (Goddess Girls Ser.: 13). (ENG., Illus.). 240p. (J). (gr. 3-7). 17.99 *(978-1-4424-8821-2(2),* Aladdin) Simon & Schuster Children's Publishing.
Lamb, Charles & Lamb, Mary. Tales from Shakespeare: "A Midsummer Night's Dream" Strang, Kay, ed. Andrews, Gary, illus. rev. ed. 2005. 39p. pap. 4.95 *(978-0-9542905-3-5(4))* Capercaillie Bks., Ltd GBR. Dist: Wilson & Assocs.
Leslie, Emma. Glaucia the Greek Slave: A Tale of Athens in the First Century. Felter & Butterworth & Heath, illus. 2007. 308p. per. 14.95 *(978-1-934671-01-6(0))* Salem Ridge Press LLC.
Maese, Fares & Shakespeare, William. A Midsummer Night's Dream, 1 vol. Esparza, Andres et al, illus. 2011. (Shakespeare Graphics Ser.). (ENG.). 88p. (gr. 2-3). pap. 7.15 *(978-1-4342-3449-0(5),* Shakespeare Graphics) Stone Arch Bks.
Marsh, Carole. The Curse of the Ancient Acropolis: Athens, Greece. 2009. (Around the World in 80 Mysteries Ser.). (Illus.). 132p. (J). lib. bdg. 18.99 *(978-0-635-07040-1(5),* Marsh, Carole Mysteries) Gallopade International.
Panayotis. Junior & Bo's Trip to the Olympics. Theophilopoulos, Andrew, illus. 2007. 104p. per. 10.95 *(978-1-934246-26-9(3))* Peppertree Pr., The.
Riggs, Sandy. Three Ancient Communities: Set Of 6. 2011. (Navigators Ser.). (J). pap. 44.00 net. *(978-1-4108-5093-5(5))* Benchmark Education Co.
Snedeker, Caroline Dale. Lysis Goes to the Play. Clark, Elizabeth Palmer, illus. 2003. 62p. (J). per. 8.95 *(978-0-9667067-4-1(9))* American Home-School Publishing, LLC.

ATHENS (GREECE)—HISTORY

Curlee, Lynn. Parthenon. Curlee, Lynn, illus. 2011. (ENG., Illus.). 40p. (J). (gr. 3-7). 19.99 *(978-1-4424-3094-5(X),* Atheneum Bks. for Young Readers) Simon & Schuster Children's Publishing.
Edwards, Roberta & dePaola, Tomie. Where Is the Parthenon? Hinderliter, John & Groff, David, illus. 2016. (Where Is? Ser.). (ENG.). 112p. (J). (gr. 3-7). 5.99 *(978-0-448-48889-9(2),* Grosset & Dunlap) Penguin Young Readers Group.
Kissock, Heather. Parthenon. 2011. (J). *(978-1-61690-434-0(8))* Weigl Pubs., Inc.
Kissock, Heather, ed. Parthenon. 2011. (J). (gr. 4-6). pap. 12.95 *(978-1-61690-772-3(X),* AV2 by Weigl); (Illus.). 24p. (gr. 2-5). 27.13 *(978-1-61690-768-6(1))* Weigl Pubs., Inc.
Kotapish, Dawn. Daily Life in Ancient & Modern Athens. Moulder, Bob, illus. 2005. (Cities Through Time Ser.). 64p. (gr. 5-12). 25.26 *(978-0-8225-3216-3(6))* Lerner Publishing Group.
Mann, Elizabeth. The Parthenon: The Height of Greek Civilization. Lee, Yuan, illus. 2006. (Wonders of the World Book Ser.). (ENG.). 48p. (J). (gr. 4-8). 22.95 *(978-1-931414-15-9(7),* 9781931414159) Mikaya Pr.

ATHLETES

see also African American Athletes
Abbey, Cherie D., ed. Biography Today: Profiles of People of Interest to Young Readers. 2003. (Biography Today Subject Ser.: 10). 200p. lib. bdg. 44.00 *(978-0-7808-0655-9(7));* 246p. lib. bdg. 44.00 *(978-0-7808-0654-2(9))* Omnigraphics, Inc.
ABDO Publishing Company Staff. Awesome Athletes. 2014. (Awesome Athletes Ser.: 12). (ENG.). 32p. (gr. 8-12). lib. bdg. 324.84 *(978-1-62403-327-8(X),* Checkerboard Library) ABDO Publishing Co.
—Extreme Sports Stars. 2014. (Extreme Sports Stars Ser.: 6). (ENG.). 32p. (gr. 8-15). lib. bdg. 162.42 *(978-1-62403-452-7(7),* SportsZone) ABDO Publishing Co.
Adler, David A. America's Champion Swimmer: Gertrude Ederle. Widener, Terry, illus. 2005. (ENG.). 32p. (J). (gr. -1-3). reprint ed. pap. 7.99 *(978-0-15-205251-5(8))* Houghton Mifflin Harcourt Publishing Co.
Aiwei, Daniel B. CM Punk: Pro Wrestling Superstar, 1 vol. 2014. (Pro Wrestling Superstars Ser.). (ENG.). 24p. (gr. 1-2). lib. bdg. 25.32 *(978-1-4765-4210-2(4),* First Facts) Capstone Press of Coughlan Cos.
—John Cena: Pro Wrestling Superstar, 1 vol. 2014. (Pro Wrestling Superstars Ser.). (ENG.). 24p. (gr. 1-2). lib. bdg. 25.32 *(978-1-4765-4207-2(4),* First Facts) Capstone Press of Coughlan Cos.
Aldridge, Rebecca. Apolo Anton Ohno. 2009. (Asian Americans of Achievement Ser.). (Illus.). 128p. (YA). (gr. 7-12). 35.00 *(978-1-60413-565-7(4))* Facts On File, Inc.
Alexander, Kwame. The Playbook: 52 Rules to Aim, Shoot, & Score in This Game Called Life. Neave, Thai, photos by. 2017. (ENG., Illus.). 176p. (J). (gr. 5-7). 14.99 *(978-0-544-57097-9(9),* HMH Books For Young Readers) Houghton Mifflin Harcourt Publishing Co.
—The Playbook: 52 Rules to Aim, Shoot, & Score in This Game Called Life. Neave, Thai, photos by. 2017. (ENG., Illus.). (J). (gr. 5-7). lib. bdg. 26.95 ***(978-0-606-39814-5(7))*** Turtleback Bks.
Allen, Kathy. Drew Brees. 2013. (Football Stars up Close Ser.). 24p. (J). (gr. k-5). lib. bdg. 23.93 *(978-1-61772-716-0(4))* Bearport Publishing Co., Inc.
—Tom Brady. 2013. (Football Stars up Close Ser.). 24p. (J). (gr. k-5). lib. bdg. 23.93 *(978-1-61772-717-7(2))* Bearport Publishing Co., Inc.
—Tony Romo. 2013. (Football Stars up Close Ser.). 24p. (J). (gr. k-5). lib. bdg. 23.93 *(978-1-61772-719-1(9))* Bearport Publishing Co., Inc.
Anderson, Jameson. Aaron Rodgers, 1 vol. 2014. (Awesome Athletes Ser.). (ENG.). 32p. (gr. 8-12). 27.07 *(978-1-62403-335-3(0))* ABDO Publishing Co.
—Colin Kaepernick, 1 vol. 2014. (Awesome Athletes Ser.). (ENG.). 32p. (gr. 8-12). 27.07 *(978-1-62403-331-5(8))* ABDO Publishing Co.
—Miguel Cabrera, 1 vol. 2014. (Awesome Athletes Ser.). (ENG.). 32p. (gr. 8-12). 27.07 *(978-1-62403-328-5(8))* ABDO Publishing Co.

—Mike Trout, 1 vol. 2014. (Awesome Athletes Ser.). (ENG.). 32p. (gr. 8-12). 27.07 *(978-1-62403-336-0(9))* ABDO Publishing Co.
—Peyton Manning, 1 vol. 2014. (Awesome Athletes Ser.). (ENG., Illus.). 32p. (gr. 8-12). 27.07 *(978-1-62403-332-2(6))* ABDO Publishing Co.
Anderson, Michael. Football & Its Greatest Players. 2011. (J). lib. bdg. 31.70 *(978-1-61530-511-7(4))* Rosen Publishing Group, Inc., The.
Apps, Roy. Cristiano Ronaldo. 2017. (EDGE: Sporting Heroes Ser.). (ENG., Illus.). 48p. (J). (gr. 2-7). 12.99 ***(978-1-4451-5318-6(1)***, Franklin Watts) Hachette Children's Group GBR. Dist: Hachette Bk. Group.
Apps, Roy. Louis Smith. King, Chris, illus. 2017. (EDGE - Dream to Win Ser.). (ENG.). 48p. (J). (gr. 2-4). pap. 9.99 *(978-1-4451-4092-6(6)*, Franklin Watts) Hachette Children's Group GBR. Dist: Hachette Bk. Group.
Armstrong, Jesse. Triple H. 2015. (Wrestling Superstars Ser.). (ENG., Illus.). 24p. (J). (gr. 3-7). lib. bdg. 25.95 *(978-1-62617-183-1(1)*, Epic Bks.) Bellwether Media.
Artell, Mike. Peyton Manning: Football Superstar, 1 vol. 2011. (Superstar Athletes Ser.). (ENG.). 24p. (gr. 1-2). lib. bdg. 25.32 *(978-1-4296-6564-3(5))* Capstone Press of Coughlan Cos.
Artell, Mike, et al. Superstar Athletes, 1 vol. 2014. (Superstar Athletes Ser.). (ENG.). 24p. (gr. 1-2). lib. bdg. 354.48 *(978-1-4765-9438-5(4))* Capstone Press of Coughlan Cos.
Bankston, John. Abby Wambach. 2013. (ENG.). 32p. (gr. 4-8). lib. bdg. 25.70 *(978-1-61228-465-1(5))* Mitchell Lane Pubs., Inc.
—Lance Armstrong. 2004. (Blue Banner Biography Ser.). (Illus.). 32p. (J). lib. bdg. 25.70 *(978-1-58415-334-4(2))* Mitchell Lane Pubs., Inc.
Barnas, Jo-Ann. Olympics Record Breakers, 1 vol. 2016. (ENG., Illus.). 48p. (J). ***(978-1-62403-849-5(2)***, 1391441, SportsZone) ABDO Publishing Co.
Barnhart, C. A. What Makes Great Athletes. 2005. (ENG., Illus.). 24p. (J). (gr. 5-5). pap. 5.97 net. *(978-0-328-13561-5(5)*, Scott Foresman) Pearson Schl.
Bednar, Chuck. Tim Duncan. 2012. (Role Model Athletes Ser.). 64p. (J). (gr. 7). 22.95 *(978-1-4222-2713-8(8))* Mason Crest.
—Tony Romo. 2013. (J). *(978-1-4222-2726-8(X))* Mason Crest.
Belval, Brian. Olympic Track & Field. 2007. (Great Moments in Olympic History Ser.). (Illus.). 48p. (YA). (gr. 5-9). lib. bdg. 29.25 *(978-1-4042-0971-8(9))* Rosen Publishing Group, Inc., The.
Benson, Michael. Lance Armstrong, Cyclist. 2003. (Ferguson Career Biographies Ser.). (Illus.). 144p. (gr. 6-12). 25.00 *(978-0-8160-5479-4(7)*, Ferguson Publishing Co.) Facts On File, Inc.
Berman, Ron. Future Stars of America. 2006. (Future Stars Ser.). (Illus.). 90p. (gr. 3-8). pap. 9.95 *(978-0-9741997-4-0(5))* Scobre Pr. Corp.
Bernstein, Ross. Shaquille O'Neal. (Amazing Athletes Ser.). 32p. 2005. (Illus.). (gr. 3-4). lib. bdg. 22.60 *(978-0-8225-3689-5(7))* 2004. (Illus.). (J). (gr. 2-5). pap. 5.95 *(978-0-8225-2042-9(7))* 2009. (ENG.). (gr. 2-5). pap. 7.95 *(978-0-7613-4489-6(6)*, First Avenue Editions) Lerner Publishing Group.
Besley, Adrian. Zlatan Ibrahimovic: The Ultimate Fan Book. 2017. (ENG., Illus.). 64p. (J). (gr. 4). pap. 9.95 *(978-1-78097-934-2(7))* Carlton Bks., Ltd. GBR. Dist: Sterling Publishing Co., Inc.
Best, Detra. Sports Edition: The Athlete. 2013. 54p. pap. 9.95 *(978-0-9854968-7-6(8))* 3G Publishing, Inc.
Big Stars, Big Pictures, 1 vol. 2010. (Time, Inc. Library-Bound Titles Ser.). (ENG.). 48p. (gr. 5-6). 31.32 *(978-1-4296-5180-6(6))* Capstone Press of Coughlan Cos.
Bingham, Jane. Sports Heroes. 2011. (20th Century Lives Ser.). (Illus.). 32p. (YA). (gr. 3-6). 26.50 *(978-1-4488-3294-1(2))* Rosen Publishing Group, Inc., The.
Bishop, Amanda. Soccer Superstars: The Best of the Best. 2013. (ENG., Illus.). 32p. (J). *(978-0-7787-0243-6(X))*; pap. *(978-0-7787-0252-8(9))* Crabtree Publishing Co.
Bodden, Valerie. Bryce Harper: Big Time. 2013. 21p. 23.09 *(978-1-60818-474-3(9))* Creative Co., The.
—Calvin Johnson. 2015. (J). *(978-1-60818-494-1(3)*, Creative Education) Creative Co., The.
—Robert Griffin III. 2013. 21p. 23.09 *(978-1-60818-475-0(7))* Creative Co., The.
Bolte, Mari. Skater Chic Style: Fun Fashions You Can Sketch, 1 vol. Rzasa, Jennifer, illus. 2013. (Drawing Fun Fashions Ser.). (ENG.). 32p. (gr. 3-4). lib. bdg. 27.99 *(978-1-62065-038-7(X)*, Snap Bks.) Capstone Press of Coughlan Cos.
Bradley, Michael. Generation Next: Superstar Kids of Superstar Athletes. 2004. (J). 3.99 *(978-1-930623-33-0(X))* Sports Illustrated For Kids.
—Yao Ming. 2004. (Benchmark All-Stars 2 Ser.). (Illus.). 48p. (gr. 4). 21.95 *(978-0-7614-1758-3(3)*, Benchmark Bks.) Marshall Cavendish Corp.
Brew, Jim. The Miz. 2012. (Pro Wrestling Champions Ser.). (ENG., Illus.). 24p. (J). (gr. 3-7). lib. bdg. 25.95 *(978-1-60014-753-1(4)*, Torque Bks.) Bellwether Media.
Brignall, Richard. Big Train: The Legendary Ironman of Sport, Lionel Conacher, 1 vol. 2009. (Lorimer Recordbooks Ser.). (ENG., Illus.). 168p. (YA). (gr. 6-12). 16.95 *(978-1-55277-451-9(1)*, 9781552774519); 9.95 *(978-1-55277-450-2(3)*, 9781552774502) Lorimer, James & Co., Ltd., Pubs. CAN. Dist: Casemate Pubs. & Bk. Distributors, LLC.
Bringle, Jennifer. The Undertaker: Master of Pain. 2011. (Slam! Stars of Wrestling Ser.). (ENG.). 48p. (YA). (gr. 5-8). pap. 11.75 *(978-1-4488-5597-1(7))*; lib. bdg. 29.25 *(978-1-4488-5536-0(5))* Rosen Publishing Group, Inc., The.
Brown, Daniel James. The Boys in the Boat (Young Readers Adaptation) The True Story of an American Team's Epic Journey to Win Gold at the 1936 Olympics. (ENG., Illus.). (J). (gr. 5). 2016. 256p. 10.99 *(978-0-14-751685-5(4)*, Puffin Books) 2015. 240p. 17.99 *(978-0-451-47592-3(5)*, Viking Books for Young Readers) Penguin Young Readers Group.
—The Boys in the Boat (Young Readers Adaptation) The True Story of an American Team's Epic Journey to Win Gold at the 1936 Olympics. 2016. lib. bdg. 22.10 *(978-0-606-39312-6(9))* Turtleback Bks.
Brown, Monica. Pelé, King of Soccer (Pelé, el Rey del Fútbol) Gayesky, Fernando, tr. Gutierrez, Rudy, illus. 2008. (SPA & ENG.). 40p. (J). (gr. -1-3). 17.99 *(978-0-06-122779-0(X)*, Rayo) HarperCollins Pubs.
Brown, Tracy. Jeff Hardy: Bound for Glory. 2011. (Slam! Stars of Wrestling Ser.). (ENG.). 48p. (gr. 5-8). (YA). pap. 11.75 *(978-1-4488-5599-5(3))*; (J). lib. bdg. 29.25 *(978-1-4488-5537-7(3))* Rosen Publishing Group, Inc., The.
—John Cena: World Wrestling Champ. 2011. (Slam! Stars of Wrestling Ser.). (ENG.). 48p. (YA). (gr. 5-8). pap. 11.75 *(978-1-4488-5593-3(4))*; lib. bdg. 29.25 *(978-1-4488-5534-6(9))* Rosen Publishing Group, Inc., The.
Bruchac, Joseph. Jim Thorpe, Original All-American. 2008. (ENG.). 288p. (YA). (gr. 7-18). 9.99 *(978-0-14-241233-6(3)*, Speak) Penguin Young Readers Group.
Bryan, Gayle. Virtual Apprentice: Professional Athlete. 2009. (Virtual Apprentice Ser.). 64p. (gr. 4-9). pap. 9.95 *(978-0-8160-7896-7(3)*, Checkmark Bks.) Facts On File, Inc.
Buckley, James. Katie Ledecky. 2017. (Amazing Americans: Olympians Ser.). (ENG.). 24p. (J). (gr. -1-3). 17.95 ***(978-1-68402-240-3(1))*** Bearport Publishing Co., Inc.
Burgan, Michael. Life as a Gladiator. 2010. (You Choose: Warriors Ser.). (ENG.). 112p. (gr. 3-4). pap. 41.70 *(978-1-4296-5725-9(1)*, You Choose Bks.) Capstone Press of Coughlan Cos.
—Life as a Gladiator: An Interactive History Adventure. 2010. (You Choose: Warriors Ser.). (ENG., 112p. (gr. 3-4). Illus.). pap. 6.95 *(978-1-4296-5638-2(7))*; 31.99 *(978-1-4296-4784-7(1))* Capstone Press of Coughlan Cos. (You Choose Bks.).
Cantwell, Lois & Smith, Pohla. Women Winners: Then & Now. 2005. (Sports Illustrated for Kids Books Ser.). (Illus.). 176p. (YA). (gr. 7-12). lib. bdg. 33.25 *(978-0-8239-3695-3(3))* Rosen Publishing Group, Inc., The.
—Women Winners: Then & Now. (J). (gr. 3-9). pap. 3.99 *(978-1-930623-09-5(7))* Sports Illustrated For Kids.
Caughey, Ellen. Eric Liddell: Gold Medal Missionary. 2006. (Heros of the Faith Ser.). 206p. (YA). (gr. 8-12). per. 2.97 *(978-1-59789-115-8(0))* Barbour Publishing, Inc.
Cefrey, Holly. Competitive Skateboarding. 2009. (Super Skateboarding Ser.). 48p. (gr. 5-8). 53.00 *(978-1-60853-207-0(0)*, Rosen Reference) Rosen Publishing Group, Inc., The.
Cheyney, Arnold B. Athletes of Purpose. 2004. (Illus.). 128p. pap. 12.95 *(978-0-673-58667-4(7))* Good Year Bks.
Childress, Boyd. 100 Most Popular Team Sports Heroes for Young Adults: Biographical Sketches & Professional Paths. 2003. (Profiles & Pathways Ser.). 500p. *(978-1-56308-738-7(3)*, Libraries Unlimited) ABC-CLIO, LLC.
Christopher, Matt. On the Bike with... Lance Armstrong. 2003. (Matt Christopher Sports Ser.). (Illus.). 116p. (J). (gr. 4-7). 12.65 *(978-0-7569-1607-7(0))* Perfection Learning Corp.
Churnin, Nancy. The William Hoy Story: How a Deaf Baseball Player Changed the Game. Tuya, Jez, illus. 2016. (ENG.). 32p. (J). (gr. -1-3). 16.99 *(978-0-8075-9192-5(0))* Whitman, Albert & Co.
Clark, Travis. Alex Rodriguez. 2010. (Role Model Athletes Ser.). (Illus.). 64p. (YA). (gr. 7-12). 22.95 *(978-1-4222-0488-7(X))* Mason Crest.
Clarkson, Stephanie. Let's Get Moving with Wenlock & Mandeville! 2012. (London 2012 Ser.). (ENG., Illus.). 32p. (J). (gr. -1-k). pap. 10.99 *(978-1-84732-645-4(5))* Carlton Bks., Ltd. GBR. Dist: Independent Pubs. Group.
Cohen, Sasha. Sasha Cohen: Autobiography of a Champion Figure Skater. Goedeken, Kathy, illus. 2005. (ENG.). 192p. (J). (gr. 3-18). pap. 9.99 *(978-0-06-072489-4(7))* HarperCollins Pubs.
Conroy, Tim. How to Become a Star Athlete. (Illus.). 88p. (Orig.). (YA). *(978-0-9636706-7-0(0))* Coach Enterprises.
Contro, Arturo. Rafael Marquez. 2009. (World Soccer Stars / Estrellas del fútbol mundial Ser.). (ENG & SPA.). 24p. (gr. 2-2). 42.50 *(978-1-60854-849-1(X)*, Editorial Buenas Letras) Rosen Publishing Group, Inc., The.
Conway, Hollis. Grasshopper: The Hollis Conway Story. 2004. 30p. (J). per. *(978-1-59196-584-8(5))* Instant Pub.
Cook, Brian & Tupper, Mark. Brian Cook: An Illini Legend. 2003. (Basketball Superstar Series; Ser.). (Illus.). 96p. (J). pap. 5.95 *(978-1-58261-731-2(7))* Sports Publishing, LLC.
Corrick, James A. Dwayne "The Rock" Johnson. 2012. (Role Model Entertainers Ser.). 64p. (J). (gr. 7). 22.95 *(978-1-4222-2716-9(2))* Mason Crest.
Crockett, Kyle A. Nutrition for Achievement in Sports & Academics. Borus, Joshua, ed. 2013. (Understanding Nutrition: a Gateway to Physical & Mental Health Ser.). (Illus.). 48p. (J). (gr. 5-18). pap. 9.95 *(978-1-4222-2990-3(4))*; 19.95 *(978-1-4222-2884-5(3))* Mason Crest.
Cronn-Mills, Kirstin & Nelson, Alex Jackson. LGBTQ+ Athletes Claim the Field: Striving for Equality. 2016. (ENG., Illus.). 104p. (YA). (gr. 7-12). 51.99 *(978-1-5124-1139-3(6)*, Twenty-First Century Bks.) Lerner Publishing Group.
—Striving for Equality: LGBTQ Athletes Claim the Field. 2016. (ENG., Illus.). 104p. (YA). (gr. 7-12). 34.65 *(978-1-4677-8012-4(X)*, Twenty-First Century Bks.) Lerner Publishing Group.
Crowe, Ellie. Surfer of the Century. Waldrep, Richard, illus. 2007. (ENG.). 48p. (J). pap. 10.95 *(978-1-60060-461-4(7))* Lee & Low Bks., Inc.
Currie, Stephen. Adrian Peterson. 2012. (Superstars of Pro Football Ser.). 64p. (J). 22.95 *(978-1-4222-2724-4(3))* Mason Crest.
Danica Patrick. 2007. (Xtreme Athletes Ser.). (Illus.). 112p. (YA). (gr. 7-12). lib. bdg. 27.95 *(978-1-59935-079-0(3))* Reynolds, Morgan Inc.
Dave Mirra. 2007. (J). pap. 5.95 *(978-0-8225-6597-0(8)*, First Avenue Editions) Lerner Publishing Group.
Davies, Ross. Andre the Giant. 2009. (Wrestling Greats Ser.). 112p. (gr. 5-5). 63.90 *(978-1-60854-861-3(9))* Rosen Publishing Group, Inc., The.
—Bobo Brazil. 2009. (Wrestling Greats Ser.). 112p. (gr. 5-5). 63.90 *(978-1-60854-863-7(5))* Rosen Publishing Group, Inc., The.
Deportistas de Poder Series: Set 1, Set. 2003. (Deportistas de Poder Ser.). (SPA & ENG., Illus.). (J). 103.50 *(978-0-8239-7197-8(X))*; lib. bdg. 103.50 *(978-0-8239-7193-0(7))* Rosen Publishing Group, Inc., The. (Editorial Buenas Letras).
Dinzeo, Paul. Sheamus. 2012. (Pro Wrestling Champions Ser.). (ENG., Illus.). 24p. (J). (gr. 3-7). lib. bdg. 25.95 *(978-1-60014-752-4(6)*, Torque Bks.) Bellwether Media.
Doeden, Matt. The Miz: Pro Wrestling Superstar, 1 vol. 2014. (Pro Wrestling Superstars Ser.). (ENG.). 24p. (gr. 1-2). lib. bdg. 25.32 *(978-1-4765-4208-9(2)*, First Facts) Capstone Press of Coughlan Cos.
—Shaun White. rev. ed. 2010. (Amazing Athletes Ser.). (ENG.). 32p. (gr. 2-5). lib. bdg. 25.26 *(978-0-7613-6859-5(0)*, Lerner Pubns.) Lerner Publishing Group.
—Stars of Basketball, 1 vol. 2014. (Sports Stars Ser.). (ENG.). 24p. (gr. k-1). lib. bdg. 26.65 *(978-1-4765-3959-1(6)*, Pebble Plus) Capstone Press of Coughlan Cos.
—Stars of Hockey, 1 vol. 2014. (Sports Stars Ser.). (ENG.). 24p. (gr. k-1). lib. bdg. 26.65 *(978-1-4765-3960-7(X)*, Pebble Plus) Capstone Press of Coughlan Cos.
—Superstar Athletes. 2012. (Superstar Athletes Ser.). (ENG.). 24p. (gr. 1-2). pap. 87.48 *(978-1-62065-632-7(9))*; pap. 14.58 *(978-1-62065-631-0(0))* Capstone Press of Coughlan Cos.
—The World's Greatest Sports Stars, 4 vols., Set. Incl. World's Greatest Basketball Players. lib. bdg. 27.99 *(978-1-4296-3923-1(7))*; World's Greatest Football Players. lib. bdg. 27.99 *(978-1-4296-3924-8(5))*; (gr. 2-3). (World's Greatest Sports Stars (Sports Illustrated for Kids) Ser.). (ENG.). 32p. 2010. Set lib. bdg. 55.98 *(978-1-4296-4419-8(2))* Capstone Press of Coughlan Cos.
Doeden, Matt & Schuh, Mari. Sport Stars, 1 vol. 2014. (Sports Stars Ser.). (ENG.). 24p. (gr. k-1). lib. bdg. 106.60 *(978-1-4765-7929-0(6)*, Pebble Plus) Capstone Press of Coughlan Cos.
Doeden, Matt & Wacholtz, Anthony. Superstar Athletes. 2012. (Superstar Athletes Ser.). (ENG.). 24p. (gr. 1-2). pap. 500.40 *(978-1-62065-633-4(7))*; lib. bdg. 227.88 *(978-1-4296-8184-1(5))* Capstone Press of Coughlan Cos.
Doeden, Matt, et al. Pro Wrestling Superstars, 1 vol. 2014. (Pro Wrestling Superstars Ser.). (ENG.). 24p. (gr. 1-2). lib. bdg. 101.28 *(978-1-4765-7926-9(1)*, First Facts) Capstone Press of Coughlan Cos.
Donovan, Sandy. Lance Armstrong. (Amazing Athletes Ser.). (Illus.). 32p. (J). 2005. (gr. 3-4). lib. bdg. 23.93 *(978-0-8225-3691-8(9))* 2004. (gr. 2-5). per. 5.95 *(978-0-8225-2039-9(7))* Lerner Publishing Group.
—Triple H: At the Top of His Game, 1 vol. 2012. (Pro Wrestling Stars Ser.). (ENG., Illus.). 48p. (gr. 3-4). lib. bdg. 31.99 *(978-1-4296-8677-8(4))* Capstone Press of Coughlan Cos.
Douglas, Gabrielle & Burford, Michelle. Grace, Gold & Glory: My Leap of Faith, 1 vol. 2013. (ENG.). 224p. pap. 16.99 *(978-0-310-74067-4(3))* 2012. (ENG.). 224p. 24.99 *(978-0-310-74061-2(4))* 2012. *(978-0-310-74200-5(5))* Zondervan.
Dublin, Anne. Bobbie Rosenfeld: The Olympian Who Could Do Everything, 1 vol. 2004. (ENG., Illus.). 148p. (J). (gr. 4-8). pap. 14.95 *(978-1-896764-82-5(7))* Second Story Pr. CAN. Dist: Orca Bk. Pubs. USA.
Dunn, Jeremy K. Ray Lewis. 2013. (J). *(978-1-4222-2722-0(7))* Mason Crest.
Dynamic Athletes & the Sports They Influenced, 6 bks. Incl. Top Teams Ever: Football, Baseball, Basketball & Hockey Winners. Ross, Dalton. lib. bdg. 33.25 *(978-0-8239-3693-9(7))*; Women Winners: Then & Now. Cantwell, Lois & Smith, Pohla. lib. bdg. 33.25 *(978-0-8239-3695-3(3))*; (YA). (gr. 7-12). (Illus.). 176p. 2005. Set lib. bdg. 169.65 *(978-0-8239-9733-6(2))* Rosen Publishing Group, Inc., The.
Eboch, M. M. Jesse Owens: Young Record Breaker. Henderson, Meryl, illus. 2008. (Childhood of Famous Americans Ser.). (ENG.). 208p. (J). (gr. 3-7). pap. 6.99 *(978-1-4169-3922-1(9)*, Aladdin) Simon & Schuster Children's Publishing.
Eli Manning. 2009. (Amazing Athletes Ser.). (gr. 2-5). pap. 6.95 *(978-0-7613-4137-6(4)*, First Avenue Editions) Lerner Publishing Group.
Ellwood, Nancy. Lance Armstrong: With a Discussion of Determination. 2004. (Values in Action Ser.). (J). *(978-1-59203-073-6(4))* Learning Challenge, Inc.
Elzaurdia, Paco. Rafael Marquez. 2012. (Superstars of Soccer ENGLISH Ser.). (Illus.). 32p. (J). (gr. 4). 19.95 *(978-1-4222-2651-3(4))* Mason Crest.
Fandel, Jennifer. CM Punk: Straight Edge Heel, 1 vol. 2012. (Pro Wrestling Stars Ser.). (ENG., Illus.). 48p. (gr. 3-4). lib. bdg. 31.99 *(978-1-4296-8693-8(6))* Capstone Press of Coughlan Cos.
—Jim Thorpe: Greatest Athlete in the World, 1 vol. Whigham, Rod, illus. 2008. (Graphic Biographies Ser.). (ENG.). 32p. (gr. 3-4). per. 8.10 *(978-1-4296-1773-4(X)*, Graphic Library) Capstone Press of Coughlan Cos.
Feldman, Heather. Hulk Hogan: Campeón de Lucha Libre (Wrestling Pro) 2009. (Superestrellas del Deporte (Superstars of Sports) Ser.). (SPA.). 24p. (gr. 1-2). 42.50 *(978-1-60853-226-1(7)*, Editorial Buenas Letras) Rosen Publishing Group, Inc., The.
Ferrara, Cos. Babe Didrikson Zaharias: Outcast & Hero. 2004. (Girls Explore, Reach for the Stars Ser.). (Illus.). 109p. (J). 20.00 *(978-0-9749456-2-0(5)*, Girls Explore) Girls Explore LLC.
Fishman, Jon M. Abby Wambach. 2014. (Amazing Athletes Ser.). (ENG., Illus.). 32p. (gr. 2-5). lib. bdg. 25.26 *(978-1-4677-2141-7(7)*, Lerner Pubns.) Lerner Publishing Group.
—Andrew Luck. 2013. (Amazing Athletes Ser.). (ENG., Illus.). 32p. (gr. 2-5). pap. 7.95 *(978-1-4677-1888-2(2))*; lib. bdg. 25.26 *(978-1-4677-1879-0(3)*, Lerner Pubns.) Lerner Publishing Group.
—Carmelo Anthony. 2013. (Amazing Athletes Ser.). (ENG., Illus.). 32p. (gr. 2-5). pap. 7.95 *(978-1-4677-2063-2(1))*; lib. bdg. 25.26 *(978-1-4677-2062-5(3)*, Lerner Pubns.) Lerner Publishing Group.
—Kevin Love. 2013. (Amazing Athletes Ser.). (ENG., Illus.). 32p. (gr. 2-5). pap. 7.95 *(978-1-4677-1891-2(2))*; lib. bdg. 25.26 *(978-1-4677-1881-3(5)*, Lerner Pubns.) Lerner Publishing Group.
Fishman, Jon M. Michael Phelps. 2017. (Sports All-Stars Ser.). (ENG.). 32p. (J). (gr. 2-5). 12.99 ***(978-1-5124-5400-0(1)***, Lerner Pubns.); 39.99 ***(978-1-5124-5397-3(8)***, Lerner Pubns.); 39.99 ***(978-1-5124-5398-0(6)***, Lerner Pubns.); (Illus.). pap. 8.99 ***(978-1-5124-5401-7(X))***; (Illus.). lib. bdg. 26.65 ***(978-1-5124-5396-6(X))*** Lerner Publishing Group.
Ford, Jeanne Marie. The 12 Most Influential Athletes of All Time. 2018. (ENG.). 32p. (gr. 3-6). 31.35 ***(978-1-63235-407-5(1)***, 12-Story Library) Pr. Room Editions LLC.
Frederick, Shane. Speed Training for Teen Athletes: Exercises to Take Your Game to the Next Level. 2012. (Sports Training Zone Ser.). (ENG.). 48p. (gr. 4-5). pap. 47.70 *(978-1-4296-8487-3(9))*; lib. bdg. 31.99 *(978-1-4296-7678-6(7))* Capstone Press of Coughlan Cos.
—Stamina Training for Teen Athletes: Exercises to Take Your Game to the Next Level, 1 vol. 2012. (Sports Training Zone Ser.). (ENG.). 48p. (gr. 4-5). pap. 8.19 *(978-1-4296-8001-1(6))*; pap. 47.70 *(978-1-4296-8489-7(5))*; lib. bdg. 31.99 *(978-1-4296-7679-3(5))* Capstone Press of Coughlan Cos.
Freedman, Jeri. Professional Wrestling: Steroids in & Out of the Ring. 2009. (Disgraced! the Dirty History of Performance-Enhancing Drugs in Sports Ser.). (Illus.). 48p. (YA). (gr. 5-9). 29.25 *(978-1-4358-5305-8(9))* Rosen Publishing Group, Inc., The.
Freedman, Russell. Babe Didrikson Zaharias: The Making of a Champion. 2014. (ENG., Illus.). 192p. (J). (gr. 5-7). pap. 10.99 *(978-0-544-10491-4(9))* Houghton Mifflin Harcourt Publishing Co.
French, Cathy. Fast Athletes. 2011. (Early Connections Ser.). (J). *(978-1-61672-229-6(0))* Benchmark Education Co.
Frew, Katherine. Gladiators: Battling in the Arena. 2005. (Way of the Warrior Ser.). (ENG., Illus.). 48p. (J). 24.50 *(978-0-516-25121-9(X)*, Children's Pr.) Scholastic Library Publishing.
Frisch, Aaron. Aaron Rodgers. 2013. (Illus.). 24 p.p. (J). 25.65 *(978-1-60818-334-0(3)*, Creative Education) Creative Co., The.
—Adrian Peterson. 2013. (Illus.). 24 p.p. (J). 25.65 *(978-1-60818-335-7(1)*, Creative Education) Creative Co., The.
Gagne, Tammy. Day by Day with Manny Machado. 2013. (ENG., Illus.). 32p. (J). (gr. -1-2). lib. bdg. 25.70 *(978-1-61228-454-5(X))* Mitchell Lane Pubs., Inc.
—Mike Trout. 2013. (ENG.). 32p. (gr. 4-8). lib. bdg. 25.70 *(978-1-61228-466-8(3))* Mitchell Lane Pubs., Inc.
Ganeri, Anita. Gladiators & Ancient Rome. 2009. (History Explorers Ser.). (ENG.). 24p. (J). (gr. k-2). pap. 5.95 *(978-1-84696-213-4(7)*, TickTock Books) Octopus Publishing Group GBR. Dist: Independent Pubs. Group.
Gerstein, Mordicai. The Man Who Walked Between the Towers. Gerstein, Mordicai, illus. 2007. (ENG., Illus.). 44p. (J). (gr. k-3). per. 7.99 *(978-0-312-36878-4(X)*, 9780312368784) Square Fish.
Gifford, Clive. Greatest Players. 2017. (Planet Football Ser.). (ENG., Illus.). 32p. (J). (gr. 4-6). pap. 12.99 *(978-1-5263-0127-7(X)*, Wayland) Hachette Children's Group GBR. Dist: Hachette Bk. Group.
—The Kingfisher Soccer Encyclopedia. 3rd rev. ed. 2014. (Kingfisher Encyclopedias Ser.). (ENG., Illus.). 144p. (J). (gr. 5-9). 19.99 *(978-0-7534-7167-8(1)*, 9780753471678, Kingfisher) Roaring Brook Pr.
—Soccer Legends. 2009. (ENG., Illus.). 32p. (J). (gr. 4-7). lib. bdg. *(978-0-7787-3777-3(2))* Crabtree Publishing Co.
Gilpin, Daniel. Record-Breaking People. 2012. (Record Breakers Ser.). (Illus.). 32p. (J). lib. bdg. 26.50 *(978-1-4488-5293-2(5)*, PowerKids Pr.) Rosen Publishing Group, Inc., The.
Gitlin, Martin. Ed Reed. 2009. (Superstars of Pro Football Ser.). (Illus.). 64p. (YA). (gr. 7-12). lib. bdg. 22.95 *(978-1-4222-0558-7(4))* Mason Crest.
—Peyton Manning: Superstar Quarterback, 1 vol. 2011. (Playmakers Ser.). (ENG., Illus.). 32p. (YA). (gr. 3-6). 27.07 *(978-1-61714-748-7(6))* ABDO Publishing Co.
—Randy Orton: A Living Legacy, 1 vol. 2012. (Pro Wrestling Stars Ser.). (ENG.). 48p. (gr. 3-4). lib. bdg. 31.99 *(978-1-4296-8675-4(8))* Capstone Press of Coughlan Cos.
—Shaun White: Snow & Skateboard Champion. 2009. (Hot Celebrity Biographies Ser.). (Illus.). 48p. (J). (gr. 5-9). pap. 8.95 *(978-0-7660-3627-7(8))*; lib. bdg. 25.27 *(978-0-7660-3212-5(4))* Enslow Pubs., Inc.
—The Stanley Cup: All about Pro Hockey's Biggest Event. 2012. (Winner Takes All Ser.). (ENG.). 32p. (gr. 3-4). pap. 41.70 *(978-1-4296-9441-4(6))* Capstone Press of Coughlan Cos.
—Tom Brady: Super Bowl Quarterback, 1 vol. 2012. (Playmakers Ser.). (ENG.). 32p. (J). (gr. 3-6). 27.07 *(978-1-61783-290-1(1))* ABDO Publishing Co.
Goddu, Krystyna Poray. What's Your Story, Wilma Rudolph? 2016. (Cub Reporter Meets Famous Americans Ser.). (ENG.). 32p. (J). (gr. k-3). 26.65 *(978-1-4677-8782-6(5))* Lerner Publishing Group.
Goldman, David J. Jewish Jocks: Athletic Stars Past & Present. 2004. (General Jewish Interest Ser.). (Illus.). 96p. (J). (gr. 6-18). pap. 8.95 *(978-1-58013-085-1(2)*, Kar-Ben Publishing) Lerner Publishing Group.
—Jewish Sports Stars: Athletic Heroes Past & Present. (Illus.). 96p. (J). (gr. 6-9). 2006. per. 9.95 *(978-1-58013-183-4(2))* 2nd rev. ed. 2013. (ENG., pap. 9.95 *(978-1-4677-1206-4(X))* Lerner Publishing Group. (Kar-Ben Publishing).
Goldsworthy, Steve. Baseball. 2011. (J). (gr. 4-6). pap. 13.95 *(978-1-61690-702-0(9)*, AV2 by Weigl); (Illus.). 32p. (YA). (gr. 2-5). 28.55 *(978-1-61690-697-9(9))* Weigl Pubs., Inc.
Golus, Carrie. Jim Thorpe. 2008. pap. 58.95 *(978-0-8225-9399-7(8))* Lerner Publishing Group.
Goodridge, Catherine. Michelle Kwan. 2011. (Early Connections Ser.). (J). *(978-1-61672-623-2(7))* Benchmark Education Co.
Grabowski, John F. Larry Fitzgerald. 2010. (Superstars of Pro Football Ser.). 64p. (J). 22.95 *(978-1-4222-2721-3(9))* Mason Crest.
Gravel, Elise. The Great Antonio, Level 3. 2016. (ENG., Illus.). 64p. (J). (gr. -1-4). 12.95 *(978-1-943145-08-9(3)*, 9781943145089) TOON Books / RAW Junior, LLC.
Grayson, Robert. John Cena. 2012. (Role Model Entertainers Ser.). 64p. (J). (gr. 7). 22.95 *(978-1-4222-2717-6(0))* Mason Crest.
Great Sports Teams, 35 bks. , Set. (Illus.). (YA). (gr. 4-10). lib. bdg. 625.35 *(978-0-89490-888-0(X))* Enslow Pubs., Inc.

Griffith, M. Christopher & Griffith, Jeana R. The Tale of Two Athletes: The Story of Jumper & the Thumper a True Story on Understanding & Combating Childhood Obesity. 2012. 60p. pap. 24.99 *(978-1-4685-4014-7(9))* AuthorHouse.

Guillain, Charlotte. Extreme Athletes: True Stories of Amazing Sporting Adventurers, 1 vol. 2014. (Ultimate Adventurers Ser.). (ENG., Illus.). 48p. (gr. 6-6). lib. bdg. 29.99 *(978-1-4109-5418-3(8))* Heinemann-Raintree.

Haerens, Margaret. Professional Athletes. Greenhaven Press Editors, ed. 2013. (Opposing Viewpoints Ser.). (ENG.). 224p. (gr. 10-12). pap. 33.80 *(978-0-7377-6069-9(9))*; lib. bdg. 48.80 *(978-0-7377-6068-2(0))* Cengage Gale. (Greenhaven Pr., Inc.).

Hanel, Rachel. Gladiators. 2007. (Fearsome Fighters Ser.). (Illus.). 48p. (YA). (gr. 3-6). lib. bdg. 31.35 *(978-1-58341-535-1(1))* Creative Co., The.

Harris, Devon & Cortés, Ricardo. Yes, I Can! The Story of the Jamaican Bobsled Team. 2008. (Illus.). *(978-0-9764082-5-3(2))* Waterhouse Publishing.

Hasday, Judy. Tiger Woods. 2008. (Black Americans of Achievement: Legacy Edition Ser.). (Illus.). 112p. (gr. 6-12). pap. 11.95 *(978-1-60413-327-1(9)*, Checkmark Bks.) Facts On File, Inc.

Hasday, Judy L. Michael Jordan. 2012. (Role Model Athletes Ser.). 64p. (J). (gr. 7). 22.95 *(978-1-4222-2711-4(1))* Mason Crest.

Haugen, Brenda. Sheamus: Pro Wrestling Superstar, 1 vol. 2014. (Pro Wrestling Superstars Ser.). (ENG.). 24p. (gr. 1-2). lib. bdg. 25.32 *(978-1-4765-4209-6(0)*, First Facts) Capstone Press of Coughlan Cos.

Hawley, Samuel. I Just Ran: Percy Williams, World's Fastest Human. 2011. (ENG., Illus.). 332p. pap. 23.95 *(978-1-55380-126-9(1))* Ronsdale Pr. CAN. Dist: SPD-Small Pr. Distribution.

Heits, Rudolph T. DeMarcus Ware. 2009. (Superstars of Pro Football Ser.). 64p. (YA). (gr. 5-18). pap. 9.95 *(978-1-4222-1985-0(2))* Mason Crest.

Heos, Bridget. Kofi Kingston: Champ of Smackdown. 2011. (Slam! Stars of Wrestling Ser.). (ENG.). 48p. (YA). (gr. 5-8). pap. 11.75 *(978-1-4488-5595-7(0))*; lib. bdg. 29.25 *(978-1-4488-5535-3(7))* Rosen Publishing Group, Inc., The.

—Rey Mysterio: Giant Killer. 2011. (Slam! Stars of Wrestling Ser.). (ENG.). 48p. (YA). (gr. 5-8). pap. 11.75 *(978-1-4488-5601-5(9))*; lib. bdg. 29.25 *(978-1-4488-5538-4(1))* Rosen Publishing Group, Inc., The.

—Triple H: No Mercy. 2011. (Slam! Stars of Wrestling Ser.). (ENG.). 48p. (YA). (gr. 5-8). pap. 11.75 *(978-1-4488-5603-9(5))*; lib. bdg. 29.25 *(978-1-4488-5539-1(X))* Rosen Publishing Group, Inc., The.

Herweck, Diana. En el Juego: La Vida de un Atleta. 2017. (TIME for Kids en Español - Level 4 Ser.). (SPA., Illus.). 48p. (gr. 4-4). lib. bdg. 31.99 *(978-1-5157-5129-8(5))* Time for Kids Inc AUS. Dist: Capstone Pub.

—In the Game: An Athlete's Life, 1 vol. 2nd rev. ed. 2013. (Nonfiction Readers Ser.). (ENG., Illus.). 48p. (J). (gr. 4-4). pap. 29.96 *(978-1-4807-1100-6(4))* Shell Educational Publishing.

—In the Game - An Athlete's Life, 1 vol. 2nd rev. ed. 2012. (Nonfiction Readers Ser.). (ENG.). 48p. (J). (gr. 4-4). pap. 9.99 *(978-1-4333-4824-2(1))* Teacher Created Materials, Inc.

Herzog, Brad. Awesome Stories of Generosity in Sports. 2014. (Count on Me: Sports Ser.). (ENG., Illus.). 96p. (J). (gr. 4-7). pap. 9.99 *(978-1-57542-477-4(0))* Free Spirit Publishing, Inc.

—Francis & Eddie: The True Story of America's Underdogs. Pullen, Zachary, illus. 2013. (ENG.). 32p. (J). (gr. 3-7). 17.95 *(978-0-9849919-2-1(1))* Why Not Bks.

—Incredible Stories of Courage in Sports. 2014. (Count on Me: Sports Ser.). (ENG., Illus.). 96p. (J). (gr. 4-7). pap. 9.99 *(978-1-57542-478-1(9))* Free Spirit Publishing, Inc.

—Powerful Stories of Perseverance in Sports. 2014. (Count on Me: Sports Ser.). (ENG., Illus.). 96p. (J). (gr. 4-7). pap. 9.99 *(978-1-57542-456-9(8))* Free Spirit Publishing, Inc.

Hicks, Peter. Lance Armstrong - Racing Hero. 2011. (Famous Lives Ser.). (Illus.). 32p. (YA). (gr. 3-6). lib. bdg. 26.50 *(978-1-4488-3289-7(6))* Rosen Publishing Group, Inc., The.

Hill, Anne E. Michelle Kwan. 2004. (Sports Heroes & Legends Ser.). (ENG., Illus.). 112p. (J). (gr. 5-12). lib. bdg. 30.60 *(978-0-8225-1795-5(7))* Lerner Publishing Group.

Hillenbrand, Laura. Unbroken: An Olympian's Journey from Airman to Castaway to Captive. 2014. (ENG., Illus.). 320p. (YA). (gr. 7). 19.99 *(978-0-385-74251-1(7))*; lib. bdg. 22.99 *(978-0-375-99062-5(3))* Random Hse. Children's Bks. (Delacorte Pr.).

Hillenbrand, Laura. Unbroken (the Young Adult Adaptation) An Olympian's Journey from Airman to Castaway to Captive. 2017. (ENG.). 320p. (YA). (gr. 7). pap. 10.99 ***(978-0-385-74252-8(5)***, Ember) Random Hse. Children's Bks.

Hillstrom & Hillstrom, Laurie C. Jackie Robinson & the Integration of Baseball. 2013. 248p. lib. bdg. 55.00 *(978-0-7808-1327-4(8))* Omnigraphics, Inc.

History's Fearless Fighters. 2015. (History's Fearless Fighters Ser.). (ENG.). 48p. (J). (gr. 5-6). pap., pap., pap. 84.30 *(978-1-4824-3481-1(4))* Stevens, Gareth Publishing LLLP.

Hoblin, Paul. Colin Kaepernick: NFL Phenom, 1 vol. 2013. (Playmakers Set 4 Ser.). (ENG.). 32p. (gr. 2-6). lib. bdg. 27.07 *(978-1-61783-701-2(6)*, SportsZone) ABDO Publishing Co.

—Gladiators, 1 vol. 2013. (Great Warriors Ser.). (ENG.). 48p. (J). (gr. 3-6). lib. bdg. 32.79 *(978-1-61783-722-7(9))*; (Illus.). pap. 15.64 *(978-1-61783-772-2(5)*, Core Library) ABDO Publishing Co.

Hoffman, Mary Ann. Shaun Alexander: Football Star. 2009. (Sports Superstars Ser.). 24p. (gr. 1-1). 42.50 *(978-1-60853-182-0(1)*, PowerKids Pr.) Rosen Publishing Group, Inc., The.

—Shaun Alexander: Football Star/Estrella del futbol Americano. 2009. (Amazing Athletes/Atletas increíbles Ser.). 24p. (gr. 1-2). 42.50 *(978-1-61511-308-8(8)*, Editorial Buenas Letras) Rosen Publishing Group, Inc., The.

Hot Shots: Grandes Idolos Set 3.Tr. of Grandes ídolos. (ENG & SPA., Illus.). (J). (gr. 3-6). 103.50 *(978-0-8239-7199-2(6)*, Editorial Buenas Letras) Rosen Publishing Group, Inc., The.

Hotchkiss, Ron. The Matchless Six: The Story of Canada's First Women's Olympic Team. 2006. (ENG., Illus.). 200p. (J). (gr. 5). pap. 16.95 *(978-0-88776-738-8(9)*, Tundra Bks.) Tundra Bks. CAN. Dist: Penguin Random Hse. LLC.

Indovino, Shaina Carmel. Kevin Durant. 2014. (Superstars in the World of Basketball Ser.: 10). 48p. (J). (gr. 5-18). 20.95 *(978-1-4222-3107-4(0))* Mason Crest.

—Lebron James. 2014. (Superstars in the World of Basketball Ser.: 10). 48p. (J). (gr. 5-18). 20.95 *(978-1-4222-3109-8(7))* Mason Crest.

Jackson, Aurelia. Carmelo Anthony. 2014. (J). *(978-1-4222-3101-2(1))* Mason Crest.

—Chris Paul. 2014. (Superstars in the World of Basketball Ser.: 10). 48p. (J). (gr. 5-18). 20.95 *(978-1-4222-3104-3(6))* Mason Crest.

—Dwyane Wade. 2014. (Superstars in the World of Basketball Ser.: 10). 48p. (J). (gr. 5-18). 20.95 *(978-1-4222-3106-7(2))* Mason Crest.

James Barter. A Roman Gladiator. 2004. lib. bdg. 27.45 *(978-1-59018-479-0(3))* Cengage Gale.

Jesse Owens. 2004. (Illus.). 112p. pap. 9.95 *(978-0-8225-5318-2(X))* Lerner Publishing Group.

Johnson, Robin. Olympic Heroes & Zeroes. 2012. (ENG.). 48p. (J). pap. *(978-0-7787-7939-1(4))* Crabtree Publishing Co.

Jones, Brenn. Learning about Resilience from the Life of Lance Armstrong. 2009. (Character Building Book Ser.). 24p. (gr. 2-3). 42.50 *(978-1-60854-967-2(4)*, PowerKids Pr.) Rosen Publishing Group, Inc., The.

Kaminsky, Marty. Uncommon Champions: Fifteen Athletes Who Battled Back. 2003. (ENG., Illus.). 152p. (J). (gr. 6-9). per. 11.95 *(978-1-59078-005-3(1))* Boyds Mills Pr.

Kelley, K. C. Quarterback Superstars 2015. 2015. (Illus.). 32p. (J). *(978-0-545-88736-6(4))* Scholastic, Inc.

Kelly Slater. 2008. (Xtreme Athletes Ser.). (Illus.). 112p. (YA). (gr. 7-12). lib. bdg. 27.95 *(978-1-59935-078-3(5))* Reynolds, Morgan Inc.

Kenney, Karen Latchana. Strength Training for Teen Athletes: Exercises to Take Your Game to the Next Level, 1 vol. 2012. (Sports Training Zone Ser.). (ENG.). 48p. (gr. 4-5). pap. 8.19 *(978-1-4296-8002-8(4))*; pap. 47.70 *(978-1-4296-8490-3(9))*; lib. bdg. 31.99 *(978-1-4296-7680-9(9))* Capstone Press of Coughlan Cos.

Knotts, Bob. Sports Superstars: 8 of Today's Hottest Athletes. (Sports Illustrated for Kids Bks). 176p. (gr. 7-12). 2009. 63.90 *(978-1-60853-154-7(6))* 2005. (Illus.). (YA). lib. bdg. 33.25 *(978-0-8239-3692-2(9))* Rosen Publishing Group, Inc., The.

Knudson, R. R. Babe Didrikson: Athlete of the Century. Lewin, Ted, illus. 2015. (Women of Our Time Ser.). (ENG.). 80p. (J). (gr. 3-7). 7.99 *(978-0-14-751465-3(7)*, Puffin Books) Penguin Young Readers Group.

Kopp, Megan. Football. 2011. (J). (gr. 4-6). pap. 13.95 *(978-1-61690-705-1(3)*, AV2 by Weigl); (Illus.). 32p. (YA). (gr. 2-5). 28.55 *(978-1-61690-700-6(2))* Weigl Pubs., Inc.

Kortemeier, Todd. WWE Superstars. 2016. (Pro Sports Superstars Ser.). (ENG., Illus.). 24p. (J). (gr. 1-4). 20.95 *(978-1-60753-943-8(8))* Amicus Publishing.

—12 Ways to Improve Athletic Performance. 2017. (Healthy Living Ser.). (ENG., Illus.). 32p. (J). (gr. 3-6). 21.95 *(978-1-63235-369-6(5))* Pr. Room Editions LLC.

Kovatch, Sarah. Record Breaking Woman. 2005. (Voices Reading Ser.). (Illus.). 16p. (J). *(978-0-7367-2914-7(3))* Zaner-Bloser, Inc.

Kramer, Barbara. Lance Armstrong: Determined to Beat the Odds. 2005. (Awesome Values in Famous Lives Ser.). (Illus.). 48p. (J). (gr. 4-7). lib. bdg. 25.27 *(978-0-7660-2377-2(X)*, Enslow Elementary) Enslow Pubs., Inc.

Krull, Kathleen. Lives of the Athletes: Thrills, Spills (and What the Neighbors Thought) Hewitt, Kathryn, illus. 2013. (Lives Of ... Ser.). (ENG.). 96p. (J). (gr. 5-7). pap. 8.99 *(978-0-544-24760-4(4))* Houghton Mifflin Harcourt Publishing Co.

Kummer, Patricia K. Athletic Trainer. 2008. (21st Century Skills Library: Cool Careers Ser.). (ENG., Illus.). 32p. (gr. 4-8). lib. bdg. 28.50 *(978-1-60279-303-3(4)*, 200142) Cherry Lake Publishing.

Lance Armstrong. 2004. (J). 31.36 *(978-0-7614-1761-3(3))* Marshall Cavendish Corp.

Lassieur, Allison. Gladiator Science: Armor, Weapons, & Arena Combat. 2016. (Warrior Science Ser.). (ENG., Illus.). 32p. (gr. 3-4). lib. bdg. 27.99 *(978-1-4914-8129-5(3)*, Edge Bks.) Capstone Press of Coughlan Cos.

LeBoutillier, Nate. Swimming. 2012. (J). 35.65 *(978-1-60818-211-4(8)*, Creative Education) Creative Co., The.

—Volleyball. 2012. (Illus.). 48p. (J). 35.65 *(978-1-60818-213-8(4)*, Creative Education) Creative Co., The.

LeBron James. 2014. (ENG., Illus.). 48p. (J). lib. bdg. 29.00 *(978-0-531-21198-4(3))* Scholastic Library Publishing.

Lee, Adrienne. Gladiators, 1 vol. 2013. (Legendary Warriors Ser.). (ENG.). 32p. (gr. 1-2). 26.65 *(978-1-4765-3114-4(5)*, Blazers) Capstone Press of Coughlan Cos.

Legendary Athletes, 8 vols., Set. Incl. Arthur Ashe: Tennis Great & Civil Rights Leader. McDougall, Chros. 34.22 *(978-1-61714-753-1(2))*; Babe Didrikson Zaharias: Groundbreaking All-Around Athlete. Lobby, Mackenzie. 34.22 *(978-1-61714-755-5(9))*; Billie Jean King: Tennis Star & Social Activist. Gitlin, Martin. 34.22 *(978-1-61714-757-9(5))*; Jesse Owens: Trailblazing Sprinter. McDougall, Chros. 34.22 *(978-1-61714-758-6(3))*; Magic Johnson: Basketball Star & Entrepreneur. Roselius, J. Chris. 34.22 *(978-1-61714-756-2(7))*; Muhammad Ali: Boxing Champ & Role Model. Owens, Thomas. 34.22 *(978-1-61714-752-4(4)*, 1324107); Wilma Rudolph: Track & Field Inspiration. Anderson, Jennifer Joline. 34.22 *(978-1-61714-759-3(1))*; (YA). (gr. 7-12). (Legendary Athletes Ser.). (Illus.). 112p. 2011. 273.76 *(978-1-61714-751-7(6)*, SportsZone) ABDO Publishing Co.

LernerClassroom Editors, ed. Amazing Athletes Set V: Classroom Library. 2008. pap. 54.95 *(978-0-8225-9997-5(X))* Lerner Publishing Group.

Libal, Joyce & Simons, Rae. Professional Athlete & Sports Official. Riggs, Ernestine G. & Gholar, Cheryl, eds. 2013. (Careers with Character Ser.: 18). 96p. (J). (gr. 7-18). 22.95 *(978-1-4222-2763-3(4))* Mason Crest.

Living Legends of Sports. 2015. (Living Legends of Sports Ser.). (ENG.). 48p. (J). (gr. 5-6). pap., pap., pap. 674.40 *(978-1-68048-146-4(0)*, Britannica Educational Publishing) Rosen Publishing Group, Inc., The.

Loader, Mandy. Amazing Young Sports People, Level 1, 1 vol., Pack. 2009. (ENG.). 48p. pap. 13.25 *(978-84-8323-568-3(4))* Cambridge Univ. Pr.

—Amazing Young Sports People Level 1 Beginner/Elementary. 2010. (ENG.). 48p. pap. 11.00 *(978-84-8323-572-0(2))* Cambridge Univ. Pr.

Lourdes-Pitt, H. H. Brett Favre. 2009. (Superstars of Pro Football Ser.). 64p. (YA). (gr. 5-18). pap. 9.95 *(978-1-4222-1982-9(8))* Mason Crest.

Lyon, Drew. Against All Odds. 2017. (Real Heroes of Sports Ser.). (ENG., Illus.). 32p. (gr. 3-4). lib. bdg. 25.99 *(978-1-5157-4380-4(2))* Capstone Press of Coughlan Cos.

Lyon, Drew, et al. Real Heroes of Sports. 2017. (Real Heroes of Sports Ser.). (ENG.). 32p. (gr. 3-4). pap. 28.76 *(978-1-5157-4464-1(7))* Capstone Press of Coughlan Cos.

MacKay, Jennifer. Tim Tebow. Greenhaven Press Editors, ed. 2013. (People in the News Ser.). (ENG., Illus.). 128p. (gr. 7-10). lib. bdg. 39.40 *(978-1-4205-0893-2(8)*, Lucent Bks.) Cengage Gale.

MacRae, Sloan. Aaron Rodgers. 2012. (Sports Heroes Ser.). (ENG., Illus.). 24p. (J). (gr. 3-6). pap. 8.25 *(978-1-4488-6280-1(9))*; lib. bdg. 22.60 *(978-1-4488-6161-3(6))* Rosen Publishing Group, Inc., The. (PowerKids Pr.).

—Carmelo Anthony. 2012. (Sports Heroes Ser.). (ENG., Illus.). 24p. (J). (gr. 3-6). pap. 8.25 *(978-1-4488-6278-8(7))*; lib. bdg. 22.60 *(978-1-4488-6160-6(8))* Rosen Publishing Group, Inc., The. (PowerKids Pr.).

—Chad Ochocinco. 2012. (Sports Heroes Ser.). (ENG., Illus.). 24p. (J). (gr. 3-6). pap. 8.25 *(978-1-4488-6282-5(5))*; lib. bdg. 22.60 *(978-1-4488-6162-0(4))* Rosen Publishing Group, Inc., The. (PowerKids Pr.).

—David Wright. 2012. (Sports Heroes Ser.). (ENG.). 24p. (J). (gr. 3-6). pap. 8.25 *(978-1-4488-6286-3(8))*; lib. bdg. 22.60 *(978-1-4488-6164-4(0))* Rosen Publishing Group, Inc., The. (PowerKids Pr.).

—Evan Longoria. 2012. (Sports Heroes Ser.). (ENG.). 24p. (J). (gr. 3-6). pap. 8.25 *(978-1-4488-6284-9(1))*; lib. bdg. 22.60 *(978-1-4488-6163-7(2))* Rosen Publishing Group, Inc., The. (PowerKids Pr.).

—Rajon Rondo. 2012. (Sports Heroes Ser.). (ENG.). 24p. (J). (gr. 3-6). pap. 8.25 *(978-1-4488-6288-7(4)*, PowerKids Pr.) Rosen Publishing Group, Inc., The.

Mahaney, Ian F. Taig Khris: In-Line Skating Champion. 2009. (Extreme Sports Biographies Ser.). 24p. (gr. 3-4). 42.50 *(978-1-61512-471-8(3)*, PowerKids Pr.) Rosen Publishing Group, Inc., The.

Malam, John. You Wouldn't Want to... Be a Roman Galdiator! Antram, David, illus. rev. ed. 2012. (ENG.). 32p. (J). lib. bdg. 29.00 *(978-0-531-27503-0(5))* Scholastic Library Publishing.

Manson, Ainslie. Boy in Motion: Rick Hansen's Story. Benoit, Renné, illus. 2009. (ENG.). 48p. (J). (gr. k-3). pap. 12.00 *(978-1-55365-427-8(7))* Greystone Books Ltd. CAN. Dist: Publishers Group West (PGW).

Marcovitz, Hal. Derek Jeter. 2007. (Role Model Athletes Ser.). (Illus.). 64p. (YA). pap. 9.95 *(978-1-4222-0770-3(6))* Mason Crest.

marcovitz, hal. How Serious a Problem Is Drug Use in Sports? 2012. (Illus.). 80p. (J). lib. bdg. *(978-1-60152-448-5(X))* ReferencePoint Pr., Inc.

Marcovitz, Hal. The Manning Brothers. 2013. (J). *(978-1-4222-2723-7(5))*; pap. *(978-1-4222-9094-1(8))* Mason Crest.

Markovics, Joyce L. Michael Phelps. 2017. (Amazing Americans: Olympians Ser.). (ENG.). 24p. (J). (gr. -1-3). 17.95 ***(978-1-68402-239-7(8))*** Bearport Publishing Co., Inc.

Martin, Isabel. Wilma Rudolph, 1 vol. 2014. (Great African-Americans Ser.). (ENG., Illus.). 24p. (gr. k-1). lib. bdg. 21.99 *(978-1-4914-0503-1(1)*, Pebble Bks.) Capstone Press of Coughlan Cos.

Mason, Paul. Extreme Sports Stars. 2012. (Celebrity Secrets Ser.). (ENG., Illus.). 24p. (J). (gr. 5-8). pap. 8.25 *(978-1-4488-7080-6(1))*; lib. bdg. 22.60 *(978-1-4488-7035-6(6))* Rosen Publishing Group, Inc., The. (PowerKids Pr.).

Mason, Paul & Eason, Sarah. Free Running. 2011. (On the Radar: Sports Ser.). (ENG., Illus.). 32p. (gr. 4-8). lib. bdg. 26.60 *(978-0-7613-7759-7(X))* Lerner Publishing Group.

Mattern, Joanne. Legendary Athletic Achievements. 2018. (ENG.). 32p. (gr. 3-6). 31.35 ***(978-1-63235-423-5(3)***, 12-Story Library) Pr. Room Editions LLC.

Mattern, Joanne & Artell, Mike. Superstar Athletes. 2011. (Superstar Athletes Ser.). (ENG.). 24p. (gr. 1-2). pap. 250.20 *(978-1-4296-7314-3(1))*; lib. bdg. 126.60 *(978-1-4296-6566-7(1))*; pap. 43.74 *(978-1-4296-7313-6(3))* Capstone Press of Coughlan Cos.

Mattern, Joanne, et al. Superstar Athletes. 2012. (Superstar Athletes Ser.). (ENG.). 24p. (gr. 1-2). lib. bdg. 253.20 *(978-1-62065-630-3(2))* Capstone Press of Coughlan Cos.

Matthews, Rupert. Gladiators. 2010. (Remarkable Man & Beast Ser.). 48p. (J). (gr. 3-18). lib. bdg. 19.95 *(978-1-4222-1970-6(4))* Mason Crest.

Maurer, Tracy Nelson. Famous Athletes. 2015. (Famous Athletes Ser.). (ENG.). 24p. (gr. k-1). 106.60 *(978-1-4914-6936-1(6)*, Pebble Plus) Capstone Press of Coughlan Cos.

McClafferty, Carla Killough. Fourth down & Inches: Concussions & Football's Make-or-Break Moment. 2013. (ENG., Illus.). 96p. (gr. 6-12). 20.95 *(978-1-4677-1067-1(9)*, Carolrhoda Bks.) Lerner Publishing Group.

McClellan, Ray. Kane. 2014. (Wrestling Superstars Ser.). (ENG., Illus.). 24p. (J). (gr. 3-7). 25.95 *(978-1-62617-142-8(4)*, Epic Bks.) Bellwether Media.

McCully, Emily Arnold. Queen of the Diamond: The Lizzie Murphy Story. 2015. (ENG., Illus.). 32p. (J). (gr. k-3). 17.99 *(978-0-374-30007-4(0)*, 9780374300074, Farrar, Straus & Giroux (BYR)) Farrar, Straus & Giroux.

McDaniel, Melissa. Pushing the Limits: A Chapter Book. 2004. (True Tales Ser.). (ENG., Illus.). 48p. (J). 22.50 *(978-0-516-23734-3(9)*, Children's Pr.) Scholastic Library Publishing.

McNeil, Niki, et al. HOCPP 1078 Gladiators. 2006. spiral bd. 19.50 *(978-1-60308-078-1(3))* In the Hands of a Child.

Michael Phelps. rev. ed. 2009. (Amazing Athletes Ser.). (gr. 2-5). pap. 6.95 *(978-0-7613-4138-3(2)*, First Avenue Editions) Lerner Publishing Group.

Miller, Calvin Craig. David Beckham. 2008. (Xtreme Athletes Ser.). (Illus.). 100p. (J). (gr. 5-13). lib. bdg. 27.95 *(978-1-59935-082-0(3))* Reynolds, Morgan Inc.

—Tom Brady. 2013. (J). *(978-1-4222-2719-0(7))* Mason Crest.

Mills, Cliff. Tony Romo. 2011. (Football Superstars Ser.). (Illus.). 128p. (gr. 6-12). 30.00 *(978-1-60413-754-5(1))* Facts On File, Inc.

Mills, Elizabeth. Ken Griffey Sr. & Ken Griffey Jr: Baseball Heroes. l.t. ed. 2012. 96p. (J). pap. *(978-1-4596-3355-1(5))* ReadHowYouWant.com, Ltd.

Monnig, Alex. Roy Halladay: Superstar Pitcher, 1 vol. 2012. (Playmakers Ser.). (ENG.). 32p. (J). (gr. 3-6). 27.07 *(978-1-61783-291-8(X))* ABDO Publishing Co.

Monroe, Judy. Steroids, Sports, & Body Image: The Risks of Performance-Enhancing Drugs. 2004. (Issues in Focus Ser.). (Illus.). 128p. (J). lib. bdg. 26.60 *(978-0-7660-2160-0(2))* Enslow Pubs., Inc.

Mooney, Carla. Asante Samuel. 2009. (Superstars of Pro Football Ser.). (Illus.). 64p. (YA). (gr. 7-12). lib. bdg. 22.95 *(978-1-4222-0542-6(8))* Mason Crest.

—Caitlyn Jenner. 2016. (Transgender Pioneers Ser.). 112p. (J). (gr. 6-6). 37.10 *(978-1-5081-7158-4(0))* Rosen Publishing Group, Inc., The.

Morganelli, Adrianna. Rick Hansen: Improving Life for People with Disabilities. 2016. (Illus.). 32p. (J). *(978-0-7787-2692-0(4))* Crabtree Publishing Co.

Morley, Jacqueline. Ancient Greek Athlete. 2005. (How to Be Ser.). (ENG., Illus.). 32p. (J). (gr. 3-7). 14.95 *(978-0-7922-7443-8(1)*, National Geographic Children's Bks.) National Geographic Society.

Mosenson, Cecil. Work Hard-Never Give Up. 2011. 32p. pap. 24.95 *(978-1-61582-829-6(X))* America Star Bks.

Murrell, Deborah Jane & Dennis, Peter. Gladiator. 2012. (Illus.). 32p. (gr. 3-5). pap. 8.95 *(978-1-926853-52-9(0))* Saunders Bk. Co. CAN. Dist: RiverStream Publishing.

Nagelhout, Ryan. The Big Show. 2013. (Superstars of Wrestling Ser.). (Illus.). 32p. (J). (gr. 3-6). 25.25 *(978-1-4339-8535-5(7))*; pap. 10.50 *(978-1-4339-8536-2(5))* Stevens, Gareth Publishing LLLP.

—Christian. 2013. (Superstars of Wrestling Ser.). (Illus.). 32p. (J). (gr. 3-6). pap. 10.50 *(978-1-4339-8518-8(7))*; lib. bdg. 25.25 *(978-1-4339-8517-1(9))* Stevens, Gareth Publishing LLLP.

—CM Punk. 2013. (Superstars of Wrestling Ser.). (Illus.). 32p. (J). (gr. 3-6). pap. 10.50 *(978-1-4339-8523-2(3))*; lib. bdg. 25.25 *(978-1-4339-8522-5(5))* Stevens, Gareth Publishing LLLP.

—Gareth's Guide to Becoming a Star Athlete. 2017. (Gareth Guides to an Extraordinary Life Ser.). 32p. (J). (gr. 4-5). pap. 63.00 ***(978-1-5382-0336-1(7))*** Stevens, Gareth Publishing LLLP.

—John Cena. 2013. (Superstars of Wrestling Ser.). (Illus.). 32p. (J). (gr. 3-6). pap. 10.50 *(978-1-4339-8528-7(4))*; lib. bdg. 25.25 *(978-1-4339-8527-0(6))* Stevens, Gareth Publishing LLLP.

—Michael Phelps: Greatest Swimmer of All Time. 2017. (Breakout Biographies Ser.). 32p. (J). (gr. 9-10). pap. 10.00 ***(978-1-5081-6066-3(X)***, PowerKids Pr.) Rosen Publishing Group, Inc., The.

Nagelhout, Ryan. Randy Orton. 2013. (Superstars of Wrestling Ser.). (Illus.). 32p. (J). (gr. 3-6). 25.25 *(978-1-4339-8531-7(4))*; pap. 10.50 *(978-1-4339-8532-4(2))* Stevens, Gareth Publishing LLLP.

Nagle, Jeanne. Top 101 Athletes, 1 vol., 1. 2014. (People You Should Know Ser.). (ENG.). 168p. (YA). (gr. 7-12). 35.25 *(978-1-62275-136-5(1))* Rosen Publishing Group, Inc., The.

Newsham, Gavin. The London 2012 Games Fact File. 2012. (London 2012 Ser.). (ENG., Illus.). 64p. (J). (gr. k-3). 13.99 *(978-1-84732-929-5(2))* Carlton Bks., Ltd. GBR. Dist: Independent Pubs. Group.

Nichols, Catherine. Record Breakers: A Chapter Book. 2004. (True Tales Ser.). (ENG.). (J). 22.50 *(978-0-516-23732-9(2)*, Children's Pr.) Scholastic Library Publishing.

Obregón, José María. Juan Pablo Ángel. 2009. (World Soccer Stars / Estrellas del fútbol mundial Ser.). (ENG & SPA.). 24p. (gr. 2-2). 42.50 *(978-1-60854-845-3(7)*, Editorial Buenas Letras) Rosen Publishing Group, Inc., The.

—Kaká. 2009. (World Soccer Stars / Estrellas del fútbol mundial Ser.). (ENG & SPA.). 24p. (gr. 2-2). 42.50 *(978-1-60854-846-0(5)*, Editorial Buenas Letras) Rosen Publishing Group, Inc., The.

O'Neal, Claire. Andrew Luck. 2013. (ENG.). (J). (gr. 1-4). lib. bdg. 25.70 *(978-1-61228-460-6(4))* Mitchell Lane Pubs., Inc.

Osier, Dan. Dirk Nowitzki. 2011. (Basketball's MVPs / Jugadores Más Valiosos Del Baloncesto Ser.). (SPA., Illus.). 24p. (J). (gr. 3-6). 22.60 *(978-1-4488-3136-4(9))* Rosen Publishing Group, Inc., The.

—Kevin Garnett. 2011. (Basketball's MVPs / Jugadores Más Valiosos Del Baloncesto Ser.). (ENG & SPA., Illus.). 24p. (J). (gr. 3-6). 22.60 *(978-1-4488-3206-4(3))* Rosen Publishing Group, Inc., The.

—LeBron James. 2011. (Basketball's MVPs Ser.). (Illus.). 24p. (J). pap. 8.85 *(978-1-4488-2629-2(2))*; (gr. 3-6). 22.60 *(978-1-4488-2522-6(9))* Rosen Publishing Group, Inc., The. (PowerKids Pr.).

—Steve Nash. 2011. (Basketball's MVPs / Jugadores Más Valiosos Del Baloncesto Ser.). (ENG & SPA., Illus.). 24p. (J). (gr. 3-6). 22.60 *(978-1-4488-3137-1(7))* Rosen Publishing Group, Inc., The.

Otten, Jack. Atletismo. 2004. (Entrenamiento Deportivo (Sports Training) Ser.). (SPA & ENG., Illus.). 24p. (J). (gr. 2-4). lib. bdg. 22.60 *(978-0-8239-6846-6(4))* Rosen Publishing Group, Inc., The.

—Track. 2009. (Sports Training Ser.). 24p. (gr. 1-2). 42.50 *(978-1-60853-190-5(2)*, PowerKids Pr.) Rosen Publishing Group, Inc., The.

Owen, Ruth. The Life of a Gladiator. 2015. (It's a Fact Ser.). (ENG.). 32p. (J). (gr. 3-6). lib. bdg. 26.60 *(978-1-909673-96-0(X))* Bearport Publishing Co., Inc.

Packard, Mary. Beating the Odds: A Chapter Book. 2004. (True Tales Ser.). (ENG.). (J). 22.50 *(978-0-516-23731-2(4)*, Children's Pr.) Scholastic Library Publishing.

Parham, Jerrill. Thrills & Spills: Fast Sports. 2007. (Shockwave: the Human Experience Ser.). (ENG., Illus.). 36p. (J). (gr. 3-5). 25.00 *(978-0-531-17762-4(9)*, Children's Pr.) Scholastic Library Publishing.

Park, Louise. Blood in the Arena: Gladiators of Ancient Rome. 2013. (Discovery Education: Ancient Civilizations Ser.). (ENG., Illus.). 32p. (J). (gr. 3-6). pap. 10.00 *(978-1-4777-0093-8(5))*; lib. bdg. 25.25 *(978-1-4777-0054-9(4))* Rosen Publishing Group, Inc., The. (PowerKids Pr.).

Payan, Michael. In the Ring with Bret Hart. 2009. (World of Wrestling Ser.). 24p. (gr. 1-1). 42.50 *(978-1-60854-342-7(0),* PowerKids Pr.) Rosen Publishing Group, Inc., The.

—In the Ring with Diamond Dallas Page. 2009. (World of Wrestling Ser.). 24p. (gr. 1-1). 42.50 *(978-1-60854-343-4(9),* PowerKids Pr.) Rosen Publishing Group, Inc., The.

—In the Ring with Goldberg. 2009. (World of Wrestling Ser.). 24p. (gr. 1-1). 42.50 *(978-1-60854-346-5(3),* PowerKids Pr.) Rosen Publishing Group, Inc., The.

—In the Ring with Kevin Nash. 2009. (World of Wrestling Ser.). 24p. (gr. 1-1). 42.50 *(978-1-60854-347-2(1),* PowerKids Pr.) Rosen Publishing Group, Inc., The.

—In the Ring with Scott Steiner. 2009. (World of Wrestling Ser.). 24p. (gr. 1-1). 42.50 *(978-1-60854-348-9(X),* PowerKids Pr.) Rosen Publishing Group, Inc., The.

—In the Ring with Sting. 2009. (World of Wrestling Ser.). 24p. (gr. 1-1). 42.50 *(978-1-60854-349-6(8),* PowerKids Pr.) Rosen Publishing Group, Inc., The.

Pearlman, Matthew. That's Great Advice: Advice from Pro Athletes for Kids, Written by a Kid. 2012. 118p. pap. 13.95 *(978-1-60746-583-6(3))* FastPencil, Inc.

Peppas, Lynn. John Cena. 2012. (ENG., Illus.). 32p. (J). *(978-0-7787-8052-6(X))*; pap. *(978-0-7787-8057-1(0))* Crabtree Publishing Co.

Perez, Mike. Lionel Messi: The Ultimate Fan Book. 2017. (ENG., Illus.). 64p. (J). (gr. 4). pap. 9.95 *(978-1-78097-921-2(5))* Carlton Bks., Ltd. GBR. Dist: Sterling Publishing Co., Inc.

Perritano, John. Performance-Enhancing Drugs: Steroids, Hormones, & Supplements, Vol. 13. Becker, Sara, ed. 2016. (Drug Addiction & Recovery Ser.). (Illus.). 64p. (J). (gr. 7). 23.95 *(978-1-4222-3609-3(9))* Mason Crest.

Petrie, Kristin. Food as Fuel: Nutrition for Athletes, 1 vol. 2012. (Mission: Nutrition Ser.). (ENG., Illus.). 32p. (YA). (gr. 3-6). 27.07 *(978-1-61783-081-5(X))* ABDO Publishing Co.

Pezzi, Bryan. Terry Fox: Ma Vie. Karvonen, Tanjah, tr. from ENG. 2011. (FRE., Illus.). 24p. (YA). (gr. 2-4). *(978-1-77071-431-1(6))* Weigl Educational Pubs. Ltd.

Piven, Hanoch. What Athletes Are Made Of. Piven, Hanoch, illus. 2015. (ENG., Illus.). 40p. (J). (gr. 1-5). 19.99 *(978-1-4814-7508-2(8),* Atheneum Bks. for Young Readers) Simon & Schuster Children's Publishing.

Playmakers, 8 vols., Set. Incl. Alex Ovechkin: NHL Superstar. McMahon, Dave. (YA). 27.07 *(978-1-61714-750-0(8))*; Derek Jeter: Yankee Great. Howell, Brian. (J). 27.07 *(978-1-61714-747-0(8))*; Drew Brees: Super Bowl Champ. Gitlin, Martin. (YA). 27.07 *(978-1-61714-743-2(5))*; Joe Mauer: All-Star Catcher. Howell, Brian. (YA). 27.07 *(978-1-61714-749-4(4))*; Kobe Bryant: NBA Champion. Gitlin, Martin. (YA). 27.07 *(978-1-61714-744-9(3))*; LeBron James: Basketball Icon. Howell, Brian. (J). 27.07 *(978-1-61714-746-3(X))*; Peyton Manning: Superstar Quarterback. Gitlin, Martin. (YA). 27.07 *(978-1-61714-748-7(6))*; Sidney Crosby: Hockey's Golden Boy. McMahon, Dave. (J). 27.07 *(978-1-61714-745-6(1))*; (gr. 3-6). (Playmakers Ser.). (Illus.). 32p. 2011. 216.56 *(978-1-61714-742-5(7),* SportsZone) ABDO Publishing Co.

Polydoros, Lori. Motocross Greats. 2011. (Best of the Best Ser.). (ENG.). 32p. (gr. 1-2). pap. 47.70 *(978-1-4296-7250-4(1),* Blazers) Capstone Press of Coughlan Cos.

—Skateboarding Greats, 1 vol. 2011. (Best of the Best Ser.). (ENG.). 32p. (gr. 1-2). pap. 8.10 *(978-1-4296-7253-5(6))*; pap. 47.70 *(978-1-4296-7254-2(4))*; lib. bdg. 26.65 *(978-1-4296-6498-1(3))* Capstone Press of Coughlan Cos. (Blazers).

Polydoros, Lori, et al. The Best of the Best. 2012. (Best of the Best Ser.). (ENG.). 32p. (gr. 1-2). lib. bdg. 53.30 *(978-1-4296-9135-2(2),* Blazers) Capstone Press of Coughlan Cos.

Porterfield, Jason. Calvin Hill & Grant Hill: One Family's Legacy in Football & Basketball. 2010. (Sports Families Ser.). 48p. (YA). (gr. 5-8). lib. bdg., E-Book 53.00 *(978-1-4488-0087-2(0))*; (ENG., Illus.). (J). pap. 11.75 *(978-1-4358-8516-5(3),* Rosen Reference); (Illus.). (YA). (gr. 4-7). lib. bdg. 29.25 *(978-1-4358-3549-8(2))* Rosen Publishing Group, Inc., The.

—Calvin Hill & Grant Hill: One Family's Legacy in Football & Basketball (Sports Families) Lt. ed. 2012. 96p. pap. *(978-1-4596-3352-0(0))* ReadHowYouWant.com, Ltd.

Powell, Jillian. Olympic Heroes. 2012. (Collins Big Cat Ser.). (ENG., Illus.). 24p. (J). (gr. k-1). pap. 6.99 *(978-0-00-746190-5(9))* HarperCollins Pubs. Ltd. GBR. Dist: Independent Pubs. Group.

Powers, J. L. Colors of the Wind: The Story of Blind Artist & Champion Runner George Mendoza. Mendoza, George, illus. 2014. (J). 18.95 *(978-1-930900-73-8(2))* Purple Hse. Pr.

Puliditor, Seth H. DeSean Jackson. 2009. (Superstars of Pro Football Ser.). 64p. (YA). (gr. 5-18). pap. 9.95 *(978-1-4222-1983-6(6))* Mason Crest.

—Drew Brees. 2013. (J). *(978-1-4222-2720-6(0))* Mason Crest.

Raatma, Lucia. John Cena: Rapping Wrestler with Attitude, 1 vol. 2012. (Pro Wrestling Stars Ser.). (ENG., Illus.). 48p. (gr. 3-4). lib. bdg. 31.99 *(978-1-4296-8676-1(6))* Capstone Press of Coughlan Cos.

Raij, Emily. Rey Mysterio. 2015. (Pro Wrestling Superstars Ser.). (ENG.). 24p. (gr. 1-2). lib. bdg. 25.32 *(978-1-4914-2057-7(X))* Capstone Press of Coughlan Cos.

Ramen, Fred. Jerry West. 2009. (Basketball Hall of Famers Ser.). 112p. (gr. 5-8). 63.90 *(978-1-61511-532-7(3),* Rosen Reference) Rosen Publishing Group, Inc., The.

Rappoport, Ken. Derek Jeter: Champion Baseball Star. 2012. (Sports Star Champions Ser.). (Illus.). 48p. (J). (gr. 5-18). 25.27 *(978-0-7660-4025-0(9))* Enslow Pubs., Inc.

—Profiles in Sports Courage, 1 vol. 2006. (ENG., Illus.). 160p. (J). (gr. 3-7). 15.95 *(978-1-56145-368-9(4))* Peachtree Pubs.

Rau, Dana Meachen. Athletic Shoes. 2007. (21st Century Skills Library: Global Products Ser.). (ENG.). 32p. (gr. 4-8). lib. bdg. 28.50 *(978-1-60279-027-8(2),* 200020) Cherry Lake Publishing.

—Sports Nutrition for Teen Athletes: Eat Right to Take Your Game to the Next Level, 1 vol. 2012. (Sports Training Zone Ser.). (ENG.). 48p. (gr. 4-5). pap. 8.19 *(978-1-4296-8000-4(8))*; pap. 47.70 *(978-1-4296-8488-0(7))*; lib. bdg. 31.99 *(978-1-4296-7681-6(7))* Capstone Press of Coughlan Cos.

Rau, Dana Meachen, et al. Sports Training Zone. 2012. (Sports Training Zone Ser.). (ENG.). 48p. (gr. 4-5). pap. 24.57 *(978-1-4296-8491-0(7))*; pap. 190.80 *(978-1-4296-8492-7(5))*; lib. bdg. 127.96 *(978-1-4296-8182-7(9))* Capstone Press of Coughlan Cos.

Richards-Ross, Sanya. Run with Me: The Story of a U. S. Olympic Champion, 1 vol. 2017. (ENG.). 224p. (J). 16.99 ***(978-0-310-76121-1(2))*** Zondervan.

Riggs, Kate. Gladiators. 2011. (Great Warriors Ser.). 24p. (J). (gr. k-2). 16.95 *(978-1-60818-000-4(X),* Creative Education); (ENG.). (gr. 1-3). pap. 9.99 *(978-0-89812-571-9(5),* Creative Paperbacks) Creative Co., The.

Riggs, Thomas. Are Althletes Good Role Models? Greenhaven Press Editors & Gale Editors, eds. 2014. (At Issue Ser.). (ENG.). 128p. (gr. 10-12). pap. 27.80 *(978-0-7377-6821-3(5))*; lib. bdg. 39.40 *(978-0-7377-6820-6(7))* Cengage Gale. (Greenhaven Pr., Inc.).

Rivkin, Jennifer. Hockey Superstars: Past, Present, & Future. 2014. (ENG., Illus.). 32p. (J). pap. *(978-0-7787-0715-8(6))* Crabtree Publishing Co.

Robinson, Tom. Game Face: Handling Sports on & off the Field, 1 vol. 2010. (Essential Health: a Guy's Guide Ser.). (ENG., Illus.). 112p. (J). (gr. 6-12). lib. bdg. 35.64 *(978-1-61613-539-3(5))* ABDO Publishing Co.

—Kevin Harvick: Racing to the Top. 2009. (Heroes of Racing Ser.). (Illus.). 128p. (J). (gr. 5-9). lib. bdg. 33.27 *(978-0-7660-3299-6(X))* Enslow Pubs., Inc.

Robison, Ken. Apolo Ohno. 2012. (Xtreme Athletes Ser.). (Illus.). 112p. (J). (gr. 7-12). 28.95 *(978-1-59935-186-5(2))* Reynolds, Morgan Inc.

Rodriguez Gonzalez, Tania. Jose Valverde. 2012. (Superstars of Baseball ENGLISH Ser.). (ENG., Illus.). 32p. (J). (gr. 4-7). lib. bdg. 19.95 *(978-1-4222-2694-0(8))* Mason Crest.

Rodríguez Gonzalez, Tania. Roberto Clemente. 2012. (Superstars of Baseball ENGLISH Ser.). 32p. (J). (gr. 4). 19.95 *(978-1-4222-2697-1(2))* Mason Crest.

—Ubaldo Jiménez. 2012. (Superstars of Baseball SPANISH Ser.). (SPA & ENG., Illus.). 32p. (J). (gr. 4). 19.95 *(978-1-4222-2627-8(1))* Mason Crest.

—Vladimir Guerrero. 2012. (Superstars of Baseball ENGLISH Ser.). (Illus.). 32p. (J). (gr. 4). 19.95 *(978-1-4222-2681-0(6))*; (SPA & ENG., 19.95 *(978-1-4222-2628-5(X))* Mason Crest.

—Yadier Molina. 2012. (Superstars of Baseball SPANISH Ser.). (SPA., Illus.). 32p. (J). (gr. 4). 19.95 *(978-1-4222-2645-2(X))* Mason Crest.

Roemhildt, Mark. Gladiators. 2012. (History's Greatest Warriors Ser.). (ENG., Illus.). 24p. (J). (gr. 3-7). lib. bdg. 25.95 *(978-1-60014-744-9(5),* Torque Bks.) Bellwether Media.

—Jack Swagger. 2012. (Pro Wrestling Champions Ser.). (ENG., Illus.). 24p. (J). (gr. 3-7). lib. bdg. 25.95 *(978-1-60014-751-7(8),* Torque Bks.) Bellwether Media.

Roselius, J. Chris. Magic Johnson: Basketball Star & Entrepreneur, 1 vol. 2011. (Legendary Athletes Ser.). (ENG., Illus.). 112p. (YA). (gr. 7-12). 34.22 *(978-1-61714-756-2(7))* ABDO Publishing Co.

Rosenberg, Aaron. Taig Khris: In-Line Skating Superstar. 2009. (Extreme Sports Biographies Ser.). 64p. (gr. 3-4). 58.50 *(978-1-61512-470-1(5),* Rosen Reference) Rosen Publishing Group, Inc., The.

Rosenstock, Barb. The Streak: How Joe DiMaggio Became America's Hero. Widener, Terry, illus. 2014. (ENG.). 32p. (J). (gr. 3). 16.95 *(978-1-59078-992-6(X),* Calkins Creek) Boyds Mills Pr.

Roza, Greg. Sidney Crosby. 2011. (Today's Sports Greats Ser.). (Illus.). 32p. (gr. 4-6). (J). pap. 10.50 *(978-1-4339-5876-2(7),* Gareth Stevens Learning Library); (YA). lib. bdg. 26.60 *(978-1-4339-5874-8(0))* Stevens, Gareth Publishing LLLP.

Ryder, Rob. Blood, Sweat & Cheers: Athletes Speak Out. 2007. 252p. per. 18.95 *(978-0-595-47393-9(8))* iUniverse, Inc.

Sandler, Michael. Daring BMXers. 2009. (X-Moves Ser.). (Illus.). 24p. (YA). (gr. 2-5). lib. bdg. 22.61 *(978-1-59716-952-3(8))* Bearport Publishing Co., Inc.

—Jean Driscoll: Dream Big, Work Hard! 2006. (Defining Moments Ser.). (Illus.). 32p. (J). (gr. 2-5). lib. bdg. 25.27 *(978-1-59716-268-5(X))* Bearport Publishing Co., Inc.

—John Cena. 2012. (Wrestling's Tough Guys Ser.). 24p. (J). (gr. 1-6). lib. bdg. 23.93 *(978-1-61772-573-9(0))* Bearport Publishing Co., Inc.

Sandler, Michael & Cohen, Eric. Randy Orton. 2012. (Wrestling's Tough Guys Ser.). 24p. (J). (gr. 1-6). lib. bdg. 23.93 *(978-1-61772-572-2(2))* Bearport Publishing Co., Inc.

—Triple H. 2012. (Wrestling's Tough Guys Ser.). 24p. (J). (gr. 1-6). lib. bdg. 23.93 *(978-1-61772-575-3(7))* Bearport Publishing Co., Inc.

Savage, Jeff. Amazing Athletes: Spring 2012 New Releases. 2012. (Amazing Athletes Ser.). 32p. (J). (gr. 2-5). lib. bdg. 75.78 *(978-0-7613-8914-9(8),* Lerner Pubns.) Lerner Publishing Group.

—Calvin Johnson. 2012. (Amazing Athletes Ser.). (ENG., Illus.). 32p. (gr. 2-5). pap. 7.95 *(978-1-4677-0285-0(4))* Lerner Publishing Group.

—Carly Patterson. 2005. (Amazing Athletes Ser.). (ENG., Illus.). 32p. (gr. 2-5). pap. 7.95 *(978-0-8225-2640-7(9))* Lerner Publishing Group.

—David Beckham. rev. ed. 2013. (Amazing Athletes Ser.). (ENG., Illus.). 32p. (gr. 2-5). pap. 7.95 *(978-1-4677-1160-9(8))*; lib. bdg. 25.26 *(978-1-4677-1159-3(4))* Lerner Publishing Group.

—Eli Manning. rev. ed. 2012. (Amazing Athletes Ser.). (ENG., Illus.). 32p. (gr. 2-5). pap. 7.95 *(978-0-7613-7684-2(4))* Lerner Publishing Group.

—LeBron James (Revised Edition) 2012. (Amazing Athletes Ser.). 32p. (J). (gr. 2-5). pap. 45.32 *(978-0-7613-9315-3(3))* Lerner Publishing Group.

—Michael Vick. rev. ed. 2011. (Amazing Athletes Ser.). (ENG.). 32p. (gr. 2-5). pap. 7.95 *(978-0-7613-8129-7(5))* Lerner Publishing Group.

—Sidney Crosby. 2009. (Amazing Athletes Ser.). (ENG.). 32p. (gr. 2-5). pap. 7.95 *(978-0-7613-4139-0(0),* First Avenue Editions) Lerner Publishing Group.

—Tim Lincecum. 2012. (Amazing Athletes Ser.). 32p. (gr. 2-5). (J). pap. 45.32 *(978-0-7613-9320-7(X))*; (ENG.). pap. 7.95 *(978-0-7613-8667-4(X))* Lerner Publishing Group.

—Usain Bolt. 2012. (Amazing Athletes Ser.). (ENG., Illus.). 32p. (gr. 2-5). lib. bdg. 25.26 *(978-1-4677-1088-6(1),* Lerner Pubns.) Lerner Publishing Group.

Scheff, Matt. Brock Lesnar. 2015. (Wrestling's Tough Guys Ser.). (ENG.). 24p. (J). (gr. 1-6). lib. bdg. 23.93 *(978-1-62724-550-0(2))* Bearport Publishing Co., Inc.

—Dolph Ziggler. 2015. (Wrestling's Tough Guys Ser.). (ENG.). 24p. (J). (gr. 1-6). lib. bdg. 23.93 *(978-1-62724-549-4(9))* Bearport Publishing Co., Inc.

—Jamie Bestwick, 1 vol. 2014. (Extreme Sports Stars Ser.). (ENG.). 32p. (gr. 8-15). lib. bdg. 27.07 *(978-1-62403-456-5(X),* SportsZone) ABDO Publishing Co.

—Tom Brady: Football Superstar. 2012. (Superstar Athletes Ser.). (ENG.). 24p. (gr. 1-2). pap. 41.70 *(978-1-4296-8496-5(8))* Capstone Press of Coughlan Cos.

Scheff, Matt & Frederick, Shane. Superstar Athletes, 1 vol. 2014. (Superstar Athletes Ser.). (ENG.). 24p. (gr. 1-2). lib. bdg. 101.28 *(978-1-4765-9437-8(6))* Capstone Press of Coughlan Cos.

Schilling, Vincent. Native Athletes in Action. 2016. (Illus.). x, 107p. (J). pap. *(978-1-939053-14-5(5))* Book Publishing Co.

—Native Athletes in Action: Sports Stars Past & Present. Peterson, Gary, illus. 2007. (Native Trailblazers Ser.). (ENG.). 128p. (YA). (gr. 3-11). pap. 9.95 *(978-0-9779183-0-0(0),* 7th Generation) Book Publishing Co.

Schuh, Mari. Aaron Rodgers. 2013. (Football Stars up Close Ser.). 24p. (J). (gr. k-5). lib. bdg. 23.93 *(978-1-61772-714-6(8))* Bearport Publishing Co., Inc.

—Famous Athletes. 2016. (Famous Athletes Ser.). (ENG.). 24p. (gr. k-1). 213.20 *(978-1-4914-8543-9(4),* Pebble Plus) Capstone Press of Coughlan Cos.

—Stars of Baseball, 1 vol. 2014. (Sports Stars Ser.). (ENG.). 24p. (gr. k-1). lib. bdg. 26.65 *(978-1-4765-3958-4(8),* Pebble Plus) Capstone Press of Coughlan Cos.

—Stars of Football, 1 vol. 2014. (Sports Stars Ser.). (ENG.). 24p. (gr. k-1). lib. bdg. 26.65 *(978-1-4765-3961-4(8),* Pebble Plus) Capstone Press of Coughlan Cos.

—Troy Polamalu. 2013. (Football Stars up Close Ser.). 24p. (J). (gr. k-5). lib. bdg. 23.93 *(978-1-61772-715-3(6))* Bearport Publishing Co., Inc.

Schuman, Michael A. Jim Thorpe: "There's No Such Thing as 'Can't'" 2009. (Americans—the Spirit of a Nation Ser.). (Illus.). 128p. (J). (gr. 5-12). lib. bdg. 33.27 *(978-0-7660-3021-3(0))* Enslow Pubs., Inc.

Schweitzer, Karen. Sheryl Swoopes. 2012. (Role Model Athletes Ser.). 64p. (J). (gr. 7). 22.95 *(978-1-4222-2712-1(X))* Mason Crest.

Sheen, Barbara, ed. Natalie Coughlin. 2013. (People in the News Ser.). (ENG., Illus.). 128p. (gr. 7-10). lib. bdg. 39.40 *(978-1-4205-0998-4(5),* Lucent Bks.) Cengage Gale.

Shone, Rob. Muhammad Ali: The Life of a Boxing Hero. 2009. (Graphic Nonfiction Biographies Ser.). (ENG.). 48p. (YA). (gr. 4-5). 58.50 *(978-1-61513-022-1(5),* Rosen Reference) Rosen Publishing Group, Inc., The.

—Spartacus: The Life of a Roman Gladiator. 2009. (Graphic Nonfiction Biographies Ser.). (ENG.). 48p. (YA). (gr. 4-5). 58.50 *(978-1-61513-028-3(4),* Rosen Reference) Rosen Publishing Group, Inc., The.

Shryer, Donna & Forschmiedt, Jodi. Peak Performance: Sports Nutrition. 2009. (Benchmark Rockets Ser.). 32p. (gr. 5-18). 28.50 *(978-0-7614-4366-7(5))* Marshall Cavendish Corp.

Shuh, Mari. Adrian Peterson. 2013. (Football Stars up Close Ser.). 24p. (J). (gr. k-5). lib. bdg. 23.93 *(978-1-61772-718-4(0))* Bearport Publishing Co., Inc.

Simmons, Matt J. Jackie Robinson: Breaking the Color Line in Baseball. 2014. (ENG., Illus.). 112p. (J). *(978-0-7787-1242-8(7))* Crabtree Publishing Co.

Skog, Jason. Kurt Angle: From Olympian to Wrestling Machine, 1 vol. 2012. (Pro Wrestling Stars Ser.). (ENG., Illus.). 48p. (gr. 3-4). lib. bdg. 31.99 *(978-1-4296-8682-2(0))* Capstone Press of Coughlan Cos.

Slade, Suzanne, et al. SI Kids Guide Books, 1 vol. 2014. (SI Kids Guide Bks.). (ENG.). 48p. (gr. 4-9). lib. bdg. 127.96 *(978-1-4765-6214-8(8))* Capstone Press of Coughlan Cos.

Smibert, Angie. 12 Ways to Improve Athletic Performance. 2016. (Healthy Living Ser.). (ENG., Illus.). 32p. (J). pap. 9.95 *(978-1-63235-387-0(3),* 12-Story Library) Pr. Room Editions LLC.

Smith, Tony. CM Punk. 2012. (Pro Wrestling Champions Ser.). (ENG., Illus.). 24p. (J). (gr. 3-7). lib. bdg. 25.95 *(978-1-60014-750-0(X),* Torque Bks.) Bellwether Media.

Snow, D. C. Champ Bailey. 2009. (Superstars of Pro Football Ser.). (Illus.). 64p. (YA). (gr. 7-12). lib. bdg. 22.95 *(978-1-4222-0544-0(4))* Mason Crest.

Solomon, Sharon. Lewis Tewanima: Born to Run, 1 vol. Fields, Lisa, illus. 2014. (ENG.). 32p. (J). (gr. k-3). 16.99 *(978-1-4556-1941-2(8))* Pelican Publishing Co., Inc.

Sommers, Annie. College Athletics: Steroids & Supplement Abuse. 2009. (Disgraced! the Dirty History of Performance-Enhancing Drugs in Sports Ser.). (Illus.). 48p. (YA). (gr. 5-9). 29.25 *(978-1-4358-5303-4(2))* Rosen Publishing Group, Inc., The.

Sommers, Michael. The NFL: Steroids & Human Growth Hormone. 2009. (Disgraced! the Dirty History of Performance-Enhancing Drugs in Sports Ser.). (Illus.). 48p. (YA). (gr. 5-9). 29.25 *(978-1-4358-5304-1(0),* 1300477) Rosen Publishing Group, Inc., The.

Sonneborn, Liz. Murder at the 1972 Olympics in Munich. 2009. (Terrorist Attacks Ser.). 64p. (gr. 5-5). 58.50 *(978-1-60853-308-4(5))* Rosen Publishing Group, Inc., The.

Sports Illustrated for Kids Books. 2005. (Illus.). 176p. (gr. 7-12). lib. bdg. 388.65 *(978-0-8239-3925-1(1))* Rosen Publishing Group, Inc., The.

Sports MVPs. 2016. (Sports MVPs Ser.). 24p. (gr. 2-1). pap. 48.90 *(978-1-4824-5344-7(4))*; lib. bdg. 135.60 *(978-1-4824-4521-3(2))* Stevens, Gareth Publishing LLLP.

Stabler, David. Kid Athletes: True Tales of Childhood from Sports Legends. Horner, Doogie, illus. 2015. (Kid Legends Ser.: 2). (ENG.). 208p. (J). (gr. 4-7). 13.95 *(978-1-59474-802-8(0))* Quirk Bks.

Stauffacher, Sue. Nothing but Trouble: The Story of Althea Gibson. Couch, Greg, illus. 2011. (ENG.). 40p. (J). (gr. -1-2). pap. 7.99 *(978-0-375-86544-2(6),* Dragonfly Bks.) Random Hse. Children's Bks.

Steele, Michael A., et al. Tony Hawk: Live2Skate, 1 vol. 2014. (Tony Hawk: Live2Skate Ser.). (ENG.). 72p. (gr. 4-5). pap. 23.80 *(978-1-4342-8956-8(7),* Tony Hawk's 900 Revolution) Stone Arch Bks.

Steps To Literacy Staff, compiled by. Amazing Athletes: Gen025. 2005. (ENG., Illus.). (J). pap. *(978-1-59564-668-2(X))* Steps To Literacy, LLC.

Sterling, Kristin. Money. 2008. pap. 22.95 *(978-0-8225-9361-4(0))* Lerner Publishing Group.

Stewart, Mark. Clutch Performers. 2009. (Ultimate 10: Sports Ser.). 48p. (ENG.). (J). (gr. 4-8). pap. 10.50 *(978-1-4339-2206-0(1))*; (YA). (gr. 5-9). lib. bdg. 31.00 *(978-0-8368-9158-4(9))* Stevens, Gareth Publishing LLLP.

—One Wild Ride: The Life of Skateboarding Superstar Tony Hawk. 2003. (Illus.). 64p. (gr. 6-18). pap. 9.95 *(978-0-7613-1689-3(2),* Twenty-First Century Bks.) Lerner Publishing Group.

Stone, Adam. Edge. 2011. (Pro Wrestling Champions Ser.). (ENG., Illus.). 24p. (J). (gr. 3-7). lib. bdg. 25.95 *(978-1-60014-635-0(X),* Torque Bks.) Bellwether Media.

—Kane. 2011. (Pro Wrestling Champions Ser.). (ENG., Illus.). 24p. (J). (gr. 3-7). lib. bdg. 25.95 *(978-1-60014-637-4(6),* Torque Bks.) Bellwether Media.

Stout, Glenn. Soldier Athletes. 2011. (Good Sports Ser.). (ENG.). 112p. (J). (gr. 5-7). pap. 6.99 *(978-0-547-41729-5(2))* Houghton Mifflin Harcourt Publishing Co.

Stradley, Don. Schooled. 2011. (J). *(978-0-531-22557-8(7))* Scholastic, Inc.

Stuckey, Rachel. Lebron James. 2013. (ENG.). 32p. (J). *(978-0-7787-1047-9(5))*; pap. *(978-0-7787-1052-3(1))* Crabtree Publishing Co.

Sundquist, Josh. We Should Hang Out Sometime: Embarrassingly, a True Story. 2014. (ENG., Illus.). 336p. (YA). (gr. 7-17). 18.00 *(978-0-316-25102-0(X))* Little Brown & Co.

Superestrellas del Deporte Series: Set 2, Set. 2003. (Superestrellas del Deporte Ser.). (Illus.). (J). (SPA & ENG.). 103.50 *(978-0-8239-7198-5(8))*; lib. bdg. 103.50 *(978-0-8239-7194-7(5))* Rosen Publishing Group, Inc., The. (Editorial Buenas Letras).

Superstars of Pro Football, 27 vols., Set. Incl. Antonio Gates. Kimmich, Ian. (Illus.). (gr. 7-12). 2009. lib. bdg. 22.95 *(978-1-4222-0553-2(3))*; Asante Samuel. Mooney, Carla. (Illus.). (gr. 7-12). 2009. lib. bdg. 22.95 *(978-1-4222-0542-6(8))*; Ben Roethlisberger. Heits, Rudolph T. (gr. 5-18). 2010. lib. bdg. 22.95 *(978-1-4222-1664-4(0))*; Brett Favre. Lourdes-Pitt, H. H. (gr. 5-18). 2010. lib. bdg. 22.95 *(978-1-4222-1662-0(4))*; Brian Urlacher. Uschan, Michael V. (Illus.). (gr. 7-12). 2009. lib. bdg. 22.95 *(978-1-4222-0555-6(X))*; Brian Westbrook. Robson, David W. (Illus.). (gr. 7-12). 2009. lib. bdg. 22.95 *(978-1-4222-0547-1(9))*; Chad Johnson. Angst, Frank. (Illus.). (gr. 5-18). 2009. lib. bdg. 22.95 *(978-1-4222-0556-3(8))*; Champ Bailey. Snow, D. C. (Illus.). (gr. 7-12). 2009. lib. bdg. 22.95 *(978-1-4222-0544-0(4))*; DeMarcus Ware. Heits, Rudolph T. (gr. 5-18). 2010. lib. bdg. 22.95 *(978-1-4222-1665-1(9))*; DeSean Jackson. Puliditor, Seth H. (gr. 5-18). 2010. lib. bdg. 22.95 *(978-1-4222-1663-7(2))*; Donovan McNabb. Chatlien, Michael. (Illus.). (gr. 7-12). 2009. lib. bdg. 22.95 *(978-1-4222-0559-4(2))*; Ed Reed. Gitlin, Martin. (Illus.). (gr. 7-12). 2009. lib. bdg. 22.95 *(978-1-4222-0558-7(4))*; Jason Witten. Heits, Rudolph T. (gr. 5-18). 2010. lib. bdg. 22.95 *(978-1-4222-1666-8(7))*; LaDanian Tomlinson. Lace, William W. (Illus.). (gr. 7-12). 2009. lib. bdg. 22.95 *(978-1-4222-0546-4(0))*; Manning Brothers. Marcovitz, Hal. (Illus.). (gr. 7-12). 2009. lib. bdg. 22.95 *(978-1-4222-0543-3(6),* 1291172); Plaxico Burress. Grayson, Robert. (Illus.). (gr. 7-12). 2009. lib. bdg. 22.95 *(978-1-4222-0552-5(5))*; Randy Moss. Robson, David. (Illus.). (gr. 7-12). 2009. lib. bdg. 22.95 *(978-1-4222-0550-1(9))*; Tony Gonzalez. Hunter, Amy N. (Illus.). (gr. 7-12). 2009. lib. bdg. 22.95 *(978-1-4222-0541-9(X))*; 64p. (YA). 2011. Set lib. bdg. 619.65 *(978-1-4222-1660-6(8))* Mason Crest.

Sutcliffe, Jane. Jesse Owens. Porter, Janice Lee, illus. 2006. (On My Own Biographies Ser.). 48p. 17.00 *(978-0-7569-6702-4(3))* Perfection Learning Corp.

Sutoski, Jennifer. Patrick Chan. 2015. (Canadian Biographies Ser.). (ENG., Illus.). 24p. (gr. k-1). lib. bdg. 26.65 *(978-1-4914-7834-9(9),* Pebble Plus) Capstone Press of Coughlan Cos.

—Terry Fox. 2015. (Canadian Biographies Ser.). (ENG., Illus.). 24p. (gr. k-1). lib. bdg. 26.65 *(978-1-4914-7836-3(5),* Pebble Plus) Capstone Press of Coughlan Cos.

Sylvester, Kevin. Game Day: Meet the People Who Make It Happen. 2nd ed. 2010. (ENG., Illus.). 192p. (J). (gr. 4-7). 21.95 *(978-1-55451-251-5(4),* 9781554512515); pap. 12.95 *(978-1-55451-250-8(6),* 9781554512508) Annick Pr., Ltd. CAN. Dist: Publishers Group West (PGW).

Tavares, Matt. Crossing Niagara: The Death-Defying Tightrope Adventures of the Great Blondin. Tavares, Matt, illus. 2016. (ENG., Illus.). 36p. (J). (gr. 1-4). 17.99 *(978-0-7636-6823-5(0))* Candlewick Pr.

Thompson, Laurie Ann. Emmanuel's Dream: The True Story of Emmanuel Ofosu Yeboah. Qualls, Sean, illus. 2015. (ENG.). 40p. (J). (gr. -1-3). 17.99 *(978-0-449-81744-5(X),* Schwartz & Wade Bks.) Random Hse. Children's Bks.

Tieck, Sarah. Eli Manning CD & Book. 2010. (Big Buddy Biographies CD+Book Ser.). 32p. (gr. 2-5). audio compact disk 57.00 *(978-1-61613-309-2(0),* Big Buddy Bks.) ABDO Publishing Co.

—Eli Manning Site CD & Book. 2010. (Big Buddy Biographies Site CD+Book Ser.). 32p. (gr. 2-5). cd-rom 85.57 *(978-1-61613-281-1(7),* Big Buddy Bks.) ABDO Publishing Co.

—Michael Phelps: Olympic Champion, 1 vol. 2009. (Big Buddy Biographies Set 2 Ser.). (ENG., Illus.). 32p. (J). (gr. 2-5). 28.50 *(978-1-60453-550-1(4))* ABDO Publishing Co.

—Michael Phelps: The Greatest Olympian, 1 vol. 2013. (Big Buddy Biographies Set 9 Ser.). (ENG.). 32p. (J). (gr. 2-5). lib. bdg. 28.50 *(978-1-61783-753-1(9),* Big Buddy Bks.) ABDO Publishing Co.

—Shaun White: Olympic Champion, 1 vol. 2010. (Big Buddy Bks.). (ENG.). 32p. (J). (gr. 2-5). 28.50 *(978-1-61613-979-7(X))* ABDO Publishing Co.

Time, Inc. Library Bound Titles [Capstone Sole Source]. 2010. (Time, Inc. Library-Bound Titles Ser.). 139.96 *(978-1-4296-5885-0(1))* Capstone Press of Coughlan Cos.

Time Out: Star Athletes Who Shine off the Field. (Illus.). 32p. (J). (gr. 3-9). pap. 3.99 *(978-1-930623-19-4(4))* Sports Illustrated For Kids.

Tony Hawk: Live 2 Skate, 1 vol. 2014. (Tony Hawk: Live2Skate Ser.). (ENG.). 72p. (gr. 4-5). 101.28 *(978-1-4342-6575-3(7),* Tony Hawk's 900 Revolution) Stone Arch Bks.

Tony Hawk: Live2Skate, 1 vol. 2014. (Tony Hawk: Live2Skate Ser.). (ENG.). 72p. (gr. 4-5). pap. 47.60 *(978-1-4342-8957-5(5),* Tony Hawk's 900 Revolution) Stone Arch Bks.

Torres, John Albert. Famous Immigrant Athletes. 2017. (J). ***(978-0-7660-9243-3(7))*** Enslow Pubs., Inc.

Torsiello, David P. Michael Phelps: Swimming for Olympic Gold. 2009. (Hot Celebrity Biographies Ser.). (Illus.). 48p. (J). (gr. 5-9). lib. bdg. 25.27 *(978-0-7660-3591-1(3))* Enslow Pubs., Inc.

—Read about Carmelo Anthony. 2011. (I Like Sports Stars! Ser.). (Illus.). 24p. (J). (gr. 1-4). lib. bdg. 22.60 *(978-0-7660-3833-2(5))* Enslow Pubs., Inc.

—Read about Eli Manning. 2011. (I Like Sports Stars! Ser.). (Illus.). 24p. (J). (gr. 1-4). lib. bdg. 22.60 *(978-0-7660-3832-5(7))* Enslow Pubs., Inc.

—Read about Kobe Bryant. 2011. (I Like Sports Stars! Ser.). (Illus.). 24p. (J). (gr. 1-4). lib. bdg. 22.60 *(978-0-7660-3830-1(0))* Enslow Pubs., Inc.

Tougas, Joe. Heroic Comeback. 2017. (Real Heroes of Sports Ser.). (ENG., Illus.). 32p. (gr. 3-4). lib. bdg. 25.99 *(978-1-5157-4436-8(1))* Capstone Press of Coughlan Cos.

Trusdell, Brian. Pel: Soccer Star & Ambassador, 1 vol. 2014. (Legendary Athletes Set 2 Ser.). (ENG.). 112p. (gr. 5-12). lib. bdg. 34.22 *(978-1-62403-132-8(3),* SportsZone) ABDO Publishing Co.

Tuma, Tomas. The Gladiators. 2011. (Shape Bks.). (ENG., Illus.). 30p. (J). (gr. 1-18). bds., bds. 16.95 *(978-1-55407-932-2(2),* 9781554079322) Firefly Bks., Ltd.

Uschan, Michael V. Brian Urlacher. (Superstars of Pro Football Ser.). 64p. (YA). (gr. 7-12). 2009. (Illus.). lib. bdg. 22.95 *(978-1-4222-0555-6(X))* 2007. pap. 9.95 *(978-1-4222-0838-0(9))* Mason Crest.

Wacholtz, Anthony & Doeden, Matt. Superstar Athletes. 2012. (Superstar Athletes Ser.). (ENG.). 24p. (gr. 1-2). pap. 29.16 *(978-1-4296-9512-1(9));* pap. 417.00 *(978-1-4296-8498-9(4));* pap. 72.90 *(978-1-4296-8497-2(6));* lib. bdg. 101.28 *(978-1-4296-8183-4(7))* Capstone Press of Coughlan Cos.

Walker, Robert. Sheamus. 2012. (ENG., Illus.). 32p. (J). *(978-0-7787-8054-0(6));* pap. *(978-0-7787-8059-5(7))* Crabtree Publishing Co.

Walters, John. Inside High School Football: A Changing Tradition, Vol. 10. 2016. (All about Professional Football Ser.: Vol. 10). (ENG., Illus.). 64p. (J). (gr. 7-12). 23.95 *(978-1-4222-3580-5(7))* Mason Crest.

Wambach, Abby. Forward: Young Reader's Edition. 224p. (J). (gr. 3-7). 2017. pap. 6.99 *(978-0-06-245793-6(4))* 2016. 16.99 *(978-0-06-245792-9(6))* HarperCollins Pubs.

Washburn, Kim. Defender of Faith: The Mike Fisher Story, 1 vol. rev. ed. 2014. (ZonderKidz Biography Ser.). (ENG., Illus.). 160p. (J). pap. 6.99 *(978-0-310-73834-3(2))* Zonderkidz.

Watkins, Christine. Sports & Athletes, No. 9. 2009. (Opposing Viewpoints Ser.). (ENG., Illus.). (gr. 10-12). 224p. 48.80 *(978-0-7377-4542-9(8),* LML01709-245987); 240p. (YA). 29.45 *(978-0-7377-4543-6(6),* LML01709-246015) Cengage Gale. (Greenhaven Pr., Inc.).

Weakland, Mark. When Wilma Rudolph Played Basketball. Duncan, Daniel, illus. 2016. (Leaders Doing Headstands Ser.). (ENG.). 32p. (gr. 2-3). lib. bdg. 27.99 *(978-1-4795-9684-3(1))* Picture Window Bks.

—When Wilma Rudolph Played Basketball. Duncan, Daniel, illus. 2017. 32p. (J). *(978-1-5158-0140-5(3))* Picture Window Bks.

Weinstein, Anna. Kevin Jones: Snowboarding Superstar. 2009. (Extreme Sports Biographies Ser.). 64p. (gr. 3-4). 58.50 *(978-1-61512-466-4(7),* Rosen Reference) Rosen Publishing Group, Inc., The.

West, David. Lots of Things You Want to Know about Gladiators: ... & Some You Don't! 2015. (Lots of Things You Want to Know About Ser.). (Illus.). 24p. (J). 28.50 *(978-1-62588-090-1(1))* Black Rabbit Bks.

Weston Woods Staff, creator. Man Who Walked Between the Towers. 2011. 38.75 *(978-0-545-14931-0(2));* 18.95 *(978-0-545-14930-3(4))* Weston Woods Studios, Inc.

—The Man Who Walked Between the Towers. 2011. 29.95 *(978-0-439-76703-3(2))* Weston Woods Studios, Inc.

Whitfield, Simon & Dheensaw, Cleve. Simon Says Gold: Simon Whitfield's Pursuit of Athletic Excellence, 1 vol. 2009. (ENG., Illus.). 128p. (J). (gr. 5-12). pap. 14.00 *(978-1-55469-141-8(9))* Orca Bk. Pubs. USA.

Whiting, Jim. David Beckham. 2012. (Role Model Athletes Ser.). 64p. (J). (gr. 7). 22.95 *(978-1-4222-2708-4(1))* Mason Crest.

—Troy Polamalu. 2012. (Superstars of Pro Football Ser.). 64p. (J). 22.95 *(978-1-4222-2725-1(1))* Mason Crest.

Wilcox, Christine. Oscar Pistorius. 2014. (People in the News Ser.). (ENG., Illus.). 128p. (gr. 7-10). 39.40 *(978-1-4205-1041-6(X),* Lucent Bks.) Cengage Gale.

—Shaun White. Greenhaven Press Editors, ed. 2013. (People in the News Ser.). (ENG., Illus.). 128p. (gr. 7-10). lib. bdg. 39.40 *(978-1-4205-0891-8(1),* Lucent Bks.) Cengage Gale.

Wingate, Brian. Tony Hawk: Skateboarding Champion. 2005. (World of Skateboarding Ser.). (Illus.). 48p. (YA). (gr. 5-8). lib. bdg. 29.25 *(978-0-8239-3651-9(1))* Rosen Publishing Group, Inc., The.

Wiseman, Blaine. Basketball. 2011. (J). (gr. 4-6). pap. 13.95 *(978-1-61690-703-7(7),* AV2 by Weigl); (Illus.). 32p. (YA). (gr. 2-5). 28.55 *(978-1-61690-698-6(7))* Weigl Pubs., Inc.

—Shaun White. 2010. (Remarkable People Ser.). (Illus.). 24p. (J). (gr. 4-6). pap. 11.95 *(978-1-60596-998-5(2));* lib. bdg. 25.70 *(978-1-60596-997-8(4))* Weigl Pubs., Inc.

Wood, Alix. Gladiators: Fighting to the Death. Wood, Alix, illus. 2013. (Illus.). 32p. (J). (gr. 4-6). 26.60 *(978-1-4339-9580-4(8));* pap. 63.00 *(978-1-4339-9582-8(4));* pap. 10.50 *(978-1-4339-9581-1(6))* Stevens, Gareth Publishing LLLP.

Woog, Adam. Reggie Bush. 2011. (Football Superstars Ser.). (Illus.). 126p. (gr. 6-12). 30.00 *(978-1-60413-756-9(8),* Chelsea Hse.) Facts On File, Inc.

World Soccer Books, 5 vols., Set. Incl. Great Moments in World Cup History. Bailey, Diane. lib. bdg. 31.95 *(978-1-4358-9139-5(2),* Rosen Reference); Great National Soccer Teams. Sommers, Annie Leah. lib. bdg. 31.95 *(978-1-4358-9138-8(4),* Rosen Reference); Top Soccer Tournaments Around the World. Velázquez de León, Mauricio. lib. bdg. 31.95 *(978-1-4358-9140-1(6),* Rosen Reference); 20 Soccer Legends. Velázquez de León, Mauricio. lib. bdg. 31.95 *(978-1-4358-9136-4(8),* Rosen Reference); 20 Soccer Superstars. Velázquez de León, Mauricio. lib. bdg. 31.95 *(978-1-4358-9137-1(6));* (YA). (gr. 5-8). (Illus.). 64p. 2010. Set lib. bdg. 146.25 *(978-1-4358-9141-8(4),* Rosen Reference) Rosen Publishing Group, Inc., The.

The World's Greatest Sports Stars. 2010. (World's Greatest Sports Stars (Sports Illustrated for Kids) Ser.). (ENG.). 32p. (gr. 2-3). pap. 17.90 *(978-1-4296-4989-6(5))* Capstone Press of Coughlan Cos.

The World's Greatest Sports Stars [Capstone Sole Source]. 2010. (World's Greatest Sports Stars (Sports Illustrated for Kids) Ser.). 32p. lib. bdg. 106.60 *(978-1-4296-5891-1(6))* Capstone Press of Coughlan Cos.

Young, Ian. Lance Armstrong: Champion for Life! 2004. (High Five Reading - Purple Ser.). (ENG., Illus.). 64p. (gr. 3-4). per. 9.00 *(978-0-7368-3850-4(3),* High Five Reading (RBL)) Capstone Press of Coughlan Cos.

—Lance Armstrong Set: Champion for Life!, 6 vols. 2004. (High Five Reading - Purple Ser.). (ENG.). 64p. (gr. 3-4). pap. 54.00 *(978-0-7368-3868-9(6),* High Five Reading (RBL)) Capstone Press of Coughlan Cos.

Young, Jeff. Shaun White. 2008. (Xtreme Athletes Ser.). (Illus.). 112p. (YA). (gr. 7-12). lib. bdg. 27.95 *(978-1-59935-081-3(5))* Reynolds, Morgan Inc.

Young, Jeff C. Dwyane Wade. 2012. (Role Model Athletes Ser.). 64p. (J). (gr. 7). 22.95 *(978-1-4222-2709-1(X))* Mason Crest.

Zuckerman, Gregory & Zuckerman, Elijah. Rising Above: How 11 Athletes Overcame Challenges in Their Youth to Become Stars. 2017. lib. bdg. 20.85 ***(978-0-606-40091-6(5))*** Turtleback Bks.

Zuckerman, Gregory, et al. Rising Above: How 10 Athletes Overcame Challenges in Their Youth to Become Stars. 2016. (ENG.). 256p. (J). (gr. 3-7). 17.99 *(978-0-399-17382-0(X));* lib. bdg. 20.99 *(978-0-399-54570-2(0))* Penguin Young Readers Group. (Philomel Bks.).

Zuehlke, Jeffrey. Michael Phelps. rev. ed. 2009. (Amazing Athletes Ser.). (ENG.). 32p. (gr. 2-5). 25.26 *(978-0-7613-4055-3(6))* Lerner Publishing Group.

ATHLETES, AFRICAN AMERICAN

see African American Athletes

ATHLETICS

see also Coaching (Athletics); Gymnastics; Olympics; Physical Education and Training; Sports; Track and Field

also names of specific athletic activities, e.g. Boxing; Rowing; etc.

Anniss, Matt. Derek Jeter in the Community, 1 vol., 1. 2014. (Making a Difference: Athletes Who Are Changing the World Ser.). (ENG.). 48p. (J). (gr. 5-8). 25.85 *(978-1-62275-185-3(X))* Rosen Publishing Group, Inc., The.

Barnhart, C. A. What Makes Great Athletes. 2005. (ENG., Illus.). 24p. (J). (gr. 5-5). pap. 5.97 net. *(978-0-328-13561-5(5),* Scott Foresman) Pearson Schl.

Bartel, Blaine. Little Black Book for Athletes. 2004. 96p. (YA). pap. 4.99 *(978-1-57794-622-9(7))* Harrison House Pubs.

Bell, Samantha. Athletic Trainer. 2015. (21st Century Skills Library: Cool STEAM Careers Ser.). (ENG., Illus.). 32p. (J). (gr. 4-7). 29.93 *(978-1-63362-555-6(9),* 206404) Cherry Lake Publishing.

Belval, Brian. Olympic Track & Field. 2009. (Great Moments in Olympic History Ser.). 48p. (gr. 5-6). 53.00 *(978-1-61513-163-1(9),* Rosen Reference) Rosen Publishing Group, Inc., The.

Clarkson, Stephanie. Let's Get Moving with Wenlock & Mandeville! 2012. (London 2012 Ser.). (ENG., Illus.). 32p. (J). (gr. -1-k). pap. 10.99 *(978-1-84732-645-4(5))* Carlton Bks., Ltd. GBR. Dist: Independent Pubs. Group.

Conklin, Wendy. No Way! Jolting Jumps. 2017. (Time for Kids Nonfiction Readers Ser.). lib. bdg. 20.85 ***(978-0-606-40292-7(6))*** Turtleback Bks.

Dintiman, George Blough. Speed Improvement for Young Athletes: How to Sprint Faster in Your Sport in 30 Workouts. rev. ed. 2006. (Illus.). 153p. pap. 17.95 *(978-0-938074-26-7(1))* National Assn. of Speed & Explosion.

Edwardes, Dan. Parkour. 2009. (ENG., Illus.). 32p. (J). (gr. 6-8). lib. bdg. *(978-0-7787-3821-3(3))* Crabtree Publishing Co.

Frisch, Aaron. The Story of Nike. 2008. (Built for Success Ser.). (YA). (gr. 5-9). 22.95 *(978-1-58341-608-2(0))* Creative Co., The.

Gigliotti, Jim. STEM in Sports. 2015. (STEM in Sports Ser.). (Illus.). 64p. (J). (gr. 7). 23.95 *(978-1-4222-3233-0(6))* Mason Crest.

Jackson, Colin. Jovenes Atletas. (SPA.). 32p. (YA). (gr. 2-18). 16.76 *(978-84-272-4966-0(7))* Molino, Editorial ESP. Dist: Lectorum Pubns., Inc.

Kamberg, Mary-Lane. A Career As an Athletic Trainer. 2012. (Essential Careers Ser.). (ENG., Illus.). 80p. (YA). (gr. 7-12). lib. bdg. 33.25 *(978-1-4488-8238-0(9))* Rosen Publishing Group, Inc., The.

KociendaGenevieve. THREE IN ONE: THE CHALLENGE OF THE TRIATHLON LOW INTERMEDIATE BOOK WITH ONLINE ACCESS. 2014. (ENG., Illus.). 24p. (J). pap. 9.50 *(978-1-107-62255-5(7))* Cambridge Univ. Pr.

Labrecque, Ellen. The Science of a Sprint. 2015. (21st Century Skills Library: Full-Speed Sports Ser.). (ENG., Illus.). 32p. (J). (gr. 4-7). 29.93 *(978-1-63362-586-0(9),* 206528) Cherry Lake Publishing.

Manley, Claudia B. Competitive Track & Field for Girls. 2009. (SportsGirl Ser.). 64p. (gr. 5-8). 58.50 *(978-1-60853-195-0(3),* Rosen Reference) Rosen Publishing Group, Inc., The.

Mason, Paul. Sports Heroes of Ancient Greece. 2010. (ENG.). 32p. (J). (gr. 3-5). *(978-0-7787-9911-5(5));* pap. *(978-0-7787-9932-0(8))* Crabtree Publishing Co.

Morley, Jacqueline. Ancient Greek Athlete. 2005. (How to Be Ser.). (ENG., Illus.). 32p. (J). (gr. 3-7). 21.90 *(978-0-7922-7495-7(4),* National Geographic Children's Bks.) National Geographic Society.

—How to Be an Ancient Greek Athlete. Antram, David, illus. 2008. (How to Be Ser.). (ENG.). 32p. (J). (gr. 3-7). pap. 5.95 *(978-1-4263-0278-7(9),* National Geographic Children's Bks.) National Geographic Society.

Newcomb, Tim. STEM in Sports: Engineering. 2015. (STEM in Sports Ser.). 64p. (J). (gr. 7). lib. bdg. 23.95 *(978-1-4222-3231-6(X))* Mason Crest.

Porterfield, Jason. Basketball in the ACC: (Atlantic Coast Conference) 2008. (Inside Men's College Basketball Ser.). (Illus.). 48p. (J). (gr. 3-7). lib. bdg. 29.25 *(978-1-4042-1380-7(5))* Rosen Publishing Group, Inc., The.

—Basketball in the ACC (Atlantic Coast Conference) 2009. (Inside Men's College Basketball Ser.). 48p. (gr. 5-5). 53.00 *(978-1-61513-543-1(X),* Rosen Reference) Rosen Publishing Group, Inc., The.

—Basketball in the Big East Conference. 2008. (Inside Men's College Basketball Ser.). (Illus.). 48p. (YA). (gr. 5-9). lib. bdg. 29.25 *(978-1-4042-1381-4(3))* Rosen Publishing Group, Inc., The.

Ryder, Rob. Blood, Sweat & Cheers: Athletes Speak Out. 2007. 252p. per. 18.95 *(978-0-595-47393-9(8))* iUniverse, Inc.

Schindler, John. Triathlons. 2005. (Extreme Sports Ser.). (Illus.). 24p. (gr. 2-5). pap. 8.15 *(978-0-8368-4551-8(X));* lib. bdg. 23.00 *(978-0-8368-4544-0(7))* Stevens, Gareth Publishing LLLP. (Gareth Stevens Learning Library).

Sommers, Michael. Basketball in the Big 12 Conference. 2009. (Inside Men's College Basketball Ser.). 48p. (gr. 5-5). 53.00 *(978-1-61513-544-8(8),* Rosen Reference) Rosen Publishing Group, Inc., The.

Sommers, Michael A. Basketball in the Big 12 Conference. 2008. (Inside Men's College Basketball Ser.). (Illus.). 48p. (YA). (gr. 5-9). lib. bdg. 29.25 *(978-1-4042-1384-5(8))* Rosen Publishing Group, Inc., The.

ATHLETICS—FICTION

Arena, Felice & Kettle, Phil. Olympics. Cox, David, illus. 2004. (J). pap. *(978-1-59336-374-1(5))* Mondo Publishing.

Aretha, David. Rounding Third, Heading Home! 2012. (Champion Sports Story Ser.). 112p. (J). (gr. 3-18). pap. 10.95 *(978-1-4644-0002-5(4))* Enslow Pubs., Inc.

Axworthy, Anni. The Dragon Who Couldn't Do Sporty Things. Axworthy, Anni, illus. 2008. (Little Dragon Ser.). (ENG., Illus.). 32p. (J). (gr. -1-k). *(978-1-84089-533-9(0))* Zero to Ten, Ltd.

Bee, Clair. Pitcher's Duel: A Chip Hilton Sports Story. 2011. 224p. (gr. 4-7). 44.95 *(978-1-258-09630-4(7))* Literary Licensing, LLC.

Boushell, Mike. Freshman Five. (J). pap. 9.99 *(978-0-88092-602-7(3))* Royal Fireworks Publishing Co.

Bowen, Fred. The Kid Coach, 1 vol. 2009. (All-Star Sports Story Ser.). (ENG., Illus.). 112p. (J). pap. 5.95 *(978-1-56145-506-5(7))* Peachtree Pubs.

—Real Hoops, 1 vol. 2011. (Fred Bowen Sports Stories Ser.). (ENG.). 128p. (J). (gr. 2-7). pap. 5.95 *(978-1-56145-566-9(0))* Peachtree Pubs.

Brouwer, Sigmund. Hurricane Power, 1 vol. 2007. (Orca Sports Ser.). (ENG.). 176p. (YA). (gr. 6-10). per. 9.95 *(978-1-55143-865-8(8))* Orca Bk. Pubs. USA.

Choat, Beth. Soccerland, 0 vols. Beck, Robert, illus. 2012. (International Sports Academy Ser.: 0). (ENG.). 242p. (YA). (gr. 7-9). pap. 8.99 *(978-0-7614-6249-1(X),* 9780761462491, Amazon Children's Publishing) Amazon Publishing.

Christopher, Matt. Play Ball! 2013. (Little League Ser.: 1). (ENG.). 240p. (J). (gr. 3-7). pap. 7.99 *(978-0-316-19975-9(3))* Little, Brown Bks. for Young Readers.

Coy, John. Crackback. 2007. 201p. (gr. 7-12). 17.00 *(978-0-7569-8274-4(X))* Perfection Learning Corp.

Crutcher, Chris. Ironman. 2004. (ENG.). 288p. (YA). (gr. 8). pap. 9.99 *(978-0-06-059840-2(9),* Greenwillow Bks.) HarperCollins Pubs.

Dawn, Nyrae, et al. Out of Play. 2013. (Entangled Teen Ser.). (ENG.). 320p. (YA). pap. 9.99 *(978-1-62266-010-0(2),* 9781622660100) Entangled Publishing, LLC.

Desclouds, Rick. My Year with the ESL Boys. 2009. 280p. pap. 22.92 *(978-1-4269-0621-3(8))* Trafford Publishing.

Dewitt, Robert. I Want to Be As Strong As Milo. 2013. 56p. *(978-1-4602-2312-3(8));* pap. *(978-1-4602-2313-0(6))* FriesenPress.

Emerson, Carl. Monster Boy's Gym Class, 1 vol. Levin, Lon, illus. 2010. (Monster Boy Set 2 Ser.). (ENG.). 32p. (J). (gr. k-3). 28.50 *(978-1-60270-781-8(2))* ABDO Publishing Co.

Fehler, Gene. Forced Out. 2012. (Travel Team Ser.). (ENG.). 128p. (gr. 6-12). pap. 7.95 *(978-0-7613-8533-2(9),* Darby Creek) Lerner Publishing Group.

Flynn, Dale Bachm. A Very Special Athlete. Soltero, Emilio, illus. 2004. 32p. (J). lib. bdg. 14.95 *(978-0-9741332-1-8(3),* 1237268) Pearl Pr.

Gilman, Grace. Dixie Wins the Race. 2012. (Dixie: I Can Read Ser.). (J). lib. bdg. 13.55 *(978-0-606-26851-6(0),* Turtleback) Turtleback Bks.

Gorman, Carol & Findley, Ron J. The Stumptown Kid, 1 vol. 2005. (ENG.). 224p. (J). (gr. 3-7). 15.95 *(978-1-56145-337-5(4))* Peachtree Pubs.

Griffith, Jeana R. The Tale of Two Athletes: the Story of Jumper & the Thumper: Workbook: Steps to Tackle Childhood Obesity. 2012. 68p. pap. 13.95 *(978-1-4772-4086-1(1))* AuthorHouse.

Harris, Richard. I'm Walking, I'm Running, I'm Jumping, I'm Hopping. Harris, R. Craig, illus. 2005. (ENG.). 32p. 16.95 *(978-0-9704504-1-8(9))* Hampton Roads Publishing Co., Inc.

Jackson, Max. Mickey Mantle: All-Star Athlete. Henderson, Meryl, illus. 2009. (Childhood of Famous Americans Ser.). (ENG.). 224p. (J). pap. 5.99 *(978-1-4169-7472-7(5),* Simon & Schuster/Paula Wiseman Bks.) Simon & Schuster/Paula Wiseman Bks.

Kenneally, Miranda. Breathe, Annie, Breathe. (Hundred Oaks Ser.: Bk. 5). (ENG.). (YA). (gr. 8-12). 2015. 336p. pap. 9.99 *(978-1-4926-0866-0(1),* 9781492608660) 2014. 320p. 16.99 *(978-1-4022-8479-3(9),* 9781402284793) Sourcebooks, Inc.

Klett, David E. Rachel & the Wizard of Lake Lure: The Lake Lure Chronicles - Book 2. 2006. (Illus.). (J). lib. bdg. 17.95 *(978-0-9779325-1-1(6))* Five Oaks Pr.

Krinsky, Lee. The Longest Fall. 2009. 228p. 25.95 *(978-0-595-71908-2(2));* pap. 15.95 *(978-0-595-42719-2(7))* iUniverse, Inc.

Lampson, Rosalie. Give Mom a Minute. 2009. 32p. pap. 13.99 *(978-1-4490-1407-0(0))* AuthorHouse.

Lubar, David. Lay Ups & Long Shots: Eight Short Stories. 2008. 128p. (YA). (gr. 5-8). 14.95 *(978-1-58196-078-5(6),* Darby Creek) Lerner Publishing Group.

Lupica, Mike. Game Changers. 2013. (Game Changers Ser.: 1). (ENG.). 224p. (J). (gr. 3-7). pap. 6.99 *(978-0-545-38179-6(7),* Scholastic Pr.) Scholastic, Inc.

Maddox, Jake. Double-Axel Doubt, 1 vol. 2011. (Jake Maddox Girl Sports Stories Ser.). (ENG.). 72p. (gr. 2-3). lib. bdg. 25.32 *(978-1-4342-2499-6(6))* Stone Arch Bks.

—Drive to the Hoop, 1 vol. Pulsar Studios Staff, illus. 2011. (Jake Maddox Girl Sports Stories Ser.). (ENG.). 72p. (gr. 2-3). 25.32 *(978-1-4342-2500-9(3))* Stone Arch Bks.

—Running Rivals. Mourning, Tuesday, illus. 2008. (Jake Maddox Girl Sports Stories Ser.). (ENG.). 72p. (gr. 2-3). 25.32 *(978-1-4342-0778-4(1))* Stone Arch Bks.

McEwan, Jamie. Scrubs Forever! Margeson, John, illus. 2008. (Darby Creek Exceptional Titles Ser.). (ENG.). 64p. (J). (gr. 2-5). lib. bdg. 14.95 *(978-1-58196-069-3(7),* Darby Creek) Lerner Publishing Group.

Moore, Stephanie Perry. Always Upbeat/All That. 2012. (Lockwood Lions Ser.). (YA). lib. bdg. 26.90 *(978-0-606-26492-1(2),* Turtleback) Turtleback Bks.

—Yell Out/Do You. 2012. (Lockwood Lions Ser.). (YA). lib. bdg. 26.90 *(978-0-606-26493-8(0),* Turtleback) Turtleback Bks.

Murray, Stuart A. P. Matty in the Goal. 2012. (Champion Sports Story Ser.). 104p. (J). (gr. 3-18). pap. 10.95 *(978-1-4644-0003-2(2));* 27.94 *(978-0-7660-3877-6(7))* Enslow Pubs., Inc.

Pearce, Richard & Story, Ken. Dorkman. 2006. (YA). mass mkt. 8.50 *(978-0-9753367-8-6(9))* Onstage Publishing, LLC.

Peters, Stephanie True & Cano, Fernando M. Track Team Titans, 1 vol. Aburto, Jesus et al, illus. 2011. (Sports Illustrated Kids Graphic Novels Ser.). (ENG.). 56p. (gr. 2-3). pap. 7.19 *(978-1-4342-3072-0(4));* lib. bdg. 26.65 *(978-1-4342-2224-4(1))* Stone Arch Bks.

Price, Roxanne M. Troy & the Championship Trophy. 2007. 20p. per. 11.95 *(978-1-4327-0613-5(6))* Outskirts Pr., Inc.

Riley, Lehman & Austin, Megan. The Life of Babe Didrikson: "Greatness Is Never Forgotten" Wallace, Joshua, illus. 2005. 47p. (J). pap. *(978-0-9760523-2-6(6))* Matter of Africa America Time.

Schraff, Anne. A Boy Called Twister, 1 vol. unabr. ed. 2010. (Urban Underground Ser.). (ENG.). 180p. (YA). (gr. 9-12). pap. 9.95 *(978-1-61651-002-2(1))* Saddleback Educational Publishing, Inc.

Scieszka, Jon. See You Later, Gladiator. McCauley, Adam, illus. 2004. (Time Warp Trio Ser.: No. 9). 87p. (J). (gr. 4-7). 12.65 *(978-0-7569-5986-9(1))* Perfection Learning Corp.

Scott, Kieran. A Non-Blonde Cheerleader in Love. 2008. (ENG.). 272p. (YA). (gr. 7-18). 8.99 *(978-0-14-241186-5(8),* Speak) Penguin Young Readers Group.

Scudamore, Beverly. Pure Fake, 1 vol. 2013. (Lorimer SideStreets Ser.). (ENG.). 136p. (YA). (gr. 9-12). 16.95 *(978-1-4594-0533-2(1),* 9781459405332); pap. 9.95 *(978-1-4594-0534-9(X),* 9781459405349) Lorimer, James & Co., Ltd., Pubs. CAN. Dist: Casemate Pubs. & Bk. Distributors, LLC.

Spinelli, Jerry. Maniac Magee. unabr. ed. 2004. 184p. (J). (gr. 4-7). pap. 36.00 incl. audio *(978-0-8072-0667-6(9),* Listening Library) Random Hse. Audio Publishing Group.

Spurr, Judy. Trapped. 2007. 84p. per. 8.95 *(978-0-595-43915-7(2))* iUniverse, Inc.

Stoudemire, Amar'e. Most Valuable. 2014. (STAT: Standing Tall & Talented Ser.: 5). lib. bdg. 16.00 *(978-0-606-35394-6(1))* Turtleback Bks.

Voigt, Cynthia. The Runner. 2005. (Tillerman Cycle Ser.: Bk. 4). 305p. (gr. 7-12). 17.00 *(978-0-7569-5506-9(8))* Perfection Learning Corp.

Wahl, Leslea. The Perfect Blindside. 2015. 280p. (YA). pap. 10.95 *(978-0-8198-6013-2(1))* Pauline Bks. & Media.

Wooden, Thomas James, Jr. Four-Hundred Meter Champion. Winston, Dennis, illus. 2003. 103p. (J). mass mkt. 12.00 *(978-0-9740195-0-5(X))* New Castle Publishing Co.

Young, Julian. The Peter Model: Understanding the Key That Unlock Maximum Kingdom Impact. 2017. (ENG.). pap. 14.99 ***(978-0-9990279-8-1(0))*** Crown Media Publishing.

Zangri, Brian. Millie Mcpree: The Athlete in Me. 2012. 24p. pap. 15.99 *(978-1-4797-2085-9(2))* Xlibris Corp.

ATLANTA BRAVES (BASEBALL TEAM)

Connery-Boyd, Peg. Atlanta Braves. 2016. (Hawk's Nest Activity Bks.: 0). (ENG.). 64p. (J). (gr. k-3). pap., act. bk. ed. 8.99 *(978-1-4926-3566-6(9))* Sourcebooks, Inc.

Epstein, Brad M. Atlanta Braves 101: My First Team-Board-Book. l.t. ed. 2007. (Illus.). 22p. (J). bds. *(978-1-932530-74-2(6),* 101 Bk.) Michaelson Entertainment.

Gilbert, Sara. Atlanta Braves. 2013. (Illus.). 24p. (J). 25.65 *(978-1-60818-258-9(4),* Creative Education) Creative Co., The.

—World Series Champs: Atlanta Braves. 2013. (World Series Champions Ser.). (ENG.). 24p. (J). (gr. 1-3). pap. 7.99 *(978-0-89812-809-3(9),* Creative Paperbacks) Creative Co., The.

Goodman, Michael E. The Story of the Atlanta Braves. 2011. 35.65 *(978-1-60818-032-5(8),* Creative Education) Creative Co., The.

Grabowski, John F. The Atlanta Braves. 2003. (Great Sports Teams Ser.). (ENG., Illus.). 112p. (J). 30.85 *(978-1-59018-304-5(5),* Lucent Bks.) Cengage Gale.

Hammer, Max. Superstars of the Atlanta Braves. 2014. (Pro Sports Superstars Ser.). 24p. (J). 27.10 *(978-1-60753-590-4(4))* Amicus Publishing.

Howell, Brian. Atlanta Braves, 1 vol. (Inside MLB Ser.). (ENG., Illus.). 48p. (gr. 3-6). 2011. (YA). lib. bdg. 32.79 *(978-1-61714-035-8(X))* 2014. (J). lib. bdg. 32.79 *(978-1-62403-461-9(6),* SportsZone) ABDO Publishing Co.

Kelley, K. C. Atlanta Braves. 2014. (Favorite Baseball Teams Ser.). (ENG.). 32p. (J). (gr. 1-4). 28.50 *(978-1-62323-973-2(7),* 206750) Child's World, Inc., The.
—Atlanta Braves. 2016. (J). ***(978-1-4896-5932-3(3),*** AV2 by Weigl) Weigl Pubs., Inc.
McRae, Sloan. The Atlanta Braves. 2012. (Illus.). 24p. (J). 49.50 *(978-1-4488-5148-5(3),* 1329145); pap. 8.25 *(978-1-4488-5147-8(5),* 1329145); lib. bdg. 22.60 *(978-1-4488-5007-5(X),* 1329145) Rosen Publishing Group, Inc., The. (PowerKids Pr.).
Robinson, Tom. Andruw Jones: All-Star on & off the Field. 2007. (Sports Stars with Heart Ser.). (Illus.). 128p. (J). (gr. 5-9). lib. bdg. 33.27 *(978-0-7660-2867-8(4))* Enslow Pubs., Inc.
Stewart, Mark. The Atlanta Braves. 2012. (Team Spirit Ser.). 48p. (J). (gr. 3-6). 29.27 *(978-1-59953-473-2(8))* Norwood Hse. Pr.

ATLANTIC COAST

Arnosky, Jim. Following the Coast. Arnosky, Jim, illus. 2004. (ENG., Illus.). 32p. (J). (gr. 3-18). 15.99 *(978-0-688-17117-9(6))* HarperCollins Pubs.
Gibbons, Gail. Surrounded by Sea: Life on a New England Fishing Island. Gibbons, Gail, illus. 2006. (ENG., Illus.). 32p. (J). (gr. -1-3). 17.95 *(978-0-8234-1941-8(X));* 6.95 *(978-0-8234-2021-6(3))* Holiday Hse., Inc.
Gonzales, Doreen. The Mighty Atlantic Ocean. 2013. (Our Earth's Oceans Ser.). 48p. (J). (gr. 3-4). 25.27 *(978-0-7660-4088-5(7))* Enslow Pubs., Inc.
Jameson, W. C. Atlantic Coast: Legends of Sunken Pirate Treasures, Mysterious Caches, & Jinxed Ships, from Maine to Florida. 2006. (Buried Treasure Ser.). (ENG.). 192p. (J). (gr. 4-17). pap. 14.95 *(978-0-87483-484-0(8))* August Hse. Pubs., Inc.
Karas, G. Brian. Atlantic. Karas, G. Brian, illus. 2004. (Rise & Shine Ser.). (ENG., Illus.). 32p. (J). (gr. -1-3). reprint ed. pap. 6.99 *(978-0-14-240027-2(0),* Puffin Books) Penguin Young Readers Group.
Karst, Ken. Enduring Mysteries: Bermuda Triangle. 2015. (Enduring Mysteries Ser.). (ENG.). 48p. (J). (gr. 5-8). pap. 12.00 *(978-1-62832-072-5(9),* Creative Paperbacks) Creative Co., The.
Milkweed Editions Staff. The South Atlantic Coast & Piedmont: A Literary Field Guide. St. Antoine, Sara, ed. Nicholson, Trudy & Mirocha, Paul, illus. 2006. (Stories from Where We Live Ser.). (ENG.). 256p. (J). (gr. 4-7). per. 10.95 *(978-1-57131-664-6(7))* Milkweed Editions.
Oachs, Emily Rose. Atlantic Ocean. 2016. (Discover the Oceans Ser.). (ENG., Illus.). 24p. (J). (gr. k-3). lib. bdg. 25.95 *(978-1-62617-331-6(1),* Blastoff! Readers) Bellwether Media.
Park, Louise. The Sinking of the Titanic. 2013. (Discovery Education: Sensational True Stories Ser.). (ENG., Illus.). 32p. (J). (gr. 3-6). pap. 10.00 *(978-1-4777-0099-0(4));* lib. bdg. 25.25 *(978-1-4777-0057-0(9))* Rosen Publishing Group, Inc., The. (PowerKids Pr.).
St. Antoine, Sara, ed. The North Atlantic Coast: A Literary Field Guide. Mirocha, Paul & Nicholson, Trudy, illus. 2004. (Stories from Where We Live Ser.). (ENG.). 288p. (J). pap., instr.'s gde. ed. 10.95 *(978-1-57131-643-1(4))* Milkweed Editions.
Yasuda, Anita. Sinking of the Titanic, 1 vol. 2013. (History's Greatest Disasters Ser.). (ENG.). 48p. (J). (gr. 3-6). lib. bdg. 32.79 *(978-1-61783-960-3(4))* ABDO Publishing Co.
Zepke, Terrance. Pirates of the Carolinas for Kids. 2009. (Carolinas for Kids Ser.). (ENG.). 71p. (J). (gr. 4-18). pap. 9.95 *(978-1-56164-459-9(5))* Pineapple Pr., Inc.

ATLANTIC STATES

Bartley, Niccole. The Mid-Atlantic. 2014. (Land That I Love: Regions of the United States Ser.). (Illus.). 32p. (J). (gr. 3-6). pap. 60.00 *(978-1-4777-6635-4(9),* PowerKids Pr.) Rosen Publishing Group, Inc., The.
Benoit, Peter. The Titanic Disaster. 2011. (True Book-Disasters Ser.). (ENG.). 48p. (J). (gr. 3-5). pap. 6.95 *(978-0-531-28996-9(6),* Children's Pr.) Scholastic Library Publishing.
Dalton, Anne. The Lenape of Pennsylvania, New Jersey, New York, Delaware, Wisconsin, Oklahoma, & Ontario. 2009. (Library of Native Americans Ser.). 64p. (gr. 4-4). 58.50 *(978-1-60853-749-5(8),* PowerKids Pr.) Rosen Publishing Group, Inc., The.
Davidson, Tish. Atlantic: North Carolina, Virginia, West Virginia, Vol. 19. 2015. (Let's Explore the States Ser.). (Illus.). 64p. (J). (gr. 5). 23.95 *(978-1-4222-3320-7(0))* Mason Crest.
Gelletly, LeeAnne. The Mid-Atlantic States: Delaware, Maryland, & Washington, D. C. 2015. (Let's Explore the States Ser.). (Illus.). 64p. (J). (gr. 5). 23.95 *(978-1-4222-3327-6(8))* Mason Crest.
Gunderson, Jessica. Your Life as a Cabin Attendant on the Titanic. Dougherty, Rachel, illus. 2012. (Way It Was Ser.). (ENG.). 32p. (gr. 2-3). pap. 8.95 *(978-1-4048-7248-6(5));* lib. bdg. 26.65 *(978-1-4048-7158-8(6))* Picture Window Bks.
Jameson, W. C. Buried Treasures of the Mid-Atlantic States: Legends of Island Treasure, Jewelry Caches & Secret Tunnels. 2006. (Buried Treasure Ser.). (ENG., Illus.). 192p. (J). (gr. 4-17). pap. 14.95 *(978-0-87483-531-1(3))* August Hse. Pubs., Inc.
Ponte, June. Fun & Simple Mid-Atlantic State Crafts. 2008. (Fun & Simple State Crafts Ser.). (Illus.). 48p. (J). (gr. 2-5). lib. bdg. 25.27 *(978-0-7660-2933-0(6))* Enslow Pubs., Inc.
Pryor, Joanne. I Spy... the Next Stop: Kids Camping the Coast from Maine to Georgia. 2004. (Illus.). 164p. (J). spiral bd. *(978-0-9735907-1-5(8))* Destination Publishing.
Rau, Dana Meachen. The Northeast. 2012. (True Book Ser.). (ENG., Illus.). 48p. (J). (gr. 3-5). 29.00 *(978-0-531-24851-5(8),* Children's Pr.) Scholastic Library Publishing.

ATLANTIS (LEGENDARY PLACE)

DeMolay, Jack. Atlántida: El Misterio de la Ciudad Perdida. Obregón, José María, tr. from ENG. 2008. (Historietas Juveniles: Misterios (Jr. Graphic Mysteries) Ser.). (SPA & ENG., Illus.). 24p. (J). (gr. 2-5). lib. bdg. 25.25 *(978-1-4358-2534-5(9))* Rosen Publishing Group, Inc., The.
—Atlántida: El misterio de la ciudad perdida (Atlantis:the Mystery of the Lost City) 2009. (Historietas Juveniles: Misterios (Jr. Graphic Mysteries) Ser.). (SPA.). 24p. (gr. 2-3). 47.90 *(978-1-61513-345-1(3),* Editorial Buenas Letras) Rosen Publishing Group, Inc., The.
—Atlantis: The Mystery of the Lost City. (Jr. Graphic Mysteries Ser.). (ENG.). 24p. 2009. (J). (gr. 2-3). 47.90 *(978-1-61513-837-1(4),* PowerKids Pr.) 2007. (Illus.). (YA). (gr. 2-5). lib. bdg. 25.25 *(978-1-4042-3407-9(1))* 2007. (Illus.). (gr. 3-8). pap. 10.60 *(978-1-4042-2160-4(3),* PowerKids Pr.) Rosen Publishing Group, Inc., The.
Hawkins, John. Atlantis & Other Lost Worlds. 2012. (Mystery Hunters Ser.). (ENG.). 32p. (J). (gr. 4-6). pap. 10.60 *(978-1-4488-6441-6(0));* lib. bdg. 25.25 *(978-1-4488-6429-4(1))* Rosen Publishing Group, Inc., The. (PowerKids Pr.).
Herbst, Judith. Lands of Mystery. 2004. (Unexplained Ser.). (Illus.). 48p. (J). pap. 7.95 *(978-0-8225-2407-6(4));* (ENG., (gr. 5-12). lib. bdg. 26.60 *(978-0-8225-1630-9(6))* Lerner Publishing Group.
Hyde, Natalie. The Lost City of Atlantis. 2016. (ENG., Illus.). 48p. (J). pap. *(978-0-7787-2237-3(6))* Crabtree Publishing Co.
Kallen, Stuart A. Atlantis. 2011. (Mysterious Encounters Ser.). (ENG.). 48p. (J). (gr. 4-8). 33.60 *(978-0-7377-5534-3(2))* Cengage Gale.
Karst, Ken. Enduring Mysteries: Atlantis. 2015. (Enduring Mysteries Ser.). (ENG.). 48p. (J). (gr. 5-8). pap. 12.00 *(978-1-62832-071-8(0),* Creative Paperbacks) Creative Co., The.
Lassieur, Allison. Is Atlantis Real? 2015. (Unexplained: What's the Evidence? Ser.). (ENG., Illus.). 32p. (J). (gr. 2-4). 19.95 *(978-1-60753-802-8(4))* Amicus Publishing.
Lewis, Ann. Atlantis. 2005. (Unsolved Mysteries: the Secret Files Ser.). (Illus.). 48p. (YA). (gr. 4-7). lib. bdg. 29.25 *(978-0-8239-3559-8(0))* Rosen Publishing Group, Inc., The.
Lewis, Anne. Atlantis. 2009. (Unsolved Mysteries: the Secret Files Ser.). 48p. (gr. 5-8). 53.00 *(978-1-60854-691-6(8),* Rosen Reference) Rosen Publishing Group, Inc., The.
Martin, Michael. Mystery of Atlantis. 2013. (Unexplained Mysteries Ser.). (ENG.). 24p. (J). (gr. 1-2). 25.32 *(978-1-4765-3096-3(3),* First Facts) Capstone Press of Coughlan Cos.
—The Unsolved Mystery of Atlantis. 2013. (Unexplained Mysteries Ser.). (ENG.). 24p. (gr. 1-2). pap. 7.95 *(978-1-4765-3441-1(1),* First Facts) Capstone Press of Coughlan Cos.
Michels, Troy. Atlantis. 2011. (Unexplained Ser.). (ENG., Illus.). 24p. (J). (gr. 3-7). lib. bdg. 25.95 *(978-1-60014-585-8(X),* Torque Bks.) Bellwether Media.
Nuzzolo, Deborah. Journey to Atlantis Funbook. 2004. (Illus.). 22p. (J). act. bk. ed. 3.99 *(978-1-893698-90-1(4),* A01) SeaWorld, Inc.
Owings, Lisa. Atlantis. 2015. (Unexplained Mysteries Ser.). (ENG., Illus.). 24p. (J). (gr. 3-7). lib. bdg. 25.95 *(978-1-62617-200-5(5),* Epic Bks.) Bellwether Media.
Roberts, Russell. The Lost Continent of Atlantis. 2006. (Natural Disasters Ser.). (Illus.). 32p. (J). (gr. 3-7). lib. bdg. 25.70 *(978-1-58415-496-9(9))* Mitchell Lane Pubs., Inc.
Shone, Rob. Atlantis & Other Lost Cities. 2009. (Graphic Mysteries Ser.). (ENG.). 48p. (YA). (gr. 5-5). 58.50 *(978-1-61512-958-4(8),* Rosen Reference) Rosen Publishing Group, Inc., The.
Snedden, Robert. Atlantis & Other Lost Worlds. 2016. (Mystery Hunters Ser.). 00048p. (J). pap. 14.05 ***(978-1-4824-5996-8(5))*** Stevens, Gareth Publishing LLLP.
Summers, Portia. Was Atlantis Real? 2017. (J). ***(978-0-7660-9201-3(1))*** Enslow Pubs., Inc.
Troupe, Thomas Kingsley. The Legend of Atlantis, 1 vol. Cressy, Mike, illus. 2012. (Legend Has It Ser.). (ENG.). 32p. (gr. 2-4). lib. bdg. 27.32 *(978-1-4048-6656-0(6))* Picture Window Bks.
Walker, Kathryn. The Mystery of Atlantis. 2009. (Unsolved! Ser.). (ENG., Illus.). 32p. (J). (gr. 3-5). pap. *(978-0-7787-4165-7(6));* (gr. 4-6). lib. bdg. *(978-0-7787-4152-7(4))* Crabtree Publishing Co.
Wolny, Philip. Investigating Atlantis & Other Lost Cities, 1 vol. 2015. (ENG.). 48p. (J). 25.85 *(978-1-62275-857-9(9),* Britannica Educational Publishing) Rosen Publishing Group, Inc., The.
World Book, Inc Staff, contrib. by. Searching for Atlantis. 2014. (J). *(978-0-7166-2662-6(4))* World Bk., Inc.

ATLANTIS (LEGENDARY PLACE)—FICTION

Barron, T. A. Atlantis in Peril. 2015. (Atlantis Saga Ser.: 2). (ENG., Illus.). 272p. (J). (gr. 5). 17.99 *(978-0-399-16804-8(4),* Philomel Bks.) Penguin Young Readers Group.
—Atlantis Lost. 2016. (Atlantis Saga Ser.: 3). (ENG.). 224p. (J). (gr. 5). 17.99 *(978-0-399-16805-5(2),* Philomel Bks.) Penguin Young Readers Group.
—Atlantis Rising. 2014. (Atlantis Saga Ser.: 1). (ENG.). 400p. (J). (gr. 5). pap. 8.99 *(978-0-14-751221-5(2),* Puffin Books) Penguin Young Readers Group.
Colfer, Eoin. Artemis Fowl & the Atlantis Complex. 2012. (ENG.). 384p. (J). (gr. 5-9). pap. 8.99 *(978-1-4231-2972-1(5))* Hyperion Pr.
—The Atlantis Complex. 2010. (Artemis Fowl Ser.: 7). (ENG.). 368p. (J). (gr. 5-9). 17.99 *(978-1-4231-2819-9(2))* Hyperion Pr.
—The Atlantis Complex. 2012. (Artemis Fowl Ser.: 7). (J). lib. bdg. 19.65 *(978-0-606-23614-0(7),* Turtleback) Turtleback Bks.
Craw, Gloria. Atlantis Quest. 2016. (Atlantis Rising Ser.: 2). (ENG.). 356p. (YA). 16.99 *(978-1-63375-283-2(6),* 9781633752832) Entangled Publishing, LLC.
De Lesseps, Ferdinand Zoticus. Oceanology: The True Account of the Voyage of the Nautilus. Steer, Dugald A. & Hawkins, Emily, eds. 2009. (Ologies Ser.: 8). (ENG., Illus.). 32p. (J). (gr. 3-7). 24.99 *(978-0-7636-4290-7(8))* Candlewick Pr.
Emerson, Kevin. The Dark Shore. 2013. (Atlanteans Ser.: 2). (ENG.). 480p. (YA). (gr. 8). 17.99 *(978-0-06-206282-6(4))* HarperCollins Pubs.
—The Far Dawn. 2014. (Atlanteans Ser.: 3). (ENG.). 368p. (YA). (gr. 8). pap. 9.99 *(978-0-06-206286-4(7),* Tegen, Katherine Bks) HarperCollins Pubs.
—The Lost Code. 2012. (Atlanteans Ser.: 1). (ENG.). 448p. (YA). (gr. 8). 17.99 *(978-0-06-206279-6(4),* Tegen, Katherine Bks) HarperCollins Pubs.
Fontes, Justine & Fontes, Ron. Casebook: Atlantis. 2009. (Top Secret Graphica Mysteries Ser.). (Illus.). 48p. (YA). (gr. 2-6). 29.25 *(978-1-60754-588-0(8));* pap. 11.75 *(978-1-60754-590-3(X))* Windmill Bks.
Hendry, Frances. Atlantis. I.t. ed. 2007. 228p. per. *(978-1-905665-20-4(2))* Pollinger In Print.
—Quest for Atlantis. I.t. ed. 2007. 228p. per. *(978-1-905665-21-1(0))* Pollinger In Print.
Jensen, Kathryn. Splash! 2007. 193p. pap. 24.95 *(978-1-4241-9903-7(4))* America Star Bks.
Kate, Lauren. Atlántida. 2015. (SPA.). 368p. pap. 10.95 *(978-1-101-91062-7(3),* Vintage Espanol) Knopf Doubleday Publishing Group.
Lerangis, Peter. The Colossus Rises, Bk. 1. Norstrand, Torstein & Reagan, Mike, illus. 2013. (Seven Wonders Ser.: 1). (ENG.). 384p. (J). (gr. 3-7). pap. 6.99 *(978-0-06-207041-8(X))* HarperCollins Pubs.
—The Colossus Rises, Bk. 1. Reagan, Mike & Norstrand, Torstein, illus. 2013. (Seven Wonders Ser.: 1). (ENG.). 368p. (J). (gr. 3-7). 17.99 *(978-0-06-207040-1(1))* HarperCollins Pubs.
—The Colossus Rises, No. 1. Lerangis, Peter, illus. 2012. (Seven Wonders Ser.). (ENG., Illus.). 112p. (J). (gr. 3-7). 2.99 *(978-0-06-223889-4(2))* HarperCollins Pubs.
—The Colossus Rises. 2013. (Seven Wonders Ser.: 1). (J). lib. bdg. 17.20 *(978-0-606-32166-2(7),* Turtleback) Turtleback Bks.
—The Legend of the Rift. 2016. (Seven Wonders Ser.: 5). (J). lib. bdg. 17.20 *(978-0-606-38738-5(2))* Turtleback Bks.
—Seven Wonders Book 5: the Legend of the Rift. Norstrand, Torstein, illus. 2016. (Seven Wonders Ser.: 5). 448p. (J). (gr. 3-7). 17.99 *(978-0-06-207052-4(5))* HarperCollins Pubs.
—Seven Wonders Journals: the Promise. 2016. (Seven Wonders Journals: 4). 112p. (J). (gr. 3-7). pap. 2.99 *(978-0-06-223895-5(7))* HarperCollins Pubs.
London, C. Alexander. We Give a Squid a Wedgie. Duddle, Jonny, illus. 2013. (Accidental Adventure Ser.: 3). (ENG.). 400p. (J). (gr. 3-7). pap. 7.99 *(978-0-14-242475-9(7),* Puffin Books) Penguin Young Readers Group.
Mayer, Kirsten. I Am Aquaman. 2013. (Justice League Classic: I Can Read! Ser.). (J). lib. bdg. 13.55 *(978-0-606-31794-8(5),* Turtleback) Turtleback Bks.
McLaren, Heather. Mythos. 2013. (ENG.). 260p. pap. 17.95 *(978-1-60619-093-7(8))* Twilight Times Bks.
Montgomery, R. A. Return to Atlantis. 2005. (Choose Your Own Adventure Ser.). (Illus.). 119p. (gr. 4-8). pap. 5.50 *(978-0-7608-9706-5(9))* Sundance/Newbridge Educational Publishing.
Myklusch, Matt. Strangers in Atlantis. 2017. (Seaborne Ser.: 2). (ENG.). 280p. (gr. 3-6). (J). 18.99 *(978-1-5124-1375-5(5));* 38.65 ***(978-1-5124-2691-5(1))*** Lerner Publishing Group. (Carolrhoda Bks.).
Nickelodeon Staff & Nickelodeon / LeapFrog. SpongeBob SquarePants: The Tour de Bikini Bottom. 2008. (J). 13.99 *(978-1-59319-926-5(0))* LeapFrog Enterprises, Inc.
O'Neill, Katrina. Protecting the Sunken City. 2007. (Illus.). 52p. (J). pap. *(978-1-4207-0724-3(8))* Sundance/Newbridge Educational Publishing.
Peters, Andrew J. The Seventh Pleiade. 2013. (ENG.). 264p. (gr. 7). pap. 11.95 *(978-1-60282-960-2(8))* Bold Strokes Bks.
Rohmer, Sax, pseud. The Orchard of Tears. 2011. 200p. 26.95 *(978-1-4638-9697-7(5))* Rodgers, Alan Bks.
Rose, Simon. The Doomsday Mask, 1 vol. 2009. (ENG., Illus.). 96p. (J). (gr. 3-7). pap. 9.95 *(978-1-896580-19-7(X))* Tradewind Bks. CAN. Dist: Orca Bk. Pubs. USA.
Roy, Philip. Journey to Atlantis. 2009. (ENG., Illus.). 224p. pap. 10.95 *(978-1-55380-076-7(1))* Ronsdale Pr. CAN. Dist: SPD-Small Pr. Distribution.
Sazaklis, John. Deep-Sea Duel, 1 vol. Baltazar, Art, illus. 2012. (DC Super-Pets Ser.). (ENG.). 56p. (gr. 2-2). pap. 4.95 *(978-1-4048-7662-0(6));* lib. bdg. 23.99 *(978-1-4048-6489-4(X))* Picture Window Bks. (DC Super-Pets).
Sherry, Kevin. Attack of the Kraken (the Yeti Files #3) 2016. (Yeti Files Ser.: 3). (ENG.). 128p. (J). (gr. 2-5). 8.99 *(978-0-545-85781-9(3),* Scholastic Pr.) Scholastic, Inc.
Stilton, Thea. The Journey to Atlantis. 2012. (Thea Stilton Special Edition Ser.). (ENG.). 320p. (J). (gr. 2-5). 14.99 *(978-0-545-44020-2(3),* Scholastic Paperbacks) Scholastic, Inc.
Sundaravej, Sittisan & Thongmoon, Kriangsak, illus. Return to Atlantis. 2007. (Choose Your Own Adventure Ser.: No. 18). 119p. (J). (gr. 4-7). per. 6.99 *(978-1-933390-18-5(2),* CHCL18) Chooseco LLC.
Sutton, Laurie S. The Curse of Atlantis. Neely, Scott, illus. 2015. (You Choose Stories: Scooby-Doo Ser.). (ENG.). 112p. (gr. 2-3). lib. bdg. 32.65 *(978-1-4965-0477-7(1))* Stone Arch Bks.
Taylor, Stuart. Austin & the Lost Kingdom of Atlantis: The Austin Chronicles Volume Iii. 2013. 286p. pap. *(978-0-9560345-7-1(8))* Exciting Stories.
Van Eekhout, Greg. Kid vs. Squid. 2010. (ENG.). 208p. (YA). (gr. 3-6). 16.99 *(978-1-59990-489-4(6),* 9781599904894, Bloomsbury USA Childrens) Bloomsbury Publishing USA.
Waring, Scott C. West's Time MacHine. 2007. 200p. 24.95 *(978-0-595-88775-0(9));* per. 14.95 *(978-0-595-41887-9(2))* iUniverse, Inc.

ATLASES

see also Bible—Geography
also names of countries, cities, etc. with the subdivision Maps, e.g. U. S.—Maps; etc.

ABDO Publishing Company Staff. Countries of the World, 1 vol., Set 1. 2011. (Countries of the World Set 1 Ser.: 16). (ENG., Illus.). 144p. (J). (gr. 6-12). lib. bdg. 593.12 *(978-1-61783-104-1(2),* Essential Library) ABDO Publishing Co.
American Map Publishing Staff. Student's Notebook Atlas. 2007. cd-rom 47.40 *(978-0-8437-0959-9(6))* Langenscheidt Publishing Group.
Anthem Press, compiled by. Modern World School Atlas: USA Edition. 2009. (ENG., Illus.). 176p. 19.95 *(978-1-84331-308-3(1),* 1843313081) Anthem Pr. GBR. Dist: Books International, Inc.
Arrowsmith, Colin. Children's World Atlas. 2004. 14.95 *(978-0-7607-5929-5(4))* Barnes & Noble, Inc.
Atlas Escolar. 2003. (SPA.). (J). 16.95 *(978-84-670-0004-7(X))* Espasa Calpe, S.A. ESP. Dist: Planeta Publishing Corp.
Atlas of the World. (Children's Reference Ser.). 256p. *(978-1-4054-9922-4(2))* Parragon, Inc.
Axelrod-Contrada, Joan. A Historical Atlas of Colonial America. 2005. (United States: Historical Atlases of the Growth of a New Nation Ser.). (Illus.). 64p. (J). (gr. 7-12). lib. bdg. 31.95 *(978-1-4042-0200-9(5))* Rosen Publishing Group, Inc., The.
AZ Books Staff. Atlas for Kids. Kazimirova, Karina, ed. 2013. (Atlas for Kids Ser.). (ENG.). 20p. (J). (gr. k-4). bds. 15.95 *(978-1-61889-145-7(6))* AZ Bks. LLC.
Big Picture Atlas. 2017. (Big Picture Books* Ser.). (ENG.). (J). 16.99 ***(978-0-7945-3904-7(1),*** Usborne) EDC Publishing.
Boyle, Bill & Hopkins, Dave. My First Atlas. (Illus.). (J). (FRE.). 21.99 *(978-0-590-24520-3(1));* 48p. pap. 18.95 *(978-0-590-24339-1(X))* Scholastic, Inc.
Brocklehurst, Ruth. Mini Children's Picture Atlas. 2005. (Illus.). 48p. (J). 7.95 *(978-0-7945-1112-8(0),* Usborne) EDC Publishing.
—Usborne Children's Picture Atlas. Edwards, Linda, illus. 2004. (Children's Picture Atlas Ser.). 48p. (J). 12.95 *(978-0-7945-0640-7(2),* Usborne) EDC Publishing.
Buckley, Susan & Leacock, Elspeth. Journeys in Time: A New Atlas of American History. Prato, Rodica, illus. 2003. (ENG.). 48p. (J). (gr. 5-7). pap. 7.99 *(978-0-618-31114-9(9))* Houghton Mifflin Harcourt Publishing Co.
Campbell, Rusty & Porter, Malcolm. Atlas of Africa. 2009. (Atlases of the World Ser.). (Illus.). 48p. (YA). (gr. 5-8). 29.25 *(978-1-4358-8454-0(X),* Rosen Reference) Rosen Publishing Group, Inc., The.
Carney, Elizabeth. Angry Birds Playground - Atlas: A Global Geographic Adventure! 2013. (ENG.). 128p. (J). (gr. -1-3). lib. bdg. 21.90 *(978-1-4263-1401-8(9),* National Geographic Children's Bks.) National Geographic Society.
Carney, Elizabeth & National Geographic Kids Staff. Angry Birds Playground - Atlas: A Global Geography Adventure. 2016. (ENG., Illus.). 128p. (J). (gr. -1-3). pap. 9.99 *(978-1-4263-2459-8(6),* National Geographic Children's Bks.) National Geographic Society.
—Atlas: A Global Geographic Adventure. 2013. (ENG., Illus.). 128p. (J). (gr. -1-3). 14.95 *(978-1-4263-1400-1(0),* National Geographic Children's Bks.) National Geographic Society.
Clifford, Clive. Atlas of Oddities. Worrall, Tracy, illus. 2016. (ENG.). 96p. (J). (gr. 2). 16.95 *(978-1-4549-2176-9(5))* Sterling Publishing Co., Inc.
Collins. Collins Fascinating Facts - The World. rev. ed. 2016. (Collins Fascinating Facts Ser.). (ENG., Illus.). 72p. (J). (gr. 1-3). pap. 10.99 *(978-0-00-816920-6(9))* HarperCollins Pubs. Ltd. GBR. Dist: Independent Pubs. Group.
Collins Maps. Collins Junior Atlas. 4th rev. ed. 2017. (Collins Primary Atlases Ser.). (ENG., Illus.). 80p. (J). (gr. 4). pap. 12.99 ***(978-0-00-820309-2(1))*** HarperCollins Pubs. Ltd. GBR. Dist: Independent Pubs. Group.
—Primary Atlas: Learn with Maps. 5th ed. 2016. (Collins Primary Atlases Ser.). (ENG., Illus.). 68p. (J). (gr. 2-6). pap. 12.99 *(978-0-00-814675-7(6))* HarperCollins Pubs. Ltd. GBR. Dist: Independent Pubs. Group.
—School Atlas: Learn with Maps. 2016. (ENG., Illus.). 104p. (J). (gr. 5-9). pap. 15.99 *(978-0-00-814676-4(4))* HarperCollins Pubs. Ltd. GBR. Dist: Independent Pubs. Group.
Cooper, Alison & McRae, Anne. The Children's Pictorial Atlas of the World. De Luca, Daniela, illus. 2008. (ENG.). 45p. (J). (gr. -1-3). 17.95 *(978-88-88166-05-6(X))* McRae Bks. Srl ITA. Dist: Independent Pubs. Group.
Corporate Contributor Staff & Rodger, Ellen. Atlas & Globe Skills. 2012. (ENG.). 32p. (J). pap. *(978-0-7787-4495-5(7));* lib. bdg. *(978-0-7787-4490-0(6))* Crabtree Publishing Co.
Crane, Nick. Barefoot Books World Atlas. Dean, David, illus. 2011. (ENG.). 52p. (J). (gr. 3-6). 19.99 *(978-1-84686-333-2(3))* Barefoot Bks., Inc.
Cullen, Dave. My First Atlas. Leeks, David, illus. 2004. 48p. (J). 7.99 *(978-1-85854-425-0(4))* Brimax Books Ltd. GBR. Dist: Byeway Bks.
Cullen, Dave & Williams, Simon. My First Atlas. Leeks, David, illus. 2004. 48p. (J). 5.99 *(978-1-85854-709-1(1))* Brimax Books Ltd. GBR. Dist: Byeway Bks.
Dalby, Elizabeth. First Atlas. 2012. (First Encyclopedias Ser.). 10p. (J). ring bd. 9.99 *(978-0-7945-3194-2(6),* Usborne) EDC Publishing.
—First Atlas - Internet Linked. 2004. (First Encyclopedias Ser.). 64p. (J). lib. bdg. 17.95 *(978-1-58086-646-0(8),* Usborne) EDC Publishing.
—First Atlas - Internet Linked. Rogers, Kirsteen, ed. 2004. (First Encyclopedias Ser.). (Illus.). 64p. (J). pap. 9.95 *(978-0-7945-0660-5(7),* Usborne) EDC Publishing.
De Luca, Daniela, illus. Meyers Bunter Weltatlas fuer Kinder. (GER.). 50p. *(978-3-411-07781-6(6))* Bibliographisches Institut & F. A. Brockhaus AG DEU. Dist: i. b. d., Ltd.
Delalandre, Benoît & Clapin, Jeremy. My Multicultural Atlas. 2013. (ENG., Illus.). 54p. (J). (gr. k-2). spiral bd. 24.99 *(978-1-85707-684-4(2))* Tango Bks. GBR. Dist: Independent Pubs. Group.
Denne, Ben. Flags Sticker Atlas. 2004. (Sticker Atlas Ser.). (Illus.). 24p. (J). pap. 8.95 *(978-0-7945-0669-8(0),* Usborne) EDC Publishing.
Doherty, Gillian. Encyclopedia of World Geography II (Reduced) 2010. (Geography Ser.). 400p. (J). pap. 19.99 *(978-0-7945-2698-6(5),* Usborne) EDC Publishing.
Dorling Kindersley Publishing Staff. Children's Illustrated Atlas. 2016. (ENG., Illus.). 128p. (J). (gr. 3-7). 15.99 *(978-1-4654-3555-2(7));* 15.99 *(978-1-4654-5961-9(8))* Dorling Kindersley Publishing, Inc. (DK Children).
—Children's Illustrated World Atlas. 2017. (ENG.). 144p. (J). (gr. 3-7). 17.99 ***(978-1-4654-6238-1(4),*** DK Children) Dorling Kindersley Publishing, Inc.
—Children's World Atlas. rev. ed. 2011. (ENG.). 144p. (J). (gr. 5-12). 17.99 *(978-0-7566-7584-4(7),* DK Children) Dorling Kindersley Publishing, Inc.
—Student Atlas, 8th Edition. 2015. (ENG.). 176p. (J). (gr. 5-12). 14.99 *(978-1-4654-3876-8(9),* DK Children) Dorling Kindersley Publishing, Inc.
—Where on Earth? Atlas. 2017. (ENG., Illus.). 160p. (J). (gr. 3-7). 19.99 *(978-1-4654-5864-3(6),* DK Children) Dorling Kindersley Publishing, Inc.
Dorling Kindersley Publishing Staff, et al. First Atlas. 2004. (ENG.). 128p. (J). (gr. 2-5). 16.99 *(978-0-7566-0231-4(9),* DK Children) Dorling Kindersley Publishing, Inc.
Draper, Allison Stark. A Historical Atlas of Egypt. 2009. (Historical Atlases of South Asia, Central Asia, & the Middle East Ser.). 64p. (gr. 6-6). 61.20 *(978-1-61513-317-8(8))* Rosen Publishing Group, Inc., The.

—A Historical Atlas of Syria. 2009. (Historical Atlases of South Asia, Central Asia, & the Middle East Ser.). 64p. (gr. 6-6). 61.20 *(978-1-61513-329-1(1))* Rosen Publishing Group, Inc., The.

Dusek, Jiri, et al. World Atlas. Hikadova, Katerina et al, illus. 2014. (ENG.). 42p. (J). (gr. 3-5). 16.95 *(978-1-4549-1235-4(9))* Sterling Publishing Co., Inc.

Encyclopaedia Britannica, Inc. Staff, compiled by. My First Britannica: Mammals. 2008. (gr. 7-12). *(978-1-59339-412-7(8))* Encyclopaedia Britannica, Inc.

Evan-Moor. The World Reference Maps & Forms, Grades 3-6. 2004. (ENG.). 112p. (J). pap. 16.99 *(978-1-55799-954-2(6),* EMC 3720) Evan-Moor Educational Pubs.

Facts on File, Inc. Staff. Maps on File. 2nd rev. ed. 2012. (Maps on File Ser.). (gr. 6-12). 250.00 *(978-0-8160-8478-4(5))* Facts On File, Inc.

Farndon, John. Children's Atlas. 2003. (Illus.). 80p. (YA). *(978-1-903954-54-6(1),* Pavilion Children's Books) Pavilion Bks.

First Atlas. 2003. (Illus.). 64p. (J). 7.98 *(978-1-4054-0518-8(X))* Parragon, Inc.

First Discovery Staff. Atlas of the Earth. 2013. (ENG., Illus.). 36p. (J). (gr. -1-3). pap. 11.99 *(978-1-85103-246-4(0))* Moonlight Publishing, Ltd. GBR. Dist: Independent Pubs. Group.

Frith, Alex. Lift the Flap Picture Atlas. 2010. (Atlases Ser.). (Illus.). 16p. (J). bds. 15.99 *(978-0-7945-2402-9(8),* Usborne) EDC Publishing.

Ganeri, Anita. Around the World: A Colorful Atlas for Kids. Corr, Christopher, illus. 2015. (ENG.). 64p. (J). (gr. -1-3). 17.99 *(978-0-8075-0443-7(2))* Whitman, Albert & Co.

Gareth Stevens editorial staff & Gareth Stevens Editorial Staff. Gareth Stevens Atlas of the World. 2004. (Gareth Stevens Atlas of the World Ser.). (Illus.). 200p. (gr. 3-6). lib. bdg. 42.00 *(978-0-8368-4091-9(7),* Gareth Stevens Learning Library) Stevens, Gareth Publishing LLLP.

Gareth Stevens Publishing Staff & Porter, Malcolm. Children's Atlas of the World. 2005. (Children's Atlas of the World Ser.). 96p. (gr. 2-6). lib. bdg. 38.00 *(978-0-8368-4989-9(2),* Gareth Stevens Learning Library) Stevens, Gareth Publishing LLLP.

Garton, Keith & Cutler, Nelida Gonzalez, eds. Time for Kids World Atlas. 2007. (Illus.). 176p. (J). reprint ed. pap. 11.00 *(978-1-4223-6807-7(6))* DIANE Publishing Co.

Green, Jen. Barron's Amazing Fact-Packed, Fold-Out Atlas of the World: With Awesome Pop-Up Map! Engel, Christiane, illus. 2014. (ENG.). 56p. (J). (gr. 3-6). 18.99 *(978-0-7641-6746-1(4))* Barron's Educational Series, Inc.

—Slide & Discover: World Atlas. 2013. (Slide & Discover Ser.). (ENG., Illus.). 24p. (J). (gr. 2). 19.95 *(978-1-60710-584-8(5),* Silver Dolphin Bks.) Readerlink Distribution Services, LLC.

Greenberger, Robert. A Historical Atlas of Pakistan. 2009. (Historical Atlases of South Asia, Central Asia, & the Middle East Ser.). 64p. (gr. 6-6). 61.20 *(978-1-61513-327-7(5))* Rosen Publishing Group, Inc., The.

Hammond, Inc, ed. World Almanac Notebk Atlas 2010. 2010. (World Almanac Ser.). 56p. pap. 6.99 *(978-0-8437-1526-2(X))* Hammond World Atlas Corp.

Hammond World Atlas Corporation Staff. Children's World Atlas. 2008. 128p. (J). (gr. 2-7). 19.95 *(978-0-8437-0972-8(3))* Hammond World Atlas Corp.

—World Almanac Notebook Atlas 2008. 2007. (World Almanac Ser.). 56p. ring bd. 6.95 *(978-0-8437-0951-3(0))* Hammond World Atlas Corp.

Hammond World Atlas Corporation Staff, creator. Discovering Maps: A Children's World Atlas. rev. ed. 2007. (Illus.). 80p. (J). 9.95 *(978-0-8437-0953-7(7))* Hammond World Atlas Corp.

—Student World Atlas. rev. ed. 2007. (Illus.). 80p. per. 9.95 *(978-0-8437-0956-8(1))* Hammond World Atlas Corp.

—Student's Notebook Atlas. 4th ed. 2007. (Hammond Student Atlases Ser.). (Illus.). 32p. cd-rom 3.95 *(978-0-8437-0949-0(9))* Hammond World Atlas Corp.

Hammond World Atlas Corporation Staff, ed. World Almanac Notebk Atlas 2009. 2008. (World Almanac Ser.). 56p. 6.95 *(978-0-8437-0973-5(1))* Hammond World Atlas Corp.

—World Passport: Atlas & Travelmate. 2nd rev. ed. 2008. 128p. 6.95 *(978-0-8437-1350-3(X))* Hammond World Atlas Corp.

Hanson III, Andrew C., ed. Ice Age Trail Atlas 2005. 2005. (Illus.). 100p. spiral bd. 25.00 *(978-0-9627079-3-3(7))* Ice Age Park and Trail Foundation, Inc.

Harpercollins Staff. Collins First Atlas. 2015. (Collins First Atlas Ser.). (ENG., Illus.). 40p. (J). (gr. -1-1). 12.99 *(978-0-00-810102-2(7))* HarperCollins Pubs. Ltd. GBR. Dist: Independent Pubs. Group.

—Collins First Atlas: Learn with Maps. 2nd ed. 2015. (Collins First Atlas Ser.). (ENG., Illus.). 32p. (J). (gr. -1-1). pap. 9.99 *(978-0-00-810101-5(9))* HarperCollins Pubs. Ltd. GBR. Dist: Independent Pubs. Group.

—Collins Student Atlas. 2015. (ENG.). 208p. (gr. 9-11). pap. 18.95 *(978-0-00-759138-1(1))* HarperCollins Pubs. Ltd. GBR. Dist: Independent Pubs. Group.

Is the World Flat? An Atlas of Cool World Maps That Teach Twenty-First Century Kids New Ways of Seeing Our Changing Earth's History, People, Environment, & Wildlife. 2006. (Illus.). 32p. (J). 19.94 *(978-0-9788138-1-9(2))* Nimble Bks. LLC.

Issac, Michael. A Historical Atlas of Oman. (Historical Atlases of South Asia, Central Asia, & the Middle East Ser.). 64p. 2009. (gr. 6-6). 61.20 *(978-1-61513-326-0(7))* 2004. (Illus.). (gr. 7-12). lib. bdg. 31.95 *(978-0-8239-4500-9(6))* Rosen Publishing Group, Inc., The.

Kemp, Richard. Atlas Visual del Mundo. Delf, Brian, illus. (SPA.). 80p. (YA). (gr. 5-8). *(978-84-216-1576-8(9),* BU4606) Bruño, Editorial ESP. Dist: Lectorum Pubns., Inc.

Khan, Aisha. A Historical Atlas of India. 2009. (Historical Atlases of South Asia, Central Asia, & the Middle East Ser.). 64p. (gr. 6-6). 61.20 *(978-1-61513-318-5(6))* Rosen Publishing Group, Inc., The.

—A Historical Atlas of Kyrgyzstan. (Historical Atlases of South Asia, Central Asia, & the Middle East Ser.). 64p. 2009. (gr. 6-6). 61.20 *(978-1-61513-324-6(0))* 2004. (Illus.). (gr. 7-12). lib. bdg. 31.95 *(978-0-8239-4499-6(9))* Rosen Publishing Group, Inc., The.

King, C. Jigsaw World Atlas. 2004. 20p. (J). 14.95 *(978-0-7945-0595-0(3))* EDC Publishing.

Kneib, Martha. A Historical Atlas of the American Revolution. 2005. (United States: Historical Atlases of the Growth of a New Nation Ser.). (Illus.). 64p. (J). (gr. 7-12). lib. bdg. 31.95 *(978-1-4042-0204-7(8))* Rosen Publishing Group, Inc., The.

Kralovansky, Susan. What Would You Do with an Atlas, 1 vol. 2013. (Library Resources Ser.). (ENG., Illus.). 32p. (J). (gr. k-4). lib. bdg. 27.07 *(978-1-61783-606-0(0),* Super SandCastle) ABDO Publishing Co.

Lake, Sam. Sticker Picture Atlas of the World. 2015. (Sticker Reference Ser.). (ENG.). 24+10p. (J). (gr. k-5). pap. 9.99 *(978-0-7945-3040-2(0),* Usborne) EDC Publishing.

Leacock, Elspeth & Buckley, Susan. Places in Time: A New Atlas of American History. Jones, Randy, illus. 2006. 48p. (J). (gr. 4-8). reprint ed. 15.00 *(978-1-4223-5555-8(1))* DIANE Publishing Co.

Leacock, Elspeth & Buckley, Susan Washburn. Places in Time: A New Atlas of American History. Jones, Randy, illus. 2003. (ENG.). 48p. (J). (gr. 5-7). pap. 6.99 *(978-0-618-31113-2(0))* Houghton Mifflin Harcourt Publishing Co.

Liberman, Sherri. A Historical Atlas of Azerbaijan. 2009. (Historical Atlases of South Asia, Central Asia, & the Middle East Ser.). 64p. (gr. 6-6). 61.20 *(978-1-61513-316-1(X))* Rosen Publishing Group, Inc., The.

Lonely Planet Publications Staff. Adventures Around the Globe - World Atlas, 1 vol. 2015. (Lonely Planet Kids Ser.). (ENG., Illus.). 60p. (J). pap. 12.99 *(978-1-74360-782-4(2),* 4985) Lonely Planet Pubns.

Los Mapas Del Mundo, 6 vols., Vol. 2. (Explorers. Exploradores Nonfiction Sets Ser.). (SPA.). 32p. (gr. 3-6). 44.95 *(978-0-7699-0646-1(X))* Shortland Pubns. (U. S. A.) Inc.

Maps & Our World: Level O, 6 vols., Vol. 2. (Explorers Ser.). 32p. (gr. 3-6). 44.95 *(978-0-7699-0610-2(9))* Shortland Pubns. (U. S. A.) Inc.

Matteson, Adrienne. Find Your Way with Atlases. 2012. (Explorer Junior Library: Information Explorer Junior Ser.). (ENG.). 24p. (J). (gr. 1-4). pap. 12.79 *(978-1-61080-395-3(7),* 201332); lib. bdg. 28.50 *(978-1-61080-370-0(1),* 201274) Cherry Lake Publishing.

Mayfield, Marilee Joy. My First Atlas. 2016. (Illus.). 52p. (J). *(978-1-4351-6296-9(X))* Barnes & Noble, Inc.

Merriam-Webster, Inc. Staff, ed. Merriam-Webster's Notebook Atlas. 2005. (ENG., Illus.). 68p. (gr. 5-18). pap. 4.95 *(978-0-87779-652-7(1),* MER-652) Merriam-Webster, Inc.

Mizielinska, Aleksandra & Mizielinski, Daniel. Maps. 2013. (ENG.). 112p. (J). (gr. k-12). 35.00 *(978-0-7636-6896-9(6),* Big Picture Press) Candlewick Pr.

Morris, Neil. Children's Picture Atlas: A First Introduction to the Countries of the World. 2012. (ENG., Illus.). 48p. (J). 15.00 *(978-1-84135-880-2(0))* Award Pubns. Ltd. GBR. Dist: Parkwest Pubns., Inc.

—Junior Atlas. 2003. (Knowledge Masters Ser.). (Illus.). 32p. (YA). pap. incl. cd-rom *(978-1-903954-50-8(9),* Pavilion Children's Books) Pavilion Bks.

National Geographic. National Geographic Kids World Atlas. 2013. (ENG.). 208p. (J). (gr. 3-7). lib. bdg. 33.90 *(978-1-4263-1404-9(3),* National Geographic Children's Bks.) National Geographic Society.

National Geographic Kids Staff. National Geographic Kids World Atlas. 2013. (ENG., Illus.). 208p. (J). (gr. 3-7). 24.99 *(978-1-4263-1405-6(1),* National Geographic Children's Bks.) National Geographic Society.

—Student World Atlas: Your Fact-Filled Reference for School & Home! 4th ed. 2014. (ENG., Illus.). 144p. (YA). (gr. 7). pap. 12.99 *(978-1-4263-1775-0(1),* National Geographic Children's Bks.) National Geographic Society.

National Geographic Staff. Beginner's World Atlas. 3rd ed. 2011. (ENG., Illus.). 64p. (J). (gr. k-4). 18.95 *(978-1-4263-0838-3(8),* National Geographic Children's Bks.) National Geographic Society.

—National Geographic Kids World Atlas. 2013. (ENG., Illus.). 208p. (J). (gr. 3-7). pap. 14.99 *(978-1-4263-1403-2(5),* National Geographic Children's Bks.) National Geographic Society.

Oleksy, Walter. Mapping the Skies. 2003. (Watts Library). (ENG., Illus.). 64p. (J). (gr. 5-7). pap. 8.95 *(978-0-531-16635-2(X),* Watts, Franklin) Scholastic Library Publishing.

—Mapping the World. 2003. (Watts Library). (ENG.). 64p. (J). (gr. 5-7). pap. 8.95 *(978-0-531-16636-9(8),* Watts, Franklin) Scholastic Library Publishing.

Oxford University Press Staff, ed. The Times Compact Atlas of the World. (Children's Reference Ser.). 256p. (J). *(978-1-4054-1708-2(0))* Parragon, Inc.

Phillips, Dee. The Atlas of My World. 2011. (ENG.). 64p. (J). (gr. 4-7). pap. 12.95 *(978-1-84898-176-8(7),* TickTock Books) Octopus Publishing Group GBR. Dist: Independent Pubs. Group.

Phillips, Larissa. A Historical Atlas of Iraq. 2009. (Historical Atlases of South Asia, Central Asia, & the Middle East Ser.). 64p. (gr. 6-6). 61.20 *(978-1-61513-320-8(8))* Rosen Publishing Group, Inc., The.

Porter, Malcolm. The Cherrytree Children's Atlas. rev. ed. (Illus.). 96p. (J). *(978-0-7451-5179-3(5))* Cherrytree Bks.

Ramen, Fred. A Historical Atlas of Iran. 2009. (Historical Atlases of South Asia, Central Asia, & the Middle East Ser.). 64p. (gr. 6-6). 61.20 *(978-1-61513-319-2(4))* Rosen Publishing Group, Inc., The.

Rand McNally. Kids' Road Atlas: Kra. 2015. (ENG.). pap. 6.99 *(978-0-528-01341-6(0))* Rand McNally.

Rand McNally Staff. Atlas Schoolhouse Beginner's Workbook. 2005. 128p. (J). pap. 7.95 *(978-0-528-93469-8(4))* Rand McNally.

—Atlas Schoolhouse Illustrated World Atlas. 2005. 112p. (J). 9.95 *(978-0-528-93458-2(9))* Rand McNally.

—Atlas Schoolhouse Intermediate World Atlas. 2005. 128p. (J). pap. 6.95 *(978-0-528-93460-5(0))* Rand McNally.

—Atlas Scoolhouse Beginner's World Atlas. 2005. 48p. (J). pap. 5.95 *(978-0-528-93463-6(5))* Rand McNally.

—Kids' Road Atlas. (Backseat Bks.). 80p. (J). pap. 3.95 *(978-0-528-96544-9(1))* Rand McNally.

Rand McNally Staff, creator. Intermediate Geography & Map Activities. 2005. (Rand McNally Schoolhouse Ser.). (Illus.). 128p. per. 7.95 *(978-0-528-93470-4(8))* Rand McNally.

Ray, Kurt. A Historical Atlas of Kuwait. 2009. (Historical Atlases of South Asia, Central Asia, & the Middle East Ser.). 64p. (gr. 6-6). 61.20 *(978-1-61513-323-9(2))* Rosen Publishing Group, Inc., The.

Romano, Amy. A Historical Atlas of Afghanistan. 2009. (Historical Atlases of South Asia, Central Asia, & the Middle East Ser.). 64p. (gr. 6-6). 61.20 *(978-1-61513-315-4(1))* Rosen Publishing Group, Inc., The.

—A Historical Atlas of Israel. 2009. (Historical Atlases of South Asia, Central Asia, & the Middle East Ser.). 64p. (gr. 6-6). 61.20 *(978-1-61513-321-5(6))* Rosen Publishing Group, Inc., The.

—A Historical Atlas of Jordan. 2004. (Historical Atlases of South Asia, Central Asia, & the Middle East Ser.). (Illus.). 64p. (gr. 7-12). lib. bdg. 31.95 *(978-0-8239-3980-0(4))* Rosen Publishing Group, Inc., The.

—A Historical Atlas of the United Arab Emirates. 2009. (Historical Atlases of South Asia, Central Asia, & the Middle East Ser.). 64p. (gr. 6-6). 61.20 *(978-1-61513-330-7(5))* Rosen Publishing Group, Inc., The.

—A Historical Atlas of United Arab Emirates. 2004. (Historical Atlases of South Asia, Central Asia, & the Middle East Ser.). (Illus.). 64p. (gr. 7-12). lib. bdg. 31.95 *(978-0-8239-4501-6(4))* Rosen Publishing Group, Inc., The.

—A Historical Atlas of Yemen. (Historical Atlases of South Asia, Central Asia, & the Middle East Ser.). 64p. 2009. (gr. 6-6). 61.20 *(978-1-61513-331-4(3))* 2004. (Illus.). (gr. 7-12). lib. bdg. 31.95 *(978-0-8239-4502-3(2))* Rosen Publishing Group, Inc., The.

Scoffham, Stephen. World in Maps. 2014. (Collins Primary Atlases Ser.). (ENG., Illus.). 16p. (J). (gr. 3). pap. 12.99 *(978-0-00-752477-8(3))* HarperCollins Pubs. Ltd. GBR. Dist: Independent Pubs. Group.

Scoffham, Stephen & Collins Maps Staff. UK in Maps. 2014. (Collins Primary Atlases Ser.). (ENG., Illus.). 24p. (J). (gr. 5-10). pap. 12.99 *(978-0-00-752476-1(5))* HarperCollins Pubs. Ltd. GBR. Dist: Independent Pubs. Group.

Shea, Therese. How Do I Use an Atlas? 2014. (Research Tools You Can Use Ser.). (Illus.). 32p. (J). (gr. 3-6). 23.45 *(978-1-62275-340-6(2))* Rosen Publishing Group, Inc., The.

Skahill, Carolyn. A Historical Atlas of Lebanon. 2004. (Historical Atlases of South Asia, Central Asia, & the Middle East Ser.). (Illus.). 64p. (gr. 7-12). lib. bdg. 31.95 *(978-0-8239-3982-4(0))* Rosen Publishing Group, Inc., The.

Skahill, Carolyn M. A Historical Atlas of Lebanon. 2009. (Historical Atlases of South Asia, Central Asia, & the Middle East Ser.). 64p. (gr. 6-6). 61.20 *(978-1-61513-325-3(9))* Rosen Publishing Group, Inc., The.

Stark Draper, Allison. A Historical Atlas of Syria. 2004. (Historical Atlases of South Asia, Central Asia, & the Middle East Ser.). (Illus.). 64p. (gr. 7-12). lib. bdg. 31.95 *(978-0-8239-3983-1(9))* Rosen Publishing Group, Inc., The.

Taylor, Barbara. Slide & Discover: Animal Atlas. 2013. (Slide & Discover Ser.). (ENG., Illus.). 24p. (J). (gr. 2). 19.95 *(978-1-60710-586-2(1),* Silver Dolphin Bks.) Readerlink Distribution Services, LLC.

Turnbull, Stephanie & Helbrough, Emma. Children's World Atlas. 2004. (Geography Ser.). (Illus.). 144p. (J). 22.95 *(978-0-7945-0318-5(7));* lib. bdg. 30.95 *(978-1-58086-489-3(9))* EDC Publishing.

—The Usborne Internet-Linked Children's World Atlas. 2005. 144p. (J). 14.99 *(978-0-7945-1079-4(5),* Usborne) EDC Publishing.

Two-Can Publishing Ltd. Staff, contrib. by. My First Trip Around the World: A Picture Atlas Adventure. 2004. (ENG., Illus.). 34p. (J). (gr. -1-3). 15.95 *(978-1-58728-515-8(0))* Cooper Square Publishing Llc.

U. S. National Geographic Society Staff. Beginner's World Atlas. 3rd rev. ed. 2011. (ENG., Illus.). 64p. (J). (gr. k-4). lib. bdg. 27.90 *(978-1-4263-0839-0(6),* National Geographic Children's Bks.) National Geographic Society.

—Our World: A Child's First Picture Atlas. 2006. (Science Quest Ser.). (ENG., Illus.). 32p. (J). (gr. -1-2). lib. bdg. 27.90 *(978-0-7922-5532-1(1));* 17.95 *(978-0-7922-5531-4(3))* National Geographic Society. (National Geographic Children's Bks.).

—Student Atlas of the World. 3rd ed. 2009. (ENG., Illus.). 144p. (J). (gr. 7-18). 19.95 *(978-1-4263-0445-3(5));* lib. bdg. 28.90 *(978-1-4263-0458-3(7))* National Geographic Society. (National Geographic Children's Bks.).

U. S. National Geographic Society Staff, creator. Beginner's World Atlas. rev. ed. 2005. (ENG., Illus.). 64p. (J). (gr. k-3). 17.95 *(978-0-7922-4205-5(X),* National Geographic Children's Bks.) National Geographic Society.

U. S. National Geographic Society Staff & National Geographic Learning Staff. United States Atlas for Young Explorers. Lamichhane, Priyanka, ed. 3rd ed. 2008. (ENG., Illus.). 176p. (J). (gr. 3-7). 24.95 *(978-1-4263-0255-8(X),* National Geographic Children's Bks.) National Geographic Society.

Van Rose, S. Atlas Visual de la Tierra. (Colección Atlas Visual). (SPA., Illus.). 310p. (YA). (gr. 5-8). *(978-84-216-2574-3(8),* BU1496) Bruño, Editorial ESP. Dist: Lectorum Pubns., Inc.

Walrus Books. Kids' Canadian Atlas. (ENG., Illus.). 40p. (J). (gr. 1-9). 14.95 *(978-1-55285-149-4(4))* Whitecap Bks., Ltd. CAN. Dist: Graphic Arts Ctr. Publishing Co.

World Book Atlas. 2005. (gr. 5-12). 55.00 *(978-0-7166-2654-1(3))* World Bk., Inc.

ATLASES, HISTORICAL

see Historical Geography—Maps

ATMOSPHERE

Here are entered works treating the body of air surrounding the earth as distinguished from the upper rarefied air. Works dealing with air as an element and of its chemical and physical properties are entered under Air.

see also Air; Meteorology

Banquieri, Eduardo. The Biosphere. 2005. (Our Planet Ser.). (Illus.). 32p. (gr. 4-6). lib. bdg. 28.00 *(978-0-7910-9008-4(6),* Chelsea Clubhouse) Facts On File, Inc.

Beaton, Kathryn. I See Rainbows. 2015. (Tell Me Why Library). (ENG.). 24p. (J). (gr. 2-5). 27.07 *(978-1-63188-997-4(4),* 205900) Cherry Lake Publishing.

Birch, Robin. How Weather Works. 2009. (Weather & Climate Ser.). 32p. (gr. 3). 28.50 *(978-0-7614-4466-4(1))* Marshall Cavendish Corp.

Bourgoing, Pascale De, et al. Earth & Sky. Peyrols, Sylvaine, illus. 2006. (ENG.). 39p. (J). (gr. k-3). pap. 11.99 *(978-1-85103-110-8(3))* Moonlight Publishing, Ltd. GBR. Dist: Independent Pubs. Group.

La Capa Ozono. (Nuestro Mundo en Peligro Ser.). (SPA.). 32p. (YA). 10.50 *(978-84-342-1930-4(1),* CAR1930) Parramon Ediciones S.A. ESP. Dist: Continental Bk. Co., Inc.

Casper, Julie Kerr. Water & Atmosphere: The Lifeblood of Natural Systems. 2007. (Natural Resources Ser.). (Illus.). 207p. (YA). (gr. 7-12). lib. bdg. 39.50 *(978-0-8160-6359-8(1))* Facts On File, Inc.

Chambers, Catherine. Are Humans Damaging the Atmosphere? 2015. (Earth Debates Ser.). (ENG.). 48p. (gr. 4-6). 33.32 *(978-1-4846-0998-9(0),* Heinemann InfoSearch) Heinemann-Raintree.

—Stickmen's Guide to Earth's Atmosphere in Layers. Dean, Venitia & De Quay, John Paul, illus. 2016. (Stickmen's Guides to This Incredible Earth Ser.). (ENG.). 32p. (J). (gr. 3-6). 26.65 *(978-1-5124-0617-7(1))* Lerner Publishing Group.

Coleman, Miriam. Using the Weather to Learn about Earth. 2015. (Earth Science Detectives Ser.). (ENG., Illus.). 24p. (J). (gr. 3-3). lib. bdg. 23.60 *(978-1-4777-5958-5(1),* PowerKids Pr.) Rosen Publishing Group, Inc., The.

Desonie, Dana. Atmosphere: Air Pollution & Its Effects. 2007. (Our Fragile Planet Ser.). (Illus.). 194p. (YA). (gr. 7-12). lib. bdg. 35.00 *(978-0-8160-6213-3(7))* Facts On File, Inc.

—Biosphere: Ecosystems & Biodiversity Loss. 2007. (Our Fragile Planet Ser.). (Illus.). 206p. (YA). (gr. 7-12). lib. bdg. 35.00 *(978-0-8160-6219-5(6))* Facts On File, Inc.

El Efecto Invernadero. (Nuestro Mundo en Peligro Ser.). (SPA.). (J). 10.50 *(978-84-342-1912-0(3),* CAR1912) Parramon Ediciones S.A. ESP. Dist: Continental Bk. Co., Inc.

Gardner, Robert. Science Fair Projects about the Atmosphere. 2016. (Hands-On Science Ser.). 48p. (J). pap. 11.70 *(978-0-7660-8220-5(2))* Enslow Pubs., Inc.

Gosman, Gillian. What Do You Know about Earth's Atmosphere? 2013. (20 Questions: Earth Science Ser.). 24p. (J). (gr. 3-6). pap. 49.50 *(978-1-4488-9857-2(9));* pap. 8.25 *(978-1-4488-9856-5(0));* lib. bdg. 22.60 *(978-1-4488-9699-8(1))* Rosen Publishing Group, Inc., The. (PowerKids Pr.).

Greek, Joe. What Is the Atmosphere & How Does It Circulate?, 1 vol. 2015. (ENG.). 32p. (J). 23.45 *(978-1-62275-783-1(1),* Britannica Educational Publishing) Rosen Publishing Group, Inc., The.

Green, Jen. Making Air Cleaner. 2011. (Sherlock Bones Looks at the Environment Ser.). (ENG., Illus.). 32p. (YA). (gr. 3-6). lib. bdg. 25.25 *(978-1-61533-345-5(2))* Windmill Bks.

Holt, Rinehart and Winston Staff. Environmental Science Chptr. 13: Atmosphere & Climate. 4th ed. Date not set. pap. 11.20 *(978-0-03-068073-1(5))* Holt McDougal.

—Holt Science & Technology Chapter 15: Earth Science: The Atmosphere. 5th ed. 2004. (Illus.). pap. 12.86 *(978-0-03-030322-7(2))* Holt McDougal.

—Holt Science Spectrum Chptr. 22: The Atmosphere. 4th ed. Date not set. pap. 11.20 *(978-0-03-068061-8(1))* Holt McDougal.

Jones, Tammy. Look at the Sky. 2009. (Sight Word Readers Set A Ser.). (J). 3.49 net. *(978-1-60719-141-4(5))* Newmark Learning LLC.

Keeping Warm! Keeping Cool! 6 Each of 1 Student Book, 6 vols. (Sunshinetm Science Ser.). 24p. (gr. 1-2). 41.95 *(978-0-7802-1410-1(2))* Wright Group/McGraw-Hill.

Keeping Warm! Keeping Cool! Big Book. (Sunshinetm Science Ser.). 24p. (gr. 1-2). 37.50 *(978-0-7802-1411-8(0))* Wright Group/McGraw-Hill.

Kissock, Heather. Rainbow. 2011. (J). *(978-1-61690-603-0(0)); (978-1-61690-957-4(9))* Weigl Pubs., Inc.

Lindeen, Mary. In the Sky. 2015. (BeginningtoRead Ser.). (ENG.). 32p. (J). (gr. k-2). pap. 11.94 *(978-1-60357-756-4(4));* (Illus.). lib. bdg. 22.60 *(978-1-59953-696-5(X))* Norwood Hse. Pr.

Meachen Rau, Dana. Air. 2008. (Earth Matters Ser.). 32p. (gr. 1-2). lib. bdg. 15.95 *(978-0-7614-3042-1(3),* Benchmark Bks.) Marshall Cavendish Corp.

—La Aire. 2008. (Planeta Es Importante Ser.). (SPA.). 32p. (gr. 1-2). lib. bdg. 15.95 *(978-0-7614-3464-1(X),* Benchmark Bks.) Marshall Cavendish Corp.

Modules: Earth Science; Earth's Atmosphere TE. 2005. (gr. 6-12). *(978-0-618-33416-2(5),* 2-01006) Holt McDougal.

Morey, Allan. The Science Behind Wonders of the Sky: Aurora Borealis, Moonbows, & St. Elmo's Fire. 2016. (Science Behind Natural Phenomena Ser.). (ENG., Illus.). 32p. (gr. 3-4). lib. bdg. 27.99 *(978-1-5157-0777-6(6),* Edge Bks.) Capstone Press of Coughlan Cos.

Morgan, Emily R. La Próxima Vez Que Veas la Puesta del Sol. 2016. (Next Time You See Ser.). (SPA., Illus.). 32p. (J). (gr. 2-4). pap. 12.95 *(978-1-68140-282-6(3))* National Science Teachers Assn.

Nadeau, Isaac. Water in the Atmosphere. (Water Cycle Ser.). 24p. 2009. (gr. 4-4). 42.50 *(978-1-60854-272-7(6))* 2003. (Illus.). (J). lib. bdg. 22.60 *(978-0-8239-6262-4(8))* Rosen Publishing Group, Inc., The. (PowerKids Pr.).

Pluckrose, Henry. Air. 2007. (Let's Explore: Elements Ser.). (Illus.). 32p. (J). (gr. 4-7). lib. bdg. 27.10 *(978-1-59771-033-6(4))* Sea-To-Sea Pubns.

Reilly, Carmel. Earth's Atmosphere. 2011. (Sky Watching Ser.). 32p. (gr. 2-4). 28.50 *(978-1-60870-580-1(3))* Marshall Cavendish Corp.

Sherman, Jill. Clean Air. 2017. (J). pap. **(978-0-7660-9143-6(0))** Enslow Pubs., Inc.

Sohn, Emily & Kentor Schmauss, Judy. Air & Weather: Where'd My Hat Go? 2011. (iScience Readers Ser.). 24p. (J). (gr. k-2). lib. bdg. 21.27 *(978-1-59953-403-9(7))* Norwood Hse. Pr.

Wilson, CeCe. All about the Sky. 2015. (Rosen REAL Readers: STEM & STEAM Collection). (ENG.). 8p. pap. 5.46 *(978-1-4994-9648-2(6),* Rosen Classroom) Rosen Publishing Group, Inc., The.

ATMOSPHERE—POLLUTION

see Air—Pollution

ATMOSPHERE, UPPER

see also Stratosphere

Shaughnessy, Mara. LEGO Man in Space: A True Story. 2013. (ENG., Illus.). 32p. (J). (gr. -1-3). 14.95 *(978-1-62087-544-5(6),* 620544, Sky Pony Pr.) Skyhorse Publishing Co., Inc.

ATOLLS

see Coral Reefs and Islands

A
B

ATOMIC BOMB

Allman, Toney. J. Robert Oppenheimer: Theoretical Physicist, Atomic Pioneer. 2005. (Giants of Science Ser.). (ENG., Illus.). 64p. (J). (gr. 3-7). lib. bdg. 28.35 *(978-1-56711-889-6(5)*, Blackbirch Pr., Inc.) Cengage Gale.

Anderson, Dale. The Atom Bomb Project. 2004. (Landmark Events in American History Ser.). (Illus.). 48p. (gr. 5-12). lib. bdg. 31.00 *(978-0-8368-5385-8(7)*, Gareth Stevens Secondary Library) Stevens, Gareth Publishing LLLP.

Bascomb, Neal. Sabotage: The Mission to Destroy Hitler's Atomic Bomb. 2016. (ENG., Illus.). 320p. (J). (gr. 7). 17.99 *(978-0-545-73243-7(3)*, Levine, Arthur A. Bks.) Scholastic, Inc.

Baxter, Roberta. The Dropping of the Atomic Bombs: A History Perspectives Book. 2014. (Perspectives Library). (ENG., Illus.). 32p. (J). (gr. 4-8). 28.50 *(978-1-62431-665-4(4)*, 203224) Cherry Lake Publishing.

Crewe, Sabrina & Anderson, Dale. The Atom Bomb Project. 2004. (Events That Shaped America Ser.). (Illus.). 32p. (gr. 3-6). lib. bdg. 26.00 *(978-0-8368-3404-8(6)*, Gareth Stevens Learning Library) Stevens, Gareth Publishing LLLP.

Elish, Dan. The Manhattan Project. 2007. (Cornerstones of Freedom Ser.). (Illus.). 48p. (J). (gr. 4-6). 26.00 *(978-0-516-23299-7(1)*, Children's Pr.) Scholastic Library Publishing.

Gonzales, Doreen. The Secret of the Manhattan Project. 2012. (Stories in American History Ser.). (Illus.). 128p. (J). (gr. 5-18). 33.27 *(978-0-7660-3954-4(4))* Enslow Pubs., Inc.

—The Secret of the Manhattan Project: Stories in American History. 2012. (Stories in American History Ser.). (Illus.). 128p. (J). (gr. 5-18). pap. 10.95 *(978-1-4644-0024-7(5))* Enslow Pubs., Inc.

Grant, R. G. Why Did Hiroshima Happen? 2010. (Moments in History Ser.). (Illus.). 48p. (YA). (gr. 5-9). lib. bdg. 31.95 *(978-1-4339-4163-4(5))*; (gr. 6-8). pap. 14.05 *(978-1-4339-4164-1(3)*, Gareth Stevens Secondary Library) Stevens, Gareth Publishing LLLP.

Kaelberer, Angie Peterson & Langley, Andrew. Hiroshima & Nagasaki. 2017. (Eyewitness to World War II Ser.). (ENG.). 112p. (gr. 5-7). lib. bdg. 35.99 ***(978-0-7565-5584-9(1)***, CPB Grades 4-8) Compass Point Bks.

Lawton, Clive A. Hiroshima: The Story of the First Atom Bomb. 60th anniv. ed. 2004. (Watts Nonfiction Ser.). (ENG., Illus.). 48p. (J). (gr. 5-18). 18.99 *(978-0-7636-2271-8(0))* Candlewick Pr.

MacCarald, Clara. The Invention of the Atomic Bomb. 2017. (Engineering That Made America Ser.). (ENG.). 32p. (J). (gr. 3-6). lib. bdg. 28.50 *(978-1-5038-1641-1(9)*, 211157) Child's World, Inc., The.

The Making of the Atomic Bomb. 2014. (Understanding World History Ser.). (ENG., Illus.). 96p. (J). lib. bdg. *(978-1-60152-686-1(5))* ReferencePoint Pr., Inc.

Orr, Tamra. The Atom Bomb: Creating & Exploding the First Nuclear Weapon. (Library of Weapons of Mass Destruction Ser.). 64p. 2009. (gr. 5-5). 58.50 *(978-1-60853-955-0(5))* 2004. (Illus.). (J). lib. bdg. 31.95 *(978-1-4042-0292-4(7))* Rosen Publishing Group, Inc., The.

Peppas, Lynn. Hiroshima & Nagasaki. 2013. (ENG., Illus.). 48p. (J). *(978-0-7787-1171-1(4))*; pap. *(978-0-7787-1179-7(X))* Crabtree Publishing Co.

Poolos, J. The Atomic Bombings of Hiroshima & Nagasaki. 2008. (Great Historic Disasters Ser.). (Illus.). 128p. (gr. 5-8). 35.00 *(978-0-7910-9738-0(2)*, Chelsea Hse.) Facts On File, Inc.

Rosinsky, Natalie M. The Story of the Atomic Bomb: How It Changed the World, 1 vol. 2010. (World Transformed Ser.). (ENG.). 64p. (gr. 6-7). lib. bdg. 33.99 *(978-0-7565-4316-7(9)*, CPB Grades 4-8) Compass Point Bks.

Ross, Stewart. Hiroshima. 2011. (Place in History Ser.). 48p. (YA). (gr. 5-9). lib. bdg. 34.25 *(978-1-84837-674-8(X))* Arcturus Publishing GBR. Dist: Black Rabbit Bks.

Scherer, Glenn & Fletcher, Marty. J. Robert Oppenheimer: The Brain Behind the Bomb. 2007. (Inventors Who Changed the World Ser.). (Illus.). 128p. (J). (gr. 5-9). lib. bdg. 34.60 *(978-1-59845-050-7(6)*, MyReportLinks.com Bks.) Enslow Pubs., Inc.

Sheinkin, Steve. Bomb: The Race to Build — & Steal — the World's Most Dangerous Weapon. 2012. (ENG., Illus.). 272p. (J). (gr. 5-9). 19.99 *(978-1-59643-487-5(2)*, 9781596434875) Roaring Brook Pr.

Smibert, Angie. 12 Incredible Facts about the Dropping of the Atomic Bombs. 2015. (Turning Points in US History Ser.). (ENG., Illus.). 32p. (J). (gr. 3-5). 19.95 *(978-1-63235-129-6(3)*, 12-Story Library) Pr. Room Editions LLC.

Stelson, Caren. Sachiko: A Nagasaki Bomb Survivor's Story. 2016. (ENG., Illus.). (gr. 5-12). 120p. 19.99 *(978-1-4677-8903-5(8))*; 144p. 38.65 *(978-1-5124-1885-9(4))*; 144p. 38.65 *(978-1-5124-0893-5(X))*; (YA). 9.99 *(978-1-5124-1884-2(6))* Lerner Publishing Group. (Carolrhoda Bks.).

Tracy, Kathleen. Top Secret: The Story of the Manhattan Project. 2005. (Monumental Milestones Ser.). (Illus.). 48p. (YA). (gr. 4-7). lib. bdg. 29.95 *(978-1-58415-399-3(7))* Mitchell Lane Pubs., Inc.

Winter, Jonah. The Secret Project. Winter, Jeanette, illus. 2017. (ENG.). 40p. (J). (gr. k-3). 17.99 *(978-1-4814-6913-5(4)*, Beach Lane Bks.) Beach Lane Bks.

Wukovits, John F. Manhattan Project. Greenhaven Press Editors, ed. 2014. (World History Ser.). (ENG., Illus.). 128p. (gr. 7-10). lib. bdg. 39.90 *(978-1-4205-0932-8(2)*, Lucent Bks.) Cengage Gale.

Yalata Communities, et al. Maralinga: The Anangu Story. 2012. (ENG., Illus.). 72p. (J). (gr. 5-9). pap. 14.99 *(978-1-74237-842-8(0))* Allen & Unwin AUS. Dist: Independent Pubs. Group.

ATOMIC BOMB—FICTION

Bauld, Jane Scoggins. Hector Saves the Moon, Vol. 2. Laronde, Gary, illus. 2003. (Hector's Escapades Ser.). 34p. (J). (gr. -1-3). per. 7.95 *(978-1-57168-312-0(7))* Eakin Pr.

Burkinshaw, Kathleen. The Last Cherry Blossom. 2016. (ENG.). 240p. (J). (gr. 5-8). 16.99 *(978-1-63450-693-9(6)*, Sky Pony Pr.) Skyhorse Publishing Co., Inc.

Reeder, Carolyn. The Secret Project Notebook. 2005. 247p. (J). 15.00 *(978-0-941232-33-3(6))* Bathtub Row Pr.

Taylor, Theodore & Taylor, Theodore. The Bomb. 2007. (ENG., Illus.). 208p. (YA). (gr. 7-12). pap. 6.95 *(978-0-15-206165-4(7))* Houghton Mifflin Harcourt Publishing Co.

Zindel, Paul & Zindel, Paul. The Gadget. 2003. (ENG., Illus.). 192p. (YA). (gr. 7). mass mkt. 6.99 *(978-0-440-22951-3(0)*, Laurel Leaf) Random Hse. Children's Bks.

ATOMIC BOMB—PHYSIOLOGICAL EFFECT

Coerr, Eleanor. Sadako & the Thousand Paper Cranes. Himler, Ronald, illus. 2004. (Puffin Modern Classics Ser.). (ENG.). 80p. (J). (gr. 3-7). pap. 6.99 *(978-0-14-240113-2(7)*, Puffin Books) Penguin Young Readers Group.

Eleanor, Coerr. Sadako & the Thousand Paper Cranes. 2014. (Puffin Modern Classics Ser.). (ENG.). 80p. (J). (gr. 3-7). 10.24 *(978-1-63245-199-6(9))* Lectorum Pubns., Inc.

ATOMIC ENERGY

see Nuclear Energy

ATOMIC NUCLEI

see Nuclear Physics

ATOMIC PILES

see Nuclear Reactors

ATOMIC POWER

see Nuclear Energy

ATOMIC SUBMARINES

see Nuclear Submarines

ATOMS

see also Electrons; Nuclear Physics

Aloian, Molly. Atoms & Molecules. 2008. (Why Chemistry Matters Ser.). (ENG., Illus.). 32p. (J). (gr. 3-7). pap. *(978-0-7787-4247-0(4))* Crabtree Publishing Co.

Bortz, Fred. The Neutron. 2009. (Library of Subatomic Particles Ser.). 64p. (gr. 6-6). 58.50 *(978-1-60853-880-5(X))* Rosen Publishing Group, Inc., The.

—The Proton. 2009. (Library of Subatomic Particles Ser.). 64p. (gr. 6-6). 58.50 *(978-1-60853-886-7(9))* Rosen Publishing Group, Inc., The.

—The Quark. 2004. (Library of Subatomic Particles Ser.). (Illus.). 64p. (gr. 7-12). lib. bdg. 31.95 *(978-0-8239-4533-7(2))* Rosen Publishing Group, Inc., The.

Campbell, Margaret Christine & Goldstein, Natalie. Discovering Atoms. 2011. (Scientist's Guide to Physics Ser.). (YA). (gr. 7-12). lib. bdg. 34.60 *(978-1-4488-4700-6(1))* Rosen Publishing Group, Inc., The.

Cregan, Elizabeth R. C. Investigating the Chemistry of Atoms, 1 vol. 2007. (Science Readers Ser.). (ENG.). 32p. (J). (gr. 4-4). pap. 8.99 *(978-0-7439-0569-5(5))* Shell Educational Publishing.

Exploring the Subatomic World. 2015. (Exploring the Subatomic World Ser.). (ENG.). 64p. (YA). (gr. 8-8). 273.68 *(978-1-5026-0370-8(5))* Cavendish Square Publishing.

Fox, Karen C. Older Than the Stars. Davis, Nancy, illus. 2011. (ENG.). 32p. (J). (gr. 2-5). pap. 7.95 *(978-1-57091-788-2(4))* Charlesbridge Publishing, Inc.

Gardner, Robert. Atoms & Molecules Experiments Using Ice, Salt, Marbles, & More: One Hour or Less Science Experiments. 2012. (Last-Minute Science Projects Ser.). 48p. (J). (gr. 5-18). 25.27 *(978-0-7660-3961-2(7))* Enslow Pubs., Inc.

Grady, Colin. Nuclear Energy. 2016. (Saving the Planet Through Green Energy Ser.). 24p. (J). pap. 9.35 *(978-0-7660-8288-5(1))* Enslow Pubs., Inc.

Hansen, Amy. Nuclear Energy: Amazing Atoms. 2010. (Powering Our World Ser.). (ENG.). 24p. (J). pap. 8.25 *(978-1-4358-9744-1(7)*, PowerKids Pr.) Rosen Publishing Group, Inc., The.

Hansen, Amy S. Nuclear Energy: Amazing Atoms. 2010. (Powering Our World Ser.). 24p. (J). (gr. 2-5). E-Book 42.50 *(978-1-4488-0201-2(6))*; (Illus.). lib. bdg. 22.60 *(978-1-4358-9328-3(X)*, PowerKids Pr.) Rosen Publishing Group, Inc., The.

Harrison Adams, Troon & Adams, Troon Harrison. Nuclear Energy: Power from the Atom. 2010. (ENG., Illus.). 32p. (J). pap. *(978-0-7787-2935-8(4))*; lib. bdg. *(978-0-7787-2921-1(4))* Crabtree Publishing Co.

Holt, Rinehart and Winston Staff. Holt Science & Technology Chapter 11: Physical Science: Introduction to Atoms. 5th ed. 2004. (Illus.). pap. 12.86 *(978-0-03-030403-3(2))* Holt McDougal.

Lepora, Nathan. Inside Atoms & Molecules. 2010. (Invisible Worlds Ser.). 48p. (gr. 4). 28.50 *(978-0-7614-4192-2(1))* Marshall Cavendish GBR. Dist: Marshall Cavendish Corp.

LernerClassroom Editors. First Step Nonfiction-States of Matter Teaching Guide. 2009. pap. 7.95 *(978-0-8225-6883-4(7))* Lerner Publishing Group.

Macfarlane, Katherine. The Father of the Atom: Democritus & the Nature of Matter. 2009. (Great Minds of Ancient Science & Math Ser.). (Illus.). 112p. (J). (gr. 4-7). lib. bdg. 33.27 *(978-0-7660-3410-5(0))* Enslow Pubs., Inc.

Manning, Phillip. Atoms, Molecules, & Compounds. 2007. (Essential Chemistry Ser.). (Illus.). 137p. (YA). (gr. 7-12). lib. bdg. 35.00 *(978-0-7910-9534-8(7))* Facts On File, Inc.

Maurer, Tracy Nelson. Atoms & Molecules. 2012. (ENG.). 24p. (gr. 4-5). pap. 8.95 *(978-1-61810-239-3(7))* Rourke Educational Media.

Monroe, Tilda. What Do You Know about Atoms & Molecules? 2010. (20 Questions: Physical Science Ser.). (ENG.). 24p. (J). pap. 8.25 *(978-1-4488-1223-3(2)*, PowerKids Pr.); (YA). (gr. 2-5). lib. bdg. 22.60 *(978-1-4488-0669-0(0))* Rosen Publishing Group, Inc., The.

Parker, Katie. Splitting the Atom. 2009. (Big Ideas in Science Ser.). (Illus.). 48p. (gr. 5-8). 31.36 *(978-0-7614-4399-5(1))* Marshall Cavendish Corp.

Saunders, Nigel. Exploring Atoms & Molecules. 2007. (Exploring Physical Science Ser.). (Illus.). 48p. (J). (gr. 4-7). lib. bdg. 26.50 *(978-1-4042-3750-6(X)*, Rosen Reference) Rosen Publishing Group, Inc., The.

Slade, Suzanne. Atoms, 1 vol., 1. 2014. (Ultimate Science: Physical Science Ser.). (ENG.). 24p. (gr. 3-6). 23.60 *(978-1-4777-6089-5(X)*, PowerKids Pr.) Rosen Publishing Group, Inc., The.

—Atoms & Chemical Reactions. (Library of Physical Science Ser.). 24p. (gr. 4-4). 2009. 42.50 *(978-1-60853-780-8(3)*, PowerKids Pr.) 2007. (ENG., Illus.). pap. 7.05 *(978-1-4042-2162-8(X)*, PowerKids Pr.) 2006. (Illus.). (YA). lib. bdg. 22.60 *(978-1-4042-3415-4(2))* Rosen Publishing Group, Inc., The.

—Looking at Atoms & Molecules. 2006. (Library of Physical Sciences). (Illus.). 24p. (J). (gr. 3-7). lib. bdg. 21.25 *(978-1-4042-3419-2(5)*, PowerKids Pr.) Rosen Publishing Group, Inc., The.

—Scientific Instruments: Looking at Atoms & Molecules. 2009. (Library of Physical Science Ser.). 24p. (gr. 4-4). 42.50 *(978-1-60853-786-0(2)*, PowerKids Pr.) Rosen Publishing Group, Inc., The.

—Scientific Instruments for Studying Atoms & Molecules. 2007. (Library of Physical Sciences). (ENG., Illus.). 24p. (gr. 4-8). pap. 7.05 *(978-1-4042-2166-6(2)*, PowerKids Pr.) Rosen Publishing Group, Inc., The.

—States of Matter. 24p. (gr. 4-4). 2009. (Library of Physical Science Ser.). 42.50 *(978-1-60853-789-1(7)*, PowerKids Pr.) 2007. (Library of Physical Sciences). (ENG., Illus.). pap. 7.05 *(978-1-4042-2163-5(8)*, PowerKids Pr.) 2006. (Library of Physical Science Ser.: Vol. 3). (Illus.). (YA). lib. bdg. 22.60 *(978-1-4042-3416-1(0))* Rosen Publishing Group, Inc., The.

—The Structure of Atoms. (Library of Physical Science Ser.). 24p. (gr. 4-4). 2009. 42.50 *(978-1-60853-795-2(1))* 2007. (ENG., Illus.). pap. 7.05 *(978-1-4042-2161-1(1))* Rosen Publishing Group, Inc., The. (PowerKids Pr.).

Trumbauer, Lisa. What Are Atoms. 2005. (Rookie Read-About Science Ser.). (ENG., Illus.). 32p. (J). (gr. 1-2). pap. 4.95 *(978-0-516-24665-9(8)*, Children's Pr.) Scholastic Library Publishing.

Walker, Denise. Materials. 2006. (Core Chemistry/Evans Brothers Ser.). (Illus.). 48p. (YA). (gr. 5-9). 34.25 *(978-1-58340-817-9(7))* Black Rabbit Bks.

Wells, Robert E. What's Smaller Than a Pygmy Shrew? 2012. (J). *(978-1-61913-158-3(7))* Weigl Pubs., Inc.

Wheeler-Toppen, Jodi. Ghosts & Atoms, 1 vol. Haus, Estudio, illus. 2011. (Monster Science Ser.). (ENG.). 32p. (gr. 3-4). pap. 8.10 *(978-1-4296-7329-7(X))*; pap. 47.70 *(978-1-4296-7330-3(3))* Capstone Press of Coughlan Cos. (Graphic Library).

Woodford, Chris & Clowes, Martin. Atoms & Molecules: Investigating the Building Blocks of Matter. 2012. (Scientific Pathways Ser.). (ENG., Illus.). 48p. (J). (gr. 5-8). lib. bdg. 27.95 *(978-1-4488-7196-4(4)*, Rosen Reference) Rosen Publishing Group, Inc., The.

ATTENDANCE, SCHOOL

see School Attendance

ATTENTION DEFICIT DISORDERS

see Attention-Deficit Hyperactivity Disorder

ATTENTION-DEFICIT HYPERACTIVITY DISORDER

Boehme, Gerry. Amphetamines. 2015. (Dangerous Drugs Ser.). (ENG.). 64p. (J). (gr. 6-6). lib. bdg. 34.21 *(978-1-5026-0560-3(0))* Cavendish Square Publishing.

Brinkerhoff, Shirley. Stuck on Fast Forward: Youth with Attention Deficit Hyper Activity Disorder. 2004. (Youth with Special Needs Ser.). (Illus.). 128p. (YA). 24.95 *(978-1-59084-728-2(8))* Mason Crest.

—Stuck on Fast Forward: Youth with Attention-Deficit/Hyperactivity Disorder. 2003. (Youth with Special Needs Ser.). (Illus.). 127p. (YA). (gr. 4-7). pap. 14.95 *(978-1-4222-0431-3(6))* Mason Crest.

Buffolano, Sandra. Coping with Tourette Syndrome: A Workbook for Kids with Tic Disorders. 2008. (Instant Help Ser.). (ENG.). 136p. (J). (gr. k-5). pap. 24.95 *(978-1-57224-673-7(1)*, Instant Help Books) New Harbinger Pubns.

Capaccio, George. ADD & ADHD. 2007. (Health Alert Ser.). (Illus.). 64p. (YA). (gr. 4-7). lib. bdg. 32.79 *(978-0-7614-2705-6(8))* Marshall Cavendish Corp.

Chara, Kathleen A. & Chara, Paul J. Sensory Smarts: A Book for Kids with ADHD or Autism Spectrum Disorders Struggling with Sensory Integration Problems. Berns, Joel M., illus. 2004. (ENG.). 80p. (J). pap. *(978-1-84310-783-5(X))* Kingsley, Jessica Pubs.

Chilman-Blair, Kim & Taddeo, John. Medikidz Explain ADHD. 2010. (Superheroes on a Medical Mission Ser.). 40p. (YA). (ENG.). pap. 11.75 *(978-1-4488-1833-4(8))*; (Illus.). (gr. 5-8). lib. bdg. 29.25 *(978-1-4358-9456-3(1))* Rosen Publishing Group, Inc., The. (Rosen Reference).

Doering Tourville, Amanda. My Friend Has ADHD, 1 vol. Sorra, Kristin, illus. 2010. (Friends with Disabilities Ser.). (ENG.). 24p. (gr. k-3). pap. 7.49 *(978-1-4048-6108-4(4))* Picture Window Bks.

—My Friend Has ADHD [Readers World]. Sorra, Kristin, illus. 2010. (Friends with Disabilities Ser.). 24p. pap. 6.00 *(978-1-4048-6701-7(5)*, Nonfiction Picture Bks.) Picture Window Bks.

Glasser, Judith M. & Kushner, Jill Menkes. Learning to Be Kind & Understand Differences: Empathy Skills for Kids with Ad/Hd. 2015. (Illus.). 96p. (J). *(978-1-4338-2043-4(9)*, Magination Pr.) American Psychological Assn.

Hoopmann, Kathy. All Dogs Have ADHD. 2008. (ENG., Illus.). 72p. 14.95 *(978-1-84310-651-7(5)*, 4468) Kingsley, Jessica Pubs. GBR. Dist: Macmillan Distribution Ltd.

Kershner, Tad. Living with ADHD, 1 vol. 2012. (Living with Health Challenges Set 1 Ser.). (ENG.). 112p. (J). (gr. 6-12). lib. bdg. 35.64 *(978-1-61783-122-5(0)*, Essential Library) ABDO Publishing Co.

Kraus, Jeanne. Cory's Stories: A Kid's Book about Living with ADHD. Martin, Whitney, illus. 2004. 32p. (J). 14.95 *(978-1-59147-148-6(6))*; pap. 9.95 *(978-1-59147-154-7(0))* American Psychological Assn. (Magination Pr.).

May, Suellen. Ritalin & Related Drugs. 2010. (Understanding Drugs Ser.). (Illus.). 120p. (YA). (gr. 9-12). 34.95 *(978-1-60413-550-3(6))* Facts On File, Inc.

Moe, Barbara A. Coping with Tourettes & Tics. rev. ed. 2005. (Coping Ser.). 192p. (J). (gr. 7-12). lib. bdg. 34.60 *(978-0-8239-4089-9(6))* Rosen Publishing Group, Inc., The.

Mooney, Carla. Teens & Adhd. 2017. (ENG.). 80p. (J). (gr. 5-12). ***(978-1-68282-120-6(X))*** ReferencePoint Pr., Inc.

Nadeau, Kathleen G. Learning to Plan & Be Organized: Enhancing Executive Function Skills in Kids with AD/HD. Beyl, Charles, illus. 2016. 120p. (J). pap. *(978-1-4338-2213-1(X)*, Magination Pr.) American Psychological Assn.

Nadeau, Kathleen G. & Dixon, Ellen B. Learning to Slow Down & Pay Attention: A Book for Kids about ADHD. Beyl, Charles, illus. 3rd ed. 2004. 96p. (J). 14.95 *(978-1-59147-149-3(4))*; pap. 12.95 *(978-1-59147-155-4(9))* American Psychological Assn. (Magination Pr.).

Peirce, Jeremy L. Attention-Deficit/Hyperactivity Disorder. Collins, Christine, ed. 2007. (Psychological Disorders Ser.). (Illus.). 118p. (YA). (gr. 7-12). lib. bdg. 37.50 *(978-0-7910-8541-7(4))* Facts On File, Inc.

Petersen, Christine. Does Everyone Have ADHD? A Teen's Guide to Diagnosis & Treatment. (ENG., Illus.). 144p. (YA). (gr. 9-13). 2007. pap. 17.95 *(978-0-531-17975-8(3))* 2006. 30.50 *(978-0-531-16794-6(1)*, Watts, Franklin) Scholastic Library Publishing.

Pomere, Jonas. Frequently Asked Questions about ADD & ADHD. (FAQ: Teen Life Ser.). 64p. 2009. (gr. 5-6). 58.50 *(978-1-61512-561-6(2))* 2006. (Illus.). (YA). (gr. 7-12). lib. bdg. 31.95 *(978-1-4042-1970-0(6))* Rosen Publishing Group, Inc., The.

Poole, H. W. Attention Deficit Hyperactivity Disorder, Vol. 13. Walters, Anne S., ed. 2015. (Mental Illnesses & Disorders: Awareness & Understanding Ser.). (Illus.). 48p. (J). (gr. 5). 20.95 *(978-1-4222-3366-5(9))* Mason Crest.

Quinn, Patricia O. Attention, Girls! A Guide to Learn All about Your AD/HD. Pearce, Carl, illus. 2009. 112p. (J). (gr. 4-7). 16.95 *(978-1-4338-0447-2(6))*; pap. 12.95 *(978-1-4338-0448-9(4))* American Psychological Assn. (Magination Pr.).

Quinn, Patricia O. & Stern, Judith M. Putting on the Brakes: Understanding & Taking Control of Your ADD or ADHD. Lee, Joe, illus. 2nd ed. 2008. 80p. (J). (gr. 3-7). pap. 12.95 *(978-1-4338-0387-1(9))*; 16.95 *(978-1-4338-0386-4(0))* American Psychological Assn. (Magination Pr.).

—Putting on the Brakes: Understanding & Taking Control of Your ADD or ADHD. 3rd rev. ed. 2012. (Illus.). 112p. (J). 16.95 *(978-1-4338-1135-7(9))*; pap. 12.95 *(978-1-4338-1134-0(0))* American Psychological Assn. (Magination Pr.).

—Putting on the Brakes Activity Book for Kids with ADD or ADHD. Lee, Joe, illus. 2nd ed. 2009. 96p. (J). (gr. 3-8). pap. 14.95 *(978-1-4338-0441-0(7)*, Magination Pr.) American Psychological Assn.

Raum, Elizabeth. I Know Someone with ADHD, 1 vol. 2011. (Understanding Health Issues Ser.). (ENG.). 32p. (gr. 1-3). 27.32 *(978-1-4329-4553-4(X)*, Heinemann First Library) Heinemann-Raintree.

Robbins, Lynette. How to Deal with ADHD. 24p. (J). 2010. (Illus.). 49.50 *(978-1-4358-3417-0(8)*, 1300428, PowerKids Pr.) 2009. (ENG.). pap. 8.25 *(978-1-4358-3416-3(X)*, PowerKids Pr.) 2009. (Illus.). (gr. 2-5). lib. bdg. 22.60 *(978-1-4042-8140-0(1))* Rosen Publishing Group, Inc., The.

Shapiro, Lawrence E. The ADHD Workbook for Kids: Helping Children Gain Self-Confidence, Social Skills, & Self-Control. 2010. (Instant Help Ser.). (ENG.). 184p. (J). (gr. k-5). pap. 17.95 *(978-1-57224-766-6(5)*, Instant Help Books) New Harbinger Pubns.

Sheen, Barbara. ADHD. 2009. (Diseases & Disorders Ser.). (Illus.). 128p. (YA). (gr. 7-12). 34.95 *(978-1-4205-0142-1(9))* Cengage Gale.

Silverstein, Alvin, et al. The ADHD Update: Understanding Attention-Deficit/Hyperactivity Disorder. 2008. (Disease Update Ser.). (Illus.). 112p. (J). (gr. 3-7). lib. bdg. 33.27 *(978-0-7660-2800-5(3))* Enslow Pubs., Inc.

Silverstein, Virginia. Handy Health Guide to ADHD. 2013. (Handy Health Guides). 48p. (J). (gr. 5-12). pap. 8.95 *(978-1-4644-0483-2(6))* Enslow Pubs., Inc.

Silverstein, Virginia B. & Nunn, Laura Silverstein. Handy Health Guide to ADHD. 2013. (Handy Health Guides). 48p. (J). (gr. 5-18). 25.27 *(978-0-7660-4270-4(7))* Enslow Pubs., Inc.

Smith, Paula. Attention-Deficit & Other Behavior Disorders. 2013. 48p. (J). *(978-0-7787-0833-9(0))*; (Illus.). pap. *(978-0-7787-0860-5(8))* Crabtree Publishing Co.

Squire, Ann O. ADHD. 2016. (True Book(tm), A — Health Ser.). (ENG., Illus.). 48p. (J). lib. bdg. 31.00 *(978-0-531-22842-5(8)*, Children's Pr.) Scholastic Library Publishing.

Stewart, Sheila. Speed Racer: Kids with Attention-Deficit/Hyperactivity Disorder. 2009. (Kids with Special Needs Ser.). 48p. (YA). (gr. 5-18). pap. 7.95 *(978-1-4222-1924-9(0))* Mason Crest.

Stewart, Sheila & Flath, Camden. Speed Racer: Kids with Attention-Deficit/Hyperactivity Disorder. 2010. (Kids with Special Needs Ser.). 48p. (YA). (gr. 5-18). lib. bdg. 19.95 *(978-1-4222-1721-4(3))* Mason Crest.

Stumpf, Tobias & Stumpf, Dawn Schaefer. Journal of an ADHD Kid: The Good, the Bad, & the Useful. 2014. (ENG., Illus.). 136p. (J). pap. 16.95 *(978-1-60613-250-0(4))* Woodbine Hse.

Tournemille, Harry. Attention Deficit Hyperactivity Disorder. 2013. (ENG., Illus.). 48p. (J). *(978-0-7787-0069-2(0))* Crabtree Publishing Co.

Tourneville, Harry. Attention-Deficit Hyperactivity Disorder. 2013. (ENG., Illus.). 48p. (J). pap. *(978-0-7787-0086-9(0))* Crabtree Publishing Co.

Tourville, Amanda Doering. My Friend Has ADHD, 1 vol. Sorra, Kristin, illus. 2010. (Friends with Disabilities Ser.). (ENG.). 24p. (gr. k-3). lib. bdg. 25.99 *(978-1-4048-5749-0(4))* Picture Window Bks.

Tourville, Amanda Doering & Sorra, Kristin. Mi Amigo Tiene ADHD. Translations.com Staff, tr. from ENG. Sorra, Kristin, illus. 2012. (Amigos con Discapacidades/Friends with Disabilities Ser.).Tr. of My Friend Has ADHD. (SPA, MUL & ENG., Illus.). 24p. (gr. k-3). lib. bdg. 25.99 *(978-1-4048-7311-7(2))* Picture Window Bks.

Vescia, Monique, et al. What You Can Do about ADHD. 2015. (Contemporary Diseases & Disorders Ser.). (ENG., Illus.). 128p. (J). (gr. 7-7). lib. bdg. 37.27 *(978-0-7660-7028-8(X)*, 1392149) Enslow Pubs., Inc.

Vincent, Annick & Guerard, Mathieu. My Brain Needs Glasses: Living with Hyperactivity. 2004. (Psychotherapy Collection). (Illus.). 43p. (J). *(978-2-922762-51-8(3)*, Spotlight Poets) Academie Impact.

Walker, Beth. Girls' Guide to Ad/Hd. 2004. (Illus.). 174p. (J). pap. 19.95 *(978-1-890627-56-0(9))* Woodbine Hse.

Yarney, Susan. Can I Tell You about ADHD? A Guide for Friends, Family & Professionals. Martin, Chris, illus. 2013. (Can I Tell You About... ? Ser.). (ENG.). 64p. pap. 13.95 *(978-1-84905-359-4(6)*, 5830) Kingsley, Jessica Pubs. GBR. Dist: Macmillan Distribution Ltd.

ATTENTION-DEFICIT HYPERACTIVITY DISORDER—FICTION

Asher, Diana Harmon. Sidetracked. 2017. (ENG.). 240p. (J). (gr. 3-7). 16.99 ***(978-1-4197-2601-9(3)***, Amulet Bks.) Abrams, Inc.

Beyer, Pamela J. & Bilbrey, Hilary. Little Jake Learns to Stop: A Heartwarming Tale about Determination & Succeeding with Attention Difficulties. Armstrong, Michelle Hartz, illus. 2006. (J). per. 9.99 *(978-0-9787074-0-8(0))* Inspired By Family.

Caffrey, Jaye Andras. First Star I See. Adamson, Lynne, illus. 2nd ed. 2010. (ENG.). 164p. (J). (gr. 2-7). pap. 12.95 *(978-1-936290-01-7(4))* Central Recovery Pr.

Cheaney, J. B. & Cheaney, Janie. The Middle of Somewhere. 2008. (ENG.). 224p. (J). (gr. 3-7). 7.99 *(978-0-440-42165-8(9)*, Yearling) Random Hse. Children's Bks.

Corman, Clifford L. & Trevino, Esther. Eukee the Jumpy Jumpy Elephant. DiMatteo, Richard A., illus. (J). 2009. (ENG.). 26p. (gr. -1-1). pap. 10.95 *(978-1-886941-75-5(0))* 2003. 24p. (gr. 1-4). 15.00 *(978-0-9621629-8-5(1))* Specialty Pr., Inc.

Crawford, Teresa. I'm Not Stupid! I'm ADHD! 2004. 23p. pap. 24.95 *(978-1-4137-3249-8(6))* PublishAmerica, Inc.

Fischer, Debbie Reed. This Is Not the Abby Show. 2016. (ENG.). 320p. (J). (gr. 4-7). 16.99 *(978-0-553-53634-8(6)*, Delacorte Bks. for Young Readers) Random Hse. Children's Bks.

French, Jennifer. Fidgets. 2007. 132p. pap. 9.95 *(978-1-59663-531-9(2)*, Castle Keep Pr.) Rock, James A. & Co. Pubs.

Gantos, Jack. Joey Pigza Loses Control. braille ed. 2003. (Joey Pigza Ser.: Bk. 2). (J). (gr. 2). spiral bd. *(978-0-616-15268-3(X))* Canadian National Institute for the Blind/Institut National Canadien pour les Aveugles.

—Joey Pigza Loses Control. unabr. ed. 2004. (Joey Pigza Ser.: Bk. 2). 195p. (J). (gr. 5-9). pap. 36.00 incl. audio *(978-0-8072-8726-2(1)*, LyA 248 SP, Listening Library) Random Hse. Audio Publishing Group.

—Joey Pigza Swallowed the Key. 2009. 8.30 *(978-0-7848-3764-1(3))*; 8.32 *(978-0-7848-1771-1(5))* Marco Bk. Co. (Everbind).

—Joey Pigza Swallowed the Key. unabr. ed. 2004. (Joey Pigza Ser.: Bk. 1). 154p. (J). (gr. 5-9). pap. 29.00 incl. audio *(978-0-8072-8166-6(2)*, YA120SP, Listening Library) Random Hse. Audio Publishing Group.

—Joey Pigza Swallowed the Key. 2007. (Joey Pigza Ser.: 1). (J). 1.25 *(978-1-4193-6006-0(X))* Recorded Bks., Inc.

—Joey Pigza Swallowed the Key. 2014. (Joey Pigza Ser.: 1). (ENG.). 176p. (J). (gr. 5-9). pap. 7.99 *(978-1-250-06168-3(7)*, 9781250061683) Square Fish.

—Joey Pigza Swallowed the Key. 2014. (Joey Pigza Ser.: 1). (J). lib. bdg. 18.40 *(978-0-606-23019-3(X)*, Turtleback) Turtleback Bks.

—The Key That Swallowed Joey Pigza. 2014. (Joey Pigza Ser.: 5). (ENG.). 160p. (J). (gr. 5-9). 16.99 *(978-0-374-30083-8(6)*, 9780374300838, Farrar, Straus & Giroux (BYR)) Farrar, Straus & Giroux.

—What Would Joey Do? 2004. (Joey Pigza Ser.). 229p. (J). (gr. 5-9). 13.65 *(978-0-7569-2597-0(5))* Perfection Learning Corp.

—What Would Joey Do? 2004. (Joey Pigza Ser.: Bk. 3). 240p. (J). (gr. 5-9). pap. 36.00 incl. audio *(978-1-4000-9020-4(2)*, Listening Library) Random Hse. Audio Publishing Group.

Gehret, Jeanne. Eagle Eyes: A Child's Guide to Paying Attention. LaDuca, Michael, illus. 4th ed. 2009. (Coping Ser.). (ENG.). 32p. (J). (gr. 1-3). 17.95 *(978-0-9821982-1-6(3))* Verbal Images Pr.

Glenn, Judith. Manassas, Please Slow Down. Colson, A. W. & Renda, Joseph, illus. 2010. 60p. pap. 21.99 *(978-1-4490-6682-6(8))* AuthorHouse.

Goldstein, Sam & Desisto, Allie. Some Kids Just Can't Sit Still! Desisto, Allie, illus. 2009. (ENG., Illus.). 32p. (J). (gr. 2-4). pap. 15.95 *(978-1-886941-73-1(4))* Specialty Pr., Inc.

Grindley, Sally. Hurricane Wills. 2012. (ENG.). 256p. (J). (gr. -1-k). pap. 6.95 *(978-1-61608-732-6(3)*, 608732, Sky Pony Pr.) Skyhorse Publishing Co., Inc.

Guest, Jacqueline. Racing Fear, 1 vol. 2004. (Lorimer SideStreets Ser.). (ENG.). 160p. (YA). (gr. 9-12). 9.95 *(978-1-55028-838-4(5)*, 9781550288384); 16.95 *(978-1-55028-839-1(3)*, 9781550288391) Lorimer, James & Co., Ltd., Pubs. CAN. Dist: Casemate Pubs. & Bk. Distributors, LLC.

Korman, Susan. Bad Deal. 2011. (Surviving Southside Ser.). (ENG.). 104p. (YA). (gr. 6-12). lib. bdg. 27.93 *(978-0-7613-6152-7(9))* Lerner Publishing Group.

Korman, Susan J. Bad Deal. 2011. (Surviving Southside Ser.). (ENG.). 104p. (YA). (gr. 6-12). pap. 7.95 *(978-0-7613-6166-4(9))* Lerner Publishing Group.

Moss, Deborah. Shelley, the Hyperactive Turtle. Schwartz, Carol, illus. 2nd ed. 2006. (ENG.). 20p. (J). (gr. -1-2). pap. *(978-1-890627-75-1(5))* Woodbine Hse.

Mostoller, Marcia. Poor William Dill. 2011. 28p. pap. 24.95 *(978-1-4626-0835-5(3))* America Star Bks.

Parker Ma Csac, Nacole A. A Day in the Life of Ruby. 2011. 28p. pap. 16.25 *(978-1-4634-1152-7(9))* AuthorHouse.

Penn, Audrey. A. D. D. Not B. A. D. Wyrick, Monica, illus. 2003. (New Child & Family Press Titles Ser.). 32p. pap. 9.95 *(978-0-87868-849-4(8)*, 8498, Child & Family Pr.) Child Welfare League of America, Inc.

—A. D. D. Not B. A. D. Wyrick, Monica Dunsky, illus. 2006. (ENG.). 32p. (J). (gr. -1-3). 7.99 *(978-0-9749303-7-4(7))* Tanglewood Pr.

Pollack, Pam & Belviso, Meg. I Can't Sit Still! Living with ADHD. Fabrega, Marta, illus. 2009. (Live & Learn Ser.). (ENG.). 36p. (J). (gr. -1-2). pap. 6.99 *(978-0-7641-4419-6(7))* Barron's Educational Series, Inc.

—¡No Puedo Estar Quieto! Mi Vida con ADHD. Fabrega, Marta, illus. 2009. (Viva y Aprende Ser.). (SPA.). 36p. (J). (gr. -1-2). pap. 6.99 *(978-0-7641-4420-2(0))* Barron's Educational Series, Inc.

Roberts, Barbara. The Adventures of Phoebe Flower: Stories of a Girl with ADHD. 2010. (ENG.). 176p. (J). (gr. 2-6). pap. 14.95 *(978-0-9714609-6-6(5))* Advantage Bks., LLC.

Rue, Nancy N. Motorcycles, Sushi & One Strange Book, 1 vol. 2010. (Real Life Ser.). (ENG.). 224p. (YA). (gr. 8-11). pap. 9.99 *(978-0-310-71484-2(2))* Zondervan.

Steinhöfel, Andreas & Wright, Chantal. The Spaghetti Detectives. 2011. (ENG.). 176p. (J). (gr. 3-7). 16.99 *(978-0-545-28975-7(0)*, Chicken Hse., The) Scholastic, Inc.

Ulch, Virginia. I Love You Anyway. 2007. 32p. per. 18.95 *(978-1-59858-433-2(2))* Dog Ear Publishing, LLC.

ATTILA, -453

Hinds, Kathryn. Huns. 2009. (Barbarians! Ser.). 80p. (gr. 6). 35.64 *(978-0-7614-4066-6(6))* Marshall Cavendish GBR. Dist: Marshall Cavendish Corp.

Price, Sean Stewart & Price, Sean. Attila the Hun: Leader of the Barbarian Hordes. 2009. (Wicked History Ser.). (ENG.). 128p. (J). (gr. 6-12). pap. 5.95 *(978-0-531-20737-6(4))*; (Illus.). 31.00 *(978-0-531-21801-3(5))* Scholastic Library Publishing. (Watts, Franklin).

Rice, Earle. The Life & Times of Attila the Hun. 2009. (Biography from Ancient Civilizations Ser.). 48p. (J). (gr. 4-8). 29.95 *(978-1-58415-741-0(0))* Mitchell Lane Pubs., Inc.

ATTITUDE (PSYCHOLOGY)

see also Public Opinion

Berry, Joy. Help Me Be Good about Whining. 2009. (ENG.). 40p. (J). (gr. k-2). pap. 7.95 *(978-1-60577-115-1(5))* Berry, Joy Enterprises.

—Help Me Be Good Whining. Bartholomew, illus. 2010. (Help Me Be Good Ser.). (ENG.). 32p. (J). (gr. -1-2). pap. 4.99 *(978-1-60577-134-2(1))* Berry, Joy Enterprises.

Berry, Joy Wilt. A Book about Being Bossy. 2005. (Illus.). (J). *(978-0-7172-8594-5(4))* Scholastic, Inc.

—A Book about Complaining. 2005. (Illus.). (J). *(978-0-7172-8595-2(2))* Scholastic, Inc.

—A Book about Whining. 2005. (Illus.). (J). *(978-0-7172-7898-5(0))* Scholastic, Inc.

Chuck, Stump & Jim, Strawn. The Sad Mad Glad Book: The Anatomy of Your Attitude. 2007. 113p. (J). pap. 14.50 *(978-0-9799315-1-2(7)*, Four Dolphins Pr.) Four Dolphins Pr., LLC.

Free Spirit Publishing Staff & Stein, Deborah Jiang. Kids' Attitude. 2009. (In a Jar(r) Ser.). (ENG.). (J). (gr. 3). 9.99 *(978-1-57542-921-2(7))* Free Spirit Publishing, Inc.

Good Attitudes Make You SHine. 2007. (Illus.). 48p. (J). pap. 15.00 *(978-0-9799440-0-0(7))* Artists On Video, LLC / (d/b/a) MN Productions.

Meiners, Cheri J. Be Positive! Allen, Elizabeth, illus. 2013. (Being the Best Me Ser.). (ENG.). 40p. (J). (gr. -1-3). 14.99 *(978-1-57542-452-1(5))*; pap. 11.99 *(978-1-57542-441-5(X))* Free Spirit Publishing, Inc.

Raatma, Lucia. Trustworthiness. 2009. (21st Century Junior Library: Character Education Ser.). (ENG.). 24p. (gr. 2-5). lib. bdg. 25.64 *(978-1-60279-319-4(0)*, 200215) Cherry Lake Publishing.

Rando, Caterina. You Can Think Differently. 2017. (Be Your Best Self Ser.). 158p. (J). (gr. 12-14). 44.60 ***(978-1-4994-6666-9(8)***, Rosen Young Adult) Rosen Publishing Group, Inc., The.

Wilbur, Regina, ed. Keys to Success: Getting Control of Mr. & Mrs Attitude & Temper (A. T.) Teacher's Guide/Students Assignments Grades 6-12. 2003. (ENG.). 48p. (YA). tchr. ed., spiral bd. 8.95 *(978-0-9710925-1-8(6)*, 0-9710925-1-6) EniCare Consulting, Inc.

The Winners. 2005. (YA). 14.95 *(978-0-9661256-4-1(9))* Youth Communication - New York Center.

ATTORNEYS

see Lawyers

ATTUCKS, CRISPUS, -1770

Beier, Anne. Crispus Attucks: Hero of the Boston Massacre. 2004. (Famous People in American History Ser.). (Illus.). 32p. (gr. 4-8). (ENG.). pap. 10.00 *(978-0-8239-4178-0(7))*; (SPA & ENG., (J). lib. bdg. 22.50 *(978-0-8239-4154-4(X))* Rosen Publishing Group, Inc., The.

—Crispus Attucks: Hero of the Boston Massacre / Héroe de la masacre de Boston. 2009. (Famous People in American History/Grandes personajes en la historia de los Estados Unidos Ser.). (ENG & SPA.). 32p. (gr. 2-3). 47.90 *(978-1-61512-541-8(8)*, Editorial Buenas Letras) Rosen Publishing Group, Inc., The.

—Crispus Attucks: Heroe de la Masacre de Boston. 2004. (Grandes Personajes en la Historia de los Estados Unidos (Famous People in American History) Ser.). (SPA & ENG., Illus.). 32p. (gr. 4-8). lib. bdg. 21.25 *(978-0-8239-4130-8(2)*, Editorial Buenas Letras) Rosen Publishing Group, Inc., The.

—Crispus Attucks: Heroe de la masacre de Boston. 2004. (Grandes personajes en la historia de los Estados Unidos Ser.). (SPA.). 32p. (gr. 3-6). pap. 10.00 *(978-0-8239-4224-4(4)*, Rosen Classroom) Rosen Publishing Group, Inc., The.

—Crispus Attucks: Héroe de la masacre de Boston (Crispus Attucks: Hero of the Boston Massacre) 2009. (Grandes personajes en la historia de los Estados Unidos (Famous People in American History) Ser.). (SPA.). 32p. (gr. 2-3). 47.90 *(978-1-61512-793-1(3)*, Editorial Buenas Letras) Rosen Publishing Group, Inc., The.

Mattern, Joanne. The Cost of Freedom: Crispus Attucks & the Boston Massacre. (Great Moments in American History Ser.). 32p. 2009. (gr. 3-3). 47.90 *(978-1-61513-153-2(1))* 2004. (Illus.). (J). (gr. 4-7). lib. bdg. 22.50 *(978-0-8239-4341-8(0))* Rosen Publishing Group, Inc., The.

McLeese, Don. Crispus Attucks. 2005. (Heroes of the American Revolution Ser.). (Illus.). 32p. (gr. 2-5). 19.95 *(978-1-59515-218-3(0))* Rourke Educational Media.

Rausch, Monica. Crispus Attucks. 2007. (Grandes personajes (Spanish- Great Americans) Ser.). 24p. (gr. 1-4). (SPA.). pap. 8.15 *(978-0-8368-7987-2(2))*; (Illus.). lib. bdg. 22.00 *(978-0-8368-7681-9(4))* Stevens, Gareth Publishing LLLP. (Weekly Reader Leveled Readers).

Rausch, Monica L. Crispus Attucks. 2007. (Grandes personajes (Great Americans) Ser.). (SPA., Illus.). 24p. (gr. 1-4). lib. bdg. 22.00 *(978-0-8368-7980-3(5)*, Weekly Reader Leveled Readers) Stevens, Gareth Publishing LLLP.

Siddons, Brian. Crispus Attucks & African American Patriots of the American Revolution. 2015. (Spotlight on American History Ser.). (ENG., Illus.). 24p. (J). (gr. 4-6). pap. 10.00 *(978-1-4994-1739-5(X)*, PowerKids Pr.) Rosen Publishing Group, Inc., The.

Taylor, Charlotte. Crispus Attucks: A Hero of the American Revolution. 2016. (Exceptional African Americans Ser.). (ENG., Illus.). 24p. (J). (gr. 3-3). 22.60 *(978-0-7660-7187-2(1))*; pap. 9.35 *(978-0-7660-7185-8(5))* Enslow Pubs., Inc.

Weiss, Lynne. Crispus Attucks & the Boston Massacre. 2013. (Jr. Graphic African American History Ser.). 24p. (J). (gr. 3-6). pap. 63.60 *(978-1-4777-1456-0(1))*; (ENG., Illus.). pap. 10.60 *(978-1-4777-1455-3(3))*; (ENG., Illus.). lib. bdg. 25.25 *(978-1-4777-1315-0(8))* Rosen Publishing Group, Inc., The. (PowerKids Pr.).

AUCTIONS

Gilbert, Sara. The Story of EBay. 2011. (Built for Success Ser.). (Illus.). 46p. (J). (gr. 5-9). 23.95 *(978-1-60818-062-2(X))* Creative Co., The.

Gilbert, Sara & MacMillian Education Australian Primary Literacy Education Staff. The Story of eBay. 2012. (Built for Success Ser.). (ENG.). 48p. (J). (gr. 4-7). pap. 12.00 *(978-0-89812-660-0(6)*, Creative Paperbacks) Creative Co., The.

Viegas, Jennifer. Pierre Omidyar: The Founder of EBay. 2009. (Internet Career Biographies Ser.). 112p. (gr. 8-8). 63.90 *(978-1-61513-596-7(0))* Rosen Publishing Group, Inc., The.

Woog, Adam. Pierre M. Omidyar: Creator of Ebay. 2007. (Innovators Ser.). (ENG., Illus.). 64p. (J). (gr. 4-8). lib. bdg. 29.95 *(978-0-7377-3864-3(2)*, LML02109-234925, Kidhaven) Cengage Gale.

AUCTIONS—FICTION

Mullarkey, Lisa. The Artsy Fartsy Auction: Book 8, 1 vol. Harris, Phyllis, illus. 2012. (Katharine the Almost Great Ser.). (ENG.). 80p. (J). (gr. 1-4). 27.07 *(978-1-61641-829-8(X))* Magic Wagon.

AUDIO-VISUAL EDUCATION

see also Motion Pictures In Education

Firth, Melissa. Behind the Scenes at a Music Video. 2014. (VIP Tours Ser.). 48p. (J). (gr. 4-6). lib. bdg. 31.36 *(978-1-62713-028-8(4))* Cavendish Square Publishing.

Furgang, Adam. Searching Online for Image, Audio, & Video Files. 2009. (Digital & Information Literacy Ser.). (Illus.). 48p. (YA). (gr. 5-8). lib. bdg. 29.25 *(978-1-4358-5318-8(0))* Rosen Publishing Group, Inc., The.

Potts, Sue. Get Fit with Video Workouts. 2014. (ENG., Illus.). 48p. (J). (gr. 4-8). 29.95 *(978-1-61228-550-4(3))* Mitchell Lane Pubs., Inc.

Steck-Vaughn Staff. Interpreting Visual Information. 2004. pap. 5.00 *(978-0-7398-9842-0(6))* Harcourt Schl. Pubs.

—Interpreting Visual Information 10-Pack. 2004. pap. 44.95 *(978-0-7398-9923-6(6))* Harcourt Schl. Pubs.

Wick, Walter. Optical Tricks. Wick, Walter, illus. 10th anniv. ed. 2008. (ENG., Illus.). 48p. (J). (gr. -1-3). 14.99 *(978-0-439-85520-4(9)*, Cartwheel Bks.) Scholastic, Inc.

AUDUBON, JOHN JAMES, 1785-1851

Burleigh, Robert. Into the Woods: John James Audubon Lives His Dream. Minor, Wendell, illus. 2011. (ENG.). 40p. (J). (gr. 1-4). pap. 19.99 *(978-1-4424-5337-1(0)*, Atheneum Bks. for Young Readers) Simon & Schuster Children's Publishing.

Davies, Jacqueline. The Boy Who Drew Birds: A Story of John James Audubon. Sweet, Melissa, illus. 2004. (ENG.). 32p. (J). (gr. -1-3). tchr. ed. 16.99 *(978-0-618-24343-3(7))* Houghton Mifflin Harcourt Publishing Co.

Mason, Miriam E. John Audubon: Young Naturalist. Morrison, Cathy, illus. 2nd rev. ed. 2006. (Young Patriots Ser.: 12). (ENG.). 120p. (J). (gr. 4-7). 15.95 *(978-1-882859-51-1(0))*; pap. 9.95 *(978-1-882859-52-8(9))* Patria Pr., Inc.

Nayer, Judy. John James Audubon. 2011. (Early Connections Ser.). (J). *(978-1-61672-554-9(0))* Benchmark Education Co.

Sherman, Patrice & Wood, Elaine. John James Audubon. 2011. (Conservation Heroes Ser.). (Illus.). 152p. (YA). (gr. 6-12). 35.00 *(978-1-60413-953-2(6)*, Chelsea Hse.) Facts On File, Inc.

AUDUBON, JOHN JAMES, 1785-1851—FICTION

Cole, Henry. A Nest for Celeste: A Story about Art, Inspiration, & the Meaning of Home. Cole, Henry, illus. (Nest for Celeste Ser.: 1). (ENG., Illus.). 352p. (J). (gr. 3-7). 2012. pap. 6.99 *(978-0-06-170412-3(1))* 2010. 16.99 *(978-0-06-170410-9(5))* HarperCollins Pubs. (Tegen, Katherine Bks).

AUGUSTINE, SAINT, BISHOP OF HIPPO, 354-430

Carr, Simonetta. Augustine of Hippo. Lowe, Wes, illus. 2009. (ENG.). 62p. (J). 18.00 *(978-1-60178-073-7(7))* Reformation Heritage Bks.

Magedanz, Stacy. St. Augustine's Confessions. 2004. (ENG.). 96p. pap. 7.49 *(978-0-7645-4480-4(2))* Houghton Mifflin Harcourt Publishing Co.

AUGUSTUS, EMPEROR OF ROME, 63 B.C.-14 A.D.

Baum, Margaux & Forsyth, Fiona. Augustus. 2016. (Leaders of the Ancient World Ser.). 00112p. (J). (gr. 6-6). 37.10 *(978-1-5081-7242-0(0))* Rosen Publishing Group, Inc., The.

Forsyth, Fiona. Augustus: The First Emperor. (Ancient Leaders Ser.). 112p. (gr. 5-8). 2009. 66.50 *(978-1-61511-419-1(X))* 2003. (Illus.). (YA). lib. bdg. 34.60 *(978-0-8239-3588-8(4))* Rosen Publishing Group, Inc., The. (Rosen Reference).

Whiting, Jim. The Life & Times of Augustus Caesar. 2005. (Biography from Ancient Civilizations Ser.). (Illus.). 48p. (J). (gr. -1-7). lib. bdg. 29.95 *(978-1-58415-336-8(9))* Mitchell Lane Pubs., Inc.

AUSTEN, JANE, 1775-1817

Bloom, Harold, ed. Jane Austen, New Edition. 2nd rev. ed. 2009. (Bloom's Modern Critical Views Ser.). 324p. (C). (gr. 9-18). 45.00 *(978-1-60413-397-4(X)*, Chelsea Hse.) Facts On File, Inc.

Johnson, Claudia. Issues of Class in Jane Austen's Pride & Prejudice. 2008. (Social Issues in Literature Ser.). (ENG., Illus.). 178p. (YA). (gr. 10-12). 28.45 *(978-0-7377-4259-6(3)*, LML02109-243174, Greenhaven Pr., Inc.) Cengage Gale.

Johnson, Claudia, ed. Issues of Class in Jane Austen's Pride & Prejudice. 2008. (Social Issues in Literature Ser.). (ENG., Illus.). 224p. (gr. 10-12). 46.40 *(978-0-7377-4258-9(5)*, LML02109-243170, Greenhaven Pr., Inc.) Cengage Gale.

Jones, Darryl. Jane Austen, 1 vol. 2004. (Critical Issues Ser.). (ENG., Illus.). x, 252p. 110.00 *(978-0-333-72743-0(6)*, 9780333727430) Palgrave Macmillan.

Kirk, Connie Ann. A Student's Guide to Jane Austen. (Lit Crit Guides). (Illus.). 2016. 176p. (J). (gr. 6-6). 39.93 *(978-0-7660-7911-3(2))* 2007. 160p. (YA). (gr. 8-12). lib. bdg. 29.27 *(978-0-7660-2439-7(3))* Enslow Pubs., Inc.

Lacey, Saskia. The Prehistoric Masters of Literature: Discover Literary History with a Prehistoric Twist! 2016. (Jurassic Classics Ser.). (ENG., Illus.). 40p. (J). (gr. 2-6). 14.95 *(978-1-63322-098-0(2))* Quarto Publishing Group USA.

Locke, Juliane. England's Jane: the Story of Jane Austen. 2006. (World Writers Ser.). (Illus.). 144p. (gr. 6-12). lib. bdg. 28.95 *(978-1-931798-82-2(6))* Reynolds, Morgan Inc.

Ruth, Amy. Jane Austen. 2005. (Biography Ser.). (Illus.). 112p. (J). (gr. 6-12). lib. bdg. 27.93 *(978-0-8225-4992-5(1))* Lerner Publishing Group.

Saddleback Educational Publishing Staff, ed. Pride & Prejudice. 2011. (Timeless Classics Ser.). (ENG.). 48p. (YA). (gr. 9-12). pupil's gde. ed. 19.95 incl. cd-rom *(978-1-61651-146-3(X))* Saddleback Educational Publishing, Inc.

Sanderson, Caroline. Jane Austen: Novelist. 2016. (History Makers Ser.). 128p. (YA). lib. bdg. 45.64 *(978-1-5026-2445-1(1))* Cavendish Square Publishing.

Thomas, Ruth. Emma: Insight Text Guide (Large Print 16pt) 2013. 86p. pap. *(978-1-4596-5995-7(3))* ReadHowYouWant.com, Ltd.

Wagner, Heather Lehr. Jane Austen. 2003. (Who Wrote That? Ser.). (Illus.). 112p. (gr. 6-12). 35.00 *(978-0-7910-7623-1(7)*, Chelsea Hse.) Facts On File, Inc.

AUSTIN, STEPHEN FULLER, 1793-1836

Isecke, Harriet. Stephen F. Austin: The Father of Texas, 1 vol. 2012. (Primary Source Readers Ser.). (ENG.). 32p. (J). (gr. 3-3). pap. 8.99 *(978-1-4333-5045-0(9))* Teacher Created Materials, Inc.

Peppas, Lynn. Why Stephen F. Austin Matters to Texas. 2014. (Illus.). 32p. (J). lib. bdg. 26.25 *(978-1-4777-0914-6(2))* Rosen Publishing Group, Inc., The.

Roberts, Russell. The Life & Times of Stephen F. Austin. 2007. (Profiles in American History Ser.). (Illus.). 48p. (J). (gr. 4-7). lib. bdg. 29.95 *(978-1-58415-531-7(0))* Mitchell Lane Pubs., Inc.

Wade, Mary Dodson. Stephen F. Austin: Keeping Promises. 2012. (Texas Heroes for Young Readers Ser.). (ENG.). 24p. (J). (gr. k-2). 16.95 *(978-1-933979-11-3(9))* Bright Sky Pr.

Wade, Mary Dodson & Finney, Pat. Stephen F. Austin: The Son Becomes Father of Texas. Finney, Pat, illus. 2009. (ENG., Illus.). 64p. (J). (gr. 4-7). 16.95 *(978-1-933979-45-8(3)*, b2874897-f07d-47b8-83fa-a611da26c6bb) Bright Sky Pr.

AUSTIN FAMILY (FICTITIOUS CHARACTERS)—FICTION

L'Engle, Madeleine. Troubling a Star. 2008. (Austin Family Ser.: 5). (ENG.). 336p. (J). (gr. 6-12). pap. 10.99 *(978-0-312-37934-6(X)*, 9780312379346) Square Fish.

AUSTRALASIA

Cooke, Tim. The Exploration of Australasia & the Pacific. 2013. (Explorers Discovering the World Ser.). (Illus.). 48p. (J). (gr. 4-6). 31.95 *(978-1-4339-8619-2(1))*; pap. 14.05 *(978-1-4339-8620-8(5))* Stevens, Gareth Publishing LLLP. (Gareth Stevens Learning Library).

AUSTRALIA

ABDO Publishing Company Staff. Australian Animals, 1 vol. 2011. (Australian Animals Ser.). (ENG., Illus.). 32p. 171.00 *(978-1-61783-009-9(7)*, Big Buddy Bks.) ABDO Publishing Co.

Aloian, Molly. Cultural Traditions in Australia. 2012. (ENG.). 32p. (J). *(978-0-7787-7516-4(X))*; (Illus.). pap. *(978-0-7787-7521-8(6))* Crabtree Publishing Co.

Alter, Judy. Discovering Australia's Land, People, & Wildlife: A MyReportLinks. com Book. 2004. (Continents of the World Ser.). (Illus.). 48p. (J). lib. bdg. 26.60 *(978-0-7660-5207-9(9)*, MyReportLinks.com Bks.) Enslow Pubs., Inc.

Anastasio, Dina. Who Was Steve Irwin? 2015. (Who Was... ? Ser.). lib. bdg. 16.00 *(978-0-606-36749-3(7))* Turtleback Bks.

Anastasio, Dina & dePaola, Tomie. Who Was Steve Irwin? Eldridge, Jim, illus. 2015. (Who Was? Ser.). (ENG.). 112p. (J). (gr. 3-7). 5.99 *(978-0-448-48838-7(8)*, Grosset & Dunlap) Penguin Young Readers Group.

Baby Australian Animals, 1 vol., Set. Incl. It's a Baby Australian Fur Seal! Hengel, Katherine. lib. bdg. 24.21 *(978-1-60453-574-7(1))*; It's a Baby Flying Fox! Hengel, Katherine. lib. bdg. 24.21 *(978-1-60453-575-4(X))*; It's a Baby Kangaroo! Doudna, Kelly. lib. bdg. 24.21 *(978-1-60453-576-1(8))*; It's a Baby Koala! Hengel, Katherine. lib. bdg. 24.21 *(978-1-60453-577-8(6))*; It's a Baby Spiny Anteater! Hengel, Katherine. lib. bdg. 24.21 *(978-1-60453-578-5(4))*; It's a Baby Tasmanian Devil! Hengel, Katherine. lib. bdg. 24.21 *(978-1-60453-579-2(2))*; (J). (gr. k-3). (Baby Australian Animals Ser.: 6). (ENG., Illus.). 24p. 2010. Set lib. bdg. 145.26 *(978-1-60453-573-0(3)*, SandCastle) ABDO Publishing Co.

Bancroft, Bronwyn. Patterns of Australia. Bancroft, Bronwyn, illus. 2005. (Illus.). 24p. *(978-1-877003-96-7(4))* Little Hare Bks. AUS. Dist: HarperCollins Pubs. Australia.

Bell, Robin. My Adventure Discovering Australia. 2007. 44p. (J). 8.99 *(978-1-59092-416-7(9))* Blue Forge Pr.

—My Adventure Discovering Australia: Advanced My Adventure. 2007. 44p. (J). pap. 8.99 *(978-1-59092-417-4(7))* Blue Forge Pr.

Benchmark Education Co., LLC. The Geography of Asia & Australia. 2014. (PRIME Ser.). (J). (gr. 6-8). pap. *(978-1-4509-9504-7(7))* Benchmark Education Co.

Bodden, Valerie. Great Barrier Reef. 2010. (Big Outdoors Ser.). 24p. (J). (gr. k-3). 16.95 *(978-1-58341-816-1(4))* Creative Co., The.

Brian, Janeen. Meet Nellie Melba. Murphy, Claire, illus. 2016. (ENG.). 32p. (J). (gr. k-2). 22.99 *(978-0-14-378029-8(8))* Random Hse. Australia AUS. Dist: Independent Pubs. Group.

Collard, Sneed B. & Collard, Sneed B., III. Australia's Cane Toads: Overrun! 2015. (They Don't Belong: Tracking Invasive Species Ser.). (ENG., Illus.). 32p. (J). (gr. 2-7). lib. bdg. 26.60 *(978-1-62724-828-0(5))* Bearport Publishing Co., Inc.

Comire, S. Joshua & Porter, Malcolm. Atlas of Australia & the Pacific. 2009. (Atlases of the World Ser.). (Illus.). 48p. (YA). (gr. 5-8). 29.25 *(978-1-4358-8456-4(6)*, Rosen Reference) Rosen Publishing Group, Inc., The.

Currie, Stephen. Australia & the Pacific Islands. 2004. (Exploration & Discovery Ser.). (ENG.). 112p. (J). (gr. 7-10). 30.85 *(978-1-59018-496-7(3)*, Lucent Bks.) Cengage Gale.

Darian-Smith, Kate. Australia, Antarctica, & the Pacific. 2005. (Continents of the World Ser.). 64p. (gr. 5-12). pap. 14.05 *(978-0-8368-5919-5(7))*; (Illus.). lib. bdg. 34.00

(978-0-8368-5912-6(X)) Stevens, Gareth Publishing LLLP. (Gareth Stevens Secondary Library).

Donaldson, Madeline. Australia. 2005. (Pull Ahead Bks.). (Illus.). 32p. (gr. k-3). (J). lib. bdg. 22.60 *(978-0-8225-4718-1(X))*; (ENG.). pap. 7.95 *(978-0-8225-2492-2(9))* Lerner Publishing Group.

Dosen, Anthony, et al. Investigating Legal Studies for Queensland. 2013. (ENG.). pap. *(978-1-107-65346-7(0))* Cambridge Univ. Pr.

Encyclopaedia Britannica, Inc. Staff, compiled by. My First Britannica: Asia, Australia, & New Zealand. 2008. (gr. 7-12). *(978-1-59339-407-3(1))* Encyclopaedia Britannica, Inc.

Encyclopaedia Britannica Publishers, Inc. Staff. Views of Asia & Australia. 2003. (Britannica Learning Library). (Illus.). 14.95 *(978-1-59339-010-5(6))* Encyclopaedia Britannica, Inc.

Friedman, Mel. Australia & Oceania. 2009. (True Bks.). (ENG.). 48p. (J). pap. 6.95 *(978-0-531-21828-0(7)*, Children's Pr.) Scholastic Library Publishing.

Germaine, Elizabeth & Burckhardt, Ann. Cooking the Australian Way. 2nd rev. ed. 2003. (Easy Menu Ethnic Cookbooks 2nd Edition Ser.). (ENG., Illus.). 72p. (gr. 5-12). 25.26 *(978-0-8225-4101-1(7))* Lerner Publishing Group.

Greder, Armin. Australia to Z. 2016. (ENG.). 32p. (J). (gr. 7-11). 22.99 *(978-1-76011-318-6(2))* Allen & Unwin AUS. Dist: Independent Pubs. Group.

Group/McGraw-Hill, Wright. Australia: Urban & Outback, 6 vols. (Book2WebTM Ser.). (gr. 4-8). 36.50 *(978-0-322-04446-3(4))* Wright Group/McGraw-Hill.

Hill, Valerie. Australia. 2004. (Ask about Asia Ser.). (Illus.). 48p. (J). (gr. 4-18). lib. bdg. 19.95 *(978-1-59084-208-9(1))* Mason Crest.

Honey, Elizabeth. Ten Blue Wrens & What a Lot of Wattle! An Absolutely Australian Counting Book. Honey, Elizabeth, illus. (ENG., Illus.). 32p. (J). (gr. -1-3). 2016. pap. 10.99 *(978-1-76029-051-1(3))* 2012. 19.99 *(978-1-74237-787-2(4))* Allen & Unwin AUS. Dist: Independent Pubs. Group.

Hovanec, Erin M. An Online Visit to Australia. 2009. (Internet Field Trips Ser.). 24p. (gr. 3-3). 45.00 *(978-1-61513-604-9(5)*, PowerKids Pr.) Rosen Publishing Group, Inc., The.

James, Otto. Focus on Australia. 2007. (World in Focus Ser.). (Illus.). 64p. (gr. 5-12). pap. 14.05 *(978-0-8368-6744-2(0))*; lib. bdg. 34.00 *(978-0-8368-6737-4(8))* Stevens, Gareth Publishing LLLP. (Gareth Stevens Secondary Library).

Jordan-Bychkov, Terry G. Australia. 2003. (Modern World Nations Ser.). (Illus.). 150p. (gr. 6-12). 35.00 *(978-0-7910-7609-5(1)*, Chelsea Hse.) Facts On File, Inc.

Kalman, Bobbie & Johnson, Robin. Spotlight on Australia. 2008. (Spotlight on my Country Ser.). (ENG., Illus.). 32p. (J). (gr. 3-7). pap. *(978-0-7787-3479-6(X))*; lib. bdg. *(978-0-7787-3453-6(6))* Crabtree Publishing Co.

Kalman, Bobbie & Sjonger, Rebecca. Explore Australia & Oceania. rev. ed. 2007. (Explore the Continents Ser.). (ENG., Illus.). 32p. (J). (gr. 1-5). pap. *(978-0-7787-3087-3(5))* Crabtree Publishing Co.

Kerns, Ann. Australia in Pictures. 2nd ed. 2003. (Visual Geography Series, Second Ser.). (ENG., Illus.). 80p. (gr. 5-12). lib. bdg. 31.93 *(978-0-8225-0932-5(6))* Lerner Publishing Group.

King, Corinne & Fenton, Corinne. Queenie: One Elephant's Story. Gouldthorpe, Peter, illus. 2013. (ENG.). 24p. (J). (gr. k-3). 16.99 *(978-0-7636-6375-9(1))* Candlewick Pr.

Leppman, Elizabeth J. Australia & the Pacific. 2005. (Modern World Cultures Ser.). (Illus.). 128p. (gr. 6-12). lib. bdg. 30.00 *(978-0-7910-8150-1(8)*, Chelsea Hse.) Facts On File, Inc.

Marsh, Carole. Australia: The Land down under for Mates of All Ages! 2009. (It's Your World Ser.). 48p. (J). (gr. 2-9). pap. 7.99 *(978-0-635-06823-1(0))* Gallopade International.

Marshall, Diana. Aboriginal Australians. 2004. (Indigenous Peoples Ser.). (J). pap. 9.95 *(978-1-59036-156-6(3))*; (Illus.). 32p. lib. bdg. 26.00 *(978-1-59036-121-4(0))* Weigl Pubs., Inc.

Mason, Paul. Sydney. Bowden, Rob, photos by. 2007. (Global Cities Ser.). (Illus.). 64p. (gr. 5-8). lib. bdg. 30.00 *(978-0-7910-8849-4(9)*, Chelsea Hse.) Facts On File, Inc.

Maule, David. What Makes a Place Special? Moscow, Egypt, Australia. 2014. (ENG., Illus.). 24p. (J). pap. 9.50 *(978-1-107-63317-9(6))* Cambridge Univ. Pr.

McCollum, Sean. Australia. 2008. pap. 40.95 *(978-0-8225-9297-6(5))* 2007. (ENG., Illus.). 48p. (gr. 2-4). lib. bdg. 29.27 *(978-0-8225-7126-1(9)*, Lerner Pubns.) Lerner Publishing Group.

McNeil, Niki, et al. Australia: Project Pack Continent Study Series, Multi-Grade Level. 2007. (In the Hands of a Child: Project Pack Continent Study Ser.). (Illus.). 141p. spiral bd. 24.00 *(978-1-60308-074-3(0))* In the Hands of a Child.

Medina, Nico. Where Is the Great Barrier Reef? Hinderliter, John, illus. 2016. (Where Is...? Ser.). (ENG.). 112p. (J). (gr. 3-7). 16.00 *(978-0-606-39316-4(1))* Turtleback Bks.

Miller, Heather. AC/DC: Hard Rock Band. 2009. (Rebels of Rock Ser.). (Illus.). 104p. (J). (gr. 7-12). lib. bdg. 33.27 *(978-0-7660-3031-2(8))* Enslow Pubs., Inc.

Mis, Melody S. How to Draw Australia's Sights & Symbols. 2009. (Kid's Guide to Drawing the Countries of the World Ser.). 48p. (gr. 4-4). 53.00 *(978-1-61511-107-7(7)*, PowerKids Pr.) Rosen Publishing Group, Inc., The.

Morreale, Marie. 5 Seconds of Summer. 2015. (Real Bios Ser.). (ENG., Illus.). 48p. (J). pap. 7.95 *(978-0-531-21662-0(4)*, Children's Pr.) Scholastic Library Publishing.

Nicola. The Lost Boomerang. 2012. 36p. pap. 22.00 *(978-1-61933-546-2(8))* FastPrncil, Inc.

Niz, Xavier. Spotlight on Australia, 1 vol. 2010. (Spotlight on the Continents Ser.). (ENG.). 24p. (gr. 1-2). lib. bdg. 25.32 *(978-1-4296-6627-5(7)*, First Facts) Capstone Press of Coughlan Cos.

Niz, Xavier W. Australia. 2016. (Seven Continents Ser.). (ENG.). 24p. (gr. 2-3). pap. 7.45 *(978-1-5157-5852-5(4)*, Bridgestone Bks.) Capstone Press of Coughlan Cos.

Oxford University Press Staff & Lindop, Christine, eds. Australia & New Zealand, Level 3. 3rd ed. 2008. (ENG., Illus.). 80p. 10.00 *(978-0-19-423390-3(1))* Oxford Univ. Pr., Inc.

Perkins, Chloe. Living in ... Australia. Woolley, Tom, illus. 2017. (Living In... Ser.). (ENG.). 32p. (J). (gr. k-2). pap. 3.99 *(978-1-4814-8092-5(8)*, Simon Spotlight) Simon Spotlight.

Popper, Garry. Kez in Australia. Johnson, Andi, illus. 2004. 36p. (gr. -1-7). 4.00 *(978-1-84161-055-9(0))* Ravette Publishing, Ltd. GBR. Dist: Parkwest Pubns., Inc.

Riggs, Sandy. Habitats of Australia: Set Of 6. 2011. (Navigators Ser.). (J). pap. 44.00 net. *(978-1-4108-5072-0(2))* Benchmark Education Co.

Rose, Elizabeth. A Primary Source Guide to Australia. (Countries of the World). 24p. 2009. (gr. 2-3). 42.50 *(978-1-61512-025-3(4))* 2004. (ENG., Illus.). (J). (gr. k-5). lib. bdg. 22.60 *(978-0-8239-6730-8(1))* Rosen Publishing Group, Inc., The. (PowerKids Pr.).

Ruth, Angie. My Adventure in Australia. 2007. 44p. (J). 8.99 *(978-1-59092-423-5(1))* Blue Forge Pr.

Sasek, Miroslav. This Is Australia. 2009. (ENG., Illus.). 62p. (J). (gr. 2-12). 17.95 *(978-0-7893-1854-1(7))* Universe Publishing.

Sayre, April Pulley. G'Day Australia! 2003. 32p. (J). (gr. 2-5). pap. 7.95 *(978-0-7613-1987-0(5))*; (Illus.). lib. bdg. 21.90 *(978-0-7613-2122-4(5))* Lerner Publishing Group. (Millbrook Pr.).

Shea, Therese. The Great Barrier Reef: Using Graphs & Charts to Solve Word Problems. 2009. (PowerMath: Advanced Proficiency Plus Ser.). 32p. (gr. 5-5). 47.90 *(978-1-60851-367-3(X)*, PowerKids Pr.) Rosen Publishing Group, Inc., The.

Sheen, Barbara. Foods of Australia. 2010. (Taste of Culture Ser.). (Illus.). 64p. (J). 30.45 *(978-0-7377-4812-3(5)*, Kidhaven) Cengage Gale.

Soffer, Ruth. Great Barrier Reef Coloring Book. 2007. (Dover Nature Coloring Book Ser.). (ENG., Illus.). 32p. (gr. 3-8). 3.99 *(978-0-486-45689-8(7))* Dover Pubns., Inc.

Somervill, Barbara A. Australia. 2003. (Geography of the World Ser.). (ENG., Illus.). 32p. (J). (gr. 3-6). 28.50 *(978-1-59296-063-7(4)*, 200257) Child's World, Inc., The.

Steele, Philip. Sydney. 2004. (Great Cities of the World Ser.). (Illus.). 48p. (gr. 5-12). lib. bdg. 31.00 *(978-0-8368-5032-1(7)*, Gareth Stevens Secondary Library) Stevens, Gareth Publishing LLLP.

Striveildi, Cheryl. Australia. 2003. (Continents Ser.). 32p. (J). (gr. 1-4). 27.07 *(978-1-57765-961-7(9))* ABDO Publishing Co.

Tan, Shaun. The Bird King: An Artist's Notebook. 2013. (ENG.). 128p. (J). (gr. 7-9). 19.99 *(978-0-545-46513-7(3)*, Levine, Arthur A. Bks.) Scholastic, Inc.

Triumph Books Staff. 5 Seconds of Summer: She Looks So Perfect. 2014. (ENG.). 112p. (YA). (gr. 7). pap. 12.95 *(978-1-62937-069-9(X))* Triumph Bks.

Turner, Pamela S. The Dolphins of Shark Bay. 2016. (Scientists in the Field Ser.). (ENG., Illus.). 80p. (J). (gr. 5-7). pap. 9.99 *(978-0-544-80909-3(2)*, HMH Books For Young Readers) Houghton Mifflin Harcourt Publishing Co.

—The Dolphins of Shark Bay. Tuason, Scott, photos by. 2013. (Scientists in the Field Ser.). (ENG., Illus.). 80p. (J). (gr. 5-7). 18.99 *(978-0-547-71638-1(9))* Houghton Mifflin Harcourt Publishing Co.

Vass, Coral. Meet... Don Bradman. Howe, Brad, illus. 2016. (ENG.). 32p. (J). (gr. k-2). 22.99 *(978-1-925324-89-1(3))* Random Hse. Australia AUS. Dist: Independent Pubs. Group.

Vierow, Wendy. Australia. 2009. (Atlas of the Seven Continents Ser.). 24p. (gr. 3-3). 42.50 *(978-1-61511-479-5(3)*, PowerKids Pr.) Rosen Publishing Group, Inc., The.

Weidenbach, Kristin. Meet Banjo Paterson. Gulliver Hancock, James, illus. 2016. (ENG.). 32p. (J). (gr. k-2). 14.99 *(978-0-85798-009-0(2))* Random Hse. Australia AUS. Dist: Independent Pubs. Group.

Weil, Ann. Meet Our New Student from Australia. 2008. (Meet Our New Student Ser.). (Illus.). 47p. (J). (gr. 3-7). lib. bdg. 29.95 *(978-1-58415-652-9(X))* Mitchell Lane Pubs., Inc.

Wunungmurra, Johnny & Wunungmurra, Helen. Djet & Nak Nak. 2003. (ENG., Illus.). 32p. pap. 8.95 *(978-0-85575-398-6(6))* Aboriginal Studies Pr. AUS. Dist: Independent Pubs. Group.

Wymarra, Elizabeth & Wymarra, Wandihnu. Wandihnu & the Old Dugong. Hodges, Benjamin, illus. 2007. (ENG.). 28p. (J). (gr. k-7). pap. 13.95 *(978-1-921248-18-4(1))* Magabala Bks. AUS. Dist: Independent Pubs. Group.

AUSTRALIA—FICTION

Abdel-Fattah, Randa. Does My Head Look Big in This? 2007. 360p. (YA). 25.66 *(978-1-4287-4610-7(2))*; 25.66 *(978-1-4287-4610-7(2))* Follett School Solutions. (Follettbound).

—Does My Head Look Big in This? 2008. (ENG.). 368p. (J). (gr. 7). pap. 9.99 *(978-0-439-92233-3(X)*, Scholastic Paperbacks) Scholastic, Inc.

Abdel-Fattah, Randa. The Lines We Cross. 2017. (ENG.). 400p. (J). (gr. 7-7). 18.99 ***(978-1-338-11866-7(8)***, Scholastic Pr.) Scholastic, Inc.

Abela, Deborah. In Search of the Time & Space Machine. Murphy, Jobi, illus. 2005. (Spy Force Ser.). 256p. (Orig.). (J). 14.95 *(978-1-74051-765-2(2)*, Simon & Schuster Bks. For Young Readers) Simon & Schuster Bks. For Young Readers.

Alden-Tirrill, Anna. The Alabaster Jar. 2013. 290p. pap. 14.95 *(978-1-885831-07-1(2))* Proclaim Publishing.

Angel, Ido. Vipo in Australia: The Koala & the Kangaroo. 2015. (AV2 Animated Storytime Ser.). (ENG.). (J). lib. bdg. 29.99 *(978-1-4896-3905-9(5)*, AV2 by Weigl) Weigl Pubs., Inc.

Apted, Violet. Tommy & Jacqui: Laughing with Kookaburras. 2011. 32p. pap. 13.00 *(978-1-61204-118-6(3)*, Eloquent Bks.) Strategic Book Publishing & Rights Agency (SBPRA).

Arrigan, Mary & Quarto Generic Staff. Esty's Gold. 2010. (ENG.). 224p. (J). (gr. 6-9). pap. 8.95 *(978-1-84507-965-9(5)*, Frances Lincoln) Quarto Publishing Group UK GBR. Dist: Hachette Bk. Group.

AZ Books, creator. Tyler Turtle Travels to Australia. 2013. (Pop-Up: Play & Listen Ser.). (ENG., Illus.). 10p. (J). (gr. -1-k). bds. 16.95 *(978-1-61889-036-8(0))* AZ Bks. LLC.

Baker, Jeannie. Mirror. Baker, Jeannie, illus. 2010. (ENG., Illus.). 48p. (J). (gr. k-4). 18.99 *(978-0-7636-4848-0(5))* Candlewick Pr.

Bancks, Tristan. Mac Slater Hunts the Cool. (Mac Slater Hunts the Cool Ser.). (ENG.). 224p. (J). (gr. 3-7). 2011. pap. 6.99 *(978-1-4169-8575-4(1))* 2010. 15.99 *(978-1-4169-8574-7(3))* Simon & Schuster Bks. For Young Readers. (Simon & Schuster Bks. For Young Readers).

—On the Run. 2015. (ENG.). 240p. (J). (gr. 5-7). 16.99 *(978-0-374-30153-8(0)*, 9780374301538, Farrar, Straus & Giroux (BYR)) Farrar, Straus & Giroux.

Barwood, Lee & Barwood, Lee. Klassic Koalas: Ancient Aboriginal Tales in New Retellings. 2007. (Illus.). 64p. (J). pap. 28.99 *(978-0-9764698-1-0(2))* Koala Jo Publishing.

Base, Graeme & Children of Gununa Staff. Our Island. 2016. (ENG.). 34p. (J). (gr. -1-k). 14.99 ***(978-0-14-350593-8(9))*** Random Hse. Australia AUS. Dist: Independent Pubs. Group.

Bates, Sonya Spreen. Topspin. 2013. 147p. (J). *(978-1-4598-0647-4(6))* Orca Bk. Pubs.

Bateson, Catherine. Being Bee. (ENG.). 136p. (J). 2008. (gr. 3-7). pap. 7.95 *(978-0-8234-2208-1(9))* 2007. (Illus.). (gr. 4-7). 16.95 *(978-0-8234-2104-6(X))* Holiday Hse., Inc.

—The Boyfriend Rules of Good Behavior. 2006. (ENG.). 192p. (YA). (gr. 8-12). 16.95 *(978-0-8234-2026-1(4))* Holiday Hse., Inc.

—Magenta Mcphee. 2010. (ENG.). 176p. (J). (gr. 3-7). pap. 16.95 *(978-0-8234-2253-1(4))* Holiday Hse., Inc.

—Millie & the Night Heron. 2005. 160p. (YA). pap. *(978-0-7022-3526-9(1))* Univ. of Queensland Pr.

—Stranded in Boringsville. (ENG.). 144p. (J). (gr. 5-9). 2007. pap. 6.95 *(978-0-8234-2113-8(9))* 2005. 16.95 *(978-0-8234-1969-2(X))* Holiday Hse., Inc.

Bauer, Michael Gerard. The Running Man. 2008. 304p. (YA). (gr. 9-18). lib. bdg. 17.89 *(978-0-06-145509-4(1)*, HarperTeen) HarperCollins Pubs.

—The Running Man. 2004. 280p. (YA). pap. *(978-1-86291-575-6(X)*, Omnibus Bks.) Scholastic Australia.

Beer, Henry, photos by. Girl Defective. 2015. (ENG., Illus.). 320p. (YA). (gr. 9). pap. 10.99 *(978-1-4424-9761-0(0))* Simon & Schuster Children's Publishing.

Berkes, Marianne. Over in Australia: Amazing Animals down Under, 1 vol. Dubin, Jill, illus. 2011. (ENG.). 32p. (J). (gr. -1-3). 16.95 *(978-1-58469-135-8(2))*; pap. 8.95 *(978-1-58469-136-5(0))* Dawn Pubns.

Bette, Grandma. The Excellent Adventures of Max & Madison: Bedtime stories for Youngsters. 2012. 116p. pap. 42.95 *(978-1-4525-0432-2(6))* Balboa Pr.

Bettinger, John & Kina. Koa Becomes a Friend. 2012. 32p. (-18). pap. 13.95 *(978-1-4497-6153-0(4)*, WestBow Pr.) Author Solutions, Inc.

Betts, A. J. Zac & Mia. 2016. (ENG.). 304p. (YA). (gr. 9). pap. 8.99 *(978-0-544-66878-2(2)*, HMH Books For Young Readers) Houghton Mifflin Harcourt Publishing Co.

Boddy, Gary. Giraffe's Holiday in Sydney. 2007. 23p. 19.95 *(978-1-84799-919-1(0))* Lulu Pr., Inc.

Boissery, Beverley. Sophie's Exile. 2008. (ENG.). 280p. (J). (gr. 5-8). pap. 12.99 *(978-1-55002-810-2(3)*, Boardwalk Bks.) Dundurn CAN. Dist: Ingram Publisher Services.

Bourke, Debra. First Day at Bouddi School. Cowley, Ray B., illus. 2012. 32p. pap. 18.00 *(978-1-4349-8469-2(9)*, RoseDog Bks.) Dorrance Publishing Co., Inc.

Broadhurst, Sherree. Bella's Adventures: Bella Rescues Gumleaf the Joey. 2010. 46p. pap. 16.50 *(978-1-60911-068-0(4)*, Eloquent Bks.) Strategic Book Publishing & Rights Agency (SBPRA).

Brown, Jeff. The Australian Boomerang Bonanza. Pamintuan, Macky, illus. 2011. (Flat Stanley's Worldwide Adventures Ser.: 8). (ENG.). 112p. (J). (gr. 2-5). 15.99 *(978-0-06-157435-1(X))* HarperCollins Pubs.

—The Australian Boomerang Bonanza No. 8. Pamintuan, Macky, illus. 2011. (Flat Stanley's Worldwide Adventures Ser.: 8). (ENG.). 112p. (J). (gr. 2-5). pap. 4.99 *(978-0-06-143018-3(8))* HarperCollins Pubs.

Bruce, Mary Grant. Back to Billabong. l.t. ed. 2006. 200p. pap. 21.99 *(978-1-4264-2197-6(4))* Creative Media Partners, LLC.

—Mates at Billabong. l.t. ed. 2006. (ENG.). 186p. pap. 21.99 *(978-1-4264-1061-1(1))* Creative Media Partners, LLC.

Burton, Rebecca. Leaving Jetty Road. 2004. 272p. *(978-0-207-20015-1(7))* HarperCollins Pubs. Australia.

Burton, Thomas. Bluey & Dingo's Outback Adventure. 2011. 40p. 15.66 *(978-1-4567-7006-8(3))* AuthorHouse.

Buzo, Laura. Love & Other Perishable Items. (ENG.). 256p. (YA). (gr. 9). 2013. pap. 8.99 *(978-0-307-92974-7(4)*, Ember) 2012. 17.99 *(978-0-375-87000-2(8)*, Knopf Bks. for Young Readers) Random Hse. Children's Bks.

Catran, Ken. Artists Are Crazy & Other Stories. (Takeaways Ser.). 160p. pap. *(978-0-7344-0475-6(1)*, Lothian Children's Bks.) Hachette Australia.

Chan, Queenie. The Dreaming Collection. 2010. (ENG., Illus.). 576p. pap. 19.99 *(978-1-4278-1871-3(1))* TOKYOPOP, Inc.

Chapman, Helen. How the Animals Got Their Colours: Tales from the Australian Dreamland. 2017. (ENG.). 32p. (J). (gr. 2-3). pap. 8.99 *(978-0-00-817934-2(4))* HarperCollins Pubs. Ltd. GBR. Dist: Independent Pubs. Group.

Chase, Diana. Angel in a Gum Tree. 2006. 32p. pap. 13.50 *(978-1-921064-77-7(3))* Fremantle Pr. AUS. Dist: Independent Pubs. Group.

Christopher, Lucy. Stolen. (ENG.). (J). 2012. 320p. (gr. 9). pap. 9.99 *(978-0-545-17094-9(X))* 2010. 304p. (gr. 7-18). 17.99 *(978-0-545-17093-2(1))* Scholastic, Inc. (Chicken Hse., The).

—Stolen. 2012. lib. bdg. 20.85 *(978-0-606-23955-4(3)*, Turtleback) Turtleback Bks.

Clarke, Judith. Al Capsella & Watchdogs. 164p. pap. *(978-0-7022-2294-8(1))* Univ. of Queensland Pr.

—One Whole & Perfect Day. (ENG.). 2013. 248p. (YA). (gr. 9-12). pap. 9.95 *(978-1-62091-025-2(X))* 2007. 250p. (J). (gr. 8-13). 16.95 *(978-1-932425-95-6(0)*, Front Street) Boyds Mills Pr.

Cleary, Jon. The Sundowners. (J). 25.95 *(978-0-88411-467-3(8))* Amereon Ltd.

Close, Johnny. The Dump. 2017. (ENG.). 128p. pap. 11.95 ***(978-1-78629-240-7(8)***, 159ddba7-410f-4899-9192-f7ee2f631b27) Austin, Stan AUS. Dist: Bookmasters Distribution.

Cohn, Rachel. The Steps. 2004. (ENG.). 144p. (J). (gr. 3-7). reprint ed. pap. 6.99 *(978-0-689-87414-7(6)*, Simon & Schuster Bks. For Young Readers) Simon & Schuster Bks. For Young Readers.

Collins, Lynette. Margie & Wolf: The Series. 2016. 260p. (gr. 1-1). 40.31 *(978-1-5245-1645-1(7))*; pap. 24.19 *(978-1-5245-1644-4(9))* Xlibris Corp.

Collins, Lynette. Margie & Wolf: When They Were Free. 2017. (ENG., Illus.). pap. 32.25 ***(978-1-5245-2168-4(X))*** Xlibris Corp.

Conn, Bruce. The Curse of Durgan's Reef. 2004. 142p. (YA). 21.95 *(978-0-595-66223-4(4))*; pap. 11.95 *(978-0-595-30935-1(6))* iUniverse, Inc.

Corr, Janice. The Aussie Time Travellers & the Cave of the Opal Eyed Snake. 2005. (Illus.). 112p. pap. 13.50 *(978-1-4120-4621-3(1))* Trafford Publishing.

Corwin, Katherine A. R. Greg the Bearded Dragon & Thomas the Sea Turtle: A Tale of Adventure, Discovery, & Friendship. 2012. 28p. pap. 19.99 *(978-1-4685-7958-1(4))* AuthorHouse.

Coughlin, Shirley. Beyond the Flood. 2011. 68p. pap. 12.50 *(978-1-60976-710-5(1)*, Eloquent Bks.) Strategic Book Publishing & Rights Agency (SBPRA).

Crane, Venessa. Duck down Under. 2008. 70p. pap. 29.95 *(978-1-4092-2376-4(0))* Lulu Pr., Inc.

Crawford, Joanne. Bilby & the Bushfire. Fielding, Grace, illus. 2007. 28p. (J). pap. *(978-1-921248-30-6(0))* Magabala Bks.

Crew, Gary. The Watertower. 2014. (ENG.). 32p. (J). (gr. 2-9). pap. 8.95 *(978-1-56656-331-4(3)*, Crocodile Bks.) Interlink Publishing Group, Inc.

Crispian. Mystery on the Tambo River. 2011. 120p. (gr. 4-6). 20.95 *(978-1-4502-6506-5(5))*; pap. 10.95 *(978-1-4502-6504-1(9))* iUniverse, Inc.

Croker, Verity. May Day Mine. (ENG., Illus.). (J). 2016. 24.99 ***(978-1-63533-048-9(3))*** 2015. 180p. pap. 14.99 *(978-1-63216-717-0(4))* Dreamspinner Pr. (Harmony Ink Pr.).

Crowley, Cath. Graffiti Moon. 2012. (ENG.). 272p. (YA). (gr. 9). pap. 8.99 *(978-0-375-87195-5(0)*, Ember); 16.99 *(978-0-375-86953-2(0)*, Knopf Bks. for Young Readers) Random Hse. Children's Bks.

—A Little Wanting Song. 2011. (ENG.). 288p. (YA). (gr. 9). pap. 8.99 *(978-0-375-85449-1(5)*, Ember) Random Hse. Children's Bks.

—Words in Deep Blue. 2017. (ENG.). 288p. (YA). (gr. 9). 17.99 *(978-1-101-93764-8(5))*; lib. bdg. 20.99 *(978-1-101-93765-5(3))* Random Hse. Children's Bks. (Knopf Bks. for Young Readers).

Cruse, Beryl, et al. Bittangabee Tribe: An Aboriginal Story from Coastal New South Wales. 2nd ed. 2011. (ENG., Illus.). 28p. (J). (gr. -1-k). pap. 17.95 *(978-0-85575-698-7(5))* Aboriginal Studies Pr. AUS. Dist: Independent Pubs. Group.

Cummings, C. R. The Cadet Under-Officer: The Army Cadets. 2nd ed. 2013. 368p. pap. *(978-0-9875975-5-7(8))* DoctorZed Publishing.

Dalton, Annie. Fogging Over: Mission - Take a Trip down Under. 2010. (Mel Beeby, Agent Angel Ser.: 5). (ENG.). 160p. (J). (gr. 4-7). pap. 7.99 *(978-0-00-720475-5(2))* HarperCollins Pubs. Ltd. GBR. Dist: HarperCollins Pubs.

Debono, Angelo. The Magic in You. 2011. 36p. pap. 13.95 *(978-1-61204-783-6(1)*, Strategic Bk. Publishing) Strategic Book Publishing & Rights Agency (SBPRA).

Dennard, Deborah. Koala Country: A Story of an Australian Eucalyptus Forest. 2005. (Soundprints' Wild Habitats Ser.). (ENG., Illus.). 32p. (J). (gr. 1-4). 8.95 *(978-1-59249-106-3(5)*, SC7018) Soundprints.

Disney Book Group Staff. Finding Nemo. 2012. (Read-Along Storybook & CD Ser.). (ENG.). 912p. (J). (gr. -1 — 1). pap. 6.99 *(978-1-4231-6028-1(2))* Disney Pr.

Divaroren, Demet. Living on Hope Street. 2017. (ENG.). 256p. (YA). (gr. 9-13). pap. 15.99 ***(978-1-76029-209-6(5))*** Allen & Unwin AUS. Dist: Independent Pubs. Group.

Dorling Kindersley Publishing Staff. Finding Nemo. 2003. (Ultimate Sticker Bks.). (ENG., Illus.). 16p. (J). (gr. k-3). pap. 6.99 *(978-0-7894-9245-6(8)*, DK Children) Dorling Kindersley Publishing, Inc.

Dowswell, Paul. Prison Ship: Adventures of a Youn Sailor. 2006. 306p. 16.95 *(978-1-58237-674-5(3))* Let's Think-kids Foundation, Inc.

Draper, Rohan. Sunny & Mayo. 2012. 146p. 46.72 *(978-1-4771-0446-0(1))*; pap. 28.03 *(978-1-4771-0445-3(3))* Xlibris Corp.

Dubosarsky, Ursula. The Golden Day. (ENG.). 160p. (YA). (gr. 7). 2015. pap. 7.99 *(978-0-7636-7679-7(9))* 2013. 15.99 *(978-0-7636-6399-5(9))* Candlewick Pr.

Dunphy, Lorraine F. An Australian Fairy Tale. 2008. 32p. pap. 14.95 *(978-1-59858-553-7(3))* Dog Ear Publishing, LLC.

Earhart, Kristin. Outback All-Stars (Race the Wild #5) 2016. (Race the Wild Ser.: 5). (ENG., Illus.). 144p. (J). (gr. 2-5). pap. 4.99 *(978-0-545-94064-1(8)*, Scholastic Paperbacks) Scholastic, Inc.

Earls, Nick. After Summer. 2005. (ENG.). 240p. (YA). (gr. 7). pap. 13.99 *(978-0-618-45781-6(X))* Houghton Mifflin Harcourt Publishing Co.

—48 Shades of Brown. 2004. (ENG.). 288p. (YA). (gr. 7-18). pap. 16.99 *(978-0-618-45295-8(8))* Houghton Mifflin Harcourt Publishing Co.

Eaton, Anthony. Nightpeople. 2005. (Darklands Ser.: Bk. 1). 392p. (Orig.). (YA). pap. *(978-0-7022-3494-1(X))* Univ. of Queensland Pr.

Edwards, Sherri L. Sally the Platypus. 2009. 48p. pap. 18.95 *(978-1-4389-5930-6(3))* AuthorHouse.

Engineering is Elementary Team. A Reminder for Emily: An Electrical Engineering Story. 2006. (J). lib. bdg. 15.99 *(978-0-9774084-3-6(4))* Engineering is Elementary.

Falkner, Brian. The Assault (Recon Team Angel #1) 2013. (Recon Team Angel Ser.: 1). (ENG.). 304p. (YA). (gr. 7). pap. 9.99 *(978-0-375-87190-0(X)*, Ember) Random Hse. Children's Bks.

—Task Force. 2013. (Recon Team Angel Ser.). (ENG., Illus.). 288p. (YA). (gr. 7). 17.99 *(978-0-449-81299-0(5)*, Random Hse. Bks. for Young Readers) Random Hse. Children's Bks.

—Task Force (Recon Team Angel #2) 2014. (Recon Team Angel Ser.). (ENG.). 416p. (YA). (gr. 7). pap. 9.99 *(978-0-449-81302-7(9)*, Ember) Random Hse. Children's Bks.

Fernandez, Nacho. La nueva era del sueno vol. 2: Los desiertos del Norte: The New Age of Dreams vol. 2: the Deserts of the North. 2007. (SPA.). 48p. 22.95 *(978-1-59497-398-7(9))* Public Square Bks.

Finke, M. e. Taconi & Claude: Double Trouble. 2011. 102p. pap. 8.95 *(978-1-61633-130-6(5))* Guardian Angel Publishing, Inc.

Fire! Individual Title Six-Packs. (Bookweb Ser.). 32p. (gr. 4-18). 34.00 *(978-0-7635-3739-5(X))* Rigby Education.

Flora, James, creator. Kangaroo for Christmas. 2011. (ENG., Illus.). 40p. (J). (gr. -1-3). 16.95 *(978-1-59270-113-1(2))* Enchanted Lion Bks., LLC.

Folau, Israel & Harding, David. Izzy Folau Bindup 1. 2016. (Izzy Folau Ser.). (ENG.). 352p. (YA). (gr. 7-9). pap. 17.99 *(978-0-14-378092-2(1))* Random Hse. Australia AUS. Dist: Independent Pubs. Group.

Foxlee, Karen. The Anatomy of Wings. 2010. (ENG.). 384p. (Orig.). (YA). (gr. 9). pap. 9.99 *(978-0-375-84761-5(8),* Knopf Bks. for Young Readers) Random Hse. Children's Bks.

Fraillon, Zana. The Bone Sparrow. 2016. (ENG.). 240p. (J). (gr. 4-7). 16.99 *(978-1-4847-8151-7(1))* Hyperion Bks. for Children.

Franco, Franco & Garcia, Eduardo. Dino-Mike & the Dinosaur Cove. Franco, Franco, illus. 2016. (Dino-Mike! Ser.). (ENG., Illus.). 128p. (J). (gr. 1-3). lib. bdg. 25.32 *(978-1-4965-2490-4(X),* Dino-Mike!) Stone Arch Bks.

Frazier, Angie. Everlasting. 2010. (ENG.). 336p. (J). (gr. 7-18). 17.99 *(978-0-545-11473-8(X),* Scholastic Pr.) Scholastic, Inc.

French, Jackie. The Camel Who Crossed Australia. 2008. 256p. *(978-0-7322-8543-2(7))* HarperCollins Pubs. Australia.

—Josephine Wants to Dance. Whatley, Bruce, illus. 2007. (ENG.). 32p. (J). (gr. -1-1). 17.95 *(978-0-8109-9431-7(3),* Abrams Bks. for Young Readers) Abrams, Inc.

—One Big Wacky Family. 2008. (Illus.). 464p. pap. *(978-0-7322-8745-0(6))* HarperCollins Pubs. Australia.

French, Jackie, et al. Pete the Sheep. 2006. (Illus.). 32p. pap. *(978-0-207-19974-5(4))* HarperCollins Pubs. Australia.

French, Simon. Where in the World, 1 vol. 2008. (J). (gr. 3-7). 2008. (ENG.). pap. 7.95 *(978-1-56145-443-3(5))* 2003. 14.95 *(978-1-56145-292-7(0,* Q34443) Peachtree Pubs.

Friday Never Leaving. 2014. (ENG., Illus.). 336p. (YA). (gr. 9). pap. 9.99 *(978-1-4424-8653-9(8),* Simon & Schuster Bks. For Young Readers) Simon & Schuster Bks. For Young Readers.

Gale, Emily. The Other Side of Summer. 2017. 336p. (J). (gr. 3-7). 16.99 *(978-0-06-265674-2(0))* HarperCollins Pubs.

Gallo, Tina. Let's Put on a Show! Style Guide Staff, illus. 2010. (Yo Gabba Gabba! Ser.). (ENG.). 16p. (J). (gr. -1-1). pap. 5.99 *(978-1-4169-9535-7(8),* Simon Scribbles) Simon Scribbles.

Ganz, Yaffa. Four in One: Four Favorites. Klineman, Harvey, illus. 2008. 24.99 *(978-1-59826-183-7(5))* Feldheim Pubs.

Gavin, Sherrie. Baptism & Boomerangs. 2015. (Illus.). (J). 14.99 *(978-1-4621-1681-2(7))* Cedar Fort, Inc./CFI Distribution.

Gervay, Susanne. Butterflies. 2012. (Fiction Ser.). (ENG.). 256p. (J). pap. 4.99 *(978-1-61067-043-2(4))* Kane Miller.

—Super Jack. Wilcox, Cathy, illus. 2003. 192p. *(978-0-207-19918-9(3))* HarperCollins Pubs. Australia.

—SuperJack. Wilcox, Cathy, illus. 2013. (ENG.). 192p. (J). pap. 5.99 *(978-1-61067-129-3(5))* Kane Miller.

Gibbs, L. Count Me In. 2017. (Netball Gems Ser.: 8). (ENG.). 160p. (J). (gr. 2-4). pap. 8.99 ***(978-0-14-378119-6(7))*** Random Hse. Australia AUS. Dist: Independent Pubs. Group.

Gillingham, Sara. In My Nest. Siminovich, Lorena, illus. 2009. (ENG.). 12p. (J). (gr. -1 — 1). bds. 8.99 *(978-0-8118-6555-5(X))* Chronicle Bks. LLC.

Gleitzman, Morris. Aristotle's Nostril. 2016. (ENG.). 144p. (J). (gr. 1-3). 14.99 ***(978-0-14-330894-2(7))*** Random Hse. Australia AUS. Dist: Independent Pubs. Group.

Gleitzman, Morris. Now. 2012. (Once Ser.: 3). (ENG.). 192p. (YA). (gr. 7). 16.99 *(978-0-8050-9378-0(8),* 9780805093780, Holt, Henry & Co. Bks. For Young Readers) Holt, Henry & Co.

—Now. 2013. (Once Ser.: 3). (ENG.). 192p. (YA). (gr. 7). pap. 9.99 *(978-1-250-03417-5(5),* 9781250034175) Square Fish.

Godwin, Jane. Falling from Grace. 2007. (ENG.). 204p. (J). (gr. 6-12). 16.95 *(978-0-8234-2105-3(8))* Holiday Hse., Inc.

Goodman, Alison. The Last Dragoneye. 2012. (Eon Ser.: 2). lib. bdg. 23.30 *(978-0-606-23648-5(1),* Turtleback) Turtleback Bks.

Gough, Erin. Get It Together, Delilah! 2017. (ENG., Illus.). 336p. (YA). 16.99 *(978-1-4521-5187-8(3))* Chronicle Bks. LLC.

Graham, Bob. Tales from the Waterhole. 2004. (Illus.). 64p. (J). *(978-0-7445-6593-5(6))* Walker Bks., Ltd.

Grandma Bette. The Excellent Adventures of Max & Madison: Bedtime Stories for Youngsters. 2013. 32p. pap. 16.95 *(978-1-4525-7268-0(2));* 36p. pap. 16.95 *(978-1-4525-7270-3(4));* 32p. pap. 16.95 *(978-1-4525-7264-2(X));* 32p. pap. 16.95 *(978-1-4525-7266-6(6))* Author Solutions, Inc. (Balboa Pr.).

Greenburg, J. C. In the Desert. Gerardi, Jan, illus. 2008. (Andrew Lost Ser.: 17). (ENG.). 96p. (J). (gr. 1-4). per. 3.99 *(978-0-375-84667-0(0),* Random Hse. Bks. for Young Readers) Random Hse. Children's Bks.

—In the Jungle. 2007. (Andrew Lost Ser.: 15). (ENG., Illus.). 96p. (J). (gr. 1-4). 3.99 *(978-0-375-83564-3(4),* Random Hse. Bks. for Young Readers) Random Hse. Children's Bks.

Gregg, Stacy. Victory & the All-Stars Academy. 2015. (Pony Club Secrets Ser.: 8). (ENG., Illus.). 288p. (J). (gr. 4-7). 6.99 *(978-0-00-727033-0(X),* HarperCollins Children's Bks.) HarperCollins Pubs. Ltd. GBR. Dist: HarperCollins Pubs.

Hamilton, Martha & Weiss, Mitch. Why Koala Has a Stumpy Tail. Wrenn, Tom, illus. 2007. (Story Cove Ser.). (ENG.). 24p. (J). (gr. -1-3). pap. 4.95 *(978-0-87483-879-4(7))* August Hse. Pubs., Inc.

Harding, David. Pushed to the Limit. Fosdike, David, illus. 2016. (Israel Folau Ser.: 3). (ENG.). 192p. (J). (gr. 4-7). pap. 9.99 *(978-0-85798-665-8(1))* Random Hse. Australia AUS. Dist: Independent Pubs. Group.

—Standing Tall. Fosdike, David, illus. 2016. (Izzy Folau Ser.: 4). (ENG.). 192p. (J). (gr. 4-7). pap. 9.99 *(978-0-85798-667-2(8))* Random Hse. Australia AUS. Dist: Independent Pubs. Group.

Harmer, Wendy. I Lost My Mobile at the Mall. 2011. (ENG.). 272p. (YA). (gr. 7-18). 10.99 *(978-1-935279-97-6(1))* Kane Miller.

Harris, Christine. Audrey Goes to Town. James, Ann, illus. 2009. (Audrey Ser.: 2). (ENG.). 192p. (J). (gr. 2-4). pap. 7.99 *(978-1-921272-67-7(8))* Little Hare Bks. AUS. Dist: Independent Pubs. Group.

Harrison, John. Fergal Onions. Harrison, John, illus. 2004. (Illus.). 36p. *(978-0-7022-3448-4(6))* Univ. of Queensland Pr.

Hartnett, Sonya. Butterfly. (ENG.). 240p. (YA). (gr. 9). 2013. pap. 7.99 *(978-0-7636-6334-6(4))* 2010. (Illus.). 16.99 *(978-0-7636-4760-5(8))* Candlewick Pr.

—Stripes of the Sidestep Wolf. 2005. (ENG.). 208p. (YA). (gr. 7-18). 16.99 *(978-0-7636-2644-0(9))* Candlewick Pr.

Harvey, Paul & Pearson Education Staff. Surfer! 2nd ed. 2008. (ENG.). 32p. pap. 11.99 *(978-1-4058-6969-0(0))* Pearson Education.

Hazell, Mark. Gift of the Wind Dancers. 2004. 140p. pap. *(978-1-84401-029-5(5))* Athena Pr.

Healey, Karen. When We Wake. 2014. (ENG.). 320p. (YA). (gr. 7-17). pap. 10.99 *(978-0-316-20077-6(8))* Little, Brown Bks. for Young Readers.

Helidoniotis, Kathy. Totally Horse Mad. 2006. 240p. *(978-0-7322-8420-6(1))* HarperCollins Pubs. Australia.

Herrick, Steven. Cold Skin. 2009. (ENG.). 279p. (YA). (gr. 9-18). 18.95 *(978-1-59078-572-0(X),* Front Street) Boyds Mills Pr.

—The Wolf. 2007. (ENG.). 216p. (J). (gr. 7-18). 17.95 *(978-1-932425-75-8(6),* Front Street) Boyds Mills Pr.

Higgins, Chris. My Funny Family down Under. 2016. (My Funny Family Ser.). (ENG., Illus.). 160p. (J). (gr. 2-4). pap. 6.99 *(978-1-4449-2577-7(6))* Hachette Children's Group GBR. Dist: Hachette Bk. Group.

Honey, Elizabeth. Hop up! Wriggle Over! 2017. (ENG., Illus.). 40p. (J). (gr. -1-3). 16.99 *(978-0-544-79084-1(7),* Clarion Bks.) Houghton Mifflin Harcourt Trade & Reference Pubs.

Horse, Harry. The Last Gold Diggers: Being as It Were, an Account of a Small Dog's Adventures, down Under. Horse, Harry, illus. 2008. (ENG., Illus.). 128p. (J). (gr. 1-5). 12.95 *(978-1-56145-435-8(4))* Peachtree Pubs.

Hulin, Pamela. Down under in Australia. Mendoza, Carlos, illus. 2007. 20p. per. 24.95 *(978-1-4241-8929-8(2))* America Star Bks.

Hunt, Elizabeth Singer. The Search for the Sunken Treasure. Williamson, Brian, illus. 2007. (Secret Agent Jack Stalwart Ser.: 2). (ENG.). 128p. (J). (gr. 1-4). per. 5.99 *(978-1-60286-002-5(5),* Weinstein Bks.) Perseus Bks. Group.

Irwin, Bindi & Black, Jess. Bushfire! 2011. (Bindi's Wildlife Adventures Ser.: 3). (ENG.). 112p. (gr. 3-6). pap. 4.99 *(978-1-4022-5520-5(9),* Sourcebooks Jabberwocky) Sourcebooks, Inc.

Irwin, Bindi & Kunz, Chris. Trouble at the Zoo. 2011. (Bindi's Wildlife Adventures Ser.: 1). (ENG.). 112p. (gr. 3-6). pap. 5.99 *(978-1-4022-5514-4(4),* Sourcebooks Jabberwocky) Sourcebooks, Inc.

Ivanoff, George. Medical Mission. 2016. (Royal Flying Doctor Service Ser.: 3). (ENG.). 192p. (J). (gr. 3-5). pap. 12.99 *(978-0-85798-880-5(8))* Random Hse. Australia AUS. Dist: Independent Pubs. Group.

—Royal Flying Doctor Service: Fast Flight. 2016. (Royal Flying Doctor Service Ser.: 4). (ENG.). 192p. (J). (gr. 3-5). pap. 12.99 *(978-0-85798-882-9(4))* Random Hse. Australia AUS. Dist: Independent Pubs. Group.

Jinks, Catherine. Evil Genius. 2007. 486p. (J). *(978-1-4287-3510-1(0))* Harcourt Trade Pubs.

—Evil Genius. 2008. (ENG., Illus.). 496p. (YA). (gr. 7). pap. 9.99 *(978-0-15-206185-2(1))* Houghton Mifflin Harcourt Publishing Co.

—Genius Squad. 2009. (ENG., Illus.). 448p. (J). (gr. 7). pap. 8.99 *(978-0-15-206650-5(0))* Houghton Mifflin Harcourt Publishing Co.

—The Genius Wars. 2011. (ENG.). 384p. (YA). (gr. 7). pap. 8.99 *(978-0-547-57727-2(3))* Houghton Mifflin Harcourt Publishing Co.

Jones, Gareth P. Ninja Meerkats (#8) Outback Attack. Finlayson, Luke, illus. 2014. (Ninja Meerkats Ser.: 8). (ENG.). 128p. (J). (gr. 2-4). pap. 5.99 *(978-1-250-04667-3(X),* 9781250046673) Square Fish.

Jonsberg, Barry. The Categorical Universe of Candice Phee. 2014. (ENG.). 242p. (J). (gr. 5-8). 16.99 *(978-1-4521-3351-5(4))* Chronicle Bks. LLC.

Jorgensen, Norman. Smuggler's Curse The. 2017. (ENG.). 356p. (J). (gr. 4-7). 8.95 ***(978-1-925164-19-0(5))*** Fremantle Pr. AUS. Dist: Independent Pubs. Group.

Keil, Melissa. Life in Outer Space, 1 vol. (ENG.). 320p. (YA). (gr. 7-11). 2016. pap. 9.95 ***(978-1-56145-975-9(5))*** 2013. 16.95 *(978-1-56145-742-7(6))* Peachtree Pubs.

Knight-Mudie, Karen. Yarns from Yandilla. 2013. 344p. pap. *(978-0-9875697-0-7(8))* Davey, Mary Stella.

Kuykendall, Roger. All Day September. 2011. 28p. 12.95 *(978-1-4638-9782-6(0));* pap. 6.95 *(978-1-4638-0109-0(2))* Rodgers, Alan Bks.

Lamond, Peter. The Rainforest Family & Those Terrible Toads. Purnell, Teresa, illus. 2011. 92p. pap. 27.25 *(978-1-60976-297-1(5),* Eloquent Bks.) Strategic Book Publishing & Rights Agency (SBPRA).

Lamperd, Laurel. Battle for Boodicuttup Creek. 2008. 64p. pap. *(978-1-84923-238-8(5))* YouWriteOn.

Lanagan, Margo. Red Spikes. 2009. (ENG.). 192p. (YA). (gr. 9). pap. 7.99 *(978-0-375-84304-4(3),* Knopf Bks. for Young Readers) Random Hse. Children's Bks.

Langeland, Deirdre. Kangaroo Island: A Story of an Australian Mallee Forest. 2005. (Soundprints' Wild Habitats Ser.). (ENG., Illus.). 32p. (J). (gr. 1-4). 8.95 *(978-1-59249-095-0(6))* Soundprints.

Larbalestier, Justine. Magic's Child. 2007. (Magic or Madness Trilogy). 291p. (YA). *(978-1-4287-3603-0(4),* Razorbill) Penguin Publishing Group.

—Razorhurst. 2016. (ENG.). 336p. (YA). (gr. 9). pap. 10.99 *(978-1-61695-625-7(9),* Soho Teen) Soho Pr., Inc.

Lee, Julia Elizabeth. Seahorses Down Under. Weiser, Robert, ed. (Defenders of Wildlife Ser.). (Illus.). 50+p. (J). (gr. k-3). lib. bdg. 9.95 *(978-0-9666857-0-1(9))* Dawn of Day Childrens Publishing Co., Inc.

Lester, Alison. The Circus Horse. Harvey, Roland, illus. 2009. (ENG.). 64p. (J). (gr. k-3). pap. 4.99 *(978-0-8118-6656-9(4))* Chronicle Bks. LLC.

Lester, Alison & Harvey, Roland. The Silver Horse Switch. 2009. (ENG., Illus.). 64p. (J). (gr. k-3). pap. 4.99 *(978-0-8118-6554-8(1))* Chronicle Bks. LLC.

Lewis, Ali. Timber Creek Station. 2016. (ENG.). 240p. (YA). (gr. 6-12). 18.99 *(978-1-4677-8117-6(7));* 35.99 *(978-1-4677-8816-8(3),* Carolrhoda Lab™) Lerner Publishing Group.

Lindsay, Norman. The Magic Pudding. 2012. (Dover Children's Classics Ser.). (ENG., Illus.). 144p. (J). (gr. 3-8). per. 8.95 *(978-0-486-45281-4(6))* Dover Pubns., Inc.

—The Magic Pudding. deluxe ed. (Illus.). 180p. 20.00 *(978-0-207-18355-3(4))* HarperCollins Pubs.

—The Magic Pudding. 2004. reprint ed. pap. 15.95 *(978-1-4191-7119-2(4));* pap. 1.99 *(978-1-4192-7119-9(9))* Kessinger Publishing, LLC.

—The Magic Pudding. Lindsay, Norman, illus. 2016. (ENG., Illus.). 184p. (J). (gr. 4-7). pap. 9.99 *(978-1-59017-994-9(3),* NYRB Kids) New York Review of Bks., Inc., The.

—The Magic Pudding: The Adventures of Bunyip Bluegum. 2008. 208p. *(978-0-7322-8432-9(5))* HarperCollins Pubs. Australia.

Linke, Glenn Colin. The Gargantuan Boy. 2011. 102p. pap. 30.50 *(978-1-60976-079-3(4),* Eloquent Bks.) Strategic Book Publishing & Rights Agency (SBPRA).

Lithgow, John. Marsupial Sue Presents the Runaway Pancake. Davis, Jack E., illus. 2008. (ENG.). 40p. (J). (gr. -1-3). 7.99 *(978-0-689-87848-0(6),* Simon & Schuster Bks. For Young Readers) Simon & Schuster Bks. For Young Readers.

Little, Lorna. The Mark of the Wagarl. Lyndon, Janice, illus. 2004. 28p. (J). *(978-1-875641-97-0(1))* Magabala Bks.

Lloyd, Alison. The Letty Stories, 4 bks. in 1. 2016. (Our Australian Girl Ser.). (ENG.). 480p. (J). (gr. 3-7). 23.99 *(978-0-670-07805-9(0))* Penguin Books Australia AUS. Dist: Independent Pubs. Group.

Lowory, Brigid. Guitar Highway Rose. 2003. (ENG.). 208p. (YA). (gr. 7-12). tchr. ed. 16.95 *(978-0-8234-1790-2(5))* Holiday Hse., Inc.

Lowry, Brigid. Follow the Blue. 2004. (ENG.). 205p. (J). (gr. 7-18). tchr. ed. 16.95 *(978-0-8234-1827-5(8))* Holiday Hse., Inc.

—Follow the Blue. 2006. (ENG.). 208p. (YA). (gr. 8-12). pap. 18.99 *(978-0-312-34297-5(7),* 9780312342975, St. Martin's Griffin) St. Martin's Pr.

—Guitar Highway Rose. 2006. (ENG.). 208p. (YA). (gr. 8-12). reprint ed. pap. 18.99 *(978-0-312-34296-8(9),* 9780312342968, St. Martin's Griffin) St. Martin's Pr.

—Things You Either Hate or Love. 2006. (ENG.). 179p. (YA). (gr. 7-12). 16.95 *(978-0-8234-2004-9(3))* Holiday Hse., Inc.

—Things You Either Hate or Love. 2007. (ENG.). 192p. (YA). (gr. 8-12). pap. 18.99 *(978-0-312-36308-6(7),* 9780312363086, St. Martin's Griffin) St. Martin's Pr.

Luck, Gail. Bumduggle Davis Beats the Boobrats or the Inauguration of the Motherless Club. 2011. 146p. pap. 12.50 *(978-1-61204-727-0(0),* Strategic Bk. Publishing) Strategic Book Publishing & Rights Agency (SBPRA).

—Bumduggle Davis Joins the Dots: Or It's All There in Black & White. 2012. 166p. pap. 13.50 *(978-1-62212-379-7(4),* Strategic Bk. Publishing) Strategic Book Publishing & Rights Agency (SBPRA).

Lumry, Amanda & Hurwitz, Laura. Riddle of the Reef. 2009. (Illus.). 32p. (J). *(978-0-545-06848-2(7),* Scholastic Pr.) Scholastic, Inc.

MacKey, Garry. Joey: The Christmas Kangaroo. 2012. 24p. pap. 9.95 *(978-1-4575-1592-7(X))* Dog Ear Publishing, LLC.

Maddox, Jake. Mountain Bike Hero, 1 vol. Tiffany, Sean, illus. 2011. (Jake Maddox Sports Stories Ser.). (ENG.). 72p. (gr. 2-3). lib. bdg. 25.32 *(978-1-4342-2536-8(4))* Stone Arch Bks.

Man-Kong, Mary. A Fin-Tastic Journey! Golden Books Staff, illus. 2012. (Color Plus Chunky Crayons Ser.). (ENG.). 48p. (J). (gr. k-k). pap. 3.99 *(978-0-307-92978-5(7),* Golden Bks.) Random Hse. Children's Bks.

Marchetta, Melina. Jellicoe Road. (ENG.). 432p. (YA). (gr. 9). 2010. pap. 9.99 *(978-0-06-143185-2(0))* 2008. 17.99 *(978-0-06-143183-8(4))* HarperCollins Pubs. (HarperTeen).

—Looking for Alibrandi. 2006. (ENG.). 320p. (YA). (gr. 7-12). reprint ed. per. 9.99 *(978-0-375-83694-7(2),* Knopf Bks. for Young Readers) Random Hse. Children's Bks.

—The Piper's Son. (ENG.). 336p. (YA). (gr. 9). 2012. pap. 7.99 *(978-0-7636-6062-8(0))* 2011. (Illus.). 17.99 *(978-0-7636-4758-2(6))* Candlewick Pr.

—Saving Francesca. 2006. (ENG.). 258p. (YA). (gr. 7-12). reprint ed. per. 8.99 *(978-0-375-82983-3(0),* Knopf Bks. for Young Readers) Random Hse. Children's Bks.

Mariconda, Barbara. Lucy at Sea. 2013. (Voyage of Lucy P. Simmons Ser.: 2). (ENG.). 320p. (J). (gr. 3-7). 16.99 *(978-0-06-211993-3(1),* Tegen, Katherine Bks) HarperCollins Pubs.

Marman, Richard. Mcalister's Spark. Marman, Richard, illus. 2013. (Illus.). 364p. pap. *(978-1-909302-21-1(X))* Abela Publishing.

Marsden, John. Tomorrow, When the War Began. 2006. (Tomorrow Ser.: 1). (ENG.). 288p. (J). (gr. 7-12). 9.99 *(978-0-439-82910-6(0),* Scholastic Paperbacks) Scholastic, Inc.

Marsh, Carole. The Mystery on the Great Barrier Reef. 2006. (Around the World in 80 Mysteries Ser.). (Illus.). 132p. (J). (gr. 3-5). per. 5.95 *(978-0-635-06206-2(2))* Gallopade International.

—The Mystery on the Great Barrier Reef: Sydney, Austrailia. 2009. (Around the World in 80 Mysteries Ser.). 132p. (J). 18.99 *(978-0-635-07015-9(4),* Marsh, Carole Mysteries) Gallopade International.

—The Mystery on the Great Barrier Reef: Sydney, Australia. 2006. (Around the World in 80 Mysteries Ser.). (Illus.). 132p. (J). (gr. 3-5). 14.95 *(978-0-635-06210-9(0))* Gallopade International.

Marshall, Kate. Mokes, Mines & Mayhem. 2008. 120p. pap. 10.95 *(978-1-60693-357-2(4),* Eloquent Bks.) Strategic Book Publishing & Rights Agency (SBPRA).

Martin, L. & Beckett, G. The Adventures of Timothy in Early New South Wales. 2012. 32p. pap. 21.10 *(978-1-4669-3144-2(2))* Trafford Publishing.

McDaniel, Lurlene. The Year of Chasing Dreams. (ENG.). 336p. (YA). (gr. 7). 2015. pap. 9.99 *(978-0-385-74174-3(X),* Ember) 2014. 16.99 *(978-0-385-74173-6(1),* Delacorte Pr.) Random Hse. Children's Bks.

McDonnell, Vincent. The Catalpa Adventure: Escape to Freedom. 2010. (ENG.). 128p. (J). pap. 12.95 *(978-1-84889-038-1(9))* Collins Pr., The IRL. Dist: Dufour Editions, Inc.

McGee, Warner, illus. Run, Run, Koala! 2010. (Go, Diego, Go! Ser.). (ENG.). 24p. (J). (gr. -1-2). pap. 3.99 *(978-1-4169-9937-9(X),* Simon Spotlight/Nickelodeon) Simon Spotlight/Nickelodeon.

Melville, Alessandra. Scavengers. 2017. (ENG.). 222p. (J). pap. 13.95 ***(978-1-78693-464-2(7),*** ca3a3b12-3706-4993-b48f-1f7018b57df9) Austin, Stan AUS. Dist: Bookmasters Distribution.

Meyer, L. A. The Wake of the Lorelei Lee: Being an Account of the Further Adventures of Jacky Faber, on Her Way to Botany Bay. (Bloody Jack Adventures Ser.: 8). (ENG.). (YA). (gr. 9). 2012. 576p. pap. 9.99 *(978-0-547-72194-1(3))* 2010. 560p. 17.00 *(978-0-547-32768-6(4))* Houghton Mifflin Harcourt Publishing Co.

—The Wake of the Lorelei Lee: Being an Account of the Further Adventures of Jacky Faber, on Her Way to Botany Bay. 2010. (Bloody Jack Adventures Ser.: Bk. 8). audio compact disk 29.95 *(978-1-59316-484-3(X))* Listen & Live Audio, Inc.

Millard, Glenda. A Small Free Kiss in the Dark. 2010. (ENG.). 192p. (YA). (gr. 7-18). pap. 16.95 *(978-0-8234-2264-7(X))* Holiday Hse., Inc.

Moriarty, Jaclyn. The Ghosts of Ashbury High. (ENG.). 496p. (J). (gr. 7). 2012. pap. 10.99 *(978-0-545-06973-1(4))* 2010. 18.99 *(978-0-545-06972-4(6))* Scholastic, Inc. (Levine, Arthur A. Bks.).

—The Murder of Bindy MacKenzie. 2008. (ENG.). 496p. (J). (gr. 7-12). pap. 9.99 *(978-0-439-74052-4(5),* Levine, Arthur A. Bks.) Scholastic, Inc.

—The Spell Book of Listen Taylor. 2007. (YA). *(978-0-439-84679-0(X),* Levine, Arthur A. Bks.) Scholastic, Inc.

Moriarty, Ros. Splosh for the Billabong. Balarinji, illus. 2015. (ENG.). 24p. (J). (— 1). 9.99 *(978-1-76011-212-7(7))* Allen & Unwin AUS. Dist: Independent Pubs. Group.

—Summer Rain. Balarinji, illus. 2016. (ENG.). 24p. (J). (gr. -1-k). 9.99 *(978-1-76011-211-0(9))* Allen & Unwin AUS. Dist: Independent Pubs. Group.

Munns, Skye. Who's at the Zoo. 2011. 24p. pap. 28.03 *(978-1-4568-5447-8(X))* Xlibris Corp.

Murray, Kirsty. Bridie's Fire. 2005. (ENG.). 264p. (J). (gr. 4-8). pap. 13.99 *(978-1-86508-727-6(0))* Allen & Unwin AUS. Dist: Independent Pubs. Group.

—Vulture's Wake. 2010. (ENG.). 256p. (YA). (gr. 7-18). pap. 17.95 *(978-0-8234-2282-1(8))* Holiday Hse., Inc.

Murray, Martine. Molly & Pim & the Millions of Stars. 2017. (ENG., Illus.). 192p. (J). (gr. 3-7). 16.99 *(978-0-399-55040-9(2),* Knopf Bks. for Young Readers) Random Hse. Children's Bks.

Murrell, Belinda. Lulu Bell & the Arabian Nights. 2015. (Lulu Bell Ser.). (ENG.). 96p. (J). (gr. 1-3). pap. 7.99 *(978-0-85798-558-3(2))* Random Hse. Australia AUS. Dist: Independent Pubs. Group.

—The River Charm. l.t. ed. 2013. 504p. pap. *(978-1-4596-6626-9(7))* ReadHowYouWant.com, Ltd.

O'Brien, May L. Wunambi the Water Snake. Wyatt, Sue, illus. 2nd ed. 2005. (ENG.). 32p. (J). (gr. k-5). pap. 17.95 *(978-0-85575-500-3(8))* Aboriginal Studies Pr. AUS. Dist: Independent Pubs. Group.

O'Callaghan, G. The Eternals. 2007. 376p. per. *(978-1-84693-055-3(3))* Best Global Publishing Ltd.

Oliver, Narelle. The Best Beak in Boonaroo Bay. Oliver, Narelle, illus. (Illus.). 48p. (YA). pap. *(978-0-85091-671-3(2),* Lothian Children's Bks.) Hachette Australia.

Ormerod, Jan. Lizzie Nonsense. 2006. (Illus.). 32p. pap. *(978-1-877003-93-6(X))* Little Hare Bks. AUS. Dist: HarperCollins Pubs. Australia.

—Lizzie Nonsense. Ormerod, Jan, illus. 2004. (Illus.). 40p. (J). *(978-1-877003-59-2(X))* Little Hare Bks. AUS. Dist: HarperCollins Pubs. Australia.

Osborne, Mary Pope. Dingoes at Dinnertime. unabr. ed. 2004. (Magic Tree House Ser.: No. 20). 71p. (J). (gr. k-3). pap. 17.00 incl. audio *(978-0-8072-0929-5(5),* S FTR 252 SP, Listening Library) Random Hse. Audio Publishing Group.

—The Mystery of the Enchanted Dog, 4 vols., Set. Murdocca, Sal, illus. 2009. (ENG.). 96p. (J). (gr. 1-4). 23.96 *(978-0-375-85811-6(3),* Random Hse. Bks. for Young Readers) Random Hse. Children's Bks.

Osborne, Mary Pope, et al. Perros Salvajes a la Hora de la Cena. Murdocca, Sal, illus. 2008. (Casa del Arbol Ser.: 20).Tr. of Dingoes at Dinnertime. (SPA.). (J). (gr. 2-4). pap. 5.99 *(978-1-933032-50-4(2))* Lectorum Pubns., Inc.

Ottley, Reginald. By the Sandhills of Yamboorah. 2003. 224p. pap. *(978-0-7022-3350-0(1))* Univ. of Queensland Pr.

Paling, Chris. The Adventures of Rumble, Tumble, & Titch: Uncertain Times. 2010. 62p. pap. 9.99 *(978-1-60911-263-9(6),* Eloquent Bks.) Strategic Book Publishing & Rights Agency (SBPRA).

Paris, Harper. The Mystery at the Coral Reef. Calo, Marcos, illus. 2015. (Greetings from Somewhere Ser.: 8). (ENG.). 128p. (J). (gr. k-4). pap. 5.99 *(978-1-4814-2370-0(3),* Little Simon) Little Simon.

Pascoe, Bruce. Fog a Dox. l.t. ed. 2013. 108p. pap. *(978-1-4596-7080-8(9))* ReadHowYouWant.com, Ltd.

Patchett, Mary Elwyn. Ajax: Golden Dog of the Australian Bush. Tansley, Eric, illus. 2011. 172p. 42.95 *(978-1-258-01103-1(4))* Literary Licensing, LLC.

Patterson, James. Middle School: Escape to Australia. Griffo, Daniel, illus. 2017. (Middle School Ser.: 9). (ENG.). 288p. (J). (gr. 3-7). 13.99 *(978-0-316-27262-9(0),* Jimmy Patterson) Little Brown & Co.

Perry, Glyn & Parry, Glyn. Invisible Girl. 2003. 160p. (YA). pap. 15.25 *(978-1-920731-48-9(2))* Fremantle Pr. AUS. Dist: Independent Pubs. Group.

Pigram, John. My Dog Jack. 2009. 20p. pap. 14.64 *(978-1-4269-2038-7(5))* Trafford Publishing.

Plamer, Anthony. Soldier's Gift. 2017. (ENG., Illus.). 44p. (J). (gr. 3-7). 14.99 ***(978-0-14-350716-1(8))*** Penguin Books Australia AUS. Dist: Independent Pubs. Group.

Ponko, Cindy A. Olive Fingers. 2006. (Illus.). (J). *(978-0-9768230-0-1(4))* Some Kids I Know.

Porter, Annaliese & Bancroft, Bronwyn. The Outback. 2005. (Illus.). 28p. (J). *(978-1-875641-86-4(6))* Magabala Bks.

Price, Kevin, ed. Ice Castles: A Born Storytellers Collection of Teen Fiction & Romance. 2013. (Illus.). 226p. pap. *(978-0-9872559-8-3(3),* Crotchet Quaver) Logorythm.

Pung, Alice. Lucy & Linh. 2016. (ENG.). 352p. (YA). (gr. 7). 17.99 *(978-0-399-55048-5(8),* Knopf Bks. for Young Readers) Random Hse. Children's Bks.

—Marly & the Goat, Bk. 3. Masciullo, Lucia, illus. 3rd ed. 2016. (Our Australian Girl Ser.: 3). (ENG.). 144p. (J). (gr. 3-7). 7.99 *(978-0-14-330851-5(3))* Penguin Books Australia AUS. Dist: Independent Pubs. Group.

Raphael, Akili & Lewis, Harriet. Malik Says, Turn off the Water! 2012. 36p. pap. 20.99 *(978-1-4772-9541-0(0))* AuthorHouse.

Ray, Michelle. A Huntsman Spider in My House... Ashford, Sylvie, illus. 2014. (ENG.). 34p. pap. 8.95 *(978-1-61448-842-2(8),* 9781614488422) Morgan James Publishing.

Rentala, Sita Kanaka Valli. Ocean Flows: In Prose: Zcumby's Judo (on Global Warming) 2010. 44p. (J). pap. 19.99 *(978-1-4490-8780-7(9))* AuthorHouse.

Richards, George. The Great Australian Super-Hero: Now You See Him, Now You Don't. 2012. 152p. pap. 12.95 *(978-1-4759-4245-3(1))* iUniverse, Inc.

Ripley's Believe It or Not Editors. Danger Underground. 2011. (Ripley RBI Ser.). 128p. (J). pap. 4.99 *(978-1-893951-64-8(2))* Ripley Entertainment, Inc.

Roberts, Roxanne. Angel Wings, Faery Dust & Other Magical Things: A Story about Guardian Angels. 2012. 16p. pap. 10.00 *(978-1-61897-252-1(9),* Eloquent Bks.) Strategic Book Publishing & Rights Agency (SBPRA).

—Angel Wings, Faery Dust & Other Magical Things: A Story about Merpeople. 2011. 24p. pap. 11.50 *(978-1-61204-588-7(X),* Strategic Bk. Publishing) Strategic Book Publishing & Rights Agency (SBPRA).

—Angel Wings, Faery Dust & Other Magical Things: A Story about Witches, Warlocks & Such. 2011. 24p. pap. 11.50 *(978-1-61204-072-1(1),* Eloquent Bks.) Strategic Book Publishing & Rights Agency (SBPRA).

Roemermann, Jennifer. The Long Grass Tunnel. 2012. 50p. pap. 18.68 *(978-1-4797-0300-5(1))* Xlibris Corp.

Rogers, Anne. PRINCE & the APPLE TREE. 2008. 32p. pap. 23.50 *(978-1-4092-1035-1(9))* Lulu Pr., Inc.

Ross, Leanna. Julie Simone. 2004. 194p. (YA). pap. 14.95 *(978-0-595-30376-2(5))* iUniverse, Inc.

Roy, Oscar. I Was Captured by Pirates. 2013. 110p. pap. 11.00 *(978-1-62212-790-0(0),* Strategic Bk. Publishing) Strategic Book Publishing & Rights Agency (SBPRA).

Russon, Penni. Breathe. 2007. (ENG., Illus.). 368p. (YA). (gr. 9-18). 16.99 *(978-0-06-079393-7(7))* HarperCollins Pubs.

Sarzin, Lisa Miranda. Stories for Simon. 2017. (ENG., Illus.). 32p. (J). (gr. 1-3). 14.99 ***(978-0-14-378425-8(0))*** Random Hse. Australia AUS. Dist: Independent Pubs. Group.

Scraper, Katherine. Save the Fairy Penguins. 2005. (J). pap. *(978-1-4108-4214-5(2))* Benchmark Education Co.

Seeary, Gary. The Beautiful Journey: A Choice between Friendship & a Chance for Love. 2017. (YA). ***(978-0-6480028-0-2(2))*** Seeary, Gary Bks.

Seib, Anke & Cameron, Emma. Out of This Place. 2013. (ENG.). 416p. (YA). (gr. 9). 17.99 *(978-0-7636-6404-6(9))* Candlewick Pr.

Shaw, Natalie. It's Nice to Meet You. Giles, Mike, illus. 2010. (Yo Gabba Gabba! Ser.). (ENG.). 24p. (J). (gr. -1-2). pap. 3.99 *(978-1-4169-9721-4(0),* Simon Spotlight) Simon Spotlight.

Shepherd, Sandra. Kangapoo & the Monster at Kakadu. 2012. 40p. pap. 32.70 *(978-1-4691-6123-5(0))* Xlibris Corp.

Silvey, Craig. Jasper Jones. 2012. 20.00 *(978-1-61383-806-8(9))* Perfection Learning Corp.

—Jasper Jones. 2012. (ENG.). 320p. (YA). (gr. 7). pap. 9.99 *(978-0-375-86627-2(2),* Ember) Random Hse. Children's Bks.

Sinclair, Gardine. Stageschool by the Sea. 2013. 176p. (J). pap. *(978-1-78299-389-6(4))* FeedARead.com.

Slade, Arthur G. Empire of Ruins. 2012. (Hunchback Assignments Ser.). (ENG.). 300p. (YA). (gr. 7). pap. 8.99 *(978-0-375-85405-7(3),* Ember) Random Hse. Children's Bks.

Spence, Eleanor. Jamberoo Road. 2007. (Living History Library). 183p. (YA). (gr. 8-12). pap. 12.95 *(978-1-932350-17-3(9))* Bethlehem Bks.

—The Switherby Pilgrims: A Tale of the Australian Bush. 2005. (Living History Library). 195p. (YA). (gr. 8-12). pap. 12.95 *(978-1-883937-99-7(X))* Bethlehem Bks.

Sretaw. Aussie Animal Friends. 2010. 36p. pap. 32.70 *(978-1-4500-7415-5(4))* Xlibris Corp.

Stevenson, Robin. Desolación, 1 vol. 2012. (Spanish Soundings Ser.). (SPA.). 160p. (YA). (gr. 8-12). pap. 9.95 *(978-1-4598-0305-3(1))* Orca Bk. Pubs. USA.

Stilton, Geronimo. Down & Out down Under. 2007. (Geronimo Stilton Ser.: 29). (ENG., Illus.). 128p. (J). (gr. 2-5). pap. 7.99 *(978-0-439-84120-7(8),* Scholastic Paperbacks) Scholastic, Inc.

—Down & Out down Under. 2007. (Geronimo Stilton Ser.: 29). lib. bdg. 18.40 *(978-1-4177-7837-9(7),* Turtleback) Turtleback Bks.

Stilton, Geronimo & Stilton, Thea. Thea Stilton & the Mountain of Fire. 2009. (Thea Stilton Ser.: 2). (ENG.). 176p. (J). (gr. 2-5). pap. 8.99 *(978-0-545-15060-6(4),* Scholastic Paperbacks) Scholastic, Inc.

—Thea Stilton & the Mountain of Fire. 2009. (Thea Stilton Ser.: 2). lib. bdg. 19.65 *(978-0-606-00232-5(4),* Turtleback) Turtleback Bks.

Stilton, Thea. Thea Stilton & the Missing Myth. 2014. (Thea Stilton Ser.: 20). (ENG.). 176p. (J). (gr. 2-5). pap. 8.99 *(978-0-545-65601-6(X),* Scholastic Paperbacks) Scholastic, Inc.

Stockdale, Stephanie. Sidney Visits Australi. 2009. 44p. pap. 18.99 *(978-1-4389-8698-2(X))* AuthorHouse.

Tan, Shaun. Tales from Outer Suburbia. 2009. (J). pap. *(978-0-545-05588-8(1),* Levine, Arthur A. Bks.) Scholastic, Inc.

—Tales from Outer Suburbia. Tan, Shaun, illus. 2009. (ENG., Illus.). 96p. (J). (gr. 7-18). 21.99 *(978-0-545-05587-1(3),* Levine, Arthur A. Bks.) Scholastic, Inc.

Taylor, Cora. Champlain & Cartier, 1 vol. 2004. (Ghost Voyages Ser.: No. 4). (ENG., Illus.). 128p. (J). (gr. 3-6). pap. 7.95 *(978-1-55050-374-6(X))* Coteau Bks. CAN. Dist: Orca Bk. Pubs. USA.

Thomas, Kerrie Annette. Jinja of the Munjyburr. Jacobs, D. K., illus. 2011. 34p. pap. 13.50 *(978-1-61204-421-7(2),* Eloquent Bks.) Strategic Book Publishing & Rights Agency (SBPRA).

Thomes, William Henry. The Bushrangers a Yankee's Adventures During His Second Visit to Australia by William H Thomes. 2006. 420p. per. 26.99 *(978-1-4255-4567-3(X))* Michigan Publishing.

Turner, Ethel. Seven Little Australians. 2005. 27.95 *(978-1-4218-0333-3(X));* 204p. pap. 12.95 *(978-1-4218-0433-0(6))* 1st World Publishing, Inc. (1st World Library - Literary Society).

—Seven Little Australians. 2007. (ENG.). 142p. pap. 18.99 *(978-1-4264-1638-5(5))* Creative Media Partners, LLC.

—Seven Little Australians. 2004. reprint ed. pap. 20.95 *(978-1-4191-4679-4(3));* pap. 1.99 *(978-1-4192-4679-1(8))* Kessinger Publishing, LLC.

Valenzuela, Kristine. A Secret Sydney. Green, Matthew, illus. 2013. 44p. (J). pap. *(978-0-9872061-6-9(8))* DoctorZed Publishing.

Vermeulen, Mariska. James & Cooper Finger Puppet Book. van de Leijgraaf, Deborah, illus. 2016. (My Best Friend & Me Ser.). (ENG.). 10p. (J). (gr. -1-k). bds. 6.99 *(978-0-7641-6830-7(4))* Barron's Educational Series, Inc.

Wakefield, Vikki. Friday Never Leaving. 2013. (ENG., Illus.). 336p. (YA). (gr. 9). 16.99 *(978-1-4424-8652-2(X),* Simon & Schuster Bks. For Young Readers) Simon & Schuster Bks. For Young Readers.

Wall, Dorothy. The Complete Adventures of Blinky Bill. 2011. (Illus.). 442p. *(978-1-84902-571-3(1))* Benediction Classics.

Wang, Gabrielle. El Jardin de la Emperatriz Casia. Holguin, Magdalena, tr. Cuellar, Olga, illus. 2004. (SPA.). 108p. (YA). 8.95 *(978-958-04-7346-6(3))* Norma S.A. COL. Dist: Distribuidora Norma, Inc.

Watson, J. R. Wizard down Under. 2009. 160p. 23.50 *(978-1-60860-138-7(2),* Eloquent Bks.) Strategic Book Publishing & Rights Agency (SBPRA).

Weingarth, Poss. Gurgle, Gurgle Splash: I'm Always in a Hurry. 2012. 36p. pap. 32.70 *(978-1-4771-4435-0(8))* Xlibris Corp.

Weston Woods Staff, creator. Possum Magic. 2011. 18.95 *(978-0-545-08634-9(5));* 38.75 *(978-0-545-14784-2(0))* Weston Woods Studios, Inc.

Whiting, Sue. Portraits of Celina. 2015. (ENG.). 352p. 16.95 *(978-1-63079-024-0(9))* Switch Pr.

Whittaker, Brian. Quest for the Kangoalaplatybat. 2010. 28p. pap. 17.99 *(978-1-4520-0844-8(2))* AuthorHouse.

Whyte, June. Murder Sucks. 2008. (ENG., Illus.). 192p. (J). pap. 12.99 *(978-1-934841-12-9(9),* Zumaya Thresholds) Zumaya Pubns. LLC.

Wilkinson, Lili. Pink. (ENG.). 320p. (YA). (gr. 8). 2012. pap. 9.99 *(978-0-06-192654-9(X))* 2011. 16.99 *(978-0-06-192653-2(1))* HarperCollins Pubs. (HarperTeen).

Will Mcallister. Sam Rivers & the Night Rustlers. 2009. 88p. pap. 9.95 *(978-0-595-46287-2(1))* iUniverse, Inc.

Wood, Fiona. Cloudwish. 2016. (ENG.). 320p. (YA). (gr. 7-17). 17.99 *(978-0-316-24212-7(8),* Poppy) Little, Brown Bks. for Young Readers.

—Six Impossible Things. 2015. (ENG.). 304p. (YA). (gr. 7-17). 18.00 *(978-0-316-24216-5(0))* Little Brown & Co.

—Six Impossible Things. 2016. (ENG.). 304p. (YA). (gr. 7-17). pap. 9.99 *(978-0-316-29941-1(3),* Poppy) Little, Brown Bks. for Young Readers.

—Wildlife. 2016. (ENG.). 416p. (YA). (gr. 10-17). pap. 9.99 *(978-0-316-24208-0(X),* Poppy) Little, Brown Bks. for Young Readers.

Wooding, Chris. Velocity. 2017. (ENG.). 336p. (J). (gr. 7). 18.99 *(978-0-545-94494-6(5),* Scholastic Pr.) Scholastic, Inc.

Zann, Paul. The Aussie Six in Australia. 2004. (J). pap. *(978-0-88887-223-4(2))* Borealis Pr.

Zorn, Claire. Protected. 2017. (ENG.). 288p. (YA). (gr. 6-12). 17.99 ***(978-1-4926-5213-7(X))*** Sourcebooks, Inc.

AUSTRALIA—HISTORY

Bailer, Darice. Australia. 2015. (One World, Many Countries Ser.). (ENG.). 32p. (J). (gr. 1-4). 28.50 *(978-1-63407-037-9(2),* 208888) Child's World, Inc., The.

Bancroft, Bronwyn. Why I Love Australia. Bancroft, Bronwyn, illus. 2016. (ENG., Illus.). 32p. (J). (gr. -1-k). 11.99 *(978-1-76012-512-7(1))* Little Hare Bks. AUS. Dist: Independent Pubs. Group.

BeaverSimon. WILD AUSTRALIA! BEGINNING BOOK WITH ONLINE ACCESS. 2014. (ENG., Illus.). 24p. (J). pap. 9.50 *(978-1-107-62165-7(8))* Cambridge Univ. Pr.

Bell, Hilary. The Marvellous Funambulist of Middle Harbour & Other Sydney Firsts. Martin, Matthew, illus. 2016. 48p. (J). 24.99 *(978-1-74223-440-3(2),* UNSW Press) NewSouth Publishing AUS. Dist: Independent Pubs. Group.

Blashfield, Jean F. Argentina. 2015. (Enchantment of the World & Trade;, Second Ser.). (ENG., Illus.). 144p. (J). lib. bdg. 40.00 *(978-0-531-21250-9(5))* Scholastic Library Publishing.

—Australia. 2012. (Enchantment of the World, Second Ser.). (ENG., Illus.). 144p. (J). (gr. 5-9). lib. bdg. 40.00 *(978-0-531-25308-3(2),* Children's Pr.) Scholastic Library Publishing.

Boddy, Alan, et al. Geography for the Australian Curriculum Year 7. 2013. (ENG.). pap. *(978-1-107-69012-7(9))* Cambridge Univ. Pr.

Bos, Samone. The Little Book of Australia's Big Things. Oehr, Alice, illus. 2015. (ENG.). 56p. (J). (gr. 2-5). 17.99 *(978-1-76012-554-7(7))* Hardie Grant Egmont Pty, Ltd. AUS. Dist: Independent Pubs. Group.

Burgan, Michael. My Teenage Life in Australia. 2017. (Custom & Cultures of the World Ser.: Vol. 12). (ENG., Illus.). (YA). (gr. 7-12). 23.95 ***(978-1-4222-3900-1(4))*** Mason Crest.

Candlewick Press, Candlewick. Australia: A 3D Expanding Country Guide. Trounce, Charlotte, illus. 2014. (Panorama Pops Ser.). (ENG.). 30p. (J). (gr. k-4). 8.99 *(978-0-7636-7505-9(9))* Candlewick Pr.

Cantor, Rachel Anne. Australia. 2017. (Countries We Come From Ser.). (ENG.). 32p. (J). (gr. k-3). 19.95 ***(978-1-68402-252-6(5))*** Bearport Publishing Co., Inc.

Chipman-Sullivan, Lois. What Does Love Mean, God? 2013. 36p. pap. 10.50 *(978-1-61286-141-8(5))* Avid Readers Publishing Group.

Colson, Mary. Australia, 1 vol. 2012. (Countries Around the World Ser.). (ENG.). 48p. (gr. 3-6). pap. 9.95 *(978-1-4329-6120-6(9),* NA-h) Heinemann-Raintree.

Costain, Meredith. You Wouldn't Want to Be an 18th-Century British Convict! A Trip to Australia You'd Rather Not Take. Antram, David, illus. 2006. (You Wouldn't Want to Ser.). (ENG.). 32p. (J). (gr. 2-5). 29.00 *(978-0-531-14973-7(0));* pap. 9.95 *(978-0-531-16998-8(7),* Watts, Franklin) Scholastic Library Publishing.

Croft, Malcolm & Besley, Preston. 5 Seconds of Summer Confidential: Over 100 Amazing Photographs of the World's Hottest Boy Band. 2015. (ENG., Illus.). 96p. (YA). (gr. 3-11). pap. 9.99 *(978-1-4380-0716-8(7))* Barron's Educational Series, Inc.

Cromarty, Jim. Great Barrier Reef Adventures. 2005. (Adventure Ser.). (ENG., Illus.). 96p. (J). (gr. 3-7). per. 8.99 *(978-1-84550-068-9(7),* 3ec344eb-b5a7-45bd-8d58-a6ba056815cc) Christian Focus Pubns. GBR. Dist: Bookmasters Distribution.

Dosen, Anthony, et al. Investigating Legal Studies for Queensland Bundle. 2013. (ENG.). pap. *(978-1-107-67198-0(1))* Cambridge Univ. Pr.

Encyclopaedia Britannica, Inc. Staff, compiled by. Views of Asia & Australia. 2003. (Illus.). 64p. 14.95 *(978-1-59339-041-9(6))* Encyclopaedia Britannica, Inc.

Fanning, Mick & Baker, Tim. Surf for Your Life: Grommets' Edition. 2011. (ENG., Illus.). 128p. (J). (gr. 7-18). pap. 14.99 *(978-1-86471-823-2(4))* Random Hse. Australia AUS. Dist: Independent Pubs. Group.

Friedman, Mel. Australia & Oceania. 2008. (True Book(tm), A — Continents Ser.). (ENG., Illus.). 48p. (J). (gr. 2-5). 31.00 *(978-0-531-16866-0(2))* Scholastic Library Publishing.

Ganeri, Anita. Australia. Isik, Sernur, illus. 2015. (Country Guides, with Benjamin Blog & His Inquisitive Dog Ser.). (ENG.). 32p. (gr. 1-3). 29.99 *(978-1-4109-6846-3(4),* Read Me!) Heinemann-Raintree.

—Introducing Australia, 1 vol. 2013. (Introducing Continents Ser.). (ENG.). 32p. (gr. 1-3). 27.32 *(978-1-4329-8041-2(6));* pap. 8.95 *(978-1-4329-8049-8(1))* Heinemann-Raintree. (Heinemann First Library).

Gitlin, Marty. Australia. 2017. (Country Profiles Ser.). (ENG., Illus.). 32p. (J). (gr. 3-8). lib. bdg. 26.95 ***(978-1-62617-675-1(2),*** Blastoff! Discovery) Bellwether Media.

Goodrich, Samuel Griswol. Peter Parleys Tales about America & Au. 2006. pap. *(978-1-4068-3320-1(7))* Echo Library.

Hakit, Ruben. Keith Urban. 2010. (Country Music Stars Ser.). (Illus.). 32p. (J). (gr. 3-8). pap. 10.50 *(978-1-4339-3605-0(4));* lib. bdg. 25.25 *(978-1-4339-3604-3(6))* Stevens, Gareth Publishing LLLP.

Hamen, Susan E. Australia, 1 vol. 2013. (Countries of the World Set 2 Ser.). (ENG.). 144p. (J). (gr. 6-12). lib. bdg. 37.07 *(978-1-61783-626-8(5),* Essential Library) ABDO Publishing Co.

Hampton, David. Living in Australia. Hampton, David, photos by. 2006. (Living In- Ser.). (Illus.). 32p. (J). (gr. 4-7). lib. bdg. 27.10 *(978-1-59771-041-1(5),* 1268834) Sea-To-Sea Pubns.

Higgins, Melissa. Julian Assange: WikiLeaks Founder, 1 vol. 2011. (Essential Lives Set 7 Ser.). (ENG., Illus.). 112p. (J). (gr. 6-12). lib. bdg. 35.64 *(978-1-61783-001-3(1))* ABDO Publishing Co.

Hirsch, Rebecca E. Australia. 2012. (Rookie Read-About Geography Ser.). (ENG., Illus.). 32p. (J). pap. 5.95 *(978-0-531-29278-5(9));* lib. bdg. 23.00 *(978-0-531-28978-5(8))* Scholastic Library Publishing.

Hudak, Heather C. Australia. 2016. ***(978-1-5105-1897-1(5))*** SmartBook Media, Inc.

—Australia. (J). 2014. *(978-1-4896-3054-4(6))* 2012. *(978-1-61913-441-6(1))* 2012. pap. *(978-1-61913-442-3(X))* 2005. (Illus.). 32p. (gr. -1-7). pap. 9.95 *(978-1-59036-326-3(4))* 2005. (Illus.). 32p. (gr. 4-6). lib. bdg. 26.00 *(978-1-59036-319-5(1))* Weigl Pubs., Inc.

Hurtig, Jennifer. Uluru: Sacred Rock of the Australian Desert. 2006. (Natural Wonders Ser.). (Illus.). 32p. (J). (gr. 3-7). 15.60 *(978-0-7569-6993-6(X))* Perfection Learning Corp.

Hyde, Natalie. Great Barrier Reef Research Journal. 2017. (Illus.). 32p. (J). ***(978-0-7787-3470-3(6))***; pap. ***(978-0-7787-3495-6(1))*** Crabtree Publishing Co.

Kalman, Bobbie. Conoce Australia. 2009. (SPA.). 32p. (J). *(978-0-7787-8191-2(7));* (gr. 2-5). pap. *(978-0-7787-8211-7(5))* Crabtree Publishing Co.

Kalman, Bobbie & Sjonger, Rebecca. Explora Australia y Oceania. 2007. (Explora Los Continentes Ser.). (SPA & ENG., Illus.). 32p. (J). (gr. 6-10). pap. *(978-0-7787-8298-8(0))* Crabtree Publishing Co.

Knight, Linsay. Australia's Greatest People & Their Achievements. 2014. (ENG., Illus.). vi, 202p. (J). (gr. 5). pap. 22.99 *(978-0-85798-020-5(3))* Random Hse. Australia AUS. Dist: Independent Pubs. Group.

Kuskowski, Alex. Super Simple Australian Art: Fun & Easy Art from Around the World, 1 vol. 2014. (Super Simple Cultural Art Set 2 Ser.). (ENG.). 32p. (gr. 5-10). lib. bdg. 27.07 *(978-1-62403-278-3(8),* Super SandCastle) ABDO Publishing Co.

Levy, Janey. Mapping Australia. 2013. 24p. (J). (gr. 2-5). 22.60 *(978-1-4339-9104-2(7))* Stevens, Gareth Publishing LLLP.

Lonely Planet Publications Staff. Australia: Everything You Ever Wanted to Know, 1 vol. 2012. (Lonely Planet Kids Ser.). (ENG., Illus.). 96p. (J). pap. 14.99 *(978-1-74321-422-0(7),* 4353) Lonely Planet Pubns.

Madison, Amelia. Predators of Asia & Australia. 2015. (J). lib. bdg. *(978-1-62713-556-6(1))* Cavendish Square Publishing.

Malley, Alex. Chris Hemsworth. 2013. (Rising Stars Ser.). 32p. (J). (gr. 3-6). 25.25 *(978-1-4339-8969-8(7));* pap. 10.50 *(978-1-4339-8970-4(0));* pap. 63.00 *(978-1-4339-8971-1(9))* Stevens, Gareth Publishing LLLP.

Mapping Australia. 2013. (Mapping the World Ser.). 24p. (J). (gr. 2-5). pap. 48.90 *(978-1-4339-9106-6(3))* Stevens, Gareth Publishing LLLP.

Marshall, Diana. Aboriginal Australians. 2012. (World Cultures Ser.). (ENG., Illus.). 32p. (J). (gr. 3-7). pap. 13.95 *(978-1-61913-528-4(0),* AV2 by Weigl) Weigl Pubs., Inc.

Mason Crest. Sydney, Vol. 8. 2016. (Major World Cities Ser.: Vol. 8). (ENG., Illus.). 48p. (J). (gr. 5-8). 20.95 *(978-1-4222-3546-1(7))* Mason Crest.

Mason Crest Publishers Staff, contrib. by. North America. 2016. (Illus.). 48p. (J). *(978-1-4222-3529-4(7))* Mason Crest.

Matthews, Sheelagh & Kissock, Heather. Sydney Opera House. 2014. (J). *(978-1-4896-2016-3(8))* Weigl Pubs., Inc.

McCartney, Tania. Australia Illustrated. 2016. (ENG., Illus.). 96p. (J). (gr. -1-3). 21.99 *(978-1-925335-21-7(6),* EK Bks.) Exisle Publishing Pty Ltd. AUS. Dist: Hachette Bk. Group.

Mes, Yvonne. Meet Sidney Nolan. Eterovic, Sandra, illus. 2016. (Meet... Ser.). (ENG.). 32p. (J). (gr. k-3). 22.99 *(978-0-85798-589-7(2))* Random Hse. Australia AUS. Dist: Independent Pubs. Group.

Moriarty, Aleta. Australia in Our World. 2010. (Countries in Our World Ser.). 32p. (YA). (gr. 3-6). lib. bdg. 28.50 *(978-1-59920-385-0(5))* Black Rabbit Bks.

Murphy, Sally. Meet Mary MacKillop. Martinez, Sonia, illus. 2013. (Meet... Ser.). (ENG.). 32p. (J). (gr. -1). 18.99 *(978-1-74275-721-6(9))* Random Hse. Australia AUS. Dist: Independent Pubs. Group.

Myers, Jenna. Australia. 2014. (J). *(978-1-4896-0946-5(6))* Weigl Pubs., Inc.

North, Peter & McKay, Susan. Australia. 2010. (Welcome to My Country Ser.). (Illus.). 48p. (J). (gr. 3). 28.50 *(978-1-60870-150-6(6))* Marshall Cavendish Corp.

Oachs, Emily Rose. Australia. (Australia Ser.). 24p. (J). (gr. k-3). 2017. pap. 6.99 ***(978-1-61891-257-2(7))*** 2016. (ENG., Illus.). lib. bdg. 25.95 *(978-1-62617-326-2(5))* Bellwether Media. (Blastoff! Readers).

O'Donnell, Kim. Australia. 2016. (Real Ser.). (ENG., Illus.). 48p. (J). (gr. 4-6). pap. 12.99 *(978-1-4451-4209-8(0),* Franklin Watts) Hachette Children's Group GBR. Dist: Hachette Bk. Group.

Oliver, Narelle. Sand Swimmers: The Secret Life of Australia's Desert Wilderness. Oliver, Narelle, illus. 2015. (ENG., Illus.). 40p. (J). (gr. 2-5). 16.99 *(978-0-7636-6761-0(7))* Candlewick Pr.

Owings, Lisa. Learning about Australia. 2015. (ENG., Illus.). 40p. (J). (gr. 3-5). 29.32 *(978-1-4677-8022-3(7),* Lerner Pubns.) Lerner Publishing Group.

Parkes, Elle. Let's Explore Australia. 2017. (Bumba Books (tm) — Let's Explore Countries Ser.). (ENG.). 24p. (J). (gr. -1-1). 25.32 ***(978-1-5124-3362-3(4))*** Lerner Publishing Group.

Peppas, Lynn. The Great Victoria Desert. 2012. (ENG.). 32p. (J). *(978-0-7787-0711-0(3));* (Illus.). pap. *(978-0-7787-0719-6(9))* Crabtree Publishing Co.

Pickwell, Linda. Australia. 2004. (QEB Travel Through Ser.). (Illus.). 32p. (J). lib. bdg. 18.95 *(978-1-59566-058-9(5))* QEB Publishing Inc.

Platt, Richard. Mapping Australia. 2016. (ENG., Illus.). 48p. (J). (gr. 3-4). pap. 9.95 *(978-0-00-816390-7(1))* HarperCollins Pubs. Ltd. GBR. Dist: Independent Pubs. Group.

Randolph, Joanne. Number Crunch Your Way Around Australia. 2015. (Math Exploration: Using Math to Learn about the Continents Ser.). (ENG., Illus.). 32p. (J). (gr. 3-4). pap. 10.00 *(978-1-4994-1243-7(6),* PowerKids Pr.) Rosen Publishing Group, Inc., The.

Reynolds, Jan. Down Under. 2007. (Vanishing Cultures Ser.). (ENG., Illus.). 32p. (J). (gr. 4-7). 8.95 *(978-1-60060-126-2(X));* 16.95 *(978-1-60060-141-5(3))* Lee & Low Bks., Inc.

Rose, Deborah Lee. Jimmy the Joey: The True Story of an Amazing Koala Rescue. Rose, Deborah Lee, photos by. 2013. (ENG., Illus.). 32p. (J). (gr. -1-3). lib. bdg. 25.90 *(978-1-4263-1372-1(1),* National Geographic Children's Bks.) National Geographic Society.

Rose, Deborah Lee & Kelly, Susan. Jimmy the Joey: The True Story of an Amazing Koala Rescue. Kelly, Susan, photos by. 2013. (ENG., Illus.). 32p. (J). (gr. -1-3). 16.95 *(978-1-4263-1371-4(3),* National Geographic Children's Bks.) National Geographic Society.

Roumanis, Alexis. Australia. 2014. (J). *(978-1-4896-3034-6(1))* Weigl Pubs., Inc.

—Exploring Continents: Australia. 2015. 24p. pap. 12.95 *(978-1-4896-3037-7(6))* Weigl Pubs., Inc.

Schwartz, Heather E. Cody Simpson: Pop Star from down Under. 2013. (Pop Culture Bios Ser.). (ENG., Illus.). 32p. (gr. 3-6). pap. 7.95 *(978-1-4677-1546-1(8));* lib. bdg. 26.60 *(978-1-4677-1305-4(8),* Lerner Pubns.) Lerner Publishing Group.

Scillian, Devin. D Is for down Under: An Australia Alphabet. Cook, Geoff, illus. 2010. (Discover the World Ser.). (ENG.). 40p. (J). (gr. 1-3). 17.95 *(978-1-58536-445-9(2),* 202170) Sleeping Bear Pr.

—D Is for down Under: An Australia Alphabet. 2016. (Av2 Fiction Readalong 2017 Ser.). (ENG.). (J). (gr. k-6). 34.28 ***(978-1-4896-5206-5(X),*** AV2 by Weigl) Weigl Pubs., Inc.

Sexton, Colleen. Australia. 2010. (Exploring Countries Ser.). (ENG., Illus.). 32p. (J). (gr. 3-7). lib. bdg. 26.95 *(978-1-60014-473-8(X),* Blastoff! Readers) Bellwether Media.

Shaffer, Jody Jensen. Liam Hemsworth. 2013. (Pop Culture Bios Ser.). (ENG., Illus.). 32p. (gr. 3-6). lib. bdg. 26.60 *(978-1-4677-0742-8(2),* Lerner Pubns.) Lerner Publishing Group.

—Liam Hemsworth: The Hunger Games' Strong Survivor. 2013. (Pop Culture Bios Ser.). (ENG., Illus.). 32p. (gr. 3-6). pap. 7.95 *(978-1-4677-0883-8(6))* Lerner Publishing Group.

Sjonger, Rebecca. L'Océanie. 2012. (FRE.). 32p. (J). pap. 9.95 *(978-2-89579-458-5(8))* Bayard Canada CAN. Dist: Crabtree Publishing Co.

Spilsbury, Richard & Spilsbury, Louise. Animals in Danger in Australia, 1 vol. 2013. (Animals in Danger Ser.). (ENG.). 32p. (gr. 1-3). pap. 8.95 *(978-1-4329-7681-1(8),* Heinemann First Library) Heinemann-Raintree.

Summerer, Eric. Wolfgang Amadeus Mozart. 2006. 36p. pap. 21.25 *(978-1-4358-3796-6(7),* PowerKids Pr.) Rosen Publishing Group, Inc., The.

Tieck, Sarah. Australia, 1 vol. 2013. (Explore the Countries Ser.). (ENG.). 40p. (J). (gr. 2-5). lib. bdg. 29.93 *(978-1-61783-804-0(7),* Big Buddy Bks.) ABDO Publishing Co.

—Liam Hemsworth: Star of the Hunger Games, 1 vol. 2013. (Big Buddy Biographies Set 9 Ser.). (ENG.). 32p. (J). (gr. 2-5). lib. bdg. 28.50 *(978-1-61783-749-4(0),* Big Buddy Bks.) ABDO Publishing Co.

Vescia, Monique. Markus Zusak, 1 vol. 2015. (ENG.). 112p. (J). 35.60 *(978-1-4777-7908-8(6),* Rosen Young Adult) Rosen Publishing Group, Inc., The.

Ward, Chris. Discover Australia. 2012. (Discover Countries Ser.). (ENG., Illus.). 32p. (J). (gr. 3-5). pap. 10.60 *(978-1-4488-7046-2(1));* lib. bdg. 26.50 *(978-1-4488-6620-5(0))* Rosen Publishing Group, Inc., The. (PowerKids Pr.).

Watson, Stephanie. Heath Ledger: Talented Actor, 1 vol. 2010. (Lives Cut Short Set 1 Ser.). (ENG.). 112p. (J). (gr. 6-12). lib. bdg. 35.64 *(978-1-60453-789-5(2))* ABDO Publishing Co.

Weil, Ann. Australia, 1 vol. 2013. (Continents Ser.). (ENG.). 48p. (J). (gr. 3-6). lib. bdg. 32.79 *(978-1-61783-931-3(0))* ABDO Publishing Co.

West, Grace. Australian Colouring Book. 2016. (ENG.). 112p. 11.95 *(978-0-670-07933-9(2))* Penguin Books Australia AUS. Dist: Independent Pubs. Group.
Wheatley, Nadia. Australians All: A History of Growing up from the Ice Age to the Apology. Searle, Ken, illus. (ENG.). 280p. (J). (gr. 5). 2015. pap. 24.99 *(978-1-76029-049-8(1))* 2013. 45.99 *(978-1-74114-637-0(2))* Allen & Unwin AUS. Dist: Independent Pubs. Group.
Woolf, Alex. Sailing the Great Barrier Reef. 2014. (Traveling Wild Ser.). 32p. (J). (gr. 3-6). pap. 63.00 *(978-1-4824-1252-9(7))* Stevens, Gareth Publishing LLLP.
Woollacott, Angela, et al. History NSW Syllabus for the Australian Curriculum Year 7 Stage 4. 2013. (ENG.). pap., stu. ed. *(978-1-107-64726-8(6))* Cambridge Univ. Pr.
—History NSW Syllabus for the Australian Curriculum Year 7 Stage 4 Workbook. 2013. (ENG.). pap., stu. ed. *(978-1-107-64127-3(6))* Cambridge Univ. Pr.
—History NSW Syllabus for the Australian Curriculum Year 9 Stage 5. 2013. (ENG.). pap., stu. ed. *(978-1-107-64473-1(9))* Cambridge Univ. Pr.
—History NSW Syllabus for the Australian Curriculum Year 9 Stage 5 Workbook. 2013. (ENG.). pap., stu. ed. *(978-1-107-68948-0(1))* Cambridge Univ. Pr.
World Book, Inc Staff, contrib. by. Aboriginal Rights Movement. 2011. (Illus.). 64p. (J). *(978-0-7166-1499-9(5))* World Bk., Inc.
—Endangered Animals of Australia, New Zealand, & Pacific Islands. 2014. *(978-0-7166-5623-4(X))* World Bk., Inc.
—Federation of Australia. 2010. (J). *(978-0-7166-1504-0(5))* World Bk., Inc.
Yalata Communities, et al. Maralinga: The Anangu Story. 2012. (ENG., Illus.). 72p. (J). (gr. 5-9). pap. 14.99 *(978-1-74237-842-8(0))* Allen & Unwin AUS. Dist: Independent Pubs. Group.

AUSTRALIAN FOOTBALL

Kirk, Brett & Kirk, Hayley S. Brave Heart: Lessons Learnt from Life. 2012. (ENG., Illus.). 244p. (J). (gr. 4-7). pap. 22.99 *(978-1-74275-325-6(6))* Random Hse. Australia AUS. Dist: Independent Pubs. Group.

AUSTRIA

Bailey, Gerry & Foster, Karen. Mozart's Wig. 2008. (Stories of Great People Ser.). (ENG., Illus.). 40p. (J). (gr. 3-6). pap. *(978-0-7787-3718-6(7))* Crabtree Publishing Co.
—Mozart's Wig. Noyes, Leighton & Radford, Karen, illus. 2008. (Stories of Great People Ser.). (ENG.). 40p. (J). (gr. 3-6). lib. bdg. *(978-0-7787-3696-7(2))* Crabtree Publishing Co.
Bodden, Valerie. The Assassination of Archduke Ferdinand. 2009. (Days of Change Ser.). 48p. (YA). (gr. 4-7). 22.95 *(978-1-58341-731-7(1))* Creative Co., The.
Cook, Diane. Wolfgang Amadeus Mozart: World-Famous Composer. 2013. (People of Importance Ser.: 21). (Illus.). 32p. (J). (gr. 4-18). 19.95 *(978-1-4222-2860-9(6))* Mason Crest.
DeCarlo, Carolyn. The Holy Roman Empire. 2017. (J). ***(978-1-68048-782-4(5))*** Rosen Publishing Group, Inc., The.
Du Bouchet, Paule. Franz Schubert, 1 vol. Voake, Charlotte, illus. 2013. (First Discovery Music Ser.). (ENG.). 28p. (J). (gr. 2-6). 19.99 *(978-1-85103-312-6(2))* Moonlight Publishing, Ltd. GBR. Dist: Independent Pubs. Group.
Dyan, Penelope. High on a Hill! a Kid's Guide to Innsbruck, Austri. Weigand, John D., photos by. 2011. (Illus.). 40p. pap. 12.95 *(978-1-935630-76-0(8))* Bellissima Publishing, LLC.
—On the Hill! a Kid's Guide to Melk, Austri. Weigand, John D., photos by. 2013. (Illus.). 34p. pap. 11.95 *(978-1-61477-074-9(3))* Bellissima Publishing, LLC.
Gillam, Scott. Sigmund Freud: Famous Neurologist, 1 vol. 2011. (Essential Lives Set 7 Ser.). (ENG., Illus.). 112p. (J). (gr. 6-12). lib. bdg. 35.64 *(978-1-61783-004-4(6))* ABDO Publishing Co.
Grahame, Deborah A. Austria. 2006. (Discovering Cultures Ser.). (Illus.). 48p. (J). (gr. 3-7). lib. bdg. 28.50 *(978-0-7614-1984-6(5),* Benchmark Bks.) Marshall Cavendish Corp.
Harel, Nirah. Lev Katan Gadol: Sipuro Shel Hertsl. (HEB., Illus.). 95p. *(978-965-403-132-5(9))* Reches Publishing Hse.
Hart, Alison. Wolfgang Puck. 2012. (J). *(978-1-61900-020-9(2)); (978-1-61900-021-6(0)); (978-1-61900-019-3(9))* Eldorado Ink.
Hughes, Helga. Cooking the Austrian Way. 2nd rev. ed. 2003. (Easy Menu Ethnic Cookbooks 2nd Edition Ser.). (ENG., Illus.). 72p. (gr. 5-12). 25.26 *(978-0-8225-4102-8(5))* Lerner Publishing Group.
Klare, Roger. Gregor Mendel: Genius of Genetics. 2015. (J). *(978-0-7660-6565-9(0))* Enslow Pubs., Inc.
Mapua, Jeff. Ludwig Van Beethoven: Classical Composer of Passion & Power. 2015. (Britannica Beginner Bios Ser.). (ENG.). 32p. (J). 23.45 *(978-1-62275-931-6(1),* Britannica Educational Publishing) Rosen Publishing Group, Inc., The.
Mazdra, Marian. Austria. 2004. (Countries of the World Ser.). (Illus.). 96p. (gr. 5-12). lib. bdg. 31.00 *(978-0-8368-3115-3(2))* Stevens, Gareth Publishing LLLP.
Owings, Lisa. Austria. 2014. (Exploring Countries Ser.). (ENG., Illus.). 32p. (J). (gr. 3-7). lib. bdg. 26.95 *(978-1-60014-983-2(9),* Blastoff! Readers) Bellwether Media.
Rusch, Elizabeth. For the Love of Music: The Remarkable Story of Maria Anna Mozart. Fancher, Lou & Johnson, Steve, illus. 2011. (ENG.). 32p. (J). (gr. k-3). 16.99 *(978-1-58246-326-1(3),* Tricycle Pr.) Random Hse. Children's Bks.
Sanna, Jeanine. Austria. 2007. (European Union Ser.). (Illus.). 88p. (YA). (gr. 3-7). lib. bdg. 21.95 *(978-1-4222-0039-1(6),* 1247981) Mason Crest.
Sanna, Jeanine & Indovino, Shaina C. Austria. Bruton, John, ed. 2012. (Major European Union Nations Ser.). 64p. (J). (gr. 7). 22.95 *(978-1-4222-2232-4(2))* Mason Crest.
Sanna, Jeanine & Indovino, Shaina Carmel. Austria. 2012. (J). pap. *(978-1-4222-2263-8(2))* Mason Crest.
Sheehan, S. & Ali, Sharifah Enayat. Afghanistan. 2013. 144p. (J). (gr. 6-9). 47.07 *(978-1-60870-866-6(7))* Cavendish Square Publishing.
Sheehan, Sean & Nevins, Debbie. Austria. 2016. (Cultures of the World (r) Ser.). (Illus.). 144p. (J). (gr. 5-5). 47.07 *(978-1-5026-1841-2(9))* Cavendish Square Publishing.
Stein, R. Conrad. Austria. 2009. (J). *(978-0-531-23119-7(4))* Scholastic, Inc.
Summerer, Eric Michael. Franz Joseph Haydn. 2009. (Primary Source Library of Famous Composers Ser.). 32p. (gr. 4-4). 42.50 *(978-1-60854-106-5(1),* PowerKids Pr.) Rosen Publishing Group, Inc., The.
—Franz Peter Schubert. 2009. (Primary Source Library of Famous Composers Ser.). 32p. (gr. 4-4). 42.50 *(978-1-60854-107-2(X),* PowerKids Pr.) Rosen Publishing Group, Inc., The.
—Wolfgang Amadeus Mozart. 2009. (Primary Source Library of Famous Composers Ser.). 32p. (gr. 4-4). 42.50 *(978-1-60854-115-7(0),* PowerKids Pr.) Rosen Publishing Group, Inc., The.
Viegas, Jennifer. Beethoven's World. 2009. (Music Throughout History Ser.). 64p. (gr. 5-6). 58.50 *(978-1-61514-682-6(2),* Rosen Reference) Rosen Publishing Group, Inc., The.
Weeks, Marcus. World History Biographies: Mozart: The Boy Who Changed the World with His Music. 2013. (National Geographic World History Biographies Ser.). (ENG., Illus.). 64p. (J). (gr. 3-7). pap. 7.99 *(978-1-4263-1451-3(5),* National Geographic Children's Bks.) National Geographic Society.

AUSTRIA—FICTION

Allen, Katherine. Gloves down Under. Allen, Katherine, illus. 2005. (Illus.). 32p. (J). 15.95 *(978-0-9747278-9-9(X))* Diakonia Publishing.
Avery, Ben. Tunnel Twist-Up, 1 vol., Vol. 4. Gaudiamo, Adi Darda, illus. 2008. (Z Graphic Novels / TimeFlyz Ser.). (ENG.). 160p. (J). (gr. 4-7). pap. 6.99 *(978-0-310-71364-7(1))* Zondervan.
Bier, Andreas. I Wish I Could Fly. Bier, Donna, illus. 2009. 20p. pap. 9.14 *(978-1-4269-0271-0(9))* Trafford Publishing.
Diller, Janelle. Mystery of the Ballerina Ghost. Turner, Adam, illus. 2013. 104p. (J). pap. 5.99 *(978-1-936376-00-1(8))* WorldTrek Publishing.
Dunlap, Susanne. The Musician's Daughter. 2009. (ENG.). 336p. (YA). (gr. 7-18). 16.99 *(978-1-59990-332-3(6),* 9781599903323, Bloomsbury USA Childrens) Bloomsbury Publishing USA.
Dunlop, Ed. Escape to Liechtenstein. 2003. (Young Refugees Ser.). 152p. (J). (gr. 3-7). per. 7.49 *(978-1-59166-013-2(0))* BJU Pr.
Heller, Silvia. The Woodman's Rose. 2005. 28p. per. 19.99 *(978-1-4208-8152-3(3))* AuthorHouse.
Jay, Basil. The Adventures of Twig. 2011. (Illus.). 120p. pap. 32.90 *(978-1-4567-8631-1(8))* AuthorHouse.
Kendall, Jane F. Maestoso Petra. Sanderson, Ruth, illus. 2010. (Horse Diaries: No. 4). (ENG.). 160p. (J). (gr. 3-7). pap. 7.99 *(978-0-375-85842-0(3),* Random Hse. Bks. for Young Readers) Random Hse. Children's Bks.
Kerz, Anna. The Gnome's Eye, 1 vol. 2010. (ENG.). 224p. (J). (gr. 4-7). pap. 9.95 *(978-1-55469-195-1(8))* Orca Bk. Pubs. USA.
Manners, Tyler. Continental Change of Heart. 2006. 65p. pap. 16.95 *(978-1-4137-9483-0(1))* PublishAmerica, Inc.
Optic, Oliver, pseud. Sunny Shores; or, Young America in Italy & Austria a Story of Travel & Adventure by William T Adams. 2006. 428p. per. 26.99 *(978-1-4255-4627-4(7))* Michigan Publishing.
Orgel, Doris. Devil in Vienna. 2004. (ENG.). 256p. (J). (gr. 3-7). 7.99 *(978-0-14-240236-8(2),* Speak) Penguin Young Readers Group.

AUTHORITARIANISM

see Totalitarianism

AUTHORS

see also African American Authors
also classes of writers (e.g. Novelists; Poets; etc.); and names of individual authors

Abbey, Cherie D., ed. Biography Today: Profiles of People of Interest to Young Readers. (Biography Today Subject Ser.: Vol. 15). 2004. 200p. (gr. 3-18). lib. bdg. 44.00 *(978-0-7808-0707-5(3))* 2003. 200p. lib. bdg. 44.00 *(978-0-7808-0652-8(2))* 2003. 228p. lib. bdg. 44.00 *(978-0-7808-0651-1(4))* Omnigraphics, Inc.
ABDO Publishing Company Staff. Children's Authors Set 6, 1 vol. 2012. (Children's Authors Set 6 Ser.: 6). (ENG., Illus.). 24p. 153.90 *(978-1-61783-044-0(5),* Checkerboard Library) ABDO Publishing Co.
About the Author: Set 2. (Illus.). (J). (gr. k-5). 112.50 *(978-0-8239-7259-3(3))* Rosen Publishing Group, Inc., The.
About the Author Set 3. (Illus.). (J). (gr. k-5). 112.50 *(978-1-4042-3291-4(5))* Rosen Publishing Group, Inc., The.
Alaniz, Valeria & Garcia, Sarah Rafael. Barrio Writers: Empowering Teens Through Creative Writing —: A Collection of Works by Teens for Teens, Teachers & Our Communities. 2012. (SPA & ENG.). 147p. (YA). pap. *(978-1-890701-32-1(7))* La Mancha Publishing Group.
Arab-American & Muslim Writers. 2010. (Multicultural Voices Ser.). (Illus.). 130p. (gr. 6-12). 35.00 *(978-1-60413-377-6(5),* Chelsea Hse.) Facts On File, Inc.
Aristizabal, Luis H. Germán Arciniegas -un joven de cien Años. 2005. (SPA.). 148p. (YA). *(978-958-30-1707-0(8))* Panamericana Editorial.
Asian-American Writers. 2010. (Multicultural Voices Ser.). (Illus.). 146p. (gr. 6-12). 35.00 *(978-1-60413-313-4(9),* Chelsea Hse.) Facts On File, Inc.
Aykroyd, Clarissa. Savage Satire: The Story of Jonathan Swift. 2006. (World Writers Ser.). (Illus.). 160p. (J). (gr. 3-7). lib. bdg. 27.95 *(978-1-59935-027-1(0))* Reynolds, Morgan Inc.
Ball, Heather. Remarkable Women Writers, 1 vol. 2006. (Women's Hall of Fame Ser.). (ENG., Illus.). 100p. (J). (gr. 4-8). pap. 10.95 *(978-1-897187-08-1(4))* Second Story Pr. CAN. Dist: Orca Bk. Pubs. USA.
Benatar, Raquel. Isabel Allende: Memories for a Story: Isabel Allende: Recuerdos para un Cuento. Petersen, Patricia, tr. Molinari, Fernando, illus. 2003. (SPA & ENG.). 32p. 16.95 *(978-1-55885-379-9(0),* Piñata Books) Arte Publico Pr.
Benatar, Raquel & Torrecilla, Pablo. Isabel Allende: Recuerdos para un Cuento. Petersen, Patricia, tr. Benatar, Raquel & Torrecilla, Pablo, illus. 2004. (ENG & SPA., Illus.). (J). 14.95 *(978-1-56492-341-7(X),* Piñata Books) Arte Publico Pr.
Bloom, Harold, ed. Bloom's Biocritiques. 2005. (Bloom's Bio Critiques Ser.). (C). (gr. 9). 665.00 *(978-0-7910-9134-0(1),* Chelsea Hse.) Facts On File, Inc.
—Bloom's Major Novelists Series, 25 vols., Set. Incl. Franz Kafka. Bloom, Harold, intro. (Illus.). 2002. 31.95 *(978-0-7910-7028-4(X),* 039975, Chelsea Hse.); Fyodor Dostoevsky. Chang, Emmy. (Illus.). 2002. 31.95 *(978-0-7910-6346-0(1),* 039964, Chelsea Hse.); Herman Melville. Piorkowski, Sue. (Illus.). 2003. 31.95 *(978-0-7910-7027-7(1),* 039976, Chelsea Hse.); Marcel Proust. Bloom, Harold, intro. 2002. 31.95 *(978-0-7910-7029-1(8),* 039977); Nathaniel Hawthorne. Hawthorne, Nathaniel. 1999. 31.95 *(978-0-7910-5253-2(2),* 039954, Chelsea Hse.); Stendhal. Bloom, Harold, intro. 2001. 31.95 *(978-0-7910-6351-4(8),* 039972, Chelsea Hse.); Thomas Hardy. Marson, Janyce. (Illus.). 2003. 31.95 *(978-0-7910-6348-4(8),* 039965, Chelsea Hse.); 120p. (C). (gr. 9-13). 573.75 *(978-0-7910-7197-7(9),* 039950S, Chelsea Hse.) Facts On File, Inc.
—Bloom's Major Short Story Writers. 2005. (Bloom's Major Short Story Writers Ser.). (C). (gr. 9). 415.35 *(978-0-7910-9135-7(X),* Chelsea Hse.) Facts On File, Inc.
Bloom, Harold, ed. & intro. Bloom's BioCritiques Series, 28 vols., Set. Bloom, Harold, intro. Incl. Ernest Hemingway. (Illus.). 112p. (C). (gr. 9-13). 2001. 35.00 *(978-0-7910-6174-9(4),* 000854, Chelsea Hse.); 726.60 *(978-0-7910-7192-2(8),* 000850S, Chelsea Hse.) Facts On File, Inc.
Bloom, Harold, et al. Bloom's Major Novelists. 2005. (Bloom's Major Novelists Ser.). (Illus.). 144p. (C). (gr. 9). 287.55 *(978-0-7910-7380-3(7))* Facts On File, Inc.
Boon, Kevin Alexander. Kurt Vonnegut. 2013. (Today's Writers & Their Works Ser.). 144p. (YA). (gr. 7-12). 42.79 *(978-1-62712-155-2(2))* Cavendish Square Publishing.
Brackett, Virginia. Restless Genius: The Story of Virginia Woolf. 2004. (World Writers Ser.). (Illus.). 144p. (YA). (gr. 6-12). 23.95 *(978-1-931798-37-2(0))* Reynolds, Morgan Inc.
Briggs, Lucy. Kate Dicamillo. 2005. (My Favorite Writer Ser.). (Illus.). 32p. (J). (gr. 5-7). lib. bdg. 26.00 *(978-1-59036-283-9(7))* Weigl Pubs., Inc.
The Britannica Guide to Authors. 2013. (Britannica Guide to Authors Ser.). (YA). (gr. 9-10). 636.00 *(978-1-62275-063-4(2));* 318.00 *(978-1-62275-017-7(9))* Rosen Publishing Group, Inc., The.
Buckley, James. Who Was Jules Verne? Harrison, Nancy & Copeland, Gregory, illus. 2016. (Who Was? Ser.). (ENG.). 112p. (J). (gr. 3-7). 5.99 *(978-0-448-48850-9(7),* Grosset & Dunlap) Penguin Young Readers Group.
Burnett, Frances Hodgson. El Pequeño Lord.Tr. of Little Lord Fauntleroy. (SPA., Illus.). (YA). 11.95 *(978-84-7281-059-4(3),* AF1059) Auriga, Ediciones S.A. ESP. Dist: Continental Bk. Co., Inc.
—El Pequeño Lord. (Coleccion Clasicos de la Juventud).Tr. of Little Lord Fauntleroy. (SPA., Illus.). 204p. (J). 12.95 *(978-84-7189-096-2(8),* ORT315) Ortells, Alfredo Editorial S.L. ESP. Dist: Continental Bk. Co., Inc.
Carlson, Cheryl. Favorite Author Bios Pack [Scholastic]. 2011. (First Biographies - Writers, Artists, & Athletes Ser.). 24p. pap. 1.50 *(978-1-4296-6320-5(0),* Pebble Bks.) Capstone Press of Coughlan Cos.
Chambers, Catherine. Count Dracula. 2015. (Autobiographies You Never Thought You'd Read! Ser.). (ENG., Illus.). 32p. (gr. 1-3). 29.99 *(978-1-4109-7963-6(6),* Read Me!) Heinemann-Raintree.
Christelow, Eileen. What Do Authors & Illustrators Do? 2013. (ENG., Illus.). 80p. (J). (gr. -1-3). 9.99 *(978-0-547-97260-2(1))* Houghton Mifflin Harcourt Publishing Co.
Clinton, Greg. Reading & Interpreting the Works of Jhumpa Lahiri. 2016. (Lit Crit Guides). 176p. (J). lib. bdg. 39.93 *(978-0-7660-8364-6(0))* Enslow Pubs., Inc.
Collins, David R. Write a Book for Me: The Story of Marguerite Henry. 2004. (World Writers Ser.). (Illus.). 112p. (YA). (gr. 6-12). 23.95 *(978-1-883846-39-8(0),* First Biographies) Reynolds, Morgan Inc.
Daudet, Alphonse. Las Aventuras Prodigiosas de Tartarin de Tarascon. (Coleccion Clasicos de la Juventud).Tr. of Tartarin de Tarascon. (SPA., Illus.). 204p. (J). 12.95 *(978-84-7189-195-2(6),* ORT324) Ortells, Alfredo Editorial S.L. ESP. Dist: Continental Bk. Co., Inc.
Davenport, John C. Dante: Poet, Author & Proud Florentine. 2005. (Makers of the Middle Ages & Renaissance Ser.). (Illus.). 136p. (J). (gr. 5-8). lib. bdg. 32.95 *(978-0-7910-8634-6(8),* Chelsea Hse.) Facts On File, Inc.
Delano, Poli. When I Was a Boy Neruda Called Me Policarpo: A Memoir, 1 vol. Higgins, Sean, tr. from SPA. Monroy, Manuel, illus. 2006. (ENG.). 96p. (J). (gr. 3-7). 15.95 *(978-0-88899-726-5(4))* Groundwood Bks. CAN. Dist: Publishers Group West (PGW).
Demi. Su Dongpo: Chinese Genius. 2015. (ENG., Illus.). 56p. (J). pap. 12.95 *(978-1-62014-232-5(5))* Lee & Low Bks., Inc.
Demi & Demi Staff. Su Dongpo. 2006. (ENG., Illus.). 56p. (J). (gr. 2-5). 24.00 *(978-1-58430-256-8(9))* Lee & Low Bks., Inc.
Doft, Tony. Nostradamus. 2011. (Unexplained Ser.). (ENG., Illus.). 24p. (J). (gr. 3-7). lib. bdg. 25.95 *(978-1-60014-584-1(1),* Torque Bks.) Bellwether Media.
Donaldson, Chelsea. Robert Munsch, 1 vol. 2014. (Canadian Biographies Ser.). (ENG.). 24p. (gr. k-1). 26.65 *(978-1-4914-1960-1(1),* Pebble Plus) Capstone Press of Coughlan Cos.
Downey, Glen R. The 10 Most Remarkable Writers. 2008. 14.99 *(978-1-55448-553-6(3))* Scholastic Library Publishing.
Edwards, Frank B. Robert Munsch: Portrait of an Extraordinary Canadian, 1 vol. 2009. (Larger Than Life Ser.). (ENG.). 71p. (J). (gr. 2-4). *(978-1-55455-138-5(2))* Fitzhenry & Whiteside, Ltd.
Ehrlich, Amy. Willa: The Story of Willa Cather, an American Writer. Minor, Wendell, illus. 2016. (ENG.). 72p. (J). (gr. 2-5). 16.99 *(978-0-689-86573-2(2),* Simon & Schuster Bks. For Young Readers) Simon & Schuster Bks. For Young Readers.
Einarson, Earl. The Moccasins. Einarson, Earl, illus. 2004. (Moccasins Ser.). (ENG., Illus.). 16p. pap. 7.95 *(978-1-894778-14-5(6))* Theytus Bks., Ltd. CAN. Dist: Univ. of Toronto Pr.
Engle, Margarita. Enchanted Air: Two Cultures, Two Wings: A Memoir. Rodriguez, Edel, illus. (ENG.). (YA). (gr. 7). 2016. 224p. pap. 10.99 *(978-1-4814-3523-9(X))* 2015. 208p. 18.99 *(978-1-4814-3522-2(1))* Simon & Schuster Children's Publishing.
Erlic, Lily. Lois Lowry. 2005. (My Favorite Writer Ser.). (Illus.). 32p. (J). (gr. 5-7). lib. bdg. 26.00 *(978-1-59036-286-0(1))* Weigl Pubs., Inc.
—Louis Sachar. 2005. (My Favorite Writer Ser.). (Illus.). 32p. (J). (gr. 5-7). lib. bdg. 26.00 *(978-1-59036-288-4(8))* Weigl Pubs., Inc.
Faulkner, Nicholas, ed. 101 Authors. 2016. (People You Should Know Ser.). 184p. (J). (gr. 8-8). lib. bdg. 36.25 *(978-1-68048-506-6(7))* Rosen Publishing Group, Inc., The.
Franco, Michou. I Can Be a Writer. 2017. (I Can Be Anything! Ser.). 24p. (gr. k-k). pap. 8.15 ***(978-1-4824-6337-8(7))*** Stevens, Gareth Publishing LLLP.
Gollub, Matthew, et al. Cool Melons — Turn to Frogs! The Life & Poems of Issa. Stone, Kazuko G., illus. 2017. (JPN & ENG.). (J). *(978-1-889910-50-5(3))* Tortuga Pr.
Great Science Writers. 2014. (Great Science Writers Ser.). 112p. (YA). (gr. 7-12). 213.60 *(978-1-4777-7773-2(3))* Rosen Publishing Group, Inc., The.
Great Writers. 2005. (Great Writers Ser.). (Illus.). 128p. (C). (gr. 9-13). 191.70 *(978-0-7910-7842-6(6),* Chelsea Hse.) Facts On File, Inc.
Henry, W., et al. Bloom's BioCritiques. (J). 934.20 *(978-0-7910-7379-7(3),* Chelsea Hse.) Facts On File, Inc.
Hispanic-American Writers. 2010. (Multicultural Voices Ser.). (Illus.). 128p. (gr. 6-12). 35.00 *(978-1-60413-312-7(0),* Chelsea Hse.) Facts On File, Inc.
Hughes, Shirley. A Life Drawing: Recollections of an Illustrator. 2007. (ENG., Illus.). 208p. (gr. 4-7). 55.00 *(978-0-370-32605-4(9))* Transworld Publishers Ltd. GBR. Dist: Independent Pubs. Group.
Hurwitz, Johanna. Astrid Lindgren: Storyteller to the World. 2016. (Women of Our Time Ser.). (ENG., Illus.). 96p. (J). (gr. 3-7). 7.99 *(978-0-14-751668-8(4),* Puffin Books) Penguin Young Readers Group.
Hustad, Douglas. Environmentalist Rachel Carson. 2016. (STEM Trailblazer Bios Ser.). (ENG., Illus.). 32p. (J). (gr. 2-5). lib. bdg. 26.65 *(978-1-5124-0787-7(9))* Lerner Publishing Group.
Hyde, Margaret O. Robert Cormier. 2005. (Who Wrote That? Ser.). (Illus.). 112p. (gr. 6-12). lib. bdg. 35.00 *(978-0-7910-8232-4(6),* Chelsea Hse.) Facts On File, Inc.
Jerome, Jerome K. & Klapka, Jerome. Tres Hombres en una Barca. (Coleccion Clasicos de la Juventud). (SPA., Illus.). 208p. (J). 12.95 *(978-84-7189-048-1(8),* ORT317) Ortells, Alfredo Editorial S.L. ESP. Dist: Continental Bk. Co., Inc.
Kilcoyne, Hope, ed. Great Authors of Popular Fiction. 2013. (Essential Authors for Children & Teens Ser.). (Illus.). 198p. (YA). (gr. 7-12). 45.00 *(978-1-62275-086-3(1))* Rosen Publishing Group, Inc., The.
Kissock, Heather. The Quirky World of Robert Munsch. 2016. (J). ***(978-1-5105-1961-9(0))*** SmartBook Media, Inc.
Kissock, Heather. Robert Munsch. 2012. (J). *(978-1-61913-056-2(4))* 2012. (J). pap. *(978-1-61913-599-4(X))* 2008. (Writers, Illus.). 32p. (YA). (gr. 5-18). pap. 8.95 *(978-1-59036-925-8(4))* 2008. (Illus.). 32p. (YA). (gr. 5-18). lib. bdg. 26.00 *(978-1-59036-924-1(6))* Weigl Pubs., Inc.
Kolpin, Molly, et al. Your Favorite Authors. Byers, Michael, illus. 2013. (Your Favorite Authors Ser.). (ENG.). 24p. (gr. 1-2). pap. 47.70 *(978-1-4765-3648-4(1));* lib. bdg. 151.92 *(978-1-4765-0372-1(9))* Capstone Press of Coughlan Cos. (First Facts).
Kovacs, Deborah & Preller, James. Meet the Authors & Illustrators. pap. 13.95 *(978-0-590-24111-3(7))* Scholastic, Inc.
Lazaro, Georgina. Jose. Sanchez, Maria, illus. 2007. (J). 14.99 *(978-1-933032-08-5(1))* Lectorum Pubns., Inc.
—Pablo. Donoso, Marcela, illus. 2008. (Cuando los Grandes Eran Pequenos Ser.). (SPA.). 32p. (J). (gr. 3-5). 14.99 *(978-1-933032-09-2(X))* Lectorum Pubns., Inc.
Lazaro, Georgina. Ruben Dario. 2016. (SPA.). (J). (gr. 4-6). 14.99 ***(978-1-63245-641-0(9))*** Lectorum Pubns., Inc.
Lázaro León, Georgina & Yockteng, Rafael. Gabriel García Márquez: Gabito. Yockteng, Rafael, illus. 2014. (SPA., Illus.). (J). 14.99 *(978-1-933032-85-6(5))* Lectorum Pubns., Inc.
Lazo, Caroline Evensen. Alice Walker: Freedom Writer. 2005. (Lerner Biographies Ser.). (Illus.). 128p. (gr. 6-12). 27.93 *(978-0-8225-4960-4(3))* Lerner Publishing Group.
Levithan, David. What We Remember, What We Forget: The Best Young Writers & Artists in America. Levithan, David, ed. 2012. (ENG.). 304p. (J). (gr. 7-7). pap. 10.99 *(978-0-545-39714-8(6),* PUSH) Scholastic, Inc.
The Library of Author Biographies, 1-4 bks., Set. 2005. (YA). (gr. 5-8). lib. bdg. 478.80 *(978-1-4042-0501-7(2))* Rosen Publishing Group, Inc., The.
The Library of Author Biographies Set 6. (YA). (gr. 5-8). 159.00 *(978-1-4042-0623-6(X),* Rosen Reference) Rosen Publishing Group, Inc., The.
Ling, Bettina. Willa Cather: Author & Critic. 2003. (Great Life Stories: Writers & Poets Ser.). (ENG., Illus.). 112p. (J). 30.50 *(978-0-531-12316-4(2),* Watts, Franklin) Scholastic Library Publishing.
Lit Crit Guides: Set 2. 2016. (Lit Crit Guides). 176p. (gr. 6-6). lib. bdg. 239.58 *(978-0-7660-7505-4(2))* Enslow Pubs., Inc.
Marcus, Leonard S. Ways of Telling: Conversations on the Art of the Picture Book. 2005. (Illus.). 247p. reprint ed. 30.00 *(978-0-7567-9704-1(7))* DIANE Publishing Co.
Martin. Dietrich Bonhoeffer. 2011. (Champion of Freedom Ser.). (gr. 7-12). 28.95 *(978-1-59935-169-8(2))* Reynolds, Morgan Inc.
Martin, Carol. Catharine Parr Traill: Backwoods Pioneer. 2004. (ENG., Illus.). 128p. (YA). pap. *(978-0-88899-495-0(8),* Libros Tigrillo) Groundwood Bks. CAN. Dist: Publishers Group West (PGW).
Molnar, Ferenc & Molnár, Ferenc. Los Muchachos de la Calle Pal. (Coleccion Clasicos de la Juventud). (SPA., Illus.). 176p. (J). 12.95 *(978-84-7189-021-4(6),* ORT303) Ortells, Alfredo Editorial S.L. ESP. Dist: Continental Bk. Co., Inc.
Nagle, Jeanne, ed. Great Authors of Children's Books. 2013. (Essential Authors for Children & Teens Ser.). (YA). (gr. 7-12). 45.00 *(978-1-62275-096-2(9))* Rosen Publishing Group, Inc., The.
—Great Authors of Classic Literature. 2013. (Essential Authors for Children & Teens Ser.). (YA). (gr. 7-12). 45.00 *(978-1-62275-084-9(5))* Rosen Publishing Group, Inc., The.
—Great Authors of Mystery, Horror & Thrillers. 2013. (Essential Authors for Children & Teens Ser.). (Illus.). 182p. (YA). (gr. 7-12). 45.00 *(978-1-62275-094-8(2))* Rosen Publishing Group, Inc., The.
—Great Authors of Nonfiction. 2013. (Essential Authors for Children & Teens Ser.). (YA). (gr. 7-12). 45.00 *(978-1-62275-092-4(6))* Rosen Publishing Group, Inc., The.

AB

—Great Poets & Playwrights. 2013. (Essential Authors for Children & Teens Ser.). (YA). (gr. 7-12). 45.00 *(978-1-62275-088-7(8))* Rosen Publishing Group, Inc., The.

Native American Writers. 2010. (Multicultural Voices Ser.). (Illus.). 126p. (gr. 6-12). 35.00 *(978-1-60413-314-1(7),* Chelsea Hse.) Facts On File, Inc.

Nault, Jennifer. The Insightful World of Judy Blume. 2016. (J). ***(978-1-5105-1953-4(X))*** SmartBook Media, Inc.

Null Petersen, Kathleen C. Writers Then & Now, 1 vol. 2006. (Primary Source Readers Ser.). (ENG.). 32p. (J). (gr. 1-1). pap. 8.99 *(978-0-7439-9380-7(2))* Shell Educational Publishing.

Owings, Lisa. Learn about Authors & Illustrators. 2013. (Library Smarts Ser.). (ENG., Illus.). 24p. (gr. -1-2). lib. bdg. 23.93 *(978-1-4677-1502-7(6),* Lerner Pubns.) Lerner Publishing Group.

Pezzi, Bryan. David Suzuki. 2010. (Illus.). 24p. *(978-1-77071-595-0(9));* pap. *(978-1-77071-601-8(7))* Weigl Educational Pubs. Ltd.

—David Suzuki: Ma Vie. Karvonen, Tanjah, tr. from ENG. 2011. (FRE., Illus.). 24p. (YA). (gr. 2-4). *(978-1-77071-429-8(4))* Weigl Educational Pubs. Ltd.

Poets & Playwrights, 5 vols., Set. Incl. Carl Sandburg. Murcia, Rebecca Thatcher. lib. bdg. 37.10 *(978-1-58415-430-3(6));* Emily Dickinson. Griskey, Michele. lib. bdg. 37.10 *(978-1-58415-429-7(2));* Langston Hughes. Gibson, Karen Bush. lib. bdg. 37.10 *(978-1-58415-431-0(4));* Tennessee Williams. Tracy, Kathleen. lib. bdg. 37.10 *(978-1-58415-427-3(6));* William Shakespeare. Whiting, Jim. lib. bdg. 37.10 *(978-1-58415-426-6(8));* (Illus.). 112p. (J). (gr. 3-7). 2007. 2007. Set lib. bdg. 185.50 *(978-1-58415-284-2(2))* Mitchell Lane Pubs., Inc.

Reed, Avery & dePaola, Tomie. Who Were the Brothers Grimm? O'brien, John, illus. 2015. (Who Was? Ser.). (ENG.). 112p. (J). (gr. 3-7). 5.99 *(978-0-448-48314-6(9),* Grosset & Dunlap) Penguin Young Readers Group.

Richardson, Gillian. Dan Gutman. 2005. (My Favorite Writer Ser.). (Illus.). 32p. (J). (gr. 5-7). lib. bdg. 26.00 *(978-1-59036-284-6(5))* Weigl Pubs., Inc.

Ridge, Judith. The Book That Made Me: A Collection of Personal Stories. 2017. (ENG.). 256p. (YA). (gr. 9). pap. 9.99 *(978-0-7636-9671-9(4))* Candlewick Pr.

Ridge, Judith, ed. The Book That Made Me. 2017. (ENG.). 256p. (YA). (gr. 9). 17.99 *(978-0-7636-9549-1(1))* Candlewick Pr.

Riggs, Kate & Fandel, Jennifer. Frank Lloyd Wright. 2017. (Odysseys in Artistry Ser.). (ENG., Illus.). 80p. (J). (gr. 7-11). pap. 14.99 *(978-1-62832-314-6(0),* Creative Paperbacks) Creative Co., The.

Rosen Publishing Staff. All about the Author: Set 3, 1 vol. 2015. (All about the Author Ser.). (ENG.). 112p. (YA). 213.60 *(978-1-4777-7916-3(7),* Rosen Young Adult) Rosen Publishing Group, Inc., The.

Salgari, Emilio & Salgari, Emilio. Los Piratas de Malasia. (Coleccion Clasicos de la Juventud). (SPA., Illus.). 200p. (J). 12.95 *(978-84-7189-058-0(5),* ORT312) Ortells, Alfredo Editorial S.L. ESP. Dist: Continental Bk. Co., Inc.

—Los Tigres de Mom Pracem. (Coleccion Clasicos de la Juventud). (SPA., Illus.). 224p. (J). 12.95 *(978-84-7189-056-6(9),* ORT318) Ortells, Alfredo Editorial S.L. ESP. Dist: Continental Bk. Co., Inc.

Sickels, Amy. Adrienne Rich. 2005. (Gay & Lesbian Writers Ser.). (Illus.). 112p. (gr. 6-12). 35.00 *(978-0-7910-8223-2(7),* Chelsea Hse.) Facts On File, Inc.

Simons, Lisa M. Bolt. Your Favorite Authors. 2017. (Your Favorite Authors Ser.). (ENG.). 24p. (gr. 1-2). 253.20 *(978-1-5157-3560-1(5),* First Facts) Capstone Press of Coughlan Cos.

Speaker-Yuan, Margaret. Avi. 2005. (Who Wrote That? Ser.). (Illus.). 112p. (gr. 6-12). lib. bdg. 35.00 *(978-0-7910-8230-0(X),* Chelsea Hse.) Facts On File, Inc.

Stathis, Roberta & Blanch, Gregory. Writers Who Inspired the World. 2003. (Explore the Ages Ser.). (Illus.). 79p. 17.00 *(978-1-55501-591-6(3))* Ballard & Tighe Pubs.

Stout, William. William Stout - Tribute to Ray Harryhausen. 2003. (Illus.). 70p. (YA). per. 20.00 *(978-0-9712716-9-2(0))* Stout, William Inc.

Ternier Gordon, Irene. Grey Owl (Junior Edition) 2007. (Amazing Stories Junior Ser.). (Illus.). 96p. pap. *(978-1-55439-723-5(5))* Altitude Publishing Canada Ltd.

Today's Writers & Their Works. 2013. (YA). (gr. 7-12). 213.95 *(978-1-62712-150-7(1))* Cavendish Square Publishing.

Tolstoi, Leo, et al. El Prisonero del Caucaso. (Coleccion Clasicos de la Juventud). (SPA., Illus.). 232p. (J). 12.95 *(978-84-7189-088-7(7),* ORT319) Ortells, Alfredo Editorial S.L. ESP. Dist: Continental Bk. Co., Inc.

Torres, John Albert. Haruki Murakami: Best-Selling Author. 2016. (Influential Asians Ser.). 128p. (gr. 7-6). 37.27 *(978-0-7660-7901-4(5))* Enslow Pubs., Inc.

Tracy, Kathleen. John Steinbeck. 2004. (Classic Storytellers Ser.). (Illus.). 48p. (J). (gr. 4-8). lib. bdg. 29.95 *(978-1-58415-271-2(0))* Mitchell Lane Pubs., Inc.

Vescia, Monique. Markus Zusak, 1 vol. 2015. (ENG.). 112p. (J). 35.60 *(978-1-4777-7908-8(6),* Rosen Young Adult) Rosen Publishing Group, Inc., The.

Wallace, Ian. The Curiosity Cabinet. 2017. (ENG., Illus.). 36p. (J). (gr. k). 19.95 ***(978-1-55498-922-5(1))*** Groundwood Bks. CAN. Dist: Publishers Group West (PGW).

Weidenbach, Kristin. Meet Banjo Paterson. Hancock, James Gulliver, illus. 2015. (Meet... Ser.: Bk. 7). (ENG.). 32p. (J). (gr. -1-k). 21.99 *(978-0-85798-008-3(4))* Random Hse. Australia AUS. Dist: Independent Pubs. Group.

Welsch, Camille-Yvette. Meg Cabot. 2008. (Who Wrote That? Ser.). 136p. (gr. 6-12). 35.00 *(978-0-7910-9631-4(9),* Chelsea Hse.) Facts On File, Inc.

Whitelaw, Nancy. Bram Stoker: Author of Dracula. rev. exp. ed. 2004. (World Writers Ser.). (Illus.). 112p. (YA). (gr. 6-12). 23.95 *(978-1-931798-33-4(8))* Reynolds, Morgan Inc.

Who Wrote That?, 6 vols., Set. (Illus.). 112p. (YA). (gr. 6-12). 137.70 *(978-0-7910-6718-5(1),* Chelsea Hse.) Facts On File, Inc.

World Writers, vols. 16, vol. 16. Incl. Best of Times: The Story of Charles Dickens. Caravantes, Peggy. (Illus.). 160p. (gr. 3-7). 2005. lib. bdg. 28.95 *(978-1-931798-68-6(0));* C. S. Lewis: Twentieth Century Pilgrim. 128p. (gr. 7-9). 2011. lib. bdg. 28.95 *(978-1-59935-112-4(9));* Dark Dreams: The Story of Stephen King. Whitelaw, Nancy. (Illus.). 128p. (YA). (gr. 8-12). 2005. lib. bdg. 26.95 *(978-1-931798-77-8(X));* Deep Woods: The Story of Robert Frost. (Illus.). 176p. (gr. 6-12). 2006. lib. bdg. 28.95 *(978-1-931798-92-1(3));* England's Jane: the Story of Jane Austen. Locke, Juliane. (Illus.). 144p. (gr. 6-12). 2006. lib. bdg. 28.95 *(978-1-931798-82-2(6));* From China to America: The Story of Amy Tan. O'Keefe, Sherry. 112p. (gr. 7-18). 2011. lib. bdg. 28.95 *(978-1-59935-138-4(2));* Gift of Imagination: The Story of Roald Dahl. Gelletly, LeeAnne. (Illus.). 160p. (gr. 6-12). 2006. lib. bdg. 27.95 *(978-1-59935-026-4(2));* Great & Sublime Fool: The Story of Mark Twain. Caravantes, Peggy. (Illus.). 176p. (YA). (gr. 8-18). 2010. lib. bdg. 28.95 *(978-1-59935-088-2(2));* Ralph Ellison: Author of Invisible Man. Rhynes, Martha E. (Illus.). 160p. (gr. 6-12). 2006. lib. bdg. 28.95 *(978-1-931798-69-3(9));* Rhythm & Folklore: The Story of Zora Neale Hurston. Sapet, Kerrily. 160p. (YA). (gr. 7-18). 2008. lib. bdg. 27.95 *(978-1-59935-067-7(X));* Savage Satire: The Story of Jonathan Swift. Aykroyd, Clarissa. (Illus.). 160p. (J). (gr. 3-7). 2006. lib. bdg. 27.95 *(978-1-59935-027-1(0));* Self Reliance: The Story of Ralph Waldo Emerson. 2011. lib. bdg. 28.95 *(978-1-59935-124-7(2));* Strange Creatures: The Story of Mary Shelley. Wells, Catherine. (J). 2009. 28.95 *(978-1-59935-092-9(0));* Tortured Noble: The Story of Leo Tolstoy. Heims, Neil. (Illus.). 144p. (gr. 9-18). 2007. lib. bdg. 27.95 *(978-1-59935-066-0(1));* Writing Is My Business: The Story of O. Henry. Caravantes, Peggy. (Illus.). 160p. (J). (gr. 3-7). 2006. lib. bdg. 27.95 *(978-1-59935-031-8(9));* 2007. Set lib. bdg. 495.20 *(978-1-59935-014-1(9))* Reynolds, Morgan Inc.

Writers & Their Works, 5 bks., Set. Incl. Arthur Miller. Andersen, Richard. 144p. lib. bdg. *(978-0-7614-1946-4(2));* Charlotte Bronte. Reiff, Raychel Haugrud. 160p. lib. bdg. *(978-0-7614-1948-8(9));* F. Scott Fitzgerald. Boon, Kevin A. 142p. lib. bdg. *(978-0-7614-1947-1(0));* Mark Twain. McArthur, Debra. 158p. lib. bdg. *(978-0-7614-1950-1(0));* Toni Morrison. Andersen, Richard. 144p. lib. bdg. *(978-0-7614-1945-7(4));* (Illus.). (YA). (gr. 8-12). 2005. *(978-0-7614-1944-0(6),* Benchmark Bks.) Marshall Cavendish Corp.

Writers & Their Works - Group 3, 4 bks., Set. Incl. Edgar Allan Poe: Tales & Poems. Reiff, Raychel Haugrud. lib. bdg. 42.79 *(978-0-7614-2963-0(8));* George Orwell: Animal Farm & Nineteen Eighty-Four. Boon, Kevin A. lib. bdg. 42.79 *(978-0-7614-2960-9(3));* John Steinbeck: The Grapes of Wrath & of Mice & Men. McArthur, Debra. (Illus.). (J). lib. bdg. 42.79 *(978-0-7614-2964-7(6));* Sylvia Plath: The Bell Jar & Poems. Reiff, Raychel Haugrud. lib. bdg. 42.79 *(978-0-7614-2962-3(X));* 144p. (gr. 7-18). 2008. Set lib. bdg. 171.14 *(978-0-7614-2957-9(3),* Benchmark Bks.) Marshall Cavendish Corp.

Zuluaga, Conrado. Gabriel Garcia Marquez: El Vicio Incurable de Contar. 2005. (100 Personajes/Autores Ser.). (SPA., Illus.). 132p. (YA). *(978-958-30-1959-3(3))* Panamericana Editorial.

AUTHORS, AFRICAN AMERICAN

see African American Authors

AUTHORS, AMERICAN

Abdo Publishing. Great American Authors, 1 vol. 2013. (Great American Authors Ser.: 6). (ENG.). 48p. (J). (gr. 3-6). lib. bdg. 196.74 *(978-1-61783-714-2(8))* ABDO Publishing Co.

Abrams, Dennis. Barbara Park. 2006. (Who Wrote That? Ser.). (Illus.). 138p. (gr. 6-12). lib. bdg. 35.00 *(978-0-7910-8969-9(X))* Facts On File, Inc.

—Gary Soto. 2008. (Who Wrote That? Ser.). (Illus.). 120p. (gr. 6-12). 35.00 *(978-0-7910-9529-4(0),* Chelsea Hse.) Facts On File, Inc.

—Maxine Hong Kingston. 2009. (Asian Americans of Achievement Ser.). (Illus.). 128p. (YA). (gr. 7-12). 35.00 *(978-1-60413-568-8(9))* Facts On File, Inc.

—S. E. Hinton. 2009. (Who Wrote That? Ser.). (Illus.). 104p. (gr. 6-12). 35.00 *(978-1-60413-088-1(1),* Chelsea Hse.) Facts On File, Inc.

Abrams, Dennis & Ludwig, Elisa. Judy Blume. 2nd rev. ed. 2009. (Who Wrote That? Ser.). 120p. (gr. 6-12). 35.00 *(978-1-60413-334-9(1),* Chelsea Hse.) Facts On File, Inc.

Adil, Janeen R. Dr. Seuss. 2004. (Robbie Reader Ser.). (Illus.). 32p. (J). (gr. 1-4). lib. bdg. 25.70 *(978-1-58415-288-0(5))* Mitchell Lane Pubs., Inc.

Adler, David A. A Picture Book of Harriet Beecher Stowe. Bootman, Colin, illus. 2003. (ENG.). 32p. (J). (gr. k-3). tchr. ed. 17.95 *(978-0-8234-1646-2(1))* Holiday Hse., Inc.

Albert, Lisa Rondinelli. Lois Lowry: The Giver of Stories & Memories. 2007. (Authors Teens Love Ser.). (Illus.). 128p. (J). (gr. 8-12). lib. bdg. 33.27 *(978-0-7660-2722-0(8))* Enslow Pubs., Inc.

—Stephenie Meyer: Author of the Twilight Saga. 2009. (Authors Teens Love Ser.). (Illus.). 112p. (J). (gr. 6-18). lib. bdg. 33.27 *(978-0-7660-3584-3(0))* Enslow Pubs., Inc.

Aller, Susan Bivin. Beyond Little Women: A Story about Louisa May Alcott. Wang, Qi Z., illus. 2004. (Creative Minds Biographies Ser.). (ENG.). 64p. (gr. 4-8). pap. 8.95 *(978-1-57505-636-4(4));* lib. bdg. 22.60 *(978-1-57505-602-9(X))* Lerner Publishing Group.

—Mark Twain. 2006. (Just the Facts Biographies Ser.). (Illus.). 112p. (J). 27.93 *(978-0-8225-3425-9(8));* (gr. 3-7). pap. 9.95 *(978-0-8225-5998-6(6))* Lerner Publishing Group. (Lerner Pubns.).

Alter, Judy & Alter, Judy. Laura Ingalls Wilder: Pioneer & Author. 2003. (Our People Ser.). (ENG., Illus.). 32p. (J). (gr. 3-6). 29.93 *(978-1-59296-007-1(3),* 200644) Child's World, Inc., The.

Amper, Susan. Bloom's How to Write about Edgar Allan Poe. 2007. (Bloom's How to Write about Literature Ser.). 232p. (C). (gr. 9-12). 45.00 *(978-0-7910-9488-4(X),* Chelsea Hse.) Facts On File, Inc.

Ancona, George. Self Portrait. Ancona, George, photos by. 2006. (Meet the Author Ser.). (Illus.). 32p. (J). 14.95 *(978-1-57274-860-6(5),* 733, Meet the Author) Owen, Richard C. Pubs., Inc.

Andersen, Richard. Abraham Rodriguez. 2013. (Today's Writers & Their Works Ser.). 144p. (YA). (gr. 7-12). pap. 22.34 *(978-1-62712-147-7(1))* Cavendish Square Publishing.

—Abraham Rodriguez. 2011. (J). *(978-1-60870-506-1(4))* Marshall Cavendish.

—Walter Dean Myers. 2014. (J). lib. bdg. *(978-1-62712-262-7(1))* Cavendish Square Publishing.

Anderson, Jennifer Joline. Langston Hughes, 1 vol. 2013. (Great American Authors Ser.). (ENG.). 48p. (J). (gr. 3-6). lib. bdg. 32.79 *(978-1-61783-718-0(0))* ABDO Publishing Co.

Anderson, Tanya. Dr. Seuss (Theodor Geisel) 2nd rev. ed. 2011. (Who Wrote That? Ser.). (Illus.). 128p. (gr. 6-12). 35.00 *(978-1-60413-750-7(9),* Chelsea Hse.) Facts On File, Inc.

Anderson, William. Laura Ingalls Wilder: A Biography. 2007. (Little House Nonfiction Ser.). (ENG., Illus.). 256p. (J). (gr. 3-7). pap. 6.99 *(978-0-06-088552-6(1),* Collins) HarperCollins Pubs.

Andre Norton. 2010. (Who Wrote That? Ser.). (Illus.). 128p. (gr. 6-12). 35.00 *(978-1-60413-682-1(0),* Chelsea Hse.) Facts On File, Inc.

Angel, Ann. Amy Tan: Weaver of Asian-American Tales. 2009. (Authors Teens Love Ser.). (Illus.). 128p. (J). (gr. 6). lib. bdg. 33.27 *(978-0-7660-2962-0(X))* Enslow Pubs., Inc.

—A Reader's Guide to Sandra Cisneros's the House on Mango Street. 2010. (Multicultural Literature Ser.). (Illus.). 128p. (YA). 33.27 *(978-0-7660-3167-8(5))* Enslow Pubs., Inc.

—Robert Cormier: Author of the Chocolate War. 2007. (Authors Teens Love Ser.). (Illus.). 104p. (J). (gr. 8-12). lib. bdg. 33.27 *(978-0-7660-2719-0(8))* Enslow Pubs., Inc.

Armentrout, David & Armentrout, Patricia. Mark Twain. 2003. (Discover the Life of an American Legend Ser.). (Illus.). 24p. (gr. 2-5). lib. bdg. *(978-1-58952-660-0(0))* Rourke Educational Media.

Arnold, Quinn M. & Riggs, Kate. Ernest Hemingway. 2017. (Odysseys in Artistry Ser.). (ENG., Illus.). 80p. (J). (gr. 7-11). pap. 14.99 *(978-1-62832-313-9(2),* Creative Paperbacks) Creative Co., The.

Arnosky, James. Whole Days Outdoors: An Autobiographical Album. Arnosky, Deanna, photos by. 2006. (Meet the Author Ser.). (ENG., Illus.). 32p. (J). 14.95 *(978-1-57274-859-0(1),* 734, Meet the Author) Owen, Richard C. Pubs., Inc.

Aronson, Deb. E. B. White. 2009. (Library of Author Biographies Ser.). 112p. (gr. 5-8). 63.90 *(978-1-60853-531-6(2),* Rosen Reference) Rosen Publishing Group, Inc., The.

Ashmore, Wayne & Nault, Jennifer. The Adventurous World of Mark Twain. 2016. (J). ***(978-1-5105-1955-8(6))*** SmartBook Media, Inc.

Ashmore, Wayne & Nault, Jennifer. Mark Twain. 2008. (My Favorite Writer Ser.). (Illus.). 32p. (YA). (gr. 5-18). pap. 9.95 *(978-1-59036-931-9(9));* lib. bdg. 26.00 *(978-1-59036-930-2(0))* Weigl Pubs., Inc.

Axelrod-Contrada, Joan. Isabel Allende. 2010. (Today's Writers & Their Works). 128p. (gr. 7-18). 42.79 *(978-0-7614-4116-8(6))* Marshall Cavendish Corp.

Bagley, Val Chadwick. My Book about Me. (J). pap. 4.95 *(978-1-57734-341-7(7),* 01113682) Covenant Communications, Inc.

Bailey, Diane. Suzanne Collins. 2012. (All about the Author Ser.). (ENG., Illus.). 112p. (J). (gr. 7-12). lib. bdg. 34.60 *(978-1-4488-6938-1(2))* Rosen Publishing Group, Inc., The.

Bankston, John. F. Scott Fitzgerald. 2004. (Classic Storytellers Ser.). (Illus.). 48p. (J). (gr. 4-8). lib. bdg. 29.95 *(978-1-58415-249-1(4))* Mitchell Lane Pubs., Inc.

—Jack London. 2004. (Classic Storytellers Ser.). (Illus.). 48p. (J). (gr. 4-8). lib. bdg. 29.95 *(978-1-58415-263-7(X))* Mitchell Lane Pubs., Inc.

—Lois Lowry. 2009. (Who Wrote That? Ser.). 128p. (gr. 6-12). 35.00 *(978-1-60413-335-6(X),* Chelsea Hse.) Facts On File, Inc.

—Ray Bradbury. 2011. (Who Wrote That? Ser.). (Illus.). 140p. (gr. 6-12). 35.00 *(978-1-60413-778-1(9),* Chelsea Hse.) Facts On File, Inc.

Banting, Erinn. Mary Pope Osbourne. 2006. (My Favorite Writer Ser.). (Illus.). 32p. (YA). (gr. 5-18). pap. 9.95 *(978-1-59036-483-3(X));* lib. bdg. 26.00 *(978-1-59036-482-6(1))* Weigl Pubs., Inc.

Baptiste, Tracey. Jerry Spinelli. 2009. (Who Wrote That? Ser.). (Illus.). 128p. (gr. 6-12). 35.00 *(978-0-7910-9572-0(X),* Chelsea Hse.) Facts On File, Inc.

—Madeleine L'Engle. 2009. (Who Wrote That? Ser.). (Illus.). 128p. (gr. 6-12). 35.00 *(978-0-7910-9573-7(8),* Chelsea Hse.) Facts On File, Inc.

—Sharon Creech. 2011. (Who Wrote That? Ser.). (Illus.). 118p. (gr. 6-12). 35.00 *(978-1-60413-774-3(6),* Chelsea Hse.) Facts On File, Inc.

—Stephenie Meyer. 2011. (Who Wrote That? Ser.). 128p. (gr. 6-12). pap. 10.95 *(978-1-60413-666-1(9),* Checkmark Bks.) Facts On File, Inc.

Barile, Mary. Alphonso Wetmore: Soldier, Adventurer, & Writer. 2015. (ENG., Illus.). 48p. (J). 24.00 *(978-1-61248-147-0(7))* Truman State Univ. Pr.

Baughan, Michael Gray. Shel Silverstein. 2008. (Who Wrote That? Ser.). (Illus.). 120p. (gr. 6-12). lib. bdg. 35.00 *(978-0-7910-9676-5(9),* Chelsea Hse.) Facts On File, Inc.

—Stephen King. 2009. (Who Wrote That? Ser.). (Illus.). 112p. (gr. 6-12). 35.00 *(978-0-7910-9852-3(4),* Chelsea Hse.) Facts On File, Inc.

Beckman, Wendy Hart. Robert Cormier: Banned, Challenged, & Censored. 2008. (Authors of Banned Bks). (Illus.). 160p. (YA). (gr. 4-7). lib. bdg. 35.94 *(978-0-7660-2691-9(4))* Enslow Pubs., Inc.

Behnke, Alison. Jack Kerouac. 2007. (Biography Ser.). (Illus.). 112p. (gr. 6-12). lib. bdg. 29.27 *(978-0-8225-6614-4(1),* Twenty-First Century Bks.) Lerner Publishing Group.

Bell, Cece. El Deafo. Lasky, David, illus. 2014. (ENG.). 248p. (J). (gr. 3-7). 21.95 *(978-1-4197-1020-9(6));* pap. 10.95 *(978-1-4197-1217-3(9))* Abrams, Inc. (Amulet Bks.).

—El Deafo. 2014. (J). lib. bdg. 22.05 *(978-0-606-36148-4(0))* Turtleback Bks.

Bennett, Doraine. Laura Ingalls Wilder: Little World Biographies. 2013. (ENG.). 24p. (gr. k-3). pap. 8.95 *(978-1-61810-293-5(1))* Rourke Educational Media.

Bernard, Catherine. E. B. White: Spinner of Webs & Tales. 2005. (Authors Teens Love Ser.). (Illus.). 104p. (J). (gr. 6-12). lib. bdg. 27.94 *(978-0-7660-2350-5(8))* Enslow Pubs., Inc.

Berne, Emma Carlson. Laura Ingalls Wilder, 1 vol. 2007. (Essential Lives Set 1 Ser.). (ENG., Illus.). 112p. (J). (gr. 6-12). lib. bdg. 35.64 *(978-1-59928-843-7(5))* ABDO Publishing Co.

Blasingame, James B. Gary Paulsen, 1 vol. 2007. (Teen Reads: Student Companions to Young Adult Literature Ser.). 184p. (C). (gr. 7). 50.00 *(978-0-313-33532-7(X),* GR3532, Greenwood) ABC-CLIO, LLC.

Bloom, Harold, ed. Catch-22 - Joseph Heller. 2nd ed. 2007. (Modern Critical Interpretations Ser.). 281p. (C). (gr. 9-18). 45.00 *(978-0-7910-9617-8(3),* Chelsea Hse.) Facts On File, Inc.

—Emerson's Essays. 2006. (Bloom's Modern Critical Interpretations Ser.). 150p. (C). (gr. 9). lib. bdg. 45.00 *(978-0-7910-8118-1(4),* Chelsea Hse.) Facts On File, Inc.

—F. Scott Fitzgerald. 2nd rev. ed. 2006. (Bloom's Modern Critical Views Ser.). 261p. (C). (gr. 9). lib. bdg. 45.00 *(978-0-7910-8570-7(8),* Chelsea Hse.) Facts On File, Inc.

—The House on Mango Street - Sandra Cisneros. 2009. (Bloom's Modern Critical Interpretations Ser.). 192p. (C). (gr. 9-18). 45.00 *(978-1-60413-586-2(7),* Chelsea Hse.) Facts On File, Inc.

—Kurt Vonnegut, New Edition. 2nd rev. ed. 2008. (Bloom's Modern Critical Views Ser.). 176p. (C). (gr. 9-18). 45.00 *(978-1-60413-167-3(5),* Chelsea Hse.) Facts On File, Inc.

—Maya Angelou, New Edition. 2nd rev. ed. 2009. (Bloom's Modern Critical Views Ser.). 200p. (C). (gr. 9-18). 45.00 *(978-1-60413-177-2(2),* Chelsea Hse.) Facts On File, Inc.

—Maya Angelou's I Know Why the Caged Bird Sings. 2nd rev. ed. 2009. (Bloom's Modern Critical Interpretations Ser.). 141p. (C). (gr. 9-18). 45.00 *(978-1-60413-187-1(X),* Chelsea Hse.) Facts On File, Inc.

—Richard Wright's Black Boy. 2006. (Bloom's Modern Critical Interpretations Ser.). 150p. (C). (gr. 9). lib. bdg. 45.00 *(978-0-7910-8585-1(6),* Chelsea Hse.) Facts On File, Inc.

Bloom, Harold, intro. Alice Walker. 2nd ed. 2007. (Modern Critical Views Ser.). 223p. (C). (gr. 9). lib. bdg. 45.00 *(978-0-7910-9611-6(4),* Chelsea Hse.) Facts On File, Inc.

Bober, Natalie S. Papa Is a Poet: A Story about Robert Frost. Gibbon, Rebecca, illus. 2013. (ENG.). 40p. (J). (gr. -1-3). 17.99 *(978-0-8050-9407-7(5),* 9780805094077, Holt, Henry & Co. Bks. For Young Readers) Holt, Henry & Co.

Bodden, Valerie. Mark Twain, 1 vol. 2013. (Great American Authors Ser.). (ENG.). 48p. (J). (gr. 3-6). lib. bdg. 32.79 *(978-1-61783-719-7(9))* ABDO Publishing Co.

Boerst, William J. Edgar Rice Burroughs: Creator of Tarzan. 2004. (World Writers Ser.). (Illus.). 112p. (J). (gr. 6-12). 23.95 *(978-1-883846-56-5(0),* First Biographies) Reynolds, Morgan Inc.

Boffa, Laura. Writing Home: The Story of Author Thomas Wolfe. 2016. (ENG., Illus.). 32p. (J). 15.95 *(978-1-63076-133-2(8))* Taylor Trade Publishing.

Boomhower, Ray E. The Sword & the Pen: A Life of Lew Wallace. 2005. (Illus.). x, 164p. (J). 15.95 *(978-0-87195-185-4(1))* Indiana Historical Society.

Boon, Kevin A. Kurt Vonnegut: Slaughterhouse-Five & Cat's Cradle. 2012. *(978-1-60870-508-5(0))* Marshall Cavendish.

Boon, Kevin Alexander. Ernest Hemingway: The Sun Also Rises & Other Works. 2007. (Writers & Their Work Ser.). (Illus.). 144p. (gr. 7-18). lib. bdg. 42.79 *(978-0-7614-2590-8(X),* Benchmark Bks.) Marshall Cavendish Corp.

Borden, Louise. The Journey That Saved Curious George Young Readers Edition: The True Wartime Escape of Margret & H. A. Rey. Drummond, Allan, illus. 2016. (Curious George Ser.). (ENG.). 96p. (J). (gr. 2-5). pap. 7.99 *(978-0-544-76345-6(9),* HMH Books For Young Readers) Houghton Mifflin Harcourt Publishing Co.

Borden, Louise & Borden, Louise W. The Journey That Saved Curious George: The True Wartime Escape of Margret & H. A. Rey. Drummond, Allan, illus. 2005. (Curious George Ser.). (ENG.). 80p. (J). (gr. 2-5). 17.99 *(978-0-618-33924-2(8))* Houghton Mifflin Harcourt Publishing Co.

Borden, Louise W. The Journey That Saved Curious George: The True Wartime Escape of Margret & H. A. Rey. Drummond, Allan, illus. 2010. (Curious George Ser.). (ENG.). 80p. (J). (gr. 2-5). pap. 8.99 *(978-0-547-41746-2(2))* Houghton Mifflin Harcourt Publishing Co.

Borus, Audrey. Reading & Interpreting the Works of Emily Dickinson. 2016. (Lit Crit Guides). (ENG., Illus.). 160p. (J). (gr. 8-8). lib. bdg. 39.93 *(978-0-7660-7344-9(0))* Enslow Pubs., Inc.

Borus, Audrey. Reading & Interpreting the Works of Maya Angelou. 2017. (Lit Crit Guides). 160p. (J). (gr. 8-8). lib. bdg. 39.93 ***(978-0-7660-8497-1(3))*** Enslow Pubs., Inc.

Bowman, Chris. Chris Van Allsburg. 2017. (Children's Storytellers Ser.). (ENG.). 24p. (J). (gr. 2-5). lib. bdg. 25.95 *(978-1-62617-549-5(7),* Blastoff! Readers) Bellwether Media.

—Christopher Paul Curtis. 2017. (Children's Storytellers Ser.). (ENG., Illus.). 24p. (J). (gr. 2-5). lib. bdg. 25.95 *(978-1-62617-550-1(0),* Blastoff! Readers) Bellwether Media.

—Dav Pilkey. 2017. (Children's Storytellers Ser.). (ENG., Illus.). 24p. (J). (gr. k-3). lib. bdg. 25.95 ***(978-1-62617-647-8(7),*** Blastoff! Readers) Bellwether Media.

—Gordon Korman. 2017. (Children's Storytellers Ser.). (ENG., Illus.). 24p. (J). (gr. k-3). lib. bdg. 25.95 ***(978-1-62617-648-5(5),*** Blastoff! Readers) Bellwether Media.

—Judy Blume. 2015. (Children's Storytellers Ser.). (ENG., Illus.). 24p. (J). (gr. 2-5). lib. bdg. 25.95 *(978-1-62617-268-5(4),* Blastoff! Readers) Bellwether Media.

—Lemony Snicket. 2017. (Children's Storytellers Ser.). (ENG.). 24p. (J). (gr. 2-5). lib. bdg. 25.95 *(978-1-62617-551-8(9),* Blastoff! Readers) Bellwether Media.

—Lois Lowry. 2016. (Children's Storytellers Ser.). (ENG., Illus.). 24p. (J). (gr. 2-5). lib. bdg. 25.95 *(978-1-62617-340-8(0),* Blastoff! Readers) Bellwether Media.

—Mary Pope Osborne. 2017. (Children's Storytellers Ser.). (ENG., Illus.). 24p. (J). (gr. k-3). lib. bdg. 25.95 ***(978-1-62617-649-2(3),*** Blastoff! Readers) Bellwether Media.

—Maurice Sendak. 2016. (Children's Storytellers Ser.). (ENG., Illus.). 24p. (J). (gr. 2-5). lib. bdg. 25.95 *(978-1-62617-341-5(9),* Blastoff! Readers) Bellwether Media.

—R. L. Stine. 2017. (Children's Storytellers Ser.). (ENG., Illus.). 24p. (J). (gr. 2-5). lib. bdg. 25.95 *(978-1-62617-552-5(7),* Blastoff! Readers) Bellwether Media.

—Shel Silverstein. 2015. (Children's Storytellers Ser.). (ENG., Illus.). 24p. (J). (gr. 2-5). lib. bdg. 25.95 *(978-1-62617-271-5(4),* Blastoff! Readers) Bellwether Media.

Brackett, Virginia. A Home in the Heart: The Story of Sandra Cisneros. 2004. (World Writers Ser.). (Illus.). 112p. (J). (gr. 6-12). 23.95 *(978-1-931798-42-6(7))* Reynolds, Morgan Inc.

Braun, Eric. John Green: Star Author, Vlogbrother, & Nerdfighter. 2015. (Gateway Biographies Ser.). (ENG., Illus.). 48p. (J). (gr. 4-8). lib. bdg. 26.60 *(978-1-4677-7244-0(5),* Lerner Pubns.) Lerner Publishing Group.

—Maurice Sendak [Scholastic]. 2011. (First Biographies - Writers, Artists, & Athletes Ser.). 24p. pap. 0.50 *(978-1-4296-6318-2(9),* Pebble Bks.) Capstone Press of Coughlan Cos.

—Tomie Depaola [Scholastic]. 2011. (First Biographies - Writers, Artists, & Athletes Ser.). 24p. pap. 0.50 *(978-1-4296-6319-9(7),* Pebble Bks.) Capstone Press of Coughlan Cos.

Brown, Monica. My Name Is Gabito: The Life of Gabriel Garcia Marquez. Colón, Raúl, illus. 2007. (ENG.). 32p. (J). (gr. -1-3). 15.95 *(978-0-87358-934-5(3))* Cooper Square Publishing Llc.

—My Name Is Gabito/Me Llamo Gabito: The Life of Gabriel Garcia Marquez/la Vida de Gabriel Garcia Marquez. Colón, Raúl, illus. 2007. (ENG, SPA & MUL.). 32p. (J). (gr. -1-3). 15.95 *(978-0-87358-908-6(4))* Cooper Square Publishing Llc.

Brown, Monica & National Geographic Learning Staff. My Name Is Gabriela/Me Llamo Gabriela: The Life of Gabriela Mistral/la Vida de Gabriela Mistral. Parra, John, illus. 2010. (Rise & Shine Ser.). (SPA, MUL & ENG.). 32p. (C). (gr. -1-3). 25.95 *(978-0-87358-859-1(2))* National Geographic School Publishing, Inc.

Brown, Tracy. Stephenie Meyer. 2012. (All about the Author Ser.). (ENG., Illus.). 112p. (J). (gr. 7-12). lib. bdg. 34.60 *(978-1-4488-6936-7(6))* Rosen Publishing Group, Inc., The.

Bryan, Ashley. Ashley Bryan: Words to My Life's Song. Bryan, Ashley, illus. McGuinness, Bill, photos by. 2009. (ENG., Illus.). 64p. (J). (gr. -1-18). 19.99 *(978-1-4169-0541-7(3),* Atheneum Bks. for Young Readers) Simon & Schuster Children's Publishing.

Buckwalter, Stephanie. Reading & Interpreting the Works of Jack London. 2017. (Lit Crit Guides). 160p. (J). (gr. 8-8). lib. bdg. 39.93 ***(978-0-7660-8491-9(4))*** Enslow Pubs., Inc.

Burlingame, Jeff. Edgar Allan Poe: Deep into That Darkness Peering. 2008. (Americans—the Spirit of a Nation Ser.). (Illus.). 128p. (J). (gr. k-5). lib. bdg. 33.27 *(978-0-7660-3020-6(2))* Enslow Pubs., Inc.

Buzzeo, Toni. Toni Buzzeo & You, 1 vol. 2005. (Author & YOU Ser.). (Illus.). 176p. (C). per. 35.00 *(978-1-59158-211-3(3),* LU2113, Libraries Unlimited) ABC-CLIO, LLC.

Byars, Betsy. The Moon & I. 2014. 112p. pap. 6.00 *(978-1-61003-379-4(5))* Center for the Collaborative Classroom.

Campbell, Kimberly. Lois Duncan: Author of I Know What You Did Last Summer. 2009. (Authors Teens Love Ser.). (Illus.). 104p. (J). (gr. 6). lib. bdg. 33.27 *(978-0-7660-2963-7(8))* Enslow Pubs., Inc.

—Richard Peck: A Spellbinding Storyteller. 2007. (Authors Teens Love Ser.). (Illus.). 112p. (J). (gr. 8-12). lib. bdg. 33.27 *(978-0-7660-2723-7(6))* Enslow Pubs., Inc.

Caravantes, Peggy. A Great & Sublime Fool: The Story of Mark Twain. 2010. (World Writers Ser.). (Illus.). 176p. (YA). (gr. 8-18). lib. bdg. 28.95 *(978-1-59935-088-2(2))* Reynolds, Morgan Inc.

—O. Henry: William Sidney Porter: Texas Cowboy Writer. 2003. (J). *(978-1-57168-768-5(8),* Eakin Pr.) Eakin Pr.

—Writing Is My Business: The Story of O. Henry. 2006. (World Writers Ser.). (Illus.). 160p. (J). (gr. 3-7). lib. bdg. 27.95 *(978-1-59935-031-8(9))* Reynolds, Morgan Inc.

Carew-Miller, Anna. Mark Twain. Di Gennaro, Andrea, illus. 2003. (Great Names Ser.). (J). 19.95 *(978-957-745-414-0(3))* Mason Crest.

Carlson, Cheryl. Dr. Seuss [Scholastic]. 2011. (First Biographies - Writers, Artists, & Athletes Ser.). 24p. pap. 0.50 *(978-1-4296-6317-5(0),* Pebble Bks.) Capstone Press of Coughlan Cos.

Carlson, Melody & Rue, Nancy N. Dear Nancy: Answers to Letters from Girls Like You, 1 vol. 2008. (Faithgirlz Ser.). (ENG.). 160p. (J). pap. 7.99 *(978-0-310-71496-5(6))* Zonderkidz.

Christopher, Dale. Behind the Desk with... Matt Christopher: The #1 Sportswriter for Kids. 2004. (ENG., Illus.). 128p. (J). (gr. 2-5). pap. 15.99 *(978-0-316-10952-9(5),* Tingley, Megan Bks.) Little, Brown Bks. for Young Readers.

Christopher Paolini. 2010. (Who Wrote That? Ser.). (Illus.). 136p. (J). (gr. 6-12). 35.00 *(978-1-60413-727-9(4),* Chelsea Hse.) Facts On File, Inc.

Clare, Cassandra, ed. Shadowhunters & Downworlders: A Mortal Instruments Reader. 2013. (ENG.). 256p. (J). (gr. 6). pap. 12.95 *(978-1-937856-22-9(4))* BenBella Bks.

Clarke, Nzingha. Karen Hesse. 2009. (Library of Author Biographies Ser.). 112p. (gr. 5-8). 63.90 *(978-1-60853-541-5(X),* Rosen Reference) Rosen Publishing Group, Inc., The.

Colich, Abby. Grace Lin, 1 vol. Byers, Michael, illus. 2013. (Your Favorite Authors Ser.). (ENG.). 24p. (gr. 1-2). 25.32 *(978-1-4765-3158-8(7));* pap. 7.95 *(978-1-4765-3445-9(4))* Capstone Press of Coughlan Cos. (First Facts).

Collard, Sneed B., III. Phillis Wheatley: She Loved Words. 2009. (American Heroes Ser.). 48p. (gr. 3-18). 29.93 *(978-0-7614-4057-4(7))* Marshall Cavendish Corp.

Collins, David R. Washington Irving: Storyteller for a New Nation. 2004. (World Writers Ser.). (Illus.). 112p. (YA). (gr. 6-12). 23.95 *(978-1-883846-50-3(1),* First Biographies) Reynolds, Morgan Inc.

Corbett, Sue. Gary Paulsen. 2013. 48p. (J). (gr. 5-8). 29.93 *(978-1-60870-934-2(5));* pap. 12.93 *(978-1-62712-142-2(0))* Cavendish Square Publishing.

—Jeff Kinney. 2013. 48p. (J). (gr. 5-8). 29.93 *(978-1-60870-932-8(9));* pap. 12.93 *(978-1-62712-140-8(4))* Cavendish Square Publishing.

—Jennifer L. Holm. 2013. 48p. (J). (gr. 5-8). 29.93 *(978-1-60870-931-1(0));* pap. 12.93 *(978-1-62712-139-2(0))* Cavendish Square Publishing.

—Kate Dicamillo. 2013. 48p. (J). (gr. 5-8). 29.93 *(978-1-60870-933-5(7));* pap. 12.93 *(978-1-62712-141-5(2))* Cavendish Square Publishing.

—Rick Riordan. 2013. 48p. (J). (gr. 5-8). 29.93 *(978-1-60870-935-9(3));* pap. 12.93 *(978-1-62712-143-9(9))* Cavendish Square Publishing.

Craats, Rennay. E. B. White. 2013. (J). *(978-1-62127-405-6(5));* pap. *(978-1-62127-411-7(X))* Weigl Pubs., Inc.

Crayton, Lisa A. Reading & Interpreting the Works of Toni Morrison. 2016. (Lit Crit Guides). (ENG., Illus.). 152p. (J). (gr. 8-8). lib. bdg. 39.93 *(978-0-7660-7352-4(1))* Enslow Pubs., Inc.

Crutcher, Chris. King of the Mild Frontier: An Ill-Advised Autobiography. 2004. (ENG.). 272p. (YA). (gr. 9). reprint ed. pap. 9.99 *(978-0-06-050251-5(7),* Greenwillow Bks.) HarperCollins Pubs.

Currie-McGhee, Leanne K. Mattie Stepanek: Inspirational Poet. 2007. (Young Heroes Ser.). (ENG., Illus.). 64p. (gr. 3-7). lib. bdg. 35.70 *(978-0-7377-3637-3(2),* Greenhaven Pr., Inc.) Cengage Gale.

Dailey, Donna. Tamora Pierce. 2006. (Who Wrote That? Ser.). (Illus.). 144p. (gr. 6-12). lib. bdg. 35.00 *(978-0-7910-8795-4(6),* Chelsea Hse.) Facts On File, Inc.

Daniel, Susanna. Karen Cushman. (Library of Author Biographies Ser.). 112p. 2009. (gr. 5-8). 63.90 *(978-1-60853-540-8(1),* Rosen Reference) 2005. (Illus.). (J). (gr. k-3). lib. bdg. 34.60 *(978-1-4042-0463-8(6))* Rosen Publishing Group, Inc., The.

—Lois Lowry. 2003. (Library of Author Biographies Ser.). (Illus.). 112p. (YA). (gr. 5-8). lib. bdg. 34.60 *(978-0-8239-3775-2(5),* Rosen Reference) Rosen Publishing Group, Inc., The.

—Paul Zindel. (Library of Author Biographies Ser.). 112p. (gr. 5-8). 2009. 63.90 *(978-1-60853-549-1(5))* 2004. (J). lib. bdg. 34.60 *(978-0-8239-4524-5(3))* Rosen Publishing Group, Inc., The. (Rosen Reference).

—Paula Fox. (Library of Author Biographies Ser.). 112p. (gr. 5-8). 2009. 63.90 *(978-1-60853-550-7(9))* 2004. (J). lib. bdg. 34.60 *(978-0-8239-4525-2(1))* Rosen Publishing Group, Inc., The. (Rosen Reference).

Darraj, Susan Muaddi. Amy Tan. 2007. (Asian Americans of Achievement Ser.). 112p. (YA). (gr. 7-12). lib. bdg. 35.00 *(978-0-7910-9269-9(0))* Facts On File, Inc.

David "Dav" Pilkey. 2010. (Who Wrote That? Ser.). (Illus.). 112p. (gr. 6-12). 35.00 *(978-1-60413-500-8(X),* Chelsea Hse.) Facts On File, Inc.

De Medeiros, Michael. Marc Brown: My Favorite Writer. 2008. (J). *(978-1-59036-927-2(0))* Weigl Pubs., Inc.

Dean, Myers Walter. Bad Boy: A Memoir. 2014. (Amistad Ser.). (ENG.). 224p. (J). 14.24 *(978-1-63245-084-5(4))* Lectorum Pubns., Inc.

Deep Woods: The Story of Robert Frost. 2006. (World Writers Ser.). (Illus.). 176p. (gr. 6-12). lib. bdg. 28.95 *(978-1-931798-92-1(3))* Reynolds, Morgan Inc.

Demuth, Patricia Brennan. Who Was Laura Ingalls Wilder? 2013. (Who Was? Ser.). (ENG., Illus.). 112p. (J). (gr. 3-7). 5.99 *(978-0-448-46706-1(2),* Grosset & Dunlap) Penguin Young Readers Group.

dePaola, Tomie. For the Duration: The War Years, 8 vols. dePaola, Tomie, illus. 2009. (26 Fairmount Avenue Book Ser.: 8). (ENG., Illus.). 80p. (J). (gr. 2-5). 17.99 *(978-0-399-25209-9(6),* G.P. Putnam's Sons Books for Young Readers) Penguin Young Readers Group.

—Here We All Are. unabr. ed. 2004. (Fairmount Avenue Ser.: Vol. 2). 80p. (J). (gr. 2-5). pap. 17.00 incl. audio *(978-0-8072-0655-3(5),* LFTR 246 SP, Listening Library) Random Hse. Audio Publishing Group.

—I'm Still Scared. 2007. (26 Fairmount Avenue Bks.). (Illus.). 83p. (gr. 2-5). 17.00 *(978-0-7569-8150-1(6))* Perfection Learning Corp.

—On My Way. unabr. ed. 2004. (Fairmount Avenue Ser.: Vol. 3). 75p. (J). (gr. 2-5). pap. 17.00 incl. audio *(978-0-8072-0656-0(3),* LFTR 247 SP, Listening Library) Random Hse. Audio Publishing Group.

—Things Will Never Be the Same. 2014. 78p. pap. 7.00 *(978-1-61003-321-3(3))* Center for the Collaborative Classroom.

—Things Will Never Be the Same. dePaola, Tomie, illus. 2004. (26 Fairmount Avenue Bks.). (Illus.). 69p. (J). (gr. 3-7). 13.65 *(978-0-7569-2951-0(2))* Perfection Learning Corp.

—What a Year. dePaola, Tomie, illus. 2003. (26 Fairmount Avenue Bks.). (Illus.). 72p. (gr. 2-5). 16.00 *(978-0-7569-1546-9(5))* Perfection Learning Corp.

—What a Year: A 26 Fairmount Avenue Book, Vol. 4. 2004. (26 Fairmount Avenue Ser.). 75p. (J). (gr. 2-5). pap. 17.00 incl. audio *(978-0-8072-0657-7(1),* Listening Library) Random Hse. Audio Publishing Group.

—26 Fairmount Avenue. dePaola, Tomie, illus. 2005. (Illus.). 58p. (J). (gr. k-4). reprint ed. 14.00 *(978-0-7567-8722-6(X))* DIANE Publishing Co.

—26 Fairmount Avenue. unabr. ed. 2004. (Fairmount Avenue Ser.: Vol. 1). 64p. (J). (gr. 2-5). pap. 17.00 incl. audio *(978-0-8072-0654-6(7),* LFTR 245 SP, Listening Library) Random Hse. Audio Publishing Group.

Diorio, Mary Ann L. A Student's Guide to Nathaniel Hawthorne. 2004. (Understanding Literature Ser.). (Illus.). 160p. (YA). lib. bdg. 29.27 *(978-0-7660-2283-6(8))* Enslow Pubs., Inc.

Ditchfield, Christin. Louisa May Alcott: Author of Little Women. 2005. (Great Life Stories Ser.). (ENG., Illus.). 111p. (J). (gr. 6-8). 30.50 *(978-0-531-12403-1(7),* Watts, Franklin) Scholastic Library Publishing.

Don, Katherine. Real Courage: The Story of Harper Lee. 2013. (Illus.). 128p. *(978-1-59935-348-7(2))* Reynolds, Morgan Inc.

Dubowski, Cathy East & Pascal, Janet. Who Was Maurice Sendak? Marchesi, Stephen & Harrison, Nancy, illus. 2013. (Who Was? Ser.). (ENG.). 112p. (J). (gr. 3-7). pap. 5.99 *(978-0-448-46500-5(0),* Grosset & Dunlap) Penguin Young Readers Group.

Dunkleberger, Amy. Reading & Interpreting the Works of Arthur Miller. 2016. (Lit Crit Guides). (ENG., Illus.). 160p. (J). (gr. 8-8). lib. bdg. 39.93 *(978-0-7660-7340-1(8))* Enslow Pubs., Inc.

—A Student's Guide to Arthur Miller. 2005. (Understanding Literature Ser.). (Illus.). 160p. (YA). (gr. 7-13). lib. bdg. 29.27 *(978-0-7660-2432-8(6))* Enslow Pubs., Inc.

Ehrlich, Amy, ed. When I Was Your Age Vol. 2: Original Stories about Growing Up. 2006. (Illus.). 187p. (YA). (gr. 8-11). reprint ed. 17.00 *(978-1-4223-5199-4(8))* DIANE Publishing Co.

—When I Was Your Age Vols. I & II: Original Stories about Growing Up. 2012. lib. bdg. 26.95 *(978-0-606-23806-9(9),* Turtleback) Turtleback Bks.

Elliot, Henry. Harriet Beecher Stowe: The Voice of Humanity in White America. 2009. (Voices for Freedom Ser.). (ENG., Illus.). 64p. (J). (gr. 5-8). pap. *(978-0-7787-4837-3(5));* lib. bdg. *(978-0-7787-4821-2(9))* Crabtree Publishing Co.

Engle, Margarita. Enchanted Air: Two Cultures, Two Wings: A Memoir. 2016. lib. bdg. 20.85 *(978-0-606-38989-1(X))* Turtleback Bks.

Ernest Hemingway: The Search for Courage. 2014. (ENG.). 236p. (J). (gr. 3-7). pap. 14.95 *(978-1-59077-352-9(7))* Evans, M. & Co., Inc.

Ernest J. Gaines. 2010. (Who Wrote That? Ser.). (Illus.). 120p. (gr. 6-12). 35.00 *(978-1-60413-683-8(9),* Chelsea Hse.) Facts On File, Inc.

Faulkner, Nicholas & Daniel, Susanna. Lois Lowry, 01 vols., 1. 2016. (All about the Author Ser.). (ENG., Illus.). 112p. (J). 35.60 *(978-1-4994-6270-8(0),* Rosen Young Adult) Rosen Publishing Group, Inc., The.

Ferguson, Melissa. Suzanne Collins: Author of the Hunger Games Trilogy. 2016. (Famous Female Authors Ser.). (ENG., Illus.). 32p. (gr. 3-4). lib. bdg. 27.99 *(978-1-5157-1326-5(1),* Snap Bks.) Capstone Press of Coughlan Cos.

Fleischman, Sid. The Trouble Begins at 8: A Life of Mark Twain in the Wild, Wild West. 2008. (Illus.). 224p. (J). (gr. 4-7). (ENG.). 18.99 *(978-0-06-134431-2(1));* lib. bdg. 19.89 *(978-0-06-134432-9(X))* HarperCollins Pubs. (Greenwillow Bks.).

Flor Ada, Alma. Island Treasures: Growing up in Cuba: Includes Where the Flame Trees Bloom, under the Royal Palms, & Five Brand New Stories. Martorell, Antonio & Rodriguez, Edel, illus. 2015. (ENG.). 240p. (J). (gr. 3-7). pap. 7.99 *(978-1-4814-2900-9(0))* Simon & Schuster Children's Publishing.

—Where the Flame Trees Bloom. 2007. (ENG.). 80p. (J). (gr. 4-6). pap. 9.95 *(978-1-4169-6840-5(7),* Simon & Schuster/Paula Wiseman Bks.) Simon & Schuster/Paula Wiseman Bks.

Florian, Douglas. See for Your Self. Florian, Douglas & Taplinger, Lee, photos by. 2005. (Meet the Author Ser.). (ENG., Illus.). 32p. (J). 14.95 *(978-1-57274-821-7(4),* 731, Meet the Author) Owen, Richard C. Pubs., Inc.

Foran, Jill. Dr. Seuss. 2012. (J). 13.95 *(978-1-61913-059-3(9));* pap. 28.55 *(978-1-61913-595-6(7))* Weigl Pubs., Inc.

Ford, Carin T. Dr. Seuss: Best-Loved Author. 2003. (People to Know Ser.). (Illus.). 112p. (J). (gr. 6-12). lib. bdg. 27.94 *(978-0-7660-2106-8(8))* Enslow Pubs., Inc.

—Laura Ingalls Wilder: Real-Life Pioneer of the Little House Books. 2003. (People to Know Ser.). (Illus.). 112p. (J). lib. bdg. 26.60 *(978-0-7660-2105-1(X))* Enslow Pubs., Inc.

Fradin, Dennis Brindell & Fradin, Judith Bloom. Zora! The Life of Zora Neale Hurston. 2012. (ENG., Illus.). 192p. (J). (gr. 5-7). 17.99 *(978-0-547-00695-6(0))* Houghton Mifflin Harcourt Publishing Co.

Frampton, David. Mr. Ferlinghetti's Poem. Frampton, David, illus. 2006. (Illus.). 32p. (J). (gr. k-4). 18.00 *(978-0-8028-5290-8(4),* Eerdmans Bks For Young Readers) Eerdmans, William B. Publishing Co.

Franklin, Joseph & Wilson, Antoine. S. E. Hinton, 01 vols., 1. 2016. (All about the Author Ser.). (ENG.). 112p. (J). 35.60 *(978-1-4994-6266-1(2),* Rosen Young Adult) Rosen Publishing Group, Inc., The.

Frisch, Aaron. Edgar Allan Poe. 2005. (Voices in Poetry Ser.). (Illus.). 48p. (J). (gr. 5-9). lib. bdg. 21.95 *(978-1-58341-344-9(8),* Creative Education) Creative Co., The.

—Edgar Allan Poe. Kelley, Gary, illus. 2014. (Voices in Poetry Ser.). 47p. (J). lib. bdg. 35.65 *(978-1-60818-324-1(6),* Creative Education) Creative Co., The.

Fromowitz, Lori. Louisa May Alcott. 2013. (ENG.). 48p. (J). pap. 15.64 *(978-1-61783-765-4(2));* (gr. 3-6). lib. bdg. 32.79 *(978-1-61783-715-9(6))* ABDO Publishing Co.

Furgang, Adam. Rick Riordan. 2012. (All about the Author Ser.). (ENG., Illus.). 112p. (J). (gr. 7-12). 34.60 *(978-1-4488-6937-4(4))* Rosen Publishing Group, Inc., The.

Gaines, Ann. Christopher Paul Curtis. 2004. (Blue Banner Biography Ser.). (Illus.). 32p. (J). lib. bdg. 25.70 *(978-1-58415-330-6(X))* Mitchell Lane Pubs., Inc.

Gantos, Jack. Hole in My Life. 2004. 18.10 *(978-0-7569-3197-1(5))* Farrar, Straus & Giroux.

—Hole in My Life. 2009. 8.89 *(978-0-7848-2463-4(0),* Everbind) Marco Bk. Co.

—Hole in My Life. 2012. (ENG.). 224p. (YA). (gr. 9-13). pap. 9.99 *(978-0-312-64157-3(5),* 9780312641573) Square Fish.

Giff, Patricia Reilly. Don't Tell the Girls: A Family Memoir. 2005. (ENG., Illus.). 144p. (J). 16.95 *(978-0-8234-1813-8(8))* Holiday Hse., Inc.

—Laura Ingalls Wilder. 2014. (Women of Our Time Ser.). (ENG., Illus.). 80p. (J). (gr. 3-7). pap. 7.99 *(978-0-14-751364-9(2),* Puffin Books) Penguin Young Readers Group.

Gigliotti, Jim. Who Was Edgar Allan Poe? Foley, Tim, illus. 2015. 105p. (J). *(978-1-4844-6178-5(9),* Grosset & Dunlap) Penguin Publishing Group.

Glaser, Linda. Emma's Poem: The Voice of the Statue of Liberty. Nivola, Claire A., illus. 2013. (ENG.). 32p. (J). (gr. -1-3). pap. 7.99 *(978-0-544-10508-9(7))* Houghton Mifflin Harcourt Publishing Co.

Goldsmith, Howard. Mark Twain at Work! Habbas, Frank, illus. 2003. (Ready-To-read COFA Ser.). (ENG.). 32p. (J). (gr. k-2). pap. 3.99 *(978-0-689-85399-9(8),* Simon Spotlight) Simon Spotlight.

Graham, Amy. Celebrated African-American Novelists. 2012. (African-American Collective Biographies Ser.). 112p. (J). pap. 10.95 *(978-1-4644-0037-7(7));* (Illus.). (gr. 5-18). 33.27 *(978-1-59845-138-2(3))* Enslow Pubs., Inc.

Grahame-Smith, Deborah. Dr. Seuss. 2014. (Spotlight on Children's Authors Ser.). 48p. (J). (gr. 4-6). lib. bdg. 29.93 *(978-1-62712-846-9(8))* Cavendish Square Publishing.

—Lois Lowry. 2014. (J). lib. bdg. *(978-1-62712-274-0(5))* Musa Publishing.

Gresh, Lois H. The Divergent Companion: The Unauthorized Guide to the Series. 2014. (ENG.). 192p. (YA). (gr. 9-12). pap. 12.99 *(978-1-250-04510-2(X),* 9781250045102, St. Martin's Griffin) St. Martin's Pr.

Griskey, Michele. Beverly Cleary. 2006. (Classic Storytellers Ser.). (Illus.). 48p. (J). (gr. 4-7). lib. bdg. 29.95 *(978-1-58415-457-0(8),* 1259543) Mitchell Lane Pubs., Inc.

—Emily Dickinson. 2007. (Poets & Playwrights Ser.). (Illus.). 112p. (J). (gr. 3-7). lib. bdg. 37.10 *(978-1-58415-429-7(2))* Mitchell Lane Pubs., Inc.

—Harriet Beecher Stowe. 2005. (Classic Storytellers Ser.). (Illus.). 48p. (J). (gr. 4-8). lib. bdg. 29.95 *(978-1-58415-375-7(X))* Mitchell Lane Pubs., Inc.

—Ray Bradbury. 2006. (Classic Storytellers Ser.). (Illus.). 48p. (J). (gr. 3-7). lib. bdg. 29.95 *(978-1-58415-455-6(1),* 1259542) Mitchell Lane Pubs., Inc.

Guillain, Charlotte. Dr. Seuss, 1 vol. 2012. (Author Biographies Ser.). (ENG.). 24p. (gr. 1-2). 23.32 *(978-1-4329-5959-3(X));* pap. 6.79 *(978-1-4329-5965-4(4))* Heinemann-Raintree. (Heinemann Read & Learn).

—Maurice Sendak, 1 vol. 2012. (Author Biographies Ser.). (ENG.). 24p. (gr. 1-2). pap. 6.79 *(978-1-4329-5967-8(0),* Heinemann Read & Learn) Heinemann-Raintree.

Gunderson, Megan M. Jeff Kinney, 1 vol. 2012. (Children's Authors Set 6 Ser.). (ENG., Illus.). 24p. (YA). (gr. 2-5). 25.65 *(978-1-61783-048-8(8))* ABDO Publishing Co.

Haggerty, Andrew. Harper Lee: To Kill a Mockingbird. 2009. (Writers & Their Works 4 Ser.). 144p. (gr. 7). 42.79 *(978-0-7614-4280-6(4))* Marshall Cavendish Corp.

Haldy, Emma E. Maya Angelou. Bane, Jeff, illus. 2017. (My Early Library: My Itty-Bitty Bio Ser.). (ENG.). 24p. (J). (gr. k-1). lib. bdg. 28.50 *(978-1-63472-153-0(5),* 209184) Cherry Lake Publishing.

Hamilton, John. The Golden Age & Beyond, 1 vol. 2006. (World of Science Fiction Ser.). (ENG., Illus.). 32p. (gr. 4-7). 27.07 *(978-1-59679-989-9(7),* Abdo & Daughters) ABDO Publishing Co.

—Modern Masters of Science Fiction, 1 vol. 2006. (World of Science Fiction Ser.). (ENG., Illus.). 32p. (gr. 4-7). 27.07 *(978-1-59679-990-5(0),* Abdo & Daughters) ABDO Publishing Co.

—Pioneers of Science Fiction, 1 vol. 2006. (World of Science Fiction Ser.). (ENG.). 32p. (gr. 4-7). 27.07 *(978-1-59679-992-9(7),* Abdo & Daughters) ABDO Publishing Co.

Hamilton, Sue L. Masters of Horror, 1 vol. 2007. (World of Horror Ser.). (ENG.). 32p. (gr. 4-8). 27.07 *(978-1-59928-770-6(6),* Abdo & Daughters) ABDO Publishing Co.

Haney, Johannah. Shel Silverstein. 2014. (J). lib. bdg. *(978-1-62712-271-9(0))* Cavendish Square Publishing.

Harkins, Susan and William. Walter Dean Myers. 2007. (YA). lib. bdg. *(978-1-58415-534-8(5))* Mitchell Lane Pubs., Inc.

Harmon, Daniel E. Cassandra Clare, 1 vol. 2015. (ENG.). 112p. (YA). 35.60 *(978-1-4777-7912-5(4),* Rosen Young Adult) Rosen Publishing Group, Inc., The.

Harness, Cheryl. The Literary Adventures of Washington Irving: American Storyteller. 2008. (ENG., Illus.). 48p. (J). (gr. 2-5). 17.95 *(978-1-4263-0438-5(2));* lib. bdg. 27.90 *(978-1-4263-0439-2(0))* National Geographic Society. (National Geographic Children's Bks.).

Harris, Laurie Lanzen. Biography for Beginners: All Authors. 2005. (Illus.). 300p. (J). lib. bdg. 50.00 *(978-1-931360-31-9(6))* Favorable Impressions.

Hart, Joyce. Native Son: The Story of Richard Wright. 2004. (World Writers Ser.). (Illus.). 128p. (YA). (gr. 6-12). 23.95 *(978-1-931798-06-8(0))* Reynolds, Morgan Inc.

Haugen, Hayley Mitchell, ed. Race in Ralph Ellison's Invisible Man. 2011. (Social Issues in Literature Ser.). (Illus.). 224p. pap. 28.45 *(978-0-7377-5812-2(0),* Greenhaven Pr., Inc.); (YA). (gr. 9-12). 40.95 *(978-0-7377-5811-5(2))* Cengage Gale.

Henneberg, Susan. James Baldwin, 1 vol. 2015. (ENG.). 112p. (YA). 35.60 *(978-1-4777-7897-5(7),* Rosen Young Adult) Rosen Publishing Group, Inc., The.

Hermann, Spring. Reading & Interpreting the Works of Eugene O'Neill. 2016. (Lit Crit Guides). 176p. (J). (gr. 6-6). 39.93 *(978-0-7660-7913-7(9))* Enslow Pubs., Inc.

Herrera, Juan Felipe. El Canto de las Palomas/Calling the Doves. 2004. (Illus.). (J). (gr. 3-6). spiral bd. *(978-0-616-14607-1(8))* Canadian National Institute for the Blind/Institut National Canadien pour les Aveugles.

Herweck Rice, Dona. Laura Ingalls Wilder: Pioneer Woman (America in The 1800s) 2017. (Primary Source Readers Ser.). (Illus.). 32p. (J). (gr. 4-5). pap. 8.99 ***(978-1-4938-3798-4(2))*** Teacher Created Materials, Inc.

—Stepping into Louisa May Alcott's World (Grade 7) 2017. (TIME for KIDS(r) Nonfiction Readers Ser.). (Illus.). 48p. (J). (gr. 7-7). pap. 9.99 ***(978-1-4938-3619-2(6))*** Teacher Created Materials, Inc.

Hicks, Kelli L. Dav Pilkey, 1 vol. Byers, Michael, illus. 2013. (Your Favorite Authors Ser.). (ENG.). 24p. (gr. 1-2). 25.32 *(978-1-4765-0221-2(8));* pap. 7.95 *(978-1-4765-3436-7(5))* Capstone Press of Coughlan Cos. (First Facts).

—Jeff Kinney, 1 vol. Byers, Michael, illus. 2013. (Your Favorite Authors Ser.). (ENG.). 24p. (gr. 1-2). 25.32 *(978-1-4765-0222-9(6));* pap. 7.95 *(978-1-4765-3437-4(3))* Capstone Press of Coughlan Cos. (First Facts).

Hill, Pamela Smith. Laura Ingalls Wilder: A Writer's Life. 2007. (South Dakota Biography Ser.). (Illus.). 244p. per. *(978-0-9777955-6-7(X),* South Dakota State Historical Society Pr.) South Dakota State Historical Society Pr.

Hillstrom, Laurie. Gabriel Garcia Marquez. 2007. (Twentieth Century's Most Influential Hispanics Ser.). (ENG., Illus.). 110p. (gr. 7-12). 39.40 *(978-1-4205-0020-2(1))* Cengage Gale.

Hinds, Maurene J. How to Analyze the Works of Toni Morrison, 1 vol. 2012. (Essential Critiques Set 3 Ser.). (ENG.). 112p. (J). (gr. 6-12). lib. bdg. 35.64 *(978-1-61783-458-5(0),* Essential Library) ABDO Publishing Co.

Hinton, Kaa Vonia. Jacqueline Woodson. 2007. (Classic Storytellers Ser.). (Illus.). 48p. (J). (gr. 4-8). lib. bdg. 29.95 *(978-1-58415-533-1(7))* Mitchell Lane Pubs., Inc.

Hodgman, Ann. How to Die of Embarrassment Every Day. Hodgman, Ann, photos by. 2011. (ENG., Illus.). 224p. (J). (gr. 3-7). 24.99 *(978-0-8050-8705-5(2),* 9780805087055, Holt, Henry & Co. Bks. For Young Readers) Holt, Henry & Co.

Hoover, Elizabeth. Suzanne Collins. 2012. (People in the News Ser.). (ENG., Illus.). 128p. (gr. 7-10). lib. bdg. 39.40 *(978-1-4205-0762-1(1),* Lucent Bks.) Cengage Gale.

Houghton, Gillian. Mildred Taylor. (Library of Author Biographies Ser.). 112p. 2009. (gr. 5-8). 63.90 *(978-1-60853-548-4(7),* Rosen Reference) 2005. (Illus.).

(YA). 34.60 *(978-1-4042-0330-3(3))* Rosen Publishing Group, Inc., The.

Hurtig, Jennifer. The Bewitching World of Maurice Sendak. 2016. (J). **(978-1-5105-1957-2(2))** SmartBook Media, Inc.

Hurtig, Jennifer. Maurice Sendak. 2007. (My Favorite Writer Ser.). (Illus.). 32p. (YA). (gr. 5-18). pap. 9.95 *(978-1-59036-485-7(6))* Weigl Pubs., Inc.

Ishizuka, Kathy. John Grisham: Best-Selling Author. 2003. (People to Know Ser.). (Illus.). 112p. (J). lib. bdg. 26.60 *(978-0-7660-2102-0(5))* Enslow Pubs., Inc.

Jackson, Constance L. Over the River: Life of Lydia Maria Child, Abolitionist for Freedom, 1802-1880. 2008. (Illus.). 160p. pap. 18.95 *(978-0-9818204-0-8(9))* Permanent Productions Publishing.

John Steinbeck: The Voice of the Land. 2014. (ENG.). 192p. (J). (gr. 3-7). pap. 13.95 *(978-1-59077-358-1(6))* Evans, M. & Co., Inc.

Jones, Jen. Judy Blume: Fearless Storyteller for Teens. 2008. (Authors Teens Love Ser.). (Illus.). 112p. (J). (gr. k-6). lib. bdg. 33.27 *(978-0-7660-2960-6(3))* Enslow Pubs., Inc.

Jordan, Denise M. Walter Dean Myers: A Biography of an Award-Winning Urban Fiction Author. 2013. (African-American Icons Ser.). 104p. (J). (gr. 6-12). pap. 10.95 *(978-1-59845-393-5(9))* Enslow Pubs., Inc.

Kaiser, Lisbeth. Maya Angelou. Salaberria, Leire, illus. 2016. (Little People, Big Dreams Ser.). (ENG.). 32p. (J). (gr. k-3). 14.99 *(978-1-84780-889-9(1),* Frances Lincoln Children's Bks.) Quarto Publishing Group UK GBR. Dist: Hachette Bk. Group.

Kamberg, Mary-Lane. Margaret Peterson Haddix. 2013. (All about the Author Ser.). 112p. (YA). (gr. 7-12). 34.60 *(978-1-4777-1765-3(X))* Rosen Publishing Group, Inc., The.

Kampff, Joseph. Louis Sachar. 2014. (J). pap. *(978-1-62712-258-0(3))* Cavendish Square Publishing.

Katherine Paterson. 2010. (Who Wrote That? Ser.). (Illus.). 128p. (gr. 6-12). 35.00 *(978-1-60413-499-5(2),* Chelsea Hse.) Facts On File, Inc.

Kerley, Barbara. A Home for Mr. Emerson. Fotheringham, Edwin, illus. 2014. (ENG.). 48p. (J). (gr. 3-7). 18.99 *(978-0-545-35088-4(3),* Scholastic Pr.) Scholastic, Inc.

Kimmel, Eric A. Tuning Up: A Visit with Eric Kimmel. Childers, Basil, photos by. 2005. (Meet the Author Ser.). (ENG., Illus.). 32p. (J). 14.95 *(978-1-57274-822-4(2),* 732, Meet the Author) Owen, Richard C. Pubs., Inc.

Kinney, Patrick. Who Is Jeff Kinney? 2015. (Who Is... ? Ser.). lib. bdg. 16.00 *(978-0-606-37553-5(8))* Turtleback Bks.

Kinney, Patrick & dePaola, Tomie. Who Is Jeff Kinney? Hinderliter, John, illus. 2015. (Who Was? Ser.). (ENG.). 112p. (J). (gr. 3-7). 5.99 *(978-0-448-48677-2(6),* Grosset & Dunlap) Penguin Young Readers Group.

Kirk, Connie Ann. Reading & Interpreting the Works of Robert Frost. 2016. (Lit Crit Guides). (ENG., Illus.). 176p. (J). (gr. 8-8). lib. bdg. 39.93 *(978-0-7660-7350-0(5))* Enslow Pubs., Inc.

Kite, L. Patricia. Maya Angelou. 2006. (Just the Facts Biographies Ser.). (Illus.). 112p. (J). (gr. 3-7). pap. 9.95 *(978-0-8225-5997-9(8));* (ENG., (gr. 5-12). lib. bdg. 27.93 *(978-0-8225-3426-6(6))* Lerner Publishing Group. (Lerner Pubns.).

Kjelle, Marylou. Katherine Paterson. 2004. (Classic Storytellers Ser.). (Illus.). 48p. (J). (gr. 4-8). lib. bdg. 29.95 *(978-1-58415-268-2(0))* Mitchell Lane Pubs., Inc.

Kjelle, Marylou Morano. Francis Scott Key. 2006. (What's So Great About... ? Ser.). (Illus.). 32p. (YA). (gr. 2-4). lib. bdg. 25.70 *(978-1-58415-474-7(8))* Mitchell Lane Pubs., Inc.

—S. E. Hinton: Author of the Outsiders. 2007. (Authors Teens Love Ser.). (Illus.). 112p. (J). (gr. 8-12). lib. bdg. 33.27 *(978-0-7660-2720-6(1))* Enslow Pubs., Inc.

Klimo, Kate. Dr. Seuss: The Great Doodler. Johnson, Steve & Fancher, Lou, illus. 2016. (Step into Reading Ser.). (ENG.). 48p. (J). (gr. k-3). 12.99 *(978-1-101-93551-4(0),* Random Hse. Bks. for Young Readers) Random Hse. Children's Bks.

—Dr. Seuss: the Great Doodler. 2016. (Step into Reading Ser.). (ENG., Illus.). 48p. (J). (gr. k-3). lib. bdg. 15.99 *(978-0-375-97376-5(1),* Random Hse. Bks. for Young Readers) Random Hse. Children's Bks.

Kolpin, Molly. Barbara Park, 1 vol. Byers, Michael, illus. 2013. (Your Favorite Authors Ser.). (ENG.). 24p. (gr. 1-2). 25.32 *(978-1-4765-0223-6(4));* pap. 7.95 *(978-1-4765-3438-1(1))* Capstone Press of Coughlan Cos. (First Facts).

—Shel Silverstein, 1 vol. Byers, Michael, illus. 2013. (Your Favorite Authors Ser.). (ENG.). 24p. (gr. 1-2). 25.32 *(978-1-4765-0224-3(2));* pap. 7.95 *(978-1-4765-3439-8(X))* Capstone Press of Coughlan Cos. (First Facts).

Komroff, Manuel. Big City, Little Boy. 2011. 188p. 42.95 *(978-1-258-06784-7(6))* Literary Licensing, LLC.

Kopp, Megan. Suzanne Collins. 2012. (J). 28.55 *(978-1-61913-054-8(8));* pap. *(978-1-61913-600-7(7))* Weigl Pubs., Inc.

Kramer, Barbara. Toni Morrison: A Biography of a Nobel Prize-Winning Writer. 2013. (African-American Icons Ser.). 104p. (J). (gr. 6-12). pap. 10.95 *(978-1-59845-392-8(0))* Enslow Pubs., Inc.

Krohn, Katherine E. Stephenie Meyer: Dreaming of Twilight. 2010. (USA TODAY Lifeline Biographies Ser.). (ENG.). 112p. (gr. 6-12). lib. bdg. 34.60 *(978-0-7613-5220-4(1))* Lerner Publishing Group.

Krull, Kathleen. The Boy on Fairfield Street: How Ted Geisel Grew up to Become Dr. Seuss. Johnson, Steve & Fancher, Lou, illus. 2010. (ENG.). 48p. (J). (gr. k-4). pap. 7.99 *(978-0-375-85550-4(5),* Dragonfly Bks.) Random Hse. Children's Bks.

—The Boy on Fairfield Street: How Ted Geisel Grew up to Become Dr. Seuss. 2010. lib. bdg. 18.40 *(978-0-606-12416-4(0),* Turtleback) Turtleback Bks.

—The Road to Oz: Twists, Turns, Bumps, & Triumphs in the Life of L. Frank Baum. Hawkes, Kevin, illus. 2008. (ENG.). 48p. (J). (gr. -1-2). 19.99 *(978-0-375-83216-1(5),* Knopf Bks. for Young Readers) Random Hse. Children's Bks.

Kudlinski, Kathleen. Dr. Seuss: Young Author & Artist. Henderson, Meryl, illus. 2005. 184p. (J). lib. bdg. 18.46 *(978-1-4242-2201-8(X))* Fitzgerald Bks.

Kurtz, Jane. Jane Kurtz & YOU, 1 vol. 2007. (Author & YOU Ser.: No. 8). (Illus.). 204p. (C). per. 35.00 *(978-1-59158-295-3(4),* LU2954, Libraries Unlimited) ABC-CLIO, LLC.

L. Frank Baum. 2010. (Who Wrote That? Ser.). (Illus.). 128p. (gr. 6-12). 35.00 *(978-1-60413-501-5(8),* Chelsea Hse.) Facts On File, Inc.

La Bella, Laura. Marissa Meyer, 01 vols., 1. 2016. (All about the Author Ser.). (ENG., Illus.). 112p. (J). 35.60 *(978-1-4994-6278-4(6),* Rosen Young Adult) Rosen Publishing Group, Inc., The.

Labrecque, Ellen. Who Was Maya Angelou? Putra, Dede, illus. 2016. 105p. (J). **(978-1-4844-6937-8(2)**, Grosset & Dunlap) Penguin Publishing Group.

—Who Was Maya Angelou? 2016. (Who Was... ? Ser.). lib. bdg. 16.00 *(978-0-606-38397-4(2))* Turtleback Bks.

Landau, Jennifer. Dr. Seuss, 01 vols., 1. 2016. (Britannica Beginner Bios Ser.). (ENG., Illus.). 32p. (J). pap. 12.90 *(978-1-5081-0063-8(2),* Britannica Educational Publishing) Rosen Publishing Group, Inc., The.

Lange, Brenda. Edward Stratemeyer. 2003. (Who Wrote That? Ser.). (Illus.). 112p. (gr. 6-12). 35.00 *(978-0-7910-7621-7(0),* Chelsea Hse.) Facts On File, Inc.

Lappi, Megan. Will Hobbs. 2006. (My Favorite Writer Ser.). (Illus.). 32p. (J). (gr. 3-7). pap. 9.95 *(978-1-59036-489-5(9));* lib. bdg. 26.00 *(978-1-59036-488-8(0))* Weigl Pubs., Inc.

Lawrence, Katherine. Laurence Yep. 2009. (Library of Author Biographies Ser.). 112p. (gr. 5-8). 63.90 *(978-1-60853-542-2(8),* Rosen Reference) Rosen Publishing Group, Inc., The.

Lawrence, Katherine Drobot. Laurence Yep. 2004. (Library of Author Biographies Ser.). 112p. (J). (gr. 5-8). lib. bdg. 34.60 *(978-0-8239-4527-6(8),* Rosen Reference) Rosen Publishing Group, Inc., The.

Leaf, Christina. Jeff Kinney. 2015. (Children's Storytellers Ser.). (ENG., Illus.). 24p. (J). (gr. 2-5). lib. bdg. 25.95 *(978-1-62617-267-8(6),* Blastoff! Readers) Bellwether Media.

—Kate Dicamillo. 2016. (Children's Storytellers Ser.). (ENG., Illus.). 24p. (J). (gr. 2-5). lib. bdg. 25.95 *(978-1-62617-339-2(7),* Blastoff! Readers) Bellwether Media.

—Rick Riordan. 2016. (Children's Storytellers Ser.). (ENG., Illus.). 24p. (J). (gr. 2-5). lib. bdg. 25.95 *(978-1-62617-342-2(7),* Blastoff! Readers) Bellwether Media.

Lemony Snicket: Daniel Handler. 2010. (Who Wrote That? Ser.). (Illus.). 120p. (YA). (gr. 6-12). 35.00 *(978-1-60413-726-2(6),* Chelsea Hse.) Facts On File, Inc.

Levin, Judy & Draper, Allison Stark. Christopher Paul Curtis. annot. ed. 2005. (Library of Author Biographies Ser.). (Illus.). 112p. (J). (gr. k-3). lib. bdg. 34.60 *(978-1-4042-0458-4(X))* Rosen Publishing Group, Inc., The.

Lew, Kristi. Laurie Halse Anderson. 2013. (All about the Author Ser.). 112p. (YA). (gr. 7-12). 34.60 *(978-1-4777-1764-6(1))* Rosen Publishing Group, Inc., The.

Litwin, Laura Baskes. E. B. White: Beyond Charlotte's Web & Stuart Little. 2003. (People to Know Ser.). (Illus.). 112p. (J). lib. bdg. 26.60 *(978-0-7660-2107-5(6))* Enslow Pubs., Inc.

—Zora Neale Hurston: I Have Been in Sorrow's Kitchen. 2007. (African-American Biography Library). (Illus.). 128p. (J). (gr. 6-12). lib. bdg. 33.27 *(978-0-7660-2536-3(5))* Enslow Pubs., Inc.

Llanas, Sheila Griffin. Contemporary American Poetry: Not the End, but the Beginning. 2010. (Poetry Rocks! Ser.). (Illus.). 160p. (YA). (gr. 9-12). 35.94 *(978-0-7660-3279-8(5))* Enslow Pubs., Inc.

—Contemporary American Poetry- Not the End, but the Beginning. 2011. (Poetry Rocks! Ser.). (Illus.). 160p. (YA). (gr. 9-18). pap. 10.95 *(978-1-59845-380-5(7))* Enslow Pubs., Inc.

—How to Analyze the Works of Suzanne Collins, 1 vol. 2012. (Essential Critiques Set 3 Ser.). (ENG.). 112p. (J). (gr. 6-12). lib. bdg. 35.64 *(978-1-61783-456-1(4),* Essential Library) ABDO Publishing Co.

Lourie, Peter. Jack London & the Klondike Gold Rush. Minor, Wendell, illus. 2017. (ENG.). 208p. (J). 18.99 *(978-0-8050-9757-3(0),* 9780805097573, Holt, Henry & Co. Bks. For Young Readers) Holt, Henry & Co.

Lusted, Marcia Amidon. How to Analyze the Works of Stephen King, 1 vol. 2010. (Essential Critiques Set 1 Ser.). (ENG.). 112p. (J). (gr. 6-12). lib. bdg. 35.64 *(978-1-61613-536-2(0),* Essential Library) ABDO Publishing Co.

—Suzanne Collins: Words on Fire. 2012. (USA TODAY Lifeline Biographies Ser.). (ENG., Illus.). 112p. (gr. 6-12). lib. bdg. 34.60 *(978-0-7613-8638-4(6))* Lerner Publishing Group.

Macken, JoAnn Early. Gary Paulsen: Voice of Adventure & Survival. 2007. (Authors Teens Love Ser.). (Illus.). 104p. (J). (gr. 8-12). lib. bdg. 33.27 *(978-0-7660-2721-3(X))* Enslow Pubs., Inc.

MacLeod, Elizabeth. Mark Twain: An American Star. 2008. (Snapshots: Images of People & Places in History Ser.). (ENG., Illus.). 32p. (J). (gr. 3-7). 14.95 *(978-1-55337-908-9(X));* pap. 6.95 *(978-1-55337-909-6(8))* Kids Can Pr., Ltd. CAN. Dist: Hachette Bk. Group.

Malaspina, Ann. Phillis Sings Out Freedom: The Story of George Washington & Phillis Wheatley. Keeter, Susan, illus. 2012. (J). 34.28 *(978-1-61913-149-1(8))* Weigl Pubs., Inc.

Maloof, Torrey. Stepping into Mark Twain's World. 2017. (TIME for KIDS(r) Nonfiction Readers Ser.). 48p. (J). (gr. 7-7). pap. 9.99 **(978-1-4938-3620-8(X))** Teacher Created Materials, Inc.

Mangal, Melina. Mildred Taylor. 2004. (Classic Storytellers Ser.). (Illus.). 48p. (J). (gr. 4-8). lib. bdg. 29.95 *(978-1-58415-311-5(3))* Mitchell Lane Pubs., Inc.

Mangrum, Allison. African American Writers Who Inspired Change. 2005. (Illus.). 79p. 17.00 *(978-1-55501-650-0(2))* Ballard & Tighe Pubs.

Mara, Wil. Laura Ingalls Wilder. 2003. (Rookie Biographies Ser.). (ENG., Illus.). 32p. (J). (gr. 1-2). 20.50 *(978-0-516-22855-6(2),* Children's Pr.) Scholastic Library Publishing.

Mara, Wil & National Geographic Learning Staff. Laura Ingalls Wilder. 2010. (Rise & Shine Ser.). (ENG.). 32p. (C). (gr. 1-2). pap. 7.95 *(978-0-516-27840-7(1))* National Geographic School Publishing, Inc.

Marcovitz, Hal. Bruce Coville. 2005. (Who Wrote That? Ser.). (Illus.). 128p. (gr. 6-12). 35.00 *(978-0-7910-8656-8(9),* Chelsea Hse.) Facts On File, Inc.

—Lawrence Yep. 2008. (Who Wrote That? Ser.). (Illus.). 136p. (gr. 6-12). 35.00 *(978-0-7910-9527-0(4),* Chelsea Hse.) Facts On File, Inc.

—R. L. Stine. 2005. (Who Wrote That? Ser.). (Illus.). 136p. (gr. 6-12). lib. bdg. 35.00 *(978-0-7910-8659-9(3),* Chelsea Hse.) Facts On File, Inc.

—Scott O'Dell. 2007. (Who Wrote That? Ser.). (Illus.). 128p. (gr. 6-12). lib. bdg. 35.00 *(978-0-7910-9526-3(6),* Chelsea Hse.) Facts On File, Inc.

—Will Hobbs. 2005. (Who Wrote That? Ser.). (Illus.). 128p. (gr. 6-12). lib. bdg. 35.00 *(978-0-7910-8657-5(7),* Chelsea Hse.) Facts On File, Inc.

Marcus, Leonard S., ed. Funny Business: Conversations with Writers of Comedy. 2009. (ENG., Illus.). 224p. (J). (gr. 5-18). 24.99 *(978-0-7636-3254-0(6))* Candlewick Pr.

Mark Twain. 2010. (Who Wrote That? Ser.). (Illus.). 128p. (YA). (gr. 6-12). 35.00 *(978-1-60413-728-6(2),* Chelsea Hse.) Facts On File, Inc.

Marsico, Katie. Zora Neale Hurston, 1 vol. 2008. (Essential Lives Set 2 Ser.). (ENG., Illus.). 112p. (J). (gr. 6-12). lib. bdg. 35.64 *(978-1-60453-036-0(7))* ABDO Publishing Co.

Mass, Wendy. Ray Bradbury: Master of Science Fiction & Fantasy. 2004. (Authors Teens Love Ser.). (Illus.). 104p. (J). lib. bdg. 27.94 *(978-0-7660-2240-9(4))* Enslow Pubs., Inc.

Mattern, Joanne. Tyler Perry. 2012. (J). lib. bdg. 25.70 *(978-1-61228-334-0(9))* Mitchell Lane Pubs., Inc.

Matthews, Sheelagh. Gordon Korman. 2012. (J). 28.55 *(978-1-61913-055-5(6));* pap. 13.95 *(978-1-61913-597-0(3))* Weigl Pubs., Inc.

McArthur, Debra. John Steinbeck: The Grapes of Wrath & of Mice & Men. 2008. (Writers & Their Work Ser.). (Illus.). 144p. (J). (gr. 7-18). lib. bdg. 42.79 *(978-0-7614-2964-7(6),* Benchmark Bks.) Marshall Cavendish Corp.

Mcarthur, Debra. Reading & Interpreting the Works of Edgar Allan Poe. 2016. (Lit Crit Guides). (ENG., Illus.). 160p. (J). (gr. 8-8). lib. bdg. 39.93 *(978-0-7660-7342-5(4))* Enslow Pubs., Inc.

—Reading & Interpreting the Works of William Faulkner. 2016. (Lit Crit Guides). (ENG., Illus.). 160p. (J). (gr. 8-8). lib. bdg. 39.93 *(978-0-7660-7354-8(8))* Enslow Pubs., Inc.

McArthur, Debra. A Student's Guide to Edgar Allan Poe. 2006. (Understanding Literature Ser.). (Illus.). 160p. (YA). (gr. 8-12). lib. bdg. 27.93 *(978-0-7660-2437-3(7))* Enslow Pubs., Inc.

McCarthy, Pat. Henry David Thoreau: Writer, Thinker, Naturalist. 2003. (Historical American Biographies Ser.). (Illus.). 128p. (J). (gr. 6-12). lib. bdg. 26.60 *(978-0-7660-1978-2(0))* Enslow Pubs., Inc.

McCormick, Lisa Wade. Christopher Paolini. 2012. (All about the Author Ser.). (ENG., Illus.). 112p. (J). (gr. 7-12). lib. bdg. 34.60 *(978-1-4488-6939-8(0))* Rosen Publishing Group, Inc., The.

McDonough, Yona Zeldis. Louisa. Andersen, Bethanne, illus. 2014. (ENG.). 48p. (J). (gr. 1-5). pap. 7.99 *(978-1-250-05047-2(2),* 9781250050472) Square Fish.

McGintry, Alice B. Cynthia Rylant. 2009. (Library of Author Biographies Ser.). 112p. (gr. 5-8). 63.90 *(978-1-60853-530-9(4),* Rosen Reference) Rosen Publishing Group, Inc., The.

McGinty, Alice B. Cynthia Rylant. 2004. (Library of Author Biographies Ser.). 112p. (YA). (gr. 5-9). lib. bdg. 34.60 *(978-0-8239-4526-9(X))* Rosen Publishing Group, Inc., The.

—Meet Daniel Pinkwater. (About the Author Ser.). 24p. 2009. (gr. 4-4). 42.50 *(978-1-61511-246-3(4),* PowerKids Pr.) 2003. (Illus.). (J). lib. bdg. 22.60 *(978-0-8239-6406-2(X))* Rosen Publishing Group, Inc., The.

—Meet Eve Bunting. (About the Author Ser.). 24p. 2009. (gr. 4-4). 42.50 *(978-1-61511-248-7(0))* 2003. (Illus.). (J). lib. bdg. 21.25 *(978-0-8239-6411-6(6))* Rosen Publishing Group, Inc., The. (PowerKids Pr.).

—Meet Jane Yolen. (About the Author Ser.). 24p. 2009. (gr. 4-4). 42.50 *(978-1-61511-252-4(9))* 2003. (Illus.). (J). lib. bdg. 22.60 *(978-0-8239-6407-9(8))* Rosen Publishing Group, Inc., The. (PowerKids Pr.).

—Meet Laurence Yep. 2003. (About the Author Ser.). (Illus.). 24p. (J). lib. bdg. 22.60 *(978-0-8239-6410-9(8),* PowerKids Pr.) Rosen Publishing Group, Inc., The.

—Sharon Creech. 2009. (Library of Author Biographies Ser.). 112p. (gr. 5-8). 63.90 *(978-1-60853-555-2(X),* Rosen Reference) Rosen Publishing Group, Inc., The.

Mcgrath, Brian S. Game Changers: Kwame Alexander. 2017. (Time for Kids Nonfiction Readers Ser.). lib. bdg. 19.65 **(978-0-606-40259-0(4))** Turtleback Bks.

McGuinness, Denis E. & Thomson, Sarah L. Gary Paulsen, 01 vols., 1. 2016. (All about the Author Ser.). (ENG., Illus.). 112p. (J). 35.60 *(978-1-4994-6268-5(9),* Rosen Young Adult) Rosen Publishing Group, Inc., The.

Meachen-Rau, Dana. Rookie Biographies: Dr. Seuss. 2014. (ENG.). 32p. lib. bdg. *(978-0-531-21060-4(X))* Children's Pr., Ltd.

—Rookie Biographies: Dr. Seuss. 2014. (ENG.). 32p. pap. *(978-0-531-24981-9(6))* Children's Pr., Ltd.

Mead, Wendy. Judy Blume. 2014. (Spotlight on Children's Authors Ser.). 48p. (J). (gr. 4-6). lib. bdg. 29.93 *(978-1-62712-843-8(3))* Cavendish Square Publishing.

—Maurice Sendak. 2014. (Spotlight on Children's Authors Ser.). 48p. (J). (gr. 4-6). 29.93 *(978-1-62712-840-7(9))* Cavendish Square Publishing.

—Sharon Creech. 2014. (J). pap. *(978-1-62712-269-6(9))* Cavendish Square Publishing.

Medina, Jane & National Geographic Learning Staff. Tomás Rivera. Martinez, Edward, illus. 2004. (Green Light Readers Level 2 Ser.). (ENG.). 24p. (J). (gr. -1-3). pap. 3.95 *(978-0-15-205145-7(7),* HMH Books For Young Readers) Houghton Mifflin Harcourt Publishing Co.

Meltzer, Milton. Edgar Allan Poe: A Biography. 2003. (Literary Greats Ser.). (ENG., Illus.). 144p. (gr. 7-12). lib. bdg. 33.26 *(978-0-7613-2910-7(2),* Twenty-First Century Bks.) Lerner Publishing Group.

—Henry David Thoreau: A Biography. 2007. (Literary Greats Ser.). (ENG., Illus.). 160p. (gr. 7-12). lib. bdg. 33.26 *(978-0-8225-5893-4(9),* Twenty-First Century Bks.) Lerner Publishing Group.

—Willa Cather: A Biography. 2008. (Literary Greats Ser.). (ENG., Illus.). 160p. (gr. 7-12). lib. bdg. 33.26 *(978-0-8225-7604-4(X))* Lerner Publishing Group.

Meyer, Susan. Gayle Forman, 01 vols., 1. 2016. (All about the Author Ser.). (ENG., Illus.). 112p. (J). 35.60 *(978-1-4994-6272-2(7),* Rosen Young Adult) Rosen Publishing Group, Inc., The.

Micklos, John, Jr. Jerry Spinelli: Master Teller of Teen Tales. 2007. (Authors Teens Love Ser.). (Illus.). 104p. (J). (gr. 8-12). lib. bdg. 33.27 *(978-0-7660-2718-3(X))* Enslow Pubs., Inc.

Miklowitz, Gloria D. Dr. Seuss. 2004. (ENG., Illus.). 26p. (J). (gr. 2-5). pap. 7.33 *(978-0-7685-1217-5(4),* Dominie Elementary) Pearson Schl.

Moonshower, Candie. Vivian Vande Velde: Author of Fantasy Fiction. 2009. (Authors Teens Love Ser.). (Illus.). 128p. (J). (gr. 6). lib. bdg. 33.27 *(978-0-7660-2964-4(6))* Enslow Pubs., Inc.

Morris, Roz. Nelle Harper Lee: Master Storyteller. 2008. (Illus.). 120p. (J). pap. 7.95 *(978-1-59421-040-2(3))* Seacoast Publishing, Inc.

Mortensen, Lori. Stephenie Meyer: Author of the Twilight Series. 2016. (Famous Female Authors Ser.). (ENG., Illus.). 32p. (gr. 3-4). lib. bdg. 27.99 *(978-1-5157-1329-6(6),* Snap Bks.) Capstone Press of Coughlan Cos.

—Veronica Roth: Author of the Divergent Trilogy. 2016. (Famous Female Authors Ser.). (ENG., Illus.). 32p. (gr. 3-4). lib. bdg. 27.99 *(978-1-5157-1327-2(X),* Snap Bks.) Capstone Press of Coughlan Cos.

Murcia, Rebecca Thatcher. E. B. White. 2004. (Classic Storytellers Ser.). (Illus.). 48p. (J). (gr. 4-8). lib. bdg. 29.95 *(978-1-58415-273-6(7))* Mitchell Lane Pubs., Inc.

Mussari, Mark. Amy Tan. 2010. (Today's Writers & Their Works). 128p. (gr. 7-18). 42.79 *(978-0-7614-4127-4(1))* Marshall Cavendish Corp.

Nagle, Jeanne & Main, Mary. Isabel Allende: Award-Winning Author. 2016. (Influential Latinos Ser.). (ENG., Illus.). 128p. (J). (gr. 7-8). lib. bdg. 37.27 *(978-0-7660-7250-3(9))* Enslow Pubs., Inc.

Nault, Jennifer. Judy Blume. 2014. (Illus.). 32p. (J). *(978-1-62127-400-1(4))* Weigl Pubs., Inc.

Neimark, Anne E. Mythmaker: The Life of J. R. R. Tolkien, Creator of the Hobbit & the Lord of the Rings. Weinman, Brad, illus. 2014. (ENG.). 144p. (J). (gr. 5-7). pap. 7.99 *(978-0-544-02324-6(2),* HMH Books For Young Readers) Houghton Mifflin Harcourt Publishing Co.

Newman, Gerald & Newman Layfield, Eleanor. Reading & Interpreting the Works of F. Scott Fitzgerald. 2016. (Lit Crit Guides). (ENG., Illus.). 160p. (J). (gr. 8-8). lib. bdg. 39.93 *(978-0-7660-7346-3(7))* Enslow Pubs., Inc.

Nichols, Susan. James Patterson, 01 vols., 1. 2016. (All about the Author Ser.). (ENG., Illus.). 112p. (J). 35.60 *(978-1-4994-6274-6(3),* Rosen Young Adult) Rosen Publishing Group, Inc., The.

Niver, Heather Moore. Henry David Thoreau: Author of Civil Disobedience. 2017. (J). **(978-1-5383-8113-7(3))**; pap. **(978-1-5383-8112-0(5))** Rosen Publishing Group, Inc., The. (Rosen Young Adult).

Niver, Heather Moore. Veronica Roth, 1 vol. 2015. (ENG.). 112p. (YA). 35.60 *(978-1-4777-7906-4(X),* Rosen Young Adult) Rosen Publishing Group, Inc., The.

Nobleman, Marc Tyler. Boys of Steel: The Creators of Superman. MacDonald, Ross, illus. 2013. (ENG.). 40p. (J). (gr. 5-6). 7.99 *(978-0-449-81063-7(1),* Dragonfly Bks.) Random Hse. Children's Bks.

North, Sterling. Rascal. 2004. (Puffin Modern Classics Ser.). (ENG., Illus.). 192p. (J). (gr. 3-7). 5.99 *(978-0-14-240252-8(4),* Puffin Books) Penguin Young Readers Group.

—Rascal, Mi Tremendo Mapache. 2003. (Cuatro Vientos Ser.: Vol. 9). (SPA.). 168p. (gr. 5-12). pap. 13.99 *(978-84-279-3109-1(3),* NG3492) Lectorum Pubns., Inc.

O'Dell, Kathryn L. American Authors E. B. White & Gary Soto. 2017. (Text Connections Guided Close Reading Ser.). (J). (gr. 2). *(978-1-4900-1851-5(4))* Benchmark Education Co.

O'Keefe, Sherry. From China to America: The Story of Amy Tan. 2011. (World Writers Ser.). 112p. (gr. 7-18). lib. bdg. 28.95 *(978-1-59935-138-4(2))* Reynolds, Morgan Inc.

Orr, Tamra. Amy Tan: Author Extraordinaire, 1 vol. 2009. (Essential Lives Set 4 Ser.). (ENG., Illus.). 112p. (J). (gr. 6-12). lib. bdg. 35.64 *(978-1-60453-705-5(1))* ABDO Publishing Co.

—Gary Soto. 2009. (Library of Author Biographies Ser.). 112p. (gr. 5-8). 63.90 *(978-1-60853-533-0(9),* Rosen Reference) Rosen Publishing Group, Inc., The.

—Stephanie Meyer. 2010. (Blue Banner Biography Ser.). (Illus.). 32p. (YA). (gr. 4-7). lib. bdg. 25.70 *(978-1-58415-907-0(3))* Mitchell Lane Pubs., Inc.

Orr, Tamra & Sommers, Michael A. Avi, 01 vols., 1. 2016. (All about the Author Ser.). (ENG., Illus.). 112p. (J). 35.60 *(978-1-4994-6276-0(X),* Rosen Young Adult) Rosen Publishing Group, Inc., The.

Owen, James A., ed. Secrets of the Dragon Riders: Your Favorite Authors on Christopher Paolini's Inheritance Cycle: Completely Unauthorized. 2010. (ENG., Illus.). 192p. (J). (gr. 7-11). pap. 12.95 *(978-1-933771-97-7(6))* BenBella Bks.

Parker-Rock, Michelle. Alma Flor Ada: An Author Kids Love. 2008. (Authors Kids Love Ser.). (Illus.). 48p. (J). (gr. 3-4). lib. bdg. 25.27 *(978-0-7660-2760-2(0),* Enslow Elementary) Enslow Pubs., Inc.

—Bruce Coville: An Author Kids Love. 2008. (Authors Kids Love Ser.). (Illus.). 48p. (J). (gr. 3-4). lib. bdg. 25.27 *(978-0-7660-2755-8(4),* Enslow Elementary) Enslow Pubs., Inc.

—Bruce Hale: An Author Kids Love. 2008. (Authors Kids Love Ser.). (Illus.). 48p. (J). (gr. 3-4). lib. bdg. 25.27 *(978-0-7660-2758-9(9),* Enslow Elementary) Enslow Pubs., Inc.

—Christopher Paul Curtis: An Author Kids Love. 2009. (Authors Kids Love Ser.). (Illus.). 48p. (J). (gr. 3-4). lib. bdg. 25.27 *(978-0-7660-3161-6(6),* Enslow Elementary) Enslow Pubs., Inc.

—Jack Gantos: An Author Kids Love. 2008. (Authors Kids Love Ser.). (Illus.). 48p. (J). (gr. 3-4). lib. bdg. 25.27 *(978-0-7660-2756-5(2),* Enslow Elementary) Enslow Pubs., Inc.

—Joseph Bruchac: An Author Kids Love. 2009. (Authors Kids Love Ser.). (Illus.). 48p. (J). (gr. 3-4). lib. bdg. 25.27 *(978-0-7660-3160-9(8),* Enslow Elementary) Enslow Pubs., Inc.

—Linda Sue Park: An Author Kids Love. 2009. (Authors Kids Love Ser.). (Illus.). 48p. (J). (gr. 3-4). lib. bdg. 25.27 *(978-0-7660-3158-6(6),* Enslow Elementary) Enslow Pubs., Inc.

—Patricia & Fredrick Mckissack: Authors Kids Love. 2008. (Authors Kids Love Ser.). (Illus.). 48p. (J). (gr. 3-4). lib. bdg. 25.27 *(978-0-7660-2759-6(7)*, Enslow Elementary) Enslow Pubs., Inc.

—Sid Fleischman: An Author Kids Love. 2008. (Authors Kids Love Ser.). (Illus.). 48p. (J). (gr. 3-4). lib. bdg. 25.27 *(978-0-7660-2757-2(0)*, Enslow Elementary) Enslow Pubs., Inc.

Pascal, Janet. Who Was Dr. Seuss? Harrison, Nancy, illus. 2011. (Who Was? Ser.). (ENG.). 112p. (J). (gr. 3-7). pap. 5.99 *(978-0-448-45585-3(4)*, Grosset & Dunlap) Penguin Young Readers Group.

—Who Was Maurice Sendak? 2013. (Who Was... ? Ser.). lib. bdg. 16.00 *(978-0-606-26962-9(2)*, Turtleback) Turtleback Bks.

Paulsen, Gary. Caught by the Sea: My Life on Boats. 2003. (Illus.). 103p. (gr. 7). 16.00 *(978-0-7569-1635-0(6))* Perfection Learning Corp.

—Caught by the Sea: My Life on Boats. 2003. (ENG., Illus.). 112p. (YA). (gr. 7). mass mkt. 5.99 *(978-0-440-40716-4(8)*, Laurel Leaf) Random Hse. Children's Bks.

—How Angel Peterson Got His Name: And Other Outrageous Tales about Extreme Sports. 2006. 108p. (gr. 5-9). per. *(978-1-905665-14-3(8))* Pollinger In Print.

—This Side of Wild. Jessell, Tim, illus. 2015. (ENG.). 144p. (J). (gr. 5). 16.99 *(978-1-4814-5150-5(2)*, Simon & Schuster Bks. For Young Readers) Simon & Schuster Bks. For Young Readers.

—This Side of Wild: Mutts, Mares, & Laughing Dinosaurs. Jessell, Tim, illus. 2016. (ENG.). 160p. (J). (gr. 5). pap. 7.99 *(978-1-4814-5151-2(0)*, Simon & Schuster Bks. For Young Readers) Simon & Schuster Bks. For Young Readers.

Peltak, Jennifer. Edgar Allan Poe. 2003. (Who Wrote That? Ser.). (Illus.). 112p. (gr. 6-12). 35.00 *(978-0-7910-7622-4(9)*, Chelsea Hse.) Facts On File, Inc.

Peterson-Hilleque, Victoria & Llanas, Sheila Griffin. How to Analyze the Works of Sylvia Plath, 1 vol. 2012. (Essential Critiques Set 3 Ser.). (ENG.). 112p. (J). (gr. 6-12). lib. bdg. 35.64 *(978-1-61783-457-8(2)*, Essential Library) ABDO Publishing Co.

Pingelton, Timothy J. Reading & Interpreting the Works of Ernest Hemingway. 2017. (Lit Crit Guides). 160p. (J). (gr. 8-8). lib. bdg. 39.93 ***(978-0-7660-8489-6(2))*** Enslow Pubs., Inc.

Pingelton, Timothy J. A Student's Guide to Ernest Hemingway. 2005. (Understanding Literature Ser.). (Illus.). 160p. (YA). (gr. 7-13). lib. bdg. 29.27 *(978-0-7660-2431-1(8))* Enslow Pubs., Inc.

Pinkney, Andrea Davis & Wells, Rosemary. A Poem for Peter: The Story of Ezra Jack Keats & the Creation of the Snowy Day. Johnson, Steve & Fancher, Lou, illus. 2016. (ENG.). 60p. (J). (gr. 2-5). bds. 18.99 *(978-0-425-28768-2(8)*, Viking Books for Young Readers) Penguin Young Readers Group.

Poolos, Christine. John Green, 1 vol. 2015. (ENG.). 112p. (YA). 35.60 *(978-1-4777-7904-0(3)*, Rosen Young Adult) Rosen Publishing Group, Inc., The.

Potter, Giselle. The Year I Didn't Go to School. Potter, Giselle, illus. 2015. (ENG., Illus.). 40p. (J). (gr. -1-3). 13.99 *(978-1-4814-7995-0(4)*, Atheneum Bks. for Young Readers) Simon & Schuster Children's Publishing.

Prince, April Jones. Who Was Mark Twain? O'Brien, John A. & Harrison, Nancy, illus. 2004. (Who Was? Ser.). (ENG.). 112p. (J). (gr. 3-7). pap. 5.99 *(978-0-448-43319-6(2)*, Grosset & Dunlap) Penguin Young Readers Group.

—Who Was Mark Twain? O'brien, John, illus. 2004. (Who Was... ? Ser.). 105p. (gr. 3-7). 16.00 *(978-0-7569-4590-9(9))* Perfection Learning Corp.

Purslow, Neil. R. L. Stine. 2006. (My Favorite Writer Ser.). (Illus.). 32p. (J). (gr. 3-7). pap. 9.95 *(978-1-59036-487-1(2))*; lib. bdg. 26.00 *(978-1-59036-486-4(4))* Weigl Pubs., Inc.

—R.L. Stine. 2014. (Illus.). 32p. (J). *(978-1-62127-404-9(7))* Weigl Pubs., Inc.

Putnam, Richelle & Aycock, John. The Inspiring Life of Eudora Welty. 2014. Orig. Title: The Inspiring Life of Eudora Welty. (ENG., Illus.). 144p. (gr. 4-7). pap. 16.99 *(978-1-62619-000-9(3)*, History Pr., The) Arcadia Publishing.

Rajczak, Kristen. Laura Ingalls Wilder in Her Own Words. 2016. (Eyewitness to History Ser.). (ENG.). 32p. (J). (gr. 4-5). pap. 10.50 *(978-1-4824-4070-6(9))* Stevens, Gareth Publishing LLLP.

Rasmussen, R. Kent. Mark Twain for Kids: His Life & Times, 21 Activities. 2004. (For Kids Ser.). (ENG., Illus.). 160p. (J). (gr. 4). pap. 14.95 *(978-1-55652-527-8(3))* Chicago Review Pr., Inc.

Rau, Dana Meachen. Who Was Harriet Beecher Stowe? 2015. (Who Was... ? Ser.). lib. bdg. 16.00 *(978-0-606-36598-7(2))* Turtleback Bks.

Rau, Dana Meachen & dePaola, Tomie. Who Was Harriet Beecher Stowe? Harrison, Nancy & Copeland, Gregory, illus. 2015. (Who Was? Ser.). (ENG.). 112p. (J). (gr. 3-7). 5.99 *(978-0-448-48301-6(7)*, Grosset & Dunlap) Penguin Young Readers Group.

Reef, Catherine. Ernest Hemingway: A Writer's Life. 2009. (ENG., Illus.). 192p. (J). (gr. 5-7). 20.00 *(978-0-618-98705-4(3))* Houghton Mifflin Harcourt Publishing Co.

Reiff, Rachel Haugrud. Sandra Cisneros. 2013. (Today's Writers & Their Works Ser.). 144p. (YA). (gr. 7-12). pap. 22.34 *(978-1-62712-145-3(5))* Cavendish Square Publishing.

Reiff, Raychel Haugrud. Sandra Cisneros. 2011. (YA). *(978-1-60870-503-0(X))* Marshall Cavendish.

Rice, Dona Herweck. Stepping into Louisa May Alcott's World. 2017. (Time for Kids Nonfiction Readers Ser.). lib. bdg. 20.85 ***(978-0-606-40262-0(4))*** Turtleback Bks.

Richardson, Gillian. Dan Gutman. 2005. (My Favorite Writer Ser.). (Illus.). 32p. (J). (gr. 3-7). per. 9.95 *(978-1-59036-290-7(X))* Weigl Pubs., Inc.

Richert, Scott P. Bill Bryson. 2010. (Today's Writers & Their Works Ser.). 128p. (gr. 7). 42.79 *(978-0-7614-4120-5(4))* Marshall Cavendish GBR. Dist: Marshall Cavendish Corp.

Riggs, Kate. Ernest Hemingway. (Illus.). (J). 2016. 80p. *(978-1-60818-717-1(9))* 2008. 48p. 22.95 *(978-1-58341-661-7(7))* Creative Co., The. (Creative Education).

Rinker, Sherri Duskey. Big Machines: The Story of Virginia Lee Burton. Rocco, John, illus. 2017. (ENG.). 48p. (J). (gr. -1-3). 17.99 ***(978-0-544-71557-8(8)***, HMH Books For Young Readers) Houghton Mifflin Harcourt Publishing Co.

Roby, Cynthia A. Zora Neale Hurston. 2016. (Artists of the Harlem Renaissance Ser.). (ENG.). 128p. (J). (gr. 9-9). lib. bdg. 45.64 *(978-1-5026-1038-6(8))* Cavendish Square Publishing.

Rubini, Julie K. Missing Millie Benson: The Secret Case of the Nancy Drew Ghostwriter & Journalist. 2015. (Biographies for Young Readers Ser.). (ENG., Illus.). 136p. (J). (gr. 1-6). 28.95 *(978-0-8214-2183-3(2))* Ohio Univ. Pr.

—Virginia Hamilton: America's Children's Book Author. 2017. (Biographies for Young Readers Ser.). (ENG., Illus.). 152p. (J). (gr. 1-6). pap. 14.95 *(978-0-8214-2269-4(3))* Ohio Univ. Pr.

Rubini, Julie K. Virginia Hamilton: Her Story. 2017. (Biographies for Young Readers Ser.). (ENG., Illus.). 152p. (J). (gr. 1-6). 28.95 ***(978-0-8214-2268-7(5))*** Ohio Univ. Pr.

Ruffin, Frances E. Meet Lois Lowry. (About the Author Ser.). 24p. 2009. (gr. 4-4). 42.50 *(978-1-61511-256-2(1)*, PowerKids Pr.) 2006. (Illus.). (YA). (gr. 2-5). lib. bdg. 22.60 *(978-1-4042-3129-0(3))* Rosen Publishing Group, Inc., The.

—Meet Patricia MacLachlan. (About the Author Ser.). 24p. 2009. (gr. 4-4). 42.50 *(978-1-61511-257-9(X)*, PowerKids Pr.) 2006. (Illus.). (YA). (gr. 2-5). lib. bdg. 22.60 *(978-1-4042-3130-6(7))* Rosen Publishing Group, Inc., The.

—Meet Paula Danziger. (About the Author Ser.). 24p. 2009. (gr. 4-4). 42.50 *(978-1-61511-258-6(8))* 2006. (Illus.). (J). (gr. -1-3). lib. bdg. 22.60 *(978-1-4042-3133-7(1))* Rosen Publishing Group, Inc., The. (PowerKids Pr.).

—Meet Sid Fleischman. (About the Author Ser.). 24p. 2009. (gr. 4-4). 42.50 *(978-1-61511-260-9(X))* 2006. (Illus.). (J). (gr. -1-3). lib. bdg. 22.60 *(978-1-4042-3132-0(3))* Rosen Publishing Group, Inc., The. (PowerKids Pr.).

Sammons, Sandra Wallus. Marjorie Kinnan Rawlings & the Florida Crackers. 2010. (Pineapple Press Biography Ser.). (ENG., Illus.). 72p. (Orig.). (J). (gr. 4-7). pap. 8.95 *(978-1-56164-473-5(0))*; 11.95 *(978-1-56164-472-8(2))* Pineapple Pr., Inc.

—Zora Neale Hurston. 2014. (ENG.). 80p. (J). (gr. 4-6). pap. 9.95 *(978-1-56164-682-1(2))* Pineapple Pr., Inc.

—Zora Neale Hurston: Wrapped in Rainbows. 2014. (Illus.). 67p. (J). pap. *(978-1-56164-611-1(3))* Pineapple Pr., Inc.

Sapet, Kerrily. Suzanne Collins. 2012. (Illus.). 112p. (J). *(978-1-59935-346-3(6))* Reynolds, Morgan Inc.

Schelly, Bill. Words of Wonder: The Life & Times of Otto Binder. 2003. *(978-0-9645669-9-6(0))* Hamster Pr.

Schnur, Steven. Henry David's House. Fiore, Peter M., illus. 2007. (ENG.). 32p. (J). (gr. k-3). pap. 7.95 *(978-0-88106-117-8(4))* Charlesbridge Publishing, Inc.

Schoell, William. Mystery & Terror: The Story of Edgar Allan Poe. 2004. (Illus.). 128p. (YA). (gr. 6-12). 23.95 *(978-1-931798-39-6(7))* Reynolds, Morgan Inc.

Schuetz, Kari. Dr. Seuss. 2015. (Children's Storytellers Ser.). (ENG., Illus.). 24p. (J). (gr. 2-5). lib. bdg. 25.95 *(978-1-62617-265-4(X)*, Blastoff! Readers) Bellwether Media.

Schumann, Marc. Ha Jin. 2011. (J). *(978-1-60870-504-7(8))* Marshall Cavendish.

Schwartz, Heather E. Marjorie Kinnan Rawlings: Writing in Rural Florida. 2016. (Primary Source Readers Ser.). 32p. (J). (gr. 4-4). pap. 8.99 *(978-1-4938-3543-0(2))* Teacher Created Materials, Inc.

Scieszka, Jon. Knucklehead: Tall Tales & Almost True Stories about Growing up Scieszka. 2008. (ENG., Illus.). 96p. (J). (gr. 3-7). 12.99 *(978-0-670-01138-4(X)*, Viking Books for Young Readers) Penguin Young Readers Group.

Self Reliance: The Story of Ralph Waldo Emerson. 2011. (World Writers Ser.). lib. bdg. 28.95 *(978-1-59935-124-7(2))* Reynolds, Morgan Inc.

Shapiro, Marc. Stephenie Meyer: The Unauthorized Biography of the Creator of the Twilight Saga. 2010. (ENG., Illus.). 224p. pap. 18.99 *(978-0-312-63829-0(9)*, 9780312638290, St. Martin's Griffin) St. Martin's Pr.

Shea, John. Outsiders. 2011. (J). *(978-0-531-22556-1(9))* Scholastic, Inc.

Shea, Therese. Kate DiCamillo: Newbery Medal-Winning Author. 2015. (Britannica Beginner Bios Ser.). (ENG., Illus.). 32p. (J). (gr. 2-3). 23.45 *(978-1-62275-936-1(2)*, Britannica Educational Publishing) Rosen Publishing Group, Inc., The.

Sheen, Barbara. Stephenie Meyer: Twilight Saga Author. 2010. (Innovators Ser.). (ENG.). 48p. (YA). (gr. 4-7). 29.95 *(978-0-7377-5066-9(9))* Cengage Gale.

Shepherd, Jodie. Maurice Sendak: King of the Wild Things. 2017. (Rookie Biographies(tm) Ser.). (ENG., Illus.). 32p. (J). lib. bdg. 25.00 *(978-0-531-22291-1(8)*, Children's Pr.) Scholastic Library Publishing.

Sherman, Josepha. Mark Twain. 2005. (Classic Storytellers Ser.). (Illus.). 48p. (J). (gr. 4-8). lib. bdg. 29.95 *(978-1-58415-374-0(1))* Mitchell Lane Pubs., Inc.

Shields, Charles J. I Am Scout: The Biography of Harper Lee. 2008. (ENG., Illus.). 256p. (J). (gr. 7-12). 19.99 *(978-0-8050-8334-7(0)*, 9780805083347, Holt, Henry & Co. Bks. For Young Readers) Holt, Henry & Co.

Shirley, David. Alex Haley: Author. 2005. (Black Americans of Achievement Ser.). (Illus.). 112p. (gr. 6-12). 35.00 *(978-0-7910-8249-2(0)*, Chelsea Hse.) Facts On File, Inc.

Sickels, Amy. Laura Ingalls Wilder. 2007. (Who Wrote That? Ser.). (Illus.). 126p. (gr. 6-12). lib. bdg. 35.00 *(978-0-7910-9525-6(8)*, Chelsea Hse.) Facts On File, Inc.

—Richard Peck. 2009. (Who Wrote That? Ser.). (Illus.). 128p. (gr. 6-12). 35.00 *(978-0-7910-9530-0(4)*, Chelsea Hse.) Facts On File, Inc.

Sierra, Judy. Imagine That! How Dr. Seuss Wrote the Cat in the Hat. Hawkes, Kevin, illus. 2017. (ENG.). 48p. (J). (gr. -1-2). lib. bdg. 20.99 *(978-0-375-97429-8(6)*, Random Hse. Bks. for Young Readers) Random Hse. Children's Bks.

Sigafus, Kim & Ernst, Lyle. Native Writers-Voices of Power, 1 vol. 2012. (Native Trailblazers Ser.). (ENG.). 128p. (YA). (gr. 6-10). pap. 9.95 *(978-0-9779183-8-6(6)*, 7th Generation) Book Publishing Co.

Silverman, Erica. Liberty's Voice: The Story of Emma Lazarus. Schuett, Stacey, illus. 2014. (ENG.). 32p. (J). (gr. 1-3). 8.99 *(978-0-14-751174-4(7)*, Puffin Books) Penguin Young Readers Group.

Silverstein, Shel. Shel Silverstein Pop-up Treasury. Silverstein, Shel, illus. 2008. (Illus.). 16p. (J). 29.99 *(978-0-06-147269-5(7))* HarperCollins Pubs.

Silverthorne, Elizabeth. Louisa May Alcott. 2nd rev. ed. 2011. (Who Wrote That? Ser.). (Illus.). 120p. (gr. 6-12). 35.00 *(978-1-60413-760-6(6)*, Chelsea Hse.) Facts On File, Inc.

Simons, Lisa M. B. Jacqueline Woodson. Byers, Michael, illus. 2017. (Your Favorite Authors Ser.). (ENG.). 24p. (gr. 1-2). lib. bdg. 25.32 *(978-1-5157-3558-8(3)*, First Facts) Capstone Press of Coughlan Cos.

Simons, Lisa M. Bolt. Jacqueline Woodson. Byers, Michael, illus. 2017. (Your Favorite Authors Ser.). (ENG.). 24p. (gr. 1-2). pap. 7.95 *(978-1-5157-3563-2(X)*, First Facts) Capstone Press of Coughlan Cos.

Sís, Peter. The Wall: Growing up Behind the Iron Curtain. Sís, Peter, illus. 2007. (ENG., Illus.). 56p. (J). (gr. 3-7). 19.99 *(978-0-374-34701-7(8)*, 9780374347017, Farrar, Straus & Giroux (BYR)) Farrar, Straus & Giroux.

Small, Cathleen. Mike Lupica. 2014. (Spotlight on Children's Authors Ser.). 48p. (J). (gr. 4-6). lib. bdg. 29.93 *(978-1-62712-849-0(2))* Cavendish Square Publishing.

Smith, Corinne Hosfeld. Henry David Thoreau for Kids: His Life & Ideas, with 21 Activities. 2016. (For Kids Ser.). (ENG., Illus.). 128p. (J). (gr. 4). pap. 16.95 *(978-1-61373-146-8(9))* Chicago Review Pr., Inc.

Sommers, Michael A. Avi. (Library of Author Biographies Ser.). 112p. (gr. 5-8). 2009. 63.90 *(978-1-60853-527-9(4)*, Rosen Reference) 2004. (YA). lib. bdg. 34.60 *(978-0-8239-4522-1(7))* Rosen Publishing Group, Inc., The.

—Chris Crutcher. 2004. (Library of Author Biographies Ser.). (Illus.). 112p. (YA). lib. bdg. 34.60 *(978-1-4042-0325-9(7))* Rosen Publishing Group, Inc., The.

Sonneborn, Liz. Harriet Beecher Stowe. 2009. (Leaders of the Civil War Era Ser.). (Illus.). 120p. (gr. 6-12). 35.00 *(978-1-60413-302-8(3)*, Chelsea Hse.) Facts On File, Inc.

—James Lincoln Collier. (Library of Author Biographies). (Illus.). 112p. 2006. (gr. 5-8). pap. 12.95 *(978-1-4042-0649-6(3))* 2005. (J). (gr. k-3). lib. bdg. 34.60 *(978-1-4042-0461-4(X))* Rosen Publishing Group, Inc., The.

—Sherman Alexie. 2012. (All about the Author Ser.). (ENG.). 112p. (YA). (gr. 7-12). lib. bdg. 34.60 *(978-1-4488-6941-1(2))* Rosen Publishing Group, Inc., The.

Sparks, Barry. Rick Riordan. 2012. (Illus.). 128p. (J). *(978-1-59935-350-0(4))* Reynolds, Morgan Inc.

Spinelli, Jerry. Knots in My Yo-Yo Strong. Gentieu, Penny, photos by. 2014. (Illus.). 158p. pap. 11.00 *(978-1-61003-375-6(2))* Center for the Collaborative Classroom.

Spring, Albert. M. E. Kerr. annot. ed. 2005. (Library of Author Biographies Ser.). (Illus.). 112p. (J). (gr. k-3). lib. bdg. 34.60 *(978-1-4042-0465-2(2))* Rosen Publishing Group, Inc., The.

Stalcup, Ann & Politi, Leo. Leo Politi: Artist of the Angels. 2004. (gr. 4). 24.95 *(978-1-893110-38-0(9))* Silver Moon Pr.

Staley, Erin. Maggie Stiefvater. 2013. (All about the Author Ser.). 112p. (YA). (gr. 7-12). 34.60 *(978-1-4777-1762-2(5))* Rosen Publishing Group, Inc., The.

Stefoff, Rebecca. Stephen King. 2010. (Today's Writers & Their Works). 128p. (gr. 7-18). 42.79 *(978-0-7614-4122-9(0))* Marshall Cavendish Corp.

Stephenie Meyer. 2010. (Who Wrote That? Ser.). (Illus.). 128p. (gr. 6-12). 35.00 *(978-1-60413-693-7(6)*, Chelsea Hse.) Facts On File, Inc.

Stine, R. L. It Came from Ohio! - My Life as a Writer. 2015. (ENG.). 176p. (J). (gr. 3-7). pap. 6.99 *(978-0-545-82890-1(2)*, Scholastic Paperbacks) Scholastic, Inc.

Streissguth, Thomas. Edgar Allan Poe. 2005. (Biography Ser.). (Illus.). 112p. (J). (gr. 6-12). lib. bdg. 27.93 *(978-0-8225-4991-8(3))* Lerner Publishing Group.

Streissguth, Tom. Edgar Allan Poe. 2007. (Just the Facts Biographies Ser.). (ENG., Illus.). 112p. (gr. 5-12). lib. bdg. 27.93 *(978-0-8225-6800-1(4)*, Lerner Pubns.) Lerner Publishing Group.

Student's Encyclopedia of Great American Writers, 5 vols., Set. 2010. (Great American Writers Ser.). 2576p. (C). (gr. 9-12). 425.00 *(978-0-8160-6087-0(8))* Facts On File, Inc.

Sullivan, Laura L. Gail Carson Levine. 2014. (Spotlight on Children's Authors Ser.). 48p. (J). (gr. 4-6). lib. bdg. 29.93 *(978-1-62712-852-0(2))* Cavendish Square Publishing.

—Jacqueline Woodson. 2014. (Spotlight on Children's Authors Ser.). (Illus.). 48p. (J). (gr. 4-6). lib. bdg. 29.93 *(978-1-62712-855-1(7))* Cavendish Square Publishing.

Sweet, Melissa. Some Writer! The Story of E. B. White. 2016. (ENG., Illus.). 176p. (J). (gr. 2-5). 18.99 *(978-0-544-31959-2(1)*, HMH Books For Young Readers) Houghton Mifflin Harcourt Publishing Co.

Tahir, Rana. Countee Cullen. 2016. (Artists of the Harlem Renaissance Ser.). (ENG.). 128p. (J). (gr. 9-9). lib. bdg. 45.64 *(978-1-5026-1068-3(X))* Cavendish Square Publishing.

Tait, Leia. Avi. 2006. (My Favorite Writer Ser.). (Illus.). 32p. (J). (gr. 3-7). pap. 9.95 *(978-1-59036-479-6(1))*; lib. bdg. 26.00 *(978-1-59036-478-9(3))* Weigl Pubs., Inc.

Taylor, Charlotte. Phillis Wheatley: Colonial African-American Poet. 2016. (Exceptional African Americans Ser.). (ENG., Illus.). 24p. (J). (gr. 3-3). 22.60 *(978-0-7660-7326-5(2))* Enslow Pubs., Inc.

Terman Cohen, Sheila. Sterling North & the Story of Rascal. 2016. (Badger Biographies Ser.). (ENG., Illus.). 128p. (J). (gr. 4-6). pap. 12.95 *(978-0-87020-735-8(0))* Wisconsin Historical Society.

Tessitore, John. Extraordinary American Writers. 2004. (Extraordinary People Ser.). (ENG., Illus.). 288p. (J). 40.00 *(978-0-516-22656-9(8)*, Children's Pr.) Scholastic Library Publishing.

Thomas, Jerry D. Who Was Ellen White? 2017. (J). pap. ***(978-0-8163-6182-3(7))*** Pacific Pr. Publishing Assn.

Tieck, Sarah. Mark Twain, 1 vol. 2010. (First Biographies Set 6 Ser.). (ENG.). 32p. (J). (gr. 1-4). 27.07 *(978-1-60453-988-2(7))* ABDO Publishing Co.

Todd, Anne M. & Bankston, John. Jacqueline Wilson. 2011. (Who Wrote That? Ser.). (Illus.). 128p. (gr. 6-12). 35.00 *(978-1-60413-773-6(8)*, Chelsea Hse.) Facts On File, Inc.

Tomljanovic, Tatiana. Megan McDonald. 2008. (My Favorite Writer Ser.). (Illus.). 32p. (YA). (gr. 5-18). pap. 9.95 *(978-1-59036-929-6(7))*; lib. bdg. 26.00 *(978-1-59036-928-9(9))* Weigl Pubs., Inc.

Tracy, Kathleen. John Steinbeck. 2004. (Classic Storytellers Ser.). (Illus.). 48p. (J). (gr. 4-8). lib. bdg. 29.95 *(978-1-58415-271-2(0))* Mitchell Lane Pubs., Inc.

—Matt Christopher. 2008. (Classic Storytellers Ser.). (Illus.). 48p. (J). (gr. 4-7). lib. bdg. 29.95 *(978-1-58415-535-5(3))* Mitchell Lane Pubs., Inc.

Ursula K. le Guin. 2010. (Who Wrote That? Ser.). (Illus.). 128p. (YA). (gr. 6-12). 35.00 *(978-1-60413-724-8(X)*, Chelsea Hse.) Facts On File, Inc.

Uschan, Michael V., ed. Tyler Perry. 2010. (People in the News Ser.). (ENG.). 96p. (YA). (gr. 7-12). 33.95 *(978-1-4205-0309-8(X))* Cengage Gale.

Wade, Mary Dodson. Joan Lowery Nixon: Masterful Mystery Writer. 2004. (Authors Teens Love Ser.). (Illus.). 128p. (J). lib. bdg. 27.94 *(978-0-7660-2194-5(7))* Enslow Pubs., Inc.

Wade McCormick, Lisa. Rick Yancey. 2013. (All about the Author Ser.). 112p. (YA). (gr. 7-12). 34.60 *(978-1-4777-1767-7(6))* Rosen Publishing Group, Inc., The.

Warrick, Karen Clemens. Sandra Cisneros: Inspiring Latina Author. 2009. (Latino Biography Library). (Illus.). 128p. (J). (gr. 6-18). lib. bdg. 33.27 *(978-0-7660-3162-3(4))* Enslow Pubs., Inc.

Watson, Galadriel Findlay. Toni Morrison. 2005. (Great African American Women for Kids Ser.). (Illus.). 24p. (J). (gr. 2-3). lib. bdg. 24.45 *(978-1-59036-334-8(5))* Weigl Pubs., Inc.

Waxman, Laura Hamilton. Dr. Seuss. 2010. (History Maker Biographies Ser.). (ENG.). 48p. (gr. 3-6). lib. bdg. 27.93 *(978-0-7613-5206-8(6)*, Lerner Pubns.) Lerner Publishing Group.

Webster, Christine. Jeff Kinney. 2012. (J). *(978-1-61913-058-6(0))*; pap. *(978-1-61913-598-7(1))* Weigl Pubs., Inc.

—Sandra Cisneros: My Favorite Writer. 2008. (J). 29.05 *(978-1-59036-933-3(5))* Weigl Pubs., Inc.

Weisbrod, Eva. A Student's Guide to F. Scott Fitzgerald. 2004. (Understanding Literature Ser.). (Illus.). 160p. (YA). lib. bdg. 29.27 *(978-0-7660-2202-7(1))* Enslow Pubs., Inc.

Weisbrod Geertz, Eva. Reading & Interpreting the Works of John Steinbeck. 2016. (Lit Crit Guides). (ENG., Illus.). 176p. (J). (gr. 8-8). lib. bdg. 39.93 *(978-0-7660-7348-7(3))* Enslow Pubs., Inc.

Welsch, Camille-Yvette. Meg Cabot. 2008. (Who Wrote That? Ser.). 136p. (gr. 6-12). 35.00 *(978-0-7910-9631-4(9)*, Chelsea Hse.) Facts On File, Inc.

Wheeler, Jill C. Alvin Schwartz, 1 vol. 2014. (Children's Authors Set 8 Ser.). (ENG.). 24p. (gr. 3-6). 25.65 *(978-1-62403-670-5(8))* ABDO Publishing Co.

—Avi, 1 vol. 2009. (Children's Authors Set 5 Ser.). (ENG.). 24p. (J). (gr. 2-5). 25.65 *(978-1-60453-075-9(8))* ABDO Publishing Co.

—Barbara Park, 1 vol. 2007. (Children's Authors Set 4 Ser.). (ENG., Illus.). 24p. (J). (gr. 2-5). 25.65 *(978-1-59679-766-6(5))* ABDO Publishing Co.

—Christopher Paolini, 1 vol. 2007. (Children's Authors Set 4 Ser.). (ENG., Illus.). 24p. (J). (gr. 2-5). 25.65 *(978-1-59679-765-9(7))* ABDO Publishing Co.

—Cynthia Kadohata, 1 vol. 2013. (Children's Authors Set 7 Ser.). (ENG.). 24p. (J). (gr. 3-6). lib. bdg. 25.65 *(978-1-61783-575-9(7)*, Checkerboard Library) ABDO Publishing Co.

—Cynthia Rylant, 1 vol. 2009. (Children's Authors Set 5 Ser.). (ENG.). 24p. (J). (gr. 2-5). 25.65 *(978-1-60453-079-7(0))* ABDO Publishing Co.

—Dav Pilkey, 1 vol. 2013. (Children's Authors Set 7 Ser.). (ENG.). 24p. (J). (gr. 3-6). lib. bdg. 25.65 *(978-1-61783-577-3(3)*, Checkerboard Library) ABDO Publishing Co.

—E. B. White, 1 vol. 2013. (Children's Authors Set 7 Ser.). (ENG.). 24p. (J). (gr. 3-6). lib. bdg. 25.65 *(978-1-61783-579-7(X)*, Checkerboard Library) ABDO Publishing Co.

—Gary Paulsen, 1 vol. 2014. (Children's Authors Set 8 Ser.). (ENG.). 24p. (J). (gr. 3-6). 25.65 *(978-1-62403-668-2(6))* ABDO Publishing Co.

—Gertrude Chandler Warner, 1 vol. 2005. (Children's Authors Set 3 Ser.). (ENG.). 24p. (gr. k-6). 25.65 *(978-1-59197-609-7(X)*, Checkerboard Library) ABDO Publishing Co.

—Grace Lin, 1 vol. 2012. (Children's Authors Set 6 Ser.). (ENG., Illus.). 24p. (J). (gr. 2-5). 25.65 *(978-1-61783-049-5(6))* ABDO Publishing Co.

—Judy Blume, 1 vol. 2005. (Children's Authors Set 3 Ser.). (ENG., Illus.). 24p. (J). (gr. 2-5). 25.65 *(978-1-59197-604-2(9))* ABDO Publishing Co.

—Julia Alvarez, 1 vol. 2012. (Children's Authors Set 6 Ser.). (ENG., Illus.). 24p. (YA). (gr. 2-5). 25.65 *(978-1-61783-045-7(3))* ABDO Publishing Co.

—Kate Dicamillo, 1 vol. 2009. (Children's Authors Set 5 Ser.). (ENG.). 24p. (J). (gr. 2-5). 25.65 *(978-1-60453-076-6(6))* ABDO Publishing Co.

—L. Frank Baum, 1 vol. 2014. (Children's Authors Set 8 Ser.). (ENG.). 24p. (gr. 3-6). 25.65 *(978-1-62403-665-1(1))* ABDO Publishing Co.

—Lemony Snicket, 1 vol. 2007. (Children's Authors Set 4 Ser.). (ENG., Illus.). 24p. (YA). (gr. 2-5). 25.65 *(978-1-59679-767-3(3))* ABDO Publishing Co.

—Margaret Wise Brown, 1 vol. 2007. (Children's Authors Set 4 Ser.). (ENG., Illus.). 24p. (J). (gr. 2-5). 25.65 *(978-1-59679-762-8(2))* ABDO Publishing Co.

—Marjorie Weinman Sharmat, 1 vol. 2005. (Children's Authors Set 3 Ser.). (ENG., Illus.). 24p. (gr. k-6). 25.65 *(978-1-59197-608-0(1)*, Checkerboard Library) ABDO Publishing Co.

—Mary Pope Osborne, 1 vol. 2007. (Children's Authors Set 4 Ser.). (ENG., Illus.). 24p. (YA). (gr. 2-5). 25.65 *(978-1-59679-764-2(9))* ABDO Publishing Co.

—Mercer Mayer, 1 vol. 2005. (Children's Authors Set 3 Ser.). (ENG., Illus.). 24p. (YA). (gr. 2-5). 25.65 *(978-1-59197-606-6(5))* ABDO Publishing Co.

—Norman Bridwell, 1 vol. 2005. (Children's Authors Set 3 Ser.). (ENG., Illus.). 24p. (J). (gr. 2-5). 25.65 *(978-1-59197-605-9(7))* ABDO Publishing Co.

—Pam Muñoz Ryan, 1 vol. 2009. (Children's Authors Set 5 Ser.). (ENG.). 24p. (J). (gr. 2-5). 25.65 *(978-1-60453-078-0(2))* ABDO Publishing Co.

—Rick Riordan, 1 vol. 2013. (Children's Authors Set 7 Ser.). (ENG.). 24p. (J). (gr. 3-6). lib. bdg. 25.65 *(978-1-61783-578-0(1)*, Checkerboard Library) ABDO Publishing Co.

A B

—Scott O'Dell, 1 vol. 2014. (Children's Authors Set 8 Ser.). (ENG.). 24p. (gr. 3-6). 25.65 (978-1-62403-669-9(4)) ABDO Publishing Co.

—Sharon Creech, 1 vol. 2014. (Children's Authors Set 8 Ser.). (ENG., Illus.). 24p. (J). (gr. 3-6). 25.65 (978-1-62403-666-8(X)) ABDO Publishing Co.

—Suzanne Collins, 1 vol. 2013. (Children's Authors Set 7 Ser.). (ENG.). 24p. (J). (gr. 3-6). lib. bdg. 25.65 (978-1-61783-574-2(9), Checkerboard Library) ABDO Publishing Co.

—Walter Dean Myers, 1 vol. 2014. (Children's Authors Set 8 Ser.). (ENG.). 24p. (gr. 3-6). 25.65 (978-1-62403-667-5(8)) ABDO Publishing Co.

—Yuyi Morales, 1 vol. 2013. (Children's Authors Set 7 Ser.). (ENG.). 24p. (J). (gr. 3-6). lib. bdg. 25.65 (978-1-61783-576-6(5), Checkerboard Library) ABDO Publishing Co.

Whiting, Jim. Edgar Allan Poe. 2005. (Classic Storytellers Ser.). (Illus.). 48p. (J). (gr. 4-8). lib. bdg. 29.95 (978-1-58415-373-3(3)) Mitchell Lane Pubs., Inc.

—Ernest Hemingway. 2005. (Classic Storytellers Ser.). (Illus.). 48p. (J). (gr. 6-8). lib. bdg. 29.95 (978-1-58415-376-4(8)) Mitchell Lane Pubs., Inc.

Wilcox, Christine. Young Adult Authors. 2016. (ENG.). 80p. (J). (gr. 5-12). lib. bdg. (978-1-68282-036-0(X)) ReferencePoint Pr., Inc.

Willems, Mo. You Can Never Find a Rickshaw When It Monsoons: The World on One Cartoon a Day. Willems, Mo, illus. 2006. (ENG., Illus.). 408p. (gr. 8-17). pap. 12.99 (978-0-7868-3747-2(0)) Hyperion Pr.

Willett, Edward. Kiera Cass, 1 vol. 2015. (ENG.). 112p. (YA). 35.60 (978-1-4777-7914-9(0), Rosen Young Adult) Rosen Publishing Group, Inc., The.

Wilson, Antoine. S. E. Hinton. 2009. (Library of Author Biographies Ser.). 112p. (gr. 5-8). 63.90 (978-1-60853-553-8(3), Rosen Reference) Rosen Publishing Group, Inc., The.

Winter, Jonah. Gertrude Is Gertrude Is Gertrude Is Gertrude. Brown, Calef, illus. 2009. (ENG.). 40p. (J). (gr. -1-3). 16.99 (978-1-4169-4088-3(X), Atheneum Bks. for Young Readers) Simon & Schuster Children's Publishing.

Wolny, Philip. Isaac Asimov. 2014. (Great Science Writers Ser.). (Illus.). 112p. (J). (gr. 7-12). 35.60 (978-1-4777-7689-6(3)) Rosen Publishing Group, Inc., The.

—James Dashner. 2013. (All about the Author Ser.). 112p. (J). (gr. 7-12). 34.60 (978-1-4777-1763-9(3)) Rosen Publishing Group, Inc., The.

—Stephen Chbosky, 1 vol. 2015. (ENG.). 112p. (J). 35.60 (978-1-4777-7910-1(8), Rosen Young Adult) Rosen Publishing Group, Inc., The.

Wolny, Philip & Green, Meg. Louis Sachar, 01 vols., 1. 2016. (All about the Author Ser.). (ENG., Illus.). 112p. (J). 35.60 (978-1-4994-6264-7(6), Rosen Young Adult) Rosen Publishing Group, Inc., The.

Wong, Janet S. Before It Wriggles Away. Lindsay, Anne, photos by. 2006. (Meet the Author Ser.). (ENG., Illus.). 32p. (J). 14.95 (978-1-57274-861-3(3), 735, Meet the Author) Owen, Richard C. Pubs., Inc.

Wooding, Sharon. Mark Twain in Nevada, a History Coloring Book for Children. l.t. ed. 2003. (Illus.). 25p. (J). (SPA.). pap. 5.95 (978-0-9727757-1-7(4)); pap. 5.95 (978-0-9727757-0-0(6)) Susy & Livy Pubns.

Woodson, Jacqueline. Brown Girl Dreaming. l.t. ed. 2017. (ENG.). 24.99 **(978-1-4328-4315-1(X))** Cengage Gale.

—Brown Girl Dreaming. (ENG.). (J). (gr. 5). 2016. 368p. pap. 10.99 (978-0-14-751582-7(3), Puffin Books) 2014. (Illus.). 336p. 17.99 (978-0-399-25251-8(7), Nancy Paulsen Books) Penguin Young Readers Group.

—Brown Girl Dreaming. 2016. (ENG.). 368p. (J). (gr. 5). 22.10 (978-0-606-39310-2(2)) Turtleback Bks.

Woog, Adam. Robert Kirkman. 2015. (People in the News Ser.). (ENG., Illus.). 128p. (J). (gr. 7-10). 39.40 (978-1-4205-1247-2(1), Lucent Bks.) Cengage Gale.

Wooldridge, Connie Nordhielm. The Brave Escape of Edith Wharton. 2010. (ENG., Illus.). 192p. (YA). (gr. 7-18). 20.00 (978-0-547-23630-8(1)) Houghton Mifflin Harcourt Publishing Co.

Wooten, Sara McIntosh. Robert Frost: The Life of America's Poet. 2006. (People to Know Today Ser.). (Illus.). 128p. (J). (gr. 4-7). lib. bdg. 33.27 (978-0-7660-2627-8(2)) Enslow Pubs., Inc.

Worth, Richard. Jack Kerouac: The Road Is Life. 2006. (American Rebels Ser.). (Illus.). 160p. (YA). (gr. 6). lib. bdg. 35.94 (978-0-7660-2448-9(2)) Enslow Pubs., Inc.

Writers & Their Times. 2014. (Writers & Their Times Ser.). 112p. (YA). (gr. 9-12). 256.74 (978-1-62713-120-9(5)) Cavendish Square Publishing.

Yaccarino, Dan. All the Way to America: The Story of a Big Italian Family & a Little Shovel. (ENG.). 40p. (J). (gr. k-4). 2014. 7.99 (978-0-375-85920-5(9), Dragonfly Bks.) 2011. 16.99 (978-0-375-86642-5(6), Knopf Bks. for Young Readers) Random Hse. Children's Bks.

Yannuzzi, Della A. The Life of Zora Neale Hurston: Author & Folklorist. 2015. (Legendary African Americans Ser.). 96p. (J). (gr. 6-12). 27.94 (978-0-7660-6275-7(9)); pap. 10.95 (978-0-7660-6276-4(7)) Enslow Pubs., Inc.

Yasuda, Anita. Rick Riordan. 2014. (Illus.). 32p. (J). (978-1-62127-403-2(9)) Weigl Pubs., Inc.

Yolen, Jane. On the Slant. Stemple, Jason, photos by. 2009. (ENG., Illus.). 56p. (J). pap. 8.00 (978-1-57274-978-8(4), Author at Work) Owen, Richard C. Pubs., Inc.

Youngblood, Wayne. Mark Twain along the Mississippi. 2006. (In the Footsteps of American Heroes Ser.). (Illus.). 64p. (gr. 5-12). pap. 14.05 (978-0-8368-6435-9(2)); lib. bdg. 34.00 (978-0-8368-6430-4(1)) Stevens, Gareth Publishing LLLP. (Gareth Stevens Secondary Library).

Zimmer, Kyle, frwd. Jane Yolen. 2005. (Who Wrote That? Ser.). (Illus.). 128p. (gr. 6-12). lib. bdg. 35.00 (978-0-7910-8660-5(7), Chelsea Hse.) Facts On File, Inc.

AUTHORS, DANISH

Fischel, Emma. Hans Christian Andersen. Ward, Nick, illus. 2010. (Famous People, Famous Lives Ser.). 38p. (J). (978-89-491-8824-9(4)) Biryongso Publishing Co.

Fradin, Dennis Brindell. Tell Us a Tale, Hans! The Life of Hans Christian Andersen. von Buhler, Cynthia, illus. 2006. (J). (978-1-59336-681-0(7)); pap. (978-1-59336-682-7(5)) Mondo Publishing.

Leslie, Roger. Isak Dinesen: Gothic Storyteller. 2004. (World Writers Ser.). (Illus.). 128p. (YA). (gr. 6-12). 23.95 (978-1-931798-17-4(6)) Reynolds, Morgan Inc.

AUTHORS, ENGLISH

Abrams, Dennis. Anthony Horowitz. 2006. (Who Wrote That? Ser.). (Illus.). 123p. (gr. 6-12). 35.00 (978-0-7910-8968-2(1), Chelsea Hse.) Facts On File, Inc.

—H. G. Wells. 2011. (Who Wrote That? Ser.). (Illus.). 128p. (gr. 6-12). 35.00 (978-1-60413-770-5(3), Chelsea Hse.) Facts On File, Inc.

Ashmore, Wayne & Nault, Jennifer. The Wonderful World of Roald Dahl. 2016. (J). **(978-1-5105-1959-6(9))** SmartBook Media, Inc.

Baker, Bill. Alan Moore on His Work & Career. 2009. (Talking with Graphic Novelists Ser.). 110p. (gr. 9-9). 61.20 (978-1-60853-259-9(3)) Rosen Publishing Group, Inc., The.

—Neil Gaiman on His Work & Career. 2009. (Talking with Graphic Novelists Ser.). 118p. (gr. 9-9). 61.20 (978-1-60853-261-2(5)) Rosen Publishing Group, Inc., The.

Benge, Janet & Benge, Geoff. Christian Heroes - Then & Now - C. S. Lewis: Master Storyteller. 2007. (Christian Heroes Ser.). (ENG.). 192p. (YA). (gr. 3-7). pap. 9.99 (978-1-57658-385-2(6)) YWAM Publishing.

Bingham, Hettie. Jeremy Clarkson. 2016. (Real-Life Stories Ser.). (ENG., Illus.). 32p. (J). (gr. 4-6). pap. 11.99 (978-0-7502-8923-8(6), Wayland) Hachette Children's Group GBR. Dist: Hachette Bk. Group.

—Richard Hammond. 2017. (Real-Life Stories Ser.). (ENG., Illus.). 32p. (J). (gr. 4-6). pap. 11.99 (978-0-7502-8924-5(4), Wayland) Hachette Children's Group GBR. Dist: Hachette Bk. Group.

Bloom, Harold, ed. Jane Austen, New Edition. 2nd rev. ed. 2009. (Bloom's Modern Critical Views Ser.). 324p. (C). (gr. 9-18). 45.00 (978-1-60413-397-4(X), Chelsea Hse.) Facts On File, Inc.

Boerst, William J. Generous Anger: The Story of George Orwell. 2004. (World Writers Ser.). (Illus.). 112p. (YA). (gr. 6-12). 23.95 (978-1-883846-74-9(9), First Biographies) Reynolds, Morgan Inc.

Boothroyd, Jennifer. Roald Dahl. 2008. pap. 40.95 (978-0-8225-9475-8(7)) Lerner Publishing Group.

—Roald Dahl: A Life of Imagination. 2008. (Pull Ahead Books-Biographies Ser.). (ENG.). 32p. (gr. k-3). pap. 7.95 (978-0-8225-8826-9(9)); (Illus.). lib. bdg. 22.60 (978-0-8225-8825-2(0), Lerner Pubns.) Lerner Publishing Group.

Boshier, Rosa. How to Analyze the Works of Virginia Woolf, 1 vol. 2012. (Essential Critiques Set 3 Ser.). (ENG.). 112p. (J). (gr. 6-12). lib. bdg. 35.64 (978-1-61783-459-2(9), Essential Library) ABDO Publishing Co.

Brackett, Virginia. Restless Genius: The Story of Virginia Woolf. 2004. (World Writers Ser.). (Illus.). 144p. (YA). (gr. 6-12). 23.95 (978-1-931798-37-2(0)) Reynolds, Morgan Inc.

Brighton, Catherine. The Brontës: Scenes from the Childhood of Charlotte, Branwell, Emily & Anne. 2004. (ENG., Illus.). 32p. (J). (gr. 1-4). pap. 7.95 (978-1-84507-334-3(7), Frances Lincoln) Quarto Publishing Group UK GBR. Dist: Hachette Bk. Group.

C. S. Lewis. 2nd rev. ed. 2010. (Who Wrote That? Ser.). (Illus.). 136p. (gr. 6-12). 35.00 (978-1-60413-725-5(8), Chelsea Hse.) Facts On File, Inc.

C. S. Lewis: Twentieth Century Pilgrim. 2011. (World Writers Ser.). 128p. (gr. 7-9). lib. bdg. 28.95 (978-1-59935-112-4(9)) Reynolds, Morgan Inc.

Caravantes, Peggy. Best of Times: The Story of Charles Dickens. 2005. (World Writers Ser.). (Illus.). 160p. (gr. 3-7). lib. bdg. 28.95 (978-1-931798-68-6(0)) Reynolds, Morgan Inc.

Collins, David R. Tales for Hard Times: A Story about Charles Dickens. Mataya, David, illus. 2007. (Creative Minds Biographies Ser.). (ENG.). 64p. (gr. 4-8). pap. 8.95 (978-0-8225-6992-3(2)) Lerner Publishing Group.

Coupe, Laurence. Marina Warner. 2006. (ENG.). 144p. (C). 80.00 (978-0-7463-1112-7(5)); pap. 19.95 (978-0-7463-0998-8(8)) Northcote Hse. Publishers, Ltd. GBR. Dist: Casemate Academic.

Dahl, Roald. Boy - Tales of Childhood. 2009. (gr. 3-6). lib. bdg. 18.40 (978-0-613-63922-4(7), Turtleback) Turtleback Bks.

—Boy & Going Solo. Blake, Quentin, illus. 2010. (ENG.). 400p. (J). (gr. 3-7). 10.99 (978-0-14-241741-6(6), Puffin Books) Penguin Young Readers Group.

—More about Boy. Blake, Quentin, illus. 2009. (ENG.). 240p. (J). (gr. 5-7). pap. 15.99 (978-0-14-241498-9(0), Puffin Books) Penguin Young Readers Group.

—More about Boy: Roald Dahl's Tales from Childhood. Blake, Quentin, illus. 2009. (ENG.). 240p. (J). (gr. 5-9). 24.99 (978-0-374-35055-0(8), 9780374350550, Farrar, Straus & Giroux (BYR)) Farrar, Straus & Giroux.

Dorling Kindersley Publishing Staff. Shakespeare. 2015. (DK Eyewitness Bks.). (ENG., Illus.). 72p. (J). (gr. 3-7). pap. 9.99 (978-1-4654-3185-1(3), DK Children) Dorling Kindersley Publishing, Inc.

Eason, Sarah. Malorie Blackman. 2016. (Real-Life Stories Ser.). (ENG., Illus.). 32p. (J). (gr. 4-6). pap. 11.99 (978-0-7502-9045-6(5), Wayland) Hachette Children's Group GBR. Dist: Hachette Bk. Group.

Edwards, Anfrew & Edwards, Fleur. Footsteps of the past: C S Lewis: The story of one of the world's most famous authors who sold over a hundred million Books. 2007. (Footsteps of the Past Ser.). 32p. pap. 6.00 (978-1-84625-091-0(9)) DayOne Pubns. GBR. Dist: Send The Light Distribution LLC.

Fabiny, Sarah. Who Was Beatrix Potter? Lacey, Mike, illus. 2015. 105p. (J). (978-1-4806-8934-3(3), Grosset & Dunlap) Penguin Publishing Group.

Fabiny, Sarah & dePaola, Tomie. Who Was Beatrix Potter? Lacey, Mike & Harrison, Nancy, illus. 2015. (Who Was? Ser.). (ENG.). 112p. (J). (gr. 3-7). 5.99 (978-0-448-48305-4(X), Grosset & Dunlap) Penguin Young Readers Group.

Ferran, Alexandri, et al. Agatha Christie. 2010. (Me Llamo... Ser.). (SPA., Illus.). 63p. (J). pap. (978-84-342-3460-4(2)) Parramon Ediciones S.A.

Fischel, Emma. The Life of Roald Dahl: A Marvellous Adventure. 2016. (ENG., Illus.). 64p. (J). (gr. 1-4). pap. 7.99 (978-1-4451-5159-5(6), Franklin Watts) Hachette Children's Group GBR. Dist: Hachette Bk. Group.

Foreman, Michael. War Boy: A Wartime Childhood. 2006. (ENG., Illus.). 96p. (J). (gr. 4-7). pap. 16.99 (978-1-84365-087-4(8)) Pavilion Bks. GBR. Dist: Independent Pubs. Group.

Gaines, Ann Graham. J. K. Rowling. 2004. (Blue Banner Biography Ser.). (Illus.). 32p. (J). (gr. 3-8). lib. bdg. 25.70 (978-1-58415-325-2(3)) Mitchell Lane Pubs., Inc.

Gelletly, LeeAnne. Gift of Imagination: The Story of Roald Dahl. 2006. (World Writers Ser.). (Illus.). 160p. (gr. 6-12). lib. bdg. 27.95 (978-1-59935-026-4(2)) Reynolds, Morgan Inc.

George Orwell 1984: The Political Pen. 2014. (ENG.). 180p. (J). (gr. 3-7). pap. 13.95 (978-1-59077-354-3(3)) Evans, M. & Co., Inc.

Gormley, Beatrice. C. S. Lewis: The Man Behind Narnia. 2nd ed. 2005. (ENG., Illus.). 192p. (gr. 8-12). per. 14.00 (978-0-8028-5301-1(3), Eerdmans Bks For Young Readers) Eerdmans, William B. Publishing Co.

Guillain, Charlotte. A. A. Milne, 1 vol. 2012. (Author Biographies Ser.). (ENG.). 24p. (gr. 1-2). 23.32 (978-1-4329-5958-6(1)); pap. 6.79 (978-1-4329-5964-7(6)) Heinemann-Raintree. (Heinemann Read & Learn).

—Beatrix Potter, 1 vol. 2012. (Author Biographies Ser.). (ENG., Illus.). 24p. (gr. 1-2). 23.32 (978-1-4329-5960-9(3)); pap. 6.79 (978-1-4329-5966-1(2)) Heinemann-Raintree. (Heinemann Read & Learn).

—Neil Gaiman: Rock Star Writer. 2010. (Culture in Action Ser.). (ENG.). 32p. (gr. 3-6). 30.65 (978-1-4109-3929-6(4), NA-r) Heinemann-Raintree.

—Roald Dahl, 1 vol. 2012. (Author Biographies Ser.). (ENG.). 24p. (gr. 1-2). pap. 6.79 (978-1-4329-5968-5(9), Heinemann Read & Learn) Heinemann-Raintree.

H. G. Wells: First Citizen of the Future. 2014. (ENG.). 192p. (J). (gr. 3-7). pap. 13.95 (978-1-59077-356-7(X)) Evans, M. & Co., Inc.

Hamilton, John. Pioneers of Science Fiction, 1 vol. 2006. (World of Science Fiction Ser.). (ENG.). 32p. (gr. 4-7). 27.07 (978-1-59679-992-9(7), Abdo & Daughters) ABDO Publishing Co.

Hamilton, Sue L. Masters of Horror, 1 vol. 2007. (World of Horror Ser.). (ENG.). 32p. (gr. 4-8). 27.07 (978-1-59928-770-6(6), Abdo & Daughters) ABDO Publishing Co.

Harmin, Karen Leigh. J. K. Rowling: Author of Harry Potter — An Unauthorized Biography. 2006. (People to Know Today Ser.). (Illus.). 128p. (J). (gr. 7-12). lib. bdg. 33.27 (978-0-7660-1850-1(4)) Enslow Pubs., Inc.

Heims, Neil. J. R. R. Tolkien. 2004. (Great Writers Ser.). (Illus.). 128p. (YA). (gr. 9-13). 31.95 (978-0-7910-7847-1(7), Chelsea Hse.) Facts On File, Inc.

Hill Nettleton, Pamela. William Shakespeare: The Inspiring Life Story of the Playwright Extraordinaire. 2016. (Inspiring Stories Ser.). (ENG., Illus.). 112p. (gr. 5-7). lib. bdg. 35.99 (978-0-7565-5163-6(3), CPB Grades 4-8) Compass Point Bks.

Hilliam, David. William Shakespeare: England's Greatest Playwright & Poet. 2009. (Rulers, Scholars, & Artists of the Renaissance Ser.). 112p. (gr. 5-8). 66.50 (978-1-60852-945-2(2), Rosen Reference) Rosen Publishing Group, Inc., The.

Hopkinson, Deborah. Beatrix Potter & the Unfortunate Tale of a Borrowed Guinea Pig. Voake, Charlotte, illus. 2016. (ENG.). 44p. (J). (gr. -1-3). 17.99 (978-0-385-37325-8(2), Schwartz & Wade Bks.) Random Hse. Children's Bks.

Houle, Michelle M. Modern British Poetry: "The World Is Never the Same" 2010. (Poetry Rocks! Ser.). (Illus.). 160p. (YA). (gr. 9-12). 35.94 (978-0-7660-3278-1(7)) Enslow Pubs., Inc.

—Roald Dahl: Author of Charlie & the Chocolate Factory. 2006. (Authors Teens Love Ser.). (Illus.). 104p. (J). (gr. 7-12). lib. bdg. 33.27 (978-0-7660-2353-6(2)) Enslow Pubs., Inc.

Hunsicker, Jennifer. J. K. Rowling: Author of the Harry Potter Series. 2016. (Famous Female Authors Ser.). (ENG., Illus.). 32p. (gr. 3-4). lib. bdg. 27.99 (978-1-5157-1328-9(8), Snap Bks.) Capstone Press of Coughlan Cos.

Hurtig, Jennifer. The Animal World of Beatrix Potter. 2016. (J). **(978-1-5105-1951-0(3))** SmartBook Media, Inc.

Hurtig, Jennifer. Beatrix Potter. (Illus.). 32p. 2014. (J). (978-1-62127-402-5(0)) 2008. (YA). (gr. 5-18). pap. 9.95 (978-1-59036-923-4(8)) 2008. (YA). (gr. 5-18). lib. bdg. 26.00 (978-1-59036-922-7(X)) Weigl Pubs., Inc.

Kelley, True. Who Was Roald Dahl? Marchesi, Stephen & Harrison, Nancy, illus. 2012. (Who Was? Ser.). (ENG.). 112p. (J). (gr. 3-7). pap. 5.99 (978-0-448-46146-5(3), Grosset & Dunlap) Penguin Young Readers Group.

—Who Was Roald Dahl? 2012. (Who Was...? Ser.). lib. bdg. 16.00 (978-0-606-26650-5(X), Turtleback) Turtleback Bks.

Kenyon, Karen Smith. Charles Dickens: A Biography. 2008. (J). lib. bdg. (978-0-8225-7532-0(9)) Twenty First Century Bks.

Kerr, Judith. Creatures: A Celebration of the Life & Work. 2013. (ENG., Illus.). 176p. (J). 24.99 (978-0-00-751321-5(6), HarperCollins Children's Bks.) HarperCollins Pubs. Ltd. GBR. Dist: HarperCollins Pubs.

Kirk, Connie Ann. A Student's Guide to Jane Austen. 2016. (Lit Crit Guides). (Illus.). 176p. (J). (gr. 6-6). 39.93 (978-0-7660-7911-3(2)) Enslow Pubs., Inc.

Klaus, Gustav. James Kelmam. 2005. (ENG., Illus.). 128p. (C). 80.00 (978-0-7463-1064-9(1)); pap. 19.95 (978-0-7463-0976-6(7)) Northcote Hse. Publishers, Ltd. GBR. Dist: Casemate Academic.

La Bella, Laura. Philip Pullman. 2013. (All about the Author Ser.). 112p. (YA). (gr. 7-12). 34.60 (978-1-4777-1766-0(8)) Rosen Publishing Group, Inc., The.

Leaf, Christina. Roald Dahl. 2015. (Children's Storytellers Ser.). (ENG., Illus.). 24p. (J). (gr. 2-5). lib. bdg. 25.95 (978-1-62617-270-8(6), Blastoff! Readers) Bellwether Media.

Lloyd, Heather. Frankenstein Worldview Guide. 2016. (J). pap. **(978-1-944503-43-7(9))** Canon Pr.

Locke, Juliane. England's Jane: the Story of Jane Austen. 2006. (World Writers Ser.). (Illus.). 144p. (gr. 6-12). lib. bdg. 28.95 (978-1-931798-82-2(6)) Reynolds, Morgan Inc.

Losure, Mary. The Fairy Ring: Or Elsie & Frances Fool the World. 2014. (ENG.). 192p. (J). (gr. 5). pap. 8.99 (978-0-7636-7495-3(8)) Candlewick Pr.

Manning, Mick & Granström, Brita. The Brontës: Children of the Moors. 2016. (ENG., Illus.). 48p. (J). (gr. 2-17). 16.99 (978-1-4451-4731-4(9), Franklin Watts) Hachette Children's Group GBR. Dist: Hachette Bk. Group.

Mannis, Celeste Davidson & Kramer, Sydelle. Who Was William Shakespeare? O'brien, John, illus. 2006. (Who Was... ? Ser.). 105p. (gr. 2-6). 15.00 (978-0-7569-6952-3(2)) Perfection Learning Corp.

Marcus, Leonard S., ed. Funny Business: Conversations with Writers of Comedy. 2009. (ENG., Illus.). 224p. (J). (gr. 5-18). 24.99 (978-0-7636-3254-0(6)) Candlewick Pr.

McAlister, Caroline. John Ronald's Dragons: the Story of J. R. R. Tolkien. Wheeler, Eliza, illus. 2017. (ENG.). 48p. (J). 18.99 (978-1-62672-092-3(4), 9781626720923) Roaring Brook Pr.

McPhail, David. Beatrix Potter & Her Paint Box. McPhail, David, illus. 2015. (ENG., Illus.). 40p. (J). (gr. -1-3). 17.99 (978-0-8050-9170-0(X), 9780805091700, Holt, Henry & Co. Bks. For Young Readers) Holt, Henry & Co.

Miller, Calvin Craig. Spirit Like a Storm: The Story of Mary Shelley. 2nd rev. ed. 2004. (World Writers Ser.). (Illus.). 144p. (YA). (gr. 6-12). 23.95 (978-1-931798-08-2(7)) Reynolds, Morgan Inc.

Mills, Cliff. Virginia Woolf. 2003. (Women in the Arts Ser.). (Illus.). 112p. (gr. 6-12). 30.00 (978-0-7910-7459-6(5), Chelsea Hse.) Facts On File, Inc.

Mittelstaedt, Walt. Reading & Interpreting the Works of William Shakespeare. 2016. (Lit Crit Guides). 176p. (J). (gr. 6-6). 39.93 (978-0-7660-7912-0(0)) Enslow Pubs., Inc.

—A Student's Guide to William Shakespeare. 2005. (Understanding Literature Ser.). (Illus.). 192p. (YA). lib. bdg. 29.27 (978-0-7660-2284-3(6)) Enslow Pubs., Inc.

Neimark, Anne E. Mythmaker: The Life of J. R. R. Tolkien, Creator of the Hobbit & the Lord of the Rings. Weinman, Brad, illus. 2012. (ENG.). 144p. (J). (gr. 5-7). 12.99 (978-0-547-99734-6(5)) Houghton Mifflin Harcourt Publishing Co.

Penguin Young Readers. The Tale of Beatrix Potter. 2016. (Penguin Young Readers, Level 4 Ser.). (ENG.). 48p. (J). (gr. 1-3). pap. 3.99 (978-0-241-24937-6(6), Penguin Young Readers) Penguin Young Readers Group.

Peterson-Hilleque, Victoria. J. K. Rowling: Extraordinary Author, 1 vol. 2010. (Essential Lives Set 5 Ser.). (ENG.). 112p. (J). (gr. 6-12). lib. bdg. 35.64 (978-1-61613-517-1(4)) ABDO Publishing Co.

Pezzi, Bryan. J. K. Rowling. 2012. (J). 28.55 (978-1-61913-057-9(2)); pap. 13.95 (978-1-61913-596-3(5)) Weigl Pubs., Inc.

Pollack, Pam & Belviso, Meg. Who Is J. K. Rowling? Marchesi, Stephen & Harrison, Nancy, illus. 2012. (Who Was? Ser.). (ENG.). 112p. (J). (gr. 3-7). pap. 5.99 (978-0-448-45872-4(1), Grosset & Dunlap) Penguin Young Readers Group.

—Who Was J. R. R. Tolkien? Moore, Jonathan & Harrison, Nancy, illus. 2015. 105p. (J). (978-1-4806-8935-0(1)) Baker & Taylor, CATS.

Pollack, Pamela & Belviso, Meg. Who Is J. K. Rowling? 2012. (Who Is...? Ser.). lib. bdg. 16.00 (978-0-606-26078-7(1), Turtleback) Turtleback Bks.

Pollack, Pamela D. & Belviso, Meg. Who Was J. R. R. Tolkien? Moore, Jonathan & Harrison, Nancy, illus. 2015. (Who Was? Ser.). (ENG.). 112p. (J). (gr. 3-7). 5.99 (978-0-448-48302-3(5), Grosset & Dunlap) Penguin Young Readers Group.

Powling, Chris. Dick King-Smith. (Illus.). 22p. (J). (978-0-237-51970-4(4)) Evans Brothers, Ltd.

Price, Joan. J. K. Rowling. 2004. (Trailblazers of the Modern World Ser.). (Illus.). 48p. (gr. 5-12). lib. bdg. 31.00 (978-0-8368-5499-2(3), Gareth Stevens Secondary Library) Stevens, Gareth Publishing LLLP.

—J.K. Rowling. 2004. (Trailblazers of the Modern World Ser.). (Illus.). 48p. (gr. 5-12). pap. 14.05 (978-0-8368-5268-4(0), Gareth Stevens Secondary Library) Stevens, Gareth Publishing LLLP.

Raum, Elizabeth. Twenty-First Century Shakespeare. 2010. (Culture in Action Ser.). (ENG.). 32p. (gr. 3-6). 30.65 (978-1-4109-3920-3(0), NA-r) Heinemann-Raintree.

Reef, Catherine. The Brontë Sisters: The Brief Lives of Charlotte, Emily, & Anne. 2012. (ENG., Illus.). 240p. (J). (gr. 5-7). 18.99 (978-0-547-57966-5(7)) Houghton Mifflin Harcourt Publishing Co.

Reiff, Raychel Haugrud. Aldous Huxley: Brave New World. 2009. (Writers & Their Works 4 Ser.). 144p. (gr. 7). 42.79 (978-0-7614-4278-3(2)) Marshall Cavendish Corp.

—William Golding. 2009. (Writers & Their Works 4 Ser.). (Illus.). 144p. (gr. 7). 42.79 (978-0-7614-4276-9(6)) Marshall Cavendish Corp.

Rice, Dona Herweck. Game Changers: A Biography of J. K. Rowling. 2017. (Time for Kids Nonfiction Readers Ser.). lib. bdg. 19.65 **(978-0-606-40264-4(0))** Turtleback Bks.

Richert, Scott P. Bill Bryson. 2010. (Today's Writers & Their Works Ser.). 128p. (gr. 7). 42.79 (978-0-7614-4120-5(4)) Marshall Cavendish GBR. Dist: Marshall Cavendish Corp.

Rosen, Michael. Dickens: His Work & His World. Ingpen, Robert R., illus. 2005. (ENG.). 96p. (YA). (gr. 7-11). 19.99 (978-0-7636-2752-2(6)) Candlewick Pr.

—Fantastic Mr. Dahl. Blake, Quentin, illus. 2012. (ENG.). 176p. (J). (gr. 3-7). pap. 6.99 (978-0-14-132213-1(6), Puffin Books) Penguin Young Readers Group.

—Shakespeare: His Work & His World. Ingpen, Robert R., illus. 2006. (ENG.). 96p. (J). (gr. 7-11). pap. 10.99 (978-0-7636-3201-4(5)) Candlewick Pr.

Ruth, Amy. Jane Austen. 2005. (Biography Ser.). (Illus.). 112p. (J). (gr. 6-12). lib. bdg. 27.93 (978-0-8225-4992-5(1)) Lerner Publishing Group.

Sage, Lorna. Angela Carter. 2nd ed. 2006. (ENG.). 96p. (C). pap. 19.95 (978-0-7463-1145-5(1)) Northcote Hse. Publishers, Ltd. GBR. Dist: Casemate Academic.

Saksena, Salini. Anthony Horowitz. 2012. (All about the Author Ser.). (ENG., Illus.). 112p. (J). (gr. 7-12). lib. bdg. 34.60 (978-1-4488-6940-4(4)) Rosen Publishing Group, Inc., The.

Sanchez Vegara, Isabel. Agatha Christie. 2017. (Little People, Big Dreams Ser.). (ENG., Illus.). (J). (gr. k-3). 14.99 **(978-1-84780-960-5(X)**, Frances Lincoln Children's Bks.) Quarto Publishing Group UK GBR. Dist: Hachette Bk. Group.

Senker, Cath. J. K. Rowling: Creator of Harry Potter. 2011. (Famous Lives Ser.). (Illus.). 32p. (YA). (gr. 3-6). lib. bdg. 26.50 (978-1-4488-3288-0(8)) Rosen Publishing Group, Inc., The.

Sexton, Colleen. J. K. Rowling. 2008. pap. 52.95 (978-1-57505-984-6(3)) Lerner Publishing Group.

Sexton, Colleen A. J. K. Rowling. 2007. (Biography Ser.). (Illus.). 112p. (J). (gr. -1). lib. bdg. 30.60 (978-0-8225-7949-6(9)) Lerner Publishing Group.
—J.K. Rowling. 2006. (Just the Facts Biographies Ser.). (Illus.). 112p. (J). 27.93 (978-0-8225-3423-5(1), Lerner Pubns.) Lerner Publishing Group.
Sexton, Colleen A. & Cosgrove, Martha. J. K. Rowling. 2006. (Just the Facts Biographies Ser.). (Illus.). 112p. (J). pap. 9.95 (978-0-8225-5995-5(1), Lerner Pubns.) Lerner Publishing Group.
Shapiro, Marc. J. K. Rowling: The Wizard Behind Harry Potter. 4th ed. 2007. (ENG., Illus.). 288p. pap. 20.99 (978-0-312-37697-0(9), 9780312376970, St. Martin's Griffin) St. Martin's Pr.
Shavick, Andrea. Roald Dahl. 2009. (True Lives Ser.). (ENG., Illus.). 32p. (J). pap. 6.99 (978-0-19-911961-5(9)) Oxford Univ. Pr., Inc.
Shipton, Paul & Pearson Education Staff. Charles Dickens, Pack. 2007. (ENG., Illus.). 64p. pap. 17.32 incl. cd-rom (978-1-4058-5211-1(9)) Pearson Education.
Sickels, Amy. Mythmaker: The Story of J. K. Rowling. 2nd rev. ed. 2008. (Who Wrote That? Ser.). (Illus.). 136p. (gr. 6-12). lib. bdg. 35.00 (978-0-7910-9632-1(7), Chelsea Hse.) Facts On File, Inc.
Smith, Rupert. Poets of World War I, 1 vol. 2014. (ENG., Illus.). 64p. (gr. 7-8). lib. bdg. 35.99 (978-1-4329-9645-1(2)) Heinemann-Raintree.
Speaker-Yuan, Margaret & Yuan, Margaret Speaker. Phillip Pullman. 2005. (Who Wrote That? Ser.). (Illus.). 120p. (gr. 6-12). lib. bdg. 35.00 (978-0-7910-8658-2(5), Chelsea Hse.) Facts On File, Inc.
Stanley, Diane & Vennema, Peter. Bard of Avon. Stanley, Diane, illus. 2015. (ENG., Illus.). 48p. (J). (gr. 1-5). pap. 7.99 (978-0-06-241925-5(0)) HarperCollins Pubs.
Streissguth, Thomas & Streissguth, Tom. Legends of Dracula. 2003. (Biography Ser.). (Illus.). 112p. (YA). (gr. 6-18). pap. 7.95 (978-0-8225-9682-0(2), Carolrhoda Bks.) Lerner Publishing Group.
Tieck, Sarah. J. K. Rowling, 1 vol. 2010. (First Biographies Set 6 Ser.). (ENG.). 32p. (J). (gr. 1-4). 27.07 (978-1-60453-987-5(9)) ABDO Publishing Co.
Twist, Clint & Wells-Cole, Catherine. Charles Dickens: England's Most Captivating Storyteller. 2011. (ENG., Illus.). 32p. (J). (gr. 3-7). 19.99 (978-0-7636-5567-9(8), Templar) Candlewick Pr.
Van Zee, Amy. How to Analyze the Works of C. S. Lewis, 1 vol. 2012. (Essential Critiques Set 3 Ser.). (ENG.). 112p. (J). (gr. 6-12). lib. bdg. 35.64 (978-1-61783-455-4(6), Essential Library) ABDO Publishing Co.
Wallner, Alexandra & Wallner, John C. J. R. R. Tolkien. 2011. (ENG., Illus.). 32p. (J). 17.95 (978-0-8234-1951-7(7)) Holiday Hse., Inc.
Walters, Tracey. Zadie Smith. 2013. (Today's Writers & Their Works Ser.). 144p. (YA). (gr. 7-12). pap. 22.34 (978-1-62712-148-4(X)) Cavendish Square Publishing.
Walters, Tracey Lorraine. Zadie Smith. 2013. (J). (978-1-60870-507-8(2)) Marshall Cavendish.
Ward, S. Meet A. A. Milne. 2009. (About the Author Ser.). 24p. (gr. 4-4). 42.50 (978-1-61511-243-2(X), PowerKids Pr.) Rosen Publishing Group, Inc., The.
—Meet J. K. Rowling. 2003. (About the Author Ser.). 24p. (J). lib. bdg. 18.75 (978-0-8239-6808-4(1), PowerKids Pr.) Rosen Publishing Group, Inc., The.
Warren, Andrea. Charles Dickens & the Street Children of London. 2011. (ENG., Illus.). 160p. (YA). (gr. 7). 18.99 (978-0-547-39574-6(4)) Houghton Mifflin Harcourt Publishing Co.
Wells, Catherine. Strange Creatures: The Story of Mary Shelley. 2009. (World Writers Ser.). (J). 28.95 (978-1-59935-092-9(0)) Reynolds, Morgan Inc.
Wheeler, Jill C. C. S. Lewis, 1 vol. 2009. (Children's Authors Set 5 Ser.). (ENG.). 24p. (YA). (gr. 2-5). 25.65 (978-1-60453-077-3(4)) ABDO Publishing Co.
—J. R. R. Tolkien, 1 vol. 2009. (Children's Authors Set 5 Ser.). (ENG.). 24p. (J). (gr. 2-5). 25.65 (978-1-60453-080-3(4)) ABDO Publishing Co.
—Roald Dahl, 1 vol. 2007. (Children's Authors Set 4 Ser.). (ENG., Illus.). 24p. (J). (gr. 2-5). 25.65 (978-1-59679-763-5(0)) ABDO Publishing Co.
Wilcox, Christine. Young Adult Authors. 2016. (ENG.). 80p. (J). (gr. 5-12). lib. bdg. (978-1-68282-036-0(X)) ReferencePoint Pr., Inc.
Willett, Edward. J. R. R. Tolkien: Master of Imaginary Worlds. 2004. (Authors Teens Love Ser.). (Illus.). 128p. (J). lib. bdg. 27.94 (978-0-7660-2246-1(3)) Enslow Pubs., Inc.
Wong, Cynthia F. Nhw:Ishiguro Kazuo 2e Pb. 2nd ed. 2005. (ENG., Illus.). 144p. (C). pap. 19.95 (978-0-7463-1142-4(7)) Northcote Hse. Publishers, Ltd. GBR. Dist: Casemate Academic.
Yasuda, Anita. A. A. Milne. 2014. (Illus.). 32p. (J). (978-1-62127-401-8(2)) Weigl Pubs., Inc.

AUTHORS, EUROPEAN

Bloom, Harold, ed. James Joyce, New Edition. 2nd rev. ed. 2009. (Bloom's Modern Critical Views Ser.). 270p. (C). (gr. 9-18). 45.00 (978-1-60413-396-7(1), Chelsea Hse.) Facts On File, Inc.
Gibbon, Monk. Pupil: A Memory of Love. 128p. 9.95 (978-0-905473-68-0(X)) Wolfhound Pr. IRL. Dist: Irish American Bk. Co.

AUTHORS—FICTION

Adams, Jennifer. Moby-Dick, 1 vol. Oliver, Alison, illus. 2013. (ENG.). 22p. (J). (gr. k-1). bds., bds. 9.99 (978-1-4236-3204-7(4)) Gibbs Smith, Publisher.
Banks, Angelica. Finding Serendipity. Lewis, Stevie, illus. 2015. (Tuesday Mcgillycuddy Adventures Ser.). (ENG.). 288p. (J). (gr. 3-7). 16.99 (978-1-62779-154-0(X), 9781627791540, Holt, Henry & Co. Bks. For Young Readers) Holt, Henry & Co.
—Finding Serendipity. Lewis, Stevie, illus. 2016. (Tuesday Mcgillycuddy Adventures Ser.). (ENG.). 304p. (J). pap. 7.99 (978-1-250-07337-2(5), 9781250073372) Square Fish.
Baratz-Logsted, Lauren. Secrets of My Suburban Life. 2008. (ENG.). 240p. (YA). (gr. 9-18). pap. 7.99 (978-1-4169-2525-5(2), Simon Pulse) Simon Pulse.
Barnett, Mac. The Ghostwriter Secret. Rex, Adam, illus. (Brixton Brothers Ser.: 2). (ENG.). (J). (gr. 3-7). 2011. 256p. pap. 7.99 (978-1-4169-7818-3(6)) 2010. 240p. 17.99 (978-1-4169-7817-6(8)) Simon & Schuster Bks. For Young Readers. (Simon & Schuster Bks. For Young Readers).
Bodeen, S. A. The Detour. 2015. (ENG.). 224p. (YA). (gr. 7). 17.99 (978-1-250-05554-5(7), 9781250055545) Feiwel & Friends.
Brown, Marc. Arthur Writes a Story. 2004. (Arthur Adventure Ser.). (J). (gr. k-3). spiral bd. (978-0-616-01604-6(2)); spiral bd. (978-0-616-01605-3(0)) Canadian National Institute for the Blind/Institut National Canadien pour les Aveugles.
—Arthur Writes a Story. 2003. (Arthur Adventure Ser.). (Illus.). 14.95 (978-1-59319-021-7(2)) LeapFrog Enterprises, Inc.
Bunting, Eve. My Special Day at Third Street School. Bloom, Suzanne, illus. 2009. (ENG.). 32p. (J). (gr. k-2). pap. 10.95 (978-1-59078-745-8(5)) Boyds Mills Pr.
Cardno, Anthony R. The Firflake: A Christmas Story. Cornue, Don, illus. 2008. 56p. pap. 8.95 (978-0-595-52468-6(0)) iUniverse, Inc.
Carpenter, Nan. Louisa May Alcott & Thoreau's Flute, Two Letters: The Huntington Library Quarterly V24, No. 1, November 1960. 2011. 8p. pap. 35.95 (978-1-258-09228-3(X)) Literary Licensing, LLC.
Chambers, Aidan. Dying to Know You. (ENG.). 288p. (YA). (gr. 9-17). 2013. pap. 9.95 (978-1-4197-0794-0(9)) 2012. 16.95 (978-1-4197-0165-8(7)) Abrams, Inc. (Amulet Bks.).
Cohn, Diana. Mr Goethes Garden. Mirocha, Paul, illus. 2003. (ENG.). 32p. (J). 17.95 (978-0-88010-521-7(6)) SteinerBooks, Inc.
Dahl, Michael. Ghost Writer, 1 vol. Kendall, Bradford, illus. 2011. (Return to the Library of Doom Ser.). (ENG.). 72p. (gr. 1-3). lib. bdg. 23.99 (978-1-4342-3230-4(1), Zone Bks.) Stone Arch Bks.
—The Viking Claw. 2011. (Finnegan Zwake Ser.: 4). (ENG.). 192p. (YA). (gr. 7). pap. 9.99 (978-1-4424-3101-0(6), Simon Pulse) Simon Pulse.
Dana, Barbara. Emily Dickinson: Fictionalized Biography. Date not set. (J). (gr. 3-7). mass mkt. 4.99 (978-0-06-440843-1(4)) HarperCollins Pubs.
—A Voice of Her Own: Becoming Emily Dickinson. 2009. (ENG.). 368p. (YA). (gr. 8). 17.99 (978-0-06-028704-7(7), HarperTeen) HarperCollins Pubs.
DeVillers, Julia. How My Private Personal Journal Became a Bestseller. 2005. (ENG.). 224p. (J). (gr. 3-7). 6.99 (978-0-14-240332-7(6), Puffin Books) Penguin Young Readers Group.
d'Lacey, Chris. Dark Fire. 2011. (Last Dragon Chronicles Ser.: 5). (ENG.). 576p. (J). (gr. 3-7). pap. 8.99 (978-0-545-10273-5(1)) Scholastic, Inc.
Eagland, Jane. The World Within: A Novel of Emily Bronte. 2015. (ENG.). 336p. (J). (gr. 7). 18.99 (978-0-545-49295-9(5)) Scholastic, Inc.
Engle, Margarita. The Lightning Dreamer: Cuba's Greatest Abolitionist. 2013. (ENG.). 192p. (YA). (gr. 7). 16.99 (978-0-547-80743-0(0)) Houghton Mifflin Harcourt Publishing Co.
Federle, Tim. The Great American Whatever. (ENG.). (YA). (gr. 9). 2017. 304p. pap. 10.99 (978-1-4814-0410-5(5)) 2016. (Illus.). 288p. E-Book (978-1-4814-0411-2(3)) 2016. (Illus.). 288p. 17.99 (978-1-4814-0409-9(1)) Simon & Schuster Bks. For Young Readers. (Simon & Schuster Bks. For Young Readers).
Fishbane, Melanie J. Maud: A Novel Inspired by the Life of L. M. Montgomery. 2017. (ENG.). 400p. (J). (gr. 7). 17.99 **(978-0-14-319125-4(X)**, Penguin Teen) Penguin Random House Canada Young Readers CAN. Dist: Penguin Random Hse. LLC.
Fogg, K. L. Diamondback Cave: A Novel. 2008. 377p. (J). (978-1-59811-512-3(X)) Covenant Communications.
Grier, Hayes. Hollywood Days with Hayes. Feiwel, Jean, ed. 2016. (ENG.). 288p. (YA). pap. 15.99 (978-1-250-13831-6(0), 9781250138316) Feiwel & Friends.
Griffiths, Andy. The 13-Story Treehouse. Denton, Terry, illus. 2013. (Treehouse Bks.: 1). (ENG.). 256p. (J). (gr. 1-5). 13.99 (978-1-250-02690-3(3), 9781250026903) Feiwel & Friends.
—The 13-Story Treehouse. Denton, Terry, illus. 2015. (Treehouse Bks.: 1). (ENG.). 272p. (J). (gr. 1-5). pap. 6.99 (978-1-250-07065-4(1), 9781250070654) Square Fish.
—The 39-Story Treehouse. Denton, Terry, illus. 2015. (Treehouse Bks.). (ENG.). 352p. (J). (gr. 1-5). 13.99 (978-1-250-02692-7(X), 9781250026927) Feiwel & Friends.
—The 39-Story Treehouse. Barcellona, Christine, ed. Denton, Terry, illus. 2016. (Treehouse Bks.: 3). (ENG.). 368p. (J). pap. 6.99 (978-1-250-07511-6(4), 9781250075116) Square Fish.
Gushue, Brenda. Through the Storm, 1 vol. 2009. 48p. pap. 12.95 (978-1-4489-8898-3(5)) PublishAmerica, Inc.
Gustafson, Scott. Eddie: The Lost Youth of Edgar Allan Poe. Gustafson, Scott, illus. (ENG., Illus.). 208p. (J). (gr. 3-7). 2012. pap. 6.99 (978-1-4169-9765-8(2)) 2011. 15.99 (978-1-4169-9764-1(4)) Simon & Schuster Bks. For Young Readers. (Simon & Schuster Bks. For Young Readers).
Gutman, Dan. Miss Suki Is Kooky! Paillot, Jim, illus. 2007. (My Weird School Ser.: 17). (J). 14.75 (978-1-4177-7430-2(4), Turtleback) Turtleback Bks.
Hayes, Karel. Snowflake Comes to Stay. 2010. (ENG.). 32p. (J). (gr. -1-3). 16.95 (978-0-89272-850-3(7)) Down East Bks.
Hopkinson, Deborah. A Boy Called Dickens. Hendrix, John, illus. 2012. (ENG.). 40p. (J). (gr. -1-3). 17.99 (978-0-375-86732-3(5), Schwartz & Wade Bks.) Random Hse. Children's Bks.
Howe, James. Bunnicula Meets Edgar Allan Crow. Fortune, Eric, illus. (Bunnicula & Friends Ser.). (ENG.). 160p. (J). (gr. 3-7). 2008. pap. 6.99 (978-1-4169-1473-0(0)) 2006. 15.95 (978-1-4169-1458-7(7)) Simon & Schuster Children's Publishing. (Atheneum Bks. for Young Readers).
Ingalls, Laura. Los Cuatro Primeros Años. 2006. (Little House Bks.). (SPA., Illus.). 126p. (gr. 5-8). pap. 12.99 (978-84-279-3259-3(6)) Lectorum Pubns., Inc.
Kaishaku. Eternal Alice Rondo, Vol. 4. 2007. (ENG., Illus.). 192p. pap. 9.95 (978-1-59796-123-3(X)) DrMaster Pubns. Inc.
Kakugawa, Frances. Wordsworth Dances the Waltz. DeSica, Melissa, illus. 2007. 32p. (J). 10.95 (978-0-9790647-3-9(2)) Watermark Publishing, LLC.
Kehoe, Tim. Furious Jones & the Assassin's Secret. 2014. (ENG., Illus.). 336p. (J). (gr. 3-7). 16.99 (978-1-4424-7337-9(1), Simon & Schuster Bks. For Young Readers) Simon & Schuster Bks. For Young Readers.
Kerley, Barbara. The Extraordinary Mark Twain (According to Susy) Fotheringham, Edwin, illus. 2010. (ENG.). 48p. (J). (gr. 2-5). 17.99 (978-0-545-12508-6(1), Scholastic Pr.) Scholastic, Inc.
—The "Extrodinary" Mark Twain (According to Susy) Fotheringham, Edwin, illus. 2010. (J). (978-0-545-12509-3(X), Scholastic Pr.) Scholastic, Inc.
Klise, Kate. Dying to Meet You. Klise, M. Sarah, illus. (43 Old Cemetery Road Ser.: Bk. 1). (ENG.). 160p. (J). (gr. 2-5). 2010. pap. 6.99 (978-0-547-39848-8(4)) 2009. 16.99 (978-0-15-205727-5(7)) Houghton Mifflin Harcourt Publishing Co.
—Greetings from the Graveyard. Klise, M. Sarah, illus. (43 Old Cemetery Road Ser.). (ENG.). 160p. (J). (gr. 2-5). 2015. pap. 6.99 (978-0-544-54010-1(7)) 2014. 15.99 (978-0-544-10567-6(2)) Houghton Mifflin Harcourt Publishing Co. (HMH Books For Young Readers).
—Over My Dead Body. Klise, M. Sarah, illus. (43 Old Cemetery Road Ser.: Bk. 2). (ENG.). 128p. (J). (gr. 2-5). 2011. pap. 6.99 (978-0-547-57713-5(3)) 2009. 15.99 (978-0-15-205734-3(X)) Houghton Mifflin Harcourt Publishing Co.
—Till Death Do Us Bark. 2012. (43 Old Cemetery Road Ser.: 3). lib. bdg. 17.20 (978-0-606-26543-0(0), Turtleback) Turtleback Bks.
Klise, Kate & Klise, M. Sarah. Till Death Do Us Bark. Klise, Kate & Klise, M. Sarah, illus. 2011. (43 Old Cemetery Road Ser.: 3). (ENG., Illus.). 144p. (J). (gr. 2-5). 16.99 (978-0-547-40036-5(5)) Houghton Mifflin Harcourt Publishing Co.
Knotoff, Karenann. The Island of Rouge. 2007. 96p. per. 19.95 (978-1-4241-7575-8(5)) America Star Bks.
Kristina Learns about Fishing. 2007. (J). (978-0-9792728-0-6(7)) Tracepaper Bks. Inc.
Leighton, Margaret. Bride of Glory: The Story of Elizabeth Bacon Custer, 1842-1933. 2011. 220p. 44.95 (978-1-258-06931-5(8)) Literary Licensing, LLC.
MacColl, Michaela. Always Emily. 2014. (ENG.). 282p. (YA). (gr. 7-17). 16.99 (978-1-4521-1174-2(X)) Chronicle Bks. LLC.
—Secrets in the Snow: A Novel of Intrigue & Romance. 2016. (ENG., Illus.). 288p. (YA). (gr. 7-12). 16.99 (978-1-4521-3358-4(1)) Chronicle Bks. LLC.
Maltbie, P. I. Bambino & Mr. Twain. Miyares, Daniel, illus. 2012. (ENG.). 40p. (J). (gr. k-3). 15.95 (978-1-58089-272-8(8)) Charlesbridge Publishing, Inc.
Maltbie, Priscilla. Bambino & Mr. Twain. 2012. 40p. 29.95 (978-0-8045-4237-1(6)) Spoken Arts, Inc.
Manushkin, Fran. Katie Woo: Star Writer. Lyon, Tammie, illus. 2013. (Katie Woo: Star Writer Ser.). (ENG.). 32p. (gr. k-2). pap. 35.70 (978-1-4795-1991-0(X)); lib. bdg. 123.90 (978-1-4048-8082-5(8)) Picture Window Bks.
Mattick, Lindsay. Finding Winnie: The True Story of the World's Most Famous Bear. Blackall, Sophie, illus. 2015. (ENG.). 56p. (J). (gr. -1-1). 18.00 (978-0-316-32490-8(6)) Little Brown & Co.
McAlpine, Gordon. Mystery Box: A Novel about the Creators of Nancy Drew & the Hardy Boys. 2003. (ENG.). 190p. (YA). 16.95 (978-0-8126-2680-3(X)) Cricket Bks.
—The Pet & the Pendulum. Zuppardi, Sam, illus. 2016. (Misadventures of Edgar & Allan Poe Ser.: 3). (ENG.). 224p. (J). (gr. 3-7). 7.99 (978-0-14-242348-6(3), Puffin Books) Penguin Young Readers Group.
McFarlane, Brian. The Hockey Book. 11th ed. 2008. (Mitchell Brothers Ser.). (ENG.). 200p. (J). (gr. 3-7). per. (978-1-55168-312-6(1)) Magma.
Montgomery, L. M. Emily Climbs. 2009. (ENG.). 376p. pap. 16.95 (978-0-7710-9382-1(9), New Can Library) McClelland & Stewart CAN. Dist: Random Hse., Inc.
—Emily's Quest. 2009. (ENG.). 272p. pap. 19.95 (978-0-7710-9383-8(7), New Can Library) McClelland & Stewart CAN. Dist: Random Hse., Inc.
Mullarkey, Lisa & Mullarkey, John. Mary Molds a Monster, 1 vol. Bernard, Courtney, illus. 2015. (ENG.). 128p. (J). (978-1-62402-088-9(7)) Magic Wagon.
—Shakespeare Saves the Globe, 1 vol. Bernard, Courtney, illus. 2015. (ENG.). 128p. (J). (978-1-62402-090-2(9)) Magic Wagon.
Nance, Andrew. Return to Daemon Hall: Evil Roots. Polhemus, Coleman, illus. 2011. (ENG.). 256p. (YA). (gr. 7-12). 18.99 (978-0-8050-8748-2(6), Holt, Henry & Co. Bks. For Young Readers) Holt, Henry & Co.
Nesbitt, Kenn. More Bears! Cummings, Troy, illus. 2017. (ENG.). 28p. (J). bds. 7.99 **(978-1-4926-5467-4(1)**, Sourcebooks Jabberwocky) Sourcebooks, Inc.
Oladokun, Alexander. Acrux Manor: The Prodigal's Curse (Hardcover) 2013. 206p. 28.50 (978-1-300-68651-4(0)) Lulu Pr., Inc.
Papp, Robert, illus. The Vanishing Passenger. 2006. (Boxcar Children Mysteries Ser.: 106). (ENG.). 128p. (J). (gr. 1-5). 14.99 (978-0-8075-1066-7(1)) Whitman, Albert & Co.
Poblocki, Dan. The Stone Child. 2010. (ENG.). 288p. (J). (gr. 3-7). pap. 7.99 (978-0-375-84255-9(1), Yearling) Random Hse. Children's Bks.
Quick, Matthew. Every Exquisite Thing. 2016. (ENG.). 272p. (YA). (gr. 10-17). 17.99 (978-0-316-37959-5(X)) Little Brown & Co.
—Every Exquisite Thing. 2017. (ENG.). 288p. (YA). (gr. 10-17). pap. 9.99 (978-0-316-37961-8(1)) Little, Brown Bks. for Young Readers.
Ray, Mary Lyn. A Lucky Author Has a Dog. Henry, Steven, illus. 2015. (ENG.). 40p. (J). (gr. -1-3). 16.99 (978-0-545-51876-5(8)) Scholastic, Inc.
Reeve, Philip. Here Lies Arthur. 2008. (ENG.). 352p. (J). (gr. 7-18). 17.99 (978-0-545-09334-7(1), Scholastic Pr.) Scholastic, Inc.
Riddell, Chris. Goth Girl & the Wuthering Fright. 2017. (Goth Girl Ser.: 3). (ENG., Illus.). 224p. (J). (gr. 2-6). 14.99 (978-1-4472-7789-7(9)) Pan Macmillan GBR. Dist: Independent Pubs. Group.
Ross, Leanna. Julie Simone. 2004. 194p. (YA). pap. 14.95 (978-0-595-30376-2(5)) iUniverse, Inc.
Rossiter, Nan Parson. The Fo'c'sle: Henry Beston's Outermost House. 2012. (Illus.). 32p. (J). (gr. 5-18). 17.95 (978-1-56792-433-6(6)) Godine, David R. Pub.
Roy, Ron. A to Z Mysteries Collection, No. 1: Gurney, John Steven, illus. 2010. (to Z Mysteries Ser.: Nos. 1-4). (ENG.). 384p. (J). (gr. 1-4). 9.99 (978-0-375-85946-5(2), Random Hse. Bks. for Young Readers) Random Hse. Children's Bks.
Sales, Leila. Tonight the Streets Are Ours. 2015. (ENG.). 352p. (YA). (gr. 7). 17.99 (978-0-374-37665-9(4), 9780374376659, Farrar, Straus & Giroux (BYR)) Farrar, Straus & Giroux.
Scott, Michael. The Magician. 2008. (Secrets of the Immortal Nicholas Flamel Ser.: 2). (ENG.). 496p. (YA). (gr. 7). 16.99 (978-0-385-73358-8(5), Delacorte Bks. for Young Readers) Random Hse. Children's Bks.
Sedgwick, Marcus. Blood Red, Snow White. 2016. (ENG.). 320p. (YA). 17.99 (978-1-62672-547-8(0), 9781626725478) Roaring Brook Pr.
Service, Pamela F. The Wizards of Wyrd World. Gorman, Mike, illus. (Way-Too-Real Aliens Ser.: 3). (ENG.). 112p. (J). (gr. 4-6). 2015. 34.65 (978-1-4677-5962-5(7), Lerner Digital) 2013. pap. 6.95 (978-0-7613-7922-5(3), Darby Creek) 2012. 15.95 (978-0-7613-7920-1(7)) Lerner Publishing Group.
Shue, Jenna. Animal Island. Herzog, Inge, illus. 2005. 27p. (J). (gr. -1-3). per. 14.95 (978-1-4259-0039-7(9)) AuthorHouse.
Smith, Andrew. 100 Sideways Miles. 2014. (ENG., Illus.). 288p. (YA). (gr. 9). 17.99 (978-1-4424-4495-9(9), Simon & Schuster Bks. For Young Readers) Simon & Schuster Bks. For Young Readers.
Snicket, Lemony, pseud. Lemony Snicket: The Unauthorized Autobiography. Helquist, Brett, illus. 2003. (Series of Unfortunate Events Ser.). (ENG.). 240p. (J). (gr. 5-6). pap. 7.99 (978-0-06-056225-0(0)) HarperCollins Pubs.
—Lemony Snicket: The Unauthorized Autobiography. 2003. (Ser. of Unfortunate Events Ser.). (J). (gr. 5-8). lib. bdg. 17.20 (978-0-613-67209-2(7), Turtleback) Turtleback Bks.
Sortland, Bjorn. The Story of the Search for the Story. Elling, Lars, illus. 2003. (Picture Bks.). 40p. (J). (gr. -1-3). 15.95 (978-1-57505-375-2(6), Carolrhoda Bks.) Lerner Publishing Group.
Stead, Philip C. Ideas Are All Around. 2016. (ENG., Illus.). 48p. (J). 18.99 (978-1-62672-181-4(5), 9781626721814) Roaring Brook Pr.
Stevenson, Robin. Escape Velocity, 1 vol. 2011. (ENG.). 240p. (YA). (gr. 8-12). pap. 12.95 (978-1-55469-866-0(9)) Orca Bk. Pubs. USA.
Stilton, Geronimo. Christmas Catastrophe. 2007. (Geronimo Stilton Ser.). (Illus.). 93p. (J). (gr. 2-5). 14.65 (978-0-7569-8804-3(7)) Perfection Learning Corp.
Thaler, Mike. The Author Visit from the Black Lagoon. Lee, Jared D., illus. 2010. 61p. (J). **(978-0-545-27327-5(7))** Scholastic, Inc.
—The Author Visit from the Black Lagoon, 1 vol. Lee, Jared, illus. 2012. (Black Lagoon Adventures Ser.: No. 2). (ENG.). 64p. (J). (gr. 2-5). 24.21 (978-1-59961-960-6(1)) Spotlight.
Thomas, Laura Michelle. Polly Wants to Be a Writer - the Junior Authors Guide to Writing & Getting Published. 2013. 232p. pap. (978-1-4602-2819-7(7)) FriesenPress.
Trumbauer, Lisa. Mountain Manor Mystery. Hawkes, Kevin, illus. 2006. 96p. (J). pap. (978-1-59034-810-9(9)) Mondo Publishing.
Warner, Gertrude Chandler, creator. The Vanishing Passenger. 2006. (Boxcar Children Mysteries Ser.: 106). (ENG., Illus.). 112p. (J). (gr. 1-5). per. 6.99 (978-0-8075-1067-4(X)) Whitman, Albert & Co.
Webb Quest, By Sara. Aydil Vice, Author of Kiski the Cat. 2008. 70p. pap. 6.96 (978-1-4357-5152-1(3)) Lulu Pr., Inc.
Wersba, Barbara. Walter: The Story of a Rat. Diamond, Donna, illus. 2012. (ENG.). 64p. (J). (gr. 4-6). pap. 8.95 (978-1-59078-948-3(2)) Boyds Mills Pr.
Wiggin, Kate Douglas. Penelope's Postscripts. 2004. reprint ed. pap. 1.99 (978-1-4192-4073-7(0)); pap. 15.95 (978-1-4191-4073-0(6)) Kessinger Publishing, LLC.
Williams, Rozanne Lanczak. The Author with the Fancy Purple Pen. Richard, Ilene, illus. (Learn to Write Ser.). 16p. (J). 2007. (gr. -1-3). pap. 8.99 (978-1-59198-346-0(0)) 2006. (gr. k-2). pap. 2.99 (978-1-59198-299-9(5), 6189) Creative Teaching Pr., Inc.
Winter, Jonah. The Fabulous Feud of Gilbert & Sullivan. Egielski, Richard, illus. 2009. (J). pap. (978-0-439-93051-2(0), Levine, Arthur A. Bks.) Scholastic, Inc.
Wolf, Elisabeth. Lulu in la la Land. 2013. (Lulu in la la Land Ser.: 1). (ENG.). 272p. (J). (gr. 3-6). pap. 6.99 (978-1-4022-8504-2(3), 9781402285042, Sourcebooks Jabberwocky) Sourcebooks, Inc.
Wyley, Enda. The Silver Notebook. 2007. (ENG.). 208p. (J). pap. 12.95 (978-1-84717-020-0(X)) O'Brien Pr., Ltd., The IRL. Dist: Dufour Editions, Inc.

AUTHORS, FRENCH

Bayer, Linda N. Elie Wiesel: Spokesman for Remembrance. 2005. (Holocaust Biographies Ser.). (Illus.). 112p. (J). (gr. 7-12). lib. bdg. 34.60 (978-0-8239-3306-8(7), HBWIES) Rosen Publishing Group, Inc., The.
Broderick, Joe. Samuel Beckett -la tragicomedia de la Vida. 2005. (SPA.). 192p. (YA). (978-958-30-1730-8(2)) Panamericana Editorial.
Buckley, James. Who Was Jules Verne? 2016. (Who Was... ? Ser.). lib. bdg. 16.00 (978-0-606-38861-0(3)) Turtleback Bks.
Elie Wiesel's Night. 2009. (Bloom's Guides). 136p. (C). (gr. 9-18). 30.00 (978-1-60413-198-7(5), Chelsea Hse.) Facts On File, Inc.
García Aguilar, Eduardo. Voltaire -el festín de la Inteligencia. 2005. (SPA.). 96p. (YA). (978-958-30-1436-9(2)) Panamericana Editorial.
Houghton, Sarah. Elie Wiesel: A Holocaust Survivor Cries Out for Peace. 2003. (High Five Reading - Green Ser.). (ENG., Illus.). 48p. (J). (gr. 3-4). per. 9.00 (978-0-7368-2833-8(8), High Five Reading (RBL)) Capstone Press of Coughlan Cos.
—Elie Wiesel Set: A Holocaust Survivor Cries Out for Peace, 6. 2003. (High Five Reading - Green Ser.). (ENG.). 48p. (gr. 3-4). pap. 54.00 (978-0-7368-2843-7(5), High Five Reading (RBL)) Capstone Press of Coughlan Cos.
Landmann, Bimba, illus. In Search of the Little Prince: The Story of Antoine de Saint-Exupéry. 2014. (ENG.). 34p. (J). 17.00 (978-0-8028-5435-3(4), Eerdmans Bks For Young Readers) Eerdmans, William B. Publishing Co.
Schoell, William. Remarkable Journeys: The Story of Jules Verne. 2004. (World Writers Ser.). (Illus.). 112p. (YA). (gr. 6-12). 23.95 (978-1-883846-92-3(7), First Biographies) Reynolds, Morgan Inc.
Sís, Peter. The Pilot & the Little Prince: The Life of Antoine de Saint-Exupéry. Sís, Peter, illus. 2014. (ENG., Illus.). 48p. (J).

(gr. k-3). 18.99 *(978-0-374-38069-4(4)*, 9780374380694, Farrar, Straus & Giroux (BYR)) Farrar, Straus & Giroux.

Tracy, Sophia Okun. A Woman Ahead of Her Time: Christine de Pizan, Defender of Womankind. 2003. (Avisson Young Adult Ser.). (Illus.). 84p. (J). pap. *(978-1-888105-57-5(7))* Avisson Pr., Inc.

AUTHORS, GERMAN

Corbett, Sue. Cornelia Funke. 2013. 48p. (J). (gr. 5-8). 29.93 *(978-1-60870-930-4(2))* Cavendish Square Publishing.

Tomljanovic, Tatiana. Cornelia Funke. 2006. (My Favorite Writer Ser.). (Illus.). 32p. (J). (gr. 3-7). lib. bdg. 26.00 *(978-1-59036-480-2(5))* Weigl Pubs., Inc.

—Cornelia Funke: My Favorite Writer. 2007. (My Favorite Writer Ser.). (Illus.). 32p. (J). (gr. 3-7). per. 9.95 *(978-1-59036-481-9(3))* Weigl Pubs., Inc.

AUTHORS, RUSSIAN

Enrique, Luque Muñoz. Fiódor Dostoievski. 2005. (SPA.). 152p. (YA). *(978-958-30-1438-3(9))* Panamericana Editorial.

AUTHORS, SCOTTISH

Yolen, Jane. Lost Boy: The Story of the Man Who Created Peter Pan. Adams, Steve, illus. 2010. (ENG.). 40p. (J). (gr. 1-3). 17.99 *(978-0-525-47886-7(8)*, Dutton Books for Young Readers) Penguin Young Readers Group.

AUTHORS, SPANISH

Iturralde, Edna. Conoce a Miguel de Cervantes: Get to Know Miguel de Cervantes. 2014. (Personajes Del Mundo Hispnico Ser.). (ENG & SPA., Illus.). 32p. (J). (gr. -1-3). 15.95 *(978-1-61435-352-2(2)*, Alfaguara) Santillana USA Publishing Co., Inc.

Lázaro, Georgina & Moreiro, Enrique S. Federico García Lorca. Moreiro, Enrique S., illus. 2009. (Cuando los Grandes Eran Pequenos Ser.). (SPA., Illus.). 32p. (J). (gr. 4-6). 14.99 *(978-1-933032-39-9(1))* Lectorum Pubns., Inc.

Parker, Barbara Keevil & Parker, Duane F. Miguel de Cervantes. 2003. (Great Hispanic Heritage Ser.). (Illus.). 112p. (gr. 6-12). 35.00 *(978-0-7910-7252-3(5)*, Chelsea Hse.) Facts On File, Inc.

AUTHORSHIP

see also Biography As a Literary Form; Drama—Technique; Fiction—Technique; Journalism; Report Writing; Versification

Grade 6. (J). (gr. 4-7). *(978-0-669-10241-3(5))* Houghton Mifflin Harcourt School Pubs.

Grade 6. (J). pap., tchr.'s training gde. ed. *(978-0-8136-1882-1(7))* Modern Curriculum Pr.

Abdo Publishing. Children's Authors Set 7, 1 vol. 2013. (Children's Authors Set 7 Ser.: 6). (ENG.). 24p. (J). (gr. 3-6). lib. bdg. 153.90 *(978-1-61783-573-5(0)*, Checkerboard Library) ABDO Publishing Co.

Abrams, Dennis. H. G. Wells. 2011. (Who Wrote That? Ser.). (Illus.). 128p. (gr. 6-12). 35.00 *(978-1-60413-770-5(3)*, Chelsea Hse.) Facts On File, Inc.

—S. E. Hinton. 2009. (Who Wrote That? Ser.). (Illus.). 104p. (gr. 6-12). 35.00 *(978-1-60413-088-1(1)*, Chelsea Hse.) Facts On File, Inc.

Abrams, Dennis & Ludwig, Elisa. Judy Blume. 2nd rev. ed. 2009. (Who Wrote That? Ser.). 120p. (gr. 6-12). 35.00 *(978-1-60413-334-9(1)*, Chelsea Hse.) Facts On File, Inc.

Albert, Lisa Rondinelli. Stephenie Meyer: Author of the Twilight Saga. 2009. (Authors Teens Love Ser.). (Illus.). 112p. (J). (gr. 6-18). lib. bdg. 33.27 *(978-0-7660-3584-3(0))* Enslow Pubs., Inc.

Anderson, Jennifer Joline. Writing Fantastic Fiction. 2015. (ENG., Illus.). 56p. (gr. 6-8). 33.32 *(978-1-4677-7908-1(3)*, Lerner Pubns.) Lerner Publishing Group.

Angel, Ann. Robert Cormier: Author of the Chocolate War. 2007. (Authors Teens Love Ser.). (Illus.). 104p. (J). (gr. 8-12). lib. bdg. 33.27 *(978-0-7660-2719-0(8))* Enslow Pubs., Inc.

Aranega, Merce. Quiero Escribir un Cuento. (SPA.). 32p. (J). *(978-84-236-5722-3(1))* Edebé ESP. Dist: Lectorum Pubns., Inc.

Aronson, Deb. E. B. White. 2009. (Library of Author Biographies Ser.). 112p. (gr. 5-8). 63.90 *(978-1-60853-531-6(2)*, Rosen Reference) Rosen Publishing Group, Inc., The.

Ashmore, Wayne & Nault, Jennifer. The Adventurous World of Mark Twain. 2016. (J). ***(978-1-5105-1955-8(6))*** SmartBook Media, Inc.

Ashmore, Wayne & Nault, Jennifer. Mark Twain. 2008. (My Favorite Writer Ser.). (Illus.). 32p. (YA). (gr. 5-18). pap. 9.95 *(978-1-59036-931-9(9))*; lib. bdg. 26.00 *(978-1-59036-930-2(0))* Weigl Pubs., Inc.

Asselin, Kristine Carlson. Think for Yourself: Avoiding Plagiarism, 1 vol. 2013. (Research Tool Kit Ser.). (ENG.). 32p. (gr. 3-4). pap. 8.10 *(978-1-62065-792-8(9))*; pap. 47.70 *(978-1-62065-793-5(7))* Capstone Press of Coughlan Cos. (Fact Finders).

Asselin, Kristine Carlson, et al. Research Tool Kit. 2013. (Research Tool Kit Ser.). (ENG.). 32p. (gr. 3-4). pap. 31.80 *(978-1-62065-794-2(5))*; pap. 190.80 *(978-1-62065-795-9(3))*; lib. bdg. 109.28 *(978-1-4296-9952-5(3))* Capstone Press of Coughlan Cos. (Fact Finders).

Athans, Sandra K. & Parente, Robin W. Tips & Tricks for Analyzing Text & Citing Evidence. 2014. (Common Core Readiness Guide to Reading Ser.). (Illus.). 80p. (J). (gr. 5-8). 32.95 *(978-1-4777-7539-4(0)*, Rosen Reference) Rosen Publishing Group, Inc., The.

Author. 2008. (Virtual Apprentice Ser.). 64p. (gr. 4-9). 29.95 *(978-0-8160-6756-5(2)*, Ferguson Publishing Co.) Facts On File, Inc.

Bailer, Darice. Will & Wendy Build a Website with Digital Tools. O'Neill, Sean, illus. 2014. (Writing Builders Ser.). (ENG.). 32p. (J). (gr. 2-4). pap. 11.94 *(978-1-60357-558-4(8))*; lib. bdg. 25.27 *(978-1-59953-584-5(X))* Norwood Hse. Pr.

Bankston, John. F. Scott Fitzgerald. 2004. (Classic Storytellers Ser.). (Illus.). 48p. (J). (gr. 4-8). lib. bdg. 29.95 *(978-1-58415-249-1(4))* Mitchell Lane Pubs., Inc.

—Jack London. 2004. (Classic Storytellers Ser.). (Illus.). 48p. (J). (gr. 4-8). lib. bdg. 29.95 *(978-1-58415-263-7(X))* Mitchell Lane Pubs., Inc.

—Lois Lowry. 2009. (Who Wrote That? Ser.). 128p. (gr. 6-12). 35.00 *(978-1-60413-335-6(X)*, Chelsea Hse.) Facts On File, Inc.

—Ray Bradbury. 2011. (Who Wrote That? Ser.). (Illus.). 140p. (gr. 6-12). 35.00 *(978-1-60413-778-1(9)*, Chelsea Hse.) Facts On File, Inc.

Baptiste, Tracey. Jerry Spinelli. 2009. (Who Wrote That? Ser.). (Illus.). 128p. (gr. 6-12). 35.00 *(978-0-7910-9572-0(X)*, Chelsea Hse.) Facts On File, Inc.

—Sharon Creech. 2011. (Who Wrote That? Ser.). (Illus.). 118p. (gr. 6-12). 35.00 *(978-1-60413-774-3(6)*, Chelsea Hse.) Facts On File, Inc.

Barnett, Mac. How This Book Was Made: Based on a True Story. Rex, Adam, illus. 2016. (ENG.). 48p. (J). (gr. -1-k). 17.99 *(978-1-4231-5220-0(4))* Disney Pr.

Barrett, Shari & Barrett, Steve. Put That in Writing Level One: Answer Key & Test Bank. 2003. 32p. 7.50 *(978-0-9728731-1-6(2))* Barrett's Bookshelf.

—Put That in Writing Level One: Mastering the Paragraph. 2003. 211p. spiral bd. 49.95 *(978-0-9728731-0-9(4))* Barrett's Bookshelf.

Barsby Ed. D., Carol. Writing Mini-Lessons Grades K-2. 2010. 48p. pap. 20.00 *(978-0-557-23273-4(2))* Lulu Pr., Inc.

Bauchner, Elizabeth. Document Analysis. Noziglia, Carla Miller & Siegel, Jay A., eds. 2013. (Solving Crimes with Science: Forensics Ser.: 12). (Illus.). 112p. (J). (gr. 7-18). 22.95 *(978-1-4222-2865-4(7))* Mason Crest.

Benke, Karen. Rip the Page! Adventures in Creative Writing. 2010. (ENG., Illus.). 256p. (J). (gr. 4-7). pap. 16.95 *(978-1-59030-812-7(3)*, Roost Books) Shambhala Pubns., Inc.

Berne, Emma Carlson. Laura Ingalls Wilder, 1 vol. 2007. (Essential Lives Set 1 Ser.). (ENG., Illus.). 112p. (J). (gr. 6-12). lib. bdg. 35.64 *(978-1-59928-843-7(5))* ABDO Publishing Co.

Beutel, Roger & Spencer, Lauren. Writing a Narrative. 2011. 77.70 *(978-1-4488-4747-1(8)*, Rosen Reference); pap. 12.95 *(978-1-4488-4689-4(7)*, Rosen Reference); (YA). (gr. 5-9). lib. bdg. 31.95 *(978-1-4488-4683-2(8))* Rosen Publishing Group, Inc., The.

—Writing about Issues. 2011. 77.70 *(978-1-4488-4746-4(X))*; pap. 12.95 *(978-1-4488-4688-7(9))*; (YA). (gr. 5-9). lib. bdg. 31.95 *(978-1-4488-4682-5(X))* Rosen Publishing Group, Inc., The.

Bidini, Dave. For Those about to Write: How I Learned to Love Books & Why I Had to Write Them. 2007. (ENG.). 136p. (J). (gr. 5-18). per. 9.95 *(978-0-88776-769-2(9)*, Tundra Bks.) Tundra Bks. CAN. Dist: Penguin Random Hse. LLC.

Blasingame, James B. Gary Paulsen, 1 vol. 2007. (Teen Reads: Student Companions to Young Adult Literature Ser.). 184p. (C). (gr. 7). 50.00 *(978-0-313-33532-7(X)*, GR3532, Greenwood) ABC-CLIO, LLC.

Bloom, Harold, intro. The Tale of Genji. 2003. (Bloom's Modern Critical Interpretations Ser.). (Illus.). 176p. (C). (gr. 9-13). 45.00 *(978-0-7910-7584-5(2)*, Chelsea Hse.) Facts On File, Inc.

Bodden, Valerie. Journalistic Articles. 2010. (Nonfiction Ser.). 48p. (YA). (gr. 5-18). 23.95 *(978-1-58341-934-2(9)*, Creative Education) Creative Co., The.

—Organized Essays. (Nonfiction Writing Ser.). 48p. 2011. (ENG., Illus.). (J). (gr. 4-7). pap. 9.99 *(978-0-89812-547-4(2))* 2010. (YA). (gr. 5-18). 23.95 *(978-1-58341-933-5(0))* Creative Co., The. (Creative Education).

—Poetry Basics: Concrete Poetry. 2011. (Poetry Basics Ser.). (ENG.). 32p. (J). (gr. 5-17). pap. 8.99 *(978-1-926722-43-6(4)*, Creative Paperbacks) Creative Co., The.

—What Are Nonfiction Genres? 2014. (Name That Text Type! Ser.). (ENG., Illus.). 32p. (gr. 2-4). lib. bdg. 26.60 *(978-1-4677-3665-7(1)*, Lerner Pubns.) Lerner Publishing Group.

Boothroyd, Jennifer. Roald Dahl: A Life of Imagination. 2008. (Pull Ahead Books-Biographies Ser.). (ENG., Illus.). 32p. (gr. k-3). lib. bdg. 22.60 *(978-0-8225-8825-2(0)*, Lerner Pubns.) Lerner Publishing Group.

Borden, Louise & Borden, Louise W. The Journey That Saved Curious George: The True Wartime Escape of Margret & H. A. Rey. Drummond, Allan, illus. 2005. (Curious George Ser.). (ENG.). 80p. (J). (gr. 2-5). 17.99 *(978-0-618-33924-2(8))* Houghton Mifflin Harcourt Publishing Co.

Borden, Louise W. The Journey That Saved Curious George: The True Wartime Escape of Margret & H. A. Rey. Drummond, Allan, illus. 2010. (Curious George Ser.). (ENG.). 80p. (J). (gr. 2-5). pap. 8.99 *(978-0-547-41746-2(2))* Houghton Mifflin Harcourt Publishing Co.

Braun, Eric. Maurice Sendak [Scholastic]. 2011. (First Biographies - Writers, Artists, & Athletes Ser.). 24p. pap. 0.50 *(978-1-4296-6318-2(9)*, Pebble Bks.) Capstone Press of Coughlan Cos.

—Tomie Depaola [Scholastic]. 2011. (First Biographies - Writers, Artists, & Athletes Ser.). 24p. pap. 0.50 *(978-1-4296-6319-9(7)*, Pebble Bks.) Capstone Press of Coughlan Cos.

Briggs, Lucy. Kate Dicamillo. 2005. (My Favorite Writer Ser.). (Illus.). 32p. (J). (gr. 5-7). lib. bdg. 26.00 *(978-1-59036-283-9(7))* Weigl Pubs., Inc.

Brocker, Susan. War Heroes: Level U, 6 vols. (Mountain Peaks Ser.). 128p. (gr. 6-18). 36.95 *(978-0-322-05893-4(7))* Wright Group/McGraw-Hill.

Bryan, Ashley. Ashley Bryan: Words to My Life's Song. Bryan, Ashley, illus. McGuinness, Bill, photos by. 2009. (ENG., Illus.). 64p. (J). (gr. -1-18). 19.99 *(978-1-4169-0541-7(3)*, Atheneum Bks. for Young Readers) Simon & Schuster Children's Publishing.

Burling, Alexis. Working in Writing. 2018. (ENG.). 32p. (gr. 3-6). ***(978-1-63235-451-8(9)***, 12-Story Library) Pr. Room Editions LLC.

Campbell, Kimberly. Lois Duncan: Author of I Know What You Did Last Summer. 2009. (Authors Teens Love Ser.). (Illus.). 104p. (J). (gr. 6). lib. bdg. 33.27 *(978-0-7660-2963-7(8))* Enslow Pubs., Inc.

Canavan, Roger. You Wouldn't Want to Live Without the Writing! Bergin, Mark, illus. 2015. (You Wouldn't Want to Live Without... Ser.). (ENG.). 32p. (J). lib. bdg. 29.00 *(978-0-531-21930-0(5)*, Watts, Franklin) Scholastic Library Publishing.

Carroll, Joyce Armstrong. Dr. JAC's Guide to Writing With Depth. 2004. 192p. 23.95 *(978-1-888842-40-1(7))* Absey & Co.

Christelow, Eileen. What Do Authors & Illustrators Do? 2013. (ENG., Illus.). 80p. (J). (gr. -1-3). 9.99 *(978-0-547-97260-2(1))* Houghton Mifflin Harcourt Publishing Co.

Christopher Paolini. 2010. (Who Wrote That? Ser.). (Illus.). 136p. (J). (gr. 6-12). 35.00 *(978-1-60413-727-9(4)*, Chelsea Hse.) Facts On File, Inc.

Clairday, Robynn. A Girl's Story: How to Write Your Autobiography. 2006. 81p. (J). (gr. 4-7). per. 7.99 *(978-0-9717119-5-2(X))* Consumer Pr., The.

Clapper, Nikki Bruno. Learning about Plagiarism. 2015. (Media Literacy for Kids Ser.). (ENG., Illus.). 24p. (gr. k-1). lib. bdg. 26.65 *(978-1-4914-6049-8(0))* Capstone Press of Coughlan Cos.

Cook, Jaye E. & Spencer, Lauren. Writing Personal Stories. 2011. (J). 77.70 *(978-1-4488-4748-8(6)*, Rosen Reference); (J). pap. 12.95 *(978-1-4488-4690-0(0)*, Rosen Reference); (YA). (gr. 5-9). lib. bdg. 31.95 *(978-1-4488-4684-9(6))* Rosen Publishing Group, Inc., The.

Corbett, Sue. Cornelia Funke. 2013. 48p. (J). (gr. 5-8). 29.93 *(978-1-60870-930-4(2))* Cavendish Square Publishing.

—Gary Paulsen. 2013. 48p. (J). (gr. 5-8). 29.93 *(978-1-60870-934-2(5))*; pap. 12.93 *(978-1-62712-142-2(0))* Cavendish Square Publishing.

—Jeff Kinney. 2013. 48p. (J). (gr. 5-8). 29.93 *(978-1-60870-932-8(9))* Cavendish Square Publishing.

—Jennifer L. Holm. 2013. 48p. (J). (gr. 5-8). 29.93 *(978-1-60870-931-1(0))* Cavendish Square Publishing.

Craats, Rennay. E. B. White. 2013. (J). *(978-1-62127-405-6(5))*; pap. *(978-1-62127-411-7(X))* Weigl Pubs., Inc.

Crutcher, Chris. King of the Mild Frontier: An Ill-Advised Autobiography. 2004. (ENG.). 272p. (YA). (gr. 9). reprint ed. pap. 9.99 *(978-0-06-050251-5(7)*, Greenwillow Bks.) HarperCollins Pubs.

Daniel, Susanna. Karen Cushman. 2009. (Library of Author Biographies Ser.). 112p. (gr. 5-8). 63.90 *(978-1-60853-540-8(1)*, Rosen Reference) Rosen Publishing Group, Inc., The.

—Paula Fox. (Library of Author Biographies Ser.). 112p. (gr. 5-8). 2009. 63.90 *(978-1-60853-550-7(9))* 2004. (J). lib. bdg. 34.60 *(978-0-8239-4525-2(1))* Rosen Publishing Group, Inc., The. (Rosen Reference).

Dawson, Willow. Lila & Ecco's Do-It-Yourself Comics Club. Dawson, Willow, illus. 2010. (ENG., Illus.). 112p. (J). (gr. 3-7). 16.95 *(978-1-55453-438-8(0))* Kids Can Pr., Ltd. CAN. Dist: Hachette Bk. Group.

De Medeiros, Michael. Marc Brown: My Favorite Writer. 2008. (J). *(978-1-59036-927-2(0))* Weigl Pubs., Inc.

Dengo, Monica, illus. Pick up Your Pen: The Art of Handwriting. 2012. (ENG.). 112p. (J). (gr. 1-4). pap. 14.95 *(978-1-926973-11-1(9))* Owlkids Bks. Inc. CAN. Dist: Publishers Group West (PGW).

Des Chenes, Elizabeth, ed. Pollution. 2007. (Writing the Critical Essay Ser.). (ENG., Illus.). 130p. (J). (gr. 3-7). lib. bdg. 33.75 *(978-0-7377-3198-9(2)*, Greenhaven Pr., Inc.) Cengage Gale.

Donaldson, Chelsea. Robert Munsch, 1 vol. 2014. (Canadian Biographies Ser.). (ENG.). 24p. (gr. k-1). 26.65 *(978-1-4914-1960-1(1)*, Pebble Plus) Capstone Press of Coughlan Cos.

Dorling Kindersley Publishing Staff. DK Workbooks: Handwriting: Cursive, Third Grade. 2016. (ENG., Illus.). 60p. (J). (gr. 3-4). pap. 6.99 *(978-1-4654-4470-7(X)*, DK Children) Dorling Kindersley Publishing, Inc.

—Handwriting - Printing, Kindergarten. 2016. (ENG., Illus.). 60p. (J). (gr. -1-1). pap. 6.99 *(978-1-4654-4469-1(6)*, DK Children) Dorling Kindersley Publishing, Inc.

—Write Your Own Book. 2016. (ENG.). 96p. (J). (gr. 3-7). 14.99 *(978-1-4654-4471-4(8)*, DK Children) Dorling Kindersley Publishing, Inc.

Dunkleberger, Amy. So You Want to Be a Film or TV Screenwriter? 2007. (Careers in Film & Television Ser.). (Illus.). 128p. (J). (gr. 6-9). lib. bdg. 33.27 *(978-0-7660-2645-2(0))* Enslow Pubs., Inc.

Dunn, Mary R. I Want to Write Books. 2009. (Dream Jobs Ser.). 24p. (gr. 2-3). 42.50 *(978-1-61512-217-2(6)*, PowerKids Pr.); (Illus.). (YA). lib. bdg. 22.60 *(978-1-4042-4474-0(3))* Rosen Publishing Group, Inc., The.

Edge, Christopher. How to Write Your Best Story Ever! Top Tips & Trade Secrets from the Experts. 2016. (ENG.). 128p. (J). (gr. 2-6). pap. 12.99 *(978-1-4380-0909-4(7))* Barron's Educational Series, Inc.

Erlic, Lily. Lois Lowry. 2005. (My Favorite Writer Ser.). (Illus.). 32p. (J). (gr. 5-7). lib. bdg. 26.00 *(978-1-59036-286-0(1))* Weigl Pubs., Inc.

—Louis Sachar. 2005. (My Favorite Writer Ser.). (Illus.). 32p. (J). (gr. 5-7). lib. bdg. 26.00 *(978-1-59036-288-4(8))* Weigl Pubs., Inc.

Family Stories: Ten Stories. 2005. (SPA & ENG., Illus.). 27p. (J). pap. *(978-0-9716580-8-0(0))* Lectura Bks.

Fandel, Jennifer. You Can Write an Amazing Journal, 1 vol. 2012. (You Can Write Ser.). (ENG., Illus.). 24p. (gr. 1-2). pap. 7.29 *(978-1-4296-9318-9(5))*; lib. bdg. 25.32 *(978-1-4296-8408-8(9))* Capstone Press of Coughlan Cos.

—You Can Write Awesome Stories, 1 vol. 2012. (You Can Write Ser.). (ENG., 24p. (gr. 1-2). Illus.). pap. 7.29 *(978-1-4296-7960-2(3))*; pap. 41.70 *(978-1-4296-8382-1(1))*; (Illus.). lib. bdg. 25.32 *(978-1-4296-7615-1(9))* Capstone Press of Coughlan Cos. (First Facts).

—You Can Write Cool Poems, 1 vol. 2012. (You Can Write Ser.). (ENG., 24p. (gr. 1-2). Illus.). pap. 7.29 *(978-1-4296-7961-9(1))*; pap. 41.70 *(978-1-4296-8383-8(X))* Capstone Press of Coughlan Cos. (First Facts).

Fandel, Jennifer & Fields, Jan. You Can Write. 2012. (You Can Write Ser.). (ENG.). 24p. (gr. 1-2). pap. 27.80 *(978-1-4296-8386-9(4))*; pap. 166.80 *(978-1-4296-8387-6(2))*; lib. bdg. 75.96 *(978-1-4296-8150-6(0))* Capstone Press of Coughlan Cos. (First Facts).

Farrell, Tish. Be a Creative Writer. 2010. (ENG.). 96p. (J). (gr. 4-7). pap. 9.95 *(978-1-84696-209-7(9)*, TickTock Books) Octopus Publishing Group GBR. Dist: Independent Pubs. Group.

Flath, Camden. Freelance & Technical Writers: Words for Sale. 2010. (New Careers for the 21st Century Ser.). 64p. (YA). (gr. 7-18). pap. 9.95 *(978-1-4222-2035-1(4))*; (Illus.). lib. bdg. 22.95 *(978-1-4222-1814-3(7))* Mason Crest.

Flatt, Lizann. How to Write Realistic Fiction. 2014. (ENG., Illus.). 32p. (J). *(978-0-7787-1656-3(2))* Crabtree Publishing Co.

Fletcher, Ralph. How to Write Your Life Story. Nagy, Ian, illus. 2007. 112p. (J). (gr. 3-7). 15.99 *(978-0-06-050770-1(5))* HarperCollins Pubs.

Francis, Barbara. Are You Misusing Other People's Words? What Plagiarism Is & How to Avoid It. 2014. (Got Issues? Ser.). (Illus.). 112p. (J). (gr. 6-12). lib. bdg. 33.27 *(978-0-7660-4321-3(5))* Enslow Pubs., Inc.

—Other People's Words: What Plagiarism Is & How to Avoid It. 2005. (Issues in Focus Today Ser.). (Illus.). 112p. (J). (gr. 6-13). lib. bdg. 33.27 *(978-0-7660-2525-7(X))* Enslow Pubs., Inc.

Frank, Vivien & Jaffe, Deborah. Make a Book: Six Different Books to Make, Write, & Illustrate. 2004. (Illus.). 32p. (J). (gr. 2-8). reprint ed. pap. 15.00 *(978-0-7567-7703-6(8))* DIANE Publishing Co.

Franklin, Joseph & Wilson, Antoine. S. E. Hinton, 01 vols., 1. 2016. (All about the Author Ser.). (ENG.). 112p. (J). 35.60 *(978-1-4994-6266-1(2)*, Rosen Young Adult) Rosen Publishing Group, Inc., The.

Freese, Susan M. Bees to Trees: Reading, Writing, & Reciting Poems about Nature, 1 vol. Westberg, Jan, illus. 2008. (Poetry Power Ser.). (ENG.). 32p. (J). (gr. 1-4). 27.07 *(978-1-60453-001-8(4))* ABDO Publishing Co.

—Buses to Books: Reading, Writing, & Reciting Poems about School, 1 vol. Westberg, Jan, illus. 2008. (Poetry Power Ser.). (ENG.). 32p. (J). (gr. 1-4). 27.07 *(978-1-60453-002-5(2))* ABDO Publishing Co.

—Carrots to Cupcakes: Reading, Writing, & Reciting Poems about Food, 1 vol. Westberg, Jan, illus. 2008. (Poetry Power Ser.). (ENG.). 32p. (J). (gr. 1-4). 27.07 *(978-1-60453-003-2(0))* ABDO Publishing Co.

—Fireworks to Fruitcake: Reading, Writing, & Reciting Poems about Holidays, 1 vol. Westberg, Jan, illus. 2008. (Poetry Power Ser.). (ENG.). 32p. (J). (gr. 1-4). 27.07 *(978-1-60453-004-9(9))* ABDO Publishing Co.

—Guppies to Puppies: Reading, Writing, & Reciting Poems about Pets, 1 vol. Westberg, Jan, illus. 2008. (Poetry Power Ser.). (ENG.). 32p. (J). (gr. 1-4). 27.07 *(978-1-60453-005-6(7))* ABDO Publishing Co.

—Nicknames to Nightmares: Reading, Writing, & Reciting Poems about Me, 1 vol. Westberg, Jan, illus. 2008. (Poetry Power Ser.). (ENG.). 32p. (J). (gr. 1-4). 27.07 *(978-1-60453-006-3(5))* ABDO Publishing Co.

Friedman, Lauri S. School Shootings. 2009. (Writing the Critical Essay Ser.). (ENG., Illus.). 128p. (J). 31.80 *(978-0-7377-4564-1(9)*, Greenhaven Pr., Inc.) Cengage Gale.

Fun to Write! Classroom Storybooks - Fiction. 2005. (J). spiral bd. 24.95 *(978-1-58970-696-5(X))* Lakeshore Learning Materials.

Fun to Write! Classroom Storybooks - Non Fiction. 2005. (J). spiral bd. 24.95 *(978-1-58970-697-2(8))* Lakeshore Learning Materials.

Gaines, Ann Graham. J. K. Rowling. 2004. (Blue Banner Biography Ser.). (Illus.). 32p. (J). (gr. 3-8). lib. bdg. 25.70 *(978-1-58415-325-2(3))* Mitchell Lane Pubs., Inc.

Ganeri, Anita. Funny Stories: Writing Stories, 1 vol. 2013. (Writing Stories Ser.). (ENG.). 32p. (gr. 1-3). 27.32 *(978-1-4329-7534-0(X))*; pap. 8.95 *(978-1-4329-7541-8(2))* Heinemann-Raintree. (Heinemann First Library).

—I Can Write. 2013. (I Can Write Ser.). (ENG.). 32p. (gr. 1-3). 163.92 *(978-1-4329-6939-4(0)*, Heinemann First Library) Heinemann-Raintree.

—I Can Write Stories, 1 vol. 2013. (I Can Write Ser.). (ENG., Illus.). 32p. (gr. 1-3). pap. 8.29 *(978-1-4329-6945-5(5))*; lib. bdg. 27.32 *(978-1-4329-6938-7(2))* Heinemann-Raintree. (Heinemann First Library).

—Scary Stories: Writing Stories, 1 vol. 2013. (Writing Stories Ser.). (ENG.). 32p. (gr. 1-3). 27.32 *(978-1-4329-7533-3(1))*; pap. 8.95 *(978-1-4329-7540-1(4))* Heinemann-Raintree. (Heinemann First Library).

—Writing Stories. 2013. (Writing Stories Ser.). (ENG.). 32p. (gr. 1-3). pap. 47.94 *(978-1-4329-7542-5(0))*; lib. bdg. 163.92 *(978-1-4329-7535-7(8))* Heinemann-Raintree. (Heinemann First Library).

Gantos, Jack. Hole in My Life. 2004. 18.10 *(978-0-7569-3197-1(5))* Farrar, Straus & Giroux.

—Hole in My Life. 2009. 8.89 *(978-0-7848-2463-4(0)*, Everbind) Marco Bk. Co.

—Hole in My Life. 2012. (ENG.). 224p. (YA). (gr. 9-13). pap. 9.99 *(978-0-312-64157-3(5)*, 9780312641573) Square Fish.

Gantos, Jack. Writing Radar: Using Your Journal to Snoop Out & Craft Great Stories. 2017. (ENG.). 224p. (J). 17.99 ***(978-0-374-30456-0(4)***, 9780374304560, Farrar, Straus & Giroux (BYR)) Farrar, Straus & Giroux.

Garstecki, Julia. Rev up Your Writing in Informational Texts. Gallagher-Cole, Mernie, illus. 2015. (Rev up Your Writing Ser.). (ENG.). 24p. (J). (gr. 2-5). 28.50 *(978-1-63407-063-8(1)*, 208898) Child's World, Inc., The.

—Rev up Your Writing in Nonfiction Narratives. Gallagher-Cole, Mernie, illus. 2015. (Rev up Your Writing Ser.). (ENG.). 24p. (J). (gr. 2-5). 28.50 *(978-1-63407-065-2(8)*, 208900) Child's World, Inc., The.

Gelletly, LeeAnne. Gift of Imagination: The Story of Roald Dahl. 2006. (World Writers Ser.). (Illus.). 160p. (gr. 6-12). lib. bdg. 27.95 *(978-1-59935-026-4(2))* Reynolds, Morgan Inc.

Gosman, Gillian. Publish It: Sharing Your Writing Online, 1 vol. 2015. (ENG., Illus.). 32p. (J). lib. bdg. 26.25 *(978-1-4777-7389-5(4)*, PowerKids Pr.) Rosen Publishing Group, Inc., The.

Gould, Judith S. & Burke, Mary F. Write Now! Mitchell, Judith, ed. Rasche, Shelly S., illus. 2005. 80p. (J). pap. 6.95 *(978-1-57310-449-4(3))* Teaching & Learning Co.

Grade 6. (J). (gr. 6). *(978-0-669-15964-6(6))* Houghton Mifflin Harcourt School Pubs.

Green, Robert. Careers If You Like Writing. 2016. (ENG.). 80p. (YA). (gr. 5-12). lib. bdg. *(978-1-68282-010-0(6))* ReferencePoint Pr., Inc.

Griskey, Michele. Ray Bradbury. 2006. (Classic Storytellers Ser.). (Illus.). 48p. (J). (gr. 3-7). lib. bdg. 29.95 *(978-1-58415-455-6(1)*, 1259542) Mitchell Lane Pubs., Inc.

The check digit for ISBN-10 appears in parentheses after the full ISBN-13

Group, Wright. Grade 6. 4th ed. (gr. 6-18). pap., tchr. ed. 12.39 *(978-0-02-688479-2(8))* SRA/McGraw-Hill.

—: Grade 6. 4th ed. Incl. 4th ed. (gr. 6-18). pap., tchr. ed. 12.39 *(978-0-02-688479-2(8))*; Set pap. 3.72 *(978-0-02-688478-5(X))* SRA/McGraw-Hill.

Guillain, Charlotte. Get Writing!, 1 vol. 2014. (Dream It, Do It! Ser.). (ENG., Illus.). 32p. (gr. 1-3). lib. bdg. 29.99 *(978-1-4109-6263-8(6),* Read Me!) Heinemann-Raintree.

—What Is a Short Story? 2015. (Connect with Text Ser.). (ENG., Illus.). 32p. (gr. 2-4). 30.65 *(978-1-4109-6828-9(6),* Raintree Perspectives) Heinemann-Raintree.

—What Is Creative Nonfiction? 2015. (Connect with Text Ser.). (ENG.). 32p. (gr. 2-4). 30.65 *(978-1-4109-8034-2(0))* Heinemann-Raintree.

—What Is Informational Writing? 2015. (Connect with Text Ser.). (ENG., Illus.). 32p. (gr. 2-4). 30.65 *(978-1-4109-8035-9(9))* Heinemann-Raintree.

—What Is Instructional Writing? 2015. (Connect with Text Ser.). (ENG., Illus.). 32p. (gr. 2-4). 30.65 *(978-1-4109-8037-3(5))* Heinemann-Raintree.

—Writing & Staging Adventure Plays. 2016. (Writing & Staging Plays Ser.). (ENG., Illus.). 48p. (gr. 4-6). lib. bdg. 33.32 *(978-1-4846-2770-9(9),* Heinemann InfoSearch) Heinemann-Raintree.

Gunderson, Megan M. Jeff Kinney, 1 vol. 2012. (Children's Authors Set 6 Ser.). (ENG., Illus.). 24p. (YA). (gr. 2-5). 25.65 *(978-1-61783-048-8(8))* ABDO Publishing Co.

Hambleton, Vicki & Greenwood, Cathleen. So, You Want to Be a Writer? How to Write, Get Published, & Maybe Even Make It Big! 2012. (Be What You Want Ser.). (ENG., Illus.). 192p. (J). (gr. 3-7). pap. 11.99 *(978-1-58270-353-4(1))* Aladdin/Beyond Words.

Hamilton, John. You Write It! Fantasy. 2009. (You Write It! Ser.). (Illus.). 32p. (gr. 5-8). 27.07 *(978-1-60453-504-4(0),* Abdo & Daughters) ABDO Publishing Co.

—You Write It! Graphic Novel. 2009. (You Write It! Ser.). (Illus.). 32p. (gr. 5-8). 27.07 *(978-1-60453-505-1(9),* Abdo & Daughters) ABDO Publishing Co.

—You Write It! Horror. 2009. (You Write It! Ser.). (Illus.). 32p. (gr. 5-8). 27.07 *(978-1-60453-506-8(7),* Abdo & Daughters) ABDO Publishing Co.

—You Write It! Screenplay. 2009. (You Write It! Ser.). (Illus.). 32p. (gr. 5-8). 27.07 *(978-1-60453-509-9(1),* Abdo & Daughters) ABDO Publishing Co.

Hamley, Harold, ed. How to Write & Sell. 4th ed. 121p. (Orig.). (YA). (gr. 9-12). reprint ed. lib. bdg. 8.95 *(978-0-9621758-0-0(3))* Raconteurs, Inc.

Heath Grammar & Composition: Grade 6. (gr. 6). (J). suppl. ed. *(978-0-669-13000-3(1))*; tchr. ed. *(978-0-669-12994-6(1))* Houghton Mifflin Harcourt School Pubs.

Hennessy, Brendan. Essay to Write? 2nd ed. 2004. 93p. pap. *(978-1-85703-835-4(5),* How To Books) Little, Brown Book Group Ltd.

Hershenhorn, Esther. S Is for Story: A Writer's Alphabet. Pullen, Zachary, illus. 2009. (ENG.). 40p. (J). (gr. 1-4). 17.95 *(978-1-58536-439-8(8),* 202167) Sleeping Bear Pr.

Hicks, Kelli L. Dav Pilkey, 1 vol. Byers, Michael, illus. 2013. (Your Favorite Authors Ser.). (ENG.). 24p. (gr. 1-2). 25.32 *(978-1-4765-0221-2(8))*; pap. 7.95 *(978-1-4765-3436-7(5))* Capstone Press of Coughlan Cos. (First Facts).

Higa, Ryan. Ryan Higa's How to Write Good. 2017. (ENG.). 208p. (YA). (gr. 7-17). 19.99 ***(978-0-316-46407-9(4)**,* Poppy) Little, Brown Bks. for Young Readers.

Higgins, Nadia. The Whole Truth: Writing Fearless Nonfiction. 2015. (Writer's Notebook Ser.). (ENG., Illus.). 64p. (gr. 4-5). 34.65 *(978-1-4914-5989-8(1))* Capstone Press of Coughlan Cos.

Hill, Pamela Smith. Laura Ingalls Wilder: A Writer's Life. 2007. (South Dakota Biography Ser.). (Illus.). 244p. per. *(978-0-9777955-6-7(X),* South Dakota State Historical Society Pr.) South Dakota State Historical Society Pr.

Hook, Sue Vander. Writing Notable Narrative Nonfiction. 2015. (ENG., Illus.). 56p. (J). (gr. 6-8). 33.32 *(978-1-4677-8084-1(7),* Lerner Pubns.) Lerner Publishing Group.

Houghton, Peggy M., et al. Houghton & Houghton Manual of Style: A Guide to Writing Research Papers. 2009. (J). *(978-0-923568-97-9(2))* Baker College Publishing Co.

Howell, Sara. How to Write a Narrative, 1 vol., 1. 2014. (Core Writing Skills Ser.). (ENG.). 24p. (J). (gr. 3-4). 23.60 *(978-1-4777-2908-3(9))*; pap. 8.25 *(978-1-4777-2997-7(6))* Rosen Publishing Group, Inc., The. (PowerKids Pr.).

—How to Write an Opinion Piece, 1 vol., 1. 2014. (Core Writing Skills Ser.). (ENG.). 24p. (J). (gr. 3-4). 23.60 *(978-1-4777-2906-9(2))*; pap. 8.25 *(978-1-4777-2995-3(X))* Rosen Publishing Group, Inc., The. (PowerKids Pr.).

Hulme, Joy N. & Guthrie, Donna. How to Write, Recite, & Delight in All Kinds of Poetry. 2003. (Single Titles Ser.: Vol. 8). 96p. (J). (gr. 3-6). pap. 9.95 *(978-0-7613-1831-6(3))* Lerner Publishing Group.

Hunsicker, Jennifer. J. K. Rowling: Author of the Harry Potter Series. 2016. (Famous Female Authors Ser.). (ENG., Illus.). 32p. (gr. 3-4). lib. bdg. 27.99 *(978-1-5157-1328-9(8),* Snap Bks.) Capstone Press of Coughlan Cos.

Hurtig, Jennifer. Beatrix Potter. 2008. (My Favorite Writer Ser.). (Illus.). 32p. (YA). (gr. 5-18). pap. 9.95 *(978-1-59036-923-4(8))*; lib. bdg. 26.00 *(978-1-59036-922-7(X))* Weigl Pubs., Inc.

—Maurice Sendak. (My Favorite Writer Ser.). (Illus.). 32p. 2007. (YA). (gr. 5-18). pap. 9.95 *(978-1-59036-485-7(6))* 2006. (J). (gr. 3-7). lib. bdg. 9.95 *(978-1-59036-484-0(8))* Weigl Pubs., Inc.

Hyde, Natalie. How to Write a Fantasy Story. 2014. (ENG., Illus.). 32p. (J). *(978-0-7787-1654-9(6))* Crabtree Publishing Co.

—How to Write an Adventure Story. 2014. (ENG., Illus.). 32p. (J). *(978-0-7787-1655-6(4))* Crabtree Publishing Co.

Infobase Publishing Staff, creator. Writing. 3rd rev. ed. 2007. (Careers in Focus Ser.). (Illus.). 224p. (gr. 6-12). lib. bdg. 32.95 *(978-0-8160-6596-7(9),* Ferguson Publishing Co.) Facts On File, Inc.

James, Sara. Writing: Stories, Poetry, Song & Rap. 2014. (Art Today! Ser.: 10). 64p. (J). (gr. 7-18). 23.95 *(978-1-4222-3177-7(1))* Mason Crest.

Jenkins, Diana R. The Stepping Stones Journals. 2010. (Illus.). 144p. (J). (gr. 3-6). pap. 9.95 *(978-0-8198-7129-9(X))* Pauline Bks. & Media.

Jones, Jen. Judy Blume: Fearless Storyteller for Teens. 2008. (Authors Teens Love Ser.). (Illus.). 112p. (J). (gr. k-6). lib. bdg. 33.27 *(978-0-7660-2960-6(3))* Enslow Pubs., Inc.

Kapai, Khyati. Express Yourself! Writing Persuasive Essays. 2013. 86p. (gr. 4-6). pap. 13.03 *(978-1-4669-2755-1(0))* Trafford Publishing.

Karlitz, Gail. Author. 2008. (Virtual Apprentice Ser.). (Illus.). 72p. (gr. 4-9). per. 9.95 *(978-0-8160-7548-5(4),* Checkmark Bks.) Facts On File, Inc.

Kassirer, Sue. Learn to Write. Date not set. (J). *(978-0-679-85297-1(2),* Random Hse. Bks. for Young Readers) Random Hse. Children's Bks.

Katherine Paterson. 2010. (Who Wrote That? Ser.). (Illus.). 128p. (gr. 6-12). 35.00 *(978-1-60413-499-5(2),* Chelsea Hse.) Facts On File, Inc.

Keats, Felicity. Dancing Pencils. 2007. (Illus.). 168p. pap. *(978-1-86900-163-6(X))* UmSinsi Pr. ZAF. Dist: Michigan State Univ. Pr.

Kemmerer, Susan. The Word Artist. 2005. per. 10.95 *(978-0-9758543-5-8(5))* Schoolhouse Publishing.

Kinney, Jeff. Do-It-Yourself. rev. ed. 2011. (Diary of a Wimpy Kid Ser.). (ENG., Illus.). 224p. (J). (gr. 3-7). 13.95 *(978-0-8109-8995-5(6),* Amulet Bks.) Abrams, Inc.

Kissock, Heather. Robert Munsch. 2012. (J). *(978-1-61913-056-2(4))*; pap. *(978-1-61913-599-4(X))* Weigl Pubs., Inc.

Kjelle, Marylou. Katherine Paterson. 2004. (Classic Storytellers Ser.). (Illus.). 48p. (J). (gr. 4-8). lib. bdg. 29.95 *(978-1-58415-268-2(0))* Mitchell Lane Pubs., Inc.

Kjelle, Marylou Morano. S. E. Hinton: Author of the Outsiders. 2007. (Authors Teens Love Ser.). (Illus.). 112p. (J). (gr. 8-12). lib. bdg. 33.27 *(978-0-7660-2720-6(1))* Enslow Pubs., Inc.

Klein, Rebecca T. Career Building Through Using Digital Publishing Tools. 2013. (Digital Career Building Ser.). (Illus.). 64p. (J). (gr. 7-12). pap. 77.70 *(978-1-4777-1742-4(0))*; pap. 12.95 *(978-1-4777-1741-7(2))*; lib. bdg. 31.95 *(978-1-4777-1724-0(2))* Rosen Publishing Group, Inc., The.

Klein, Rebecca T. & Asselin, Janelle. Cool Careers Without College for People Who Love Reading & Research. 2017. (Cool Careers Without College Ser.). (ENG.). 112p. (gr. 12-12). 38.45 ***(978-1-5081-7542-1(X)**,* Rosen Young Adult) Rosen Publishing Group, Inc., The.

Kopp, Megan. How to Write Science Fiction. 2014. (ENG., Illus.). 32p. (J). *(978-0-7787-1657-0(0))* Crabtree Publishing Co.

—Suzanne Collins. 2012. (J). 28.55 *(978-1-61913-054-8(8))*; pap. *(978-1-61913-600-7(7))* Weigl Pubs., Inc.

Krasner, Barbara. 12 Great Tips on Writing a Script. 2017. (Great Tips on Writing Ser.). (ENG.). 32p. (J). (gr. 3-6). 21.95 *(978-1-63235-276-7(1))* Pr. Room Editions LLC.

Krohn, Katherine E. Stephenie Meyer: Dreaming of Twilight. 2010. (USA TODAY Lifeline Biographies Ser.). (ENG.). 112p. (gr. 6-12). lib. bdg. 34.60 *(978-0-7613-5220-4(1))* Lerner Publishing Group.

Krull, Kathleen. The Boy on Fairfield Street: How Ted Geisel Grew up to Become Dr. Seuss. Johnson, Steve & Fancher, Lou, illus. 2010. (ENG.). 48p. (J). (gr. k-4). pap. 7.99 *(978-0-375-85550-4(5),* Dragonfly Bks.) Random Hse. Children's Bks.

—The Boy on Fairfield Street: How Ted Geisel Grew up to Become Dr. Seuss. 2010. lib. bdg. 18.40 *(978-0-606-12416-4(0),* Turtleback) Turtleback Bks.

Kumon Publishing, ed. My Book of Amazing Tracing. 2012. (Illus.). (J). 80p. pap. 7.95 *(978-4-7743-0007-8(1))*; (ENG., 78p. pap. 7.95 *(978-1-935800-43-9(4))* Kumon Publishing North America, Inc.

Kuprin, Alexander. To Chekhov's Memory. 2004. reprint ed. pap. 15.95 *(978-1-4191-9023-0(7))*; pap. 1.99 *(978-1-4192-9023-7(1))* Kessinger Publishing, LLC.

Kurtz, Jane. Jane Kurtz & YOU, 1 vol. 2007. (Author & YOU Ser.: No. 8). (Illus.). 204p. (C). per. 35.00 *(978-1-59158-295-3(4),* LU2954, Libraries Unlimited) ABC-CLIO, LLC.

L. Frank Baum. 2010. (Who Wrote That? Ser.). (Illus.). 128p. (gr. 6-12). 35.00 *(978-1-60413-501-5(8),* Chelsea Hse.) Facts On File, Inc.

LaBaff, Stephanie. Draw Animals in 4 Easy Steps: Then Write a Story. LaBaff, Tom, illus. 2012. (Drawing in 4 Easy Steps Ser.). 48p. (J). (gr. 3-18). 25.27 *(978-0-7660-3840-0(8))* Enslow Pubs., Inc.

Labaff, Stephanie. Draw Animals in 4 Easy Steps: Then Write a Story. LaBaff, Tom, illus. 2012. (Drawing in 4 Easy Steps Ser.). 48p. (J). (gr. 3-18). pap. 8.95 *(978-1-4644-0013-1(X),* Enslow Elementary) Enslow Pubs., Inc.

LaBaff, Stephanie. Draw Superheroes in 4 Easy Steps: Then Write a Story. LaBaff, Tom, illus. 2012. (Drawing in 4 Easy Steps Ser.). 48p. (J). (gr. 3-18). 25.27 *(978-0-7660-3842-4(4))* Enslow Pubs., Inc.

Laminack, Lester & Laminack, Lester L. Cracking Open the Author's Craft: Teaching the Art of Writing. 2007. (ENG., Illus.). 96p. pap. 31.99 *(978-0-439-91964-7(9))* Scholastic, Inc.

Landon, Lucinda. Meg Mackintosh's Mystery Writing Handbook: For Young Authors & Illustrators. 2012. (Meg Mackintosh Mystery Ser.). 48p. pap. 6.95 *(978-1-888695-13-7(7))* Secret Passage Pr.

Langston-George, Rebecca, et al. Encounter: Narrative Nonfiction Stories. 2017. (Encounter: Narrative Nonfiction Stories Ser.). (ENG.). 157.27 *(978-1-5157-6333-8(1))* Encounter Bks.

Larson, Mark H. & Boone, Robert S. Moe's Cafe: 48 Decidedly Different Creative Writing Prompts. 2006. (Illus.). 124p. (YA). (gr. 8-12). per. 14.95 *(978-1-59647-088-0(7))* Good Year Bks.

Learning to Write: 4-Month Academic Access Version. 2003. (Illus.). (C). E-Book incl. cd-rom *(978-0-9726808-1-3(0))* MEIER Enterprises Inc.

Lee, Frank. Telling the Story in Your Graphic Novel. 2012. (How to Draw Your Own Graphic Novel Ser.). (ENG., Illus.). 32p. (J). (gr. 4-6). pap. 12.30 *(978-1-4488-6453-9(4))*; lib. bdg. 26.50 *(978-1-4488-6434-8(8))* Rosen Publishing Group, Inc., The. (PowerKids Pr.).

Lee, Naomi Davis & LaRue, Nicole. Write Here, Write Now. 2015. (ENG., Illus.). 144p. (J). (gr. 3-7). 14.95 *(978-1-4521-2939-6(8))* Chronicle Bks. LLC.

Leedy, Loreen. Look at My Book! How Kids Can Write & Illustrate Terrific Books. 2005. (ENG., Illus.). 32p. (J). 8.99 *(978-0-8234-1959-3(2))* Holiday Hse., Inc.

—Look at My Book! How Kids Can Write & Illustrate Terrific Books. Leedy, Loreen, tr. 2005. (ENG., Illus.). 32p. (J). (gr. -1-3). tchr. ed. 17.95 *(978-0-8234-1590-8(2))* Holiday Hse., Inc.

Leusted, Marcia Amidon & Amidon Lusted, Marcia. Money-Making Opportunities for Teens Who Like to Write. 2013. 80p. (YA). (gr. 7-12). 33.25 *(978-1-4488-9386-7(0))* Rosen Publishing Group, Inc., The.

Levine, Gail Carson. Writer to Writer: From Think to Ink. 2014. (ENG.). 304p. (J). (gr. 3-7). 16.99 *(978-0-06-227530-1(5))*; pap. 6.99 *(978-0-06-227529-5(1))* HarperCollins Pubs.

—Writing Magic: Creating Stories That Fly. 2014. (ENG.). 176p. (J). (gr. 3). pap. 7.99 *(978-0-06-236717-4(X))* HarperCollins Pubs.

Levine, Gail Carson & Levine, Gail C. Writing Magic: Creating Stories That Fly. 2006. (ENG.). 176p. (J). (gr. 3-7). 16.99 *(978-0-06-051961-2(4),* Collins) HarperCollins Pubs.

Lewis, Catherine. Thrice Told Tales: Three Mice Full of Writing Advice. Swarte, Joost, illus. 2013. (ENG.). 144p. (YA). (gr. 7). 17.99 *(978-1-4169-5784-3(7))* Simon & Schuster Children's Publishing.

Lierman, Jane. Cursive Writing Practice - Inspiring Quotes: Reproducible Activity Pages with Motivational & Character-Building Quotes That Make Handwriting Practice Meaningful. 2009. (ENG.). 48p. pap. 10.99 *(978-0-545-09437-5(2),* Teaching Resources) Scholastic, Inc.

Lieurance, Suzanne. Write a Romance in 5 Simple Steps. 2012. (Creative Writing in 5 Simple Steps Ser.). (Illus.). 48p. (J). (gr. 5-9). 25.27 *(978-0-7660-3837-0(8))* Enslow Pubs., Inc.

Litton, Jonathan. Touch & Trace Farm. Rumiz, Susanna, illus. 2016. (ENG.). 26p. (J). (gr. -1-k). bds. 8.99 *(978-1-58925-220-2(9))* Tiger Tales.

Litwin, Laura Baskes. Write Horror Fiction in 5 Simple Steps. 2012. (Creative Writing in 5 Simple Steps Ser.). (Illus.). 48p. (J). (gr. 5-9). 25.27 *(978-0-7660-3836-3(X))* Enslow Pubs., Inc.

Llanas, Sheila Griffin. Picture Yourself Writing Fiction: Using Photos to Inspire Writing, 1 vol. 2011. (See It, Write It Ser.). (ENG., 32p. (gr. 3-4). Illus.). pap. 8.10 *(978-1-4296-7205-4(6),* 1330421); pap. 47.70 *(978-1-4296-7206-1(4))* Capstone Press of Coughlan Cos. (Fact Finders).

Loewen, Nancy. It's All about You: Writing Your Own Journal, 1 vol. Lyles, Christopher & Ouren, Todd, illus. 2009. (Writer's Toolbox Ser.). (ENG.). 32p. (gr. 2-4). pap. 8.95 *(978-1-4048-5698-1(6))* Picture Window Bks.

—Make Me Giggle: Writing Your Own Silly Story, 1 vol. Doerrfeld, Cori & Lyles, Christopher, illus. 2009. (Writer's Toolbox Ser.). (ENG.). 32p. (gr. 2-4). pap. 8.95 *(978-1-4048-5704-9(4))* Picture Window Bks.

—Once upon a Time: Writing Your Own Fairy Tale, 1 vol. Lyles, Christopher, illus. 2009. (Writer's Toolbox Ser.). (ENG.). 32p. (gr. 2-4). pap. 8.95 *(978-1-4048-5336-2(7))*; lib. bdg. 27.32 *(978-1-4048-5335-5(9))* Picture Window Bks.

—Share a Scare: Writing Your Own Scary Story, 1 vol. Lyles, Christopher, illus. 2009. (Writer's Toolbox Ser.). (ENG.). 32p. (gr. 2-4). pap. 8.95 *(978-1-4048-5700-1(1))* Picture Window Bks.

—Show Me a Story: Writing Your Own Picture Book, 1 vol. Lyles, Christopher, illus. 2009. (Writer's Toolbox Ser.). (ENG.). 32p. (gr. 2-4). pap. 8.95 *(978-1-4048-5342-3(1))*; lib. bdg. 27.32 *(978-1-4048-5341-6(3))* Picture Window Bks.

—Words, Wit, & Wonder: Writing Your Own Poem, 1 vol. Lyles, Christopher, illus. 2010. (Writer's Toolbox Ser.). (ENG.). 32p. (gr. 2-4). pap. 8.95 *(978-1-4048-5345-4(6))* Picture Window Bks.

—Writer's Toolbox: Learn How to Write Letters, Fairy Tales, Scary Stories, Journals, Poems, & Reports, 1 vol. Lyles, Christopher et al, illus. 2009. (Writer's Toolbox Ser.). (ENG.). 192p. (gr. 2-4). pap. 14.95 *(978-1-4048-5905-0(5))* Picture Window Bks.

Lynette, Rachel. Ben & Bailey Build a Book Report. Chewning, Randy, illus. 2012. (Writing Builders Ser.). 32p. (J). (gr. 2-4). lib. bdg. 25.27 *(978-1-59953-506-7(8))* Norwood Hse. Pr.

—Frank & Fiona Build a Fictional Story. Lieffering, Jan, illus. 2014. (Writing Builders Ser.). (ENG.). 32p. (J). (gr. 2-4). pap. 11.94 *(978-1-60357-561-4(8))*; lib. bdg. 25.27 *(978-1-59953-587-6(4))* Norwood Hse. Pr.

Macken, JoAnn Early. Gary Paulsen: Voice of Adventure & Survival. 2007. (Authors Teens Love Ser.). (Illus.). 104p. (J). (gr. 8-12). lib. bdg. 33.27 *(978-0-7660-2721-3(X))* Enslow Pubs., Inc.

Mahaney, Ian F. Author, 1 vol. 2015. (Best Job Ever Ser.). (ENG.). 24p. (J). 23.60 *(978-1-4994-0106-6(X),* PowerKids Pr.) Rosen Publishing Group, Inc., The.

Malam, John. Journey of a Book, 1 vol. 2012. (Journey of A... Ser.). (ENG.). 32p. (gr. 1-3). pap. 8.29 *(978-1-4329-6607-2(3))*; lib. bdg. 27.32 *(978-1-4329-6600-3(6))* Heinemann-Raintree. (Heinemann First Library).

Marcovitz, Hal. R. L. Stine. 2005. (Who Wrote That? Ser.). (Illus.). 136p. (gr. 6-12). lib. bdg. 35.00 *(978-0-7910-8659-9(3),* Chelsea Hse.) Facts On File, Inc.

—Scott O'Dell. 2007. (Who Wrote That? Ser.). (Illus.). 128p. (gr. 6-12). lib. bdg. 35.00 *(978-0-7910-9526-3(6),* Chelsea Hse.) Facts On File, Inc.

Marcus, Leonard S., ed. Funny Business: Conversations with Writers of Comedy. 2009. (ENG., Illus.). 224p. (J). (gr. 5-18). 24.99 *(978-0-7636-3254-0(6))* Candlewick Pr.

Matthews, Sheelagh. Gordon Korman. 2012. (J). 28.55 *(978-1-61913-055-5(6))*; pap. 13.95 *(978-1-61913-597-0(3))* Weigl Pubs., Inc.

McCurry, Kristen. Pick a Picture, Write a Poem!, 1 vol. 2014. (Little Scribe Ser.). (ENG.). 32p. (gr. 1-2). lib. bdg. 27.32 *(978-1-4765-4237-9(6),* Aplus Bks.) Capstone Press of Coughlan Cos.

—Pick a Picture, Write a Story!, 1 vol. 2014. (Little Scribe Ser.). (ENG.). 32p. (gr. 1-2). lib. bdg. 27.32 *(978-1-4765-4238-6(4),* Aplus Bks.) Capstone Press of Coughlan Cos.

—Pick a Picture, Write an Opinion!, 1 vol. 2014. (Little Scribe Ser.). (ENG.). 32p. (gr. 1-2). lib. bdg. 27.32 *(978-1-4765-4240-9(6),* Aplus Bks.) Capstone Press of Coughlan Cos.

McGinty, Alice B. Cynthia Rylant. 2004. (Library of Author Biographies Ser.). 112p. (YA). (gr. 5-9). lib. bdg. 34.60 *(978-0-8239-4526-9(X))* Rosen Publishing Group, Inc., The.

—Meet Daniel Pinkwater. 2003. (About the Author Ser.). (Illus.). 24p. (J). lib. bdg. 22.60 *(978-0-8239-6406-2(X))* Rosen Publishing Group, Inc., The.

—Meet Eve Bunting. 2009. (About the Author Ser.). 24p. (gr. 4-4). 42.50 *(978-1-61511-248-7(0),* PowerKids Pr.) Rosen Publishing Group, Inc., The.

—Meet Jane Yolen. 2003. (About the Author Ser.). (Illus.). 24p. (J). lib. bdg. 22.60 *(978-0-8239-6407-9(8),* PowerKids Pr.) Rosen Publishing Group, Inc., The.

—Meet Laurence Yep. 2003. (About the Author Ser.). (Illus.). 24p. (J). lib. bdg. 22.60 *(978-0-8239-6410-9(8),* PowerKids Pr.) Rosen Publishing Group, Inc., The.

McGuinness, Denis E. & Spencer, Lauren. Writing to Describe. 2011. (Illus.). 64p. (J). 77.70 *(978-1-4488-4744-0(3),* Rosen Reference); (J). pap. 12.95 *(978-1-4488-4686-3(2),* Rosen Reference); (YA). (gr. 5-9). lib. bdg. 31.95 *(978-1-4488-4680-1(3))* Rosen Publishing Group, Inc., The.

McKay, Laura Lee. Write Fantasy Fiction in 5 Simple Steps. 2012. (Creative Writing in 5 Simple Steps Ser.). (Illus.). 48p. (J). (gr. 5-9). 25.27 *(978-0-7660-3834-9(3))* Enslow Pubs., Inc.

McLachlan, Brian & Owlkids Books Inc. Staff. Draw Out the Story: Ten Secrets to Creating Your Own Comics. 2013. (ENG., Illus.). 144p. (J). (gr. 2-7). pap. 11.95 *(978-1-77147-003-2(8))*; (gr. 3-7). 18.95 *(978-1-926973-83-8(6))* Owlkids Bks. Inc. CAN. (Owlkids). Dist: Publishers Group West (PGW).

Mead, Wendy. Judy Blume. 2014. (Spotlight on Children's Authors Ser.). 48p. (J). (gr. 4-6). lib. bdg. 29.93 *(978-1-62712-843-8(3))* Cavendish Square Publishing.

Micklos, John, Jr. Jerry Spinelli: Master Teller of Teen Tales. 2007. (Authors Teens Love Ser.). (Illus.). 104p. (J). (gr. 8-12). lib. bdg. 33.27 *(978-0-7660-2718-3(X))* Enslow Pubs., Inc.

Minden, Cecilia & Roth, Kate. How to Write a Fairy Tale. 2012. (Explorer Junior Library: Language Arts Explorer Junior Ser.). (ENG.). 24p. (gr. 1-4). lib. bdg. 25.64 *(978-1-61080-309-0(4),* 201282) Cherry Lake Publishing.

—How to Write a News Article. 2012. (Explorer Junior Library: Language Arts Explorer Junior Ser.). (ENG., Illus.). 24p. (gr. 1-4). lib. bdg. 25.64 *(978-1-61080-308-3(6),* 201276) Cherry Lake Publishing.

—How to Write a Review. 2012. (Explorer Junior Library: Language Arts Explorer Junior Ser.). (ENG.). 24p. (gr. 1-4). lib. bdg. 25.64 *(978-1-61080-310-6(8),* 201285) Cherry Lake Publishing.

—How to Write an Essay. 2012. (Explorer Junior Library: Language Arts Explorer Junior Ser.). (ENG.). 24p. (gr. 1-4). 25.64 *(978-1-61080-492-9(9),* 202102); pap. 12.79 *(978-1-61080-666-4(2),* 202276) Cherry Lake Publishing.

Minden, Cecilia, et al. How to Write a Fairy Tale. 2012. (Explorer Junior Library: Language Arts Explorer Junior Ser.). (ENG.). 24p. (gr. 1-4). pap. 12.79 *(978-1-61080-319-9(1),* 201284) Cherry Lake Publishing.

—How to Write a News Article. 2012. (Explorer Junior Library: Language Arts Explorer Junior Ser.). (ENG., Illus.). 24p. (gr. 1-4). pap. 12.79 *(978-1-61080-318-2(3),* 201278) Cherry Lake Publishing.

—How to Write a Review. 2012. (Explorer Junior Library: Language Arts Explorer Junior Ser.). (ENG.). 24p. (gr. 1-4). pap. 12.79 *(978-1-61080-320-5(5),* 201287) Cherry Lake Publishing.

Moonshower, Candie. Vivian Vande Velde: Author of Fantasy Fiction. 2009. (Authors Teens Love Ser.). (Illus.). 128p. (J). (gr. 6). lib. bdg. 33.27 *(978-0-7660-2964-4(6))* Enslow Pubs., Inc.

Mortensen, Lori. Veronica Roth: Author of the Divergent Trilogy. 2016. (Famous Female Authors Ser.). (ENG., Illus.). 32p. (gr. 3-4). lib. bdg. 27.99 *(978-1-5157-1327-2(X),* Snap Bks.) Capstone Press of Coughlan Cos.

Mullins, Matt. Scriptwriter. 2011. (21st Century Skills Library: Cool Arts Careers Ser.). (ENG.). 32p. (gr. 4-8). lib. bdg. 28.50 *(978-1-61080-135-5(0),* 201148) Cherry Lake Publishing.

Murray, Jennifer. Twas a Dark & Stormy Night... Why Writers Write. 2007. (Shockwave: Life Stories Ser.). (ENG., Illus.). 36p. (J). (gr. 3-5). 25.00 *(978-0-531-17773-0(4),* Children's Pr.) Scholastic Library Publishing.

—'Twas a Dark & Stormy Night- Why Writers Write. 2008. (Illus.). 36p. (J). pap. *(978-0-531-15543-1(9))* Children's Pr., Ltd.

Myers, Walter Dean. Just Write: Here's How! 2012. (ENG.). 176p. (YA). (gr. 9). 17.99 *(978-0-06-220389-2(4))*; pap. 7.99 *(978-0-06-220390-8(8))* HarperCollins Pubs. (Collins).

Nagle, Jeanne. What Is Nonfiction?, 1 vol. 2015. (ENG., Illus.). 32p. (J). 23.45 *(978-1-62275-656-8(8),* Britannica Educational Publishing) Rosen Publishing Group, Inc., The.

Nash, Kimberley. Creative Writing Textbook: A one-year Course. 2007. (ENG., Illus.). 188p. (YA). spiral bd., wbk. ed. 33.00 *(978-0-9792338-3-8(6))* Resurrection Resources LLC.

Nayeri, Daniel. How to Tell a Story: Read the Book, Roll the Blocks, Build Adventures! Won, Brian, illus. 2015. (ENG.). 144p. (J). (gr. 3-7). pap. 19.95 *(978-0-7611-8457-7(0))* Workman Publishing Co., Inc.

Niver, Heather Moore. Veronica Roth, 1 vol. 2015. (ENG.). 112p. (YA). 35.60 *(978-1-4777-7906-4(X),* Rosen Young Adult) Rosen Publishing Group, Inc., The.

Otfinoski, Steven. Extraordinary Short Story Writing. 2005. (F.W. Prep Ser.). (ENG., Illus.). 128p. (YA). (gr. 8-13). lib. bdg. 31.00 *(978-0-531-16760-1(7),* Watts, Franklin) Scholastic Library Publishing.

Owings, Lisa. Learn about Authors & Illustrators. 2013. (Library Smarts Ser.). (ENG., Illus.). 24p. (gr. -1-2). lib. bdg. 23.93 *(978-1-4677-1502-7(6),* Lerner Pubns.) Lerner Publishing Group.

—Rev up Your Writing in Blogs. Gallagher-Cole, Mernie, illus. 2015. (Rev up Your Writing Ser.). (ENG.). 24p. (J). (gr. 2-5). 28.50 *(978-1-63407-061-4(5),* 208896) Child's World, Inc., The.

Parker-Rock, Michelle. Bruce Coville: An Author Kids Love. 2008. (Authors Kids Love Ser.). (Illus.). 48p. (J). (gr. 3-4). lib. bdg. 25.27 *(978-0-7660-2755-8(4),* Enslow Elementary) Enslow Pubs., Inc.

—Joseph Bruchac: An Author Kids Love. 2009. (Authors Kids Love Ser.). (Illus.). 48p. (J). (gr. 3-4). lib. bdg. 25.27 *(978-0-7660-3160-9(8),* Enslow Elementary) Enslow Pubs., Inc.

Parks, Peggy J. Writer. 2003. (Illus.). 48p. (J). 26.20 *(978-0-7377-2069-3(7),* Greenhaven Pr., Inc.) Cengage Gale.

Pascal, Francine. Haciendo Novelas. Orig. Title: Playing Hockey. (SPA.). 120p. (J). 6.95 *(978-84-272-3790-2(1))* Molino, Editorial ESP. Dist: AIMS International Bks., Inc.

Pearson, Kim. You Can Be an Author, Even If You're Not A Writer: The 1-2-3 of Creating a Book. 2005. 64p. pap. 6.95 *(978-1-881849-06-3(6))* Primary Sources.

Pearson, Yvonne. Rev up Your Writing in Fictional Stories. Gallagher-Cole, Mernie, illus. 2015. (Rev up Your Writing Ser.). (ENG.). 24p. (J). (gr. 2-5). 28.50 *(978-1-63407-062-1(3),* 208897) Child's World, Inc., The.

—12 Great Tips on Writing Poetry. 2017. (Great Tips on Writing Ser.). (ENG., Illus.). 32p. (J). (gr. 3-6). 21.95 *(978-1-63235-275-0(3))* Pr. Room Editions LLC.

Pellegrino, Victor C. A Writer's Guide to Powerful Paragraphs. Magee, Christopher, illus. 2003. 187p. (YA). (gr. 7-18). pap. 18.95 *(978-0-945045-05-2(0))* Maui Arthoughts Co.

Pelleschi, Andrea. Neil & Nan Build Narrative Nonfiction. Han, Yu-Mei, illus. 2014. (Writing Builders Ser.). (ENG.). 32p. (J). (gr. 2-4). pap. 11.94 *(978-1-60357-560-7(X));* lib. bdg. 25.27 *(978-1-59953-586-9(6))* Norwood Hse. Pr.

Pelos, Rebecca & Roza, Greg. Cool Careers Without College for People Who Love Writing & Blogging. 2017. (Cool Careers Without College Ser.). 112p. (gr. 12-12). 38.45 ***(978-1-5081-7546-9(2),*** Rosen Young Adult) Rosen Publishing Group, Inc., The.

Peters, Jeffrey Edward. Write a Graphic Novel in 5 Simple Steps. 2012. (Creative Writing in 5 Simple Steps Ser.). (Illus.). 48p. (J). (gr. 5-9). 25.27 *(978-0-7660-3888-2(2))* Enslow Pubs., Inc.

Peterson-Hilleque, Victoria. Ana & Adam Build & Acrostic. Barnum-Newman, Winifred, illus. 2011. (Poetry Builders Ser.). 32p. (J). (gr. 2-4). lib. bdg. 25.27 *(978-1-59953-433-6(9))* Norwood Hse. Pr.

—J. K. Rowling: Extraordinary Author, 1 vol. 2010. (Essential Lives Set 5 Ser.). (ENG.). 112p. (J). (gr. 6-12). lib. bdg. 35.64 *(978-1-61613-517-1(4))* ABDO Publishing Co.

Pezzi, Bryan. J. K. Rowling. (J). 2012. 28.55 *(978-1-61913-057-9(2))* 2012. pap. 13.95 *(978-1-61913-596-3(5))* 2005. (Illus.). 32p. (gr. 5-7). lib. bdg. 26.00 *(978-1-59036-287-7(X))* Weigl Pubs., Inc.

Pierce, Mark & Jennings, Karen. Wright Fright: A Guide to Writing Scary Stories. 2004. 88p. pap. 10.95 *(978-0-673-58655-1(3))* Good Year Bks.

Pipe, Jim. Make a Movie! 2013. (Find Your Talent Ser.). 32p. (gr. 5-8). 28.50 *(978-1-84858-573-7(X))* Arcturus Publishing GBR. Dist: Black Rabbit Bks.

Potter, Ellen & Mazer, Anne. Spilling Ink: A Young Writer's Handbook. Phelan, Matt, illus. 2010. (ENG.). 288p. (YA). (gr. 4-9). pap., instr.'s hndbk. ed. 11.99 *(978-1-59643-628-2(X),* 9781596436282) Square Fish.

Price, Joan. J. K. Rowling. 2004. (Trailblazers of the Modern World Ser.). (Illus.). 48p. (gr. 5-12). lib. bdg. 31.00 *(978-0-8368-5499-2(3),* Gareth Stevens Secondary Library) Stevens, Gareth Publishing LLLP.

—J.K. Rowling. 2004. (Trailblazers of the Modern World Ser.). (Illus.). 48p. (gr. 5-12). pap. 14.05 *(978-0-8368-5268-4(0),* Gareth Stevens Secondary Library) Stevens, Gareth Publishing LLLP.

Reeves, Diane Lindsey & Clasen, Lindsey. Career Ideas for Kids Who Like Writing. Bond, Nancy, illus. 2nd rev. ed. 2007. (Career Ideas for Kids Ser.). 208p. (gr. 4-9). 32.95 *(978-0-8160-6555-4(1),* Ferguson Publishing Co.) Facts On File, Inc.

Richardson, Gillian. Dan Gutman. 2005. (My Favorite Writer Ser.). (Illus.). 32p. (J). (gr. 5-7). lib. bdg. 26.00 *(978-1-59036-284-6(5))* Weigl Pubs., Inc.

Rinker, Sherri Duskey. Big Machines: The Story of Virginia Lee Burton. Rocco, John, illus. 2017. (ENG.). 48p. (J). (gr. -1-3). 17.99 ***(978-0-544-71557-8(8),*** HMH Books For Young Readers) Houghton Mifflin Harcourt Publishing Co.

Ripley, Ellen. What Are Rules & Laws? 2012. (I'm an American Citizen Ser.). (ENG., Illus.). 24p. (J). (gr. 1-3). 22.60 *(978-1-4488-8585-5(X),* PowerKids Pr.) Rosen Publishing Group, Inc., The.

Rock Spring Elementary. Roadrunner Writing Rocks! 2013. 210p. pap. 15.00 *(978-0-9859367-2-3(X))* Pen & Publish Inc.

Rollins, Brenda. How to Write an Essay: 80 Interactive Screen Pages. 2011. (Writing Skills Ser.). (J). (gr. 3-8). pap. 39.95 *(978-1-55319-507-8(8),* Classroom Complete Pr.) Rainbow Horizons Publishing, Inc.

Rosen Publishing Staff. Creating Comics, 1 vol. 2015. (Creating Comics Ser.). (ENG.). 32p. (J). 165.00 *(978-1-4777-5724-6(4),* PowerKids Pr.) Rosen Publishing Group, Inc., The.

Roy, Jennifer Rozines. Sharpen Your Story or Narrative Writing Skills. 2011. (Sharpen Your Writing Skills Ser.). (Illus.). 64p. (J). (gr. 6-18). pap. 8.95 *(978-1-59845-340-9(8));* lib. bdg. 29.27 *(978-0-7660-3901-8(3))* Enslow Pubs., Inc.

—You Can Write a Story or Narrative. 2003. (You Can Write Ser.). (Illus.). 64p. (J). (gr. 6-12). lib. bdg. 23.94 *(978-0-7660-2085-6(1))* Enslow Pubs., Inc.

Roy, Jennifer Rozines & Haney, Johannah. You Can Write an Essay. 2004. (You Can Write Ser.). (Illus.). 64p. (J). lib. bdg. 23.94 *(978-0-7660-2091-7(6))* Enslow Pubs., Inc.

Roza, Greg. What Is Fiction?, 1 vol. 2015. (ENG., Illus.). 32p. (J). 23.45 *(978-1-62275-660-5(6),* Britannica Educational Publishing) Rosen Publishing Group, Inc., The.

Ruffin, Frances E. Meet Patricia MacLachlan. 2006. (About the Author Ser.). (Illus.). 24p. (YA). (gr. 2-5). lib. bdg. 22.60 *(978-1-4042-3130-6(7))* Rosen Publishing Group, Inc., The.

—Meet Sid Fleischman. 2009. (About the Author Ser.). 24p. (gr. 4-4). 42.50 *(978-1-61511-260-9(X),* PowerKids Pr.) Rosen Publishing Group, Inc., The.

Rustad, Martha E. H. How Books Are Made, 1 vol. 2013. (Wonderful World of Reading Ser.). (ENG.). 24p. (gr. k-1). lib. bdg. 26.65 *(978-1-62065-095-0(9),* Pebble Plus) Capstone Press of Coughlan Cos.

—Learning about Fiction, 1 vol. Doerrfeld, Cori, illus. 2014. (Language Arts Ser.). (ENG.). 24p. (gr. k-1). 26.65 *(978-1-4914-0578-9(3),* Pebble Plus) Capstone Press of Coughlan Cos.

—Learning about Folktales, Fables, & Fairy Tales, 1 vol. 2014. (Language Arts Ser.). (ENG.). 24p. (gr. k-1). 26.65 *(978-1-4914-0577-2(5),* Pebble Plus) Capstone Press of Coughlan Cos.

—Learning about Nonfiction, 1 vol. 2014. (Language Arts Ser.). (ENG.). 24p. (gr. k-1). 26.65 *(978-1-4914-0579-6(1),* Pebble Plus) Capstone Press of Coughlan Cos.

Salas, Laura Purdie. Picture Yourself Writing Poetry: Using Photos to Inspire Writing, 1 vol. 2011. (See It, Write It Ser.). (ENG.). 32p. (gr. 3-4). pap. 8.10 *(978-1-4296-7209-2(9));* pap. 47.70 *(978-1-4296-7210-8(2))* Capstone Press of Coughlan Cos. (Fact Finders).

Schuman, Michael & Schuman, Michael A. Write Science Fiction in 5 Simple Steps. 2012. (Creative Writing in 5 Simple Steps Ser.). (Illus.). 48p. (J). (gr. 5-9). 25.27 *(978-0-7660-3844-8(0))* Enslow Pubs., Inc.

Schwartz, Tina P. Writing & Publishing: The Ultimate Teen Guide. 2009. (It Happened to Me Ser.: 27). (ENG.). 282p. (gr. 9-18). instr.'s gde. ed. 50.00 *(978-0-8108-5647-9(6))* Scarecrow Pr., Inc.

See It, Write It. 2011. (See It, Write It Ser.). (ENG.). 32p. (gr. 3-4). pap. 190.80 *(978-1-4296-7212-2(9));* pap. 16.20 *(978-1-4296-7211-5(0));* lib. bdg. 54.64 *(978-1-4296-6128-7(3))* Capstone Press of Coughlan Cos. (Fact Finders).

Segall, Miriam. Career Building Through Fan Fiction Writing: New Work Based on Favorite Fiction. 2009. (Digital Career Building Ser.). 64p. (gr. 6-6). 58.50 *(978-1-61512-166-3(8))* Rosen Publishing Group, Inc., The.

Senker, Cath. J. K. Rowling: Creator of Harry Potter. 2011. (Famous Lives Ser.). (Illus.). 32p. (YA). (gr. 3-6). lib. bdg. 26.50 *(978-1-4488-3288-0(8))* Rosen Publishing Group, Inc., The.

Shapiro, Marc. J. K. Rowling: The Wizard Behind Harry Potter. 4th ed. 2007. (ENG., Illus.). 288p. pap. 20.99 *(978-0-312-37697-0(9),* 9780312376970, St. Martin's Griffin) St. Martin's Pr.

—Stephenie Meyer: The Unauthorized Biography of the Creator of the Twilight Saga. 2010. (ENG., Illus.). 224p. pap. 18.99 *(978-0-312-63829-0(9),* 9780312638290, St. Martin's Griffin) St. Martin's Pr.

Shaskan, Trisha Speed. Art Panels, BAM! Speech Bubbles, POW! Writing Your Own Graphic Novel, 1 vol. Shaskan, Stephen, illus. 2010. (Writer's Toolbox Ser.). (ENG.). 32p. (gr. 2-4). pap. 8.95 *(978-1-4048-6393-4(1))* Picture Window Bks.

Shawntel, Ashley. The Heart's Flames. 2005. (Fresh Voices Ser.). (ENG.). 163p. (J). (gr. 7-17). pap. 5.95 *(978-1-932802-99-3(1),* Holy Macro! Bks.) Tickling Keys, Inc.

Sheen, Barbara. Stephenie Meyer: Twilight Saga Author. 2010. (Innovators Ser.). (ENG.). 48p. (YA). (gr. 4-7). 29.95 *(978-0-7377-5066-9(9))* Cengage Gale.

Shepherd, Jodie. Maurice Sendak: King of the Wild Things. 2017. (Rookie Biographies(tm) Ser.). (ENG., Illus.). 32p. (J). lib. bdg. 25.00 *(978-0-531-22291-1(8),* Children's Pr.) Scholastic Library Publishing.

Sickels, Amy. Richard Peck. 2009. (Who Wrote That? Ser.). (Illus.). 128p. (gr. 6-12). 35.00 *(978-0-7910-9530-0(4),* Chelsea Hse.) Facts On File, Inc.

Silverstein, Shel. Shel Silverstein Pop-up Treasury. Silverstein, Shel, illus. 2008. (Illus.). 16p. (J). 29.99 *(978-0-06-147269-5(7))* HarperCollins Pubs.

Simons, Lisa M. Bolt. Rev up Your Writing in Letters & E-Mails. Gallagher-Cole, Mernie, illus. 2015. (Rev up Your Writing Ser.). (ENG.). 24p. (J). (gr. 2-5). 28.50 *(978-1-63407-064-5(X),* 208899) Child's World, Inc., The.

—Rev up Your Writing in Opinion Pieces. Gallagher-Cole, Mernie, illus. 2015. (Rev up Your Writing Ser.). (ENG.). 24p. (J). (gr. 2-5). 28.50 *(978-1-63407-066-9(6),* 208901) Child's World, Inc., The.

Slade, Suzanne. A Bill's Journey into Law, 1 vol. Trimmer, Tony, illus. 2011. (Follow It! Ser.). (ENG.). 24p. (gr. 1-3). pap. 7.49 *(978-1-4048-7027-7(X))* Picture Window Bks.

Smith, Paula. Understanding Metaphors. 2015. (Figuratively Speaking Ser.). (ENG., Illus.). 32p. (J). *(978-0-7787-1776-8(3))* Crabtree Publishing Co.

—Understanding Personification. 2015. (Figuratively Speaking Ser.). (ENG., Illus.). 32p. (J). *(978-0-7787-1777-5(1))* Crabtree Publishing Co.

Snider, Brandon T. Write It Out! Hundreds of Writing Prompts to Inspire Creative Thinking. 2016. (ENG.). 248p. (J). (gr. 3). pap. 14.95 *(978-1-4549-1935-3(3))* Sterling Publishing Co., Inc.

Sommers, Michael A. Avi. (Library of Author Biographies Ser.). 112p. (gr. 5-8). 2009. 63.90 *(978-1-60853-527-9(4),* Rosen Reference) 2004. (YA). lib. bdg. 34.60 *(978-0-8239-4522-1(7))* Rosen Publishing Group, Inc., The.

Sonnebom, Liz. Frequently Asked Questions about Plagiarism. 2011. (FAQ: Teen Life Ser.). (ENG.). 64p. (YA). lib. bdg. 31.95 *(978-1-4488-1330-8(1))* Rosen Publishing Group, Inc., The.

Spine Shivers, 4 vols. 2015. (Spine Shivers Ser.). (ENG.). 128p. (gr. 3-4). 106.60 *(978-1-4965-1994-8(9))* Stone Arch Bks.

St. John, Amanda. Bridget & Bo Build a Blog. McDee, Katie, illus. 2012. (Writing Builders Ser.). 32p. (J). (gr. 2-4). lib. bdg. 25.27 *(978-1-59953-507-4(6))* Norwood Hse. Pr.

—Evan & Erin Build an Essay. Rooney, Ronnie, illus. 2012. (Writing Builders Ser.). 32p. (J). (gr. 2-4). lib. bdg. 25.27 *(978-1-59953-508-1(4))* Norwood Hse. Pr.

Stephenie Meyer. 2010. (Who Wrote That? Ser.). (Illus.). 128p. (gr. 6-12). 35.00 *(978-1-60413-693-7(6),* Chelsea Hse.) Facts On File, Inc.

StJohn, Amanda. Bridget & Bo Build a Blog. McDee, Katie, illus. 2012. (Writing Builders Ser.). 32p. (J). (gr. 2-4). pap. 11.94 *(978-1-60357-387-0(9))* Norwood Hse. Pr.

—Evan & Erin Build an Essay. Rooney, Ronnie, illus. 2012. (Writing Builders Ser.). 32p. (J). (gr. 2-4). pap. 11.94 *(978-1-60357-388-7(7))* Norwood Hse. Pr.

Storm, Wilda. Write up A Storm! ¿ Practice for Proficiency: Student Handbook 3rd Grade. 2007. ring bd. *(978-0-9772935-8-2(0))* DoveTail Hse., Inc.

—Write up A Storm! ¿ Practice for Proficiency: Student Handbook 4th Grade. 2007. ring bd. *(978-0-9772935-9-9(9))* DoveTail Hse., Inc.

—Write up A Storm! ¿ Writing Tools: A Student Guide ¿ Grade 2-3. 2007. ring bd. *(978-0-9772935-5-1(6))* DoveTail Hse., Inc.

—Write up A Storm! Take Rewarding Revisions by Storm. 2007. ring bd. *(978-0-9772935-2-0(1))* DoveTail Hse., Inc.

Tait, Leia. Avi. 2006. (My Favorite Writer Ser.). (Illus.). 32p. (J). (gr. 3-7). pap. 9.95 *(978-1-59036-479-6(1));* lib. bdg. 26.00 *(978-1-59036-478-9(3))* Weigl Pubs., Inc.

Think Aloud Trade Book Package. 2003. 165.50 *(978-0-673-75203-1(8))* Modern Curriculum Pr.

Thomas, Marian. Adventure Writer. (J). (gr. 4-6). pap. *(978-1-875739-93-6(9))* Wizard Bks.

—Comedy Writer. (Illus.). 48p. (J). (gr. 3-6). pap. *(978-1-875739-84-4(X))* Wizard Bks.

—Fantasy Writer. (Illus.). (J). (gr. 3-6). pap. *(978-1-876367-11-4(3))* Wizard Bks.

—Mystery Writer. (Illus.). 48p. (J). (gr. 4-6). pap. *(978-1-876367-00-8(8))* Wizard Bks.

Thompson, Kristin & Grigsby, Ann, creators. Creating a Legacy: Leave More Than Money. 2003. 20p. per. 6.00 *(978-0-9745923-0-5(7))* Editorial Resources, Inc.

Thomson, Ruth. Adventure Stories: Writing Activities to Brong Out Your Senses of Adventure! 2013. (Illus.). 32p. (J). lib. bdg. 28.50 *(978-1-59771-405-1(4))* Sea-To-Sea Pubns.

—Fairy Tales: Writing Activities with Your Favorite Fairy Tale Characters. 2013. (Illus.). 32p. (J). lib. bdg. 28.50 *(978-1-59771-406-8(2))* Sea-To-Sea Pubns.

Today's Writers & Their Works. 2013. (YA). (gr. 7-12). 213.95 *(978-1-62712-150-7(1))* Cavendish Square Publishing.

Todd, Anne M. & Bankston, John. Jacqueline Wilson. 2011. (Who Wrote That? Ser.). (Illus.). 128p. (gr. 6-12). 35.00 *(978-1-60413-773-6(8),* Chelsea Hse.) Facts On File, Inc.

Tomljanovic, Tatiana. Cornelia Funke. 2006. (My Favorite Writer Ser.). (Illus.). 32p. (J). (gr. 3-7). lib. bdg. 26.00 *(978-1-59036-480-2(5))* Weigl Pubs., Inc.

—Cornelia Funke: My Favorite Writer. 2007. (My Favorite Writer Ser.). (Illus.). 32p. (J). (gr. 3-7). per. 9.95 *(978-1-59036-481-9(3))* Weigl Pubs., Inc.

Townsend, Beth. Publishing, 1 vol. 2011. (Inside the Industry Ser.). (ENG., Illus.). 112p. (J). (gr. 6-12). lib. bdg. 35.64 *(978-1-61714-803-3(2),* Essential Library) ABDO Publishing Co.

Tracy, Kathleen. John Steinbeck. 2004. (Classic Storytellers Ser.). (Illus.). 48p. (J). (gr. 4-8). lib. bdg. 29.95 *(978-1-58415-271-2(0))* Mitchell Lane Pubs., Inc.

—Matt Christopher. 2008. (Classic Storytellers Ser.). (Illus.). 48p. (J). (gr. 4-7). lib. bdg. 29.95 *(978-1-58415-535-5(3))* Mitchell Lane Pubs., Inc.

Tucker, Shelley. Painting the Sky. 2nd ed. 2006. 160p. pap. 15.95 *(978-1-59647-012-5(7))* Good Year Bks.

Turrell, Linda. Everyday Writing - How to Master Basic Writing Skills Student Activities Book. Matthews, Douglas L., ed. 2003. (Illus.). stu. ed., wbk. ed. *(978-1-931680-83-7(3),* Expert Systems for Teachers) Teaching Point, Inc.

Vankyan, Arpine & Wallace, Dejuanna. From the Inside Out. 2004. (ENG.). 80p. (YA). per. *(978-0-595-33149-9(1))* iUniverse, Inc.

Ward, S. Meet A. A. Milne. 2009. (About the Author Ser.). 24p. (gr. 4-4). 42.50 *(978-1-61511-243-2(X),* PowerKids Pr.) Rosen Publishing Group, Inc., The.

Waxman, Laura Hamilton. Dr. Seuss. 2010. (History Maker Biographies Ser.). (ENG.). 48p. (gr. 3-6). lib. bdg. 27.93 *(978-0-7613-5206-8(6),* Lerner Pubns.) Lerner Publishing Group.

Webster, Christine. Jeff Kinney. 2012. (J). *(978-1-61913-058-6(0));* pap. *(978-1-61913-598-7(1))* Weigl Pubs., Inc.

—Sandra Cisneros: My Favorite Writer. 2008. (J). 29.05 *(978-1-59036-933-3(5))* Weigl Pubs., Inc.

Wheeler, Jill C. Alvin Schwartz, 1 vol. 2014. (Children's Authors Set 8 Ser.). (ENG.). 24p. (gr. 3-6). 25.65 *(978-1-62403-670-5(8))* ABDO Publishing Co.

—Avi, 1 vol. 2009. (Children's Authors Set 5 Ser.). (ENG.). 24p. (J). (gr. 2-5). 25.65 *(978-1-60453-075-9(8))* ABDO Publishing Co.

—E. B. White, 1 vol. 2013. (Children's Authors Set 7 Ser.). (ENG.). 24p. (J). (gr. 3-6). lib. bdg. 25.65 *(978-1-61783-579-7(X),* Checkerboard Library) ABDO Publishing Co.

—Gertrude Chandler Warner, 1 vol. 2005. (Children's Authors Set 3 Ser.). (ENG.). 24p. (gr. k-6). 25.65 *(978-1-59197-609-7(X),* Checkerboard Library) ABDO Publishing Co.

—Judy Blume, 1 vol. 2005. (Children's Authors Set 3 Ser.). (ENG., Illus.). 24p. (J). (gr. 2-5). 25.65 *(978-1-59197-604-2(9))* ABDO Publishing Co.

—Lemony Snicket, 1 vol. 2007. (Children's Authors Set 4 Ser.). (ENG., Illus.). 24p. (YA). (gr. 2-5). 25.65 *(978-1-59679-767-3(3))* ABDO Publishing Co.

—Mercer Mayer, 1 vol. 2005. (Children's Authors Set 3 Ser.). (ENG., Illus.). 24p. (YA). (gr. 2-5). 25.65 *(978-1-59197-606-6(5))* ABDO Publishing Co.

—Norman Bridwell, 1 vol. 2005. (Children's Authors Set 3 Ser.). (ENG., Illus.). 24p. (J). (gr. 2-5). 25.65 *(978-1-59197-605-9(7))* ABDO Publishing Co.

—Yuyi Morales, 1 vol. 2013. (Children's Authors Set 7 Ser.). (ENG.). 24p. (J). (gr. 3-6). lib. bdg. 25.65 *(978-1-61783-576-6(5),* Checkerboard Library) ABDO Publishing Co.

Williams, Rozanne Lanczak. This Is My Story. Maio, Barbara & Faulkner, Stacey, eds. Burris, Priscilla, illus. 2006. (J). per. 6.99 *(978-1-59198-331-6(2))* Creative Teaching Pr., Inc.

—Two Stories, Two Friends. Maio, Barbara, ed. Allen, Joy, illus. 2006. (J). per. 8.99 *(978-1-59198-343-9(6))* Creative Teaching Pr., Inc.

—When You Go Walking. Maio, Barbara, ed. Briles, Patty, illus. 2006. (J). per. 8.99 *(978-1-59198-345-3(2))* Creative Teaching Pr., Inc.

—Writing about Books. Maio, Barbara & Faulkner, Stacey, eds. Schneider, Christine, illus. 2006. (J). per. 6.99 *(978-1-59198-340-8(1))* Creative Teaching Pr., Inc.

—Writing Dino-Mite Poems. Adnet, Bernard, illus. 2008. (Learn to Write Ser.). 8p. (J). (gr. -1-3). pap. 6.99 *(978-1-59198-336-1(3))* Creative Teaching Pr., Inc.

Willis, Meredith Sue. Blazing Pencils. 2nd ed. 2013. 126p. pap. 14.95 *(978-1-932727-14-2(0))* Montemayor Pr.

Wilson, Antoine. S. E. Hinton. 2009. (Library of Author Biographies Ser.). 112p. (gr. 5-8). 63.90 *(978-1-60853-553-8(3),* Rosen Reference) Rosen Publishing Group, Inc., The.

Write Right! 2013. (Write Right! Ser.). 24p. (J). (gr. 2-5). 135.60 *(978-1-4339-9676-4(6));* pap. 293.40 *(978-1-4339-9762-4(2));* pap. 48.90 *(978-1-4339-9761-7(4))* Stevens, Gareth Publishing LLLP.

Writing. 2004. (Practice Makes Perfect Ser.). 24p. (J). (gr. k-2). 4.99 *(978-1-85997-980-8(7))* Byeway Bks.

Writing in the Ancient World. (Illus.). (J). (gr. 3-6). 103.50 *(978-0-8239-7291-3(7),* Reading Power) Rosen Publishing Group, Inc., The.

Yates, Irene. How to Be a Wizard at Writing Stories. 48p. (J). (gr. 3-6). pap. *(978-1-875739-67-7(X))* Wizard Bks.

Yomtov, Nel. How to Write a Comic Book. Petelinsek, Kathleen, illus. 2013. (Explorer Junior Library: How to Write Ser.). (ENG.). 24p. (J). (gr. 1-4). pap. 12.79 *(978-1-62431-319-6(1),* 203074) Cherry Lake Publishing.

—How to Write a Fractured Fairy Tale. Petelinsek, Kathleen, illus. 2013. (Explorer Junior Library: How to Write Ser.). (ENG.). 24p. (J). (gr. 1-4). 25.64 *(978-1-62431-186-4(5),* 203068); pap. 12.79 *(978-1-62431-318-9(3),* 203070) Cherry Lake Publishing.

—How to Write a Lab Report. Petelinsek, Kathleen, illus. 2013. (Explorer Junior Library: How to Write Ser.). (ENG.). 24p. (J). (gr. 1-4). 25.64 *(978-1-62431-185-7(7),* 203064); pap. 12.79 *(978-1-62431-317-2(5),* 203066) Cherry Lake Publishing.

—How to Write a Memoir. Petelinsek, Kathleen, illus. 2013. (Explorer Junior Library: How to Write Ser.). (ENG.). 24p. (J). (gr. 1-4). 25.64 *(978-1-62431-188-8(1),* 203076); pap. 12.79 *(978-1-62431-320-2(5),* 203078) Cherry Lake Publishing.

Yomtov, Nelson. How to Write a Comic Book. Petelinsek, Kathleen, illus. 2013. (Explorer Junior Library: How to Write Ser.). (ENG.). 24p. (J). (gr. 1-4). lib. bdg. 25.64 *(978-1-62431-187-1(3),* 203072) Cherry Lake Publishing.

Young, Judy. R Is for Rhyme: A Poetry Alphabet. Juhasz, Victor, illus. rev. ed. 2006. (Art & Culture Ser.). (ENG.). 40p. (J). (gr. -1-3). 17.95 *(978-1-58536-240-0(9))* Sleeping Bear Pr.

Zee, Amy Van. Rev up Your Writing in Procedural Texts. Gallagher-Cole, Mernie, illus. 2015. (Rev up Your Writing Ser.). (ENG.). 24p. (J). (gr. 2-5). 28.50 *(978-1-63407-067-6(4),* 208902) Child's World, Inc., The.

AUTHORSHIP—FICTION

Almond, David. The Savage. McKean, Dave, illus. 2008. (ENG.). 80p. (J). (gr. 7). 17.99 *(978-0-7636-3932-7(X))* Candlewick Pr.

Amato, Mary. Please Write in This Book. Brace, Eric, illus. (ENG.). (J). (gr. 4-7). 2008. 97p. pap. 7.99 *(978-0-8234-2138-1(4))* 2006. 112p. 16.95 *(978-0-8234-1932-6(0))* Holiday Hse., Inc.

Auch, Mary Jane. The Plot Chickens. Auch, Mary Jane & Auch, Herm, illus. (ENG.). 32p. (J). (gr. -1-3). 2010. pap. 7.99 *(978-0-8234-2307-1(7))* 2009. 17.95 *(978-0-8234-2087-2(6))* Holiday Hse., Inc.

Auch, Mary Jane & Auch, Herm. The Buk Buk Buk Festival. 2015. (ENG., Illus.). 32p. (J). (gr. -1-3). 16.95 *(978-0-8234-3201-1(7))* Holiday Hse., Inc.

Avi. A Beginning, a Muddle, & an End: The Right Way to Write Writing. Tusa, Tricia, illus. 2008. (ENG.). 176p. (J). (gr. 2-5). 14.95 *(978-0-15-205555-4(X))* Houghton Mifflin Harcourt Publishing Co.

Banks, Angelica. Finding Serendipity. Lewis, Stevie, illus. 2015. (Tuesday Mcgillycuddy Adventures Ser.). (ENG.). 288p. (J). (gr. 3-7). 16.99 *(978-1-62779-154-0(X),* 9781627791540, Holt, Henry & Co. Bks. For Young Readers) Holt, Henry & Co.

—Finding Serendipity. Lewis, Stevie, illus. 2016. (Tuesday Mcgillycuddy Adventures Ser.). (ENG.). 304p. (J). pap. 7.99 *(978-1-250-07337-2(5),* 9781250073372) Square Fish.

Barnett, Mac. Chloe & the Lion. Rex, Adam, illus. 2012. (ENG.). 48p. (J). (gr. -1-k). 16.99 *(978-1-4231-1334-8(9))* Hyperion Pr.

Bateson, Catherine. Magenta Mcphee. 2010. (ENG.). 176p. (J). (gr. 3-7). pap. 16.95 *(978-0-8234-2253-1(4))* Holiday Hse., Inc.

Bick, Ilsa J. White Space, Bk. 1. 2015. (Dark Passages Ser.: Bk. 1). (ENG.). 560p. (gr. 9). pap. 9.99 *(978-1-60684-565-3(9),* Carolrhoda Lab™) Lerner Publishing Group.

Birney, Betty G. Imagination According to Humphrey. 2015. (Humphrey Ser.: 11). (ENG.). 128p. (J). (gr. 2-4). 15.99 *(978-0-399-25797-1(7),* G.P. Putnam's Sons Books for Young Readers) Penguin Young Readers Group.

Bloom, M. Beth. Don't Ever Change. 2015. (ENG.). 368p. (YA). (gr. 9). 17.99 *(978-0-06-203688-9(2),* HarperTeen) HarperCollins Pubs.

Borden, Louise & Gustavson, Adam. The Day Eddie Met the Author. 2004. (ENG., Illus.). 44p. (J). (gr. 2-5). 7.99 *(978-0-689-86720-0(4),* McElderry, Margaret K. Bks.) McElderry, Margaret K. Bks.

Bosch, Pseudonymous. Write This Book: A Do-It-Yourself Mystery. (Secret Ser.). (ENG., Illus.). (J). (gr. 3-7). 2014. 304p. pap. 8.99 *(978-0-316-20780-5(2))* 2013. 288p. 16.99 *(978-0-316-20781-2(0))* Little, Brown Bks. for Young Readers.

Bruel, Nick. Bad Kitty Drawn to Trouble. 2014. (Bad Kitty Ser.). (ENG., Illus.). 128p. (J). (gr. 2-5). 13.99 *(978-1-59643-671-8(9),* 9781596436718) Roaring Brook Pr.

Bulion, Leslie. Uncharted Waters, 1 vol. (ENG.). 192p. (J). (gr. 3-7). 2009. pap. 7.95 *(978-1-56145-485-3(0))* 2006. 14.95 *(978-1-56145-365-8(X))* Peachtree Pubs.

Bullard, Lisa. Nina & Nolan Build a Nonsense Poem. Girourard, Patrick, illus. 2011. (Poetry Builders Ser.). 32p. (J). (gr. 2-4). lib. bdg. 25.27 *(978-1-59953-437-4(1))* Norwood Hse. Pr.

Bushnell, Candace. The Carrie Diaries. (Carrie Diaries: 1). (ENG.). (YA). (gr. 9). 2011. 416p. pap. 9.99 *(978-0-06-172892-1(6))* 2010. 400p. 18.99 *(978-0-06-172891-4(8))* 2012. 416p. pap. 10.99 *(978-0-06-223684-5(9))* HarperCollins Pubs.

Butler, Dori Hillestad. Trading Places with Tank Talbott. 2003. (ENG.). 144p. (J). (gr. 3-7). 15.99 *(978-0-8075-1708-6(9))* Whitman, Albert & Co.

Cabot, Meg. Forever Princess, Vol. X. 2009. (Princess Diaries: 10). (ENG.). 416p. (YA). (gr. 8). pap. 9.99 *(978-0-06-123294-7(7),* HarperTeen) HarperCollins Pubs.

Capucilli, Alyssa Satin. Tulip & Rex Write a Story. Massini, Sarah, illus. 2015. (ENG.). 32p. (J). (gr. -1-3). 17.99 *(978-0-06-209416-2(5))* HarperCollins Pubs.

Carlson, Nancy. Henry's Amazing Imagination. 2010. (ENG.). 32p. (J). (gr. -1-1). pap. 6.99 *(978-0-14-241605-1(3),* Puffin Books) Penguin Young Readers Group.

Chambers, Aidan. Breaktime. 2008. (ENG.). 192p. (YA). (gr. 9-17). pap. 9.95 *(978-0-8109-7262-9(X),* Amulet Bks.) Abrams, Inc.

Child, Lauren. Clarice Bean Spells Trouble. Child, Lauren, illus. 2006. (Clarice Bean Ser.). (Illus.). 189p. (J). (gr. 3-6). 13.65 *(978-0-7569-7919-5(6))* Perfection Learning Corp.

—Spells Trouble. Child, Lauren, illus. 2006. (Clarice Bean Ser.). (ENG., Illus.). 192p. (J). (gr. 3-7). pap. 6.99 *(978-0-7636-2903-8(0))* Candlewick Pr.

Clements, Andrew. Lunch Money. Selznick, Brian, illus. 2007. (ENG.). 240p. (J). (gr. 3-7). pap. 7.99 *(978-0-689-86685-2(2),* Atheneum Bks. for Young Readers) Simon & Schuster Children's Publishing.

—Lunch Money. 2007. 17.20 *(978-1-4177-8116-4(5),* Turtleback) Turtleback Bks.

—The School Story. unabr. ed. 2004. (Middle Grade Cassette Librariestm Ser.). 224p. (J). (gr. 3-7). pap. 29.00 incl. audio *(978-0-8072-1000-0(5),* S YA 352 SP, Listening Library) Random Hse. Audio Publishing Group.

Coakley, Lena. Worlds of Ink & Shadow. 2016. (ENG.). 352p. (YA). (gr. 8-17). 17.95 *(978-1-4197-1034-6(6),* Amulet Bks.) Abrams, Inc.

Cofer, Judith Ortiz. The Poet Upstairs. Ortiz, Oscar, illus. 2012. (J). (gr. 5-9). 16.95 *(978-1-55885-704-9(4),* Piñata Books) Arte Publico Pr.

—La Poeta Del Piso de Arriba. Baeza Ventura, Gabriela, tr. from ENG. Ortiz, Oscar, illus. 2014. (SPA.). (J). 17.95 *(978-1-55885-788-9(5),* Piñata Books) Arte Publico Pr.

Cooney, Caroline B. Janie Face to Face. 2013. (ENG.). 352p. (YA). (gr. 7). 17.99 *(978-0-385-74206-1(1),* Delacorte Bks. for Young Readers) Random Hse. Children's Bks.

Cornwell, Autumn. Carpe Diem. 2009. (ENG.). 368p. (YA). (gr. 7-12). pap. 12.99 *(978-0-312-56129-1(6),* 9780312561291) Square Fish.

Crimi, Carolyn. Henry & the Crazed Chicken Pirates. Manders, John, illus. 2010. (ENG.). 40p. (J). (gr. -1-3). pap. 7.99 *(978-0-7636-4999-9(6))* Candlewick Pr.

Davis, Katie. The Curse of Addy Mcmahon. 2008. (ENG., Illus.). 288p. (J). (gr. 5-9). 16.99 *(978-0-06-128711-4(3),* Greenwillow Bks.) HarperCollins Pubs.

—The Curse of Addy McMahon. 2008. (Illus.). 288p. (J). (gr. 5-9). lib. bdg. 17.89 *(978-0-06-128712-1(1),* Greenwillow Bks.) HarperCollins Pubs.

Davis, Terry. If Rock & Roll Were a Machine. 2015. (ENG., Illus.). 256p. (YA). (gr. 7). pap. 10.99 *(978-1-4814-5632-6(6),* Simon & Schuster Bks. For Young Readers) Simon & Schuster Bks. For Young Readers.

De felice, Cynthia. The Strange Night Writing of Jessamine Colter. 2008. (ENG.). 56p. (J). (gr. 5-9). pap. 5.99 *(978-1-4169-7908-1(5),* Atheneum Bks. for Young Readers) Simon & Schuster Children's Publishing.

Dee, Barbara. Just Another Day in My Insanely Real Life. 2007. (Mix Ser.). (ENG.). 256p. (J). (gr. 4-8). pap. 7.99 *(978-1-4169-4739-4(6),* Aladdin) Simon & Schuster Children's Publishing.

DiSalvo-Ryan, DyAnne. The Sloppy Copy Slipup. 2005. (ENG., Illus.). 128p. (J). (gr. 2-6). 16.95 *(978-0-8234-1947-0(9))* Holiday Hse., Inc.

d'Lacey, Chris. Dark Fire. 2010. (Last Dragon Chronicles Ser.: 5). (ENG.). 576p. (J). (gr. 3-7). 17.99 *(978-0-545-10272-8(3),* Orchard Bks.) Scholastic, Inc.

—Fire Star. 2008. (Last Dragon Chronicles Ser.: 3). (ENG.). 560p. (J). (gr. 3-7). 8.99 *(978-0-439-90185-7(5),* Orchard Bks.) Scholastic, Inc.

—The Fire Within. 2007. (Last Dragon Chronicles Ser.: 1). (ENG.). 352p. (J). (gr. 3-7). pap. 8.99 *(978-0-439-67244-3(9),* Orchard Bks.) Scholastic, Inc.

—Icefire. d'Lacey, Chris, illus. 2007. (Last Dragon Chronicles Ser.: 2). (Illus.). lib. bdg. 19.65 *(978-1-4177-9138-5(1),* Turtleback) Turtleback Bks.

Dubose, Sarah. Uncharted Waters. 2013. 440p. pap. *(978-1-4596-6282-7(2))* ReadHowYouWant.com, Ltd.

Durant, Alan. That's Not Right! McEwen, Katharine, illus. 2004. (Flying Foxes Ser.). 48p. (J). (gr. k-2). 13.10 *(978-0-7569-3057-8(X))* Perfection Learning Corp.

—That's Not Right. McEwen, Katharine, illus. 2003. (Flying Foxes Ser.). (ENG.). 48p. (J). *(978-0-7787-1532-0(9));* lib. bdg. *(978-0-7787-1486-6(1))* Crabtree Publishing Co.

Echols, Jennifer. Love Story. 2011. (ENG.). 256p. pap. 11.00 *(978-1-4391-7832-4(1),* MTV Bks.) MTV Books.

Edge, Christopher. The Black Crow Conspiracy. 2015. (Penelope Tredwell Mysteries Ser.: 3). (ENG.). 272p. (J). (gr. 3-7). 16.99 *(978-0-8075-0780-3(6))* Whitman, Albert & Co.

—Shadows of the Silver Screen. 2014. (Penelope Tredwell Mysteries Ser.: 2). (ENG.). 256p. (J). (gr. 3-7). 16.99 *(978-0-8075-7319-8(1))* Whitman, Albert & Co.

—Twelve Minutes to Midnight. 2014. (Penelope Tredwell Mysteries Ser.: Book 1). (ENG.). 256p. (J). (gr. 3-7). 16.99 *(978-0-8075-8133-9(X))* Whitman, Albert & Co.

Farley, Brianne. Ike's Incredible Ink. Farley, Brianne, illus. 2013. (ENG., Illus.). 32p. (J). (gr. -1-3). 16.99 *(978-0-7636-6296-7(8))* Candlewick Pr.

Freedman, Deborah. By Mouse & Frog. Freedman, Deborah, illus. 2015. (ENG., Illus.). 32p. (J). (gr. -1-k). 16.99 *(978-0-670-78490-5(7),* Viking Books for Young Readers) Penguin Young Readers Group.

Funke, Cornelia. Inkheart. Bell, Anthea, tr. 2005. (Inkheart Trilogy Ser.: Bk. 1).Tr. of Tintenherz. (ENG., Illus.). 576p. (J). (gr. 3-7). pap. 10.99 *(978-0-439-70910-1(5))* Scholastic, Inc.

—Inkheart Trilogy Boxed Set: Inkheart, Inkspell, Inkdeath. 2003. (Inkheart Trilogy: Bks. 1-3). 544p. (J). 60.00 *(978-0-439-61671-3(9),* Chicken Hse., The) Scholastic, Inc.

—Inkspell. Bell, Anthea, tr. from GER. 2007. (Illus.). 653p. (gr. 3-7). 21.00 *(978-0-7569-7917-1(X))* Perfection Learning Corp.

—Inkspell. Bell, Anthea, tr. 2007. (Inkheart Trilogy Ser.: Bk. 2). (ENG., Illus.). 672p. (J). (gr. 3-7). pap. 10.99 *(978-0-439-55401-5(2),* Chicken Hse., The) Scholastic, Inc.

—Inkspell. 2007. (Inkheart Trilogy Ser.: 2). lib. bdg. 22.10 *(978-1-4177-7471-5(1),* Turtleback) Turtleback Bks.

Grindley, Sally. Bravo, Max! Ross, Tony, illus. 2007. (ENG.). 160p. (J). (gr. 1-4). pap. 8.99 *(978-1-4169-3645-9(9),* Simon & Schuster/Paula Wiseman Bks.) Simon & Schuster/Paula Wiseman Bks.

Grindley, Sally & Lucas, D J. Dear Max. Ross, Tony, illus. 2007. (ENG.). 144p. (J). (gr. 1-4). pap. 7.99 *(978-1-4169-3443-1(X),* Simon & Schuster/Paula Wiseman Bks.) Simon & Schuster/Paula Wiseman Bks.

Haddix, Margaret Peterson. Dexter the Tough. Elliott, Mark, illus. 2008. (ENG.). 144p. (J). (gr. 2-5). pap. 6.99 *(978-1-4169-1170-8(7))* 2007. 141p. pap. 7.99 *(978-0-15-377020-3(1))* 2007. (ENG.). 144p. (J). (gr. 2-5). 17.99 *(978-1-4169-1159-3(6))* Simon & Schuster Bks. For Young Readers. (Simon & Schuster Bks. For Young Readers).

Hahn, Mary Downing. Daphne's Book. 2008. (ENG., Illus.). 192p. (J). (gr. 5-7). pap. 7.99 *(978-0-547-01641-2(7))* Houghton Mifflin Harcourt Publishing Co.

Haskell, Merrie. Handbook for Dragon Slayers. 2013. (ENG.). 336p. (J). (gr. 3-7). 16.99 *(978-0-06-200816-9(1))* HarperCollins Pubs.

Haughey, Jennifer. NOT a Stupid Baby Book: Top Secret: Boys Only! 2010. (ENG.). 26p. pap. 9.25 *(978-1-4505-1212-1(7))* CreateSpace Independent Publishing Platform.

Heiden, Pete. Penelope & Pip Build a Prose Poem. Huntington, Amy, illus. 2011. (Poetry Builders Ser.). 32p. (J). (gr. 2-4). lib. bdg. 25.27 *(978-1-59953-438-1(X))* Norwood Hse. Pr.

Helgeson, Kat & Moskowitz, Hannah. Gena/Finn. 2016. (ENG., Illus.). (YA). (gr. 7-12). 17.99 *(978-1-4521-3839-8(7))* Chronicle Bks. LLC.

Hemphill, Stephanie. Hideous Love: The Story of the Girl Who Wrote Frankenstein. 2013. (ENG.). 320p. (YA). (gr. 8). 17.99 *(978-0-06-185331-9(3))* HarperCollins Pubs.

Hills, Tad. Rocket Writes a Story. Hills, Tad, illus. 2012. (ENG., Illus.). 40p. (J). (gr. -1-3). 17.99 *(978-0-375-87086-6(5),* Schwartz & Wade Bks.) Random Hse. Children's Bks.

Hinton, S. E. Taming the Star Runner. 2013. (ENG.). 192p. (YA). (gr. 7). pap. 7.99 *(978-0-385-37666-2(9),* Delacorte Pr.) Random Hse. Children's Bks.

Hobbie, Holly. Fanny & Annabelle. 2009. (Fanny Ser.: 2). (ENG., Illus.). 40p. (J). (gr. -1-3). 16.99 *(978-0-316-16688-1(X))* Little, Brown Bks. for Young Readers.

Holub, Joan. Little Red Writing. Sweet, Melissa, illus. (ENG.). 36p. (J). (gr. k-3). 2016. pap. 7.99 *(978-1-4521-5209-7(8))* 2013. 16.99 *(978-0-8118-7869-2(4))* Chronicle Bks. LLC.

Howe, James. Bud Barkin, Private Eye. Helquist, Brett, illus. (Tales from the House of Bunnicula Ser.: 5). (ENG.). (J). (gr. 2-5). 2004. 112p. pap. 5.99 *(978-0-689-86989-1(4))* 2003. 96p. 13.99 *(978-0-689-85632-7(6))* Simon & Schuster Children's Publishing. (Atheneum Bks. for Young Readers).

—Howie Monroe & the Doghouse of Doom. Helquist, Brett, illus. 2003. (Tales from the House of Bunnicula Ser.: 3). (ENG.). 112p. (J). (gr. 2-4). pap. 5.99 *(978-0-689-83952-8(9),* Atheneum Bks. for Young Readers) Simon & Schuster Children's Publishing.

—Howie Monroe & the Doghouse of Doom. 2004. (Tales from the House of Bunnicula Ser.). 85p. (J). (gr. 3-6). pap. 17.00 incl. audio *(978-1-4000-8634-4(5),* Listening Library) Random Hse. Audio Publishing Group.

—Invasion of the Mind Swappers from Asteroid 6! 2004. (Tales from the House of Bunnicula Ser.). 112p. (J). (gr. 3-6). pap. 17.00 incl. audio *(978-1-4000-8633-7(7),* Listening Library) Random Hse. Audio Publishing Group.

—Invasion of the Mind Swappers from Asteroid 6! Helquist, Brett, illus. 2003. (Tales from the House of Bunnicula Ser.). 89p. (J). (gr. 2-5). 11.65 *(978-0-7569-2814-8(1))* Perfection Learning Corp.

—Invasion of the Mind Swappers from Asteroid 6! Helquist, Brett, illus. 2003. (Tales from the House of Bunnicula Ser.: 2). (ENG.). 112p. (J). (gr. 2-5). pap. 5.99 *(978-0-689-83950-4(2),* Simon & Schuster/Paula Wiseman Bks.) Simon & Schuster/Paula Wiseman Bks.

—It Came from Beneath the Bed! 2004. (Tales from the House of Bunnicula Ser.). 112p. (J). (gr. 3-6). pap. 17.00 incl. audio *(978-1-4000-8632-0(9),* Listening Library) Random Hse. Audio Publishing Group.

—The Odorous Adventures of Stinky Dog. Helquist, Brett, illus. 2003. (Tales from the House of Bunnicula Ser.: 6). (ENG.). 112p. (J). (gr. 2-5). 13.99 *(978-0-689-85633-4(4),* Atheneum Bks. for Young Readers) Simon & Schuster Children's Publishing.

—Screaming Mummies of the Pharaoh's Tomb II. Helquist, Brett, illus. 2003. (Tales from the House of Bunnicula Ser.: 4). (ENG.). 112p. (J). (gr. 2-4). 13.99 *(978-0-689-83953-5(7),* Atheneum Bks. for Young Readers) Simon & Schuster Children's Publishing.

Jenkins, Jerry B. & Fabry, Chris. Phantom Writer. 2005. (Red Rock Mysteries Ser.: 6). (ENG.). 256p. (YA). pap. 5.99 *(978-1-4143-0145-7(6),* Tyndale Kids) Tyndale Hse. Pubs.

Jennings, Sharon. Home Free, 1 vol. 2009. (Gutsy Girl Ser.). (ENG., Illus.). 160p. (J). (gr. 4-7). pap. 8.95 *(978-1-897187-55-5(6))* Second Story Pr. CAN. Dist: Orca Bk. Pubs. USA.

Johnson, Maureen. Suite Scarlett. 2009. (ENG.). 368p. (J). (gr. 3-7). 8.99 *(978-0-545-09632-4(4))* Scholastic, Inc.

Johnson, Peter. The Amazing Adventures of John Smith, Jr. Aka Houdini. 2012. (ENG.). 176p. (J). (gr. 3-7). 16.99 *(978-0-06-198890-5(1))* HarperCollins Pubs.

—The Amazing Adventures of John Smith, Jr. AKA Houdini. 2014. (ENG.). 192p. (J). (gr. 3-7). pap. 6.99 *(978-0-06-198891-2(X))* HarperCollins Pubs.

Joyce, William. Billy's Booger. Joyce, William, illus. 2015. (ENG., Illus.). 40p. (J). (gr. -1-3). 17.99 *(978-1-4424-7351-5(7))* Simon & Schuster Children's Publishing.

Kalman, Maira. Max Makes a Million. 2017. (ENG., Illus.). 48p. (J). (gr. k-3). 18.95 ***(978-1-68137-170-2(7),*** NYR Children's Collection) New York Review of Bks., Inc., The.

Kanakia, Rahul. Enter Title Here. 2016. (ENG., Illus.). 352p. (YA). (gr. 9-17). 17.99 *(978-1-4847-2387-6(2))* Hyperion Bks. for Children.

Kanninen, Barbara. A Story with Pictures. Reed, Lynn Rowe, illus. 2007. (ENG.). 32p. (J). (gr. -1-3). 16.95 *(978-0-8234-2049-0(3))* Holiday Hse., Inc.

Kerley, Barbara. The Extraordinary Mark Twain (According to Susy) Fotheringham, Edwin, illus. 2010. (ENG.). 48p. (J). (gr. 2-5). 17.99 *(978-0-545-12508-6(1),* Scholastic Pr.) Scholastic, Inc.

—The "Extrodinary" Mark Twain (According to Susy) Fotheringham, Edwin, illus. 2010. (J). *(978-0-545-12509-3(X),* Scholastic Pr.) Scholastic, Inc.

Kimmel, Elizabeth Cody. Lily B. on the Brink of Cool. 2005. 245p. (J). (gr. 5-9). 14.65 *(978-0-7569-5653-0(6))* Perfection Learning Corp.

—Lily B. on the Brink of Love. 2005. (ENG.). 192p. (J). 15.99 *(978-0-06-075541-6(5))* HarperCollins Pubs.

Kirk, Daniel. Library Mouse, No. 1. 2007. (ENG., Illus.). 32p. (J). (gr. 1-4). 17.95 *(978-0-8109-9346-4(5),* Abrams Bks. for Young Readers) Abrams, Inc.

—Library Mouse. 2010. (ENG., Illus.). 32p. (J). (gr. 1-4). pap. 7.95 *(978-0-8109-8929-0(8))* UK Abrams Bks. for Young Readers.

—Library Mouse Bk. 2: A Friend's Tale. 2009. (ENG., Illus.). 32p. (J). (gr. 1-4). 17.95 *(978-0-8109-8927-6(1),* Abrams Bks. for Young Readers) Abrams, Inc.

—Library Mouse No. 2: A Friend's Tale. 2010. (ENG., Illus.). 32p. (J). (gr. 1-4). pap. 7.95 *(978-0-8109-8930-6(1))* UK Abrams Bks. for Young Readers.

Klise, Kate. Dying to Meet You. Klise, M. Sarah, illus. (43 Old Cemetery Road Ser.: Bk. 1). (ENG.). 160p. (J). (gr. 2-5). 2010. pap. 6.99 *(978-0-547-39848-8(4))* 2009. 16.99 *(978-0-15-205727-5(7))* Houghton Mifflin Harcourt Publishing Co.

Koertge, Ronald. Shakespeare Bats Cleanup. 2006. 116p. (gr. 7-12). 16.00 *(978-0-7569-6571-6(3))* Perfection Learning Corp.

Kroll, Steven. Patches Lost & Found, 0 vols. Gott, Barry, illus. 2005. (ENG.). 32p. (J). (gr. k-4). pap. 5.95 *(978-0-7614-5217-1(6),* 9780761452171, Amazon Children's Publishing) Amazon Publishing.

Kuipers, Alice. The Best-Ever Bookworm Book. Murguia, Bethanie Deeney, illus. 2014. (ENG.). 40p. (J). (gr. -1-3). 17.00 *(978-0-316-21200-7(8))* Little, Brown Bks. for Young Readers.

—Violet & Victor Write the Most Fabulous Fairy Tale. 2016. (ENG., Illus.). 40p. (J). (gr. -1-3). 17.00 *(978-0-316-21202-1(4))* Little Brown & Co.

Lagercrantz, Rose. When I Am Happiest. Eriksson, Eva, illus. 2015. (ENG.). 128p. (J). (gr. k-3). 16.99 *(978-1-927271-90-2(8))* Gecko Pr. NZL. Dist: Lerner Publishing Group.

Lehrhaupt, Adam. This Is a Good Story. Le Huche, Magali, illus. 2017. (ENG.). 40p. (J). (gr. k-3). 17.99 ***(978-1-4814-2935-1(3),*** Simon & Schuster/Paula Wiseman Bks.) Simon & Schuster/Paula Wiseman Bks.

Leveen, Tom. Manicpixiedreamgirl. 2014. (ENG.). 256p. (YA). (gr. 9). pap. 8.99 *(978-0-375-87021-7(0),* Ember) Random Hse. Children's Bks.

Levy, Dana Alison. This Would Make a Good Story Someday. 2017. (ENG.). 320p. (J). (gr. 4-7). 16.99 ***(978-1-101-93817-1(X));*** lib. bdg. 19.99 ***(978-1-101-93818-8(8))*** Random Hse. Children's Bks. (Delacorte Bks. for Young Readers).

Liniers. Written & Drawn by Henrietta. 2015. (ENG., Illus.). 64p. (J). (gr. k). 12.95 *(978-1-935179-90-0(X))* TOON Books / RAW Junior, LLC.

Lubar, David. Sleeping Freshmen Never Lie. 2007. (ENG.). 288p. (YA). (gr. 7-18). 10.99 *(978-0-14-240780-6(1),* Speak) Penguin Young Readers Group.

Ludwig, Trudy. Confessions of a Former Bully. Adams, Beth, illus. (ENG.). 48p. (J). 2012. (gr. 3-7). pap. 7.99 *(978-0-307-93113-9(7),* Dragonfly Bks.) 2010. (gr. 1-4). 15.99 *(978-1-58246-309-4(3),* Tricycle Pr.) Random Hse. Children's Bks.

—Confessions of a Former Bully. 2012. lib. bdg. 18.40 *(978-0-606-26382-5(9),* Turtleback) Turtleback Bks.

Mackall, Dandi Daley. Larger-Than-Life Lara. 2016. (ENG.). 176p. 14.99 *(978-1-4964-1429-8(2))* Tyndale Hse. Pubs.

MacLachlan, Patricia. Someone Like Me. Sheban, Chris, illus. 2017. (ENG.). 32p. (J). 16.99 *(978-1-62672-334-4(6),* 9781626723344) Roaring Brook Pr.

—Word after Word after Word. 2010. (ENG.). 128p. (J). (gr. 1-5). 16.99 *(978-0-06-027971-4(0),* Tegen, Katherine Bks) HarperCollins Pubs.

Manushkin, Fran. What Happens Next, Katie? Writing a Narrative with Katie Woo, 1 vol. Lyon, Tammie, illus. 2013. (Katie Woo: Star Writer Ser.). (ENG.). 32p. (J). (gr. k-2). pap. 6.95 *(978-1-4795-1924-8(3));* lib. bdg. 20.65 *(978-1-4048-8129-7(8))* Picture Window Bks.

Matson, Stacey. A Year in the Life of a Complete & Total Genius. 2015. (Arthur Bean Stories Ser.: 0). (ENG.). 272p. (J). (gr. 3-7). 15.99 *(978-1-4926-2074-7(2),* 9781492620747, Sourcebooks Jabberwocky) Sourcebooks, Inc.

McLaughlin, Tom. The Story Machine. 2015. (ENG., Illus.). 32p. (J). (gr. -1-1). 12.99 *(978-1-4088-3934-8(2),* 9781408839348, Bloomsbury USA Childrens) Bloomsbury Publishing USA.

McNamara, Margaret. A Poem in Your Pocket. Karas, G. Brian, illus. 2015. (Mr. Tiffin's Classroom Ser.). (ENG.). 40p. (J). (gr. -1-3). 16.99 *(978-0-307-97947-6(4),* Schwartz & Wade Bks.) Random Hse. Children's Bks.

Mills, Claudia. Write This Down. 2016. (ENG.). 256p. (J). 15.99 *(978-0-374-30164-4(6),* 9780374301644, Farrar, Straus & Giroux (BYR)) Farrar, Straus & Giroux.

Montgomery, L. M. Emily Climbs: Emily of New Moon Series. 2014. (Emily Ser.: 2). (ENG.). 368p. (YA). (gr. 5-12). pap. 8.99 *(978-1-4022-8915-6(4))* Sourcebooks, Inc.

—Emily's Quest. 2014. (Emily Ser.: 3). (ENG.). 256p. (YA). (gr. 5-12). pap. 8.99 *(978-1-4022-8918-7(9))* Sourcebooks, Inc.

Moritzky, Sager. The Super Bad Slime Ball from Outer Space. 2011. 28p. pap. 14.99 *(978-1-4389-8652-4(1))* AuthorHouse.

Mullarkey, Lisa & Mullarkey, John. Mary Molds a Monster, 1 vol. Bernard, Courtney, illus. 2015. (ENG.). 128p. (J). *(978-1-62402-088-9(7))* Magic Wagon.

Muntean, Michaela. Do Not Open This Book. Lemaître, Pascal, illus. 2006. (ENG.). 40p. (J). (gr. -1-3). 17.99 *(978-0-439-69839-9(1),* Scholastic Pr.) Scholastic, Inc.

Murphy, T. M. Saving Santa's Seals. Taylor, Adam, illus. 2009. (LeapKids Ser.). (ENG.). 170p. (J). (gr. 1-5). pap. 10.95 *(978-0-9815148-8-8(X))* Leapfrog Pr.

Myers, Walter Dean. Darius & Twig. 2013. 208p. (YA). (gr. 8). (ENG.). 17.99 *(978-0-06-172823-5(3));* lib. bdg. 18.89 *(978-0-06-172824-2(1))* HarperCollins Pubs. (Amistad).

Nance, Andrew. Return to Daemon Hall: Evil Roots. Polhemus, Coleman, illus. 2011. (ENG.). 256p. (YA). (gr. 7-12). 18.99 *(978-0-8050-8748-2(6),* Holt, Henry & Co. Bks. For Young Readers) Holt, Henry & Co.

Nelson, Theresa. Ruby Electric. 2004. 264p. (J). (gr. 5-7). 13.65 *(978-0-7569-3530-6(X))* Perfection Learning Corp.

—Ruby Electric. 2004. (ENG.). 272p. (J). (gr. 5-7). reprint ed. pap. 12.99 *(978-0-689-87146-7(5),* Atheneum Bks. for Young Readers) Simon & Schuster Children's Publishing.

Nixon, Joan Lowery. If You Were a Writer. Degen, Bruce, illus. 2014. 32p. pap. 7.00 *(978-1-61003-353-4(1))* Center for the Collaborative Classroom.

O'Malley, Kevin. Once upon a Cool Motorcycle Dude. O'Malley, Kevin et al, illus. 2005. (ENG.). 32p. (J). (gr. 1-5). 16.99 *(978-0-8027-8947-1(1),* 9780802789471, Bloomsbury USA Childrens) Bloomsbury Publishing USA.

Palatini, Margie. Under a Pig Tree: A History of the Noble Fruit. Groenink, Chuck, illus. 2015. (ENG.). 40p. (J). (gr. -1-3). 16.95 *(978-1-4197-1488-7(0),* Abrams Bks. for Young Readers) Abrams, Inc.

Park, Linda Sue. Project Mulberry. 2007. 225p. (gr. 4-7). 17.00 *(978-0-7569-7921-8(8))* Perfection Learning Corp.

—Project Mulberry. 2007. (ENG.). 240p. (J). (gr. 3-7). 6.99 *(978-0-440-42163-4(2),* Yearling) Random Hse. Children's Bks.

Pett, Mark, illus. This Is My Book. 2016. (ENG.). 40p. (J). (gr. -1-2). 17.99 *(978-1-101-93790-7(4),* Knopf Bks. for Young Readers) Random Hse. Children's Bks.

Polacco, Patricia & McPike, Elizabeth. An A from Miss Keller. Polacco, Patricia, illus. 2015. (ENG., Illus.). 40p. (J). (gr. k-3). bds. 17.99 *(978-0-399-16691-4(2),* G.P. Putnam's Sons Books for Young Readers) Penguin Young Readers Group.

Russell, Ching Yeung. Tofu Quilt. (ENG.). 136p. (J). 2016. (gr. 4-7). pap. 10.95 ***(978-1-62014-354-4(2))*** 2009. (gr. 3-8). 16.95 *(978-1-60060-423-2(4))* Lee & Low Bks., Inc.

Russell, Natalie. Lost for Words, 1 vol. Russell, Natalie, illus. 2014. (ENG., Illus.). 32p. (J). (gr. -1-3). 16.95 *(978-1-56145-739-7(6))* Peachtree Pubs.

Rylant, Cynthia. Mr. Putter & Tabby Write the Book. Howard, Arthur, illus. 2005. (Mr. Putter & Tabby Ser.). (ENG.). 44p. (J). (gr. 1-4). pap. 5.99 *(978-0-15-200242-8(1))* Houghton Mifflin Harcourt Publishing Co.

—Mr. Putter & Tabby Write the Book. Howard, Arthur, illus. 2005. (Mr. Putter & Tabby Ser.). 36p. (J). (gr. 1-4). 13.60 *(978-0-7569-5446-8(0))* Perfection Learning Corp.

Salisbury, Linda G. The Mysterious Jamestown Suitcase: A Bailey Fish Adventure. Grotke, Christopher A., illus. 2006. (Bailey Fish Adventures Ser.). 191p. (J). (gr. 3-7). per. 8.95 *(978-1-881539-43-8(1))* Tabby Hse. Bks.

Saltzberg, Barney. Inside This Book. 2015. (ENG., Illus.). 40p. (J). (gr. -1-1). 15.95 *(978-1-4197-1487-0(2))* Abrams, Inc.

Schotter, Roni. Nothing Ever Happens on 90th Street. Brooker, Kyrsten, illus. 2014. 32p. pap. 7.00 *(978-1-61003-316-9(7))* Center for the Collaborative Classroom.

Service, Pamela F. Escape from Planet Yastol. Gorman, Mike, illus. (Way-Too-Real Aliens Ser.: 1). (ENG.). 112p. (J). (gr. 4-6). 2015. 34.65 *(978-1-4677-5960-1(0),* Lerner Digital)No. 1. 2011. 15.95 *(978-0-7613-7918-8(5),* Darby Creek)No. 1. 2011. pap. 5.95 *(978-0-7613-7921-8(5),* Darby Creek) Lerner Publishing Group.

Snyder, Zilpha Keatley. The Bronze Pen. (ENG.). 208p. (J). (gr. 3-7). 2009. pap. 5.99 *(978-1-4169-4208-5(4))* 2008. 16.99 *(978-1-4169-4201-6(7))* Simon & Schuster Children's Publishing. (Atheneum Bks. for Young Readers).

Spinelli, Eileen. The Best Story. Wilsdorf, Anne, illus. 2008. (ENG.). 32p. (J). (gr. 1-3). 17.99 *(978-0-8037-3055-7(1),* Dial Bks) Penguin Young Readers Group.

—The Best Story. 2009. (J). (gr. 1-3). 27.95 incl. audio *(978-0-8045-6980-4(0))* Spoken Arts, Inc.

Spizman, Robyn Freedman & Johnston, Mark. Secret Agent. 2006. (ENG.). 240p. (J). (gr. 4-7). pap. 11.99 *(978-1-4169-1862-2(0),* Atheneum Bks. for Young Readers) Simon & Schuster Children's Publishing.

Stead, Philip C. Ideas Are All Around. 2016. (ENG., Illus.). 48p. (J). 18.99 *(978-1-62672-181-4(5),* 9781626721814) Roaring Brook Pr.

StJohn, Amanda. Sophie & Sadie Build a Sonnet. Marten, Luanne, illus. 2011. (Poetry Builders Ser.). 32p. (J). (gr. 2-4). lib. bdg. 25.27 *(978-1-59953-440-4(1))* Norwood Hse. Pr.

The Storybook. 2004. 224p. per. 6.95 *(978-0-9703729-3-2(0))* Missing Piece Pr.

Studio Mouse Staff. Tinkerbell's Magic Story Writer. rev. ed. 2008. (ENG.). 30p. (J). 14.99 *(978-1-59069-616-3(6))* Studio Mouse LLC.

Tan, Susan. Cilla Lee-Jenkins: Future Author Extraordinaire. Wulfekotte, Dana, illus. 2017. (Cilla Lee-Jenkins Ser.). (ENG.). 256p. (J). 16.99 *(978-1-62672-551-5(9),* 9781626725515) Roaring Brook Pr.

Thomas, Laura Michelle. Polly Wants to Be a Writer - the Junior Authors Guide to Writing & Getting Published. 2013. 232p. pap. *(978-1-4602-2819-7(7))* FriesenPress.

Trooboff, Rhoda. A Book for Elie. Radjou, Anna Nazaretz, illus. 2008. (ENG.). 31p. pap. 15.00 *(978-0-9773536-1-3(3))* Univ. of Toledo Pr.

Tu, Stella. Follow your Dream: Asian American Essay. 2009. (Illus.). 58p. (YA). pap. 20.00 *(978-1-4276-4473-2(X))* Aardvark Global Publishing.

Westerfeld, Scott. Afterworlds. 2014. (ENG., Illus.). 608p. (YA). (gr. 9). 19.99 *(978-1-4814-2234-5(0),* Simon Pulse) Simon Pulse.

—Afterworlds. 2015. lib. bdg. 24.50 *(978-0-606-37860-4(X))* Turtleback Bks.

Weston, Carol. Ava & Pip. (Ava & Pip Ser.: 1). (ENG.). 224p. (J). (gr. 5-7). 2015. pap. 6.99 *(978-1-4926-0183-8(7))* 2014. 15.99 *(978-1-4022-8870-8(0),* 9781402288708) Sourcebooks, Inc. (Sourcebooks Jabberwocky).

Williams, Rozanne Lanczak. My Picture Story. Mahan, Benton, illus. 2006. (Learn to Write Ser.). 8p. (J). (gr. k-2). pap. 3.49 *(978-1-59198-281-4(2),* 6175) Creative Teaching Pr., Inc.

—My Picture Story. Maio, Barbara & Faulkner, Stacey, eds. Mahan, Benton, illus. 2006. (J). per. 6.99 (978-1-59198-332-3(0)) Creative Teaching Pr., Inc.

—Special Memories. 2006. (Learn to Write Ser.). (Illus.). 16p. (J). (gr. k-2). pap. 2.99 (978-1-59198-302-6(9), 6196) Creative Teaching Pr., Inc.

—Special Memories. Maio, Barbara, ed. Nobens, C. A., illus. 2006. (J). per. 8.99 (978-1-59198-360-6(6)) Creative Teaching Pr., Inc.

Wittlinger, Ellen. Love & Lies: Marisol's Story. (ENG.). (YA). 2009. 272p. (gr. 7). pap. 8.99 (978-1-4169-7914-2(X)) 2008. 256p. (gr. 9-18). 16.99 (978-1-4169-1623-9(7)) Simon & Schuster Bks. For Young Readers. (Simon & Schuster Bks. For Young Readers).

Wizner, Jake. Spanking Shakespeare. Ewing, Richard, illus. 2008. (ENG.). 304p. (YA). (gr. 9). pap. 8.99 (978-0-375-85594-8(7), Ember) Random Hse. Children's Bks.

—Spanking Shakespeare. 2007. (YA). (978-0-375-84086-9(9)) Random Hse. Children's Bks.

Yeh, Kat. The Way to Bea. 2017. (ENG.). 352p. (J). (gr. 3-7). 16.99 **(978-0-316-23667-6(5))** Little, Brown Bks. for Young Readers.

Young, Judy. A Pet for Miss Wright. Wesson, Andrea, illus. 2011. (ENG.). 40p. (J). (gr. 1-4). lib. bdg. 15.95 (978-1-58536-509-8(2), 202202) Sleeping Bear Pr.

AUTISM

Adams, Sue. A Book about What Autism Can Be Like. 2008. (ENG., Illus.). 48p. pap. 13.95 **(978-1-84310-940-2(9)**, 1029) Kingsley, Jessica Pubs. GBR. Dist: Macmillan Distribution Ltd.

Allman, Toney. Asperger's Syndrome. 2009. (Diseases & Disorders Ser.). (ENG., Illus.). 128p. (gr. 7-10). lib. bdg. 39.90 (978-1-4205-0111-7(9), LML02109-245422, Lucent Bks.) Cengage Gale.

Amenta, Charles A. Russell's World: A Story for Kids about Autism. 2011. (Illus.). 40p. (J). (gr. -1-3). pap. 9.95 (978-1-4338-0976-7(1), Magination Pr.) American Psychological Assn.

—Russell's World: A Story for Kids about Autism. Pollak, Monika, illus. 2011. 40p. (J). (gr. -1-3). 14.95 (978-1-4338-0975-0(3), Magination Pr.) American Psychological Assn.

Attwood, Sarah. Making Sense of Sex: A Forthright Guide to Puberty, Sex & Relationships for People with Asperger's Syndrome. Powell, Jonathan, illus. 2008. (ENG.). 320p. (J). (gr. 4-12). pap. 21.95 (978-1-84310-374-5(5), 1254) Kingsley, Jessica Pubs. GBR. Dist: Macmillan Distribution Ltd.

Atwood, Megan. Living with Autism, 1 vol. 2012. (Living with Health Challenges Set 1 Ser.). (ENG.). 112p. (J). (gr. 6-12). lib. bdg. 35.64 (978-1-61783-123-2(9), Essential Library) ABDO Publishing Co.

Autism. 2009. (Psychological Disorders Ser.). (Illus.). 112p. (YA). (gr. 7-12). 37.50 (978-1-60413-425-4(9)) Facts On File, Inc.

Baker, Jed. The Social Skills Picture Book: For High School & Beyond. 2006. (ENG., Illus.). 177p. (J). (gr. 9-12). pap. 39.95 (978-1-932565-35-5(3)) Future Horizons, Inc.

Balestrieri, James, et al. Meltdown: Aspergers Disorder, Challenging Behavior, & a Families Journey Toward Hope. 2013. (ENG.). 132p. pap. 13.99 (978-1-939418-02-9(X)) RTC Publishing.

Bardhan-Quallen, Sudipta. Autism. 2005. (Understanding Diseases & Disorders Ser.). (ENG., Illus.). 48p. (J). (gr. 4-8). lib. bdg. 27.50 (978-0-7377-2167-6(7), Greenhaven Pr., Inc.) Cengage Gale.

Baretz, Susie. You Would Be Surprised. Wulfing, Amy J., illus. 2010. (ENG.). 32p. (J). 16.95 (978-0-9759850-9-0(4)) Maple Leaf Ctr.

Barraclough, Sue. I Know Someone with Autism, 1 vol. 2011. (Understanding Health Issues Ser.). (ENG.). 32p. (gr. 1-3). 27.32 (978-1-4329-4563-3(7), Heinemann First Library) Heinemann-Raintree.

Barrette, Melanie. Welcome to School: Helping Friends with Autism. James, Colin, ed. Crestan, David, illus. James, Colin & Newton, Jennifer, photos by. 2005. 16p. (J). (gr. k-6). pap. 12.00 (978-1-928598-11-4(0)) Pyramid Educational Products, Inc.

Becklund, Annette L. Warren Is Wonderful. Gulzeth, Ray, illus. 2009. 52p. pap. 12.95 (978-1-4401-2042-8(0)) iUniverse, Inc.

Bonnice, Sherry. Autism. Albers, Lisa et al, eds. 2014. (Living with a Special Need Ser.: 16). 128p. (J). (gr. 7-18). 25.95 (978-1-4222-3029-9(5)) Mason Crest.

—The Hidden Child: Youth with Autism. 2004. (Youth with Special Needs Ser.). (Illus.). 128p. (YA). 24.95 (978-1-59084-736-7(9)) Mason Crest.

—The Hidden Child: Youth with Autism. 2003. (Youth with Special Needs Ser.). (Illus.). 127p. (YA). pap. 14.95 (978-1-4222-0424-5(3)) Mason Crest.

Brill, Marlene Targ. Autism. 2007. (Health Alert Ser.). (Illus.). 64p. (YA). (gr. 4-7). lib. bdg. 32.79 (978-0-7614-2700-1(7)) Marshall Cavendish Corp.

Brunnström, Åse & Lindström, Emma. Robin & the White Rabbit. Lindström, Emma, illus. 2017. (ENG., Illus.). 48p. (J). 16.95 **(978-1-78592-290-9(4)**, 9190) Kingsley, Jessica Pubs. GBR. Dist: Macmillan Distribution Ltd.

Buron, Kari D. & Buron, Kari Dunn. When My Worries Get Too Big! A Relaxation Book for Children Who Live with Anxiety. 2006. (Illus.). 124p. pap. 16.95 (978-1-931282-92-5(7)) Autism Asperger Publishing Co.

Cain, Barbara S. Autism, the Invisible Cord: A Sibling's Diary. 2012. 112p. (J). 14.95 (978-1-4338-1191-3(X)); pap. 9.95 (978-1-4338-1192-0(8)) American Psychological Assn. (Magination Pr.).

Carlson, Jr. Autism Coloring Book. Carlson, Kevin, illus. 2009. 50p. pap. 9.95 (978-1-60264-383-3(0)) Virtualbookworm.com Publishing, Inc.

Casanueva, Idilian. I Like to Flap My Hands. 2009. 32p. pap. 12.95 (978-1-60844-001-6(X)) Dog Ear Publishing, LLC.

Chastain, Zachary & Livingston, Phyllis. Youth with Asperger's Syndrome: A Different Drummer. 2009. (Helping Youth with Mental, Physical, & Social Challenges Ser.). (Illus.). 128p. (YA). (gr. 7-18). lib. bdg. 24.95 (978-1-4222-0137-4(6)) Mason Crest.

Cheray, Toni. My Friend Zac. 2011. 16p. pap. 10.99 (978-1-4634-1831-1(0)) AuthorHouse.

Chilman-Blair, Kim. Superheroes on a Medical Mission, 6 vols., Set 2. Incl. Medikidz Explain ADHD. Taddeo, John. lib. bdg. 29.25 (978-1-4358-9456-3(1)); Medikidz Explain Autism. Taddeo, John. lib. bdg. 29.25 (978-1-4358-9460-0(X)); Medikidz Explain Depression. Deloache, Shawn. lib. bdg. 29.25 (978-1-4358-9455-6(3)); Medikidz Explain HIV. Taddeo, John. lib. bdg. 29.25 (978-1-4358-9458-7(8)); Medikidz Explain Sleep Apnea. Deloache, Shawn. lib. bdg. 29.25 (978-1-4358-9459-4(6)); Medikidz Explain Swine Flu. lib. bdg. 29.25 (978-1-4358-9457-0(X)); (YA). (gr. 5-8). (Illus.). 40p. 2010. Set lib. bdg. 175.50 (978-1-4358-9570-6(3), Rosen Reference) Rosen Publishing Group, Inc., The.

Chilman-Blair, Kim & Taddeo, John. Medikidz Explain Autism. 2010. (Superheroes on a Medical Mission Ser.). (Illus.). 40p. (YA). pap. 11.75 (978-1-4488-1835-8(4)); (gr. 5-8). lib. bdg. 29.25 (978-1-4358-9460-0(X)) Rosen Publishing Group, Inc., The. (Rosen Reference).

Coe, Julie L. The Friendship Puzzle: Helping Kids Learn about Accepting & Including Kids with Autism. Brassel, Sondra, illus. 2009. 24p. (J). (gr. k-2). 14.95 (978-0-9789182-4-8(X)) Larstan Publishing, Inc.

Crissey, Pat. Personal Hygiene? What's That Got to Do with Me? Crissey, Noah, illus. 2004. (ENG.). 96p. pap. 19.95 (978-1-84310-796-5(1), 2100) Kingsley, Jessica Pubs. GBR. Dist: Macmillan Distribution Ltd.

Doering Tourville, Amanda. My Friend Has Autism, 1 vol. Sorra, Kristin, illus. 2010. (Friends with Disabilities Ser.). (ENG.). 24p. (gr. k-3). pap. 7.49 (978-1-4048-6109-1(2)) Picture Window Bks.

—My Friend Has Autism [Readers World]. Sorra, Kristin, illus. 2010. (Friends with Disabilities Ser.). 24p. pap. 6.00 (978-1-4048-6702-4(3), Nonfiction Picture Bks.) Picture Window Bks.

Edward, Justine. Shine. 2013. 28p. pap. 13.95 (978-1-4525-7531-5(2), Balboa Pr.) Author Solutions, Inc.

Elder, Jennifer. Autistic Planet. Elder, Jennifer & Thomas, Marc, illus. 2007. (ENG.). 48p. (gr. -1-k). 21.95 (978-1-84310-842-9(9), 3058) Kingsley, Jessica Pubs. GBR. Dist: Macmillan Distribution Ltd.

—Different Like Me: My Book of Autism Heroes. Elder, Jennifer & Thomas, Marc, illus. 2005. (ENG.). 48p. 16.95 (978-1-84310-815-3(1), 2390) Kingsley, Jessica Pubs. GBR. Dist: Macmillan Distribution Ltd.

Farrington Wilson, Lynda. Autistic? How Silly Is That! I Don't Need Any Labels at All. 2012. (ENG., Illus.). 32p. pap. 9.95 (978-1-935274-59-9(7), 9781935274599) Future Horizons, Inc.

Feuer, Bonnie. I Hear a Red Crayon: A Child's Perspective of Her Brother's Autism. Boemmels, Kayleigh, illus. Lt. ed. 2015. (ENG.). 36p. (gr. 3-12). 19.95 (978-0-9825468-9-5(0)) Connecticut Pr., The.

Fredericks, Carrie. Autism. 2007. (Perspectives on Diseases & Disorders Ser.). (ENG., Illus.). 168p. (YA). (gr. 10-12). lib. bdg. 38.95 (978-0-7377-3869-8(3), LML02109-235106, Greenhaven Pr., Inc.) Cengage Gale.

Freedman, Jeri. Autism. 2009. (Genetic & Developmental Diseases & Disorders Ser.). 64p. (gr. 4-6). 58.50 (978-1-61512-658-3(9)) Rosen Publishing Group, Inc., The.

Gast, Christy & Krug, Jane. Caring for Myself: A Social Skills Storybook. 2007. (ENG., Illus.). 96p. (gr. 3-7). 39.95 (978-1-84310-872-6(0), 3483) Kingsley, Jessica Pubs. GBR. Dist: Macmillan Distribution Ltd.

Goodwine, Lashayla. My Mind Has Many Colors. 2012. 24p. pap. 24.95 (978-1-4626-9503-4(5)) America Star Bks.

Harrison, Anne-Marie. Babies Are Noisy: A Book for Big Brothers & Sisters Including Those on the Autism Spectrum. Byrne, Beth, illus. 2013. (ENG.). 40p. (J). 15.95 (978-1-84905-459-1(2), 4085) Kingsley, Jessica Pubs. GBR. Dist: Macmillan Distribution Ltd.

Hartman, Davida. The Growing up Book for Boys: What Boys on the Autism Spectrum Need to Know! Suggs, Margaret Anne, illus. 2015. (Growing Up Ser.). (ENG.). 68p. (J). 16.95 (978-1-84905-575-8(0), 4099) Kingsley, Jessica Pubs. GBR. Dist: Macmillan Distribution Ltd.

—The Growing up Guide for Girls: What Girls on the Autism Spectrum Need to Know! Suggs, Margaret Anne, illus. 2015. (Growing Up Ser.). (ENG.). 72p. (J). 16.95 (978-1-84905-574-1(2), 2878) Kingsley, Jessica Pubs. GBR. Dist: Macmillan Distribution Ltd.

Hickerson, Brandy. My Brother & Me. 2008. 60p. pap. 31.99 (978-1-4363-1635-4(9)) Xlibris Corp.

Jaffe, Amy V. & Gardner, Luci. My Book Full of Feelings: How to Control & React to the Size of Your Emotions. 2006. (Illus.). 70p. spiral bd. 27.95 (978-1-931282-83-3(8)) Autism Asperger Publishing Co.

Jane, Christy Gast, et al. Caring for Myself. 2007. (ENG., Illus.). 96p. pap. 24.95 **(978-1-84310-887-0(9)**, 2643) Kingsley, Jessica Pubs. GBR. Dist: Macmillan Distribution Ltd.

Jessum, Jeffrey E. Diary of a Social Detective: Real-life tales of mystery, intrigue & interpersonal Adventure. 2011. (ENG., Illus.). 293p. (YA). pap. 19.95 (978-1-934575-71-0(2)) Autism Asperger Publishing Co.

Kats, Jewel. The Princess & the Ruby: An Autism Fairy Tale. Kinra, Richa, illus. 2013. 42p. 26.95 (978-1-61599-193-8(X)); (J). (gr. 3-7). pap. 16.95 (978-1-61599-175-4(1)) Loving Healing Pr., Inc.

Keating-Velasco, Joanna. In His Shoes, A Short Journey Through Autism. 2008. (YA). pap. 18.95 (978-1-934575-26-0(7)) Autism Asperger Publishing Co.

Keating-Velasco, Joanna L. A Is for Autism, F Is for Friend: A Kid's Book on Making Friends with a Child Who Has Autism. 2007. (Illus.). 54p. per. 12.95 (978-1-931282-43-7(9)) Autism Asperger Publishing Co.

Kluth, Paula & Schwarz, Patrick. Pedro's Whale, 1 vol. 2010. (ENG., Illus.). 32p. (J). 18.95 (978-1-59857-160-8(5)) Brookes Publishing.

Larson, Elaine M., et al. I Am Utterly Unique: Celebrating the Strengths of Children with Asperger Syndrome & High-Functioning Autism. Strand, Vivian, illus. 2006. 56p. (J). (gr. -1-3). 18.95 (978-1-931282-89-5(7)) Autism Asperger Publishing Co.

Larson, Elaine Marie. The Chameleon Kid: Controlling Meltdown Before He Controls You. 2008. (ENG.). 41p. (J). 17.95 (978-1-934575-22-2(4)) Autism Asperger Publishing Co.

—The Kaleidoscope Kid: Focusing on the Strengths of Children with Asperger Syndrome & High-Functioning Autism. Strand, Vivian, illus. 2007. 35p. 17.95 (978-1-931282-41-3(2)) Autism Asperger Publishing Co.

Lazar, Michelle & Jensen, Jeremy. Tuned in to Learning Vol. 1: Social Skills & Pragmatics for Autism & Related Needs, 11 vols. 2005. (J). spiral bd. 59.95 incl. audio compact disk (978-0-9768881-3-0(0)) Tuned in to Learning.

Levine, Michelle. Autism. 2015. (Living With... Ser.). (Illus.). 32p. (J). lib. bdg. 28.50 (978-1-60753-479-2(7)) Amicus Publishing.

Love. Why Do I Take Vitamins? a Book for Children with Autism. 2010. 20p. pap. 9.99 (978-1-60911-169-4(9), Eloquent Bks.) Strategic Book Publishing & Rights Agency (SBPRA).

Manasco, Hunter. The Way to A: Empowering Children with Autism Spectrum & Other Neurological Disorders to Monitor & Replace Aggression & Tantrum Behavior. Manasco, Katharine, illus. 2006. 19p. spiral bd., wbk. ed. 18.95 (978-1-931282-87-1(0)) Autism Asperger Publishing Co.

Marks, Elizabeth. Growing Together Across the Autism Spectrum: A Kid's Guide to Living with, Learning from, & Loving a Parent with Autism Spectrum Disorder. Marks, Elizabeth, illus. 2015. (ENG., Illus.). 47p. (J). pap. 19.95 (978-1-942197-08-9(X)) Autism Asperger Publishing Co.

Mccracken, Heather. That's What's Different about Me! Helping Children Understand Autism Spectrum Disorders - Story & Coloring BK. Robbins, Kathryn, illus. 2006. (J). pap. 3.00 (978-1-931282-97-0(8)) Autism Asperger Publishing Co.

McHenry, Irene & Moog, Carol. The Autism Playbook for Teens: Imagination-Based Mindfulness Activities to Calm Yourself, Build Independence, & Connect with Others. 2014. (Instant Help Solutions Ser.). (ENG.). 168p. (YA). (gr. 5-12). pap. 16.95 (978-1-62625-009-3(X)) New Harbinger Pubns.

McKracken, Heather. That's What's Different about Me: Helping Children Understand Autism Spectrum Disorders. Robbins, Kathryn, illus. 2006. (J). pap. 59.95 (978-1-931282-96-3(X)) Autism Asperger Publishing Co.

Montgomery, Sy. Temple Grandin: How the Girl Who Loved Cows Embraced Autism & Changed the World, 1 vol. 2012. 49.95 (978-0-7927-9012-9(X)) Audio Bookshelf.

Montgomery, Sy & Grandin, Temple. Temple Grandin: How the Girl Who Loved Cows Embraced Autism & Changed the World. 2012. (ENG., Illus.). 160p. (J). (gr. 5-7). 18.99 (978-0-547-44315-7(3)) Houghton Mifflin Harcourt Publishing Co.

Mosca, Isabelle. Adventure to Autism Planet. 2011. (ENG., Illus.). 32p. (YA). 15.00 (978-1-935232-36-0(3)) ComteQ Publishing.

Mulstay, Linda Muratore. Autism & PDD Answering Questions, Level 1. 2006. (J). per. 29.95 (978-0-7606-0673-5(0)) LinguiSystems, Inc.

Muratore, Linda Mulstay. Autism & PDD Answering Questions, Level 2. 2006. (J). per. 29.95 (978-0-7606-0674-2(9)) LinguiSystems, Inc.

Naff, Clay Farris. Why Is Autism on Rise? Gale, ed. 2014. (At Issue Ser.). (ENG.). 128p. (gr. 10-12). lib. bdg. 39.40 (978-0-7377-6870-1(3), Greenhaven Pr., Inc.) Cengage Gale.

Ovalles, Misty Haney. Picture the Place. 2011. 50p. pap. 24.95 (978-1-4560-3417-7(0)) PublishAmerica, Inc.

Peete, Holly Robinson, et al. Same but Different: Teen Life on the Autism Express. 2016. (ENG.). 224p. (J). (gr. 7). 17.99 (978-0-545-09468-9(2), Scholastic Pr.) Scholastic, Inc.

Perner, Lars, ed. Scholars with Autism Achieving Dreams. 2012. (ENG., Illus.). 182p. (J). 26.95 (978-0-9825785-3-7(9)); pap. 19.95 (978-0-9825785-1-3(2)) Auricle Ink Pubs.

Poole, H. W. Autism Spectrum Disorders, Vol. 13. Walters, Anne S., ed. 2015. (Mental Illnesses & Disorders: Awareness & Understanding Ser.). (Illus.). 48p. (J). (gr. 5). 20.95 (978-1-4222-3367-2(7)) Mason Crest.

Rafail, Dyllan. Super Senses. 2009. (J). pap. 10.95 (978-1-61623-086-9(X)) Independent Pub.

Rawlins, Abi. Is It OK to Ask Questions about Autism? 2017. (ENG., Illus.). 96p. (C). 17.95 (978-1-78592-170-4(3), 8735) Kingsley, Jessica Pubs. GBR. Dist: Macmillan Distribution Ltd.

Reese, Pam Britton & Challenner, Nena C. Autism & PDD Expanding Social Options, 2 vols. 2003. (Illus.). (YA). per. 21.95 (978-0-7606-0499-1(1)) LinguiSystems, Inc.

Respess, Beth. Autism & PDD Opposites Buddy Bear & Bonnie Bear. 2004. (J). spiral bd. (978-0-7606-0579-0(3)) LinguiSystems, Inc.

—Autism & PDD Opposites Buddy Bear's Animals. 2004. (J). spiral bd. (978-0-7606-0576-9(9)) LinguiSystems, Inc.

—Autism & PDD Opposites Buddy Bear's Clothes. 2004. (J). spiral bd. (978-0-7606-0575-2(0)) LinguiSystems, Inc.

—Autism & PDD Opposites Buddy Bear's Food. 2004. (J). spiral bd. (978-0-7606-0578-3(5)) LinguiSystems, Inc.

—Autism & PDD Opposites Buddy Bear's Toys. 2004. (J). spiral bd. (978-0-7606-0577-6(7)) LinguiSystems, Inc.

Respess, Beth, et al. Autism & PDD Concepts What Shape Is it, Becca Bunny? 2004. (J). spiral bd. (978-0-7606-0591-2(2)) LinguiSystems, Inc.

Respess, Beth W. Autism & PDD Associations Buddy Bear Gets Ready for School. 2004. (J). spiral bd. (978-0-7606-0567-7(X)) LinguiSystems, Inc.

—Autism & PDD Associations Buddy Bear Goes on a Picnic. 2004. (J). spiral bd. (978-0-7606-0569-1(6)) LinguiSystems, Inc.

—Autism & PDD Associations Buddy Bear Has Fun. 2004. (J). spiral bd. (978-0-7606-0566-0(1)) LinguiSystems, Inc.

—Autism & PDD Associations Buddy Bear Helps Mama Bear. 2004. (J). spiral bd. (978-0-7606-0568-4(8)) LinguiSystems, Inc.

—Autism & PDD Associations Buddy Bear Likes Animals. 2004. (J). spiral bd. (978-0-7606-0565-3(3)) LinguiSystems, Inc.

—Autism & PDD Categories Buddy Bear in the House. 2004. (J). spiral bd. (978-0-7606-0560-8(2)) LinguiSystems, Inc.

—Autism & PDD Categories Buddy Bear in the Kitchen. 2004. (J). spiral bd. (978-0-7606-0562-2(9)) LinguiSystems, Inc.

—Autism & PDD Categories Buddy Bear in the Yard. 2004. (J). spiral bd. (978-0-7606-0561-5(0)) LinguiSystems, Inc.

—Autism & PDD Categories Buddy Bear on Vacation. 2004. (J). spiral bd. (978-0-7606-0563-9(7)) LinguiSystems, Inc.

—Autism & PDD Categories Buddy Bear Plays. 2004. (J). spiral bd. (978-0-7606-0564-6(5)) LinguiSystems, Inc.

—Autism & PDD Comparatives/Superlatives What Buddy Bear Does. 2004. (J). spiral bd. (978-0-7606-0572-1(6)) LinguiSystems, Inc.

—Autism & PDD Comparatives/Superlatives What Buddy Bear Finds. 2004. (J). spiral bd. (978-0-7606-0571-4(8)) LinguiSystems, Inc.

—Autism & PDD Comparatives/Superlatives What Buddy Bear Has. 2004. (J). spiral bd. (978-0-7606-0570-7(X)) LinguiSystems, Inc.

—Autism & PDD Comparatives/Superlatives What Buddy Bear Likes. 2004. (J). spiral bd. (978-0-7606-0574-5(2)) LinguiSystems, Inc.

—Autism & PDD Comparatives/Superlatives What Buddy Bear Sees. 2004. (J). spiral bd. (978-0-7606-0573-8(4)) LinguiSystems, Inc.

—Autism & PDD Yes/No Questions Buddy Bear at Home. 2004. (J). spiral bd. (978-0-7606-0557-8(2)) LinguiSystems, Inc.

—Autism & PDD Yes/No Questions Buddy Bear at School. 2004. (J). spiral bd. (978-0-7606-0555-4(6)) LinguiSystems, Inc.

—Autism & PDD Yes/No Questions Buddy Bear at the Beach. 2004. (J). (978-0-7606-0556-1(4)) LinguiSystems, Inc.

—Autism & PDD Yes/No Questions Buddy Bear at the Grocery Store. 2004. (J). spiral bd. (978-0-7606-0558-5(0)) LinguiSystems, Inc.

—Autism & PDD Yes/No Questions Buddy Bear at the Park. 2004. (J). spiral bd. (978-0-7606-0554-7(8)) LinguiSystems, Inc.

Robbins, Lynette. How to Deal with Autism. 2009. (Kids' Health Ser.). 24p. (J). (ENG.). pap. 8.25 (978-1-4358-3421-7(6), PowerKids Pr.); (Illus.). (gr. 2-5). lib. bdg. 22.60 (978-1-4042-8142-4(8)) Rosen Publishing Group, Inc., The.

Rodger, Marguerite. Autism Spectrum Disorder. 2013. (ENG., Illus.). 48p. (J). (978-0-7787-0081-4(X)); pap. (978-0-7787-0087-6(9)) Crabtree Publishing Co.

Rodriguez, Ana Maria. Autism & Asperger's Syndrome. 2008. (Twenty-First Century Medical Library). (YA). (gr. 7-12). lib. bdg. 33.26 (978-0-8225-7291-6(5)) Twenty First Century Bks.

—Autism Spectrum Disorders. 2011. (USA TODAY Health Reports: Diseases & Disorders Ser.). (ENG.). 128p. (gr. 6-12). lib. bdg. 34.60 (978-0-7613-5883-1(8)) Lerner Publishing Group.

Rosaler, Maxine. Coping with Asperger Syndrome. (Coping Ser.). (gr. 7-12). 2009. 196p. 63.90 (978-1-61511-991-2(4)) 2005. 192p. (J). lib. bdg. 34.60 (978-0-8239-4482-8(4)) Rosen Publishing Group, Inc., The.

Rose, Jennifer. It's Not a Perfect World but I'll Take It: 50 Life Lessons for Teens Like Me - Who Are Kind of (You Know) Autistic. 2016. (ENG.). 136p. (gr. 6). 12.99 (978-1-5107-0549-4(X)) Skyhorse Publishing Co., Inc.

Rosenberg, Marsha Sarah. Coping When a Brother or Sister Is Autistic. (Coping Ser.). 192p. (gr. 7-12). 2009. 63.90 (978-1-61511-986-8(8)) 2005. (Illus.). (YA). lib. bdg. 34.60 (978-0-8239-3194-1(3)) Rosen Publishing Group, Inc., The.

—Everything You Need to Know When a Brother or Sister Is Autistic. 2005. (Need to Know Library). (Illus.). 64p. (YA). (gr. 7-12). lib. bdg. 31.95 (978-0-8239-3123-1(4), NTAUTI) Rosen Publishing Group, Inc., The.

Rustad, Martha E. H. Algunos Niños Tienen Autismo. 2010. (Comprendiendo Las Diferencias/Understanding Differences Ser.).Tr. of Some Kids Have Autism. (MUL, SPA & ENG.). 24p. (gr. k-1). lib. bdg. 21.99 (978-1-4296-4593-5(8)) Capstone Press of Coughlan Cos.

—Some Kids Have Autism, 1 vol. Saunders-Smith, Gail, ed. 2008. (Understanding Differences Ser.). (ENG., Illus.). 24p. (gr. k-1). 21.99 (978-1-4296-1230-2(4), Pebble Bks.) Capstone Press of Coughlan Cos.

Santomauro, Josie. The ASD Zoo of Kalamazoo. 2014. (ENG., Illus.). 52p. (J). lib. bdg. 10.77 net. (978-1-937473-98-3(8)) Autism Asperger Publishing Co.

—Your Special Friend: A Book for Peers of Children Diagnosed with Asperger Syndrome. Marino, Carla, illus. 2009. (ENG.). 32p. (C). pap. 12.95 (978-1-84310-661-6(2), 6669) Kingsley, Jessica Pubs. GBR. Dist: Macmillan Distribution Ltd.

Scherer, Lauri S. Autism. Greenhaven Press Editors, ed. 2014. (Introducing Issues with Opposing Viewpoints Ser.). (ENG., Illus.). 144p. (gr. 7-10). lib. bdg. 42.00 (978-0-7377-6920-3(3), Greenhaven Pr., Inc.) Cengage Gale.

Shanta, N. D. He's My Brother. 2006. 24p. (J). 19.95 (978-1-58909-380-5(1)) Bookstand Publishing.

Shaul, Joel. The ASD & Me Picture Book: A Visual Guide to Understanding Challenges & Strengths. 2017. (ENG., Illus.). 96p. (C). 24.95 (978-1-78592-723-2(X), 8570) Kingsley, Jessica Pubs. GBR. Dist: Macmillan Distribution Ltd.

—Our Brains Are Like Computers! Exploring Social Skills & Social Cause & Effect with Children on the Autism Spectrum. 2016. (ENG., Illus.). 80p. (J). 24.95 (978-1-84905-716-5(8), 8164) Kingsley, Jessica Pubs. GBR. Dist: Macmillan Distribution Ltd.

Sherman, Rebecca. Autism & Other Developmental Disabilities. 2017. (J). **(978-1-4222-3751-9(6))** Mason Crest.

Smith, Paula. Autism & Other Pervasive Developmental Disorders. 2013. 48p. (J). (978-0-7787-0832-2(2)); (Illus.). pap. (978-0-7787-0859-9(4)) Crabtree Publishing Co.

Squire, Ann O. Autism. 2015. (ENG., Illus.). 48p. (J). lib. bdg. (978-0-531-21473-2(7), Orchard Bks.) Scholastic, Inc.

Stewart, Sheila. The Hidden Child: Kids with Autism. 2009. (Kids with Special Needs Ser.). 48p. (YA). (gr. 5-18). pap. 7.95 (978-1-4222-1927-0(5)) Mason Crest.

Stewart, Sheila & Flath, Camden. The Hidden Child: Kids with Autism. 2010. (Kids with Special Needs Ser.). (Illus.). 48p. (YA). (gr. 5-18). lib. bdg. 19.95 (978-1-4222-1724-5(8)) Mason Crest.

Stontz, Karen & Malone, Kelly. Autism & PDD Concepts How Many, Becca Bunny. 2004. (J). spiral bd. (978-0-7606-0593-6(9)) LinguiSystems, Inc.

—Autism & PDD Concepts What Time Is it, Becca Bunny. 2004. (J). spiral bd. *(978-0-7606-0592-9(0))* LinguiSystems, Inc.

—Autism & PDD Concepts Where are they Hiding, Becca Bunny? 2004. (J). spiral bd. *(978-0-7606-0595-0(5))* LinguiSystems, Inc.

Sundem, Garth. Real Kids, Real Stories, Real Change: Courageous Actions Around the World. 2010. (ENG.). 176p. (J). (gr. 4-8). pap. 9.99 *(978-1-57542-350-0(2))* Free Spirit Publishing, Inc.

—Real Kids, Real Stories, Real Character: Choices That Matter Around the World. 2016. (ENG., Illus.). 176p. (J). (gr. 3-8). pap. 9.99 *(978-1-63198-026-8(2))* Free Spirit Publishing, Inc.

Thalhamer, Ellen Viola. I'm a Daddy: I Love to Pretend! 2010. 36p. pap. 16.49 *(978-1-4490-7489-0(8))* AuthorHouse.

—Let's Play Doctor: I Love to Pretend! 2010. 36p. pap. 15.99 *(978-1-4490-7487-6(1))* AuthorHouse.

Thomas, Pat. I See Things Differently: A First Look at Autism. 2014. (First Look At... Ser.). (Illus.). 32p. (J). (gr. -1-2). pap. 7.99 *(978-1-4380-0479-2(6))* Barron's Educational Series, Inc.

Tourville, Amanda Doering. My Friend Has Autism, 1 vol. Sorra, Kristin, illus. 2010. (Friends with Disabilities Ser.). (ENG.). 24p. (gr. k-3). lib. bdg. 25.99 *(978-1-4048-5750-6(8))* Picture Window Bks.

Tyree, Debi. Jessica's Little Sister: A Story about Autism. 2004. 35p. pap. 24.95 *(978-1-4137-1724-2(1))* PublishAmerica, Inc.

VanDerTuuk-Perkins, Jennifer E. Life with Gabriel. VanDerTuuk-Perkins, Jennifer E. & Perkins, Rodney R., illus. l.t. ed. 2004. 22p. (J). per. 9.95 *(978-0-9749862-0-3(8))* Theragogy.com.

Verdick, Elizabeth & Reeve, Elizabeth. The Survival Guide for Kids with Autism Spectrum Disorders (and Their Parents) 2012. (ENG.). 240p. (J). (gr. 2-8). pap. 16.99 *(978-1-57542-385-2(5))* Free Spirit Publishing, Inc.

Welton, Jude. Can I Tell You about Asperger Syndrome? A Guide for Friends & Family. Telford, Jane, illus. 2003. (Can I Tell You About... ? Ser.). (ENG.). 48p. pap. 13.95 *(978-1-84310-206-9(4)*, 5357) Kingsley, Jessica Pubs. GBR. Dist: Macmillan Distribution Ltd.

What It Is to Be Me! An Asperger Kid Book. 2005. (J). 9.95 *(978-1-59352-199-8(5))* Christian Services Publishing.

Yacio, Jennifer Gilpin. Temple Did It, & I Can, Too! Wilson, Lynda Farrington, illus. 2015. (ENG.). 32p. (J). 14.95 *(978-1-935567-52-3(7))* Sensory Resources.

AUTISM—FICTION

Abdullah, Shaila. A Manual for Marco: Living, Learning, & Laughing with an Autistic Sibling. Tejpar, Iman, illus. 2015. (J). *(978-1-61599-248-5(0))* Loving Healing Pr., Inc.

Allen, Gregory G. Chicken Boy: The Amazing Adventures of a Super Hero with Autism. Culver, Dennis, illus. 2012. 32p. pap. 9.99 *(978-0-9853441-0-8(5))* ASD Publishing.

Arnold, Elana K. A Boy Called Bat. Santoso, Charles, illus. 2017. 208p. (J). (gr. 1-5). 16.99 *(978-0-06-244582-7(0)*, Waldon Pond Pr.) HarperCollins Pubs.

Autismfighter. The Smunkarellies: Through the Eyes of Children. 2011. (ENG.). 23p. (J). pap. 13.95 *(978-1-4327-7137-9(X))* Outskirts Pr., Inc.

Baskin, Nora Raleigh. Anything but Typical. (ENG.). 208p. (J). (gr. 5-9). 2010. pap. 8.99 *(978-1-4169-9500-5(5))* 2009. (Illus.). 17.99 *(978-1-4169-6378-3(2))* Simon & Schuster Bks. For Young Readers. (Simon & Schuster Bks. For Young Readers).

Beynon, Veronica. My Sister Has Autism & That's Okay. 2013. 24p. pap. *(978-1-4602-2066-5(8))* FriesenPress.

Birch, Sue. Dead Puzzling. 2009. 100p. pap. *(978-1-84923-891-5(X))* YouWriteOn.

Bitner, Amanda Marie. Baby Sister. 2012. 28p. pap. 24.95 *(978-1-4626-8684-1(2))* America Star Bks.

Boehm, Patricia. Does Noah's Kitten Have Autism Too? Kelly, Robert, illus. 2013. 16p. pap. 24.95 *(978-1-62709-877-9(1))* America Star Bks.

Brown, Jahla. Nathan Is Nathan. 2009. (ENG., Illus.). 20p. (J). pap. 19.95 *(978-0-9778083-8-0(6))* Everlasting Publishing.

Bulhak-Paterson, Danuta. I Am an Aspie Girl: A Book for Young Girls with Autism Spectrum Conditions. Ferguson, Teresa, illus. 2015. (ENG.). 32p. 15.95 *(978-1-84905-634-2(X)*, 7811) Kingsley, Jessica Pubs. GBR. Dist: Macmillan Distribution Ltd.

Burford, Dinah. If I Could Talk, I Would Say the Adventures of Miss Pink. 2011. 28p. pap. 13.99 *(978-1-4634-4181-4(9))* AuthorHouse.

Burkhardt, Melissa K. Exceptionally Good Friends: Building Relationships with Autism. 2012. (ENG., Illus.). 56p. (J). pap. 14.99 *(978-0-9884707-0-5(5))* EMC Publishing.

Chilman-Blair, Kim & Deloache, Shawn. Medikidz Explain Autism: What's up with Ben? 2010. (Illus.). 32p. (J). pap. *(978-1-906935-28-3(9))* Medikidz Ltd.

Choldenko, Gennifer. Al Capone Does My Homework. 2013. Bk. 3. (ENG.). 224p. (J). (gr. 5). 17.99 *(978-0-8037-3472-2(7)*, Dial Bks) Penguin Publishing Group.

—Al Capone Does My Homework. 2014. (ENG.). 240p. (J). (gr. 5). pap. 7.99 *(978-0-14-242522-0(2)*, Puffin Books) Penguin Young Readers Group.

—Al Capone Does My Homework. 2014. (Tale from Alcatraz (Al Capone) Ser.: 3). lib. bdg. 18.40 *(978-0-606-35714-2(9))* Turtleback Bks.

—Al Capone Does My Shirts. (Tales from Alcatraz Ser.). (ENG., Illus.). (J). (gr. 5-18). 2004. 240p. 17.99 *(978-0-399-23861-1(1)*, G.P. Putnam's Sons Books for Young Readers) 2006. 288p. reprint ed. pap. 7.99 *(978-0-14-240370-9(9)*, Puffin Books) Penguin Young Readers Group.

—Al Capone Does My Shirts. 2006. (Illus.). 317p. (J). (gr. 4-7). per. 10.95 *(978-0-7862-8927-1(9))* Thorndike Pr.

—Al Capone Shines My Shoes. (ENG.). (J). (gr. 5-18). 2011. 304p. 7.99 *(978-0-14-241718-8(1)*, Puffin Books) 2009. 288p. 17.99 *(978-0-8037-3460-9(3)*, Dial Bks) Penguin Young Readers Group.

—Al Capone Shines My Shoes. 2011. (Tale from Alcatraz (Al Capone) Ser.: 2). lib. bdg. 18.40 *(978-0-606-23072-8(6)*, Turtleback) Turtleback Bks.

Clark, Joan. Ann Drew Jackson. Clark, Nathan, illus. 2007. 122p. per. 17.95 *(978-1-931282-45-1(5))* Autism Asperger Publishing Co.

Cocca-Leffler, Maryann. Janine. Cocca-Leffler, Maryann, illus. 2015. (ENG., Illus.). 32p. (J). (gr. -1-3). 16.99 *(978-0-8075-3754-1(3))* Whitman, Albert & Co.

Cowhey, Sharon P. Shy Harold & His Hiding Place, 1 vol. 2010. 48p. pap. 16.95 *(978-1-4489-4348-7(5))* America Star Bks.

Cozzo, Karole. How to Say I Love You Out Loud. 2015. (ENG.). 240p. (YA). (gr. 7). pap. 9.99 *(978-1-250-06359-5(0))* Feiwel & Friends.

Crisp, Lisa. Stewart & His Fish Tank. 2011. 28p. pap. 24.95 *(978-1-4560-1007-2(7))* America Star Bks.

Currinder, Michael. Running Full Tilt. 2017. (ENG.). 336p. (YA). (gr. 7). lib. bdg. 17.99 ***(978-1-58089-802-7(5)***, Charlesbridge Teen) Charlesbridge Publishing, Inc.

Davis, Mandy. Superstar. 2017. 336p. (J). (gr. 3-7). 16.99 *(978-0-06-237777-7(9))* HarperCollins Pubs.

Demonia, Lori. Leah's Voice. Turchan, Monique, illus. 2012. 28p. pap. 12.95 *(978-1-61244-089-7(4))* Halo Publishing International.

Dowd, Siobhan. The London Eye Mystery. 2009. (ENG.). 336p. (J). (gr. 3-7). 7.99 *(978-0-385-75184-1(2)*, Yearling) Random Hse. Children's Bks.

—The London Eye Mystery. 2009. lib. bdg. 18.40 *(978-0-606-14413-1(7)*, Turtleback) Turtleback Bks.

Duane, Diane. A Wizard Alone. 2003. (Young Wizards Ser.: 6). (ENG.). 352p. (J). (gr. 5-7). pap. 8.99 *(978-0-15-204911-9(8))* Houghton Mifflin Harcourt Publishing Co.

Duyvis, Corinne. On the Edge of Gone. 2016. (ENG.). 464p. (J). (gr. 8-17). 17.95 *(978-1-4197-1903-5(3)*, Amulet Bks.) Abrams, Inc.

Edwards, Becky & Armitage, David. My Brother Sammy Is Special. Armitage, David, illus. 2012. (ENG., Illus.). 32p. (J). (gr. -1-k). 16.95 *(978-1-61608-480-6(4)*, 608480, Sky Pony Pr.) Skyhorse Publishing Co., Inc.

El Khatiri, Basma. Momma's Song. Kala, Sabah, illus. 2016. (Stories & Fables from Around the World Ser.). (ENG.). 24p. (J). (gr. 2-1). lib. bdg. 24.60 *(978-1-4777-5694-2(9)*, Windmill Bks.) Rosen Publishing Group, Inc., The.

Ellis, Marvie. Keisha's Doors Bk. 1: An Autism Story. l.t. ed. 2005.Tr. of Las Puertas de Keisha. (SPA., Illus.). 32p. (J). per. 16.95 *(978-1-933319-00-1(3))* Speech Kids Texas Pr.

—Tacos Anyone? Bk. 2: An Autism Story Book. l.t. ed. 2005.Tr. of Alguien quiere Tacos? (SPA., Illus.). 32p. (J). per. 16.95 *(978-1-933319-01-8(1))* Speech Kids Texas Pr.

Ennis, Ryan R. The September Surprise: A Story about Kids & Autism. 2012. 112p. pap. 10.95 *(978-0-9849360-2-1(5))* G Publishing LLC.

—The Thursday Surprise: A Story about Kids & Autism. Stroud, Brenda, illus. 2011. 86p. pap. 9.95 *(978-0-9843426-7-9(2))* G Publishing LLC.

Erskine, Kathryn. Mockingbird. (ENG.). (J). (gr. 5-18). 2011. 256p. 7.99 *(978-0-14-241775-1(0)*, Puffin Books) 2010. 240p. 16.99 *(978-0-399-25264-8(9)*, Philomel Bks.) Penguin Young Readers Group.

—Mockingbird. (J). 2012. 1.25 *(978-1-4407-4671-0(0))* 2010. 74.75 *(978-1-4407-4665-9(6))* 2010. 72.75 *(978-1-4407-4667-3(2))* 2010. (SPA.). 62.75 *(978-1-4407-4663-5(X))* 2010. 64.75 *(978-1-4407-4661-1(3))* 2010. 210.75 *(978-1-4407-4662-8(1))* Recorded Bks., Inc.

—Mockingbird. 2011. lib. bdg. 18.40 *(978-0-606-15356-0(X)*, Turtleback) Turtleback Bks.

Farrington Wilson, Lynda. Squirmy Wormy: How I Learned to Help Myself. 2009. (ENG., Illus.). 32p. (gr. 1). pap. 14.95 *(978-1-935567-18-9(7)*, 9781935567189) Sensory Resources.

Feuerbach, Jennifer. Chef Philip Has Autism. Wroth, Dean, illus. 2014. 32p. (J). pap. 10.49 *(978-0-944727-61-4(1)*, Turtle Bks.) Jason & Nordic Pubs.

Flowers, Natasha. Sammy the Snail. 2006. 10.00 *(978-0-8059-9158-1(1))* Dorrance Publishing Co., Inc.

Gennifer, Choldenko. Al Capone Does My Shirts. 2014. (ENG.). 240p. (J). (gr. 6-12). 12.24 *(978-1-63245-251-1(0))* Lectorum Pubns., Inc.

Gerlach, Elizabeth K. Apples for Cheyenne: A Story about Autism, Horses & Friendship. 2010. (ENG., Illus.). 44p. (J). (gr. k-4). pap. 11.95 *(978-1-935274-22-3(8))* Future Horizons, Inc.

Gomez, Nicole. The Missing Piece. 2011. 24p. pap. *(978-1-4269-6452-7(8))* Trafford Publishing (UK) Ltd.

Haddon, Mark. The Curious Incident of the Dog in the Night-Time. 2007. (ENG., Illus.). 320p. mass mkt. *(978-1-4000-2535-0(4)*, Seal Bks) Doubleday Canada, Ltd. CAN. Dist: Random Hse., Inc.

Hunter, Sara Hoagland. Every Turtle Counts. Spellman, Susan, illus. 2014. (ENG.). 36p. (J). 16.95 *(978-1-931807-25-8(6))* Randall, Peter E. Pub.

Hurtado, Patricia. The Magical Feline & the White Haven. 2009. 142p. pap. 10.95 *(978-1-60594-325-1(8)*, Llumina Pr.) Aeon Publishing Inc.

Jacobs, Karen & Miller, Leah. How Full Is Sophia's Backpack? Hewitt, Elizabeth, illus. 2012. 40p. pap. 11.95 *(978-0-9850440-0-8(4))* Jacobs, Karen.

Johnson, Angela. A Certain October. (ENG.). 176p. (YA). (gr. 9). 2013. pap. 9.99 *(978-0-689-87065-1(5))* 2012. 16.99 *(978-0-689-86505-3(8))* Simon & Schuster Bks. For Young Readers. (Simon & Schuster Bks. For Young Readers).

Johnson, Celeste. The Beez Brothers: Baby Brother Has Autism. 2013. 36p. pap. 18.41 *(978-1-4669-9767-7(2))* Trafford Publishing.

Juwayriyah, Umm & Ayed, Juwayriyah. Hind's Hands: A Story about Autism. Apple, Emma, illus. 2013. 16p. (J). pap. 6.00 *(978-1-935437-76-5(3)*, As Sabr Pubns.) Imago Pr.

Kamateros, Litsa & Morfonios, Nia. Sarah's Socks: My World of Autism. 2010. 24p. pap. 10.95 *(978-1-61633-023-1(6))* Guardian Angel Publishing, Inc.

Kavan, Barbara. Trainman: Gaining Acceptance ... & Friends ... Through Special Interests. 2010. (Illus.). 40p. (J). pap. 17.95 *(978-1-934575-70-3(4))* Autism Asperger Publishing Co.

Kehoe, Stasia Ward. The Sound of Letting Go. 2014. (ENG.). 400p. (YA). (gr. 7). 17.99 *(978-0-670-01553-5(9)*, Viking Books for Young Readers) Penguin Young Readers Group.

Kelly, Deborah. The Chalk Rainbow. Jones, Gwynneth, illus. 2017. (ENG.). 32p. (J). (gr. -1-3). 17.99 ***(978-1-925335-45-3(3)***, EK Bks.) Exisle Publishing Pty Ltd. AUS. Dist: Hachette Bk. Group.

Kleinman, Estelle. Al Capone Does My Shirts. Friedland, Joyce & Kessler, Rikki, eds. 2007. (Al Capone on Alcatraz Ser.: Bk. 1). (Illus.). 38p. pap. 16.95 *(978-0-7675-3758-2(0))* Learning Links Inc.

Krukar, Jeff, et al. Melting Down: A Comic for Kids with Asperger's Disorder & Challenging Behavior (the Orp Library) 2013. 74p. pap. 12.99 *(978-1-939418-20-3(8))* Writer of the Round Table Pr.

Lawrence, Eve Pollard. My Friend Eddie. 2012. 30p. pap. 19.99 *(978-1-4685-7632-0(1))* AuthorHouse.

Lazebnik, Claire. Things I Should Have Known. 2017. (ENG.). 320p. (YA). (gr. 7). 17.99 *(978-0-544-82969-5(7)*, HMH Books For Young Readers) Houghton Mifflin Harcourt Publishing Co.

Lehman-Wilzig, Tami & Katzman, Nicole. Nathan Blows Out the Hanukkah Candles. Tugeau, Jeremy, illus. 2011. (Hanukkah Ser.). (ENG.). 32p. (J). (gr. k-3). pap. 7.95 *(978-0-7613-6658-4(X)*, Kar-Ben Publishing) Lerner Publishing Group.

Lord, Cynthia. Rules. 2009. 8.44 *(978-0-7848-2921-9(7)*, Everbind) Marco Bk. Co.

—Rules. 2008. (Illus.). 200p. (gr. 4-7). 17.00 *(978-0-7569-8283-6(9))* Perfection Learning Corp.

—Rules. (J). 2008. 77.49 *(978-1-4361-5837-4(0))* 2007. 220.75 *(978-1-4281-5209-0(1))* 2007. 74.75 *(978-1-4281-5208-3(3))* 2007. 89.75 *(978-1-4281-5212-0(1))* 2007. 87.75 *(978-1-4281-5214-4(8))* 2007. (SPA.). 72.75 *(978-1-4281-5210-6(5))* Recorded Bks., Inc.

—Rules. (ENG.). (J). (gr. 3-7). 2008. 224p. pap. 7.99 *(978-0-439-44383-8(0)*, Scholastic Paperbacks) 2006. 208p. 15.99 *(978-0-439-44382-1(2)*, Scholastic Pr.) Scholastic, Inc.

—Rules. rev. l.t. ed. 2007. (Literacy Bridge Middle Reader Ser.). 191p. (J). (gr. 4-7). 23.95 *(978-0-7862-9559-3(7))* Thorndike Pr.

—Rules. 2008. lib. bdg. 17.20 *(978-1-4178-2956-9(7))* Turtleback Bks.

Mammay, Judith. It's Time. Fargo, Todd, illus. l.t. ed. 2007. 32p. (J). pap. 9.95 *(978-0-944727-20-1(4))*; lib. bdg. 15.95 *(978-0-944727-21-8(2))* Jason & Nordic Pubs. (Turtle Bks.).

—Knowing Joseph. (ENG., Illus.). 256p. (J). (gr. 2-7). 2009. pap. 8.95 *(978-1-933831-06-0(5))* 2008. 13.95 *(978-1-933831-05-3(7))* Blooming Tree Pr.

—Ryan's Victory. Fargo, Todd, illus. 2009. 32p. (J). pap. 9.95 *(978-0-944727-53-9(0))*; lib. bdg. 15.95 *(978-0-944727-54-6(9))* Jason & Nordic Pubs. (Turtle Bks.).

Mandarino, Gene. What's Autism? 2006. pap. 25.00 *(978-0-9786795-0-7(4))* Charlie's Gift.

Mannering, Rose. Boo's Beard. Straker, Bethany, illus. 2015. (ENG.). 32p. (J). (gr. -1-k). 16.99 *(978-1-63450-207-8(8)*, Sky Pony Pr.) Skyhorse Publishing Co., Inc.

Marin, Victoria. Aiden's Waltz. 2012. 24p. pap. 15.99 *(978-1-4691-6271-3(7))* Xlibris Corp.

Martin, Ann M. Rain Reign. 2014. (ENG.). 240p. (J). (gr. 4-7). 16.99 *(978-0-312-64300-3(4)*, 9780312643003) Feiwel & Friends.

Mathieu, Jennifer. Afterward. 2016. (ENG.). 320p. (YA). 17.99 *(978-1-62672-238-5(2)*, 9781626722385) Roaring Brook Pr.

—Afterward. 2017. (ENG.). 336p. (YA). pap. 9.99 ***(978-1-250-12962-8(1)***, 9781250129628) Square Fish.

—Afterward. 2017. (YA). lib. bdg. 20.85 ***(978-0-606-40590-4(9))*** Turtleback Bks.

Matlin, Marlee & Cooney, Doug. Nobody's Perfect. 2006. (ENG., Illus.). 240p. (J). (gr. 3-7). 15.95 *(978-0-689-86986-0(X)*, Simon & Schuster Bks. For Young Readers) Simon & Schuster Bks. For Young Readers.

Mayes, Joanne. I'm Isaac: My Brain Is Green. 2008. 27p. pap. 24.95 *(978-1-60563-984-0(2))* America Star Bks.

Mazer, Harry & Lerangis, Peter. Somebody, Please Tell Me Who I Am. (ENG.). 160p. (YA). (gr. 7). 2013. pap. 9.99 *(978-1-4169-3896-5(6))* 2012. (Illus.). 15.99 *(978-1-4169-3895-8(8))* Simon & Schuster Bks. For Young Readers. (Simon & Schuster Bks. For Young Readers).

McGregor, Janet C. Happy for a Honk & a Wave. Craft, Donna, illus. 2010. 20p. pap. 12.95 *(978-1-936343-04-1(5))* Peppertree Pr., The.

Meadows, Daisy. Rainbow Magic Special Edition: Autumn the Falling Leaves Fairy. 2013. (Rainbow Magic Special Edition Ser.). (ENG.). 176p. (J). (gr. 2-5). pap. 6.99 *(978-0-545-48495-4(2)*, Scholastic Paperbacks) Scholastic, Inc.

Mignano, Regina. Autism - A Holistic View, 2nd Edition. 2008. 173p. pap. 14.95 *(978-0-557-00420-1(9))* Lulu Pr., Inc.

Mueller, Dagmar H. David's World: A Picture Book about Living with Autism. Ballhaus, Verena, illus. 2012. (ENG.). 28p. (J). (gr. -1-k). 16.95 *(978-1-61608-962-7(8)*, 608962, Sky Pony Pr.) Skyhorse Publishing Co., Inc.

Murrell, Diane. Friends Learn about Tobin. Murrell, Diane, illus. 2007. (ENG., Illus.). 29p. (J). (gr. -1-3). 16.95 *(978-1-932565-41-6(8))* Future Horizons, Inc.

Myers, Walter Dean. A Star Is Born. 2012. (Cruisers Ser.: Bk. 3). (J). *(978-0-439-91631-8(3))*; (ENG.). 176p. (gr. 5-9). 17.99 *(978-0-439-91628-8(3))* Scholastic, Inc.

Nappi, Frank. Welcome to the Show. 2016. (Mickey Tussler Ser.). (ENG.). 288p. (J). (gr. 6). pap. 9.99 *(978-1-63450-829-2(7)*, Sky Pony Pr.) Skyhorse Publishing Co., Inc.

Notarfrancesco, Lisa Christiano & Padovano, Chris. Catherine the Caterpillar & Friends Coloring Book: A Children's Guide to Autism. 2014. (ENG.). 72p. pap. 1.95 *(978-1-63443-539-0(7))* Primedia eLaunch LLC.

of Limpsfield Grange School, The Students & Martin, Vicky. M in the Middle: Secret Crushes, Mega-Colossal Anxiety & the People's Republic of Autism. 2016. (ENG., Illus.). 352p. (J). pap. 16.95 *(978-1-78592-034-9(0)*, 8350) Kingsley, Jessica Pubs. GBR. Dist: Macmillan Distribution Ltd.

Ogaz, Nancy. Wishing on the Midnight Star: My Asperger Brother. 2003. (ENG.). 144p. (J). pap. 22.95 *(978-1-84310-757-6(0)*, 4318) Kingsley, Jessica Pubs. GBR. Dist: Macmillan Distribution Ltd.

Orr, Peter. Now I Get It - Angry & Sharing: Social Stories for children with Autism. 2007. (Illus.). 20p. (J). 9.95 *(978-0-9778866-2-3(X))* Natural Learning Concepts, Inc.

Osborn. Understanding Jason. Mills, illus. 2009. 24p. pap. 11.49 *(978-1-4389-4403-6(9))* AuthorHouse.

Peck, Lisa J. A Challenge for Brittany: CTR Club - Book One, 4 bks. 2005. (J). pap. 6.95 *(978-0-9749241-5-1(6))* Golden Wings Enterprises.

Peete, Holly Robinson & Peete, Ryan Elizabeth. My Brother Charlie. Evans, Shane W., illus. 2010. (ENG.). 40p. (J). (gr. 2-5). 17.99 *(978-0-545-09466-5(6)*, Scholastic Pr.) Scholastic, Inc.

Pen, Chenda. Dara Learns How to Ride a Bike! An Autism Story. 2010. 24p. pap. 14.99 *(978-1-4490-6943-8(6))* AuthorHouse.

Peterson, Kathryn. Reilly's Leap of Faith, 1 vol. 2010. 48p. pap. 16.95 *(978-1-4512-0154-3(0))* America Star Bks.

Pinto, Mindee & Cohen, Judy. Mikey. Fairbanks, Mark, illus. 2013. 32p. pap. 9.99 *(978-1-937165-41-3(8))* Orange Hat Publishing.

Potash, Dorothy. Sam & Me. 2012. 28p. pap. 19.99 *(978-1-4772-5585-8(0))* AuthorHouse.

Raines, Gary. My Brother's Blue. 2009. 32p. pap. 14.49 *(978-1-4490-4185-4(X))* AuthorHouse.

Reish, Kathleen. Matthew's Box. Leonhard, Herb, illus. 2005. 48p. (J). 21.95 *(978-0-9762664-0-2(7)*, 3000) KBR Mutti's Pubns.

Reiss, I. The Boy in the Invisible Box. Katz, Avi, illus. 2007. 24p. per. 9.95 *(978-965-7344-30-9(1))* Mazo Pubs.

Rorby, Ginny. How to Speak Dolphin. (ENG.). 272p. (J). (gr. 3-7). 2017. pap. 6.99 *(978-0-545-67607-6(X))* 2015. 16.99 *(978-0-545-67605-2(3))* Scholastic, Inc. (Scholastic Pr.).

Roy, Jennifer. Mindblind, 0 vols. unabr. ed. 2013. (ENG.). 254p. (J). (gr. 7-9). pap. 9.99 *(978-1-4778-1712-4(3)*, 9781477817124, Amazon Children's Publishing) Amazon Publishing.

Rozanski, Bonnie. Borderline. 2007. (ENG.). 208p. (YA). (gr. 10). pap. 22.95 *(978-0-88984-293-9(0))* Porcupine's Quill, Inc. CAN. Dist: Univ. of Toronto Pr.

Rudner, Barry. Silent Voice. Trabalka, Pegy, illus. l.t. ed. 2013. (ENG.). 30p. (J). 14.99 *(978-1-940775-00-5(0))* Nick Of Time Media, Inc.

Rudolph, Shaina & Royer, Danielle. All My Stripes: A Story for Children with Autism. Zivoin, Jennifer, illus. 2014. (J). pap. *(978-1-4338-1917-9(1)*, Magination Pr.) American Psychological Assn.

Saleem-Muhammad, Rasheedah. My Friend Michael: A Short Story about Autism - A Pedro Collection. Harris, - Crystal, illus. 2011. 30p. 19.95 *(978-1-4575-0295-8(X))*; pap. 14.95 *(978-1-4575-0037-4(X))* Dog Ear Publishing, LLC.

Scholastic, Inc. Staff. Peppa's Windy Fall Day. Scholastic, Inc. Staff, illus. 2015. (Peppa Pig Ser.). (ENG., Illus.). 24p. (J). (gr. -1-k). 3.99 *(978-0-545-84818-3(0))* Scholastic, Inc.

Shally, Celeste. Since We're Friends: An Autism Picture Book. Harrington, David, illus. 2007. 32p. (J). (gr. -1-3). per. 8.99 *(978-0-9794713-0-8(3))* Awaken Specialty Pr.

—Since We're Friends: An Autism Picture Book. Harrington, David, illus. 2012. (ENG.). 32p. (J). (gr. -1-3). 12.95 *(978-1-61608-656-5(4)*, 608656, Sky Pony Pr.) Skyhorse Publishing Co., Inc.

Siddoway, Richard M. The Cottage Park Puzzle. 2015. 200p. (YA). pap. 14.99 *(978-1-4621-1562-4(4))* Cedar Fort, Inc./CFI Distribution.

Spencer, Leslie. Social Stories for Children with Disabilities, 1 vol. 2010. 46p. 24.95 *(978-1-4512-0917-4(7))* PublishAmerica, Inc.

Stork, Francisco X. Marcelo in the Real World. 2011. 9.64 *(978-0-7848-3609-5(4)*, Everbind) Marco Bk. Co.

—Marcelo in the Real World. (ENG.). 320p. (J). (gr. 7-7). 2011. pap. 9.99 *(978-0-545-05690-8(X)*, Scholastic Paperbacks) 2009. (Illus.). 17.99 *(978-0-545-05474-4(5)*, Levine, Arthur A. Bks.) Scholastic, Inc.

—Marcelo in the Real World. l.t. ed. 2010. (ENG.). 420p. 23.99 *(978-1-4104-2751-9(X))* Thorndike Pr.

Thalhamer, Ellen Viola. Let's Play Cashier: I Love to Pretend! 2011. 36p. pap. 15.49 *(978-1-4490-7488-3(X))* AuthorHouse.

The Students of Limpsfield Grange School & Martin, Vicky. M Is for Autism. 2015. (ENG., Illus.). 96p. (J). pap. 14.95 *(978-1-84905-684-7(6)*, 8117) Kingsley, Jessica Pubs. GBR. Dist: Macmillan Distribution Ltd.

Tice, Kimberly & Litvack, Venita. Lou Knows What to Do: Supermarket. Kerry, Andre, illus. 2017. (Lou Knows What to Do Ser.: 1). (ENG.). 32p. (J). (gr. -1-6). pap. 10.95 ***(978-1-944882-14-3(6))*** Boys Town Pr.

Varin-Mignano, Regina, Lcsw. Autism: A Holistic View, Hard Cover Edition. 2008. 173p. 32.00 *(978-0-557-00421-8(7))* Lulu Pr., Inc.

Vernick, Shirley Reva. Remember Dippy. 2013. (ENG.). 176p. (J). (gr. 5-10). 16.95 *(978-1-935955-48-1(9))*; pap. 9.95 *(978-1-935955-58-0(6))* Cinco Puntos Pr.

Walsh, Melanie. Isaac & His Amazing Asperger Superpowers! Walsh, Melanie, illus. 2016. (ENG., Illus.). 32p. (J). (gr. -1-2). 16.99 *(978-0-7636-8121-0(0))* Candlewick Pr.

Watson, Cristy. On Cue. 2016. (Orca Currents Ser.). lib. bdg. 20.80 *(978-0-606-38695-1(5))* Turtleback Bks.

Welton, Jude. Tomas Loves... A Rhyming Book about Fun, Friendship - & Autism. Telford, Jane, illus. 2015. (ENG.). 32p. 15.95 *(978-1-84905-544-4(0)*, 7155) Kingsley, Jessica Pubs. GBR. Dist: Macmillan Distribution Ltd.

Werlin, Nancy. Are You Alone on Purpose? 2007. (ENG.). 208p. (YA). (gr. 7-18). 7.99 *(978-0-14-240777-6(1)*, Speak) Penguin Young Readers Group.

Werner, Michael. Aspey's Adventures with Asperger's. 2012. 32p. pap. 21.99 *(978-1-4771-0800-0(9))* Xlibris Corp.

Westendorf, Sandra. The World According to August: One Good Friend. Rand, Tracy, illus. 2011. *(978-0-9868424-0-5(0))* Purple Birch Publishing.

Williams-Hines, Jacqueline. Joshua, That's Sooo Slimming! 2009. 28p. pap. 13.99 *(978-1-4389-0342-2(1))* AuthorHouse.

Zolty, Meredith. Ben Has Autism. Ben Is Awesome. Rivard, Rebecca, illus. 2011. 32p. (J). pap. 9.95 *(978-0-944727-41-6(7)*, Turtle Bks.) Jason & Nordic Pubs.

—Ben Has Autism. Ben Is Awesome. Rebecca, Rivard, illus. 2011. 32p. (J). lib. bdg. 15.95 *(978-0-944727-40-9(9)*, Turtle Bks.) Jason & Nordic Pubs.

AUTO COURTS

see Hotels, Motels, etc.

AUTOBIOGRAPHIES

Abbey, Cherie, ed. 2009 Biography Today Annual Cumulation. 2009. (Biography Today General Ser.). 525p. lib. bdg. 73.00 *(978-0-7808-1055-6(4))* Omnigraphics, Inc.

Bodden, Valerie. Nonfiction - Writing for Fact & Argument: Truthful Biographies. 2010. (Nonfiction Ser.). 48p. (YA). (gr.

5-18). 23.95 *(978-1-58341-932-8(2)*, Creative Education) Creative Co., The.

Calabazza, Della & Monckeberg, Paulina. Ludovico & Ooops 2006. 2005. (Pascualina Family of Products Ser.). (ENG., Illus.). 240p. (J). (gr. 3-7). spiral bd. 11.99 *(978-956-8222-23-9(5))* Pascualina Producciones S.A.

Cook, Jaye E. & Spencer, Lauren. Writing Personal Stories. 2011. (J). 77.70 *(978-1-4488-4748-8(6)*, Rosen Reference); (J). pap. 12.95 *(978-1-4488-4690-0(0)*, Rosen Reference); (YA). (gr. 5-9). lib. bdg. 31.95 *(978-1-4488-4684-9(6))* Rosen Publishing Group, Inc., The.

Dormer, Cindy. Hold That Thought for Kids: Capturing Precious Memories Through Fun Questions, Images & Conversations. 2005. (Hold that Thought Keepsake Conversation Journals). (Illus.). 145p. (J). 19.95 *(978-0-9743720-0-6(5))* Brightside Co.

Fandel, Jennifer. You Can Write an Amazing Journal, 1 vol. 2012. (You Can Write Ser.). (ENG., Illus.). 24p. (gr. 1-2). pap. 7.29 *(978-1-4296-9318-9(5))*; lib. bdg. 25.32 *(978-1-4296-8408-8(9))* Capstone Press of Coughlan Cos.

Ganeri, Anita. I Can Write Journals & Narratives, 1 vol. 2013. (I Can Write Ser.). (ENG., Illus.). 32p. (gr. 1-3). lib. bdg. 27.32 *(978-1-4329-6933-2(1)*, Heinemann First Library) Heinemann-Raintree.

—Journals & Narratives. 2013. (I Can Write Ser.). (ENG., Illus.). 32p. (gr. 1-3). pap. 8.29 *(978-1-4329-6940-0(4)*, Heinemann First Library) Heinemann-Raintree.

Jenkins, Diana R. The Stepping Stones Journals. 2010. (Illus.). 144p. (J). (gr. 3-6). pap. 9.95 *(978-0-8198-7129-9(X))* Pauline Bks. & Media.

Kalman, Bobbie. I Can Write a Book about My Life. 2012. (ENG.). 32p. (J). *(978-0-7787-7993-3(9))*; pap. *(978-0-7787-8002-1(3))* Crabtree Publishing Co.

Loewen, Nancy. It's All about You: Writing Your Own Journal, 1 vol. Lyles, Christopher & Ouren, Todd, illus. 2009. (Writer's Toolbox Ser.). (ENG.). 32p. (gr. 2-4). pap. 8.95 *(978-1-4048-5698-1(6))*; lib. bdg. 27.32 *(978-1-4048-5520-5(3))* Picture Window Bks.

Lynette, Rachel. Jesse & Jasmine Build a Journal. Aon, Carlos, illus. 2014. (Writing Builders Ser.). (ENG.). 32p. (J). (gr. 2-4). pap. 11.94 *(978-1-60357-559-1(6))*; lib. bdg. 25.27 *(978-1-59953-585-2(8))* Norwood Hse. Pr.

Minden, Cecilia & Roth, Kate. How to Write a Journal. 2011. (Explorer Junior Library: Language Arts Explorer Junior Ser.). (ENG.). 24p. (gr. 1-4). lib. bdg. 25.64 *(978-1-60279-994-3(6)*, 200988) Cherry Lake Publishing.

Monckeberg, Paulina. Pascualina 2006. 2005. (Pascualina Family of Products Ser.). (ENG., Illus.). 272p. (J). spiral bd. 16.99 *(978-956-8222-28-4(6))* Pascualina Producciones S.A.

—Rosamunda Della Calabazza 2006 Agenda & Stationary 2006: The Youngest & Most Dangerous Sister of Pascualina. 2005. (Pascualina Family of Products Ser.). (ENG., Illus.). 228p. (J). spiral bd. 11.99 *(978-956-8222-21-5(9))* Pascualina Producciones S.A.

Plaja, Luisa. Write Your Own Blog. 2013. (Quick Expert's Guide Ser.). 64p. (J). (gr. 5-8). 31.95 *(978-1-4777-2819-2(8))*; pap. 77.70 *(978-1-4777-2822-2(8))*; pap. 12.95 *(978-1-4777-2821-5(X))* Rosen Publishing Group, Inc., The. (Rosen Reference).

Russell, Rachel Renée. OMG!:All about Me Diary! Russell, Rachel Renée, illus. 2013. (Dork Diaries). (ENG., Illus.). 272p. (J). (gr. 4-8). 12.99 *(978-1-4424-8771-0(2)*, Aladdin) Simon & Schuster Children's Publishing.

Spence, Kelly & Burns, Kylie. Be a Diary Detective. 2017. (Be a Document Detective Ser.). (ENG., Illus.). 24p. (J). ***(978-0-7787-3053-8(0))*** Crabtree Publishing Co.

Townsley, Janet Howe. Dakota Dreams: Fannie Sabra Howe's Own Story, 1881-1884. 2003. (Illus.). 77p. (J). 19.95 *(978-0-9715171-4-1(2))* South Dakota State Historical Society Pr.

Turnbull, Stephanie. Diaries & Keepsakes: Style Secrets for Girls. 2013. (Girl Talk Ser.). 32p. (gr. 4-7). 31.35 *(978-1-59920-945-6(4))* Black Rabbit Bks.

Yan, Ma & Haski, Pierre. The Diary of Ma Yan: The Struggles & Hopes of a Chinese Schoolgirl. 2009. (ENG.). 192p. (J). (gr. 5). pap. 5.99 *(978-0-06-076498-2(8)*, Collins) HarperCollins Pubs.

Young, Jay, creator. Secret Ziga Zaga. 2003. (Ziga Zaga Ser.). 192p. (YA). *(978-1-84347-034-2(9)*, Pavilion Children's Books) Pavilion Bks.

Zimmerman, Bill. Pocketdoodles for Kids, 1 vol. 2009. (ENG., Illus.). 272p. (J). (gr. 1). 9.99 *(978-1-4236-0465-5(2))* Gibbs Smith, Publisher.

AUTOMATIC COMPUTERS

see Computers

AUTOMATIC CONTROL

see also Automation

O'Neill, Terence & Williams, Josh. Arduino. 2013. (21st Century Skills Innovation Library: Makers As Innovators Ser.). (ENG.). 32p. (J). (gr. 4-8). 28.50 *(978-1-62431-137-6(7)*, 202868); pap. 14.21 *(978-1-62431-269-4(1)*, 202870) Cherry Lake Publishing.

Rauf, Don. Getting the Most Out of Makerspaces to Explore Arduino & Electronics. 2014. (Makerspaces Ser.). 64p. (J). (gr. 6-12). 32.95 *(978-1-4777-7815-9(2)*, Rosen Reference) Rosen Publishing Group, Inc., The.

AUTOMATIC DATA PROCESSING

see Electronic Data Processing

AUTOMATIC INFORMATION RETRIEVAL

see Information Storage and Retrieval Systems

AUTOMATION

see also Systems Engineering

Allman, Toney. The Next Robot. 2009. (Great Idea Ser.). (Illus.). 48p. (J). (gr. 4-6). lib. bdg. 26.60 *(978-1-59953-342-1(1))* Norwood Hse. Pr.

Ceceri, Kathy. Robotics: Discover the Science & Technology of the Future with 20 Projects. Carbaugh, Sam, illus. 2012. (Build It Yourself Ser.). (ENG.). 128p. (J). (gr. 3-7). 21.95 *(978-1-936749-76-8(9))* Open City Bks.

Espejo, Roman. What Is the Impact of Automation? 2007. (At Issue Ser.). (ENG., Illus.). 128p. (gr. 10-12). pap. 27.80 *(978-0-7377-3945-9(2)*, Greenhaven Pr., Inc.); lib. bdg. 39.40 *(978-0-7377-3944-2(4))* Cengage Gale.

Foran, Racquel. Robotics: From Automatons to the Roomba, 1 vol. 2014. (History of Science Ser.). (ENG., Illus.). 112p. (YA). (gr. 6-12). lib. bdg. 35.64 *(978-1-62403-564-7(7)*, Essential Library) ABDO Publishing Co.

Forest, Christopher. Robot Competitions. 2013. (Robots Ser.). (ENG.). 32p. (gr. 3-4). pap. 47.70 *(978-1-62065-783-6(X))*; lib. bdg. 27.99 *(978-1-4296-9920-4(5))*; (Illus.). pap. 8.29 *(978-1-62065-782-9(1))* Capstone Press of Coughlan Cos. (Edge Bks.).

Forest, Christopher, et al. Robots. 2013. (Robots Ser.). (ENG.). 32p. (gr. 3-4). pap. 190.80 *(978-1-62065-785-0(6))*; pap. 31.80 *(978-1-62065-784-3(8))*; lib. bdg. 111.96 *(978-1-4296-9921-1(3))* Capstone Press of Coughlan Cos. (Edge Bks.).

Gray, Peter. Robots. 2009. (Drawing Manga Ser.). 32p. (gr. 4-4). 50.50 *(978-1-61512-201-1(X))* Rosen Publishing Group, Inc., The.

Hubbard, Ben. Hi Tech World: High Level Security. 2010. (ENG., Illus.). 32p. (J). pap. *(978-0-7787-7552-2(6))*; lib. bdg. *(978-0-7787-7530-0(5))* Crabtree Publishing Co.

Hulick, Kathryn. Careers in Robotics. 2017. (ENG.). 80p. (J). (gr. 5-12). *(978-1-68282-118-3(8))* ReferencePoint Pr., Inc.

Kupperberg, Paul. Careers in Robotics. 2009. (Cutting-Edge Careers Ser.). 64p. (gr. 7-7). 55.90 *(978-1-61512-101-4(3))* Rosen Publishing Group, Inc., The.

Mara, Wil. Robotics: From Concept to Consumer. 2015. (ENG., Illus.). 64p. (J). pap. 8.95 *(978-0-531-21237-0(8)*, Orchard Bks.) Scholastic Library Publishing.

O'Hearn, Michael. Awesome Space Robots. 2013. (Robots Ser.). (ENG.). 32p. (gr. 3-4). pap. 47.70 *(978-1-62065-779-9(1)*, Edge Bks.); lib. bdg. 27.99 *(978-1-4296-9918-1(3))*; (Illus.). pap. 8.29 *(978-1-62065-778-2(3))* Capstone Press of Coughlan Cos.

Pflugfelder, Bob & Hockensmith, Steve. Robot Army Rampage: A Mystery with Hoverbots, Bristle Bots, & Other Robots You Can Build Yourself. 2014. (Nick & Tesla Ser.: 2). (ENG., Illus.). 224p. (J). (gr. 4-7). 12.95 *(978-1-59474-649-9(4))* Quirk Bks.

Price, Sean Stewart. Amazing Military Robots. 2013. (Robots Ser.). (ENG.). 32p. (gr. 3-4). pap. 47.70 *(978-1-62065-777-5(5)*, Edge Bks.) Capstone Press of Coughlan Cos.

Randolph, Ryan P. Robotics. 2009. (Real Life Readers Ser.). 32p. (gr. 4-5). pap. 10.00 *(978-1-4358-0157-8(1)*, Rosen Classroom); 32p. (gr. 4-4). 47.90 *(978-1-60853-039-7(6)*, PowerKids Pr.); lib. bdg. 25.25 *(978-1-4358-2987-9(5)*, PowerKids Pr.) Rosen Publishing Group, Inc., The.

Rau, Dana Meachen. Robots. 2010. (Bookworms Chapter Books: Surprising Science Ser.). 24p. (gr. 2-3). 22.79 *(978-0-7614-4871-6(3))* Marshall Cavendish Corp.

Smibert, Angie. Building Better Robots. 2017. (Illus.). 32p. (J). *(978-1-62143-515-0(6))* Pr. Room Editions LLC.

Smibert, Angie & Ringstad, Arnold. Building Better Robots. 2016. (Science Frontiers Ser.). (ENG., Illus.). 32p. (J). pap. 9.95 *(978-1-63235-391-7(1))* Pr. Room Editions LLC.

AUTOMATION—VOCATIONAL GUIDANCE

Baum, Margaux & Payment, Simone. Building a Career in Robotics. 2017. (J). pap. ***(978-1-4994-3880-2(X))*** Rosen Publishing Group, Inc., The.

Mozer, Mindy. Getting a Job in Automotive Care & Service. 2013. 80p. (YA). (gr. 9-12). 33.25 *(978-1-4488-9609-7(6))* Rosen Publishing Group, Inc., The.

AUTOMOBILE ACCIDENTS

see Traffic Accidents

AUTOMOBILE DRIVERS

Abbot, Henry. I Want to Drive an Ambulance. 2016. (At the Wheel Ser.). 00024p. (J). (gr. 1-1). pap. 8.25 *(978-1-4994-2762-2(X)*, PowerKids Pr.) Rosen Publishing Group, Inc., The.

Aksomitis, Linda. Teen Driving. 2008. (Issues That Concern You Ser.). (ENG., Illus.). 116p. (YA). (gr. 7-10). lib. bdg. 35.75 *(978-0-7377-4187-2(2)*, LML02109-243088, Greenhaven Pr., Inc.) Cengage Gale.

Allen, K. Kurt Busch. 2009. (NASCAR Champions Ser.). 24p. (gr. 1-2). 42.50 *(978-1-61514-781-6(0)*, PowerKids Pr.) Rosen Publishing Group, Inc., The.

Allen, Kenny. Kurt Busch. 2007. (NASCAR Champions Ser.). (Illus.). 24p. (J). (gr. 1-3). lib. bdg. 22.60 *(978-1-4042-3457-4(8))* Rosen Publishing Group, Inc., The.

Allman, Toney. Distracted Driving. 2015. (Hot Topics Ser.). (ENG.). 128p. (J). (gr. 7-10). 39.40 *(978-1-4205-1233-5(1)*, Lucent Bks.) Cengage Gale.

Anderson, Wayne. Tony Stewart: NASCAR Driver. 2009. (Behind the Wheel Ser.). 48p. (gr. 5-5). 53.00 *(978-1-61511-560-0(9)*, Rosen Reference) Rosen Publishing Group, Inc., The.

Anderson, Wayne A. Tony Stewart: NASCAR Driver. 2006. (Behind the Wheel Ser.). (Illus.). 48p. (YA). (gr. 5-9). lib. bdg. 29.25 *(978-1-4042-0984-8(0))* Rosen Publishing Group, Inc., The.

Anniss, Matt. Jeff Gordon in the Community, 1 vol., 1. 2014. (Making a Difference: Athletes Who Are Changing the World Ser.). (ENG.). 48p. (J). (gr. 5-8). 25.85 *(978-1-62275-190-7(6))* Rosen Publishing Group, Inc., The.

Apelqvist, Eva. Getting Ready to Drive. 2011. (Life—a How-To Guide Ser.). (Illus.). 128p. (J). lib. bdg. 33.27 *(978-0-7660-3443-3(7))*; (gr. 6-18). pap. 10.95 *(978-1-59845-314-0(9))* Enslow Pubs., Inc.

Basen, Ryan. Jeff Burton: Chasing the Championship. 2009. (Heroes of Racing Ser.). (Illus.). 128p. (J). (gr. 5-9). lib. bdg. 33.27 *(978-0-7660-3301-6(5))* Enslow Pubs., Inc.

—Kyle Busch: Gifted & Giving Racing Star. 2010. (Sports Stars Who Give Back Ser.). (Illus.). 128p. (J). (gr. 5-9). 33.27 *(978-0-7660-3589-8(1))* Enslow Pubs., Inc.

—Tony Stewart: Rocket on the Racetrack. 2008. (Heroes of Racing Ser.). (Illus.). 128p. (J). (gr. 3-7). lib. bdg. 33.27 *(978-0-7660-2998-9(0))* Enslow Pubs., Inc.

Benatar, Raquel & Rubio, Adrian. Go, Milka, Go! The Life of Milka Duno. Benatar, Raquel & Rubio, Adrian, illus. 2008.Tr. of Corre, Milka, Corre! (SPA & ENG., Illus.). 32p. (J). 19.95 *(978-1-56492-360-8(6))* Laredo Publishing Co., Inc.

Biking Safely: Fourth Grade Guided Comprehension Level K. (On Our Way to English Ser.). (gr. 4-18). 34.50 *(978-0-7578-7149-8(6))* Rigby Education.

Braidich, V. Dale Earnhardt. 2009. (NASCAR Champions Ser.). 24p. (gr. 1-2). 42.50 *(978-1-61514-762-5(4)*, PowerKids Pr.) Rosen Publishing Group, Inc., The.

Braidich, Victoria. Dale Earnhardt. 2007. (NASCAR Champions Ser.). (Illus.). 24p. (J). (gr. 1-3). lib. bdg. 22.60 *(978-1-4042-3512-0(4))* Rosen Publishing Group, Inc., The.

Brennan, Kristine. Danica Patrick. 2010. (Role Model Athletes Ser.). (Illus.). 64p. (YA). (gr. 7-12). 22.95 *(978-1-4222-0487-0(1))* Mason Crest.

Brezina, Corona. I've Gotten a DWI/DUI, Now What? 2015. (Teen Life 411 Ser.). (ENG., Illus.). 112p. (J). (gr. 6-7). 35.60 *(978-1-4994-6146-6(1)*, Rosen Young Adult) Rosen Publishing Group, Inc., The.

Briggs, Raymond. Jimmy Murphy & the White Duesenberg. 2006. (Illus.). (J). *(978-0-9766683-0-5(0))* Racemaker Pr.

—Nuvolari & the Alfa Romeo. 2006. (Illus.). (J). *(978-0-9766683-1-2(9))* Racemaker Pr.

Caviezel, Giovanni. Race Car Driver. Mesturini, Cristina, illus. 2009. (Mini People Shape Bks.). (ENG.). 12p. (J). (gr. -1-2). bds. 5.99 *(978-0-7641-6217-6(9))* Barron's Educational Series, Inc.

Cefrey, Holly. Race Car Drivers: Life on the Fast Track. 2009. (Extreme Careers Ser.). 64p. (gr. 5-5). 58.50 *(978-1-61512-402-2(0)*, Rosen Reference) Rosen Publishing Group, Inc., The.

Christopher, Matt. Dale Earnhardt Sr: Matt Christopher Legends in Sports. 2007. (ENG., Illus.). 128p. (J). (gr. 3-7). per. 15.99 *(978-0-316-01114-3(2))* Little, Brown Bks. for Young Readers.

Colich, Abby. Danica Patrick. 2016. (Women in Sports Ser.). (ENG., Illus.). 24p. (gr. k-1). pap. 6.95 *(978-1-4914-8567-5(1)*, Pebble Plus) Capstone Press of Coughlan Cos.

Crisp, Dan. Little Drivers Going Places! 2006. (Little Drivers Ser.). (ENG., Illus.). 14p. (J). (gr. 1-1). bds. *(978-1-904550-96-9(7))* Child's Play International Ltd.

Crisp, Dan, illus. To the Rescue! 2006. (Little Drivers Ser.). (ENG.). 14p. (J). bds. *(978-1-904550-97-6(5))* Child's Play International Ltd.

Dayton, Connor. Denny Hamlin. 2009. (NASCAR Champions/Campeones de NASCAR Ser.). 24p. (gr. 1-2). (ENG & SPA.). 42.50 *(978-1-61514-789-2(6)*, Editorial Buenas Letras); 42.50 *(978-1-61514-767-0(5)*, PowerKids Pr.) Rosen Publishing Group, Inc., The.

—Greg Biffle. 2009. (NASCAR Champions Ser.). 24p. (gr. 1-2). 42.50 *(978-1-61514-768-7(3)*, PowerKids Pr.); (ENG & SPA.). 42.50 *(978-1-61514-790-8(X)*, Editorial Buenas Letras) Rosen Publishing Group, Inc., The.

—Greg Biffle. Alaman, Eduardo, tr. 2007. (NASCAR Champions / Campeones de NASCAR Ser.). (SPA., Illus.). 24p. (J). (gr. 1-3). lib. bdg. 22.60 *(978-1-4042-7646-8(7))* Rosen Publishing Group, Inc., The.

—Greg Biffle. 2007. (NASCAR Champions Ser.: Vol. 2). (Illus.). 24p. (J). (gr. 1-3). lib. bdg. 22.60 *(978-1-4042-3816-9(6))* Rosen Publishing Group, Inc., The.

—Jamie Mcmurray. 24p. (gr. 1-2). 2009. (NASCAR Champions Ser.). 42.50 *(978-1-61514-769-4(1)*, PowerKids Pr.) 2009. (NASCAR Champions/Campeones de NASCAR Ser.). (ENG & SPA.). 42.50 *(978-1-61514-791-5(8)*, Editorial Buenas Letras) 2007. (NASCAR Champions Ser.: Vol. 2). (Illus.). (J). lib. bdg. 22.60 *(978-1-4042-3813-8(1))* Rosen Publishing Group, Inc., The.

—Jamie Mcmurray. Alaman, Eduardo, tr. 2007. (NASCAR Champions / Campeones de NASCAR Ser.). (SPA., Illus.). 24p. (J). (gr. 1-3). lib. bdg. 22.60 *(978-1-4042-7643-7(2))* Rosen Publishing Group, Inc., The.

—Jeff Burton. 2009. (NASCAR Champions/Campeones de NASCAR Ser.). 24p. (gr. 1-2). (ENG & SPA.). 42.50 *(978-1-61514-792-2(6)*, Editorial Buenas Letras); 42.50 *(978-1-61514-770-0(5)*, PowerKids Pr.) Rosen Publishing Group, Inc., The.

—Jeff Burton. Alaman, Eduardo, tr. 2007. (NASCAR Champions / Campeones de NASCAR Ser.). (SPA., Illus.). 24p. (J). (gr. 1-3). lib. bdg. 22.60 *(978-1-4042-7642-0(4))* Rosen Publishing Group, Inc., The.

—Jeff Burton. 2007. (NASCAR Champions Ser.: Vol. 2). (Illus.). 24p. (J). (gr. 1-3). lib. bdg. 22.60 *(978-1-4042-3812-1(3))* Rosen Publishing Group, Inc., The.

—Kasey Kahne. 2009. (NASCAR Champions/Campeones de NASCAR Ser.). 24p. (gr. 1-2). (ENG & SPA.). 42.50 *(978-1-61514-793-9(4)*, Editorial Buenas Letras); 42.50 *(978-1-61514-777-9(2)*, PowerKids Pr.) Rosen Publishing Group, Inc., The.

—Kasey Kahne. Alaman, Eduardo, tr. 2007. (NASCAR Champions / Campeones de NASCAR Ser.). (SPA., Illus.). 24p. (J). (gr. 1-3). lib. bdg. 22.60 *(978-1-4042-7645-1(9))* Rosen Publishing Group, Inc., The.

—Kasey Kahne. 2007. (NASCAR Champions Ser.: Vol. 2). (Illus.). 24p. (J). (gr. 1-3). lib. bdg. 22.60 *(978-1-4042-3815-2(8))* Rosen Publishing Group, Inc., The.

—Kyle Busch. 2009. (NASCAR Champions/Campeones de NASCAR Ser.). 24p. (gr. 1-2). (ENG & SPA.). 42.50 *(978-1-61514-794-6(2)*, Editorial Buenas Letras); 42.50 *(978-1-61514-782-3(9)*, PowerKids Pr.) Rosen Publishing Group, Inc., The.

—Kyle Busch. Alaman, Eduardo, tr. 2007. (NASCAR Champions / Campeones de NASCAR Ser.). (SPA., Illus.). 24p. (J). (gr. 1-3). lib. bdg. 22.60 *(978-1-4042-7647-5(5))* Rosen Publishing Group, Inc., The.

—Kyle Busch. 2007. (NASCAR Champions Ser.: Vol. 2). (Illus.). 24p. (J). (gr. 1-3). lib. bdg. 22.60 *(978-1-4042-3817-6(4))* Rosen Publishing Group, Inc., The.

El Nabli, Dina. Danica Patrick. 2009. (People We Should Know Ser.). 32p. (J). (gr. 3-5). pap. 10.50 *(978-1-4339-0158-4(7))*; lib. bdg. 31.00 *(978-1-4339-0018-1(1))* Stevens, Gareth Publishing LLLP. (Gareth Stevens Learning Library).

Ertle-Rickard, Stephen. Formula 1: Life at the Edge. 2008. (321 Go! Ser.). (ENG., Illus.). 36p. pap. *(978-1-84167-783-5(3))* Ransom Publishing Ltd.

Farmer, Emily. Jimmie Johnson: NASCAR Driver. 2009. (Behind the Wheel Ser.). 48p. (gr. 5-5). 53.00 *(978-1-61511-545-7(5)*, Rosen Reference) Rosen Publishing Group, Inc., The.

Figorito, M. Matt Kenseth. 2009. (NASCAR Champions Ser.). 24p. (gr. 1-2). 42.50 *(978-1-61514-783-0(7)*, PowerKids Pr.) Rosen Publishing Group, Inc., The.

Fleischman, Bill. Dale Earnhardt JR. collector's ed. 2005. (Race Car Legends Ser.). (Illus.). 72p. (YA). (gr. 5-9). lib. bdg. 25.00 *(978-0-7910-8671-1(2))* Facts On File, Inc.

Ford, Michael. Dale Earnhardt, Jr. 2010. (Superstars of NASCAR Ser.). (ENG.). 32p. (J). (gr. 3-8). pap. 10.50 *(978-1-4339-3948-8(7))*; lib. bdg. 25.25 *(978-1-4339-3947-1(9))* Stevens, Gareth Publishing LLLP.

Franks, Katie. I Want to Be a Race Car Driver. (Dream Jobs Ser.). 24p. (gr. 2-3). 2009. 42.50 *(978-1-61512-208-0(7)*, PowerKids Pr.) 2007. (Illus.). (J). lib. bdg. 22.60 *(978-1-4042-3623-3(6))* Rosen Publishing Group, Inc., The.

—Quiero Ser Piloto de Carreras. 2009. (Trabajos de ensueño (Dream Jobs) Ser.). (SPA.). 24p. pap. 8.25 *(978-1-4358-8603-2(8))*; (Illus.). (J). (gr. 2-4). 22.60 *(978-1-4042-8157-8(6))* Rosen Publishing Group, Inc., The. (PowerKids Pr.).

Gaines, Ann Graham. Kenny Irwin JR. rev. collector's ed. 2005. (Race Car Legends Ser.). (Illus.). 64p. (YA). (gr. 5-9). lib. bdg. 25.00 *(978-0-7910-8766-4(2))* Facts On File, Inc.

Ganchy, Sally. Mark Martin: NASCAR Driver. 2009. (Behind the Wheel Ser.). (gr. 5-8). (ENG., Illus.). 48p. (J). pap. 11.75 *(978-1-4358-5407-9(1))*; 48p. 53.00 *(978-1-61511-553-2(6)*, Rosen Reference); (YA). lib. bdg. 29.25 *(978-1-4042-1952-6(8))* Rosen Publishing Group, Inc., The.

Garfield, Ken. Dale Earnhardt, Jr: Born to Race. 2005. (Sports Leaders Ser.). (Illus.). 104p. (J). (gr. 5-13). lib. bdg. 27.94 *(978-0-7660-2424-3(5))* Enslow Pubs., Inc.

Gerdes, Louise. Teen Driving. 2008. (At Issue Ser.). (ENG., Illus.). 80-128p. (J). (gr. 10-12). 24.45 *(978-0-7377-3941-1(X)*, Greenhaven Pr., Inc.); (YA). (gr. 9-12). pap. 34.45 *(978-0-7377-3940-4(1))* Cengage Gale.

Gillis, Jennifer B. Jobs on Wheels. 2006. (My Neighborhood Ser.). (Illus.). 24p. (J). (gr. -1-3). 16.15 *(978-0-7569-6928-8(X))* Perfection Learning Corp.

Gitlin, Martin. Darrell Waltrip: Racing Legend. 2009. (Heroes of Racing Ser.). (Illus.). 128p. (J). (gr. 5-9). lib. bdg. 33.27 *(978-0-7660-3300-9(7))* Enslow Pubs., Inc.

—Jeff Gordon: Racing's Brightest Star. 2008. (Heroes of Racing Ser.). (Illus.). 128p. (J). (gr. 3-7). lib. bdg. 33.27 *(978-0-7660-2997-2(2))* Enslow Pubs., Inc.

—Jimmie Johnson: Racing Champ. 2008. (Heroes of Racing Ser.). (Illus.). 128p. (J). (gr. 3-7). lib. bdg. 33.27 *(978-0-7660-2999-6(9))* Enslow Pubs., Inc.

Glaser, Jason. Danica Patrick. 2009. (Sports Idols Ser.). 24p. (gr. 2-3). 42.50 *(978-1-60853-140-0(6)*, PowerKids Pr.) Rosen Publishing Group, Inc., The.

Goddard, Jennifer S. On the Road: The Savvy Girl's Guide to Cars. 2006. (Illus.). 49p. (J). pap. *(978-0-88441-701-9(8))* Girl Scouts of the USA.

Gordon, Nick. Monster Trucks. 2013. (Monster Machines Ser.). (ENG., Illus.). 24p. (J). (gr. k-3). lib. bdg. 25.95 *(978-1-60014-940-5(5)*, Blastoff! Readers) Bellwether Media.

Grosshandler, Janet. Drugs & Driving. (Drug Abuse Prevention Library). 64p. 2009. (gr. 5-5). 58.50 *(978-1-60853-429-6(4))* 2005. (Illus.). (YA). (gr. 7-12). lib. bdg. 31.95 *(978-0-8239-3459-1(4))* Rosen Publishing Group, Inc., The.

Harper, John. Denny Hamlin. 2010. (Superstars of NASCAR Ser.). (ENG.). 32p. (J). (gr. 3-8). pap. 10.50 *(978-1-4339-3951-8(7))*; lib. bdg. 25.25 *(978-1-4339-3950-1(9))* Stevens, Gareth Publishing LLLP.

Hillstrom, Kevin & Hillstrom, Laurie Collier. Dale Earnhardt, Jr. 2008. (People in the News Ser.). (ENG., Illus.). 128p. (gr. 7-12). lib. bdg. 39.40 *(978-1-4205-0088-2(0)*, LML02109-242092) Cengage Gale.

Hofer, Charles. Race Cars. 2009. (World's Fastest Machines Ser.). 24p. (gr. 2-3). 42.50 *(978-1-60854-854-5(6)*, PowerKids Pr.) Rosen Publishing Group, Inc., The.

Hoffman, Mary Ann. Jeff Gordon. 2010. (Superstars of NASCAR Ser.). (ENG.). 32p. (J). (gr. 3-8). pap. 10.50 *(978-1-4339-3954-9(1))*; lib. bdg. 25.25 *(978-1-4339-3953-2(3))* Stevens, Gareth Publishing LLLP.

—Kyle Busch. 2010. (Superstars of NASCAR Ser.). (ENG.). 32p. (J). (gr. 3-8). pap. 10.50 *(978-1-4339-3963-1(0))*; lib. bdg. 25.25 *(978-1-4339-3962-4(2))* Stevens, Gareth Publishing LLLP.

Holmes, Bill. Mark Martin. 2010. (Superstars of NASCAR Ser.). (ENG.). 32p. (J). (gr. 3-8). pap. 10.50 *(978-1-4339-3966-2(5))*; lib. bdg. 25.25 *(978-1-4339-3965-5(7))* Stevens, Gareth Publishing LLLP.

Horn, Geoffrey M. Dale Earnhardt, Jr. 2006. (Today's Superstars). (Illus.). 32p. (gr. 5-8). lib. bdg. 31.95 *(978-0-8368-6182-2(5))* Stevens, Gareth Publishing LLLP.

Howse, Jennifer. NASCAR Sprint Cup. 2012. (J). 28.55 *(978-1-61913-616-8(3))* 2012. (J). pap. 13.95 *(978-1-61913-618-2(X))* 2009. 32p. (YA). (gr. 4-7). lib. bdg. 26.00 *(978-1-60596-636-6(3))* Weigl Pubs., Inc.

Hubbard-Brown, Janet. The Labonte Brothers. rev. collector's ed. 2005. (Race Car Legends Ser.). (Illus.). 72p. (YA). (gr. 5-9). lib. bdg. 25.00 *(978-0-7910-8767-1(0))* Facts On File, Inc.

Jacques, Michele Siuda. Teen Driving. 2012. (At Issue Ser.). (ENG.). 128p. (gr. 10-12). pap. 27.80 *(978-0-7377-6419-2(8))*; lib. bdg. 39.40 *(978-0-7377-6418-5(X))* Cengage Gale. (Greenhaven Pr., Inc.).

James, L. Dale Jarrett. 2009. (NASCAR Champions Ser.). 24p. (gr. 1-2). 42.50 *(978-1-61514-766-3(7)*, PowerKids Pr.) Rosen Publishing Group, Inc., The.

James, Lincoln. Dale Jarrett. 2007. (NASCAR Champions Ser.). (Illus.). 24p. (J). (gr. 1-3). lib. bdg. 22.60 *(978-1-4042-3459-8(4))* Rosen Publishing Group, Inc., The.

Keith, Ted. Matt Kenseth. 2008. (World of NASCAR Ser.). (ENG., Illus.). 32p. (J). (gr. 3-6). 28.50 *(978-1-60253-077-5(7)*, 200995) Child's World, Inc., The.

Kirkpatrick, Rob. Dale Earnhardt Jr: NASCAR Road Racer / Piloto de NASCAR. 2009. (Hot Shots/Grandes idolos Ser.). (ENG & SPA.). 24p. (gr. 1-1). 42.50 *(978-1-61513-413-7(1)*, Editorial Buenas Letras) Rosen Publishing Group, Inc., The.

—Dale Earnhardt Jr: Piloto de NASCAR (NASCAR Road Racer) 2009. (Grandes Idolos (Hot Shots) Ser.). (SPA.). 24p. (gr. 1-1). 42.50 *(978-1-61512-735-1(6)*, Editorial Buenas Letras) Rosen Publishing Group, Inc., The.

—Dale Earnhardt Jr. , NASCAR Road Racer/Piloto de NASCAR. De Leon, Mauricio Velzaquez, tr. 2008. (Reading Power Ser.). (ENG., Illus.). 24p. (gr. 1-6). per. 8.85 *(978-1-4042-7539-3(8))* Rosen Publishing Group, Inc., The.

—Jeff Gordon: Campeón de NASCAR (NASCAR Champion) 2009. (Grandes Idolos (Hot Shots) Ser.). (SPA.). 24p. (gr. 1-1). 42.50 *(978-1-61512-737-5(2)*, Editorial Buenas Letras) Rosen Publishing Group, Inc., The.

—Jeff Gordon: NASCAR Champion / Campeón de NASCAR. 2009. (Hot Shots/Grandes ídolos Ser.). (ENG & SPA.). 24p. (gr. 1-1). 42.50 *(978-1-61513-415-1(8),* Editorial Buenas Letras) Rosen Publishing Group, Inc., The.

Kopp, Megan. NASCAR. 2013. (J). *(978-1-62127-503-9(5));* pap. *(978-1-62127-506-0(X))* Weigl Pubs., Inc.

Kortemeier, Todd. Superstars of NASCAR. 2016. (Pro Sports Superstars Ser.). (ENG., Illus.). 24p. (J). (gr. 1-4). 20.95 *(978-1-60753-940-7(3))* Amicus Publishing.

La Bella, Laura. Carl Edwards: NASCAR Driver. 2009. (Behind the Wheel Ser.). (ENG., Illus.). 48p. (YA). (gr. 5-8). pap. 11.75 *(978-1-4358-5405-5(5))* Rosen Publishing Group, Inc., The.

Levy, Janey. Kurt Busch. 2007. (High Interest Bks.). (ENG., Illus.). 48p. (J). (gr. 4-7). pap. 6.95 *(978-0-531-18714-2(4))* Scholastic Library Publishing.

MacDonald, James. Dale Earnhardt, Jr. Racing's Living Legacy. 2008. (Heroes of Racing Ser.). (Illus.). 128p. (J). (gr. 3-7). lib. bdg. 33.27 *(978-0-7660-2996-5(4))* Enslow Pubs., Inc.

Martin, Bob. Tony Stewart. 2010. (Superstars of NASCAR Ser.). (ENG.). 32p. (J). (gr. 3-8). pap. 10.50 *(978-1-4339-3969-3(X));* lib. bdg. 25.25 *(978-1-4339-3968-6(1))* Stevens, Gareth Publishing LLLP.

McCarthy, Meghan. Daredevil: The Daring Life of Betty Skelton. McCarthy, Meghan, illus. 2013. (ENG., Illus.). 48p. (J). (gr. -1-3). 17.99 *(978-1-4424-2262-9(9),* Simon & Schuster/Paula Wiseman Bks.) Simon & Schuster/Paula Wiseman Bks.

Meachen Rau, Dana. Driving. 2006. (On the Move Ser.). (ENG & SPA., Illus.). 24p. (gr. k-1). lib. bdg. 15.95 *(978-0-7614-2316-4(8),* Benchmark Bks.) Marshall Cavendish Corp.

Mello, Tara Baukus. Rusty Wallace. rev. collector's ed. 2005. (Race Car Legends Ser.). (Illus.). 72p. (YA). (gr. 5-9). lib. bdg. 25.00 *(978-0-7910-8669-8(0))* Facts On File, Inc.

Miller, Connie Colwell. Carl Edwards, 1 vol. 2013. (NASCAR Heroes Ser.). (ENG.). 32p. (J). (gr. 3-9). lib. bdg. 27.07 *(978-1-61783-662-6(1),* SportsZone) ABDO Publishing Co.

—Dale Earnhardt, Jr, 1 vol. 2013. (NASCAR Heroes Ser.). (ENG.). 32p. (J). (gr. 3-9). lib. bdg. 27.07 *(978-1-61783-661-9(3),* SportsZone) ABDO Publishing Co.

—Danica Patrick, 1 vol. 2013. (NASCAR Heroes Ser.). (ENG.). 32p. (J). (gr. 3-9). lib. bdg. 27.07 *(978-1-61783-666-4(4),* SportsZone) ABDO Publishing Co.

—Jimmie Johnson, 1 vol. 2013. (NASCAR Heroes Ser.). (ENG.). 32p. (J). (gr. 3-9). lib. bdg. 27.07 *(978-1-61783-664-0(8),* SportsZone) ABDO Publishing Co.

—Matt Kenseth, 1 vol. 2013. (NASCAR Heroes Ser.). (ENG.). 32p. (J). (gr. 3-9). lib. bdg. 27.07 *(978-1-61783-665-7(6),* SportsZone) ABDO Publishing Co.

Mooney, Carla. Thinking Critically: Distracted Driving. 2015. (ENG., Illus.). 80p. (J). lib. bdg. *(978-1-60152-780-6(2))* ReferencePoint Pr., Inc.

Murray, Stuart A. P. Score with Race Car Math. 2013. (Score with Sports Math Ser.). 48p. (J). lib. bdg. 25.27 *(978-0-7660-4177-6(8),* Enslow Elementary) Enslow Pubs., Inc.

Nagelhout, Ryan. Talk Like a Race Car Driver. 2016. (Let's Talk Sports! Ser.). 00032p. (J). pap. 10.50 ***(978-1-4824-5708-7(3))*** Stevens, Gareth Publishing LLLP.

NASCAR Champions, 6 vols., Set 1. 2008. (J). (gr. 1-6). lib. bdg. 127.50 *(978-1-4042-3549-6(3))* Rosen Publishing Group, Inc., The.

Payment, Simone. Kyle Busch: NASCAR Driver. 2009. (Behind the Wheel Ser.). 48p. (gr. 5-8). (ENG., Illus.). (J). pap. 11.75 *(978-1-4358-5403-1(9));* 53.00 *(978-1-61511-550-1(1),* Rosen Reference) Rosen Publishing Group, Inc., The.

—Ryan Newman: NASCAR Driver. (Behind the Wheel Ser.). 48p. (gr. 5-5). 2009. 53.00 *(978-1-61511-559-4(5),* Rosen Reference) 2006. (Illus.). (YA). lib. bdg. 29.25 *(978-1-4042-0983-1(2))* Rosen Publishing Group, Inc., The.

PC Treasures Staff, ed. Tony Stewart. 2009. (Nascar Drivers Coloring Book Ser.). (ENG., Illus.). 96p. (J). pap. 2.99 *(978-1-60072-160-1(5))* PC Treasures, Inc.

Poolos, J. Jeff Gordon: NASCAR Driver. (Behind the Wheel Ser.). 48p. (gr. 5-5). 2009. 53.00 *(978-1-61511-544-0(7),* Rosen Reference) 2006. (Illus.). (YA). lib. bdg. 29.25 *(978-1-4042-0980-0(8))* Rosen Publishing Group, Inc., The.

Porterfield, Jason. Kurt Busch: NASCAR Driver. 2009. (Behind the Wheel Ser.). 48p. (gr. 5-5). 53.00 *(978-1-61511-549-5(8),* Rosen Reference) Rosen Publishing Group, Inc., The.

Pratt, Laura. Danica Patrick. 2012. (J). *(978-1-61913-534-5(5));* pap. 12.95 *(978-1-61913-589-5(2))* Weigl Pubs., Inc.

Priddy, Roger. Let's Pretend Race Driver Set. 2009. (Let's Pretend Ser.). (ENG.). 8p. (J). (gr. -1 — 1). 14.95 *(978-0-312-50717-6(8),* Priddy Bks.) St. Martin's Pr.

Pristash, Nicole. Carl Edwards. 2009. (NASCAR Champions Ser.). 24p. (gr. 1-2). 42.50 *(978-1-61514-759-5(4));* (Illus.). (J). lib. bdg. 22.60 *(978-1-4042-4449-8(2))* Rosen Publishing Group, Inc., The. (PowerKids Pr.).

—Dale Earnhardt Jr. 2009. (NASCAR Champions Ser.). 24p. (gr. 1-2). 42.50 *(978-1-61514-763-2(2),* PowerKids Pr.) Rosen Publishing Group, Inc., The.

—Jeff Gordon. 2009. (NASCAR Champions Ser.). 24p. (gr. 1-2). 42.50 *(978-1-61514-771-7(3),* PowerKids Pr.) Rosen Publishing Group, Inc., The.

—Jimmie Johnson. 2009. (NASCAR Champions Ser.). 24p. (gr. 1-2). 42.50 *(978-1-61514-774-8(8));* (Illus.). (J). lib. bdg. 22.60 *(978-1-4042-4447-4(6))* Rosen Publishing Group, Inc., The. (PowerKids Pr.).

—Kevin Harvick. 2009. (NASCAR Champions Ser.). 24p. (gr. 1-2). 42.50 *(978-1-61514-778-6(0),* PowerKids Pr.); (Illus.). (J). lib. bdg. 22.60 *(978-1-4042-4448-1(4))* Rosen Publishing Group, Inc., The.

—Ryan Newman. 2009. (NASCAR Champions Ser.). 24p. (Illus.). (gr. 1-6). pap. 8.25 *(978-1-4042-4546-4(4),* Rosen Classroom); (gr. 1-2). 42.50 *(978-1-61514-784-7(5),* PowerKids Pr.); (Illus.). lib. bdg. 22.60 *(978-1-4042-4450-4(6),* PowerKids Pr.) Rosen Publishing Group, Inc., The.

Race Car Legends. 2008. (Race Car Legends Ser.). (gr. 5-8). 625.00 *(978-0-7910-9816-5(8),* Chelsea Hse.) Facts On File, Inc.

Rappoport, Ken. Dale Earnhardt, Jr. A Car Racer Who Cares. 2011. (Sports Stars Who Care Ser.). (Illus.). 48p. (J). (gr. 3-18). pap. 8.95 *(978-1-59845-228-0(2),* Enslow Elementary); (gr. 2-5). lib. bdg. 25.27 *(978-0-7660-3777-9(0))* Enslow Pubs., Inc.

Robinson, Tom. Mark Martin: Master Behind the Wheel. 2008. (Heroes of Racing Ser.). (Illus.). 128p. (J). (gr. 3-7). lib. bdg. 33.27 *(978-0-7660-3001-5(6))* Enslow Pubs., Inc.

Roselius, J. Chris. Danica Patrick: Racing to History. 2009. (Heroes of Racing Ser.). (Illus.). 128p. (J). (gr. 5-9). lib. bdg. 33.27 *(978-0-7660-3302-3(3))* Enslow Pubs., Inc.

—Matt Kenseth: Speeding to Victory. 2008. (Heroes of Racing Ser.). (Illus.). 128p. (J). (gr. 3-7). lib. bdg. 33.27 *(978-0-7660-3000-8(8))* Enslow Pubs., Inc.

Roza, Greg. Dale Earnhardt Jr. NASCAR Driver. 2006. (Behind the Wheel Ser.). (Illus.). 48p. (YA). (gr. 5-9). lib. bdg. 29.25 *(978-1-4042-0979-4(4))* Rosen Publishing Group, Inc., The.

—Dale Earnhardt Jr: NASCAR Driver. 2009. (Behind the Wheel Ser.). 48p. (gr. 5-5). 53.00 *(978-1-61511-540-2(4),* Rosen Reference) Rosen Publishing Group, Inc., The.

—Kevin Harvick: NASCAR Driver. 2009. (Behind the Wheel Ser.). (gr. 5-5). 48p. 53.00 *(978-1-61511-546-4(3),* Rosen Reference); (YA). lib. bdg. 29.25 *(978-1-4042-1899-4(8))* Rosen Publishing Group, Inc., The.

—Tony Stewart. 2009. (NASCAR Champions Ser.). 24p. (gr. 1-2). 42.50 *(978-1-61514-788-5(8),* PowerKids Pr.) Rosen Publishing Group, Inc., The.

Sapet, Kerrily. Jeff Gordon. 2012. (Role Model Athletes Ser.). 64p. (J). (gr. 7). 22.95 *(978-1-4222-2710-7(3))* Mason Crest.

Savage, Jeff. Auto Racing Super Stats. 2017. (Pro Sports Stats Ser.). (ENG.). 32p. (J). (gr. 3-6). 27.99 ***(978-1-5124-3412-5(4))*** Lerner Publishing Group.

—Dale Earnhardt Jr. 2005. (Amazing Athletes Ser.). (Illus.). 32p. (J). (gr. 4-7). per. 5.95 *(978-0-8225-2953-8(X))* Lerner Publishing Group.

—Dale Earnhardt Jr. (Revised Edition) 2009. pap. 40.95 *(978-0-7613-4775-0(5))* Lerner Publishing Group.

—Danica Patrick. (Amazing Athletes Ser.). 32p. 2006. (Illus.). (J). (gr. 4). pap. 6.95 *(978-0-8225-6012-8(7),* First Avenue Editions) 2010. (ENG.). (gr. 2-5). lib. bdg. 25.26 *(978-0-7613-5750-6(5),* Lerner Pubns.) Lerner Publishing Group.

—James Stewart. 2007. (Amazing Athletes Ser.). (ENG., Illus.). 32p. (gr. 2-5). per. 7.95 *(978-0-8225-7662-4(7),* First Avenue Editions) Lerner Publishing Group.

Sawyer, Sarah. Denny Hamlin: NASCAR Driver. 2009. (Behind the Wheel Ser.). 48p. (gr. 5-5). 53.00 *(978-1-61511-541-9(2),* Rosen Reference) Rosen Publishing Group, Inc., The.

Scheff, Matt. Jeff Gordon, 1 vol. 2013. (NASCAR Heroes Ser.). (ENG.). 32p. (J). (gr. 3-9). lib. bdg. 27.07 *(978-1-61783-663-3(X),* SportsZone) ABDO Publishing Co.

—Kyle Busch, 1 vol. 2013. (NASCAR Heroes Ser.). (ENG.). 32p. (J). (gr. 3-9). lib. bdg. 27.07 *(978-1-61783-660-2(5),* SportsZone) ABDO Publishing Co.

—Tony Stewart, 1 vol. 2013. (NASCAR Heroes Ser.). (ENG.). 32p. (J). (gr. 3-9). lib. bdg. 27.07 *(978-1-61783-667-1(2),* SportsZone) ABDO Publishing Co.

Sheen, Barbara. Danica Patrick. 2009. (People in the News Ser.). (ENG.). 128p. (gr. 7-12). 39.40 *(978-1-4205-0155-1(0))* Cengage Gale.

—Janet Guthrie: Racing Pioneer. 2010. (Innovators Ser.). (Illus.). 64p. (J). 29.95 *(978-0-7377-5050-8(2),* Kidhaven) Cengage Gale.

Spaulding, Jeffrey. Matt Kenseth: NASCAR Driver. 2009. (Behind the Wheel Ser.). (gr. 5-5). 48p. 53.00 *(978-1-61511-556-3(0),* Rosen Reference); (YA). lib. bdg. 29.25 *(978-1-4042-1897-0(1))* Rosen Publishing Group, Inc., The.

—The Most Victorious Cars of NASCAR Racing. (Highlights of NASCAR Racing Ser.). 48p. (gr. 5-5). 2009. 53.00 *(978-1-61513-302-4(X),* Rosen Reference) 2008. (Illus.). (YA). lib. bdg. 29.25 *(978-1-4042-1398-2(8))* Rosen Publishing Group, Inc., The.

Stinson, Rick. Kyle Busch: NASCAR Driver. 2009. (Behind the Wheel Ser.). (YA). (gr. 5-9). lib. bdg. 29.25 *(978-1-4042-1896-3(3))* Rosen Publishing Group, Inc., The.

Studio Mouse Staff. Cars on the Road to Learning: Flat Learn & Carry 4 Board Books & CD. rev. ed. 2007. (ENG.). 80p. 12.99 *(978-1-59069-549-4(6))* Studio Mouse LLC.

Sutherland, Adam. Being a Formula One Driver. 2012. (On the Radar: Awesome Jobs Ser.). (ENG., Illus.). 32p. (gr. 4-8). lib. bdg. 26.60 *(978-0-7613-7781-8(6),* Lerner Pubns.) Lerner Publishing Group.

Teitelbaum, Michael. Tony Stewart. 2008. (World of NASCAR Ser.). (ENG., Illus.). 32p. (J). (gr. 3-6). 28.50 *(978-1-60253-083-6(1),* 201001) Child's World, Inc., The.

Thompson, Gary. What Every Teen Should Know Before Getting Behind the Wheel Alone: A Guide to Increasing Your Child's Safety While Reducing Your Auto Repair Expenses. 2004. 131p. (YA). per. 9.95 *(978-0-9749763-1-0(8))* Guiding Horizons.

Tieck, Sarah. Jimmie Johnson: NASCAR Champion, 1 vol. 2009. (Big Buddy Biographies Set 3 Ser.). (ENG., Illus.). 32p. (J). (gr. 2-5). 28.50 *(978-1-60453-709-3(4))* ABDO Publishing Co.

West, David. Race Car Drivers. 2009. (Graphic Careers Ser.). (ENG.). 48p. (YA). (gr. 5-5). 58.50 *(978-1-61512-888-4(3),* Rosen Reference) Rosen Publishing Group, Inc., The.

Wilson, Walt. Jimmie Johnson. 2010. (Superstars of NASCAR Ser.). (ENG.). 32p. (J). (gr. 3-6). pap. 10.50 *(978-1-4339-3957-0(6));* lib. bdg. 25.25 *(978-1-4339-3956-3(8))* Stevens, Gareth Publishing LLLP.

Winters, Adam. Everything You Need to Know about Being a Teen Driver. 2005. (Need to Know Library). (Illus.). 64p. (YA). (gr. 7-12). 31.95 *(978-0-8239-3287-0(7),* NTTEDR) Rosen Publishing Group, Inc., The.

Woods, Bob. Want to Be a NASCAR Driver? 2008. (World of NASCAR Ser.). (ENG., Illus.). 32p. (J). (gr. 3-6). 28.50 *(978-1-60253-084-3(X),* 201002) Child's World, Inc., The.

Woods, Bob & Willis, John. Racer Girls. 2017. (Illus.). 32p. (J). ***(978-1-4896-4782-5(1))*** Weigl Pubs., Inc.

Wright, Marcy. Juan Pablo Montoya. 2010. (Superstars of NASCAR Ser.). (ENG.). 32p. (J). (gr. 3-8). pap. 10.50 *(978-1-4339-3960-0(6));* lib. bdg. 25.25 *(978-1-4339-3959-4(2))* Stevens, Gareth Publishing LLLP.

AUTOMOBILE DRIVERS—FICTION

Bauer, Joan. Rules of the Road. 2005. (ENG.). 208p. (YA). (gr. 7-7). pap. 8.99 *(978-0-14-240425-6(X),* Speak) Penguin Young Readers Group.

Brouwer, Sigmund. Scarlet Thunder, 1 vol. 2008. (Orca Sports Ser.). (ENG.). 176p. (YA). (gr. 6-10). pap. 9.95 *(978-1-55143-911-2(5))* Orca Bk. Pubs. USA.

Brown, Joe. Race to the Rescue. Marchesi, Stephen, illus. 2009. (J). *(978-0-545-13473-6(0))* Scholastic, Inc.

DiCamillo, Kate. Mercy Watson Goes for a Ride. Van Dusen, Chris, illus. 2006. (Mercy Watson Ser.: 2). (ENG.). 80p. (J). (gr. k-4). 14.99 *(978-0-7636-2332-6(6))* Candlewick Pr.

—Mercy Watson Goes for a Ride. 2012. 16.00 *(978-1-61383-702-3(X))* Perfection Learning Corp.

—Mercy Watson Goes for a Ride. Van Dusen, Chris, illus. 2009. (Mercy Watson Ser.: 2). (ENG.). 80p. (J). (gr. 1-4). pap. 5.99 *(978-0-7636-4505-2(2))* Candlewick Pr.

—Mercy Watson Goes for a Ride. 2009. (Mercy Watson Ser.: Bk. 2). lib. bdg. 16.00 *(978-0-606-06699-0(3),* Turtleback) Turtleback Bks.

Hall, Kirsten. Zoom, Zoom, Zoom. Garofoli, Viviana, illus. 2004. (My First Reader Ser.). (ENG.). 32p. (J). (gr. k-1). pap. 3.95 *(978-0-516-25509-5(6),* Children's Pr.) Scholastic Library Publishing.

Harper, Jamie. Miles to Go. Harper, Jamie, illus. 2010. (ENG., Illus.). 32p. (J). (gr. -1-2). 12.99 *(978-0-7636-3598-5(7))* Candlewick Pr.

Hill, David. Coming Back. 2007. (ENG.). 200p. per. 18.95 *(978-0-9542330-2-0(6))* Aurora Metro Pubns. Ltd. GBR. Dist: Consortium Bk. Sales & Distribution.

Johnson, Maureen. The Key to the Golden Firebird. 2004. (ENG.). 304p. (J). (gr. 7-18). 15.99 *(978-0-06-054138-5(5))* HarperCollins Pubs.

Marchesi, Stephen, illus. The Flights of Marceau: Week One. 2007. (ENG.). 56p. (J). 16.95 *(978-0-9797495-0-6(6))* Majestic Eagle Publishing.

Perlman, Rhea. Water Balloon Doom. Santat, Dan, illus. 2006. (Otto Undercover Ser.: No. 3). 124p. (J). (gr. 2-6). 14.99 *(978-0-06-075500-3(8),* Tegen, Katherine Bks) HarperCollins Pubs.

Porter, Alan J. Cars: The Rookie. Carreres, Albert, illus. 2009. (World of Cars Ser.). (ENG.). 112p. (J). 24.99 *(978-1-60886-522-2(3))* Boom! Studios.

—Cars: the Rookie. Carreres, Albert, illus. 2009. (World of Cars Ser.). (ENG.). 112p. (J). pap. 9.99 *(978-1-934506-84-4(2))* Boom! Studios.

Publications International Ltd. Staff. Steering Wheel Sound Elmo Away We Go. 2008. 12p. (J). bds. 17.98 *(978-1-4127-8948-6(6),* PIL Kids) Publications International, Ltd.

Scott, Jerry. Zits Vol. 7: Carretera y Manta. 2007. (SPA., Illus.). 128p. reprint ed. pap. 19.95 *(978-1-59497-337-6(7))* Public Square Bks.

Tali Drives His Car. (Pebble Soup Explorations Ser.). 16p. (gr. -1-18). 31.00 *(978-0-7578-1663-5(0))* Rigby Education.

Tali Drives His Car: Small Book. (Pebble Soup Explorations Ser.). 16p. (gr. -1-18). 5.00 *(978-0-7578-1703-8(3))* Rigby Education.

Tillworth, Mary. Licensed to Drive. 2014. (Barbie Step into Reading Level 3 Ser.). lib. bdg. 13.55 *(978-0-606-35992-4(3))* Turtleback Bks.

Villeneuve, Anne. The Red Scarf. 2010. (ENG., Illus.). 40p. (J). (gr. k-3). 17.95 *(978-0-88776-989-4(6),* Tundra Bks.) Tundra Bks. CAN. Dist: Penguin Random Hse. LLC.

Walsh, Patrick M., Jr. Who Says Timmy Can't Play: The Derby: A Timmy Wallings Story. McGriff, Aaron, ed. WFM Services, illus. 2011. 135p. (J). *(978-0-9842929-3-6(4))* Daddy Bean Bks.

Yoshida, Tatsuo. Speed Racer Set: Mach Go Go Go, 2 vols. 2008. (ENG., Illus.). 700p. (YA). (gr. 8). 39.95 *(978-1-56970-731-9(6),* 9781569707319) Digital Manga Publishing.

AUTOMOBILE DRIVING

see Automobile Drivers

AUTOMOBILE ENGINES

see Automobiles—Engines

AUTOMOBILE INDUSTRY AND TRADE

Armstrong, Linda. Henry Ford. 2009. pap. 13.25 *(978-1-60559-062-2(2))* Hameray Publishing Group, Inc.

Bell, Lonnie. The Story of the Ford Motor Company. 2003. (Built for Success Ser.). (Illus.). 48p. (J). 28.50 *(978-1-58340-293-1(4))* Black Rabbit Bks.

Bow, James. Aston Martin. 2012. (ENG.). 64p. (J). *(978-0-7787-2099-7(3));* pap. *(978-0-7787-2104-8(3))* Crabtree Publishing Co.

Brown, Jonatha A. Henry Ford. 2005. (People to Know Ser.). (Illus.). 24p. (gr. 1-4). pap. 8.15 *(978-0-8368-4473-3(4));* lib. bdg. 22.00 *(978-0-8368-4466-5(1))* Stevens, Gareth Publishing LLLP. (Weekly Reader Leveled Readers).

Burgan, Michael. Who Was Henry Ford? Hammond, Ted, illus. 2014. 105p. (J). lib. bdg. *(978-1-4844-3671-4(7),* Grosset & Dunlap) Penguin Publishing Group.

Crum, Colin. Mustang vs. Corvette, 1. 2014. (Ultimate Car Battles Ser.). (ENG.). 32p. (J). (gr. 3-6). 26.25 *(978-1-4777-9007-6(1),* Windmill Bks.) Rosen Publishing Group, Inc., The.

Davis, Lynn. Henry Ford, 1 vol. 2016. (ENG., Illus.). 24p. (J). *(978-1-62403-724-5(0))* ABDO Publishing Co.

Ferguson. Careers in Focus: Automotives. 2009. (Careers in Focus Ser.). 188p. (gr. 6-12). 32.95 *(978-0-8160-7300-9(7),* Ferguson Publishing Co.) Facts On File, Inc.

Ford, Carin T. Henry Ford: The Car Man. 2003. (Famous Inventors Ser.). (Illus.). 32p. (J). (gr. 1-4). lib. bdg. 22.60 *(978-0-7660-2179-2(3))* Enslow Pubs., Inc.

Freedman, Jeri. The U.S. Auto Industry: American Carmakers & the Economic Crisis. 2010. (In the News Ser.). (ENG.). 64p. (YA). pap. 12.95 *(978-1-4488-1680-4(7));* (gr. 7-12). lib. bdg. 31.95 *(978-1-4358-9448-8(0))* Rosen Publishing Group, Inc., The.

Gagne, Tammy. General Motors. 2017. (J). ***(978-1-5105-2368-5(5))*** SmartBook Media, Inc.

Green, Robert. Cars. 2008. (21st Century Skills Library: Global Products Ser.). (ENG., Illus.). 32p. (gr. 4-8). lib. bdg. 28.50 *(978-1-60279-028-5(0),* 200199) Cherry Lake Publishing.

James, Emily. Henry Ford. 2017. (Great Scientists & Inventors Ser.). (ENG.). 24p. (gr. k-1). lib. bdg. 26.65 *(978-1-5157-3880-0(9),* Pebble Plus) Capstone Press of Coughlan Cos.

Kulling, Monica. Eat My Dust! Henry Ford's First Race. Walz, Richard, illus. 2004. (Step into Reading Ser.). 48p. (J). (gr. 1-3). 11.65 *(978-0-7569-3231-2(9))* Perfection Learning Corp.

—Eat My Dust! Henry Ford's First Race. Walz, Richard, illus. 2004. (Step into Reading Ser.). (ENG.). 48p. (J). (gr. k-3). pap. 3.99 *(978-0-375-81510-2(4),* Random Hse. Bks. for Young Readers) Random Hse. Children's Bks.

Macy, Sue. Motor Girls. 2017. (ENG., Illus.). 96p. (J). (gr. 5). 18.99 *(978-1-4263-2697-4(1),* National Geographic Children's Bks.) National Geographic Society.

Mara, Wil. Henry Ford: Automotive Innovator. 2017. (Rookie Biographies Ser.). (ENG.). 32p. (J). lib. bdg. 25.00 ***(978-0-531-23225-5(5),*** Children's Pr.) Scholastic Library Publishing.

Marsico, Katie. Self-Driving Cars. 2016. (True Book(tm) — Engineering Wonders Ser.). (ENG., Illus.). 48p. (J). pap. 6.95 *(978-0-531-22272-0(1),* Children's Pr.) Scholastic Library Publishing.

McDowell, Pamela. Henry Ford. 2014. (Illus.). 24p. (J). *(978-1-62127-306-6(7))* Weigl Pubs., Inc.

Musolf, Nell. The Story of Ford. 2008. (Built for Success Ser.). (Illus.). 46p. (YA). (gr. 5-9). 22.95 *(978-1-58341-604-4(8))* Creative Co., The.

Nagelhout, Ryan. Henry Ford in His Own Words. 2014. (Eyewitness to History Ser.). 32p. (J). (gr. 4-6). pap. 63.00 *(978-1-4824-1218-5(7))* Stevens, Gareth Publishing LLLP.

Oachs, Emily Rose. Aston Martin DB9. 2017. (Car Crazy Ser.). (ENG., Illus.). 24p. (J). (gr. 3-7). lib. bdg. 25.95 *(978-1-62617-575-4(6),* Torque Bks.) Bellwether Media.

—Chevrolet Camaro Z28. 2017. (Car Crazy Ser.). (ENG., Illus.). 24p. (J). (gr. 3-7). lib. bdg. 25.95 *(978-1-62617-576-1(4),* Torque Bks.) Bellwether Media.

—Ford Mustang Shelby GT350. 2017. (Car Crazy Ser.). (ENG., Illus.). 24p. (J). (gr. 3-7). lib. bdg. 25.95 *(978-1-62617-579-2(9),* Torque Bks.) Bellwether Media.

—Lykan HyperSport. 2017. (Car Crazy Ser.). (ENG., Illus.). 24p. (J). (gr. 3-7). lib. bdg. 25.95 *(978-1-62617-580-8(2),* Torque Bks.) Bellwether Media.

Quinlan, Julia J. Alfa Romeo. 2012. (Speed Machines Ser.). (ENG., Illus.). 32p. (J). (gr. 3-6). 25.25 *(978-1-4488-7461-3(0));* pap. 10.00 *(978-1-4488-7533-7(1))* Rosen Publishing Group, Inc., The. (PowerKids Pr.).

—Corvette. 2012. (Speed Machines Ser.). (ENG., Illus.). 32p. (J). (gr. 3-6). 25.25 *(978-1-4488-7460-6(2));* pap. 10.00 *(978-1-4488-7532-0(3))* Rosen Publishing Group, Inc., The. (PowerKids Pr.).

—Lamborghini. 2012. (Speed Machines Ser.). (ENG., Illus.). 32p. (J). (gr. 3-6). 25.25 *(978-1-4488-7458-3(0));* pap. 10.00 *(978-1-4488-7530-6(7))* Rosen Publishing Group, Inc., The. (PowerKids Pr.).

—Mustang. 2012. (Speed Machines Ser.). (ENG., Illus.). 32p. (J). (gr. 3-6). 25.25 *(978-1-4488-7459-0(9));* pap. 10.00 *(978-1-4488-7531-3(5))* Rosen Publishing Group, Inc., The. (PowerKids Pr.).

Reis, Ronald A. Henry Ford for Kids: His Life & Ideas, with 21 Activities. 2016. (For Kids Ser.). (ENG., Illus.). 144p. (J). (gr. 4). pap. 16.95 *(978-1-61373-090-4(X))* Chicago Review Pr., Inc.

Rice, D. M. A Visit to a Car Factory, 1 vol. 2nd rev. ed. 2014. (TIME for KIDS(r) Nonfiction Readers Ser.). (ENG., Illus.). 24p. (J). (gr. 2-2). pap. 23.96 *(978-1-4807-1034-4(2))* Shell Educational Publishing.

—A Visit to a Car Factory, 1 vol. 2nd rev. ed. 2011. (Nonfiction Readers Ser.). (ENG.). 24p. (J). (gr. 2-2). pap. 6.99 *(978-1-4333-3607-2(3))* Teacher Created Materials, Inc.

Roberts, Steven. Henry Ford. 2013. (Jr. Graphic American Inventors Ser.). (ENG., Illus.). 24p. (J). (gr. 3-6). pap. 10.60 *(978-1-4777-0143-0(5));* lib. bdg. 25.25 *(978-1-4777-0079-2(X))* Rosen Publishing Group, Inc., The. (PowerKids Pr.).

Roop, Peter & Roop, Connie. Let's Drive, Henry Ford! 2004. (Before I Made History Ser.). (Illus.). 59p. (J). pap. *(978-0-439-67624-3(X))* Scholastic, Inc.

Venezia, Mike. Henry Ford: Big Wheel in the Auto Industry. Venezia, Mike, illus. 2009. (Getting to Know the World's Greatest Inventors & Scientists Ser.). (ENG., Illus.). 32p. (J). (gr. 3-4). pap. 6.95 *(978-0-531-21335-3(8),* Children's Pr.); (gr. 2-5). 28.00 *(978-0-531-23726-7(5))* Scholastic Library Publishing.

York, M. J. Henry Ford: Manufacturing Mogul, 1 vol. 2010. (Essential Lives Set 5 Ser.). (ENG.). 112p. (J). (gr. 6-12). lib. bdg. 35.64 *(978-1-61613-514-0(X))* ABDO Publishing Co.

Young, Jeff C. Henry Ford: Genius Behind the Affordable Car. 2007. (Inventors Who Changed the World Ser.). (Illus.). 128p. (J). (gr. 4-7). lib. bdg. 34.60 *(978-1-59845-053-8(0),* MyReportLinks.com Bks.) Enslow Pubs., Inc.

Zuehlke, Jeffrey. Henry Ford. 2007. (History Maker Bios Ser.). (Illus.). 48p. (J). (gr. 3-7). lib. bdg. 26.60 *(978-0-8225-6583-3(8),* Lerner Pubns.) Lerner Publishing Group.

AUTOMOBILE INDUSTRY AND TRADE—HISTORY

Gregory, Josh. Henry Ford: Father of the Auto Industry. 2013. (True Book(tm), a — Great American Business Ser.). (ENG.). 48p. (J). 31.00 *(978-0-531-24777-8(5));* pap. 6.95 *(978-0-531-28463-6(8))* Scholastic Library Publishing.

Rivera, Sheila. Thunderbird, 1 vol. 2004. (Ultimate Cars Ser.). (ENG.). 32p. (gr. 3-8). 27.07 *(978-1-59197-583-0(2),* Abdo & Daughters) ABDO Publishing Co.

Roza, Greg. Henry Ford: Pioneer of Modern Industry. 2009. (Real Life Readers Ser.). 24p. (gr. 3-4). pap. 8.25 *(978-1-4358-0137-0(7),* Rosen Classroom) Rosen Publishing Group, Inc., The.

AUTOMOBILE RACING

see also Karts and Karting

Aloian, Molly & Kalman, Bobbie. Race Cars: Start Your Engines! rev. ed. 2007. (Vehicles on the Move Ser.). (ENG., Illus.). 32p. (J). (gr. 1-5). pap. *(978-0-7787-3057-6(3))* Crabtree Publishing Co.

—Racecars: Start Your Engines! 2007. (Vehicles on the Move Ser.). (ENG., Illus.). 32p. (J). (gr. 3-7). lib. bdg. *(978-0-7787-3043-9(3))* Crabtree Publishing Co.

Alvarez, Carlos & Finn, Denny Von. Salt Flat Racers. 2010. (World's Fastest Ser.). (ENG., Illus.). 24p. (J). (gr. 3-7). lib. bdg. 25.95 *(978-1-60014-334-2(2))* Bellwether Media.

Anderson, Jameson. Danica Patrick, 1 vol. 2014. (Awesome Athletes Ser.). (ENG., Illus.). 32p. (J). (gr. 8-12). lib. bdg. 27.07 (978-1-62403-339-1(3), Checkerboard Library) ABDO Publishing Co.

Arroyo, Sheri, et al. How Race Car Drivers Use Math. 2009. (Math in the Real World Ser.). 32p. (gr. 4-6). 28.00 (978-1-60413-609-8(X), Chelsea Clubhouse) Facts On File, Inc.

AZ Books, creator. Cool Races. 2012. (Lively Machines Ser.). (ENG., Illus.). 10p. (J). (gr. -1-k). bds. 10.95 (978-1-61889-323-9(8)) AZ Bks. LLC.

Bach, Rachel. The Car Race. 2017. (Let's Race Ser.). (ENG., Illus.). 16p. (J). (gr. -1-1). pap. 7.99 (978-1-68152-131-2(8)) Amicus.

—The Car Race. 2016. (Let's Race Ser.). (ENG., Illus.). 16p. (J). (gr. k-3). 17.95 (978-1-60753-912-4(8)) Amicus Publishing.

—The Go-Kart Race. 2017. (Let's Race Ser.). (ENG., Illus.). 16p. (J). (gr. -1-1). pap. 7.99 (978-1-68152-132-9(6)) Amicus.

—The Go-Kart Race. 2016. (Let's Race Ser.). (ENG., Illus.). 16p. (J). (gr. k-3). 17.95 (978-1-60753-913-1(6)) Amicus Publishing.

Bechtel, Mark. NASCAR Race Day: Behind the Scenes. 2003. (J). 3.99 (978-1-930623-28-6(3)) Sports Illustrated For Kids.

Bentley, Dawn. Speedy Little Race Cars. Cahoon, Heather, illus. 2004. 20p. 10.99 (978-0-9755195-1-6(4)) MELJAMES, Inc.

Blomquist, Christopher. Motocross in the X Games. 2009. (Kid's Guide to the X Games Ser.). 24p. (gr. 3-3). 42.50 (978-1-61511-209-8(X), PowerKids Pr.) Rosen Publishing Group, Inc., The.

Brooklyn, Billie. Sports Car Racing, 1 vol. 2015. (ENG., Illus.). 32p. (J). lib. bdg. 26.25 (978-1-4994-0160-8(4), PowerKids Pr.) Rosen Publishing Group, Inc., The.

Bullard, Lisa. Stock Cars. 2004. (Pull Ahead Books-Mighty Movers Ser.). (ENG., Illus.). 32p. (gr. k-3). pap. 7.95 (978-0-8225-9922-7(8)); lib. bdg. 22.60 (978-0-8225-0694-2(7)) Lerner Publishing Group.

Busby, Barbara Sheen. Car Racing. Greenhaven Press Editors, ed. 2014. (Science Behind Sports Ser.). (ENG., Illus.). 128p. (gr. 7-10). lib. bdg. 39.40 (978-1-4205-1152-9(1), Lucent Bks.) Cengage Gale.

Car Racing. (J). (978-0-8118-4879-4(5)) Chronicle Bks. LLC.

Carney, Larry. Joe Gibbs Racing 2008. 2008. (ENG., Illus.). 200p. (J). pap., act. bk. ed. 14.95 (978-1-60072-108-3(7)) PC Treasures, Inc.

—NASCAR Hendrick Motorsports 2008. 2008. (ENG., Illus.). 200p. (J). pap., act. bk. ed. 14.95 (978-1-60072-104-5(4)) PC Treasures, Inc.

—NASCAR Petty Racing 2008. 2009. (ENG., Illus.). 200p. pap. 14.95 (978-1-60072-107-6(9)) PC Treasures, Inc.

Casanova, Karen. Danica Patrick. 2010. (USA TODAY Lifeline Biographies Ser.). (ENG.). 112p. (gr. 6-12). lib. bdg. 34.60 (978-0-7613-5222-8(8)) Lerner Publishing Group.

Castellano, Peter. Motocross. 2015. (Daredevil Sports Ser.). (ENG., Illus.). 32p. (J). (gr. 1-1). pap. 10.50 (978-1-4824-2984-8(5)) Stevens, Gareth Publishing LLLP.

Caviezel, Giovanni. Race Car Driver. Mesturini, Cristina, illus. 2009. (Mini People Shape Bks.). (ENG.). 12p. (J). (gr. -1-2). bds. 5.99 (978-0-7641-6217-6(9)) Barron's Educational Series, Inc.

Cefrey, Holly. The Biggest NASCAR Races. 2008. (Highlights of NASCAR Racing Ser.). (Illus.). 48p. (YA). (gr. 5-9). lib. bdg. 29.25 (978-1-4042-1399-9(6)) Rosen Publishing Group, Inc., The.

—Race Car Drivers: Life on the Fast Track. 2005. (Extreme Careers Ser.). (Illus.). 64p. (YA). (gr. 5-8). 31.95 (978-0-8239-3367-9(9)) Rosen Publishing Group, Inc., The.

Challen, Paul. The Checkered Flag, 1 vol. 2015. (Checkered Flag Ser.). (ENG.). 32p. (J). 60.00 (978-1-4994-0312-1(7), PowerKids Pr.) Rosen Publishing Group, Inc., The.

Challen, Paul C. Formula 1 Racing, 1 vol. 2015. (ENG., Illus.). 32p. (J). lib. bdg. 26.25 (978-1-4994-0161-5(2), PowerKids Pr.) Rosen Publishing Group, Inc., The.

—NASCAR Racing, 1 vol. 2015. (ENG., Illus.). 32p. (J). lib. bdg. 26.25 (978-1-4994-0164-6(7), PowerKids Pr.) Rosen Publishing Group, Inc., The.

Chapman, Giles. Racing Driver: How to Drive Racing Cars Step by Step. 2014. (ENG., Illus.). 48p. (J). (gr. 3-5). pap. 14.95 (978-0-500-65026-4(8), 565026) Thames & Hudson.

Christopher, Matt. Great Moments in American Auto Racing. 2011. (ENG., Illus.). 144p. (J). (gr. 3-7). pap. 4.99 (978-0-316-10297-1(0)) Little, Brown Bks. for Young Readers.

Clayton, David. NASCAR Blast. 2008. (Crabtree Contact Ser.). (ENG., Illus.). 32p. (J). (gr. 3-7). lib. bdg. (978-0-7787-3810-7(8)) Crabtree Publishing Co.

Clearwater, Gary. Colors at the Races. 2017. (Wonderful World of Colors Ser.). 24p. (gr. 4-6). pap. 8.25 **(978-1-5081-6167-7(4),** PowerKids Pr.) Rosen Publishing Group, Inc., The.

Clement, Nathan. Speed. Clement, Nathan, illus. 2013. (ENG., Illus.). 32p. (J). (gr. k). 16.95 (978-1-59078-937-7(7)) Boyds Mills Pr.

Collins, Luke. Stock Cars. 2017. (Gearhead Garage Ser.). (ENG., Illus.). 32p. (gr. 3-7). 31.35 **(978-1-68072-035-8(X))** Black Rabbit Bks.

Dahl, Michael. Una Bandera a Cuadros: Un Libro para Contar Sobre Carreras de Autos. Alderman, Derrick & Shea, Denise, illus. 2010. (Apréndete Tus Números/Know Your Numbers Ser.).Tr. of One Checkered Flag - A Counting Book about Racing. (SPA & MUL.). 24p. (gr. -1-2). lib. bdg. 26.65 (978-1-4048-6295-1(1)) Picture Window Bks.

Daniel, P. K. IndyCar Racing, 1 vol. 2014. (Inside the Speedway Ser.). (ENG., Illus.). 48p. (J). (gr. 3-6). lib. bdg. 32.79 (978-1-62403-404-6(7), SportsZone) ABDO Publishing Co.

David, Jack. Go-Kart Racing. 2008. (Action Sports Ser.). (ENG., Illus.). 24p. (J). (gr. 3-7). lib. bdg. 25.95 (978-1-60014-123-2(4)) Bellwether Media.

—Indy Cars. 2008. (Cool Rides Ser.). (ENG., Illus.). 24p. (J). (gr. 3-7). lib. bdg. 25.95 (978-1-60014-148-5(X)) Bellwether Media.

—Stock Cars. 2008. (Cool Rides Ser.). (ENG., Illus.). 24p. (J). (gr. 3-7). lib. bdg. 25.95 (978-1-60014-153-9(6)) Bellwether Media.

Daynes, K. M. Race Cars II. 2011. (Discovery Adventures Ser.). 80p. (J). pap. 8.99 (978-0-7945-2202-5(5), Usborne) EDC Publishing.

Dayton, Connor. Denny Hamlin. 2009. (NASCAR Champions/Campeones de NASCAR Ser.). 24p. (gr. 1-2). (ENG & SPA.). 42.50 (978-1-61514-789-2(6), Editorial Buenas Letras); 42.50 (978-1-61514-767-0(5), PowerKids Pr.) Rosen Publishing Group, Inc., The.

Doeden, Matt. Sports Car Racing. 2009. pap. 52.95 (978-0-7613-4794-1(1)); (ENG.). 48p. (gr. 4-7). 26.60 (978-0-8225-9429-1(3)) Lerner Publishing Group.

—Stock Cars. 2006. (Motor Mania Ser.). (ENG., Illus.). 48p. (gr. 4-7). lib. bdg. 26.60 (978-0-8225-3530-0(0)) Lerner Publishing Group.

Donovan, Sandy. Cool Stock Car Racing Facts, 1 vol. (Cool Sports Facts Ser.). (ENG., 24p. (gr. k-1). 2011. Illus.). pap. 7.29 (978-1-4296-6202-4(6)) 2011. pap. 41.70 (978-1-4296-6371-7(5)) 2010. lib. bdg. 26.65 (978-1-4296-5302-2(7)) Capstone Press of Coughlan Cos. (Pebble Plus).

Dooling, Michael. The Great Horse-Less Carriage Race. Dooling, Michael, illus. 2005. (ENG., Illus.). 32p. (J). (gr. k-3). tchr. ed. 16.95 (978-0-8234-1640-0(2)) Holiday Hse., Inc.

Dorling Kindersley Publishing Staff. Disney Pixar Cars 3. 2017. (Ultimate Sticker Bks.). (ENG.). 16p. (J). (gr. k-4). pap. 6.99 **(978-1-4654-5560-4(4),** DK Children) Dorling Kindersley Publishing, Inc.

—Disney Pixar Cars 3: the Essential Guide. 2017. (ENG.). 64p. (J). (gr. 1-4). 12.99 **(978-1-4654-5559-8(0),** DK Children) Dorling Kindersley Publishing, Inc.

Downey, Glen R. The 10 Most Unforgettable NASCAR Moments. 2008. 14.99 (978-1-55448-515-4(0)) Scholastic Library Publishing.

Eagen, Rachel. Nascar. 2006. (Automania! Ser.). (ENG., Illus.). 32p. (J). (gr. 4-7). pap. (978-0-7787-3029-3(8)); lib. bdg. (978-0-7787-3007-1(7)) Crabtree Publishing Co.

Egan, Erin. Hottest Race Cars. 2007. (Wild Wheels! Ser.). (Illus.). 48p. (J). (gr. 3-7). lib. bdg. 25.27 (978-0-7660-2871-5(2)) Enslow Pubs., Inc.

Ertle-Rickard, Stephen. Drag Race. 2008. (321 Go! Ser.). (ENG., Illus.). 36p. pap. (978-1-84167-759-0(0)) Ransom Publishing Ltd.

—Formula 1: Life at the Edge. 2008. (321 Go! Ser.). (ENG., Illus.). 36p. pap. (978-1-84167-783-5(3)) Ransom Publishing Ltd.

Farndon, John. Megafast Trucks. Edwards, Mat & Pyke, Jeremy, illus. 2016. (Megafast Ser.). (ENG.). 32p. (J). (gr. 3-6). lib. bdg. 26.65 (978-1-4677-9366-7(3)) Lerner Publishing Group.

Finn, Denny Von. Formula 1 Cars. 2009. (Cool Rides Ser.). (ENG., Illus.). 24p. (J). (gr. 3-7). lib. bdg. 25.95 (978-1-60014-195-9(1)) Bellwether Media.

—Indy Cars. 2011. (World's Fastest Ser.). (ENG., Illus.). 24p. (J). (gr. 3-7). lib. bdg. 25.95 (978-1-60014-588-9(4), Torque Bks.) Bellwether Media.

—Sprint Cars. 2009. (Cool Rides Ser.). (ENG., Illus.). 24p. (J). (gr. 3-7). lib. bdg. 25.95 (978-1-60014-257-4(5)) Bellwether Media.

—Stock Cars. 2011. (World's Fastest Ser.). (ENG., Illus.). 24p. (J). (gr. 3-7). lib. bdg. 25.95 (978-1-60014-589-6(2), Torque Bks.) Bellwether Media.

—Top Fuel Dragsters. 2009. (World's Fastest Ser.). (ENG., Illus.). 24p. (J). (gr. 3-7). lib. bdg. 25.95 (978-1-60014-288-8(5), Torque Bks.) Bellwether Media.

Francis, Jim. Great NASCAR Champions. 2008. (NASCAR Ser.). (ENG., Illus.). 32p. (J). (gr. 3-7). pap. (978-0-7787-3195-5(2)); lib. bdg. (978-0-7787-3187-0(1)) Crabtree Publishing Co.

—The History of NASCAR. 2008. (NASCAR Ser.). (ENG., Illus.). 32p. (J). (gr. 3-7). pap. (978-0-7787-3194-8(4)); lib. bdg. (978-0-7787-3186-3(3)) Crabtree Publishing Co.

Franks, Katie. I Want to Be a Race Car Driver. (Dream Jobs Ser.). 24p. (gr. 2-3). 2009. 42.50 (978-1-61512-208-0(7), PowerKids Pr.) 2007. (Illus.). (J). lib. bdg. 22.60 (978-1-4042-3623-3(6)) Rosen Publishing Group, Inc., The.

—Quiero Ser Piloto de Carreras. 2009. (Trabajos de ensueño (Dream Jobs) Ser.). (SPA.). 24p. pap. 8.25 (978-1-4358-8603-2(8)); (Illus.). (J). (gr. 2-4). 22.60 (978-1-4042-8157-8(6)) Rosen Publishing Group, Inc., The. (PowerKids Pr.).

Gaines, Ann Graham. Famous Finishes. rev. collector's ed. 2005. (Race Car Legends Ser.). (Illus.). 64p. (YA). (gr. 5-9). lib. bdg. 25.00 (978-0-7910-8758-9(1)) Facts On File, Inc.

Ganchy, Sally. Mark Martin: NASCAR Driver. 2009. (Behind the Wheel Ser.). (gr. 5-8). (ENG., Illus.). 48p. (J). pap. 11.75 (978-1-4358-5407-9(1)); (YA). lib. bdg. 29.25 (978-1-4042-1952-6(8)) Rosen Publishing Group, Inc., The.

Georgiou, Tyrone. Formula 1. 2011. (Fast Lane: Open-Wheel Racing Ser.). 24p. (J). (gr. 2-5). pap. 8.15 (978-1-4339-5752-9(3)); lib. bdg. 22.60 (978-1-4339-5750-5(7)) Stevens, Gareth Publishing LLLP. (Gareth Stevens Learning Library).

—Funny Car Dragsters. 2011. (Fast Lane: Drag Racing Ser.). (Illus.). 24p. (gr. 2-5). pap. 8.15 (978-1-4339-4696-7(3)); (J). 22.60 (978-1-4339-4695-0(5)) Stevens, Gareth Publishing LLLP. (Gareth Stevens Learning Library).

—Indy Cars. 2011. (Fast Lane: Open-Wheel Racing Ser.). (Illus.). 24p. (J). (gr. 2-5). lib. bdg. 22.60 (978-1-4339-5754-3(X), Gareth Stevens Learning Library) Stevens, Gareth Publishing LLLP.

—Pro Stock Dragsters. 2011. (Fast Lane: Drag Racing Ser.). (Illus.). 24p. (gr. 2-5). pap. 8.15 (978-1-4339-4700-1(5)); (J). 22.60 (978-1-4339-4699-8(8)) Stevens, Gareth Publishing LLLP. (Gareth Stevens Learning Library).

—Pro Stock Motorcycle Dragsters. 2011. (Fast Lane: Drag Racing Ser.). (Illus.). 24p. (J). (gr. 2-5). lib. bdg. 22.60 (978-1-4339-4703-2(X), Gareth Stevens Learning Library) Stevens, Gareth Publishing LLLP.

—Top Fuel Dragsters. 2011. (Fast Lane: Drag Racing Ser.). (Illus.). 24p. (J). (gr. 2-5). pap. 8.15 (978-1-4339-4708-7(0)); lib. bdg. 22.60 (978-1-4339-4707-0(2)) Stevens, Gareth Publishing LLLP. (Gareth Stevens Learning Library).

Gifford, Clive. Extreme Motorcycle Racing. 2010. (Extreme! Ser.). (ENG.). 32p. (gr. 3-4). pap. 47.70 (978-1-4296-5113-4(X), Fact Finders) Capstone Press of Coughlan Cos.

Gigliotti, Jim. Amazing NASCAR Races. 2008. (NASCAR Ser.). (ENG., Illus.). 32p. (J). (gr. 3-7). pap. (978-0-7787-3199-3(5)) Crabtree Publishing Co.

—Famous NASCAR Tracks. 2008. (NASCAR Ser.). (ENG., Illus.). 32p. (J). (gr. 3-7). pap. (978-0-7787-3196-2(0)); lib. bdg. (978-0-7787-3188-7(X)) Crabtree Publishing Co.

—Fantastic Finishes. 2008. (World of NASCAR Ser.). (ENG., Illus.). 32p. (J). (gr. 3-6). 28.50 (978-1-60253-075-1(0), 200993) Child's World, Inc., The.

—Great NASCAR Teams. 2008. (NASCAR Ser.). (ENG., Illus.). 32p. (J). (gr. 3-7). pap. (978-0-7787-3198-6(7)); lib. bdg. (978-0-7787-3190-0(1)) Crabtree Publishing Co.

—Hottest Dragsters & Funny Cars. 2007. (Wild Wheels! Ser.). (Illus.). 48p. (J). (gr. 3-7). lib. bdg. 25.27 (978-0-7660-2870-8(4)) Enslow Pubs., Inc.

—Off-Road Racing. 2009. (Racing Mania Ser.). 48p. (gr. 4-18). lib. bdg. 31.36 (978-0-7614-4388-9(6)) Marshall Cavendish Corp.

—Teamwork at the Track. 2008. (World of NASCAR Ser.). (ENG., Illus.). 32p. (J). (gr. 3-6). 28.50 (978-1-60253-082-9(3), 201000) Child's World, Inc., The.

Glaser, Jason. Danica Patrick. 2009. (Sports Idols Ser.). 24p. (gr. 2-3). 42.50 (978-1-60853-140-0(6), PowerKids Pr.) Rosen Publishing Group, Inc., The.

Glave, Tom. Sprint Car Racing, 1 vol. 2014. (Inside the Speedway Ser.). (ENG., Illus.). 48p. (J). (gr. 3-6). lib. bdg. 32.79 (978-1-62403-407-7(1), SportsZone) ABDO Publishing Co.

Goldsworthy, Steve. Scorching Supercars. 2015. (Dream Cars Ser.). (ENG., Illus.). 32p. (gr. 3-4). lib. bdg. 27.99 (978-1-4914-2014-0(6)) Capstone Press of Coughlan Cos.

Gordon, Nick. Monster Cars. 2013. (Monster Machines Ser.). (ENG., Illus.). 24p. (J). (gr. k-3). lib. bdg. 25.95 (978-1-60014-935-1(9), Blastoff! Readers) Bellwether Media.

Gould, Robert. Racers. Gould, Robert, photos by. 2005. (Big Stuff Ser.). (ENG., Illus.). 16p. (J). bds. 7.95 (978-1-929945-52-8(3)) Big Guy Bks., Inc.

Graham, Ian. Fast Cars. 2009. (How Machines Work Ser.). (Illus.). 32p. (J). pap. (978-1-897563-43-4(4)) Saunders Bk. Co.

The Great Race: Fight to the Finish. 2017. (Great Race: Fight to the Finish Ser.). 48p. (gr. 4-5). pap. 84.30 **(978-1-5382-0834-2(2))**; lib. bdg. 191.70 **(978-1-5382-0828-1(8))** Stevens, Gareth Publishing LLLP.

Gunn, Richard. Racing Cars. 2006. (Cool Wheels Ser.). (Illus.). 32p. (gr. 2-6). lib. bdg. 26.00 (978-0-8368-6829-6(3), Gareth Stevens Learning Library) Stevens, Gareth Publishing LLLP.

Hamilton, John. Drag Racers. 2012. (Speed Zone Ser.). 32p. (J). (gr. 3-9). lib. bdg. 27.07 (978-1-61783-526-1(9), A&D Xtreme) ABDO Publishing Co.

—Formula One Cars. 2012. (Speed Zone Ser.). (Illus.). 32p. (J). (gr. 3-9). lib. bdg. 27.07 (978-1-61783-527-8(7), A&D Xtreme) ABDO Publishing Co.

—Motocross. 2014. (Action Sports Ser.). (ENG., Illus.). 32p. (J). (gr. 3-8). lib. bdg. 27.07 (978-1-62403-442-8(X), A&D Xtreme) ABDO Publishing Co.

—Sports Cars. 2012. (Speed Zone Ser.). 32p. (J). (gr. 3-9). lib. bdg. 27.07 (978-1-61783-530-8(7), A&D Xtreme) ABDO Publishing Co.

—Stock Cars. 2012. (Speed Zone Ser.). 32p. (J). (gr. 3-9). lib. bdg. 27.07 (978-1-61783-531-5(5), A&D Xtreme) ABDO Publishing Co.

Hamilton, S. L. Indianapolis 500. 2013. (Xtreme Races Ser.). 32p. (J). (gr. 3-9). lib. bdg. 27.07 (978-1-61783-694-7(X), Abdo & Daughters) ABDO Publishing Co.

Hantula, Richard. Science at Work in Auto Racing. 2011. (Benchmark Rockets: Sports Science Ser.). 32p. (gr. 4). 28.50 (978-1-60870-586-3(2)) Marshall Cavendish GBR. Dist: Marshall Cavendish Corp.

Harrison, Paul. Racing Supercars. 2015. 32p. (gr. 1-5). lib. bdg. 31.35 (978-1-78404-075-8(4)) Arcturus Publishing GBR. Dist: Black Rabbit Bks.

—Speed Machines. (Up Close Ser.). 24p. 2009. (gr. 3-3). 47.90 (978-1-60854-705-0(1)) 2008. (Illus.). (J). (gr. 4-7). lib. bdg. 25.25 (978-1-4042-4222-7(8)) Rosen Publishing Group, Inc., The. (PowerKids Pr.).

—Supercars. 2013. (Illus.). 32p. (J). (978-1-84858-564-5(0)) Arcturus Pubs., Inc.

Hawley, Rebecca. Corvette. 2009. (Superfast Cars Ser.). 24p. (gr. 2-3). 42.50 (978-1-60853-231-5(3), PowerKids Pr.) Rosen Publishing Group, Inc., The.

Herzog, Brad. R Is for Race: A Stock Car Alphabet. Bready, Jane Gilltrap, illus. 2006. (Sports Ser.). (ENG.). 40p. (J). (gr. -1-5). 16.95 (978-1-58536-272-1(7)) Sleeping Bear Pr.

—R Is for Race: A Stock Car Alphabet. Bready, Jane Gilltrap, illus. 2015. (Av2 Fiction Readalong 2016 Ser.). (ENG.). (J). (gr. 1-4). lib. bdg. 34.28 (978-1-4896-3762-8(1), AV2 by Weigl) Weigl Pubs., Inc.

Hoblin, Paul. Rock Crawling: Tearing It Up. 2014. (Dirt & Destruction Sports Zone Ser.). (ENG., Illus.). 32p. (gr. 4-8). lib. bdg. 26.60 (978-1-4677-2119-6(0), Lerner Pubns.) Lerner Publishing Group.

Hofer, Charles. Motorcycles. 2009. (World's Fastest Machines Ser.). 24p. (gr. 2-3). 42.50 (978-1-60854-853-8(8), PowerKids Pr.) Rosen Publishing Group, Inc., The.

—Race Cars. 2008. (World's Fastest Machines Ser.). (Illus.). 24p. (J). (gr. 3-7). lib. bdg. 22.60 (978-1-4042-4175-6(2), PowerKids Pr.) Rosen Publishing Group, Inc., The.

Holter, James. Dirt Bike Racers. 2010. (Kid Racers Ser.). (Illus.). 48p. (J). pap. 8.95 (978-0-7660-3752-6(5)) Enslow Pubs., Inc.

Horn, Geoffrey M. Pit Crew Worker. 2010. (Benchmark Rockets: Dirty & Dangerous Jobs Ser.). 32p. (J). (gr. 3-6). 28.50 (978-1-60870-177-3(8)) Marshall Cavendish Corp.

Howard, Melanie A. Stock Cars, 1 vol. 2010. (Full Throttle Ser.). (ENG.). 32p. (gr. 3-4). lib. bdg. 27.99 (978-1-4296-4752-6(3), Edge Bks.) Capstone Press of Coughlan Cos.

Howell, Brian. Demolition Derby: Tearing It Up. 2014. (Dirt & Destruction Sports Zone Ser.). (ENG., Illus.). 32p. (gr. 4-8). lib. bdg. 26.60 (978-1-4677-2122-6(0), Lerner Pubns.) Lerner Publishing Group.

—Mud Truck Racing: Tearing It Up. 2014. (Dirt & Destruction Sports Zone Ser.). (ENG., Illus.). 32p. (gr. 4-8). lib. bdg. 26.60 (978-1-4677-2118-9(2), Lerner Pubns.) Lerner Publishing Group.

—Rally Car Racing: Tearing It Up. 2014. (Dirt & Destruction Sports Zone Ser.). (ENG., Illus.). 32p. (gr. 4-8). lib. bdg. 26.60 (978-1-4677-2121-9(2), Lerner Pubns.) Lerner Publishing Group.

Howse, Jennifer. NASCAR Sprint Cup. 2012. (J). 28.55 (978-1-61913-616-8(3)) 2012. (J). pap. 13.95 (978-1-61913-618-2(X)) 2009. 32p. (YA). (gr. 4-7). lib. bdg. 26.00 (978-1-60596-636-6(3)) Weigl Pubs., Inc.

Ikids Staff. Race Cars. Randazzo, Tony, illus. 2009. (ENG.). 10p. (J). (gr. -1-1). 15.99 (978-1-58476-939-2(4)) Innovative Kids.

James, Brant. Formula One Racing, 1 vol. 2014. (Inside the Speedway Ser.). (ENG., Illus.). 48p. (J). (gr. 3-6). lib. bdg. 32.79 (978-1-62403-403-9(9), SportsZone) ABDO Publishing Co.

James, L. Dale Jarrett. 2009. (NASCAR Champions Ser.). 24p. (gr. 1-2). 42.50 (978-1-61514-766-3(7), PowerKids Pr.) Rosen Publishing Group, Inc., The.

Jefferis. Racing Cars 6-Pack. 2004. (Illus.). (J). pap. 48.35 (978-1-4109-0835-3(6)) Harcourt Schl. Pubs.

Johnson, Ben. Motocross. 2008. (Crabtree Contact Ser.). (ENG., Illus.). 32p. (J). (gr. 3-7). pap. (978-0-7787-3786-5(1)); lib. bdg. (978-0-7787-3764-3(0)) Crabtree Publishing Co.

Johnstone, Michael. NASCAR. 2005. (Need for Speed Ser.). (Illus.). 32p. (gr. 3-5). lib. bdg. 23.93 (978-0-8225-0389-7(1)) Lerner Publishing Group.

—Nascar. 2003. (Need for Speed Ser.). (Illus.). 32p. (YA). (gr. 3-6). 7.95 (978-0-8225-0392-7(1), Carolrhoda Bks.) Lerner Publishing Group.

Jordan, Christopher. ABC. 2012. (My First NASCAR Racing Ser.). (ENG., Illus.). 30p. (J). (gr. k-k). bds. 7.95 (978-1-77049-429-9(4), Fenn-Tundra) Tundra Bks. CAN. Dist: Penguin Random Hse. LLC.

—NASCAR 123. 2012. (My First NASCAR Racing Ser.). (ENG., Illus.). 24p. (J). (gr. k-k). bds. 7.95 (978-1-77049-428-2(6), Fenn-Tundra) Tundra Bks. CAN. Dist: Penguin Random Hse. LLC.

—NASCAR Colors. 2012. (My First NASCAR Racing Ser.). (ENG., Illus.). 26p. (J). (gr. k-k). bds. 7.95 (978-1-77049-430-5(8), Fenn-Tundra) Tundra Bks. CAN. Dist: Penguin Random Hse. LLC.

—NASCAR Shapes. 2012. (My First NASCAR Racing Ser.). (ENG., Illus.). 28p. (J). (-k). bds. 7.95 (978-1-77049-431-2(6), Fenn-Tundra) Tundra Bks. CAN. Dist: Penguin Random Hse. LLC.

Kalman, Bobbie, et al. Autos de Carrera: lenciendan Sus Motores! 2007. (Vehículos en Acción Ser.). (SPA & ENG., Illus.). 32p. (J). (gr. 3-7). pap. (978-0-7787-8315-2(4)) Crabtree Publishing Co.

Kelley, K. C. Drag Racing. 2009. (Racing Mania Ser.). 48p. (gr. 4-18). lib. bdg. 31.36 (978-0-7614-4384-1(3)) Marshall Cavendish Corp.

—Hottest NASCAR Machines. 2007. (Wild Wheels! Ser.). (Illus.). 48p. (J). (gr. 3-7). lib. bdg. 25.27 (978-0-7660-2869-2(0)) Enslow Pubs., Inc.

—NASCAR. 2009. (Racing Mania Ser.). 48p. (gr. 4-18). lib. bdg. 31.36 (978-0-7614-4387-2(8)) Marshall Cavendish Corp.

—Pit Stop Secrets. 2008. (World of NASCAR Ser.). (ENG., Illus.). 32p. (J). (gr. 3-6). 28.50 (978-1-60253-080-5(7), 200997) Child's World, Inc., The.

—Smokin' Race Cars. 2013. (Fast Wheels! Ser.). 48p. (J). (gr. 4-18). 14.95 (978-1-62285-095-2(5)) Enslow Pubs., Inc.

Kenney, Karen Latchana. The Science of Car Racing, 1 vol. 2014. (Science of Speed Ser.). (ENG.). 48p. (gr. 3-4). lib. bdg. 31.99 (978-1-4765-3910-2(3)) Capstone Press of Coughlan Cos.

—The Science of Race Cars: Studying Forces & Motion, 1 vol. 2016. (Science in Action Ser.). (ENG., Illus.). 32p. (J). (gr. 3-6). 27.07 (978-1-62403-963-8(4)) ABDO Publishing Co.

Kirkpatrick, Rob. Dale Earnhardt Jr: NASCAR Road Racer / Piloto de NASCAR. 2009. (Hot Shots/Grandes ídolos Ser.). (ENG & SPA.). 24p. (gr. 1-1). 42.50 (978-1-61513-413-7(1), Editorial Buenas Letras) Rosen Publishing Group, Inc., The.

—Dale Earnhardt Jr: Piloto de NASCAR (NASCAR Road Racer) 2009. (Grandes Idolos (Hot Shots) Ser.). (SPA.). 24p. (gr. 1-1). 42.50 (978-1-61512-735-1(6), Editorial Buenas Letras) Rosen Publishing Group, Inc., The.

Kulling, Monica. Eat My Dust! Henry Ford's First Race. Walz, Richard, illus. 2004. (Step into Reading Ser.). 48p. (J). (gr. 1-3). 11.65 (978-0-7569-3231-2(9)) Perfection Learning Corp.

—Eat My Dust! Henry Ford's First Race. Walz, Richard, illus. 2004. (Step into Reading Ser.). (ENG.). 48p. (J). (gr. k-3). pap. 3.99 (978-0-375-81510-2(4), Random Hse. Bks. for Young Readers) Random Hse. Children's Bks.

Labrecque, Ellen C. BMX Racers. 2010. (Kid Racers Ser.). (Illus.). 48p. (J). pap. 8.95 (978-0-7660-3753-3(3)) Enslow Pubs., Inc.

LaDow, William. Conversations with a Winner — the Ray Nichels Story. 2004. 54.95 (978-0-9723623-0-6(4)) LaDow Publishing.

Latham, Donna. Superfast Trucks. 2006. (Ultimate Speed Ser.). (Illus.). 32p. (J). (gr. 3-6). lib. bdg. 25.27 (978-1-59716-253-1(1)) Bearport Publishing Co., Inc.

Lawson, Lela. Building a Race Car: Checking Your Work. 2017. (Computer Science for the Real World Ser.). 12p. (gr. 6-7). pap. 7.05 **(978-1-5383-5160-4(9),** Rosen Classroom) Rosen Publishing Group, Inc., The.

LernerClassroom Editors. The Science of Nascar Teaching Guide. 2009. pap. 7.95 (978-0-8225-9345-4(9)) Lerner Publishing Group.

LernerClassroom Editors, ed. Motor Mania Set Iii Classroom Library. 2008. pap. 34.95 (978-1-58013-708-9(3)) Lerner Publishing Group.

—Motor Mania Set Iii Complete Library. 2008. pap. 210.95 (978-1-58013-710-2(5)) Lerner Publishing Group.

Levy, Janey. Dale Earnhardt, Jr. 2006. (High Interest Bks.). (ENG., Illus.). 48p. (J). (gr. 4-7). lib. bdg. 24.50 (978-0-531-16805-9(0)) Scholastic Library Publishing.

—Dale Earnhardt, Jr. 2007. (High Interest Bks.). (ENG., Illus.). 48p. (J). (gr. 4-7). pap. 6.95 (978-0-531-18713-5(6)) Scholastic Library Publishing.

—Motocross. 2009. (Motocross Ser.). 32p. (gr. 4-5). 47.90 (978-1-61514-663-5(6), PowerKids Pr.) Rosen Publishing Group, Inc., The.

—Motocross Races. 2009. (Motocross Ser.). 32p. (gr. 4-5). 47.90 *(978-1-61514-666-6(0)*, PowerKids Pr.) Rosen Publishing Group, Inc., The.

—Motocross Superstars. 2009. (Motocross Ser.). 32p. (gr. 4-5). 47.90 *(978-1-61514-667-3(9)*, PowerKids Pr.) Rosen Publishing Group, Inc., The.

—Motocross Tricks. 2009. (Motocross Ser.). 32p. (gr. 4-5). 47.90 *(978-1-61514-668-0(7)*, PowerKids Pr.) Rosen Publishing Group, Inc., The.

—Racing Through History: Stock Cars Then to Now. 2007. (High Interest Bks.). (ENG., Illus.). 48p. (J). (gr. 4-7). pap. 6.95 *(978-0-531-18716-6(0)*, Children's Pr.) Scholastic Library Publishing.

—Supercross. 2009. (Motocross Ser.). 32p. (gr. 4-5). 47.90 *(978-1-61514-669-7(5)*, PowerKids Pr.) Rosen Publishing Group, Inc., The.

Long, Dustin. Daytona 500, 1 vol. 2013. (Sports' Great Championships Ser.). (ENG.). 64p. (J). (gr. 4-6). lib. bdg. 32.79 *(978-1-61783-669-5(9)*, SportsZone) ABDO Publishing Co.

—NASCAR Racing, 1 vol. 2014. (Inside the Speedway Ser.). (ENG.). 48p. (J). (gr. 3-6). lib. bdg. 32.79 *(978-1-62403-406-0(3)*, SportsZone) ABDO Publishing Co.

Luke, Andrew. All-Terrain Sports. 2017. (Illus.). 48p. (J). ***(978-1-4222-3706-9(0))*** Mason Crest.

Luke, Andrew. Auto Racing, Vol. 13. 2016. (Inside the World of Sports Ser.: Vol. 13). (ENG., Illus.). 80p. (J). (gr. 7-12). 24.95 *(978-1-4222-3456-3(8))* Mason Crest.

Lupo, Tamar. Moto X: X Games. 2008. (Extreme Ser.). (Illus.). 32p. (J). (gr. 4-6). lib. bdg. 26.00 *(978-1-59036-914-2(9))* Weigl Pubs., Inc.

Lupo, Tamar & Hudak, Heather C. Moto X: X Games. 2008. (Extreme Ser.). (Illus.). 32p. (J). (gr. 4-6). pap. 9.95 *(978-1-59036-915-9(7))* Weigl Pubs., Inc.

MacArthur, Collin. Inside a Drag Racer. 2014. (Life in the Fast Lane Ser.). 48p. (J). (gr. 4-6). lib. bdg. 31.36 *(978-1-62713-049-3(7))* Cavendish Square Publishing.

—Inside a Formula 1 Car. 2014. (Life in the Fast Lane Ser.). 48p. (J). (gr. 4-6). lib. bdg. 31.36 *(978-1-62713-034-9(9))* Cavendish Square Publishing.

Mason, Jennifer. Crazy Road Races. 2017. (Great Race: Fight to the Finish Ser.). 48p. (gr. 4-5). pap. 84.30 ***(978-1-5382-0805-2(9))*** Stevens, Gareth Publishing LLLP.

Mason, Paul. Formula 1. 2010. (Motorsports Ser.). 32p. (J). (gr. 3-6). 28.50 *(978-1-60753-117-3(8))* Amicus Publishing.

—Formula 1 Driver: Lewis Hamilton vs Nico Rosberg. 2016. (EDGE: the Inside Track Ser.). (ENG., Illus.). 32p. (J). (gr. 2-4). 16.99 *(978-1-4451-4504-4(9)*, Franklin Watts) Hachette Children's Group GBR. Dist: Hachette Bk. Group.

—Indy Cars. 2010. (Motorsports Ser.). 32p. (J). (gr. 3-6). 28.50 *(978-1-60753-118-0(6))* Amicus Publishing.

—Kart Racer: Lando Norris vs Callum Ilott. 2016. (EDGE: the Inside Track Ser.). (ENG., Illus.). 32p. (J). (gr. 2-4). 16.99 *(978-1-4451-4696-6(7)*, Franklin Watts) Hachette Children's Group GBR. Dist: Hachette Bk. Group.

—Karting. 2010. (Motorsports Ser.). 32p. (J). (gr. 3-6). 28.50 *(978-1-60753-119-7(4))* Amicus Publishing.

—Monster Trucks. 2010. (Motorsports Ser.). 32p. (J). (gr. 3-6). 28.50 *(978-1-60753-120-3(8))* Amicus Publishing.

—Moto Gp Rider: Marc Marquez vs Valentino Rossi. 2016. (EDGE: the Inside Track Ser.). (ENG., Illus.). 32p. (J). (gr. 2-4). 16.99 *(978-1-4451-4699-7(1)*, Franklin Watts) Hachette Children's Group GBR. Dist: Hachette Bk. Group.

—Stock Cars. 2010. (Motorsports Ser.). 32p. (J). (gr. 3-6). 28.50 *(978-1-60753-122-7(4))* Amicus Publishing.

Maurer, Tracy Nelson. Go-Kart Racing, 1 vol. 2013. (Super Speed Ser.). (ENG., Illus.). 32p. (gr. 1-2). lib. bdg. 26.65 *(978-1-4296-9998-3(1))* Capstone Press of Coughlan Cos.

—NASCAR Racers. 2003. (Illus.). 48p. (J). 29.93 *(978-1-58952-751-5(8))* Rourke Educational Media.

—Outrageous Car Racing Rivalries. 2015. (Sports Rivalries Ser.). (ENG.). 32p. (gr. 3-4). lib. bdg. 27.99 *(978-1-4914-2025-6(1))* Capstone Press of Coughlan Cos.

—Truck Racing, 1 vol. 2013. (Super Speed Ser.). (ENG.). 32p. (gr. 1-2). 26.65 *(978-1-4765-0118-5(1)*, Blazers) Capstone Press of Coughlan Cos.

McClellan, Ray & Finn, Denny Von. Dragsters. 2008. (Cool Rides Ser.). (ENG., Illus.). 24p. (J). (gr. 3-7). lib. bdg. 25.95 *(978-1-60014-209-3(5))* Bellwether Media.

McClellan, Ray & Von Finn, Denny. Rally Cars. 2008. (Cool Rides Ser.). (ENG., Illus.). 24p. (J). (gr. 3-7). lib. bdg. 25.95 *(978-1-60014-212-3(5))* Bellwether Media.

McCollum, Sean. Dragsters, 1 vol. 2010. (Full Throttle Ser.). (ENG.). 32p. (gr. 3-4). lib. bdg. 27.99 *(978-1-4296-3941-5(5)*, Edge Bks.) Capstone Press of Coughlan Cos.

—Indy Cars, 1 vol. 2010. (Full Throttle Ser.). (ENG.). 32p. (gr. 3-4). lib. bdg. 27.99 *(978-1-4296-3942-2(3)*, Edge Bks.) Capstone Press of Coughlan Cos.

—Racecars: The Ins & Outs of Stock Cars, Dragsters, & Open-Wheelers. 2010. (Rpm Ser.). (ENG.). 48p. (gr. 3-4). pap. 59.70 *(978-1-4296-5128-8(8))* Capstone Press of Coughlan Cos.

—The World's Fastest Cars. 2016. (World Record Breakers Ser.). (ENG., Illus.). 32p. (gr. 3-4). lib. bdg. 27.99 *(978-1-4914-8177-6(3)*, Edge Bks.) Capstone Press of Coughlan Cos.

Mead, Sue. Off Road Racing. rev. collector's ed. 2005. (Race Car Legends Ser.). (Illus.). 72p. (YA). (gr. 5-9). lib. bdg. 25.00 *(978-0-7910-8690-2(9))* Facts On File, Inc.

Mello, Tara Baukus. The Pit Crew. rev. ed. 2007. (Race Car Legends Ser.). (Illus.). 68p. (YA). (gr. 5-9). lib. bdg. 25.00 *(978-0-7910-8665-0(8))* Facts On File, Inc.

Mercer, Bobby. The Racecar Book: Build & Race Mousetrap Cars, Dragsters, Tri-Can Haulers & More. 2013. (Science in Motion Ser.). (ENG., Illus.). 216p. (J). (gr. 4). pap. 14.95 *(978-1-61374-714-8(4))* Chicago Review Pr., Inc.

Mezzanotte, Jim. Flat Track. 2006. (Motorcycle Racing: the Fast Track Ser.). (Illus.). 24p. (gr. 5-8). lib. bdg. 23.00 *(978-0-8368-6421-2(2))* Stevens, Gareth Publishing LLLP.

—Hillclimb. 2006. (Motorcycle Racing: the Fast Track Ser.). (Illus.). 24p. (gr. 5-8). lib. bdg. 23.00 *(978-0-8368-6422-9(0))* Stevens, Gareth Publishing LLLP.

Miller, Dean. Becoming a Pro Auto Racer. 2015. (Going Pro Ser.). (ENG.). 32p. (J). (gr. 3-4). pap. 10.50 *(978-1-4824-2078-4(3))*; (Illus.). 26.60 *(978-1-4824-2079-1(1))* Stevens, Gareth Publishing LLLP.

Miller, Tim. Vroom! Motoring into the Wild World of Racing. 2006. (ENG., Illus.). 58p. (J). (gr. 4-7). pap. 17.95 *(978-0-88776-755-5(9)*, Tundra Bks.) Tundra Bks. CAN. Dist: Penguin Random Hse. LLC.

Monnig, Alex. Drag Racing, 1 vol. 2014. (Inside the Speedway Ser.). (ENG., Illus.). 48p. (J). (gr. 3-6). lib. bdg. 32.79 *(978-1-62403-402-2(0)*, SportsZone) ABDO Publishing Co.

—Motocross Racing, 1 vol. 2014. (Inside the Speedway Ser.). (ENG.). 48p. (J). (gr. 3-6). lib. bdg. 32.79 *(978-1-62403-405-3(5)*, SportsZone) ABDO Publishing Co.

Morey, Allan. Race Cars. 2014. (Illus.). 24p. (J). lib. bdg. 25.65 *(978-1-62031-105-9(4)*, Bullfrog Bks.) Jump! Inc.

Mountain Bike Mania: Individual Title Six-Packs. (Action Packs Ser.). 104p. (gr. 3-5). 44.00 *(978-0-7635-2999-4(0))* Rigby Education.

Murray, Robb. A Daredevil's Guide to Car Racing, 1 vol. 2013. (Daredevils' Guides). (ENG.). 48p. (gr. 3-4). 31.99 *(978-1-4296-9986-0(8))* Capstone Press of Coughlan Cos.

Murray, Robb & Leavitt, Amie Jane. A Daredevil's Guide. 2013. (Daredevils' Guides). (ENG.). 48p. (gr. 3-4). lib. bdg. 127.96 *(978-1-4296-9988-4(4))* Capstone Press of Coughlan Cos.

Murray, Stuart A. P. Score with Race Car Math. 2013. (Score with Sports Math Ser.). 48p. (J). lib. bdg. 25.27 *(978-0-7660-4177-6(8))*; (gr. 3-4). pap. 8.95 *(978-1-4644-0293-7(0))* Enslow Pubs., Inc. (Enslow Elementary).

Nagelhout, Ryan. 20 Fun Facts about Auto Racing. 2016. (Fun Fact File: Sports! Ser.). (ENG., Illus.). 32p. (J). (gr. 2-3). pap. 10.50 *(978-1-4824-3963-2(8))* Stevens, Gareth Publishing LLLP.

National Geographic. Things That Go! Collection. 2015. (Readers Ser.). (ENG., Illus.). 120p. (J). (gr. k-3). lib. bdg. 16.90 *(978-1-4263-1973-0(8)*, National Geographic Children's Bks.) National Geographic Society.

National Geographic Staff. Things That Go Collection: Readers That Grow With You. 2015. (Readers Ser.). (ENG.). 120p. (J). (gr. k-3). pap. 7.99 *(978-1-4263-1972-3(X)*, National Geographic Children's Bks.) National Geographic Society.

Niver, Heather Moore. Racing's Greatest Records, 1 vol. 2015. (ENG., Illus.). 32p. (J). lib. bdg. 26.25 *(978-1-4994-0229-2(5)*, PowerKids Pr.) Rosen Publishing Group, Inc., The.

Noble, Jonathan & Owen, Ruth. Pole Position! 2010. (Top Score Maths Ser.). (Illus.). 32p. pap. *(978-0-237-54283-2(8))* Evans Brothers, Ltd.

Norman, Tony. Auto Racing. 2006. (Action Sports Ser.). (Illus.). 32p. (gr. 3-6). lib. bdg. 26.00 *(978-0-8368-6365-9(8)*, Gareth Stevens Learning Library) Stevens, Gareth Publishing LLLP.

Norville, Alison G. Kart Racers. 2010. (Kid Racers Ser.). (Illus.). 48p. (J). pap. 8.95 *(978-0-7660-3754-0(1))*; (gr. 5-9). 25.27 *(978-0-7660-3482-2(8))* Enslow Pubs., Inc.

Orme, David. Formula One. 2007. (Trailblazers Ser.). (ENG., Illus.). 36p. pap. *(978-1-84167-428-5(1))* Ransom Publishing Ltd.

Parker, Steve. On the Race Track. 2010. (J). 28.50 *(978-1-59920-287-7(5))* Black Rabbit Bks.

Parr, Ann. The Allisons. 2007. (Race Car Legends Ser.). (Illus.). 77p. (YA). (gr. 5-9). lib. bdg. 25.00 *(978-0-7910-8694-0(1))* Facts On File, Inc.

—Lowriders. rev. collector's ed. 2005. (Race Car Legends Ser.). (Illus.). 64p. (YA). (gr. 5-9). lib. bdg. 25.00 *(978-0-7910-8673-5(9))* Facts On File, Inc.

Payment, Simone. Kyle Busch: NASCAR Driver. 2009. (Behind the Wheel Ser.). (ENG., Illus.). 48p. (J). (gr. 5-8). pap. 11.75 *(978-1-4358-5403-1(9))* Rosen Publishing Group, Inc., The.

—Ryan Newman: NASCAR Driver. 2009. (Behind the Wheel Ser.). 48p. (gr. 5-5). 53.00 *(978-1-61511-559-4(5)*, Rosen Reference) Rosen Publishing Group, Inc., The.

Pearce, Al. Famous Tracks. collector's ed. 2005. (Race Car Legends Ser.). (Illus.). 80p. (J). (gr. 5-9). lib. bdg. 25.00 *(978-0-7910-8692-6(5))* Facts On File, Inc.

Performance Racing Car. 2004. (Press-Out & Build Ser.). (Illus.). 24p. (J). per. *(978-1-84229-722-3(8))* Top That! Publishing PLC.

Perritano, John. Mx Bikes: Evolution from Primitive Street Machines to State of the Art Off-Road Machines. 2008. (MXplosion! Ser.). (ENG., Illus.). 32p. (J). (gr. 3-7). pap. *(978-0-7787-4001-8(3))*; lib. bdg. *(978-0-7787-3988-3(0))* Crabtree Publishing Co.

Peterson, Megan Cooley. Stock Car Drivers. 2017. (Rank It! Ser.). (ENG.). 32p. (gr. 3-7). 31.35 ***(978-1-68072-062-4(7)***, Bolt) Black Rabbit Bks.

Phillips, Hamilton. Inside a Sprint Car. 2014. (Life in the Fast Lane Ser.). 48p. (J). (gr. 4-6). lib. bdg. 31.36 *(978-1-62713-052-3(7))* Cavendish Square Publishing.

—Inside a Stock Car. 2014. (Life in the Fast Lane Ser.). 48p. (J). (gr. 4-6). lib. bdg. 31.36 *(978-1-62713-040-0(3))* Cavendish Square Publishing.

Picthall, Chez. Racers. Gunzi, Christiane, ed. 2015. (ENG., Illus.). 12p. (J). pap. 7.99 *(978-1-907604-80-5(4))* Award Pubns. Ltd. GBR. Dist: Parkwest Pubns., Inc.

Piehl, Janet. Formula One Race Cars. (Motor Mania Ser.). (ENG., Illus.). 2006. 48p. (gr. 4-7). lib. bdg. 26.60 *(978-0-8225-5929-0(3)*, Lerner Pubns.) 2004. 32p. (gr. k-3). pap. 7.95 *(978-0-8225-9920-3(1))* 2004. 32p. (gr. k-3). lib. bdg. 22.60 *(978-0-8225-0693-5(9))* Lerner Publishing Group.

—Formula One Race Cars on the Move. 2010. pap. 45.32 *(978-0-7613-6938-7(4))*; (ENG.). 32p. pap. 7.95 *(978-0-7613-6117-6(0))*; (ENG., Illus.). 32p. lib. bdg. 26.60 *(978-0-7613-3920-5(5))* Lerner Publishing Group.

Pimm, Nancy Roe. The Daytona 500: The Thrill & Thunder of the Great American Race. 2011. (Spectacular Sports Ser.). (ENG.). 64p. (gr. 5-12). lib. bdg. 33.27 *(978-0-7613-6677-5(6))* Lerner Publishing Group.

—Indy 500: The Inside Track. 2004. (ENG., Illus.). 64p. (gr. 3-6). per. 8.95 *(978-1-58196-023-5(9)*, Darby Creek) Lerner Publishing Group.

Polydoros, Lori. Drag Racing, 1 vol. 2013. (Super Speed Ser.). (ENG.). 32p. (gr. 1-2). lib. bdg. 26.65 *(978-1-4296-9996-9(5))* Capstone Press of Coughlan Cos.

—Indy Car Racing, 1 vol. 2013. (Super Speed Ser.). (ENG.). 32p. (gr. 1-2). lib. bdg. 26.65 *(978-1-4296-9995-2(7))* Capstone Press of Coughlan Cos.

Polydoros, Lori & Maurer, Tracy Nelson. Super Speed. 2013. (Super Speed Ser.). (ENG.). 32p. (gr. 1-2). lib. bdg. 79.95 *(978-1-4296-9999-0(X)*, Blazers) Capstone Press of Coughlan Cos.

Poolos, J. Dragsters. Alaman, Eduardo, tr. from ENG. 2007. (Wild Rides / Autos de Locura Ser.). (SPA., Illus.). 24p. (J). (gr. 2-5). lib. bdg. 22.60 *(978-1-4042-7637-6(8))* Rosen Publishing Group, Inc., The.

—Wild about Dragsters. (Wild Rides Ser.). 24p. (gr. 2-3). 2009. 42.50 *(978-1-60854-798-2(1)*, PowerKids Pr.) 2009. (SPA.). 42.50 *(978-1-60854-803-3(1)*, Editorial Buenas Letras) 2007. (Illus.). (J). lib. bdg. 22.60 *(978-1-4042-3792-6(5))* Rosen Publishing Group, Inc., The.

—Wild about Hot Rods. 2009. (Wild Rides/Autos de locura Ser.). 24p. (gr. 2-3). (SPA.). 42.50 *(978-1-60854-806-4(6)*, Editorial Buenas Letras); 42.50 *(978-1-60854-799-9(X)*, PowerKids Pr.) Rosen Publishing Group, Inc., The.

—Wild about Lowriders. 2007. (Wild Rides Ser.). (Illus.). 24p. (J). (gr. 2-5). lib. bdg. 22.60 *(978-1-4042-3789-6(5))* Rosen Publishing Group, Inc., The.

Pratt, Laura. Danica Patrick. 2012. (J). *(978-1-61913-534-5(5))*; pap. 12.95 *(978-1-61913-589-5(2))* Weigl Pubs., Inc.

Priddy, Roger. Let's Pretend Race Driver Set. 2009. (Let's Pretend Ser.). (ENG.). 8p. (J). (gr. -1 — 1). 14.95 *(978-0-312-50717-6(8)*, Priddy Bks.) St. Martin's Pr.

Pristash, Nicole. Dale Earnhardt Jr. 2009. (NASCAR Champions Ser.). 24p. (gr. 1-2). 42.50 *(978-1-61514-763-2(2)*, PowerKids Pr.) Rosen Publishing Group, Inc., The.

—Jeff Gordon. 2009. (NASCAR Champions Ser.). (Illus.). 24p. (ENG.). (gr. 1-6). pap. 8.25 *(978-1-4042-4542-6(1))*; (J). lib. bdg. 22.60 *(978-1-4042-4446-7(8))* Rosen Publishing Group, Inc., The. (PowerKids Pr.).

—Jimmie Johnson. 2009. (NASCAR Champions Ser.). 24p. (gr. 1-6). (ENG., Illus.). pap. 8.25 *(978-1-4042-4543-3(X))*; 42.50 *(978-1-61514-774-8(8))* Rosen Publishing Group, Inc., The. (PowerKids Pr.).

—Kevin Harvick. 2009. (NASCAR Champions Ser.). (Illus.). 24p. (J). (ENG.). (gr. 1-6). pap. 8.25 *(978-1-4042-4544-0(8))*; lib. bdg. 22.60 *(978-1-4042-4448-1(4))* Rosen Publishing Group, Inc., The.

Publications International Ltd. Staff, ed. Look & Find - Animals. 2011. 24p. (J). 3.75 net. *(978-1-4508-2115-5(4))* Publications International, Ltd.

—Look & Find - Cars, Vol. 2. 2011. 24p. (J). 3.75 net. *(978-1-4508-0921-4(9))* Phoenix International Publications, Inc.

Raby, Philip. Racing Cars. 2003. (Need for Speed Ser.). (Illus.). 32p. (J). (gr. 3-6). pap. 7.95 *(978-0-8225-9853-4(1))* Lerner Publishing Group.

Race Car Legends. 2008. (Race Car Legends Ser.). (gr. 5-8). 625.00 *(978-0-7910-9816-5(8)*, Chelsea Hse.) Facts On File, Inc.

Race Cars: Science Technology Engineering. 2014. (Calling All Innovators: a Career for You Ser.). (ENG.). 64p. (J). lib. bdg. 32.00 *(978-0-531-20614-0(9))* Scholastic Library Publishing.

Racing Mania, 6 bks., Set. Incl. Drag Racing. Kelley, K. C. lib. bdg. 31.36 *(978-0-7614-4384-1(3))*; Monster Trucks. Gigliotti, Jim. lib. bdg. 31.36 *(978-0-7614-4385-8(1))*; Motorcross. Stealey, Bryan. lib. bdg. 31.36 *(978-0-7614-4386-5(X))*; NASCAR. Kelley, K. C. lib. bdg. 31.36 *(978-0-7614-4387-2(8))*; Off-Road Racing. Gigliotti, Jim. lib. bdg. 31.36 *(978-0-7614-4388-9(6))*; Wild Racers. Woods, Bob. lib. bdg. 31.36 *(978-0-7614-4389-6(4))*; 48p. (gr. 4-18). (Racing Mania Ser.). 2009. Set lib. bdg. 188.16 o.p. *(978-0-7614-4380-3(0))* Marshall Cavendish Corp.

Regis, Natalie. NASCAR & Its Greatest Drivers, 1 vol. 2015. (ENG.). 80p. (J). 31.70 *(978-1-62275-590-5(1)*, Britannica Educational Publishing) Rosen Publishing Group, Inc., The.

Richards, Jon, text. Race Cars. 2003. (Microfacts Ser.). (Illus.). 48p. (J). *(978-0-439-62757-3(5))* Scholastic, Inc.

A Ride, 6 Packs. (Sails Literacy Ser.). 16p. (gr. k-18). 27.00 *(978-0-7635-4386-0(1))* Rigby Education.

Riggs, Kate. Indy Cars. 2015. (J). *(978-1-60818-520-7(6)*, Creative Education) Creative Co., The.

—Seedlings: Stock Cars. 2015. (Seedlings Ser.). (ENG.). 24p. (J). (gr. -1-1). pap. 7.99 *(978-1-62832-124-1(5)*, Creative Paperbacks) Creative Co., The.

—Stock Cars. (J). 2015. *(978-1-60818-524-5(9))* 2010. 24p. (gr. -1-3). 16.95 *(978-1-58341-916-8(0))* Creative Co., The. (Creative Education).

Robinson, Matthew. The Greatest NASCAR Tracks. (Highlights of NASCAR Racing Ser.). 48p. (gr. 5-5). 2009. 53.00 *(978-1-61513-301-7(1)*, Rosen Reference) 2008. (Illus.). (YA). lib. bdg. 29.25 *(978-1-4042-1400-2(3))* Rosen Publishing Group, Inc., The.

Rosen Publishing Staff. The Checkered Flag, 1 vol. 2015. (Checkered Flag Ser.). (ENG.). 32p. (J). 157.50 *(978-1-4777-5742-0(2)*, PowerKids Pr.) Rosen Publishing Group, Inc., The.

Roza, Greg. Kevin Harvick: NASCAR Driver. 2009. (Behind the Wheel Ser.). (gr. 5-8). (ENG., Illus.). 48p. (J). pap. 11.75 *(978-1-4358-5406-2(3))*; (YA). lib. bdg. 29.25 *(978-1-4042-1899-4(8))* Rosen Publishing Group, Inc., The.

—Terry Labonte. 2009. (NASCAR Champions Ser.). 24p. (gr. 1-2). 42.50 *(978-1-61514-787-8(X)*, PowerKids Pr.) Rosen Publishing Group, Inc., The.

Ryan, Pat. Car Racing Greats. 2011. (Best of the Best Ser.). (ENG.). 32p. (gr. 1-2). pap. 47.70 *(978-1-4296-7246-7(3)*, Blazers) Capstone Press of Coughlan Cos.

Sandler, Michael. Dynamic Drag Racers. 2011. (Fast Rides Ser.). 24p. (YA). (gr. 2-5). lib. bdg. 22.61 *(978-1-61772-138-0(7))* Bearport Publishing Co., Inc.

—Electrifying Eco Race Cars. 2011. (Fast Rides Ser.). 24p. (J). (gr. 2-5). lib. bdg. 22.61 *(978-1-61772-137-3(9))* Bearport Publishing Co., Inc.

—Enter the Speed Zone. 2006. (Illus.). 16p. (J). pap. *(978-0-439-73908-5(X))* Scholastic, Inc.

—Hot Hot Rods. 2011. (Fast Rides Ser.). 24p. (J). (gr. 2-5). lib. bdg. 22.61 *(978-1-61772-139-7(5))* Bearport Publishing Co., Inc.

—Rally Car Dudes. 2009. (X-Moves Ser.). (Illus.). 24p. (YA). (gr. 2-5). lib. bdg. 22.61 *(978-1-59716-948-6(X))* Bearport Publishing Co., Inc.

Sandler, Michael & McNessor, Mike. Electrifying Eco-Race Cars. 2016. (Fast Rides Ser.). (ENG.). 24p. (J). (gr. 1-6). pap. 7.95 *(978-1-944998-57-8(8))* Bearport Publishing Co., Inc.

Savage, Jeff. Dale Earnhardt Jr. 2005. (Amazing Athletes Ser.). (Illus.). 32p. (J). (gr. 4-7). per. 5.95 *(978-0-8225-2953-8(X))* Lerner Publishing Group.

—Dale Earnhardt Jr. (Revised Edition) 2009. pap. 40.95 *(978-0-7613-4775-0(5))* Lerner Publishing Group.

—Danica Patrick. (Amazing Athletes Ser.). 32p. 2006. (Illus.). (J). (gr. 4). pap. 6.95 *(978-0-8225-6012-8(7)*, First Avenue Editions) 2010. (ENG.). (gr. 2-5). pap. 7.95 *(978-0-7613-5760-5(2))* Lerner Publishing Group.

—Monster Trucks, 1 vol. 2010. (Full Throttle Ser.). (ENG.). 32p. (gr. 3-4). lib. bdg. 27.99 *(978-1-4296-3943-9(1)*, Edge Bks.) Capstone Press of Coughlan Cos.

—Travis Pastrana. 2006. (Amazing Athletes Ser.). (ENG., Illus.). 32p. (gr. 2-5). lib. bdg. 25.26 *(978-0-8225-3428-0(2))* Lerner Publishing Group.

Savery, Annabel. Supercars. 2012. (It's Amazing Ser.). (Illus.). 32p. (gr. 3-6). lib. bdg. 31.35 *(978-1-59920-691-2(9))* Black Rabbit Bks.

Sawyer, Sarah. Denny Hamlin: NASCAR Driver. 2009. (Behind the Wheel Ser.). 48p. (gr. 5-5). 53.00 *(978-1-61511-541-9(2)*, Rosen Reference) Rosen Publishing Group, Inc., The.

Schuh, Mari C. The Tractor Race. 2017. (Let's Race Ser.). (ENG., Illus.). 16p. (J). (gr. -1-1). pap. 7.99 *(978-1-68152-136-7(9))* Amicus.

Schwartz, Heather E. The Science of a Race Car: Reactions in Action. 2010. (Action Science Ser.). (ENG.). 32p. (gr. 3-4). pap. 47.70 *(978-1-4296-5074-8(5)*, Fact Finders) Capstone Press of Coughlan Cos.

Sechrist, Darren. Supercross & Arenacross: Taking MX Indoors. 2008. (MXplosion! Ser.). (ENG., Illus.). 32p. (J). (gr. 3-7). pap. *(978-0-7787-4004-9(8))*; lib. bdg. *(978-0-7787-3991-3(0))* Crabtree Publishing Co.

Sexton, Susan. Sprint Car Racing: Unleashing the Power. 2003. (Cover-To-Cover Books). (Illus.). 68p. pap. 8.95 *(978-0-7891-5884-0(1))* Perfection Learning Corp.

—Sprint Car Racing: Unleashing the Power. 2003. (Cover-to-Cover Informational Ser.). (Illus.). 68p. (J). (gr. 4-7). lib. bdg. 17.95 *(978-0-7569-1144-7(3))* Perfection Learning Corp.

—Stock Car Racing: Running with the Big Boys. 2003. (Cover-To-Cover Books). (Illus.). 64p. pap. 8.95 *(978-0-7891-5922-9(8))*; (J). (gr. 4-7). lib. bdg. 17.95 *(978-0-7569-1189-8(3))* Perfection Learning Corp.

Shoup, Kate. Danica Patrick: Breaking Speed Barriers. 2017. (J). ***(978-1-5026-2833-6(3))*** Cavendish Square Publishing.

Silverman, Buffy. How Do Formula One Race Cars Work? 2016. (Lightning Bolt Books (tm) — How Vehicles Work Ser.). (ENG.). 32p. (J). (gr. 1-3). lib. bdg. 26.65 *(978-1-4677-9503-6(8))* Lerner Publishing Group.

Simon and Schuster Staff. NASCAR Jeff Gordon: Stock Car Superstar. 2005. (Nascar Ser.). (J). 59.94 *(978-0-7944-0345-4(X))*; 59.94 *(978-0-7944-0344-7(1))* Studio Fun International. (Reader's Digest Children's Bks.).

—NASCAR Tony Stewart: Racing to Victory Lane. 2005. (Nascar Ser.). (J). 59.95 *(978-0-7944-0346-1(8))*; 59.95 *(978-0-7944-0347-8(6))* Studio Fun International. (Reader's Digest Children's Bks.).

Sodaro, Craig. Blazing Hot Rods: By Craig Sodaro. 2015. (Dream Cars Ser.). (ENG.). 32p. (gr. 3-4). lib. bdg. 27.99 *(978-1-4914-2011-9(1))* Capstone Press of Coughlan Cos.

Sodomka, Martin & Lacey, Saskia. How to Build a Car. 2015. (Technical Tales Ser.). (ENG., Illus.). 64p. (J). (gr. 1-3). 14.95 *(978-1-63322-040-9(0))* Quarto Publishing Group USA.

Spalding, Lee-Anne T. Go-Kart Racing. 2008. (Thrill of Racing Ser.). (Illus.). 24p. (YA). (gr. 4-7). 27.07 *(978-1-60472-371-7(8))* Rourke Educational Media.

Spaulding, Jeffrey. Matt Kenseth: NASCAR Driver. 2009. (Behind the Wheel Ser.). (YA). (gr. 5-9). lib. bdg. 29.25 *(978-1-4042-1897-0(1))* Rosen Publishing Group, Inc., The.

Sports Illustrated for Kids Editors. Race Day: Behind the Scenes at NASCAR. 2004. (Sports Illustrated for Kids Ser.). (Illus.). 96p. pap. 9.99 *(978-1-931933-65-0(0))* Time Inc. Bks.

Starfall Education. Car Race. Starfall Education, ed. 2004. (ENG., Illus.). 8p. (J). pap. *(978-1-59577-012-7(7))* Starfall Education.

—Dune Buggy. Starfall Education, ed. 2004. (ENG., Illus.). 8p. (J). pap. *(978-1-59577-010-3(0))* Starfall Education.

Starke, John. Speed Machines: Mission Xtreme 3D. 2004. (Mission Xtreme 3D Ser.). (Illus.). 18p. (J). pap. 5.95 *(978-1-902626-50-5(8))* Red Bird Publishing GBR. Dist: Weatherhill, Inc.

Stealey, Bryan. The Powerhouse MX Nations: USA, Belgium, UK, Netherlands, France, & Germany. 2008. (MXplosion! Ser.). (ENG., Illus.). 32p. (J). (gr. 3-7). lib. bdg. *(978-0-7787-3990-6(2))* Crabtree Publishing Co.

—The Powerhouse MX Nations: USA, Belgium, UK, Netherlands, France & Germany. 2008. (MXplosion! Ser.). (ENG.). 32p. (J). (gr. 3-7). pap. *(978-0-7787-4003-2(X))* Crabtree Publishing Co.

Steele, Cameron. Funny Cars. 2011. (World's Fastest Ser.). (ENG., Illus.). 24p. (J). (gr. 3-7). lib. bdg. 25.95 *(978-1-60014-587-2(6)*, Torque Bks.) Bellwether Media.

Stewart, Mark & Kennedy, Mike. NASCAR at the Track. 2008. (Science of NASCAR Ser.). (ENG.). 48p. (gr. 4-7). lib. bdg. 27.93 *(978-0-8225-8741-5(6))* Lerner Publishing Group.

—Nascar at the Track. 2009. pap. 52.95 *(978-0-8225-9275-4(4))* Lerner Publishing Group.

—NASCAR Behind the Scenes. 2008. (Science of NASCAR Ser.). (Illus.). 48p. (YA). (gr. 4-7). lib. bdg. 27.93 *(978-0-8225-8743-9(2))* Lerner Publishing Group.

—Nascar Behind the Scenes. 2009. pap. 52.95 *(978-0-8225-9277-8(0))* Lerner Publishing Group.

—NASCAR Designed to Win. 2008. (Science of NASCAR Ser.). (Illus.). 48p. (YA). (gr. 4-7). lib. bdg. 27.93 *(978-0-8225-8736-1(X))* Lerner Publishing Group.

—Nascar Designed to Win. 2009. pap. 52.95 *(978-0-8225-9283-9(5))* Lerner Publishing Group.

—NASCAR in the Driver's Seat. 2008. (Science of NASCAR Ser.). (ENG., Illus.). 48p. (gr. 4-7). lib. bdg. 27.93 *(978-0-8225-8737-8(8))* Lerner Publishing Group.

—Nascar in the Driver's Seat. 2008. (Science of NASCAR Ser.). (ENG.). (gr. 4-7). pap. 51.01 *(978-0-8225-9290-7(8))* Lerner Publishing Group.

—NASCAR in the Pits. 2008. (Science of NASCAR Ser.). (ENG., Illus.). 48p. (gr. 4-7). lib. bdg. 27.93 *(978-0-8225-8738-5(6))* Lerner Publishing Group.

A
B

—Nascar in the Pits. 2008. (Science of NASCAR Ser.). (ENG.). (gr. 4-7). pap. 51.01 (978-0-8225-9337-9(8)) Lerner Publishing Group.
—The Science of Nascar. 2009. (Science of NASCAR Ser.). (ENG.). (gr. 4-7). pap. 17.01 (978-0-8225-9341-6(6)); pap. 102.03 (978-1-58013-277-0(4)) Lerner Publishing Group.
—The Science of NASCAR, 6 vols., Set. Incl. NASCAR at the Track. lib. bdg. 27.93 (978-0-8225-8741-5(6)); NASCAR Behind the Scenes. (Illus.). (YA). lib. bdg. 27.93 (978-0-8225-8743-9(2)); NASCAR Designed to Win. (Illus.). (YA). lib. bdg. 27.93 (978-0-8225-8736-1(X)); NASCAR in the Driver's Seat. (Illus.). lib. bdg. 27.93 (978-0-8225-8737-8(8)); NASCAR in the Pits. (Illus.). lib. bdg. 27.93 (978-0-8225-8738-5(6)); 48p. (gr. 4-7). 2008. (Science of NASCAR Ser.). (ENG.). 2008. Set lib. bdg. 55.86 (978-0-8225-8735-4(1)) Lerner Publishing Group.
Stinson, Rick. Kyle Busch: NASCAR Driver. 2009. (Behind the Wheel Ser.). (YA). (gr. 5-9). lib. bdg. 29.25 (978-1-4042-1896-3(3)) Rosen Publishing Group, Inc., The.
Stock Cars. (Illus.). 24p. (978-2-7643-0250-7(9)) Phidal Publishing, Inc./Editions Phidal, Inc.
Sutherland, Adam. Being a Formula One Driver. 2012. (On the Radar: Awesome Jobs Ser.). (ENG., Illus.). 32p. (gr. 4-8). lib. bdg. 26.60 (978-0-7613-7781-8(6), Lerner Pubns.) Lerner Publishing Group.
Tieck, Sarah. Dragsters, 1 vol. 2011. (Amazing Vehicles Set 2 Ser.). (ENG., Illus.). 32p. (J). (gr. 2-5). 28.50 (978-1-61714-696-1(X)) ABDO Publishing Co.
Timblin, Stephen. Race Week: Seven Crazy Days. 2008. (World of NASCAR Ser.). (ENG., Illus.). 32p. (J). (gr. 3-6). 28.50 (978-1-60253-079-9(3), 200998) Child's World, Inc., The.
Tomljanovic, Tatiana. Rallying. 2009. (Extreme Ser.). (Illus.). 32p. (J). (gr. 4-6). pap. 9.95 (978-1-60596-133-0(7)); lib. bdg. 26.00 (978-1-60596-132-3(9)) Weigl Pubs., Inc.
Tuchman, Gail. Race Day. 2015. (National Geographic Readers: Pre-Reader Ser.). (ENG.). (gr. -1-k). 19.95 (978-1-4301-1886-2(5)) Live Oak Media.
—Race Day. 2010. (Readers Ser.). (ENG., Illus.). 24p. (J). (gr. -1-k). pap. 3.99 (978-1-4263-0612-9(1)); lib. bdg. 13.90 (978-1-4263-0613-6(X)) National Geographic Society. (National Geographic Children's Bks.).
Weber, M. Wild Moments of Sports Car Racing. 2017. (Wild Moments of Motorsports Ser.). (ENG.). 32p. (gr. 3-4). lib. bdg. 27.99 **(978-1-5157-7405-1(8)**, Edge Bks.) Capstone Press of Coughlan Cos.
West, David. Speedsters. 2015. (Mechanic Mike's Machines (continuation) Ser.). (Illus.). 24p. (J). (gr. k-3). 27.10 (978-1-62588-059-8(6)) Black Rabbit Bks.
West, David, illus. Race Cars. 2017. (What's Inside? Ser.). 24p. (gr. k-3). lib. bdg. 28.50 (978-1-62588-403-9(6)) Black Rabbit Bks.
Woods, Bob. Hottest Motorcycles. 2007. (Wild Wheels! Ser.). (Illus.). 48p. (J). (gr. 3-7). lib. bdg. 25.27 (978-0-7660-2874-6(7)) Enslow Pubs., Inc.
—Hottest Sports Cars. 2007. (Wild Wheels! Ser.). (Illus.). 48p. (J). (gr. 3-7). lib. bdg. 25.27 (978-0-7660-2873-9(9)) Enslow Pubs., Inc.
—Motocross History: From Local Scrambling to World Championship MX to Freestyle. 2008. (MXplosion! Ser.). (ENG., Illus.). 32p. (J). (gr. 3-7). pap. (978-0-7787-4000-1(5)); lib. bdg. (978-0-7787-3987-6(2)) Crabtree Publishing Co.
—NASCAR Tech. 2008. (World of NASCAR Ser.). (ENG., Illus.). 32p. (J). (gr. 3-6). 28.50 (978-1-60253-078-2(5), 200996) Child's World, Inc., The.
—Talkin' NASCAR. 2008. (World of NASCAR Ser.). (ENG., Illus.). 32p. (J). (gr. 3-6). 28.50 (978-1-60253-081-2(5), 200999) Child's World, Inc., The.
—Want to Be a NASCAR Driver? 2008. (World of NASCAR Ser.). (ENG., Illus.). 32p. (J). (gr. 3-6). 28.50 (978-1-60253-084-3(X), 201002) Child's World, Inc., The.
—Wild Racers. 2009. (Racing Mania Ser.). 48p. (gr. 4-18). lib. bdg. 31.36 (978-0-7614-4389-6(4)) Marshall Cavendish Corp.
Worms, Penny. Race Cars. 2016. (Motormania Ser.). 32p. (gr. 2-7). 31.35 (978-1-59920-992-0(6), Smart Apple Media) Black Rabbit Bks.
Xtreme Races. 2013. (Xtreme Races Ser.: 6). 32p. (J). (gr. 3-9). lib. bdg. 162.42 (978-1-61783-691-6(5), Abdo & Daughters) ABDO Publishing Co.
Young, Jeff C. Dropping the Flag: Auto Racing, 1 vol. 2011. (Adrenaline Adventure Ser.). (ENG., Illus.). 32p. (YA). (gr. 3-6). 27.07 (978-1-61613-548-5(4)) ABDO Publishing Co.
Zobel, Derek. Race Cars. 2009. (Mighty Machines Ser.). (ENG., Illus.). 24p. (J). (gr. k-3). lib. bdg. 25.95 (978-1-60014-193-5(5)) Bellwether Media.
Zuehlke, Jeffrey. Drag Racers. 2008. pap. 52.95 (978-1-58013-662-4(1)); (ENG., Illus.). 48p. (gr. 4-7). lib. bdg. 26.60 (978-0-8225-7287-9(7)) Lerner Publishing Group.
—Motorcycle Road Racing. 2009. (Motor Mania Ser.). (YA). (gr. 3-6). 26.60 (978-0-8225-9427-7(7)) Lerner Publishing Group.
—Rally Cars. 2009. (Motor Mania Ser.). (YA). (gr. 3-6). 26.60 (978-0-8225-9428-4(5)); pap. 52.95 (978-0-7613-4793-4(3)) Lerner Publishing Group.
—Supercross. 2008. (Motor Mania Ser.). (ENG., Illus.). 48p. (gr. 4-7). lib. bdg. 26.60 (978-0-8225-7286-2(9)) Lerner Publishing Group.

AUTOMOBILE RACING—BIOGRAPHY

Allen, K. Kurt Busch. 2009. (NASCAR Champions Ser.). 24p. (gr. 1-2). 42.50 (978-1-61514-781-6(0), PowerKids Pr.) Rosen Publishing Group, Inc., The.
Allen, Kenny. Kurt Busch. 2007. (NASCAR Champions Ser.). (Illus.). 24p. (J). (gr. 1-3). lib. bdg. 22.60 (978-1-4042-3457-4(8)) Rosen Publishing Group, Inc., The.
Anderson, Wayne. Tony Stewart: NASCAR Driver. 2009. (Behind the Wheel Ser.). 48p. (gr. 5-5). 53.00 (978-1-61511-560-0(9), Rosen Reference) Rosen Publishing Group, Inc., The.
Anderson, Wayne A. Tony Stewart: NASCAR Driver. 2006. (Behind the Wheel Ser.). (Illus.). 48p. (YA). (gr. 5-9). lib. bdg. 29.25 (978-1-4042-0984-8(0)) Rosen Publishing Group, Inc., The.
Basen, Ryan. Jeff Burton: Chasing the Championship. 2009. (Heroes of Racing Ser.). (Illus.). 128p. (J). (gr. 5-9). lib. bdg. 33.27 (978-0-7660-3301-6(5)) Enslow Pubs., Inc.
—Kyle Busch: Gifted & Giving Racing Star. 2010. (Sports Stars Who Give Back Ser.). (Illus.). 128p. (J). (gr. 5-9). 33.27 (978-0-7660-3589-8(1)) Enslow Pubs., Inc.
—Tony Stewart: Rocket on the Racetrack. 2008. (Heroes of Racing Ser.). (Illus.). 128p. (J). (gr. 3-7). lib. bdg. 33.27 (978-0-7660-2998-9(0)) Enslow Pubs., Inc.
Benatar, Raquel & Rubio, Adrian. Go, Milka, Go! The Life of Milka Duno. Benatar, Raquel & Rubio, Adrian, illus. 2008.Tr. of Corre, Milka, Corre! (SPA & ENG., Illus.). 32p. (J). 19.95 (978-1-56492-360-8(6)) Laredo Publishing Co., Inc.
Bentley, Karen. The Unsers. rev. collector's ed. 2005. (Race Car Legends Ser.). (Illus.). 72p. (YA). (gr. 5-9). lib. bdg. 25.00 (978-0-7910-8764-0(6)) Facts On File, Inc.
Book & Car. 2004. (Nascar Ser.). 24p. (J). 9.99 (978-0-7944-0410-9(3)); 9.99 (978-0-7944-0409-3(X)) Studio Fun International. (Reader's Digest Children's Bks.).
Braidich, V. Dale Earnhardt. 2009. (NASCAR Champions Ser.). 24p. (gr. 1-2). 42.50 (978-1-61514-762-5(4), PowerKids Pr.) Rosen Publishing Group, Inc., The.
Briggs, Raymond. Jimmy Murphy & the White Duesenberg. 2006. (Illus.). (J). (978-0-9766683-0-5(0)) Racemaker Pr.
—Nuvolari & the Alfa Romeo. 2006. (Illus.). (J). (978-0-9766683-1-2(9)) Racemaker Pr.
Buckley, James, Jr. Jimmie Johnson. 2008. (World of NASCAR Ser.). (ENG., Illus.). 32p. (J). (gr. 3-6). 28.50 (978-1-60253-076-8(9), 200994) Child's World, Inc., The.
Carney, Larry. Jeff Gordon. PC Treasures Staff, ed. Houghton, Chris & Morrison, Jeff, illus. 2009. (Nascar Drivers Coloring/Sticker Book Ser.). (ENG.). 96p. (J). pap. 6.95 (978-1-60072-162-5(1)) PC Treasures, Inc.
—Tony Stewart. PC Treasures Staff, ed. Morrison, Jeff, illus. 2009. (Nascar Drivers Coloring/Sticker Book Ser.). (ENG.). 96p. (J). pap. 6.95 (978-1-60072-166-3(4)) PC Treasures, Inc.
Colich, Abby. Danica Patrick. 2016. (Women in Sports Ser.). (ENG., Illus.). 24p. (gr. k-1). pap. 6.95 (978-1-4914-8567-5(1), Pebble Plus) Capstone Press of Coughlan Cos.
Danica Patrick. 2007. (Xtreme Athletes Ser.). (Illus.). 112p. (YA). (gr. 7-12). lib. bdg. 27.95 (978-1-59935-079-0(3)) Reynolds, Morgan Inc.
Dayton, Connor. Denny Hamlin. Alaman, Eduardo, tr. 2007. (NASCAR Champions / Campeones de NASCAR Ser.). (SPA., Illus.). 24p. (J). (gr. 1-3). lib. bdg. 22.60 (978-1-4042-7644-4(0)) Rosen Publishing Group, Inc., The.
—Denny Hamlin. 2007. (NASCAR Champions Ser.: Vol. 2). (Illus.). 24p. (J). (gr. 1-3). lib. bdg. 22.60 (978-1-4042-3814-5(X)) Rosen Publishing Group, Inc., The.
—Greg Biffle. 2009. (NASCAR Champions Ser.). 24p. (gr. 1-2). 42.50 (978-1-61514-768-7(3), PowerKids Pr.); (ENG & SPA.). 42.50 (978-1-61514-790-8(X), Editorial Buenas Letras) Rosen Publishing Group, Inc., The.
—Jeff Burton. 2009. (NASCAR Champions/Campeones de NASCAR Ser.). 24p. (gr. 1-2). (ENG & SPA.). 42.50 (978-1-61514-792-2(6), Editorial Buenas Letras); 42.50 (978-1-61514-770-0(5), PowerKids Pr.) Rosen Publishing Group, Inc., The.
—Kyle Busch. 2009. (NASCAR Champions Ser.). 24p. (gr. 1-2). 42.50 (978-1-61514-782-3(9), PowerKids Pr.); (ENG & SPA.). 42.50 (978-1-61514-794-6(2), Editorial Buenas Letras) Rosen Publishing Group, Inc., The.
Doeden, Matt. Dale Earnhardt Jr. 2005. (Sports Heroes & Legends Ser.). (Illus.). 106p. (J). (gr. 3-7). lib. bdg. 27.93 (978-0-8225-3067-1(8), Lerner Pubns.) Lerner Publishing Group.
El Nabli, Dina. Danica Patrick. 2009. (People We Should Know Ser.). 32p. (J). (gr. 3-5). pap. 10.50 (978-1-4339-0158-4(7)); lib. bdg. 31.00 (978-1-4339-0018-1(1)) Stevens, Gareth Publishing LLLP. (Gareth Stevens Learning Library).
Evans, Andy. Three to Go Mario! Morgan-Magee, Mary, ed. 2009. (ENG., Illus.). 37p. (J). 25.00 (978-1-935240-01-3(3)) Racemaker Pr.
Farmer, Emily. Jimmie Johnson: NASCAR Driver. 2006. (Behind the Wheel Ser.). (Illus.). 48p. (YA). (gr. 5-9). lib. bdg. 29.25 (978-1-4042-0981-7(6)) Rosen Publishing Group, Inc., The.
Figorito, M. Matt Kenseth. 2009. (NASCAR Champions Ser.). 24p. (gr. 1-2). 42.50 (978-1-61514-783-0(7), PowerKids Pr.) Rosen Publishing Group, Inc., The.
Figorito, Marcus. Matt Kenseth. 2007. (NASCAR Champions Ser.). (Illus.). 24p. (J). (gr. 1-3). lib. bdg. 22.60 (978-1-4042-3458-1(6)) Rosen Publishing Group, Inc., The.
Fleischman, Bill. Jimmie Johnson. collector's ed. 2005. (Race Car Legends Ser.). (Illus.). 64p. (YA). (gr. 5-9). lib. bdg. 25.00 (978-0-7910-8672-8(0)) Facts On File, Inc.
Ford, June. Jeff Burton. rev. collector's ed. 2005. (Race Car Legends Ser.). (Illus.). 64p. (YA). (gr. 5-9). lib. bdg. 25.00 (978-0-7910-8699-5(2)) Facts On File, Inc.
Ford, Michael. Dale Earnhardt, Jr. 2010. (Superstars of NASCAR Ser.). (ENG.). 32p. (J). (gr. 3-8). pap. 10.50 (978-1-4339-3948-8(7)); lib. bdg. 25.25 (978-1-4339-3947-1(9)) Stevens, Gareth Publishing LLLP.
Ganchy, Sally. Mark Martin: NASCAR Driver. 2009. (Behind the Wheel Ser.). 48p. (gr. 5-5). 53.00 (978-1-61511-553-2(6), Rosen Reference) Rosen Publishing Group, Inc., The.
Garfield, Ken. Jeff Gordon: Rewriting the Record Book. 2003. (Superstar Ser.). (Illus.). 96p. (J). (gr. 4-7). pap. 4.95 (978-1-58382-055-1(8)) Sports Publishing, LLC.
Gigliotti, Jim. Dale Earnhardt Jr. 2008. (World of NASCAR Ser.). (ENG., Illus.). 32p. (J). (gr. 3-6). 28.50 (978-1-60253-074-4(2), 200992) Child's World, Inc., The.
Gitlin, Martin. Darrell Waltrip: Racing Legend. 2009. (Heroes of Racing Ser.). (Illus.). 128p. (J). (gr. 5-9). lib. bdg. 33.27 (978-0-7660-3300-9(7)) Enslow Pubs., Inc.
—Jimmie Johnson: Racing Champ. 2008. (Heroes of Racing Ser.). (Illus.). 128p. (J). (gr. 3-7). lib. bdg. 33.27 (978-0-7660-2999-6(9)) Enslow Pubs., Inc.
Glaser, Jason. Danica Patrick. 2008. (Sports Idols Ser.). (Illus.). 24p. (J). (gr. 2-5). lib. bdg. 22.60 (978-1-4042-4180-0(9)) Rosen Publishing Group, Inc., The.
Hand, Jimmie, told to. Jimmy Spencer: Don't Ever Quit! 2004. (YA). pap. 19.95 (978-0-9754755-0-8(9)) Strong Corner Publishing, LCC.
Harper, John. Denny Hamlin. 2010. (Superstars of NASCAR Ser.). (ENG.). 32p. (J). (gr. 3-8). pap. 10.50 (978-1-4339-3951-8(7)); lib. bdg. 25.25 (978-1-4339-3950-1(9)) Stevens, Gareth Publishing LLLP.
Hoffman, Mary Ann. Jeff Gordon. 2010. (Superstars of NASCAR Ser.). (ENG.). 32p. (J). (gr. 3-8). pap. 10.50 (978-1-4339-3954-9(1)); lib. bdg. 25.25 (978-1-4339-3953-2(3)) Stevens, Gareth Publishing LLLP.
Holmes, Bill. Mark Martin. 2010. (Superstars of NASCAR Ser.). (ENG.). 32p. (J). (gr. 3-8). pap. 10.50 (978-1-4339-3966-2(5)); lib. bdg. 25.25 (978-1-4339-3965-5(7)) Stevens, Gareth Publishing LLLP.
James, Lincoln. Dale Jarrett. 2007. (NASCAR Champions Ser.). (Illus.). 24p. (J). (gr. 1-3). lib. bdg. 22.60 (978-1-4042-3459-8(4)) Rosen Publishing Group, Inc., The.
Keith, Ted. Matt Kenseth. 2008. (World of NASCAR Ser.). (ENG., Illus.). 32p. (J). (gr. 3-6). 28.50 (978-1-60253-077-5(7), 200995) Child's World, Inc., The.
Kirkpatrick, Rob. Dale Earnhardt Jr: NASCAR Road Racer. rev. ed. 2003. (Buenas Letras Bilingual Ser.). 24p. (J). lib. bdg. 17.25 (978-0-8239-7540-2(1), Editorial Buenas Letras) Rosen Publishing Group, Inc., The.
—Dale Earnhardt Jr. , NASCAR Road Racer/Piloto de NASCAR. De Leon, Mauricio Velzaquez, tr. 2008. (Reading Power Ser.). (ENG., Illus.). 24p. (gr. 1-6). per. 8.85 (978-1-4042-7539-3(8)) Rosen Publishing Group, Inc., The.
—Jeff Gordon: Campeón de NASCAR (NASCAR Champion) 2009. (Grandes Idolos (Hot Shots) Ser.). (SPA.). 24p. (gr. 1-1). 42.50 (978-1-61512-737-5(2), Editorial Buenas Letras) Rosen Publishing Group, Inc., The.
—Jeff Gordon: NASCAR Champion / Campeón de NASCAR. 2009. (Hot Shots/Grandes idolos Ser.). (ENG & SPA.). 24p. (gr. 1-1). 42.50 (978-1-61513-415-1(8), Editorial Buenas Letras) Rosen Publishing Group, Inc., The.
Kortemeier, Todd. Superstars of NASCAR. 2016. (Pro Sports Superstars Ser.). (ENG., Illus.). 24p. (J). (gr. 1-4). 20.95 (978-1-60753-940-7(3)) Amicus Publishing.
Krumenauer, Heidi. Jimmie Johnson. 2009. (Robbie Reader Ser.). (Illus.). 32p. (YA). (gr. 2-5). lib. bdg. 25.70 (978-1-58415-756-4(9)) Mitchell Lane Pubs., Inc.
La Bella, Laura. Carl Edwards: NASCAR Driver. 2009. (Behind the Wheel Ser.). (ENG., Illus.). 48p. (YA). (gr. 5-8). pap. 11.75 (978-1-4358-5405-5(5)) Rosen Publishing Group, Inc., The.
Levy, Janey. Dale Earnhardt, Jr. 2006. (High Interest Bks.). (ENG., Illus.). 48p. (J). (gr. 4-7). lib. bdg. 24.50 (978-0-531-16805-9(0)) Scholastic Library Publishing.
—Dale Earnhardt, Jr. 2007. (High Interest Bks.). (ENG., Illus.). 48p. (J). (gr. 4-7). pap. 6.95 (978-0-531-18713-5(6)) Scholastic Library Publishing.
—Kurt Busch. 2007. (High Interest Bks.). (ENG., Illus.). 48p. (J). (gr. 4-7). pap. 6.95 (978-0-531-18714-2(4)) Scholastic Library Publishing.
MacDonald, James. Dale Earnhardt, Sr. The Intimidator. 2009. (Heroes of Racing Ser.). (Illus.). 128p. (J). (gr. 5-9). lib. bdg. 33.27 (978-0-7660-3297-2(3)) Enslow Pubs., Inc.
Mantell, Paul. Dale Earnhardt Jr: Young Race Car Driver. Henderson, Meryl, illus. 2006. 216p. (J). lib. bdg. 18.46 (978-1-4242-2205-6(2)) Fitzgerald Bks.
Martin, Bob. Tony Stewart. 2010. (Superstars of NASCAR Ser.). (ENG.). 32p. (J). (gr. 3-8). pap. 10.50 (978-1-4339-3969-3(X)); lib. bdg. 25.25 (978-1-4339-3968-6(1)) Stevens, Gareth Publishing LLLP.
Maruszewski, Kelley. Matt Kenseth: Midwest Racing Sensation. 2003. (Racing Superstar Ser.). (Illus.). 93p. mass mkt. 4.95 (978-1-58261-653-7(1)) Sports Publishing, LLC.
Mello, Tara Baukus. Danica Patrick. 2007. (Race Car Legends Ser.). (Illus.). 71p. (YA). (gr. 5-9). lib. bdg. 25.00 (978-0-7910-9126-5(0)) Facts On File, Inc.
—Mark Martin. rev. ed. 2007. (Race Car Legends Ser.). (Illus.). 72p. (YA). (gr. 5-9). lib. bdg. 25.00 (978-0-7910-8664-3(X)) Facts On File, Inc.
—The Need for Speed. rev. ed. 2007. (Race Car Legends Ser.). (Illus.). 64p. (YA). (gr. 5-9). lib. bdg. 25.00 (978-0-7910-8667-4(4)) Facts On File, Inc.
—Tony Stewart. rev. collector's ed. 2005. (Race Car Legends Ser.). (Illus.). 64p. (YA). (gr. 5-9). lib. bdg. 25.00 (978-0-7910-8670-4(4)) Facts On File, Inc.
Miller, Connie Colwell. Dale Earnhardt, Jr, 1 vol. 2013. (NASCAR Heroes Ser.). (ENG.). 32p. (J). (gr. 3-9). lib. bdg. 27.07 (978-1-61783-661-9(3), SportsZone) ABDO Publishing Co.
—Danica Patrick, 1 vol. 2013. (NASCAR Heroes Ser.). (ENG.). 32p. (J). (gr. 3-9). lib. bdg. 27.07 (978-1-61783-666-4(4), SportsZone) ABDO Publishing Co.
NASCAR Champions, 6 vols., Set 1. 2008. (J). (gr. 1-6). lib. bdg. 127.50 (978-1-4042-3549-6(3)) Rosen Publishing Group, Inc., The.
Payment, Simone. Kyle Busch: NASCAR Driver. 2009. (Behind the Wheel Ser.). 48p. (gr. 5-5). 53.00 (978-1-61511-550-1(1), Rosen Reference) Rosen Publishing Group, Inc., The.
PC Treasures Staff, ed. Dale Earnhardt Jr. 2009. (Nascar Drivers Coloring Book Ser.). (ENG., Illus.). 96p. (J). 2.99 (978-1-60072-150-2(8)); 6.95 (978-1-60072-163-2(X)) PC Treasures, Inc.
—Jeff Gordon. 2009. (Nascar Drivers Coloring Book Ser.). (ENG., Illus.). 96p. (J). 2.99 (978-1-60072-151-9(6)) PC Treasures, Inc.
—Jimmie Johnson. 2009. (Nascar Drivers Coloring Book Ser.). (ENG., Illus.). 96p. (J). pap. 2.99 (978-1-60072-152-6(4)); Vol. 48. 6.95 (978-1-60072-161-8(3)) PC Treasures, Inc.
—Kyle Busch. 2010. (Nascar Drivers Coloring/Sticker Book Ser.). (ENG., Illus.). 96p. (J). 6.95 (978-1-60072-165-6(6)) PC Treasures, Inc.
—NASCAR Drivers Coloring Book: Kyle Busch. 2010. (Illus.). 96p. (J). pap. 2.99 incl. cd-rom (978-1-60072-153-3(2)) PC Treasures, Inc.
—Tony Stewart. 2009. (Nascar Drivers Coloring Book Ser.). (ENG., Illus.). 96p. (J). pap. 2.99 (978-1-60072-160-1(5)) PC Treasures, Inc.
Persinger, Kathy. Mark Martin: Ozark Original. 2004. (Illus.). 96p. (J). (gr. 4-7). per. 5.95 (978-1-58261-654-4(X)) Sports Publishing, LLC.
Poolos, J. Jeff Gordon: NASCAR Driver. 2009. (Behind the Wheel Ser.). 48p. (gr. 5-5). 53.00 (978-1-61511-544-0(7), Rosen Reference) Rosen Publishing Group, Inc., The.
Porterfield, Jason. Kurt Busch: NASCAR Driver. (Behind the Wheel Ser.). 48p. (gr. 5-5). 2009. 53.00 (978-1-61511-549-5(8), Rosen Reference) 2006. (Illus.). (YA). lib. bdg. 29.25 (978-1-4042-0982-4(4)) Rosen Publishing Group, Inc., The.
Prentzas, G. S. Mario Andretti. rev. ed. 2007. (Race Car Legends Ser.). (Illus.). 80p. (YA). (gr. 5-9). lib. bdg. 25.00 (978-0-7910-8755-8(7)) Facts On File, Inc.
Pristash, Nicole. Carl Edwards. 2009. (NASCAR Champions Ser.). (Illus.). 24p. (J). lib. bdg. 22.60 (978-1-4042-4449-8(2), PowerKids Pr.) Rosen Publishing Group, Inc., The.
—Dale Earnhardt Jr. 2009. (NASCAR Champions Ser.). (Illus.). 24p. (gr. 1-6). pap. 8.25 (978-1-4042-4541-9(3), Rosen Classroom); (J). lib. bdg. 22.60 (978-1-4042-4445-0(X), PowerKids Pr.) Rosen Publishing Group, Inc., The.
—Jeff Gordon. 2009. (NASCAR Champions Ser.). 24p. (gr. 1-2). 42.50 (978-1-61514-771-7(3), PowerKids Pr.) Rosen Publishing Group, Inc., The.
—Ryan Newman. 2009. (NASCAR Champions Ser.). 24p. (Illus.). (gr. 1-6). pap. 8.25 (978-1-4042-4546-4(4), Rosen Classroom); (gr. 1-2). 42.50 (978-1-61514-784-7(5), PowerKids Pr.); (Illus.). lib. bdg. 22.60 (978-1-4042-4450-4(6), PowerKids Pr.) Rosen Publishing Group, Inc., The.
Robinson, Tom. Kevin Harvick: Racing to the Top. 2009. (Heroes of Racing Ser.). (Illus.). 128p. (J). (gr. 5-9). lib. bdg. 33.27 (978-0-7660-3299-6(X)) Enslow Pubs., Inc.
—Mark Martin: Master Behind the Wheel. 2008. (Heroes of Racing Ser.). (Illus.). 128p. (J). (gr. 3-7). lib. bdg. 33.27 (978-0-7660-3001-5(6)) Enslow Pubs., Inc.
Roselius, J. Chris. Danica Patrick: Racing to History. 2009. (Heroes of Racing Ser.). (Illus.). 128p. (J). (gr. 5-9). lib. bdg. 33.27 (978-0-7660-3302-3(3)) Enslow Pubs., Inc.
—Matt Kenseth: Speeding to Victory. 2008. (Heroes of Racing Ser.). (Illus.). 128p. (J). (gr. 3-7). lib. bdg. 33.27 (978-0-7660-3000-8(8)) Enslow Pubs., Inc.
—Richard Petty: The King of Racing. 2009. (Heroes of Racing Ser.). (Illus.). 128p. (J). (gr. 5-9). lib. bdg. 33.27 (978-0-7660-3298-9(1)) Enslow Pubs., Inc.
Roza, Greg. Dale Earnhardt Jr: NASCAR Driver. 2009. (Behind the Wheel Ser.). 48p. (gr. 5-5). 53.00 (978-1-61511-540-2(4), Rosen Reference) Rosen Publishing Group, Inc., The.
—Terry Labonte. 2007. (NASCAR Champions Ser.: Vol. 3). (Illus.). 24p. (J). (gr. 1-3). lib. bdg. 22.60 (978-1-4042-3501-4(9)) Rosen Publishing Group, Inc., The.
—Tony Stewart. 2009. (NASCAR Champions Ser.). 24p. (gr. 1-2). 42.50 (978-1-61514-788-5(8), PowerKids Pr.) Rosen Publishing Group, Inc., The.
Sapet, Kerrily. Jeff Gordon. 2012. (Role Model Athletes Ser.). 64p. (J). (gr. 7). 22.95 (978-1-4222-2710-7(3)) Mason Crest.
Savage, Jeff. Auto Racing Super Stats. 2017. (Pro Sports Stats Ser.). (ENG.). 32p. (J). (gr. 3-6). 27.99 **(978-1-5124-3412-5(4))** Lerner Publishing Group.
—Dale Earnhardt, Jr. 2005. (Amazing Athletes Ser.). (ENG., Illus.). 32p. (gr. 2-5). lib. bdg. 25.26 (978-0-8225-2946-0(7)) Lerner Publishing Group.
—Dale Earnhardt Jr. (Amazing Athletes Ser.). (gr. 2-5). rev. ed. 2009. pap. 6.95 (978-0-7613-4430-8(6), First Avenue Editions) 2nd ed. 2015. (ENG., Illus.). 32p. (J). pap. 7.95 (978-1-4677-7583-0(5), Lerner Pubns.) Lerner Publishing Group.
—Danica Patrick. 2006. (Amazing Athletes Ser.). (Illus.). 32p. (J). (gr. 2-5). lib. bdg. 23.93 (978-0-8225-5954-2(4), Lerner Pubns.) Lerner Publishing Group.
—Danica Patrick (Revised Edition) 2010. pap. 39.62 (978-0-7613-6966-0(X)) Lerner Publishing Group.
—Jeff Gordon. (Amazing Athletes Ser.). 2007. (J). pap. 6.95 (978-0-8225-6802-5(0), Lerner Pubns.) 2005. (Illus.). 32p. (gr. 3-4). lib. bdg. 22.60 (978-0-8225-1339-1(0)) 2007. (ENG., Illus.). 32p. (gr. 2-5). lib. bdg. 25.26 (978-0-8225-8962-4(1)) Lerner Publishing Group.
—Travis Pastrana. 2006. (Amazing Athletes Ser.). (ENG., Illus.). 32p. (gr. 2-5). lib. bdg. 25.26 (978-0-8225-3428-0(2)) Lerner Publishing Group.
Sawyer, Sarah. Denny Hamlin: NASCAR Driver. 2009. (Behind the Wheel Ser.). (gr. 5-8). (ENG., Illus.). 48p. (J). pap. 11.75 (978-1-4358-5402-4(0)); (YA). lib. bdg. 29.25 (978-1-4042-1895-6(5)) Rosen Publishing Group, Inc., The.
Schuh, Mari C. Stars of Stock Car Racing, 1 vol. 2014. (Sports Stars Ser.). (ENG.). 24p. (gr. k-1). 26.65 (978-1-4914-0593-2(7), Pebble Plus) Capstone Press of Coughlan Cos.
Sheen, Barbara. Danica Patrick. 2009. (People in the News Ser.). (ENG.). 128p. (gr. 7-12). 39.40 (978-1-4205-0155-1(0)) Cengage Gale.
—Janet Guthrie: Racing Pioneer. 2010. (Innovators Ser.). (Illus.). 64p. (J). 29.95 (978-0-7377-5050-8(2), Kidhaven) Cengage Gale.
Spaulding, Jeffrey. Matt Kenseth: NASCAR Driver. 2009. (Behind the Wheel Ser.). 48p. (gr. 5-5). 53.00 (978-1-61511-556-3(0), Rosen Reference) Rosen Publishing Group, Inc., The.
Stewart, Mark. Dale Earnhardt, Jr. Driven by Destiny. 2003. (Auto Racing's New Wave Ser.: up). (Illus.). 48p. (gr. 4-18). lib. bdg. 22.90 (978-0-7613-2908-4(0), Millbrook Pr.) Lerner Publishing Group.
Teitelbaum, Michael. Tony Stewart. 2008. (World of NASCAR Ser.). (ENG., Illus.). 32p. (J). (gr. 3-6). 28.50 (978-1-60253-083-6(1), 201001) Child's World, Inc., The.
Tieck, Sarah. Jimmie Johnson: NASCAR Champion, 1 vol. 2009. (Big Buddy Biographies Set 3 Ser.). (ENG., Illus.). 32p. (J). (gr. 2-5). 28.50 (978-1-60453-709-3(4)) ABDO Publishing Co.
Weatherford, Carole Boston. Racing Against the Odds: The Story of Wendell Scott, Stock Car Racing's African-American Champion. 0 vols. 2009. (ENG., Illus.). 40p. (J). (gr. -1-2). 17.99 (978-0-7614-5465-6(9), 9780761454656, Amazon Children's Publishing) Amazon Publishing.
Weber, Terri Smith. Jeff Gordon: Racing to Win. 2003. (J). pap. (978-0-9740180-2-7(3)); lib. bdg. (978-0-9740180-0-3(7)) Panda Publishing, L.L.C. (Bios for Kids).
Wilker, Josh & Prentzas, G. S., texts. A. J. Foyt. rev. ed. 2007. (Race Car Legends Ser.). (Illus.). 72p. (YA). (gr. 5-9). lib. bdg. 25.00 (978-0-7910-8759-6(X)) Facts On File, Inc.
Wilner, Barry. Best Auto Racers of All Time, 1 vol. 2014. (Sports' Best Ever Ser.). (ENG., Illus.). 64p. (J). (gr. 3-6). lib. bdg. 32.79 (978-1-62403-617-0(1), SportsZone) ABDO Publishing Co.
Wilson, Walt. Jimmie Johnson. 2010. (Superstars of NASCAR Ser.). (ENG.). 32p. (J). (gr. 3-8). pap. 10.50

(978-1-4339-3957-0(6)); lib. bdg. 25.25 (978-1-4339-3956-3(8)) Stevens, Gareth Publishing LLLP.

Woods, Bob. Racer Girls. 2006. (Reading Rocks! Ser.). (ENG., Illus.). 32p. (J). (gr. 2-5). 28.50 (978-1-59296-742-1(6), 200732) Child's World, Inc., The.

—Racer Girls. 2016. (Illus.). 32p. (J). (978-1-4896-4781-8(3)) Weigl Pubs., Inc.

Wright, Marcy. Juan Pablo Montoya. 2010. (Superstars of NASCAR Ser.). (ENG.). 32p. (J). (gr. 3-8). pap. 10.50 (978-1-4339-3960-0(6)); lib. bdg. 25.25 (978-1-4339-3959-4(2)) Stevens, Gareth Publishing LLLP.

AUTOMOBILE RACING—FICTION

Abdo Publishing. Nascar Heroes, 1 vol. 2013. (NASCAR Heroes Ser.: 8). (ENG.). 32p. (J). (gr. 3-9). lib. bdg. 216.56 (978-1-61783-659-6(1), SportsZone) ABDO Publishing Co.

Accord Publishing Staff. Ready, Set, Go! 2011. (ENG., Illus.). 12p. (J). 9.99 (978-1-4494-0833-6(8)) Andrews McMeel Publishing.

Ahmad, M. I. Aldebaram. 2009. 95p. pap. 13.00 (978-0-557-08323-7(0)) Lulu Pr., Inc.

Amos, Eduardo & Pearson Education Staff. Amazon Rally. 2007. (ENG.). 24p. pap. 17.32 incl. cd-rom (978-1-4058-5199-2(6)) Pearson Education.

Arena, Felice & Kettle, Phil. Race Car Dreamers. Cox, David, illus. 2004. (J). pap. (978-1-59336-375-8(3)) Mondo Publishing.

Auerbach, Annie & Berrios, Frank. Off-Road Racers!/Crash Course! Random House Disney Staff, illus. 2010. (Pictureback(R) Ser.). (ENG.). 32p. (J). (gr. -1-2). pap. 4.99 (978-0-7364-2650-3(7), RH/Disney) Random Hse. Children's Bks.

Berrios, Frank. The Easter Buggy. 2014. lib. bdg. 14.75 (978-0-606-35543-8(X)) Turtleback Bks.

—Let's Cruise!, 4 vols. 2006. (Illus.). (J). (978-0-7364-2436-3(9)); (978-0-7364-2433-2(4)); (978-0-7364-2434-9(2)); (978-0-7364-2435-6(0)) Random Hse. Children's Bks.

—Radiator Springs 500. RH Disney Staff, illus. deluxe ed. 2015. (Pictureback(R) Ser.). (ENG.). 24p. (J). (gr. -1-2). 4.99 (978-0-7364-3281-8(7), RH/Disney) Random Hse. Children's Bks.

Brouwer, Sigmund. Scarlet Thunder, 1 vol. 2008. (Orca Sports Ser.). (ENG.). 176p. (YA). (gr. 6-10). pap. 9.95 (978-1-55143-911-2(5)) Orca Bk. Pubs. USA.

Burroughs, Caleb. Cars. 2006. (Look & Find Ser.). (Illus.). 18p. (J). (gr. -1-3). pap. 24.98 (978-1-4127-3775-3(3), 7269900) Phoenix International Publications, Inc.

Carmine's Big Race. 2009. (ENG.). 24p. pap. 3.99 (978-1-4231-1688-2(7)) Disney Pr.

Cars & Disney Book Group Staff. Cars. 2010. (Read-Along Storybook & CD Ser.). (ENG.). 32p. (J). (gr. -1 — 1). pap. 6.99 (978-1-4231-3332-2(3)) Disney Pr.

Colorful Cars. 2017. (Colorful Cars Ser.). 24p. (gr. 4-6). 70.80 **(978-1-5081-6176-9(3))**; pap. 24.75 **(978-1-5081-6178-3(X))** Rosen Publishing Group, Inc., The. (PowerKids Pr.).

Cooper, Ann Goode. Zebordee Goes to the Races. Jessee, Diana, illus. 2005. 32p. (J). (gr. -1-3). (978-1-933251-01-1(8)) Parkway Pubs., Inc.

Cousins, Lucy. Maisy's Race Car: A Go with Maisy Board Book. Cousins, Lucy, illus. 2015. (Maisy Ser.). (ENG., Illus.). 18p. (J). (— 1). bds. 5.99 (978-0-7636-8011-4(7)) Candlewick Pr.

Crow, Melinda Melton. Road Race, 1 vol. Rooney, Ronnie, illus. 2009. (Truck Buddies Ser.). (ENG.). 32p. (gr. -1-1). pap. 6.25 (978-1-4342-1754-7(X)) Stone Arch Bks.

Dempsey, Kristy. Mini Racer. Strevens-Marzo, Bridget, illus. 2011. (ENG.). 32p. (J). (gr. -1-k). 17.89 (978-1-59990-591-4(4), 9781599905914, Bloomsbury USA Childrens) Bloomsbury Publishing USA.

Depken, Kristen L. Pit Crew Pups. Jackson, Mike, illus. 2015. (Step into Reading Ser.). (ENG.). 24p. (J). (gr. -1-1). 4.99 (978-0-553-50853-6(9), Random Hse. Bks. for Young Readers) Random Hse. Children's Bks.

Disney Book Group. Cars 3 Read-Along Storybook & CD. Disney Storybook Art Team, illus. 2017. (Read-Along Storybook & CD Ser.). (ENG.). 32p. (J). (gr. 1-3). pap. 6.99 (978-1-4847-8134-0(1)) Disney Pr.

Disney Book Group Staff. Disney*Pixar Storybook Collection. Disney Storybook Art Team, illus. 2011. (Storybook Collection). (ENG.). 312p. (J). (gr. -1 — 1). 15.99 (978-1-4231-2423-8(5)) Disney Pr.

Disney Press Staff & Disney Book Group Staff. Cars 2. 2011. (Read-Along Storybook & CD Ser.). (ENG.). 32p. (J). (gr. -1-2). pap. 6.99 (978-1-4231-4179-2(2)) Disney Pr.

Disney/Pixar 6. 2010. bds. 12.99 (978-1-4231-2789-5(7)) Disney Pr.

Dixon, Franklin W. Double Jeopardy. 2003. (Hardy Boys Ser.: 181). (ENG.). 160p. (J). (gr. 3-7). pap. 5.99 (978-0-689-85780-5(2), Aladdin) Simon & Schuster Children's Publishing.

Donovan, Kyle. CurBee Races the NasBee 500: The Do'Bees. 2007. (J). 15.95 net. (978-0-9767670-2-2(3)) WannaBees Media LLC.

Dotlich, Rebecca Kai. Race Car Count. Slack, Michael, illus. 2015. (ENG.). 32p. (J). (gr. -1-k). 14.99 (978-1-62779-009-3(8), 9781627790093, Holt, Henry & Co. Bks. For Young Readers) Holt, Henry & Co.

Early Bird Books Staff. The Race. Date not set. (J). 1.95 (978-0-394-86703-8(3), Random Hse. Bks. for Young Readers) Random Hse. Children's Bks.

Elliott, Craig. Racer Buddies-Opening Day at Daytona. William, Harper, illus. 2004. 40p. (J). per. 12.95 (978-0-9746445-0-9(1), 1234022) Powerband, LLC.

Everheart, Chris. Sprint. 2016. (Tartan House Ser.). (ENG.). 96p. (YA). (gr. 5-12). (978-1-63235-167-8(6), 12-Story Library) Pr. Room Editions LLC.

Felsen, Henry Gregor. Fever Heat. Welch, Holly Felsen, illus. 2013. 230p. pap. 15.00 (978-1-62272-002-6(4)) Felsen Ink.

—Henry Gregor Felsen Street Rod Collection. Welch, Holly Felsen, illus. 2013. 75.00 (978-1-62272-005-7(9)) Felsen Ink.

—Rag Top. Felsen, Holly, illus. 2013. 212p. pap. 15.00 (978-1-62272-001-9(6)) Felsen Ink.

—Road Rocket. 2013. 260p. pap. 15.00 (978-1-62272-004-0(0)) Felsen Ink.

Fliess, Sue. Race! Taylor, Edwardian, illus. 2017. (ENG.). 32p. (J). (gr. -1-3). 16.99 (978-1-4998-0237-5(4)) Little Bee Books Inc.

Floca, Brian. The Racecar Alphabet. Floca, Brian, illus. 2003. (ENG., Illus.). 40p. (J). (gr. -1-2). 18.99 (978-0-689-85091-2(3), Atheneum/Richard Jackson Bks.) Simon & Schuster Children's Publishing.

Fox, Christyan & Fox, Diane. Enzo the Racing Car. Fox, Christyan & Fox, Diane, illus. 2008. (Wheelyworld Ser.). (ENG., Illus.). 32p. (J). (gr. -1-k). pap. 8.95 (978-1-4052-2742-1(7)) Egmont Bks., Ltd. GBR. Dist: Independent Pubs. Group.

—Monty the Rally Car. Fox, Christyan & Fox, Diane, illus. 2008. (Wheelyworld Ser.). (ENG., Illus.). 32p. (J). (gr. -1-k). pap. 8.95 (978-1-4052-2743-8(5)) Egmont Bks., Ltd. GBR. Dist: Independent Pubs. Group.

Gamble, Adam & Jasper, Mark. Good Night Race Cars. Veno, Joe, illus. 2015. (Good Night Our World Ser.). (ENG.). 20p. (J). (— 1). bds. 9.95 (978-1-60219-228-7(6), 1396132) Good Night Bks.

Garcia, Kami. The Lovely Reckless. 2016. (ENG.). 384p. (YA). 18.99 (978-1-250-07919-0(5), 9781250079190) Imprint IND. Dist: Macmillan.

Golden Books. Full Speed Ahead! (Blaze & the Monster Machines) Golden Books, illus. 2015. (Color Plus Crayons & Sticker Ser.). (ENG., Illus.). 48p. (J). (gr. -1-2). pap. 4.99 (978-0-553-52455-0(0), Golden Bks.) Random Hse. Children's Bks.

Golden Books Staff. Cars. Golden Books Staff, illus. 2009. (Make Your Own Little Golden Book Ser.). (ENG., Illus.). 16p. (J). (gr. -1-2). 5.99 (978-0-375-84597-0(6), Golden Bks.) Random Hse. Children's Bks.

Graudin, Ryan. Wolf by Wolf. 2015. (Wolf by Wolf Ser.). (ENG.). 400p. (YA). (gr. 10-17). 18.00 (978-0-316-40512-6(4)) Little Brown & Co.

Haesche, Richard, Sr. The Big Race. 2007. (ENG.). 222p. (J). per. 10.49 (978-0-9798536-1-6(3)) Kreative X-Pressions Pubns.

Hampshire, Anthony. Fast Track. 2004. (Redline Racing Ser.: Bk. 1). (Illus.). 104p. (YA). pap. 3.99 (978-1-55305-007-0(X)) Cygnet Publishing Group, Inc./Coolreading.com CAN. Dist: Orca Bk. Pubs. USA.

—Full Throttle. 2004. (Redline Racing Ser.: Bk. 2). (Illus.). 108p. (YA). pap. 3.99 (978-1-55305-008-7(8)) Cygnet Publishing Group, Inc./Coolreading.com CAN. Dist: Orca Bk. Pubs. USA.

—On the Limit. 2004. (Redline Racing Ser.: Bk. 3). 144p. (YA). pap. 3.99 (978-1-55305-025-4(8)) Cygnet Publishing Group, Inc./Coolreading.com CAN. Dist: Orca Bk. Pubs. USA.

—Title Run. 2004. (Redline Racing Ser.: Bk. 4). 148p. (YA). pap. 3.99 (978-1-55305-026-1(6)) Cygnet Publishing Group, Inc./Coolreading.com CAN. Dist: Orca Bk. Pubs. USA.

Harris, Patricia. Race Cars Can Go. 2017. (Colorful Cars Ser.). 24p. (gr. 4-6). pap. 8.25 **(978-1-5383-2091-4(6)**, PowerKids Pr.) Rosen Publishing Group, Inc., The.

—A Thrilling Race. 2017. (Colorful Cars Ser.). 24p. (gr. 4-6). pap. 8.25 **(978-1-5383-2083-9(5)**, PowerKids Pr.) Rosen Publishing Group, Inc., The.

Harvey, Pam & Panckridge, Michael. Taking the Chequered Flag. 2008. 208p. (978-0-207-20062-5(9)) HarperCollins Pubs. Australia.

Hunt, Elizabeth Singer. Peril at the Grand Prix - Italy, Bk. 8. 2009. (Secret Agent Jack Stalwart Ser.: 8). (ENG.). 144p. (J). (gr. 1-4). pap. 5.99 (978-1-60286-019-3(X), Weinstein Bks.) Perseus Bks. Group.

Jones, Patrick. Drift: Nissan Skyline. 2013. (Turbocharged Ser.). (ENG.). 112p. (gr. 6-12). pap. 7.95 (978-1-4677-1474-7(7)); lib. bdg. 27.93 (978-1-4677-1242-2(6)) Lerner Publishing Group. (Darby Creek).

—Slammed: Honda Civic. 2013. (Turbocharged Ser.). (ENG.). 96p. (gr. 6-12). pap. 7.95 (978-1-4677-1478-5(X)); lib. bdg. 27.93 (978-1-4677-1245-3(0)) Lerner Publishing Group. (Darby Creek).

Just for Boys. 2008. (Amazing Body Growing Up Ser.). 96p. (978-1-4075-1570-0(5)) Parragon, Inc.

Karre, Elizabeth. Blind Curve: Acura Integra. 2013. (Turbocharged Ser.). (ENG.). 96p. (YA). (gr. 6-12). pap. 7.95 (978-1-4677-1477-8(1)); lib. bdg. 27.93 (978-1-4677-1244-6(2)) Lerner Publishing Group. (Darby Creek).

Kay, Ross. The Go Ahead Boys & the Racing Motor Boat. 2007. 104p. per. (978-1-4068-1923-6(9)) Echo Library.

Knife & Packer. Desert Dustup. 2015. (Illus.). 93p. (J). (978-1-61067-431-7(6)) Kane Miller.

—Spooky Smackdown. 2015. (Illus.). 93p. (J). (978-1-61067-432-4(4)) Kane Miller.

Knife & Packer. Desert Dustup: Wheelnuts! Knife & Packer, illus. 2016. (Illus.). 96p. (J). pap. 6.99 (978-1-61067-395-2(6)) Kane Miller.

—Spash Mash. Knife & Packer, illus. 2016. (Illus.). 93p. (J). pap. 6.99 (978-1-61067-397-6(2)) Kane Miller.

—Spooky Smackdown: Wheelnuts! Knife & Packer, illus. 2016. (Illus.). 96p. (J). pap. 6.99 (978-1-61067-396-9(4)) Kane Miller.

Knife & Packer, creator. Deep-Sea Dash. 2016. (Illus.). 93p. (J). pap. 6.99 (978-1-61067-398-3(0)) Kane Miller.

—Rain Forest Rumble. 2016. (Illus.). 94p. (J). pap. 6.99 (978-1-61067-399-0(9)) Kane Miller.

Lagonegro, Melissa. Secret Agent Mater. Random House Disney Staff, illus. 2011. (Step into Reading Ser.). (ENG.). 32p. (J). (gr. k-3). pap. 3.99 (978-0-7364-8095-6(1), RH/Disney) Random Hse. Children's Bks.

Lagonegro, Melissa & Random House Disney Staff. Roadwork! Mawhinney, Art, illus. 2008. (Step into Reading Ser.). (ENG.). 32p. (J). (gr. k-3). pap. 3.99 (978-0-7364-2516-2(0), RH/Disney) Random Hse. Children's Bks.

Landers, Ace. Cave Race! White, Dave, illus. 2010. 32p. (J). (978-0-545-20871-0(8)) Scholastic, Inc.

—Hot Wheels: Wild Rides. White, Dave, illus. 2009. 32p. (J). (978-0-545-15347-8(6)) Scholastic, Inc.

—Shark Attack. 2013. (Scholastic Reader Level 1 Ser.). lib. bdg. 13.55 (978-0-606-32391-8(0), Turtleback) Turtleback Bks.

—Start Your Engines. White, Dave, illus. 2007. (Scholastic Reader Ser.). (J). pap. (978-0-545-02017-6(4)) Scholastic, Inc.

Leary, Sean & Leary, Jackson. Go, Racecars Go! 2013. 30p. pap. 11.00 (978-0-9772819-9-2(X)) Dingobi Publishing.

Lipsyte, Robert. Yellow Flag. 2009. (ENG.). 256p. (YA). (gr. 8). pap. 9.99 (978-0-06-055709-6(5), Tegen, Katherine Bks) HarperCollins Pubs.

Lord, Cynthia. Hot Rod Hamster. Anderson, Derek, illus. 2010. (ENG.). 40p. (J). (gr. -1-k). 18.99 (978-0-545-03530-9(9), Scholastic Pr.) Scholastic, Inc.

Maddox, Jake. On the Speedway, 1 vol. Tiffany, Sean, illus. 2011. (Jake Maddox Sports Stories Ser.). (ENG.). 208p. (gr. 2-3). pap. 7.95 (978-1-4342-3030-0(9)) Stone Arch Bks.

—Pit Crew Crunch, 1 vol. Tiffany, Sean, illus. 2009. (Jake Maddox Sports Stories Ser.). (ENG.). 72p. (gr. 2-3). 25.32 (978-1-4342-1600-7(4)) Stone Arch Bks.

—Race Car Rival, 1 vol. Tiffany, Sean, illus. 2009. (Jake Maddox Sports Stories Ser.). (ENG.). 72p. (gr. 2-3). 25.32 (978-1-4342-1601-4(2)) Stone Arch Bks.

—Speed Camp, 1 vol. Tiffany, Sean, illus. 2009. (Jake Maddox Sports Stories Ser.). (ENG.). 72p. (gr. 2-3). 25.32 (978-1-4342-1602-1(0)) Stone Arch Bks.

—Speedway Switch. Tiffany, Sean, illus. 2007. (Jake Maddox Sports Stories Ser.). (ENG.). 72p. (gr. 2-3). pap. 5.95 (978-1-59889-416-5(1)); lib. bdg. 25.32 (978-1-59889-321-2(1)) Stone Arch Bks.

—Stock Car Sabotage, 1 vol. Tiffany, Sean, illus. 2009. (Jake Maddox Sports Stories Ser.). (ENG.). 72p. (gr. 2-3). 25.32 (978-1-4342-1603-8(9)) Stone Arch Bks.

Martin, Jenny. Marked. 2016. (ENG.). 368p. (YA). (gr. 7). 17.99 (978-0-525-42871-8(2), Dial Bks) Penguin Young Readers Group.

—Tracked. 2015. (ENG.). 400p. (YA). (gr. 7). 17.99 (978-0-8037-4012-9(3), Dial Bks) Penguin Young Readers Group.

Matheis, Mickie. Balloon Blast! (Rusty Rivets) Flowers, Luke, illus. 2017. (Little Golden Book Ser.). (ENG.). 24p. (J). (-k). 4.99 **(978-1-5247-1672-1(3)**, Golden Bks.) Random Hse. Children's Bks.

McMorrine, David. Tim, Sherri & Formula One. 2003. 140p. (YA). pap. 7.95 (978-0-9639940-4-2(2)) Morgan Publishing Co.

Meddaugh, Susan. Martha Go, Go, Goes Green! 2013. (Martha Speaks Ser.). (ENG., Illus.). 24p. (J). (gr. -1-3). pap. 3.99 (978-0-547-97017-2(X)) Houghton Mifflin Harcourt Publishing Co.

—Martha Speaks: Martha Go, Go, Goes Green! (Reader) 2013. (Martha Speaks Ser.). (ENG., Illus.). 24p. (J). (gr. -1-3). 12.99 (978-0-547-99547-2(4)) Houghton Mifflin Harcourt Publishing Co.

Montgomery, R. A. Behind the Wheel. 2010. 144p. pap. 6.99 (978-1-933390-35-2(2)) Chooseco LLC.

—Race Forever. 2005. (Illus.). 122p. (J). (978-0-7608-9695-2(X)) Sundance/Newbridge Educational Publishing.

—Race Forever. Sundaravej, Sittisan, illus. 2006. (Choose Your Own Adventure Ser.: No. 7). 144p. (J). (gr. 4-8). per. 6.99 (978-1-933390-07-9(7), CHCL07) Chooseco LLC.

Moore, Tessa. Dad & the Mad Cow Roundabout. 2007. (ENG.). 64p. (J). pap. 10.95 (978-1-901737-54-7(3)) Anvil Bks., Ltd. IRL. Dist: Dufour Editions, Inc.

Narayanan, Manjula. The Red Red Car. 2009. (Illus.). 32p. pap. 14.49 (978-1-4490-3366-8(0)) AuthorHouse.

Orpinas, Jean-Paul & Tilley, Scott, illus. Cars. 2006. (Little Golden Book Ser.). (ENG.). 24p. (J). (gr. -1-2). 4.99 (978-0-7364-2347-2(8), Golden/Disney) Random Hse. Children's Bks.

O'Ryan, Ray. Ready, Set, Blast Off! Kraft, Jason, illus. 2017. (Galaxy Zack Ser.: 15). (ENG.). 128p. (J). (gr. k-4). pap. 5.99 (978-1-4814-8595-1(4), Little Simon) Little Simon.

Oxley, Jennifer & Aronson, Billy. The Race Car Problem. 2016. (Peg + Cat Ser.). (ENG.). 32p. (J). (gr. -1-2). 5.99 (978-0-7636-9083-0(X), Candlewick Entertainment) Candlewick Pr.

Packer. Deep-Sea Dash. Knife, illus. 2016. 93p. (J). (978-1-61067-478-2(2)) Kane Miller.

—Rain Forest Rumble. Knife, illus. 2016. 94p. (J). (978-1-61067-479-9(0)) Kane Miller.

—Space Mash. Knife, illus. 2016. 93p. (J). (978-1-61067-477-5(4)) Kane Miller.

Peck, Richard. Here Lies the Librarian. 2007. (ENG.). 160p. (J). (gr. 5-18). 7.99 (978-0-14-240908-4(1), Puffin Books) Penguin Young Readers Group.

—Here Lies the Librarian. 2007. 145p. (J). (gr. 4-7). 14.65 (978-0-7569-8193-8(X)) Perfection Learning Corp.

—Here Lies the Librarian. rev. l.t. ed. 2007. (Thorndike Literacy Bridge Ser.). 173p. (J). (gr. 5-9). 23.95 (978-0-7862-9183-0(4)) Thorndike Pr.

Perlman, Rhea. Born to Drive. Santat, Dan, illus. 2006. (Otto Undercover Ser.). 127p. (J). (gr. 4-7). 14.99 (978-0-06-075496-9(6), Tegen, Katherine Bks) HarperCollins Pubs.

Phoenix Books Staff, illus. Disney(r) PIXAR Cars! Can Drive! 2015. 11p. (J). bds. (978-1-4508-8633-8(7), 1450886337) Publications International, Ltd.

Pizzoli, Greg. Number One Sam. Pizzoli, Greg, illus. 2014. (ENG., Illus.). 40p. (J). (gr. -1-k). 16.99 (978-1-4231-7111-9(X)) Hyperion Bks. for Children.

Porter, Alan J. Rally Race. Magic Eye Studios, illus. 2010. (Cars Ser.). (ENG.). 112p. (J). (gr. 3-6). pap. 9.99 (978-1-60886-517-8(7)) Boom! Studios.

Priddy, Roger. The Great Turkey Race. 2014. (Shaped Board Bks.). (ENG., Illus.). 6p. (J). (gr. -1-k). bds. 6.99 (978-0-312-51719-9(X), 9780312517199, Priddy Bks.) St. Martin's Pr.

Pruett, Scott, et al. Rookie Racer. Morgan, Rick, illus. 2005. (J). (978-0-9670600-2-6(8)) Word Weaver Bks., Inc.

Publications International Ltd. Staff, ed. Disney Pixar Cars: (Stereo Play-a-Sound) 2010. 24p. (J). 19.98 (978-1-60553-857-0(4)) Publications International, Ltd.

—Disney Pixar Cars - Mater's Manners, Vol. 2. 2011. 12p. (J). bds. (978-1-4508-0400-4(4)) Phoenix International Publications, Inc.

—Disney Pixar Cars; Cruising' Cool. 2011. 12p. (J). bds. 10.98 (978-1-4508-0915-3(4)) Publications International, Ltd.

—Little Carry Case Spa Cars 8 Bks. 2009. 8p. 9.98 (978-1-4127-6434-6(3), PIL Kids) Publications International, Ltd.

—Mater Saves the Day. 2011. 12p. (J). bds. 10.98 (978-1-4508-0695-4(3)) Phoenix International Publications, Inc.

—Zoom! 2010. 14p. (J). bds. 17.98 (978-1-4127-4594-9(2)) Phoenix International Publications, Inc.

The Race Car: Individual Title Six-Packs. (Sails Literacy Ser.). 16p. (gr. k-18). 27.00 (978-0-7635-4438-6(8)) Rigby Education.

Random House. Racing Colors! (Blaze & the Monster Machines) Random House, illus. 2016. (ENG., Illus.). 24p. (J). (gr. -1 — 1). bds. 6.99 (978-0-553-53892-2(6), Random Hse. Bks. for Young Readers) Random Hse. Children's Bks.

Random House Disney Staff. Good Night, Lightning (Disney/Pixar Cars) Random House Disney Staff, illus. 2013. (Glow-In-the-Dark Board Book Ser.). (ENG., Illus.). 12p. (J). (gr. -1-2). bds. 7.99 (978-0-7364-2976-4(X), RH/Disney) Random Hse. Children's Bks.

—Super Spies. Random House Disney Staff, illus. 2011. (Step into Reading Ser.). (ENG., Illus.). 32p. (J). (gr. k-3). pap. 3.99 (978-0-7364-2807-1(0), RH/Disney) Random Hse. Children's Bks.

—Taking the Lead. Random House Disney Staff, illus. 2011. (Puzzle Book Ser.). (ENG., Illus.). 8p. (J). (gr. -1-2). 7.99 (978-0-7364-2822-4(4), RH/Disney) Random Hse. Children's Bks.

Random House Disney Staff, illus. The Cars Story Collection. 2011. (Step into Reading Ser.). (ENG.). 160p. (J). (gr. k-3). pap. 7.99 (978-0-7364-2813-2(5), RH/Disney) Random Hse. Children's Bks.

Random House Staff. UmiCar's Big Race (Team Umizoomi) Random House Staff & Aikins, David, illus. 2013. (Pictureback(R) Ser.). (ENG.). 16p. (J). (gr. -1-2). pap. 3.99 (978-0-449-81386-7(X), Random Hse. Bks. for Young Readers) Random Hse. Children's Bks.

Rao, Lisa. Blaze & the Monster Machines: We're Movin' 2016. (ENG.). 10p. (J). (gr. -1-k). bds. 10.99 (978-0-7944-3762-6(1), Reader's Digest Children's Bks.) Studio Fun International.

Reilly, Matthew. Full Throttle. Raimondi, Pablo, illus. 2006. (ENG.). 224p. (J). (gr. 5-9). pap. 10.99 (978-1-4169-0228-7(7), Simon & Schuster/Paula Wiseman Bks.) Simon & Schuster/Paula Wiseman Bks.

RH Disney. Back on Track. RH Disney, illus. 2017. (Step into Reading Ser.). (ENG., Illus.). 24p. (J). (gr. -1-1). pap. 4.99 **(978-0-7364-3680-9(4))**; lib. bdg. 12.99 **(978-0-7364-8198-4(2))** Random Hse. Children's Bks. (RH/Disney).

—Taken by Storm/How to Be a Great Racer. RH Disney, illus. 2017. (Pictureback(R) Ser.). (ENG., Illus.). 48p. (J). (gr. -1-2). pap. 5.99 **(978-0-7364-3727-1(4)**, RH/Disney) Random Hse. Children's Bks.

RH Disney & Keane, Dave. Storm Chasing: Cars Origins. RH Disney, illus. 2017. (Stepping Stone Book(TM) Ser.). (ENG., Illus.). 128p. (J). (gr. 1-4). 5.99 **(978-0-7364-3821-6(1))**; lib. bdg. 12.99 **(978-0-7364-8257-8(1))** Random Hse. Children's Bks. (RH/Disney).

—Struck by Lightning. RH Disney, illus. 2017. (Stepping Stone Book Ser.). (ENG., Illus.). 128p. (J). (gr. 1-4). lib. bdg. 12.99 **(978-0-7364-8256-1(3)**, RH/Disney) Random Hse. Children's Bks.

RH Disney Staff. Cars 2 Little Golden Book (Disney/Pixar Cars 2) RH Disney Staff, illus. 2011. (Little Golden Book Ser.). (ENG., Illus.). 24p. (J). (gr. -1-2). 3.99 (978-0-7364-2781-4(3), Golden/Disney) Random Hse. Children's Bks.

—Let's Cruise! Disney Storybook Artists Staff, illus. 2017. (Friendship Box Ser.). (ENG.). 12p. (J). (gr. k — 1). bds. 10.99 (978-0-7364-2391-5(5), RH/Disney) Random Hse. Children's Bks.

Scarry, Richard & Farber, Erica. Go, Huckle, Go! Scarry, Huck, illus. 2011. (Richard Scarry's Great Big Schoolhouse Ser.). (ENG.). 24p. (J). (gr. -1-k). pap. 3.95 (978-1-4027-7316-7(1)) Sterling Publishing Co., Inc.

Shulevitz, Uri. Troto & the Trucks. 2015. (ENG., Illus.). 32p. (J). (gr. -1-1). 17.99 (978-0-374-30080-7(1), 9780374300807, Farrar, Straus & Giroux (BYR)) Farrar, Straus & Giroux.

Soo, Kean, illus. March Grand Prix: The Fast & the Furriest. 2015. (March Grand Prix Ser.). (ENG.). 144p. (gr. 1-3). pap. 14.95 (978-1-62370-171-0(6)) Capstone Young Readers of Coughlan Cos.

—The Race at Harewood. 2015. (March Grand Prix Ser.). (ENG.). 48p. (gr. 1-3). lib. bdg. 33.32 (978-1-4342-9639-9(3)) Capstone Young Readers of Coughlan Cos.

Spanyol, Jessica. Keith & His Super-Stunt Rally Racer. Spanyol, Jessica, illus. 2008. (MiniBug Bks.). (ENG., Illus.). 24p. (J). (gr. k-k). 5.99 (978-0-7636-3742-2(4)) Candlewick Pr.

Sporteller Staff. Race to Win (Auto Racing) 64p. (YA). (gr. 6-12). pap. 10.95 (978-0-8224-6479-2(9)) Globe Fearon Educational Publishing.

Stein, Garth. Enzo - Races in the Rain! Alley, R. W., illus. 2014. (ENG.). 40p. (J). (gr. -1-3). 17.99 (978-0-06-229533-0(0)) HarperCollins Pubs.

—Racing in the Rain: My Life as a Dog. 2011. (ENG., Illus.). 304p. (J). (gr. 3-7). 16.99 (978-0-06-201574-7(5)); pap. 6.99 (978-0-06-201576-1(1)) HarperCollins Pubs.

Stevens, Eric. The Classic: '69 Chevy Camaro. 2013. (Turbocharged Ser.). (ENG.). 96p. (gr. 6-12). pap. 7.95 (978-1-4677-1479-2(8)); lib. bdg. 27.93 (978-1-4677-1247-7(7)) Lerner Publishing Group. (Darby Creek).

—Jacked: Ford Focus ST. 2013. (Turbocharged Ser.). (ENG.). 96p. (gr. 6-12). pap. 7.95 (978-1-4677-1475-4(5)); lib. bdg. 27.93 (978-1-4677-1246-0(9)) Lerner Publishing Group. (Darby Creek).

Stierle, Cynthia. Cars 2 CarryAlong(r) Play Book. Disney Artists Staff, illus. 2011. (Carry along Play Book Ser.). (ENG.). 14p. (J). (gr. -1-k). bds. 14.99 (978-0-7944-2323-0(X)) Reader's Digest Assn., Inc., The.

—Grand Prix Garage: Storybook & Garage. 2011. (Storybook & Playset Ser.). (ENG., Illus.). 24p. (J). (gr. -1-1). 19.99 (978-0-7944-2311-7(6)) Reader's Digest Assn., Inc., The.

Suen, Anastasia. Test Drive: A Robot & Rico Story. Laughead, Mike, illus. 2010. (Robot & Rico Ser.). (ENG.). 32p. (gr. 1-2). pap. 6.25 *(978-1-4342-2303-6(5))* Stone Arch Bks.

Tashiro, Chisato. Five Nice Mice & the Great Car Race. Tashiro, Chisato, illus. 2014. (Five Nice Mice Ser.). (ENG., Illus.). 40p. (J). (gr. k-2). 17.99 *(978-988-8240-73-9(0))* Neugebauer, Michael (Publishing) Limited HKG. Dist: Independent Pubs. Group.

Walters, Eric. Overdrive. 2004. (Orca Soundings Ser.). 102p. (gr. 8-12). 19.95 *(978-0-7569-4320-2(5))* Perfection Learning Corp.

Weaver, Will. Checkered Flag Cheater. 2010. (Motor Novels Ser.: 3). (ENG.). 208p. (YA). (gr. 7-12). 19.99 *(978-0-374-35062-8(0)*, 9780374350628, Farrar, Straus & Giroux (BYR)) Farrar, Straus & Giroux.

—Saturday Night Dirt. 2009. (Motor Novels Ser.: 1). (ENG.). 192p. (YA). (gr. 7-12). pap. 14.99 *(978-0-312-56131-4(8)*, 9780312561314) Square Fish.

Welling, Peter J. Justin Potemkin & the 500-Mile Race, 1 vol. Welling, Peter J., illus. 2004. (ENG., Illus.). 32p. (J). (gr. k-3). 16.99 *(978-1-58980-149-3(0))* Pelican Publishing Co., Inc.

Wheeler, Lisa. Dino-Racing. Gott, Barry, illus. 2016. (ENG.). 32p. (gr. k-3). (J). lib. bdg. 17.99 *(978-1-5124-0314-5(8))*; 35.99 *(978-1-5124-0886-7(7))* Lerner Publishing Group. (Carolrhoda Bks.).

Wielkiewicz, Richard M. Okay, Riders, Set 'Em Up: A Nate Walker BMX Adventure. Dwyer, Corinne et al, illus. 2005. 140p. (J). pap. 12.95 *(978-0-9774129-0-7(3))* Main Event Pr.

Wooding, Chris. Velocity. 2017. (ENG.). 336p. (J). (gr. 7). 18.99 *(978-0-545-94494-6(5)*, Scholastic Pr.) Scholastic, Inc.

Yoshida, Tatsuo. Speed Racer Set: Mach Go Go Go, 2 vols. 2008. (ENG., Illus.). 700p. (YA). (gr. 8). 39.95 *(978-1-56970-731-9(6)*, 9781569707319) Digital Manga Publishing.

AUTOMOBILE TOURING

see Automobile Travel

AUTOMOBILE TRAILERS

see Automobiles—Trailers

AUTOMOBILE TRAVEL

see also Games for Travelers

Ashley, Susan. Going by Car. 2003. (Weekly Reader Early Learning Library). (Illus.). 24p. (gr. 1-4). pap. 8.15 *(978-0-8368-3835-0(1)*, Weekly Reader Leveled Readers) Stevens, Gareth Publishing LLLP.

Chanko, Pamela. Totally Wacky Roadside Attractions. 2017. (Rookie Amazing America(tm) Ser.). (ENG., Illus.). 32p. (J). pap. 5.95 *(978-0-531-22592-9(5)*, Children's Pr.) Scholastic Library Publishing.

Clissold, Caroline. Let's Go. 2007. (Trackers-Math Ser.). (gr. 2-5). pap. 5.00 *(978-1-59055-915-4(0))* Pacific Learning, Inc.

Figorito, C. Go Far in the Car: Learning the AR Sound. 2009. (PowerPhonics Ser.). 24p. (gr. 1-1). 39.90 *(978-1-60851-444-1(7)*, PowerKids Pr.) Rosen Publishing Group, Inc., The.

Hamilton, Robert M. In a Car. 2012. (Going Places Ser.). (ENG.). 24p. (J). (gr. k-2). pap. 8.15 *(978-1-4339-6263-9(2))*; lib. bdg. 22.60 *(978-1-4339-6261-5(6))* Stevens, Gareth Publishing LLLP.

Hanson, Anders. Let's Go by Car, 1 vol. 2008. (Let's Go Ser.). (ENG., Illus.). 24p. (J). (gr. k-3). lib. bdg. 24.21 *(978-1-59928-897-0(4)*, SandCastle) ABDO Publishing Co.

Macy, Sue. Motor Girls. 2017. (ENG., Illus.). 96p. (J). (gr. 5). 18.99 *(978-1-4263-2697-4(1)*, National Geographic Children's Bks.) National Geographic Society.

Morris, Juddi. Route 66: Main Street of America. 2006. (J). pap. *(978-1-59336-716-9(3))* Mondo Publishing.

National Geographic Kids Staff. 125 Wacky Roadside Attractions: See All the Weird, Wonderful, & Downright Bizarre Landmarks from Around the World! 2016. (ENG., Illus.). 112p. (J). (gr. 3-7). pap. 12.99 *(978-1-4263-2407-9(3)*, National Geographic Children's Bks.) National Geographic Society.

Parker, Steven. On Land. 2011. (Future Transport Ser.). (Illus.). 32p. (J). (gr. 4). 28.50 *(978-1-60870-779-9(2))* Marshall Cavendish Corp.

Proudfit, Benjamin. The Oregon Trail. 2016. (Road Trip Ser.). (Illus.). 24p. (J). (gr. 3-2). pap. 8.15 *(978-1-4824-4675-3(8))* Stevens, Gareth Publishing LLLP.

—The Pacific Coast Highway. 2016. (Road Trip Ser.). (Illus.). 24p. (J). (gr. 3-2). 22.60 *(978-1-4824-4667-8(7))* Stevens, Gareth Publishing LLLP.

AUTOMOBILE TRAVEL—FICTION

Alsaid, Adi. Let's Get Lost. 2015. (ENG.). 384p. (YA). pap. 9.99 *(978-0-373-21149-4(X)*, Harlequin Teen) Harlequin Enterprises, Ltd. CAN. Dist: HarperCollins Pubs.

Anderson, Jodi Lynn. My Diary from the Edge of the World. 2015. (ENG., Illus.). 432p. (J). (gr. 3-7). 16.99 *(978-1-4424-8387-3(3)*, Aladdin) Simon & Schuster Children's Publishing.

—My Diary from the Edge of the World. 2017. (ENG., Illus.). 448p. (J). (gr. 3-7). pap. 7.99 *(978-1-4424-8388-0(1)*, Simon & Schuster/Paula Wiseman Bks.) Simon & Schuster/Paula Wiseman Bks.

Arnold, Tedd. Fly High, Fly Guy! Arnold, Tedd, illus. 2008. (Fly Guy Ser.: 5). (ENG., Illus.). 32p. (J). (gr. -1-3). 6.99 *(978-0-545-00722-1(4))* Scholastic, Inc.

Barnholdt, Lauren. Right of Way. (ENG., Illus.). (YA). (gr. 9). 2014. 336p. pap. 9.99 *(978-1-4424-5128-5(9))* 2013. 320p. 16.99 *(978-1-4424-5127-8(0))* Simon Pulse. (Simon Pulse).

—Two-Way Street. 2013. (ENG., Illus.). 320p. (YA). (gr. 9). 17.99 *(978-1-4424-8952-3(9)*, Simon Pulse) Simon Pulse.

Berenstain, Stan & Berenstain, Jan. The Berenstain Bears & Too Much Car Trip. Berenstain, Stan & Berenstain, Jan, illus. 2006. (Berenstain Bears Ser.). (Illus.). 32p. (J). (gr. -1-2). 10.99 *(978-0-06-057400-0(3))*; (ENG., pap. 3.99 *(978-0-06-057384-3(8))* HarperCollins Pubs. (HarperFestival).

Berenstain, Stan, et al. The Berenstain Bears & the Big Spelling Bee, No. 6. Berenstain, Stan et al, illus. 2007. (Berenstain Bears Ser.). (ENG.). 32p. (J). (gr. -1-2). pap. 3.99 *(978-0-06-057386-7(4)*, HarperFestival) HarperCollins Pubs.

—The Berenstain Bears Hug & Make Up. Berenstain, Stan & Berenstain, Jan, illus. 2006. (Berenstain Bears Ser.). (ENG.). 32p. (J). (gr. -1-2). pap. 3.99 *(978-0-06-057385-0(6)*, HarperFestival) HarperCollins Pubs.

Berger, Carin. Ok Go. Berger, Carin, illus. 2009. (ENG., Illus.). 32p. (J). (gr. -1-k). 17.99 *(978-0-06-157666-9(2)*, Greenwillow Bks.) HarperCollins Pubs.

Berrios, Frank & Random House Disney Staff. Travel Buddies. Golden Books Staff, illus. 2012. (Little Golden Book Ser.). (ENG.). 24p. (J). (gr. k-k). 3.99 *(978-0-7364-2911-5(5)*, Golden/Disney) Random Hse. Children's Bks.

Blackwood, Gary. Around the World in 100 Days. 2011. (ENG.). 368p. (J). (gr. 5-18). 7.99 *(978-0-14-241963-2(X)*, Puffin Books) Penguin Young Readers Group.

Blakemore, Megan Frazer. Good & Gone. 2017. 304p. (YA). (gr. 8). 17.99 ***(978-0-06-234842-5(6)***, HarperTeen) HarperCollins Pubs.

Borris, Albert. Crash into Me. (ENG.). 272p. (YA). (gr. 9). 2010. pap. 9.99 *(978-1-4169-9827-3(6))* 2009. 16.99 *(978-1-4169-7435-2(0))* Simon Pulse. (Simon Pulse).

Bray, Libba. Going Bovine. 2010. (ENG.). 496p. (YA). (gr. 9). pap. 10.99 *(978-0-385-73398-4(4)*, Ember) Random Hse. Children's Bks.

Brown, Jennifer. Perfect Escape. 2012. (ENG.). 368p. (YA). (gr. 7-17). 17.99 *(978-0-316-18557-8(4))* Little, Brown Bks. for Young Readers.

Burch, Christian. Hit the Road, Manny: A Manny Files Novel. 2008. (ENG.). 240p. (J). (gr. 3-7). 16.99 *(978-1-4169-2812-6(X)*, Atheneum Bks. for Young Readers) Simon & Schuster Children's Publishing.

Calonita, Jen. Battle of the Bands. 2016. (VIP Ser.: 2). (ENG., Illus.). 320p. (J). (gr. 3-7). 16.99 *(978-0-316-25977-4(2))* Little, Brown Bks. for Young Readers.

Cerato, Mattia. Mom's New Friend. Cerato, Mattia, illus. 2014. (Family Snaps Ser.). (ENG., Illus.). 32p. (J). (gr. k-2). pap. 6.95 *(978-1-939656-61-2(3))* Red Chair Pr.

Cheaney, J. B. & Cheaney, Janie. The Middle of Somewhere. 2008. (ENG.). 224p. (J). (gr. 3-7). 7.99 *(978-0-440-42165-8(9)*, Yearling) Random Hse. Children's Bks.

Clark, Kristin Elizabeth. Jess, Chunk, & the Road Trip to Infinity. 2016. (ENG.). 272p. (YA). 17.99 *(978-0-374-38006-9(6)*, 9780374380069, Farrar, Straus & Giroux (BYR)) Farrar, Straus & Giroux.

Cooney, Caroline B. Hit the Road. rev. l.t. ed. 2007. (Thorndike Literacy Bridge Ser.). 259p. (YA). (gr. 7-12). 23.95 *(978-0-7862-9429-9(9))* Thorndike Pr.

Damaged. 2014. (ENG., Illus.). 384p. (YA). (gr. 8). 17.99 *(978-1-4424-5699-0(X)*, Simon Pulse) Simon Pulse.

Davis, Tanita S. Mare's War. 2011. (ENG.). 352p. (YA). (gr. 7). pap. 9.99 *(978-0-375-85077-6(5)*, Knopf Bks. for Young Readers) Random Hse. Children's Bks.

Dawn, Nyrae. The History of Us. (ENG., Illus.). 2016. (YA). (gr. 9-12). 24.99 ***(978-1-63477-968-5(1))*** 2015. 184p. (J). pap. 14.99 *(978-1-63476-179-6(0))* Dreamspinner Pr. (Harmony Ink Pr.).

Depken, Kristen L. Driving School (Disney/Pixar Cars) RH Disney Staff, illus. 2013. (Step into Reading Ser.). (ENG.). 24p. (J). (gr. -1-1). 3.99 *(978-0-7364-2982-5(4)*, RH/Disney) Random Hse. Children's Bks.

Doller, Trish. The Devil You Know. 2016. (ENG.). 256p. (YA). pap. 9.99 *(978-1-68119-022-8(2)*, 9781681190228, Bloomsbury USA Childrens) Bloomsbury Publishing USA.

Dooley, Sarah. Ashes to Asheville. 2017. (ENG.). 256p. (J). (gr. 5). 16.99 *(978-0-399-16504-7(5)*, G.P. Putnam's Sons Books for Young Readers) Penguin Young Readers Group.

Downing, Erin. Drive Me Crazy. 2009. (Romantic Comedies Ser.). (ENG.). 240p. (YA). (gr. 7-18). mass mkt. 6.99 *(978-1-4169-7484-0(9)*, Simon Pulse) Simon Pulse.

Driscoll, Laura. Super Specs. Gott, Barry, illus. 2005. (Math Matters Ser.). (ENG.). 32p. (J). (gr. -1-3). pap. 5.95 *(978-1-57565-145-3(9))* Kane Press, Inc.

Eastman, Peter. Fred & Ted's Road Trip. 2011. (Beginner Books(R) Ser.). (ENG., Illus.). 48p. (J). (gr. -1-2). 9.99 *(978-0-375-86764-4(3)*, Random Hse. Bks. for Young Readers) Random Hse. Children's Bks.

Elya, Susan Middleton. Oh No, Gotta Go! Karas, G. Brian, illus. 2005. 29p. (J). (gr. k-4). reprint ed. 15.00 *(978-0-7567-8946-6(X))* DIANE Publishing Co.

Emerson, Kevin. The Fellowship for Alien Detection. 2013. (ENG.). 432p. (J). (gr. 3-7). 16.99 *(978-0-06-207185-9(8)*, Waldon Pond Pr.) HarperCollins Pubs.

Engle, Margarita. All the Way to Havana. Curato, Mike, illus. 2017. (ENG.). 40p. (J). 17.99 *(978-1-62779-642-2(8)*, 9781627796422, Holt, Henry & Co. Bks. For Young Readers) Holt, Henry & Co.

Feiffer, Kate. My Side of the Car. Feiffer, Jules, illus. 2011. (ENG.). 32p. (J). (gr. -1-3). 16.99 *(978-0-7636-4405-5(6))* Candlewick Pr.

Friedman, Laurie. On the Road with Mallory. Kalis, Jennifer, illus. 2016. (Mallory Ser.: 25). (ENG.). 160p. (gr. 2-5). (J). 15.95 *(978-1-4677-5029-5(8))*; 31.99 *(978-1-4677-9567-8(4))* Lerner Publishing Group. (Darby Creek).

Furniss, Clare. How Not to Disappear. 2017. (ENG., Illus.). 448p. (YA). (gr. 7). 17.99 *(978-1-4814-2102-7(6)*, McElderry, Margaret K. Bks.) McElderry, Margaret K. Bks.

Graham, Bob. Home in the Rain. Graham, Bob, illus. 2017. (ENG., Illus.). 32p. (J). (gr. -1-2). 16.99 *(978-0-7636-9269-8(7))* Candlewick Pr.

Graham, Hilary Weisman. Reunited. (ENG., 336p. (YA). (gr. 7). 2013. Illus.). pap. 9.99 *(978-1-4424-0687-2(9))* 2012. 16.99 *(978-1-4424-3984-9(X))* Simon & Schuster Bks. For Young Readers. (Simon & Schuster Bks. For Young Readers).

Gutman, Dan. From Texas with Love. 2014. (Genius Files Ser.: 4). (ENG.). 304p. (J). (gr. 3-7). pap. 6.99 *(978-0-06-182775-4(4))* HarperCollins Pubs.

—From Texas with Love. 2014. (Genius Files Ser.: 4). (J). lib. bdg. 17.20 *(978-0-606-36462-1(5))* Turtleback Bks.

Hallowell, George & Holub, Joan. Wagons Ho! Avril, Lynne, illus. 2011. (ENG.). 32p. (J). (gr. 1-3). 16.99 *(978-0-8075-8612-9(9))* Whitman, Albert & Co.

Harper, Jamie. Miles to Go. Harper, Jamie, illus. (ENG., Illus.). 32p. (J). (gr. -1-2). 2013. pap. 4.99 *(978-0-7636-6469-5(3))* 2010. 12.99 *(978-0-7636-3598-5(7))* Candlewick Pr.

Hawkins, Rachel. Lady Renegades: A Rebel Belle Novel. 2016. (Rebel Belle Ser.: 3). (ENG.). 272p. (YA). (gr. 7). 17.99 *(978-0-399-25695-0(4)*, G.P. Putnam's Sons Books for Young Readers) Penguin Young Readers Group.

Hendershot, Eric. At Season's End. 2012. pap. 13.99 *(978-1-59955-995-7(1))* Cedar Fort, Inc./CFI Distribution.

Homel, David & Gay, Marie-Louise. Travels with My Family, 1 vol. 2007. (ENG., Illus.). 120p. (J). (gr. 1-5). pap. 8.95 *(978-0-88899-833-0(3))* Groundwood Bks. CAN. Dist: Publishers Group West (PGW).

Hope, Laura Lee. Bunny Brown & His Sister Sue on an Aut. 2006. 26.95 *(978-1-4218-2976-0(2))*; pap. 11.95 *(978-1-4218-3076-6(0))* 1st World Publishing, Inc.

Hopgood, Sally. A Trip to Busy Town: A Pull-The-Tab Book. Hinton, Stephanie, illus. 2014. (J). *(978-1-4351-5690-6(0))* Barnes & Noble, Inc.

Jenkins, A. M. Night Road. (ENG.). 368p. (YA). (gr. 8). 2010. pap. 8.99 *(978-0-06-054606-9(9))*No. 1. 2008. 16.99 *(978-0-06-054604-5(2))* HarperCollins Pubs. (HarperTeen).

Jones, Sam. Yolo. 2014. (ENG., Illus.). 224p. (YA). (gr. 9). pap. 9.99 *(978-1-4814-1548-4(4)*, Simon Pulse) Simon Pulse.

Kernan, Elizabeth. Dolly Takes a Drive. 2006. (Neighborhood Readers Ser.). (ENG., Illus.). 12p. (gr. -1-3). pap. 5.90 *(978-1-4042-6754-1(9)*, Rosen Classroom) Rosen Publishing Group, Inc., The.

Kinney, Jeff. The Long Haul. Kinney, Jeff, illus. 2014. (Diary of a Wimpy Kid Ser.: Bk. 9). (ENG., Illus.). 224p. (J). (gr. 3-7). 13.95 *(978-1-4197-1189-3(X)*, Amulet Bks.) Abrams, Inc.

—The Long Haul. (CHI.). (J). 2015. 368p. (gr. 4-8). pap. *(978-986-6104-59-6(1))* 2014. *(978-986-6104-52-7(4))* DaskoviK, Izdatel'sko-torgovaja korporacija.

—The Long Haul. 2014. (JPN.). 221p. (J). *(978-4-591-14196-0(9))* Poplar Publishing.

—The Long Haul. 2013. (Diary of a Wimpy Kid Ser.: 9). (J). 43.75 *(978-1-4906-4058-7(4))*; 40.75 *(978-1-4906-4383-0(4))* Recorded Bks., Inc.

—The Long Haul. 2014. (Diary of a Wimpy Kid Ser.: 9). (J). lib. bdg. 25.70 *(978-0-606-36074-6(3))* Turtleback Bks.

Kirby, Jessi. In Honor. (ENG., (YA). (gr. 9). 2013. Illus.). 256p. pap. 9.99 *(978-1-4424-1698-7(X))* 2012. 240p. 16.99 *(978-1-4424-1697-0(1))* Simon & Schuster Bks. For Young Readers. (Simon & Schuster Bks. For Young Readers).

Kreie, Chris. Blood Moon. 2017. (Midnight Ser.). (ENG.). 96p. (YA). (gr. 6-12). 26.65 *(978-1-5124-2772-1(1))*; 12.99 ***(978-1-5124-3483-5(3)***, Darby Creek); 39.99 ***(978-1-5124-2792-9(6)***, Darby Creek); 39.99 ***(978-1-5124-3482-8(5)***, Darby Creek) Lerner Publishing Group.

LaCour, Nina. The Disenchantments. (ENG.). (YA). (gr. 9). 2013. 336p. pap. 10.99 *(978-0-14-242391-2(2)*, Speak) 2012. 320p. 16.99 *(978-0-525-42219-8(6)*, Dutton Books for Young Readers) Penguin Young Readers Group.

Laden, Nina. Are We There Yet? McCauley, Adam, illus. 2016. (ENG.). 36p. (J). (gr. -1-k). 16.99 *(978-1-4521-3155-9(4))* Chronicle Bks. LLC.

Lake, Nick. There Will Be Lies. 2015. (ENG.). 464p. (YA). (gr. 9-12). 17.99 *(978-1-61963-440-4(6)*, 9781619634404, Bloomsbury USA Childrens) Bloomsbury Publishing USA.

LaMarche, Una & Loftin, Nikki. Don't Fail Me Now. 2015. (ENG.). 288p. (YA). (gr. 7). 17.99 *(978-1-59514-817-9(5)*, Razorbill) Penguin Young Readers Group.

Lansdale, Joe R. All the Earth, Thrown to the Sky. 2012. (ENG.). 252p. (YA). (gr. 7). pap. 8.99 *(978-0-385-73932-0(X)*, Ember) Random Hse. Children's Bks.

Lockhart, E., et al. How to Be Bad. 2008. 325p. (YA). (gr. 9-12). lib. bdg. 17.89 *(978-0-06-128423-6(8)*, HarperTeen) HarperCollins Pubs.

Love, Jessica. In Real Life: A Novel. 2016. (ENG.). 240p. (YA). 18.99 *(978-1-250-06471-4(6)*, 9781250064714, St. Martin's Griffin) St. Martin's Pr.

Lumley, Jemima. The Journey Home from Grandpa's. Fatus, Sophie, illus. (ENG.). 24p. (J). 2012. (gr. -1-2). 16.99 *(978-1-84686-898-6(X))* 2006. pap. 6.99 *(978-1-84686-029-4(6))* 2006. (gr. -1-k). 9.99 *(978-1-84686-026-3(1))* 2006. (gr. -1-3). 16.99 *(978-1-905236-37-4(9))* Barefoot Bks., Inc.

Lumley, Jemima & Penner, Fred. The Journey Home from Grandpa's. Fatus, Sophie, illus. 2011. (ENG.). 24p. (J). (gr. -1-2). 9.99 *(978-1-84686-658-6(8))* Barefoot Bks., Inc.

Mackler, Carolyn. Guyaholic. 2009. (ENG., Illus.). 192p. (YA). (gr. 9). pap. 7.99 *(978-0-7636-2801-7(8))* Candlewick Pr.

Matson, Morgan. Amy & Roger's Epic Detour. (ENG.). (YA). (gr. 7). 2011. 384p. pap. 10.99 *(978-1-4169-9066-6(6))* 2010. 352p. 19.99 *(978-1-4169-9065-9(8))* Simon & Schuster Bks. For Young Readers. (Simon & Schuster Bks. For Young Readers).

McDonald, Megan. Stink & the Great Guinea Pig Express, Bk. 4. Reynolds, Peter H., illus. 2013. (Stink Ser.: 4). (ENG.). (J). (gr. 1-4). 128p. 12.99 *(978-0-7636-6391-9(3))*; 144p. pap. 4.99 *(978-0-7636-6421-3(9))* Candlewick Pr.

—Stink & the Great Guinea Pig Express. Reynolds, Peter H., illus. 2010. (Stink Ser.: No. 4). 128p. (J). (gr. k-4). 24.21 *(978-1-59961-683-4(1))* Spotlight.

—Stink & the Great Guinea Pig Express. 2013. (Stink Ser.: 4). lib. bdg. 14.75 *(978-0-606-31590-6(X)*, Turtleback) Turtleback Bks.

McKay, Sindy. We Both Read-My Car Trip. Johnson, Meredith, illus. 2005. (We Both Read Ser.). 48p. (J). (gr. -1-2). lib. bdg. 7.99 *(978-1-891327-63-6(1))*; per. 4.99 *(978-1-891327-64-3(X))* Treasure Bay, Inc.

McPhail, David. Pig Pig Returns. McPhail, David, illus. 2011. (ENG., Illus.). 32p. (J). (gr. -1-3). 15.95 *(978-1-58089-356-5(2))* Charlesbridge Publishing, Inc.

McRee Turner, Amber. Sway. 2013. (ENG.). 320p. (J). (gr. 4-7). pap. 6.99 *(978-1-4231-3784-9(1))* Hyperion Pr.

McVoy, Terra Elan. Drive Me Crazy. 2015. (ENG.). 288p. (J). (gr. 3-7). 16.99 *(978-0-06-232243-2(5)*, Tegen, Katherine Bks) HarperCollins Pubs.

Monninger, Joseph. Finding Somewhere. 2012. (ENG.). 240p. (YA). (gr. 7). pap. 8.99 *(978-0-375-89755-9(0)*, Ember) Random Hse. Children's Bks.

Moss, Marissa. Amelia's Are-We-There-Yet Longest Ever Car Trip. Moss, Marissa, illus. (Amelia Ser.). (ENG., Illus.). 40p. (J). (gr. 2-5). 2012. pap. 6.99 *(978-1-4169-1287-3(8))* 2006. 10.99 *(978-1-4169-0906-4(0))* Simon & Schuster/Paula Wiseman Bks. (Simon & Schuster/Paula Wiseman Bks.).

Murphy, Stuart J. Tally O'Malley. Jabar, Cynthia, illus. 2004. (MathStart Ser.). 40p. (J). (gr. 1-18). 15.99 *(978-0-06-053162-1(2))*; (ENG.). pap. 5.99 *(978-0-06-053164-5(9))* HarperCollins Pubs.

Myracle, Lauren, et al. How to Be Bad. 2015. (ENG.). 352p. (YA). (gr. 9). pap. 9.99 *(978-0-06-240568-5(3)*, HarperTeen) HarperCollins Pubs.

Neri, Greg. Surf Mules. 2104. (ENG.). 288p. (YA). pap. *(978-1-4677-4238-2(4))* Lerner Publishing Group.

Norman, Kim. This Old Van. Conahan, Carolyn Digby, illus. 2015. (ENG.). 30p. (J). (gr. -1-2). 14.95 *(978-1-4549-1063-3(1))* Sterling Publishing Co., Inc.

Osterhold, Jared, illus. OLIVIA Takes a Trip. 2010. (Olivia TV Tie-In Ser.). (ENG.). 24p. (J). (gr. -1-1). 16.99 *(978-1-4424-1381-8(6)*, Simon Spotlight) Simon Spotlight.

Ostrovski, Emil. The Paradox of Vertical Flight. 2014. (ENG.). 272p. (YA). (gr. 9). pap. 9.99 *(978-0-06-223853-5(1)*, Greenwillow Bks.) HarperCollins Pubs.

Parish, Herman. Amelia Bedelia Chapter Book #3: Amelia Bedelia Road Trip! (Special Edition) 2013. (ENG., Illus.). 160p. (J). *(978-0-06-227057-3(5)*, Collins Design) HarperCollins Pubs.

—Amelia Bedelia Road Trip! 2013. (Amelia Bedelia Chapter Book Ser.: 3). (J). lib. bdg. 14.75 *(978-0-606-32453-3(4)*, Turtleback) Turtleback Bks.

Patterson, James & Raymond, Emily. First Love. 2017. (ENG., Illus.). 384p. mass mkt. 7.99 ***(978-1-4555-8500-7(9)***, Jimmy Patterson) Little Brown & Co.

—First Love. Illingworth, Sasha, photos by. 2015. (ENG., Illus.). 336p. (YA). (gr. 10-17). pap. 9.99 *(978-0-316-20703-4(9)*, Jimmy Patterson) Little Brown & Co.

—First Love. 2014. (ENG.). 560p. (YA). pap. 16.00 *(978-1-4555-8501-4(7)*, Jimmy Patterson) Little Brown & Co.

—First Love. 2014. (YA). lib. bdg. 28.20 *(978-0-606-35894-1(3))* Turtleback Bks.

Paulsen, Gary & Paulsen, Jim. Field Trip. 2015. (ENG.). 128p. (J). (gr. 5). 12.99 *(978-0-553-49674-1(3)*, Lamb, Wendy Bks.) Random Hse. Children's Bks.

—Road Trip. 2014. (ENG.). 128p. (J). (gr. 5). pap. 6.99 *(978-0-307-93086-6(6)*, Yearling) Random Hse. Children's Bks.

Penrose, Margaret. The Motor Girls on a Tour. 2006. pap. *(978-1-84702-440-4(8))* Echo Library.

Peschke, M. Vacation Queen. Mourning, Tuesday, illus. 2016. (Kylie Jean Ser.). (ENG.). 112p. (gr. 2-3). 8.95 *(978-1-5158-0059-0(8))* Picture Window Bks.

Peschke, Marci. Vacation Queen. Mourning, Tuesday, illus. 2016. (Kylie Jean Ser.). (ENG.). 112p. (gr. 2-3). lib. bdg. 22.65 *(978-1-5158-0058-3(X))* Picture Window Bks.

Philpot, Chelsey. Be Good Be Real Be Crazy. 2016. 272p. (YA). (gr. 8). 17.99 *(978-0-06-229372-5(9)*, HarperTeen) HarperCollins Pubs.

Ponti, Claude. En El Coche. 2003. (SPA.). 32p. 15.95 *(978-84-95150-08-0(5))* Corimbo, Editorial S.L. ESP. Dist: Distribooks, Inc.

Priddy, Roger. Little Friends: Big Adventure. 2015. (Little Friends Ser.). (ENG., Illus.). 12p. (J). (gr. -1 — 1). bds. 14.99 *(978-0-312-51869-1(2)*, 9780312518691, Priddy Bks.) St. Martin's Pr.

Publications International Ltd. Staff, ed. Disney Pixar Cars: Road Trip Adventure. 2010. (J). 10.98 *(978-1-4508-0387-8(3))* Phoenix International Publications, Inc.

Rabb, Margo. Kissing in America. 2015. (ENG.). 400p. (YA). (gr. 9). 17.99 *(978-0-06-232237-1(0))* HarperCollins Pubs.

Resau, Laura. Red Glass. 2009. (ENG.). 304p. (YA). (gr. 7). pap. 8.99 *(978-0-440-24025-9(5)*, Delacorte Bks. for Young Readers) Random Hse. Children's Bks.

Rex, Adam. The True Meaning of Smekday. Rex, Adam, illus. 2015. (ENG., Illus.). 432p. (J). (gr. 3-7). pap. 7.99 *(978-1-4847-2946-5(3))* Hyperion Bks. for Children.

—The True Meaning of Smekday. Rex, Adam, illus. 2009. (Smek Smeries Ser.). (ENG., Illus.). 432p. (J). (gr. 3-7). pap. 7.99 *(978-0-7868-4901-7(0))* Hyperion Pr.

—The True Meaning of Smekday. 2009. (Illus.). 423p. 18.00 *(978-1-60686-525-5(0))* Perfection Learning Corp.

Ribay, Randy. An Infinite Number of Parallel Universes. 2015. (ENG.). 240p. (YA). 17.99 *(978-1-4405-8814-3(7)*, Simon Pulse) Simon Pulse.

Robins, Eleanor. Broken Promise, 1 vol. unabr. ed. 2011. (Choices Ser.). (ENG.). 50p. (YA). (gr. 9-12). 7.95 *(978-1-61651-591-1(0))* Saddleback Educational Publishing, Inc.

Rockliff, Mara. Around America to Win the Vote: Two Suffragists, a Kitten, & 10,000 Miles. Hooper, Hadley, illus. 2016. (ENG.). 40p. (J). (gr. k-3). 16.99 *(978-0-7636-7893-7(7))* Candlewick Pr.

Rosen, Michael J. A Drive in the Country. Burckhardt, Marc, illus. 2007. (ENG.). 32p. (J). (gr. k-4). 16.99 *(978-0-7636-2140-7(4))* Candlewick Pr.

Roux, Madeleine. Catacomb. 2015. (Asylum Ser.: 3). (ENG.). 336p. (YA). (gr. 9). 17.99 *(978-0-06-236405-0(7))* HarperCollins Pubs.

Rylant, Cynthia. Annie & Snowball & the Surprise Day. Stevenson, Suçie, illus. (Annie & Snowball Ser.: 11). (ENG.). 40p. (J). (gr. k-2). 2013. pap. 3.99 *(978-1-4169-3948-1(2))* 2012. 16.99 *(978-1-4169-3944-3(X))* Simon Spotlight. (Simon Spotlight).

Sanchez, Alex. Rainbow Road. 2007. (ENG., Illus.). 266p. (YA). (gr. 7-12). pap. 11.99 *(978-1-4169-1191-3(X)*, Simon & Schuster Bks. For Young Readers) Simon & Schuster Bks. For Young Readers.

Sanchez, Alex & Louth, Jack. Rainbow Road. 2005. (ENG., Illus.). 256p. (J). (gr. 7). 16.95 *(978-0-689-86565-7(1)*, Simon & Schuster Bks. For Young Readers) Simon & Schuster Bks. For Young Readers.

Santat, Dan, illus. Are We There Yet? 2016. (ENG.). 40p. (J). (gr. -1-3). 17.99 *(978-0-316-19999-5(0))* Little Brown & Co.

Scott, Jerry. Shredded. Borgman, Jim, illus. 2014. (Zits Ser.: 2). (ENG.). 224p. (YA). (gr. 8). pap. 9.99 *(978-0-06-222853-6(6)*, HarperTeen) HarperCollins Pubs.

Soup, Cuthbert. A Whole Nother Story. Timmins, Jeffrey Stewart, illus. 2010. (Whole Nother Story Ser.). (ENG.). 288p. (YA). (gr. 3-6). pap. 7.99 *(978-1-59990-518-1(3)*, 9781599905181, Bloomsbury USA Childrens) Bloomsbury Publishing USA.

Thrash, Maggie. Honor Girl. Thrash, Maggie, illus. 2017. (ENG., Illus.). 272p. (YA). (gr. 9). pap. 14.99 *(978-0-7636-8755-7(3))* Candlewick Pr.

The Trolley Ride: 6 Small Books. (gr. k-3). 24.00 *(978-0-7635-6233-5(5))* Rigby Education.

van Lieshout, Maria. Backseat A-B-See. (ENG., Illus.). (J). (gr. -1-k). 2014. 26p. bds. 7.99 *(978-1-4521-3732-2(3))* 2012. 40p. 14.99 *(978-1-4521-0664-9(9))* Chronicle Bks. LLC.

Walters, Virginia. Are We There Yet, Daddy? Schindler, S. D., illus. 2005. 27p. (J). (gr. k-4). reprint ed. 16.00 *(978-0-7567-9708-9(X))* DIANE Publishing Co.

Willems, Mo. Let's Go for a Drive! Willems, Mo, illus. 2012. (Elephant & Piggie Book Ser.). (ENG., Illus.). 64p. (J). (gr. -1-k). 9.99 *(978-1-4231-6482-1(2))* Hyperion Pr.

Williams, Carol Lynch. Signed, Skye Harper. 2014. (ENG., Illus.). 304p. (YA). (gr. 7). 17.99 *(978-1-4814-0032-9(0),* Simon & Schuster/Paula Wiseman Bks.) Simon & Schuster/Paula Wiseman Bks.

Winfield, Arthur M. Rover Boys on A Tour or Last Days at Bri. 2006. pap. 31.95 *(978-1-4286-4389-5(3))* Kessinger Publishing, LLC.

Winkler, Henry & Oliver, Lin. Barfing in the Backseat: How I Survived My Family Road Trip. Watson, Jesse Joshua, illus. 2007. (Hank Zipzer Ser.: No. 12). 152p. (gr. 4-7). 15.00 *(978-0-7569-8162-4(X))* Perfection Learning Corp.

Woolston, Blythe. Troutzilla. 2012. (Carolrhoda YA Ser.). (ENG.). 216p. (YA). (gr. 9-12). 17.95 *(978-0-7613-7755-9(7),* Carolrhoda Lab™) Lerner Publishing Group.

Wunder, Wendy. The Museum of Intangible Things. 2015. (ENG.). 256p. (YA). (gr. 7). pap. 9.99 *(978-1-59514-576-5(1),* Razorbill) Penguin Young Readers Group.

AUTOMOBILE TRUCKS

see Trucks

AUTOMOBILES

see also Buses; Trucks

also names of automobiles, e.g. Ford Automobile

Abbott, Simon. Pop & Play: Things That Go. 2013. (ENG., Illus.). 10p. (J). (gr. -1-k). bds. 7.99 *(978-0-7534-7162-3(0),* 9780753471623, Kingfisher) Roaring Brook Pr.

Abramovitz, Melissa. Big Cars, 1 vol. 2013. (Cars, Cars, Cars Ser.). (ENG.). 24p. (gr. k-1). pap. 7.29 *(978-1-62065-869-7(0));* pap. 41.70 *(978-1-62065-870-3(4));* lib. bdg. 26.65 *(978-1-62065-088-2(6))* Capstone Press of Coughlan Cos. (Pebble Plus).

—Famous Cars, 1 vol. 2013. (Cars, Cars, Cars Ser.). (ENG.). 24p. (gr. k-1). pap. 7.29 *(978-1-62065-871-0(2));* pap. 41.70 *(978-1-62065-872-7(0));* lib. bdg. 26.65 *(978-1-62065-091-2(6))* Capstone Press of Coughlan Cos. (Pebble Plus).

—Silly Cars, 1 vol. 2013. (Cars, Cars, Cars Ser.). (ENG.). 24p. (gr. k-1). pap. 7.29 *(978-1-62065-877-2(1));* pap. 41.70 *(978-1-62065-878-9(X));* lib. bdg. 26.65 *(978-1-62065-089-9(4))* Capstone Press of Coughlan Cos. (Pebble Plus).

Abramovitz, Melissa & Alpert, Barbara. Cars, Cars, Cars. 2013. (Cars, Cars, Cars Ser.). (ENG.). 24p. (gr. k-1). lib. bdg. 159.90 *(978-1-62065-092-9(4),* Pebble Plus) Capstone Press of Coughlan Cos.

Abramovitz, Melissa & Clay, Kathryn. Wild about Wheels. 2015. (Wild about Wheels Ser.). (ENG.). 24p. (gr. k-1). lib. bdg. 106.60 *(978-1-4914-2572-5(5),* Pebble Plus) Capstone Press of Coughlan Cos.

Aloian, Molly. Bugatti. 2012. (ENG.). 64p. (J). *(978-0-7787-2100-0(0));* pap. *(978-0-7787-2105-5(1))* Crabtree Publishing Co.

—Ferrari. 2010. (Superstar Cars Ser.). (ENG.). 64p. (J). pap. *(978-0-7787-2149-9(3))* Crabtree Publishing Co.

Alpert, Barbara. Fast Cars, 1 vol. 2013. (Cars, Cars, Cars Ser.). (ENG.). 24p. (gr. k-1). pap. 7.29 *(978-1-62065-873-4(9));* pap. 41.70 *(978-1-62065-874-1(7));* lib. bdg. 26.65 *(978-1-62065-086-8(X))* Capstone Press of Coughlan Cos. (Pebble Plus).

—Small Cars. 2013. (Cars, Cars, Cars Ser.). (ENG.). 24p. (gr. k-1). pap. 41.70 *(978-1-62065-880-2(1));* pap. 7.29 *(978-1-62065-879-6(8));* lib. bdg. 26.65 *(978-1-62065-087-5(8))* Capstone Press of Coughlan Cos. (Pebble Plus).

Alpert, Barbara & Abramovitz, Melissa. Cars, Cars, Cars. 2013. (Cars, Cars, Cars Ser.). (ENG.). 24p. (gr. k-1). pap. 41.70 *(978-1-62065-881-9(X));* pap. 250.20 *(978-1-62065-882-6(8))* Capstone Press of Coughlan Cos. (Pebble Plus).

Amazing Cars. 2013. (ENG.). 14p. (J). 16.95 *(978-1-78212-216-6(8))* Arcturus Publishing GBR. Dist: Bookmasters Distribution.

Amoroso, Cynthia. Tow Trucks. 2014. (Big Machines at Work Ser.). (ENG.). 24p. (J). (gr. -1-2). 25.64 *(978-1-62323-970-1(2),* 206745) Child's World, Inc., The.

Amstutz, L. J. & Amstutz, Lisa J. How Can We Reduce Transportation Pollution? 2016. (Searchlight Books — What Can We Do About Pollution? Ser.). (ENG., Illus.). 40p. (J). (gr. 3-5). lib. bdg. 30.65 *(978-1-4677-9515-9(1))* Lerner Publishing Group.

Arnold, Nick. How Cars Work: The Interactive Guide to Mechanisms That Make a Car Move. 2013. (ENG., Illus.). 24p. (gr. k). 19.95 *(978-0-7624-4726-8(5),* Running Pr. Kids) Running Pr. Bk. Pubs.

Ashley, Susan. En Carro. 2003. (Weekly Reader Early Learning Library).Tr. of Going by Car). (SPA., Illus.). 24p. (gr. 1-4). pap. 8.15 *(978-0-8368-3840-4(8),* Weekly Reader Leveled Readers) Stevens, Gareth Publishing LLLP.

Aston Martin. 2013. (Speed Machines Ser.). 32p. (J). (gr. 3-6). pap. 60.00 *(978-1-4777-0987-0(8),* PowerKids Pr.) Rosen Publishing Group, Inc., The.

At the Wheel. 2016. (At the Wheel Ser.). 00024p. (J). (gr. 1-1). 94.40 *(978-1-4994-2624-3(0),* PowerKids Pr.) Rosen Publishing Group, Inc., The.

Audi. 2013. (Speed Machines Ser.). 32p. (J). (gr. 3-6). pap. 60.00 *(978-1-4777-0993-1(2),* PowerKids Pr.) Rosen Publishing Group, Inc., The.

Augarde, Steve. Garage: A Pop-up Book. Augarde, Steve, illus. 2005. (Illus.). 10p. (J). (gr. k-4). reprint ed. 15.00 *(978-0-7567-9299-2(1))* DIANE Publishing Co.

AZ Books Staff. Fast Cars. Tulup, Natasha, ed. 2012. (Workshop Ser.). (ENG.). 10p. (J). (gr. -1-k). bds. 10.95 *(978-1-61889-161-7(8))* AZ Bks. LLC.

—Making Machines. Sisoj, Natalja, ed. 2012. (Modeling Clay Bks.). (ENG.). 12p. (J). (gr. -1-2). bds. 10.95 *(978-1-61889-198-3(7))* AZ Bks. LLC.

Bailey, Devon. Supercars, Vol. 8. 2015. (Classic Cars & Bikes Collection). (Illus.). 64p. (J). (gr. 7). lib. bdg. 23.95 *(978-1-4222-3283-5(2))* Mason Crest.

Bailey, Katharine. Muscle Cars. 2006. (Automania! Ser.). (ENG., Illus.). 32p. (J). (gr. 4-7). pap. *(978-0-7787-3032-3(8));* lib. bdg. *(978-0-7787-3010-1(7))* Crabtree Publishing Co.

—Sweet Rides. 2006. (Automania! Ser.). (ENG., Illus.). 32p. (J). (gr. 4-7). pap. *(978-0-7787-3030-9(1));* lib. bdg. *(978-0-7787-3008-8(5))* Crabtree Publishing Co.

Barrington, Richard. Bmw: Ultimate Riding Experience. 2013. (Motorcycles: a Guide to the World's Best Bikes Ser.). (Illus.). 48p. (J). (gr. 5-8). 29.95 *(978-1-4777-1857-5(5));* pap. 11.75 *(978-1-4777-1868-1(0))* Rosen Publishing Group, Inc., The. (Rosen Reference).

Barton, Byron. My Car/Mi Auto. Barton, Byron, illus. 2016. (SPA & ENG., Illus.). 40p. (J). (gr. -1-3). 17.99 *(978-0-06-245545-1(1),* Greenwillow Bks.) HarperCollins Pubs.

—My Car/Mi Auto (Spanish/English Bilingual Edition) Barton, Byron, illus. 2016. (SPA & ENG., Illus.). 40p. (J). (gr. -1-3). pap. 7.99 *(978-0-06-245544-4(3),* Greenwillow Bks.) HarperCollins Pubs.

Bearce, Stephanie. All about Electric & Hybrid Cars. 2009. (Tell Your Parents Ser.). (Illus.). 48p. (J). (gr. 4-7). lib. bdg. 25.70 *(978-1-58415-763-2(1))* Mitchell Lane Pubs., Inc.

Bender, Lionel. Cars & Motorcycles. 2006. (J). *(978-1-59389-262-3(4))* Chrysalis Education.

Bergin, Mark. Cars. 2009. (How to Draw Ser.). (ENG., Illus.). 32p. (J). (gr. 4-6). pap. 11.75 *(978-1-4358-2649-6(3),* PowerKids Pr.) Rosen Publishing Group, Inc., The.

Blackford, Cheryl. Powerful Muscle Cars. 2015. (Dream Cars Ser.). (ENG.). 32p. (gr. 3-4). lib. bdg. 27.99 *(978-1-4914-2012-6(X))* Capstone Press of Coughlan Cos.

Bmw: Ultimate Riding Experience. 2013. (Motorcycles: a Guide to the World's Best Bikes Ser.). (Illus.). 48p. (J). (gr. 5-8). pap. 70.50 *(978-1-4777-1869-8(9),* Rosen Reference) Rosen Publishing Group, Inc., The.

Bodden, Valerie. Ambulances. 2011. (Rescue Vehicles Ser.). 24p. (J). (ENG.). (gr. 1-3). pap. 5.99 *(978-0-89812-575-7(8),* Creative Paperbacks); (gr. k-2). 16.95 *(978-1-60818-004-2(2))* Creative Co., The.

Bodensteiner, Peter. Formula 1 Cars. 2017. (Gearhead Garage Ser.). (ENG., Illus.). 32p. (gr. 3-7). 31.35 ***(978-1-68072-029-7(5))*** Black Rabbit Bks.

—Indy Cars. 2017. (Gearhead Garage Ser.). (ENG., Illus.). 32p. (gr. 3-7). 31.35 ***(978-1-68072-031-0(7))*** Black Rabbit Bks.

—Super Cars. 2017. (Gearhead Garage Ser.). (ENG., Illus.). 32p. (gr. 3-7). 31.35 ***(978-1-68072-036-5(8))*** Black Rabbit Bks.

Bow, James. Lamborghini. Crabtree, ed. 2010. (Superstar Cars Ser.). (ENG., Illus.). 64p. (J). pap. *(978-0-7787-2151-2(5))* Crabtree Publishing Co.

Bowman, Chris. Rally Car Racing. 2016. (Extreme Sports Ser.). (ENG., Illus.). 24p. (J). (gr. 3-7). lib. bdg. 25.95 *(978-1-62617-352-1(4),* Epic Bks.) Bellwether Media.

Bradley, Michael. Cars, 6 bks., Set. Incl. Corvette. (Illus.). (J). lib. bdg. 28.50 *(978-0-7614-2976-0(X));* Ferrari. lib. bdg. 28.50 *(978-0-7614-2978-4(6));* Ford Truck. lib. bdg. 28.50 *(978-0-7614-2979-1(4));* Hummer. (Illus.). (J). lib. bdg. 28.50 *(978-0-7614-2981-4(6));* Mustang. lib. bdg. 28.50 *(978-0-7614-2982-1(4));* Thunderbird. lib. bdg. 28.50 *(978-0-7614-2983-8(2));* 32p. (gr. 3-18). (Cars Ser.). 2008. Set lib. bdg. 171.00 *(978-0-7614-2975-3(1),* Benchmark Bks.) Marshall Cavendish Corp.

—The Corvette. 2008. (Cars Ser.). (Illus.). 32p. (J). (gr. 3-18). lib. bdg. 28.50 *(978-0-7614-2976-0(X),* Benchmark Bks.) Marshall Cavendish Corp.

—Ferrari. 2008. (Cars Ser.). 32p. (gr. 3-18). lib. bdg. 28.50 *(978-0-7614-2978-4(6),* Benchmark Bks.) Marshall Cavendish Corp.

—Lamborghini. 2009. (Cars 2 Ser.). 32p. (gr. 3). 28.50 *(978-0-7614-4109-0(3))* Marshall Cavendish Corp.

—Mustang. 2008. (Cars Ser.). 32p. (gr. 3-18). lib. bdg. 28.50 *(978-0-7614-2982-1(4),* Benchmark Bks.) Marshall Cavendish Corp.

—Prius. 2009. (Cars 2 Ser.). (Illus.). 32p. (gr. 3). 28.50 *(978-0-7614-4114-4(X))* Marshall Cavendish Corp.

—Thunderbird. 2008. (Cars Ser.). 32p. (gr. 3-18). lib. bdg. 28.50 *(978-0-7614-2983-8(2),* Benchmark Bks.) Marshall Cavendish Corp.

Brain Quest Editors. Brain Quest for the Car: 1100 Questions, 1100 Answers, All about America. rev. ed. 2013. (ENG.). 152p. (J). (gr. 2-6). 11.95 *(978-0-7611-7401-1(X),* 17401) Workman Publishing Co., Inc.

Braun, Eric. Hot Rods. 2009. pap. 8.95 *(978-0-8225-6663-2(X))* 2006. (ENG., Illus.). 48p. (gr. 4-7). lib. bdg. 26.60 *(978-0-8225-3531-7(9))* Lerner Publishing Group.

Bridges, Sarah. Muscle Cars, 1 vol. 2010. (Rev It Up! Ser.). (ENG.). 24p. (gr. k-1). lib. bdg. 26.65 *(978-1-4296-5316-9(7),* Pebble Plus) Capstone Press of Coughlan Cos.

—Sports Cars, 1 vol. 2010. (Rev It Up! Ser.). (ENG.). 24p. (gr. k-1). lib. bdg. 26.65 *(978-1-4296-5318-3(3),* Pebble Plus) Capstone Press of Coughlan Cos.

Brooks, Felicity. Build a Picture Cars Sticker Book. Lovell, Katie, illus. 2013. (Build a Picture Sticker Bks.). (ENG.). (J). (gr. -1-3). 6.99 *(978-0-7945-3376-2(0),* Usborne) EDC Publishing.

—Cars. Newell, Keith, illus. 2008. (Usborne Lift & Look Ser.). 12p. (J). (gr. -1-3). bds. 9.99 *(978-0-7945-1958-2(X),* Usborne) EDC Publishing.

Bullard, Lisa. Lowriders. 2007. (Pull Ahead Books-Mighty Movers Ser.). (ENG., Illus.). 32p. (gr. k-3). pap. 7.95 *(978-0-8225-6423-2(8),* First Avenue Editions); lib. bdg. 22.60 *(978-0-8225-6379-2(7),* Lerner Pubns.) Lerner Publishing Group.

Bulleman, Curtis David. Car Crazy Super Sticker Book. 2011. (Dover Sticker Bks.). (ENG., Illus.). 4p. (J). (gr. k-6). 7.99 *(978-0-486-48377-1(0))* Dover Pubns., Inc.

—Let's Color Together — Cool Cars. 2014. (ENG., Illus.). 64p. (J). (gr. -1-3). pap. 3.99 *(978-0-486-77971-3(8))* Dover Pubns., Inc.

Burch, Lynda S. Wicky Wacky Things that Go! Automobiles 1. Burch, Lynda S. & Roberts, MarySue, photos by. 2004. (Illus.). 30p. (J). E-Book 9.95 incl. cd-rom *(978-1-933090-12-2(X))* Guardian Angel Publishing, Inc.

Caballero, D., tr. Que? Como? Por Que?: Autos y Camiones. Weller, Ursula, illus. 2007. (Junior (Silver Dolphin) Ser.). 16p. (J). (gr. -1). *(978-970-718-490-9(6),* Silver Dolphin en Español) Advanced Marketing, S. de R. L. de C. V.

Callery, Sean. Victor Wouk: The Father of the Hybrid Car. 2009. (Voices for Green Choices Ser.). (ENG., Illus.). 48p. (J). (gr. 5-9). pap. *(978-0-7787-4677-5(1));* lib. bdg. *(978-0-7787-4664-5(X))* Crabtree Publishing Co.

Carlson Berne, Emma. Run Your Own Car Wash. 2014. (Young Entrepreneurs Ser.). 32p. (J). (gr. 4-6). pap. 10.00 *(978-1-4777-3009-6(5));*1. (ENG.). 26.25 *(978-1-4777-2920-5(8))* Rosen Publishing Group, Inc., The. (PowerKids Pr.).

Carmichael, L. E. Hybrid & Electric Vehicles, 1 vol. 2013. (Innovative Technologies Ser.). (ENG.). 112p. (J). (gr. 6-12). lib. bdg. 35.64 *(978-1-61783-463-9(7),* Essential Library) ABDO Publishing Co.

Cars & Trucks. Date not set. (Illus.). (J). bds. 9.98 *(978-0-7525-9892-5(9))* Parragon, Inc.

Cars in America, 6 vols. (Book2WebTM Ser.). (gr. 4-8). 36.50 *(978-0-322-02992-7(9))* Wright Group/McGraw-Hill.

Challen, Paul C. Formula 1 Racing, 1 vol. 2015. (ENG., Illus.). 32p. (J). lib. bdg. 26.25 *(978-1-4994-0161-5(2),* PowerKids Pr.) Rosen Publishing Group, Inc., The.

—Mighty Tanks. 2010. (Vehicles on the Move Ser.). (ENG.). 32p. (J). (gr. k-3). pap. *(978-0-7787-3063-7(8))* Crabtree Publishing Co.

Chambers, Jo. All about Cars. 2007. (Trackers-Math Ser.). (gr. 2-5). pap. 5.00 *(978-1-59055-923-9(1))* Pacific Learning, Inc.

Clark, Willow. Cars on the Move. 2010. (Transportation Station Ser.). 24p. (J). (ENG.). pap. 8.25 *(978-1-4358-9754-0(4));* (Illus.). (gr. 2-5). lib. bdg. 22.60 *(978-1-4358-9333-7(6))* Rosen Publishing Group, Inc., The. (PowerKids Pr.).

Cockerham, Paul H. Bmw: Performance & Precision. 2017. (Speed Rules! Inside the World's Hottest Cars Ser.: Vol. 8). (ENG., Illus.). (YA). (gr. 7-12). 25.95 ***(978-1-4222-3829-5(6))*** Mason Crest.

—Ferrari: Pure Passion & Power. 2017. (Speed Rules! Inside the World's Hottest Cars Ser.: Vol. 8). (ENG., Illus.). (YA). (gr. 7-12). 25.95 ***(978-1-4222-3831-8(8))*** Mason Crest.

—Jaguar: A Tradition of Luxury & Style. 2017. (Speed Rules! Inside the World's Hottest Cars Ser.: Vol. 8). (ENG., Illus.). (YA). (gr. 7-12). 25.95 ***(978-1-4222-3832-5(6))*** Mason Crest.

—Lamborghini: A Fusion of Technology & Power. 2017. (Speed Rules! Inside the World's Hottest Cars Ser.: Vol. 8). (ENG., Illus.). (YA). (gr. 7-12). 25.95 ***(978-1-4222-3833-2(4))*** Mason Crest.

—Mercedes-Benz: German Engineering Excellence. 2017. (Speed Rules! Inside the World's Hottest Cars Ser.: Vol. 8). (ENG., Illus.). (YA). (gr. 7-12). 25.95 ***(978-1-4222-3834-9(2))*** Mason Crest.

—Porsche: The Ultimate Speed Machine. 2017. (Speed Rules! Inside the World's Hottest Cars Ser.: Vol. 8). (ENG., Illus.). (YA). (gr. 7-12). 25.95 ***(978-1-4222-3836-3(9))*** Mason Crest.

Colins, Luke. Stock Cars. 2017. (Gearhead Garage Ser.). (ENG., Illus.). 32p. (gr. 3-7). 31.35 ***(978-1-68072-035-8(X))*** Black Rabbit Bks.

Collier, James Lincoln. The Automobile. 2005. (Great Inventions Ser.). (Illus.). 112p. (J). (gr. 3-7). lib. bdg. *(978-0-7614-1877-1(6),* Benchmark Bks.) Marshall Cavendish Corp.

Colson, Rob. SUVs & Offroaders. 2016. (Top Marques Ser.). (ENG., Illus.). 32p. (J). (gr. 2-4). pap. 11.99 *(978-0-7502-9797-4(2),* Wayland) Hachette Children's Group GBR. Dist: Hachette Bk. Group.

Colson, Rob Scott. Aston Martin. 2010. (Ultimate Cars Ser.). (ENG.). 24p. (YA). (gr. 4-7). lib. bdg. 22.60 *(978-1-61532-620-4(0))* Rosen Publishing Group, Inc., The.

—BMW. 2010. (Ultimate Cars Ser.). (ENG.). 24p. (YA). (gr. 4-7). lib. bdg. 22.60 *(978-1-61532-624-2(3))* Rosen Publishing Group, Inc., The.

—Ferrari. 2010. (Ultimate Cars Ser.). (ENG.). 24p. (YA). (gr. 4-7). lib. bdg. 22.60 *(978-1-61532-854-3(8))* Rosen Publishing Group, Inc., The.

—Jaguar. 2010. (Ultimate Cars Ser.). (ENG.). 24p. (YA). (gr. 4-7). lib. bdg. 22.60 *(978-1-61532-622-8(7))* Rosen Publishing Group, Inc., The.

—Lamborghini. 2010. (Ultimate Cars Ser.). (ENG.). 24p. (YA). (gr. 4-7). lib. bdg. 22.60 *(978-1-61532-621-1(9))* Rosen Publishing Group, Inc., The.

—Porsche. 2010. (Ultimate Cars Ser.). (ENG.). 24p. (YA). (gr. 4-7). lib. bdg. 22.60 *(978-1-61532-623-5(5))* Rosen Publishing Group, Inc., The.

¿Como Funciona un Auto? (SPA.). (J). (gr. 1-3). pap. *(978-950-724-554-1(5),* LMA8231) Lumen ARG. Dist: Lectorum Pubns., Inc.

Coppendale, Jean & Graham, Ian. Cars. 2010. (Mighty Machines Ser.). (ENG., Illus.). 24p. (J). (gr. -1-2). pap. 5.95 *(978-1-55407-627-7(7),* 9781554076277) Firefly Bks., Ltd.

—The Great Big Book of Mighty Machines. 2009. (Mighty Machines Ser.). (ENG., Illus.). 160p. (J). (gr. -1-2). 19.95 *(978-1-55407-521-8(1),* 9781554075218) Firefly Bks., Ltd.

Crabtree Staff, illus. Mustang. 2010. (Superstar Cars Ser.). (ENG.). 64p. (J). pap. *(978-0-7787-2152-9(3))* Crabtree Publishing Co.

Crane, Cody. Race Cars. 2017. (True Book — Behind the Scenes Ser.). (ENG.). 48p. (J). lib. bdg. 31.00 ***(978-0-531-23502-7(5),*** Children's Pr.) Scholastic Library Publishing.

Creese, Sarah. Mad about Tractors Trucks Digger & Dumpers. 2009. (Mad About Ser.). (ENG., Illus.). 24p. (J). (gr. -1-3). pap. 3.99 *(978-1-84879-003-2(1))* Make Believe Ideas GBR. Dist: Nelson, Thomas Inc.

Crum, Colin. Alfa Romeo vs. Maserati, 1. 2014. (Ultimate Car Battles Ser.). (ENG.). 32p. (J). (gr. 3-6). 26.25 *(978-1-4777-9019-9(5),* Windmill Bks.) Rosen Publishing Group, Inc., The.

—BMW vs. Mercedes, 1. 2014. (Ultimate Car Battles Ser.). (ENG.). 32p. (J). (gr. 3-6). 26.25 *(978-1-4777-9011-3(X),* Windmill Bks.) Rosen Publishing Group, Inc., The.

—Ferrari vs. Lamborghini, 1. 2014. (Ultimate Car Battles Ser.). (ENG.). 32p. (J). (gr. 3-6). pap. 10.00 *(978-1-4777-9000-7(4),* Windmill Bks.) Rosen Publishing Group, Inc., The.

—Jaguar vs. Aston Martin, 1. 2014. (Ultimate Car Battles Ser.). (ENG.). 32p. (J). (gr. 3-6). 26.25 *(978-1-4777-9015-1(2),* Windmill Bks.) Rosen Publishing Group, Inc., The.

—Porsche vs. Lotus, 1. 2014. (Ultimate Car Battles Ser.). (ENG.). 32p. (J). (gr. 3-6). 26.25 *(978-1-4777-9003-8(9),* Windmill Bks.) Rosen Publishing Group, Inc., The.

Cruz, Calvin. Bentley Continental GT. 2015. (Car Crazy Ser.). (ENG., Illus.). 24p. (J). (gr. 3-7). lib. bdg. 25.95 *(978-1-62617-278-4(1),* Torque Bks.) Bellwether Media.

—Bugatti Veyron. 2015. (Car Crazy Ser.). (ENG., Illus.). 24p. (J). (gr. 3-7). lib. bdg. 25.95 *(978-1-62617-279-1(X),* Torque Bks.) Bellwether Media.

—Chevrolet Corvette Z06. 2015. (Car Crazy Ser.). (ENG., Illus.). 24p. (J). (gr. 3-7). lib. bdg. 25.95 *(978-1-62617-280-7(3),* Torque Bks.) Bellwether Media.

—Dodge Viper SRT. 2015. (Car Crazy Ser.). (ENG., Illus.). 24p. (J). (gr. 3-7). lib. bdg. 25.95 *(978-1-62617-281-4(1),* Torque Bks.) Bellwether Media.

—Ferrari 458 Italia. 2015. (Car Crazy Ser.). (ENG., Illus.). 24p. (J). (gr. 3-7). lib. bdg. 25.95 *(978-1-62617-282-1(X),* Torque Bks.) Bellwether Media.

—Lamborghini Aventador. 2015. (Car Crazy Ser.). (ENG., Illus.). 24p. (J). (gr. 3-7). lib. bdg. 25.95 *(978-1-62617-283-8(8),* Torque Bks.) Bellwether Media.

—McLaren 12C. 2015. (Car Crazy Ser.). (ENG., Illus.). 24p. (J). (gr. 3-7). lib. bdg. 25.95 *(978-1-62617-284-5(6),* Torque Bks.) Bellwether Media.

—Porsche 918 Spyder. 2015. (Car Crazy Ser.). (ENG., Illus.). 24p. (J). (gr. 3-7). lib. bdg. 25.95 *(978-1-62617-285-2(4),* Torque Bks.) Bellwether Media.

Dan's Old Van: Set B Individual Title Six-Packs. (Supersonic Phonics Ser.). (gr. k-3). 29.00 *(978-0-7635-0537-0(4))* Rigby Education.

David, Jack. Tuner Cars. 2008. (Cool Rides Ser.). (ENG., Illus.). 24p. (J). (gr. 3-7). lib. bdg. 25.95 *(978-1-60014-154-6(4))* Bellwether Media.

Daynes, Katie. Cars. Larkum, A., illus. 2005. 64p. (J). (gr. 2-18). pap. 5.95 *(978-0-7945-0999-6(1),* Usborne) EDC Publishing.

Disney & Disney / LeapFrog. The World of Cars: L'escapade Nocturne. 2008. (J). 20.79 *(978-1-59319-945-6(7))* LeapFrog Enterprises, Inc.

Disney Staff, contrib. by. Write, Slide & Learn Disney Pixar Cars: Numbers. 2011. (Disney Write, Slide & Learn Ser.). 12p. (J). 9.99 *(978-1-74183-851-0(7))* Hinkler Bks. Pty. Ltd. AUS. Dist: Ideals Pubns.

Doeden, Matt. Crazy Cars. 2007. (Motor Mania Ser.). (Illus.). 48p. (J). pap. 8.95 *(978-0-8225-6869-8(1),* Lerner Pubns.); (ENG., (gr. 4-7). lib. bdg. 26.60 *(978-0-8225-6565-9(X))* Lerner Publishing Group.

—Custom Cars. Uranas, Chuck, photos by. 2008. (Motor Mania Ser.). (Illus.). 48p. (J). (gr. 3-6). lib. bdg. 26.60 *(978-0-8225-7289-3(3))* Lerner Publishing Group.

—Custom Cars. 2008. pap. 52.95 *(978-1-58013-663-1(X))* Lerner Publishing Group.

—Lowriders. 2006. (Motor Mania Ser.). (ENG., Illus.). 48p. (J). (gr. 4-7). lib. bdg. 26.60 *(978-0-8225-6042-5(9),* Lerner Pubns.) Lerner Publishing Group.

—Stock Cars. 2006. (Motor Mania Ser.). (ENG., Illus.). 48p. (gr. 4-7). lib. bdg. 26.60 *(978-0-8225-3530-0(0))* Lerner Publishing Group.

Doman, Mary Kate. Cool Cars. 2011. (All about Big Machines Ser.). (Illus.). 24p. (J). (gr. -1-18). pap. 7.95 *(978-1-59845-242-6(8),* Enslow Elementary); (gr. k-3). lib. bdg. 22.60 *(978-0-7660-3930-8(7))* Enslow Pubs., Inc.

Donovan, Sandra. Sports Cars. 2006. (Motor Mania Ser.). (Illus.). 48p. (J). (gr. 3-7). lib. bdg. 26.60 *(978-0-8225-5928-3(5),* Lerner Pubns.) Lerner Publishing Group.

Dorling Kindersley Publishing Staff. Cars. 2014. (Eye Wonder Ser.). (ENG.). 56p. (J). (gr. k-4). 10.99 *(978-1-4654-1692-6(7),* DK Children) Dorling Kindersley Publishing, Inc.

—Diggers & Dumpers. Parsons, Jayne, ed. 2005. (Ultimate Sticker Bks.). (ENG.). 16p. (J). (gr. k-3). pap. 6.99 *(978-0-7566-0974-0(7),* DK Children) Dorling Kindersley Publishing, Inc.

—Disney Pixar Cars 3: the Essential Guide. 2017. (ENG.). 64p. (J). (gr. 1-4). 12.99 ***(978-1-4654-5559-8(0),*** DK Children) Dorling Kindersley Publishing, Inc.

—Fast & Cool Cars. 2015. (DK Adventures Ser.). (ENG., Illus.). 128p. (J). (gr. 3-7). 16.99 *(978-1-4654-2935-3(2),* DK Children) Dorling Kindersley Publishing, Inc.

—Pocket Genius: Cars. 2016. (Pocket Genius Ser.). (ENG., Illus.). 160p. (J). (gr. 3-7). pap. 4.99 *(978-1-4654-4237-6(5),* DK Children) Dorling Kindersley Publishing, Inc.

—Sports Car. 2003. (Wheelie Bks.). (ENG., Illus.). 12p. (J). (gr. -1-k). bds. 6.99 *(978-0-7894-9711-6(5),* DK Children) Dorling Kindersley Publishing, Inc.

—Ultimate Sticker Book: Things That Go. 2016. (ENG.). 32p. (J). (gr. k-4). pap. 6.99 *(978-1-4654-4720-3(2),* DK Children) Dorling Kindersley Publishing, Inc.

Downey, Glen R. & Malara, Maria. The 10 Hottest Hollywood Cars. 2007. 14.99 *(978-1-55448-526-0(6))* Scholastic Library Publishing.

Dream Cars. (Cool Creations CD Rom Activity Books Ser.). 32p. *(978-1-4054-9517-2(0))* Parragon, Inc.

Dubowski, Mark. Superfast Cars. 2005. (Ultimate Speed Ser.). (Illus.). 32p. (J). (gr. 3-6). lib. bdg. 25.27 *(978-1-59716-080-3(6))* Bearport Publishing Co., Inc.

Eason, Sarah. How Does a Car Work? 2010. (How Does It Work? Ser.). (Illus.). 32p. (J). (gr. 3-6). pap. 10.50 *(978-1-4339-3463-6(9));* lib. bdg. 26.00 *(978-1-4339-3462-9(0))* Stevens, Gareth Publishing LLLP. (Gareth Stevens Learning Library).

Edison, Erin. Crush It!, 1 vol. 2013. (Destruction Ser.). (ENG., Illus.). 12p. (J). (gr. k-1). bds. 9.99 *(978-1-4765-3528-9(0),* Pebble Plus) Capstone Press of Coughlan Cos.

Editors of Kingfisher. Fast Cars. 2016. (It's All About... Ser.). (ENG.). 32p. pap. 5.99 *(978-0-7534-7284-2(8),* 9780753472842, Kingfisher) Roaring Brook Pr.

Edmonston, Phil & Sawa, Maureen. Car Smarts: Hot Tips for the Car Crazy. Sauve, Gordon, illus. 2003. (ENG.). 80p. (J). (gr. 4-7). pap. 15.95 *(978-0-88776-646-6(3),* Tundra Bks.) Tundra Bks. CAN. Dist: Penguin Random Hse. LLC.

Egan, Erin. Smokin' Open-Wheel Race Cars. 2014. (Fast Wheels! Ser.). 48p. (J). (gr. 4-9). pap. 8.95 *(978-1-62285-101-0(3))* Enslow Pubs., Inc.

Elish, Dan. Insight. 2010. (Green Cars Ser.). 48p. (J). (gr. 3-6). 28.50 *(978-1-60870-010-3(0))* Marshall Cavendish Corp.

—Prius. 2010. (Green Cars Ser.). (Illus.). 48p. (J). (gr. 3-6). 28.50 (978-1-60870-011-0(9)) Marshall Cavendish Corp.

Enz, Tammy. Batmobiles & Batcycles: The Engineering Behind Batman's Vehicles, 1 vol. 2014. (Batman Science Ser.). (ENG.). 32p. (gr. 3-4). 27.32 (978-1-4765-3940-9(5), DC Super Heroes) Stone Arch Bks.

Espejo, Roman. Cars in America. 2010. (Opposing Viewpoints Ser.). (Illus.). 240p. (J). 42.95 (978-0-7377-4759-1(5)); pap. 29.45 (978-0-7377-4760-7(9)) Cengage Gale. (Greenhaven Pr., Inc.).

Famighetti, Robert, et al. How Do Hybrid Cars Work? 2009. (Science in the Real World Ser.). (Illus.). 32p. (gr. 4-6). 28.00 (978-1-60413-476-6(3), Chelsea Clubhouse) Facts On File, Inc.

Farndon, John. Megafast Cars. Edwards, Mat & Pyke, Jeremy, illus. 2016. (Megafast Ser.). (ENG.). 32p. (J). (gr. 3-6). lib. bdg. 26.65 (978-1-4677-9363-6(9)) Lerner Publishing Group.

Feldman, Thea & Oxlade, Chris. Cars. 2013. (Kingfisher Readers Ser.). (ENG., Illus.). 32p. (J). (gr. k-3). pap. 3.99 (978-0-7534-6929-3(4), 9780753469293, Kingfisher) Roaring Brook Pr.

Figorito, C. Go Far in the Car: Learning the AR Sound. 2009. (PowerPhonics Ser.). 24p. (gr. 1-1). 39.90 (978-1-60851-444-1(7), PowerKids Pr.) Rosen Publishing Group, Inc., The.

Finn, Denny Von. Funny Cars. 2009. (Cool Rides Ser.). (ENG., Illus.). 24p. (J). (gr. 3-7). lib. bdg. 25.95 (978-1-60014-255-0(9)) Bellwether Media.

—Muscle Cars. 2009. (Cool Rides Ser.). (ENG., Illus.). 24p. (J). (gr. 3-7). lib. bdg. 25.95 (978-1-60014-272-7(9)) Bellwether Media.

Firefly Books Staff & Worek, Michael. My Little Book of Cars. 2013. (ENG., Illus.). 160p. (J). (gr. -1-k). 9.95 (978-1-77085-230-3(1), 9781770852303) Firefly Bks., Ltd.

Flammang, James M. & Green, Robert. Cars. 2008. (21st Century Skills Innovation Library: Innovation in Transportation Ser.). (ENG., Illus.). 32p. (gr. 4-8). lib. bdg. 28.50 (978-1-60279-231-9(3), 200022) Cherry Lake Publishing.

Flounders, Anne. Cars. 2013. (Machines in Motion Ser.). 48p. (J). (gr. 3-5). pap. 84.30 (978-1-4339-9598-9(0)); (ENG., Illus.). lib. bdg. 31.95 (978-1-4339-9596-5(4)) Stevens, Gareth Publishing LLLP.

Francis, Jim. Stock Car Secrets. 2008. (NASCAR Ser.). (ENG., Illus.). 32p. (J). (gr. 3-7). pap. (978-0-7787-3197-9(9)); lib. bdg. (978-0-7787-3189-4(8)) Crabtree Publishing Co.

Franks, Katie. I Want to Be a Race Car Driver. 2007. (Dream Jobs Ser.). (Illus.). 24p. (J). (gr. 2-5). lib. bdg. 22.60 (978-1-4042-3623-3(6)) Rosen Publishing Group, Inc., The.

Full Throttle. 2010. (Full Throttle Ser.). 32p. lib. bdg. 159.90 (978-1-4296-5858-4(4), Edge Bks.) Capstone Press of Coughlan Cos.

Full Throttle, 6 vols., Set. Incl. Choppers. Savage, Jeff. lib. bdg. 27.99 (978-1-4296-3939-2(3)); Dirt Bikes. Polydoros, Lori. lib. bdg. 27.99 (978-1-4296-3940-8(7)); Dragsters. McCollum, Sean. lib. bdg. 27.99 (978-1-4296-3941-5(5)); Indy Cars. McCollum, Sean. lib. bdg. 27.99 (978-1-4296-3942-2(3)); Monster Trucks. Savage, Jeff. lib. bdg. 27.99 (978-1-4296-3943-9(1)); Sports Cars. McCollum, Sean. lib. bdg. 27.99 (978-1-4296-3944-6(X)); (gr. 3-4). (Full Throttle Ser.). (ENG.). 32p. 2010. Set lib. bdg. 167.94 (978-1-4296-4445-7(1), Edge Bks.) Capstone Press of Coughlan Cos.

Gale Editor & MacKay, Jennifer, eds. Electric Cars. 2011. (Technology 360 Ser.). (Illus.). 128p. (J). (gr. 9-12). lib. bdg. 34.95 (978-1-4205-0612-9(9)) Cengage Gale.

Georgiou, Tyrone. Formula 1. 2011. (Fast Lane: Open-Wheel Racing Ser.). 24p. (J). (gr. 2-5). pap. 8.15 (978-1-4339-5752-9(3)); lib. bdg. 22.60 (978-1-4339-5750-5(7)) Stevens, Gareth Publishing LLLP. (Gareth Stevens Learning Library).

Gerdes, Louise, ed. Hybrid & Electric Cars. 2014. (At Issue Ser.). (ENG.). 128p. (gr. 10-12). lib. bdg. 39.40 (978-0-7377-6838-1(X), Greenhaven Pr., Inc.) Cengage Gale.

Gibbs, Lynne & Morris, Neil. Mega Book of Cars. 2003. (Illus.). 32p. (YA). pap. (978-1-903954-56-0(8), Pavilion Children's Books) Pavilion Bks.

Gifford, Clive. Car World: The Most Amazing Automobiles on Earth. 2016. (ENG., Illus.). 80p. (J). (gr. 3). 19.95 (978-1-78312-141-0(6)) Carlton Kids GBR. Dist: Sterling Publishing Co., Inc.

—Cars. 2012. (ENG.). 24p. (J). (978-0-7787-7474-7(0)); (Illus.). pap. (978-0-7787-7479-2(1)) Crabtree Publishing Co.

Gigliotti, Jim. Smokin' Dragsters & Funny Cars. 2014. (Fast Wheels! Ser.). 48p. (J). (gr. 4-9). pap. 8.95 (978-1-62285-071-6(8)) Enslow Pubs., Inc.

Gilpin, Daniel. Record-Breaking Cars. 2012. (Record Breakers Ser.). (Illus.). 32p. (J). lib. bdg. 26.50 (978-1-4488-5289-5(7), PowerKids Pr.) Rosen Publishing Group, Inc., The.

Glaser, Rebecca Stromstad. Cars Zoom. 2016. (ENG., Illus.). 14p. (J). (gr. -1 — 1). bds. 7.99 (978-1-68152-121-3(0)) Amicus.

Glover, David & Glover, Penny. Cars in Action. 2008. (On the Go Ser.). (Illus.). 24p. (J). (gr. 3-7). lib. bdg. 22.60 (978-1-4042-4306-4(2), PowerKids Pr.) Rosen Publishing Group, Inc., The.

Graham, Ian. Amazing Vehicles: Foldout Book. 2005. (Illus.). 14p. (J). (gr. k-4). reprint ed. 10.00 (978-0-7567-8777-6(7)) DIANE Publishing Co.

—Build Your Own Cool Cars. 2004. (Illus.). 48p. (978-0-439-67662-5(2)) Scholastic, Inc.

—Cars. 2009. (Mighty Machines Ser.). (Illus.). 31p. (J). (gr. 4-7). pap. 7.95 (978-1-59920-253-2(0)) Black Rabbit Bks.

—Cars & Bikes. 2008. (QEB Machines at Work Ser.). (Illus.). 36p. (YA). (gr. 4-7). 19.95 (978-1-59566-317-7(7)) QEB Publishing Inc.

—Mighty Machines, CARS, Scholastic BF Edition. 2008. 24p. (J). (978-1-59566-133-3(6)) QEB Publishing Inc.

Green Android. Customized Cars: Mean Machines. Green Android, ed. 2017. (Illus.). 32p. (J). pap. 6.99 (978-1-61067-419-5(7)) Kane Miller.

Greve, Meg. From Tow Truck to Auto Body Shop. 2015. (ENG.). 24p. (gr. k-2). 28.50 (978-1-63430-062-9(9)) Rourke Educational Media.

Group/McGraw-Hill, Wright. On the Move: Level H, 6 vols. (First Explorers Ser.). 24p. (gr. 1-2). 29.95 (978-0-7699-1449-7(7)) Shortland Pubns. (U. S. A.) Inc.

Gunston, Bill Tudor & Parker, Steve. Fasten Your Seatbelt! Mind-Boggling Machines. 2010. (ENG.). 96p. (J). (gr. 2-4). pap. 9.95 (978-1-84696-205-9(6), TickTock Books) Octopus Publishing Group GBR. Dist: Independent Pubs. Group.

Hamilton, John. Muscle Cars. 2012. (Speed Zone Ser.). 32p. (J). (gr. 3-9). lib. bdg. 27.07 (978-1-61783-529-2(3), A&D Xtreme) ABDO Publishing Co.

Hamilton, Robert M. In a Car. 2012. (Going Places Ser.). (ENG.). 24p. (J). (gr. k-2). pap. 8.15 (978-1-4339-6263-9(2)) Stevens, Gareth Publishing LLLP.

Harmon, Daniel E. Smart Strategies for Buying a Car. 2014. (Financial Security & Life Success for Teens Ser.). 80p. (YA). (gr. 7-12). 34.25 (978-1-4777-7622-3(2)) Rosen Publishing Group, Inc., The.

Harrison, Paul. Mega Machines: Roar into Action with These Super-Charged Racers! 2012. (ENG., Illus.). 128p. (J). pap. 9.95 (978-1-84858-652-9(3)) Arcturus Publishing GBR. Dist: Bookmasters Distribution.

Harrison, Peter. Cars: An Amazing Fact File & Hands-On Project Book. 2016. (ENG., Illus.). 64p. (J). (gr. -1-12). 12.99 (978-1-86147-642-5(6), Armadillo) Anness Publishing GBR. Dist: National Bk. Network.

Hawley, Rebecca. Corvette. 2007. (Superfast Cars Ser.). (Illus.). 24p. (J). (gr. 3-6). lib. bdg. 22.60 (978-1-4042-3643-1(0)) Rosen Publishing Group, Inc., The.

—Lamborghini. 2007. (Superfast Cars Ser.). (Illus.). 24p. (J). (gr. 3-6). lib. bdg. 22.60 (978-1-4042-3642-4(2)) Rosen Publishing Group, Inc., The.

—Mustang. (Superfast Cars Ser.). 24p. 2009. (gr. 2-3). 42.50 (978-1-60853-234-6(8), PowerKids Pr.) 2007. (Illus.). (J). (gr. 3-6). lib. bdg. 22.60 (978-1-4042-3645-5(7)) Rosen Publishing Group, Inc., The.

—Porsche. (Superfast Cars Ser.). 24p. 2009. (gr. 2-3). 42.50 (978-1-60853-235-3(6), PowerKids Pr.) 2007. (Illus.). (J). (gr. 3-6). lib. bdg. 22.60 (978-1-4042-3641-7(4)) Rosen Publishing Group, Inc., The.

—Superfast Cars, 6 bks., Set. Incl. Corvette. lib. bdg. 22.60 (978-1-4042-3643-1(0)); Ferrari. lib. bdg. 22.60 (978-1-4042-3640-0(6)); Lamborghini. lib. bdg. 22.60 (978-1-4042-3642-4(2)); Mustang. lib. bdg. 22.60 (978-1-4042-3645-5(7)); Porsche. lib. bdg. 22.60 (978-1-4042-3641-7(4)); Viper. lib. bdg. 22.60 (978-1-4042-3644-8(9)); (Illus.). 24p. (J). (gr. 3-6). 2007. 2007. Set lib. bdg. 127.50 (978-1-4042-3602-8(3)) Rosen Publishing Group, Inc., The.

—Viper. (Superfast Cars Ser.). 24p. 2009. (gr. 2-3). 42.50 (978-1-60853-236-0(4), PowerKids Pr.) 2007. (Illus.). (J). (gr. 3-6). lib. bdg. 22.60 (978-1-4042-3644-8(9)) Rosen Publishing Group, Inc., The.

Hayes, Amy. Why Do Cars Need Gas? And Other FAQs about Machines. 2016. (Q & a: Life's Mysteries Solved! Ser.). 32p. (J). (gr. 4-3). pap. 10.50 (978-1-4824-4773-6(8)) Stevens, Gareth Publishing LLLP.

Herrington, Lisa M. Car Safety. 2012. (Rookie Read-About(tm) Safety Ser.). (ENG., Illus.). 32p. (J). lib. bdg. 25.00 (978-0-531-28969-3(9)); (gr. -1-1). pap. 5.95 (978-0-531-29271-6(1)) Scholastic Library Publishing.

Hewitt, Sally. Cars. 2006. (Illus.). 24p. (YA). (gr. 1-18). lib. bdg. 22.80 (978-1-931983-55-6(0)) Chrysalis Education.

Hoffman, Kurt. How Cars Changed the World. 2009. (Real Life Readers Ser.). 16p. (gr. 2-3). pap. 7.05 (978-1-4358-0119-6(9), Rosen Classroom) Rosen Publishing Group, Inc., The.

Hosley, Maria. Cars, 1 vol. 2007. (First Drawings Ser.). (ENG., Illus.). 24p. (J). (gr. -1-3). lib. bdg. 25.65 (978-1-59679-800-7(9), Buddy Bks.) ABDO Publishing Co.

How things Work: Level Q, 6 vols., Vol. 3. (Explorers Ser.). 32p. (gr. 3-6). 44.95 (978-0-7699-0620-1(6)) Shortland Pubns. (U. S. A.) Inc.

Hughes, Mónica. Cars. 2005. (Big Cat Ser.). (gr. k-2). pap. 6.50 (978-1-60457-026-7(1)) Pacific Learning, Inc.

Hunter, Nick. How Electric & Hybrid Cars Work. 2013. (EcoWorks Ser.). 32p. (J). (gr. 3-5). 26.60 (978-1-4339-9560-6(3)); pap. 63.00 (978-1-4339-9562-0(X)); pap. 10.50 (978-1-4339-9561-3(1)) Stevens, Gareth Publishing LLLP.

Izumo, Rebecca. Colorful Race Cars. 2017. (Wonderful World of Colors Ser.). 24p. (gr. 4-6). pap. 8.25 **(978-1-5383-2095-2(9)**, PowerKids Pr.) Rosen Publishing Group, Inc., The.

Jackson, Tom. Car. 2015. (Technology Timelines Ser.). (Illus.). 32p. (gr. 3-6). 31.35 (978-1-78121-235-6(X)) Brown Bear Bks.

Jacobs, David H. Corvette: The Classic American Sports Car. 2017. (Speed Rules! Inside the World's Hottest Cars Ser.: Vol. 8). (ENG., Illus.). (YA). (gr. 7-12). 25.95 **(978-1-4222-3830-1(X))** Mason Crest.

Jaguar. 2013. (Speed Machines Ser.). 32p. (J). (gr. 3-6). pap. 60.00 (978-1-4777-1193-4(7), PowerKids Pr.) Rosen Publishing Group, Inc., The.

Johanson, Carl, illus. All Kinds of Cars. 2017. (ENG.). 40p. (J). (gr. -1-k). 16.95 (978-1-911171-01-0(1)) Flying Eye Bks. GBR. Dist: Consortium Bk. Sales & Distribution.

Johnson, Robin. Jaguar. Crabtree, ed. 2010. (Superstar Cars Ser.). (ENG., Illus.). 64p. (J). pap. (978-0-7787-2150-5(7)) Crabtree Publishing Co.

Johnstone, Michael. Cars. (Illus.). 32p. (J). mass mkt. 8.99 (978-0-590-24423-7(X)) Scholastic, Inc.

Jones, Rob Lloyd. Flip Flap Cars. 2010. (Flip Flap Board Bks). 14p. (J). (gr. 1). bds. 14.99 (978-0-7945-2554-5(7), Usborne) EDC Publishing.

—Look Inside Cars. 2011. (Look Inside Board Bks). 14p. (J). ring bd. 15.99 (978-0-7945-3232-1(2), Usborne) EDC Publishing.

Jones, Tammy. I Go! 2009. (Sight Word Readers Set A Ser.). (J). 3.49 net. (978-1-60719-143-8(1)) Newmark Learning LLC.

Kamberg, Mary-Lane. Working As a Mechanic in Your Community. 2015. (Careers in Your Community Ser.). (ENG., Illus.). 80p. (J). (gr. 7-8). 34.25 (978-1-4994-6113-8(5), Rosen Young Adult) Rosen Publishing Group, Inc., The.

Katirgis, Jane. STEM Jobs with Cars. 2014. (ENG.). 48p. (gr. 4-8). 35.64 (978-1-62717-702-3(7)) Rourke Educational Media.

Kelley, K. C. Smokin' Race Cars. 2014. (Fast Wheels! Ser.). 48p. (J). (gr. 4-9). pap. 8.95 (978-1-62285-096-9(3)) Enslow Pubs., Inc.

Kenney, Karen Latchana. Shop Tech: The Science of Cars, 1 vol. 2011. (Everyday Science Ser.). (ENG.). 64p. (gr. 5-7). pap. 9.10 (978-0-7565-4506-2(4), CPB Grades 4-8) Compass Point Bks.

—Thrilling Sports Cars. 2015. (Dream Cars Ser.). (ENG.). 32p. (gr. 3-4). lib. bdg. 27.99 (978-1-4914-2013-3(8)) Capstone Press of Coughlan Cos.

Kerrod, Robin. Transportation. 2004. (21st Century Science Ser.). (Illus.). 44p. (J). lib. bdg. 28.50 (978-1-58340-507-9(0)) Black Rabbit Bks.

Kniffke, Sophie, et al. El Coche. (Coleccion Mundo Maravilloso). (SPA., Illus.). 40p. (J). (gr. 2-4). (978-84-348-3472-9(3), SM5465) SM Ediciones.

Kuskowski, Alex & Craig, Diane. Super Simple Automobile Projects: Inspiring & Educational Science Activities, 1 vol. 2016. (ENG., Illus.). 32p. (J). 18.95 (978-1-62403-729-0(1)) ABDO Publishing Co.

Labrecque, Ellen. Auto Technician. 2016. (21st Century Skills Library: Cool Vocational Careers Ser.). (ENG., Illus.). 32p. (J). (gr. 4-7). 29.93 (978-1-63471-058-9(4), 208312) Cherry Lake Publishing.

Ladybird. Cars. 2016. (Read It Yourself with Ladybird Ser.). (ENG.). 32p. (J). 5.99 (978-0-241-24444-9(7)) Penguin Bks., Ltd. GBR. Dist: Independent Pubs. Group.

—Cars, Level 1. 2016. (Read It Yourself with Ladybird Ser.). (ENG.). 32p. (J). (gr. 2-4). pap. 9.99 (978-0-241-24443-2(9)) Penguin Bks., Ltd. GBR. Dist: Independent Pubs. Group.

Lafferty, Peter. Cars. 2016. (Wise Up Ser.). 32p. (gr. 2-6). 31.35 (978-1-62588-338-4(2), Smart Apple Media) Black Rabbit Bks.

LaFontaine, Bruce. Classic Cars Coloring Book. 2007. (Dover History Coloring Book Ser.). (ENG., Illus.). 112p. (gr. 3-8). 9.95 (978-0-486-46067-3(3)) Dover Pubns., Inc.

—Luxury Cars Coloring Book. 2005. (Dover History Coloring Book Ser.). (ENG., Illus.). 32p. (gr. 3-5). per. 3.99 (978-0-486-44436-9(8)) Dover Pubns., Inc.

—Shiny Fast Cars Stickers. 2004. (Dover Little Activity Books Stickers Ser.). (ENG., Illus.). 2p. (J). (gr. 1-4). 1.50 (978-0-486-43535-0(0)) Dover Pubns., Inc.

Landes, Andi. Trace Race: Things That Go. Hawkins, Klara, illus. 2017. (ENG.). 12p. (J). (gr. -1). bds. 9.99 (978-1-62686-964-6(2), Silver Dolphin Bks.) Readerlink Distribution Services, LLC.

Lang, Sheri. Reed Makes a Race Car: Checking Your Work. 2017. (Computer Science for the Real World Ser.). 12p. (gr. 6-7). pap. 7.05 **(978-1-5383-5158-1(7)**, Rosen Classroom) Rosen Publishing Group, Inc., The.

Lew, Kristi. Volt. 2010. (Green Cars Ser.). 48p. (J). (gr. 3-6). 28.50 (978-1-60870-013-4(5)) Marshall Cavendish Corp.

Lichtenheld, Tom. Everything I Know about Cars. Lichtenheld, Tom, illus. 2005. (ENG., Illus.). 40p. (J). (gr. -1-3). 18.99 (978-0-689-84382-2(8), Simon & Schuster Bks. For Young Readers) Simon & Schuster Bks. For Young Readers.

Light, Steve. Cars Go. 2016. (ENG., Illus.). 16p. (J). (gr. -1 — 1). bds. 9.99 (978-1-4521-5067-3(2)) Chronicle Bks. LLC.

Lotus. 2013. (Speed Machines Ser.). 32p. (J). (gr. 3-6). pap. 60.00 (978-1-4777-0985-6(1), PowerKids Pr.) Rosen Publishing Group, Inc., The.

Lunis, Natalie. Cars. 2011. (Early Connections Ser.). (J). (978-1-61672-630-0(X)) Benchmark Education Co.

Machajewski, Sarah. All about Cars. 2016. (Let's Find Out! Ser.). 32p. (J). (gr. 3-2). lib. bdg. 24.45 (978-1-68048-440-3(0), Britannica Educational Publishing) Rosen Publishing Group, Inc., The.

Manolis, Kay. Taxis. 2008. (Mighty Machines Ser.). (ENG., Illus.). 24p. (J). (gr. k-3). lib. bdg. 25.95 (978-1-60014-232-1(X), Blastoff! Readers) Bellwether Media.

Mara, Wil. What Should I Do? In the Car. 2011. (Community Connections: What Should I Do? Ser.). (ENG.). 24p. (gr. 2-5). lib. bdg. 25.64 (978-1-61080-052-5(4), 201046) Cherry Lake Publishing.

Maserati. 2013. (Speed Machines Ser.). 32p. (J). (gr. 3-6). pap. 60.00 (978-1-4777-0989-4(4), PowerKids Pr.) Rosen Publishing Group, Inc., The.

Mason, Paul. Rally Driver: Sébastien Ogier vs Sébastien Loeb. 2016. (EDGE: the Inside Track Ser.). (ENG., Illus.). 32p. (J). (gr. 2-4). 16.99 (978-1-4451-4702-4(5), Franklin Watts) Hachette Children's Group GBR. Dist: Hachette Bk. Group.

Mattern, Joanne. Staying Safe in the Car. 2007. (Safety First Ser.). (Illus.). 24p. (gr. k-3). pap. 8.15 (978-0-8368-7800-4(0)); lib. bdg. 22.00 (978-0-8368-7793-9(4)) Stevens, Gareth Publishing LLLP. (Weekly Reader Leveled Readers).

—Staying Safe in the Car (la Seguridad en el Auto) 2007. (Safety First / la Seguridad Es lo Primero Ser.). (ENG & SPA., Illus.). 24p. (gr. k-3). lib. bdg. 22.00 (978-0-8368-8058-8(7), Weekly Reader Leveled Readers) Stevens, Gareth Publishing LLLP.

—Staying Safe in the Car (la seguridad en el Auto) 2007. (Safety First / la Seguridad Es lo Primero Ser.). (ENG & SPA.). 24p. (gr. k-3). pap. 8.15 (978-0-8368-8065-6(X), Weekly Reader Leveled Readers) Stevens, Gareth Publishing LLLP.

Matthews, Derek. Tráfico: Con Graciosos Sonidos de vehículos. 2005. (Escucha y Aprende Ser.). (SPA., Illus.). 10p. (J). (gr. -1-1). (978-970-718-297-4(0), Silver Dolphin en Español) Advanced Marketing, S. de R. L. de C. V.

Maurer, Tracy Nelson. Lamborghini. 2006. (Full Throttle Ser.). (Illus.). 32p. (J). (gr. -1-3). lib. bdg. 28.50 (978-1-60044-224-7(2)) Rourke Educational Media.

Mayo, Margaret. Dig Dig Digging. Ayliffe, Alex, illus. 2006. (ENG.). 24p. (J). (gr. -1-k). bds. 7.99 (978-0-8050-7985-2(8), 9780805079852, Holt, Henry & Co. Bks. For Young Readers) Holt, Henry & Co.

McCollum, Sean. Custom Cars: The Ins & Outs of Tuners, Hot Rods, & Other Muscle Cars. 2010. (Rpm Ser.). (ENG.). 48p. (gr. 3-4). pap. 59.70 (978-1-4296-5126-4(1)) Capstone Press of Coughlan Cos.

—Sports Cars, 1 vol. 2010. (Full Throttle Ser.). (ENG.). 32p. (gr. 3-4). lib. bdg. 27.99 (978-1-4296-3944-6(X), Edge Bks.) Capstone Press of Coughlan Cos.

McKenzie, Precious. Grand Theft Safari. 2015. (ENG.). 96p. (gr. 3-6). 31.36 (978-1-63430-391-0(1)) Rourke Educational Media.

Meachen Rau, Dana. Driving. 2006. (On the Move Ser.). (ENG & SPA., Illus.). 24p. (gr. k-1). lib. bdg. 15.95 (978-0-7614-2316-4(8), Benchmark Bks.) Marshall Cavendish Corp.

Mean Machines: Customized Cars. 2015. (Illus.). 32p. (J). **(978-1-61067-429-4(4))** Kane Miller.

Mellet, Peter, et al, trs. Cars. 2003. (All About...Ser.). (ENG., Illus.). 64p. (J). (gr. 3-7). pap. 7.99 (978-1-84215-893-7(7)) Anness Publishing GBR. Dist: National Bk. Network.

Mercedes. 2013. (Speed Machines Ser.). 32p. (J). (gr. 3-6). pap. 60.00 (978-1-4777-0991-7(6), PowerKids Pr.) Rosen Publishing Group, Inc., The.

Mezzanotte, Jim. The Story of the Ford Mustang. 2005. (Classic Cars Ser.). (Illus.). 24p. (gr. 1-4). lib. bdg. 23.00 (978-0-8368-4534-1(X), Gareth Stevens Learning Library) Stevens, Gareth Publishing LLLP.

Miller, Reagan & Aloian, Molly. Ferrari. 2010. (ENG.). 64p. (J). lib. bdg. (978-0-7787-2142-0(6)) Crabtree Publishing Co.

Miller, Reagan & Bow, James. Lamborghini. 2010. (ENG., Illus.). 64p. (J). lib. bdg. (978-0-7787-2144-4(2)) Crabtree Publishing Co.

Miller, Reagan & Peppas, Lynn. Mustang. 2010. (ENG., Illus.). 64p. (J). lib. bdg. (978-0-7787-2145-1(0)) Crabtree Publishing Co.

Miller, Reagan & Walker, Robert. Porsche. 2010. (ENG.). 64p. (J). lib. bdg. (978-0-7787-2146-8(9)) Crabtree Publishing Co.

Minden, Cecilia & Minden-Zins, Mary. Auto Mechanics. 2014. (People in Our Community Ser.). (ENG.). 24p. (J). (gr. k-3). 27.07 (978-1-62687-009-3(8), 206799) Child's World, Inc., The.

Mitton, Tony & Parker, Ant. Cool Cars. (Amazing Machines Ser.). (ENG., Illus.). 24p. (J). (gr. -1-k). 2014. 4.99 (978-0-7534-7207-1(4), 9780753472071) 2005. 9.99 (978-0-7534-5802-0(0), 9780753458020) Roaring Brook Pr. (Kingfisher).

—Cool Cars. 2014. (Amazing Machines Ser.). (J). lib. bdg. 14.75 (978-0-606-36132-3(4)) Turtleback Bks.

Morgan, Charlie. Classic American Cars, Vol. 8. 2015. (Classic Cars & Bikes Collection). (Illus.). 64p. (J). (gr. 7). lib. bdg. 23.95 (978-1-4222-3276-7(X)) Mason Crest.

Morganelli, Adrianna. Formula One. 2006. (Automania! Ser.). (ENG., Illus.). 32p. (J). (gr. 4-7). lib. bdg. (978-0-7787-3009-5(3)) Crabtree Publishing Co.

Mullins, Matt. Think Like a Scientist in the Car. 2011. (Explorer Junior Library: Science Explorer Junior Ser.). (ENG.). 32p. (gr. 4-8). lib. bdg. 28.50 (978-1-61080-164-5(4), 201098) Cherry Lake Publishing.

Murray, Julie. Carros. 2015. (Medios de Transporte Ser.). (SPA., Illus.). 24p. (gr. k-1). pap. 7.95 (978-1-4966-0491-0(1)) Capstone Classroom.

—Cars, 1 vol. 2014. (Transportation Ser.). (ENG., Illus.). 24p. (J). (gr. 4-8). lib. bdg. 28.50 (978-1-62970-079-3(7), 1375346) ABDO Publishing Co.

Nagle, Jeanne. Reducing Your Carbon Footprint at School. 2009. (Your Carbon Footprint Ser.). 48p. (gr. 5-5). 53.00 (978-1-60854-911-5(9), Rosen Reference) Rosen Publishing Group, Inc., The.

Nicholls, Paul. Wind-up Race Cars. 2010. (Wind-up Bks). 14p. (J). bds. 29.99 (978-0-7945-2657-3(8), Usborne) EDC Publishing.

Niver, Heather. Midget Cars. 2011. (Fast Lane: Open-Wheel Racing Ser.). (Illus.). 24p. (gr. 2-5). 22.60 (978-1-4339-5762-8(0)); pap. 8.15 (978-1-4339-5764-2(7)) Stevens, Gareth Publishing LLLP. (Gareth Stevens Learning Library).

—Porsches. 2011. (Wild Wheels Ser.). (Illus.). 32p. (J). (gr. 3-6). 26.60 (978-1-4339-5838-0(4)); pap. 10.50 (978-1-4339-5840-3(6)) Stevens, Gareth Publishing LLLP. (Gareth Stevens Learning Library).

Niver, Heather Moore. Camaros. 2011. (Wild Wheels Ser.). (Illus.). 32p. (J). (gr. 3-6). pap. 10.50 (978-1-4339-4736-0(6)); lib. bdg. 26.60 (978-1-4339-4735-3(8)) Stevens, Gareth Publishing LLLP. (Gareth Stevens Learning Library).

—Corvettes. 2011. (Wild Wheels Ser.). 32p. (J). (gr. 3-6). pap. 10.50 (978-1-4339-5820-5(1)); lib. bdg. 26.60 (978-1-4339-5818-2(X)) Stevens, Gareth Publishing LLLP. (Gareth Stevens Learning Library).

—GTOs. 2011. (Wild Wheels Ser.). (Illus.). 32p. (J). (gr. 3-6). pap. 10.50 (978-1-4339-4748-3(X)); lib. bdg. 26.60 (978-1-4339-4747-6(1)) Stevens, Gareth Publishing LLLP. (Gareth Stevens Learning Library).

Nixon, James. Cars. 2010. (Machines on the Move Ser.). 32p. (J). 28.50 (978-1-60753-057-2(0)) Amicus Publishing.

—Cars. 2012. (Illus.). 32p. (gr. 1-3). pap. 8.95 (978-1-926722-67-2(1)) Saunders Bk. Co. CAN. Dist: RiverStream Publishing.

Oachs, Emily Rose. Dodge Challenger SRT Hellcat. 2017. (Car Crazy Ser.). (ENG., Illus.). 24p. (J). (gr. 3-7). lib. bdg. 25.95 (978-1-62617-577-8(2), Torque Bks.) Bellwether Media.

Oachs, Emilyi Rose. Dodge Charger R/T. 2017. (Car Crazy Ser.). (ENG., Illus.). 24p. (J). (gr. 3-7). lib. bdg. 25.95 (978-1-62617-578-5(0), Torque Bks.) Bellwether Media.

Off-Road Racers. (Mighty MacHines Ser.). 16p. (J). (978-2-7643-0173-9(1)) Phidal Publishing, Inc./Editions Phidal, Inc.

Omoth, Tyler. Incredible Car Stunts. 2015. (Wild Stunts Ser.). (ENG., Illus.). 32p. (gr. 3-4). lib. bdg. 27.99 (978-1-4914-4254-8(9), Edge Bks.) Capstone Press of Coughlan Cos.

Otfinoski, Steven. Here We Go!, 4 bks., Set, Group 1. Incl. Behind the Wheel: Cars Then & Now. lib. bdg. 22.79 (978-0-7614-0403-3(1)); Into the Wind: Sailboats Then & Now. lib. bdg. 22.79 (978-0-7614-0405-7(8)); Pedaling Along: Bikes Then & Now. lib. bdg. 22.79 (978-0-7614-0402-6(3)); Taking Off: Planes Then & Now. lib. bdg. 22.79 (978-0-7614-0407-1(4)); 32p. (J). (gr. 1-12). 1996. (Illus.). lib. bdg. (978-0-7614-0401-9(5), Benchmark Bks.) Marshall Cavendish Corp.

Out & About: Level Q, 6 vols., Vol. 2. (Explorers Ser.). 32p. (gr. 3-6). 44.95 (978-0-7699-0608-9(7)) Shortland Pubns. (U. S. A.) Inc.

Oxlade, Chris. Cars Inside & Out. 2009. (Machines Inside Out Ser.). (ENG.). 32p. (J). (gr. 4-6). pap. 10.00

(978-1-4358-2939-8(5), PowerKids Pr.); (YA). (gr. 3-6). lib. bdg. 25.25 (978-1-4358-2861-2(5)) Rosen Publishing Group, Inc., The.

—Sports Cars 6-Pack. 2004. (Mean Machines Ser.). (Illus.). (J). pap. 48.30 (978-1-4109-1204-6(3)) Harcourt Schl. Pubs.

Paine, Jed. Ferrari, Vol. 8. 2015. (Classic Cars & Bikes Collection). 64p. (J). (gr. 7). lib. bdg. 23.95 (978-1-4222-3279-8(4)) Mason Crest.

—Porsche, Vol. 8. 2015. (Classic Cars & Bikes Collection). (Illus.). 64p. (J). (gr. 7). lib. bdg. 23.95 (978-1-4222-3281-1(6)) Mason Crest.

Parker, Felicity. Big Machines to Spot. 2009. (Spotter's Cards Ser.). 50p. (J). 9.99 (978-0-7945-2645-0(4), Usborne) EDC Publishing.

Parker, Steve. Cars. Sweet, Stephen, illus. 2005. (Twenty4Sevens Ser.). 48p. (J). pap. (978-0-439-78528-0(6)) Scholastic, Inc.

—Cars Trucks & Bikes. 2010. (How It Works Ser.). (Illus.). 40p. (J). (gr. 3-18). lib. bdg. 19.95 (978-1-4222-1792-4(2), 1317905) Mason Crest.

Pedal to the Metal: A History of Cars. 2005. (Book Treks Ser.). (J). 37.95 (978-0-7652-3249-6(9)) Celebration Pr.

Peppas, Lynn. Camaro. 2012. (ENG.). 64p. (J). pap. (978-0-7787-2106-2(X)) Crabtree Publishing Co.

—Corvette. Crabtree Staff, ed. 2010. (ENG.). 64p. (J). pap. (978-0-7787-2148-2(5)) Crabtree Publishing Co.

Petrie, Kristin. Automobiles, 1 vol. 2009. (Everyday Inventions Ser.). (ENG., Illus.). 32p. (gr. 3-6). 27.07 (978-1-60453-083-4(9), Checkerboard Library) ABDO Publishing Co.

Petty, Kate. The Encyclopedia of Awesome Machines. Watton, Ross & Moore, Jo, illus. 2003. 112p. (J). (gr. 4-8). reprint ed. 15.00 (978-0-7567-6963-5(9)) DIANE Publishing Co.

Phillips, Hamilton. Inside a Stock Car. 2014. (Life in the Fast Lane Ser.). 48p. (J). (gr. 4-6). lib. bdg. 31.36 (978-1-62713-040-0(3)) Cavendish Square Publishing.

Picthall, Chez & Gunzi. My Favourite Cars Sticker Book. Rayner, Katy, ed. rev. ed. 2015. (ENG., Illus.). 12p. (J). pap. 7.99 (978-1-907604-01-0(4)) Award Pubns. Ltd. GBR. Dist: Parkwest Pubns., Inc.

Piehl, Janet. Indy Race Cars. 2007. (Illus.). 48p. (J). pap. 8.95 (978-0-8225-6870-4(5)); (ENG., (gr. 4-7). lib. bdg. 26.60 (978-0-8225-6566-6(8)) Lerner Publishing Group.

Polydoros, Lori & Maurer, Tracy Nelson. Super Speed. 2013. (Super Speed Ser.). (ENG.). 32p. (gr. 1-2). lib. bdg. 186.55 (978-1-4765-0319-6(2)); lib. bdg. 106.60 (978-1-4765-0318-9(4)) Capstone Press of Coughlan Cos. (Blazers).

Poolos, J. Hot Rods. Alaman, Eduardo, tr. from ENG. 2007. (Wild Rides / Autos de Locura Ser.). (SPA., Illus.). 24p. (J). (gr. 2-5). lib. bdg. 22.60 (978-1-4042-7638-3(6)) Rosen Publishing Group, Inc., The.

—Lowriders. Alaman, Eduardo, tr. from ENG. 2007. (Wild Rides / Autos de Locura Ser.). (SPA., Illus.). 24p. (YA). (gr. 2-5). lib. bdg. 22.60 (978-1-4042-7636-9(X)) Rosen Publishing Group, Inc., The.

—Muscle Cars/Autos de Poder. Alaman, Eduardo, tr. from ENG. 2007. (Wild Rides / Autos de Locura Ser.). (SPA., Illus.). 24p. (J). (gr. 2-5). lib. bdg. 22.60 (978-1-4042-7639-0(4)) Rosen Publishing Group, Inc., The.

—Wild about Hot Rods. 2007. (Wild Rides Ser.). (Illus.). 24p. (J). (gr. 2-5). lib. bdg. 22.60 (978-1-4042-3790-2(9)) Rosen Publishing Group, Inc., The.

—Wild about Muscle Cars. 2007. (Wild Rides Ser.). (Illus.). 24p. (J). (gr. 2-5). lib. bdg. 22.60 (978-1-4042-3788-9(7)) Rosen Publishing Group, Inc., The.

—Wild about Muscle Cars/Autos de Poder. 2009. (Wild Rides/Autos de locura Ser.). (SPA.). 24p. (gr. 2-3). 42.50 (978-1-60854-809-5(0), Editorial Buenas Letras) Rosen Publishing Group, Inc., The.

Porter, Steve. Sports Cars. 2014. (You Can Draw It! Ser.). (ENG., Illus.). 24p. (J). (gr. 3-8). lib. bdg. 25.95 (978-1-62617-099-5(1), Express Bks.) Bellwether Media.

Portman, Michael. Chargers. 2011. (Wild Wheels Ser.). (Illus.). 32p. (J). (gr. 3-6). lib. bdg. 26.60 (978-1-4339-4739-1(0), Gareth Stevens Learning Library) Stevens, Gareth Publishing LLLP.

—Mustangs. 2011. (Wild Wheels Ser.). (Illus.). 32p. (J). (gr. 3-6). lib. bdg. 26.60 (978-1-4339-4751-3(X), Gareth Stevens Learning Library) Stevens, Gareth Publishing LLLP.

Power, Bob. Dodge Vipers. 2011. (Wild Wheels Ser.). 32p. (J). (gr. 3-6). pap. 10.50 (978-1-4339-5824-3(4)); lib. bdg. 26.60 (978-1-4339-5822-9(8)) Stevens, Gareth Publishing LLLP. (Gareth Stevens Learning Library).

—Lamborghinis. 2011. (Wild Wheels Ser.). (Illus.). 32p. (J). (gr. 3-6). 26.60 (978-1-4339-5830-4(9)); pap. 10.50 (978-1-4339-5832-8(5)) Stevens, Gareth Publishing LLLP. (Gareth Stevens Learning Library).

—Maseratis. 2011. (Wild Wheels Ser.). (Illus.). 32p. (J). (gr. 3-6). 26.60 (978-1-4339-5834-2(1)); pap. 10.50 (978-1-4339-5836-6(8)) Stevens, Gareth Publishing LLLP. (Gareth Stevens Learning Library).

Prior, Jennifer. Zoom! How Cars Move, 1 vol. 2nd rev. ed. 2014. (TIME for KIDS(r) Nonfiction Readers Ser.). (ENG., Illus.). 28p. (J). (gr. 3-3). pap. 25.96 (978-1-4807-1072-6(5)) Shell Educational Publishing.

—Zoom! How Cars Move, 1 vol. 2nd rev. ed. 2011. (Nonfiction Readers Ser.). (ENG.). 28p. (J). (gr. 3-3). pap. 8.99 (978-1-4333-3657-7(X)) Teacher Created Materials, Inc.

Publications International Ltd. Staff. First Look & Find Cars Fast Friends. 2008. 16p. (J). bds. 9.98 (978-1-4127-9344-5(0)) Phoenix International Publications, Inc.

—Yesterday & Today Nascar. 2010. 144p. 18.98 (978-1-60553-336-0(X)) Publications International, Ltd.

Publications International Ltd. Staff, ed. Cars My First Look & Find. 2014. 16p. (J). bds. (978-1-4508-8210-1(2), 1450882102) Phoenix International Publications, Inc.

—Yesterday & Today: Chevrolet. 2009. (Illus.). 160p. (978-1-60553-337-7(8), 1605533378) Publications International, Ltd.

Quinlan, Julia J. Aston Martin. 2013. (Speed Machines Ser.). 32p. (J). (gr. 3-6). 25.25 (978-1-4777-0807-1(3)); pap. 10.00 (978-1-4777-0986-3(X)) Rosen Publishing Group, Inc., The. (PowerKids Pr.).

—Audi. 2013. (Speed Machines Ser.). 32p. (J). (gr. 3-6). 25.25 (978-1-4777-0810-1(3)); pap. 10.00 (978-1-4777-0992-4(4)) Rosen Publishing Group, Inc., The. (PowerKids Pr.).

—Ferrari. 2012. (Speed Machines Ser.). (ENG., Illus.). 32p. (J). (gr. 3-6). 25.25 (978-1-4488-7457-6(2)); pap. 10.00 (978-1-4488-7529-0(3)) Rosen Publishing Group, Inc., The. (PowerKids Pr.).

—Jaguar. 2013. (Speed Machines Ser.). 32p. (J). (gr. 3-6). 25.25 (978-1-4777-0806-4(5)); pap. 10.00 (978-1-4777-1192-7(9)) Rosen Publishing Group, Inc., The. (PowerKids Pr.).

—Lotus. 2013. (Speed Machines Ser.). 32p. (J). (gr. 3-6). pap. 10.00 (978-1-4777-0984-9(3)); (ENG., Illus.). lib. bdg. 25.25 (978-1-4777-0805-7(7)) Rosen Publishing Group, Inc., The. (PowerKids Pr.).

—Maserati. 2013. (Speed Machines Ser.). 32p. (J). (gr. 3-6). 25.25 (978-1-4777-0808-8(1)); pap. 10.00 (978-1-4777-0988-7(6)) Rosen Publishing Group, Inc., The. (PowerKids Pr.).

—Mercedes. 2013. (Speed Machines Ser.). 32p. (J). (gr. 3-6). 25.25 (978-1-4777-0809-5(X)); pap. 10.00 (978-1-4777-0990-0(8)) Rosen Publishing Group, Inc., The. (PowerKids Pr.).

Race Cars: Science Technology Engineering. 2014. (Calling All Innovators: a Career for You Ser.). (ENG.). 64p. (J). lib. bdg. 32.00 (978-0-531-20614-0(9)) Scholastic Library Publishing.

Randolph, Joanne. Police Cars. 2009. (To the Rescue! Ser.). 24p. (gr. 1-1). 42.50 (978-1-60854-398-4(6), PowerKids Pr.) Rosen Publishing Group, Inc., The.

—Police Cars/Patrullas. 2009. (To the Rescue! / ¡Al rescate! Ser.). (ENG & SPA.). 24p. (gr. 1-1). 42.50 (978-1-60854-404-2(4), Editorial Buenas Letras) Rosen Publishing Group, Inc., The.

—Tow Trucks. 2008. (To the Rescue! Ser.). (Illus.). 24p. (J). (gr. -1-3). lib. bdg. 22.60 (978-1-4042-4154-1(X), PowerKids Pr.) Rosen Publishing Group, Inc., The.

—Tow Trucks/Gruas. Alaman, Eduardo, tr. from ENG. 2008. (To the Rescue! / ¡Al Rescate! Ser.). (Illus.). 24p. (J). (gr. 4-7). lib. bdg. 22.60 (978-1-4042-7675-8(0), Editorial Buenas Letras) Rosen Publishing Group, Inc., The.

Random House. 1 2 3 Blaze! (Blaze & the Monster Machines) Pixel Mouse House LLC, illus. 2016. (ENG.). 24p. (J). (— 1). bds. 6.99 (978-1-101-93679-5(7), Random Hse. Bks. for Young Readers) Random Hse. Children's Bks.

Rau, Dana Meachen. Cars. 2009. (Bookworms Ser.). 24p. (gr. k-1). 15.95 (978-0-7614-4078-9(X)) Marshall Cavendish Corp.

—Cars/En Carros. 2009. (Bookworms Ser.). (SPA & ENG.). 24p. (gr. k-1). lib. bdg. 15.95 (978-0-7614-4769-6(5)) Marshall Cavendish Corp.

Richards, Jon. Design It Yourself Supercars. Araujo, Paige Krul, ed. 2005. (Design It Yourself Ser.). (ENG., Illus.). 32p. (J). (gr. 4-7). pap. 9.99 (978-0-439-71607-9(1)) Scholastic, Inc.

Riggs, Kate. Seedlings: Indy Cars. 2015. (Seedlings Ser.). (ENG.). 24p. (J). (gr. -1-1). pap. 7.99 (978-1-62832-120-3(2), Creative Paperbacks) Creative Co., The.

—Stock Cars. 2010. (Now That's Fast! Ser.). 24p. (J). (gr. -1-3). 16.95 (978-1-58341-916-8(0), Creative Education) Creative Co., The.

Rosario, Miguel. Car Math. 2015. (J). lib. bdg. (978-1-62713-442-2(5)) Cavendish Square Publishing.

Rose, Simon. Mechanic. 2014. (J). (978-1-4896-2990-6(4)) Weigl Pubs., Inc.

Rowe, Barry & Doyle, Garry. Atmosphere & Light: The Automotive Paintings of Barry Rowe. 2004. (Illus.). 224p. 125.00 (978-1-893618-34-3(X)) Bull, David Publishing, Inc.

Ruck, Colleen. Cars. 2011. (My Favorite Machines Ser.). 24p. (gr. 2-5). 28.50 (978-1-59920-673-8(0)) Black Rabbit Bks.

Salzmann, Mary Elizabeth. Automobile, 1 vol. 2016. (ENG., Illus.). 24p. (J). (978-1-62403-708-5(9)) ABDO Publishing Co.

Sandler, Michael. Fast Rides, 4 vols., Set. Incl. Dynamic Drag Racers. (YA). lib. bdg. 22.61 (978-1-61772-138-0(7)); Electrifying Eco Race Cars. (J). lib. bdg. 22.61 (978-1-61772-137-3(9)); Hot Hot Rods. (J). lib. bdg. 22.61 (978-1-61772-139-7(5)); Jet-Powered Speed. (YA). lib. bdg. 22.61 (978-1-61772-136-6(0)); (gr. 2-5). 24p. 2011. Set lib. bdg. 90.44 (978-1-61772-135-9(2)) Bearport Publishing Co., Inc.

—Jet-Powered Speed. 2011. (Fast Rides Ser.). 24p. (YA). (gr. 2-5). lib. bdg. 22.61 (978-1-61772-136-6(0)) Bearport Publishing Co., Inc.

Sautter, Aaron. How to Draw Incredible Cars, 1 vol. Bascle, Brian, illus. 2007. (Drawing Cool Stuff Ser.). (ENG.). 32p. (gr. 3-4). 27.99 (978-1-4296-0077-4(2), Edge Bks.) Capstone Press of Coughlan Cos.

Savage, Jeff. Tuner Cars, 1 vol. 2010. (Full Throttle Ser.). (ENG.). 32p. (gr. 3-4). lib. bdg. 27.99 (978-1-4296-4750-2(7), Edge Bks.) Capstone Press of Coughlan Cos.

Scheff, Matt. Indy Cars, 1 vol. 2014. (Speed Machines Ser.). (ENG.). 32p. (gr. 3-6). lib. bdg. 27.07 (978-1-62403-611-8(2), SportsZone) ABDO Publishing Co.

Scholastic, Inc. Staff, contrib. by. Counting Cars & Trucks. 2016. (Rookie Toddlers Ser.). (ENG.). 12p. (J). bds. 6.95 (978-0-531-22453-3(8), Children's Pr.) Scholastic Library Publishing.

Sexton, Susan. Sprint Car Racing: Unleashing the Power. 2003. (Cover-To-Cover Books). (Illus.). 68p. pap. 8.95 (978-0-7891-5884-0(1)) Perfection Learning Corp.

—Sprint Car Racing: Unleashing the Power. 2003. (Cover-to-Cover Informational Ser.). (Illus.). 68p. (J). (gr. 4-7). lib. bdg. 17.95 (978-0-7569-1144-7(3)) Perfection Learning Corp.

Sharkey, Alex. Classic Cars, Vol. 8. 2015. (Classic Cars & Bikes Collection). 64p. (J). (gr. 7). lib. bdg. 23.95 (978-1-4222-3278-1(6)) Mason Crest.

Shelly, Jeff. Cars & Trucks: Step by Step Instructions for 28 Different Vehicles. 2004. (Learn to Draw Ser.). (ENG., Illus.). 40p. (J). (gr. 1-3). per. 4.95 (978-1-56010-819-1(3), 1560108193) Quarto Publishing Group USA.

Silverman, Buffy. How Do Formula One Race Cars Work? 2016. (Lightning Bolt Books (tm) — How Vehicles Work Ser.). (ENG.). 32p. (J). (gr. 1-3). lib. bdg. 26.65 (978-1-4677-9503-6(8)) Lerner Publishing Group.

Sodaro, Craig, et al. Dream Cars. 2015. (Dream Cars Ser.). (ENG.). 32p. (gr. 3-4). lib. bdg. 111.96 (978-1-4914-2549-7(0), Edge Bks.) Capstone Press of Coughlan Cos.

Spaulding, Jeffrey. The Most Victorious Cars of NASCAR Racing. (Highlights of NASCAR Racing Ser.). 48p. (gr. 5-5). 2009. 53.00 (978-1-61513-302-4(X), Rosen Reference) 2008. (Illus.). (YA). lib. bdg. 29.25 (978-1-4042-1398-2(8)) Rosen Publishing Group, Inc., The.

Steedman, Scott. Cars. 2015. (Wonderwise Ser.). (Illus.). 32p. (gr. 2-6). 31.35 (978-1-62588-359-9(5)) Black Rabbit Bks.

Sterling Publishing Co., Inc. Things That Go. 2012. (Say & Play Ser.). (ENG., Illus.). 28p. (J). (gr. k — 1). bds. 4.95 (978-1-4027-9894-8(6)) Sterling Publishing Co., Inc.

Storey, Rita. How to Build Cars. 2017. (Illus.). 32p. (J). **(978-0-7787-3393-5(9))** Crabtree Publishing Co.

Tagnetti, Stefano & Watt, Fiona. Busy Car. 2011. (Pull-Back Bks). 10p. (J). ring bd. 24.99 (978-0-7945-3071-6(0), Usborne) EDC Publishing.

Tatge, Cathy. Cars. 2007. (My First Look at: Vehicles Ser.). (Illus.). 24p. (J). (gr. -1-3). lib. bdg. 24.25 (978-1-58341-527-6(0), Creative Education) Creative Co., The.

Tejido, Jomike, illus. Things That Go. 2017. (Jumbo Stickers for Little Hands Ser.). (ENG.). 24p. (J). (gr. -1-k). pap. 7.95 (978-1-63322-157-4(1), Moondance) Quarto Publishing Group USA.

Tieck, Sarah. Indy Cars, 1 vol. 2009. (Amazing Vehicles Ser.). (ENG., Illus.). 32p. (gr. 2-5). 28.50 (978-1-60453-542-6(3), Big Buddy Bks.) ABDO Publishing Co.

Tiner, John Hudson. Cars. (Illus.). 32p. 2004. pap. 8.95 (978-0-89812-388-3(7), Creative Paperbacks) 2003. (J). lib. bdg. 18.95 (978-1-58341-256-5(5), Creative Education) Creative Co., The.

Top That Publishing Staff, ed. Fast Cars. 2005. (Illus.). 24p. (978-1-84510-536-5(2)) Top That! Publishing PLC.

Top That! Kids, creator. Things That Go. 2008. (Magnetic Play & Learn Ser.). (ENG., Illus.). 12p. (J). (gr. -1-k). (978-1-84510-726-0(8)) Top That! Publishing PLC.

Troupe, Thomas Kingsley. Crush It!, 1 vol. 2013. (Destruction Ser.). (ENG.). 24p. (gr. k-1). lib. bdg. 26.65 (978-1-4765-2088-9(7), Pebble Plus) Capstone Press of Coughlan Cos.

Trucks & Cars. 2003. 32p. 12.98 (978-1-4054-2006-8(5)) Parragon, Inc.

Tudhope, Simon. Build Your Own Cars Sticker Book. Shirley, John, illus. 2013. (ENG.). 23p. (J). (gr. -1-3). 8.99 (978-0-7945-3379-3(5), Usborne) EDC Publishing.

Turner, Tracy. Supercars. 2015. (Head-To-Head Ser.). (ENG., Illus.). 24p. (gr. 3-8). 28.50 (978-1-62588-150-2(9)) Black Rabbit Bks.

Von Finn, Denny. Concept Cars. 2009. (Cool Rides Ser.). (ENG., Illus.). 24p. (J). (gr. 3-7). lib. bdg. 25.95 (978-1-60014-276-5(1)) Bellwether Media.

—Sprint Cars. 2009. (Torque Ser.). (ENG.). 24p. (J). (gr. 3-7). 20.00 (978-0-531-21740-5(X), Children's Pr.) Scholastic Library Publishing.

—Super Cars. 2009. (World's Fastest Ser.). (ENG., Illus.). 24p. (J). (gr. 3-7). lib. bdg. 25.95 (978-1-60014-289-5(3), Torque Bks.) Bellwether Media.

—Torque: Funny Cars. 2009. (Torque Ser.). (ENG.). 24p. (J). (gr. 3-7). 20.00 (978-0-531-21738-2(8), Children's Pr.) Scholastic Library Publishing.

—Torque - Cool Rides, 4 vols., Set. Incl. Snowmobiles. 20.00 (978-0-531-21739-9(6)); Sprint Cars. 20.00 (978-0-531-21740-5(X)); Torque: 4X4 Trucks. 20.00 (978-0-531-21741-2(8)); Torque: Funny Cars. 20.00 (978-0-531-21738-2(8)); 24p. (J). (gr. 3-7). 2009. 2009. Set lib. bdg. 80.00 (978-0-531-26136-1(0), Children's Pr.) Scholastic Library Publishing.

Walker, Robert. Maserati. 2012. (ENG.). 64p. (J). (978-0-7787-2102-4(7)); pap. (978-0-7787-2107-9(8)) Crabtree Publishing Co.

—Porsche. Crabtree, ed. 2010. (Superstar Cars Ser.). (ENG.). 64p. (J). pap. (978-0-7787-2153-6(1)) Crabtree Publishing Co.

Walt Disney Company Staff & Phidal Publishing Staff, contrib. by. Cars. 2006. (Illus.). 24p. (978-2-7643-0261-3(4)) Phidal Publishing, Inc./Editions Phidal, Inc.

Ward, Ian. Cars & How They Work. (Magic Machines Ser.). 10p. (978-1-4054-9137-2(X)) Parragon, Inc.

Warhol, Tom. Aptera. 2010. (Green Cars Ser.). 48p. (J). (gr. 3-6). 28.50 (978-1-60870-008-0(9)) Marshall Cavendish Corp.

—Smart Car. 2010. (Green Cars Ser.). (Illus.). 48p. (J). (gr. 3-6). 28.50 (978-1-60870-012-7(7)) Marshall Cavendish Corp.

Watson, Stephanie. What Is the Future of Self-Driving Cars? 2016. (ENG.). 80p. (J). (gr. 5-12). (978-1-68282-064-3(5)) ReferencePoint Pr., Inc.

Watt, Fiona. That's Not My Car. Wells, Rachel, illus. 2004. (Touchy-Feely Board Books Ser.). 10p. (J). 7.95 (978-0-7945-0636-0(4), Usborne) EDC Publishing.

Waxman, Laura Hamilton. Terrific Transportation Inventions. 2013. (Awesome Inventions You Use Every Day Ser.). (ENG., Illus.). 32p. (gr. 3-6). lib. bdg. 26.60 (978-1-4677-1096-1(2), Lerner Pubns.) Lerner Publishing Group.

Weber, Belinda & Butterfield, Moira. I Wonder Why Cars Go Fast. 2014. (I Wonder Why Ser.). (ENG., Illus.). 24p. (J). (gr. k-3). act. bk. ed. 6.99 (978-0-7534-7141-8(8), 9780753471418, Kingfisher) Roaring Brook Pr.

Weiss, Ellen. Math in the Car. 2007. (Scholastic News Nonfiction Readers Ser.). (ENG., Illus.). 24p. (J). (gr. 1-2). 22.00 (978-0-531-18530-8(3)) Scholastic Library Publishing.

Werther, Scott P. Long Limosines / Limosinas Largas. 2009. (Extreme Machines / Máquinas extremas Ser.). (ENG & SPA.). 24p. (gr. 1-2). 42.50 (978-1-61512-447-3(0), Editorial Buenas Letras) Rosen Publishing Group, Inc., The.

West, David. Race Cars. 2015. (Mechanic Mike's Machines (continuation) Ser.). (Illus.). 24p. (J). (gr. k-3). 27.10 (978-1-62588-065-9(0)) Black Rabbit Bks.

Wick, Walter. Trucks & Cars. Wick, Walter, photos by. 2007. (Can You See What I See? Ser.). (ENG., Illus.). 16p. (J). (gr. k — 1). bds. 5.99 (978-0-439-86230-1(2), Cartwheel Bks.) Scholastic, Inc.

Winget, Mary. Taxis. 2007. (Pull Ahead Bks.). (ENG., Illus.). 32p. (J). pap. 5.95 (978-0-8225-6425-6(4), First Avenue Editions) Lerner Publishing Group.

Winget, Mary & Winget, W. Bryan. Tow Trucks. 2006. (Pull Ahead Books-Mighty Movers Ser.). (ENG., Illus.). 32p. (gr. k-3). lib. bdg. 22.60 (978-0-8225-6006-7(2), Lerner Pubns.) Lerner Publishing Group.

Woods, Bob. Hottest Muscle Cars. 2007. (Wild Wheels! Ser.). (Illus.). 48p. (J). (gr. 4-10). lib. bdg. 25.27 (978-0-7660-2872-2(0)) Enslow Pubs., Inc.

—Smokin' Muscle Cars. (Fast Wheels! Ser.). 48p. (J). (gr. 4-9). 2014. pap. 8.95 (978-1-62285-091-4(2)) 2013. 14.95 (978-1-62285-090-7(4)) Enslow Pubs., Inc.

—Smokin' Sports Cars. (Fast Wheels! Ser.). 48p. (J). (gr. 4-9). 2014. pap. 8.95 (978-1-62285-106-5(4)) 2013. 14.95 (978-1-62285-105-8(6)) Enslow Pubs., Inc.

Worms, Penny. Eco Cars. 2016. (Motormania Ser.). 32p. (gr. 2-7). 31.35 (978-1-59920-994-4(2), Smart Apple Media) Black Rabbit Bks.

—Sports Cars. 2016. (Motormania Ser.). 32p. (gr. 2-7). 31.35 (978-1-59920-993-7(4), Smart Apple Media) Black Rabbit Bks.

Wright, Nicky. Mustang: The American Muscle Car. 2017. (Speed Rules! Inside the World's Hottest Cars Ser.: Vol. 8). (ENG., Illus.). (YA). (gr. 7-12). 25.95 **(978-1-4222-3835-6(0))** Mason Crest.

Yoyo Books, creator. Vroom. 2011. (Baby's First Library). (ENG., Illus.). 38p. (gr. -1-k). bds. (978-90-8622-910-9(7)) YoYo Bks.

Zabludoff, Marc. Ebox. 2010. (Green Cars Ser.). 48p. (J). (gr. 3-6). 28.50 (978-1-60870-009-7(7)) Marshall Cavendish Corp.

Zronik, John Paul & Zronik, John. Street Cred. 2006. (Automania! Ser.). (ENG., Illus.). 32p. (J). (gr. 4-7). pap. (978-0-7787-3028-6(X)); lib. bdg. (978-0-7787-3006-4(9)) Crabtree Publishing Co.

Zuehlke, Jeffrey. Concept Cars. 2007. (Motor Mania Ser.). (Illus.). 48p. (J). pap. 8.95 (978-0-8225-6868-1(3), Lerner Pubns.); (ENG., (gr. 4-7). lib. bdg. 26.60 (978-0-8225-6568-0(4)) Lerner Publishing Group.

—Muscle Cars. 2006. (Motor Mania Ser.). (Illus.). 48p. (J). (gr. 3-7). lib. bdg. 26.60 (978-0-8225-5927-6(7), Lerner Pubns.) Lerner Publishing Group.

AUTOMOBILES—ACCIDENTS

see Traffic Accidents

AUTOMOBILES—DESIGN AND CONSTRUCTION

Aloian, Sam. How a Car Is Made. 2016. (Engineering Our World Ser.). (ENG.). 24p. (J). (gr. 2-3). pap. 8.15 (978-1-4824-3923-6(9)) Stevens, Gareth Publishing LLLP.

Balmer, Alden J. Mousetrap Racers: The Complete Builder's Manual - Science Secrets You'll Need to Win. 2008. (ENG., Illus.). 144p. (gr. 7-18). pap. 14.95 (978-1-56523-359-1(X), 3591D) Fox Chapel Publishing Co., Inc.

Banting, Erinn. Inventing the Automobile. 2006. (Breakthrough Inventions Ser.). (ENG., Illus.). 32p. (J). (gr. 3-7). pap. (978-0-7787-2834-4(X)) Crabtree Publishing Co.

Car Designer. 2008. (Cool Creations Style Folder Ser.). 32p. pap. (978-1-4075-1650-9(7)) Parragon, Inc.

Currie, Stephen. Self-Driving Car. 2016. (Tech Bytes Ser.). (ENG.). 48p. (J). (gr. 4-6). pap. 13.26 (978-1-60357-870-7(6)); (Illus.). lib. bdg. 26.60 (978-1-59953-762-7(1)) Norwood Hse. Pr.

DeBoard, Will. Building a Stock Car. 2008. (World of NASCAR Ser.). (ENG., Illus.). 32p. (J). (gr. 3-6). 28.50 (978-1-60253-073-7(4), 200991) Child's World, Inc., The.

Economy, Peter. We Both Read-New Car Design. 2010. (Illus.). 44p. (J). (ENG.). 9.95 (978-1-60115-243-5(4)); pap. 4.99 (978-1-60115-244-2(2)) Treasure Bay, Inc.

Gardner, Jane P. Car Science, Vol. 11. Lewin, Russ, ed. 2015. (Science 24/7 Ser.). (Illus.). 48p. (J). (gr. 5). 20.95 (978-1-4222-3406-8(1)) Mason Crest.

Graham, Ian. Cars, 1 vol. 2013. (Design & Engineering for STEM Ser.). (ENG., Illus.). 56p. (gr. 6-8). pap. 9.99 (978-1-4329-7035-2(6), NA-h); lib. bdg. 34.65 (978-1-4329-7030-7(5)) Heinemann-Raintree.

—Fast Cars. 2009. (How Machines Work Ser.). (Illus.). 32p. (J). pap. (978-1-897563-43-4(4)) Saunders Bk. Co.

Green, Robert. Cars. 2008. (21st Century Skills Library: Global Products Ser.). (ENG., Illus.). 32p. (gr. 4-8). lib. bdg. 28.50 (978-1-60279-028-5(0), 200199) Cherry Lake Publishing.

Hammelef, Danielle S. Building a Car, 1 vol. 2014. (See How It's Made Ser.). (ENG.). 32p. (gr. 1-2). lib. bdg. 26.65 (978-1-4765-3976-8(6), Blazers) Capstone Press of Coughlan Cos.

Hammond, Richard & Dorling Kindersley Publishing Staff. Car Science. 2008. (ENG.). 96p. (J). (gr. 2-5). 19.99 (978-0-7566-4026-2(1), DK Children) Dorling Kindersley Publishing, Inc.

Kenney, Karen Latchana. The Science of Car Racing, 1 vol. 2014. (Science of Speed Ser.). (ENG.). 48p. (gr. 3-4). lib. bdg. 31.99 (978-1-4765-3910-2(3)) Capstone Press of Coughlan Cos.

Knudsen, Shannon. From Iron to Car. 2013. (Start to Finish, Second Series: Everyday Products Ser.). (ENG., Illus.). 24p. (gr. k-3). lib. bdg. 23.93 (978-0-7613-9182-1(7), Lerner Pubns.) Lerner Publishing Group.

Llewellyn, Claire. Making a Car. Jonatronix, illus. 2016. (Cambridge Reading Adventures Ser.). (ENG.). 16p. pap. 6.56 (978-1-107-57597-4(4)) Cambridge Univ. Pr.

Morris, Neil. Transportation, 1 vol. 2010. (From Fail to Win! Learning from Bad Ideas Ser.). (ENG., Illus.). 56p. (gr. 5-8). 34.65 (978-1-4109-3911-1(1), Raintree Freestyle) Heinemann-Raintree.

Oxlade, Chris. Design Line: Planes, Trains, & Automobiles. Lemanski, Mike, illus. 2014. (ENG.). 16p. (J). (gr. k-12). 17.99 (978-0-7636-7121-1(5), Big Picture Press) Candlewick Pr.

Petruccio, Steven James. Cars: Doodle, Design & Draw. 2011. (Dover Doodle Bks.). (ENG., Illus.). 64p. (J). (gr. 3-5). pap. 5.99 (978-0-486-48055-8(0)) Dover Pubns., Inc.

Sodomka, Martin & Lacey, Saskia. How to Build a Car. 2015. (Technical Tales Ser.). (ENG., Illus.). 64p. (J). (gr. 1-3). 14.95 (978-1-63322-040-9(0)) Quarto Publishing Group USA.

Stewart, Mark & Kennedy, Mike. The Science of NASCAR, 6 vols., Set. Incl. NASCAR at the Track. lib. bdg. 27.93 (978-0-8225-8741-5(6)); NASCAR Behind the Scenes. (Illus.). (YA). lib. bdg. 27.93 (978-0-8225-8743-9(2));

NASCAR Designed to Win. (Illus.). (YA). lib. bdg. 27.93 *(978-0-8225-8736-1(X))*; NASCAR in the Driver's Seat. (Illus.). lib. bdg. 27.93 *(978-0-8225-8737-8(8))*; NASCAR in the Pits. (Illus.). lib. bdg. 27.93 *(978-0-8225-8738-5(6))*; 48p. (gr. 4-7). 2008. (Science of NASCAR Ser.). (ENG.). 2008. Set lib. bdg. 55.86 *(978-0-8225-8735-4(1))* Lerner Publishing Group.

Townsend, John. Cars & Motorcycles, 1 vol. 2011. (Sci-Hi: Science & Technology Ser.). (ENG., Illus.). 48p. (gr. 4-4). pap. 9.95 *(978-1-4109-4278-4(3)*, Sci-Hi) Heinemann-Raintree.

Zemlicka, Shannon. From Iron to Car. (Start to Finish, Second Series: Everyday Products Ser.). (ENG., Illus.). 24p. (gr. k-3). 2013. pap. 6.95 *(978-1-4677-0795-4(3))* 2003. 19.93 *(978-0-8225-0943-1(1)*, Lerner Pubns.) Lerner Publishing Group.

AUTOMOBILES—DRIVING

see Automobile Drivers

AUTOMOBILES—ENGINES

Bankston, John. Karl Benz & the Single Cylinder Engine. 2004. (Uncharted, Unexplored, & Unexplained Ser.). (Illus.). 48p. (J). (gr. 4-8). lib. bdg. 29.95 *(978-1-58415-244-6(3))* Mitchell Lane Pubs., Inc.

Nagle, Jeanne. Reducing Your Carbon Footprint at School. 2008. (Your Carbon Footprint Ser.). (Illus.). 48p. (YA). (gr. 5-9). lib. bdg. 29.25 *(978-1-4042-1774-4(6)*, 1284467) Rosen Publishing Group, Inc., The.

Porter, Esther. Peeking under the Hood. Lozano, Andres, illus. 2016. (What's Beneath Ser.). (ENG.). 32p. (gr. -1-3). lib. bdg. 27.32 *(978-1-4795-8667-7(6))* Picture Window Bks.

World Book, Inc Staff, contrib. by. Green Transportation. 2008. (J). *(978-0-7166-1405-0(7))* World Bk., Inc.

AUTOMOBILES—FICTION

Alexander, Jenny. Taxi about Town. 2010. (ENG., Illus.). 64p. (J). *(978-0-340-98149-8(0)*, Hodder Children's Books) Hachette Children's Group GBR. Dist: Hachette Bk. Group.

Appleton, Victor. Tom Swift & His Electric Runabout. 2007. 224p. 29.95 *(978-1-4344-9462-7(4))*; per. 19.95 *(978-1-4344-9461-0(6))* Wildside Pr., LLC.

—Tom Swift & His Electric Runabout or T. 2006. pap. *(978-1-4065-0901-4(9))* Dodo Pr.

—Tom Swift & his War Tank. 2005. 212p. pap. 12.95 *(978-1-4218-1605-0(9)*, 1st World Library - Literary Society) 1st World Publishing, Inc.

Aroner, Miriam. Clink Clank Clunk! Catalano, Dominic, illus. 2006. (ENG.). 32p. (J). (gr. -1-1). 15.95 *(978-1-59078-270-5(4))* Boyds Mills Pr.

AZ Books Staff. Fast Vehicles Moving & Talking. Harko, Lubov, ed. 2012. (Funny Trails Ser.). (ENG.). 10p. (J). (gr. -1-k). bds. 9.95 *(978-1-61889-177-8(4))* AZ Bks. LLC.

—Sam the Auto Mechanic. Boroda, Janna, ed. 2012. (Little Master Ser.). (ENG.). 10p. (J). (gr. -1-k). bds. 10.95 *(978-1-61889-148-8(0))* AZ Bks. LLC.

Barbot, Daniel. El Auto del Sr. Pulga. Mas, Maribel, illus. 2004. (SPA.). 28p. (J). pap. 6.99 *(978-980-257-260-1(8))* Ekare, Ediciones VEN. Dist: Lectorum Pubns., Inc.

Barton, Byron. My Car. Barton, Byron, illus. (Illus.). (J). (gr. -1-3). 2016. 40p. pap. 6.99 *(978-0-06-239960-1(8))* 2003. (ENG., 36p. bds. 7.99 *(978-0-06-056045-4(2))* 2004. (ENG., 40p. reprint ed. pap. 6.99 *(978-0-06-058940-0(X))* HarperCollins Pubs. (Greenwillow Bks.).

—My Car. 2004. (Illus.). 32p. (gr. -1-1). 17.00 *(978-0-7569-4589-3(5))* Perfection Learning Corp.

Baxter, Nicola. Chase That Car! A First Reading Adventure Book. Glover, Peter, illus. 2016. (ENG.). 24p. (J). (gr. -1-12). pap. 6.99 *(978-1-86147-756-9(2)*, Armadillo) Anness Publishing GBR. Dist: National Bk. Network.

Bee, William. And the Cars Go... Bee, William, illus. 2013. (ENG., Illus.). 32p. (J). (-k). 15.99 *(978-0-7636-6580-7(0))* Candlewick Pr.

Bell, Babs. Sputter, Sputter, Sput! Staake, Bob, illus. 2008. 32p. (J). (gr. -1-k). lib. bdg. 17.89 *(978-0-06-056223-6(4))* HarperCollins Pubs.

Bender, Carol. The Doctor's Little Stowaway. 2009. 28p. pap. 13.99 *(978-1-4490-3711-6(9))* AuthorHouse.

Beresford, Elisabeth. Wombles Buggy Trouble. (Illus.). 15p. (J). (gr. k-6). pap. *(978-0-340-74670-7(X))* Hodder & Stoughton.

Berresford, J. R. Gerald Giraffe's Garage. Parmelee, George, illus. 2013. (ENG.). 32p. (J). (gr. -1-3). 11.95 *(978-0-9860321-0-3(7))* Tuscarora Publishing Company.

Berrios, Frank. Deputy Mater Saves the Day! (Disney/Pixar Cars) Random House Disney Staff, illus. 2013. (Little Golden Book Ser.). (ENG.). 24p. (J). (-k). 3.99 *(978-0-7364-2979-5(4)*, Golden/Disney) Random Hse. Children's Bks.

—The Easter Buggy. 2014. lib. bdg. 14.75 *(978-0-606-35543-8(X))* Turtleback Bks.

—The Easter Buggy (Disney/Pixar Cars) Random House Disney Staff, illus. 2014. (Pictureback(R) Ser.). (ENG.). 16p. (J). (gr. -1-2). 4.99 *(978-0-7364-3139-2(X)*, RH/Disney) Random Hse. Children's Bks.

—Lightning Loves Racing! (Disney/Pixar Cars) Random House Disney Staff, illus. 2013. (Pictureback(R) Ser.). (ENG.). 16p. (J). (gr. -1-2). 4.99 *(978-0-7364-3138-5(1)*, RH/Disney) Random Hse. Children's Bks.

—Lights Out!; Tow Truck Trouble. RH Disney Staff, illus. 2010. (Pictureback(R) Ser.). (ENG.). 32p. (J). (gr. -1-2). pap. 4.99 *(978-0-7364-2713-5(9)*, RH/Disney) Random Hse. Children's Bks.

—Mater to the Rescue! (Disney/Pixar Cars) Random House Disney Staff, illus. 2012. (Pictureback(R) Ser.). (ENG.). 16p. (J). (gr. -1-2). pap. 4.99 *(978-0-7364-2863-7(1)*, RH/Disney) Random Hse. Children's Bks.

—Time Travel Mater (Disney/Pixar Cars) RH Disney Staff, illus. 2013. (Pictureback(R) Ser.). (ENG.). 16p. (J). (gr. -1-2). 3.99 *(978-0-7364-3107-1(1)*, RH/Disney) Random Hse. Children's Bks.

—To Protect & Serve. Random House Disney Staff, illus. 2015. (Step into Reading Ser.). (ENG.). 24p. (J). (gr. -1-1). 4.99 *(978-0-7364-3282-5(5)*, RH/Disney) Random Hse. Children's Bks.

—To Protect & Serve. 2015. (Cars Step into Reading Ser.). lib. bdg. 14.75 *(978-0-606-36393-8(9))* Turtleback Bks.

Berrios, Frank & RH Disney Staff. Shapes, Colors, Counting & More! (Disney/Pixar Cars) RH Disney Staff, illus. 2013. (Friendship Box Ser.). (ENG., Illus.). 48p. (J). (gr. -1-2). bds. 10.99 *(978-0-7364-3105-7(5)*, RH/Disney) Random Hse. Children's Bks.

Biggs, Brian. Everything Goes: Henry in a Jam. Biggs, Brian & Abbott, Simon, illus. 2012. (My First I Can Read Ser.). (ENG.). 32p. (J). (gr. -1-3). 16.99 *(978-0-06-195819-9(0))* HarperCollins Pubs.

—Everything Goes: Henry in a Jam. 2012. (My First I Can Read Ser.). (J). lib. bdg. 13.55 *(978-0-606-23549-5(3)*, Turtleback) Turtleback Bks.

—Henry Goes Skating. Abbott, Simon, illus. 2012. (My First I Can Read Ser.). (J). lib. bdg. 13.55 *(978-0-606-26852-3(9)*, Turtleback) Turtleback Bks.

—Henry in a Jam. Biggs, Brian & Abbott, Simon, illus. 2012. (My First I Can Read Ser.). (ENG.). 32p. (J). (gr. -1-3). pap. 3.99 *(978-0-06-195818-2(2))* HarperCollins Pubs.

Biggs, Brian. Henry in a Jam. Abbott, Simon, illus. 2013. 32p. (J). ***(978-1-4351-5057-7(0))*** Barnes & Noble, Inc.

Billet, Marion. My First Camper Van. 2016. (Whizzy Wheels Ser.). (ENG., Illus.). 10p. (J). (— 1). bds. 11.99 *(978-1-5098-0426-9(9))* Pan Macmillan GBR. Dist: Independent Pubs. Group.

Biro, Val. Gumdrop All at Sea. 2015. (ENG., Illus.). 32p. (J). pap. 9.99 *(978-1-78270-046-3(3))* Award Pubns. Ltd. GBR. Dist: Parkwest Pubns., Inc.

—Gumdrop & the Secret Switches. 2015. (ENG., Illus.). 32p. (J). pap. 9.99 *(978-1-78270-047-0(1))* Award Pubns. Ltd. GBR. Dist: Parkwest Pubns., Inc.

Blackburn, Sheila M. Stewie Scraps & the Easy Rider. 2008. 72p. pap. *(978-1-903853-85-6(0))* Brilliant Pubns.

Blake, Quentin. Mrs. Armitage, Queen of the Road. Blake, Quentin, illus. 2003. (ENG., Illus.). 32p. (J). (gr. k-3). 15.95 *(978-1-56145-287-3(4))* Peachtree Pubs.

Bloom, Suzanne. Nuestro Autobus. 2008.Tr. of Bus for Us. (ENG & SPA., Illus.). 32p. (J). (gr. k-2). pap. 8.95 *(978-1-59078-629-1(7))* Boyds Mills Pr.

Boles, Jim. Ivan the Invacar Helps Big Dog. Cunningham, Bob, illus. 2012. 56p. pap. 19.95 *(978-0-9845983-5-9(9))* People Ink Pr.

Boles, S. Ivan the Invacar Saves the Wobbly Hubcap. Cunningham, Bob, illus. 2014. (J). pap. 7.95 *(978-0-9893267-3-5(X))* People Ink Pr.

Boyce, Frank Cottrell. Chitty Chitty Bang Bang & the Race Against Time. Berger, Joe, illus. (Chitty Chitty Bang Bang Ser.). (ENG.). 240p. (J). (gr. 4-7). 2014. pap. 6.99 *(978-0-7636-6931-7(8))* 2013. 15.99 *(978-0-7636-5982-0(7))* Candlewick Pr.

—Chitty Chitty Bang Bang Flies Again. Berger, Joe, illus. (Chitty Chitty Bang Bang Ser.). (ENG.). (J). (gr. 4-7). 2013. 224p. pap. 6.99 *(978-0-7636-6353-7(0))* 2012. 192p. 15.99 *(978-0-7636-5957-8(6))* Candlewick Pr.

—Chitty Chitty Bang Bang over the Moon. Berger, Joe, illus. (Chitty Chitty Bang Bang Ser.). (ENG.). (J). (gr. 4-7). 2015. 304p. pap. 6.99 *(978-0-7636-7666-7(7))* 2014. 240p. 15.99 *(978-0-7636-5983-7(5))* Candlewick Pr.

—Framed. (J). (gr. 3). 2008. (Illus.). 320p. per. 8.99 *(978-0-06-073404-6(3))* 2006. 306p. lib. bdg. 17.89 *(978-0-06-073403-9(5))* HarperCollins Pubs.

Bracken, Beth. Henry Helps Wash the Car, 1 vol. Busby, Ailie, illus. 2012. (Henry Helps Ser.). (ENG.). 24p. (gr. -1 — 1). pap. 5.95 *(978-1-4048-7671-2(5))*; lib. bdg. 22.65 *(978-1-4048-7304-9(X))* Picture Window Bks. (Henry Helps).

Brezenoff, Steve. Curses for Sale, 1 vol. Percival, Tom, illus. 2012. (Ravens Pass Ser.). (ENG.). 96p. (gr. 2-3). pap. 6.15 *(978-1-4342-4209-9(9))*; lib. bdg. 25.32 *(978-1-4342-3763-7(X))* Stone Arch Bks.

Brouillette, Peter. The Adventures of Old Henry: Nobody Cares. Lee, Williams, illus. 2004. (J). per. 19.99 *(978-0-9760419-3-1(6))* ThatsMyLife Co.

Bruna, Dick. On My Scooter. 2013. (ENG., Illus.). 28p. (J). (gr. -1-1). 7.95 *(978-1-84976-216-8(3))* Tate Publishing, Ltd. GBR. Dist: Abrams, Inc.

Calmenson, Stephanie. No Honking Allowed. Ferrari, Antongionata, illus. 2017. (ENG.). 40p. (J). 16.95 ***(978-0-8234-3672-9(1))*** Holiday Hse., Inc.

Carlson, Claudia, illus. Avi the Ambulance Goes to School. 2015. (J). *(978-0-87441-941-2(7))* Behrman Hse., Inc.

Christelow, Eileen. Five Little Monkeys Wash the Car. 2004. (Five Little Monkeys Story Ser.). (ENG., Illus.). 40p. (J). (gr. -1-3). 6.99 *(978-0-618-48602-1(X))* Houghton Mifflin Harcourt Publishing Co.

Clark, Betsy Huhn. Lizzie's Extraordinary Adventure. 2006. (Illus.). 24p. (J). 9.99 *(978-1-4276-0116-2(X))* Aardvark Global Publishing.

Clark, Carol. Eternity Express. 2009. 32p. pap. 10.95 *(978-0-9818488-6-0(9))* Ajoyin Publishing, Inc.

Colorful Cars. 2017. (Colorful Cars Ser.). 24p. (gr. 4-6). 70.80 ***(978-1-5081-6176-9(3)***, PowerKids Pr.) Rosen Publishing Group, Inc., The.

Cosson, M. J. The Mystery of the Old Car. 2005. (Cover-to-Cover Kooties Club Mysteries Ser.). (Illus.). 56p. (J). (gr. k-3). lib. bdg. 14.95 *(978-0-7569-4606-7(9))* Perfection Learning Corp.

Cowley, Joy. Mrs. WishyWashy & the Big Wash Big Book. 2010. 48.25 *(978-1-60559-247-3(1))* Hameray Publishing Group, Inc.

Crimi, Carolyn. Pugs in a Bug. Buscema, Stephanie, illus. 2012. (ENG.). 32p. (J). (gr. -1-k). 16.99 *(978-0-8037-3320-6(8)*, Dial Bks) Penguin Young Readers Group.

Cunningham, Darrell. The Adventures of Stan: Book One the Awakening. 2011. (Illus.). 80p. (gr. 4-6). pap. 29.00 *(978-1-4567-7918-4(4))* AuthorHouse.

Curry, Peter, illus. Cars & Trucks. 2016. (ENG.). 12p. (J). (gr. -1 — 1). bds. 4.99 *(978-1-4998-0199-6(8))* Little Bee Books Inc.

Dahl, Michael. Dragon Theft Auto, 1 vol. Evans, Mark & Kun Rong, Yap, illus. 2009. (Dragonblood Ser.). (ENG.). 40p. (gr. 1-3). 23.99 *(978-1-4342-1264-1(5)*, Zone Bks.) Stone Arch Bks.

Dale, Decisive. The Determined Dream Cars. 2008. 48p. pap. 19.95 *(978-1-4389-1484-8(9))* AuthorHouse.

Dale, Penny. Dinosaur Zoom! Dale, Penny, illus. 2014. (ENG., Illus.). 24p. (J). (-k). bds. 6.99 *(978-0-7636-7394-9(3)*, Nosy Crow) Candlewick Pr.

Daniels, Dominique. Mike & the Bike: Money Doesn't Grow on Trees. 2010. (Illus.). 20p. pap. 13.50 *(978-1-4490-1768-2(1))* AuthorHouse.

D'Aulaire, Ingri & D'Aulaire, Edgar Parin. The Two Cars. 2007. (ENG., Illus.). 32p. (J). (gr. -1-2). 14.95 *(978-1-59017-234-6(5)*, NYR Children's Collection) New York Review of Bks., Inc., The.

Davis, Trevor. The Adventures of Charley Mcchoochoo: Danny & the Whistling Engine. Davis, Natalie, ed. Anderson, Lochlin, illus. 2012. 34p. pap. 9.99 *(978-0-9853650-5-9(6))* Mindstir Media.

Day, K. The Silver Bullet: Tour of the Universe. 2010. 120p. pap. 12.49 *(978-1-4490-6534-8(1))* AuthorHouse.

Dean, James. Go, Pete, Go. 2016. (Pete the Cat (HarperCollins) Ser.). (J). lib. bdg. 14.75 *(978-0-606-38759-0(5))* Turtleback Bks.

Dembinski, Chris. Maxi the Taxi. 2011. 28p. pap. 24.95 *(978-1-4512-8509-3(4))* America Star Bks.

Dempsey, Kristy. Mini Racer. Strevens-Marzo, Bridget, illus. 2011. (ENG.). 32p. (J). (gr. -1-k). 16.99 *(978-1-59990-170-1(6)*, 9781599901701, Bloomsbury USA Childrens) Bloomsbury Publishing USA.

Denice, Sonia. Chow-E-Chowz: Saved by a Whistle. 2011. 44p. pap. 18.46 *(978-1-4567-1020-0(6))* AuthorHouse.

Denise, Anika. Monster Trucks. Wragg, Nate, illus. 2016. 32p. (J). (gr. -1-3). 17.99 *(978-0-06-234522-6(2))* HarperCollins Pubs.

Depken, Kristen L. Driving School. 2013. (Cars Step into Reading Ser.). lib. bdg. 13.55 *(978-0-606-31932-4(8)*, Turtleback) Turtleback Bks.

DePrisco, Dorothea. Willie & Buster Take the Train. Ansley, Frank, illus. 2003. (Stories to Share Ser.). 10p. (J). 10.95 *(978-1-58117-183-9(8)*, Intervisual/Piggy Toes) Bendon, Inc.

Disney Book Group. Meet the Cars. Disney Storybook Art Team, illus. 2017. (ENG.). 144p. (J). (gr. -1-k). 12.99 ***(978-1-368-00783-2(X))*** Disney Pr.

Disney Book Group & Landers, Ace. Lead the Way. Disney Storybook Art Team & Taylor, Garrett, illus. 2017. (ENG.). 40p. (J). (gr. 1-3). 16.99 *(978-1-4847-8127-2(9))* Disney Pr.

Disney Book Group Staff. 5-Minute Racing Stories. Disney Storybook Art Team Staff, illus. 2017. (5-Minute Stories Ser.). (ENG.). 192p. (J). (gr. 1-3). 12.99 *(978-1-368-00075-8(4))* Disney Pr.

Disney, Pixar Cars, ed. Red Light, Green Light: Action Opposites. 2009. (ENG.). 20p. 9.99 *(978-1-59069-780-1(4))* Studio Mouse LLC.

—Rhymes on the Go. 2009. (ENG.). 24p. 4.99 *(978-1-59069-776-4(6))* Studio Mouse LLC.

Disney Pixar Staff. Rescue Mater: And Other Tall Tales. 2013. (Fold-Out Figure Ser.: 1). (ENG.). 32p. (J). (gr. -1-2). 14.99 *(978-0-7944-2815-0(0))* Reader's Digest Assn., Inc., The.

Disney Press Staff & Disney Book Group Staff. Cars 2. 2011. (Read-Along Storybook & CD Ser.). (ENG.). 32p. (J). (gr. -1-2). pap. 6.99 *(978-1-4231-4179-2(2))* Disney Pr.

Disney Storybook Artists Staff, ed. Disney/Pixar Cars Drawing Book & Kit. 2008. 32p. pap. 10.95 *(978-1-60058-102-1(1))* Quarto Publishing Group USA.

Dotlich, Rebecca Kai. Race Car Count. Slack, Michael, illus. 2017. (ENG.). 32p. (J). bds. 7.99 *(978-1-62779-934-8(6)*, 9781627799348, Holt, Henry & Co. Bks. For Young Readers) Holt, Henry & Co.

Duncan, Hall F. Those Tires Have Got to Go! 2004. (Woodpecker Sunroom Ser.: No. 3). (Illus.). 30p. (J). *(978-0-9677844-4-1(1))* Humor & Communication.

DuPrau, Jeanne. Car Trouble. 2005. 288p. (J). 15.99 *(978-0-06-073672-9(0))*; lib. bdg. 16.89 *(978-0-06-073674-3(7))* HarperCollins Pubs.

Durand, Hallie. Mitchell Goes Driving. Fucile, Tony, illus. 2013. (ENG.). 40p. (J). (gr. -1-2). pap. 6.99 *(978-0-7636-6737-5(4))* Candlewick Pr.

—Mitchell's License. Fucile, Tony, illus. 2011. (ENG.). 40p. (J). (gr. -1-2). 15.99 *(978-0-7636-4496-3(X))* Candlewick Pr.

Elya, Susan Middleton. Oh No, Gotta Go! Karas, G. Brian, illus. 2003. (SPA & ENG.). 32p. (J). (gr. -1-2). 15.99 *(978-0-399-23493-4(4)*, G.P. Putnam's Sons Books for Young Readers) Penguin Young Readers Group.

Ernst, Lisa Campbell. This Is the Van That Dad Cleaned. Ernst, Lisa Campbell, illus. 2005. (ENG., Illus.). 40p. (J). (gr. -1-3). 18.99 *(978-0-689-86190-1(7)*, Simon & Schuster Bks. For Young Readers) Simon & Schuster Bks. For Young Readers.

Estes, Don. Willy: The Little Jeep Who Wanted to Be a Fire Truck. Garrison, Sue, illus. 2003. 46p. (J). lib. bdg. 14.95 *(978-1-883551-47-6(1)*, ASP-471, Attic Studio Pr.) Attic Studio Publishing Hse.

—Willy & Friends traveling through the Seasons: The continuing story of Willy the little fire Jeep. Glass, Eric, illus. 2006. (J). *(978-1-883551-75-9(7)*, Maple Corners Press) Attic Studio Publishing Hse.

Everheart, Chris. Sprint. 2016. (Tartan House Ser.). (ENG.). 96p. (YA). (gr. 5-12). *(978-1-63235-167-8(6)*, 12-Story Library) Pr. Room Editions LLC.

Evolution [4 Pack]. 2004. (gr. 7-18). 99.95 incl. DVD *(978-1-57807-856-1(3)*, WG35469) WGBH Boston Video.

Feldman, Thea. Things That Go. 2006. 3p. 5.99 *(978-1-932915-31-0(1))* Sandvik Publishing.

Finkelstein, Chaim. The Burksfield Bike Club, Book 2: Lost & Found. Jennings, R. W., illus. 2007. 224p. (J). 15.95 *(978-1-932443-69-1(X)*, BBC1H) Judaica Pr., Inc., The.

Fisher-Price Little People, Fisher-Price Little. Fisher-Price Little People Planes, Cars, Trucks & Trains! 2015. (Lift-The-Flap Ser.: 24). (ENG.). 10p. (J). (gr. -1-k). bds. 9.99 *(978-0-7944-3468-7(1))* Reader's Digest Assn., Inc., The.

Fishman, Cathy Goldberg. Car Wash Kid. Gott, Barry, illus. 2003. (Rookie Reader Skill Set Ser.). (ENG.). (J). (gr. k-2). pap. 4.95 *(978-0-516-27811-7(8)*, Children's Pr.) Scholastic Library Publishing.

Fitzhugh, Percy K. Roy Blakeley on the Mohawk Trail. 2005. (Illus.). pap. 24.95 *(978-1-885529-76-3(7))* Stevens Publishing.

Fleming, Ian. Chitty Chitty Bang Bang. Berger, Joe, illus. 2013. (Chitty Chitty Bang Bang Ser.). (ENG.). 160p. (J). (gr. 4-7). pap. 6.99 *(978-0-7636-6666-8(1))* Candlewick Pr.

Fliess, Sue. Calling All Cars. Beise, Sarah, illus. 2016. (ENG.). 32p. (J). (-3). 14.99 *(978-1-4926-1881-2(0)*, 9781492618812, Sourcebooks Jabberwocky) Sourcebooks, Inc.

—Race! Taylor, Edwardian, illus. 2017. (ENG.). 32p. (J). (gr. -1-3). 16.99 *(978-1-4998-0237-5(4))* Little Bee Books Inc.

Fox, Christyan & Fox, Diane. Enzo the Racing Car. Fox, Christyan & Fox, Diane, illus. 2008. (Wheelyworld Ser.). (ENG., Illus.). 32p. (J). (gr. -1-k). pap. 8.95 *(978-1-4052-2742-1(7))* Egmont Bks., Ltd. GBR. Dist: Independent Pubs. Group.

—Monty the Rally Car. Fox, Christyan & Fox, Diane, illus. 2008. (Wheelyworld Ser.). (ENG., Illus.). 32p. (J). (gr. -1-k). pap. 8.95 *(978-1-4052-2743-8(5))* Egmont Bks., Ltd. GBR. Dist: Independent Pubs. Group.

Galvin, Laura Gates. What Am I? A Guessing Game. 2009. (CARs Audio Tales). (ENG.). 20p. (J). (gr. -1). 8.99 *(978-1-59069-773-3(1))* Studio Mouse LLC.

Garcia, Emma. Tip Tip Dig Dig. 2013. (ENG., Illus.). 26p. (J). (— 1). bds. 6.95 *(978-1-906250-82-9(0))* Boxer Bks., Ltd. GBR. Dist: Sterling Publishing Co., Inc.

—Toot Toot Beep Beep. 2013. (ENG., Illus.). 26p. (J). (— 1). bds. 6.95 *(978-1-906250-84-3(7))* Boxer Bks., Ltd. GBR. Dist: Sterling Publishing Co., Inc.

Garis, Howard Roger. Uncle Wiggily's Automobile. Date not set. 192p. (J). 20.95 *(978-0-8488-2276-7(5))* Amereon Ltd.

Garland, Michael. Car Goes Far. Garland, Michael, illus. 2014. (I Like to Read(r) Ser.). (ENG., Illus.). 24p. (J). (gr. -1-3). 6.99 *(978-0-8234-3058-1(8))* Holiday Hse., Inc.

Gilbert, Wendy June. Our Beds Are Cars. 2008. 44p. per. 24.95 *(978-1-60441-749-4(8))* America Star Bks.

Golden Books. Start Your Engines! (Bubble Guppies) Golden Books, illus. 2015. (Color Plus Crayons & Sticker Ser.). (ENG., Illus.). 48p. (J). (gr. -1-2). pap. 4.99 *(978-0-553-49764-9(2)*, Golden Bks.) Random Hse. Children's Bks.

Goldsack, Gaby. Fire Engine. Lawson, Peter, illus. 2009. (Turn the Wheel Ser.). (ENG.). 10p. (J). (gr. -1-k). bds. 5.95 *(978-0-7892-1022-7(3)*, Abbeville Kids) Abbeville Pr., Inc.

—Fishing Boat. Lawson, Peter, illus. 2009. (Turn the Wheel Ser.). (ENG.). 10p. (J). (gr. -1-k). bds. 5.95 *(978-0-7892-1025-8(8)*, Abbeville Kids) Abbeville Pr., Inc.

Goldstein, William. My Blood Feet. 2011. 90p. 24.99 *(978-1-4568-8233-4(3))*; pap. 15.99 *(978-1-4568-8232-7(5))* Xlibris Corp.

Gottesfeld, Jeff. Chopped! 2013. (Robinson's Hood Ser.: 3). lib. bdg. 19.60 *(978-0-606-27020-5(5)*, Turtleback) Turtleback Bks.

Gould, Robert. Big Rigs. 2004. (Big Stuff Ser.). (ENG., Illus.). 16p. (J). bds. 7.95 *(978-1-929945-41-2(8))* Big Guy Bks., Inc.

—Giant Earth Movers. 2004. (Big Stuff Ser.). (ENG., Illus.). 16p. (J). bds. 7.95 *(978-1-929945-42-9(6))* Big Guy Bks., Inc.

Grace, N. B. Rev It Up! 9th ed. 2010. (Wizards of Waverly Place Ser.: No. 9). 128p. (J). (gr. 3-7). pap. 4.99 *(978-1-4231-2676-8(9))* Disney Pr.

Greenwell, Jessica. This Is My Car. 2009. (Touchy-Feely Board Bks). 10p. (J). bds. 16.99 *(978-0-7945-2545-3(8)*, Usborne) EDC Publishing.

Grimm, Kristi. Mommy, Tell Me a Story about a Car, 2nd Edition. Grimm, Dave, illus. 2nd ed. 2013. 32p. pap. 13.99 *(978-0-9855699-9-0(9))* Richer Life, LLC.

Guest, Jacqueline. Dream Racer, 1 vol. 2006. (Lorimer SideStreets Ser.). (ENG.). 136p. (YA). (gr. 9-12). 16.95 *(978-1-55028-945-9(4)*, 9781550289459); 9.95 *(978-1-55028-942-8(X)*, 9781550289428) Lorimer, James & Co., Ltd., Pubs. CAN. Dist: Casemate Pubs. & Bk. Distributors, LLC.

Gutman, Dan. Never Say Genius. 2012. (Genius Files Ser.: 2). (ENG.). 304p. (J). (gr. 3-7). pap. 6.99 *(978-0-06-182769-3(X))* HarperCollins Pubs.

—You Only Die Twice. 2013. (Genius Files Ser.: 3). (ENG.). 320p. (J). (gr. 3-7). pap. 6.99 *(978-0-06-182772-3(X))* HarperCollins Pubs.

Hagen, Carol L. The Night Henry Ford Met Santa. Faulkner, Matt, illus. 2006. (ENG.). 32p. (J). (gr. k-6). 17.95 *(978-1-58536-132-8(1))* Sleeping Bear Pr.

Harper, Benjamin. Hot Wheels: To the Extreme. Wisinski, Ed & White, Dave, illus. 2007. (Scholastic Reader Ser.). 30p. (J). pap. *(978-0-545-02019-0(0))* Scholastic, Inc.

Harris, Patricia. The Car of Many Colors. 2017. (Colorful Cars Ser.). 24p. (gr. 4-6). pap. 8.25 ***(978-1-5383-2087-7(8)***, PowerKids Pr.) Rosen Publishing Group, Inc., The.

Harvey, Irene J. William the Fairground Car. 2008. 116p. pap. 30.95 *(978-1-60693-210-0(1)*, Eloquent Bks.) Strategic Book Publishing & Rights Agency (SBPRA).

Haskett, J. A. Morgan & Friends. 2011. (Illus.). 40p. pap. 16.76 *(978-1-4389-3657-4(5))* AuthorHouse.

Hawksley, Gerald, illus. Danny Dog's Car: Press Out Parts Make a Car Carrying Danny Dog! 2009. (Toddler Make & Play Ser.). 10p. (J). bds. 6.95 *(978-1-59496-184-7(0))* Teora USA LLC.

Hearn, Sam. Beep! Beep! Hearn, Sam, illus. 2016. (ENG., Illus.). 12p. (J). (gr. -1-k). 10.99 *(978-0-545-79958-4(9)*, Cartwheel Bks.) Scholastic, Inc.

Highlights for Children, Highlights for & Jordan, Karen. Things That Go. Meisel, Paul, illus. 2015. (Highlights(tm) Find It! Padded Board Bks.). (ENG.). 14p. (J). (— 1). bds. 7.99 *(978-1-62979-414-3(7)*, Highlights) Boyds Mills Pr.

Hillert, Margaret. The Birthday Car. Girouard, Patrick, illus. 2016. (BeginningtoRead Ser.). (ENG.). 32p. (J). (gr. -1-2). pap. 11.94 *(978-1-60357-936-0(2))*; (gr. k-2). 22.60 *(978-1-59953-795-5(8))* Norwood Hse. Pr.

Hirsch, Jennifer. The Bitty Twins on the Go. Lohmann, Renate, illus. 2006. (J). *(978-1-59369-188-2(2))* American Girl Publishing, Inc.

Hissom, Jennie. Wheels on the Move: Driving with Andy. Catusanu, Mircea, illus. 2006. (J). *(978-1-58987-141-0(3))* Kindermusik International.

Hoffman, Mary Ann. Caleb's Car Wash. 2006. (Neighborhood Readers Ser.). (ENG.). 16p. (gr. 1-3). pap. 6.50 *(978-1-4042-6998-9(3)*, Rosen Classroom) Rosen Publishing Group, Inc., The.

Holden, Pam. Tin Lizzy, 6 pack. Hawley, Kelvin, illus. 2009. (Red Rocket Readers Ser.). (ENG.). 16p. (gr. 2-2). pap. *(978-1-877363-86-3(3))* Flying Start Bks.

Holliday, Susan. Riding the Storm. I.t. ed. 2007. 164p. per. *(978-1-905665-22-8(9))* Pollinger In Print.

Homberg, Ruth. Racing for Good. 2014. (Cars Step into Reading Ser.). lib. bdg. 13.55 *(978-0-606-36007-4(7))* Turtleback Bks.

Hubbard, Sharron/Y. Rosie's New Bike. Schleihs, Kristin, illus. 2006. (J). bds. 7.95 *(978-0-9762434-1-0(5))* Link & Rosie Pr.

Hubbell, Patricia. Cars: Rushing! Honking! Zooming!, 0 vols. Halsey, Megan & Addy, Sean, illus. 2010. (ENG.). 32p. (J). (gr. -1-1). pap. 6.99 *(978-0-7614-5616-2(3),* 9780761456162, Amazon Children's Publishing) Amazon Publishing.

Jennings, Sharon. Franklin & the Scooter. Gagnon, Celeste et al, illus. 2004. 32p. (J). lib. bdg. 15.38 *(978-1-4242-1169-2(7))* Fitzgerald Bks.

Jiang, Eva. Eric Loved Fire Trucks. 2013. 28p. pap. 16.09 *(978-1-4669-7117-2(7))* Trafford Publishing.

JibJab Bros Studios. Cars Are Cool! JibJab Bros Studios, illus. 2017. (ENG., Illus.). 24p. (J). (— 1). bds. 7.99 ***(978-1-5247-1823-7(8),*** Random Hse. Bks. for Young Readers) Random Hse. Children's Bks.

Jones, Patrick. Drift: Nissan Skyline. 2013. (Turbocharged Ser.). (ENG.). 112p. (gr. 6-12). pap. 7.95 *(978-1-4677-1474-7(7));* lib. bdg. 27.93 *(978-1-4677-1242-2(6))* Lerner Publishing Group. (Darby Creek).

—Slammed: Honda Civic. 2013. (Turbocharged Ser.). (ENG.). 96p. (gr. 6-12). pap. 7.95 *(978-1-4677-1478-5(X));* lib. bdg. 27.93 *(978-1-4677-1245-3(0))* Lerner Publishing Group. (Darby Creek).

Jordan, Apple. Fast Kart, Slow Kart. 2013. (Step into Reading Level 1 Ser.). lib. bdg. 13.55 *(978-0-606-26980-3(0),* Turtleback) Turtleback Bks.

Keller, Holly. The Van. 2008. (Green Light Readers Level 1 Ser.). (ENG., Illus.). 24p. (J). (gr. -1-1). pap. 3.95 *(978-0-15-206587-4(3))* Houghton Mifflin Harcourt Publishing Co.

Kelly, J. M. Speed of Life. 2016. (ENG.). 352p. (YA). (gr. 9). 17.99 *(978-0-544-74782-1(8),* HMH Books For Young Readers) Houghton Mifflin Harcourt Publishing Co.

Knowlton, Dwight. The Little Red Racing Car: A Father/Son/Car Story. Knowlton, Dwight, illus. 2013. (ENG., Illus.). (J). 21.99 *(978-0-9892949-0-4(0))* Carpe Viam Productions, LLC.

Lagonegro, Melissa. Go, Go, Go! Cohee, Ron, illus. 2011. (Step into Reading Ser.). (ENG.). 32p. (J). (gr. k-3). pap. 3.99 *(978-0-7364-2765-4(1));* lib. bdg. 12.99 *(978-0-7364-8091-8(9))* Random Hse. Children's Bks. (RH/Disney).

—Go, Go, Go! 2011. (Cars Step into Reading Ser.). lib. bdg. 13.55 *(978-0-606-15226-6(1),* Turtleback) Turtleback Bks.

—Mater's Birthday Surprise. 2012. (Cars Step into Reading Ser.). lib. bdg. 13.55 *(978-0-606-23724-6(0),* Turtleback) Turtleback Bks.

—Mater's Birthday Surprise (Disney/Pixar Cars) Random House Disney Staff, illus. 2012. (Step into Reading Ser.). (ENG.). 32p. (J). (gr. -1-1). pap. 3.99 *(978-0-7364-2858-3(5),* RH/Disney) Random Hse. Children's Bks.

—Secret Agent Mater. Random House Disney Staff, illus. 2011. (Step into Reading Ser.). (ENG.). 32p. (J). (gr. k-3). pap. 3.99 *(978-0-7364-8095-6(1),* RH/Disney) Random Hse. Children's Bks.

Lagonegro, Melissa & Random House Disney Staff. Roadwork! Mawhinney, Art, illus. 2008. (Step into Reading Ser.). (ENG.). 32p. (J). (gr. k-3). pap. 3.99 *(978-0-7364-2516-2(0),* RH/Disney) Random Hse. Children's Bks.

Lagonegro, Melissa & RH Disney Staff. Old, New, Red, Blue! 2006. (Step into Reading Ser.). (ENG., Illus.). 32p. (J). (gr. k-3). pap. 3.99 *(978-0-7364-2410-3(5),* RH/Disney) Random Hse. Children's Bks.

Lakin, Patricia. Muddy, Mud, Bud. Atkinson, Cale, illus. 2014. (Penguin Young Readers, Level 1 Ser.). (ENG.). 32p. (J). (gr. k-1). pap. 3.99 *(978-0-448-47989-7(3),* Penguin Young Readers) Penguin Young Readers Group.

Landers, Ace. Race for Treasure. White, Dave, illus. 2011. 32p. (J). pap. *(978-0-545-33454-9(3))* Scholastic, Inc.

LaRochelle, David. Moo! Wohnoutka, Mike, illus. 2013. (ENG.). 40p. (J). (gr. -1-1). 16.99 *(978-0-8027-3409-9(X),* 9780802734099, Bloomsbury USA Childrens) Bloomsbury Publishing USA.

Larsen, Kirsten, et al. Mater & the Easter Buggy. Disney Storybook Art Team, illus. 2012. (ENG.). 48p. (J). (gr. -1-k). 12.99 *(978-1-4231-3875-4(9))* Disney Pr.

Lawson, Peter. Tractor. 2009. (Turn the Wheel Ser.). (ENG., Illus.). 10p. (J). (gr. -1-k). bds. 5.95 *(978-0-7892-1023-4(1),* Abbeville Kids) Abbeville Pr., Inc.

Lawson, Peter & Smith, Kathryn. Animal Ambulance. 2009. (Turn the Wheel Ser.). (ENG., Illus.). 10p. (J). (gr. -1-k). bds. 5.95 *(978-0-7892-1026-5(6),* Abbeville Kids) Abbeville Pr., Inc.

Leonard, Nellie M. Grand Daddy Whiskers, M. D. 2004. reprint ed. pap. 1.99 *(978-1-4192-2227-6(9));* pap. 15.95 *(978-1-4191-2227-9(4))* Kessinger Publishing, LLC.

Little Bee Books Staff. On the Move: A Touch-and-Feel Book. 2015. (ENG.). 12p. (J). (gr. -1 — 1). bds. 6.99 *(978-1-4998-0013-5(4))* Little Bee Books Inc.

Litton, Jonathan. Red Car, Blue Car. Verrall, Lisa, illus. 2015. (My Little World Ser.). (ENG.). 12p. (J). (gr. -1-2). bds. 8.99 *(978-1-68010-506-3(X))* Tiger Tales.

Litz, Amanda. Sam & Pam Can & You Can Too! We Can Ride Our Bikes. Garcia, Cynthia, illus. 2011. 32p. (J). pap. 3.99 *(978-0-9841496-2-9(7))* Traveler's Trunk Publishing LLC.

Lombardi, Kristine & Disney Storybook Artists Staff. Disney Cars Carry along Treasury. 2010. (Carry along Bks.). (ENG., Illus.). 20p. (J). (gr. -1). bds. 14.99 *(978-0-7944-1947-9(X))* Reader's Digest Assn., Inc., The.

Long, Ethan. Clara & Clem Take a Ride. 2012. (Penguin Young Readers Level 1 Ser.). lib. bdg. 13.55 *(978-0-606-26639-0(9),* Turtleback) Turtleback Bks.

Lord, Cynthia. Hot Rod Hamster. Anderson, Derek, illus. 2010. (ENG.). 40p. (J). (gr. -1-k). 18.99 *(978-0-545-03530-9(9),* Scholastic Pr.) Scholastic, Inc.

Lynn, Sarah. 1-2-3 Va-Va-Vroom! A Counting Book, 0 vols. Griffo, Daniel, illus. 2012. (ENG.). 32p. (J). (gr. -1-3). 16.99 *(978-0-7614-6162-3(0),* 9780761461623, Amazon Children's Publishing) Amazon Publishing.

Martin, LaJoyce. The Silver Ghost. 2004. (Illus.). 161p. (J). pap. 9.99 *(978-1-56722-643-0(4))* Word Aflame Pr.

McAllister, Cameron. The Tin Snail. Usher, Sam, illus. 2016. (ENG.). 288p. (J). (gr. 4-7). 16.99 *(978-0-553-53638-6(9),* Delacorte Bks. for Young Readers) Random Hse. Children's Bks.

McCormick, Shawn R. Zoey & the Zones: A Story for Children with Asthma. 2003. per. 8.95 *(978-0-9718120-8-6(X))* HealthSprings, LLC.

Medina, Meg. Tía Isa Quiere un Carro. Munoz, Claudio, illus. 2012.Tr. of Tia Isa Wants a Car. (SPA.). 32p. (J). (gr. -1-2). pap. 6.99 *(978-0-7636-5751-2(4))* Candlewick Pr.

—Tía Isa Quiere un Carro. 2012.Tr. of Tia Isa Wants a Car. (SPA.). lib. bdg. 17.20 *(978-0-606-23801-4(8),* Turtleback) Turtleback Bks.

—Tia Isa Wants a Car. Munoz, Claudio, illus. 2016. (ENG.). 32p. (J). (gr. -1-2). 6.99 *(978-0-7636-5752-9(2))* Candlewick Pr.

—Tia Isa Wants a Car. Muñoz, Claudio, illus. 2011. (ENG.). 32p. (J). (gr. -1-2). 15.99 *(978-0-7636-4156-6(1))* Candlewick Pr.

Meister, Cari. Buzz Beaker & the Super Fast Car, 1 vol. McGuire, Bill, illus. 2011. (Buzz Beaker Bks.). (ENG.). 32p. (gr. 2-3). pap. 6.25 *(978-1-4342-3058-4(9))* Stone Arch Bks.

Merlin, Christophe. Under the Hood. 2011. (ENG., Illus.). 14p. (J). (gr. -1-2). 14.99 *(978-0-7636-5535-8(X))* Candlewick Pr.

Mermelstein, Yael. A Car That Goes Far. Rosenfeld, Dina, ed. Romanenko, Vitaliy & Romanenko, Vasilisa, illus. 2009. 30p. (J). (gr. 1-3). 12.95 *(978-1-929628-47-6(1))* Hachai Publishing.

Michalak, Jamie. Joe & Sparky Get New Wheels. Remkiewicz, Frank, illus. 2013. (Candlewick Sparks Ser.). (ENG.). 48p. (J). (gr. k-4). pap. 3.99 *(978-0-7636-6641-5(6))* Candlewick Pr.

Mitchell, Julie & Rinkel, Ken. Slow down, Mrs. Brown! 2008. (Rigby Focus Forward: Level F Ser.). (Illus.). 24p. (J). (gr. 4-7). pap. *(978-1-4190-3700-9(5),* Rigby) Pearson Education Australia.

Moloney, James. Black Taxi. 2005. 272p. (J). (gr. 7-18). 15.99 *(978-0-06-055937-3(3))* HarperCollins Pubs.

—Black Taxi. 2003. 288p. *(978-0-207-19989-9(2))* HarperCollins Pubs. Australia.

Murray, Kiel. Mater Saves Christmas. 2009. (ENG.). 48p. (J). (gr. -1-2). 12.99 *(978-1-4231-1695-0(X))* Disney Pr.

My Little Library of Things That do. 2008. (Pocket Libraries Ser.). 5p. bds. *(978-1-4075-3192-2(1))* Parragon, Inc.

My Visit to the Car Factory. 2004. (J). ring bd. 4.50 *(978-0-9762740-7-0(8),* Flat Kids) Smart Smiles Co., The.

Neale, R. W. Harry the Rally Car: The Beginning. 2010. 28p. pap. 12.99 *(978-1-60911-046-8(3),* Eloquent Bks.) Strategic Book Publishing & Rights Agency (SBPRA).

Neill, Grace. Luke & His Motorbike. 2011. 28p. pap. 15.99 *(978-1-4568-6926-7(4))* Xlibris Corp.

Neuschwander, Angel & Johnston, Becky. Gretchen Asks, How Do Cars Work? 2009. 24p. pap. 12.99 *(978-1-4389-2886-9(6))* AuthorHouse.

Newton-Perry, Linda. The Little Red Car & Bigfoot. 2009. 70p. pap. 15.95 *(978-0-557-08449-4(0))* Lulu Pr., Inc.

Nugent, Cynthia. Francesca & the Magic Bike. 2005. 4p. (J). pap., tchr. ed. *(978-1-55192-825-8(6))* Raincoast Bk. Distribution CAN. Dist: Publishers Group West (PGW).

Olds, Laurie. Cars on Vacation. 2009. 24p. pap. 12.25 *(978-1-4490-1633-3(2))* AuthorHouse.

Olszewski, Raymond VanCe. Chucky the Car: A Children's Story & Coloring Book. 2010. (Illus.). 20p. 12.95 *(978-1-4490-6821-9(9))* AuthorHouse.

Oxenbury, Helen. En El Auto.Tr. of In the Car. (SPA.). 24p. (J). 7.50 *(978-84-261-2000-7(8))* Juventud, Editorial ESP. Dist: AIMS International Bks., Inc.

Oxley, Jennifer & Aronson, Billy. Peg + Cat: The Race Car Problem. 2015. (Peg + Cat Ser.). (ENG., Illus.). 32p. (J). (gr. -1-2). 12.99 *(978-0-7636-7558-5(X),* Candlewick Entertainment) Candlewick Pr.

P, Michael. Daniel's Ride/el Paseo de Daniel. Ballard, Lee, illus. 2nd ed. 2006. (ENG.). 32p. (J). (gr. -1-7). 18.95 *(978-0-86719-641-2(6))* Last Gasp of San Francisco.

Parvensky Barwell, Catherine A. Tommi Goes Camping, 4 vols. Barwell, Matthew W. et al, eds. Parvensky Barwell, Catherine A., illus. 2006. (Illus.). 40p. (J). 14.95 *(978-0-9774409-3-1(1),* TL004) ILT Publishing.

—Tommi Goes to the Beach, 4 vols. Barwell, Matthew W. & Parvensky, Mary T., eds. 2006. (Illus.). 40p. (J). *(978-0-9774409-2-4(3),* TL003) ILT Publishing.

—Tommi Lance Grows Up, 4 vols. 2006. (Illus.). 30p. (J). *(978-0-9774409-0-0(7),* TL001) ILT Publishing.

—Tommi's First Snowfall, 4 vols. 2006. (Illus.). 32p. (J). *(978-0-9774409-1-7(5),* TL002) ILT Publishing.

Paulsen, Gary. The Car. 2006. (ENG., Illus.). 192p. (YA). (gr. 7-12). pap. 7.99 *(978-0-15-205827-2(3))* Houghton Mifflin Harcourt Publishing Co.

—The Car. 2006. 182p. (gr. 7-12). 17.00 *(978-0-7569-6685-0(X))* Perfection Learning Corp.

Peck, Richard. Here Lies the Librarian. 2007. (ENG.). 160p. (J). (gr. 5-18). 7.99 *(978-0-14-240908-4(1),* Puffin Books) Penguin Young Readers Group.

—Here Lies the Librarian. 2007. 145p. (J). (gr. 4-7). 14.65 *(978-0-7569-8193-8(X))* Perfection Learning Corp.

—Here Lies the Librarian. rev. l.t. ed. 2007. (Thorndike Literacy Bridge Ser.). 173p. (J). (gr. 5-9). 23.95 *(978-0-7862-9183-0(4))* Thorndike Pr.

Pen, Chenda. Dara Learns How to Ride a Bike! An Autism Story. 2010. 24p. pap. 14.99 *(978-1-4490-6943-8(6))* AuthorHouse.

Penrose, Margaret. The Motor Girls on a Tour. 2007. 152p. pap. 19.99 *(978-1-4346-5779-4(5));* 172p. pap. 21.99 *(978-1-4346-5780-0(9))* Creative Media Partners, LLC.

Perlman, Rhea. Canyon Catastrophe. Santat, Dan, illus. 2006. (Otto Undercover Ser.). 128p. (J). (gr. 4-7). 14.99 *(978-0-06-075498-3(2))* HarperCollins Pubs.

Piggy Toes Press, creator. Cars 2. 2011. (Splish-Splash Bks.). (ENG., Illus.). (gr. -1-k). 5.95 *(978-1-61524-418-8(2),* Intervisual/Piggy Toes) Bendon, Inc.

Pilkons, Alyssa. Confessions of a Teenage Lima Bean. 2009. 232p. pap. 14.98 *(978-1-4303-1132-4(0))* Lulu Pr., Inc.

The Pillow Sale: KinderWords Individual Title Six-Packs. (Kinderstarters Ser.). 8p. (gr. -1-1). 21.00 *(978-0-7635-8707-9(9))* Rigby Education.

Porter, Alan J. Cars: Radiator Springs. Carreres, Albert, illus. 2010. (World of Cars Ser.). (ENG.). 112p. (J). pap. 9.99 *(978-1-60886-502-4(9))* Boom! Studios.

—Cars: Route 66 Dash! Gladfelter, Allen, illus. 2010. (Cars Ser.). (ENG.). 112p. (J). (gr. 3-6). pap. 9.99 *(978-1-60886-585-7(1))* Boom! Studios.

—Cars Vol. 2: Radiator Springs. Carreres, Albert, illus. 2010. (World of Cars Ser.). (ENG.). 112p. (J). 24.99 *(978-1-60886-528-4(2))* Boom! Studios.

—Rally Race. Magic Eye Studios, illus. 2010. (Cars Ser.). (ENG.). 112p. (J). (gr. 3-6). pap. 9.99 *(978-1-60886-517-8(7))* Boom! Studios.

Poulter, David. Morris & Mini Minor & Friends: A Day at the Seaside. 2010. (ENG., Illus.). 50p. pap. *(978-1-84748-774-2(2))* Athena Pr.

Priddy, Roger. On the Go. 2013. (Hello Baby Ser.). (ENG., Illus.). 16p. (J). (gr. -1 — 1). bds. 4.99 *(978-0-312-51599-7(5),* 9780312515997, Priddy Bks.) St. Martin's Pr.

Prochovnic, Dawn Babb. Watch Me Go! Sign Language for Vehicles, 1 vol. Bauer, Stephanie, illus. 2009. (Story Time with Signs & Rhymes Ser.). (ENG.). 32p. (gr. -1-3). 28.50 *(978-1-60270-673-6(5),* Looking Glass Library) ABDO Publishing Co.

Publications International Ltd. Staff. Giant Look & Find Disney Pixar Cars. 2008. 24p. (J). 15.98 *(978-1-4127-8967-7(2),* PIL Kids) Publications International, Ltd.

—Steering Wheel Sound Cars. 2007. 12p. (J). 17.98 *(978-1-4127-5884-0(X))* Phoenix International Publications, Inc.

—Thomas & Friends: First Look & Find. 2010. 18p. 7.98 *(978-1-4508-1139-2(6))* Phoenix International Publications, Inc.

Publications International Ltd. Staff, creator. Disney Pixar Cars Tour the Town. 2007. (Steering Wheel Sound Ser.). (Illus.). (gr. -1-k). 16.98 *(978-1-4127-8804-5(8))* Publications International, Ltd.

Publications International Ltd. Staff, ed. Cars. 2010. 18p. (J). bds. 10.98 *(978-1-60553-465-7(X),* PIL Kids) Publications International, Ltd.

—Cars: Fun with Friends. 2010. (J). bds. 5.98 *(978-1-60553-038-3(7))* Phoenix International Publications, Inc.

—Cars (Musical Treasury) 2011. 40p. (J). bds. 15.98 *(978-1-4508-1085-2(3))* Publications International, Ltd.

—Disney Pixar Cars: First Look & Find & Shaped Puzzle Box Set. 2010. (J). 22.98 *(978-1-4508-0136-2(6))* Publications International, Ltd.

—Disney Pixar Cars (book Block) 2010. (J). 10.98 *(978-1-4508-0671-8(6))* Phoenix International Publications, Inc.

—Disney Pixar Cars: Mater the Greater & More Tall Tales! (Look & Find) 2010. 24p. (J). 7.98 *(978-1-60553-634-7(2))* Publications International, Ltd.

—Disney Pixar Cars My First Look & Find & Shaped Puzzle. 2010. (J). 22.98 *(978-1-4508-0801-9(8))* Phoenix International Publications, Inc.

—Disney Pixar Cars Ride-along Songs. 2010. 14p. (J). bds. 19.98 *(978-1-4127-5368-5(6))* Phoenix International Publications, Inc.

—Elmo. 2007. (J). 9.98 *(978-1-4127-8301-9(1))* Phoenix International Publications, Inc.

—Flashlight Book Disney Pixar Cars. 2008. (J). 17.10 *(978-1-4127-8958-5(3))* Phoenix International Publications, Inc.

—Look & Find: Disney Pixar Cars. 2013. 24p. (J). 7.98 *(978-1-4508-7916-3(0),* 1450879160) Phoenix International Publications, Inc.

—Steering Wheel Spa Cars. 2009. 14p. 16.98 *(978-1-4127-9241-7(X))* Phoenix International Publications, Inc.

—What's Different? 2010. 24p. (J). 7.98 *(978-1-60553-039-0(5),* PIL Kids) Publications International, Ltd.

—The World of Cars, Welcome to the Pit Crew. 2008. 14p. (J). bds. 17.98 *(978-1-4127-7597-7(3),* PIL Kids) Publications International, Ltd.

Pyne, Jane. Billy the Banger Racer. 2013. 32p. pap. *(978-1-909593-23-7(0))* Legend Pr.

Rae, Lisa. A Distinguished Old Bentley Drove down to the Sea, 1 vol. Pickersgill, Peter, illus. 2007. (ENG.). 28p. (J). (gr. -1-2). pap. 8.95 *(978-1-897174-05-0(5),* Tuckamore Bks) Creative Bk. Publishing CAN. Dist: Orca Bk. Pubs. USA.

Ramesh, Serita. Jason & the Ingenious Number Trick: A Story about Patterns. 2010. 28p. pap. 15.49 *(978-1-4490-4740-5(8))* AuthorHouse.

Random House Disney Staff. Five Tales from the Road (Disney/Pixar Cars) Random House Disney Staff, illus. 2013. (Step into Reading Ser.). (ENG., Illus.). 160p. (J). (gr. -1-1). pap. 7.99 *(978-0-7364-3108-8(X),* RH/Disney) Random Hse. Children's Bks.

—Good Night, Lightning (Disney/Pixar Cars) Random House Disney Staff, illus. 2013. (Glow-In-the-Dark Board Book Ser.). (ENG., Illus.). 12p. (J). (gr. -1-2). bds. 7.99 *(978-0-7364-2976-4(X),* RH/Disney) Random Hse. Children's Bks.

—Look Out for Mater! Random House Disney Staff, illus. 2009. (Little Golden Book Ser.). (ENG., Illus.). 24p. (J). (gr. -1-2). 4.99 *(978-0-7364-2582-7(9),* Golden/Disney) Random Hse. Children's Bks.

—Race Around the World. Random House Disney Staff, illus. 2011. (Step into Reading Ser.). (ENG., Illus.). 32p. (J). (gr. k-3). pap. 3.99 *(978-0-7364-2808-8(9),* RH/Disney) Random Hse. Children's Bks.

Random House Disney Staff, illus. Cars Little Golden Book Library (Disney/Pixar Cars), 5 vols. 2012. (ENG.). 24p. (J). (gr. -1-2). 22.95 *(978-0-7364-3008-1(3),* Golden/Disney) Random Hse. Children's Bks.

Random House Staff. Demolition Derby/Class Confusion (SpongeBob SquarePants) Aikins, Dave, illus. 2013. (Pictureback(R) Ser.). (ENG.). 32p. (J). (gr. -1-2). 4.99 *(978-0-449-81756-8(3),* Random Hse. Bks. for Young Readers) Random Hse. Children's Bks.

Random House Staff & Disney Editors. Five Tales from the Road. 2013. (Cars Step into Reading Ser.). lib. bdg. 18.40 *(978-0-606-32198-3(5),* Turtleback) Turtleback Bks.

Reader's Digest Staff. Cars - Movie Theater. rev. ed. 2009. (Movie Theater Ser.). (ENG., Illus.). 48p. (J). (gr. -1-3). 19.99 *(978-0-7944-1767-3(1))* Reader's Digest Assn., Inc., The.

Rey, H. A. On the Go! 2011. (Curious George Ser.). (ENG., Illus.). 10p. (J). (gr. -1 — 1). bds. 6.99 *(978-0-547-55151-7(7))* Houghton Mifflin Harcourt Publishing Co.

Reynolds, Luke. Bedtime Blast-Off! Yamada, Mike, illus. 2016. (ENG.). 40p. (J). (gr. -1-1). 16.99 *(978-0-545-77855-8(7),* Orchard Bks.) Scholastic, Inc.

RH Disney. Cars 3 Deluxe Junior Novelization (Disney/Pixar Cars 3) RH Disney, illus. 2017. (Junior Novel Ser.). (ENG., Illus.). 144p. (J). (gr. 2-5). 9.99 ***(978-0-7364-3725-7(8),*** RH/Disney) Random Hse. Children's Bks.

—Cars 3 Junior Novelization (Disney/Pixar Cars 3) RH Disney, illus. 2017. (Junior Novel Ser.). (ENG., Illus.). 144p. (J). (gr. 2-5). 6.99 ***(978-0-7364-3726-4(6),*** RH/Disney) Random Hse. Children's Bks.

—Cars 3 Little Golden Book (Disney/Pixar Cars 3) RH Disney, illus. 2017. (Little Golden Book Ser.). (ENG., Illus.). 24p. (J). (-k). 4.99 ***(978-0-7364-3730-1(4),*** Golden/Disney) Random Hse. Children's Bks.

—Driven to Win! RH Disney, illus. 2017. (Step into Reading Ser.). (ENG., Illus.). 32p. (J). (gr. -1-1). pap. 4.99 ***(978-0-7364-3682-3(0));*** lib. bdg. 12.99 ***(978-0-7364-8199-1(0))*** Random Hse. Children's Bks. (RH/Disney).

RH Disney & Keane, Dave. Cars Origins: Struck by Lightning. RH Disney, illus. 2017. (Stepping Stone Book(TM) Ser.). (ENG., Illus.). 128p. (J). (gr. 1-4). 5.99 ***(978-0-7364-3820-9(3),*** RH/Disney) Random Hse. Children's Bks.

RH Disney Staff. Cars 2 Little Golden Book (Disney/Pixar Cars 2) RH Disney Staff, illus. 2011. (Little Golden Book Ser.). (ENG., Illus.). 24p. (J). (gr. -1-2). 3.99 *(978-0-7364-2781-4(3),* Golden/Disney) Random Hse. Children's Bks.

Richter, Abigail. Mike the Bike. 2006. (Neighborhood Readers Ser.). (ENG.). 16p. (gr. 1-3). pap. 6.50 *(978-1-4042-7168-5(6),* Rosen Classroom) Rosen Publishing Group, Inc., The.

Roberts, Daniel. Harrison & His Dinosaur Robot & the Super-Fast Race Car. 2009. (Illus.). 32p. pap. 14.95 *(978-1-4389-2847-0(5))* AuthorHouse.

Rockwell, Anne. Truck Stop. Iwai, Melissa, illus. 2013. (ENG.). 32p. (J). (gr. -1-k). 16.99 *(978-0-670-06261-4(8),* Viking Books for Young Readers) Penguin Young Readers Group.

Roehm, R. Curtis. My Dad's Gto. 2011. 36p. pap. 18.99 *(978-1-4634-4379-5(X))* AuthorHouse.

Root, Phyllis. Rattletrap Car. Barton, Jill, illus. 2004. (ENG.). 40p. (J). (gr. -1-3). reprint ed. pap. 7.99 *(978-0-7636-2007-3(6))* Candlewick Pr.

—Rattletrap Car Big Book. Barton, Jill, illus. 2009. (ENG.). 40p. (J). (gr. -1-3). pap. 24.99 *(978-0-7636-4139-9(1))* Candlewick Pr.

Rouse, Betty Munn. The Adventures of the Phillyfab Family. 2011. 68p. pap. 12.95 *(978-1-4567-3005-5(3))* AuthorHouse.

Rylant, Cynthia. Brownie & Pearl Go for a Spin. Biggs, Brian, illus. 2012. (Brownie & Pearl Ser.). (ENG.). 24p. (J). (gr. -1-3). 14.99 *(978-1-4169-8633-1(2),* Beach Lane Bks.) Beach Lane Bks.

—Brownie & Pearl Go for a Spin. Biggs, Brian, illus. 2015. (Brownie & Pearl Ser.). (ENG.). 24p. (J). (gr. -1-k). pap. 3.99 *(978-1-4814-2570-4(6),* Simon Spotlight) Simon Spotlight.

Sacks, Nathan. The Duel: Mitsubishi Eclipse. 2013. (Turbocharged Ser.). (ENG.). 104p. (gr. 6-12). pap. 7.95 *(978-1-4677-1476-1(3));* (YA). lib. bdg. 27.93 *(978-1-4677-1243-9(4))* Lerner Publishing Group. (Darby Creek).

Sargent, Dave & Sargent, Pat. Goober: (Silver Dapple) Appreciate Others, 30 vols., Vol. 29. Lenoir, Jane, illus. 2003. (Saddle up Ser.: Vol. 29). 42p. (J). lib. bdg. 23.60 *(978-1-56763-689-5(6))* Ozark Publishing.

—Goober: (Silver Dapple) Appreciate Others, 30 vols., Vol. 29. Lenoir, Jane, illus. 2004. (Saddle up Ser.: Vol. 29). 42p. (J). pap. 10.95 *(978-1-56763-690-1(X))* Ozark Publishing.

Sargent, Dave, et al. Grubby: (Smutty Olive Grullo) Have a Good Disposition, 30 vols., Vol. 31. 2003. (Saddle up Ser.: Vol. 31). (Illus.). 42p. (J). pap. 10.95 *(978-1-56763-692-5(6))* Ozark Publishing.

Scarry, Richard. Richard Scarry's Cars. 2015. (ENG., Illus.). 24p. (J). (— 1). bds. 4.99 *(978-0-385-38926-6(4),* Golden Bks.) Random Hse. Children's Bks.

—Richard Scarry's Mixed-Up Cars & Trucks. 2014. (ENG., Illus.). 34p. (J). (gr. -1-2). 12.95 *(978-1-4027-7220-7(3))* Sterling Publishing Co., Inc.

Scheets, Sonny. At the Car Show. 2007. 20p. 13.95 *(978-0-615-17522-5(8))* Southern Acres Academy.

Scheidies, Carolyn R. Let's Fly Away Little Blue Car. 2008. 60p. pap. 30.98 *(978-0-557-01064-6(0))* Lulu Pr., Inc.

Shaw, Nancy E. Sheep in a Jeep. Apple, Margot, illus. 2009. (ENG.). 26p. (J). (gr. -1 — 1). bds. 12.99 *(978-0-547-23775-6(8))* Houghton Mifflin Harcourt Publishing Co.

Shealy, Dennis R. The Noisy Garage. 2016. (Little Golden Book Ser.). (ENG., Illus.). 24p. (J). (-k). 4.99 *(978-1-101-93439-5(5),* Golden Bks.) Random Hse. Children's Bks.

Shulevitz, Uri. Troto & the Trucks. 2015. (ENG., Illus.). 32p. (J). (gr. -1-1). 17.99 *(978-0-374-30080-7(1),* 9780374300807, Farrar, Straus & Giroux (BYR)) Farrar, Straus & Giroux.

Silver Dolphin en Español Staff. Figuras magicas: Cars: Magical Magnets: Cars, Spanish-Language Edition. 2006. (Illus.). 8p. (J). bds. *(978-970-718-388-9(8),* Silver Dolphin en Español) Advanced Marketing, S. de R. L. de C. V.

Silver Dolphin en Español Staff, ed. Cine en casa: Cars: Movie Theater: Cars. 2007. (Cine en casa Disney Ser.). (Illus.). 46p. (J). *(978-970-718-508-1(2),* Silver Dolphin en Español) Advanced Marketing, S. de R. L. de C. V.

Spalding, Esta. Look Out for the Fitzgerald-Trouts. Smith, Sydney, illus. 2016. (ENG.). 256p. (J). (gr. 3-7). 16.99 *(978-0-316-29858-2(1))* Little, Brown Bks. for Young Readers.

Sparks, Jake. Monty Wins the Cup. Scott, Kimberley, illus. 2016. (Reading Ladder Ser.). (ENG.). 48p. (J). (gr. k-2). pap. 7.99 *(978-1-4052-8247-5(9))* Egmont Bks., Ltd. GBR. Dist: Independent Pubs. Group.

Standish, Burt L. Frank Merriwell's Auto. Rudman, Jack, ed. 2003. (Frank Merriwell Ser.). 29.95 *(978-0-8373-9350-6(7));* pap. 9.95 *(978-0-8373-9050-5(8))* Merriwell, Frank Inc.

Stanley, George Edward. The Case of the Dirty Clue. Murdocca, Sal, illus. 2005. (Ready-for-Chapters Ser.). (J). lib. bdg. 15.00 *(978-1-59054-898-1(1))* Fitzgerald Bks.

Stein, Peter. Cars Galore. Staake, Bob, illus. (ENG.). (J). (gr. -1-3). 2012. 30p. bds. 6.99 *(978-0-7636-6148-9(1))* 2011. 32p. 15.99 *(978-0-7636-4743-8(8))* Candlewick Pr.

—Little Red's Riding 'Hood. Gall, Chris, illus. 2015. (ENG.). 40p. (J). (gr. -1-k). 16.99 *(978-0-545-60969-2(0))* Scholastic, Inc.

Stevens, Eric. The Classic: '69 Chevy Camaro. 2013. (Turbocharged Ser.). (ENG.). 96p. (gr. 6-12). pap. 7.95 *(978-1-4677-1479-2(8))*; lib. bdg. 27.93 *(978-1-4677-1247-7(7))* Lerner Publishing Group. (Darby Creek).

Stilton, Geronimo. Get into Gear, Stilton! 2013. (Geronimo Stilton Ser.: 54). lib. bdg. 18.40 *(978-0-606-31999-7(9),* Turtleback) Turtleback Bks.

Sutherland, Harry A. Dad's Car Wash. 2013. (ENG., Illus.). 32p. (J). (gr. -1-3). 16.99 *(978-1-4814-2170-6(0),* Simon & Schuster/Paula Wiseman Bks.) Simon & Schuster/Paula Wiseman Bks.

Tango Books Staff. Car. Abbott, Simon, illus. 2012. (Noisy Pops! Ser.). (ENG.). 10p. (J). (gr. -1-k). 11.99 *(978-1-85707-802-2(0))* Tango Bks. GBR. Dist: Independent Pubs. Group.

Tekenteam, illus. My Favorite Safari. 2011. (My Favorite Vehicles Ser.). (ENG.). 12p. (J). (gr. -1-k). bds. 5.99 *(978-0-7641-6412-5(0))* Barron's Educational Series, Inc.

Tessin, Kit Elaine. My Little Pinto, 1 vol. Bates, Brenda J. et al, illus. 2010. 26p. pap. 24.95 *(978-1-4489-9173-0(0))* PublishAmerica, Inc.

Thomas Nelson. Fit & Feel Vroom. 2015. (ENG.). 12p. (gr. -1). bds. *(978-1-78393-437-9(9))* Make Believe Ideas.

Tiger Tales Staff, creator. Things That Go. 2014. (My First Jumbo Tab Bks.). (ENG., Illus.). 12p. (J). (gr. -1). bds. 8.99 *(978-1-58925-589-0(5))* Tiger Tales.

Tim, Fireball. Big Book of Wacky Rides! 2013. (ENG.). 32p. (J). (gr. -1). 17.95 *(978-1-933492-81-0(3))* Design Studio Pr.

Timmers, Leo. Who Is Driving? Timmers, Leo, illus. 2014. (ENG., Illus.). 30p. (J). (gr. -1-1). bds. 7.99 *(978-1-61963-169-4(5),* 9781619631694, Bloomsbury USA Childrens) Bloomsbury Publishing USA.

Top That, ed. Let's Play Magnetic Play Scene Diggers. 2008. *(978-1-84666-605-6(8))* Top That! Publishing PLC.

Toy Box Innovations, creator. Disney/Pixar: Volume 2. abr. ed. 2006. (Disney's Read along Collection Ser.). (ENG.). 24p. (J). (gr. -1-3). pap. *(978-0-7634-2181-6(2))* Walt Disney Records.

Trueman, Terry. No Right Turn. 2009. (ENG.). 176p. (YA). (gr. 9). pap. 8.99 *(978-0-06-057493-2(3),* HarperTeen) HarperCollins Pubs.

Turbo Powers! Individual Title Six-Packs. (Bookweb Ser.). 32p. (gr. 6-18). 34.00 *(978-0-7578-0903-3(0))* Rigby Education.

Turn-the-Wheel, 4 bks., Set. Incl. Animal Ambulance. Lawson, Peter & Smith, Kathryn. bds. 5.95 *(978-0-7892-1026-5(6))*; Fire Engine. Goldsack, Gaby. Lawson, Peter, illus. bds. 5.95 *(978-0-7892-1022-7(3))*; Fishing Boat. Goldsack, Gaby. Lawson, Peter, illus. bds. 5.95 *(978-0-7892-1025-8(8))*; Tractor. Lawson, Peter. bds. 5.95 *(978-0-7892-1023-4(1))*; 10p. (J). (gr. -1-k). (Turn the Wheel Ser.). (ENG., Illus.). 40p. 2009. Set bds. 22.95 *(978-0-7892-1027-2(4),* Abbeville Kids) Abbeville Pr., Inc.

The Van. 2005. (Georgie Giraffe Set 1 Ser.). (J). 7.33 *(978-1-932570-40-3(3))* Pioneer Valley Bks.

Van Dusen, Chris. If I Built a Car. Van Dusen, Chris, illus. (ENG., Illus.). (J). 2007. 40p. (gr. k-k). pap. 7.99 *(978-0-14-240825-4(5),* Puffin Books) 2005. 32p. (gr. -1-k). 17.99 *(978-0-525-47400-5(5),* Dutton Books for Young Readers) Penguin Young Readers Group.

—If I Built a Car. Van Dusen, Chris, illus. 2007. (Illus.). (gr. -1-3). lib. bdg. 17.00 *(978-0-7569-8149-5(2))* Perfection Learning Corp.

Various, illus. Cars Little Golden Book Favorites (Disney/Pixar Cars) 2017. (Little Golden Book Favorites Ser.). (ENG.). 80p. (J). (-k). 7.99 ***(978-0-7364-3679-3(0),*** Golden/Disney) Random Hse. Children's Bks.

Wadsworth, Wallace. The Modern Story Book. Eger, Caroline Ruth, illus. 2010. (Dover Read & Listen Ser.). (ENG.). 112p. (J). (gr. 1-5). pap. 14.99 incl. audio compact disk *(978-0-486-47844-9(0))* Dover Pubns., Inc.

Watt, Fiona. Beep Beep. 2009. (Stroller Bks). 8p. (J). 7.99 *(978-0-7945-2498-2(2),* Usborne) EDC Publishing.

—Cars. 2011. (Luxury Touchy-Feely Board Books Ser.). 10p. (J). ring bd. 15.99 *(978-0-7945-2568-2(7),* Usborne) EDC Publishing.

Watts, Debra G. Carter Car & His Wild & Carazy Birthday. 2011. 40p. pap. 21.99 *(978-1-4628-4864-5(8))* Xlibris Corp.

Webster, Christy. Scooter Trouble (Pocoyo) Random House Staff, illus. 2013. (Step into Reading Ser.). (ENG.). 32p. (J). (gr. -1-1). 3.99 *(978-0-449-81541-0(2),* Random Hse. Bks. for Young Readers) Random Hse. Children's Bks.

Willis, Jeanne. The Cow Tripped over the Moon: a Nursery Rhyme Emergency. Stewart, Joel, illus. 2015. (ENG.). 32p. (J). (gr. -1-2). 15.99 *(978-0-7636-7402-1(8))* Candlewick Pr.

Wilson, Debra. 65 Mustang: A Novel. 2011. 300p. pap. *(978-1-934922-47-7(1))* IBJ Custom Publishing.

Woodard, Amy. The Day the Teacher Rode a Horse to School. 2008. 24p. pap. 24.95 *(978-1-60441-736-4(6))* America Star Bks.

Woodbury, Mary. The Ghost in the Machine. 2005. 222p. (J). (gr. 6-9). pap. 7.95 *(978-1-55050-227-5(1))* Coteau Bks. CAN. Dist: Fitzhenry & Whiteside, Ltd.

Woolley, Bryan. Mr. Green's Magnificent Machine. Arbuckle, Scott, illus. 2003. 32p. 15.95 *(978-1-57168-606-0(1))* Eakin Pr.

Wright, Neville. Cop Car: And the Phantom Street Gang. 2010. 16p. 8.49 *(978-1-4520-2881-1(8))* AuthorHouse.

Wyre, Yvonne. The Further Adventures of Cuthbert the Coal Lorry & all His Friends. 2007. (Illus.). 204p. pap. *(978-1-84401-801-7(6))* Athena Pr.

AUTOMOBILES—HISTORY

ABDO Publishing Company. Ultimate Cars Set II, 6 vols. 2004. (Ultimate Cars Set 2 Ser.). (gr. 3-8). 162.42 *(978-1-59197-577-9(8),* Abdo & Daughters) ABDO Publishing Co.

Abramovitz, Melissa. Old Cars. 2013. (Cars, Cars, Cars Ser.). (ENG.). 24p. (gr. k-1). pap. 41.70 *(978-1-62065-876-5(3))*; pap. 7.29 *(978-1-62065-875-8(5))*; lib. bdg. 26.65 *(978-1-62065-090-5(8))* Capstone Press of Coughlan Cos. (Pebble Plus).

Banting, Erinn. Inventing the Automobile. 2006. (Breakthrough Inventions Ser.). (ENG., Illus.). 32p. (J). (gr. 3-7). pap. *(978-0-7787-2834-4(X))* Crabtree Publishing Co.

Baxter, Roberta. The First Cars, 1 vol. 2014. (Famous Firsts Ser.). (ENG., Illus.). 24p. (gr. k-1). 26.65 *(978-1-4914-0574-1(0),* Pebble Plus) Capstone Press of Coughlan Cos.

Beyer, Mark. Autos Del Pasado. 2004. (Transporte Ayer y Hoy (Transportation Through the Ages) Ser.). (SPA & ENG., Illus.). 24p. (J). (gr. 2-4). lib. bdg. 22.60 *(978-0-8239-6851-0(0))* Rosen Publishing Group, Inc., The.

—Autos del pasado (Cars of the Past) 2009. (transporte ayer y hoy (Transportation Through the Ages) Ser.). 24p. (gr. 1-2). 42.50 *(978-1-61512-251-6(6),* Editorial Buenas Letras) Rosen Publishing Group, Inc., The.

—Cars of the Past. 2009. (Transportation Through the Ages Ser.). 24p. (gr. 1-1). 42.50 *(978-1-60854-588-9(1),* PowerKids Pr.) Rosen Publishing Group, Inc., The.

Bradley, Michael. GTO. 2009. (Cars 2 Ser.). 32p. (gr. 3). 28.50 *(978-0-7614-4112-0(3))* Marshall Cavendish GBR. Dist: Marshall Cavendish Corp.

Cheetham, Craig. American Cars Before 1950. 2007. (American Cars Through the Decades Ser.). (Illus.). 32p. (gr. 3-6). lib. bdg. 26.00 *(978-0-8368-7723-6(3),* Gareth Stevens Learning Library) Stevens, Gareth Publishing LLLP.

—American Cars of The 1950s. 2007. (American Cars Through the Decades Ser.). (Illus.). 32p. (gr. 3-6). lib. bdg. 26.00 *(978-0-8368-7724-3(1),* Gareth Stevens Learning Library) Stevens, Gareth Publishing LLLP.

—American Cars of The 1960s. 2007. (American Cars Through the Decades Ser.). (Illus.). 32p. (gr. 3-6). lib. bdg. 26.00 *(978-0-8368-7725-0(X),* Gareth Stevens Learning Library) Stevens, Gareth Publishing LLLP.

—American Cars of The 1970s. 2007. (American Cars Through the Decades Ser.). (Illus.). 32p. (gr. 3-6). lib. bdg. 26.00 *(978-0-8368-7726-7(8),* Gareth Stevens Learning Library) Stevens, Gareth Publishing LLLP.

—American Cars of The 1980s. 2007. (American Cars Through the Decades Ser.). (Illus.). 32p. (gr. 3-6). lib. bdg. 26.00 *(978-0-8368-7727-4(6),* Gareth Stevens Learning Library) Stevens, Gareth Publishing LLLP.

Conley, Robyn. The Automobile. 2006. (Inventions That Shaped the World Ser.). (Illus.). 80p. (gr. 5-8). 19.95 *(978-0-7569-6853-3(4))* Perfection Learning Corp.

Corbett, David. A History of Cars. 2006. (From Past to Present Ser.). (Illus.). 36p. (gr. 3-7). lib. bdg. 26.00 *(978-0-8368-6286-7(4),* Gareth Stevens Learning Library) Stevens, Gareth Publishing LLLP.

Cowdery, Ray. All American Wonder, Vol 2, Vol. II. 4th ed. 2003. (Illus.). 144p. pap. 29.95 *(978-0-9700567-3-3(7))* Victory WW 2 Publishing Ltd.

Dooling, Michael. The Great Horse-Less Carriage Race. Dooling, Michael, illus. 2005. (ENG., Illus.). 32p. (J). (gr. k-3). tchr. ed. 16.95 *(978-0-8234-1640-0(2))* Holiday Hse., Inc.

Farndon, John. Stickmen's Guide to Trains & Automobiles. Paul de Quay, John, illus. 2016. (Stickmen's Guides to How Everything Works). (ENG.). 32p. (J). (gr. 3-6). 30.65 *(978-1-4677-9590-6(9))* Lerner Publishing Group.

Fitzpatrick, Anne. The Automobile. 2003. 24p. (J). lib. bdg. 21.35 *(978-1-58340-319-8(1))* Black Rabbit Bks.

Fletcher, Robert A. Jeeps at War. Naples, Thomas R. et al, eds. Fletcher, Robert A., illus. 2008. (Illus.). 36p. (J). 19.95 *(978-0-9722961-1-3(5))* Iron Mountain Pr.

Georgano, G. N. Cars of the Seventies & Eighties: Hatchbacks for the Sportsman. 2004. (World of Wheels Ser.). (Illus.). 104p. (YA). (gr. 7-18). lib. bdg. 22.95 *(978-1-59084-488-5(2))* Mason Crest.

Gibbs, Lynne. Mega Book of Motorcycles. 2003. (Illus.). 32p. (YA). pap. *(978-1-903954-57-7(6),* Pavilion Children's Books) Pavilion Bks.

Gibbs, Lynne & Morris, Neil. Mega Book of Cars. 2003. (Illus.). 32p. (YA). pap. *(978-1-903954-56-0(8),* Pavilion Children's Books) Pavilion Bks.

Hawley, Rebecca. Ferrari. (Superfast Cars Ser.). 24p. 2009. (gr. 2-3). 42.50 *(978-1-60853-232-2(1),* PowerKids Pr.) 2007. (Illus.). (J). (gr. 3-6). lib. bdg. 22.60 *(978-1-4042-3640-0(6))* Rosen Publishing Group, Inc., The.

—Lamborghini. 2009. (Superfast Cars Ser.). 24p. (gr. 2-3). 42.50 *(978-1-60853-233-9(X),* PowerKids Pr.) Rosen Publishing Group, Inc., The.

Levinson, Nancy Smiler. Cars: A Holiday House Reader, Level 2. Rogers, Jacqueline, tr. Rogers, Jacqueline, illus. 2004. (ENG.). 32p. (J). (gr. k-3). tchr. ed. 14.95 *(978-0-8234-1614-1(3))* Holiday Hse., Inc.

Maurer, Tracy Nelson. Maserati. 2007. (Full Throttle 2 (High Interest) Ser.). (Illus.). 32p. (J). (gr. 3-7). lib. bdg. 28.50 *(978-1-60044-573-6(X))* Rourke Educational Media.

Mezzanotte, Jim. The Story of the Cadillac Eldorado. 2005. (Classic Cars Ser.). (Illus.). 24p. (gr. 1-4). lib. bdg. 23.00 *(978-0-8368-4532-7(3),* Gareth Stevens Learning Library) Stevens, Gareth Publishing LLLP.

Morris, Neil. Cars. (Past & Present Ser.). (Illus.). 32p. lib. bdg. 24.25 *(978-1-931983-36-5(4))* Chrysalis Education.

Morton, Norman & Mort, Norm. Classic Cars, 1931-1980. rev. ed. 2007. (Automania! Ser.). (ENG., Illus.). 32p. (J). (gr. 2-9). pap. *(978-0-7787-3034-7(4))* Crabtree Publishing Co.

Mulligan, Simon. Porsche. 2012. (Speed Machines Ser.). (ENG., Illus.). 32p. (J). (gr. 3-6). pap. 10.00 *(978-1-4488-7528-3(5))*; lib. bdg. 25.25 *(978-1-4488-7456-9(4))* Rosen Publishing Group, Inc., The. (PowerKids Pr.).

Nagelhout, Ryan. The Problem with Early Cars. 2015. (Bloopers of Invention Ser.). (ENG., Illus.). 24p. (J). (gr. 2-3). pap. 8.15 *(978-1-4824-2760-8(5))* Stevens, Gareth Publishing LLLP.

Nielsen, L. Michelle & Neilsen, L. Michelle. Vintage Cars. 2006. (Automania! Ser.). (ENG., Illus.). 32p. (J). (gr. 4-7). lib. bdg. *(978-0-7787-3011-8(5))* Crabtree Publishing Co.

—Vintage Cars, 1919-1930. 2006. (Automania! Ser.). (ENG., Illus.). 32p. (J). (gr. 4-7). pap. *(978-0-7787-3033-0(6))* Crabtree Publishing Co.

Oxlade, Chris & Farndon, John. Stickmen's Guide to Trains & Automobiles. Pyke, Jerry & Quay, John Paul de, illus. 2016. (Stickmen's Guides to How Everything Works). (ENG.). 32p. (J). (gr. 3-6). lib. bdg. 26.65 *(978-1-4677-9360-5(4))* Lerner Publishing Group.

Oxlade, Chris & Ganeri, Anita. The Car, 1 vol. 2010. (Tales of Invention Ser.). (ENG.). 32p. (gr. 3-5). 30.65 *(978-1-4329-3827-7(4))*; pap. 8.95 *(978-1-4329-3834-5(7))* Heinemann-Raintree. (NA-h).

Power, Bob. Ferraris. 2011. (Wild Wheels Ser.). (Illus.). 32p. (J). (gr. 3-6). pap. 10.50 *(978-1-4339-5828-1(7))*; lib. bdg. 26.60 *(978-1-4339-5826-7(0))* Stevens, Gareth Publishing LLLP. (Gareth Stevens Learning Library).

Publications International Ltd. Staff. Cars Of 60's. 2007. 192p. 12.98 *(978-1-4127-1391-7(9),* PIL Kids) Publications International, Ltd.

—Cars of The 50's. 2007. 192p. 12.98 *(978-1-4127-1390-0(0),* PIL Kids) Publications International, Ltd.

—Cars of the Fabulous 40's Landscape. 2008. 192p. 12.98 *(978-1-4127-7205-1(2))* Publications International, Ltd.

Publications International Ltd. Staff, ed. Cars of the Sizzling 60s. 2008. 416p. lthr. 29.98 *(978-1-4127-7119-1(6))* Publications International, Ltd.

Publications International Ltd. Staff & Flamming, James A. Cars 70s. 2008. 416p. 29.98 *(978-1-4127-7117-7(X))* Publications International, Ltd.

—Cars of The 50s. 2008. 416p. lthr. 29.98 *(978-1-4127-7118-4(8))* Publications International, Ltd.

Speed Machines: Sets 1 - 2. 2013. (Speed Machines Ser.). 32p. (J). (gr. 3-6). 303.00 *(978-1-4777-1153-8(8))*; pap. 720.00 *(978-1-4777-1246-7(1))*; pap. 120.00 *(978-1-4777-1245-0(3))* Rosen Publishing Group, Inc., The. (PowerKids Pr.).

Spilsbury, Richard. Great Car Designs 1900-Today. 2015. (Iconic Designs Ser.). (ENG., Illus.). 48p. (gr. 4-6). pap. 8.99 *(978-1-4846-2622-1(2),* Heinemann InfoSearch) Heinemann-Raintree.

Transportation Zone. 2011. (Transportation Zone Ser.). (ENG.). 24p. (gr. 1-2). lib. bdg. 126.60 *(978-1-4296-6834-7(2),* First Facts) Capstone Press of Coughlan Cos.

Volkswagen History to Hobby: All the Facts - All the Fun. 2005. (YA). lib. bdg. 24.99 net. *(978-0-9765261-0-0(7))* Jersey Classic Publishing.

Wheeler, Jill C. Beetle, 1 vol. 2004. (Ultimate Cars Ser.). (ENG.). 32p. (gr. 3-8). 27.07 *(978-1-59197-578-6(6),* Abdo & Daughters) ABDO Publishing Co.

—Camaro, 1 vol. 2004. (Ultimate Cars Ser.). (ENG.). 32p. (gr. 3-8). 27.07 *(978-1-59197-579-3(4),* Abdo & Daughters) ABDO Publishing Co.

—Maserati, 1 vol. 2004. (Ultimate Cars Ser.). (ENG., Illus.). 32p. (gr. 3-8). 27.07 *(978-1-59197-580-9(8),* Abdo & Daughters) ABDO Publishing Co.

—Mercedes-Benz, 1 vol. 2004. (Ultimate Cars Ser.). (ENG.). 32p. (gr. 3-8). 27.07 *(978-1-59197-581-6(6),* Abdo & Daughters) ABDO Publishing Co.

—Rolls Royce, 1 vol. 2004. (Ultimate Cars Ser.). (ENG.). 32p. (gr. 3-8). 27.07 *(978-1-59197-582-3(4),* Abdo & Daughters) ABDO Publishing Co.

AUTOMOBILES—MODELS

Bradley, Michael. Camaro. 2009. (Cars 2 Ser.). 32p. (gr. 3). 28.50 *(978-0-7614-4104-5(2))* Marshall Cavendish GBR. Dist: Marshall Cavendish Corp.

—Jaguar. 2009. (Cars 2 Ser.). 32p. (gr. 3). 28.50 *(978-0-7614-4105-2(0))* Marshall Cavendish Corp.

Kenney, Sean. Cool Cars & Trucks. Kenney, Sean, illus. Barrett, John E., photos by. 2009. (ENG., Illus.). 32p. (J). (gr. -1-3). 12.99 *(978-0-8050-8761-1(3),* 9780805087611, Holt, Henry & Co. Bks. For Young Readers) Holt, Henry & Co.

Publications International Ltd. Staff, ed. Muscle Car Classics. 2008. 128p. (J). 10.98 *(978-1-4127-7658-5(9))* Publications International, Ltd.

Rigsby, Mike. Amazing Rubber Band Cars: Easy-to-build Wind-up Racers, Models, & Toys. 2007. (ENG., Illus.). 136p. (J). (gr. 4-18). pap. 14.95 *(978-1-55652-736-4(5))* Chicago Review Pr., Inc.

Rothrock, Megan H. The LEGO Adventure Book Vol. 2: Spaceships, Pirates, Dragons & More! 2013. (ENG., Illus.). 196p. (gr. 5). 24.95 *(978-1-59327-512-9(9),* 9781593275129) No Starch Pr., Inc.

Scholastic, Inc. Staff, contrib. by. Hot Wheels: The Collector's Handbook. 2014. (ENG.). 96p. (J). *(978-0-545-76912-9(4))* Scholastic, Inc.

Sobey, Ed, ed. Radio-Controlled Car Experiments. 2011. (Cool Science Projects with Technology Ser.). (Illus.). 128p. (J). (gr. 5-18). lib. bdg. 33.27 *(978-0-7660-3304-7(X))* Enslow Pubs., Inc.

Speed Machines: Sets 1 - 2. 2013. (Speed Machines Ser.). 32p. (J). (gr. 3-6). 303.00 *(978-1-4777-1153-8(8))*; pap. 720.00 *(978-1-4777-1246-7(1))*; pap. 120.00 *(978-1-4777-1245-0(3))* Rosen Publishing Group, Inc., The. (PowerKids Pr.).

Thorne, Troy. Getting Started in Pinewood Derby: Step-by-Step Workbook to Building Your First Car. 2011. (ENG., Illus.). 96p. pap. 12.95 *(978-1-56523-617-2(3),* 6172) Fox Chapel Publishing Co., Inc.

AUTOMOBILES—MOTORS

see Automobiles—Engines

AUTOMOBILES—POETRY

Lewis, J. Patrick & Florian, Douglas. Poem-Mobiles: Crazy Car Poems. Holmes, Jeremy, illus. 2014. (ENG.). 40p. (J). (gr. -1-3). 17.99 *(978-0-375-86690-6(6),* Schwartz & Wade Bks.) Random Hse. Children's Bks.

Townsend, Una Belle. Racecar Driver's Night Before Christmas, 1 vol. Anderson, Rick, illus. 2008. (Night Before Christmas Ser.). (ENG.). 32p. (gr. 1-3). 16.99 *(978-1-58980-565-1(8))* Pelican Publishing Co., Inc.

AUTOMOBILES—RACING

see Automobile Racing

AUTOMOBILES—REPAIRING

Marlowe, Christie. Car Mechanic. 2013. (Earning $50,000 - $100,000 with a High School Diploma or Less Ser.: 14). 64p. (J). (gr. 7-18). 22.95 *(978-1-4222-2889-0(4))* Mason Crest.

Mozer, Mindy. Getting a Job in Automotive Care & Service. 2013. 80p. (YA). (gr. 9-12). 33.25 *(978-1-4488-9609-7(6))* Rosen Publishing Group, Inc., The.

Thompson, Gary. What Every Teen Should Know Before Getting Behind the Wheel Alone: A Guide to Increasing Your Child's Safety While Reducing Your Auto Repair Expenses. 2004. 131p. (YA). per. 9.95 *(978-0-9749763-1-0(8))* Guiding Horizons.

AUTOMOBILES—REPAIRING—VOCATIONAL GUIDANCE

Jozefowicz, Chris. Auto Technician. 2009. (Cool Careers: Cutting Edge Ser.). (ENG.). 32p. (J). (gr. 5-8). pap. 10.50 *(978-1-4339-2154-4(5))*; lib. bdg. 26.00 *(978-1-4339-1955-8(9))* Stevens, Gareth Publishing LLLP.

Marsico, Katie. Auto Technician. 2010. (21st Century Skills Library: Cool Careers Ser.). (ENG.). 32p. (gr. 4-8). lib. bdg. 28.50 *(978-1-60279-937-0(7),* 200619) Cherry Lake Publishing.

Orr, Tamra. A Career as an Auto Mechanic. 2010. (Essential Careers Ser.). (ENG.). 80p. (YA). lib. bdg. 33.25 *(978-1-4358-9471-6(5))* Rosen Publishing Group, Inc., The.

AUTOMOBILES—TOURING

see Automobile Travel

AUTOMOBILES—TRAILERS

Bender, Lionel. Trucks & Trailers. 2006. (J). *(978-1-59389-270-8(5))* Chrysalis Education.

Hanson, Anders. Let's Go by RV, 1 vol. 2008. (Let's Go Ser.). (ENG., Illus.). 24p. (J). (gr. k-3). lib. bdg. 24.21 *(978-1-59928-902-1(4),* SandCastle) ABDO Publishing Co.

Ransom, Candice & Brill, Marlene Targ. Big Rigs. (Pull Ahead Bks.). (Illus.). 32p. (J). (gr. k-2). 2005. lib. bdg. 22.60 *(978-0-8225-1537-1(7))* 2004. pap. 6.95 *(978-0-8225-2379-6(5))* Lerner Publishing Group.

AUTOSUGGESTION

see Hypnotism

AUTUMN

Aloian, Molly. How Do We Know It's Fall? 2013. (ENG., Illus.). 24p. (J). *(978-0-7787-0961-9(2))*; pap. *(978-0-7787-0965-7(5))* Crabtree Publishing Co.

Amoroso, Cynthia & Noyed, Robert B. Fall. 2014. (Seasons of the Year Ser.). (ENG.). 24p. (J). (gr. -1-2). 25.64 *(978-1-62687-022-2(5),* 206821) Child's World, Inc., The.

Anderson, Sheila. Are You Ready for Fall? 2010. (Lightning Bolt Books (tm) — Our Four Seasons Ser.). (ENG.). 32p. (gr. k-2). pap. 7.95 *(978-0-7613-5672-1(X))*; lib. bdg. 26.60 *(978-0-7613-4586-2(8))* Lerner Publishing Group.

Appleby, Alex. Qu Sucede en Otoo? / What Happens in Fall?, Vol. 1. 2014. (Cuatro Estaciones Estupendas / Four Super Seasons Ser.). (SPA & BYN.). 24p. (J). (gr. k-k). 22.60 *(978-1-4824-0101-1(0))* Stevens, Gareth Publishing LLLP.

Barklem, Jill. Autumn Story. Barklem, Jill, illus. 2011. (Brambly Hedge Ser.). (ENG., Illus.). 32p. (J). 9.99 *(978-0-00-183739-3(7),* HarperCollins Children's Bks.) HarperCollins Pubs. Ltd. GBR. Dist: HarperCollins Pubs.

Barnham, Kay. Fall. 2010. (Seasons Ser.). (ENG.). 24p. (J). lib. bdg. 22.60 *(978-1-61532-567-2(0),* PowerKids Pr.) Rosen Publishing Group, Inc., The.

Brennan, Linda Crotta. Leaves Change Color. 2014. (Tell Me Why Library). (ENG., Illus.). 24p. (J). (gr. 2-5). 25.64 *(978-1-63188-008-7(X),* 205439) Cherry Lake Publishing.

Brode, Robyn. October. 2nd rev. ed. 2009. (Months of the Year Ser.). 24p. (J). (gr. -1-3). pap. 8.15 *(978-1-4339-2103-2(0))*; lib. bdg. 22.00 *(978-1-4339-1926-8(5))* Stevens, Gareth Publishing LLLP. (Weekly Reader Leveled Readers).

—October;octubre. 2009. (Months of the Year/Meses del año Ser.). (ENG & SPA.). 24p. (J). (gr. -1-3). pap. 8.15 *(978-1-4339-2115-5(4),* Weekly Reader Leveled Readers) Stevens, Gareth Publishing LLLP.

—October/Octubre. 2009. (Months of the Year/Meses del año Ser.). (ENG & SPA.). 24p. (J). (gr. -1-3). lib. bdg. 22.00 *(978-1-4339-1938-1(9),* Weekly Reader Leveled Readers) Stevens, Gareth Publishing LLLP.

—September;septiembre. 2009. (Months of the Year/Meses del año Ser.). (ENG & SPA.). 24p. (J). (gr. -1-3). pap. 8.15 *(978-1-4339-2114-8(6),* Weekly Reader Leveled Readers) Stevens, Gareth Publishing LLLP.

—September/Septiembre. 2009. (Months of the Year/Meses del año Ser.). (ENG & SPA.). 24p. (J). (gr. -1-3). lib. bdg. 22.00 *(978-1-4339-1937-4(0),* Weekly Reader Leveled Readers) Stevens, Gareth Publishing LLLP.

Brode, Robyn & Nations, Susan. September. 2nd rev. ed. 2009. (Months of the Year Ser.). (ENG.). 24p. (J). (gr. -1-3). pap. 8.15 *(978-1-4339-2102-5(2))*; lib. bdg. 22.00 *(978-1-4339-1925-1(7))* Stevens, Gareth Publishing LLLP. (Weekly Reader Leveled Readers).

Bryant, Margaret A., et al. Learning about Fall with Children's Literature: Cross-Curricular Units Based on the Works of Eric Carle, Robert Kalan, Ludwig Bemelmans, & More. 2006. (ENG., Illus.). 160p. (J). (gr. k-3). pap. 14.95 *(978-1-55976-204-2(X))* Chicago Review Pr., Inc.

Bullard, Lisa. Busy Animals: Learning about Animals in Autumn, 1 vol. Takvorian, Nadine, illus. 2010. (Autumn Ser.). (ENG.). 24p. (gr. 1-2). lib. bdg. 26.65 *(978-1-4048-6014-8(2))* Picture Window Bks.

—Leaves Fall Down: Learning about Autumn Leaves, 1 vol. Takvorian, Nadine, illus. 2010. (Autumn Ser.). (ENG.). 24p. (gr. 1-2). pap. 8.95 *(978-1-4048-6390-3(7))*; lib. bdg. 26.65 *(978-1-4048-6013-1(4))* Picture Window Bks.

Butterworth Moira. Fall. James, Helen, illus. 2005. (Seasons (Smart Apple Media) Ser.). 32p. (YA). (gr. 2-4). lib. bdg. 27.10 *(978-1-58340-616-8(6))* Black Rabbit Bks.

DeGezelle, Terri. Exploring Fall, 1 vol. 2012. (Exploring the Seasons Ser.). (ENG.). 24p. (gr. k-1). pap. 7.29 *(978-1-4296-7908-4(5))*; pap. 41.70 *(978-1-4296-8350-0(3))* Capstone Press of Coughlan Cos. (Pebble Plus).

Dils, Tracey E. Falling Leaves 1,2,3: A Farm Counting Book. 2015. (1, 2, 3... Count with Me Ser.). (ENG., Illus.). 24p. (J). (gr. k-2). 19.95 *(978-1-60753-719-9(2))* Amicus Publishing.

Dolphin, Colleen. Signs of Autumn, 1 vol. 2012. (Signs of the Seasons Ser.). (ENG.). 24p. (J). (gr. k-3). lib. bdg. 24.21 *(978-1-61783-392-2(4),* SandCastle) ABDO Publishing Co.

Ely, Lisa & Glassman, Michael. Kinder Gardens: Autumn Fun, 1 vol. 2011. (ENG., Illus.). 64p. (J). pap. 16.99 *(978-0-7643-3853-3(6),* 9780764338533, Schiffer Publishing Ltd) Schiffer Publishing, Ltd.

Enslow, Brian. Fall Colors. 2011. (All about Colors of the Seasons Ser.). (Illus.). 24p. (J). (gr. -1-18). pap. 7.95 *(978-1-59845-264-8(9),* Enslow Elementary) Enslow Pubs., Inc.

Felix, Rebecca. How's the Weather in Fall? 2013. (21st Century Basic Skills Library: Let's Look at Fall Ser.). (ENG.). 24p. (J). (gr. k-3). 22.79 *(978-1-61080-902-3(5),* 202587); pap. 12.79 *(978-1-61080-927-6(0),* 202589) Cherry Lake Publishing.

—How's the Weather in Fall?/Rebecca Felix. 2013. (J). (978-1-61080-977-1(7)) Cherry Lake Publishing.

—We Harvest Apples in Fall. 2013. (Illus.). 24p. (J). (978-1-61080-980-1(7)); (ENG., 22.79 (978-1-61080-905-4(X), 202599); (ENG., pap. 12.79 (978-1-61080-930-6(0), 202601) Cherry Lake Publishing.

—We Harvest Pumpkins in the Fall. 2013. 24p. (J). (978-1-61080-981-8(5)); (ENG.). 22.79 (978-1-61080-906-1(8), 202603); (ENG.). pap. 12.79 (978-1-61080-931-3(9), 202605) Cherry Lake Publishing.

—What Do Animals Do in Fall? 2013. (J). (978-1-61080-982-5(3)); (ENG.). 24p. 22.79 (978-1-61080-907-8(6), 202607); (ENG.). 24p. pap. 12.79 (978-1-61080-932-0(7), 202609) Cherry Lake Publishing.

—What Do People Do in Fall? 2013. (J). (978-1-61080-983-2(1)); (ENG.). 24p. 22.79 (978-1-61080-908-5(4), 202611); (ENG.). 24p. pap. 12.79 (978-1-61080-933-7(5), 202613) Cherry Lake Publishing.

—What Happens to Leaves in Fall? 2013. (J). (978-1-61080-984-9(X)); (ENG.). 24p. 22.79 (978-1-61080-909-2(2), 202615); (ENG.). 24p. pap. 12.79 (978-1-61080-934-4(3), 202617) Cherry Lake Publishing.

Flatt, Lizann. Counting on Fall. Barron, Ashley & Owlkids Books Inc. Staff, illus. 2012. (Math in Nature Ser.: 1). (ENG.). 32p. (J). (gr. k-2). 15.95 (978-1-926973-36-4(4), Owlkids) Owlkids Bks. Inc. CAN. Dist: Publishers Group West (PGW).

Glaser, Rebecca. Fall. 2012. (ENG., Illus.). 24p. (J). lib. bdg. 25.65 (978-1-62031-016-8(3)) Jump! Inc.

Gleisner, Jenna Lee. Weather in Fall. 2017. (Welcome, Fall! Ser.). (ENG.). 24p. (J). (gr. -1-2). lib. bdg. 27.07 (978-1-5038-1665-7(6), 211501) Child's World, Inc., The.

Goldstone, Bruce. Awesome Autumn. Goldstone, Bruce, photos by. 2012. (ENG., Illus.). 48p. (J). (gr. -1-3). 17.99 (978-0-8050-9210-3(2), 9780805092103, Holt, Henry & Co. Bks. For Young Readers) Holt, Henry & Co.

Green, Emily K. & Herriges, Ann. Fall. 2006. (Seasons Ser.). (ENG., Illus.). 24p. (J). (gr. k-3). lib. bdg. 25.95 (978-1-60014-033-4(5)) Bellwether Media.

Griswold, Cliff. Fall Leaves. 2015. (Fun in Fall Ser.). (ENG.). 24p. (J). (gr. k-k). lib. bdg. 22.60 (978-1-4824-1776-0(6)) Stevens, Gareth Publishing LLLP.

—Let's Go on a Hayride! 2015. (Fun in Fall Ser.). (ENG., Illus.). 24p. (J). (gr. k-k). pap. 8.15 (978-1-4824-1786-9(3)) Stevens, Gareth Publishing LLLP.

Hawk, Fran. Count down to Fall, 1 vol. Neidigh, Sherry, illus. 2009. (ENG.). 32p. (J). (gr. -1-3). 16.95 (978-1-934359-94-5(7)) Arbordale Publishing.

Hedlund, Stephanie. Autumn. Bauer, Stephanie, illus. 2013. (Seasons Ser.). 24p. (J). (gr. k-4). lib. bdg. 27.07 (978-1-61641-992-9(X), Looking Glass Library- Nonfiction) Magic Wagon.

Here Comes Fall! 2003. (J). per. (978-1-57657-970-1(0)) Paradise Pr., Inc.

Herriges, Ann. Fall. 2011. (Blastoff! Readers Ser.). 24p. (J). pap. 5.95 (978-0-531-26246-7(4), Children's Pr.) Scholastic Library Publishing.

Herrington, Lisa M. How Do You Know It's Fall? 2013. (ENG.). 32p. (J). 23.00 (978-0-531-29946-3(5)); pap. 5.95 (978-0-531-22575-2(5)) Scholastic Library Publishing.

Jeffries, Joyce. Dinosaurs in the Fall. 2014. (Dinosaur School Ser.). 24p. (J). (gr. -1-1). 22.60 (978-1-4824-0710-5(8)) Stevens, Gareth Publishing LLLP.

Kalz, Jill. Fall. 2005. (My First Look at Seasons Ser.). (Illus.). 24p. (J). (gr. k-3). lib. bdg. 15.95 (978-1-58341-362-3(6), Creative Education) Creative Co., The.

Koontz, Robin. Apples, Apples Everywhere! Learning about Apple Harvests, 1 vol. Takvorian, Nadine, illus. 2010. (Autumn Ser.). (ENG.). 24p. (gr. 1-2). pap. 8.95 (978-1-4048-6388-0(5)) Picture Window Bks.

Lapenta, Marilyn. Fall Shakes to Harvest Bakes. 2013. (Yummy Tummy Recipes: Seasons Ser.). 24p. (J). (gr. 1-6). lib. bdg. 23.93 (978-1-61772-742-9(3)) Bearport Publishing Co., Inc.

Latta, Sara L. ¿Qué Pasa en el Otoño? What Happens in Fall? 2010. (SPA.). (J). 23.94 (978-0-7660-3241-5(8), Enslow Elementary) Enslow Pubs., Inc.

—What Happens in Fall? 2006. (I Like the Seasons! Ser.). (Illus.). 24p. (J). (gr. 1-3). lib. bdg. 22.60 (978-0-7660-2417-5(2), Enslow Elementary) Enslow Pubs., Inc.

—Why Is It Fall? 2012. (Why Do We Have Seasons? Ser.). (Illus.). 24p. (J). (gr. k-18). pap. 7.95 (978-1-59845-388-1(2), Enslow Elementary); 22.60 (978-0-7660-3985-8(4)) Enslow Pubs., Inc.

Lim, Annalees. 10-Minute Seasonal Crafts for Autumn. 2014. (10-Minute Seasonal Crafts Ser.). (Illus.). 24p. (J). (gr. k-3). lib. bdg. 26.25 (978-1-4777-9214-8(7)) Windmill Bks.

Lindeen, Mary. Fall! 2015. (BeginningtoRead Ser.). (ENG., Illus.). 32p. (J). (gr. k-2). lib. bdg. 22.60 (978-1-59953-681-1(1)) Norwood Hse. Pr.

—Fall. 2015. (BeginningtoRead Ser.). (ENG., Illus.). 32p. (J). (gr. k-2). pap. 11.94 (978-1-60357-741-0(6)) Norwood Hse. Pr.

—I Eat Apples in Fall. 2016. (First Step Nonfiction — Observing Fall Ser.). (ENG., Illus.). 24p. (J). (gr. k-2). 23.99 (978-1-5124-0793-8(3)) Lerner Publishing Group.

—I Watch Fall Harvests. 2016. (First Step Nonfiction — Observing Fall Ser.). (ENG., Illus.). 24p. (J). (gr. k-2). 23.99 (978-1-5124-0794-5(1)) Lerner Publishing Group.

Mackall, Dandi. The Fantastic Gifts of Fall. 2017. (Seasons Ser.). (ENG., Illus.). 32p. (J). (gr. -1-3). pap. 3.99 **(978-1-4627-4517-3(2)**, B&H Kids) B&H Publishing Group.

Macken, JoAnn Early. Autumn. 2006. (Seasons of the Year Ser.). (Illus.). 16p. (gr. -1-2). pap. 5.30 (978-0-8368-6358-1(5)); lib. bdg. 19.00 (978-0-8368-6353-6(4)) Stevens, Gareth Publishing LLLP. (Weekly Reader Leveled Readers).

—Autumn (Otoño) 2006. (Seasons of the Year/Las Estaciones del Ano Ser.). (ENG & SPA., Illus.). 16p. (gr. -1-2). lib. bdg. 19.00 (978-0-8368-6532-5(4), Weekly Reader Leveled Readers) Stevens, Gareth Publishing LLLP.

—Autumn/Otoño. 2006. (Seasons of the Year/ Las estaciones del ano Ser.). (ENG & SPA., Illus.). 16p. (gr. -1-2). pap. 5.30 (978-0-8368-6537-0(5), Weekly Reader Leveled Readers) Stevens, Gareth Publishing LLLP.

McGee, Randel. Fun & Festive Fall Crafts: Leaf Rubbings, Dancing Scarecrows, & Pinecone Turkeys. 2014. (Fun & Festive Crafts for the Seasons Ser.). (Illus.). 48p. (J). (gr. 3-4). lib. bdg. 25.27 (978-0-7660-4320-6(7), Enslow Elementary) Enslow Pubs., Inc.

Meister, Cari. Fall Is Fun, 1 vol. Lingenfelter, Jim, illus. 2010. (First Graphics: Seasons Ser.). (ENG.). 24p. (gr. 1-2). pap. 6.29 (978-1-4296-5623-8(9)); pap. 35.70 (978-1-4296-5692-4(1)); lib. bdg. 23.99 (978-1-4296-4731-1(0)) Capstone Press of Coughlan Cos.

Moon, Walt K. ¡El Otoño Es Divertido! 2017. (Bumba Books (tm) en Español — Diviértete con Las Estaciones (Season Fun) Ser.). (SPA., Illus.). 24p. (J). (gr. -1-1). 25.32 (978-1-5124-2860-5(4)) Lerner Publishing Group.

—Fall Is Fun! 2016. (Bumba Books (tm) — Season Fun Ser.). (ENG., Illus.). 24p. (J). (gr. -1-1). 25.32 (978-1-5124-1409-7(3)) Lerner Publishing Group.

Murray, Julie. Fall, 1 vol. 2016. (ENG., Illus.). 24p. (J). (978-1-62970-919-2(0), 1391198) ABDO Publishing Co.

—El Otono. 2016. (Las Estaciones Ser.). (SPA.). 24p. (J). (gr. k-5). pap. 7.95 (978-1-4966-0707-2(4)) Capstone Classroom.

Owen, Ruth. How Do You Know It's Fall? (Signs of the Seasons Ser.). 24p. (J). 2016. (ENG.). (gr. k-3). pap. 7.95 (978-1-944998-48-6(9)) 2012. (gr. -1-3). lib. bdg. 23.93 (978-1-61772-396-4(7)) Bearport Publishing Co., Inc.

Pfeffer, Wendy. We Gather Together: Celebrating the Harvest Season. Bleck, Linda, illus. 2014. (ENG.). 32p. (J). (gr. 1-4). 8.99 (978-0-14-751282-6(4), Puffin Books) Penguin Young Readers Group.

René, Ellen. Investigating Why Leaves Change Their Color. 2009. (Science Detectives Ser.). 24p. (gr. 2-3). 42.50 (978-1-60853-017-5(5), PowerKids Pr.) Rosen Publishing Group, Inc., The.

Roca, Nuria. Fall. 2004. (Seasons Ser.). (ENG., Illus.). 36p. (J). pap. 6.95 (978-0-7641-2729-8(2)) Barron's Educational Series, Inc.

Ross, Kathy. Crafts to Make in the Fall. Enright, Vicky, illus. 2003. (Crafts for All Seasons Ser.). (ENG.). 64p. (J). (gr. k-3). pap. 9.95 (978-0-7613-0335-0(9), First Avenue Editions) Lerner Publishing Group.

Rustad, Martha E. Las Personas en Otoño. 2009. (Todo Acerca Del Otoño/All about Fall Ser.).Tr. of People in Fall. (SPA, ENG & MUL.). 24p. (gr. k-1). 26.65 (978-1-4296-3261-4(5)) Capstone Press of Coughlan Cos.

Rustad, Martha E. H. Animals in Fall: Preparing for Winter. Enright, Amanda, illus. 2011. (Fall's Here! Ser.). pap. 39.62 (978-0-7613-8643-8(2), Millbrook Pr.); (ENG.). 24p. (J). lib. bdg. 23.93 (978-0-7613-5066-8(7)); (ENG.). 24p. pap. 6.95 (978-0-7613-8506-6(1), Millbrook Pr.) Lerner Publishing Group.

—Fall Leaves: Colorful & Crunchy. Enright, Amanda, illus. 2011. (Fall's Here! Ser.). pap. 39.62 (978-0-7613-8646-9(7), Millbrook Pr.); (ENG.). 24p. pap. 6.95 (978-0-7613-8505-9(3), Millbrook Pr.); (ENG.). 24p. lib. bdg. 23.93 (978-0-7613-5062-0(4)) Lerner Publishing Group.

—Fall Weather: Cooler Temperatures. Enright, Amanda, illus. 2011. (Fall's Here! Ser.). pap. 39.62 (978-0-7613-8648-3(3), Millbrook Pr.); (ENG.). 24p. pap. 6.95 (978-0-7613-8510-3(X), Millbrook Pr.); (ENG.). 24p. lib. bdg. 23.93 (978-0-7613-5063-7(2)) Lerner Publishing Group.

Rustad, Martha E. H. & Rustad, Martha E. People in Fall, 1 vol. Saunders-Smith, Gail, ed. 2007. (All about Fall Ser.). (ENG., Illus.). 24p. (gr. k-1). 26.65 (978-1-4296-0025-5(X), Pebble Plus) Capstone Press of Coughlan Cos.

Salas, Laura Purdie. Colors of Fall. (Colors All Around Ser.). (ENG.). 32p. (gr. 1-2). 2011. pap. 47.70 (978-1-4296-6152-2(6)) 2010. lib. bdg. 27.32 (978-1-4296-5256-8(X)) Capstone Press of Coughlan Cos. (Aplus Bks.).

Sayre, April Pulley. Full of Fall. 2017. (ENG., Illus.). 40p. (J). (gr. -1-3). 17.99 **(978-1-4814-7984-4(9)**, Beach Lane Bks.) Beach Lane Bks.

Schuh, Mari. Animals in Fall. 2013. (ENG., Illus.). 24p. (J). lib. bdg. 25.65 (978-1-62031-056-4(2)) Jump! Inc.

—Apples in Fall. 2013. (ENG., Illus.). 24p. (J). lib. bdg. 25.65 (978-1-62031-057-1(0)) Jump! Inc.

—Harvest in Fall. 2013. (ENG., Illus.). 24p. (J). lib. bdg. 25.65 (978-1-62031-058-8(9)) Jump! Inc.

—Leaves in Fall. 2013. (ENG., Illus.). 24p. (J). lib. bdg. 25.65 (978-1-62031-059-5(7)) Jump! Inc.

—Pumpkins in Fall. 2013. (ENG., Illus.). 24p. (J). lib. bdg. 25.65 (978-1-62031-060-1(0)) Jump! Inc.

—Weather in Fall. 2013. (ENG., Illus.). 24p. (J). lib. bdg. 25.65 (978-1-62031-061-8(9)) Jump! Inc.

Schuh, Mari C. I Feel Fall Weather. 2016. (First Step Nonfiction — Observing Fall Ser.). (ENG., Illus.). 24p. (J). (gr. k-2). 23.99 (978-1-5124-0797-6(6)) Lerner Publishing Group.

—I Notice Animals in Fall. 2016. (First Step Nonfiction — Observing Fall Ser.). (ENG., Illus.). 24p. (J). (gr. k-2). 23.99 (978-1-5124-0792-1(5)) Lerner Publishing Group.

—I See Fall Leaves. 2016. (First Step Nonfiction — Observing Fall Ser.). (ENG., Illus.). 24p. (J). (gr. k-2). 23.99 (978-1-5124-0795-2(X)) Lerner Publishing Group.

Serio, Marie L. Hello Autumn Goodbye Autumn. 2011. (Illus.). 16p. (gr. 1-2). pap. 9.75 (978-1-4634-0215-0(5)) AuthorHouse.

Shores, Erika L. Apples. 2015. (Celebrate Fall Ser.). (ENG., Illus.). 24p. (gr. k-1). lib. bdg. 21.99 (978-1-4914-6001-6(6), Pebble Bks.) Capstone Press of Coughlan Cos.

—Celebrate Fall. 2015. (Celebrate Fall Ser.). (ENG.). 24p. (gr. k-1). 87.96 (978-1-4914-6917-0(X), Pebble Bks.) Capstone Press of Coughlan Cos.

—Harvest Time. 2015. (Celebrate Fall Ser.). (ENG., Illus.). 24p. (gr. k-1). lib. bdg. 21.99 (978-1-4914-6002-3(4), Pebble Bks.) Capstone Press of Coughlan Cos.

—Leaves. 2015. (Celebrate Fall Ser.). (ENG., Illus.). 24p. (gr. k-1). lib. bdg. 21.99 (978-1-4914-6003-0(2), Pebble Bks.) Capstone Press of Coughlan Cos.

—Pumpkins. 2015. (Celebrate Fall Ser.). (ENG., Illus.). 24p. (gr. k-1). lib. bdg. 21.99 (978-1-4914-6004-7(0), Pebble Bks.) Capstone Press of Coughlan Cos.

Smith, Sian. What Can You See in Fall?, 1 vol. 2014. (Seasons Ser.). (ENG.). 24p. (gr. -1-1). pap. 5.99 (978-1-4846-0353-6(2), Acorn) Heinemann-Raintree.

Thayer, Tanya. Fall. 2005. (First Step Nonfiction Ser.). (Illus.). 24p. (gr. k-2). lib. bdg. 17.27 (978-0-8225-1987-4(9)) Lerner Publishing Group.

Turnbull, Stephanie. Fall. 2013. (Seasons Ser.). (Illus.). 24p. (J). (gr. 1-4). 25.65 (978-1-59920-849-7(0)) Black Rabbit Bks.

Wearing, Judy. Fall. 2010. (World of Wonder Ser.). (Illus.). 24p. (J). (gr. 2-4). lib. bdg. 25.70 (978-1-61690-044-1(X)) Weigl Pubs., Inc.

—Fall: WOW Study of Day & Seasons. 2010. (J). pap. (978-1-60596-768-4(8)); (Illus.). 24p. pap. 9.95 (978-1-61690-048-9(2)) Weigl Pubs., Inc.

AUTUMN—POETRY

Barker, Cicely Mary. Flower Fairies of the Autumn. 2008. (Flower Fairies Ser.). (ENG.). 56p. (J). (gr. -1-2). 7.99 (978-0-7232-6317-3(5), Warne) Penguin Young Readers Group.

AVALANCHES

Bullard, Lisa. Avalanches. 2009. pap. 40.95 (978-0-7613-4765-1(8)) 2008. (ENG.). 32p. 22.60 (978-0-8225-8827-6(7), Lerner Pubns.) Lerner Publishing Group.

Duden, Jane. Avalanche! The Deadly Slide. 2005. (Cover-to-Cover Informational Ser.). (Illus.). 56p. (gr. 4-7). lib. bdg. 17.95 (978-0-7569-4750-7(2)) Perfection Learning Corp.

Garbe, Suzanne. The Worst Avalanches of All Time, 1 vol. 2012. (Epic Disasters Ser.). (ENG., Illus.). 32p. (gr. 3-4). lib. bdg. 27.99 (978-1-4296-8417-0(8)) Capstone Press of Coughlan Cos.

Green, Sara. Snow Search Dogs. 2013. (Dogs to the Rescue! Ser.). (ENG., Illus.). 24p. (J). (gr. 3-8). lib. bdg. 25.95 (978-1-60014-959-7(6), Pilot Bks.) Bellwether Media.

Hamilton, John. Avalanches, 1 vol. 2006. (Nature's Fury Ser.). (ENG., Illus.). 32p. (gr. 3-8). 27.07 (978-1-59679-328-6(7), Abdo & Daughters) ABDO Publishing Co.

Hand, Carol. The Science of an Avalanche. 2015. (21st Century Skills Library: Disaster Science Ser.). (ENG., Illus.). 32p. (J). (gr. 4-8). pap. 14.21 (978-1-63362-500-6(1), 206845) Cherry Lake Publishing.

Katirgis, Jane & Drohan, Michele Ingber. Awful Avalanches. 2015. (Earth's Natural Disasters Ser.). (ENG., Illus.). 32p. (J). (gr. 3-4). 25.27 (978-0-7660-6791-2(2)) Enslow Pubs., Inc.

Katirgis, Jane & Ingber Drohan, Michele. Awful Avalanches. 2015. (Earth's Natural Disasters Ser.). (ENG., Illus.). 32p. (J). (gr. 3-4). pap. 10.52 (978-0-7660-6789-9(0)) Enslow Pubs., Inc.

Kopp, Megan. Avalanches. 2015. (Illus.). 32p. (J). (978-1-5105-0074-7(X)) SmartBook Media, Inc.

—Avalanches. 2014. (J). (978-1-4896-3264-7(6)) Weigl Pubs., Inc.

Lanier, Wendy. Avalanches, 1 vol. 2013. (Earth in Action Ser.). (ENG., Illus.). 48p. (J). (gr. 3-6). lib. bdg. 32.79 (978-1-61783-936-8(1)) ABDO Publishing Co.

Merrick, Patrick. Avalanches. 2015. (Forces of Nature Ser.). (ENG.). 24p. (J). (gr. 2-5). 27.07 (978-1-63143-762-5(3), 208602) Child's World, Inc., The.

Otfinoski, Steven. Avalanches. 2016. (True Book(tm), a — Extreme Earth Ser.). (ENG., Illus.). 48p. (J). lib. bdg. 31.00 (978-0-531-22294-2(2), Children's Pr.) Scholastic Library Publishing.

Perish, Patrick. Survive an Avalanche. 2017. (Survival Zone Ser.). (ENG., Illus.). 24p. (J). (gr. 3-7). lib. bdg. 25.95 (978-1-62617-583-9(7), Torque Bks.) Bellwether Media.

Schuh, Mari C. Avalanches. 2016. (Earth in Action Ser.). (ENG.). 24p. pap. 6.95 (978-1-5157-6205-8(X), Pebble Plus) Capstone Press of Coughlan Cos.

ShackletonCaroline. AVALANCHE! HIGH INTERMEDIATE BOOK WITH ONLINE ACCESS, 1 vol. 2014. (ENG., Illus.). 28p. pap. 9.50 (978-1-107-62157-2(7)) Cambridge Univ. Pr.

Shone, Rob. Avalanches & Landslides. (Graphic Natural Disasters Ser.). (ENG.). 48p. (gr. 5-5). 2009. (YA). 58.50 (978-1-61512-994-2(4), Rosen Reference) 2007. (Illus.). (J). lib. bdg. 31.95 (978-1-4042-1992-2(7)) Rosen Publishing Group, Inc., The.

—Avalanches & Mudslides. 2007. (Graphic Natural Disasters Ser.). (ENG., Illus.). 48p. (gr. 5-8). pap. 14.05 (978-1-4042-1983-0(8)) Rosen Publishing Group, Inc., The.

Spilsbury, Louise. The Science of Avalanches. 2013. (Nature's Wrath: the Science Behind Natural Disasters Ser.). (Illus.). 48p. (J). (gr. 4-6). 31.95 (978-1-4339-8651-2(5)); pap. 14.05 (978-1-4339-8652-9(3)) Stevens, Gareth Publishing LLLP. (Gareth Stevens Learning Library).

Suen, Anastasia. Avalanches. 2015. (ENG.). 48p. (gr. 3-6). 35.64 (978-1-63430-424-5(1)) Rourke Educational Media.

Trueit, Trudi Strain. Detecting Avalanches. 2017. (Detecting Disasters (hardcover) Ser.). (ENG., Illus.). 32p. (J). (gr. 4-7). lib. bdg. 28.50 **(978-1-63517-000-9(1)**, Focus Readers) North Star Editions.

Woods, Michael & Woods, Mary B. Avalanches. 2007. (Disasters up Close Ser.). (ENG., Illus.). 64p. (gr. 4-8). lib. bdg. 27.93 (978-0-8225-6577-2(3), Lerner Pubns.) Lerner Publishing Group.

AVIATION

see Aeronautics

AVIATORS

see Air Pilots

AZTECS

see Indians of Mexico—Aztecs

B

BABAR (FICTITIOUS CHARACTER)—FICTION

de Brunhoff, Jean. The Babar Collection: Five Classic Stories. 2017. (ENG., Illus.). 240p. (J). (gr. -1-k). pap. 22.99 **(978-1-4052-7989-5(3))** Egmont Bks., Ltd. GBR. Dist: Independent Pubs. Group.

de Brunhoff, Jean. Classic Tales of Babar. 2014. (ENG., Illus.). 112p. (J). (gr. -1-1). 19.99 (978-1-4052-6420-4(9)) Egmont Bks., Ltd. GBR. Dist: Independent Pubs. Group.

de Brunhoff, Laurent. L' Anniversaire de Babar. (Babar Ser.). (FRE., Illus.). (J). (gr. -1-3). pap. (978-2-01-002551-8(2)) Hachette Groupe Livre.

—B Is for Babar: An Alphabet Book. 2012. (ENG., Illus.). 30p. (J). (gr. -1 — 1). bds. 7.95 (978-1-4197-0298-3(X), Abrams Appleseed) Abrams, Inc.

—Babar & the Ghost. 2012. (ENG., Illus.). 40p. (J). (gr. k-2). 15.95 (978-1-4197-0380-5(3), Abrams Bks. for Young Readers) Abrams, Inc.

—Babar dans l'Ile aux Oiseaux.Tr. of Babar in the Jungle. (FRE., Illus.). (J). pap. 16.95 (978-2-211-09806-9(1)) Archimede Editions FRA. Dist: Distribooks, Inc.

—Babar dans l'Ile aux Oiseaux. (Babar Ser.).Tr. of Babar in the Jungle. (FRE., Illus.). 29p. (J). (gr. -1-3). 15.95 (978-0-7859-0681-0(9), F2002) French & European Pubns., Inc.

—Babar et la Vieille Dame. (Babar Ser.). (FRE., Illus.). (J). (gr. -1-3). pap. 15.95 (978-0-7859-0614-8(2), FC254) French & European Pubns., Inc.

—Babar et le Wouly-Wouly. (Babar Ser.).Tr. of Babar & the Wully-Wully. (FRE., Illus.). 26p. (J). (gr. -1-3). 15.95 (978-0-7859-0682-7(7), M11805) French & European Pubns., Inc.

—Babar et ses Amis a la Ferme. (Babar Ser.). (FRE., Illus.). 48p. (J). (gr. -1-3). 19.95 (978-0-7859-8805-2(X)) French & European Pubns., Inc.

—Babar et ses Amis a la Fete. (Babar Ser.). (FRE., Illus.). 48p. (J). (gr. -1-3). 19.95 (978-0-7859-8806-9(8)) French & European Pubns., Inc.

—Babar et ses Amis a la Maison. (Babar Ser.). (FRE., Illus.). 48p. (J). (gr. -1-3). 19.95 (978-0-7859-8804-5(1)) French & European Pubns., Inc.

—Babar et ses Amis a la Ville. (Babar Ser.). (FRE., Illus.). 48p. (J). (gr. -1-3). 19.95 (978-0-7859-8809-0(2)) French & European Pubns., Inc.

—Babar et ses Amis a L'Ecole. (Babar Ser.). (FRE., Illus.). 48p. (J). (gr. -1-3). 19.95 (978-0-7859-8802-1(5)) French & European Pubns., Inc.

—Babar et ses Amis au Spectacle. (Babar Ser.). (FRE., Illus.). 48p. (J). (gr. -1-3). 19.95 (978-0-7859-8803-8(3)) French & European Pubns., Inc.

—Babar et ses Amis en Foret. (Babar Ser.). (FRE., Illus.). 48p. (J). (gr. -1-3). 19.95 (978-0-7859-8811-3(4)) French & European Pubns., Inc.

—Babar et ses Amis en Vacances. (Babar Ser.). (FRE., Illus.). 48p. (J). (gr. -1-3). 19.95 (978-0-7859-8808-3(4)) French & European Pubns., Inc.

—Babar et ses Amis Font les Courses. (Babar Ser.). (FRE., Illus.). 48p. (J). (gr. -1-3). 19.95 (978-0-7859-8810-6(6)) French & European Pubns., Inc.

—Babar et ses Amis Visitent le Royaume. (Babar Ser.). (FRE., Illus.). 48p. (J). (gr. -1-3). 19.95 (978-0-7859-8807-6(6)) French & European Pubns., Inc.

—Babar les 500 Premiers Mots. (Babar Ser.). (FRE., Illus.). 48p. (J). (gr. -1-3). 19.95 (978-0-7859-8812-0(2)) French & European Pubns., Inc.

—Babar pour Chaque Soir de la Semaine. 15.95 (978-2-01-223932-6(3)) Hachette Groupe Livre FRA. Dist: Distribooks, Inc.

—Babar Raconte Flore Reporter. (Babar Ser.). (FRE., Illus.). 48p. (J). (gr. -1-3). 19.95 (978-0-7859-8813-7(0)) French & European Pubns., Inc.

—Babar Raconte Halte a la Pollution. (Babar Ser.). (FRE., Illus.). 48p. (J). (gr. -1-3). 19.95 (978-0-7859-8816-8(5)) French & European Pubns., Inc.

—Babar Raconte la Course a la Lune. (Babar Ser.). (FRE., Illus.). 48p. (J). (gr. -1-3). 19.95 (978-0-7859-8820-5(3)) French & European Pubns., Inc.

—Babar Raconte l'Affaire de la Couronne. (Babar Ser.). (FRE., Illus.). 48p. (J). (gr. -1-3). 19.95 (978-0-7859-8818-2(1)) French & European Pubns., Inc.

—Babar Raconte l'Arrivee du Bebe Elephant. (Babar Ser.). (FRE., Illus.). 48p. (J). (gr. -1-3). 19.95 (978-0-7859-8815-1(7)) French & European Pubns., Inc.

—Babar Raconte le Fantome. (Babar Ser.). (FRE., Illus.). 48p. (J). (gr. -1-3). 19.95 (978-0-7859-8819-9(X)) French & European Pubns., Inc.

—Babar Raconte le Meilleur Ami des Elephants. (Babar Ser.). (FRE., Illus.). 48p. (J). (gr. -1-3). 19.95 (978-0-7859-8823-6(8)) French & European Pubns., Inc.

—Babar Raconte le Pianiste. (Babar Ser.). (FRE., Illus.). 48p. (J). (gr. -1-3). 19.95 (978-0-7859-8822-9(X)) French & European Pubns., Inc.

—Babar Raconte le Plus Beau Cadeau du Monde. (Babar Ser.). (FRE., Illus.). 48p. (J). (gr. -1-3). 19.95 (978-0-7859-8821-2(1)) French & European Pubns., Inc.

—Babar Raconte Que la Fete Continue. (Babar Ser.). (FRE., Illus.). 48p. (J). (gr. -1-3). 19.95 (978-0-7859-8824-3(6)) French & European Pubns., Inc.

—Babar Raconte un Diner Chez Rataxes. (Babar Ser.). (FRE., Illus.). 48p. (J). (gr. -1-3). 19.95 (978-0-7859-8817-5(3)) French & European Pubns., Inc.

—Babar Raconte Zephir Fait le Singe. (Babar Ser.). (FRE., Illus.). 48p. (J). (gr. -1-3). 19.95 (978-0-7859-8814-4(9)) French & European Pubns., Inc.

—Babar's Little Girl. rev. ed. 2012. (ENG., Illus.). 40p. (J). (gr. k-2). 16.95 (978-1-4197-0340-9(4), Abrams Bks. for Young Readers) Abrams, Inc.

—Babar's Museum of Art, 65 vols. 2003. (ENG., Illus.). 48p. (J). (gr. -1-17). 19.99 (978-0-8109-4597-5(5)) Abrams, Inc.

—Meet Babar & His Family. (Babar Ser.). (Illus.). 32p. (J). (gr. -1-3). Random Hse. Children's Bks.

—Il Re Babar. pap. 12.95 (978-88-04-44195-3(X)) Mondadori ITA. Dist: Distribooks, Inc.

—Storia de Babar l'elefantino. pap. 12.95 (978-88-04-44508-1(4)) Mondadori ITA. Dist: Distribooks, Inc.

Viagem de Babar. pap. 19.95 (978-85-85466-78-7(2)) Companhia das Letras BRA. Dist: Distribooks, Inc.

BABIES

see Infants

BABOONS

Bluemel Oldfield, Dawn. Baboon. 2016. (J). lib. bdg. (978-1-62724-823-5(4)) Bearport Publishing Co., Inc.

Borgert-Spaniol, Megan. Baboons. 2012. (Animal Safari Ser.). (ENG., Illus.). 24p. (J). (gr. k-3). lib. bdg. 25.95 (978-1-60014-767-8(4), Blastoff! Readers) Bellwether Media.

Doudna, Kelly. It's a Baby Baboon!, 1 vol. 2009. (Baby African Animals Ser.). (ENG., Illus.). 24p. (J). (gr. k-3). lib. bdg. 24.21 (978-1-60453-150-3(9), SandCastle) ABDO Publishing Co.

Gosman, Gillian. Baboons. 2012. (Illus.). 24p. (J). 49.50 (978-1-4488-5178-2(5), PowerKids Pr.); (J). pap. 8.25 (978-1-4488-5177-5(7), PowerKids Pr.); (YA). lib. bdg. 22.60 (978-1-4488-5022-8(3)) Rosen Publishing Group, Inc., The.

McCarthy, Cecilia Pinto. Baboons, 1 vol. 2013. (Monkeys Ser.). (ENG.). 24p. (gr. k-1). lib. bdg. 26.65 (978-1-62065-109-4(2), Pebble Plus) Capstone Press of Coughlan Cos.

Murray, Julie. Baboons, 1 vol. 2003. (Animal Kingdom Ser.). (ENG., Illus.). 24p. (J). (gr. 1-4). 25.65 (978-1-57765-711-8(X)) ABDO Publishing Co.

Roumanis, Alexis. Baboons. 2014. (Illus.). 24p. (J). (978-1-4896-2866-4(5)) Weigl Pubs., Inc.

Spilsbury, Louise. Baboon, 1 vol. 2011. (Day in the Life: Grassland Animals Ser.). (ENG., Illus.). 24p. (gr. k-2). 23.32 (978-1-4329-4727-9(3)); pap. 6.79 (978-1-4329-4737-8(0)) Heinemann-Raintree. (Heinemann Read & Learn).

Stewart, Melissa. Baboons. 2007. (Nature Watch Ser.). (ENG., Illus.). 48p. (gr. 4-8). lib. bdg. 27.93 (978-1-57505-868-9(5), Lerner Pubns.) Lerner Publishing Group.

Walden, Katherine. Baboons. 2009. (Safari Animals Ser.). (Illus.). 24p. (J). (gr. k-3). pap. 8.25 (978-1-4358-3063-9(6)); 24p. (gr. 1-1). 42.50 (978-1-60852-946-9(0)); (J). lib. bdg. 22.60 (978-1-4358-2689-2(2)) Rosen Publishing Group, Inc., The. (PowerKids Pr.).

Wilsdon, Christina. Baboons. 2010. (Amazing Animals Ser.). (ENG.). 48p. (J). (gr. 2-6). pap. 10.50 (978-1-4339-4005-7(1)); lib. bdg. 28.00 (978-1-4339-4004-0(3)) Stevens, Gareth Publishing LLLP. (Gareth Stevens Learning Library).

—Baboons. 2007. (J). (978-1-59939-124-3(4), Reader's Digest Young Families, Inc.) Studio Fun International.

BABY ANIMALS

see Animals—Infancy

BABY SITTERS

see Babysitters

BABYLONIA

see also Sumer

Bryant, Tamera. The Life & Times of Hammurabi. 2005. (Biography from Ancient Civilizations Ser.). (Illus.). 48p. (J). (gr. -1-7). lib. bdg. 29.95 (978-1-58415-338-2(5), 1244807) Mitchell Lane Pubs., Inc.

Gibson, Karen. Ancient Babylon. 2012. (Explore Ancient Worlds Ser.). (J). lib. bdg. 29.95 (978-1-61228-278-7(4)) Mitchell Lane Pubs., Inc.

Levin, Judith. Hammurabi. 2008. (Ancient World Leaders Ser.). (Illus.). 120p. (gr. 6-12). 30.00 (978-0-7910-9603-1(3), Chelsea Hse.) Facts On File, Inc.

Mayfield, Christine & Quinn, Kristine M. Hammurabi: Babylonian Ruler, 1 vol. 2007. (Primary Source Readers Ser.). (ENG.). 32p. (J). (gr. 4-4). pap. 8.99 (978-0-7439-0441-4(9)) Shell Educational Publishing.

Rustad, Martha E. H. & Hiti, Samuel. The Babylonians: Life in Ancient Babylon. 2009. (Life in Ancient Civilizations Ser.). (Illus.). 48p. (J). (gr. 3-6). lib. bdg. 29.27 (978-0-8225-8682-1(7), Millbrook Pr.) Lerner Publishing Group.

BABYLONIA—FICTION

Booth, Bradley. Prince of Dreams. 2008. (J). pap. 10.99 (978-0-8163-2253-4(8)) Pacific Pr. Publishing Assn.

Dorison, Xavier & Nury, Fabian. Century Club. Ross, C., illus. 2012. (Spooks Ser.: 2). (ENG.). 56p. (J). (gr. 10-12). pap. 13.95 (978-1-84918-129-7(2)) CineBook GBR. Dist: National Bk. Network.

Focus on the Family Staff & Hering, Marianne. Light in the Lions' Den. 2017. (AIO Imagination Station Bks.: 19). (ENG.). 144p. (J). pap. 4.99 (978-1-58997-878-2(1)) Focus on the Family Publishing.

Howard, Annabelle. Hammurabi's Law & Order. 2005. (J). pap. (978-1-4108-4233-6(9)) Benchmark Education Co.

Lerangis, Peter. Lost in Babylon. Norstrand, Torstein, illus. 2014. (Seven Wonders Ser.: 2). (ENG.). 400p. (J). (gr. 3-7). pap. 6.99 (978-0-06-207044-9(4)) HarperCollins Pubs.

—Lost in Babylon. 2013. (Seven Wonders Ser.). (ENG., Illus.). 384p. (J). (gr. 3-7). 17.99 (978-0-06-207043-2(6)) HarperCollins Pubs.

—Lost in Babylon. 2014. (Seven Wonders Ser.: 2). (J). lib. bdg. 17.20 (978-0-606-35483-7(2)) Turtleback Bks.

BABYSITTERS

Babysitting 101. . . Your Complete Guide to Becoming the Best Babysitter! 2003. (YA). stu. ed. (978-0-9729706-2-4(2)); (978-0-9729706-1-7(4)) Production 101, Inc.

Buckley, Annie. Be a Better Babysitter. 2006. (Reading Rocks! Ser.). (ENG., Illus.). 32p. (J). (gr. 2-5). 28.50 (978-1-59296-740-7(X), 200727) Child's World, Inc., The.

—Be a Better Babysitter. 2016. (Illus.). 32p. (J). (978-1-4896-4773-3(2)) Weigl Pubs., Inc.

Carlson Berne, Emma. Run Your Own Babysitting Business, 1 vol., 1. 2014. (Young Entrepreneurs Ser.). (ENG.). 32p. (J). (gr. 4-6). 26.25 (978-1-4777-2922-9(4), PowerKids Pr.) Rosen Publishing Group, Inc., The.

Colich, Abby. A Babysitter's Guide to Keeping the Kids Entertained. 2017. (Go-To Guides). (ENG., Illus.). 32p. (gr. 3-4). lib. bdg. 27.99 (978-1-5157-3664-6(4), Snap Bks.) Capstone Press of Coughlan Cos.

Higgins, Melissa. Start Your Babysitting Business. 2017. (Build Your Business Ser.). (ENG.). 32p. (gr. 3-4). lib. bdg. 27.99 **(978-1-5157-6691-9(8))** Capstone Press of Coughlan Cos.

Higgins, Melissa & Rissman, Rebecca. The Babysitter's Backpack: Everything You Need to Be a Safe, Smart, & Skilled Babysitter, 1 vol. 2014. (ENG.). 128p. (gr. 3-4). pap. 12.95 (978-1-62370-134-5(1)) Capstone Young Readers of Coughlan Cos.

Martin, Ann M. Dawn on the Coast. (Baby-Sitters Club Ser.: No. 23). 10p. (J). (gr. 3-7). pap. 3.95 (978-0-590-42007-5(0)) Scholastic, Inc.

Pascal, Francine. My First Love & Other Disasters: My First Love & Other Disasters; Love & Betrayal & Hold the Mayo; My Mother Was Never a Kid. 2014. (ENG., Illus.). 672p. (YA). (gr. 7). pap. 12.99 (978-1-4814-0168-5(8), Simon Pulse) Simon Pulse.

Powell, Jillian. My New Babysitter. 2012. (New Beginnings Ser.). (ENG., Illus.). 24p. (J). (gr. k-3). 21.25 (978-1-4488-6636-6(7), PowerKids Pr.) Rosen Publishing Group, Inc., The.

Rissman, Rebecca. No Running in the House: Safety Tips Every Babysitter Needs to Know, 1 vol. 2014. (Babysitter's Backpack Ser.). (ENG., Illus.). 32p. (gr. 3-4). 27.99 (978-1-4914-0765-3(4), Snap Bks.) Capstone Press of Coughlan Cos.

—You're Hired! Business Basics Every Babysitter Needs to Know, 1 vol. 2014. (Babysitter's Backpack Ser.). (ENG., Illus.). 32p. (gr. 3-4). 27.99 (978-1-4914-0766-0(2), Snap Bks.) Capstone Press of Coughlan Cos.

Weintraub, Aileen. Everything You Need to Know about Being a Baby-sitter: A Teen's Guide to Responsible Child Care. 2009. (Need to Know Library). 64p. (gr. 5-5). 58.50 (978-1-60854-054-9(5)) Rosen Publishing Group, Inc., The.

—Everything You Need to Know about Being a Babysitter: A Teen's Guide to Responsible Child Care. rev. ed. 2005. (Need to Know Library). (Illus.). 64p. (YA). (gr. 4-6). lib. bdg. 31.95 (978-0-8239-3770-7(4)) Rosen Publishing Group, Inc., The.

BABYSITTERS—FICTION

Alexander's First Babysitter. 2004. (J). 5.00 (978-1-882541-38-6(3)) Food Allergy & Anaphylaxis Network.

Allen, Elise & Conners, Daryle. Gabby Duran, Book 2 Gabby Duran: Troll Control. (Gabby Duran Ser.). (ENG.). (J). (gr. 3-7). 2017. 256p. pap. 7.99 **(978-1-4847-2540-5(9))** 2016. (Illus.). 240p. 16.99 (978-1-4847-0936-8(5)) Hyperion Bks. for Children.

—Gabby Duran, Book 3 Gabby Duran: Multiple Mayhem. 2017. (Gabby Duran Ser.). (ENG.). 224p. (J). (gr. 3-7). 16.99 **(978-1-4847-0937-5(3))** Hyperion Bks. for Children.

—Troll Control. 2017. (Gabby Duran Ser.: 2). (J). lib. bdg. 18.40 **(978-0-606-39970-8(4))** Turtleback Bks.

Allen, Elise & Daryle Connors. Gabby Duran & the Unsittables. 2016. (Gabby Duran Ser.: 1). (J). lib. bdg. 18.40 (978-0-606-39443-7(5)) Turtleback Bks.

Anderson, Peggy Perry. Time for Bed, the Babysitter Said. 2012. (Green Light Readers Level 1 Ser.). (ENG., Illus.). 32p. (J). (gr. -1-3). pap. 3.99 (978-0-547-85061-0(1)) Houghton Mifflin Harcourt Publishing Co.

—Time for Bed, the Babysitter Said. 2012. (Green Light Readers — Level 1 Ser.). lib. bdg. 13.55 (978-0-606-26607-9(0), Turtleback) Turtleback Bks.

Ballarini, Joe. A Babysitter's Guide to Monster Hunting #1. To, Vivienne, illus. 2017. (Babysitter's Guide to Monsters Ser.: 1). 352p. (J). (gr. 3-7). 13.99 (978-0-06-243783-9(6), Tegen, Katherine Bks) HarperCollins Pubs.

Baltazar, Franco & Art Baltazar Comic Book Staff. Field Trippin, Vol. 5. 2011. (ENG., Illus.). 160p. (J). (gr. 2-5). pap. 12.99 (978-1-4012-3173-6(X)) DC Comics.

Barkley, Callie. Marion Takes Charge. Riti, Marsha, illus. 2015. (Critter Club Ser.: 12). (ENG.). 128p. (J). (gr. k-4). pap. 5.99 (978-1-4814-2408-0(4), Little Simon) Little Simon.

Barrows, Annie. Ivy + Bean Take Care of the Babysitter. Blackall, Sophie, illus. (Ivy & Bean Ser.: IVYB). (ENG.). 2008. 128p. (J). (gr. 1-5). pap. 5.99 (978-0-8118-6584-5(3)) 2007. pap., tchr. ed. (978-0-8118-8667-3(0)) Chronicle Bks. LLC.

Barrows, Annie & Blackall, Sophie. Ivy + Bean Take Care of the Babysitter, 1 vol. 2011. (Ivy & Bean Ser.). (ENG., Illus.). 128p. (J). (gr. 1-4). 24.21 (978-1-59961-931-6(8)) Spotlight.

Benjamin, A. H. Baa! Moo! What Will We Do? Chapman, Jane, tr. Chapman, Jane, illus. 2003. 32p. (J). pap. 6.95 (978-1-58925-381-0(7)) Tiger Tales.

Bourgeois, Paulette. Franklin & the Baby-Sitter. 2004. (Illus.). (J). (gr. k-3). spiral bd. (978-0-616-11098-0(7)); spiral bd. (978-0-616-11097-3(9)) Canadian National Institute for the Blind/Institut National Canadien pour les Aveugles.

Brewer, Jo Ann. Miss Q-Cee Baby Sits. 2011. 28p. pap. 15.99 (978-1-4535-8183-4(9)) Xlibris Corp.

Brown, Marc. Arthur's Mystery Babysitter. Brown, Marc, illus. 2004. (ENG., Illus.). 24p. (J). (gr. -1-1). pap. 3.99 (978-0-316-73394-6(6), Tingley, Megan Bks.) Little, Brown Bks. for Young Readers.

Capucilli, Alyssa Satin. Katy Duck Meets the Babysitter. Cole, Henry, illus. 2012. (Katy Duck Ser.). (ENG.). 24p. (J). (gr. -1-1). 15.99 (978-1-4424-5242-8(0)); pap. 3.99 (978-1-4424-5241-1(2)) Simon Spotlight. (Simon Spotlight).

Chaconas, Dori. The Babysitters. McCue, Lisa, illus. 2014. (Cork & Fuzz Ser.: 6). (ENG.). 32p. (J). (gr. 1-3). pap. 3.99 (978-0-448-48050-3(6), Penguin Young Readers) Penguin Young Readers Group.

Child, Lauren. Guess Who's Babysitting? Child, Lauren, illus. 2010. (Clarice Bean Ser.). (ENG., Illus.). 32p. (J). (gr. 1-4). pap. 8.99 (978-0-7636-4797-1(7)) Candlewick Pr.

Christelow, Eileen. Five Little Monkeys Play Hide & Seek. 2010. (Five Little Monkeys Story Ser.). (ENG., Illus.). 40p. (J). (gr. -1-3). pap. 6.99 (978-0-547-33787-6(6)) Houghton Mifflin Harcourt Publishing Co.

—Five Little Monkeys Play Hide & Seek. 2010. (Five Little Monkeys Story Ser.). lib. bdg. 17.20 (978-0-606-14479-7(X), Turtleback) Turtleback Bks.

—Five Little Monkeys Trick-Or-Treat. 2013. (Five Little Monkeys Story Ser.). (ENG., Illus.). 40p. (J). (gr. -1-3). 16.99 (978-0-547-85893-7(0)) Houghton Mifflin Harcourt Publishing Co.

Dahl, Michael. Penguin Misses Mom. Vidal, Oriol, illus. 2016. (Hello Genius Ser.). (ENG.). 20p. (gr. 1-2). bds. 7.99 (978-1-4795-8739-1(7)) Picture Window Bks.

Darke, J. A. The Grin in the Dark. Evergreen, Nelson, illus. 2015. (Spine Shivers Ser.). (ENG.). 128p. (gr. 3-4). lib. bdg. 26.65 (978-1-4965-0217-9(5)) Stone Arch Bks.

Dasilva, D. Mom Has Left & Gone to Vegas. Craig, Dan, illus. 2008. 32p. pap. 19.95 (978-1-59858-603-9(3)) Dog Ear Publishing, LLC.

Day, Alexandra. Carl's Snowy Afternoon. Day, Alexandra, illus. 2009. (Carl Ser.). (ENG., Illus.). 32p. (J). (gr. -1-1). 13.99 (978-0-374-31086-8(6), 9780374310868, Farrar, Straus & Giroux (BYR)) Farrar, Straus & Giroux.

DeCamp, Alison. My Near-Death Adventures: I Almost Died. Again. 2016. (ENG., Illus.). 288p. (J). (gr. 3-7). 16.99 (978-0-385-39048-4(3), Crown Books For Young Readers) Random Hse. Children's Bks.

Deriso, C. H. Elisabeth & the Unwanted Advice. 2016. (Babysitter Chronicles Ser.). (ENG., Illus.). 160p. (gr. 4-7). lib. bdg. 26.65 (978-1-4965-2757-8(7)) Stone Arch Bks.

Deriso, Christine Hurley. Elisabeth & the Unwanted Advice. 2016. (Babysitter Chronicles Ser.). (ENG., Illus.). 160p. (gr. 4-7). pap. 6.95 (978-1-4914-8864-5(6)) Stone Arch Bks.

Disney Book Group. The Lion Guard Babysitter Bunga. Disney Storybook Art Team, illus. 2017. (ENG.). 24p. (J). (gr. -1-k). pap. 4.99 (978-1-4847-8868-4(0)) Disney Pr.

Farrell, Liam. Goldilocks the Babysitter from Hell. 2007. (ENG.). 64p. (J). pap. 11.95 (978-1-901737-57-8(8)) Anvil Bks., Ltd. IRL. Dist: Dufour Editions, Inc.

Fisher, Isla. Why Follow the Rules When You Cam Invent Your Own? Ceulemans, Eglantine, illus. 2017. (Marge in Charge Ser.: 1). 176p. (J). (gr. 3-7). 15.99 **(978-0-06-266218-7(X))** HarperCollins Pubs.

Fox, Mem. Good Night, Sleep Tight. Horacek, Judy, illus. 2013. (ENG.). 32p. (J). (gr. -1-k). 16.99 (978-0-545-53370-6(8), Orchard Bks.) Scholastic, Inc.

Friedman, Laurie. Mallory McDonald, Super Snoop. Kalis, Jennifer, illus. (Mallory Ser.: 18). (ENG.). 152p. (J). (gr. 2-5). 2013. pap. 5.95 (978-1-4677-0929-3(8), Darby Creek) 2012. 15.95 (978-0-7613-6073-5(5)) Lerner Publishing Group.

Friedman, Laurie B. McDonald, Super Sitter. Kalis, Jennifer, illus. 2017. (Mallory Ser.: 27). (ENG.). 160p. (J). (gr. 2-5). 15.95 (978-1-4677-5031-8(X)) Lerner Publishing Group.

Gallagher, Diana G. Beach Blues: The Complicated Life of Claudia Cristina Cortez, 1 vol. Garvey, Brann, illus. 2008. (Claudia Cristina Cortez Ser.). (ENG.). 88p. (gr. 2-3). pap. 6.10 (978-1-4342-0869-9(9), Claudia Cristina Cortez) Stone Arch Bks.

—Monica & the Weekend of Drama, 1 vol. 2011. (Monica Ser.). (ENG.). 88p. (gr. 2-3). lib. bdg. 26.65 (978-1-4342-2557-3(7)) Stone Arch Bks.

Gliori, Debi. Babysits. 2015. (ENG., Illus.). 32p. (J). (gr. -1-k). pap. 10.99 (978-1-4083-3635-9(9)) Hodder & Stoughton GBR. Dist: Hachette Bk. Group.

Gorbachev, Valeri. Ms. Turtle the Babysitter. Gorbachev, Valeri, illus. 2005. (I Can Read Bks.). (Illus.). 64p. (J). (gr. k-3). (ENG.). 15.99 (978-0-06-058073-5(9)); lib. bdg. 16.89 (978-0-06-058074-2(7)) HarperCollins Pubs.

Graff, Lisa. Absolutely Almost. 2014. (ENG.). 304p. (J). (gr. 3-7). 16.99 (978-0-399-16405-7(7), Philomel Bks.) Penguin Young Readers Group.

Graves, Annie. The Demon Babysitter. McElhinney, Glenn, illus. 2015. (Nightmare Club Ser.: 7). (ENG.). 64p. (J). (gr. 2-5). pap. 6.99 (978-1-4677-6041-6(2), Darby Creek); lib. bdg. 25.32 (978-1-4677-4355-6(0)) Lerner Publishing Group.

Gray, Kes. Nelly, the Monster Sitter. Hanson, Stephen, illus. 2009. (ENG.). 272p. (J). (gr. 3-7). 8.99 (978-1-59514-259-7(2), Razorbill) Penguin Young Readers Group.

Greenwald, Tom. My Dog Is Better Than Your Dog. Stower, Adam, illus. 2015. 198p. (J). pap. (978-0-545-91669-1(0), Scholastic Pr.) Scholastic, Inc.

Greenwald, Tommy. My Dog Is Better Than Your Dog (Crimebiters! #1) Stower, Adam, illus. 2015. (Crimebiters Ser.: 1). (ENG.). 208p. (J). (gr. 3-7). 12.99 (978-0-545-77332-4(6), Scholastic Pr.) Scholastic, Inc.

Gunderson, Jessica. Olivia Bitter, Spooked-Out Sitter! 2016. (Babysitter Chronicles Ser.). (ENG.). 160p. (gr. 4-7). pap. 6.95 (978-1-4914-8862-1(X)) Stone Arch Bks.

Hapka, Cathy, pseud & Titlebaum, Ellen. How Not to Babysit Your Brother. Palen, Debbie, illus. 2005. (Step into Reading Ser.). (ENG.). 48p. (J). (gr. 2-4). pap. 3.99 (978-0-375-82856-0(7), Random Hse. Bks. for Young Readers) Random Hse. Children's Bks.

Hastings, Suanne. Many Moods of Maddie: Bossy Boots. Crabtree, Andy, illus. 2006. (Baby Sitter Ser.). 24p. (J). (gr. -1-3). (978-0-9769348-0-6(9)) Tastica, Suanne Creations Inc.

Hershenhorn, Esther. Chicken Soup by Heart. Litzinger, Rosanne, illus. 2010. (ENG.). 40p. (J). (gr. -1-3). 16.99 (978-1-4424-2197-4(5), Simon & Schuster Bks. For Young Readers) Simon & Schuster Bks. For Young Readers.

Hirschmann, Kris. Triple Trouble Time. 2014. (Tickety Toc Ser.). (ENG.). 32p. (J). (gr. -1-k). pap. 3.99 (978-0-545-61473-3(2)) Scholastic, Inc.

Holm, Jennifer L. & Holm, Matthew. Bad Babysitter. Holm, Jennifer L. & Holm, Matthew, illus. 2015. (Babymouse Ser.: 19). (ENG., Illus.). 96p. (J). (gr. 2-5). pap. 6.99 (978-0-307-93162-7(5), Random Hse. Bks. for Young Readers) Random Hse. Children's Bks.

Hooper, Mary. The Revolting Baby. Vayssiere, Frederique, illus. 2008. (Katie Ser.). (ENG.). 96p. (J). (gr. 2-4). pap. 8.95 (978-0-7475-8613-5(6)) Bloomsbury Publishing Plc GBR. Dist: Independent Pubs. Group.

Horvath, Polly. My One Hundred Adventures. 2010. (My One Hundred Adventures Ser.). (ENG., Illus.). 272p. (J). (gr. 3-7). 7.99 (978-0-375-85526-9(2), Yearling) Random Hse. Children's Bks.

Hughes, Shirley. Don't Want to Go! Hughes, Shirley, illus. 2010. (ENG., Illus.). 32p. (J). (gr. -1-2). 16.99 (978-0-7636-5091-9(9)) Candlewick Pr.

—An Evening at Alfie's. Hughes, Shirley, illus. 2009. (Alfie Ser.). (ENG., Illus.). 32p. (J). (gr. k-k). pap. 11.99 (978-1-86230-786-5(5), Red Fox) Random House Children's Books GBR. Dist: Independent Pubs. Group.

Jordan, Apple. Merida Is Our Babysitter (Disney Princess) RH Disney, illus. 2016. (Little Golden Book Ser.). (ENG.). 24p. (J). (-k). 4.99 (978-0-7364-3614-4(6), Golden/Disney) Random Hse. Children's Bks.

Kann, Victoria. Pinkalicious & the Babysitter. Kann, Victoria, illus. 2017. (I Can Read Level 1 Ser.). (Illus.). 32p. (J). (gr. -1-3). pap. 3.99 **(978-0-06-256688-1(1))** HarperCollins Pubs.

Katz, Alan. The Day the Mustache Took Over. Easler, Kris, illus. (Mustache Ser.: 1). (ENG.). 208p. 2016. (J). pap. 6.99 (978-1-68119-148-5(2), 9781681191485) 2015. (YA). (gr. 2-4). 13.99 (978-1-61963-558-6(5), 9781619635586) Bloomsbury Publishing USA. (Bloomsbury USA Childrens).

Kehret, Peg. Stolen Children. 2010. (ENG.). 176p. (J). (gr. 3-7). 6.99 (978-0-14-241513-9(8), Puffin Books) Penguin Young Readers Group.

Kelley, Jane. Sol-Ray Man & the Freaky Flood. 2017. (Escapades of Clint Mccool Ser.: 2). lib. bdg. 16.00 **(978-0-606-40112-8(1))** Turtleback Bks.

Kirby, Stan. Captain Awesome vs. the Evil Babysitter. O'Connor, George, illus. 2014. (Captain Awesome Ser.: 11). (ENG.). 128p. (J). (gr. k-4). pap. 5.99 (978-1-4814-0446-4(6), Little Simon) Little Simon.

Konigsburg, E. L. Silent to the Bone. unabr. ed. 2004. (Middle Grade Cassette Librariestm Ser.). 272p. (J). (gr. 5-9). pap. 38.00 incl. audio (978-0-8072-8741-5(5), S YA 253 SP, Listening Library) Random Hse. Audio Publishing Group.

—Silent to the Bone. 2004. (ENG.). 272p. (YA). (gr. 7). mass mkt. 7.99 (978-0-689-86715-6(8), Simon Pulse) Simon Pulse.

London, Jonathan. Froggy's Best Babysitter. Remkiewicz, Frank, illus. 2011. (Froggy Ser.). (ENG.). 32p. (J). (gr. -1-k). pap. 6.99 (978-0-14-241899-4(4), Puffin Books) Penguin Young Readers Group.

Long, Melinda. Pirates Don't Change Diapers. Shannon, David, illus. 2007. (ENG.). 44p. (J). (gr. -1-3). 17.99 (978-0-15-205353-6(0)) Houghton Mifflin Harcourt Publishing Co.

Maddox, Jake. Skateboard Struggle, 1 vol. Tiffany, Sean, illus. 2011. (Jake Maddox Sports Stories Ser.). (ENG.). 72p. (gr. 2-3). pap. 5.95 (978-1-4342-3424-7(X)) Stone Arch Bks.

Mancusi, Mari. Princesses, Inc. 2017. (Mix Ser.). (ENG., Illus.). 320p. (J). (gr. 4-8). pap. 7.99 **(978-1-4814-7900-4(8),** Aladdin) Simon & Schuster Children's Publishing.

Marshall, Carly. The Babysitter & the Critter Hunt. 2012. 38p. 24.95 (978-1-4626-9407-5(1)); 40p. pap. 24.95 (978-1-4626-7516-6(6)) America Star Bks.

—The Babysitter & the Hot Rainy Days. 2012. 48p. 24.95 (978-1-4626-7515-9(8)); pap. 24.95 (978-1-4626-9644-4(9)) America Star Bks.

—The Babysitter & the Six Pack. 2013. 24p. 24.95 (978-1-63000-617-4(3)); pap. 24.95 (978-1-63000-540-5(1)) America Star Bks.

—The Babysitter Takes Us to Church. 2012. 44p. 24.95 (978-1-4626-9519-5(1)); pap. 24.95 (978-1-4626-7514-2(X)) America Star Bks.

Martin, Ann M. Bsls Box Set, No. 9. 2003. (J). 11.80 (978-0-590-66716-6(5)) Scholastic, Inc.

Martin Ann, M. Claudia & Mean Janine. Telgemeier, Raina, illus. 2016. (Baby-Sitters Club Graphix Ser.: 4). (ENG.). 176p. (J). (gr. 3-7). 24.99 (978-0-545-88623-9(6), Graphix) Scholastic, Inc.

Martin, Ann M. Claudia & Mean Janine. Telgemeier, Raina, illus. rev. ed. 2016. (Baby-Sitters Club Graphix Ser.: 4). (ENG.). 176p. (J). (gr. 3-7). pap. 10.99 (978-0-545-88622-2(8), Graphix) Scholastic, Inc.

—Claudia & the Phantom Phone Calls. 2010. (Baby-Sitters Club Ser.: 2). (ENG.). 176p. (J). (gr. 3-7). 6.99 (978-0-545-17476-3(7), Scholastic Paperbacks) Scholastic, Inc.

—Dawn on the Coast. (Baby-Sitters Club Ser.: No. 23). 10p. (J). (gr. 3-7). pap. 3.95 (978-0-590-42007-5(0)) Scholastic, Inc.

—Kristy's Great Idea. 2010. (Baby-Sitters Club Ser.: 1). (ENG.). 176p. (J). (gr. 3-7). 6.99 (978-0-545-17475-6(9), Scholastic Paperbacks) Scholastic, Inc.

—Kristy's Great Idea. Telgemeier, Raina, illus. rev. ed. 2015. (Baby-Sitters Club Graphix Ser.: 1). (ENG.). 192p. (J). (gr. 3-7). 24.99 (978-0-545-81386-0(7), Graphix) Scholastic, Inc.

—Mary Anne Saves the Day. Telgemeier, Raina, illus. rev. ed. 2015. (Baby-Sitters Club Graphix Ser.: 3). (ENG.). 160p. (J). (gr. 3-7). 24.99 (978-0-545-88617-8(1)); pap. 10.99 (978-0-545-88621-5(X)) Scholastic, Inc. (Graphix).

—The Truth about Stacey. 2010. (Baby-Sitters Club Ser.: 3). (ENG.). 176p. (J). (gr. 3-7). 6.99 (978-0-545-17477-0(5), Scholastic Paperbacks) Scholastic, Inc.

—The Truth about Stacey. Telgemeier, Raina, illus. rev. ed. 2015. (Baby-Sitters Club Graphix Ser.: 2). (ENG.). 144p. (J). (gr. 3-7). 24.99 (978-0-545-81388-4(3)); pap. 10.99 (978-0-545-81389-1(1)) Scholastic, Inc. (Graphix).

—The Truth about Stacey. 2015. (Baby-Sitters Club Graphix Ser.: 2). lib. bdg. 22.10 (978-0-606-37027-1(7)) 2010. (Baby-Sitters Club Ser.: 3). lib. bdg. 17.20 (978-0-606-14789-7(6), Turtleback) Turtleback Bks.

Martin, Ann M. & Martin Ann, M. Claudia & Mean Janine. Telgemeier, Raina, illus. 2016. (Baby-Sitters Club Graphix Ser.: 4). (ENG.). 176p. (J). (gr. 3-7). lib. bdg. 22.10 (978-0-606-38056-0(6)) Turtleback Bks.

Martin, Ann M. & Telgemeier, Raina. Baby-Sitters Club Graphix, Bks. 1-4, Set. Telgemeier, Raina, illus. 2016. (Baby-Sitters Club Graphix Ser.). (ENG., Illus.). 192p. (J). (gr. 3-7). pap. 43.96 (978-1-338-11898-8(6)) Scholastic, Inc.

Meadows, Daisy. Rainbow Magic Special Edition: Bailey the Babysitter Fairy. 2014. (Rainbow Magic Special Edition Ser.). (ENG.). 176p. (J). (gr. 2-5). pap. 6.99 (978-0-545-60539-7(3), Scholastic Paperbacks) Scholastic, Inc.

Melling, David. The Three Wishes. Melling, David, illus. 2008. (ENG., Illus.). 32p. (J). (gr. -1-k). pap. 10.99 (978-0-340-93153-0(1)) Hodder & Stoughton GBR. Dist: Hachette Bk. Group.

Metz, Melinda. Bri's Big Crush. 2016. (Babysitter Chronicles Ser.). (ENG.). 160p. (gr. 4-7). lib. bdg. 26.65 (978-1-4965-2756-1(9), 1400591) Stone Arch Bks.

Metz, Melinda, et al. The Babysitter Chronicles. 2016. (Babysitter Chronicles Ser.). (ENG.). 160p. (gr. 4-7). 106.60 (978-1-4965-2768-4(2)) Stone Arch Bks.

Miller-Johnston, Renee. Courtney Logan Kennedy Presents Zoe. 2008. 76p. pap. 19.95 (978-1-60703-558-9(8)) America Star Bks.

Moss, Marissa. Amelia's Back-to-School Survival Guide: Vote 4 Amelia - Amelia's Guide to Babysitting. Moss, Marissa, illus. 2012. (Amelia Ser.). (ENG., Illus.). 160p. (J). (gr. 5-8). 12.99 (978-1-4424-4349-5(9), Simon & Schuster/Paula Wiseman Bks.) Simon & Schuster/Paula Wiseman Bks.

—Amelia's Guide to Babysitting. Moss, Marissa, illus. 2008. (Amelia Ser.). (ENG., Illus.). 80p. (J). (gr. 5-8). 9.99 (978-1-4169-5051-6(6), Simon & Schuster/Paula Wiseman Bks.) Simon & Schuster/Paula Wiseman Bks.

Nickel, Scott. Back to the Ice Age. Corts, Enrique, illus. 2008. (Graphic Sparks Ser.). (ENG.). 40p. (gr. 1-3). pap. 5.95 (978-1-4342-0500-1(2), Graphic Sparks) Stone Arch Bks.

O'Connor, Jane. Fancy Nancy & the Sensational Babysitter. Glasser, Robin Preiss et al, illus. 2010. (Fancy Nancy Ser.). (ENG.). 24p. (J). (gr. -1-3). pap. 3.99 (978-0-06-170378-2(8), HarperFestival) HarperCollins Pubs.

—Fancy Nancy & the Sensational Babysitter. 2010. (Fancy Nancy Picture Bks.). (J). lib. bdg. 13.55 (978-0-606-14840-5(X), Turtleback) Turtleback Bks.

Orr, Leah. Messy Tessy. 2009. 36p. pap. 17.99 (978-1-4389-9398-0(6)) AuthorHouse.

Orshoski, Paul. We Both Read-My Sitter Is a T-Rex! (Level 1-2) Ebbeler, Jeffrey, illus. 2011. (ENG.). 44p. (J). 9.95

(978-1-60115-253-4(1)); pap. 4.99 (978-1-60115-254-1(X)) Treasure Bay, Inc.

Parish, Herman. Amelia Bedelia under Construction. Sweat, Lynn, illus. (I Can Read Level 2 Ser.). 64p. (J). (gr. k-3). 2007. (ENG.). pap. 3.99 (978-0-06-084346-5(2)) 2006. (ENG.). 15.99 (978-0-06-084344-1(6)) 2006. lib. bdg. 16.89 (978-0-06-084345-8(4)) HarperCollins Pubs. (Greenwillow Bks.).

—Amelia Bedelia under Construction. Sweat, Lynn, illus. 2007. (I Can Read Bks.). 64p. (gr. k-3). 14.00 (978-0-7569-8054-2(2)) Perfection Learning Corp.

Pascal, Francine. My First Love & Other Disasters. 2011. (ENG.). 256p. (YA). (gr. 4-9). pap. 11.99 (978-1-4424-5234-3(X), Simon Pulse) Simon Pulse.

Peterson, Lois. Meeting Miss 405, 1 vol. 2008. (Orca Young Readers Ser.). (ENG.). 112p. (J). (gr. 3-6). pap. 7.95 (978-1-55469-015-2(3)) Orca Bk. Pubs. USA.

Pinkwater, Daniel M. Mrs. Noodlekugel. Stower, Adam, illus. 2012. (Mrs. Noodlekugel Ser.). (ENG.). 80p. (J). (gr. k-4). 14.99 (978-0-7636-5053-7(6)) Candlewick Pr.

—Mrs. Noodlekugel & Drooly the Bear. Stower, Adam, illus. 2015. (Mrs. Noodlekugel Ser.). (ENG.). 96p. (J). (gr. k-4). 14.99 (978-0-7636-6645-3(9)) Candlewick Pr.

—Mrs. Noodlekugel & Four Blind Mice. Stower, Adam, illus. 2015. (Mrs. Noodlekugel Ser.). (ENG.). 96p. (J). (gr. k-4). pap. 5.99 (978-0-7636-7658-2(6)) Candlewick Pr.

Reagan, Jean. How to Babysit a Grandma, 2 vols. (ENG.). 32p. (J). (gr. k-3). 2016. 33.98 (978-1-5247-1435-2(6)) 2014. (Illus.). 16.99 (978-0-385-75384-5(5)) Random Hse. Children's Bks. (Knopf Bks. for Young Readers).

—How to Babysit a Grandpa. Wildish, Lee, illus. 2012. (ENG.). 32p. (J). (gr. k-3). 16.99 (978-0-375-86713-2(9), Knopf Bks. for Young Readers) Knopf, Alfred A. Inc.

RH Disney Staff & Posner-Sanchez, Andrea. Cinderella Is My Babysitter (Disney Princess) RH Disney Staff et al, illus. 2015. (Little Golden Book Ser.). (ENG.). 24p. (J). (-k). 3.99 (978-0-7364-3324-2(4), Golden/Disney) Random Hse. Children's Bks.

Rippin, Sally. The Circus Lesson. Spartels, Stephanie, illus. 2013. 41p. (J). (978-1-61067-236-8(4)) Kane Miller.

—The Circus Lesson: Hey Jack! Spartels, Stephanie, illus. 2014. (ENG.). 48p. (J). pap. 4.99 (978-1-61067-186-6(4)) Kane Miller.

Roberts, Willo Davis. Baby-Sitting Is a Dangerous Job. 2016. (ENG., Illus.). 224p. (J). (gr. 3-7). pap. 6.99 (978-1-4814-3704-2(6), Aladdin) Simon & Schuster Children's Publishing.

—Baby-Sitting Is a Dangerous Job. 2016. (ENG., Illus.). 224p. (J). (gr. 3-7). 17.99 (978-1-4814-3705-9(4), Simon & Schuster/Paula Wiseman Bks.) Simon & Schuster/Paula Wiseman Bks.

Rylant, Cynthia. Henry & Mudge & Mrs. Hopper's House. Bracken, Carolyn, illus. 2004. (Ready-to-Read Ser.). 40p. (gr. k-2). 14.00 (978-0-7569-2200-9(3)) Perfection Learning Corp.

—Henry & Mudge & Mrs. Hopper's House. Bracken, Carolyn, illus. (Henry & Mudge Ser.: 22). (ENG.). 40p. (J). (gr. k-2). 2004. pap. 3.99 (978-0-689-83446-2(2)) 2003. 15.99 (978-0-689-81153-1(5)) Simon Spotlight. (Simon Spotlight).

Sage, Angie. Ghostsitters. Pickering, Jimmy, illus. 2009. (Araminta Spookie Ser.: 5). (ENG.). 224p. (J). (gr. 1-5). pap. 6.99 (978-0-06-144925-3(3), Tegen, Katherine Bks) HarperCollins Pubs.

Schaefer, Carole Lexa. Monkey & Elephant & the Babysitting Adventure. Bernstein, Galia, illus. 2016. (ENG.). 48p. (J). (gr. k-4). 14.99 (978-0-7636-6535-7(5)) Candlewick Pr.

Schwartz, Amy. Willie & Uncle Bill. (ENG.). 40p. (J). (gr. -1-3). 2013. pap. 6.99 (978-0-8234-2907-3(5)) 2012. 16.95 (978-0-8234-2203-6(8)) Holiday Hse., Inc.

Sévigny, Eric, illus. Caillou: Watches Rosie. rev. ed. 2008. (Playtime Ser.). (ENG.). 24p. (J). (gr. -1-1). pap. 4.95 (978-2-89450-635-6(X)) Caillouet, Gerry.

Sheth, Kashmira. Tiger in My Soup, 1 vol. Ebbeler, Jefferey, illus. 2015. (ENG.). 32p. (J). (gr. -1-3). pap. 7.95 (978-1-56145-890-5(2)) Peachtree Pubs.

—Tiger in My Soup, 1 vol. Ebbeler, Jeffrey, illus. 2013. (ENG.). 32p. (J). (gr. -1-3). 15.95 (978-1-56145-696-3(9)) Peachtree Pubs.

Simon, Coco. Emma All Stirred Up! 2013. (Cupcake Diaries: 7). (ENG., Illus.). 160p. (J). (gr. 3-7). 17.99 (978-1-4424-8567-9(1), Simon Spotlight) Simon Spotlight.

Smith, Jane Denitz. Fairy Dust. Date not set. (J). (gr. 3-7). mass mkt. 4.99 (978-0-06-440961-2(9)) HarperCollins Pubs.

Smith, Sherri. Where's the Baby??? 2012. (ENG.). 39p. pap. 11.95 (978-1-4327-9609-9(7)) Outskirts Pr., Inc.

Sternberg, Julie. Like Pickle Juice on a Cookie. Cordell, Matthew, illus. (Eleanor Ser.). (ENG.). (J). 2016. 144p. (gr. 1-4). pap. 6.95 (978-1-4197-2050-5(3)) 2011. 128p. (gr. 3-7). 15.95 (978-0-8109-8424-0(5)) Abrams, Inc. (Amulet Bks.).

Stine, R. L. Don't Stay up Late: A Fear Street Novel. 2015. (Fear Street Ser.). (ENG.). 304p. (YA). (gr. 7-12). 17.99 (978-1-250-05162-2(2), 9781250051622, St. Martin's Griffin) St. Martin's Pr.

—Fear Street Super Thriller: Party Games & Don't Stay up Late. 2015. (Fear Street Ser.). (ENG.). 592p. (YA). (gr. 7-12). pap. 11.99 (978-1-250-07693-9(5), 9781250076939, St. Martin's Griffin) St. Martin's Pr.

Sullivan, Kevin & Goldman, Leslie. Anne's Babysitting Blues. 2010. (Anne of Green Gables for Young Readers Ser.). (ENG.). 64p. (J). (gr. 2-4). pap. 4.95 (978-0-9736803-1-7(8)) Davenport Pr. CAN. Dist: Independent Pubs. Group.

Tomasi, Joseph. Miss Wheezer Comes to Stay. 2006. 48p. pap. 16.95 (978-1-4241-3703-9(9)) PublishAmerica, Inc.

Travers, P. L. Mary Poppins. (Mary Poppins Ser.: No. 1). 202p. (J). (gr. 3-5). pap. 6.00 (978-0-8072-1536-4(8), Listening Library) Random Hse. Audio Publishing Group.

Urbanovic, Jackie. Sitting Duck. Urbanovic, Jackie, illus. 2010. (Illus.). 40p. (J). (gr. -1-2). (ENG.). 17.99 (978-0-06-176583-4(X)); lib. bdg. 18.89 (978-0-06-176584-1(8)) HarperCollins Pubs.

Vernick, Audrey. Water Balloon. 2011. (ENG.). 320p. (J). (gr. 5-7). 16.99 (978-0-547-59554-2(9), Clarion Bks.) Houghton Mifflin Harcourt Trade & Reference Pubs.

Viorst, Judith. Lulu's Mysterious Mission. Smith, Lane, illus. 2015. (ENG.). 192p. (J). (gr. 1-5). pap. 7.99 (978-1-4424-9747-4(5)) Simon & Schuster Children's Publishing.

Wagner, Anke. Help, I Don't Want a Babysitter! Behl, Anne-Kathrin, illus. 2015. (ENG.). 32p. (J). 17.95 (978-0-7358-4214-4(0)) North-South Bks., Inc.

Welchlin, Jewell. Babysitting Grandmama. 2013. (ENG.). 24p. (J). pap. 12.95 (978-1-4787-2554-1(0)) Outskirts Pr., Inc.

Wetterer, Charles M. When Grandad Babysat. 2012. 24p. pap. 14.93 (978-1-4669-5627-8(5)) Trafford Publishing.

Wolff, Virginia Euwer. Make Lemonade. unabr. ed. 2004. (Make Lemonade Trilogy: No. 1). 200p. (J). (gr. 7-18). pap. 36.00 incl. audio (978-0-8072-0793-2(4), S YA 348 SP, Listening Library) Random Hse. Audio Publishing Group.

—Make Lemonade. 2006. (ENG.). 208p. (YA). (gr. 5-9). pap. 8.99 (978-0-8050-8070-4(8), 9780805080704) Square Fish.

Young, Janet Ruth. The Babysitter Murders. 2011. (ENG., Illus.). 336p. (YA). (gr. 9-18). 16.99 (978-1-4169-5944-1(0), Atheneum Bks. for Young Readers) Simon & Schuster Children's Publishing.

Zimmerman, Mary. The Secret in the Wings. 2014. (ENG., Illus.). 128p. pap. 16.00 (978-0-8101-2987-0(6)) Northwestern Univ. Pr.

BACH, JOHANN SEBASTIAN, 1685-1750

Bobb, Barry L. Hero of Faith - Johann Sebastian Bach. 2011. 64p. pap. 7.99 (978-0-7586-2829-9(3)) Concordia Publishing Hse.

Getzinger, Donna & Felsenfeld, Daniel. Johann Sebastian Bach & the Art of Baroque Music. 2004. (Classical Composers Ser.). (Illus.). 144p. (YA). (gr. 6-12). lib. bdg. 26.95 (978-1-931798-22-8(2)) Reynolds, Morgan Inc.

JOHANN SEBASTIAN BACH. 2007. (Descubrimos a Los Músicos Ser.). (ENG., Illus.). 24p. (J). (gr. 2-4). 14.95 (978-84-9825-162-3(1)) Combel Editorial, S.A. ESP. Dist: Independent Pubs. Group.

Khoury, Marielle D. & du Bouchet, Paule. Bach, 1 vol. Voake, Charlotte, illus. 2012. (ENG.). 28p. (J). (gr. 2-6). 22.99 (978-1-85103-319-5(X)) Moonlight Publishing, Ltd. GBR. Dist: Independent Pubs. Group.

Leonard, Tom. Becoming Bach. 2017. (ENG., Illus.). 40p. (J). 17.99 (978-1-62672-286-6(2), 9781626722866) Roaring Brook Pr.

Summerer, Eric Michael. Johann Sebastian Bach. (Primary Source Library of Famous Composers Ser.). 32p. 2009. (gr. 4-4). 42.50 (978-1-60854-109-6(6)) 2006. (Illus.). (J). (gr. -1-3). lib. bdg. 21.25 (978-1-4042-2770-5(9)) Rosen Publishing Group, Inc., The. (PowerKids Pr.).

Venezia, Mike. Johann Sebastian Bach (Revised Edition) 2017. (Getting to Know the World's Greatest Composers Ser.). (ENG., Illus.). 40p. (J). lib. bdg. 29.00 (978-0-531-22060-3(5), Children's Pr.) Scholastic Library Publishing.

BACILLI

see Bacteriology

BACKPACKING

McKinney, John. Hiking & Backpacking, Vol. 10. 2016. (Great Outdoors! Ser.). (Illus.). 48p. (J). (gr. 5). 20.95 (978-1-4222-3569-0(6)) Mason Crest.

BACTERIA

see also Bacteriology

Bacteria up Close. 2013. (Under the Microscope Ser.). 32p. (J). (gr. 4-6). pap. 70.20 (978-1-4339-8336-8(2)) Stevens, Gareth Publishing LLLP.

Barker, David M. Archaea. 2010. (Class of Their Own Ser.). (ENG., Illus.). 48p. (J). (gr. 5-8). lib. bdg. (978-0-7787-5373-5(5)) Crabtree Publishing Co.

—Archaea: Salt-Lovers, Methane-Makers, Thermophiles, & Other Archaeans. 2010. (Class of Their Own Ser.). (ENG., Illus.). 48p. (J). (gr. 5-8). pap. (978-0-7787-5387-2(5)) Crabtree Publishing Co.

Berger, Melvin. Germs Make Me Sick! Hafner, Marylin, illus. 2015. (Let's-Read-And-Find-Out Science 2 Ser.). (ENG.). 32p. (J). (gr. -1-3). pap. 6.99 (978-0-06-238187-3(3)) HarperCollins Pubs.

—Germs Make Me Sick! 2015. (Let's Read & Find Out Science Stage 2 Ser.). (J). lib. bdg. 17.20 (978-0-606-37742-3(5)) Turtleback Bks.

Biskup, Agnieszka, et al. The Surprising World of Bacteria with Max Axiom, Super Scientist, 1 vol. 2010. (Graphic Science Ser.). (ENG.). 32p. (gr. 3-4). pap. 8.10 (978-1-4296-4863-9(5)); lib. bdg. 30.65 (978-1-4296-3975-0(X)) Capstone Press of Coughlan Cos. (Graphic Library).

Canavan, Roger. You Wouldn't Want to Live Without Bacteria! Bergin, Mark, illus. 2015. (You Wouldn't Want to Live Without... Ser.). (ENG.). 32p. (J). lib. bdg. 29.00 (978-0-531-21363-6(3), Watts, Franklin) Scholastic Library Publishing.

Cline-Ransome, Lesa. Germs: Sickness, Bad Breath, & Pizza. Ransome, James, illus. 2017. (ENG.). 40p. (J). 17.99 (978-0-8050-7915-9(7), 9780805079159, Holt, Henry & Co. Bks. For Young Readers) Holt, Henry & Co.

Close, Edward. Germ Warfare, 1 vol., 1. 2014. (Discovery Education: How It Works). (ENG.). 32p. (gr. 3-6). pap. 10.00 (978-1-4777-6301-8(5), PowerKids Pr.) Rosen Publishing Group, Inc., The.

Crewe, Sabrina. In Your Body. 2010. (Under the Microscope Ser.). 32p. (gr. 2-4). 30.00 (978-1-60413-825-2(4), Chelsea Clubhouse) Facts On File, Inc.

DiConsiglio, John. Superbugs, 1 vol. 2012. (Hot Topics Ser.). (ENG.). 64p. (gr. 7-8). 34.65 (978-1-4329-6037-7(7)); pap. 10.95 (978-1-4329-6045-2(8)) Heinemann-Raintree. (NA-h).

Eamer, Claire. Inside Your Insides: A Guide to the Microbes That Call You Home. Tremblay, Marie-Eve, illus. 2016. (ENG.). 36p. (J). (gr. 3-7). 17.95 (978-1-77138-332-5(1)) Kids Can Pr., Ltd. CAN. Dist: Hachette Bk. Group.

Eaton, Louise & Rogers, Kara. Examining Viruses & Bacteria. 2017. (J). lib. bdg. (978-1-5383-0009-1(5)) Rosen Publishing Group, Inc., The.

Favor, Lesli J. & Baum, Margaux. Bacteria. 2016. (Germs: Disease Causing Organisms Ser.). 48p. (J). (gr. 5-5). pap. 11.75 (978-1-4777-8836-3(0), Rosen Reference) Rosen Publishing Group, Inc., The.

Flynn, Wes. What Makes Me Stinky?, Vol. 1. 2014. (My Body Does Strange Stuff! Ser.). 24p. (J). (gr. 1-2). (ENG.). pap. 8.15 (978-1-4824-0304-6(8)); 22.60 (978-1-4824-0301-5(3)) Stevens, Gareth Publishing LLLP.

Gardy, Jennifer. It's Catching: The Infectious World of Germs & Microbes. Holinaty, Josh, illus. 2014. (ENG.). 64p. (J). (gr. 3-7). pap. 13.95 (978-1-77147-053-7(4), Owlkids) Owlkids Bks. Inc. CAN. Dist: Publishers Group West (PGW).

Halvorson, Karin. Inside Your Germs, 1 vol. 2016. (Super Simple Body Set 2 Ser.). (ENG., Illus.). 32p. (J). (gr. k-4). 27.07 (978-1-62403-944-7(8)) ABDO Publishing Co.

Herrington, Lisa M. I Have a Cold. 2015. (Rookie Read-About(tm) Health Ser.). (ENG., Illus.). 32p. (J). lib. bdg. 25.00 (978-0-531-21012-3(X)) Scholastic Library Publishing.

Hollar, Sherman. A Closer Look at Bacteria, Algae, & Protozoa. 2011. (Illus.). 88p. (J). lib. bdg. 31.70 (978-1-61530-534-6(3)) Rosen Publishing Group, Inc., The.

Holt, Rinehart and Winston Staff. Holt Science & Technology Chapter 10: Life Science: Bacteria & Viruses. 5th ed. 2004. (Illus.). pap. 12.86 (978-0-03-030206-0(4)) Holt McDougal.

Kawa, Katie. We Need Bacteria. 2015. (Creatures We Can't Live Without Ser.). (ENG., Illus.). 24p. (J). (gr. 3-4). pap. 8.25 (978-1-4994-0978-9(8), PowerKids Pr.) Rosen Publishing Group, Inc., The.

Klosterman, Lorrie. Drug-Resistant Diseases & Superbugs. 2009. (Health Alert 6 Ser.). 64p. (gr. 4). 32.79 (978-0-7614-3981-3(1)) Marshall Cavendish GBR. Dist: Marshall Cavendish Corp.

Kornberg, Arthur. Germ Stories. Alaniz, Adam, illus. Kolter, Roberto, photos by. 2007. 70p. (J). (gr. 3-7). 34.00 (978-1-891389-51-1(3)) Univ. Science Bks.

Kroll, Jennifer. Pequeños Poderosos: Cosas Diminutas - Grandes Resultados. 2016. (TIME for Kids en Español - Level 5 Ser.). (SPA.). 64p. (gr. 5-5). lib. bdg. 31.99 (978-1-5157-2926-6(5)) Time for Kids Inc AUS. Dist: Capstone Pub.

Latta, Sara L. The Good, the Bad, the Slimy: The Secret Life of Microbes. Kunkel, Dennis, photos by. 2006. (Prime (Middle/Senior) Ser.). (Illus.). 128p. (J). (gr. 4-9). lib. bdg. 33.27 (978-0-7660-1294-3(8)) Enslow Pubs., Inc.

Leet, Karen M. Food Intruders: Invisible Creatures Lurking in Your Food. 2011. (Tiny Creepy Creatures Ser.). (ENG.). 32p. (gr. 3-4). pap. 47.70 (978-1-4296-7274-0(9)); lib. bdg. 27.99 (978-1-4296-6532-2(7)) Capstone Press of Coughlan Cos. (Edge Bks.).

—Yard Monsters: Invisible Creatures Lurking in Your Backyard. 2011. (Tiny Creepy Creatures Ser.). (ENG.). 32p. (gr. 3-4). pap. 47.70 (978-1-4296-7278-8(1)); lib. bdg. 27.99 (978-1-4296-6533-9(5)) Capstone Press of Coughlan Cos. (Edge Bks.).

Levy, Janey. The World of Microbes: Bacteria, Viruses, & Other Microorganisms. 2010. (Understanding Genetics Ser.). (ENG.). 80p. (YA). lib. bdg. 33.25 (978-1-4358-9536-2(3)) Rosen Publishing Group, Inc., The.

Markovics, Joyce L. Tiny Invaders! Deadly Microorganisms, 1 vol. 2013. (Nature's Invaders Ser.). (ENG.). 32p. (gr. 3-4). lib. bdg. 27.99 (978-1-4765-0142-0(4)) Capstone Press of Coughlan Cos.

Oetting, Judy. Germs. Herr, Tad, illus. 2011. (Rookie Ready to Learn Ser.). 40p. (J). (gr. -1-k). (ENG.). pap. 5.95 (978-0-531-26732-5(6)); lib. bdg. 23.00 (978-0-531-26500-0(5), Children's Pr.) Scholastic Library Publishing.

Ollhoff, Jim. The Germ Detectives, 1 vol. 2009. (History of Germs Ser.). (ENG., Illus.). 32p. (YA). (gr. 5-9). 27.07 (978-1-60453-499-3(0)) ABDO Publishing Co.

—What Are Germs?, 1 vol. 2009. (History of Germs Ser.). (ENG., Illus.). 32p. (YA). (gr. 5-9). 27.07 (978-1-60453-502-0(4)) ABDO Publishing Co.

Orr, Tamra B. Antibiotics. 2016. (True Book(tm), a — Greatest Discoveries & Discoverers Ser.). (ENG., Illus.). 48p. (J). lib. bdg. 31.00 (978-0-531-21860-0(0), Children's Pr.) Scholastic Library Publishing.

Owen, Ruth. Disgusting Food Invaders. 2016. (Up Close & Gross: Microscopic Creatures Ser.). (ENG.). 24p. (J). (gr. 1-6). pap. 7.95 (978-1-944998-70-7(5)) Bearport Publishing Co., Inc.

Rake, Jody Sullivan. Why Feet Smell & Other Gross Facts about Your Body, 1 vol. 2012. (Gross Me Out Ser.). (ENG.). 24p. (gr. 1-2). pap. 7.29 (978-1-4296-7955-8(7)); pap. 41.70 (978-1-4296-8377-7(5)); lib. bdg. 25.32 (978-1-4296-7610-6(8)) Capstone Press of Coughlan Cos. (First Facts).

Romanek, Trudee. Achoo! Cowles, Rose, illus. 2003. (Mysterious You Ser.). (ENG.). 40p. (J). (gr. 4-9). pap. 8.95 (978-1-55337-451-0(7)) Kids Can Pr., Ltd. CAN. Dist: Hachette Bk. Group.

Roza, Greg. Bacteria up Close. 2013. 32p. (J). (gr. 4-6). 26.60 (978-1-4339-8334-4(6)); pap. 11.70 (978-1-4339-8335-1(4)) Stevens, Gareth Publishing LLLP.

Sherman, Josepha. The War Against Germs. (Germs: the Library of Disease-Causing Organisms Ser.). 48p. 2009. (gr. 5-5). 53.00 (978-1-61512-718-4(6)) 2004. (Illus.). (gr. 7-12). lib. bdg. 29.25 (978-0-8239-4495-8(6)) Rosen Publishing Group, Inc., The.

Sherman, Josepha & Baum, Margaux. The Fight Against Germs. 2016. (Germs: Disease Causing Organisms Ser.). 48p. (J). (gr. 5-5). pap. 11.75 (978-1-4777-8851-6(4), Rosen Reference) Rosen Publishing Group, Inc., The.

Simione, Ruth. Mike the Microbe. Simione, Allen, illus. Date not set. 38p. (J). (gr. 4-8). pap. 14.70 (978-1-877960-23-9(3)) Kemtec Educational Corp.

Smith, Tara C. Streptococcus (Group B) Alcamo, I. Edward, ed. 2007. (Deadly Diseases & Epidemics Ser.). (Illus.). 112p. (YA). (gr. 9-12). lib. bdg. 34.95 (978-0-7910-9243-9(7)) Facts On File, Inc.

Stewart, Melissa. Do People Really Have Tiny Insects Living in Their Eyelashes? And Other Questions about the Microscopic World. 2010. (Is That a Fact? Ser.). (ENG.). 40p. (gr. 4-6). lib. bdg. 26.60 (978-0-7613-4916-7(2)) Lerner Publishing Group.

—Germ Wars! The Secrets of the Immune System. 2010. (Gross & Goofy Body 2 Ser.). 48p. (gr. 3). 29.93 (978-0-7614-4165-6(4)) Marshall Cavendish Corp.

Swanson, Jennifer. Body Bugs: Invisible Creatures Lurking Inside You. 2011. (Tiny Creepy Creatures Ser.). (ENG.). 32p. (gr. 3-4). pap. 47.70 (978-1-4296-7272-6(2)); lib. bdg. 27.99 (978-1-4296-6530-8(0)) Capstone Press of Coughlan Cos. (Edge Bks.).

Tilden, Thomasine E. Lewis. Flesh Wound: A Minor Injury Takes a Deadly Turn. 2011. (J). pap. (978-0-545-32806-7(3)) Scholastic, Inc.

Verdick, Elizabeth. Germs Are Not for Sharing. Heinlen, Marieka, illus. 2006. (Best Behavior Ser.).Tr. of Germenes No Son para Compartir. (ENG.). (J). (gr. -1-2). 24p. 7.95 (978-1-57542-196-4(8)); 40p. pap. 11.95 (978-1-57542-197-1(6)) Free Spirit Publishing, Inc.

Verdick, Elizabeth & Heinlen, Marieka. Germs Are Not for Sharing. 2011. (Best Behavior Ser.).Tr. of Germenes No Son para Compartir. (SPA, ENG & MUL.). 24p. (J). (gr. k — 1). 7.95 (978-1-57542-369-2(3)) Free Spirit Publishing, Inc.

—Germs Are Not for Sharing/Los Gérmenes No Son Para Compartir. 2011. (Best Behavior Ser.). (SPA & ENG.). 40p. (J). (gr. -1-2). pap. 11.95 (978-1-57542-368-5(5)) Free Spirit Publishing, Inc.

Weakland, Mark. Gut Bugs, Dust Mites, & Other Microorganisms You Can't Live Without. (Nasty (but Useful!) Science Ser.). (ENG.). 32p. (gr. 3-4). 2011. pap. 8.10 (978-1-4296-6346-5(4)) 2011. pap. 47.70 (978-1-4296-6472-1(X)) 2010. lib. bdg. 27.32 (978-1-4296-4538-6(5)) Capstone Press of Coughlan Cos. (Fact Finders).

Wearing, Judy. Bacteria: Staph, Strep, Clostridium, & Other Bacteria. 2010. (Class of Their Own Ser.). (ENG., Illus.). 48p. (J). (gr. 5-8). pap. (978-0-7787-5388-9(3)); lib. bdg. (978-0-7787-5374-2(3)) Crabtree Publishing Co.

BACTERIOLOGY

see also Immunity; Microorganisms

Cole, Joanna. The Magic School Bus Inside Ralphie. Speirs, John & Degen, Bruce, illus. 2010. (ENG.). 32p. (C). (gr. -1-3). pap. 10.95 (978-0-590-40025-1(8)) National Geographic School Publishing, Inc.

Germ Theory. 2010. (Science Foundations Ser.). (Illus.). 128p. (gr. 6-12). 35.00 (978-1-60413-041-6(5), Chelsea Hse.) Facts On File, Inc.

GIANTmicrobes(r). GIANTmicrobes — Germs & Microbes Coloring Book. Cutting, David, illus. 2014. (ENG.). 32p. (J). (gr. k-5). pap. 3.99 (978-0-486-78018-4(X)) Dover Pubns., Inc.

Martin, Sherri. Bye-Bye, Germs. 2012. 32p. pap. 14.51 (978-1-4669-1397-4(5)) Trafford Publishing.

McNeil, Niki, et al. HOCPP 1140 Germs. 2007. spiral bd. 16.00 (978-1-60308-140-5(2)) In the Hands of a Child.

Nadler, Beth. The Magic School Bus Inside Ralphie. Duchesne, Lucie, tr. (Magic School Bus Ser.). (FRE., Illus.). 32p. (J). (gr. 1-4). pap. 5.99 (978-0-590-24658-3(5)) Scholastic, Inc.

Rooke, Thom. A Germ's Journey, 1 vol. Trimmer, Tony, illus. (Follow It! Ser.). (ENG.). 24p. (gr. 1-3). 2011. pap. 7.49 (978-1-4048-6710-9(4)) 2010. lib. bdg. 26.65 (978-1-4048-6268-5(4)) Picture Window Bks.

BAD DREAMS

see Nightmares

BADEN-POWELL OF GILWELL, ROBERT STEPHENSON SMYTH BADEN-POWELL, BARON, 1857-1941

Baden-Powell, Robert. My Adventures as a Spy. 2014. (ENG., Illus.). 128p. pap. 13.95 (978-1-4456-3610-8(7)) Amberley Publishing GBR. Dist: Independent Pubs. Group.

BADGERS

Brexel, Bernadette. A Badger's Burrow, 1 vol. 2015. (Rosen Real Readers: STEAM Collection). (ENG.). 12p. (J). pap. 6.33 (978-1-4994-9298-9(7), Rosen Classroom) Rosen Publishing Group, Inc., The.

Gates, Margo. Honey Badgers. 2013. (Animal Safari Ser.). (ENG., Illus.). 24p. (J). (gr. k-3). lib. bdg. 25.95 (978-1-60014-909-2(X), Blastoff! Readers) Bellwether Media.

Heos, Bridget. Do You Really Want to Meet a Badger? Fabbri, Daniele, illus. 2017. (Do You Really Want to Meet... Wild Animals? Ser.). (ENG.). 24p. (J). (gr. 1-3). pap. 8.99 (978-1-68152-115-2(6)) Amicus.

—Do You Really Want to Meet a Badger? Fabbri, Daniele, illus. 2016. (Do You Really Want to Meet... Wild Animals? Ser.). (ENG.). 24p. (J). (gr. k-3). 20.95 (978-1-60753-944-5(6)) Amicus Publishing.

Klobuchar, Lisa. Badgers & Other Mustelids. 2005. (World Book's Animals of the World Ser.). (Illus.). 64p. (J). (978-0-7166-1265-0(8)) World Bk., Inc.

Kyler, Inge Logenburg. Search for a House. 2010. 24p. 11.49 (978-1-4520-2007-5(8)) AuthorHouse.

Leach, Michael. Badger. 2009. (Animal Neighbors Ser.). 32p. (gr. k-5). pap. 10.60 (978-1-4042-4571-6(5), Rosen Classroom); (Illus.). (J). lib. bdg. 25.25 (978-1-4358-4994-5(9), PowerKids Pr.) Rosen Publishing Group, Inc., The.

Maximus, Sofia. Badgers in the Dark. 2012. (Creatures of the Night Ser.). (Illus.). 24p. (J). (gr. 1-3). pap. 8.15 (978-1-4339-6362-9(0)); lib. bdg. 22.60 (978-1-4339-6480-0(5)) Stevens, Gareth Publishing LLLP.

Moore Niver, Heather. Badgers after Dark. 2016. (Animals of the Night Ser.). (ENG.). 32p. (J). (gr. 3-3). pap. 10.52 (978-0-7660-7166-7(9)) Enslow Pubs., Inc.

Niver, Heather Moore. Badgers after Dark. 2016. (Animals of the Night Ser.). (ENG., Illus.). 32p. (J). (gr. 3-3). 25.27 (978-0-7660-7168-1(5)) Enslow Pubs., Inc.

Petz, Moritz. The Day Everything Went Wrong. Jackowski, Amélie, illus. 2015. (ENG.). 32p. (J). 17.95 (978-0-7358-4209-0(4)) North-South Bks., Inc.

Phillips, Dee. Badger's Burrow. 2013. (Science Slam: the Hole Truth! Underground Animal Life Ser.). 24p. (J). (gr. -1-3). lib. bdg. 23.93 (978-1-61772-745-0(8)) Bearport Publishing Co., Inc.

Quinlan, Julia J. Honey Badgers. 2013. (Ferocious Fighting Animals Ser.). (ENG., Illus.). 24p. (J). (gr. k-5). pap. 8.25 (978-1-4488-9800-8(5)); lib. bdg. 22.60 (978-1-4488-9671-4(1)) Rosen Publishing Group, Inc., The. (PowerKids Pr.).

Sebastian, Emily. Badgers. 2012. (Illus.). 24p. (J). 49.50 (978-1-4488-5061-7(4), PowerKids Pr.); pap. 8.25 (978-1-4488-5060-0(6), PowerKids Pr.); lib. bdg. 22.60 (978-1-4488-4955-0(1)) Rosen Publishing Group, Inc., The.

Zobel, Derek. Badgers. 2011. (Backyard Wildlife Ser.). (ENG., Illus.). 24p. (J). (gr. k-3). lib. bdg. 25.95 (978-1-60014-595-7(7), Blastoff! Readers) Bellwether Media.

BADGERS—FICTION

Bagley, Jessixa. Laundry Day. 2017. (ENG., Illus.). 32p. (J). 17.99 (978-1-62672-317-7(6), 9781626723177) Roaring Brook Pr.

Base, Graeme, et al. Dinosaurs in Your Backyard: The Coolest, Scariest Creatures Ever Found in the USA! 2009. (ENG., Illus.). 32p. (J). (gr. 1-4). 16.95 *(978-0-8109-7099-1(6)*, Abrams Bks. for Young Readers) Abrams, Inc.

Bean, Margo Cronbaugh. Buffaloed Badger. Perry, Aumi Kauffman, illus. 2012. 24p. 19.95 *(978-1-61633-239-6(5))*; pap. 11.95 *(978-1-61633-240-2(9))* Guardian Angel Publishing, Inc.

Boelts, Maribeth. Beaver & Badger. 2016. (Spring Forward Ser.). (J). (gr. 2). *(978-1-4900-9422-9(9))* Benchmark Education Co.

Chiew, Suzanne. That's What Friends Are For. Pedler, Caroline, illus. 2017. (ENG.). 32p. (J). (gr. -1-2). 16.99 ***(978-1-68010-040-2(8))*** Tiger Tales.

Dearing, Rodney. Brilliant Mr. Badger & the Seaplane Treasure. 2013. (Illus.). 98p. (J). pap. 16.95 *(978-0-7552-1585-0(0))* Authors OnLine, Ltd. GBR. Dist: Printondemand-worldwide.com.

Díaz, Katacha. Badger at Sandy Ridge Road. Kest, Kristin, illus. 2005. (Smithsonian's Backyard Ser.). (ENG.). 32p. (J). (gr. -1-2). 15.95 *(978-1-59249-420-0(X)*, B5028); 4.95 *(978-1-59249-421-7(8)*, B5078); pap. 6.95 *(978-1-59249-422-4(6)*, S5028) Soundprints.

Diaz, Katacha. Badger at Sandy Ridge Road. Kest, Kristin, illus. 2005. (Smith Sonian's Backyard Ser.). (ENG.). 32p. (J). (gr. 2-2). 8.95 *(978-1-59249-423-1(4)*, SC5028); 19.95 *(978-1-59249-424-8(2)*, BC5028) Soundprints.

Dougherty, John. Stinkbomb & Ketchup-Face & the Badness of Badgers. Ricks, Sam, illus. 2017. (Stinkbomb & Ketchup-Face Ser.). (ENG.). 144p. (J). (gr. 3-7). 15.99 *(978-1-101-99662-1(5)*, G.P. Putnam's Sons Books for Young Readers) Penguin Young Readers Group.

Gravett, Emily. Tidy. Gravett, Emily, illus. 2017. (ENG., Illus.). 40p. (J). (gr. -1-3). 17.99 *(978-1-4814-8019-2(7)*, Simon & Schuster Bks. For Young Readers) Simon & Schuster Bks. For Young Readers.

Hamley, Dennis. Badger's Fate. 2006. (ENG., Illus.). 112p. per. *(978-1-904529-19-4(4)*, Back to Front) Solidus.

Hiscock, Bruce. Coyote & Badger: Desert Hunters of the Southwest. 2003. (ENG., Illus.). 32p. (J). (gr. 2-4). 15.95 *(978-1-56397-848-7(2))* Boyds Mills Pr.

Hoban, Russell. A Bargain for Frances. Hoban, Lillian, illus. l.t. ed. 2003. (I Can Read Level 2 Ser.). (ENG.). 64p. (J). (gr. k-3). pap. 3.99 *(978-0-06-444001-1(X))* HarperCollins Pubs.

—Best Friends for Frances. braille ed. 2004. (Illus.). (J). (gr. k-3). spiral bd. *(978-0-616-01674-9(3))* Canadian National Institute for the Blind/Institut National Canadien pour les Aveugles.

—Best Friends for Frances. Hoban, Lillian, illus. 2016. (ENG.). 32p. (J). (gr. -1-3). pap. 5.99 *(978-0-06-239244-2(1)*, HarperFestival) HarperCollins Pubs.

—A Birthday for Frances. Hoban, Lillian, illus. 2012. (I Can Read Level 2 Ser.). (ENG.). 48p. (J). (gr. k-3). 16.99 *(978-0-06-083795-2(0))* HarperCollins Pubs.

—A Birthday for Frances. 2012. (I Can Read! Level 2 Ser.). (J). lib. bdg. 13.55 *(978-0-606-26850-9(2)*, Turtleback) Turtleback Bks.

—Bread & Jam for Frances. Hoban, Lillian, illus. 2008. (I Can Read Level 2 Ser.). (ENG.). 48p. (J). (gr. k-3). 16.99 *(978-0-06-083798-3(5))*; pap. 3.99 *(978-0-06-083800-3(0))* HarperCollins Pubs.

Hunter, Erin. Twilight. Richardson, Owen & Stevenson, Dave, illus. 2015. (Warriors: the New Prophecy Ser.: 5). (ENG.). 368p. (J). (gr. 3-7). pap. 7.99 *(978-0-06-236706-8(4))* HarperCollins Pubs.

—Twilight. Stevenson, Dave, illus. 2006. (Warriors: the New Prophecy Ser.: 5). (ENG.). 336p. (J). (gr. 3-7). 16.99 *(978-0-06-082764-9(5))* HarperCollins Pubs.

Jacques, Brian. Eulalia! 2010. (Redwall Ser.). (ENG.). 400p. (J). (gr. 5-18). 8.99 *(978-0-14-241495-8(6)*, Firebird) Penguin Young Readers Group.

—Lord Brocktree. Fangorn, illus. 2005. (Redwall Ser.). (ENG.). 384p. (J). (gr. 5-7). pap. 8.99 *(978-0-14-250110-8(7)*, Firebird) Penguin Young Readers Group.

Jones, Allan. The Six Crowns: Trundle's Quest. Chalk, Gary, illus. 2011. (Six Crowns Ser.: 1). 176p. (J). (gr. 2-5). pap. 5.99 *(978-0-06-200625-7(8)*, Greenwillow Bks.) HarperCollins Pubs.

Jones, Allan Frewin. Fire over Swallowhaven. Chalk, Gary, illus. 2012. (Six Crowns Ser.: 3). 160p. (J). (gr. 2-5). 15.99 *(978-0-06-200629-5(0)*, Greenwillow Bks.) HarperCollins Pubs.

—Trundle's Quest. Chalk, Gary, illus. 2011. (Six Crowns Ser.: 1). 160p. (J). (gr. 2-5). 15.99 *(978-0-06-200623-3(1)*, Greenwillow Bks.) HarperCollins Pubs.

Kasza, Keiko. Badger's Fancy Meal. 2009. (ENG.). 32p. (J). (gr. -1-3). pap. 6.99 *(978-0-14-241271-8(6)*, Puffin Books) Penguin Young Readers Group.

Lester, Helen & Munsinger, Lynn. Boris & the Worrisome Wakies. Lester, Helen & Munsinger, Lynn, illus. 2017. (ENG., Illus.). 32p. (J). (gr. -1-3). 16.99 *(978-0-544-64094-8(2)*, HMH Books For Young Readers) Houghton Mifflin Harcourt Publishing Co.

Luciani, Brigitte. The Carnival. Tharlet, Eve, illus. 2014. (ENG.). 32p. (J). pap. 6.95 *(978-1-4677-4204-7(X))*; lib. bdg. 25.26 *(978-1-4677-4203-0(1)*, Graphic Universe™) Lerner Publishing Group.

—A Hubbub. Gauvin, Edward, tr. from FRE. Tharlet, Eve, illus. 2010. (Mr. Badger & Mrs. Fox Ser.: 2). (ENG.). 32p. (J). (gr. k-3). pap. 6.95 *(978-0-7613-5632-5(0)*, Graphic Universe™);Bk. 2. 25.26 *(978-0-7613-5626-4(6))* Lerner Publishing Group.

—The Meeting. Burrell, Carol, tr. from FRE. Tharlet, Eve, illus. 2010. (Mr. Badger & Mrs. Fox Ser.: 1). (ENG.). 32p. (J). (gr. k-3). lib. bdg. 25.26 *(978-0-7613-5625-7(8))* Lerner Publishing Group.

—The Meeting. Burrell, Carol, tr. from FRE. Tharlet, Eve, illus. 2010. 1. (ENG.). 32p. (C). (gr. k-3). pap. 10.95 *(978-0-7613-5631-8(2))* National Geographic School Publishing, Inc.

—Peace & Quiet. Burrell, Carol, tr. Tharlet, Eve, illus. 2012. (Mr. Badger & Mrs. Fox Ser.: 4). (ENG.). 32p. (J). (gr. k-3). pap. 6.95 *(978-0-8225-9163-4(4))*; lib. bdg. 25.26 *(978-0-7613-8520-2(7))* Lerner Publishing Group. (Graphic Universe™).

—What a Team! Gauvin, Edward, tr. from FRE. Tharlet, Eve, illus. 2011. (Mr. Badger & Mrs. Fox Ser.: 3). (ENG.). 32p. (J). (gr. k-3). 25.26 *(978-0-7613-5627-1(4))*; pap. 6.95 *(978-0-7613-5633-2(9)*, Graphic Universe™) Lerner Publishing Group.

Martell, Ray. Brox the Bungling Badger. 2012. (Illus.). 88p. pap. 15.50 *(978-1-78035-345-6(6)*, Fastprint Publishing) Upfront Publishing Ltd. GBR. Dist: Printondemand-worldwide.com.

McSorley, Paul J. & Bearss, Patricia. The Adventures of Forealdo: Finding Millie. 2012. 34p. 24.95 *(978-1-4626-6721-5(X))* America Star Bks.

Sargent, Dave & Sargent, Pat. Buddy Badger: I'm a Little Bully, 15 vols., Vol. 17. Huff, Jeane, illus. 2nd rev. ed. 2003. (Animal Pride Ser.: 17). 42p. (J). pap. 10.95 *(978-1-56763-792-2(2))*; lib. bdg. 20.95 *(978-1-56763-791-5(4))* Ozark Publishing.

Varley, Susan. Badger's Parting Gifts. (Illus.). 32p. (J). (gr. -1-3). (BEN, ENG, URD, ARA & VIE.). *(978-1-85430-528-2(X))*; (ENG, URD, ARA, VIE & CHI., *(978-1-85430-527-5(1))* Little Tiger Pr. Group.

BADMINTON

Dann, Sarah & Kantor, Katherine. Le Badminton. 2012. (FRE.). 32p. (J). pap. 9.95 *(978-2-89579-479-0(0))* Bayard Canada CAN. Dist: Crabtree Publishing Co.

BAGGINS, BILBO (FICTITIOUS CHARACTER)—FICTION

Tolkien, J. R. R. El Hobbit. 2003. (Lord of the Rings Ser.). (SPA.). 320p. (YA). 17.95 *(978-84-450-7141-0(6)*, MQ9001) Minotauro Ediciones ESP. Dist: Distribooks, Inc.

—The Hobbit. Tolkien, J. R. R., illus. 70th anniv. ed. 2011. (ENG., Illus.). 400p. mass mkt. *(978-0-261-10221-7(4))* HarperCollins Pubs. Ltd.

—The Hobbit. movie tie-in ed. 2012. lib. bdg. 19.65 *(978-0-606-26240-8(7)*, Turtleback) Turtleback Bks.

BAGGINS, FRODO (FICTITIOUS CHARACTER)—FICTION

Tolkien, J. R. R. Senhor dos Aneis. pap. 36.95 *(978-85-336-1337-9(7))* Livraria Martins Editora BRA. Dist: Distribooks, Inc.

BAHAI FAITH

Betts, Bambi. Basic Truths 1-3. 2008. (ENG., Illus.). 58p. pap. 9.95 *(978-0-85398-523-5(5))* Ronald, George Pub., Ltd.

Hosack, Leona. Kamal's Day. 2014. (J). *(978-0-87743-717-8(3))* Baha'i Publishing Trust, U.S.

Ring, Phyllis Edgerly. Jamila Does Not Want a Bat in Her House. Hosack, Leona, illus. 2016. 30p. (J). ***(978-0-87743-718-5(1))*** Baha'i Publishing Trust, U.S.

Tunick, I. Walter. Spiritual Journey: The Bahandaacute;'andiacute; Faith. 2007. 296p. 24.95 *(978-1-4251-6740-0(3))* Trafford Publishing.

Von Kitzing, Constanze. Pearls of Wisdom. 2014. (Illus.). (J). *(978-1-61851-069-3(X))* Baha'i Publishing.

White, Bender Richardson, et al. Baha'i Faith. 3rd rev. ed. 2009. (World Religions Ser.). (Illus.). 144p. (gr. 6-12). 40.00 *(978-1-60413-104-8(7)*, Chelsea Hse.) Facts On File, Inc.

BAHAISM

see Bahai Faith

BAHAMAS

Barlas, Robert & Yong, Jui Lin. Bahamas. 2nd rev. ed. 2010. (Cultures of the World 20 Ser.). 144p. (gr. 6). 42.79 *(978-1-60870-021-9(6))* Marshall Cavendish GBR. Dist: Marshall Cavendish Corp.

Colleen Madonna Flood Williams. The Bahamas, Vol. 11. Henderson, James D., ed. 2015. (Discovering the Caribbean: History, Politics, & Culture Ser.). (Illus.). 64p. (J). (gr. 7). lib. bdg. 22.95 *(978-1-4222-3316-0(2))* Mason Crest.

Hintz, Martin. The Bahamas. 2012. (ENG.). 144p. (J). lib. bdg. 40.00 *(978-0-531-27541-2(8))* Scholastic Library Publishing.

Williams, Colleen Madonna Flood. The Bahamas. 2010. (Caribbean Today Ser.). (Illus.). 64p. (YA). (gr. 7-18). 21.95 *(978-1-4222-0620-1(3))* Mason Crest.

BAHAMAS—FICTION

Cooper, Susan. Green Boy. (ENG., Illus.). 208p. (J). 2013. (gr. 3-7). 17.99 *(978-1-4424-8081-0(5))* 2003. (gr. 4-7). pap. 7.99 *(978-0-689-84760-8(2))* McElderry, Margaret K. Bks. (McElderry, Margaret K. Bks.).

Cooper, Susan & National Geographic Learning Staff. Green Boy. 2013. (ENG., Illus.). 208p. (J). (gr. 3-7). pap. 7.99 *(978-1-4424-8082-7(3)*, McElderry, Margaret K. Bks.) McElderry, Margaret K. Bks.

Herlong, M. H. The Great Wide Sea. 2010. (ENG.). 288p. (YA). (gr. 7-18). 8.99 *(978-0-14-241670-9(3)*, Puffin Books) Penguin Young Readers Group.

Lagrou, Patrick. Born among the Dolphins. 2008. (Born among the Dolphins Ser.: 1). (ENG & DUT.). 154p. (J). (gr. 3-18). 19.95 *(978-1-60537-022-4(3))* Clavis Publishing.

Rabley, Stephen & Pearson Education Staff. Maisie & the Dolphin. 2nd ed. 2009. (ENG.). 20p. pap. 11.99 *(978-1-4058-6954-6(2))* Pearson Education.

Simms, Abigail & Gabrielle. Let's Turn Our World Upside Down. 2013. 28p. pap. 16.09 *(978-1-4669-8156-0(3))* Trafford Publishing.

Stevenson, Robin. A Thousand Shades of Blue, 1 vol. 2008. (ENG.). 240p. (YA). (gr. 7-12). pap. 12.95 *(978-1-55143-921-1(2))* Orca Bk. Pubs. USA.

Sullivan, Carolyn. Cutter the Crab: Spring Break. 2012. pap. 11.95 *(978-0-7414-7391-2(7))* Infinity Publishing.

Sutton, Laurie S. The Curse of Atlantis. Neely, Scott, illus. 2015. (You Choose Stories: Scooby-Doo Ser.). (ENG.). 112p. (gr. 2-3). lib. bdg. 32.65 *(978-1-4965-0477-7(1))* Stone Arch Bks.

Wohlford, Martha Crikelair. Splash: The Staniel Cay Cat. 2006. (Illus.). (J). per. 21.95 *(978-0-9787981-0-9(4))* Serenity Pr.

BAILEY SCHOOL KIDS (FICTITIOUS CHARACTERS)—FICTION

The Abominable Snowman Doesn't Roast Marshmallows, 6 bks., Pack. 2005. 96p. (J). pap. 3.99 *(978-0-439-86573-9(5))* Scholastic, Inc.

Dadey, Debbie & Jones, Marcia Thornton. Monsters Don't Scuba Dive. (Adventures of the Bailey School Kids Ser.: No. 14). (FRE., Illus.). 80p. (J). (gr. 2-4). pap. 5.99 *(978-0-590-24550-0(3))* Scholastic, Inc.

Jones, Marcia Thornton & Dadey, Debbie. Dragons Do Eat Homework. Dreidemy, Joëlle, illus. 2007. 64p. (J). *(978-0-545-00234-9(6))* Scholastic, Inc.

—Ghosts Do Splash in Puddles. Dreidemy, Joëlle, illus. 2006. 64p. (J). pap. *(978-0-439-87629-2(X))* Scholastic, Inc.

—Wizards Do Roast Turkeys. Dreidemy, Joëlle, illus. 2007. 64p. (J). pap. *(978-0-545-00235-6(4))* Scholastic, Inc.

BAJA CALIFORNIA (MEXICO: PENINSULA)—FICTION

Cruz, Maria Colleen. Border Crossing. 2003. 128p. (J). pap. 9.95 *(978-1-55885-405-5(3)*, Piñata Books) Arte Publico Pr.

Gill, Shelley. Big Blue. Barrow, Ann, illus. 2005. (ENG.). 32p. (J). (gr. k-3). 7.95 *(978-1-57091-667-0(5))* Charlesbridge Publishing, Inc.

Irwin, Bindi, et al. Surfing with Turtles: Bindi Wildlife Adventures. 2013. (Bindi's Wildlife Adventures Ser.: 8). (ENG.). 112p. (J). (gr. 3-6). pap. 4.99 *(978-1-4022-8094-8(7)*, Sourcebooks Jabberwocky) Sourcebooks, Inc.

O'Dell, Scott. The Black Pearl. 2009. 9.00 *(978-0-7848-3610-1(8)*, Everbind) Marco Bk. Co.

Semionov, Vladimir, illus. Silver Wings. 2007. (Choose Your Own Adventure Ser.: No. 23). 107p. (J). (gr. 4-7). pap. 6.99 *(978-1-933390-23-9(9))* Chooseco LLC.

BAKERS AND BAKERIES

Jeffries, Joyce. Meet the Baker. 2012. (People Around Town Ser.). (Illus.). 24p. (J). (gr. k-2). pap. 8.15 *(978-1-4339-7321-5(9)*, 1344186); lib. bdg. 22.60 *(978-1-4339-7320-8(0)*, 1344186) Stevens, Gareth Publishing LLLP.

McConnell, S. What a Baker Makes: Learning the Long A Sound. 2009. (PowerPhonics Ser.). 24p. (gr. 1-1). 39.90 *(978-1-60851-477-9(3)*, PowerKids Pr.) Rosen Publishing Group, Inc., The.

Meachen Rau, Dana. Un Panadero. 2007. (En el Trabajo Ser.). (SPA., Illus.). 24p. (gr. k-1). lib. bdg. 15.95 *(978-0-7614-2781-0(3)*, Benchmark Bks.) Marshall Cavendish Corp.

Pohl, Kathleen. What Happens at a Bakery? 2006. (Where People Work Ser.). (Illus.). 24p. (gr. -1-3). pap. 8.15 *(978-0-8368-6891-3(9))*; lib. bdg. 22.00 *(978-0-8368-6884-5(6))* Stevens, Gareth Publishing LLLP. (Weekly Reader Leveled Readers).

BAKING

see also Bread; Cake; Pastry

ABDO Publishing Company Staff. Cool Cupcakes & Muffins. 2014. (Cool Cupcakes & Muffins Ser.: 6). (ENG.). 32p. (gr. 8-12). lib. bdg. 171.00 *(978-1-62403-298-1(2)*, Checkerboard Library) ABDO Publishing Co.

Beech, Linda Ward. The Magic School Bus Gets Baked in a Cake: A Book about Kitchen Chemistry. Duchesne, Lucie, tr. from ENG. Degen, Bruce, illus. (Magic School Bus Ser.). (FRE.). 32p. (J). (gr. 1-4). pap. 5.99 *(978-0-590-24660-6(7))* Scholastic, Inc.

Besel, Jennifer M. Baking Bliss! Baked Desserts to Make & Devour, 1 vol. 2014. (Custom Confections Ser.). (ENG., Illus.). 48p. (gr. 4-5). lib. bdg. 31.99 *(978-1-4914-0859-9(6))* Capstone Press of Coughlan Cos.

Boon, Fiona, ed. The Great Fairy Baking Competition. Ede, Lara, illus. Snaith, Andy, photos by. 2013. (ENG.). 64p. (J). 12.99 *(978-1-78235-591-5(X))* Make Believe Ideas GBR. Dist: Nelson, Thomas Inc.

Brash, Lorna. Professor Cook's Mind-Blowing Baking. 2013. (Professor Cook's... Ser.). 32p. (J). (gr. 4-12). pap. 7.95 *(978-1-4644-0551-8(4))*; (Illus.). lib. bdg. 23.94 *(978-0-7660-4303-9(7))* Enslow Pubs., Inc.

Carlson Berne, Emma. Run Your Own Bake Sale. 2014. (Young Entrepreneurs Ser.). 32p. (J). (gr. 4-6). pap. 10.00 *(978-1-4777-3007-2(9)*, PowerKids Pr.) Rosen Publishing Group, Inc., The.

Collister, Linda. Baking with Kids. Wreford, Polly, photos by. 2006. (ENG., Illus.). 128p. (J). (gr. 3-7). *(978-1-84597-220-2(1))* Ryland Peters & Small.

Cook, Deanna F. Baking Class: 50 Fun Recipes Kids Love to Bake & Eat! 2017. (ENG., Illus.). 144p. (J). spiral bd. 18.95 ***(978-1-61212-855-9(6))*** Storey Publishing, LLC.

Cornell, Kari. Sweet Cookies & Bars. Cohen, Brie, photos by. 2013. (You're the Chef Ser.). (ENG., Illus.). 32p. (gr. 3-5). lib. bdg. 26.60 *(978-0-7613-6638-6(5)*, Millbrook Pr.) Lerner Publishing Group.

Dorling Kindersley Publishing Staff. Mommy & Me Bake. 2015. (ENG.). 80p. (J). (gr. k-4). 15.99 *(978-1-4654-2896-7(8)*, DK Children) Dorling Kindersley Publishing, Inc.

Dresser, Cathryn. Let's Bake! 2016. (ENG., Illus.). 144p. (J). (gr. 2-17). pap. 10.99 *(978-1-4440-1082-4(4)*, Orion Children's Bks.) Hachette Children's Group GBR. Dist: Hachette Bk. Group.

From Father to Son: 6 Small Books. (Greetings Ser.: Vol. 1). 24p. (gr. 3-5). 31.00 *(978-0-7635-1748-9(8))* Rigby Education.

From Father to Son: Big Book. (Greetings Ser.: Vol. 1). 24p. (gr. 3-5). 31.00 *(978-0-7635-3135-5(9))* Rigby Education.

Goodman, Susan E. All in Just One Cookie. Bush, Timothy, illus. 2006. (ENG.). 32p. (J). (gr. -1-4). 17.99 *(978-0-06-009092-0(8)*, Greenwillow Bks.) HarperCollins Pubs.

Hoffmann, Sara E. Nia Bakes Cookies. Strange, Katie, illus. 2013. (My Reading Neighborhood: First-Grade Sight Word Stories Ser.). (ENG.). 16p. (gr. -1-1). pap. 5.95 *(978-1-4677-1172-2(1))* Lerner Publishing Group.

Jeffries, Joyce. Meet the Baker. 2012. (People Around Town Ser.). (Illus.). 24p. (gr. k-2). 69.20 *(978-1-4339-8058-9(4))*; (J). pap. 8.15 *(978-1-4339-7321-5(9)*, 1344186); (J). lib. bdg. 22.60 *(978-1-4339-7320-8(0)*, 1344186) Stevens, Gareth Publishing LLLP.

—Meet the Baker / Te Presento A Los Panaderos. 2012. (People Around Town / Gente de mi ciudad Ser.). (SPA & ENG., Illus.). 24p. (J). (gr. k-2). 22.60 *(978-1-4339-7382-6(0))* Stevens, Gareth Publishing LLLP.

Joyal, Kristen. Baking with Mommy Cookbook: Recipes for Kid-Size Ovens 10th Anniversary Edition. 2011. 121p. (J). spiral bd. 13.95 *(978-0-9718515-6-6(5))* Straight Forward Technologies.

Khan, Ramla. Fairy Tale Baking: More Than 50 Enchanting Cakes,bakes, & Decorations. 2015. (ENG., Illus.). 192p. (J). 25.00 *(978-1-56656-078-8(0)*, Crocodile Bks.) Interlink Publishing Group, Inc.

Kleven, Elisa. Sun Bread. 2004. (ENG., Illus.). 32p. (J). (gr. -1-k). reprint ed. pap. 6.99 *(978-0-14-240073-9(4)*, Puffin Books) Penguin Young Readers Group.

Kuskowski, Alex. Cool Healthy Muffins: Fun & Easy Baking Recipes for Kids!, 1 vol. 2014. (Cool Cupcakes & Muffins Ser.). (ENG.). 32p. (gr. 8-12). 28.50 *(978-1-62403-302-5(4))* ABDO Publishing Co.

—Cool Savory Muffins: Fun & Easy Baking Recipes for Kids!, 1 vol. 2014. (Cool Cupcakes & Muffins Ser.). (ENG.). 32p. (gr. 8-12). 28.50 *(978-1-62403-303-2(2))* ABDO Publishing Co.

—Cool Sweet Muffins: Fun & Easy Baking Recipes for Kids!, 1 vol. 2014. (Cool Cupcakes & Muffins Ser.). (ENG.). 32p. (gr. 8-12). 28.50 *(978-1-62403-304-9(0))* ABDO Publishing Co.

—Super Simple Bar Cookies: Easy Cookie Recipes for Kids!, 1 vol. 2016. (Super Simple Cookies Ser.). (ENG., Illus.). 32p. (J). (gr. k-4). 27.07 *(978-1-62403-946-1(4))* ABDO Publishing Co.

—Super Simple Classic Cookies: Easy Cookie Recipes for Kids!, 1 vol. 2016. (Super Simple Cookies Ser.). (ENG., Illus.). 32p. (J). (gr. k-4). 27.07 *(978-1-62403-947-8(2))* ABDO Publishing Co.

—Super Simple Healthy Cookies: Easy Cookie Recipes for Kids!, 1 vol. 2016. (Super Simple Cookies Ser.). (ENG., Illus.). 32p. (J). (gr. k-4). 27.07 *(978-1-62403-948-5(0))* ABDO Publishing Co.

—Super Simple Specialty Cookies: Easy Cookie Recipes for Kids!, 1 vol. 2016. (Super Simple Cookies Ser.). (ENG., Illus.). 32p. (J). (gr. k-4). 27.07 *(978-1-62403-951-5(0))* ABDO Publishing Co.

Lewis, Sarah. Kids' Baking: 60 Delicious Recipes for Children to Make. 2013. (ENG.). 144p. (gr. -1-17). pap. 12.99 *(978-0-600-62516-2(8)*, Hamlyn) Octopus Publishing Group GBR. Dist: Hachette Bk. Group.

Lidstrom, Clara & Nyberg, Annakarin. Let' Bake: A Step by Step Introduction. 2015. (ENG., Illus.). 48p. (J). (gr. k-4). 19.95 *(978-3-89955-751-0(4))* Die Gestalten Verlag DEU. Dist: Penguin Random Hse. LLC.

Loh-Hagan, Virginia. Bake Sale. 2016. (D. I. Y. Make It Happen Ser.). (ENG., Illus.). 32p. (J). (gr. 4-8). 29.93 *(978-1-63471-101-2(7)*, 208515, 45th Parallel Press) Cherry Lake Publishing.

McConnell, S. What a Baker Makes: Learning the Long A Sound. 2009. (PowerPhonics Ser.). 24p. (gr. 1-1). 39.90 *(978-1-60851-477-9(3)*, PowerKids Pr.) Rosen Publishing Group, Inc., The.

Meachen Rau, Dana. Baker. 2007. (Jobs in Town Ser.). (SPA., Illus.). 24p. (gr. k-1). lib. bdg. 15.95 *(978-0-7614-2623-3(X)*, Benchmark Bks.) Marshall Cavendish Corp.

—Un Panadero. 2007. (En el Trabajo Ser.). (SPA., Illus.). 24p. (gr. k-1). lib. bdg. 15.95 *(978-0-7614-2781-0(3)*, Benchmark Bks.) Marshall Cavendish Corp.

Midnight Bakery: Individual Title Six-Packs. (Bookweb Ser.). 32p. (gr. 5-18). 34.00 *(978-0-7635-3793-7(4))* Rigby Education.

Nathan, Helen. Flossie Crums & the Enchanted Cookie Tree: A Flossie Crums Baking Adventure. Stevenson, Daryl, illus. 2012. (Flossie Crums Ser.). (ENG.). 56p. (J). (gr. k-2). pap. 8.99 *(978-1-84365-197-0(1)*, Pavilion Children's Books) Pavilion Bks. GBR. Dist: Independent Pubs. Group.

Panik, Alison Saeger. Angel Cake's Cupcake Book. 2004. (Strawberry Shortcake Crafts Club Ser.). (Illus.). 39p. (J). *(978-0-439-70311-6(5))* Scholastic, Inc.

Paré, Jean. Kids Do Baking: Sweet & Savoury Baked Delights, 1 vol. 2009. (Original Ser.). (ENG., Illus.). 160p. (J). spiral bd. 16.99 *(978-1-897069-99-8(5)*, 1897069995) Company's Coming Publishing, Ltd. CAN. Dist: Lone Pine Publishing USA.

Patchett, Fiona, et al. Children's Book of Baking. Allman, Howard, photos by. 2007. (Children's Cooking Ser.). (ENG., Illus.). 96p. (J). 17.99 *(978-0-7945-1438-9(3)*, Usborne) EDC Publishing.

Pohl, Kathleen. What Happens at a Bakery? 2006. (Where People Work Ser.). (Illus.). 24p. (gr. -1-3). pap. 8.15 *(978-0-8368-6891-3(9))*; lib. bdg. 22.00 *(978-0-8368-6884-5(6))* Stevens, Gareth Publishing LLLP. (Weekly Reader Leveled Readers).

—What Happens at a Bakery (¿Qué pasa en una Panadería?) 2006. (Where People Work/Dónde Trabaja la Gente? Ser.). (ENG & SPA., Illus.). 24p. (gr. -1-3). pap. 8.15 *(978-0-8368-7392-4(0)*, Weekly Reader Leveled Readers) Stevens, Gareth Publishing LLLP.

—What Happens at a Bakery?/¿Qué Pasa en una Panadería? 2006. (Where People Work/Dónde Trabaja la Gente? Ser.). (SPA & ENG., Illus.). 24p. (J). (gr. -1-3). lib. bdg. 22.00 *(978-0-8368-7385-6(8)*, Weekly Reader Leveled Readers) Stevens, Gareth Publishing LLLP.

Quinlivan, Ada. Blake the Baker: Develop Understanding of Fractions & Numbers. 2014. (Rosen Common Core Math Readers Ser.). (ENG.). 24p. (J). (gr. 3-4). pap. 8.25 *(978-1-4777-4930-2(6)*, PowerKids Pr.) Rosen Publishing Group, Inc., The.

Shannon, George. Who Put the Cookies in the Cookie Jar? Paschkis, Julie, illus. 2013. (ENG.). 32p. (J). (gr. -1-1). 17.99 *(978-0-8050-9197-7(1)*, 9780805091977, Holt, Henry & Co. Bks. For Young Readers) Holt, Henry & Co.

Smith, Dineen. So, You Think I Am Too Little To Bake! 2013. 50p. 25.99 *(978-0-615-80672-3(4))* Sweet 76 Bakery.

Sullivan, Jaclyn. What's in Your Pizza? 2012. (What's in Your Fast Food Ser.). (ENG., Illus.). 24p. (J). (gr. 2-5). pap. 8.25 *(978-1-4488-6377-8(5)*, PowerKids Pr.); lib. bdg. 22.60 *(978-1-4488-6209-2(4))* Rosen Publishing Group, Inc., The.

Sur La Table Staff & Mushet, Cindy. Baking Kids Love. 2009. (ENG.). 128p. 20.00 *(978-0-7407-8345-6(9))* Andrews McMeel Publishing.

Thomas, Mary Ann. Bonnie's Bakery. 2006. (Neighborhood Readers Ser.). (ENG.). 12p. (gr. 1-3). pap. 5.90 *(978-1-4042-6843-2(X)*, Rosen Classroom) Rosen Publishing Group, Inc., The.

Turnbull, Stephanie. Baking. 2015. (Try This! Ser.). (ENG., Illus.). 24p. (gr. 2-6). 27.10 *(978-1-62588-370-4(6))* Black Rabbit Bks.

—Cool Stuff to Bake. 2015. (ENG., Illus.). 32p. (J). pap. 9.95 *(978-1-77092-220-4(2))* RiverStream Publishing.

Turnbull, Stephaniel & Turnbull, Stephanie. Cool Stuff to Bake. 2014. (Cool Stuff Ser.). 32p. (gr. 2-5). 31.35 *(978-1-62588-186-1(X))* Black Rabbit Bks.

Walton, Ruth. Let's Bake a Cake. 2013. (Let's Find Out Ser.). (Illus.). 32p. (gr. k-5). 28.50 *(978-1-59771-386-3(4))* Sea-To-Sea Pubns.

826 Valencia Writing Project Student Staff. A Time to Eat Cake. 2012. (ENG., Illus.). 73p. (J). (gr. k). pap. 12.00 *(978-1-934750-27-8(1))* 826 Valencia.

BAKING—FICTION

Abbott, Simon, illus. Happy Street: Bakery. 2016. (Happy Street Ser.). (ENG.). 10p. (J). (gr. -1). bds. 9.99 *(978-1-4052-7521-7(9))* Egmont Bks., Ltd. GBR. Dist: Independent Pubs. Group.

Archer, Nick & McDonald, Megan. Rule of Three. 2010. (Sisters Club Ser.: 2). (ENG., Illus.). 240p. (J). (gr. 3-7). pap. 5.99 *(978-0-7636-4830-5(2))* Candlewick Pr.

—Rule of Three. Consolazio, Pamela A., illus. 2009. (Sisters Club Ser.: 2). (ENG.). 240p. (J). (gr. 3-7). 15.99 *(978-0-7636-4153-5(7))* Candlewick Pr.

Armas, Teresa. Remembering Grandma / Recordando a Abuela. Ventura, Gabriela Baeza, tr. from ENG. Rodriguez Howard, Pauline, illus. 2003. (ENG & SPA.). 32p. (J). 16.95 *(978-1-55885-344-7(8)*, Piñata Books) Arte Publico Pr.

Aylesworth, Jim. The Gingerbread Man. McClintock, Barbara, illus. 2010. (ENG.). 32p. (J). (gr. k — 1). bds. 6.99 *(978-0-545-23514-3(6)*, Cartwheel Bks.) Scholastic, Inc.

Baicker-McKee, Carol, illus. An Apple Pie for Dinner, 0 vols. 2009. (ENG.). 32p. (J). (gr. k-3). 17.99 *(978-0-7614-5452-6(7)*, 9780761454526, Amazon Children's Publishing) Amazon Publishing.

Bauer, Joan. Close to Famous. 2012. (ENG.). 272p. (J). (gr. 5-18). 7.99 *(978-0-14-242017-1(4)*, Puffin Books) Penguin Young Readers Group.

Berk, Sheryl & Berk, Carrie. Baby Cakes. 2014. (Cupcake Club Ser.: 5). (ENG.). 160p. (J). (gr. 3-6). pap. 6.99 *(978-1-4022-8330-7(X)*, Sourcebooks Jabberwocky) Sourcebooks, Inc.

—Bakers on Board. 2016. (Cupcake Club Ser.: 9). (ENG.). 128p. (J). (gr. 3-7). pap. 7.99 *(978-1-4926-2085-3(8)*, 9781492620853, Sourcebooks Jabberwocky) Sourcebooks, Inc.

—Icing on the Cake. 2013. (Cupcake Club Ser.: 4). (ENG.). 160p. (J). (gr. 3-6). pap. 6.99 *(978-1-4022-8327-7(X)*, Sourcebooks Jabberwocky) Sourcebooks, Inc.

—Royal Icing: The Cupcake Club. 2014. (Cupcake Club Ser.: 6). (ENG.). 144p. (J). (gr. 3-7). pap. 6.99 *(978-1-4022-8333-8(4)*, Sourcebooks Jabberwocky) Sourcebooks, Inc.

—Sugar & Spice: The Cupcake Club. 2015. (Cupcake Club Ser.: 7). (ENG.). 160p. (J). (gr. 3-7). pap. 6.99 *(978-1-4022-8336-9(9)*, Sourcebooks Jabberwocky) Sourcebooks, Inc.

—Sweet Victory. 2015. (Cupcake Club Ser.: 8). (ENG.). 128p. (J). (gr. 3-7). pap. 6.99 *(978-1-4926-2082-2(3)*, Sourcebooks Jabberwocky) Sourcebooks, Inc.

Billings, David Joseph. Road Trip with Rabbit & Squash. Billings, David Joseph, illus. 2006. (Illus.). 48p. (J). per. *(978-0-9789036-0-2(9))* Billings, David J.

Bracken, Beth. Henry Helps Make Cookies, 1 vol. Busby, Ailie, illus. 2012. (Henry Helps Ser.). (ENG.). 24p. (gr. -1 — 1). pap. 5.95 *(978-1-4048-7669-9(3))*; lib. bdg. 22.65 *(978-1-4048-7303-2(1))* Picture Window Bks. (Henry Helps).

Brett, Jan. Gingerbread Baby. Brett, Jan, illus. 2003. (ENG., Illus.). 32p. (J). (gr. -1 — 1). bds. 7.99 *(978-0-399-24166-6(3)*, G.P. Putnam's Sons Books for Young Readers) Penguin Young Readers Group.

Burfoot, Ella. How to Bake a Book. 2014. (ENG., Illus.). 32p. (J). (-2). 16.99 *(978-1-4926-0651-2(0)*, 9781492606512, Sourcebooks Jabberwocky) Sourcebooks, Inc.

Cacciapuoti, Aurora. Baking with Dad. Cacciapuoti, Aurora, illus. 2016. (Child's Play Library). (ENG., Illus.). 32p. (J). pap. *(978-1-84643-754-0(7))* Child's Play International Ltd.

Carle, Eric. Pancakes, Pancakes! Carle, Eric, illus. 2004. (World of Eric Carle Ser.). (ENG., Illus.). 32p. (J). (gr. -1-3). bds. 8.99 *(978-0-689-87148-1(1)*, Little Simon) Little Simon.

—Walter the Baker. Carle, Eric, illus. 2012. (World of Eric Carle Ser.). (ENG., Illus.). 34p. (J). (gr. -1 — 1). bds. 7.99 *(978-1-4424-4941-1(1)*, Little Simon) Little Simon.

Carlson, Nancy. Harriet & George's Christmas Treat. Carlson, Nancy, illus. 2005. (Picture Bks.). (Illus.). 32p. (J). (gr. k-2). 15.95 *(978-1-57505-506-0(6))* Lerner Publishing Group.

—Harriet & George's Christmas Treat. 2003. (ENG., Illus.). 32p. (J). (gr. k-2). pap. 9.95 *(978-1-57505-639-5(9))* Lerner Publishing Group.

Cavanaugh, Wendy. Pumpkin in the Sky: Let's bake a pie together, you & I, with Auntie Wendy. Cavanaugh, Wendy & LeVesque, Sherry, photos by. 2011. (Illus.). 32p. (J). spiral bd. 20.00 *(978-0-9743121-1-8(8))* Eastlight Pr.

Christelow, Eileen. Cinco Monitos Hacen un Pastel de Cumpleanos. 2014. (Five Little Monkeys Story Ser.).Tr. of Five Little Monkeys Bake a Birthday Cake. (ENG & SPA., Illus.). 30p. (J). (— 1). bds. 7.99 *(978-0-544-08899-3(9)*, HMH Books For Young Readers) Houghton Mifflin Harcourt Publishing Co.

—Five Little Monkeys Bake a Birthday Cake. 2005. (Five Little Monkeys Story Ser.). (ENG., Illus.). 32p. (J). (gr. -1-3). pap. 6.99 *(978-0-618-49648-8(3))* Houghton Mifflin Harcourt Publishing Co.

Corderoy, Tracey. The Great Granny Cake Contest! Hubble Bubble. Berger, Joe, illus. 2017. (ENG.). 128p. (J). (gr. 1-4). pap. 6.99 *(978-0-7636-8849-3(5)*, Nosy Crow) Candlewick Pr.

Covey, Sean. Lily & the Yucky Cookies. Curtis, Stacy, illus. 2013. (7 Habits of Happy Kids Ser.: 5). (ENG.). 32p. (J). (gr. -1-1). 7.99 *(978-1-4424-7649-3(4)*, Simon & Schuster Bks. For Young Readers) Simon & Schuster Bks. For Young Readers.

Denise, Anika. Baking Day at Grandma's. Denise, Christopher, illus. 2014. (ENG.). 32p. (J). (gr. -1-k). 16.99 *(978-0-399-24244-1(9)*, Philomel Bks.) Penguin Young Readers Group.

Dower, Laura. Kiki Takes the Cake. Lazuli, Lilly, illus. 2016. (Dessert Diaries). (ENG.). 160p. (gr. 4-5). lib. bdg. 26.65 *(978-1-4965-3120-9(5))* Stone Arch Bks.

Dunbar, Joyce. Pat-A-Cake Baby. Dunbar, Polly, illus. 2015. (ENG.). 40p. (J). (-k). 15.99 *(978-0-7636-7577-6(6))* Candlewick Pr.

Eilrich, Dinah Kay. Teeny Tessie's Big Baking Adventure. 2009. 28p. pap. 13.99 *(978-1-4490-2277-8(4))* AuthorHouse.

Emch, Christiana M. Donut Cat's Bakery. 2010. 16p. pap. 9.30 *(978-1-935125-67-9(2))* Robertson Publishing.

Fergus, Maureen. Recipe for Disaster. 2009. (ENG.). 256p. (J). (gr. 5-9). 8.95 *(978-1-55453-320-6(1))*; 18.95 *(978-1-55453-319-0(8))* Kids Can Pr., Ltd. CAN. Dist: Hachette Bk. Group.

Fiford, Tanya. How to Bake Grandm. 2009. (Illus.). 16p. pap. 8.49 *(978-1-4389-6352-5(1))* AuthorHouse.

Florence, Tyler. Tyler Makes a Birthday Cake! Frazier, Craig, illus. 2014. (J). lib. bdg. *(978-0-06-204761-8(2))* Harper & Row Ltd.

Forest, Heather. The Baker's Dozen. Gaber, Susan, illus. 2013. (ENG.). 32p. (J). (gr. -1-3). 8.95 *(978-1-939160-70-6(7))* August Hse. Pubs., Inc.

Gehl, Laura. Koala Challah. Mola, Maria, illus. 2017. (ENG.). 24p. (gr. -1-1). 17.99 ***(978-1-5124-2087-6(5))***; pap. 7.99 ***(978-1-5124-2088-3(3))*** Lerner Publishing Group. (Kar-Ben Publishing).

Gershator, David & Gershator, Phillis. Bread Is for Eating. Shaw-Smith, Emma, illus. 2003. (ENG & SPA.). 25p. (J). (gr. k-4). reprint ed. 16.00 *(978-0-7567-9033-2(6))* DIANE Publishing Co.

Graff, Lisa. A Tangle of Knots. 2013. (ENG.). 240p. (J). (gr. 3-7). 16.99 *(978-0-399-25517-5(6)*, Philomel Bks.) Penguin Young Readers Group.

Graves, Sue. A Cake for Dinner. 2011. (Tadpoles Ser.: No. 26). (ENG., Illus.). 24p. (J). (gr. k-3). pap. *(978-0-7787-0583-3(8))* Crabtree Publishing Co.

Green, Poppy. The Maple Festival. Bell, Jennifer A., illus. 2015. (Adventures of Sophie Mouse Ser.: 5). (ENG.). 128p. (J). (gr. k-4). pap. 5.99 *(978-1-4814-4196-4(5)*, Little Simon) Little Simon.

Grogan, Shannon. From Where I Watch You. 2015. (ENG.). 304p. (YA). (gr. 9). 18.99 *(978-1-61695-554-0(6)*, Soho Teen) Soho Pr., Inc.

Hacker, Erin. The Baker of Sweet City, 1 vol. 2010. 36p. pap. 24.95 *(978-1-4489-2550-6(9))* PublishAmerica, Inc.

Hannigan, Kate. Summer Showers. Hughes, Brooke Boynton, illus. (Cupcake Cousins Ser.: Bk. 2). (ENG.). (J). (gr. 3-7). 2016. 256p. pap. 6.99 *(978-1-4847-2362-3(7))*Bk. 2. 2015. 240p. 16.99 *(978-1-4847-1662-5(0))* Hyperion Bks. for Children.

—Winter Wonders. Hughes, Brooke Boynton, illus. 2016. (Cupcake Cousins Ser.: Bk. 3). (ENG.). 240p. (J). (gr. 3-7). 16.99 *(978-1-4847-1663-2(9))* Hyperion Bks. for Children.

Harvey, Keith. Tiberius & the Chocolate Cake. Kirk, Heather, illus. 2010. (Tiberius Tales Ser.). 24p. (J). (gr. -1-2). pap. 8.15 *(978-1-60754-836-2(4))*; lib. bdg. 22.60 *(978-1-60754-832-4(1))* Windmill Bks.

Herman, Charlotte. My Chocolate Year: A Novel with 12 Recipes. Pham, LeUyen, illus. 2008. (ENG.). 176p. (J). (gr. 3-7). 15.99 *(978-1-4169-3341-0(7)*, Simon & Schuster Bks. For Young Readers) Simon & Schuster Bks. For Young Readers.

Hill, Eric. Spot Bakes a Cake. Hill, Eric, illus. 2003. (ENG., Illus.). 22p. (J). (gr. -1-1). bds. 7.99 *(978-0-399-24013-3(6))* Penguin Publishing Group.

Hobbs, Leigh. Old Tom, Man of Mystery. Hobbs, Leigh, illus. 2017. (Old Tom Ser.). (ENG., Illus.). 32p. (J). (gr. -1-k). 10.99 ***(978-1-877003-53-0(0))*** Little Hare Bks. AUS. Dist: Independent Pubs. Group.

Howland, Naomi. The Better-Than-Best Purim, 0 vols. 2012. (ENG.). 32p. (J). (gr. -1-2). 16.99 *(978-0-7614-6203-3(1)*, 9780761462033, Amazon Children's Publishing) Amazon Publishing.

Hunt, Debbie Colleen. The Dinosaur Who Loved to Bake & Eat Cakes. Hunt, Craig J. S., illus. 2012. 32p. 24.95 *(978-1-4626-3213-8(0))* America Star Bks.

Jacobson, Darlene Beck. Wheels of Change. 2014. (ENG., Illus.). 180p. (J). (gr. 2-8). 12.95 *(978-1-939547-13-2(X))* Creston Bks.

Jordan, Apple. A Cake to Bake. 2014. (Disney Princess Step into Reading Ser.). lib. bdg. 13.55 *(978-0-606-36005-0(0))* Turtleback Bks.

Kertell, Lynn Maslen. Cupcake Surprise! Hendra, Sue, illus. 2012. (Scholastic Reader Level 1 Ser.). (ENG.). 32p. (J). (gr. -1-3). pap. 3.99 *(978-0-545-38269-4(6))* Scholastic, Inc.

Kimmel, Eric A. Little Red Rosie. Gutiérrez, Mónica, illus. 2016. (J). *(978-1-68115-518-0(4))* Behrman Hse., Inc.

Kleven, Elisa, illus. The Horribly Hungry Gingerbread Boy: A San Francisco Story. 2016. 40p. (J). *(978-1-59714-352-3(9))* Heyday.

Lindman. Flicka, Ricka, Dicka Bake a Cake. Lindman, illus. 2013. (Flicka, Ricka, Dicka Ser.). (ENG., Illus.). 32p. (J). (gr. k-3). 9.99 *(978-0-8075-2506-7(5))* Whitman, Albert & Co.

Lowenthal, Ambur & Werner, Joe. Shirley's Cakes, 1 vol. 2012. (ENG., Illus.). 32p. (J). 12.99 *(978-0-7643-4005-5(0)*, 9780764340055) Schiffer Publishing, Ltd.

Magnin, Joyce. Cake: Love, Chickens, & a Taste of Peculiar, 1 vol. Ivanov, Alexsey & Ivanov, Olga, illus. 2013. (ENG.). 224p. (J). 14.99 *(978-0-310-73333-1(2))* Zonderkidz.

Malbrough, Mike. Marigold Bakes a Cake. Malbrough, Mike, illus. 2017. (ENG., Illus.). 40p. (J). (gr. -1-2). 17.99 ***(978-1-5247-3738-2(0)***, Philomel Bks.) Penguin Young Readers Group.

Man-Kong, Mary, et al. I Can Be a Pastry Chef/I Can Be a Lifeguard (Barbie) RH Disney Staff & Random House Staff, illus. 2012. (Pictureback(R) Ser.). (ENG.). 32p. (J). (gr. -1-2). pap. 4.99 *(978-0-307-93114-6(5)*, Random Hse. Bks. for Young Readers) Random Hse. Children's Bks.

Marshall, Carly. The Babysitter & Little Miss Bossy. 2013. 26p. 24.95 *(978-1-63000-618-1(1))*; 28p. pap. 24.95 *(978-1-63000-541-2(X))* America Star Bks.

May, Eleanor. Albert the Muffin-Maker. Melmon, Deborah, illus. 2014. (Mouse Math Ser.). 32p. (gr. -1-1). lib. bdg. 22.60 *(978-1-57565-631-1(0))* Kane Press, Inc.

May, Kyla. Coco: My Delicious Life. 2013. (Lotus Lane Ser.: 2). (ENG., Illus.). 96p. (J). (gr. 1-3). 15.99 *(978-0-545-49615-5(2))*; pap. 4.99 *(978-0-545-44514-6(0))* Scholastic, Inc.

—Coco: My Delicious Life. 2013. (Lotus Lane Ser.: 2). lib. bdg. 14.75 *(978-0-606-31978-2(6)*, Turtleback) Turtleback Bks.

McOmber, Rachel B., ed. McOmber Phonics Storybooks: The Cake. rev. ed. (Illus.). (J). *(978-0-944991-44-2(0))* Swift Learning Resources.

Meadows, Daisy. Roxie the Baking Fairy. 2015. (Magical Crafts Fairies Ser.: 7). (ENG., Illus.). 80p. (J). (gr. 2-5). pap. 4.99 *(978-0-545-70835-7(4)*, Scholastic Paperbacks) Scholastic, Inc.

Meadows, Michelle. Piggies in the Kitchen. Hoyt, Ard, illus. 2011. (ENG.). 32p. (J). (gr. -1-2). 14.99 *(978-1-4169-3787-6(0)*, Simon & Schuster Bks. For Young Readers) Simon & Schuster Bks. For Young Readers.

Meddaugh, Susan. Martha Bakes a Cake. 2012. (Martha Speaks Ser.). (ENG., Illus.). 24p. (J). (gr. -1-3). 12.99 *(978-0-547-68102-3(X))*; pap. 3.99 *(978-0-547-68113-9(5))* Houghton Mifflin Harcourt Publishing Co.

—Martha Bakes a Cake (Martha Hornea un Pastel) 2012. (Martha Speaks Ser.). (ENG & SPA., Illus.). 24p. (J). (gr. -1-3). pap. 3.99 *(978-0-547-71896-5(9))* Houghton Mifflin Harcourt Publishing Co.

Mills, Susan & Shara, Diana. Frankie & Her Little Pals - Stir It Up. 2007. (J). 7.95 *(978-0-9790690-0-0(9))* Lucky Red Pr., LLC.

Moore, Stephanie Perry. Icing on the Cake. 2014. (Sharp Sisters Ser.: 5). (ENG.). 160p. (YA). (gr. 6-12). pap. 7.95 *(978-1-4677-4487-4(5)*, Darby Creek); lib. bdg. 27.93 *(978-1-4677-3728-9(3))* Lerner Publishing Group.

Morel, John Henry. Little Button Annie. 2009. 48p. pap. 14.99 *(978-1-935436-94-2(5))* Rodaian Pr.

Mullican, Judy. Mary & Marsha Make Cookies. Storch, Ellen N., illus. I.t. ed. 2005. 18p. (J). (gr. -1-k). pap. 10.95 *(978-1-57332-346-8(2)*, HighReach Learning, Incorporated) Carson-Dellosa Publishing, LLC.

Nakagawa, Chihiro. Who Made This Cake? Koyose, Junji, illus. 2008. (ENG.). 32p. (J). (gr. -1-2). 16.95 *(978-1-59078-595-9(9)*, Front Street) Boyds Mills Pr.

Nash, Margaret. Dad's Cake. 2009. (Tadpoles Ser.). (ENG., Illus.). 24p. (J). (gr. -1-2). pap. *(978-0-7787-3896-1(5))* Crabtree Publishing Co.

Nathan, Helen. Flossie Crums & the Fairies' Cupcake Ball. Stevenson, Daryl, illus. 2012. (Flossie Crums Ser.). (ENG.). 56p. (J). (gr. k-2). pap. 8.99 *(978-1-84365-196-3(3)*, Pavilion Children's Books) Pavilion Bks. GBR. Dist: Independent Pubs. Group.

Nelson, Suzanne. Cake Pop Crush. (J). 2016. (ENG.). 256p. (gr. 4-7). pap. 6.99 *(978-0-545-85734-5(1)*, Scholastic Paperbacks) 2013. 247p. *(978-0-545-50389-1(2))* Scholastic, Inc.

Neuschwander, Cindy. Sir Cumference & the off-The-Charts Dessert. Geehan, Wayne, illus. 2013. (ENG.). 32p. (J). (gr. 3-7). pap. 7.95 *(978-1-57091-199-6(1))* Charlesbridge Publishing, Inc.

—Sir Cumference & the off-The-Charts Dessert. 2013. (Sir Cumference Ser.). lib. bdg. 18.40 *(978-0-606-34743-3(7)*, Turtleback) Turtleback Bks.

Nicholson, Doris. A Day with Grandma. 2006. 9.00 *(978-0-8059-9914-3(0))* Dorrance Publishing Co., Inc.

Numeroff, Laura Joffe. The Best Mouse Cookie. Bond, Felicia, illus. 2006. (If You Give... Ser.). (ENG.). 32p. (J). (gr. -1-2). 9.99 *(978-0-06-113760-0(X))* HarperCollins Pubs.

O'Connor, Jane. Fancy Nancy & the Delectable Cupcakes. Glasser, Robin Preiss & Enik, Ted, illus. 2010. (I Can Read Level 1 Ser.). (ENG.). 32p. (J). (gr. -1-3). 16.99 *(978-0-06-188269-2(0))*; pap. 3.99 *(978-0-06-188268-5(2))* HarperCollins Pubs.

O'Connor, Jane. Fancy Nancy: Jojo & Daddy Bake a Cake. Glasser, Robin Preiss, illus. 2017. (My First I Can Read Ser.). 32p. (J). (gr. -1-3). pap. 3.99 ***(978-0-06-237801-9(5))*** HarperCollins Pubs.

Ostrove, Karen. Rise & Shine: A Challah-Day Tale. Scott, Kimberley, illus. 2013. (Shabbat Ser.). (ENG.). 24p. (J). (gr. -1-3). 7.95 *(978-0-7613-7500-5(7))*; lib. bdg. 17.95 *(978-0-7613-7499-2(X))* Lerner Publishing Group. (Kar-Ben Publishing).

Papademetriou, Lisa. Confectionately Yours #2: Taking the Cake! 2012. (Confectionately Yours Ser.: 2). (ENG.). 240p. (J). (gr. 3-7). pap. 5.99 *(978-0-545-22229-7(X)*, Scholastic Paperbacks) Scholastic, Inc.

—Save the Cupcake! 2012. (Confectionately Yours Ser.: 1). (J). (ENG.). 240p. (gr. 3-7). pap. 6.99 *(978-0-545-22228-0(1)*, Scholastic Paperbacks); 231p. *(978-0-545-46039-2(5))* Scholastic, Inc.

—Taking the Cake! 2012. (Confectionately Yours Ser.: Bk. 2). 223p. (J). *(978-0-545-49391-8(9))* Scholastic, Inc.

Parish, Herman. Amelia Bedelia Bakes Off. Sweat, Lynn, illus. 2010. (I Can Read Level 2 Ser.). 64p. (J). (gr. k-3). (ENG.). pap. 3.99 *(978-0-06-084360-1(8))*; (ENG.). 17.99 *(978-0-06-084358-8(6))*; lib. bdg. 18.89 *(978-0-06-084359-5(4))* HarperCollins Pubs. (Greenwillow Bks.).

—Amelia Bedelia's First Apple Pie. Avril, Lynne, illus. 2012. (Amelia Bedelia Ser.). (ENG.). 32p. (J). (gr. -1-3). pap. 6.99 *(978-0-06-196411-4(5)*, Greenwillow Bks.) HarperCollins Pubs.

Paulin, Chrita. Let's Bake a Family. Burns, Rosalyn, ed. Richards, Tanya, illus. 2009. (ENG.). 32p. (J). pap. 12.95 *(978-0-9763400-1-0(1))* Coal Under Pressure Pubns.

Paulson, Michael William. The Baker Street Bunch & the Missing Pie Mystery. 2005. (J). per. *(978-0-9754241-9-3(X))* MiMar Publishing.

Peschke, Marci. Cupcake Queen. Mourning, Tuesday, illus. (Kylie Jean Ser.). (ENG.). 112p. (gr. 2-3). 2015. pap. 5.95 *(978-1-4795-6753-9(1))* 2013. 8.95 *(978-1-4048-8102-0(6))* 2013. lib. bdg. 22.65 *(978-1-4048-7580-7(8))* Picture Window Bks. (Kylie Jean).

Peyo. Smurf Cake. Peyo, illus. 2013. (Smurfs Classic Ser.). (ENG., Illus.). 32p. (J). (gr. k-2). 16.99 *(978-1-4424-8493-1(4))*; pap. 3.99 *(978-1-4424-8492-4(6))* Simon Spotlight. (Simon Spotlight).

Pham, LeUyen. A Piece of Cake. Pham, LeUyen, illus. 2014. (ENG., Illus.). 40p. (J). (gr. -1-3). 16.99 *(978-0-06-199264-3(X))* HarperCollins Pubs.

Phillips, Ruby Ann. Fortune Cookie Fiasco. Isik, Semur, illus. 2015. (Krystal Ball Ser.). (ENG.). 112p. (gr. 2-3). lib. bdg. 25.32 *(978-1-4795-5874-2(5))* Picture Window Bks.

Platt, Cynthia. Little Bit of Love. Whitty, Hannah, illus. 2011. (ENG.). 32p. (J). (gr. -1-2). pap. 7.95 *(978-1-58925-426-8(0))* Tiger Tales.

—A Little Bit of Love. Whitty, Hannah, illus. 2011. (ENG.). 32p. (J). (gr. -1-2). 15.95 *(978-1-58925-095-6(8))* Tiger Tales.

Priceman, Marjorie. How to Make a Cherry Pie & See the U. S. A. Priceman, Marjorie, illus. 2013. (ENG., Illus.). 40p. (J). (gr. k-3). 7.99 *(978-0-385-75293-0(8)*, Dragonfly Bks.) Random Hse. Children's Bks.

—How to Make a Cherry Pie & See the U. S. A. 2013. lib. bdg. 18.40 *(978-0-606-32190-7(X)*, Turtleback) Turtleback Bks.

Provantini, Silvia, illus. The Runaway Pancake. 2006. (First Reading Level 4 Ser.). 48p. (J). (gr. 1-4). 8.99 *(978-0-7945-1276-7(3)*, Usborne) EDC Publishing.

Rabe, Tish. Cooking with the Grinch (Dr. Seuss) Brannon, Tom, illus. 2017. (Step into Reading Ser.). (ENG.). 32p. (J). (gr. -1-1). pap. 4.99 ***(978-1-5247-1462-8(3))***; lib. bdg. 12.99 ***(978-1-5247-1463-5(1))*** Random Hse. Children's Bks. (Random Hse. Bks. for Young Readers).

Roques, Dominique. Anna Banana & the Chocolate Explosion. Dormal, Alexis, illus. 2015. (Anna Banana Ser.). (ENG.). 28p. (J). (gr. k-2). 15.99 *(978-1-62672-020-6(7)*, 9781626720206, First Second Bks.) Roaring Brook Pr.

Rosenthal, Amy Krouse. One Smart Cookie: Bite-Size Lessons for the School Years & Beyond. Dyer, Jane & Dyer, Brooke, illus. 2010. (ENG.). 40p. (J). (gr. k-5). 12.99 *(978-0-06-142970-5(8))* HarperCollins Pubs.

—Sugar Cookies: Sweet Little Lessons on Love. Dyer, Jane & Dyer, Brooke, illus. 2009. (ENG.). 40p. (J). (gr. k-5). 12.99 *(978-0-06-174072-5(1))* HarperCollins Pubs.

Rosenthal, Betsy R. It's Not Worth Making a Tzimmes Over! Rivers, Ruth, illus. 2006. 32p. (J). (gr. k-3). lib. bdg. 16.99 *(978-0-8075-3677-3(6))* Whitman, Albert & Co.

Safer, Catherine Hogan. What If Your Mom Made Raisin Buns?, 1 vol. Rose, Hilda, illus. 2007. (ENG.). 32p. (J). (gr. -1-2). pap. 8.95 *(978-1-897174-03-6(9)*, Tuckamore Bks) Creative Bk. Publishing CAN. Dist: Orca Bk. Pubs. USA.

Santillo, LuAnn. Jane. Santillo, LuAnn, ed. 2003. (Half-Pint Kids Readers Ser.). (Illus.). 7p. (J). (gr. -1-1). pap. 1.00 *(978-1-59256-099-8(7))* Half-Pint Kids, Inc.

Scarry, Richard & Farber, Erica. Cake Soup. Scarry, Huck, illus. 2011. (Richard Scarry's Great Big Schoolhouse Ser.). (ENG.). 24p. (J). (gr. -1-k). pap. 3.95 *(978-1-4027-7317-4(X))* Sterling Publishing Co., Inc.

Schmidt, Kristina Edelkamp. Miss Flavia & the Cookie Cottage. Cologne, Starla, illus. 2009. 28p. pap. 7.99 *(978-1-935125-61-7(3))* Robertson Publishing.

Schroeder, Lisa. Frosting & Friendship. 2013. (ENG., Illus.). 224p. (J). (gr. 3-7). 15.99 *(978-1-4424-7396-6(7)*, Aladdin) Simon & Schuster Children's Publishing.

Shulman, Goldie. Way Too Much Challah Dough. 2006. (ENG., Illus.). 30p. (J). 12.95 *(978-1-929628-23-0(4))* Hachai Publishing.

Skead, Robert. Elves Can't Kick. 2005. 84p. per. 7.99 *(978-1-929478-66-8(6))* Cross Training Publishing.

Slater, David Michael. Flour Girl: A Recipe for Disaster, 1 vol. Brooks, S. G., illus. 2007. (Missy Swiss & More Ser.). (ENG.). 32p. (gr. -1-4). 28.50 *(978-1-60270-009-3(5)*, Looking Glass Library) ABDO Publishing Co.

Smothers, Ethel Footman. Auntee Edna. Clay, Wil, illus. 2004. 32p. (J). pap. 8.00 *(978-0-8028-5246-5(7))*; 16.00 *(978-0-8028-5154-3(1))* Eerdmans, William B. Publishing Co.

Staniszewski, Anna. The Prank List. 2014. (Dirt Diary Ser.: 2). (ENG.). 256p. (J). (gr. 5-9). pap. 6.99 *(978-1-4022-8639-1(2)*, 9781402286391, Sourcebooks Jabberwocky) Sourcebooks, Inc.

Sutton, Katisha Barner. Caring & Sharing. 2011. 26p. pap. 12.50 *(978-1-60976-177-6(4)*, Strategic Bk. Publishing) Strategic Book Publishing & Rights Agency (SBPRA).

Tachikawa, Carter. Half-Baked Kate. 2013. 20p. pap. 24.95 *(978-1-63000-444-6(8))* America Star Bks.

Thorpe, Kiki. A Pinch of Magic. Christy, Jana, illus. 2014. (Never Girls Ser.: No. 7). (ENG.). 128p. (J). (gr. 1-4). 5.99 *(978-0-7364-3097-5(0)*, RH/Disney) Random Hse. Children's Bks.

—A Pinch of Magic. 2014. (Never Girls Ser.: 7). lib. bdg. 16.00 *(978-0-606-36008-1(5))* Turtleback Bks.

Vince Crandall, Vince. The Village Baker. 2011. 40p. pap. 16.95 *(978-1-257-16195-9(4))* Lulu Pr., Inc.

Wallace, Lizzie. Sam the Baker & the Buns of Courage. 2012. (Illus.). 16p. pap. 15.99 *(978-1-4678-8280-4(1))* AuthorHouse.

Warner, Gertrude Chandler, creator. The Boxcar Children, 12 bks. 2010. (Boxcar Children Mysteries Ser.: 1). (ENG.). 1p. (J). (gr. 1-5). pap. 59.99 *(978-0-8075-0855-8(1))* Whitman, Albert & Co.

Weeks, Sarah. Pie. 2013. (ENG.). 192p. (J). (gr. 3-7). pap. 6.99 *(978-0-545-27012-0(X)*, Scholastic Paperbacks) Scholastic, Inc.

Wells, Rosemary. Bunny Cakes. Wells, Rosemary, illus. 2014. (Max & Ruby Ser.). (ENG & SPA., Illus.). 32p. (J). (gr. -1-k). 7.99 *(978-0-14-751586-5(6)*, Puffin Books) Penguin Young Readers Group.

Weston Woods Staff, creator. In the Night Kitchen. 2011. 29.95 *(978-0-439-73480-6(0))*; 18.95 *(978-0-439-72723-5(5))*; 38.75 *(978-0-439-72728-0(6))* Weston Woods Studios, Inc.

Williams, Katina T. Jeremiah Pie. 2011. 36p. pap. 24.95 *(978-1-4626-2332-7(8))* America Star Bks.

Wilson, Jacqueline. Cookie. Sharratt, Nick, illus. 2010. (ENG.). 352p. (J). (gr. 4-7). pap. 11.99 *(978-0-312-64290-7(3)*, 9780312642907) Square Fish.

Winston, Sherri. President of the Whole Fifth Grade. 2012. (President Ser.: 1). (ENG.). 288p. (J). (gr. 3-7). pap. 8.00 *(978-0-316-11433-2(2))* Little, Brown Bks. for Young Readers.

Wurzburg, Robert. Who Took the Cake? 2006. (I'm Going to Read(r) Ser.). (ENG., Illus.). 24p. (J). (gr. -1-k). pap. 3.95 *(978-1-4027-3344-4(5))* Sterling Publishing Co., Inc.

Zahler, Diane. Baker's Magic. Price, Mina, illus. 2016. (Middle-Grade Novels Ser.). (ENG.). 336p. (gr. 4-7). lib. bdg. 26.65 *(978-1-4965-2724-0(0))* Stone Arch Bks.

BALANCE OF NATURE

see Ecology

BALBOA, VASCO NUNEZ DE, 1475-1519

Molzahn, Arlene Bourgeois. Vasco Nunez de Balboa: Explorer to the Pacific Ocean. 2004. (Explorers! Ser.). (Illus.). 48p. (J). lib. bdg. 25.27 *(978-0-7660-2142-6(4))* Enslow Pubs., Inc.

Petrie, Kristin. Vasco Núñez de Balboa, 1 vol. 2007. (Explorers Set 2 Ser.). (ENG., Illus.). 32p. (J). (gr. 4-7). 27.07 *(978-1-59679-740-6(1)*, Checkerboard Library) ABDO Publishing Co.

BALI ISLAND (INDONESIA)

Hawker, Frances & Resi, Putu. Hinduism in Bali. Campbell, Bruce, photos by. 2009. (ENG., Illus.). 32p. (J). (gr. 3-6).

(978-0-7787-5008-6(6)); pap. (978-0-7787-5025-3(6)) Crabtree Publishing Co.

BALI ISLAND (INDONESIA)—FICTION

Noensie, Pamela & Lamore, Garretta. Tari: the Little Balinese Dancer. 2013. (ENG., Illus.). 32p. (J). (gr. k-3). 14.95 (978-0-8048-4387-4(2)) Tuttle Publishing.

BALKAN PENINSULA

Daniels, Jimmy. The Dusty Road. 2008. (ENG.). 26p. pap. 11.00 (978-1-4196-2664-7(7)) CreateSpace Independent Publishing Platform.

Docalavich, Heather. Slovenia. 2007. (European Union Ser.). (Illus.). 88p. (YA). (gr. 3-7). lib. bdg. 21.95 (978-1-4222-0061-2(2)) Mason Crest.

The European Union: Political, Social, & Economic Cooperation, 26 vols., Set. Incl. Austria. Sanna, Jeanine. (gr. 3-7). lib. bdg. 21.95 (978-1-4222-0039-1(6), 1247981); Belgium. Walker, Ida. (gr. 3-7). lib. bdg. 21.95 (978-1-4222-0040-7(X), 1247982); Cyprus. Etingoff, Kim. (gr. 5-18). lib. bdg. 21.95 (978-1-4222-0041-4(8), 1247983); Denmark. Docalavich, Heather. (gr. 3-7). lib. bdg. 21.95 (978-1-4222-0043-8(4)); Finland. Sia, Nicole. (gr. 3-7). lib. bdg. 21.95 (978-1-4222-0046-9(9), 1247998); Germany. Walker, Ida. (gr. 3-7). lib. bdg. 21.95 (978-1-4222-0048-3(5), 1248000); Hungary. Docalavich, Heather. (gr. 3-7). lib. bdg. 21.95 (978-1-4222-0050-6(7), 1248003); Ireland. Walker, Ida. (gr. 4-7). lib. bdg. 21.95 (978-1-4222-0051-3(5)); Luxembourg. Simons, Rae. (gr. 3-7). lib. bdg. 21.95 (978-1-4222-0055-1(8)); Malta. Stafford, James. (gr. 3-7). lib. bdg. 21.95 (978-1-4222-0056-8(6)); Netherlands. Docalavich, Heather. (gr. 4-7). lib. bdg. 21.95 (978-1-4222-0057-5(4)); Portugal. Etingoff, Kim. (gr. 3-7). lib. bdg. 21.95 (978-1-4222-0059-9(0)); Slovenia. Docalavich, Heather. (gr. 3-7). lib. bdg. 21.95 (978-1-4222-0061-2(2)); Sweden. Docalavich, Heather. (gr. 3-7). lib. bdg. 21.95 (978-1-4222-0063-6(9)); (YA). 2007. (Illus.). 88p. 2006. lib. bdg. (978-1-4222-0038-4(8), 1247983) Mason Crest.

Hintz, Martin. Croatia. 2004. (Enchantment of the World Ser.). (ENG., Illus.). 144p. (YA). (gr. 5-9). 37.00 (978-0-516-24253-8(9), Children's Pr.) Scholastic Library Publishing.

Kalman, Bobbie & Jeffrey, Gary. Gallipoli & the Southern Theaters. 2013. (ENG.). 48p. (J). (978-0-7787-0911-4(6)) Crabtree Publishing Co.

BALKAN PENINSULA—FICTION

Hayes, Clair W. The Boy Allies in the Balkan Campaign. 2007. 208p. per. (978-1-4065-4395-7(0)) Dodo Pr.

—The Boy Allies in the Balkan Campaign or the Struggle to Save a Nation. 2007. 128p. per. (978-1-4068-1714-0(7)) Echo Library.

Uncle Markie. Piglettè & Bobo Winter in Zagreb. 2003. (YA). ring bd. 9.95 (978-1-933129-11-2(5)) Studio 403.

BALL GAMES

see names of games, e.g. Baseball; Soccer

Bowker, Paul. Girls' Lacrosse, 1 vol. 2013. (Girls' SportsZone Ser.). (ENG., Illus.). 48p. (J). (gr. 3-6). lib. bdg. 32.79 (978-1-61783-988-7(4), SportsZone) ABDO Publishing Co.

Day, Meredith & Augustyn, Adam. Lacrosse & Its Greatest Players, 1 vol. 2015. (ENG.). 80p. (J). 31.70 (978-1-62275-592-9(8), Britannica Educational Publishing) Rosen Publishing Group, Inc., The.

Gifford, Clive. Ball Sports. 2011. (Olympic Sports Ser.). 32p. (YA). (gr. 4-7). 19.95 (978-1-60753-188-3(7)) Amicus Publishing.

—Basketball & Other Ball Sports. 2011. (ENG., Illus.). 32p. (J). pap. 10.95 (978-1-77092-035-4(8)) Saunders Bk. Co. CAN. Dist: RiverStream Publishing.

—The Kingfisher Soccer Encyclopedia. 3rd rev. ed. 2014. (Kingfisher Encyclopedias Ser.). (ENG., Illus.). 144p. (J). (gr. 5-9). 19.99 (978-0-7534-7167-8(1), 9780753471678, Kingfisher) Roaring Brook Pr.

Holden, Pam. Let's Play Ball, 6 pack. Webb, Philip, illus. 2009. (Red Rocket Readers Ser.). (ENG.). 16p. (gr. -1-1). pap. (978-1-877363-17-7(0), Red Rocket Readers) Flying Start Bks.

Ingham, Anne. The Ball Book. 2012. 28p. pap. 21.99 (978-1-4691-8747-1(7)) Xlibris Corp.

Jones, Cameron. An Insider's Guide to Lacrosse, 1 vol. 2015. (ENG.). 48p. (J). 30.25 (978-1-4777-8077-0(7), Rosen Reference) Rosen Publishing Group, Inc., The.

Kalman, Bobbie. I Like to Play. 2011. (ENG.). 16p. (J). (978-0-7787-9549-0(7)); pap. (978-0-7787-9574-2(8)) Crabtree Publishing Co.

Kortemeier, Todd. 12 Reasons to Love Lacrosse. 2018. (ENG.). 32p. (gr. 3-6). 31.35 **(978-1-63235-429-7(2),** 12-Story Library) Pr. Room Editions LLC.

Laughlin, Kara L. Dodgeball. 2016. (Beginning Sports Ser.). (ENG.). 24p. (J). (gr. k-3). 27.07 (978-1-5038-0773-0(8), 210601) Child's World, Inc., The.

—T-Ball. 2016. (Beginning Sports Ser.). (ENG.). 24p. (J). (gr. k-3). 27.07 (978-1-5038-0781-5(9), 210609) Child's World, Inc., The.

Page, Jason. Basketball, Soccer, & Other Ball Games. 2008. (Olympic Sports Ser.). (ENG., Illus.). 32p. (J). (gr. 4-7). pap. (978-0-7787-4029-2(3)); lib. bdg. (978-0-7787-4012-4(9)) Crabtree Publishing Co.

Play Ball! Level O, 6 vols., Vol. 3. (Explorers Ser.). 32p. (gr. 3-6). 44.95 (978-0-7699-0624-9(9)) Shortland Pubns. (U. S. A.) Inc.

Rosen, Michael J. Balls! Round 2. Margeson, John, illus. 2008. (Darby Creek Exceptional Titles Ser.). (ENG.). 80p. (gr. 4-8). 18.95 (978-1-58196-066-2(2), Darby Creek) Lerner Publishing Group.

Rosenthal, Cynthia. Matt Does Math at the Ball Game. 2012. (InfoMax Readers Ser.). (ENG., Illus.). 24p. (J). (gr. 1-2). pap. 8.25 (978-1-4488-9028-6(4), Rosen Classroom) Rosen Publishing Group, Inc., The.

Salzmann, Mary Elizabeth. Balls, Birdies & Pucks, 1 vol. 2012. (Sports Gear Ser.). (ENG., Illus.). 24p. (J). (gr. k-3). lib. bdg. 24.21 (978-1-61714-822-4(9)) ABDO Publishing Co.

Smolka, Bo. Girls Play to Win Lacrosse. 2011. (Girls Play to Win Ser.). 64p. (J). (gr. 3-6). lib. bdg. 27.93 (978-1-59953-463-3(0)) Norwood Hse. Pr.

Stillinger, Doug. Ball Games. 2005. (ENG., Illus.). 52p. (J). (gr. 1-18). 14.95 (978-1-57054-254-1(6)) Klutz.

—Ball Games 6 Copy Pack. 2005. (ENG.). 52p. (J). 89.70 (978-1-57054-255-8(4)) Klutz.

Tometich, Annabelle. Lacrosse, 1 vol. 2012. (ENG.). 64p. 32.79 (978-1-61783-145-4(X), SportsZone) ABDO Publishing Co.

Ubberball, R. The Wham-O Superball. Copeland, Cynthia L., illus. 2008. (ENG.). 80p. (J). (gr. 3). pap. 12.95 (978-1-60433-049-6(X), Applesauce Pr.) Cider Mill Pr. Bk. Pubs., LLC.

Vanderhoof, Gabrielle. Lacrosse. 2010. (Getting the Edge Ser.). 96p. (YA). lib. bdg. 24.95 (978-1-4222-1737-5(X)) Mason Crest.

Wells, Don. Lacrosse. 2010. (In the Zone Ser.). (Illus.). 32p. (J). (gr. 3-5). pap. 11.95 (978-1-61690-019-9(9)); lib. bdg. 25.70 (978-1-61690-018-2(0)) Weigl Pubs., Inc.

Williams, Nancy Noel. Have a Ball. 2010. (J). (978-1-60617-123-3(2)) Teaching Strategies, LLC.

BALLADS

see also Folk Songs

Murphy, Claire Rudolf. My Country, 'Tis of Thee: How One Song Reveals the History of Civil Rights. Collier, Bryan, illus. 2014. (ENG.). 48p. (J). (gr. k-4). 17.99 (978-0-8050-8226-5(3), 9780805082265, Holt, Henry & Co. Bks. For Young Readers) Holt, Henry & Co.

BALLET

Adelman, Heidi. Beautiful Ballerinas. 2016. (Illus.). 32p. (J). (978-1-4896-4775-7(9)) Weigl Pubs., Inc.

Appleby, Alex. Puedo Ser una Bailarina / I Can Be a Ballerina. 2014. (Cuando Sea Grande / When I Grow Up Ser.). (SPA.). 24p. (J). (gr. k-2). 22.60 (978-1-4824-0857-7(0)) Stevens, Gareth Publishing LLLP.

Ballerina: Eine Einführung ins Ballett. 2003. (Illus.). 32p. (J). 12.98 (978-1-4054-1296-4(8)) Parragon, Inc.

Ballet. 2nd rev. ed. 2010. (World of Dance Ser.). (Illus.). 120p. (C). (gr. 9-18). 35.00 (978-1-60413-479-7(8), Chelsea Hse.) Facts On File, Inc.

Barringer, Janice & Schlesinger, Sarah. The Pointe Book: Shoes, Training, Technique. 3rd ed. 2012. (ENG., Illus.). 368p. pap. 29.95 (978-0-87127-355-0(1)) Princeton Bk. Co. Pubs.

Barton, Chris. The Nutcracker Comes to America: How Three Ballet-Loving Brothers Created a Holiday Tradition. Gendron, Cathy, illus. 2015. (ENG.). 36p. (J). (gr. 2-5). 19.99 (978-1-4677-8848-9(1), Millbrook Pr.) Lerner Publishing Group.

Bell-Myers, Darcy. The Animal Babies ABC Book of Ballet. 2013. (Dover Coloring Bks.). (ENG.). 32p. (J). (gr. -1-3). pap. 3.99 (978-0-486-49814-0(X)) Dover Pubns., Inc.

Bicknell, Joanna & Page, Nick. Look at Me! I'm a Ballerina! Snaith, Andy, photos by. 2005. (Illus.). 23p. (J). (gr. -1-3). (978-1-905051-72-4(7)) Make Believe Ideas.

Blackledge, Annabel. I Want to Be a Ballerina. 2005. (DK Readers Ser.). (ENG., Illus.). 32p. (J). (gr. k-2). pap. 3.99 (978-0-7566-1696-0(4), DK Children) Dorling Kindersley Publishing, Inc.

Bussell, Darcey & Dorling Kindersley Publishing Staff. The Ballet Book. 2006. (ENG., Illus.). 72p. (J). (gr. 2-5). pap. 6.99 (978-0-7566-1933-6(5), DK Children) Dorling Kindersley Publishing, Inc.

Cady, Jennifer. José Limón. 2009. (Library of American Choreographers Ser.). 48p. (gr. 5-8). 53.00 (978-1-60853-459-3(6), Rosen Reference) Rosen Publishing Group, Inc., The.

Capucilli, Alyssa Satin. My First Ballet Class: A Book with Foldout Pages. Jensen, Leyah, illus. Jensen, Leyah, photos by. 2011. (My First Ser.). (ENG.). 14p. (J). (gr. -1-k). 9.99 (978-1-4424-0895-1(2), Little Simon) Little Simon.

Castle, Kate. The Ballerina's Handbook. Allsopp, Sophie, illus. 2009. (Genuine & Moste Authentic Guide Ser.). (ENG.). 22p. (J). (gr. 1-4). 14.99 (978-0-7636-4552-6(4), Templar) Candlewick Pr.

Castor, H. Ballet for Beginners. 2009. (Kid Kits Ser.). 32p. (J). 19.99 (978-1-60130-159-8(6)); 19.99 (978-1-60130-160-4(X)) EDC Publishing. (Usborne).

Castor, Harriet. Ballet Magic, Vol. 1. Fisher, Chris, illus. 64p. (J). pap. 7.95 (978-0-14-038479-6(0)) Penguin Publishing Group.

Clay, Kathryn. Ballet Dancing, 1 vol. 2010. (Dance, Dance, Dance Ser.). (ENG., Illus.). 24p. (gr. k-1). lib. bdg. 26.65 (978-1-4296-4002-2(2), 1308539, Pebble Plus) Capstone Press of Coughlan Cos.

Clibbon, Meg. Ballerina. Clibbon, Lucy, illus. 2008. (Imagine You're A ... Ser.). (ENG.). 32p. (J). pap. 9.99 (978-1-84089-453-0(9)) Meg and Lucy Bks. GBR. Dist: Independent Pubs. Group.

—Imagine You're a Ballerina. Clibbon, Lucy, illus. 2006. (ENG.). 32p. (J). (gr. -1-4). 19.95 (978-1-55451-020-7(1), 9781554510207) Annick Pr., Ltd. CAN. Dist: Publishers Group West (PGW).

—My Beautiful Ballet Pack. Clibbon, Lucy, illus. 2008. (Imagine You're A ... Ser.). (ENG.). 32p. (J). 15.99 (978-1-84089-485-1(7)) Meg and Lucy Bks. GBR. Dist: Independent Pubs. Group.

Daynes, Katie & Davidson, Susannah. Ballet Treasury. 2005. (Ballet Treasury Ser.). 96p. (J). 19.95 (978-0-7945-0936-1(3), Usborne) EDC Publishing.

Dorling Kindersley Publishing Staff. Ballet. 2004. (Ultimate Sticker Bks.). (ENG.). 16p. (J). (gr. k-3). pap. 6.99 (978-0-7566-0233-8(5), DK Children) Dorling Kindersley Publishing, Inc.

Dowd, Olympia. A Young Dancer's Apprenticeship: On Tour with the Moscow City Ballet. 2003. (Single Titles Ser.). (ENG., Illus.). 128p. (gr. 7-12). lib. bdg. 25.26 (978-0-7613-2917-6(X), Twenty-First Century Bks.) Lerner Publishing Group.

Dunn, Mary R. I Want to Be a Ballet Dancer. 2009. (Dream Jobs Ser.). 24p. (gr. 2-3). 42.50 (978-1-61512-202-8(8), PowerKids Pr.); (Illus.). (YA). lib. bdg. 22.60 (978-1-4042-4469-6(7)) Rosen Publishing Group, Inc., The.

Gemwitch, Ruby. Tayanna's Ballet Tutorial for Tiny Tots. 2011. 24p. pap. 24.95 (978-1-4626-1948-1(7)) America Star Bks.

Geras, Adèle & McNicholas, Shelagh. Tilly Tutu. McNicholas, Shelagh, illus. 2004. (ESP & SPA., Illus.). 28p. (J). 14.99 (978-84-8488-091-2(5)) Serres, Ediciones, S. L. ESP. Dist: Lectorum Pubns., Inc.

Goodman, Joan Elizabeth. Ballet Bunnies, 0 vols. 2013. (ENG.). 40p. (J). (gr. k-3). pap. 9.99 (978-1-4778-1028-6(5), 9781477810286, Amazon Children's Publishing) Amazon Publishing.

Grigorovich, Yuri, et al. The Authorized Bolshoi Ballet Book of Romeo & Juliet. 2006. (Illus.). 95p. (YA). (gr. 4-8). reprint ed. 22.00 (978-1-4223-5261-8(7)) DIANE Publishing Co.

Hackett, Jane & Dorling Kindersley Publishing Staff. Ballerina: A Step-by-Step Guide to Ballet. Handley, David, photos by. 2007. (ENG., Illus.). 80p. (J). (gr. 3-7). 17.99 (978-0-7566-2668-6(4), DK Children) Dorling Kindersley Publishing, Inc.

Herweck, Diana. A Day in the Life of a Ballet Dancer, 1 vol. 2nd rev. ed. 2011. (Nonfiction Readers Ser.). (ENG.). 28p. (J). (gr. 3-3). pap. 8.99 (978-1-4333-3650-8(2)) Teacher Created Materials, Inc.

Herweck, Dona. A Day in the Life of a Ballet Dancer, 1 vol. 2nd rev. ed. 2014. (TIME for KIDS(r) Nonfiction Readers Ser.). (ENG., Illus.). 28p. (J). (gr. 3-3). pap. 25.96 (978-1-4807-1065-8(2)) Shell Educational Publishing.

I Want to be a Ballerina. 2008. (Magnetic Board Books Ser.). 7p. bds. (978-1-4075-1414-7(8)) Parragon, Inc.

I'm Going to be the Best Ballerina Ever! 2008. (I'm Going to be Storybooks... Ser.). 32p. (978-1-4075-1706-3(6)) Parragon, Inc.

Isadora, Rachel. On Your Toes: A Ballet ABC. 2006. pap. (978-0-06-050242-3(8)) HarperCollins Canada, Ltd.

Lee, Laura. A Child's Introduction to Ballet: The Stories, Music, & Magic of Classical Dance. Hamilton, Meredith, illus. 2007. (ENG.). 96p. (J). (gr. -1-17). 19.99 (978-1-57912-699-5(5), 81699, Black Dog & Leventhal Pubs. Inc.) Hachette Bks.

Levy, Barbara Soloff. How to Draw Ballet Pictures. 2009. (Dover How to Draw Ser.). (ENG., Illus.). 64p. (J). (gr. 1-5). pap. 4.99 (978-0-486-47055-9(5)) Dover Pubns., Inc.

Mellow, Mary Kate & Troeller, Stephanie. Ballet for Beginners. 2011. (ENG., Illus.). 80p. (J). (gr. -1-3). pap. 7.95 (978-1-936140-45-9(4)) Charlesbridge Publishing, Inc.

Miles, Lisa. Ballet Spectacular: A Young Ballet Lover's Guide & an Insight into a Magical World. (Illus.). (J). 2015. 79p. **(978-1-4380-0681-9(0))** 2014. (ENG., 80p. (gr. 3-9). 18.99 (978-0-7641-6745-4(6)) Barron's Educational Series, Inc.

Miller, Eileen Rudisill. Ballet Dancers Paper Dolls. 2010. (Dover Paper Dolls Ser.). (ENG., Illus.). 32p. (J). (gr. 1-3). pap. 7.99 (978-0-486-47920-0(X)) Dover Pubns., Inc.

Mitchell, Missy. Ballet: Pointe by Pointe. 2004. (Curtain Call Library of Dance Ser.). (Illus.). 48p. (YA). (gr. 5-9). lib. bdg. 29.25 (978-0-8239-4555-9(3)) Rosen Publishing Group, Inc., The.

Morris, Ann. Dancing to America. Kolnik, Paul, photos by. 2004. (Illus.). 40p. (YA). (gr. 7-10). 16.00 (978-0-7567-7577-3(9)) DIANE Publishing Co.

Regan, Lisa. Ballet Dancer. 2012. (Stage School Ser.). (ENG., Illus.). 32p. (J). (gr. 3-6). 25.25 (978-1-4488-8091-1(2)); pap. 10.00 (978-1-4488-8150-5(1)) Windmill Bks.

Rodriguez, Sonia. T Is for Tutu: A Ballet Alphabet. Browning, Kurt, illus. 2015. (Av2 Fiction Readalong 2016 Ser.). (ENG.). (J). (gr. 1-4). lib. bdg. 34.28 (978-1-4896-3768-0(0), AV2 by Weigl) Weigl Pubs., Inc.

Royston, Angela. Ballet, 1 vol. 2013. (Love to Dance Ser.). (ENG.). 32p. (gr. 1-3). 29.99 (978-1-4109-4920-2(6)); pap. 8.29 (978-1-4109-4925-7(7)) Heinemann-Raintree. (Read Me!).

Schuette, Sarah L. A Ballerina Cookbook: Simple Recipes for Kids, 1 vol. 2012. (First Cookbooks Ser.). (ENG.). 24p. (gr. 1-2). lib. bdg. 25.32 (978-1-4296-7622-9(1), First Facts) Capstone Press of Coughlan Cos.

Spatt, Leslie E. The Sleeping Beauty: Behind the Scenes at the Ballet. (Illus.). (J). pap. 19.99 (978-0-590-24536-4(8)) Scholastic, Inc.

Sterling Publishing Co., Inc. My First Dance: Ballet. 2016. (ENG., Illus.). 22p. (J). (— 1). bds. 6.95 (978-1-4549-1873-8(X)) Sterling Publishing Co., Inc.

Tatchell, Judy. World of Ballet. Miles, Lisa, ed. Safarewicz, Evie, illus. 2006. (Kid Kits Ser.). 64p. (J). (gr. 5). lib. bdg. 17.95 (978-1-58086-514-2(3)) EDC Publishing.

—World of Ballet. 2004. (Kid Kits Ser.). (Illus.). 64p. (J). pap. 9.95 (978-0-7945-0403-8(5)) EDC Publishing.

—The World of Ballet: Internet-Linked. Miles, Lisa, ed. Safarewicz, Evie & Smith, Guy, illus. rev. ed. 2007. (World of Ballet Ser.). 64p. (J). (gr. 4-7). per. 9.99 (978-0-7945-1060-2(4), Usborne) EDC Publishing.

Uralskaia, Valeria, et al. Tales of Classical Ballet Talmi, Mary, ed. Loutchinina, Ekaterina, tr. from RUS. Dmitriev, Sergei, illus. 2004. 40p. (J). (978-0-9743082-1-0(8), Moscow Ballet) Sports Marketing International, Inc.

Vaughan, Carolyn. Invitation to Ballet: A Celebration of Dance & Degas. Isadora, Rachel, illus. 2012. (ENG.). 32p. (J). (gr. 1-4). 16.95 (978-1-4197-0260-0(2), Abrams Bks. for Young Readers) Abrams, Inc.

Watt, Fiona. Little Ballerina Dancing Book. Cascio, Maria Cristina Lo & McNicholas, Shelagh, illus. 2007. (Little Ballerina Dancing Book Ser.). 12p. (J). bds. 15.99 incl. audio compact disk (978-0-7945-1520-1(7), Usborne) EDC Publishing.

BALLET—FICTION

Albon, Lucie, illus. Little Ballerina: A Children's Book Inspired by Edgar Degas. 2011. (ENG.). 32p. (J). (gr. -1-3). 14.95 (978-3-7913-7081-1(2)) Prestel Verlag GmbH & Co KG. DEU. Dist: Penguin Random Hse. LLC.

Allen, Debbie. Dancing in the Wings. Nelson, Kadir, illus. 2003. (ENG.). 32p. (J). (gr. -1-3). 7.99 (978-0-14-250141-2(7), Puffin Books) Penguin Young Readers Group.

—Dancing in the Wings. Nelson, Kadir, illus. 2003. (J). (gr. -1-3). 14.65 (978-0-7569-7022-2(9)) Perfection Learning Corp.

Andrew, Carol B. My Beautiful Ballets. 2006. (Illus.). (J). (978-1-933577-04-3(5)) Learning Wood, LLC.

Andrews, Julie & Hamilton, Emma Walton. The Very Fairy Princess Takes the Stage. 2011. (Very Fairy Princess Ser.). (ENG., Illus.). 32p. (J). (gr. -1-3). 16.99 (978-0-316-04052-5(5)) Little Brown & Co.

Atwood, Megan. The Cursed Ballet. 2013. (Dario Quincy Academy of Dance Ser.: 3). (ENG.). 104p. (gr. 6-12). (J). lib. bdg. 27.93 (978-1-4677-0932-3(8)); (YA). pap. 7.95 (978-1-4677-1485-3(2)) Lerner Publishing Group. (Darby Creek).

August, Elaine. Fira Gani: An Earthly Fable. 2012. 40p. pap. 24.95 (978-1-4626-7589-0(1)) America Star Bks.

Balducci, Rita. The Nutcracker. Beckett, Sheilah, illus. 2014. (Little Golden Book Ser.). (ENG.). 24p. (J). (-k). 4.99 (978-0-385-36993-0(X), Golden Bks.) Random Hse. Children's Bks.

Ballerina Magic Shoes. (Ballerina Charm Book Ser.). (Illus.). 32p. (J). (978-1-4054-1144-8(9)) Parragon, Inc.

Barrows, Annie. Ivy + Bean Doomed to Dance. Blackall, Sophie, illus. 2010. (ENG.). 136p. (J). (gr. 1-5). pap. 5.99 (978-0-8118-7666-7(7)) Chronicle Bks. LLC.

Barrows, Annie & Blackall, Sophie. Ivy + Bean Doomed to Dance, 1 vol. 2011. (Ivy & Bean Ser.). (ENG., Illus.). 136p. (J). (gr. 1-4). 24.21 (978-1-59961-933-0(4)) Spotlight.

Baxter, Nicola. My Ballet Theatre: Peek Inside the 3-D Windows. Chaffey, Samantha, illus. 2014. (ENG.). 24p. (J). (gr. -1-12). 16.99 (978-1-84322-949-0(8), Armadillo) Anness Publishing GBR. Dist: National Bk. Network.

—A Sparkly Ballet Story. Pedler, Caroline, illus. 2014. (ENG.). 14p. (J). (gr. -1-1). bds. 7.99 (978-1-84322-546-1(8), Armadillo) Anness Publishing GBR. Dist: National Bk. Network.

Bentley, Sue. Sparkling Steps. 7th ed. 2007. (ENG., Illus.). 128p. (J). pap. (978-0-14-132155-4(5), Puffin) Penguin Publishing Group.

—Sparkling Steps #7, 7 vols. Farley, Andrew & Swan, Angela, illus. 2009. (Magic Kitten Ser.: 7). (ENG.). 128p. (J). (gr. 1-3). pap. 5.99 (978-0-448-45063-6(1), Grosset & Dunlap) Penguin Young Readers Group.

Beylon, Cathy. I Love Ballet/Me Encanta el Ballet: Bilingual Coloring Book. Gongora, Oscar, tr. 2011. (Dover Children's Bilingual Coloring Book Ser.). (ENG & SPA., Illus.). 32p. (J). (gr. k-5). pap. 3.99 (978-0-486-47815-9(7)) Dover Pubns., Inc.

Black, Yelena. Dance of Shadows. (Dance of Shadows Ser.). (ENG., Illus.). 384p. (YA). (gr. 7). 2014. pap. 9.99 (978-1-61963-185-4(7), 9781619631854) 2013. 17.99 (978-1-59990-940-0(5), 9781599909400) Bloomsbury Publishing USA. (Bloomsbury USA Childrens).

Bound, Samantha-Ellen. Breaking Pointe. 2015. (Silver Shoes Ser.: 3). (ENG.). 144p. (J). (gr. 4-7). pap. 8.99 (978-0-85798-374-9(1)) Random Hse. Australia AUS. Dist: Independent Pubs. Group.

Bramsen, Kirsten. The Yellow Tutu. Bramsen, Carin, illus. 2013. (ENG.). 40p. (J). (-k). pap. 7.99 (978-0-375-84393-8(0), Dragonfly Bks.) Random Hse. Children's Bks.

Broad, Michael. Spooky Ballet!, No. 4. Broad, Michael, illus. 2011. (Agent Amelia Ser.: 4). (ENG., Illus.). 144p. (J). (gr. 2-5). pap. 5.95 (978-0-7613-8064-1(7), Darby Creek); lib. bdg. 22.60 (978-0-7613-8059-7(0)) Lerner Publishing Group.

—#4 Spooky Ballet! 2011. (Agent Amelia Ser.). pap. 33.92 (978-0-7613-8344-4(1), Darby Creek) Lerner Publishing Group.

Brooke, Samantha. Best Friends Forever. 2011. (Strawberry Shortcake Ser.). (ENG.). 24p. (J). (gr. -1-k). pap. 4.99 (978-0-448-45721-5(0), Grosset & Dunlap) Penguin Young Readers Group.

Brown, Monica. Lola Levine & the Ballet Scheme. 2016. (Lola Levine Ser.: 3). (ENG., Illus.). 112p. (J). (gr. 1-5). pap. 5.99 (978-0-316-25847-0(4)); 14.99 (978-0-316-25844-9(X)) Little, Brown Bks. for Young Readers.

Bryant, Ann. Ballet Magic. 2007. (Ballerina Dreams Ser.). (Illus.). 322p. (J). (gr. 4-7). per. 7.99 (978-0-7945-1740-3(4), Usborne) EDC Publishing.

—The Christmas Nutcracker. 2006. (Ballerina Dreams Ser.). (Illus.). 181p. (J). per. 4.99 (978-0-7945-1369-6(7)); (gr. 5). lib. bdg. 12.99 (978-1-58086-919-5(X)) EDC Publishing. (Usborne).

—Dancing Forever. 2006. (Ballerina Dreams Ser.). (Illus.). 105p. (J). (gr. 5). lib. bdg. 12.99 (978-1-58086-920-1(3), Usborne) EDC Publishing.

—Dancing Forever. Benton, Tim, illus. 2006. (Ballerina Dreams Ser.). 105p. (J). lib. bdg. 4.99 (978-0-7945-1299-6(2), Usborne) EDC Publishing.

—Dancing Friends. 2007. (Ballerina Dreams Ser.). (Illus.). 326p. (J). (gr. 4-7). per. 7.99 (978-0-7945-1741-0(2), Usborne) EDC Publishing.

—Dancing Princess. 2006. (Ballerina Dreams Ser.). (Illus.). 103p. (J). (gr. 5). lib. bdg. 12.99 (978-1-58086-921-8(1), Usborne) EDC Publishing.

—Dancing Princess. Benton, Tim, illus. 2006. (Ballerina Dreams Ser.). 102p. (J). per. 4.99 (978-0-7945-1297-2(6), Usborne) EDC Publishing.

—Dancing with the Stars. Benton, Tim, illus. 2006. (Ballerina Dreams Ser.). 107p. (J). per. 4.99 (978-0-7945-1298-9(4), Usborne) EDC Publishing.

—Jasmine's Lucky Star. 2006. (Ballerina Dreams Ser.). (Illus.). 104p. (J). (gr. 5). lib. bdg. 12.99 (978-1-58086-923-2(8), Usborne) EDC Publishing.

—Rose's Big Decision. 2006. (Ballerina Dreams Ser.). (Illus.). 103p. (J). (gr. 5). lib. bdg. 12.99 (978-1-58086-925-6(4), Usborne) EDC Publishing.

Burgess, Melvyn & Pearson Education Staff. Billy Elliot 'A Writer of the Hightest Quality with Exceptional Powers of Insight' 2nd ed. 2008. (ENG., Illus.). 64p. pap. 11.99 (978-1-4058-8176-0(3)) Pearson Education.

Bussell, Darcey. Delphie & the Glass Slippers, 4. 2008. (Magic Ballerina Ser.: 4). (ENG., Illus.). 96p. (J). (gr. k-2). pap. 6.99 (978-0-00-728617-1(1), HarperCollins Children's Bks.) HarperCollins Pubs. Ltd. GBR. Dist: HarperCollins Pubs.

—Delphie & the Masked Ball, 3. 2008. (Magic Ballerina Ser.: 3). (ENG., Illus.). 96p. (J). (gr. k-2). pap. 6.99 (978-0-00-728610-2(4), HarperCollins Children's Bks.) HarperCollins Pubs. Ltd. GBR. Dist: HarperCollins Pubs.

Capucilli, Alyssa Satin. Katy Duck. Cole, Henry, illus. 2007. (Katy Duck Ser.). (ENG.). 16p. (J). (gr. -1-k). bds. 7.99 (978-1-4169-1901-8(5), Little Simon) Little Simon.

—Katy Duck & the Tip-Top Tap Shoes. Cole, Henry, illus. 2013. (Katy Duck Ser.). (ENG.). 24p. (J). (gr. -1-1). 16.99 (978-1-4424-5246-6(3)); pap. 3.99 (978-1-4424-5245-9(5)) Simon Spotlight. (Simon Spotlight).

Carlson, Nancy. Harriet's Recital. 2006. (Illus.). (J). 15.95 (978-1-57505-898-6(7), Carolrhoda Bks.); (ENG., 32p. per. 9.95 (978-1-57505-929-7(0), First Avenue Editions) Lerner Publishing Group.

Carr, Jan. Toe Shoe Mouse. Bell, Jennifer, illus. 2014. (ENG.). 32p. (J). (gr. -1-3). 16.95 (978-0-8234-2406-1(5)) Holiday Hse., Inc.

Cheng, Andrea. Brushing Mom's Hair. Wong, Nicole, illus. 2009. (ENG.). 64p. (J). (gr. 5-8). 17.95 *(978-1-59078-599-7(1),* Front Street) Boyds Mills Pr.

Ciesa, Mary E. Dina Prima the Ballerina. 2013. 36p. pap. 16.99 *(978-1-4525-8313-6(7),* Balboa Pr.) Author Solutions, Inc.

Cleary, Beverly. Ellen Tebbits. Darling, Louis & Dockray, Tracy, illus. 2008. (Avon Camelot Bks.). (ENG.). 192p. (J). (gr. 3-7). pap. 6.99 *(978-0-380-70913-7(9))* HarperCollins Pubs.

—Ellen Tebbits. 160p. (J). (gr. 2-4). pap. 4.99 *(978-0-8072-1397-1(7),* Listening Library) Random Hse. Audio Publishing Group.

Conway, Celeste. Unlovely. 2015. (ENG.). 254p. (YA). 17.99 *(978-1-4405-8279-0(3),* Simon Pulse) Simon Pulse.

Coulman, Valerie. Je Suis Ballerine! Duchesne, Christiane, tr. from ENG. Lamb, Sandra, illus. (FRE.). 32p. (J). pap. 6.95 *(978-2-922435-05-4(9))* Editions Homard CAN. Dist: Univ. of Toronto Pr.

Dakota, Heather. Emma's Very Busy Week. Panaccione, Nancy, illus. 2009. 31p. (J). *(978-0-545-17227-1(6))* Scholastic, Inc.

DePalma, Mary Newell. The Nutcracker Doll. 2007. (ENG., Illus.). 32p. (J). (gr. -1-3). 16.99 *(978-0-439-80242-0(3),* Levine, Arthur A. Bks.) Scholastic, Inc.

Duchess of York Staff & Ferguson, Sarah. Ballerina Rosie. Goode, Diane, illus. 2012. (ENG.). 32p. (J). (gr. -1-3). 16.99 *(978-1-4424-3066-2(4),* Simon & Schuster/Paula Wiseman Bks.) Simon & Schuster/Paula Wiseman Bks.

Duncan Edwards, Pamela. Honk! Cole, Henry, illus. 2014. 32p. pap. 8.00 *(978-1-61003-226-1(8))* Center for the Collaborative Classroom.

Espluga, Maria. I Am a Ballerina. 2009. (I Am A... (Alphabet Soup) Ser.). (Illus.). 24p. (J). (gr. k-1). pap. 8.15 *(978-1-60754-252-0(8));* lib. bdg. 22.60 *(978-1-60754-251-3(X))* Windmill Bks.

Evans, Cordelia. Olivia Takes Ballet: From the Fancy Keepsake Collection. Spaziante, Patrick, illus. 2013. (Olivia TV Tie-In Ser.). (ENG.). 28p. (J). (gr. -1-2). 6.99 *(978-1-4424-7394-2(0),* Simon Spotlight) Simon Spotlight.

Falligant, Erin. Into the Spotlight. Studios, Arcana, illus. 2011. (ENG.). 120p. (YA). (gr. 3-18). pap. 8.95 *(978-1-59369-835-5(6))* American Girl Publishing, Inc.

Farley, Robin. Mia & the Big Sister Ballet. Ivanov, Olga & Ivanov, Aleksey, illus. 2012. (My First I Can Read Ser.). (ENG.). 32p. (J). (gr. -1-3). pap. 3.99 *(978-0-06-173307-9(5))* HarperCollins Pubs.

—Mia & the Big Sister Ballet. 2012. (Mia I Can Read Bks.). (J). lib. bdg. 13.55 *(978-0-606-26282-8(2),* Turtleback) Turtleback Bks.

—Mia & the Daisy Dance. 2012. (Mia I Can Read Bks.). (J). lib. bdg. 13.55 *(978-0-606-23595-2(7),* Turtleback) Turtleback Bks.

—Mia & the Tiny Toe Shoes. 2012. (Mia I Can Read Bks.). (J). lib. bdg. 13.55 *(978-0-606-26863-9(4),* Turtleback) Turtleback Bks.

—Mia's Nutcracker Ballet. Ivanov, Olga & Ivanov, Aleksey, illus. 2013. (Mia Ser.). (ENG.). 32p. (J). (gr. -1-3). 9.99 *(978-0-06-223830-6(2))* HarperCollins Pubs.

—The Snow Day Ballet. Ivanov, Olga & Ivanov, Aleksey, illus. 2014. (Mia Ser.). (ENG.). 24p. (J). (gr. -1-k). pap. 4.99 *(978-0-06-210015-3(7),* HarperFestival) HarperCollins Pubs.

Fay, Nicole. Brittney & Beario Become Ballerinas. 2009. 16p. pap. 9.50 *(978-1-4389-1058-1(4))* AuthorHouse.

Feldman, Thea. My Day of Ballet. Mayberry, Maranda, illus. 2007. (Magnix Imagination Activity Bks.). 6p. (J). (gr. -1-3). bds. 5.99 *(978-1-932915-41-9(9))* Sandvik Innovations, LLC.

Flack, Sophie. Bunheads. 2012. (ENG.). 320p. (YA). (gr. 7-17). pap. 10.99 *(978-0-316-12654-0(3),* Poppy) Little, Brown Bks. for Young Readers.

Fliess, Sue. I'm a Ballerina! Chou, Joey, illus. 2015. (Little Golden Book Ser.). (ENG.). 24p. (J). (-k). 4.99 *(978-0-553-49758-8(8),* Golden Bks.) Random Hse. Children's Bks.

Ford, Bernette. Ballet Kitty: Christmas Recital. Williams, Sam, illus. 2012. (ENG.). 32p. (J). (gr. -1-1). 16.95 *(978-1-907152-12-2(1))* Boxer Bks., Ltd. GBR. Dist: Sterling Publishing Co., Inc.

Frank, Hannah. The Ballet Shoes. 2008. 44p. pap. 18.49 *(978-1-4389-1025-3(8))* AuthorHouse.

Franklin, Cathy. The Magical Ballet Shoes: A Pinta & Polly Story, 1 vol. Watkins, Tammy, illus. 2009. 25p. pap. 24.95 *(978-1-4489-2007-5(8))* America Star Bks.

French, Jackie. Josephine Wants to Dance. Whatley, Bruce, illus. 2007. (ENG.). 32p. (J). (gr. -1-1). 17.95 *(978-0-8109-9431-7(3),* Abrams Bks. for Young Readers) Abrams, Inc.

Gallegos, Jacqueline C. The Night the Princesses Danced. 2009. 40p. pap. 18.00 *(978-1-4389-4514-9(0))* AuthorHouse.

Garn, Laura Aimee. Bella Basset Ballerina. Sokolova, Valerie, illus. 2006. 32p. (J). (gr. -1-3). 15.95 *(978-0-9759378-0-8(4))* Pretty Please Pr., Inc.

Goldberg, Whoopi. Dancing Diva. Roos, Maryn, illus. 2012. (ENG.). 160p. (J). (gr. 1-5). pap. 4.99 *(978-0-7868-5265-9(8),* Jump at the Sun) Hyperion Bks. for Children.

—Perfectly Prima, No. 3. Roos, Maryn, illus. 2010. (ENG.). 160p. (J). (gr. 1-17). pap. 4.99 *(978-0-7868-5262-8(3),* Jump at the Sun) Hyperion Bks. for Children.

—Terrible Terrel. Roos, Maryn, illus. 2010. (ENG.). 160p. (J). (gr. 1-17). pap. 4.99 *(978-0-7868-5263-5(1),* Jump at the Sun) Hyperion Bks. for Children.

Golden Books. Ballet Wishes (Barbie) 2016. (Hologramatic Sticker Book Ser.). (ENG.). 64p. (J). (gr. -1-2). pap. 4.99 *(978-1-101-93993-2(1),* Golden Bks.) Random Hse. Children's Bks.

Golden Books Staff. Barbie Loves Ballet/Fashion Show Fun!, 2 bks. in 1. Golden Books Staff, illus. 2009. (Pictureback(R) Ser.). (ENG., Illus.). 32p. (J). (gr. -1-2). pap. 4.99 *(978-0-375-85148-3(8),* Golden Bks.) Random Hse. Children's Bks.

Gravel, Elise. The Cranky Ballerina. Gravel, Elise, illus. 2016. (Illus.). 32p. (J). (gr. -1-3). 17.99 *(978-0-06-235124-1(9),* Tegen, Katherine Bks) HarperCollins Pubs.

Greenberg, Jan & Jordan, Sandra. Ballet for Martha: Making Appalachian Spring. Floca, Brian, illus. 2010. (ENG.). 48p. (J). (gr. 1-5). 18.99 *(978-1-59643-338-0(8),* 9781596433380) Roaring Brook Pr.

Greene, Stephanie. Princess Posey & the First Grade Ballet. Sisson, Stéphanie Roth, illus. 2014. (Princess Posey, First Grader Ser.: 9). (ENG.). 96p. (J). (gr. k-3). pap. 5.99 *(978-0-14-751292-5(1),* Puffin Books) Penguin Young Readers Group.

Grindley, Sally & Dorling Kindersley Publishing Staff. Little Ballerina, Level 2. 2013. (DK Readers Ser.). (ENG.). 32p. (J). (gr. 1-3). pap. 3.99 *(978-1-4654-0942-3(4),* DK Children) Dorling Kindersley Publishing, Inc.

Grover, Lorie Ann. On Pointe. 2008. (ENG.). 320p. (J). (gr. 3-7). pap. 14.99 *(978-1-4169-7826-8(7),* McElderry, Margaret K. Bks.) McElderry, Margaret K. Bks.

Guillian, Adam & Guillain, Charlotte. Emma Peror's New Clothes. Waters, Erica-Jane, illus. 2015. (Fairy Tales Today Ser.). (ENG.). 24p. (J). (gr. 1-2). 23.99 *(978-1-4795-8617-2(X))* Picture Window Bks.

Hall, Kirsten. Ballerina Girl. 2004. (My First Reader Ser.). (ENG.). 32p. (J). (gr. k-1). pap. 3.95 *(978-0-516-24623-9(2),* Children's Pr.) Scholastic Library Publishing.

Hegarty, Pat. If I Were a... Ballerina. Pope, Liz & Pope, Kate, illus. 2008. (If I Were A Ser.). 10p. (J). (gr. -1-k). bds. 6.95 *(978-1-58925-834-1(7))* Tiger Tales.

Hillert, Margaret. The Magic Nutcracker. Osterhold, Jared, illus. 2016. (BeginningtoRead Ser.). (ENG.). 32p. (J). (gr. 1-2). 22.60 *(978-1-59953-802-0(4))* Norwood Hse. Pr.

Hoffmann, E. T. A. & Ventura, Paola Fratalocchi. The Nutcracker. 2010. (ENG., Illus.). 32p. (J). 14.99 *(978-0-7944-2044-4(3))* Reader's Digest Assn., Inc., The.

Holub, Joan. Ballet Stars. McNicholas, Shelagh, illus. 2012. (Step into Reading Ser.). (ENG.). 24p. (J). (gr. -1-1). pap. 3.99 *(978-0-375-86909-9(3),* Random Hse. Bks. for Young Readers) Random Hse. Children's Bks.

—Ballet Stars. 2012. (Step into Reading Level 1 Ser.). lib. bdg. 13.55 *(978-0-606-26398-6(5),* Turtleback) Turtleback Bks.

Howe, James. Brontorina. Cecil, Randy, illus. 2013. (ENG.). 32p. (J). (gr. -1-3). 6.99 *(978-0-7636-5323-1(3))* Candlewick Pr.

Howell, Jessica. Lilly Lu & the Pink Tutu. 2007. 29p. pap. 24.95 *(978-1-4241-8398-2(7))* America Star Bks.

Isadora, Rachel. Bea at Ballet. Isadora, Rachel, illus. (ENG., Illus.). 32p. (J). (gr. -1 — 1). 2014. bds. 7.99 *(978-0-399-16844-4(3))* 2012. 12.99 *(978-0-399-25409-3(9))* Penguin Young Readers Group. (Nancy Paulsen Books).

—Bea in the Nutcracker. Isadora, Rachel, illus. 2015. (ENG., Illus.). 32p. (J). (gr. -1-k). 16.99 *(978-0-399-25231-0(2),* Nancy Paulsen Books) Penguin Young Readers Group.

James, Annabelle. Abigail's Ballet Class. Beckes, Shirley, illus. 2004. 10p. (J). (gr. -1-k). 12.49 *(978-1-883043-54-4(9))* Straight Edge Pr., The.

Jane, Pamela. Noelle of the Nutcracker. Brett, Jan, illus. 2003. (ENG.). 64p. (J). (gr. 5-7). pap. 8.95 *(978-0-618-36922-5(8))* Houghton Mifflin Harcourt Publishing Co.

Jordan, Apple & RH Disney Staff. Barbie: On Your Toes. Wolcott, Karen, illus. 2005. (Step into Reading Ser.: No. 1). (ENG.). 32p. (J). (gr. -1-1). pap. 3.99 *(978-0-375-83142-3(8),* Random Hse. Bks. for Young Readers) Random Hse. Children's Bks.

Kahaney, Amelia. The Brokenhearted. 2014. (Brokenhearted Ser.: 1). (ENG.). 368p. (YA). (gr. 8). pap. 9.99 *(978-0-06-223093-5(X),* HarperTeen) HarperCollins Pubs.

Kann, Victoria. Pinkalicious: Tutu-Rrific. Kann, Victoria, illus. 2017. (I Can Read Level 1 Ser.). (Illus.). 40p. (J). (gr. -1-3). 9.99 ***(978-0-06-257278-3(4))*** HarperCollins Pubs.

—Tutu-Rrific! 2014. (Pinkalicious I Can Read Ser.). (J). lib. bdg. 13.55 *(978-0-606-35958-0(3))* Turtleback Bks.

—Tutu-Rrific! Pinkalicious. Kann, Victoria, illus. 2014. (I Can Read Level 1 Ser.). (ENG., Illus.). 32p. (J). (gr. -1-3). pap. 3.99 *(978-0-06-218795-6(3))* HarperCollins Pubs.

Keene, Carolyn. The Cinderella Ballet Mystery, 1 vol. Pamintuan, Macky, illus. 2007. (Nancy Drew & the Clue Crew Ser.). (ENG.). 83p. (gr. 1-4). 24.21 *(978-1-59961-345-1(X))* Spotlight.

—The Red Slippers. 2015. (Nancy Drew Diaries: 11). (ENG., Illus.). 192p. (J). (gr. 3-7). pap. 6.99 *(978-1-4814-3813-1(1),* Aladdin) Simon & Schuster Children's Publishing.

Kemp, Anna. Dogs Don't Do Ballet. Ogilvie, Sara, illus. 2010. (ENG.). 32p. (J). (gr. -1-3). 17.99 *(978-1-4169-9839-6(X),* Simon & Schuster Bks. For Young Readers) Simon & Schuster Bks. For Young Readers.

—Dogs Don't Do Ballet. Ogilvie, Sara, illus. 2010. (ENG.). 32p. pap. *(978-1-84738-474-4(9))* Simon & Schuster, Ltd.

Kent, Allegra. Ballerina Gets Ready. Stock, Catherine, illus. (ENG.). 40p. (J). (gr. -1-3). 2017. 6.99 *(978-0-8234-3765-8(5))* 2016. 16.95 *(978-0-8234-3563-0(6))* Holiday Hse., Inc.

—Ballerina Swan. McCully, Emily Arnold, illus. 2012. (ENG.). 32p. (J). (gr. -1-3). 16.95 *(978-0-8234-2373-6(5))* Holiday Hse., Inc.

—Ballerina Swan. McCully, Emily Arnold, illus. 2013. (ENG.). 32p. (J). (gr. -1-3). pap. 6.99 *(978-0-8234-2906-6(7))* Holiday Hse., Inc.

Keyser, Amber J. Pointe, Claw. 2017. (Fiction — Young Adult Ser.). (ENG.). 288p. (YA). (gr. 8-12). 9.99 ***(978-1-5124-3431-6(0));*** 38.65 ***(978-1-5124-0895-9(6));*** 38.65 ***(978-1-5124-3432-3(9))*** Lerner Publishing Group. (Carolrhoda Lab™).

—Pointe, Claw. Burrell, Carol klio, tr. 2017. (ENG.). 288p. (YA). (gr. 8-12). 18.99 *(978-1-4677-7591-5(6))* Lerner Publishing Group.

Klem, Elizabeth. Hider, Seeker, Secret Keeper. 2014. (Bolshoi Saga Ser.). (ENG., Illus.). 264p. (YA). (gr. 9). 17.99 *(978-1-61695-412-3(4),* Soho Teen) Soho Pr., Inc.

Kovalkova-McKenna, Svetlana & McKenna, Alexandra. The Fairy Book. 2009. 52p. pap. 7.58 *(978-0-557-06160-0(1))* Lulu Pr., Inc.

Laframboise, Tammy. Popsy in Ballet My Way. 2012. 50p. pap. 14.99 *(978-0-9848749-0-3(9))* Raspberry Bks.

Lagonegro, Melissa & RH Disney Staff. Ballerina Princess. Harding, Niall, illus. 2007. (Step into Reading Ser.). (ENG.). 32p. (J). (gr. k-3). pap. 3.99 *(978-0-7364-2428-8(8),* RH/Disney) Random Hse. Children's Bks.

LaMarche, Una. You in Five Acts. 2016. (ENG.). 352p. (YA). (gr. 7). 17.99 *(978-1-101-99893-9(8),* Razorbill) Penguin Young Readers Group.

Lasky, Kathryn. Dancing Through Fire. 2005. 172p. (J). *(978-1-4156-3323-6(1))* Scholastic, Inc.

Luraschi, Anna, illus. The Nutcracker. 2007. 24p. (J). 9.99 *(978-0-7945-1515-7(0),* Usborne) EDC Publishing.

Maccarone, Grace. Miss Lina's Ballerinas. Davenier, Christine, illus. 2010. (ENG.). 40p. (J). (gr. -1-1). 17.99 *(978-0-312-38243-8(X),* 9780312382438) Feiwel & Friends.

—Miss Lina's Ballerinas & the Wicked Wish. Davenier, Christine, illus. 2012. (ENG.). 40p. (J). (gr. k-1). 16.99 *(978-1-250-00580-9(9),* 9781250005809) Feiwel & Friends.

Mack, Lorrie. DK Adventures: Ballet Academy: Ballet Academy. 2014. (DK Adventures Ser.). (ENG., Illus.). 128p. (J). (gr. 3-7). 16.99 *(978-1-4654-1970-5(5),* DK Children) Dorling Kindersley Publishing, Inc.

Mack, Lorrie & Dorling Kindersley Publishing Staff. Ballet Academy. 2014. (DK Adventures Ser.). (ENG., Illus.). 128p. (J). (gr. 3-7). pap. 5.99 *(978-1-4654-1969-9(1),* DK Children) Dorling Kindersley Publishing, Inc.

Maddox, Jake. Dancing Solo, 1 vol. Wood, Katie, illus. 2014. (Jake Maddox Girl Sports Stories Ser.). (ENG.). 72p. (gr. 2-3). 25.32 *(978-1-4342-4142-9(4))* Stone Arch Bks.

Maddox, Jake & Berne, Emma Carlson. Ballet Bullies, 1 vol. Mourning, Tuesday, illus. 2009. (Jake Maddox Girl Sports Stories Ser.). (ENG.). 72p. (gr. 2-3). 25.32 *(978-1-4342-1604-5(7))* Stone Arch Bks.

Mahoney, Jean. Swan Lake Ballet Theatre. Seddon, Viola Anne, illus. 2009. (ENG.). 16p. (J). (gr. 1-4). 24.99 *(978-0-7636-4396-6(3))* Candlewick Pr.

Martin, Denise R. Alicia's Dance. 2009. 72p. pap. 12.99 *(978-1-4389-4194-3(3))* AuthorHouse.

Mayhew, James. Ella Bella Ballerina & Swan Lake. 2011. (Ella Bella Ballerina Ser.). 32p. (J). (gr. -1-3). 14.99 *(978-0-7641-6407-1(4))* Barron's Educational Series, Inc.

—Ella Bella Ballerina & the Midsummer Night's Dream. 2015. (Ella Bella Ballerina Ser.). (ENG., Illus.). 32p. (J). (gr. -1-3). 14.99 *(978-0-7641-6797-3(9))* Barron's Educational Series, Inc.

—The Magic Toyshop. 2017. (Ella Bella Ballerina Ser.). (ENG.). 32p. (J). (gr. -1-3). 14.99 ***(978-1-4380-5005-8(4))*** Barron's Educational Series, Inc.

—Nutcracker. 2012. (Ella Bella Ballerina Ser.). (ENG., Illus.). 32p. (J). (gr. 1-3). 14.99 *(978-0-7641-6581-8(X))* Barron's Educational Series, Inc.

—The Sleeping Beauty. 2008. (Ella Bella Ballerina Ser.). (ENG., Illus.). 32p. (J). (gr. -1-3). 14.99 *(978-0-7641-6118-6(0))* Barron's Educational Series, Inc.

McClintock, Barbara. Emma & Julia Love Ballet. 2016. (ENG., Illus.). 32p. (J). (gr. -1-3). 17.99 *(978-0-439-89401-2(8),* Scholastic Pr.) Scholastic, Inc.

McDoogle, Farrah. Olivia the Ballerina. Spaziante, Patrick, illus. 2013. (Olivia TV Tie-In Ser.). (ENG.). 24p. (J). (gr. -1-1). 16.99 *(978-1-4424-8515-0(9),* Simon Spotlight) Simon Spotlight.

Meadows, Daisy. A Fairy Ballet. 2011. (Scholastic Reader, Level 2 Ser.). (ENG.). 32p. (J). (gr. 1-3). pap. 3.99 *(978-0-545-22294-5(X),* Cartwheel Bks.) Scholastic, Inc.

—Giselle the Christmas Ballet Fairy. 2016. (Rainbow Magic Special Edition Ser.). (ENG.). 176p. (J). (gr. 2-5). pap. 6.99 *(978-0-545-85203-6(X),* Scholastic Paperbacks) Scholastic, Inc.

Mendle, Jane. My Ultimate Sister Disaster: A Novel. 2010. (ENG.). 208p. (YA). (gr. 7-18). pap. 18.99 *(978-0-312-36904-0(2),* 9780312369040, St. Martin's Griffin) St. Martin's Pr.

Michaels, Kitty. Ballet Friends #1 Toe-tally Fabulous. 2011. (ENG.). 102p. pap. 9.99 *(978-1-4392-0019-3(X))* CreateSpace Independent Publishing Platform.

—Ballet Friends #3 Birthday at the Ballet. 2011. (ENG.). 102p. pap. 9.99 *(978-1-4392-0021-6(1))* CreateSpace Independent Publishing Platform.

—Ballet Friends #4 Nowhere to Turn. 2011. (ENG.). 102p. pap. 9.99 *(978-1-4392-0022-3(X))* CreateSpace Independent Publishing Platform.

—Ballet Friends #5 Waiting in the Wings. 2011. (ENG.). 102p. pap. 9.99 *(978-1-4392-0023-0(8))* CreateSpace Independent Publishing Platform.

Mitchard, Jacquelyn. Starring Prima! The Mouse of the Ballet Jolie. Tusa, Tricia, illus. 2004. 160p. (J). (gr. 3-18). 16.89 *(978-0-06-057357-7(0));* (ENG.). 15.99 *(978-0-06-057356-0(2))* HarperCollins Pubs.

Moss, Alexandra. Lara's Leap of Faith. 2005. (Royal Ballet School Diaries). 138p. (J). 12.65 *(978-0-7569-5894-7(6))* Perfection Learning Corp.

Moss, Alexandra, pseud. Ellie's Chance to Dance. 2005. (Royal Ballet School Diaries: 1). (ENG.). 144p. (J). (gr. 3-7). mass mkt. 5.99 *(978-0-448-43535-0(7),* Grosset & Dunlap) Penguin Young Readers Group.

—Lara's Leap of Faith. 2005. (Royal Ballet School Diaries: 2). (ENG.). 144p. (J). (gr. 3-7). mass mkt. 5.99 *(978-0-448-43536-7(5),* Grosset & Dunlap) Penguin Young Readers Group.

New York City Ballet, New York. George Balanchine's the Nutcracker. Docampo, Valeria, illus. 2016. (ENG.). 40p. (J). (gr. -1-3). 17.99 *(978-1-4814-5829-0(9),* Little Simon) Little Simon.

Newman, Lesléa. Miss Tutu's Star. Armstrong-Ellis, Carey, illus. 2010. (ENG.). 32p. (J). (gr. k-2). 17.95 *(978-0-8109-8396-0(6),* Abrams Bks. for Young Readers) Abrams, Inc.

O'Connor, Jane. Budding Ballerina. 2013. (Fancy Nancy Picture Bks.). (J). lib. bdg. 13.55 *(978-0-606-32158-7(6),* Turtleback) Turtleback Bks.

—Fancy Nancy & the Mermaid Ballet. Glasser, Robin Preiss & Bracken, Carolyn, illus. 2012. (Fancy Nancy Ser.). (ENG.). 32p. (J). (gr. -1-2). 17.99 *(978-0-06-170381-2(8))* HarperCollins Pubs.

Ohrt, Kate. Dancing Dreams. Valiant, Kristi, illus. 2014. (ENG.). 18p. (J). bds. 8.99 *(978-1-4494-3554-7(8))* Andrews McMeel Publishing.

Pace, Anne Marie. Vampirina Ballerina. Pham, LeUyen, illus. 2012. (Vampirina Ser.). (ENG.). 40p. (J). (gr. -1-k). 16.99 *(978-1-4231-5753-3(2))* Hyperion Pr.

Padian, Maria. Jersey Tomatoes Are the Best. 2012. (ENG.). 352p. (YA). (gr. 7). pap. 9.99 *(978-0-375-86563-3(2),* Ember) Random Hse. Children's Bks.

Peschke, Marci. Dancing Queen, 1 vol. Mourning, Tuesday, illus. 2012. (Kylie Jean Ser.). (ENG.). 112p. (gr. 2-3). pap. 5.95 *(978-1-4048-7209-7(4));* lib. bdg. 22.65 *(978-1-4048-6798-7(8))* Picture Window Bks. (Kylie Jean).

Peyo. Smurfette & the Beast: A Smurftastic Pop-Up Book. Peyo, illus. 2013. (Smurfs Classic Ser.). (ENG., Illus.). 12p. (J). (gr. -1-3). 17.99 *(978-1-4424-8317-0(2),* Simon Spotlight) Simon Spotlight.

Piggy Toes Press. Our Ballet Recital. Maddocks, Maria, illus. 2005. (ENG.). 12p. (J). (gr. -1-3). 12.95 *(978-1-58117-425-0(X),* Intervisual/Piggy Toes) Bendon, Inc.

Pinkwater, Daniel M. Dancing Larry, 1 vol. Pinkwater, Jill, illus. 2006. (ENG.). 32p. (J). (gr. -1-3). 16.95 *(978-0-7614-5220-1(6))* Marshall Cavendish Corp.

Quin-Harkin, Janet. Toe Shoe Trouble. 2014. (Tgif Ser.: 5). (ENG., Illus.). 128p. (J). (gr. 3-7). pap. 13.99 *(978-1-4814-2883-5(7),* Simon & Schuster/Paula Wiseman Bks.) Simon & Schuster/Paula Wiseman Bks.

Random House Staff. Ballet Dreams. Random House Staff, illus. 2013. (Step into Reading Ser.). (ENG., Illus.). 32p. (J). (gr. -1-1). pap. 3.99 *(978-0-307-98115-8(0),* Random Hse. Bks. for Young Readers) Random Hse. Children's Bks.

Ravera, Giuseppe. My Ballet Bag. Pagnoni, Roberta et al, illus. 2015. (ENG.). 8p. (J). (gr. -1-k). bds. 6.99 *(978-0-7641-6786-7(3))* Barron's Educational Series, Inc.

Reaves, Esther R. Gammy's Snow Queen. 2011. 24p. pap. 12.79 *(978-1-4520-7158-9(6))* AuthorHouse.

RH Disney Staff & Random House Editors. Ballet Dreams. 2013. (Barbie Step into Reading Level 2 Ser.). lib. bdg. 13.55 *(978-0-606-31561-6(6),* Turtleback) Turtleback Bks.

Roberts, Angela. Barbie Loves Ballet. Wolcott, Karen, illus. Dias, Joe et al, photos by. 2010. (Barbie Ser.). (J). 14.10 *(978-0-7569-7778-8(9))* Perfection Learning Corp.

Rubin, Sarah. Someday Dancer. 2012. (J). *(978-0-545-39379-9(5));* (ENG.). 256p. (gr. 7-7). 16.99 *(978-0-545-39378-2(7),* Chicken Hse., The) Scholastic, Inc.

Saab, Julie. Little Lola Saves the Show. Gothard, David, illus. 2016. 32p. (J). (gr. -1-3). 17.99 *(978-0-06-227453-3(8),* Greenwillow Bks.) HarperCollins Pubs.

Sanders, Rob. Ruby Rose, Big Bravos. Ohi, Debbie Ridpath, illus. 2017. 40p. (J). (gr. -1-3). 15.99 ***(978-0-06-223571-8(0))*** HarperCollins Pubs.

Schaefer, Elizabeth. Ballet Lesson. 2014. (Peppa Pig Ser.). (ENG.). 24p. (J). (gr. -1-k). pap. 3.99 *(978-0-545-74775-2(9))* Scholastic, Inc.

Scoon, Saska. Miss Rosie's Academy of Ballet. 2016. (ENG., Illus.). 64p. (J). (gr. 1-2). 14.99 *(978-1-74257-811-8(X))* New Holland Pubs. Pty, Ltd. AUS. Dist: Midpoint Trade Bks., Inc.

Scott, Kate. Spies in Disguise: Boy in a Tutu. 2016. (ENG., Illus.). 192p. (J). (gr. 1-5). pap. 7.99 *(978-1-63450-695-3(2),* Sky Pony Pr.) Skyhorse Publishing Co., Inc.

Shaw, Natalie. Olivia Leaps! Osterhold, Jared, illus. 2010. (Olivia TV Ser.). (ENG.). 12p. (J). bds. 8.99 *(978-1-84738-612-0(1))* Simon & Schuster Children's Publishing.

Shea, Bob. Ballet Cat: The Totally Secret Secret. Shea, Bob, illus. 2016. (Ballet Cat Ser.). (ENG., Illus.). 56p. (J). (gr. 1-3). bds. 9.99 *(978-1-4847-1379-2(6))* Disney Pr.

Simon, Jenne. The Ballet Recital. 2012. (Scholastic Reader Level 2 Ser.). lib. bdg. 13.55 *(978-0-606-23962-2(6),* Turtleback) Turtleback Bks.

—Lalaloopsy: the Ballet Recital. 2012. (Lalaloopsy Ser.). (ENG.). 32p. (J). (gr. -1-3). pap. 3.99 *(978-0-545-39216-7(0))* Scholastic, Inc.

Sinclair, Gardine. Mystery at Stageschool. 2013. 190p. (J). pap. *(978-1-78299-388-9(6))* FeedARead.com.

Singer, Marilyn. Tallulah's Nutcracker. Boiger, Alexandra, illus. 2013. (ENG.). 48p. (J). (gr. -1-3). 16.99 *(978-0-547-84557-9(X))* Houghton Mifflin Harcourt Publishing Co.

—Tallulah's Toe Shoes. Boiger, Alexandra, illus. 2013. (ENG.). 48p. (J). (gr. -1-3). 16.99 *(978-0-547-48223-1(X))* Houghton Mifflin Harcourt Publishing Co.

—Tallulah's Tutu. Boiger, Alexandra, illus. 2011. (ENG.). 40p. (J). (gr. -1-3). 16.99 *(978-0-547-17353-5(9))* Houghton Mifflin Harcourt Publishing Co.

Sís, Peter. Ballerina! 2005. (ENG., Illus.). 30p. (J). (gr. -1-1). bds. 7.99 *(978-0-06-075966-7(6),* Greenwillow Bks.) HarperCollins Pubs.

Steigvilas, Nemira. Mini Eva Lovvves Ballet. 2013. 44p. pap. 15.95 *(978-1-4525-7341-0(7),* Balboa Pr.) Author Solutions, Inc.

Stevenson, Robin. Attitude, 1 vol. 2013. (Orca Limelights Ser.). (ENG.). 144p. (J). (gr. 6-9). pap. 9.95 *(978-1-4598-0382-4(5))* Orca Bk. Pubs. USA.

Stilton, Thea. Thea Stilton & the Dancing Shadows. 2013. (Thea Stilton Ser.: 14). lib. bdg. 19.65 *(978-0-606-31528-9(4),* Turtleback) Turtleback Bks.

Stout, Shawn K. Fiona Finkelstein, Big-Time Ballerina!! Martini, Angela, illus. 2010. (ENG.). 192p. (J). pap. 4.99 *(978-1-4169-7109-2(2),* Simon & Schuster/Paula Wiseman Bks.) Simon & Schuster/Paula Wiseman Bks.

Strathy, Glen C. Dancing on the Inside. 2013. 236p. pap. 15.95 *(978-1-938908-28-6(7),* iUniverse Star) iUniverse, Inc.

Suma, Nova Ren. The Walls Around Us. (ENG.). 336p. (YA). (gr. 9-12). 2016. pap. 9.95 *(978-1-61620-590-4(3))* 2015. 17.95 *(978-1-61620-372-6(2))* Algonquin Bks. of Chapel Hill.

—The Walls Around Us. 2016. lib. bdg. 20.80 *(978-0-606-37957-1(6))* Turtleback Bks.

Thomas, Isabel. Emma Peror's New Clothes. Waters, Erica-Jane, illus. 2016. (Fairy Tales Today Ser.). (ENG.). 24p. (gr. 1-2). 9.95 *(978-1-4795-8751-3(6))* Picture Window Bks.

Tillworth, Mary. Backyard Ballet (Shimmer & Shine) Hee, Liana, illus. 2016. (Little Golden Book Ser.). (ENG.). 24p. (J). (gr. -1-2). 4.99 *(978-0-553-52202-0(7),* Golden Bks.) Random Hse. Children's Bks.

—It's Time for Ballet! (Bubble Guppies) MJ Illustrations, illus. 2015. (Glitter Picturebook Ser.). (ENG.). 16p. (J). (gr. -1-2). 5.99 *(978-0-553-52117-7(9),* Random Hse. Bks. for Young Readers) Random Hse. Children's Bks.

Ure, Jean. Dazzling Danny. Donnelly, Karen, illus. 2011. (ENG.). 96p. (J). pap. 5.99 *(978-0-00-713370-3(7))* HarperCollins Pubs. Ltd. GBR. Dist: HarperCollins Pubs.

Vail, Rachel. Please, Please, Please. 2014. (Friendship Ring Ser.: 2). (ENG.). 176p. (J). (gr. 5). pap. 7.99 *(978-0-14-751119-5(4),* Puffin Books) Penguin Young Readers Group.

Van Scoyoc, Pam. The Ballerina with Webbed Feet/la Bailarina Palmipeda. Teichman, Diane E., tr. from ENG. Lewis, R. J., illus. l.t. ed. 2004. (ENG & SPA.). 40p. (J). (gr.

k-2). lib. bdg. 16.98 (978-0-9663629-2-3(6)) By Grace Enterprises.

Wethington, Constance. The Butterfly's Ball. 2013. 20p. pap. 24.95 (978-1-4626-8640-7(0)) America Star Bks.

Weyn, Suzanne. The Phantom Music Box. 2014. (Hauntings: the Haunted Museum Ser.: 2). lib. bdg. 17.20 (978-0-606-36036-4(0)) Turtleback Bks.

BALLETS—STORIES, PLOTS, ETC.

Dewhurst, Carin. The Nutcracker. Howland, Naomi, illus. 2006. 24p. (J). (gr. 4-8). reprint ed. 20.00 (978-1-4223-5524-4(1)) DIANE Publishing Co.

Hautzig, Deborah & Goode, Diane. The Story of the Nutcracker Ballet. Goode, Diane, illus. 2006. (Pictureback(R) Ser.). (ENG., Illus.). 32p. (J). (gr. -1-2). pap. 3.99 (978-0-394-88178-2(8), Random Hse. Bks. for Young Readers) Random Hse. Children's Bks.

Herman, Mark & Apter, Ronnie, trs. from RUS. Moscow Ballet Great Russian Nutcracker. Fedorov, Valentin, illus. 2003. 32p. (J). (978-0-9743082-0-3(X)) Sports Marketing International, Inc.

Kain, Karen. The Nutcracker. Kupesic, Rajka, illus. 2005. (ENG.). 32p. (J). (gr. k-12). 18.95 (978-0-88776-696-1(X), Tundra Bks.) Tundra Bks. CAN. Dist: Penguin Random Hse. LLC.

Orchid Publishing, prod. The Sleeping Beauty Ballet by Aleksandra. 2011. (ENG., Illus.). 36p. (J). 19.95 (978-0-9831641-2-8(6)) Orchid Publishing, Inc.

Yolen, Jane, et al. The Barefoot Book Stories from the Ballet. Guay, Rebecca, illus. 2004. (ENG.). 96p. (J). 19.99 (978-1-84148-229-3(3)) Barefoot Bks., Inc.

BALLOONS

see also Aeronautics

Bach, Rachel. The Hot Air Balloon Race. 2017. (Let's Race Ser.). (ENG.). 16p. (J). (gr. -1-1). pap. 7.99 (978-1-68152-133-6(4)) Amicus.

Burch, Lynda S. Wicky Wacky Things that Go! Hot Air Balloons. Roberts, MarySue, photos by. 2004. (Illus.). 28p. (J). E-Book 9.95 incl. cd-rom (978-1-933090-08-5(1)) Guardian Angel Publishing, Inc.

Crazy Creatures Balloon Modeling. 2004. (Fun Kits Ser.). (Illus.). 48p. (J). (978-1-84229-732-2(5)) Top That! Publishing PLC.

Doudna, Kelly. Super Simple Things to Do with Balloons: Fun & Easy Science for Kids, 1 vol. 2011. (Super Simple Science Ser.). (ENG., Illus.). 24p. (J). (gr. k-3). lib. bdg. 25.65 (978-1-61714-672-5(2)) ABDO Publishing Co.

Hanson, Anders. Let's Go by Hot Air Balloon, 1 vol. 2008. (Let's Go Ser.). (ENG., Illus.). 24p. (J). (gr. k-3). lib. bdg. 24.21 (978-1-59928-899-4(0), SandCastle) ABDO Publishing Co.

Hicks, Kelli Shay. Hot Air Ballooning. 2009. (Illus.). 24p. (J). lib. bdg. 27.07 (978-1-60694-358-8(8)) Rourke Educational Media.

Hinkler Books Staff. Balloon Animals. 2004. (ENG., Illus.). 48p. (J). 6.95 (978-1-86515-644-6(2)) Hinkler Bks. Pty, Ltd. AUS. Dist: Penton Overseas, Inc.

Hosford, William. ABalloonC. Hosford, William, illus. 2007. (Illus.). 32p. (J). per. 10.00 (978-0-9776562-1-9(7)) WGH Arts LLC.

Kekewich, Deborah. Balloons. 2004. (ENG., Illus.). 16p. (J). (gr. 2-2). pap. 10.92 (978-0-7652-5173-2(6), Celebration Pr.) Pearson Schl.

Masters, Nancy Robinson. How Does It Fly? Hot Air Balloon. 2011. (Community Connections: How Does It Fly? Ser.). (ENG.). 24p. (gr. 2-5). lib. bdg. 25.64 (978-1-61080-068-6(0), 201062) Cherry Lake Publishing.

Mattern, Joanne & Rainsford, Blair. Hot Air Balloons. 2015. (Rookie Read-About(tm) Science: How Things Work Ser.). (ENG.). 32p. (J). lib. bdg. 25.00 (978-0-531-21370-4(6), Children's Pr.) Scholastic Library Publishing.

O'Brien, Joan. Hot Air Balloons Stickers. 2006. (Dover Stickers Ser.). (ENG., Illus.). 4p. (gr. -1). 1.99 (978-0-486-44855-8(X)) Dover Pubns., Inc.

Obrochta, Dale. Faces, Faces, Balloon Faces. 2003. (Illus.). 32p. (YA). (978-0-9728793-0-9(7)) DEO Consulting, Inc.

Outrageous Monster Balloons. 2004. (How 2 Kits Ser.). (Illus.). 48p. (J). (978-1-84229-960-9(3)) Top That! Publishing PLC.

Priceman, Marjorie. Hot Air: The (Mostly) True Story of the First Hot-Air Balloon Ride. Priceman, Marjorie, illus. 2005. (ENG., Illus.). 40p. (J). (gr. -1-3). 18.99 (978-0-689-82642-9(7), Atheneum Bks. for Young Readers) Simon & Schuster Children's Publishing.

Rau, Dana Meachen. Hot Air Balloons. 2010. (Bookworms Chapter Books: Surprising Science Ser.). 24p. (gr. 2-3). 22.79 (978-0-7614-4873-0(X)) Marshall Cavendish GBR. Dist: Marshall Cavendish Corp.

Really Cool Balloon Modeling. 2004. (How 2 Kits Ser.). (Illus.). 48p. (J). (978-1-84229-937-1(9)) Top That! Publishing PLC.

Ross, Dev. We Both Read Bilingual Edition-Frank & the Giant/Sapi y el Globo. Reinhart, Larry, illus. 2011. (ENG & SPA.). 44p. (J). pap. 4.99 (978-1-60115-042-4(3)) Treasure Bay, Inc.

Ross, Dev & Canetti, Yanitzia. Frank & the Balloon: Sapi y el Globo. Reinhart, Larry, illus. 2010. (SPA & ENG.). 41p. (J). (978-1-60115-041-7(5)) Treasure Bay, Inc.

Shaughnessy, Mara. LEGO Man in Space: A True Story. 2013. (ENG., Illus.). 32p. (J). (gr. -1-3). 14.95 (978-1-62087-544-5(6), 620544, Sky Pony Pr.) Skyhorse Publishing Co., Inc.

Silverman, Buffy. How Do Hot Air Balloons Work? 2013. (Lightning Bolt Books (tm) — How Flight Works). (ENG., Illus.). 32p. (gr. k-2). lib. bdg. 26.60 (978-0-7613-8969-9(5), Lerner Pubns.) Lerner Publishing Group.

Thompson, Gare. My Balloon Ride. 2006. (Nonfiction Reading & Writing Workshops Ser.). (ENG., Illus.). 24p. (J). pap. 13.95 (978-0-7922-8501-4(8)) CENGAGE Learning.

Top That Publishing Staff, ed. Brilliant Balloon Modeling. 2004. (Fun Kits Ser.). (Illus.). 48p. (J). (978-1-84510-247-0(9)) Top That! Publishing PLC.

Trusty, Brad & Trusty, Cindy. The Kids' Guide to Balloon Twisting, 1 vol. 2010. (Kids' Guides). (ENG.). 32p. (gr. 3-4). lib. bdg. 27.99 (978-1-4296-5444-9(9), Edge Bks.) Capstone Press of Coughlan Cos.

BALLOONS, DIRIGIBLE

see Airships

BALLOONS—FICTION

Avia. Sunshine & Ladybug: In Angel Balloons. 2013. 32p. pap. 17.25 (978-1-4669-6380-1(8)) Trafford Publishing.

The Balloon Ride, 6, Pack. (Sails Literacy Ser.). 16p. (gr. k-18). 27.00 (978-0-7635-4427-0(2)) Rigby Education.

The Balloon Ride: KinderConcepts Individual Title Six-Packs. (Kinderstarters Ser.). 8p. (gr. -1-1). 21.00 (978-0-7635-8736-9(2)) Rigby Education.

Balloons. Date not set. 5.95 (978-0-89868-343-1(2)) ARO Publishing Co.

Bentley, Sue. Cloud Capers, 3 vols. Swan, Angela & Farley, Andrew, illus. 2009. (Magic Puppy Ser.: 3). (ENG.). 128p. (J). (gr. 1-3). pap. 5.99 (978-0-448-45046-9(1), Grosset & Dunlap) Penguin Young Readers Group.

Bevans, Ph. D. Don't Do That, Harry! The Balloon Story. 2009. 20p. pap. 10.49 (978-1-4490-2926-5(4)) AuthorHouse.

Bird, Helen. The Balloon Launch. Dimitri, Simona, illus. 2005. 32p. (J). lib. bdg. 9.00 (978-1-4242-0887-6(4)) Fitzgerald Bks.

—Big Yellow Balloon. Dimitri, Simona, illus. 2009. (Get Set Readers Ser.). 32p. (J). (gr. -1-2). lib. bdg. 22.60 (978-1-60754-268-1(4)) Windmill Bks.

Bois, William Pene du. The Twenty-One Balloons. 2005. (Puffin Modern Classics Ser.). (ENG., Illus.). 192p. (J). (gr. 3-7). pap. 7.99 (978-0-14-240330-3(X), Puffin Books) Penguin Young Readers Group.

Bolo the Balloon. Bolo the Balloon. 2007. (Illus.). 22p. (J). per. 10.00 (978-0-9797549-0-6(9)) DeKruyff, Ruth.

Bonner, Janet L. Balloon Wishes. 2010. 28p. pap. 13.99 (978-1-4520-4109-4(1)) AuthorHouse.

Burke, Ellinor Rozecki. Susana Worrywart & the Magical Teddy Bear Balloon. Perciopelo, illus. 2003. 32p. (J). 17.99 (978-0-9741586-3-1(1)) Comfort Tales, LLC.

—Susana Worrywart & the Magical Teddy Bear Balloon: With CD for Relaxation. Perciopelo, illus. 2003. 32p. (J). 27.00 incl. audio compact disk (978-0-9741586-0-0(7)) Comfort Tales, LLC.

Burroughs, Scott, illus. Balloon Blow-Up. 2013. (Hardy Boys: the Secret Files Ser.: 13). (ENG.). 112p. (J). (gr. 1-4). pap. 5.99 (978-1-4424-5371-5(0), Aladdin) Simon & Schuster Children's Publishing.

Cassidy, Anne. Wizard Balloon, 1 vol. Remphry, Martin, illus. 2013. (Start Reading Ser.). (ENG.). 24p. (gr. k-1). pap. 7.95 (978-1-4765-4145-7(0)) Capstone Press of Coughlan Cos.

Cliffe, Kara. Jeff & His Magic Hot Air Balloon. Campbell, Ken, illus. 2013. 44p. pap. 15.50 (978-1-62212-186-1(4), Strategic Bk. Publishing) Strategic Book Publishing & Rights Agency (SBPRA).

Cummings, Troy. Rise of the Balloon Goons. 2013. (Notebook of Doom Ser.: 1). lib. bdg. 14.75 (978-0-606-31981-2(6), Turtleback) Turtleback Bks.

Dailey, Reid. Ross the Reader & the Great Balloon Race. Stacy, Alan F., illus. 2011. 46p. pap. 13.95 (978-1-4575-0154-8(6)) Dog Ear Publishing, LLC.

Dale, Jay. Big Balloon, 1 vol. Meldrum, Ned, photos by. 2012. (Engage Literacy Yellow Ser.). (ENG., Illus.). 32p. (gr. k-2). pap. 5.99 (978-1-4296-8962-5(5), Engage Literacy) Capstone Press of Coughlan Cos.

Das, Christina. The Red Spotted Balloon. I.t. ed. 2005. (Illus.). 32p. (J). 15.95 (978-0-9763082-3-2(1), A JuneOne Production) JuneOne Publishing Hub.

Davis, Elena. Where Do the Balloons Go? Jurinich, Anna, illus. 2006. (ENG.). 32p. (J). (gr. -1-3). 16.95 (978-0-9714372-3-4(8)) Red Rock Pr., Inc.

de Beer, Hans, pseud. Little Polar Bear & the Big Balloon. Lanning, Rosemary, tr. from GER. 2006. (Illus.). 22p. (J). (gr. k-4). reprint ed. 16.00 (978-0-7567-9875-8(2)) DIANE Publishing Co.

Dematons, Charlotte. Yellow Balloon. 2004. (ENG., Illus.). 32p. (J). 15.95 (978-1-932425-01-7(2), Lemniscaat) Boyds Mills Pr.

DiSalle, Zanita. Sofia's Pink Balloon. 2008. (Illus.). 32p. 15.95 (978-0-9735663-4-5(5)) APG Sales & Distribution Services.

Disney Book Group Staff, et al. Minnie Minnie's Winter Bow Show. Disney Storybook Artists Staff, illus. 2014. (ENG.). 24p. (J). (gr. -1-k). pap. 5.99 (978-1-4231-8070-8(4)) Disney Pr.

du Bois, William Pène. Twenty-One Balloons. du Bois, William Pène, illus. 2005. (Illus.). 180p. (J). lib. bdg. 15.00 (978-1-4242-2270-4(2)) Fitzgerald Bks.

Fenske, Jonathan. Love Is in the Air. Fenske, Jonathan, illus. 2012. (Penguin Young Readers, Level 2 Ser.). (ENG., Illus.). 32p. (J). (gr. 1-2). mass mkt. 3.99 (978-0-448-49647-4(X), Penguin Young Readers) Penguin Young Readers Group.

Fernandez, Joyce & Marsh, Laura. Um Is One. 2009. 22p. 15.95 (978-0-557-05629-3(2)) Lulu Pr., Inc.

Fine, Anne. Big Red Balloon. Pankhurst, Kate, illus. 2013. (Blue Bananas Ser.). (ENG.). 48p. (J). (gr. k-2). pap. 5.99 (978-1-4052-5433-5(5)) Egmont Bks., Ltd. GBR. Dist: Independent Pubs. Group.

—Big Red Balloon. Pankhurst, Kate, illus. 2nd ed. 2016. (Reading Ladder Ser.). (ENG.). 48p. (J). (gr. k-2). 7.99 (978-1-4052-8212-3(6)) Egmont Bks., Ltd. GBR. Dist: Independent Pubs. Group.

Galbraith, Bree. Once upon a Balloon, 1 vol. Malenfant, Isabelle, illus. 2013. (ENG.). 32p. (J). (gr. -1-3). 19.95 (978-1-4598-0324-4(8)) Orca Bk. Pubs. USA.

Gathorne-Hardy, Jonathan. Jane's Adventures: Jane's Adventures in & Out of the Book; Jane's Adventures on the Island of Peeg; Jane's Adventures in a Balloon. Hill, Nicolas, illus. 2006. (ENG.). 588p. (gr. 4-13). 27.95 (978-1-58567-798-6(1), 856798) Overlook Pr., The.

Gibert, Bruno. A King Seen from the Sky. 2015. (ENG., Illus.). 32p. (J). 16.95 (978-1-60606-460-3(6), J. Paul Getty Museum) Getty Pubns.

Gilman, Phoebe. The Balloon Tree. 2004. (J). (gr. k-3). spiral bd. (978-0-616-01650-3(6)) Canadian National Institute for the Blind/Institut National Canadien pour les Aveugles.

Giulieri, Anne. Max & the Balloons, 1 vol. Bailey, Martin, illus. 2012. (Engage Literacy Yellow Ser.). (ENG.). 32p. (gr. k-2). pap. 5.99 (978-1-4296-8960-1(9), Engage Literacy) Capstone Press of Coughlan Cos.

Graves, Sue. Ben & the Big Balloon. Jakson, Helen, illus. 2008. (Tadpoles Ser.). (ENG.). 24p. (J). (gr. -1-3). pap. (978-0-7787-3891-6(4)) Crabtree Publishing Co.

Guerrero, Rhonda. It's Me, Penny! The Hot Air Balloon Adventure. Leech, Jacob, illus. 2011. 28p. pap. 24.95 (978-1-4489-7070-4(9)) America Star Bks.

Gummelt, Donna & Melchiorre, Dondino. I'm All Blown Up. Wall, Randy Hugh, ed. Varela, Juan D., tr. Varela, Juan D., illus. 2006.Tr. of Ya Creci. (SPA.). 34p. (J). 14.95 (978-0-9764798-4-0(2)) Story Store Collection Publishing.

Hassett, Ann & Hassett, John. Come Back, Ben. Hassett, Ann & Hassett, John, illus. 2014. (I Like to Read(r) Ser.). (ENG., Illus.). 24p. (J). (gr. -1-3). pap. 6.99 (978-0-8234-3181-6(9)) Holiday Hse., Inc.

Hassett, John & Hassett, Ann. Come Back, Ben. 2013. (I Like to Read(r) Ser.). (ENG., Illus.). 24p. (J). (gr. -1-3). 14.95 (978-0-8234-2599-0(1)) Holiday Hse., Inc.

Hincher, Theresa B. Baldy the Balloon. 2005. 16p. (J). (gr. -1). per. 13.95 (978-0-933767-06-5(4)) Pex Publishing Co.

Hinkler Books Staff, reader. Barney's Big Balloon. 2004. 32p. (J). 9.99 incl. audio compact disk (978-1-86515-997-3(2)) Hinkler Bks. Pty, Ltd. AUS. Dist: Penton Overseas, Inc.

Holden, Pam. Balloons Fly By. 2015. (ENG., Illus.). 16p. (-1). pap. (978-1-77654-106-5(5), Red Rocket Readers) Flying Start Bks.

—The Flying Monkey, 6 pack. East, Jacqueline, illus. 2009. (Red Rocket Readers Ser.). (ENG.). 16p. (gr. -1-1). pap. (978-1-877363-29-0(4), Red Rocket Readers) Flying Start Bks.

Hooray for Boys & Girls! 2006. (J). 15.95 (978-0-9776837-0-3(2)) West Woods Pr.

Hopgood, Tim. UnpOppable. 2013. (ENG., Illus.). 32p. (J). (gr. -1-k). pap. 8.99 (978-0-330-51740-9(6)) Pan Macmillan GBR. Dist: Independent Pubs. Group.

Hopkins, Douglas. Princess June & the Shadow Pirates, 1 vol. 2007. (ENG., Illus.). 32p. (J). (gr. -1-2). per. 8.95 (978-1-894294-88-1(2), Tuckamore Bks) Creative Bk. Publishing CAN. Dist: Orca Bk. Pubs. USA.

Huneck, Stephen. Sally's Great Balloon Adventure. 2010. (ENG., Illus.). 32p. (J). 16.95 (978-0-8109-8331-1(1), Abrams Bks. for Young Readers) Abrams, Inc.

Jay, Eli. Poppy & the Fat Puppy. 2013. (ENG.). 40p. (J). pap. 19.95 (978-1-4787-0003-6(3)) Outskirts Pr., Inc.

—Poppy & the Stranger. 2012. (ENG.). 41p. (J). pap. 21.95 (978-1-4327-9752-2(2)) Outskirts Pr., Inc.

—Poppy, the Wandering Balloon. 2011. 33p. (J). pap. 19.95 (978-1-4327-6855-3(7)) Outskirts Pr., Inc.

Jenkins, Celeste. The Lost (and Found) Balloon. Bogade, Maria, illus. 2013. (ENG.). 32p. (J). (gr. -1-3). 16.99 (978-1-4424-6697-5(9), Aladdin) Simon & Schuster Children's Publishing.

Johnson, Angela. The Day Ray Got Away. LaMarca, Luke, illus. 2010. (ENG.). 40p. (J). (gr. k-3). 16.99 (978-0-689-87375-1(1), Simon & Schuster Bks. For Young Readers) Simon & Schuster Bks. For Young Readers.

Kimball, Angela. Of All the Silly Things. 2011. 52p. (gr. -1 — 1). pap. 25.49 (978-1-4567-2259-3(X)) AuthorHouse.

Koehn, Wendel. Love Problematic: And Other Stories. 2012. 24p. pap. 14.93 (978-1-4669-1851-1(9)) Trafford Publishing.

Lee, Jc. Clara's Red Balloon. Park, Kathy, illus. 2011. 40p. pap. 24.95 (978-1-4560-2491-8(4)) America Star Bks.

Liniers. The Big Wet Balloon (El Globo Grande y Mojado) Liniers, illus. 2013. (ENG & SPA., Illus.). 32p. (J). (gr. -1-3). 12.95 (978-1-935179-40-5(3)) TOON Books / RAW Junior, LLC.

—The Big Wet Balloon (El Globo Grande y Mojado) Liniers, illus. 2013. (ENG & SPA., Illus.). 32p. (J). (gr. -1-3). pap. 4.99 (978-1-935179-39-9(X)) TOON Books / RAW Junior, LLC.

Liniers, Ricardo. The Big Wet Balloon. Liniers, Ricardo, illus. 2013. (ENG., Illus.). 32p. (J). (gr. -1-3). 12.95 (978-1-935179-32-0(2)) TOON Books / RAW Junior, LLC.

Lipka, Francine. Balloon Babies Inside Our Rainbows. 2009. 32p. (gr. -1). pap. 14.49 (978-1-4490-3118-3(8)) AuthorHouse.

Lisa Darby And Rachel Darby. When Balloons Go Bye-Bye. 2008. 28p. pap. 21.99 (978-1-4257-7068-6(1)) Xlibris Corp.

Lodge, Jo. Little Roar's Round Balloon. 2013. (ENG., Illus.). 20p. (J). (gr. -1-k). 5.99 (978-1-4449-0483-3(3)) Hodder & Stoughton GBR. Dist: Hachette Bk. Group.

Lund, Wendy E. The Fly Away Balloon. 2010. 50p. pap. 16.50 (978-1-60911-660-6(7), Eloquent Bks.) Strategic Book Publishing & Rights Agency (SBPRA).

Mac Killian, Caroline. Travels of the Zephyr: An Interactive Journey Around the World. 2010. (ENG., Illus.). 88p. (J). (gr. 3-7). 24.95 (978-0-8109-8974-0(3), Abrams Bks. for Young Readers) Abrams, Inc.

Marie, Jill Jana. Balloon Blessing. Zamboni, David, illus. 2008. 28p. pap. 12.95 (978-0-9820479-7-2(5)) Peppertree Pr., The.

Matthias, Catherine. Too Many Balloons. Sharp, Gene, illus. 2011. (Rookie Ready to Learn Ser.). 40p. (J). (gr. -1-k). pap. 5.95 (978-0-531-26749-3(0)); lib. bdg. 23.00 (978-0-531-26449-2(1)) Scholastic Library Publishing. (Children's Pr.).

Matthias, Catherine & Sharp, Gene. Demasiados Globos. Sharp, Gene, illus. 2011. (Rookie Ready to Learn Español Ser.). (SPA., Illus.). 40p. (J). pap. 5.95 (978-0-531-26792-9(X)); lib. bdg. 23.00 (978-0-531-26124-8(7)) Scholastic Library Publishing. (Children's Pr.).

Milgrim, David. See Pip Point. Milgrim, David, illus. 2016. (Adventures of Otto Ser.). (ENG., Illus.). 32p. (J). (gr. -1-k). pap. 3.99 (978-1-4814-6784-1(0), Simon Spotlight) Simon Spotlight.

Na, Il Sung. Bird, Balloon, Bear. 2017. (ENG.). 32p. (J). (-k). 17.99 (978-0-399-55155-0(7), Knopf Bks. for Young Readers) Random Hse. Children's Bks.

Nolen, T. K. The Magical Fantastical Big Red Balloon. 2009. 20p. pap. 11.49 (978-1-4389-5183-6(3)) AuthorHouse.

Nora, David, Jr. Happy Balloon to You. 2005. 9.00 (978-0-8059-9870-2(5)) Dorrance Publishing Co., Inc.

Oelrich, Ryan. The Grand Adventures of Carson the Balloonatic! A Peculiar Hero Story for Children & Adults Who Are Brave Enough to Believe in the Unbelievable. 2011. 36p. 16.99 (978-1-4567-0030-0(8)) AuthorHouse.

Okada, Toshihiko. The Balloon. 2008. 48p. pap. 18.50 (978-1-60693-089-2(3), Eloquent Bks.) Strategic Book Publishing & Rights Agency (SBPRA).

Oldfield, Rachel. Up up Up. Reed, Susan, illus. 2011. (ENG.). 24p. (J). (gr. -1-2). 9.99 (978-1-84686-550-3(6)) Barefoot Bks., Inc.

Pasca, Pamela. If I Lived in a Balloon. 2009. 24p. pap. 12.99 (978-1-4389-2242-3(6)) AuthorHouse.

Phifer, Larry & Phifer. World on a String. 2013. (ENG.). 17.95 (978-0-9886984-0-6(4)) Storytime Works.

Publications International Ltd. Staff, ed. Dora the Explorer: Sounds All Around! 2011. 24p. (J). 20.98 (978-1-4508-0011-2(4)) Phoenix International Publications, Inc.

Quinn, Timothy. Marvelous Miriam's Magnificent Hawaiian Adventure. 2011. 56p. pap. 16.95 (978-1-4560-9630-4(3)) America Star Bks.

Reed, Susan. Up, up, Up! Oldfield, Rachel, illus. 2010. (ENG.). 24p. (J). (gr. -1-2). 16.99 (978-1-84686-369-1(4)) Barefoot Bks., Inc.

Reinertson, Bob. The Mysterious Visitor. 2012. 28p. pap. 21.99 (978-1-4771-0006-6(7)) Xlibris Corp.

Rey, H. A. Curious George & the Hot Air Balloon. 2011. (Curious George Ser.). (ENG., Illus.). 24p. (J). (gr. -1-3). pap. 4.99 (978-0-547-54745-9(5)) Houghton Mifflin Harcourt Publishing Co.

—Up, Up, & Away. 2009. (Curious George Ser.). (ENG., Illus.). 24p. (J). (gr. -1-3). pap. 4.99 (978-0-547-11966-3(6)) Houghton Mifflin Harcourt Publishing Co.

Rey, H. A. & Rey, Margret. Curious George Goes Bowling (CGTV Lift-The-Flap 8x8) 2009. (Curious George Ser.). (ENG., Illus.). 18p. (J). (gr. -1-3). 5.99 (978-0-618-80041-4(7)) Houghton Mifflin Harcourt Publishing Co.

Richards, Dan. Can One Balloon Make an Elephant Fly? Newman, Jeff, illus. 2016. (ENG.). 40p. (J). (gr. -1-3). 17.99 (978-1-4424-5215-2(3)) Simon & Schuster Bks. For Young Readers.

Roberts, Daniel. Mouse & His Balloon. 2011. 32p. pap. 14.95 (978-1-4634-2090-1(0)) AuthorHouse.

Ross, Dev. We Both Read-Frank & the Balloon: Level K-1. Reinhart, Larry, illus. (We Both Read Ser.). 44p. (J). (gr. -1-2). 2008. per. 4.99 (978-1-60115-012-7(1)) 2007. 7.99 (978-1-60115-011-0(3)) Treasure Bay, Inc.

Rylant, Cynthia. The High-Rise Private Eye: The\Case of the Troublesome Turtle. Karas, G. Brian, illus. 2003. (High-Rise Private Eyes Ser.: No. 4). (J). (gr. k-3). 25.95 incl. audio (978-1-59112-202-9(3)) Live Oak Media.

Sakai, Komako. Emily's Balloon. 2015. (ENG., Illus.). 44p. (J). (gr. -1-7). pap. 7.99 (978-1-4521-4567-9(9)) Chronicle Bks. LLC.

Schmid, Paul. Perfectly Percy. Schmid, Paul, illus. 2013. (ENG., Illus.). 40p. (J). (gr. -1-3). 17.99 (978-0-06-180436-6(3)) HarperCollins Pubs.

Shankman, Ed. The Boston Balloonies. O'Neill, Dave, illus. (Shankman & O'Neill Ser.). (J). (gr. -1-3). 2012. (ENG.). 40p. pap. 12.95 (978-1-933212-66-1(7)) 2008. 36p. 14.95 (978-1-933212-76-0(4)) Applewood Bks. (Commonwealth Editions).

Smith-Eubanks, Jennifer. Balloons for Grandpa, 1 vol. Schneider, Robin, illus. 2010. 20p. pap. 24.95 (978-1-4489-5282-3(4)) PublishAmerica, Inc.

Solomon, Philippa. Settle down for Storytime. 2009. (Illus.). 64p. pap. 23.49 (978-1-4389-6032-6(8)) AuthorHouse.

Stead, Philip C. Sebastian & the Balloon. Stead, Philip C., illus. 2014. (ENG., Illus.). 40p. (J). (gr. -1-2). 17.99 (978-1-59643-930-6(0), 9781596439306) Roaring Brook Pr.

Turner, Mary. Colored Balloons & Clowns. 2012. 28p. pap. 21.99 (978-1-4771-0004-2(0)) Xlibris Corp.

Underwood, Deborah. A Balloon for Isabel. Rankin, Laura, illus. 2010. (ENG.). 32p. (J). (gr. -1-2). 16.99 (978-0-06-177987-9(3), Greenwillow Bks.) HarperCollins Pubs.

Voght, Victor A. Fun with Huff & Puff, 1 vol. 2009. 15p. pap. 24.95 (978-1-60749-853-7(7)) America Star Bks.

Walz, Susan. Balloons to the Moon. 2008. 29p. pap. 24.95 (978-1-60474-586-3(X)) America Star Bks.

White, June. The Amazing Adventure of Tiptoe & the Yellow Balloon. Starkey, Fiona, illus. 2011. 32p. pap. (978-0-7552-1345-0(9)) Authors OnLine, Ltd.

Wilson, Liesl-Yvette. A Balloon & a Bear. 2009. 48p. pap. 20.90 (978-0-9559752-4-0(7)) Tallulah & Bear GBR. Dist: Lulu Pr., Inc.

Wolchansky, Molly Kay. The Cactus & the Balloon. 2009. 24p. pap. 12.99 (978-1-4490-1037-9(7)) AuthorHouse.

Wood, Audrey. Balloonia. Wood, Audrey, illus. 2005. (Child's Play Library). (ENG., Illus.). 32p. (J). (gr. 1-2). pap. (978-1-904550-49-5(5)) Child's Play International Ltd.

BALLOT

see Elections

BALLROOM DANCING

Gagne, Tammy. Derek Hough. 2017. lib. bdg. 25.70 (978-1-68020-118-5(2)) Mitchell Lane Pubs., Inc.

Learn to Dance. 2008. 96p. (978-1-4075-1141-2(6)) Parragon, Inc.

Royston, Angela. Ballroom, 1 vol. 2013. (Love to Dance Ser.). (ENG.). 32p. (gr. 1-3). 29.99 (978-1-4109-4921-9(4)); pap. 8.29 (978-1-4109-4926-4(5)) Heinemann-Raintree. (Read Me!).

—Read Me! Love to Dance: Ballroom. 2013. (ENG., Illus.). 32p. (J). (gr. 3-5). pap. 47.94 (978-1-4109-4931-8(1)) Heinemann-Raintree.

BALTIMORE (MD.)

Dans, Peter E. Sergeant Bill & His Horse Bob. Corpus, Mary Grace, illus. 2015.Tr. of 28. (ENG.). (J). 17.95 (978-1-933822-97-6(X)) Camino Bks., Inc.

Ingram, Scott. The Writing of The Star-Spangled Banner. 2004. (Landmark Events in American History Ser.). (Illus.). 48p. (gr. 5-12). pap. 14.05 (978-0-8368-5418-3(7), Gareth Stevens Secondary Library) Stevens, Gareth Publishing LLLP.

Landau, Elaine. The National Anthem. 2007. (True Book(tm), a — American History Ser.). (ENG., Illus.). 48p. (J). (gr. 3-5). lib. bdg. 31.00 (978-0-531-12633-2(1), Children's Pr.) Scholastic Library Publishing.

Maynard, Charles W. Fort McHenry. 2009. (Famous Forts Throughout American History Ser.). 24p. (gr. 3-4). 42.50 (978-1-61512-519-7(1), PowerKids Pr.) Rosen Publishing Group, Inc., The.

Pingry, Patricia A. O Little Town of Bethlehem. 2008. (ENG., Illus.). 16p. (J). bds. 12.99 *(978-0-8249-6566-2(3),* Ideal Pubns.) Worthy Publishing.

RJF Publishing Staff & Burgan, Michael. Fort McHenry. 2009. (Symbols of American Freedom Ser.). 48p. (gr. 4-6). 30.00 *(978-1-60413-520-6(4),* Chelsea Clubhouse) Facts On File, Inc.

BALTIMORE (MD.)—FICTION

Conly, Jane Leslie. Impetuous R. , Secret Agent. Leick, Bonnie, illus. 2008. (ENG.). 240p. (gr. 3-7). 16.99 *(978-1-4231-0418-6(8))* Hyperion Pr.

Couloumbis, Audrey. Jake. 2011. (ENG.). 176p. (J). (gr. 3-7). pap. 6.99 *(978-0-375-85631-0(5),* Yearling) Random Hse. Children's Bks.

Dans, Peter E. Perry's Baltimore Adventure: A Bird's-Eye View of Charm City. Harrell, Kim, illus. 2007. (ENG.). 32p. (J). (gr. -1-1). 14.95 *(978-1-933822-08-2(2))* Camino Bks., Inc.

—Perry's Baltimore Adventure: A Bird's-Eye View of Charm City. Harrell, Kim, illus. 2003. 30p. (J). 11.95 *(978-0-87033-540-2(5),* Cornell Maritime Pr./Tidewater Pubs.) Schiffer Publishing, Ltd.

Dorman, Brandon, illus. The Slippery Map. 2007. 288p. (J). (gr. 3-7). lib. bdg. 17.89 *(978-0-06-079109-4(8))* HarperCollins Pubs.

Fuqua, Jonathon Scott. The Reappearance of Sam Webber. 2010. (ENG.). 250p. pap. 12.95 *(978-1-890862-60-2(6))* Bancroft Pr.

Gattis, Ryan. Air. 2016. (ENG.). 320p. (YA). 17.99 *(978-0-9864484-2-3(7))* Adaptive Studios.

Hahn, Mary Downing. Mister Death's Blue-Eyed Girls. (ENG.). 336p. (YA). (gr. 7). 2012. 16.99 *(978-0-547-76062-9(0))* 2013. pap. 8.99 *(978-0-544-02224-9(6))* Houghton Mifflin Harcourt Publishing Co.

Howard, Elizabeth Fitzgerald. Aunt Flossie's Hats (and Crab Cakes Later) Ransome, James, illus. 2015. 32p. pap. 8.00 *(978-1-61003-491-3(0))* Center for the Collaborative Classroom.

—Chita's Christmas Tree. 2007. (ENG.). 32p. (J). (gr. -1-3). 13.99 *(978-1-4169-6156-7(9),* Simon & Schuster/Paula Wiseman Bks.) Simon & Schuster/Paula Wiseman Bks.

Moore, Wes & Goodman, Shawn. This Way Home. 2015. (ENG.). 256p. (YA). (gr. 9). 20.99 *(978-0-375-99019-9(4),* Delacorte Pr.) Random Hse. Children's Bks.

Proimos, James. 12 Things to Do Before You Crash & Burn. 2011. (ENG.). 128p. (YA). (gr. 9-13). 14.99 *(978-1-59643-595-7(X))* Roaring Brook Pr.

Ripken, Cal, Jr. & Cowherd, Kevin. Super Slugger. 2013. (ENG.). 200p. (YA). (gr. 3-7). pap. 6.99 *(978-1-4231-4004-7(4))* Hyperion Pr.

Smallman, Steve. Santa Is Coming to Baltimore. Dunn, Robert, illus. 2015. (ENG.). 32p. (J). (-3). 9.99 *(978-1-4926-2652-7(X),* Sourcebooks Jabberwocky) Sourcebooks, Inc.

Smith-Ready, Jeri. Shade. (ENG.). (YA). (gr. 9). 2011. 336p. pap. 9.99 *(978-1-4169-9407-7(6))* 2010. 320p. 17.99 *(978-1-4169-9406-0(8))* Simon Pulse. (Simon Pulse).

—Shift. (ENG.). (YA). (gr. 9). 2012. 400p. pap. 9.99 *(978-1-4169-9409-1(2))* 2011. 384p. 17.99 *(978-1-4169-9408-4(4))* Simon Pulse. (Simon Pulse).

Snyder, Laurel. Seven Stories Up. 2014. (ENG.). 288p. (J). (gr. 3-7). 16.99 *(978-0-375-86917-4(4),* Random Hse. Bks. for Young Readers) Random Hse. Children's Bks.

Standiford, Natalie. Confessions of the Sullivan Sisters. 2012. (ENG.). 320p. (J). (gr. 9). pap. 9.99 *(978-0-545-10711-2(3),* Scholastic Paperbacks) Scholastic, Inc.

—How to Say Goodbye in Robot. 2009. (ENG.). 288p. (J). (gr. 7-18). 17.99 *(978-0-545-10708-2(3),* Scholastic Pr.) Scholastic, Inc.

Sternberg, Libby. Finding the Forger. 2004. 192p. (YA). 19.95 *(978-1-890862-32-9(0));* (ENG.). pap. 14.95 *(978-1-890862-37-4(1))* Bancroft Pr.

Verne, Jules. Topsy-Turvy. Ogilvie, J. G., tr. 2009. 108p. 22.95 *(978-1-60664-685-4(0));* pap. 9.95 *(978-1-60664-314-3(2))* Rodgers, Alan Bks.

BALTIMORE ORIOLES (BASEBALL TEAM)

Connery-Boyd, Peg. Baltimore Orioles. 2016. (Hawk's Nest Activity Bks.: 0). (ENG.). 64p. (J). (gr. k-3). pap., act. bk. ed. 8.99 *(978-1-4926-3361-7(5))* Sourcebooks, Inc.

Doeden, Matt. Cal Ripken, Jr. 2008. (Sports Heroes & Legends Ser.). (YA). (gr. 7-12). lib. bdg. 29.27 *(978-0-8225-9040-8(9))* Twenty First Century Bks.

—Cal Ripken Jr. 2009. pap. 58.95 *(978-0-7613-4807-8(7))* Lerner Publishing Group.

Frager, Ray. Baltimore Orioles, 1 vol. (Inside MLB Ser.). (ENG., 48p. (gr. 3-6). 2011. Illus.). (YA). lib. bdg. 32.79 *(978-1-61714-036-5(8))* 2014. lib. bdg. 32.79 *(978-1-62403-462-6(4),* SportsZone) ABDO Publishing Co.

Frisch, Aaron. Baltimore Orioles. 2009. (World Series Champions Ser.). (Illus.). 23p. (J). (gr. 2-3). 24.25 *(978-1-58341-692-1(7),* Creative Education) Creative Co., The.

Gilbert, Sara. Baltimore Orioles. 2013. (Illus.). 24p. (J). 25.65 *(978-1-60818-259-6(2),* Creative Education) Creative Co., The.

—The Story of the Baltimore Orioles. 2011. (Illus.). 48p. (J). 35.65 *(978-1-60818-033-2(6),* Creative Education) Creative Co., The.

—World Series Champs: Baltimore Orioles. 2013. (World Series Champions Ser.). (ENG., Illus.). 24p. (J). (gr. 1-3). pap. 7.99 *(978-0-89812-810-9(2),* Creative Paperbacks) Creative Co., The.

Omoth, Tyler. The Story of the Baltimore Orioles. 2007. (Baseball, the Great American Game Ser.). (Illus.). 48p. (YA). (gr. 4-7). lib. bdg. 32.80 *(978-1-58341-480-4(0))* Creative Co., The.

Stewart, Mark. The Baltimore Orioles. 2012. (Team Spirit Ser.). 48p. (J). (gr. 3-6). lib. bdg. 29.27 *(978-1-59953-474-9(6))* Norwood Hse. Pr.

BAMBI (FICTITIOUS CHARACTER)—FICTION

Bambi: A Little Spring Shower. unabr. ed. Date not set. (My First Read Along Ser.). (Illus.). 18p. (J). 7.99 incl. audio *(978-1-55723-749-1(2))* Walt Disney Records.

Cooke, Marjorie Benton. Bambi. 2004. reprint ed. pap. 1.99 *(978-1-4192-0885-0(3));* pap. 27.95 *(978-1-4191-0885-3(9))* Kessinger Publishing, LLC.

Disney Staff. Bambi. (FRE.). 96p. (J). (gr. k-5). pap. 9.95 *(978-0-7859-8850-2(5))* French & European Pubns., Inc.

Disney Staff, creator. Bambi. 2005. (Illus.). 96p. pap. 14.99 *(978-1-59532-715-4(0),* Tokyopop Kids) TOKYOPOP, Inc.

RH Disney Staff. Bambi. (FRE.). (J). (gr. 3-8). 13.95 *(978-0-7859-0613-1(4),* S26622) French & European Pubns., Inc.

—Bambi. unabr. ed. (Read-Along Ser.). (J). 7.99 incl. audio *(978-1-55723-008-9(0))* Walt Disney Records.

RH Disney Staff & Posner-Sanchez, Andrea. Bambi's Hide-and-Seek. Mones, Isidre, illus. 2013. (Step into Reading Ser.). (ENG.). 32p. (J). (gr. -1-1). pap. 3.99 *(978-0-7364-1347-3(2),* RH/Disney) Random Hse. Children's Bks.

Salten, Felix. Bambi - Life in the Woods. (J). 20.95 *(978-0-8488-1467-0(3))* Amereon Ltd.

Studio Mouse Staff. Walt Disney Bambi Learning Library. rev. ed. 2007. (ENG.). 60p. 12.99 *(978-1-59069-612-5(3))* Studio Mouse LLC.

BANANA

Blue Bananas. 2005. (J). *(978-1-59564-735-1(X))* Steps To Literacy, LLC.

Eagen, Rachel. The Biography of Bananas. 2005. (How did That Get There? Ser.). (ENG., Illus.). 32p. (J). (gr. 4-5). pap. *(978-0-7787-2519-0(7));* lib. bdg. *(978-0-7787-2483-4(2))* Crabtree Publishing Co.

Griego, Margarita. Monkeys Like Bananas! a Los Monos les Gustan Los Platanos! 2012. 52p. pap. 24.99 *(978-1-4685-4537-1(0))* AuthorHouse.

Ray, Liz. Bananas: From Farm to Home, 6 vols. 2004. (Phonics Readers Books 37-72 Ser.). (ENG.). 8p. (gr. k-1). pap. 35.70 *(978-0-7368-4068-2(0),* Phonics Readers) Capstone Press of Coughlan Cos.

BANDITS

see Robbers and Outlaws

BANDS (MUSIC)

Bailey, Ellen & Williams, Imogen. 5 Seconds of Summer: 100% Unofficial. 2014. (ENG., Illus.). 24p. (J). (gr. 3-7). pap. 7.99 *(978-1-4814-4365-4(8),* Aladdin) Simon & Schuster Children's Publishing.

Emmer, Rae. Band. 2009. (School Activities Ser.). 24p. (gr. 1-1). 42.50 *(978-1-60852-992-6(4),* PowerKids Pr.) Rosen Publishing Group, Inc., The.

—Band / Banda. 2009. (School Activities / Actividades escolares Ser.). (ENG & SPA.). 24p. (gr. 1-2). 42.50 *(978-1-60853-000-7(0),* Editorial Buenas Letras) Rosen Publishing Group, Inc., The.

French, Holly. One Direction. 2015. (Pop Icons Ser.). (Illus.). 64p. (J). (gr. 7). lib. bdg. 23.95 *(978-1-4222-3249-1(2))* Mason Crest.

Garty, Judy. Marching Band Competition. 2004. (Let's Go Team Ser.). (Illus.). 64p. (YA). (gr. 5-18). lib. bdg. 19.95 *(978-1-59084-539-4(0))* Mason Crest.

George, Gale. We're in the Band: Develop Understanding of Fractions & Numbers. 2014. (Rosen Common Core Math Readers Ser.). (ENG., Illus.). 24p. (J). (gr. 3-4). pap. 8.25 *(978-1-4777-4927-2(6),* Rosen Classroom) Rosen Publishing Group, Inc., The.

Harvey, M. A. Wannabes Pop Diva: For Girls Who Know What They Want to Be. 2004. (Illus.). 128p. (J). pap. *(978-1-84458-049-1(0),* Pavilion Children's Books) Pavilion Bks.

Owen, Ruth. I Can Start a Band! 2017. (Kids Can Do It! Ser.). 32p. (gr. 8-8). 28.50 ***(978-1-4994-8347-5(3),*** Windmill Bks.) Rosen Publishing Group, Inc., The.

Peppas, Lynn. One Direction. 2013. (ENG., Illus.). 32p. (J). *(978-0-7787-1049-3(1));* pap. *(978-0-7787-1053-0(X))* Crabtree Publishing Co.

Salazar, Sam. One Direction. 2013. (Rising Stars Ser.). 32p. (J). (gr. 3-6). 25.25 *(978-1-4339-8985-8(9));* pap. 10.50 *(978-1-4339-8986-5(7));* pap. 63.00 *(978-1-4339-8987-2(5))* Stevens, Gareth Publishing LLLP.

Usilton, Theresa A. Let's Go team: Cheer, Dance, & March, 12 vols., Set. 2003. (Let's Go Team Ser.). (Illus.). 64p. (YA). (gr. 5-18). lib. bdg. *(978-1-59084-529-5(3))* Mason Crest.

BANDS (MUSIC)—FICTION

Abdo, Kenny. Duck, Dive, Rock & Roll, 1 vol. Doucet, Bob, illus. 2013. (Haven't Got a Clue! Ser.). (ENG.). 80p. (J). (gr. 3-6). lib. bdg. 27.07 *(978-1-61641-952-3(0),* Calico Chapter Bks) Magic Wagon.

Anderson, Peggy Perry. Chuck's Band. 2017. (Green Light Readers Level 1 Ser.). (ENG., Illus.). 32p. (J). (gr. -1-3). 12.99 *(978-0-544-92620-2(X),* HMH Books For Young Readers) Houghton Mifflin Harcourt Publishing Co.

Andrews, Jesse. The Haters. (ENG.). 336p. (YA). (gr. 8-17). 2017. pap. 9.95 *(978-1-4197-2370-4(7))* 2016. 18.95 *(978-1-4197-2078-9(3))* Abrams, Inc. (Amulet Bks.).

—The Haters. 2017. (YA). lib. bdg. 20.80 ***(978-0-606-39688-2(8))*** Turtleback Bks.

Arena, Felice & Kettle, Phil. Rock Star. Gordon, Gus, illus. 2004. (J). pap. *(978-1-59336-368-0(0))* Mondo Publishing.

Beaudoin, Sean. Wise Young Fool. 2013. (ENG.). 448p. (YA). (gr. 9-17). 18.00 *(978-0-316-20379-1(3))* Little, Brown Bks. for Young Readers.

Beaufrand, M. J. The Rise & Fall of the Gallivanters. 2015. (ENG., Illus.). 288p. (YA). (gr. 9-17). 16.95 *(978-1-4197-1495-5(3),* Amulet Bks.) Abrams, Inc.

Benator, Eileen. A Marching Band for Bears. Benator, Seth, illus. 2004. 32p. (J). lib. bdg. 15.95 *(978-0-9748478-5-6(2))* Lion's Tale Pr., LLC.

Bowe, Julie. Face the Music. 2015. (Victoria Torres, Unfortunately Average Ser.). (ENG.). 160p. (gr. 4-4). pap. 5.95 *(978-1-4965-0538-5(7))* Stone Arch Bks.

Briant, Ed. I Am (Not) the Walrus. 2012. (ENG.). 288p. (YA). pap. 9.95 *(978-0-7387-3246-6(X),* Flux) North Star Editions.

Brooks, Kevin. Naked '76. 2016. (ENG.). 424p. (gr. 9-12). 18.99 *(978-1-5124-0418-0(7),* Carolrhoda Bks.); (YA). 38.65 *(978-1-5124-0445-6(4),* Carolrhoda Lab™) Lerner Publishing Group.

Burroughs, Scott, illus. A Rockin' Mystery. 2012. (Hardy Boys: the Secret Files Ser.: 10). (ENG.). 96p. (J). (gr. 1-4). pap. 5.99 *(978-1-4424-1671-0(8),* Aladdin) Simon & Schuster Children's Publishing.

Calonita, Jen. Battle of the Bands. 2016. (VIP Ser.: 2). (ENG., Illus.). 320p. (J). (gr. 3-7). 16.99 *(978-0-316-25977-4(2))* Little, Brown Bks. for Young Readers.

—VIP: Battle of the Bands. 2017. (VIP Ser.: 2). (ENG.). 320p. (J). (gr. 3-7). pap. 6.99 *(978-0-316-25978-1(0))* Little, Brown Bks. for Young Readers.

Carlson, Melody. Road Trip. 2003. (Diary of a Teenage Girl Ser.: Bk. 7). (ENG.). 304p. (J). (gr. 7). pap. 14.99 *(978-1-59052-142-7(0),* Multnomah) Doubleday Religious Publishing Group, The.

—Sold Out. 2003. (Diary of a Teenage Girl Ser.: Bk. 6). (ENG.). 288p. (YA). (gr. 7). pap. 14.99 *(978-1-59052-141-0(2),* Multnomah Bks.) Crown Publishing Group.

Carlson, Nancy. Loudmouth George & the Comet. rev. ed. 2004. (Carolrhoda Picture Books Ser.). (ENG., Illus.). 32p. (J). (gr. k-2). pap. 9.95 *(978-1-57505-725-5(5))* Lerner Publishing Group.

Cobb, Amy. Dude, Where's My Saxophone?, 1 vol. Cattish, Anna, illus. 2015. (ENG.). 112p. (J). *(978-1-62402-073-5(9))* Magic Wagon.

—First Chair, 1 vol. Cattish, Anna, illus. 2015. (ENG.). 112p. (J). *(978-1-62402-074-2(7))* Magic Wagon.

—Notes from a Pro, 1 vol. Cattish, Anna, illus. 2015. (ENG.). 112p. (J). *(978-1-62402-075-9(5))* Magic Wagon.

—Settling the Score. 2016. (Band Geeks Set 2 Ser.). (ENG.). (J). (gr. 3-6). lib. bdg. 27.07 ***(978-1-62402-175-6(1))*** ABDO Publishing Co.

—Shredding with the Geeks, 1 vol. Cattish, Anna, illus. 2015. (ENG.). 112p. (J). *(978-1-62402-076-6(3))* Magic Wagon.

—Snaring the Trumpet, 1 vol. Cattish, Anna, illus. 2015. (ENG.). 112p. (J). *(978-1-62402-077-3(1))* Magic Wagon.

—Swing Vote for Solo, 1 vol. Cattish, Anna, illus. 2015. (ENG.). 112p. (J). *(978-1-62402-078-0(X))* Magic Wagon.

Cofer, Judith Ortiz. ¡A Bailar! / Let's Dance! Rodriguez, Christina Ann, illus. 2011. (ENG & SPA.). (J). 16.95 *(978-1-55885-698-1(6),* Piñata Books) Arte Publico Pr.

Costello, David Hyde. Little Pig Joins the Band. Costello, David Hyde, illus. 2014. (ENG., Illus.). 32p. (J). (gr. -1-3). pap. 7.95 *(978-1-58089-265-0(5))* Charlesbridge Publishing, Inc.

Cotugno, Katie. Fireworks. 2017. 336p. (YA). (gr. 8). 17.99 *(978-0-06-241827-2(0))* HarperCollins Pubs.

Curry, Kenneth. Fuzzy & the All Bear Band. 2007. (Illus.). 22p. (J). 10.95 *(978-0-9798364-8-0(4))* Curry Brothers Publishing Group.

Denman, K. L. Battle of the Bands, 1 vol. 2006. (Orca Soundings Ser.). (ENG.). 128p. (YA). (gr. 8-12). per. 9.95 *(978-1-55143-540-4(3))* Orca Bk. Pubs. USA.

Denman, K. L. & Fernández, Queta. La Guerra de las Bandas, 1 vol. 2008. (Spanish Soundings Ser.). (SPA.). 112p. (YA). (gr. 8-12). pap. 9.95 *(978-1-55143-998-3(0))* Orca Bk. Pubs. USA.

Dowell, Frances O'Roark. Ten Miles Past Normal. 2012. (ENG., Illus.). 224p. (YA). (gr. 7). pap. 9.99 *(978-1-4169-9586-9(2),* Atheneum Bks. for Young Readers) Simon & Schuster Children's Publishing.

Emberley, Rebecca. The Ant & the Grasshopper. Emberley, Ed, illus. 2012. (ENG.). 28p. (J). (gr. -1-2). 18.99 *(978-1-59643-493-6(7),* 9781596434936) Roaring Brook Pr.

Emerson, Kevin. Breakout. 2015. (ENG.). 304p. (YA). (gr. 7). 17.99 *(978-0-385-39112-2(9),* Crown Books For Young Readers) Random Hse. Children's Bks.

—Encore to an Empty Room. (Exile Ser.: 2). (YA). (gr. 9). 2016. 336p. pap. 9.99 *(978-0-06-213399-1(3))* 2015. (ENG.). 320p. 17.99 *(978-0-06-213398-4(5))* HarperCollins Pubs. (Tegen, Katherine Bks).

—Exile. (Exile Ser.: 1). (ENG.). (YA). (gr. 9). 2015. 336p. pap. 9.99 *(978-0-06-213396-0(9))* 2014. 320p. 17.99 *(978-0-06-213395-3(0))* HarperCollins Pubs. (Tegen, Katherine Bks).

—Finding Abbey Road. 2017. 256p. (J). pap. 9.99 ***(978-0-06-213402-8(7))*** 2016. (Exile Ser.: 3). 240p. (YA). (gr. 9). 17.99 *(978-0-06-213401-1(9))* HarperCollins Pubs. (Tegen, Katherine Bks).

England, Linda. 3 Kids Dreamin' Schutzer, Dena, illus. 2011. (ENG.). 32p. (J). (gr. 4-6). 6.99 *(978-1-4424-2944-4(5),* McElderry, Margaret K. Bks.) McElderry, Margaret K. Bks.

Falconer, Ian. Olivia Forma una Banda. Mlawer, Teresa, tr. from ENG. Falconer, Ian, illus. 2007. (SPA., Illus.). 39p. (J). (gr. -1-3). 17.99 *(978-1-933032-23-8(5))* Lectorum Pubns., Inc.

—Olivia Forms a Band. Falconer, Ian, illus. 2009. (ENG., Illus.). 50p. (J). (gr. -1-3). 12.99 *(978-1-4169-8037-7(7),* Atheneum Bks. for Young Readers) Simon & Schuster Children's Publishing.

Friedman, Laurie. Play It Again, Mallory. Kalis, Jennifer, illus. (Mallory Ser.: 20). (ENG.). 160p. (J). (gr. 2-5). 2014. pap. 5.95 *(978-1-4677-0936-1(0))* 2013. 15.95 *(978-0-7613-6075-9(1))* Lerner Publishing Group. (Darby Creek).

Frosting & Friendship. 2014. (ENG., Illus.). 240p. (J). (gr. 3-7). pap. 6.99 *(978-1-4424-7397-3(5),* Aladdin) Simon & Schuster Children's Publishing.

Gallagher, Diana G. Monica & the Sweetest Song, 1 vol. 2011. (Monica Ser.). (ENG.). 88p. (gr. 2-3). lib. bdg. 26.65 *(978-1-4342-2556-6(9))* Stone Arch Bks.

Gerber, Carole. A Band of Babies. Dyer, Jane, illus. 2017. 32p. (J). (gr. -1-3). 17.99 *(978-0-06-168955-0(6))* HarperCollins Pubs.

Gershenson, Harold P. Freddy Flamingo & the Kindertown Five. Mills, Christopher, illus. 2005. 27p. (J). *(978-1-58987-070-3(0))* Kindermusik International.

Grace, N. B. Battle of the Bands. 2007. (High School Musical Stories from East High Ser.). 142p. (J). (gr. 3-7). 12.65 *(978-0-7569-8337-6(1))* Perfection Learning Corp.

Haston, Meg. How to Rock Best Friends & Frenemies. 2013. (How to Rock Ser.: 2). (ENG.). 352p. (J). (gr. 3-7). pap. 8.00 *(978-0-316-06827-7(6),* Poppy) Little, Brown Bks. for Young Readers.

—How to Rock Braces & Glasses. 2011. (How to Rock Ser.: 1). (ENG.). 336p. (J). (gr. 3-7). 16.99 *(978-0-316-06825-3(X),* Poppy) Little, Brown Bks. for Young Readers.

—How to Rock Braces & Glasses. 2012. (How to Rock Ser.: 1). (ENG.). 352p. (J). (gr. 3-7). pap. 8.00 *(978-0-316-06824-6(1),* Poppy) Little, Brown Bks. for Young Readers.

Herbach, Geoff. Fat Boy vs. the Cheerleaders. 2014. (ENG.). 320p. (YA). (gr. 7-12). 16.99 *(978-1-4022-9141-8(8),* 9781402291418) Sourcebooks, Inc.

—Gabe Johnson Takes Over. 2015. (ENG.). 352p. (YA). (gr. 6-12). pap. 9.99 *(978-1-4926-0865-3(3))* Sourcebooks, Inc.

Howarth, Kylie. Fish Jam. 2015. (ENG., Illus.). 40p. (J). (gr. -1-2). 16.99 *(978-1-4998-0098-2(3))* Little Bee Books Inc.

Huang, Charlotte. For the Record. (ENG.). 320p. (YA). (gr. 7). 2016. pap. 9.99 *(978-0-553-51185-7(8),* Ember) 2015. 17.99 *(978-0-553-51182-6(3),* Delacorte Pr.) Random Hse. Children's Bks.

Hughes, Mark Peter. Lemonade Mouth Puckers Up. 2013. (ENG.). 300p. (YA). (gr. 7). pap. 9.99 *(978-0-385-73713-5(0),* Ember) Random Hse. Children's Bks.

Hurd, Thacher. Mama Don't Allow. 2003. (Illus.). (J). (gr. -1-2). pap. 35.95 incl. audio compact disk *(978-1-59112-605-8(3))* Live Oak Media.

Hurd, Thacher & Hurd. Mama Don't Allow. Hurd, Thacher, illus. 25th anniv. ed. 2008. (Trophy Picture Bks.). (ENG., Illus.). 40p. (J). (gr. -1-3). pap. 6.99 *(978-0-06-443078-4(2))* HarperCollins Pubs.

Hurd, Thacher & Hurd, T. Mama Don't Allow. 2008. (Illus.). (J). (gr. -1-2). 17.20 *(978-0-8085-3698-7(2),* Turtleback) Turtleback Bks.

Ignatow, Amy. The Awesomely Awful Melodies of Lydia Goldblatt & Julie Graham-Chang. 2013. (Popularity Papers). (ENG., Illus.). 208p. (J). (gr. 3-7). 16.95 *(978-1-4197-0536-6(9),* Amulet Bks.) Abrams, Inc.

Jaimet, Kate. Dunces Rock, 1 vol. 2014. (ENG.). 224p. (J). (gr. 4-7). pap. 9.95 *(978-1-4598-0585-9(2))* Orca Bk. Pubs. USA.

Jarrell, Pamela R. Caillou's Musical Band. Gray, Stacy A., illus. l.t. ed. 2005. (HRL Board Book Ser.). (J). (gr. -1-k). 10.95 *(978-1-57332-311-6(X),* HighReach Learning, Incorporated) Carson-Dellosa Publishing, LLC.

John, Antony. Five Flavors of Dumb. 2011. (ENG.). 368p. (YA). (gr. 7-18). 8.99 *(978-0-14-241943-4(5),* Speak) Penguin Young Readers Group.

Johnson, Angela. Violet's Music. Huliska-Beith, Laura & Laura, Huliska-beith, illus. 2004. (ENG.). 32p. (J). (gr. -1-3). 17.99 *(978-0-8037-2740-3(2),* Dial Bks) Penguin Young Readers Group.

Jones, Harmony. The High Note. 2017. (ENG.). 240p. (J). 16.99 *(978-1-61963-949-2(1),* 9781619639492, Bloomsbury USA Childrens) Bloomsbury Publishing USA.

Jones, Patrick. Friend or Foe. 2016. (Unbarred Ser.). (ENG.). 120p. (YA). (gr. 6-12). lib. bdg. 27.99 *(978-1-5124-0005-2(X),* Darby Creek) Lerner Publishing Group.

—Friend or Foe. 2016. (Unbarred Ser.). (ENG.). 120p. (YA). (gr. 6-12). pap. 7.99 *(978-1-5124-0095-3(5),* Darby Creek) Lerner Publishing Group.

—Friend or Foe. 2016. (Unbarred Ser.). (ENG.). 120p. (YA). (gr. 6-12). 42.65 *(978-1-5124-0096-0(3),* Darby Creek) Lerner Publishing Group.

Kamata, Suzanne. Screaming Divas. 2014. (ENG.). 208p. (YA). 17.99 *(978-1-4405-7279-1(8),* Simon Pulse) Simon Pulse.

Kelley, Marty. Fame, Fortune, & the Bran Muffins of Doom. Kelley, Marty, illus. 2012. (ENG., Illus.). 144p. (J). 16.95 *(978-0-8234-2606-5(8))* Holiday Hse., Inc.

Korman, Gordon. Born to Rock. 2008. (ENG.). 272p. (J). (gr. 7-17). per. 8.99 *(978-0-7868-0921-9(3))* Hyperion Pr.

—Born to Rock. 2011. 10.36 *(978-0-7848-3479-4(2),* Everbind) Marco Bk. Co.

Kunze, Nansi. Kill the Music. l.t. ed. 2013. 330p. pap. *(978-1-4596-6983-3(5))* ReadHowYouWant.com, Ltd.

LaCour, Nina. The Disenchantments. (ENG.). (YA). (gr. 9). 2013. 336p. pap. 10.99 *(978-0-14-242391-2(2),* Speak) 2012. 320p. 16.99 *(978-0-525-42219-8(6),* Dutton Books for Young Readers) Penguin Young Readers Group.

Lee, WonKyeong. The Chirping Band. Jang, EunJoo, illus. 2014. (MySELF Bookshelf Ser.). (ENG.). 32p. (J). (gr. k-2). pap. 11.94 *(978-1-60357-698-7(3));* lib. bdg. 25.27 *(978-1-59953-663-7(3))* Norwood Hse. Pr.

London, Jonathan. Froggy Plays in the Band. Remkiewicz, Frank & Frank, Remkiewicz, illus. 2004. (Froggy Ser.). (ENG.). 32p. (J). (gr. -1-k). 6.99 *(978-0-14-240051-7(3),* Puffin Books) Penguin Young Readers Group.

—Froggy Plays in the Band. Remkiewicz, Frank, illus. 2004. (Froggy Ser.). (J). (gr. -1-3). 13.65 *(978-0-7569-2955-8(5))* Perfection Learning Corp.

McGowan, Jayme. One Bear Extraordinaire. 2015. (ENG., Illus.). 32p. (J). (gr. -1-3). 16.95 *(978-1-4197-1654-6(9),* Abrams Bks. for Young Readers) Abrams, Inc.

McVoy, Terra Elan. Being Friends with Boys. (ENG., (YA). (gr. 9). 2013. Illus.). 384p. pap. 10.99 *(978-1-4424-2160-8(6))* 2012. 368p. 16.99 *(978-1-4424-2159-2(2))* Simon Pulse. (Simon Pulse).

Milanes, Janelle. The Victoria in My Head. 2017. (ENG., Illus.). 400p. (YA). (gr. 7). 17.99 ***(978-1-4814-8089-5(8),*** Simon Pulse) Simon Pulse.

Moldavsky, Goldy. Kill the Boy Band. (ENG.). 320p. (J). (gr. 9). 2017. pap. 9.99 *(978-0-545-86750-4(9))* 2016. 17.99 *(978-0-545-86747-4(9))* Scholastic, Inc.

—Kill the Boy Band. 2017. lib. bdg. 20.85 ***(978-0-606-39701-8(9))*** Turtleback Bks.

Moskal, Greg. Give the Band a Hand. 2006. (Neighborhood Readers Ser.). (ENG.). 12p. (gr. 1-3). pap. 5.90 *(978-1-4042-6859-3(6),* Rosen Classroom) Rosen Publishing Group, Inc., The.

Murphy, Stuart J. Left, Right, Emma! 2012. (I See I Learn Ser.). (ENG., Illus.). 32p. (J). (-k). 14.95 *(978-1-58089-472-2(0));* pap. 6.95 *(978-1-58089-473-9(9))* Charlesbridge Publishing, Inc.

Nichols, Travis. Matthew Meets the Man. 2012. (ENG., Illus.). 176p. (YA). (gr. 6-9). 24.99 *(978-1-59643-545-2(3),* 9781596435452) Roaring Brook Pr.

Nowlin, Laura. This Song Is (Not) for You. 2016. (ENG.). 240p. (YA). (gr. 8-12). pap. 9.99 *(978-1-4926-0290-3(6),* 9781492602903) Sourcebooks, Inc.

Osmond, Jimmy. The Awesome Possum Family Band. 2014. (ENG., Illus.). 40p. (J). (gr. -1-3). 16.99 *(978-1-62157-211-4(0),* Regnery Kids) Regnery Publishing, Inc., An Eagle Publishing Co.

Palumbo, Mary Lou. Skippy the Dog in the Band. Mikle, Toby, illus. 2009. 48p. pap. 19.49 *(978-1-4389-9218-1(1))* AuthorHouse.

Pérez, Celia C. The First Rule of Punk. 2017. (ENG., Illus.). 336p. (J). (gr. 4-7). 16.99 ***(978-0-425-29040-8(9),*** Viking Books for Young Readers) Penguin Young Readers Group.

Perez, Marlene. Dead Is a Killer Tune. 2012. (Dead Is Ser.: 7). lib. bdg. 18.40 *(978-0-606-26623-9(2),* Turtleback) Turtleback Bks.

Perry, Pete. The Saints in Paradise: Another Crazy Story for Crazy Kids. 2009. (Illus.). 76p. pap. 24.99 *(978-1-4490-1311-0(2))* AuthorHouse.

Phillips, Dee. Scout, 1 vol. unabr. ed. 2011. (Right Now! Ser.). (ENG., Illus.). 45p. (YA). (gr. 9-12). pap. 8.95 *(978-1-61651-252-1(0))* Saddleback Educational Publishing, Inc.

Raskin, Joyce. My Misadventures As a Teenage Rock Star. Chu, Carol, illus. 2011. (ENG.). 112p. (YA). (gr. 7-18). pap. 8.99 *(978-0-547-39311-7(3))* Houghton Mifflin Harcourt Publishing Co.

Rich, Jamie S. Love the Way You Love. Ellerby, Marc, illus. 2006. (J). *(978-1-932664-52-2(1))* Oni Pr., Inc.

Rivers, Olivia. Tone Deaf. 2016. (ENG.). 288p. (YA). (gr. 8). 17.99 *(978-1-63450-707-3(X)*, Sky Pony Pr.) Skyhorse Publishing Co., Inc.

Rose, Sue. Starstruck. 2006. (Unfabulous! Ser.). (Illus.). 105p. (J). *(978-1-4156-5353-1(4))* Scholastic, Inc.

Russell, Rachel Renée. Tales from a Not-So-Glam TV Star. Russell, Rachel Renée, illus. 2014. (Dork Diaries: 7). (ENG., Illus.). 336p. (J). (gr. 4-8). 13.99 *(978-1-4424-8767-3(4)*, Aladdin) Simon & Schuster Children's Publishing.

—Tales from a Not-So-Glam TV Star. 2014. (Dork Diaries: 7). lib. bdg. 25.75 *(978-0-606-36240-5(1))* Turtleback Bks.

Saft, Lauren. Those Girls. 2016. (ENG.). 336p. (YA). (gr. 10-17). pap. 9.99 *(978-0-316-26016-9(9)*, Poppy) Little, Brown Bks. for Young Readers.

Scarsbrook, Richard. Featherless Bipeds. 2006. (ENG.). 224p. per. 15.95 *(978-1-897235-05-8(4))* Thistledown Pr., Ltd. CAN. Dist: Univ. of Toronto Pr.

Schusterman, Michelle. Friends, Fugues, & Fortune Cookies. Kote, Genevieve, illus. 2014. (I Heart Band Ser.: 2). (ENG.). 208p. (J). (gr. 3-7). 6.99 *(978-0-448-45684-3(2)*, Grosset & Dunlap) Penguin Young Readers Group.

—I Heart Band #1. Kote, Genevieve, illus. 2014. (I Heart Band Ser.: 1). (ENG.). 208p. (J). (gr. 3-7). 6.99 *(978-0-448-45683-6(4)*, Grosset & Dunlap) Penguin Young Readers Group.

Schusterman, Michelle & Kote, Geneviève. Sleepovers, Solos, & Sheet Music. 2014. (I Heart Band Ser.: 3). (ENG.). 208p. (J). (gr. 3-7). 6.99 *(978-0-448-45685-0(0)*, Grosset & Dunlap) Penguin Young Readers Group.

Scotton, Rob. Splat the Cat with a Bang & a Clang. Scotton, Rob, illus. 2013. (I Can Read Level 1 Ser.). (ENG., Illus.). 32p. (J). (gr. -1-3). 16.99 *(978-0-06-209021-8(6))* HarperCollins Pubs.

—Splat the Cat with a Bang & a Clang. 2013. (Splat the Cat: I Can Read Ser.). (J). lib. bdg. 13.55 *(978-0-606-27148-6(1)*, Turtleback) Turtleback Bks.

Skovron, Jon. Struts & Frets. (ENG.). 304p. (YA). 2011. (gr. 9-17). pap. 7.95 *(978-1-4197-0028-6(6))* 2009. (gr. 7-11). 16.95 *(978-0-8109-4174-8(0))* Abrams, Inc. (Amulet Bks.).

Smethurst, Julia. Finclucky from Kentucky: A Picture Book. 2013. (J). *(978-1-938905-36-0(9))* Acclaim Pr., Inc.

Strom, Yale. The Wedding That Saved a Town. Prosmitsky, Jenya, illus. 2008. (J). (gr. -1). 17.95 *(978-0-8225-7376-0(8))*; (ENG.). 32p. (gr. 2-4). pap. 7.95 *(978-0-8225-7380-7(6))* Lerner Publishing Group. (Kar-Ben Publishing).

Stuchner, Joan Betty. The Kugel Valley Klezmer Band. Row, Richard, illus. 2005. 30p. (J). (gr. 2-6). reprint ed. 16.00 *(978-0-7567-8605-2(3))* DIANE Publishing Co.

Takemori, Lianne K. The Four Dog Blues Band, or How Chester Boy, Dog in the Fog, & Diva Took the Big City by Storm. Dietrick, Robin C. & Klein, Bradley S., eds. 2010. (ENG., Illus.). 48p. 15.95 *(978-1-887422-13-0(7))* Mississippi Museum of Art.

Tracy, Blaise. The Inside Out & Upside Town. 2008. 24p. pap. 17.95 *(978-1-4327-2484-9(3))* Outskirts Pr., Inc.

Vlahos, Len. The Scar Boys. 2014. (ENG.). 256p. (J). (gr. 9). 17.99 *(978-1-60684-439-7(3))* Lerner Publishing Group.

—Scar Girl. 2016. (ENG.). 280p. (YA). (gr. 9-12). 17.99 *(978-1-60684-607-0(8))*; 35.99 *(978-1-5124-0164-6(1))* Lerner Publishing Group. (Carolrhoda Lab™).

Weeks, Sarah. Catfish Kate & the Sweet Swamp Band. Smith, Elwood H., illus. 2009. (ENG.). 32p. (J). (gr. -1-3). 17.99 *(978-1-4169-4026-5(X)*, Atheneum Bks. for Young Readers) Simon & Schuster Children's Publishing.

Wissinger, Tamera Will. This Old Band. Loveridge, Matt, illus. 2014. (ENG.). 32p. (J). (gr. -1-k). 16.95 *(978-1-62873-595-6(3)*, Sky Pony Pr.) Skyhorse Publishing Co., Inc.

Zamora, Nancy. Back in the Band. 2007. 94p. pap. 19.95 *(978-1-60441-818-7(4))* America Star Bks.

BANGLADESH

Adamson, Heather. Bangladesh. 2016. (Exploring Countries Ser.). (ENG., Illus.). 32p. (J). (gr. 3-7). lib. bdg. 26.95 *(978-1-62617-343-9(5)*, Blastoff! Readers) Bellwether Media.

Barker, Amanda. Bangladesh. (World Focus Ser.). (Illus.). 32p. pap. 3.99 *(978-0-431-07257-9(4))* Oxfam Publishing GBR. Dist: Stylus Publishing, LLC.

London, Ellen. Bangladesh. 2004. (Countries of the World Ser.). (Illus.). 96p. (gr. 5-12). lib. bdg. 31.00 *(978-0-8368-3107-8(1))* Stevens, Gareth Publishing LLLP.

Montgomery, Sy. The Man-Eating Tigers of Sundarbans. Briggs, Eleanor, photos by. 2004. (Illus.). 57p. (J). 14.60 *(978-0-7569-5180-1(1))* Perfection Learning Corp.

Orr, Tamra. Bangladesh. 2010. (Explorer Library: Social Studies Explorer Ser.). (ENG.). 48p. (gr. 4-8). lib. bdg. 31.36 *(978-1-60279-829-8(X)*, 200524) Cherry Lake Publishing.

Phillips, Douglas A. Bangladesh. 2007. (Modern World Nations Ser.). (Illus.). 107p. (YA). (gr. 7-12). lib. bdg. 35.00 *(978-0-7910-9251-4(8))* Facts On File, Inc.

Rahman, Urmi & Quarto Generic Staff. B Is for Bangladesh. Das, Prodeepta, photos by. 2009. (World Alphabets Ser.). (ENG., Illus.). 32p. (J). (gr. -1-2). 16.95 *(978-1-84507-918-5(3)*, Frances Lincoln) Quarto Publishing Group UK GBR. Dist: Hachette Bk. Group.

Streissguth, Thomas. Bangladesh. 2008. (Visual Geography Ser.). (YA). (gr. 7-12). lib. bdg. 31.93 *(978-0-8225-8577-0(4))* Twenty First Century Bks.

Thomson, Ruth. Living in Bangladesh. Matthews, Jenny, photos by. 2006. (Living In- Ser.). (Illus.). 32p. (J). (gr. 4-7). lib. bdg. 27.10 *(978-1-59771-045-9(8))* Sea-To-Sea Pubns.

Valliant, Doris. Bangladesh. 2006. (Growth & Influence of Islam in the Nations of Asia & Central Asia Ser.). (Illus.). 128p. (YA). lib. bdg. 25.95 *(978-1-59084-879-1(9))* Mason Crest.

Whyte, Mariam & Yong, Jui Lin. Bangladesh. 2nd rev. ed. 2009. (Cultures of the World 17 Ser.). 144p. (gr. 6). lib. bdg. 42.79 *(978-0-7614-4475-6(0))* Marshall Cavendish Corp.

Yoo, Paula. Twenty-Two Cents: Muhammad Yunus & the Village Bank. Akib, Jamel, illus. 2014. (ENG.). 40p. (J). 18.95 *(978-1-60060-658-8(X))* Lee & Low Bks., Inc.

BANKING

see Banks and Banking

BANKRUPTCY

Allen, Sandra. Bankruptcy Law. 2008. (Point/Counterpoint Ser.). (Illus.). 99p. (C). (gr. 9). 35.00 *(978-0-7910-9713-7(7)*, Chelsea Hse.) Facts On File, Inc.

Bezdecheck, Bethany. Bailout! Government Intervention in Business. 2010. (In the News Ser.). (ENG.). 64p. (YA). pap. 12.95 *(978-1-4488-1681-1(5))*; (gr. 7-12). lib. bdg. 31.95 *(978-1-4358-9449-5(9))* Rosen Publishing Group, Inc., The.

Casil, Amy Sterling. Why Banks Fail. 2010. (Real World Economics Ser.). (Illus.). 80p. (YA). (gr. 7-18). lib. bdg. 33.25 *(978-1-4358-9462-4(6))* Rosen Publishing Group, Inc., The.

Freedman, Jeri. The U.S. Auto Industry: American Carmakers & the Economic Crisis. 2010. (In the News Ser.). (ENG.). 64p. (YA). pap. 12.95 *(978-1-4488-1680-4(7))*; (gr. 7-12). lib. bdg. 31.95 *(978-1-4358-9448-8(0))* Rosen Publishing Group, Inc., The.

Hamilton, Jill. Bankruptcy. 2010. (Introducing Issues with Opposing Viewpoints Ser.). (Illus.). 144p. (J). 36.95 *(978-0-7377-4852-9(4)*, Greenhaven Pr., Inc.) Cengage Gale.

BANKS AND BANKING

see also Credit; Investments; Money

Allman, Barbara. Banking. 2005. (How Economics Works). (ENG., Illus.). 48p. (gr. 4-6). lib. bdg. 25.26 *(978-0-8225-2148-8(2)*, Lerner Pubns.) Lerner Publishing Group.

Andrade, J. Jack. Mom, Dad, Tell Me about Money: A Primer. 2004. 68p. (YA). per. 19.95 *(978-0-9759494-0-5(3)*, 2004-money01) Thundermist Consulting and Research Co.

Apel, Melani. The Federal Reserve Act: Making the American Banking System Stronger. 2009. (Progressive Movement 1900-1920: Efforts to Reform America's New Industrial Society Ser.). 32p. (gr. 3-4). 47.90 *(978-1-60854-172-0(X))* Rosen Publishing Group, Inc., The.

Apel, Melanie Ann. The Federal Reserve Act: Making the American Banking System Stronger. 2004. (Progressive Movement, 1900-1920 Ser.). (Illus.). 32p. (YA). (gr. 5-9). lib. bdg. 22.50 *(978-1-4042-0196-5(3))* Rosen Publishing Group, Inc., The.

Armentrout, David & Armentrout, Patricia. The Bank. 2008. (Illus.). 24p. (J). lib. bdg. 22.79 *(978-1-60472-335-9(1))* Rourke Educational Media.

Bellamy, Adam. This Is My Bank. 2016. (All about My World Ser.). 24p. (J). pap. 9.35 *(978-0-7660-8106-2(0))* Enslow Pubs., Inc.

Biz Kid$ & Kotsiovos, Jean. Banking & Financial Systems. 2012. (ENG.). 136p. (gr. 9-12). pap. 22.00 *(978-1-60525-780-8(X))* Goodheart-Willcox Pub.

Biz Kids Staff. Banking & Financial Systems. 2012. (ENG., Illus.). 425p. (gr. 9-12). 90.00 *(978-1-60525-778-5(8))* Goodheart-Willcox Pub.

Bodden, Valerie. Federal Reserve System. 2016. (Agents of Government Ser.). (ENG., Illus.). 48p. (J). (gr. 5-9). pap. 12.00 *(978-1-62832-147-0(4)*, Creative Paperbacks) Creative Co., The.

Brezina, Corona. Understanding the Federal Reserve & Monetary Policy. 2011. (Real World Economics Ser.). (ENG.). 80p. (J). (gr. 7-12). lib. bdg. 33.25 *(978-1-4488-5567-4(5))* Rosen Publishing Group, Inc., The.

Brown, Lisa, illus. Baby Do My Banking. 2006. (ENG.). 12p. 6.95 *(978-1-932416-55-8(2))* McSweeney's Publishing.

Caravantes, Peggy. Guarding the Federal Reserve Bank of New York. 2016. (Highly Guarded Places Ser.). (ENG.). 24p. (J). (gr. 2-5). 28.50 *(978-1-5038-0811-9(4)*, 210645) Child's World, Inc., The.

Casil, Amy Sterling. Why Banks Fail. 2010. (Real World Economics Ser.). (Illus.). 80p. (YA). (gr. 7-18). lib. bdg. 33.25 *(978-1-4358-9462-4(6))* Rosen Publishing Group, Inc., The.

Connolly, Sean. Banks & Banking. 2010. (World Economy Explained Ser.). 48p. (YA). (gr. 7-12). 35.65 *(978-1-60753-077-0(5))* Amicus Publishing.

—Banks & Banking. 2012. (Illus.). 48p. (gr. 6-10). pap. 9.95 *(978-1-926722-75-7(2))* Saunders Bk. Co. CAN. Dist: RiverStream Publishing.

Connolly, Sean & Pipe, Jim. Banks & Banking. 2011. (On the Edge Ser.). 32p. (YA). (gr. 3-6). 28.50 *(978-1-59920-517-5(3))* Black Rabbit Bks.

Crompton, Samuel Willard. McCulloch V. Maryland: Implied Powers of the Federal Government. 2007. (Great Supreme Court Decisions Ser.). (Illus.). 136p. (YA). (gr. 5-9). lib. bdg. 32.95 *(978-0-7910-9262-0(3))* Facts On File, Inc.

Cuthbert, Megan & Siemens, Jared. Bank. 2016. (J). ***(978-1-5105-1879-7(7))*** SmartBook Media, Inc.

Dougherty, Terri. Tyra Banks. 2009. (People in the News Ser.). (Illus.). 128p. (YA). (gr. 7-12). 33.95 *(978-1-4205-0161-2(5))* Cengage Gale.

Einspruch, Andrew. The Money System. 2012. (Money Sense Ser.). (Illus.). 32p. (gr. 4-6). lib. bdg. 28.50 *(978-1-59920-429-1(0))* Black Rabbit Bks.

Fischer, James. Banking Basics. 2010. (Junior Library of Money). 64p. (YA). (gr. 7-18). lib. bdg. 22.95 *(978-1-4222-1761-0(2))* Mason Crest.

Godfrey, Neale S. Check It Out: The Book about Banking: Classroom Set. 2003. (One & Only Common Sense/cents Ser.). 486.95 *(978-0-7652-0811-8(3))* Modern Curriculum Pr.

Gunderson, Megan M. Banks & Banking, 1 vol. 2012. (Economy in Action! Ser.). (ENG.). 32p. (J). (gr. 3-6). lib. bdg. 27.07 *(978-1-61783-485-1(8)*, Checkerboard Library) ABDO Publishing Co.

Haddock, Patricia. Careers in Banking & Finance. 2009. (Career Resource Library). 192p. (gr. 7-12). 63.90 *(978-1-60853-398-5(0))* Rosen Publishing Group, Inc., The.

Hall, Margaret. Banks. 2016. (Earning, Saving, Spending Ser.). (ENG.). 32p. (gr. 1-3). pap. 7.99 *(978-1-4846-3641-1(4)*, NA-h) Heinemann-Raintree.

Haugen, David M. Should the Federal Government Bail Out Private Industry? 2010. (At Issue Ser.). (Illus.). 128p. (J). 34.45 *(978-0-7377-4656-3(4))*; pap. 24.45 *(978-0-7377-4657-0(2))* Cengage Gale. (Greenhaven Pr., Inc.).

Hollander, Barbara. How the World Bank & International Monetary Fund Work. 2012. (Real World Economics Ser.). (ENG., Illus.). 80p. (J). (gr. 7-12). lib. bdg. 33.25 *(978-1-4488-6787-5(8))* Rosen Publishing Group, Inc., The.

Houghton, Gillian. Balancing a Checkbook. 2009. (Invest Kids Ser.). 24p. (gr. 2-3). 42.50 *(978-1-61513-608-7(8)*, PowerKids Pr.) Rosen Publishing Group, Inc., The.

—How Banks Work. 2009. (Invest Kids Ser.). 24p. (gr. 2-5). (ENG., Illus.). (J). pap. 8.25 *(978-1-4358-3205-3(1)*, 1291646); 42.50 *(978-1-61513-620-9(7))*; (J). lib. bdg. 22.60 *(978-1-4358-2770-7(8))* Rosen Publishing Group, Inc., The. (PowerKids Pr.).

Hudak, Heather C. Banking. 2017. (J). ***(978-1-5105-1939-8(4))*** SmartBook Media, Inc.

—Banking. 2009. (Everyday Economics Ser.). (Illus.). 32p. (J). (gr. 4-6). pap. 9.95 *(978-1-60596-652-6(5))*; lib. bdg. 26.00 *(978-1-60596-651-9(7))* Weigl Pubs., Inc.

Kawa, Katie. My First Trip to the Bank. Livingston, Jessica, illus. 2012. (My First Adventures Ser.). (ENG.). 24p. (J). (gr. k-2). pap. 8.15 *(978-1-4339-6238-7(1))*; lib. bdg. 22.60 *(978-1-4339-6236-3(5))* Stevens, Gareth Publishing LLLP.

—My First Trip to the Bank: Mi Primera Visita Al Banco. Livingston, Jessica, illus. 2012. (My First Adventures / Mis primeras aventuras Ser.). (ENG & SPA.). 24p. (J). (gr. k-2). lib. bdg. 22.60 *(978-1-4339-6625-5(5))* Stevens, Gareth Publishing LLLP.

Larson, Jennifer S. Where Do We Keep Money? How Banks Work. 2010. (Lightning Bolt Books — Exploring Economics Ser.). (ENG., Illus.). 32p. (gr. k-2). pap. 7.95 *(978-0-7613-5663-9(0)*, Lerner Pubns.); lib. bdg. 26.60 *(978-0-7613-3911-3(6))* Lerner Publishing Group.

Loewen, Nancy. In the Money: A Book about Banking, 1 vol. Fitzpatrick, Brad, illus. 2010. (Money Matters Ser.). (ENG.). 32p. lib. bdg. 9.95 *(978-1-4048-6036-0(3))*, Nonfiction Picture Bks.) Picture Window Bks.

Machajewski, David. John Pierpont Morgan & the Banking Industry. 2016. (Great Entrepreneurs in U. S. History Ser.). (Illus.). 32p. (J). (gr. 5-5). pap. 11.75 *(978-1-4994-2127-9(3)*, PowerKids Pr.) Rosen Publishing Group, Inc., The.

Marsico, Katie. Working at a Bank. 2008. (21st Century Junior Library: Careers Ser.). (ENG.). 24p. (gr. 2-5). lib. bdg. 25.64 *(978-1-60279-270-8(4)*, 200175) Cherry Lake Publishing.

McAlpine, Margaret. Working in Banking & Finance. 2005. (My Future Career Ser.). (Illus.). 64p. (J). (gr. 3-7). lib. bdg. 27.00 *(978-0-8368-4772-7(5)*, Gareth Stevens Learning Library) Stevens, Gareth Publishing LLLP.

Meachen Rau, Dana. ¿Qué es un banco? (What Is a Bank?) 2010. (Dinero y los Bancos (Money & Banks) Ser.). (SPA., Illus.). 24p. (gr. 2-5). pap. 8.15 *(978-1-4339-3727-9(1))* Stevens, Gareth Publishing LLLP.

—What Is a Bank? 2010. (Money & Banks Ser.). (Illus.). 24p. (gr. 2-5). pap. 8.15 *(978-1-4339-3393-6(4))* Stevens, Gareth Publishing LLLP.

Parker, Lewis K. J. Pierpont Morgan & Wall Street. 2003. (American Tycoons Ser.). (Illus.). 24p. (J). lib. bdg. 22.60 *(978-0-8239-6449-9(3)*, PowerKids Pr.) Rosen Publishing Group, Inc., The.

Pettifor, Bonnie & Petit, Charles E. McCulloch V. Maryland: When State & Federal Powers Conflict. 2004. (Landmark Supreme Court Cases Ser.). (Illus.). 128p. (J). lib. bdg. 27.94 *(978-0-7660-1887-7(3))* Enslow Pubs., Inc.

Rau, Dana Meachen. ?Que Es un Banco? 2010. (Dinero y los Bancos (Money & Banks) Ser.). (SPA., Illus.). 24p. (J). (gr. 2-5). lib. bdg. 22.00 *(978-1-4339-3726-2(3))* Stevens, Gareth Publishing LLLP.

—What Is a Bank? 2010. (Money & Banks Ser.). (Illus.). 24p. (J). (gr. 2-5). lib. bdg. 22.00 *(978-1-4339-3392-9(6))* Stevens, Gareth Publishing LLLP.

Schwartz, Heather E. Bank Wisely. 2015. (Money Smarts Ser.). (ENG., Illus.). 32p. (J). (gr. 2-4). 19.95 *(978-1-60753-792-2(3))* Amicus Publishing.

SHARP Literacy, compiled by. Banking on Your Future: A Blueprint for Entrepreneurial, Technical & Trade Careers. 2010. (SPA & ENG., Illus.). 124p. (J). pap. 18.00 *(978-0-9770816-9-1(9))* SHARP Literacy, Inc.

Sieplinga, Drew. Paint Your Own Piggy Bank. 2007. (Illus.). 32p. (J). *(978-0-545-02112-8(X))* Scholastic, Inc.

Simons, Rae. A Guide to Teaching Young Adults about Money. 2010. (Junior Library of Money). 64p. (YA). (gr. 7-18). pap. 9.95 *(978-1-4222-1884-6(8))*; lib. bdg. 22.95 *(978-1-4222-1765-8(5))* Mason Crest.

Smith, Kathy & National Geographic Learning Staff. Let's Go to the Bank. 2010. (Rise & Shine Ser.). (ENG., Illus.). 12p. (C). (gr. 1-2). pap. 9.95 *(978-0-8239-8119-9(3))* National Geographic School Publishing, Inc.

Spath, Carolyn E. W. Savvy Saving. 2015. (J). lib. bdg. *(978-1-62713-304-3(6))* Cavendish Square Publishing.

Thompson, Helen. Banking Math. 2013. (Math 24/7 Ser.: 10). 48p. (J). (gr. 5-18). 19.95 *(978-1-4222-2902-6(5))* Mason Crest.

Wallach, Jonah M. & Tattersall, Clare. Money & Banking. 2011. (J). 77.70 *(978-1-4488-4752-5(4)*, Rosen Reference); (J). pap. 12.95 *(978-1-4488-4720-4(6)*, Rosen Reference); (YA). (gr. 5-9). lib. bdg. 31.95 *(978-1-4488-4713-6(3))* Rosen Publishing Group, Inc., The.

BANKS AND BANKING—FICTION

Bain, Michelle. The Adventures of Thumbs up Johnnie Banker Bill's Guide to Common Cents: Banker Bill's Guide to Common Cents. Lizana, Lorenzo, illus. 2007. (J). 14.95 *(978-0-9761421-9-5(8))* Pixie Stuff LLC.

Coman, Carolyn. The Memory Bank. Shepperson, Rob, illus. 2010. (J). 263p. pap. *(978-0-545-21067-6(4))*; (ENG.). 288p. (gr. 3-7). 16.99 *(978-0-545-21066-9(6))* Scholastic, Inc. (Levine, Arthur A. Bks.).

Heflick, LaMonte. The Story of Boney & Clyde. 2004. (Illus.). 64p. pap. 3.99 *(978-1-56175-911-8(2))* Remedia Pubns.

Higginson, Sheryl. Dilbert's Pets, 1 vol. 2010. 94p. pap. 19.95 *(978-1-4489-5757-6(5))* America Star Bks.

Hillert, Margaret. Dear Dragon Goes to the Bank. Schimmell, David, illus. 2012. (BeginningtoRead Ser.). 32p. (J). (-2). lib. bdg. 22.60 *(978-1-59953-502-9(5))* Norwood Hse. Pr.

—Querido Dragón Va Al Banco. Fernandez, Queta, tr. from ENG. Schimmell, David, illus. 2014. (BeginningtoRead Ser.).Tr. of Dear Dragon Goes to the Bank. (ENG & SPA.). 32p. (J). (-2). lib. bdg. 22.60 *(978-1-59953-614-9(5))* Norwood Hse. Pr.

Jo, Eun-jeong. Grandfather Whisker's Table. Landmann, Bimba, illus. 2017. (J). ***(978-0-8028-5474-2(5)**,* Eerdmans Bks For Young Readers) Eerdmans, William B. Publishing Co.

Manushkin, Fran. Piggy Bank Problems, 1 vol. Lyon, Tammie, illus. 2013. (Katie Woo Ser.). (ENG.). 32p. (gr. k-2). pap. 5.95 *(978-1-4048-8048-1(8))*; lib. bdg. 21.32 *(978-1-4048-7654-5(5))* Picture Window Bks.

Regan, Peter. Riverside: Exit Point. 2009. (ENG., Illus.). 128p. (J). pap. 10.95 *(978-1-901737-59-2(4))* Anvil Bks., Ltd. IRL. Dist: Dufour Editions, Inc.

Roza, Greg. A Piggy Bank for Pedro. 2006. (Neighborhood Readers Ser.). (ENG.). 8p. (gr. -1-3). pap. 5.15 *(978-1-4042-5714-6(4)*, Rosen Classroom) Rosen Publishing Group, Inc., The.

Sander, Sonia. Calling All Cars! 2010. (Lego City Ser.). (ENG.). 32p. (J). (gr. -1-k). pap. 3.99 *(978-0-545-15523-6(1))* Scholastic, Inc.

Webster, Frank V. Dick the Bank Boy. 2007. (ENG.). 184p. per. 11.95 *(978-1-4218-3331-6(X))* 1st World Publishing, Inc.

—Dick the Bank Boy: Or A Missing Fortune. 2007. (ENG.). 142p. pap. 18.99 *(978-1-4264-9526-7(9))*; 158p. pap. 21.99 *(978-1-4264-9907-4(8))* Creative Media Partners, LLC.

Williams, Teri. I Got Bank! What My Granddad Taught Me about Money. 2010. (ENG., Illus.). 88p. (J). pap. 14.95 *(978-0-9827943-7-1(1))* Beckham Pubns. Group, Inc.

BANKS AND BANKING—VOCATIONAL GUIDANCE

Haddock, Patricia. Careers in Banking & Finance. rev. ed. 2005. (Career Resource Library). (Illus.). 192p. (YA). (gr. 7-12). lib. bdg. 34.60 *(978-0-8239-3446-1(2))* Rosen Publishing Group, Inc., The.

BANNEKER, BENJAMIN, 1731-1806

Keller, Shana. Ticktock Banneker's Clock. Gardner, David C., illus. 2016. (ENG.). 32p. (J). (gr. 1-4). 16.99 *(978-1-58536-956-0(X)*, 204114) Sleeping Bear Pr.

Litwin, Laura Baskes. The Life of Benjamin Banneker: Astronomer & Mathematician. 2014. (Legendary African Americans Ser.). (Illus.). 96p. (J). (gr. 6-12). 27.94 *(978-0-7660-6112-5(4))* Enslow Pubs., Inc.

Marsh, Carole. Benjamin Banneker. 2003. 12p. (gr. k-4). 2.95 *(978-0-635-02129-8(3))* Gallopade International.

Martin, Isabel. Benjamin Banneker, 1 vol. 2014. (Great African-Americans Ser.). (ENG.). 24p. (gr. k-1). pap. 5.95 *(978-1-4914-0506-2(6)*, Pebble Bks.) Capstone Press of Coughlan Cos.

Shaffer, Jody Jensen. Benjamin Banneker: Self-Made Man. 2016. (Primary Source Readers Ser.). (Illus.). 32p. (J). (gr. 4-5). pap. 8.99 *(978-1-4938-3082-4(1))* Teacher Created Materials, Inc.

Soentpiet, Chris K., et al. Molly Bannaky. 2009. (ENG., Illus.). 32p. (J). (gr. -1-3). pap. 6.99 *(978-0-547-07676-8(2))* Houghton Mifflin Harcourt Publishing Co.

Wadsworth, Ginger. Benjamin Banneker: Pioneering Scientist. Orback, Craig, illus. 2003. (On My Own Biography Ser.). (ENG.). 48p. (gr. 2-4). 25.26 *(978-0-87614-916-4(6))*; per. 6.95 *(978-0-87614-104-5(1)*, Carolrhoda Bks.) Lerner Publishing Group.

—Benjamin Banneker: Pioneering Scientist. Orback, Craig, illus. 2006. (On My Own Biographies Ser.). 47p. (gr. 2-5). 17.00 *(978-0-7569-6705-5(8))* Perfection Learning Corp.

Welch, Catherine A. Benjamin Banneker. 2008. (History Maker Biographies Ser.). (Illus.). 48p. (J). (gr. 3-7). lib. bdg. 26.60 *(978-0-8225-7167-4(6)*, Lerner Pubns.); pap. 52.95 *(978-0-8225-9386-7(6))* Lerner Publishing Group.

BANNERS

see Flags

BANTING, FREDERICK GRANT, SIR, 1891-1941

Downey, Glen. Miracle Men. Brennan, Anthony, illus. 2007. (Timeline Ser.). 48p. pap. 8.99 *(978-1-4190-4410-6(9))* Steck-Vaughn.

BAPTISM

Baptism in the Holy Spirit. 2003. (YA). 1.50 *(978-0-9673342-4-0(1))* Saints Of Glory Church.

Beckstead, Lene, illus. Color Me Baptized. 2009. 32p. pap. 6.95 *(978-0-88494-335-8(6))* Deseret Bk. Co.

Bowman, Peg. Welcomed by Name: Our Child's Baptism. 2003. (ENG.). 32p. pap. 3.95 *(978-0-8294-1798-2(2))* Loyola Pr.

Consuegra, Claudio & Consuegra, Pamela. Making Jesus My Best Friend: Baptism Preparation for Younger Children (Ages 8-10) 2005. (Illus.). 95p. (J). (gr. 4-7). per. 8.99 *(978-0-8280-1836-4(7))* Review & Herald Publishing Assn.

Daybell, Chad G. Baptism: Entering the Path to Eternal Life. 2004. 72p. (J). pap. 7.95 *(978-1-932898-18-7(2)*, 98182) Spring Creek Bk. Co.

Donahue, Laurie. God's Plan My Response. Rittenhouse, Ralph, ed. 2003. (Illus.). 100p. pap. 10.99 *(978-0-9718306-0-8(6))* LifeSong Pubs.

Donahue, Laurie & Rittenhouse, Ralph. God... Should I Be Baptized? 2003. (Illus.). 96p. (gr. 4-6). pap. 11.99 *(978-0-9718306-1-5(4))* LifeSong Pubs.

Durrant, George D. Seven Years Old & Preparing for Baptism. 2007. (Illus.). 68p. (J). pap. 7.95 *(978-1-932898-74-3(3))* Spring Creek Bk. Co.

Elkins, Stephen. Tell Me about Baptism. 2014. (Train 'Em Up Ser.). (ENG.). 24p. (J). pap. 4.99 *(978-1-4143-9682-8(1))* Tyndale Hse. Pubs.

Hall, Annalisa. I Want to Be Baptized. Egbert, Corey, illus. 2015. (J). 10.99 *(978-1-4621-1670-6(1)*, Horizon Pubs.) 2014. 14.99 *(978-1-4621-1461-0(X))* Cedar Fort, Inc./CFI Distribution.

Hanna, Heather. Daniel Asks about Baptism & Communion. 2005. (Illus.). 32p. (J). 3.97 *(978-0-8163-2083-7(7))* Pacific Pr. Publishing Assn.

Olive, Phyllis Carol. The Gift of the Holy Ghost. Olive, Phyllis Carol, illus. unabr. ed. 2003. (Illus.). 25p. (J). (gr. k-4). 12.95 *(978-1-932280-08-1(1)*, 80081) Granite Publishing & Distribution.

Piper, Sophie. Bible Promises for Baby's Baptism. Woodward, Antonia, illus. 2015. (ENG.). 32p. (J). (— 1). 9.99 *(978-0-7459-6554-3(7))* Lion Hudson PLC GBR. Dist: Independent Pubs. Group.

—Bible Promises for Baby's Christening. Woodward, Antonia, illus. 2015. (ENG.). 32p. (J). (— 1). 9.99

(978-0-7459-7620-4(4)) Lion Hudson PLC GBR. Dist: Independent Pubs. Group.
—Bible Promises for Baby's Dedication. Woodward, Antonia, illus. 2015. (ENG.). 32p. (J). (— 1). 9.99 (978-0-7459-7606-8(9)) Lion Hudson PLC GBR. Dist: Independent Pubs. Group.
—My Baptism Book. Kolanovic, Dubravka, illus. 2007. (ENG.). 64p. (J). (gr. -1-1). 14.95 (978-1-55725-535-8(0)) Paraclete Pr., Inc.
Riggs, Kate. Fairy Godmothers. 2013. (Illus.). 24p. (J). 25.65 (978-1-60818-241-1(X), Creative Education) Creative Co., The.
Rock, Lois. A Gift for Baby's Christening. Rescek, Sanja, illus. 2014. (ENG.). 48p. (J). (— 1). 9.99 (978-0-7459-6490-4(7)) Lion Hudson PLC GBR. Dist: Independent Pubs. Group.
Setzer, Lee Ann. I Am Ready for Baptism. 2006. 30p. (J). pap. 4.99 (978-1-55517-944-1(4)) Cedar Fort, Inc./CFI Distribution.
Spear, Kevin. What's a Bathtub Doing in My Church? Fifteen Questions Kids Ask about Baptism, Salvation & Snorkels. Spear, Kevin, illus. 2006. (ENG., Illus.). 32p. (J). per. 5.99 (978-1-59317-155-1(2)) Warner Pr., Inc.
Staker, Sara. My Baptism Keepsake. 2009. (Illus.). (J). (978-1-59811-837-7(4)) Covenant Communications, Inc.
Stanton, Sue. Child's Guide to Baptism. Blake, Anne Catharine, illus. 2006. (Child's Guide Ser.). 32p. (J). (gr. 3-7). 9.95 (978-0-8091-6728-9(X), 6728-x) Paulist Pr.
Steenwyk, Carrie & Witvliet, John D. At Your Baptism. 2011. (ENG.). 10p. (YA). (gr. -1). 8.00 (978-0-8028-5381-3(1), Eerdmans Bks For Young Readers) Eerdmans, William B. Publishing Co.
Stiegemeyer, Julie. Things I See at Baptism. Mitter, Kathryn, illus. 2007. 20p. (J). (gr. -1-3). bds. 5.49 (978-0-7586-1246-5(X)) Concordia Publishing Hse.
Todd, Richard E. Baptism: A Bible Study Wordbook for Kids. 2009. (Children's Wordbooks Ser.). (ENG., Illus.). 32p. (gr. 4-7). pap. 5.99 (978-1-60066-194-5(7)) WingSpread Publishers.
Walker, Joni. Holy Baptism. Walker, Joni, illus. 2005. (Follow & Do Ser.). (Illus.). 32p. (J). 7.49 (978-0-7586-0800-0(4)) Concordia Publishing Hse.
Wittenback, Janet. God Makes Me His Child in Baptism. McDonnell, Janet, illus. rev. ed. 2007. 32p. (J). (gr. -1-k). pap. 6.49 (978-0-7586-1305-9(9)) Concordia Publishing Hse.
Wood Lake Books Staff & Novalis Staff. Your Child's Baptism: Roman Catholic. Date not set. 16p. (Orig.). (J). pap. 2.50 (978-2-89088-669-8(7)) Logos Productions, Inc.

BAPTISTS

see also Mennonites

Bader, Bonnie. Who Was Martin Luther King, Jr. ? Wolf, Elizabeth & Harrison, Nancy, illus. 2007. (Who Was? Ser.). (ENG.). 112p. (J). (gr. 3-7). pap. 5.99 (978-0-448-44723-0(1), Grosset & Dunlap) Penguin Young Readers Group.
—Who Was Martin Luther King, Jr. ? Wolf, Elizabeth, illus. 2008. (Who Was... ? Ser.). 105p. (J). (gr. 2-5). 12.65 (978-0-7569-8935-4(3)) Perfection Learning Corp.
Bailey, Gerry & Foster, Karen. Martin Luther King Jr.'s Microphone. Radford, Karen & Noyes, Leighton, illus. 2008. (Stories of Great People Ser.). (ENG.). 40p. (J). (gr. 3-8). pap. (978-0-7787-3711-7(X)); lib. bdg. (978-0-7787-3689-9(X)) Crabtree Publishing Co.
Bolden, Tonya. M. L. K. The Journey of a King. Adelman, Bob, ed. 2007. (ENG., Illus.). 128p. (J). (gr. 5-9). 27.95 (978-0-8109-5476-2(1), Abrams Bks. for Young Readers) Abrams, Inc.
Boyd, Herb. Martin Luther King, Jr. Marcos, Pablo, illus. 2005. (Heroes of America Ser.). 239p. (gr. 3-8). 27.07 (978-1-59679-258-6(2), Abdo & Daughters) ABDO Publishing Co.
Brown, Jonatha A. Martin Luther King, Jr. 2005. (People We Should Know Ser.). (Illus.). 24p. (gr. 1-4). pap. 8.15 (978-0-8368-4474-0(2)); (ENG & SPA., lib. bdg. 22.00 (978-0-8368-4583-9(8)); lib. bdg. 22.00 (978-0-8368-4467-2(X)) Stevens, Gareth Publishing LLLP. (Weekly Reader Leveled Readers).
Bull, Angela. The Story of Martin Luther King, Level 4. 2009. (DK Readers Ser.). (ENG.). 48p. (J). (gr. 3-7). 3.99 (978-0-7566-5615-7(X), DK Children) Dorling Kindersley Publishing, Inc.
Carson, Mary Kay. What Was Your Dream, Dr. King? And Other Questions About... Martin Luther King, Jr. Madsen, Jim, illus. 2013. (Good Question! Ser.). (ENG.). 32p. (J). (gr. 2). pap. 5.95 (978-1-4027-9045-4(7)) Sterling Publishing Co., Inc.
Colbert, David. Martin Luther King Jr. 2008. (10 Days Ser.). (ENG.). 160p. (J). (gr. 3-8). pap. 7.99 (978-1-4169-6805-4(9), Aladdin) Simon & Schuster Children's Publishing.
DeRubertis, Barbara. Let's Celebrate Martin Luther King, Jr. Day. Griffith, Gershom, illus. 2013. (Holidays & Heroes Ser.). 32p. (gr. 1-3). pap. 7.95 (978-1-57565-638-0(8)) Kane Press, Inc.
Dunn, Joeming W. Martin Luther King, Jr, 1 vol. Allen, Chris, illus. 2008. (Bio-Graphics Ser.). (ENG.). 32p. 28.50 (978-1-60270-175-5(X), Graphic Planet- Nonfiction) ABDO Publishing Co.
Fandel, Jennifer. Martin Luther King, Jr. 2005. (Genius Ser.). (Illus.). 48p. (J). (gr. 5-9). lib. bdg. 21.95 (978-1-58341-329-6(4), Creative Education) Creative Co., The.
—Martin Luther King, Jr: Great Civil Rights Leader, 1 vol. Bascle, Brian, illus. 2006. (Graphic Biographies Ser.). (ENG.). 32p. (gr. 3-4). 30.65 (978-0-7368-6498-5(9), Graphic Library) Capstone Press of Coughlan Cos.
Feinstein, Stephen. Lee sobre Martin Luther King, Jr. 2006. (I Like Biographies! Bilingual Ser.).Tr. of Read about Martin Luther King, Jr. (ENG & SPA., Illus.). 24p. (J). (gr. 1-3). lib. bdg. 22.60 (978-0-7660-2745-9(7), Enslow Elementary) Enslow Pubs., Inc.
—Read about Martin Luther King, Jr. 2004. (I Like Biographies! Ser.). (Illus.). 24p. (J). lib. bdg. 24.95 (978-0-7660-2300-0(1)) Enslow Pubs., Inc.
Fine, Edith Hope. Martin Luther King, Jr: Champion of Civil Rights. 2006. (Heroes of American History Ser.). (Illus.). 32p. (J). (gr. 3-7). lib. bdg. 23.94 (978-0-7660-2466-3(0), Enslow Elementary) Enslow Pubs., Inc.
Fleming, Alice. Martin Luther King, Jr. A Dream of Hope. 2008. (Sterling Biographies(r) Ser.). (ENG., Illus.). 128p. (J). (gr. 5). pap. 5.95 (978-1-4027-4439-6(0)) Sterling Publishing Co., Inc.
Flowers, Arthur. I See the Promised Land: A Life of Martin Luther King, Jr., 1 vol. Chitrakar, Manu, illus. rev. ed. 2013. (ENG.). 156p. (J). (gr. 6). 16.95 (978-1-55498-328-5(2)) Groundwood Bks. CAN. Dist: Publishers Group West (PGW).
Flynn, Riley. Martin Luther King Jr, 1 vol. 2014. (Great African-Americans Ser.). (ENG.). 24p. (gr. k-1). lib. bdg. 21.99 (978-1-4765-3953-9(7), Pebble Bks.) Capstone Press of Coughlan Cos.
Gosman, Gillian. Martin Luther King, Jr. 2011. (Life Stories Ser.). (Illus.). 24p. (J). pap. 8.25 (978-1-4488-2755-8(8), PowerKids Pr.); (gr. 1-4). lib. bdg. 22.60 (978-1-4488-2583-7(0), PowerKids Pr.); (ENG & SPA., (gr. 1-4). lib. bdg. 22.60 (978-1-4488-3217-0(9)) Rosen Publishing Group, Inc., The.
Gotsch, Patrice. Martin Luther King, Jr: Changing Lives. Arreola, Gil, illus. 2006. 19p. pap. 6.30 (978-1-55501-779-8(7)) Ballard & Tighe Pubs.
Gregory, Josh. Martin Luther King Jr. 2015. (ENG., Illus.). 48p. (J). pap. 6.95 (978-0-531-21208-0(4), Orchard Bks.) Scholastic Library Publishing.
Hall, M. C. Martin Luther King, Jr. Civil Rights Leader, 1 vol. Soud, illus. 2008. (Beginner Biographies Ser.). (ENG.). 32p. (gr. -1-3). 28.50 (978-1-60270-251-6(9), Looking Glass Library- Nonfiction) Magic Wagon.
Hinton, KaaVonia. Martin Luther King, Jr. 2008. (What's So Great About... ? Ser.). (Illus.). 32p. (YA). (gr. 2-4). lib. bdg. 25.70 (978-1-58415-724-3(0)) Mitchell Lane Pubs., Inc.
Jakoubek, Robert E. Martin Luther King, Jr. Civil Rights Leader. 2004. (Black Americans of Achievement Ser.). (Illus.). 112p. (gr. 6-12). 35.00 (978-0-7910-8161-7(3), Chelsea Hse.) Facts On File, Inc.
Jeffrey, Gary. Martin Luther King Jr: The Life of a Civil Rights Leader. 2009. (Graphic Nonfiction Biographies Ser.). (ENG.). 48p. (YA). (gr. 4-5). 58.50 (978-1-61513-021-4(7), Rosen Reference) Rosen Publishing Group, Inc., The.
—Martin Luther King Jr: The Life of a Civil Rights Leader. Forsey, Chris, illus. 2007. (Graphic Nonfiction Biographies Ser.). (ENG.). 48p. (YA). (gr. 4-7). lib. bdg. 31.95 (978-1-4042-0858-2(5)) Rosen Publishing Group, Inc., The.
—Martin Luther King Jr: The Life of a Civil Rights Leader. Forsey, Christopher, illus. 2007. (Graphic Biographies Ser.). (ENG.). 48p. (gr. 5-8). pap. 14.05 (978-1-4042-0921-3(2)) Rosen Publishing Group, Inc., The.
Jones, Rob Lloyd. Martin Luther King, Jr. 2006. (Illus.). 62p. (J). pap. (978-0-439-02299-6(1)) Scholastic, Inc.
Linde, Barbara M. Martin Luther King Jr. 2011. (Civil Rights Crusaders Ser.). (Illus.). 24p. (gr. 2-5). (J). pap. 8.15 (978-1-4339-5692-8(6), Gareth Stevens Learning Library); (YA). lib. bdg. 22.60 (978-1-4339-5690-4(X)) Stevens, Gareth Publishing LLLP.
Linney, Susan. Martin Luther King, Jr: With a Discussion of Responsibility. 2004. (Values in Action Ser.). (J). (978-1-59203-069-9(6)) Learning Challenge, Inc.
Long, Julie Whidden. Portraits of Courage: Stories of Baptist Heroes. 2008. (Illus.). 128p. (J). pap. 16.00 (978-0-88146-109-1(1)) Mercer Univ. Pr.
MacMillan, Dianne M. Martin Luther King, Jr. Day. rev. ed. 2008. (Best Holiday Bks.). (Illus.). 48p. (J). (gr. 3-7). lib. bdg. 25.27 (978-0-7660-3043-5(1)) Enslow Pubs., Inc.
Manheimer, Ann S. Martin Luther King Jr: Dreaming of Equality. 2004. (Trailblazer Biographies Ser.). (ENG., Illus.). 112p. (gr. 5-9). 31.93 (978-1-57505-627-2(5), Carolrhoda Bks.) Lerner Publishing Group.
Mara, Wil. Martin Luther King Jr. 2013. (Rookie Biographies(r) Ser.). (ENG.). 32p. (J). pap. 5.95 (978-0-531-24704-4(X)); lib. bdg. 23.00 (978-0-531-24738-9(4)) Scholastic Library Publishing.
Marsh, Carole. Roger Williams. 2003. 12p. (gr. k-4). 2.95 (978-0-635-02361-2(X)) Gallopade International.
Mis, Melody S. Meet Martin Luther King Jr. 2009. (Civil Rights Leaders Ser.). 24p. (gr. 2-3). 42.50 (978-1-61511-854-0(3), PowerKids Pr.) Rosen Publishing Group, Inc., The.
—Meet Martin Luther King Jr. 2008. (Civil Rights Leaders Ser.). (Illus.). 24p. (YA). (gr. 2-5). lib. bdg. 22.60 (978-1-4042-4209-8(0)) Rosen Publishing Group, Inc., The.
Moore, Johnny Ray. The Story of Martin Luther King Jr. Wummer, Amy, illus. 2016. (J). (978-0-8249-1974-0(2), Ideal Pubns.) Worthy Publishing.
Murcia, Rebecca Thatcher. The Civil Rights Movement. 2005. (Monumental Milestones Ser.). (Illus.). 48p. (YA). (gr. 4-7). lib. bdg. 29.95 (978-1-58415-401-3(2)) Mitchell Lane Pubs., Inc.
Myers, Walter Dean. I've Seen the Promised Land: The Life of Dr. Martin Luther King, Jr. Jenkins, Leonard, illus. 2012. (ENG.). 40p. (J). (gr. -1-3). pap. 6.99 (978-0-06-225002-5(7), Amistad) HarperCollins Pubs.
Nichols, Kaitlyn. Martin Luther King. 2009. pap. 13.25 (978-1-60559-065-3(7)) Hameray Publishing Group, Inc.
Ponto, Joanna & Gnojewski, Carol. Martin Luther King Jr. Day. 2016. (Story of Our Holidays Ser.). (Illus.). 32p. (J). pap. 10.52 (978-0-7660-8340-0(3)) Enslow Pubs., Inc.
Rivera, Sheila. Martin Luther King Jr: A Life of Determination. 2006. (Pull Ahead Bks.). (Illus.). 32p. (J). (gr. 3-7). lib. bdg. 22.60 (978-0-8225-3477-8(0), Lerner Pubns.) Lerner Publishing Group.
Schraff, Anne E. Martin Luther King, Jr: We Shall Overcome. 2005. (African-American Biography Library). (Illus.). 128p. (J). (gr. 6-13). lib. bdg. 33.27 (978-0-7660-1774-0(5)) Enslow Pubs., Inc.
Schuldt, Lori Meek. Martin Luther King, Jr: With Profiles of Mohandas K. Gandhi & Nelson Mandela. 2006. (Biographical Connections Ser.). (Illus.). 112p. (J). (978-0-7166-1822-5(2)) World Bk., Inc.
Schuman, Michael A. The Life of Martin Luther King, Jr: Leader for Civil Rights. 2014. (Legendary African Americans Ser.). (Illus.). 96p. (J). (gr. 6-12). 27.94 (978-0-7660-6147-7(7)) Enslow Pubs., Inc.
Schuman, Michael A. & Schraff, Anne E. Martin Luther King Jr: Fighting for Civil Rights. 2017. (Rebels with a Cause Ser.). 128p. (gr. 8-8). lib. bdg. 37.27 **(978-0-7660-8511-4(2))** Enslow Pubs., Inc.
Seiling, Rebecca. Plant a Seed of Peace. Rothshank, Brooke, illus. 2007. 115p. (J). (gr. 3-7). per. 15.99 (978-0-8361-9397-8(0)) Faith & Life Pr.
Staley, Erin. Martin Luther King Jr. & the Speech That Inspired the World. 2014. (Celebration of the Civil Rights Movement Ser.). 80p. (YA). (gr. 7-12). 34.25 (978-1-4777-7745-9(8)) Rosen Publishing Group, Inc., The.
Vogel, Cara Lynn. The Lottie & Annie Upside-down Book. Adkins, Loretta B., illus. 2003. 16p. (J). 8.99 (978-1-56309-627-3(7)) Woman's Missionary Union.
Ward, Jill. Martin Luther King, Jr: Georgia, My State Biographies. I.t. ed. 2008. (ENG., Illus.). 24p. (J). (gr. k-2). 22.60 (978-1-935077-01-5(5)); pap. 22.60 (978-1-935077-08-4(2)) State Standards Publishing, LLC.
Watkins, Angela Farris. My Uncle Martin's Big Heart. Velasquez, Eric, illus. 2010. (ENG.). 32p. (J). (gr. k-2). 19.95 (978-0-8109-8975-7(1), Abrams Bks. for Young Readers) Abrams, Inc.
Weakland, Mark. When Martin Luther King Jr. Wore Roller Skates. Ballesteros, Patrick, illus. 2017. 31p. (J). (978-1-5158-0141-2(1)) 2016. (ENG.). 32p. (gr. 2-3). lib. bdg. 27.99 (978-1-4795-9685-0(X)) Picture Window Bks.
Weaver, Lisa & Weaver, J. Denny. Living the Anabaptist Story: A Guide to Early Beginnings with Questions for Today. 2015. (ENG., Illus.). 112p. (J). (gr. 7-12). pap. 19.95 (978-1-68027-004-4(4)) Cascadia Publishing Hse., LLC.
Weston Woods Staff, creator. Martin's Big Words. 2011. 18.95 (978-0-545-15251-8(8)); 38.75 (978-0-545-15256-3(9)) Weston Woods Studios, Inc.
Winget, Mary. Martin Luther King, Jr. 2004. (History Maker Bios Ser.). (Illus.). 48p. (J). pap. 8.95 (978-0-8225-4804-1(6), Lerner Pubns.) Lerner Publishing Group.

BAR

see Lawyers

BARBADOS

Elias, Marie Louise & Elias, Josie. Barbados. 2nd rev. ed. 2009. (Cultures of the World 19 Ser.). 144p. (gr. 6). 42.79 (978-0-7614-4853-2(5)) Marshall Cavendish GBR. Dist: Marshall Cavendish Corp.
Johnson, Robin. Rihanna. 2013. (ENG., Illus.). 32p. (J). (978-0-7787-1051-6(3)); pap. (978-0-7787-1055-4(6)) Crabtree Publishing Co.
Orr, Tamra. Barbados. 2010. (Caribbean Today Ser.). (Illus.). 64p. (YA). (gr. 9-12). 21.95 (978-1-4222-0621-8(1)) Mason Crest.
—Barbados, Vol. 11. Henderson, James D., ed. 2015. (Discovering the Caribbean: History, Politics, & Culture Ser.). (Illus.). 64p. (J). (gr. 7). lib. bdg. 22.95 (978-1-4222-3308-5(1)) Mason Crest.
Saddleback Educational Publishing Staff. Rihanna. 2013. (Hip-Hop Biographies (Saddleback Publishing) Ser.). (YA). lib. bdg. 23.25 (978-0-606-31489-3(X), Turtleback) Turtleback Bks.

BARBADOS—FICTION

Henry, Beresford. The Gaulin & the Dove. 2008. 128p. (J). pap. (978-0-435-89938-7(4)) Pearson Education, Ltd.
Literature Connections English: The Witch of Blackbird Pond. 2004. (gr. 6-12). (978-0-395-78592-8(8), 2-70293) Holt McDougal.
Matthews, Annette. Mischievous Molly. 2006. (Illus.). x, 48p. pap. 13.00 (978-1-4120-9693-5(6)) Trafford Publishing.

BARBARY CORSAIRS

see Pirates

BARBARY STATES

see Africa, North

BARBECUE COOKING

see Outdoor Cooking

BARBIE (FICTITIOUS CHARACTER)—FICTION

Barbie. Barbie Dreamhouse Party/ Una Fiesta de Ensueno: An English/Spanish Flap Book. 2013. (Lift-The Flap Ser.: 1). (ENG & SPA.). 10p. (J). (gr. -1-k). bds. 9.99 (978-0-7944-2874-7(6)) Reader's Digest Assn., Inc., The.
—Barbie Fall Movie Sliding Tab. 2015. (Barbie Movie Tie-In Ser.: 1). (ENG.). 12p. (J). (gr. -1-1). bds. 10.99 (978-0-7944-3529-5(7)) Studio Fun International.
—Barbie Find Your Talent: Book with Microphone. 2013. (Book with Microphone Ser.: 1). (ENG.). 32p. (J). (gr. -1-1). 17.99 (978-0-7944-2914-0(9), Reader's Digest Children's Bks.) Studio Fun International.
—Barbie in Rock 'N Royals. 2015. (Book & Jewelry Ser.: 1). (ENG.). 10p. (J). (gr. -1-1). bds. 9.99 (978-0-7944-3556-1(4), Reader's Digest Children's Bks.) Studio Fun International.
Barbie: a Special Christmas. 2014. (ENG.). 16p. (J). (gr. -1-1). bds. 8.99 (978-0-7944-3231-7(X), Reader's Digest Children's Bks.) Studio Fun International.
Barbie As Rapunzel, Vol. 1. 7.99 (978-1-59532-717-8(7)) TOKYOPOP, Inc.
Barbie First Play a Sound Barb. pap. 7.98 (978-0-7853-3332-6(0)) Publications International, Ltd.
Barbie Loves Lacey/Adora a Lacey. 2014.Tr. of English/Spanish Book. (SPA., Illus.). 10p. (J). (gr. -1-k). bds. 8.99 (978-0-7944-3208-9(5)) Studio Fun International.
Barbie Music Player Storybook. 2014. (Music Player Storybook Ser.). (ENG.). 32p. (J). (gr. -1-1). 19.99 (978-0-7944-3075-7(9)) Studio Fun International.
Barbie of Swan Lake. 10p. 9.98 (978-0-7853-9372-6(2)) Publications International, Ltd.
Barbie Staff. Barbie Mariposa & the Fairy Princess. 2013. (Panorama Sticker Storybook Ser.: 1). (ENG.). 20p. (J). (gr. -1-1). pap. 7.99 (978-0-7944-2837-2(1)) Reader's Digest Assn., Inc., The.
—Barbie Mariposa & the Fairy Princess Storybook. 2013. (Storybook with Jewelry Ser.: 1). (ENG.). 24p. (J). (gr. -1-3). 11.99 (978-0-7944-2838-9(X)) Reader's Digest Assn., Inc., The.
Depken, Kristen L. Dream Closet. 2013. (Barbie Step into Reading Level 3 Ser.). lib. bdg. 13.55 (978-0-606-32194-5(2), Turtleback) Turtleback Bks.
—I Can Be a Baby Doctor. 2013. (Barbie Step into Reading Level 2 Ser.). lib. bdg. 13.55 (978-0-606-26968-1(1), Turtleback) Turtleback Bks.
—I Can Be... a Baby Doctor (Barbie) Das Grup, illus. 2013. (Step into Reading Ser.). (ENG.). 32p. (J). (gr. -1-1). pap. 3.99 (978-0-307-98112-7(6), Random Hse. Bks. for Young Readers) Random Hse. Children's Bks.
—I Can Be a Gymnast (Barbie) 2014. (Step into Reading Ser.). (ENG., Illus.). 32p. (J). (gr. -1-1). lib. bdg. 12.99 (978-0-375-97347-5(8), Random Hse. Bks. for Young Readers) Random Hse. Children's Bks.
—Little Lost Dolphin. 2014. (Barbie Step into Reading Level 2 Ser.). lib. bdg. 13.55 (978-0-606-35191-1(4)) Turtleback Bks.
Depken, Kristen L. & Tillworth, Mary. The Dream-Tastic Story Collection (Barbie) 2015. (Step into Reading Ser.). (ENG., Illus.). 160p. (J). (gr. k-3). pap. 7.99 (978-0-553-52337-9(6), Random Hse. Bks. for Young Readers) Random Hse. Children's Bks.
Eberly, Chelsea. Surf Princess. Random House Staff, illus. 2012. (Step into Reading Ser.). (ENG.). 32p. (J). (gr. -1-1). pap. 3.99 (978-0-307-93004-0(1), Random Hse. Bks. for Young Readers) Random Hse. Children's Bks.
—Surf Princess. 2012. (Barbie Step into Reading Level 2 Ser.). lib. bdg. 13.55 (978-0-606-23718-5(6), Turtleback) Turtleback Bks.
Fontes, Justine. Barbie in the Pink Shoes. 2013. (Book & Jewelry Ser.: 1). (ENG.). 24p. (J). (gr. -1-3). 10.99 (978-0-7944-2785-6(5)) Reader's Digest Assn., Inc., The.
Frazer, Rebecca. Barbie Loves Pets. An, Jiyoung, illus. 2007. (Pictureback(R) Ser.). (ENG.). 16p. (J). (gr. -1-2). pap. 3.99 (978-0-375-84797-4(9), Golden Bks.) Random Hse. Children's Bks.
—An Egg-Cellent Easter! (Barbie) Riley, Kellee, illus. 2012. (Pictureback(R) Ser.). (ENG.). 16p. (J). (gr. -1-2). pap. 3.99 (978-0-307-93025-5(4), Random Hse. Bks. for Young Readers) Random Hse. Children's Bks.
Giddy Up Staff, contrib. by. Barbie Surprize Ink Book 2. 2009. 6.99 (978-1-932125-27-6(2)) Giddy Up, LLC.
Golden Books. Barbie Dreamtopia Deluxe Paintbox Book (Barbie Dreamtopia) 2017. (Paint Box Book Ser.). (ENG.). 128p. (J). (gr. -1-2). pap. 7.99 (978-1-5247-1439-0(9), Golden Bks.) Random Hse. Children's Bks.
—Barbie Fall 2016 Holiday Movie Hologramatic Sticker Book (Barbie) 2016. (Hologramatic Sticker Book Ser.). (ENG.). 64p. (J). (gr. -1-2). pap. 4.99 (978-0-399-54957-1(9), Golden Bks.) Random Hse. Children's Bks.
—Barbie: My Book of Bunnies (Barbie) 2017. (Little Golden Book Ser.). (ENG., Illus.). 24p. (J). (-k). 4.99 (978-0-399-55695-1(8), Golden Bks.) Random Hse. Children's Bks.
—Barbie: My Book of Ponies (Barbie) 2016. (Little Golden Book Ser.). (ENG., Illus.). 24p. (J). (-k). 4.99 (978-0-399-54960-1(9), Golden Bks.) Random Hse. Children's Bks.
—Barbie: My Book of Puppies (Barbie) 2017. (Little Golden Book Ser.). (ENG., Illus.). 24p. (J). (-k). 4.99 **(978-1-5247-1508-3(5)**, Golden Bks.) Random Hse. Children's Bks.
—My Book of Kittens. 2016. (Little Golden Book Ser.). (ENG., Illus.). 24p. (J). (gr. -1-k). 4.99 (978-0-553-53919-6(1), Golden Bks.) Random Hse. Children's Bks.
—Show Your Style (Barbie) Amati, Susanna, illus. 2017. (ENG.). 24p. (J). (gr. -1-2). pap. 9.99 **(978-1-5247-1644-8(8)**, Golden Bks.) Random Hse. Children's Bks.
—Twinkle & Twirl. 2016. (Deluxe Paint Box Book Ser.). (ENG.). 128p. (J). (gr. -1-2). pap. 7.99 (978-1-101-93752-5(1), Golden Bks.) Random Hse. Children's Bks.
—The World of Barbie. Golden Books, illus. 50th anniv. ed. 2012. (Little Golden Book Ser.). (ENG., Illus.). 24p. (J). (gr. -1-2). 4.99 (978-0-307-98090-8(1), Golden Bks.) Random Hse. Children's Bks.
Golden Books, illus. Barbie 9 Favorite Fairy Tales (Barbie) 2013. (Little Golden Book Treasury Ser.). (ENG.). 224p. (J). (-k). 10.99 (978-0-449-81861-9(6), Golden Bks.) Random Hse. Children's Bks.
Golden Books Staff. Barbie & the Three Musketeers. 2009. (Little Golden Book Ser.). (ENG., Illus.). 24p. (J). (gr. -1-2). 3.99 (978-0-375-85448-4(7), Golden Bks.) Random Hse. Children's Bks.
—Barbie & the Three Musketeers. Golden Books Staff, illus. 2009. (Pictureback(R) Ser.). (ENG., Illus.). 16p. (J). (gr. -1-2). pap. 3.99 (978-0-375-85446-0(0), Golden Bks.) Random Hse. Children's Bks.
—Barbie Loves Ballet/Fashion Show Fun!, 2 bks. in 1. Golden Books Staff, illus. 2009. (Pictureback(R) Ser.). (ENG., Illus.). 32p. (J). (gr. -1-2). pap. 4.99 (978-0-375-85148-3(8), Golden Bks.) Random Hse. Children's Bks.
—Beautiful Barbie. Golden Books Staff, illus. 2009. (Super Stickerific Ser.). (ENG., Illus.). 64p. (J). (gr. -1-2). pap. 12.99 (978-0-375-85553-5(X), Golden Bks.) Random Hse. Children's Bks.
—Princess Stories: A Collection to Color. 2007. (Jumbo Coloring Book Ser.). (ENG., Illus.). 224p. (J). (gr. -1-2). 4.99 (978-0-375-83971-9(2), Golden Bks.) Random Hse. Children's Bks.
Golden Books Staff & Man-Kong, Mary. Barbie Bedtime Story Collection (Barbie) 2014. (ENG., Illus.). 320p. (J). (gr. -1-2). 15.99 (978-0-385-38784-2(9), Random Hse. Bks. for Young Readers) Random Hse. Children's Bks.
Golden Books Staff & Tillworth, Mary. Barbie Spy Squad. 2016. (Big Golden Book Ser.). (ENG., Illus.). 48p. (J). (gr. -1-2). 9.99 (978-0-553-53917-2(5), Golden Bks.) Random Hse. Children's Bks.
Gordh, Bill & Pugliano-Martin, Carol. Barbie. Wolcott, Karen, illus. 2006. (Step into Reading Ser.). (ENG.). 192p. (J). (gr. -1-1). pap. 8.99 (978-0-375-84124-8(5), Random Hse. Bks. for Young Readers) Random Hse. Children's Bks.
Hamilton, Tisha, adapted by. Barbie Fairytopia: A Junior Novelization. 2005. (Illus.). 74p. (J). pap. (978-0-439-74086-9(X)) Scholastic, Inc.
Jordan, Apple. I Can Be a Farm Vet. 2016. (Barbie Step into Reading Level 2 Ser.). lib. bdg. 14.75 (978-0-606-38473-5(1)) Turtleback Bks.
—I Can Be a Farm Vet (Barbie) Riley, Kellee, illus. 2016. (Step into Reading Ser.). (ENG.). 24p. (J). (gr. -1-1). 4.99 (978-1-101-93245-2(7), Random Hse. Bks. for Young Readers) Random Hse. Children's Bks.
—Star Song. 2016. (Step into Reading Ser.). (ENG., Illus.). 24p. (J). (gr. -1-1). 4.99 (978-1-101-93986-4(9), Random Hse. Bks. for Young Readers) Random Hse. Children's Bks.
Lagonegro, Melissa. Barbie in Princess Power - Saving the Day! 2015. (Step into Reading Ser.). (ENG., Illus.). 24p. (J). (gr. -1-1). 4.99 (978-0-553-50890-1(3), Random Hse. Bks. for Young Readers) Random Hse. Children's Bks.

Landolf, Diane Wright. Thumbelina. Random House Audio Publishing Group Staff, illus. 2009. (Step into Reading Ser.). (ENG.). 32p. (J). (gr. -1-1). pap. 3.99 *(978-0-375-85690-7(0),* Random Hse. Bks. for Young Readers) Random Hse. Children's Bks.

Lichtwardt, Rita, illus. Barbie - A Perfect Christmas. 2011. (Book & Jewelry Ser.). (ENG.). 24p. (J). (gr. -1-1). 10.99 *(978-0-7944-2319-3(1),* Reader's Digest Children's Bks.) Studio Fun International.

Lombardi, Kristine. Barbie What Shall I Be? Mattel, illus. 2010. (Vinyl Shaped Purse Ser.). (ENG.). 72p. (J). (gr. -1-k). bds. 14.99 *(978-0-7944-2034-5(6))* Reader's Digest Assn., Inc., The.

—It's a Surprise Playhouse Storybook. Mattel Inc. Staff, illus. 2010. (Storybook & Playset Ser.). (ENG.). 16p. (J). (gr. -1-2). bds. 15.99 *(978-0-7944-2005-5(2))* Reader's Digest Assn., Inc., The.

Man-Kong, Mary. Barbie: A Fairy Secret. Golden Books Staff, illus. 2011. (Little Golden Book Ser.). (ENG.). 24p. (J). (gr. -1-2). 3.99 *(978-0-375-86540-4(3),* Golden Bks.) Random Hse. Children's Bks.

—Barbie - Fashion Fairytale. Random House Value Publishing Staff, illus. 2010. (Step into Reading Ser.). (ENG.). 32p. (J). (gr. -1-1). pap. 3.99 *(978-0-375-86697-5(3),* Random Hse. Bks. for Young Readers) Random Hse. Children's Bks.

—Barbie -Fairy Secret. Random House Staff, illus. 2011. (Pictureback(R) Ser.). (ENG.). 16p. (J). (gr. -1-2). pap. 3.99 *(978-0-375-86555-8(1),* Random Hse. Bks. for Young Readers) Random Hse. Children's Bks.

—Barbie & the Diamond Castle. Rainmaker Entertainment Staff & Rainmaker Entertainment, illus. 2008. (Little Golden Book Ser.). (ENG.). 24p. (J). (gr. -1-2). 3.99 *(978-0-375-87508-3(5),* Golden Bks.) Random Hse. Children's Bks.

—Barbie & the Diamond Castle: A Storybook. Golden Books Staff, illus. 2008. (Pictureback(R) Ser.). (ENG.). 24p. (J). (gr. -1-2). pap. 3.99 *(978-0-375-87505-2(0),* Golden Bks.) Random Hse. Children's Bks.

—Barbie & the Three Musketeers. Random House Staff, illus. 2009. (Step into Reading Ser.). (ENG.). 32p. (J). (gr. -1-1). pap. 3.99 *(978-0-375-86007-2(X),* Random Hse. Bks. for Young Readers) Random Hse. Children's Bks.

—Barbie as the Island Princess. 2007. (Pictureback(R) Ser.). (ENG., Illus.). 24p. (J). (gr. -1-2). pap. 3.99 *(978-0-375-84218-4(7),* Random Hse. Bks. for Young Readers) Random Hse. Children's Bks.

—Barbie in a Christmas Carol. Random House Editors, illus. 2010. (Pictureback(R) Ser.). (ENG.). 24p. (J). (gr. -1-2). pap. 3.99 *(978-0-375-86482-7(2),* Random Hse. Bks. for Young Readers) Random Hse. Children's Bks.

—Barbie in a Mermaid Tale. Golden Books Staff, illus. 2010. (Little Golden Book Ser.). (ENG.). (J). (gr. -1-2). 24p. 4.99 *(978-0-375-85733-1(8),* Golden Bks.); 16p. pap. 3.99 *(978-0-375-85735-5(4),* Random Hse. Bks. for Young Readers) Random Hse. Children's Bks.

—Barbie Loves Horses (Barbie) Duarte, Pamela, illus. 2013. (Color Plus Stencil Ser.). (ENG.). 64p. (J). (gr. -1-2). pap. 5.99 *(978-0-449-81612-7(5),* Golden Bks.) Random Hse. Children's Bks.

—Barbie Spring 2016 Movie Pictureback. 2016. (Pictureback(R) Ser.). (ENG., Illus.). 16p. (J). (gr. -1-2). 4.99 *(978-0-553-53914-1(0),* Random Hse. Bks. for Young Readers) Random Hse. Children's Bks.

—A Boo-Tiful Halloween! Riley, Kellee, illus. 2013. (Pictureback(R) Ser.). (ENG.). 16p. (J). (gr. -1-2). 4.99 *(978-0-449-81860-2(8),* Random Hse. Bks. for Young Readers) Random Hse. Children's Bks.

—Code Racers. 2017. (Pictureback(R) Ser.). (ENG., Illus.). 24p. (J). (gr. -1-2). pap. 4.99 *(978-0-399-55932-7(9),* Random Hse. Bks. for Young Readers) Random Hse. Children's Bks.

—Dazzling Duet. 2015. (Deluxe Paint Box Book Ser.). (ENG.). 128p. (J). (gr. -1-2). pap. 7.99 *(978-0-553-52164-1(0),* Golden Bks.) Random Hse. Children's Bks.

—Fairy Dreams. Random House Staff, illus. 2013. (Step into Reading Ser.). (ENG.). 32p. (J). (gr. -1-1). 3.99 *(978-0-449-81628-8(1),* Random Hse. Bks. for Young Readers) Random Hse. Children's Bks.

—Feel the Music. 2015. (Color Plus Crayons & Sticker Ser.). (ENG.). 48p. (J). (gr. -1-2). pap. 4.99 *(978-0-553-53718-5(0),* Golden Bks.) Random Hse. Children's Bks.

—Friends, Fashion, & Fun! (Barbie) Golden Books Staff & Das Group Staff, illus. 2012. (Jumbo Coloring Book Ser.). (ENG.). 224p. (J). (gr. -1-2). pap. 5.99 *(978-0-375-87358-4(9),* Golden Bks.) Random Hse. Children's Bks.

—Get Your Glam On! (Barbie) 2015. (Super Jumbo Coloring Book Ser.). (ENG.). 416p. (J). (gr. -1-2). pap. 10.99 *(978-0-553-52165-8(9),* Golden Bks.) Random Hse. Children's Bks.

—Hair-Tastic! 2015. (Color Plus Hair Extension Ser.). (ENG.). 48p. (J). (gr. -1-2). pap. 5.99 *(978-0-553-50905-2(5),* Golden Bks.) Random Hse. Children's Bks.

—Holiday Style (Barbie) 2014. (Big Coloring Book Ser.). (ENG.). 48p. (J). (gr. -1-2). pap. 6.99 *(978-0-385-38339-4(8),* Golden Bks.) Random Hse. Children's Bks.

—I Can Be a Horse Rider. 2012. (Barbie Step into Reading Level 1 Ser.). lib. bdg. 13.55 *(978-0-606-23721-5(6),* Turtleback) Turtleback Bks.

—I Can Be a Horse Rider (Barbie) RH Disney Staff & An, Jiyoung, illus. 2012. (Step into Reading Ser.). (ENG.). 32p. (J). (gr. -1-1). pap. 3.99 *(978-0-375-97030-6(4),* Random Hse. Bks. for Young Readers) Random Hse. Children's Bks.

—I Can Be a Pet Vet. An, Jiyoung, illus. 2010. (Step into Reading Ser.). (ENG.). 32p. (J). (gr. -1-1). pap. 3.99 *(978-0-375-86581-7(0),* Random Hse. Bks. for Young Readers) Random Hse. Children's Bks.

—I Can Be a Rock Star. Golden Books Staff, illus. 2010. (Pictureback(R) Ser.). (ENG.). 16p. (J). (gr. -1-2). pap. 3.99 *(978-0-375-86545-9(4),* Golden Bks.) Random Hse. Children's Bks.

—I Can Be a Teacher (Barbie) Golden Books Staff & Riley, Kellee, illus. 2011. (Step into Reading Ser.). (ENG.). 32p. (J). (gr. -1-1). pap. 3.99 *(978-0-375-86927-3(1),* Random Hse. Bks. for Young Readers) Random Hse. Children's Bks.

—I Can Be... Anything I Want to Be. Golden Books Staff & An, Jiyoung, illus. 2011. (Paper Doll Book Ser.). (ENG.). 32p. (J). (gr. -1-2). pap. 5.49 *(978-0-375-87260-0(4),* Golden Bks.) Random Hse. Children's Bks.

—It's Sparkle Time! 2015. (Color Plus Crayons & Sticker Ser.). (ENG., Illus.). 48p. (J). (gr. -1-2). pap. 4.99 *(978-0-553-50744-7(3),* Golden Bks.) Random Hse. Children's Bks.

—Listen to Your Heart! 2015. (Pictureback(R) Ser.). (ENG., Illus.). 16p. (J). (gr. -1-2). 4.99 *(978-0-553-52341-6(4),* Random Hse. Bks. for Young Readers) Random Hse. Children's Bks.

—Magic of the Rainbow. 2007. (Pictureback(R) Ser.). (ENG., Illus.). 16p. (J). (gr. -1-2). pap. 3.99 *(978-0-375-83985-6(2),* Golden Bks.) Random Hse. Children's Bks.

—Magical Mermaid Adventure. 2014. (Pictureback(R) Ser.). (ENG., Illus.). 16p. (J). (gr. -1-2). 3.99 *(978-0-385-37308-1(2),* Random Hse. Bks. for Young Readers) Random Hse. Children's Bks.

—Mariposa. 2008. (Pictureback(R) Ser.). (ENG., Illus.). 16p. (J). (gr. -1-2). pap. 3.99 *(978-0-375-84798-1(7),* Golden Bks.) Random Hse. Children's Bks.

—My Fabulous Friends! Golden Books Staff, illus. 2009. (Pictureback(R) Ser.). (ENG.). 16p. (J). (gr. -1-2). pap. 3.99 *(978-0-375-85789-8(3),* Random Hse. Bks. for Young Readers) Random Hse. Children's Bks.

—My First Visit to the Doctor. Riley, Kellee, illus. 2017. (Pictureback(R) Ser.). (ENG.). 16p. (J). (gr. -1-2). pap. 4.99 *(978-0-399-55810-8(1),* Random Hse. Bks. for Young Readers) Random Hse. Children's Bks.

—Princess to the Rescue! 2015. (Pictureback(R) Ser.). (ENG., Illus.). 16p. (J). (gr. -1-2). 4.99 *(978-0-553-50737-9(0),* Random Hse. Bks. for Young Readers) Random Hse. Children's Bks.

—Sleepover Fun! 2014. (Pictureback(R) Ser.). (ENG., Illus.). 16p. (J). (gr. -1-2). 4.99 *(978-0-385-38478-0(5),* Random Hse. Bks. for Young Readers) Random Hse. Children's Bks.

—Snow Much Fun! (Barbie) 2015. (Pictureback(R) Ser.). (ENG., Illus.). 16p. (J). (gr. -1-2). 5.99 *(978-0-553-52338-6(4),* Random Hse. Bks. for Young Readers) Random Hse. Children's Bks.

—Spring into Style. Golden Books Staff, illus. 2011. (Color Plus Flocked Stickers Ser.). (ENG.). 64p. (J). (gr. -1-2). pap. 4.99 *(978-0-375-86813-9(5),* Golden Bks.) Random Hse. Children's Bks.

—Star Power. Random House Staff, illus. 2012. (Step into Reading Ser.). (ENG.). 32p. (J). (gr. -1-1). pap. 3.99 *(978-0-307-93196-2(X),* Random Hse. Bks. for Young Readers) Random Hse. Children's Bks.

—Star Power. 2012. (Barbie Step into Reading Level 2 Ser.). lib. bdg. 13.55 *(978-0-606-26550-8(3),* Turtleback) Turtleback Bks.

—The Sweetest Halloween (Barbie) Golden Books Staff & Duarte, Pamela, illus. 2012. (Glow-In-the-Dark Sticker Book Ser.). (ENG.). 48p. (J). (gr. -1-2). pap. 3.99 *(978-0-307-93115-3(3),* Golden Bks.) Random Hse. Children's Bks.

—Travel in Style (Barbie) 2015. (Color Plus Chunky Crayons Ser.). (ENG.). 48p. (J). (gr. -1-2). pap. 4.99 *(978-0-553-49941-4(6),* Golden Bks.) Random Hse. Children's Bks.

—Wedding Party! (Barbie) Riley, Kellee, illus. 2013. (Pictureback(R) Ser.). (ENG.). 16p. (J). (gr. -1-2). pap. 3.99 *(978-0-307-93116-0(1),* Random Hse. Bks. for Young Readers) Random Hse. Children's Bks.

Man-Kong, Mary & Inches, Alison. Pink Boots & Ponytails. Random House Staff, illus. 2013. (Pictureback(R) Ser.). (ENG.). 16p. (J). (gr. -1-2). 3.99 *(978-0-449-81637-0(0),* Random Hse. Bks. for Young Readers) Random Hse. Children's Bks.

Man-Kong, Mary & Random House. A Surprise for a Friend (Barbie) 2015. (Pictureback(R) Ser.). (ENG., Illus.). 16p. (J). (gr. -1-2). 4.99 *(978-0-553-50942-7(X),* Random Hse. Bks. for Young Readers) Random Hse. Children's Bks.

Man-Kong, Mary & Tillworth, Mary. A Perfect Christmas (Barbie) Golden Books Staff, illus. 2011. (Pictureback(R) Ser.). (ENG.). 16p. (J). (gr. -1-2). pap. 3.99 *(978-0-375-87363-8(5),* Random Hse. Bks. for Young Readers) Random Hse. Children's Bks.

—Princess Charm School (Barbie) Golden Books Staff, illus. 2011. (Little Golden Book Ser.). (ENG.). 24p. (J). (gr. -1-2). 3.99 *(978-0-375-87361-4(9),* Golden Bks.) Random Hse. Children's Bks.

Man-Kong, Mary, et al. I Can Be a Pastry Chef/I Can Be a Lifeguard (Barbie) RH Disney Staff & Random House Staff, illus. 2012. (Pictureback(R) Ser.). (ENG.). 32p. (J). (gr. -1-2). pap. 4.99 *(978-0-307-93114-6(5),* Random Hse. Bks. for Young Readers) Random Hse. Children's Bks.

Mattel Inc. Staff, illus. Barbie Always in Style. 2011. (Storybook & Playset Ser.). (ENG.). 24p. (J). (gr. -1-1). 19.99 *(978-0-7944-2316-2(7))* Reader's Digest Assn., Inc., The.

McGuire Woods, Molly. Barbie & Her Sisters in a Puppy Chase. 2016. (Barbie Chapters Ser.). (ENG., Illus.). 64p. (J). (gr. 1-4). 5.99 *(978-0-399-55136-9(0),* Random Hse. Bks. for Young Readers) Random Hse. Children's Bks.

—Barbie Fall 2014 DVD Junior Novelization (Barbie) 2014. (Junior Novel Ser.). (ENG., Illus.). 128p. (J). (gr. 3-7). 5.99 *(978-0-385-38627-2(3),* Random Hse. Bks. for Young Readers) Random Hse. Children's Bks.

—Barbie in Rock 'n Royals. 2015. (Barbie Chapters Ser.). (ENG.). 64p. (J). (gr. 1-4). 5.99 *(978-0-553-52435-2(6),* Random Hse. Bks. for Young Readers) Random Hse. Children's Bks.

—The Pearl Princess. 2014. (Junior Novel Ser.). (ENG.). 128p. (J). (gr. 3-7). 5.99 *(978-0-385-37517-7(4),* Random Hse. Bks. for Young Readers) Random Hse. Children's Bks.

Publications International Ltd. Staff. Barbie & the Magic of Pegasus. 2005. (Play-a-Sound Ser.). (Illus.). 10p. (J). (gr. -1-k). bds. 10.50 *(978-1-4127-3763-0(X),* 7269300) Publications International, Ltd.

—Little Sound Barbie Fairytopia. 2007. 12p. (J). 10.98 *(978-1-4127-6770-5(9),* PIL Kids) Publications International, Ltd.

Publications International Ltd. Staff, creator. Barbie as the Island Princess. 2007. (Play-A-Sound Bks.). (Illus.). 9.98 *(978-1-4127-7413-0(6))* Publications International, Ltd.

Random House. Barbie 5-Minute Stories: the Sister Collection (Barbie) 2016. (ENG., Illus.). 160p. (J). (gr. -1-2). 12.99 *(978-0-399-55209-0(X),* Random Hse. Bks. for Young Readers) Random Hse. Children's Bks.

—Barbie Dreamtopia Step into Reading (Barbie) 2017. (Step into Reading Ser.). (ENG.). 24p. (J). (gr. -1-1). lib. bdg. 12.99 ***(978-1-5247-1639-4(1));*** (Illus.). pap. 4.99 ***(978-1-5247-1638-7(3))*** Random Hse. Children's Bks. (Random Hse. Bks. for Young Readers).

—Barbie Star Light Adventure. 2016. (Barbie Chapters Ser.). (ENG., Illus.). 64p. (J). (gr. 1-4). 5.99 *(978-1-101-94020-4(4),* Random Hse. Bks. for Young Readers) Random Hse. Children's Bks.

—Barbie Summer 2016 Chapter Book (Barbie) 2016. (Barbie Chapters Ser.). (ENG., Illus.). 64p. (J). (gr. 1-4). lib. bdg. 12.99 *(978-1-101-94021-1(2),* Random Hse. Bks. for Young Readers) Random Hse. Children's Bks.

—Barbie Summer 2016 Movie Pictureback (Barbie) 2016. (Pictureback(R) Ser.). (ENG., Illus.). 24p. (J). (gr. -1-2). 4.99 *(978-1-101-93750-1(5),* Random Hse. Bks. for Young Readers) Random Hse. Children's Bks.

—Barbie You Can Be 5-Minute Stories (Barbie) 2017. (ENG., Illus.). 160p. (J). (gr. -1-2). 12.99 ***(978-1-5247-1505-2(0),*** Random Hse. Bks. for Young Readers) Random Hse. Children's Bks.

—Best Sisters Ever!(Barbie) 2016. (Pictureback(R) Ser.). (ENG., Illus.). 24p. (J). (gr. -1-2). pap. 6.99 *(978-1-101-93796-9(3),* Random Hse. Bks. for Young Readers) Random Hse. Children's Bks.

—Great Island Adventure. 2016. (Pictureback(R) Ser.). (ENG., Illus.). 24p. (J). (gr. -1-2). 4.99 *(978-0-399-55098-0(4),* Random Hse. Bks. for Young Readers) Random Hse. Children's Bks.

—Happy Howl-O-ween! (Barbie) 2016. (Pictureback(R) Ser.). (ENG., Illus.). 16p. (J). (gr. -1-2). 4.99 *(978-1-101-93748-8(3),* Random Hse. Bks. for Young Readers) Random Hse. Children's Bks.

—It's All about Me! 2017. (ENG.). 128p. (J). (gr. -1-2). 12.99 *(978-1-5247-1405-5(4),* Random Hse. Bks. for Young Readers) Random Hse. Children's Bks.

—Let's Pick Apples! (Barbie) Dynamo Limited, illus. 2017. (Step into Reading Ser.). (ENG.). 24p. (J). (gr. -1-1). pap. 4.99 ***(978-1-5247-6477-7(9));*** lib. bdg. 12.99 ***(978-1-5247-6478-4(7))*** Random Hse. Children's Bks. (Random Hse. Bks. for Young Readers).

—The Loose Tooth (Barbie) 2015. (Pictureback(R) Ser.). (ENG., Illus.). 16p. (J). (gr. -1-2). 4.99 *(978-0-553-51130-7(0),* Random Hse. Bks. for Young Readers) Random Hse. Children's Bks.

—My First Pet (Barbie) 2016. (Pictureback(R) Ser.). (ENG., Illus.). 16p. (J). (gr. -1-2). 4.99 *(978-1-101-93729-7(7),* Random Hse. Bks. for Young Readers) Random Hse. Children's Bks.

—Sisters on Safari (Barbie) Riley, Kellee, illus. 2014. (Pictureback Ser.). (ENG.). 16p. (J). (gr. -1-2). 4.99 *(978-0-385-37410-1(0),* Random Hse. Bks. for Young Readers) Random Hse. Children's Bks.

—Somebunny Loves You (Barbie) 2016. (Pictureback(R) Ser.). (ENG., Illus.). 16p. (J). (gr. -1-2). 4.99 *(978-1-101-93195-0(7),* Random Hse. Bks. for Young Readers) Random Hse. Children's Bks.

Random House & Man-Kong, Mary. Happy Birthday, Barbie! Riley, Kellee, illus. 2014. (Pictureback(R) Ser.). (ENG.). 24p. (J). (gr. -1-2). 5.99 *(978-0-385-37320-3(1),* Random Hse. Bks. for Young Readers) Random Hse. Children's Bks.

Random House Editors & Random House Staff. I Can Be a Movie Star. Random House Editors & Random House Staff, illus. 2010. (Pictureback Favorites Ser.). (ENG., Illus.). 80p. (J). (gr. -1-2). 7.99 *(978-0-375-86089-8(4),* Random Hse. Bks. for Young Readers) Random Hse. Children's Bks.

Random House Staff. I Can Be... A Zoo Vet/I Can Be... A Cheerleader. Riley, Kellee, illus. 2011. (Pictureback(R) Ser.). (ENG.). 32p. (J). (gr. -1-2). pap. 4.99 *(978-0-375-87265-5(5),* Random Hse. Bks. for Young Readers) Random Hse. Children's Bks.

Random House Staff, illus. Barbie Fairytale Collection. 2011. (Step into Reading Ser.). (ENG.). 160p. (J). (gr. -1-1). pap. 7.99 *(978-0-375-87255-6(8),* Random Hse. Bks. for Young Readers) Random Hse. Children's Bks.

—I Can Be... Story Collection (Barbie) 2013. (Step into Reading Ser.). (ENG.). 160p. (J). (gr. -1-2). 7.99 *(978-0-449-81666-0(4),* Random Hse. Bks. for Young Readers) Random Hse. Children's Bks.

Random House Staff & Depken, Kristen L. Dream Closet. 2013. (Step into Reading Ser.). (ENG., Illus.). 48p. (J). (gr. k-3). 3.99 *(978-0-385-37121-6(7),* Golden Bks.) Random Hse. Children's Bks.

Reader's Digest Editors & Rosenblum, Jill. Barbie Dreamhouse Party. 2012. (Lift-The-Flap Ser.). (ENG., Illus.). 10p. (J). (gr. -1-k). bds. 9.99 *(978-0-7944-2720-7(0))* Reader's Digest Assn., Inc., The.

Redbank, Tennant. The Beach Bandit. 2016. (Barbie Chapters Ser.). (ENG., Illus.). 64p. (J). (gr. 1-4). lib. bdg. 12.99 *(978-0-375-97413-7(X),* Random Hse. Bks. for Young Readers) Random Hse. Children's Bks.

—The Secret Sea Monster. 2016. (Barbie Chapters Ser.). (ENG., Illus.). 64p. (J). (gr. 1-4). 5.99 *(978-1-101-93844-7(7),* Random Hse. Bks. for Young Readers) Random Hse. Children's Bks.

RH Disney Staff & Random House Editors. Ballet Dreams. 2013. (Barbie Step into Reading Level 2 Ser.). lib. bdg. 13.55 *(978-0-606-31561-6(6),* Turtleback) Turtleback Bks.

Roberts, Angela. Barbie Loves Ballet. Wolcott, Karen, illus. Dias, Joe et al, photos by. 2010. (Barbie Ser.). (J). 14.10 *(978-0-7569-7778-8(9))* Perfection Learning Corp.

Saxon, Victoria. Message in a Bottle. 2016. (Barbie Chapters Ser.). (ENG., Illus.). 64p. (J). (gr. 1-4). 5.99 *(978-0-399-54962-5(5),* Random Hse. Bks. for Young Readers) Random Hse. Children's Bks.

Silk, Courtney. Barbie - From the Heart. Duarte, Pamela, illus. 2014. (Panorama Sticker Storybook Ser.: 1). (ENG.). 16p. (J). (gr. -1-1). 5.99 *(978-0-7944-3315-4(4))* Reader's Digest Assn., Inc., The.

Tillworth, Mary. Barbie in Princess Power. 2015. (Little Golden Book Ser.). (ENG., Illus.). 24p. (J). (-k). 4.99 *(978-0-553-50741-6(9),* Golden Bks.) Random Hse. Children's Bks.

—Barbie in the Pink Shoes. Golden Books, illus. 2013. (Little Golden Book Ser.). (ENG.). 24p. (J). (-k). 3.99 *(978-0-307-98108-0(8),* Golden Bks.) Random Hse. Children's Bks.

—Cupcake Challenge! (Barbie: Life in the Dreamhouse) 2015. (Step into Reading Ser.). (ENG., Illus.). 48p. (J). (gr. k-3). 3.99 *(978-0-553-50745-4(1),* Random Hse. Bks. for Young Readers) Random Hse. Children's Bks.

—Licensed to Drive. 2014. (Barbie Step into Reading Level 3 Ser.). lib. bdg. 13.55 *(978-0-606-35992-4(3))* Turtleback Bks.

—Mariposa & the Fairy Princess (Barbie) Golden Books, illus. 2013. (Little Golden Book Ser.). (ENG.). 24p. (J). (-k). 3.99 *(978-0-449-81633-2(8),* Golden Bks.) Random Hse. Children's Bks.

Turner, Patrenia. Barbie In The Queen Patrenialla Fairy - Tale. Turner, Keeng Troyius, ed. 2014. (Illus.). 31p. pap. *(978-0-578-14812-0(9))* Patrenialla Turner, Queen.

Ulkutay Design Group Staff & Random House Children's Books Staff, contrib. by. My Book of Kittens. 2016. (Illus.). (J). *(978-1-4806-9710-2(9),* Golden Bks.) Random Hse. Children's Bks.

Webster, Christy. Barbie: A Fairy Secret. Random House Staff, illus. 2011. (Step into Reading Ser.). (ENG.). 32p. (J). (gr. -1-1). pap. 3.99 *(978-0-375-86775-0(9),* Random Hse. Bks. for Young Readers) Random Hse. Children's Bks.

—Barbie in a Mermaid Tale. Random House Editors, illus. 2010. (Step into Reading Ser.). (ENG.). 32p. (J). (gr. -1-1). pap. 3.99 *(978-0-375-86450-6(4),* Random Hse. Bks. for Young Readers) Random Hse. Children's Bks.

—Barbie in a Mermaid Tale. 2010. (Barbie Step into Reading Level 2 Ser.). lib. bdg. 13.55 *(978-0-606-07031-7(1),* Turtleback) Turtleback Bks.

—I Can Be a Ballerina. Random House Staff & Riley, Kellee, illus. 2011. (Step into Reading Ser.). (ENG.). 32p. (J). (gr. -1-1). pap. 3.99 *(978-0-375-86839-9(9),* Random Hse. Bks. for Young Readers) Random Hse. Children's Bks.

—A Perfect Christmas. Random House Staff, illus. 2011. (Step into Reading Ser.). (ENG.). 32p. (J). (gr. -1-1). pap. 3.99 *(978-0-375-86932-7(8),* Random Hse. Bks. for Young Readers) Random Hse. Children's Bks.

Weinberg, Jennifer Liberts. Pretty Pearl Mermaid. 2014. (Step into Reading Ser.). (ENG., Illus.). 32p. (J). (gr. -1-1). 3.99 *(978-0-385-37307-4(4),* Random Hse. Bks. for Young Readers) Random Hse. Children's Bks.

Wooster, Devin Ann. Barbie & Her Sisters in the Great Puppy Adventure. 2015. (Barbie Chapters Ser.). (ENG.). 64p. (J). (gr. 1-4). pap. 5.99 *(978-0-553-53764-2(4),* Random Hse. Bks. for Young Readers) Random Hse. Children's Bks.

—Barbie Fall 2016 Holiday Movie Deluxe Step into Reading (Barbie) 2016. (Step into Reading Ser.). (ENG., Illus.). 24p. (J). (gr. -1-1). pap. 4.99 *(978-1-101-93995-6(8),* Random Hse. Bks. for Young Readers) Random Hse. Children's Bks.

BARCELONA (SPAIN)

Burlingame, Jeff. Soccer Star AndrS Iniesta. 2014. (Goal! Latin Stars of Soccer Ser.). 48p. 14.95 *(978-1-62285-225-3(7))* Enslow Pubs., Inc.

Cormand, Bernat. Barcelona, Tell Us about Gaudi. Kliczkowski, H., ed. Rifa, Fina, illus. 80p. *(978-84-89439-29-0(X))* A. Asppan, S.L. Distribuidora Internacional de Libros y Revistas.

—Barcelona, Tell Us about Yourself. (SPA., Illus.). 80p. *(978-84-96048-36-2(5))* A. Asppan, S.L. Distribuidora Internacional de Libros y Revistas.

Torres, John Albert. Soccer Star Lionel Messi. 2014. (Goal! Latin Stars of Soccer Ser.). 48p. 14.95 *(978-1-62285-221-5(4))* Enslow Pubs., Inc.

BARNAVELT, LEWIS (FICTITIOUS CHARACTER)—FICTION

Bellairs, John. The House with a Clock in Its Walls. Gorey, Edward, illus. 2004. (Lewis Barnavelt Ser.: Bk. 1). (ENG.). 192p. (J). (gr. 3-7). pap. 6.99 *(978-0-14-240257-3(5),* Puffin Books) Penguin Young Readers Group.

—The House with a Clock in Its Walls. (Lewis Barnavelt Ser.: Bk. 1). 179p. (J). (gr. 4-6). pap. 4.50 *(978-0-8072-1423-7(X),* Listening Library) Random Hse. Audio Publishing Group.

BARNEY (FICTITIOUS CHARACTER)—FICTION

Hinkler Books Staff, reader. Barney Says "Play Safely" 2004. 32p. (J). 9.99 incl. audio compact disk *(978-1-86515-998-0(0))* Hinkler Bks. Pty, Ltd. AUS. Dist: Penton Overseas, Inc.

—Barney's Big Balloon. 2004. 32p. (J). 9.99 incl. audio compact disk *(978-1-86515-997-3(2))* Hinkler Bks. Pty, Ltd. AUS. Dist: Penton Overseas, Inc.

—Barney's Outer Space Adventure. 2004. (J). 9.99 incl. audio compact disk *(978-1-86515-996-6(4))* Hinkler Bks. Pty, Ltd. AUS. Dist: Penton Overseas, Inc.

—Come on over Barneys House. 2004. 32p. (J). 9.99 incl. audio compact disk *(978-1-86515-999-7(9))* Hinkler Bks. Pty, Ltd. AUS. Dist: Penton Overseas, Inc.

Publications International Ltd. Staff, ed. Barney & Friends Book Box & Plush. 2011. 8p. (J). 14.98 *(978-1-4508-0854-5(9))* Publications International, Ltd.

BARNUM, P. T. (PHINEAS TAYLOR), 1810-1891

Fleming, Candace. The Great & Only Barnum: The Tremendous, Stupendous Life of Showman P. T. Barnum. Fenwick, Ray, illus. 2009. (ENG.). 160p. (J). (gr. 3-7). 19.99 *(978-0-375-84197-2(0),* Schwartz & Wade Bks.) Random Hse. Children's Bks.

Streissguth, Tom. P. T. Barnum: Every Crowd Has a Silver Lining. 2009. (Americans—the Spirit of a Nation Ser.). (Illus.). 128p. (J). (gr. 5). lib. bdg. 33.27 *(978-0-7660-3022-0(9))* Enslow Pubs., Inc.

BAROMETER

Hanson, Anders. Meteorologist's Tools, 1 vol. 2011. (Professional Tools Ser.). (ENG., Illus.). 24p. (J). (gr. 3-5). lib. bdg. 25.65 *(978-1-61613-580-5(8),* Super SandCastle) ABDO Publishing Co.

BARRISTERS

see Lawyers

BARROWS

see Mounds and Mound Builders

BARRY, JOHN, 1745-1803

Anderson, Floyd. Father of the American Navy: John Barry. Orban, Paul, illus. 2011. 188p. 42.95 *(978-1-258-07454-8(0))* Literary Licensing, LLC.

BARTHOLDI, FREDERIC AUGUSTE, 1834-1904

Curlee, Lynn. Liberty. Curlee, Lynn, illus. 2003. (ENG., Illus.). 48p. (J). (gr. 2-7). 9.99 *(978-0-689-85683-9(0)*, Atheneum Bks. for Young Readers) Simon & Schuster Children's Publishing.

Fandel, Jennifer. The Statue of Liberty. 2005. (What in the World? Ser.). (Illus.). 48p. (J). (gr. 5-9). lib. bdg. 21.95 *(978-1-58341-377-7(4)*, Creative Education) Creative Co., The.

Shea, Pegi Deitz. Liberty Rising: The Story of the Statue of Liberty. Zahares, Wade, illus. 2013. (ENG.). 44p. (J). (gr. k-4). 8.99 *(978-1-250-02720-7(9)*, 9781250027207) Square Fish.

BARTON, CLARA, 1821-1912

Benge, Janet & Benge, Geoff. Heroes of History - Clara Barton: Courage under Fire. 2003. (ENG.). 189p. (YA). pap. 9.99 *(978-1-883002-50-3(8))* Emerald Bks.

Connors, Kathleen. The Life of Clara Barton, Vol. 1. 2014. (Famous Lives Ser.). (ENG.). 24p. (J). (gr. 1-2). 22.60 *(978-1-4824-0375-6(7))* Stevens, Gareth Publishing LLLP.

Crompton, Samuel Willard. Clara Barton. 2009. (Women of Achievement Ser.). (Illus.). 144p. (J). (gr. 6-12). 35.00 *(978-1-60413-492-6(5)*, Chelsea Hse.) Facts On File, Inc.

Ditchfield, Christin. Clara Barton: Founder of the American Red Cross. 2004. (Great Life Stories Ser.). (ENG., Illus.). 111p. (J). 30.50 *(978-0-531-12276-1(X)*, Watts, Franklin) Scholastic Library Publishing.

Dubowski, Cathy East. Clara Barton: I Want to Help! 2005. (Defining Moments Ser.). (Illus.). 32p. (J). (gr. 2-5). lib. bdg. 25.27 *(978-1-59716-075-9(X))* Bearport Publishing Co., Inc.

Dunn, Joeming W. Clara Barton, 1 vol. Espinosa, Rod, illus. 2008. (Bio-Graphics Ser.). (ENG.). 32p. (gr. 3-5). 28.50 *(978-1-60270-170-0(9)*, Graphic Planet- Nonfiction) ABDO Publishing Co.

Edison, Erin. Clara Barton. 2013. (Great Women in History Ser.). (ENG.). 24p. (gr. k-1). pap. 35.70 *(978-1-62065-858-1(5))*; pap. 6.29 *(978-1-62065-857-4(7))*; (Illus.). lib. bdg. 21.99 *(978-1-62065-076-9(2))* Capstone Press of Coughlan Cos. (Pebble Bks.).

Ford, Carin T. Clara Barton: Brave Nurse. 2006. (Heroes of American History Ser.). (Illus.). 32p. (J). (gr. 3-7). lib. bdg. 23.94 *(978-0-7660-2602-5(7)*, Enslow Elementary) Enslow Pubs., Inc.

Hamen, Susan E. Clara Barton: Civil War Hero & American Red Cross Founder, 1 vol. 2010. (Military Heroes Ser.). (ENG.). 112p. (J). (gr. 6-12). lib. bdg. 35.64 *(978-1-60453-960-8(7))* ABDO Publishing Co.

Harkins, Susan Sales & Harkins, William H. The Life & Times of Clara Barton. 2008. (Profiles in American History Ser.). (Illus.). 48p. (J). (gr. 4-8). lib. bdg. 29.95 *(978-1-58415-667-3(8))* Mitchell Lane Pubs., Inc.

Kramer, Candice. Clara Barton: Angel of the Battlefield. 2004. (Reader's Theater Ser.). (J). pap. *(978-1-4108-1136-3(0))* Benchmark Education Co.

Lakin, Patricia. Clara Barton: Spirit of the American Red Cross. Sullivan, Simon, illus. 2004. (Ready-To-Read SOFA Ser.). (ENG.). 48p. (J). (gr. 1-3). pap. 3.99 *(978-0-689-86513-8(9)*, Simon Spotlight) Simon Spotlight.

—Clara Barton Spirit of the American Red Cross. Sullivan, Simon, illus. 2005. (Ready-to-Read Ser.). 48p. (J). lib. bdg. 15.00 *(978-1-59054-958-2(9))* Fitzgerald Bks.

Mara, Wil. Clara Barton. 2003. (Rookie Biographies Ser.). (ENG., Illus.). 32p. (J). (gr. 1-2). pap. 4.95 *(978-0-516-27339-6(6)*, Children's Pr.) Scholastic Library Publishing.

Marko, Eve. Clara Barton & the American Red Cross. Marcos, Pablo, illus. 2005. (Heroes of America Ser.). 237p. (gr. 3-8). 27.07 *(978-1-59679-255-5(8)*, Abdo & Daughters) ABDO Publishing Co.

Marsh, Carole. Clara Barton. 2003. 12p. (gr. k-4). 2.95 *(978-0-635-02353-7(9))* Gallopade International.

Meloche, Renee Taft. Heroes of History for Young Readers - Clara Barton: Courage to Serve. Pollard, Bryan, illus. 2006. (Heroes of History for Young Readers Ser.). (ENG.). 32p. (gr. -1). 8.99 *(978-1-932096-33-0(7))* Emerald Bks.

Nardo, Don. Clara Barton: Face Danger, but Never Fear It. 2008. (Americans—the Spirit of a Nation Ser.). (Illus.). 128p. (J). (gr. 3-7). lib. bdg. 33.27 *(978-0-7660-3024-4(5))* Enslow Pubs., Inc.

Polacco, Patricia. Clara & Davie. 2014. (ENG.). 40p. (J). (gr. -1-k). 18.99 *(978-0-545-35477-6(3)*, Scholastic Pr.) Scholastic, Inc.

Ransom, Candice. Clara Barton. 2003. (History Maker Bios Ser.). (Illus.). 48p. (J). (gr. 3-5). lib. bdg. 26.60 *(978-0-8225-4677-1(9))* Lerner Publishing Group.

Rose, Mary Catherine. Clara Barton: Soldier of Mercy. Johnson, E. Harper, illus. 2011. 80p. 37.95 *(978-1-258-07364-0(1))* Literary Licensing, LLC.

Ruffin, Frances E. Clara Barton. 2009. (American Legends Ser.). 24p. (gr. 3-3). 42.50 *(978-1-61511-379-8(7)*, PowerKids Pr.) Rosen Publishing Group, Inc., The.

Spinner, Stephanie. Who Was Clara Barton? Harrison, Nancy & Groff, David, illus. 2014. (Who Was? Ser.). (ENG.). 112p. (J). (gr. 3-7). 5.99 *(978-0-448-47953-8(2)*, Grosset & Dunlap) Penguin Young Readers Group.

—Who Was Clara Barton? 2014. (Who Was... ? Ser.). lib. bdg. 16.00 *(978-0-606-35695-4(9))* Turtleback Bks.

Time for Kids Editors. Clara Barton: Angel of the Battlefield. 2008. (Time for Kids Ser.). (ENG., Illus.). 48p. (J). (gr. 2-4). pap. 3.99 *(978-0-06-057622-6(7)*, Collins) HarperCollins Pubs.

Wade, Mary Dodson. Amazing Civil War Nurse Clara Barton. (Amazing Americans Ser.). (Illus.). 24p. (J). 2013. (gr. k-3). pap. 7.95 *(978-0-7660-5977-1(4)*, Enslow Elementary) 2009. (gr. 1-3). lib. bdg. 22.60 *(978-0-7660-3281-1(7))* Enslow Pubs., Inc.

BARTON, CLARA, 1821-1912—FICTION

Hood, Ann. Clara Barton: Angel of the Battlefield. Kwasney, Karl et al, illus. 2012. (Treasure Chest Ser.: 1). (ENG.). 208p. (J). (gr. 3-7). pap. 6.99 *(978-0-448-45467-2(X)*, Grosset & Dunlap) Penguin Young Readers Group.

Hood, Ann & Altmann, Scott. Angel of the Battlefield. Kwasney, Karl & Zilber, Denis, illus. 2012. (Treasure Chest Ser.: 1). (ENG.). 240p. (J). (gr. 3-7). 15.99 *(978-0-448-45471-9(8)*, Grosset & Dunlap) Penguin Young Readers Group.

Osborne, Mary Pope. Civil War on Sunday. unabr. ed. 2004. (Magic Tree House Ser.: No. 21). 76p. (J). (gr. k-3). pap. 17.00 incl. audio *(978-0-8072-0930-1(9)*, S FTR 253 SP, Listening Library) Random Hse. Audio Publishing Group.

BASEBALL

see also Softball

ABDO. Inside MLB, 1 vol. 2014. (Inside MLB Ser.: 30). (ENG.). 48p. (gr. 3-6). lib. bdg. 984.00 *(978-1-62403-459-6(4)*, SportsZone) ABDO Publishing Co.

Abrams, Dennis. Ty Cobb. 2007. (Baseball Superstars Ser.). (Illus.). 130p. (YA). (gr. 7-12). lib. bdg. 30.00 *(978-0-7910-9439-6(1))* Facts On File, Inc.

Adams, Michelle. Cliff Lee. 2011. (Robbie Reader Ser.). (Illus.). 32p. (J). (gr. 2-5). lib. bdg. 25.70 *(978-1-61228-065-3(X))* Mitchell Lane Pubs., Inc.

Adamson, Thomas K. Baseball: The Math of the Game, 1 vol. 2011. (Sports Math Ser.). (ENG.). 48p. (gr. 5-6). pap. 8.19 *(978-1-4296-7315-0(X))*; pap. 47.70 *(978-1-4296-7316-7(8))*; lib. bdg. 31.99 *(978-1-4296-6569-8(6))* Capstone Press of Coughlan Cos.

—The Technology of Baseball, 1 vol. 2013. (High-Tech Sports Ser.). (ENG.). 48p. (gr. 3-9). pap. 8.95 *(978-1-62065-906-9(9))*; pap. 53.70 *(978-1-62065-907-6(7))*; (Illus.). lib. bdg. 31.99 *(978-1-4296-9955-6(8))* Capstone Press of Coughlan Cos.

Aretha, David. Top 10 Greatest Hitters in Baseball. 2016. (Sports Greats Ser.). (ENG., Illus.). 48p. (J). (gr. 5-6). 27.93 *(978-0-7660-7396-8(3))* Enslow Pubs., Inc.

—Top 10 Moments in Baseball. 2016. (Sports Greats Ser.). (ENG., Illus.). 48p. (J). (gr. 5-6). pap. 11.70 *(978-0-7660-7402-6(1))* Enslow Pubs., Inc.

—Top 10 Pitchers in Baseball. 2016. (Sports Greats Ser.). (ENG., Illus.). 48p. (J). (gr. 5-6). 27.93 *(978-0-7660-7408-8(0))* Enslow Pubs., Inc.

—Top 25 Baseball Skills, Tips, & Tricks. 2011. (Top 25 Sports Skills, Tips, & Tricks Ser.). (Illus.). 48p. (J). (gr. 2-5). lib. bdg. 25.27 *(978-0-7660-3859-2(9))*; (gr. 4-18). pap. 8.95 *(978-1-59845-360-7(2))* Enslow Pubs., Inc.

Baron, Jessica. Trading Baseball Cards: Learning the Symbols +, -, And = 2009. (Math for the REAL World Ser.). 12p. (gr. 1-2). pap. 5.90 *(978-0-8239-8865-5(1)*, Rosen Classroom) Rosen Publishing Group, Inc., The.

Behrens, Janice. Let's Talk Baseball. 2008. (Scholastic News Nonfiction Readers Ser.). (ENG.). 24p. (J). (gr. 1-2). pap. 6.95 *(978-0-531-20427-6(8))*; (Illus.). (gr. k-1). lib. bdg. 22.00 *(978-0-531-13827-4(5)*, Children's Pr.) Scholastic Library Publishing.

Benjamin, Lisa. Baseball Dreams: The Story of Roberto Clemente. (Voices Reading Ser.). (Illus.). 32p. (J). *(978-0-7367-2912-3(7))* Zaner-Bloser, Inc.

Bennett, Carson. A Dozen Ways to Play Baseball Without the Ball & Bat. 2007. 48p. 7.56 *(978-1-4116-3102-1(1))* Lulu Pr., Inc.

Berra, Lawrence Yogi & Ferdenzi, Til. Behind the Plate. 2011. 190p. 42.95 *(978-1-258-00202-2(7))* Literary Licensing, LLC.

Bertoletti, John C., et al. How Baseball Managers Use Math. 2009. (Math in the Real World Ser.). 32p. (gr. 4-6). 28.00 *(978-1-60413-604-3(9)*, Chelsea Clubhouse) Facts On File, Inc.

Bonnet, Robert L. & Keen, Dan. Home Run! Science Projects with Baseball & Softball. 2009. (Score! Sports Science Projects Ser.). (Illus.). 104p. (J). (gr. 5-9). lib. bdg. 33.27 *(978-0-7660-3365-8(1))* Enslow Pubs., Inc.

Boone, Mary. Tim Lincecum. 2011. (Robbie Reader Ser.). (Illus.). 32p. (J). (gr. 2-5). lib. bdg. 25.70 *(978-1-61228-058-5(7))* Mitchell Lane Pubs., Inc.

Borden, Louise. Baseball Is... Colón, Raúl, illus. 2014. (ENG.). 48p. (J). (gr. 2-5). 17.99 *(978-1-4169-5502-3(X)*, McElderry, Margaret K. Bks.) McElderry, Margaret K. Bks.

Bow, James. Baseball Science. 2008. (Sports Science Ser.). (ENG., Illus.). 32p. (J). (gr. 4-6). pap. *(978-0-7787-4551-8(1))* Crabtree Publishing Co.

Bratton, Deboral B. & Bratton, Ashley D. Record-a-Sport Baseball & Softball Organizer. Bratton, Deborah B. & Bratton, Ashley D., eds. Bratton, Deborah B. & Bratton, Ashley D., illus. 2003. (Illus.). (gr. 1-18). 18.95 *(978-1-931746-03-8(6))* Sport Your Stuff Corp.

Braun, Eric. If I Were a Major League Baseball Player. Harmer, Sharon, illus. 2009. (Dream Big! Ser.). (ENG.). 24p. (gr. k-3). lib. bdg. 26.65 *(978-1-4048-5536-6(X))* Picture Window Bks.

—Super Baseball Infographics. 2015. (Super Sports Infographics Ser.). (ENG., Illus.). 32p. (J). (gr. 3-5). pap. 8.99 *(978-1-4677-7574-8(6))*; lib. bdg. 26.65 *(978-1-4677-5232-9(0))* Lerner Publishing Group. (Lerner Pubns.).

Brown, Jim. A Bridge to Cross. 2003. 234p. (YA). 25.95 *(978-0-595-74894-5(5))*; pap. 15.95 *(978-0-595-28773-4(5))* iUniverse, Inc.

Brown, Jordan D. The Innings & Outs of Baseball. Kennedy, Kelly & Downey, Dagney, illus. 2015. (Science of Fun Stuff Ser.). (ENG.). 48p. (J). (gr. 1-3). 16.99 *(978-1-4814-2862-0(4))*; pap. 3.99 *(978-1-4814-2861-3(6))* Simon Spotlight. (Simon Spotlight).

Bryant, Howard. Legends: The Best Players, Games, & Teams in Baseball. 2016. (ENG., Illus.). 256p. (J). (gr. 3-7). 8.99 *(978-0-14-751262-8(X)*, Puffin Books) Penguin Young Readers Group.

Buckley, James, Jr. Baseball: Facts, Stats, Stars, & Stuff. 2010. (Scholastic Ultimate Guides). (ENG., Illus.). 160p. (J). (gr. 6-18). pap. 7.99 *(978-0-531-21021-5(9)*, Watts, Franklin) Scholastic Library Publishing.

Burdick, Mason. Baseball. 2012. (On the Team Ser.). (ENG.). 24p. (J). (gr. 2-5). pap. 8.15 *(978-1-4339-6434-3(1))*; lib. bdg. 22.60 *(978-1-4339-6432-9(5))* Stevens, Gareth Publishing LLLP. (Gareth Stevens Learning Library).

Challen, Paul. What Does a Catcher Do? 2016. (Baseball Smarts Ser.). 00032p. (J). (gr. 3-3). pap. 10.00 *(978-1-4994-3280-0(1)*, PowerKids Pr.) Rosen Publishing Group, Inc., The.

—What Does a Pitcher Do? 2016. (Baseball Smarts Ser.). 00032p. (J). (gr. 3-3). pap. 10.00 *(978-1-4994-3289-3(5)*, PowerKids Pr.) Rosen Publishing Group, Inc., The.

—What Does an Infielder Do? 2016. (Baseball Smarts Ser.). 00032p. (J). (gr. 3-3). pap. 10.00 *(978-1-4994-3282-4(8)*; PowerKids Pr.) Rosen Publishing Group, Inc., The.

—What Does an Outfielder Do? 2016. (Baseball Smarts Ser.). 00032p. (J). (gr. 3-3). pap. 10.00 *(978-1-4994-3285-5(2)*, PowerKids Pr.) Rosen Publishing Group, Inc., The.

Chandler, Matt. The Science of Baseball: The Top Ten Ways Science Affects the Game. 2016. (Top 10 Science Ser.). (ENG., Illus.). 32p. (gr. 3-4). lib. bdg. 27.99 *(978-1-4914-8218-6(4))* Capstone Press of Coughlan Cos.

Cho, Alan. The World Series. 2016. (Illus.). 32p. ***(978-1-5105-0861-3(9))*** Lightbox, The.

Christopher, Matt. Albert Pujols: On the Field With... 2009. (ENG., Illus.). 128p. (J). (gr. 3-7). pap. 15.99 *(978-0-316-02701-4(4))* Little Brown & Co.

—At the Plate with... Ichiro. 2003. (ENG., Illus.). 112p. (J). (gr. 5-8). pap. 15.99 *(978-0-316-13679-2(4))* Little, Brown Bks. for Young Readers.

—On the Mound with... Curt Schilling. 2004. (Matt Christopher Sports Ser.). (Illus.). 106p. (gr. 3-7). 15.00 *(978-0-7569-3023-3(5))* Perfection Learning Corp.

—The World Series: Legendary Sports Events. 2007. (ENG., Illus.). 128p. (J). (gr. 3-7). per. 15.99 *(978-0-316-01117-4(7))* Little, Brown Bks. for Young Readers.

Clay, Kathryn. Cool Baseball Facts. 2011. (Cool Sports Facts Ser.). (ENG.). 24p. (gr. k-1). pap. 41.70 *(978-1-4296-7378-5(8)*, Pebble Plus) Capstone Press of Coughlan Cos.

—Cool Baseball Facts (Datos Geniales Sobre Béisbol) Strictly Spanish Translation Services Staff, tr. from SPA. 2012. (Datos Geniales Sobre Deportes/Cool Sports Facts Ser.). (ENG & MUL.). 24p. (gr. k-1). lib. bdg. 26.65 *(978-1-4296-9217-5(0))* Capstone Press of Coughlan Cos.

Cohen, Marina. Polygons. 2010. (ENG.). 24p. (J). *(978-0-7787-6784-8(1))*; pap. *(978-0-7787-6793-0(0))* Crabtree Publishing Co.

Connery-Boyd, Peg. Big Book of Major League Baseball Activities. 2016. (Hawk's Nest Activity Bks.: 0). (ENG.). 176p. (J). (gr. k-3). pap. 12.99 *(978-1-4926-3380-8(1))* Sourcebooks, Inc.

—Major League Baseball 2016 World Series Champions: Big Book of Activities. 2016. (Hawk's Nest Activity Bks.: 0). (ENG., Illus.). 64p. (J). (-3). pap. 12.99 *(978-1-4926-5021-8(8)*, 9781492650218, Sourcebooks Jabberwocky) Sourcebooks, Inc.

—Milwaukee Brewers. 2016. (Hawk's Nest Activity Bks.: 0). (ENG.). 64p. (J). (gr. k-3). pap., act. bk. ed. 8.99 *(978-1-4926-3366-2(6))* Sourcebooks, Inc.

—St. Louis Cardinals. 2016. (Hawk's Nest Activity Bks.: 0). (ENG.). 64p. (J). (gr. k-3). pap., act. bk. ed. 8.99 *(978-1-4926-3371-6(2))* Sourcebooks, Inc.

Cook, Sally & Charlton, James. Hey Batta Batta Swing! The Wild Old Days of Baseball. MacDonald, Ross, illus. 2007. (ENG.). 56p. (J). (gr. 1-5). 19.99 *(978-1-4169-1207-1(X)*, McElderry, Margaret K. Bks.) McElderry, Margaret K. Bks.

Craats, Rennay. Baseball. 2009. (In the Zone Ser.). 24p. (J). (gr. 3-5). pap. 8.95 *(978-1-60596-123-1(X))*; (Illus.). lib. bdg. 24.45 *(978-1-60596-122-4(1))* Weigl Pubs., Inc.

—For the Love of Baseball. Craats, Rennay & Kissock, Heather, eds. 2003. (For the Love of Sports Ser.). (Illus.). 32p. (J). pap. 8.95 *(978-1-59036-068-2(0))* Weigl Pubs., Inc.

Curlee, Lynn. Ballpark: The Story of America's Baseball Fields. Curlee, Lynn, illus. (ENG., Illus.). 48p. (J). 2008. (gr. -1-3). 8.99 *(978-1-4169-5360-9(4))* 2005. (gr. 3-7). 19.99 *(978-0-689-86742-2(5))* Simon & Schuster Children's Publishing. (Atheneum Bks. for Young Readers).

Dann, Sarah & Crossingham, John. Le Baseball. 2010. (FRE., Illus.). 32p. (J). pap. 9.95 *(978-2-89579-289-5(5))* Bayard Canada Livres CAN. Dist: Crabtree Publishing Co.

—Béisbol en Acción. 2005. (Deportes en Acción Ser.). (SPA., Illus.). 32p. (J). pap. *(978-0-7787-8617-7(X))* Crabtree Publishing Co.

Davis, Mo'ne. Mo'ne Davis: Remember My Name: My Story from First Pitch to Game Changer. 2016. 208p. (J). (gr. 3-7). pap. 6.99 *(978-0-06-239754-6(0))* HarperCollins Pubs.

DeGezelle, Terri. ¡Vamos a Jugar Al Béisbol! (Let's Play Baseball!) 2012. (Deportes y Actividades/Sports & Activities Ser.). (MUL & SPA.). 24p. (gr. k-1). lib. bdg. 26.65 *(978-1-4296-8247-3(7))* Capstone Press of Coughlan Cos.

Derr, Aaron. Baseball: An Introduction to Being a Good Sport. Angle, Scott, illus. 2017. (Start Smart (tm) — Sports Ser.). (ENG.). 32p. (J). (gr. k-3). lib. bdg. 26.65 *(978-1-63440-129-6(8))*; 39.99 ***(978-1-63440-141-8(7))*** Red Chair Pr.

Dicicco, Joe. Planet Baseball, Japanese Edition, Volume 1: Making the Play, Vol. 1. Jimenez, Ruben D., tr. Dicicco, Joe, illus. l.t. ed. 2009. (JPN & ENG., Illus.). 14p. (J). (gr. -1-3). 7.95 *(978-1-929528-03-5(5))* Punta Gorda Pr.

Dobrow, Larry & Jeter, Derek. Derek Jeter's Ultimate Baseball Guide 2015. Jones, Damien, illus. 2015. (Jeter Publishing Ser.). (ENG.). 96p. (J). (gr. 3-5). pap. 9.99 *(978-1-4814-2318-2(5)*, Little Simon) Little Simon.

Douglas, Peter. Baseball & Softball: Success on the Diamond. 2017. (Preparing for Game Day Ser.: Vol. 10). (ENG.). (YA). (gr. 7-12). 24.95 ***(978-1-4222-3913-1(6))*** Mason Crest.

Dreier, David. Baseball: How It Works. 2010. (Science of Sports (Sports Illustrated for Kids) Ser.). (ENG.). 48p. (gr. 3-4). pap. 59.70 *(978-1-4296-5106-6(7))* Capstone Press of Coughlan Cos.

Dreier, David L. The Science of Baseball with Max Axiom, Super Scientist. Aranda, Tom, illus. 2015. (Science of Sports with Max Axiom Ser.). (ENG.). 32p. (gr. 3-4). lib. bdg. 30.65 *(978-1-4914-6083-2(0)*, Graphic Library) Capstone Press of Coughlan Cos.

Durrie, Karen. Al Béisbol. 2012. (J). *(978-1-61913-198-9(6))* Weigl Pubs., Inc.

—Baseball. 2011. (J). *(978-1-61690-937-6(4))*; *(978-1-61690-583-5(2))* Weigl Pubs., Inc.

Dzidrums, Christine. Mike Trout: Baseball Sensation. Dzidrums, Joseph, photos by. 2013. (Illus.). 64p. pap. 9.99 *(978-1-938438-28-8(0))* Creative Media Publishing.

Edwards, Ethan. Meet Albert Pujols: Baseball's Power Hitter. 2009. (All-Star Players Ser.). (Illus.). 32p. (YA). (gr. 4-7). lib. bdg. 25.25 *(978-1-4042-4487-0(5))* Rosen Publishing Group, Inc., The.

—Meet Derek Jeter: Captain of the New York Yankees. 2009. (All-Star Players Ser.). (Illus.). 32p. (YA). (gr. 4-7). lib. bdg. 25.25 *(978-1-4042-4488-7(3))* Rosen Publishing Group, Inc., The.

Epstein, Brad. Arizona Diamondbacks 101: My First Team-Board-Book. 2008. Orig. Title: 2008. (Illus.). 22p. (J). bds. *(978-1-932530-79-7(7)*, 101 Bk.) Michaelson Entertainment.

—Chicago White Sox 101. 2013. (My First Team-Board-Book Ser.). (ENG., Illus.). 24p. (J). bds. *(978-1-60730-298-8(5)*, 101 Bk.) Michaelson Entertainment.

—Chicago White Sox ABC. 2013. (My First Alphabet Books (Michaelson Entertainment) Ser.). (ENG., Illus.). (J). bds. 11.95 *(978-1-60730-204-9(7))* Michaelson Entertainment.

—Colorado Rockies 101: My First Team-Board-Book. 2008. Orig. Title: 2008. (Illus.). 22p. (J). bds. *(978-1-932530-94-0(0))* Michaelson Entertainment.

—Los Angeles Angels of Anaheim 101: My First Team-Board-Book. 2008. Orig. Title: 2008. (ENG., Illus.). 22p. (J). bds. *(978-1-932530-70-4(3)*, 101 Bk.) Michaelson Entertainment.

—New York Mets 101. 2013. (My First Team-Board-Book Ser.). (ENG., Illus.). 24p. (J). bds. *(978-1-60730-285-8(3)*, 101 Bk.) Michaelson Entertainment.

—New York Mets ABC. 2013. (My First Alphabet Books (Michaelson Entertainment) Ser.). (ENG., Illus.). 28p. (J). bds. *(978-1-60730-208-7(X)*, ABC Bk.) Michaelson Entertainment.

—Philadelphia Phillies 101: My First Team-Board-Book. 2008. Orig. Title: 2008. (ENG., Illus.). 22p. (J). bds. *(978-1-932530-89-6(4)*, 101 Bk.) Michaelson Entertainment.

—Seattle Mariners 101: My First Team-Board-Book. 2008. (ENG., Illus.). 22p. (J). bds. *(978-1-932530-83-4(5)*, 101 Bk.) Michaelson Entertainment.

Flynn, Brendan. Baseball Time! 2016. (Bumba Books (tm) — Sports Time! Ser.). (ENG.). 24p. (J). (gr. -1-1). 25.32 *(978-1-5124-1431-8(X))* Lerner Publishing Group.

—¡Hora de Béisbol! 2017. (Bumba Books (tm) en Español — ¡Hora de Deportes! (Sports Time!) Ser.). (SPA., Illus.). 24p. (J). (gr. -1-1). 25.32 *(978-1-5124-2870-4(1))* Lerner Publishing Group.

Franchino, Vicky. Roberto Clemente. 2007. (21st Century Skills Library: Life Skills Biographies Ser.). (ENG.). 48p. (gr. 4-8). lib. bdg. 31.36 *(978-1-60279-073-5(6)*, 200047) Cherry Lake Publishing.

Franks, Katie. I Want to Be a Baseball Player. (Dream Jobs Ser.). 24p. (gr. 2-3). 2009. 42.50 *(978-1-61512-203-5(6)*, PowerKids Pr.) 2007. (Illus.). (J). lib. bdg. 22.60 *(978-1-4042-3622-6(8))* Rosen Publishing Group, Inc., The.

—Quiero Ser Beisbolista. 2009. (Trabajos de ensueño (Dream Jobs) Ser.). (SPA & ENG.). 24p. pap. 8.25 *(978-1-4358-3431-6(3))*; (Illus.). 22.60 *(978-1-4042-8159-2(2))* Rosen Publishing Group, Inc., The. (PowerKids Pr.).

Fredrickson, Anne. The Baseball Brothers. 2008. lib. bdg. 12.95 *(978-0-615-20146-7(6))* Fredrickson, Anne.

Gagne, Eric & Brown, Greg. Eric Gagne: Break Barriers. 2004. (Illus.). 48p. (J). 15.95 *(978-0-9634650-6-1(6))* Positively for Kids, Inc.

Gagne, Tammy. Roy Halladay. 2011. (Robbie Reader Ser.). (Illus.). 32p. (J). (gr. 2-5). lib. bdg. 25.70 *(978-1-61228-061-5(7))* Mitchell Lane Pubs., Inc.

Geng, Don & King, Andy. Baseball. 2003. (Play-by-Play Ser.). (Illus.). 80p. (J). (gr. 5-18). pap. 7.95 *(978-0-8225-9880-0(9))* Lerner Publishing Group.

Get Inside Series. Incl. Baseball. Almonte, Paul. 80p. 14.95 *(978-1-881889-55-7(6))*; Ranch. Morgenroth, Barbara. 64p. 14.95 *(978-1-881889-56-4(4))*; (Illus.). (J). 1994. 29.90 *(978-1-881889-79-3(3))* Silver Moon Pr.

Gilbert, Sara. World Series Champs: la Angels of Anaheim. 2013. (World Series Champions Ser.). (ENG.). 24p. (J). (gr. 1-3). pap. 7.99 *(978-0-89812-816-1(1)*, Creative Paperbacks) Creative Co., The.

—World Series Champs: Miami Marlins. 2013. (World Series Champions Ser.). (ENG.). 24p. (J). (gr. 1-3). pap. 7.99 *(978-0-89812-815-4(3)*, Creative Paperbacks) Creative Co., The.

Glaser, Jason. Batter. 2011. (Play Ball: Baseball Ser.). (Illus.). 48p. (J). (gr. 4-8). lib. bdg. 31.95 *(978-1-4339-4619-6(X))* Stevens, Gareth Publishing LLLP.

—Batters. 2011. (Play Ball: Baseball Ser.). (Illus.). 48p. (J). (gr. 4-8). pap. 14.05 *(978-1-4339-4620-2(3))* Stevens, Gareth Publishing LLLP.

—Catcher. 2011. (Play Ball: Baseball Ser.). (Illus.). 48p. (J). (gr. 4-8). pap. 14.05 *(978-1-4339-4484-0(7))*; lib. bdg. 31.95 *(978-1-4339-4483-3(9))* Stevens, Gareth Publishing LLLP.

—Infielders. 2011. (Play Ball: Baseball Ser.). (Illus.). 48p. (J). (gr. 4-8). pap. 14.05 *(978-1-4339-4488-8(X))*; (J). 31.95 *(978-1-4339-4487-1(1))* Stevens, Gareth Publishing LLLP.

—Outfielders. 2011. (Play Ball: Baseball Ser.). (Illus.). 48p. (J). (gr. 4-8). lib. bdg. 31.95 *(978-1-4339-4491-8(X))* Stevens, Gareth Publishing LLLP.

—Pitcher. 2011. (Play Ball: Baseball Ser.). (Illus.). 48p. (J). (gr. 4-8). lib. bdg. 31.95 *(978-1-4339-4495-6(2))* Stevens, Gareth Publishing LLLP.

Golenbock, Peter. ABCs of Baseball. Andreasen, Dan, illus. 2012. (ENG.). 48p. (J). (gr. 1-3). 16.99 *(978-0-8037-3711-2(4)*, Dial Bks) Penguin Young Readers Group.

Grant, Elaine Y. & Elliott, Sharon M. The Little Book of Baseball. 2003. (Illus.). 168p. (J). spiral bd. 12.95 *(978-0-9729676-0-0(5)*, LBOB) Presence Publishing.

Graubart, Norman D. The Science of Baseball. 2015. (Sports Science Ser.). (ENG.). 32p. (J). (gr. 4-5). 26.25 *(978-1-4994-1122-5(7)*, PowerKids Pr.) Rosen Publishing Group, Inc., The.

Gutman, Dan. Jackie Robinson & the Big Game. Garvin, Elaine, illus. 2006. 32p. (J). lib. bdg. 15.00 *(978-1-4242-0957-6(9))* Fitzgerald Bks.

Hantula, Richard. Science at Work in Baseball. 2011. (Benchmark Rockets: Sports Science Ser.). (Illus.). 32p. (J). (gr. 4). 28.50 *(978-1-60870-587-0(0))* Marshall Cavendish GBR. Dist: Marshall Cavendish Corp.

Hardman, Lizabeth. Baseball. 2010. (Science Behind Sports Ser.). (ENG., Illus.). 128p. (gr. 7-10). 39.40 *(978-1-4205-0262-6(X))* Cengage Gale.

Herzog, Brad. Full Count: A Baseball Number Book. Langton, Bruce, illus. 2009. (ENG.). 40p. (J). (gr. k-6). 17.95 *(978-1-58536-429-9(0))* Sleeping Bear Pr.

—H Is for Home Run: A Baseball Alphabet. Rose, Melanie, illus. (Alphabet-Sports Ser.). (ENG.). 40p. 2009. (gr. k-6). pap. 7.95 *(978-1-58536-475-6(4))* 2004. (J). (gr. -1-5). 16.95 *(978-1-58536-219-6(0))* Sleeping Bear Pr.

—H Is for Home Run: A Baseball Alphabet. Rose, Melanie, illus. 2015. (Av2 Fiction Readalong 2016 Ser.). (ENG.). (J).

(gr. 1-4). lib. bdg. 34.28 *(978-1-4896-3744-4(3)*, AV2 by Weigl) Weigl Pubs., Inc.

—I Spy with My Little Eye: Baseball. Milne, David, illus. 2011. (I Spy Ser.). (ENG.). 32p. (J). (gr. 3-6). 13.95 *(978-1-58536-496-1(7))* Sleeping Bear Pr.

—Little Baseball. Bowles, Doug, illus. 2011. (Little Sports Ser.). (ENG.). 22p. (J). 7.95 *(978-1-58536-547-0(5))* Sleeping Bear Pr.

Herzog, Brad. Murphy's Ticket: The Goofy Start & Glorious End of the Chicago Cubs Billy Goat Curse. Leonard, David, illus. 2017. (ENG.). 32p. (J). (gr. 1-4). 16.99 ***(978-1-58536-387-2(1)***, 204331) Sleeping Bear Pr.

Hetrick, Hans. Baseball's Record Breakers. 2017. (Record Breakers Ser.). (ENG., Illus.). 32p. (gr. 3-4). pap. 8.95 *(978-1-5157-3764-3(0))*; lib. bdg. 27.32 *(978-1-5157-3760-5(8))* Capstone Press of Coughlan Cos.

—Play Baseball Like a Pro: Key Skills & Tips. 2010. (Play Like the Pros (Sports Illustrated for Kids) Ser.). (ENG.). 32p. (gr. 3-4). pap. 7.19 *(978-1-4296-5644-3(1))*; pap. 41.70 *(978-1-4296-5957-4(2))*; lib. bdg. 26.65 *(978-1-4296-4824-0(4))* Capstone Press of Coughlan Cos.

Hinnant, Jamal. Top 10 Bloopers in Baseball. 2016. (Sports Greats Ser.). (ENG., Illus.). 48p. (J). (gr. 5-6). lib. bdg. 27.93 *(978-0-7660-7392-0(0))* Enslow Pubs., Inc.

—Top 10 Injuries in Baseball. 2016. (Sports Greats Ser.). (ENG., Illus.). 48p. (J). (gr. 5-6). 27.93 *(978-0-7660-7400-2(5))* Enslow Pubs., Inc.

Hoena, Blake. Baseball. 2015. (J). lib. bdg. 25.65 *(978-1-62031-176-9(3)*, Bullfrog Bks.) Jump! Inc.

Hoffman, Mary Ann. David Ortiz: Baseball Star/Estrella del Beisbol. 2009. (Amazing Athletes/Atletas increibles Ser.). (ENG & SPA.). 24p. (gr. 1-2). 42.50 *(978-1-61511-304-0(5)*, Editorial Buenas Letras) Rosen Publishing Group, Inc., The.

Howell, Brian. Playing Pro Baseball. 2014. (Playing Pro Sports Ser.). (ENG., Illus.). 64p. (gr. 4-8). lib. bdg. 26.60 *(978-1-4677-3846-0(8)*, Lerner Pubns.) Lerner Publishing Group.

Hughes, Morgan. Baseball. 2005. (Junior Sports Ser.). (Illus.). 32p. (gr. 2-4). 19.95 *(978-1-59515-188-9(5))* Rourke Educational Media.

Hurley, Michael. Baseball, 1 vol. 2013. (Fantastic Sports Facts Ser.). (ENG., Illus.). 32p. (gr. 1-3). pap. 8.29 *(978-1-4109-5114-4(6)*, Read Me!) Heinemann-Raintree.

Inside MLB, 30 vols., Set. Incl. Arizona Diamondbacks. Tricchinelli, Rob. (YA). lib. bdg. 32.79 *(978-1-61714-034-1(1))*; Atlanta Braves. Howell, Brian. (YA). lib. bdg. 32.79 *(978-1-61714-035-8(X))*; Baltimore Orioles. Frager, Ray. (YA). lib. bdg. 32.79 *(978-1-61714-036-5(8))*; Boston Red Sox. Freedman, Lew. (YA). lib. bdg. 32.79 *(978-1-61714-037-2(6))*; Chicago Cubs. Castle, George. (YA). lib. bdg. 32.79 *(978-1-61714-038-9(4))*; Chicago White Sox. Castle, George. (YA). lib. bdg. 32.79 *(978-1-61714-039-6(2))*; Cincinnati Reds. Gitlin, Martin. (YA). lib. bdg. 32.79 *(978-1-61714-040-2(6))*; Cleveland Indians. Gitlin, Martin. (YA). lib. bdg. 32.79 *(978-1-61714-041-9(4))*; Colorado Rockies. Howell, Brian. (YA). lib. bdg. 32.79 *(978-1-61714-042-6(2))*; Detroit Tigers. Gerstner, Joanne. (YA). lib. bdg. 32.79 *(978-1-61714-043-3(0))*; Florida Marlins. Smolka, Bo. (YA). 31.35 *(978-1-61714-044-0(9))*; Houston Astros. Roselius, J. Chris. (YA). lib. bdg. 32.79 *(978-1-61714-045-7(7))*; Kansas City Royals. Bowker, Paul. (YA). lib. bdg. 32.79 *(978-1-61714-046-4(5))*; Los Angeles Angels. Wilson, Bernie. (J). lib. bdg. 32.79 *(978-1-61714-047-1(3))*; Los Angeles Dodgers. Gitlin, Martin. (YA). lib. bdg. 32.79 *(978-1-61714-048-8(1))*; Milwaukee Brewers. Derong, Gary. (YA). lib. bdg. 32.79 *(978-1-61714-049-5(X))*; Minnesota Twins. Bissen, Joe. (YA). lib. bdg. 32.79 *(978-1-61714-050-1(3))*; New York Mets. Knobel, Andy. (YA). lib. bdg. 32.79 *(978-1-61714-051-8(1))*; New York Yankees. Howell, Brian. (YA). lib. bdg. 32.79 *(978-1-61714-052-5(X))*; Oakland Athletics. Howell, Brian. (YA). lib. bdg. 32.79 *(978-1-61714-053-2(8))*; Philadelphia Phillies. Jackson, Dave. (YA). lib. bdg. 32.79 *(978-1-61714-054-9(6))*; Pittsburgh Pirates. Frager, Ray. (YA). lib. bdg. 32.79 *(978-1-61714-055-6(4))*; San Diego Padres. Wilson, Bernie. (YA). lib. bdg. 32.79 *(978-1-61714-057-0(0))*; San Francisco Giants. Gitlin, Martin. (YA). lib. bdg. 32.79 *(978-1-61714-058-7(9))*; Seattle Mariners. Freedman, Lew. (YA). lib. bdg. 32.79 *(978-1-61714-059-4(7))*; St. Louis Cardinals. Gitlin, Martin. (YA). lib. bdg. 32.79 *(978-1-61714-056-3(2))*; Tampa Bay Rays. Bowker, Paul. (YA). lib. bdg. 32.79 *(978-1-61714-060-0(0))*; Texas Rangers. Basen, Ryan. (YA). lib. bdg. 32.79 *(978-1-61714-061-7(9))*; Toronto Blue Jays. Gerstner, Joanne. (YA). lib. bdg. 32.79 *(978-1-61714-062-4(7))*; Washington Nationals. Goessling, Ben. (YA). lib. bdg. 32.79 *(978-1-61714-063-1(5))*; (gr. 3-6). (Inside MLB Ser.). (ENG., Illus.). 48p. 2011. Set lib. bdg. 983.70 *(978-1-61714-033-4(3)*, SportsZone) ABDO Publishing Co.

Jacobs, Greg. The Everything Kids' Baseball Book: Today's Superstars, Great Teams, Legends — and Tips on Playing Like a Pro. 4th ed. 2006. (Everything Ser.). (ENG., Illus.). 144p. (J). (gr. 3-7). per. 7.95 *(978-1-59337-614-7(6))* Adams Media Corp.

Jennison, Christopher. Baseball Math: Grandslam Activities & Projects. 3rd ed. 2005. (Illus.). 104p. (J). (gr. 4-8). per. 12.95 *(978-1-59647-007-1(0))* Good Year Bks.

Jones, Tammy. Count at the Baseball Field. 2009. (Sight Word Readers Set A Ser.). (J). 3.49 net. *(978-1-60719-156-8(3))* Newmark Learning LLC.

Jordan, Christopher. Baseball Animals. 2014. (Major League Baseball: First Base Bks.). (ENG., Illus.). 24p. (gr. -1-2). 12.99 *(978-1-77049-474-9(X)*, Fenn-Tundra) Tundra Bks. CAN. Dist: Penguin Random Hse. LLC.

—Baseball Opposites. 2014. (Major League Baseball: First Base Bks.). (ENG., Illus.). 32p. (gr. -1-2). 12.99 *(978-1-77049-518-0(5)*, Fenn-Tundra) Tundra Bks. CAN. Dist: Penguin Random Hse. LLC.

Jorgensen, Katrina. Ballpark Cookbooks: Recipes Inspired by Baseball Stadium Foods. 2016. (Ballpark Cookbooks Ser.). (ENG.). 64p. (gr. 3-4). 63.98 *(978-1-4914-8697-9(X))* Capstone Press of Coughlan Cos.

Kalman, Bobbie & Crossingham, John. Batter up Baseball. 2007. (Sports Starters Ser.). (ENG., Illus.). 32p. (J). (gr. 3-7). lib. bdg. *(978-0-7787-3136-8(7))*; (gr. -1-3). pap. *(978-0-7787-3168-9(5))* Crabtree Publishing Co.

Kalman, Bobbie & Dyer, Hadley. Turno al Bate en el Béisbol. 2008.Tr. of Batter up Baseball. (SPA.). 32p. (J). lib. bdg. *(978-0-7787-8640-5(4))* Crabtree Publishing Co.

Kalman, Bobbie, et al. Turno al Bate en el Béisbol. 2008.Tr. of Batter up Baseball. (SPA.). 32p. (J). pap. *(978-0-7787-8649-8(8))* Crabtree Publishing Co.

Kawa, Katie. My First Trip to a Baseball Game. 2012. (My First Adventures Ser.). (Illus.). 24p. (J). (gr. k-2). pap. 8.15 *(978-1-4339-7304-8(9))*; lib. bdg. 22.60 *(978-1-4339-7307-9(3))* Stevens, Gareth Publishing LLLP.

—My First Trip to A Baseball Game. 2012. (My First Adventures Ser.). (Illus.). 24p. (gr. k-2). 69.20 *(978-1-4339-8048-0(7))* Stevens, Gareth Publishing LLLP.

—My First Trip to a Baseball Game: Mi Primer Partido de Béisbol. 2012. (My First Adventures / Mis primeras aventuras Ser.). (SPA., Illus.). 24p. (J). (gr. k-2). lib. bdg. 22.60 *(978-1-4339-7374-1(X))* Stevens, Gareth Publishing LLLP.

Kelley, James E. & Buckley, James. Baseball. 2010. (DK Eyewitness Bks.). (ENG., Illus.). 72p. (J). (gr. 3-7). 16.99 *(978-0-7566-5934-9(5)*, DK Children) Dorling Kindersley Publishing, Inc.

Kelly, David A. Miracle Mud: Lena Blackburne & the Secret Mud That Changed Baseball. Dominguez, Oliver, illus. 2013. (ENG.). 32p. (J). (gr. 2-5). lib. bdg. 16.95 *(978-0-7613-8092-4(2)*, Millbrook Pr.) Lerner Publishing Group.

Kortemeier, Todd. Pro Baseball by the Numbers. 2016. (Illus.). 32p. pap. *(978-1-4914-9072-3(1))* Capstone Press of Coughlan Cos.

Kortemeier, Tom. Pro Baseball by the Numbers. 2016. (Pro Sports by the Numbers Ser.). (ENG., Illus.). 32p. (gr. 3-4). lib. bdg. 27.99 *(978-1-4914-9059-4(4)*, Edge Bks.) Capstone Press of Coughlan Cos.

Krasner, Steven. Play Ball Like the Hall of Famers: Tips for Kids from 19 Baseball Greats, 1 vol. Neely, Keith, illus. 2005. (ENG.). 208p. (J). (gr. 5-9). pap. 14.95 *(978-1-56145-339-9(0))* Peachtree Pubs.

—Play Ball Like the Pros: Tips for Kids from 20 Big League Stars, 1 vol. 2nd rev. ed. 2010. (ENG., Illus.). 208p. (J). pap. 13.95 *(978-1-56145-535-5(0))* Peachtree Pubs.

Lake, Kirsten. A Trip to the Ball Game. 2016. (PowerKids Readers: My Community Ser.). 00024p. (J). (gr. k-k). pap. 8.25 *(978-1-4994-2782-0(4)*, PowerKids Pr.) Rosen Publishing Group, Inc., The.

Latimer, Clay. VIP Pass to a Pro Baseball Game Day: From the Locker Room to the Press Box (and Everything in Between), 1 vol. (Game Day (Sports Illustrated for Kids) Ser.). (ENG.). 32p. (gr. 3-4). 2011. pap. 8.19 *(978-1-4296-6283-3(2))* 2011. pap. 47.70 *(978-1-4296-6447-9(9))* 2010. lib. bdg. 27.99 *(978-1-4296-5462-3(7))* Capstone Press of Coughlan Cos.

LeBoutillier, Nate. Play Baseball Like a Pro: Key Skills & Tips. 2010. (Play Like the Pros (Sports Illustrated for Kids) Ser.). (ENG.). 32p. (gr. 3-4). pap. 41.70 *(978-1-4296-5958-1(0))* Capstone Press of Coughlan Cos.

Little League's Official How-to-Play Baseball. 2007. 210p. 39.95 incl. DVD *(978-1-55919-997-1(0))* MasterVision.

Mackin, Bob & Mackin, B. Record-Breaking Baseball Trivia: Games, Puzzles, Quizzes. 2003. (ENG., Illus.). 128p. pap. 6.95 *(978-1-55054-757-3(7))* Greystone Books Ltd. CAN. Dist: Publishers Group West (PGW).

MacRae, Sloan. David Wright. 2012. (Sports Heroes Ser.). (ENG.). 24p. (J). (gr. 3-6). pap. 8.25 *(978-1-4488-6286-3(8))*; lib. bdg. 22.60 *(978-1-4488-6164-4(0))* Rosen Publishing Group, Inc., The. (PowerKids Pr.).

—Meet Manny Ramirez: Baseball's Grand Slam Hitter. 2009. (All-Star Players Ser.). 32p. (J). lib. bdg. 25.25 *(978-1-4358-2708-0(2)*, PowerKids Pr.) Rosen Publishing Group, Inc., The.

—Meet Vladimir Guerrero: Baseball's Super Vlad. 2009. (All-Star Players Ser.). (Illus.). 32p. (J). lib. bdg. 25.25 *(978-1-4358-2707-3(4)*, PowerKids Pr.) Rosen Publishing Group, Inc., The.

Mahaney, Ian F. The Math of Baseball. 2011. (J). 49.50 *(978-1-4488-2693-3(4)*, PowerKids Pr.); pap. 8.25 *(978-1-4488-2692-6(6)*, PowerKids Pr.); (gr. 2-5). lib. bdg. 22.60 *(978-1-4488-2554-7(7))* Rosen Publishing Group, Inc., The.

Mandel, Peter. Say Hey! A Song of Willie Mays. Tate, Don, illus. 2004. 30p. (J). (gr. k-2). reprint ed. 16.00 *(978-0-7567-8162-0(0))* DIANE Publishing Co.

Mara, Wil. Tee Ball. 2012. (Rookie Read-about Ser.). (ENG.). 32p. (J). pap. 5.95 *(978-0-531-20926-4(1))*; (gr. -1-1). lib. bdg. 23.00 *(978-0-531-20857-1(5))* Scholastic Library Publishing. (Children's Pr.).

Mason, Tyler. 12 Reasons to Love Baseball. 2018. (ENG.). 32p. (gr. 3-6). 31.35 ***(978-1-63235-425-9(X)***, 12-Story Library) Pr. Room Editions LLC.

Mattern, Joanne. Derek Jeter: Baseball Superstar, 1 vol. 2011. (Superstar Athletes Ser.). (ENG.). 24p. (gr. 1-2). pap. 7.29 *(978-1-4296-7303-7(6))*; pap. 41.70 *(978-1-4296-7304-4(4))* Capstone Press of Coughlan Cos.

—I Know Baseball. 2013. (21st Century Basic Skills Library: I Know Sports Ser.). (ENG., Illus.). 24p. (J). (gr. k-3). 22.79 *(978-1-62431-397-4(3)*, 202708); pap. 12.79 *(978-1-62431-473-5(2)*, 202710) Cherry Lake Publishing.

—I Use Math at the Game. 2005. (I Use Math Ser.). (Illus.). 24p. (gr. k-3). pap. 8.15 *(978-0-8368-4862-5(4))*; lib. bdg. 22.00 *(978-0-8368-4855-7(1))* Stevens, Gareth Publishing LLLP. (Weekly Reader Leveled Readers).

McClellan, Ray. Baseball. 2009. (My First Sports Ser.). (ENG., Illus.). 24p. (J). (gr. 2-5). lib. bdg. 25.95 *(978-1-60014-277-2(X)*, Blastoff! Readers) Bellwether Media.

McFee, Shane. Let's Play Baseball. (Let's Get Active Ser.). 24p. 2009. (gr. 2-3). 42.50 *(978-1-61514-251-4(7))* 2008. (Illus.). lib. bdg. 22.60 *(978-1-4042-4194-7(9))* Rosen Publishing Group, Inc., The. (PowerKids Pr.).

McMahon, Dave. Baseball Skills: How to Play Like a Pro. 2008. (How to Play Like a Pro Ser.). (Illus.). 48p. (J). (gr. 3-6). lib. bdg. 25.27 *(978-0-7660-3204-0(3))* Enslow Pubs., Inc.

Mills, Cliff. Clayton Kershaw. 2014. (Illus.). 32p. (J). (gr. 1-4). 25.70 *(978-1-61228-636-5(4))* Mitchell Lane Pubs., Inc.

Minden, Cecilia. Baseball. 2008. (21st Century Skills Library: Real World Math Ser.). (ENG., Illus.). 32p. (gr. 4-8). lib. bdg. 28.50 *(978-1-60279-243-2(7)*, 200194) Cherry Lake Publishing.

Morey, Allan. Fantasy Baseball Math: Using Stats to Score Big in Your League. 2016. (Fantasy Sports Math Ser.). (ENG., Illus.). 32p. (gr. 3-4). lib. bdg. 27.99 *(978-1-5157-2167-3(1))* Capstone Press of Coughlan Cos.

Murray, Stuart A. P. Score with Baseball Math. 2013. (Score with Sports Math Ser.). 48p. (J). lib. bdg. 25.27 *(978-0-7660-4174-5(3))*; (gr. 3-4). pap. 8.95 *(978-1-4644-0287-6(6))* Enslow Pubs., Inc. (Enslow Elementary).

Nagelhout, Ryan. Baseball: Who Does What? 2017. (Sports: What's Your Position? Ser.). 32p. (J). (gr. 3-4). pap. 63.00 ***(978-1-5382-0410-8(X))***; pap. 10.50 ***(978-1-5382-0409-2(6))*** Stevens, Gareth Publishing LLLP.

—Discovering STEM at the Baseball Game. 2015. (STEM in the Real World Ser.). (ENG., Illus.). 24p. (J). (gr. 2-3). pap. 8.25 *(978-1-4994-0916-1(8)*, PowerKids Pr.) Rosen Publishing Group, Inc., The.

—I Love Baseball. 2014. (My Favorite Sports Ser.). (Illus.). 24p. (J). (gr. k-2). 22.60 *(978-1-4824-0719-8(1))* Stevens, Gareth Publishing LLLP.

—Me Encanta el Béisbol / I Love Baseball. 2014. (My Favorite Sports Ser.). (SPA & ENG., Illus.). 24p. (J). (gr. k-2). 22.60 *(978-1-4824-0846-1(5))* Stevens, Gareth Publishing LLLP.

—Talk Like a Baseball Player. 2016. (Let's Talk Sports! Ser.). 00032p. (J). pap. 10.50 ***(978-1-4824-5689-9(3))*** Stevens, Gareth Publishing LLLP.

Nagelhout, Ryan. 20 Fun Facts about Baseball. 2016. (Fun Fact File: Sports! Ser.). (ENG., Illus.). 32p. (J). (gr. 2-3). pap. 10.50 *(978-1-4824-3965-6(4))* Stevens, Gareth Publishing LLLP.

Nash, Ogden. Lineup for Yesterday. Payne, C. F., illus. 2011. (ENG.). 56p. (J). (gr. 1-3). 24.99 *(978-1-56846-212-7(3)*, Creative Editions) Creative Co., The.

—Lineup for Yesterday ABC Baseball Cards. Payne, C. F., illus. 2013. (ENG.). (J). (gr. 1-3). 12.99 *(978-1-56846-249-3(2)*, Creative Editions) Creative Co., The.

Nelson, Robin. Baseball Is Fun! 2013. (First Step Nonfiction - Sports Are Fun! Ser.). (ENG., Illus.). 24p. (gr. k-2). pap. 6.95 *(978-1-4677-1535-5(2))*; lib. bdg. 23.93 *(978-1-4677-1101-2(2)*, Lerner Pubns.) Lerner Publishing Group.

—From Wood to Baseball Bat. 2014. (Start to Finish: Sports Gear Ser.). (Illus.). 24p. (gr. k-3). pap. 6.95 *(978-1-4677-4561-1(8))*; (ENG., lib. bdg. 23.93 *(978-1-4677-3891-0(3)*, Lerner Pubns.) Lerner Publishing Group.

Nevius, Carol. Baseball Hour, 0 vols. Thomson, Bill, illus. 2008. (ENG.). 32p. (J). (gr. -1-3). lib. bdg. 16.99 *(978-0-7614-5380-2(6)*, 9780761453802, Amazon Children's Publishing) Amazon Publishing.

Omoth, Tyler. First Source to Baseball: Rules, Equipment, & Key Playing Tips. 2016. (First Sports Source Ser.). (ENG., Illus.). 24p. (gr. 1-2). lib. bdg. 25.32 *(978-1-4914-8420-3(9)*, First Facts) Capstone Press of Coughlan Cos.

Orr, Tamra B. The Science of a Fastball. 2015. (21st Century Skills Library: Full-Speed Sports Ser.). (ENG., Illus.). 32p. (J). (gr. 4-7). 29.93 *(978-1-63362-582-2(6)*, 206512) Cherry Lake Publishing.

Otten, Jack. Beisbol. 2004. (Entrenamiento Deportivo (Sports Training) Ser.). (SPA & ENG., Illus.). 24p. (J). (gr. 2-4). lib. bdg. 22.60 *(978-0-8239-6845-9(6))* Rosen Publishing Group, Inc., The.

—Béisbol (Baseball) 2009. (Entrenamiento deportivo (Sports Training) Ser.). (SPA.). 24p. (gr. 1-2). 42.50 *(978-1-61512-268-4(0)*, Editorial Buenas Letras) Rosen Publishing Group, Inc., The.

Ovations. Incl. Barry Bonds. Goodman, Michael E. lib. bdg. 21.30 *(978-0-88682-694-9(2))*; Grant Hill. Goodman, Michael E. lib. bdg. *(978-0-88682-831-8(7))*; Hillary Rodham Clinton. Loewen, Nancy. lib. bdg. *(978-0-88682-636-9(5))*; Jeff Gordon. Bach, Julie S. pap. *(978-0-88682-939-1(9))*; Monica Seles. Goodman, Michael E. lib. bdg. 21.30 *(978-0-88682-699-4(3))*; Shaquille O'Neal. Goodman, Michael E. lib. bdg. *(978-0-88682-633-8(0))*; Spike Lee. Chapman, Ferguson. lib. bdg. *(978-0-88682-697-0(7))*; Whoopi Goldberg. DeBoer, Andy. 21.30 *(978-0-88682-696-3(9))*; (Illus.). 32p. (YA). (gr. 4-7). 1998. 59.80 *(978-0-88682-693-2(4)*, Creative Education) Creative Co., The.

Pallotta, Jerry. F Is for Fenway Park: America's Oldest Major League Ballpark. 2012. (Discover the World Ser.). (ENG., Illus.). 40p. (YA). (gr. 2-5). 16.95 *(978-1-58536-788-7(5))* Sleeping Bear Pr.

Panchyk, Richard. Baseball History for Kids: America at Bat from 1900 to Today, with 21 Activities. 2016. (For Kids Ser.). (ENG.). 160p. (J). (gr. 4). pap. 16.95 *(978-1-61374-779-7(9))* Chicago Review Pr., Inc.

Patrick, Denise Lewis. Jackie Robinson Strong Inside & Out. 2005. 44p. (J). lib. bdg. 15.00 *(978-1-4242-0850-0(5))* Fitzgerald Bks.

Patrick, Jean L. S. The Baseball Adventure of Jackie Mitchell, Girl Pitcher vs. Babe Ruth. Hammond, Ted & Carbajal, Richard, illus. 2011. (History's Kid Heroes Ser.). 32p. pap. 51.02 *(978-0-7613-7635-4(6))*; (ENG.). (gr. 3-5). pap. 8.95 *(978-0-7613-7072-7(2))* Lerner Publishing Group. (Graphic Universe™).

—The Baseball Adventure of Jackie Mitchell, Girl Pitcher vs. Babe Ruth. Trover, Zachary et al, illus. 2011. (History's Kid Heroes Ser.). (ENG.). 32p. (gr. 3-5). 26.60 *(978-0-7613-6180-0(4))* Lerner Publishing Group.

Porterfield, Jason. Baseball: Rules, Tips, Strategy, & Safety. (Sports from Coast to Coast Ser.). 48p. 2009. (gr. 6-6). 53.00 *(978-1-60853-121-9(X)*, Rosen Reference) 2006. (Illus.). (J). (gr. 5-8). lib. bdg. 29.25 *(978-1-4042-0991-6(3))* Rosen Publishing Group, Inc., The.

—Major League Baseball: The Great Steroid Scandals. 2009. (Disgraced! the Dirty History of Performance-Enhancing Drugs in Sports Ser.). (Illus.). 48p. (YA). (gr. 5-9). 29.25 *(978-1-4358-5302-7(4)*, 1300476) Rosen Publishing Group, Inc., The.

Price, Roger & Stern, Leonard. Grand Slam Mad Libs. 2009. (Mad Libs Ser.). (ENG.). 48p. (J). (gr. 3-7). 4.99 *(978-0-8431-3355-4(4)*, Mad Libs) Penguin Young Readers Group.

Puckett & Gutelle. K Puckett's Baseball Game. 2004. pap. 111.60 *(978-0-7611-0494-0(1)*, 20494) Algonquin Bks. of Chapel Hill.

Rappoport, Ken. David Wright: A Baseball Star Who Cares. 2011. (Sports Stars Who Care Ser.). (Illus.). 48p. (J). (gr. 3-18). pap. 8.95 *(978-1-59845-229-7(0)*, Enslow Elementary) Enslow Pubs., Inc.

Rice, Dona Herweck. Batter Up! History of Baseball, 1 vol. 2nd rev. ed. 2014. (TIME for KIDS(r) Nonfiction Readers Ser.). (ENG., Illus.). 32p. (J). (gr. 3-3). pap. 25.96 *(978-1-4807-1088-7(1))* Shell Educational Publishing.

—Batter Up! History of Baseball, 1 vol. 2nd rev. ed. 2012. (TIME for KIDS(r) Nonfiction Readers Ser.). (ENG.). 32p. (J). (gr. 3-3). pap. 8.99 *(978-1-4333-3679-9(0))* Teacher Created Materials, Inc.

Roberts, Kelly. Baseball Book for Kids. 2006. 24.95 *(978-0-9777764-4-3(1))* Arbor Bks.

Roberts, Russell. C. C. Sabathia. 2011. (Blue Banner Biography Ser.). (Illus.). 32p. (YA). (gr. 4-7). lib. bdg. 25.70 *(978-1-61228-053-0(6))* Mitchell Lane Pubs., Inc.

Robinson, Sharon. Jackie Robinson: American Hero. 2013. (ENG.). 48p. (J). (gr. -1-3). pap. 4.99 *(978-0-545-54006-3(2)*, Scholastic Paperbacks) Scholastic, Inc.

Rodda, Bob. For the Fun of It: The Story of the 2001 Wooster, Ohio, Williamsport Little League Team's Tournament Run to the State Playoffs. 2003. 152p. (YA). pap. 14.00 *(978-1-59098-190-0(1))* Wooster Bk. Co., The.

Rosenstock, Barb. The Streak: How Joe DiMaggio Became America's Hero. Widener, Terry, illus. 2014. (ENG.). 32p. (J). (gr. 3). 16.95 *(978-1-59078-992-6(X)*, Calkins Creek) Boyds Mills Pr.

Rosero, Tucidides Perea. Reglamento Oficial Ilustrado Beisbol. 2003. (SPA., Illus.). 232p. per. *(978-958-30-0068-3(X))* Panamericana Editorial.

Ross, Dalton. The Top Teams Ever: Football, Baseball, Basketball, & Hockey Winners. 2009. (Sports Illustrated for Kids Bks). 176p. (gr. 7-12). 63.90 *(978-1-60853-156-1(2))* Rosen Publishing Group, Inc., The.

Royston, Angela. Wood: Let's Look at a Sports Bat. 2005. (J). *(978-1-4109-1819-2(X))*; (ENG.). 24p. pap. *(978-1-4109-1828-4(9))* Steck-Vaughn.

Rumaner, Marc. Play Ball! Incl. 2 1/2" Baseball. (Illus.). 12p. (J). (gr. -1-1). bds. *(978-1-56021-372-7(8)*, 219) W.J. Fantasy, Inc.

Saddleback Educational Publishing Staff, ed. Babe Ruth, 1 vol. unabr. ed. 2008. (Graphic Biographies Ser.). (ENG., Illus.). 25p. (YA). (gr. 9-12). pap. 7.95 *(978-1-59905-215-1(6))* Saddleback Educational Publishing, Inc.

Sanna, Gabriel. Baseball & Softball. 2010. (Getting the Edge Ser.). 96p. (YA). lib. bdg. 24.95 *(978-1-4222-1730-6(2))* Mason Crest.

Savage, Jeff. David Ortiz. 2006. (Illus.). (J). pap. 6.95 *(978-0-8225-3594-2(7)*, First Avenue Editions) Lerner Publishing Group.

Scheff, Matt. Incredible Baseball Records. 2016. (Incredible Sports Records Ser.). (ENG.). 24p. (J). (gr. 2-5). 28.50 *(978-1-5038-0886-7(6)*, 210675) Child's World, Inc., The.

Schuh, Mari C. Baseball. 2017. (Spot Sports Ser.). (ENG.). 16p. (gr. k-3). 17.95 ***(978-1-68151-085-9(5))*** Amicus Publishing.

Silverstone, Michael. Latino Legends Set: Hispanics in Major League Baseball, 6 vols. 2003. (High Five Reading - Green Ser.). (ENG.). 48p. (gr. 3-4). pap. 54.00 *(978-0-7368-2842-0(7)*, High Five Reading (RBL)) Capstone Press of Coughlan Cos.

Smolka, Bo. Baseball, 1 vol. 2012. (ENG.). 64p. 32.79 *(978-1-61783-140-9(9)*, Super SandCastle) ABDO Publishing Co.

Sommer, Shelley. Hammerin' Hank Greenberg: Baseball Pioneer. 2011. (ENG., Illus.). 136p. (J). (gr. 5-18). 17.95 *(978-1-59078-452-5(9)*, Calkins Creek) Boyds Mills Pr.

Sports Illustrated Kids Pro Files: Baseball, 1 vol. 2012. (Time, Inc. Library-Bound Titles Ser.). (ENG.). 48p. (gr. 5-6). 31.32 *(978-1-4296-9187-1(5))* Capstone Press of Coughlan Cos.

Spradlin, Michael P. Baseball from A to Z. Pamintuan, Macky, illus. 2010. (ENG.). 32p. (J). (gr. -1-3). 16.99 *(978-0-06-124081-2(8))* HarperCollins Pubs.

Stanley, Glen F. & Porterfield, Jason. An Insider's Guide to Baseball. 2014. (Sports Tips, Techniques, & Strategies Ser.). 48p. (YA). (gr. 5-8). pap. 11.75 *(978-1-4777-8578-2(7)*, Rosen Reference) Rosen Publishing Group, Inc., The.

Sterling Children's, Sterling. My First Baseball Book. 2015. (First Sports Ser.). (ENG., Illus.). 22p. (J). (— 1). bds. 6.95 *(978-1-4549-1486-0(6))* Sterling Publishing Co., Inc.

Stewart, John. The Baseball Clinic: A Handbook for Players & Coaches. 2004. (Illus.). 146p. (J). (gr. 4-8). reprint ed. 20.00 *(978-0-7567-7637-4(6))* DIANE Publishing Co.

Stewart, Mark. Baseball. 2009. (Ultimate 10: Sports Ser.). (ENG.). 48p. (J). (gr. 4-8). pap. 10.50 *(978-1-4339-2203-9(7))* Stevens, Gareth Publishing LLLP.

Stewart, Mark & Kennedy, Mike. Long Ball: The Legend & Lore of the Home Run. 2006. (Spectacular Sports Ser.). (ENG., Illus.). 64p. (gr. 5-12). lib. bdg. 33.27 *(978-0-7613-2779-0(7))* Lerner Publishing Group.

Stone, Lynn M. Pitchers. 2007. (Playmakers (High Interest) Ser.). (Illus.). 24p. (YA). (gr. 3-6). lib. bdg. 27.07 *(978-1-60044-594-1(2))* Rourke Educational Media.

Storden, Thom. Amazing Baseball Records, 1 vol. 2014. (Epic Sports Records Ser.). (ENG.). 32p. (gr. 1-2). lib. bdg. 26.65 *(978-1-4914-0740-0(9))* Capstone Press of Coughlan Cos.

Stout, Glenn & Williams, Ike. From Hardships to Championships. 2013. (Good Sports Ser.). (ENG., Illus.). 144p. (J). (gr. 5-7). pap. 5.99 *(978-0-547-88735-7(3))* Houghton Mifflin Harcourt Publishing Co.

Stuckey, Rachel. Play Ball! Baseball Tips & Tricks. 2015. (ENG., Illus.). 32p. (J). *(978-0-7787-1478-1(0))* Crabtree Publishing Co.

Sullivan, Erin. Baseball Math. 2011. (Early Connections Ser.). (J). *(978-1-61672-626-3(1))* Benchmark Education Co.

Sylvester, Kevin. Baseballogy: Tons of Things You Never Knew. 2015. (ENG., Illus.). 72p. (J). (gr. 3-7). pap. 14.95 *(978-1-55451-707-7(9)*, 9781554517077) Annick Pr., Ltd. CAN. Dist: Publishers Group West (PGW).

Tallarico, Tony J., Jr. Baseball Facts & Fun Activity Book. 2017. (Dover Children's Activity Bks.). (ENG.). 48p. (J). (gr. 1-4). pap. 4.99 *(978-0-486-81442-1(4))* Dover Pubns., Inc.

Tavares, Matt. Henry Aaron's Dream. Tavares, Matt, illus. (Candlewick Biographies Ser.). (ENG., Illus.). (J). 2015. 48p. (gr. k-3). 14.99 (978-0-7636-7653-7(5)) 2012. 40p. (gr. 3-7). pap. 6.99 (978-0-7636-5820-5(0)) Candlewick Pr.

Taylor, Trace. Baseball. Taylor, Trace, illus. 2009. (2G Sports Ser.). (ENG., Illus.). 16p. (J). (gr. k-2). pap. 5.99 (978-1-59301-877-1(0)) American Reading Co.

Taylor, Trace & SáNchez, LucíA M. Bélsbol (Baseball) 2011. (ARC Press / el poder de 100 - Deportes (Power 100 - Sports) Ser.). (SPA.). pap. 33.92 (978-1-61541-470-3(3)) American Reading Co.

Teitelbaum, Michael. Baseball. 2008. (21st Century Skills Innovation Library: Innovation in Sports Ser.). (ENG., Illus.). 32p. (gr. 4-8). lib. bdg. 28.50 (978-1-60279-255-5(0), 200122) Cherry Lake Publishing.

Thayer, Ernest L. & Gardner, Martin. Casey at the Bat. Hull, Jim, illus. 2012. (Dover Children's Classics Ser.). (ENG.). 72p. (J). (gr. 2-5). pap. 6.99 (978-0-486-48510-2(2)) Dover Pubns., Inc.

The Editors of Sports Illustrated Kids. My First Book of Baseball: A Rookie Book. 2016. (Sports Illustrated Kids Rookie Bks.). (ENG., Illus.). 48p. (J). (gr. -1-1). 11.99 (978-1-61893-167-2(9)) Time Inc. Bks.

Trussell-Cullen, Alan. Jackie Robinson. 2009. pap. 13.25 (978-1-60559-063-9(0)) Hameray Publishing Group, Inc.

Tustison, Matt. Sacramento Kings, 1 vol. 2011. (Inside the NBA Ser.). (ENG., Illus.). 48p. (YA). (gr. 3-6). lib. bdg. 32.79 (978-1-61783-174-4(3)) ABDO Publishing Co.

Vigue, Jim, ed. Peak Power Baseball: How to Turn Your Little League Dream into Major League Reality. 2003. (Illus.). 238p. (YA). (gr. 7-18). pap. 17.95 (978-0-9724194-0-6(3)) Power Pubns., Inc.

Wacholtz, Anthony. Picture a Home Run: A Baseball Drawing Book, 1 vol. Haya, Erwin, illus. 2013. (Drawing with Sports Illustrated Kids Ser.). (ENG.). 64p. (gr. 5-7). 33.99 (978-1-4765-3106-9(4)) Capstone Press of Coughlan Cos.

—The Ultimate Collection of Pro Baseball Records. 2012. (For the Record Ser.). (ENG.). 64p. (gr. 4-6). pap. 53.70 (978-1-4296-9429-2(7)); (Illus.). lib. bdg. 34.65 (978-1-4296-8714-0(2)) Capstone Press of Coughlan Cos.

Wark, Laurie & Ritchie, Scot. Baseball. (FRE., Illus.). (J). pap. 5.99 (978-0-590-24305-6(5)) Scholastic, Inc.

Washington, Joi. Baseball (2Y) 2010. (1-3Y Sports Ser.). (ENG.). 16p. (J). pap. 5.99 (978-1-61541-532-8(7)) American Reading Co.

West, David Anthony. Baseball: Secrets of the Know 'n Go Game. l.t. ed. 2006. (Illus.). 224p. (J). per. 17.95 (978-0-9769478-5-1(4)) Aztec 5 Publishing.

Whiting, Jim. The Science of Hitting a Home Run: Forces & Motion in Action. 2010. (Action Science Ser.). (ENG.). 32p. (gr. 3-4). pap. 47.70 (978-1-4296-5076-2(1), Fact Finders) Capstone Press of Coughlan Cos.

Winter, Jonah, photos by. ¡Beisbol! Latino Baseball Pioneers & Legends. 2013. (ENG., Illus.). 32p. (J). (gr. 3-6). pap. 9.95 (978-1-58430-234-6(8)) Lee & Low Bks., Inc.

Wiseman, Blaine. Baseball. 2010. (Record Breakers Ser.). (Illus.). 24p. (YA). (gr. 3-6). lib. bdg. 27.13 (978-1-61690-109-7(8)); (J). (gr. 4-6). pap. 12.95 (978-1-61690-110-3(1)) Weigl Pubs., Inc.

Wright, John. Baseball. 2005. (Sports Injuries Ser.). (Illus.). 64p. (YA). lib. bdg. 19.95 (978-1-59084-626-1(5)) Mason Crest.

Young, Jeff C. Albert Pujols: A Baseball Star Who Cares. 2013. (Sports Stars Who Care Ser.). 48p. (J). lib. bdg. 25.27 (978-0-7660-4228-5(6)) Enslow Pubs., Inc.

Zuehlke, Jeffrey. Curt Schilling. 2007. (Amazing Athletes Ser.). 32p. (ENG.). (gr. 2-5). pap. 7.95 (978-0-8225-3596-6(3), First Avenue Editions); (Illus.). (J). (gr. 3-7). lib. bdg. 23.93 (978-0-8225-3431-0(2), Lerner Pubns.) Lerner Publishing Group.

—Joe Mauer. 2008. pap. 40.95 (978-0-8225-9490-1(0)) Lerner Publishing Group.

BASEBALL—BIOGRAPHY

Abramson, Danny. Andruw Jones. (Baseball Superstars Ser.). 2009. 120p. (gr. 6-12). pap. 11.95 (978-0-7910-9899-8(0), Checkmark Bks.) 2008. (Illus.). 114p. (YA). (gr. 7-12). lib. bdg. 30.00 (978-0-7910-9647-5(5)) Facts On File, Inc.

Anderson, Jameson. Miguel Cabrera, 1 vol. 2014. (Awesome Athletes Ser.). (ENG.). 32p. (gr. 8-12). 27.07 (978-1-62403-328-5(8)) ABDO Publishing Co.

—Mike Trout, 1 vol. 2014. (Awesome Athletes Ser.). (ENG.). 32p. (gr. 8-12). 27.07 (978-1-62403-336-0(9)) ABDO Publishing Co.

Anderson, Sheila. Roberto Clemente. 2008. pap. 40.95 (978-0-8225-9476-5(5)) Lerner Publishing Group.

—Roberto Clemente: A Life of Generosity. 2008. (Pull Ahead Bks.). (Illus.). 32p. (J). (gr. -1-3). lib. bdg. 22.60 (978-0-8225-8586-2(3), Lerner Pubns.) Lerner Publishing Group.

Aretha, David. Ichiro Suzuki: Baseball's Most Valuable Player. 2016. (Influential Asians Ser.). (Illus.). 128p. (J). (gr. 7-6). 37.27 (978-0-7660-7902-1(3)) Enslow Pubs., Inc.

—José Altuve: Champion Baseball Star. 2017. (Sports Star Champions Ser.). 48p. (J). (gr. 5-6). lib. bdg. 27.93 **(978-0-7660-8690-6(9))** Enslow Pubs., Inc.

—Top 10 Hitters in Baseball. 2016. (Sports Greats Ser.). (ENG., Illus.). 48p. (J). (gr. 5-6). pap. 11.70 (978-0-7660-7394-4(7)) Enslow Pubs., Inc.

—Top 10 Pitchers in Baseball. 2016. (Sports Greats Ser.). (ENG., Illus.). 48p. (J). (gr. 5-6). pap. 11.70 (978-0-7660-7406-4(4)) Enslow Pubs., Inc.

—Top 10 Teams in Baseball. 2016. (Sports Greats Ser.). (ENG.). 48p. (J). (gr. 5-6). pap. 11.70 (978-0-7660-7410-1(2)) Enslow Pubs., Inc.

Bailey, Budd. Ichiro Suzuki: A League of His Own. 2017. (J). **(978-1-5026-2760-5(4))** Musa Publishing.

Bailey, Budd. Jackie Robinson: Breaking Baseball's Color Barrier. 2016. (Game-Changing Athletes Ser.). (ENG.). 112p. (J). (gr. 9-9). lib. bdg. 42.79 (978-1-5026-1056-0(6)) Cavendish Square Publishing.

Bankston, John. What It's Like to Be Mariano Rivera. 2012. (Illus.). 32p. (J). lib. bdg. 25.70 (978-1-61228-320-3(9)) Mitchell Lane Pubs., Inc.

Bednar, Chuck. Derek Jeter: All-Star Major League Baseball Player. 2012. (Transcending Race Ser.). 64p. (J). (gr. 5). 22.95 (978-1-4222-2728-2(6)) Mason Crest.

Benjamin, Lisa. Jackie Robinson: Changing the Game. 2005. (Voices Reading Ser.). (Illus.). 32p. (J). (978-0-7367-2937-6(2)) Zaner-Bloser, Inc.

Bennett, Doraine. Jackie Robinson. 2008. (J). pap. (978-1-935077-11-4(2)); (ENG., Illus.). 24p. lib. bdg. 19.93 (978-1-935077-04-6(X)) State Standards Publishing, LLC.

Berne, Emma Carlson. What's Your Story, Jackie Robinson? 2015. (ENG., Illus.). 32p. (J). (gr. k-3). 26.65 (978-1-4677-7964-7(4)) Lerner Publishing Group.

Bernstein, Ross. Barry Bonds. 2004. (Sports Heroes & Legends Ser.). (ENG., Illus.). 112p. (gr. 5-12). lib. bdg. 30.60 (978-0-8225-1791-7(4)) Lerner Publishing Group.

Bildner, Phil. The Shot Heard 'Round the World. Payne, C. F., illus. 2010. (ENG.). 32p. (J). (gr. k-3). 16.99 (978-1-4424-2195-0(9), Simon & Schuster Bks. For Young Readers) Simon & Schuster Bks. For Young Readers.

—The Unforgettable Season: Joe Dimaggio, Ted Williams & the Record-Setting Summer of 1941. Schindler, S. D., illus. 2011. (ENG.). 32p. (J). (gr. 2-4). 16.99 (978-0-399-25501-4(X), G.P. Putnam's Sons Books for Young Readers) Penguin Young Readers Group.

Billus, Kathleen. Judy Johnson. 2009. (Baseball Hall of Famers of the Negro Leagues Ser.). 112p. (gr. 5-8). 63.90 (978-1-61511-524-2(2), Rosen Reference) Rosen Publishing Group, Inc., The.

Boehme, Gerry. Roberto Clemente: The Pride of Puerto Rico. 2016. (Game-Changing Athletes Ser.). (ENG., Illus.). 112p. (J). (gr. 9-9). lib. bdg. 42.79 (978-1-5026-1058-4(2)) Cavendish Square Publishing.

Boone, Mary. David Wright. 2010. (Blue Banner Biography Ser.). (Illus.). 32p. (YA). (gr. 4-7). lib. bdg. 25.70 (978-1-58415-910-0(3)) Mitchell Lane Pubs., Inc.

Boothroyd, Jennifer. Lou Gehrig. 2008. pap. 40.95 (978-0-8225-9473-4(0)) Lerner Publishing Group.

—Lou Gehrig: A Life of Dedication. 2008. (Pull Ahead Bks.). (Illus.). 32p. (J). (gr. -1-3). lib. bdg. 22.60 (978-0-8225-8587-9(1), Lerner Pubns.) Lerner Publishing Group.

Bowen, Fred. No Easy Way: The Story of Ted Williams & the Last .400 Season. Pyle, Charles S. & Pyle, Chuck, illus. 2010. (ENG.). 32p. (J). (gr. k-3). 16.99 (978-0-525-47877-5(9), Dutton Books for Young Readers) Penguin Young Readers Group.

Bradley, Michael. Derek Jeter. 2004. (Benchmark All-Stars Ser.). (Illus.). 48p. (gr. 4-18). lib. bdg. 27.07 (978-0-7614-1626-5(9), Benchmark Bks.) Marshall Cavendish Corp.

Braun, Eric. Pro Baseball's Underdogs: Players & Teams Who Shocked the Baseball World. 2017. (Sports Shockers! Ser.). (ENG.). 32p. (gr. 3-4). lib. bdg. 27.99 **(978-1-5157-8047-2(3))** Capstone Press of Coughlan Cos.

Brignall, Richard. Big League Dreams: Baseball Hall of Fame's First African-Canadian, Fergie Jenkins, 1 vol. 2010. (Lorimer Recordbooks Ser.). (ENG., Illus.). 152p. (gr. 8-12). 9.95 (978-1-55277-486-1(4), 9781552774861) Lorimer, James & Co., Ltd., Pubs. CAN. Dist: Casemate Pubs. & Bk. Distributors, LLC.

Brooks, Aaron & Brown, Greg. Aaron Brooks: Rise Above. 2004. (Illus.). 48p. (J). 15.95 (978-0-9634650-9-2(0)) Positively for Kids, Inc.

Brown, Jonatha A. Jackie Robinson. Acosta, Tatiana & Gutierrez, Guillermo, trs. 2004. (Gente Que Hay Que Conocer Ser.). (SPA., Illus.). 24p. (gr. 1-4). lib. bdg. 22.00 (978-0-8368-4353-8(3), Weekly Reader Leveled Readers) Stevens, Gareth Publishing LLLP.

Brown, Jonatha A. & Raatma, Lucia. Jackie Robinson. 2004. (People We Should Know Ser.). (Illus.). 24p. (gr. 1-4). pap. 8.15 (978-0-8368-4318-7(5)); lib. bdg. 22.00 (978-0-8368-4311-8(8)) Stevens, Gareth Publishing LLLP. (Weekly Reader Leveled Readers).

Bryant, Howard & Mack, Jeff. Legends: The Best Players, Games, & Teams in Baseball. 2015. (ENG., Illus.). 240p. (J). (gr. 3-7). bds. 16.99 (978-0-399-16903-8(2), Philomel Bks.) Penguin Young Readers Group.

Bubar, Joe. Go Mo'! Mo'Ne Davis: The Girl Who Changed Baseball History. 2015. (Illus.). 32p. (J). pap. (978-0-545-83753-8(7)) Scholastic, Inc.

Buckley, James, Jr. Home Run Heroes: Big Mac, Sammy & Junior. 2004. (Illus.). 48p. (J). (gr. k-4). reprint ed. pap. 10.00 (978-0-7567-7273-4(7)) DIANE Publishing Co.

Burgan, Michael. Daring Play: How a Courageous Jackie Robinson Transformed Baseball. 2016. (Captured History Sports Ser.). (ENG.). 64p. (gr. 5-7). lib. bdg. 34.65 (978-0-7565-5291-6(5), CPB Grades 4-8) Compass Point Bks.

Burleigh, Robert. Stealing Home: Jackie Robinson: Against the Odds. Wimmer, Mike, illus. 2007. (ENG.). 32p. (J). (gr. 1-4). 17.99 (978-0-689-86276-2(8), Simon & Schuster/Paula Wiseman Bks.) Simon & Schuster/Paula Wiseman Bks.

Castle, George. Sammy Sosa: Slammin' Sammy. Rains, Rob, ed. 2003. (Superstar Ser.). (Illus.). 96p. (J). (gr. 4-7). pap. 4.95 (978-1-58261-029-0(0)) Sports Publishing, LLC.

Chandler, Matt. Side-By-Side Baseball Stars: Comparing Pro Baseball's Greatest Players, 1 vol. 2014. (Side-By-Side Sports Ser.). (ENG.). 48p. (gr. 4-6). lib. bdg. 27.99 (978-1-4765-6167-7(2)) Capstone Press of Coughlan Cos.

—Who's Who of Pro Baseball: A Guide to the Game's Greatest Players. 2015. (Who's Who of Pro Sports Ser.). (ENG., Illus.). 32p. (gr. 3-4). lib. bdg. 27.99 (978-1-4914-0892-6(8)) Capstone Press of Coughlan Cos.

Christopher, Matt. At the Plate with... Ichiro. 2003. (Matt Christopher Sports Bio Bookshelf Ser.). (Illus.). 101p. (J). (gr. 4-7). 12.65 (978-0-7569-1606-0(2)) Perfection Learning Corp.

—Babe Ruth. 2006. (Matt Christopher Legends in Sports Ser.). (Illus.). 91p. (gr. 3-7). 15.00 (978-0-7569-6922-6(0)) Perfection Learning Corp.

—En El Campo de Juego Con... Derek Jeter. 2005.Tr. of On the Field with... Derek Jeter. (SPA., Illus.). 144p. (J). (gr. 5-8). pap. 16.99 (978-0-316-73770-8(4)) Little Brown & Co.

—Great Americans in Sports: Babe Ruth. 2015. (ENG., Illus.). 128p. (J). (gr. 3-7). pap. 5.99 (978-0-316-26097-8(5)) Little, Brown Bks. for Young Readers.

Christopher, Matt & Stout, Glenn. On the Mound With... Curt Schilling. 2004. (ENG., Illus.). 112p. (J). (gr. 3-7). pap. 15.99 (978-0-316-60736-0(3)) Little, Brown Bks. for Young Readers.

Churnin, Nancy. The William Hoy Story: How a Deaf Baseball Player Changed the Game. Tuya, Jez, illus. 2016. (ENG.). 32p. (J). (gr. -1-3). 16.99 (978-0-8075-9192-5(0)) Whitman, Albert & Co.

Cline-Ransome, Lesa. Satchel Paige. Ransome, James E., illus. 2004. 31p. (J). (gr. k-4). reprint ed. pap. 7.00 (978-0-7567-7799-9(2)) DIANE Publishing Co.

—Satchel Paige. Ransome, James E., illus. 2003. (ENG.). 40p. (J). (gr. 1-5). 8.99 (978-0-689-85681-5(4), Simon & Schuster/Paula Wiseman Bks.) Simon & Schuster/Paula Wiseman Bks.

Cockcroft, James D. Latinos in Beisbol. 2004. (Illus.). 207p. (J). (gr. 4-9). reprint ed. pap. 10.00 (978-0-7567-7347-2(4)) DIANE Publishing Co.

Collins, Tracy Brown. Babe Ruth. (Baseball Superstars Ser.). (gr. 6-12). 2009. 128p. pap. 11.95 (978-0-7910-9897-4(4), Checkmark Bks.) 2008. (Illus.). 122p. lib. bdg. 30.00 (978-0-7910-9570-6(3), Chelsea Hse.) Facts On File, Inc.

Crisp, Victor. Jackie Robinson: Breaking Barriers. 2013. (InfoMax Readers Ser.). (ENG.). 24p. (J). (gr. 3-4). pap. 49.50 (978-1-4777-2632-7(2)); (Illus.). pap. 8.25 (978-1-4777-2631-0(4)) Rosen Publishing Group, Inc., The. (Rosen Classroom).

Darraj, Susan Muaddi. Jackie Robinson. 2007. (Baseball Superstars Ser.). (Illus.). 122p. (YA). (gr. 7-12). lib. bdg. 30.00 (978-0-7910-9442-6(1)) Facts On File, Inc.

Davis, Mo'ne & TBD Staff. Mo'Ne - Remember My Name: My Story from First Pitch to Game Changer. 2015. (ENG., Illus.). 208p. (J). (gr. 3-7). 16.99 (978-0-06-239752-2(4)) HarperCollins Pubs.

De Marco, Tony. Jackie Robinson. 2009. (Journey to Freedom Ser.). (ENG., Illus.). 32p. (J). (gr. 4-7). 29.93 (978-1-60253-125-3(0), 200391) Child's World, Inc., The.

Doeden, Matt. Cal Ripken Jr. 2009. pap. 58.95 (978-0-7613-4807-8(7)) Lerner Publishing Group.

—Miguel Cabrera: Baseball Superstar, 1 vol. 2014. (Superstar Athletes Ser.). (ENG.). 24p. (gr. 1-2). pap. 7.29 (978-1-4765-9431-6(7)); lib. bdg. 25.32 (978-1-4765-8602-1(0)) Capstone Press of Coughlan Cos.

—The Negro Leagues: Celebrating Baseball's Unsung Heroes. 2017. (Spectacular Sports Ser.). (ENG.). 64p. (J). (gr. 5-12). 16.99 **(978-1-5124-3881-9(2))**; 50.65 **(978-1-5124-3882-6(0))**; (Illus.). 50.65 **(978-1-5124-2845-2(0))** Lerner Publishing Group. (Millbrook Pr.).

—Sandy Koufax. 2007. (YA). pap. 9.95 (978-0-8225-6692-2(3)) 2006. (Illus.). 106p. (J). (gr. 3-7). lib. bdg. 27.93 (978-0-8225-5961-0(7), Twenty-First Century Bks.) Lerner Publishing Group.

—Willie Mays. 2010. (Sports Heroes & Legends Ser.). (ENG.). 120p. (gr. 5-12). lib. bdg. 30.60 (978-0-7613-5370-6(4)) Lerner Publishing Group.

—The World's Greatest Baseball Players. 2010. (World's Greatest Sports Stars (Sports Illustrated for Kids) Ser.). (ENG.). 32p. (gr. 2-3). pap. 53.70 (978-1-4296-5102-8(4)) Capstone Press of Coughlan Cos.

Donovan, Sandy. Derek Jeter. 2011. 32p. (gr. 2-5). 25.26 (978-0-7613-7203-5(2)) 2008. pap. 40.95 (978-1-58013-718-8(0)) 2004. 32p. (J). (gr. 2-5). pap. 6.95 (978-0-8225-2038-2(9)) 2004. (Illus.). 32p. (J). (gr. 3-4). lib. bdg. 23.93 (978-0-8225-3674-1(9)) 2011. (ENG.). 32p. (gr. 2-5). pap. 7.95 (978-0-7613-7067-3(6)) Lerner Publishing Group.

—Derek Jeter (Revised Edition) 2011. (Amazing Athletes Ser.). 32p. (J). pap. 45.32 (978-0-7613-7652-1(6)) Lerner Publishing Group.

Dougherty, Terri. Ichiro Suzuki. 2004. (Awesome Athletes Ser.). 32p. (J). (gr. k-6). lib. bdg. 25.65 (978-1-59197-483-3(6), Checkerboard Library) ABDO Publishing Co.

Dunn, Joe. Jackie Robinson, 1 vol. Espinosa, Rod, illus. 2007. (Bio-Graphics Ser.). (ENG.). 32p. (gr. 3-6). 28.50 (978-1-60270-068-0(0), Graphic Planet- Nonfiction) ABDO Publishing Co.

Eckstein, David & Brown, Greg. Have Heart. 2nd rev. ed. 2006. (Illus.). 120p. (J). per. (978-0-9791504-0-1(X)) Builders' Stone Publishing, LLC.

Edwards, Ethan. Buster Posey: Baseball's Superstar Catcher, 1 vol., 1. 2014. (All-Star Players Ser.). (ENG.). 32p. (J). (gr. 3-6). 26.25 (978-1-4777-2915-1(1), PowerKids Pr.) Rosen Publishing Group, Inc., The.

—Josh Hamilton: Baseball's Unbelievable Comeback, 1 vol., 1. 2014. (All-Star Players Ser.). (ENG.). 32p. (J). (gr. 3-6). 26.25 (978-1-4777-2914-4(3), PowerKids Pr.) Rosen Publishing Group, Inc., The.

—Meet Albert Pujols: Baseball's Power Hitter. 2009. (All-Star Players Ser.). 32p. (gr. 4-5). 47.90 (978-1-61511-273-9(1), PowerKids Pr.) Rosen Publishing Group, Inc., The.

—Meet Derek Jeter: Baseball's Superstar Shortstop. 2009. (All-Star Players Ser.). 32p. (gr. 4-5). 47.90 (978-1-61511-279-1(0), PowerKids Pr.) Rosen Publishing Group, Inc., The.

Eisenstark, Reyna. Baseball's Stars: The Negro League. 2005. (Voices Reading Ser.). (Illus.). 16p. (J). (978-0-7367-2927-7(5)) Zaner-Bloser, Inc.

Elish, Dan. Jackie Robinson. 2005. (Cornerstones of Freedom Ser.). (ENG., Illus.). 48p. (YA). (gr. 4-7). lib. bdg. 26.00 (978-0-516-23635-3(0)) Scholastic Library Publishing.

Feinstein, Stephen. Read about Jackie Robinson. 2005. (I Like Biographies! Ser.). (Illus.). 24p. (J). lib. bdg. 22.60 (978-0-7660-2592-9(6), Enslow Elementary) Enslow Pubs., Inc.

Feldman, Heather. Derek Jeter: Baseball's Best / Estrella del Béisbol. 2009. (Superstars of Sports/Superestrellas del deporte Ser.). (ENG & SPA.). 24p. (gr. 1-2). 42.50 (978-1-60853-237-7(2), Editorial Buenas Letras) Rosen Publishing Group, Inc., The.

—Derek Jeter: Estrella del Béisbol (Baseball's Best) 2009. (Superestrellas del Deporte (Superstars of Sports) Ser.). (SPA.). 24p. (gr. 1-2). 42.50 (978-1-60853-225-4(9), Editorial Buenas Letras) Rosen Publishing Group, Inc., The.

—Derek Jeter, Baseball's Best/Estrella del Beisbol. De Leon, Mauricio Velzaquez, tr. 2008. (Reading Power Ser.). (ENG., Illus.). 24p. (gr. 1-6). pap. 8.85 (978-0-8239-6213-6(X)) Rosen Publishing Group, Inc., The.

Fischer, David. Roberto Clemente. 2004. (Trailblazers of the Modern World Ser.). (Illus.). 48p. (gr. 5-12). pap. 14.05 (978-0-8368-5264-6(8)); lib. bdg. 31.00 (978-0-8368-5495-4(0)) Stevens, Gareth Publishing LLLP. (Gareth Stevens Secondary Library).

Fishman, Cathy Goldberg. When Jackie & Hank Met, 0 vols. Elliott, Mark, illus. 2012. (ENG.). 40p. (J). (gr. 2-5). 17.99 (978-0-7614-6140-1(X), 9780761461401, Amazon Children's Publishing) Amazon Publishing.

Fishman, Jon. Andrew Mccutchen. 2015. (Amazing Athletes Ser.). (ENG., Illus.). 32p. (gr. 2-5). pap. 7.95 (978-1-4677-8158-9(4)) Lerner Publishing Group.

—Dustin Pedroia. 2015. (Amazing Athletes Ser.). (ENG., Illus.). 32p. (J). (gr. 2-5). lib. bdg. 25.26 (978-1-4677-5743-0(8), Lerner Pubns.) Lerner Publishing Group.

Fishman, Jon. Jose Altuve. 2017. (Sports All-Stars Ser.). (ENG.). (J). (gr. 2-5). 32p. pap. 8.99 **(978-1-5124-5615-8(2))**; (Illus.). lib. bdg. 26.65 **(978-1-5124-3923-6(1))** Lerner Publishing Group.

Fishman, Jon M. Andrew McCutchen. 2015. (Amazing Athletes Ser.). (ENG., Illus.). 32p. (J). (gr. 2-5). 25.26 (978-1-4677-8157-2(6), Lerner Pubns.) Lerner Publishing Group.

—Bryce Harper. 2014. (Amazing Athletes Ser.). (ENG., Illus.). 32p. (gr. 2-5). lib. bdg. 25.26 (978-1-4677-2143-1(3), Lerner Pubns.) Lerner Publishing Group.

—Buster Posey. 2016. (Amazing Athletes Ser.). (ENG., Illus.). 32p. (J). (gr. 2-5). 26.65 (978-1-4677-9384-1(1)) Lerner Publishing Group.

—Clayton Kershaw. 2015. (Amazing Athletes Ser.). (ENG., Illus.). 32p. (J). (gr. 2-5). lib. bdg. 25.26 (978-1-4677-5745-4(4), Lerner Pubns.) Lerner Publishing Group.

—Mariano Rivera. 2014. (Amazing Athletes Ser.). (ENG., Illus.). 32p. (gr. 2-5). lib. bdg. 25.26 (978-1-4677-2144-8(1), Lerner Pubns.) Lerner Publishing Group.

—Miguel Cabrera. 2013. (Amazing Athletes Ser.). (ENG., Illus.). 32p. (gr. 2-5). pap. 7.95 (978-1-4677-1559-1(X)); lib. bdg. 25.26 (978-1-4677-1558-4(1), Lerner Pubns.) Lerner Publishing Group.

—Mike Trout. 2014. (Amazing Athletes Ser.). (ENG., Illus.). 32p. (gr. 2-5). pap. 7.95 (978-1-4677-2183-7(2)); lib. bdg. 25.26 (978-1-4677-2142-4(5), Lerner Pubns.) Lerner Publishing Group.

—Robinson Cano. 2016. (Amazing Athletes Ser.). (ENG., Illus.). 32p. (J). (gr. 2-5). 26.65 (978-1-4677-9385-8(X), Lerner Pubns.) Lerner Publishing Group.

Flynn, Brendan. Andrew Mccutchen: National League MVP. 2015. (Today's MVPs & Champions Ser.). (ENG.). 24p. (J). (gr. 2-5). 27.07 (978-1-63143-734-2(8), 208569) Child's World, Inc., The.

—Miguel Cabrera: MVP & Triple Crown Winner. 2015. (Today's MVPs & Champions Ser.). (ENG.). 24p. (J). (gr. 2-5). 27.07 (978-1-63143-736-6(4), 208572) Child's World, Inc., The.

Ford, Carin T. Jackie Robinson: All I Ask Is That You Respect Me as a Human Being. 2005. (African-American Biography Library). (Illus.). 128p. (J). (gr. 6-12). lib. bdg. 33.27 (978-0-7660-2461-8(X)) Enslow Pubs., Inc.

—Jackie Robinson: Hero of Baseball. 2006. (Heroes of American History Ser.). (Illus.). 32p. (J). (gr. -1-3). lib. bdg. 23.94 (978-0-7660-2600-1(0), Enslow Elementary) Enslow Pubs., Inc.

—Roberto Clemente: Baseball Legend. 2005. (Latino Biography Library). (Illus.). 128p. (J). (gr. 6-12). lib. bdg. 33.27 (978-0-7660-2485-4(7)) Enslow Pubs., Inc.

Friedman, Nick. Mike Piazza. 2007. (Baseball Superstars Ser.). (Illus.). 130p. (YA). (gr. 7-12). lib. bdg. 30.00 (978-0-7910-9493-8(6)) Facts On File, Inc.

Frisch, Aaron. Albert Pujols. 2013. (Illus.). 24 p.p. (J). 25.65 (978-1-60818-336-4(X), Creative Education) Creative Co., The.

Gaab, Carol. Felipe Alou: From the Valleys to the Mountains. 2012. (Illus.). 98p. (J). (978-1-935575-79-5(1)) TPRS Publishing, Inc.

Gagne, Tammy. Day by Day with Manny Machado. 2013. (ENG., Illus.). 32p. (J). (gr. -1-2). lib. bdg. 25.70 (978-1-61228-454-5(X)) Mitchell Lane Pubs., Inc.

—Dustin Pedroia. 2014. 32p. (J). (gr. 1-4). 25.70 (978-1-61228-638-9(0)) Mitchell Lane Pubs., Inc.

—Mike Trout. 2013. (ENG.). 32p. (gr. 4-8). lib. bdg. 25.70 (978-1-61228-466-8(3)) Mitchell Lane Pubs., Inc.

García, Luis. Johan Santana. 2012. (Superstars of Baseball ENGLISH Ser.). 32p. (J). (gr. 4). 19.95 (978-1-4222-2695-7(6)); (SPA., Illus.). 19.95 (978-1-4222-2642-1(5)) Mason Crest.

Gaspar, Joe. Albert Pujols. 2010. (Reading Power: Baseball's MVPs Ser.). (Illus.). 24p. (J). pap. 8.85 (978-1-4488-1782-5(X), PowerKids Pr.) Rosen Publishing Group, Inc., The.

—Albert Pujols: Amazing Hitter. 2010. (Baseball's MVPs Ser.). (ENG.). 24p. (J). (gr. 3-6). lib. bdg. 22.60 (978-1-4488-0629-4(1)) Rosen Publishing Group, Inc., The.

—Alex Rodriguez. 2010. (Reading Power: Baseball's MVPs Ser.). (Illus.). 24p. (J). pap. 8.85 (978-1-4488-1793-1(5), PowerKids Pr.); (gr. 3-6). lib. bdg. 22.60 (978-1-4488-0634-8(8)) Rosen Publishing Group, Inc., The.

—Dustin Pedroia. 2010. (Reading Power: Baseball's MVPs Ser.). (Illus.). 24p. (J). pap. 8.85 (978-1-4488-1784-9(6), PowerKids Pr.) Rosen Publishing Group, Inc., The.

—Dustin Pedroia: Rising Star. 2010. (Baseball's MVPs Ser.). (ENG.). 24p. (J). (gr. 3-6). lib. bdg. 22.60 (978-1-4488-0630-0(5)) Rosen Publishing Group, Inc., The.

—Jimmy Rollins. 2010. (Baseball's MVPs Ser.). 24p. (J). (ENG.). (gr. 3-6). lib. bdg. 22.60 (978-1-4488-0631-7(3)); (Illus.). pap. 8.85 (978-1-4488-1786-3(2), PowerKids Pr.) Rosen Publishing Group, Inc., The.

—Justin Morneau. 2010. (Baseball's MVPs Ser.). 24p. (J). (ENG.). (gr. 3-6). lib. bdg. 22.60 (978-1-4488-0633-1(X)); (Illus.). pap. 8.85 (978-1-4488-1790-0(0), PowerKids Pr.) Rosen Publishing Group, Inc., The.

—Ryan Howard. 2010. (Reading Power: Baseball's MVPs Ser.). (Illus.). 24p. (J). pap. 8.85 (978-1-4488-1788-7(9), PowerKids Pr.) Rosen Publishing Group, Inc., The.

Gatto, Kimberly. Derek Jeter: A Baseball Star Who Cares. 2013. (Sports Stars Who Care Ser.). 48p. (J). (gr. 3-4). pap. 8.95 (978-1-4644-0541-9(7), Enslow Elementary) Enslow Pubs., Inc.

Gibson, Karen. What It's Like to Be Vladimir Guerrero. de la Vega, Eida, tr. 2011. (What It's Like to Be... = Que Se Sienta

Al Ser... Ser.). (ENG & SPA., Illus.). 32p. (J). (gr. -1-2). lib. bdg. 25.70 *(978-1-58415-992-6(8))* Mitchell Lane Pubs., Inc.

Giglio, James N. Stan Musial: Baseball Hero. 2015. (ENG., Illus.). 48p. (J). pap. 24.00 *(978-1-61248-151-7(5))* Truman State Univ. Pr.

Gigliotti, Jim. I Am #8: Roberto Clemente. 2013. (I Am Ser.: 8). (ENG.). 128p. (J). (gr. 2-5). pap. 5.99 *(978-0-545-53381-2(3))*, Scholastic Paperbacks) Scholastic, Inc.

—Power Pitchers. 2007. (Reading Rocks! Ser.). (ENG., Illus.). 32p. (J). (gr. 2-5). 28.50 *(978-1-59296-860-2(0))*, 200748) Child's World, Inc., The.

Giordano, Geraldine. Sandy Koufax. (Baseball Hall of Famers Ser.). 112p. (gr. 5-8). 2009. 63.90 *(978-1-61511-516-7(1))* 2003. (Illus.). lib. bdg. 34.60 *(978-0-8239-3603-8(1))* Rosen Publishing Group, Inc., The. (Rosen Reference).

Gitlin, Martin. David Wright: Gifted & Giving Baseball Star. 2010. (Sports Stars Who Give Back Ser.). (Illus.). 128p. (J). (gr. 5-9). 33.27 *(978-0-7660-3588-1(3))* Enslow Pubs., Inc.

Gitlin, Marty. Baseball Legends in the Making, 1 vol. 2014. (Legends in the Making Ser.). (ENG.). 32p. (gr. 3-4). lib. bdg. 27.99 *(978-1-4765-4062-7(4))* Capstone Press of Coughlan Cos.

—Bryce Harper: Baseball Star. 2017. (Biggest Names in Sports (paperback) Ser.). (ENG., Illus.). 32p. (J). (gr. 4-7). pap. 9.95 ***(978-1-63517-097-9(4)***, Focus Readers) North Star Editions.

—Kris Bryant: Baseball Star. 2017. (Biggest Names in Sports (paperback) Ser.). (ENG., Illus.). 32p. (J). (gr. 4-7). pap. 9.95 ***(978-1-63517-095-5(8)***, Focus Readers) North Star Editions.

Gitlin, Marty, et al. Legends in the Making, 1 vol. 2014. (Legends in the Making Ser.). (ENG.). 32p. (gr. 3-4). pap. 35.80 *(978-1-4765-6222-3(9))* Capstone Press of Coughlan Cos.

Glaser, Jason. Jackie Robinson: Baseball's Great Pioneer, 1 vol. Lentz, Bob et al, illus. 2005. (Graphic Biographies Ser.). (ENG.). 32p. (gr. 3-4). 30.65 *(978-0-7368-4633-2(6))*, Graphic Library) Capstone Press of Coughlan Cos.

—Tim Lincecum. 2011. (Today's Sports Greats Ser.). (Illus.). 32p. (gr. 4-6). (J). pap. 10.50 *(978-1-4339-5880-9(5)*, Gareth Stevens Learning Library); (YA). lib. bdg. 26.60 *(978-1-4339-5878-6(3))* Stevens, Gareth Publishing LLLP.

Goldsworthy, Steve. Baseball. 2011. (J). (gr. 4-6). pap. 13.95 *(978-1-61690-702-0(9)*, AV2 by Weigl); (Illus.). 32p. (YA). (gr. 2-5). 28.55 *(978-1-61690-697-9(9))* Weigl Pubs., Inc.

Golus, Carrie. Josh Gibson. 2010. (Sports Heroes & Legends Ser.). (ENG.). 120p. (gr. 5-12). lib. bdg. 30.60 *(978-0-7613-5367-6(4))* Lerner Publishing Group.

Gomez, Rebecca. Jackie Robinson, 1 vol. 2003. (First Biographies Ser.). (ENG., Illus.). 32p. (gr. k-4). 27.07 *(978-1-57765-949-5(X)*, Buddy Bks.) ABDO Publishing Co.

Greenberg, Doreen & Greenberg, Michael. A Drive to Win: The Story of Nancy Lieberman-Cline. 2003. (Anything You Can Do. . .Ser.: Vol. 1). (Illus.). 112p. (J). (gr. 2-5). pap. 9.95 *(978-1-930546-40-0(8))* Wish Publishing.

Greenberg, Keith Elliot. Derek Jeter. 2005. (Sports Heroes & Legends Ser.). (Illus.). 106p. (J). (gr. 3-7). lib. bdg. 27.93 *(978-0-8225-3068-8(6))*, Lerner Pubns.) Lerner Publishing Group.

—Derek Jeter: Spectacular Shortstop. 2011. (USA TODAY Lifeline Biographies Ser.). (ENG.). 112p. (gr. 6-12). 34.60 *(978-0-7613-6422-1(6))* Lerner Publishing Group.

Greenberger, Robert. Lou Gehrig. (Baseball Hall of Famers Ser.). 112p. (gr. 5-8). 2009. 63.90 *(978-1-61511-512-9(9))* 2004. (Illus.). lib. bdg. 34.60 *(978-0-8239-3781-3(X))* Rosen Publishing Group, Inc., The. (Rosen Reference).

Gregory, Josh. Jackie Robinson. 2015. (ENG., Illus.). 48p. (J). lib. bdg. *(978-0-531-21598-2(9))* Children's Pr., Ltd.

—Jackie Robinson. 2015. (True Book(tm) — Biographies Ser.). (ENG.). 48p. (J). pap. 6.95 *(978-0-531-21760-3(4)*, Children's Pr.) Scholastic Library Publishing.

Haidy, Emma E. Jackie Robinson. Bane, Jeff, illus. 2016. (My Early Library: My Itty-Bitty Bio Ser.). (ENG.). 24p. (J). (gr. k-1). 28.50 *(978-1-63471-021-3(5)*, 208164) Cherry Lake Publishing.

Hanft, J. & Zukowski/Faust, Jean. Jackie Robinson. 2006. (Heinle Reading Library: Biography Collection). (ENG.). 240p. pap. 16.95 ***(978-1-4240-0564-2(7))*** Cengage Heinle.

Hanft, Joshua E. Jackie Robinson. Marcos, Pablo, illus. 2005. (Heroes of America Ser.). 238p. (gr. 3-8). 27.07 *(978-1-59679-259-3(0)*, Abdo & Daughters) ABDO Publishing Co.

Hansen, Grace. Jackie Robinson: Baseball Legend, 1 vol. 2014. (History Maker Biographies Ser.). (ENG., Illus.). 24p. (J). (gr. 2-4). lib. bdg. 28.50 *(978-1-62970-701-3(5))* ABDO Publishing Co.

Herman, Gail. Who Is Derek Jeter? 2015. (Who Is... ? Ser.). lib. bdg. 16.00 *(978-0-606-37552-8(X))* Turtleback Bks.

—Who Was Jackie Robinson? Harrison, Nancy & O'brien, John, illus. 2010. (Who Was? Ser.). (ENG.). 112p. (J). (gr. 3-7). pap. 5.99 *(978-0-448-45557-0(9)*, Grosset & Dunlap) Penguin Young Readers Group.

Hillstrom & Hillstrom, Laurie C. Jackie Robinson & the Integration of Baseball. 2013. 248p. lib. bdg. 55.00 *(978-0-7808-1327-4(8))* Omnigraphics, Inc.

Hinnant, Jamal. Top 10 Injuries in Baseball. 2016. (Sports Greats Ser.). (ENG.). 48p. (J). (gr. 5-6). pap. 11.70 *(978-0-7660-7398-2(X))* Enslow Pubs., Inc.

Hoblin, Paul. Mike Trout: MLB Superstar, 1 vol. 2016. (ENG., Illus.). 32p. (J). *(978-1-62403-842-6(5)*, 1391431, SportsZone) ABDO Publishing Co.

Hoffman, Mary Ann. Alex Rodriguez: Baseball Star. 2007. (Sports Superstars Ser.). (Illus.). 24p. (J). (gr. 1-3). lib. bdg. 22.60 *(978-1-4042-3533-5(7))* Rosen Publishing Group, Inc., The.

—Alex Rodriguez: Baseball Star/Estrella del Beisbol. Alaman, Eduardo, tr. 2007. (Amazing Athletes/Atletas increíbles Ser.). (SPA., Illus.). 24p. (J). (gr. 2-5). lib. bdg. 22.60 *(978-1-4042-7598-0(3))* Rosen Publishing Group, Inc., The.

—David Ortiz: Baseball Star. (Sports Superstars Ser.). 24p. (gr. 1-1). 2009. 42.50 *(978-1-60853-174-5(0)*, PowerKids Pr.) 2007. (Illus.). (J). lib. bdg. 22.60 *(978-1-4042-3534-2(5))* Rosen Publishing Group, Inc., The.

—David Ortiz: Baseball Star/Estrella del Beisbol. Alaman, Eduardo, tr. 2007. (Amazing Athletes/Atletas increíbles Ser.). (SPA., Illus.). 24p. (J). (gr. 2-5). lib. bdg. 22.60 *(978-1-4042-7599-7(1))* Rosen Publishing Group, Inc., The.

Holub, Joan. Who Was Babe Ruth? Hammond, Ted & Harrison, Nancy, illus. 2012. (Who Was? Ser.). (ENG.). 112p. (J). (gr. 3-7). pap. 5.99 *(978-0-448-45586-0(2)*, Grosset & Dunlap) Penguin Young Readers Group.

Horn, Geoffrey M. Albert Pujols. 2006. (Today's Superstars). (Illus.). 32p. (gr. 5-8). lib. bdg. 31.95 *(978-0-8368-6185-3(X))* Stevens, Gareth Publishing LLLP.

Howell, Brian. Joe Mauer: All-Star Catcher, 1 vol. 2011. (Playmakers Ser.). (ENG., Illus.). 32p. (YA). (gr. 3-6). 27.07 *(978-1-61714-749-4(4))* ABDO Publishing Co.

Hubbard, Crystal. Catching the Moon: The Story of a Young Girl's Baseball Dream, 1 vol. Duburke, Randy, illus. 2005. (ENG.). 32p. (J). (gr. 1-5). 16.95 *(978-1-58430-243-8(7))* Lee & Low Bks., Inc.

Jarnow, Jesse. Johnny Bench. (Baseball Hall of Famers Ser.). 112p. (gr. 5-8). 2009. 63.90 *(978-1-61511-511-2(0))* 2004. (Illus.). lib. bdg. 34.60 *(978-0-8239-3780-6(1))* Rosen Publishing Group, Inc., The. (Rosen Reference).

Joltin' Joe DiMaggio. 2014. (ENG., Illus.). 48p. (J). (gr. -1-3). 17.99 *(978-1-4169-4080-7(4)*, Atheneum Bks. for Young Readers) Simon & Schuster Children's Publishing.

Kappes, Serena. Alex Rodriguez. 2006. (Sports Heroes & Legends Ser.). (Illus.). 106p. (J). (gr. 3-7). lib. bdg. 27.93 *(978-0-8225-5963-4(3)*, Lerner Pubns.) Lerner Publishing Group.

—Alex Rodriguez: Hot Corner, Hot Shot. 2012. (USA TODAY Lifeline Biographies Ser.). (ENG.). 112p. (gr. 6-12). lib. bdg. 34.60 *(978-0-7613-8155-6(4))* Lerner Publishing Group.

Kelley, K. C. Baseball Superstars 2015. 2015. (ENG.). 32p. (J). (gr. 2-5). pap. 5.99 *(978-0-545-83898-6(3)*, Scholastic Paperbacks) Scholastic, Inc.

—Baseball Superstars 2016. 2016. (ENG.). 32p. (J). (gr. 2-5). pap. 5.99 *(978-1-338-03276-5(3))* Scholastic, Inc.

Kellogg, David. True Stories of Baseball's Hall of Famers. 2015. (ENG., Illus.). 100p. (J). pap. 8.95 *(978-0-912517-41-4(7))* Bluewood Bks.

Kennedy, Mike. Derek Jeter. 2009. (Today's Superstars Ser.). 48p. (J). (gr. 5-8). pap. 14.05 *(978-1-4339-2162-9(6))*; lib. bdg. 31.95 *(978-1-4339-1969-5(9))* Stevens, Gareth Publishing LLLP.

Kirkpatrick, Rob. Mark Mcgwire: Record Breaker/Rompe Records. 2009. (Power Players / Deportistas de Poder Ser.). (ENG & SPA.). 24p. (gr. 1-2). 42.50 *(978-1-60851-332-1(7)*, Editorial Buenas Letras) Rosen Publishing Group, Inc., The.

—Mark Mcgwire: Rompe Récords (Record Breaker) 2009. (Deportistas de Poder (Power Players) Ser.). (SPA.). 24p. (gr. 1-1). 42.50 *(978-1-61512-159-5(5)*, Editorial Buenas Letras) Rosen Publishing Group, Inc., The.

—Mark Mcgwire: The Home Run King. 2009. (Great Record Breakers in Sports Ser.). 24p. (gr. 3-3). 42.50 *(978-1-61513-188-4(4)*, PowerKids Pr.) Rosen Publishing Group, Inc., The.

—Sammy Sosa: Bateador de Home Runs (Home-Run Hitter) 2009. (Deportistas de Poder (Power Players) Ser.). (SPA.). 24p. (gr. 1-1). 42.50 *(978-1-61512-160-1(9)*, Editorial Buenas Letras) Rosen Publishing Group, Inc., The.

—Sammy Sosa: Home Run Hitter/Bateador de home Runs. 2009. (Power Players / Deportistas de Poder Ser.). (ENG & SPA.). 24p. (gr. 1-2). 42.50 *(978-1-60851-333-8(5)*, Editorial Buenas Letras) Rosen Publishing Group, Inc., The.

—Sammy Sosa, Home Run Hitter/Bateador de Home Runs. De Leon, Mauricio Velzaquez, tr. 2008. (Reading Power Ser.). (ENG., Illus.). 24p. (gr. 1-6). pap. 8.85 *(978-1-4042-7541-6(X))* Rosen Publishing Group, Inc., The.

Kisseloff, Jeff. Who Is Baseball's Greatest Pitcher? 2003. (ENG., Illus.). 160p. (J). (gr. 5-7). 17.95 *(978-0-8126-2685-8(0))* Cricket Bks.

Kjelle, Marylou Morano. Alex Rodriguez: Professional Baseball Player. 2005. (Robbie Reader Ser.). (Illus.). 32p. (J). (gr. 4-8). lib. bdg. 25.70 *(978-1-58415-394-8(6))* Mitchell Lane Pubs., Inc.

Koestler-Grack, Rachel A. Kirby Puckett. 2007. (Baseball Superstars Ser.). (Illus.). 122p. (YA). (gr. 7-12). lib. bdg. 30.00 *(978-0-7910-9497-6(9))* Facts On File, Inc.

Kramer, S. A. Baseball's Greatest Hitters. 2016. (Step into Reading Ser.). (ENG., Illus.). 48p. (J). (gr. 2-4). 3.99 *(978-0-553-53910-3(8)*, Random Hse. Bks. for Young Readers) Random Hse. Children's Bks.

Kratz, Marilyn. Umpire in a Skirt: The Amanda Clement Story. Currie, Hector, illus. 2011. 44p. (J). pap. 9.95 *(978-0-9845041-2-1(5)*, South Dakota State Historical Society Pr.) South Dakota State Historical Society Pr.

Lace, William W. Nolan Ryan: Hall of Fame Baseball Superstar. (Hall of Fame Sports Greats Ser.). 64p. (J). (gr. 4-9). 2014. pap. 9.95 *(978-1-62285-026-6(2))* 2013. 15.95 *(978-1-62285-025-9(4))* Enslow Pubs., Inc.

LeBoutillier, Nate. The Best of Everything Baseball Book, 1 vol. 2011. (All-Time Best of Sports Ser.). (ENG.). 64p. (gr. 3-4). pap. 8.95 *(978-1-4296-6288-6(3))*; pap. 53.70 *(978-1-4296-6452-3(5))* Capstone Press of Coughlan Cos.

LeBron James. 2014. (ENG., Illus.). 48p. (J). lib. bdg. 29.00 *(978-0-531-21198-4(3))* Scholastic Library Publishing.

Leigh, David S. Ichiro Suzuki. 2004. (Sports Heroes & Legends Ser.). (ENG., Illus.). 112p. (gr. 5-12). lib. bdg. 30.60 *(978-0-8225-1792-4(2))* Lerner Publishing Group.

Leventhal, Josh. Albert Pujols. 2017. (Béisbol! Latino Heroes of Major League Baseball Ser.). (ENG., Illus.). 32p. (J). (gr. 3-7). 31.35 ***(978-1-68072-049-5(X))*** Black Rabbit Bks.

—Felix Hernandez. 2017. (Béisbol! Latino Heroes of Major League Baseball Ser.). (ENG., Illus.). 32p. (gr. 3-7). 31.35 ***(978-1-68072-047-1(3))*** Black Rabbit Bks.

—Jose Altuve. 2017. (Béisbol! Latino Heroes of Major League Baseball Ser.). (ENG., Illus.). 32p. (gr. 3-7). 31.35 ***(978-1-68072-044-0(9))*** Black Rabbit Bks.

—Miguel Cabrera. 2017. (Béisbol! Latino Heroes of Major League Baseball Ser.). (ENG., Illus.). 32p. (J). (gr. 3-7). 31.35 ***(978-1-68072-045-7(7))*** Black Rabbit Bks.

—Nelson Cruz. 2017. (Béisbol! Latino Heroes of Major League Baseball Ser.). (ENG., Illus.). 32p. (gr. 3-7). 31.35 ***(978-1-68072-046-4(5))*** Black Rabbit Bks.

Levin, Judith. Ichiro Suzuki. (Baseball Superstars Ser.). (Illus.). 2008. 144p. (gr. 6-12). pap. 11.95 *(978-0-7910-9849-3(4)*, Checkmark Bks.) 2007. 135p. (YA). (gr. 7-12). lib. bdg. 30.00 *(978-0-7910-9440-2(5))* Facts On File, Inc.

—Mariano Rivera. (Baseball Superstars Ser.). 2009. 136p. (gr. 6-12). pap. 11.95 *(978-0-7910-9901-8(6)*, Checkmark Bks.) 2008. 130p. (YA). (gr. 7-12). 30.00 *(978-0-7910-9599-7(1))* Facts On File, Inc.

Macnow, Glen. Cal Ripken, Jr: Hall of Fame Baseball Superstar. (Hall of Fame Sports Greats Ser.). 64p. (J). (gr. 4-9). 2014. pap. 9.95 *(978-1-62285-021-1(1))* 2013. 15.95 *(978-1-62285-020-4(3))* Enslow Pubs., Inc.

MacRae, Sloan. Meet Manny Ramirez: Baseball's Grand Slam Hitter. 2009. 32p. (gr. 4-6). (Illus.). (J). pap. 10.00 *(978-1-4358-3100-1(4))*; 47.90 *(978-1-61511-290-6(1))* Rosen Publishing Group, Inc., The. (PowerKids Pr.).

—Meet Vladimir Guerrero: Baseball's Super Vlad. 2009. 32p. (gr. 4-6). (Illus.). (J). pap. 10.00 *(978-1-4358-3099-8(7))*; 47.90 *(978-1-61511-300-2(2))* Rosen Publishing Group, Inc., The. (PowerKids Pr.).

Malone, Julio. Sammy Sosa en 9 Innings. 2nd exp. ed. 2004. (SPA.). (YA). pap. 12.95 net. *(978-0-9671705-0-3(8))* Editorial Miglo Inc.

—Sammy Sosa in 9 Innings. 2004. (YA). pap. 12.95 *(978-0-9671705-1-0(6))* Editorial Miglo Inc.

Manny Ramirez. 2010. (Great Hispanic Heritage Ser.). (Illus.). 128p. (gr. 6-12). 35.00 *(978-1-60413-730-9(4)*, Chelsea Hse.) Facts On File, Inc.

Manoloff, Dennis. Omar Vizquel: The Man with the Golden Glove. Rains, Rob, ed. 2003. (Super Star Ser.). (Illus.). 96p. (J). (gr. 4-7). pap. 4.95 *(978-1-58261-045-0(2))* Sports Publishing, LLC.

Marcovitz, Hal. Derek Jeter. 2010. (Modern Role Models Ser.). (Illus.). 64p. (YA). (gr. 7-12). lib. bdg. 22.95 *(978-1-4222-0482-5(0))* Mason Crest.

Mattern, Joanne. Albert Pujols: Baseball Superstar, 1 vol. 2011. (Superstar Athletes Ser.). (ENG.). 24p. (gr. 1-2). pap. 7.29 *(978-1-4296-7301-3(X))*; pap. 41.70 *(978-1-4296-7302-0(8))* Capstone Press of Coughlan Cos.

—David Ortiz. 2007. (Blue Banner Biography Ser.). (Illus.). 32p. (YA). (gr. 4-7). lib. bdg. 25.70 *(978-1-58415-620-8(1))* Mitchell Lane Pubs., Inc.

—Day by Day with Adam Jones. 2014. (Illus.). 32p. (J). (gr. -1-2). 25.70 *(978-1-61228-632-7(1))* Mitchell Lane Pubs., Inc.

—Derek Jeter: Baseball Superstar, 1 vol. 2011. (Superstar Athletes Ser.). (ENG.). 24p. (gr. 1-2). lib. bdg. 25.32 *(978-1-4296-6560-5(2))* Capstone Press of Coughlan Cos.

—Miguel Tejada. 2006. (Blue Banner Biography Ser.). (Illus.). 32p. (YA). (gr. 4-7). lib. bdg. 25.70 *(978-1-58415-505-8(1))* Mitchell Lane Pubs., Inc.

Maurer, Tracy Nelson. Mike Trout. 2015. (Famous Athletes Ser.). (ENG., Illus.). 24p. (gr. k-1). lib. bdg. 26.65 *(978-1-4914-6237-9(X))* Capstone Press of Coughlan Cos.

McCormack, Shaun. Ted Williams. 2009. (Baseball Hall of Famers Ser.). 112p. (gr. 5-8). 63.90 *(978-1-61511-517-4(X)*, Rosen Reference) Rosen Publishing Group, Inc., The.

McCully, Emily Arnold. Queen of the Diamond: The Lizzie Murphy Story. 2015. (ENG., Illus.). 32p. (J). (gr. k-3). 17.99 *(978-0-374-30007-4(0)*, 9780374300074, Farrar, Straus & Giroux (BYR)) Farrar, Straus & Giroux.

McPherson, Stephanie Sammartino. Jackie Robinson. 2010. (J). lib. bdg. 27.93 *(978-0-7613-5207-5(4)*, Lerner Pubns.) Lerner Publishing Group.

Michelson, Richard. Lipman Pike: America's First Home Run King. Pullen, Zachary, illus. 2011. (ENG.). 32p. (J). (gr. 1-4). 16.95 *(978-1-58536-465-7(7)*, 202186) Sleeping Bear Pr.

Mills, Clifford W. Bernie Williams. 2007. (Baseball Superstars Ser.). (Illus.). 122p. (YA). (gr. 7-12). 30.00 *(978-0-7910-9468-6(5))* Facts On File, Inc.

—Curt Schilling. 2008. (Baseball Superstars Ser.). (Illus.). 121p. (YA). (gr. 7-12). lib. bdg. 30.00 *(978-0-7910-9635-2(1))* Facts On File, Inc.

—Derek Jeter. (Baseball Superstars Ser.). (Illus.). 2008. 128p. (gr. 6-12). pap. 11.95 *(978-0-7910-9846-2(X)*, Checkmark Bks.) 2007. 122p. (YA). (gr. 7-12). lib. bdg. 30.00 *(978-0-7910-9422-8(7))* Facts On File, Inc.

Mills, J. Elizabeth. Ken Griffey Sr. & Ken Griffey Jr: Baseball Heroes. 2010. (Sports Families Ser.). (ENG., Illus.). 48p. (J). pap. 11.75 *(978-1-4358-8514-1(7)*, Rosen Reference) Rosen Publishing Group, Inc., The.

—Ken Griffey Sr. & Ken Griffey Jr. Baseball Heroes. 2010. (Sports Families Ser.). 48p. (YA). (gr. 5-8). lib. bdg., E-Book 53.00 *(978-1-4488-0122-0(2))*; (Illus.). (gr. 4-7). lib. bdg. 29.25 *(978-1-4358-3554-2(9))* Rosen Publishing Group, Inc., The.

Monnig, Alex. Albert Pujols: Groundbreaking Slugger, 1 vol. 2012. (Playmakers Ser.). (ENG.). 32p. (J). (gr. 3-6). 27.07 *(978-1-61783-294-9(4))* ABDO Publishing Co.

—Roy Halladay: Superstar Pitcher, 1 vol. 2012. (Playmakers Ser.). (ENG.). 32p. (J). (gr. 3-6). 27.07 *(978-1-61783-291-8(X))* ABDO Publishing Co.

Morreale, Marie. Mike Trout. 2016. (Real Bios Ser.). (ENG.). 48p. (J). pap. 7.95 *(978-0-531-22564-6(X))*; (Illus.). lib. bdg. 29.00 *(978-0-531-22380-2(9))* Scholastic Library Publishing. (Children's Pr.).

Morrison, Jessica. Hank Aaron: Home Run Hero. 2010. (Crabtree Groundbreaker Biographies Ser.). (ENG., Illus.). 112p. (J). pap. *(978-0-7787-2547-3(2))*; (gr. 5-8). lib. bdg. *(978-0-7787-2538-1(3))* Crabtree Publishing Co.

Morrison, John. Sammy Sosa. 2006. (Great Hispanic Heritage Ser.). (Illus.). 112p. (gr. 6-12). lib. bdg. 35.00 *(978-0-7910-8845-6(6)*, Chelsea Hse.) Facts On File, Inc.

Moss, Marissa. Barbed Wire Baseball. 2016. (J). lib. bdg. 20.80 *(978-0-606-38199-4(6))* Turtleback Bks.

Murphy, Frank. Babe Ruth Saves Baseball! Walz, Richard, illus. 2005. (Step into Reading Ser.: Vol. 3). (ENG.). 48p. (J). (gr. k-3). pap. 3.99 *(978-0-375-83048-8(0)*, Random Hse. Bks. for Young Readers) Random Hse. Children's Bks.

—Babe Ruth Saves Baseball. Walz, Richard, illus. 2005. (Step into Reading Ser.). 46p. (gr. 1-3). 14.00 *(978-0-7569-5161-0(5))* Perfection Learning Corp.

Nagelhout, Ryan. David Ortiz: World Series Champion. 2015. (Living Legends of Sports Ser.). (ENG.). 48p. (J). (gr. 5-6). pap. 14.05 *(978-1-68048-100-6(2))*; (Illus.). 25.85 *(978-1-68048-099-3(5))* Rosen Publishing Group, Inc., The. (Britannica Educational Publishing).

Needham, Tom. Albert Pujols: MVP on & off the Field. 2007. (Sports Stars with Heart Ser.). (Illus.). 128p. (J). (gr. 5-9). lib. bdg. 33.27 *(978-0-7660-2866-1(6))* Enslow Pubs., Inc.

Nicholson, Lois. Cal Ripken, Jr. Quiet Hero, 1 vol. 2nd rev. ed. 2009. (ENG., Illus.). 128p. (J). (gr. 4-8). 13.95 *(978-0-87033-481-8(6)*, 9780870334818, Cornell Maritime Pr./Tidewater Pubs.) Schiffer Publishing, Ltd.

Nicholson, Lois P. From Maryland to Cooperstown: Seven Maryland Natives in Baseball's Hall of Fame, 1 vol. 2010. (ENG., Illus.). 144p. (J). (gr. 4-8). 19.95 *(978-0-87033-494-8(8)*, 9780870334948, Cornell Maritime Pr./Tidewater Pubs.) Schiffer Publishing, Ltd.

Noble, Marty. Mike Piazza: Mike & the Mets. Rains, Rob, ed. 2003. (Superstar Ser.). (Illus.). 96p. (J). (gr. 4-7). pap. 4.95 *(978-1-58261-051-1(7))* Sports Publishing, LLC.

Nolan, Arthea. Whitey Ford. (Baseball Hall of Famers Ser.). 112p. (gr. 5-8). 2009. 63.90 *(978-1-61511-518-1(8))* 2004. (Illus.). lib. bdg. 34.60 *(978-0-8239-3784-4(4))* Rosen Publishing Group, Inc., The. (Rosen Reference).

O'Connell, Jack. Derek Jeter: The Yankee Kid. Rains, Rob, ed. 2003. (Super Star Ser.). 96p. (J). pap. 4.95 *(978-1-58261-043-6(6))* Sports Publishing, LLC.

O'Hern, Kerri & Raatma, Lucia. Jackie Robinson. 2006. (Graphic Biographies Ser.). (Illus.). 32p. (gr. 5-8). pap. 10.50 *(978-0-8368-6250-8(3))* Stevens, Gareth Publishing LLLP.

Omoth, Tyler. Six Degrees of David Ortiz: Connecting Baseball Stars. 2015. (Six Degrees of Sports Ser.). (ENG.). 48p. (gr. 3-4). lib. bdg. 31.99 *(978-1-4914-2142-0(8))* Capstone Press of Coughlan Cos.

O'Neal, Claire. Cole Hamels. 2009. (Blue Banner Biography Ser.). (Illus.). 32p. (YA). (gr. 4-7). lib. bdg. 25.70 *(978-1-58415-776-2(3))* Mitchell Lane Pubs., Inc.

Osier, Dan. Dirk Nowitzki. 2011. (Basketball's MVPs Ser.). 24p. (J). (ENG.). pap. 8.85 *(978-1-4488-2632-2(2))*; (Illus.). (gr. 3-6). lib. bdg. 22.60 *(978-1-4488-2524-0(5))* Rosen Publishing Group, Inc., The. (PowerKids Pr.).

Patrick, Denise Lewis & Time for Kids Editors. Jackie Robinson - Strong Inside & Out. 2005. (Time for Kids Ser.). (ENG., Illus.). 48p. (J). (gr. 2-4). pap. 3.99 *(978-0-06-057600-4(6))* HarperCollins Pubs.

Payment, Simone. Buck Leonard. 2009. (Baseball Hall of Famers of the Negro Leagues Ser.). 112p. (gr. 5-8). 63.90 *(978-1-61511-521-1(8)*, Rosen Reference) Rosen Publishing Group, Inc., The.

Pellowski, Michael J. Super Sports Star Mike Piazza. 2004. (Super Sports Star Ser.). (Illus.). 48p. (J). lib. bdg. 25.27 *(978-0-7660-2159-4(9))* Enslow Pubs., Inc.

Perdomo, Willie. Clemente! Collier, Bryan, illus. 2010. (ENG.). 32p. (J). (gr. 1-5). 17.99 *(978-0-8050-8224-1(7)*, 9780805082241, Holt, Henry & Co. Bks. For Young Readers) Holt, Henry & Co.

Peterson, Megan Cooley. Baseball's Sluggers. 2017. (Rank It! Ser.). (ENG.). 32p. (gr. 3-7). 31.35 ***(978-1-68072-058-7(9)***, Bolt) Black Rabbit Bks.

Pina, Andrew. Becoming a Pro Baseball Player. 2015. (Going Pro Ser.). (ENG.). 32p. (J). (gr. 3-4). pap. 10.50 *(978-1-4824-2054-8(6))* Stevens, Gareth Publishing LLLP.

Prince, April Jones. Jackie Robinson - He Led the Way. Casilla, Robert, illus. 2007. (Penguin Young Readers, Level 3 Ser.). (ENG.). 48p. (J). (gr. 1-3). mass mkt. 3.99 *(978-0-448-44721-6(5)*, Penguin Young Readers) Penguin Young Readers Group.

Raatma, Lucia & O'Hern, Kerri. Jackie Robinson. Campbell, Alex & Spay, Anthony, illus. (Biografías Gráficas (Graphic Biographies) Ser.). 32p. (gr. 5-8). 2007. (SPA.). pap. 10.50 *(978-0-8368-7889-9(2))* 2006. lib. bdg. 27.00 *(978-0-8368-6198-3(1))* Stevens, Gareth Publishing LLLP.

Rains, Rob & Smith, Ozzie. Cardinals Sports Heroes Block: City Block St. Louis: Mark Mcgwire, Ozzie Smith. 2004. (Illus.). 5.98 *(978-1-58261-858-6(5))* Sports Publishing, LLC.

Rappoport, Ken. Alex Rodriguez: Champion Baseball Star. 2012. (Sports Star Champions Ser.). (Illus.). 48p. (J). (gr. 5-18). 25.27 *(978-0-7660-4026-7(7))* Enslow Pubs., Inc.

—Baseball's Top 10 Home Run Hitters. 2010. (Top 10 Sports Stars Ser.). 48p. (J). (gr. 5-9). 25.27 *(978-0-7660-3465-5(8))* Enslow Pubs., Inc.

—Baseball's Top 10 Pitchers. 2010. (Top 10 Sports Stars Ser.). (Illus.). 48p. (J). (gr. 5-9). 25.27 *(978-0-7660-3466-2(6))* Enslow Pubs., Inc.

—David Wright: A Baseball Star Who Cares. 2011. (Sports Stars Who Care Ser.). (Illus.). 48p. (J). (gr. 2-5). lib. bdg. 25.27 *(978-0-7660-3775-5(4))* Enslow Pubs., Inc.

—Super Sports Star Alex Rodriguez. 2004. (Super Sports Star Ser.). (Illus.). 48p. (J). lib. bdg. 25.27 *(978-0-7660-2138-9(6))* Enslow Pubs., Inc.

—Super Sports Star Derek Jeter. 2004. (Super Sports Star Ser.). (Illus.). 48p. (J). lib. bdg. 25.27 *(978-0-7660-2139-6(4))* Enslow Pubs., Inc.

—Super Sports Star Ichiro Suzuki. 2004. (Super Sports Star Ser.). (Illus.). 48p. (J). lib. bdg. 25.27 *(978-0-7660-2137-2(8))* Enslow Pubs., Inc.

Rauf, Don. Miguel Cabrera: Triple Crown Winner. 2015. (Living Legends of Sports Ser.). (ENG., Illus.). 48p. (J). (gr. 5-6). 25.85 *(978-1-68048-094-8(4)*, Britannica Educational Publishing) Rosen Publishing Group, Inc., The.

Raum, Elizabeth. Bryce Harper. 2017. (Pro Sports Biographies Ser.). (ENG.). 24p. (gr. 1-4). 20.95 ***(978-1-68151-135-1(5))*** Amicus Publishing.

—Pro Sports Biographies: Bryce Harper. 2017. (Pro Sports Biographies Ser.). (ENG.). 24p. (J). (gr. 1-3). pap. 8.99 ***(978-1-68152-166-4(0))*** Amicus.

—Pro Sports Biographies: Cam Newton. 2017. (Pro Sports Biographies Ser.). (ENG.). 24p. (J). (gr. 1-3). pap. 8.99 ***(978-1-68152-168-8(7))*** Amicus.

Reis, Ronald A. Lou Gehrig. 2009. (Baseball Superstars Ser.). 136p. (gr. 6-12). pap. 11.95 *(978-0-7910-9898-1(2)*, Checkmark Bks.) Facts On File, Inc.

—Mickey Mantle. 2009. (Baseball Superstars Ser.). 136p. (gr. 6-12). pap. 11.95 *(978-0-7910-9900-1(8)*, Checkmark Bks.) Facts On File, Inc.

Rice, Dona. Jackie Robinson: Hometown Hero. 2016. (Primary Source Readers Ser.). (Illus.). 32p. (gr. 2-2). 8.99 *(978-1-4938-2560-8(7))* Teacher Created Materials, Inc.

—Roberto Clemente, 1 vol. 2nd rev. ed. 2014. (TIME for KIDS(r) Nonfiction Readers Ser.). (ENG., Illus.). 32p. (J). (gr. 3-3). pap. 25.96 *(978-1-4807-1092-4(X))* Shell Educational Publishing.

Rice, William & Rice, Dona. Roberto Clemente. 2017. (TIME for Kids en Español - Level 3 Ser.). (SPA.). 32p. (gr. 3-3). lib. bdg. 31.99 ***(978-1-5157-5190-8(2))*** Time for Kids Inc AUS. Dist: Capstone Pub.

Rivera, Mariano. The Closer: Young Readers Edition. (ENG.). (J). (gr. 3-7). 2016. 336p. pap. 7.99 (978-0-316-28413-4(0)) 2014. 432p. 19.00 (978-0-316-40962-9(6)) Little, Brown Bks. for Young Readers.

Rivkin, Jennifer. Baseball's Best: All-Time Greats. 2015. (ENG., Illus.). 32p. (J). (978-0-7787-1475-0(6)) Crabtree Publishing Co.

Roberts, Jerry. Roberto Clemente: Baseball Player. 2005. (Ferguson Career Biographies Ser.). (Illus.). 128p. (gr. 6-12). 25.00 (978-0-8160-6072-6(X), Ferguson Publishing Co.) Facts On File, Inc.

Robinson, Tom. Andruw Jones: All-Star on & off the Field. 2007. (Sports Stars with Heart Ser.). (Illus.). 128p. (J). (gr. 5-9). lib. bdg. 33.27 (978-0-7660-2867-8(4)) Enslow Pubs., Inc.

—Derek Jeter: Captain on & off the Field. 2006. (Sports Stars with Heart Ser.). (Illus.). 128p. (J). (gr. 5-9). lib. bdg. 33.27 (978-0-7660-2819-7(4)) Enslow Pubs., Inc.

Rodríguez Gonzalez, Tania. Adrián Beltré. 2012. (Superstars of Baseball SPANISH Ser.). 32p. (J). (gr. 4). (SPA.). 19.95 (978-1-4222-2629-2(8)); 19.95 (978-1-4222-2682-7(4)) Mason Crest.

—Albert Pujols. 2012. (Superstars of Baseball ENGLISH Ser.). 32p. (J). (gr. 4). 19.95 (978-1-4222-2676-6(X)); (SPA., Illus.). 19.95 (978-1-4222-2623-0(9)) Mason Crest.

—Alex Rodriguez. 2012. (Superstars of Baseball ENGLISH Ser.). 32p. (J). (gr. 4). 19.95 (978-1-4222-2674-2(3)); (SPA., Illus.). 19.95 (978-1-4222-2621-6(2)) Mason Crest.

—Alfonso Soriano. 2012. (Superstars of Baseball ENGLISH Ser.). 32p. (J). (gr. 4). 19.95 (978-1-4222-2673-5(5)) Mason Crest.

—Aramis Ramirez. 2012. (ENG & SPA., Illus.). 32p. (J). (978-1-4222-2617-9(4)) Mason Crest.

—Bartolo Colón. 2012. (Superstars of Baseball ENGLISH Ser.). 32p. (J). (gr. 4). 19.95 (978-1-4222-2687-2(5)); (SPA., Illus.). 19.95 (978-1-4222-2634-6(4)) Mason Crest.

—Carlos Beltrán. 2012. (Superstars of Baseball ENGLISH Ser.). 32p. (J). (gr. 4). 19.95 (978-1-4222-2699-5(9)); (SPA., Illus.). 19.95 (978-1-4222-2646-9(8)) Mason Crest.

—Carlos Peña. 2012. (Superstars of Baseball SPANISH Ser.). (SPA.). 32p. (J). (gr. 4). 19.95 (978-1-4222-2625-4(5)) Mason Crest.

—David Ortiz. 2012. (Superstars of Baseball SPANISH Ser.). 32p. (J). (gr. 4). (SPA.). 19.95 (978-1-4222-2626-1(3)); 19.95 (978-1-4222-2679-7(4)) Mason Crest.

—Francisco Cordero. 2012. (Superstars of Baseball ENGLISH Ser.). 32p. (J). (gr. 4). 19.95 (978-1-4222-2690-2(5)); (SPA.). 19.95 (978-1-4222-2637-7(9)) Mason Crest.

—Francisco Liriano. 2012. (Superstars of Baseball ENGLISH Ser.). 32p. (J). (gr. 4). 19.95 (978-1-4222-2692-6(1)); (SPA., Illus.). 19.95 (978-1-4222-2639-1(5)) Mason Crest.

—Hanley Ramirez. 2012. (Superstars of Baseball ENGLISH Ser.). 32p. (J). (gr. 4). 19.95 (978-1-4222-2675-9(1)); (SPA., Illus.). 19.95 (978-1-4222-2622-3(0)) Mason Crest.

—Jhonny Peralta. 2012. (Superstars of Baseball ENGLISH Ser.). 32p. (J). (gr. 4). 19.95 (978-1-4222-2686-5(7)); (SPA., Illus.). 19.95 (978-1-4222-2633-9(6)) Mason Crest.

—José Bautista. 2012. (Superstars of Baseball ENGLISH Ser.). 32p. (J). (gr. 4). 19.95 (978-1-4222-2685-8(9)); (SPA., Illus.). 19.95 (978-1-4222-2632-2(8)) Mason Crest.

—José Reyes. 2012. (Superstars of Baseball ENGLISH Ser.). 32p. (J). (gr. 4). 19.95 (978-1-4222-2684-1(0)); (SPA., Illus.). 19.95 (978-1-4222-2631-5(X)) Mason Crest.

—José Valverde. 2012. (Superstars of Baseball SPANISH Ser.). (SPA., Illus.). 32p. (J). (gr. 4). 19.95 (978-1-4222-2641-4(7)) Mason Crest.

Rodriguez Gonzalez, Tania. Jose Valverde. 2012. (Superstars of Baseball ENGLISH Ser.). (ENG., Illus.). 32p. (J). (gr. 4-7). lib. bdg. 19.95 (978-1-4222-2694-0(8)) Mason Crest.

Rodríguez Gonzalez, Tania. Juan Uribe. 2012. (Superstars of Baseball ENGLISH Ser.). 32p. (J). (gr. 4). 19.95 (978-1-4222-2671-1(9)); (SPA., Illus.). 19.95 (978-1-4222-2618-6(2)) Mason Crest.

—Miguel Batista. 2012. (Superstars of Baseball ENGLISH Ser.). 32p. (J). (gr. 4). 19.95 (978-1-4222-2689-6(1)); (SPA., Illus.). 19.95 (978-1-4222-2636-0(0)) Mason Crest.

—Miguel Tejada. 2012. (Superstars of Baseball ENGLISH Ser.). 32p. (J). (gr. 4). 19.95 (978-1-4222-2672-8(7)); (SPA., Illus.). 19.95 (978-1-4222-2619-3(0)) Mason Crest.

—Nelson Cruz. 2012. (Superstars of Baseball ENGLISH Ser.). 32p. (J). (gr. 4). 19.95 (978-1-4222-2691-9(3)); (SPA., Illus.). 19.95 (978-1-4222-2638-4(7)) Mason Crest.

—Placido Polanco. 2012. (Superstars of Baseball SPANISH Ser.). (SPA.). 32p. (J). (gr. 4). 19.95 (978-1-4222-2624-7(7)) Mason Crest.

—Rafael Furcal. 2012. (Superstars of Baseball ENGLISH Ser.). 32p. (J). (gr. 4). 19.95 (978-1-4222-2688-9(3)); (SPA., Illus.). 19.95 (978-1-4222-2635-3(2)) Mason Crest.

—Roberto Clemente. 2012. (Superstars of Baseball ENGLISH Ser.). 32p. (J). (gr. 4). 19.95 (978-1-4222-2697-1(2)); (SPA., Illus.). 19.95 (978-1-4222-2644-5(1)) Mason Crest.

—Robinson Canó. 2012. (Superstars of Baseball ENGLISH Ser.). 32p. (J). (gr. 4). 19.95 (978-1-4222-2683-4(2)); (SPA., Illus.). 19.95 (978-1-4222-2630-8(1)) Mason Crest.

—Ubaldo Jiménez. 2012. (Superstars of Baseball ENGLISH Ser.). 32p. (J). (gr. 4). 19.95 (978-1-4222-2680-3(8)); (SPA & ENG., Illus.). 19.95 (978-1-4222-2627-8(1)) Mason Crest.

—Vladimir Guerrero. 2012. (Superstars of Baseball SPANISH Ser.). (Illus.). 32p. (J). (gr. 4). (SPA & ENG.). 19.95 (978-1-4222-2628-5(X)); 19.95 (978-1-4222-2681-0(6)) Mason Crest.

—Yadier Molina. 2012. (Superstars of Baseball ENGLISH Ser.). 32p. (J). (gr. 4). 19.95 (978-1-4222-2698-8(0)); (SPA., Illus.). 19.95 (978-1-4222-2645-2(X)) Mason Crest.

Rodríguez Gonzalez, Tania & Rodriguez, Tania. Placido Polanco. 2012. (Superstars of Baseball ENGLISH Ser.). 32p. (J). (gr. 4). 19.95 (978-1-4222-2677-3(8)) Mason Crest.

Rodríguez Salazar, Tania. Aramis Ramirez. 2012. 32p. (J). (Illus.). (978-1-4222-2670-4(0)); (gr. 4). 19.95 (978-1-4222-2693-3(X)) Mason Crest.

—Carlos Peña. 2012. (Superstars of Baseball ENGLISH Ser.). 32p. (J). (gr. 4). 19.95 (978-1-4222-2678-0(6)) Mason Crest.

Rodriguez, Tia. Jackie Robinson: Baseball Legend. 2013. (Rosen Readers Ser.). (ENG.). 24p. (J). (gr. 3-4). pap. 49.50 (978-1-4777-2569-6(5)); pap. 8.25 (978-1-4777-2568-9(7)) Rosen Publishing Group, Inc., The. (Rosen Classroom).

Rolfe, John. Ken Griffey, Jr: Superstar Centerfielder. 2009. (Sports Illustrated for Kids Bks). 176p. (gr. 7-12). 63.90 (978-1-60853-149-3(X)) Rosen Publishing Group, Inc., The.

Rolfe, John, et al. Ken Griffey, Jr: Superstar Centerfielder. 2005. (Sports Illustrated for Kids Books Ser.). (Illus.). 176p. (YA). (gr. 7-12). lib. bdg. 33.25 (978-0-8239-3687-8(2)) Rosen Publishing Group, Inc., The.

Saddleback Educational Publishing Staff, ed. Jackie Robinson, 1 vol. unabr. ed. 2008. (Graphic Biographies Ser.). (ENG., Illus.). 25p. (YA). (gr. 9-12). pap. 7.95 (978-1-59905-225-0(3)) Saddleback Educational Publishing, Inc.

Sakany, Lois. Joe DiMaggio. 2004. (Baseball Hall of Famers Ser.). (Illus.). 112p. (gr. 5-8). lib. bdg. 34.60 (978-0-8239-3779-0(8), Rosen Reference) Rosen Publishing Group, Inc., The.

Salqueiro, Adolfo. Carlos Gonzalez. 2012. (Superstars of Baseball SPANISH Ser.). 32p. (J). (gr. 4). (SPA.). 19.95 (978-1-4222-2643-8(3)); 19.95 (978-1-4222-2696-4(4)) Mason Crest.

Sandler, Michael. Derek Jeter & the New York Yankees: 2000 World Series. 2008. (World Series Superstars). (Illus.). 24p. (J). (gr. 1-4). lib. bdg. 22.61 (978-1-59716-641-6(3)) Bearport Publishing Co., Inc.

—Jermaine Dye & the Chicago White Sox: 2005 World Series. 2008. (World Series Superstars). (Illus.). 24p. (J). (gr. 1-4). lib. bdg. 22.61 (978-1-59716-637-9(5)) Bearport Publishing Co., Inc.

—Josh Beckett & the Florida Marlins: 2003 World Series. 2008. (World Series Superstars). (Illus.). 24p. (J). (gr. 1-4). lib. bdg. 22.61 (978-1-59716-639-3(1)) Bearport Publishing Co., Inc.

—Manny Ramirez & the Boston Red Sox: 2004 World Series. 2008. (World Series Superstars). (Illus.). 24p. (J). (gr. 1-4). lib. bdg. 22.61 (978-1-59716-628-7(6)) Bearport Publishing Co., Inc.

—Mike Lowell & the Boston Red Sox: 2007 World Series. 2008. (World Series Superstars). (Illus.). 24p. (J). (gr. 1-4). lib. bdg. 22.61 (978-1-59716-739-0(8), 1284374) Bearport Publishing Co., Inc.

—Randy Johnson & the Arizona Diamondbacks: 2001 World Series. 2008. (World Series Superstars). (Illus.). 24p. (J). (gr. 1-4). lib. bdg. 22.61 (978-1-59716-638-6(3)) Bearport Publishing Co., Inc.

—Troy Glaus & the Anaheim Angels: 2002 World Series. 2008. (World Series Superstars). (Illus.). 24p. (J). (gr. 1-4). lib. bdg. 22.61 (978-1-59716-640-9(5)) Bearport Publishing Co., Inc.

Savage, Jeff. Albert Pujols. 2007. (Amazing Athletes Ser.). (ENG.). 32p. (gr. 2-5). 25.26 (978-0-8225-6849-0(7)); (Illus.). pap. 7.95 (978-0-8225-6850-6(0), First Avenue Editions) Lerner Publishing Group.

—Barry Bonds. 2008. pap. 40.95 (978-1-58013-717-1(2)) 2004. (ENG., Illus.). 32p. (gr. 2-5). lib. bdg. 25.26 (978-0-8225-3688-8(9)) 2008. (Illus.). 32p. (J). (gr. 3-7). lib. bdg. 23.93 (978-1-58013-611-2(7), Lerner Pubns.) Lerner Publishing Group.

—Barry Bonds: Record Breaker. 2nd rev. ed. 2003. (Sports Achievers Biographies Ser.). (Illus.). 64p. (J). (gr. 4-9). 5.95 (978-0-8225-0472-6(3), Carolrhoda Bks.) Lerner Publishing Group.

—David Ortiz. (Amazing Athletes Ser.). 32p. 2015. (ENG., Illus.). (J). (gr. 2-5). pap. 7.95 (978-1-4677-7584-7(3), Lerner Pubns.) 2006. (Illus.). (J). (gr. 3-7). lib. bdg. 22.60 (978-0-8225-3429-7(0), Lerner Pubns.) 2009. (ENG.). (gr. 2-5). pap. 7.95 (978-0-7613-4922-8(7), First Avenue Editions) 2009. (ENG., Illus.). (gr. 2-5). 25.26 (978-0-7613-4920-4(0)) Lerner Publishing Group.

—Dwight Howard. 2010. (Amazing Athletes Ser.). (ENG.). 32p. (gr. 2-5). lib. bdg. 25.26 (978-0-7613-5748-3(3)) Lerner Publishing Group.

—Ichiro Suzuki. (Amazing Athletes Ser.). 2007. (J). pap. 6.95 (978-0-8225-7266-4(4), Lerner Pubns.) 2005. (Illus.). 32p. (gr. 3-4). lib. bdg. 22.60 (978-0-8225-1344-5(7)) 2nd rev. ed. 2014. (ENG., Illus.). 32p. (gr. 2-5). pap. 7.95 (978-1-4677-2641-2(9)) Lerner Publishing Group.

—Josh Hamilton. 2009. (Amazing Athletes Ser.). (J). (gr. 2-5). 23.93 (978-0-7613-4603-6(1)); pap. 40.95 (978-0-7613-4782-8(8)); (ENG.). 32p. (gr. 2-5). pap. 7.95 (978-0-7613-4604-3(X), First Avenue Editions) Lerner Publishing Group.

—Justin Verlander. 2013. (Amazing Athletes Ser.). (ENG., Illus.). 32p. (gr. 2-5). pap. 7.95 (978-1-4677-1107-4(1)); lib. bdg. 25.26 (978-1-4677-1099-2(7), Lerner Pubns.) Lerner Publishing Group.

—Mark McGwire: Home Run King. 2003. (Sports Achievers Biographies Ser.). (Illus.). 64p. (YA). (gr. 4-9). pap. 5.95 (978-0-8225-9845-9(0), Carolrhoda Bks.) Lerner Publishing Group.

—Prince Fielder. 2013. (Amazing Athletes Ser.). (ENG., Illus.). 32p. (gr. 2-5). lib. bdg. 25.26 (978-0-7613-8668-1(8)) Lerner Publishing Group.

—Roy Halladay. 2011. 32p. 25.26 (978-0-7613-7696-5(8)); (J). pap. 45.32 (978-0-7613-7709-2(3)); (ENG.). (gr. 2-5). 25.26 (978-0-7613-7690-3(9), Lerner Pubns.); (ENG.). (gr. 2-5). pap. 7.95 (978-0-7613-7695-8(X)) Lerner Publishing Group.

—Ryan Howard. (Amazing Athletes Ser.). 2008. (Illus.). 32p. (J). (gr. -1). per. 6.95 (978-0-8225-8978-5(8), First Avenue Editions) 2008. (Illus.). 32p. (J). (gr. 3-7). lib. bdg. 23.93 (978-0-8225-8833-7(1), Lerner Pubns.) 2008. pap. 40.95 (978-0-8225-9488-8(9)) 2012. (ENG.). 32p. (gr. 2-5). pap. 7.95 (978-0-7613-8670-4(X)) 2012. (ENG., Illus.). 32p. (gr. 2-5). lib. bdg. 25.26 (978-0-7613-8669-8(6)) Lerner Publishing Group.

—Ryan Howard (Revised Edition) 2012. (Amazing Athletes Ser.). 32p. (J). (gr. 2-5). pap. 45.32 (978-0-7613-9318-4(8)) Lerner Publishing Group.

—Sammy Sosa. 2005. (Amazing Athletes Ser.). (Illus.). 32p. (gr. 2-5). (J). per. 5.95 (978-0-8225-2041-2(9)); (ENG., lib. bdg. 25.26 (978-0-8225-3672-7(2)) Lerner Publishing Group.

—Sammy Sosa: Home Run Hero. (Sports Achievers Biographies Ser.). (Illus.). 2005. (SPA.). 80p. (gr. 7-12). lib. bdg. 22.60 (978-0-8225-3681-9(1)) 2003. 64p. (J). (gr. 4-9). 5.95 (978-0-8225-9858-9(2), Carolrhoda Bks.) Lerner Publishing Group.

—Stephen Strasburg. 2013. (Amazing Athletes Ser.). (ENG., Illus.). 32p. (gr. 2-5). pap. 7.95 (978-1-4677-1115-9(2)); lib. bdg. 25.26 (978-1-4677-1100-5(4)) Lerner Publishing Group.

—Tim Lincecum. 2012. (Amazing Athletes Ser.). 32p. (gr. 2-5). (J). pap. 45.32 (978-0-7613-9320-7(X)); (ENG.). pap. 7.95 (978-0-7613-8667-4(X)); (ENG.). lib. bdg. 25.26 (978-0-7613-8636-0(X)) Lerner Publishing Group.

Scheff, Matt. Baseball's Greatest Stars. 2016. (Baseball's Greatest Stars Ser.: 6). (ENG.). 32p. (J). (gr. 3-9). lib. bdg. 162.42 (978-1-68078-073-4(5), SportsZone) ABDO Publishing Co.

Schwarz, Alan. Baseball All-Stars: Today's Greatest Players. 2009. (Sports Illustrated for Kids Bks). 176p. (gr. 7-12). 63.90 (978-1-60853-146-2(5)) Rosen Publishing Group, Inc., The.

—Rising Stars: The 10 Best Young Players in Baseball. 2005. (Sports Illustrated for Kids Books Ser.). (Illus.). 176p. (YA). (gr. 7-12). lib. bdg. 33.25 (978-0-8239-3576-5(0)) Rosen Publishing Group, Inc., The.

Sexton, Colleen. Jackie Robinson: A Life of Determination. 2007. (People of Character Ser.). (ENG., Illus.). 24p. (J). (gr. 2-5). lib. bdg. 25.95 (978-1-60014-089-1(0)) Bellwether Media.

Shalin, Mike. Nomar Garciaparra: High 5! Rains, Rob, ed. 2003. (Superstar Ser.). (Illus.). 96p. (J). (gr. 4-7). pap. 4.95 (978-1-58261-053-5(3)) Sports Publishing, LLC.

—Pedro Martinez: Throwing Strikes. Rains, Rob, ed. 2003. (Superstar Ser.). (Illus.). 96p. (J). (gr. 4-7). pap. 4.95 (978-1-58261-047-4(9)) Sports Publishing, LLC.

Shea, Therese. CC Sabathia. 2010. (Today's Superstars Ser.). (ENG.). 48p. (J). (gr. 5-8). pap. 14.05 (978-1-4339-3987-7(8)); lib. bdg. 31.95 (978-1-4339-3986-0(X)) Stevens, Gareth Publishing LLLP.

Sherman, Patrice & Murica, Rebecca Thatcher. What It's Like to Be Ryan Howard: Como Es Ser Ryan Howard. de la Vega, Eida, tr. from ENG. Rasemas, Joe, illus. 2009. (What It's Like to Be Ser.). (SPA & ENG.). 32p. (J). (gr. -1-2). 25.70 (978-1-58415-845-5(X)) Mitchell Lane Pubs., Inc.

Silverstone, Michael. Latino Legends: Hispanics in Major League Baseball. 2003. (High Five Reading - Green Ser.). (ENG., Illus.). 48p. (gr. 3-4). per. 9.00 (978-0-7368-2832-1(X), High Five Reading (RBL)) Capstone Press of Coughlan Cos.

Skead, Robert. Something to Prove: Rookie Joe Dimaggio vs. the Great Satchel Paige. Cooper, Floyd, illus. 2013. (ENG.). 32p. (J). (gr. 2-5). lib. bdg. 16.95 (978-0-7613-6619-5(9), Carolrhoda Bks.) Lerner Publishing Group.

Skipper, John C. Frank Robinson: A Baseball Biography, 1 vol. 2014. (ENG., Illus.). 220p. pap. 25.00 (978-0-7864-7561-2(7), efd5081f-d54f-4da6-bb69-aad22ed14bb9) McFarland & Co., Inc. Pubs.

Smithwick, John. Meet Alex Rodriguez: Baseball's Lightning Rod. (All-Star Players Ser.). 32p. (gr. 4-5). 2009. 47.90 (978-1-61511-274-6(X), PowerKids Pr.) 2007. (Illus.). (YA). lib. bdg. 25.25 (978-1-4042-3636-3(8)) Rosen Publishing Group, Inc., The.

—Meet David Ortiz: Baseball's Top Slugger. (All-Star Players Ser.). 32p. (gr. 4-5). 2009. 47.90 (978-1-61511-278-4(2), PowerKids Pr.) 2007. (Illus.). (YA). lib. bdg. 25.25 (978-1-4042-3637-0(6)) Rosen Publishing Group, Inc., The.

Smolka, Bo. Jackie Robinson Breaks the Color Barrier, 1 vol. 2014. (Greatest Events in Sports History Ser.). (ENG.). 48p. (gr. 3-6). lib. bdg. 32.79 (978-1-62403-594-4(9), SportsZone) ABDO Publishing Co.

Spencer, Lauren. Hank Aaron. (Baseball Hall of Famers Ser.). 112p. (gr. 5-8). 2009. 63.90 (978-1-61511-509-9(9)) 2003. (Illus.). lib. bdg. 34.60 (978-0-8239-3600-7(7)) Rosen Publishing Group, Inc., The. (Rosen Reference).

Stewart, Mark. Sammy Sosa: Touching All the Bases. 2004. (American Literary Greats Ser.). (Illus.). 64p. (J). (gr. 5-18). lib. bdg. 25.26 (978-0-7613-2778-3(9), Millbrook Pr.) Lerner Publishing Group.

Stewart, Mark & Kennedy, Mike. Latino Baseball's Finest Fielders/Las Mas Destacados Guantes del Beisbol Latino. Kalmanovitz, Manuel, tr. from ENG. 2003. (En Fuego Ser.). (ENG & SPA., Illus.). 48p. (J). (gr. 5-18). pap. 9.95 (978-0-7613-1749-4(X)) Lerner Publishing Group.

—Latino Baseball's Hottest Hitters. Kalmanovitz, Manuel, tr. 2003. (En Fuego Ser.). (SPA & ENG., Illus.). 48p. (J). (gr. 5-18). pap. 9.95 (978-0-7613-1775-3(9)) Lerner Publishing Group.

Stille, Darlene R. Jackie Robinson: Amazing Athlete & Activist, 1 vol. Sterguiz, Richard, illus. 2013. (Beginner Biographies Set 2 Ser.). (ENG.). 32p. (J). (gr. -1-4). 28.50 (978-1-61641-940-0(7)) Magic Wagon.

Stone, Lynn M. Shortstops. 2007. (Playmakers (High Interest) Ser.). (Illus.). 24p. (YA). (gr. 3-6). lib. bdg. 27.07 (978-1-60044-597-2(7)) Rourke Educational Media.

Stout, Glenn. Able to Play: Overcoming Physical Challenges. 2012. (Good Sports Ser.). (ENG., Illus.). 112p. (J). (gr. 5-7). pap. 5.99 (978-0-547-41733-2(0)) Houghton Mifflin Harcourt Publishing Co.

—Baseball Heroes. 2010. (Good Sports Ser.). (ENG., Illus.). 128p. (J). (gr. 2-5). pap. 6.99 (978-0-547-41708-0(X)) Houghton Mifflin Harcourt Publishing Co.

Stradley, Don. Schooled. 2011. (J). (978-0-531-22557-8(7)) Scholastic, Inc.

Sullivan, George. Baseball's Boneheads, Bad Boys & Just Plain Crazy. 2003. (Single Titles Ser.). (Illus.). 64p. (gr. 5-8). lib. bdg. 23.90 (978-0-7613-2321-1(X), Millbrook Pr.) Lerner Publishing Group.

Tavares, Matt. Becoming Babe Ruth. Tavares, Matt, illus. (Candlewick Biographies Ser.). (ENG., Illus.). (J). (gr. k-3). 2016. 48p. 14.99 (978-0-7636-8767-0(7)) 2013. 40p. 16.99 (978-0-7636-5646-1(1)) Candlewick Pr.

—Growing up Pedro: How the Martinez Brothers Made It from the Dominican Republic All the Way to the Major Leagues. Tavares, Matt, illus. (Candlewick Biographies Ser.). (ENG., Illus.). (J). (gr. 3-7). 2017. 48p. 14.99 (978-0-7636-9310-7(3)) 2015. 40p. 16.99 (978-0-7636-6824-2(9)) Candlewick Pr.

—Henry Aaron's Dream. Tavares, Matt, illus. 2010. (ENG., Illus.). 40p. (J). (gr. 3-7). 16.99 (978-0-7636-3224-3(4)) Candlewick Pr.

—There Goes Ted Williams: The Greatest Hitter Who Ever Lived. Tavares, Matt, illus. 2015. (Candlewick Biographies Ser.). (ENG., Illus.). 48p. (J). (gr. 1-4). 14.99 (978-0-7636-7655-1(1)) Candlewick Pr.

Teitelbaum, Michael. Jackie Robinson: Champion for Equality. 2010. (Sterling Biographies(r) Ser.). (ENG., Illus.). 128p. (J). (gr. 5-18). pap. 5.95 (978-1-4027-6362-5(X)) Sterling Publishing Co., Inc.

Thornley, Stew. Derek Jeter: Daring to Dream. 2004. (Sports Leaders Ser.). (Illus.). 104p. (J). lib. bdg. 27.94 (978-0-7660-2035-1(5)) Enslow Pubs., Inc.

—Roberto Clemente. 2006. (Sports Heroes & Legends Ser.). (ENG., Illus.). 120p. (gr. 5-12). lib. bdg. 30.60 (978-0-8225-5962-7(5)) Lerner Publishing Group.

—Super Sports Star Barry Bonds. 2004. (Super Sports Star Ser.). (Illus.). 48p. (J). lib. bdg. 23.93 (978-0-7660-2132-7(7)) Enslow Pubs., Inc.

—Super Sports Star Chipper Jones. 2004. (Super Sports Star Ser.). (Illus.). 48p. (J). lib. bdg. 25.27 (978-0-7660-2134-1(3)) Enslow Pubs., Inc.

—Super Sports Star Ken Griffey, Jr. 2004. (Super Sports Star Ser.). (Illus.). 48p. (J). lib. bdg. 25.27 (978-0-7660-2133-4(5)) Enslow Pubs., Inc.

Todd, Anne M. Roger Maris. 2008. (Baseball Superstars Ser.). (Illus.). 121p. (YA). (gr. 7-12). lib. bdg. 30.00 (978-0-7910-9734-2(X)) Facts On File, Inc.

Torres, John Albert. Derek Jeter. 2004. (Blue Banner Biography Ser.). (Illus.). 32p. (J). lib. bdg. 25.70 (978-1-58415-333-7(4)) Mitchell Lane Pubs., Inc.

—Dwight Howard: A Basketball Star Who Cares. 2013. (Sports Stars Who Care Ser.). 48p. (J). (gr. 3-4). pap. 8.95 (978-1-4644-0533-4(6), Enslow Elementary) Enslow Pubs., Inc.

—Sports Great Sammy Sosa. 2003. (Sports Great Bks.). (Illus.). 64p. (J). (gr. 4-10). lib. bdg. 23.94 (978-0-7660-2065-8(7)) Enslow Pubs., Inc.

Torsiello, David P. Read about Alex Rodriguez. 2011. (I Like Sports Stars! Ser.). (Illus.). 24p. (J). (gr. k-18). pap. 7.95 (978-1-59845-302-7(5), Enslow Elementary); (gr. 1-4). lib. bdg. 22.60 (978-0-7660-3828-8(9)) Enslow Pubs., Inc.

—Read about Derek Jeter. 2011. (I Like Sports Stars! Ser.). (Illus.). 24p. (J). (gr. k-18). pap. 7.95 (978-1-59845-301-0(7), Enslow Elementary); (gr. 1-4). lib. bdg. 22.60 (978-0-7660-3829-5(7)) Enslow Pubs., Inc.

Triumph Books Staff. Baseball All-Stars. 2013. (ENG.). 48p. (J). (gr. 4-7). pap. 5.99 (978-1-60078-832-1(7)) Triumph Bks.

Twemlow, Nick. Josh Gibson. 2009. (Baseball Hall of Famers of the Negro Leagues Ser.). 112p. (gr. 5-8). 63.90 (978-1-61511-523-5(4), Rosen Reference) Rosen Publishing Group, Inc., The.

Uschan, Michael V. Alex Rodriguez. 2011. (People in the News Ser.). 128p. (YA). (gr. 7-12). lib. bdg. 33.95 (978-1-4205-0350-0(2)) Cengage Gale.

Viola, Kevin. Joe Dimaggio. 2005. (Sports Heroes & Legends Ser.). (Illus.). 106p. (YA). (gr. 7-12). lib. bdg. 27.93 (978-0-8225-3081-7(3)) Lerner Publishing Group.

Vizquel, Omar & Dyer, Bob. Omar! My Life on & off the Field. 2003. (Illus.). 272p. pap. 13.95 (978-1-886228-59-7(0)) Gray and Company, Publishers.

Wacholtz, Anthony. Joe Mauer: Baseball Superstar, 1 vol. 2012. (Superstar Athletes Ser.). (ENG.). 24p. (gr. 1-2). pap. 7.29 (978-1-4296-8003-5(2)); pap. 41.70 (978-1-4296-8493-4(3)); lib. bdg. 25.32 (978-1-4296-7683-0(3)) Capstone Press of Coughlan Cos.

Walker, Sally M. Jackie Robinson. Translations.com Staff, tr. Pate, Rodney S., illus. 2005. (Yo Solo: Biografías (on My Own Biographies) Ser.). (SPA & ENG.). 48p. (gr. 2-4). lib. bdg. 25.26 (978-0-8225-3126-5(7), Ediciones Lerner) Lerner Publishing Group.

Weber, Terri Smith. Alex Rodrigues: Improving His Game. 2004. (J). pap. (978-1-932724-19-6(2), Bios for Kids) Panda Publishing, L.L.C.

—Alex Rodriguez: Improving His Game. 2004. (J). lib. bdg. (978-1-932724-18-9(4), Bios for Kids) Panda Publishing, L.L.C.

—Alex Rodriguez: Mejorando Su Juego. 2003. (SPA.). (J). pap. (978-0-9740180-6-5(6)); lib. bdg. (978-0-9740180-5-8(8)) Panda Publishing, L.L.C. (Bios for Kids).

Weinstein, Howard. Mickey Mantle. (Baseball Hall of Famers Ser.). 112p. (gr. 5-8). 2009. 63.90 (978-1-61511-513-6(7)) 2004. (Illus.). lib. bdg. 34.60 (978-0-8239-3782-0(8)) Rosen Publishing Group, Inc., The. (Rosen Reference).

Williams, Doug. Baseball Record Breakers, 1 vol. 2016. (ENG., Illus.). 48p. (J). **(978-1-62403-845-7(X)**, SportsZone) ABDO Publishing Co.

Wilmore, Kathy. Jackie Robinson: With a Discussion of Respect. 2004. (Values in Action Ser.). (J). (978-1-59203-071-2(8)) Learning Challenge, Inc.

Winter, Jonah. Mickey Mantle: The Commerce Comet. Payne, C. F., illus. 2017. (ENG.). 40p. (J). (gr. -1-3). 17.99 (978-1-101-93352-7(6), Schwartz & Wade Bks.) Random Hse. Children's Bks.

—Roberto Clemente: Pride of the Pittsburgh Pirates. Colón, Raúl, illus. 2008. (ENG.). 40p. (J). (gr. -1-3). 7.99 (978-1-4169-5082-0(6), Atheneum Bks. for Young Readers) Simon & Schuster Children's Publishing.

—You Never Heard of Casey Stengel?! Blitt, Barry, illus. 2016. (ENG.). 40p. (J). (gr. -1-3). 20.99 (978-0-375-97013-9(4)); 17.99 (978-0-375-87013-2(X)) Random Hse. Children's Bks. (Schwartz & Wade Bks.).

—You Never Heard of Sandy Koufax?! Carrilho, Andre, illus. 2016. (ENG.). 40p. (J). (gr. -1-3). 7.99 (978-0-553-49842-4(8), Dragonfly Bks.) Random Hse. Children's Bks.

—You Never Heard of Willie Mays?! Widener, Terry, illus. 2016. (ENG.). 40p. (J). (gr. -1-3). 7.99 (978-1-101-93421-0(2), Dragonfly Bks.) Random Hse. Children's Bks.

Wise, Bill. Louis Sockalexis: Native American Baseball Pioneer, 1 vol. Farnsworth, Bill, illus. 2007. (ENG.). 32p. (J). (gr. 1-7). 16.95 (978-1-58430-269-8(0)) Lee & Low Bks., Inc.

Wood, Kerry & Muskat, Carrie. All You Can Be: Learning & Growing Through Sports. 2012. (All You Can Be Ser.). (ENG., Illus.). 48p. (gr. 2-4). 16.95 (978-1-60078-689-1(8)) Triumph Bks.

Wukovits, John F. Jackie Robinson & the Integration of Baseball. 2005. (Lucent Library of Black History). (ENG., Illus.). 104p. (J). (gr. 3-7). lib. bdg. 33.45 (978-1-59018-913-9(2), Lucent Bks.) Cengage Gale.

Yomtov, Nel. The Bambino: The Story of Babe Ruth's Legendary 1927 Season, 1 vol. Foley, Tim, illus. 2011.

(American Graphic Ser.). (ENG.). 32p. (gr. 3-4). pap. 8.10 (978-1-4296-6265-9(4)); pap. 47.70 (978-1-4296-6433-2(9)) Capstone Press of Coughlan Cos. (Graphic Library).
Yomtov, Nelson. The Bambino: The Story of Babe Ruth's Legendary 1927 Season, 1 vol. Foley, Tim, illus. 2010. (American Graphic Ser.). (ENG.). 32p. (gr. 3-4). lib. bdg. 30.65 (978-1-4296-5473-9(2), Graphic Library) Capstone Press of Coughlan Cos.
Young, Jeff C. Albert Pujols: A Baseball Star Who Cares. 2013. (Sports Stars Who Care Ser.). 48p. (J). (gr. 3-4). pap. 8.95 (978-1-4644-0399-6(6), Enslow Elementary) Enslow Pubs., Inc.
Zuehlke, Jeffrey. Alex Rodriguez. (Amazing Athletes Ser.). 32p. 2005. (Illus.). (J). (gr. 2-5). per. 5.95 (978-0-8225-2311-6(6)) 2005. (Illus.). (J). (gr. 3-7). lib. bdg. 23.93 (978-0-8225-2427-4(9)) 2009. (ENG.). (gr. 2-5). 25.26 (978-0-8225-8871-9(4)) 2009. (ENG.). (gr. 2-5). pap. 7.95 (978-0-8225-8872-6(2), First Avenue Editions) Lerner Publishing Group.
—Alex Rodriguez (Revised Edition) 2009. pap. 40.95 (978-0-7613-4773-6(9)) Lerner Publishing Group.
—Joe Mauer. (Amazing Athletes Ser.). 32p. 2008. (Illus.). (J). (gr. 3-7). per. 6.95 (978-0-8225-8976-1(1), First Avenue Editions) 2008. (Illus.). (J). (gr. 2-5). lib. bdg. 23.93 (978-0-8225-8835-1(8)) 2011. (ENG.). (gr. 2-5). 25.26 (978-0-7613-7066-6(8)) Lerner Publishing Group.
—Johan Santana. 2007. (Amazing Athletes Ser.). (ENG.). 32p. (gr. 2-5). 25.26 (978-0-8225-6592-5(7)); (Illus.). pap. 7.95 (978-0-8225-6596-3(X), First Avenue Editions) Lerner Publishing Group.

BASEBALL—COLLECTIBLES

Wong, Stephen. Baseball Treasures. Einstein, Susan, illus. 2007. 58p. (J). (gr. 4-7). lib. bdg. 17.89 (978-0-06-114473-8(8)) HarperCollins Pubs.

BASEBALL—DICTIONARIES

Suzy. Game Day Youth: Learning Baseball's Lingo. 2010. (Illus.). iii, 84p. (J). pap. (978-1-4507-0952-1(4), 1315692) Independent Pub.
Trust, Richard. Baseball Pictionary. 2005. 48p. (J). (978-0-7868-0064-3(X)) Hyperion Pr.

BASEBALL—FICTION

Ablondi, Richard. The Ball, the Bat, & the Unforgiving BRAT. 2013. 46p. pap. 13.99 (978-1-62509-956-3(8)) Salem Author Services.
Abrahams, Peter. Quacky Baseball. Morrison, Frank, illus. 2011. (ENG.). 32p. (J). (gr. -1-3). 16.99 (978-0-06-122978-7(4)) HarperCollins Pubs.
Adachi, Mitsuru. Cross Game, Vol. 2. Adachi, Mitsuri, illus. 2011. (ENG., Illus.). 376p. pap. 14.99 (978-1-4215-3766-5(4)) Viz Media.
Adachi, Mitsuru. Cross Game, Vol. 4. Adachi, Mitsuru, illus. 2011. (ENG., Illus.). 376p. pap. 14.99 (978-1-4215-3768-9(0)) Viz Media.
Adkins, Kurt. The Summer of Mucus Mcbain. 2013. 188p. (gr. 4-6). pap. 13.99 (978-1-4582-1138-5(X), Abbott Pr.) Author Solutions, Inc.
Adler, David A. The Babe & I. Widener, Terry, illus. 2006. 28p. (gr. 1-4). 18.00 (978-0-7569-6560-0(8)) Perfection Learning Corp.
—The Babe & I. Widener, Terry, illus. 2004. (ENG.). 32p. (J). (gr. -1-3). reprint ed. pap. 7.99 (978-0-15-205026-9(4)) Houghton Mifflin Harcourt Publishing Co.
—Danny's Doodles: The Donut Dilemma. 2014. (Danny's Doodles Ser.: 2). (ENG., Illus.). 144p. (J). (gr. 2-5). pap. 4.99 (978-1-4022-8728-2(3), 9781402287282, Sourcebooks Jabberwocky) Sourcebooks, Inc.
—Danny's Doodles: The Jelly Bean Experiment. 2013. (Danny's Doodles Ser.: 1). (ENG.). 112p. (J). (gr. 2-5). pap. 5.99 (978-1-4022-8721-3(6), 9781402287213, Sourcebooks Jabberwocky) Sourcebooks, Inc.
—Get a Hit, Mo! Ricks, Sam, illus. (Mo Jackson Ser.: bk.2). (ENG.). 32p. (J). (gr. 1-2). 2017. pap. 3.99 (978-0-448-48010-7(7)) 2016. 14.99 (978-0-670-01632-7(2)) Penguin Young Readers Group. (Penguin Young Readers).
Adler, David A. Yom Kippur Shortstop. Ceolin, Andre, illus. 2017. (J). (978-1-68115-521-0(4)) Behrman Hse., Inc.
All Pro Base Star 82. Date not set. (J). pap. 46.80 (978-0-590-39611-0(0)) Scholastic, Inc.
Amerikaner, Susan. Goofy at Bat. 2013. (Mickey & Friends World of Reading Ser.). (J). lib. bdg. 13.55 (978-0-606-27117-2(1), Turtleback) Turtleback Bks.
Appel, Marty. Pinstripe Pride: The Inside Story of the New York Yankess. 2016. lib. bdg. 24.50 (978-0-606-38275-5(5)) Turtleback Bks.
Aretha, David. Foul Ball Frame-Up at Wrigley Field: The Baseball Geeks Adventures Book 2. 2014. (Baseball Geeks Adventures Ser.). (Illus.). 96p. (J). (gr. 4-9). 17.95 (978-1-62285-123-2(4)) Enslow Pubs., Inc.
—A Hall Lot of Trouble at Cooperstown: The Baseball Geeks Adventures Book 1. 2014. (Baseball Geeks Adventures Ser.). (Illus.). 96p. (J). (gr. 4-9). 17.95 (978-1-62285-118-8(8)) Enslow Pubs., Inc.
—Rounding Third, Heading Home! 2012. (Champion Sports Story Ser.). 112p. (J). (gr. 3-18). pap. 10.95 (978-1-4644-0002-5(4)); 27.94 (978-0-7660-3876-9(9)) Enslow Pubs., Inc.
—The Treasure Hunt Stunt at Fenway Park: The Baseball Geeks Adventures Book 3. 2014. (Baseball Geeks Adventures Ser.). (Illus.). 96p. (J). (gr. 4-9). 17.95 (978-1-62285-128-7(5)) Enslow Pubs., Inc.
Aryal, Aimee. Let's Go, White Sox! De Angel, Miguel & Moore, D., illus. 2007. 24p. (J). lib. bdg. 14.95 (978-1-932888-87-4(X)) Mascot Bks., Inc.
Baggott, Julianna. The Prince of Fenway Park. 2011. (ENG.). 352p. (J). (gr. 3-7). pap. 6.99 (978-0-06-087244-1(6)) HarperCollins Pubs.
Bancroft, Greg. Betsy's Day at the Game. Blackmore, Katherine, illus. 2013. (ENG.). 40p. (gr. k-5). pap. 13.95 (978-1-938063-01-5(5), Mighty Media Kids) Mighty Media Pr.
Barber, Tiki & Barber, Ronde. Extra Innings. 2014. (Barber Game Time Bks.). (ENG., Illus.). 160p. (J). (gr. 3-7). 16.99 (978-1-4424-5726-3(0), Simon & Schuster/Paula Wiseman Bks.) Simon & Schuster/Paula Wiseman Bks.
Bartlett, Adam. The Littlest Giant. 2010. 32p. pap. 19.95 (978-1-4520-9840-1(9)) AuthorHouse.
Barwin, Steven. Hardball, 1 vol. 2014. (Orca Sports Ser.). (ENG.). 192p. (YA). (gr. 6-10). pap. 9.95 (978-1-4598-0441-8(4)) Orca Bk. Pubs. USA.
—Hurricane Heat, 1 vol. 2013. (Orca Sports Ser.). (ENG.). 176p. (YA). (gr. 6-10). pap. 9.95 (978-1-4598-0213-1(6)) Orca Bk. Pubs. USA.
Bauer, Joan. Soar. 2016. (ENG.). 304p. (J). (gr. 5). 16.99 (978-0-451-47034-8(6), Viking Books for Young Readers) Penguin Young Readers Group.
—Soar. 2017. lib. bdg. 18.40 **(978-0-606-39793-3(0))** Turtleback Bks.
Bee, Clair. Clutch Hitter. (J). 17.95 (978-0-8488-1246-1(8)) Amereon Ltd.
—Dugout Jinx. (J). 17.95 (978-0-8488-1247-8(6)) Amereon Ltd.
—Dugout Jinx: A Chip Hilton Sports Story. 2011. 222p. (gr. 4-7). 44.95 (978-1-258-07860-7(0)) Literary Licensing, LLC.
—No Hitter: A Chip Hilton Sports Story. 2011. 192p. (gr. 3-8). 42.95 (978-1-258-09702-8(8)) Literary Licensing, LLC.
—Pay-off Pitch: A Chip Hilton Sports Story. 2011. 192p. (gr. 3-8). 42.95 (978-1-258-09970-1(5)) Literary Licensing, LLC.
—Pitcher's Duel: A Chip Hilton Sports Story. 2011. 224p. (gr. 4-7). 44.95 (978-1-258-09630-4(7)) Literary Licensing, LLC.
—Tournament Crisis: A Chip Hilton Sports Story. 2011. 224p. (gr. 3-8). 44.95 (978-1-258-09892-6(X)) Literary Licensing, LLC.
Beeuwsaert, Matt. I Got Game. Beeuwsaert, Matt, illus. 2003. (Illus.). 176p. per. 14.95 (978-0-9724358-0-2(8)) Beex Art Bks.
Berenstain, Mike. The Berenstain Bears: We Love Baseball! Berenstain, Mike, illus. 2017. (I Can Read Level 1 Ser.). (Illus.). 32p. (J). (gr. -1-3). pap. 3.99 (978-0-06-235028-2(5)) HarperCollins Pubs.
Berenstain, Mike. We Love Baseball! 2017. (Berenstain Bears — I Can Read Ser.). (J). lib. bdg. 13.55 **(978-0-606-39630-1(6))** Turtleback Bks.
Berenstain, Mike & Berenstain, Jan. The Berenstain Bears Say Their Prayers, 1 vol. 2008. (Berenstain Bears/Living Lights Ser.). (ENG., Illus.). 32p. (J). (gr. -1-2). pap. 3.99 (978-0-310-71246-6(7)) Zonderkidz.
Berenstain, Stan & Berenstain, Jan. The Berenstain Bears Play T-Ball. 2005. (Berenstain Bears Ser.). (Illus.). 32p. (J). 11.65 (978-0-7569-5228-0(X)) Perfection Learning Corp.
Berk, Josh. Say It Ain't So. (Lenny & the Mikes Ser.). (ENG.). 288p. (J). (gr. 3-7). 2015. pap. 7.99 (978-0-307-93007-1(6), Yearling) 2014. 16.99 (978-0-375-87009-5(1), Knopf Bks. for Young Readers) Random Hse. Children's Bks.
—Strike Three, You're Dead. 2014. (Lenny & the Mikes Ser.). (ENG.). 272p. (J). (gr. 3-7). 6.99 (978-0-307-93006-4(8), Yearling) Random Hse. Children's Bks.
Berra, Yogi. Let's Go, Yankees! Moore, Danny, illus. 2006. 24p. (J). 17.95 (978-1-932888-81-2(0)) Mascot Bks., Inc.
Biedrzycki, David. Ace Lacewing, Bug Detective: The Big Swat. Biedrzycki, David, illus. 2010. (ENG., Illus.). 44p. (J). (gr. k-4). 16.95 (978-1-57091-747-9(7)) Charlesbridge Publishing, Inc.
—Ace Lacewing Bug Detective: The Big Swat. Biedrzycki, David, illus. 2012. (ENG., Illus.). 44p. (J). (gr. k-4). pap. 8.95 (978-1-57091-748-6(5)) Charlesbridge Publishing, Inc.
Bildner, Phil. Derek Jeter Presents Night at the Stadium. Booth, Tom, illus. 2016. (Jeter Publishing Ser.). (ENG.). 32p. (J). (gr. -1-3). 17.99 (978-1-4814-2655-8(9), Aladdin) Simon & Schuster Children's Publishing.
—Playing the Field. 2013. (ENG., Illus.). 192p. (YA). (gr. 7). pap. 13.99 (978-1-4814-2172-0(7), Simon & Schuster Bks. For Young Readers) Simon & Schuster Bks. For Young Readers.
—Shoeless Joe & Black Betsy. Payne, C. F., illus. 2006. (ENG.). 40p. (J). (gr. k-3). reprint ed. 8.99 (978-0-689-87437-6(5), Simon & Schuster Bks. For Young Readers) Simon & Schuster Bks. For Young Readers.
Bildner, Phil & Long, Loren. Game 3. Long, Loren, illus. 2008. (ENG., Illus.). 208p. (J). (gr. 2-5). 10.99 (978-1-4169-1865-3(5), Simon & Schuster Bks. For Young Readers) Simon & Schuster Bks. For Young Readers.
Bishop, Jenn. The Distance to Home. (ENG.). 240p. (J). (gr. 3-7). 2017. 6.99 **(978-1-101-93874-4(9)**, Yearling) 2016. 16.99 (978-1-101-93871-3(4), Knopf Bks. for Young Readers) Random Hse. Children's Bks.
Bitterman, Kevin. BD's Big Hit, 1 vol. 2009. (ENG.). 63p. pap. 19.95 (978-1-60836-366-7(X)) America Star Bks.
Blackmon, Rodney Allan. A Kitten Named Buddy: Buddy Stays Clean. 2013. 20p. pap. 24.95 (978-1-62709-675-1(2)) America Star Bks.
Blumenthal, Scott & Hodus, Brett. The Road to the Majors. 2005. (Dream Ser.). (ENG.). 147p. (gr. 3-8). pap. 9.95 (978-0-9708992-0-0(3)) Scobre Pr. Corp.
Bottiglieri, Tim. Robber Raccoon, 1 vol. Bishop, John E., illus. 2009. 16p. pap. 24.95 (978-1-61546-432-6(8)) America Star Bks.
Bowen, Fred. Dugout Rivals, 1 vol. 2010. (Fred Bowen Sports Stories Ser.). (ENG.). 128p. (J). (gr. 2-7). pap. 6.95 (978-1-56145-515-7(6)) Peachtree Pubs.
—The Golden Glove, 1 vol. 2009. (Fred Bowen Sports Story Ser.). (ENG., Illus.). 112p. (J). (gr. 3). pap. 6.95 (978-1-56145-505-8(9)) Peachtree Pubs.
—The Kid Coach, 1 vol. 2009. (All-Star Sports Story Ser.). (ENG., Illus.). 112p. (J). pap. 5.95 (978-1-56145-506-5(7)) Peachtree Pubs.
—Perfect Game, 1 vol. 2013. (Fred Bowen Sports Stories Ser.). (ENG.). 144p. (J). (gr. 2-6). 14.95 (978-1-56145-701-4(9)); pap. 5.95 (978-1-56145-625-3(X)) Peachtree Pubs.
—Playoff Dreams, 1 vol. 2009. (All-Star Sports Story Ser.). (ENG., Illus.). 112p. (J). pap. 5.95 (978-1-56145-507-2(5)) Peachtree Pubs.
—T. J.'s Secret Pitch, 1 vol. 2009. (All-Star Sports Story Ser.). (ENG., Illus.). 112p. (J). pap. 5.95 (978-1-56145-504-1(0)) Peachtree Pubs.
—Throwing Heat, 1 vol. 2010. (ENG.). 128p. (J). (gr. 2-7). pap. 6.95 (978-1-56145-540-9(7)) Peachtree Pubs.
—Winners Take All, 1 vol. 2009. (All-Star Sports Story Ser.). (ENG., Illus.). 112p. (J). pap. 5.95 (978-1-56145-512-6(1)) Peachtree Pubs.
Boyer, Allen B. Roberto's Bat. 2003. (Summit Books Ser.). (Illus.). 128p. (gr. 3-6). lib. bdg. 13.95 (978-0-7569-1642-8(9)) Perfection Learning Corp.
Boyer, Allen B. & Hatala, Dan. Roberto's Bat. 2003. (Illus.). 128p. 6.95 (978-0-7891-6149-9(4)) Perfection Learning Corp.
Bradford James Nolan. The Mouse Who Lived in Fenway Park. Jim Connelly, illus. 2009. 36p. pap. 19.99 (978-1-4389-4491-3(8)) AuthorHouse.
Brasch, Nicolas. A Baseball Giant, 1 vol. rev. ed. 2013. (Fiction Readers Ser.). (ENG., Illus.). 32p. (J). (gr. 3-3). pap. 8.99 (978-1-4333-5644-5(9)) Shell Educational Publishing.
Breslin, Jud. If the Ball's in the Air a Season in Tee-Ball. 2007. (Illus.). 48p. (gr. 3-7). per. 17.95 (978-1-59858-275-8(5)) Dog Ear Publishing, LLC.
Brezenoff, Steve. Ballgame with No One at Bat. 2013. (Field Trip Mysteries Ser.). (ENG.). 88p. (gr. 2-3). pap. 35.70 (978-1-4342-6230-1(8)) Stone Arch Bks.
—The Ballgame with No One at Bat. Calo, Marcos, illus. 2013. (Field Trip Mysteries Ser.). (ENG.). 88p. (gr. 2-3). pap. 6.10 (978-1-4342-6211-0(1)); lib. bdg. 25.32 (978-1-4342-5978-3(1)) Stone Arch Bks.
Bridwell, Norman. Clifford Makes the Team. Bridwell, Norman, illus. 2011. (Scholastic Reader Level 1 Ser.). (ENG., Illus.). 32p. (J). (gr. -1-2). pap. 3.99 (978-0-545-23141-1(8)) Scholastic, Inc.
Brooks, Walter R. Freddy & the Baseball Team from Mars. Wiese, Kurt, illus. 2011. (ENG.). 256p. 10.99 (978-1-59020-696-6(7), 902696) Overlook Pr., The.
Brophy, Mary-Beth. The Last Stop Before Home. 2004. 166p. (YA). pap. 12.95 (978-0-595-30436-3(2)) iUniverse, Inc.
Brown, Jeff. Flat Stanley at Bat. Pamintuan, Macky, illus. 2012. (I Can Read Level 2 Ser.). (ENG.). 32p. (J). (gr. k-3). 16.99 (978-0-06-143010-7(2)); pap. 3.99 (978-0-06-143012-1(9)) HarperCollins Pubs.
—Flat Stanley at Bat. 2012. (Flat Stanley: I Can Read Ser.). (J). lib. bdg. 13.55 (978-0-606-23584-6(1), Turtleback) Turtleback Bks.
Burleigh, Robert. Home Run: The Story of Babe Ruth. Plimpton, George, ed. Wimmer, Mike, illus. 2003. (ENG.). 32p. (J). (gr. -1-3). pap. 7.99 (978-0-15-204599-9(6)) Houghton Mifflin Harcourt Publishing Co.
Burroughs, Scott, illus. The Missing Mitt. 2010. (Hardy Boys: the Secret Files Ser.: 2). (ENG.). 112p. (J). (gr. 1-4). pap. 5.99 (978-1-4169-9394-0(0), Aladdin) Simon & Schuster Children's Publishing.
Butler, Dori Hillestad. Sliding into Home, 1 vol. 2005. (ENG.). 192p. (J). (gr. 3-7). pap. 7.95 (978-1-56145-341-2(2)) Peachtree Pubs.
—Sliding into Home, 1 vol. Casale, Paul, illus. 2003. (Peachtree Junior Publication Ser.). (ENG.). 192p. (J). (gr. 3-7). 14.95 (978-1-56145-222-4(X)) Peachtree Pubs.
Byrne, Marlene F. & Graber, Jesse. Just a Baseball Game. 2009. (Illus.). 52p. (J). 14.99 (978-0-9777135-2-3(0)) Celtic Marketing Inc.
Carlson, Ron. The Speed of Light. 2003. (Illus.). 288p. (J). 16.89 (978-0-06-029825-8(1)); (ENG.). 15.99 (978-0-380-97837-3(7)) HarperCollins Pubs. (HarperTeen).
Carter, Lara. Crusher Field Opening Day. 2009. 28p. pap. 12.49 (978-1-4389-3389-4(4)) AuthorHouse.
CC Claus: A Baseball Christmas Story. 2014. (ENG.). 40p. 16.99 (978-0-06-231841-1(1), Ecco) HarperCollins Pubs.
Cervasio, Mark. Life's a Ball with Billy the Baseball. 2007. (J). 12.95 (978-1-59526-758-0(1)) Aeon Publishing Inc.
Chabon, Michael. Summerland. l.t. ed. 2003. 615p. (J). 25.95 (978-0-7862-5143-8(3)) Thorndike Pr.
Christopher, Matt. All-Star Fever. Dewdney, Anna, illus. 2009. (New Peach Street Mudders Sports Library). 64p. (J). (gr. 2-4). lib. bdg. 23.93 (978-1-59953-315-5(4)) Norwood Hse. Pr.
—Baseball Flyhawk. 2010. (Matt Christopher Sports Library). (Illus.). 128p. (J). (gr. 4-6). lib. bdg. 26.60 (978-1-59953-354-4(5)) Norwood Hse. Pr.
—Baseball Turnaround. 2005. (Sports Classics I Ser.). 123p. (J). lib. bdg. 15.00 (978-1-59054-747-2(0)) Fitzgerald Bks.
—Baseball World Series. (Little League Ser.: 5). (ENG., 208p. (J). (gr. 3-7). 2015. Illus.). pap. 7.00 (978-0-316-21295-3(4)) 2014. 16.00 (978-0-316-22046-0(9)) Little, Brown Bks. for Young Readers.
—Centerfield Ballhawk. Beier, Ellen, illus. 2009. (New Peach Street Mudders Sports Library). 64p. (J). (gr. 2-4). lib. bdg. 23.93 (978-1-59953-317-9(0)) Norwood Hse. Pr.
—District Doubleheader. 2014. (Little League Ser.: 1). (ENG.). 224p. (J). (gr. 3-7). pap. 7.00 (978-0-316-19915-5(X)) Little, Brown Bks. for Young Readers.
—The Dog That Called the Pitch. Vasconcellos, Dan, illus. 2010. (Matt Christopher Sports Readers Ser.). 48p. (J). (gr. 1-3). lib. bdg. 23.93 (978-1-59953-353-7(7)) Norwood Hse. Pr.
—The Dog That Pitched a No-Hitter. 2013. (Passport to Reading Level 3 Ser.). (ENG., Illus.). 48p. (J). (gr. 1-4). 4.99 (978-0-316-21848-1(0)) Little, Brown Bks. for Young Readers.
—The Dog That Pitched a No-Hitter. Vasconcellos, Dan, illus. 2010. (Matt Christopher Sports Readers Ser.). 48p. (J). (gr. 1-3). lib. bdg. 23.93 (978-1-59953-351-3(0)) Norwood Hse. Pr.
—The Dog That Stole Home. Vasconcellos, Dan, illus. 2010. (Matt Christopher Sports Readers Ser.). 48p. (J). (gr. 1-3). lib. bdg. 23.93 (978-1-59953-352-0(9)) Norwood Hse. Pr.
—Double Play at Short. 2005. (Sports Classics I Ser.). 137p. (J). lib. bdg. 15.00 (978-1-59054-754-0(3)) Fitzgerald Bks.
—The Hit-Away Kid. Ulrich, George, illus. 2009. (New Peach Street Mudders Sports Library). 64p. (J). (gr. 2-4). lib. bdg. 23.93 (978-1-59953-318-6(9)) Norwood Hse. Pr.
—The Home Run Kid Races On. 2010. (ENG.). 128p. (J). (gr. 3-7). pap. 5.99 (978-0-316-04481-3(4)) Little, Brown Bks. for Young Readers.
—The Kid Who Only Hit Homers. l.t. ed. 2007. (New Matt Christopher Sports Library). 144p. (J). (gr. 4-6). lib. bdg. 26.60 (978-1-59953-107-6(0)) Norwood Hse. Pr.
—Little Lefty. 2009. (J). pap. 7.95 (978-1-933523-38-5(7)) Bella Rosa Bks.
—The Lucky Baseball Bat. Henneberger, Robert, illus. 2005. 123p. (gr. -1-3). 16.00 (978-0-7569-4890-0(8)) Perfection Learning Corp.
—The Lucky Baseball Bat: 50th Anniversary Commemorative Edition. Henneberger, Robert, illus. anniv. ed. 2004. (ENG.). 128p. (J). (gr. -1-17). pap. 5.99 (978-0-316-01012-2(X)) Little, Brown Bks. for Young Readers.
—Man Out at First. Beier, Ellen, illus. 2009. (New Peach Street Mudders Sports Library). 64p. (J). (gr. 2-4). lib. bdg. 23.93 (978-1-59953-319-3(7)) Norwood Hse. Pr.
—Miracle at the Plate. 2005. (Sports Classics I Ser.). 119p. (J). lib. bdg. 15.00 (978-1-59054-763-2(2)) Fitzgerald Bks.
—El Muchacho Que Bateaba Solo Jonrones.Tr. of Kid Who Only Hit Homers. 145p. (J). (gr. 3-5). pap. 145.00 (978-0-8072-1464-0(7), Listening Library) Random Hse. Audio Publishing Group.
—Out at Second. 2011. (Playaway Top Children's Picks Ser.). (J). 49.99 (978-1-60941-973-8(1)) Findaway World, LLC.
—Out at Second. 2011. (ENG.). 144p. (J). (gr. 3-7). pap. 4.99 (978-0-316-08481-9(6)) Little, Brown Bks. for Young Readers.
—Perfect Game. 2014. (Little League Ser.: 4). (ENG., Illus.). 192p. (J). (gr. 3-7). 15.00 (978-0-316-22045-3(0)) Little, Brown Bks. for Young Readers.
—Play Ball! 2013. (Little League Ser.: 1). (ENG.). (J). (gr. 3-7). 240p. pap. 7.99 (978-0-316-19975-9(3)); 224p. 14.99 (978-0-316-21994-5(0)) Little, Brown Bks. for Young Readers.
—Power Pitcher. 2010. (Matt Christopher Sports Library). 112p. (J). (gr. 4-6). lib. bdg. 26.60 (978-1-59953-356-8(1)) Norwood Hse. Pr.
—Return of the Home Run Kid. 2005. (Sports Classics I Ser.). 152p. (J). lib. bdg. 15.00 (978-1-59054-766-3(7)) Fitzgerald Bks.
—Return of the Home Run Kid. 2008. (New Matt Christopher Sports Library). 160p. (J). (gr. 4-6). lib. bdg. 26.60 (978-1-59953-213-4(1)) Norwood Hse. Pr.
—Shadow over Second. Dewdney, Anna, illus. 2009. (New Peach Street Mudders Sports Library). 64p. (J). (gr. 2-4). lib. bdg. 23.93 (978-1-59953-320-9(0)) Norwood Hse. Pr.
—Shoot for the Hoop. 2010. (Matt Christopher Sports Library). 128p. (J). (gr. 4-6). lib. bdg. 26.60 (978-1-59953-357-5(X)) Norwood Hse. Pr.
—Slide, Danny, Slide. 2010. (ENG.). 138p. (YA). pap. 9.95 (978-1-933523-39-2(5)) Bella Rosa Bks.
—The Spy on Third Base. Ulrich, George, illus. 2009. (New Peach Street Mudders Sports Library). 64p. (J). (gr. 2-4). lib. bdg. 23.93 (978-1-59953-321-6(9)) Norwood Hse. Pr.
—State Show-Down. 2013. (Little League Ser.: 3). (ENG.). 192p. (J). (gr. 3-7). 15.00 (978-0-316-22044-6(2)) Little, Brown Bks. for Young Readers.
—State Showdown. 2014. (Little League Ser.: 3). (ENG., Illus.). 208p. (J). (gr. 3-7). pap. 7.99 (978-0-316-19916-2(8)) Little, Brown Bks. for Young Readers.
—Stealing Home. 2004. (ENG.). 144p. (J). (gr. 3-7). pap. 5.99 (978-0-316-60742-1(8)) Little, Brown Bks. for Young Readers.
—Stranger in Right Field. Dodson, Bert, illus. 2009. (New Peach Street Mudders Sports Library). 64p. (J). (gr. 2-4). lib. bdg. 23.93 (978-1-59953-322-3(7)) Norwood Hse. Pr.
—The Submarine Pitch. 2005. (Sports Classics I Ser.). 124p. (J). lib. bdg. 15.00 (978-1-59054-775-5(6)) Fitzgerald Bks.
—Zero's Slider. Delaney, Molly, illus. 2009. (New Peach Street Mudders Sports Library). 64p. (J). (gr. 2-4). lib. bdg. 23.93 (978-1-59953-323-0(5)) Norwood Hse. Pr.
Ciencin, Scott & Cano, Fernando. Power at the Plate, 1 vol. Esparza, Andres et al, illus. 2011. (Sports Illustrated Kids Graphic Novels Ser.). (ENG.). 56p. (gr. 2-3). pap. 7.19 (978-1-4342-3400-1(2)); lib. bdg. 26.65 (978-1-4342-2239-8(X)) Stone Arch Bks.
Clark, Seneca & Giardi, Sandy. Frankie Goes to Fenway: The Tale of the Faithful, Red Sox-Loving Mouse. Decedue, Julie, illus. 2008. 56p. (J). 18.95 (978-0-9767276-3-7(3)) Three Bean Pr.
Coates, Doug. Pitching for Success: Character Lessons, the Joe Nuxhall Way. 2014. (ENG.). 16.95 (978-1-939710-09-3(X)) Orange Frazer Pr.
Cochrane, Mick. The Girl Who Threw Butterflies. 2010. (ENG.). 192p. (J). (gr. 3-7). 6.99 (978-0-375-84610-6(7), Yearling) Random Hse. Children's Bks.
Conkling, Ken. Glove of Their Own. Lambiase, Lauren, illus. 2008. 32p. 15.95 (978-0-9760469-5-0(4)) Franklin Mason Pr.
Cooney, Doug. I Know Who Likes You. Bernardin, James, illus. 2005. (ENG.). 224p. (J). (gr. 3-7). pap. 10.99 (978-1-4169-0261-4(9), Simon & Schuster Bks. For Young Readers) Simon & Schuster Bks. For Young Readers.
Corbett, Sue. Free Baseball. 2008. (ENG.). 160p. (J). (gr. 3-7). 6.99 (978-0-14-241080-6(2), Puffin Books) Penguin Young Readers Group.
Corey, Shana. Players in Pigtails. Gibbon, Rebecca, illus. 2010. (Rise & Shine Ser.). (ENG.). 40p. (C). (gr. -1-3). per. 17.95 (978-0-439-18306-2(5)) National Geographic School Publishing, Inc.
—Players in Pigtails. Gibbon, Rebecca, illus. 2003. (ENG.). 40p. (J). (gr. -1-3). 21.99 (978-0-439-18305-5(7)) Scholastic, Inc.
Coy, John. Top of the Order. 2010. (4 For 4 Ser.: 1). (ENG.). 208p. (J). (gr. 3-7). pap. 8.99 (978-0-312-61111-8(0), 9780312611118) Square Fish.
Crowe, Chris. Just as Good: How Larry Doby Changed America's Game. Benny, Mike, illus. 2012. (ENG.). 32p. (J). (gr. 1-4). 16.99 (978-0-7636-5026-1(9)) Candlewick Pr.
Curtis, Gavin. The Bat Boy & His Violin. Lewis, E. B., illus. 2015. 32p. pap. 8.00 (978-1-61003-618-4(2)) Center for the Collaborative Classroom.
Curtis, Jennifer Keats. Baby Owl's Rescue, 1 vol. Jacques, Laura, illus. 2009. (ENG.). 32p. (J). (gr. -1-3). 16.95 (978-1-934359-95-2(5), 9781934359952) Arbordale Publishing.
Cutler, Stephen. Rally Caps. 2007. 88p. per. 19.95 (978-1-4241-7381-5(7)) America Star Bks.
Cyr, Liz. Pete-O Burrito & the Lucky Stripes. Cyr, Christopher & Cyr, James, illus. 2012. 28p. 24.95 (978-1-4626-5566-3(1)) America Star Bks.
Dahl, Michael. Goodnight Baseball. Forshay, Christina, illus. 2013. (Sports Illustrated Kids Bedtime Bks.). (ENG.). 32p. (gr. -1-2). pap. 6.95 (978-1-4795-4975-7(4)) Capstone Press of Coughlan Cos.
—Goodnight Baseball, 1 vol. Forshay, Christina E., illus. 2013. (Sports Illustrated Kids Bedtime Bks.). (ENG.). 32p. (gr. -1-2). 14.95 (978-1-62370-000-3(0)) Capstone Press of Coughlan Cos.
—Goodnight Baseball, 1 vol. Forshay, Christina, illus. 2013. (Sports Illustrated Kids Bedtime Bks.). (ENG.). 32p. (gr. -1-2).

lib. bdg. 22.60 *(978-1-4048-7979-9(X))* Capstone Press of Coughlan Cos.

Day, Alexandra. Frank & Ernest Play Ball. 2011. (ENG., illus.). 40p. 15.95 *(978-1-59583-438-6(9))*, 9781595834386, Green Tiger Pr.) Laughing Elephant.

Day, Karen. No Cream Puffs. 2010. (ENG.). 224p. (J). (gr. 3-7). 6.99 *(978-0-375-83776-0(0)*, Yearling) Random Hse. Children's Bks.

De Fonte', Desiree. Gaining the Heart of a Man: A Story of Hope & Forgiveness. 2011. 28p. pap. 24.95 *(978-1-4626-0274-2(6))* America Star Bks.

De la Peña, Matt. Mexican WhiteBoy. 2010. (ENG.). 256p. (YA). (gr. 9). pap. 9.99 *(978-0-440-23938-3(9)*, Ember) Random Hse. Children's Bks.

—Mexican WhiteBoy. 2010. lib. bdg. 20.85 *(978-0-606-12316-7(4)*, Turtleback) Turtleback Bks.

Dean, James. Play Ball! Dean, James, illus. 2013. (My First I Can Read Ser.). (ENG., illus.). 32p. (J). (gr. -1-3). 16.99 *(978-0-06-211067-1(5))* HarperCollins Pubs.

—Play Ball! 2013. (Pete the Cat I Can Read Ser.). (J). lib. bdg. 13.55 *(978-0-606-27145-5(7)*, Turtleback) Turtleback Bks.

DeFillipis, Nunzio & Weir, Christina. Play Ball. 2012. (ENG., illus.). 144p. 19.99 *(978-1-934964-79-8(4)*, 9781934964798) Oni Pr., Inc.

Delaney, Ned. Two Strikes, Four Eyes. Date not set. (J). pap. *(978-0-679-84172-2(5))*; lib. bdg. *(978-0-679-94172-9(X))* Random Hse. Children's Bks. (Random Hse. Bks. for Young Readers).

Delsante, Vito. Babe Ruth. Martínez, Andrés Vera, illus. 2009. (Before They Were Famous Ser.). (ENG.). 128p. (J). (gr. 3-7). pap. 8.99 *(978-1-4169-5071-4(0)*, Simon & Schuster/Paula Wiseman Bks.) Simon & Schuster/Paula Wiseman Bks.

Deuker, Carl. Heart of a Champion. 2007. (ENG.). 208p. (YA). (gr. 7-17). per. 9.99 *(978-0-316-06726-3(1))* Little, Brown Bks. for Young Readers.

—High Heat. 2005. (ENG.). 352p. (J). (gr. 8-18). pap. 8.99 *(978-0-06-057248-8(5)*, HarperTeen) HarperCollins Pubs.

Dickey, R. A. Knuckleball Ned. Bowers, Tim, illus. 2014. (ENG.). 32p. (J). (gr. -1-k). 17.99 *(978-0-8037-4038-9(7)*, Dial Bks) Penguin Young Readers Group.

Dixon, Franklin W. The Missing Playbook. David, Matt, illus. 2016. (Hardy Boys Clue Book Ser.: 2). (ENG.). 96p. (J). (gr. 1-4). 16.99 *(978-1-4814-5178-9(2))*; pap. 5.99 *(978-1-4814-5177-2(4))* Simon & Schuster Children's Publishing. (Aladdin).

Doyle, Bill. The Werewolf at Home Plate. Lee, Jared D., illus. 2012. (Scream Team Ser.: 1). (ENG.). 96p. (J). (gr. 2-5). pap. 4.99 *(978-0-545-34198-1(1)*, Scholastic Paperbacks) Scholastic, Inc.

Dreams Will Come, Dreams Will Go. 2008. (Illus.). 28p. (J). per. 11.99 *(978-0-615-17947-6(9))* Play Ball Publishing.

Driscoll, Laura & Rey, H. A. Curious George at the Baseball Game. Hines, Anna Grossnickle, illus. 2006. (Curious George Ser.). (ENG.). 24p. (J). (gr. -1-3). pap. 4.99 *(978-0-618-66375-0(4))* Houghton Mifflin Harcourt Publishing Co.

Driscoll, Laura, et al. Curious George at the Baseball Game. Hines, Anna Grossnickle, illus. 2006. (Curious George Ser.). (ENG.). 24p. (J). (gr. -1-3). 13.99 *(978-0-618-66374-3(6))* Houghton Mifflin Harcourt Publishing Co.

Dunrea, Olivier. Peedie. 2008. (Gossie & Friends Ser.). (ENG., illus.). 32p. (J). (gr. -1 — 1). bds. 6.95 *(978-0-618-75506-6(3))* Houghton Mifflin Harcourt Publishing Co.

Dyan, Penelope. Three Strikes — -Doesn't Really Mean You Are Out. Dyan, Penelope, illus. 2008. (Illus.). 44p. pap. 11.95 *(978-1-935118-39-8(0))* Bellissima Publishing, LLC.

Dzidrums, Christine. Timmy Adopts a Girl Dog. Lopez, Lyle & Dzidrums, Joseph, illus. 2012. 48p. pap. 6.99 *(978-1-938438-03-5(5))* Creative Media Publishing.

—Timmy & the Baseball Birthday Party. Lopez, Lyle, illus. 2012. 50p. pap. 6.99 *(978-0-9835393-8-4(3))* Creative Media Publishing.

Edman Lamote, Lisa. Don't Judge a Book by Its Cover. Wilson, Alisha, illus. 2006. (Bookmann Family Presents Ser.). 32p. (J). (gr. k-3). 15.99 *(978-1-933673-01-1(X)*, BookMann Pr.) Mann Publishing Group.

Ellery, Amanda. If I Were a Jungle Animal. Ellery, Tom, illus. 2009. (ENG.). 40p. (J). (gr. -1-3). 17.99 *(978-1-4169-3778-4(1)*, Simon & Schuster Bks. For Young Readers) Simon & Schuster Bks. For Young Readers.

Ellis, Jesse. Kyle Learns Baseball. 2013. 36p. pap. 24.95 *(978-1-63004-169-4(6))* America Star Bks.

English, Travis. Knights of Paris. 2004. (J). per. 11.95 *(978-0-9759903-1-5(4))* Blue Tiger Publishing.

Erskine, Kevin L. Derek's Dream Team, 1 vol. 2010. 48p. pap. 24.95 *(978-1-4489-5947-1(0))* PublishAmerica, Inc.

Farley, Colby King. A Warm Familiar Feeling. 2nd ed. 2003. (YA). per. 13.50 *(978-0-943864-48-8(8))* Davenport, May Pubs.

Fehler, Gene. Beanball. 2011. (ENG.). 144p. (YA). (gr. 7). pap. 7.99 *(978-0-547-55001-5(4))* Houghton Mifflin Harcourt Publishing Co.

—Cutoff Play. 2012. (Travel Team Ser.). (ENG.). 128p. (gr. 6-12). lib. bdg. 27.93 *(978-0-7613-8321-5(2))* Lerner Publishing Group.

—Forced Out. 2012. (Travel Team Ser.). (ENG.). 128p. (gr. 6-12). pap. 7.95 *(978-0-7613-8533-2(9)*, Darby Creek) Lerner Publishing Group.

—Never Blame the Umpire, 1 vol. 2010. (ENG.). 192p. (J). (gr. 4-7). 12.99 *(978-0-310-71941-0(0))* Zonderkidz.

Fein, Eric & Fuentes, Benny. Wild Pitch, 1 vol. Sandoval, Gerardo, illus. 2011. (Sports Illustrated Kids Graphic Novels Ser.). (ENG.). 56p. (gr. 2-3). pap. 7.19 *(978-1-4342-3073-7(2))*; lib. bdg. 26.65 *(978-1-4342-2221-3(7))* Stone Arch Bks.

Feinstein, John. Change-Up. 2010. (Sports Beat Ser.). (ENG.). 336p. (J). (gr. 5). 8.99 *(978-0-375-84759-2(6)*, Yearling) Random Hse. Children's Bks.

—The DH (the Triple Threat, 3) 2016. (Triple Threat Ser.). (ENG.). 304p. (YA). (gr. 5). 16.99 *(978-0-553-53582-2(X)*, Knopf Bks. for Young Readers) Random Hse. Children's Bks.

Ferguson, Donald. Chums of Scranton High. 2006. 25.95 *(978-1-4218-2935-7(5))*; pap. 10.95 *(978-1-4218-3035-3(3))* 1st World Publishing, Inc.

—The Chums of Scranton High, or, Hugh Morgan's Uphill Fight. 2007. 136p. per. *(978-1-4065-2362-1(3))* Dodo Pr.

Finnegan, Evelyn M. My Little Friend Goes to a Baseball Game. Houghton, Diane R., illus. 2006. 32p. (J). (gr. -1-3). reprint ed. pap. 7.00 *(978-1-4223-5403-2(2))* DIANE Publishing Co.

Fitzmaurice, Kathryn. A Diamond in the Desert. (ENG.). 272p. (J). (gr. 5). 2013. pap. 6.99 *(978-0-14-242437-7(4)*, Puffin Books) 2012. 16.99 *(978-0-670-01292-3(0)*, Viking Books for Young Readers) Penguin Young Readers Group.

Fitzsimmons, Kakie. Bur Bur Throws Out the First Pitch: An Exciting Baseball Experience. VanDeWeghe, Lindsay & Bohnet, Christopher, illus. 2007. (Bur Bur & Friends Ser.). (ENG.). 30p. (J). (gr. -1-3). lib. bdg. *(978-0-9777121-4-4(1))* IGI Pr.

Freeman, Martha. Who Stole Uncle Sam? 2008. (Chickadee Court Mystery Ser.). (ENG., illus.). 128p. (J). (gr. 3-7). 16.95 *(978-0-8234-2091-9(4))* Holiday Hse., Inc.

Frisch, Aaron. Pirates at the Plate. Summers, Mark, illus. 2012. (ENG.). 32p. (J). (gr. 1-3). 17.99 *(978-1-56846-210-3(7)*, Creative Editions) Creative Co., The.

Funari Willever, Lisa. Nicky Fifth on 32 Dandelion Court. 2003. 160p. pap. 5.95 *(978-0-9679227-7-5(1)*, 329-008) Franklin Mason Pr.

Gaetz, Dayle Campbell. No Problem, 1 vol. 2003. (Orca Soundings Ser.). (ENG.). 128p. (YA). (gr. 8-12). pap. 9.95 *(978-1-55143-231-1(5))* Orca Bk. Pubs. USA.

Gal, Dakota. Jaffy Gaffy. 2009. 60p. pap. 12.00 *(978-1-4389-8336-3(0))* AuthorHouse.

Gantos, Jack. Joey Pigza Loses Control. braille ed. 2003. (Joey Pigza Ser.: Bk. 2). (J). (gr. 2). spiral bd. *(978-0-616-15268-3(X))* Canadian National Institute for the Blind/Institut National Canadien pour les Aveugles.

—Joey Pigza Loses Control. unabr. ed. 2004. (Joey Pigza Ser.: Bk. 2). 195p. (J). (gr. 5-9). pap. 36.00 incl. audio *(978-0-8072-8726-2(1)*, LyA 248 SP, Listening Library) Random Hse. Audio Publishing Group.

—Joey Pigza Loses Control. 2014. (Joey Pigza Ser.: 2). (J). lib. bdg. 18.40 *(978-0-606-36561-1(3))* Turtleback Bks.

Garfield, Henry. Tartabull's Throw. 2015. (ENG., illus.). 272p. (YA). (gr. 7). pap. 12.99 *(978-1-4814-7510-5(X)*, Atheneum Bks. for Young Readers) Simon & Schuster Children's Publishing.

Gayken, D. Rae. Grandma's Baseball Card: A Braynard Family Story. 2007. 60p. per. 8.95 *(978-0-595-45439-6(9))* iUniverse, Inc.

Geddes, Diana E. Baseball Fun. Kaeden Corp. Staff, ed. Palmer, Kate S., illus. 2003. (ENG.). 12p. (gr. k-2). pap. 7.95 *(978-1-879835-72-6(X)*, Kaeden Bks.) Kaeden Corp.

Gibney, Shannon. See No Color. 2015. (ENG.). 192p. (YA). (gr. 7-12). 18.99 *(978-1-4677-8814-4(7)*, Carolrhoda Lab™); 18.99 *(978-1-4677-7682-0(3))* Lerner Publishing Group.

Gill, Amber. Joseph's Summer. 2006. 71p. pap. 16.95 *(978-1-4241-0122-1(0))* PublishAmerica, Inc.

Glaser, Jason. The Prospect. 2012. (Travel Team Ser.). (ENG.). 120p. (gr. 6-12). pap. 7.95 *(978-0-7613-8540-0(1)*, Darby Creek); lib. bdg. 27.93 *(978-0-7613-8325-3(5))* Lerner Publishing Group.

Gordon, Amy. The Gorillas of Gill Park. 2003. (ENG., illus.). 256p. (J). (gr. 4-6). tchr. ed. 16.95 *(978-0-8234-1751-3(4))* Holiday Hse., Inc.

Gorin, Leslie. Elly & the Smelly Sneaker: A Riches to Rags Story. Vamos, Lesley, illus. 2017. (ENG.). 40p. (J). (gr. -1). 14.95 *(978-1-4549-1817-2(9))* Sterling Publishing Co., Inc.

Gorman, Carol & Findley, Ron J. The Stumptown Kid, 1 vol. 2005. (ENG.). 224p. (J). (gr. 3-7). 15.95 *(978-1-56145-337-5(4))* Peachtree Pubs.

Gratz, Alan. The Brooklyn Nine. 2010. (ENG.). 320p. (J). (gr. 3-7). 8.99 *(978-0-14-241544-3(8)*, Puffin Books) Penguin Young Readers Group.

—Fantasy Baseball. 2012. (ENG.). 336p. (J). (gr. 3-7). 7.99 *(978-0-14-242018-8(2)*, Puffin Books) Penguin Young Readers Group.

—Samurai Shortstop. 2008. (ENG.). 288p. (YA). (gr. 7-18). 7.99 *(978-0-14-241099-8(3)*, Speak) Penguin Young Readers Group.

Green, Teri & Taylor, Sue. The Littlest Soldier, 1 vol. 2009. 94p. pap. 19.95 *(978-1-4489-2714-2(5))* America Star Bks.

Green, Tim. Baseball Great. (Baseball Great Ser.: 1). (ENG.). (J). (gr. 3-7). 2010. 272p. pap. 6.99 *(978-0-06-162688-3(0))* 2009. 256p. 16.99 *(978-0-06-162686-9(4))* HarperCollins Pubs.

—Baseball Great. 2010. (Baseball Great Ser.: 1). (J). lib. bdg. 17.20 *(978-0-606-10356-5(2)*, Turtleback) Turtleback Bks.

—Force Out. 2013. (ENG.). 288p. (J). (gr. 3-7). 16.99 *(978-0-06-208959-5(5))* HarperCollins Pubs.

—Home Run. 2016. (Baseball Great Ser.: 4). 352p. (J). (gr. 3-7). 16.99 *(978-0-06-231711-7(3))* HarperCollins Pubs.

—Lost Boy. 2015. (ENG.). 304p. (J). (gr. 3-7). 16.99 *(978-0-06-231708-7(3))* HarperCollins Pubs.

—New Kid. 2014. (ENG.). 320p. (J). (gr. 3-7). 16.99 *(978-0-06-220872-9(1))* HarperCollins Pubs.

—Pinch Hit. (ENG.). (J). (gr. 3-7). 2013. 336p. pap. 6.99 *(978-0-06-201247-0(9))* 2012. 320p. 16.99 *(978-0-06-201246-3(0))* HarperCollins Pubs.

—Rivals: A Baseball Great Novel. (Baseball Great Ser.: 2). (ENG.). (J). (gr. 3-7). 2011. 288p. pap. 6.99 *(978-0-06-162694-4(5))* 2010. 272p. 16.99 *(978-0-06-162692-0(9))* HarperCollins Pubs.

Green, Tim & Jeter, Derek. Baseball Genius. 2017. (Jeter Publishing Ser.). (ENG., illus.). 352p. (J). (gr. 3-7). 16.99 *(978-1-4814-6864-0(2)*, Simon & Schuster/Paula Wiseman Bks.) Simon & Schuster/Paula Wiseman Bks.

—Baseball Genius. 2018. lib. bdg. 18.40 ***(978-0-606-40847-9(9))*** Turtleback Bks.

Grey, Zane. The Redheaded Outfield. 302p. (J). reprint ed. lib. bdg. 22.95 *(978-0-89190-759-6(9)*, Rivercity Pr.) Amereon Ltd.

Griffiths, Sara. Thrown a Curve. 2007. 151p. (ENG.). (gr. 6-10). pap. 13.99 *(978-1-890862-49-7(5))*; (J). (gr. 5-13). 16.95 *(978-1-890862-48-0(7))* Bancroft Pr.

Griswold, Melissa. Friends, Like You: Educator's Guide. 2007. 12p. *(978-0-979287-5-4(4))* Mainstream Ctr., Schl. for the Deaf, The.

Grogan, John & Hill, Susan. Strike Three, Marley! Cowdrey, Richard & Beier, Ellen, illus. 2010. (I Can Read Level 2 Ser.). (ENG.). 32p. (J). (gr. k-3). pap. 3.99 *(978-0-06-185386-9(0))* HarperCollins Pubs.

Gutman, Dan. Abner & Me. 2007. (Baseball Card Adventures Ser.). (ENG., illus.). 176p. (J). (gr. 5-9). pap. 5.99 *(978-0-06-053445-5(1))* HarperCollins Pubs.

—Abner & Me. 2007. (Baseball Card Adventures Ser.). (illus.). 166p. (gr. 5-9). 16.00 *(978-0-7569-7920-1(X))* Perfection Learning Corp.

—Honus & Me. 2003. (Baseball Card Adventures Ser.). (ENG., illus.). 144p. (J). (gr. 5-9). pap. 6.99 *(978-0-380-78878-1(0))* HarperCollins Pubs.

—Honus & Me. 2003. (Baseball Card Adventures Ser.). (J). (gr. 3-6). lib. bdg. 16.00 *(978-0-613-07982-2(5)*, Turtleback) Turtleback Bks.

—Jackie & Me. 2005. (Baseball Card Adventures Ser.). (illus.). 145p. (YA). (gr. 4-8). reprint ed. 20.00 *(978-0-7567-9569-6(9))* DIANE Publishing Co.

—Jim & Me. 2010. (Baseball Card Adventures Ser.). (ENG.). 224p. (J). (gr. 5-9). pap. 6.99 *(978-0-06-059496-1(9))* HarperCollins Pubs.

—Jim & Me. 2010. (Baseball Card Adventures Ser.). (J). lib. bdg. 17.20 *(978-0-606-09536-5(5)*, Turtleback) Turtleback Bks.

—Mickey & Me. 2004. (Baseball Card Adventures Ser.). (ENG., illus.). 160p. (J). (gr. 5-9). pap. 5.99 *(978-0-06-447258-6(2))* HarperCollins Pubs.

—Mickey & Me. 2004. (Baseball Card Adventures Ser.). (J). lib. bdg. 16.00 *(978-0-613-99233-6(4)*, Turtleback) Turtleback Bks.

—Ray & Me. (Baseball Card Adventures Ser.). (ENG.). 192p. (J). (gr. 5-9). 2011. pap. 6.99 *(978-0-06-123483-5(4))* 2009. (illus.). 16.99 *(978-0-06-123481-1(8))* HarperCollins Pubs.

—Roberto & Me. (Baseball Card Adventures Ser.). (ENG.). 192p. (J). (gr. 5-9). 2012. pap. 5.99 *(978-0-06-123486-6(9))* 2010. 16.99 *(978-0-06-123484-2(2))* HarperCollins Pubs.

—Roberto & Me. 2012. (Baseball Card Adventures Ser.). (J). lib. bdg. 16.00 *(978-0-606-23591-4(4)*, Turtleback) Turtleback Bks.

—Satch & Me. (Baseball Card Adventures Ser.). (ENG.). 192p. (J). (gr. 5-9). 2009. pap. 5.99 *(978-0-06-059493-0(4))* 2006. (illus.). 16.99 *(978-0-06-059491-6(8))* HarperCollins Pubs. (Amistad).

—Satch & Me. 2009. (Baseball Card Adventures Ser.). (J). lib. bdg. 16.00 *(978-0-606-00023-9(2)*, Turtleback) Turtleback Bks.

—Shoeless Joe & Me. 2003. (Baseball Card Adventures Ser.). (ENG., illus.). 176p. (J). (gr. 5-9). pap. 6.99 *(978-0-06-447259-3(0))* HarperCollins Pubs.

—Shoeless Joe & Me. 2003. (Baseball Card Adventures Ser.). (illus.). 163p. (gr. 3-7). 16.00 *(978-0-7569-1438-7(8))* Perfection Learning Corp.

—Shoeless Joe & Me. 2003. (Baseball Card Adventures Ser.). (J). (gr. 3-6). lib. bdg. 16.00 *(978-0-613-61816-8(5)*, Turtleback) Turtleback Bks.

—Ted & Me. 2012. (Baseball Card Adventures Ser.). (illus.). 208p. (J). (gr. 5-9). (ENG.). 15.99 *(978-0-06-123487-3(7))*; lib. bdg. 16.89 *(978-0-06-123488-0(5))* HarperCollins Pubs.

—Willie & Me. (Baseball Card Adventures Ser.). 176p. (J). (gr. 3-7). 2016. pap. 5.99 *(978-0-06-170406-2(7))* 2015. (ENG.). 16.99 *(978-0-06-170404-8(0))* HarperCollins Pubs.

H & T Imaginations Unlimited, Inc. Home Run Derby with Professor Woodpecker. 2009. 12p. pap. 8.49 *(978-1-4389-5926-9(5))* AuthorHouse.

Hairston, Kennard Lee. Rosie Bear Plays Baseball. 2009. 48p. pap. 19.49 *(978-1-4389-7343-2(8))* AuthorHouse.

Hall, Kenneth. Johnny & the Heaters. 2008. 49p. pap. 24.50 *(978-0-615-19649-7(7))* Hall, Kenneth.

Hammond, John, as told by. Lucky in Life. 2003. 150p. (YA). per. 13.95 *(978-1-885631-76-3(6))* Hutchison, G.F. Pr.

Hancock, H. Irving. The Grammar School Boys in Summer Athletics. rev. ed. 2006. 216p. 27.95 *(978-1-4218-1748-4(9))*; pap. 12.95 *(978-1-4218-1848-1(5))* 1st World Publishing, Inc. (1st World Library - Literary Society).

—The Grammar School Boys in Summer Athletics. 2007. 184p. per. *(978-1-4065-1982-2(0))* Dodo Pr.

—The High School Pitcher. rev. ed. 2006. 212p. 27.95 *(978-1-4218-1743-9(8))*; pap. 12.95 *(978-1-4218-1843-6(4))* 1st World Publishing, Inc. (1st World Library - Literary Society).

—The High School Pitcher. 2007. 176p. per. *(978-1-4065-1990-7(1))* Dodo Pr.

Harms, Carol. What If? 2010. 20p. 10.49 *(978-1-4520-8463-3(7))* AuthorHouse.

Haven, Paul. Two Hot Dogs with Everything. Jessell, Tim, illus. 2007. (ENG.). 320p. (J). (gr. 3-7). per. 7.99 *(978-0-375-83349-6(8)*, Yearling) Random Hse. Children's Bks.

Hawaii Winter Baseball. Major Mynah & Da Menehune Crew. 2007. (Illus.). 18p. (J). pap. 4.99 *(978-0-9796769-5-6(9))* Watermark Publishing, LLC.

Heller, Alyson. Time for T-Ball. Björkman, Steve, illus. 2010. (After-School Sports Club Ser.). (ENG.). 32p. (J). (gr. -1-1). pap. 3.99 *(978-1-4169-9412-1(2)*, Simon Spotlight) Simon Spotlight.

Heller, Pete. Peppy Learns to Play Baseball. Kinsey, Thomas D., ed. Schaeffer, Bob, illus. (Peppy Learns to Play Ser.). 32p. (J). (gr. k-5). pap. 3.95 *(978-0-932423-00-9(0))* Summa Bks.

Hellman, Charles. Adventures in Sportsand - the Baseball Bully (with accompanying CD) The Baseball Bully. Tiritilli, Robert, illus. 2008. (Adventures in SportsLand: the Bully Ser.). 32p. pap. 19.95 *(978-0-935938-27-2(3))* Stogo, Malcolm Assocs.

Hellman, Charles & Tiritilli, Robert. Beisbol Humor. 2008. (Illus.). 32p. (J). (gr. -1-3). pap. 4.95 *(978-0-935938-43-2(5))* Williams, Michael.

Hellman, Charles S. The Baseball Bully. Tiritilli, Robert A., illus. 2013. 34p. pap. 9.25 *(978-0-935938-19-7(2))* LuckySports.

—The Baseball Challenge: Defenders of Sportsland. Tiritilli, Robert A., illus. 2013. 54p. pap. 11.25 *(978-0-935938-52-4(4))* LuckySports.

Hello, Phillie Phanatic! 2007. (J). 17.95 *(978-1-932888-85-0(3))* Mascot Bks., Inc.

Hengel, Katherine. Hit Just Right, 1 vol. unabr. ed. 2011. (District 13 Ser.). (ENG.). 48p. (YA). (gr. 9-12). 7.95 *(978-1-61651-584-3(8))* Saddleback Educational Publishing, Inc.

—Wings, 1 vol. unabr. ed. 2011. (District 13 Ser.). (ENG.). 48p. (YA). (gr. 9-12). pap. 7.95 *(978-1-61651-280-4(6))* Saddleback Educational Publishing, Inc.

Henighan, Tom. The Boy from Left Field. 2012. (ENG.). 216p. (J). (gr. 5-5). pap. 12.99 *(978-1-4597-0060-4(0))* Dundurn CAN. Dist: Ingram Publisher Services.

Hennessy, James. Shane's Game. 2003. 184p. 23.95 *(978-0-595-74739-9(6))*; pap. 13.95 *(978-0-595-28112-1(5))* iUniverse, Inc.

Hernandez, Keith. First-Base Hero: A Lift-the-Flap Pop-up Book. Manders, John, illus. 2005. 12p. (J). (gr. k-4). reprint ed. 13.00 *(978-0-7567-8543-7(X))* DIANE Publishing Co.

Higgins, Carter. A Rambler Steals Home. 2017. (ENG.). 224p. (J). (gr. 5-7). 16.99 *(978-0-544-60201-4(3)*, HMH Books For Young Readers) Houghton Mifflin Harcourt Publishing Co.

Higgins, M. G. Power Hitter. 2012. (Travel Team Ser.). (ENG.). 128p. (J). (gr. 6-12). lib. bdg. 27.93 *(978-0-7613-8324-6(7))* Lerner Publishing Group.

Higgins, M. g. & Higgins, M. G. Power Hitter. 2012. (Travel Team Ser.). (ENG.). 128p. (gr. 6-12). pap. 7.95 *(978-0-7613-8539-4(8)*, Darby Creek) Lerner Publishing Group.

Hoban, Russell. Best Friends for Frances. Hoban, Lillian, illus. 2009. (I Can Read Level 2 Ser.). (ENG.). 48p. (J). (gr. k-3). pap. 3.99 *(978-0-06-083803-4(5))* HarperCollins Pubs.

Hoff, Syd. The Littlest Leaguer. Hoff, Syd, illus. 2008. (I Can Read Level 1 Ser.). (ENG., illus.). 48p. (J). (gr. -1-3). pap. 3.99 *(978-0-06-053774-6(4))* HarperCollins Pubs.

Holden, Pam. Watch the Ball, 6 pack. Whimp, Pauline, illus. 2009. (Red Rocket Readers Ser.). (ENG.). 16p. (gr. 2-2). pap. *(978-1-877363-80-1(4))* Flying Start Bks.

Holland, Robert. The Ghost Who Came to Tea: A Novel of Sports & Mystery. 2006. (illus.). 204p. (J). *(978-0-9794273-4-3(7))* Frost Hollow Pubs., LLC.

Holtzen, Mark. A Ticket to the Pennant: A Tale of Baseball in Seattle. Skewes, John, illus. 2016. (ENG.). 32p. (J). (gr. -1-3). 17.99 *(978-1-63217-003-3(5)*, Little Bigfoot) Sasquatch Bks.

Honsinger, Laura. Mike's New Friends. 2005. 35p. (J). pap. 5.92 *(978-1-4116-3070-3(X))* Lulu Pr., Inc.

Hopkinson, Deborah. Girl Wonder. Widener, Terry, illus. 2015. 40p. pap. 8.00 *(978-1-61003-606-1(9))* Center for the Collaborative Classroom.

—Girl Wonder: A Baseball Story in Nine Innings. Widener, Terry, illus. 2006. (ENG.). 40p. (J). (gr. k-3). reprint ed. 7.99 *(978-1-4169-1393-1(9)*, Aladdin) Simon & Schuster Children's Publishing.

Horatio Alger Jr. The Cash Boy. l.t. ed. 2007. 186p. pap. 19.99 *(978-1-4264-7014-1(2))* Creative Media Partners, LLC.

Houghton, Jackolyn. Detective Billy Pears & the Missing Hat. 2008. 36p. pap. 24.95 *(978-1-60474-543-6(6))* America Star Bks.

Howard, Lee. Scooby-Doo & the Unnatural, 1 vol. 2016. (Scooby-Doo Comic Readers Ser.). (ENG.). 32p. (J). (gr. k-3). lib. bdg. 24.21 *(978-1-61479-453-0(7)*, Graphic Planet) Magic Wagon.

Howard, Ryan & Howard, Krystle. The Best Bat. Madrid, Erwin, illus. 2015. (Little Rhino Ser.: 2). (ENG.). 112p. (J). (gr. 2-5). 16.99 *(978-0-545-67494-2(8))*; pap. 4.99 *(978-0-545-67493-5(X))* Scholastic, Inc. (Scholastic Paperbacks).

—Dugout Hero. Madrid, Erwin, illus. 2015. (Little Rhino Ser.: 3). (ENG.). 112p. (J). (gr. 2-5). pap. 4.99 *(978-0-545-67496-6(4)*, Scholastic Paperbacks) Scholastic, Inc.

—My New Team. Madrid, Erwin, illus. 2015. (Little Rhino Ser.: 1). (ENG.). 112p. (J). (gr. 2-5). pap. 4.99 *(978-0-545-67490-4(5)*, Scholastic Paperbacks) Scholastic, Inc.

Hubbard, Crystal. Catching the Moon: The Story of a Young Girl's Baseball Dream. DuBurke, Randy, illus. 2005. (ENG.). 32p. (J). pap. 9.95 *(978-1-60060-572-7(9))* Lee & Low Bks., Inc.

Hughes, Dean. Missing in Action. 2010. (ENG.). 240p. (J). (gr. 5-9). 16.99 *(978-1-4169-1502-7(8)*, Atheneum Bks. for Young Readers) Simon & Schuster Children's Publishing.

Hyde, Margaret. Mo Smells the Ballpark. Chaudhary, Aman, illus. 2014. (ENG.). 24p. (J). (gr. -1-k). 14.95 *(978-1-62873-668-7(2)*, Sky Pony Pr.) Skyhorse Publishing Co., Inc.

Hyman, Zachary. The Bambino & Me. Pullen, Zachary, illus. (ENG.). 48p. (J). (gr. 1-4). 2015. pap. 7.99 *(978-1-77049-628-6(9))* 2014. 17.99 *(978-1-77049-627-9(0))* Tundra Bks. CAN. (Tundra Bks.). Dist: Penguin Random Hse. LLC.

Jackson, Max. Mickey Mantle: All-Star Athlete. Henderson, Meryl, illus. 2009. (Childhood of Famous Americans Ser.). (ENG.). 224p. (J). pap. 5.99 *(978-1-4169-7472-7(5)*, Simon & Schuster/Paula Wiseman Bks.) Simon & Schuster/Paula Wiseman Bks.

Jacobson, Ryan. Caught in a Pickle, 1 vol. Garcia, Eduardo & Ferrara, Eduardo, illus. 2011. (B-Team Ser.). (ENG.). 40p. (gr. 1-3). lib. bdg. 23.99 *(978-1-4342-2606-8(9)*, Graphic Sparks) Stone Arch Bks.

Jasper, Rick & Reece, Richard. The Catch. 2012. (Travel Team Ser.). (ENG.). 120p. (gr. 6-12). pap. 7.95 *(978-0-7613-8532-5(0)*, Darby Creek); lib. bdg. 27.93 *(978-0-7613-8320-8(4))* Lerner Publishing Group.

—Out of Control. 2012. (Travel Team Ser.). (ENG.). 120p. (gr. 6-12). pap. 7.95 *(978-0-7613-8538-7(X)*, Darby Creek); lib. bdg. 27.93 *(978-0-7613-8323-9(9))* Lerner Publishing Group.

Jeter, Derek. Change Up. 2016. (Jeter Publishing Ser.). (ENG., illus.). 176p. (J). (gr. 3-7). 16.99 *(978-1-4814-6445-1(0)*, Simon & Schuster/Paula Wiseman Bks.) Simon & Schuster/Paula Wiseman Bks.

—The Contract. 2016. (Jeter Publishing Ser.). (ENG., illus.). 192p. (J). (gr. 3-7). pap. 7.99 *(978-1-4814-2313-7(4)*, Simon & Schuster/Paula Wiseman Bks.) Simon & Schuster/Paula Wiseman Bks.

—Hit & Miss. 2015. (Jeter Publishing Ser.). (ENG., illus.). 192p. (J). (gr. 3-7). 16.99 *(978-1-4814-2315-1(0)*, Simon & Schuster/Paula Wiseman Bks.) Simon & Schuster/Paula Wiseman Bks.

Jeter, Derek & Mantell, Paul. The Contract. 2014. (Jeter Publishing Ser.). (ENG., illus.). 176p. (J). (gr. 3-7). 16.99 *(978-1-4814-2312-0(6)*, Simon & Schuster/Paula Wiseman Bks.) Simon & Schuster/Paula Wiseman Bks.

Johnson, Angela. Just Like Josh Gibson. Peck, Beth, illus. 2007. (J). 14.65 *(978-0-7569-8068-7(7))* Perfection Learning Corp.

—Just Like Josh Gibson. Peck, Beth, illus. (ENG.). 32p. (J). 2004. (gr. -1-2). 17.99 *(978-0-689-82628-3(1))* 2007. (gr. k-2). reprint ed. 7.99 *(978-1-4169-2728-0(X))* Simon & Schuster Bks. For Young Readers. (Simon & Schuster Bks. For Young Readers).

Johnson, Sandi. Baseball Billy. Johnson, Britt, ed. Nadaskay, Lori, illus. l.t. ed. 2003. 12p. (J). (gr. k-5). spiral bd. 5.99 *(978-1-929063-30-7(X)*, 320) Moons & Stars Publishing For Children.

Jones, Patrick. Returning to Normal. 2015. (J). 104p. 9.99 *(978-1-4677-7700-1(5))*; (ENG.). 112p. (gr. 6-12). lib. bdg. 27.99 *(978-1-4677-5799-7(3))* Lerner Publishing Group.

Jordan, Deloris. Michael's Golden Rules. Nelson, Kadir, illus. 2007. (ENG.). 32p. (J). (gr. 1-5). 17.99 *(978-0-689-87016-3(7)*, Simon & Schuster/Paula Wiseman Bks.) Simon & Schuster/Paula Wiseman Bks.

Joven, C. C. Baseball Buzz. Shems, Ed, illus. 2017. (Sports Illustrated Kids Starting Line Readers Ser.). (ENG.). 32p. (gr. -1-1). pap. 3.95 *(978-1-4965-4259-5(2))*; lib. bdg. 22.65 *(978-1-4965-4252-6(5))* Capstone Press of Coughlan Cos.

Kalkowski, John. Red Cell. 2010. 164p. 21.95 *(978-1-4502-1209-0(3))*; pap. 11.95 *(978-1-4502-1207-6(7))* iUniverse, Inc.

Karen & Kary. Little Wizard. 2004. 21p. pap. 24.95 *(978-1-4137-2956-6(8))* PublishAmerica, Inc.

Karre, Andrew. High Heat. 2012. (Travel Team Ser.). (ENG.). 120p. (gr. 6-12). pap. 7.95 *(978-0-7613-8534-9(7)*, Darby Creek); lib. bdg. 27.93 *(978-0-7613-8322-2(0))* Lerner Publishing Group.

Keith, Doug, illus. B Is for Baseball: Alphabet Cards. 2011. (ENG.). 26p. (J). 12.95 *(978-1-897476-55-0(8))* Simply Read Bks. CAN. Dist: Ingram Publisher Services.

Kelly, David A. The All-Star Joker. Meyers, Mark, illus. 2012. (Ballpark Mysteries Ser.: 5). (ENG.). 112p. (J). (gr. 1-4). 4.99 *(978-0-375-86884-9(4)*, Random Hse. Bks. for Young Readers) Random Hse. Children's Bks.

—The All-Star Joker. Meyers, Mark, illus. 2012. (Ballpark Mysteries Ser.: Bk. 5). lib. bdg. 14.75 *(978-0-606-26401-3(9)*, Turtleback) Turtleback Bks.

—The Astro Outlaw. Meyers, Mark, illus. 2012. (Ballpark Mysteries Ser.: Bk. 4). (ENG.). 112p. (J). (gr. 1-4). pap. 4.99 *(978-0-375-86883-2(6)*, Random Hse. Bks. for Young Readers) Random Hse. Children's Bks.

—The Astro Outlaw. 2012. (Ballpark Mysteries Ser.: Bk. 4). lib. bdg. 14.75 *(978-0-606-23861-8(1)*, Turtleback) Turtleback Bks.

—The Fenway Foul-Up. Meyers, Mark, illus. 2011. (Ballpark Mysteries Ser.: Bk. 1). (ENG.). 112p. (J). (gr. 1-4). pap. 4.99 *(978-0-375-86703-3(1)*, Random Hse. Bks. for Young Readers) Random Hse. Children's Bks.

—The L. A. Dodger. Meyers, Mark, illus. 2011. (Ballpark Mysteries Ser.: Bk. 3). (ENG.). 112p. (J). (gr. 1-4). 4.99 *(978-0-375-86885-6(2)*, Random Hse. Bks. for Young Readers) Random Hse. Children's Bks.

—The Philly Fake. Meyers, Mark, illus. 2014. (Ballpark Mysteries Ser.: Bk. 9). (ENG.). 112p. (J). (gr. 1-4). 4.99 *(978-0-307-97785-4(4)*, Random Hse. Bks. for Young Readers) Random Hse. Children's Bks.

—The Philly Fake. 2014. (Ballpark Mysteries Ser.: Bk. 9). lib. bdg. 14.75 *(978-0-606-35566-7(9))* Turtleback Bks.

—The Pinstripe Ghost. Meyers, Mark, illus. 2011. (Ballpark Mysteries Ser.: 2). (ENG.). 112p. (J). (gr. 1-4). 4.99 *(978-0-375-86704-0(X)*, Random Hse. Bks. for Young Readers) Random Hse. Children's Bks.

—The Rangers Rustlers. Meyers, Mark, illus. 2016. (Ballpark Mysteries Ser.: Bk. 12). (ENG.). 112p. (J). (gr. 1-4). pap. 4.99 *(978-0-385-37881-9(5)*, Random Hse. Bks. for Young Readers) Random Hse. Children's Bks.

—The Rookie Blue Jay. Meyers, Mark, illus. 2015. (Ballpark Mysteries Ser.: 10). (ENG.). 112p. (J). (gr. 1-4). 4.99 *(978-0-385-37875-8(0)*, Random Hse. Bks. for Young Readers) Random Hse. Children's Bks.

—The Rookie Blue Jay. 2015. (Ballpark Mysteries Ser.: Bk. 10). lib. bdg. 14.75 *(978-0-606-36413-3(7))* Turtleback Bks.

—The San Francisco Splash. Meyers, Mark, illus. 2013. (Ballpark Mysteries Ser.: Bk. 7). (ENG.). 112p. (J). (gr. 1-4). pap. 4.99 *(978-0-307-97779-3(X)*, Random Hse. Bks. for Young Readers) Random Hse. Children's Bks.

—The San Francisco Splash. 2013. (Ballpark Mysteries Ser.: Bk. 7). lib. bdg. 14.75 *(978-0-606-31940-9(9)*, Turtleback) Turtleback Bks.

—The Tiger Troubles. Meyers, Mark, illus. 2015. (Ballpark Mysteries Ser.: 11). (ENG.). 112p. (J). (gr. 1-4). pap. 4.99 *(978-0-385-37878-9(5)*, Random Hse. Bks. for Young Readers) Random Hse. Children's Bks.

—The World Series Curse. Meyers, Mark, illus. 2016. (Ballpark Mysteries Ser.: 13). (ENG.). 144p. (J). (gr. 1-4). 5.99 *(978-0-385-37884-0(X)*, Random Hse. Bks. for Young Readers) Random Hse. Children's Bks.

—The Wrigley Riddle. Meyers, Mark, illus. 2013. (Ballpark Mysteries Ser.: Bk. 6). (ENG.). 112p. (J). (gr. 1-4). pap. 4.99 *(978-0-307-97776-2(5)*, Random Hse. Bks. for Young Readers) Random Hse. Children's Bks.

—The Wrigley Riddle. 2013. (Ballpark Mysteries Ser.: Bk. 6). lib. bdg. 14.75 *(978-0-606-26998-8(3)*, Turtleback) Turtleback Bks.

Kemp, Dane. Imaginary Tales. 2011. 186p. pap. 24.95 *(978-1-4560-4686-6(1))* America Star Bks.

Kinerk, Robert. Clorinda Plays Baseball! Kellogg, Steven, illus. 2012. (ENG.). 40p. (J). (gr. -1-3). 16.99 *(978-0-689-86865-8(0)*, Simon & Schuster/Paula Wiseman Bks.) Simon & Schuster/Paula Wiseman Bks.

Knudson, Mike & Wilkinson, Steve. Bases Loaded. 2011. (Raymond & Graham Ser.). (ENG.). 160p. (J). (gr. 3-7). 6.99 *(978-0-14-241751-5(3)*, Puffin Books) Penguin Young Readers Group.

Koertge, Ron. Shakespeare Makes the Playoffs. 2012. (ENG., Illus.). 176p. (YA). (gr. 7). pap. 6.99 *(978-0-7636-5852-6(9))* Candlewick Pr.

Koertge, Ronald. Shakespeare Bats Cleanup. 2006. (ENG.). 128p. (YA). (gr. 7-12). reprint ed. per. 6.99 *(978-0-7636-2939-7(1))* Candlewick Pr.

—Shakespeare Bats Cleanup. 2006. 116p. (gr. 7-12). 16.00 *(978-0-7569-6571-6(3))* Perfection Learning Corp.

—Shakespeare Makes the Playoffs. 2010. (ENG., Illus.). 176p. (YA). (gr. 7-18). 15.99 *(978-0-7636-4435-2(8))* Candlewick Pr.

Konigsburg, E. L. About the B'nai Bagels. Konigsburg, E. L., illus. 2008. (ENG., Illus.). 208p. (J). (gr. 3-7). pap. 7.99 *(978-1-4169-5798-0(7)*, Atheneum Bks. for Young Readers) Simon & Schuster Children's Publishing.

Korba, Joanna. Cindy Eller Plays Ball: A Modern-Day Cinderella Tale. 2006. (J). pap. *(978-1-4108-6164-1(3))* Benchmark Education Co.

Korman, Gordon. Swindle. 2009. (ENG.). 256p. (J). (gr. 3-7). 6.99 *(978-0-439-90345-5(9)*, Scholastic Paperbacks) Scholastic, Inc.

Kreie, Chris, et al. Battle for Home Plate, 1 vol. Aburtov, Jesus Aburto, illus. 2010. (Sports Illustrated Kids Graphic Novels Ser.). (ENG.). 56p. (gr. 2-3). pap. 7.19 *(978-1-4342-2290-9(X))* Stone Arch Bks.

—Battle for Home Plate, 1 vol. Aburto, Jesus, illus. 2010. (Sports Illustrated Kids Graphic Novels Ser.). (ENG.). 56p. (gr. 2-3). 26.65 *(978-1-4342-1913-8(5))* Stone Arch Bks.

Krensky, Stephen. Play Ball, Jackie! Morse, Joe, illus. 2011. (Single Titles Ser.). (ENG.). 32p. (J). (gr. 2-5). lib. bdg. 16.95 *(978-0-8225-9030-9(1)*, Millbrook Pr.) Lerner Publishing Group.

Larsen, Angela Sage. Broken Record, Bk. 4. 2013. (Fifties Chix Ser.: 4). (ENG., Illus.). 200p. (YA). pap. 9.95 *(978-1-60746-446-4(2)*, Premiere) FastPencil, Inc.

—Till the End of Time. 2013. (Fifties Chix Ser.: 5). (ENG.). 200p. (YA). pap. 9.95 *(978-1-60746-468-6(3)*, Premiere) FastPencil, Inc.

Lawrence, David. Home Run. 2013. 132p. pap. *(978-1-922168-94-8(7))* Connor Court Publishing Pty Ltd.

Lester, Helen. Batter up Wombat. Munsinger, Lynn, illus. 2006. (ENG.). 32p. (J). (gr. k-3). 24.80 *(978-1-4287-0160-1(5)*, Follettbound) Follett School Solutions.

Levine, Bdette M. The Talking Baseball. 2007. (Illus.). 22p. (J). pap. 12.99 net. *(978-0-9721094-1-3(2))* Levine, Bette M.

Lewman, David & Gomez, Yuliana. Batter up!/¡a Batear!(SpongeBob SquarePants) Random House, illus. 2014. (Pictureback Ser.). (ENG.). 24p. (J). (gr. -1-2). 3.99 *(978-0-385-38436-0(X)*, Random Hse. Bks. for Young Readers) Random Hse. Children's Bks.

Lies, Brian. Bats at the Ballgame. 2010. (Bat Book Ser.). (ENG., Illus.). 32p. (J). (gr. -1-3). 16.99 *(978-0-547-24970-4(5))* Houghton Mifflin Harcourt Publishing Co.

Lieurance, Suzanne. The Lucky Baseball: My Story in a Japanese-American Internment Camp. 2009. (Historical Fiction Adventures (HFA) Ser.). (Illus.). 160p. (J). (gr. 3-6). lib. bdg. 29.27 *(978-0-7660-3311-5(2))* Enslow Pubs., Inc.

Lilienstein, Jennel. First Ball Game/Sports! 2003. 36p. (J). 8.99 *(978-0-9741215-2-9(5))* Stories of My Life, The.

Lipsyte, Robert. Center Field. 2010. (ENG.). 288p. (YA). (gr. 8-18). 17.99 *(978-0-06-055704-1(4)*, HarperTeen) HarperCollins Pubs.

Long, Loren & Bildner, Phil. Blastin' the Blues. Long, Loren, illus. 2011. (Sluggers Ser.: 5). (ENG., Illus.). 448p. (J). (gr. 3-7). pap. 8.99 *(978-1-4169-1891-2(4)*, Simon & Schuster Bks. For Young Readers) Simon & Schuster Bks. For Young Readers.

—Great Balls of Fire. Long, Loren, illus. 2009. (Sluggers Ser.: 3). (ENG., Illus.). 224p. (J). (gr. 3-7). pap. 7.99 *(978-1-4169-1889-9(2)*, Simon & Schuster Bks. For Young Readers) Simon & Schuster Bks. For Young Readers.

—Home of the Brave. Long, Loren, illus. (Sluggers Ser.: 6). (ENG., Illus.). 336p. (J). (gr. 3-7). 2011. pap. 8.99 *(978-1-4169-1892-9(2))* 2010. 15.99 *(978-1-4169-1868-4(X))* Simon & Schuster Bks. For Young Readers. (Simon & Schuster Bks. For Young Readers).

—Magic in the Outfield. Long, Loren, illus. 2009. (Sluggers Ser.: 1). (ENG., Illus.). 160p. (J). (gr. 3-7). pap. 8.99 *(978-1-4169-1884-4(1)*, Simon & Schuster Bks. For Young Readers) Simon & Schuster Bks. For Young Readers.

—Water, Water Everywhere. Long, Loren, illus. (Sluggers Ser.: 4). (ENG., Illus.). (J). (gr. 3-7). 2010. 288p. pap. 7.99 *(978-1-4169-1890-5(6))* 2009. 272p. 14.99 *(978-1-4169-1866-0(3))* Simon & Schuster Bks. For Young Readers. (Simon & Schuster Bks. For Young Readers).

Lorbiecki, Marybeth. Jackie's Bat. Pinkney, Brian, illus. 2006. (ENG.). 40p. (J). (gr. k-3). 17.99 *(978-0-689-84102-6(7)*, Simon & Schuster Bks. For Young Readers) Simon & Schuster Bks. For Young Readers.

Lorenzi, Natalie Dias. A Long Pitch Home. 2016. (ENG.). 256p. (J). (gr. 4-7). lib. bdg. 16.95 *(978-1-58089-713-6(4))* Charlesbridge Publishing, Inc.

Lupica, Mike. The Batboy. 2011. (ENG.). 272p. (J). (gr. 5-18). 7.99 *(978-0-14-241782-9(3)*, Puffin Books) Penguin Young Readers Group.

—The Batboy. 2011. lib. bdg. 18.40 *(978-0-606-15352-2(7)*, Turtleback) Turtleback Bks.

—The Big Field. 2009. (ENG.). 272p. (J). (gr. 3-7). 7.99 *(978-0-14-241910-6(9)*, Puffin Books) Penguin Young Readers Group.

—Heat. 2007. 220p. (gr. 5-9). 18.00 *(978-0-7569-8131-0(X))* Perfection Learning Corp.

—Heavy Hitters. 2015. (Game Changers Ser.: 3). (ENG.). 240p. (J). (gr. 3-7). pap. 6.99 *(978-0-545-38181-9(9)*, Scholastic Paperbacks) Scholastic, Inc.

—The Only Game. 2015. (Home Team Ser.). (ENG., Illus.). 320p. (J). (gr. 3-7). 16.99 *(978-1-4814-0995-7(6)*, Simon & Schuster Bks. For Young Readers) Simon & Schuster Bks. For Young Readers.

—The Only Game. 2016. (Home Team Ser.). lib. bdg. 18.40 *(978-0-606-38252-6(6))* Turtleback Bks.

—Safe at Home. 2009. (Comeback Kids Ser.). (ENG.). 192p. (J). (gr. 3-7). 6.99 *(978-0-14-241460-6(3)*, Puffin Books) Penguin Young Readers Group.

—Safe at Home, 1 vol. 2012. (Comeback Kids Ser.). (ENG.). 192p. (J). (gr. 4-8). lib. bdg. 27.07 *(978-1-59961-177-8(5))* Spotlight.

—Travel Team & the Big Field. 2011. (ENG.). 544p. (J). (gr. 5-18). 8.99 *(978-0-14-241984-7(2)*, Puffin Books) Penguin Young Readers Group.

Lyga, Barry. Boy Toy. 2009. (ENG.). 416p. (YA). (gr. 9). pap. 9.99 *(978-0-547-07634-8(7))* Houghton Mifflin Harcourt Publishing Co.

Mackall, Dandi Daley. A Girl Named Dan. Graef, Renee, illus. 2008. (ENG.). 32p. (J). (gr. k-6). 16.95 *(978-1-58536-351-3(0))* Sleeping Bear Pr.

MacLachlan, Patricia. Edward's Eyes. 2009. (ENG.). 128p. (J). (gr. 3-7). pap. 7.99 *(978-1-4169-2744-0(1)*, Atheneum Bks. for Young Readers) Simon & Schuster Children's Publishing.

—Edward's Eyes. l.t. ed. 2008. (Literacy Bridge Middle Reader Ser.). 139p. (J). (gr. 3-7). 23.95 *(978-1-4104-0436-7(6))* Thorndike Pr.

Maddox, Jake. Batter Up!, 1 vol. Tiffany, Sean, illus. 2008. (Jake Maddox Sports Stories Ser.). (ENG.). 72p. (gr. 2-3). lib. bdg. 25.32 *(978-1-4342-0465-3(0))*; per. 5.95 *(978-1-4342-0515-5(0))* Stone Arch Bks.

—Behind the Plate, 1 vol. Tiffany, Sean, illus. 2012. (Jake Maddox Sports Stories Ser.). (ENG.). 72p. (gr. 2-3). pap. 5.95 *(978-1-4342-4205-1(6))*; lib. bdg. 25.32 *(978-1-4342-4010-1(X))* Stone Arch Bks.

—Caught Stealing. Aburtov, Jesus Aburto, illus. 2015. (Jake Maddox Sports Stories Ser.). (ENG.). 72p. (gr. 2-3). lib. bdg. 25.32 *(978-1-4965-0493-7(3))* Stone Arch Bks.

—Comeback Catcher. Muniz, Berenice, illus. 2017. (Jake Maddox Graphic Novels Ser.). (ENG.). 72p. (gr. 2-5). lib. bdg. 26.65 *(978-1-4965-3700-3(9))* Stone Arch Bks.

—El Lanzador Bajo Presión. Heck, Claudia M., tr. from ENG. Tiffany, Sean, illus. 2012. (Jake Maddox en Español Ser.). (SPA.). 72p. (gr. 2-3). 25.32 *(978-1-4342-3815-3(6))* Stone Arch Bks.

—Mr. Strike Out, 1 vol. Tiffany, Sean, illus. 2006. (Jake Maddox Sports Stories Ser.). (ENG.). 72p. (gr. 2-3). 25.32 *(978-1-59889-061-7(1))* Stone Arch Bks.

—Outfield Outcast, 1 vol. Ray, Mike, illus. 2014. (Jake Maddox JV Ser.). (ENG.). 96p. (gr. 3-4). 25.99 *(978-1-4342-9153-0(7))* Stone Arch Bks.

—Pitcher Pressure, 1 vol. Tiffany, Sean, illus. 2009. (Jake Maddox Sports Stories Ser.). (ENG.). 72p. (gr. 2-3). 25.32 *(978-1-4342-1596-3(2))* Stone Arch Bks.

Madison, Alan. Pecorino Plays Ball. Cantone, AnnaLaura, illus. 2006. (ENG.). 40p. (J). (gr. -1-3). 15.95 *(978-0-689-86522-0(8)*, Atheneum Bks. for Young Readers) Simon & Schuster Children's Publishing.

Mammano, Julie. Rhinos Who Play Baseball. Mammano, Julie, illus. 2006. (Illus.). 24p. (J). (gr. k-4). reprint ed. 14.00 *(978-0-7567-9995-3(3))* DIANE Publishing Co.

Markey, Kevin. Rainmaker. 2012. (Illus.). (J). 230p. lib. bdg. 16.89 *(978-0-06-115229-0(3))*; (ENG.). 240p. (gr. 3-7). 15.99 *(978-0-06-115228-3(5))* HarperCollins Pubs.

—Slumpbuster. Fitzgerald, Royce, illus. 2010. (Super Sluggers Ser.). (ENG.). 208p. (J). (gr. 3-7). pap. 6.99 *(978-0-06-115220-7(X))* HarperCollins Pubs.

—Wall Ball. 2011. (Super Sluggers Ser.). (ENG.). 208p. (J). (gr. 3-7). pap. 5.99 *(978-0-06-115223-8(4))* HarperCollins Pubs.

—Wing Ding. 2012. (Super Sluggers Ser.). (ENG.). 224p. (J). (gr. 3-7). pap. 5.99 *(978-0-06-115227-6(7))* HarperCollins Pubs.

Marsh, Carole. The Baseball Bully. 2006. 64p. (gr. 2-4). 14.95 *(978-0-635-06221-5(6))*; pap. 3.99 *(978-0-635-06215-4(1))* Gallopade International.

Marsh, Robert. Monster in the Outfield, 1 vol. Percival, Tom, illus. 2009. (Monster & Me Ser.). (ENG.). 40p. (gr. 1-3). lib. bdg. 23.99 *(978-1-4342-1590-1(3)*, Graphic Sparks) Stone Arch Bks.

Maruno, Jennifer. Cherry Blossom Baseball: A Cherry Blossom Book. 2015. (Cherry Blossom Book Ser.: 3). (ENG.). 184p. (J). pap. 11.99 *(978-1-4597-3166-0(2))* Dundurn CAN. Dist: Ingram Publisher Services.

—Cherry Blossom Winter. 2012. (Cherry Blossom Book Ser.: 2). (ENG.). 176p. (J). pap. 9.99 *(978-1-4597-0211-0(5))* Dundurn CAN. Dist: Ingram Publisher Services.

—Cherry Blossom Winter. 2013. 208p. pap. *(978-1-4596-6307-7(1))* ReadHowYouWant.com, Ltd.

Mason, Jane B. Battle Bugs of Outer Space, 1 vol. Baltazar, Art, illus. 2011. (DC Super-Pets Ser.). (ENG.). 56p. (gr. 2-2). pap. 4.95 *(978-1-4048-6848-9(8))*; lib. bdg. 23.99 *(978-1-4048-6482-5(2))* Picture Window Bks. (DC Super-Pets).

Masterson, Hoss. Owl Ball. Alves, Josh, illus. 2017. (Animal All-Stars Ser.). (ENG.). 56p. (gr. 1-3). lib. bdg. 25.32 *(978-1-4965-4309-7(2))* Stone Arch Bks.

Mathewson, Christy. Catcher Craig. Relyea, Charles M., illus. 2011. 360p. 51.95 *(978-1-258-06942-1(3))* Literary Licensing, LLC.

Mazeroski, Kelly. Maz, You're Up! Lauso, Judith, illus. 2010. 24p. (J). pap. 12.95 *(978-0-936340-18-0(5))* Historical Society of Western Pennsylvania.

Mazurak, Tena. Harley Hits a Homer. 2010. 24p. pap. 12.99 *(978-1-4490-9977-0(7))* AuthorHouse.

McCaffrey, Debra. Fly...Ball: Illustrated by 2nd Grade Students of Mrs. Young's 2KY at Mohansic Elementary School. 2007. pap. 20.00 *(978-0-8059-8781-2(9))* Dorrance Publishing Co., Inc.

McCormick, Wilfred. Bases Loaded: A Bronc Burnett Story. 2011. 190p. 42.95 *(978-1-258-06779-3(X))* Literary Licensing, LLC.

—Fielder's Choice: A Bronc Burnett Story. 2011. 188p. 42.95 *(978-1-258-07457-9(5))* Literary Licensing, LLC.

—The Three-Two Pitch: A Bronc Burnett Story. 2011. 192p. 42.95 *(978-1-258-10008-7(8))* Literary Licensing, LLC.

McFarlane, Brian. The Baseball Thief. 8th ed. 2007. (Mitchell Brothers Ser.: Bk. 8). (ENG.). 200p. (J). (gr. 3-7). pap. *(978-1-55168-276-1(1))* Magma.

—Daredevil over Niagara. 7th ed. 2007. (Mitchell Brothers Ser.). (ENG.). 200p. (J). (gr. 3-7). pap. *(978-1-55168-275-4(3))* Magma.

McKay, Sindy & Johnson, Meredith. We Both Read-Baseball Fever. 2003. (We Both Read Ser.). (Illus.). 44p. (J). (gr. 1-2). 7.99 *(978-1-891327-45-2(3))* Treasure Bay, Inc.

McKissack, Patricia C. The Home-Run King. 2009. (Scraps of Time Ser.). (ENG.). 112p. (J). (gr. 3-7). 6.99 *(978-0-14-241459-0(X)*, Puffin Books) Penguin Young Readers Group.

McKnight, Marty. Jim Nasium Is a Strikeout King. Jones, Chris, illus. 2016. (Jim Nasium Ser.). (ENG.). 88p. (gr. 2-3). lib. bdg. 25.32 *(978-1-4965-3025-7(X))* Stone Arch Bks.

McOmber, Rachel B., ed. McOmber Phonics Storybooks: Everyone Knows a Pitcher. rev. ed. (Illus.). (J). *(978-0-944991-79-4(3))* Swift Learning Resources.

Meltzer Kleinhenz, Sydnie. Bats in My Attic. Stromoski, Rick, illus. 2005. (Rookie Readers Ser.). (ENG.). 32p. (J). (gr. k-2). lib. bdg. 19.50 *(978-0-516-24865-3(0)*, Children's Pr.) Scholastic Library Publishing.

Mercado, Nancy, ed. Baseball Crazy: Ten Stories That Cover All the Bases. 2009. (ENG.). 192p. (J). (gr. 3-7). 6.99 *(978-0-14-241371-5(2)*, Puffin Books) Penguin Young Readers Group.

Meshon, Aaron. Take Me Out to the Yakyu. Meshon, Aaron, illus. 2013. (ENG., Illus.). 40p. (J). (gr. -1-3). 16.99 *(978-1-4424-4177-4(1)*, Atheneum Bks. for Young Readers) Simon & Schuster Children's Publishing.

Michelson, Richard. Across the Alley. Lewis, E. B., illus. 2006. (ENG.). 32p. (J). (gr. -1-3). 16.99 *(978-0-399-23970-0(7)*, G.P. Putnam's Sons Books for Young Readers) Penguin Young Readers Group.

Minton, Ross. Baseball, from the Street to the Diamond, 1 vol. 2010. 94p. pap. 19.95 *(978-1-4489-4918-2(1))* America Star Bks.

Mishica, Claire. Superstar Charlie. 2014. (Happy Day Ser.). (ENG.). 16p. (J). pap. 2.49 *(978-1-4143-9518-0(3))* Tyndale Hse. Pubs.

Mochizuki, Ken. Baseball Saved Us. 97th rev. ed. 2014. (ENG.). 30p. (J). (gr. k-12). 15.65 *(978-1-63245-249-8(9))* Lectorum Pubns., Inc.

—Baseball Saved Us. Lee, Dom, illus. (Picture Book Readalong Ser.). pap. 39.95 incl. audio compact disk *(978-1-59112-917-2(6))*; 2004. (J). (gr. -1-2). 25.95 incl. audio *(978-1-59112-456-6(5))* Live Oak Media.

—El Beisbol Nos Salvo. 2004. (SPA., Illus.). (J). (gr. k-4). spiral bd. *(978-0-616-03090-5(8))* Canadian National Institute for the Blind/Institut National Canadien pour les Aveugles.

Moldovan, Deborah, et al. A Glove of Their Own. Lambiase, Lauren, illus. 2015. (ENG.). 32p. pap. 9.95 *(978-1-63047-415-7(0))* Morgan James Publishing.

Montgomery, Lewis B. The Case of the Stinky Socks. Wummer, Amy, illus. 2009. (Milo & Jazz Mysteries Ser.). 96p. (J). (gr. 2-5). 22.60 *(978-1-57565-288-7(9))*; (ENG.). pap. 6.95 *(978-1-57565-285-6(4))* Kane Press, Inc.

Montgomery, Robert. Gary Carter's Iron Mask: Home Run! 2013. 160p. pap. 13.95 *(978-1-59687-948-5(3))* ibooks, Inc.

Morrison, Kevin. Stitches. Nixon, John, illus. 2003. 32p. (J). 12.95 *(978-1-929039-15-9(8))* Ambassador Bks., Inc.

Mullen, Paul Michael. The Day I Hit a Home Run at Great American Ball Park. 2007. 146p. (J). *(978-1-933197-30-2(7))* Orange Frazer Pr.

—Swinging for the Fences at Citizens Bank Park. 2012. 194p. pap. 12.95 *(978-0-9831950-7-8(2))* Day I Hit a Home Run Enterprise, The.

Munro, Ken. The Mysterious Baseball Scorecard: Sammy & Brian Mystery Series #17. 2005. (Sammy & Brian Mystery Ser.: 17). pap. 6.95 *(978-1-932864-31-1(8))* Masthof Pr.

Myers, Walter Dean. Down to the Last Out: The Journal of Biddy Owens, the Negro Leagues, Birmingham, Alabama, 1948. 2013. (ENG.). 144p. (J). (gr. 3-7). pap. 6.99 *(978-0-545-53050-7(4)*, Scholastic Paperbacks) Scholastic, Inc.

Nappi, Frank. The Legend of Mickey Tussler. 2012. (ENG.). 304p. (YA). (gr. 6-11). pap. 17.99 *(978-1-61608-658-9(0)*, 608658, Sky Pony Pr.) Skyhorse Publishing Co., Inc.

—Sophomore Campaign: A Mickey Tussler Novel. 2012. (ENG.). 280p. (YA). (gr. 6-11). pap. 12.95 *(978-1-61608-663-3(7)*, 608663, Sky Pony Pr.) Skyhorse Publishing Co., Inc.

—Welcome to the Show. 2016. (Mickey Tussler Ser.). (ENG.). 288p. (J). (gr. 6). pap. 9.99 *(978-1-63450-829-2(7)*, Sky Pony Pr.) Skyhorse Publishing Co., Inc.

Naylor, Phyllis Reynolds. Boys in Control. 2005. (Boys Against Girls Ser.: No. 9). 143p. (J). (gr. 4-7). 13.65 *(978-0-7569-5094-1(5))* Perfection Learning Corp.

—Boys in Control. 2005. (Boy/Girl Battle Ser.: No. 9). (ENG.). 160p. (J). (gr. 3-7). 6.99 *(978-0-440-41681-4(7)*, Yearling) Random Hse. Children's Bks.

New, William. Sam Swallow & the Riddleworld League, 1 vol. Yayo, illus. 2013. (ENG.). 144p. (J). (gr. 3-5). pap. 12.95 *(978-1-896580-98-2(X))* Tradewind Bks. CAN. Dist: Orca Bk. Pubs. USA.

Newman, C. Edward. The Little Leaguer Wore #7. 2008. 76p. pap. 19.95 *(978-1-60563-347-3(X))* America Star Bks.

Newman, Jeff. The Boys. Newman, Jeff, illus. 2010. (ENG., Illus.). 40p. (J). (gr. -1-2). 17.99 *(978-1-4169-5012-7(5)*, Simon & Schuster Bks. For Young Readers) Simon & Schuster Bks. For Young Readers.

Norman, Rick. Fielder's Choice. 2006. (ENG.). 196p. (J). (gr. 6-17). pap. 12.95 *(978-0-87483-204-4(7))* August Hse. Pubs., Inc.

Northrop, Michael. Plunked. 2014. (ENG.). 256p. (J). (gr. 3-7). pap. 7.99 *(978-0-545-29715-8(X)*, Scholastic Paperbacks) Scholastic, Inc.

Norworth, Jack. Take Me Out to the Ball Game. Hirao, Amiko, illus. 2016. (ENG.). 24p. (J). (— 1). bds. 7.95 *(978-1-62354-071-5(2))* Charlesbridge Publishing, Inc.

—Take Me Out to the Ball Game. Huntington, Amy, illus. 2011. (Favorite Children's Songs Ser.). (ENG.). 16p. (J). (gr. -1-2). lib. bdg. 25.64 *(978-1-60954-294-8(0)*, 200098) Child's World, Inc., The.

—Take Me Out to the Ball Game. Meyers, Mark, illus. 2011. 16p. (J). (gr. -1-k). bds. 10.99 *(978-0-8249-1852-1(5)*, Ideal Pubns.) Worthy Publishing.

Nussbaum, Ben. Grand Old Flag. Pamintuan, Macky, illus. 2006. (American Favorites Ser.). (ENG.). 32p. (J). (gr. -1-3). 9.85 *(978-1-59249-593-1(1))*; 14.95 *(978-1-59249-572-6(9))* Soundprints.

—Take Me Out to the Ballgame. Studio Mouse Staff, ed. rev. ed. 2007. (ENG.). 24p. 4.99 *(978-1-59069-603-3(4))* Studio Mouse LLC.

O'Hara, Susan. Christie Plays Softball. Barrett, Rebecca, illus. 2013. 48p. pap. 15.97 *(978-1-62516-519-0(6)*, Strategic Bk. Publishing) Strategic Book Publishing & Rights Agency (SBPRA).

Okimoto, Jean Davies. Dear Ichiro. Keith, Doug, illus. 2006. 29p. (J). (gr. 4-8). reprint ed. 17.00 *(978-1-4223-5803-0(8))* DIANE Publishing Co.

Olker, Constance. The Punctuation Pals Go to the Baseball Park. Guzman, Minerva, illus. 2005. (Punctuation Pals Ser.). 44p. (J). per. 18.95 *(978-1-933449-15-9(2))* Nightengale Pr.

—The Punctuation Pals Go to the Baseball Park. l.t. ed. 2005. (Illus.). 22p. (J). per. 17.95 *(978-0-9761289-8-4(5))* Nightengale Pr.

O'Neal, Shaquille. Little Shaq. Taylor, Theodore, illus. 2016. (ENG.). 80p. (J). pap. 6.99 *(978-1-61963-722-1(7),* 9781619637221, Bloomsbury USA Childrens) Bloomsbury Publishing USA.

Osborne, Mary Pope. A Big Day for Baseball. Murdocca, Sal, illus. 2017. (Magic Tree House Ser.: 29). (ENG.). (J). (gr. 1-4). 80p. 13.99 ***(978-1-5247-1308-9(2))***; 96p. lib. bdg. 16.99 ***(978-1-5247-1309-6(0))*** Random Hse. Children's Bks. (Random Hse. Bks. for Young Readers).

Osterweil, Adam & Smith, Craig. The Baseball Card Kid. Smith, Craig, illus. 2009. (ENG., Illus.). 199p. (J). (gr. 3-7). 17.95 *(978-1-59078-526-3(6),* Front Street) Boyds Mills Pr.

Palmer, Iva-Marie. Gabby Garcia's Ultimate Playbook. 2017. (Gabby Garcia's Ultimate Playbook Ser.: 1). 304p. (J). (gr. 3-7). 12.99 *(978-0-06-239180-3(1),* Tegen, Katherine Bks) HarperCollins Pubs.

Palmer, Kristine. Eigenoids Episode 2: Momentum Sphere Coaster. 2013. 134p. pap. 19.95 *(978-1-63000-928-1(8))* America Star Bks.

Papp, Robert, illus. The Spy in the Bleachers. 2010. (Boxcar Children Mysteries Ser.: 122). (ENG.). 128p. (J). (gr. 1-5). 14.99 *(978-0-8075-7606-9(9))*;No. 122. pap. 6.99 *(978-0-8075-7607-6(7))* Whitman, Albert & Co.

Park, Barbara. Skinnybones. 2016. (ENG.). 160p. (J). (gr. 3-7). 12.99 *(978-0-394-94988-8(9),* Yearling) Random Hse. Children's Bks.

Park, Linda Sue. Keeping Score. 2010. (ENG.). 224p. (J). (gr. 2-5). pap. 7.99 *(978-0-547-24897-4(0))* Houghton Mifflin Harcourt Publishing Co.

Parkinson, Ethelyn. Good Old Archibald. Stevens, Mary, illus. 2014. 145p. (J). pap. 14.95 *(978-1-932350-42-5(X))* Bethlehem Bks.

Pearson, Susan. Slugger, 0 vols. Slonim, David, illus. 2013. (ENG.). 32p. (J). (gr. -1-2). 14.99 *(978-1-4778-1641-7(0),* 9781477816417, Amazon Children's Publishing) Amazon Publishing.

Peirce, Lincoln. Big Nate: Revenge of the Cream Puffs. 2016. (Big Nate Ser.: 15). (ENG.). 184p. (J). (gr. 3-7). pap. 9.99 *(978-1-4494-6228-4(6))* Andrews McMeel Publishing.

Petrillo, Genevieve & Lyon, Lea. Keep Your Ear on the Ball, 1 vol. Lyon, Lea07/, illus. 2009. (ENG.). 32p. (J). (gr. 2-6). pap. 7.95 *(978-0-88448-324-3(X),* 884324) Tilbury Hse. Pubs.

Petrucci, Lou. Heart of the Hide. 2008. 320p. 22.95 *(978-1-4401-0102-1(7),* iUniverse Star) iUniverse, Inc.

Pollock, Hal. Monster at the Bat. 2009. (ENG.). 32p. (J). (gr. 4-7). 15.95 *(978-1-59687-884-6(3))* IBks., Inc.

Poole, Catherine Cheyenne. Batboy's Crazy Day. Murphy, Fredrick, illus. 2008. 24p. pap. 8.95 *(978-1-935105-18-3(3))* Avid Readers Publishing Group.

Posada, Jorge. Play Ball! Colón, Raúl, illus. 2010. (ENG.). 32p. (J). (gr. 1-5). 6.99 *(978-1-4169-9825-9(X),* Simon & Schuster/Paula Wiseman Bks.) Simon & Schuster/Paula Wiseman Bks.

—Sí, Puedes. Colón, Raúl, illus. 2010.Tr. of Play Ball! (SPA.). 32p. (J). (gr. 1-5). 6.99 *(978-1-4169-9826-6(8),* Simon & Schuster/Paula Wiseman Bks.) Simon & Schuster/Paula Wiseman Bks.

Potok, Chaim. The Chosen: And Related Readings. 2006. (McDougal Littell Literature Connections Ser.). (ENG.). 416p. (gr. 6-8). 18.50 *(978-0-395-88145-3(5),* 2-70858) Great Source Education Group, Inc.

Potter, Noel Gyro. Dibble Can't Dribble, 1 vol. Cannon, Joseph, illus. 2008. (Adventures of Marshall & Art Ser.). (ENG.). 32p. (gr. -1-4). 28.50 net. *(978-1-60270-197-7(0),* Looking Glass Library) ABDO Publishing Co.

Preller, James. Six Innings. 2010. (ENG.). 176p. (YA). (gr. 4-9). pap. 7.99 *(978-0-312-60240-6(5),* 9780312602406) Square Fish.

Purciello, Gerard. The Year They Won: A Tale of the Boston Red Sox. 2005. 112p. (J). (gr. 5-9). per. *(978-0-9746481-5-6(9))* Brown Barn Bks.

Raczka, Bob. Joy in Mudville. Dibley, Glin, illus. 2014. (ENG.). 32p. (J). (gr. -1-3). 17.95 *(978-0-7613-6015-5(8),* Carolrhoda Bks.) Lerner Publishing Group.

Rae, Kristin. What You Always Wanted: An If Only Novel. 2016. (If Only... Ser.). (ENG.). 320p. (YA). pap. 9.99 *(978-1-61963-345-2(0),* 9781619633452, Bloomsbury USA Childrens) Bloomsbury Publishing USA.

Raven, Margot Theis. Let Them Play. Ellison, Chris, illus. 2005. (ENG.). 32p. (J). (gr. 1-4). 17.99 *(978-1-58536-260-8(3),* 202075) Sleeping Bear Pr.

Remy, Jerry. Hello, Wally! Boston Red Sox. Moore, Danny, illus. 2006. 24p. (J). lib. bdg. 17.95 *(978-1-932888-80-5(2))* Mascot Bks., Inc.

—Wally the Green Monster & His Journey Through Red Sox Nation. Moore, Danny, illus. 2007. 24p. (J). 14.95 *(978-1-932888-89-8(6))* Mascot Bks., Inc.

Rey, H. A. Curious George at the Baseball Game (Jorge el Curioso en el Partido de Beisbol) 2011. (Curious George Ser.). (SPA & ENG., Illus.). 24p. (J). (gr. -1-3). pap. 4.99 *(978-0-547-51500-7(6))* Houghton Mifflin Harcourt Publishing Co.

—Curious George Home Run (Jorge el Curioso el Jonrón) 2012. (Curious George Ser.). (ENG & SPA., Illus.). 24p. (J). (gr. -1-3). pap. 3.99 *(978-0-547-69114-5(9))* Houghton Mifflin Harcourt Publishing Co.

—Home Run. 2012. (Curious George Ser.). (ENG., Illus.). 24p. (J). (gr. -1-3). pap. 3.99 *(978-0-547-69118-3(1))* Houghton Mifflin Harcourt Publishing Co.

—Jorge el Curioso en el Partido de Beisbol. 2011. (Curious George Ser.).Tr. of Curious George at the Baseball Game. (SPA & ENG., Illus.). 24p. (J). (gr. -1-3). 12.99 *(978-0-547-54746-6(3))* Houghton Mifflin Harcourt Publishing Co.

Rey, H. A. & Rey, Margret. Home Run. 2012. (Curious George TV Tie-In Early Reader Ser.). lib. bdg. 13.55 *(978-0-606-23985-1(5),* Turtleback) Turtleback Bks.

Rickis, Andrew. The Magic Oak: (A Baseball Story) A Novel for Young Adults. 2003. 114p. pap. 19.95 *(978-1-4137-0665-9(7))* America Star Bks.

Riley, Zach. Down for the Count. Ricci, Andrés, illus. 2012. (Zach Riley Ser.). 80p. (J). (gr. 3-6). lib. bdg. 27.07 *(978-1-61783-533-9(1))* Magic Wagon.

Ripken, Cal. Cal Ripken, Jr. 's All-Stars Squeeze Play. 2015. (Cal Ripken, Jr. 's All Stars Ser.). (ENG.). 224p. (J). (gr. 3-7). pap. 6.99 *(978-1-4231-9465-1(9))* Hyperion Bks. for Children.

Ripken, Cal, Jr. Hothead. aut. ed. 2011. 16.99 *(978-1-4231-5168-5(2))* Disney Pr.

—Hothead. 2011. (Playaway Children Ser.). (J). (gr. 4-6). 44.99 *(978-1-61707-430-1(6))* Random Hse., Inc.

Ripken, Cal. Wild Pitch. Cowherd, Kevin, illus. 2014. (Cal Ripken, Jr. 's All Stars Ser.). (ENG.). 224p. (J). (gr. 3-7). pap. 6.99 *(978-1-4231-4005-4(2))* Hyperion Bks. for Children.

Ripken, Cal, Jr. & Cowherd, Kevin. Hothead. 2012. (ENG.). 160p. (J). (gr. 3-7). pap. 6.99 *(978-1-4231-4003-0(6))* Hyperion Pr.

—Super Slugger. 2013. (ENG.). 200p. (YA). (gr. 3-7). pap. 6.99 *(978-1-4231-4004-7(4))* Hyperion Pr.

Ripken, Cal, et al. Cal Ripken, Jr. 's All-Stars the Closer. 2016. (Cal Ripken, Jr. 's All Stars Ser.). (ENG.). 208p. (J). (gr. 3-7). 16.99 *(978-1-4231-7868-2(8))* Hyperion Bks. for Children.

Ripken Jr., Cal. Cal Ripken, Jr. 's All-Stars Out at Home. 2015. (Cal Ripken, Jr. 's All Stars Ser.). (ENG.). 208p. (J). (gr. 3-7). 16.99 *(978-1-4231-7867-5(X))* Hyperion Bks. for Children.

—Cal Ripken, Jr. 's All Stars the Closer. 2017. (Cal Ripken, Jr. 's All Stars Ser.). (ENG.). 208p. (J). (gr. 3-7). pap. 6.99 *(978-1-4847-2788-1(6))* Hyperion Bks. for Children.

Ritter, John H. The Boy Who Saved Baseball. 2005. (ENG.). 224p. (J). (gr. 3-7). pap. 7.99 *(978-0-14-240286-3(9),* Puffin Books) Penguin Young Readers Group.

—Desperado Who Stole Baseball. 2010. (ENG.). 288p. (J). (gr. 5-18). 7.99 *(978-0-14-241507-8(3),* Puffin Books) Penguin Young Readers Group.

—Fenway Fever. 2013. (ENG.). 256p. (J). (gr. 5). pap. 7.99 *(978-0-14-242491-9(9),* Puffin Books) Penguin Young Readers Group.

Roberts, Kelly. Baseball Boy. 2007. 17.95 *(978-0-9792147-0-7(X))* Beau Francis Pr.

Roberts, Ken. Thumb on a Diamond, 1 vol. Franson, Leanne, illus. 2007. (ENG.). 128p. (J). (gr. 2-5). pap. 7.95 *(978-0-88899-705-0(1))* Groundwood Bks. CAN. Dist: Publishers Group West (PGW).

—Thumb on a Diamond. 2013. 112p. pap. *(978-1-4596-6492-0(2))* ReadHowYouWant.com, Ltd.

Robins, Eleanor. The Right Kind of Win. 2004. (Carter High Chronicles (High-Interest Readers) Ser.). (Illus.). 48p. (J). per. 3.95 *(978-1-56254-691-5(0),* SP6910) Saddleback Educational Publishing, Inc.

—Right Kind of Win, 1 vol. unabr. ed. 2011. (Carter High Chronicles Ser.). (ENG.). 50p. (YA). (gr. 9-12). pap. 7.95 *(978-1-61651-311-5(X))* Saddleback Educational Publishing, Inc.

Robinson, Sharon. The Hero Two Doors Down: A Story of Friendship Between a Boy & a Baseball Legend. (ENG.). 208p. (J). (gr. 3-7). 2017. pap. 6.99 ***(978-0-545-80452-3(3),*** Scholastic Paperbacks) 2016. 16.99 *(978-0-545-80451-6(5),* Scholastic Pr.) Scholastic, Inc.

Robinson, Sharon. Testing the Ice: A True Story about Jackie Robinson. Nelson, Kadir, illus. 2009. (ENG.). 40p. (J). (gr. 2-5). 18.99 *(978-0-545-05251-1(3),* Scholastic Pr.) Scholastic, Inc.

Rocky the Mudhen: We're Talkin' Baseball. 2004. (J). lib. bdg. 14.95 *(978-0-9748922-0-7(3))* Rabbit Ears Pr. & Co.

Rodriguez, Alex. Out of the Ballpark. Morrison, Frank, illus. 2012. (ENG.). 32p. (J). (gr. -1-3). pap. 6.99 *(978-0-06-115196-5(3))* HarperCollins Pubs.

Rotman, Stuart. Welcome to Trashtown. 2007. 192p. 34.95 *(978-1-4303-2662-5(X))*; pap. 14.95 *(978-1-4303-1179-9(7))* Lulu Pr., Inc.

Roy, Ron. The Unwilling Umpire. Gurney, John Steven, illus. 2004. (to Z Mysteries Ser.: 21). (ENG.). 96p. (J). (gr. 1-4). 4.99 *(978-0-375-81370-2(5),* Random Hse. Bks. for Young Readers) Random Hse. Children's Bks.

—The Unwilling Umpire. Gurney, John Steven, illus. 2004. (to Z Mysteries Ser.: 21). (gr. k-3). lib. bdg. 14.75 *(978-0-613-82496-5(2),* Turtleback) Turtleback Bks.

Russell, Nancy L. M., et al. So Long, Jackie Robinson. rev. ed. 2007. (ENG.). 224p. (J). (gr. 4-7). 7.95 *(978-1-55263-863-7(4))* Leaf Storm Pr.

Rutherford, Kris. Batting Ninth. 2012. (Champion Sports Story Ser.). 104p. (J). (gr. 3-18). pap. 10.95 *(978-1-4644-0001-8(6))*; lib. bdg. 27.94 *(978-0-7660-3886-8(6))* Enslow Pubs., Inc.

Rylant, Cynthia. Mr. Putter & Tabby Drop the Ball. Howard, Arthur, illus. 2014. (Mr. Putter & Tabby Ser.). (ENG.). 44p. (J). (gr. 1-4). pap. 5.99 *(978-0-544-34115-9(5),* HMH Books For Young Readers) Houghton Mifflin Harcourt Publishing Co.

—Mr. Putter & Tabby Drop the Ball. 2014. (Mr. Putter & Tabby Ser.). lib. bdg. 16.00 *(978-0-606-35985-6(0))* Turtleback Bks.

Santos, Dennis. Earl the Pearl. 2007. 28p. per. 10.95 *(978-1-59526-833-4(2),* Llumina Kids) Aeon Publishing Inc.

Satera, Diane. The Angel of Wild Springs: Jaiden & the Sacred Stones. 2010. 168p. 23.99 *(978-1-4520-3460-7(5))*; pap. 11.99 *(978-1-4520-3461-4(3))* AuthorHouse.

Scaletta, Kurtis. Batter Up! Beavers, Ethen, illus. 2013. (Topps Ser.). (ENG.). 112p. (J). (gr. 1-4). pap. 5.95 *(978-1-4197-0727-8(2),* Amulet Bks.) Abrams, Inc.

—Jinxed! Wight, Eric, illus. 2012. (Topps Ser.). (ENG.). 112p. (J). (gr. 1-4). pap. 5.95 *(978-1-4197-0261-7(0),* Amulet Bks.) Abrams, Inc.

—Mudville. 2010. (ENG.). 272p. (J). (gr. 3-7). 8.99 *(978-0-375-84472-0(4),* Yearling) Random Hse. Children's Bks.

—Rooting for Rafael Rosales. 2017. (ENG.). 288p. (J). (gr. 3-7). 16.99 ***(978-0-8075-6742-5(6))*** Whitman, Albert & Co.

—Steal That Base! Wight, Eric, illus. 2012. (Topps Ser.). (ENG.). 112p. (J). (gr. 1-4). pap. 5.95 *(978-1-4197-0262-4(9),* Amulet Bks.) Abrams, Inc.

—A Topps League Story: Book Three: Zip It! Wight, Eric, illus. 2012. (Topps Ser.). (ENG.). 112p. (J). (gr. 1-4). pap. 5.95 *(978-1-4197-0437-6(0),* Amulet Bks.) Abrams, Inc.

—You're Out! Beavers, Ethen, illus. 2013. (Topps Ser.). (ENG.). 112p. (J). (gr. 1-4). pap. 5.95 *(978-1-4197-0659-2(4),* Amulet Bks.) Abrams, Inc.

—The 823rd Hit Bk. 4, Bk. 4. Wight, Eric, illus. 2012. (Topps Ser.). (ENG.). 112p. (J). (gr. 1-4). pap. 5.95 *(978-1-4197-0445-1(1),* Amulet Bks.) Abrams, Inc.

Scattergood, Augusta. The Way to Stay in Destiny. 2015. (ENG.). 192p. (J). (gr. 3-7). 16.99 *(978-0-545-53824-4(6),* Scholastic Pr.) Scholastic, Inc.

Schnell, David. The Night Before Baseball at the Park by the Bay. Pamintuan, Macky, illus. 2013. (ENG.). 32p. 0.00 *(978-0-9891043-0-2(3))* Prospect Palo Alto Publishing.

Schraff, Anne. The Brothers. 2017. (Red Rhino Ser.). lib. bdg. 18.40 ***(978-0-606-40323-8(X))*** Turtleback Bks.

Schrenk, Kathleen. A Dog Steals Home, 1 vol. 2017. (ENG.). 128p. (J). (gr. 3-7). pap. 8.95 *(978-1-4556-2228-3(1))* Pelican Publishing Co., Inc.

Schulz, Charles & Scott, Vicki. It's Tokyo, Charlie Brown! Braddock, Paige, illus. 2012. (Peanuts Ser.). (ENG.). 96p. (J). (gr. 2). pap. 9.99 *(978-1-60886-270-2(4))* Boom! Studios.

Schulz, Charles M. Batter up, Charlie Brown! 2014. (ENG., Illus.). 64p. 9.99 *(978-1-60699-725-3(4),* 699725) Fantagraphics Bks.

Schwartz, Ellen. Stealing Home. 2006. (ENG.). 224p. (J). (gr. 4-7). pap. 9.95 *(978-0-88776-765-4(6),* Tundra Bks.) Tundra Bks. CAN. Dist: Penguin Random Hse. LLC.

Sewell, Kele. Beewee & Meager to the Rescue! the Underbed Entertainment Network. 2008. 28p. pap. 12.50 *(978-1-60693-326-8(4),* Eloquent Bks.) Strategic Book Publishing & Rights Agency (SBPRA).

Shane, Sam. Rocky the Mudhen: Baseball & Humble Pie. 2006. (Illus.). (J). lib. bdg. 15.95 *(978-0-9748922-1-4(1))* Rabbit Ears Pr. & Co.

Shang, Wendy Wan-Long. The Way Home Looks Now. 2015. (ENG.). 272p. (J). (gr. 3-7). 16.99 *(978-0-545-60956-2(9),* Scholastic Pr.) Scholastic, Inc.

Shanks, Melanie. The Squints. 2007. 116p. per. 10.95 *(978-0-595-44849-4(6))* iUniverse, Inc.

Shannon, David. How Georgie Radbourn Saved Baseball. Shannon, David, illus. 2012. (ENG., Illus.). 32p. (J). (gr. -1-3). 17.99 *(978-0-545-38178-9(9),* Blue Sky Pr., The) Scholastic, Inc.

Shannon, Terry Miller. Family Baseball Star. 2016. (Spring Forward Ser.). (J). (gr. 2). *(978-1-4900-9412-0(1))* Benchmark Education Co.

Sharp, Paul. Pablo el Lanzador. Sharp, Paul, illus. 2011. (Rookie Ready to Learn Español Ser.). (SPA., Illus.). 40p. (J). pap. 5.95 *(978-0-531-26781-3(4))*; lib. bdg. 23.00 *(978-0-531-26113-2(1))* Scholastic Library Publishing. (Children's Pr.).

Sharp, Paul, illus. Paul the Pitcher. 2011. (Rookie Ready to Learn — All about Me! Ser.). 40p. (J). (gr. -1-k). lib. bdg. 25.00 *(978-0-531-26426-3(2))*; (ENG.). pap. 5.95 *(978-0-531-26651-9(6))* Scholastic Library Publishing. (Children's Pr.).

Shaw, Mary. Brady Brady & the Ballpark Bark. Temple, Chuck, illus. 2007. (J). *(978-1-897169-10-0(8))* Brady Brady, Inc.

Sheehan, P. J. Gabby's Big Game. 2006. (Neighborhood Readers Ser.). (ENG.). 12p. (gr. -1-3). pap. 5.90 *(978-1-4042-6758-9(1),* Rosen Classroom) Rosen Publishing Group, Inc., The.

Sherman, Harold M. Strike Him Out. 2005. pap. 26.95 *(978-1-4191-1422-9(0))* Kessinger Publishing, LLC.

Sherman, Harold Morrow & Townsend, Ernest N. Batter Up: A Story of American Legion Junior Baseball. 2011. 328p. 50.95 *(978-1-258-07856-0(2))* Literary Licensing, LLC.

Shultz, Charles M. & Bailer, Darice. Make a Trade, Charlie Brown!, 1 vol. Lo Bianco, Peter, illus. 2011. (Peanuts Ready-To-Reads Ser.). (ENG.). 32p. (gr. -1-2). lib. bdg. 24.21 *(978-1-59961-806-7(0))* Spotlight.

Shultz, Charles M. & Katschke, Judy. It's a Home Run, Charlie Brown!, 1 vol. Lo Bianco, Nick, illus. 2011. (Peanuts Ready-To-Reads Ser.). (ENG.). 32p. (gr. -1-2). lib. bdg. 24.21 *(978-1-59961-801-2(X))* Spotlight.

Silva, Kenny. The Card. 2007. 84p. per. 19.95 *(978-1-60441-320-5(4))* America Star Bks.

Silver Dolphin en Español Editors. Magical Magnets: Chicken Little. 2006. (SPA., Illus.). 8p. (J). bds. 12.95 *(978-970-718-318-6(7))* Readerlink Distribution Services, LLC.

Simkins, Aron. Dream Big: The Journey of the Jazz Bear. 2012. 15.99 *(978-1-59955-945-2(5),* Bonneville Bks.) Cedar Fort, Inc./CFI Distribution.

Simon, Carly. Take Me Out to the Ball Game. Hirao, Amiko, illus. 2011. (ENG.). 26p. (J). (gr. k-12). 17.95 *(978-1-936140-26-8(8))* Charlesbridge Publishing, Inc.

Skiles, Janet. Just Ducky! Stickers. 2017. (Dover Little Activity Books Stickers Ser.). (ENG., Illus.). 8p. (J). (gr. k-3). pap. 1.99 *(978-0-486-81455-1(6))* Dover Pubns., Inc.

Slote, Alfred. Hang Tough, Paul Mather. 2013. 146p. pap. 11.99 *(978-0-9886988-3-3(8))* Arborville Bks.

—Jake. 2013. 160p. pap. 11.99 *(978-0-9886988-2-6(X))* Arborville Bks.

Smith, Charles. Out at First. 2010. 111p. pap. 11.95 *(978-0-557-60419-7(2))* Lulu Pr., Inc.

Smith, Jennifer E. The Comeback Season. 2008. (ENG.). 256p. (YA). (gr. 8). 15.99 *(978-1-4169-3847-7(8),* Simon & Schuster Bks. For Young Readers) Simon & Schuster Bks. For Young Readers.

Smith, Michelle. Play On. 2015. (Lewis Creek Ser.: 1). (ENG.). 296p. (YA). (gr. 10-12). pap. 9.95 *(978-1-939392-59-6(4),* Spencer Hill Contemporary) Spencer Hill Pr.

Spence, Tom. Tough Day at the Plate. 2004. 39p. (J). (gr. -1-7). per. 5.95 *(978-1-59353-241-3(5))* Mountain Valley Publishing, LLC.

Spreng, Robert. Goin' Great in the Lone Star State. 2010. 39p. pap. 7.95 *(978-0-557-58803-9(0))* Lulu Pr., Inc.

Standish, Burt L. Frank Merriwell's Baseball Victories. Rudman, Jack, ed. 2003. (Frank Merriwell Ser.). 29.95 *(978-0-8373-9348-3(5))*; pap. 9.95 *(978-0-8373-9048-2(6))* Merriwell, Frank Inc.

Stanek, Robert, pseud. The Bugville Critters Play Their First Big Game. 2008. (ENG., Illus.). (J). 32p. per. 9.95 *(978-1-57545-149-7(2))*; 52p. per. 16.95 *(978-1-57545-127-5(1))* RP Media.

Staub, Rusty. Hello, Mr. Met. Moore, Danny, illus. 2006. 24p. (J). lib. bdg. 17.95 *(978-1-932888-82-9(9))* Mascot Bks., Inc.

Steiner, Matt. Mission Possible. 2011. 108p. (gr. 4-6). 20.95 *(978-1-4620-0028-9(2))*; pap. 10.95 *(978-1-4620-0027-2(4))* iUniverse, Inc.

Stewart, Chuck. Angels at Rickwood. 2009. (J). pap. 10.00 *(978-1-61584-842-3(8))* Independent Pub.

Stinson, Aimee. The Championship Game, 1 vol. 2009. 52p. pap. 16.95 *(978-1-60813-645-2(0))* PublishAmerica, Inc.

Strike Two (Baseball) 64p. (YA). (gr. 6-12). pap. 10.95 *(978-0-8224-6481-5(0))* Globe Fearon Educational Publishing.

Sullivan, Derek E. Biggie. 2015. (ENG.). 272p. (YA). (gr. 8-12). 16.99 *(978-0-8075-0727-8(X))* Whitman, Albert & Co.

Swango, Lynn. No Baseball in Fairview. 2003. (ENG., Illus.). 104p. (J). per. 12.95 *(978-1-878044-95-2(8))* Mayhaven Publishing, Inc.

Tavares, Matt. Mudball. Tavares, Matt, illus. 2011. (ENG., Illus.). 32p. (J). (gr. 1-4). pap. 6.99 *(978-0-7636-4136-8(7))* Candlewick Pr.

—Oliver's Game. Tavares, Matt, illus. (Tavares Baseball Bks.). (ENG., Illus.). 32p. (J). (gr. 1-4). 2009. pap. 6.99 *(978-0-7636-4137-5(5))* 2004. 15.99 *(978-0-7636-1852-0(7))* Candlewick Pr.

—Zachary's Ball. Tavares, Matt, illus. anniv. ed. 2012. (Tavares Baseball Bks.). (ENG., Illus.). 32p. (J). (gr. 1-4). 15.99 *(978-0-7636-5033-9(1))*; pap. 6.99 *(978-0-7636-5977-6(0))* Candlewick Pr.

Taylor, Jeannie St. John & St. John Taylor, Jeannie. Out at Home: A Novel. 2004. 144p. (J). pap. 7.99 *(978-0-8254-3724-3(5))* Kregel Pubns.

Tellier, Derek. Anderson's Heat. 2016. (What's Your Dream? Ser.). (ENG.). 96p. (gr. 3-4). lib. bdg. 25.32 *(978-1-4965-3441-5(7))* Capstone Press of Coughlan Cos.

Terrell, Brandon. 8-Bit Baseball, 1 vol. Ferrara, Eduardo, illus. 2014. (Sports Illustrated Kids Graphic Novels Ser.). (ENG.). 72p. (gr. 2-5). 26.65 *(978-1-4342-4164-1(5))* Stone Arch Bks.

Testa, Maria. Becoming Joe Dimaggio. Hunt, Scott, illus. 2005. (ENG.). 64p. (J). (gr. 5-9). reprint ed. pap. 6.99 *(978-0-7636-2444-6(6))* Candlewick Pr.

Thaler, Mike. The Little League Team from the Black Lagoon. Lee, Jared D., illus. 2009. (Black Lagoon Adventures Ser.: 10). (ENG.). 64p. (J). (gr. 2-5). 4.99 *(978-0-439-87162-4(X),* Scholastic Paperbacks) Scholastic, Inc.

—The Little League Team from the Black Lagoon, 1 vol. Lee, Jared, illus. 2011. (Black Lagoon Adventures Ser.: No. 1). (ENG.). 64p. (J). (gr. 3-6). 24.21 *(978-1-59961-813-5(3))* Spotlight.

—Little League Team from the Black Lagoon. 2009. (Black Lagoon Adventures Ser.: 10). lib. bdg. 14.75 *(978-0-606-05316-7(6),* Turtleback) Turtleback Bks.

Tiffany, Sean & Maddox, Jake. Mr. Strike Out, 1 vol. Tiffany, Sean, illus. 2006. (Jake Maddox Sports Stories Ser.). (ENG., Illus.). 72p. (gr. 2-3). per. 5.95 *(978-1-59889-239-0(8))* Stone Arch Bks.

Time, Nicholas O. Going, Going, Gone. 2016. (In Due Time Ser.: 1). (ENG., Illus.). 160p. (J). (gr. 3-7). pap. 6.99 *(978-1-4814-6729-2(8),* Simon Spotlight) Simon Spotlight.

Tocher, Timothy. Bill Pennant, Babe Ruth, & Me. 2009. (ENG.). 184p. (J). (gr. 3-7). 17.95 *(978-0-8126-2755-8(5))* Cricket Bks.

—Chief Sunrise, John McGraw, & Me. 2004. (ENG.). 168p. (J). (gr. 4-8). 16.95 *(978-0-8126-2711-4(3))* Cricket Bks.

Tooke, Wes. King of the Mound: My Summer with Satchel Paige. (ENG.). 160p. (J). (gr. 3-7). 2013. pap. 7.99 *(978-1-4424-3347-2(7))* 2012. (Illus.). 17.99 *(978-1-4424-3346-5(9))* Simon & Schuster Bks. For Young Readers. (Simon & Schuster Bks. For Young Readers).

—Lucky: Maris, Mantle, & My Best Summer Ever. (ENG.). 192p. (J). (gr. 3-7). 2011. pap. 6.99 *(978-1-4169-8664-5(2))* 2010. 15.99 *(978-1-4169-8663-8(4))* Simon & Schuster Bks. For Young Readers. (Simon & Schuster Bks. For Young Readers).

Travel Team. 2012. (Travel Team Ser.). (ENG.). 120p. (gr. 6-12). lib. bdg. 167.58 *(978-0-7613-8897-5(4),* Darby Creek) Lerner Publishing Group.

Travis, Allison J. Bundy. One More Wake Up: With Faith All Things Are Possible-Even Surviving the Loss of a Loved One. 2012. 34p. 24.95 *(978-1-4626-5862-6(8))* America Star Bks.

Tunis, John Roberts. Keystone Kids. 2006. (Odyssey/Harcourt Young Classic Ser.). 239p. (J). (gr. 3). 13.65 *(978-0-7569-7102-1(0))* Perfection Learning Corp.

—The Kid from Tomkinsville. 2006. (Odyssey/Harcourt Young Classic Ser.). 278p. (J). (gr. 3). 13.60 *(978-0-7569-6556-3(X))* Perfection Learning Corp.

—Rookie of the Year. 2006. (Odyssey/Harcourt Young Classic Ser.). 220p. (J). (gr. 3). 13.60 *(978-0-7569-7215-8(9))* Perfection Learning Corp.

Tunis, John Roberts & Tunis, John R. The Kid from Tomkinsville. 2006. (ENG., Illus.). 300p. (J). (gr. 2-5). pap. 15.95 *(978-0-15-205641-4(6))* Houghton Mifflin Harcourt Publishing Co.

—Rookie of the Year. 2006. (ENG., Illus.). 240p. (J). (gr. 2-5). pap. 15.95 *(978-0-15-205648-3(3))* Houghton Mifflin Harcourt Publishing Co.

Uhlberg, Myron. Dad, Jackie, & Me, 1 vol. Bootman, Colin, illus. (ENG.). 32p. (J). 2010. pap. 8.95 *(978-1-56145-531-7(8))* 2005. 16.95 *(978-1-56145-329-0(3))* Peachtree Pubs.

Van Dusen, Chris. Randy Riley's Really Big Hit. Van Dusen, Chris, illus. (ENG., Illus.). (J). (gr. -1-3). 2016. 7.99 *(978-0-7636-8774-8(X))* 2012. 32p. 15.99 *(978-0-7636-4946-3(5))* Candlewick Pr.

Van Riper, Guernsey, Jr. Babe Ruth. Fleishman, Seymour, illus. 2015. (History's All-Stars Ser.). (ENG.). 208p. (J). (gr. 3-7). pap. 6.99 *(978-1-4814-2507-0(2),* Aladdin) Simon & Schuster Children's Publishing.

Vernick, Audrey. Screaming at the Ump. 2014. (ENG.). 272p. (J). (gr. 5-7). 16.99 *(978-0-544-25208-0(X),* Clarion Bks.) Houghton Mifflin Harcourt Trade & Reference Pubs.

Volponi, Paul & Wells, Rosemary. Game Seven. 2015. (ENG.). 256p. (YA). (gr. 7). bds. 17.99 *(978-0-670-78518-6(0),* Viking Books for Young Readers) Penguin Young Readers Group.

Waldman, Neil. Say-Hey & the Babe: Two Mostly True Baseball Stories. Waldman, Neil, illus. 2006. (ENG., Illus.). 40p. (J). (gr. 4-7). 16.95 *(978-0-8234-1857-2(X))* Holiday Hse., Inc.

Wallace, Rich. Curveball, No. 9. 2008. (Winning Season Ser.). (ENG.). 128p. (J). (gr. 3-7). 5.99 *(978-0-14-241092-9(6),* Puffin Books) Penguin Young Readers Group.

—No Relief, 1 vol. Heitz, Tim, illus. 2016. (Game Face Ser.). (ENG.). 112p. (J). (gr. 3-7). 27.07 *(978-1-62402-134-3(4))* Magic Wagon.

—Southpaw. 2006. 105p. (J). lib. bdg. 15.38 *(978-1-4242-2166-0(8))* Fitzgerald Bks.

—Southpaw. 6th ed. 2007. (Winning Season Ser.). (ENG.). 128p. (J). (gr. 3-7). 5.99 *(978-0-14-240785-1(2)*, Puffin Books) Penguin Young Readers Group.

Weston Woods Staff, creator. Players in Pigtails. 2004. 29.95 *(978-0-7882-0518-7(8))* Weston Woods Studios, Inc.

Wheeler, Lisa. Dino-Baseball. Gott, Barry, illus. 2010. (ENG.). 32p. (J). (gr. k-3). lib. bdg. 16.95 *(978-0-7613-4429-2(2)*, Carolrhoda Bks.) Lerner Publishing Group.

White, Ellen Emerson. A Season of Daring Greatly. 2017. 432p. (YA). (gr. 8). 17.99 *(978-0-06-246321-0(7)*, Greenwillow Bks.) HarperCollins Pubs.

Wight, Eric. Frankie Pickle & the Pine Run 3000. Wight, Eric, illus. 2010. (Frankie Pickle Ser.). (ENG., Illus.). 96p. (J). (gr. 2-5). 9.99 *(978-1-4169-6485-8(1)*, Simon & Schuster Bks. For Young Readers) Simon & Schuster Bks. For Young Readers.

Wiles, Deborah. The Aurora County All-Stars. (ENG., Illus.). 256p. (J). 2009. (gr. 2-5). pap. 7.99 *(978-0-15-206626-0(8))* 2007. (gr. 5-7). 16.00 *(978-0-15-206068-8(5))* Houghton Mifflin Harcourt Publishing Co.

Williams, Alan. Little Teammate. 2017. (ENG.). 38p. (J). (gr. -1-4). 18.95 ***(978-1-68350-201-2(9))*** Morgan James Publishing.

Williamson, A. M. The Castle of the Shadows. 2007. (ENG.). 164p. pap. 19.99 *(978-1-4346-3410-8(8))* Creative Media Partners, LLC.

Willis, Janet, illus. A Dad's Delight. 2006. *(978-0-9785077-0-1(3))*; pap. *(978-0-9785077-1-8(1))* Khesed Foundation.

Wittenstein, Barry & Ladd, London. Waiting for Pumpsie. 2017. (ENG., Illus.). 32p. (J). (gr. k-3). lib. bdg. 16.99 *(978-1-58089-545-3(X))* Charlesbridge Publishing, Inc.

Yasuda, Anita. First Base Blues. 1 vol. Harpster, Steve, illus. 2012. (My First Graphic Novel Ser.). (ENG.). 32p. (gr. k-2). pap. 6.25 *(978-1-4342-3863-4(6))*; lib. bdg. 24.65 *(978-1-4342-3279-3(4))* Stone Arch Bks. (My First Graphic Novel).

—There's No Crying in Baseball. 1 vol. Santillan, Jorge H., illus. 2011. (Sports Illustrated Kids Victory School Superstars Ser.). (ENG.). 56p. (gr. 1-3). pap. 5.95 *(978-1-4342-3077-5(5))*; lib. bdg. 26.65 *(978-1-4342-2226-8(8))* Stone Arch Bks.

Yavin, T. S. All-Star Season. 2006. 160p. (J). (gr. 3-7). lib. bdg. 15.95 *(978-1-58013-211-4(1)*, Kar-Ben Publishing) Lerner Publishing Group.

BASEBALL—HISTORY

ABDO Publishing Company Staff. Major League Baseball's Best Ever. 2014. (Major League Baseball's Best Ever Ser.: 6). (ENG.). 64p. (gr. 3-6). lib. bdg. 196.74 *(978-1-62403-112-0(9)*, SportsZone) ABDO Publishing Co.

Aretha, David. Top 10 Moments in Baseball. 2016. (Sports Greats Ser.). (ENG., Illus.). 48p. (J). (gr. 5-6). 27.93 *(978-0-7660-7404-0(8))* Enslow Pubs., Inc.

Baseball: The Great American Game, 30 bks. (Illus.). (J). 478.50 *(978-0-88682-929-2(1)*, Creative Education) Creative Co., The.

Bildner, Phil. The Unforgettable Season: Joe Dimaggio, Ted Williams & the Record-Setting Summer of 1941. Schindler, S. D., illus. 2011. (ENG.). 32p. (J). (gr. 2-4). 16.99 *(978-0-399-25501-4(X)*, G.P. Putnam's Sons Books for Young Readers) Penguin Young Readers Group.

Borth, Teddy. Baseball: Great Moments, Records, & Facts. 1 vol. 2014. (Great Sports Ser.). (ENG., Illus.). 24p. (J). (gr. 2-4). lib. bdg. 28.50 *(978-1-62970-687-0(6))* ABDO Publishing Co.

Bryant, Howard & Mack, Jeff. Legends: The Best Players, Games, & Teams in Baseball. 2015. (ENG., Illus.). 240p. (J). (gr. 3-7). bds. 16.99 *(978-0-399-16903-8(2)*, Philomel Bks.) Penguin Young Readers Group.

Chandler, Matt. Wacky Baseball Trivia: Fun Facts for Every Fan. 2016. (Wacky Sports Trivia Ser.). (ENG., Illus.). 32p. (gr. 3-4). lib. bdg. 27.99 *(978-1-5157-1995-3(2))* Capstone Press of Coughlan Cos.

Cho, Alan. World Series. (J). 2012. *(978-1-61913-063-0(7))* 2012. pap. *(978-1-61913-625-0(2))* 2007. (Illus.). 32p. (gr. 4-6). lib. bdg. 26.00 *(978-1-59036-699-8(9))* 2007. (Illus.). 32p. (gr. 4-7). per. 9.95 *(978-1-59036-700-1(6))* Weigl Pubs., Inc.

Cockcroft, James D. Latinos in Beisbol. 2004. (Illus.). 207p. (J). (gr. 4-9). reprint ed. pap. 10.00 *(978-0-7567-7347-2(4))* DIANE Publishing Co.

Coleman, Janet Wyman & Warren, Elizabeth V. Baseball for Everyone: Stories from the Great Game. 2006. (Illus.). 51p. (J). (gr. 4-8). reprint ed. 17.00 *(978-0-7567-9972-4(4))* DIANE Publishing Co.

Coombs, Charles. Young Infield Rookie. Geer, Charles H., illus. 2011. 190p. 42.95 *(978-1-258-10529-7(2))* Literary Licensing, LLC.

De Marco, Tony. Jackie Robinson. 2009. (Journey to Freedom Ser.). (ENG., Illus.). 32p. (J). (gr. 4-7). 29.93 *(978-1-60253-125-3(0)*, 200391) Child's World, Inc., The.

Dicicco, Joe. Planet Baseball, Dominican Republic Edition, Volume 1: Making the Play, Vol. 1. Jimenez, Ruben D., tr. Dicicco, Joe, illus. l.t. ed. 2009.Tr. of Beisbol de Planeta. (ENG & SPA., Illus.). 14p. (J). (gr. -1-3). 7.95 *(978-1-929528-01-1(9))* Punta Gorda Pr.

—Planet Baseball, Puerto Rico: Volume 1, Making the Play, Vol. 1. Jimenez, Ruben D., tr. Dicicco, Joe, illus. l.t. ed. 2009.Tr. of Beisbol de Planeta. (ENG & SPA., Illus.). 14p. (J). (gr. -1-3). 7.95 *(978-1-929528-02-8(7))* Punta Gorda Pr.

Doeden, Matt. All about Baseball. 2015. (All about Sports Ser.). (ENG.). 32p. (gr. 1-2). lib. bdg. 27.32 *(978-1-4914-1993-9(8)*, Aplus Bks.) Capstone Press of Coughlan Cos.

Dzidrums, Christine & Rendon, Leah. Matt Kemp: True Blue Baseball Star. 2013. 72p. pap. 9.99 *(978-1-938438-25-7(6))* Creative Media Publishing.

Elish, Dan. The Black Sox Scandal of 1919. 2008. (Cornerstones of Freedom Ser.). (ENG.). 48p. (J). pap. 5.95 *(978-0-531-20828-1(1)*, Children's Pr.) Scholastic Library Publishing.

Frisch, Aaron. Los Angeles Dodgers. 2009. (World Series Champions Ser.). (Illus.). 23p. (J). (gr. 2-3). 24.25 *(978-1-58341-689-1(7)*, Creative Education) Creative Co., The.

—New York Knicks. 2012. (NBA Champions Ser.). (ENG., Illus.). 24p. (J). (gr. 1-3). pap. 9.99 *(978-0-89812-714-0(9)*, Creative Paperbacks) Creative Co., The.

Frystak, Timothy D. Jackie Robinson: With Profiles of Satchel Paige & & Branch Rickey. 2006. (Biographical Connections Ser.). (Illus.). 112p. (J). *(978-0-7166-1828-7(1))* World Bk., Inc.

Grabowski, John F. The Atlanta Braves. 2003. (Great Sports Teams Ser.). (ENG., Illus.). 112p. (J). 30.85 *(978-1-59018-304-5(5)*, Lucent Bks.) Cengage Gale.

Hawkins, Jeff. World Series, 1 vol. 2013. (Sports' Great Championships Ser.). (ENG.). 64p. (J). (gr. 4-6). lib. bdg. 32.79 *(978-1-61783-676-3(1)*, SportsZone) ABDO Publishing Co.

Herman, Gail. What Is the World Series? Kenyon, David Grayson, illus. 2015. 108p. (J). ***(978-1-4844-5712-2(9)***, Grosset & Dunlap) Penguin Publishing Group.

Hillstrom & Hillstrom, Laurie C. Jackie Robinson & the Integration of Baseball. 2013. 248p. lib. bdg. 55.00 *(978-0-7808-1327-4(8))* Omnigraphics, Inc.

Hinnant, Jamal. Top 10 Bloopers in Baseball. 2016. (Sports Greats Ser.). (ENG., Illus.). 48p. (J). (gr. 5-6). pap. 11.70 *(978-0-7660-7390-6(4))* Enslow Pubs., Inc.

Hoblin, Paul. Great Pitchers of the Negro Leagues, 1 vol. 2012. (Negro Baseball Leagues Ser.). (ENG.). 64p. (J). (gr. 5-8). lib. bdg. 32.79 *(978-1-61783-508-7(0)*, SportsZone) ABDO Publishing Co.

Inside Major League Baseball, 5 vols., Set. 2009. (Inside Major League Baseball Ser.). (Illus.). 48p. (YA). (gr. 5-8). lib. bdg. 159.00 *(978-1-4358-5214-3(1)*, Rosen Reference) Rosen Publishing Group, Inc., The.

Kelly, David A. Babe Ruth & the Baseball Curse. Jessell, Tim, illus. 2009. (Totally True Adventures Ser.). (ENG.). 112p. (J). (gr. 2-5). 4.99 *(978-0-375-85603-7(X)*, Random Hse. Bks. for Young Readers) Random Hse. Children's Bks.

Meltzer, Brad. I Am Jackie Robinson. Eliopoulos, Christopher, illus. 2015. (Ordinary People Change the World Ser.). (ENG.). 40p. (J). (gr. k-3). 14.99 *(978-0-8037-4086-0(7)*, Dial Bks) Penguin Young Readers Group.

Moss, Marissa. Barbed Wire Baseball. Shimizu, Yuko, illus. 2013. (ENG.). 48p. (J). (gr. 1-4). 19.95 *(978-1-4197-0521-2(0)*, Abrams Bks. for Young Readers) Abrams, Inc.

—Mighty Jackie: The Strike-Out Queen. Payne, C. F., tr. Payne, C. F., illus. 2004. (ENG.). 32p. (J). (gr. k-3). 18.99 *(978-0-689-86329-5(2)*, Simon & Schuster/Paula Wiseman Bks.) Simon & Schuster/Paula Wiseman Bks.

Murphy, Frank. Babe Ruth Saves Baseball! Walz, Richard, illus. 2005. (Step into Reading Ser.: Vol. 3). (ENG.). 48p. (J). (gr. k-3). pap. 3.99 *(978-0-375-83048-8(0)*, Random Hse. Bks. for Young Readers) Random Hse. Children's Bks.

—Babe Ruth Saves Baseball. Walz, Richard, illus. 2005. (Step into Reading Ser.). 46p. (gr. 1-3). 14.00 *(978-0-7569-5161-0(5))* Perfection Learning Corp.

Nelson, Kadir. We Are the Ship: The Story of Negro League Baseball. 2009. 88p. (J). 19.00 *(978-1-4379-6953-5(4))* DIANE Publishing Co.

—We Are the Ship: The Story of Negro League Baseball. Nelson, Kadir, illus. 2008. (ENG., Illus.). 96p. (J). (gr. 3-7). 19.99 *(978-0-7868-0832-8(2)*, Jump at the Sun) Hyperion Bks. for Children.

Patrick, Jean L. S. La Nina Que Poncho A Babe Ruth. Reeves, Jeni, illus. 2007. (Yo Solo - Historia (on My Own - History) Ser.). 48p. (J). (gr. 4-7). per. 6.95 *(978-0-8225-7788-1(7))* Lerner Publishing Group.

—La Niña Que Ponchó a Babe Ruth. Translations.com Staff, tr. from ENG. Reeves, Jeni, illus. 2007. (Yo Solo - Historia (on My Own - History) Ser.).Tr. of Girl Who Struck Out Babe Ruth. (SPA.). 48p. (gr. 2-4). lib. bdg. 25.26 *(978-0-8225-7785-0(2))* Lerner Publishing Group.

—La Nina Que Poncho a Babe Ruth; the Girl Who Struck Out Babe Ruth. 2008. pap. 40.95 *(978-0-8225-9725-4(X))* Lerner Publishing Group.

Pellowski, Michael J. The Chicago Black Sox Baseball Scandal. 2003. (Headline Court Cases Ser.). (Illus.). 128p. (J). (gr. 6-12). lib. bdg. 26.60 *(978-0-7660-2044-3(4))* Enslow Pubs., Inc.

Peters, Gregory N. The Negro Leagues, 1 vol. 2014. (Sports & Recreation Ser.). (ENG.). 48p. (gr. 4-12). 31.99 *(978-1-4765-8015-9(4))* Capstone Press of Coughlan Cos.

Pina, Andrew. Baseball's Greatest Records, 1 vol. 2015. (ENG., Illus.). 32p. (J). lib. bdg. 26.25 *(978-1-4994-0230-8(9)*, PowerKids Pr.) Rosen Publishing Group, Inc., The.

Rausch, David. Major League Baseball. 2014. (Major League Sports Ser.). (ENG., Illus.). 24p. (J). (gr. 3-7). 25.95 *(978-1-62617-133-6(5)*, Epic Bks.) Bellwether Media.

Rice, Dona. ¡Al Bate! Historia Del Béisbol. 2017. (TIME for Kids en Español - Level 3 Ser.). (SPA.). 32p. (gr. 3-3). lib. bdg. 31.99 ***(978-1-5157-5186-1(4))*** Capstone Press of Coughlan Cos.

Ritter, Lawrence S. Leagues Apart: The Men & Times of the Negro Baseball Leagues. Merkin, Richard, illus. 2004. 35p. (J). (gr. k-4). reprint ed. pap. 12.00 *(978-0-7567-7714-2(3))* DIANE Publishing Co.

Savage, Jeff. Baseball Super Stats. 2017. (Pro Sports Stats Ser.). (ENG., Illus.). 32p. (J). (gr. 3-6). 27.99 ***(978-1-5124-3407-1(8)***, Lerner Pubns.) Lerner Publishing Group.

Shaughnessy, Dan. The Legend of the Curse of the Bambino. Payne, C. F., illus. 2005. (ENG.). 32p. (J). (gr. k-3). 16.95 *(978-0-689-87235-8(6)*, Simon & Schuster/Paula Wiseman Bks.) Simon & Schuster/Paula Wiseman Bks.

Smith, Charles R., Jr. Stars in the Shadows: The Negro League All-Star Game of 1934. Morrison, Frank, illus. 2012. (ENG.). 112p. (J). (gr. 3-7). 14.99 *(978-0-689-86638-8(0)*, Atheneum Bks. for Young Readers) Simon & Schuster Children's Publishing.

Smolka, Bo. The Negro Leagues' Integration Era, 1 vol. 2012. (Negro Baseball Leagues Ser.). (ENG.). 64p. (J). (gr. 5-8). lib. bdg. 32.79 *(978-1-61783-509-4(9)*, SportsZone) ABDO Publishing Co.

—The Story of the Negro Leagues, 1 vol. 2012. (Negro Baseball Leagues Ser.). (ENG.). 64p. (J). (gr. 5-8). lib. bdg. 32.79 *(978-1-61783-510-0(2)*, SportsZone) ABDO Publishing Co.

Stewart, Mark. The Atlanta Hawks. 2009. (Team Spirit Ser.). 48p. (J). (gr. 3-6). lib. bdg. 26.60 *(978-1-59953-281-3(6))* Norwood Hse. Pr.

—Baseball. 2009. (Ultimate 10 Ser.). 48p. (J). (gr. 5-9). lib. bdg. 31.00 *(978-0-8368-9156-0(2))* Stevens, Gareth Publishing LLLP.

—The Georgetown Hoyas. 2009. (Team Spirit Ser.). (ENG.). 48p. (J). (gr. 3-6). lib. bdg. 26.60 *(978-1-59953-364-3(2))* Norwood Hse. Pr.

Stewart, Mark & Kennedy, Mike. Latino Baseball's Finest Fielders/Las Mas Destacados Guantes del Beisbol Latino. Kalmanovitz, Manuel, tr. from ENG. 2003. (En Fuego Ser.). (ENG & SPA., Illus.). 48p. (J). (gr. 5-18). pap. 9.95 *(978-0-7613-1749-4(X))* Lerner Publishing Group.

Suen, Anastasia. La Historia del Beisbol. Spanish Educational Publishers Staff, tr. 2004. (Historia de Los Deportes (Sports History) Ser.). (SPA.). 24p. (J). (gr. 3-6). lib. bdg. 22.60 *(978-0-8239-6873-2(1)*, Editorial Buenas Letras) Rosen Publishing Group, Inc., The.

—La historia del béisbol (the Story of Baseball) 2009. (Historia de los deportes (Sports History) Ser.). (SPA.). 24p. (gr. 2-2). 42.50 *(978-1-61513-310-9(0)*, Editorial Buenas Letras) Rosen Publishing Group, Inc., The.

—The Story of Baseball. 2009. (Sports History Ser.). 24p. (gr. 2-2). 42.50 *(978-1-60853-136-3(8)*, PowerKids Pr.) Rosen Publishing Group, Inc., The.

Sullivan, George. Baseball's Boneheads, Bad Boys & Just Plain Crazy. 2003. (Single Titles Ser.). (Illus.). 64p. (gr. 5-8). lib. bdg. 23.90 *(978-0-7613-2321-1(X)*, Millbrook Pr.) Lerner Publishing Group.

—Baseball's Boneheads, Bad Boys, & Just Plain Crazy Guys. Green, Anne Canevari, illus. 2003. 64p. (J). (gr. 5-8). pap. 8.95 *(978-0-7613-1928-3(X)*, Millbrook Pr.) Lerner Publishing Group.

Tometich, Annabelle. Superstars of the St. Louis Cardinals. 2014. (Pro Sports Superstars Ser.). 24p. (J). 27.10 *(978-1-60753-597-3(1))* Amicus Publishing.

Ward, Geoffrey C., et al. Who Invented the Game? Baseball: the American Epic. 2004. (Illus.). 80p. (J). (gr. 6-10). reprint ed. 15.00 *(978-0-7567-7571-1(X))* DIANE Publishing Co.

Weatherford, Carole Boston. A Negro League Scrapbook. 2005. (ENG., Illus.). 48p. (J). (gr. 2-7). 19.95 *(978-1-59078-091-6(4))* Boyds Mills Pr.

Windwalker, Stephen. The 100 Greatest Baseball Games of All Time: Box Scores & Game Stories of Baseball's Unforgettable Moments. 2003. 160p. per. 21.95 *(978-0-9715778-1-7(1)*, Harvard Perspectives in American Sports) Harvard Perspectives Pr.

Winters, Jaime. Center Field: The History of Baseball. 2015. (ENG., Illus.). 32p. (J). *(978-0-7787-1476-7(4))* Crabtree Publishing Co.

Wong, Stephen. Baseball Treasures. Einstein, Susan, illus. 2007. 58p. (J). (gr. 4-7). lib. bdg. 17.89 *(978-0-06-114473-8(8))* HarperCollins Pubs.

Yomtov, Nel. The Bambino: The Story of Babe Ruth's Legendary 1927 Season. Foley, Tim, illus. 2011. (American Graphic Ser.). (ENG.). 32p. (gr. 3-4). pap. 47.70 *(978-1-4296-6433-2(9)*, Graphic Library) Capstone Press of Coughlan Cos.

BASEBALL—POETRY

Florian, Douglas. Poem Runs: Baseball Poems & Paintings. Jones, Noah, illus. 2012. (ENG.). 32p. (J). (gr. 1-4). 16.99 *(978-0-547-68838-1(5))* Houghton Mifflin Harcourt Publishing Co.

Shane, Bill. Hey Batter Batter: A Collection of Baseball Poems for Kids. 2003. (Illus.). 88p. (J). (gr. k-9). pap. 7.95 *(978-1-931643-20-7(2))* Seven Locks Pr.

Shore, Diane ZuHone & Alexander, Jessica. This Is the Game. Smith, Owen, illus. 2011. (ENG.). 32p. (J). (gr. -1-3). 16.99 *(978-0-06-055522-1(X))* HarperCollins Pubs.

Thayer, Ernest L. Casey at the Bat. Morse, Joe, illus. 2010. (Visions in Poetry Ser.). (ENG.). 48p. (J). (gr. 5-9). pap. 9.95 *(978-1-55453-458-6(5))* Kids Can Pr., Ltd. CAN. Dist: Hachette Bk. Group.

—Casey at the Bat: A Ballad of the Republic Sung in the Year 1888. Payne, C. F., illus. 2003. (ENG.). 40p. (J). (gr. -1-3). 17.99 *(978-0-689-85494-1(3)*, Simon & Schuster Bks. For Young Readers) Simon & Schuster Bks. For Young Readers.

Thayer, Ernest Lawrence. Casey at the Bat: A Ballad of the Republic, Sung in the Year 1888. 2009. 30p. 17.00 *(978-1-4379-6644-2(6))* DIANE Publishing Co.

BASEBALL CLUBS

see Baseball Teams

BASEBALL TEAMS

Dobrow, Larry & Jeter, Derek. Derek Jeter's Ultimate Baseball Guide 2015. Jones, Damien, illus. 2015. (Jeter Publishing Ser.). (ENG.). 96p. (J). (gr. 3-5). pap. 9.99 *(978-1-4814-2318-2(5)*, Little Simon) Little Simon.

Doeden, Matt. The Negro Leagues. 2017. (Spectacular Sports Ser.). (ENG., Illus.). 64p. (J). (gr. 5-12). 33.32 *(978-1-5124-2753-0(5)*, Millbrook Pr.) Lerner Publishing Group.

Eck, Ed. Baseball in the American League West Division. 2009. (Inside Major League Baseball Ser.). 48p. (gr. 5-5). 53.00 *(978-1-61513-531-8(6)*, Rosen Reference) Rosen Publishing Group, Inc., The.

—Baseball in the National League Central Division. 2009. (Inside Major League Baseball Ser.). 48p. (gr. 5-8). (ENG., Illus.). (J). pap. 11.75 *(978-1-4358-5419-2(5))*; 53.00 *(978-1-61513-534-9(0)*, Rosen Reference); (Illus.). (J). lib. bdg. 29.25 *(978-1-4358-5045-3(9))* Rosen Publishing Group, Inc., The.

—Baseball in the National League West. 2009. (Inside Major League Baseball Ser.). (Illus.). 48p. (J). (gr. 5-8). (ENG.). pap. 11.75 *(978-1-4358-5418-5(7))*; lib. bdg. 29.25 *(978-1-4358-5044-6(0))* Rosen Publishing Group, Inc., The.

—Baseball in the National League West Division. 2009. (Inside Major League Baseball Ser.). 48p. (gr. 5-5). 53.00 *(978-1-61513-540-0(5)*, Rosen Reference) Rosen Publishing Group, Inc., The.

Eck, Edward. Baseball in the American League West Division. 2009. (Inside Major League Baseball Ser.). (Illus.). 48p. (J). (gr. 5-8). (ENG.). pap. 11.75 *(978-1-4358-5415-4(2))*; lib. bdg. 29.25 *(978-1-4358-5041-5(6))* Rosen Publishing Group, Inc., The.

Epstein, Brad. Miami Marlins 101. 2013. (My First Team-Board-Book Ser.). (ENG., Illus.). 24p. (J). bds. *(978-1-60730-284-1(5)*, 101 Bk.) Michaelson Entertainment.

Finoli, David. Classic Bucs: The 50 Greatest Games in Pittsburgh Pirates History. 2013. (Classic Sports Ser.). (ENG., Illus.). 272p. pap. 18.00 *(978-1-60635-160-4(5)*, 9781606351604, Black Squirrel Bks.) Kent State Univ. Pr.

Frisch, Aaron. Atlanta Hawks. 2011. (J). 25.65 *(978-1-60818-130-8(8)*, Creative Education) Creative Co., The.

—Boston Celtics. 2011. (J). 25.65 *(978-1-60818-131-5(6)*, Creative Education) Creative Co., The.

—Chicago Bulls. 2011. (J). 25.65 *(978-1-60818-132-2(4)*, Creative Education) Creative Co., The.

—Detroit Pistons. 2011. (J). 25.65 *(978-1-60818-133-9(2)*, Creative Education) Creative Co., The.

—Golden State Warriors. 2011. (J). 25.65 *(978-1-60818-134-6(0)*, Creative Education) Creative Co., The.

—Houston Rockets. 2011. (J). 25.65 *(978-1-60818-135-3(9)*, Creative Education) Creative Co., The.

—Los Angeles Lakers. 2011. (J). 25.65 *(978-1-60818-136-0(7)*, Creative Education) Creative Co., The.

Giglio, James N. Stan Musial: Baseball Hero. 2015. (ENG., Illus.). 48p. (J). pap. 24.00 *(978-1-61248-151-7(5))* Truman State Univ. Pr.

Gilbert, Sara. The Story of the Florida Marlins. 2012. (Baseball: the Great American Game Ser.). (ENG.). 48p. (J). (gr. 4-7). pap. 9.99 *(978-0-89812-639-6(8)*, Creative Paperbacks) Creative Co., The.

—The Story of the Los Angeles Angels of Anaheim. 2012. (Baseball: the Great American Game Ser.). (ENG.). 48p. (J). (gr. 4-7). pap. 9.99 *(978-0-89812-642-6(8)*, Creative Paperbacks) Creative Co., The.

—The Story of the Milwaukee Brewers. 2012. (Baseball: the Great American Game Ser.). (ENG.). 48p. (J). (gr. 4-7). pap. 9.99 *(978-0-89812-644-0(4)*, Creative Paperbacks) Creative Co., The.

—The Story of the Texas Rangers. 2012. (Baseball: the Great American Game Ser.). (ENG.). 48p. (J). (gr. 4-7). pap. 12.00 *(978-0-89812-656-3(8)*, Creative Paperbacks) Creative Co., The.

Goodman, Michael E. The Story of the New York Mets. 2012. (Baseball: the Great American Game Ser.). (ENG.). 48p. (J). (gr. 4-7). pap. 9.99 *(978-0-89812-646-4(0)*, Creative Paperbacks) Creative Co., The.

Kelley, K. C. St. Louis Cardinals. 2016. (J). ***(978-1-4896-5950-7(1)***, AV2 by Weigl) Weigl Pubs., Inc.

LeBoutillier, Nate. The Story of the Seattle Mariners. 2012. (Baseball: the Great American Game Ser.). (ENG.). 48p. (J). (gr. 4-7). pap. 9.99 *(978-0-89812-654-9(1)*, Creative Paperbacks) Creative Co., The.

—The Ultimate Guide to Pro Baseball Teams. 2010. (Ultimate Pro Team Guides (Sports Illustrated for Kids) Ser.). (ENG.). 72p. (gr. 3-4). pap. 53.70 *(978-1-4296-5733-4(2))* Capstone Press of Coughlan Cos.

Monning, Alex. Texas Rangers. 2016. (J). ***(978-1-4896-5953-8(6)***, AV2 by Weigl) Weigl Pubs., Inc.

Monteverde, Matt. Baseball in the American League East Division. 2009. (Inside Major League Baseball Ser.). 48p. (gr. 5-5). 53.00 *(978-1-61513-528-8(6)*, Rosen Reference) Rosen Publishing Group, Inc., The.

Monteverde, Matthew. Baseball in the American League East Division. 2009. (Inside Major League Baseball Ser.). (Illus.). 48p. (J). (gr. 5-8). (ENG.). pap. 11.75 *(978-1-4358-5414-7(4))*; lib. bdg. 29.25 *(978-1-4358-5040-8(8))* Rosen Publishing Group, Inc., The.

Porterfield, Jason. Baseball in the American League Central Division. 2009. (Inside Major League Baseball Ser.). 48p. (gr. 5-5). 53.00 *(978-1-61513-525-7(1)*, Rosen Reference) Rosen Publishing Group, Inc., The.

—Baseball in the National League East Division. 2009. (Inside Major League Baseball Ser.). 48p. (gr. 5-8). (ENG., Illus.). (J). pap. 11.75 *(978-1-4358-5417-8(9))*; 53.00 *(978-1-61513-539-4(1)*, Rosen Reference); (Illus.). (J). lib. bdg. 29.25 *(978-1-4358-5043-9(2))* Rosen Publishing Group, Inc., The.

Ross, Dalton. The Top Teams Ever: Football, Baseball, Basketball & Hockey Winners. 2005. (Sports Illustrated for Kids Books Ser.). (Illus.). 176p. (YA). (gr. 7-12). lib. bdg. 33.25 *(978-0-8239-3693-9(7))* Rosen Publishing Group, Inc., The.

Silverman, Drew. Atlanta Hawks, 1 vol. 2011. (Inside the NBA Ser.). (ENG., Illus.). 48p. (YA). (gr. 3-6). lib. bdg. 32.79 *(978-1-61783-149-2(2))* ABDO Publishing Co.

Smolka, Bo. Miami Marlins, 1 vol. 2014. (Inside MLB Ser.). (ENG., Illus.). 48p. (J). (gr. 3-6). lib. bdg. 32.79 *(978-1-62403-470-1(5)*, SportsZone) ABDO Publishing Co.

Vernick, Audrey. Brothers at Bat: The True Story of an Amazing All-Brother Baseball Team. Salerno, Steven, illus. 2012. (ENG.). 40p. (J). (gr. -1-3). 17.99 *(978-0-547-38557-0(9)*, Clarion Bks.) Houghton Mifflin Harcourt Trade & Reference Pubs.

Wyner, Zach. Atlanta Hawks. 2014. (On the Hardwood Ser.). (gr. 3-8). pap. 8.95 *(978-1-61570-897-0(9))* Scobre Pr. Corp.

BASHFULNESS

Berry, Joy. Let's Talk about Being Shy. Smith, Maggie, illus. 2010. (Let's Talk About Ser.). (ENG.). 32p. (J). (gr. -1-k). pap. 4.99 *(978-1-60577-220-2(8))* Berry, Joy Enterprises.

Brozovich, Richard & Chase, Linda. Say Goodbye to Being Shy: A Workbook to Help Kids Overcome Shyness. 2008. (Instant Help Ser.). (ENG., Illus.). 120p. (J). (gr. k-5). pap. 20.95 *(978-1-57224-609-6(X)*, Instant Help Books) New Harbinger Pubns.

Carducci, Bernardo J. & Fields, Teesue H. Shyness Workbook for Teens. 2006. (ENG.). 156p. (YA). pap. 16.95 *(978-0-87822-583-5(8)*, 5286) Research Pr.

Orr, Tamra B. Shyness. 2016. (21st Century Basic Skills Library: Feelings Ser.). (ENG., Illus.). 24p. (J). (gr. k-3). 24.21 *(978-1-63471-047-3(9)*, 208268) Cherry Lake Publishing.

Thomas, Isabel. Dealing with Feeling... Shy. 2013. (Dealing with Feeling... Ser.). (ENG.). 24p. (gr. 1-2). pap. 6.79 *(978-1-4329-7118-2(2))*; lib. bdg. 23.32 *(978-1-4329-7109-0(3))* Heinemann-Raintree. (Heinemann Read & Learn).

BASHFULNESS—FICTION

Aboff, Marcie. The Giant Jelly Bean Jar. Billin-Frye, Paige, illus. 2013. (Puffin Young Readers, L3 Ser.). (ENG.). 32p. (J). (gr. -1-3). pap. 3.99 *(978-0-448-46624-8(4),* Puffin) Penguin Publishing Group.

Aboff, Marcie, et al. The Giant Jelly Bean Jar. Billin-Frye, Paige, illus. 2004. (Puffin Easy-to-Read Ser.). 32p. (gr. k-3). 14.00 *(978-0-7569-2824-7(9))* Perfection Learning Corp.

Alsenas, Linas. The Princess of 8th Street. 2012. (ENG., Illus.). 32p. (J). (gr. k-2). 16.95 *(978-0-8109-8972-6(7),* Abrams Bks. for Young Readers) Abrams, Inc.

Asquith, Ros & Good, Andi. Boo! 2004. (ENG., Illus.). 32p. (J). (gr. -1-k). pap. 11.00 *(978-0-00-711267-8(X))* HarperCollins Pubs. Ltd. GBR. Dist: Independent Pubs. Group.

Bechtold, Lisze. Buster the Very Shy Dog. 2015. (Green Light Readers Level 3 Ser.). (ENG., Illus.). 32p. (J). (gr. 1-4). pap. 3.99 *(978-0-544-33606-3(2),* HMH Books For Young Readers) Houghton Mifflin Harcourt Publishing Co.

—Buster the Very Shy Dog Finds a Kitten. 2015. (Green Light Readers Level 3 Ser.). (ENG., Illus.). 32p. (J). (gr. 1-4). 12.99 *(978-0-544-33604-9(6));* pap. 3.99 *(978-0-544-33605-6(4))* Houghton Mifflin Harcourt Publishing Co. (HMH Books For Young Readers).

Bracken, Beth. Too Shy for Show-And-Tell, 1 vol. Bell, Jennifer A., illus. 2012. (Little Boost Ser.). (ENG.). 32p. (gr. k-3). 7.95 *(978-1-4048-7418-3(6),* Little Boost) Picture Window Bks.

Burkhart, Kiersi & Keyser, Amber J. Shy Girl & Shy Guy. 2017. (Quartz Creek Ranch Ser.). (ENG.). 240p. (gr. 4-8). 27.99 *(978-1-4677-9253-0(5),* Carolrhoda Bks.) Lerner Publishing Group.

Button, Lana. Willow's Whispers, 0 vols. Howells, Tania, illus. 2014. (Willow Ser.). (ENG.). 32p. (J). (gr. -1-2). pap. 7.95 *(978-1-55453-744-0(4))* Kids Can Pr., Ltd. CAN. Dist: Hachette Bk. Group.

Cooper, Ilene. Look at Lucy! Merrell, David, illus. 2009. (Lucy Ser.: No. 3). (ENG.). 112p. (J). (gr. 1-4). 4.99 *(978-0-375-85558-0(0),* Random Hse. Bks. for Young Readers) Random Hse. Children's Bks.

Crowley, Cath. A Little Wanting Song. 2011. (ENG.). 288p. (YA). (gr. 9). pap. 8.99 *(978-0-375-85449-1(5),* Ember) Random Hse. Children's Bks.

Desbordes, Astrid. Edmond, the Moonlit Party. Boutavant, Marc, illus. 2015. (ENG.). 32p. (J). (gr. -1-3). 17.95 *(978-1-59270-174-2(4))* Enchanted Lion Bks., LLC.

Desir, C. & Perry, Jolene. Love Blind. 2016. (ENG., Illus.). 320p. (YA). (gr. 9). 17.99 *(978-1-4814-1693-1(6),* Simon Pulse) Simon Pulse.

Finger, Mary E. Charlotte Bakeman Has Her Say. Batti, Kimberly Rose, illus. 2007. 96p. (J). 16.00 *(978-0-9746911-2-1(7))* Little Pear Pr.

Fredericks, Mariah. Life. Watkins, Liselotte, illus. 2009. (In the Cards Ser.: No. 3). (ENG.). 272p. (J). pap. 5.99 *(978-0-689-87659-2(9),* Simon & Schuster/Paula Wiseman Bks.) Simon & Schuster/Paula Wiseman Bks.

Gibbs, Lynne. Molly Mouse Is Shy: A Story of Shyness. Mitchell, Melanie, illus. 2009. (Let's Grow Together Ser.). 32p. (J). (gr. -1-2). pap. 10.55 *(978-1-60754-761-7(9));* lib. bdg. 22.60 *(978-1-60754-756-3(2))* Windmill Bks.

Goldfinger, Jennifer P. Hello, My Name Is Tiger. Goldfinger, Jennifer P., illus. 2016. (Illus.). 40p. (J). (gr. -1-3). 17.99 *(978-0-06-239951-9(9))* HarperCollins Pubs.

Hodgkinson, Jo. A Big Day for Migs. Hodgkinson, Jo, illus. 2014. (ENG., Illus.). 32p. (J). (gr. -1-3). 16.95 *(978-1-4677-5014-1(X))* Lerner Publishing Group.

Hughes, Susan. Bijou. 2017. (Puppy Pals Ser.: 4). (ENG.). 112p. (J). (gr. 2-5). pap. 5.99 *(978-1-4926-3403-4(4),* 9781492634034, Sourcebooks Jabberwocky) Sourcebooks, Inc.

Jarman, Julia. Two Shy Pandas. Varley, Susan, illus. 2013. (ENG.). 32p. (J). (gr. -1-3). 16.95 *(978-1-4677-1141-8(1))* Andersen Pr. GBR. Dist: Lerner Publishing Group.

Jeong, SoYun. Lulu the Shy Piglet. Orsolini, Laura, illus. rev. ed. 2014. (MySELF Bookshelf Ser.). (ENG.). 32p. (J). (gr. k-2). pap. 11.94 *(978-1-60357-654-3(1));* lib. bdg. 25.27 *(978-1-59953-645-3(5))* Norwood Hse. Pr.

Jones, Birdy. Blossom Plays Possum: (Because She's Shy) McDonnell, Janet, illus. 2017. 32p. (J). 15.95 ***(978-1-4338-2735-8(2),*** Magination Pr.) American Psychological Assn.

Jones, Harmony. The High Note. 2017. (ENG.). 240p. (J). 16.99 *(978-1-61963-949-2(1),* 9781619639492, Bloomsbury USA Childrens) Bloomsbury Publishing USA.

Jones, Jen. Faith & the Dance Drama: #5, 1 vol. 2013. (Team Cheer Ser.). (ENG.). 112p. (gr. 4-4). pap. 7.19 *(978-1-4342-4263-1(3),* Team Cheer) Stone Arch Bks.

Joseph, Danielle. Shrinking Violet. 2009. (ENG.). 320p. pap. 19.99 *(978-1-4165-9696-7(8),* MTV Bks.) MTV Books.

Kay, Regina. I Just Want to Be Liked. Kinard, Brandi, illus. 2013. (J). 19.95 *(978-1-56411-592-8(5),* CB Publishing & Design) UBUS Communications Systems.

Keyser, Amber J. & Burkhart, Kiersi. Shy Girl & Shy Guy. 2017. (Quartz Creek Ranch Ser.). (ENG.). 240p. (gr. 4-8). 35.99 ***(978-1-4677-9569-2(0),*** Darby Creek) Lerner Publishing Group.

Kirk, Daniel. Library Mouse Bk. 2: A Friend's Tale. 2009. (ENG., Illus.). 32p. (J). (gr. 1-4). 17.95 *(978-0-8109-8927-6(1),* Abrams Bks. for Young Readers) Abrams, Inc.

Lakritz, Deborah. Say Hello, Lily. Avilés, Martha, illus. 2010. (Jewish Identity Ser.). 32p. (J). (gr. -1-3). lib. bdg. 17.95 *(978-0-7613-4511-4(6));* (ENG.). pap. 7.95 *(978-0-7613-4512-1(4))* Lerner Publishing Group. (Kar-Ben Publishing).

Levine, Kristin. The Lions of Little Rock. (ENG.). (J). (gr. 5-9). 2013. 320p. pap. 7.99 *(978-0-14-242435-3(8),* Puffin Books) 2012. 304p. 16.99 *(978-0-399-25644-8(X),* G.P. Putnam's Sons Books for Young Readers) Penguin Young Readers Group.

Lipp, Frederick J. Bread Song. Gaillard, Jason, tr. Gaillard, Jason, illus. 2004. (J). 15.95 *(978-1-59336-000-9(2));* pap. *(978-1-59336-001-6(0))* Mondo Publishing.

Longo, Sharon. My Friend Daniel Doesn't Talk. 2007. (ENG., Illus.). 28p. (C). pap. 13.95 *(978-0-86388-562-4(4),* Y329914, Routledge) Taylor & Francis Group GBR. Dist: Taylor & Francis Group.

Lucas, David. Halibut Jackson. 2016. (ENG., Illus.). 32p. (J). (gr. -1-k). pap. 10.99 *(978-1-84270-371-7(4))* Andersen Pr. GBR. Dist: Independent Pubs. Group.

Martin, Alison J. Charlie, the Brave Monkey. Martin, Alison J., illus. 2013. (Illus.). 24p. pap. 13.97 *(978-1-62516-155-0(7),* Strategic Bk. Publishing) Strategic Book Publishing & Rights Agency (SBPRA).

McKee, David. Elmer & Rose. McKee, David, illus. 2010. (ENG., Illus.). 32p. (J). (gr. -1-3). 16.95 *(978-0-7613-5493-2(X))* Lerner Publishing Group.

Miller, Pat Zietlow. Sophie's Squash Go to School. Wilsdorf, Anne, illus. 2016. (ENG.). 40p. (J). (gr. -1-2). 17.99 *(978-0-553-50944-1(6),* Schwartz & Wade Bks.) Random Hse. Children's Bks.

Nagus, Kari. Congratulations Q & U. 2010. 16p. 8.49 *(978-1-4520-5153-6(4))* AuthorHouse.

Newman, Jeff. The Boys. Newman, Jeff, illus. 2010. (ENG., Illus.). 40p. (J). (gr. -1-2). 17.99 *(978-1-4169-5012-7(5),* Simon & Schuster Bks. For Young Readers) Simon & Schuster Bks. For Young Readers.

Norris, Christine. The Talisman of Zandria. 2013. 240p. pap. 14.99 *(978-1-61271-220-8(7))* Zumaya Pubns. LLC.

Peters, Suzanne. Misee Mouse. 2011. 36p. pap. 15.49 *(978-1-4269-5738-3(6))* Trafford Publishing.

Poydar, Nancy. Brave Santa. 2004. (ENG., Illus.). 32p. (J). (gr. k-3). tchr. ed. 16.95 *(978-0-8234-1821-3(9))* Holiday Hse., Inc.

Puttock, Simon. Mouse's First Night at Moonlight School. Pye, Ali, illus. 2015. (ENG.). 32p. (J). (gr. -1-2). 16.99 *(978-0-7636-7607-0(1),* Nosy Crow) Candlewick Pr.

Raschka, Chris. Clammy Clam. Raschka, Chris, illus. 2014. (Thingy Things Ser.). (ENG., Illus.). 24p. (J). (gr. -1-k). 6.95 *(978-1-4197-1201-2(2),* Abrams Appleseed) Abrams, Inc.

Ryan, Jeanne. Charisma. 2015. (ENG.). 384p. (YA). (gr. 7). 17.99 *(978-0-8037-3966-6(4),* Dial Bks) Penguin Young Readers Group.

Shyness Isn't a Minus: How to Turn Bashfulness into a Plus. 2006. (Elf-Help Books for Kids Ser.). (Illus.). (J). (gr. -1-3). per. 7.95 *(978-0-87029-403-7(2))* Abbey Pr.

Small, Lily. Poppy the Pony. 2016. (Fairy Animals of Misty Wood Ser.). (ENG., Illus.). 144p. (J). pap. 5.99 *(978-1-62779-734-4(3),* 9781627797344, Holt, Henry & Co. Bks. For Young Readers) Holt, Henry & Co.

Srinivasan, Divya. Octopus Alone. 2013. (ENG., Illus.). 40p. (J). (gr. -1-k). 16.99 *(978-0-670-78515-5(6),* Viking Books for Young Readers) Penguin Young Readers Group.

Stine, R. L. How I Met My Monster. 2013. (Goosebumps: Most Wanted Ser.: 3). (ENG.). 160p. (J). (gr. 3-7). pap. 6.99 *(978-0-545-41800-3(3),* Scholastic Paperbacks) Scholastic, Inc.

—How I Met My Monster. 2013. (Goosebumps Most Wanted Ser.: 3). lib. bdg. 17.20 *(978-0-606-31534-0(9),* Turtleback) Turtleback Bks.

Taylor, Robin. Shy Jenny & Her Special Ears. 2013. 36p. pap. 18.41 *(978-1-4669-9732-5(X))* Trafford Publishing.

Thompson, Lauren. Little Lamb. Butler, John, illus. 2014. (J). *(978-1-4351-5352-3(9),* Simon & Schuster Bks. For Young Readers) Simon & Schuster Bks. For Young Readers.

—Wee Little Lamb. Butler, John, illus. 2009. (Wee Little Ser.). (ENG.). 32p. (J). (gr. -1-3). 16.99 *(978-1-4169-3469-1(3),* Simon & Schuster Bks. For Young Readers) Simon & Schuster Bks. For Young Readers.

Twohy, Mike. Poindexter Makes a Friend. Twohy, Mike, illus. 2011. (ENG., Illus.). 32p. (J). (gr. -1-3). 15.99 *(978-1-4424-0965-1(7),* Simon & Schuster/Paula Wiseman Bks.) Simon & Schuster/Paula Wiseman Bks.

Weinstone, David. Music Class Today! Vogel, Vin, illus. 2015. (ENG.). 40p. (J). (gr. -1 — 1). 17.99 *(978-0-374-35131-1(7),* 9780374351311, Farrar, Straus & Giroux (BYR)) Farrar, Straus & Giroux.

Wilson, Karma. Bear's New Friend. Chapman, Jane, illus. 2009. (Bear Bks.). (ENG.). 34p. (J). (gr. -1-2). bds. 7.99 *(978-1-4169-5438-5(4),* Little Simon) Little Simon.

—Bear's New Friend. Chapman, Jane, illus. 2006. (Bear Bks.). (ENG.). 40p. (J). (gr. -1-3). 17.99 *(978-0-689-85984-7(8),* McElderry, Margaret K. Bks.) McElderry, Margaret K. Bks.

Winston, Sherri. The Sweetest Sound. 2017. (ENG.). 272p. (J). (gr. 3-7). 17.99 *(978-0-316-30295-1(3))* Little Brown & Co.

Wojtowycz, David. Fizz the Fire Engine! 2003. (Illus.). (J). pap. *(978-0-439-82852-9(X))* Scholastic, Inc.

BASKET MAKING

McNutt, Nan. The Twined Basket. Youso, Justin & Kaino, Kim, illus. 2011. (Native American Art Activity Book Ser.). (ENG.). 56p. (J). (gr. 5-7). pap. 9.95 *(978-0-88240-760-9(0),* West Winds Pr.) Graphic Arts Ctr. Publishing Co.

BASKETBALL

Adams, Sean. Tim Duncan. 2004. (Sports Heroes & Legends Ser.). (ENG., Illus.). 112p. (gr. 5-12). lib. bdg. 30.60 *(978-0-8225-1793-1(0))* Lerner Publishing Group.

Adamson, Thomas K. Basketball: The Math of the Game. 2011. (Sports Math Ser.). (ENG.). 48p. (gr. 5-6). pap. 47.70 *(978-1-4296-7318-1(4))* Capstone Press of Coughlan Cos.

Adamson, Thomas K. & Wacholtz, Anthony. Basketball: The Math of the Game, 1 vol. 2011. (Sports Math Ser.). (ENG.). 48p. (gr. 5-6). pap. 8.19 *(978-1-4296-7317-4(6));* lib. bdg. 31.99 *(978-1-4296-6568-1(8))* Capstone Press of Coughlan Cos.

Aretha, David. Top 10 Dunks in Basketball. 2016. (Sports Greats Ser.). (Illus.). 48p. (J). (gr. 6-5). pap. 11.70 *(978-0-7660-7580-1(X))* Enslow Pubs., Inc.

—Top 10 Towers of Power in Basketball. 2016. (Sports Greats Ser.). (Illus.). 48p. (J). (gr. 6-5). pap. 11.70 *(978-0-7660-7573-3(7))* Enslow Pubs., Inc.

Aryal, Aimee. Hello, Testudo! Goh, Tai Hwa, illus. 2004. 24p. (J). 18.95 *(978-0-9743442-1-8(4))* Mascot Bks., Inc.

Augustyn, Adam. The Britannica Guide to Basketball. 2011. (Illus.). xvii, 221p. (J). lib. bdg. 46.75 *(978-1-61530-528-5(9))* Rosen Publishing Group, Inc., The.

Balog, Cyn. Unnatural Deeds. 2016. (ENG.). 288p. (YA). (gr. 9-12). 17.99 *(978-1-4926-3579-6(0),* 9781492635796) Sourcebooks, Inc.

Barth, Katrin & Boesing, Lothar. Learning Basketball. 2008. (Illus.). 152p. pap. 14.95 *(978-1-84126-250-5(1))* Meyer & Meyer Sport, Ltd. GBR. Dist: Cardinal Pubs. Group.

Basketball Smarts. 2016. (Basketball Smarts Ser.). 32p. (gr. 3-3). 131.25 *(978-1-4994-2249-8(0));* pap. 50.00 *(978-1-4994-2470-6(1))* Rosen Publishing Group, Inc., The. (PowerKids Pr.).

Bethea, Nikole Brooks. The Science of Basketball with Max Axiom, Super Scientist. 2015. (Science of Sports with Max Axiom Ser.). (ENG., Illus.). 32p. (gr. 3-4). lib. bdg. 30.65 *(978-1-4914-6084-9(9))* Capstone Press of Coughlan Cos.

—The Science of Basketball with Max Axiom, Super Scientist. Aranda, Tomás, illus. 2015. (Science of Sports with Max Axiom Ser.). (ENG.). 32p. (gr. 3-4). pap. 7.95 *(978-1-4914-6088-7(1),* Graphic Library) Capstone Press of Coughlan Cos.

Bird, Sue & Brown, Greg. Sue Bird: Be Yourself. 2004. (Illus.). 48p. (J). 15.95 *(978-0-9634650-5-4(8))* Positively for Kids, Inc.

Birle, Pete. Boston Celtics. 2013. (On the Hardwood Ser.). (ENG., Illus.). 47p. (gr. 3-8). pap. 8.95 *(978-1-61570-832-1(4))* Scobre Pr. Corp.

—Cleveland Cavaliers. 2014. (On the Hardwood Ser.). (gr. 3-8). pap. 8.95 *(978-1-61570-901-4(0))* Scobre Pr. Corp.

Birle, Peter. Cleveland Cavaliers. 2014. (On the Hardwood Ser.). 48p. (gr. 3-8). 27.93 *(978-1-61570-902-1(9))* Scobre Pr. Corp.

Blaxland, Wendy. Basketballs. 2009. (How Are They Made? Ser.). (Illus.). 32p. (gr. 4-6). lib. bdg. 18.56 *(978-0-7614-4751-1(2))* Marshall Cavendish Corp.

Boone, Mary. Sue Bird. 2011. (Robbie Reader Ser.). (Illus.). 32p. (J). (gr. 2-5). lib. bdg. 25.70 *(978-1-61228-062-2(5))* Mitchell Lane Pubs., Inc.

The Boston Celtics. rev. ed. 2014. (Team Spirit Ser.). (ENG.). 48p. (J). (gr. 3-6). lib. bdg. 29.27 *(978-1-59953-630-9(7))* Norwood Hse. Pr.

Bradley, Michael. Yao Ming. 2004. (Benchmark All-Stars 2 Ser.). (Illus.). 48p. (gr. 4). 21.95 *(978-0-7614-1758-3(3),* Benchmark Bks.) Marshall Cavendish Corp.

Bratton, Deboral B. & Bratton, Ashley D. Record-a-Sport Basketball Sport Organizer. Bratton, Deboral B. & Bratton, Ashley D., eds. 2003. (Illus.). (gr. 1-18). 18.95 *(978-1-931746-02-1(8))* Sport Your Stuff Corp.

Brown, Jonatha A. Basketball. 2004. (My Favorite Sport Ser.). (Illus.). 24p. (gr. 1-4). lib. bdg. 22.00 *(978-0-8368-4338-5(X),* Weekly Reader Leveled Readers) Stevens, Gareth Publishing LLLP.

Buckley, James, Jr. NBA on the Inside. 2003. (NBA Ser.). (ENG.). 32p. (J). pap. 5.99 *(978-0-439-57974-2(0))* Scholastic, Inc.

Campbell, Forest G. & Ramen, Fred. An Insider's Guide to Basketball. 2014. (Sports Tips, Techniques, & Strategies Ser.). (Illus.). 48p. (J). (gr. 5-8). 30.25 *(978-1-4777-8581-2(7),* Rosen Reference) Rosen Publishing Group, Inc., The.

Chandler, Matt. The Science of Basketball: The Top Ten Ways Science Affects the Game. 2016. (Top 10 Science Ser.). (ENG., Illus.). 32p. (gr. 3-4). lib. bdg. 27.99 *(978-1-4914-8220-9(6))* Capstone Press of Coughlan Cos.

—Wacky Basketball Trivia: Fun Facts for Every Fan. 2016. (Wacky Sports Trivia Ser.). (ENG., Illus.). 32p. (gr. 3-4). lib. bdg. 27.99 *(978-1-5157-1994-6(4))* Capstone Press of Coughlan Cos.

Clay, Jonathan. At the Basketball Game. 2013. (Core Math Skills: Operations & Algebraic Thinking Ser.). 24p. (J). (gr. 1-2). 22.60 *(978-1-4777-2234-3(3));* (ENG.). pap. 8.25 *(978-1-4777-2088-2(X))* Rosen Publishing Group, Inc., The. (Rosen Classroom).

—At the Basketball Game: Work with Addition & Subtraction Equations. 2013. (Rosen Math Readers Ser.). (ENG.). 24p. (J). (gr. 1-2). pap. 49.50 *(978-1-4777-2089-9(8),* Rosen Classroom) Rosen Publishing Group, Inc., The.

Cooper, Floyd. Jump! From the Life of Michael Jordan. Cooper, Floyd, illus. 2004. (ENG., Illus.). 40p. (J). (gr. 1-4). 17.99 *(978-0-399-24230-4(9),* Philomel Bks.) Penguin Young Readers Group.

Craats, Rennay. Basketball. 2009. (In the Zone Ser.). 24p. (J). (gr. 3-5). pap. 8.95 *(978-1-60596-129-3(9));* (Illus.). lib. bdg. 24.45 *(978-1-60596-128-6(0))* Weigl Pubs., Inc.

Crossingham, John & Dann, Sarah. Basquetbol en Acción. 2005. (Deportes en Accion Ser.). (SPA., Illus.). 32p. (J). (gr. 6-9). pap. *(978-0-7787-8618-4(8))* Crabtree Publishing Co.

—Basquetbol en Accion. 2005. (Serie Deportes en Accion Ser.). (FRE & SPA., Illus.). 32p. (J). (gr. 3-4). lib. bdg. *(978-0-7787-8572-9(6))* Crabtree Publishing Co.

Crouch, Cheryl. Trouble in East Timor. 2010. (Illus.). 56p. (J). *(978-0-8341-2488-2(2))* Beacon Hill Pr. of Kansas City.

Czeskleba, Abby. Cool Basketball Facts. 2011. (Cool Sports Facts Ser.). (ENG.). 24p. (gr. k-1). pap. 41.70 *(978-1-4296-7382-2(6),* Pebble Plus) Capstone Press of Coughlan Cos.

Daniel, P. K. Magic vs. Bird in the NCAA Final, 1 vol. 2014. (Greatest Events in Sports History Ser.). (ENG., Illus.). 48p. (J). (gr. 3-6). lib. bdg. 32.79 *(978-1-62403-596-8(5),* SportsZone) ABDO Publishing Co.

Derr, Aaron. Basketball: An Introduction to Being a Good Sport. Angle, Scott, illus. 2017. (Start Smart (tm) — Sports Ser.). (ENG.). 32p. (J). (gr. k-3). lib. bdg. 26.65 *(978-1-63440-130-2(1));* 39.99 ***(978-1-63440-142-5(5))*** Red Chair Pr.

DiPrimio, Pete. Dwyane Wade. 2011. (Robbie Reader Ser.). 32p. (J). (gr. 2-5). lib. bdg. 25.70 *(978-1-61228-063-9(3))* Mitchell Lane Pubs., Inc.

Doeden, Matt. Fantasy Basketball Math: Using Stats to Score Big in Your League. 2016. (Fantasy Sports Math Ser.). (ENG., Illus.). 32p. (gr. 3-4). lib. bdg. 27.99 *(978-1-5157-2163-5(9))* Capstone Press of Coughlan Cos.

Douglas, Peter. Basketball: Strategy on the Hardwood. 2017. (Preparing for Game Day Ser.: Vol. 10). (ENG.). (YA). (gr. 7-12). 24.95 ***(978-1-4222-3914-8(4))*** Mason Crest.

Durrie, Karen. Al Baloncesto. 2012. (J). *(978-1-61913-199-6(4))* Weigl Pubs., Inc.

—Basketball. 2011. (J). *(978-1-61690-938-3(2));* *(978-1-61690-584-2(0))* Weigl Pubs., Inc.

Edwards, Ethan. Meet Kevin Garnett: Basketball's Big Ticket. 2009. (All-Star Players Ser.). (Illus.). 32p. (YA). (gr. 4-7). lib. bdg. 25.25 *(978-1-4042-4490-0(5))* Rosen Publishing Group, Inc., The.

—Meet Steve Nash: Basketball's Ultimate Team Player. 2009. (All-Star Players Ser.). (Illus.). 32p. (J). (gr. 4-6). lib. bdg. 23.95 *(978-1-4042-4489-4(1),* PowerKids Pr.) Rosen Publishing Group, Inc., The.

Ervin, Phil. 12 Reasons to Love Basketball. 2018. (ENG.). 32p. (gr. 3-6). ***(978-1-63235-426-6(8),*** 12-Story Library) Pr. Room Editions LLC.

Figorito, Marcus. Let's Play Basketball! Learning Addition Facts to 10. 2009. (Math for the REAL World Ser.). 12p. (gr. 1-2). pap. 5.90 *(978-0-8239-8866-2(X),* Rosen Classroom) Rosen Publishing Group, Inc., The.

Flynn, Brendan. Basketball Time! 2016. (Bumba Books (tm) — Sports Time! Ser.). (ENG., Illus.). 24p. (J). (gr. -1-1). 25.32 *(978-1-5124-1432-5(8))* Lerner Publishing Group.

—¡Hora de Baloncesto! 2017. (Bumba Books (tm) en Español — ¡Hora de Deportes! (Sports Time!) Ser.). (SPA., Illus.). 24p. (J). (gr. -1-1). 25.32 *(978-1-5124-2871-1(X))* Lerner Publishing Group.

Fowler, Josh. Indiana Pacers, 1 vol. 2011. (Inside the NBA Ser.). (ENG., Illus.). 48p. (YA). (gr. 3-6). lib. bdg. 32.79 *(978-1-61783-159-1(X))* ABDO Publishing Co.

Frager, Ray. Dallas Mavericks, 1 vol. 2011. (Inside the NBA Ser.). (ENG., Illus.). 48p. (YA). (gr. 3-6). lib. bdg. 32.79 *(978-1-61783-154-6(9))* ABDO Publishing Co.

Franks, Katie. I Want to Be a Basketball Player. (Dream Jobs Ser.). 24p. (gr. 2-3). 2009. 42.50 *(978-1-61512-204-2(4),* PowerKids Pr.) 2007. (Illus.). (J). lib. bdg. 22.60 *(978-1-4042-3621-9(X))* Rosen Publishing Group, Inc., The.

Frederick, Shane. Basketball's Record Breakers. 2017. (Record Breakers Ser.). (ENG., Illus.). 32p. (gr. 3-4). lib. bdg. 27.32 *(978-1-5157-3759-9(4))* Capstone Press of Coughlan Cos.

—The Story of the Los Angeles Lakers. 2014. (J). *(978-1-60818-434-7(X),* Creative Education) Creative Co., The.

—The Story of the Miami Heat. 2014. (J). *(978-1-60818-436-1(6),* Creative Education) Creative Co., The.

—The Story of the New Orleans Pelicans. 2014. (J). *(978-1-60818-440-8(4),* Creative Education) Creative Co., The.

—The Story of the San Antonio Spurs. 2014. (J). *(978-1-60818-448-4(X),* Creative Education) Creative Co., The.

Friedman, Laura, et al. Let's Talk Basketball. 2008. (ENG., Illus.). 24p. (J). (gr. k-1). lib. bdg. 22.00 *(978-0-531-13829-8(1),* Children's Pr.) Scholastic Library Publishing.

Frisch, Nate. The Story of the Chicago Bulls. 2014. (J). *(978-1-60818-425-5(0),* Creative Education) Creative Co., The.

—The Story of the Cleveland Cavaliers. 2014. (J). *(978-1-60818-426-2(9),* Creative Education) Creative Co., The.

—The Story of the Dallas Mavericks. 2014. (J). *(978-1-60818-427-9(7),* Creative Education) Creative Co., The.

—The Story of the Golden State Warriors. 2014. (J). *(978-1-60818-430-9(7),* Creative Education) Creative Co., The.

—The Story of the Houston Rockets. 2014. (J). *(978-1-60818-431-6(5),* Creative Education) Creative Co., The.

—The Story of the Indiana Pacers. 2014. (J). *(978-1-60818-432-3(3),* Creative Education) Creative Co., The.

—The Story of the Memphis Grizzlies. 2014. (J). *(978-1-60818-435-4(8),* Creative Education) Creative Co., The.

Gagne, Tammy. Day by Day with Elena Delle Donne. 2014. (Illus.). 32p. (J). (gr. -1-2). 25.70 *(978-1-61228-634-1(8))* Mitchell Lane Pubs., Inc.

Gerstner, Joanne C. Detroit Pistons, 1 vol. 2011. (Inside the NBA Ser.). (ENG., Illus.). 48p. (YA). (gr. 3-6). lib. bdg. 32.79 *(978-1-61783-156-0(5))* ABDO Publishing Co.

Gettelman, Elizabeth. Competitive Basketball for Girls. 2005. (SportsGirl Ser.). (Illus.). 64p. (YA). (gr. 5-8). lib. bdg. 31.95 *(978-0-8239-3402-7(0))* Rosen Publishing Group, Inc., The.

Gifford, Clive. Basketball. 2009. (Tell Me about Sports Ser.). 32p. (gr. 3-18). 28.50 *(978-0-7614-4455-8(6))* Marshall Cavendish Corp.

—Basketball. 2008. (Personal Best Ser.). (Illus.). 32p. (YA). (gr. 3-6). lib. bdg. 26.50 *(978-1-4042-4444-3(1))* Rosen Publishing Group, Inc., The.

—Basketball & Other Ball Sports. 2011. (ENG., Illus.). 32p. (J). pap. 10.95 *(978-1-77092-035-4(8))* Saunders Bk. Co. CAN. Dist: RiverStream Publishing.

Gitlin, Martin. Playing Pro Basketball. 2014. (Playing Pro Sports Ser.). (ENG., Illus.). 64p. (gr. 4-8). lib. bdg. 26.60 *(978-1-4677-3845-3(X),* Lerner Pubns.) Lerner Publishing Group.

Glaser, Jason. Point Guard. 2010. (Tip-off: Basketball Ser.). (ENG.). 48p. (J). (gr. 4-8). pap. 14.05 *(978-1-4339-3975-4(4));* lib. bdg. 31.95 *(978-1-4339-3974-7(6))* Stevens, Gareth Publishing LLLP.

—Power Forward. 2010. (Tip-off: Basketball Ser.). (ENG.). 48p. (J). (gr. 4-8). pap. 14.05 *(978-1-4339-3978-5(9));* lib. bdg. 31.95 *(978-1-4339-3977-8(0))* Stevens, Gareth Publishing LLLP.

—Tim Duncan. 2008. (Sports Idols Ser.). (Illus.). 24p. (J). (gr. 2-5). lib. bdg. 22.60 *(978-1-4042-4183-1(3))* Rosen Publishing Group, Inc., The.

Graubart, Norman D. The Science of Basketball. 2015. (Sports Science Ser.). (ENG., Illus.). 32p. (J). (gr. 4-5). pap. 10.00 *(978-1-4994-1064-8(6),* PowerKids Pr.) Rosen Publishing Group, Inc., The.

Hantula, Richard. Science at Work in Basketball. 2011. (Benchmark Rockets: Sports Science Ser.). 32p. (gr. 4). 28.50 *(978-0-76870-588-7(9))* Marshall Cavendish GBR. Dist: Marshall Cavendish Corp.

Harrow, Jeremy. Basketball in the Pac-10 Conference. (Inside Men's College Basketball Ser.). 48p. (gr. 5-5). 2009. 53.00 *(978-1-61513-547-9(2),* Rosen Reference) 2008. (Illus.). (YA). lib. bdg. 29.25 *(978-1-4042-1385-2(6))* Rosen Publishing Group, Inc., The.

Herzog, Brad. Little Basketball. Bowles, Doug, illus. 2011. (Little Sports Ser.). (ENG.). 22p. 9.95 *(978-1-58536-181-6(X))* Sleeping Bear Pr.

Hinnant, Jamal. Top 10 Injuries in Basketball. 2016. (Sports Greats Ser.). 48p. (J). (gr. 6-5). pap. 11.70 *(978-0-7660-7567-2(2))* Enslow Pubs., Inc.

Hoena, Blake. Basketball. 2015. (J). lib. bdg. 25.65 (978-1-62031-177-6(1), Bullfrog Bks.) Jump! Inc.

Hoffman, Mary Ann. LeBron James: Basketball Star. 2009. (Sports Superstars Ser.). 24p. (gr. 1-1). 42.50 (978-1-60853-178-3(3), PowerKids Pr.) Rosen Publishing Group, Inc., The.

—LeBron James: Basketball Star/Estrella del Baloncesto. 2009. (Amazing Athletes/Atletas increibles Ser.). (ENG & SPA.). 24p. (gr. 1-2). 42.50 (978-1-61511-306-4(1), Editorial Buenas Letras) Rosen Publishing Group, Inc., The.

Hollar, Sherman. Basketball & Its Greatest Players. 2011. (J). lib. bdg. 31.70 (978-1-61530-509-4(2)) Rosen Publishing Group, Inc., The.

Hughes, Morgan. Basketball. 2005. (Junior Sports Ser.). (Illus.). 32p. (gr. 2-4). 19.95 (978-1-59515-189-6(3)) Rourke Educational Media.

Hurley, Michael. Basketball, 1 vol. 2013. (Fantastic Sports Facts Ser.). (ENG., Illus.). 32p. (gr. 1-3). pap. 8.29 (978-1-4109-5111-3(1)); lib. bdg. 29.99 (978-1-4109-5104-5(9)) Heinemann-Raintree. (Read Me!).

Indovino, Shaina Carmel. Kobe Bryant. 2014. (Superstars in the World of Basketball Ser.: 10). 48p. (J). (gr. 5-18). 20.95 (978-1-4222-3108-1(9)) Mason Crest.

Inside Men's College Basketball, 6 vols., Set. 2008. (YA). (gr. 5-8). lib. bdg. 159.00 (978-1-4042-1483-5(6)) Rosen Publishing Group, Inc., The.

Jackson, Aurelia. Rajon Rondo. 2014. (Superstars in the World of Basketball Ser.: 10). 48p. (J). (gr. 5-18). 20.95 (978-1-4222-3111-1(9)) Mason Crest.

James, Lebron, et al. Lebron James. 2015. (Quotes from the Greatest Athletes Ser.). (ENG., Illus.). 24p. (J). lib. bdg. 12.95 (978-1-4896-3361-3(8), AV2 by Weigl) Weigl Pubs., Inc.

Jordan, Michael. Michael Jordan. 2015. (Quotes from the Greatest Athletes Ser.). (ENG., Illus.). 24p. (J). lib. bdg. 12.95 (978-1-4896-3369-9(3), 1393457, AV2 by Weigl) Weigl Pubs., Inc.

Joyce, Dru, II. Beyond Championships Teen Edition: A Playbook for Winning at Life, 1 vol. 2015. (ENG., Illus.). 192p. (J). pap. 14.99 (978-0-310-74615-7(9)) Zondervan.

Kalman, Bobbie & Crossingham, John. Baloncesto Espectacular. 2008.Tr. of Slam Dunk Basketball. (SPA.). 32p. (J). pap. (978-0-7787-8646-7(3)); lib. bdg. (978-0-7787-8637-5(4)) Crabtree Publishing Co.

—Slam Dunk Basketball. 2007. (Sports Starters Ser.). (ENG., Illus.). 32p. (J). (gr. 3-7). lib. bdg. (978-0-7787-3139-9(1)); (gr. -1-3). pap. (978-0-7787-3171-9(5)) Crabtree Publishing Co.

Kaplan, Coach Bobby. Bball Basics for Kids: A Basketball Handbook. 2012. 146p. (gr. 4-6). pap. 19.95 (978-1-4620-4373-6(9)) iUniverse, Inc.

Kaufman, Gabriel. Basketball in the Big Ten Conference. (Inside Men's College Basketball Ser.). 48p. (gr. 5-5). 2009. 53.00 (978-1-61513-546-2(4), Rosen Reference) 2008. (Illus.). (YA). lib. bdg. 29.25 (978-1-4042-1383-8(X)) Rosen Publishing Group, Inc., The.

Kirkpatrick, Rob. Grant Hill: Basketball All-Star. 2003. (Power Players Ser.). (Illus.). 24p. (J). 22.60 (978-0-8239-6818-3(9), PowerKids Pr.) Rosen Publishing Group, Inc., The.

Kortemeier, Todd. Pro Basketball by the Numbers. 2016. (Illus.). 32p. (J). pap. (978-1-4914-9071-6(3)) Capstone Press of Coughlan Cos.

Kortemeier, Tom. Pro Basketball by the Numbers. 2016. (Pro Sports by the Numbers Ser.). (ENG., Illus.). 32p. (gr. 3-4). lib. bdg. 27.99 (978-1-4914-9058-7(6), Edge Bks.) Capstone Press of Coughlan Cos.

Labrecque, Ellen. Basketball. 2008. (21st Century Skills Innovation Library: Innovation in Sports Ser.). (ENG., Illus.). 32p. (gr. 4-8). lib. bdg. 28.50 (978-1-60279-256-2(9), 200124) Cherry Lake Publishing.

Ladewski, Paul & Smallwood, John. Playmaker. 2008. (ENG., Illus.). 32p. (J). (gr. 2-5). pap. 5.99 (978-0-545-00666-8(X), Scholastic) Scholastic, Inc.

Latimer, Clay. VIP Pass to a Pro Basketball Game Day: From the Locker Room to the Press Box (and Everything in Between), 1 vol. (Game Day (Sports Illustrated for Kids) Ser.). (ENG.). 32p. (gr. 3-4). 2011. pap. 8.19 (978-1-4296-6284-0(0)) 2011. pap. 47.70 (978-1-4296-6448-6(7)) 2010. lib. bdg. 27.99 (978-1-4296-5463-0(5)) Capstone Press of Coughlan Cos.

Latta, Sara L. Who Invented Basketball? James Naismith. 2012. (I Like Inventors! Ser.). 24p. (J). (gr. k-3). 22.60 (978-0-7660-3965-0(X), Enslow Elementary) Enslow Pubs., Inc.

Laughlin, Kara L. Basketball. 2016. (Beginning Sports Ser.). (ENG.). 24p. (J). (gr. k-3). 27.07 (978-1-5038-0771-6(1), 210599) Child's World, Inc., The.

LeBoutillier, Nate. The Best of Everything Basketball Book, 1 vol. 2010. (All-Time Best of Sports Ser.). (ENG.). 64p. (gr. 3-4). lib. bdg. 34.65 (978-1-4296-5468-5(6)) Capstone Press of Coughlan Cos.

—Play Basketball Like a Pro: Key Skills & Tips, 1 vol. 2010. (Play Like the Pros (Sports Illustrated for Kids) Ser.). (ENG.). 32p. (gr. 3-4). pap. 7.19 (978-1-4296-5645-0(X)); lib. bdg. 26.65 (978-1-4296-4826-4(0)) Capstone Press of Coughlan Cos.

—The Story of the Denver Nuggets. 2014. (J). (978-1-60818-428-6(5), Creative Education) Creative Co., The.

—The Story of the Minnesota Timberwolves. 2014. (J). (978-1-60818-438-5(2), Creative Education) Creative Co., The.

—The Story of the Portland Trail Blazers. 2014. (J). (978-1-60818-446-0(3), Creative Education) Creative Co., The.

—The Story of the Utah Jazz. 2014. (J). (978-1-60818-450-7(1), Creative Education) Creative Co., The.

—The Ultimate Guide to Pro Basketball Teams, 1 vol. 2010. (Ultimate Pro Team Guides (Sports Illustrated for Kids) Ser.). (ENG.). 72p. (gr. 3-4). lib. bdg. 34.65 (978-1-4296-4821-9(X)) Capstone Press of Coughlan Cos.

Lindeen, Carol K. ¡Vamos a Jugar al Básquetbol! 2012. (Deportes y Actividades/Sports & Activities Ser.).Tr. of Let's Play Basketball! (MUL & SPA.). 24p. (gr. k-1). lib. bdg. 26.65 (978-1-4296-8246-6(9)) Capstone Press of Coughlan Cos.

Lindeen, Mary. Let's Play Basketball. 2015. (BeginningtoRead Ser.). (ENG.). 32p. (J). (gr. k-2). lib. bdg. 22.60 (978-1-59953-685-9(4)); (Illus.). pap. 11.94 (978-1-60357-745-8(9)) Norwood Hse. Pr.

Mableton, Barry & Gettelman, Elizabeth. Basketball: Girls Rocking It, 01 vols., 1. 2016. (Title IX Rocks! Ser.). (ENG., Illus.). 64p. (J). 32.95 (978-1-5081-7035-8(5), Rosen Young Adult) Rosen Publishing Group, Inc., The.

MacRae, Sloan. Meet Dirk Nowitzki: Basketball's Blond Bomber. 2009. (All-Star Players Ser.). (J). lib. bdg. 25.25 (978-1-4358-2709-7(0), PowerKids Pr.) Rosen Publishing Group, Inc., The.

Mahaney, Ian F. The Math of Basketball. 2011. (J). 49.50 (978-1-4488-2695-7(0), PowerKids Pr.); (J). pap. 8.25 (978-1-4488-2694-0(2), PowerKids Pr.); (YA). (gr. 2-5). lib. bdg. 22.60 (978-1-4488-2593-6(8)) Rosen Publishing Group, Inc., The.

Marcovitz, Hal. LeBron James. 2008. (Pop Culture Ser.). (Illus.). 64p. (YA). (gr. 3-7). lib. bdg. 22.95 (978-1-4222-0205-0(4)) Mason Crest.

Mason, Tyler. Incredible Basketball Records. 2016. (Incredible Sports Records Ser.). (ENG.). 24p. (J). (gr. 2-5). 28.50 (978-1-5038-0887-4(4), 210676) Child's World, Inc., The.

Mattern, Joanne. Dwight Howard: Basketball Superstar, 1 vol. 2011. (Superstar Athletes Ser.). (ENG.). 24p. (gr. 1-2). pap. 7.29 (978-1-4296-7307-5(9)); pap. 41.70 (978-1-4296-7308-2(7)) Capstone Press of Coughlan Cos.

McClellan, Ray. Basketball. 2009. (My First Sports Ser.). (ENG., Illus.). 24p. (J). (gr. 2-5). lib. bdg. 25.95 (978-1-60014-279-6(6), Blastoff! Readers) Bellwether Media.

McFee, Shane. Let's Play Basketball. (Let's Get Active Ser.). 24p. 2009. (gr. 2-3). 42.50 (978-1-61514-252-1(5)) 2008. (Illus.). lib. bdg. 22.60 (978-1-4042-4193-0(0)) Rosen Publishing Group, Inc., The. (PowerKids Pr.).

Minden, Cecilia. Basketball. 2008. (21st Century Skills Library: Real World Math Ser.). (ENG., Illus.). 32p. (gr. 4-8). lib. bdg. 28.50 (978-1-60279-245-6(3), 200196) Cherry Lake Publishing.

Morey, Allan. Basketball. 2016. (Summer Olympic Sports Ser.). (ENG., Illus.). 32p. (J). (gr. 2-4). pap. 9.99 (978-1-68152-047-6(8)) Amicus.

—Basketball. 2015. (Summer Olympic Sports Ser.). (ENG., Illus.). 32p. (J). (gr. 2-4). 19.95 (978-1-60753-806-6(7)) Amicus Publishing.

Mullin, Chris. Jovenes Jugadores de Baloncesto. (SPA.). 46p. (YA). (gr. 2-18). 16.76 (978-84-272-4985-1(3)) Molino, Editorial ESP. Dist: Lectorum Pubns., Inc.

Murray, Stuart A. P. Score with Basketball Math. 2013. (Score with Sports Math Ser.). 48p. (J). lib. bdg. 25.27 (978-0-7660-4178-3(6)); (gr. 3-4). pap. 8.95 (978-1-4644-0295-1(7)) Enslow Pubs., Inc. (Enslow Elementary).

Nagelhout, Ryan. Basketball: Who Does What? 2017. (Sports: What's Your Position? Ser.). 32p. (gr. 3-4). lib. bdg. 26.60 **(978-1-5382-0422-1(3))** Stevens, Gareth Publishing LLLP.

—Basketball's Greatest Records, 1 vol. 2015. (ENG., Illus.). 32p. (J). lib. bdg. 26.25 (978-1-4994-0220-9(1), PowerKids Pr.) Rosen Publishing Group, Inc., The.

—I Love Basketball. 2014. (My Favorite Sports Ser.). 24p. (J). (gr. k-2). 22.60 (978-1-4824-0722-8(1)) Stevens, Gareth Publishing LLLP.

—Me Encanta el Baloncesto / I Love Basketball. 2014. (My Favorite Sports Ser.). (SPA & ENG., Illus.). 24p. (J). (gr. k-2). 22.60 (978-1-4824-0848-5(1)) Stevens, Gareth Publishing LLLP.

—Talk Like a Basketball Player. 2016. (Let's Talk Sports! Ser.). 00032p. (J). pap. 10.50 (978-1-4824-5696-7(6)) Stevens, Gareth Publishing LLLP.

—20 Fun Facts about Basketball. 2016. (Fun Fact File: Sports! Ser.). (ENG., Illus.). 32p. (J). (gr. 2-3). pap. 10.50 (978-1-4824-3969-4(7)) Stevens, Gareth Publishing LLLP.

Nelson, Robin. Basketball Is Fun! 2013. (First Step Nonfiction - Sports Are Fun! Ser.). (ENG., Illus.). 24p. (gr. k-2). pap. 6.95 (978-1-4677-1536-2(0)); lib. bdg. 23.93 (978-1-4677-1102-9(0), Lerner Pubns.) Lerner Publishing Group.

—From Leather to Basketball Shoes. 2014. (Start to Finish: Sports Gear Ser.). (Illus.). 24p. (gr. k-3). pap. 6.95 (978-1-4677-4559-8(6)); (ENG., lib. bdg. 23.93 (978-1-4677-3893-4(X), Lerner Pubns.) Lerner Publishing Group.

Omoth, Tyler. First Source to Basketball: Rules, Equipment, & Key Playing Tips. 2016. (First Sports Source Ser.). (ENG., Illus.). 24p. (gr. 1-2). lib. bdg. 25.32 (978-1-4914-8422-7(5), First Facts) Capstone Press of Coughlan Cos.

—The Ultimate Collection of Pro Basketball Records. 2012. (For the Record Ser.). (ENG.). 64p. (gr. 4-6). pap. 53.70 (978-1-4296-9431-5(9)); (Illus.). lib. bdg. 34.65 (978-1-4296-8653-2(7)) Capstone Press of Coughlan Cos.

Omoth, Tyler Dean. The Ultimate Collection of Pro Basketball Records, 1 vol. 2012. (For the Record Ser.). (ENG.). 64p. (gr. 4-6). pap. 8.95 (978-1-4296-9430-8(0)) Capstone Press of Coughlan Cos.

Osier, Dan. Basketball's MVPs, 6 vols., Set. Incl. Dirk Nowitzki. lib. bdg. 22.60 (978-1-4488-2524-0(5)); Kevin Garnett. lib. bdg. 22.60 (978-1-4488-2526-4(1)); Kobe Bryant. lib. bdg. 22.60 (978-1-4488-2523-3(7)); LeBron James. 22.60 (978-1-4488-2522-6(9)); Steve Nash. lib. bdg. 22.60 (978-1-4488-2525-7(3)); Tim Duncan. lib. bdg. 22.60 (978-1-4488-2527-1(X)); (J). (gr. 3-6). (Basketball's MVPs Ser.). (Illus.). 24p. 2011. Set lib. bdg. 127.50 (978-1-4488-2906-4(2), PowerKids Pr.) Rosen Publishing Group, Inc., The.

—Dirk Nowitzki. 2011. (Basketball's MVPs / Jugadores Más Valiosos Del Baloncesto Ser.). (SPA., Illus.). 24p. (J). (gr. 3-6). 22.60 (978-1-4488-3136-4(9)) Rosen Publishing Group, Inc., The.

—Steve Nash. 2011. (Basketball's MVPs / Jugadores Más Valiosos Del Baloncesto Ser.). (ENG & SPA., Illus.). 24p. (J). (gr. 3-6). 22.60 (978-1-4488-3137-1(7)) Rosen Publishing Group, Inc., The.

Otten, Jack. Baloncesto. 2004. (Entrenamiento Deportivo (Sports Training) Ser.). (SPA & ENG., Illus.). 24p. (J). (gr. 2-4). lib. bdg. 22.60 (978-0-8239-6849-7(9)) Rosen Publishing Group, Inc., The.

—Baloncesto (Basketball) 2009. (Entrenamiento deportivo (Sports Training) Ser.). (SPA.). 24p. (gr. 1-2). 42.50 (978-1-61512-267-7(2), Editorial Buenas Letras) Rosen Publishing Group, Inc., The.

Page, Jason. Basketball, Soccer, & Other Ball Games. 2008. (Olympic Sports Ser.). (ENG., Illus.). 32p. (J). (gr. 4-7). pap. (978-0-7787-4029-2(3)); lib. bdg. (978-0-7787-4012-4(9)) Crabtree Publishing Co.

Peters, Gregory N. The Best of College Basketball, 1 vol. 2014. (Sports & Recreation Ser.). (ENG.). 48p. (gr. 4-12). 31.99 (978-1-4765-8521-5(0)) Capstone Press of Coughlan Cos.

Porterfield, Jason. Basketball in the Big East Conference. 2009. (Inside Men's College Basketball Ser.). 48p. (gr. 5-5). 53.00 (978-1-61513-545-5(6), Rosen Reference) Rosen Publishing Group, Inc., The.

Ramen, Fred. Basketball: Rules, Tips, Strategy, & Safety. (Sports from Coast to Coast Ser.). 48p. 2009. (gr. 6-6). 53.00 (978-1-60853-122-6(8), Rosen Reference) 2007. (Illus.). (J). (gr. 3-7). lib. bdg. 29.25 (978-1-4042-0992-3(1)) Rosen Publishing Group, Inc., The.

Rissman, Rebecca. Top Basketball Tips. 2017. (Top Sports Tips Ser.). (ENG., Illus.). 32p. (gr. 3-4). lib. bdg. 27.99 (978-1-5157-4719-2(0), Snap Bks.) Capstone Press of Coughlan Cos.

Robinson, Tom. Basketball Skills: How to Play Like a Pro. 2008. (How to Play Like a Pro Ser.). (Illus.). 48p. (J). (gr. 3-6). lib. bdg. 25.27 (978-0-7660-3205-7(1)) Enslow Pubs., Inc.

—Girls Play to Win Basketball. 2010. (Girls Play to Win Ser.). 64p. (J). (gr. 3-6). lib. bdg. 27.93 (978-1-59953-388-9(X)) Norwood Hse. Pr.

Roselius, J. Chris. Houston Rockets, 1 vol. 2011. (Inside the NBA Ser.). (ENG., Illus.). 48p. (YA). (gr. 3-6). lib. bdg. 32.79 (978-1-61783-158-4(1)) ABDO Publishing Co.

Ross, Dalton. The Top Teams Ever: Football, Baseball, Basketball & Hockey Winners. 2005. (Sports Illustrated for Kids Books Ser.). (Illus.). 176p. (YA). (gr. 7-12). lib. bdg. 33.25 (978-0-8239-3693-9(7)) Rosen Publishing Group, Inc., The.

—The Top Teams Ever: Football, Baseball, Basketball, & Hockey Winners. 2009. (Sports Illustrated for Kids Bks). 176p. (gr. 7-12). 63.90 (978-1-60853-156-1(2)) Rosen Publishing Group, Inc., The.

Roza, Greg. Basketball in the SEC (Southeastern Conference) (Inside Men's College Basketball Ser.). 48p. (gr. 5-5). 2009. 53.00 (978-1-61513-548-6(0), Rosen Reference) 2008. (Illus.). (YA). lib. bdg. 29.25 (978-1-4042-1382-1(1)) Rosen Publishing Group, Inc., The.

Salzmann, Mary Elizabeth. Basketball by the Numbers, 1 vol. 2010. (Team Sports by the Numbers Ser.). (ENG.). 24p. (J). (gr. k-3). lib. bdg. 24.21 (978-1-60453-768-0(X), SandCastle) ABDO Publishing Co.

Savage, Jeff. Dwight Howard. 2010. pap. 39.62 (978-0-7613-6968-4(6)) Lerner Publishing Group.

—LeBron James. 2005. (Amazing Athletes Ser.). (Illus.). 32p. (J). (gr. 3-7). pap. 6.95 (978-0-8225-2954-5(8)) Lerner Publishing Group.

—Super Basketball Infographics. Schuster, Rob, illus. 2015. (Super Sports Infographics Ser.). (ENG.). 32p. (J). (gr. 3-5). pap. 8.99 (978-1-4677-7575-5(4)); lib. bdg. 26.65 (978-1-4677-5233-6(9)) Lerner Publishing Group. (Lerner Pubns.).

—Tim Duncan. 2009. (Amazing Athletes Ser.). (ENG.). 32p. (gr. 2-5). pap. 7.95 (978-1-58013-794-2(6), First Avenue Editions) Lerner Publishing Group.

Schrier, Allyson Valentine, et al. Get in the Game. 2012. (Get in the Game Ser.). (ENG.). 32p. (gr. 3-4). lib. bdg. 55.98 (978-1-4296-8221-3(3), Snap Bks.) Capstone Press of Coughlan Cos.

Schuh, Mari C. Basketball. 2017. (Spot Sports Ser.). (ENG.). 16p. (gr. k-3). 17.95 **(978-1-68151-084-2(7))** Amicus Publishing.

Schulte, Mary E. The Final Four: All about College Basketball's Biggest Event, 1 vol. 2012. (Winner Takes All Ser.). (ENG., 32p. (gr. 3-4). Illus.). pap. 7.19 (978-1-4296-9438-4(6)); pap. 41.70 (978-1-4296-9439-1(4)); (Illus.). lib. bdg. 27.99 (978-1-4296-6572-8(6)) Capstone Press of Coughlan Cos.

Shea, Therese. Becoming a Pro Basketball Player. 2015. (Going Pro Ser.). (ENG.). 32p. (J). (gr. 3-4). pap. 10.50 (978-1-4824-2058-6(9)); (Illus.). lib. bdg. 26.60 (978-1-4824-2059-3(7)) Stevens, Gareth Publishing LLLP.

Silverman, Drew. Basketball, 1 vol. 2012. (ENG.). 64p. 32.79 (978-1-61783-141-6(7), SportsZone) ABDO Publishing Co.

—Nba Finals, 1 vol. 2013. (Sports' Great Championships Ser.). (ENG., Illus.). 64p. (J). (gr. 4-6). lib. bdg. 32.79 (978-1-61783-671-8(0), SportsZone) ABDO Publishing Co.

Skogen, J. M. Memphis Grizzlies. 2014. (On the Hardwood Ser.). 48p. (gr. 3-8). pap. 8.95 (978-1-61570-917-5(7)) Scobre Pr. Corp.

—Washington Wizards. 2014. (On the Hardwood Ser.). (gr. 3-8). pap. 8.95 (978-1-61570-925-0(8)) Scobre Pr. Corp.

Skogen, J. m. & Skogen, J. M. Memphis Grizzlies. 2014. (On the Hardwood Ser.). (gr. 3-8). 27.93 (978-1-61570-918-2(5)) Scobre Pr. Corp.

Slade, Suzanne. Basketball: How It Works. 2010. (Science of Sports (Sports Illustrated for Kids) Ser.). (ENG.). 48p. (gr. 3-4). pap. 59.70 (978-1-4296-5107-3(5)) Capstone Press of Coughlan Cos.

—The Technology of Basketball, 1 vol. 2013. (High-Tech Sports Ser.). (ENG.). 48p. (gr. 3-9). pap. 8.95 (978-1-62065-908-3(5)); pap. 53.70 (978-1-62065-909-0(3)); lib. bdg. 31.99 (978-1-4296-9956-3(6)) Capstone Press of Coughlan Cos.

Sommers, Michael. Basketball in the Big 12 Conference. 2009. (Inside Men's College Basketball Ser.). 48p. (gr. 5-5). 53.00 (978-1-61513-544-8(8), Rosen Reference) Rosen Publishing Group, Inc., The.

Sommers, Michael A. Basketball in the Big 12 Conference. 2008. (Inside Men's College Basketball Ser.). (Illus.). 48p. (YA). (gr. 5-9). lib. bdg. 29.25 (978-1-4042-1384-5(8)) Rosen Publishing Group, Inc., The.

Sterling Children's, Sterling. My First Basketball Book. 2015. (First Sports Ser.). (ENG., Illus.). 22p. (J). (— 1). bds. 6.95 (978-1-4549-1487-7(4)) Sterling Publishing Co., Inc.

Stewart, Mark. Basketball. 2009. (Ultimate 10: Sports Ser.). 48p. (ENG.). (J). (gr. 4-8). pap. 10.50 (978-1-4339-2204-6(5)); (YA). (gr. 5-9). lib. bdg. 31.00 (978-0-8368-9157-7(0)) Stevens, Gareth Publishing LLLP.

—Los Lakers de Los Ángeles. Kalmanovitz, Manuel, tr. from ENG. 2007. (Espíritu de Equipo Ser.). (SPA., Illus.). 48p. (J). (gr. 3-6). lib. bdg. 26.60 (978-1-59953-100-7(3)) Norwood Hse. Pr.

—Los Heat de Miami. Kalmanovitz, Manuel, tr. from ENG. 2007. (Espíritu de Equipo Ser.). (SPA.). 48p. (J). (gr. 3-6). lib. bdg. 26.60 (978-1-59953-102-1(X)) Norwood Hse. Pr.

—The NBA Finals. Kennedy, Mike, ed. 2003. (Watts History of Sports Ser.). (ENG., Illus.). 128p. (J). 34.50 (978-0-531-11955-6(6)) Scholastic Library Publishing.

Stewart, Mark & Zeysing, Matt. The Syracuse Orange. 2010. (Team Spirit Ser.). (ENG.). 48p. (J). (gr. 3-6). lib. bdg. 26.60 (978-1-59953-377-3(4)) Norwood Hse. Pr.

Stone, Danton. Basketball. 2012. (Rookie Read-about Ser.). (ENG., Illus.). 32p. (J). (gr. -1-1). pap. 5.95 (978-0-531-20935-6(0)); lib. bdg. 23.00 (978-0-531-20866-3(4)) Scholastic Library Publishing. (Children's Pr.).

Storden, Thom. Amazing Basketball Records, 1 vol. 2014. (Epic Sports Records Ser.). (ENG.). 32p. (gr. 1-2). lib. bdg. 26.65 (978-1-4914-0741-7(7)) Capstone Press of Coughlan Cos.

Stuckey, Rachel. Full Court Press: Basketball Skills & Drills. 2015. (ENG., Illus.). 32p. (J). (978-0-7787-1536-8(1)) Crabtree Publishing Co.

Sweeny, Sheila. Wacky Basketball Facts to Bounce Around. Wolf, Cathrine, ed. rev. ed. Date not set. (Illus.). 32p. (J). (gr. k-3). pap. 2.50 (978-1-886749-38-2(8)) Sports Illustrated For Kids.

Swope, Bob. Teach'n Beginning Defensive Basketball Drills, Plays, & Games Free Flow Handbook. 2013. 150p. pap. 16.95 (978-0-9911151-8-1(X)) Jacobob Pr., LLC.

—Teach'n Beginning Offensive Basketball Drills, Plays, & Games Free Flow Handbook. 2013. 80p. pap. 19.95 (978-0-9911151-0-5(4)) Jacobob Pr., LLC.

Taylor, Trace & SáNchez, LucíA M. BáSquetbol (Basketball) 2011. (ARC Press / el poder de 100 - Deportes (Power 100 - Sports) Ser.). (SPA.). pap. 33.92 (978-1-61541-468-0(1)) American Reading Co.

Tometich, Annabelle. I Know Basketball. 2013. (21st Century Basic Skills Library: I Know Sports Ser.). (ENG., Illus.). 24p. (J). (gr. k-3). 22.79 (978-1-62431-398-1(1), 202712); pap. 12.79 (978-1-62431-474-2(0), 202714) Cherry Lake Publishing.

Torres, John Albert. Dwight Howard: A Basketball Star Who Cares. 2013. (Sports Stars Who Care Ser.). 48p. (J). 25.27 (978-0-7660-4294-0(4)) Enslow Pubs., Inc.

—Top 25 Basketball Skills, Tips, & Tricks. 2011. (Top 25 Sports Skills, Tips, & Tricks Ser.). (Illus.). 48p. (J). (gr. 2-5). lib. bdg. 25.27 (978-0-7660-3857-8(2)); (gr. 4-18). pap. 8.95 (978-1-59845-356-0(4)) Enslow Pubs., Inc.

Triano, Jay. Basketball Basics: How to Play Like the Pros, 1 vol. 2009. (ENG., Illus.). 80p. pap. 17.95 (978-1-55365-451-3(X)) Greystone Books Ltd. CAN. Dist: Publishers Group West (PGW).

Ulmer, Michael. J Is for Jump Shot: A Basketball Alphabet. Braught, Mark, illus. 2005. (Sports Alphabet Ser.). (ENG.). 40p. (J). (gr. -1-5). 16.95 (978-1-58536-229-5(8)) Sleeping Bear Pr.

—J Is for Jump Shot: A Basketball Alphabet. Braught, Mark, illus. 2015. (Av2 Fiction Readalong 2016 Ser.). (ENG.). (J). (gr. 1-4). lib. bdg. 34.28 (978-1-4896-3753-6(2), AV2 by Weigl) Weigl Pubs., Inc.

Ulmer, Mike. J Is for Jump Shot: A Basketball Alphabet. Braught, Mark, illus. rev. ed. 2006. (Sports Ser.). (ENG.). 40p. (J). (gr. k-5). pap. 7.95 (978-1-58536-338-4(3)) Sleeping Bear Pr.

Ultimate Sports Force Staff. Super Squad: Basketball's Superstars. 2003. (Illus.). 56p. (J). pap. 7.95 (978-1-57243-601-5(8)) Triumph Bks.

Vanderhoof, Gabrielle. Basketball. 2010. (Getting the Edge Ser.). 96p. (YA). lib. bdg. 24.95 (978-1-4222-1731-3(0)) Mason Crest.

Wacholtz, Anthony. Picture a Slam Dunk: A Basketball Drawing Book, 1 vol. Haya, Erwin, illus. 2013. (Drawing with Sports Illustrated Kids Ser.). (ENG.). 64p. (gr. 5-7). 33.99 (978-1-4765-3107-6(2)) Capstone Press of Coughlan Cos.

Weierbach, Jane & Phillips-Hershey, Elizabeth. Mind over Basketball: Coach Yourself to Handle Stress. Beyl, Charles, illus. 2007. (Coach Yourself to Handle Stress Ser.). 48p. (J). (gr. 3-7). 14.95 (978-1-4338-0135-8(3), 4418006); per. 9.95 (978-1-4338-0136-5(1), 4418007) American Psychological Assn. (Magination Pr.).

We're a Team! Individual Title Six-Packs. (gr. -1-2). 27.00 (978-0-7635-9482-4(2)) Rigby Education.

Whiting, Jim. Memphis Grizzlies. 2nd ed. 2017. (NBA: a History of Hoops Ser.). (ENG.). 48p. (J). (gr. 5-7). pap. 12.00 **(978-1-62832-452-5(X)**, Creative Paperbacks) Creative Co., The.

—Milwaukee Bucks. 2017. (J). **(978-1-60818-851-2(5)**, Creative Education) Creative Co., The.

—Minnesota Timberwolves. 2017. (J). **(978-1-60818-852-9(3)**, Creative Education) Creative Co., The.

—The NBA: a History of Hoops: Atlanta Hawks. 2nd ed. 2017. (NBA: a History of Hoops Ser.). (ENG.). 48p. (J). (gr. 5-7). pap. 12.00 **(978-1-62832-438-9(4)**, Creative Paperbacks) Creative Co., The.

—The NBA: a History of Hoops: Boston Celtics. 2nd ed. 2017. (NBA: a History of Hoops Ser.). (ENG.). 48p. (J). (gr. 5-7). pap. 12.00 **(978-1-62832-439-6(2)**, Creative Paperbacks) Creative Co., The.

—The NBA: a History of Hoops: Brooklyn Nets. 2nd ed. 2017. (NBA: a History of Hoops Ser.). (ENG.). 48p. (J). (gr. 5-7). pap. 12.00 **(978-1-62832-440-2(6)**, Creative Paperbacks) Creative Co., The.

—The NBA: a History of Hoops: Charlotte Hornets. 2nd ed. 2017. (NBA: a History of Hoops Ser.). (ENG.). 48p. (J). (gr. 5-7). pap. 12.00 **(978-1-62832-441-9(4)**, Creative Paperbacks) Creative Co., The.

—The NBA: a History of Hoops: Dallas Mavericks. 2nd ed. 2017. (NBA: a History of Hoops Ser.). (ENG.). 48p. (J). (gr. 5-7). pap. 12.00 **(978-1-62832-444-0(9)**, Creative Paperbacks) Creative Co., The.

—The NBA: a History of Hoops: Denver Nuggets. 2nd ed. 2017. (NBA: a History of Hoops Ser.). (ENG.). 48p. (J). (gr. 5-7). pap. 12.00 **(978-1-62832-445-7(7)**, Creative Paperbacks) Creative Co., The.

—The NBA: a History of Hoops: Detroit Pistons. 2nd ed. 2017. (NBA: a History of Hoops Ser.). (ENG.). 48p. (J). (gr. 5-7).

pap. 12.00 *(978-1-62832-446-4(5)*, Creative Paperbacks) Creative Co., The.

—The NBA: a History of Hoops: Houston Rockets. 2nd ed. 2017. (NBA: a History of Hoops Ser.). (ENG.). 48p. (J). (gr. 5-7). pap. 12.00 ***(978-1-62832-448-8(1)***, Creative Paperbacks) Creative Co., The.

—The NBA: a History of Hoops: Indiana Pacers. 2nd ed. 2017. (NBA: a History of Hoops Ser.). (ENG.). 48p. (J). (gr. 5-7). pap. 12.00 ***(978-1-62832-449-5(X)***, Creative Paperbacks) Creative Co., The.

—The NBA: a History of Hoops: Los Angeles Clippers. 2nd ed. 2017. (NBA: a History of Hoops Ser.). (ENG.). 48p. (J). (gr. 5-7). pap. 12.00 ***(978-1-62832-450-1(3)***, Creative Paperbacks) Creative Co., The.

—The NBA: a History of Hoops: Los Angeles Lakers. 2nd ed. 2017. (NBA: a History of Hoops Ser.). (ENG.). 48p. (J). (gr. 5-7). pap. 12.00 ***(978-1-62832-451-8(1)***, Creative Paperbacks) Creative Co., The.

—The NBA: a History of Hoops: Miami Heat. 2nd ed. 2017. (NBA: a History of Hoops Ser.). (ENG.). 48p. (J). (gr. 5-7). pap. 12.00 ***(978-1-62832-453-2(8)***, Creative Paperbacks) Creative Co., The.

—The NBA: a History of Hoops: Milwaukee Bucks. 2nd ed. 2017. (NBA: a History of Hoops Ser.). (ENG.). 48p. (J). (gr. 5-7). pap. 12.00 ***(978-1-62832-454-9(6)***, Creative Paperbacks) Creative Co., The.

—The NBA: a History of Hoops: the Story of the Atlanta Hawks. 2015. (NBA: a History of Hoops Ser.). (ENG.). 48p. (J). (gr. 5-8). pap. 12.00 *(978-1-62832-008-4(7)*, Creative Paperbacks) Creative Co., The.

—New Orleans Pelicans. 2017. (J). ***(978-1-60818-853-6(1)***, Creative Education) Creative Co., The.

—New York Knicks. 2017. (J). ***(978-1-60818-854-3(X)***, Creative Education) Creative Co., The.

—Oklahoma City Thunder. 2017. (J). ***(978-1-60818-855-0(8)***, Creative Education) Creative Co., The.

—Orlando Magic. 2017. (J). ***(978-1-60818-856-7(6)***, Creative Education) Creative Co., The.

—Philadelphia 76ers. 2017. (J). ***(978-1-60818-857-4(4)***, Creative Education) Creative Co., The.

—Phoenix Suns. 2017. (J). ***(978-1-60818-858-1(2)***, Creative Education) Creative Co., The.

—Portland Trail Blazers. 2017. (J). ***(978-1-60818-859-8(0)***, Creative Education) Creative Co., The.

—Sacramento Kings. 2017. (J). ***(978-1-60818-860-4(4)***, Creative Education) Creative Co., The.

—San Antonio Spurs. 2017. (J). ***(978-1-60818-861-1(2)***, Creative Education) Creative Co., The.

—The Story of the Atlanta Hawks. 2014. (J). *(978-1-60818-422-4(6)*, Creative Education) Creative Co., The.

—The Story of the Boston Celtics. 2014. (J). *(978-1-60818-423-1(4)*, Creative Education) Creative Co., The.

—The Story of the Detroit Pistons. 2014. (J). *(978-1-60818-429-3(3)*, Creative Education) Creative Co., The.

—The Story of the Los Angeles Clippers. 2014. (J). *(978-1-60818-433-0(1)*, Creative Education) Creative Co., The.

—The Story of the Orlando Magic. 2014. (J). *(978-1-60818-443-9(9)*, Creative Education) Creative Co., The.

—The Story of the Pphiladelphia 76ers. 2014. (J). *(978-1-60818-444-6(7)*, Creative Education) Creative Co., The.

—The Story of the Sacramento Kings. 2014. (J). *(978-1-60818-447-7(1)*, Creative Education) Creative Co., The.

—The Story of the Washington Wizards. 2014. (J). *(978-1-60818-451-4(X)*, Creative Education) Creative Co., The.

Williams, Doug. Girls' Basketball, 1 vol. 2013. (Girls' SportsZone Ser.). (ENG., Illus.). 48p. (J). (gr. 3-6). lib. bdg. 32.79 *(978-1-61783-984-9(1)*, SportsZone) ABDO Publishing Co.

Winters, Jaime. Ruling the Court: Basketball's Biggest Wins. 2015. (ENG., Illus.). 32p. (J). *(978-0-7787-1537-5(X))* Crabtree Publishing Co.

Wiseman, Blaine. Basketball. 2011. (J). (gr. 4-6). pap. 13.95 *(978-1-61690-703-7(7)*, AV2 by Weigl); (Illus.). 32p. (YA). (gr. 2-5). 28.55 *(978-1-61690-698-6(7))* Weigl Pubs., Inc.

Woods, Mark & Owen, Ruth. Slam Dunk! 2010. (Top Score Maths Ser.). (Illus.). 32p. pap. *(978-0-237-54278-8(1))* Evans Brothers, Ltd.

Wright, John. Basketball. 2005. (Sports Injuries Ser.). (Illus.). 64p. (YA). lib. bdg. 19.95 *(978-1-59084-627-8(3))* Mason Crest.

Wyatt, James. Basketball. 2012. (On the Team Ser.). (ENG.). 24p. (J). (gr. 2-5). pap. 8.15 *(978-1-4339-6438-1(4))*; lib. bdg. 22.60 *(978-1-4339-6436-7(8))* Stevens, Gareth Publishing LLLP. (Gareth Stevens Learning Library).

Wyner, Zach. Denver Nuggets. 2014. (On the Hardwood Ser.). (gr. 3-8). pap. 8.95 *(978-1-61570-905-2(3))* Scobre Pr. Corp.

—Detroit Pistons. 2014. (On the Hardwood Ser.). (gr. 3-8). 27.93 *(978-1-61570-910-6(X))* Scobre Pr. Corp.

—Golden State Warriors. 2014. (On the Hardwood Ser.). (gr. 3-8). pap. 8.95 *(978-1-61570-913-7(4))* Scobre Pr. Corp.

—Indiana Pacers. 2013. (On the Hardwood Ser.). (ENG., Illus.). 48p. (gr. 3-8). pap. 8.95 *(978-1-61570-836-9(7))* Scobre Pr. Corp.

—Phoenix Suns. 2014. (On the Hardwood Ser.). (gr. 3-8). pap. 8.95 *(978-1-61570-921-2(5))* Scobre Pr. Corp.

Yancey, Diane. Basketball. 2011. (Science Behind Sports Ser.). 128p. (YA). (gr. 7-12). 34.45 *(978-1-4205-0293-0(X))* Cengage Gale.

Young, Jeff C. Burning up the Court - The Miami Heat. 2007. (Sensational Sports Teams Ser.). (Illus.). 128p. (J). (gr. 5). lib. bdg. 34.60 *(978-1-59845-049-1(2)*, MyReportLinks.com Bks.) Enslow Pubs., Inc.

Zuehlke, Jeffrey. Kevin Garnett. 2004. (Amazing Athletes Ser.). (Illus.). 32p. (gr. 2-5). (J). pap. 5.95 *(978-0-8225-2224-9(1))*; (ENG., lib. bdg. 25.26 *(978-0-8225-2429-8(5))* Lerner Publishing Group.

BASKETBALL—BIOGRAPHY

Aaseng, Nathan. Michael Jordan: Hall of Fame Basketball Superstar. (Hall of Fame Sports Greats Ser.). 64p. (J). (gr. 4-9). 2014. pap. 9.95 *(978-1-62285-036-5(X))* 2013. 15.95 *(978-1-62285-035-8(1))* Enslow Pubs., Inc.

Anderson, Jameson. Kevin Durant, 1 vol. 2014. (Awesome Athletes Ser.). (ENG.). 32p. (gr. 8-12). lib. bdg. 27.07 *(978-1-62403-329-2(6)*, Checkerboard Library) ABDO Publishing Co.

Aretha, David. Superstars of the Chicago Bulls. 2015. (Pro Sports Superstars (NBA) Ser.). (ENG.). 24p. (J). (gr. 1-4). 19.95 *(978-1-60753-766-3(4))* Amicus Publishing.

Bailey, Peter. Steve Nash: Most Valuable Player. 2007. (ENG., Illus.). 104p. pap. *(978-1-55168-319-5(9))* Magma.

Basen, Ryan. Dwight Howard: Gifted & Giving Basketball Star. 2010. (Sports Stars Who Give Back Ser.). (Illus.). 128p. (YA). (gr. 5-9). 33.27 *(978-0-7660-3586-7(7))* Enslow Pubs., Inc.

—Steve Nash: Leader on & off the Court. 2007. (Sports Stars with Heart Ser.). (Illus.). 128p. (J). (gr. 5-9). lib. bdg. 33.27 *(978-0-7660-2868-5(2))* Enslow Pubs., Inc.

Bednar, Chuck. Tim Duncan. (Role Model Athletes Ser.). 64p. 2012. (J). (gr. 7). 22.95 *(978-1-4222-2713-8(8))* 2007. (Illus.). (YA). pap. 9.95 *(978-1-4222-0768-0(4))* Mason Crest.

—Tony Parker. (Modern Role Models Ser.). (Illus.). 64p. (YA). 2010. (gr. 7-12). 22.95 *(978-1-4222-0486-3(3))* 2007. pap. 9.95 *(978-1-4222-0774-1(9))* Mason Crest.

Bernstein, Ross. Shaquille O'Neal. rev. ed. 2009. (Amazing Athletes Ser.). (ENG.). 32p. (gr. 2-5). 25.26 *(978-0-7613-4488-9(8))* Lerner Publishing Group.

—Shaquille O'Neal (Revised Edition) 2009. pap. 40.95 *(978-0-7613-4779-8(8))* Lerner Publishing Group.

Beyer, Mark. Larry Bird. 2009. (Basketball Hall of Famers Ser.). 112p. (gr. 5-8). 63.90 *(978-1-61511-534-1(X)*, Rosen Reference) Rosen Publishing Group, Inc., The.

Bodden, Valerie. The Big Time: Kevin Durant. 2014. (Big Time Ser.). (ENG., Illus.). 24p. (J). (gr. 1-3). pap. 9.99 *(978-1-62832-077-0(X)*, Creative Paperbacks) Creative Co., The.

—Kevin Durant. 2015. (J). *(978-1-60818-495-8(1)*, Creative Education) Creative Co., The.

Braun, Eric. Pro Basketball's Underdogs: Players & Teams Who Shocked the Basketball World. 2017. (Sports Shockers! Ser.). (ENG.). 32p. (gr. 3-4). lib. bdg. 27.99 ***(978-1-5157-8046-5(5))*** Capstone Press of Coughlan Cos.

—Stephen Curry. 2017. (Sports All-Stars Ser.). (ENG.). 32p. (J). (gr. 2-5). 12.99 ***(978-1-5124-3796-6(4)***, Lerner Pubns.); 39.99 ***(978-1-5124-2828-5(0)***, Lerner Pubns.); 39.99 ***(978-1-5124-3794-2(8)***, Lerner Pubns.); (Illus.). 26.65 *(978-1-5124-2583-3(4))* Lerner Publishing Group.

Bryant, Howard. Legends: The Best Players, Games, & Teams in Basketball. 2016. (ENG., Illus.). 368p. (J). (gr. 3-7). 17.99 *(978-0-399-16905-2(9)*, Philomel Bks.) Penguin Young Readers Group.

Buckley, James, Jr. Bill Bradley. 2009. (Basketball Hall of Famers Ser.). 112p. (gr. 5-8). 63.90 *(978-1-61511-529-7(3)*, Rosen Reference) Rosen Publishing Group, Inc., The.

Buckley, James. Kevin Durant. 2017. (Amazing Americans: Olympians Ser.). (ENG.). 24p. (J). (gr. -1-3). 17.95 ***(978-1-68402-242-7(8))*** Bearport Publishing Co., Inc.

Byman, Jeremy. Tim Duncan. 2004. (Great Athletes Ser.). (Illus.). 64p. (J). (gr. 5-18). 18.95 *(978-1-883846-43-5(9)*, First Biographies) Reynolds, Morgan Inc.

Christopher, Matt. Blake Griffin. 2015. (Great Americans in Sports Ser.). (J). lib. bdg. 16.00 *(978-0-606-37524-5(4))* Turtleback Bks.

—Great Americans in Sports: Blake Griffin. 2015. (ENG., Illus.). 160p. (J). (gr. 3-7). pap. 5.99 *(978-0-316-29663-2(5))* Little, Brown Bks. for Young Readers.

—Michael Jordan: Legends in Sports. rev. ed. 2008. (ENG., Illus.). 176p. (gr. 3-7). pap. 6.99 *(978-0-316-02380-1(9))* Little, Brown Bks. for Young Readers.

—On the Court with... Dwight Howard. 2010. (ENG., Illus.). 144p. (J). (gr. 3-7). pap. 5.99 *(978-0-316-08480-2(8))* Little, Brown Bks. for Young Readers.

—On the Court with... Lebron James. 2008. (ENG., Illus.). 176p. (J). (gr. 3-7). pap. 6.99 *(978-0-316-01630-8(6))* Little, Brown Bks. for Young Readers.

—On the Court With... Shaquille O'Neil. 2003. (ENG., Illus.). 112p. (J). (gr. 3-7). pap. 16.99 *(978-0-316-16473-3(9))* Little, Brown Bks. for Young Readers.

—On the Court with... Stephen Curry. 2017. (ENG., Illus.). 128p. (J). (gr. 3-7). pap. 6.99 ***(978-0-316-50958-9(2))*** Little, Brown Bks. for Young Readers.

Christopher, Matt. On the Court with... Yao Ming. 2004. (ENG., Illus.). 112p. (J). (gr. 5-8). pap. 15.99 *(978-0-316-73574-2(4)*, Tingley, Megan Bks.) Little, Brown Bks. for Young Readers.

Ciovacco, Justine. LeBron James: NBA Champion. 2015. (Living Legends of Sports Ser.). (ENG., Illus.). 48p. (J). (gr. 5-6). 25.85 *(978-1-68048-104-4(5)*, Britannica Educational Publishing) Rosen Publishing Group, Inc., The.

Clark, Travis. Portland Trail Blazers, 1 vol. 2011. (Inside the NBA Ser.). (ENG., Illus.). 48p. (YA). (gr. 3-6). lib. bdg. 32.79 *(978-1-61783-173-7(5))* ABDO Publishing Co.

—Yao Ming. 2010. (Modern Role Models Ser.). (Illus.). 64p. (YA). (gr. 7-12). lib. bdg. 22.95 *(978-1-4222-0484-9(7))* Mason Crest.

Cohen, Joel H. Oscar Robertson. 2009. (Basketball Hall of Famers Ser.). 112p. (gr. 5-8). 63.90 *(978-1-61511-535-8(8)*, Rosen Reference) Rosen Publishing Group, Inc., The.

Cook, Brian & Tupper, Mark. Brian Cook: An Illini Legend. 2003. (Basketball Superstar Series; Ser.). (Illus.). 96p. (J). pap. 5.95 *(978-1-58261-731-2(7))* Sports Publishing, LLC.

Corporate Contributor. Steve Nash. 2012. (ENG.). 32p. (J). *(978-0-7787-7618-5(2))*; pap. *(978-0-7787-7631-4(X))* Crabtree Publishing Co.

Dakers, Diane. Magic Johnson: Basketball Legend, Entrepreneur, & HIV/AIDS Activist. 2016. (Crabtree Groundbreaker Biographies Ser.). (ENG.). 112p. (J). (gr. 5-8). *(978-0-7787-2608-1(8))* Crabtree Publishing Co.

Damon - Beyond the Glory. l.t. ed. 2003. (Illus.). 152p. per. 14.95 *(978-0-9724033-2-0(9))* Backroads Pr.

Dayton, Connor. Kobe Bryant: NBA Scoring Sensation. 2015. (Living Legends of Sports Ser.). (ENG., Illus.). 48p. (J). (gr. 5-6). 25.85 *(978-1-68048-109-9(6)*, Britannica Educational Publishing) Rosen Publishing Group, Inc., The.

De Medeiros, Michael. Steve Nash. 2011. 24p. (YA). (gr. 2-4). *(978-1-77071-649-0(1))*; pap. *(978-1-77071-653-7(X))* Weigl Educational Pubs. Ltd.

—Steve Nash. 2008. (Remarkable People Ser.). (Illus.). 24p. (J). (gr. 4-6). pap. 8.95 *(978-1-59036-991-3(2))*; lib. bdg. 24.45 *(978-1-59036-990-6(4))* Weigl Pubs., Inc.

DiPrimio, Pete. Jeremy Lin. 2012. (J). lib. bdg. 25.70 *(978-1-61228-403-3(5))* Mitchell Lane Pubs., Inc.

Doeden, Matt. Basketball Legends in the Making, 1 vol. 2014. (Legends in the Making Ser.). (ENG.). 32p. (gr. 3-4). lib. bdg. 27.99 *(978-1-4765-4063-4(2))* Capstone Press of Coughlan Cos.

—Dwyane Wade: Basketball Superstar, 1 vol. 2014. (Superstar Athletes Ser.). (ENG.). 24p. (gr. 1-2). pap. 7.29 *(978-1-4765-9429-3(5))*; lib. bdg. 25.32 *(978-1-4765-8599-4(7))* Capstone Press of Coughlan Cos.

—Jeremy Lin: Basketball Superstar. 2012. (Superstar Athletes Ser.). (ENG.). 24p. (gr. 1-2). pap. 41.70 *(978-1-62065-628-0(0))*; (Illus.). pap. 7.29 *(978-1-62065-627-3(2))*; (Illus.). lib. bdg. 25.32 *(978-1-62065-626-6(4))* Capstone Press of Coughlan Cos.

—Kevin Durant: Basketball Superstar, 1 vol. 2012. (Superstar Athletes Ser.). (ENG.). 24p. (gr. 1-2). pap. 7.29 *(978-1-4296-8004-2(0))*; lib. bdg. 25.32 *(978-1-4296-7682-3(5))* Capstone Press of Coughlan Cos.

—Russell Westbrook. 2017. (Sports All-Stars Ser.). (ENG.). 32p. (J). (gr. 2-5). 12.99 ***(978-1-5124-3792-8(1)***, Lerner Pubns.); 39.99 ***(978-1-5124-3791-1(3)***, Lerner Pubns.); 39.99 ***(978-1-5124-2827-8(2)***, Lerner Pubns.); (Illus.). 26.65 *(978-1-5124-2581-9(8))* Lerner Publishing Group.

—Wilt Chamberlain. 2010. (Sports Heroes & Legends Ser.). (ENG.). 120p. (gr. 5-12). lib. bdg. 30.60 *(978-0-7613-5369-0(0))* Lerner Publishing Group.

—The World's Greatest Basketball Players, 1 vol. 2010. (World's Greatest Sports Stars (Sports Illustrated for Kids) Ser.). (ENG.). 32p. (gr. 2-3). pap. 8.95 *(978-1-4296-4869-1(4))*; pap. 53.70 *(978-1-4296-5103-5(2))*; lib. bdg. 27.99 *(978-1-4296-3923-1(7))* Capstone Press of Coughlan Cos.

—Yao Ming. 2009. (Sports Heroes & Legends Ser.). (ENG.). 120p. (gr. 5-12). 30.60 *(978-0-7613-4227-4(3))* Lerner Publishing Group.

Dunn, Mary R. & Davin, Rose. Candace Parker. 2016. (Women in Sports Ser.). (ENG., Illus.). 24p. (gr. k-1). lib. bdg. 26.65 *(978-1-4914-7975-9(2)*, Pebble Plus) Capstone Press of Coughlan Cos.

Edwards, Ethan. Blake Griffin: Basketball's Slam Dunk King, 1 vol., 1. 2014. (All-Star Players Ser.). (ENG.). 32p. (J). (gr. 3-6). 26.25 *(978-1-4777-2913-7(5)*, PowerKids Pr.) Rosen Publishing Group, Inc., The.

—Chris Paul: Basketball's CP3, 1 vol., 1. 2014. (All-Star Players Ser.). (ENG.). 32p. (J). (gr. 3-6). 26.25 *(978-1-4777-2912-0(7)*, PowerKids Pr.) Rosen Publishing Group, Inc., The.

—Meet Kevin Garnett: Basketball's Big Ticket. 2009. (All-Star Players Ser.). 32p. (gr. 4-5). 47.90 *(978-1-61511-287-6(1)*, PowerKids Pr.) Rosen Publishing Group, Inc., The.

—Meet Steve Nash: Basketball's Ultimate Team Player. 2009. (All-Star Players Ser.). 32p. (gr. 4-5). 47.90 *(978-1-61511-295-1(2)*, PowerKids Pr.) Rosen Publishing Group, Inc., The.

Ervin, Phil. Maya Moore: WNBA Champion, 1 vol. 2016. (ENG., Illus.). 32p. (J). *(978-1-62403-840-2(9)*, 1391429, SportsZone) ABDO Publishing Co.

Fedorko, Jamie. Charles Barkley. (Sharing the American Dream Ser.). 64p. (YA). (gr. 7-12). 2009. 22.95 *(978-1-4222-0576-1(2))* 2007. pap. 9.95 *(978-1-4222-0737-6(4))* Mason Crest.

—Kevin Garnett. (Sharing the American Dream Ser.). 64p. (YA). (gr. 7-12). 2009. (Illus.). 22.95 *(978-1-4222-0575-4(4))* 2007. pap. 9.95 *(978-1-4222-0746-8(3))* Mason Crest.

Feinstein, Stephen. LeBron James. 2008. (African-American Heroes Ser.). (Illus.). 24p. (J). (gr. 1-3). lib. bdg. 22.60 *(978-0-7660-2898-2(4)*, Enslow Elementary) Enslow Pubs., Inc.

Fishman, Jon. Blake Griffin. 2014. (Amazing Athletes Ser.). (ENG., Illus.). 32p. (gr. 2-5). pap. 7.95 *(978-1-4677-4580-2(4))* Lerner Publishing Group.

—Derrick Rose. 2014. (Amazing Athletes Ser.). (Illus.). 32p. (gr. 2-5). lib. bdg. 25.26 *(978-1-4677-3677-0(5)*, Lerner Pubns.) Lerner Publishing Group.

Fishman, Jon M. Anthony Davis. 2015. (Amazing Athletes Ser.). (ENG., Illus.). 32p. (gr. 2-5). pap. 7.95 *(978-1-4677-9369-8(8))* Lerner Publishing Group.

—Blake Griffin. 2014. (Amazing Athletes Ser.). (ENG.). 32p. (gr. 2-5). lib. bdg. 25.26 *(978-1-4677-4505-5(7)*, Lerner Pubns.) Lerner Publishing Group.

—Carmelo Anthony. 2013. (Amazing Athletes Ser.). (ENG., Illus.). 32p. (gr. 2-5). pap. 7.95 *(978-1-4677-2063-2(1))*; lib. bdg. 25.26 *(978-1-4677-2062-5(3)*, Lerner Pubns.) Lerner Publishing Group.

—James Harden. 2015. (Amazing Athletes Ser.). (ENG., Illus.). 32p. (gr. 2-5). pap. 7.95 *(978-1-4677-8113-8(4))*; (J). 26.65 *(978-1-4677-7922-7(9)*, Lerner Pubns.) Lerner Publishing Group.

—John Wall. 2015. (Amazing Athletes Ser.). (ENG., Illus.). 32p. (J). (gr. 2-5). pap. 7.95 *(978-1-4677-9405-3(8))* Lerner Publishing Group.

—Kevin Durant. 2017. (Sports All-Stars Ser.). (ENG.). 32p. (J). (gr. 2-5). 26.65 ***(978-1-5124-3453-8(1))*** Lerner Publishing Group.

—Kyrie Irving. 2016. (Amazing Athletes Ser.). (ENG., Illus.). 32p. (J). (gr. 2-5). lib. bdg. 26.65 *(978-1-5124-1336-6(4)*, Lerner Pubns.) Lerner Publishing Group.

—LeBron James. 2017. (Sports All-Stars Ser.). (ENG.). 32p. (J). (gr. 2-5). pap. 8.99 ***(978-1-5124-5617-2(9))***; (Illus.). 26.65 ***(978-1-5124-3452-1(3)***, Lerner Pubns.) Lerner Publishing Group.

Fishman, Jon M. Stephen Curry. 2015. (Amazing Athletes Ser.). (ENG., Illus.). 32p. (J). (gr. 2-5). pap. 7.95 *(978-1-4677-8112-1(6)*, Lerner Pubns.) Lerner Publishing Group.

Forest, Christopher. Side-By-Side Basketball Stars: Comparing Pro Basketball's Greatest Players, 1 vol. 2014. (Side-By-Side Sports Ser.). (ENG.). 48p. (gr. 4-6). lib. bdg. 27.99 *(978-1-4765-6164-6(8))* Capstone Press of Coughlan Cos.

Frisaro, Joe. Reggie Miller: From Downtown. 2003. (Superstar Ser.: Vol. 6). (Illus.). 96p. (gr. 4-7). pap. 4.95 *(978-1-58261-180-8(7))* Sports Publishing, LLC.

Frisch, Aaron. Lebron James. 2013. (Illus.). 24p. (J). 25.65 *(978-1-60818-337-1(8)*, Creative Education) Creative Co., The.

Frisch, Aaron & Bodden, Valerie. The Big Time: Lebron James. 2014. (Big Time Ser.). (ENG.). 24p. (J). (gr. 1-3). pap. 9.99 *(978-1-62832-063-3(X)*, Creative Paperbacks) Creative Co., The.

Gatto, Kimberly. Kevin Garnett: A Basketball Star Who Cares. 2011. (Sports Stars Who Care Ser.). (Illus.). 48p. (J). (gr. 3-18). pap. 8.95 *(978-1-59845-230-3(4)*, Enslow Elementary); (gr. 2-5). lib. bdg. 25.27 *(978-0-7660-3772-4(X))* Enslow Pubs., Inc.

—LeBron James: A Basketball Star Who Cares. 2011. (Sports Stars Who Care Ser.). (Illus.). 48p. (J). (gr. 3-18). pap. 8.95 *(978-1-59845-231-0(2)*, Enslow Elementary); (gr. 2-5). lib. bdg. 25.27 *(978-0-7660-3776-2(2))* Enslow Pubs., Inc.

Gerstner, Joanne C. Toronto Raptors, 1 vol. 2011. (Inside the NBA Ser.). (ENG., Illus.). 48p. (J). (gr. 3-6). lib. bdg. 32.79 *(978-1-61783-176-8(X))* ABDO Publishing Co.

Gilliam, Nancy, creator. LeBron James: King of the Court Companion Study Guide. 2005. 94p. (YA). pap. 10.00 *(978-0-9771113-0-5(X)*, SpringTree) Forest Hill Publishing, LLC.

Gitlin, Martin. Dirk Nowitzki: NBA Champion, 1 vol. 2012. (Playmakers Ser.). (ENG.). 32p. (J). (gr. 3-6). 27.07 *(978-1-61783-292-5(8))* ABDO Publishing Co.

—Jeremy Lin: Basketball Phenom, 1 vol. 2012. (Playmakers Set 3 Ser.). (ENG.). 32p. (J). (gr. 2-6). lib. bdg. 27.07 *(978-1-61783-548-3(X)*, SportsZone) ABDO Publishing Co.

—Kevin Durant: NBA Superstar, 1 vol. 2012. (Playmakers Set 3 Ser.). (ENG.). 32p. (J). (gr. 2-6). lib. bdg. 27.07 *(978-1-61783-547-6(1)*, SportsZone) ABDO Publishing Co.

—Kobe Bryant: NBA Champion, 1 vol. 2011. (Playmakers Ser.). (ENG., Illus.). 32p. (YA). (gr. 3-6). 27.07 *(978-1-61714-744-9(3))* ABDO Publishing Co.

—Los Angeles Lakers, 1 vol. 2011. (Inside the NBA Ser.). (ENG., Illus.). 48p. (YA). (gr. 3-6). lib. bdg. 32.79 *(978-1-61783-161-4(1))* ABDO Publishing Co.

—Memphis Grizzlies, 1 vol. 2011. (Inside the NBA Ser.). (ENG., Illus.). 48p. (YA). (gr. 3-6). lib. bdg. 32.79 *(978-1-61783-162-1(X))* ABDO Publishing Co.

Gitlin, Marty. Carmelo Anthony. 2015. (Basketball Heroes Making a Difference Ser.). (ENG.). 24p. (J). (gr. 1-6). lib. bdg. 23.93 *(978-1-62724-546-3(4))* Bearport Publishing Co., Inc.

—Chris Paul. 2015. (Basketball Heroes Making a Difference Ser.). (ENG.). 24p. (J). (gr. 1-6). lib. bdg. 23.93 *(978-1-62724-547-0(2))* Bearport Publishing Co., Inc.

—Kevin Durant: Basketball Star. 2017. (Biggest Names in Sports (paperback) Ser.). (ENG., Illus.). 32p. (J). (gr. 4-7). pap. 9.95 ***(978-1-63517-096-2(6)***, Focus Readers) North Star Editions.

Gitlin, Marty. Kevin Love. 2015. (Basketball Heroes Making a Difference Ser.). (ENG.). 24p. (J). (gr. 1-6). lib. bdg. 23.93 *(978-1-62724-548-7(0))* Bearport Publishing Co., Inc.

Glaser, Jason. Tim Duncan. 2009. (Sports Idols Ser.). 24p. (gr. 2-3). 42.50 *(978-1-60853-144-8(9)*, PowerKids Pr.) Rosen Publishing Group, Inc., The.

Graves, Will. Basketball Record Breakers, 1 vol. 2016. (ENG., Illus.). 48p. (J). ***(978-1-62403-846-4(8)***, SportsZone) ABDO Publishing Co.

Gregory, Josh. Blake Griffin. 2014. (Basketball Heroes Making a Difference Ser.). 24p. (J). (gr. 1-6). lib. bdg. 23.93 *(978-1-62724-081-9(0))* Bearport Publishing Co., Inc.

—Lebron James. 2014. (Basketball Heroes Making a Difference Ser.). 24p. (J). (gr. 1-6). lib. bdg. 23.93 *(978-1-62724-082-6(9))* Bearport Publishing Co., Inc.

Hammer, Max. Superstars of the Miami Heat. 2015. (Pro Sports Superstars (NBA) Ser.). (ENG., Illus.). 24p. (J). (gr. 1-4). 19.95 *(978-1-60753-770-0(2))* Amicus Publishing.

—Superstars of the Oklahoma City Thunder. (Illus.). 24p. (J). 2016. pap. *(978-1-68152-022-3(2))* 2015. (ENG., (gr. 1-4). 19.95 *(978-1-60753-768-7(0))* Amicus Publishing.

Hammer, Maxwell. LeBron James: NBA MVP & Champion. 2015. (Today's MVPs & Champions Ser.). (ENG.). 24p. (J). (gr. 2-5). 27.07 *(978-1-63143-737-3(2)*, 208571) Child's World, Inc., The.

Harasymiw, Malcolm J. Dwight Howard: Emerging Basketball Superstar. 2010. (Inspiring Lives Ser.). (Illus.). 32p. (J). (gr. 5-8). pap. 10.50 *(978-1-4339-3641-8(0))*; lib. bdg. 25.25 *(978-1-4339-3640-1(2)*, 1309369) Stevens, Gareth Publishing LLLP.

Hareas, John. NBA Slam Dunk 3-D. 2006. (J). pap. *(978-0-439-78814-4(5))* Scholastic, Inc.

Hareas, John & Smallwood, John. Steve Nash. 2008. (NBA Reader Ser.). (ENG., Illus.). 32p. (J). (gr. 2-5). pap. 3.99 *(978-0-545-03411-1(6)*, Scholastic) Scholastic, Inc.

Hasday, Judy L. Michael Jordan. 2012. (Role Model Athletes Ser.). 64p. (J). (gr. 7). 22.95 *(978-1-4222-2711-4(1))* Mason Crest.

Hayhurst, Chris. Bill Russell. 2009. (Basketball Hall of Famers Ser.). 112p. (gr. 5-8). 63.90 *(978-1-61511-530-3(7)*, Rosen Reference) Rosen Publishing Group, Inc., The.

Hill, Anne E. Lebron James: King of Shots. 2012. (USA TODAY Lifeline Biographies Ser.). (ENG., Illus.). 112p. (gr. 6-12). lib. bdg. 34.60 *(978-0-7613-8641-4(6))* Lerner Publishing Group.

Hill, Z. B. Players & the Game Around the World. 2014. (Superstars in the World of Basketball Ser.: 10). 48p. (J). (gr. 5-18). 20.95 *(978-1-4222-3110-4(0))* Mason Crest.

Hoblin, Paul. Carmelo Anthony: Superstar Scorer, 1 vol. 2012. (Playmakers Ser.). (ENG.). 32p. (J). (gr. 3-6). 27.07 *(978-1-61783-289-5(8))* ABDO Publishing Co.

—Derrick Rose: NBA's Youngest MVP, 1 vol. 2012. (Playmakers Ser.). (ENG.). 32p. (J). (gr. 3-6). 27.07 *(978-1-61783-296-3(0))* ABDO Publishing Co.

—Superstars of the New York Knicks. 2015. (Pro Sports Superstars (NBA) Ser.). (ENG., Illus.). 24p. (J). (gr. 1-4). 19.95 *(978-1-60753-771-7(0))* Amicus Publishing.

—Superstars of the San Antonio Spurs. 2015. (Pro Sports Superstars (NBA) Ser.). (ENG., Illus.). 24p. (J). (gr. 1-4). 19.95 *(978-1-60753-772-4(9))* Amicus Publishing.

Hoffman, Mary Ann. Dwayne Wade: Basketball Star. (Sports Superstars Ser.). 24p. (gr. 1-1). 2009. 42.50 *(978-1-60853-176-9(7)*, PowerKids Pr.) 2007. (Illus.). (J). lib. bdg. 22.60 *(978-1-4042-3536-6(1))* Rosen Publishing Group, Inc., The.

—Dwayne Wade: Basketball Star/Estrella del Baloncesto. 2009. (Amazing Athletes/Atletas increíbles Ser.). (ENG & SPA.). 24p. (gr. 1-2). 42.50 *(978-1-61511-305-7(3)*, Editorial Buenas Letras) Rosen Publishing Group, Inc., The.

—Dwayne Wade: Basketball Star/Estrella del Baloncesto. Alaman, Eduardo, tr. 2007. (Amazing Athletes/Atletas increíbles Ser.). (SPA., Illus.). 24p. (J). (gr. 2-5). lib. bdg. 22.60 *(978-1-4042-7602-4(5))* Rosen Publishing Group, Inc., The.

—Lebron James: Basketball Star. 2007. (Sports Superstars Ser.). (Illus.). 24p. (J). (gr. 1-3). lib. bdg. 22.60 *(978-1-4042-3535-9(3))* Rosen Publishing Group, Inc., The.

—Lebron James: Basketball Star/Estrella del Baloncesto. Alaman, Eduardo, tr. from ENG. 2007. (Amazing Athletes/Atletas increíbles Ser.). (SPA & ENG., Illus.). 24p. (J). (gr. 2-5). lib. bdg. 22.60 *(978-1-4042-7600-0(9))* Rosen Publishing Group, Inc., The.

Howell, Brian. Duke Blue Devils, 1 vol. 2012. (Inside College Basketball Set 1 Ser.). (ENG.). 48p. lib. bdg. 32.79 *(978-1-61783-281-9(2)*, SportsZone) ABDO Publishing Co.

—LeBron James: Basketball Icon, 1 vol. 2011. (Playmakers Ser.). (ENG., Illus.). 32p. (J). (gr. 3-6). 27.07 *(978-1-61714-746-3(X))* ABDO Publishing Co.

Indovino, Shaina Carmel. Blake Griffin. 2014. (Superstars in the World of Basketball Ser.: 10). 48p. (J). (gr. 5-18). 20.95 *(978-1-4222-3102-9(X))* Mason Crest.

—Dwight Howard. 2014. (Superstars in the World of Basketball Ser.: 10). 48p. (J). (gr. 5-18). 20.95 *(978-1-4222-3105-0(4))* Mason Crest.

—Kevin Durant. 2014. (Superstars in the World of Basketball Ser.: 10). 48p. (J). (gr. 5-18). 20.95 *(978-1-4222-3107-4(0))* Mason Crest.

—Lebron James. 2014. (Superstars in the World of Basketball Ser.: 10). 48p. (J). (gr. 5-18). 20.95 *(978-1-4222-3109-8(7))* Mason Crest.

Jackson, Aurelia. Carmelo Anthony. 2014. (J). *(978-1-4222-3101-2(1))* Mason Crest.

—Chris Paul. 2014. (Superstars in the World of Basketball Ser.: 10). 48p. (J). (gr. 5-18). 20.95 *(978-1-4222-3104-3(6))* Mason Crest.

—Dwyane Wade. 2014. (Superstars in the World of Basketball Ser.: 10). 48p. (J). (gr. 5-18). 20.95 *(978-1-4222-3106-7(2))* Mason Crest.

James, Lebron, et al. Lebron James. 2015. (Quotes from the Greatest Athletes Ser.). (ENG., Illus.). 24p. (J). lib. bdg. 28.55 *(978-1-4896-3360-6(X)*, AV2 by Weigl) Weigl Pubs., Inc.

Jordan, Michael. Michael Jordan. 2015. (Quotes from the Greatest Athletes Ser.). (ENG., Illus.). 24p. (J). lib. bdg. 28.55 *(978-1-4896-3368-2(5)*, 1393457, AV2 by Weigl) Weigl Pubs., Inc.

Kampff, Joseph. Kobe Bryant: All-Star Shooting Guard. 2016. (Exceptional African Americans Ser.). (ENG.). 24p. (J). (gr. 3-3). pap. 9.35 *(978-0-7660-7256-5(8))*; (Illus.). 22.60 *(978-0-7660-7258-9(4))* Enslow Pubs., Inc.

Kavanagh, Jack. Larry Bird: Hall of Fame Basketball Superstar. (Hall of Fame Sports Greats Ser.). 64p. (J). (gr. 4-9). 2014. pap. 9.95 *(978-1-62285-031-0(9))* 2013. 15.95 *(978-1-62285-030-3(0))* Enslow Pubs., Inc.

Kelley, K. C. Basketball Superstars 2015. 2014. (ENG.). 32p. (J). (gr. 1-3). pap. 5.99 *(978-0-545-80858-3(8)*, Scholastic Paperbacks) Scholastic, Inc.

—Basketball Superstars 2017. 2016. (ENG.). 32p. (J). (gr. 1-3). pap. 5.99 *(978-1-338-09865-5(9))* Scholastic, Inc.

Kennedy, Mike. Lebron James. 2009. (People We Should Know Ser.). 32p. (gr. 3-5). (J). lib. bdg. 31.00 *(978-1-4339-0016-7(5))*; pap. 10.50 *(978-1-4339-0161-4(7))* Stevens, Gareth Publishing LLLP. (Gareth Stevens Learning Library).

Kimmich, Ian. Steve Nash. (Role Model Athletes Ser.). (Illus.). 64p. (YA). 2010. (gr. 7-12). 22.95 *(978-1-4222-0485-6(5))* 2007. pap. 9.95 *(978-1-4222-0773-4(0))* Mason Crest.

Kirkpatrick, Rob. Grant Hill: Basketball All-Star. (Power Players Ser.). 24p. (gr. 1-1). 2009. 42.50 *(978-1-60851-328-4(9))* 2003. (Illus.). (J). lib. bdg. 17.25 *(978-0-8239-5538-1(9))* Rosen Publishing Group, Inc., The. (PowerKids Pr.).

—Grant Hill: Basketball Star/Estrella del Basketball. 2009. (Power Players / Deportistas de Poder Ser.). (ENG & SPA.). 24p. (gr. 1-2). 42.50 *(978-1-60851-330-7(0)*, Editorial Buenas Letras) Rosen Publishing Group, Inc., The.

—Grant Hill: Estrella del Basketball (Basketball All-Star) 2009. (Deportistas de Poder (Power Players) Ser.). (SPA.). 24p. (gr. 1-1). 42.50 *(978-1-61512-157-1(9)*, Editorial Buenas Letras) Rosen Publishing Group, Inc., The.

—Kobe Bryant: Campeón de Slam Dunk (Slam Dunk Champion) 2009. (Deportistas de Poder (Power Players) Ser.). (SPA.). 24p. (gr. 1-1). 42.50 *(978-1-61512-158-8(7)*, Editorial Buenas Letras) Rosen Publishing Group, Inc., The.

—Kobe Bryant: Slam Dunk Champion / Campeón de Slam Dunk. 2009. (Power Players / Deportistas de Poder Ser.). (ENG & SPA.). 24p. (gr. 1-2). 42.50 *(978-1-60851-331-4(9)*, Editorial Buenas Letras) Rosen Publishing Group, Inc., The.

—Kobe Bryant, Slam Dunk Champion/Campeon del Slam Dunk. De Leon, Mauricio Velzaquez, tr. 2008. (Reading Power Ser.). (ENG., Illus.). 24p. (gr. 1-6). pap. 8.85 *(978-1-4042-7544-7(4))* Rosen Publishing Group, Inc., The.

—Michael Jordan: Basketball Superstar. 2009. (Great Record Breakers in Sports Ser.). 24p. (gr. 3-3). 42.50 *(978-1-61513-190-7(6)*, PowerKids Pr.) Rosen Publishing Group, Inc., The.

Kirkpatrick, Robert. Bob Cousy. 2009. (Basketball Hall of Famers Ser.). 112p. (gr. 5-8). 63.90 *(978-1-61511-531-0(5)*, Rosen Reference) Rosen Publishing Group, Inc., The.

Kneib, Martha. Kareem Abdul-Jabbar. 2009. (Basketball Hall of Famers Ser.). 112p. (gr. 5-8). 63.90 *(978-1-61511-533-4(1)*, Rosen Reference) Rosen Publishing Group, Inc., The.

Kramer, S. A. Basketball's Greatest Players. 2015. (Step into Reading Ser.). (ENG., Illus.). 48p. (J). (gr. 2-4). pap. 3.99 *(978-0-553-53394-1(0)*, Random Hse. Bks. for Young Readers) Random Hse. Children's Bks.

Krawiec, Richard. Yao Ming: Gentle Giant of Basketball. 2003. (Avisson Young Adult Ser.). (Illus.). 108p. (J). 19.95 *(978-1-888105-63-6(1))* Avisson Pr., Inc.

Labrecque, Ellen. Magic Johnson. 2007. (21st Century Skills Library: Life Skills Biographies Ser.). (ENG.). 48p. (gr. 4-8). lib. bdg. 31.36 *(978-1-60279-071-1(X)*, 200044) Cherry Lake Publishing.

Latta, Sara L. Who Invented Basketball? James Naismith. 2012. (I Like Inventors! Ser.). (Illus.). 24p. (J). (gr. k-3). pap. 7.95 *(978-1-4644-0131-2(4)*, Enslow Elementary) Enslow Pubs., Inc.

LeBoutillier, Nate. Basketball. 2012. (J). 35.65 *(978-1-60818-208-4(8)*, Creative Education) Creative Co., The.

Lohre, Mike. Six Degrees of Lebron James: Connecting Basketball Stars. 2015. (Six Degrees of Sports Ser.). (ENG.). 48p. (gr. 3-4). lib. bdg. 31.99 *(978-1-4914-2144-4(4))* Capstone Press of Coughlan Cos.

Macnow, Glen. Sports Great Allen Iverson. 2003. (Sports Great Bks.). (Illus.). 64p. (J). (gr. 4-10). lib. bdg. 22.60 *(978-0-7660-2063-4(0))* Enslow Pubs., Inc.

MacRae, Sloan. Carmelo Anthony. 2012. (Sports Heroes Ser.). (ENG., Illus.). 24p. (J). (gr. 3-6). pap. 8.25 *(978-1-4488-6278-8(7))*; lib. bdg. 22.60 *(978-1-4488-6160-6(8))* Rosen Publishing Group, Inc., The. (PowerKids Pr.).

—The Los Angeles Lakers. (J). 2010. pap. 8.25 *(978-1-4358-3398-2(8))* 2009. (Illus.). 24p. lib. bdg. 22.60 *(978-1-4042-8132-5(0))* Rosen Publishing Group, Inc., The. (PowerKids Pr.).

—Meet Dirk Nowitzki: Basketball's Blond Bomber. 2009. (All-Star Players Ser.). 32p. (gr. 4-6). (Illus.). (J). pap. 10.00 *(978-1-4358-3101-8(2))*; 47.90 *(978-1-61511-280-7(4))* Rosen Publishing Group, Inc., The. (PowerKids Pr.).

—Meet Tony Parker: Basketball's Famous Point Guard. 2009. (Illus.). 32p. (J). (gr. 4-6). pap. 10.00 *(978-1-4358-3102-5(0))*; 32p. (gr. 4-5). 47.90 *(978-1-61511-297-5(9))*; (J). lib. bdg. 25.25 *(978-1-4358-2710-3(4))* Rosen Publishing Group, Inc., The. (PowerKids Pr.).

—Rajon Rondo. 2012. (Sports Heroes Ser.). (ENG.). 24p. (J). (gr. 3-6). lib. bdg. 22.60 *(978-1-4488-6165-1(9)*, PowerKids Pr.) Rosen Publishing Group, Inc., The.

—The San Antonio Spurs. (J). 2010. pap. 8.25 *(978-1-4358-3400-2(3))* 2009. (Illus.). 24p. lib. bdg. 22.60 *(978-1-4042-8133-2(9))* Rosen Publishing Group, Inc., The. (PowerKids Pr.).

Macy, Sue. Basketball Belles: How Two Teams & One Scrappy Player Put Women's Hoops on the Map. Collins, Matt & Matt, Collins, illus. 2011. (ENG.). 32p. (J). (gr. 1-5). 17.95 *(978-0-8234-2163-3(5))* Holiday Hse., Inc.

Magic Johnson: Athlete. 2010. (Black Americans of Achievement Legacy Edition Ser.). (Illus.). 120p. (gr. 6-12). 35.00 *(978-1-60413-684-5(7))* Facts On File, Inc.

Martin, Annabelle T. Superstars of the Boston Celtics. 2015. (Pro Sports Superstars (NBA) Ser.). (ENG., Illus.). 24p. (J). (gr. 1-4). 19.95 *(978-1-60753-765-6(6))* Amicus Publishing.

—Superstars of the Cleveland Cavaliers. 2015. (Pro Sports Superstars (NBA) Ser.). (ENG.). 24p. (J). (gr. 1-4). 19.95 *(978-1-60753-767-0(2))* Amicus Publishing.

—Superstars of the Los Angeles Lakers. 2015. (Pro Sports Superstars (NBA) Ser.). (ENG., Illus.). 24p. (J). (gr. 1-4). 19.95 *(978-1-60753-769-4(9))* Amicus Publishing.

Martin, Isabel. Jackie Robinson, 1 vol. 2014. (Great African-Americans Ser.). (ENG., Illus.). 24p. (J). (gr. k-1). pap. 5.95 *(978-1-4914-0508-6(2)*, Pebble Bks.) Capstone Press of Coughlan Cos.

Marvis, Barbara. Day by Day with Lebron James. 2010. (Randy's Corner Ser.). (Illus.). 32p. (YA). (gr. -1-2). lib. bdg. 25.70 *(978-1-58415-858-5(1))* Mitchell Lane Pubs., Inc.

Mattern, Joanne. Dwight Howard: Basketball Superstar, 1 vol. 2011. (Superstar Athletes Ser.). (ENG.). 24p. (gr. 1-2). lib. bdg. 25.32 *(978-1-4296-6563-6(7))* Capstone Press of Coughlan Cos.

—James Harden. 2017. lib. bdg. 25.70 ***(978-1-68020-122-2(0))*** Mitchell Lane Pubs., Inc.

Mattern, Joanne. LeBron James: Basketball Superstar, 1 vol. 2011. (Superstar Athletes Ser.). (ENG.). 24p. (gr. 1-2). pap. 7.29 *(978-1-4296-7309-9(5))*; pap. 41.70 *(978-1-4296-7310-5(9))*; lib. bdg. 25.32 *(978-1-4296-6562-9(9))* Capstone Press of Coughlan Cos.

Maurer, Tracy Nelson. LeBron James. 2015. (Famous Athletes Ser.). (ENG., Illus.). 24p. (gr. k-1). lib. bdg. 26.65 *(978-1-4914-6236-2(1))* Capstone Press of Coughlan Cos.

Miller, Ray. Shaquille O'Neal. 2003. (Stars of Sports Ser.). (ENG., Illus.). 48p. (J). 27.50 *(978-0-7377-1422-7(0)*, Kidhaven) Cengage Gale.

Miller, Raymond H. Kobe Bryant. 2003. (Stars of Sports Ser.). (ENG., Illus.). 48p. (J). 27.50 *(978-0-7377-1538-5(3)*, Greenhaven Pr., Inc.) Cengage Gale.

Mosenson, Cecil. Work Hard-Never Give Up. 2011. 32p. pap. 24.95 *(978-1-61582-829-6(X))* America Star Bks.

Murray, Laura K. Stephen Curry. 2016. (Illus.). (J). *(978-1-60818-672-3(5)*, Creative Education) Creative Co., The.

—Stephen Curry: The Big Time. 2016. (Big Time Ser.). (ENG.). 24p. (J). (gr. 1-3). pap. 9.99 *(978-1-62832-268-2(3)*, Creative Paperbacks) Creative Co., The.

Nagelhout, Ryan. Kevin Durant: Champion Basketball Star. 2017. (Sports Star Champions Ser.). 48p. (J). (gr. 5-6). lib. bdg. 27.93 ***(978-0-7660-8692-0(5))*** Enslow Pubs., Inc.

Nagelhout, Ryan & Wallace Sharp, Anne. Lebron James: Basketball's King. 2017. (People in the News Ser.). 104p. (YA). (gr. 7-7). lib. bdg. 39.40 ***(978-1-5345-6029-1(7)***, Lucent Pr.) Greenhaven Publishing LLC.

Norwich, Grace. I Am #12: Lebron James. 2014. (I Am Ser.: 12). (ENG.). 128p. (J). (gr. 3-7). pap. 5.99 *(978-0-545-67350-1(X)*, Scholastic Paperbacks) Scholastic, Inc.

—I Am Lebron James. Simon, Ute, illus. 2014. 127p. (J). *(978-0-545-79428-2(5))* Scholastic, Inc.

Offutt, Jason. Helen Stephens: The Fulton Flash. Hare, John, illus. 2014. (ENG.). 48p. (J). lib. bdg. 24.00 *(978-1-61248-114-2(0))* Truman State Univ. Pr.

Omoth, Tyler. Who's Who of Pro Basketball: A Guide to the Game's Greatest Players. 2015. (Who's Who of Pro Sports Ser.). (ENG., Illus.). 32p. (gr. 3-4). lib. bdg. 27.99 *(978-1-62065-926-7(3))* Capstone Press of Coughlan Cos.

Osier, Dan. Kevin Garnett. 2011. (Basketball's MVPs Ser.). 24p. (J). (ENG.). pap. 8.85 *(978-1-4488-2636-0(5)*, PowerKids Pr.); (ENG & SPA., Illus.). (gr. 3-6). 22.60 *(978-1-4488-3206-4(3))*; (Illus.). (gr. 3-6). lib. bdg. 22.60 *(978-1-4488-2526-4(1)*, PowerKids Pr.) Rosen Publishing Group, Inc., The.

—LeBron James. 2011. (Basketball's MVPs Ser.). (Illus.). 24p. (J). pap. 8.85 *(978-1-4488-2629-2(2))*; (gr. 3-6). 22.60 *(978-1-4488-2522-6(9))* Rosen Publishing Group, Inc., The. (PowerKids Pr.).

—Steve Nash. 2011. (Basketball's MVPs Ser.). 24p. (J). (ENG.). pap. 8.85 *(978-1-4488-2634-6(9))*; (Illus.). (gr. 3-6). lib. bdg. 22.60 *(978-1-4488-2525-7(3))* Rosen Publishing Group, Inc., The. (PowerKids Pr.).

Peterson, Megan Cooley. Basketball's Great Players. 2017. (Rank It! Ser.). (ENG., Illus.). 32p. (J). (gr. 3-7). 31.35 ***(978-1-68072-059-4(7)***, Bolt) Black Rabbit Bks.

Porterfield, Jason. Calvin Hill & Grant Hill: One Family's Legacy in Football & Basketball. 2010. (Sports Families Ser.). (Illus.). 48p. (ENG.). (J). pap. 11.75 *(978-1-4358-8516-5(3)*, Rosen Reference); (YA). (gr. 4-7). lib. bdg. 29.25 *(978-1-4358-3549-8(2))* Rosen Publishing Group, Inc., The.

—Calvin Hill & Grant Hill: One Family's Legacy in Football & Basketball (Sports Families) l.t. ed. 2012. 96p. pap. *(978-1-4596-3352-0(0))* ReadHowYouWant.com, Ltd.

Quinlan, Don. Rick Hansen: Larger Than Life, 1 vol. 2013. (ENG.). 64p. (J). *(978-1-55455-195-8(1))* Fitzhenry & Whiteside, Ltd.

Raber, Thomas R. Michael Jordan: Returning Champion. 4th rev. ed. 2005. (Sports Achievers Biographies Ser.). (Illus.). 80p. (gr. 7-12). pap. 5.95 *(978-0-8225-0473-3(1))* Lerner Publishing Group.

Rappoport, Ken. Basketball's Top 10 Slam Dunkers. 2010. (Top 10 Sports Stars Ser.). (Illus.). 48p. (J). (gr. 5-9). 25.27 *(978-0-7660-3467-9(4))* Enslow Pubs., Inc.

—Jason Kidd: Leader on the Court. 2004. (Sports Leaders Ser.). (Illus.). 104p. (J). lib. bdg. 27.94 *(978-0-7660-2214-0(5))* Enslow Pubs., Inc.

—LeBron James: King on & off the Court. 2006. (Sports Stars with Heart Ser.). (Illus.). 128p. (J). (gr. 5-9). lib. bdg. 33.27 *(978-0-7660-2420-5(2))* Enslow Pubs., Inc.

Raum, Elizabeth. Lebron James. 2017. (Pro Sports Biographies Ser.). (ENG.). 24p. (gr. 1-4). 20.95 ***(978-1-68151-138-2(X))*** Amicus Publishing.

—Maya Moore. 2017. (Pro Sports Biographies Ser.). (ENG.). 24p. (J). (gr. 1-4). 20.95 ***(978-1-68151-133-7(9)***, Amicus High Interest) Amicus Publishing.

—Pro Sports Biographies: Lebron James. 2017. (Pro Sports Biographies Ser.). (ENG.). 24p. (J). (gr. 1-3). pap. 8.99 ***(978-1-68152-169-5(5))*** Amicus.

—Pro Sports Biographies: Maya Moore. 2017. (Pro Sports Biographies Ser.). (ENG.). 24p. (J). (gr. 1-3). pap. 8.99 ***(978-1-68152-164-0(4))*** Amicus.

Rivkin, Jennifer. All Ball: Basketball's Greatest Players. 2015. (ENG., Illus.). 32p. (J). *(978-0-7787-1534-4(5))* Crabtree Publishing Co.

Robinson, B. J. LeBron James: King of the Court. 2005. (Illus.). x, 195p. (YA). pap. 15.00 *(978-0-9759251-5-7(6))* Forest Hill Publishing, LLC.

Robinson, Tom. Shaquille O'Neal: Giant on & off the Court. 2006. (Sports Stars with Heart Ser.). (Illus.). 128p. (J). (gr. 5-9). lib. bdg. 33.27 *(978-0-7660-2823-4(2))* Enslow Pubs., Inc.

—Today's 12 Hottest NBA Superstars. 2015. (ENG., Illus.). 32p. (J). *(978-1-63235-021-3(1))* Pr. Room Editions LLC.

Roselius, J. Chris. Kevin Garnett: All-Star on & off the Court. 2007. (Sports Stars with Heart Ser.). (Illus.). 128p. (J). (gr. 5-9). lib. bdg. 33.27 *(978-0-7660-2863-0(1))* Enslow Pubs., Inc.

—Magic Johnson: Basketball Star & Entrepreneur, 1 vol. 2011. (Legendary Athletes Ser.). (ENG., Illus.). 112p. (YA). (gr. 7-12). 34.22 *(978-1-61714-756-2(7))* ABDO Publishing Co.

—San Antonio Spurs, 1 vol. 2011. (Inside the NBA Ser.). (ENG., Illus.). 48p. (YA). (gr. 3-6). lib. bdg. 32.79 *(978-1-61783-175-1(1))* ABDO Publishing Co.

—Tim Duncan: Champion on & off the Court. 2006. (Sports Stars with Heart Ser.). (Illus.). 128p. (J). (gr. 5-9). lib. bdg. 33.27 *(978-0-7660-2821-0(6))* Enslow Pubs., Inc.

Sandler, Michael. Basketball: The Return of Bernard King. 2006. (Upsets & Comebacks Ser.). (Illus.). 32p. (J). (gr. 3-6). lib. bdg. 25.27 *(978-1-59716-166-4(7))* Bearport Publishing Co., Inc.

—LeBron James: I Love Challenges! 2009. (Defining Moments Ser.). (Illus.). 32p. (YA). (gr. 2-5). lib. bdg. 25.27 *(978-1-59716-856-4(4))* Bearport Publishing Co., Inc.

Sandler, Michael & Zegers, Charlie. Amar'E Stoudemire. 2012. (Basketball Heroes Making a Difference Ser.). 24p. (J). (gr. 1-6). lib. bdg. 23.93 *(978-1-61772-442-8(4))* Bearport Publishing Co., Inc.

—Derrick Rose. 2012. (Basketball Heroes Making a Difference Ser.). 24p. (J). (gr. 1-6). lib. bdg. 23.93 *(978-1-61772-439-8(4))* Bearport Publishing Co., Inc.

—Dwyane Wade. 2012. (Basketball Heroes Making a Difference Ser.). 24p. (J). (gr. 1-6). lib. bdg. 23.93 *(978-1-61772-441-1(6))* Bearport Publishing Co., Inc.

—Kevin Durant. 2012. (Basketball Heroes Making a Difference Ser.). 24p. (J). (gr. 1-6). lib. bdg. 23.93 *(978-1-61772-440-4(8))* Bearport Publishing Co., Inc.

Savage, Jeff. Chris Paul. 2009. (Amazing Athletes Ser.). (ENG.). 32p. (gr. 2-5). 25.26 *(978-0-7613-4254-0(0))*; pap. 7.95 *(978-0-7613-4462-9(4)*, First Avenue Editions) Lerner Publishing Group.

—Dwight Howard. 2010. (Amazing Athletes Ser.). (ENG.). 32p. (gr. 2-5). pap. 7.95 *(978-0-7613-5756-8(4))* Lerner Publishing Group.

—Dwyane Wade. 2006. (Amazing Athletes Ser.). (Illus.). 32p. (J). (gr. 4). pap. 6.95 *(978-0-8225-6013-5(5)*, First Avenue Editions); (ENG., (gr. 2-5). lib. bdg. 25.26 *(978-0-8225-5955-9(2)*, Lerner Pubns.) Lerner Publishing Group.

—Jeremy Lin. 2012. (Illus.). 112p. (J). *(978-1-59935-352-4(0))* Reynolds, Morgan Inc.

—Kevin Durant. 2011. (Amazing Athletes Ser.). (ENG.). 32p. (gr. 2-5). pap. 7.95 *(978-0-7613-7819-8(7))* Lerner Publishing Group.

—Kobe Bryant. (Amazing Athletes Ser.). 32p. (gr. 2-5). 2005. (Illus.). (YA). lib. bdg. 22.60 *(978-0-8225-1300-1(5))* 2003. (Illus.). (J). pap. 6.95 *(978-0-8225-9849-7(3))* 2010. (ENG.). pap. 7.95 *(978-0-7613-5752-0(1)*, Lerner Pubns.) Lerner Publishing Group.

—Kobe Bryant: Basketball Big Shot. (Sports Achievers Biographies Ser.). (Illus.). (J). 2005. 80p. (gr. 7-12). lib. bdg. 22.60 *(978-0-8225-3680-2(3))* 2003. 64p. (gr. 4-9). pap. 5.95 *(978-0-8225-9860-2(4))* Lerner Publishing Group.

—Kobe Bryant (Revised Edition) 2010. pap. 39.62 *(978-0-7613-6970-7(8))* Lerner Publishing Group.

—Lebron James. (Amazing Athletes Ser.). (Illus.). 32p. (gr. 2-5). 2012. (J). pap. 7.95 *(978-0-7613-9098-5(7))* 2005. (ENG., lib. bdg. 25.26 *(978-0-8225-2947-7(5)*, Lerner Pubns.) 2nd rev. ed. 2014. (ENG., pap. 7.95 *(978-1-4677-3853-8(0))* Lerner Publishing Group.

—LeBron James (3rd Revised Edition) 2016. (Amazing Athletes Ser.). (ENG., Illus.). 32p. (J). (gr. 2-5). pap. 7.95 *(978-1-5124-0416-6(0))*; 39.99 *(978-1-5124-0417-3(9)*, Lerner Pubns.) Lerner Publishing Group.

—LeBron James (Revised Edition) 2012. (Amazing Athletes Ser.). 32p. (J). (gr. 2-5). pap. 45.32 *(978-0-7613-9315-3(3))* Lerner Publishing Group.

—Lisa Leslie: Slam Dunk Queen. 2005. (Sports Leaders Ser.). (Illus.). 104p. (J). lib. bdg. 27.94 *(978-0-7660-2423-6(7))* Enslow Pubs., Inc.

—Maya Moore. 2012. (Amazing Athletes Ser.). 32p. (gr. 2-5). (J). pap. 45.32 *(978-0-7613-9316-0(1))*; (ENG.). pap. 7.95 *(978-0-7613-8666-7(1))*; (ENG., Illus.). lib. bdg. 25.26 *(978-0-7613-8637-7(8))* Lerner Publishing Group.

—Steve Nash. 2006. (Amazing Athletes Ser.). (ENG., Illus.). 32p. (gr. 2-5). pap. 7.95 *(978-0-8225-6014-2(3)*, First Avenue Editions); lib. bdg. 25.26 *(978-0-8225-5956-6(0)*, Lerner Pubns.) Lerner Publishing Group.

—Tim Duncan. 2009. (Amazing Athletes Ser.). (ENG.). 32p. (gr. 2-5). 25.26 *(978-0-8225-9993-7(7))* Lerner Publishing Group.

—Yao Ming. (Amazing Athletes Ser.). 2005. (Illus.). 32p. (J). (gr. 3-4). lib. bdg. 23.93 *(978-0-8225-2432-8(5))* 2004. (Illus.). 32p. (J). (gr. 4-7). per. 5.95 *(978-0-8225-2225-6(X))* 2009. (gr. 2-5). pap. 6.95 *(978-0-7613-3893-2(4)*, Lerner Pubns.) Lerner Publishing Group.

—Yao Ming (Revised Edition) 2009. pap. 40.95 *(978-0-7613-4781-1(X))* Lerner Publishing Group.

Schuh, Mari C. Stephen Curry. 2016. (Famous Athletes Ser.). (ENG., Illus.). 24p. (gr. k-1). lib. bdg. 26.65 *(978-1-4914-8509-5(4))* Capstone Press of Coughlan Cos.

Schweitzer, Karen. Sheryl Swoopes. (Role Model Athletes Ser.). 64p. 2012. (J). (gr. 7). 22.95 *(978-1-4222-2712-1(X))* 2010. (Illus.). (YA). (gr. 7-12). 22.95 *(978-1-4222-0491-7(X))* 2007. (Illus.). (YA). pap. 9.95 *(978-1-4222-0778-9(1))* Mason Crest.

Sharp, Anne Wallace. Lebron James. 2007. (People in the News Ser.). (ENG., Illus.). 128p. (YA). (gr. 7-12). lib. bdg. 33.95 *(978-1-4205-0014-1(7)*, LML02109-234934) Cengage Gale.

Shea, Therese. Stephen Curry: Basketball's MVP. 2016. (Junior Biographies Ser.). (Illus.). 24p. (J). pap. 9.35 *(978-0-7660-8173-4(7))* Enslow Pubs., Inc.

—Yao Ming: International Basketball Star. 2006. (Tony Stead Nonfiction Independent Reading Collection). (ENG.). (gr. 3-6). pap. 8.85 *(978-1-4042-5538-8(9))* Rosen Publishing Group, Inc., The.

Shuster, Rachel. LeBron James: King of the Court. 2017. (J). ***(978-1-5026-2836-7(8))*** Cavendish Square Publishing.

Sibila, Tom. LeBron James: King of the Court. 2005. (High Five Reading - Blue Ser.). (ENG., Illus.). 48p. (gr. 3-4). per. 9.00 *(978-0-7368-5747-5(8)*, High Five Reading (RBL)) Capstone Press of Coughlan Cos.

Smith, Pohla. Shaquille O'Neal: Superhero at Center. 2009. (Sports Illustrated for Kids Bks). 176p. (gr. 7-12). 63.90 *(978-1-60853-153-0(8))* Rosen Publishing Group, Inc., The.

Smith, Pohla & Wilson, Steve. Shaquille O'Neal: Superhero at Center. 2005. (Sports Illustrated for Kids Books Ser.). (Illus.). 176p. (YA). (gr. 7-12). lib. bdg. 33.25 *(978-0-8239-3577-2(9))* Rosen Publishing Group, Inc., The.

Smithwick, John. Meet Dwyane Wade: Basketball's Rising Star. (All-Star Players Ser.). 32p. (gr. 4-5). 2009. 47.90 *(978-1-61511-283-8(9)*, PowerKids Pr.) 2007. (Illus.). (YA). lib. bdg. 25.25 *(978-1-4042-3639-4(2))* Rosen Publishing Group, Inc., The.

—Meet Lebron James: Basketball's King James. (All-Star Players Ser.). 32p. (gr. 4-5). 2009. 47.90 *(978-1-61511-289-0(8)*, PowerKids Pr.) 2007. (Illus.). (YA). lib. bdg. 25.25 *(978-1-4042-3638-7(4))* Rosen Publishing Group, Inc., The.

Stewart, Mark. The Brooklyn Nets. rev. ed. 2014. (Team Spirit Ser.). (ENG.). 48p. (J). (gr. 3-6). lib. bdg. 29.27 *(978-1-59953-637-8(4))* Norwood Hse. Pr.

—The Dallas Mavericks. rev. ed. 2014. (Team Spirit Ser.). (ENG.). 48p. (J). (gr. 3-6). lib. bdg. 29.27 *(978-1-59953-632-3(3))* Norwood Hse. Pr.

—The Detroit Pistons. rev. ed. 2014. (Team Spirit Ser.). (ENG., Illus.). 48p. (J). (gr. 3-6). lib. bdg. 29.27 *(978-1-59953-633-0(1))* Norwood Hse. Pr.

—The Los Angeles Lakers. rev. ed. 2014. (Team Spirit Ser.). (ENG.). 48p. (J). (gr. 3-6). lib. bdg. 29.27 *(978-1-59953-635-4(8))* Norwood Hse. Pr.

—The Miami Heat. rev. ed. 2014. (Team Spirit Ser.). (ENG.). 48p. (J). (gr. 3-6). lib. bdg. 29.27 *(978-1-59953-636-1(6))* Norwood Hse. Pr.

Stewart, Mark & Kennedy, Mike. Swish: The Quest for Basketball's Perfect Shot. 2009. (Spectacular Sports Ser.). (ENG.). 64p. (gr. 5-12). 33.27 *(978-0-8225-8752-1(1))* Lerner Publishing Group.

Stradley, Don. Schooled. 2011. (J). *(978-0-531-22557-8(7))* Scholastic, Inc.

Stuckey, Rachel. Lebron James. 2013. (ENG.). 32p. (J). *(978-0-7787-1047-9(5))*; pap. *(978-0-7787-1052-3(1))* Crabtree Publishing Co.

Taylor, Charlotte & Feinstein, Stephen. Lebron James: Basketball Champion. 2015. (Exceptional African Americans Ser.). (ENG., Illus.). 24p. (J). (gr. 3-4). 22.60 *(978-0-7660-6660-1(6))* Enslow Pubs., Inc.

—LeBron James: Basketball Champion. 2015. (Exceptional African Americans Ser.). (ENG.). 24p. (J). (gr. 3-4). pap. 9.35 *(978-0-7660-6658-8(4))* Enslow Pubs., Inc.

Thomas, William David. Pete Thompson & the Long Road Home. 2003. 80p. pap. 19.95 *(978-1-4137-1620-7(2))* America Star Bks.

Thornley, Stew. Kevin Garnett: Champion Basketball Star. 2012. (Sports Star Champions Ser.). (Illus.). 48p. (J). (gr. 5-18). 25.27 *(978-0-7660-4028-1(3))* Enslow Pubs., Inc.

Tieck, Sarah. LeBron James: Basketball Superstar, 1 vol. 2009. (Big Buddy Biographies Set 3 Ser.). (ENG., Illus.). 32p. (J). (gr. 2-5). 28.50 *(978-1-60453-708-6(6))* ABDO Publishing Co.

Torres, John. Carmelo Anthony. 2012. (J). lib. bdg. 25.70 *(978-1-61228-333-3(0))* Mitchell Lane Pubs., Inc.

Torres, John Albert. Allen Iverson: Never Give Up. 2004. (Sports Leaders Ser.). (Illus.). 104p. (J). lib. bdg. 27.94 *(978-0-7660-2174-7(2))* Enslow Pubs., Inc.

—Kevin Garnett: "Da Kid" 2003. (Sports Achievers Biographies Ser.). (Illus.). 64p. (J). (gr. 4-9). pap. 5.95 *(978-0-8225-9843-5(4)*, Carolrhoda Bks.) Lerner Publishing Group.

—Shaquille O'Neal: Gentle Giant. 2004. (Sports Leaders Ser.). (Illus.). 104p. (J). lib. bdg. 27.94 *(978-0-7660-2175-4(0))* Enslow Pubs., Inc.

—Vince Carter: Slam Dunk Artist. 2004. (Sports Leaders Ser.). (Illus.). 104p. (J). lib. bdg. 26.60 *(978-0-7660-2173-0(4))* Enslow Pubs., Inc.

Torsiello, David P. Read about Carmelo Anthony. 2011. (I Like Sports Stars! Ser.). (Illus.). 24p. (J). (gr. k-18). pap. 7.95 *(978-1-59845-297-6(5)*, Enslow Elementary) Enslow Pubs., Inc.

—Read about Kobe Bryant. 2011. (I Like Sports Stars! Ser.). (Illus.). 24p. (J). (gr. k-18). pap. 7.95 *(978-1-59845-300-3(9)*, Enslow Elementary); (gr. 1-4). lib. bdg. 22.60 *(978-0-7660-3830-1(0))* Enslow Pubs., Inc.

Tustison, Matt. Kyrie Irving. 2017. (Illus.). 32p. (J). ***(978-1-68079-809-8(X)***, SportsZone) ABDO Publishing Co.

Ward, S. Meet E. B. White. 2009. (About the Author Ser.). 24p. (gr. 4-4). 42.50 *(978-1-61511-247-0(2)*, PowerKids Pr.) Rosen Publishing Group, Inc., The.

Wearing, Judy & Yasuda, Anita. Lebron James. 2011. (J). (gr. 4-6). pap. 12.95 *(978-1-61690-674-0(X)*, AV2 by Weigl); (Illus.). 24p. (YA). (gr. 3-6). 27.13 *(978-1-61690-669-6(3))* Weigl Pubs., Inc.

Weber, Terri Smith. Lebron James: Rising Star. 2004. (J). pap. *(978-1-932724-23-3(0))*; lib. bdg. *(978-1-932724-22-6(2))* Panda Publishing, L.L.C. (Bios for Kids).

Whiting, Jim. Atlanta Hawks. 2017. (J). ***(978-1-60818-835-2(3)***, Creative Education) Creative Co., The.

—Boston Celtics. 2017. (J). ***(978-1-60818-836-9(1)***, Creative Education) Creative Co., The.

—Brooklyn Nets. 2017. (J). ***(978-1-60818-837-6(X)***, Creative Education) Creative Co., The.

—Charlotte Hornets. 2017. (J). ***(978-1-60818-838-3(8)***, Creative Education) Creative Co., The.

—Chicago Bulls. 2017. (J). ***(978-1-60818-839-0(6)***, Creative Education) Creative Co., The.

—Cleveland Cavaliers. 2017. (J). ***(978-1-60818-840-6(X)***, Creative Education) Creative Co., The.

—Dallas Mavericks. 2017. (J). ***(978-1-60818-841-3(8)***, Creative Education) Creative Co., The.

—Denver Nuggets. 2017. (J). ***(978-1-60818-842-0(6)***, Creative Education) Creative Co., The.

—Detroit Pistons. 2017. (J). ***(978-1-60818-843-7(4)***, Creative Education) Creative Co., The.

—Golden State Warriors. 2017. (J). ***(978-1-60818-844-4(2)***, Creative Education) Creative Co., The.

—Houston Rockets. 2017. (J). ***(978-1-60818-845-1(0)***, Creative Education) Creative Co., The.

—Indiana Pacers. 2017. (J). ***(978-1-60818-846-8(9)***, Creative Education) Creative Co., The.

—Los Angeles Clippers. 2017. (J). ***(978-1-60818-847-5(7)***, Creative Education) Creative Co., The.

—Los Angeles Lakers. 2017. (J). ***(978-1-60818-848-2(5)***, Creative Education) Creative Co., The.

—Memphis Grizzlies. 2017. (J). ***(978-1-60818-849-9(3)***, Creative Education) Creative Co., The.

—Miami Heat. 2017. (J). ***(978-1-60818-850-5(7)***, Creative Education) Creative Co., The.

—The NBA: a History of Hoops: Portland Trail Blazers. 2nd ed. 2017. (NBA: a History of Hoops Ser.). (ENG.). 48p. (J). (gr. 5-7). pap. 12.00 ***(978-1-62832-462-4(7)***, Creative Paperbacks) Creative Co., The.

—The NBA: a History of Hoops: Sacramento Kings. 2nd ed. 2017. (NBA: a History of Hoops Ser.). (ENG.). 48p. (J). (gr. 5-7). pap. 12.00 ***(978-1-62832-463-1(5)***, Creative Paperbacks) Creative Co., The.

—The NBA: a History of Hoops: San Antonio Spurs. 2nd ed. 2017. (NBA: a History of Hoops Ser.). (ENG.). 48p. (J). (gr. 5-7). pap. 12.00 ***(978-1-62832-464-8(3)***, Creative Paperbacks) Creative Co., The.

—The NBA: a History of Hoops: Toronto Raptors. 2nd ed. 2017. (NBA: a History of Hoops Ser.). (ENG.). 48p. (J). (gr. 5-7). pap. 12.00 ***(978-1-62832-465-5(1)***, Creative Paperbacks) Creative Co., The.

—The NBA: a History of Hoops: Utah Jazz. 2nd ed. 2017. (NBA: a History of Hoops Ser.). (ENG.). 48p. (J). (gr. 5-7). pap. 12.00 ***(978-1-62832-466-2(X)***, Creative Paperbacks) Creative Co., The.

—The NBA: a History of Hoops: Washington Wizards. 2nd ed. 2017. (NBA: a History of Hoops Ser.). (ENG.). 48p. (J). (gr. 5-7). pap. 12.00 ***(978-1-62832-467-9(8)***, Creative Paperbacks) Creative Co., The.

—Russell Westbrook. 2017. (J). lib. bdg. 25.70 ***(978-1-68020-133-8(6))*** Mitchell Lane Pubs., Inc.

Wilner, Barry. Basketball's Top 10 Scorers. 2010. (Top 10 Sports Stars Ser.). 48p. (J). (gr. 5-9). 25.27 *(978-0-7660-3470-9(4))* Enslow Pubs., Inc.

Wilson, Wayne. Allen Iverson. 2004. (Blue Banner Biography Ser.). (Illus.). 32p. (J). lib. bdg. 25.70 *(978-1-58415-328-3(8))* Mitchell Lane Pubs., Inc.

Wiseman, Blaine. Basketball. 2010. (Record Breakers Ser.). (Illus.). 24p. (YA). (gr. 3-6). lib. bdg. 27.13 *(978-1-61690-118-9(7))*; (J). (gr. 4-6). pap. 12.95 *(978-1-61690-119-6(5))* Weigl Pubs., Inc.

Woog, Adam. Derrick Rose. 2010. (People in the News Ser.). (Illus.). 128p. (J). 33.95 *(978-1-4205-0233-6(6)*, Lucent Bks.) Cengage Gale.

Worthy, Shanya. LeBron James: Basketball Legend. 2010. (Inspiring Lives Ser.). 32p. (J). (gr. 5-8). lib. bdg. 25.25 *(978-1-4339-3637-1(2))*; (Illus.). pap. 10.50 *(978-1-4339-3638-8(0))* Stevens, Gareth Publishing LLLP.

Yorkey, Mike & Florea, Jesse. Linspired: The Jeremy Lin Story, 1 vol. 2012. (ZonderKidz Biography Ser.). (ENG.). 144p. (J). pap. 6.99 *(978-0-310-73523-6(8))* Zonderkidz.

Young, Jeff C. Dwyane Wade. 2012. (Role Model Athletes Ser.). 64p. (J). (gr. 7). 22.95 *(978-1-4222-2709-1(X))* Mason Crest.

—Yao Ming: Basketball's Big Man. 2005. (Sports Leaders Ser.). (Illus.). 104p. (J). lib. bdg. 27.94 *(978-0-7660-2422-9(9))* Enslow Pubs., Inc.

Zuehlke, Jeffrey. Dirk Nowitzki. 2008. pap. 40.95 *(978-0-8225-9285-3(1))* 2007. (Illus.). 32p. (J). (gr. -1-3). per. 6.95 *(978-0-8225-7666-2(X)*, First Avenue Editions) 2012. (ENG., Illus.). 32p. (gr. 2-5). pap. 7.95 *(978-0-7613-9005-3(7))* Lerner Publishing Group.

—Dirk Nowitzki (Revised Edition) 2012. (Amazing Athletes Ser.). 32p. (J). (gr. 2-5). pap. 45.32 *(978-0-7613-9314-6(5))* Lerner Publishing Group.

—Kevin Garnett. rev. ed. 2010. (Amazing Athletes Ser.). (ENG.). 32p. (gr. 2-5). pap. 7.95 *(978-0-7613-5595-3(2))*; (Illus.). lib. bdg. 25.26 *(978-0-7613-5594-6(4))* Lerner Publishing Group.

—Kevin Garnett (Revised Edition) 2010. pap. 39.62 *(978-0-7613-6969-1(4))* Lerner Publishing Group.

BASKETBALL—FICTION

Abdul-Jabbar, Kareem. Streetball Crew Book One Sasquatch in the Paint. 2015. (Streetball Crew Ser.). (ENG.). 288p. (J). (gr. 3-7). pap. 7.99 *(978-1-4231-9254-1(0))* Hyperion Bks. for Children.

Abdul-Jabbar, Kareem & Obstfeld, Raymond. Sasquatch in the Paint. 2013. (Streetball Crew Ser.). (ENG.). 272p. (J). (gr. 3-7). 16.99 *(978-1-4231-7870-5(X))* Hyperion Pr.

Aboff, Marcie. The Hot Shots. Manning, Maurie, illus. 2003. (ENG.). 56p. (J). (gr. 6-8). pap. 7.97 net. *(978-0-7652-3275-5(8)*, Celebration Pr.) Pearson Schl.

Adler, David A. The Basketball Mystery, 29 vols., No. 29. Allen, Joy, illus. 2010. (Cam Jansen Ser.: 29). (ENG.). 64p. (J). (gr. 2-5). 4.99 *(978-0-14-241671-6(1)*, Puffin Books) Penguin Young Readers Group.

Ahmad, Kamil. Up, up, up! the Tale of a Magical Basket. 2017. (Text Connections Guided Close Reading Ser.). (J). (gr. 1). *(978-1-4900-1821-8(2))* Benchmark Education Co.

Aker, Don. One on One. 2014. 144p. (J). (gr. 3-7). pap. 8.99 *(978-0-06-231353-9(3))* HarperCollins Pubs.

Alexander, Kwame. The Crossover. 2014. (ENG.). (J). (gr. 4-7). E-Book 16.99 *(978-1-306-46985-2(6))* Harcourt Trade Pubs.

—The Crossover. 2014. (ENG.). 240p. (J). (gr. 4-7). 16.99 *(978-0-544-10771-7(3)*, HMH Books For Young Readers) Houghton Mifflin Harcourt Publishing Co.

—The Crossover. 2014. lib. bdg. 29.40 *(978-0-606-37975-5(4))* Turtleback Bks.

Alonge, L. J. Janae. Allen, Raul, illus. 2016. (Blacktop Ser.: 2). (ENG.). 144p. (YA). (gr. 7). mass mkt. 6.99 *(978-1-101-99564-8(5)*, Grosset & Dunlap) Penguin Young Readers Group.

—Justin. Allen, Raul, illus. 2016. (Blacktop Ser.: 1). (ENG.). 144p. (YA). (gr. 7). mass mkt. 6.99 *(978-1-101-99562-4(9)*, Grosset & Dunlap) Penguin Young Readers Group.

Alonge, L. J. & dePaola, Tomie. Janae #2. Allen, Raul, illus. 2016. (Blacktop Ser.: 2). (ENG.). 144p. (YA). (gr. 7). bds. 15.99 *(978-0-399-54276-3(0)*, Grosset & Dunlap) Penguin Young Readers Group.

—Justin #1. Allen, Raul, illus. 2016. (Blacktop Ser.: 1). (ENG.). 144p. (YA). (gr. 7). bds. 15.99 *(978-0-399-54275-6(2)*, Grosset & Dunlap) Penguin Young Readers Group.

Alphin, Elaine Marie. The Perfect Shot. (Carolrhoda YA Ser.). (ENG.). 360p. (YA). (gr. 6-12). 2011. pap. 9.95 *(978-0-7613-8138-9(4)*, Carolrhoda Lab™) 2005. 16.95 *(978-1-57505-862-7(6)*, Carolrhoda Bks.) Lerner Publishing Group.

Andracki, Zenon. Dear Ashley: A Middle Grade Novel. 2006. (ENG.). 84p. per. 19.95 *(978-1-4241-6168-3(1))* America Star Bks.

Arena, Felice. Sporty Kids: Basketball! Jellett, Tom, illus. 5th ed. 2017. (Sporty Kids Ser.). (ENG.). 80p. (J). (gr. 1-3). 7.99 ***(978-0-14-330889-8(0))*** Random Hse. Australia AUS. Dist: Independent Pubs. Group.

Arena, Felice & Kettle, Phil. Basketball Buddies. Gordon, Gus, illus. 2004. (J). pap. *(978-1-59336-369-7(9))* Mondo Publishing.

Arena, Jacqueline. Basketball Showdown. Foye, Lloyd, illus. 2005. (Girlz Rock! Ser.). (J). pap. *(978-1-59336-704-6(X))* Mondo Publishing.

Aronson, Marc & Smith, Charles R., Jr., eds. Pick-Up Game: A Full Day of Full Court. Smith, Charles R., Jr., illus. (ENG., Illus.). 176p. (YA). (gr. 9). 2012. pap. 7.99 *(978-0-7636-6068-0(X))* 2011. 15.99 *(978-0-7636-4562-5(1))* Candlewick Pr.

Barber, Barbara E. Allie's Basketball Dream. Ligasan, Darryl, illus. 2013. (ENG.). 32p. (J). (gr. 2-2). pap. 9.95 *(978-1-880000-72-4(5))* Lee & Low Bks., Inc.

Barber, Tiki & Barber, Ronde. Jump Shot. 2013. (Barber Game Time Bks.). (ENG., Illus.). 160p. (J). (gr. 3-7). 16.99 *(978-1-4424-5729-4(5)*, Simon & Schuster/Paula Wiseman Bks.) Simon & Schuster/Paula Wiseman Bks.

Baskin, Nora Raleigh. Basketball (or Something Like It) 176p. (J). 2007. (ENG.). (gr. 4-7). pap. 6.99 *(978-0-06-059612-5(0))* 2005. (ENG.). 15.99 *(978-0-06-059610-1(4))* 2005. lib. bdg. 16.89 *(978-0-06-059611-8(2))* HarperCollins Pubs.

Bee, Clair. Buzzer Basket: A Chip Hilton Sports Story. 2011. 184p. (gr. 4-7). 42.95 *(978-1-258-06936-0(9))* Literary Licensing, LLC.

—Hardcourt Upset: A Chip Hilton Sports Story. 2011. 190p. (gr. 3-8). 42.95 *(978-1-258-08011-2(7))* Literary Licensing, LLC.

Bernard, Teko & Wilson, Wayne L. The Hoop Kid from Elmdale Park. Diaz, Gabriel, illus. 2013. 126p. pap. 7.99 *(978-0-9860593-0-8(7))* Elmdale Park Books.

Bildner, Phil. Tournament of Champions. Probert, Tim, illus. 2017. (Rip & Red Ser.: 3). (ENG.). 256p. (J). 16.99 *(978-0-374-30507-9(2)*, 9780374305079, Farrar, Straus & Giroux (BYR)) Farrar, Straus & Giroux.

Birdsall, Bridget. Double Exposure. 2014. (ENG.). 304p. (J). (gr. 6). 16.95 *(978-1-62914-606-5(4)*, Sky Pony Pr.) Skyhorse Publishing Co., Inc.

Blumenthal, Scott & Hodus, Brett. Hoop City. 2005. (Dream Ser.). 145p. (gr. 3-8). pap. 9.95 *(978-0-9708992-1-7(1))* Scobre Pr. Corp.

Bongiovanni, Debbie. Kindness Pays Off, 1 vol. 2010. 58p. pap. 16.95 *(978-1-4489-6320-1(6))* America Star Bks.

Bowen, Fred. The Final Cut, 1 vol. 2009. (All-Star Sports Story Ser.). (ENG., Illus.). 112p. (J). pap. 6.95 *(978-1-56145-510-2(5))* Peachtree Pubs.

—Full Court Fever, 1 vol. 2009. (All-Star Sports Story Ser.). (ENG., Illus.). 112p. (J). pap. 5.95 *(978-1-56145-508-9(3))* Peachtree Pubs.

—Hardcourt Comeback, 1 vol. 2010. (Fred Bowen Sports Stories Ser.). (ENG., Illus.). 144p. (J). (gr. 2-7). pap. 5.95 *(978-1-56145-516-4(4)*, Peachtree Junior) Peachtree Pubs.

—Off the Rim, 1 vol. 2009. (All-Star Sports Story Ser.). (ENG., Illus.). 112p. (J). pap. 5.95 *(978-1-56145-509-6(1))* Peachtree Pubs.

—On the Line, 1 vol. 2nd ed. 2009. (Fred Bowen Sports Story Ser.). (ENG., Illus.). 112p. (J). pap. 6.95 *(978-1-56145-511-9(3))* Peachtree Pubs.

—Outside Shot, 1 vol. 2017. (Fred Bowen Sports Story Ser.). (ENG.). 144p. (J). (gr. 2-6). pap. 6.95 *(978-1-56145-956-8(9))*; 14.95 *(978-1-56145-955-1(0))* Peachtree Pubs.

—Perfect Game, 1 vol. 2013. (Fred Bowen Sports Stories Ser.). (ENG.). 144p. (J). (gr. 2-6). 14.95 *(978-1-56145-701-4(9))*; pap. 5.95 *(978-1-56145-625-3(X))* Peachtree Pubs.

—Real Hoops, 1 vol. 2011. (Fred Bowen Sports Stories Ser.). (ENG.). 128p. (J). (gr. 2-7). pap. 5.95 *(978-1-56145-566-9(0))* Peachtree Pubs.

Britton, Faith. If You'D Only Believe. 2009. 24p. pap. 12.99 *(978-1-4490-1741-5(X))* AuthorHouse.

Brooks, Bruce. The Moves Make the Man. 2003. (ENG.). 256p. (YA). (gr. 8-18). pap. 8.99 *(978-0-06-447022-3(9)*, HarperTeen) HarperCollins Pubs.

—The Moves Make the Man. (J). pap., stu. ed. *(978-0-13-017518-2(8))* Prentice Hall (Schl. Div.).

Brouwer, Sigmund. Titan Clash, 1 vol. 2007. (Orca Sports Ser.). (ENG.). 176p. (YA). (gr. 6-10). per. 9.95 *(978-1-55143-721-7(X))* Orca Bk. Pubs. USA.

Buffington, Cecil. High School Super-Star: The Junior Year. 2008. 244p. pap. 16.95 *(978-0-595-51914-9(8))* iUniverse, Inc.

Butler, Jeremy. Hello, Zippy! 2008. (YA). 14.95 *(978-1-932888-71-3(3))* Mascot Bks., Inc.

Bylsma, Dan & Bylsma, Jay M. Slam Dunks Not Allowed! 2003. (Illus.). 238p. (YA). *(978-0-938682-72-1(5))*; pap. *(978-0-938682-77-6(6))* River Road Pubns., Inc.

Casey, C. A. Top of the Key. 2006. 120p. (J). 20.95 *(978-0-9759555-3-6(5))*; per. 8.95 *(978-0-9759555-4-3(3))* Bedazzled Ink Publishing Co.

Christopher, Matt. The Basket Counts. 2008. (New Matt Christopher Sports Library). 96p. (J). (gr. 4-6). lib. bdg. 26.60 *(978-1-59953-212-7(3))* Norwood Hse. Pr.

—Center Court Sting. 2005. (Sports Classics II Ser.). 140p. (J). lib. bdg. 15.00 *(978-1-59054-749-6(7))* Fitzgerald Bks.

—Center Court Sting. l.t. ed. 2007. (New Matt Christopher Sports Library). 160p. (J). (gr. 4-6). lib. bdg. 26.60 *(978-1-59953-106-9(2))* Norwood Hse. Pr.

—Hook Shot Hero: A Nothin' but Net Sequel. 2011. (ENG.). 144p. (J). (gr. 3-7). pap., pap. 5.99 *(978-0-316-10296-4(2))* Little, Brown Bks. for Young Readers.

—Hot Shot. 2010. (ENG.). 128p. (J). (gr. 3-7). pap. 5.99 *(978-0-316-04482-0(2))* Little, Brown Bks. for Young Readers.

—Johnny Long Legs. 2005. (Sports Classics II Ser.). 117p. (J). lib. bdg. 15.00 *(978-1-59054-760-1(8))* Fitzgerald Bks.

—Nothin' but Net. 2003. (ENG.). 144p. (J). (gr. 3-7). pap. 16.99 *(978-0-316-13344-9(2))* Little, Brown Bks. for Young Readers.

—Slam Dunk. 2004. (ENG., Illus.). 128p. (J). (gr. 3-7). pap. 5.99 *(978-0-316-60762-9(2))* Little, Brown Bks. for Young Readers.

—Slam Dunk. 2004. (Matt Christopher Sports Ser.). 118p. (gr. 3-7). 15.00 *(978-0-7569-3046-2(4))* Perfection Learning Corp.

Ciencin, Scott & Fuentes, Benny. Full Court Flash, 1 vol. Sandoval, Gerardo, illus. 2011. (Sports Illustrated Kids Graphic Novels Ser.). (ENG.). 56p. (gr. 2-3). pap. 7.19 *(978-1-4342-3074-4(0))*; lib. bdg. 26.65 *(978-1-4342-2225-1(X))* Stone Arch Bks.

Ciencin, Scott, et al. Hoop Rat, 1 vol. Aburto, Jesus & Cano, Fernando M., illus. 2011. (Sports Illustrated Kids Graphic Novels Ser.). (ENG.). 56p. (gr. 2-3). pap. 7.19 *(978-1-4342-3069-0(4))*; lib. bdg. 26.65 *(978-1-4342-2223-7(3))* Stone Arch Bks.

Coburn, Jake. Lovesick. 2007. (ENG.). 240p. (YA). (gr. 9-18). 7.99 *(978-0-14-240802-5(6)*, Speak) Penguin Young Readers Group.

Cooke, Bruce. Tubby's Magic Socks. 2010. 48p. pap. 18.68 *(978-1-4535-1220-3(9))* Xlibris Corp.

Coy, John. Take Your Best Shot. 2012. (4 For 4 Ser.: 4). (ENG.). 192p. (J). (gr. 3-7). 16.99 *(978-0-312-37332-0(5)*, 9780312373320) Feiwel & Friends.

Coy, John & Reonegro, Antonio. Around the World, 1 vol. 2015. (ENG.). 32p. (J). pap. 10.95 *(978-1-62014-224-0(4))* Lee & Low Bks., Inc.

—Around the World. Lynch, Tom, illus. 2005. (ENG.). 32p. (J). (gr. 1-7). 17.95 *(978-1-58430-244-5(5))* Lee & Low Bks., Inc.

Craig, Sherryn. Locura de Medianoche en el Zoológico, 1 vol. Jones, Karen, illus. 2016. (SPA.). 32p. (J). (gr. k-3). pap. 9.95 *(978-1-62855-744-2(3))* Arbordale Publishing.

—Midnight Madness at the Zoo, 1 vol. Jones, Karen, illus. 2016. (ENG & SPA.). 32p. (J). (gr. k-3). 17.95 *(978-1-62855-730-5(3))* Arbordale Publishing.

Cumyn, Alan. Tilt. 2013. 260p. pap. *(978-1-4596-6448-7(5))* ReadHowYouWant.com, Ltd.

Damerau, Diane Deci. The Petoskey Stones, 1 vol. 2009. 135p. pap. 24.95 *(978-1-60749-903-9(7))* America Star Bks.

Dawn, Nyrae. The History of Us. (ENG., Illus.). 2016. (YA). (gr. 9-12). 24.99 ***(978-1-63477-968-5(1))*** 2015. 184p. (J). pap. 14.99 *(978-1-63476-179-6(0))* Dreamspinner Pr. (Harmony Ink Pr.).

De la Peña, Matt. Ball Don't Lie. 2007. (ENG.). 288p. (YA). (gr. 9-12). pap. 9.99 *(978-0-385-73425-7(5)*, Ember) Random Hse. Children's Bks.

Depue, Anne. The Basketball Game. 2016. (Spring Forward Ser.). (J). (gr. k). *(978-1-4900-3709-7(8))* Benchmark Education Co.

Deuker, Carl. Night Hoops. 2009. (ENG.). 224p. (YA). (gr. 7). pap. 8.99 *(978-0-547-24891-2(1))* Houghton Mifflin Harcourt Publishing Co.

—Night Hoops. 2009. 250p. (gr. 7-12). lib. bdg. 19.65 *(978-0-613-61919-6(6)*, Turtleback) Turtleback Bks.

—On the Devil's Court. 2008. (ENG.). 208p. (YA). (gr. 7-17). pap. 10.99 *(978-0-316-06727-0(X))* Little, Brown Bks. for Young Readers.

—Swagger. (ENG.). 304p. (YA). (gr. 7). 2015. pap. 9.99 *(978-0-544-33619-3(4)*, HMH Books For Young Readers) 2013. 17.99 *(978-0-547-97459-0(0))* Houghton Mifflin Harcourt Publishing Co.

Erikson, Harvey. Basketball Fever... Bring It On! 2014. 206p. pap. 11.95 *(978-1-62652-583-2(8)*, Mill City Press, Inc) Salem Author Services.

Feinstein, John. Foul Trouble. (ENG.). (YA). (gr. 7). 2014. 416p. pap. 9.99 *(978-0-375-87169-6(1)*, Ember) 2013. 400p. 16.99 *(978-0-375-86964-8(6)*, Knopf Bks. for Young Readers) Random Hse. Children's Bks.

—Last Shot - Mystery at the Final Four. 2006. (Sports Beat Ser.). (ENG.). 272p. (J). (gr. 7-9). reprint ed. per. 8.99 *(978-0-553-49460-0(0)*, Yearling) Random Hse. Children's Bks.

—The Sixth Man. 2016. (Triple Threat Ser.: 2). (ENG.). 304p. (J). (gr. 5). 18.40 *(978-0-606-39342-3(0))* Turtleback Bks.

—The Sixth Man (the Triple Threat, 2) 2015. (Triple Threat Ser.). (ENG.). 304p. (YA). (gr. 5). 16.99 *(978-0-385-75350-0(0)*, Knopf Bks. for Young Readers) Random Hse. Children's Bks.

Ferrell, Phil. Bernie Books Makes the Team. 2007. 86p. 16.95 *(978-1-4241-4991-9(6))* PublishAmerica, Inc.

Flower, Jessie Graham. Grace Harlowe's Sophomore Year at High School. 2007. 256p. 29.95 *(978-1-4344-9678-2(3))*; per. 19.95 *(978-1-4344-9677-5(5))* Wildside Pr., LLC.

Forrey, B. J. Basketball's My Favorite. 2004. 20p. pap. 24.95 *(978-1-4137-2991-7(6))* PublishAmerica, Inc.

Fowler, Marie. Long Shot. 2005. (Dream Ser.). 160p. (gr. 3-8). pap. 9.95 *(978-0-9708992-6-2(2))* Scobre Pr. Corp.

Frederiksen, Barbara. Rippen Ricky Loves the Game: A Book of Perseverance. 2011. 24p. pap. 15.99 *(978-1-4628-2999-6(6))* Xlibris Corp.

Friedman, Laurie B. Game Time, Mallory! Kalis, Jennifer, illus. 2015. (J). 15.99 *(978-1-4677-6188-8(5))* Lerner Publishing Group.

Furr, L. David. Hoops & Me. Simonton, Tom, illus. 2005. (ENG.). 16p. (J). 5.75 *(978-1-57274-751-7(X)*, 2746, Bks. for Young Learners) Owen, Richard C. Pubs., Inc.

Gabolinscy, Jack & Harrison, Brian. Not Again. 2008. (Rigby Focus Forward: Level P Ser.). (Illus.). 24p. (J). (gr. 4-7). pap. *(978-1-4190-3859-4(1)*, Rigby) Pearson Education Australia.

Gallegos, Bryan. Ghost Train. 2012. (ENG.). 163p. pap. 12.95 *(978-1-4327-7290-1(2))* Outskirts Pr., Inc.

Game On. 13th ed. 2009. (ENG.). 128p. (J). pap. 4.99 *(978-1-4231-0972-3(4))* Disney Pr.

Garland, Michael. Hooray José!, 1 vol. Garland, Michael, illus. 2007. (ENG., Illus.). 32p. (J). (gr. -1-3). 16.99 *(978-0-7614-5345-1(8))* Marshall Cavendish Corp.

Gassman, Julie A. Nobody Wants to Play with a Ball Hog, 1 vol. Santillan, Jorge H., illus. 2010. (Sports Illustrated Kids Victory School Superstars Ser.). (ENG.). 56p. (gr. 1-3). 26.65 *(978-1-4342-2056-1(7))*; pap. 5.95 *(978-1-4342-2806-2(1))* Stone Arch Bks.

Geddes, Diana E. Let's Play Basketball. Kaeden Corp. Staff, ed. Palmer, Kate S., illus. 2005. (ENG.). 16p. (gr. k-1). pap. 7.95 *(978-1-879835-55-9(X)*, Kaeden Bks.) Kaeden Corp.

Goode, John. Going the Distance. (YA). 2016. (ENG., Illus.). (gr. 8-12). 24.99 ***(978-1-63533-020-5(3)***, Harmony Ink Pr.) 2015. lib. bdg. *(978-1-63216-620-3(8))* Dreamspinner Pr.

Gourlay, Candy. Tall Story. 2012. (ENG.). 304p. (J). (gr. 5). 6.99 *(978-0-385-75233-6(4)*, Yearling) Random Hse. Children's Bks.

Greene, Janice. Blood & Basketball. 2005. (Quickreads Ser.). (Illus.). 32p. (J). pap. 2.95 *(978-1-56254-739-4(9)*, SP7399) Saddleback Educational Publishing, Inc.

Grimes, Nikki. Planet Middle School. 2011. (ENG.). 160p. (YA). 15.99 *(978-1-59990-284-5(2)*, 9781599902845, Bloomsbury USA Childrens) Bloomsbury Publishing USA.

Gunderson, Jessica & Gonzalez, Jorge. Full Court Pressure, 1 vol. Ruiz, Alfonso, illus. 2010. (Sports Illustrated Kids Graphic Novels Ser.). (ENG.). 56p. (gr. 2-3). pap. 7.19 *(978-1-4342-2291-6(8))*; 26.65 *(978-1-4342-1911-4(9))* Stone Arch Bks.

Gunnery, Sylvia. Personal Best, 1 vol. 2005. (Lorimer Sports Stories Ser.). (ENG.). 112p. (J). (gr. 4-8). 16.95 *(978-1-55028-897-1(0)*, 9781550288971) Lorimer, James & Co., Ltd., Pubs. CAN. Dist: Casemate Pubs. & Bk. Distributors, LLC.

Gutman, Dan. The Million Dollar Shot. 2nd rev. ed. 2006. (ENG.). 128p. (J). (gr. 3-7). pap. 5.99 *(978-1-4231-0084-3(0))* Hyperion Pr.

Hallinan, P. K. Let's Play As a Team. 2003. (ENG., Illus.). 28p. (J). 8.75 *(978-0-8249-5452-9(1)*, Ideal Pubns.) Worthy Publishing.

Harkrader, L. D. Airball: My Life in Briefs. 2008. (ENG.). 208p. (J). (gr. 3-7). per. 9.99 *(978-0-312-37382-5(1)*, 9780312373825) Square Fish.

Hawkins, Jyren. The Shot to Victory. 2012. 24p. pap. 15.99 *(978-1-4771-1833-7(0))* Xlibris Corp.

Heldring, Thatcher. Toby Wheeler: Eighth Grade Benchwarmer. 2008. (ENG.). 224p. (J). (gr. 3-7). 6.99 *(978-0-440-42183-2(7)*, Yearling) Random Hse. Children's Bks.

Hellman, Charles. Adventures in SportsLand - the Basketball Bully (with accompanying CD) Tintilli, Robert, illus. 2008. (Adventures in SportsLand: the Bully Ser.). 32p. (J). (gr. -1-3). 19.95 *(978-0-935938-28-9(1))* Stogo, Malcolm Assocs.

Hengel, Katherine. Taking Control, 1 vol. unabr. ed. 2011. (District 13 Ser.). (ENG.). 48p. (YA). (gr. 9-12). pap. 7.95 *(978-1-61651-276-7(8))* Saddleback Educational Publishing, Inc.

Hicks, Betty. Basketball Bats / Goof-Off Goalie. McCauley, Adam, illus. 2009. (Gym Shorts Ser.). (ENG.). 128p. (J). (gr. 2-5). pap. 10.99 *(978-0-312-58247-0(1)*, 9780312582470) Square Fish.

Hillert, Margaret. Up, up, up, Dear Dragon. Schimmell, David, illus. 2012. (BeginningtoRead Ser.). 32p. (J). (-2). lib. bdg. 22.60 *(978-1-59953-545-6(9))* Norwood Hse. Pr.

Hoblin, Paul & Hueller, Patrick. Foul. 2011. (Night Fall Ser.). (ENG.). 120p. (YA). (gr. 6-12). pap. 7.95 *(978-0-7613-7813-6(8))*; lib. bdg. 27.93 *(978-0-7613-7746-7(8))* Lerner Publishing Group.

Hoffmeister, Peter Brown. This Is the Part Where You Laugh. 2016. (ENG.). 336p. (YA). (gr. 9). 17.99 *(978-0-553-53810-6(1)*, Knopf Bks. for Young Readers) Random Hse. Children's Bks.

Holroyd, Irene. Slam Dunk State Side. 2010. 36p. pap. 13.95 *(978-1-60911-135-9(4)*, Eloquent Bks.) Strategic Book Publishing & Rights Agency (SBPRA).

Hunter, Muata. Check Up. 2009. 94p. pap. 24.99 *(978-0-557-04443-6(X))* Lulu Pr., Inc.

I Can't Play Basketball, I'm Only Four Feet Tall. 2003. (J). 10.95 *(978-0-9745798-1-8(5))* Pen & Sword Publishing Co., The.

Jacobs, Evan. Emoji of Doom, 1 vol. 2017. (White Lightning Ser.). (ENG.). 91p. (J). (gr. 6-8). pap. 8.95 ***(978-1-68021-354-6(7))*** Saddleback Educational Publishing, Inc.

Jaimet, Kate. Slam Dunk, 1 vol. 2009. (Orca Sports Ser.). (ENG.). 176p. (YA). (gr. 6-10). pap. 9.95 *(978-1-55469-132-6(X))* Orca Bk. Pubs. USA.

Johnson, Lauren. Beastly Basketball, 1 vol. Garcia, Eduardo, illus. 2014. (Sports Illustrated Kids Graphic Novels Ser.). (ENG.). 72p. (gr. 2-5). lib. bdg. 26.65 *(978-1-4342-6490-9(4))* Stone Arch Bks.

Johnson, Temeka & Phillips, Quency. Decisions, Decisions, Decisions. 2010. 32p. 19.99 *(978-1-4520-5758-3(3))* AuthorHouse.

Jones, Patrick. At the Center. 2016. (Bounce Ser.). (ENG.). 104p. (YA). (gr. 6-12). 26.65 *(978-1-5124-1122-5(1))* Lerner Publishing Group.

—On Guard. 2016. (Bounce Ser.). (ENG.). 104p. (YA). (gr. 6-12). lib. bdg. 26.65 *(978-1-5124-1123-2(X)*, Darby Creek) Lerner Publishing Group.

—Pass It Forward. 2016. (Bounce Ser.). (ENG.). 104p. (YA). (gr. 6-12). lib. bdg. 26.65 *(978-1-5124-1125-6(6)*, Darby Creek) Lerner Publishing Group.

—To the Point. 2016. (Bounce Ser.). (ENG.). 96p. (YA). (gr. 6-12). lib. bdg. 26.65 *(978-1-5124-1124-9(8)*, Darby Creek) Lerner Publishing Group.

Jones, Patrick & Chartier, Brent. Collateral Damage. 2015. (ENG.). 128p. (YA). (gr. 6-12). pap. 7.99 *(978-1-4677-8091-9(X))* Lerner Publishing Group.

Jordan, Deloris. Dream Big: Michael Jordan & the Pursuit of Excellence. Root, Barry, illus. 2014. (ENG.). 32p. (J). (gr. -1-3). 7.99 *(978-1-4424-1270-5(4)*, Simon & Schuster/Paula Wiseman Bks.) Simon & Schuster/Paula Wiseman Bks.

—Dream Big: Michael Jordan & the Pursuit of Olympic Gold. Root, Barry, illus. 2012. (ENG.). 32p. (J). (gr. -1-3). 16.99 *(978-1-4424-1269-9(0)*, Simon & Schuster/Paula Wiseman Bks.) Simon & Schuster/Paula Wiseman Bks.

Jordan, Deloris & Jordan, Roslyn M. Salt in His Shoes: Michael Jordan in Pursuit of a Dream. Nelson, Kadir, illus. 2003. (ENG.). 32p. (J). (gr. -1-3). pap. 7.99 *(978-0-689-83419-6(5)*, Simon & Schuster Bks. For Young Readers) Simon & Schuster Bks. For Young Readers.

—Salt in His Shoes: Michael Jordan in Pursuit of a Dream. Nelson, Kadir, illus. 2003. lib. bdg. 18.40 *(978-0-613-89001-4(9)*, Turtleback) Turtleback Bks.

Joseph, Danielle. Pure Red. 2011. (ENG.). 240p. (YA). pap. 9.95 *(978-0-7387-2743-1(1)*, Flux) North Star Editions.

Joven, C. C. Basketball Break. Lopez, Alex, illus. 2017. (Sports Illustrated Kids Starting Line Readers Ser.). (ENG.). 32p. (gr. -1-1). lib. bdg. 22.65 *(978-1-4965-4253-3(3))* Capstone Press of Coughlan Cos.

Jump Shot. 2014. (Barber Game Time Bks.). (ENG., Illus.). 160p. (J). (gr. 3-7). pap. 7.99 *(978-1-4424-5730-0(9)*, Simon & Schuster/Paula Wiseman Bks.) Simon & Schuster/Paula Wiseman Bks.

Kalkipsakis, Thalia. Basketball Blues. Oswald, Ash, illus. 2008. (Go Girl! Ser.: 11). (ENG.). 96p. (Orig.). (J). (gr. 2-4). pap. 5.99 *(978-0-312-34646-1(8)*, 9780312346461) Feiwel & Friends.

Kantar, Andrew. Game Face. Keleher, Fran, illus. 2013. 160p. pap. 12.95 *(978-1-61160-566-2(0))* Whiskey Creek Restorations.

Kelly, Allison Palmer. The Power of Words. 2013. 202p. 24.95 *(978-1-4759-6745-6(4))*; pap. 14.95 *(978-1-4759-6743-2(8))* iUniverse, Inc.

Kelly, David A. The Basketball Blowout. Brundage, Scott, illus. 2017. (Most Valuable Players Ser.: 4). (ENG.). 128p. (J). (gr. 1-4). 4.99 *(978-0-553-51328-8(1)*, Random Hse. Bks. for Young Readers) Random Hse. Children's Bks.

Kindig, Tess Eileen. Slam Dunk Set, 8 vols. (Slam Dunk Ser.). (J). 38.99 *(978-0-7586-0014-1(3))* Concordia Publishing Hse.

Kline, Trish & Donev, Mary. Hoops in the Coop: KA Reader 7. 2007. (Illus.). 32p. (J). per. 20.00 *(978-1-934307-00-7(9))* Ghost Hunter Productions.

Kolb, Joseph J. Reservation Dreams. 2004. 185p. pap. 24.95 *(978-1-4137-3054-8(X))* America Star Bks.

Krech, Bob. Rebound, 0 vols. 2009. (ENG.). 276p. (YA). (gr. 7-9). pap. 9.99 *(978-0-7614-5543-1(4)*, 9780761455431, Amazon Children's Publishing) Amazon Publishing.

Kreie, Chris & Maese, Fares. Shot Clock Slam. Aburto, Jesus & Esparza, Andres, illus. 2010. (Sports Illustrated Kids Graphic Novels Ser.). (ENG.). 56p. (gr. 2-3). pap. 7.19 *(978-1-4342-2786-7(3))* Stone Arch Bks.

Kropp, Paul. Foul Shot. Doherty, Catherine, illus. 96p. pap. *(978-1-897039-25-0(5))* High Interest Publishing (HIP).

Laconi, Kristin. Karma the Kangaroo Takes the Court. 2010. 24p. pap. 12.99 *(978-1-4490-3227-2(3))* AuthorHouse.

Lawrence, David. Ball Stars. 2017. (Ball Stars Ser.: 4). (ENG.). 144p. (J). (gr. 1-3). 12.99 ***(978-0-14-378169-1(3))*** Random Hse. Australia AUS. Dist: Independent Pubs. Group.

—Ball Stars 3. 2017. (Ball Stars Ser.: 3). (ENG.). 144p. (J). (gr. 1-3). 12.99 ***(978-0-14-378167-7(7))*** Random Hse. Australia AUS. Dist: Independent Pubs. Group.

—Basketball Australia 2: The Bench Warmers vs the Raptors. 2017. (Ball Stars Ser.). (ENG.). 144p. (J). (gr. 1-3). 12.99 ***(978-0-14-378165-3(0))*** Random Hse. Australia AUS. Dist: Independent Pubs. Group.

—The Bench Warmers. 2017. (Ball Stars Ser.). (ENG.). 144p. (J). (gr. 1-3). 12.99 ***(978-0-14-378163-9(4))*** Random Hse. Australia AUS. Dist: Independent Pubs. Group.

Leipold, Judith. Hoops. Giddens, Jake, illus. 2013. 24p. 23.95 *(978-1-61493-223-9(9))* Peppertree Pr., The.

Lemke, Amy J. Too Short for the Court, 1 vol. Harpster, Steve, illus. 2012. (My First Graphic Novel Ser.). (ENG.). 32p. (gr. k-2). pap. 6.25 *(978-1-4342-3862-7(8))*; lib. bdg. 24.65 *(978-1-4342-3282-3(4))* Stone Arch Bks. (My First Graphic Novel).

Lovell, Whitney. The Game of the Season. 2012. 28p. pap. 24.95 *(978-1-4626-9978-0(2))* America Star Bks.

Lupica, Mike. Fast Break. 2015. (ENG.). 272p. (J). (gr. 5-8). 17.99 *(978-0-399-25606-6(7)*, Philomel Bks.) Penguin Publishing Group.

—Fast Break. 2016. (ENG.). 288p. (J). (gr. 5). pap. 8.99 *(978-1-101-99783-3(4)*, Puffin Books) Penguin Young Readers Group.

—Fast Break. 2016. (ENG.). 288p. (J). (gr. 5). 19.65 *(978-0-606-39313-3(7))* Turtleback Bks.

—Hot Hand. 2009. (Comeback Kids Ser.). (ENG.). 192p. (J). (gr. 3-7). pap. 6.99 *(978-0-14-241441-5(7)*, Puffin Books) Penguin Young Readers Group.

—Hot Hand, 1 vol. 2012. (Comeback Kids Ser.). (ENG.). 176p. (J). (gr. 4-8). lib. bdg. 27.07 *(978-1-59961-175-4(9))* Spotlight.

—Long Shot, 1 vol. 2012. (Comeback Kids Ser.). (ENG.). 192p. (J). (gr. 4-8). lib. bdg. 27.07 *(978-1-59961-176-1(7))* Spotlight.

—Miracle on 49th Street. 2007. (ENG.). 272p. (J). (gr. 5-18). 7.99 *(978-0-14-240942-8(1)*, Puffin Books) Penguin Young Readers Group.

—Miracle on 49th Street. 2007. 246p. (gr. 5-9). 18.00 *(978-0-7569-8157-0(3))* Perfection Learning Corp.

—Play Makers. 2014. (Game Changers Ser.: 2). (ENG.). 224p. (J). (gr. 3-7). pap. 6.99 *(978-0-545-38180-2(0)*, Scholastic Pr.) Scholastic, Inc.

—Point Guard. 2017. (Home Team Ser.). (ENG., Illus.). 272p. (J). (gr. 3-7). 16.99 *(978-1-4814-1003-8(2)*, Simon & Schuster Bks. For Young Readers) Simon & Schuster Bks. For Young Readers.

—Summer Ball. 2008. (ENG.). 272p. (J). (gr. 3-7). 7.99 *(978-0-14-241153-7(1)*, Puffin Books) Penguin Young Readers Group.

—Summer Ball. 2008. (Illus.). 244p. (gr. 5-9). 18.00 *(978-0-7569-8825-8(X))* Perfection Learning Corp.

—Travel Team. (ENG.). (J). (gr. 3-7). 2005. 304p. pap. 7.99 *(978-0-14-240462-1(4)*, Puffin Books) 2004. 288p. 17.99 *(978-0-399-24150-5(7)*, Philomel Bks.) Penguin Young Readers Group.

—Travel Team. l.t. ed. 2005. (Thorndike Literacy Bridge Ser.). 400p. (J). (gr. 4-7). lib. bdg. 23.95 *(978-0-7862-7415-4(8))* Thorndike Pr.

—Travel Team & the Big Field. 2011. (ENG.). 544p. (J). (gr. 5-18). 8.99 *(978-0-14-241984-7(2)*, Puffin Books) Penguin Young Readers Group.

—True Legend. (ENG.). (J). (gr. 5). 2013. 320p. pap. 7.99 *(978-0-14-242650-0(4)*, Puffin Books) 2012. 304p. 17.99 *(978-0-399-25227-3(4)*, Philomel Bks.) Penguin Young Readers Group.

Mack, W. C. Athlete vs. Mathlete. 2013. (Athlete vs. Mathlete Ser.). (ENG.). (YA). (gr. 3-6). 192p. 16.99 *(978-1-61963-129-8(6)*, 9781619631298); 192p. pap. 7.99 *(978-1-59990-938-7(3)*, 9781599909387); 208p. 16.99 *(978-1-59990-915-8(4)*, 9781599909158); (Illus.). 208p. pap. 7.99 *(978-1-59990-858-8(1)*, 9781599908588) Bloomsbury Publishing USA. (Bloomsbury USA Childrens).

—Time-Out. 2014. (Athlete vs. Mathlete Ser.). (ENG.). 208p. (YA). (gr. 3-6). 16.99 *(978-1-61963-301-8(9)*, 9781619633018, Bloomsbury USA Childrens) Bloomsbury Publishing USA.

Mackel, Kathy. Boost. 2010. (ENG.). 256p. (YA). (gr. 7-18). 7.99 *(978-0-14-241539-9(1)*, Speak) Penguin Young Readers Group.

Maddox, Jake. Bad-Luck Basketball, 1 vol. Ray, Mike, illus. 2014. (Jake Maddox JV Ser.). (ENG.). 96p. (gr. 3-4). 25.99 *(978-1-4342-9156-1(1))* Stone Arch Bks.

—Basketball Breakdown. 2016. (Jake Maddox JV Girls Ser.). (ENG.). 96p. (gr. 3-4). lib. bdg. 25.99 *(978-1-4965-3166-7(3))* Stone Arch Bks.

—Drive to the Hoop, 1 vol. Pulsar Studios Staff, illus. 2011. (Jake Maddox Girl Sports Stories Ser.). (ENG.). 72p. (gr. 2-3). 25.32 *(978-1-4342-2500-9(3))* Stone Arch Bks.

—Free Throw, 1 vol. Tiffany, Sean, illus. 2006. (Jake Maddox Sports Stories Ser.). (ENG.). 72p. (gr. 2-3). pap. 5.95 *(978-1-59889-238-3(X))*; lib. bdg. 25.32 *(978-1-59889-060-0(3))* Stone Arch Bks.

—Full Court Dreams. Mourning, Tuesday, illus. 2008. (Jake Maddox Girl Sports Stories Ser.). (ENG.). 72p. (gr. 2-3). lib. bdg. 25.32 *(978-1-4342-0469-1(3))*; per. 5.95 *(978-1-4342-0519-3(3))* Stone Arch Bks.

—Hoop Hotshot, 1 vol. Tiffany, Sean, illus. 2009. (Jake Maddox Sports Stories Ser.). (ENG.). 72p. (gr. 2-3). lib. bdg. 25.32 *(978-1-4342-1202-3(5))* Stone Arch Bks.

—Hoop Hustle. Aburto, Jesus, illus. 2015. (Jake Maddox Sports Stories Ser.). (ENG.). 72p. (gr. 2-3). lib. bdg. 25.32 *(978-1-4965-0494-4(1))* Stone Arch Bks.

—Off the Bench, 1 vol. Tiffany, Sean, illus. 2010. (Team Jake Maddox Sports Stories Ser.). (ENG.). 72p. (gr. 2-3). pap. 5.95 *(978-1-4342-2278-7(0))*; lib. bdg. 25.32 *(978-1-4342-1922-0(4))* Stone Arch Bks.

—On Guard, 1 vol. Tiffany, Sean, illus. 2010. (Team Jake Maddox Sports Stories Ser.). (ENG.). 72p. (gr. 2-3). pap. 5.95 *(978-1-4342-2279-4(9))*; lib. bdg. 25.32 *(978-1-4342-1920-6(8))* Stone Arch Bks.

—Playing Forward. Tiffany, Sean, illus. 2010. (Team Jake Maddox Sports Stories Ser.). (ENG.). 72p. (gr. 2-3). pap. 5.95 *(978-1-4342-2280-0(2))* Stone Arch Bks.

—Point Guard Prank, 1 vol. Tiffany, Sean, illus. 2012. (Jake Maddox Sports Stories Ser.). (ENG.). 72p. (gr. 2-3). pap. 5.95 *(978-1-4342-4207-5(2))*; 25.32 *(978-1-4342-4009-5(6))* Stone Arch Bks.

—Slam Dunk Shoes, 1 vol. Tiffany, Sean, illus. 2007. (Jake Maddox Sports Stories Ser.). (ENG.). 72p. (gr. 2-3). 25.32 *(978-1-59889-842-2(6))*; per. 5.95 *(978-1-59889-894-1(9))* Stone Arch Bks.

—Tiro Libre, 1 vol. Heck, Claudia M., tr. from ENG. Tiffany, Sean, illus. 2012. (Jake Maddox en Español Ser.). (SPA.). 72p. (gr. 2-3). 25.32 *(978-1-4342-3812-2(1))* Stone Arch Bks.

—Wildcats Slam Dunk, 1 vol. Tiffany, Sean, illus. 2010. (Team Jake Maddox Sports Stories Ser.). (ENG.). 208p. (gr. 3-6). pap. 7.95 *(978-1-4342-2886-4(X))* Stone Arch Bks.

—Win or Lose. Tiffany, Sean, illus. 2010. (Team Jake Maddox Sports Stories Ser.). (ENG.). 72p. (gr. 2-3). pap. 5.95 *(978-1-4342-2281-7(0))* Stone Arch Bks.

Maddox, Jake & Berne, Emma Carlson. Hoop Doctor, 1 vol. Mourning, Tuesday, illus. 2009. (Jake Maddox Girl Sports Stories Ser.). (ENG.). 72p. (gr. 2-3). 25.32 *(978-1-4342-1605-2(5))* Stone Arch Bks.

—Rebound Time, 1 vol. Wood, Katie, illus. 2013. (Jake Maddox Girl Sports Stories Ser.). (ENG.). 72p. (gr. 2-3). pap. 5.95 *(978-1-4342-4202-0(1))*; lib. bdg. 25.32 *(978-1-4342-4013-2(4))* Stone Arch Bks.

Mantell, Paul, text. Nothin' but Net. 2003. (Matt Christopher Sports Ser.). 136p. (J). (gr. 3-7). 12.65 *(978-0-7569-3021-9(9))* Perfection Learning Corp.

Marbury, Stephon & Dean, Marshall. The Adventures of Young Starbury: Practice Makes Perfect. Nakai, Ryan, illus. 2007. 36p. (J). 12.99 *(978-0-9798250-0-2(8))* Godspeed Pr.

Marsh, Carole. The Baskerville Basketball. 2006. 64p. (gr. 2-4). 14.95 *(978-0-635-06222-2(4))*; pap. 3.99 *(978-0-635-06216-1(X))* Gallopade International.

Masterson, Hoss. Ball Hog. Alves, Josh, illus. 2017. (Animal All-Stars Ser.). (ENG.). 56p. (gr. 1-3). lib. bdg. 25.32 *(978-1-4965-4308-0(4))* Stone Arch Bks.

McGirr, Randel W. Bible Camp. 2007. 176p. per. 13.95 *(978-0-595-44663-6(9))* iUniverse, Inc.

McGowan, Angel. Stomp Out the Bullying! 2011. (ENG.). 28p. (J). pap. 14.95 *(978-1-4327-7994-8(X))* Outskirts Pr., Inc.

McKnight, Marty. Jim Nasium Is a Basket Case. Jones, Chris B., illus. 2015. (Jim Nasium Ser.). (ENG.). 88p. (gr. 2-3). pap. 5.95 *(978-1-4965-0526-2(3))* Stone Arch Bks.

Meadows, Daisy. Brittany the Basketball Fairy. 2010. (Sports Fairies Ser.: 4). (ENG.). 80p. (J). (gr. 2-5). 4.99 *(978-0-545-20255-8(8)*, Scholastic Paperbacks) Scholastic, Inc.

Millett, Peter & Texidor, Dee. On the Team. 2008. (Rigby Focus Forward: Level F Ser.). (Illus.). 24p. (J). (gr. 4-7). pap. *(978-1-4190-3698-9(X)*, Rigby) Pearson Education Australia.

Mills, Claudia. Basketball Disasters. Francis, Guy, illus. 2013. (Mason Dixon Ser.). (ENG.). 176p. (J). (gr. 2-5). pap. 6.99 *(978-0-375-87276-1(0)*, Yearling) Random Hse. Children's Bks.

Mills, Lamonte. Franklin Basketball, 1 vol. 2009. 48p. pap. 16.95 *(978-1-61582-066-5(3))* America Star Bks.

Moore, Wes & Goodman, Shawn. This Way Home. 2015. (ENG.). 256p. (YA). (gr. 9). 20.99 *(978-0-375-99019-9(4)*, Delacorte Pr.) Random Hse. Children's Bks.

Morgan, Cliff. Like You, Like Me, 1 vol. Taylor, Stephen, illus. 2010. 20p. 24.95 *(978-1-4489-5140-6(2))* PublishAmerica, Inc.

Mullarkey, Lisa. TJ Zaps the Smackdown: Stopping a Physical Bully #6, 1 vol. LaCoste, Gary, illus. 2012. (TJ Trapper, Bully Zapper Ser.). (ENG.). 80p. (J). (gr. 2-5). lib. bdg. 27.07 *(978-1-61641-910-3(5)*, Calico Chapter Bks) Magic Wagon.

Murdock, Catherine Gilbert. Front & Center. (ENG.). (YA). (gr. 7). 2011. 288p. pap. 8.99 *(978-0-547-40305-2(4))* 2009. 272p. 16.00 *(978-0-618-95982-2(3))* Houghton Mifflin Harcourt Publishing Co.

Myers, Christopher. H. O. R. S. E. A Game of Basketball & Imagination. Myers, Christopher, illus. 2012. (ENG., Illus.). 32p. (J). (gr. k-12). 18.99 *(978-1-60684-218-8(8)*, Carolrhoda Bks.) Lerner Publishing Group.

Myers, Walter Dean. Game. (ENG.). (YA). (gr. 8). 2009. 240p. pap. 9.99 *(978-0-06-058296-8(0))* 2008. 224p. 17.99 *(978-0-06-058294-4(4))* HarperCollins Pubs. (HarperTeen).

—Game. 2011. 10.36 *(978-0-7848-3476-3(8)*, Everbind) Marco Bk. Co.

—Hoops. 2012. (ENG.). 224p. (YA). (gr. 7). pap. 9.99 *(978-0-307-97611-6(4)*, Ember) Random Hse. Children's Bks.

—Hoops. 2012. lib. bdg. 20.85 *(978-0-606-24821-1(8)*, Turtleback) Turtleback Bks.

—Slam! 2008. (ENG.). 288p. (J). (gr. 7). pap. 8.99 *(978-0-545-05574-1(1)*, Scholastic Paperbacks) Scholastic, Inc.

—Slam! 2008. (Point Signature Ser.). 266p. (gr. 7-12). lib. bdg. 19.65 *(978-0-613-12111-8(2)*, Turtleback) Turtleback Bks.

Nabors, V. L. Mad Craze Middle School; the Case of the Crumpled Balls. 2010. 215p. pap. 16.95 *(978-0-557-44140-2(4))* Lulu Pr., Inc.

Noble, Trinka Hakes. Jimmy's Boa & the Bungee Jump Slam Dunk. Kellogg, Steven, illus. 2005. 28p. (gr. -1-3). 16.00 *(978-0-7569-5765-0(6))* Perfection Learning Corp.

O'Malley, Kevin. Mount Olympus Basketball. 2004. (Illus.). 32p. (J). (gr. 2-6). 16.85 *(978-0-8027-8845-0(9))* Walker & Co.

Parker, Robert. Edenville Owls. 2008. 194p. (gr. 4-6). 18.00 *(978-0-7569-8920-0(5))* Perfection Learning Corp.

Patterson, C. Marie. Little Dinky's Love for Basketball. 2009. 24p. pap. 15.99 *(978-1-4415-1255-0(1))* Xlibris Corp.

Paul, Chris. Long Shot: Never Too Small to Dream Big. Morrison, Frank, illus. 2009. (ENG.). 32p. (J). (gr. -1-3). 17.99 *(978-1-4169-5079-0(6)*, Simon & Schuster Bks. For Young Readers) Simon & Schuster Bks. For Young Readers.

Paul, Volponi. Black & White. 2014. (ENG.). 208p. (YA). 11.24 *(978-1-63245-196-5(4))* Lectorum Pubns., Inc.

Pavlik, Al. Battles in the Backcourt. 2003. 120p. (J). per. 9.97 *(978-0-9722906-2-3(1))* AP Publishing.

Pee-Wee Basketball. 2003. (J). per. *(978-1-57657-939-8(5))* Paradise Pr., Inc.

Perry, Phyllis Jean. The Alien, the Giant, & Rocketman. Francis, Guy, illus. 2006. (J). pap. *(978-1-59336-723-7(6))* Mondo Publishing.

Peschke, Marci. Hoop Queen, 1 vol. Mourning, Tuesday, illus. 2011. (Kylie Jean Ser.). (ENG.). 112p. (gr. 2-3). lib. bdg. 22.65 *(978-1-4048-5962-3(4)*, Kylie Jean) Picture Window Bks.

—Hoop Queen, 1 vol. Mourning, Tuesday, illus. 2011. (Kylie Jean Ser.). (ENG.). 112p. (gr. 2-3). pap. 5.95 *(978-1-4048-6617-1(5)*, Kylie Jean) Picture Window Bks.

Pippenger, Jack G. The Young Rebel. 2007. 292p. 27.95 *(978-0-595-86314-3(0))*; per. 17.95 *(978-0-595-41077-4(4))* iUniverse, Inc.

Potter, Noel Gyro. Dibble Can't Dribble, 1 vol. Cannon, Joseph, illus. 2008. (Adventures of Marshall & Art Ser.). (ENG.). 32p. (gr. -1-4). 28.50 net. *(978-1-60270-197-7(0)*, Looking Glass Library) ABDO Publishing Co.

Priebe, Val. Basketball Breakdown. 2016. (Jake Maddox JV Girls Ser.). (ENG.). 96p. (gr. 3-4). pap. 5.95 *(978-1-4965-3676-1(2))* Stone Arch Bks.

—Five Fouls & You're Out!, 1 vol. Santillan, Jorge H., illus. 2011. (Sports Illustrated Kids Victory School Superstars Ser.). (ENG.). 56p. (gr. 1-3). pap. 5.95 *(978-1-4342-3075-1(9))*; lib. bdg. 26.65 *(978-1-4342-2228-2(4))* Stone Arch Bks.

Quick, Matthew. Boy21. 2013. (ENG.). 272p. (YA). (gr. 7-17). pap. 10.99 *(978-0-316-12796-7(5))* Little, Brown Bks. for Young Readers.

Reed, Ken. Sara's Big Challenge: Who's the Real Me? A Sara Thompson Sports Book. 2008. 188p. (J). pap. 9.95 *(978-1-4327-0624-1(1))* Outskirts Pr., Inc.

Richardson, Charisse K. & Richardson, Charisse. The Real Lucky Charm. Velasquez, Eric, illus. 2005. (ENG.). 80p. (J). (gr. 2-5). 5.99 *(978-0-14-240431-7(4)*, Puffin Books) Penguin Young Readers Group.

Robins, E. The Easy Way. 2004. (Carter High Chronicles (High-Interest Readers) Ser.). (Illus.). 48p. (J). per. 4.95 *(978-1-56254-683-0(X)*, SP683X) Saddleback Educational Publishing, Inc.

Robins, Eleanor. The Easy Way, 1 vol. unabr. ed. 2011. (Carter High Chronicles Ser.). (ENG.). 51p. (YA). (gr. 9-12). pap. 7.95 *(978-1-61651-307-8(1))* Saddleback Educational Publishing, Inc.

Robinson, Kerby Mae. Give 'N Go. 2010. 84p. pap. 8.95 *(978-1-4502-5075-7(0))* iUniverse, Inc.

Rockwell, Anne F. & Rockwell, Brendan & Belinda & the Slam Dunk! Meisel, Paul, illus. 2007. (Good Sports Ser.). 40p. (J). (gr. -1-1). 15.99 *(978-0-06-028443-5(9))* HarperCollins Pubs.

Rousselow, Jeff. Bury the Dead. 2009. 244p. pap. 15.26 *(978-0-557-07129-6(1))* Lulu Pr., Inc.

Rud, Jeff. Centerville. 2016. (Orca Sports Ser.). lib. bdg. 20.80 *(978-0-606-38688-3(2))* Turtleback Bks.

—Crossover, 1 vol. 2008. (Orca Sports Ser.). (ENG.). 176p. (YA). (gr. 6-10). pap. 9.95 *(978-1-55143-981-5(6))* Orca Bk. Pubs. USA.

—In the Paint: South Side Sports, 1 vol. 2005. (ENG., Illus.). 176p. (J). (gr. 4-7). per. 7.95 *(978-1-55143-337-0(0))* Orca Bk. Pubs. USA.

Safren, Hannah. Dive: The Life & Fight of Reba Tutt. 2013. (ENG.). 154p. pap. 15.00 *(978-1-938912-28-3(4))* Write Bloody Publishing.

Sasturain, Juan. Brooklin y Medio. (SPA.). (YA). 9.95 *(978-958-04-6876-9(1))* Norma S.A. COL. Dist: Distribuidora Norma, Inc.

Shamsiddeen, Abdul. Long Jeffery & the Backboard. 2012. 28p. pap. 19.99 *(978-1-4685-6862-2(0))* AuthorHouse.

Sharing Turf. 2004. (Illus.). (YA). mass mkt. 19.95 *(978-0-9753663-0-1(0))* Ballad Productions.

Sherman, Harold M. Get 'Em Mayfield. Anderson, Harold, illus. 2011. 272p. 47.95 *(978-1-258-06451-8(0))* Literary Licensing, LLC.

Shuert, Randy. Randy Ray & Easy Jay: Court Day Adventure. 2011. 28p. pap. 21.99 *(978-1-4568-8393-5(3))* Xlibris Corp.

Sitomer, Alan Lawrence. The Hoopster, 4 vols. unabr. ed. 2005. (GER.). (YA). 57.75 *(978-1-4025-7027-8(9)*, 41853) Recorded Bks., Inc.

Skead, Robert & Simmel, Mike. Mighty Mike Bounces Back: A Boy's Life with Epilepsy. 2011. 64p. (J). 14.95 *(978-1-4338-1043-5(3))*; pap. 9.95 *(978-1-4338-1042-8(5))* American Psychological Assn. (Magination Pr.).

Stevens, Eric & Maddox, Jake. Playing Forward. Tiffany, Sean, illus. 2010. (Jake Maddox Sports Story Ser.). 72p. pap. 0.60 *(978-1-4342-3206-9(9)*, Impact Bks.) Stone Arch Bks.

Stoudemire, Amar'e. Double Team. Jessell, Tim, illus. 2012. (STAT: Standing Tall & Talented Ser.: No. 2). (ENG.). 144p. (J). (gr. 3-7). pap. 5.99 *(978-0-545-38760-6(4)*, Scholastic Paperbacks) Scholastic, Inc.

—Double Team. Jessell, Tim, illus. 2012. (STAT: Standing Tall & Talented Ser.: 2). lib. bdg. 16.00 *(978-0-606-26762-5(X)*, Turtleback) Turtleback Bks.

—Home Court. Jessell, Tim, illus. 2012. (STAT: Standing Tall & Talented Ser.: 1). (ENG.). 144p. (J). (gr. 3-7). pap. 5.99 *(978-0-545-38759-0(0)*, Scholastic Pr.) Scholastic, Inc.

—Most Valuable. 2014. (STAT: Standing Tall & Talented Ser.: 5). lib. bdg. 16.00 *(978-0-606-35394-6(1))* Turtleback Bks.

—Schooled. 2013. (STAT: Standing Tall & Talented Ser.: 4). lib. bdg. 16.00 *(978-0-606-32378-9(3)*, Turtleback) Turtleback Bks.

—Slam Dunk. 2013. (STAT: Standing Tall & Talented Ser.: 3). lib. bdg. 16.00 *(978-0-606-31531-9(4)*, Turtleback) Turtleback Bks.

—Slam Dunk: Standing Tall & Talented. Jessell, Tim, illus. 2013. (Stat Ser.: 3). (ENG.). 144p. (J). (gr. 3-7). pap. 5.99 *(978-0-545-38761-3(2)*, Scholastic Paperbacks) Scholastic, Inc.

—Standing Tall & Talented - Most Valuable. 2014. (ENG.). 144p. (J). (gr. 3-7). pap. 5.99 *(978-0-545-60613-4(6)*, Scholastic Paperbacks) Scholastic, Inc.

—STAT #4: Schooled. 2013. (ENG.). 144p. (J). (gr. 3-7). pap. 5.99 *(978-0-545-60607-3(1)*, Scholastic Paperbacks) Scholastic, Inc.

Suen, Anastasia. Loose Tooth. Eitzen, Allan, illus. 2004. 28p. (gr. -1-3). 14.00 *(978-0-7569-1955-9(X))* Perfection Learning Corp.

Taddonio, Lea. Book 2: First Date. 2016. (Head over Heels Ser.). (ENG.). (J). (gr. 2-8). lib. bdg. 28.50 ***(978-1-62402-193-0(X))*** ABDO Publishing Co.

Talley, Rebecca Cornish. Heaven Scent. 2008. 229p. (gr. 8-12). pap. 15.99 *(978-1-59955-100-5(4))* Cedar Fort, Inc./CFI Distribution.

Taylor, Thomas. Superstar Coach. 2004. (Sport Story Ser.: 1). 202p. (J). 9.95 *(978-0-9702216-0-5(6))* Sport Story Publishing.

Terrell, Brandon. Double Scribble. 2017. (Jake Maddox Graphic Novels Ser.). (ENG., Illus.). 72p. (gr. 2-5). lib. bdg. 26.65 *(978-1-4965-3701-0(7))* Stone Arch Bks.

Tetrick, Chase. A Hot Dog Who Wanted to Play Basketball. 2009. 16p. pap. 12.50 *(978-1-4490-2078-1(X))* AuthorHouse.

Tillworth, Mary. All-Star Pups! (Paw Patrol) Petrossi, Fabrizio, illus. 2016. (Little Golden Book Ser.). (ENG.). 24p. (J). (-k).

4.99 *(978-1-101-93685-6(1)*, Golden Bks.) Random Hse. Children's Bks.
Toombs, Tom. The Way to Be a Winner: Little Tommy Learns a Lesson in Working Together. Wells Smith, Abby, illus. 2012. 32p. pap. 12.95 *(978-1-61314-034-5(7))* Innovo Publishing, LLC.
Volponi, Paul. The Final Four. (ENG.). (YA). (gr. 7). 2013. 272p. pap. 9.99 *(978-0-14-242385-1(8)*, Speak) 2012. 256p. 16.99 *(978-0-670-01264-0(5)*, Viking Books for Young Readers) Penguin Young Readers Group.
—Rucker Park Setup. 2008. (ENG.). 160p. (YA). (gr. 7-18). 6.99 *(978-0-14-241207-7(4)*, Speak) Penguin Young Readers Group.
Wachtel, Shirley Russak. Brad Sureshot — Coach-Detective: The Baffling Case of the Disappearing Dribbler. 2007. 76p. per. 8.95 *(978-0-595-47266-6(4))* iUniverse, Inc.
Wallace, Rich. Dunk under Pressure, Vol. 7. 7th ed. 2007. (Winning Season Ser.). (ENG.). 120p. (J). (gr. 3-7). 5.99 *(978-0-14-240858-2(1)*, Puffin Books) Penguin Young Readers Group.
—Pressure Point, 1 vol. Heitz, Tim, illus. 2016. (Game Face Ser.). (ENG.). 112p. (J). (gr. 3-7). 27.07 *(978-1-62402-135-0(2))* Magic Wagon.
—Second-String Center. 2008. (Winning Season Ser.: 10). (ENG.). 128p. (J). (gr. 3-7). 5.99 *(978-0-14-241216-9(3)*, Puffin Books) Penguin Young Readers Group.
—Technical Foul. 2nd ed. 2005. (Winning Season Ser.). (ENG.). 128p. (J). (gr. 3-7). pap. 5.99 *(978-0-14-240444-7(6)*, Puffin Books) Penguin Young Readers Group.
Walters, Eric. Home Team, 1 vol. 2010. (Orca Young Readers Ser.). (ENG.). 176p. (J). (gr. 3-6). pap. 7.95 *(978-1-55469-218-7(0))* Orca Bk. Pubs. USA.
—Off Season, 1 vol. 2003. (Orca Young Readers Ser.). (ENG., Illus.). 176p. (J). (gr. 3-6). pap. 6.95 *(978-1-55143-237-3(4))* Orca Bk. Pubs. USA.
—Underdog, 1 vol. 2004. (Orca Young Readers Ser.). (ENG., Illus.). 176p. (J). (gr. 3-6). pap., tchr. ed. 6.95 *(978-1-55143-302-8(8)*, 1234544) Orca Bk. Pubs. USA.
Walters, Eric & Williams, Jerome. Triple Threat, 1 vol. 2004. (Orca Young Readers Ser.). (ENG., Illus.). 144p. (J). (gr. 3-6). pap. 6.95 *(978-1-55143-359-2(1))* Orca Bk. Pubs. USA.
Waltman, Kevin. Next. 2013. (D-Bow High School Hoops Ser.). (ENG.). 216p. (J). 16.95 *(978-1-935955-64-1(0))*; pap. 11.95 *(978-1-935955-65-8(9))* Cinco Puntos Pr.
—Pull. 2016. (D-Bow High School Hoops Ser.). (ENG.). 216p. (gr. 6). 16.95 *(978-1-941026-26-7(5))* Cinco Puntos Pr.
—Quicks. 2016. (D-Bow High School Hoops Ser.). (ENG.). 216p. (J). (gr. 6). 16.95 *(978-1-941026-61-8(3))* Cinco Puntos Pr.
—Slump. 2014. (D-Bow High School Hoops Ser.). (ENG.). 216p. (J). 16.95 *(978-1-941026-00-7(1))* Cinco Puntos Pr.
Warner, Sally. EllRay Jakes Stands Tall. Biggs, Brian, illus. 2016. (EllRay Jakes Ser.). (ENG.). 176p. (J). (gr. 1-3). 5.99 *(978-0-14-751253-6(0)*, Puffin Books) Penguin Young Readers Group.
Wheeler, Lisa. Dino-Basketball. Gott, Barry, illus. 2011. (Carolrhoda Picture Bks.). (ENG.). 32p. (J). (gr. k-3). 16.95 *(978-0-7613-6393-4(9))* Lerner Publishing Group.
Wrong Way, Mallory! 2015. (Mallory Ser.: 23). (ENG., Illus.). 160p. (J). (gr. 2-5). 15.95 *(978-1-4677-0923-1(9))* Lerner Publishing Group.
Yarnell, Duane. The Winning Basket. 2005. pap. 26.95 *(978-1-4191-5930-5(5))* Kessinger Publishing, LLC.
Yee, Lisa. Stanford Wong Flunks Big-Time. 2007. (Apple Signature Edition Ser.). (ENG., Illus.). 320p. (J). (gr. 3-7). per. 6.99 *(978-0-439-62248-6(4)*, Levine, Arthur A. Bks.) Scholastic, Inc.
4RV Publishing LLC Staff. Case of the Missing Coach. 2007. (Illus.). 144p. (J). per. 18.99 *(978-0-9797513-1-8(4))* 4RV Publishing, LLC.

BASKETBALL—HISTORY

ABDO Publishing Company Staff. Inside College Basketball Set 2, 1 vol. 2013. (Inside College Basketball Set 2 Ser.: 4). (ENG.). 48p. (gr. 3-6). lib. bdg. 131.16 *(978-1-61783-913-9(2)*, SportsZone) ABDO Publishing Co.
—NBA's Best Ever. 2014. (NBA's Best Ever Ser.: 6). (ENG.). 64p. (gr. 8-12). lib. bdg. 196.74 *(978-1-62403-408-4(X)*, SportsZone) ABDO Publishing Co.
America's Most Winning Teams: Set 2. 2013. (America's Most Winning Teams Ser.). 48p. (J). (gr. 5-8). 175.50 *(978-1-4488-9410-9(7))* Rosen Publishing Group, Inc., The.
America's Most Winning Teams: Sets 1 - 2. 2013. (America's Most Winning Teams Ser.). 48p. (J). (gr. 5-8). 351.00 *(978-1-4777-0613-8(5))*; pap. 141.00 *(978-1-4777-2683-9(7))*; pap. 846.00 *(978-1-4777-2684-6(5))* Rosen Publishing Group, Inc., The.
Anderson, Jameson. Lebron James, 1 vol. 2014. (Awesome Athletes Ser.). (ENG.). 32p. (gr. 8-12). 27.07 *(978-1-62403-330-8(X))* ABDO Publishing Co.
Anderson, Josh. Los Angeles Clippers. 2012. (On the Hardwood Ser.). (ENG., Illus.). 47p. (gr. 3-8). pap. 8.95 *(978-1-61570-510-8(4))*; lib. bdg. 27.93 *(978-1-61570-511-5(2))* Scobre Pr. Corp.
—Miami Heat. 2012. (On the Hardwood Ser.). (ENG., Illus.). 47p. (gr. 3-8). pap. 8.95 *(978-1-61570-500-9(7))*; lib. bdg. 27.93 *(978-1-61570-501-6(5))* Scobre Pr. Corp.
Aretha, David. Top 10 Moments in Basketball. 2016. (Sports Greats Ser.). (Illus.). 48p. (J). (gr. 6-5). pap. 11.70 *(978-0-7660-7590-0(7))* Enslow Pubs., Inc.
—Top 10 Shooters & Scorers in Basketball. 2016. (Sports Greats Ser.). (Illus.). 48p. (J). (gr. 6-5). pap. 11.70 *(978-0-7660-7561-0(3))* Enslow Pubs., Inc.
Bailey, Diane. Kansas Basketball. 2013. (America's Most Winning Teams Ser.). 48p. (J). (gr. 5-8). 29.25 *(978-1-4488-9405-5(0))*; pap. 11.75 *(978-1-4488-9429-1(8))* Rosen Publishing Group, Inc., The.
Basen, Ryan. Georgetown Hoyas, 1 vol. 2012. (Inside College Basketball Set 1 Ser.). (ENG.). 48p. lib. bdg. 32.79 *(978-1-61783-282-6(0)*, SportsZone) ABDO Publishing Co.
Bekkering, Annalise. NCAA Basketball. 2013. (J). *(978-1-62127-366-0(0))*; pap. *(978-1-62127-371-4(7))* Weigl Pubs., Inc.
—NCAA Basketball Championships. 2009. (Sporting Championships Ser.). 32p. (gr. 4-6). (J). pap. 9.95 *(978-1-60596-635-9(5))*; (Illus.). (YA). lib. bdg. 26.00 *(978-1-60596-634-2(7))* Weigl Pubs., Inc.
Berman, Ron. Houston Rockets. 2013. (On the Hardwood Ser.). (ENG., Illus.). 48p. (gr. 3-8). pap. 8.95 *(978-1-61570-837-6(5))* Scobre Pr. Corp.
—Los Angeles Lakers. 2012. (On the Hardwood Ser.). (ENG., Illus.). 47p. (gr. 3-8). pap. 8.95 *(978-1-61570-502-3(3))*; lib. bdg. 27.93 *(978-1-61570-503-0(1))* Scobre Pr. Corp.
Birle, Pete. Chicago Bulls. 2012. (On the Hardwood Ser.). (ENG., Illus.). 47p. (gr. 3-8). pap. 8.95 *(978-1-61570-504-7(X))*; lib. bdg. 27.93 *(978-1-61570-505-4(8))* Scobre Pr. Corp.
—Minnesota Timberwolves. 2012. (On the Hardwood Ser.). (ENG., Illus.). 47p. (gr. 3-8). pap. 8.95 *(978-1-61570-506-1(6))*; lib. bdg. 27.93 *(978-1-61570-507-8(4))* Scobre Pr. Corp.
—New York Knicks. 2013. (On the Hardwood Ser.). (ENG., Illus.). 48p. (gr. 3-8). pap. 8.95 *(978-1-61570-834-5(0))* Scobre Pr. Corp.
—San Antonio Spurs. 2012. (On the Hardwood Ser.). (ENG., Illus.). 47p. (gr. 3-8). pap. 8.95 *(978-1-61570-508-5(2))*; lib. bdg. 27.93 *(978-1-61570-509-2(0))* Scobre Pr. Corp.
Borth, Teddy. Basketball: Great Moments, Records, & Facts, 1 vol. 2014. (Great Sports Ser.). (ENG., Illus.). 24p. (J). (gr. 2-4). lib. bdg. 28.50 *(978-1-62970-688-7(4))* ABDO Publishing Co.
Bowker, Paul D. New Orleans Pelicans, 1 vol. 2011. (Inside the NBA Ser.). (ENG., Illus.). 48p. (C). (gr. 4-6). lib. bdg. 32.79 *(978-1-61783-167-6(0))* ABDO Publishing Co.
Braun, Eric. Basketball Stats & the Stories Behind Them: What Every Fan Needs to Know. 2016. (Sports Stats & Stories Ser.). (ENG., Illus.). 48p. (gr. 4-6). lib. bdg. 31.99 *(978-1-4914-8216-2(8))* Capstone Press of Coughlan Cos.
Buckley, James, Jr. Bill Bradley. 2009. (Basketball Hall of Famers Ser.). 112p. (gr. 5-8). 63.90 *(978-1-61511-529-7(3)*, Rosen Reference) Rosen Publishing Group, Inc., The.
Caffrey, Scott. The Story of the Boston Celtics. 2010. (NBA — A History of Hoops Ser.). 48p. (YA). (gr. 5-18). 23.95 *(978-1-58341-937-3(3)*, Creative Education) Creative Co., The.
—The Story of the Chicago Bulls. 2010. (J). 23.95 *(978-1-58341-939-7(X)*, Creative Education) Creative Co., The.
—The Story of the Detroit Pistons. 2010. (NBA — A History of Hoops Ser.). 48p. (YA). (gr. 5-18). 23.95 *(978-1-58341-943-4(8)*, Creative Education) Creative Co., The.
Christopher, Matt. Great Moments in Basketball History. 2009. (ENG., Illus.). 144p. (J). (gr. 3-7). pap. 6.99 *(978-0-316-04483-7(0))* Little, Brown Bks. for Young Readers.
Coy, John. Game Changer: John McLendon & the Secret Game. DuBurke, Randy, illus. 2015. (ENG.). 32p. (J). (gr. 2-5). 17.99 *(978-1-4677-8810-6(4)*, Carolrhoda Bks.); 17.99 *(978-1-4677-9055-0(9)*, Carolrhoda Bks.); 9.99 *(978-1-4677-9056-7(7)*, Carolrhoda Bks.); 17.99 *(978-1-4677-2604-7(4))* Lerner Publishing Group.
—Hoop Genius: How a Desperate Teacher & a Rowdy Gym Class Invented Basketball. Morse, Joe, illus. 2013. (ENG.). 32p. (J). (gr. 2-5). lib. bdg. 16.95 *(978-0-7613-6617-1(2)*, Carolrhoda Bks.) Lerner Publishing Group.
De Medeiros, Michael. The NBA. 2007. (Sporting Championships Ser.). (Illus.). 32p. (J). (gr. 4-6). lib. bdg. 26.00 *(978-1-59036-691-2(3))*; per. 9.95 *(978-1-59036-692-9(1))* Weigl Pubs., Inc.
—NBA. 2012. (J). *(978-1-61913-060-9(2))*; pap. 28.55 *(978-1-61913-622-9(8))* Weigl Pubs., Inc.
Disney & Me. 2012. *(978-0-7948-3763-1(8))* Whitman Publishing LLC.
Dittmer, Lori. The Story of the Orlando Magic. 2010. (NBA — A History of Hoops Ser.). 48p. (YA). (gr. 5-18). 23.95 *(978-1-58341-956-4(X)*, Creative Education) Creative Co., The.
Doeden, Matt. All about Basketball. 2015. (All about Sports Ser.). (ENG.). 32p. (gr. 1-2). lib. bdg. 27.32 *(978-1-4914-1994-6(6)*, Aplus Bks.) Capstone Press of Coughlan Cos.
—The Final Four: The Pursuit of College Basketball Glory. 2016. (Spectacular Sports Ser.). (ENG.). 64p. (J). (gr. 5-12). 33.32 *(978-1-4677-8780-2(9))*; (Illus.). 50.65 *(978-1-4677-9730-6(8))* Lerner Publishing Group. (Millbrook Pr.).
Donnelly, Patrick. Best NBA Centers of All Time, 1 vol. 2014. (NBA's Best Ever Ser.). (ENG., Illus.). 64p. (J). (gr. 8-12). lib. bdg. 32.79 *(978-1-62403-409-1(8)*, SportsZone) ABDO Publishing Co.
—Best NBA Forwards of All Time, 1 vol. 2014. (NBA's Best Ever Ser.). (ENG.). 64p. (gr. 8-12). lib. bdg. 32.79 *(978-1-62403-411-4(X)*, SportsZone) ABDO Publishing Co.
Fishman, Jon M. Anthony Davis. 2015. (ENG., Illus.). 32p. (J). (gr. 2-5). 26.65 *(978-1-4677-9367-4(1)*, Lerner Pubns.) Lerner Publishing Group.
Frager, Ray. Oklahoma City Thunder, 1 vol. 2011. (Inside the NBA Ser.). (ENG., Illus.). 48p. (YA). (gr. 3-6). lib. bdg. 32.79 *(978-1-61783-169-0(7))* ABDO Publishing Co.
—Washington Wizards, 1 vol. 2011. (Inside the NBA Ser.). (ENG., Illus.). 48p. (YA). (gr. 3-6). lib. bdg. 32.79 *(978-1-61783-178-2(6))* ABDO Publishing Co.
Frederick, Shane. The NBA: a History of Hoops: the Story of the Los Angeles Lakers. 2015. (NBA: a History of Hoops Ser.). (ENG.). 48p. (J). (gr. 5-8). pap. 9.99 *(978-1-62832-021-3(4)*, Creative Paperbacks) Creative Co., The.
—The NBA: a History of Hoops: the Story of the Miami Heat. 2015. (NBA: a History of Hoops Ser.). (ENG.). 48p. (J). (gr. 5-8). pap. 12.00 *(978-1-62832-023-7(0)*, Creative Paperbacks) Creative Co., The.
—The NBA: a History of Hoops: the Story of the Milwaukee Bucks. 2015. (NBA: a History of Hoops Ser.). (ENG.). 48p. (J). (gr. 5-8). pap. 12.00 *(978-1-62832-024-4(9)*, Creative Paperbacks) Creative Co., The.
—The NBA: a History of Hoops: the Story of the New Orleans Pelicans. 2015. (NBA: a History of Hoops Ser.). (ENG.). 48p. (J). (gr. 5-8). pap. 12.00 *(978-1-62832-026-8(5)*, Creative Paperbacks) Creative Co., The.
—The NBA: a History of Hoops: the Story of the New York Knicks. 2015. (NBA: a History of Hoops Ser.). (ENG.). 48p. (J). (gr. 5-8). pap. 12.00 *(978-1-62832-027-5(3)*, Creative Paperbacks) Creative Co., The.
—The NBA: a History of Hoops: the Story of the San Antonio Spurs. 2015. (NBA: a History of Hoops Ser.). (ENG.). 48p. (J). (gr. 5-8). pap. 12.00 *(978-1-62832-034-3(6)*, Creative Paperbacks) Creative Co., The.
—The Story of the New York Knicks. 2014. (J). *(978-1-60818-441-5(2)*, Creative Education) Creative Co., The.
Frisch, Aaron. Boston Celtics. 2012. (NBA Champions Ser.). (ENG., Illus.). 24p. (J). (gr. 1-3). pap. 9.99 *(978-0-89812-706-5(8)*, Creative Paperbacks) Creative Co., The.
—Chicago Bulls. 2012. (NBA Champions Ser.). (ENG.). 24p. (J). (gr. 1-3). pap. 9.99 *(978-0-89812-707-2(6)*, Creative Paperbacks) Creative Co., The.
—Los Angeles Lakers. 2012. (NBA Champions Ser.). (ENG., Illus.). 24p. (J). (gr. 1-3). pap. 9.99 *(978-0-89812-711-9(4)*, Creative Paperbacks) Creative Co., The.
—Miami Heat. 2012. (NBA Champions Ser.). (Illus.). 24p. (J). (ENG.). (gr. 1-3). pap. 9.99 *(978-0-89812-712-6(2)*, Creative Paperbacks); 25.65 *(978-1-60818-137-7(5)*, Creative Education) Creative Co., The.
—Milwaukee Bucks. 2012. (J). 25.65 *(978-1-60818-138-4(3)*, Creative Education) Creative Co., The.
—Oklahoma City Thunder. 2012. (Illus.). 24p. (J). 25.65 *(978-1-60818-144-5(8)*, Creative Education) Creative Co., The.
—Philadelphia 76ers. 2012. (J). 25.65 *(978-1-60818-140-7(5)*, Creative Education) Creative Co., The.
—Portland Trail Blazers. 2012. (Illus.). 24p. (J). 25.65 *(978-1-60818-141-4(3)*, Creative Education) Creative Co., The.
—San Antonio Spurs. 2012. (Illus.). 24p. (J). 25.65 *(978-1-60818-143-8(X)*, Creative Education) Creative Co., The.
—The Story of the Dallas Mavericks. 2006. (Pro Basketball Today Ser.). (Illus.). 32p. (J). lib. bdg. 18.95 *(978-1-58341-404-0(5)*, Creative Education) Creative Co., The.
—The Story of the Indiana Pacers. 2006. (Pro Basketball Today Ser.). (Illus.). 32p. (J). lib. bdg. 18.95 *(978-1-58341-409-5(6)*, Creative Education) Creative Co., The.
—The Story of the Los Angeles Clippers. (J). 2010. 23.95 *(978-1-58341-947-2(0))* 2006. (Illus.). 32p. lib. bdg. 18.95 *(978-1-58341-410-1(X))* Creative Co., The. (Creative Education).
—The Story of the Phoenix Suns. 2006. (Pro Basketball Today Ser.). (Illus.). 32p. (J). lib. bdg. 18.95 *(978-1-58341-421-7(5)*, Creative Education) Creative Co., The.
—The Story of the Portland Trail Blazers. 2006. (Pro Basketball Today Ser.). (Illus.). 32p. (J). lib. bdg. 18.95 *(978-1-58341-422-4(3)*, Creative Education) Creative Co., The.
—The Story of the Washington Wizards. 2006. (NBA — A History of Hoops Ser.). (Illus.). 32p. (J). lib. bdg. 18.95 *(978-1-58341-428-6(2)*, Creative Education) Creative Co., The.
—Washington Wizards. 2012. (Illus.). 24p. (J). 25.65 *(978-1-60818-145-2(6)*, Creative Education) Creative Co., The.
Frisch, Nate. The NBA: a History of Hoops: the Story of the Brooklyn Nets. 2015. (NBA: a History of Hoops Ser.). (ENG.). 48p. (J). (gr. 5-8). pap. 12.00 *(978-1-62832-010-7(9)*, Creative Paperbacks) Creative Co., The.
—The NBA: a History of Hoops: the Story of the Chicago Bulls. 2015. (NBA: a History of Hoops Ser.). (ENG.). 48p. (J). (gr. 5-8). pap. 12.00 *(978-1-62832-012-1(5)*, Creative Paperbacks) Creative Co., The.
—The NBA: a History of Hoops: the Story of the Cleveland Cavaliers. 2015. (NBA: a History of Hoops Ser.). (ENG.). 48p. (J). (gr. 5-8). pap. 12.00 *(978-1-62832-013-8(3)*, Creative Paperbacks) Creative Co., The.
—The NBA: a History of Hoops: the Story of the Dallas Mavericks. 2015. (NBA: a History of Hoops Ser.). (ENG.). 48p. (J). (gr. 5-8). pap. 12.00 *(978-1-62832-014-5(1)*, Creative Paperbacks) Creative Co., The.
—The NBA: a History of Hoops: the Story of the Golden State Warriors. 2015. (NBA: a History of Hoops Ser.). (ENG.). 48p. (J). (gr. 5-8). pap. 12.00 *(978-1-62832-017-6(6)*, Creative Paperbacks) Creative Co., The.
—The NBA: a History of Hoops: the Story of the Houston Rockets. 2015. (NBA: a History of Hoops Ser.). (ENG.). 48p. (J). (gr. 5-8). pap. 12.00 *(978-1-62832-018-3(4)*, Creative Paperbacks) Creative Co., The.
—The NBA: a History of Hoops: the Story of the Indiana Pacers. 2015. (NBA: a History of Hoops Ser.). (ENG.). 48p. (J). (gr. 5-8). pap. 12.00 *(978-1-62832-019-0(2)*, Creative Paperbacks) Creative Co., The.
—The NBA: a History of Hoops: the Story of the Memphis Grizzlies. 2015. (NBA: a History of Hoops Ser.). (ENG.). 48p. (J). (gr. 5-8). pap. 12.00 *(978-1-62832-022-0(2)*, Creative Paperbacks) Creative Co., The.
—The NBA: a History of Hoops: the Story of the Phoenix Suns. 2015. (NBA: a History of Hoops Ser.). (ENG.). 48p. (J). (gr. 5-8). pap. 12.00 *(978-1-62832-031-2(1)*, Creative Paperbacks) Creative Co., The.
—The NBA: a History of Hoops: the Story of the Toronto Raptors. 2015. (NBA: a History of Hoops Ser.). (ENG.). 48p. (J). (gr. 5-8). pap. 12.00 *(978-1-62832-035-0(4)*, Creative Paperbacks) Creative Co., The.
—The Story of the Brooklyn Nets. 2014. (J). *(978-1-60818-439-2(0)*, Creative Education) Creative Co., The.
—The Story of the Cleveland Cavaliers. 2010. (NBA — A History of Hoops Ser.). 48p. (YA). (gr. 5-18). 23.95 *(978-1-58341-940-3(3)*, Creative Education) Creative Co., The.
—The Story of the Houston Rockets. 2010. (NBA — A History of Hoops Ser.). 48p. (YA). (gr. 5-18). 23.95 *(978-1-58341-945-8(4)*, Creative Education) Creative Co., The.
—The Story of the Phoenix Suns. 2014. (J). *(978-1-60818-445-3(5)*, Creative Education) Creative Co., The.
—The Story of the Toronto Raptors. 2014. (J). *(978-1-60818-449-1(8)*, Creative Education) Creative Co., The.
Gilbert, Sara. The Story of the Los Angeles Lakers. 2010. (NBA — A History of Hoops Ser.). 48p. (YA). (gr. 5-18). 23.95 *(978-1-58341-948-9(9)*, Creative Education) Creative Co., The.
—The Story of the Memphis Grizzlies. 2006. (Pro Basketball Today Ser.). (Illus.). 32p. (J). lib. bdg. 18.95 *(978-1-58341-412-5(6)*, Creative Education) Creative Co., The.
—The Story of the Miami Heat. 2006. (Pro Basketball Today Ser.). (Illus.). 32p. (J). lib. bdg. 18.95 *(978-1-58341-413-2(4)*, Creative Education) Creative Co., The.
—The Story of the Milwaukee Bucks. 2010. (NBA — A History of Hoops Ser.). 48p. (YA). (gr. 5-18). 23.95 *(978-1-58341-951-9(9)*, Creative Education) Creative Co., The.
—The Story of the Minnesota Timberwolves. 2006. (Pro Basketball Today Ser.). (Illus.). 32p. (J). lib. bdg. 18.95 *(978-1-58341-415-6(0)*, Creative Education) Creative Co., The.
—The Story of the New Orleans Hornets. 2006. (Pro Basketball Today Ser.). (Illus.). 32p. (J). lib. bdg. 18.95 *(978-1-58341-417-0(7)*, Creative Education) Creative Co., The.
—The Story of the Orlando Magic. 2006. (Pro Basketball Today Ser.). (Illus.). 32p. (J). lib. bdg. 18.95 *(978-1-58341-419-4(3)*, Creative Education) Creative Co., The.
—The Story of the Philadelphia 76ers. 2010. (NBA — A History of Hoops Ser.). 48p. (YA). (gr. 5-18). 23.95 *(978-1-58341-957-1(8)*, Creative Education) Creative Co., The.
—The Story of the Toronto Raptors. 2006. (Pro Basketball Today Ser.). (Illus.). 32p. (J). lib. bdg. 18.95 *(978-1-58341-426-2(6)*, Creative Education) Creative Co., The.
Gitlin, Martin. Boston Celtics, 1 vol. 2011. (Inside the NBA Ser.). (ENG., Illus.). 48p. (YA). (gr. 3-6). lib. bdg. 32.79 *(978-1-61783-150-8(6))* ABDO Publishing Co.
—Connecticut Huskies, 1 vol. 2012. (Inside College Basketball Set 1 Ser.). (ENG.). 48p. lib. bdg. 32.79 *(978-1-61783-280-2(4)*, SportsZone) ABDO Publishing Co.
—Louisville Cardinals, 1 vol. 2013. (Inside College Basketball Set 2 Ser.). (ENG., Illus.). 48p. (J). (gr. 3-6). lib. bdg. 32.79 *(978-1-61783-916-0(7)*, SportsZone) ABDO Publishing Co.
Goessling, Ben. Minnesota Timberwolves, 1 vol. 2011. (Inside the NBA Ser.). (ENG., Illus.). 48p. (YA). (gr. 3-6). lib. bdg. 32.79 *(978-1-61783-165-2(4))* ABDO Publishing Co.
Goodman, Michael E. The Story of the New Jersey Nets. 2010. (NBA — A History of Hoops Ser.). 48p. (YA). (gr. 5-18). 23.95 *(978-1-58341-953-3(5)*, Creative Education) Creative Co., The.
—The Story of the New York Knicks. 2010. (NBA — A History of Hoops Ser.). 48p. (YA). (gr. 5-18). 23.95 *(978-1-58341-955-7(1)*, Creative Education) Creative Co., The.
Graves, Will. Best NBA Guards of All Time, 1 vol. 2014. (NBA's Best Ever Ser.). (ENG.). 64p. (gr. 8-12). lib. bdg. 32.79 *(978-1-62403-412-1(8)*, SportsZone) ABDO Publishing Co.
—Best NBA Teams of All Time, 1 vol. 2014. (NBA's Best Ever Ser.). (ENG.). 64p. (gr. 8-12). lib. bdg. 32.79 *(978-1-62403-414-5(4)*, SportsZone) ABDO Publishing Co.
Hetrick, Hans. The Story of the Miami Heat. 2010. (NBA — A History of Hoops Ser.). 48p. (YA). (gr. 5-18). 23.95 *(978-1-58341-950-2(0)*, Creative Education) Creative Co., The.
—The Story of the San Antonio Spurs. 2010. (NBA — A History of Hoops Ser.). 48p. (YA). (gr. 5-18). 23.95 *(978-1-58341-961-8(6)*, Creative Education) Creative Co., The.
Hinnant, Jamal. Top 10 Teams in Basketball. 2016. (Sports Greats Ser.). 48p. (J). (gr. 6-5). pap. 11.70 *(978-0-7660-7599-3(0))* Enslow Pubs., Inc.
Hofstetter, Adam. Olympic Basketball. 2007. 52p. pap. 26.50 *(978-1-4358-3778-2(9))* Rosen Publishing Group, Inc., The.
Hofstetter, Adam B. Olympic Basketball. (Great Moments in Olympic History Ser.). 48p. (gr. 5-6). 2009. 53.00 *(978-1-61513-157-0(4)*, Rosen Reference) 2007. (Illus.). (YA). lib. bdg. 29.25 *(978-1-4042-0967-1(0))* Rosen Publishing Group, Inc., The.
Holmes, Parker. Lakers vs. Celtics. (J). 2014. pap. *(978-1-4777-2786-7(8))* 2013. (gr. 2-5). 22.60 *(978-1-4777-2785-0(X))* Rosen Publishing Group, Inc., The. (PowerKids Pr.).
Howell, Brian. Florida Gators, 1 vol. 2013. (Inside College Basketball Set 2 Ser.). (ENG., Illus.). 48p. (J). (gr. 3-6). lib. bdg. 32.79 *(978-1-61783-914-6(0)*, SportsZone) ABDO Publishing Co.
—Kentucky Wildcats, 1 vol. 2012. (Inside College Basketball Set 1 Ser.). (ENG.). 48p. lib. bdg. 32.79 *(978-1-61783-284-0(7)*, SportsZone) ABDO Publishing Co.
—Utah Jazz, 1 vol. 2011. (Inside the NBA Ser.). (ENG., Illus.). 48p. (YA). (gr. 3-6). lib. bdg. 32.79 *(978-1-61783-177-5(8))* ABDO Publishing Co.
Jackson, Dave. Philadelphia 76ers, 1 vol. 2011. (Inside the NBA Ser.). (ENG., Illus.). 48p. (YA). (gr. 3-6). lib. bdg. 32.79 *(978-1-61783-171-3(9))* ABDO Publishing Co.
Kamberg, Mary-Lane. North Carolina Basketball. 2013. (America's Most Winning Teams Ser.). 48p. (J). (gr. 5-8). 29.25 *(978-1-4488-9404-8(2))*; pap. 70.50 *(978-1-4488-9444-4(1))*; pap. 11.75 *(978-1-4488-9435-2(2))* Rosen Publishing Group, Inc., The.
Knobel, Andy. New York Knicks, 1 vol. 2011. (Inside the NBA Ser.). (ENG., Illus.). 48p. (YA). (gr. 3-6). lib. bdg. 32.79 *(978-1-61783-168-3(9))* ABDO Publishing Co.
Lannin, Joanne. A History of Basketball for Girls & Women: From Bloomers to Big Leagues. (Sports Legacy Ser.). (Illus.). 144p. (gr. 7-12). 2005. lib. bdg. 26.63 *(978-0-8225-3331-3(6))* 2003. (J). pap. 9.95 *(978-0-8225-9863-3(9))* Lerner Publishing Group.
LeBoutillier, Nate. The NBA: a History of Hoops: the Story of the Denver Nuggets. 2015. (NBA: a History of Hoops Ser.). (ENG.). 48p. (J). (gr. 5-8). pap. 12.00 *(978-1-62832-015-2(X)*, Creative Paperbacks) Creative Co., The.

—The NBA: a History of Hoops: the Story of the Minnesota Timberwolves. 2015. (NBA: a History of Hoops Ser.). (ENG.). 48p. (J). (gr. 5-8). pap. 12.00 (978-1-62832-025-1(7), Creative Paperbacks) Creative Co., The.

—The NBA: a History of Hoops: the Story of the Oklahoma City Thunder. 2015. (NBA: a History of Hoops Ser.). (ENG.). 48p. (J). (gr. 5-8). pap. 12.00 (978-1-62832-028-2(1), Creative Paperbacks) Creative Co., The.

—The NBA: a History of Hoops: the Story of the Portland Trail Blazers. 2015. (NBA: a History of Hoops Ser.). (ENG.). 48p. (J). (gr. 5-8). pap. 12.00 (978-1-62832-032-9(X), Creative Paperbacks) Creative Co., The.

—The NBA: a History of Hoops: the Story of the Utah Jazz. 2015. (NBA: a History of Hoops Ser.). (ENG.). 48p. (J). (gr. 5-8). pap. 12.00 (978-1-62832-036-7(2), Creative Paperbacks) Creative Co., The.

Leboutillier, Nate. Seattle Supersonics. 2006. (NBA — A History of Hoops Ser.). (Illus.). 32p. (J). lib. bdg. 18.95 (978-1-58341-425-5(8), Creative Education) Creative Co., The.

—The Story of the Boston Celtics. 2006. (Pro Basketball Today Ser.). (Illus.). 32p. (J). lib. bdg. 18.95 (978-1-58341-400-2(2), Creative Education) Creative Co., The.

—The Story of the Chicago Bulls. 2006. (Pro Basketball Today Ser.). (Illus.). 32p. (J). lib. bdg. 18.95 (978-1-58341-402-6(9), Creative Education) Creative Co., The.

—The Story of the Cleveland Cavaliers. 2006. (Pro Basketball Today Ser.). (Illus.). 32p. (J). lib. bdg. 18.95 (978-1-58341-403-3(7), Creative Education) Creative Co., The.

—The Story of the Denver Nuggets. 2006. (Pro Basketball Today Ser.). (Illus.). 32p. (J). lib. bdg. 18.95 (978-1-58341-405-7(3), Creative Education) Creative Co., The.

LeBoutillier, Nate. The Story of the Denver Nuggets. 2010. (J). 23.95 (978-1-58341-942-7(X), Creative Education) Creative Co., The.

Leboutillier, Nate. The Story of the Detroit Pistons. 2006. (Pro Basketball Today Ser.). (Illus.). 32p. (J). lib. bdg. 18.95 (978-1-58341-406-4(1), Creative Education) Creative Co., The.

—The Story of the Golden State Warriors. 2006. (Pro Basketball Today Ser.). (Illus.). 32p. (J). lib. bdg. 18.95 (978-1-58341-407-1(X), Creative Education) Creative Co., The.

—The Story of the Houston Rockets. 2006. (Pro Basketball Today Ser.). (Illus.). 32p. (J). lib. bdg. 18.95 (978-1-58341-408-8(8), Creative Education) Creative Co., The.

—The Story of the Los Angeles Lakers. 2006. (Pro Basketball Today Ser.). (Illus.). 32p. (YA). (gr. 4-7). lib. bdg. 18.95 (978-1-58341-411-8(8)) Creative Co., The.

—The Story of the Milwaukee Bucks. 2006. (Pro Basketball Today Ser.). (Illus.). 32p. (J). lib. bdg. 18.95 (978-1-58341-414-9(2), Creative Education) Creative Co., The.

LeBoutillier, Nate. The Story of the Minnesota Timberwolves. 2010. (NBA — A History of Hoops Ser.). 48p. (YA). (gr. 5-18). 23.95 (978-1-58341-952-6(7), Creative Education) Creative Co., The.

Leboutillier, Nate. The Story of the New Jersey Nets. 2006. (Pro Basketball Today Ser.). (Illus.). 32p. (J). lib. bdg. 18.95 (978-1-58341-416-3(9), Creative Education) Creative Co., The.

—The Story of the New York Knicks. 2006. (Pro Basketball Today Ser.). (Illus.). 32p. (J). lib. bdg. 18.95 (978-1-58341-418-7(5), Creative Education) Creative Co., The.

LeBoutillier, Nate. The Story of the Oklahoma City Thunder. 2010. (NBA — A History of Hoops Ser.). 48p. (YA). (gr. 5-18). 23.95 (978-1-58341-962-5(4), Creative Education) Creative Co., The.

Leboutillier, Nate. The Story of the Philadelphia 76ers. 2006. (Pro Basketball Today Ser.). (Illus.). 32p. (J). lib. bdg. 18.95 (978-1-58341-420-0(7), Creative Education) Creative Co., The.

LeBoutillier, Nate. The Story of the Portland Trail Blazers. 2010. (NBA — A History of Hoops Ser.). 48p. (YA). (gr. 5-18). 23.95 (978-1-58341-959-5(4), Creative Education) Creative Co., The.

Leboutillier, Nate. The Story of the Sacramento Kings. 2006. (Pro Basketball Today Ser.). (Illus.). 32p. (J). lib. bdg. 18.95 (978-1-58341-423-1(1), Creative Education) Creative Co., The.

—The Story of the San Antonio Spurs. 2006. (NBA — A History of Hoops Ser.). (Illus.). 32p. (J). lib. bdg. 18.95 (978-1-58341-424-8(X), Creative Education) Creative Co., The.

—The Story of the Utah Jazz. 2006. (Pro Basketball Today Ser.). (Illus.). 32p. (J). lib. bdg. 18.95 (978-1-58341-427-9(4), Creative Education) Creative Co., The.

LeBoutillier, Nate. The Story of the Utah Jazz. 2010. (NBA — A History of Hoops Ser.). 48p. (YA). (gr. 5-18). 23.95 (978-1-58341-964-9(0), Creative Education) Creative Co., The.

MacRae, Sloan. Rajon Rondo. 2012. (Sports Heroes Ser.). (ENG.). 24p. (J). (gr. 3-6). pap. 8.25 (978-1-4488-6288-7(4), PowerKids Pr.) Rosen Publishing Group, Inc., The.

Monnig, Alex. North Carolina Tar Heels, 1 vol. 2012. (Inside College Basketball Set 1 Ser.). (ENG.). 48p. lib. bdg. 32.79 (978-1-61783-286-4(3), SportsZone) ABDO Publishing Co.

Mooney, Carla. Duke Basketball. 2013. (America's Most Winning Teams Ser.). 48p. (J). (gr. 5-8). 29.25 (978-1-4488-9406-2(9)); pap. 11.75 (978-1-4488-9427-7(1)); pap. 70.50 (978-1-4488-9428-4(X)) Rosen Publishing Group, Inc., The.

Nichols, John. The Story of the Charlotte Bobcats. 2006. (Pro Basketball Today Ser.). (Illus.). 32p. (J). lib. bdg. 18.95 (978-1-58341-401-9(0), Creative Education) Creative Co., The.

—The Story of the Toronto Raptors. 2010. (NBA — A History of Hoops Ser.). (Illus.). 48p. (J). (gr. 5-18). 23.95 (978-1-58341-963-2(2), 1316689, Creative Education) Creative Co., The.

Omoth, Tyler. The Story of the Atlanta Hawks. 2010. (NBA — A History of Hoops Ser.). 48p. (YA). (gr. 5-18). 23.95 (978-1-58341-936-6(5), Creative Education) Creative Co., The.

—The Story of the Dallas Mavericks. 2010. (NBA — A History of Hoops Ser.). 48p. (YA). (gr. 5-18). 23.95 (978-1-58341-941-0(1), Creative Education) Creative Co., The.

—The Story of the Golden State Warriors. 2010. (NBA — A History of Hoops Ser.). 48p. (YA). (gr. 5-18). 23.95 (978-1-58341-944-1(6), Creative Education) Creative Co., The.

—The Story of the New Orleans Hornets. 2010. (NBA — A History of Hoops Ser.). 48p. (YA). (gr. 5-18). 23.95 (978-1-58341-954-0(3), Creative Education) Creative Co., The.

Pattinson, Darcy. Kentucky Basketball. 2013. (America's Most Winning Teams Ser.). 48p. (J). (gr. 5-8). pap. 70.50 (978-1-4488-9432-1(8)) Rosen Publishing Group, Inc., The.

Pattison, Darcy. Kentucky Basketball. 2013. (America's Most Winning Teams Ser.). 48p. (J). (gr. 5-8). 29.25 (978-1-4488-9403-1(4)); pap. 11.75 (978-1-4488-9431-4(X)) Rosen Publishing Group, Inc., The.

Porterfield, Jason. Basketball in the ACC: (Atlantic Coast Conference) 2008. (Inside Men's College Basketball Ser.). (Illus.). 48p. (J). (gr. 3-7). lib. bdg. 29.25 (978-1-4042-1380-7(5)) Rosen Publishing Group, Inc., The.

—Basketball in the ACC (Atlantic Coast Conference) 2009. (Inside Men's College Basketball Ser.). 48p. (gr. 5-5). 53.00 (978-1-61513-543-1(X), Rosen Reference) Rosen Publishing Group, Inc., The.

—Basketball in the Big East Conference. 2008. (Inside Men's College Basketball Ser.). (Illus.). 48p. (YA). (gr. 5-9). lib. bdg. 29.25 (978-1-4042-1381-4(3)) Rosen Publishing Group, Inc., The.

Pueschner, Gordon. The Story of the Charlotte Bobcats. 2010. (NBA — A History of Hoops Ser.). 48p. (YA). (gr. 5-18). 23.95 (978-1-58341-938-0(1), Creative Education) Creative Co., The.

—The Story of the Memphis Grizzlies. 2010. (NBA — A History of Hoops Ser.). 48p. (YA). (gr. 5-18). 23.95 (978-1-58341-949-6(7), Creative Education) Creative Co., The.

Rausch, David. National Basketball Association. 2014. (Major League Sports Ser.). (ENG.). 24p. (J). (gr. 3-7). 25.95 (978-1-62617-135-0(1), Epic Bks.) Bellwether Media.

Rogers, Amy B. Girls Play Basketball. 2016. (Girls Join the Team Ser.). 24p. (J). (gr. 3-3). pap. 8.25 (978-1-4994-2093-7(5), PowerKids Pr.) Rosen Publishing Group, Inc., The.

Roselius, J. Chris. Michigan State Spartans, 1 vol. 2012. (Inside College Basketball Set 1 Ser.). (ENG.). 48p. lib. bdg. 32.79 (978-1-61783-285-7(5), SportsZone) ABDO Publishing Co.

Savage, Jeff. Basketball Super Stats. 2017. (Pro Sports Stats Ser.). (ENG.). 32p. (J). (gr. 3-6). 27.99 **(978-1-5124-3410-1(8))** Lerner Publishing Group.

Savage, Jeff. Kevin Durant. 2011. (Amazing Athletes Ser.). (ENG., Illus.). 32p. (gr. 2-5). lib. bdg. 25.26 (978-0-7613-7671-2(2)) Lerner Publishing Group.

Shea, John M. Syracuse Basketball. 2013. (America's Most Winning Teams Ser.). 48p. (J). (gr. 5-8). 29.25 (978-1-4488-9407-9(7)); pap. 70.50 (978-1-4488-9441-3(7)); pap. 11.75 (978-1-4488-9440-6(9)) Rosen Publishing Group, Inc., The.

Silverman, Drew. Indiana Hoosiers, 1 vol. 2013. (Inside College Basketball Set 2 Ser.). (ENG., Illus.). 48p. (gr. 3-6). lib. bdg. 32.79 (978-1-61783-915-3(9), SportsZone) ABDO Publishing Co.

—Kansas Jayhawks, 1 vol. 2012. (Inside College Basketball Set 1 Ser.). (ENG.). 48p. lib. bdg. 32.79 (978-1-61783-283-3(9), SportsZone) ABDO Publishing Co.

—Orlando Magic, 1 vol. 2011. (Inside the NBA Ser.). (ENG., Illus.). 48p. (YA). (gr. 3-6). lib. bdg. 32.79 (978-1-61783-170-6(0)) ABDO Publishing Co.

—Syracuse Orange, 1 vol. 2013. (Inside College Basketball Set 2 Ser.). (ENG.). 48p. (gr. 3-6). lib. bdg. 32.79 (978-1-61783-917-7(5), SportsZone) ABDO Publishing Co.

—UCLA Bruins, 1 vol. 2012. (Inside College Basketball Set 1 Ser.). (ENG.). 48p. lib. bdg. 32.79 (978-1-61783-287-1(1), SportsZone) ABDO Publishing Co.

Silverman, Steve. The Story of the Indiana Pacers. 2010. (NBA — A History of Hoops Ser.). 48p. (YA). (gr. 5-18). 23.95 (978-1-58341-946-5(2), Creative Education) Creative Co., The.

—The Story of the Phoenix Suns. 2010. (NBA — A History of Hoops Ser.). 48p. (YA). (gr. 5-18). 23.95 (978-1-58341-958-8(6), Creative Education) Creative Co., The.

—The Story of the Sacramento Kings. 2010. (NBA — A History of Hoops Ser.). 48p. (YA). (gr. 5-18). 23.95 (978-1-58341-960-1(8), Creative Education) Creative Co., The.

—The Story of the Washington Wizards. 2010. (NBA — A History of Hoops Ser.). 48p. (YA). (gr. 5-18). 23.95 (978-1-58341-965-6(9), Creative Education) Creative Co., The.

Skogen, J. M. Dallas Mavericks. 2012. (On the Hardwood Ser.). (ENG., Illus.). 47p. (gr. 3-8). pap. 8.95 (978-1-61570-512-2(0)); lib. bdg. 27.93 (978-1-61570-513-9(9)) Scobre Pr. Corp.

—Oklahoma City Thunder. 2012. (On the Hardwood Ser.). (ENG., Illus.). 47p. (gr. 3-8). pap. 8.95 (978-1-61570-514-6(7)); lib. bdg. 27.93 (978-1-61570-515-3(5)) Scobre Pr. Corp.

—Portland Trail Blazers. 2013. (On the Hardwood Ser.). (ENG., Illus.). 47p. (gr. 3-8). pap. 8.95 (978-1-61570-838-3(3)) Scobre Pr. Corp.

—Utah Jazz. 2013. (On the Hardwood Ser.). (ENG., Illus.). 48p. (gr. 3-8). pap. 8.95 (978-1-61570-833-8(2)) Scobre Pr. Corp.

Stewart, Mark. The Charlotte Bobcats. 2007. (Team Spirit Ser.). (Illus.). 48p. (J). (gr. 3-6). lib. bdg. 26.60 (978-1-59953-123-6(2)) Norwood Hse. Pr.

—The Chicago Bulls. rev. ed. 2014. (Team Spirit Ser.). (ENG.). 48p. (J). (gr. 3-6). lib. bdg. 29.27 (978-1-59953-631-6(5)) Norwood Hse. Pr.

—The Cleveland Cavaliers. 2009. (Team Spirit Ser.). 48p. (J). (gr. 3-6). lib. bdg. 26.60 (978-1-59953-288-2(3)) Norwood Hse. Pr.

—The Golden State Warriors. 2009. (Team Spirit Ser.). (Illus.). 48p. (J). (gr. 3-6). lib. bdg. 26.60 (978-1-59953-324-7(3)) Norwood Hse. Pr.

—The Illinois Fighting Illini. 2010. (Team Spirit Ser.). (ENG.). 48p. (J). (gr. 3-6). lib. bdg. 26.60 (978-1-59953-365-0(0)) Norwood Hse. Pr.

—The Indiana Pacers. rev. ed. 2014. (Team Spirit Ser.). (ENG.). 48p. (J). (gr. 3-6). lib. bdg. 29.27 (978-1-59953-634-7(X)) Norwood Hse. Pr.

—The Los Angeles Clippers. 2009. (Team Spirit Ser.). (Illus.). 48p. (J). (gr. 3-6). lib. bdg. 26.60 (978-1-59953-290-5(5)) Norwood Hse. Pr.

—The Memphis Grizzlies. 2009. (Team Spirit Ser.). (Illus.). 48p. (J). (gr. 3-6). lib. bdg. 26.60 (978-1-59953-284-4(0)) Norwood Hse. Pr.

—The Milwaukee Bucks. 2006. (Team Spirit Ser.). (Illus.). 48p. (J). (gr. 3-6). lib. bdg. 26.60 (978-1-59953-062-8(7)) Norwood Hse. Pr.

—The Minnesota Timberwolves. 2009. (Team Spirit Ser.). 48p. (J). (gr. 3-6). lib. bdg. 26.60 (978-1-59953-291-2(3)) Norwood Hse. Pr.

—The New Orleans Hornets. 2009. (Team Spirit Ser.). (Illus.). 48p. (J). (gr. 3-6). lib. bdg. 26.60 (978-1-59953-286-8(7)) Norwood Hse. Pr.

—The New York Knicks. rev. ed. 2014. (Team Spirit Ser.). (ENG.). 48p. (J). (gr. 3-6). lib. bdg. 29.27 (978-1-59953-638-5(2)) Norwood Hse. Pr.

—The Oklahoma City Thunder. rev. ed. 2014. (Team Spirit Ser.). (ENG.). 48p. (J). (gr. 3-6). lib. bdg. 29.27 (978-1-59953-639-2(0)) Norwood Hse. Pr.

—The Orlando Magic. 2009. (Team Spirit Ser.). (Illus.). 48p. (J). (gr. 3-6). lib. bdg. 26.60 (978-1-59953-326-1(X)) Norwood Hse. Pr.

—The Philadelphia 76ers. rev. ed. 2014. (Team Spirit Ser.). (ENG.). 48p. (J). (gr. 3-6). lib. bdg. 29.27 (978-1-59953-640-8(4)) Norwood Hse. Pr.

—The Phoenix Suns. 2006. (Team Spirit Ser.). (Illus.). 48p. (J). (gr. 3-6). lib. bdg. 26.60 (978-1-59953-010-9(4)) Norwood Hse. Pr.

—The Portland Trail Blazers. 2007. (Team Spirit Ser.). (Illus.). 48p. (J). (gr. 3-6). lib. bdg. 26.60 (978-1-59953-126-7(7)) Norwood Hse. Pr.

—The Sacramento Kings. 2009. (Team Spirit Ser.). (Illus.). 48p. (J). (gr. 3-6). lib. bdg. 26.60 (978-1-59953-285-1(9)) Norwood Hse. Pr.

—The San Antonio Spurs. rev. ed. 2014. (Team Spirit Ser.). (ENG.). 48p. (J). (gr. 3-6). lib. bdg. 29.27 (978-1-59953-641-5(2)) Norwood Hse. Pr.

—The Toronto Raptors. 2009. (Team Spirit Ser.). 48p. (J). (gr. 3-6). 26.60 (978-1-59953-292-9(1)) Norwood Hse. Pr.

—The Utah Jazz. 2007. (Team Spirit Ser.). (Illus.). 48p. (J). (gr. 3-6). lib. bdg. 26.60 (978-1-59953-127-4(5)) Norwood Hse. Pr.

—The Washington Wizards. 2009. (Team Spirit Ser.). 48p. (J). (gr. 3-6). 26.60 (978-1-59953-287-5(5)) Norwood Hse. Pr.

Stewart, Mark & Kennedy, Mike. Swish: The Quest for Basketball's Perfect Shot. 2009. (Spectacular Sports Ser.). (ENG.). 64p. (gr. 5-12). 33.27 (978-0-8225-8752-1(1)) Lerner Publishing Group.

Suen, Anastasia. La Historia Del Baloncesto. 2004. (Historia de Los Deportes (Sports History) Ser.). (SPA & ENG., Illus.). 24p. (J). (gr. 3-6). lib. bdg. 22.60 (978-0-8239-6868-8(5), Editorial Buenas Letras) Rosen Publishing Group, Inc., The.

—La historia del baloncesto (the Story of Basketball) 2009. (Historia de los deportes (Sports History) Ser.). (SPA.). 24p. (gr. 2-2). 42.50 (978-1-61513-309-3(7), Editorial Buenas Letras) Rosen Publishing Group, Inc., The.

—The Story of Basketball. 2009. (Sports History Ser.). 24p. (gr. 2-2). 42.50 (978-1-60853-137-0(6), PowerKids Pr.) Rosen Publishing Group, Inc., The.

Tricchinelli, Rob. Golden State Warriors, 1 vol. 2011. (Inside the NBA Ser.). (ENG., Illus.). 48p. (YA). (gr. 3-6). lib. bdg. 32.79 (978-1-61783-157-7(3)) ABDO Publishing Co.

Trogdon, Wendell. Who Killed Hoosier Hysteria? Sport Survives amid Fading Fervor. l.t. ed. 2004. (Illus.). 168p. (YA). pap. (978-0-9724033-3-7(7)) Backroads Pr.

Ucla Basketball. 2013. (America's Most Winning Teams Ser.). 48p. (J). (gr. 5-8). pap. 70.50 (978-1-4488-9446-8(8)) Rosen Publishing Group, Inc., The.

Wade McCormick, Lisa. Ucla Basketball. 2013. (America's Most Winning Teams Ser.). 48p. (J). (gr. 5-8). 29.25 (978-1-4488-9408-6(5)); pap. 11.75 (978-1-4488-9443-7(3)) Rosen Publishing Group, Inc., The.

Whiting, Jim. The NBA: a History of Hoops: Minnesota Timberwolves. 2nd ed. 2017. (NBA: a History of Hoops Ser.). (ENG.). 48p. (J). (gr. 5-7). pap. 12.00 **(978-1-62832-455-6(4)**, Creative Paperbacks) Creative Co., The.

—The NBA: a History of Hoops: New Orleans Pelicans. 2nd ed. 2017. (NBA: a History of Hoops Ser.). (ENG.). 48p. (J). (gr. 5-7). pap. 12.00 **(978-1-62832-456-3(2)**, Creative Paperbacks) Creative Co., The.

—The NBA: a History of Hoops: New York Knicks. 2nd ed. 2017. (NBA: a History of Hoops Ser.). (ENG.). 48p. (J). (gr. 5-7). pap. 12.00 **(978-1-62832-457-0(0)**, Creative Paperbacks) Creative Co., The.

—The NBA: a History of Hoops: Oklahoma City Thunder. 2nd ed. 2017. (NBA: a History of Hoops Ser.). (ENG.). 48p. (J). (gr. 5-7). pap. 12.00 **(978-1-62832-458-7(9)**, Creative Paperbacks) Creative Co., The.

—The NBA: a History of Hoops: Orlando Magic. 2nd ed. 2017. (NBA: a History of Hoops Ser.). (ENG.). 48p. (J). (gr. 5-7). pap. 12.00 **(978-1-62832-459-4(7)**, Creative Paperbacks) Creative Co., The.

—The NBA: a History of Hoops: Philadelphia 76ers. 2nd ed. 2017. (NBA: a History of Hoops Ser.). (ENG.). 48p. (J). (gr. 5-7). pap. 12.00 **(978-1-62832-460-0(0)**, Creative Paperbacks) Creative Co., The.

—The NBA: a History of Hoops: Phoenix Suns. 2nd ed. 2017. (NBA: a History of Hoops Ser.). (ENG.). 48p. (J). (gr. 5-7). pap. 12.00 **(978-1-62832-461-7(9)**, Creative Paperbacks) Creative Co., The.

—The NBA: a History of Hoops: the Story of the Boston Celtics. 2015. (NBA: a History of Hoops Ser.). (ENG.). 48p. (J). (gr. 5-8). pap. 9.99 (978-1-62832-009-1(5), Creative Paperbacks) Creative Co., The.

—The NBA: a History of Hoops: the Story of the Detroit Pistons. 2015. (NBA: a History of Hoops Ser.). (ENG.). 48p. (J). (gr. 5-8). pap. 12.00 (978-1-62832-016-9(8), Creative Paperbacks) Creative Co., The.

—The NBA: a History of Hoops: the Story of the Los Angeles Clippers. 2015. (NBA: a History of Hoops Ser.). (ENG.). 48p. (J). (gr. 5-8). pap. 12.00 (978-1-62832-020-6(6), Creative Paperbacks) Creative Co., The.

—The NBA: a History of Hoops: the Story of the Orlando Magic. 2015. (NBA: a History of Hoops Ser.). (ENG.). 48p. (J). (gr. 5-8). pap. 12.00 (978-1-62832-029-9(X), Creative Paperbacks) Creative Co., The.

—The NBA: a History of Hoops: the Story of the Philadelphia 76ers. 2015. (NBA: a History of Hoops Ser.). (ENG.). 48p. (J). (gr. 5-8). pap. 12.00 (978-1-62832-030-5(3), Creative Paperbacks) Creative Co., The.

—The NBA: a History of Hoops: the Story of the Sacramento Kings. 2015. (NBA: a History of Hoops Ser.). (ENG.). 48p. (J). (gr. 5-8). pap. 12.00 (978-1-62832-033-6(8), Creative Paperbacks) Creative Co., The.

—The NBA: a History of Hoops: the Story of the Washington Wizards. 2015. (NBA: a History of Hoops Ser.). (ENG.). 48p. (J). (gr. 5-8). pap. 12.00 (978-1-62832-037-4(0), Creative Paperbacks) Creative Co., The.

—The NBA: a History of Hoops: Toronto Raptors. 2nd ed. 2017. (NBA: a History of Hoops Ser.). (ENG.). 48p. (J). (gr. 5-7). pap. 12.00 **(978-1-62832-465-5(1)**, Creative Paperbacks) Creative Co., The.

—The NBA: a History of Hoops: Utah Jazz. 2nd ed. 2017. (NBA: a History of Hoops Ser.). (ENG.). 48p. (J). (gr. 5-7). pap. 12.00 **(978-1-62832-466-2(X)**, Creative Paperbacks) Creative Co., The.

—The NBA: a History of Hoops: Washington Wizards. 2nd ed. 2017. (NBA: a History of Hoops Ser.). (ENG.). 48p. (J). (gr. 5-7). pap. 12.00 **(978-1-62832-467-9(8)**, Creative Paperbacks) Creative Co., The.

—The Story of the Charlotte Hornets. (NBA: a History of Hoops Ser.). (ENG.). 48p. (J). 2015. (gr. 5-8). pap. 12.00 (978-1-62832-011-4(7), Creative Paperbacks) 2014. (Illus.). (978-1-60818-424-8(2), Creative Education) Creative Co., The.

—Toronto Raptors. 2017. (J). **(978-1-60818-862-8(0)**, Creative Education) Creative Co., The.

—Utah Jazz. 2017. (J). **(978-1-60818-863-5(9)**, Creative Education) Creative Co., The.

—Washington Wizards. 2017. (J). **(978-1-60818-864-2(7)**, Creative Education) Creative Co., The.

Williams, Doug. Great Moments in Olympic Basketball, 1 vol. 2014. (Great Moments in Olympic Sports Ser.). (ENG.). 64p. (gr. 10-14). lib. bdg. 32.79 (978-1-62403-393-3(8), SportsZone) ABDO Publishing Co.

Wilner, Barry. Best NBA Dunkers of All Time, 1 vol. 2014. (NBA's Best Ever Ser.). (ENG.). 64p. (gr. 8-12). lib. bdg. 32.79 (978-1-62403-410-7(1), SportsZone) ABDO Publishing Co.

—Best NBA Shooters of All Time, 1 vol. 2014. (NBA's Best Ever Ser.). (ENG., Illus.). 64p. (J). (gr. 8-12). lib. bdg. 32.79 (978-1-62403-413-8(6), SportsZone) ABDO Publishing Co.

Winters, Jaime. Center Court: The History of Basketball. 2015. (Basketball Source Ser.). (ENG., Illus.). 32p. (J). (gr. 3-6). pap. (978-0-7787-1539-9(6)) Crabtree Publishing Co.

Woods, Mark & Gifford, Clive. Basketball Legends. 2009. (ENG., Illus.). 32p. (J). (gr. 4-7). lib. bdg. (978-0-7787-3774-2(8)) Crabtree Publishing Co.

Wyckoff, Edwin Brit. The Man Who Invented Basketball: James Naismith & His Amazing Game. 2007. (Genius at Work! Great Inventor Biographies Ser.). (Illus.). 32p. (J). (gr. 3-7). lib. bdg. 23.94 (978-0-7660-2846-3(1), Enslow Elementary) Enslow Pubs., Inc.

—The Man Who Invented Basketball: The Genius of James Naismith. 2013. (Genius Inventors & Their Great Ideas Ser.). (Illus.). 48p. (J). (gr. 3-18). 25.27 (978-0-7660-4142-4(5), Enslow Elementary) Enslow Pubs., Inc.

—The Man Who Invented the Game of Basketball: The Genius of James Naismith. 2013. (Genius Inventors & Their Great Ideas Ser.). 48p. (J). (gr. 3-4). pap. 8.95 (978-1-4644-0212-8(4), Enslow Elementary) Enslow Pubs., Inc.

Wyner, Zach. Brooklyn Nets. 2013. (On the Hardwood Ser.). (ENG., Illus.). 48p. (gr. 3-8). pap. 8.95 (978-1-61570-835-2(9)) Scobre Pr. Corp.

—Philadelphia 76ers. 2013. (On the Hardwood Ser.). (ENG., Illus.). 48p. (gr. 3-8). pap. 8.95 (978-1-61570-831-4(6)) Scobre Pr. Corp.

Ybarra, Andres. Phoenix Suns, 1 vol. 2011. (Inside the NBA Ser.). (ENG., Illus.). 48p. (YA). (gr. 3-6). lib. bdg. 32.79 (978-1-61783-172-0(7)) ABDO Publishing Co.

Yomtov, Nel. Being Your Best at Basketball. 2016. (True Book(tm), a — Sports & Entertainment Ser.). (ENG., Illus.). 48p. (J). lib. bdg. 31.00 (978-0-531-23260-6(3), Children's Pr.) Scholastic Library Publishing.

BASKETBALL CLUBS

Basen, Ryan. Charlotte Bobcats, 1 vol. 2011. (Inside the NBA Ser.). (ENG., Illus.). 48p. (YA). (gr. 3-6). lib. bdg. 32.79 (978-1-61783-151-5(4)) ABDO Publishing Co.

Derong, Gary. Milwaukee Bucks, 1 vol. 2011. (Inside the NBA Ser.). (ENG., Illus.). 48p. (YA). (gr. 3-6). lib. bdg. 32.79 (978-1-61783-164-5(6)) ABDO Publishing Co.

Frager, Ray. New Jersey Nets, 1 vol. 2011. (Inside the NBA Ser.). (ENG., Illus.). 48p. (YA). (gr. 3-6). lib. bdg. 32.79 (978-1-61783-166-9(2)) ABDO Publishing Co.

Frederick, Shane. The Story of the Milwaukee Bucks. 2014. (J). (978-1-60818-437-8(4), Creative Education) Creative Co., The.

Frisch, Aaron. Sacramento Kings. 2012. (J). 25.65 (978-1-60818-142-1(1), Creative Education) Creative Co., The.

Gitlin, Martin. Cleveland Cavaliers, 1 vol. 2011. (Inside the NBA Ser.). (ENG., Illus.). 48p. (YA). (gr. 3-6). lib. bdg. 32.79 (978-1-61783-153-9(0)) ABDO Publishing Co.

Howell, Brian. Chicago Bulls, 1 vol. 2011. (Inside the NBA Ser.). (ENG., Illus.). 48p. (YA). (gr. 3-6). lib. bdg. 32.79 (978-1-61783-152-2(2)) ABDO Publishing Co.

—Denver Nuggets, 1 vol. 2011. (Inside the NBA Ser.). (ENG., Illus.). 48p. (YA). (gr. 3-6). lib. bdg. 32.79 *(978-1-61783-155-3(7))* ABDO Publishing Co.

LeBoutillier, Nate. The Story of the Oklahoma City Thunder. 2014. (J). *(978-1-60818-442-2(0),* Creative Education) Creative Co., The.

Wilson, Bernie. Los Angeles Clippers, 1 vol. 2011. (Inside the NBA Ser.). (ENG., Illus.). 48p. (YA). (gr. 3-6). lib. bdg. 32.79 *(978-1-61783-160-7(3))* ABDO Publishing Co.

Wyner, Zach. Detroit Pistons. 2014. (On the Hardwood Ser.). 48p. (gr. 3-8). pap. 8.95 *(978-1-61570-909-0(6))* Scobre Pr. Corp.

BAT

see Bats

BATES, KATHARINE LEE, 1859-1929

Wesolowski, Harriet. The Songs We Sing: Honoring Our Country. 2012. (I'm an American Citizen Ser.). (ENG., Illus.). 24p. (J). (gr. 1-3). 22.60 *(978-1-4488-8581-7(7),* PowerKids Pr.) Rosen Publishing Group, Inc., The.

Younger, Barbara. Purple Mountain Majesties: The Story of Katharine Lee Bates & America the Beautiful. Schuett, Stacey, illus. 2005. 29p. (J). reprint ed. 16.00 *(978-0-7567-8984-8(2))* DIANE Publishing Co.

BATHS—FICTION

Anderson, Derek. Ten Pigs: An Epic Bath Adventure. Anderson, Derek, illus. 2015. (ENG., Illus.). 40p. (J). (gr. -1-k). 16.99 *(978-0-545-16846-5(5))* Scholastic, Inc.

Anderson, Peggy Perry. To the Tub. 2012. (Green Light Readers Level 1 Ser.). (ENG., Illus.). 32p. (J). (gr. -1-3). pap. 3.99 *(978-0-547-85053-5(0))* Houghton Mifflin Harcourt Publishing Co.

—To the Tub. Anderson, Peggy Perry, illus. 2004. (Illus.). 52p. (gr. -1-3). 17.00 *(978-0-7569-4258-8(6))* Perfection Learning Corp.

—To the Tub. 2012. (Green Light Readers — Level 1 Ser.). lib. bdg. 13.55 *(978-0-606-26608-6(9)),* Turtleback) Turtleback Bks.

Arnold, Marsha Diane. Baby Animals Take a Bath. Tildes, Phyllis Limbacher, illus. 2017. (ENG.). 10p. (J). (— 1). bds. 6.99 *(978-1-58089-538-5(7))* Charlesbridge Publishing, Inc.

Babin, Claire. Gus Is a Fish. Bedrick, Claudia Z., tr. from FRE. Tallec, Olivier & Sorman, Joy, illus. 2008. (ENG.). 32p. (J). (gr. -1-2). 14.95 *(978-1-59270-101-8(9))* Enchanted Lion Bks., LLC.

Barchers, Suzanne I. Gus in the Tub, 1 vol. 2011. (Targeted Phonics Ser.). (ENG., Illus.). 16p. (J). (gr. k-2). pap. 5.99 *(978-1-4333-2419-2(9))* Teacher Created Materials, Inc.

The Bath: Set C Individual Title Six-Packs. (Smart Start Ser.). (gr. k-1). 23.00 *(978-0-7635-0431-1(9))* Rigby Education.

Beaumont, Karen. Dini Dinosaur. Roode, Daniel, illus. 2012. (ENG.). 32p. (J). (gr. -1-k). 14.99 *(978-0-06-207299-3(4),* Greenwillow Bks.) HarperCollins Pubs.

Bell, S. Towel Tales: Tub Time. 2011. 24p. pap. 15.99 *(978-1-4568-8050-7(0))* Xlibris Corp.

Boyd, Colin. The Bath Monster. Ross, Tony, illus. 2016. (ENG.). 32p. (J). (gr. -1-3). 17.99 *(978-1-5124-0426-5(8))* Lerner Publishing Group.

Boykins, Corinthia. Too Big for the Tub. 2008. 36p. per. 14.95 *(978-1-4327-1456-7(2))* Outskirts Pr., Inc.

Boynton. Bath Time! 2007. 10p. pap. 7.95 *(978-0-7611-4780-0(2))* Workman Publishing Co., Inc.

Boza, Eduardo Robles. Mi Amigo - Banarse (My Friend Doesn't Like - Baths) (SPA.). (J). 4.95 *(978-970-05-0209-0(0))* Grijalbo, Editorial MEX. Dist: AIMS International Bks., Inc.

Brignaud, Pierre, illus. Caillou Takes a Bath. 2014. (Step by Step Ser.). (ENG.). 24p. (J). (gr. -1 — 1). bds. 5.99 *(978-2-89718-138-3(9))* Caillouet, Gerry.

Bringsvaerd, Tor Age. When Two Take a Bath. Soli, Tina, illus. 2009. (When Two Ser.). 36p. (J). (gr. -1-3). 14.95 *(978-0-9815761-1-4(7))* Mackenzie Smiles, LLC.

Briscoe, Holly. The Boy in the Shower. 2008. 25p. 16.50 *(978-1-4357-1506-6(3))* Lulu Pr., Inc.

Brouillard, Anne. The Bathtub Prima Donna. Brouillard, Anne, illus. 2004. (Illus.). 24p. (J). (gr. k-4). reprint ed. 13.00 *(978-0-7567-7755-5(0))* DIANE Publishing Co.

Bruel, Nick. Bad Kitty Gets a Bath. Bruel, Nick, illus. 2008. (Bad Kitty Ser.). (ENG., Illus.). 128p. (J). (gr. 2-5). 15.99 *(978-1-59643-341-0(8),* 9781596433410) Roaring Brook Pr.

—Bad Kitty Gets a Bath. Bruel, Nick, illus. 2009. (Bad Kitty Ser.). (ENG., Illus.). 144p. (J). (gr. 2-5). pap. 6.99 *(978-0-312-58138-1(6),* 9780312581381) Square Fish.

Carter, Angela C. Momma, Why Do We Have to Take a Bath? 2012. 36p. pap. 24.95 *(978-1-4626-7547-0(6))* America Star Bks.

Christelow, Eileen. Five Little Monkeys Jump in the Bath. 2012. (Five Little Monkeys Story Ser.). (ENG., Illus.). 20p. (J). (gr. k — 1). bds. 7.99 *(978-0-547-87527-9(4))* Houghton Mifflin Harcourt Publishing Co.

Clarke, Jane. How to Bathe Your Little Dino. Birkett, Georgie, illus. 2017. 16p. (J). bds. 8.99 *(978-1-61067-495-9(2))* Kane Miller.

Colvin, Layne. Augustus' Bath. 2008. 16p. pap. 8.49 *(978-1-4389-3482-2(3))* AuthorHouse.

Dad's Bathtime: Individual Title Six-Packs. (Literatura 2000 Ser.). (gr. 1-2). 28.00 *(978-0-7635-0128-0(X))* Rigby Education.

Dahl, Michael. Pig Takes a Bath, 1 vol. Vidal, Oriol, illus. 2010. (Hello Genius Ser.). (ENG.). 20p. (gr. 1-2). bds. 7.99 *(978-1-4048-5729-2(X))* Picture Window Bks.

Danis, Naomi. Splish-Splash, into the Bath! Kreloff, Elliot, illus. 2007. 16p. (J). *(978-1-59354-609-0(2))* Handprint Bks.

Dannenbring-Eichstadt, Lana. Bubble. Harvey, Kathleen, illus. 2004. 24p. (J). *(978-1-57579-282-8(6))* Pine Hill Pr.

Demarest, Chris L. My Blue Boat. 20th ed. 2014. (J). 18.95 *(978-1-930900-76-9(7))* Purple Hse. Pr.

DePrisco, Dorothea. Tub-A-Tub. 2006. (Illus.). 10p. (J). (gr. -1-k). 9.95 *(978-1-58117-463-2(2),* Intervisual/Piggy Toes) Bendon, Inc.

Disney Book Group. World of Reading: Doc Mcstuffins Peaches Pie, Take a Bath! Level Pre-1. Disney Storybook Art Team, illus. 2015. (World of Reading Ser.). (ENG.). 32p. (J). (gr. -1-k). pap. 3.99 *(978-1-4847-1591-8(8))* Disney Pr.

Disney Press Editors. Peaches Pie, Take a Bath! 2015. (World of Reading Ser.). (J). lib. bdg. 13.55 *(978-0-606-36900-8(7))* Turtleback Bks.

Donaldson, Julia. The Flying Bath. Roberts, David, illus. 2016. (ENG.). 32p. (J). (gr. -1-k). pap. 9.99 *(978-1-4472-7711-8(2))* Pan Macmillan GBR. Dist: Independent Pubs. Group.

Dorling Kindersley Publishing Staff. Bathtime Peekaboo! 2005. (ENG., Illus.). 12p. (J). (gr. -1-k). bds. 6.99 *(978-0-7566-1145-3(8),* DK Children) Dorling Kindersley Publishing, Inc.

ETA/Cuisenaire Staff. Ben's Bath. 2003. (SunSprouts Big Bk Ser.). (ENG.). (gr. -1-3). pap. 33.50 *(978-0-7406-2018-8(5),* SunSprouts) ETA hand2mind.

Evans, Yvette Kemp. If I Take a Shower. 2008. 32p. pap. 24.95 *(978-1-4241-9953-2(0))* America Star Bks.

Fernandes, Eugenie. Waves in the Bathtub. 2015. (ENG., Illus.). 32p. (J). (gr. -1-k). 16.99 *(978-1-63220-429-5(0),* Sky Pony Pr.) Skyhorse Publishing Co., Inc.

Ficocelli, Elizabeth. Kid Tea, 0 vols. Dibley, Glin, illus. 2013. (ENG.). 36p. (J). (gr. -1-k). pap. 9.99 *(978-1-4778-4738-1(3),* 9781477847381, Amazon Children's Publishing) Amazon Publishing.

—Kid Tea. Dibley, Glin, illus. 2009. 32p. (J). (gr. -1). bds. 7.99 *(978-0-7614-5533-2(7))* Marshall Cavendish Corp.

Fox, Tamar. No Baths at Camp. Vasquez, Natalia, illus. 2013. (ENG.). 32p. (J). (gr. -1-3). pap. 7.95 *(978-0-7613-8121-1(X));* lib. bdg. 17.95 *(978-0-7613-8120-4(1))* Lerner Publishing Group. (Kar-Ben Publishing).

Friden, Chris. Bathtime with Bubbles. 2008. (Illus.). 27p. (J). bds. 14.99 *(978-0-9758785-6-9(5))* Haydenburri Lane.

—Bathtime with Bubbles. Zapater Oliva, Carlos & Depew, Robert, illus. 2008. (J). *(978-0-9801849-2-1(4))* Haydenburri Lane.

Garton, Sam. Otter: Oh No, Bath Time! Garton, Sam, illus. 2016. (My First I Can Read Ser.). (Illus.). 32p. (J). (gr. -1-3). pap. 3.99 *(978-0-06-236657-3(2))* HarperCollins Pubs.

George, Kallie. Duck, Duck, Dinosaur: Bubble Blast. Vidal, Oriol, illus. 2017. (My First I Can Read Ser.). 32p. (J). (gr. -1-3). pap. 3.99 *(978-0-06-235311-5(X))* HarperCollins Pubs.

Gershator, Phillis. Time for a Bath. Walker, David, illus. 2016. (Snuggle Time Stories Ser.). (ENG.). 22p. (J). (— 1). bds. 6.95 *(978-1-4549-2069-4(6))* Sterling Publishing Co., Inc.

Gershator, Phillis & Walker, David. Time for a Bath. 2014. (Snuggle Time Stories Ser.). (ENG., Illus.). 24p. (J). (gr. -1-k). 9.95 *(978-1-4549-1032-9(1))* Sterling Publishing Co., Inc.

Gerver, Jane E. Bath Time. Ovresat, Laura, illus. 2004. (My First Reader Ser.). 31p. (J). 18.50 *(978-0-516-24677-2(1),* Children's Pr.) Scholastic Library Publishing.

Gilmore, Cathy. Bubbles & Fun. 2011. 24p. pap. 24.95 *(978-1-4560-4179-3(7))* America Star Bks.

Goodman, Peggy. Ritzi's Bath. Bunker, Thomas, illus. 2012. 28p. 24.95 *(978-1-4560-4138-0(X))* America Star Bks.

Goss, Shelia M. & Hughes, Vi. Once upon a Bathtime, 1 vol. Shefrin, Sima Elizabeth, illus. 2011. (ENG.). 32p. (J). (gr. -1-k). 17.95 *(978-1-896580-54-8(8))* Tradewind Bks. CAN. Dist: Orca Bk. Pubs. USA.

Gurney, Stella. Sally Sets Sail. Worsley, Belinda, illus. 2009. (Get Ready (Windmill Books) Ser.). 32p. (J). (gr. k-2). lib. bdg. 22.60 *(978-1-60754-261-2(7))* Windmill Bks.

Hanna, Virginie. Rosy Posey Is Not Dirty! Desmoineaux, Christel, illus. 2012. (My Little Picture Book Ser.). (ENG.). 32p. (J). pap. 6.95 *(978-2-7338-1947-0(X))* Auzou, Philippe Editions FRA. Dist: Consortium Bk. Sales & Distribution.

Harper, Jamie. Splish Splash, Baby Bundt: A Recipe for Bath Time. Harper, Jamie, illus. 2007. (ENG., Illus.). 24p. (J). (— 1). bds. 6.99 *(978-0-7636-3240-3(6))* Candlewick Pr.

Hartley, Alicia Byrd. I Like Being Me. 2012. 24p. pap. 15.50 *(978-1-4772-9088-0(5))* AuthorHouse.

Hayes, Geoffrey. Patrick Eats His Peas & Other Stories. Hayes, Geoffrey, illus. 2013. (ENG., Illus.). 32p. (J). (gr. -1-3). 12.95 *(978-1-935179-34-4(9))* TOON Books / RAW Junior, LLC.

HB Staff. What a Shower! 97th ed. 2003. (First-Place Reading Ser.). (gr. 1-18). pap. 16.50 *(978-0-15-308124-8(4))* Harcourt Schl. Pubs.

Hillert, Margaret. Away Go the Boats. Kelleher, Kathie, illus. 2016. (BeginningtoRead Ser.). (ENG.). 32p. (J). (gr. -1-2). pap. 11.94 *(978-1-60357-933-9(8));* (gr. -1-2). 22.60 *(978-1-59953-792-4(3))* Norwood Hse. Pr.

Hines, Thomas, illus. The Bubble Machine. l.t. ed. 2003. 26p. (J). per. *(978-1-887636-02-5(1))* Creative Writing & Publishing Co.

Innovative Kids Staff, creator. Playful Penguins. 2012. (ENG.). 6p. (J). (gr. -1 — 1). 14.99 *(978-1-60169-266-5(8))* Innovative Kids.

Jones, Anna, illus. Scrub-a-Dub Froggy: Bath Mitt & Book Set. 2013. (ENG.). 8p. (J). (gr. -1 — 1). 9.99 *(978-1-4380-7439-9(5))* Barron's Educational Series, Inc.

Kate Smith Designs, illus. Who's Playing on the Farm? 2011. (Magic Bath Bks.). (ENG.). 8p. (J). (gr. -1-3). 5.99 *(978-1-4380-7179-4(5))* Barron's Educational Series, Inc.

—Who's Playing Outdoors? 2011. (Magic Bath Bks.). (ENG.). 8p. (J). (gr. -1-3). 5.99 *(978-1-4380-7178-7(7))* Barron's Educational Series, Inc.

Katz, Karen. Splish, Splash, Baby! Katz, Karen, illus. 2015. (ENG., Illus.). 14p. (J). (gr. -1 — 1). bds. 6.99 *(978-1-4814-1789-1(4),* Little Simon) Little Simon.

Knight, Deidre Denise. The Wash Cloth & the Turtle. Milosevic, Tamara, illus. 2013. 36p. 17.95 *(978-0-9893091-2-7(6))* Cube Marketing.

Kreloff, Elliot, illus. Counting Duckies. 2010. 16p. (J). bds. *(978-1-60906-007-7(5))* Begin Smart LLC.

Lambert, Lydia. Scrub-A-Dub Santa: Bath Mitt & Bath Book Set. Jones, Anna, illus. 2015. (Scrub-A-Dub Bath Mitt & Bath Book Sets Ser.). (ENG.). 8p. (J). (gr. -1 — 1). 9.99 *(978-1-4380-7585-3(5))* Barron's Educational Series, Inc.

Lilibeth, Ethel. Princesses Take Baths Too! 2009. 44p. pap. 18.60 *(978-1-4389-6626-7(1))* AuthorHouse.

Lindahl, Inger. Bertil & the Bathroom Elephants. Dyssegaard, Elisabeth Kallick, tr. Lindstrom, Eva, illus. 2003. 28p. (J). 15.00 *(978-91-29-65944-3(2))* R & S Bks. SWE. Dist: Macmillan.

Lock, Brian. There's a Hippo in My Bathtub. 2007. (ENG.). 76p. per. 19.95 *(978-1-4241-7331-0(0))* America Star Bks.

Macaluso, Jennifer. Where Do the Bubbles Go? O'Shaughnessy, Nancy, illus. 2006. (ENG.). 40p. (J). (gr. -1-3). pap. 21.99 *(978-1-4259-3929-8(5))* AuthorHouse.

Mack, Jeff. Who Needs a Bath? Mack, Jeff, illus. 2015. (ENG., Illus.). 40p. (J). (gr. -1-3). 17.99 *(978-0-06-222028-8(4))* HarperCollins Pubs.

Mader, Jan. Time for a Bath! World of Discovery II. Maizel, Karen, illus. l.t. ed. 2005. (ENG.). 8p. (gr. k-1). pap. 7.95 *(978-1-879835-46-7(0),* Kaeden Bks.) Kaeden Corp.

Mahy, Margaret. The Green Bath. Kellogg, Steven, illus. 2013. (J). pap. *(978-0-545-20668-6(5));* (ENG.). 40p. (gr. -1-3). 16.99 *(978-0-545-20667-9(7))* Scholastic, Inc. (Levine, Arthur A. Bks.).

Mamakas, Stavroula & Lagoutaris, Maria Mamakas. Mama Lagoo: Bath Time Battle. 2011. 28p. pap. 14.95 *(978-1-4634-1524-2(9))* AuthorHouse.

Marciano, John Bemelmans. Madeline & Her Dog. 2011. (Madeline Ser.). (ENG.). 32p. (J). (gr. 1-2). pap. 3.99 *(978-0-448-45438-2(6),* Penguin Young Readers) Penguin Young Readers Group.

McAnulty, Stacy. 101 Reasons Why I'm Not Taking a Bath. Ang, Joy, illus. 2016. (ENG.). 40p. (J). (gr. -1-2). lib. bdg. 20.99 *(978-0-375-97365-9(6),* Random Hse. Bks. for Young Readers) Random Hse. Children's Bks.

Meddaugh, Susan. Martha Speaks: Martha Stinks! (Reader) 2013. (Martha Speaks Ser.). (ENG., Illus.). 24p. (J). (gr. -1-3). 12.99 *(978-0-544-09662-2(2))* Houghton Mifflin Harcourt Publishing Co.

—Martha Stinks! 2013. (Martha Speaks Ser.). (ENG., Illus.). 24p. (J). (gr. -1-3). pap. 3.99 *(978-0-544-10012-1(3))* Houghton Mifflin Harcourt Publishing Co.

Messer, Claire. Grumpy Pants. Messer, Claire, illus. 2016. (ENG., Illus.). 32p. (J). (gr. -1-3). 16.99 *(978-0-8075-3075-7(1))* Whitman, Albert & Co.

Miramontes, Arturo J. & Miramontes, Arthur J. There's an Elephant in My Bathtub. 2010. 28p. pap. 16.95 *(978-1-4520-7522-8(0))* AuthorHouse.

Mitchell, Dawn. A Bird in a Bathing Suit. 2010. 24p. (J). pap. 12.95 *(978-1-4327-5404-4(1))* Outskirts Pr., Inc.

Montgomery, Margaret, illus. The Adventures of Anna Banana Shoeshine: Anna Banana Takes a Bath. 2006. 40p. (J). *(978-1-930401-49-5(3))* Central Coast Bks./Pr.

Mortensen, Lori. Cowpoke Clyde & Dirty Dawg. Austin, Michael Allen, illus. 2013. (ENG.). 32p. (J). (gr. -1-3). 16.99 *(978-0-547-23993-4(9))* Houghton Mifflin Harcourt Publishing Co.

Mühle, Jörg. Bathtime for Little Rabbit. Mühle, Jörg, illus. 2017. (ENG., Illus.). 20p. (J). (gr. -1-k). bds. 9.99 ***(978-1-77657-137-6(1))*** Gecko Pr. NZL. Dist: Lerner Publishing Group.

Muller, Carrie & Halsey, Jacqueline. The Terrible, Horrible, Smelly Pirate, 1 vol. Orchard, Eric, illus. 2008. (ENG.). 32p. (J). (gr. k-3). pap. 11.95 *(978-1-55109-655-1(2))* Nimbus Publishing, Ltd. CAN. Dist: Orca Bk. Pubs. USA.

Nevels, Lourene. A Dog's Life. 2011. (Illus.). 52p. pap. 19.95 *(978-1-4575-0538-6(X))* Dog Ear Publishing, LLC.

nicklin, philip. The Belly Button Fluff Pixie. 2009. (Illus.). 31p. 25.50 *(978-0-9561561-1-2(8))* de Fosseway, Marquis GBR. Dist: Lulu Pr., Inc.

Nosy Crow Staff. Get Out of My Bath! Teckentrup, Britta, illus. 2015. (ENG.). 24p. (J). (gr. -1-2). 15.99 *(978-0-7636-8006-0(0),* Nosy Crow) Candlewick Pr.

Ojo, Loyce. Bath Time. 2015. (ENG.). 35p. (J). mass mkt. 13.95 *(978-1-78554-304-3(0),* 9fd86c2b-11cf-4b00-9409-3a9c56e1bdc5) Austin, Stan AUS. Dist: Bookmasters Distribution.

Pack, Sherri. Little Cat, 1 vol. 2009. 20p. pap. 24.95 *(978-1-60813-706-0(6))* America Star Bks.

Parenteau, Shirley. Bears in the Bath. Walker, David, illus. (ENG.). (J). (— 1). 2016. 30p. bds. 6.99 *(978-0-7636-7946-0(1))* 2014. 32p. 15.99 *(978-0-7636-6418-3(9))* Candlewick Pr.

Parker, Emma. Bath Time. 2010. (Illus.). pap. *(978-1-877547-83-6(2))* First Edition Ltd.

—Billy & the Deep Sea Monster. 2010. (Illus.). 20p. pap. *(978-1-877561-57-3(6))* First Edition Ltd.

Patricelli, Leslie. Tubby. Patricelli, Leslie, illus. 2010. (Leslie Patricelli Board Bks.). (ENG., Illus.). 28p. (J). (— 1). bds. 6.99 *(978-0-7636-4567-0(2))* Candlewick Pr.

—Tubby / Bañito. Patricelli, Leslie, illus. 2017. (Leslie Patricelli Board Bks.). (ENG & SPA., Illus.). 28p. (J). (— 1). bds. 6.99 *(978-0-7636-9316-9(2))* Candlewick Pr.

Petrarca, Natalie. Stinky the Cat. 2009. 24p. pap. 13.95 *(978-1-4327-1184-9(9))* Outskirts Pr., Inc.

Pope, Mildred. But I Don't Wanna Take a Bath! A Mike & Tyke Series. 2011. 36p. (gr. -1). 15.95 *(978-1-4567-3939-3(5))* AuthorHouse.

Posner-Sanchez, Andrea. Bath Time with Ariel (Disney Princess) DiCicco, Sue, illus. 2015. (Board Book Ser.). (ENG.). 24p. (J). (— 1). bds. 6.99 *(978-0-7364-3310-5(4),* RH/Disney) Random Hse. Children's Bks.

Powell, Richard. Bear. Gardner, Louise, illus. 2014. (Bathing Beauties Ser.). (ENG.). 8p. (J). (gr. -1 — 1). 7.99 *(978-1-4380-7441-2(7))* Barron's Educational Series, Inc.

Prince, April Jones. Dive In! Berg, Michelle, illus. 2013. (ENG.). 14p. (J). (gr. -1 — 1). bds. 7.95 *(978-1-4197-0523-6(7))* Abrams, Inc.

Quintanilla, Billie. Never Again a Homeless Christmas! 2012. 28p. pap. 24.95 *(978-1-4626-5197-9(6))* America Star Bks.

Ransom, Nicole. Mimi: Takes a Bath. 2010. 16p. 8.49 *(978-1-4490-0420-0(2))* AuthorHouse.

Real, F. A. Casey & the Car Wash. 2008. 20p. pap. 24.95 *(978-1-4241-9091-1(6))* America Star Bks.

Riccobono, Michael P. Billy Balonie & the Belly Buttonie. 2010. (Illus.). 28p. pap. 19.00 *(978-1-4490-3119-0(6))* AuthorHouse.

Rivers-Moore, Debbie. Let's Go - Tractor! Backhouse, Carolyn, illus. 2011. (Let's Go Bath Bks.). (ENG.). 8p. (J). (gr. -1-k). 6.99 *(978-1-4380-7117-6(5))* Barron's Educational Series, Inc.

—Scrub-A-Dub Ducky: Bath Mitt & Bath Book Set. Jones, Anna, illus. 2014. (ENG.). 8p. (J). (gr. -1 — 1). 9.99 *(978-1-4380-7530-3(8))* Barron's Educational Series, Inc.

Robinson, Michelle. How to Wash a Woolly Mammoth. Hindley, Kate, illus. 2014. (ENG.). 32p. (J). (gr. -1-3). 16.99 *(978-0-8050-9966-9(2),* 9780805099669, Holt, Henry & Co. Bks. For Young Readers) Holt, Henry & Co.

Rodriguez, Edarissa. The Girl Who Took a Shower. Santiago, Claribel, ed. Rodriguez, Edarissa, illus. 2003. (Illus.). (J). pap. 13.99 *(978-0-9744726-0-7(3))* Santiago, Claribel.

Rose, Andrea. A Home for Abby. 2011. 24p. pap. 12.79 *(978-1-4634-2121-2(4))* AuthorHouse.

Ross, Tony. Hora de Dormir. 2006. (Little Princess Ser.) Tr. of Bedtime. (SPA.). (J). (gr. -1-k). bds. 7.95 *(978-968-19-1488-2(0),* AT33282) Lectorum Pubns., Inc.

Rylant, Cynthia & Mones, Isidre. Puppy Mudge Takes a Bath. Mones, Isidre, illus. 2004. (Puppy Mudge Ser.). (ENG., Illus.). 32p. (J). (gr. -1-k). pap. 3.99 *(978-0-689-86621-0(6),* Simon Spotlight) Simon Spotlight.

Scheffler, Axel. Freddy the Frog. Scheffler, Axel, illus. 2014. (Noisy Bath Bks.). (ENG., Illus.). 12p. (J). (— 1). 13.99 *(978-1-4472-6804-8(0))* Pan Macmillan GBR. Dist: Independent Pubs. Group.

Seltzer, Jerry Joe. There Are Fairies in My Tub. Seltzer, Jerry Joe, illus. 2013. (Illus.). 20p. (J). 12.95 *(978-1-60131-175-7(3),* Castlebridge Bks.) Big Tent Bks.

Shaffer, Jennifer. I Want to Play! 2012. 26p. 24.95 *(978-1-4626-5779-7(6))* America Star Bks.

Shea, Therese. Digger Has a Bath. 2006. (Neighborhood Readers Ser.). (ENG.). 12p. (gr. -1-3). pap. 5.90 *(978-1-4042-6467-0(1),* Rosen Classroom) Rosen Publishing Group, Inc., The.

Shyba, Jessica. Bathtime with Theo & Beau. 2016. (ENG., Illus.). 40p. (J). 16.99 *(978-1-250-05907-9(0),* 9781250059079) Feiwel & Friends.

Slegers, Liesbet. Bathing. 2011. (Clavis Toddler: Daily Life Ser.). (ENG.). 12p. (J). (gr. k — 1). bds. 5.95 *(978-1-60537-092-7(4))* Cobblestone Publishing Co.

Smalls, Irene. I Can't Take a Bath! Boyd, Aaron, illus. 2004. (Just for You Ser.). (ENG.). 32p. (J). (gr. 1-1). pap. 3.99 *(978-0-439-56852-4(8))* Scholastic, Inc.

Smart Kidz, creator. This Is the Way We Take a Bath. 2013. (Sing N Play Songs Ser.). (ENG., Illus.). (gr. -1). bds. 12.99 *(978-1-891100-08-6(4),* Smart Kids) Penton Overseas, Inc.

Smith, Michael. My Ducky Buddy. Oliva, Octavio, illus. 2011. 23p. (J). *(978-0-9821675-4-0(7))* East West Discovery Pr.

—My Ducky Buddy/Mi Amigo el Pato. Oliva, Octavio, illus. 2011. (ENG & SPA.). 24p. (J). (gr. -1-3). 12.95 *(978-0-9821675-5-7(5))* East West Discovery Pr.

Smith, Michael & Wang, Emily. My Ducky Buddy. Oliva, Octavio, illus. 2011. (CHI & ENG.). 23p. (J). *(978-0-9821675-7-1(1))* East West Discovery Pr.

Spinelli, Eileen & Spinelli. Bath Time, 1 vol. Pedersen, Janet, illus. 2003. (ENG.). 32p. (J). 14.95 *(978-0-7614-5117-4(X))* Marshall Cavendish Corp.

Stewart, Amber & Rankin, Laura. Rabbit Ears. Rankin, Laura, illus. 2012. (ENG., Illus.). 32p. (J). (gr. -1-1). pap. 8.99 *(978-1-59990-740-6(2),* 9781599907406, Bloomsbury USA Childrens) Bloomsbury Publishing USA.

Trasler, Janee. Bathtime for Chickies. Trasler, Janee, illus. 2015. (Chickies Ser.). (ENG., Illus.). 24p. (J). (gr. -1 — 1). bds. 8.99 *(978-0-06-234229-4(0),* HarperFestival) HarperCollins Pubs.

Van Laan, Nancy. Scrubba Dub. Pons, Bernadette, illus. 2008. (ENG.). 32p. (J). (gr. -1-1). 8.99 *(978-1-4169-7859-6(3),* Simon & Schuster/Paula Wiseman Bks.) Simon & Schuster/Paula Wiseman Bks.

Vogel, Elizabeth. ¡Al agua patos! (Taking My Bath) 2009. (Limpieza y salud todo el día (Clean & Healthy All Day Long) Ser.). (SPA.). 24p. (gr. 1-1). 37.50 *(978-1-61514-294-1(0),* Editorial Buenas Letras) Rosen Publishing Group, Inc., The.

—Taking My Bath. 2009. (Clean & Healthy All Day Long Ser.). 24p. (gr. 1-1). 37.50 *(978-1-61511-868-7(3),* PowerKids Pr.) Rosen Publishing Group, Inc., The.

—Taking My Bath / ¡Al agua Patos! 2009. (Clean & Healthy All Day Long / Limpieza y salud todo el día Ser.). (ENG & SPA.). 24p. (gr. 1-1). 37.50 *(978-1-61511-873-1(X),* Editorial Buenas Letras) Rosen Publishing Group, Inc., The.

Warnes, Tim & Sykes, Julie. Bathtime, Little Tiger! Warnes, Tim, illus. 2003. (Little Tiger Lift-the-Flap Ser.). (Illus.). 12p. (J). 5.95 *(978-1-58925-693-4(X))* Tiger Tales.

Watt, Fiona. Water Baby. 2011. (Snuggletime Board Books Ser.). 10p. (J). ring bd. 8.99 *(978-0-7945-2038-0(3),* Usborne) EDC Publishing.

Weiss, Ellen. Bathtime for Twins. Williams, Sam, illus. 2012. (ENG.). 30p. (J). (gr. -1 — 1). bds. 7.99 *(978-1-4424-3026-6(5),* Little Simon) Little Simon.

Westaway, Kylie. A Whale in the Bathtub. Jellett, Tom, illus. 2016. (ENG.). 40p. (J). (gr. -1-3). 16.99 *(978-0-544-53535-0(9))* Houghton Mifflin Harcourt Publishing Co.

When Bath Time Comes. 2004. (J). per. *(978-1-57657-470-6(9))* Paradise Pr., Inc.

Willems, Mo. The Pigeon Needs a Bath! Willems, Mo, illus. 2014. (Pigeon Ser.). (ENG., Illus.). 40p. (J). (gr. -1-k). 16.99 *(978-1-4231-9087-5(4))* Hyperion Bks. for Children.

Wilson, Karma. Hogwash! McMullan, Jim, illus. 2011. (ENG.). 40p. (J). (gr. -1-3). 17.99 *(978-0-316-98840-7(5))* Little, Brown Bks. for Young Readers.

Witkowski, Teri. The Bitty Bunch Bath Book. Ackley, Peggy Jo, illus. 2006. (J). *(978-1-59369-080-9(0))* American Girl Publishing, Inc.

Wood, Audrey. King Bidgood's in the Bathtub. Wood, Don, illus. 2010. (ENG.). 32p. (J). (gr. -1-3). pap. 7.99 *(978-0-15-205435-9(9))* Houghton Mifflin Harcourt Publishing Co.

BATHYSCAPHE

Bodden, Valerie. To the Ocean Deep. 2012. (Great Expeditions Ser.). (ENG.). 48p. (J). (gr. 4-7). pap. 12.00 *(978-0-89812-665-5(7),* Creative Paperbacks) Creative Co., The.

BATMAN (FICTITIOUS CHARACTER)—FICTION

Ameet Studio Staff. Enter the Dark Knight. 2016. (LEGO DC Super Heroes Ser.). (ENG.). 32p. (J). (gr. 2-5). pap., act. bk. ed. 8.99 *(978-1-338-11411-9(5))* Scholastic, Inc.

Aptekar, Devan. Darkseid's Revenge. Gordon, Eric A. & Gordon, Steven E., illus. 2012. (ENG.). 24p. (J). (gr. -1-3). pap. 3.99 *(978-0-06-188533-4(9),* HarperFestival) HarperCollins Pubs.

—Darkseid's Revenge. Gordon, Eric A. & Gordon, Steven E., illus. 2012. (Justice League Classic 8X8 Ser.). (J). lib. bdg. 13.55 *(978-0-606-23566-2(3),* Turtleback) Turtleback Bks.

Batman: Comic Chapter Books, 1 vol. 2014. (Batman: Comic Chapter Bks.). (ENG.). 32p. (gr. k-2). pap. 11.90 *(978-1-4342-9534-7(6),* DC Super Heroes) Stone Arch Bks.

Batman vs. Superman: Their Greatest Battles. 2015. lib. bdg. 20.85 *(978-0-606-37886-4(3))* Turtleback Bks.

Beatty, Scott. Scarecrow's Panic Plot. Vecchio, Luciano, illus. 2015. (Batman: Comic Chapter Bks.). (ENG.). 88p. (gr. 3-7). lib. bdg. 21.32 *(978-1-4965-0512-5(3))* Stone Arch Bks.

Beatty, Scott, et al. In the Mouth of the Whale. Vecchio, Luciano, illus. 2015. (Beware the Batman Ser.). (ENG.). 32p. (gr. 2-3). lib. bdg. 22.60 *(978-1-4342-9740-2(3))* Stone Arch Bks.

Berrios, Frank. Batman's Birthday Surprise! (DC Super Friends) Random House & Doescher, Erik, illus. 2016. (Pictureback(R) Ser.). (ENG.). 16p. (J). (gr. -1-2). 4.99 *(978-0-553-53983-7(3)*, Random Hse. Bks. for Young Readers) Random Hse. Children's Bks.

Black, Jake. Attack of the Man-Bat! Vecchio, Luciano, illus. 2015. (Batman: Comic Chapter Bks.). (ENG.). 88p. (gr. 3-7). lib. bdg. 21.32 *(978-1-4965-0513-2(1))* Stone Arch Bks.

—Batman Classic: Coin Toss. Tong, Andie, illus. 2016. 24p. (J). (gr. -1-3). pap. 3.99 *(978-0-06-234491-5(9)*, HarperFestival) HarperCollins Pubs.

—Coin Toss. 2016. (Batman 8X8 Storybooks Ser.). (J). lib. bdg. 13.55 *(978-0-606-38197-0(X))* Turtleback Bks.

Black, Jake & Beatty, Scott. Batman: Comic Chapter Books, 2 vols. 2015. (Batman: Comic Chapter Bks.). (ENG., Illus.). 88p. (gr. 3-7). 42.64 *(978-1-4965-1997-9(3))* Stone Arch Bks.

Black, Jake & Meredith Books Staff. Race Against Crime. Wallace, Loston, illus. 2008. 24p. (J). pap. 3.99 *(978-0-696-23958-8(2))* Meredith Bks.

Bright, J. E. Batman Unlimited: Heroes of Gotham City. Spaziante, Patrick, illus. 2016. (Simon & Schuster Ready-To-Read Level 2 Ser.). (ENG.). 32p. (J). (gr. k-2). lib. bdg. 13.55 *(978-0-606-39245-7(9))* Turtleback Bks.

—Batman Versus Man-Bat. Gordon, Steven E. & Gordon, Eric A., illus. 2012. (I Can Read Level 2 Ser.). (ENG.). 32p. (J). (gr. -1-3). pap. 3.99 *(978-0-06-188523-5(1))* HarperCollins Pubs.

—Batman Versus Man-Bat. 2012. (Batman: I Can Read Ser.). (J). lib. bdg. 13.55 *(978-0-606-26846-2(4)*, Turtleback) Turtleback Bks.

—Batman vs. Catwoman, 1 vol. Levins, Tim, illus. 2013. (DC Super Heroes Ser.). (ENG.). 56p. (gr. 2-3). lib. bdg. 26.65 *(978-1-4342-6013-0(5))* Stone Arch Bks.

—Better Call Batman! 2016. (Simon & Schuster Ready-To-Read Level 2 Ser.). lib. bdg. 13.55 ***(978-0-606-39753-7(1))*** Turtleback Bks.

—Joker on the High Seas, 1 vol. McManus, Shawn, illus. 2012. (DC Super-Villains Ser.). (ENG.). 56p. (gr. 2-3). pap. 5.95 *(978-1-4342-3895-5(4)*, DC Super-villains) Stone Arch Bks.

—The Joker's Magic Mayhem. Vecchio, Luciano, illus. 2016. (Batman & Robin Adventures Ser.). (ENG.). 88p. (gr. 2-3). lib. bdg. 26.65 *(978-1-4965-2538-3(8)*, DC Super Heroes) Stone Arch Bks.

—Scarecrow's Nightmare Maze. Vecchio, Luciano, illus. 2016. (Batman & Robin Adventures Ser.). (ENG.). 88p. (gr. 2-3). lib. bdg. 26.65 *(978-1-4965-2537-6(X)*, DC Super Heroes) Stone Arch Bks.

—Seed Bank Heist. Beavers, Ethen, illus. 2015. (You Choose Stories: Batman Ser.). (ENG.). 112p. (gr. 2-3). pap. 6.95 *(978-1-4342-9709-9(8))* Stone Arch Bks.

Bright, J. E. & Loughridge, Lee. Joker on the High Seas, 1 vol. McManus, Shawn, illus. 2012. (DC Super-Villains Ser.). (ENG.). 56p. (gr. 2-3). lib. bdg. 26.65 *(978-1-4342-3794-1(X)*, DC Super-villains) Stone Arch Bks.

Bright, J. E., et al. You Choose Stories: Batman. Beavers, Ethen, illus. 2015. (You Choose Stories: Batman Ser.). (ENG.). 112p. (gr. 2-3). 130.60 *(978-1-4965-0245-2(0)*, DC Super Heroes) Stone Arch Bks.

Cohen, Ivan, et al. Beware the Batman. Vecchio, Luciano & Brizuela, Dario, illus. 2015. (Beware the Batman Ser.). (ENG.). 32p. (gr. 2-3). 90.40 *(978-1-4965-0302-2(3))* Stone Arch Bks.

—Law & Disorder. Vecchio, Luciano, illus. 2015. (Beware the Batman Ser.). (ENG.). 32p. (gr. 2-3). lib. bdg. 22.60 *(978-1-4342-9738-9(1))* Stone Arch Bks.

—The Son of the Man-Bat. Vecchio, Luciano, illus. 2015. (Beware the Batman Ser.). (ENG.). 32p. (gr. 2-3). lib. bdg. 22.60 *(978-1-4342-9741-9(1))* Stone Arch Bks.

Cosentino, Ralph. Batman: The Story of the Dark Knight. Cosentino, Ralph, illus. 2008. (ENG., Illus.). 40p. (J). (gr. -1-2). 16.99 *(978-0-670-06255-3(3)*, Viking Books for Young Readers) Penguin Young Readers Group.

Cregg, R. J. Batman Strikes Back. Spaziante, Patrick, illus. 2016. (Batman Unlimited Ser.). (ENG.). 24p. (J). (gr. -1-2). 13.55 *(978-0-606-39249-5(1))* Turtleback Bks.

Dahl, Michael. Bedtime for Batman. Beavers, Ethen, illus. 2016. (DC Super Heroes Ser.). (ENG.). 32p. (gr. -1-2). 15.95 *(978-1-62370-732-3(3))*; lib. bdg. 22.65 *(978-1-5158-0652-3(9))* Stone Arch Bks. (DC Super Heroes).

—The Clown Prince of Cards. Vecchio, Luciano, illus. 2016. (Batman Tales of the Batcave Ser.). (ENG.). 40p. (gr. 1-3). lib. bdg. 24.65 *(978-1-4965-4013-3(1)*, DC Super Heroes) Stone Arch Bks.

—The Crushing Coin. Vecchio, Luciano, illus. 2016. (Batman Tales of the Batcave Ser.). (ENG.). 40p. (gr. 1-3). lib. bdg. 24.65 *(978-1-4965-4014-0(X)*, DC Super Heroes) Stone Arch Bks.

—Dino Death-Trap. Vecchio, Luciano, illus. 2016. (Batman Tales of the Batcave Ser.). (ENG.). 40p. (gr. 1-3). lib. bdg. 24.65 *(978-1-4965-4015-7(8)*, DC Super Heroes) Stone Arch Bks.

—The Penguin's Power Parasol. Vecchio, Luciano, illus. 2016. (Batman Tales of the Batcave Ser.). (ENG.). 40p. (gr. 1-3). lib. bdg. 24.65 *(978-1-4965-4012-6(3)*, DC Super Heroes) Stone Arch Bks.

—Tales of the BatCave. Vecchio, Luciano, illus. 2016. (Batman Tales of the Batcave Ser.). (ENG.). 40p. (gr. 1-3). 98.60 *(978-1-4965-4032-4(8)*, DC Super Heroes) Stone Arch Bks.

Dahl, Michael, et al. Five Riddles for Robin, 1 vol. Schigiel, Gregg, illus. 2013. (Batman Ser.). (ENG.). 56p. (gr. 2-3). pap. 4.95 *(978-1-4342-1366-2(8)*, DC Super Heroes) Stone Arch Bks.

Davies, Beth. Batman's Missions. 2015. (DK Reader Level 3 Ser.). lib. bdg. 13.55 *(978-0-606-36692-2(X))* Turtleback Bks.

Dc Comics Editors. Batman Arkham Poison Ivy. 2016. lib. bdg. 33.05 *(978-0-606-39204-4(1))* Turtleback Bks.

DC Comics Staff. Batman Jumbo Color & Activity Book. Meredith Books Staff et al, eds. 2005. 400p. (J). pap. 5.99 *(978-0-696-22722-6(3))* Meredith Bks.

Dewin, Howie. Batman's Guide to Being Cool. Scholastic, illus. 2016. (LEGO Batman Movie Ser.). (ENG.). 128p. (J). (gr. 2-5). 9.99 *(978-1-338-11210-8(4))* Scholastic, Inc.

Dini, Paul. The Batman & Robin Adventures Vol. 1. 2016. (ENG., Illus.). 240p. (J). (gr. 2-5). pap. 19.99 *(978-1-4012-6783-4(1))* DC Comics.

—Men of Steel, 1 vol. Burchett, Rick & Austin, Terry, illus. 2012. (Superman Adventures Ser.). (ENG.). 32p. (gr. 2-3). lib. bdg. 22.60 *(978-1-4342-4549-6(7))* Stone Arch Bks.

Dorling Kindersley Publishing Staff. Amazing Battles! 2015. (DK Readers Ser.). (ENG., Illus.). 48p. (J). (gr. 1-3). pap. 3.99 *(978-1-4654-3011-3(3)*, DK Children) Dorling Kindersley Publishing, Inc.

—Batman's Missions. 2015. (DK Readers Ser.). (ENG.). 64p. (J). (gr. 2-4). pap. 3.99 *(978-1-4654-3014-4(8)*, DK Children) Dorling Kindersley Publishing, Inc.

—DK Readers L3: LEGO DC Comics Super Heroes: Batman's Missions: LEGO DC Comics Super Heroes: Batman's Missions. 2015. (DK Readers Ser.). (ENG.). 64p. (J). (gr. 2-4). 14.99 *(978-1-4654-3013-7(X)*, DK Children) Dorling Kindersley Publishing, Inc.

Dorling Kindersley Publishing Staff. The LEGO Batman Movie. 2016. (LEGO DC Universe DK Readers Ser.). lib. bdg. 13.55 ***(978-0-606-39895-4(3))*** Turtleback Bks.

Dorling Kindersley Publishing Staff & Taylor, Victoria. Ready for Action! 2013. (DK Readers Ser.). (ENG., Illus.). 32p. (J). (gr. k-4). pap. 3.99 *(978-1-4654-0174-8(1)*, DK Children) Dorling Kindersley Publishing, Inc.

Duggan, Gerry. Batman: Arkham Manor Vol. 1. 2015. lib. bdg. 26.95 *(978-0-606-37250-3(4))* Turtleback Bks.

Esquivel, Eric. Carnival Capers! Wang, Sean, illus. 2016. (LEGO DC Super Heroes Ser.). (ENG.). 32p. (J). (gr. -1-3). pap. 3.99 *(978-0-545-86815-0(7))* Scholastic, Inc.

Finnegan, Delphine. Batman Classic: I Am Batman. Tong, Andie, illus. 2016. (I Can Read Level 2 Ser.). 32p. (J). (gr. -1-3). pap. 3.99 *(978-0-06-236087-8(6))* HarperCollins Pubs.

—I Am Batman. Tong, Andie, illus. 2016. (Batman Classic I Can Read Level 2 Ser.). (ENG.). 32p. (J). (gr. -1-3). 13.55 *(978-0-606-39268-6(8))* Turtleback Bks.

Fisch, Sholly & Age, Heroic. Who Is the Mystery Bat-Squad?, 1 vol. Clugston, Chynna, illus. 2014. (DC Super Friends Ser.). (ENG.). 32p. (gr. 1-2). 22.60 *(978-1-4342-9224-7(X))* Stone Arch Bks.

Fisch, Sholly, et al. The All-New Batman: the Brave & the Bold. 2015. (All-New Batman: the Brave & the Bold Ser.). (ENG., Illus.). 32p. (gr. 2-3). lib. bdg. 90.40 *(978-1-4965-0544-6(1))* Stone Arch Bks.

—Bottle of the Planets. 2015. (All-New Batman: the Brave & the Bold Ser.). (ENG., Illus.). 32p. (gr. 2-3). lib. bdg. 22.60 *(978-1-4342-9658-0(X))* Stone Arch Bks.

—The Bride & the Bold. 2015. (All-New Batman: the Brave & the Bold Ser.). (ENG., Illus.). 32p. (gr. 2-3). lib. bdg. 22.60 *(978-1-4342-9661-0(X))* Stone Arch Bks.

—Clobbered by Clayface! 2015. (All-New Batman: the Brave & the Bold Ser.). (ENG., Illus.). 32p. (gr. 2-3). lib. bdg. 22.60 *(978-1-4342-9663-4(6))* Stone Arch Bks.

—Manhandled by Manhunters! 2015. (All-New Batman: the Brave & the Bold Ser.). (ENG., Illus.). 32p. (gr. 2-3). lib. bdg. 22.60 *(978-1-4342-9662-7(8))* Stone Arch Bks.

—That Holiday Feeling. 2015. (All-New Batman: the Brave & the Bold Ser.). (ENG., Illus.). 32p. (gr. 2-3). lib. bdg. 22.60 *(978-1-4342-9659-7(8))* Stone Arch Bks.

—Through the Looking Glass! 2015. (All-New Batman: the Brave & the Bold Ser.). (ENG., Illus.). 32p. (gr. 2-3). lib. bdg. 22.60 *(978-1-4342-9660-3(1))* Stone Arch Bks.

Hoena, Blake. The Riddler's Ransom. Beavers, Ethen, illus. 2015. (You Choose Stories: Batman Ser.). (ENG.). 112p. (gr. 2-3). lib. bdg. 32.65 *(978-1-4342-9706-8(3))* Stone Arch Bks.

Hoena, Blake A., et al. Poison Ivy's Deadly Garden, 1 vol. (Batman Ser.). (ENG., Illus.). 56p. (gr. 2-3). 2013. pap. 4.95 *(978-1-4342-1368-6(4))* 2009. lib. bdg. 26.65 *(978-1-4342-1152-1(5))* Stone Arch Bks. (DC Super Heroes).

Huelin, Jodi. Batman & the Toxic Terror. Gordon, Steven E., illus. 2011. (ENG.). 24p. (J). (gr. -1-3). pap. 3.99 *(978-0-06-188530-3(4)*, HarperFestival) HarperCollins Pubs.

—Batman Versus Bane. Tong, Andie, illus. 2012. (I Can Read Book 2 Ser.). (ENG.). 32p. (J). (gr. -1-3). pap. 3.99 *(978-0-06-213224-6(5))* HarperCollins Pubs.

Hult, Gene & Bright, J. E. Cat Commander. Vecchio, Luciano, illus. (Dark Knight Ser.). (ENG.). 88p. (gr. 2-3). 2013. pap. 5.95 *(978-1-4342-4214-3(5))* 2012. 26.65 *(978-1-4342-4088-0(6))* Stone Arch Bks.

Jurgens, Dan. Brave New Worlds. 2016. (Batman Beyond Ser.: 1). lib. bdg. 26.95 *(978-0-606-38627-2(0))* Turtleback Bks.

Kane, Bob. Comic con & Labor Day. Nguyen, Dustin, illus. 2015. (Batman: Li'l Gotham Ser.). (ENG.). 32p. (gr. 2-3). lib. bdg. 22.60 *(978-1-4342-9736-5(5))* Stone Arch Bks.

—Month of Waters & Independence Day. Nguyen, Dustin, illus. 2015. (Batman: Li'l Gotham Ser.). (ENG.). 32p. (gr. 2-3). lib. bdg. 22.60 *(978-1-4342-9666-5(0))* Stone Arch Bks.

—Sandwich Day & Our Family Album. Nguyen, Dustin, illus. 2015. (Batman: Li'l Gotham Ser.). (ENG.). 32p. (gr. 2-3). lib. bdg. 22.60 *(978-1-4342-9737-2(3))* Stone Arch Bks.

—Tropical Getaway & Bird Watching. Nguyen, Dustin, illus. 2015. (Batman: Li'l Gotham Ser.). (ENG.). 32p. (gr. 2-3). lib. bdg. 22.60 *(978-1-4342-9735-8(7))* Stone Arch Bks.

Kiernan, Kenny, illus. Save the Day! 2013. (J). *(978-1-4844-0146-0(8))* Scholastic, Inc.

King, Trey. Friends & Foes! Wang, Sean, illus. 2015. (LEGO DC Super Heroes Ser.: 1). (ENG.). 24p. (J). (gr. -1-3). pap. 3.99 *(978-0-545-78504-4(9))* Scholastic, Inc.

—The Last Laugh! Kiernan, Kenny, illus. 2013. (LEGO DC Superheroes Ser.). (ENG.). 32p. (J). (gr. -1-3). pap. 3.99 *(978-0-545-48029-1(9))* Scholastic, Inc.

—Save the Day! Kiernan, Kenny, illus. 2013. (LEGO DC Superheroes Ser.). (ENG.). 32p. (J). (gr. -1-3). pap. 3.99 *(978-0-545-48028-4(0))* Scholastic, Inc.

Lagonegro, Melissa. Beauty & the Beast. 2017. (Disney Princess Step into Reading Ser.). lib. bdg. 14.75 ***(978-0-606-39855-8(4))*** Turtleback Bks.

Lane, Jeanette. Junior Novel. 2016. (LEGO Batman Movie Ser.). (ENG.). 176p. (J). (gr. 2-5). pap. 6.99 *(978-1-338-11221-4(X))* Scholastic, Inc.

Lemke, Donald. Batman - Who Is Clayface? Gordon, Steven E. & Gordon, Eric A., illus. 2013. (I Can Read Level 2 Ser.). (ENG.). 32p. (J). (gr. -1-3). pap. 3.99 *(978-0-06-188525-9(8))* HarperCollins Pubs.

—Batman - Winter Wasteland. Gordon, Steven E. & Gordon, Eric A., illus. 2014. (I Can Read Level 2 Ser.). (ENG.). 32p. (J). (gr. -1-3). pap. 3.99 *(978-0-06-221004-3(1))* HarperCollins Pubs.

—Batman Classic: Batman Versus the Riddler. Gordon, Steven E. & Gordon, Eric A., illus. 2014. (I Can Read Level 2 Ser.). (ENG.). 32p. (J). (gr. -1-3). pap. 3.99 *(978-0-06-221008-1(4))* HarperCollins Pubs.

—Batman Classic - The Joker's Ice Scream. Tong, Andie, illus. 2015. (I Can Read Level 2 Ser.). (ENG.). 32p. (J). (gr. -1-3). pap. 3.99 *(978-0-06-234492-2(7))* HarperCollins Pubs.

—Batman Classic: Battle in the Batcave. 2014. (ENG.). 24p. (J). (gr. -1-3). pap. 3.99 *(978-0-06-220998-6(1)*, HarperFestival) HarperCollins Pubs.

—Batman Classic: Dino Dilemma. Tong, Andie, illus. 2017. (I Can Read Level 2 Ser.). 32p. (J). (gr. -1-3). pap. 3.99 ***(978-0-06-236091-5(4))*** HarperCollins Pubs.

—Batman Classic: Rat Trap. Tong, Andie, illus. 2016. 24p. (J). (gr. -1-3). pap. 3.99 *(978-0-06-236073-1(6)*, HarperFestival) HarperCollins Pubs.

—Batman Versus the Riddler. 2014. (Batman Classic I Can Read Level 2 Ser.). (J). lib. bdg. 13.55 *(978-0-606-35474-5(3))* Turtleback Bks.

—Nightmare in Gotham City. Tong, Andie, illus. 2015. (ENG.). 24p. (J). (gr. -1-3). pap. 3.99 *(978-0-06-234486-1(2)*, HarperFestival) HarperCollins Pubs.

—Nightmare in Gotham City. 2015. (Batman 8X8 Storybooks Ser.). (J). lib. bdg. 13.55 *(978-0-606-36952-7(X))* Turtleback Bks.

—The Penguin's Arctic Adventure. Roberts, Jeremy, illus. 2014. (ENG.). 24p. (J). (gr. -1-3). pap. 3.99 *(978-0-06-221000-5(9)*, HarperFestival) HarperCollins Pubs.

—The Penguin's Arctic Adventure. 2014. (Batman 8X8 Storybooks Ser.). (J). lib. bdg. 13.55 *(978-0-606-36457-7(9))* Turtleback Bks.

—Who Is Clayface? 2013. (Justice League Classic: I Can Read! Ser.). (J). lib. bdg. 13.55 *(978-0-606-31790-0(2)*, Turtleback) Turtleback Bks.

—Winter Wasteland. 2014. (Batman Classic I Can Read Level 2 Ser.). (J). lib. bdg. 13.55 *(978-0-606-36458-4(7))* Turtleback Bks.

Lemke, Donald B., et al. Fun House of Evil, 1 vol. 2013. (Batman Ser.). (ENG., Illus.). 56p. (gr. 2-3). pap. 4.95 *(978-1-4342-1367-9(6)*, DC Super Heroes) Stone Arch Bks.

Lipkowitz, Daniel & Dorling Kindersley Publishing Staff. Batman, Visual Dictionary. 2012. (ENG.). 96p. (J). (gr. 2-5). 21.99 *(978-0-7566-9787-7(5)*, DK Children) Dorling Kindersley Publishing, Inc.

Manning, Matthew K. Batman & the Flock of Fear. Vecchio, Luciano, illus. 2013. (Dark Knight Ser.). (ENG.). 88p. (gr. 2-3). pap. 5.95 *(978-1-4342-4217-4(X))* Stone Arch Bks.

—Batman Tangles with Terror. Beavers, Ethen, illus. 2017. (DC Super Hero Stories Ser.). (ENG.). 56p. (gr. 1-3). lib. bdg. 25.32 *(978-1-4965-4632-6(6)*, DC Super Heroes) Stone Arch Bks.

—Catwoman's Nine Lives, 1 vol. Vecchio, Luciano, illus. 2014. (Batman: Comic Chapter Bks.). (ENG.). 88p. (gr. 3-7). 21.32 *(978-1-4342-9132-5(4))* Stone Arch Bks.

—Scarecrow's Flock of Fear, 1 vol. Vecchio, Luciano, illus. 2012. (Dark Knight Ser.). (ENG.). 88p. (gr. 2-3). lib. bdg. 26.65 *(978-1-4342-4090-3(8))* Stone Arch Bks.

Manning, Matthew K., et al. The Rule of Three. Brizuela, Dario, illus. 2015. (Beware the Batman Ser.). (ENG.). 32p. (gr. 2-3). lib. bdg. 22.60 *(978-1-4342-9739-6(X))* Stone Arch Bks.

Matheny, Bill, et al. Alfred to the Rescue?! 2015. (Batman Strikes! Ser.). (ENG., Illus.). 32p. (gr. 2-3). lib. bdg. 22.60 *(978-1-4342-9664-1(4))* Stone Arch Bks.

—Bane on the Rampage!, 1 vol. 2014. (Batman Strikes! Ser.). (ENG., Illus.). 32p. (gr. 2-3). 22.60 *(978-1-4342-4788-9(0))* Stone Arch Bks.

—Bane's Breaking In! 2015. (Batman Strikes! Ser.). (ENG., Illus.). 32p. (gr. 2-3). lib. bdg. 22.60 *(978-1-4342-9665-8(2))* Stone Arch Bks.

—The Batman Is on Fire!, 1 vol. 2014. (Batman Strikes! Ser.). (ENG., Illus.). 32p. (gr. 2-3). 22.60 *(978-1-4342-9229-2(0))* Stone Arch Bks.

—Batman Strikes!, 1 vol. 2014. (Batman Strikes! Ser.). (ENG., Illus.). 32p. (gr. 2-3). 90.40 *(978-1-4342-9518-7(4))*; 90.40 *(978-1-4342-8928-5(1))* Stone Arch Bks.

—Batman Strikes. (Batman Strikes! Ser.). (ENG., Illus.). 32p. (gr. 2-3). 2015. 271.20 *(978-1-4965-0292-6(2))* 2014. 180.80 *(978-1-4342-9600-9(8))* Stone Arch Bks.

—Catwoman Gets Busted by the Batman, 1 vol. 2014. (Batman Strikes! Ser.). (ENG., Illus.). 32p. (gr. 2-3). 22.60 *(978-1-4342-9211-7(8))* Stone Arch Bks.

—Frozen Solid by Mr. Freeze!, 1 vol. 2014. (Batman Strikes! Ser.). (ENG., Illus.). 32p. (gr. 2-3). 22.60 *(978-1-4342-9212-4(6))* Stone Arch Bks.

—Going... Batty!, 1 vol. 2014. (Batman Strikes! Ser.). (ENG., Illus.). 32p. (gr. 2-3). 22.60 *(978-1-4342-6484-8(X))* Stone Arch Bks.

—In the Clutches of the Penguin!, 1 vol. 2014. (Batman Strikes! Ser.). (ENG., Illus.). 32p. (gr. 2-3). 22.60 *(978-1-4342-6483-1(1))* Stone Arch Bks.

—Joker's Wild!, 1 vol. 2014. (Batman Strikes! Ser.). (ENG., Illus.). 32p. (gr. 2-3). 22.60 *(978-1-4342-6485-5(8))* Stone Arch Bks.

—Man-Bat's Sneak Attack! 2015. (Batman Strikes! Ser.). (ENG., Illus.). 32p. (gr. 2-3). lib. bdg. 22.60 *(978-1-4342-9655-9(5))* Stone Arch Bks.

—Sanity Plea! 2015. (Batman Strikes! Ser.). (ENG., Illus.). 32p. (gr. 2-3). lib. bdg. 22.60 *(978-1-4342-9743-3(8))* Stone Arch Bks.

—Scarface Is Gonna Go Boom!, 1 vol. 2014. (Batman Strikes! Ser.). (ENG., Illus.). 32p. (gr. 2-3). 22.60 *(978-1-4342-9210-0(X))* Stone Arch Bks.

Meredith Books Staff. Batman Activity Kit. 2008. (Illus.). 32p. (J). 14.99 *(978-0-696-23961-8(2))* Meredith Bks.

—Batman Sticker Story Adventure. 2008. (Illus.). 16p. (J). pap. 5.99 *(978-0-696-23960-1(4))* Meredith Bks.

Peterson, Scott. The Joker Virus, 1 vol. Cavallaro, Mike, illus. 2012. (Dark Knight Ser.). (ENG.). 88p. (gr. 2-3). lib. bdg. 26.65 *(978-1-4342-4096-5(7))* Stone Arch Bks.

Petranek, Michael. Being Batman. 2017. (LEGO Batman Movie Ser.: 2). (ENG.). 24p. (J). (gr. -1-3). pap. 4.99 *(978-1-338-11817-9(X))* Scholastic, Inc.

—The Joker's Big Break. 2016. (LEGO Batman Movie Ser.). (ENG.). 24p. (J). (gr. -1-3). pap. 4.99 *(978-1-338-11217-7(1))* Scholastic, Inc.

Publications International Ltd. Staff, ed. Batman: The Brave & the Bold (My First Library) 2010. 10p. (J). bds. 12.98 *(978-1-60553-856-3(6))* Phoenix International Publications, Inc.

Puckett, Kelley. Batman's Dark Secret. Muth, Jon J., illus. 2015. (ENG.). 32p. (J). (gr. k-2). 17.99 *(978-0-545-86755-9(X)*, Scholastic Pr.) Scholastic, Inc.

Random House Staff. Riddle Me This! Random House Staff, illus. 2010. (Pictureback(R) Ser.). (ENG., Illus.). 24p. (J). (gr. -1-2). pap. 3.99 *(978-0-375-84747-9(2)*, Random Hse. Bks. for Young Readers) Random Hse. Children's Bks.

Rosen, Lucy. Batman Phonics Fun! Farley, Rick et al, illus. 2011. (My First I Can Read Ser.). (ENG.). 36p. (J). (gr. -1-3). pap. 12.99 *(978-0-06-188542-6(8))* HarperCollins Pubs.

Sazaklis, John. Batman: An Origin Story. Baltazar, Art & Vecchio, Luciano, illus. 2015. (DC Super Heroes Origins Ser.). (ENG.). 48p. (gr. k-2). lib. bdg. 23.99 *(978-1-4342-9727-3(6))* Stone Arch Bks.

—Batman Classic: Dawn of the Dynamic Duo. Gordon, Eric A. & Gordon, Steven E., illus. 2011. (I Can Read Level 2 Ser.). (ENG.). 32p. (J). (gr. -1-3). pap. 3.99 *(978-0-06-188520-4(7))* HarperCollins Pubs.

—Batman Classic: Gotham's Villains Unleashed! Mada Design Staff, illus. 2009. (ENG.). 24p. (J). (gr. -1-3). pap. 3.99 *(978-0-06-187856-5(1)*, HarperFestival) HarperCollins Pubs.

—Batman Classic - Eternal Enemies. Tong, Andie, illus. 2013. (ENG.). 24p. (J). (gr. -1-3). pap. 3.99 *(978-0-06-220997-9(3)*, HarperFestival) HarperCollins Pubs.

—Battle - Battle in Metropolis. Smith, Andy & Vancata, Brad, illus. 2013. (ENG.). 24p. (J). (gr. -1-3). pap. 3.99 *(978-0-06-188537-2(1)*, HarperFestival) HarperCollins Pubs.

—Battle in Metropolis. 2013. (Justice League Classic 8X8 Ser.). lib. bdg. 13.55 *(978-0-606-31827-3(5)*, Turtleback) Turtleback Bks.

—Clayface Returns. Beavers, Ethen, illus. 2016. (You Choose Stories: Batman Ser.). (ENG.). 112p. (gr. 2-3). lib. bdg. 32.65 *(978-1-4965-3089-9(6)*, DC Super Heroes) Stone Arch Bks.

—The Lazarus Plan. Beavers, Ethen, illus. 2016. (You Choose Stories: Batman Ser.). (ENG.). 112p. (gr. 2-3). lib. bdg. 32.65 *(978-1-4965-3088-2(8)*, DC Super Heroes) Stone Arch Bks.

—Super-Villain Smackdown! Beavers, Ethen, illus. 2015. (You Choose Stories: Batman Ser.). (ENG.). 112p. (gr. 2-3). lib. bdg. 32.65 *(978-1-4965-0528-6(X))* Stone Arch Bks.

—You Choose Stories: Batman. Beavers, Ethen, illus. 2016. (You Choose Stories: Batman Ser.). (ENG.). 112p. (gr. 2-3). 261.20 *(978-1-4965-3100-1(0)*, DC Super Heroes) Stone Arch Bks.

Sazaklis, John & Merkel, Joe F. Day of the Undead. Tong, Andie, illus. 2013. (ENG.). 24p. (J). (gr. -1-3). pap. 3.99 *(978-0-06-220999-3(X)*, HarperFestival) HarperCollins Pubs.

Sazaklis, John & Roberts, Jeremy. Fright Club. Farley, Rick & Smith, Andy, illus. 2012. (ENG.). 24p. (J). (gr. -1-2). pap. 3.99 *(978-0-06-188534-1(7)*, HarperFestival) HarperCollins Pubs.

Scholastic Editors & Marsham, Liz. Harley Quinn: Wild Card. 2016. (Backstories Ser.). (ENG., Illus.). 128p. (J). (gr. 3-7). 16.00 *(978-0-606-39148-1(7))* Turtleback Bks.

Scholastic, Inc. Staff & Kogge, Michael. Cross Fire. 2016. (Batman vs. Superman: Dawn of Justice Ser.). (ENG.). 144p. (J). (gr. 2-5). pap. 5.99 *(978-0-545-91630-1(5))* Scholastic, Inc.

—Cross Fire. 2016. (Batman vs. Superman: Dawn of Justice Ser.). (ENG.). 144p. (J). (gr. 2-5). lib. bdg. 16.00 *(978-0-606-38097-3(3))* Turtleback Bks.

Shealy, Dennis & Random House Staff. Heroes United! - Attack of the Robot! Doescher, Erik et al, illus. 2008. (Pictureback(R) Ser.). (ENG.). 32p. (J). (gr. -1-2). pap. 4.99 *(978-0-375-84409-6(0)*, Random Hse. Bks. for Young Readers) Random Hse. Children's Bks.

Siegel, Jerry, et al. Adventures of Superman. Gordon, Steven E. et al, illus. 2013. 125p. (J). *(978-1-4351-5063-8(5))* Barnes & Noble, Inc.

Simonson, Louise. Harley Quinn's Crazy Creeper Caper. Vecchio, Luciano, illus. 2017. (Batman & Robin Adventures Ser.). (ENG.). 88p. (gr. 2-3). lib. bdg. 26.65 ***(978-1-4965-5347-8(0)***, DC Super Heroes) Stone Arch Bks.

Slott, Dan & Templeton, Ty. Batman Adventures. Templeton, Ty, illus. 2013. (Batman Adventures Ser.). (ENG., Illus.). 32p. (gr. 2-3). 158.20 *(978-1-4342-8837-0(4))* Stone Arch Bks.

Slott, Dan, et al. Masquerade in Red!, 1 vol. 2013. (Batman Adventures Ser.). (ENG.). 32p. (gr. 2-3). 22.60 *(978-1-4342-6036-9(4))* Stone Arch Bks.

—Phantasm Strikes!, 1 vol. Burchett, Rick, illus. 2013. (Batman Adventures Ser.). (ENG.). 32p. (gr. 2-3). 22.60 *(978-1-4342-6035-2(6))* Stone Arch Bks.

—Playing with Matches, 1 vol. Burchett, Rick, illus. 2013. (Batman Adventures Ser.). (ENG.). 32p. (gr. 2-3). 22.60 *(978-1-4342-6034-5(8))* Stone Arch Bks.

—Target: Deadshot!, 1 vol. Templeton, Ty, illus. 2013. (Batman Adventures Ser.). (ENG.). 32p. (gr. 2-3). 22.60 *(978-1-4342-6033-8(X))* Stone Arch Bks.

Snyder, Scott. Zero Year - Dark City, Vol. 5. 2015. (Batman: the New 52 Ser.: 5). lib. bdg. 29.40 *(978-0-606-37111-7(7))* Turtleback Bks.

Sonneborn, Scott. Batman & the Villainous Voyage. Vecchio, Luciano, illus. 2013. (Dark Knight Ser.). (ENG.). 88p. (gr. 2-3). pap. 5.95 *(978-1-4342-4216-7(1))* Stone Arch Bks.

—Danger on Deck!, 1 vol. Vecchio, Luciano & DC Comics Staff, illus. 2013. (Dark Knight Ser.). (ENG.). 88p. (gr. 2-3). 26.65 *(978-1-4342-4092-7(4))* Stone Arch Bks.

—Partners in Peril. Smith, Andy & Vancata, Brad, illus. 2013. (ENG.). 24p. (J). (gr. -1-3). pap. 3.99 *(978-0-06-221007-4(6)*, HarperFestival) HarperCollins Pubs.

—Prisoner of the Penguin!, 1 vol. Vecchio, Luciano, illus. 2014. (Batman: Comic Chapter Bks.). (ENG.). 88p. (gr. 3-7). 21.32 *(978-1-4342-9131-8(6))* Stone Arch Bks.

Spaziante, Patrick, illus. Creatures of Crime: A Guide to the Bad Guys. 2016. (Batman Ser.). (ENG.). 24p. (J). (gr. -1-2).

pap. 3.99 *(978-1-4814-7837-3(0),* Simon Spotlight) Simon Spotlight.

Stephens, Sarah Hines. Catwoman's Purrfect Plot. Vecchio, Luciano, illus. 2017. (Batman & Robin Adventures Ser.). (ENG.). 88p. (gr. 2-3). lib. bdg. 26.65 ***(978-1-4965-5349-2(7),*** DC Super Heroes) Stone Arch Bks.

—Poison Ivy's Rainforest Revenge. Levins, Tim, illus. 2017. (Batman & Robin Adventures Ser.). (ENG.). 88p. (gr. 2-3). lib. bdg. 26.65 ***(978-1-4965-5352-2(7),*** DC Super Heroes) Stone Arch Bks.

Stevens, Eric, et al. The Revenge of Clayface, 1 vol. Schigiel, Gregg, illus. (Batman Ser.). (ENG.). 56p. (gr. 2-3). 2013. pap. 4.95 *(978-1-4342-1369-3(2))* 2009. lib. bdg. 26.65 *(978-1-4342-1149-1(5))* Stone Arch Bks. (DC Super Heroes).

Stewart, Yale. Battle of the Super Heroes!, 1 vol. Stewart, Yale, illus. 2014. (Amazing Adventures of Superman! Ser.). (ENG., Illus.). 32p. (gr. k-2). 25.32 *(978-1-4795-5731-8(5),* DC Super Heroes) Stone Arch Bks.

Stone Arch Books. April Showers & Cinco de Mayo, 1 vol. Nguyen, Dustin, illus. 2014. (Batman: Li'l Gotham Ser.). (ENG.). 32p. (gr. 2-3). 22.60 *(978-1-4342-9220-9(7))* Stone Arch Bks.

—Batman: Li'l Gotham, 1 vol. Nguyen, Dustin Tri, illus. 2014. (Batman: Li'l Gotham Ser.). (ENG.). 32p. (gr. 2-3). 135.60 *(978-1-4342-9529-3(X))* Stone Arch Bks.

—Christmas & New Year's Eve, 1 vol. Nguyen, Dustin, illus. 2014. (Batman: Li'l Gotham Ser.). (ENG.). 32p. (gr. 2-3). 22.60 *(978-1-4342-9217-9(7))* Stone Arch Bks.

—Halloween & Thanksgiving, 1 vol. Nguyen, Dustin, illus. 2014. (Batman: Li'l Gotham Ser.). (ENG.). 32p. (gr. 2-3). 22.60 *(978-1-4342-9208-7(8))* Stone Arch Bks.

—Mother's Day & Father's Day, 1 vol. Nguyen, Dustin, illus. 2014. (Batman: Li'l Gotham Ser.). (ENG.). 32p. (gr. 2-3). 22.60 *(978-1-4342-9221-6(5))* Stone Arch Bks.

—St. Patrick's Day & Easter, 1 vol. Nguyen, Dustin, illus. 2014. (Batman: Li'l Gotham Ser.). (ENG.). 32p. (gr. 2-3). 22.60 *(978-1-4342-9219-3(3))* Stone Arch Bks.

—Valentine's Day & the Lunar New Year, 1 vol. Nguyen, Dustin, illus. 2014. (Batman: Li'l Gotham Ser.). (ENG.). 32p. (gr. 2-3). 22.60 *(978-1-4342-9218-6(5))* Stone Arch Bks.

Stone Arch Books & Fisch, Sholly. DC Super Friends, 1 vol. 2014. (DC Super Friends Ser.). (ENG.). 32p. (gr. 1-2). 90.40 *(978-1-4342-9526-2(5))* Stone Arch Bks.

Stone Arch Books Staff, et al. Batman: Comic Chapter Books, 1 vol. Vecchio, Luciano, illus. 2014. (Batman: Comic Chapter Bks.). (ENG.). 32p. (gr. k-2). 42.64 *(978-1-4342-9377-0(7),* DC Super Heroes) Stone Arch Bks.

Style Guide, Style, illus. Animal Instincts. 2016. (Batman Ser.). (ENG.). 144p. (J). (gr. 3-7). pap. 6.99 *(978-1-4814-7731-4(5),* Simon Spotlight) Simon Spotlight.

Sudduth, Brent & Meredith Books Staff. Heads or Tails. Mada Design Staff, illus. 2008. 20p. (J). pap. 3.99 *(978-0-696-23959-5(0))* Meredith Bks.

Sutton, Laurie S. Batman Battles the Penguin. Style Guide, illus. 2016. (Batman Unlimited Ser.). (ENG.). 64p. (J). (gr. k-4). 16.00 *(978-0-606-39248-8(3))* Turtleback Bks.

—Batman vs. the Penguin. Vecchio, Luciano, illus. 2013. (Dark Knight Ser.). (ENG.). 88p. (gr. 2-3). pap. 5.95 *(978-1-4342-4825-1(9))* Stone Arch Bks.

—Cheetah & the Purrfect Crime, 1 vol. Vecchio, Luciano, illus. 2012. (DC Super-Villains Ser.). (ENG.). 56p. (gr. 2-3). pap. 5.95 *(978-1-4342-3900-6(4));* lib. bdg. 26.65 *(978-1-4342-3799-6(0))* Stone Arch Bks. (DC Super-villains).

—Clayface's Slime Spree. Vecchio, Luciano, illus. 2016. (Batman & Robin Adventures Ser.). (ENG.). 88p. (gr. 2-3). lib. bdg. 26.65 *(978-1-4965-2536-9(1),* DC Super Heroes) Stone Arch Bks.

—The Dark Knight: the Penguin's Crime Wave. Vecchio, Luciano, illus. 2013. (ENG.). (J). (gr. 4-7). pap. 35.70 *(978-1-4342-4872-5(0))* Stone Arch Bks.

—Going Ape. Gordon, Eric A. & Gordon, Steven E., illus. 2012. (I Can Read Level 2 Ser.). (ENG.). 32p. (J). (gr. -1-3). pap. 3.99 *(978-0-06-188522-8(3))* HarperCollins Pubs.

—Going Ape. 2012. (Justice League Classic: I Can Read! Ser.). (J). lib. bdg. 13.55 *(978-0-606-26260-6(1),* Turtleback) Turtleback Bks.

—The Joker's Dozen. Beavers, Ethen, illus. 2015. (You Choose Stories: Batman Ser.). (ENG.). 112p. (gr. 2-3). lib. bdg. 32.65 *(978-1-4342-9707-5(1))* Stone Arch Bks.

—Killer Croc of Doom! Vecchio, Luciano, illus. (Dark Knight Ser.). (ENG.). 88p. (gr. 2-3). 2013. pap. 5.95 *(978-1-4342-4215-0(3))* 2012. 26.65 *(978-1-4342-4097-2(5))* Stone Arch Bks.

—The Penguin's Crime Wave, 1 vol. Vecchio, Luciano, illus. 2013. (Dark Knight Ser.). (ENG.). 88p. (gr. 2-3). lib. bdg. 26.65 *(978-1-4342-4485-7(7))* Stone Arch Bks.

—The Terrible Trio. Beavers, Ethen, illus. 2015. (You Choose Stories: Batman Ser.). (ENG.). 112p. (gr. 2-3). lib. bdg. 32.65 *(978-1-4965-0529-3(8))* Stone Arch Bks.

—Two-Face Face-Off. Vecchio, Luciano, illus. 2016. (Batman & Robin Adventures Ser.). (ENG.). 88p. (gr. 2-3). lib. bdg. 26.65 *(978-1-4965-2535-2(3),* DC Super Heroes) Stone Arch Bks.

Sutton, Laurie S. & Sazaklis, John. You Choose Stories: Batman, 2 vols. 2015. (You Choose Stories: Batman Ser.). (ENG., Illus.). 112p. (gr. 2-3). 65.30 *(978-1-4965-2001-2(7))* Stone Arch Bks.

Teitelbaum, Michael. Meet the Super Heroes. 2009. (Justice League Classic: I Can Read! Ser.). (J). lib. bdg. 13.55 *(978-0-606-06941-0(0),* Turtleback) Turtleback Bks.

Templeton, Ty & Slott, Dan. Free Man, 1 vol. Templeton, Ty, illus. 2012. (Batman Adventures Ser.). (ENG., Illus.). 32p. (gr. 2-3). lib. bdg. 22.60 *(978-1-4342-4558-8(6))* Stone Arch Bks.

—My Boyfriend's Back, 1 vol. Templeton, Ty, illus. 2012. (Batman Adventures Ser.). (ENG., Illus.). 32p. (gr. 2-3). lib. bdg. 22.60 *(978-1-4342-4559-5(4))* Stone Arch Bks.

—Need to Know, 1 vol. Templeton, Ty, illus. 2012. (Batman Adventures Ser.). (ENG., Illus.). 32p. (gr. 2-3). lib. bdg. 22.60 *(978-1-4342-4560-1(8))* Stone Arch Bks.

—No Asylum, 1 vol. Templeton, Ty, illus. 2012. (Batman Adventures Ser.). (ENG., Illus.). 32p. (gr. 2-3). lib. bdg. 22.60 *(978-1-4342-4557-1(8))* Stone Arch Bks.

Terrell, Brandon. Summer Freeze! Beavers, Ethen, illus. 2015. (You Choose Stories: Batman Ser.). (ENG.). 112p. (gr. 2-3). lib. bdg. 32.65 *(978-1-4342-9708-2(X))* Stone Arch Bks.

Torres, J. Batman: the Brave & the Bold. Beatty, Terry et al, illus. 2013. (Batman: the Brave & the Bold Ser.). (ENG.). 32p. (gr. 2-3). 90.40 *(978-1-4342-4857-2(7));* 180.80 *(978-1-4342-4858-9(5))* Stone Arch Bks.

—Batman Versus the Yeti!, 1 vol. Barberi, Carlo & Beatty, Terry, illus. 2013. (Batman: the Brave & the Bold Ser.). (ENG.). 32p. (gr. 2-3). 22.60 *(978-1-4342-4708-7(2))* Stone Arch Bks.

—The Case of the Fractured Fairy Tale, 1 vol. Barberi, Carlo & Beatty, Terry, illus. 2013. (Batman: the Brave & the Bold Ser.). (ENG.). 32p. (gr. 2-3). 22.60 *(978-1-4342-4705-6(8))* Stone Arch Bks.

—Charge of the Army Eternal, 1 vol. Davis, Dan & Suriano, Andy, illus. 2013. (Batman: the Brave & the Bold Ser.). (ENG.). 32p. (gr. 2-3). 22.60 *(978-1-4342-4706-3(6))* Stone Arch Bks.

—The Secret of the Doomsday Design!, 1 vol. Bone, J., illus. 2013. (Batman: the Brave & the Bold Ser.). (ENG.). 32p. (gr. 2-3). 22.60 *(978-1-4342-4707-0(4))* Stone Arch Bks.

Tulien, Sean. The Black Masquerade. Vecchio, Luciano, illus. 2013. (Dark Knight Ser.). (ENG.). 88p. (gr. 2-3). pap. 5.95 *(978-1-4342-4824-4(0));* lib. bdg. 26.65 *(978-1-4342-4486-4(5))* Stone Arch Bks.

Turner, Katharine. Reptile Rampage. Gordon, Eric A. & Gordon, Steven E., illus. 2012. (I Can Read Level 2 Ser.). (ENG.). 32p. (J). (gr. -1-3). pap. 3.99 *(978-0-06-188521-1(5))* HarperCollins Pubs.

—Reptile Rampage. 2012. (Justice League Classic: I Can Read! Ser.). (J). lib. bdg. 13.55 *(978-0-606-23593-8(0),* Turtleback) Turtleback Bks.

Unknown. Villains on the Loose. 2011. (Batman: the Brave & the Bold Ser.). (ENG.). 16p. (J). (gr. 1-3). pap. 6.99 *(978-0-448-45608-9(7),* Grosset & Dunlap) Penguin Publishing Group.

Various, illus. 5-Minute Batman Stories. 2015. (ENG.). 192p. (J). (gr. -1-3). 12.99 *(978-0-06-235798-4(0),* HarperFestival) HarperCollins Pubs.

Vivinetto, Gina. With Superman & Wonder Woman. Farley, Rick & Tripp, Kanila, illus. 2011. (ENG.). 24p. (J). (gr. -1-3). pap. 3.99 *(978-0-06-188531-0(2),* HarperFestival) HarperCollins Pubs.

Wayne, Matt. Attack of the Virtual Villains. Moy, Philip, illus. 2012. (Batman: the Brave & the Bold Ser.). (ENG.). 32p. (gr. 2-3). lib. bdg. 22.60 *(978-1-4342-4546-5(2))* Stone Arch Bks.

—Menace of the Time Thief, 1 vol. Suriano, Andy & Davis, Dan W., illus. 2012. (Batman: the Brave & the Bold Ser.). (ENG.). 32p. (gr. 2-3). lib. bdg. 22.60 *(978-1-4342-4548-9(9))* Stone Arch Bks.

—Panic of the Composite Creatures. Suriano, Andy & Davis, Dan W., illus. 2012. (Batman: the Brave & the Bold Ser.). (ENG.). 32p. (gr. 2-3). lib. bdg. 22.60 *(978-1-4342-4545-8(4))* Stone Arch Bks.

—President Batman, 1 vol. Suriano, Andy & Davis, Dan W., illus. 2012. (Batman: the Brave & the Bold Ser.). (ENG.). 32p. (gr. 2-3). lib. bdg. 22.60 *(978-1-4342-4547-2(0))* Stone Arch Bks.

Wayne, Matt & Torres, J. Batman - The Brave & the Bold. 2010. (ENG., Illus.). 128p. (YA). pap. 12.99 *(978-1-4012-2650-3(7))* DC Comics.

Weissburg, Paul. Batman Undercover. Levins, Tim, illus. 2013. (Dark Knight Ser.). (ENG.). 88p. (gr. 2-3). pap. 5.95 *(978-1-4342-4213-6(7))* Stone Arch Bks.

—Batman Undercover, 1 vol. Levins, Tim & DC Comics Staff, illus. 2013. (Dark Knight Ser.). (ENG.). 88p. (gr. 2-3). 26.65 *(978-1-4342-4094-1(0))* Stone Arch Bks.

Wrecks, Billy. Batman: Adventures of the Dark Knight. 2016. (DK Adventures Ser.). lib. bdg. 16.00 *(978-0-606-38229-8(1))* Turtleback Bks.

—Batman! (DC Super Friends) Schoening, Dan & Beavers, Ethen, illus. 2012. (Little Golden Book Ser.). (ENG.). 24p. (J). (gr. k-k). 4.99 *(978-0-307-93103-0(X),* Golden Bks.) Random Hse. Children's Bks.

—Batman's Hero Files. 2015. (Step into Reading Level 2 Ser.). lib. bdg. 14.75 *(978-0-606-36382-2(3))* Turtleback Bks.

—Batman's Hero Files (DC Super Friends) Random House Editors et al, illus. 2015. (Step into Reading Ser.). (ENG.). 24p. (J). (gr. -1-1). 4.99 *(978-0-553-50808-6(3),* Random Hse. Bks. for Young Readers) Random Hse. Children's Bks.

—Bizarro Day! 2013. (Step into Reading Level 2 Ser.). lib. bdg. 13.55 *(978-0-606-26971-1(1),* Turtleback) Turtleback Bks.

—Bizarro Day! (DC Super Friends) Legramandi, Francesco, illus. 2013. (Step into Reading Ser.). (ENG.). 32p. (J). (gr. k-3). pap. 3.99 *(978-0-307-98119-6(3),* Random Hse. Bks. for Young Readers) Random Hse. Children's Bks.

—Catch Catwoman! DeCarlo, Mike & Tanguay, David D., illus. 2013. (Step into Reading Ser.). (ENG.). 32p. (J). (gr. -1-1). 3.99 *(978-0-449-81616-5(8),* Random Hse. Bks. for Young Readers) Random Hse. Children's Bks.

—DK Adventures: DC Comics: Batman: Adventures of the Dark Knight. 2016. (DK Adventures Ser.). (ENG., Illus.). 96p. (J). (gr. 3-7). 16.99 *(978-1-4654-4608-4(7),* DK Children) Dorling Kindersley Publishing, Inc.

—Green Lantern vs. the Meteor Monster! Random House Staff, illus. 2011. (Pictureback Ser.). (ENG.). 24p. (J). (gr. -1-2). pap. 3.99 *(978-0-375-87297-6(3),* Random Hse. Bks. for Young Readers) Random Hse. Children's Bks.

—Heroes! Golden Books Staff, illus. 2011. (Hologramatic Sticker Book Ser.). (ENG.). 48p. (J). (gr. -1-2). pap. 3.99 *(978-0-375-85331-9(6),* Golden Bks.) Random Hse. Children's Bks.

—Shark Attack! Doescher, Erik, illus. 2017. 24p. (J). ***(978-1-5182-2649-6(3))*** Random Hse., Inc.

—Skyscraper Showdown. Schoening, Dan, illus. 2012. (Pictureback(R) Ser.). (ENG.). 16p. (J). (gr. -1-2). pap. 4.99 *(978-0-375-87299-0(X),* Random Hse. Bks. for Young Readers) Random Hse. Children's Bks.

—X-Ray Vision! (DC Super Friends) Borkowski, Michael, illus. 2014. (Pictureback Ser.). (ENG.). 16p. (J). (gr. -1-2). 4.99 *(978-0-385-38718-7(0),* Random Hse. Bks. for Young Readers) Random Hse. Children's Bks.

You Choose Stories: Batman. 2016. (You Choose Stories: Batman Ser.). (ENG.). 112p. (gr. 2-3). pap. 55.60 *(978-1-4965-3104-9(3));* pap. 13.90 *(978-1-4965-3103-2(5))* Stone Arch Bks. (DC Super Heroes).

BATS

Arnold, Tedd. Bats. 2015. (Scholastic Reader, Level 2 Ser.). (ENG., Illus.). 32p. (J). (gr. k-2). pap. 3.99 *(978-0-545-77813-8(1),* Scholastic Reference) Scholastic, Inc.

Ball, Jacqueline A. Animales Migratorios: Por Aire. 2007. (En marcha: Migraciones animales (Spanish- on the Move: Animal Migration) Ser.). (SPA.). 24p. (gr. 1-4). pap. 8.15 *(978-0-8368-8432-6(9));* (Illus.). lib. bdg. 22.00 *(978-0-8368-8427-2(2))* Stevens, Gareth Publishing LLLP. (Weekly Reader Leveled Readers).

—Migrating Animals of the Air. 2007. (On the Move: Animal Migration Ser.). 24p. (gr. 1-4). pap. 8.15 *(978-0-8368-8422-7(1));* (Illus.). lib. bdg. 22.00 *(978-0-8368-8417-3(5))* Stevens, Gareth Publishing LLLP. (Weekly Reader Leveled Readers).

Bats. 2006. (Ugly Animals Ser.). (Illus.). 24p. (J). (gr. 3-7). lib. bdg. 22.60 *(978-1-4042-3525-0(6),* PowerKids Pr.) Rosen Publishing Group, Inc., The.

Beer, Amy-Jane. Bats. 2008. (Nature's Children Ser.). (Illus.). 52p. (J). *(978-0-7172-6247-2(2))* Grolier, Ltd.

Bekkering, Annalise. Bats. 2009. (Backyard Animals Ser.). (Illus.). 24p. (J). (gr. 3-5). pap. 8.95 *(978-1-60596-077-7(2));* lib. bdg. 24.45 *(978-1-60596-076-0(4))* Weigl Pubs., Inc.

Berman, Ruth. Let's Look at Bats. (Lightning Bolt Books (tm) — Animal Close-Ups Ser.). (ENG., Illus.). 32p. 2015. (gr. 2-3). E-Book 39.99 *(978-1-5124-1053-2(5),* 9781512410532) 2009. (gr. k-2). pap. 7.95 *(978-0-7613-5007-1(1))* 2009. (gr. k-2). lib. bdg. 26.60 *(978-0-7613-3885-7(3))* Lerner Publishing Group. (Lerner Pubns.).

Boynton, Bibi. Bats, 6 vols., Set. 2003. (Phonics Readers 1-36 Ser.). (ENG.). 8p. (gr. k-1). pap. 29.70 *(978-0-7368-3199-4(1),* Phonics Readers) Capstone Press of Coughlan Cos.

Bradley, James V. The Bat. 2006. (Nature Walk Ser.). (Illus.). 64p. (gr. 4-6). lib. bdg. 28.00 *(978-0-7910-9117-3(1),* Chelsea Hse.) Facts On File, Inc.

Braun, Eric. Simply Sound: Science Adventures with Jasper the Origami Bat, 1 vol. Christoph, Jamey, illus. 2014. (Origami Science Adventures Ser.). (ENG.). 24p. (gr. 3-4). lib. bdg. 27.32 *(978-1-4795-2187-6(6))* Picture Window Bks.

Britton, Tamara L. Dog-Faced Bats, 1 vol. 2011. (Bats Set 1 *2011 Ser.). (ENG.). 24p. 25.65 *(978-1-61613-390-0(2),* Checkerboard Library) ABDO Publishing Co.

—Fisherman Bats, 1 vol. 2011. (Bats Set 1 *2011 Ser.). (ENG., Illus.). 24p. 25.65 *(978-1-61613-391-7(0),* Checkerboard Library) ABDO Publishing Co.

—Flying Fox Bats, 1 vol. 2011. (Bats Set 1 *2011 Ser.). (ENG., Illus.). 24p. 25.65 *(978-1-61613-392-4(9),* Checkerboard Library) ABDO Publishing Co.

—Spear-Nosed Bats, 1 vol. 2011. (Bats Set 1 *2011 Ser.). (ENG.). 24p. 25.65 *(978-1-61613-393-1(7),* Checkerboard Library) ABDO Publishing Co.

—Vampire Bats, 1 vol. 2011. (Bats Set 1 *2011 Ser.). (ENG., Illus.). 24p. 25.65 *(978-1-61613-394-8(5),* Checkerboard Library) ABDO Publishing Co.

—Wrinkle-Faced Bats, 1 vol. 2011. (Bats Set 1 *2011 Ser.). (ENG., Illus.). 24p. 25.65 *(978-1-61613-395-5(3),* Checkerboard Library) ABDO Publishing Co.

Brown, Laaren. Icky Sticky - Bats. 2016. (Scholastic Reader, Level 2 Ser.). (ENG.). 32p. (J). (gr. 1-3). pap. 4.99 *(978-0-545-93550-0(4),* Scholastic Nonfiction) Scholastic, Inc.

Burgan, Michael. Bat Researcher. 2010. (Benchmark Rockets: Dirty & Dangerous Jobs Ser.). 32p. (J). (gr. 3-6). 28.50 *(978-1-60870-170-4(0))* Marshall Cavendish Corp.

Carney, Elizabeth. Bats. 2010. (Readers Ser.). (ENG., Illus.). 32p. (J). (gr. k-3). lib. bdg. 13.90 *(978-1-4263-0711-9(X),* National Geographic Children's Bks.) National Geographic Society.

Carney, Elizabeth & National Geographic Kids Staff. Bats. 2010. (Readers Ser.). (Illus.). 32p. (J). (gr. k-3). pap. 3.99 *(978-1-4263-0710-2(1),* National Geographic Children's Bks.) National Geographic Society.

Carson, Mary Kay. The Bat Scientists. Uhlman, Tom, photos by. (Scientists in the Field Ser.). (ENG., Illus.). 80p. (J). (gr. 5-7). 2013. pap. 9.99 *(978-0-544-10493-8(5))* 2010. 18.99 *(978-0-547-19956-6(2))* Houghton Mifflin Harcourt Publishing Co.

Coste, Marion. The Hawaiian Bat: Ope'ape'a. Maxner, Pearl, illus. 2005. (Latitude 20 Bks.). 30p. (J). (gr. 4-18). 14.99 *(978-0-8248-2797-7(X))* Univ. of Hawaii Pr.

Crowther, Robert. Deep down under Ground: A Pop-up Book of Amazing Facts & Feats. Crowther, Robert, illus. 2004. (Illus.). 18p. (J). (gr. 3-8). reprint ed. pap. 22.00 *(978-0-7567-7179-9(X))* DIANE Publishing Co.

Davies, Nicola. Bat Loves the Night. Fox-Davies, Sarah, illus. 2008. (Read, Listen, & Wonder Ser.). (ENG.). 32p. (J). (gr. -1-3). pap. 8.99 *(978-0-7636-3863-4(3))* Candlewick Pr.

Dibble, Traci. Bats. (Predator Animals Ser.). 16p. 2011. pap. 39.62 *(978-1-61541-300-3(6))* 2010. (ENG.). (J). pap. 5.99 *(978-1-61541-299-0(9))* American Reading Co.

Dibble, Traci & Sánchez, Lucía M. MurciéLagos: Bats. 2011. (2Y Animales Depredador Ser.). (SPA.). 16p. (J). (gr. k-2). pap. 6.99 *(978-1-61541-443-7(6))* American Reading Co.

Dibble, Traci & Sanchez, Lucia M. Murciélagos (Bats) 2011. (Animales depredadores Ser.). (SPA.). 16p. pap. 39.62 *(978-1-61541-444-4(4))* American Reading Co.

Dieker, Wendy Strobel. Bats. 2017. (Spot Backyard Animals Ser.). (ENG.). 16p. (gr. k-3). 17.95 ***(978-1-68151-090-3(1))*** Amicus Publishing.

—El Murciélago. 2017. (Spot Backyard Animals Ser.). (SPA & ENG.). 16p. (gr. k-3). 17.95 ***(978-1-68151-270-9(X))*** Amicus Publishing.

Dittrich, Tina & Morrison, Kathryn. Stellaluna: An Study of Birds & Bats. 2005. pap. 10.95 *(978-1-931334-85-3(4))* Pieces of Learning.

Donovan, Sandy. A Bat in Its Cave. 2003. (Where Do Animals Live? Ser.). (J). lib. bdg. *(978-1-58417-188-1(X))* Lake Street Pubs.

Dorling Kindersley Publishing Staff & Jenner, Caryn. DK Readers L1: All about Bats. 2017. (DK Readers Ser.). (ENG., Illus.). 24p. (J). (-k). pap. 3.99 *(978-1-4654-5746-2(1),* DK Children) Dorling Kindersley Publishing, Inc.

Dornfeld, Margaret. Bats. 2004. (Animals Animals Ser.). (Illus.). 48p. (YA). (gr. 3-6). 29.93 *(978-0-7614-1754-5(0))* Marshall Cavendish Corp.

Forrester, Anna. Bat Count: A Citizen Science Story, 1 vol. Detwiler, Susan, illus. 2017. (ENG & SPA.). 32p. (J). (gr. k-3). 17.95 *(978-1-62855-894-4(6))* Arbordale Publishing.

—Contando Los Murciélagos: Una Historia de Ciencias para Los Ciudadanos. Detwiler, Susan, illus. 2017. (SPA.). 32p. (J). (gr. k-3). pap. 9.95 *(978-1-62855-896-8(2))* Arbordale Publishing.

Gish, Melissa. Bats. 2011. (Living Wild Ser.). (ENG., Illus.). 48p. (J). (gr. 4-7). pap. 12.00 *(978-0-89812-549-8(9),* Creative Paperbacks) Creative Co., The.

—Living Wild - Bats. 2010. (Living Wild Ser.). 46p. (YA). (gr. 5-18). 23.95 *(978-1-58341-966-3(7),* Creative Education) Creative Co., The.

Gonzales, Doreen. Bats in the Dark. 2009. (Creatures of the Night Ser.). (Illus.). 24p. (J). (ENG.). pap. 8.25 *(978-1-4358-3249-7(3),* PowerKids Pr.); (gr. 1-3). lib. bdg. 22.60 *(978-1-4042-8096-0(0))* Rosen Publishing Group, Inc., The.

Gray, Susan Heinrichs. Bats Sleep Upside Down. 2015. (Tell Me Why Library). (ENG., Illus.). 24p. (J). (gr. 2-5). 27.07 *(978-1-63362-608-9(3),* 206616) Cherry Lake Publishing.

Guillain, Charlotte. Bats, 1 vol. 2013. (Animal Abilities Ser.). (ENG., Illus.). 32p. (gr. 2-4). 29.99 *(978-1-4109-5236-3(3));* pap. 8.95 *(978-1-4109-5243-1(6))* Heinemann-Raintree. (Raintree Perspectives).

Halfmann, Janet. Home in the Cave, 1 vol. Bersani, Shennen, illus. 2012. (ENG.). 32p. (J). (gr. -1-4). 17.95 *(978-1-60718-522-2(9));* pap. 9.95 *(978-1-60718-531-4(8))* Arbordale Publishing.

Hengel, Katherine. It's a Baby Flying Fox!, 1 vol. 2010. (Baby Australian Animals Ser.). (ENG., Illus.). 24p. (J). (gr. k-3). lib. bdg. 24.21 *(978-1-60453-575-4(X),* SandCastle) ABDO Publishing Co.

Hirsch, Rebecca E. Vampire Bats: Nighttime Flying Mammals. 2015. (Comparing Animal Traits Ser.). (ENG., Illus.). 32p. (J). (gr. 2-4). pap. 8.99 *(978-1-4677-6066-9(8));* lib. bdg. 26.65 *(978-1-4677-5879-6(5))* Lerner Publishing Group. (Lerner Pubns.).

Honders, Jamie. Flying Foxes Are Not Foxes! 2014. (Confusing Creature Names Ser.). 24p. (J). (gr. 1-3). 22.60 *(978-1-4824-0783-9(3))* Stevens, Gareth Publishing LLLP.

Jenner, Caryn. All about Bats. 2017. (Illus.). 23p. (J). ***(978-1-5182-2632-8(9))*** Dorling Kindersley Publishing, Inc.

Jennings, Rosemary. Cuevas de Murciélagos (Inside Bat Caves) 2015. (Las Casas de Los Animales (Inside Animal Homes) Ser.). (ENG & SPA.). 24p. (J). (gr. 2-3). 23.60 *(978-1-4994-0598-9(7),* PowerKids Pr.) Rosen Publishing Group, Inc., The.

—Inside Bat Caves. 2015. (Inside Animal Homes Ser.). (ENG.). 24p. (J). (gr. 2-3). 23.60 *(978-1-4994-0913-0(3),* PowerKids Pr.) Rosen Publishing Group, Inc., The.

Johnson, J. Angelique. Bats. 2011. (Nocturnal Animals Ser.). (ENG.). 24p. (gr. k-1). pap. 41.70 *(978-1-4296-6359-5(6),* Pebble Plus) Capstone Press of Coughlan Cos.

Kalman, Bobbie & Levigne, Heather. Les Chauves-Souris. 2003. (Petit Monde Vivant Ser.). (FRE., Illus.). 32p. (J). pap. 9.95 *(978-2-920660-83-0(7))* Bayard Canada Livres CAN. Dist: Crabtree Publishing Co.

—¿Qué Son los Murciélagos? 2005. (Ciencia de los Seres Vivos Ser.). (SPA., Illus.). 32p. (J). (gr. 3-4). pap. *(978-0-7787-8809-6(1));* lib. bdg. *(978-0-7787-8763-1(X))* Crabtree Publishing Co.

Kalman, Bobbie & Lundblad, Kristina. Endangered Bats. 2006. (Earth's Endangered Animals Ser.). (ENG., Illus.). 32p. (J). (gr. -1-3). pap. *(978-0-7787-1912-0(X))* Crabtree Publishing Co.

Kenan, Tessa. Es un Murciélago Vampiro! 2017. (Bumba Books (tm) en Español — Animales de la Selva Tropical (Rain Forest Animals) Ser.). (SPA.). 24p. (J). (gr. -1-1). 25.32 ***(978-1-5124-4129-1(5))*** Lerner Publishing Group.

Kenan, Tessa. It's a Vampire Bat! 2017. (Bumba Books (tm) — Rain Forest Animals Ser.). (ENG.). 24p. (J). (gr. -1-1). 12.99 ***(978-1-5124-3762-1(X),*** Lerner Pubns.); 38.65 ***(978-1-5124-2762-2(4),*** Lerner Pubns.); 38.65 ***(978-1-5124-3761-4(1),*** Lerner Pubns.); (Illus.). 25.32 *(978-1-5124-2570-3(2))* Lerner Publishing Group.

Koch, Falynn. Science Comics: Bats: Learning to Fly. Koch, Falynn, illus. 2017. (Science Comics Ser.). (ENG., Illus.). 128p. (J). pap. 12.99 *(978-1-62672-408-2(3),* 9781626724082, First Second Bks.) Roaring Brook Pr.

Kopp, Megan. Real-Life Vampires, 1 vol. 2010. (Vampires Ser.). (ENG.). 32p. (gr. 3-4). lib. bdg. 27.99 *(978-1-4296-4578-2(4),* Edge Bks.) Capstone Press of Coughlan Cos.

Landau, Elaine. Bats: Hunters of the Night. 2007. (Animals after Dark Ser.). (Illus.). 32p. (J). (gr. 2-4). lib. bdg. 23.94 *(978-0-7660-2772-5(4),* Enslow Elementary) Enslow Pubs., Inc.

Lane, Jeanette & Cole, Joanna. The Magic School Bus in the Bat Cave. Cuddy, Robbin & Cole, Joanna, illus. 2006. (J). pap. *(978-0-439-89934-5(6))* Scholastic, Inc.

Leaf, Christina. Brown Bats. 2015. (North American Animals Ser.). (ENG., Illus.). 24p. (J). (gr. k-3). lib. bdg. 25.95 *(978-1-62617-258-6(7),* Blastoff! Readers) Bellwether Media.

Lunde, Darrin. Hello, Bumblebee Bat. Wynne, Patricia J., illus. 2007. (J). (gr. -1-1). 14.60 *(978-0-7569-8048-1(8))* Perfection Learning Corp.

Lunde, Darrin P. Hello, Bumblebee Bat. Wynne, Patricia J., illus. 2016. (ENG.). 14p. (J). (— 1). bds. 6.95 *(978-1-58089-526-2(3))* Charlesbridge Publishing, Inc.

Lynette, Rachel. Vampire Bats. 2013. (Monsters of the Animal Kingdom Ser.). (ENG., Illus.). 24p. (J). (gr. k-5). pap. 8.25 *(978-1-4488-9716-2(5));* lib. bdg. 22.60 *(978-1-4488-9629-5(0))* Rosen Publishing Group, Inc., The. (PowerKids Pr.).

Macken, JoAnn Early. The Life Cycle of a Bat. 2006. (Things with Wings Ser.). (Illus.). 24p. (gr. k-3). pap. 8.15 *(978-0-8368-6386-4(0));* lib. bdg. 22.00 *(978-0-8368-6379-6(8))* Stevens, Gareth Publishing LLLP. (Weekly Reader Leveled Readers).

Mara, Wil. Bats. 2014. 32p. 28.50 *(978-1-62712-295-5(8))* Cavendish Square Publishing.

Markle, Sandra. Bats: Biggest! Littlest! 2013. (Biggest! Littlest! Ser.). (ENG., Illus.). 32p. (J). (gr. k-2). 16.95 *(978-1-59078-952-0(0))* Boyds Mills Pr.

—The Case of the Vanishing Little Brown Bats: A Scientific Mystery. 2014. (ENG., Illus.). 48p. (gr. 4-6). lib. bdg. 29.27

(978-1-4677-1463-1(1), Millbrook Pr.) Lerner Publishing Group.

Markovics, Joyce L. The Bat's Cave: A Dark City. 2009. (Spectacular Animal Towns Ser.). (Illus.). 32p. (J). (gr. 2-7). lib. bdg. 25.27 *(978-1-59716-871-7(8))* Bearport Publishing Co., Inc.

—Little Brown Bats. 2015. (Illus.). 24p. (J). lib. bdg. *(978-1-62724-315-5(1))* Bearport Publishing Co., Inc.

—Los Pequeños Murciélagos Café. 2014. (¿a dónde Van en Invierno? Ser.). (SPA.). 24p. (J). (gr. -1-3). lib. bdg. 23.93 *(978-1-62724-457-2(3))* Bearport Publishing Co., Inc.

Mason, Adrienne. Bats. Ogle, Nancy Gray & Ogle, Nancy, illus. 2003. (Kids Can Press Wildlife Ser.). (ENG.). 32p. (J). (gr. k-5). 5.95 *(978-1-55337-525-8(4))* Kids Can Pr., Ltd. CAN. Dist: Hachette Bk. Group.

Mattern, Joanne. Bats Are Night Animals. 2007. (Night Animals Ser.). (Illus.). 24p. (gr. k-3). pap. 8.15 *(978-0-8368-7852-3(3));* lib. bdg. 22.00 *(978-0-8368-7845-5(0))* Stevens, Gareth Publishing LLLP. (Weekly Reader Leveled Readers).

—Bats Are Night Animals: Los Murciélagos Son Animales Nocturnos. 2007. (Night Animals/ Animales Nocturnos Ser.). (ENG & SPA., Illus.). 24p. (gr. k-3). pap. 8.15 *(978-0-8368-8049-6(8),* Weekly Reader Leveled Readers) Stevens, Gareth Publishing LLLP.

—Bats Are Night Animals/Los Murcielagos Son Animales Nocturnos. 2007. (Night Animals/ Animales Nocturnos Ser.). (ENG & SPA., Illus.). 24p. (gr. k-3). lib. bdg. 22.00 *(978-0-8368-8042-7(0),* Weekly Reader Leveled Readers) Stevens, Gareth Publishing LLLP.

—It's a Good Thing There Are Bats. 2014. (Rookie Read-About(r) Science — It's a Good Thing... Ser.). (ENG.). 32p. (J). pap. 5.95 *(978-0-531-22834-0(7));* lib. bdg. 25.00 *(978-0-531-22362-8(0))* Scholastic Library Publishing.

McKay, Sindy. We Both Read Bilingual Edition-About Bats/Acerca de Los Murcielagos. Canetti, Yanitzia, tr. Smith, Wendy, illus. 2014. (We Both Read - Level K-1 (Quality) Ser.). (ENG & SPA.). 44p. (J). (gr. k-1). pap. 4.99 *(978-1-60115-060-8(1))* Treasure Bay, Inc.

Miles, Victoria, et al. Henry Chow & Other Stories, 1 vol. Juhasz, George, illus. 2010. (ENG.). 134p. (YA). (gr. 8-11). pap. 12.95 *(978-1-896580-33-3(5))* Tradewind Bks. CAN. Dist: Orca Bk. Pubs. USA.

Mitchell, Susan K. Biggest vs. Smallest Things with Wings. 2010. (Biggest vs. Smallest Animals Ser.). (Illus.). 24p. (J). 22.60 *(978-0-7660-3578-2(6),* Enslow Elementary) Enslow Pubs., Inc.

Morgan, Sally. Bats: Animal Lives Series. 2008. (J). lib. bdg. 18.95 *(978-1-59566-535-5(8))* QEB Publishing Inc.

Los Murciélagos. (Fascinante Mundo de... Ser.).Tr. of Fascinating World of Bats. (Illus.). 8.95 *(978-958-04-3230-2(9))* Norma S.A. COL. Dist: Distribuidora Norma, Inc.

Murcielagos y mas Murcielagos. 2006. (Real Readers en español Ser.). (J). pap. 24.95 *(978-1-4042-2484-1(X),* Rosen Classroom) Rosen Publishing Group, Inc., The.

Murray, Julie. Vampire Bats, 1 vol. 2005. (Animal Kingdom Set li Ser.). (ENG., Illus.). 24p. (gr. k-4). 25.65 *(978-1-59197-313-3(9),* Buddy Bks.) ABDO Publishing Co.

—Wrinkle-Faced Bats, 1 vol. 2003. (Animal Kingdom Ser.). (ENG.). 24p. (gr. k-4). 25.65 *(978-1-57765-710-1(1),* Buddy Bks.) ABDO Publishing Co.

National Geographic Editors. Creepy Crawly Collection. 2012. lib. bdg. 18.40 *(978-0-606-26822-6(7),* Turtleback) Turtleback Bks.

Niver, Heather Moore. We Need Bats. 2015. (Creatures We Can't Live Without Ser.). (ENG., Illus.). 24p. (J). (gr. 3-4). pap. 8.25 *(978-1-4994-0979-6(6),* PowerKids Pr.) Rosen Publishing Group, Inc., The.

—20 Fun Facts about Bats. 2012. (Fun Fact File: Animals! Ser.). (ENG.). 32p. (J). (gr. 2-5). pap. 10.50 *(978-1-4339-6507-4(0));* lib. bdg. 25.25 *(978-1-4339-6505-0(4))* Stevens, Gareth Publishing LLLP. (Gareth Stevens Learning Library).

O'Donnell, Kerri. Bats. 2009. (Ugly Animals Ser.). 24p. (gr. 2-3). 42.50 *(978-1-60854-598-8(9),* PowerKids Pr.) Rosen Publishing Group, Inc., The.

Olearczyk, Erin A. Bats, Bats, Bats. 2006. (Rosen Real Readers Big Bookstm Ser.). (ENG.). 8p. (gr. k-1). 29.95 *(978-1-4042-6207-2(5))* Rosen Publishing Group, Inc., The.

O'Shaughnessy, Ruth. Bats after Dark. 2015. (Animals of the Night Ser.). (ENG.). 32p. (J). (gr. 3-4). pap. 10.52 *(978-0-7660-6750-9(5));* (Illus.). 25.27 *(978-0-7660-6752-3(1))* Enslow Pubs., Inc.

PRESS, Celebration. Hanging Around Bats. 2003. (ENG.). (J). (gr. 2-5). pap., stu. ed. 34.95 *(978-0-673-62834-3(5),* Celebration Pr.) Pearson Schl.

Pringle, Laurence. Bats! Strange & Wonderful. Henderson, Meryl, illus. 2009. (Strange & Wonderful Ser.). (ENG.). 32p. (J). (gr. 1-4). pap. 9.95 *(978-1-59078-781-6(1))* Boyds Mills Pr.

Raabe, Emily. Bulldog Bats. (Library of Bats Ser.). 24p. 2009. (gr. 3-3). 42.50 *(978-1-60853-561-3(4))* 2003. (Illus.). (J). lib. bdg. 22.60 *(978-0-8239-6326-3(8))* Rosen Publishing Group, Inc., The. (PowerKids Pr.).

—Flying Foxes. (Library of Bats Ser.). 24p. 2009. (gr. 3-3). 42.50 *(978-1-60853-562-0(2))* 2003. (Illus.). (J). lib. bdg. 22.60 *(978-0-8239-6324-9(1))* Rosen Publishing Group, Inc., The. (PowerKids Pr.).

—Free-Tailed Bats. (Library of Bats Ser.). 24p. 2009. (gr. 3-3). 42.50 *(978-1-60853-563-7(0))* 2003. (Illus.). (J). lib. bdg. 22.60 *(978-0-8239-6325-6(X))* Rosen Publishing Group, Inc., The. (PowerKids Pr.).

—Horseshoe Bats. (Library of Bats Ser.). 24p. 2009. (gr. 3-3). 42.50 *(978-1-60853-564-4(9))* 2003. (Illus.). (J). lib. bdg. 22.60 *(978-0-8239-6327-0(6))* Rosen Publishing Group, Inc., The. (PowerKids Pr.).

—Plain-Nosed Bats. (Library of Bats Ser.). 24p. 2009. (gr. 3-3). 42.50 *(978-1-60853-565-1(7))* 2003. (Illus.). (J). lib. bdg. 22.60 *(978-0-8239-6323-2(3))* Rosen Publishing Group, Inc., The. (PowerKids Pr.).

—Vampire Bats. (Library of Bats Ser.). 24p. 2009. (gr. 3-3). 42.50 *(978-1-60853-566-8(5))* 2003. (Illus.). (J). lib. bdg. 22.60 *(978-0-8239-6322-5(5))* Rosen Publishing Group, Inc., The. (PowerKids Pr.).

Rafferty, John P. Rats, Bats, & Xenarthrans. 2011. (Britannica Guide to Predators & Prey Ser.). (Illus.). 256p. (YA). (gr. 9-12). lib. bdg. 51.70 *(978-1-61530-332-8(4))* Rosen Publishing Group, Inc., The.

Rafferty, John P., ed. Rats, Bats, & Xenarthrans. 2011. (Britannica Guide to Predators & Prey Ser.). (Illus.). 256p. (YA). 103.40 *(978-1-61530-456-1(8))* Rosen Publishing Group, Inc., The.

Riggs, Kate. Amazing Animals: Bats. 2012. (Amazing Animals Ser.). (ENG., Illus.). 24p. (J). (gr. 1-3). pap. 8.99 *(978-0-89812-690-7(8),* Creative Paperbacks) Creative Co., The.

—Bats. 2012. (Illus.). 24p. (J). 25.65 *(978-1-60818-105-6(7),* Creative Education) Creative Co., The.

Riley, Joelle. Bats. 2005. (Early Bird Nature Bks.). (ENG., Illus.). 48p. (gr. 2-5). lib. bdg. 26.60 *(978-0-8225-2416-8(3))* Lerner Publishing Group.

Rissman, Rebecca. Bats: Nocturnal Flyers, 1 vol. 2014. (Night Safari Ser.). (ENG., Illus.). 24p. (gr. k-2). 23.32 *(978-1-4846-0309-3(5),* Heinemann Read & Learn) Heinemann-Raintree.

Robb, Jackie & Stringle, Berny. The Story of Bat. Duncan, Karen & Stringle, Sam, illus. 2003. (Bang on the Door Ser.). 32p. (YA). pap. *(978-1-85602-316-0(8),* Pavilion Children's Books) Pavilion Bks.

Robbins, Maureen. El Hábitat de los Murciélagos. 2012.Tr. of Habitat for Bats. (SPA & ENG.). 24p. (gr. 2-3). pap. 8.95 *(978-1-61810-546-2(9))* Rourke Educational Media.

—Habitat for Bats. Reese, Bob, illus. 2011. (ENG.). 24p. (gr. 2-3). pap. 8.95 *(978-1-61236-037-9(8))* Rourke Educational Media.

Rodriguez, Ana Maria. The Secret of the Scuba Diving Spider... & More! 2017. (Animal Secrets Revealed! Ser.). 48p. (J). (gr. 4-4). lib. bdg. 27.93 ***(978-0-7660-8629-6(1))*** Enslow Pubs., Inc.

Rudolph, Jessica. MIS Colmillos Son Blancos y Afilados. 2015. (Pistas de Animales Ser.). (SPA.). 24p. (J). (gr. -1-3). lib. bdg. 23.93 *(978-1-62724-580-7(4))* Bearport Publishing Co., Inc.

—My Fangs Are White & Sharp (Vampire Bat) 2014. (Zoo Clues Ser.). 24p. (J). (gr. -1-3). lib. bdg. 23.93 *(978-1-62724-116-8(7))* Bearport Publishing Co., Inc.

Rustad, Marthe E. H. Bats. 2013. (ENG., Illus.). 24p. (J). lib. bdg. 25.65 *(978-1-62031-068-7(6))* Jump! Inc.

Ryndak, Rob. Bats. 2015. (Jungle Animals Ser.). (ENG., Illus.). 24p. (J). (gr. k-k). 22.60 *(978-1-4824-1744-9(6))* Stevens, Gareth Publishing LLLP.

Salzmann, Mary Elizabeth. What Has Wings?, 1 vol. 2007. (Creature Features Ser.). (ENG., Illus.). 24p. (J). (gr. -1-3). lib. bdg. 25.65 *(978-1-59928-876-5(1),* Super SandCastle) ABDO Publishing Co.

Savage, Stephen. British Animals - Bat. 2009. (Animal Neighbors Ser.). (gr. k-5). 32p. pap. 10.60 *(978-1-4042-4572-3(3),* Rosen Classroom); (J). lib. bdg. 25.25 *(978-1-4358-4995-2(7),* PowerKids Pr.) Rosen Publishing Group, Inc., The.

Schimel, Lawrence. Is That a Bat? 2008. (ENG., Illus.). 22p. (J). (gr. -1-1). 9.99 *(978-1-58476-735-0(9))* Innovative Kids.

Schuetz, Kari. Bats. 2012. (Backyard Wildlife Ser.). (ENG., Illus.). 24p. (J). (gr. k-3). lib. bdg. 25.95 *(978-1-60014-720-3(8),* Blastoff! Readers) Bellwether Media.

Shaw, Nancy J. Bats. (Illus.). 32p. pap. 8.95 *(978-0-89812-318-0(6))* Creative Co., The.

Shea, Therese. Bloodsucking Vampire Bats. 2016. (Real-Life Vampires Ser.). (ENG., Illus.). 24p. (J). (gr. 2-3). pap. 8.15 *(978-1-4824-3959-5(X))* Stevens, Gareth Publishing LLLP.

Simon, Seymour. Vampire Bats: Extreme Animals. 2009. (Illus.). 32p. (J). *(978-0-545-16193-0(2))* Scholastic, Inc.

Sjonger, Rebecca & Kalman, Bobbie. The Life Cycle of a Bat. 2005. (Life Cycle Ser.). (ENG., Illus.). 32p. (J). (gr. 2-3). pap. *(978-0-7787-0701-1(6));* lib. bdg. *(978-0-7787-0671-7(0))* Crabtree Publishing Co.

Smith, J. Batty about Texas, 1 vol. Coates, Kathy, illus. 2008. (ENG.). 32p. (J). (gr. k-3). 16.99 *(978-1-58980-582-8(8))* Pelican Publishing Co., Inc.

Somervill, Barbara A. Vampire Bats: Hunting for Blood. (Bloodsuckers Ser.). 24p. (gr. 2-3). 2009. 42.50 *(978-1-61511-637-9(0),* PowerKids Pr.) 2007. (Illus.). (J). lib. bdg. 22.60 *(978-1-4042-3804-6(2))* Rosen Publishing Group, Inc., The.

Stewart, Melissa. How Do Bats Fly in the Dark? 2008. (Tell Me Why, Tell Me How Ser.). (Illus.). 32p. (gr. 3-18). lib. bdg. 29.93 *(978-0-7614-2924-1(7),* Benchmark Bks.) Marshall Cavendish Corp.

—A Place for Bats, 1 vol. Bond, Higgins, illus. 2012. (ENG.). 32p. (J). 16.95 *(978-1-56145-624-6(1))* Peachtree Pubs.

—A Place for Bats, Revised Edition, 1 vol. Bond, Higgins, illus. rev. ed. 2017. (Place For. . Ser.). (ENG.). 32p. (J). (gr. 1-5). 16.95 *(978-1-56145-762-5(0))* Peachtree Pubs.

Stout, Frankie. Bats: Nature's Night Flyers. 2009. (Things with Wings Ser.). 24p. (gr. 2-3). 42.50 *(978-1-60854-350-2(1));* (Illus.). (J). lib. bdg. 22.60 *(978-1-4042-4496-2(4))* Rosen Publishing Group, Inc., The. (PowerKids Pr.).

Taschek, Karen. Hanging with Bats: Ecobats, Vampires, & Movie Stars. 2008. (World's of Wonder Ser.). (ENG., Illus.). 104p. (J). (gr. 3-18). 19.95 *(978-0-8263-4403-8(8))* Univ. of New Mexico Pr.

Time for Kids Editors. Bats! 2005. (Time for Kids Ser.). (ENG., Illus.). 32p. (J). (gr. 1-3). pap. 3.99 *(978-0-06-057638-7(3))* HarperCollins Pubs.

Time for Kids Magazine Staff, ed. Bats! 2005. (Time for Kids Science Scoops Ser.). (Illus.). 32p. 14.00 *(978-0-7569-5434-5(7))* Perfection Learning Corp.

Vogel, Julia. Bats. Recher, Andrew, illus. 2007. (Our Wild World Ser.). (ENG.). 48p. (J). (gr. 2-5). 10.95 *(978-1-55971-968-1(0));* pap. 7.95 *(978-1-55971-969-8(9))* Cooper Square Publishing Llc.

Watt, Fiona. Bats: Internet- Referenced. 2009. (Beginner's Nature Ser.). 32p. (J). 4.99 *(978-0-7945-2541-5(5),* Usborne) EDC Publishing.

We Both Read-About Bats. 2014. (Illus.). 44p. (J). 9.95 *(978-1-60115-267-1(1))* Treasure Bay, Inc.

What Is Bat?, 6 Packs. (Literatura 2000 Ser.). (gr. 1-2). 28.00 *(978-0-7635-0118-1(2))* Rigby Education.

Wheeler, Jill C. Bumblebee Bats, 1 vol. 2006. (Bats Set 2 Ser.). (ENG., Illus.). 24p. (gr. k-6). 25.65 *(978-1-59679-320-0(1),* Checkerboard Library) ABDO Publishing Co.

—Fringe-Lipped Bats, 1 vol. 2006. (Bats Set 2 Ser.). (ENG., Illus.). 24p. (gr. k-6). 25.65 *(978-1-59679-321-7(X),* Checkerboard Library) ABDO Publishing Co.

—Ghost-Faced Bats, 1 vol. 2006. (Bats Set 2 Ser.). (ENG., Illus.). 24p. (gr. k-6). 25.65 *(978-1-59679-322-4(8),* Checkerboard Library) ABDO Publishing Co.

—Honduran White Bats, 1 vol. 2006. (Bats Set 2 Ser.). (ENG., Illus.). 24p. (gr. k-6). 25.65 *(978-1-59679-324-8(4),* Checkerboard Library) ABDO Publishing Co.

—Slit-Faced Bats, 1 vol. 2006. (Bats Set 2 Ser.). (ENG., Illus.). 24p. (gr. k-6). 25.65 *(978-1-59679-323-1(6),* Checkerboard Library) ABDO Publishing Co.

Wilson, Natashya. Bats. 2009. (My World of Animals Ser.). 24p. (gr. 1-1). 37.50 *(978-1-61514-709-0(8),* PowerKids Pr.) Rosen Publishing Group, Inc., The.

Windsor, Jo. Bats in Blankets: Early Level Satellite Individual Title Six-Packs. (Sails Literacy Ser.). 16p. (gr. 1-2). 27.00 *(978-0-7578-2939-0(2))* Rigby Education.

World Book, Inc. Staff, contrib. by. Flying Foxes & Other Bats. 2005. (World Book's Animals of the World Ser.). (Illus.). 64p. (J). *(978-0-7166-1262-9(3))* World Bk., Inc.

Zeiger, Jennifer. Bats. 2012. (ENG.). 48p. (J). lib. bdg. 28.00 *(978-0-531-26830-8(6));* (gr. 3-5). pap. 6.95 *(978-0-531-25475-2(5))* Scholastic Library Publishing.

BATS—FICTION

Alikhan, Salima. The Pied Piper of Austin, 1 vol. Alikhan, Salima, illus. 2009. (ENG., Illus.). 32p. (J). (gr. k-3). 16.99 *(978-1-58980-629-0(8))* Pelican Publishing Co., Inc.

Appelt, Kathi. Bat Jamboree. Sweet, Melissa, illus. 2004. 17.00 *(978-0-7569-4074-4(5))* Perfection Learning Corp.

Avi. Poppy & Ereth. Floca, Brian, illus. 2011. (Poppy Stories Ser.). (ENG.). 224p. (J). (gr. 3-7). pap. 6.99 *(978-0-06-111971-2(7))* HarperCollins Pubs.

Avion And Matt. Bronsky the Bat. 2013. (Illus.). 24p. pap. 19.82 *(978-1-4817-8333-0(5))* AuthorHouse.

Bad Bat. 2012. (Collins Big Cat Ser.). (ENG.). 16p. (J). pap., wbk. ed. 4.99 *(978-0-00-747282-6(X))* HarperCollins Pubs. Ltd. GBR. Dist: Independent Pubs. Group.

Bash, Barbara. Shadows of Night: The Hidden World of the Little Brown Bat, 1 vol. Bash, Barbara, illus. 2004. (ENG., Illus.). 32p. (J). (gr. -1-3). pap. 7.95 *(978-0-87156-440-5(8))* Sierra Club Bks. for Children.

Bauld, Jane Scoggins. Hector Saves the Moon, Vol. 2. Laronde, Gary, illus. 2003. (Hector's Escapades Ser.). 34p. (J). (gr. -1-3). per. 7.95 *(978-1-57168-312-0(7))* Eakin Pr.

—Hector Visits His Country Cousin, Vol. 3. Laronde, Gary, illus. 2003. (Hector's Escapades Ser.). 25p. (gr. -1). per. 7.95 *(978-1-57168-676-3(2))* Eakin Pr.

Beeson, Jan. Mysterious World of the Puffins the Treasure Hunt Book 1. 2013. 74p. pap. 19.99 *(978-0-9890482-0-0(9))* Beeson, Jan.

Berk, Ari. Nightsong. Long, Loren, illus. 2012. (ENG.). 48p. (J). (gr. -1-3). 17.99 *(978-1-4169-7886-2(0),* Simon & Schuster Bks. For Young Readers) Simon & Schuster Bks. For Young Readers.

Bright, J. E. Batman Versus Man-Bat. 2012. (Batman: I Can Read Ser.). (J). lib. bdg. 13.55 *(978-0-606-26846-2(4),* Turtleback) Turtleback Bks.

Cannon, Janell. Stellaluna. 2017. (ENG., Illus.). 48p. (J). *(978-0-544-87435-0(8))* Harcourt.

—Stellaluna. 2007. (ENG., Illus.). 42p. (J). (gr. -1-3). bds. 7.99 *(978-0-15-206287-3(4))* Houghton Mifflin Harcourt Publishing Co.

Carr, Matt. Superbat. 2017. (ENG.). 32p. (J). (gr. -1-k). 16.99 ***(978-1-338-16052-9(4),*** Scholastic Pr.) Scholastic, Inc.

Clarke, Jane. The Amazing Adventures of Batbird. Schon, Nick, illus. 2005. (Collins Big Cat Ser.). (ENG.). 32p. (J). (gr. 2-3). pap. 7.99 *(978-0-00-718637-2(1))* HarperCollins Pubs. Ltd. GBR. Dist: Independent Pubs. Group.

Colandro, Lucille. There Was an Old Lady Who Swallowed a Bat! Lee, Jared D., illus. 2009. (ENG.). (J). (gr. -1-3). 9.99 *(978-0-545-16353-8(6))* Scholastic, Inc.

Colby, Rebecca. It's Raining Bats & Frogs. Henry, Steven, illus. 2015. (ENG.). 40p. (J). (gr. -1-k). 16.99 *(978-1-250-04992-6(X),* 9781250049926) Feiwel & Friends.

Coombes, Patrick. The Witch's Assistant. 2013. 34p. pap. *(978-1-909593-74-9(5))* Legend Pr.

Danziger, Paula. There's a Bat in Bunk Five. 160p. (J). pap. 160.00 *(978-0-8072-1369-8(1),* Listening Library) Random Hse. Audio Publishing Group.

Davies, Nicola. Bat Loves the Night. Fox-Davies, Sarah, illus. 2006. (Read & Wonder Ser.). 17.00 *(978-0-7569-6561-7(6))* Perfection Learning Corp.

—Bat Loves the Night: Read & Wonder. Fox-Davies, Sarah, illus. 2004. (Read & Wonder Ser.). (ENG.). 32p. (J). (gr. -1-3). pap. 6.99 *(978-0-7636-2438-5(1))* Candlewick Pr.

Davis, Mike. Pirates, Bats, & Dragons. Simpson, William, illus. 2004. 174p. (J). 15.95 *(978-0-9747078-2-2(1))* Perceval Pr.

Dias, Denise. Burton & Isabelle Pipistrelle: Out of the Bat Cave. Winterhalt, Tara, illus. 2010. (ENG.). 32p. 19.99 *(978-0-88854-485-8(5))* Royal Ontario Museum CAN. Dist: Univ. of Toronto Pr.

Dragonwagon, Crescent. Bat in the Dining Room, 1 vol. Schindler, S. D., illus. 2005. (ENG.). 32p. (J). pap. 5.95 *(978-0-7614-5146-4(3))* Marshall Cavendish Corp.

Elliott, Rebecca. Baxter Is Missing. 2017. (Owl Diaries — Branches Ser.: 6). lib. bdg. 14.75 ***(978-0-606-40189-0(X))*** Turtleback Bks.

—Baxter Is Missing - A Branches Book. Elliott, Rebecca, illus. 2017. (Owl Diaries: 6). (ENG., Illus.). 80p. (J). (gr. k-2). pap. 4.99 ***(978-1-338-04284-9(X))*** Scholastic, Inc.

Ferguson, Alane & Skurzynski, Gloria. Running Scared. 2008. (Mysteries in Our National Park Ser.). (ENG., Illus.). 160p. (J). (gr. 3-7). mass mkt. 4.99 *(978-1-4263-0182-7(0),* National Geographic Children's Bks.) National Geographic Society.

Ferris, Margaret Ann. Bart the Batronaut. Gove, Frank Stanley, illus. 2011. (ENG.). 32p. (J). pap. *(978-0-9832819-8-6(X))* BookCrafters.

Fitzpatrick, Marie-Louise. Owl Bat Bat Owl. Fitzpatrick, Marie-Louise, illus. 2017. (ENG., Illus.). 32p. (J). (gr. -1-2). 15.99 *(978-0-7636-9161-5(5))* Candlewick Pr.

Freeman, David. The Batty Bat. Beers, Robert Lee, illus. 2012. 24p. pap. 24.95 *(978-1-4241-0177-1(8))* PublishAmerica, Inc.

Goss, Michael Anthony. The Bat Who Wore Glasses. Longabough, Kristen, illus. 2005. (J). pap. *(978-1-933156-13-2(9));* per. 16.99 *(978-1-933156-06-4(6))* GSVQ Publishing. (VisionQuest Kids).

Greenburg, J. C. With the Bats. Gerardi, Jan, illus. 2006. (Andrew Lost Ser.: 14). (ENG.). 96p. (J). (gr. 1-4). 3.99 *(978-0-375-83563-6(6),* Random Hse. Bks. for Young Readers) Random Hse. Children's Bks.

Gresham, P. A. Anything Could Be Any Thing. 2005. 128p. pap. 12.95 *(978-1-4116-4353-6(4))* Lulu Pr., Inc.

Guiza, Vic, illus. Bat in the Bunk: Summer Camp Stories Seires. 2015. (ENG.). 32p. (J). (gr. 1-18). 19.99 *(978-0-9863743-0-2(X))* Summer Camp Stories LLC.

Halfmann, Janet. Red Bat at Sleep Hollow Lane. Stegos, Daniel, illus. 2005. (ENG.). 32p. (J). (gr. -1-2). 19.95 *(978-1-59249-343-2(2),* BC5027); 15.95 *(978-1-59249-340-1(8),* B5027); 4.95 *(978-1-59249-342-5(4),* B5077) Soundprints.

—Red Bat at Sleep Hollow Lane. Buchs, Thomas, illus. 2004. (ENG.). 32p. (J). (gr. -1-2). 9.95 *(978-1-59249-345-6(9),* PB5027) Soundprints.

—Red Bat at Sleepy Hollow Lane. Stegos, Daniel, illus. 2005. (Smithsonian's Backyard Ser.). (ENG.). 32p. (J). (gr. -1-2). pap. 6.95 *(978-1-59249-341-8(6),* S5027) Soundprints.

Hamlett, Martha. Bats in the Air, Bats in My Hair. 2008. 32p. pap. 13.99 *(978-1-4389-2358-1(9))* AuthorHouse.

Holub, Joan. Bed, Bats, & Beyond. Gallagher-Cole, Mernie, illus. (Darby Creek Exceptional Titles Ser.). 64p. (J). 2010. (ENG.). (gr. 1-3). pap. 6.95 *(978-0-7613-6451-1(X))* 2008. (gr. -1-1). 14.95 *(978-1-58196-077-8(8),* Darby Creek) Lerner Publishing Group.

Hughes, Devon. Escape from Lion's Head. 2017. (Unnaturals Ser.: 2). 384p. (J). (gr. 3-7). 16.99 *(978-0-06-225757-4(9),* Tegen, Katherine Bks) HarperCollins Pubs.

Hull, Claire. Isn;T That Silly. 2012. 82p. pap. 15.95 *(978-0-9846558-7-8(5))* Taylor and Seale Publishing, LLC.

Ingalls, Ann. Biggety Bat: Chow down, Biggety! Zenz, Aaron, illus. 2015. (Scholastic Reader, Level 1 Ser.). (ENG.). 32p. (J). (gr. -1-1). pap. 3.99 *(978-0-545-66264-2(8))* Scholastic, Inc.

—Scholastic Reader Level 1: Biggety Bat: Hot Diggety, It's Biggety! Zenz, Aaron, illus. 2014. (Scholastic Reader Level 1 Ser.). (ENG.). 32p. (J). (gr. -1-2). pap. 3.99 *(978-0-545-66263-5(X))* Scholastic, Inc.

Irbinskas, Heather. Pauly the Adventurous Pallid Bat. Anthis, Brian, illus. Tuttle, Merlin D., photos by. 2003. 32p. (J). pap. 7.95 *(978-1-58369-032-1(8))* Western National Parks Assn.

Jennings, Patrick. Bat & Rat. Cordell, Matthew, illus. 2012. (ENG.). 40p. (J). (gr. k-2). 16.95 *(978-1-4197-0160-3(6),* Abrams Bks. for Young Readers) Abrams, Inc.

Karpes, H. R. Morris... the Downside-Up Bat. 2013. (ENG., Illus.). 32p. (J). (gr. -1-k). 11.95 *(978-1-62087-987-0(5),* 620987, Sky Pony Pr.) Skyhorse Publishing Co., Inc.

Kim, Melissa. A Little Brown Bat Story, 1 vol. Fitch, Jada, illus. 2015. (ENG.). 24p. (J). bds. 10.95 *(978-1-939017-70-3(X),* 7f78678a-9b76-46c9-94f1-ff6d96df81bf) Islandport Pr., Inc.

Knudsen, Michelle. El Caso de Vivian la Vampira. Wummer, Amy, illus. 2008. (Science Solves It! en Espanol Ser.). (SPA.). 32p. (J). (gr. -1-3). pap. 5.95 *(978-1-57565-277-1(3))* Kane Press, Inc.

—El Caso de Vivian la Vampira (the Case of Vampire Vivian) Wummer, Amy, illus. 2009. (Science Solves It! (r) en Espanol Ser.). (SPA.). (gr. 1-3). pap. 33.92 *(978-0-7613-4800-9(X))* Lerner Publishing Group.

Knudson, Michelle. The Case of Vampire Vivian. Wummer, Amy, illus. 2003. (Science Solves It! Ser.). 32p. (J). pap. 5.95 *(978-1-57565-127-9(0))* Kane Press, Inc.

Krulik, Nancy. Going Batty. John and Wendy Staff, illus. 2009. (Katie Kazoo, Switcheroo Ser.: 32). (ENG.). 80p. (J). (gr. 2-4). pap. 4.99 *(978-0-448-45042-1(9),* Grosset & Dunlap) Penguin Young Readers Group.

LeBaron, Cecilia. The Cap. 2007. (Illus.). 16p. (J). 5.95 *(978-0-9798869-2-8(9))* Crush Publishing.

Lederer, Ryan. The Adventures of Captain Candy. 2007. (Illus.). 48p. (J). (gr. 4-7). 15.95 *(978-0-9795852-1-0(X))* Seven Locks Pr.

Lies, Brian. Bats at the Ballgame. 2010. (Bat Book Ser.). (ENG., Illus.). 32p. (J). (gr. -1-3). 16.99 *(978-0-547-24970-4(5))* Houghton Mifflin Harcourt Publishing Co.

—Bats at the Beach. (Bat Book Ser.). (ENG., Illus.). 32p. (J). (gr. -1 — 1). 2011. bds. 11.99 *(978-0-547-55437-2(0))* 2006. 17.99 *(978-0-618-55744-8(X))* Houghton Mifflin Harcourt Publishing Co.

—Bats at the Library. 2014. (Bat Book Ser.). (ENG., Illus.). 32p. (J). (gr. -1-3). pap. 7.99 *(978-0-544-33920-0(7),* HMH Books For Young Readers) Houghton Mifflin Harcourt Publishing Co.

—Bats at the Library. Lies, Brian, illus. 2008. (Bat Book Ser.). (ENG., Illus.). 32p. (J). (gr. -1-3). 17.99 *(978-0-618-99923-1(X))* Houghton Mifflin Harcourt Publishing Co.

—Bats in the Band. Lies, Brian, illus. 2014. (Bat Book Ser.). (ENG., Illus.). 32p. (J). (gr. -1-3). 17.99 *(978-0-544-10569-0(9),* HMH Books For Young Readers) Houghton Mifflin Harcourt Publishing Co.

Marsh, Carole. Dear Bats: The Creepy Cave Caper Mystery. 2007. (Postcard Mysteries Ser.). (Illus.). 115p. (J). (gr. 2-9). per. 5.99 *(978-0-635-06342-7(5))* Gallopade International.

Matheny, Bill, et al. Going... Batty!, 1 vol. 2014. (Batman Strikes! Ser.). (ENG., Illus.). 32p. (gr. 2-3). 22.60 *(978-1-4342-6484-8(X))* Stone Arch Bks.

Mc Shane, Mary. Karena the Fairy & the Bat Colony. 2011. 344p. (gr. 4-6). pap. 19.95 *(978-1-4620-5295-0(9))* iUniverse, Inc.

Meisel, Paul, illus. Good Night, Bat! Good Morning, Squirrel! 2016. (ENG.). 40p. (J). (gr. -1-3). 16.95 *(978-1-62979-495-2(3))* Boyds Mills Pr.

Meltzer Kleinhenz, Sydnie. Bats in My Attic. Stromoski, Rick, illus. 2005. (Rookie Readers Ser.). (ENG.). 32p. (J). (gr. k-2). lib. bdg. 19.50 *(978-0-516-24865-3(0),* Children's Pr.) Scholastic Library Publishing.

Mitchard, Jacquelyn. Baby Bat's Lullaby. Noonan, Julia, illus. 2004. 32p. (J). (gr. -1-1). lib. bdg. 16.89 *(978-0-06-050761-9(6))* HarperCollins Pubs.

Naylor, Phyllis Reynolds. Bernie Magruder & the Bats in the Belfry. 2004. (ENG., Illus.). 144p. (J). (gr. 3-7). pap. 7.99 *(978-0-689-85067-7(0),* Atheneum Bks. for Young Readers) Simon & Schuster Children's Publishing.

Nickel, Scott. Billions of Bats. Smith, Andy J., illus. 2007. (Graphic Sparks Ser.). (ENG.). 40p. (gr. 1-3). per. 5.95 *(978-1-59889-408-0(0),* Graphic Sparks) Stone Arch Bks.

Oppel, Kenneth. Darkwing. Thompson, Keith, illus. 2007. (Silverwing Ser.: 1). 432p. (J). (gr. 5-9). 17.99 *(978-0-06-085054-8(X))* HarperCollins Pubs.

—Firewing. (Silverwing Trilogy Ser.). (ENG.). (J). (gr. 3-7). 2008. 336p. pap. 7.99 *(978-1-4169-4999-2(2))* 2003. (Illus.). 272p. 19.99 *(978-0-689-84993-0(1))* Simon & Schuster Bks. For Young Readers. (Simon & Schuster Bks. For Young Readers).

—Silverwing. braille ed. 2003. (Silverwing Saga: Bk. 1). (J). (gr. 2). spiral bd. *(978-0-616-15274-4(4))* Canadian National Institute for the Blind/Institut National Canadien pour les Aveugles.

—Silverwing. 2007. (Silverwing Trilogy Ser.). (ENG.). 224p. (J). (gr. 3-7). per. 7.99 *(978-1-4169-4998-5(4),* Simon & Schuster Bks. For Young Readers) Simon & Schuster Bks. For Young Readers.

—Sunwing. 2008. (Silverwing Trilogy Ser.). (ENG.). 336p. (J). (gr. 3-7). pap. 7.99 *(978-1-4169-4997-8(6),* Simon & Schuster Bks. For Young Readers) Simon & Schuster Bks. For Young Readers.

Ortiz, Gilberto Rendon. Tuiiiii el Murcielago. (Barril Sin Fondo Ser.). (SPA.). (J). (gr. 3-5). pap. *(978-968-6465-22-8(7))* Casa de Estudios de Literatura y Talleres Artisticos Amaquemecan A.C. MEX. Dist: Lectorum Pubns., Inc.

Park, Linda Sue. Forest of Wonders. Madsen, Jim, illus. 2016. (Wing & Claw Ser.: 1). 352p. (J). (gr. 3-7). 16.99 *(978-0-06-232738-3(0))* HarperCollins Pubs.

Parkinson, Helen. How Well Can Wombats Bat? 2012. 28p. pap. 32.70 *(978-1-4797-2235-8(9))* Xlibris Corp.

Paulding, Steve. The Wonderful Adventures of Bradley the Bat. Schmidt, Caleb & Schmidt, Carter, illus. 2013. 70p. pap. 18.95 *(978-0-615-74591-6(1))* Slow on the Draw Productions.

Pavanello, Roberto. The Chilly Mammoth, 1 vol. Zeni, Marco, tr. from ITA. Pisapia, Blasco & Brughera, Pamela, illus. 2013. (Echo & the Bat Pack Ser.). (ENG.). 128p. (gr. 2-3). 9.95 *(978-1-4342-4889-3(5))* Stone Arch Bks.

—The Dancing Vampire. Zeni, Marco, tr. from ITA. Pisapia, Blasco & Brughera, Pamela, illus. 2012. (Echo & the Bat Pack Ser.). (ENG.). 128p. (gr. 2-3). 25.32 *(978-1-4342-3837-5(7),* Echo & the Bat Pack) Stone Arch Bks.

—The Ghost of Dr. Mold. Zeni, Marco, tr. from ITA. Pisapia, Blasco & Brughera, Pamela, illus. 2012. (Echo & the Bat Pack Ser.). (ENG.). 128p. (gr. 2-3). 25.32 *(978-1-4342-3834-4(2),* Echo & the Bat Pack) Stone Arch Bks.

—King Tut's Grandmother, 1 vol. Zeni, Marco, tr. from ITA. Pisapia, Blasco & Brughera, Pamela, illus. 2012. (Echo & the Bat Pack Ser.). (ENG.). 128p. (gr. 2-3). 9.95 *(978-1-4342-4245-7(5));* lib. bdg. 25.32 *(978-1-4342-3823-8(7),* Echo & the Bat Pack) Stone Arch Bks.

—The Midnight Witches, 1 vol. Zeni, Marco, tr. from ITA. Pisapia, Blasco & Brughera, Pamela, illus. 2012. (Echo & the Bat Pack Ser.). (ENG.). 128p. (gr. 2-3). 9.95 *(978-1-4342-4246-4(3));* lib. bdg. 25.32 *(978-1-4342-3822-1(9),* Echo & the Bat Pack) Stone Arch Bks.

—The Pirate with the Golden Tooth, 1 vol. Zeni, Marco, tr. from ITA. Pisapia, Blasco & Brughera, Pamela, illus. (Echo & the Bat Pack Ser.). (ENG.). 128p. (gr. 2-3). 2013. 9.95 *(978-1-4342-4888-6(7))* 2012. 25.32 *(978-1-4342-3836-8(9),* Echo & the Bat Pack) Stone Arch Bks.

—The Thing in the Sewers, 1 vol. Zeni, Marco, tr. from ITA. Pisapia, Blasco & Brughera, Pamela, illus. 2012. (Echo & the Bat Pack Ser.). (ENG.). 128p. (gr. 2-3). 9.95 *(978-1-4342-4247-1(1));* 25.32 *(978-1-4342-3824-5(5),* Echo & the Bat Pack) Stone Arch Bks.

—Treasure in the Graveyard, 1 vol. Zeni, Marco, tr. from ITA. Pisapia, Blasco & Brughera, Pamela, illus. 2012. (Echo & the Bat Pack Ser.). (ENG.). 128p. (gr. 2-3). 9.95 *(978-1-4342-4248-8(X))* Stone Arch Bks.

Pottie, Marjolein & Auzary-Luton, Sylvie. Going Batty! Special Glow-in-the-Dark Surprise Pictures. Auzary-Luton, Sylvie, illus. 2005. (Illus.). 32p. (J). 15.95 *(978-0-689-04635-3(9),* Milk & Cookies) ibooks, Inc.

Prieto, Rafaela. Myvera's Love of Sunshine. 2011. 20p. pap. 16.95 *(978-1-4626-2930-5(X))* America Star Bks.

Ralph, Brian. Cave In. 2013. (ENG., Illus.). 96p. (J). (gr. 7-12). pap. 14.95 *(978-1-77046-094-2(2),* 9781770460942) Drawn & Quarterly Pubns. CAN. Dist: Macmillan.

Rand, Jonathan. Michigan Chillers #14 Bionic Bats Bay City. 2007. 208p. (J). pap. 5.99 *(978-1-893699-65-6(X))* AudioCraft Publishing, Inc.

Ricci, Christine. Puppy Takes a Bath. Mangano, Tom, illus. 2006. (Dora the Explorer Ser.: 10). (ENG.). 24p. (J). (gr. 3-7). pap. 3.99 *(978-1-4169-1483-9(8),* Simon Spotlight/Nickelodeon) Simon Spotlight/Nickelodeon.

Sargemt, Dave & Sargent, Pat. Batley Needs Glasses, 10 vols., Vol. 12. Robinson, Laura, illus. 2004. (Learn to Read Ser.: 10). 18p. (J). lib. bdg. 20.95 *(978-1-56763-819-6(8))* Ozark Publishing.

Sargent, Dave & Sargent, Pat. Batley Needs Glasses, 10 vols., Vol. 12. Robinson, Laura, illus. 2004. (Learn to Read Ser.: 10).Tr. of Batley Necesita Anteojos. 18p. (J). pap. 10.95 *(978-1-56763-820-2(1))* Ozark Publishing.

Searle, Gleneta E. Mr. Tedd Fredd: The Intellectual Pioneer from Phew. 2013. 80p. pap. 9.95 *(978-1-4908-0973-1(2),* WestBow Pr.) Author Solutions, Inc.

Sherry, Kevin. I'm the Scariest Thing in the Castle. 2011. (ENG.). 28p. (J). (gr. -1 — 1). bds. 6.99 *(978-0-8037-3390-9(9),* Dial Bks) Penguin Young Readers Group.

Sloan, William. Of Bees & Bats of Crocodiles & Cats. 2009. 73p. pap. 14.95 *(978-1-4092-9470-2(6))* Lulu Pr., Inc.

Spalding, Brenda M. Just Batty. Teagle, Caitlyn, illus. 2011. 26p. pap. 12.00 *(978-1-61204-156-8(6),* Strategic Bk. Publishing) Strategic Book Publishing & Rights Agency (SBPRA).

Sullivan, William J. About Black Bat. 2003. (Illus.). 32p. (J). per. 7.95 *(978-0-9708066-7-3(1))* Painted Horse Pubns., Inc.

Tauiliili, Pemerika L. The Rat & the Bat: And Other Short Stories. 2009. 88p. pap. 16.99 *(978-1-4490-4389-6(5));* pap. 32.49 *(978-1-4389-2700-8(2))* AuthorHouse.

Thomas-Christensen, Sheelagh. Morus Yr Ystlum. Thomas, Dylan, illus. 2005. (Cyfres Llyfrau Llawen Ser.: Vol. 1). (WEL.). 36p. pap. *(978-0-86243-396-3(7))* Y Lolfa.

Ungerer, Tomi. Rufus. 2015. (ENG.). 32p. (gr. -1-2). 16.95 *(978-0-7148-7049-6(8))* Phaidon Pr., Inc.

—Rufus: The Bat Who Loved Colours. 2015. (ENG., Illus.). 32p. 16.95 *(978-0-7148-6972-8(4))* Phaidon Pr., Inc.

Vernon, Ursula. Dani Bocafuego. la Cueva Del Murcielago Gigante. 2012. (SPA.). 204p. (J). (gr. 4-6). pap. 20.99 *(978-84-246-3599-2(X))* La Galera, S.A. Editorial ESP. Dist: Lectorum Pubns., Inc.

—Lair of the Bat Monster. 4th ed. (Dragonbreath Ser.: 4). (ENG.). 208p. (J). (gr. 3-7). 2014. pap. 6.99 *(978-0-14-751320-5(0),* Puffin Books) 2011. 12.99 *(978-0-8037-3525-5(1),* Dial Bks) Penguin Young Readers Group.

—Lair of the Bat Monster. 2014. (Dragonbreath Ser.: 4). lib. bdg. 17.20 *(978-0-606-35711-1(4))* Turtleback Bks.

Von Buhler, Cynthia. But Who Will Bell the Cats? Von Buhler, Cynthia, illus. 2009. (ENG., Illus.). 32p. (J). (gr. -1-3). 17.00 *(978-0-618-99718-3(0))* Houghton Mifflin Harcourt Publishing Co.

Voskuil, Hannah. Horus & the Curse of Everlasting Regret. 2016. (ENG.). 224p. (J). (gr. 3-7). 16.99 *(978-1-101-93333-6(X),* Knopf Bks. for Young Readers) Random Hse. Children's Bks.

Waring, Geoff. Oscar & the Bat: A Book about Sound. Waring, Geoff, illus. 2009. (Start with Science Ser.). (ENG., Illus.). 32p. (J). (gr. -1-3). pap. 6.99 *(978-0-7636-4513-7(3))* Candlewick Pr.

Weston Woods Staff, creator. Ready, Freddy! #3: Homework Hassles. 2011. 20.95 *(978-0-545-05007-4(3))* Weston Woods Studios, Inc.

Williams, Paul. How the Bat Got Its Wings & Young Bear's Lesson: Two Cherokee Stories. 2003. (Illus.). 47p. (J). per. 14.95 *(978-0-9630310-6-8(6))* Will Hall Bks.

Willis, Jeanne. Daft Bat. Ross, Tony, illus. 2007. (ENG.). 32p. (J). (gr. k-2). 16.95 *(978-1-84270-476-9(1))* Transworld Publishers Ltd. GBR. Dist: Independent Pubs. Group.

Wilson, Steve. Hedgehugs: Autumn Hide-And-Squeak. Tapper, Lucy, illus. 2017. (Hedgehugs Ser.). (ENG.). 32p. (J). 16.99 ***(978-1-250-11248-4(6),*** 9781250112484, Holt, Henry & Co. Bks. For Young Readers) Holt, Henry & Co.

Young, Justin. A Most Vivid Day! 2010. (ENG., Illus.). 40p. (J). (gr. k-2). 16.95 *(978-0-9785418-1-1(2))* Dream Character, Inc.

BATTLE OF BRITAIN, 1940

see Britain, Battle of, Great Britain, 1940

BATTLE SHIPS

see Warships

BATTLES

see also Naval Battles

also names of wars with the subdivision Campaigns and Battles, e.g. World War, 1939-1945—Campaigns and Battles; and names of individual battles, e.g. Ardennes, Battle of the, 1944-1945

ABDO Publishing Company Staff. Great Battles. 2014. (Great Battles Ser.: 6). (ENG.). 32p. (gr. 5-9). lib. bdg. 162.42 *(978-1-62403-202-8(8),* Abdo & Daughters) ABDO Publishing Co.

La Batalla de 5 de Mayo. 2005. (SPA.). (J). pap. *(978-968-7381-12-1(4))* Tecolote, Ediciones, S.A. de C.V.

Baxter, Roberta. Battles for Gold & Glory: Civil War Skirmishes in New Mexico Territory. 2012. (ENG.). 81p. pap. 11.95 *(978-1-4327-8643-4(1))* Outskirts Pr., Inc.

Big Battles of World War II. 2014. (ENG.). 48p. (J). lib. bdg. 29.00 *(978-0-531-20494-8(4))* Scholastic Library Publishing.

Bizarre Beast Battles. 2015. (Bizarre Beast Battles Ser.). (ENG.). 24p. (J). (gr. 2-3). pap., pap., pap. 293.40 *(978-1-4824-3440-8(7))* Stevens, Gareth Publishing LLLP.

Bobrick, Benson. The Battle of Nashville. 2010. (ENG., Illus.). 144p. (J). (gr. 3-7). 19.99 *(978-0-375-84887-2(8),* Knopf Bks. for Young Readers) Random Hse. Children's Bks.

Booth, Jack. The 10 Most Gripping 20th Century War Stories. 2008. 14.99 *(978-1-55448-497-3(9))* Scholastic Library Publishing.

Chambers, Catherine. Fierce Fighters. Bustamante, Maryin & Juta, Jason, illus. 2016. (Warriors! Ser.). (ENG.). 32p. (J). (gr. 3-6). 26.65 *(978-1-4677-9357-5(4))* Lerner Publishing Group.

Chambers, Catherine. A King's Guide. Pentney, Ryan, illus. 2017. (How-To Guides for Fiendish Rulers Ser.). (ENG.). 32p. (J). (gr. 3-6). lib. bdg. 26.65 *(978-1-5124-1550-6(2));* 7.99 ***(978-1-5124-3624-2(0));*** 39.99 ***(978-1-5124-3623-5(2));*** 39.99 ***(978-1-5124-2706-6(3))*** Lerner Publishing Group.

Chapman, Caroline. Battles & Weapons: Exploring History Through Art. 2007. (Picture That Ser.). (ENG., Illus.). 64p. (J). (gr. 3-17). 19.95 *(978-1-58728-588-2(6))* Cooper Square Publishing Llc.

Colson, Rob. Battles: 12 Epic Battles on Land, Sea & in the Air. 2017. (Epic! Ser.). (ENG., Illus.). 32p. (J). (gr. 4-6). pap. 11.99 *(978-0-7502-9731-8(X),* Wayland) Hachette Children's Group GBR. Dist: Hachette Bk. Group.

Corporate Contibutor Staff & Clarke, Gordon. Significant Battles of the American Revolution. 2012. (ENG.). 48p. (J). *(978-0-7787-0806-3(3))* Crabtree Publishing Co.

Doeden, Matt. The Battle of the Alamo, 1 vol. Barnett, Charles, III & Miller, Phil, illus. 2005. (Graphic History Ser.). (ENG.). 32p. (gr. 3-4). per. 8.10 *(978-0-7368-5242-5(5),* Graphic Library) Capstone Press of Coughlan Cos.

Donaldson, Madeline. Deadly Bloody Battles. 2013. (ShockZone — Deadly & Dangerous Ser.). (ENG., Illus.). 32p. (gr. 5-8). pap. 8.95 *(978-1-4677-0889-0(5));* lib. bdg. 26.60 *(978-1-4677-0601-8(9),* Lerner Pubns.) Lerner Publishing Group.

Dorling Kindersley Publishing Staff & Bray, Adam. Into Battle! 2015. (DK Adventures Ser.). (ENG.). 128p. (J). (gr. 3-7). pap. 5.99 *(978-1-4654-3534-7(4),* DK Children) Dorling Kindersley Publishing, Inc.

Downey, Glen R. The 10 Most Decisive Battles. 2007. 14.99 *(978-1-55448-507-9(X))* Scholastic Library Publishing.

Gunston, Bill Tudor & Guy, John. Battle Machines. 2009. (ENG.). 112p. (J). (gr. 4-7). pap. 12.95 *(978-1-84696-201-1(3),* TickTock Books) Octopus Publishing Group GBR. Dist: Independent Pubs. Group.

Hallett, R. B. The 10 Most Decisive Battles on American Soil. 2008. 14.99 *(978-1-55448-538-3(X))* Scholastic Library Publishing.

Hama, Larry. The Battle of Antietam: The Bloodiest Day of Battle. (Graphic Civil War Battles Ser.). (ENG.). 48p. 2009. (YA). (gr. 4-5). 58.50 *(978-1-61512-897-6(2),* Rosen Reference) 2007. (Illus.). (gr. 5-8). pap. 14.05 *(978-1-4042-6475-5(2),* Rosen Classroom) Rosen Publishing Group, Inc., The.

—The Battle of First Bull Run: The War Begins! 2007. (Graphic Battles: Civil War Ser.). (ENG., Illus.). 48p. (gr. 5-6). pap. 14.05 *(978-1-4042-6476-2(0),* Rosen Classroom) Rosen Publishing Group, Inc., The.

—The Battle of Shiloh: Surprise Attack! 2007. (Graphic Battles: Civil War Ser.). (ENG., Illus.). 48p. (gr. 5-8). pap. 14.05 *(978-1-4042-6478-6(7),* Rosen Classroom) Rosen Publishing Group, Inc., The.

Hamilton, John. Battles of World War I, 1 vol. 2004. (World War I Ser.). (ENG.). 32p. 27.07 *(978-1-57765-913-6(9),* Abdo & Daughters) ABDO Publishing Co.

—World War II: Early Battles, 1 vol. 2011. (World War II Ser.). (ENG., Illus.). 32p. (YA). (gr. 5-9). 27.07 *(978-1-61783-059-4(3))* ABDO Publishing Co.

Holmes, Richard. Battle. 2009. (DK Eyewitness Bks.). (ENG.). 72p. (J). (gr. 3-7). 16.99 *(978-0-7566-5027-8(5),* DK Children) Dorling Kindersley Publishing, Inc.

Martin, Christopher. Great Battles. 2008. 48p. (gr. 10-11). pap. 21.50 *(978-0-340-96630-3(0))* Hodder Education Group GBR. Dist: Trans-Atlantic Pubns., Inc.

Matthews, Rupert & Dorling Kindersley Publishing Staff. Battle at the Castle. 2014. (DK Readers Ser.). (ENG., Illus.). 32p. (J). (gr. 1-3). pap. 3.99 *(978-1-4654-2005-3(3),* DK Children) Dorling Kindersley Publishing, Inc.

Nardo, Don. Bad Days in Battle. 2017. (Whoops! a History of Bad Days Ser.). (ENG., Illus.). 48p. (gr. 5-8). lib. bdg. 33.32 *(978-1-4109-8562-0(8))* Heinemann-Raintree.

Oxlade, Chris. The Top Ten Battles That Changed the World. 2009. (J). 60.00 *(978-1-4358-9178-4(3),* PowerKids Pr.); (J). pap. 10.00 *(978-1-4358-9177-7(5),* PowerKids Pr.); (Illus.). 32p. (YA). (gr. 3-6). 26.50 *(978-1-4358-9176-0(7))* Rosen Publishing Group, Inc., The.

Perritano, John & Spears, James. National Geographic Kids Everything Battles: Arm Yourself with Fierce Photos & Fascinating Facts. 2013. (National Geographic Kids Everything Ser.). (ENG.). 64p. (J). (gr. 3-7). lib. bdg. 25.90 *(978-1-4263-1101-7(X));* (Illus.). pap. 12.95 *(978-1-4263-1100-0(1))* National Geographic Society. (National Geographic Children's Bks.).

Sabin, Edwin L. Boys' Book of Border Battles. 2013. (ENG., Illus.). 352p. pap. 14.95 *(978-1-62087-158-4(0),* 620158) Skyhorse Publishing Co., Inc.

Sepahban, Lois. Spartan Warriors. 2015. (Ancient Warriors Ser.). (ENG.). 32p. (J). (gr. 2-5). 28.50 *(978-1-63143-760-1(7),* 208592) Child's World, Inc., The.

Turner, Tracey. Hard As Nails in Wars & Battles. Lenman, Jamie, illus. 2015. (ENG.). 64p. (J). pap. *(978-0-7787-1526-9(4))* Crabtree Publishing Co.

Vierow, Wendy. The Battle of Trenton. 2009. (Atlas of Famous Battles of the American Revolution Ser.). 24p. (gr. 3-3). 42.50 *(978-1-60853-331-2(X),* PowerKids Pr.) Rosen Publishing Group, Inc., The.

Waldman, Scott P. The Battle of Monmouth. (Atlas of Famous Battles of the American Revolution Ser.). 24p. 2009. (gr. 3-3). 42.50 *(978-1-60853-329-9(8))* 2003. (Illus.). (J). lib. bdg. 22.60 *(978-0-8239-6330-0(6))* Rosen Publishing Group, Inc., The. (PowerKids Pr.).

Wood, Alix. Haunted Battlefields. 2016. (World's Scariest Places Ser.). 00032p. (J). pap. 10.50 ***(978-1-4824-5908-1(6))*** Stevens, Gareth Publishing LLLP.

Yasuda, Anita. The 12 Most Amazing American Battles. 2014. (ENG., Illus.). 32p. (J). *(978-1-63235-006-0(8))* Pr. Room Editions LLC.

BATTLESHIPS

see Warships

BAY OF PIGS INVASION

see Cuba—History

BAYEUX TAPESTRY

Lemaresquier, D. & Pivard, G. The Story of a Conquest: The Bayeux Tapestry Narrated to Children. 2007. (Illus.). 48p. *(978-2-915762-15-0(5))* OREP Edition & Communication.

BAZAARS

see Fairs

BEACHES

see Seashore

BEACONSFIELD, BENJAMIN DISRAELI, 1ST EARL OF, 1804-1881

see Disraeli, Benjamin, Earl of Beaconsfield, 1804-1881

BEADWORK

Annie's. I Can Bead. Frank, Sharon, ed. 2012. (I Can Ser.). (ENG., Illus.). 32p. (J). (gr. 4-7). pap. 7.95 *(978-1-59635-562-0(X),* Annie's) Annie's Publishing, LLC.

Beaded Bracelets: Easy to Make & Fun to Wear! 2013. (Craft Box Kids Ser.). (ENG., Illus.). 48p. (J). *(978-1-77132-083-2(4))* SpiceBox Products Ltd.

Boase, Petra. Friendship Bracelets & Beading Fun: 25 Knotty, Dotty, Stripey & Sparkly Designs to Make! 2014. (ENG., Illus.). 64p. (J). (gr. -1-6). 9.99 *(978-1-84322-944-5(7),* Armadillo) Anness Publishing GBR. Dist: National Bk. Network.

Collings, Julie. Creaturas. 2005. (SPA., Illus.). 92p. (J). spiral bd. 20.95 *(978-968-5528-01-6(2))* Klutz Latino MEX. Dist: Independent Pubs. Group.

Etchison, Denise. Kids! Picture Yourself Making Jewelry. 2008. (Picture Yourself Ser.). (ENG.). 104p. pap. 12.99 *(978-1-59863-526-3(3))* Course Technology.

Fantastic Beads. 2004. (Whizz Kits Ser.). (Illus.). 48p. (J). *(978-1-84229-948-7(4))* Top That! Publishing PLC.

Friendship Bracelets. 2013. (Kits for Kids Ser.). (ENG., Illus.). 64p. (J). (gr. 3-7). *(978-1-894722-49-0(3))* SpiceBox Products Ltd.

Johnson, Anne Akers. Loop Loom Bracelets: Make Super-Stretchy Beaded Bracelets. 2014. (ENG.). 40p. (J). (gr. 3). 21.99 *(978-0-545-70318-5(2))* Klutz.

—Pulseras Rusticas. 2005. (SPA., Illus.). 32p. (J). (gr. 1). 17.95 *(978-968-5528-11-5(X))* Klutz Latino MEX. Dist: Independent Pubs. Group.

Johnson, Anne Akers & Klutz Editors. Brilliant Bead Rings. 2011. (ENG.). 50p. (J). (gr. 5-9). 16.99 *(978-0-545-34617-7(7))* Klutz.

Limós, Anna. Easy Bead Crafts in 5 Steps. 2008. (Easy Crafts in 5 Steps Ser.). (Illus.). 32p. (J). (gr. 3-7). lib. bdg. 23.94 *(978-0-7660-3082-4(2),* Enslow Elementary) Enslow Pubs., Inc.

—Easy Bead Crafts in 5 Steps. 2010. (Easy Crafts in 5 Steps Ser.). (Illus.). 32p. (J). pap. 7.95 *(978-0-7660-3757-1(6),* Enslow Elementary) Enslow Pubs., Inc.

Miles, L. Hair Braiding Kid Kit. rev. ed. 2005. 32p. (J). 10.99 *(978-1-58086-858-7(4),* Usborne) EDC Publishing.

Murray, Patricia. Make It & Pray It. Murray, Patricia, illus. gif. ed. 2005. (Illus.). 110p. (J). (gr. 3-7). 22.00 *(978-0-88489-895-5(4))* St. Mary's Pr. of MN.

Nunn, Daniel. Buttons & Beads, 1 vol. 2011. (From Trash to Treasures Ser.). (ENG.). 24p. (gr. k-2). 23.32 *(978-1-4329-5152-8(1),* Heinemann Read & Learn) Heinemann-Raintree.

Ross, Kathy. Beautiful Beads. In Den Bosch, Nicole, illus. 2009. (Girl Crafts Ser.). 48p. (J). (gr. 2-6). pap. 7.95 *(978-1-58013-884-0(5),* First Avenue Editions) Lerner Publishing Group.

—Beautiful Beads. Bosch, Nicole in den, illus. 2009. (Girl Crafts Ser.). (ENG.). 48p. (gr. 2-5). 26.60 *(978-0-8225-9214-3(2),* Millbrook Pr.) Lerner Publishing Group.

Sadler, Judy Ann. Beads.Tr. of Perles. (FRE., Illus.). (J). pap. 7.99 *(978-0-590-24194-6(X))* Scholastic, Inc.

Sadler, Judy Ann & Sadler, Judy. Hemp Jewelry. Bradford, June, illus. 2005. (Kids Can Do It Ser.). (ENG.). 40p. (J). (gr. 3-7). 6.95 *(978-1-55337-775-7(3))* Kids Can Pr., Ltd. CAN. Dist: Hachette Bk. Group.

Speechley, Greta. Bead Crafts. 2010. (Creative Crafts for Kids Ser.). 32p. (J). (gr. 2-5). lib. bdg. 28.00 *(978-1-4339-3549-7(X));* (Illus.). pap. 10.50 *(978-1-4339-3550-3(3))* Stevens, Gareth Publishing LLLP. (Gareth Stevens Learning Library).

Top That! Kids, creator. Brilliant Beads & Bracelets. 2006. (Creative Studio Ser.). (Illus.). 48p. (J). (gr. -1-3). *(978-1-905359-85-1(3))* Top That! Publishing PLC.

—Fabulous Footware. 2006. (Creative Studio Ser.). (Illus.). 48p. (J). (gr. -1-3). *(978-1-905359-84-4(5))* Top That! Publishing PLC.

BEAGLE (DOG BREED)

Albright, Rosie. Bedbug-Sniffing Beagles & Other Scent Hounds. 2012. (Animal Detectives Ser.). (ENG., Illus.). 24p. (J). (gr. k-3). pap. 8.25 *(978-1-4488-6264-1(7));* lib. bdg. 22.60 *(978-1-4488-6152-1(7))* Rosen Publishing Group, Inc., The. (PowerKids Pr.).

—Bedbug-Sniffing Beagles & Other Scent Hounds: Beagles Cazadores de Chinches y Otros Sabuesos. Alamán, Eduardo, tr. from ENG. 2012. (Animal Detectives / Detectives Del Reino Animal Ser.). (SPA & ENG., Illus.). 24p. (J). (gr. k-3). lib. bdg. 22.60 *(978-1-4488-6726-4(6),* PowerKids Pr.) Rosen Publishing Group, Inc., The.

Beal, Abigail. I Love My Beagle. 2011. (Top Dogs Ser.). (Illus.). 24p. (J). pap. 8.25 *(978-1-4488-2664-3(0));* lib. bdg. 22.60 *(978-1-4488-2540-0(7))* Rosen Publishing Group, Inc., The. (PowerKids Pr.).

Bodden, Valerie. Beagles. 2014. (J). 25.65 *(978-1-60818-360-9(2),* Creative Education) Creative Co., The.

—Fetch!: Beagles. 2014. (Fetch! Ser.). (ENG., Illus.). 24p. (J). (gr. 1-3). pap. 7.99 *(978-0-89812-939-7(7),* Creative Paperbacks) Creative Co., The.

Bozzo, Linda. I Like Beagles! 2012. (Discover Dogs with the American Canine Association Ser.). (Illus.). 24p. (J). (gr. k-3). pap. 7.95 *(978-1-4644-0123-7(3),* Enslow Elementary) Enslow Pubs., Inc.

Finne, Stephanie. Beagles, 1 vol. 2014. (Dogs Set 12 Ser.). (ENG.). 24p. (J). (gr. 3-6). 25.65 *(978-1-62403-672-9(4))* ABDO Publishing Co.

George, Charles & George, Linda. Beagle. 2010. (J). 26.00 *(978-0-531-23242-2(5))* Scholastic Library Publishing.

Gray, Susan H. Beagles. 2008. (Domestic Dogs Ser.). (ENG., Illus.). 32p. (J). (gr. 2-5). 28.50 *(978-1-59296-961-6(5),* 200135) Child's World, Inc., The.

Green, Sara. Beagles. 2008. (Dog Breeds Ser.). (ENG., Illus.). 24p. (J). (gr. 2-5). lib. bdg. 25.95 *(978-1-60014-217-8(6))* Bellwether Media.

Heit Schwaeber, Barbie. Bailey & the Beagle Brigade. Neidigh, Sherry, illus. 2011. (ENG.). 32p. (J). 6.95 *(978-1-60727-218-2(0))* Soundprints.

Johnson, Jinny. Beagle. 2013. (My Favorite Dogs Ser.). (Illus.). 24p. (gr. k-3). 28.50 *(978-1-59920-839-8(3))* Black Rabbit Bks.

Landau, Elaine. Beagles Are the Best! 2009. (Best Dogs Ever Ser.). (ENG.). 32p. (gr. 2-4). lib. bdg. 25.26 *(978-1-58013-559-7(5),* Lerner Pubns.) Lerner Publishing Group.

Riggs, Kate. Beagles. 2016. (Seedlings Ser.). 24p. (J). (gr. k-2). (ENG.). pap. 7.99 *(978-1-62832-246-0(2),* Creative Paperbacks); (Illus.). 28.50 *(978-1-60818-661-7(X),* Creative Education) Creative Co., The.

Searl, Duncan. Beagle: A Howling Good Time. 2009. (Little Dogs Rock! Ser.). (Illus.). 32p. (YA). (gr. 2-5). lib. bdg. 25.27 *(978-1-59716-749-9(5))* Bearport Publishing Co., Inc.

Shores, Erika L. All about Beagles, 1 vol. 2012. (Dogs, Dogs, Dogs Ser.). (ENG., Illus.). 24p. (gr. k-1). lib. bdg. 26.65 *(978-1-4296-8722-5(3),* Pebble Plus) Capstone Press of Coughlan Cos.

BEAGLE EXPEDITION (1831-1836)

Ashby, Ruth. Young Charles Darwin & the Voyage of the Beagle, 1 vol. Duranceau, Suzanne, illus. 2009. (ENG.). 128p. (J). (gr. 2-5). 12.95 *(978-1-56145-478-5(8),* Peachtree Junior) Peachtree Pubs.

MacDonald, Fiona. Inside the Beagle with Charles Darwin. Bergin, Mark, illus. 2005. (ENG.). 48p. (J). (gr. 3-6). 19.95 *(978-1-59270-041-7(1))* Enchanted Lion Bks., LLC.

Weaver, Anne H. The Voyage of the Beetle: A Journey Around the World with Charles Darwin & the Search for the Solution to the Mystery of Mysteries, as Narrated by Rosie, an Articulate Beetle. Lawrence, George, illus. 2007. (ENG.).

80p. (J). (gr. 5-8). 19.95 *(978-0-8263-4304-8(X))* Univ. of New Mexico Pr.

BEAGLE EXPEDITION (1831-1836)—FICTION

Meyer, Carolyn. The True Adventures of Charley Darwin. 2011. (ENG., Illus.). 336p. (YA). (gr. 7). pap. 9.99 *(978-0-547-41564-2(8))* Houghton Mifflin Harcourt Publishing Co.

Weaver, Anne H. The Voyage of the Beetle: A Journey Around the World with Charles Darwin & the Search for the Solution to the Mystery of Mysteries, As Narrated by Rosie, an Articulate Beetle. Lawrence, George, tr. Lawrence, George, illus. 2004. (Roman Mysteries Ser.). 80p. (J). (gr. 5-8). lib. bdg. 26.90 *(978-0-7613-2923-7(4))*, Millbrook Pr.) Lerner Publishing Group.

BEAGLES (DOGS)

see Beagle (Dog Breed)

BEARD, DANIEL CARTER, 1850-1941

Seibert, Jerry. Dan Beard: Boy Scout Pioneer. Bjorklung, Lorence, illus. 2012. 192p. 42.95 *(978-1-258-25301-1(1))*; pap. 27.95 *(978-1-258-25517-6(0))* Literary Licensing, LLC.

BEARS

Aboff, Marcie. Do You Really Want to Meet a Polar Bear? Fabbri, Daniele, illus. 2015. (Do You Really Want to Meet... ? Ser.). 24p. (J). 27.10 *(978-1-60753-455-6(X))* Amicus Publishing.

Alinsky, Shelby. National Geographic Readers: Sleep, Bear! 2015. (Readers Ser.). (ENG., Illus.). 24p. (J). (-k). pap. 3.99 *(978-1-4263-1959-4(2)*, National Geographic Children's Bks.) National Geographic Society.

—Sleep, Bear! (1 Hardcover/1 CD) 2017. (National Geographic Kids Ser.). (ENG.). (J). 29.95 ***(978-1-4301-2649-2(3))*** Live Oak Media.

—Sleep, Bear! (1 Paperback/1 CD) 2017. (National Geographic Kids Ser.). (ENG.). (J). pap. 19.95 ***(978-1-4301-2648-5(5))*** Live Oak Media.

—Sleep, Bear! (4 Paperbacks/1 CD), 4 vols. 2017. (National Geographic Kids Ser.). (ENG.). (J). pap., pap. 31.95 ***(978-1-4301-2650-8(7))*** Live Oak Media.

All Kinds of Bears, 6 vols. (Book2WebTM Ser.). (gr. 4-8). 36.50 *(978-0-322-02972-9(4))* Wright Group/McGraw-Hill.

Allen, Kathy. Polar Bears, 1 vol. 2012. (Endangered & Threatened Animals Ser.). (ENG., Illus.). 32p. (gr. 3-4). lib. bdg. 27.99 *(978-1-4296-8432-3(1)*, Snap Bks.) Capstone Press of Coughlan Cos.

Anderson, Jill. Polar Bears. 2007. (Wild Ones Ser.). (ENG.). 24p. (J). (gr. 2-5). 12.95 *(978-1-55971-974-2(5))* Cooper Square Publishing Llc.

Antill, Sara. A Bear's Life. 2012. (Illus.). 24p. (J). 49.50 *(978-1-4488-5102-7(5)*, 1329314, PowerKids Pr.); pap. 8.25 *(978-1-4488-5101-0(7)*, 1329314, PowerKids Pr.); lib. bdg. 22.60 *(978-1-4488-4977-2(2)*, 1329314) Rosen Publishing Group, Inc., The.

—Red Panda. 2010. (Unusual Animals Ser.). (Illus.). 24p. (J). (gr. k-3). (ENG.). pap. 8.15 *(978-1-61533-003-4(8))*; lib. bdg. 22.60 *(978-1-60754-994-9(8))* Windmill Bks.

Arnold, Caroline. A Polar Bear's World, 1 vol. Arnold, Caroline, illus. 2010. (Caroline Arnold's Animals Ser.). (ENG., Illus.). 24p. (gr. k-2). lib. bdg. 27.99 *(978-1-4048-5743-8(5))* Picture Window Bks.

Arnold, Quinn M. Brown Bears. 2017. (J). ***(978-1-60818-866-6(3)***, Creative Education) Creative Co., The.

—Seedlings: Brown Bears. 2017. (Seedlings Ser.). (ENG.). 24p. (J). (gr. -1-1). pap. 7.99 ***(978-1-62832-481-5(3)***, Creative Paperbacks) Creative Co., The.

Bailer, Darice. Why Do Bears Hibernate? 2009. (Tell Me Why, Tell Me How Ser.). 32p. (gr. 3-18). 29.93 *(978-0-7614-3990-5(0))* Marshall Cavendish Corp.

Baines, Becky. A Den Is a Bed for a Bear. 2008. (ZigZag Ser.). (ENG., Illus.). 32p. (J). (gr. k-3). 14.95 *(978-1-4263-0309-8(2))*; lib. bdg. 19.90 *(978-1-4263-0310-4(6))* National Geographic Society. (National Geographic Children's Bks.).

Baines, Rebecca, et al. Arctic Tale: Companion to the Major Motion Picture. 2007. (ENG., Illus.). 32p. (J). (gr. -1-3). lib. bdg. 22.90 *(978-1-4263-0085-1(9))*; per. 5.95 *(978-1-4263-0084-4(0))* National Geographic Society. (National Geographic Children's Bks.).

Barner, Bob & Chronicle Books Staff. Bears! Bears! Bears! 2010. (ENG., Illus.). 32p. (J). (gr. -1-3). 14.99 *(978-0-8118-7057-3(X))* Chronicle Bks. LLC.

Barnes, Julia. The Secret Lives of Brown Bears. 2007. (Secret Lives of Animals Ser.). (Illus.). 32p. (gr. 2-6). lib. bdg. 26.00 *(978-0-8368-7655-0(5)*, Gareth Stevens Learning Library) Stevens, Gareth Publishing LLLP.

—101 Facts about Polar Bears. 2004. (One Hundred One Facts about Predators Ser.). (Illus.). 32p. (gr. 1-4). lib. bdg. 26.00 *(978-0-8368-4038-4(0)*, Gareth Stevens Learning Library) Stevens, Gareth Publishing LLLP.

Barry, Holly, et al. Wisdom of Bear. Du Houx, E. M. Cornell, illus. 2006. 63p. (J). per. 6.95 *(978-1-882190-50-8(5))* Polar Bear & Co.

Bears. (Eyes on Nature Ser.). 32p. (J). (gr. 1). pap. *(978-1-882210-75-6(1))* Action Publishing, Inc.

Bears, Vol. 4. 2005. (Animals, Animals, Animals Ser.). (YA). (gr. k-3). 118.80 *(978-0-7368-4210-5(1)*, Pebble Bks.) Capstone Press of Coughlan Cos.

The Bears: Individual Title Six-Packs. (Sails Literacy Ser.). 16p. (gr. k-18). 27.00 *(978-0-7635-4433-1(7))* Rigby Education.

Bears for Kids: Amazing Pictures & Fun Fact Children Book. 2013. 32p. pap. 12.97 *(978-1-63022-034-1(5))* Speedy Publishing LLC.

Bear's House. Date not set. (Illus.). (J). bds. 4.98 *(978-1-4054-0784-7(0))* Parragon, Inc.

Bears of the World. 2016. (Bears of the World Ser.). 24p. (gr. 3-3). 94.40 *(978-1-5081-4899-9(6))*; pap. 33.00 *(978-1-5081-5249-1(7))* Rosen Publishing Group, Inc., The. (PowerKids Pr.).

Becker, John. Grizzly Bears. 2003. (Returning Wildlife Ser.). (Illus.). 48p. (J). (gr. 3-5). 23.70 *(978-0-7377-1534-7(0)*, Kidhaven) Cengage Gale.

Beckett, Leslie. Polar Bears. 2016. (Bears of the World Ser.). 24p. (J). (gr. 3-3). pap. 8.25 *(978-1-4994-2042-5(0)*, PowerKids Pr.) Rosen Publishing Group, Inc., The.

Benchmark Education Co., LLC. What Do Bears Eat? Big Book. 2014. (Shared Reading Foundations Ser.). (J). (gr. -1). *(978-1-4509-9433-0(4))* Benchmark Education Co.

Berenstain, Jan & Berenstain, Stan. The Berenstain Bears Giant Coloring & Activity Book. 2013. (ENG.). 272p. (J). (gr. -1-2). pap. 7.99 *(978-0-486-49341-1(5))* Dover Pubns., Inc.

Berger, Melvin & Berger, Gilda. Bears. 2010. (Illus.). 16p. (J). pap. *(978-0-545-24439-8(0))* Scholastic, Inc.

—Polar Bears. 2010. (Illus.). 16p. (J). *(978-0-545-16081-0(2))* Scholastic, Inc.

Berman, Ruth. Let's Look at Brown Bears. (Lightning Bolt Books (tm) — Animal Close-Ups Ser.). (ENG., Illus.). 32p. 2015. (gr. 2-3). E-Book 39.99 *(978-1-5124-1054-9(3)*, 9781512410549, Lerner Pubns.) 2009. (gr. k-2). pap. 7.95 *(978-0-7613-5006-4(3))* 2009. (gr. k-2). lib. bdg. 26.60 *(978-0-7613-3890-1(X)*, Lerner Pubns.) Lerner Publishing Group.

Biel, Timothy Levi. Osos Polares. Rountree, Monica, tr. 2003. (Zoobooks Ser.). Orig. Title: Polar Bears. (SPA., Illus.). 24p. (J). (gr. k-6). lib. bdg. 15.95 *(978-1-888153-77-4(6))* Wildlife Education, Ltd.

Bissell, Robert, illus. Robert Bissell's Rabbits & Bears. 2013. (ENG.). (J). 7.95 *(978-0-7649-6476-3(3))* Pomegranate Communications, Inc.

Black Bears. 2013. (American Animals Ser.). 24p. (J). (gr. k-5). pap. 49.50 *(978-1-4777-0955-9(X)*, PowerKids Pr.) Rosen Publishing Group, Inc., The.

Bodden, Valerie. Amazing Animals: Polar Bears. 2011. (ENG.). 24p. (J). (gr. 1-17). pap. 5.99 *(978-1-926722-26-9(4)*, Creative Paperbacks) Creative Co., The.

—Amazing Animals: Polar Bears. 2011. (Amazing Animals Ser.). (ENG.). 24p. (J). (gr. 1-3). pap. 8.99 *(978-0-89812-752-2(1)*, Creative Paperbacks) Creative Co., The.

—Polar Bears. 2010. (Amazing Animals Ser.). 24p. (J). (gr. -1-3). 16.95 *(978-1-58341-811-6(3)*, Creative Education) Creative Co., The.

Boehm, Barbara. Bears I'd Like to Meet! A Bear's-Eye View of 101 Notable Figures in History. 2008. (Illus.). 48p. (YA). 15.95 *(978-0-9728061-7-6(2))* HNB Publishing.

Borgert-Spaniol, Megan. Black Bears. 2015. (North American Animals Ser.). (ENG., Illus.). 24p. (J). (gr. k-3). lib. bdg. 25.95 *(978-1-62617-186-2(6)*, Blastoff! Readers) Bellwether Media.

—Grizzly Bears. 2015. (North American Animals Ser.). (ENG., Illus.). 24p. (J). (gr. k-3). lib. bdg. 25.95 *(978-1-62617-190-9(4)*, Blastoff! Readers) Bellwether Media.

Brannon, Cecelia H. Baby Polar Bears at the Zoo. 2016. (All about Baby Zoo Animals Ser.). (ENG.). 24p. (J). (gr. k-1). pap. 9.35 *(978-0-7660-7154-4(5))*; (Illus.). lib. bdg. 22.60 *(978-0-7660-7156-8(1))* Enslow Pubs., Inc.

Brett, Jeannie. Wild about Bears. Brett, Jeannie, illus. 2014. (ENG., Illus.). 32p. (J). (gr. 1-4). pap. 7.95 *(978-1-58089-419-7(4))* Charlesbridge Publishing, Inc.

Bright, Michael. Exploring Nature - Bears & Pandas: An Intriguing Insight into the Lives of Brown Bears, Polar Bears, Black Bears, Pandas & Others, with 190 Exciting Images: Bears & Pandas: Bears & Pandas. 2015. (ENG., Illus.). 64p. (J). (gr. -1-2). 12.99 *(978-1-86147-389-9(3)*, Armadillo) Anness Publishing GBR. Dist: National Bk. Network.

Brisville, J. C. Invierno en Vid - Grand Oso (Winter - Life of Big Bear) (SPA.). 32p. (J). 17.50 *(978-84-305-6104-9(6))* Susaeta Ediciones, S.A. ESP. Dist: AIMS International Bks., Inc.

Byerly, Robbie & Warren, Heather. Brown Bear or Black Bear. 2011. (ARC Press / Power 100 - Predator Animals Ser.). pap. 45.32 *(978-1-61541-497-0(5))* American Reading Co.

Camm, Martin, illus. Meyers Buch der Baeren. (GER.). 48p. *(978-3-411-07461-7(2))* Bibliographisches Institut & F. A. Brockhaus AG DEU. Dist: i. b. d., Ltd.

Carney, Elizabeth, et al. Face to Face with Polar Bears. 2009. (Face to Face with Animals Ser.). (ENG., Illus.). 32p. (J). (gr. 2-5). pap. 6.95 *(978-1-4263-0548-1(6)*, National Geographic Children's Bks.) National Geographic Society.

Christian, Peggy. Chocolate, a Glacier Grizzly. Cottone-Kolthoff, Carol, illus. (Humane Society of the United States Animal Tales Ser.). 32p. (J). (gr. 1-5). 34.95 incl. audio *(978-1-882728-64-0(5))*; pap. 9.95 incl. audio *(978-1-882728-67-1(X))*; pap. 19.95 incl. audio *(978-1-882728-69-5(6))* Benefactory, Inc., The.

Ciovacco, Justine. Saving the Endangered Grizzly Bear, 01 vols., 1. 2016. (Conservation of Endangered Species Ser.). (ENG., Illus.). 32p. (J). pap. 12.90 *(978-1-5081-0054-6(3)*, Britannica Educational Publishing) Rosen Publishing Group, Inc., The.

Clarke, Catriona. The Life Cycle of a Polar Bear. 2017. (ENG., Illus.). 48p. (J). pap. 8.99 ***(978-0-00-820881-3(6))*** HarperCollins Pubs. Ltd. GBR. Dist: Independent Pubs. Group.

Cotton, Jacqueline S. Polar Bears. 2004. (Pull Ahead Bks.). (J). 22.60 *(978-0-8225-3776-2(1)*, Carolrhoda Bks.); (ENG.). 32p. pap. 7.95 *(978-0-8225-9890-9(6))* Lerner Publishing Group.

Courtauld, Sarah. Bears. Furukawa, Masumi, illus. 2010. (First Reading Level 2 Ser.). 32p. (J). 6.99 *(978-0-7945-2735-8(3)*, Usborne) EDC Publishing.

Curtis, Jennifer Keats. La Historia de Kali: El Rescate de un Oso Polar Huérfano. Gomes, John, illus. 2014.Tr. of Kali's Story: an Orphaned Polar Bear Rescue. (SPA.). 32p. (J). (gr. 1-4). pap. 9.95 *(978-1-62855-226-3(3))* Arbordale Publishing.

—Kali's Story: An Orphaned Polar Bear Rescue, 1 vol. Gomes, John, photos by. 2014. (ENG., Illus.). 32p. (J). (gr. 1-4). 17.95 *(978-1-62855-208-9(5))* Arbordale Publishing.

Daly, Timothy M. Black Bears. 2012. (Nature's Children Ser.). (ENG.). 48p. (J). pap. 6.95 *(978-0-531-25476-9(3))*; lib. bdg. 28.00 *(978-0-531-26831-5(4))* Scholastic Library Publishing.

Davies, Nicola. Ice Bear: In the Steps of the Polar Bear. Blythe, Gary, illus. 2008. (Read & Wonder Ser.). (ENG.). 32p. (J). (gr. -1-3). pap. 6.99 *(978-0-7636-4149-8(9))* Candlewick Pr.

—Ice Bear with Audio, Peggable: Read, Listen, & Wonder: in the Steps of the Polar Bear. Blythe, Gary, illus. 2009. (Read, Listen, & Wonder Ser.). (ENG.). 32p. (J). (gr. -1-3). pap. 9.99 *(978-0-7636-4441-3(2))* Candlewick Pr.

de Hugo, Pierre. Polar Bears. de Hugo, Pierre, illus. 2013. (ENG., Illus.). 36p. (J). (gr. -1-k). 12.99 *(978-1-85103-418-5(8))* Moonlight Publishing, Ltd. GBR. Dist: Independent Pubs. Group.

De la Bédoyère, Camilla. The Wild Life of Bears, 1 vol. 2015. (ENG., Illus.). 24p. (J). lib. bdg. 23.60 *(978-1-4777-5514-3(4)*, Windmill Bks.) Rosen Publishing Group, Inc., The.

De Medeiros, Michael. Polar Bears. 2008. (Amazing Animals Ser.). (Illus.). 24p. (J). (gr. 2-4). pap. 8.95 *(978-1-59036-965-4(3))*; lib. bdg. 24.45 *(978-1-59036-964-7(5))* Weigl Pubs., Inc.

de Seve, Karen & Castaldo, Nancy F. National Geographic Kids Mission: Polar Bear Rescue: All about Polar Bears & How to Save Them. 2014. (NG Kids Mission: Animal Rescue Ser.). (ENG., Illus.). 128p. (J). (gr. 5). lib. bdg. 21.90 *(978-1-4263-1732-3(8)*, National Geographic Children's Bks.) National Geographic Society.

Desmond, Jenni, creator. The Polar Bear. 2016. (ENG., Illus.). 48p. (J). (gr. -1-3). 17.95 *(978-1-59270-200-8(7))* Enchanted Lion Bks., LLC.

Dibble, Traci. Brown Bears. 2011. (Predator Animals Ser.). 16p. pap. 39.62 *(978-1-61541-376-8(6))* American Reading Co.

—Brown Bears. Dibble, Traci, illus. 2010. (1-3Y Animals Ser.). (ENG., Illus.). 16p. (J). (gr. k-2). pap. 5.99 *(978-1-61541-375-1(8))* American Reading Co.

Dibble, Traci & Sánchez, Lucía M. Osos Pardos. 2011. (2Y Animales Depredador Ser.).Tr. of Brown Bears. (SPA.). 16p. (J). (gr. k-2). pap. 6.99 *(978-1-61541-377-5(4))* American Reading Co.

Dineen, Jacqueline. Grizzly Bears. (Amazing Animals Ser.). (Illus.). 24p. (J). 2009. (gr. 2-4). pap. 8.95 *(978-1-60596-642-7(8))* 2009. (gr. 2-4). lib. bdg. 24.45 *(978-1-60596-158-3(2))* 2003. lib. bdg. 21.35 *(978-1-58340-229-0(2))* Weigl Pubs., Inc.

Doudna, Kelly. It's a Baby Black Bear!, 1 vol. 2008. (Baby Mammals Ser.). (ENG., Illus.). 24p. (J). (gr. k-3). lib. bdg. 24.21 *(978-1-60453-023-0(5))* ABDO Publishing Co.

Duden, Jane. Why Do Bears Sleep All Winter? [Chicago]: A Book about Hibernation. 2010. (Why in the World? Ser.). (ENG.). 24p. pap. 6.95 *(978-1-4296-5183-7(0)*, First Facts) Capstone Press of Coughlan Cos.

Durrie, Karen. I Am a Grizzly Bear. 2012. (J). 27.13 *(978-1-61913-225-2(7))*; pap. 12.95 *(978-1-61913-226-9(5))* Weigl Pubs., Inc.

—Oso Gris. 2013. (SPA.). (J). *(978-1-62127-569-5(8))* Weigl Pubs., Inc.

Eason, Sarah. Save the Polar Bear. Geeson, Andrew & Veldhoven, Marijke, illus. 2009. (Save the... Ser.). 32p. (J). (gr. 2-5). lib. bdg. 25.25 *(978-1-4358-2810-0(0))* Rosen Publishing Group, Inc., The.

Edwards, Roberta. Polar Bears: In Danger. Johnson, Pamela, illus. 2008. (Penguin Young Readers, Level 3 Ser.). (ENG.). 48p. (J). (gr. 1-3). mass mkt. 3.99 *(978-0-448-44924-1(2)*, Penguin Young Readers) Penguin Young Readers Group.

Elora, Grace. Bear Cubs. 2011. (Cute & Cuddly: Baby Animals Ser.). (Illus.). 24p. (gr. k-2). 69.20 *(978-1-4339-6148-9(2))*; (J). pap. 8.15 *(978-1-4339-4500-7(2))*; (J). lib. bdg. 22.60 *(978-1-4339-4499-4(5))* Stevens, Gareth Publishing LLLP.

Emily Rose Townsend. Polar Bears [Scholastic]. 2009. (Polar Animals Ser.). 24p. (gr. k-1). pap. 0.34 *(978-1-4296-4225-5(4)*, Pebble Bks.) Capstone Press of Coughlan Cos.

Eszterhas, Suzi. Eye on the Wild: Lion. 2012. (Eye on the Wild Ser.: 3). (Illus.). 32p. (J). *(978-1-84780-310-8(5)*, Frances Lincoln) Quarto Publishing Group UK.

Feldman, Thea. Kingfisher Readers L1: Bears. 2017. (Kingfisher Readers Ser.). (ENG.). 32p. (J). 12.99 *(978-0-7534-7339-9(9)*, 9780753473399, Kingfisher) Roaring Brook Pr.

Fitzgerald, Lee. Brown Bears. 2016. (Bears of the World Ser.). 24p. (J). (gr. 3-3). pap. 8.25 *(978-1-4994-2036-4(6)*, PowerKids Pr.) Rosen Publishing Group, Inc., The.

Flaherty, William. Polar Bear, 1 vol. Christopher, Danny, illus. 2016. (Animals Illustrated Ser.). (ENG.). 24p. (J). (gr. -1-k). 15.95 *(978-1-77227-079-2(2))* Inhabit Media Inc. CAN. Dist: Independent Pubs. Group.

Gagne, Tammy. Black Bears. 2015. (Wild Bears Ser.). (ENG., Illus.). 24p. (J). (gr. 1-4). 19.95 *(978-1-60753-773-1(7))* Amicus Publishing.

—Sloth Bears. 2015. (Wild Bears Ser.). (ENG., Illus.). 24p. (J). (gr. 1-4). 19.95 *(978-1-60753-777-9(X))* Amicus Publishing.

—Spectacled Bears. 2015. (Wild Bears Ser.). (ENG., Illus.). 24p. (J). (gr. 1-4). 19.95 *(978-1-60753-778-6(8))* Amicus Publishing.

—Sun Bears. 2015. (Wild Bears Ser.). (ENG., Illus.). 24p. (J). (gr. 1-4). 19.95 *(978-1-60753-779-3(6))* Amicus Publishing.

Gaines, Richard Marshall. When Bears Attack! 2006. (When Wild Animals Attack! Ser.). (Illus.). 48p. (J). (gr. 4-10). lib. bdg. 25.27 *(978-0-7660-2669-8(8))* Enslow Pubs., Inc.

Gareth Stevens Publishing Staff, contrib. by. Polar Bear. 2004. (All about Wild Animals Ser.). (Illus.). 32p. (gr. k-4). lib. bdg. 26.00 *(978-0-8368-4187-9(5)*, Gareth Stevens Learning Library) Stevens, Gareth Publishing LLLP.

George, Jean Craighead. Winter Moon. 2003. (J). (gr. 3-7). 20.75 *(978-0-8446-7244-1(0))* Smith, Peter Pub., Inc.

Gibbons, Gail. Grizzly Bears. Gibbons, Gail, illus. 2003. (ENG., Illus.). 32p. (J). (gr. k-3). tchr. ed. 17.95 *(978-0-8234-1793-3(X))* Holiday Hse., Inc.

Gilbert, Sara. Giant Short-Faced Bears. 2017. (Illus.). 24p. (J). *(978-1-60818-766-9(7)*, Creative Education) Creative Co., The.

Gilbert, Sara. Ice Age Mega Beasts: Giant Short-Faced Bears. 2017. (Ice Age Mega Beasts Ser.). (ENG., Illus.). 24p. (J). (gr. 1-3). pap. 8.99 ***(978-1-62832-374-0(4)***, Creative Paperbacks) Creative Co., The.

Gish, Melissa. Brown Bears. 2014. 48p. *(978-1-60818-415-6(3)*, Creative Education) Creative Co., The.

—Living Wild: Brown Bears. 2015. (Living Wild Ser.). (ENG.). 48p. (J). (gr. 5-8). pap. 12.00 *(978-1-62832-001-5(X)*, Creative Paperbacks) Creative Co., The.

Goecke, Michael P. Short-Faced Bear, 1 vol. 2003. (Prehistoric Animals Set II Ser.). (ENG.). 24p. (gr. k-4). 25.65 *(978-1-57765-976-1(7)*, Buddy Bks.) ABDO Publishing Co.

Goldish, Meish. Brown Bear: The Biggest Meat-Eater on Land. 2010. (More SuperSized! Ser.). (Illus.). 24p. (J). (gr. k-3). lib. bdg. 22.61 *(978-1-936087-25-9(1))* Bearport Publishing Co., Inc.

Gray, Susan H. Bears Hibernate. 2015. (Tell Me Why Library). (ENG., Illus.). 24p. (J). (gr. 2-5). pap. 12.79 *(978-1-63362-029-2(8)*, 205873) Cherry Lake Publishing.

Great Big Grizzlies. 2013. (Great Big Animals Ser.). 24p. (J). (gr. k-2). pap. 48.90 *(978-1-4339-9434-0(8))* Stevens, Gareth Publishing LLLP.

Green, Emily. Bears. 2010. (Backyard Wildlife Ser.). (ENG., Illus.). 24p. (J). (gr. k-3). lib. bdg. 25.95 *(978-1-60014-437-0(3)*, Blastoff! Readers) Bellwether Media.

Green, Jen. Bears. 2011. (Amazing Animal Hunters Ser.). (Illus.). 32p. (J). 28.50 *(978-1-60753-044-2(9))* Amicus Publishing.

—Bears. 2012. (Illus.). 32p. (gr. 3-5). pap. 8.95 *(978-1-926722-48-1(5))* Saunders Bk. Co. CAN. Dist: RiverStream Publishing.

Greene, Jacqueline Dembar. Grizzly Bears: Saving the Silvertip. 2007. (America's Animal Comebacks Ser.). (Illus.). 32p. (YA). (gr. 2-5). lib. bdg. 25.27 *(978-1-59716-533-4(6))* Bearport Publishing Co., Inc.

Gregory, Josh. Polar Bears. 2012. (21st Century Basic Skills Library: Baby Zoo Animals Ser.). (ENG.). 24p. (gr. k-3). (J). 22.79 *(978-1-61080-459-2(7)*, 202069); pap. 12.79 *(978-1-61080-633-6(6)*, 202243) Cherry Lake Publishing.

Guiberson, Brenda Z. Moon Bear. Young, Ed, illus. 2010. (ENG.). 40p. (J). (gr. -1-3). 16.99 *(978-0-8050-8977-6(2)*, 9780805089776, Holt, Henry & Co. Bks. For Young Readers) Holt, Henry & Co.

Guidoux, Valerie. Little Bears. 2006. (Born to Be Wild Ser.). (Illus.). 24p. (gr. k-3). lib. bdg. 23.00 *(978-0-8368-6696-4(7)*, Gareth Stevens Learning Library) Stevens, Gareth Publishing LLLP.

—Little Polar Bears. 2005. (Born to Be Wild Ser.). (Illus.). 24p. (gr. k-3). lib. bdg. 23.00 *(978-0-8368-4739-0(3)*, Gareth Stevens Learning Library) Stevens, Gareth Publishing LLLP.

—Ositos. 2006. (Nacidos para Ser Salvajes Ser.). (SPA., Illus.). 24p. (gr. k-3). lib. bdg. 23.00 *(978-0-8368-7424-2(2)*, Gareth Stevens Learning Library) Stevens, Gareth Publishing LLLP.

Guillain, Charlotte. Powerful Polar Bears, 1 vol. 2013. (Walk on the Wild Side Ser.). (ENG.). 32p. (gr. 1-3). 29.99 *(978-1-4109-5218-9(5))*; pap. 8.95 *(978-1-4109-5225-7(8))* Heinemann-Raintree. (Read Me!).

Gunderson, Megan M. Bears: Level 1. Keimig, Candice, illus. 2014. (Magic Readers Ser.). (ENG.). 24p. (J). (gr. 5-9). 24.21 *(978-1-62402-057-5(7))* ABDO Publishing Co.

—Bears Eat & Grow: Level 2. Keimig, Candice, illus. 2014. (Magic Readers Ser.). (ENG.). 24p. (J). (gr. 5-9). 24.21 *(978-1-62402-058-2(5))* ABDO Publishing Co.

—Bears in the Mountains: Level 3. Keimig, Candice, illus. 2014. (Magic Readers Ser.). (ENG.). 24p. (J). (gr. 5-9). 24.21 *(978-1-62402-059-9(3))* ABDO Publishing Co.

Hall, Katharine. Osos Polares y Pingüinos: Un Libro de Comparación y Contraste. 2014.Tr. of Polar Bears & Penguins: a Compare & Contrast Book. (SPA.). 32p. (J). (gr. -1-3). pap. 9.95 *(978-1-62855-227-0(1))* Arbordale Publishing.

Hall, Katherine. Polar Bears & Penguins: A Compare & Contrast Book, 1 vol. 2014. (Compare & Contrast Ser.). (ENG., Illus.). 32p. (J). (gr. -1-3). 17.95 *(978-1-62855-209-6(3))* Arbordale Publishing.

Hamilton, S. L. Bears. 2010. (Xtreme Predators Ser.). 32p. (gr. 3-9). 27.07 *(978-1-60453-990-5(9)*, A&D Xtreme) ABDO Publishing Co.

Hamilton, Sue. Mauled by a Bear, 1 vol. 2010. (Close Encounters of the Wild Kind Ser.). (ENG.). 32p. (YA). (gr. 4-7). 27.07 *(978-1-60453-932-5(1))* ABDO Publishing Co.

Hanel, Rachael. Polar Bears. 2009. (Living Wild Ser.). 48p. 22.95 *(978-1-58341-741-6(9)*, Creative Education) Creative Co., The.

Harkrader, Lisa. The Grizzly Bear: A MyReportLinks.com Book. 2005. (Endangered & Threatened Animals Ser.). (Illus.). 48p. (J). (gr. 4-10). lib. bdg. 26.60 *(978-0-7660-5066-2(1)*, MyReportLinks.com Bks.) Enslow Pubs., Inc.

Hatkoff, Craig. Knut: How One Little Polar Bear Captivated the World. 2007. (J). pap. 16.99 *(978-0-545-04717-3(X)*, Scholastic Pr.) Scholastic, Inc.

Haywood, Karen Diane. Bears. 2008. (Endangered! Ser.). 48p. (gr. 3-18). lib. bdg. 29.93 *(978-0-7614-2987-6(5)*, Benchmark Bks.) Marshall Cavendish Corp.

Helbrough, Emma. Bears. Kushii, Tetsuo & Larkum, Adam, illus. 2006. (Beginners Nature: Level 1 Ser.). 32p. (J). (gr. k-2). 4.99 *(978-0-7945-1393-1(X))*; (gr. 1). lib. bdg. 12.99 *(978-1-58086-941-6(6))* EDC Publishing. (Usborne).

Herriott, Charlotte. Boa Constrictor vs. Grizzly Bear. 2015. (Bizarre Beast Battles Ser.). (ENG., Illus.). 24p. (J). (gr. 2-3). pap. 8.15 *(978-1-4824-2780-6(X))* Stevens, Gareth Publishing LLLP.

Hirsch, Rebecca E. Grizzly Bears: Huge Hibernating Mammals. 2015. (Comparing Animal Traits Ser.). (ENG., Illus.). 32p. (gr. 2-4). 39.99 *(978-1-4677-8924-0(0)*, Lerner Digital); (J). pap. 8.99 *(978-1-4677-6061-4(7)*, Lerner Pubns.); (J). lib. bdg. 26.65 *(978-1-4677-5578-8(8)*, Lerner Pubns.) Lerner Publishing Group.

—Top 50 Reasons to Care about Polar Bears: Animals in Peril. 2010. (Top 50 Reasons to Care about Endangered Animals Ser.). (Illus.). 104p. (J). (gr. 5-9). 33.27 *(978-0-7660-3458-7(5))* Enslow Pubs., Inc.

Hirschi, Ron. Searching for Grizzlies. Cooper, Deborah, illus. Mangelsen, Thomas, photos by. 2005. (ENG.). 32p. (J). (gr. 2-7). 16.95 *(978-1-59078-014-5(0))* Boyds Mills Pr.

—Searching for Grizzlies. Mangelsen, Thomas D. & Cooper, Deborah, illus. Mangelsen, Thomas D., photos by. 2005. (J). *(978-1-4156-2797-6(5))* Boyds Mills Pr.

Hodge, Deborah. Looking at Bears. Stephens, Pat, illus. 2008. (Kids Can Read Ser.). (ENG.). 32p. (J). (gr. k-1). pap. 3.95 *(978-1-55453-250-6(7))* Kids Can Pr., Ltd. CAN. Dist: Hachette Bk. Group.

Hoff, Mary King. Polar Bears. 2005. (Wild World of Animals (Creative Education) Ser.). (Illus.). 32p. (J). (gr. 2-5). lib. bdg. 18.95 *(978-1-58341-353-1(7)*, Creative Education) Creative Co., The.

Holloway, Jamie. All about Bears. 2015. (Rosen REAL Readers: STEM & STEAM Collection). (ENG.). 8p. pap. 5.46 *(978-1-4994-9687-1(7)*, Rosen Classroom) Rosen Publishing Group, Inc., The.

Howse, Jennifer. Spirit Bears. 2010. (Illus.). 24p. (978-1-55388-662-4(3)); pap. (978-1-55388-663-1(1)) Weigl Educational Pubs. Ltd.

Hudak, Heather C. Bears. 2008. (Backyard Animals Ser.). (Illus.). 24p. (J). (gr. 4-7). lib. bdg. 24.45 (978-1-60596-000-5(4)) Weigl Pubs., Inc.

Hudak, Heather C., ed. Bears. 2008. (Backyard Animals Ser.). (Illus.). 24p. (J). (gr. 4-7). pap. 8.95 (978-1-60596-006-7(3)) Weigl Pubs., Inc.

Hunt, Joni Phelps & London Town Press Staff. A Band of Bears: The Rambling Life of a Lovable Loner. León, Vicki, ed. 2nd ed. 2006. (Jean-Michel Cousteau Presents Ser.). (ENG., Illus.). 48p. (J). (gr. 4-9). pap. 8.95 (978-0-9766134-5-9(X)) London Town Pr.

Hutchison, Patricia & Peterson, Sheryl. Polar Bears. 2015. (Endangered Animals Ser.). (ENG.). 24p. (J). (gr. 1-4). 27.07 (978-1-63143-970-4(7), 208805) Child's World, Inc., The.

Jackson, Tom. Black Bears. 2008. (Nature's Children Ser.). (Illus.). 52p. (J). (978-0-7172-6250-2(2)) Grolier, Ltd.

Jeffries, Joyce. Black Bears. 2016. (Bears of the World Ser.). 24p. (J). (gr. 3-3). pap. 8.25 (978-1-4994-2032-6(3), PowerKids Pr.) Rosen Publishing Group, Inc., The.

Johnson, Gee. Polar Bears. 2011. (ARC Press / Predator Animals Ser.). pap. 39.62 (978-1-61541-482-6(7)); 24p. (J). pap. 6.95 (978-1-61541-395-9(2)) American Reading Co.

—Polar Bears. Johnson, Gee, illus. 2011. (1-3Y Marine Life Exploration Ser.). (ENG., Illus.). 16p. (J). (gr. k-2). pap. 5.99 (978-1-61541-481-9(9)) American Reading Co.

Johnson, Jinny. Brown Bear. 2014. (North American Mammals Ser.). 24p. (gr. 2-5). 28.50 (978-1-62588-032-1(4)) Black Rabbit Bks.

—Brown Bear. 2014. (North American Mammals Ser.). (ENG., Illus.). 24p. (J). (gr. -1-4). pap. 8.95 (978-1-77092-167-2(2)) Saunders Bk. Co. CAN. Dist: RiverStream Publishing.

—Polar Bear. Rosewarne, Graham, illus. 2007. (Zoo Animals in the Wild Ser.). 32p. (J). (gr. -1-3). lib. bdg. 28.50 (978-1-58340-901-5(7)) Black Rabbit Bks.

Kalman, Bobbie. Baby Bears. 2008. (It's Fun to Learn about Baby Animals Ser.). (ENG., Illus.). 24p. (J). (gr. 3-7). pap. (978-0-7787-3968-5(6)); lib. bdg. (978-0-7787-3949-4(X)) Crabtree Publishing Co.

—Baby Polar Bears. 2010. (Fun to Learn about Baby Animals Ser.). (ENG.). 24p. (J). (gr. k-3). (978-0-7787-4894-6(4)); (Illus.). pap. (978-0-7787-4899-1(5)) Crabtree Publishing Co.

—Polar Bear Family Adventures. 2016. (ENG., Illus.). 32p. (J). (978-0-7787-2228-1(7)) Crabtree Publishing Co.

Kalman, Bobbie & Burns, Kylie. Endangered Bears. 2007. (Earth's Endangered Animals Ser.). (ENG., Illus.). 32p. (J). (gr. 1-5). lib. bdg. (978-0-7787-1861-1(1)); pap. (978-0-7787-1907-6(3)) Crabtree Publishing Co.

Kalman, Bobbie & Crossingham, John. Les Ours. 2003. (Petit Monde Vivant Ser.). (FRE., Illus.). 32p. (J). pap. 9.95 (978-2-89579-007-5(8)) Bayard Canada Livres CAN. Dist: Crabtree Publishing Co.

Kavanagh, James. The World of Bears. 2014. (Jeff Corwin's Explorer Ser.). (ENG., Illus.). 12p. 7.95 (978-1-58355-818-8(7)) Western National Parks Assn.

Kissock, Heather. Black Bears. 2016. (J). **(978-1-4896-5390-1(2))** Weigl Pubs., Inc.

Kolpin, Molly. American Black Bears, 1 vol. 2011. (Bears Ser.). (ENG., 24p. (gr. 1-2). Illus.). pap. 7.29 (978-1-4296-7183-5(1)); pap. 41.70 (978-1-4296-7184-2(X)); (Illus.). lib. bdg. 25.32 (978-1-4296-6131-7(3)) Capstone Press of Coughlan Cos. (First Facts).

—Bears. 2011. (Bears Ser.). (ENG.). 24p. (gr. 1-2). pap. 166.80 (978-1-4296-7192-7(0)); pap. 21.87 (978-1-4296-7191-0(2)); lib. bdg. 101.28 (978-1-4296-6133-1(X)) Capstone Press of Coughlan Cos. (First Facts).

—Grizzly Bears, 1 vol. (North American Animals Ser.). (ENG.). 24p. 2012. (gr. k-1). lib. bdg. 26.65 (978-1-4296-8740-9(1), Pebble Plus) 2011. (gr. 1-2). pap. 7.29 (978-1-4296-7187-3(4), First Facts) 2011. (gr. 1-2). pap. 41.70 (978-1-4296-7188-0(2), First Facts) 2011. (gr. 1-2). lib. bdg. 25.32 (978-1-4296-6129-4(1), First Facts) Capstone Press of Coughlan Cos.

—Polar Bears. 2011. (Bears Ser.). (ENG.). 24p. (gr. 1-2). pap. 41.70 (978-1-4296-7190-3(4)); lib. bdg. 25.32 (978-1-4296-6130-0(5)) Capstone Press of Coughlan Cos. (First Facts).

Kras, Sara Louise. The Hunted: Polar Prey. 2014. 64p. (J). 15.95 (978-1-62285-080-8(7)) Enslow Pubs., Inc.

Kuskowski, Alex. Bears, 1 vol. 2014. (Zoo Animals Ser.). (ENG.). 24p. (J). (gr. k-3). lib. bdg. 24.21 (978-1-62403-271-4(0), SandCastle) ABDO Publishing Co.

Kvatum, Lia. Saving Yasha: The Incredible True Story of an Adopted Moon Bear. Pokrovskaya, Liya, photos by. 2012. (ENG., Illus.). 32p. (J). (gr. -1-3). lib. bdg. 25.90 (978-1-4263-1076-8(5), National Geographic Children's Bks.) National Geographic Society.

Lackner, Michelle Myers. Finding Hope, 1 vol. North American Bear Center Staff, photos by. 2013. (ENG., Illus.). 40p. (J). (gr. -1-3). pap. 14.95 (978-1-59193-373-1(0)) Adventure Pubns.

Lake, G. G. North American Black Bears. 2016. (Woodland Wildlife Ser.). (ENG., Illus.). 24p. (gr. k-1). lib. bdg. 26.65 (978-1-5157-0814-8(4), Pebble Plus) Capstone Press of Coughlan Cos.

Landau, Elaine. Polar Bears: Hunters of the Snow & Ice. 2010. (Animals of the Snow & Ice Ser.). (Illus.). 32p. (J). (gr. 1-3). 23.94 (978-0-7660-3461-7(5)) Enslow Pubs., Inc.

Leathers, Dan. Polar Bears on the Hudson Bay. 2007. (On the Verge of Extinction Ser.). (Illus.). 32p. (YA). (gr. 2-5). lib. bdg. 25.70 (978-1-58415-586-7(8)) Mitchell Lane Pubs., Inc.

LeChance, Polly. Bears & Cubs. 2017. (Animal Family Ser.). 24p. (gr. k-k). pap. 8.15 **(978-1-4824-6369-9(5))** Stevens, Gareth Publishing LLLP.

The Life of a Bear: His Birth, Education & Adventure. 2004. reprint ed. pap. 27.95 (978-1-4179-4276-3(2)) Kessinger Publishing, LLC.

Lindeen, Mary. Polar Bears. 2013. (ENG., Illus.). 24p. (J). lib. bdg. 25.65 (978-1-62031-067-0(8)) Jump! Inc.

Llanas, Sheila Griffin. Grizzly Bears, 1 vol. 2013. (Animal Icons Ser.). (ENG.). 32p. (J). (gr. 3-6). lib. bdg. 27.07 (978-1-61783-572-8(2), Checkerboard Library) ABDO Publishing Co.

Lourie, Peter. The Polar Bear Scientist. 2015. (Scientists in the Field Ser.). lib. bdg. 20.85 (978-0-606-37373-9(X)) Turtleback Bks.

Lukas, Catherine. Bears. 2006. (J). 7.99 (978-1-59939-036-9(1)) Cornerstone Pr.

—Bears. 2009. (Amazing Animals Ser.). 48p. (J). (gr. 2-6). pap. 10.50 (978-1-4339-2021-9(2), Gareth Stevens Learning Library); (gr. 3-6). lib. bdg. 28.00 (978-0-8368-9104-1(X)) Stevens, Gareth Publishing LLLP.

Mack, Dinah & van Gageldonk, Mack. Vicks, the Polar Bear Cub. 2013. (ENG.). 32p. (J). (gr. -1-k). 15.95 (978-1-60537-154-2(8)) Cobblestone Publishing Co.

Macken, JoAnn Early. Black Bears. 2nd rev. ed. 2009. (Animals That Live in the Forest Ser.). (ENG.). 24p. (J). (gr. -1-3). pap. 8.15 (978-1-4339-2478-1(1)); lib. bdg. 22.60 (978-1-4339-2402-6(1)) Stevens, Gareth Publishing LLLP.

—Black Bears: Osos Negros. 2nd rev. ed. 2009. (Animals That Live in the Forest/Animales del bosque Ser.). (ENG & SPA.). 24p. (J). (gr. -1-3). pap. 8.15 (978-1-4339-2485-9(4)); lib. bdg. 22.60 (978-1-4339-2434-7(X)) Stevens, Gareth Publishing LLLP. (Weekly Reader Leveled Readers).

Macleod, Steve. Giant Panda. 2011. (J). 27.13 (978-1-61690-756-3(8)); pap. 12.95 (978-1-61690-763-1(0)) Weigl Pubs., Inc.

—Polar Bear. 2011. (J). 27.13 (978-1-61690-759-4(2)); pap. 12.95 (978-1-61690-852-2(1)) Weigl Pubs., Inc.

—Soy el Oso Polar. 2012. (SPA.). (J). (978-1-61913-178-1(1)) Weigl Pubs., Inc.

Maday, Gregory. Hunting with Grizzly Bears. 2012. (Animal Attack! Ser.). (Illus.). 24p. (J). (gr. 2-5). 22.60 (978-1-4339-7079-5(1)); pap. 8.15 (978-1-4339-7080-1(5)) Stevens, Gareth Publishing LLLP. (Gareth Stevens Learning Library).

Magby, Meryl. Black Bears. 2013. 24p. (J). (gr. k-5). 22.60 (978-1-4777-0791-3(3)); pap. 8.25 (978-1-4777-0954-2(1)) Rosen Publishing Group, Inc., The. (PowerKids Pr.).

Markle, Sandra. Grizzly Bears. 2009. (Animal Predators Ser.). (ENG.). 40p. (gr. 3-6). 26.60 (978-1-58013-537-5(4)) Lerner Publishing Group.

—Polar Bears. (Animal Predators Ser.). 40p. 2005. (J). (gr. 4-6). pap. 7.95 (978-1-57505-746-0(8)) 2004. (ENG., Illus.). (gr. 3-6). lib. bdg. 26.60 (978-1-57505-730-9(1)) Lerner Publishing Group.

—Waiting for Ice. Marks, Alan, illus. 2012. (ENG.). 32p. (J). (gr. -1-3). 15.95 (978-1-58089-255-1(8)) Charlesbridge Publishing, Inc.

Marquardt, Meg. Polar Bears on the Hunt. 2017. (Searchlight Books (tm) — Predators Ser.). (ENG.). (J). (gr. 3-5). pap. 9.99 **(978-1-5124-5611-0(X))**; (Illus.). lib. bdg. 30.65 **(978-1-5124-3397-5(7))** Lerner Publishing Group.

Marsh, Laura. National Geographic Readers: Polar Bears. 2013. (Readers Ser.). (ENG., Illus.). 32p. (J). (gr. -1-1). lib. bdg. 13.90 (978-1-4263-1105-5(2), National Geographic Children's Bks.) National Geographic Society.

—Polar Bears. 2013. (Readers Ser.). (ENG., Illus.). 32p. (J). (gr. -1-1). pap. 3.99 (978-1-4263-1104-8(4), National Geographic Children's Bks.) National Geographic Society.

Marsico, Katie. Bears. 2017. (True Book(tm) — The Most Endangered Ser.). (ENG., Illus.). 48p. (J). lib. bdg. 31.00 (978-0-531-22725-1(1), Children's Pr.) Scholastic Library Publishing.

—Polar Bear, 1 vol. 2011. (Day in the Life: Polar Animals Ser.). (ENG.). 24p. (gr. k-2). pap. 6.79 (978-1-4329-5335-5(4), Heinemann Read & Learn) Heinemann-Raintree.

Mason, Conrad. Polar Bears: Internet-Referenced. Howarth, Daniel, illus. 2009. (First Reading Level 4 Ser.). 48p. (J). 6.99 (978-0-7945-2457-9(5), Usborne) EDC Publishing.

McBratney, Sam. Todos Son Mis Favoritos. Jeram, Anita, illus. 2004.Tr. of You're All My Favorites. (SPA.). 32p. (J). 16.99 (978-84-88342-67-6(5)) S.A. Kokinos ESP. Dist: Lectorum Pubns., Inc.

McDowell, Pamela. Black Bear. 2012. (J). 27.13 (978-1-61913-267-2(2)); pap. 27.13 (978-1-61913-271-9(0)) Weigl Pubs., Inc.

—Osos Negros. 2013. (Animales en Mi Patio Ser.). (SPA., Illus.). 24p. (J). (gr. -1-3). lib. bdg. 27.13 (978-1-62127-595-4(7), AV2 by Weigl) Weigl Pubs., Inc.

McRae, Anne & Morris, Neil. Mattie the Polar Bear. De Luca, Daniela, illus. 2017. (J). **(978-0-7166-3526-0(7))** World Bk., Inc.

Meinking, Mary. Polar Bear vs. Seal, 1 vol. 2011. (Predator vs. Prey Ser.). (ENG., Illus.). 32p. (gr. 1-2). pap. 8.29 (978-1-4109-3948-7(0), Read Me!) Heinemann-Raintree.

Meister, Cari. Brown Bears. 2015. (J). lib. bdg. 25.65 (978-1-62031-166-0(6), Bullfrog Bks.) Jump! Inc.

Merritt, Robin. The Life Cycle of a Polar Bear. 2011. (Life Cycles Ser.). (ENG., Illus.). 32p. (J). (gr. k-3). lib. bdg. 29.93 (978-1-60973-190-8(5), 201176) Child's World, Inc., The.

Middleton, Don. Polar Bears. 2012. (Animals on the Brink Ser.). (ENG., Illus.). 48p. (J). (gr. 4-7). lib. bdg. 29.99 (978-1-61913-429-4(2), AV2 by Weigl) Weigl Pubs., Inc.

—Polar Bears with Code. 2012. (Animals on the Brink Ser.). (ENG., Illus.). 48p. (J). (gr. 4-7). pap. 14.95 (978-1-61913-430-0(6), AV2 by Weigl) Weigl Pubs., Inc.

Miller, Debbie S. Grizzly Bears of Alaska: Explore the Wild World of Bears. Endres, Patrick J., photos by. 2014. (Paws IV Ser.). (ENG., Illus.). 32p. (J). (gr. k-3). pap. 10.99 (978-1-57061-932-8(8), Little Bigfoot) Sasquatch Bks.

—A Polar Bear Journey. Van Zyle, Jon, illus. 2005. (ENG.). 32p. (J). (gr. 1-4). pap. 8.99 (978-0-8027-7715-7(5), 9780802777157, Bloomsbury USA Childrens) Bloomsbury Publishing USA.

Miller, Sara Swan. Polar Bears of the Arctic. 2009. (Brrr! Polar Animals Ser.). (Illus.). 24p. (J). (gr. k-5). pap. 8.25 (978-1-4358-3145-2(4), PowerKids Pr.); 24p. (gr. 2-3). 42.50 (978-1-61511-751-2(2), PowerKids Pr.); (J). (gr. k-3). lib. bdg. 22.60 (978-1-4358-2741-7(4)) Rosen Publishing Group, Inc., The.

Milton, Joyce. Bears Are Curious. Santoro, Christopher, illus. 2015. (Step into Reading Ser.). (ENG.). 32p. (J). (gr. -1-1). pap. 3.99 (978-0-679-85301-5(4), Random Hse. Bks. for Young Readers) Random Hse. Children's Bks.

Mineo, Kate. Compare with Bears. 2011. (Animal Math Ser.). (Illus.). 24p. (J). (gr. 1-3). pap. 8.15 (978-1-4339-5660-7(8)); lib. bdg. 22.60 (978-1-4339-5658-4(6)) Stevens, Gareth Publishing LLLP.

Morgan, Sally. Bears. 2004. (QEB Animal Lives Ser.). (Illus.). 32p. (J). lib. bdg. 18.95 (978-1-59566-033-6(X)) QEB Publishing Inc.

Murray, Julie. Black Bears, 1 vol. 2005. (Animal Kingdom Set Ii Ser.). (ENG., Illus.). 24p. (gr. k-4). 25.65 (978-1-59197-302-7(3), Buddy Bks.) ABDO Publishing Co.

—Grizzly Bears, 1 vol. 2003. (Animal Kingdom Ser.). (ENG.). 24p. (gr. k-4). 25.65 (978-1-57765-715-6(2), Buddy Bks.) ABDO Publishing Co.

—Polar Bears, 1 vol. (Arctic Animals Ser.). (ENG.). 2013. 32p. (J). (gr. 2-5). lib. bdg. 28.50 (978-1-61783-799-9(7), Big Buddy Bks.) 2005. (Illus.). 24p. (gr. k-4). 25.65 (978-1-59197-332-4(5), Buddy Bks.) ABDO Publishing Co.

—Sloth Bears, 1 vol. 2013. (Asian Animals Ser.). (ENG.). 32p. (J). (gr. 2-5). lib. bdg. 28.50 (978-1-61783-557-5(9), Big Buddy Bks.) ABDO Publishing Co.

Nagda, Ann Whitehead & Bickel, Cindy. Polar Bear Math: Learning about Fractions from Klondike & Snow. 2007. (ENG., Illus.). 32p. (J). (gr. -1-3). per. 8.99 (978-0-312-37749-6(5), 9780312377496) Square Fish.

Nagelhout, Ryan. Great Big Grizzlies. 2013. (Great Big Animals Ser.). 24p. (J). (gr. k-2). pap. 8.15 (978-1-4339-9433-3(X)); (ENG., Illus.). lib. bdg. 22.60 (978-1-4339-9432-6(1)) Stevens, Gareth Publishing LLLP.

—Great Big Grizzlies / Enormes Osos Pardos. 2013. (Great Big Animals / Superanimales Ser.). (SPA.). 24p. (J). (gr. k-2). 22.60 (978-1-4339-9442-5(9)) Stevens, Gareth Publishing LLLP.

National Geographic Kids. National Geographic Readers: Bears. 2016. (Readers Ser.). (ENG., Illus.). 48p. (J). (gr. 1-4). pap. 3.99 (978-1-4263-2444-4(8), National Geographic Children's Bks.) National Geographic Society.

National Geographic Kids Staff. Bears. (Readers Ser.). (ENG., (J). 2016. Illus.). 48p. (gr. 1-4). lib. bdg. 13.90 (978-1-4263-2445-1(6)) 2015. 24p. (-k). bds. 6.99 (978-1-4263-1875-7(8)) National Geographic Society. (National Geographic Children's Bks.).

Nault, Jennifer. Project Polar Bear. Kissock, Heather & Marshall, Diana, eds. 2003. (Zoo Life Ser.). (Illus.). 24p. (J). pap. 8.95 (978-1-59036-060-6(5)) Weigl Pubs., Inc.

Neal, Chuck. Grizzlies in the Mist. 2003. (Illus.). 160p. pap. 14.95 (978-0-943972-75-6(2), 75-2) Homestead Publishing.

Newman, Aline Alexander. Rascally Rabbits! And More True Stories of Animals Behaving Badly! 2016. (NGK Chapters Ser.). (ENG., Illus.). 112p. (J). (gr. 2-5). pap. 5.99 (978-1-4263-2308-9(5), National Geographic Children's Bks.) National Geographic Society.

Newman, Mark. Moon Bears. 2015. (ENG., Illus.). 32p. (J). (gr. -1-3). 18.99 (978-0-8050-9344-5(3), 9780805093445, Holt, Henry & Co. Bks. For Young Readers) Holt, Henry & Co.

—Polar Bears. 2015. 32p. pap. 8.00 (978-1-61003-613-9(1)) Center for the Collaborative Classroom.

—Polar Bears. Newman, Mark, illus. 2010. (ENG., Illus.). 32p. (J). (gr. -1-3). 16.99 (978-0-8050-8999-8(3), 9780805089998, Holt, Henry & Co. Bks. For Young Readers) Holt, Henry & Co.

—Polar Bears. 2015. (J). lib. bdg. 17.20 (978-0-606-37974-8(6)) Turtleback Bks.

Niebergall, Jane Sutherland. Bears to Barely Bears. 2005. (Cross-Curricular/Thematic Studies). (gr. 6-18). 9.95 (978-1-878051-12-7(1)) Circumpolar Pr.

Olson, Gillia M. Polar Bears' Search for Ice: A Cause & Effect Investigation, 1 vol. 2010. (Animals on the Edge Ser.). (ENG.). 32p. (gr. 3-4). lib. bdg. 27.32 (978-1-4296-4532-4(6), Fact Finders) Capstone Press of Coughlan Cos.

Omoth, Tyler. American Black Bears. 2017. (Animals of North America (paperback) Ser.). (ENG., Illus.). 32p. (J). (gr. 3-5). pap. 9.95 **(978-1-63517-086-3(9)**, Focus Readers) North Star Editions.

Orme, Helen. Polar Bears in Danger. 2006. (Wildlife Survival Ser.). (Illus.). 32p. (J). (gr. 2-5). lib. bdg. 25.27 (978-1-59716-264-7(7)) Bearport Publishing Co., Inc.

Orr, Tamra B. Polar Bears. 2013. (Nature's Children Ser.). (ENG.). 48p. (J). 28.00 (978-0-531-20980-6(6)); pap. 6.95 (978-0-531-24306-0(0)) Scholastic Library Publishing. (Children's Pr.).

Los Osos. (Fascinante Mundo de... Ser.). 8.95 (978-958-04-3229-6(5)) Norma S.A. COL. Dist: Distribuidora Norma, Inc.

Owen, Ruth. Brawny Bears. 2012. (Eye to Eye with Animals Ser.). (ENG., Illus.). 32p. (J). (gr. k-5). 25.25 (978-1-4488-8068-3(8)); pap. 10.00 (978-1-4488-8104-8(8)) Windmill Bks.

—Grizzly Bears. 2012. (Dr. Bob's Amazing World of Animals Ser.). (Illus.). 32p. (J). (gr. k-5). pap. 11.75 (978-1-61533-562-6(5)); lib. bdg. 26.50 (978-1-61533-551-0(X)) Windmill Bks.

—Polar Bear Cubs. 2011. (Wild Baby Animals Ser.). 24p. (J). (gr. k-3). lib. bdg. 19.96 (978-1-61772-157-1(3)); lib. bdg., E-Book 39.93 (978-1-61772-241-7(3)) Bearport Publishing Co., Inc.

—Polar Bears. 2012. (Dr. Bob's Amazing World of Animals Ser.). (ENG.). 32p. (J). (gr. k-5). pap. 11.75 (978-1-61533-552-7(8)); lib. bdg. 26.50 (978-1-61533-546-6(3)) Windmill Bks.

Owings, Lisa. Bear Attack. 2012. (Animal Attacks Ser.). (ENG., Illus.). 24p. (J). (gr. 3-7). lib. bdg. 25.95 (978-1-60014-786-9(0), Torque Bks.) Bellwether Media.

—The Grizzly Bear. 2012. (Nature's Deadliest Ser.). (ENG., Illus.). 24p. (J). (gr. 3-8). lib. bdg. 25.95 (978-1-60014-742-5(9), Pilot Bks.) Bellwether Media.

—The Grizzly Bear. 2012. (ENG., Illus.). 24p. 23.00 (978-0-531-20881-6(8), Children's Pr.) Scholastic Library Publishing.

—The Polar Bear. 2013. (Nature's Deadliest Ser.). (ENG., Illus.). 24p. (J). (gr. 3-8). lib. bdg. 25.95 (978-1-60014-882-8(4), Pilot Bks.) Bellwether Media.

Pallotta, Jerry. Polar Bear vs. Grizzly Bear. Bolster, Rob, illus. 2015. (Who Would Win? Ser.). (ENG.). 32p. (J). (gr. 1-3). pap. 3.99 (978-0-545-17572-2(0)) Scholastic, Inc.

Parker, Steve. Bears. Morandi, Andrea, illus. 2010. (I Love Animals Ser.). (ENG.). 24p. (J). (gr. 1-5). pap. 8.15 (978-1-61533-232-8(4)); lib. bdg. 22.60 (978-1-61533-226-7(X)) Windmill Bks.

Pearl, Norman. Grizzly Bears: Wild & Strong. 2009. (Powerful Predators Ser.). 24p. (gr. 2-3). 42.50 (978-1-60851-346-8(7)); (Illus.). (J). lib. bdg. 22.60 (978-1-4042-4506-8(5)) Rosen Publishing Group, Inc., The. (PowerKids Pr.).

—Polar Bears: Arctic Hunters. 2009. (Powerful Predators Ser.). 24p. (gr. 2-3). 42.50 (978-1-60851-348-2(3)); (Illus.). (J). lib. bdg. 22.60 (978-1-4042-4510-5(3)) Rosen Publishing Group, Inc., The. (PowerKids Pr.).

Pearson, Debora. Polar Bear Alert! 2007. (DK Readers Ser.). (ENG., Illus.). 48p. (J). (gr. 2-4). pap. 3.99 (978-0-7566-3140-6(8), DK Children) Dorling Kindersley Publishing, Inc.

Pelusey, Michael & Pelusey, Jane. Bears. 2008. (Zoo Animals Ser.). 32p. (gr. 2-3). lib. bdg. 18.56 (978-0-7614-3147-3(0), Benchmark Bks.) Marshall Cavendish Corp.

Person, Stephen. Polar Bear: Shrinking Ice. (Built for Cold: Arctic Animals Ser.). 2016. (ENG.). 32p. (J). (gr. 2-7). pap. 8.95 **(978-1-944998-66-0(7))** 2011. 32p. (YA). (gr. 1-4). lib. bdg. 25.27 (978-1-61772-129-8(8)) 2011. (J). (gr. 4-5). lib. bdg., E-Book 49.22 (978-1-61772-221-9(9)) Bearport Publishing Co., Inc.

Phillips, Dee. Polar Bear. 2015. (Arctic Animals: Life Outside the Igloo Ser.). (ENG.). 24p. (J). (gr. -1-3). lib. bdg. 23.93 (978-1-62724-526-5(X)) Bearport Publishing Co., Inc.

Pighin, Marcel. Tickles the Bear, 1 bk. Pighin, Marcel & Daggett, Irma, illus. 2005. 92p. (J). per. 7.99 (978-0-9717947-5-7(8)) MP2ME Enterprise.

Plourde, Lynn. Baby Bear's Not Hibernating, Vol. Weidner, Teri, illus. 2016. (ENG.). 40p. (J). 16.95 (978-1-60893-622-9(8)) Down East Bks.

Poitier, Anton. Once I Was a Cardboard Box... But Now I'm a Book about Polar Bears. Evans, Melvyn, illus. 2010. 24p. (J). (gr. k-3). 7.99 (978-0-8416-7200-0(8)) Hammond World Atlas Corp.

Polar Bears, 6 bks. 2005. (Animal Predators Ser.). (Illus.). 40p. (J). (gr. 3-6). pap. 46.95 (978-0-8225-5489-9(5)) Lerner Publishing Group.

Polar Bears: Individual Title Six-Packs. (Story Steps Ser.). (gr. k-2). 32.00 (978-0-7635-9612-5(4)) Rigby Education.

Polar Bears: Level M, 6 vols. (Wonder Worldtm Ser.). 16p. 34.95 (978-0-7802-4593-8(8)); 26.50 (978-0-7802-7006-0(1)) Wright Group/McGraw-Hill.

Polydoros, Lori. Grizzly Bears: Built for the Hunt. 2015. (Predator Profiles Ser.). (ENG., Illus.). 24p. (gr. 1-2). lib. bdg. 25.32 (978-1-4914-5043-7(6)) Capstone Press of Coughlan Cos.

Priddy, Roger. B Is for Bear. 2007. (ENG., Illus.). 26p. (J). (gr. -1 — 1). bds. 12.95 (978-0-312-49918-1(3), 9780312499181, Priddy Bks.) St. Martin's Pr.

Rake, Jody Sullivan. Polar Bears: On the Hunt, 1 vol. 2010. (Killer Animals Ser.). (ENG.). 32p. (gr. 1-2). lib. bdg. 26.65 (978-1-4296-3927-9(X), Blazers) Capstone Press of Coughlan Cos.

Raum, Elizabeth. Bears Make Dens. Romina Martí, illus. 2017. (Animal Builders Ser.). (ENG.). 24p. (J). (gr. 1-4). 20.95 **(978-1-68151-171-9(1)**, Amicus Illustrated) Amicus Publishing.

—Los Pájaros y Sus Nidos (Birds Build Nests) Romina Martí, illus. 2017. (Animal Builders Ser.). (ENG & SPA.). 24p. (J). (gr. 1-4). 20.95 **(978-1-68151-281-5(5)**, Amicus Illustrated) Amicus Publishing.

Read, Nicholas. A Bear's Life, 1 vol. McAllister, Ian, photos by. 2017. (My Great Bear Rainforest Ser.). (ENG., Illus.). 32p. (J). (gr. k-3). 19.95 **(978-1-4598-1270-3(0))** Orca Bk. Pubs. USA.

Read, Nicholas. The Salmon Bears: Giants of the Great Bear Rainforest, 1 vol. McAllister, Ian, photos by. 2010. (ENG., Illus.). 96p. (J). (gr. 3-9). 18.95 (978-1-55469-205-7(9)) Orca Bk. Pubs. USA.

Rettore. Nighty Night Bear. 2016. (ENG.). 8p. (J). (gr. -1 — 1). 16.99 (978-1-4380-7757-4(2)) Barron's Educational Series, Inc.

Richards, Mose, et al. Arctic Tale: Official Companion to the Major Motion Picture. 2007. (ENG., Illus.). 160p. 30.00 (978-1-4262-0065-6(X)) National Geographic Society.

Riggs, Kate. Amazing Animals: Brown Bears. 2015. (Amazing Animals Ser.). (ENG.). 24p. (J). (gr. 1-3). pap. 8.99 (978-1-62832-087-9(7), Creative Paperbacks) Creative Co., The.

—Brown Bears. 2015. (J). (978-1-60818-487-3(0), Creative Education) Creative Co., The.

—Polar Bears. 2015. (J). (978-1-60818-515-3(X), Creative Education) Creative Co., The.

—Seedlings: Polar Bears. 2015. (Seedlings Ser.). (ENG.). 24p. (J). (gr. -1-1). pap. 7.99 (978-1-62832-115-9(6), Creative Paperbacks) Creative Co., The.

Ring, Susan. Polar Bear Babies. McCue, Lisa, illus. 2016. (Step into Reading Ser.). (ENG.). 32p. (J). (gr. -1-1). 3.99 (978-0-399-54954-0(4), Random Hse. Bks. for Young Readers) Random Hse. Children's Bks.

Ritchey, Kate & Bader, Bonnie. Lion, Tiger, & Bear, Level 4. 2015. (Penguin Young Readers, Level 4 Ser.). (ENG., Illus.). 48p. (J). (gr. 3-4). pap. 3.99 (978-0-448-48336-8(X), Penguin Young Readers) Penguin Young Readers Group.

Robinson, Jill & Bekoff, Marc. Jasper's Story: Saving Moon Bears. Frankenhuyzen, Gijsbert van, illus. 2013. (ENG.). 40p. (J). (gr. 1-4). 16.99 (978-1-58536-798-6(2), 202359) Sleeping Bear Pr.

Rocket Bear. (Buggy Buddies with Flaps Ser.). (Illus.). (YA). bds. 3.00 net. (978-1-56021-392-5(2)) W.J. Fantasy, Inc.

Rosing, Norbert. Polar Bears. 2010. (ENG., Illus.). 56p. (J). (gr. 3-7). 19.95 (978-1-55407-599-7(8), 9781554075997); pap. 9.95 (978-1-55407-623-9(4), 9781554076239) Firefly Bks., Ltd.

Rosing, Norbert & Carney, Elizabeth. Face to Face with Polar Bears. 2007. (Face to Face with Animals Ser.). (ENG., Illus.). 32p. (J). (gr. 2-5). lib. bdg. 25.90 (978-1-4263-0140-7(5), National Geographic Children's Bks.) National Geographic Society.

Royston, Angela. Polar Bears & Their Homes. 2010. (Big Picture: Climate Ser.). (ENG.). 24p. (gr. 1-2). pap. 41.70 (978-1-4296-5824-9(X), First Facts) Capstone Press of Coughlan Cos.

Rustad, Martha E. H. A Baby Polar Bear Story. 2011. (Baby Animals Ser.). (ENG.). 24p. (gr. k-1). pap. 41.70 (978-1-4296-7099-9(1), Pebble Plus) Capstone Press of Coughlan Cos.

Ryder, Joanne. A Pair of Polar Bears: Twin Cubs Find a Home at the San Diego Zoo. San Diego Zoological Society Staff, photos by. 2006. (ENG., Illus.). 32p. (J). (gr. -1-3). 17.99 (978-0-689-85871-0(X), Simon & Schuster Bks. For Young Readers) Simon & Schuster Bks. For Young Readers.

—Panda Kindergarten. 2009. (J). lib. bdg. (978-0-06-057851-0(3), Collins) HarperCollins Pubs. Ltd.

Sackett-Smith, Lucy. Grizzly Bears: Fierce Hunters. 2009. (Mighty Mammals Ser.). (Illus.). 24p. (J). (gr. k-3). 22.60 (978-1-4042-8106-6(1)) Rosen Publishing Group, Inc., The.

Salzmann, Mary Elizabeth. Baby Polar Bears, 1 vol. 2014. (Baby Animals Set 2 Ser.). (ENG.). 24p. (J). (gr. -1-3). 24.21 (978-1-62403-511-1(6)) ABDO Publishing Co.

Sartore, Joel. Face to Face with Grizzlies. 2009. (Face to Face with Animals Ser.). (ENG., Illus.). 32p. (J). (gr. 2-5). 6.95 (978-1-4263-0474-3(9), National Geographic Children's Bks.) National Geographic Society.

—Face to Face with Grizzlies. Sartore, Joel, illus. 2007. (Face to Face with Animals Ser.). (ENG., Illus.). 32p. (J). (gr. 2-5). 16.95 (978-1-4263-0050-9(6)); lib. bdg. 25.90 (978-1-4263-0051-6(4)) National Geographic Society. (National Geographic Children's Bks.).

Schindel, John. Busy Bear Cubs. Husar, Lisa & Husar, Mike, photos by. 2009. (Busy Book Ser.). (ENG., Illus.). 20p. (J). (gr. k — 1). bds. 6.99 (978-1-58246-302-5(6), Tricycle Pr.) Random Hse. Children's Bks.

Schreiber, Anne, et al. National Geographic Readers: Cutest Animals Collection. 2014. (Readers Ser.). (ENG.). 128p. (J). (gr. k-3). pap. 7.99 (978-1-4263-1522-0(8), National Geographic Children's Bks.) National Geographic Society.

Schuetz, Kari. Baby Bears. 2013. (Super Cute! Ser.). (ENG., Illus.). 24p. (J). (gr. k-3). lib. bdg. 25.95 (978-1-60014-922-1(7), Blastoff! Readers) Bellwether Media.

Schuh, Mari. Polar Bears. 2017. (Black & White Animals Ser.). (ENG., Illus.). 24p. (gr. k-1). lib. bdg. 21.99 (978-1-5157-3621-9(0), Pebble Bks.) Capstone Press of Coughlan Cos.

Schwabacher, Martin & Shannon, Terry Miller. Bears. 2009. (Benchmark Rockets Ser.). 24p. (gr. 1-18). 24.21 (978-0-7614-3820-5(3)) Marshall Cavendish Corp.

Schwaeber, Barbie Heit. Alphabet of Bears. Nelson, Will et al, illus. 2011. (Alphabet Bks.). (ENG.). 40p. (J). (gr. -1-3). 17.95 (978-1-60727-668-5(2)) Soundprints.

—Alphabet of Bears. Nelson, Will et al, illus. 2007. (Alphabet Of... Ser.). (ENG.). 40p. (J). 15.95 (978-1-59249-689-1(X)) Soundprints.

Scott, Jonathan & Scott, Angela. Kings of the Wild. Scott, Jonathan & Scott, Angela, illus. 2007. (Collins Big Cat Ser.). (ENG., Illus.). 384p. (J). (gr. 2-4). pap. 8.99 (978-0-00-723085-3(0)) HarperCollins Pubs. Ltd. GBR. Dist: Independent Pubs. Group.

Scott, Keith. The Bear Man. Hill, Steve, illus. 2010. 32p. (J). pap. 5.95 (978-0-88839-655-6(4)) Hancock Hse. Pubs.

Shaffer, Jody Jensen. Grizzly Bear, 1 vol. 2013. (Great Predators Ser.). (ENG., Illus.). 48p. (J). (gr. 3-6). lib. bdg. 32.79 (978-1-61783-948-1(5)) ABDO Publishing Co.

—Grizzly Bear Paperback. 2013. (Illus.). 48p. (J). pap. 15.64 (978-1-62403-013-0(0), Core Library) ABDO Publishing Co.

Shea, Therese. Bears. (Big Bad Biters Ser.). 24p. 2009. (gr. 2-3). 42.50 (978-1-61511-561-7(7)) 2006. (Illus.). (J). (gr. 3-7). lib. bdg. 22.60 (978-1-4042-3524-3(8)) Rosen Publishing Group, Inc., The. (PowerKids Pr.).

—Grizzly Bears. 2010. (Animals That Live in the Tundra Ser.). (ENG.). 24p. (J). (gr. -1-3). pap. 8.15 (978-1-4339-3900-6(2)); lib. bdg. 22.60 (978-1-4339-3899-3(5)) Stevens, Gareth Publishing LLLP.

Shively, Julie. Baby Polar Bear. Johnson, Meredith, illus. 2005. (San Diego Zoo Animal Library: Vol. 10). (ENG.). 24p. (J). bds. 6.95 (978-0-8249-6576-1(0), Ideal Pubns.) Worthy Publishing.

Sisk, Maeve T. Hunting with Polar Bears, Vol. 1. 2014. (Animal Attack! Ser.). (ENG., Illus.). 32p. (J). (gr. 2-3). 22.60 (978-1-4824-0526-2(1), 1368256) Stevens, Gareth Publishing LLLP.

—Polar Bears. 2010. (Animals That Live in the Tundra Ser.). (ENG.). 24p. (J). (gr. -1-3). pap. 8.15 (978-1-4339-3906-8(1)); lib. bdg. 22.60 (978-1-4339-3905-1(3)) Stevens, Gareth Publishing LLLP.

Sjonger, Rebecca & Kalman, Bobbie. The Life Cycle of a Polar Bear. 2005. (Life Cycle Ser.). (ENG., Illus.). 32p. (J). (gr. 2-3). pap. (978-0-7787-0698-4(2)); lib. bdg. (978-0-7787-0668-7(0)) Crabtree Publishing Co.

Smith, Lucy. Grizzly Bears: Fierce Hunters. 2009. 24p. (YA). pap. 8.25 (978-1-4358-3283-1(3)) Rosen Publishing Group, Inc., The.

Somervill, Barbara. Grizzly Bear. 2009. (21st Century Skills Library: Road to Recovery Ser.). (ENG.). 32p. (gr. 4-8). lib. bdg. 28.50 (978-1-60279-315-6(8), 200211) Cherry Lake Publishing.

Spezialy, Millie. Binky's Trophy. (J). 14.95 (978-0-9654200-2-0(7)) Six Suns Publishing.

Spilsbury, Louise. Polar Bear. 2013. (Top of the Food Chain Ser.). 32p. (J). (gr. k-5). 25.25 (978-1-61533-739-2(3)); pap. 10.00 (978-1-61533-795-8(4)) Windmill Bks.

—Polar Bear: Killer King of the Arctic. 2013. (Top of the Food Chain Ser.). 32p. (J). (gr. k-5). pap. 60.00 (978-1-61533-796-5(2)) Windmill Bks.

Stamper, Judith. Polar Bear Patrol. Haefele, Steve, illus. 2010. (Magic School Bus Science Chapter Bks.). (KOR.). 106p. (J). (978-89-491-5321-6(1)) Biryongso Publishing Co.

Stanley, Joseph. Grizzly Bear, 01 vols., 1. 2016. (North America's Biggest Beasts Ser.). (ENG., Illus.). 24p. (J). pap. 8.25 (978-1-5081-4294-2(7), PowerKids Pr.) Rosen Publishing Group, Inc., The.

Stefoff, Rebecca. Polar Bears. 2014. (Giant Animals Ser.). 48p. (J). (gr. 4-6). lib. bdg. 31.36 (978-1-62712-963-3(4)) Cavendish Square Publishing.

—Polar Bears. 2015. (Illus.). 48p. (J). pap. (978-1-62712-964-0(2)) Musa Publishing.

Stone, Lynn M. Grizzlies. Stone, Lynn M., photos by. rev. ed. 2007. (Nature Watch Ser.). (ENG., Illus.). 48p. (gr. 4-8). lib. bdg. 27.93 (978-0-8225-6601-4(X), Lerner Pubns.) Lerner Publishing Group.

Stone, Tanya Lee. Polar Bears. 2003. (Wild Wild World Ser.). 24p. (YA). 24.94 (978-1-56711-820-9(8), Blackbirch Pr., Inc.) Cengage Gale.

Sundance/Newbridge LLC Staff. The Big Bears. 2007. (Early Science Ser.). (gr. k-3). 18.95 (978-1-4007-6278-1(2)); pap. 6.10 (978-1-4007-6274-3(X)) Sundance/Newbridge Educational Publishing.

Swinburne, Stephen R. Black Bear: North America's Bear. 2009. (ENG., Illus.). 32p. (J). (gr. 1). pap. 10.95 (978-1-59078-798-4(6)) Boyds Mills Pr.

Tagliaferro, Linda. Animals Babies Pack [Scholastic]. 2011. (Animal Offspring Ser.). 24p. pap. 2.00 (978-1-4296-6297-0(2), Pebble Plus) Capstone Press of Coughlan Cos.

—Bears & Their Cubs [Scholastic]. 2011. (Animal Offspring Ser.). 24p. pap. 0.50 (978-1-4296-6294-9(8), Pebble Plus) Capstone Press of Coughlan Cos.

—Bears & Their Dens [Scholastic]. 2010. (Animal Homes Ser.). 24p. pap. 0.49 (978-1-4296-5793-8(6), Pebble Plus) Capstone Press of Coughlan Cos.

Tara, Stephanie Lisa. Snowy White World to Save. Walton, Alex, illus. 2007. 32p. (J). (gr. -1-3). 16.95 (978-1-933285-89-4(3)) Brown Books Publishing Group.

Taylor, Trace & Sánchez, Lucía M. Osos Pardos. 2009. (1G Animales Depredador Ser.). (SPA., Illus.). 32p. (J). (gr. k-2). pap. 6.99 (978-1-61541-053-8(8)) American Reading Co.

Thomas, Keltie. Bear Rescue: Changing the Future for Endangered Wildlife. 2006. (Firefly Animal Rescue Ser.). (ENG., Illus.). 64p. (J). (gr. 5-12). 19.95 (978-1-55297-922-8(9), 9781552979228); pap. 9.95 (978-1-55297-921-1(0), 9781552979211) Firefly Bks., Ltd.

Thomson, Sarah L. Where Do Polar Bears Live? Chin, Jason, illus. 2009. (Let's-Read-And-Find-Out Science 2 Ser.). (ENG.). 40p. (J). (gr. k-4). 16.99 (978-0-06-157518-1(6)); pap. 5.99 (978-0-06-157517-4(8)) HarperCollins Pubs. (Collins).

Time for Kids Editors & Iorio, Nicole. Bears! 2005. (Time for Kids Ser.). (ENG., Illus.). 32p. (J). (gr. 1-3). pap. 3.99 (978-0-06-078196-5(3)) HarperCollins Pubs.

Tokuda, Wendy. Samson the Hot Tub Bear: A True Story. 2005. 32p. pap. 9.95 (978-1-58979-215-9(7)) Taylor Trade Publishing.

Trapani, Iza. Sing along with Iza & Friends: Row Row Row Your Boat. Trapani, Iza, illus. 2004. (Illus.). 32p. (J). pap. 11.95 incl. audio compact disk (978-1-58089-102-8(0)) Charlesbridge Publishing, Inc.

Troupe, Thomas Kingsley. What's with the Long Naps, Bears? Learning about Hibernation with the Garbage Gang. Toye, Derek, illus. 2015. (Garbage Gang's Super Science Questions Ser.). (ENG.). 24p. (gr. k-2). lib. bdg. 26.65 (978-1-4795-7056-0(7)) Picture Window Bks.

Trueit, Trudi Strain. Grizzly Bears. 2015. (Wild Bears Ser.). (ENG., Illus.). 24p. (J). (gr. 1-4). 19.95 (978-1-60753-775-5(3)) Amicus Publishing.

—Polar Bears. 2015. (Wild Bears Ser.). (ENG., Illus.). 24p. (J). (gr. 1-4). 19.95 (978-1-60753-776-2(1)) Amicus Publishing.

Turnbull, Stephanie. Polar Bear. 2013. (Big Beasts Ser.). (Illus.). 24p. (gr. k-3). 28.50 (978-1-59920-836-7(9)) Black Rabbit Bks.

Twine, Alice. Bears. 2009. (Baby Animals Ser.). 24p. (gr. 1-1). 42.50 (978-1-61511-487-0(4), PowerKids Pr.) Rosen Publishing Group, Inc., The.

—Bears/Osos. 2009. (Baby Animals/Animales bebé Ser.). (ENG & SPA.). 24p. (gr. 1-1). 42.50 (978-1-61511-498-6(X), Editorial Buenas Letras) Rosen Publishing Group, Inc., The.

—Bears/Osos. Obregon, Jose Maria, tr. 2007. (Baby Animals / Animales Bebé Ser.). (ENG & SPA., Illus.). 24p. (J). (gr. -1-3). lib. bdg. 22.60 (978-1-4042-7634-5(3), Editorial Buenas Letras) Rosen Publishing Group, Inc., The.

Varela, Barry, et al. Arctic Tale. movie tie-in ed. 2007. (ENG., Illus.). 132p. (J). (gr. 3-7). per. 4.99 (978-1-4263-0106-3(5), National Geographic Children's Bks.) National Geographic Society.

Vastola, P. Huge Animals: Learning the Long U Sound. 2009. (PowerPhonics Ser.). 24p. (gr. 1-1). 39.90 (978-1-60851-445-8(5), PowerKids Pr.) Rosen Publishing Group, Inc., The.

Walker, Rachel. Polar Bear Survival. 2015. (ENG., Illus.). 16p. (-2). pap. (978-1-77654-141-6(3), Red Rocket Readers) Flying Start Bks.

Walker, Sally M. Winnie: The True Story of the Bear Who Inspired Winnie-the-Pooh. Voss, Jonathan D., illus. 2015. (ENG.). 40p. (J). (gr. -1-3). 17.99 (978-0-8050-9715-3(5), 9780805097153, Holt, Henry & Co. Bks. For Young Readers) Holt, Henry & Co.

Wallace, Karen. Bears in the Forest: Read & Wonder. Firth, Barbara, illus. 2009. (Read & Wonder Ser.). (ENG.). 32p. (J). (gr. -1-3). pap. 6.99 (978-0-7636-4522-9(2)) Candlewick Pr.

Ward, Finn. Osos Polares / Polar Bears at the Zoo. 2015. (Animales Del Zoológico / Zoo Animals Ser.). (ENG & SPA.). 24p. (J). (gr. k-k). lib. bdg. 22.60 (978-1-4824-3239-8(0)) Stevens, Gareth Publishing LLLP.

—Polar Bears at the Zoo. 2015. (Zoo Animals Ser.). (ENG., Illus.). 24p. (J). (gr. k-k). pap. 8.15 (978-1-4824-2609-0(9)) Stevens, Gareth Publishing LLLP.

Watt, Fiona. Polar Bears. Chiara, Francesca De, illus. 2010. (Luxury Touchy-Feely Board Bks). 10p. (J). bds. 15.99 (978-0-7945-2544-6(X), Usborne) EDC Publishing.

Welvaert, Scott R. A Bear in Its Den. 2003. (Where Do Animals Live? Ser.). (J). (978-1-58417-184-3(7)); pap. (978-1-58417-185-0(5)) Lake Street Pubs.

Wendorff, Anne. Bear Cubs. 2009. (Watch Animals Grow Ser.). (ENG., Illus.). 24p. (J). (gr. k-3). lib. bdg. 25.95 (978-1-60014-238-3(9)) Bellwether Media.

—Bear Cubs. 2009. (Blastoff! Readers Ser.). (ENG., Illus.). 24p. (J). (gr. k-3). 20.00 (978-0-531-21626-2(8), Children's Pr.) Scholastic Library Publishing.

Wexo, John Bonnett. Bears. rev. ed. 2003. (Illus.). 24p. (J). (gr. 1-12). 10.95 (978-1-888153-90-3(3), Zoo Bks.) Wildlife Education, Ltd.

—Osos. Rountree, Monica, tr. 2003. (Zoobooks Ser.). Orig. Title: Bears. (SPA., Illus.). 24p. (J). (gr. 1-7). lib. bdg. 15.95 (978-1-888153-73-6(3)) Wildlife Education, Ltd.

Wicker, Jan Lee. Those Big Bears. 2011. (Those Amazing Animals Ser.). (ENG., Illus.). 56p. (J). (gr. k-4). pap. 8.95 (978-1-56164-492-6(7)); lib. bdg. 14.95 (978-1-56164-491-9(9)) Pineapple Pr., Inc.

Wildlife Education. Polar Bears. 2007. (Illus.). 10p. (J). pap. 5.99 (978-1-932396-32-4(2), Critters Up Close) Wildlife Education, Ltd.

Wilsdon, Christina. Polar Bears. 2009. (Amazing Animals Ser.). 48p. (J). (gr. 2-6). pap. 10.50 (978-1-4339-2027-1(1), Gareth Stevens Learning Library); (gr. 3-6). lib. bdg. 28.00 (978-0-8368-9110-2(4)) Stevens, Gareth Publishing LLLP.

—Polar Bears. 2006. (J). (978-1-59939-116-8(3), Reader's Digest Young Families, Inc.) Studio Fun International.

Wilson, Natashya. Bears. 2009. (My World of Animals Ser.). 24p. (gr. 1-1). 37.50 (978-1-61514-710-6(1), PowerKids Pr.) Rosen Publishing Group, Inc., The.

—Bears: Osos. Beullens, Nathalie, tr. 2004. (My World of Animals Ser.). (ENG & SPA., Illus.). 24p. (J). (gr. k-1). lib. bdg. 16.00 (978-1-4042-7518-8(5), PowerKids Pr.) Rosen Publishing Group, Inc., The.

—Bears / Osos. 2009. (My World of Animals / Yo y los animales Ser.). (ENG & SPA.). 24p. (gr. 1-1). 37.50 (978-1-61514-716-8(0), Editorial Buenas Letras) Rosen Publishing Group, Inc., The.

Woodward, John. Grizzly Bears. 2008. (Nature's Children Ser.). (Illus.). 52p. (J). (978-0-7172-6255-7(3)) Grolier, Ltd.

BEARS—FICTION

Adair, Dick. The Story of Aloha Bear. Britt, Stephanie, illus. 2008. 24p. (J). 12.95 (978-1-59700-492-3(8)) Island Heritage Publishing.

Adele, Oroma. Berry Bear. 2013. 28p. pap. 24.95 (978-1-62709-096-4(7)) America Star Bks.

Adelson, Leone. The Mystery Bear: A Purim Story. Howland, Naomi, tr. Howland, Naomi, illus. 2004. 32p. (J). (gr. -1-2). 15.00 (978-0-618-33727-9(X), Clarion Bks.) Houghton Mifflin Harcourt Trade & Reference Pubs.

Aesop. Two Travelers & a Bear. 2012. (J). (978-1-61913-102-6(1)) Weigl Pubs., Inc.

Agee, Jon. Milo's Hat Trick. 2017. (ENG., Illus.). 40p. (J). (gr. k-3). 17.99 **(978-0-7352-2987-7(2)**, Dial Bks) Penguin Young Readers Group.

Ahlberg, Allan. The Goldilocks Variations: A Pop-Up Book. Ahlberg, Jessica, illus. 2012. (ENG.). 40p. (J). (gr. k-4). 17.99 (978-0-7636-6268-4(2)) Candlewick Pr.

Alderson, Sue Ann. Wherever Bears Be. Johnson, Arden, illus. 2003. 32p. (J). (gr. -1-3). 14.95 (978-1-883672-77-5(5), Tricycle Pr.) Ten Speed Pr.

Alexie, Oscar. How the Bear Lost This Tail. Sloat, Teri, illus. 2004. (J). pap. 14.00 (978-1-58084-222-8(4)) Lower Kuskokwim Schl. District.

Allan-Meyer, Kathleen. Play Fair, Little Bear. Garvin, Elaine, illus. 2003. (Little Bear Adventure Ser.: Vol. 7). 28p. (J). (gr. -1-1). pap. 6.49 (978-1-57924-887-1(X)) BJU Pr.

Allen, Elise & Stanford, Halle. Winter's Flurry Adventure. Pooler, Paige, illus. 2014. (Enchanted Sisters Ser.). (ENG.). 128p. (YA). (gr. 2-4). pap. 5.99 (978-1-61963-267-7(5), 9781619632677, Bloomsbury USA Childrens) Bloomsbury Publishing USA.

—Winter's Flurry Adventure. Pooler, Paige, illus. 2014. (Enchanted Sisters Ser.: 2). (YA). lib. bdg. 16.00 (978-0-606-36217-7(7)) Turtleback Bks.

Altés, Marta. My Grandpa. 2013. (ENG., Illus.). 32p. (J). (gr. k-2). 16.95 (978-1-4197-0588-5(1), Abrams Bks. for Young Readers) Abrams, Inc.

Ambrosio, Michael. It Takes a Lot of Love. Awes, Jennifer, illus. 2007. 32p. (J). 14.95 (978-0-9716085-4-2(7)) LionX Publishing.

Amery, Heather. Goldilocks & the Three Bears. Tyler, Jenny, ed. 2004. (Usborne First Stories Ser.). (Illus.). 16p. (J). (gr. -1-3). lib. bdg. 12.95 (978-1-58086-619-4(0), Usborne) EDC Publishing.

And Bean. Pronouns on the Farm. 2011. 32p. pap. 21.99 (978-1-4568-4235-2(8)) Xlibris Corp.

Anderson, Derek. Romeo & Lou Blast Off. Anderson, Derek, illus. 2014. (ENG., Illus.). 32p. (J). (gr. -1-3). 16.99 (978-1-4814-1932-1(3), Simon & Schuster Bks. For Young Readers) Simon & Schuster Bks. For Young Readers.

Anderson, Jeannine. Nightlight. Johnson, Nikki, illus. 2004. 32p. (J). pap. 7.95 (978-0-89317-057-8(7), WW-0577); lib. bdg. 16.95 (978-0-89317-056-1(9), WW-0569) Finney Co., Inc. (Windward Publishing).

Anderson, T. N. Chiko & the Butterfly. 2009. 70p. pap. 7.00 (978-0-557-10395-9(9)) Lulu Pr., Inc.

Anderson, Wayne R. Paula's Perilous Adventure. 2006. 48p. (YA). 12.95 (978-0-9773478-0-3(X)); 19.95 incl. DVD (978-0-9773478-2-7(6)) IMAGECRAFTERS.

Andreae, Giles. Heaven Is Having You. Cabban, Vanessa, illus. (Padded Board Bks.). (J). 2007. 18p. (gr. -1-1). bds. 7.95 (978-1-58925-820-4(7)) 2004. 32p. reprint ed. pap. 6.95 (978-1-58925-388-9(4)) Tiger Tales.

—Love Is a Handful of Honey. Cabban, Vanessa, illus. 2004. 32p. (J). (gr. -1-k). 5.95 (978-1-58925-353-7(1)); tchr. ed. 15.95 (978-1-58925-003-1(6)) Tiger Tales.

Andrews, Jackie. Goldilocks & the Three Bears. Taylor, Lawrie, illus. 2012. (ENG.). 32p. (J). pap. 6.50 (978-1-84135-191-9(1)) Award Pubns. Ltd. GBR. Dist: Parkwest Pubns., Inc.

Archambault, Douglas J. The Adventures of Little Buddy & Grizz, 1 vol. 2009. 64p. pap. 19.95 (978-1-60836-159-5(4)) America Star Bks.

Armstrong, Kim. Frosty the Snowbear. 2009. 48p. pap. 12.99 (978-1-935436-96-6(1)) Rodaian Pr.

Aruego, Jose & Dewey, Ariane. Splash! 2003. (Green Light Readers Level 2 Ser.). (ENG., Illus.). 32p. (J). (gr. -1-3). pap. 3.95 (978-0-15-204832-7(4)) Houghton Mifflin Harcourt Publishing Co.

Asch, Frank. Bread & Honey. 2015. lib. bdg. 18.40 (978-0-606-36290-0(8)) Turtleback Bks.

—Happy Birthday, Moon. Asch, Frank, illus. 2014. (Moonbear Ser.). (ENG., Illus.). 32p. (J). (gr. -1-3). 7.99 (978-1-4424-9400-8(X), Aladdin) Simon & Schuster Children's Publishing.

—Just Like Daddy. Asch, Frank, illus. 2015. (Frank Asch Bear Book Ser.). (ENG., Illus.). 32p. (J). (gr. -1-3). 6.99 (978-1-4814-2207-9(3), Aladdin) Simon & Schuster Children's Publishing.

—Milk & Cookies. Asch, Frank, illus. 2015. (Frank Asch Bear Book Ser.). (ENG., Illus.). 40p. (J). (gr. -1-3). 17.99 (978-1-4424-6672-2(3), Aladdin) Simon & Schuster Children's Publishing.

—Moonbear's Bargain. Asch, Frank, illus. 2014. (Moonbear Ser.). (ENG., Illus.). 32p. (J). (gr. -1-3). 17.99 (978-1-4424-9436-7(0), Aladdin) Simon & Schuster Children's Publishing.

—Moonbear's Pet. Asch, Frank, illus. 2014. (Moonbear Ser.). (ENG., Illus.). 32p. (J). (gr. -1-3). 17.99 (978-1-4424-9430-5(1), Simon & Schuster/Paula Wiseman Bks.) Simon & Schuster/Paula Wiseman Bks.

—Moonbear's Shadow. Asch, Frank, illus. 2014. (Moonbear Ser.). (ENG., Illus.). 32p. (J). (gr. -1-3). 7.99 (978-1-4424-9426-8(3), Aladdin) Simon & Schuster Children's Publishing.

—Moonbear's Skyfire. Asch, Frank, illus. 2014. (Moonbear Ser.). (ENG., Illus.). 32p. (J). (gr. -1-3). 7.99 (978-1-4424-9409-1(3), Aladdin) Simon & Schuster Children's Publishing.

—Moonbear's Sunrise. Asch, Frank, illus. (Moonbear Ser.). (ENG., Illus.). 32p. (J). (gr. -1-3). 2016. 7.99 (978-1-4424-6648-7(0)) 2014. 16.99 (978-1-4424-6647-0(2)) Simon & Schuster Children's Publishing. (Aladdin).

—Mooncake. Asch, Frank, illus. 2014. (Moonbear Ser.). (ENG., Illus.). 32p. (J). (gr. -1-3). 7.99 (978-1-4424-9403-9(4), Aladdin) Simon & Schuster Children's Publishing.

—Moondance. Asch, Frank, illus. 2014. (Moonbear Ser.). (ENG., Illus.). 32p. (J). (gr. -1-3). 17.99 (978-1-4424-6659-3(6), Aladdin) Simon & Schuster Children's Publishing.

—Pizza. Asch, Frank, illus. (Frank Asch Bear Book Ser.). (ENG., Illus.). 32p. (J). (gr. -1-3). 2016. 7.99 (978-1-4424-6676-0(6)) 2015. 16.99 (978-1-4424-6675-3(8)) Simon & Schuster Children's Publishing. (Aladdin).

—Popcorn. Asch, Frank, illus. 2015. (Frank Asch Bear Book Ser.). (ENG., Illus.). 40p. (J). (gr. -1-3). 16.99 (978-1-4424-6662-3(6), Aladdin) Simon & Schuster Children's Publishing.

—Popcorn. 2015. lib. bdg. 17.20 (978-0-606-36289-4(4)) Turtleback Bks.

Asch, Frank & Asch, Frank. Happy Birthday, Moon. Asch, Frank & Asch, Frank, illus. 2005. (Stories to Go! Ser.). (ENG., Illus.). 32p. (J). 4.99 (978-1-4169-0307-9(0), Simon & Schuster/Paula Wiseman Bks.) Simon & Schuster/Paula Wiseman Bks.

Ashby, Lenore. The Magic of the Bear. 2003. (Illus.). 162p. (YA). per. 7.95 (978-0-9728535-0-7(2), 853502) Grandma Chubby's Bks.

Ashley, Brook, et al. The Lonely Doll Makes New Friends. 2006. (ENG., Illus.). 44p. per. 17.99 (978-1-4257-0410-0(7)) Xlibris Corp.

Atkinson, Cale. Explorers of the Wild. Atkinson, Cale, illus. 2016. (ENG., Illus.). 40p. (J). (gr. -1-k). 16.99 (978-1-4847-2340-1(6)) Disney Pr.

Atkinson, Ruth & Atkinson, Brett. Story Templates. Atkinson, Ruth & Atkinson, Brett, illus. (Illus.). (J). (gr. k-2). pap. (978-1-875739-73-8(4)) Wizard Bks.

Austin, Rikey. Captain's Treasure: Alice's Bear Shop. 2012. 28p. pap. (978-1-78092-149-5(7)) MX Publishing, Ltd.

—Cobby Goes for a Swim: Alice's Bear Shop. 2012. 28p. pap. (978-1-78092-164-8(0)) MX Publishing, Ltd.

—Sandy Paints a Picture: Alice's Bear Shop. 2012. 28p. pap. (978-1-78092-155-6(1)) MX Publishing, Ltd.

—Tat Gets a Patch: Alice's Bear Shop. 2012. 28p. pap. (978-1-78092-161-7(6)) MX Publishing, Ltd.

—Tilly & the Magic Wand: Alice's Bear Shop. 2012. 28p. pap. (978-1-78092-146-4(2)) MX Publishing, Ltd.

—Ting Finds a Bell: Alice's Bear Shop. 2012. 28p. pap. (978-1-78092-158-7(6)) MX Publishing, Ltd.

—Woodroffe Growls Again: Alice's Bear Shop. 2012. (Illus.). 32p. pap. (978-1-78092-085-6(7)) MX Publishing, Ltd.

Averiss, Corrinne. A Dot in the Snow. Woodcock, Fiona, illus. 2016. (ENG.). 32p. (J). (gr. -1-2). 14.95 (978-1-4549-2101-1(3)) Sterling Publishing Co., Inc.

Award, Anna. The Story of Goldilocks. 2012. (ENG.). 24p. (J). pap. 9.95 (978-1-84135-517-7(8)) Award Pubns. Ltd. GBR. Dist: Parkwest Pubns., Inc.

Award, Anna & Biro, Val. The Bear & the Travellers & the Ducks & the Tortoise. 2014. (ENG.). 24p. (J). pap. 6.95 (978-1-84135-959-5(9)) Award Pubns. Ltd. GBR. Dist: Parkwest Pubns., Inc.

Award Publications Staff. Read along with Me. 2012. (ENG., Illus.). 24p. (J). pap. 6.50 (978-1-84135-159-9(8)) Award Pubns. Ltd. GBR. Dist: Parkwest Pubns., Inc.

Aylesworth, Jim. Goldilocks & the Three Bears. McClintock, Barbara, illus. 2003. (ENG.). 32p. (J). (gr. -1-3). 17.99 (978-0-439-39545-8(3), Scholastic Pr.) Scholastic, Inc.

AZ Books Staff. Hello, I'm Bear! Gorbachenok, Ekaterina, ed. 2012. (Who Lives in the Book? Ser.). (ENG.). 10p. (J). (-k). bds. 11.95 (978-1-61889-070-2(0)) AZ Bks. LLC.

—Who Is the Bear Looking For? Sharipovas, Alesja, ed. 2012. (Who Is There Ser.). (ENG.). 10p. (J). (-k). bds. 11.95 (978-1-61889-039-9(5)) AZ Bks. LLC.

Azevedo, Eric. Why Is Blue Bear So Blue? The Adventures of Blue Bear. 2012. 28p. pap. 16.95 (978-1-4582-0674-9(2), Abbott Pr.) Author Solutions, Inc.

Baby Bear Sees Blue. 2014. (Baby Bear Ser.). (ENG., Illus.). 42p. (J). (gr. -1 — 1). bds. 7.99 (978-1-4814-1503-3(4), Little Simon) Little Simon.

Bailer, Darice & Domínguez, Madelca. Ricitos de Oro y Los Tres Osos. Espluga, Maria, illus. 2007. (SPA & ENG.). 28p. (J). (978-0-545-02447-1(1)) Scholastic, Inc.

Bailey, Arthur Scott. Sleepy-Time Tales: The Tale of Cuffy Bea. 2006. (Illus.). pap. (978-1-4065-0448-4(3)) Dodo Pr.

Baker, Barbara. One Saturday Evening. Duke, Kate, illus. 2007. (J). (978-0-525-47850-8(7), Dutton Juvenile) Penguin Publishing Group.

Baker, Sara, illus. Ready to Read Goldilocks & the Three Bears. 2007. (Ready to Read Ser.). 31p. (J). (gr. k-2). (978-1-84610-440-4(8)) Make Believe Ideas.

Banks, Kate. The Bear in the Book, 1 vol. Hallensleben, Georg, illus. 2012. (ENG.). 36p. (J). (gr. -1-1). 16.99 (978-0-374-30591-8(9), 9780374305918, Farrar, Straus & Giroux (BYR)) Farrar, Straus & Giroux.

Barlow, Ben. Mimi's Bears. 2006. 24p. 13.76 (978-1-4116-7984-9(9)) Lulu Pr., Inc.

Barske, Dianne. Two Bears There: The Story of Alpun & Oreo. 2003. (J). 14.95 (978-1-888125-49-8(7)) Publication Consultants.

Bart, Kathleen. Town Teddy & Country Bear Go Global. Bart, Kathleen, illus. 2011. (Illus.). (J). (gr. k-3). 16.95 (978-1-932485-60-8(0)) Reverie Publishing Co.

—Town Teddy Country Bear. 2004. (Illus.). 32p. (J). (978-1-932485-19-6(8)) Reverie Publishing Co.

Bateson-Hill, Margaret. Goldilocks & the Three Bears. Slater, Kate, illus. 2015. (J). *(978-1-84686-890-0(4))* Barefoot Bks., Inc.

Bauer, Marion Dane. Baby Bear Discovers the World, 1 vol. Tekiela, Stan, photos by. 2006. (Wildlife Picture Bks.). (ENG., Illus.). 64p. (J). (gr. -1-3). 14.95 *(978-1-59193-165-2(7))* Adventure Pubns.

Baxter, Nicola & Ladybird Books Staff. Goldilocks & the Three Bears. 2015. (First Favourite Tales Ser.). (ENG., Illus.). 32p. (J). (-k). 7.99 *(978-1-4093-0629-0(1))* Penguin Bks., Ltd. GBR. Dist: Independent Pubs. Group.

Be Kind, Be Friendly, Be Thankful: The Adventures of Brisky Bear & Trooper Dog. 2007. Orig. Title: Friends for Always. (J). pap. 7.95 incl. audio compact disk *(978-0-9795127-0-4(0))* Glory Be Collectibles.

Bear Story Board Books 800655, 5. 2005. (J). bds. *(978-1-59794-007-8(0))* Environments, Inc.

Bears, Bears, Bears, 6 Packs. (Story Steps Ser.). (gr. k-2). 23.00 *(978-0-7635-9608-8(6))* Rigby Education.

The Bears of Blue River. 2008. 100p. pap. 10.95 *(978-1-60459-531-4(0))* Wilder Pubns., Corp.

Beck, Ian. Getting Dressed. 2004. (Little Brown Bear Ser.). (Illus.). 12p. (J). bds. 4.99 *(978-1-85854-650-5(8))* Brimax Books Ltd. GBR. Dist: Byeway Bks.

—Let's Pretend. 2004. (Little Brown Bear Ser.). (Illus.). 12p. (J). bds. 4.99 *(978-1-85854-649-0(4))* Brimax Books Ltd. GBR. Dist: Byeway Bks.

—Playtime. 2004. (Little Brown Bear Ser.). (Illus.). 12p. (J). bds. 4.99 *(978-1-85854-648-3(6))* Brimax Books Ltd. GBR. Dist: Byeway Bks.

Becker, Bonny. A Bedtime for Bear. Denton, Kady MacDonald, illus. 2010. (J). (Bear & Mouse Ser.: 3). (ENG.). 48p. (gr. -1-2). 16.99 *(978-0-7636-4101-6(4))*; *(978-0-7636-5364-4(0))* Candlewick Pr.

—A Birthday for Bear. Denton, Kady MacDonald, illus. (Candlewick Sparks Ser.). (ENG.). (J). 2013. 56p. (gr. k-4). pap. 3.99 *(978-0-7636-6861-7(3))* 2012. 48p. (gr. -1-2). 16.99 *(978-0-7636-5823-6(5))* Candlewick Pr.

—A Library Book for Bear. Denton, Kady MacDonald, illus. 2014. (Bear & Mouse Ser.). (ENG.). 32p. (J). 16.99 *(978-0-7636-4924-1(4))* Candlewick Pr.

—The Sniffles for Bear. Denton, Kady MacDonald, illus. 2011. (Bear & Mouse Ser.). (ENG.). 32p. (J). (gr. -1-2). 16.99 *(978-0-7636-4756-8(X))* Candlewick Pr.

—A Visitor for Bear. Denton, Kady MacDonald, illus. (Bear & Mouse Ser.). (ENG.). 56p. (J). 2012. (gr. k-k). pap. 6.99 *(978-0-7636-4611-0(3))* 2008. (gr. -1-2). 16.99 *(978-0-7636-2807-9(7))* Candlewick Pr.

—A Visitor for Bear. Denton, Kady MacDonald, illus. 2012. lib. bdg. 17.20 *(978-0-606-26930-8(4)*, Turtleback) Turtleback Bks.

Beckstrand, Karl. Crumbs on the Stairs - Migas en Las Escaleras: A Mystery. Beckstrand, Karl, illus. 2011. (Mini-Mysteries for Minors Ser.: 2).Tr. of Migas en Las Escaleras. (ENG & SPA., Illus.). 24p. (J). pap. 14.95 *(978-0-9776065-9-7(7)*, Gozo Bks.) Premio Publishing & Gozo Bks., LLC.

A Bed for Bear. 2014. (ENG., Illus.). 32p. (J). (gr. -1-3). 17.99 *(978-0-06-223705-7(5))* HarperCollins Pubs.

Bedford, David. Big Bear Little Bear. Chapman, Jane, illus. 2005. (Storytime Board Bks.). 18p. (J). (gr. -1-k). bds. 6.95 *(978-1-58925-770-2(7))* Tiger Tales.

—Big Bears Can! Hansen, Gaby, illus. 2007. (Storytime Board Bks.). 16p. (J). (gr. -1-k). bds. 6.95 *(978-1-58925-826-6(6))* Tiger Tales.

—I've Seen Santa! Warnes, Tim, illus. 32p. 2008. pap. 6.95 *(978-1-58925-411-4(2))* 2006. (J). (gr. -1-3). 15.95 *(978-1-58925-058-1(3))* Tiger Tales.

Bell, A. L. The Adventures of Captain Zero: I'm the Hero (Special Edition Cover) 2005. 45p. 17.00 *(978-1-4116-3732-0(1))* Lulu Pr., Inc.

Bell, Karen. Cookie's Victorian. 2010. 84p. pap. 31.95 *(978-1-4497-0558-9(8)*, WestBow Pr.) Author Solutions, Inc.

Benator, Eileen. A Marching Band for Bears. Benator, Seth, illus. 2004. 32p. (J). lib. bdg. 15.95 *(978-0-9748478-5-6(2))* Lion's Tale Pr., LLC.

Bennett, Bonnie. Meet Cinnamon Bear. 2009. 48p. pap. 16.95 *(978-1-60749-496-6(5))* America Star Bks.

Bennett, David. The Lost Teddy. 2004. (Ben & Friends Ser.). (Illus.). 24p. (J). pap. 4.99 *(978-1-85854-691-9(5))* Brimax Books Ltd. GBR. Dist: Byeway Bks.

Bennicke, Rune Brandt. The Mystery Hat. Jensen, Jakob Hjort, illus. 2014. (ENG.). 32p. (J). (gr. -1-k). 16.95 *(978-1-62914-621-8(8)*, Sky Pony Pr.) Skyhorse Publishing Co., Inc.

Bentley, Dawn. Fuzzy Bear Goes to School. Nagy, Krisztina, illus. 2005. (Fuzzy Bear Ser.). 10p. (J). 10.95 *(978-1-58117-124-2(2)*, Intervisual/Piggy Toes) Bendon, Inc.

—Goodnight Bear: A Book & Night Light. Couri, Kathryn A., illus. 2005. (Stories to Share Ser.). 12p. (J). 12.95 *(978-1-58117-034-4(3)*, Intervisual/Piggy Toes) Bendon, Inc.

—Wake up, Black Bear! Stover, Beth, illus. 2003. (ENG.). 32p. (J). (gr. -1-17). pap. 4.35 *(978-1-59249-007-3(7)*, S2020); 12.95 *(978-1-59249-008-0(5)*, PS2070) Soundprints.

Bentley, Jonathan, illus. Where Is Bear? 2017. (ENG.). 32p. (J). (gr. -1-2). 16.99 *(978-0-399-55593-0(5)*, Doubleday Bks. for Young Readers) Random Hse. Children's Bks.

Bently, Peter. National Geographic Kids Wild Tales: Twin Trouble: A Lift-The-flap Story about Bears. 2013. (ENG.). 20p. (J). (gr. -1-2). bds. 9.99 *(978-1-4263-1361-5(6)*, National Geographic Children's Bks.) National Geographic Society.

Bently, Peter & McPhillips, Robert, illus. Say Please, Little Bear. 2013. (J). *(978-1-4351-4727-0(8))* Barnes & Noble, Inc.

Benton, Jim. The End (Almost) Benton, Jim, illus. 2014. (ENG., Illus.). 40p. (J). (gr. -1-k). 16.99 *(978-0-545-17731-3(6)*, Scholastic Pr.) Scholastic, Inc.

—The End (Almost) 2014. (Illus.). (J). *(978-0-545-67536-9(7)*, Scholastic Pr.) Scholastic, Inc.

Berardy, Lloyd, 1st. A Tropical Bear in Hawaii Goes Underwater. 2006. (J). 12.95 *(978-1-4276-0212-1(3))* Aardvark Global Publishing.

Berenstain, Jan & Berenstain, Mike. All Things Bright & Beautiful, 1 vol. 2012. (Berenstain Bears/Living Lights Ser.). (ENG., Illus.). 32p. (J). pap. 4.99 *(978-0-310-72088-1(5))* Zonderkidz.

—Bear Country Blessings, 1 vol. 2013. (Berenstain Bears/Living Lights Ser.). (ENG.). 96p. (J). 7.99 *(978-0-310-73503-8(3))* Zonderkidz.

—The Berenstain Bears & a Job Well Done, 1 vol. Berenstain, Stan, illus. 2010. (Berenstain Bears/Living Lights Ser.). (ENG.). 32p. (J). (gr. -1-2). pap. 3.99 *(978-0-310-71254-1(8))* Zonderkidz.

—The Berenstain Bears & Mama for Mayor! Berenstain, Jan & Berenstain, Mike, illus. 2012. (I Can Read Level 1 Ser.). (ENG., Illus.). 32p. (J). (gr. k-3). 16.99 *(978-0-06-207528-4(4))*; pap. 3.99 *(978-0-06-207527-7(6))* HarperCollins Pubs.

—Berenstain Bears & the Forgiving Tree, 1 vol. 2011. (Berenstain Bears/Living Lights Ser.). (ENG.). 32p. (J). pap. 3.99 *(978-0-310-72084-3(2))* Zonderkidz.

—Berenstain Bears & the Gift of Courage, 1 vol. Berenstain, Stan, illus. 2010. (Berenstain Bears/Living Lights Ser.). (ENG.). 32p. (J). (gr. -1-2). pap. 3.99 *(978-0-310-71256-5(4))* Zonderkidz.

—The Berenstain Bears & the Joy of Giving, 1 vol. 2010. (Berenstain Bears/Living Lights Ser.). (ENG.). 32p. (J). (gr. -1-2). pap. 3.99 *(978-0-310-71255-8(6))* Zonderkidz.

—The Berenstain Bears & the Little Lost Cub, 1 vol. 2011. (I Can Read! / Berenstain Bears / Good Deed Scouts / Living Lights Ser.). (ENG.). 32p. (J). pap. 3.99 *(978-0-310-72100-0(8))* Zonderkidz.

—The Berenstain Bears & the Nutcracker. Berenstain, Jan & Berenstain, Mike, illus. 2011. (Berenstain Bears Ser.). (ENG., Illus.). 32p. (J). (gr. -1-3). pap. 3.99 *(978-0-06-057396-6(1)*, HarperFestival) HarperCollins Pubs.

—The Berenstain Bears & the Tooth Fairy. Berenstain, Jan & Berenstain, Mike, illus. 2012. (Berenstain Bears Ser.). (ENG., Illus.). 24p. (J). (gr. -1-3). pap. 3.99 *(978-0-06-207549-9(7)*, HarperFestival) HarperCollins Pubs.

—The Berenstain Bears & the Trouble with Things, 1 vol. 2013. (Berenstain Bears/Living Lights Ser.). (ENG., Illus.). 32p. (J). pap. 4.99 *(978-0-310-72091-1(5))* Zonderkidz.

—The Berenstain Bears at the Aquarium. Berenstain, Jan & Berenstain, Mike, illus. 2012. (I Can Read Level 1 Ser.). (ENG., Illus.). 32p. (J). (gr. k-3). 16.99 *(978-0-06-207525-3(X))*; pap. 3.99 *(978-0-06-207524-6(1))* HarperCollins Pubs.

—The Berenstain Bears' Baby Easter Bunny. Berenstain, Jan & Berenstain, Mike, illus. 2008. (Berenstain Bears Ser.). (ENG., Illus.). 16p. (J). (gr. -1-1). pap. 6.99 *(978-0-06-057420-8(8)*, HarperFestival) HarperCollins Pubs.

—The Berenstain Bears Bear Country Fun Sticker & Activity Book, 1 vol. 2016. (Berenstain Bears/Living Lights Ser.). (ENG., Illus.). 32p. (J). pap. 6.99 *(978-0-310-75336-0(8))* Zonderkidz.

—The Berenstain Bears' Class Trip. Berenstain, Jan & Berenstain, Mike, illus. 2009. (I Can Read Level 1 Ser.). (ENG., Illus.). 32p. (J). (gr. k-3). 16.99 *(978-0-06-168973-4(4))*;No. 4. pap., act. bk. ed. 3.99 *(978-0-06-057416-1(X))* HarperCollins Pubs.

—The Berenstain Bears Come Clean for School. Berenstain, Jan & Berenstain, Mike, illus. 2011. (Berenstain Bears Ser.). (ENG., Illus.). 32p. (J). (gr. -1-3). pap. 3.99 *(978-0-06-057395-9(3)*, HarperFestival) HarperCollins Pubs.

—The Berenstain Bears' Computer Trouble. Berenstain, Jan & Berenstain, Mike, illus. 2010. (Berenstain Bears Ser.). (ENG., Illus.). 32p. (J). (gr. -1-3). 10.99 *(978-0-06-057410-9(0))*; pap. 3.99 *(978-0-06-057394-2(5))* HarperCollins Pubs. (HarperFestival).

—The Berenstain Bears' Dinosaur Dig. Berenstain, Jan & Berenstain, Mike, illus. 2012. (Berenstain Bears Ser.). (ENG., Illus.). 24p. (J). (gr. -1-3). pap. 3.99 *(978-0-06-207548-2(9)*, HarperFestival) HarperCollins Pubs.

—The Berenstain Bears' Dinosaur Dig. 2012. (Berenstain Bears Ser.). (J). lib. bdg. 13.55 *(978-0-606-26290-3(3)*, Turtleback) Turtleback Bks.

—The Berenstain Bears Go Out to Eat. Berenstain, Jan & Berenstain, Mike, illus. 2009. (Berenstain Bears Ser.). (ENG., Illus.). 32p. (J). (gr. -1-2). pap. 3.99 *(978-0-06-057393-5(7)*, HarperFestival) HarperCollins Pubs.

—The Berenstain Bears Go Out to Eat. 2009. (Berenstain Bears Ser.). (J). lib. bdg. 13.55 *(978-0-606-09291-3(9)*, Turtleback) Turtleback Bks.

—The Berenstain Bears' Old-Fashioned Christmas. Berenstain, Jan & Berenstain, Mike, illus. 2012. (Berenstain Bears Ser.). (ENG., Illus.). 32p. (J). (gr. -1-3). 12.99 *(978-0-06-057443-7(7))* HarperCollins Pubs.

—The Berenstain Bears' Really Big Pet Show. Berenstain, Jan & Berenstain, Mike, illus. 2008. (Berenstain Bears Ser.). (Illus.). 32p. (J). (gr. -1-2). 8.99 *(978-0-06-057406-2(2))*; (ENG., pap. 3.99 *(978-0-06-057390-4(2))* HarperCollins Pubs. (HarperFestival).

—The Berenstain Bears Say Please & Thank You. Berenstain, Jan & Berenstain, Mike, illus. 2011. (Berenstain Bears Ser.). (ENG., Illus.). 32p. (J). (gr. -1-3). 12.99 *(978-0-06-057437-6(2))* HarperCollins Pubs.

—The Berenstain Bears' Sleepover. Berenstain, Jan & Berenstain, Mike, illus. 2008. (I Can Read Level 1 Ser.). (ENG., Illus.). 32p. (J). (gr. k-3). 16.99 *(978-0-06-168974-1(2))* HarperCollins Pubs.

—The Berenstain Bears, the Very First Christmas, 1 vol. 2015. (Berenstain Bears/Living Lights Ser.). (ENG., Illus.). 24p. (J). pap. 3.99 *(978-0-310-75102-1(0))* Zonderkidz.

—The Berenstain Bears Trim the Tree. Berenstain, Jan & Berenstain, Mike, illus. 2007. (Berenstain Bears Ser.). (ENG., Illus.). 16p. (J). (gr. -1-1). pap. 6.99 *(978-0-06-057417-8(8)*, HarperFestival) HarperCollins Pubs.

—The Berenstain Bears' Valentine Party. 2008. (Berenstain Bears Ser.). (ENG., Illus.). 16p. (J). (gr. -1-3). pap. 6.99 *(978-0-06-057425-3(9)*, HarperFestival) HarperCollins Pubs.

—The Berenstain Bears' Winter Wonderland. Berenstain, Jan & Berenstain, Mike, illus. 2011. (Berenstain Bears Ser.). (ENG., Illus.). 16p. (J). (gr. -1-1). pap. 6.99 *(978-0-06-057427-7(5)*, HarperFestival) HarperCollins Pubs.

—God Bless Our Home, 1 vol. 2012. (Berenstain Bears/Living Lights Ser.). (ENG., Illus.). 32p. (J). pap. 3.99 *(978-0-310-72089-8(3))* Zonderkidz.

—God Made the Colors, 1 vol. 2013. (I Can Read! / Berenstain Bears / Living Lights Ser.). (ENG.). 32p. (J). pap. 3.99 *(978-0-310-72507-7(0))* Zonderkidz.

—Help the Homeless, 1 vol. 2012. (I Can Read! / Berenstain Bears / Good Deed Scouts / Living Lights Ser.). (ENG., Illus.). 32p. (J). pap. 3.99 *(978-0-310-72102-4(4))* Zonderkidz.

—Honey Hunt Helpers, 1 vol. 2012. (I Can Read! / Berenstain Bears / Good Deed Scouts / Living Lights Ser.). (ENG., Illus.). 32p. (J). pap. 3.99 *(978-0-310-72101-7(6))* Zonderkidz.

—Kitten Rescue, 1 vol. 2011. (I Can Read! / Berenstain Bears / Good Deed Scouts / Living Lights Ser.). (ENG.). 32p. (J). (gr. -1-2). pap. 3.99 *(978-0-310-72097-3(4))* Zonderkidz.

—Let the Bible Be Your Guide. 2011. (Berenstain Bears/Living Lights Ser.). (ENG., Illus.). 40p. (J). 6.99 *(978-0-310-72714-9(6))* Zonderkidz.

—Mama's Helpers, 1 vol. 2011. (I Can Read! / Berenstain Bears / Good Deed Scouts / Living Lights Ser.). (ENG.). 32p. (J). pap. 3.99 *(978-0-310-72099-7(0))* Zonderkidz.

—A Neighbor in Need, 1 vol. 2011. (I Can Read! / Berenstain Bears / Good Deed Scouts / Living Lights Ser.). (ENG.). 32p. (J). (gr. -1-2). pap. 3.99 *(978-0-310-72098-0(2))* Zonderkidz.

—Safe & Sound! Berenstain, Jan & Berenstain, Mike, illus. 2009. (Berenstain Bears Ser.). (ENG., Illus.). 32p. (J). (gr. -1-3). pap. 3.99 *(978-0-06-057391-1(0)*, HarperFestival) HarperCollins Pubs.

—Sick Days. Berenstain, Jan & Berenstain, Mike, illus. 2009. (Berenstain Bears Ser.). (ENG., Illus.). 32p. (J). (gr. -1-3). pap. 3.99 *(978-0-06-057392-8(9)*, HarperFestival) HarperCollins Pubs.

—We Love Our Dad! Berenstain, Jan & Berenstain, Mike, illus. 2013. (Berenstain Bears Ser.). (ENG., Illus.). 24p. (J). (gr. -1-3). pap. 3.99 *(978-0-06-207551-2(9)*, HarperFestival) HarperCollins Pubs.

—We Love Our Mom! Berenstain, Jan & Berenstain, Mike, illus. 2012. (Berenstain Bears Ser.). (ENG., Illus.). 24p. (J). (gr. -1-3). pap. 3.99 *(978-0-06-207547-5(0)*, HarperFestival) HarperCollins Pubs.

—We Love Our Mom! 2012. (Berenstain Bears Ser.). (J). lib. bdg. 13.55 *(978-0-606-23578-5(7)*, Turtleback) Turtleback Bks.

—We Love Trucks! Berenstain, Jan & Berenstain, Mike, illus. 2013. (I Can Read Level 1 Ser.). (ENG., Illus.). 32p. (J). (gr. -1-3). 16.99 *(978-0-06-207536-9(5))* HarperCollins Pubs.

Berenstain, Jan & Berenstain, Stan. The Big Book of Berenstain Bears Beginner Books. 2011. (Beginner Books(R) Ser.). (ENG., Illus.). 320p. (J). (gr. -1-2). 16.99 *(978-0-375-87366-9(X)*, Random Hse. Bks. for Young Readers) Random Hse. Children's Bks.

Berenstain, Jan, et al. Berenstain Bears. 2009. (I Can Read Level 1 Ser.). (J). (gr. k-3). pap. 9.99 *(978-0-06-171904-2(8))* HarperCollins Pubs.

—The Berenstain Bears — a Bear Country Alphabet Coloring Book. 2014. (ENG.). 48p. (J). (gr. -1). pap. 4.99 *(978-0-486-49470-8(5))* Dover Pubns., Inc.

—The Berenstain Bears' Family Reunion. Berenstain, Jan & Berenstain, Mike, illus. 2009. (I Can Read Level 1 Ser.). (ENG.). 32p. (J). (gr. k-3). pap. 3.99 *(978-0-06-058360-6(6))* HarperCollins Pubs.

—The Berenstain Bears Get Involved, 1 vol. 2012. (Berenstain Bears/Living Lights Ser.). (ENG.). 32p. (J). pap. 3.99 *(978-0-310-72090-4(7))* Zonderkidz.

—The Berenstain Bears Go on Vacation. Berenstain, Jan & Berenstain, Mike, illus. 2010. (Berenstain Bears Ser.). (ENG.). 32p. (J). (gr. -1-3). pap. 6.99 *(978-0-06-057433-8(X))* HarperCollins Pubs.

—The Berenstain Bears' New Kitten. Berenstain, Jan et al, illus. 2007. (I Can Read Level 1 Ser.). (ENG.). 32p. (J). (gr. k-3). 16.99 *(978-0-06-058356-9(8))*; pap. 3.99 *(978-0-06-058357-6(6))* HarperCollins Pubs.

—The Berenstain Bears Play a Good Game, 1 vol. 2009. (Berenstain Bears/Living Lights Ser.). (ENG., Illus.). 32p. (J). (gr. -1-2). pap. 3.99 *(978-0-310-71252-7(1))* Zonderkidz.

—The Berenstain Bears Save Christmas. Berenstain, Mike, illus. 2003. (Berenstain Bears Ser.). (ENG.). 48p. (J). (gr. -1-3). 14.99 *(978-0-06-052670-2(X)*, HarperFestival) HarperCollins Pubs.

—The Big Bedtime Book. Berenstain, Jan & Berenstain, Stan, illus. 2008. (Berenstain Bears Ser.). (ENG.). 48p. (J). (gr. -1-3). 12.99 *(978-0-06-057434-5(8)*, HarperFestival) HarperCollins Pubs.

—Kindness Counts, 1 vol. 2010. (Berenstain Bears/Living Lights Ser.). (ENG.). 32p. (J). (gr. -1-2). pap. 3.99 *(978-0-310-71257-2(2))* Zonderkidz.

Berenstain, Mike. The Berenstain Bears & the Biggest Brag, 1 vol. 2014. (Berenstain Bears/Living Lights Ser.). (ENG.). 24p. (J). pap. 3.99 *(978-0-310-73479-6(7))* Zonderkidz.

—The Berenstain Bears & the Christmas Angel, 1 vol. 2016. (Berenstain Bears/Living Lights Ser.). (ENG.). 24p. (J). pap. 3.99 *(978-0-310-74924-0(7))* Zonderkidz.

—The Berenstain Bears Blessed Are the Peacemakers, 1 vol. 2014. (Berenstain Bears/Living Lights Ser.). (ENG.). 24p. (J). pap. 3.99 *(978-0-310-73481-9(9))* Zonderkidz.

—The Berenstain Bears' Lemonade Stand. 2014. (Berenstain Bears: I Can Read! Ser.). (J). lib. bdg. 13.55 *(978-0-606-35072-3(1)*, Turtleback) Turtleback Bks.

—The Berenstain Bears' Night Before Christmas. Berenstain, Mike, illus. 2013. (Berenstain Bears Ser.). (ENG., Illus.). 24p. (J). (gr. -1-3). pap. 3.99 *(978-0-06-207553-6(5)*, HarperFestival) HarperCollins Pubs.

—The Berenstain Bears Phonics Fun. Berenstain, Mike, illus. 2013. (My First I Can Read Ser.). (ENG., Illus.). 100p. (J). (gr. -1-3). pap. 12.99 *(978-0-06-222346-3(1))* HarperCollins Pubs.

—The Berenstain Bears under the Sea. 2016. (Illus.). (J). ***(978-1-5182-2637-3(X))*** Baker & Taylor, CATS.

—The Berenstain Bears: Welcome to Bear Country. Berenstain, Mike, illus. 2017. (Berenstain Bears Ser.). (Illus.). 24p. (J). (gr. -1-3). pap. 3.99 *(978-0-06-235026-8(9)*, HarperFestival) HarperCollins Pubs.

—The Berenstain Bears: When I Grow Up. Berenstain, Mike, illus. 2015. (Berenstain Bears Ser.). (ENG., Illus.). 24p. (J). (gr. -1-3). pap. 3.99 *(978-0-06-235005-3(6)*, HarperFestival) HarperCollins Pubs.

—God Made You Special, 1 vol. 2014. (Berenstain Bears/Living Lights Ser.). (ENG.). 24p. (J). pap. 3.99 *(978-0-310-73483-3(5))* Zonderkidz.

—Gone Fishin'! 2014. (Berenstain Bears: I Can Read! Ser.). (J). lib. bdg. 13.55 *(978-0-606-35476-9(X))* Turtleback Bks.

—We Love Soccer! 2016. (Berenstain Bears: I Can Read! Ser.). (J). lib. bdg. 13.55 *(978-0-606-38123-9(6))* Turtleback Bks.

Berenstain, Mike. Welcome to Bear Country. 2017. (Berenstain Bears Ser.). (J). lib. bdg. 13.55 ***(978-0-606-39641-7(1))*** Turtleback Bks.

Berenstain, Mike, illus. The Berenstain Bears: Easter Blessings. 2016. (J). *(978-0-8249-1967-2(X)*, Ideal Pubns.) Worthy Publishing.

—The Berenstain Bears Love One Another. 2016. (J). *(978-0-8249-1983-2(1)*, Ideal Pubns.) Worthy Publishing.

—The Berenstain Bears' Please & Thank You Book. 2015. (J). *(978-0-8249-1945-0(9)*, Ideal Pubns.) Worthy Publishing.

—The Berenstain Bears' Sleepy Time Book. 2015. (J). *(978-0-8249-1946-7(7)*, Ideal Pubns.) Worthy Publishing.

Berenstain, Mike & Berenstain, Jan. The Berenstain Bears Go to Sunday School, 1 vol. 2008. (Berenstain Bears/Living Lights Ser.). (ENG., Illus.). 32p. (J). (gr. -1-2). pap. 3.99 *(978-0-310-71248-0(3))* Zonderkidz.

—The Berenstain Bears Lose a Friend. Berenstain, Mike & Berenstain, Jan, illus. 2007. (Berenstain Bears Ser.). (Illus.). 32p. (J). (gr. -1-1). 8.99 *(978-0-06-057405-5(4)*, HarperFestival) HarperCollins Pubs.

—The Berenstain Bears Say Their Prayers, 1 vol. 2008. (Berenstain Bears/Living Lights Ser.). (ENG., Illus.). 32p. (J). (gr. -1-2). pap. 3.99 *(978-0-310-71246-6(7))* Zonderkidz.

Berenstain, Mike & Berenstain, Stan. The Berenstain Bears God Bless Our Country, 1 vol. 2015. (Berenstain Bears/Living Lights Ser.). (ENG.). 24p. (J). pap. 4.99 *(978-0-310-73485-7(1))* Zonderkidz.

Berenstain, Mike, et al. The Berenstain Bears & the Golden Rule, 1 vol. 2008. (Berenstain Bears/Living Lights Ser.). (ENG., Illus.). 32p. (J). (gr. -1-2). pap. 3.99 *(978-0-310-71247-3(5))* Zonderkidz.

—The Berenstain Bears Give Thanks, 1 vol. Berenstain, Stan, illus. 2009. (Berenstain Bears/Living Lights Ser.). (ENG.). 32p. (J). (gr. -1-2). pap. 3.99 *(978-0-310-71251-0(3))* Zonderkidz.

—The Berenstain Bears(r) Visit the Firehouse. 2016. (Illus.). (J). ***(978-1-5182-1125-6(9))*** Baker & Taylor, CATS.

—Faithful Friends, 1 vol. Berenstain, Stan, illus. 2009. (Berenstain Bears/Living Lights Ser.). (ENG.). 32p. (J). (gr. -1-2). pap. 3.99 *(978-0-310-71253-4(X))* Zonderkidz.

—5-Minute Berenstain Bears Stories. Berenstain, Mike, illus. 2015. (Berenstain Bears Ser.). (ENG., Illus.). 192p. (J). (gr. -1-3). 12.99 *(978-0-06-236018-2(3)*, HarperFestival) HarperCollins Pubs.

Berenstain, Stan & Berenstain, Jan. Bears on Wheels. 2014. (Step into Reading Level 1 Ser.). lib. bdg. 13.55 *(978-0-606-35994-8(X))* Turtleback Bks.

—The Berenstain Bears. 2007. (Berenstain Bears Ser.). (ENG., Illus.). 160p. (J). (gr. -1-2). 10.99 *(978-0-375-84214-6(4)*, Random Hse. Bks. for Young Readers) Random Hse. Children's Bks.

—The Berenstain Bears & the Baby Chipmunk. Berenstain, Stan & Berenstain, Jan, illus. 2005. (I Can Read Level 1 Ser.). (ENG., Illus.). 32p. (J). (gr. k-3). pap. 3.99 *(978-0-06-058413-9(0))* HarperCollins Pubs.

—The Berenstain Bears & the Bad Dream. 2004. (Berenstain Bears First Time Bks.). (J). (gr. -1-2). spiral bd. *(978-0-616-01555-1(0))*; spiral bd. *(978-0-616-01556-8(9))* Canadian National Institute for the Blind/Institut National Canadien pour les Aveugles.

—The Berenstain Bears & the Big Blooper. 2004. (Berenstain Bears First Time Bks.). (J). (gr. k-3). spiral bd. *(978-0-616-07216-5(3))*; spiral bd. *(978-0-616-07217-2(1))* Canadian National Institute for the Blind/Institut National Canadien pour les Aveugles.

—The Berenstain Bears & the Blame Game. 2004. (Berenstain Bears First Time Bks.). (Illus.). (J). (gr. k-3). spiral bd. *(978-0-616-14560-9(8))*; spiral bd. *(978-0-616-14559-3(4))* Canadian National Institute for the Blind/Institut National Canadien pour les Aveugles.

—The Berenstain Bears & the Mama's Day Surprise. 2004. (First Time Books Ser.). (ENG., Illus.). 32p. (J). (gr. -1-2). pap. 4.99 *(978-0-375-81132-6(X)*, Random Hse. Bks. for Young Readers) Random Hse. Children's Bks.

—The Berenstain Bears & the Papa's Day Surprise. 2003. (First Time Books(R) Ser.). (ENG., Illus.). 32p. (J). (gr. -1-2). pap. 4.99 *(978-0-375-81129-6(X)*, Random Hse. Bks. for Young Readers) Random Hse. Children's Bks.

—The Berenstain Bears(r) & the Talent Show. 2014. (ENG.). 32p. (J). (-3). 9.99 *(978-1-4022-9095-4(0)*, Sourcebooks Jabberwocky) Sourcebooks, Inc.

—The Berenstain Bears & the Trouble with Chores. Berenstain, Jan, illus. 2005. (Berenstain Bears Ser.). (ENG., Illus.). 32p. (J). (gr. -1-3). pap. 3.99 *(978-0-06-057382-9(1)*, HarperFestival) HarperCollins Pubs.

—The Berenstain Bears & the Wishing Star. Berenstain, Stan & Berenstain, Jan, illus. 2005. (I Can Read Level 1 Ser.). (ENG., Illus.). 32p. (J). (gr. k-3). pap. 3.99 *(978-0-06-058347-7(9))* HarperCollins Pubs.

—The Berenstain Bears & Too Much Car Trip. Berenstain, Stan & Berenstain, Jan, illus. 2006. (Berenstain Bears Ser.). (Illus.). 32p. (J). (gr. -1-2). 10.99 *(978-0-06-057400-0(3))*; (ENG., pap. 3.99 *(978-0-06-057384-3(8))* HarperCollins Pubs. (HarperFestival).

—The Berenstain Bears' Bedtime Battle. Berenstain, Stan & Berenstain, Jan, illus. 2004. (Berenstain Bears Ser.). (ENG., Illus.). 32p. (J). (gr. -1-3). pap. 3.99 *(978-0-06-057381-2(3)*, HarperFestival) HarperCollins Pubs.

—The Berenstain Bears Clean House. 2005. (Berenstain Bears Ser.). (Illus.). 32p. (J). (gr. k-3). 16.99 *(978-0-06-058334-7(7))* HarperCollins Pubs.

—The Berenstain Bears Clean House. Berenstain, Stan & Berenstain, Jan, illus. 2004. (I Can Read Level 1 Ser.). (ENG., Illus.). 32p. (J). (gr. k-3). pap. 3.99 *(978-0-06-058335-4(5))* HarperCollins Pubs.

—The Berenstain Bears Clean House. 2005. (I Can Read Bks.). (Illus.). (J). (gr. -1-3). 14.00 *(978-0-7569-5227-3(1))* Perfection Learning Corp.

—The Berenstain Bears down on the Farm. Berenstain, Stan & Berenstain, Jan, illus. 2006. (I Can Read Level 1 Ser.). (ENG., Illus.). 32p. (J). (gr. k-3). pap. 3.99 *(978-0-06-058351-4(7))* HarperCollins Pubs.

A
B

—The Berenstain Bears' Family Reunion. 2009. (Berenstain Bears — I Can Read Ser.). (J). lib. bdg. 13.55 (978-0-606-04776-0(X), Turtleback) Turtleback Bks.
—The Berenstain Bears Go on a Ghost Walk. Berenstain, Jan, illus. 2005. (Berenstain Bears Ser.). (ENG., Illus.). 32p. (J). (gr. -1-2). 10.99 (978-0-06-057399-7(6)); pap. 3.99 (978-0-06-057383-6(X)) HarperCollins Pubs. (HarperFestival).
—The Berenstain Bears Go to School. 2004. (Berenstain Bears First Time Bks.). (J). (gr. k-3). spiral bd. (978-0-616-01551-3(8)); spiral bd. (978-0-616-01552-0(6)) Canadian National Institute for the Blind/Institut National Canadien pour les Aveugles.
—The Berenstain Bears Happy Halloween! 2013. (First Time Books(R) Ser.). (ENG., Illus.). 96p. (J). (gr. -1-2). 9.99 (978-0-385-37191-9(8), Random Hse. Bks. for Young Readers) Random Hse. Children's Bks.
—Berenstain Bears' Home Sweet Tree. 2013. (ENG.). 32p. (J). (-3). 9.99 (978-1-4022-9085-5(3), Sourcebooks Jabberwocky) Sourcebooks, Inc.
—The Berenstain Bears' New Pup. Berenstain, Jan, illus. 2005. (I Can Read Level 1 Ser.). (ENG., Illus.). 32p. (J). (gr. k-3). pap. 3.99 (978-0-06-058344-6(4)) HarperCollins Pubs.
—The Berenstain Bears' Pet Show. 2014. (ENG.). 32p. (J). (-3). 9.99 (978-1-4022-9090-9(X), Sourcebooks Jabberwocky) Sourcebooks, Inc.
—The Berenstain Bears Play T-Ball. Berenstain, Stan & Berenstain, Jan, illus. Berenstain, Mike, illus. (I Can Read Level 1 Ser.). (ENG.). 32p. (J). (gr. k-3). 2005. 16.99 (978-0-06-058337-8(1)) 2004. pap. 3.99 (978-0-06-058338-5(X)) HarperCollins Pubs.
—The Berenstain Bears Play T-Ball. 2005. (Berenstain Bears Ser.). (Illus.). 32p. (J). 11.65 (978-0-7569-5228-0(X)) Perfection Learning Corp.
—The Berenstain Bears' Report Card Trouble. 2004. (Berenstain Bears First Time Bks.). (J). (gr. k-3). spiral bd. (978-0-616-11095-9(2)); spiral bd. (978-0-616-11096-6(0)) Canadian National Institute for the Blind/Institut National Canadien pour les Aveugles.
—The Berenstain Bears Save Christmas. Berenstain, Mike, illus. 2005. (Berenstain Bears Ser.). 48p. (J). (gr. -1-3). pap. 6.99 (978-0-06-052672-6(6), HarperFestival) HarperCollins Pubs.
—The Berenstain Bears' Seashore Treasure. Berenstain, Jan, illus. 2005. (I Can Read Level 1 Ser.). (ENG., Illus.). 32p. (J). (gr. k-3). pap. 3.99 (978-0-06-058341-5(X)) HarperCollins Pubs.
—The Berenstain Bears' Sleepover, 7 vols., Date not set. (Early Childhood First Bks.). (Illus.). (J). (gr. -1-2). lib. bdg. 97.65 (978-1-56674-942-8(5)) Forest Hse. Publishing Co., Inc.
—The Berenstain Bears' Storytime Treasury. 2012. (ENG., Illus.). 104p. (J). (gr. k-3). pap. 12.99 (978-0-486-49836-2(0)) Dover Pubns., Inc.
—The Berenstain Bears' Trouble with Pets. Berenstain, Stan & Berenstain, Jan, illus. 2012. (Berenstain First Time Chapter Bks.). (ENG., Illus.). 32p. (J). (gr. -1-3). pap. 3.99 (978-0-679-80848-0(5), Random Hse. Bks. for Young Readers) Random Hse. Children's Bks.
—Los Osos Berenstain y Demasiada Fiesta. 2004.Tr. of Berenstain Bears & Too Much Birthday. (SPA., Illus.). (J). (gr. k-3). spiral bd. (978-0-616-14610-1(8)) Canadian National Institute for the Blind/Institut National Canadien pour les Aveugles.
—We Like Kites. 2004. (Step into Reading Ser.). (ENG., Illus.). 32p. (J). (gr. -1-1). pap. 3.99 (978-0-679-89231-1(1), Random Hse. Bks. for Young Readers) Random Hse. Children's Bks.
—We Like Kites. 2004. (Step into Reading Level 1 Ser.). (gr. -1-2). lib. bdg. 13.55 (978-0-613-87779-4(9), Turtleback) Turtleback Bks.
Berenstain, Stan, et al. The Berenstain Bears. 2012. (Dover Paper Dolls Ser.). (ENG.). 32p. (J). (gr. 1-5). pap. 9.99 (978-0-486-49835-5(2)) Dover Pubns., Inc.
—The Berenstain Bears & the Bad Influence. Berenstain, Stan et al, illus. 2008. (Berenstain Bears Ser.). 32p. (J). (gr. -1-2). 8.99 (978-0-06-057404-8(6)); (ENG.). pap. 3.99 (978-0-06-057388-1(0)) HarperCollins Pubs. (HarperFestival).
—The Berenstain Bears & the Big Spelling Bee, No. 6. Berenstain, Stan et al, illus. 2007. (Berenstain Bears Ser.). (ENG.). 32p. (J). (gr. -1-2). pap. 3.99 (978-0-06-057386-7(4), HarperFestival) HarperCollins Pubs.
—The Berenstain Bears & the Haunted House. 2010. (Berenstain Bears Ser.). (ENG., Illus.). 16p. (J). (gr. -1-1). pap. 6.99 (978-0-06-057426-0(7), HarperFestival) HarperCollins Pubs.
—The Berenstain Bears & the Papa's Day Surprise. 2003. (Berenstain Bears First Time Bks.). (gr. k-3). lib. bdg. 14.75 (978-0-613-64152-4(3), Turtleback) Turtleback Bks.
—The Berenstain Bears' Big Bedtime Book. Berenstain, Stan & Berenstain, Jan, illus. 2011. (Berenstain Bears Ser.). (ENG.). 48p. (J). (gr. -1-3). pap. 6.99 (978-0-06-057436-9(4)) HarperCollins Pubs.
—The Berenstain Bears' Big Bedtime Book. Berenstain, Jan & Berenstain, Mike, illus. 2008. (Berenstain Bears Ser.). 48p. (J). (gr. -1-3). 13.89 (978-0-06-057435-2(6)) HarperCollins Pubs.
—The Berenstain Bears' Christmas Tree, 1 vol. 2009. (Berenstain Bears/Living Lights Ser.). (ENG., Illus.). 72p. (J). (gr. -1-2). 9.99 (978-0-310-71940-3(2)) Zonderkidz.
—The Berenstain Bears Discover God's Creation, 1 vol. 2010. (Berenstain Bears/Living Lights Ser.). (ENG.). 40p. (J). (gr. -1-2). 6.99 (978-0-310-71936-6(4)) Zonderkidz.
—The Berenstain Bears Do Their Best, 1 vol. 2010. (Berenstain Bears/Living Lights Ser.). (ENG.). 40p. (J). (gr. -1-2). 6.99 (978-0-310-71937-3(2)) Zonderkidz.
—The Berenstain Bears Go Back to School. Berenstain, Mike, illus. (Berenstain Bears Ser.). (ENG.). 32p. (J). (gr. -1-3). 2009. pap. 6.99 (978-0-06-052675-7(0)) 2005. 15.99 (978-0-06-052673-3(4)) HarperCollins Pubs. (HarperFestival).
—The Berenstain Bears Hug & Make Up. Berenstain, Stan & Berenstain, Jan, illus. 2006. (Berenstain Bears Ser.). (ENG.). 32p. (J). (gr. -1-2). pap. 3.99 (978-0-06-057385-0(6), HarperFestival) HarperCollins Pubs.
—The Berenstain Bears Learn to Share, 1 vol. 2010. (Berenstain Bears/Living Lights Ser.). (ENG.). 40p. (J). (gr. -1-2). 6.99 (978-0-310-71939-7(9)) Zonderkidz.
—Berenstain Bears Love Their Neighbors, 1 vol. Berenstain, Stan, illus. 2009. (Berenstain Bears/Living Lights Ser.). (ENG., Illus.). 32p. (J). (gr. -1-2). pap. 3.99 (978-0-310-71249-7(1)) Zonderkidz.
—The Berenstain Bears Save Christmas. Berenstain, Stan et al, illus. 2003. (Berenstain Bears Ser.). (J). (gr. k-3). 129.90 (978-0-06-056995-2(6)) HarperCollins Pubs.
—The Berenstain Bears Storybook Treasury. Berenstain, Stan & Berenstain, Jan, illus. 2012. (Berenstain Bears Ser.). (ENG.). 192p. (J). 11.99 (978-0-06-212014-4(X)) HarperCollins Pubs.
—Do Not Fear, God Is Near, 1 vol. 2013. (I Can Read! / Berenstain Bears / Living Lights Ser.). (ENG.). 32p. (J). pap. 3.99 (978-0-310-72511-4(9)) Zonderkidz.
—God Loves You!, 1 vol. 2008. (Berenstain Bears/Living Lights Ser.). (ENG., Illus.). 32p. (J). pap. 3.99 (978-0-310-71250-3(5)) Zonderkidz.
—Jobs Around Town, 1 vol. 2011. (Berenstain Bears/Living Lights Ser.). (ENG.). 32p. (J). (gr. -1-2). pap. 3.99 (978-0-310-72286-1(1)) Zonderkidz.
Bergen, Lara. Polar Bears' Home: A Story about Global Warming. Nguyen, Vincent, illus. 2008. (Little Green Bks.). (ENG.). 24p. (J). (gr. -1-1). pap. 3.99 (978-1-4169-6787-3(7), Little Simon) Little Simon.
Berger, Carin. Finding Spring. Berger, Carin, illus. 2015. (ENG., Illus.). 40p. (J). (gr. -1-3). 17.99 (978-0-06-225019-3(1), Collins Design) HarperCollins Pubs.
Bergren, Lisa T. God Gave Us Angels. Bryant, Laura J., illus. 2014. (ENG.). 40p. (J). (gr. -1-2). 10.99 (978-1-60142-661-1(5), WaterBrook Pr.) Crown Publishing Group.
—God Gave Us Christmas. 2006. (God Gave Us Ser.). (ENG., Illus.). 40p. (J). (gr. -1-k). 10.99 (978-1-4000-7175-3(5), WaterBrook Pr.) Crown Publishing Group.
—God Gave Us Love. Bryant, Laura J., illus. 2011. (ENG.). 22p. (J). (gr. k — 1). bds. 6.99 (978-0-307-73027-5(1), WaterBrook Pr.) Crown Publishing Group.
—God Gave Us Love. 2009. (ENG., Illus.). 40p. (gr. -1-2). 10.99 (978-1-4000-7447-1(9), WaterBrook Pr.) Crown Publishing Group.
—God Gave Us So Much: A Limited-Edition Three-Book Treasury. Bryant, Laura J., illus. 2010. (ENG.). 112p. 19.99 (978-0-307-44629-9(8), WaterBrook Pr.) Crown Publishing Group.
—God Gave Us the World. Bryant, Laura J., illus. 2011. (ENG.). 40p. (gr. -1-2). 10.99 (978-1-4000-7448-8(7), WaterBrook Pr.) Crown Publishing Group.
Bergren, Lisa Tawn. God Gave Us Heaven. 2008. (ENG., Illus.). 40p. (J). (gr. -1-2). 10.99 (978-1-4000-7446-4(0), WaterBrook Pr.) Crown Publishing Group.
—God Gave Us Sleep. Bryant, Laura J., illus. 2015. (ENG.). 40p. (J). (gr. -1-2). 10.99 (978-1-60142-663-5(1), WaterBrook Pr.) Crown Publishing Group.
Berkes, Marianne. El árbol Que Trepó el Oso, 1 vol. Rietz, Kathleen, illus. 2012. (SPA.). 32p. (J). (gr. -1-3). 17.95 (978-1-60718-679-3(9)) Arbordale Publishing.
—The Tree That Bear Climbed, 1 vol. Rietz, Kathleen, illus. 2012. 32p. (J). (gr. -1-3). (ENG & SPA.). 17.95 (978-1-60718-528-4(8)); (ENG & SPA.). pap. 9.95 (978-1-60718-537-6(7)); (SPA.). pap. 9.95 (978-1-62855-426-7(6)) Arbordale Publishing.
Bersani, Shennen. Achoo! Why Pollen Counts, 1 vol. 2015. (ENG., Illus.). 32p. (J). (gr. k-3). 17.95 (978-1-62855-550-9(5)) Arbordale Publishing.
Betts, McKenzie Leigh. Blue Bear Finds a Rainbow. Abbott, Candy, ed. Desautels, Stacie, illus. 2011. 24p. (J). 15.00 (978-1-886068-51-3(8)) Fruitbearer Publishing, LLC.
—Pink Bear's Journey: I Love Me, Who Do You Love? Desautels, Stacie, illus. 2013. (ENG.). 48p. (J). 15.00 (978-1-886068-72-8(0)) Fruitbearer Publishing, LLC.
Bianchi, John. Bear Can Jump. 2016. (1-3Y Bird, Bunny & Bear Ser.). (ENG., Illus.). 16p. (J). pap. 5.99 (978-1-63437-488-0(6)) American Reading Co.
Bianchi. John. Go, Bear, Go! 2016. (1-3Y Bird, Bunny & Bear Ser.). (ENG., Illus.). 16p. (J). pap. 5.99 (978-1-63437-416-3(9)) American Reading Co.
Bianchi, John. If & But. 2015. (2G Bird, Bunny & Bear Ser.). (ENG., Illus.). 16p. (J). pap. 5.99 (978-1-63437-157-5(7)) American Reading Co.
Bianchi, John, illus. Bear Gets a Hat. 2012. (Bird, Bunny, & Bear Ser.). (ENG.). 12p. (J). pap. 5.99 (978-1-61406-305-6(2)) American Reading Co.
Biddulph, Rob. The Grizzly Bear Who Lost His GRRRRR! Biddulph, Rob, illus. 2016. (Illus.). 40p. (J). (gr. -1-3). 17.99 (978-0-06-236725-9(0)) HarperCollins Pubs.
Bieber, Hartmut. Busy Bear Around the House. 2003. (Loveable Busy Bear Is Back in Two New Adventures! Ser.). (Illus.). 14p. (J). 5.99 (978-1-59384-005-1(5)) Parklane Publishing.
—Busy Bear Celebrates Christmas. 2003. (Illus.). (J). 5.99 (978-1-59384-006-8(3)) Parklane Publishing.
—Busy Bear Goes to Kindergarten. 2004. (Illus.). 14p. (J). 5.99 (978-1-59384-049-5(7)) Parklane Publishing.
—Busy Bear Goes to the Beach. 2004. (Illus.). 14p. (J). 5.99 (978-1-59384-050-1(0)) Parklane Publishing.
Biedrzycki, David. Breaking News: Bear Alert. Biedrzycki, David, illus. (Breaking News Ser.). (ENG., Illus.). 32p. (J). (gr. -1-3). 2016. lib. bdg. 17.95 (978-1-58089-624-5(3)) 2014. 17.95 (978-1-58089-663-4(4)) Charlesbridge Publishing, Inc.
Bier, Erich & Bier, Donna. Lester the Bear. 2013. (ENG., Illus.). 22p. (J). (gr. -1-3). 14.95 (978-1-62086-297-1(2)) Mascot Bks., Inc.
Billings, David Joseph. Road Trip with Rabbit & Squash. Billings, David Joseph, illus. 2006. (Illus.). 48p. (J). per. (978-0-9789036-0-2(9)) Billings, David J.
Bills, Taylor, illus. Goldilocks & the Three Bears. 2009. 24p. 12.95 (978-0-9776845-2-6(0)) 3D Alley, Inc.
Binder, Anita. Bananas & Bears, 1 vol. Binder, Lenore, illus. 2010. 24p. 24.95 (978-1-4489-5946-4(2)) PublishAmerica, Inc.
Birchfield, Elaine. Wilbur Two the Woodland Road. 2012. pap. 12.95 (978-1-4675-2830-6(7)) Independent Pub.
Blackburn, Katie. Dozy Bear & the Secret of Sleep. Smythe, Richard, illus. 2017. 32p. (J). (gr. -1-3). 17.99 (978-0-06-256426-9(9)) HarperCollins Pubs.
Blackford, Andy. Jack & the Hungry Bear, 1 vol. Van Veldhoven, Marijke, illus. 2013. (Start Reading Ser.). (ENG.). 24p. (gr. k-1). pap. 7.95 (978-1-4765-4107-5(8)) Capstone Press of Coughlan Cos.
Blackman, Malorie. Sinclair, Wonder Bear. Allwright, Deborah, illus. 2005. (Blue Go Bananas Ser.). (ENG.). 48p. (J). (gr. 1-2). (978-0-7787-2653-1(3)) Crabtree Publishing Co.
Blackstone, Stella. Bear about Town / Ours en Ville. Harter, Debbie, illus. rev. ed. 2017. (ENG & FRE.). 24p. (J). (gr. -1-1). pap. 6.99 **(978-1-78285-329-9(4))** Barefoot Bks., Inc.
—Bear about Town (Oso en las Ciudad) Harter, Debbie, illus. 2010. (ENG, SPA & FRE.). 24p. (J). (gr. -1-1). pap. 6.99 (978-1-84686-377-6(5)) Barefoot Bks., Inc.
—Bear at Home (Oso en Casa) Harter, Debbie, illus. 2010. (ENG & SPA.). 24p. (J). (gr. -1-1). pap. 6.99 (978-1-84686-422-3(4)) Barefoot Bks., Inc.
—Bear at Work. Harter, Debbie, illus. 2011. (ENG & SPA.). 24p. (J). (gr. -1-k). pap. 6.99 (978-1-84686-554-1(9)) Barefoot Bks., Inc.
—Bear at Work (Oso en el Trabajo) 2012. (ENG & SPA., Illus.). (J). 6.99 (978-1-84686-769-9(X)) Barefoot Bks., Inc.
—Bear in a Square / Ours Dans un Carré. Harter, Debbie, illus. rev. ed. 2017. (ENG & FRE.). 24p. (J). (gr. -1-1). pap. 6.99 **(978-1-78285-330-5(8))** Barefoot Bks., Inc.
—Bear in Sunshine / Ours Au Soleil. Harter, Debbie, illus. rev. ed. 2017. (ENG & FRE.). 24p. (J). (gr. -1-1). pap. 6.99 **(978-1-78285-331-2(6))** Barefoot Bks., Inc.
—Bear on a Bike / Ours À Vélo. Harter, Debbie, illus. 2017. (ENG & FRE.). 32p. (J). (gr. -1-1). pap. 6.99 **(978-1-78285-328-2(6))** Barefoot Bks., Inc.
—Bear Takes a Trip (Oso Se Va de Viaje) Harter, Debbie, illus. 2013. (ENG & SPA.). 24p. (J). (gr. k-1). 6.99 (978-1-84686-945-7(5)) Barefoot Bks., Inc.
—Bear's Birthday. Harter, Debbie, illus. 2011.Tr. of El Cumpleanos de Oso. (ENG.). 24p. (J). (gr. -1-1). pap. 6.99 (978-1-84686-515-2(8)) Barefoot Bks., Inc.
—Bear's Birthday (L'Anniversaire de l'Ours) Harter, Debbie, illus. 2013. (ENG & FRE.). 24p. (J). (gr. k-1). pap. 6.99 (978-1-84686-944-0(7)) Barefoot Bks., Inc.
—Bear's Birthday/El Cumpleanos de Oso. Harter, Debbie, illus. 2013. (ENG & SPA.). 24p. (J). (gr. k-1). 6.99 (978-1-84686-943-3(9)) Barefoot Bks., Inc.
—La Familia Activa de Oso. Sarfatti, Esther, tr. Harter, Debbie, illus. 2003. (Bear Ser.). (SPA.). 24p. (J). pap. 6.99 (978-1-84148-777-9(5)) Barefoot Bks., Inc.
—La Familia Ocupada de Oso. 2012. (ENG & SPA.). (J). 6.99 (978-1-84686-771-2(1)) Barefoot Bks., Inc.
—La Famille Active de l'Ours. 2012.Tr. of Bear's Busy Family. (FRE & ENG.). (J). pap. 6.99 (978-1-84686-772-9(X)) Barefoot Bks., Inc.
—L'Ours au Travail. 2012.Tr. of Bear at Work. (FRE & ENG.). (J). 6.99 (978-1-84686-770-5(3)) Barefoot Bks., Inc.
—Oso Bajo el Sol. Sarfatti, Esther, tr. Harter, Debbie, illus. 2003. (Bear Ser.). (SPA.). 24p. (J). pap. 6.99 (978-1-84148-778-6(3)) Barefoot Bks., Inc.
—Oso en Bicicleta. Sarfatti, Esther, tr. Harter, Debbie, illus. 2003. (Bear Ser.). (SPA.). 32p. (J). pap. 6.99 (978-1-84148-775-5(9)) Barefoot Bks., Inc.
—Oso en Casa. Sarfatti, Esther, tr. Harter, Debbie, illus. 2003. (Bear Ser.). (SPA.). 24p. (J). pap. 6.99 (978-1-84148-779-3(1)) Barefoot Bks., Inc.
—Oso en la Ciudad. Sarfatti, Esther, tr. Harter, Debbie, illus. 2003. (Bear Ser.). (SPA.). 24p. (J). pap. 6.99 (978-1-84148-776-2(7)) Barefoot Bks., Inc.
—Oso en un Cuadrado. Sarfatti, Esther, tr. Harter, Debbie, illus. 2003. (Bear Ser.). (SPA.). 24p. (J). pap. 6.99 (978-1-84148-774-8(0)) Barefoot Bks., Inc.
Blackstone, Stella & Barefoot Books. Bear on a Bike (Oso en Bicicleta) Harter, Debbie, illus. 2014. (ENG & SPA.). 32p. (J). (gr. -1-1). pap. 6.99 (978-1-78285-079-3(1)) Barefoot Bks., Inc.
Blackstone, Stella & Harter, Debbie. Bear at Work. Harter, Debbie, illus. 2008. (Bear Ser.). (ENG., Illus.). 24p. (J). (gr. -1-1). pap. 6.99 (978-1-84686-110-9(1)) Barefoot Bks., Inc.
—Bear in Sunshine. 2003. (ENG., Illus.). 24p. (J). 6.99 (978-1-84148-700-7(7)) Barefoot Bks., Inc.
—Bear Takes a Trip. 2012. (ENG., Illus.). 24p. (J). (gr. -1-1). pap. 6.99 (978-1-84686-756-9(8)) Barefoot Bks., Inc.
Blackstone, Stella & Meza-Riedewald, Leticia. Oso Bajo el Sol. Harter, Debbie, illus. 2009. (SPA & ENG.). 24p. (J). (gr. -1-1). pap. 6.99 (978-1-84686-389-9(9)) Barefoot Bks., Inc.
—Oso en un Cuadrado. Harter, Debbie, illus. 2009. (SPA & ENG.). 24p. (J). (gr. -1-k). pap. 6.99 (978-1-84686-387-5(2)) Barefoot Bks., Inc.
Blackstone, Stella & Parker, Elizabeth. L'Ours Fait un Voyage. Harter, Debbie, illus. 2013.Tr. of Bear Takes a Trip. (FRE & ENG.). 24p. (J). (gr. k-1). pap. 6.99 (978-1-84686-946-4(3)) Barefoot Bks., Inc.
Blackstone, Stella, et al. Bear at Home. Harter, Debbie, illus. 2003. (Avenues Ser.). (ENG.). 24p. (C). (gr. -1). pap. 12.95 (978-1-84148-701-4(5)) National Geographic School Publishing, Inc.
Blake, Adriana L. Benjamin Bear's Naughtiest Night Ever! 2011. 60p. pap. 24.00 (978-1-4567-5252-1(9)) AuthorHouse.
Bland, Nick. The Very Brave Bear. 2013. (Illus.). (J). pap. (978-0-545-65137-0(9)) Scholastic, Inc.
—The Very Cranky Bear. Bland, Nick, illus. 2014. (ENG., Illus.). 32p. (J). (gr. -1-k). 16.99 (978-0-545-61269-2(1), Orchard Bks.) Scholastic, Inc.
Blecha, Aaron. Good Morning, Grizzle Grump! Blecha, Aaron, illus. 2017. (Illus.). 32p. (J). (gr. -1-3). 17.99 (978-0-06-229749-5(X)) HarperCollins Pubs.
—Goodnight, Grizzle Grump! Blecha, Aaron, illus. 2015. (ENG., Illus.). 32p. (J). (gr. -1-3). 17.99 (978-0-06-229746-4(5)) HarperCollins Pubs.
Blevins, Wiley. Bear's Bad Day: Bullies Can Change. Clegg, Dave, illus. 2015. (ENG.). 24p. (J). (gr. k-2). lib. bdg. 19.99 (978-1-63440-012-1(7)) Red Chair Pr.
Bloom, Suzanne. Alone Together. Bloom, Suzanne, illus. 2014. (Goose & Bear Stories Ser.). (ENG., Illus.). 32p. (J). (gr. -1-k). 16.95 (978-1-62091-736-7(X)) Boyds Mills Pr.
—Fox Forgets. Bloom, Suzanne, illus. 2013. (Goose & Bear Stories Ser.). (ENG., Illus.). 32p. (J). (gr. -1-1). 16.95 (978-1-59078-996-4(2)) Boyds Mills Pr.
—Oh! What a Surprise! 2012. (Goose & Bear Stories Ser.). (ENG.). 32p. (J). (gr. -1-k). 16.95 (978-1-59078-892-9(3)) Boyds Mills Pr.
—A Splendid Friend, Indeed. Bloom, Suzanne, illus. 2009. (Goose & Bear Stories Ser.). (ENG., Illus.). 32p. (J). (gr. -1-k). pap. 7.95 (978-1-59078-488-4(X)) Boyds Mills Pr.
—A Splendid Friend, Indeed. 2005. (Goose & Bear Stories Ser.). (ENG., Illus.). 32p. (J). (gr. -1-k). 16.95 (978-1-59078-286-6(0)) Boyds Mills Pr.
—Treasure. (Goose & Bear Stories Ser.). (ENG.). 32p. (J). (gr. -1-1). 2012. pap. 7.95 (978-1-59078-920-9(2)) 2007. (Illus.). 15.95 (978-1-59078-457-0(X)) Boyds Mills Pr.
—What about Bear? (Goose & Bear Stories Ser.). (ENG., Illus.). 32p. (J). (gr. -1-1). 2012. pap. 7.95 (978-1-59078-913-1(X)) 2010. 16.95 (978-1-59078-528-7(2)) Boyds Mills Pr.
Bloom, Suzanne, illus. Bear Can Dance! 2015. (Goose & Bear Stories Ser.). (ENG.). 40p. (J). (-k). 16.95 (978-1-62979-442-6(2)) Boyds Mills Pr.
—A Splendid Friend, Indeed. 2015. (Goose & Bear Stories Ser.). (ENG.). 32p. (J). (— 1). bds. 7.99 (978-1-62979-408-2(2)) Boyds Mills Pr.
Blosser, Connie S. A Bear Named Blue. 2013. 20p. pap. 24.95 (978-1-4626-9340-5(7)) America Star Bks.
Boase, Wendy. Los Tres Osos. Bull, Carolyn, illus. (Primeros Cuentos Ser.). (SPA.). 28p. (J). (gr. k-3). pap. 7.95 (978-1-56014-475-5(0)) Santillana USA Publishing Co., Inc.
Boelts, Maribeth. Polar Bear Almost There. 2016. (Spring Forward Ser.). (J). (gr. k). (978-1-4900-6027-9(8)) Benchmark Education Co.
—Stay Awake, Bear! 2016. (Spring Forward Ser.). (J). (gr. 2). (978-1-4900-9451-9(2)) Benchmark Education Co.
Bogan, Paulette. Virgil & Owen. 2015. (ENG., Illus.). 32p. (J). (gr. k-3). 16.99 (978-1-61963-372-8(8), 9781619633728, Bloomsbury USA Childrens) Bloomsbury Publishing USA.
—Virgil & Owen Stick Together. Bogan, Paulette, illus. 2016. (ENG., Illus.). 32p. (J). 16.99 (978-1-61963-373-5(6), 9781619633735, Bloomsbury USA Childrens) Bloomsbury Publishing USA.
Boland, Gerry. Marco: Master of Disguise. McGuinness, Áine, illus. 2012. (ENG.). 64p. (J). 12.95 (978-1-84717-273-0(3)) O'Brien Pr., Ltd., The IRL. Dist: Dufour Editions, Inc.
—Marco Moves In. McGuinness, Áine, illus. 2012. (Rather Remarkable Grizzly Be Ser.). (ENG.). 64p. (J). 12.95 (978-1-84717-229-7(6)) O'Brien Pr., Ltd., The IRL. Dist: Dufour Editions, Inc.
Bolger, Kevin. Lazy Bear, Crazy Bear. Hodson, Ben, illus. 2015. (ENG.). 40p. (J). (gr. -1-3). 7.99 (978-0-06-228598-0(X)) HarperCollins Pubs.
Bombay, Cal & Sharpe, Margaret. Slave, Brave & Free, 10 bks. 2003. 256p. (J). per. 12.99 (978-1-929125-41-8(0), Multnomah) Doubleday Religious Publishing Group, The.
Bond, Michael. Love from Paddington. Fortnum, Peggy & Alley, R. W., illus. 2016. (Paddington Ser.). 144p. (J). (gr. 3-7). pap. 5.99 (978-0-06-242526-3(9)) HarperCollins Pubs.
—More about Paddington. Fortnum, Peggy, illus. 2015. (Paddington Ser.). 176p. (J). (gr. 3-7). 9.99 (978-0-06-231220-4(0)) HarperCollins Pubs.
—Paddington. Alley, R. W., illus. 2014. (Paddington Ser.). (ENG.). 32p. (J). (gr. -1-3). 17.99 (978-0-06-231719-3(9)) HarperCollins Pubs.
—Paddington Abroad. Fortnum, Peggy, illus. 2015. (Paddington Ser.). 176p. (J). (gr. 3-7). 9.99 (978-0-06-231222-8(7)) HarperCollins Pubs.
—Paddington at the Beach. Alley, R. W., illus. 2009. (Paddington Ser.). 32p. (J). (gr. -1-3). 17.99 (978-0-06-168767-9(7)) HarperCollins Pubs.
—Paddington Bear All Day. braille ed. 2004. (Illus.). (J). (gr. 1). spiral bd., bds. (978-0-616-01860-6(6)) Canadian National Institute for the Blind/Institut National Canadien pour les Aveugles.
—Paddington Bear All Day. Alley, R. W., illus. 2014. (Paddington Ser.). (ENG.). 14p. (J). (gr. -1-3). bds. 6.99 (978-0-06-231721-6(0), HarperFestival) HarperCollins Pubs.
—Paddington Bear All Day. Alley, R. W., illus. 2004. 12p. (J). (978-1-85269-442-5(4)); (978-1-85269-443-2(2)); (978-1-85269-444-9(0)); (978-1-85269-445-6(9)); (978-1-85269-456-2(4)) Mantra Lingua.
—Paddington Bear Goes to Market. Alley, R. W., illus. 2014. (Paddington Ser.). (ENG.). 14p. (J). (gr. -1-3). bds. 6.99 (978-0-06-231722-3(9), HarperFestival) HarperCollins Pubs.
—Paddington Bear Goes to Market. Alley, R. W., illus. 2004. 12p. (J). (978-1-85269-455-5(6)); (978-1-85269-451-7(3)) Mantra Lingua.
—Paddington Here & Now. Alley, R. W., illus. 176p. (J). 2009. pap. 5.99 (978-0-06-147366-1(9)) 2008. (ENG.). (gr. 3-7). 15.99 (978-0-06-147364-7(2)) HarperCollins Pubs.
—Paddington in the Garden. Alley, R. W., illus. 2015. (Paddington Ser.). (ENG.). 32p. (J). (gr. -1-3). 17.99 (978-0-06-231844-2(6)) HarperCollins Pubs.
Bonnell, Kris. Where Is a Bear? 2007. (J). pap. 6.95 (978-1-933727-63-9(2)) Reading Reading Bks., LLC.
Bonnett-Rampersaud, Louise. Never Ask a Bear. Barrette, Doris, illus. 2009. (ENG.). 32p. (J). (gr. -1-1). 16.99 (978-0-06-112876-9(7)) HarperCollins Pubs.
Book Buddy: Polar Bear with Story Book. Orig. Title: Child's Play. (Illus.). 10p. (J). (gr. -1-3). reprint ed. (978-1-881469-48-3(4)) Safari, Ltd.
Boucles d'Or et les Trois Ours.Tr. of Goldilocks & the Three Bears. (FRE.). 48p. pap. 12.95 incl. audio compact disk (978-2-89558-061-4(8)) Coffragants CAN. Dist: Penton Overseas, Inc.
Bour, Daniele. Petit ours brun aime Noel. pap. 12.95 (978-2-227-70915-7(4)) Bayard Editions FRA. Dist: Distribooks, Inc.
—Petit ours brun fait un Cauche. pap. 12.95 (978-2-227-70921-8(9)) Bayard Editions FRA. Dist: Distribooks, Inc.
—Petit ours brun repond au Teleph. pap. 12.95 (978-2-227-74805-7(2)) Bayard Editions FRA. Dist: Distribooks, Inc.
Bourgeois, Paulette & Clark, Brenda. Franklin Snoops. 2003. (Franklin TV Storybook Ser.). (ENG., Illus.). 32p. (J). (gr. -1-3). 4.95 (978-1-55337-365-0(0)) Kids Can Pr., Ltd. CAN. Dist: Hachette Bk. Group.

Bourne, C. L. Sam the Big Blue Bear, Vol. 1. Bourne, C. L., illus. Date not set. (Illus.). 24p. (J). (gr. k-4). pap. *(978-0-9651281-4-8(8))* Beach Front Bks.

Bradford, Wilson D. The Bear & the Price. Abby, Mitchell, illus. 2012. 48p. (-18). pap. 12.00 *(978-0-9848651-2-3(8))* True Path Pubs.

Bradman, Tony. Mr. Bear Gets Alarmed, 1 vol. Warburton, Sarah, illus. 2014. (After Happily Ever After Ser.). (ENG.). 56p. (gr. 2-3). lib. bdg. 25.32 *(978-1-4342-7948-4(0)*, After Happily Ever After) Stone Arch Bks.

Bramble Bear; Can I Help. 2006. (Alphabet & Counting Ser.). (J). per. 3.99 *(978-1-934004-10-4(3))* Byeway Bks.

Bramble Bear; I Wish I Was... 2006. (J). per. 3.99 *(978-1-934004-11-1(1))* Byeway Bks.

Bramble Bear; Pretends to Be... 2006. (J). per. 3.99 *(978-1-934004-13-5(8))* Byeway Bks.

Bramble bear; the Missing Necklace. 2006. (J). per. 3.99 *(978-1-934004-12-8(X))* Byeway Bks.

Brandon, Wendy. Cinderbear: Board Book & Puppet Theater. Winter, Janet, illus. 2004. (J). *(978-1-883043-47-6(6))* Straight Edge Pr., The.

—Cinderbear: (Imagination in a Box) Winter, Janet, illus. 2004. 10p. (J). bds. 17.99 *(978-1-883043-50-6(6)*, 6020) Straight Edge Pr., The.

Brandt-Taylor, Diane. The Bunny, the Bear, the Bug & the Bee. Brandt, Michael, illus. 2005. (J). cd-rom 9.88 *(978-0-9773236-0-9(9))* TaySysCo Publishing.

Brasch, Nicolas. Hot Springs & Brown Bears, 1 vol. rev. ed. 2013. (Fiction Readers Ser.). (ENG., Illus.). 32p. (J). (gr. 3-3). pap. 8.99 *(978-1-4333-5637-7(6))* Shell Educational Publishing.

Braun, Sebastien. I Love My Daddy. Braun, Sebastien, illus. 2004. (ENG., Illus.). 32p. (J). (gr. -1-2). 12.99 *(978-0-06-054311-2(6))* HarperCollins Pubs.

—On Our Way Home. 2009. (ENG., Illus.). 32p. (J). (gr. -1-k). 14.95 *(978-1-906250-59-1(6))* Boxer Bks., Ltd. GBR. Dist: Sterling Publishing Co., Inc.

—One Sleepy Night. 2013. (Padded Board Books Ser.). (ENG.). 20p. (J). bds. 8.95 *(978-1-58925-619-4(0))* Tiger Tales Pubns.

Braunns, Melissa. Big Bear Cares. 2009. 24p. pap. 11.50 *(978-1-60860-636-8(8)*, Strategic Bk. Publishing) Strategic Book Publishing & Rights Agency (SBPRA).

Breckwoldt. The Story of Craig Winston: An Adopted Bear. 2009. 36p. pap. 21.99 *(978-1-4389-9636-3(5))* AuthorHouse.

Brecon, Connah. Frank! 2014. (ENG., Illus.). 32p. (J). (gr. -1-17). 16.95 *(978-0-7624-5423-5(7)*, Running Pr. Kids) Running Pr. Bk. Pubs.

Brett, Jan. The Three Snow Bears. Brett, Jan, illus. (ENG., Illus.). (J). (gr. -1 — 1). 2013. 36p. bds. 14.99 *(978-0-399-16326-5(3))* 2012. 34p. bds. 8.99 *(978-0-399-26009-4(9))* 2007. 40p. 17.99 *(978-0-399-24792-7(0))* Penguin Young Readers Group. (G.P. Putnam's Sons Books for Young Readers).

Bristow, Frank. The Bears of Bopplestone - Book 1 with Tails. 2016. (ENG.). 182p. (J). pap. 16.95 *(978-1-78612-107-3(7)*, 92231f3a-9a27-40be-be66-8e4f5a7c4318) Austin, Stan AUS. Dist: Bookmasters Distribution.

Britto, Romero. Where Is Friendship Bear? Britto, Romero, illus. 2010. (ENG., Illus.). 16p. (J). (gr. -1-k). 12.99 *(978-1-4169-9623-1(0)*, Little Simon) Little Simon.

Brock-Jaurequi, Dawn. From Little Brother to Big Brother, 1 vol. 2009. 45p. pap. 24.95 *(978-1-60836-891-4(2))* America Star Bks.

Broekstra, Lorette. Baby Bbear Goes to the Farm. 2004. (Baby-Bear Ser.). (Illus.). 32p. (J). 5.99 *(978-1-85854-488-5(2))* Brimax Books Ltd. GBR. Dist: Byeway Bks.

—Baby Bear Goes Camping. 2004. (Baby Bear Ser.). (Illus.). 32p. (J). 5.99 *(978-1-85854-408-3(4))* Brimax Books Ltd. GBR. Dist: Byeway Bks.

Brooks, Erik. Polar Opposites, 0 vols. 2010. (ENG., Illus.). 32p. (J). (gr. -1-3). 16.99 *(978-0-7614-5685-8(6)*, 9780761456858, Amazon Children's Publishing) Amazon Publishing.

Brorsen, Jens. Red Face Bear. 2008. 20p. pap. 12.49 *(978-1-4389-3384-9(3))* AuthorHouse.

Brothers Grimm. Snow White & Rose Red: A Grimms' Fairy Tale. Marshall, Denise, illus. 2008. 28p. (J). 17.95 *(978-0-88010-591-0(7)*, Bell Pond Bks.) SteinerBooks, Inc.

Broutin & Stehr. Baldomero Va A la Escuela. (SPA.). 26p. *(978-84-95150-47-9(6))* Corimbo, Editorial S.L.

Brown, Margaret Wise. Little Fur Family. Williams, Garth, illus. 2005. (ENG.). 32p. (J). (gr. -1-1). bds. 7.99 *(978-0-06-075960-5(7)*, HarperFestival) HarperCollins Pubs.

Brown, Peter. Children Make Terrible Pets. 2010. (Starring Lucille Beatrice Bear Ser.). (ENG., Illus.). 40p. (J). (gr. -1-3). 17.99 *(978-0-316-01548-6(2))* Little, Brown Bks. for Young Readers.

—You Will Be My Friend! 2011. (Starring Lucille Beatrice Bear Ser.). (ENG., Illus.). 40p. (J). (gr. -1-3). 18.00 *(978-0-316-07030-0(0))* Little, Brown Bks. for Young Readers.

Brown, Petra. When the Wind Blew. Brown, Petra, illus. 2017. (ENG., Illus.). 32p. (J). (gr. k-3). 16.99 *(978-1-58536-969-0(1)*, 204234) Sleeping Bear Pr.

Brown, Staci. Beary Bad Trouble. 2010. 44p. pap. 18.99 *(978-1-4490-6440-2(X))* AuthorHouse.

Browne, Anthony. The Little Bear Book. Browne, Anthony, illus. 2014. (ENG., Illus.). 24p. (J). (gr. -1-2). 15.99 *(978-0-7636-7007-8(3))* Candlewick Pr.

Browne, Anthony & Bartholin, Hanne. Frida & Bear Play the Shape Game! 2016. (ENG.). 32p. (J). (gr. -1-2). 15.99 *(978-0-7636-7837-1(6))* Candlewick Pr.

Bruchac, Joseph. Bearwalker. Comport, Sally Wern, illus. 2010. (ENG.). 240p. (J). (gr. 5). pap. 6.99 *(978-0-06-112315-3(3))* HarperCollins Pubs.

—How Chipmunk Got His Stripes. 2003. (gr. k-3). lib. bdg. 17.20 *(978-0-613-61631-7(6)*, Turtleback) Turtleback Bks.

Brundage, Frances, illus. The Three Bears. 2004. (Shape Bks.). (ENG.). 16p. (J). (gr. -1-3). 9.95 *(978-1-883211-94-3(8)*, 9781883211943) Laughing Elephant.

Bryan, Sean & Thomas, Evan. A Bear & His Boy. Murphy, Tom, illus. 2011. (ENG.). 32p. (J). (gr. -1-k). 14.95 *(978-1-61145-027-9(6)*, 611027, Arcade Publishing) Skyhorse Publishing Co., Inc.

Bryant, Phoebe. What Is That in the Air? A play date with Sayde. 2009. (Illus.). 28p. pap. 12.99 *(978-1-4490-2209-9(X))* AuthorHouse.

Budds, Laura. Have You Ever Seen a Bear with a Purple Smile? Zimmerman, Kadie, illus. 2013. 16p. (J). 16.95 *(978-1-59152-114-3(9))* Farcountry Pr.

Buehner, Caralyn. Goldilocks & the Three Bears. Buehner, Mark, illus. 2009. (ENG.). 32p. (J). (gr. -1-k). pap. 6.99 *(978-0-14-241275-6(9)*, Puffin Books) Penguin Young Readers Group.

Bunting, Eve. Big Bear's Big Boat. Carpenter, Nancy, illus. 2013. (ENG.). 32p. (J). (gr. -1-3). 12.99 *(978-0-618-58537-3(0))* Houghton Mifflin Harcourt Publishing Co.

Burach, Ross. Pine & Boof: the Lucky Leaf. Burach, Ross, illus. 2017. (Illus.). 40p. (J). (gr. -1-3). 17.99 **(978-0-06-241850-0(5))** HarperCollins Pubs.

Burchett, Jan & Vogler, Sara. Polar Meltdown, 1 vol. Le Feyer, Diane, illus. 2012. (Wild Rescue Ser.). (ENG.). 152p. (gr. 3-6). 9.95 *(978-1-4342-4594-6(2))*; lib. bdg. 25.32 *(978-1-4342-3769-9(9))* Stone Arch Bks.

Burchett, Loni R. Bear & Katie in a Day at Nestlenook Farm. l.t. ed. 2004. (Illus.). 76p. (J). per. 11.95 *(978-0-9742815-1-3(4))* Black Lab Publishing LLC.

—Bear & Katie in a Day with Friends, Vol. 3. l.t. ed. 2005. (Illus.). 68p. (J). per. 11.95 *(978-0-9742815-2-0(2)*, bk003) Black Lab Publishing LLC.

—Bear & Katie in the Great Searsport Caper. l.t. ed. 2004. (Illus.). 81p. (J). per. 12.95 *(978-0-9742815-0-6(6))* Black Lab Publishing LLC.

Burgess, Thornton W. The Adventures of Buster Bear. 2008. 108p. (gr. 4-7). 22.95 *(978-1-60664-950-3(7))*; per. 9.95 *(978-1-60312-500-0(0))* Aegypan.

—The Adventures of Buster Bear. (J). 19.95 *(978-0-8488-0354-4(X))* Amereon Ltd.

—The Adventures of Buster Bear. 2011. 108p. 23.95 *(978-1-4638-9555-6(0))* Rodgers, Alan Bks.

—The Adventures of Buster Bear. 2007. 192p. (gr. 4-7). 29.95 *(978-1-4344-8855-8(1))*; per. 14.95 *(978-1-4344-8854-1(3))* Wildside Pr., LLC.

—Big Book of Animal Stories. 2011. (Dover Children's Classics Ser.). (ENG., Illus.). 272p. (J). (gr. 3-8). 9.95 *(978-0-486-41980-0(0))* Dover Pubns., Inc.

—Buster Bear's Twins. (J). 19.95 *(978-0-8488-0396-4(5))* Amereon Ltd.

Burk, Rachelle. Don't Turn the Page! Downing, Julie, illus. 2014. (ENG.). 32p. (J). (gr. -1-3). 16.95 *(978-1-939547-06-4(7))* Creston Bks.

Burke, David. Goldilocks & the 3 Bears: Level 2: Learn Spanish Through Fairy Tales. Sandoval, Migs, illus. 2006. (Learn Spanish Through Fairy Tales Ser.). (ENG & SPA.). 29p. (J). (gr. -1-3). pap. 14.95 incl. audio compact disk *(978-1-891888-80-9(3))* Slangman Publishing.

—Goldilocks (English to German - Level 2) Learn GERMAN Through Fairy Tales. 2007. (Learn German Through Fairy Tales Ser.). (ENG & GER., Illus.). 29p. (J). per. 14.95 incl. audio compact disk *(978-1-891888-83-0(8))* Slangman Publishing.

—Goldilocks (English to Italian - Level 2) Learn ITALIAN Through Fairy Tales. 2007. (Learn Italian Through Fairy Tales Ser.). (ENG & ITA., Illus.). (J). per. 14.95 incl. audio compact disk *(978-1-891888-82-3(X))* Slangman Publishing.

Burke, David, adapted by. GOLDILOCKS (English to Chinese - Level 2) Learn MANDARIN CHINESE Through Fairy Tales. 2007. (Learn Chinese Through Fairy Tales Ser.). (ENG & CHI., Illus.). (J). per. 14.95 incl. audio compact disk *(978-1-891888-85-4(4))* Slangman Publishing.

Burris, Shana Renee. Bailey the Bear: Sees Stars Everywhere! 2012. (ENG.). 31p. (J). pap. 12.95 *(978-1-4327-9011-0(0))* Outskirts Pr., Inc.

Busch, Jean. Cheyenne & the Indian Spirit. 2011. 28p. pap. 16.95 *(978-1-4560-5651-3(4))* America Star Bks.

Busy Bear Book Set 800938, 4 vols. 2005. (J). bds. *(978-1-59794-097-9(6))* Environments, Inc.

Butler, M. Christina. Who's Been Eating My Porridge? Howarth, Daniel, illus. 2004. 32p. (J). (gr. -1). tchr. ed. 15.95 *(978-1-58925-040-6(0))* Tiger Tales.

Cali, Davide. The Bear with the Sword. Foli, Gianluca, illus. 2010. (ENG.). 32p. (J). (gr. -1-3). 15.99 *(978-0-9806070-4-8(3))* Wilkins Farago Pty, Ltd. AUS. Dist: Independent Pubs. Group.

Callahan, Sean. The Bear Hug. 2015. (Illus.). 24p. (J). *(978-1-4896-3852-6(0))* Weigl Pubs., Inc.

Callahan, Susan. The Fighter. 2012. 16p. pap. 15.99 *(978-1-4685-7190-5(7))* AuthorHouse.

Calmes, Nikki. The Adorable Bears & the New Arrival. 2012. 32p. pap. 19.99 *(978-1-4670-4092-1(4))* AuthorHouse.

Calvani, Mayra. A Bad Mad Sad Day for Mama Bear. Snider, K. C., illus. 2013. 24p. 19.95 *(978-1-61633-434-5(7))* Guardian Angel Publishing, Inc.

Candlewick. My Little Bear Library. 2004. (J). 4.50 *(978-0-7636-2808-6(5))* Candlewick Pr.

Capstone Press. Jelly Bear Christmas Surprise, 1 vol. 2015. (Jelly Bear Ser.). (ENG.). 10p. (gr. -1 — 1). bds. 12.99 *(978-1-62370-247-2(X))* Capstone Young Readers of Coughlan Cos.

Capucilli, Alyssa Satin. My Dad & Me. Mitchell, Susan, illus. 2009. (ENG.). 16p. (J). (gr. -1-1). 7.99 *(978-1-4169-5828-4(2)*, Little Simon) Little Simon.

—Not This Bear: A First Day of School Story. Hussey, Lorna, illus. 2015. (ENG.). 32p. (J). (gr. -1-1). 16.99 *(978-0-8050-9896-9(8)*, 9780805098969, Holt, Henry & Co. Bks. For Young Readers) Holt, Henry & Co.

—This Bear's Birthday. Hussey, Lorna, illus. 2017. (ENG.). 32p. (J). 16.99 *(978-1-62779-701-6(7)*, 9781627797016, Holt, Henry & Co. Bks. For Young Readers) Holt, Henry & Co.

Carey-Costa, Denise. A Tale of Three Tails. Sjostrom, Nicole & Iseminger, Jonathon, illus. 2009. 81p. 10.99 *(978-1-4251-8492-6(8))* Trafford Publishing.

Carle, Eric. Ours Blanc Dis Moi. pap. 15.95 *(978-2-87142-190-0(0))* Mijade Editions BEL. Dist: Distribooks, Inc.

Carle, Eric & Chronicle Books Staff. Stage & Play: Brown Bear, Brown Bear, What Do You See? 2015. (ENG., Illus.). 8p. (J). (gr. -1-1). 16.99 *(978-1-4521-4320-0(X))* Chronicle Bks. LLC.

Carlstrom, Nancy White. Climb the Family Tree, Jesse Bear! Degen, Bruce, illus. 2004. (Jesse Bear Ser.). (ENG.). 32p. (J). (gr. -1-1). 18.99 *(978-0-689-80701-5(5)*, Simon & Schuster Bks. For Young Readers) Simon & Schuster Bks. For Young Readers.

—Guess Who's Coming, Jesse Bear. Degen, Bruce, illus. 2012. (ENG.). 32p. (J). (gr. -1-1). 16.99 *(978-0-689-84820-9(X)*, Aladdin) Simon & Schuster Children's Publishing.

—Jesse Bear, What Will You Wear? braille ed. 2004. (Illus.). (J). (gr. 1). spiral bd., bds. *(978-0-616-01861-3(4))* Canadian National Institute for the Blind/Institut National Canadien pour les Aveugles.

—Jesse Bear, What Will You Wear? Degen, Bruce, illus. 2nd ed. 2005. (ENG.). 32p. (J). (gr. -1-1). 4.99 *(978-1-4169-0834-0(X)*, Simon & Schuster/Paula Wiseman Bks.) Simon & Schuster/Paula Wiseman Bks.

—What a Scare, Jesse Bear. Degen, Bruce, illus. 2012. (ENG.). 32p. (J). (gr. -1-1). 16.99 *(978-0-689-85190-2(1)*, Simon & Schuster/Paula Wiseman Bks.) Simon & Schuster/Paula Wiseman Bks.

—Where Is Christmas, Jesse Bear? Degen, Bruce, illus. 2003. (ENG.). 32p. (J). (gr. -1-1). 13.99 *(978-0-689-86233-5(4)*, Aladdin) Simon & Schuster Children's Publishing.

Carnesi, Mônica. Sleepover with Beatrice & Bear. Carnesi, Mônica, illus. 2014. (ENG., Illus.). 32p. (J). (gr. -1-k). 15.99 *(978-0-399-25667-7(9)*, Nancy Paulsen Books) Penguin Young Readers Group.

Carney, Larry, adapted by. The Three Bears Christmas. 2009. (ENG., Illus.). 24p. (J). 6.95 *(978-1-60072-112-0(5))* PC Treasures, Inc.

Carrick, Carol. The Polar Bears Are Hungry. 2004. (Illus.). (J). (gr. -1-3). spiral bd. *(978-0-616-14567-8(5))* Canadian National Institute for the Blind/Institut National Canadien pour les Aveugles.

Carroll, James Christopher. Papa's Backpack. Carroll, James Christopher, illus. 2015. (ENG., Illus.). 32p. (J). (gr. 1-3). pap. 15.99 *(978-1-58536-613-2(7)*, 203942) Sleeping Bear Pr.

Carroll, Michael Shane. Brewster's New School. Carroll, Katie, illus. 2012. 24p. pap. 5.00 *(978-1-937260-13-2(5))* Sleepytown Pr.

—Bye-Bye Brewster. Carroll, Katie, illus. 2012. 20p. pap. 5.00 *(978-1-937260-14-9(3))* Sleepytown Pr.

Carson, Jeanelle. Lexi Lou Meets Jadie Bear. 2010. 36p. pap. 15.49 *(978-1-4520-9449-6(7))* AuthorHouse.

Casale, Roberto, illus. Little Binky Bear. 2009. (ENM & ENG.). 18p. (J). 7.99 *(978-0-9825700-0-5(7))* Siebler Corp.

Casale, Roberto, illus. El Osito Binky. 2017.Tr. of Little Binky Bear. (J). 7.99 **(978-0-9986498-0-1(5))** Show n' Tell Publishing.

Chambers, Mark. Brian the Smelly Bear. 2013. (Illus.). (J). *(978-1-4351-4728-7(6))* Barnes & Noble, Inc.

Chandler, Pauline. Mr. Rabbit the Farmer. Smith, Eric, illus. 2005. (ENG.). 24p. (J). lib. bdg. 23.65 *(978-1-59646-736-1(3))* Dingles & Co.

Chapman, Jane. Hands off My Honey! Warnes, Tim, illus. 2013. (ENG.). 32p. (J). (gr. -1-1). 12.95 *(978-1-58925-142-7(3))* Tiger Tales.

—Is It Christmas Yet? Chapman, Jane, illus. (ENG., Illus.). (J). 2015. 22p. (gr. -1-2). bds. 8.99 *(978-1-58925-553-1(4))* 2013. 32p. *(978-1-58925-149-6(0))* Tiger Tales.

Chappell, Billie-Jean & Williams, Frederick C. Happiness Colouring Book. Williams, Frederick C., illus. 2012. (Illus.). 36p. pap. *(978-0-9566564-2-1(0))* Dreamality Bks.

Chaud, Benjamin. The Bear's Sea Escape. 2014. (ENG., Illus.). 32p. (J). (gr. -1-k). 17.99 *(978-1-4521-2743-9(3))* Chronicle Bks. LLC.

—The Bear's Song. 2013. (ENG., Illus.). 32p. (J). (gr. -1-k). 17.99 *(978-1-4521-1424-8(2))* Chronicle Bks. LLC.

—The Bear's Surprise. 2015. (ENG., Illus.). 32p. (J). (gr. -1-k). 17.99 *(978-1-4521-4028-5(6))* Chronicle Bks. LLC.

Chaud, Benjamin, illus. The Bear's Song Matching Game. 2015. (ENG.). 60p. (J). (gr. -1-1). bds. 14.99 *(978-1-4521-4183-1(5))* Chronicle Bks. LLC.

Chernesky, Felicia Sanzari. Sugar White Snow & Evergreens: A Winter Wonderland of Color. Swan, Susan, illus. 2014. (ENG.). 32p. (J). (gr. -1-3). 16.99 *(978-0-8075-7234-4(9))* Whitman, Albert & Co.

Chichester Clark, Emma. Bears Don't Read! Chichester Clark, Emma, illus. 2016. (Illus.). 32p. (J). 12.99 *(978-1-61067-366-2(2))* Kane Miller.

—Minty & Tink. Chichester Clark, Emma, illus. 2008. (ENG., Illus.). 32p. (J). (gr. -1-k). 19.95 *(978-1-84270-713-5(2))* Andersen Pr. GBR. Dist: Independent Pubs. Group.

Children, Highlights for & Highlights for Children, inc Staff, creators. Bear's Day. 2016. (Story Puzzle Fun Ser.). (ENG.). 24p. (J). (gr. -1-k). pap. 4.99 *(978-1-62979-546-1(1)*, Highlights) Boyds Mills Pr.

Christmas in Beartown. 2003. (J). bds. 4.99 *(978-1-59384-010-5(1))* Bk. Club of America.

Ciardi, John. Someone Could Win a Polar Bear. Gorey, Edward, illus. 2003. (ENG.). 64p. (J). (gr. 2-4). 9.95 *(978-1-59078-012-1(4))* Boyds Mills Pr.

Clara Roddy-Worsham. Bear Baby Ran a Race. 2012. 34p. 24.95 *(978-1-4626-8182-2(4))* America Star Bks.

Clark, Maxine. Build-A-Bear Workshop Furry Friends Hall of Fame: The Official Collector's Guide. 2005. (Illus.). 159p. (J). (gr. 4-7). *(978-1-59258-142-9(0))* Hylas Publishing.

Clarke, Christie. Star Spirit. 2013. 118p. pap. *(978-0-9917348-2-5(3))* RedemptionHse. Publishing.

Clarke, Jane. Runny Honey. Zlatic, Tomislav, illus. 2008. (Tadpoles Ser.). (ENG.). 24p. (J). (gr. -1-3). pap. *(978-0-7787-3893-0(0))*; lib. bdg. *(978-0-7787-3862-6(0))* Crabtree Publishing Co.

Clements, Becky. A Picnic with Friends: Alaska Adventure Bears. 2003. (Alaska Adventure Bears Ser.). 16p. (J). pap. 9.95 *(978-1-888125-87-0(X))* Publication Consultants.

Clynes, Kate. Goldilocks & the Three Bears. Daykin, Louise, illus. 32p. (J). 2004. (ENG & URD.). pap. *(978-1-84444-048-1(6))* 2004. (ENG & POL.). pap. *(978-1-84444-051-1(6))* 2004. (ENG & HIN.). pap. *(978-1-84444-059-7(1))* 2004. (ENG & POR.). pap. *(978-1-84444-044-3(3))* 2004. (ENG & PAN.). pap. *(978-1-84444-043-6(5))* 2004. (FRE & ENG.). pap. *(978-1-84444-040-5(0))* 2004. (ENG & ARA.). pap. *(978-1-84444-036-8(2))* 2003. (RUS & ENG.). pap. *(978-1-84444-052-8(4))* 2003. (BEN & ENG.). pap. *(978-1-84444-037-5(0))* 2003. (CHI & ENG.). pap. *(978-1-84444-038-2(9))* Mantra Lingua.

—Goldilocks & the Three Bears. Daykin, Louise, tr. Daykin, Louise, illus. 2003. (VIE & ENG.). 32p. (J). pap. 12.95 *(978-1-84444-055-9(9))* Mantra Lingua GBR. Dist: Chinasprout, Inc.

Coats, Vivian. His Special Love. 2009. 32p. pap. 12.99 *(978-1-4490-1915-0(3))* AuthorHouse.

—In His Love. 2009. 32p. pap. 12.99 *(978-1-4389-4104-2(8))* AuthorHouse.

—Safe in His Love. 2009. 28p. pap. 12.99 *(978-1-4490-0377-7(X))* AuthorHouse.

Cochard, David, illus. The Legend of Honey Hollow. 2008. 46p. (J). 16.99 *(978-0-9799444-0-6(6))* Joey Publishing.

Cohn, Karen & Cohn, Brian. The Polar Bear Who Couldn't, Wouldn't Swim. 2013. (J). 14.95 *(978-1-62086-335-0(9))* Mascot Bks., Inc.

Cole, Joanna & Van Horn, William. Ca C'est Chez Moi.Tr. of This is the Place for Me. (FRE.). (J). 6.99 *(978-0-590-71919-3(X))* Scholastic, Inc.

Colleen, Marcie. Super Happy Party Bears: Knock Knock on Wood. James, Steve, illus. 2016. (Super Happy Party Bears Ser.: 2). (ENG.). 144p. (J). pap. 5.99 *(978-1-250-09808-5(4)*, 9781250098085) Imprint IND. Dist: Macmillan.

Colors All Day. (J). 26.20 *(978-0-8136-8399-7(8))*; (gr. -1-3). 59.50 *(978-0-8136-7918-1(4))* Modern Curriculum Pr.

Cook, Jacqueline. The Little Bear Who Worried Too Much: Suzie Bear & the Music Festival. 2010. 32p. pap. 13.00 *(978-1-60860-529-3(9)*, Strategic Bk. Publishing) Strategic Book Publishing & Rights Agency (SBPRA).

—The Little Bear Who Worried Too Much: Suzie Bear & the Social Studies Test. 2012. 28p. pap. 13.97 *(978-1-62212-027-7(2)*, Strategic Bk. Publishing) Strategic Book Publishing & Rights Agency (SBPRA).

—The Little Bear Who Worried Too Much: Suzie Bear Goes to London. 2011. 34p. (gr. 1-4). pap. 13.50 *(978-1-60976-875-1(2)*, Eloquent Bks.) Strategic Book Publishing & Rights Agency (SBPRA).

Coombs, Bob. Ted P Bear - A Bitter Tale. 2005. 83p. (YA). pap. 8.69 *(978-1-4116-4260-7(0))* Lulu Pr., Inc.

Cooper, Doris Marie. Ben Bear's Eventful Day. 2010. (Illus.). 40p. 20.99 *(978-1-4389-0839-7(3))* AuthorHouse.

Cooper, Elisha. Bear Dreams. Cooper, Elisha, illus. 2006. (ENG., Illus.). 40p. (J). (gr. -1-2). 16.99 *(978-0-06-087428-5(7)*, Greenwillow Bks.) HarperCollins Pubs.

Corderoy, Tracey. Flower in the Snow. Allsopp, Sophie, illus. 2012. (ENG.). 32p. (J). (-3). 16.99 *(978-1-4022-7740-5(7)*, 1350490, Sourcebooks Jabberwocky) Sourcebooks, Inc.

—It's Potty Time! Pedler, Caroline, illus. 2014. (ENG.). 22p. (J). (gr. -1-k). bds. 8.99 *(978-1-58925-574-6(7))* Tiger Tales.

Cordier, Claire. The POLAR BEAR in CENTRAL PARK. 2010. 32p. pap. 23.50 *(978-0-557-08167-7(X))* Lulu Pr., Inc.

Corke, Estelle, illus. Goldilocks & the Three Bears. 2005. (Flip-Up Fairy Tales Ser.). (ENG.). 24p. (J). (gr. 1-2). pap. *(978-1-904550-19-8(3))* Child's Play International Ltd.

Cosgrove, Stephen. Fiddler T. Bear. Edelson, Wendy, illus. 2015. (Barely There Ser.). (ENG.). 32p. (J). (gr. k-4). pap. 7.95 *(978-1-941437-44-5(3))* Heritage Builders, LLC.

—Gabriel Faintheart. Edelson, Wendy, illus. 2015. (Barely There Ser.). (ENG.). 32p. (J). (gr. k-4). pap. 7.95 *(978-1-941437-46-9(X))* Heritage Builders, LLC.

—The Grumpling. James, Robin, illus. 2003. (Serendipity Bks.). (Orig.). (J). (gr. k-4). 12.65 *(978-0-7569-5259-4(X))* Perfection Learning Corp.

Costamagna, Beatrice, illus. Polar Bear Munch! 2016. (Crunchy Board Bks.). (ENG.). 12p. (J). (gr. -1 — 1). bds. 6.99 *(978-1-4998-0345-7(1))* Little Bee Books Inc.

Costantino, Eric. Beeboo Bear Dreamed A Dream. 2004. 31p. pap. 24.95 *(978-1-4137-3649-6(1))* PublishAmerica, Inc.

Coudray, Philippe. Benjamin Bear in Bright Ideas! 2013. (Benjamin Bear Ser.). (ENG., Illus.). 32p. (J). (gr. -1-3). 12.95 *(978-1-935179-22-1(5))* TOON Books / RAW Junior, LLC.

—Benjamin Bear in Fuzzy Thinking. 2011. (Benjamin Bear Ser.). (ENG., Illus.). 32p. (J). (gr. -1-3). 12.95 *(978-1-935179-12-2(8))* TOON Books / RAW Junior, LLC.

—Benjamin Bear in Fuzzy Thinking. 2013. (Toon Books Level 2 Ser.). lib. bdg. 14.75 *(978-0-606-31596-8(9)*, Turtleback) Turtleback Bks.

Covey, Sean. Goob & His Grandpa. Curtis, Stacy, illus. 2013. (7 Habits of Happy Kids Ser.: 7). (ENG.). 32p. (J). (gr. -1-1). 7.99 *(978-1-4424-7653-0(2)*, Simon & Schuster Bks. For Young Readers) Simon & Schuster Bks. For Young Readers.

Cowan, Charlotte. Katie Caught a Cold. Bratun, Katy, illus. 2007. (ENG.). 32p. (J). (gr. 3-7). 17.95 *(978-0-9753516-3-5(X))* Hippocratic Pr., The.

Cowley, Joy. Big Bear & Little Bear: Buttons. Lam, Amy, illus. 2013. (ENG.). 8p. pap. *(978-1-927186-33-6(1)*, Joy Cowley Club) Flying Start Bks.

—Big Bear & Little Bear: Cold Feet. Lam, Amy, illus. 2013. (ENG.). 8p. pap. *(978-1-927186-27-5(7)*, Joy Cowley Club) Flying Start Bks.

—Big Bear & Little Bear: Cookies. Lam, Amy, illus. 2013. (ENG.). 8p. pap. *(978-1-927186-29-9(3)*, Joy Cowley Club) Flying Start Bks.

—Big Bear & Little Bear: Egg. Lam, Amy, illus. 2013. (ENG.). 8p. pap. *(978-1-927186-32-9(3)*, Joy Cowley Club) Flying Start Bks.

—Big Bear & Little Bear: Ice Cream. Lam, Amy, illus. 2013. (ENG.). 8p. pap. *(978-1-927186-21-3(8)*, Joy Cowley Club) Flying Start Bks.

—Big Bear & Little Bear: Jackets. Lam, Amy, illus. 2013. (ENG.). 8p. pap. *(978-1-927186-26-8(9)*, Joy Cowley Club) Flying Start Bks.

—Big Bear & Little Bear: Lemonade. Lam, Amy, illus. 2013. (ENG.). 8p. pap. *(978-1-927186-28-2(5)*, Joy Cowley Club) Flying Start Bks.

—Big Bear & Little Bear: Lollipop. Lam, Amy, illus. 2013. (ENG.). 8p. pap. *(978-1-927186-30-5(7)*, Joy Cowley Club) Flying Start Bks.

—Big Bear & Little Bear: Puddle. Lam, Amy, illus. 2013. (ENG.). 8p. pap. *(978-1-927186-34-3(X)*, Joy Cowley Club) Flying Start Bks.

A B

—Big Bear & Little Bear: Race. Lam, Amy, illus. 2013. (ENG.). 8p. pap. (978-1-927186-22-0(6), Joy Cowley Club) Flying Start Bks.

—Big Bear & Little Bear: Singing. Lam, Amy, illus. 2013. (ENG.). 8p. pap. (978-1-927186-25-1(0), Joy Cowley Club) Flying Start Bks.

—Big Bear & Little Bear: Story. Lam, Amy, illus. 2013. (ENG.). 8p. pap. (978-1-927186-23-7(4), Joy Cowley Club) Flying Start Bks.

—Big Bear & Little Bear: Wind. Lam, Amy, illus. 2013. (ENG.). 8p. pap. (978-1-927186-20-6(X), Joy Cowley Club) Flying Start Bks.

—Freddy Bear & the Green Peas. Webb, Philip, illus. 2016. (Freddy Bear Ser.). (ENG.). 20p. (J). (gr. -1-k). bds. 12.99 (978-1-927262-57-3(7)) Upstart Pr. NZL. Dist: Independent Pubs. Group.

Cox, Phil Roxbee & Cartwright, S. Ted in a Red Bed. 2004. (Phonics Board Bks.). 10p. (J). 4.95 (978-0-7945-0061-0(7), Usborne) EDC Publishing.

Cratzius, Barbara & Thonissen, Uta. Good Morning, Sunshine. 2004. (Illus.). 16p. (J). 5.99 (978-1-59384-041-9(1)) Parklane Publishing.

Crichlow, Giselle. Just Call Me Shaun. 2010. 24p. 11.99 (978-1-4490-5222-5(3)) AuthorHouse.

Cuffaro, Anna. Gatwick Bear & the Secret Plans. Anguissola, Anna, illus. 2009. (ENG.). 189p. (J). 18.00 (978-1-907230-02-8(5)) Sparkling Bks. GBR. Dist: Silvermine International Bks., LLC.

Cullison, Martha J. The Adventures of the Culli Bear Boys. 2011. 32p. pap. 21.99 (978-1-4628-8029-4(0)) Xlibris Corp.

Curry, Kenneth. Fuzzy & the All Bear Band. 2007. (Illus.). 22p. (J). 10.95 (978-0-9798364-8-0(4)) Curry Brothers Publishing Group.

Curtis, Shelly. Shellbear's Adventures. 2012. 56p. pap. (978-1-4602-0601-0(0)) FriesenPress.

Dadey, Debbie. The Polar Bear Express. Avakyan, Tatevik, illus. 2015. (Mermaid Tales Ser.: 11). (ENG.). 128p. (J). (gr. 1-4). pap. 5.99 (978-1-4814-0260-6(9), Aladdin) Simon & Schuster Children's Publishing.

Dahl, Michael. Bear Says Thank You, 1 vol. Vidal, Oriol, illus. 2011. (Hello Genius Ser.). (ENG.). 20p. (gr. 1-2). bds. 7.99 (978-1-4048-6786-4(4)) Picture Window Bks.

—Thumbs up, Brown Bear. Vidal, Oriol, illus. 2015. (Hello Genius Ser.). (ENG.). 20p. (gr. 1-2). bds. 7.99 (978-1-4795-5794-3(3)) Picture Window Bks.

Dailey, Reid. Ross the Reader & the Great Balloon Race. Stacy, Alan F., illus. 2011. 46p. pap. 13.95 (978-1-4575-0154-8(6)) Dog Ear Publishing, LLC.

Dale, Jay. Grumpy Old Bear, 1 vol. East, Jacqueline, illus. 2012. (Wonder Words Ser.). (ENG.). 32p. (gr. k-2). pap. 5.99 (978-1-4296-8918-2(8), Engage Literacy) Capstone Press of Coughlan Cos.

Dalrymple, Lisa. If It's No Trouble... a Big Polar Bear, 1 vol. Pratt, Lizz, illus. 2012. (ENG.). 32p. (J). (gr. k-3). 12.95 (978-1-897174-95-1(0), Tuckamore Bks) Creative Bk. Publishing CAN. Dist: Orca Bk. Pubs. USA.

Daniell, G. Dusty & Albert's Beaver Tales. 2009. 50p. pap. 24.00 (978-0-557-08541-5(1)) Lulu Pr., Inc.

D'Ath, Justin. Grizzly Trap. 2015. (ENG.). 144p. (J). pap. 4.99 (978-1-61067-359-4(X)) Kane Miller.

David, Erica. Anna & Elsa #5: the Polar Bear Piper (Disney Frozen) Robinson, William et al, illus. 2015. (Stepping Stone Book Ser.: 5). (ENG.). 128p. (J). (gr. 1-4). 9.99 (978-0-7364-3436-2(4), RH/Disney) Random Hse. Children's Bks.

—Anna & Elsa #8. Random House Disney Staff et al, illus. 2016. (Stepping Stone Book(TM) Ser.: 8). (ENG.). 128p. (J). (gr. 1-4). 9.99 (978-0-7364-3476-8(3), RH/Disney) Random Hse. Children's Bks.

—Anna & Elsa: Books 5-8 (Disney Frozen), 4 vols. RH Disney, illus. 2016. (ENG.). 512p. (J). (gr. 1-4). 39.96 (978-0-7364-3631-1(6), RH/Disney) Random Hse. Children's Bks.

Davidson, Susanna, retold by. East of the Sun, West of the Moon. 2009. (Young Reading Ser.). 64p. (J). 6.99 (978-0-7945-2274-2(2), Usborne) EDC Publishing.

—Goldilocks & the Three Bears (Picture Book) 2008. (Picture Book Classics Ser.). 24p. (J). 9.99 (978-0-7945-2251-3(3), Usborne) EDC Publishing.

Davis, Andrea Nicek. Rex Polar Bear. 2008. 40p. pap. 24.95 (978-1-60474-962-5(8)) PublishAmerica, Inc.

Davis, Angie & Davis, Storm. Make That a Table For: A Grizzly Family Story. 2010. 20p. pap. 11.49 (978-1-4490-7273-5(9)) AuthorHouse.

Davis, Heather. Lam & the Pickle-Eating Bear. 2008. 24p. pap. 24.95 (978-1-60474-332-6(8)) America Star Bks.

Davis, Kerry. Plumple. 2009. (Illus.). 20p. pap. 12.49 (978-1-4389-9362-1(5)) AuthorHouse.

Day, Alexandra. Frank & Ernest. 2010. (ENG., Illus.). 40p. (J). 15.95 (978-1-59583-424-9(9), 9781595834249, Green Tiger Pr.) Laughing Elephant.

—Frank & Ernest Play Ball. 2011. (ENG., Illus.). 40p. 15.95 (978-1-59583-438-6(9), 9781595834386, Green Tiger Pr.) Laughing Elephant.

Daykin, Louise, illus. Goldilocks & the Three Bears. 2004. 32p. (J). (SER & ENG.). (978-1-84444-053-5(2)); (978-1-84444-042-9(7)); (GER & ENG.). (978-1-84444-041-2(9)); (978-1-84444-039-9(7)); (ALB & ENG.). (978-1-84444-035-1(4)); (ENG & SPA.). (978-1-84444-046-7(X)); (TUR & ENG.). (978-1-84444-047-4(8)); (CZE & ENG.). (978-1-84444-049-8(4)); (978-1-84444-054-2(0)); (SOM & ENG.). (978-1-84444-045-0(1)); (ITA & ENG.). (978-1-84444-050-4(8)) Mantra Lingua.

Daykin, Louise, tr. & illus. Goldilocks & the Three Bears. Daykin, Louise, illus. 2004. 31p. (J). (978-1-84444-057-3(5)) Mantra Lingua.

de Beer, Hans, pseud. Kleiner eisbar wohin fahrst Du. pap. 17.95 (978-3-423-07954-9(1)) Deutscher Taschenbuch Verlag GmbH & Co KG DEU. Dist: Distribooks, Inc.

—Little Polar Bear. 2016. (ENG., Illus.). 32p. (J). 16.95 (978-0-7358-4264-9(7)) North-South Bks., Inc.

—The Little Polar Bear. 2011. (Little Polar Bear Ser.). (ENG., Illus.). 32p. (J). (gr. -1-3). pap. 7.95 (978-0-7358-4052-2(0)) North-South Bks., Inc.

—Little Polar Bear & the Big Balloon. Lanning, Rosemary, tr. from GER. 2006. (Illus.). 22p. (J). (gr. k-4). reprint ed. 16.00 (978-0-7567-9875-8(2)) DIANE Publishing Co.

—The Little Polar Bear Lars & the Husky Pup. 2012. (Little Polar Bear Ser.). (ENG., Illus.). 32p. (J). (gr. -1-2). pap. 7.95 (978-0-7358-4078-2(4)) North-South Bks., Inc.

De Jong, Riet M. W. I. Little Freebie & All His Friends. 2011. 124p. pap. 42.75 (978-1-4269-5243-2(0)) Trafford Publishing.

de Las Casas, Dianne. Beware, Beware of the Big Bad Bear!, 1 vol. Gentry, Marita, illus. 2012. (ENG.). 32p. (J). (gr. k-3). 16.99 (978-1-4556-1690-9(7)) Pelican Publishing Co., Inc.

de Vries, Maggie. Fraser Bear: A Cub's Life. Benoit, Renné, illus. 2012. (ENG.). 48p. (J). (gr. k-4). pap. 10.95 (978-1-926812-95-3(6)) Greystone Books Ltd. CAN. Dist: Publishers Group West (PGW).

Degen, Bruce. Jamberry. Degen, Bruce, illus. 25th enl. anniv. ed. 2008. (I Can Read Bks.). (ENG., Illus.). 32p. (J). (gr. -1-3). pap. 7.99 (978-0-06-443068-5(5)) HarperCollins Pubs.

—Jamberry. 2006. (Illus.). (J). (gr. -1-3). 28.95 incl. audio compact disk (978-1-59519-362-9(6)); pap. 39.95 incl. audio compact disk (978-1-59519-323-0(5)) Live Oak Media.

—Jamberry Padded Board Book. Degen, Bruce, illus. 2017. (Illus.). 34p. (J). (gr. -1 — 1). bds. 9.99 (978-0-06-264379-7(7), HarperFestival) HarperCollins Pubs.

Delval, Marie-Hélène. Voici les trois freres Ours. (FRE.). pap. 14.95 (978-2-227-75607-6(1)) Bayard Editions FRA. Dist: Distribooks, Inc.

DePrisco, Dorothea. Mini Snowbears Winter Day. 2006. (ENG.). 10p. (J). 4.95 (978-1-58117-506-6(X), Intervisual/Piggy Toes) Bendon, Inc.

—Snowbear's Winter Day: A Winter Wonder Book. Fehlau, Dagmar, illus. 2005. 18p. (J). (gr. -1). 9.95 (978-1-58117-133-4(1), Intervisual/Piggy Toes) Bendon, Inc.

Derkez, Linda. Chip's Sharing Day. Doehring, Phoebe, illus. 2012. 16p. pap. 9.95 (978-1-61633-245-7(X)) Guardian Angel Publishing, Inc.

Derrick Patricia. Beaser the Bear's Rocky Mountain Christmas. Hoch, Doug, illus. 2007. 32p. (J). (gr. -1-3). 18.95 incl. audio compact disk (978-1-933818-09-2(3)) Animalations.

Derrick, Patricia. Rickity & Snickity at the Balloon Fiesta. Martinez, J-P Loppo, illus. 2007. 32p. (J). (gr. -1-3). 18.95 incl. audio compact disk (978-1-933818-11-5(5)) Animalations.

deRubertis, Barbara. Corky Cub's Crazy Caps. Alley, R. W., illus. 2010. (Animal Antics A to Z Ser.). 32p. (J). lib. bdg. 22.60 (978-1-57565-306-8(0)); (ENG.). (gr. -1-3). pap. 7.95 (978-1-57565-302-0(8)) Kane Press, Inc.

deRubertis, Barbara & DeRubertis, Barbara. Corky Cub's Crazy Caps. Alley, R. W., illus. 2012. (Animal Antics A to Z Ser.). 32p. (J). (gr. 2 — 1). cd-rom 7.95 (978-1-57565-396-9(6)) Kane Press, Inc.

Deshone, Jerry Michael. Bear in Mind. 2011. 24p. pap. 24.95 (978-1-4626-2973-2(3)) America Star Bks.

Dewey, Ariane & Aruego, Jose. Splash! 2003. (Green Light Readers Level 2 Ser.). (Illus.). (J). (gr. k-2). 11.60 (978-0-7569-0534-7(6)) Perfection Learning Corp.

deYonge, Sandra. The Last Bit Bear: A Fable. 20th anniv. ed. 2004. (ENG., Illus.). 48p. (J). (gr. -1-17). pap. 8.95 (978-1-57098-431-0(X)) Rinehart, Roberts Pubs.

Un Día de Escuela de Oso. 2014. (SPA., Illus.). (J). (978-1-78285-087-8(2)) Barefoot Bks., Inc.

Dickens, Ned. By a Thread, 1 vol. Ross, Graham, illus. 2005. (ENG.). 32p. (J). (gr. -1-3). 16.95 (978-1-55143-325-7(7)) Orca Bk. Pubs. USA.

Disney Book Group. Goldie & Bear Training of the Broom. 2017. (ENG.). 24p. (J). (gr. -1-k). pap. 4.99 **(978-1-368-00856-3(9))** Disney Pr.

d'Lacey, Chris. Fire Star. 2008. (Last Dragon Chronicles Ser.: 3). (ENG.). 560p. (J). (gr. 3-7). 8.99 (978-0-439-90185-7(5), Orchard Bks.) Scholastic, Inc.

—Frankin's Bear. Taylor, Thomas, illus. 2005. (Red Go Bananas Ser.). (ENG.). 48p. (J). (gr. 2-3). (978-0-7787-2696-8(7)) Crabtree Publishing Co.

—Icefire. 2007. (Last Dragon Chronicles Ser.: 2). (ENG.). 432p. (J). (gr. 3-7). pap. 8.99 (978-0-439-67246-7(5), Orchard Bks.) Scholastic, Inc.

Dodd, Emma. When I Grow Up. Dodd, Emma, illus. 2015. (Emma Dodd's Love You Bks.). (ENG., Illus.). 24p. (J). (-k). 12.99 (978-0-7636-7985-9(2), Templar) Candlewick Pr.

Dompierre, Judith. Little Bear's & Friend's Summer Trip. 32p. 2012. 29.95 (978-1-4626-9272-9(9)) 2011. pap. 24.95 (978-1-4512-6624-5(3)) America Star Bks.

Dompierre, Judith E. Little Bear's & Friend's Summer Trip. 2012. 32p. pap. 24.95 (978-1-4626-9325-2(3)) America Star Bks.

Don, Lari. Masha & the Bear: A Story from Russia. Williamson, Melanie, illus. 2013. (Animal Stories Ser.). (ENG.). 48p. (J). (gr. 1-4). pap. 8.99 (978-1-84686-874-0(2)) Barefoot Bks., Inc.

Donaki & Rosenberry, Donald. Spectacular Journey. Rosenberry, Akiko & Rosenberry, Susan, illus. 2006. (J). per. 20.00 (978-0-9771482-6-4(2), Ithaca Pr.) Authors & Artists Publishers of New York, Inc.

Donovan, Kevin. Billy & His Friends Rescue a Baby Bear. 2003. (Illus.). 32p. 10.95 (978-0-9641338-4-6(9)) Billy the Bear & His Friends, Inc.

—Billy & His Friends Rescue Betsy Bear. 2003. (Illus.). 28p. 10.95 (978-0-9641338-3-9(0)) Billy the Bear & His Friends, Inc.

Dorémus, Gaëtan, creator. Bear Despair. 2012. (Stories Without Words Ser.). (ENG., Illus.). 32p. (J). (gr. -1-2). 14.95 (978-1-59270-125-4(6)) Enchanted Lion Bks., LLC.

Dorling Kindersley Publishing Staff. Winnie the Pooh. 2004. (Ultimate Sticker Bks.). (ENG.). 16p. (J). (gr. k-3). pap. 6.99 (978-0-7894-9996-7(7), DK Children) Dorling Kindersley Publishing, Inc.

Douglass, Mary E. An Unusually Happy Bear. 2012. 16p. pap. 9.00 (978-1-4575-1333-6(1)) Dog Ear Publishing, LLC.

Downey, Glen. Ice Journey. Brucker, Glenn, illus. 2007. 48p. (J). lib. bdg. 23.08 (978-1-4242-1618-5(4)) Fitzgerald Bks.

Draper, Tricia. Bobby Bear Learns to Be a Cowboy. Babinski, Michael, illus. 2004. 36p. (gr. -1-3). per. 14.95 (978-1-58961-246-4(9)) PageFree Publishing, Inc.

Dube, Pierrette. Searching for Sleep. Godbout, Genevieve, illus. 2018. (ENG.). 40p. (J). (gr. -1-3). 16.95 (978-1-77229-021-9(1)) Simply Read Bks. CAN. Dist: Ingram Publisher Services.

Duchéne, Mique. The Mystery of Foo & the Great Chasm. 2012. 32p. (-18). pap. 17.99 (978-1-4772-7211-4(9)) AuthorHouse.

Dudas, Gergely. Bear's Merry Book of Hidden Things. Dudas, Gergely, illus. 2017. (Illus.). 32p. (J). (gr. -1-3). 14.99 **(978-0-06-257078-9(1))** HarperCollins Pubs.

Due, Kirsten L. Bearen Bear & the Bunbury Tales. Berends, Jenny, illus. 2013. 194p. pap. (978-0-9884916-3-2(X)) Roxby Media Ltd.

Duey, Kathleen. Nanuq: A Baby Polar Bear's Story. Gurin, Lara, illus. 2008. (ENG.). 32p. (J). (gr. -1-3). 12.99 (978-0-8249-1818-7(5), Ideal Pubns.) Worthy Publishing.

Dunbar, Polly. Hello, Tilly. Dunbar, Polly, illus. 2008. (Tilly & Friends Ser.). (ENG., Illus.). 32p. (J). (gr. -1-2). 12.99 (978-0-7636-4109-2(X)) Candlewick Pr.

Durst, Sarah Beth. Ice. (ENG.). (YA). (gr. 7). 2010. 336p. pap. 8.99 (978-1-4169-8644-7(8)) 2009. 320p. 16.99 (978-1-4169-8643-0(X)) McElderry, Margaret K. Bks. (McElderry, Margaret K. Bks.).

Duval, Kathy. A Bear's Year. Turley, Gerry, illus. 2015. (ENG.). 40p. (J). (gr. -1-2). 17.99 (978-0-385-37011-0(3), Schwartz & Wade Bks.) Random Hse. Children's Bks.

—The Three Bears' Christmas. Meisel, Paul, illus. (ENG.). 32p. (J). (gr. -1-3). 2006. 6.95 (978-0-8234-2039-1(6)) 2005. 16.95 (978-0-8234-1871-8(5)) Holiday Hse., Inc.

—The Three Bears' Christmas. Meisel, Paul, illus. 2007. (J). (978-0-545-05421-8(4)) Scholastic, Inc.

—The Three Bears' Halloween. Meisel, Paul, illus. 2007. (ENG.). 32p. (J). (gr. -1-3). 16.95 (978-0-8234-2032-2(9)) Holiday Hse., Inc.

Dyckman, Ame. Horrible Bear! OHora, Zachariah, illus. 2016. (ENG.). 40p. (J). (gr. -1-3). 17.99 (978-0-316-28283-3(9)) Little Brown & Co.

—Tea Party Rules. Campbell, K. G., illus. 2013. (ENG.). 36p. (J). (gr. -1-k). 16.99 (978-0-670-78501-8(6), Viking Books for Young Readers) Penguin Young Readers Group.

Dyer, Howard Wayne. The Itty Bitty Bear. 2006. 11.00 (978-0-9760691-0-2(5)) Itty Bitty Bks.

Dziekan, Jennifer Ellen. The Wishing Bear. l.t. ed. 2006. (Illus.). 40p. (J). per. 7.50 (978-0-9772231-0-7(8)) Kidstory Pr.

Eagle, Golden. You've Got to Know When to Lead. 2005. (Illus.). 20p. (J). per. 12.99 (978-1-59879-025-2(0)) Lifevest Publishing, Inc.

Earl, David G. Koala Koala, I'm Not a Bear, I'm a Koala. Gentry, T. Kyle, illus. 2009. 32p. pap. 12.95 (978-1-936051-22-9(2)) Peppertree Pr., The.

Eaton, Seymour. The Roosevelt Bears Travels Adventures. 2013. (ENG.). 186p. pap. 17.95 (978-1-4290-9805-2(8)) New-York Historical Society.

Edgell, Ernest. The Cowbears of Texas: The Hero. Haycraft, Marilynn J., illus. 2004. 25p. pap. 24.95 (978-1-4137-3507-9(X)) PublishAmerica, Inc.

Eldred, Delmer. Cubby & Scotty. 2012. 28p. pap. 19.99 (978-1-4772-6579-6(1)) AuthorHouse.

Elliott, David. What the Grizzly Knows. Grafe, Max, illus. 2008. (ENG.). 32p. (J). (gr. -1-2). 16.99 (978-0-7636-2778-2(X)) Candlewick Pr.

Elwell, Peter. A Most Remarkable Bear. Elwell, Peter, illus. Date not set. (Illus.). 32p. (J). (gr. k-3). 15.95 (978-0-7614-5008-5(4), Benchmark Bks.) Marshall Cavendish Corp.

Emerson, Darcie. One Sock. 2012. 24p. pap. 24.95 (978-1-4626-7763-4(0)) America Star Bks.

Enderlin, Lisa. Dad, There's a Bear in the Pool!!! 2012. 24p. pap. 24.95 (978-1-4626-8263-8(4)) America Star Bks.

Erb Iii, Walter J. Junior's Fishpond: A Financial Fable. 2012. 38p. pap. 15.95 (978-1-4497-5434-1(1), WestBow Pr.) Author Solutions, Inc.

Erin, K. c. Blueberry Pie: The Adventures of Blueberry Bear & Her Friends. Sloane, Roxy, illus. 2009. 40p. pap. 16.99 (978-1-4389-7592-4(9)) AuthorHouse.

—The Carnival. 2009. 60p. pap. 23.99 (978-1-4389-7048-6(X)) AuthorHouse.

Erlbruch, Wolf. The Miracle of Bears. Reynolds, Michael, tr. from GER. 2006. (ENG., Illus.). 32p. 14.95 (978-1-933372-21-1(4)) Europa Editions, Inc.

Ernst, Lisa Campbell. Goldilocks Returns. Ernst, Lisa Campbell, illus. 2003. (ENG., Illus.). 40p. (J). (gr. -1-3). pap. 7.99 (978-0-689-85705-8(5), Simon & Schuster Bks. For Young Readers) Simon & Schuster Bks. For Young Readers.

Esparza-Vela, Mary. Bearly Learning about Water. Morris, Alexander, illus. 2012. 16p. pap. 9.95 (978-1-61633-288-4(3)) Guardian Angel Publishing, Inc.

Espinoza, Carlota D. God Made a Very Big Big Bang! Espinoza, Gabbi & EspinoZa, Carlota D., illus. 2011. 32p. pap. 24.95 (978-1-4560-9582-6(X)) America Star Bks.

Eubank, Patti Reeder. Count Your Blessings! 2004. (ENG., Illus.). 14p. (J). bds. 9.95 (978-0-8249-6544-0(2), Ideal Pubns.) Worthy Publishing.

Ewashen, Julie. Life in the Arctic with Nina & Nikita. 2013. 56p. pap. (978-1-4602-2727-5(1)) FriesenPress.

Fairley, Melissa. Ding! Dong! Harland, Jackie, illus. 2011. (ENG.). 12p. (J). (gr. -1-k). 15.95 (978-1-84898-362-5(X), TickTock Books) Octopus Publishing Group GBR. Dist: Independent Pubs. Group.

Famous, Howard B. Bobby Bear & Other Stories. 2005. reprint ed. pap. 19.95 (978-1-4179-3376-1(3)) Kessinger Publishing, LLC.

Fanger, Rolf & Moltgen, Ulrike. Moonbeam Bear. 2004. (Illus.). 32p. (J). 10.99 (978-1-59384-015-0(2)) Parklane Publishing.

Farkle, Sandy. The Day the Gummies Wrecked: Square Bears Race the Fakers. 2011. 88p. pap. 19.95 (978-1-4560-4242-4(4)) America Star Bks.

Farnsworth, Frances. Cubby in Wonderland. 2005. pap. 20.95 (978-1-4179-8778-8(2)) Kessinger Publishing, LLC.

Farnsworth, Frances Joyce. Tike & Tiny in the Tetons. 2007. (Illus.). 172p. (J). pap. 14.95 (978-0-943972-79-4(5)) Homestead Publishing.

Farrell, Darren. Stop Following Me, Moon! 2016. (ENG., Illus.). 40p. (J). (-k). 17.99 (978-0-8037-4159-1(6), Dial Bks) Penguin Young Readers Group.

Farrell, Liam. Goldilocks the Babysitter from Hell. 2007. (ENG.). 64p. (J). pap. 11.95 (978-1-901737-57-8(8)) Anvil Bks., Ltd. IRL. Dist: Dufour Editions, Inc.

Fast, Suellen M. Golden-Brown Baby Bear & the Three Sisters. Serman, Gina L., ed. 30p. (Orig.). (J). (gr. -1-18). pap. 4.00 (978-0-935281-11-8(8)) Daughter Culture Pubns.

Ferguson, Don. Winnie the Pooh's A to ZZZZ. Wakeman, Bill & Langley, Bill, illus. 2009. 32p. (gr. -1-2). pap. 4.99 (978-0-7868-4094-6(3)) Disney Pr.

Ferrell, Annie K. Benny the Burro Bears His Burden. 2004. 24p. pap. 24.95 (978-1-4137-2495-0(7)) PublishAmerica, Inc.

Ferrell, Claudine L. In the Valley of the Grizzly. 2011. (ENG.). 184p. (J). (gr. 8-8). pap. 12.95 (978-0-88240-770-8(8), Alaska Northwest Bks.) Graphic Arts Ctr. Publishing Co.

Ferri, Francesca, illus. Good Night, Teddy. 2003. (ENG.). 8p. (J). 15.99 (978-0-7641-2595-9(8)) Barron's Educational Series, Inc.

Ferrier, Charlotte. Goldilocks & the Three Bears. 2016. (Fairytale Cottages Ser.). (ENG., Illus.). 12p. (J). (gr. -1-k). bds. 8.99 (978-0-7641-6817-8(7)) Barron's Educational Series, Inc.

Fett, Ruth E. Goldilocks & the Three Bears: Baxter Bee Teaches about Respect. 2011. 24p. (gr. 1-2). 13.99 (978-1-4567-6192-9(7)) AuthorHouse.

Fianko, Sandra. Sunnie Meets the Bears. 2013. 46p. 26.99 (978-1-4582-0769-2(2)); pap. 20.99 (978-1-4582-0770-8(6)) Author Solutions, Inc. (Abbott Pr.).

Filipek, Nina. Goldilocks & the Three Bears. O'Toole, Jeanette, illus. 2009. (Fairy Tale Firsts Ser.). 12p. (J). (gr. -1-k). bds. 11.40 (978-1-60754-689-4(2)) Windmill Bks.

Finke, Margot. Mama Grizzly Bear. Swan, Gloria, illus. 2012. 16p. (-18). pap. 9.95 (978-1-61633-304-1(9)) Guardian Angel Publishing, Inc.

Floersch, Chris. Mr Charlie. 2011. 16p. pap. 11.99 (978-1-4357-9607-2(1)) Lulu Pr., Inc.

Flor Ada, Alma. Dear Peter Rabbit. Tryon, Leslie, illus. 2006. (Stories to Go! Ser.). (J). (gr. k-3). 12.65 (978-0-7569-7322-3(8)) Perfection Learning Corp.

Florian, Douglas. The Curious Cares of Bears. Sánchez, Sonia, illus. 2017. (ENG.). 32p. (J). (gr. -1-3). 16.99 **(978-1-4998-0462-1(8))** Little Bee Books Inc.

Foley, Greg. Thank You Bear. Foley, Greg, illus. 2007. (ENG., Illus.). 32p. (J). (gr. -1-k). 15.99 (978-0-670-06165-5(4), Viking Books for Young Readers) Penguin Young Readers Group.

—Thank You Bear Board Book. Foley, Greg, illus. 2012. (ENG., Illus.). 28p. (J). (gr. -1-k). bds. 6.99 (978-0-670-78507-0(5), Viking Books for Young Readers) Penguin Young Readers Group.

Foley, James. Danny & the Blue Cloud: Coping with Childhood Depression. Ng-Benitez, Shirley, illus. 2016. 32p. (J). (978-1-4338-2103-5(6), Magination Pr.) American Psychological Assn.

Follett, Ross C. Beebear 2. Sievers, Lee, illus. 2013. (ENG.). 52p. (J). (gr. -1-3). 15.95 (978-0-9881748-0-1(4), OddInt Media) Greenwood Hill Pr.

Forbush, Kyle. Who Is Alaska's Favorite Bear? Forbush, Lisa, illus. 2003. (J). bds. 6.95 (978-1-57833-211-3(7)) Todd Communications.

Forde, Catherine. Tug of War. 2008. (ENG.). 320p. (YA). (gr. 7). pap. 9.99 (978-1-4052-3967-7(0)) Egmont Bks., Ltd. GBR. Dist: Independent Pubs. Group.

Foreman, Michael. I Love You, Too! Foreman, Michael, illus. 2014. (ENG., Illus.). 32p. (J). (gr. -1-3). 16.95 (978-1-4677-3451-6(9)) Lerner Publishing Group.

Forte, Lauren. Masha & the Bear: Scary Movies Are Bad for Bedtime! 2017. (ENG., Illus.). 24p. (J). (gr. -1-3). pap. 4.99 **(978-0-316-43621-2(6))** Little, Brown Bks. for Young Readers.

—Masha & the Bear: Kidding Around. 2017. (ENG.). 32p. (J). (gr. -1-3). 12.99 (978-0-316-50489-8(0)) Little, Brown Bks. for Young Readers.

Forte, Lauren. Masha & the Bear: the Girl Who Cried Wolf. 2017. (Passport to Reading Level 1 Ser.). (ENG., Illus.). 32p. (J). (gr. -1-3). pap. 4.99 **(978-0-316-43620-5(8))** Little, Brown Bks. for Young Readers.

Foust, Cindy G. Benny Bear: Having A Baby Sister Isn't Fair. Revoir, Joyce, illus. 2004. (J). 12.95 (978-0-9749220-1-0(3)) Alpha-kidZ.

Fox, Frances Margaret. Little Bear at Work & at Play. 2004. reprint ed. pap. 1.99 (978-1-4192-3071-4(9)); pap. 15.95 (978-1-4191-3071-7(4)) Kessinger Publishing, LLC.

Fox, Mem. Sleepy Bears. 2004. (Illus.). (J). (gr. -1-2). spiral bd. (978-0-616-04554-1(9)); spiral bd. (978-0-616-03033-2(9)) Canadian National Institute for the Blind/Institut National Canadien pour les Aveugles.

Fraggalosch, Audrey & Eberhart, Donald G. Grizzly Bear Family. 2005. (Amazing Animal Adventures Ser.). (ENG., Illus.). 36p. (J). (gr. -1-2). 15.95 (978-1-59249-048-6(4), B7103); pap. 6.95 (978-1-59249-049-3(2), S7103) Soundprints.

Fraggalosch, Audrey M. Grizzly Bear Family. Eberhart, Donald G., illus. (Soundprints' Amazing Animal Adventures! Ser.). (ENG.). (J). 2005. 36p. (gr. -1-2). 8.95 (978-1-59249-395-1(5), SC7103) 2005. 32p. (gr. 2-2). 19.95 (978-1-59249-394-4(7), BC7103) 2003. 36p. (gr. -1-3). 9.95 (978-1-59249-059-2(X), PS7153) 2003. 36p. (gr. -1-k). pap. 2.95 (978-1-59249-050-9(6), S7153) Soundprints.

Francis, Jamaine. The Adventures of Pb & Brown Bear: Lost & Found. 2009. 28p. pap. 12.88 (978-1-4490-1817-7(3)) AuthorHouse.

Franklin, Cathy. The Magical Ballet Shoes: A Pinta & Polly Story, 1 vol. Watkins, Tammy, illus. 2009. 25p. pap. 24.95 (978-1-4489-2007-5(8)) America Star Bks.

—Pinta & Polly Go to the Moon, 1 vol. Poole, Tracy, illus. 2009. 27p. pap. 24.95 (978-1-60813-861-6(5)) America Star Bks.

Fraser, Frank. The Bible Amigos: Jonah & the Bear. 2014. (ENG., Illus.). 48p. (J). 7.99 (978-1-62416-887-1(6)) Barbour Publishing, Inc.

Frati, Dorothy. Friendly Bubbles. 2012. 24p. pap. 17.99 (978-1-4772-6447-8(7)) AuthorHouse.

Freedman, Claire. Good Night, Sleep Tight! Tyger, Rory, illus. 2007. 32p. (J). (gr. -1-1). pap. 6.95 (978-1-58925-405-3(8)) Tiger Tales.

—Goodnight, Sleep Tight! Tyger, Rory, illus. 2013. (ENG.). 32p. (J). (gr. -1). pap. 3.99 (978-1-58925-440-4(6)) Tiger Tales.

—Little Bear's Special Friend. Kolanovic, Dubravka, illus. 2007. (J). (978-0-545-06757-7(X)) Scholastic, Inc.

—My Precious Little Bear. Scott, Gavin, illus. 2011. (ENG.). 20p. (J). (gr. k — 1). bds. 8.99 *(978-0-545-27432-6(X),* Cartwheel Bks.) Scholastic, Inc.

Freeman, Don. Beady Bear: With the Never-Before-Seen Story Beady's Pillow. 2015. (ENG., Illus.). 96p. (J). (gr. k-4). pap. 12.99 *(978-0-486-79713-7(9))* Dover Pubns., Inc.

—Corduroy Goes to the Doctor. McCue, Lisa, illus. 2005. (Corduroy Ser.). (ENG.). 14p. (J). (gr. -1 — 1). bds. 5.99 *(978-0-670-06031-3(3),* Viking Books for Young Readers) Penguin Young Readers Group.

—Corduroy's Day. McCue, Lisa, illus. 2005. (Corduroy Ser.). (ENG.). 14p. (J). (gr. -1 — 1). bds. 5.99 *(978-0-670-06030-6(5),* Viking Books for Young Readers) Penguin Young Readers Group.

—Halloween Is Here, Corduroy! McCue, Lisa & Kong, Emilie, illus. 2007. (Corduroy Ser.). (ENG.). 16p. (J). (gr. -1-k). pap. 5.99 *(978-0-448-44563-2(8),* Grosset & Dunlap) Penguin Young Readers Group.

—A Pocket for Corduroy. 1 vol. 2008. (Corduroy Ser.). (ENG., Illus.). 32p. (J). (gr. -1-k). 10.99 *(978-0-14-241040-0(3),* Puffin Books) Penguin Young Readers Group.

—Spring Is Here, Corduroy! McCue, Lisa, illus. 2007. (Corduroy Ser.). (ENG.). 16p. (J). (gr. -1-k). 6.99 *(978-0-448-44461-1(5),* Grosset & Dunlap) Penguin Young Readers Group.

French, Jackie. My Pa the Polar Bear. 2015. (Wacky Families Ser.: 08). 128p. 5.99 *(978-0-207-20078-6(5))* HarperCollins Pubs. Australia AUS. Dist: HarperCollins Pubs.

Friden, Chris. Pajamatime with P.J. Zapater Oliva, Carlos & Glazier, Garth, illus. 2008. (J). *(978-0-9758785-9-0(X));* *(978-0-9801849-5-2(9))* Haydenburri Lane.

Frith, Nicholas John. Hector & Hummingbird. Frith, Nicholas John, illus. 2016. (ENG., Illus.). 32p. (J). (gr. -1-3). 17.99 *(978-0-545-85701-7(5))* Scholastic, Inc.

Fronte, Kathy. Bella's Bow Tie Bears: Three Magnificent Tales of Adventure, Dreams & Magic. 2006. (Illus.). 36p. (J). pap. 12.95 *(978-0-9727725-0-1(2))* Fronte, Kathy.

Gabriel, Andrea. My Favorite Bear. 2014. 32p. pap. 8.00 *(978-1-61003-310-7(8))* Center for the Collaborative Classroom.

—My Favorite Bear. Gabriel, Andrea, illus. 2004. (ENG., Illus.). 32p. (J). (-k). pap. 7.95 *(978-1-58089-039-7(3))* Charlesbridge Publishing, Inc.

Galdone, Paul. The Three Bears. 2011. (Folk Tale Classics Ser.). (ENG., Illus.). 40p. (J). (gr. -1-3). 8.99 *(978-0-547-37019-4(9))* Houghton Mifflin Harcourt Publishing Co.

—The Three Bears Big Book. 2014. (Paul Galdone Classics Ser.). (ENG., Illus.). 32p. (J). (gr. -1-3). 26.99 *(978-0-544-33913-2(4),* HMH Books For Young Readers) Houghton Mifflin Harcourt Publishing Co.

Galdone, Paul, illus. The Three Bears. 2011. (J). pap. ***(978-0-547-86831-8(6))*** Harcourt.

Gallo, Tina. Master of Manners. 2016. (Kung Fu Panda 8x8 Ser.). lib. bdg. 13.55 *(978-0-606-38996-9(2))* Turtleback Bks.

—Thankfulness Is Awesomeness. 2016. (Kung Fu Panda Ready-To-Read Ser.). (ENG., Illus.). 32p. (J). (gr. k-2). 13.55 *(978-0-606-39243-3(2))* Turtleback Bks.

Galvin, Laura Gates. Baby Polar Bear Learns to Swim. 2008. (Smithsonian Baby Animals Ser.). (ENG., Illus.). 16p. (gr. -1-k). 13.95 *(978-1-59249-786-7(1));* (J). 6.95 *(978-1-59249-785-0(3))* Soundprints.

—Black Bear Cub at Sweet Berry Trail. 2008. (ENG., Illus.). 32p. (J). (gr. k-2). 9.95 *(978-1-59249-779-9(9))* Soundprints.

—Black Bear Cub at Sweet Berry Trail. Nelson, Will, illus. 2008. (ENG.). 32p. (J). (gr. k-2). 6.95 *(978-1-59249-775-1(6));* pap. 8.95 *(978-1-59249-777-5(2));* 19.95 *(978-1-59249-776-8(4));* 16.95 *(978-1-59249-773-7(X));* pap. 6.95 *(978-1-59249-774-4(8))* Soundprints.

Gammon, Bob. Orange Polar Bears Don't Cry. 2008. 36p. pap. 18.50 *(978-1-60693-393-0(0),* Eloquent Bks.) Strategic Book Publishing & Rights Agency (SBPRA).

Gansle, Sherry. Oops, a Curious Horse Big Book. Light, Carol, illus. 2003. 56p. (J). *(978-0-9745803-6-4(8))* Little Big Tomes.

—Oops, a Curious Horse Little Book. Light, Carol, illus. 2003. 52p. (J). *(978-0-9745803-7-1(6))* Little Big Tomes.

Garland, Sally. Tig & Tog's Dinosaur Discovery. 2015. (ENG., Illus.). 32p. (J). (gr. -1-3). 16.99 *(978-1-4998-0155-2(6))* Little Bee Books Inc.

Garton, Sam. Otter Loves Halloween! Garton, Sam, illus. 2015. (ENG., Illus.). 32p. (J). (gr. -1-3). 9.99 *(978-0-06-236666-5(1),* Balzer & Bray) HarperCollins Pubs.

Gavin, Ciara. Bear Is Not Tired. 2016. (ENG., Illus.). 32p. (J). (gr. -1-2). 16.99 *(978-0-385-75476-7(0),* Knopf Bks. for Young Readers) Random Hse. Children's Bks.

—Bear Likes Jam. 2017. (ENG., Illus.). 32p. (J). (gr. -1-2). 16.99 *(978-0-399-55179-6(4),* Knopf Bks. for Young Readers) Random Hse. Children's Bks.

—Room for Bear. 2015. (ENG., Illus.). 32p. (J). (gr. -1-2). 16.99 *(978-0-385-75473-6(6),* Knopf Bks. for Young Readers) Random Hse. Children's Bks.

Gebhart, Ryan. There Will Be Bears. 2014. (ENG.). 224p. (J). (gr. 5). 16.99 *(978-0-7636-6521-0(5))* Candlewick Pr.

Gehrmann, Katja, illus. Goose the Bear. 2014. (ENG.). 40p. (J). (gr. -1-3). 16.95 *(978-1-62636-384-7(6),* Sky Pony Pr.) Skyhorse Publishing Co., Inc.

George, Jean Craighead. The Last Polar Bear. Minor, Wendell, illus. (ENG.). 32p. (J). (gr. -1-2). 2014. pap. 6.99 *(978-0-06-124069-0(9))* 2009. 16.99 *(978-0-06-124067-6(2))* HarperCollins Pubs.

Gerver, Jane E. Good Night. Flint, Gillian, illus. 2015. (ENG.). 14p. (J). (— 1). bds. 4.99 *(978-1-62979-415-0(5),* Highlights) Boyds Mills Pr.

Getti, C. Bear's Prayer. 2011. 28p. pap. 15.99 *(978-1-4568-7228-1(1))* Xlibris Corp.

Ghigna, Charles. Bobby Bear. East, Jacqueline, illus. 2015. (Tiny Tales Ser.). (ENG.). 64p. (gr. -1-2). lib. bdg. 23.99 *(978-1-4795-6531-3(8))* Tiny Tales.

Gi Gi. The Adventures of Trueword the Bear. 2012. 28p. pap. 24.95 *(978-1-4626-8042-9(9))* America Star Bks.

Giesler, Dagmar & Geisler, Dagmar. Max juega en la Arena. 2004. (Coleccion Max Max Ser.). (SPA.). (J). bds. 11.95 *(978-84-261-3295-6(2))* Juventud, Editorial ESP. Dist: Distribooks, Inc.

Gili, Phillida. The Lost Ears. 25th annot. anniv. ed. 2006. (Illus.). 32p. (J). (gr. -1-1). 12.95 *(978-1-905417-18-6(7))* Boxer Bks., Ltd. GBR. Dist: Sterling Publishing Co., Inc.

Girvan, Gregor. A Trial for Iris. 2013. 32p. pap. 3.95 *(978-1-78035-666-2(8),* Fastprint Publishing) Upfront Publishing Ltd. GBR. Dist: Printondemand-worldwide.com.

Glendenning, Debra Morgan. Little Lost Baxter. 2009. 28p. pap. 24.95 *(978-1-60749-256-6(3))* America Star Bks.

Glori, Debi. Little Bear & the Wish Fish. (Illus.). 32p. (J). (gr. -1-2). pap. *(978-0-7112-0986-2(3))* ReiseArt Buchhandlung GmbH.

Glitterpony, Jessica Noelle. The Warkak & Snoozle. 2013. 42p. pap. 9.87 *(978-1-939896-16-2(9))* Levity Pr.

Godley, Marie. The Special Christmas Bear. 2007. (Illus.). 52p. per. *(978-1-84748-005-7(5))* Athena Pr.

Godwin, Jane & Wagner, Michael. Bear Make Den. Joyner, Andrew, illus. 2017. (ENG.). 40p. (J). (gr. -1-3). 16.99 ***(978-0-7636-9061-8(9))*** Candlewick Pr.

Goggins, Jean. The Adventures of Boo & Koty: Snow. 2009. 36p. pap. 21.99 *(978-1-4415-4670-8(7))* Xlibris Corp.

Goldilocks: 6 Small Books. (gr. k-2). 23.00 *(978-0-7635-8512-9(2))* Rigby Education.

Goldilocks & the Three Bears. 2004. (My First Fairy Tales Ser.). (Illus.). 24p. (J). pap. 3.99 *(978-1-85854-686-5(9))* Brimax Books Ltd. GBR. Dist: Byeway Bks.

Goldilocks & the Three Bears. 2005. (J). bds. 3.99 *(978-1-933200-09-5(X))* Family Bks. at Home.

Goldilocks & the Three Bears. (Ladybird Bks.). (ARA., Illus.). 52p. (J). 12.95 incl. audio *(978-0-86685-254-8(9),* LDL109C) International Bk. Ctr., Inc.

Goldilocks & the Three Bears: Take-Home Book. 2005. (Emergent Library: Vol. 2). (YA). (gr. -1-1). 12.60 *(978-0-8215-7260-3(1))* Sadlier, William H. Inc.

GoldilocksThree Bears. 2004. (J). E-Book incl. cd-rom *(978-1-84444-460-1(0))* Mantra Lingua.

Gonzalo, Angela. The Pig, Bear, & the Pear: The Pear Meets the Pig & Bear. 2013. 44p. pap. 17.45 *(978-1-4624-0576-3(2),* Inspiring Voices) Author Solutions, Inc.

Gorbachev, Valeri. Me Too! Gorbachev, Valeri, illus. 2014. (I Like to Read(r) Ser.). (ENG., Illus.). 24p. (J). (gr. -1-3). 6.99 *(978-0-8234-3179-3(7))* Holiday Hse., Inc.

—Me Too! 2013. (I Like to Read(r) Ser.). (ENG., Illus.). 24p. (J). (gr. -1-3). 14.95 *(978-0-8234-2744-4(7))* Holiday Hse., Inc.

—Not Me! Gorbachev, Valeri, illus. 2016. (ENG., Illus.). 24p. (J). 14.95 *(978-0-8234-3546-3(6));* pap. 6.99 *(978-0-8234-3547-0(4))* Holiday Hse., Inc.

Gorbachev, Valeri, illus. Goldilocks & the Three Bears. 2015. (ENG.). 40p. (J). 15.95 *(978-0-7358-4211-3(6))* North-South Bks., Inc.

Gordon, Mike, illus. Goldilocks & the Three Bears. 2007. (First Reading Level 4 Ser.). 48p. (J). (gr. -1-3). 8.99 *(978-0-7945-1708-3(0),* Usborne) EDC Publishing.

Grandma Sue. Bubba the Bear. 2010. 12p. pap. 8.49 *(978-1-4490-1813-9(0))* AuthorHouse.

Gravett, Emily. Bear & Hare Go Fishing. Gravett, Emily, illus. 2015. (Bear & Hare Ser.). (ENG., Illus.). 32p. (J). (gr. -1-3). 15.99 *(978-1-4814-2289-5(8),* Simon & Schuster Bks. For Young Readers) Simon & Schuster Bks. For Young Readers.

—Bear & Hare Snow! Gravett, Emily, illus. 2015. (Bear & Hare Ser.). (ENG., Illus.). 32p. (J). (gr. -1-3). 16.99 *(978-1-4814-4514-6(6),* Simon & Schuster Bks. For Young Readers) Simon & Schuster Bks. For Young Readers.

—Orange Pear Apple Bear. Gravett, Emily, illus. 2011. (Classic Board Bks.). (ENG., Illus.). 24p. (J). (gr. -1 — 1). bds. 7.99 *(978-1-4424-2003-8(0),* Little Simon) Little Simon.

—Orange Pear Apple Bear. Gravett, Emily, illus. 2007. (ENG., Illus.). 32p. (J). (gr. -1 — 1). 12.99 *(978-1-4169-3999-3(7),* Simon & Schuster Bks. For Young Readers) Simon & Schuster Bks. For Young Readers.

—Share! Gravett, Emily, illus. 2016. (Bear & Hare Ser.). (ENG., Illus.). 32p. (J). (gr. -1-3). 16.99 *(978-1-4814-6217-4(2),* Simon & Schuster Bks. For Young Readers) Simon & Schuster Bks. For Young Readers.

—Where's Bear? Gravett, Emily, illus. 2016. (Bear & Hare Ser.). (ENG., Illus.). 32p. (J). (gr. -1-3). 16.99 *(978-1-4814-5615-9(6),* Simon & Schuster Bks. For Young Readers) Simon & Schuster Bks. For Young Readers.

Gray, Diane. The Bears with Unruly Hairs. 2011. 28p. pap. 15.99 *(978-1-4568-8129-0(9))* Xlibris Corp.

Great, Alex. Balkan Tales. 2009. 134p. pap. 18.36 *(978-1-4452-4363-4(6))* Lulu Pr., Inc.

Greene, Carol. The Cat & the Bear. 2005. 32p. (J). pap. *(978-0-7868-1175-5(7))* Hyperion Bks. for Children.

Greene, Rhonda Gowler. Firebears, the Rescue Team. Andreasen, Dan, illus. 2015. (ENG.). 30p. (J). (gr. -1 — 1). bds. 7.99 *(978-1-62779-240-0(6),* 9781627792400, Holt, Henry & Co. Bks. For Young Readers) Holt, Henry & Co.

Greiner, Gail. Patchwork Helps a Friend. Schmidt, Jacqueline, illus. 2013. (ENG.). 40p. (J). (gr. -1-2). 17.95 *(978-1-57687-642-8(X),* powerHouse Bks.) powerHouse Cultural Entertainment, Inc.

Gresham, Joel. The Bible Bears: Featuring the Imagination Bears. 2007. 19.95 *(978-0-9708446-2-0(X))* Gresham, Joel.

Grey, Erika. The Alphabet Bears: Spook-Tales Collection. Grey, Erika, illus. 2010. (Illus.). 127p. (YA). pap. 24.95 *(978-0-9790199-3-7(1))* PeDante Pr.

Grey, Mini. Biscuit Bear. 2004. (Illus.). 32p. (J). *(978-0-224-06496-5(7),* Jonathan Cape) Random Hse.

Grindley, Sally. Keep Out! Bears About! 2015. (ENG., Illus.). 32p. (J). (gr. -1-k). pap. 12.99 *(978-1-4449-1416-0(2))* Hodder & Stoughton GBR. Dist: Hachette Bk. Group.

Groth, Lynn. Buttons' Bouquet of Flowers. 2003. (Illus.). (J). pap. 5.99 *(978-0-8100-1334-6(7))* Northwestern Publishing Hse.

—Buttons in the Dark. 2003. (Illus.). pap. 5.99 *(978-0-8100-1333-9(9))* Northwestern Publishing Hse.

—Buttons' Picnic. 2003. (Illus.). (J). pap. 5.99 *(978-0-8100-1331-5(2))* Northwestern Publishing Hse.

—Buttons Visits Grandma. 2003. (Illus.). pap. 5.99 *(978-0-8100-1332-2(0))* Northwestern Publishing Hse.

Grumpy Bear: 3-in-1 Package. (Sails Literacy Ser.). 24p. (gr. k-18). 57.00 *(978-0-7578-3196-6(6))* Rigby Education.

Grumpy Bear: Big Book Only. (Sails Literacy Ser.). 24p. (gr. k-18). 27.00 *(978-0-7635-6988-4(7))* Rigby Education.

Guarnaccia, Steven. Goldilocks & the Three Bears: A Tale Moderne. 2010. (ENG., Illus.). 32p. (J). (gr. k-3). 19.95 *(978-0-8109-8966-5(2),* Abrams Bks. for Young Readers) Abrams, Inc.

Guiberson, Brenda Z. Moon Bear. Young, Ed, illus. 2010. (ENG.). 40p. (J). pap. 7.99 *(978-0-8050-9258-5(7))* Holt, Henry & Co.

Guillain, Charlotte. Red Riding Hood Meets the Three Bears. West, Karl, illus. 2016. (Fairy Tale Mix-Ups Ser.). (ENG.). 24p. (gr. k-2). lib. bdg. 23.32 *(978-1-4109-8304-6(8))* Heinemann-Raintree.

GüRth, Per-Henrik. When Wishes Come True. l.t. ed. 2012. 57p. (J). pap. *(978-1-4596-3456-5(X))* ReadHowYouWant.com, Ltd.

Guy, Ginger Foglesong & Guy, Ginger F. Siesta Board Book. Moreno, Rene King, illus. 2009. (SPA & ENG.). 34p. (J). (gr. -1 — 1). bds. 7.99 *(978-0-06-168884-3(3),* Greenwillow Bks.) HarperCollins Pubs.

Guy, Glen. The Adventure Fire: Adventures of Dusty Sourdough. 2003. (YA). pap. 9.95 *(978-1-59433-006-3(9))* Publication Consultants.

Gwent (Wales), Staff Development Unit Staff & Acen Staff, contrib. by. Nos Da, Arthur. 2005. (WEL., Illus.). 8p. pap. *(978-1-874049-31-9(9))* Acen Limited.

Haggarty, S. Little Muddy Bear. 2009. 52p. pap. 11.99 *(978-1-4389-4071-7(8))* AuthorHouse.

Hainsworth, B. R. Boris the Lost Badger. Perkins, Mair, illus. 2012. 42p. pap. *(978-1-78148-585-9(2))* Grosvenor Hse. Publishing Ltd.

Halfman, Janet. Polar Bear Horizon. Chesterman, Adrian, illus. 2006. (Smithsonian Oceanic Collection). (ENG.). 32p. (J). 19.95 *(978-1-59249-568-9(0));* (gr. -1-3). 9.95 *(978-1-59249-570-2(2))* Soundprints.

Halfmann, Janet. Polar Bear Horizon. Chesterman, Adrian, illus. (Smithsonian Oceanic Collection). (J). 2009. 24.95 incl. audio compact disk *(978-1-59249-665-5(2))* 2006. (ENG.). 32p. 8.95 *(978-1-59249-569-6(9))* 2006. (ENG.). 32p. 4.95 *(978-1-59249-567-2(2))* 2006. (ENG.). 32p. (gr. -1-3). 15.95 *(978-1-59249-565-8(6))* 2006. (ENG.). 32p. (gr. -1-3). mass mkt. 6.95 *(978-1-59249-566-5(4))* Soundprints.

Halfmann, Janet & Smithsonian Institution Staff. El horizonte del Oso Polar: Polar Bear Horizon. 2008. (MUL.). 16p. 14.95 *(978-1-59249-852-9(3))* Soundprints.

Hall, Gladys, illus. Red Riding Hood. 2007. (Shape Bks.). (ENG.). (J). (gr. -1-3). pap. 9.95 *(978-1-59583-133-0(9),* 9781595831330, Green Tiger Pr.) Laughing Elephant.

Hamilton, Elizabeth L. Cubby Bear's Big Responsibility. 2004. (Character Critters Ser.: No. 8). (Illus.). 32p. (J). per. 5.95 *(978-0-9754629-4-2(6),* Character-in-Action) Quiet Impact, Inc.

Hand, Reuben. The Jumping Jack: Drill Sergeant Bear Volume 1. 2009. 20p. pap. 24.95 *(978-1-60749-876-6(6))* America Star Bks.

—The Knee Bender: Drill Sergeant Bear Volume 3, 1 vol. Fiebiger, John, illus. 2009. 17p. pap. 24.95 *(978-1-61582-706-0(4))* America Star Bks.

—The Push Up: Drill Sergeant Bear Volume 2. Fiebiger, John, illus. 2009. 20p. pap. 24.95 *(978-1-61546-234-6(1))* America Star Bks.

—The Turn & Bounce, 1 vol. Fiebiger, John, illus. 2010. 18p. 24.95 *(978-1-4489-5185-7(2))* PublishAmerica, Inc.

Hansen, Tevin. Alexia Versus the Birthday Bear. Hansen, Tevin, illus. 2016. (Illus.). (J). pap. 5.99 *(978-1-941429-37-2(8))* Handersen Publishing.

Hapka, Catherine, pseud & Disney Book Group Staff. Pooh's Secret Garden. Disney Storybook Art Team, illus. 2012. (ENG.). 24p. (J). (gr. -1-k). pap. 4.99 *(978-1-4231-4845-6(2))* Disney Pr.

—Sweet Dreams, Roo. Disney Storybook Art Team, illus. 2012. (ENG.). 24p. (J). (gr. -1-k). bds. 6.99 *(978-1-4231-4843-2(6))* Disney Pr.

Harbo, Gary. The Northern Woods Adventure: Early Reader. Harbo, Gary, illus. l.t. ed. 2004. (If You Want to Succeed, You Need to Read! Ser.: 6). (Illus.). 33p. (J). 10.95 *(978-1-884149-16-0(2))* Kutie Kari Bks., Inc.

Hardin, Becky. Shug E Bear. 2008. 24p. pap. 19.99 *(978-1-4389-3247-7(2))* AuthorHouse.

Harker, Jillian. I Love You, Grandma. (I Love... Ser.). pap. *(978-1-4054-6660-8(X))* Parragon, Inc.

Harley, Bill. Bear's All-Night Party. Ferreira, Melissa, illus. 2005. (ENG.). 32p. (J). (gr. -1-2). 15.95 *(978-0-87483-572-4(0))* August Hse. Pubs., Inc.

Harper Collins & Auerbach, Annie. Meet Paddington. 2014. (Paddington — I Can Read Ser.). (J). lib. bdg. 13.55 *(978-0-606-35966-5(4))* Turtleback Bks.

HarperCollins Publishers Ltd. Staff & Auerbach, Annie. Paddington: Paddington's Adventures. 2014. (I Can Read Level 1 Ser.). (ENG., Illus.). 32p. (J). (gr. -1-3). pap. 3.99 *(978-0-06-235001-5(3))* HarperCollins Pubs.

HarperCollins Publishers Ltd. Staff, et al. Paddington: Paddington's World. 2014. (Paddington Ser.). (ENG., Illus.). 24p. (J). (gr. -1-3). pap. 3.99 *(978-0-06-234997-2(X))* HarperCollins Pubs.

Hartley Bellows, Carol. Icabog Bear. 2009. 24p. pap. 15.50 *(978-1-4389-3856-1(X))* AuthorHouse.

Harvey, M. A. The Riddle of Bear Cave: Dare to Take the Test. 2004. (Illus.). 128p. (J). pap. *(978-1-84458-146-7(2),* Pavilion Children's Books) Pavilion Bks.

Harvey, Tom. Creature Teachers. 2013. 72p. pap. 24.27 *(978-1-4669-9417-1(7))* Trafford Publishing.

Hatley, A. L. Little Pinky's Day. 2010. 53p. pap. 22.95 *(978-1-4327-5754-0(7))* Outskirts Pr., Inc.

Hats: Individual Title Six-Packs. (Sails Literacy Ser.). 16p. (gr. k-18). 27.00 *(978-0-7635-4443-0(4))* Rigby Education.

Hawkins, Denise. The Plight of Sanna, the Polar Bear, 1 vol. 2010. 106p. pap. 19.95 *(978-1-60441-672-5(6))* America Star Bks.

Hayes, Karel. The Summer Visitors, 10 vols. Hayes, Karel, illus. 2011. (ENG., Illus.). 32p. (gr. -1-3). 17.95 *(978-0-89272-918-0(X))* Down East Bks.

—The Winter Visitors. 2007. (ENG., Illus.). 32p. (J). (gr. -1-3). 17.95 *(978-0-89272-750-6(0))* Down East Bks.

Heap, Sue. Espera y Veras. (SPA.). pap. 7.95 *(978-950-07-2025-0(6))* Editorial Sudamericana S.A. ARG. Dist: Distribooks, Inc.

Heder, Thyra. The Bear Report. 2015. (ENG., Illus.). 48p. (J). (gr. -1-3). 17.95 *(978-1-4197-0783-4(3),* Abrams Bks. for Young Readers) Abrams, Inc.

Hegarty, Patricia. Bear's Truck Is Stuck! 2015. (Amazing Changing Pictures! Ser.). (ENG.). 14p. (J). (gr. -1-3). 12.99 *(978-1-68010-001-3(7))* Tiger Tales.

Hegarty, Patricia. Bug Bear. Saldana, Carmen, illus. 2017. (ENG.). 32p. (J). (gr. -1-2). 16.99 ***(978-1-68010-053-2(X))*** Tiger Tales.

Heinz, Brian J. Nanuk, Lord of the Ice. Manchess, Gregory, illus. 2005. (J). *(978-0-936335-13-1(0));* pap. *(978-0-936335-14-8(9))* Ballyhoo BookWorks, Inc.

Heling, Kathryn & Hembrook, Deborah. Bear's Big Ideas. Walz, Richard, illus. 2005. (Step into Reading Ser.: Vol. 2). (ENG.). 32p. (J). (gr. -1-1). per. 3.99 *(978-0-375-83391-5(9),* Random Hse. Bks. for Young Readers) Random Hse. Children's Bks.

Helmrath, M. O. & Bartlett, J. L. Bobby Bear Series, 18 bks. (Illus.). (J). (gr. -1-1). lib. bdg. 189.60 *(978-0-87783-163-1(7));*Set. 63.52 *(978-0-87783-181-5(5))* Oddo Publishing, Inc.

Helquist, Brett. Bedtime for Bear. Helquist, Brett, illus. 2010. (ENG., Illus.). 32p. (J). (gr. -1-2). 16.99 *(978-0-06-050205-8(3))* HarperCollins Pubs.

Henkes, Kevin. Old Bear. Henkes, Kevin, illus. 2008. (Illus.). 32p. (J). (gr. -1-5). (ENG.). 17.99 *(978-0-06-155205-2(4));* lib. bdg. 18.89 *(978-0-06-155206-9(2))* HarperCollins Pubs. (Greenwillow Bks.).

—Old Bear Board Book. Henkes, Kevin, illus. 2011. (ENG., Illus.). 28p. (J). (gr. -1 — 1). bds. 7.99 *(978-0-06-208963-2(3),* Greenwillow Bks.) HarperCollins Pubs.

Henn, Sophy. Where Bear? Henn, Sophy, illus. 2015. (ENG., Illus.). 32p. (J). (gr. k-3). 16.99 *(978-0-399-17158-1(4),* Philomel Bks.) Penguin Young Readers Group.

Hest, Amy. Are You Sure, Mother Bear? Tobia, Lauren, illus. 2016. (ENG.). 32p. (J). (-k). 15.99 *(978-0-7636-7207-2(6))* Candlewick Pr.

—Un Beso de Buenas Noches. Rubio, Esther, tr. Jeram, Anita, illus. (SPA.). (J). 16.00 *(978-1-930332-04-1(1),* LC3294) Lectorum Pubns., Inc.

—Don't You Feel Well, Sam? Jeram, Anita, illus. 2007. (Sam Bks.). (ENG.). 32p. (J). (gr. -1-k). 4.99 *(978-0-7636-2408-8(X))* Candlewick Pr.

—Kiss Good Night. Jeram, Anita, illus. (Sam Bks.). (ENG.). (J). (gr. k-12). 2006. 32p. pap. 4.99 *(978-0-7636-2114-8(5))* 2004. 30p. bds. 6.99 *(978-0-7636-2094-3(7))* Candlewick Pr.

—Kiss Good Night: Book & Toy Gift Set. Jeram, Anita, illus. gif. ed. 2004. (Sam Bks.). (ENG.). 30p. (J). (gr. k-12). bds. 15.99 *(978-0-7636-2524-5(8))* Candlewick Pr.

—Kiss Good Night Lap-Size Board Book. Jeram, Anita, illus. 2014. (Sam Bks.). (ENG.). 32p. (J). (— 1). bds. 12.99 *(978-0-7636-4748-3(9))* Candlewick Pr.

—You Can Do It, Sam. Jeram, Anita, illus. 2007. (Sam Bks.). (ENG.). 32p. (J). (gr. -1-k). pap. 4.99 *(978-0-7636-3688-3(6))* Candlewick Pr.

Hickner, Hayden. A Bear & the Bees. 2010. 36p. 15.49 *(978-1-4520-5087-4(2))* AuthorHouse.

Higgins, Ryan T. Hotel Bruce. Higgins, Ryan T., illus. 2016. (Mother Bruce Ser.). (ENG., Illus.). 48p. (J). (gr. -1-k). 17.99 *(978-1-4847-4362-1(8))* Hyperion Bks. for Children.

—Mother Bruce. Higgins, Ryan T., illus. 2015. (Mother Bruce Ser.). (ENG., Illus.). 48p. (J). (gr. -1-k). 17.99 *(978-1-4847-3088-1(7))* Disney Pr.

Hillenbrand, Will. All for a Dime! A Bear & Mole Story. (ENG.). 32p. (J). (gr. -1-1). 2016. 7.99 *(978-0-8234-3684-2(5))* 2015. (Illus.). 16.95 *(978-0-8234-2946-2(6))* Holiday Hse., Inc.

—Kite Day: A Bear & Mole Story. Hillenbrand, Will, illus. (ENG., Illus.). 32p. (J). 2013. pap. 6.99 *(978-0-8234-2758-1(7))* 2012. 16.95 *(978-0-8234-1603-5(8))* Holiday Hse., Inc.

—Off We Go! A Bear & Mole Story. Hillenbrand, Will, illus. 2014. (Bear & Mole Ser.). (ENG., Illus.). 32p. (J). (gr. -1-1). pap. 7.99 *(978-0-8234-3172-4(X))* Holiday Hse., Inc.

—Off We Go! A Bear & Mole Story. 2013. (Bear & Mole Ser.). (ENG., Illus.). 32p. (J). (gr. -1-1). 16.95 *(978-0-8234-2520-4(7))* Holiday Hse., Inc.

—Spring Is Here. Hillenbrand, Will, illus. 2012. (ENG., Illus.). 32p. (J). pap. 7.99 *(978-0-8234-2431-3(6))* Holiday Hse., Inc.

Hillert, Margaret. The Three Bears. Undercuffler, Gary, illus. 2016. (BeginningtoRead Ser.). (ENG.). 32p. (J). (gr. -1-2). pap. 11.94 *(978-1-60357-913-1(3))* Norwood Hse. Pr.

Hillert, Margaret. Los Tres Osos. Jack Pullan & Undercuffler, Gary, illus. 2017. (BeginningtoRead Ser.).Tr. of Three Bears. (ENG & SPA.). 32p. (J). (-2). 22.60 ***(978-1-59953-850-1(4))*** Norwood Hse. Pr.

Hiris, Monica. Sleepy Polar Bear. Harston, Jerry, illus. l.t. ed. 2006. (ENG.). 24p. (gr. k-2). pap. 8.95 *(978-1-57874-072-7(X),* Kaeden Bks.) Kaeden Corp.

Hobbs, Will. Beardream. Kastner, Jill, illus. 2014. 32p. pap. 8.00 *(978-1-61003-340-4(X))* Center for the Collaborative Classroom.

—Never Say Die. 224p. (J). (gr. 3-7). 2014. (ENG.). pap. 6.99 *(978-0-06-170880-0(1))* 2013. (ENG.). 16.99 *(978-0-06-170878-7(X))* 2013. lib. bdg. 17.89 *(978-0-06-170879-4(8))* HarperCollins Pubs.

Hodge, Deborah. Bear's Winter Party, 1 vol. Cinar, Lisa, illus. 2016. (ENG.). 32p. (J). (gr. -1-2). 16.95 *(978-1-55498-853-2(5))* Groundwood Bks. CAN. Dist: Publishers Group West (PGW).

Hodges, Ronald. Buff Bears. 2011. 68p. (gr. -1). pap. 11.99 *(978-1-4567-9437-8(X))* AuthorHouse.

Hodgkinson, Leigh. Goldilocks & Just One Bear. Hodgkinson, Leigh, illus. 2012. (ENG., Illus.). 32p. (J). (gr. -1-2). 15.99 *(978-0-7636-6172-4(4),* Nosy Crow) Candlewick Pr.

Hofmann, Ginnie. One Teddy Bear Is Enough! 2003. (Illus.). 32p. (Orig.). (J). pap. *(978-1-932485-02-8(3))* Reverie Publishing Co.

—Who Wants an Old Teddy Bear?, 5 vols. Hofmann, Ginnie, illus. 2003. (Illus.). 32p. (J). pap. 5.95 *(978-1-932485-00-4(7))* Reverie Publishing Co.

Hofmann-Maniyar, Ariane. Ice in the Jungle. Hofmann-Maniyar, Ariane, illus. 2015. (Child's Play Library). (ENG., Illus.). 32p. (J). *(978-1-84643-731-1(8))* Child's Play International Ltd.

Hofstrand, Skip. Tears for Nanertak: Text & Watercolors by Skip Hofstrand. 2012. (ENG.). 31p. (J). pap. 29.95 *(978-1-4787-2081-2(6))* Outskirts Pr., Inc.

Holden, Pam. Bear Gets Stuck. Whimp, Pauline, illus. 2015. (ENG.). 16p. (-1). pap. *(978-1-77654-127-0(8)*, Red Rocket Readers) Flying Start Bks.

—Knock, Knock!, 6 pack. Holt, Richard, illus. 2009. (Red Rocket Readers Ser.). (ENG.). 16p. (gr. 2-2). pap. *(978-1-877363-60-3(X)*, Red Rocket Readers) Flying Start Bks.

Holtei, Christa. Nanuk Flies Home. Vohwinkel, Astrid, illus. 2008. 26p. (J). (gr. 4-7). 16.00 *(978-0-8028-5342-4(0))* Eerdmans, William B. Publishing Co.

Holub, Joan & Williams, Suzanne. Goldilocks Breaks In. 2015. 179p. (J). *(978-1-4242-6104-8(X))* Scholastic, Inc.

Hopkins, Jackie Mims. Goldie Socks & the Three Libearians. Manders, John, illus. 2007. (J). *(978-1-932146-68-4(7)*, Upstart Bks.) Highsmith Inc.

Hopper, Bobby E. Bleep the Purple Bear. Hopper, Andy Lee, illus. 2009. 36p. pap. 18.99 *(978-1-4389-1908-9(5))* AuthorHouse.

Horowitz, Jeanine. Latch Key Kid. 2006. 75p. (YA). lib. bdg. 12.99 *(978-1-934190-10-4(1))* Ocean Front Bk. Publishing, Inc.

House, Megan. The Big Black Bear. 2008. 32p. per. 24.95 *(978-1-4241-9315-8(X))* America Star Bks.

Hovaguimian, Vroni. Deep in the Woods. 2011. 32p. pap. 13.00 *(978-0-557-70332-6(8))* Lulu Pr., Inc.

Howse, Jennifer. Les Ours Esprit: Les Animaux du Canada. Karvonen, Tanjah, tr. from ENG. 2011. (FRE.). 24p. (gr. 3-6). *(978-1-77071-415-1(4))* Weigl Educational Pubs. Ltd.

Huang, Yu-Hsuan, illus. Baby Bear: Finger Puppet Book. 2016. (ENG.). 12p. (J). (gr. -1 — 1). bds. 6.99 *(978-1-4521-4235-7(1))* Chronicle Bks. LLC.

Hudson, Katy. Bear & Duck. Hudson, Katy, illus. 2015. (ENG., Illus.). 32p. (J). (gr. -1-3). 17.99 *(978-0-06-232051-3(3))* HarperCollins Pubs.

Hungry Bear, 6 Packs. (Chiquilibros Ser.). (gr. k-1). 23.00 *(978-0-7635-0424-3(6))* Rigby Education.

Hunter, Erin. The Burning Horizon. 2015. (Seekers: Return to the Wild Ser.: 5). (ENG., Illus.). 304p. (J). (gr. 3-7). 16.99 *(978-0-06-199646-7(7))* HarperCollins Pubs.

—Fire in the Sky. 2011. (Seekers Ser.: 5). (ENG.). 288p. (J). (gr. 3-7). pap. 6.99 *(978-0-06-087136-9(9))* HarperCollins Pubs.

—Forest of Wolves. (Seekers: Return to the Wild Ser.: 4). (ENG.). (J). (gr. 3-7). 2015. 304p. pap. 6.99 *(978-0-06-199645-0(9))* 2014. 288p. 16.99 *(978-0-06-199643-6(2))* HarperCollins Pubs.

—Forest of Wolves. 2015. (Seekers: Return to the Wild Ser.: 4). (J). lib. bdg. 17.20 *(978-0-606-36472-0(2))* Turtleback Bks.

—Great Bear Lake. (Seekers Ser.: 2). (ENG.). 320p. (J). (gr. 3-7). 2010. pap. 6.99 *(978-0-06-087127-7(X))* 2009. 16.99 *(978-0-06-087125-3(3))* HarperCollins Pubs.

—Island of Shadows. (Seekers: Return to the Wild Ser.: 1). 320p. (J). (gr. 3-7). 2013. (ENG.). pap. 6.99 *(978-0-06-199636-8(X))* 2012. (ENG.). 16.99 *(978-0-06-199634-4(3))* 2012. lib. bdg. 17.89 *(978-0-06-199635-1(1))* HarperCollins Pubs.

—Island of Shadows. 2013. (Seekers: Return to the Wild Ser.: 1). (J). lib. bdg. 17.20 *(978-0-606-27127-1(9)*, Turtleback) Turtleback Bks.

—Kallik's Adventure. Kurkoski, Bettina M., illus. 2011. (Seekers Manga Ser.). (ENG.). 112p. (J). (gr. 3-7). pap. 7.99 *(978-0-06-172383-4(5))* HarperCollins Pubs.

—The Last Wilderness. (Seekers Ser.: 4). (J). 2011. (ENG.). 288p. (gr. 3-7). pap. 6.99 *(978-0-06-087133-8(4))* 2010. (ENG.). 288p. (gr. 3-7). 16.99 *(978-0-06-087131-4(8))* 2010. (Illus.). 265p. 9.99 *(978-0-06-198681-9(X))* HarperCollins Pubs.

—The Longest Day. 2017. (Seekers: Return to the Wild Ser.: 6). (J). lib. bdg. 18.40 *(978-0-606-39613-4(6))* Turtleback Bks.

—The Melting Sea. (Seekers: Return to the Wild Ser.: 2). (J). (gr. 3-7). 2013. (ENG.). 304p. pap. 6.99 *(978-0-06-199639-9(4))* 2012. (ENG., Illus.). 288p. 16.99 *(978-0-06-199637-5(8))* 2012. (Illus.). 288p. lib. bdg. 17.89 *(978-0-06-199638-2(6))* HarperCollins Pubs.

—The Melting Sea. 2013. (Seekers: Return to the Wild Ser.: 2). (J). lib. bdg. 17.20 *(978-0-606-31816-7(X)*, Turtleback) Turtleback Bks.

—The Quest Begins. Chalk, Gary, illus. 2008. (Seekers Ser.: 1). (ENG.). 320p. (J). (gr. 3-7). 16.99 *(978-0-06-087122-2(9))* HarperCollins Pubs.

—The Quest Begins. l.t. ed. 2008. (Seekers Ser.: No. 1). 372p. (J). pap. 16.99 *(978-0-06-170951-7(4))* HarperCollins Pubs.

—River of Lost Bearsrs No. 3. 2013. (Seekers: Return to the Wild Ser.: 3). (ENG., Illus.). 320p. (J). (gr. 3-7). 16.99 *(978-0-06-199640-5(8))* HarperCollins Pubs.

—Smoke Mountain. (Seekers Ser.: 3). (ENG.). 288p. (J). (gr. 3-7). 2010. pap. 6.99 *(978-0-06-087130-7(X))* 2009. 16.99 *(978-0-06-087128-4(8))* HarperCollins Pubs.

—Spirits in the Stars. (Seekers Ser.: 6). (ENG.). 304p. (J). (gr. 3-7). 2012. pap. 6.99 *(978-0-06-087142-0(3))* 2011. 16.99 *(978-0-06-087140-6(7))* HarperCollins Pubs.

Hutchins, Hazel J. It's Raining, Yancy & Bear. 2004. (Illus.). (J). (gr. k-3). spiral bd. *(978-0-616-01678-7(6))*; spiral bd. *(978-0-616-01679-4(4))* Canadian National Institute for the Blind/Institut National Canadien pour les Aveugles.

Huven, Kim. The Birthday Bears. Padron, Alicia, illus. 2010. 10p. bds. 10.95 *(978-1-60747-774-7(2)*, Pickwick Pr.) Phoenix Bks., Inc.

Ilagan, Roland Michael. Baba the Bear. 5000th ed. 2007. (Illus.). 32p. (J). (gr. -1-3). pap. 16.00 *(978-0-9773809-0-9(4))* Wonderbooks Publishing.

ImageBooks Staff & Mulligan, Lenz. Little Polar Bear Finger Puppet Book. 2009. (Little Finger Puppet Board Bks.: FING). (ENG., Illus.). 12p. (J). (gr. -1 — 1). bds. 6.99 *(978-0-8118-6974-4(1))* Chronicle Bks. LLC.

Impey, Rose. The Three Angry Bears. McEwen, Katharine, illus. (Sir Lance-A-Little Ser.). (ENG.). 32p. (J). (gr. k-2). 2017. pap. 9.99 ***(978-1-4083-2527-8(6))*** 2016. 9.99 *(978-1-4083-2521-6(7))* Hachette Children's Group GBR. (Orchard Bks.). Dist: Hachette Bk. Group.

Inkpen, Mick. Bear. (Illus.). 34p. (J). (gr. -1-2). (BEN, ENG, URD, VIE & SPA.). *(978-1-85430-546-6(8))*; (ENG, URD, VIE, SPA & CHI., *(978-1-85430-550-3(6))* Little Tiger Pr. Group.

Inkpen, Mick. Silly Big Bear. 2017. (Wibbly Pig Ser.). (ENG., Illus.). 32p. (J). (gr. -1-k). pap. 8.99 ***(978-1-4449-3125-9(3))*** Hachette Children's Group GBR. Dist: Hachette Bk. Group.

Irwin, Daniel. The Adventures of Tylor Bear & Mana. 2004. 144p. pap. 24.95 *(978-1-4137-5580-0(1))* America Star Bks.

Irwin, John P. The Cubby Files; Tales of a Pennsylvania Black Bear Growing Up. 2009. 96p. pap. 15.99 *(978-1-4415-0209-4(2))* Xlibris Corp.

Iverson-Noel, Gayle. Brown Beary's Adventures with Jon-Paul. 2011. 32p. pap. 21.99 *(978-1-4628-9875-6(0))* Xlibris Corp.

Jacquemain, Patti. Journey of the Great Bear: Through California's Golden Past. Jacquemain, Patti, illus. 2006. (Illus.). (J). *(978-0-929702-10-0(7))* Mission Creek Studios.

James, Ann. Bird & Bear. James, Ann, illus. 2015. (ENG., Illus.). 40p. (J). (gr. -1-2). 16.99 *(978-1-4998-0037-1(1))* Little Bee Books Inc.

James, Suzi. Matilda Bear & Father Bear: I Love You Father Bear. 2012. (Illus.). 52p. pap. 23.95 *(978-1-4525-4822-7(6))* Balboa Pr.

Janosch. Yo Te Curare, Dijo el Pequeno Oso. Janosch, illus. 2003. (SPA., Illus.). 48p. (J). (gr. k-3). pap. 8.95 *(978-958-24-0110-8(9))* Santillana USA Publishing Co., Inc.

—Zampano y Su Oso. Janosch, illus. (Coleccion el Faro Azul). (SPA., Illus.). (J). 8.95 *(978-84-348-1571-1(0)*, SM004) SM Ediciones ESP. Dist: Continental Bk. Co., Inc.

Jennie Lyon Wood. Bath Time Bears Have So Much Fun. Kristie Kryssing, illus. 2009. 24p. pap. 12.99 *(978-1-4389-4420-3(9))* AuthorHouse.

Jennings, Sharon. Bearcub & Mama. Watt, Mélanie, illus. 2007. (ENG.). 32p. (J). (gr. -1-2). 6.95 *(978-1-55453-162-2(4))* Kids Can Pr., Ltd. CAN. Dist: Hachette Bk. Group.

Jennings, Sharon, et al, adapted by. Franklin Snoops. 2003. (Franklin TV Storybook Ser.). (ENG., Illus.). 32p. (J). (gr. -1-3). 10.95 *(978-1-55337-364-3(2))* Kids Can Pr., Ltd. CAN. Dist: Hachette Bk. Group.

Jensen, Olivia. Thomas & the Bully. 2009. 16p. pap. 8.49 *(978-1-4389-1848-8(8))* AuthorHouse.

Job. Yakari & the Grizzly. Dérib, illus. 2007. (Yakari Ser.: 4). (ENG.). 46p. (J). (gr. 4-7). per. 9.99 *(978-1-905460-16-8(3))* CineBook GBR. Dist: National Bk. Network.

John, Jory. Goodnight Already! Davies, Benji, illus. 2014. (ENG.). 32p. (J). (gr. -1-3). 17.99 *(978-0-06-228620-8(X))* HarperCollins Pubs.

—I Love You Already! Davies, Benji, illus. 2015. 32p. (J). (gr. -1-3). 17.99 *(978-0-06-237095-2(2))* HarperCollins Pubs.

Johnson, D. B. Henry Hikes to Fitchburg. 2006. (ENG., Illus.). 32p. (J). (gr. -1-3). reprint ed. 7.99 *(978-0-618-73749-9(9))* Houghton Mifflin Harcourt Publishing Co.

—Henry Hikes to Fitchburg. Johnson, D. B., illus. 2006. (Illus.). (gr. -1-3). 16.95 *(978-0-7569-6798-7(8))* Perfection Learning Corp.

Jones, Carolyn. Theodora Bear, 1 vol. Spurll, Barbara, illus. 2007. (Orca Echoes Ser.). (ENG.). 64p. (J). (gr. 2-3). per. 4.99 *(978-1-55143-496-4(2))* Orca Bk. Pubs. USA.

Jones, Dennis. Fruitiebears: Yorkies Birthday Today: Book 1. 2010. 36p. pap. 18.99 *(978-1-4520-7037-7(7))* AuthorHouse.

Jones, Frankie. Bedtime: Trace the Trails with Your Finger to Get to Bed! Galloway, Fhiona, illus. 2016. (ENG.). 10p. (J). (gr. -1 — 1). bds. 7.99 *(978-1-4998-0267-2(6))* Little Bee Books Inc.

Jones, Janey Louise. Basil the Bear Cub. Poh, Jennie, illus. 2016. (Superfairies Ser.). (ENG.). 56p. (gr. k-3). lib. bdg. 23.99 *(978-1-4795-8641-7(2))* Picture Window Bks.

Jones, Nick. Food-head Makes a Pie. 2008. 28p. pap. 24.95 *(978-1-60610-225-1(7))* America Star Bks.

Jordan, Apple. Oh, Brother! 2012. (Disney Princess Step into Reading Ser.). lib. bdg. 13.55 *(978-0-606-26560-7(0)*, Turtleback) Turtleback Bks.

Jordan, Dana Hall. Clang Went the Cymbals: An Onomatopoeia Alphabet Book. Burma, Willingham, illus. 2008. 32p. (J). 15.99 *(978-0-9798664-0-1(5))* Capture Bks.

The Journals of Punkin Bear Volume One. 2006. (J). per. 12.00 *(978-0-9778471-0-5(1))* Bayliss, Erin.

Joyce, Melanie. Goldilocks. 2009. (Fairydust Fairytales Ser.). (ENG.). 5p. (J). (gr. -1-k). bds. 6.95 *(978-1-84696-962-1(X)*, TickTock Books) Octopus Publishing Group GBR. Dist: Independent Pubs. Group.

Kaeden Books, compiled by. Joy Cowley Big & Little Bear Collection. 2014. (ENG.). (gr. k-2). pap. *(978-1-61181-451-4(0)*, Kaeden Bks.) Kaeden Corp.

Kananen, Barbara L. Fairies in My Garden. 2007. 106p. (YA). (gr. 2-2). per. 10.95 *(978-0-595-45082-4(2))* iUniverse, Inc.

—Fairies in My Garden. 2007. 106p. (YA). (gr. 2-2). 20.95 *(978-0-595-91014-4(9))* iUniverse, Inc.

Kasza, Keiko. The Mightiest. 2003. (ENG., Illus.). 32p. (J). (gr. -1-k). pap. 5.99 *(978-0-14-250185-6(9)*, Puffin Books) Penguin Young Readers Group.

—No Te Rias, Pepe. (Buenas Noches Ser.). (SPA.). (J). (gr. k-3). *(978-958-04-3623-2(1))* Norma S.A.

Kathryn Aartman-Weed. The Little Brown Bear. 2009. 36p. pap. 15.49 *(978-1-4389-4968-0(5))* AuthorHouse.

Keith, Donna. I Love You All the Same, 1 vol. Edgson, Allison, illus. 2014. (ENG.). 20p. (J). bds. 9.99 *(978-0-529-10204-1(8))* Nelson, Thomas Inc.

—I Love You Just Because, 1 vol. 2016. (ENG., Illus.). 20p. (J). bds. 9.99 *(978-0-7180-8853-8(0))* Nelson, Thomas Inc.

Kelley, Gerald. Please Please the Bees. Kelley, Gerald, illus. 2017. (ENG., Illus.). 32p. (J). (gr. -1-3). 16.99 ***(978-0-8075-5183-7(X))*** Whitman, Albert & Co.

Ken Lindstrom To Ken Lindstrom. Ollie & Grampa Go to the Zoo: How the Polar Bear Got to the Zoo. Jones., Amber, illus. 2011. 28p. pap. 12.49 *(978-1-4520-1529-3(5))* AuthorHouse.

Kennedy, Jimmy. The Teddy Bears' Picnic. Day, Alexandra, illus. 2015. (Classic Board Bks.). (ENG.). 34p. (J). (gr. -1-k). bds. 7.99 *(978-1-4814-2274-1(X)*, Little Simon) Little Simon.

Kenner, Crystal R. The King of All Tickle Bugs & Other Stories. 2011. (Illus.). 124p. (gr. -1). pap. 10.95 *(978-1-4502-9466-9(9))* iUniverse, Inc.

Ketteman, Helen. If Beaver Had a Fever, 0 vols. O'Malley, Kevin, illus. 2011. (ENG.). 32p. (J). (gr. -1-3). 16.99 *(978-0-7614-5951-4(0)*, 9780761459514, Amazon Children's Publishing) Amazon Publishing.

Keylock, Joanna Murray. Pupazzo's Colorful World. Pelayo, Ruben, tr. Murray, Paula, illus. 2006.Tr. of colorido mundo de Pupazzo. (J). 10.00 *(978-1-889289-62-5(0))* Ye Olde Font Shoppe.

Kherdian, David. Come Back, Moon. Hogrogian, Nonny, illus. 2013. (ENG.). 32p. (J). (gr. -1-3). 16.99 *(978-1-4424-5887-1(9)*, Beach Lane Bks.) Beach Lane Bks.

Kim, YunYeong. Brown Bear's Dream. Kim, KyeMahn, illus. rev. ed. 2014. (MySELF Bookshelf Ser.). (ENG.). 32p. (J). (gr. k-2). pap. 11.94 *(978-1-60357-655-0(X))*; lib. bdg. 25.27 *(978-1-59953-646-0(3))* Norwood Hse. Pr.

Kimmel, Eric A. Hanukkah Bear. Wohnoutka, Mike, illus. (ENG.). 32p. (J). (gr. -1-3). 2014. 6.99 *(978-0-8234-3169-4(X))* 2013. 17.95 *(978-0-8234-2855-7(9))* Holiday Hse., Inc.

Kimmel, Eric A. & Trueman, Matthew. Simon & the Bear: A Hanukkah Tale. 2014. (ENG., Illus.). 40p. (J). (gr. -1-k). 16.99 *(978-1-4231-4355-0(8))* Hyperion Bks. for Children.

Kinney, Kendall. Tiger Tails. 2004. 68p. (J). per. 10.95 *(978-1-932196-21-4(8))* WordWright.biz, Inc.

Kirk, Trish. I Think There's a Bear Out There. 2009. 36p. pap. 16.99 *(978-1-4389-6097-5(2))* AuthorHouse.

Klassen, Jon. I Want My Hat Back. Klassen, Jon, illus. 2011. (ENG., Illus.). 40p. (J). (gr. -1-3). 16.99 *(978-0-7636-5598-3(8))* Candlewick Pr.

—I Want My Hat Back. 2012. (CHI.). 40p. (J). (gr. k-3). *(978-7-5332-6789-6(3))* Mingtian Chubanshe.

Kneen, Maggie. The First Christmas: An Angel Came to Nazareth. 2010. (ENG., Illus.). 24p. (J). (gr. -1-1). 9.99 *(978-0-8118-7662-9(4))* Chronicle Bks. LLC.

Kolar, Bob. Big Kicks. Kolar, Bob, illus. 2008. (ENG., Illus.). 40p. (J). (gr. -1-1). 16.99 *(978-0-7636-3390-5(9))* Candlewick Pr.

Kolar, Marsha. Little Brave Bear. Di Marco, Audrey, illus. 2005. 17p. (J). per. *(978-0-9766804-0-6(8))* CottonWood Publishing Co.

Kono, Erin Eitter. Every Color. 2016. (ENG., Illus.). 32p. (J). (gr. -1-3). 16.99 *(978-0-8037-4132-4(4)*, Dial Bks) Penguin Young Readers Group.

Kormos, Lawrence A. What Is Love Mama? 2007. (Illus.). (J). *(978-1-55452-190-6(4))* Essence Publishing.

Kovalski, Maryann. Omar on Ice. 2004. (J). (gr. k-3). spiral bd. *(978-0-616-01690-9(5))*; spiral bd. *(978-0-616-01691-6(3))* Canadian National Institute for the Blind/Institut National Canadien pour les Aveugles.

Krakower, Harold. Sugarland: Volume 2 Trouble in Sugarland. 2009. 28p. pap. 12.50 *(978-1-4490-1880-1(7))* AuthorHouse.

Kras, Sara Louise. The Hunted: Polar Prey. 2014. 64p. (J). (gr. 3-4). pap. 9.95 *(978-1-62285-081-5(5))* Enslow Pubs., Inc.

Krauss, Ruth. Bears. Sendak, Maurice, illus. 2005. (ENG.). 24p. (J). 21.99 *(978-0-06-027994-3(X))* HarperCollins Pubs.

Krensky, Stephen. Chaucer's First Winter. Cole, Henry, illus. (ENG.). 32p. (J). (gr. -1-1). 2010. 9.99 *(978-1-4424-1658-1(0))* 2009. 17.99 *(978-1-4169-9026-0(7))* Simon & Schuster Bks. For Young Readers. (Simon & Schuster Bks. For Young Readers).

Krutop, Lee, creator. Go Out to Play. 2008. (Illus.). 10p. (J). (gr. -1-1). bds. *(978-1-74178-572-2(3))* Brimax Books Ltd.

Kulikovsky-Romanoff, Grand Duchess Olga Alexandrovna, illus. The Adventures of Three White Bears. 2011. 26p. (J). pap. *(978-0-9716365-2-1(4)*, St. Nicholas Pr.) CrossBearers Publishing.

Kunkel, Mike. Herobear & the Kid Vol. 1: The Inheritance. 2003. (ENG., Illus.). 230p. 49.95 *(978-0-9721259-0-1(6)*, 9780972125901) Astonish Comics.

—The Inheritance. 2003. (Illus.). 208p. pap. 19.95 *(978-0-9721259-1-8(4))* Astonish Comics.

Kurtz, Carmen. Brun. (SPA.). 128p. (YA). (gr. 5-8). *(978-84-279-3367-5(3))* Noguer y Caralt Editores, S. A. ESP. Dist: Lectorum Pubns., Inc.

Kurtz, John. JATS Fairytale Classics - Goldilocks & the Three Bears. Kurtz, John, illus. 2004. (Illus.). 24p. (J). lib. bdg. 8.00 *(978-1-4242-0635-3(9))* Fitzgerald Bks.

Lammers, Elizabeth A. & McKinney, Dan. The Tale of the Black Igloo: Another Adventure of Pepe & Pierre, 1 vol. Epstein, Gabriela, illus. 2010. 26p. pap. 24.95 *(978-1-60610-433-0(0))* PublishAmerica, Inc.

Landry, Leo. Grin & Bear It. Landry, Leo, illus. (ENG., Illus.). 48p. (J). (gr. k-3). 2014. pap. 5.95 *(978-1-57091-746-2(9))* 2011. 12.95 *(978-1-57091-745-5(0))* Charlesbridge Publishing, Inc.

Lansky, Bruce. Polar BRRR Delivers. Wummer, Amy, illus. 2010. 10p. (J). bds. 6.99 *(978-1-4169-9318-6(5))* Meadowbrook Pr.

Lasky, Kathryn. Frost Wolf. 2011. (Wolves of the Beyond Ser.: 4). (ENG.). 288p. (J). (gr. 3-7). 17.99 *(978-0-545-09316-3(3)*, Scholastic Pr.) Scholastic, Inc.

Latter, Kym & Stroud, Cassie. The Trouble with Bear Hugs: A Story about Asthma. 2012. (Illus.). 32p. (J). pap. *(978-0-9873747-0-7(2))* Latter, Kym.

Lavie, Oren. The Bear Who Wasn't There & the Fabulous Forest. Erlbruch, Wolf, illus. 2016. (ENG.). 48p. (J). (gr. -1-2). 17.95 *(978-1-61775-490-6(0)*, Black Sheep) Akashic Bks.

Law, Felicia. Benjamin the Bear: A Tale of Selfishness. Spoor, Mike, illus. 2010. (Animal Fair Values Ser.). (ENG.). 32p. (J). (gr. -1-3). pap. 10.55 *(978-1-60754-915-4(8))*; lib. bdg. 22.60 *(978-1-60754-905-5(0))* Windmill Bks.

Lean, Chris Mac. BearWild. 2012. (ENG.). (J). pap. *(978-1-4675-3980-7(5))* Independent Pub.

Leatherman, Greg & Harris Wilson, P. Moving the Clouds: Tales of Priscilla. 2011. pap. 14.95 *(978-0-578-09100-6(3))* Gene Caven.

Lecis, Alessandro & Shirtiffe, Leanne. I Am Not Little Red Riding Hood. Wolfsgruber, Linda, illus. 2013. (ENG.). 32p. (J). (gr. -1-1). 16.95 *(978-1-62087-985-6(9)*, 620985, Sky Pony Pr.) Skyhorse Publishing Co., Inc.

Lee, Jamie. Washaka: The Bear Dreamer. 2007. (Illus.). 238p. per. 12.95 *(978-0-9729002-4-9(1))* Many Kites Pr.

Lee, Michelle. Play with Me! Lee, Michelle, illus. 2017. (ENG., Illus.). 32p. (J). (-k). 16.99 *(978-0-399-54601-3(4)*, G.P. Putnam's Sons Books for Young Readers) Penguin Young Readers Group.

Leffler, Silke & Janisch, Heinz. "I Have a Little Problem" Said the Bear. 2012. (ENG., Illus.). 32p. (J). (gr. -1-3). pap. 8.95 *(978-0-7358-4094-2(6))* North-South Bks., Inc.

Leist, Christina, illus. Jack the Bear. 2009. (ENG.). 40p. (J). (gr. -1-3). 16.95 *(978-1-894965-97-2(3))* Simply Read Bks. CAN. Dist: Ingram Publisher Services.

Lemieux, Michele. What's That Noise? 2004. (J). (gr. k-3). spiral bd. *(978-0-616-01698-5(0))*; spiral bd. *(978-0-616-01699-2(9))* Canadian National Institute for the Blind/Institut National Canadien pour les Aveugles.

Leone, Dee. Bizz & Buzz Make Honey Buns. Maritie, illus. 2014. (Penguin Core Concepts Ser.). (ENG.). 32p. (J). (gr. -1-k). 3.99 *(978-0-448-47927-9(3)*, Grosset & Dunlap) Penguin Young Readers Group.

Lepp, Royden. Happy Birthday Barnabas, 1 vol. Lepp, Royden, illus. 2008. (I Can Read! / Barnabas Ser.). (ENG., Illus.). 32p. (J). (gr. -1-1). pap. 3.99 *(978-0-310-71586-3(5))* Zonderkidz.

Lester, Helen. Tacky Goes to Camp. Munsinger, Lynn, illus. 2009. (Tacky the Penguin Ser.). (ENG.). 32p. (J). (gr. -1-3). 16.00 *(978-0-618-98812-9(2))* Houghton Mifflin Harcourt Publishing Co.

—Tacky Goes to Camp. 2012. (Tacky the Penguin Ser.). lib. bdg. 17.20 *(978-0-606-23992-9(8)*, Turtleback) Turtleback Bks.

Levin, Amy. A Bear's Year, 6 vols., Set. 2003. (Phonics Readers 1-36 Ser.). (ENG.). 8p. (gr. k-1). pap. 29.70 *(978-0-7368-3200-7(9)*, Phonics Readers) Capstone Press of Coughlan Cos.

Levin, Freddie. Goodnight Stained Glass Coloring Book. 2009. (Dover Stained Glass Coloring Book Ser.). (ENG., Illus.). 32p. (J). (gr. -1-2). pap. 6.99 *(978-0-486-47293-5(0))* Dover Pubns., Inc.

Levine, Arthur A. The Very Beary Tooth Fairy. Brannen, Sarah S., illus. 2013. (J). *(978-0-439-47404-7(3)*, Scholastic Pr.) Scholastic, Inc.

Levis, Caron. Ida, Always. Santoso, Charles, illus. 2016. (ENG.). 40p. (J). (gr. -1-3). 17.99 *(978-1-4814-2640-4(0))* Simon & Schuster Children's Publishing.

Lewis, Anne Margaret. Sleeping Bear: Journey of the Cub Book 1. 2012. (ENG.). (J). pap. 8.00 *(978-1-4675-5260-8(7))* Independent Pub.

—Sleeping Bear: The Legend. Grant, Sarah, illus. 2007. (ENG.). 40p. (J). (gr. -1-2). 16.95 *(978-1-934133-15-6(9)*, Mackinac Island Press, Inc.) Charlesbridge Publishing, Inc.

Lewis, Carolyn & DeVince, James. The Hairy Beary Adventure Series, 3 bks. DeVince, James, ed. Porcheron, Tammy, illus. 2005. 122p. (J). pap. 24.95 *(978-0-9712641-3-7(9))* J M D's Business Services.

—Hairy Beary Book Three: The Blue Ribbon Hero, 3 bks., Vol. 3. DeVince, James, ed. Porcheron, Tammy, illus. 2003. (Hairy Beary Ser.: 3). 46p. (J). pap. 9.95 *(978-0-9712641-2-0(0))* J M D's Business Services.

Lewis, Gill. Moon Bear. Gottardo, Alessandro, illus. 2015. (ENG.). 384p. (J). (gr. 3-7). 16.99 *(978-1-4814-0094-7(0))* Simon & Schuster Children's Publishing.

Lewis, Paeony. I'll Always Love You. Ives, Penny, illus. (J). 2013. (ENG.). 32p. pap. *(978-1-58925-441-1(4))* 2008. 12p. (gr. -1-3). bds. 7.95 *(978-1-58925-833-4(9))* 2004. 32p. pap. 5.95 *(978-1-58925-360-5(4))* Tiger Tales.

Library Bear. Date not set. 9.95 *(978-0-89868-293-9(2))*; pap. 0.95 *(978-0-89868-292-2(4))* ARO Publishing Co.

Libster, Bernard. The Bonsai Bear. Cheung, Aries, illus. 2006. 31p. (J). (gr. k-4). reprint ed. 16.00 *(978-1-4223-5857-3(7))* DIANE Publishing Co.

Lichfield, Walter C. Fanciful Bear Stories for Small Kids & Factual Bear Stories for Big Kids. 2003. (Illus.). 84p. per. *(978-1-931456-47-0(X))* Athena Pr.

Light, Carol. Chickensing Big Book. Light, Carol, illus. 2003. (Illus.). (J). *(978-0-9745803-2-6(5))* Little Big Tomes.

Lincoln, Hazel. Little Snow Bear, 1 vol. Lincoln, Hazel, illus. 2004. (ENG., Illus.). 32p. (J). pap. 17.95 *(978-0-86315-454-6(9))* Floris Bks. GBR. Dist: SteinerBooks, Inc.

Linderman, Frank B., et al. Big Jinny: The Story of a Grizzly Bear. Lochrie, Elizabeth, illus. 2005. (ENG.). 130p. pap. 16.95 *(978-0-8032-8044-1(0)*, LINBIX, Bison Bks.) Univ. of Nebraska Pr.

Litchfield, David. The Bear & the Piano. 2016. (ENG., Illus.). 40p. (J). (gr. -1-3). 16.99 *(978-0-544-67454-7(5))* Houghton Mifflin Harcourt Publishing Co.

Litchfield, Jo, contrib. by. Goldilocks & the Three Bears. 2008. (Usborne First Fairytales Ser.). (Illus.). 10p. (J). bds. 9.99 *(978-0-7945-1962-9(8)*, Usborne) EDC Publishing.

Little Bear. 2003. (Goodnight Mr. Moon Ser.). (Illus.). (J). bds. 2.98 *(978-0-7525-4740-4(2))* Parragon, Inc.

little bee books, little bee & Llewhellin, Gareth. Jump into Fall! 2016. (ENG., Illus.). 12p. (J). (gr. -1 — 1). bds. 6.99 *(978-1-4998-0298-6(6))* Little Bee Books Inc.

Little Golden Books Staff. The Three Bears. Rojankovsky, Feodor, illus. 2012. (Little Golden Book Ser.). (ENG.). 24p. (J). (gr. k-k). 4.99 *(978-0-307-02140-3(8)*, Golden Bks.) Random Hse. Children's Bks.

The Little Prayer Bear. 2004. lib. bdg. 12.95 *(978-0-9748558-0-6(4))* Rainbow Valley Publishing Co.

Litton, Jonathan. Planet Pop-Up: Bear's Merry Christmas. Anderson, Nicola, illus. 2015. (Planet Pop-Up Ser.). (ENG.). 12p. (J). (gr. -1). 12.95 *(978-1-62686-486-3(1)*, Silver Dolphin Bks.) Readerlink Distribution Services, LLC.

Liu, Cynthea. Bike on, Bear! Litten, Kristyna, illus. 2015. (ENG.). 32p. (J). (gr. -1-2). 17.99 *(978-1-4814-0506-5(3)*, Aladdin) Simon & Schuster Children's Publishing.

Livingston, A. A. B. Bear & Lolly: Off to School. Chou, Joey, illus. 2014. (ENG.). 32p. (J). (gr. -1-3). 15.99 *(978-0-06-219788-7(6))* HarperCollins Pubs.

—B. Bear & Lolly: Catch That Cookie! Chou, Joey, illus. 2015. (ENG.). 32p. (J). (gr. -1-3). 15.99 *(978-0-06-219791-7(6))* HarperCollins Pubs.

Lobel, Arnold. The Arnold Lobel Treasury. 2014. (ENG., Illus.). 160p. (J). (gr. 1-4). pap. 14.99 *(978-0-486-78078-8(3))* Dover Pubns., Inc.

Lobel, Gill. Little Bear's Special Wish. Hansen, Gaby, illus. (Storytime Board Bks.). (J). 2005. 16p. (gr. -1-k). bds. 6.95 *(978-1-58925-769-6(3))* 2004. 32p. tchr. ed. 16.95 *(978-1-58925-034-5(6))* Tiger Tales.

Loewen, Nancy. Believe Me, Goldilocks Rocks! The Story of the Three Bears As Told by Baby Bear. Avakyan, Tatevik, illus. 2013. (Other Side of the Story Ser.). (ENG.). 24p. (gr. 2-3). 9.95 *(978-1-4795-1939-2(1))* Picture Window Bks.

Lomando, Suzanne. My Buddy Bear, Tales: Buddy Bear's First Storybook. 2005. 10.00 *(978-0-8059-9755-2(5))* Dorrance Publishing Co., Inc.

Lomba, Ana. Boucle d'or et les Trois Ours. Wenzel, Dominique, tr. Cornejo, Santiago, illus. 2006.Tr. of Goldilocks & the Three Bears. (FRE & ENG.). 48p. (gr. -1-3). 17.00 *(978-0-07-146173-3(6)*, 0071461736) McGraw-Hill Cos., The.

London, Jonathan. Honey Paw & Lightfoot. Van Zyle, Jon, illus. 2014. (ENG.). 32p. (J). 16.99 *(978-1-941821-10-7(3)*, Alaska Northwest Bks.) Graphic Arts Ctr. Publishing Co.

Loney, Andrea J. Bunnybear. Saldaña, Carmen, illus. 2017. (ENG.). 32p. (J). (gr. -1-3). 16.99 *(978-0-8075-0938-8(8))* Whitman, Albert & Co.

Long, Ethan. Lion & Tiger & Bear: Tag! You're It! 2016. (Lion & Tiger & Bear Ser.). (ENG., Illus.). 40p. (J). (gr. k-2). 14.95 *(978-1-4197-1896-0(7))* Abrams, Inc.

Lopez, Horacio. La Funcion de Teatro. Wright, Douglas, illus. 2003. (SPA.). 38p. (J). (gr. k-3). pap. 8.95 *(978-950-511-622-5(5))* Santillana USA Publishing Co., Inc.

Lorraine, Florido. Dezzer the Gasser. Shami, Susan & Crossman, Keith, eds. Ewing, John, illus. 2009. 32p. (J). 15.99 *(978-0-9818449-0-9(1))* Thinkus Pubs.

Love, Pamela. A Cub Explores. Sykes, Shannon, illus. 2004. (ENG.). 32p. (J). (gr. -1-17). 15.95 *(978-0-89272-593-9(1))* Down East Bks.

Lucas, David. A Letter for Bear. 2013. (ENG., Illus.). 32p. (J). (gr. -1-2). 14.95 *(978-1-909263-13-0(3))* Flying Eye Bks. GBR. Dist: Consortium Bk. Sales & Distribution.

Luedtke, Courtney. Baby Boo: The Happy Beginning. 2009. (Illus.). 72p. pap. 27.49 *(978-1-4389-2696-4(0))* AuthorHouse.

Lumry, Amanda & Hurwitz, Laura. Operation Orangutan. 2007. (Adventures of Riley (Unnumberd) Ser.). (Illus.). 36p. (J). (gr. -1-3). 18.95 *(978-0-9748411-7-5(X))* Eaglemont Pr.

—Polar Bear Puzzle. 2007. (Adventures of Riley Ser.). (Illus.). (J). (gr. -1-3). 33p. 15.95 *(978-1-60040-004-9(3))*; 36p. 18.95 *(978-1-60040-005-6(1))* Eaglemont Pr.

Luther, Jacqueline. Polar Bear Cub. Trachock, Cathy, illus. 2006. (ENG.). 32p. (J). pap. 3.95 *(978-1-59249-589-4(3))* Soundprints.

Luther, Jacqueline & Lind, Alan. Black Bear Cub. Trachock, Cathy, illus. 2006. (ENG.). 32p. (J). pap. 3.95 *(978-1-59249-587-0(7))* Soundprints.

Maccarone, Grace. The Three Bears ABC. Hibbert, Hollie, illus. 2013. (ENG.). 32p. (J). (gr. -1-3). 16.99 *(978-0-8075-7904-6(1))* Whitman, Albert & Co.

MacDonald, Steven. Just Clowning Around: Two Stories. McPhail, David, illus. 2003. (Green Light Readers Level 1 Ser.). (ENG.). 24p. (J). (gr. -1-3). pap. 3.95 *(978-0-15-204856-3(1))* Houghton Mifflin Harcourt Publishing Co.

—Just Clowning Around: Two Stories. McPhail, David, illus. 2003. (Green Light Readers — Level 1 Ser.). 20p. (gr. -1-3). lib. bdg. 13.50 *(978-0-613-66362-5(4)*, Turtleback) Turtleback Bks.

MacGregor, Helen & Chadwick, Stephen. Goldilocks & the Three Bears: An Impeccable Judged Musical, 1 vol. Lowe, Harriet et al, eds. Eccles, Jane, illus. 2005. (and C Black Musicals Ser.). (ENG.). 56p. (J). (gr. 2-6). pap. 42.95 ***(978-0-7136-7085-1(1))*** HarperCollins Pubs. Ltd. GBR. Dist: Independent Pubs. Group.

Machas, Dimi, illus. Tsaani: The Grizzly Bear Story. 2nd ed. 2005. 28p. (YA). 10.00 *(978-0-9767217-0-3(8))* Chickaloon Village Publishing.

Mack. The Legend of the Lonesome Bear: Level O, 6 vols. (Take-Twostm Ser.). 32p. 38.95 *(978-0-322-04486-9(3))* Wright Group/McGraw-Hill.

Mack, Jeff. Hush Little Polar Bear. Mack, Jeff, illus. (ENG., Illus.). (J). (gr. -1-1). 2013. 36p. bds. 7.99 *(978-1-59643-945-0(9)*, 9781596439450) 2008. 40p. 17.99 *(978-1-59643-368-7(X)*, 9781596433687) Roaring Brook Pr.

—Who Needs a Bath? Mack, Jeff, illus. 2015. (ENG., Illus.). 40p. (J). (gr. -1-3). 17.99 *(978-0-06-222028-8(4))* HarperCollins Pubs.

—Who Wants a Hug? Mack, Jeff, illus. 2015. (ENG., Illus.). 40p. (J). (gr. -1-3). 17.99 *(978-0-06-222026-4(8))* HarperCollins Pubs.

MacKenzie, Maryellen. Sneekie & Snookie: And the Honey Tree. 2012. 24p. (-18). pap. 17.99 *(978-1-4772-7651-8(3))* AuthorHouse.

MacKey, Esther L. Little Bear & Honey Bee. Mackey, Kaitlin L., illus. 2012. 28p. 14.95 *(978-1-937260-10-1(0))* Sleepytown Pr.

Mackey, Stephen. Miki, Set. Mackey, Stephen, illus. 2012. (ENG., Illus.). 48p. (J). (gr. -1-k). 16.99 *(978-1-4449-0651-6(8))* Hodder & Stoughton GBR. Dist: Hachette Bk. Group.

Magoun, James. There's a Bear in My Chair. Magnuson, Diana, illus. 2004. (ENG.). 20p. (gr. k-2). pap. 8.95 *(978-1-57874-080-2(0)*, Kaeden Bks.) Kaeden Corp.

Magsamen, Sandra. I Love You Beary Much. 2014. (Earisistables Ser.). (ENG., Illus.). 14p. (J). (gr. -1 — 1). bds. 7.99 *(978-0-316-25516-5(5))* Little, Brown Bks. for Young Readers.

Maguire, Thomas Aquinas. A Growling Place. 2007. (ENG., Illus.). 32p. (J). (gr. -1-3). 16.95 *(978-1-894965-74-3(4))* Simply Read Bks. CAN. Dist: Ingram Publisher Services.

Maithya, Susan M. Struffel Cares: Struffel's New Pet. 2012. 40p. pap. 20.99 *(978-1-4772-3323-8(7))* AuthorHouse.

Make Believe Ideas. B Is for Breakdancing Bear Alphabet Sticker Activity Book. 2015. (ENG.). 110p. (J). pap. 9.99 *(978-1-78393-442-3(5))* Make Believe Ideas GBR. Dist: Nelson, Thomas Inc.

—Bear Hugs. 2013. (ENG.). 8p. (J). 12.99 *(978-1-78235-690-5(8))* Make Believe Ideas GBR. Dist: Nelson, Thomas Inc.

—Goldilocks & the Three Bears. 2014. (ENG.). 12p. (J). bds. 9.99 *(978-1-78235-907-4(9))* Make Believe Ideas GBR. Dist: Nelson, Thomas Inc.

Malak, Annabel, illus. Goldilocks & the Three Bears. (Classic Stories Ser.). 48p. (J). audio, audio compact disk *(978-2-921997-84-3(3))* Coffragants.

Malinowski, Carrie. The Hand-Me-Down Bear. 2012. (ENG., Illus.). 28p. (J). pap. 12.99 *(978-1-937008-15-4(0))* Heart to Heart Publishing, Inc.

Mallat, Kathy. Brave Bear. 2004. (Illus.). 24p. (J). (gr. -1-k). 15.95 *(978-0-8027-8704-0(5))* Walker & Co.

Mallory, Gail. The Bear Went over the Mountain. 2008. 27p. pap. 24.95 *(978-1-60563-902-4(8))* America Star Bks.

Marcero, Deborah, illus. Ursa's Light. 2016. (J). *(978-1-4413-1881-7(X))* Peter Pauper Pr. Inc.

Marsh, Carole. The Mystery at Grizzly Graveyard. 2014. (Real Kids, Real Places Ser.: Vol. 3). (ENG., Illus.). 158p. (J). (gr. 3-5). pap. 7.99 *(978-0-635-11187-6(X)*, Marsh, Carole Mysteries) Gallopade International.

Martin, Bill, Jr. Baby Bear, Baby Bear, What Do You See? Carle, Eric, illus. (Brown Bear & Friends Ser.). (ENG.). (J). (gr. -1-k). 2014. 28p. bds. 12.99 *(978-0-8050-9949-2(2)*, 9780805099492) 2011. 40p. 8.99 *(978-0-8050-9291-2(9)*, 9780805092912) 2009. 28p. bds. 7.99 *(978-0-8050-8990-5(X)*, 9780805089905) 2007. 32p. 17.99 *(978-0-8050-8336-1(7)*, 9780805083361) Holt, Henry & Co. (Holt, Henry & Co. Bks. For Young Readers).

—Baby Bear, Baby Bear, What Do You See? 10th Anniversary Edition with Audio CD. Carle, Eric, illus. 2016. (Brown Bear & Friends Ser.). (ENG.). 32p. (J). 19.99 *(978-1-62779-731-3(9)*, 9781627797313, Holt, Henry & Co. Bks. For Young Readers) Holt, Henry & Co.

—Baby Bear, Baby Bear, What Do You See? Big Book. Carle, Eric, illus. 2011. (Brown Bear & Friends Ser.). (ENG.). 32p. (J). (gr. -1-k). pap. 27.99 *(978-0-8050-9345-2(1)*, 9780805093452, Holt, Henry & Co. Bks. For Young Readers) Holt, Henry & Co.

—Brown Bear & Friends. Carle, Eric, illus. unabr. ed. 2011. (Brown Bear & Friends Ser.). (ENG.). (J). (gr. -1-k). 39.99 *(978-1-4272-1448-5(4)*, 9781427214485) Macmillan Audio.

—Brown Bear Book & CD Storytime Set. Carle, Eric, illus. unabr. ed. 2013. (ENG.). (J). (gr. -1-k). 12.99 *(978-1-4272-3510-7(4)*, 9781427235107) Macmillan Audio.

—Brown Bear, Brown Bear, What Do You See? Date not set. (J). bds. 12.95 *(978-0-8050-7209-9(8)*, Holt, Henry & Co. Bks. For Young Readers) Holt, Henry & Co.

—Brown Bear, Brown Bear, What Do You See? Carle, Eric, illus. (J). 2004. (ALB & ENG.). 26p. pap. *(978-1-84444-115-0(6))* 2004. (ENG & ARA.). 32p. pap. *(978-1-84444-116-7(4))* 2004. (PER & ENG.). 32p. pap. *(978-1-84444-120-4(2))* 2004. (GUJ & ENG.). 32p. pap. *(978-1-84444-121-1(0))* 2004. (ENG & HIN.). 32p. pap. *(978-1-84444-122-8(9))* 2004. (PAN & ENG.). 32p. pap. *(978-1-84444-123-5(7))* 2004. (SOM & ENG.). 27p. pap. *(978-1-84444-125-9(3))* 2004. (TAM & ENG.). 32p. pap. *(978-1-84444-126-6(1))* 2004. (ENG & TUR.). 27p. pap. *(978-1-84444-127-3(X))* 2004. (YOR & ENG.). 25p. pap. *(978-1-84444-129-7(6))* 2004. (KUR & ENG.). 26p. pap. *(978-1-84444-158-7(X))* 2004. (ENG & POR.). 32p. pap. *(978-1-84444-159-4(8))* 2003. (CHI & ENG.). 32p. pap. *(978-1-84444-118-1(0))* 2003. (URD & ENG.). 32p. pap. *(978-1-84444-128-0(8))* Mantra Lingua.

—Brown Bear, Brown Bear, What Do You See? Carle, Eric, illus. 2003. (VIE & ENG.). 32p. (J). pap. 12.95 *(978-1-84444-124-2(5))* Mantra Lingua GBR. Dist: Chinasprout, Inc.

—Brown Bear, Brown Bear, What Do You See? 50th Anniversary Edition with Audio CD. Carle, Eric, illus. 2016. (Brown Bear & Friends Ser.). (ENG.). 32p. (J). 19.99 *(978-1-62779-721-4(1)*, 9781627797214, Holt, Henry & Co. Bks. For Young Readers) Holt, Henry & Co.

Martin, Bill. Lift-the-Tab: Baby Bear, Baby Bear, What Do You See? Carle, Eric, illus. 2016. (Brown Bear & Friends Ser.). (ENG.). 28p. (J). bds. 6.99 *(978-1-62779-724-5(6)*, 9781627797245, Holt, Henry & Co. Bks. For Young Readers) Holt, Henry & Co.

—Lift-The-Tab: Brown Bear, Brown Bear, What Do You See? 50th Anniversary Edition. Carle, Eric, illus. 2016. (Brown Bear & Friends Ser.). (ENG.). 28p. (J). bds. 9.99 *(978-1-62779-723-8(8)*, 9781627797238, Holt, Henry & Co. Bks. For Young Readers) Holt, Henry & Co.

Martin, Bill, Jr. Polar Bear Book & CD Storytime Set. Carle, Eric, illus. unabr. ed. 2012. (ENG.). (J). (gr. -1-k). 12.99 *(978-1-4272-3256-4(3)*, 9781427232564) Macmillan Audio.

Martin, David. Shh! Bears Sleeping. Johnson, Steve & Fancher, Lou, illus. 2016. (ENG.). 32p. (J). (gr. -1-2). 16.99 *(978-0-670-01718-8(3)*, Viking Books for Young Readers) Penguin Young Readers Group.

—Three Little Bears Play All Day. Gutierrez, Akemi, illus. 2010. (Brand New Readers Ser.). (ENG.). 48p. (J). (gr. -1-3). pap. 5.99 *(978-0-7636-4230-3(4))* Candlewick Pr.

Mason, Chad. Wake up, Bertha Bear! Wallace, Chad, illus. 2006. (ENG.). 32p. (J). (gr. -1-3). 15.95 *(978-0-89272-655-4(5))* Down East Bks.

Mason, Jane B. Stella & the Berry Thief, 1 vol. Koopmans, Loek, tr. Koopmans, Loek, illus. 2004. (ENG.). 32p. (J). 16.95 *(978-0-7614-5123-5(4))* Marshall Cavendish Corp.

Mathews, Leslie. I Am a Bear. Dumont, Jean-françois, illus. 2015. (ENG.). 34p. (J). 16.00 *(978-0-8028-5447-6(8)*, Eerdmans Bks For Young Readers) Eerdmans, William B. Publishing Co.

Mattern, Joanne. The Tricky Garden. 2005. (J). pap. *(978-1-4108-4191-9(X))* Benchmark Education Co.

Matthews, Curtis. Boots Meets the Grizzly Bears. 2007. 164p. per. 13.95 *(978-1-4343-3372-8(8))* AuthorHouse.

Mattick, Lindsay. Finding Winnie: The True Story of the World's Most Famous Bear. Blackall, Sophie, illus. 2015. (ENG.). 56p. (J). (gr. -1-1). 18.00 *(978-0-316-32490-8(6))* Little Brown & Co.

Maurer, Eileen. The Bear Who Needs Your Help. 2009. 16p. pap. 8.49 *(978-1-4389-5146-1(9))* AuthorHouse.

Mawhinney, Art, illus. Diego's Arctic Rescue. 2009. (Go, Diego, Go! Ser.). (ENG.). 24p. (J). (gr. -1-2). pap. 3.99 *(978-1-4169-8504-4(2)*, Simon Spotlight/Nickelodeon) Simon Spotlight/Nickelodeon.

—Look & Find Open Season. 2007. 32p. (J). (gr. -1-3). lib. bdg. 7.98 *(978-1-4127-8889-2(7))* Publications International, Ltd.

McAllister, Angela. A Mouse So Small. Pedler, Caroline, illus. 2015. (ENG.). 32p. (J). (gr. -1-3). 16.99 *(978-1-58925-194-6(6))* Tiger Tales.

McBratney, Sam. There, There. Bates, Ivan, illus. (ENG.). (J). 2015. 32p. (-k). bds. 7.99 *(978-0-7636-7565-3(2))* 2013. 40p. (gr. -1-2). 15.99 *(978-0-7636-6702-3(1))* Candlewick Pr. (Templar).

—You're All My Favorites. Jeram, Anita, illus. 2008. (ENG.). 32p. (J). (gr. k-k). bds. 7.99 *(978-0-7636-4297-6(5))* Candlewick Pr.

McCloskey, Robert. Blueberries for Sal, 1 vol. 2010. (Puffin Storytime Ser.). (ENG.). 15p. (J). (gr. -1-k). 9.99 *(978-0-14-241643-3(6)*, Puffin Books) Penguin Young Readers Group.

—Blueberries for Sal. (J). (gr. -1-k). pap. 12.95 incl. audio. 2004. 29.95 *(978-1-55592-841-4(2))*; 2004. (J). 18.95 *(978-1-55592-799-8(8))*; 2004. (J). 38.75 *(978-1-55592-816-2(1))* Weston Woods Studios, Inc.

McCreadie, Sandi. Thistle Fables. 2013. 64p. pap. 23.99 *(978-1-4808-0313-8(8))* Archway Publishing.

McCue, Gil. Buzzy the Honey Bee. 2009. 36p. pap. 14.95 *(978-1-4269-1933-6(6))* Trafford Publishing.

McDonagh, Christelle, et al. Mission Magic Bubble. 2009. (Illus.). 56p. pap. 23.99 *(978-1-4389-0640-9(4))* AuthorHouse.

McEwen, Katharine. Bear Hug. McEwen, Katharine, illus. 2014. (ENG., Illus.). 32p. (J). (gr. -1-2). 15.99 *(978-0-7636-6630-9(0)*, Templar) Candlewick Pr.

McGee, Marni. Bear Can't Sleep! Julian, Sean, illus. 2015. (ENG.). 32p. (J). (gr. -1-3). 16.99 *(978-1-58925-189-2(X))* Tiger Tales.

McGee, Warner, illus. Diego's Egyptian Expedition. 2009. (Go, Diego, Go! Ser.). (ENG.). 24p. (J). pap. 3.99 *(978-1-4169-6870-2(9)*, Simon Spotlight/Nickelodeon) Simon Spotlight/Nickelodeon.

McGuire, Roberta Libby. The Adventures of the Cape Cod Bear. 2012. 24p. pap. 15.99 *(978-1-4771-5266-9(0))* Xlibris Corp.

McIntosh Williams, Samantha. The Last Bear on Brandywine Crick. 2013. 276p. pap. 11.99 *(978-1-4575-1960-4(7))* Dog Ear Publishing, LLC.

McMillan, J. Ann. Billy Bob Bear's Six Wishes. 2009. 20p. pap. 12.99 *(978-1-4389-8785-9(4))* AuthorHouse.

McPhail, David. Big Brown Bear. 2003. (Green Light Readers Level 1 Ser.). (ENG., Illus.). 24p. (J). (gr. -1-3). pap. 3.95 *(978-0-15-204858-7(8))* Houghton Mifflin Harcourt Publishing Co.

—Big Brown Bear. 2003. (Green Light Readers — Level 1 Ser.). (gr. -1-2). lib. bdg. 13.50 *(978-0-613-64462-4(X)*, Turtleback) Turtleback Bks.

—Big Brown Bear/El Gran Oso Pardo. Flor Ada, Alma & Campoy, F. Isabel, trs. 2007. (Green Light Readers Level 1 Ser.). (ENG & SPA., Illus.). 28p. (J). (gr. -1-3). pap. 3.95 *(978-0-15-205970-5(9))* Houghton Mifflin Harcourt Publishing Co.

—Big Brown Bear's up & down Day. McPhail, David, illus. 2005. (Illus.). 42p. (J). (gr. -1-3). reprint ed. 16.00 *(978-0-7567-8542-0(1))* DIANE Publishing Co.

—Budgie & Boo. 2009. (ENG., Illus.). 32p. (J). (gr. -1-k). 15.95 *(978-0-8109-8324-3(9)*, Abrams Bks. for Young Readers) Abrams, Inc.

—I Promise. 2017. (ENG., Illus.). 40p. (J). (gr. -1-3). 16.99 *(978-0-316-29787-5(9))* Little Brown & Co.

—Rick Is Sick. 2004. (Green Light Readers Level 1 Ser.). (ENG., Illus.). 24p. (J). (gr. -1-3). pap. 3.95 *(978-0-15-205092-4(2))* Houghton Mifflin Harcourt Publishing Co.

—Rick Is Sick. 2004. (Green Light Readers — Level 1 Ser.). 13.50 *(978-0-613-97286-4(4)*, Turtleback) Turtleback Bks.

Mcwherter, Barbara. I Should Have Been a Bear. McWherter, Seth, illus. 2011. 24p. pap. 24.95 *(978-1-4626-3532-0(6))* America Star Bks.

Meadows, Daisy. Caitlin the Ice Bear Fairy. 2012. (Illus.). 65p. (J). *(978-0-545-42602-2(2))* Scholastic, Inc.

—Rosie the Honey Bear Fairy. 2015. (Baby Animal Rescue Fairies Ser.: 6). (ENG.). 80p. (J). (gr. 2-5). pap. 4.99 *(978-0-545-70855-5(9)*, Scholastic Paperbacks) Scholastic, Inc.

Mejuto, Eva. Run Pumpkin, Run. 2007. (ENG., Illus.). 36p. (J). 17.95 *(978-84-96788-88-6(1))* OQO, Editora ESP. Dist: Baker & Taylor Bks.

Melling, David. Dont Worry Douglas. Melling, David, illus. 2011. (ENG., Illus.). 32p. 12.95 *(978-1-58925-106-9(7))* Tiger Tales.

—Hugless Douglas & the Big Sleepover. 2013. (ENG., Illus.). 32p. (J). *(978-1-58925-116-8(4))* Tiger Tales.

—Hugless Dougless. Melling, David, illus. 2010. (ENG., Illus.). 32p. (J). (gr. -1-2). 15.95 *(978-1-58925-098-7(2))* Tiger Tales.

Menard, James. The Bees & the Bears. Menard, John C., illus. 2008. 36p. pap. 16.99 *(978-1-4389-2150-1(0))* AuthorHouse.

Meyer, Brigit. Merry Christmas, Little Bear. Mussenbrock, Anne, illus. 2004. 10p. (J). bds. 5.99 *(978-1-59384-062-4(4))* Parklane Publishing.

M.H.Pruitt. The Adventures of Rexie the Bear. 2009. 16p. pap. 8.99 *(978-1-4490-4211-0(2))* AuthorHouse.

Michalak, Jamie. The Coziest Place. Davis, Jon, illus. 2013. (ENG.). 32p. (J). (gr. -1-k). 14.99 *(978-1-58925-121-2(0))* Tiger Tales.

Mikaelsen, Ben. Touching Spirit Bear. l.t. ed. 2017. (Spirit Bear Ser.). (ENG.). 310p. 22.99 ***(978-1-4328-3843-0(1))*** Cengage Gale.

Miki Sos: (Little Bear) 2007.Tr. of Little Bear. (Illus.). 26p. (J). spiral bd. 14.95 *(978-0-9795400-0-4(3))* NANUQ Publishing.

Milios, Rita. Bears, Bears, Everywhere. Motoyama, Keiko, illus. rev. ed. 2003. (Rookie Reader Español Ser.). (ENG.). 32p. (J). (gr. k-2). pap. 4.95 *(978-0-516-27830-8(4)*, Children's Pr.) Scholastic Library Publishing.

Miller, Jay. Bingo the Banjo Picking Bear. 2007. 40p. (YA). per. 14.95 *(978-1-4327-0739-2(6))* Outskirts Pr., Inc.

Miller, Jennifer. Run, Rasputin, Run! Trials & Friendships (Book 2) 2006. (ENG., Illus.). 172p. per. 14.85 *(978-1-4120-8494-9(6))* Trafford Publishing.

Miller, Lois. The Last Three Tall Tales. 2010. 72p. pap. 8.95 *(978-0-557-09181-2(0))* Lulu Pr., Inc.

Miller, Marie. The Great Complaint: Oh! What a Day! 2012. 20p. pap. 17.99 *(978-1-4772-2439-7(4))* AuthorHouse.

Miller, Pat. We're Going on a Book Hunt. Bernard Westcott, Nadine, illus. 2008. (J). (gr. -1). 17.95 *(978-1-60213-034-0(5)*, Upstart Bks.) Highsmith Inc.

Miller, Sara F. Pooh's Honey Trouble. 2012. (ENG.). 16p. (J). (gr. -1-1). bds. 6.99 *(978-1-4231-3579-1(2))* Disney Pr.

Milne, A. A. The House at Pooh Corner. Set. Shepard, Ernest H., illus. (J). incl. audio *(978-1-57375-653-2(9)*, 71524) Audioscope.

—Winnie Puh. Meddemmen, John, tr. Shepard, Ernest H., illus.Tr. of Winnie the Pooh. (ITA.). 164p. pap. 29.95 *(978-88-7782-278-9(3))* Salani ITA. Dist: Distribooks, Inc.

—Winnie the Pooh & When We Were Young, Boxed set. Shepard, Ernest H., illus. 32p. (J). pap. incl. audio compact disk *(978-1-57375-583-2(4)*, 71512) Audioscope.

—The World of Pooh: The Complete Winnie-the-Pooh & the House at Pooh Corner. Shepard, Ernest H., illus. 2010. (Winnie-The-Pooh Ser.). (ENG.). 384p. (J). (gr. 3-7). 25.99 *(978-0-525-44447-3(5)*, Dutton Books for Young Readers) Penguin Young Readers Group.

Minarik, Else Holmelund. Los Amigos de Osito. Benavides, Rosa, tr. Sendak, Maurice, illus. 2nd ed. (Infantil Alfaguara Ser.: 32).Tr. of Little Bear's Friends. (SPA.). 64p. (J). 7.95 *(978-84-204-3049-2(8))* Santillana USA Publishing Co., Inc.

—Un Beso para Osito. Benavides, Rosa, tr. Sendak, Maurice, illus. 2003. (Infantil Alfaguara Ser.: 31).Tr. of Kiss for Little Bear. (SPA.). 36p. (J). (gr. k-3). 11.95 *(978-84-204-3050-8(1)*, AF1633) Ediciones Alfaguara ESP. Dist: Lectorum Pubns., Inc., Santillana USA Publishing Co., Inc.

—Un Beso para Osito. Sendak, Maurice, tr. Sendak, Maurice, illus.Tr. of Kiss for Little Bear. (SPA.). 34p. (J). (gr. k-3). pap. 8.95 *(978-84-204-4827-5(3))* Santillana USA Publishing Co., Inc.

—Little Bear. Sendak, Maurice, illus. 2003. (I Can Read Level 1 Ser.). (ENG.). 64p. (J). (gr. k-3). pap. 3.95 *(978-0-06-444004-2(4))* HarperCollins Pubs.

—Little Bear. 2003. (Little Bear: I Can Read! Ser.). (J). (gr. k-3). lib. bdg. 13.55 *(978-0-8085-2618-6(9)*, Turtleback) Turtleback Bks.

—Little Bear & the Marco Polo. Doubleday, Dorothy, illus. 2010. (I Can Read Level 1 Ser.). (ENG.). 32p. (J). (gr. k-3). 16.99 *(978-0-06-085485-0(5))*; pap. 3.99 *(978-0-06-085487-4(1))* HarperCollins Pubs.

—Little Bear's Visit. Sendak, Maurice, illus. (J). pap. 12.95 incl. audio Weston Woods Studios, Inc.

—Osito. Aguilar, Joaquina, tr. Sendak, Maurice, illus. 2003. (Infantil Alfaguara Ser.: 25).Tr. of Little Bear. (SPA.). 60p. (J). (gr. k-3). pap. 8.95 *(978-84-204-3044-7(7)*, AF1346) Santillana USA Publishing Co., Inc.

—Papa Oso Vuelve a Casa. Benavides, Rosa, tr. Sendak, Maurice, illus. 2nd ed. 2003. (Infantil Alfaguara Ser.: 29).Tr. of Father Bear Comes Home. (SPA.). 63p. (J). (gr. -1-3). pap. *(978-84-204-3048-5(X)*, AF1359) Ediciones Alfaguara ESP. Dist: Santillana USA Publishing Co., Inc.

—La Visita de Osito. Puncel, María, tr. Sendak, Maurice, illus. 2006. (Osito / Little Bear Ser.).Tr. of Little Bear's Visit. (SPA.). 64p. (gr. k-3). pap. 8.95 *(978-968-19-0623-8(3)*, AF1060) Santillana USA Publishing Co., Inc.

Minarik, Else Holmelund & Tashlin, Frank. El Oso Que No lo Era. Sendak, Maurice, illus. 2003. (Infantil Ser.).Tr. of Bear That Wasn't. (SPA.). 62p. (J). (gr. k-3). pap. 8.95 *(978-958-24-0002-6(1))* Santillana USA Publishing Co., Inc.

Ming, Markay. Bear's Great Adventure, 1 vol. 2010. 32p. 24.95 *(978-1-4489-5792-7(3))* PublishAmerica, Inc.

Minor, Florence F. If You Were a Panda Bear. Minor, Wendell, illus. 2013. (ENG.). 32p. (J). (gr. -1-3). 17.99 *(978-0-06-195090-2(4)*, Tegen, Katherine Bks) HarperCollins Pubs.

Mitcham Davis, Zipporah. The Fox & Emily's Long Migration. 2008. 28p. pap. 13.99 *(978-1-4389-0326-2(X))* AuthorHouse.

Mitchell, Melanie, illus. Who Do You Love? 2008. (ENG.). 6p. (J). bds. 5.95 *(978-1-58117-707-7(0)*, Intervisual/Piggy Toes) Bendon, Inc.

Mitchell, Stan R. Oskar & Myer at the Lake. 2013. 24p. pap. 24.95 *(978-1-63000-414-9(6))* America Star Bks.

Mitton, Tony. Snowy Bear. Brown, Alison, illus. (ENG.). (J). 2016. 26p. bds. 7.99 *(978-1-68119-084-6(2)*, 9781681190846) 2015. 32p. (gr. -1-1). 16.99 *(978-1-61963-905-8(X)*, 9781619639058) Bloomsbury Publishing USA. (Bloomsbury USA Childrens).

M.J.Higgy. The Bombay Bear. 2012. (Illus.). 16p. pap. 18.30 *(978-1-4685-8193-5(7))* AuthorHouse.

Modugno, Maria. Santa Claus & the Three Bears. Dyer, Jane & Dyer, Brooke, illus. 2013. (ENG.). 40p. (J). (gr. -1-3). 17.99 *(978-0-06-170023-1(1))* HarperCollins Pubs.

Moerbeck, Kees, illus. & des. Goldilocks. Moerbeck, Kees, des. 2006. (Roly Poly Box Bks.). (ENG.). 24p. (J). *(978-1-84643-017-6(8))* Child's Play International Ltd.

Mohler, Marie. The Habit of Rabbits. 2008. 32p. 18.95 *(978-1-4357-1992-7(1))* Lulu Pr., Inc.

Moncure, Jane Belk. The Biggest Snowball of All: A Book about Sizes. Rooney, Ronnie, illus. 2013. (Magic Castle Readers Ser.). (ENG.). 32p. (J). (gr. -1-2). 25.64 *(978-1-62323-578-9(2)*, 206315) Child's World, Inc., The.

—Here We Go 'Round the Year: A Book about the Months. Billin-Frye, Paige, illus. 2013. (Magic Castle Readers Ser.). (ENG.). 32p. (J). (gr. -1-2). 25.64 *(978-1-62323-582-6(0)*, 206318) Child's World, Inc., The.

—Where Is Baby Bear? A Book about Animal Homes. Billin-Frye, Paige, illus. 2013. (Magic Castle Readers Ser.). (ENG.). 32p. (J). (gr. -1-2). 25.64 *(978-1-62323-585-7(5)*, 206320) Child's World, Inc., The.

Monkman, Olga. Dos Perros y una Abuela. Calderon, Marcela, illus. 2003. (SPA.). 31p. (J). (gr. k-3). pap. 9.95 *(978-950-511-642-3(X))* Santillana USA Publishing Co., Inc.

Moore, Ann C. Looking for a Place to Take a Long Winter Nap. 2009. 32p. pap. 14.49 *(978-1-4490-0852-9(6))* AuthorHouse.

Moore, Bonnie S. Honey Bear & the Honey Horde: Bear Tales. 2007. (J). per. 6.00 *(978-1-59872-823-1(7))* Instant Pub.

Moore, Natascha. Little Bear Kleiner Bär. 2012. 28p. pap. 19.99 *(978-1-4772-6055-5(2))* AuthorHouse.

Morey, Walt. Gentle Ben. Schoenherr, John, illus. l.t. ed. 2004. (LRS Large Print Cornerstone Ser.). 264p. (J). lib. bdg. 33.95 *(978-1-58118-119-7(1))* LRS.

—Gentle Ben. Schoenherr, John, illus. 2006. (ENG.). 192p. (J). (gr. 3-7). 6.99 *(978-0-14-240551-2(5)*, Puffin Books) Penguin Young Readers Group.

Moroney, Trace. Bathtime: Baxter Bear Chubby. Moroney, Trace, illus. 2008. (Baxter Bear Collection). (Illus.). 10p. (J). (gr. -1-1). bds. *(978-1-86463-175-3(9))* Brimax Books Ltd.

Morrison, Maria. Why Bears Don't Live in Humble, 1 vol. Morrison, Cameron & Morrison, Connor, illus. 2010. 26p. pap. 24.95 *(978-1-4489-9748-0(8))* PublishAmerica, Inc.

Morrow, Dj. Two Bears Short. 2013. 28p. pap. 24.95 *(978-1-62709-822-9(4))* America Star Bks.

Morton, Christine. No Te Preocupes, Guille. McMullen, Nigel, illus. (Buenas Noches Ser.). (SPA.). 26p. (J). (gr. k-3). 8.95 *(978-958-04-5088-7(9))* Norma S.A. COL. Dist: Distribuidora Norma, Inc.

Moss, Miriam. Bare Bear. McQuillan, Mary, illus. 2005. (ENG.). 32p. (J). 16.95 *(978-0-8234-1934-0(7))* Holiday Hse., Inc.

—Matty in a Mess! Simmons, Jane, illus. 2010. (Matty & Milly Ser.). (ENG.). 32p. (J). (gr. k-k). pap. 9.99 *(978-1-84270-946-7(1))* Andersen Pr. GBR. Dist: Independent Pubs. Group.

Mouse Works Staff. Winnie the Pooh's Touch & Feel Book. 2nd ed. 2005. 10p. (J). 6.99 *(978-0-7364-1021-2(X))* Hyperion Pr.

Mueller, Ruth Ann. Bumpy Bear's Escape. 2011. 48p. pap. 17.49 *(978-1-4389-5711-1(4))* AuthorHouse.

Murray, Marjorie Dennis. Don't Wake up the Bear!, 0 vols. Wittmann, Patricia, illus. unabr. ed. 2006. (ENG.). 34p. (J). (gr. -1-2). per. 9.99 *(978-0-7614-5330-7(X)*, 9780761453307, Amazon Children's Publishing) Amazon Publishing.

Murray, Ross. Goldilocks & the Three Polar Bears. 2016. (ENG., Illus.). 36p. (J). (gr. 2-4). 15.99 *(978-1-940052-23-6(8))* Craigmore Creations.

Muth, Jon J. Zen Shorts. Muth, Jon J., illus. 2005. (ENG., Illus.). 40p. (J). (gr. -1-3). 17.99 *(978-0-439-33911-7(1))* Scholastic, Inc.

Na, Il Sung. Bird, Balloon, Bear. 2017. (ENG.). 32p. (J). (-k). 17.99 *(978-0-399-55155-0(7)*, Knopf Bks. for Young Readers) Random Hse. Children's Bks.

—Welcome Home, Bear. 2016. (ENG., Illus.). 24p. (J). (— 1). bds. 7.99 *(978-1-101-93549-1(9)*, Knopf Bks. for Young Readers) Random Hse. Children's Bks.

Na, Il Sung, illus. Welcome Home, Bear: A Book of Animal Habitats. 2015. (ENG.). 32p. (J). (— 1). lib. bdg. 19.99 *(978-0-385-75376-0(4)*, Knopf Bks. for Young Readers) Random Hse. Children's Bks.

Namm, Diane. Goldilocks & the Three Bears. Graegin, Stephanie, illus. 2013. (Silver Penny Stories Ser.). (ENG.). 48p. (J). (gr. -1-1). 4.95 *(978-1-4027-8430-9(9))* Sterling Publishing Co., Inc.

—Little Bear. McCue, Lisa, illus. (My First Reader Ser.). (ENG.). 32p. (J). (gr. k-1). 2004. pap. 3.95 *(978-0-516-24633-8(X))* 2003. 18.50 *(978-0-516-22931-7(1))* Scholastic Library Publishing. (Children's Pr.).

Napolitano, Gretchen. Christopher Lee & Bozzie Bear's First Day of School. 2012. (ENG.). 56p. 27.95 *(978-1-4327-9443-9(4))*; pap. 20.95 *(978-1-4327-8487-4(0))* Outskirts Pr., Inc.

Nastanlieva, Vanya. Mo & Beau. 2015. (ENG., Illus.). 36p. (J). (gr. -1-3). 15.95 *(978-1-927018-63-7(3))* Simply Read Bks. CAN. Dist: Ingram Publisher Services.

Nastro, Caroline. The Bear Who Couldn't Sleep. Nastanlieva, Vanya, illus. 2016. (ENG.). 32p. 17.95 *(978-0-7358-4268-7(X))* North-South Bks., Inc.

Natalini, Sandro & Baruzzi, Agnese. The True Story of Goldilocks. Natalini, Sandro & Baruzzi, Agnese, illus. 2009. (ENG., Illus.). 18p. (J). (gr. -1-3). 14.99 *(978-0-7636-4475-8(7)*, Templar) Candlewick Pr.

Nawashani. Stepping Stones to the Sun. Wiles, Pat, illus. 2013. 68p. pap. 11.95 *(978-1-4787-0445-4(4))* Outskirts Pr., Inc.

Naylor, Phyllis Reynolds. Please Do Feed the Bears. Escriva, Ana Lopez, illus. 2007. (ENG.). 40p. (J). (gr. -1-2). 11.99 *(978-1-4169-6750-7(8)*, Simon & Schuster/Paula Wiseman Bks.) Simon & Schuster/Paula Wiseman Bks.

Nebesky, Donna Martin. Beatrice the Bear Cub. 2012. 16p. pap. 15.99 *(978-1-4685-6264-4(9))* AuthorHouse.

Neely, Judith. Goodnight Honey Bear. 2009. 24p. pap. 11.49 *(978-1-4490-1622-7(7))* AuthorHouse.

Neff, Ethel Maxine. Pokey, the Runaway Bear. 2004. (Illus.). 39p. 5.99 *(978-0-8163-2060-8(8))* Pacific Pr. Publishing Assn.

Nelson, Kadir. Baby Bear. Nelson, Kadir, illus. 2014. (ENG., Illus.). 40p. (J). (gr. -1-3). 17.99 *(978-0-06-224172-6(9))* HarperCollins Pubs.

Nelson, Sheila K. The Backpack Bears' Adventure: Friendship. 2009. 24p. pap. 16.50 *(978-1-4490-0554-2(3))* AuthorHouse.

Nesbitt, Kenn. More Bears! Cummings, Troy, illus. (ENG.). (J). 2017. 28p. bds. 7.99 ***(978-1-4926-5467-4(1))*** 2010. 32p. 14.99 *(978-1-4022-3835-2(5))* Sourcebooks, Inc. (Sourcebooks Jabberwocky).

Newman, Lesléa. Where Is Bear? Gorbachev, Valeri, illus. 2006. (ENG.). 44p. (J). (gr. -1 — 1). pap. 6.99 *(978-0-15-205918-7(0))* Houghton Mifflin Harcourt Publishing Co.

Newton, Jill. Don't Wake Mr Bear! Newton, Jill, illus. 2011. (ENG., Illus.). 32p. (J). (gr. -1). 17.99 *(978-1-4052-4965-2(X))*; pap. 9.99 *(978-1-4052-4966-9(8))* Egmont Bks., Ltd. GBR. Dist: Independent Pubs. Group.

Niddrie, June. Quiet Queenie. 2010. 36p. pap. 17.30 *(978-0-557-31868-1(8))* Lulu Pr., Inc.

Nivens, Karen. Benjamin P. Blizzard: Welcome to Christmastown. Grisham, Jason, illus. 2007. 48p. (J). per. *(978-0-9798154-1-6(X))* Living Waters Publishing Co.

Nolan, J. & Moffatt, J. Floaties: Teddy Bear Teddy Bear. 2003. (J). 9.95 *(978-1-929766-60-4(2))* Handprint Bks.

Nolte, Nancy. The Gingerbread Man. Scarry, Richard, illus. 2004. (Big Little Golden Book Ser.). (ENG.). 32p. (J). (gr. -1-2). 8.99 *(978-0-375-82589-7(4)*, Golden Bks.) Random Hse. Children's Bks.

Nord, Kristin Magnuson. Moosh & Grizzle. 2011. 28p. (gr. 1-2). 13.95 *(978-1-4269-6167-0(7))* Trafford Publishing.

Nosy Crow Staff. Bizzy Bear: Deep-Sea Diver. Davies, Benji, illus. 2016. (Bizzy Bear Ser.). (ENG.). 8p. (J). (— 1). bds. 6.99 *(978-0-7636-8647-5(6)*, Nosy Crow) Candlewick Pr.

—Bizzy Bear: Dinosaur Safari. Davies, Benji, illus. 2015. (Bizzy Bear Ser.). (ENG.). 8p. (J). (— 1). bds. 6.99 *(978-0-7636-8170-8(9)*, Nosy Crow) Candlewick Pr.

—Bizzy Bear: Do-It-Yourself Day. Davies, Benji, illus. 2017. (Bizzy Bear Ser.). (ENG.). 8p. (J). (— 1). bds. 6.99 *(978-0-7636-9328-2(6)*, Nosy Crow) Candlewick Pr.

—Bizzy Bear: Knights' Castle. Davies, Benji, illus. 2015. (Bizzy Bear Ser.). (ENG.). 8p. (J). (— 1). bds. 6.99 *(978-0-7636-7602-5(0)*, Nosy Crow) Candlewick Pr.

—Bizzy Bear: Let's Get to Work! Davies, Benji, illus. 2012. (Bizzy Bear Ser.). (ENG.). 8p. (J). (gr. k — 1). bds. 6.99 *(978-0-7636-5899-1(5)*, Nosy Crow) Candlewick Pr.

—Bizzy Bear: off We Go! Davies, Benji, illus. 2012. (Bizzy Bear Ser.). (ENG.). 8p. (J). (gr. k — 1). bds. 6.99 *(978-0-7636-5900-4(2)*, Nosy Crow) Candlewick Pr.

—Bizzy Bear: Space Rocket. Davies, Benji, illus. 2015. (Bizzy Bear Ser.). (ENG.). 8p. (J). (— 1). bds. 6.99 *(978-0-7636-8003-9(6)*, Nosy Crow) Candlewick Pr.

—Bizzy Bear: Spooky House. Davies, Benji, illus. 2017. (Bizzy Bear Ser.). (ENG.). 8p. (J). (— 1). bds. 6.99 ***(978-0-7636-9327-5(8)***, Nosy Crow) Candlewick Pr.

—Bizzy Bear: Zookeeper. Davies, Benji, illus. 2015. (Bizzy Bear Ser.). (ENG.). 8p. (J). (— 1). bds. 6.99 *(978-0-7636-7603-2(9)*, Nosy Crow) Candlewick Pr.

—Fire Rescue! Davies, Benji, illus. 2013. (Bizzy Bear Ser.). (ENG.). 8p. (J). (— 1). bds. 6.99 *(978-0-7636-6518-0(5)*, Nosy Crow) Candlewick Pr.

—Pirate Adventure. Davies, Benji, illus. 2013. (Bizzy Bear Ser.). (ENG.). 8p. (J). (— 1). bds. 6.99 *(978-0-7636-6519-7(3)*, Nosy Crow) Candlewick Pr.

Novak, Matt. Jazzbo, Vol. 4. 2007. (ENG.). 32p. (J). (gr. -1-17). 12.99 *(978-0-7868-0592-1(7))* Hyperion Pr.

Numeroff, Laura Joffe. A Bear a Brownie. Bond, Felicia, illus. 2016. (If You Give... Ser.). 32p. (J). (gr. -1-3). lib. bdg. 18.89 *(978-0-06-027572-3(3))* HarperCollins Pubs.

—If You Give a Bear a Brownie: Book & Doll. Bond, Felicia, illus. Date not set. (J). 19.99 *(978-0-694-01423-1(0))* HarperCollins Pubs.

Nyeu, Tao. Bunny Days. Nyeu, Tao, illus. 2010. (ENG., Illus.). 48p. (J). (gr. -1-k). 16.99 *(978-0-8037-3330-5(5)*, Dial Bks) Penguin Young Readers Group.

—Wonder Bear. 2008. (ENG., Illus.). 48p. (J). (gr. -1-k). 18.99 *(978-0-8037-3328-2(3)*, Dial Bks) Penguin Young Readers Group.

Ocean Front Books. Coloring Book. I.t. ed. 2006. (Illus.). (J). lib. bdg. *(978-1-934190-02-9(0))* Ocean Front Bk. Publishing, Inc.

Ochoa, Mary Lou. Andy's Arctic Party. 2009. 20p. pap. 9.14 *(978-1-4269-0943-6(8))* Trafford Publishing.

O'Dare, Helen. Love. O'Byrne, Nicola, illus. 2016. (ENG.). 26p. (J). bds. 6.99 *(978-1-62686-677-5(5)*, Silver Dolphin Bks.) Readerlink Distribution Services, LLC.

O'Dea, Kendra J. Polar Bear Pond. 2007. (Illus.). 62p. (J). per. 11.95 *(978-0-9799162-0-5(8))* Shortbread Hill Bk. Co.

OHora, Zachariah. The Not So Quiet Library. 2016. (ENG., Illus.). 40p. (J). (-k). 17.99 *(978-0-8037-4140-9(5)*, Dial Bks) Penguin Young Readers Group.

Oldland, Nicholas. Big Bear Hug. 2009. (J). (gr. k-2). pap. *(978-1-55453-482-1(8))* Kids Can Pr., Ltd.

—Big Bear Hug. Oldland, Nicholas, illus. (Life in the Wild Ser.). (ENG., Illus.). 32p. (J). (gr. -1-2). 2014. 7.95 *(978-1-77138-151-2(5))* 2009. 16.95 *(978-1-55453-464-7(X))* Kids Can Pr., Ltd. CAN. Dist: Hachette Bk. Group.

Oliver, Carmen. Bears Make the Best Reading Buddies. Claude, Jean, illus. 2016. (Fiction Picture Bks.). (ENG.). 32p. (gr. -1-1). lib. bdg. 21.27 *(978-1-4795-9181-7(5)*, Fiction Picture Bks.) Picture Window Bks.

O'Mara, Robert J. Friends Are Special, 1 vol. 2009. 26p. pap. 24.95 *(978-1-60749-087-6(0))* America Star Bks.

Once upon a Time Spanish Version-the Three Bears. 2005. (J). *(978-1-57022-563-5(X))* ECS Learning Systems, Inc.

Ondrias, Rachel. Kolby, the Skating Bear: A Kalamazoo Christmas. Scarborough, Casey, illus. 2007. (ENG.). 32p. (J). 16.95 *(978-1-933660-29-5(5)*, Tadpole Pr. 4 Kids) Smooth Sailing Pr., LLC.

—Kolby, the Skating Bear from Kalamazoo! 2006. (ENG., Illus.). 28p. (J). 16.95 *(978-1-933660-00-4(7)*, Tadpole Pr. 4 Kids) Smooth Sailing Pr., LLC.

Opal, Paola. Perry. 2010. (ENG., Illus.). 24p. (J). (gr. -1-3). bds. 7.95 *(978-1-897476-47-5(7))* Simply Read Bks. CAN. Dist: Ingram Publisher Services.

Ordiway, Clipper Zane. There's a Bear on the Porch & There's a Bear on the Hill! 2004. 51p. (J). pap. 16.95 *(978-1-4137-3121-7(X))* America Star Bks.

Osborne, Mary Pope. Osos Polares Despues de la Medianoche. 2005. (Casa del Arbol Ser.: 12).Tr. of Polar Bears Past Bedtime. (SPA.). (J). pap. 5.99 *(978-1-930332-99-7(8))* Lectorum Pubns., Inc.

—Polar Bears Past Bedtime. unabr. ed. 2004. (Magic Tree House Ser.: No. 12). 71p. (J). (gr. k-3). pap. 17.00 incl. audio *(978-0-8072-0537-2(0)*, Listening Library) Random Hse. Audio Publishing Group.

Un Oso con Hambre, 6 Packs. (Chiquilibros Ser.). (SPA.). (gr. k-1). 23.00 *(978-0-7635-8598-3(X))* Rigby Education.

Oso Se Va de Viaje. 2014. (ENG & SPA., Illus.). (J). *(978-1-78285-088-5(0))* Barefoot Bks., Inc.

Ostermeyer Photography. Frosty & Snowy's Arctic Adventures. 2011. (Illus.). 18.95 *(978-0-9794228-5-0(X))* Ostermeyer Photography.

Ostrow, Kim. Bear in the Big Blue House. 2003. (Ready-to-Read Ser.: Vol. 2). (Illus.). (J). mass mkt. 3.99 *(978-0-689-83814-9(X)*, Little Simon) Little Simon.

Owen, Anna. A Day Out. Hammond, Andy, illus. 2005. (Collins Big Cat Ser.). (ENG.). 80p. (J). (gr. -1-k). pap. 5.99 *(978-0-00-718555-9(3))* HarperCollins Pubs. Ltd. GBR. Dist: Independent Pubs. Group.

Owings, Lisa. The Constellation Ursa Major: The Story of the Big Bear. Morrow, J. T., illus. 2013. (Constellations Ser.). (ENG.). 32p. (J). (gr. 2-5). 29.93 *(978-1-62323-489-8(1)*, 206257) Child's World, Inc., The.

—The Constellation Ursa Minor: The Story of the Little Bear. Morrow, J. T., illus. 2013. (Constellations Ser.). (ENG.). 32p. (J). (gr. 2-5). 29.93 *(978-1-62323-490-4(5)*, 206258) Child's World, Inc., The.

Oxenbury, Helen, illus. We're Going on a Bear Hunt. 2004. 33p. (J). *(978-1-85269-713-6(X))*; *(978-1-85269-719-8(9))*; (ENG & ARA.). pap. *(978-1-85269-707-5(5))* Mantra Lingua.

Page, Rhonda G. The Most Important Thing to Have. 2003. pap. 8.00 *(978-0-8059-5438-8(4))* Dorrance Publishing Co., Inc.

Painter, Grace. The Harry Bear Story. Kacer, Stephen, illus. 2011. 28p. pap. 24.95 *(978-1-4626-3327-2(7))* America Star Bks.

Paling, Chris. The Adventures of Rumble, Tumble, & Titch: Uncertain Times. 2010. 62p. pap. 9.99 *(978-1-60911-263-9(6)*, Eloquent Bks.) Strategic Book Publishing & Rights Agency (SBPRA).

Parenteau, Shirley. Bears in Beds. Walker, David, illus. 2012. (ENG.). 32p. (J). (gr. k-k). 15.99 *(978-0-7636-5338-5(1))* Candlewick Pr.

—Bears in the Bath. Walker, David, illus. (ENG.). (J). (— 1). 2016. 30p. bds. 6.99 *(978-0-7636-7946-0(1))* 2014. 32p. 15.99 *(978-0-7636-6418-3(9))* Candlewick Pr.

—Bears in the Snow. Walker, David, illus. 2016. (ENG.). 32p. (J). (-k). 15.99 *(978-0-7636-8148-7(2))* Candlewick Pr.

—Bears on Chairs. Walker, David, illus. 2009. (ENG.). 32p. (J). (gr. -1-k). 15.99 *(978-0-7636-3588-6(X))* Candlewick Pr.

—Bears on Chairs. Walker, David, illus. 2011. (ENG.). 32p. (J). (gr. -1 — 1). bds. 6.99 *(978-0-7636-5092-6(7))* Candlewick Pr.

—Bears on Chairs: Book & Toy Gift Set. Walker, David, illus. 2016. (ENG.). (J). (— 1). bds. 15.99 *(978-0-7636-8878-3(9))* Candlewick Pr.

Parenteau Shirley, Shirley. Bears in a Band. Walker, David, illus. 2016. (ENG.). 32p. (J). (-k). 15.99 *(978-0-7636-8147-0(4))* Candlewick Pr.

Parker, Emma. There's a Bear in My Bed. 2010. (Illus.). pap. *(978-1-877547-97-3(2))* First Edition Ltd.

Parkins, Joanne. The Adventures of Little Bear: Little Bear & the Potty. 2012. (Illus.). 12p. pap. 18.30 *(978-1-4772-2673-5(7))* AuthorHouse.

Parry, Linda & Parry, Alan. Christmastime with Mr Bear. 2006. 12p. (J). bds. 11.99 *(978-0-7847-1469-0(X)*, 04389) Standard Publishing.

Partridge, Helen L. Blinky: The Bear Who Wouldn't Hibernate. 2008. 32p. per. 24.95 *(978-1-4241-9261-8(7))* America Star Bks.

Pastis, Stephan. Mistakes Were Made. Pastis, Stephan, illus. 2013. (Timmy Failure Ser.: No. 1). (ENG., Illus.). 304p. (J). (gr. 3-7). 14.99 *(978-0-7636-6050-5(7))*; 100.00 *(978-0-7636-6689-7(0))* Candlewick Pr.

—Mistakes Were Made. 2015. (Timmy Failure Ser.: 1). lib. bdg. 18.40 *(978-0-606-36864-3(7))* Turtleback Bks.

—Now Look What You've Done. Pastis, Stephan, illus. 2014. (Timmy Failure Ser.: No. 2). (ENG., Illus.). 288p. (J). (gr. 3-7). 14.99 *(978-0-7636-6051-2(5))* Candlewick Pr.

—Sanitized for Your Protection. Pastis, Stephan, illus. 2015. (Timmy Failure Ser.: 4). (ENG., Illus.). 288p. (J). (gr. 3-7). 14.99 *(978-0-7636-8092-3(3))* Candlewick Pr.

—Timmy Failure: We Meet Again. Pastis, Stephan, illus. 2016. (Timmy Failure Ser.). (ENG., Illus.). 288p. (J). (gr. 3-7). pap. 7.99 *(978-0-7636-9106-6(2))* Candlewick Pr.

Patrick, Rudolph. Mulligan's Rainbow. 2010. 24p. pap. 13.98 *(978-1-4490-4980-5(X))* AuthorHouse.

Patterson, Ann Elizabeth. Rocking Chair Bear. 2009. 32p. pap. 12.99 *(978-1-4343-9331-9(3))* AuthorHouse.

Patterson, Ellie. Baby Bear & the Big, Wide World. Kolanovic, Dubravka, illus. 2013. (J). *(978-1-4351-4929-8(7))* Barnes & Noble, Inc.

Pattou, Edith. East. 2005. (ENG.). 528p. (YA). (gr. 7-12). pap. 8.95 *(978-0-15-205221-8(6))* Houghton Mifflin Harcourt Publishing Co.

—East. 2005. 507p. (YA). (gr. 7-12). 16.60 *(978-0-7569-5054-5(6))* Perfection Learning Corp.

Paul & Lady Jan. Wesley the Wobbly Bear. Beeson, Jan, illus. 2013. 38p. pap. 12.99 *(978-0-9890482-4-8(1))* Beeson, Jan.

Paulsen, Gary. Brian's Hunt. 2005. 103p. (YA). (gr. 4-8). reprint ed. 15.00 *(978-0-7567-9570-2(2))* DIANE Publishing Co.

Pavelka, Joe. Ned: The Story of Bear Six Nine Three, 1 vol. Huras, Lynne, illus. 2007. (ENG.). 32p. (J). (gr. -1-1). *(978-1-894765-95-4(8))* RMB Rocky Mountain Bks.

Paver, Michelle. HERMANO LOBO: CRÓNICAS DE LA PREHISTORIA I. 2005. (SPA., Illus.). 222p. 17.25 *(978-84-7888-933-4(7))* Emece Editores ESP. Dist: Ediciones Universal.

—Wolf Brother. Taylor, Geoff, illus. 2006. (Chronicles of Ancient Darkness Ser.: 1). 320p. (J). (gr. 5-9). reprint ed. per. 6.99 *(978-0-06-072827-4(2)*, Tegen, Katherine Bks) HarperCollins Pubs.

—Wolf Brother, 6 vols. 2005. (Chronicles of Ancient Darkness Ser.: 1). (J). 89.75 *(978-1-4193-3811-3(0))*; 91.75 *(978-1-4193-3809-0(9))*; 76.75 *(978-1-4193-2628-8(7))*; 73.75 *(978-1-4193-2630-1(9))* Recorded Bks., Inc.

PC Treasures Staff, prod. Goldilocks & the Three Bears. 2007. (J). *(978-1-60072-034-5(X))* PC Treasures, Inc.

—Little Red Riding Hood. 2007. (J). *(978-1-60072-031-4(5))* PC Treasures, Inc.

Pearson, Anthony. Baby Bear Eats the Night, 0 vols. Leick, Bonnie, illus. 2012. (ENG.). 32p. (J). (gr. k-3). 16.99 *(978-0-7614-6103-6(5)*, 9780761461036, Amazon Children's Publishing) Amazon Publishing.

Penn, M. W. Square Bear Meets Round Hound: A Fairytale of Shapes. Firos, Daphne, illus. 2012. (ENG.). 38p. (J). pap. 11.95 *(978-0-9840425-8-6(X))* MathWord Pr., LLC.

Penner, Lucille Recht. Osos en la Mente; Bears on the Brain. 2008. pap. 34.95 *(978-1-58013-769-0(5))* Kane Press, Inc.

Percival, Tom. Herman's Letter. 2014. (ENG., Illus.). 32p. (J). (gr. -1-1). 17.99 *(978-1-61963-423-7(6)*, 9781619634237, Bloomsbury USA Childrens) Bloomsbury Publishing USA.

—Herman's Vacation. 2016. (ENG., Illus.). 32p. (J). 17.99 *(978-1-61963-990-4(4)*, 9781619639904, Bloomsbury USA Childrens) Bloomsbury Publishing USA.

Perl, Erica S. Goatilocks & the Three Bears. Howard, Arthur, illus. 2014. (ENG.). 40p. (J). (gr. -1-3). 17.99 *(978-1-4424-0168-6(0)*, Beach Lane Bks.) Beach Lane Bks.

Peters, Andrew Fusek. Bear & Turtle & the Great Lake Race. Edgson, Alison, illus. 2005. (Traditional Tales with a Twist Ser.). (ENG.). 32p. (J). (gr. 2-2). per. *(978-1-904550-91-4(6))* Child's Play International Ltd.

Pfeffer, Wendy. Sounds All Around. Chernyshova, Anna, illus. 2016. (Let's-Read-And-Find-Out Science 1 Ser.). 40p. (J). (gr. -1-3). pap. 6.99 *(978-0-06-238669-4(7))* HarperCollins Pubs.

Pham, LeUyen. The Bear Who Wasn't There. Pham, LeUyen, illus. 2016. (ENG., Illus.). 40p. (J). 16.99 *(978-1-59643-970-2(X)*, 9781596439702) Roaring Brook Pr.

Phillips, Jan. Just for Today. Shapiro, Alison Bonds, illus. 2005. (ENG.). 32p. (J). (gr. -1-5). 15.95 *(978-1-932073-07-2(8))* Kramer, H.J. Inc.

Phyllarry (Rittmueller), Kathryn. Beauregart the Bear. 2009. (ENG., Illus.). 64p. (J). 12.95 *(978-0-943972-80-0(9))* Homestead Publishing.

Pickering, Lynne. James & the Naughty Seagull. Pickering, Lynne, illus. 2013. (Illus.). 32p. pap. 13.50 *(978-1-62857-333-6(3)*, Strategic Bk. Publishing) Strategic Book Publishing & Rights Agency (SBPRA).

Pighin, Marcel. Tickles the Bear Goes on a Cruise, 1 bk. Mitchell, Hazel, illus. 2006. 48p. (J). per. 10.49 *(978-0-9776679-7-0(9))* MP2ME Enterprise.

Pilutti, Deb. Bear & Squirrel Are Friends ... Yes, Really! Pilutti, Deb, illus. 2015. (ENG., Illus.). 40p. (J). (gr. -1-3). 17.99 *(978-1-4814-2913-9(2)*, Simon & Schuster Bks. For Young Readers) Simon & Schuster Bks. For Young Readers.

Pinder, Eric. How to Build a Snow Bear. Graegin, Stephanie, illus. 2016. (ENG.). 40p. (J). 16.99 *(978-0-374-30020-3(8)*, 9780374300203, Farrar, Straus & Giroux (BYR)) Farrar, Straus & Giroux.

—How to Share with a Bear. Graegin, Stephanie, illus. 2015. (ENG.). 40p. (J). (gr. -1-1). 17.99 *(978-0-374-30019-7(4)*, 9780374300197, Farrar, Straus & Giroux (BYR)) Farrar, Straus & Giroux.

Pinkwater, Daniel. Sleepover Larry, 0 vols. 2013. (ENG.). 34p. (J). (gr. -1-3). pap. 9.99 *(978-1-4778-4765-7(0)*, 9781477847657, Amazon Children's Publishing) Amazon Publishing.

Pinkwater, Daniel M. Bear & Bunny. Hillenbrand, Will, illus. 2015. (ENG.). 40p. (J). 15.99 *(978-0-7636-7153-2(3))* Candlewick Pr.

—Bear in Love. Hillenbrand, Will, illus. 2012. (ENG.). 40p. (J). (gr. k-k). 15.99 *(978-0-7636-4569-4(9))* Candlewick Pr.

—Dancing Larry, 1 vol. Pinkwater, Jill, illus. 2006. (ENG.). 32p. (J). (gr. -1-3). 16.95 *(978-0-7614-5220-1(6))* Marshall Cavendish Corp.

—Irving & Muktuk: Two Bad Bears. 2004. (Illus.). (J). (gr. k-3). spiral bd. *(978-0-616-11137-6(1))*; spiral bd. *(978-0-616-11136-9(3))* Canadian National Institute for the Blind/Institut National Canadien pour les Aveugles.

—Mrs. Noodlekugel & Drooly the Bear. Stower, Adam, illus. 2015. (Mrs. Noodlekugel Ser.). (ENG.). 96p. (J). (gr. k-4). 14.99 *(978-0-7636-6645-3(9))* Candlewick Pr.

—Sleepover Larry. 2007. (Illus.). 32p. 16.99 *(978-0-7614-5335-2(0))* Marshall Cavendish Corp.

—Young Larry, 1 vol. Pinkwater, Jill, illus. 2005. (ENG.). 32p. (J). pap. 5.95 *(978-0-7614-5177-8(3))* Marshall Cavendish Corp.

Pinkwater, Daniel M. & Pinkwater, Jill. Bongo Larry, 1 vol. 2005. (ENG., Illus.). 32p. (J). pap. 5.95 *(978-0-7614-5189-1(7))* Marshall Cavendish Corp.

Pisarik, Michael E. Ursus: A Bear's Story. 2005. (YA). per. *(978-1-59872-564-3(5))* Instant Pub.

Pish, Kathryn & Crider, Darcy R. Bubble Trouble. 2009. 32p. pap. 12.99 *(978-1-4389-9208-2(4))* AuthorHouse.

Pledger, Maurice. Bobby Bear & the Honeybees. Pledger, Maurice, illus. 2014. (Friendship Tales Ser.). (ENG., Illus.). 16p. (J). (gr. -1). bds. 10.95 *(978-1-62686-189-3(7)*, Silver Dolphin Bks.) Readerlink Distribution Services, LLC.

Plitt, Kay. Why Isn't Bobby Like Me, Mom? 2010. 32p. 14.75 *(978-1-4269-4038-5(6))* Trafford Publishing.

Polar Bear & the Rainbow. (Glitter Books... Ser.). 24p. *(978-1-4054-7605-8(2))* Parragon, Inc.

Pollock, J. A. Titus & Otis & the Arctic Adventure. 2009. 151p. pap. 12.00 *(978-0-557-03427-7(2))* Lulu Pr., Inc.

Posner, Renee & Quinton, Sasha. Suzy Season Loves Spring. D'Argo, Laura, illus. (Be Mine Bears Ser.). (J). bds. 4.99 *(978-1-58209-350-5(4))* Bks. Are Fun, Ltd.

—Suzy Season Loves Summer. D'Argo, Laura, illus. (Be Mine Bears Ser.). (J). bds. 4.99 *(978-1-58209-351-2(2))* Bks. Are Fun, Ltd.

Powell, Richard. Bear. Gardner, Louise, illus. 2014. (Bathing Beauties Ser.). (ENG.). 8p. (J). (gr. -1 — 1). 7.99 *(978-1-4380-7441-2(7))* Barron's Educational Series, Inc.

Prasadam-halls, Smriti. I Love You Night & Day. Brown, Alison, illus. 2014. (ENG.). 32p. (J). (gr. -1-1). 16.99 *(978-1-61963-222-6(5)*, 9781619632226, Bloomsbury USA Childrens) Bloomsbury Publishing USA.

Pratcher, Roger & Pratcher, Birgit. June Bear Adventures: The Missing Pies. 2007. 236p. per. 11.95 *(978-1-4327-0352-3(8))* Outskirts Pr., Inc.

Price, Diane J. Tiny Story, Vol. 1. Csavas, Sally, illus. 2008. 28p. (J). 9.00 *(978-0-9789637-0-5(9))* Price, Diane Joan.

Priddy, Roger. Little Friends: Sleepy Time. 2014. (Little Friends Ser.). (ENG.). 6p. (J). (gr. -1 — 1). 9.99 *(978-0-312-51681-9(9)*, 9780312516819, Priddy Bks.) St. Martin's Pr.

Priddy, Roger, adapted by. Baby Bear, Baby Bear, What Do You See? 2012. (ENG., Illus.). 8p. (J). (gr. -1 — 1). 12.99 *(978-0-312-51501-0(4)*, 9780312515010, Priddy Bks.) St. Martin's Pr.

Proimos, James, Jr. Knuckle & Potty Destroy Happy World. Proimos, James, Jr., illus. 2012. (ENG., Illus.). 80p. (J). (gr. 2-5). 12.99 *(978-0-8050-9155-7(6)*, 9780805091557, Holt, Henry & Co. Bks. For Young Readers) Holt, Henry & Co.

Pruett, Candace. A Visit with My Uncle Ted. 2003. (J). per. 16.95 *(978-1-930859-68-5(6))* Elderberry Press, Inc.

Publications International Ltd. Staff, ed. Good Night, Little Bear: A Sleepy Time Tale. 2010. (J). bds. 7.98 *(978-1-60553-435-0(8))* Phoenix International Publications, Inc.

—Record Story Goldilocks 3 Bears. 2011. 18p. 17.98 *(978-1-4508-1909-1(5))* Phoenix International Publications, Inc.

Pugliano-Martin, Carol. See You in Spring! 2006. (Early Explorers Ser.). (J). pap. *(978-1-4108-6105-4(8))* Benchmark Education Co.

Pwob. The Search for the Missing Ball: Norman G. Bear. Finnell-Acosta, B. C., illus. 2010. 64p. pap. 25.49 *(978-1-4520-3952-7(6))* AuthorHouse.

Pym, Tasha & Pichon, Liz. Colour Bears. 2006. (Collins Big Cat Ser.). (ENG., Illus.). 56p. (J). (gr. -1-k). pap. 5.99 *(978-0-00-718652-5(5))* HarperCollins Pubs. Ltd. GBR. Dist: Independent Pubs. Group.

Quinn, Susan. Little Bear & the Butterflies. Pedler, Caroline, illus. 2014. 24p. (J). ***(978-1-4351-5922-8(5))*** Barnes & Noble, Inc.

Quintart, Natalie. Mama Bear. Blanchart, Stephanie, illus. 2005. (Tiger Tales Ser.). 32p. (J). (gr. -1-2). 6.95 *(978-1-58925-394-0(9))* Tiger Tales.

Rabideau, Dianna. A Den for Ben. 2009. 24p. pap. 12.99 *(978-1-4490-0886-4(0))* AuthorHouse.

Rains, Deborah Jane. 2011's New Year with Cuddles & Snuggles. 2011. 20p. pap. 24.95 *(978-1-4489-4424-8(4))* America Star Bks.

Ramos, Marielly. The Fast Getting Married Ugly Changing Bear. 2012. 24p. pap. 17.99 *(978-1-4772-8581-7(4))* AuthorHouse.

Ramsey, Charmaine J. Frollica & Frenzi: New York City Friends. Steinlage, Kelly, illus. 2009. 36p. pap. 15.49 *(978-1-4490-0487-3(3))* AuthorHouse.

Random House Disney Staff. Big Bear, Little Bear. Random House Disney Staff, illus. 2012. (Step into Reading Ser.). (ENG., Illus.). 32p. (J). (gr. -1-1). pap. 3.99 *(978-0-7364-2915-3(8)*, RH/Disney) Random Hse. Children's Bks.

Ranes, Robert. The Bear with the Square Nose. 2010. 24p. 14.49 *(978-1-4520-0310-8(6))* AuthorHouse.

Ransom, Candice & Lyon, Tammie. Goldilocks & the Three Bears, Grades Pk - 3 (Ricitos de Oro y los Tres Osos) 2005. (Keepsake Stories Ser.). (ENG & SPA., Illus.). 32p. (gr. -1-3). pap. 3.99 *(978-0-7696-3815-7(5)*, Brighter Child) Carson-Dellosa Publishing, LLC.

Ranson, Erin. One Little Bear & Her Friends. Gévry, Claudine, illus. 2007. 10p. (J). (gr. -1-k). bds. *(978-1-84666-354-3(7)*, Tide Mill Pr.) Top That! Publishing PLC.

Raye, Rebekah. Bear-Ly There. Raye, Rebekah, illus. 2009. (ENG., Illus.). 32p. (gr. 3-6). 16.95 *(978-0-88448-314-4(2)*, 884314) Tilbury Hse. Pubs.

Rayner, Catherine. The Bear Who Shared. 2011. (ENG.). 32p. (J). (gr. -1-k). 16.99 *(978-0-8037-3576-7(6)*, Dial Bks) Penguin Young Readers Group.

Reasoner, Charles, illus. Bear Hugs. 2015. (J). *(978-1-4795-5944-2(X))* Picture Window Bks.

Rebein, Alyssa Chase & Chase, Andra. Stanley's "This Is the Life!" Chase, Andra, illus. 2008. (Illus.). (J). *(978-1-55942-570-4(9))* Witcher Productions.

Redenbaugh, Vicki. Skar's Picnic ... A Bear's Tale. Redenbaugh, Vicki, illus. 2005. (Illus.). (J). 14.95 *(978-1-59091-034-4(6))* Eastern National.

Reed, Lynn Rowe. Bear's Big Breakfast. Helquist, Brett, illus. 2016. 32p. (J). (gr. -1-3). 17.99 *(978-0-06-226455-8(9))* HarperCollins Pubs.

Reese, Jacob. Copperweight. 2008. 231p. pap. 24.95 *(978-1-60813-240-9(4))* America Star Bks.

Rewalt, Nancy E. Lost & Found: Goldilocks & the Three Bears Revisited. Cranford, Darren, illus. 2012. 64p. (J). pap. 6.95 *(978-0-9821110-2-4(9))* Ronan Enterprises, Inc.

Rey, H. A. A Winter's Nap. 2010. (Curious George Ser.). (ENG., Illus.). 24p. (J). (gr. -1-3). pap. 3.99 *(978-0-547-23590-5(9))* Houghton Mifflin Harcourt Publishing Co.

Rhodes, Tim W. The Story of the Bed Bear. 2007. (Illus.). (J). 14.95 *(978-1-60131-009-5(9))* Big Tent Bks.

Richemont, Enid. Brownilocks & the Three Bowls of Cornflakes. 2016. (ENG., Illus.). 32p. (J). *(978-0-7787-2459-9(X))* Crabtree Publishing Co.

Richter, Bernd & Richter, Susan. The Little Bear Who Didn't Want to Hibernate. Green, Sue, illus. 2003. 42p. pap. 9.95 *(978-1-931353-10-6(7))* Saddle Pal Creations, Inc.

—There Was a Little Bear. 2008. (ENG., Illus.). 22p. (J). bds. 8.95 *(978-1-931353-43-4(3))* Saddle Pal Creations, Inc.

Ricitos de Oro y los tres osos: Goldilocks & the Three Bears. 2005. (Take-Home Bks.). (SPA.). (YA). (gr. -1-3). 15.75 *(978-0-8215-1205-0(6))* Sadlier, William H. Inc.

Ricitos de Oro y los tres osos/Goldilocks & the Three Bears. 2005. (Libros en Espanol Para Ninos Ser.). (SPA.). (YA). (gr. -1-1). 11.97 *(978-0-8215-0995-1(0))* Sadlier, William H. Inc.

Rigby Education Staff. Goldilocks: Jumbled Tumble. (gr. k-2). 26.00 *(978-0-7635-2418-0(2))* Rigby Education.

Rigo, L., illus. Little Panda. 2010. (Look at Me Bks.). (ENG.). 10p. (J). (gr. -1-k). 8.99 *(978-0-7641-6339-5(6))* Barron's Educational Series, Inc.

—Little Panda Bear. 2014. (Mini Look at Me Bks.). (ENG.). 10p. (J). (gr. -1 — 1). bds. 4.99 *(978-0-7641-6739-3(1))* Barron's Educational Series, Inc.

—Little Polar Bear. 2010. (Look at Me Bks.). (ENG.). 10p. (J). (gr. -1-k). bds. 8.99 *(978-0-7641-6325-8(6))* Barron's Educational Series, Inc.

Rigo, Laura, illus. Little Polar Bear. 2017. (Mini Look at Me Bks.). (ENG.). 10p. (J). (gr. -1 — 1). bds. 4.99 *(978-0-7641-6880-2(0))* Barron's Educational Series, Inc.

Rim, Sujean. Chee-Kee: A Panda in Bearland. 2017. (ENG., Illus.). 40p. (J). (gr. -1-3). 17.99 *(978-0-316-40744-1(5))* Little Brown & Co.

Rissman, Angelica. Julius & the Lost Letter to Santa. 2003. (J). 7.99 *(978-1-59384-019-8(5))* Parklane Publishing.

Ritchie, Alison. Me & My Dad! Edgson, Alison, illus. 2007. (J). pap. *(978-0-545-02064-0(6))* Scholastic, Inc.

Robaard, Jedda. The Little Bear Who Lost Her Way. 2015. (ENG., Illus.). 10p. (J). (gr. -1-k). 7.99 *(978-1-4998-0092-0(4))* Little Bee Books Inc.

Roberts, Daniel. The Good Night Book: A Book of Animal Sounds. 2009. 36p. pap. 16.99 *(978-1-4389-8278-6(X))* AuthorHouse.

—The Penguin & the Polar Bear. 2009. 32p. pap. 14.95 *(978-1-4389-2845-6(9))* AuthorHouse.

Roberts, Tom. Goldilocks, 1 vol. Kubinyi, Laszlo, illus. 2005. (Rabbit Ears: A Classic Tale Ser.). (ENG.). 28p. (gr. 2-7). 25.65 *(978-1-59197-748-3(7))* Spotlight.

Robinson, Fay. Bear's Icicles. 2016. (Spring Forward Ser.). (J). (gr. 2). *(978-1-4900-9419-9(9))* Benchmark Education Co.

Robinson, Michelle. A Beginner's Guide to Bear Spotting. Roberts, David, illus. 2016. (ENG.). 32p. (J). 16.99 *(978-1-68119-026-6(5)*, 9781681190266, Bloomsbury USA Childrens) Bloomsbury Publishing USA.

Robinson, Rachaell. Princess Karakul: The Runaway Bear. 2003. 22.00 *(978-0-8059-6188-1(7))* Dorrance Publishing Co., Inc.

Rocha, K. E. Battle for Bearhaven. 2017. (Secrets of Bearhaven Ser.: 4). (ENG.). 240p. (J). (gr. 3-7). 14.99 ***(978-0-545-81306-8(9)***, Scholastic Pr.) Scholastic, Inc.

—Mission to Moon Farm. 2016. (J). *(978-0-545-81316-7(6)*, Scholastic Pr.) Scholastic, Inc.

—Mission to Moon Farm (Secrets of Bearhaven #2) 2016. (Secrets of Bearhaven Ser.: 2). (ENG.). 224p. (J). (gr. 3-7). 14.99 *(978-0-545-81304-4(2)*, Scholastic Pr.) Scholastic, Inc.

—Secrets of Bearhaven. 2016. (Bearhaven Ser.: 1). (ENG.). 256p. (J). (gr. 3-7). 14.99 *(978-0-545-81303-7(4)*, Scholastic Pr.) Scholastic, Inc.

Rock, Brian. With All My Heart. Banta, Susan, illus. 2012. (ENG.). 24p. (J). *(978-1-58925-648-4(4))* Tiger Tales.

Rockhill, Dennis. Polar Slumber. 2008. (ENG., Illus.). 32p. (J). (gr. -1-3). pap. 7.95 *(978-1-932748-73-4(3)*, Raven Tree Pr.,Csi) Continental Sales, Inc.

—Polar Slumber. Rockhill, Dennis, illus. 2007. (ENG., Illus.). 32p. (J). (gr. -1-3). 16.95 *(978-0-9741992-8-3(1)*, Raven Tree Pr.,Csi) Continental Sales, Inc.

—Polar Slumber/Sueño Polar. Raven Tree Press Staff, ed. de la Vega, Eida, tr. Rockhill, Dennis, illus. 2004.Tr. of Sueño Polar. (SPA & ENG., Illus.). 32p. (J). (gr. -1-3). 16.95 *(978-0-9724973-1-2(5)*, 1234791, Raven Tree Pr.,Csi) Continental Sales, Inc.

—Sueno Polar. 2008. 32p. (J). (gr. -1-3). (ENG.). 16.95 *(978-1-932748-76-5(8))*; (SPA & ENG.). pap. 7.95 *(978-1-932748-77-2(6))* Continental Sales, Inc. (Raven Tree Pr.,Csi).

—Sueno Polar. 2008. 32p. 16.95 *(978-1-932746-76-1(5))* Sacred Garden Fellowship.

Roddy, Lee. The City Bear's Adventures. 2008. (D. J. Dillon Adventure Ser.: No. 2). (J). 7.99 *(978-0-88062-266-0(0))* Mott Media.

—The Hair-Pulling Bear Dog. 2008. (D. J. Dillon Adventure Ser.: No. 1). (J). 7.99 *(978-0-88062-265-3(2))* Mott Media.

Roddy-Worsham, Clara. Bear Baby & New Baby Forever. 2012. 24p. 24.95 *(978-1-4626-4672-2(7))* America Star Bks.

—Bear Baby Goes Fishing. 2013. 24p. 24.95 *(978-1-63004-070-3(3))* America Star Bks.

—Bear Baby's Birthday Gift. 2013. 24p. 24.95 *(978-1-4626-9940-7(5))* America Star Bks.

Rodgers, Phillip W. When Was God Born?, 1 vol. 2008. (Discovering God Ser.). 32p. (J). 12.99 *(978-0-8254-3608-6(7))* Kregel Pubns.

Rodriguez, AJ. Theodore Da Baer Ii: A New Beginning. 2006. 207p. pap. 24.95 *(978-1-4241-1125-1(0))* America Star Bks.

Rogers, Alan. Ours Vert. 2003. (Little Giants Ser.). (SPA., Illus.). 16p. (J). (gr. -1-k). 5.95 *(978-1-58728-180-8(5)*, Two-Can Publishing) T&N Children's Publishing.

Rogger. The Fifty-Fifth Bear & the Awkward Rabbits: An Amazing Thick Blue Wood Bear Adventure. 2009. (Illus.). 60p. pap. 21.99 *(978-1-4389-1672-9(8))* AuthorHouse.

Roosa, Bertha. The Hobert Bears' Great Ideas. 2007. (Illus.). 80p. (J). *(978-0-9639391-2-8(2))* Pine Hill Pr.

Rosen, Michael. Bear Flies High. Reynolds, Adrian, illus. 2009. (ENG.). 32p. (J). (gr. -1-1). 16.99 *(978-1-59990-386-6(5)*, 9781599903866, Bloomsbury USA Childrens) Bloomsbury Publishing USA.

—Bear's Day Out. Reynolds, Adrian, illus. (ENG.). (J). 2009. 26p. (gr. -1 — 1). bds. 7.99 *(978-1-59990-391-0(1)*, 9781599903910) 2007. 32p. (gr. k-3). 16.95 *(978-1-59990-007-0(6)*, 9781599900070) Bloomsbury Publishing USA. (Bloomsbury USA Childrens).

—Bob the Bursting Bear. Ross, Tony, illus. 2013. (ENG.). 32p. (J). (gr. -1-k). 17.99 *(978-1-84939-440-6(7))* Andersen Pr. GBR. Dist: Independent Pubs. Group.

—We're Going on a Bear Hunt. Oxenbury, Helen, illus. 2004. (J). 32p. *(978-1-85269-720-4(2))*; 32p. *(978-1-85269-718-1(0))*; 32p. *(978-1-85269-716-7(4))*; 32p. *(978-1-85269-711-2(3))*; 32p. *(978-1-85269-710-5(5))*; 32p. *(978-1-85269-706-8(7))*; (ENG & BEN.). 33p. pap. *(978-1-85269-708-2(3))*; (ENG & PAN.). 33p. pap. *(978-1-85269-714-3(8))*; (ENG & URD.). 33p. pap. *(978-1-85269-721-1(0))* Mantra Lingua.

—We're Going on a Bear Hunt. Oxenbury, Helen, illus. 2003. (ENG.). 36p. (J). (gr. -1-3). pap. 7.99 *(978-0-689-85349-4(1)*, McElderry, Margaret K. Bks.) McElderry, Margaret K. Bks.

—We're Going on a Bear Hunt. Oxenbury, Helen, illus. 2003. (gr. k-3). 18.40 *(978-0-613-61665-2(0)*, Turtleback) Turtleback Bks.

—We're Going on a Bear Hunt: Anniversary Edition of a Modern Classic. Oxenbury, Helen, illus. 2009. (Classic Board Bks.). (ENG.). 36p. (J). (gr. -1-k). bds. 9.99 *(978-1-4169-8712-3(6)*, Little Simon) Little Simon.

—We're Going on a Bear Hunt: Anniversary Edition of a Modern Classic. Oxenbury, Helen, illus. 2009. (ENG.). 40p. (J). (gr. -1-3). 18.99 *(978-1-4169-8711-6(8)*, McElderry, Margaret K. Bks.) McElderry, Margaret K. Bks.

—We're Going on a Bear Hunt: Sound Book. Oxenbury, Helen, illus. 2014. (ENG.). 40p. (J). (gr. -1-2). 19.99 *(978-0-7636-7702-2(7))* Candlewick Pr.

Rosenberg, Michael. Chilly Goes to Hong Kong & China: Another Chilly the Toy Polar Bear Adventure. 2013. 36p. pap. 13.95 *(978-1-62212-841-9(9)*, Strategic Bk. Publishing) Strategic Book Publishing & Rights Agency (SBPRA).

—The Little Lost Tune: More Adventures from Bendalot. 2010. 30p. pap. 13.00 *(978-1-60911-881-5(2)*, Eloquent Bks.) Strategic Book Publishing & Rights Agency (SBPRA).

Ross, Michael Elsohn. Baby Bear Isn't Hungry. Powell, Consie, illus. 2006. (ENG.). 26p. (J). (gr. -1-4). 10.95 *(978-1-930238-24-4(X))* Yosemite Assn.

Ross, Tony & Ross, Tony. Goldilocks & the Three Bears. 40th ed. 2017. (ENG., Illus.). 32p. (J). (-k). 14.99 ***(978-1-78344-469-4(X))*** Andersen Pr. GBR. Dist: Independent Pubs. Group.

Roth, Megan. Bright Books: Baby Bear's Busy Day. Hayashi, Emiri, illus. 2016. (Bright Bks.). (ENG.). 12p. (J). bds. 14.99 *(978-1-62686-717-8(8)*, Silver Dolphin Bks.) Readerlink Distribution Services, LLC.

Rouillard, Wendy W. Barnaby's Tree House. 2005. (Illus.). 30p. (J). *(978-0-9651070-4-4(3))* Barnaby & Co.

Rowold, Shirley. Big Bear. 2010. 42p. pap. 15.50 *(978-1-60860-851-5(4)*, Eloquent Bks.) Strategic Book Publishing & Rights Agency (SBPRA).

Rubio, Gabriela. Terrible/Terrible. 2006. (Jardin de los Ninos (Ediciones Ekare) Ser.). (SPA., Illus.). 22p. (J). (gr. 3-5). *(978-84-933060-7-6(X))* Ekare, Ediciones.

Rueda, Claudia. No, 1 vol. Amado, Elisa, tr. from SPA. 2010. (ENG., Illus.). 40p. (J). (gr. k-k). 18.95 *(978-0-88899-991-7(7))* Groundwood Bks. CAN. Dist: Publishers Group West (PGW).

Ruiz, Emilio. Waluk. 2013. 56p. pap. 23.95 *(978-1-4677-2057-1(7))* Lerner Publishing Group.

—Waluk. Oliverio, Daniel, tr. Miralles, Ana, illus. 2013. (ENG.). 56p. (J). (gr. 2-5). pap. 7.95 *(978-1-4677-1606-2(5))*; lib. bdg. 26.60 *(978-1-4677-1598-0(0))* Lerner Publishing Group. (Graphic Universe™).

Rusling, Annette. No Time for Bed! Edgson, Alison, illus. 2014. (ENG.). 18p. (J). (gr. -1-k). 12.99 *(978-1-58925-529-6(1))* Tiger Tales.

Ruzzier, Sergio. Bear & Bee. Ruzzier, Sergio, illus. 2013. (Bear & Bee Ser.). (ENG., Illus.). 48p. (J). (gr. -1-k). 14.99 *(978-1-4231-5957-5(8))* Hyperion Pr.

—Too Busy. Ruzzier, Sergio, illus. 2014. (Bear & Bee Ser.). (ENG., Illus.). 48p. (J). (gr. -1-k). 14.99 *(978-1-4231-5961-2(6))* Disney Pr.

Ryder, Joanne. Bear of My Heart. Moore, Margie, illus. 2009. (ENG.). 32p. (J). (gr. -1 — 1). bds. 9.99 *(978-1-4169-5472-9(4)*, Little Simon) Little Simon.

Rylant, Cynthia. The Case of the Baffled Bear. Karas, G. Brian, illus. 2006. (I Can Read Level 2 Ser.: No. 7). (ENG.). 48p. (J). (gr. k-3). per. 3.99 *(978-0-06-053450-9(8)*, Greenwillow Bks.) HarperCollins Pubs.

SACHS, Andrew. Teddybear Tales. 2013. (ENG., Illus.). 32p. (J). (gr. -1-1). 5.99 *(978-1-84322-811-0(4)*, Armadillo) Anness Publishing GBR. Dist: National Bk. Network.

Sachs, Marilyn. The Bears' House. 2008. 80p. (gr. 4-7). pap. 8.95 *(978-0-595-53553-8(4))* iUniverse, Inc.

Saddleback Educational Publishing Staff, ed. Camp, 1 vol. unabr. ed. 2011. (Heights Ser.). (ENG.). 50p. (gr. 5-8). pap. 7.95 *(978-1-61651-284-2(9))* Saddleback Educational Publishing, Inc.

Sagendorph, Jean. Starry Night, Hold Me Tight. Siebold, Kim, illus. 2015. (ENG.). 18p. (J). (gr. -1-17). bds. 6.95 *(978-0-7624-5853-0(4)*, Running Pr. Kids) Running Pr. Bk. Pubs.

Salzano, Tammi. One Sunny Day. 2013. pap. *(978-0-545-53655-4(3))* Scholastic, Inc.

Salzano, Tammi J. One Sunny Day. Wood, Hannah, illus. 2012. (ENG.). 20p. (J). bds. *(978-1-58925-871-6(1))* Tiger Tales.

Sandage, Charley. ALL AROUND ARKANSAS Big Book. 2005. (Illus.). (J). pap. *(978-0-9794044-2-9(8))* Archeological Assessments, Inc.

—ALL AROUND ARKANSAS student Edition. 2005. (Illus.). (J). pap. *(978-0-9638956-5-3(6))* Archeological Assessments, Inc.

—Big Bear's Arkansas ABCs. Przybylek, Leslie, illus. 2004. 56p. (J). (gr. k-2). pap. 14.95 *(978-0-9638956-9-1(9))* Archeological Assessments, Inc.

—Big Bear's Arkansas ABCs Big Book. 2005. (Illus.). (J). pap. *(978-0-9794044-1-2(X))* Archeological Assessments, Inc.

—I can tell you stories, if you gather round Big Book. 2005. (Illus.). (J). pap. *(978-0-9794044-3-6(6))* Archeological Assessments, Inc.

Sandall, Ellie. Copycat Bear! Sandall, Ellie, illus. 2013. (ENG., Illus.). 32p. (J). (gr. -1-k). 14.99 *(978-1-58925-120-5(2))* Tiger Tales.

Sandoval, Migs, illus. Goldilocks & the 3 Bears: Level 2: Learn French Through Fairy Tales. 2006. (Learn French Through Fairy Tales Ser.). (ENG & FRE.). 29p. (J). (gr. -1-3). pap. 14.95 incl. audio compact disk *(978-1-891888-81-6(1))* Slangman Publishing.

Sangha Mitra, Ms Janice. Golden Bear: The Story of a Flowering Heart. Sangha Mitra, Ms Janice, illus. 4th ed. 2013. (ENG., Illus.). 38p. pap. *(978-0-9805945-2-2(9))* Little Bear Values.

Sanschagrin, Joceline. El Osito de Peluche. 2004. (Caillou Ser.).Tr. of Where's Teddy? (SPA & ENG., Illus.). 24p. (J). (gr. -1-17). bds. 5.95 *(978-1-58728-404-5(9))* Cooper Square Publishing Llc.

Sansone, V. K. Katie Bear: Fun Days at School. WillowRaven, Aidana, illus. 2007. 84p. pap. 16.95 *(978-0-9798154-7-8(9))* Living Waters Publishing Co.

—Katie Bear & Friends (Book One) 2009. 36p. pap. 16.97 *(978-0-557-09358-8(9))* Lulu Pr., Inc.

—Katie Bear & Friends (Book Three) 2009. 36p. pap. 16.97 *(978-0-557-09331-1(7))* Lulu Pr., Inc.

—Katie Bear & Friends (Book Two) 2009. 40p. pap. 18.00 *(978-0-557-09393-9(7))* Lulu Pr., Inc.

—Pandora's Incredible Journey. 2009. 32p. pap. 8.98 *(978-0-557-07374-0(X))* Lulu Pr., Inc.

Sarcone-Roach, Julia. The Bear Ate Your Sandwich. 2015. (ENG., Illus.). 40p. (J). (gr. -1-2). 16.99 *(978-0-375-85860-4(1))*; lib. bdg. 19.99 *(978-0-375-95860-1(6))* Random Hse. Children's Bks. (Knopf Bks. for Young Readers).

Sargent, Dave & Sargent, David, Jr. Pinkie Flamingo: Leaving Home, 19 vols., Vol. 15. Lenoir, Jane, illus. 2003. (Feather Tales Ser.: 15). 42p. (J). pap. 10.95 *(978-1-56763-748-9(5))* Ozark Publishing.

Sargent, Dave & Sargent, Pat. Brutus the Bear: Show Respect, 15 vols., Vol. 4. Huff, Jeane, illus. 2nd rev. ed. 2003. (Animal Pride Ser.: 4). 42p. (J). pap. 6.95 *(978-1-56763-766-3(3))*; lib. bdg. 20.95 *(978-1-56763-765-6(5))* Ozark Publishing.

Sargent, Pat L. The Grizzly, 6 vols., Vol. 1. Lenoir, Jane, illus. 2004. (Barney the Bear Killer Ser.: No. 1). 129p. (YA). pap. 10.95 *(978-1-56763-964-3(X))* Ozark Publishing.

Sayre, April Pulley. Eat Like a Bear. Jenkins, Steve, illus. 2013. (ENG.). 32p. (J). (gr. -1-3). 16.99 *(978-0-8050-9039-0(8)*, 9780805090390, Holt, Henry & Co. Bks. For Young Readers) Holt, Henry & Co.

Scarry, Patricia M. The Sweet Smell of Christmas. Miller, J. P., illus. 2003. (Scented Storybook Ser.). (ENG.). 36p. (J). (gr. -1-2). 9.99 *(978-0-375-82643-6(2)*, Golden Bks.) Random Hse. Children's Bks.

Scarry, Patsy. Richard Scarry's Good Night, Little Bear. Scarry, Richard, illus. 2014. (Big Golden Book Ser.). (ENG.). 32p. (J). (-k). 9.99 *(978-0-385-38729-3(6)*, Golden Bks.) Random Hse. Children's Bks.

Scarry, Richard. Richard Scarry's Good Night, Little Bear. 2015. lib. bdg. 14.75 *(978-0-606-36400-3(5))* Turtleback Bks.

Schaaf, Ron. BearClaw: Finding Courage Within. 2007. (J). *(978-0-9787555-1-5(0))* Hickory Tales Publishing.

Scheffrin-Falk, Gladys. Another Celebrated Dancing Bear. Garrison, Barbara, illus. (J). 2007. 32p. (gr. -1-3). 18.95 *(978-1-930900-35-6(X))* 20th ed. 2011. 28p. 18.95 *(978-1-930900-50-9(3))* Purple Hse. Pr.

Schertle, Alice. Very Hairy Bear. Phelan, Matt, illus. 2012. lib. bdg. 17.20 *(978-0-606-26605-5(4)*, Turtleback) Turtleback Bks.

Scheunemann, Pam. Bear Claws, 1 vol. Chawla, Neena, illus. 2006. (Animal Tales Ser.). 24p. (J). (gr. k-3). (ENG.). lib. bdg. 24.21 *(978-1-59679-925-7(0)*, SandCastle); pap. 48.42 *(978-1-59679-926-4(9))* ABDO Publishing Co.

Schlembach, Audrey. Stinky Winky Bear. 2011. 20p. (gr. 1-2). pap. 12.99 *(978-1-4567-2704-8(4))* AuthorHouse.

Schoenherr, Ian. Don't Spill the Beans! Schoenherr, Ian, illus. 2010. (Illus.). 32p. (J). (gr. -1 — 1). (ENG.). 16.99 *(978-0-06-172457-2(2))*; lib. bdg. 17.89 *(978-0-06-172458-9(0))* HarperCollins Pubs. (Greenwillow Bks.).

Schwartz, Corey Rosen & Coulton, Beth. Goldi Rocks & the Three Bears. Wragg, Nate, illus. 2014. (ENG.). 32p. (J). (gr. k-3). 17.99 *(978-0-399-25685-1(7)*, G.P. Putnam's Sons Books for Young Readers) Penguin Young Readers Group.

Schwartz, Staci J. The New Bear on the Block. 2006. (J). pap. 12.95 *(978-0-9766889-2-1(1))* ComteQ Publishing.

Scott, Liz. Bear Story: Just a Silly Man Who Wears a Fur Coat & Needs a Shave. 2012. (Illus.). 40p. (gr. k-3). pap. 18.49 *(978-1-4678-8714-4(5))* AuthorHouse.

Scott, William. Bouncy Bear. 2013. 32p. pap. 24.95 *(978-1-4626-9757-1(7))* America Star Bks.

Scripture Teachers: Solomon & Friends Learn about Being Wonderfully Made. 2003. pap. *(978-0-9712894-3-7(3))* Lighthouse Christian Products Co.

Scripture Teachers: Solomon & Friends Learn about Forgiveness. 2003. pap. *(978-0-9712894-1-3(7))* Lighthouse Christian Products Co.

Scripture Teachers: Solomon & Friends Learn about Prayer. 2003. pap. *(978-0-9712894-0-6(9))* Lighthouse Christian Products Co.

Scripture Teachers: Solomon & Friends Learn about the Christmas Story. 2003. pap. *(978-0-9712894-4-4(1))* Lighthouse Christian Products Co.

Scripture Teachers: Solomon & Friends Learn about Trusting God. 2003. pap. *(978-0-9712894-2-0(5))* Lighthouse Christian Products Co.

Searcy, Margaret Zehmer. The Charm of the Bearclaw Necklace. Brough, Hazel, illus. 80p. (J). (gr. 3-7). pap. 7.95 *(978-1-56554-777-3(2))* Pelican Publishing Co., Inc.

Seeger, Laura Vaccaro. Bear in the Chair. 2017. (Dog & Bear Ser.). (ENG., Illus.). 18p. (J). bds. 5.99 *(978-1-62672-497-6(0)*, 9781626724976) Roaring Brook Pr.

—Dog & Bear, Level 2: Two Friends, Three Stories. Seeger, Laura Vaccaro, illus. 2012. (My Readers Ser.). (ENG., Illus.). 32p. (J). (gr. k-2). pap. 3.99 *(978-0-312-54799-8(4)*, 9780312547998) Square Fish.

—Two Friends, Three Stories. Seeger, Laura Vaccaro, illus. 2007. (Dog & Bear Ser.). (ENG., Illus.). 32p. (J). (gr. -1-3). 15.99 *(978-1-59643-053-2(2)*, 9781596430532) Roaring Brook Pr.

Seltzer, Eric. Granny Doodle Day. Seltzer, Eric, illus. 2006. (Doodle Dog Ser.). (ENG., Illus.). 32p. (J). (gr. -1-1). pap. 3.99 *(978-0-689-85911-3(2)*, Simon & Schuster/Paula Wiseman Bks.) Simon & Schuster/Paula Wiseman Bks.

Seltzer, Jerry Joe. There Are Fairies in My Tub. Seltzer, Jerry Joe, illus. 2013. (Illus.). 20p. (J). 12.95 *(978-1-60131-175-7(3)*, Castlebridge Bks.) Big Tent Bks.

Seton, Ernest Thompson. The Biography of a Grizzly. 2008. 48p. per. *(978-1-4065-9175-0(0))* Dodo Pr.

—Biography of a Grizzly. Seton-Thompson, Grace Gallatin, illus. 2008. 72p. pap. *(978-1-4099-1427-3(5))* Dodo Pr.

—The Biography of a Grizzly & Drawing. 2009. 170p. 26.99 *(978-1-110-54606-0(8))*; pap. 20.75 *(978-1-110-54605-3(X))* Creative Media Partners, LLC.

—Johnny Bear. 2004. reprint ed. pap. 1.99 *(978-1-4192-2787-5(4))* Kessinger Publishing, LLC.

—Monarch, the Big Bear of Tallac. 2009. 220p. 28.99 *(978-1-110-87583-2(5))*; 220p. pap. 23.75 *(978-1-110-87580-1(0))*; 104p. pap. 18.75 *(978-0-559-09409-5(4))* Creative Media Partners, LLC.

—Monarch, the Big Bear of Tallac. 2004. reprint ed. pap. 1.99 *(978-1-4192-3486-6(2))* Kessinger Publishing, LLC.

—Monarch, the Big Bear of Tallac. 2008. 216p. pap. *(978-1-4086-8818-2(2))* Read Bks.

Sgarlato, Dawn. Big Sister. 2012. 24p. pap. 17.99 *(978-1-4685-9426-3(5))* AuthorHouse.

Shakespeare, Nancy. Benjamin the Bear. Clouette, Katie, illus. 2013. (Benjamin the Bear Ser.). (ENG.). (J). (gr. -1-3). 14.95 *(978-1-62086-312-1(X))* Mascot Bks., Inc.

—Benjamin the Bear Gets a Sister. Clouette, Katie, illus. 2013. (Benjamin the Bear Ser.). (ENG.). (J). (gr. -1-3). 14.95 *(978-1-62086-316-9(2))* Mascot Bks., Inc.

—Benjamin the Bear Goes on a Picnic. Clouette, Katie, illus. 2013. (Benjamin the Bear Ser.). (ENG.). (J). (gr. -1-3). 14.95 *(978-1-62086-314-5(6))* Mascot Bks., Inc.

—Benjamin the Bear Goes to Kindergarten. Clouette, Katie, illus. 2013. (Benjamin the Bear Ser.). (ENG.). (J). (gr. -1-k). 14.95 *(978-1-62086-320-6(0))* Mascot Bks., Inc.

—Benjamin the Bear Rides on an Airplane. Clouette, Katie, illus. 2013. (Benjamin the Bear Ser.). (ENG.). (J). (gr. -1-3). 14.95 *(978-1-62086-318-3(9))* Mascot Bks., Inc.

Sharmat, Mitchell. Berkley, the Terrible Sleeper. Kurilla, Renée, illus. 2015. (Ready-To-Reads Ser.). (ENG.). 32p. (J). (gr. k-2). pap. 3.99 *(978-1-4814-3832-2(8)*, Simon Spotlight) Simon Spotlight.

Shea, Bob. Ballet Cat: The Totally Secret Secret. Shea, Bob, illus. 2016. (Ballet Cat Ser.). (ENG., Illus.). 56p. (J). (gr. 1-3). bds. 9.99 *(978-1-4847-1379-2(6))* Disney Pr.

Shea, Therese. Bear Likes to Share. 2006. (Neighborhood Readers Ser.). (ENG.). 8p. (gr. -1-3). pap. 5.15 *(978-1-4042-5696-5(2)*, Rosen Classroom) Rosen Publishing Group, Inc., The.

Shelton, Dave. A Boy & a Bear in a Boat. 2013. (ENG.). 304p. (J). (gr. 2-5). 6.99 *(978-0-449-81060-6(7)*, Yearling) Random Hse. Children's Bks.

Shields, Gillian. The Perfect Bear. Blythe, Gary, illus. 2008. (ENG.). 32p. (J). (gr. -1-3). 16.99 *(978-1-4169-5363-0(9)*, Simon & Schuster Bks. For Young Readers) Simon & Schuster Bks. For Young Readers.

Shields, Vicki. Mooshka the Bear. 2012. 52p. pap. *(978-1-909040-47-2(9))* Athena Pr.

Shoshan, Beth. That's When I'm Happy. East, Jacqueline, illus. 2011. *(978-1-4351-3618-2(7))* Barnes & Noble, Inc.

Shoulders, Michael. Goodnight Baby Bear. Weidner, Teri, illus. 2010. (ENG.). 32p. (J). (gr. -1-k). 15.95 *(978-1-58536-471-8(1))* Sleeping Bear Pr.

—Say Daddy! Weidner, Teri, illus. (ENG.). (J). 2013. 26p. (gr. -1-k). 8.99 (978-1-58536-863-1(6), 202383) 2008. 32p. (gr. k-6). 15.95 (978-1-58536-354-4(5)) Sleeping Bear Pr.
Siemens, Cindy Louetta. The Adventures of Mr Grizz. 2011. 24p. pap. 15.99 (978-1-4568-4816-3(X)) Xlibris Corp.
Silbaugh, Michael John. Crosseyed Puzzle. 2009. 28p. pap. 15.99 (978-1-4415-8779-4(9)) Xlibris Corp.
Simkins, Aron. Dream Big: The Journey of the Jazz Bear. 2012. 15.99 (978-1-59955-945-2(5), Bonneville Bks.) Cedar Fort, Inc./CFI Distribution.
Simon, Mary Manz. Bear Obeys. Clearwater, Linda & Couri, Kathy, illus. 2006. (First Virtues for Toddlers Ser.). 20p. (J). 5.99 (978-0-7847-1416-4(9), 04068) Standard Publishing.
Sinfield, Irene. Julia & her Bears on Holiday. 2009. (Illus.). 150p. pap. (978-1-84748-662-2(2)) Athena Pr.
Sissung, Ingrid. The Hiccup. 2014. (ENG., Illus.). 32p. (J). (gr. -1-k). 16.95 (978-1-62636-387-8(0), 263387, Sky Pony Pr.) Skyhorse Publishing Co., Inc.
Skead, Robert. Elves Can't Kick. 2005. 84p. per. 7.99 (978-1-929478-66-8(6)) Cross Training Publishing.
Skevington, Andrea. Little Red Riding Hood. Hersey, Bob, illus. 2003. 48p. (J). (978-0-439-57189-0(8)) Scholastic, Inc.
Skiing: KinderConcepts Individual Title Six-Packs. (Kinderstarters Ser.). 8p. (gr. -1-1). 21.00 (978-0-7635-8718-5(4)) Rigby Education.
Skofield, James. Bear & Bird. Thermes, Jennifer, illus. 2014. (ENG.). 40p. (J). (gr. 1-3). 15.99 (978-1-58536-835-8(0), 203012) Sleeping Bear Pr.
Skurzynski, Gloria & Ferguson, Alane. Night of the Black Bear: A Mystery in Great Smoky Mountains National Park. 2007. (Mysteries in Our National Park Ser.). (ENG., Illus.). 160p. (J). (gr. 3-7). 4.99 (978-1-4263-0094-3(8)); 18.90 (978-1-4263-0105-6(7)) National Geographic Society. (National Geographic Children's Bks.).
Slater, David Michael. Westley the Wicked & the Rascally Ring Bear. Brooks, S. G., illus. 2012. 36p. pap. 10.95 (978-1-61413-028-4(0)) Puddletown Publishing Group, Inc.
Slater, Teddy. Goldilocks & the Three Bears: Pop-up Storybook Theater. Yerkes, Lane, illus. 2004. 10p. (J). (gr. k-4). reprint ed. 17.00 (978-0-7567-8224-5(4)) DIANE Publishing Co.
Smallman, Steve. Bear's Big Bottom, 1 vol. Yarlett, Emma, illus. 2014. (ENG.). 32p. (gr. -1-2). 14.95 (978-1-62370-118-5(X)) Capstone Young Readers of Coughlan Cos.
Smart, Jamie. Bear, Vol. 1. 2004. (ENG., Illus.). 144p. pap. 14.95 (978-1-59362-001-1(2), 9781593620011) Slave Labor Bks.
Smedes, Marty. Goldie Bear & the Three Lockes. 2009. 24p. pap. 12.99 (978-1-4389-7216-9(4)) AuthorHouse.
Smiley, Lucy Ireland. Bass-Fishing Bears. 2006. (J). pap. 8.00 (978-0-8059-7017-3(7)) Dorrance Publishing Co., Inc.
Smith, Ben Bailey. I Am Bear. Akyüz, Sav, illus. 2016. (ENG.). (J). (-k). 15.99 (978-0-7636-7743-5(4), Candlewick Entertainment) Candlewick Pr.
Smith, Bryan L. The Bear That 8 My Flashlight. 2013. 12p. pap. 10.67 (978-1-4669-8196-6(2)) Trafford Publishing.
Smith, Carrie. Goldilocks & the Three Bears: Classic Tales Edition. Greenhead, Bill, illus. 2011. (Classic Tales Ser.). (J). (978-1-936258-61-1(7)) Benchmark Education Co.
Smith, Laura Rountree. Snubby Nose & Tippy Toes. 2004. reprint ed. pap. 15.95 (978-1-4191-4792-0(7)); pap. 1.99 (978-1-4192-4792-7(1)) Kessinger Publishing, LLC.
Smith, Ruth. Buddy Bear: Visits Michigan Lighthouses. 2010. 28p. pap. 13.99 (978-1-4490-8363-2(3)) AuthorHouse.
Sobel, Gerrie. Jacob & His Magical Flying Bears. Torres, Dottie, illus. 2009. 32p. pap. 12.95 (978-1-936051-16-8(8)) Peppertree Pr., The.
—Jacob & His Magical Flying Bears, a Halloween Story. Torres, Dottie, illus. 2009. 32p. pap. 12.95 (978-1-936051-42-7(7)) Peppertree Pr., The.
Solomon, Chad. Adventures of Rabbit & Bear Paws: The Voyageurs. 2008. (ENG.). 32p. pap. (978-0-9739906-2-1(7)) Little Spirit Bear Productions CAN. Dist: Lone Pine Publishing.
Soman, David. Three Bears in a Boat. Soman, David, illus. 2014. (ENG., Illus.). 40p. (J). (gr. -1-k). 17.99 (978-0-8037-3993-2(1), Dial Bks) Penguin Publishing Group.
Sommer, Carl. Can You Help Me Find My Smile? 2003. (Another Sommer-Time Story Ser.). (Illus.). 48p. (J). (gr. k-4). lib. bdg. 23.95 incl. audio (978-1-57537-757-5(8)) Advance Publishing, Inc.
—Can You Help Me Find My Smile? Budwine, Greg, illus. 2003. (Another Sommer-Time Story Ser.). (ENG.). 48p. (J). (gr. k-4). lib. bdg. 23.95 incl. audio compact disk (978-1-57537-707-0(1)) Advance Publishing, Inc.
—Can You Help Me Find My Smile? 2003. (Another Sommer-Time Story Ser.). (Illus.). 48p. (J). (gr. 1-4). 16.95 incl. audio (978-1-57537-556-4(7)) Advance Publishing, Inc.
—Can You Help Me Find My Smile? Budwine, Greg, illus. 2003. (Another Sommer-Time Story Ser.). (ENG.). 48p. (J). (gr. 1-4). 16.95 incl. audio compact disk (978-1-57537-507-6(9)) Advance Publishing, Inc.
—Can You Help Me Find My Smile? Me Puedes Ayudar a Encontrar Mi Sonrisa? Budwine, Greg, illus. 2009. (Another Sommer-Time Story Bilingual Ser.). (SPA & ENG.). 48p. (J). lib. bdg. 16.95 (978-1-57537-150-4(2)) Advance Publishing, Inc.
—Lost & Found. Budwine, Greg, illus. 2009. (Quest for Success Ser.). 56p. (YA). pap. 4.95 (978-1-57537-280-8(0)); lib. bdg. 12.95 (978-1-57537-255-6(X)) Advance Publishing, Inc.
—Lost & Found(Perdida y Encontrada) Budwine, Greg, illus. 2009. (Quest for Success Bilingual Ser.). (ENG & SPA.). 96p. (YA). lib. bdg. 14.95 (978-1-57537-229-7(0)) Advance Publishing, Inc.
—You Move You Lose. James, Kennon, illus. 2014. (J). pap. (978-1-57537-972-2(4)) Advance Publishing, Inc.
—You Move You Lose(El Que Se Mueva, Pierde) James, Kennon, illus. 2009. (Another Sommer-Time Story Bilingual Ser.). (SPA & ENG.). 48p. (J). lib. bdg. 16.95 (978-1-57537-172-6(3)) Advance Publishing, Inc.
Sontag, Mary G. Bruno's Adventures. 2009. 128p. pap. 38.49 (978-1-4490-1769-9(X)) AuthorHouse.
Soundprints. Grizzly Bear Cub's First Fish: Wilderness Adventures. 2012. (ENG.). 32p. (J). pap. 3.95 (978-1-60727-873-3(1)) Soundprints.
—Polar Bear Cub & Mommy: Wilderness Adventures. 2012. (ENG.). 32p. (J). pap. 3.95 (978-1-60727-871-9(5)) Soundprints.
Southey, Robert. Goldilocks & the Three Bears. 2005. (Classics Illustrated Junior Ser.). (Illus.). 32p. per. 5.99 (978-1-894998-21-5(9)) Lake, Jack Productions, Inc. CAN. Dist: Hushion Hse. Publishing, Ltd.
Sowerby, Dale. The Adventures of Baggy & Paxton: Trouble in Dawlish Warren. 2010. (ENG., Illus.). 48p. pap. (978-1-84748-704-9(1)) Athena Pr.
Spanos, Seva, retold by. Goldilocks & the Three Bears. 2004. (Treasure Tree Ser.). (J). (978-0-7166-1603-0(3)) World Bk., Inc.
Sparrow, Leilani. My First Day. Taylor, Dan, illus. 2015. (ENG.). 32p. (J). (gr. -1-k). 16.99 (978-1-4998-0111-8(4)) Little Bee Books Inc.
—My New Shoes. Taylor, Dan, illus. 2016. (ENG.). 32p. (J). (gr. -1-k). 16.99 (978-1-4998-0363-1(X)) Little Bee Books Inc.
Spelman, Cornelia. When I Feel Scared. Parkinson, Kathy, illus. 2012. (J). (978-1-61913-141-5(2)) Weigl Pubs., Inc.
Spelman, Cornelia Maude. When I Feel Jealous. Parkinson, Kathy, illus. 2003. (Way I Feel Bks.). (ENG.). 24p. (J). (gr. -1-3). 6.99 (978-0-8075-8902-1(0)) Whitman, Albert & Co.
—When I Feel Scared. Parkinson, Kathy, illus. 2010. (ENG.). 16p. (J). (gr. -1 — 1). bds. 7.99 (978-0-8075-8905-2(5)) Whitman, Albert & Co.
Sperring, Mark. How Many Sleeps 'til Christmas? Braun, Sebastien, illus. 2014. (ENG.). 32p. (J). (gr. -1-3). 16.99 (978-1-58925-160-1(1)) Tiger Tales.
—How Many Sleeps 'Til My Birthday? Braun, Sebastien, illus. 2016. (ENG.). 32p. (J). (gr. -1-2). 16.99 (978-1-68010-009-9(2)) Tiger Tales.
Spetzler, Carl. Goldilocks Meets Desidero. Meyers, Mark, illus. 2011. 36p. pap. 16.86 (978-1-4634-2684-2(4)) AuthorHouse.
Spirin, Gennady. Goldilocks & the Three Bears, 0 vols. Spirin, Gennady, illus. 2009. (ENG., Illus.). 32p. (J). (gr. -1-2). 17.99 (978-0-7614-5596-7(5), 9780761455967, Amazon Children's Publishing) Amazon Publishing.
Spitzer, Linda. A Friend in Freezeville. 2005. 23p. (J). 10.95 (978-1-4116-4968-2(0)) Lulu Pr., Inc.
Sprecher, John. Zoe & the Very Unmerry Bear. Forrest, James, illus. l.t. ed. Date not set. (Special Kids "Special Message" Book Ser.). 32p. (J). (gr. k-4). pap. 10.00 (978-1-892186-03-4(9), SKPB4) Anythings Possible, Inc.
Springer, Susan Woodward. Seldovia Sam & the Blueberry Bear, Vol. 4. Meissner, Amy, illus. 2005. (Misadventures of Seldovia Sam Ser.). (ENG.). 64p. (J). (gr. -1-4). per. 6.95 (978-0-88240-603-9(5), Alaska Northwest Bks.) Graphic Arts Ctr. Publishing Co.
St. Jean, Alan. The Legend of OinkADoodleMoo. St. Jean, Alan, ed. Krock, Libby Carruth, illus. 2013. 32p. 19.95 (978-0-9777272-9-2(7)) Oren Village, LLC.
Stafford, Liliana. Snow Bear. Davis, Lambert, illus. 32p. (J). pap. (978-0-88899-441-7(9)) Groundwood Bks.
Stamper, Judith B. Polar Bear Patrol. Haefele, Steve, illus. 2003. (Magic School Bus Science Chapter Bks.). 91p. (J). (gr. 2-5). 12.65 (978-0-7569-1577-3(5)) Perfection Learning Corp.
Stanley, Diane. Goldie & the Three Bears. Stanley, Diane, illus. 2007. (ENG., Illus.). 40p. (J). (gr. k-3). pap. 7.99 (978-0-06-113611-5(5)) HarperCollins Pubs.
Stanton, Andy. Mr Gum & the Dancing Bear. Tazzyman, David, illus. 2015. (Mr Gum Ser.: 5). (ENG.). 256p. (J). (gr. 2-4). pap. 8.99 (978-1-4052-7496-8(4)) Egmont Bks., Ltd. GBR. Dist: Independent Pubs. Group.
Starin, Liz. Splashdance. Starin, Liz, illus. 2016. (ENG., Illus.). 32p. (J). 16.99 (978-0-374-30098-2(4), 9780374300982, Farrar, Straus & Giroux (BYR)) Farrar, Straus & Giroux.
Stead, Philip C. Bear Has a Story to Tell. Stead, Erin E., illus. 2012. (ENG.). 32p. (J). (gr. -1-1). 16.99 (978-1-59643-745-6(6), 9781596437456) Roaring Brook Pr.
Stein, David Ezra. Leaves. Stein, David Ezra, illus. (ENG., Illus.). (J). (gr. -1 — 1). 2010. 30p. bds. 6.99 (978-0-399-25497-0(8)) 2007. 32p. 16.99 (978-0-399-24636-4(3)) Penguin Young Readers Group. (G.P. Putnam's Sons Books for Young Readers).
—Ol' Mama Squirrel. Stein, David Ezra, illus. 2013. (ENG., Illus.). 32p. (J). (gr. -1-k). 16.99 (978-0-399-25672-1(5), Nancy Paulsen Books) Penguin Young Readers Group.
Stephens, Melissa. Little Miss & Spirit Bear's Kiss: A Simple Story of Rediscovering One's Light. 2012. 16p. pap. 15.50 (978-1-4389-7851-2(0)) AuthorHouse.
Sterling, Amber. Little Mud Bear. 2006. (Illus.). 44p. (J). per. (978-0-9803058-1-4(0)) Carpe Diem Publishing.
Steven, Kenneth C. The Biggest Thing in the World. Mitchell, Melanie, illus. 2013. (ENG.). 32p. (J). (gr. -1-k). 6.99 (978-0-7459-6402-7(8)) Lion Hudson PLC GBR. Dist: Independent Pubs. Group.
Stevens, Jennifer. Love You More. 2013. 24p. pap. 24.95 (978-1-63004-655-2(8)) America Star Bks.
Stihler, Cherie B. Polar Polka: Counting Polar Bears in Alaska. Brooks, Erik, illus. 2008. (Paws IV Ser.). (ENG.). 32p. (J). (gr. -1-2). pap. 10.95 (978-1-57061-520-7(9), Little Bigfoot) Sasquatch Bks.
Stinson, Aimee & Somson, Kathy. The Bearless City, 1 vol. 2009. 22p. pap. 24.95 (978-1-60749-406-5(X)) America Star Bks.
Stone, Julia. Little Bear's Sparkly Christmas. Muss, Angela, illus. 2014. (ENG.). 6p. (J). (gr. -1-k). 8.99 (978-0-7459-6262-7(9)) Lion Hudson PLC GBR. Dist: Independent Pubs. Group.
Stoop, Naoko. Red Knit Cap Girl to the Rescue. 2013. (ENG., Illus.). 40p. (J). (gr. -1-3). 17.00 (978-0-316-22885-5(0)) Little, Brown Bks. for Young Readers.
Stott, Dorothy, illus. Ten in the Bed. 2010. (Padded Board Book W/CD Ser.). 8p. (J). (gr. k-2). bds. 10.99 incl. audio compact disk (978-1-59922-578-4(6)) Twin Sisters IP, LLC.
Stower, Adam. Silly Doggy! Stower, Adam, illus. 2012. (ENG., Illus.). 40p. (J). (gr. -1-k). 16.99 (978-0-545-37323-4(9), Orchard Bks.) Scholastic, Inc.
Stratton, Bart. Arctic Mall Adventure. Riddle, Scott, illus. 2010. 28p. pap. 15.95 (978-1-60844-558-5(5)) Dog Ear Publishing, LLC.
Straub-Martin, Susan M. Legends, Loves & Great Lakes. 2013. 28p. pap. 15.00 (978-0-9830321-6-8(5)) Strauberry Studios.
Stubbs, Lisa. Grumpy Feet. Stubbs, Lisa, illus. 2017. (Lily & Bear Ser.). (ENG., Illus.). 32p. (J). (gr. -1-3). 17.99 (978-1-4814-7167-1(8), Simon & Schuster/Paula Wiseman Bks.) Simon & Schuster/Paula Wiseman Bks.
—Lily & Bear. Stubbs, Lisa, illus. 2015. (Lily & Bear Ser.). (ENG., Illus.). 32p. (J). (gr. -1-3). 17.99 (978-1-4814-4416-3(6), Simon & Schuster Bks. For Young Readers) Simon & Schuster Bks. For Young Readers.
Subramaniam, Manasi. Dancing Bear. Gwangjo & Park, Jung-a, illus. 2013. (ENG.). 32p. (J). (gr. k). pap. 9.95 (978-81-8190-200-9(9)) Karadi Tales Co. Pvt. Ltd. IND. Dist: Consortium Bk. Sales & Distribution.
Sutherland, Paul H. Mani & Pitouee: The True Legend of Sleeping Bear Dunes. Gibbons, Timothy M., illus. 2006. 36p. (J). (gr. -1-3). 20.00 (978-0-9661060-3-9(2)) Utopia Pr.
Swanson, Maggie, illus. Goldilocks & the Three Bears: A Tale about Respecting Others. 2006. (J). 6.99 (978-1-59939-006-2(X)) Cornerstone Pr.
Swift, Melanie. Rioc & Elber's Arctic Adventure. 2011. 120p. pap. (978-1-84549-511-4(X), Swirl) arima publishing.
Tafuri, Nancy. Mama's Little Bears. 2004. (J). bds. 7.99 (978-0-439-57357-3(2)) Scholastic, Inc.
Tak, Bibi Dumon & Dumon Tak, Bibi. Soldier Bear. Hopman, Philip, illus. 2011. (ENG.). 158p. (J). 13.00 (978-0-8028-5375-2(7), Eerdmans Bks For Young Readers) Eerdmans, William B. Publishing Co.
Takahashi, Kazue. Kuma-Kuma Chan's Home. 2016. (Kuma-Kuma Chan Ser.). (ENG., Illus.). 52p. (J). (gr. -1-k). 12.99 (978-1-940842-09-7(3)) Museyon.
Tanwar, Rajesh, illus. Goldilocks & the Three Bears. 2010. (J). (978-1-60617-147-9(X)) Teaching Strategies, LLC.
Tashlin, Frank. The Bear That Wasn't. 2010. (ENG., Illus.). 64p. (J). (gr. -1-3). 16.95 (978-1-59017-344-2(9), NYR Children's Collection) New York Review of Bks., Inc., The.
Tattum, Stephan. Bear Cub. 2005. (J). 4.95 (978-1-59792-008-7(8)) F.A.S.T. Learning LLC.
Taylor, Arthur Charles. Bears Like Us. 2007. 52p. per. 10.00 (978-1-4257-3733-7(1)) Xlibris Corp.
Taylor, Sean. A Brave Bear. Hughes, Emily, illus. 2016. (ENG.). 32p. (J). (-k). 16.99 (978-0-7636-8224-8(1)) Candlewick Pr.
Taylor, Sean & Quarto Generic Staff. Grizzly Bear with the Frizzly Hair. Shaw, Hannah, illus. 2011. (ENG.). 32p. (J). (gr. -1-1). pap. 8.95 (978-1-84780-144-9(7), Frances Lincoln) Quarto Publishing Group UK GBR. Dist: Hachette Bk. Group.
Taylor, Theodore. The Weirdo. 2006. (Illus.). 292p. (gr. 7-12). 18.00 (978-0-7569-6752-9(X)) Perfection Learning Corp.
Taylor, Theodore & Taylor, Theodore. The Weirdo. 2006. (ENG., Illus.). 304p. (YA). (gr. 7-12). pap. 8.99 (978-0-15-205666-7(1)) Houghton Mifflin Harcourt Publishing Co.
Teckentrup, Britta. Sleep Tight, Little Bear. 2014. (ENG., Illus.). 40p. (J). 17.95 (978-0-7358-4180-2(2)) North-South Bks., Inc.
Ted in a Red Bed Kid Kit. 2004. (Kid Kits Ser.). (Illus.). 10p. (J). bds. 9.95 (978-1-58086-404-6(X)) EDC Publishing.
Teddy Tender-Heart: Paper Doll Cut-Out Book. 2006. (J). pap. 5.95 (978-0-9787319-6-0(4)) Kolluri, Alina M.
Teel, Julie. The Biggest Bear in the World: As Told by Grandpa Kingsford. 2009. 36p. pap. 16.99 (978-1-4389-7983-0(5)) AuthorHouse.
Temairik, Jaime. Alice & Lucy Will Work for Bunk Beds. Temairik, Jaime, illus. 2016. (ENG., Illus.). 40p. (J). (gr. -1-k). 16.99 (978-1-4847-0816-3(4)) Disney Publishing Worldwide.
Thebo, Mimi. Dreaming the Bear. 2017. (YA). pap. (978-0-399-55753-8(9)) Earthscan Canada.
Thomas, Deborah E. The Bramble Thicket. l.t. ed. 2004. (Illus.). 88p. 27.95 (978-0-9742805-0-9(X)) Gypsy Hill Publishing.
Thomas Nelson. Playdate Pals Bear Learns to Share. 2016. (ENG.). 24p. (J). (gr. -1-7). pap. (978-1-78598-477-8(2)) Make Believe Ideas.
Thompson, Aron. The Biography of a Grizzly. 2008. (Illus.). 176p. (YA). pap. 16.95 (978-0-9728155-1-2(1)) CONVERPAGE.
Thompson, Berine. Tedi the Bear & His Pals Adventure at the Zoo! 2005. 44p. per. 21.99 (978-1-4208-1007-3(3)) AuthorHouse.
Thompson, Kim Mitzo & Thompson, Bailey. I Love You More. 2011. (J). (gr. k-1). bds. 9.99 incl. audio compact disk (978-1-59922-841-9(6)) Twin Sisters IP, LLC.
Thompson, Lauren. Polar Bear Morning. Savage, Stephen, illus. 2013. (ENG.). 32p. (J). (gr. -1-k). 16.99 (978-0-439-69885-6(5), Scholastic Pr.) Scholastic, Inc.
—Polar Bear Night. Savage, Stephen, illus. (ENG.). 32p. (J). (gr. -1 — 1). 2013. bds. 8.99 (978-0-545-48558-6(4), Cartwheel Bks.) 2004. 17.99 (978-0-439-49524-0(5), Scholastic Pr.) Scholastic, Inc.
Thompson, Michael. Los Otros Osos, 1 vol. Thompson, Michael, illus. 2013. (SPA., Illus.). 32p. (J). pap. 6.99 (978-1-59572-664-3(0)) Star Bright Bks., Inc.
—Los Otros Osos / the Other Bears. Thompson, Michael, illus. 2013. (ENG & SPA., Illus.). (J). 16.99 (978-1-59572-644-5(6)) Star Bright Bks., Inc.
—The Other Bears, 1 vol. Thompson, Michael, illus. 2013.Tr. of Os Outros Ursos. (ENG., Illus.). 32p. (J). 16.99 (978-1-59572-638-4(1)); pap. 6.99 (978-1-59572-639-1(X)) Star Bright Bks., Inc.
Thomson, Sarah L. Cub's Big World. Cepeda, Joe, illus. 2013. (ENG.). 32p. (J). (gr. -1-3). 16.99 (978-0-544-05739-5(2)) Houghton Mifflin Harcourt Publishing Co.
Thong, Roseanne Greenfield. Cuddly Bear Cubs Carnival. 2006. (ENG.). 12p. 14.95 (978-1-58117-478-6(0), Intervisual/Piggy Toes) Bendon, Inc.
The Three Bears. 2004. (Folk Tales Set 1 Ser.). (J). 4.00 (978-1-58453-275-0(0)) Pioneer Valley Bks.
Tidholm, Anna-Clara. Knock! Knock! Bradley, MaryChris, tr. 2009. (Illus.). 32p. (J). (gr. -1). 9.95 (978-0-9815761-6-9(8)) Mackenzie Smiles, LLC.
Timbers, James. Salmon & Fuzz in Helping a Friend. 2004. 30p. pap. 24.95 (978-1-4137-2602-2(X)) PublishAmerica, Inc.
Toh, Irene. Kumi the Bear. Hagan, Stacy, illus. 2008. (ENG.). 24p. pap. 12.75 (978-1-4389-1368-1(0)) AuthorHouse.
Tolman, Marije & Tolman, Ronald. The Island. 2012. (ENG., Illus.). 32p. (J). (gr. -1). 17.95 (978-1-935954-19-4(9), 9781935954194) Lemniscaat USA.
—The Tree House. 2010. (ENG., Illus.). 32p. (J). (gr. -1-1). 17.95 (978-1-59078-806-6(0), Lemniscaat) Boyds Mills Pr.
Tomlin, Chris & Barrett, Pat. Good Good Father, 1 vol. 2016. (ENG.). 32p. (J). 16.99 (978-0-7180-8695-4(3)) Nelson, Thomas Inc.
Tommy. Bubba & Cecil. 2009. 52p. pap. 16.95 (978-1-60836-860-0(2)) America Star Bks.
Toms, Kate. The Bear Who Dares. 2008. (Kate Toms Ser.). (Illus.). 26p. (gr. -1-k). bds. 7.99 (978-1-84610-819-8(5)) Make Believe Ideas GBR. Dist: Nelson, Thomas Inc.
—The Bear Who Dares Book & Plush. 2008. (Illus.). 26p. (gr. -1-k). bds. (978-1-84610-855-6(1)) Make Believe Ideas.
Top That, ed. Night Light Sleepy Bear. 2008. (Night Light Book Ser.). 10p. (J). (gr. -1). (978-1-84666-607-0(4), Tide Mill Pr.) Top That! Publishing PLC.
Top That Publishing Staff, ed. Goldilocks & Three Bears. 2006. (Illus.). 10p. bds. (978-1-905359-93-6(4)) Top That! Publishing PLC.
—There Were Ten Bears in a Bed: A Count-and-Feel Book. Atkins, Alison, illus. 2007. (Story Book Ser.). 22p. (J). (gr. -1). bds. (978-1-84666-130-3(7), Tide Mill Pr.) Top That! Publishing PLC.
Top That!, creator. Counting with Billy the Bear. 2012. (Learn with Magnets Ser.). (ENG., Illus.). 10p. (gr. -1-k). (978-1-84956-669-8(0)) Top That! Publishing PLC.
Tower, Cory L. The Adventures of Courtney, Morgan & the Magic Toy Bears Book 2: In the Beginning. 2012. 24p. pap. 24.95 (978-1-4626-8395-6(9)) America Star Bks.
ToyBox Innovations, creator. Disney's Instant Classics: Chicken Little/Lilo & Stitch/Brother Bear. unabr. abr. ed. 2005. (Disney's Read along Collection). (ENG., Illus.). (J). pap. (978-0-7634-1148-0(5)) Walt Disney Records.
Toynton, Ian. Hooligan Bear Home. Dietrich, Andrea, illus. 2012. 32p. (J). 15.95 (978-1-60131-108-5(7)) Big Tent Bks.
—Hooligan Bear New Friends. Dietrich, Andrea, illus. 2012. 34p. (J). 15.95 (978-1-60131-107-8(9)) Big Tent Bks.
Trent, Rodney. Sadie Mae's Big Adventure. 2012. 28p. pap. 19.99 (978-1-4772-6536-9(8)) AuthorHouse.
Tripp, Jenny. Pete & Fremont. Manders, John, illus. 2008. (ENG.). 192p. (J). (gr. 3-7). pap. 12.95 (978-0-15-206238-5(6)) Houghton Mifflin Harcourt Publishing Co.
Tripp, Patricia. The Bears That Lived in Evergreen Forest. 2006. 18p. (J). spiral bd. 10.76 (978-1-4116-5835-6(3)) Lulu Pr., Inc.
A Tropical Bear in Hawaii. 2005. (Illus.). 32p. (J). (gr. 1-2). 12.95 (978-1-59779-002-4(8)) Reece, Kim Taylor Prodns. LLC.
A Tropical Bear Learns to Surf. 2005. 32p. (J). (gr. 1-2). 12.95 (978-1-59779-003-1(6)) Reece, Kim Taylor Prodns. LLC.
Tucker, Stephen. Goldilocks, 2 vols. Sharratt, Nick, illus. 2017. (Lift-The-Flap Fairy Tales Ser.). (ENG.). 24p. (J). (gr. -1-k). 10.99 **(978-1-5098-2818-0(4))** Pan Macmillan GBR. Dist: Independent Pubs. Group.
Tugman, Etta. Smokey Mountain Bears. 2006. 9.00 (978-0-8059-8189-6(6)) Dorrance Publishing Co., Inc.
Tupera, Tupera. Polar Bear's Underwear. 2015. (ENG., Illus.). 32p. (J). (gr. -1-k). 16.99 (978-1-4521-4199-2(1)) Chronicle Bks. LLC.
Tyrer, Robert. Ralphie the Polar Bear. 2011. 28p. pap. 16.95 (978-1-4560-5635-3(2)) PublishAmerica, Inc.
Ulch, Virginia. Love You, Teddy - a Tail of Loss & Hope. Burkert, Howard, photos by. 2007. (Illus.). 32p. per. 18.95 (978-1-59858-354-0(9)) Dog Ear Publishing, LLC.
Umansky, Kaye. Belinda & the Bears & the New Chair. Jevons, Chris, illus. 2016. (Early Reader Ser.). (ENG.). 80p. (J). (gr. k-2). 6.99 (978-1-4440-1351-1(3), Orion Children's Bks.) Hachette Children's Group GBR. Dist: Hachette Bk. Group.
—Belinda & the Bears Go Shopping. Jevons, Chris, illus. 2016. (Early Reader Ser.). (ENG.). 64p. (J). (gr. k-2). 6.99 (978-1-4440-1354-2(8), Orion Children's Bks.) Hachette Children's Group GBR. Dist: Hachette Bk. Group.
Umina, Lisa. Milo & the Green Wagon. 2008. (Illus.). 32p. 15.95 (978-0-9797429-4-1(3)) Halo Publishing International.
—Milo Finds His Best Friend. Thompson, Chad, illus. 2013. 30p. 15.95 (978-1-61244-182-5(3)) Halo Publishing International.
Underwood, Deborah. The Loud Book! Liwska, Renata, illus. 2011. (ENG.). 32p. (J). (gr. -1-3). 12.99 (978-0-547-39008-6(4)) Houghton Mifflin Harcourt Publishing Co.
V., Patti. My Na Na Stories. 2005. 18.00 (978-0-8059-9806-1(3)) Dorrance Publishing Co., Inc.
Van Buren, David. I Love You As Big As the World. Warnes, Tim, illus. 2013. (ENG.). 22p. (J). bds. (978-1-58925-603-3(4)) Tiger Tales.
Van Dusen, Chris. A Camping Spree with Mr. Magee. 2003. (Mr. Mcgee Ser.: MCGE). (ENG., Illus.). 36p. (J). (gr. -1-7). 15.99 (978-0-8118-3603-6(7)) Chronicle Bks. LLC.
van Genechten, Guido. Because I Love You So Much. (Illus.). (J). 2006. 12p. (gr. -1-3). 15.95 (978-1-58925-794-8(4)) 2004. 32p. tchr. ed. 15.95 (978-1-58925-039-0(7)) Tiger Tales.
—Porque Te Quiero Tanto. 2003. (SPA., Illus.). 28p. (J). (gr. k-3). 15.95 (978-970-29-0912-5(0)) Santillana USA Publishing Co., Inc.
—Snowy's Special Secret. van Genechten, Guido, illus. 2005. (Illus.). 32p. (J). (gr. -1-2). 15.95 (978-1-58925-049-9(4)) Tiger Tales.
VanRiper, Gary & VanRiper, Justin. The Final Daze of Summer. 2010. (Adirondack Kids Ser.: Vol. 10). 96p. (J). (gr. 2-7). pap. 9.95 (978-0-9826250-0-2(6)) Adirondack Kids Pr.
Vasquez, Paula. I Spy with My Little Eye, 1 vol. 2017. (ENG., Illus.). 40p. (J). bds. 8.99 (978-1-4236-4687-7(8)) Gibbs Smith, Publisher.
Vaughan, Richard & Crews, Marcia. Three Bears of the Pacific Northwest. Trammell, Jeremiah, illus. 2016. (ENG.). 20p. (J). (— 1). bds. 9.99 (978-1-63217-076-7(0), Little Bigfoot) Sasquatch Bks.
Vaughan, Richard Lee & Vaughan, Marcia. Three Bears of the Pacific Northwest. Trammell, Jeremiah, illus. 2011. (ENG.). 32p. (J). (gr. -1-2). 17.99 (978-1-57061-684-6(1), Little Bigfoot) Sasquatch Bks.
Vayenas, Christina. Snozo, the Polar Bear. 2012. 24p. pap. 28.03 (978-1-4771-5662-9(3)) Xlibris Corp.

Verburg, Bonnie. The Kiss Box. Cole, Henry, illus. 2011. (ENG.). 32p. (J). (gr. -1-k). 16.99 *(978-0-545-11284-0(2),* Orchard Bks.) Scholastic, Inc.

Vermeulen, Mariska. Anton & Boris Finger Puppet Book. van de Liejgraaf, Deborah, illus. 2016. (My Best Friend & Me Ser.). (ENG.). 10p. (J). (gr. -1-k). bds., bds. 6.99 *(978-0-7641-6831-4(2))* Barron's Educational Series, Inc.

Vicuna, Claudio Orrego. The Surprising Adventures of Balthazar. 2011. (Peace, Justice, Human Rights, & Freedom in Latin America Ser.). (SPA & ENG.). 160p. 15.00 *(978-1-58966-218-6(0))* Univ. of Scranton Pr.

Vorndran, Judith Clay. Mr. Bear Lives There. l.t. ed. 2005. (Illus.). 11p. (J). pap. 7.98 *(978-0-9772439-0-7(7))* Vorndran, Judith Clay.

Vuillamy, Clara. The Bear with Sticky Paws Won't Go to Bed. Vuillamy, Clara, illus. 2010. (ENG., Illus.). 32p. (J). (gr. -1-2). 15.95 *(978-1-58925-087-1(7))* Tiger Tales.

Vulliamy, Claire, illus. The Bear with Sticky Paws. 2008. (Tiger Tales Ser.). 24p. (J). (gr. -1-2). 15.95 *(978-1-58925-070-3(2))* Tiger Tales.

Vulliamy, Clara. Bear with Sticky Paws Goes to School. Vulliamy, Clara, illus. 2010. (ENG., Illus.). 32p. pap. 7.95 *(978-1-58925-424-4(4))* Tiger Tales.

Waddell, Martin. Bears, Bears, Bears! Wildish, Lee, illus. 2013. (J). *(978-1-4351-4999-1(8))* Barnes & Noble, Inc.

—Can't You Sleep, Little Bear? (CHI & ENG., Illus.). 32p. (J). *(978-1-85430-315-8(5),* 93445) Little Tiger Pr. Group.

—Can't You Sleep, Little Bear?: Candlewick Storybook Animations. Firth, Barbara, illus. 2008. (Candlewick Storybook Animations Ser.). (ENG.). 32p. (J). (gr. k-k). 14.99 *(978-0-7636-3537-4(5))* Candlewick Pr.

—Let's Go Home, Little Bear. 2004. (Illus.). (J). (gr. k-3). spiral bd. *(978-0-616-01805-7(3));* spiral bd. *(978-0-616-01804-0(5))* Canadian National Institute for the Blind/Institut National Canadien pour les Aveugles.

—Muy Bien, Osito. 2003.Tr. of Good. (SPA., Illus.). (J). *(978-84-88342-26-3(8),* KK5127) S.A. Kokinos ESP. Dist: Lectorum Pubns., Inc.

—Non Dormi Piccolo Orso. pap. 19.95 *(978-88-7782-378-6(X))* Salani ITA. Dist: Distribooks, Inc.

—You & Me, Little Bear. 2004. (Illus.). (J). (gr. -1-2). spiral bd. *(978-0-616-01803-3(7));* spiral bd. *(978-0-616-01802-6(9))* Canadian National Institute for the Blind/Institut National Canadien pour les Aveugles.

Wahl, Jan. Bear Dance. Felix, Monique, illus. 2008. (ENG.). 32p. (J). (gr. k-17). 19.95 *(978-1-56846-199-1(2),* Creative Editions) Creative Co., The.

Walden, Pamela Charlene. Puff Bear Goes to the Hospital. 2013. 44p. pap. 9.99 *(978-1-62839-470-2(6))* Salem Author Services.

Waldman, David K. How Teddy Bears Find Their Homes. Danner, Maggie, illus. 2nd ed. 2015. (ENG.). 154p. (gr. k-2). pap. 38.40 *(978-0-945522-02-7(9))* Bk.Baby Print.

Walker, Lane. Terror at Deadwood Lake. 2014. (Hometown Hunters Collection: Vol. 3). (ENG.). 137p. (YA). (gr. 7-13). pap. 9.99 *(978-1-58169-519-9(5),* Evergreen Pr.) Genesis Communications, Inc.

Walker, Melissa & Walker, Richard. A Place for Delta. 2010. (Illus.). 266p. (J). 16.95 *(978-0-9824784-0-0(2))* Whale Tale Pr.

Walker, Susan Eileen. I Know the Quigglebush Heroes. 2008. 53p. pap. 16.95 *(978-1-60672-587-0(4))* America Star Bks.

Wallace, Nancy Elizabeth. Apples, Apples, Apples, 0 vols. 2004. (ENG., Illus.). 32p. (J). (gr. -1-3). pap. 5.95 *(978-0-7614-5181-5(1),* 9780761451815, Amazon Children's Publishing) Amazon Publishing.

—Leaves! Leaves! Leaves!, 1 vol. 2003. (ENG., Illus.). 32p. (J). 16.95 *(978-0-7614-5140-2(4))* Marshall Cavendish Corp.

—Seeds! Seeds! Seeds!, 0 vols. Wallace, Nancy Elizabeth, illus. 2007. (ENG., Illus.). 40p. (J). (gr. -1-3). 7.99 *(978-0-7614-5366-6(0),* 9780761453666, Amazon Children's Publishing) Amazon Publishing.

—Shells! Shells! Shells!, 0 vols. 2013. (ENG.). 40p. (J). (gr. k-3). pap. 9.99 *(978-1-4778-1679-0(8),* 9781477816790, Amazon Children's Publishing) Amazon Publishing.

Wallen, Virginia. Boo Boo Bear. 2005. 17.00 *(978-0-8059-9886-3(1))* Dorrance Publishing Co., Inc.

Walluk, Wilbur, illus. The Alaskan Ten-Footed Bear & Other Legends. 2013. 44p. pap. 9.95 *(978-1-61646-201-7(9))* Coachwhip Pubns.

Wampol, Pam & Woodard, Heather. Oscar's Dreamzz: The Story of Santa's First Elf. 2013. 40p. pap. *(978-1-4602-0414-6(X))* FriesenPress.

Ward, Lindsay. Please Bring Balloons. 2013. (ENG., Illus.). 32p. (J). (gr. -1-k). 16.99 *(978-0-8037-3878-2(1),* Dial Bks) Penguin Young Readers Group.

Wargin, Kathy-jo & Bendall-Brunello, John, illus. Scare a Bear. 2010. (ENG.). 32p. (J). (gr. -1-3). 15.95 *(978-1-58536-430-5(4))* Sleeping Bear Pr.

Warnes, Tim, illus. Sweet Dreams, Little Bear. 2013. (ENG.). 18p. (gr. -1). bds. 8.95 *(978-1-58925-604-0(2))* Tiger Tales.

Warren, George A. Bob Chase after Grizzly Bears. 2005. (Illus.). pap. 24.95 *(978-1-885529-40-4(6))* Stevens Publishing.

Washakie, John. Yuse: The Bully & the Bear. Cox, Jon, illus. 2nd ed. 2004. 47p. (J). 14.95 *(978-0-9759806-0-6(2))* Painted Pony, Inc.

Waterhouse, Raymond & Lawrie, Gabrielle. Yoppi A Bear Story. 2007. 158p. pap. 19.50 *(978-1-84753-876-5(2))* Lulu Pr., Inc.

Watt, Fiona. That's Not My Polar Bear. 2009. (Touchy-Feely Board Bks). 10p. (J). bds. 8.99 *(978-0-7945-2551-4(2),* Usborne) EDC Publishing.

Watt, Fiona & Wells, R. That's Not My Bear. 2004. 10p. (J). 7.99 *(978-0-7945-0363-5(2))* EDC Publishing.

Watts, Frances. Kisses for Daddy. Legge, David, illus. 2008. 24p. (J). bds. *(978-1-921272-56-1(2))* Little Hare Bks. AUS. Dist: HarperCollins Pubs. Australia.

—Kisses for Daddy. Legge, David, illus. 2010. (ENG.). 26p. (J). (gr. -1-k). bds. 7.99 *(978-1-4169-8721-5(5),* Little Simon) Little Simon.

We Meet Again. 2014. (Timmy Failure Ser.: No. 3). (ENG., Illus.). 272p. (J). (gr. 3-7). 14.99 *(978-0-7636-7375-8(7))* Candlewick Pr.

Weaver, Joyce A. Mckissick. The Adventures of Mopey Bear & His Two Brothers, 1 vol. 2009. 48p. pap. 16.95 *(978-1-60813-775-6(9))* America Star Bks.

—Chubby Bear & His Two Brothers. 2008. 28p. per. 24.95 *(978-1-4241-9047-8(9))* America Star Bks.

Webb-King, Marian. Sweet Dreams Bear Cub: My Life As a Cricket. 2011. 20p. 11.49 *(978-1-4520-0979-7(1))* AuthorHouse.

Weck, Peter. Lima Bear's Halloween. DiSalvo, Len, illus. 2012. (Lima Bear Stories Ser.). 40p. (J). 15.95 *(978-1-933872-16-2(0))* Lima Bear Pr LLC, The.

Weiss, Bobbi & Weiss, David. Twisted Tales II, Vol. 7. 2009. (ENG., Illus.). 24p. (J). (gr. 1-17). pap. 3.99 *(978-1-58476-815-9(0))* Innovative Kids.

Weiss, Nicki. Where Does the Brown Bear Go. Date not set. (Illus.). 32p. (J). 5.95 *(978-0-06-051534-8(1))* HarperCollins Pubs.

Wellesley, Rosie. Moonlight Bear. Wellesley, Rosie, illus. 2015. (ENG., Illus.). 32p. (J). (gr. -1-3). pap. 9.99 *(978-1-84365-292-2(7),* Pavilion) Pavilion Bks. GBR. Dist: Independent Pubs. Group.

Wells, Rosemary. Eduardo: Cumpleanos en la Piscina. 2003. Orig. Title: Edward's Big Splash. (SPA., Illus.). 22p. (J). (gr. -1-k). 12.95 *(978-1-56014-664-3(8))* Santillana USA Publishing Co., Inc.

—Eduardo: El Primer Dia de Colegio. 2003. Orig. Title: Edward's First Day at School. (SPA., Illus.). 22p. (J). (gr. -1-k). 12.95 *(978-1-56014-620-9(6))* Santillana USA Publishing Co., Inc.

Wells-Sanders, Glenora. Trinny Bear & Dallas. Wells, Quierra LaQuelle, illus. 2012. 24p. pap. 11.50 *(978-1-61897-763-2(6),* Strategic Bk. Publishing) Strategic Book Publishing & Rights Agency (SBPRA).

Welty, Lauresta. The Best Place in the World, 1 vol. 2010. 40p. 24.95 *(978-1-4512-9690-7(8))* PublishAmerica, Inc.

Wendling, Peter. Matthew Leads the Animal Parade, 1 vol. 2010. 30p. 24.95 *(978-1-4512-1836-7(2))* PublishAmerica, Inc.

Went, Jannetje Van. The Wishing Bear: The Impossible Wish. 2012. 24p. pap. 15.99 *(978-1-4771-1038-6(0))* Xlibris Corp.

We're Going on a Bear Hunt: Lap Edition. 2014. (ENG., Illus.). 36p. (J). (gr. -1-k). bds. 12.99 *(978-1-4814-1924-6(2),* Little Simon) Little Simon.

Weston Woods Staff, creator. The Biggest Bear. 2011. 29.95 *(978-0-439-74008-1(8));* 38.75 *(978-0-439-78362-0(3))* Weston Woods Studios, Inc.

—Children Make Terrible Pets. 2011. 29.95 *(978-0-545-40221-7(2))* Weston Woods Studios, Inc.

—Goldilocks & the Three Bears. 2011. 29.95 *(978-0-439-73471-4(1));* 38.75 *(978-0-439-72682-5(4));* 18.95 *(978-0-439-72679-5(4))* Weston Woods Studios, Inc.

—Happy Birthday Moon. 2004. 29.95 *(978-1-55592-842-1(0));* (J). 38.75 *(978-1-55592-822-3(6));* (J). 18.95 *(978-1-55592-805-6(6))* Weston Woods Studios, Inc.

—Henry Hikes to Fitchburg. 2011. 38.75 *(978-0-439-90698-2(9));* 18.95 *(978-0-439-90696-8(2))* Weston Woods Studios, Inc.

—I Lost My Bear. 2004. 29.95 *(978-1-55592-704-2(1));* 18.95 *(978-1-55592-707-3(6))* Weston Woods Studios, Inc.

—Little Bear's Visit. 2011. 18.95 *(978-0-439-72741-9(3));* 29.95 *(978-0-439-73484-4(3));* 38.75 *(978-0-439-72743-3(X))* Weston Woods Studios, Inc.

Wheeler, Lisa. One Dark Night. Bates, Ivan, illus. 2006. (ENG.). 32p. (J). (gr. -1-3). reprint ed. pap. 6.99 *(978-0-15-205888-3(5))* Houghton Mifflin Harcourt Publishing Co.

—Ugly Pie. Solomon, Heather, illus. (ENG.). 32p. (J). (gr. -1-3). 2014. pap. 7.99 *(978-0-544-23961-6(X),* HMH Books For Young Readers) 2010. 16.99 *(978-0-15-216754-7(4))* Houghton Mifflin Harcourt Publishing Co.

White, Marsha. Bear's New Classes. White, Marsha, illus. (Illus.). 16p. (J). 10.95 *(978-1-58117-294-2(X),* Intervisual/Piggy Toes) Bendon, Inc.

White, Pam. Buddy Goes to the Beach. 2010. 20p. 12.50 *(978-1-4520-3065-4(0))* AuthorHouse.

Whited, Melissa F. The Bear Brothers' Big Adventure, 1 vol. 2009. 23p. pap. 24.95 *(978-1-60749-258-0(X))* America Star Bks.

Whitfield, Peter. No Presents Please. Bevington, Nancy, illus. 2005. (Zen Tails Ser.). (ENG.). 28p. (J). (gr. -1-3). 15.95 *(978-1-894965-23-1(X))* Simply Read Bks. CAN. Dist: Ingram Publisher Services.

Whitley-Kinzett, Sara. Grumpy Ted: The Teds Volume One. Ellams, Victoria, illus. 2009. 16p. pap. 10.65 *(978-1-4251-0051-3(1))* Trafford Publishing.

Whybrow, Ian. The Bedtime Bear. Scheffler, Axel, illus. 2016. (ENG.). 12p. (J). (gr. -1-2). pap. 9.99 *(978-1-5098-0695-9(4))* Pan Macmillan GBR. Dist: Independent Pubs. Group.

—Bedtime Bear. Scheffler, Axel, illus. 4th ed. 2004. (ENG.). 12p. (J). (gr. -1-k). pap. 13.99 *(978-1-4050-4993-1(6))* Pan Macmillan GBR. Dist: Independent Pubs. Group.

Widgen, Susan. A Caring Deed for Becky. Novak, Steven, illus. 2012. 36p. pap. 8.99 *(978-1-60820-579-0(7))* MLR Pr., LLC.

Wiley, Melissa. Fox & Crow Are Not Friends. Braun, Sebastien, illus. 2012. (Step into Reading Ser.). (ENG.). 48p. (J). (gr. k-3). pap. 3.99 *(978-0-375-86982-2(4),* Random Hse. Bks. for Young Readers) Random Hse. Children's Bks.

—Fox & Crow Are Not Friends. 2012. (Step into Reading Level 3 Ser.). lib. bdg. 13.55 *(978-0-606-26806-6(5),* Turtleback) Turtleback Bks.

Wilhite, Kenneth. Little Black Bear's Lunch. 2009. (J). spiral bd. 8.85 *(978-1-61584-370-1(1))* Independent Pub.

Willard, Nancy. A Starlit Snowfall. Pinkney, Jerry, illus. 2011. (ENG.). 32p. (J). (gr. -1-3). 6.99 *(978-0-316-18366-6(0))* Little Brown & Co.

Willey, Margaret. The 3 Bears & Goldilocks. Solomon, Heather M., illus. 2008. (ENG.). 32p. (J). (gr. -1-3). 17.99 *(978-1-4169-2494-4(9),* Atheneum Bks. for Young Readers) Simon & Schuster Children's Publishing.

William H. Sadlier Staff. Goldilocks & the Three Bears. 2005. (Emergent Library: Vol. 2). (gr. -1-1). 24.00 net. *(978-0-8215-8930-4(X))* Sadlier, William H. Inc.

Williams, Paul. How the Bat Got Its Wings & Young Bear's Lesson: Two Cherokee Stories. 2003. (Illus.). 47p. (J). per. 14.95 *(978-0-9630310-6-8(6))* Will Hall Bks.

Williams, Rozanne Lanczak. All about Real Bears. Christensen, David, illus. 2006. (Learn to Write Ser.). 8p. (J). (gr. k-2). pap. 3.49 *(978-1-59198-288-3(X),* 6182) Creative Teaching Pr., Inc.

—All about Real Bears. Maio, Barbara & Faulkner, Stacey, eds. Christensen, David, illus. 2006. (J). per. 6.99 *(978-1-59198-339-2(8))* Creative Teaching Pr., Inc.

—Postcards from Barney Bear. Maio, Barbara & Faulkner, Stacey, eds. Thelen, Mary, illus. 2006. (Learn to Write Ser.). 8p. (J). pap. 3.49 *(978-1-59198-287-6(1),* 6181) Creative Teaching Pr., Inc.

Willis, Jeanne. El Nino y los Osos de Pelucke. (SPA.). (J). 8.95 *(978-958-04-7344-2(7))* Norma S.A. COL. Dist: Distribuidora Norma, Inc.

Wilson, Henrike, illus. I Am So Bored! 2016. (ENG.). 32p. (J). (gr. -1-k). 16.99 *(978-1-5107-0676-7(3),* Sky Pony Pr.) Skyhorse Publishing Co., Inc.

Wilson, Karma. Bear Counts. Chapman, Jane, illus. 2015. (Bear Bks.). (ENG.). 32p. (J). (gr. -1-2). 16.99 *(978-1-4424-8092-6(0),* McElderry, Margaret K. Bks.) McElderry, Margaret K. Bks.

—Bear Feels Scared. Chapman, Jane, illus. 2011. (Bear Bks.). (ENG.). 34p. (J). (gr. -1 — 1). bds. 7.99 *(978-1-4424-2755-6(8),* Little Simon) Little Simon.

—Bear Feels Scared. Chapman, Jane, illus. 2008. (Bear Bks.). (ENG.). 40p. (J). (gr. -1-3). 17.99 *(978-0-689-85986-1(4),* McElderry, Margaret K. Bks.) McElderry, Margaret K. Bks.

—Bear Feels Sick. Chapman, Jane, illus. 2012. (Bear Bks.). (ENG.). 34p. (J). (gr. -1-2). bds. 7.99 *(978-1-4424-4093-7(7),* Little Simon) Little Simon.

—Bear Feels Sick. Chapman, Jane, illus. 2007. (Bear Bks.). (ENG.). 40p. (J). (gr. -1-3). 17.99 *(978-0-689-85985-4(6),* McElderry, Margaret K. Bks.) McElderry, Margaret K. Bks.

—Bear Says Thanks. Chapman, Jane, illus. 2012. (Bear Bks.). (ENG.). 40p. (J). (gr. -1-3). 17.99 *(978-1-4169-5856-7(8),* McElderry, Margaret K. Bks.) McElderry, Margaret K. Bks.

—Bear Sees Colors. Chapman, Jane, illus. 2014. (Bear Bks.). (ENG.). 32p. (J). (gr. -1-2). 16.99 *(978-1-4424-6536-7(0),* McElderry, Margaret K. Bks.) McElderry, Margaret K. Bks.

—Bear Snores On. Chapman, Jane, illus. 2005. (Bear Bks.). (ENG.). 34p. (J). (gr. -1-k). bds. 7.99 *(978-1-4169-0272-0(4),* Little Simon) Little Simon.

—Bear Stays up for Christmas. Chapman, Jane, illus. 2011. (Bear Bks.). (ENG.). 34p. (J). (gr. -1 — 1). bds. 7.99 *(978-1-4424-2790-7(6),* Little Simon) Little Simon.

—Bear Stays up for Christmas. Chapman, Jane, illus. (Bear Bks.). (ENG.). 40p. (J). (gr. -1-3). 2008. 9.99 *(978-1-4169-5896-3(7))* 2004. 17.99 *(978-0-689-85278-7(9))* McElderry, Margaret K. Bks. (McElderry, Margaret K. Bks.).

—Bear Wants More. Chapman, Jane, illus. 2008. (Bear Bks.). (ENG.). 34p. (J). (gr. -1-2). bds. 7.99 *(978-1-4169-4922-0(4),* Little Simon) Little Simon.

—Bear Wants More. Chapman, Jane, illus. 2003. (Bear Bks.). (ENG.). 40p. (J). (gr. -1-3). 17.99 *(978-0-689-84509-3(X),* McElderry, Margaret K. Bks.) McElderry, Margaret K. Bks.

—Bear's Loose Tooth. Chapman, Jane, illus. 2014. (Bear Bks.). (ENG.). 34p. (J). (gr. -1-k). bds. 7.99 *(978-1-4424-8936-3(7),* Little Simon) Little Simon.

—Bear's Loose Tooth. Chapman, Jane, illus. 2011. (Bear Bks.). (ENG.). 40p. (J). (gr. -1-3). 17.99 *(978-1-4169-5855-0(X),* McElderry, Margaret K. Bks.) McElderry, Margaret K. Bks.

—Bear's New Friend. Chapman, Jane, illus. 2009. (Bear Bks.). (ENG.). 34p. (J). (gr. -1-2). bds. 7.99 *(978-1-4169-5438-5(4),* Little Simon) Little Simon.

—Bear's New Friend. Chapman, Jane, illus. 2006. (Bear Bks.). (ENG.). 40p. (J). (gr. -1-3). 17.99 *(978-0-689-85984-7(8),* McElderry, Margaret K. Bks.) McElderry, Margaret K. Bks.

—Big Bear, Small Mouse. Chapman, Jane, illus. 2016. (Bear Bks.). (ENG.). 32p. (J). (gr. -1-2). 16.99 *(978-1-4814-5971-6(6),* McElderry, Margaret K. Bks.) McElderry, Margaret K. Bks.

—Mama, Why? Mendez, Simon, illus. 2011. (ENG.). 40p. (J). (gr. -1-2). 16.99 *(978-1-4169-4205-4(X),* McElderry, Margaret K. Bks.) McElderry, Margaret K. Bks.

Wilson, Liesl-Yvette. A Balloon & a Bear. 2009. 48p. pap. 20.90 *(978-0-9559752-4-0(7))* Tallulah & Bear GBR. Dist: Lulu Pr., Inc.

Wilson, W. Shane. Gavin the Gnome. 2010. 100p. pap. 11.99 *(978-0-557-50370-4(1))* Lulu Pr., Inc.

Winnie the Pooh. (Sing-Along Ser.). (J). 11.99 incl. audio *(978-1-55723-933-4(9))* Walt Disney Records.

Winnie the Pooh & a Day for Eeyore (Read-Along Ser.). (J). 7.99 incl. audio *(978-1-55723-176-5(1))* Walt Disney Records.

Winslow, Theresa. Katie the Bear & Her Adventure for Honey, 1 vol. 2009. 20p. pap. 24.95 *(978-1-60836-893-8(9))* America Star Bks.

Winter, Jeanette. Nanuk the Ice Bear. Winter, Jeanette, illus. 2016. (ENG., Illus.). 48p. (J). (gr. -1-3). 17.99 *(978-1-4814-4667-9(3),* Beach Lane Bks.) Beach Lane Bks.

Witkowski, Teri. Bitty Bear, Flower Girl. Ackley, Peggy Jo, illus. 2009. (J). *(978-1-59369-564-4(0),* American Girl) American Girl Publishing, Inc.

—Bitty Bear's Birthday Treats. Ackley, Peggy Jo, illus. 2008. (J). *(978-1-59369-384-8(2),* American Girl) American Girl Publishing, Inc.

—Bitty Bear's New Friend. Ackley, Peggy Jo, illus. 2005. (J). *(978-1-59369-021-2(5))* American Girl Publishing, Inc.

—Bitty Bear's Snowflake Dreams. Ackley, Peggy Jo, illus. 2006. (J). *(978-1-59369-166-0(1))* American Girl Publishing, Inc.

—Bitty Bear's Valentines. Ackley, Peggy Jo, illus. 2004. (J). *(978-1-58485-837-9(0))* American Girl Publishing, Inc.

—Bitty Bear's Walk in the Woods. Ackley, Peggy Jo, illus. 2006. (J). *(978-1-59369-156-1(4))* American Girl Publishing, Inc.

—Bitty Bunny's Bedtime. Ackley, Peggy Jo, illus. 2004. (J). *(978-1-58485-921-5(0))* American Girl Publishing, Inc.

—Happy Birthday, Bitty Bear! Ackley, Peggy Jo, illus. 2005. (J). *(978-1-58485-959-8(8))* American Girl Publishing, Inc.

—It's Spring, Bitty Bear! Ackley, Peggy Jo, illus. 2007. (J). *(978-1-59369-242-1(0))* American Girl Publishing, Inc.

Wittenbach, Jennie. Little Stories for Little Folks. 2011. 36p. pap. 21.99 *(978-1-4628-8818-4(6))* Xlibris Corp.

Wojtowycz, David, illus. What Will You Wear, Claude? 2004. 10p. (J). (gr. -1-3). reprint ed. 8.00 *(978-0-7567-8259-7(7))* DIANE Publishing Co.

Wolff, Ashley. Baby Bear Counts One. Wolff, Ashley, illus. 2013. (Baby Bear Ser.). (ENG., Illus.). 40p. (J). (gr. -1-1). 16.99 *(978-1-4424-4158-3(5),* Beach Lane Bks.) Beach Lane Bks.

—Baby Bear Sees Blue. Wolff, Ashley, illus. 2012. (Baby Bear Ser.). (ENG., Illus.). 40p. (J). (gr. -1-1). 17.99 *(978-1-4424-1306-1(9),* Beach Lane Bks.) Beach Lane Bks.

Woo, Melissa. Cooper's Big Bear Hug. Couch, Crista, illus. 2012. 32p. (J). 9.95 *(978-1-59530-352-3(9))* Hallmark Card, Inc.

Wood, Debra. William Warrior Bear. Blake, Joshua Aaron, illus. l.t. ed. 2005. 30p. (J). per. 12.95 *(978-1-59879-001-6(3))* Lifevest Publishing, Inc.

Wood, Gillian W. Bumbles Barely a Bear & His 4000 Mile Journey. 2011. 40p. (gr. -1). pap. 18.46 *(978-1-4567-4976-7(5))* AuthorHouse.

Wood, Gillian Wheeler. Bumble an Interesting Bear. 2004. 156p. 24.45 *(978-1-4140-4695-2(2))* AuthorHouse.

Wooden, Walter. Little Bear's Journey. 2011. 32p. pap. 21.99 *(978-1-4628-4440-1(5))* Xlibris Corp.

Wooten, Arthur. Wise Bear William: A New Beginning. Santora, Bud, illus. 2012. 44p. pap. 12.99 *(978-0-9850529-1-1(0))* Galaxias Productions.

Wright, Maureen. Sleep, Big Bear, Sleep!, 0 vols. Hillenbrand, Will, illus. 2009. (ENG.). 32p. (J). (gr. -1-3). 16.99 *(978-0-7614-5560-8(4),* 9780761455608, Amazon Children's Publishing) Amazon Publishing.

—Sneeze, Big Bear, Sneeze!, 0 vols. Hillenbrand, Will, illus. 2011. (ENG.). 32p. (J). (gr. -1-3). 16.99 *(978-0-7614-5959-0(6),* 9780761459590, Amazon Children's Publishing) Amazon Publishing.

Wu, Nicholas. The Bears' Story by Baldwin B. Bear, 1 vol. rev. ed. 2013. (Fiction Readers Ser.). (ENG., Illus.). 20p. (J). (gr. 1-1). pap. 15.96 *(978-1-4807-1147-1(0));* pap. 4.99 *(978-1-4333-5491-5(8))* Shell Educational Publishing.

Yarrow, Peter. Day Is Done. Sweet, Melissa, illus. 2014. (ENG.). 24p. (J). (— 1). bds. 7.95 *(978-1-4549-1147-0(6))* Sterling Publishing Co., Inc.

Yelchin, Eugene & Kuryla, Mary. The Next Door Bear. Yelchin, Eugene & Kuryla, Mary, illus. 2011. (ENG., Illus.). 40p. (J). (gr. -1-3). 16.99 *(978-0-06-125925-8(X))* HarperCollins Pubs.

Yeoman, John. The Bear's Water Picnic. Blake, Quentin, illus. 2011. (ENG.). 40p. (J). (gr. k-k). pap. 12.99 *(978-1-84939-004-0(5))* Andersen Pr. GBR. Dist: Independent Pubs. Group.

—The Bear's Winter House. Blake, Quentin, illus. 2012. (J). *(978-1-4351-4374-6(4))* Barnes & Noble, Inc.

—Bear's Winter House. Blake, Quentin, illus. 2010. (ENG.). 32p. (J). (gr. k-k). pap. 12.99 *(978-1-84270-916-0(X))* Andersen Pr. GBR. Dist: Independent Pubs. Group.

Yolen, Jane. Sister Bear: A Norse Tale, 0 vols. Linda, Graves & Graves, Linda, illus. 2011. (ENG.). 32p. (J). (gr. k-3). 17.99 *(978-0-7614-5958-3(8),* 9780761459583, Amazon Children's Publishing) Amazon Publishing.

Yoon, Salina. Bear's Big Day. 2017. (ENG., Illus.). 32p. (J). bds. 7.99 *(978-1-68119-436-3(8),* 9781681194363, Bloomsbury USA Childrens) Bloomsbury Publishing USA.

—Found. Yoon, Salina, illus. 2014. (ENG., Illus.). 40p. (J). (gr. -1-1). 14.99 *(978-0-8027-3559-1(2),* 9780802735591, Bloomsbury USA Childrens) Bloomsbury Publishing USA.

—Stormy Night. 2015. (ENG., Illus.). 40p. (J). (gr. -1-1). 14.99 *(978-0-8027-3780-9(3),* 9780802737809, Bloomsbury USA Childrens) Bloomsbury Publishing USA.

Young, Judy. The Missing Grizzly Cubs. 2016. (Wild World of Buck Bray Ser.). (ENG.). 240p. (J). (gr. 3-6). 16.99 *(978-1-58536-970-6(5),* 204107) Sleeping Bear Pr.

Zak, Faith. Naptime Adventures: Christmas Tree. 2012. 24p. pap. 24.95 *(978-1-4626-5279-2(4))* America Star Bks.

—Naptime Adventures: Train. 2012. 24p. 24.95 *(978-1-4626-5000-2(7))* America Star Bks.

Zapp, et al. Baby Bear's Read-Along Goldilocks & the Three Bears. (Illus.). *(978-2-7641-0516-0(9))* Tormont Pubns.

Zepf, Máire. Don't Go to School! Krüse, Tarsila, illus. 2017. (ENG.). 40p. (J). (gr. -1). 14.95 ***(978-1-4549-2359-6(8))*** Sterling Publishing Co., Inc.

Zolotow, Charlotte. Growing up Stories for 5-6 Year Olds. 114p. (J). (gr. -1-17). 19.99 *(978-0-7868-0519-8(6))* Disney Pr.

Zolty, H. Calli the Bear: the Story of a Little Bear Who Explores California & Helps Children Learn about the Golden State. 2006. 56p. pap. 19.98 *(978-1-4116-4889-0(7))* Lulu Pr., Inc.

—Calli the Bear: the Story of a Little Bear Who Teaches Children about the Power of Friendship. 2005. 36p. 16.19 *(978-1-4116-7135-5(X))* Lulu Pr., Inc.

Zschock, Martha Day. Hello, Rockies! 2014. (Hello! Ser.). (ENG., Illus.). 16p. (J). (gr. -1-k). bds. 9.95 *(978-1-938700-21-7(X),* 9781938700217, Commonwealth Editions) Applewood Bks.

BEARS—PICTORIAL WORKS

Hairston, Kennard. World's Best Recreational Activity Bears. 2003. (Illus.). 24p. (J). (gr. 2-4). spiral bd. 7.00 *(978-0-8059-4498-3(2))* Dorrance Publishing Co., Inc.

BEARS—POETRY

Bradley, Timothy J. Osito, Osito di Buenas Noches, 1 vol. rev. ed. 2010. (Early Childhood Themes Ser.). (SPA., Illus.). 16p. (J). (gr. -1-2). pap. 6.99 *(978-1-4333-1946-4(2))* Shell Educational Publishing.

—Osito, Osito, Di Buenas Noches: Teddy Bear, Teddy Bear, Say Good Night, 1 vol. rev. ed. 2010. (Early Childhood Themes Ser.). (SPA., Illus.). 16p. (J). (gr. -1-2). pap. 19.99 *(978-1-4333-1947-1(0))* Shell Educational Publishing.

Canetti, Yanitzia. A Lullaby for My Teddy Bear. 2010. 32p. (J). pap. 6.99 *(978-1-59835-259-7(8),* BrickHouse Education) Cambridge BrickHouse, Inc.

BEASTS

see Animals

BEATLES

Beatles. Date not set. 384p. (J). 5.98 *(978-1-4054-0716-8(6))* Parragon, Inc.

Burlingame, Jeff. John Lennon: "Imagine" 2010. (American Rebels Ser.). 160p. (YA). (gr. 7-12). 35.94 *(978-0-7660-3675-8(8))* Enslow Pubs., Inc.

Dakers, Diane. The Beatles: Leading the British Invasion. 2013. (ENG., Illus.). 112p. (J). *(978-0-7787-1035-6(1));* pap. *(978-0-7787-1045-5(9))* Crabtree Publishing Co.

Edgers, Geoff. Who Were the Beatles? Tageau, Jerry, illus. 2006. (Who Was... ? Ser.). 106p. (J). *(978-0-448-43907-5(7),* Grosset & Dunlap) Penguin Publishing Group.

—Who Were the Beatles? Tugeau, Jeremy, illus. 2006. (Who Was? Ser.). (ENG.). 112p. (J). (gr. 3-7). pap. 5.99 *(978-0-448-43906-8(9)*, Grosset & Dunlap) Penguin Young Readers Group.

Gallagher, James. The Beatles. 2008. (Pop Rock Ser.). (Illus.). 64p. (YA). (gr. 4-7). lib. bdg. 22.95 *(978-1-4222-0186-2(4))* Mason Crest.

Hajeski, Nancy J. The Beatles: Here, There & Everywhere. 2014. (ENG., Illus.). 320p. 34.95 *(978-1-62686-088-9(2)*, Thunder Bay Pr.) Readerlink Distribution Services, LLC.

Kallen, Stuart A. The Beatles. 2011. (Innovators Ser.). (ENG., Illus.). 48p. (gr. 4-8). lib. bdg. 34.60 *(978-0-7377-5868-9(6))* Cengage Gale.

Little Monster Records, et al. All Together Now. 2006. (Illus.). (J). bds. 13.98 incl. audio compact disk *(978-1-4243-1410-2(0))* Independent Publisher Services.

Manning, Mick & Granström, Brita. The Beatles. 2014. (ENG., Illus.). 48p. (J). (gr. 3-7). 18.99 *(978-1-84780-451-8(9)*, Frances Lincoln) Quarto Publishing Group UK GBR. Dist: Hachette Bk. Group.

Roberts, Jeremy. The Beatles. (Biography Ser.). (Illus.). 112p. (J). (gr. 6-12). 2005. lib. bdg. 27.93 *(978-0-8225-4998-7(0))* 2003. pap. 7.95 *(978-0-8225-5002-0(4))* Lerner Publishing Group.

Saddleback Educational Publishing Staff, ed. The Beatles, 1 vol. unabr. ed. 2008. (Graphic Biographies Ser.). (ENG., Illus.). 25p. (YA). (gr. 9-12). pap. 7.95 *(978-1-59905-216-8(4))* Saddleback Educational Publishing, Inc.

Sandler, Martin W. How the Beatles Changed the World. 2014. (ENG., Illus.). 176p. (J). (gr. 5-8). 20.99 *(978-0-8027-3565-2(7)*, 9780802735652, Bloomsbury USA Childrens) Bloomsbury Publishing USA.

Sierra i Fabra, Jordi. John Lennon - Imagina que esto fue Real. 2005. (SPA.). 168p. (YA). *(978-958-30-1702-5(7))* Panamericana Editorial.

Tougas, Joe. The Beatles: Defining Rock 'n' Roll. 2015. (Legends of Rock Ser.). (ENG.). 32p. (gr. 3-4). lib. bdg. 27.99 *(978-1-4914-1816-1(8))* Capstone Press of Coughlan Cos.

Venezia, Mike. The Beatles (Revised Edition) Venezia, Mike, illus. 2017. (Getting to Know the World's Greatest Composers Ser.). (ENG., Illus.). 40p. (J). pap. 7.95 *(978-0-531-22243-0(8)*, Children's Pr.) Scholastic Library Publishing.

—Beatles, the (Revised Edition) 2017. (Getting to Know the World's Greatest Composers Ser.). (ENG., Illus.). 40p. (J). lib. bdg. 29.00 *(978-0-531-22061-0(3)*, Children's Pr.) Scholastic Library Publishing.

Wentzel, Jim. The Beatles. (Rock & Roll Hall of Famers Ser.). 112p. (gr. 5-8). 2009. 63.90 *(978-1-60852-477-8(9)*, Rosen Reference) 2006. (Illus.). (YA). lib. bdg. 34.60 *(978-0-8239-3526-0(4))* Rosen Publishing Group, Inc., The.

Wimmer, Teresa. The Beatles' Sgt. Pepper's Lonely Hearts Club Band. 2008. (What in the World? Ser.). 22.95 *(978-1-58341-651-8(X)*, Creative Education) Creative Co., The.

BEAUTY, PERSONAL

see also Cosmetics; Costume; Hair

Andrus, Aubre. Botanical Beauty: 80 Essential Recipes for Natural Spa Products. 2017. (ENG., Illus.). 160p. (gr. 9-12). pap. 14.95 *(978-1-63079-075-2(3))* Switch Pr.

Beautiful Nail & Body Art. 2004. (How 2 Kits Ser.). (Illus.). 32p. (J). *(978-1-84229-932-6(8))* Top That! Publishing PLC.

Beery, Barbara. Spa Princess Cookbook, 1 vol. 2008. (ENG., Illus.). 64p. (J). (gr. 1). spiral bd. 14.99 *(978-1-4236-0502-7(0))* Gibbs Smith, Publisher.

Beker, Jeanne. The Big Night Out. Dion, Nathalie, illus. 2005. (ENG.). 80p. (J). (gr. 4-7). pap. 15.95 *(978-0-88776-719-7(2)*, Tundra Bks.) Tundra Bks. CAN. Dist: Penguin Random Hse. LLC.

Berne, Emma Carlson. Nail Care Tips & Tricks. Heschke, Elena, illus. 2015. (Style Secrets Ser.). (ENG.). 32p. (gr. 4-8). 26.65 *(978-1-4677-8655-3(1)*, Lerner Pubns.) Lerner Publishing Group.

Bliss, John. Preening, Painting, & Piercing: Body Art. 2010. (Culture in Action Ser.). (ENG.). 32p. (gr. 3-6). 30.65 *(978-1-4109-3924-1(3)*, NA-r) Heinemann-Raintree.

Body Art. 2004. (Formula Fun Ser.). (Illus.). 48p. (J). *(978-1-84229-585-4(3))*; (ENG., 32p. *(978-1-84229-983-8(2))* Top That! Publishing PLC.

Body Crayons. 2004. (Whizz Kits Ser.). (Illus.). 48p. (J). *(978-1-84229-942-5(5))* Top That! Publishing PLC.

Boehne, Jacob A. Two Long Ears, 1 vol. 2016. (ENG., Illus.). 24p. (J). bds. 9.99 *(978-0-7643-5039-9(0)*, 9780764350399) Schiffer Publishing, Ltd.

Bokram, Karen, ed. Head-to-Toe Guide to You. Thomas, Bill, illus. 2010. (ENG.). 128p. (J). (gr. 5-9). pap. 8.99 *(978-0-545-20236-7(1)*, Scholastic Paperbacks) Scholastic, Inc.

Boleman-Herring, Elizabeth. The First of Everso. 2005. (Illus.). (J). pap. *(978-0-9759042-0-6(5))* Literate Chigger Pr., Ink, Inc., The.

Boritzer, Etan. What Is Beautiful? Forrest, Nancy, illus. 2004. (gr. -1-5). 40p. 14.95 *(978-0-9637597-6-4(0))*; 32p. pap. *(978-0-9637597-7-1(9))* Lane, Veronica Bks.

Bourke, Kenna. So Cute! Beginning Book with Online Access. 2014. (ENG.). 24p. pap. 9.50 *(978-1-107-64649-0(9))* Cambridge Univ. Pr.

Bratz Fashion Funktivity Books. 2004. (J). 1.49 *(978-0-7666-1223-5(6)*, 99215); 1.49 *(978-0-7666-1222-8(8)*, 99215); 1.49 *(978-0-7666-1224-2(4)*, 99215) Modern Publishing.

Burningham, Sarah O'Leary. Girl to Girl: Honest Talk about Growing up & Your Changing Body. Arnold, Ali, illus. 2013. (ENG.). 136p. (J). (gr. 3-7). 12.99 *(978-1-4521-0242-9(2))* Chronicle Bks. LLC.

Carmindy. Bloom: A Girl's Guide to Growing up Gorgeous. 2014. (ENG., Illus.). 160p. (gr. k-12). pap. 20.00 *(978-0-399-16659-4(9)*, TarcherPerigee) Penguin Publishing Group.

Conrad, Lauren. Lauren Conrad Style. 2012. (ENG.). 240p. (YA). (gr. 8). pap. 12.99 *(978-0-06-198969-8(X))* HarperCollins Pubs.

Conrad, Lauren, et al. Beauty. 2012. (ENG., Illus.). 288p. (YA). (gr. 9). 21.99 *(978-0-06-212845-4(0))* HarperCollins Pubs.

Davies, Monika. Surprising Things We Do for Beauty. 2017. (Time for Kids Nonfiction Readers Ser.). lib. bdg. 22.10 ***(978-0-606-40274-3(8))*** Turtleback Bks.

Design your own Body Art. 2004. (How 2 Kits Ser.). (Illus.). 48p. (J). *(978-1-84229-926-5(3))* Top That! Publishing PLC.

DiPiazza, Francesca. Remaking the John: The Invention & Reinvention of the Toilet. 2014. (Illus.). 64p. (J). (gr. 6-12). lib. bdg. 34.60 *(978-1-4677-2645-0(1)*, Twenty-First Century Bks.) Lerner Publishing Group.

Donovan, Sandy. Stay Clear! What You Should Know about Skin Care. 2009. pap. 52.95 *(978-0-7613-4686-9(4))* Lerner Publishing Group.

—Stay Clear! What You Should Know about Skin Care. Desrocher, Jack, illus. 2008. (Health Zone Ser.). (ENG.). 64p. (gr. 4-7). lib. bdg. 30.60 *(978-0-8225-7550-4(7))* Lerner Publishing Group.

Dorling Kindersley Publishing Staff. Fashion. 2014. (ENG.). 96p. (J). (gr. 2-4). pap. 12.99 *(978-1-4654-1653-7(6)*, DK Children) Dorling Kindersley Publishing, Inc.

—The Fashion Book. 2014. (ENG.). 160p. (YA). (gr. 8-12). 15.99 *(978-1-4654-2284-2(6)*, DK Children) Dorling Kindersley Publishing, Inc.

Espejo, Roman. Culture of Beauty. 2009. (Opposing Viewpoints Ser.). (ENG., Illus.). 240p. (J). 29.45 *(978-0-7377-4509-2(0))*; pap. 42.95 *(978-0-7377-4508-5(8))* Cengage Gale.

Fabulous Hair & Groovy Nails. 2004. (How 2 Kits Ser.). (Illus.). 48p. (J). *(978-1-84229-958-6(1))* Top That! Publishing PLC.

Faithgirlz! and Girls' Life Magazine Editors. Best Hair Book Ever! Cute Cuts, Sweet Styles & Tons of Tress Tips, 1 vol. 2015. (Faithgirlz Ser.). (ENG., Illus.). 128p. (J). pap. 14.99 *(978-0-310-74622-5(1))* Zonderkidz.

Feltö, Raphaël. The Toilet. 2016. (Little Inventions Ser.). (ENG., Illus.). 32p. (J). (gr. 3-5). 9.95 *(978-1-77085-750-6(8)*, 9781770857506) Firefly Bks., Ltd.

Ferguson Publishing Staff, creator. Cosmetology. 4th rev. ed. 2008. (Careers in Focus Ser.). (Illus.). 185p. (gr. 6-12). 32.95 *(978-0-8160-7271-2(X)*, Ferguson Publishing Co.) Facts On File, Inc.

Friends & Trends. 2004. (Bratz). (J). 2.49 *(978-0-7666-1303-4(8)*, 49315) Modern Publishing.

Funky Body Crayons. 2004. (Fun Kits Ser.). (Illus.). 48p. (J). *(978-1-84229-860-2(7))* Top That! Publishing PLC.

Ganchy, Sally. A Career As a Cosmetologist. 2012. (Essential Careers Ser.). (ENG., Illus.). 80p. (YA). (gr. 7-12). lib. bdg. 33.25 *(978-1-4488-8240-3(0))* Rosen Publishing Group, Inc., The.

Gano, Debra. Beauty's Secret. Pitre, Dawn, illus. 2008. (Heartlight Girls Ser.). 54p. (J). 17.95 *(978-0-9787689-0-4(6))* Heartlight Girls.

Glassman, Bruce S. Fairness. 2008. (Illus.). 48p. (J). pap. 9.95 *(978-1-60108-505-4(2)*, Bearing Bks.); (YA). (gr. 3-6). lib. bdg. 29.25 *(978-1-60108-504-7(4))* Red Cygnet Pr.

Gordon, Stephen G. Expressing the Inner Wild: Tattoos, Piercings, Jewelry, & Other Body Art. 2014. (Illus.). 56p. (J). (gr. 6-12). lib. bdg. 33.26 *(978-1-4677-1467-9(4)*, Twenty-First Century Bks.) Lerner Publishing Group.

Grabis, Bettina, et al. Nail Decorating. 2004. (Illus.). 62p. pap. *(978-1-59412-033-6(1))* Mud Puddle, Inc.

Gresh, Dannah. It's Great to Be a Girl! A Guide to Your Changing Body. 2015. (Secret Keeper Girl(r) Ser.). (ENG., Illus.). 128p. (J). pap. 11.99 *(978-0-7369-6007-6(4))* Harvest Hse. Pubs.

Haab, Sherri. Unas Divertidas. 2005. (SPA., Illus.). 59p. (J). (gr. 4-7). 23.95 *(978-968-5528-12-2(8))* Klutz Latino MEX. Dist: Independent Pubs. Group.

Haberman, Lia. About Face: Beauty Tricks & Tips. 2005. (Illus.). 48p. (J). *(978-0-439-80297-0(0))* Scholastic, Inc.

Hair Designer. 2004. (Whizz Kits Ser.). (Illus.). 48p. (J). *(978-1-84229-941-8(7))*; pap. *(978-1-84229-584-7(5))* Top That! Publishing PLC.

Harris, Destiny. Beauty Secrets for Girls. 2004. (J). per. *(978-0-9754380-2-2(6)*, 100) Harris, Pleshette Communications Inc. Publishing.

Harris, Lisa Delmedico. The Official Princess Handbook: A Little Girl's Guide to Beauty, Poise, & Righteousness. 2010. (ENG.). 96p. (J). pap. 9.99 *(978-1-60683-025-3(2))* Harrison House Pubs.

Harrison, Emma. From Head to Toe: The Girls' Life Guide to Taking Care of You. Montagna, Frank, illus. 2004. 124p. (J). *(978-0-439-44983-0(9))* Scholastic, Inc.

Harrison, Paul. Ancient Roman Clothes. 2010. (Ancient Communities: Roman Life Ser.). 32p. (J). (ENG.). pap. 10.60 *(978-1-61532-308-1(2))*; (Illus.). (gr. 3-6). lib. bdg. 26.50 *(978-1-61532-304-3(X))* Rosen Publishing Group, Inc., The. (PowerKids Pr.).

Harvey, Joanna & Crabtree, Marc. Meet My Neighbor, the Hair Stylist. 2010. (ENG., Illus.). 24p. (J). pap. *(978-0-7787-4584-6(8))*; lib. bdg. *(978-0-7787-4574-7(0))* Crabtree Publishing Co.

Heos, Bridget. A Career as a Hairstylist. 2010. (Essential Careers Ser.). (ENG.). 80p. (YA). lib. bdg. 33.25 *(978-1-4358-9474-7(X))* Rosen Publishing Group, Inc., The.

—Getting a Job in Hair Care & Makeup. 2013. 80p. (YA). (gr. 9-12). 33.25 *(978-1-4488-9611-0(8))* Rosen Publishing Group, Inc., The.

Higgins, Nadia. Brilliant Beauty Inventions. 2013. (Awesome Inventions You Use Every Day Ser.). (ENG., Illus.). 32p. (gr. 3-6). lib. bdg. 26.60 *(978-1-4677-1089-3(X)*, Lerner Pubns.) Lerner Publishing Group.

Horstschaefer, Felicitas. Paper Style: Hairdos. 2014. (ENG., Illus.). 15p. (J). (gr. 3-7). 16.99 *(978-1-4521-2031-7(5))* Chronicle Bks. LLC.

Houghton, Gillian. Creating a Budget. 2009. (Invest Kids Ser.). 24p. (gr. 2-3). 42.50 *(978-1-61513-614-8(2)*, PowerKids Pr.) Rosen Publishing Group, Inc., The.

Hurley, Jo. Looking Good! How to Get Stylin' with Your Friends. Morley, Taia, illus. 2007. 64p. (J). *(978-0-439-02013-8(1))* Scholastic, Inc.

Kauchak, Therese. Real Beauty: 101 Ways to Feel Great about You. Yoshizumi, Carol, illus. 2008. (American Girl Library). (ENG.). 120p. (J). pap. 9.95 *(978-1-58485-908-6(3))* American Girl Publishing, Inc.

Kenney, Karen Latchana. Skin Care & Makeup Tips & Tricks. Heschke, Elena, illus. 2015. (ENG.). 32p. (gr. 4-8). (J). lib. bdg. 26.65 *(978-1-4677-5219-0(3))*; 26.65 *(978-1-4677-8656-0(X))* Lerner Publishing Group. (Lerner Pubns.).

Kiesbye, Stefan. Body Piercing & Tattoos. 2008. (Social Issues Firsthand Ser.). (ENG., Illus.). 97p. (YA). (gr. 10-12). lib. bdg. 33.75 *(978-0-7377-4249-7(6)*, LML02109-243161, Greenhaven Pr., Inc.) Cengage Gale.

Klutz Editors. Nail Charms. 2016. (ENG.). 76p. (J). (gr. 3-7). 21.99 *(978-1-338-03753-1(6))* Klutz.

Laughlin, Kara L. Hip Hair Accessories for the Crafty Fashionista, 1 vol. 2011. (Fashion Craft Studio Ser.). (ENG.). 32p. (gr. 3-4). lib. bdg. 27.99 *(978-1-4296-6551-3(3)*, Snap Bks.) Capstone Press of Coughlan Cos.

Levin, Judith. Tattoos & Indigenous Peoples. 2008. (Tattooing Ser.). (Illus.). 64p. (YA). (gr. 9-12). lib. bdg. 31.95 *(978-1-4042-1828-4(9))* Rosen Publishing Group, Inc., The.

Libal, Autumn. Can I Change the Way I Look? A Teen's Guide to the Health Implications of Cosmetic Surgery, Makeovers, & Beyond. 2006. (Science of Health Ser.). (Illus.). 128p. (YA). 24.95 *(978-1-59084-843-2(8))* Mason Crest.

—Health Implications of Cosmetic Surgery, Makeovers, & Body Alterations. McDonnell, Mary Ann & Forman, Sara, eds. 2013. (Young Adult's Guide to the Science of Health Ser.: 15). 128p. (J). (gr. 7-18). 24.95 *(978-1-4222-2811-1(8))* Mason Crest.

Llewellyn, Claire. Your Hair. 2008. (Look after Yourself Ser.). (Illus.). 30p. (J). (gr. 1-4). lib. bdg. 28.50 *(978-1-59771-097-8(0))* Sea-To-Sea Pubns.

Macdonald, Fiona. You Wouldn't Want to Live Without Toilets! Antram, David, illus. 2014. (You Wouldn't Want to Live Without... Ser.). (ENG.). 32p. (J). lib. bdg. 29.00 *(978-0-531-21215-8(7)*, Watts, Franklin) Scholastic Library Publishing.

Marlowe, Christie. Cosmetologist. 2013. (Earning $50,000 - $100,000 with a High School Diploma or Less Ser.: 14). 64p. (J). (gr. 7-18). 22.95 *(978-1-4222-2891-3(6))* Mason Crest.

Martin, Mari. The Amazing Hairstyles Book. 2008. (Reading Rocks! Ser.). (ENG., Illus.). 32p. (J). (gr. 2-5). 28.50 *(978-1-60253-093-5(9)*, 200765) Child's World, Inc., The.

—The Amazing Hairstyles Book. 2016. 32p. (J). *(978-1-4896-4771-9(6))* Weigl Pubs., Inc.

Mattern, Joanne. Toilets. 2015. (Rookie Read-About(tm) Science: How Things Work Ser.). (ENG.). 32p. (J). lib. bdg. 25.00 *(978-0-531-21372-8(2)*, Children's Pr.) Scholastic Library Publishing.

Mooney, Carla. STEM Jobs in Fashion & Beauty. 2014. (ENG., Illus.). 48p. (gr. 4-8). 35.64 *(978-1-62717-700-9(0))* Rourke Educational Media.

Naik, Anita. Think Yourself Gorgeous: How to Feel Good - Inside & Out. 2012. (ENG., Illus.). 176p. (YA). (gr. 7). pap. 11.99 *(978-0-7499-5244-0(X)*, Piatkus Bks.) Little, Brown Book Group Ltd. GBR. Dist: Independent Pubs. Group.

Natterson, Cara. The Care & Keeping of You 2: The Body Book for Older Girls. Masse, Josée, illus. 2013. lib. bdg. 24.50 *(978-0-606-31576-0(4)*, Turtleback) Turtleback Bks.

Olsen, Mary-Kate & Olsen, Ashley. Mary-Kate & Ashley Yearbook. 2005. (Illus.). 96p. *(978-0-00-720729-9(8))* HarperCollins Pubs. Australia.

Park, Louise. Extreme Fashions. 2013. (Discovery Education: Sensational True Stories Ser.). (ENG., Illus.). 32p. (J). (gr. 3-6). pap. 10.00 *(978-1-4777-0107-2(9))*; lib. bdg. 25.25 *(978-1-4777-0061-7(7))* Rosen Publishing Group, Inc., The.

Petty, Kate. Hair. 2006. (World Show-And-Tell Ser.). (ENG., Illus.). 32p. (J). (gr. -1-1). 14.95 *(978-1-58728-531-8(2))* Cooper Square Publishing Llc.

Pinkney, Sandra L. & Pinkney, Myles C. I Am Latino: The Beauty in Me. 2007. (ENG., Illus.). 32p. (J). (gr. -1-3). 17.99 *(978-0-316-16009-4(1))* Little, Brown Bks. for Young Readers.

Platt, Richard. They Wore What?! The Weird History of Fashion & Beauty. 2007. (Weird History Ser.). (ENG.). 48p. (J). (gr. 3-6). 16.95 *(978-1-58728-582-0(7))*; pap. 9.95 *(978-1-58728-584-4(3))* Cooper Square Publishing Llc.

Priddy, Roger. Nail Art! 2015. (Make It! Ser.). (ENG.). 64p. (J). (gr. k-3). pap. 12.99 *(978-0-312-51846-2(3)*, 9780312518462, Priddy Bks.) St. Martin's Pr.

Rasmussen, Kitrisha. Dumb Bunny's Guide to Basic Hair Bows. 2012. (ENG.). 43p. (J). pap. 17.95 *(978-1-4327-9663-1(1))* Outskirts Pr., Inc.

Reybold, Laura. Todo lo que necesitas saber sobre Los peligros del tatuaje y el body piercing (Everything You Need to Know about the Dangers of Tattooing & Piercing) 2009. (Todo lo que necesitas (the Need to Know Library) Ser.). (SPA.). 64p. (gr. 6-6). 58.50 *(978-1-60854-412-7(5)*, Editorial Buenas Letras) Rosen Publishing Group, Inc., The.

Rowlands, Caroline. Do It Yourself Beauty Diary: With Pretty Stickers, Body Art Stencils, & a Skin Color Guide. 2015. (ENG.). 80p. (J). (gr. 4-8). pap. 12.99 *(978-1-4380-0616-1(0))* Barron's Educational Series, Inc.

Rue, Nancy N. The Skin You're In: Discovering True Beauty, 1 vol. 2010. (Faithgirlz Ser.). (ENG.). 144p. (J). (gr. 4-7). pap. 7.99 *(978-0-310-71999-1(2))* Zonderkidz.

Sawyer, Sarah. Body Piercing & Tattooing: The Hidden Dangers of Body Art. 2009. (Coping in a Changing World Ser.). 112p. (gr. 7-7). 63.90 *(978-1-61512-019-2(X))* Rosen Publishing Group, Inc., The.

—Frequently Asked Questions about Body Piercing & Tattooing. (FAQ: Teen Life Ser.). 64p. 2009. (gr. 5-6). 58.50 *(978-1-61512-567-8(1))* 2008. (Illus.). (YA). (gr. 7-12). lib. bdg. 31.95 *(978-1-4042-1812-3(2))* Rosen Publishing Group, Inc., The.

Schaefer, Valorie. The Care & Keeping of You Vol. 1: The Body Book for Younger Girls. 2013. lib. bdg. 24.50 *(978-0-606-31575-3(6)*, Turtleback) Turtleback Bks.

Shaw, Holly & Gluck, Leanne. Mirror, Mirror: Discover Your Inner Beauty, a Guide for Girls 14-17. 2007. (Uniquely Me! Ser.: Vol. 4). (Illus.). 84p. (J). pap. *(978-0-88441-706-4(9))* Girl Scouts of the USA.

Simons, Rae. At Home in Your Body: Care for the Shape You're In. 2010. (Kids & Obesity Ser.). 48p. (YA). lib. bdg. 19.95 *(978-1-4222-1715-3(9))* Mason Crest.

—Healthy Skin. McDonnell, Mary Ann & Forman, Sara, eds. 2013. (Young Adult's Guide to the Science of Health Ser.: 15). 128p. (J). (gr. 7-18). 24.95 *(978-1-4222-2812-8(6))* Mason Crest.

Snow, Todd. You Are Beautiful. Strong, Melodee, illus. 2007. (You Are Important Ser.). (ENG.). 24p. (J). (gr. -1-k). bds. 7.99 *(978-1-934277-10-2(X))* Maren Green Publishing, Inc.

Sommers, Annie Leah. Everything You Need to Know about Looking & Feeling Your Best: A Guide for Girls. 2005. (Need to Know Library). (Illus.). 64p. (YA). (gr. 7-12). lib. bdg. 31.95 *(978-0-8239-3079-1(3)*, NTGUWO) Rosen Publishing Group, Inc., The.

Sommers, Michael A. Everything You Need to Know about Looking & Feeling Your Best: A Guide for Guys. 2005. (Need to Know Library). (Illus.). 64p. (YA). (gr. 7-12). lib. bdg. 31.95 *(978-0-8239-3080-7(7)*, NTGUGU) Rosen Publishing Group, Inc., The.

Speregen, Debra Newberger. Girl Style: Get Your Glam On. 2008. (Illus.). 48p. (J). *(978-0-545-04095-2(7))* Scholastic, Inc.

Stardoll. Stardoll: Style Bible. 2014. (Stardoll Ser.). (ENG., Illus.). 304p. (J). (gr. 4-6). pap. 12.99 *(978-0-85751-101-0(7))* Transworld Publishers Ltd. GBR. Dist: Independent Pubs. Group.

Steele-Saccio, Eva. Nail Style Studio: Simple Steps to Painting 25 Stunning Designs. 2013. (ENG.). 60p. (J). (gr. 5). 24.99 *(978-0-545-56163-1(9))* Klutz.

Sutherland, Adam. Body Decoration. 2012. (On the Radar: Street Style Ser.). (ENG., Illus.). 32p. (gr. 4-8). lib. bdg. 26.60 *(978-0-7613-7769-6(7)*, Lerner Pubns.) Lerner Publishing Group.

Teague Meyer, Terry. Female Genital Cutting. 2015. (Confronting Violence Against Women Ser.). (ENG., Illus.). 80p. (J). (gr. 6-7). 32.95 *(978-1-4994-6050-6(3)*, Rosen Young Adult) Rosen Publishing Group, Inc., The.

Telgemeier, Raina. Smile. 2010. 21.00 *(978-1-60686-896-6(9))* Perfection Learning Corp.

—Smile. 2010. (ENG.). 224p. (J). (gr. 3-7). 24.99 *(978-0-545-13205-3(3))*; (Illus.). pap. 10.99 *(978-0-545-13206-0(1))* Scholastic, Inc. (Graphix).

—Smile. 2010. lib. bdg. 22.10 *(978-0-606-14082-9(4)*, Turtleback) Turtleback Bks.

Temporary Tattoos. 2004. (Whizz Kits Ser.). (Illus.). 48p. (J). *(978-1-84229-947-0(6))* Top That! Publishing PLC.

Top That Publishing Staff, ed. Fabulous Facials. 2004. (Cachet Ser.). (ENG., Illus.). 48p. (YA). *(978-1-84510-330-9(0))* Top That! Publishing PLC.

Toselli, Leigh. Pro Nail Care: Salon Secrets of the Professionals. 2009. (ENG., Illus.). 256p. spiral bd. 29.95 *(978-1-55407-478-5(9)*, 9781554074785) Firefly Bks., Ltd.

Tremlin, Samantha & Waite, Sarah. Pretty Hands & Sweet Feet: Paint Your Way Through a Colorful Variety of Crazy-Cute Nail Art Designs, Step by Step. 2016. (DIY Ser.). (ENG., Illus.). 128p. (J). (gr. 3-8). 34.65 *(978-1-942875-12-3(6)*, Walter Foster Jr) Quarto Publishing Group USA.

Turnbull, Stephanie. Beauty Blitz. 2016. (Sleepover Secrets Ser.). 24p. (gr. 2-6). 28.50 *(978-1-62588-376-6(5)*, Smart Apple Media) Black Rabbit Bks.

—Looking Good: Style Secrets for Girls. 2013. (Girl Talk Ser.). 32p. (gr. 4-7). 31.35 *(978-1-59920-948-7(9))* Black Rabbit Bks.

—Looking Good: Style Secrets for Girls. 2014. (Girl Talk Ser.). (ENG., Illus.). 32p. (J). (gr. 4-8). pap. 9.95 *(978-1-77092-205-1(9))* Saunders Bk. Co. CAN. Dist: RiverStream Publishing.

Vision, David & Vision, Mutiya. What Makes Me Beautiful? ¿Qué Es lo Que Me Hace Hermoso? 2013.Tr. of ¿Qué Es lo Que Me Hace Hermoso? (Illus.). 24p. (J). 17.00 *(978-0-9816254-1-6(X)*, Vision Works Publishing) Soul Vision Works Publishing.

Wadeson, Jacki. Brilliant Braids, Beads & Bows: 25 Fantastic Hairstyles That You Can Create Yourself! 2014. (ENG., Illus.). 64p. (J). (gr. 2-6). 9.99 *(978-1-84322-757-1(6)*, Armadillo) Anness Publishing GBR. Dist: National Bk. Network.

Weiss, S. I. Coping with the Beauty Myth: A Guide for Real Girls. 2009. (Coping Ser.). 192p. (gr. 7-12). 63.90 *(978-1-61512-014-7(9))* Rosen Publishing Group, Inc., The.

Weiss, Stefanie Iris. Coping with the Beauty Myth: A Guide for Real Girls. 2005. (Coping Ser.). (Illus.). 192p. (YA). (gr. 7-12). lib. bdg. 34.60 *(978-0-8239-3757-8(7))* Rosen Publishing Group, Inc., The.

BEAUTY CONTESTS

Roleff, Tamara L. Beauty Pageants. Greenhaven Press Editors, ed. 2014. (At Issue Ser.). (ENG.). 128p. (gr. 10-12). pap. 27.80 *(978-0-7377-6825-1(8))*; lib. bdg. 39.40 *(978-0-7377-6824-4(X))* Cengage Gale. (Greenhaven Pr., Inc.).

BEAUTY CONTESTS—FICTION

Adeleke, Abraham Ajibade. Beauty Contest in the Animal Kingdom. 2011. 40p. pap. 16.46 *(978-1-4269-5773-4(4))* Trafford Publishing.

Barry, Maureen. Miss Fairfield's Beauty Pageant. 2006. (J). pap. 20.00 net. *(978-1-60402-176-9(4))* Independent Pub.

Bradman, Tony. It Came from Outer Space. Wright, Carol, illus. 2004. 25p. (J). *(978-1-85269-393-0(2))*; *(978-1-85269-336-7(3))* Mantra Lingua.

Bray, Libba. Beauty Queens. (ENG.). 400p. (J). (gr. 7). 2012. pap. 10.99 *(978-0-439-89598-9(7)*, Scholastic Paperbacks) 2011. 18.99 *(978-0-439-89597-2(9)*, Scholastic Pr.) Scholastic, Inc.

Cherry, Alison. Red. 2014. (ENG.). 336p. (YA). (gr. 7). pap. 9.99 *(978-0-385-74294-8(0)*, Ember) Random Hse. Children's Bks.

Dockray, Tracy. My Life Story. Dockray, Tracy, illus. 2003. (Illus.). 40p. (J). lib. bdg. 15.95 *(978-1-58717-218-2(6)*, SeaStar Bks.) Chronicle Bks. LLC.

Eulberg, Elizabeth. Revenge of the Girl with the Great Personality. 2014. (ENG.). 272p. (J). (gr. 7). pap. 10.99 *(978-0-545-47700-0(X)*, Scholastic Paperbacks) Scholastic, Inc.

Gorgas, Paula Blais. Little Lost Leprechaun. 2007. (Illus.). 20p. (J). per. 11.99 *(978-0-9797574-5-7(2))* Dragonfly Publishing, Inc.

Juby, Susan. Miss Smithers. 2004. (Illus.). 336p. (J). 15.99 *(978-0-06-051546-1(5)*, HarperTeen) HarperCollins Pubs.

Levine, Gail Carson. Fairest. 2006. 326p. (J). (gr. 3-7). lib. bdg. 18.89 *(978-0-06-073409-1(4))* HarperCollins Pubs.

London, Kelli. Star Power. 2013. (Charly's Epic Fiascos Ser.). (ENG., Illus.). 224p. (YA). (gr. 9). pap. 9.95 *(978-0-7582-8699-4(6)*, K-Teen/Dafina) Kensington Publishing Corp.

Michael, Todd. Texas State Bird Pageant. Randall, Lee Brandt, illus. 2005. 32p. (J). (gr. -1-3). 16.95 (978-1-893062-75-7(9)) Quail Ridge Pr., Inc.

Murphy, Julie. Dumplin. (YA). (gr. 8). 2017. 400p. pap. 9.99 (978-0-06-232719-2(4)) 2015. (ENG.). 384p. 17.99 (978-0-06-232718-5(6)) HarperCollins Pubs.

—Dumplin. 2017. (YA). lib. bdg. 20.85 **(978-0-606-39647-9(0))** Turtleback Bks.

Peschke, Marci. Blueberry Queen, 1 vol. Mourning, Tuesday, illus. 2011. (Kylie Jean Ser.). (ENG.). 112p. (gr. 2-3). pap. 5.95 (978-1-4048-6615-7(9)); lib. bdg. 22.65 (978-1-4048-6756-7(2)) Picture Window Bks. (Kylie Jean).

Quinn, Stephanie. The Miss Medieval Beauty Pageant. 2008. (J). per. 6.99 (978-0-9773099-3-1(2)) Quinn Entertainment.

Ransom, Candice. Rebel Mckenzie. 2013. (ENG.). 288p. (J). (gr. 3-7). pap. 7.99 (978-1-4231-6388-6(5)) Hyperion Pr.

Sayres, Brianna Caplan. Tiara Saurus Rex. Boldt, Mike, illus. 2015. (ENG.). 32p. (J). (gr. -1-1). 16.99 (978-1-61963-263-9(2), 9781619632639, Bloomsbury USA Childrens) Bloomsbury Publishing USA.

Scott, Lisa Ann. School of Charm. 2014. (ENG.). 304p. (J). (gr. 3-7). 16.99 (978-0-06-220758-6(X), Tegen, Katherine Bks) HarperCollins Pubs.

Vision, David & Vision, Mutiya Sahar. What Makes Me Beautiful? Alcantara, Ignacio, illus. 2009. 24p. 16.00 (978-0-9659538-4-9(X)) Von Curtis Publishing.

Zuckerman, Lilla & Zuckerman, Nora. Beauty Queen Blowout. 2003. (ENG.). 240p. pap. 15.99 (978-0-7432-3846-5(X), Touchstone) Touchstone.

BEAUTY SHOPS

Harvey, Joanna & Crabtree, Marc. Meet My Neighbor, the Hair Stylist. 2010. (ENG., Illus.). 24p. (J). pap. (978-0-7787-4584-6(8)); lib. bdg. (978-0-7787-4574-7(0)) Crabtree Publishing Co.

BEAVERS

Arnold, Quinn M. Beavers. 2017. (J). **(978-1-60818-865-9(5)**, Creative Education) Creative Co., The.

—Seedlings: Beavers. 2017. (Seedlings Ser.). (ENG.). 24p. (J). (gr. -1-1). pap. 7.99 **(978-1-62832-480-8(5)**, Creative Paperbacks) Creative Co., The.

Berger, Melvin & Berger, Gilda. Beavers. 2010. (Illus.). 16p. (J). (978-0-545-24438-1(2)) Scholastic, Inc.

Borgert-Spaniol, Megan. American Beavers. 2015. (North American Animals Ser.). (ENG., Illus.). 24p. (J). (gr. k-3). lib. bdg. 25.95 (978-1-62617-256-2(0), Blastoff! Readers) Bellwether Media.

Buckingham, Suzanne. Meet the Beaver. 2009. (Scales & Tails Ser.). 24p. (gr. 2-3). 42.50 (978-1-60852-981-0(9)); (Illus.). (J). lib. bdg. 22.60 (978-1-4042-4502-0(2)) Rosen Publishing Group, Inc., The. (PowerKids Pr.).

Crewe, Sabrina. Beavers. 2015. (Canadian Symbols Ser.). (ENG.). 24p. (gr. k-1). 26.65 (978-1-4914-7091-6(7)) Capstone Press of Coughlan Cos.

de Nijs, Erika. A Beaver's Lodge. 2016. (Animal Builders Ser.). 24p. (J). pap. 8.22 (978-1-5026-2067-5(7)) Cavendish Square Publishing.

Donovan, Sandy. A Beaver in Its Lodge. 2003. (Where Do Animals Live? Ser.). (J). pap. (978-1-58417-183-6(9)); lib. bdg. (978-1-58417-182-9(0)) Lake Street Pubs.

Doudna, Kelly. It's a Baby Beaver!, 1 vol. 2008. (Baby Mammals Ser.). (ENG., Illus.). 24p. (J). (gr. k-3). lib. bdg. 24.21 (978-1-60453-022-3(7)) ABDO Publishing Co.

George, Lynn. Beavers: Dam Builders. 2010. (Animal Architects Ser.). (ENG.). 24p. (J). pap. 8.25 (978-1-4488-1357-5(3)); lib. bdg. 22.60 (978-1-4488-0698-0(4)) Rosen Publishing Group, Inc., The. (PowerKids Pr.).

Gibbons, Gail. Beavers. Gibbons, Gail, illus. 2014. (ENG., Illus.). 32p. (J). (gr. -1-3). 7.99 (978-0-8234-3184-7(3)) Holiday Hse., Inc.

—Beavers. 2013. (ENG.). 32p. (J). 17.95 (978-0-8234-2412-2(X)) Holiday Hse., Inc.

Gish, Melissa. Beavers. 2014. 46p. (978-1-60818-414-9(5), Creative Education) Creative Co., The.

—Living Wild: Beavers. 2015. (Living Wild Ser.). (ENG.). 48p. (J). (gr. 5-8). pap. 12.00 (978-1-62832-000-8(1), Creative Paperbacks) Creative Co., The.

Goddard, Jolyon. Beavers. 2008. (Nature's Children Ser.). (Illus.). 52p. (J). (978-0-7172-6248-9(0)) Grolier, Ltd.

Graubart, Norman D. Beavers in American History. 2014. (How Animals Shaped History Ser.). (Illus.). 24p. (J). (gr. k-5). pap. 8.25 (978-1-4777-6754-2(1), PowerKids Pr.) Rosen Publishing Group, Inc., The.

Green, Emily. Beavers. 2011. (Backyard Wildlife Ser.). (ENG., Illus.). 24p. (J). (gr. k-3). lib. bdg. 25.95 (978-1-60014-560-5(4), Blastoff! Readers) Bellwether Media.

Green, Emily K. Beavers. 2011. (Backyard Wildlife Ser.). (Illus.). 24p. (J). (gr. k-1). lib. bdg. 22.00 (978-0-531-20136-7(8), Children's Pr.) Scholastic Library Publishing.

Gurtler, Janet. Beaver. 2011. 24p. (YA). (gr. 2-4). (978-1-77071-662-9(9)); pap. (978-1-77071-668-1(8)) Weigl Educational Pubs. Ltd.

Holland, Mary. The Beavers' Busy Year, 1 vol. 2014. (SPA.). 32p. (J). (gr. 1-4). pap. 9.95 (978-1-62855-222-5(0), 9781628552225) Arbordale Publishing.

—The Beavers' Busy Year, 1 vol. Holland, Mary, photos by. 2014. (ENG., Illus.). 32p. (J). (gr. 1-4). pap. 9.95 (978-1-62855-213-3(1)) Arbordale Publishing.

Jacobs, Lee. Beaver. 2003. (Wild America Ser.). (Illus.). 24p. (J). 24.94 (978-1-56711-566-6(7), Blackbirch Pr., Inc.) Cengage Gale.

Johnson, Jinny. Beaver. 2014. (North American Mammals Ser.). (Illus.). 24p. (gr. 2-5). 28.50 (978-1-62588-031-4(6)) Black Rabbit Bks.

—Beaver. 2014. (North American Mammals Ser.). (ENG., Illus.). 24p. (J). (gr. -1-4). pap. 8.95 (978-1-77092-166-5(4)) Saunders Bk. Co. CAN. Dist: RiverStream Publishing.

Kalman, Bobbie. Les Castors. Briere, Marie-Josee, tr. from ENG. 2008. (Petit Monde Vivant Ser.). (FRE., Illus.). 32p. (J). pap. 9.95 (978-2-89579-181-2(3)) Bayard Canada Livres CAN. Dist: Crabtree Publishing Co.

—The Life Cycle of a Beaver. 2006. (Life Cycle Ser.). (ENG., Illus.). 32p. (J). (gr. -1-3). pap. (978-0-7787-0702-8(4)); lib. bdg. (978-0-7787-0628-1(1)) Crabtree Publishing Co.

Klepeis, Alicia Z. American Beavers. 2017. (Animals of North America (hardcover) Ser.). (ENG., Illus.). 32p. (J). (gr. 3-5). lib. bdg. 28.50 **(978-1-63517-028-3(1)**, Focus Readers) North Star Editions.

Mara, Wil. Beavers. 2007. (Animals Animals Ser.). (Illus.). 48p. (gr. 3-7). lib. bdg. 29.93 (978-0-7614-2524-3(1), Benchmark Bks.) Marshall Cavendish Corp.

Marie, Christian. Little Beavers. 2005. (Born to Be Wild Ser.). (Illus.). 24p. (gr. k-3). lib. bdg. 23.00 (978-0-8368-4734-5(2), Gareth Stevens Learning Library) Stevens, Gareth Publishing LLLP.

Mary Holland. The Beavers' Busy Year, 1 vol. 2014. (ENG., Illus.). 32p. (J). (gr. 1-4). 17.95 (978-1-62855-204-1(2)) Arbordale Publishing.

Meredith, Susan Markowitz. Bitsy the Beaver. 2011. (Early Connections Ser.). (J). (978-1-61672-574-7(5)) Benchmark Education Co.

Oldland, Nicholas. The Busy Beaver. Oldland, Nicholas, illus. 2011. (Life in the Wild Ser.). (ENG., Illus.). 32p. (J). (gr. -1-2). 16.95 (978-1-55453-749-5(5)) Kids Can Pr., Ltd. CAN. Dist: Hachette Bk. Group.

O'Sullivan, Elizabeth. Beavers. 2007. (Early Bird Nature Books). (Illus.). 48p. (J). (gr. 3-7). lib. bdg. 25.26 (978-0-8225-6465-2(3), Lerner Pubns.) Lerner Publishing Group.

Owen, Ruth. Beaver Kits. 2011. (Wild Baby Animals Ser.). 24p. (J). (gr. k-3). lib. bdg. 19.96 (978-1-61772-155-7(7)); lib. bdg., E-Book 39.93 (978-1-61772-239-4(1)) Bearport Publishing Co., Inc.

Polinsky, Paige V. Beaver: Master Builder. 2016. (ENG., Illus.). 24p. (J). (978-1-68078-146-5(4)) ABDO Publishing Co.

Raum, Elizabeth. Beavers Build Lodges. Romina Martí, illus. 2017. (Animal Builders Ser.). (ENG.). 24p. (J). (gr. 1-4). 20.95 **(978-1-68151-168-9(1)**, Amicus Illustrated) Amicus Publishing.

Reingold, Adam. The Beaver's Lodge: Building with Leftovers. 2009. (Spectacular Animal Towns Ser.). (Illus.). 32p. (J). (gr. 2-7). lib. bdg. 25.27 (978-1-59716-872-4(6)) Bearport Publishing Co., Inc.

Riggs, Kate. Amazing Animals: Beavers. 2015. (Amazing Animals Ser.). (ENG.). 24p. (J). (gr. 1-3). pap. 8.99 (978-1-62832-086-2(9), Creative Paperbacks) Creative Co., The.

—Beavers. 2015. (J). (978-1-60818-486-6(2), Creative Education) Creative Co., The.

Roza, Greg. Beavers. 2014. (Animals of Mass Destruction Ser.). 32p. (J). (gr. 2-5). 25.25 (978-1-4824-0796-9(5)) Stevens, Gareth Publishing LLLP.

Rudolph, Jessica. Beaver. 2016. (J). lib. bdg. (978-1-62724-822-8(6)) Bearport Publishing Co., Inc.

Schuh, Mari. Beavers. 2015. (J). lib. bdg. 25.65 (978-1-62031-173-8(9), Bullfrog Bks.) Jump! Inc.

Wilson, Emily. Inside Beaver Lodges. 2015. (Inside Animal Homes Ser.). (ENG.). 24p. (J). (gr. 2-3). pap. 8.25 (978-1-4994-0872-0(2), PowerKids Pr.) Rosen Publishing Group, Inc., The.

—Madrigueras de Castores (Inside Beaver Lodges) 2015. (Las Casas de Los Animales (Inside Animal Homes) Ser.). (ENG & SPA.). 24p. (J). (gr. 2-3). 23.60 (978-1-4994-0569-9(3), PowerKids Pr.) Rosen Publishing Group, Inc., The.

Wiseman, Blaine. Beavers. 2010. (Illus.). 24p. (J). (978-1-60596-879-7(X)); (J). (gr. 2-4). pap. 11.95 (978-1-60596-878-0(1)); (YA). (gr. 2-5). lib. bdg. 25.70 (978-1-60596-877-3(3)) Weigl Pubs., Inc.

World Book, Inc. Staff, contrib. by. Ben the Beaver. 2017. (J). **(978-0-7166-3520-8(8))** World Bk., Inc.

Wykes, Gerald. A Beaver Tale: The Castors of Conners Creek. 2016. (Great Lakes Books Ser.). (ENG., Illus.). 56p. (J). 18.99 (978-0-8143-4181-0(0), 3988) Wayne State Univ. Pr.

BEAVERS—FICTION

Altiero, Carl. Alvora & Vulture Mountain. 2011. 86p. pap. 19.95 (978-1-4512-8263-4(X)) America Star Bks.

Bailey, Arthur Scott. Sleepy-Time Tales: The Tale of Brownie B. 2006. (Illus.). pap. (978-1-4065-0447-7(5)) Dodo Pr.

Baley, Arthur. The Tale of Brownie Beaver. 2007. 128p. per. 16.95 (978-1-60466-001-2(5)) Capricorn Hse. Publishing.

Belaney, Archibald Stansfeld. Beavers: Pages from the Writings of Grey Owl. Reynolds, E. E., ed. 2011. (ENG.). 130p. pap. 21.99 (978-1-107-60028-7(6)) Cambridge Univ. Pr.

Bennett, Earl. The Legend of Bucky the Beaver. 2009. 44p. pap. 12.95 (978-1-4269-1669-4(8)) Trafford Publishing.

Bentley, Dawn. Busy Little Beaver. Stover, Beth, illus. 2003. (ENG.). 32p. (J). (gr. -1-1). pap. 3.95 (978-1-59249-011-0(5), S2029); 12.95 (978-1-59249-012-7(3), PS2079) Soundprints.

Bloxam, Frances. Beau Beaver Goes to Town. Sollers, Jim, illus. 2009. (ENG.). 32p. (J). (gr. -1-3). 16.95 (978-0-89272-792-6(6)) Down East Bks.

Boelts, Maribeth. Beaver & Badger. 2016. (Spring Forward Ser.). (J). (gr. 2). (978-1-4900-9422-9(9)) Benchmark Education Co.

Bowman, Andy. Bobby Beaver Learns a Lesson. Travis, Stephanie, illus. 26p. (J). (gr. k-5). pap. 6.95 (978-1-931650-10-6(1)); lib. bdg. 14.95 (978-1-931650-11-3(X)) Coastal Publishing Carolina, Inc.

Burgess, Thornton W. The Adventures of Paddy the Beaver. 2008. 108p. (gr. 4-7). 22.95 (978-1-60664-952-7(3)); per. 9.95 (978-1-60312-502-4(7)) Aegypan.

—The Adventures of Paddy the Beaver. (J). 18.95 (978-0-8488-0379-7(5)) Amereon Ltd.

—The Adventures of Paddy the Beaver. 2004. reprint ed. pap. 1.99 (978-1-4192-5156-6(2)); pap. 15.95 (978-1-4191-5156-9(8)) Kessinger Publishing, LLC.

—The Adventures of Paddy the Beaver. 2011. 108p. 23.95 (978-1-4638-9557-0(7)) Rodgers, Alan Bks.

Calvani, Mayra. Humberto, the Bookworm Hamster. Grady, Kit, illus. 2009. 20p. pap. 10.95 (978-1-935137-92-4(1)) Guardian Angel Publishing, Inc.

Carlson, Nancy. Take Time to Relax! Carlson, Nancy, illus. 2012. (Nancy Carlson Picture Bks). (Illus.). 32p. (J). (gr. k-2). (ENG.). 9.95 (978-0-7613-8949-1(0)); 56.72 (978-0-7613-9304-7(8)) Lerner Publishing Group. (Carolrhoda Bks.).

Cole, Charmaine W. Barky, a Very Special Beaver. 2012. 28p. (-18). pap. 24.95 (978-1-4626-9528-7(0)) America Star Bks.

Dalrymple, Marilyn. Bartholomew's Buttons. 2006. 18p. (J). 9.73 (978-1-4116-9200-8(4)) Lulu Pr., Inc.

Diehl, Jean Heilprin. Three Little Beavers, 1 vol. Morrison, Cathy, illus. 2012. (ENG.). 32p. (J). (gr. -1-3). 17.95 (978-1-60718-524-6(5)); pap. 9.95 (978-1-60718-533-8(4)) Arbordale Publishing.

Dobrina, Elena. The Beaver Kid's Adventures. 2007. (Illus.). 120p. (J). pap. 88.00 (978-0-8059-7451-5(2)) Dorrance Publishing Co., Inc.

Eaton, Maxwell, III. Birds vs. Bunnies. 2013. (Flying Beaver Brothers Ser.). (ENG., Illus.). 96p. (J). (gr. 1-4). pap. 7.99 (978-0-449-81022-4(4), Knopf Bks. for Young Readers) Random Hse. Children's Bks.

—Birds vs. Bunnies. 2013. (Flying Beaver Brothers Ser.: 4). lib. bdg. 18.40 (978-0-606-32234-8(5), Turtleback) Turtleback Bks.

—The Flying Beaver Brothers & the Crazy Critter Race. 2015. (Flying Beaver Brothers Ser.). (ENG., Illus.). 96p. (J). (gr. 1-4). pap. 7.99 (978-0-385-75469-9(8), Knopf Bks. for Young Readers) Random Hse. Children's Bks.

—The Flying Beaver Brothers & the Evil Penguin Plan. 2012. (Flying Beaver Brothers Ser.). (ENG.). 96p. (J). (gr. 1-4). pap. 7.99 (978-0-375-86447-6(4), Knopf Bks. for Young Readers) Random Hse. Children's Bks.

—The Flying Beaver Brothers & the Evil Penguin Plan. 2012. (Flying Beaver Brothers Ser.: 1). lib. bdg. 17.20 (978-0-606-23869-4(7), Turtleback) Turtleback Bks.

—The Flying Beaver Brothers & the Fishy Business. 2012. (Flying Beaver Brothers Ser.: 2). lib. bdg. 18.40 (978-0-606-23870-0(0), Turtleback) Turtleback Bks.

—The Flying Beaver Brothers & the Hot Air Baboons. 2014. (Flying Beaver Brothers Ser.). (ENG., Illus.). 96p. (J). (gr. 1-4). pap. 6.99 (978-0-385-75466-8(3), Knopf Bks. for Young Readers) Random Hse. Children's Bks.

—The Flying Beaver Brothers & the Mud-Slinging Moles. 2013. (Flying Beaver Brothers Ser.). (ENG., Illus.). 96p. (J). (gr. 1-4). pap. 7.99 (978-0-449-81019-4(4), Knopf Bks. for Young Readers) Random Hse. Children's Bks.

—The Flying Beaver Brothers & the Mud-Slinging Moles. 2013. (Flying Beaver Brothers Ser.: 3). lib. bdg. 17.20 (978-0-606-32233-1(7), Turtleback) Turtleback Bks.

Folmsbee, Judi. Bubba, the Busy Beaver. Benton, Marilyn, illus. 2013. (ENG.). 48p. (J). 20.00 (978-1-886068-68-1(2)) Fruitbearer Publishing, LLC.

Heim, Barbara. The Hudson Beavers & the New Neighbourhood. 2012. (ENG.). 42p. (J). pap. 11.95 (978-1-938586-36-1(0)) Writer's Cramp, Inc.

—The Hudson Beavers Build a Lodge. 2013. (ENG.). 44p. (J). 13.95 (978-1-938586-45-3(X)) Writer's Cramp, Inc.

Hoban, Russell. Charlie the Tramp. Hoban, Lillian, illus. 2016. (ENG.). 48p. (J). 16.00 (978-0-87486-780-0(0)) Plough Publishing Hse.

Holloway, Jamie. Beaver Works On. 2015. (Rosen REAL Readers: STEM & STEAM Collection). (ENG.). 8p. pap. 5.46 (978-1-4994-9489-1(0), Rosen Classroom) Rosen Publishing Group, Inc., The.

Job, et al. Yakari & the Beavers. 2007. (Yakari Ser.: 3). (ENG., Illus.). 48p. (J). (gr. 4-7). per. 11.95 (978-1-905460-09-0(0)) CineBook GBR. Dist: National Bk. Network.

Johnson, Amy Crane. Mason Moves Away. Mommaerts, Robb, illus. 2009. (ENG.). 32p. (J). (gr. 4-7). 16.95 (978-1-934960-56-1(X), Raven Tree Pr.,Csi) Continental Sales, Inc.

—Mason Moves Away/Mason se Muda: A Solomon Raven Story: un cuento del cuervo Salomon, 4 vols. de la Vega, Eida, tr. Mommaerts, Robb, illus. 2004. (Solomon Raven Ser.: 4).Tr. of Mason se Muda. (SPA & ENG.). 32p. (J). (gr. -1-3). 16.95 (978-0-9720192-3-1(5), 626999, Raven Tree Pr.,Csi) Continental Sales, Inc.

Jordan, Christopher. The Little Beaver. Boey, Stephanie, illus. 2008. (ENG.). 24p. (J). (gr. k-3). (978-1-55168-249-5(4)) Magma.

Kim, YunYeong. Brown Bear's Dream. Kim, KyeMahn, illus. rev. ed. 2014. (MySELF Bookshelf Ser.). (ENG.). 32p. (J). (gr. k-2). pap. 11.94 (978-1-60357-655-0(X)); lib. bdg. 25.27 (978-1-59953-646-0(3)) Norwood Hse. Pr.

Kline, Trish & Donev, Mary. Coming Home: KA Reader 8. 2007. (Illus.). 32p. (J). per. 20.00 (978-1-934307-01-4(7)) Ghost Hunter Productions.

Klinting, Lars. Beaver the Tailor: A How-to Picture Book. Klinting, Lars, illus. 2004. Orig. Title: Castor Syr.. (Illus.). 32p. (J). (gr. k-3). reprint ed. 17.00 (978-0-7567-7213-0(3)) DIANE Publishing Co.

Lee, WonKyeong. Green River. Yang, HyeWon, illus. 2014. (MySELF Bookshelf Ser.). (ENG.). 32p. (J). (gr. k-2). pap. 11.94 (978-1-60357-695-6(9)); lib. bdg. 25.27 (978-1-59953-660-6(9)) Norwood Hse. Pr.

Legrand, H J, III. Paddle Tail's First Winter Adventure. Fair, Patricia Anne, illus. 2006. 64p. (J). per. 7.95 (978-1-59466-082-5(4), Growing Years) Port Town Publishing.

Lemon, Keith. The Beaver & the Elephant. 2016. (Anholt Family Favourites Ser.). (ENG.). 96p. (J). (gr. -1-k). 12.99 (978-1-4440-1300-9(9)) Orion Publishing Group, Ltd. GBR. Dist: Hachette Bk. Group.

Little Airplane Productions & Fogarty, Alexandria, illus. Baby Beaver Rescue. 2009. (Wonder Pets! Ser.). (ENG.). 24p. (J). (gr. -1-2). pap. 3.99 (978-1-4169-8499-3(2), Simon Spotlight/Nickelodeon) Simon Spotlight/Nickelodeon.

Long, Heather & Long, Ethan. Max & Milo Go to Sleep! Long, Ethan, illus. 2013. (ENG., Illus.). 32p. (J). (gr. -1-3). 14.99 (978-1-4424-5143-8(2), Aladdin) Simon & Schuster Children's Publishing.

—Max & Milo the Mixed-Up Message. Long, Ethan, illus. 2013. (ENG., Illus.). 32p. (J). (gr. -1-3). 14.99 (978-1-4424-5140-7(8), Simon & Schuster/Paula Wiseman Bks.) Simon & Schuster/Paula Wiseman Bks.

Markle, Sandra. Build, Beaver, Build! Life at the Longest Beaver Dam. Hocking, Deborah, illus. 2016. (ENG.). 32p. (gr. k-3). (J). 26.65 (978-1-4677-4900-8(1)); 39.99 (978-1-4677-9725-2(1)) Lerner Publishing Group. (Millbrook Pr.).

Markowitz, Susan Meredith. Bitsy the Beaver & Bitsy el Castor: 6 English, 6 Spanish Adaptations. 2011. (ENG & SPA.). (J). 75.00 net. (978-1-4108-5646-3(1)) Benchmark Education Co.

Marquez, Athena. Leave It to Beaver's. 2013. 28p. pap. 24.95 (978-1-63000-638-9(6)) America Star Bks.

Meredith-Markowitz, Susan. Bitsy the Beaver: Set Of 6. 2011. (Early Connections Ser.). (J). pap. 37.00 net. (978-1-4108-1364-0(9)) Benchmark Education Co.

Nitto, Tomio. The Red Rock: A Graphic Fable, 1 vol. 2006. (ENG., Illus.). 32p. (J). (gr. -1-4). 15.95 (978-0-88899-669-5(1)) Groundwood Bks. CAN. Dist: Publishers Group West (PGW).

O'Mara, Robert J. Friends Are Special, 1 vol. 2009. 26p. pap. 24.95 (978-1-60749-087-6(0)) America Star Bks.

Opal, Paola. Bitsy. 2012. (Simply Small Ser.). (ENG., Illus.). 76p. (J). (gr. k — 1). bds. 7.95 (978-1-897476-65-9(5)) Simply Read Bks. CAN. Dist: Ingram Publisher Services.

Owl, Grey. The Adventures of Sajo & Her Beaver People. 2011. 164p. (978-1-84902-465-5(0)) Benediction Classics.

Parasciuc, Natalia. Beaverlini & Rodney Are Having Fun! 2011. 28p. pap. 12.99 (978-0-557-84882-9(2)) Lulu Pr., Inc.

Plourde, Lynn. Only Cows Allowed!, 1 vol. Sollers, Jim & Reed, Rebecca Harrison, illus. 2011. (ENG.). 32p. (gr. -1-3). 16.95 (978-0-89272-790-2(X)) Down East Bks.

Reasoner, Charles. Number Munch! 2009. (Bite Bks.). (Illus.). (J). bds. 7.99 (978-1-934650-14-1(5)) Just For Kids Pr., LLC.

Sargent, Dave & Sargent, Pat. Billy Beaver: A New Beginning, 15 vols., Vol. 2. Huff, Jeane, illus. 2nd rev. ed. 2003. (Animal Pride Ser.: 2). 42p. (J). pap. 6.95 (978-1-56763-762-5(0)); lib. bdg. 20.95 (978-1-56763-761-8(2)) Ozark Publishing.

Simpson, Caroll. The First Beaver, 1 vol. rev. ed. 2009. (ENG., Illus.). 32p. (J). (978-1-894974-50-9(6)) Heritage Hse.

—The First Beaver, 1 vol. Simpson, Caroll, illus. 2015. (Coastal Spirit Tales Ser.). (ENG., Illus.). 32p. (J). (gr. k-3). pap. 12.95 **(978-1-77203-062-4(7))** Heritage Hse. CAN. Dist: Orca Bk. Pubs. USA.

Stokes, Brenda. Bella's Blessings. DesRosiers, Trisha, illus. 2012. (ENG.). 50p. (J). (gr. -1-3). 17.95 (978-1-897476-61-1(2)) Simply Read Bks. CAN. Dist: Ingram Publisher Services.

Walters, Eric. Saving Sammy, 1 vol. Meissner, Amy, illus. 2014. (Orca Echoes Ser.). (ENG.). 64p. (J). (gr. 2-3). pap. 6.95 (978-1-4598-0499-9(6)) Orca Bk. Pubs. USA.

Weinberg, Steven. Fred & the Lumberjack. Weinberg, Steven, illus. 2017. (ENG., Illus.). 40p. (J). (gr. -1-3). 17.99 **(978-1-4814-2983-2(3)**, McElderry, Margaret K. Bks.) McElderry, Margaret K. Bks.

Williams, Chase. The Tale of the Beaver. 2012. 36p. pap. 21.99 (978-1-4691-7984-1(9)) Xlibris Corp.

Wingart, Ramona A. Where Is Brother Beaver?, 1 vol. 2010. 30p. 24.95 (978-1-4489-4773-7(1)) PublishAmerica, Inc.

Wong, Gabriel, illus. Patches the Beaver: Welcome to Harmony Woods. 2008. 36p. (978-0-9783398-0-7(0)) Gauthier, Shane.

BECKWOURTH, JAMES PIERSON, 1798-1867

Demund, Tom. From Slave to Superstar of the Wild West: The Awesome Story of Jim Beckwourth. 2007. (Illus.). 154p. (J). 18.95 (978-0-9786904-0-3(0)) Legends of the West Publishing Co.

Manheimer, Ann S. James Beckwourth: Legendary Mountain Man. 2005. (Trailblazer Biographies Ser.). (ENG., Illus.). 112p. (gr. 5-9). lib. bdg. 31.93 (978-1-57505-892-4(8), Twenty-First Century Bks.) Lerner Publishing Group.

Whiting, Jim. Jim Beckwourth: The Man Who Opened the West. 2007. (Illus.). 144p. (YA). (gr. 6-18). lib. bdg. 25.95 (978-1-59556-027-8(0)) OTTN Publishing.

BEDELIA, AMELIA (FICTITIOUS CHARACTER)—FICTION

see Amelia-Bedelia (Fictitious Character)—Fiction

BEDOUINS

Losleben, Elizabeth. The Bedouin of the Middle East. 2005. (First Peoples Ser.). (Illus.). 48p. (gr. 4-8). lib. bdg. 23.95 (978-0-8225-0663-8(7)) Lerner Publishing Group.

BEDOUINS—FICTION

Cohen, Deborah Bodin. Engineer Ari & the Hanukkah Mishap. Kober, Shahar, illus. 2011. (Hanukkah Ser.). (ENG.). 32p. (J). (gr. k-3). pap. 7.95 (978-0-7613-5146-7(9)); lib. bdg. 17.95 (978-0-7613-5145-0(0)) Lerner Publishing Group. (Kar-Ben Publishing).

Hapka, Catherine, pseud. Yatimah. Sanderson, Ruth, illus. 2011. (Horse Diaries). (ENG.). 176p. (J). (gr. 3-7). pap. 7.99 (978-0-375-86719-4(8), Random Hse. Bks. for Young Readers) Random Hse. Children's Bks.

LaFevers, R. L. Flight of the Phoenix Bk. 1. Murphy, Kelly, illus. 2010. (Nathaniel Fludd, Beastologist Ser.: 1). (ENG.). 144p. (J). (gr. 1-4). pap. 5.99 (978-0-547-40845-3(5)) Houghton Mifflin Harcourt Publishing Co.

BEDTIME

Beaton, Clare, illus. Mrs. Moon: Lullabies for Bedtime. 2003. 48p. (J). 19.99 incl. audio compact disk (978-1-84148-176-0(9)) Barefoot Bks., Inc.

Behrens, Janice & Butler, Marybeth. I'm Not Tired! A Bedtime Routine Book. 2017. (Rookie Toddler(tm) Ser.). (ENG.). 12p. (J). bds. 6.95 (978-0-531-22978-1(5), Children's Pr.) Scholastic Library Publishing.

Berry, Joy. Teach Me about Bedtime. 2009. (ENG.). 40p. (J). (gr. k — 1). bds. 7.95 (978-1-60577-010-9(8)) Berry, Joy Enterprises.

Berry, Ron & Sharp, Chris. It's Bedtime. Sharp, Chris & Currant, Gary, illus. 2003. (It's Time to Ser.). (ENG.). 14p. (J). (gr. -1-k). bds. 6.95 (978-1-891100-61-1(0)) Smart Kidz Media, Inc.

Boynton, Sandra. Buenas Noches a Todos. Boynton, Sandra, illus. 2004.Tr. of Going to Bed Book. (SPA., Illus.). 14p. (J). (gr. -1 — 1). bds. 5.99 (978-0-689-86652-4(6), Libros Para Ninos) Libros Para Ninos.

Darens, Cat. My Bedtime Angel. Oliver, Julia, illus. 2010. 18p. (J). (gr. -1-k). 7.95 (978-0-8091-6745-6(X), Ambassador Bks.) Paulist Pr.

David C. Cook Publishing Company Staff. Land of Milk & Honey, Bk. 4. 2007. (LMH Ser.). 16p. (J). (gr. 1-3). 6.99 (978-0-7814-4527-6(2)) Cook, David C.

Dorling Kindersley Publishing Staff, ed. Buenas Noches, Bebe! / Good Night, Baby! 2004. (Soft-To-Touch Bks.). (SPA & ENG., Illus.). 18p. (J). (gr. -1-k). bds. 5.99 (978-0-7566-0438-7(9), DK Children) Dorling Kindersley Publishing, Inc.

Everyday Signs for Bed Time. 2007. (J). bds. (978-0-9791059-2-0(7)) Dakitab, Inc.

Farquharson, Jerome. Playtime to Bedtime: Memories That Last Forever... 2011. (Illus.). 24p. (J). pap. 10.95 (978-0-615-45886-1(6)) JFAR Bks.

Gamble, Adam & Jasper, Mark. Good Night Dinosaur. Kelly, Cooper, illus. 2013. (Good Night Our World Ser.). (ENG.). 28p. (J). (— 1). bds. 9.95 *(978-1-60219-078-8(X))* Good Night Bks.

Janisch, Heinz & Bansch, Helga. Good Night Giants. 2011. (Illus.). 32p. (J). (gr. -1-3). 14.95 *(978-1-4338-0950-7(8))*; pap. 9.95 *(978-1-4338-0951-4(6))* American Psychological Assn. (Magination Pr.).

Jones, Stephanie, illus. Bedtime. 2007. (Luxury Look & Say Board Bks.). 12p. (J). (gr. -1-k). bds. 12.99 *(978-0-7945-1461-7(8),* Usborne) EDC Publishing.

Keonna-E'nea. Momzilla, 1 vol. Joane', E'nea, illus. 2009. 18p. pap. 24.95 *(978-1-60749-607-6(0))* America Star Bks.

Lindeen, Mary. Getting Ready for Bed. 2015. (BeginningtoRead Ser.). (ENG.). 32p. (J). (gr. k-2). pap. 11.94 *(978-1-60357-761-8(0))*; (Illus.). lib. bdg. 22.60 *(978-1-59953-701-6(X))* Norwood Hse. Pr.

Matheny, B. K. Goodnight Baby, 1 vol. 2009. 20p. pap. 24.95 *(978-1-61546-281-0(3))* America Star Bks.

Organic Baby Sleep. 2008. (Illus.). (J). (gr. -1-3). bds. *(978-0-312-50270-6(2))* Priddy Bks.

Picthall, Chez. Bedtime. Hewett, Angela, illus. 2015. (ENG.). 10p. (J). 11.99 *(978-1-909763-43-2(8))* Award Pubns. Ltd. GBR. Dist: Parkwest Pubns., Inc.

Piper, Sophie. Goodnight Prayers. Moriuchi, Mique, illus. 2009. (ENG.). 64p. (J). (gr. -1-k). 9.99 *(978-0-7459-6065-4(0))* Lion Hudson PLC GBR. Dist: Independent Pubs. Group.

Priddy, Roger. It's Time to Sleep. 2013. (Bright Baby Ser.). (ENG.). 10p. (J). (gr. -1 — 1). bds. 4.99 *(978-0-312-51635-2(5),* 9780312516352, Priddy Bks.) St. Martin's Pr.

Razo, Rebecca J. The Monsters under My Bed. Fisher, Diana, illus. 2014. 24p. (J). (gr. k-2). 23.93 *(978-1-939581-37-2(0))* Quarto Publishing Group USA.

Reynolds, D. G. Moon Beam Walking: Dream Space Books, 1 vol. Ward, Scott, illus. 2009. 14p. pap. 19.95 *(978-1-61546-726-6(2))* PublishAmerica, Inc.

Roche, Maite. My First Bedtime Prayers. 2011. (ENG., Illus.). 14p. (gr. -1). bds. 6.99 *(978-1-58617-503-0(3))* Ignatius Pr.

Smart Kids Publishing Staff. My Snuggle up Bedtime Book. Smart Kids Publishing Staff, illus. 2007. (Illus.). 16p. 14.99 *(978-0-8249-6695-9(3),* Ideal Pubns.) Worthy Publishing.

Stohs, Anita Reith. Hush, Little One: A Lullaby for God's Children. Kanzler, John, tr. Kanzler, John, illus. 2004. 32p. (J). 12.99 *(978-0-570-07144-0(5))* Concordia Publishing Hse.

Verdick, Elizabeth. Bedtime. Heinlen, Marieka, illus. 2010. (Toddler Tools Ser.). (ENG.). 24p. (J). (gr. -1). 7.95 *(978-1-57542-315-9(4))* Free Spirit Publishing, Inc.

Walters, Eric. Bedtime 123, 1 vol. Bisaillon, Josée, illus. 2017. (ENG.). 26p. (J). (gr. -1-k). bds. 9.95 ***(978-1-4598-1073-0(2))*** Orca Bk. Pubs. USA.

Wong, Alice & Tabori, Lena, eds. The Goodnight Book for Moms & Little Ones. 2010. (ENG., Illus.). 224p. 17.95 *(978-1-59962-084-8(7),* Welcome Bks) Rizzoli International Pubns., Inc.

BEDTIME—FICTION

ABDO Publishing Company Staff. Story Time for Little Monsters. 2014. (Story Time for Little Monsters Ser.: 4). 24p. (J). (gr. -1-4). lib. bdg. 108.28 *(978-1-62402-019-3(4),* Looking Glass Library) Magic Wagon.

Adams, David J. Good Night Vancouver. Veno, Joe & Rosen, Anne, illus. 2010. (Good Night Our World Ser.). (ENG.). 20p. (J). (gr. k — 1). bds. 9.95 *(978-1-60219-039-9(9))* Good Night Bks.

Adams, Diane. I Can Do It Myself!, 1 vol. Hayashi, Nancy, illus. (ENG.). 32p. (J). (gr. -1-1). 2013. 7.95 *(978-1-56145-725-0(6))* 2009. 15.95 *(978-1-56145-471-6(0))* Peachtree Pubs.

Adams, Michael. The Little King & the Honeybee. 2005. (J). per. 9.95 *(978-1-58597-327-9(0))* Leathers Publishing.

Adelman, Nechama Dina. Bedtime. Blau, Nicole, illus. 2003. 30p. (J). 10.95 *(978-1-929628-12-4(9))* Hachai Publishing.

Adler, David A. It's Time to Sleep, It's Time to Dream. Chorao, Kay, illus. 2009. (ENG.). 32p. (J). (gr. -1-k). 16.95 *(978-0-8234-1924-1(X))* Holiday Hse., Inc.

Ajmera, Maya. Global Baby Bedtimes. 2015. (ENG., Illus.). 16p. (J). (— 1). bds. 6.95 *(978-1-58089-708-2(8))* Charlesbridge Publishing, Inc.

Akers, Darla G. The Man, the Moon, & the Star. 2008. 24p. per. 24.95 *(978-1-60474-030-1(2))* PublishAmerica, Inc.

Albee, Sarah. Off to Bed. Ebert, Len, illus. 2006. (Step-By-Step Readers Ser.). (J). pap. *(978-1-59939-060-4(4),* Reader's Digest Young Families, Inc.) Studio Fun International.

—Time for Bed, Elmo! (Sesame Street) Swanson, Maggie, illus. 2014. (Little Golden Book Ser.). (ENG.). 24p. (J). (-k). 4.99 *(978-0-385-37138-4(1),* Golden Bks.) Random Hse. Children's Bks.

Alborozo, Gabriel. Good Night, Firefly. Alborozo, Gabriel, illus. 2015. (ENG., Illus.). 32p. (J). (gr. -1-2). 16.99 *(978-1-62779-222-6(8),* 9781627792226, Holt, Henry & Co. Bks. For Young Readers) Holt, Henry & Co.

Aliaga, Roberto. A Night Time Story. 2012. (ENG., Illus.). 24p. (J). (gr. k-2). *(978-84-15241-98-0(4))* D P & G Military Pubs.

All the Stars. 2008. (Looney Tunes Giant Floor Pad Ser.). 80p. pap. *(978-1-4075-2897-7(1))* Parragon, Inc.

Allen, Carolyn. My Bedtime Prayer. 2009. pap. 8.99 *(978-1-61584-240-7(3))* Independent Pub.

Allen, Jonathan. I'm Not Sleepy! 2012. (Baby Owl Ser.). (ENG., Illus.). 26p. (J). (gr. k — 1). bds. 6.95 *(978-1-907967-37-5(0))* Boxer Bks., Ltd. GBR. Dist: Sterling Publishing Co., Inc.

Allen, Lisa & Sharp, Julis. Time for Bed - The Secret of Shadows: Shadow Theater Inside. Johnson, Vickie, illus. 26p. (J). (gr. -1-2). pap. *(978-1-56021-355-0(8),* 206) W.J. Fantasy, Inc.

Alvord, David Myron. Albert & His Journey Through the Mountains. 2006. 76p. pap. 16.95 *(978-1-4241-2423-7(9))* PublishAmerica, Inc.

Anders, Bill. Becoming Noah. 2004. 114p. (J). pap. 7.95 *(978-0-9762059-0-6(4))* Leaping Antelope Productions.

Anderson, Peggy Perry. La Niñera Dijo: "Es Hora de Ir a la Cama" 2017. (Green Light Readers Level 1 Ser.). (ENG., Illus.). 32p. (J). (gr. -1-3). pap. 3.99 *(978-0-544-80895-9(9),* HMH Books For Young Readers) Houghton Mifflin Harcourt Publishing Co.

—Time for Bed, the Babysitter Said. 2012. (Green Light Readers — Level 1 Ser.). lib. bdg. 13.55 *(978-0-606-26607-9(0),* Turtleback) Turtleback Bks.

Andreae, Giles. Keep Love in Your Heart, Little One. Vulliamy, Clara, illus. 2007. 32p. (J). (gr. -1-3). 15.95 *(978-1-58925-066-6(4))* Tiger Tales.

Andrews McMeel Publishing Staff & Wang, Dorthea Deprisco. Five Minutes until Bed. Vaux, Patricia, illus. 2009. (ENG.). 14p. (J). (gr. 4-7). 14.99 *(978-0-7407-8428-6(5))* Andrews McMeel Publishing.

Anything Is Possible. 2006. (J). 12.00 *(978-0-9769827-1-5(4))* Wren Song Pr.

Arai, Hiroyuki. Everyone Says Goodnight. 2016. (ENG., Illus.). 28p. (J). (gr. -1 — 1). 14.99 *(978-1-4521-5139-7(3))* Chronicle Bks. LLC.

Armstrong, Robert W. The Big Blue Lake. Broxon, Janet, illus. 2015. (ENG.). 32p. (J). (gr. -1). 13.95 *(978-0-9801468-3-7(6))* All About Kids Publishing.

Arnold, Tedd. No Jumping on the Bed! 25th anniv. ed. 2012. (ENG., Illus.). 32p. (J). (gr. -1-1). 16.99 *(978-0-8037-3563-7(4),* Dial Bks) Penguin Young Readers Group.

Arnold, Tedd, et al. Noodlehead Nightmares. Arnold, Tedd, illus. 2016. (ENG., Illus.). 48p. (J). (gr. 1-5). 15.95 *(978-0-8234-3566-1(0))* Holiday Hse., Inc.

Arthur, Tish. Pretty Little Face, 1 vol. 2009. 16p. pap. 24.95 *(978-1-60836-179-3(9))* America Star Bks.

Asch, Frank. Moonbear's Sunrise. Asch, Frank, illus. 2014. (Moonbear Ser.). (ENG., Illus.). 32p. (J). (gr. -1-3). 16.99 *(978-1-4424-6647-0(2),* Aladdin) Simon & Schuster Children's Publishing.

Ashman, Linda. How to Make a Night. Tusa, Tricia, illus. Date not set. 32p. (J). (gr. -1-3). pap. 5.99 *(978-0-06-443699-1(3))* HarperCollins Pubs.

—Sailing off to Sleep. Winter, Susan, illus. 2010. (ENG.). 32p. (J). (gr. -1-1). pap. 9.99 *(978-1-4424-1435-8(9),* Simon & Schuster Bks. For Young Readers) Simon & Schuster Bks. For Young Readers.

Asim, Jabari. Boy of Mine. Pham, LeUyen, illus. 2010. (ENG.). 20p. (J). (gr. -1 — 1). bds. 6.99 *(978-0-316-73577-3(9))* Little, Brown Bks. for Young Readers.

—Girl of Mine. Pham, LeUyen, illus. 2010. (ENG.). 20p. (J). (gr. -1 — 1). bds. 6.99 *(978-0-316-73578-0(7))* Little, Brown Bks. for Young Readers.

Awdry, Wilbert V. Good Night, Thomas (Thomas & Friends) Random House Staff, illus. 2012. (Glow-In-the-Dark Board Book Ser.). (ENG.). 12p. (J). (gr. k-k). bds. 6.99 *(978-0-307-97697-0(1),* Random Hse. Bks. for Young Readers) Random Hse. Children's Bks.

Bach, Annie. Night-Night, Forest Friends. Bach, Annie, illus. 2013. (ENG., Illus.). 24p. (J). (gr. -1-k). bds. 8.99 *(978-0-8431-7278-2(9),* Grosset & Dunlap) Penguin Young Readers Group.

Bada, Shizzer. Bedtime Stories. 2013. 90p. pap. *(978-1-907402-45-6(4))* Ministry In Art.

Bader, Bonnie. Go to Bed, Blue. Robertson, Michael, illus. 2014. (Penguin Young Readers, Level 1 Ser.). (ENG.). 32p. (J). (gr. k-1). pap. 3.99 *(978-0-448-48219-4(3),* Penguin Young Readers) Penguin Young Readers Group.

Bailey, Arthur Scott. Sleepy Time Tales the Tale of Fatty Coon. 2004. reprint ed. pap. 15.95 *(978-1-4191-4779-1(X))*; pap. 1.99 *(978-1-4192-4779-8(4))*; pap. 15.95 *(978-1-4191-4779-1(X))*; pap. 1.99 *(978-1-4192-4779-8(4))* Kessinger Publishing, LLC.

Bailey, Linda & Masse, Josée. Goodnight, Sweet Pig. Masse, Josée, illus. 2007. (ENG., Illus.). 32p. (J). (gr. -1-k). 18.95 *(978-1-55337-844-0(X))* Kids Can Pr., Ltd. CAN. Dist: Hachette Bk. Group.

Bajaj, Varsha. How Many Kisses Do You Want Tonight? Bates, Ivan, illus. 2007. (ENG.). 26p. (J). (gr. -1 — 1). bds. 6.99 *(978-0-316-06735-5(0))* Little, Brown Bks. for Young Readers.

Balmes, Santi. I Will Fight Monsters for You. Lyona, illus. 2015. (ENG.). 32p. (J). (gr. -1-3). 16.99 *(978-0-8075-9056-0(8))* Whitman, Albert & Co.

Banks, Kate. The Bear in the Book, 1 vol. Hallensleben, Georg, illus. 2012. (ENG.). 36p. (J). (gr. -1-1). 16.99 *(978-0-374-30591-8(9),* 9780374305918, Farrar, Straus & Giroux (BYR)) Farrar, Straus & Giroux.

Barcelo, François. My Mommy's Hands. Mongeau, Marc, illus. 2009. (My First Stories Ser.). 24p. (J). (gr. -1-3). 22.60 *(978-1-60754-362-6(1))*; pap. 8.15 *(978-1-60754-365-7(6))* Windmill Bks.

Barchers, Suzanne I. Get to Bed, Ren!, 1 vol. 2011. (Targeted Phonics Ser.). (ENG.). 16p. (J). (gr. k-2). pap. 5.99 *(978-1-4333-2416-1(4))* Teacher Created Materials, Inc.

Bardhan-Quallen, Sudipta. Brobot Bedtime. Campbell, Scott, illus. 2017. (ENG.). 32p. (J). (gr. k-2). 16.95 *(978-1-4197-2290-5(5),* Abrams Bks. for Young Readers) Abrams, Inc.

—Chicks Run Wild. Jenkins, Ward, illus. 2011. (ENG.). 32p. (J). (gr. -1-1). 15.99 *(978-1-4424-0673-5(9),* Simon & Schuster Bks. For Young Readers) Simon & Schuster Bks. For Young Readers.

Barnett, Mac. Noisy Night. Biggs, Brian, illus. 2017. (ENG.). 32p. (J). 16.99 *(978-1-59643-967-2(X),* 9781596439672) Roaring Brook Pr.

Barron Dc, Philip. Daddy Can't Play Now: A bedtime story of understanding & an introduction to Chiropractic Care. 2009. (Illus.). 20p. pap. 10.99 *(978-1-4490-1818-4(1))* AuthorHouse.

Barry, Bridget. Sweet Dreams. 2010. 24p. pap. 12.99 *(978-1-4490-6905-6(3))* AuthorHouse.

Bartgen M.S. Cco-Slp-L, Katie Foy. Around the World in a Dream. 2012. 20p. pap. 13.77 *(978-1-4669-0262-6(0))* Trafford Publishing.

Barton, Jen. If Chocolate Were Purple. Matsuoka, Yoko, illus. gif. ed. 2013. (ENG.). 28p. (J). pap., instr.'s hndbk. ed. 10.89 *(978-0-615-78343-7(0),* Flickerfawn) Barton Bks.

Bass, L. G. & Geringer, Laura. Boom Boom Go Away! Ibatoulline, Bagram, illus. 2010. (ENG.). 40p. (J). (gr. -1-1). 15.99 *(978-0-689-85093-6(X),* Atheneum Bks. for Young Readers) Simon & Schuster Children's Publishing.

Bateman, Julie. Bath, Book, Bed, 1 vol. 2010. 20p. 24.95 *(978-1-4489-6162-7(9))* PublishAmerica, Inc.

Baxter, Nicola. Bedtime Tales. Press, Jenny, illus. 2013. (ENG.). 80p. (J). (gr. -1-k). pap. 9.99 *(978-1-84322-952-0(8))* Anness Publishing GBR. Dist: National Bk. Network.

—Book of Five-Minute Farmyard Tales. Press, Jenny, illus. 2013. (ENG.). 80p. (J). (gr. -1-k). pap. 9.99 *(978-1-84322-953-7(6))* Anness Publishing GBR. Dist: National Bk. Network.

—A Book of Five-Minute Teddy Bear Tales: A Treasury of over 35 Bedtime Stories. Press, Jenny, illus. 2013. (ENG.). 80p. pap. 9.99 *(978-1-84322-889-9(0))* Anness Publishing GBR. Dist: National Bk. Network.

—My First Bedtime Stories. Allen, Marie, illus. 2016. (ENG.). 16p. (J). (gr. -1-12). bds. 10.99 *(978-0-85723-809-2(4),* Armadillo) Anness Publishing GBR. Dist: National Bk. Network.

—My Little Treasury of Bedtime Stories. Press, Jenny, illus. 2013. (ENG.). 320p. (J). (gr. -1-k). 12.99 *(978-1-84322-729-8(0))* Anness Publishing GBR. Dist: National Bk. Network.

—My Wonderful Treasury of Five-Minute Stories. Press, Jenny, illus. 2012. (ENG.). 256p. (J). (gr. k-4). 18.99 *(978-1-84322-805-9(X))* Anness Publishing GBR. Dist: National Bk. Network.

Baxter, Nicola & Siewert, Pauline. Sweet Dreams: Soothing Stories for Peaceful Bedtimes. 2012. (ENG., Illus.). 210p. (J). (gr. -1-12). pap. 7.99 *(978-1-84322-817-2(3),* Armadillo) Anness Publishing GBR. Dist: National Bk. Network.

BeachHouse Publishing. Geckos Go to Bed. Murakami, Jon, illus. 2008. (ENG.). 24p. (J). (gr. -1-k). bds. 8.95 *(978-1-933067-26-1(8))* Beachhouse Publishing, LLC.

Beander, Lillian. Mylah's Bedtime Stories, 1 vol. 2009. 48p. pap. 16.95 *(978-1-61546-981-9(8))* America Star Bks.

Beaty, Andrea. Hush, Baby Ghostling. Lemaître, Pascal, illus. 2009. (ENG.). 32p. (J). (gr. -1-3). 14.99 *(978-1-4169-2545-3(7),* McElderry, Margaret K. Bks.) McElderry, Margaret K. Bks.

Beaudoin, Beau. The Url King. 2010. (Illus.). 56p. (J). per. 15.95 *(978-0-9788401-0-5(0))* Red Ink Pr.

Beaumont, Karen. Crybaby. Yelchin, Eugene, illus. 2015. (ENG.). 40p. (J). (gr. -1-1). 17.99 *(978-0-8050-8974-5(8),* 9780805089745, Holt, Henry & Co. Bks. For Young Readers) Holt, Henry & Co.

—Dini Dinosaur. Roode, Daniel, illus. 2012. (ENG.). 32p. (J). (gr. -1-k). 14.99 *(978-0-06-207299-3(4),* Greenwillow Bks.) HarperCollins Pubs.

Becker, Bonny. A Bedtime for Bear. Denton, Kady MacDonald, illus. 2010. (J). (Bear & Mouse Ser.: 3). (ENG.). 48p. (gr. -1-2). 16.99 *(978-0-7636-4101-6(4))*; *(978-0-7636-5364-4(0))* Candlewick Pr.

Beckman, Amy. The Good Night Book. Ahern, Frank, illus. 2006. 28p. per. 16.95 *(978-1-59858-255-0(0))* Dog Ear Publishing, LLC.

A Bed for Bear. 2014. (ENG., Illus.). 32p. (J). (gr. -1-3). 17.99 *(978-0-06-223705-7(5))* HarperCollins Pubs.

Bedtime. 2014. (Touch & Feel Ser.). (ENG.). 12p. (J). (gr. -1-k). bds. 6.99 *(978-1-4654-1693-3(5),* DK Children) Dorling Kindersley Publishing, Inc.

Bedtime Peeksboo! 2008. (Baby Gold Stars Die-Cut Board Ser.). 6p. bds. *(978-1-4075-1557-1(8))* Parragon, Inc.

Bedtime with Mothergoose. 2005. (J). bds. *(978-1-4194-0089-6(4))* Paradise Pr., Inc.

Beinstein, Phoebe. Los Deseos de Dora. Ziegler, Argentina Palacios, tr. from ENG. Roper, Robert, illus. 2008. (Dora la Exploradora Ser.).Tr. of Dora's Bedtime Wishes. (ENG.). 14p. (J). (gr. -1). bds. 4.99 *(978-1-4169-5036-3(2),* Libros Para Ninos) Libros Para Ninos.

Bell-Jackson, Sylvia. Bree's Bubble Gum Adventures: The Pajamas from the Bahamas. 2012. 36p. pap. 13.97 *(978-1-61204-299-2(6),* Strategic Bk. Publishing) Strategic Book Publishing & Rights Agency (SBPRA).

Bell, Liz. Chickee Chickee Chew & Whoo Whoo. 2011. 16p. pap. 24.95 *(978-1-4626-3588-7(1))* America Star Bks.

Bencivengo, Mary Ann. The Man in the Moon. 2011. 56p. pap. *(978-1-77067-302-1(4))* FriesenPress.

Bennetts, Nancy. Bed Head. 2003. (Illus.). 48p. (J). 16.95 *(978-0-9726004-1-5(8))* Big Valley Publishing.

Bentley, Bernard E. Little Ben's Pledge. 2013. (ENG.). 33p. pap. 9.95 *(978-1-4787-1737-9(8))* Outskirts Pr., Inc.

Bentley, Dawn. Fuzzy Bear's Bedtime. Nagy, Krisztina, illus. 2005. (Fuzzy Bear Ser.). 10p. (J). (gr. -1-k). act. bk. ed. 10.95 *(978-1-58117-055-9(6),* Intervisual/Piggy Toes) Bendon, Inc.

—Goodnight Bear: A Book & Night Light. Couri, Kathryn A., illus. 2005. (Stories to Share Ser.). 12p. (J). 12.95 *(978-1-58117-034-4(3),* Intervisual/Piggy Toes) Bendon, Inc.

Bentley, Jonathan, illus. Where Is Bear? 2017. (ENG.). 32p. (J). (gr. -1-2). 16.99 *(978-0-399-55593-0(5),* Doubleday Bks. for Young Readers) Random Hse. Children's Bks.

Bently, Peter. A Recipe for Bedtime. Massini, Sarah, illus. 2016. (ENG.). 32p. (J). (— 1). 16.99 *(978-0-399-17625-8(X),* G.P. Putnam's Sons Books for Young Readers) Penguin Young Readers Group.

Bercowetz, Cynthia. Grandpa Herman's Petting Zoo. 2007. (Illus.). 48p. (J). per. 14.95 *(978-0-9708430-9-8(7))* Uitti, Daniel.

Berenstain, Mike, illus. The Berenstain Bears' Sleepy Time Book. 2015. (J). *(978-0-8249-1946-7(7),* Ideal Pubns.) Worthy Publishing.

Berenstain, Stan & Berenstain, Jan. The Berenstain Bears' Bedtime Battle. Berenstain, Stan & Berenstain, Jan, illus. 2004. (Berenstain Bears Ser.). (ENG., Illus.). 32p. (J). (gr. -1-3). pap. 3.99 *(978-0-06-057381-2(3),* HarperFestival) HarperCollins Pubs.

Berg, Ray. Sailing Duck. 2005. 15p. (J). 9.33 *(978-1-4116-3554-8(X))* Lulu Pr., Inc.

Berger, Carin. Good Night! Good Night! Berger, Carin, illus. 2017. (Illus.). 40p. (J). (gr. -1-3). 17.99 *(978-0-06-240884-6(4),* Greenwillow Bks.) HarperCollins Pubs.

Bergman, Mara. Oliver Who Would Not Sleep! Maland, Nick, illus. 2007. (J). *(978-0-439-92827-4(3),* Levine, Arthur A. Bks.) Scholastic, Inc.

Bergren, Lisa Tawn. God Gave Us Sleep. Bryant, Laura J., illus. 2015. (ENG.). 40p. (J). (gr. -1-2). 10.99 *(978-1-60142-663-5(1),* WaterBrook Pr.) Crown Publishing Group.

Berne, Jennifer. Nighty-Night, Sleep Tight. Walker, David, illus. 2015. (Snuggle Time Stories Ser.). (ENG.). 24p. (J). (gr. -1-k). bds. 6.95 *(978-1-4549-1390-0(8))* Sterling Publishing Co., Inc.

Beston, Henry. Chimney Farm Bedtime Stories. 2006. (Illus.). 80p. (J). pap. 13.95 *(978-0-942396-93-5(6))* Blackberry Maine.

Betts, Joan D. Bagley B. Butterfield: A Dog Book for People. 2011. 24p. pap. 16.99 *(978-1-4520-9280-5(X))* AuthorHouse.

Bewley, Elizabeth. The Moon Followed Me Home. Furukawa, Masumi, illus. 2007. (ENG.). 6p. (J). (gr. -1-3). 12.95 *(978-1-58117-598-1(1),* Intervisual/Piggy Toes) Bendon, Inc.

Bibi, Zarina. The Bright Night Sky. 2012. 24p. pap. 15.49 *(978-1-4685-4566-1(3))* AuthorHouse.

Big Davie. The Lady & Her Cat As Told by Bigdavie: A simple easy reading bedtime story that will leave children with delightful images while drifting off to S. 2009. (Illus.). 28p. pap. 12.49 *(978-1-4389-3124-1(7))* AuthorHouse.

Binder, Mark. Genies, Giants & a Walrus. 2012. 132p. pap. 14.99 *(978-0-9824707-9-4(7))* Light Pubns.

—Kings, Wolves, Princesses & Lions: 28 Illustrated Stories for Young Readers. 2012. (ENG., Illus.). 122p. (J). pap. 14.99 *(978-0-9824707-8-7(9))* Light Pubns.

Bingham, Frances. Bedtime Stories for the Inner Child: Reuniting with & Nurturing Your Inner Child. 2009. 68p. pap. 10.49 *(978-1-4389-3185-2(9))* AuthorHouse.

Biro, Sharon. Snaggleloopus. 2008. (Illus.). 36p. pap. 24.95 *(978-1-60474-118-6(X))* America Star Bks.

Blackall, Sophie. Are You Awake? Blackall, Sophie, illus. 2011. (ENG., Illus.). 40p. (J). (gr. -1-k). 12.99 *(978-0-8050-7858-9(4),* 9780805078589, Holt, Henry & Co. Bks. For Young Readers) Holt, Henry & Co.

Blake, Chris & Charismalife. Hover Get's His Wings. 2004. 24p. (J). (gr. k-3). 9.99 *(978-1-59185-452-4(0),* Charisma Kids) Charisma Media.

Blakeslee, S. E. Once upon a Blue Moon: The Chronicles of the Blue Moon. Blakeslee, S. E., illus. 2007. (ENG., Illus.). 32p. (J). 17.95 *(978-0-9789031-0-7(2))* Blaumond Pr.

Blitz, Shmuel. Bedtime Stories to Make You Smile. 2003. (ArtScroll Youth Ser.). 14.99 *(978-1-57819-745-3(7),* BEDS) Mesorah Pubns., Ltd.

—A Treasury of Shabbos Bedtime Stories. 2004. (ArtScroll Youth Ser.). (Illus.). 48p. (J). 14.99 *(978-1-57819-431-5(8),* BESH) Mesorah Pubns., Ltd.

Bloom, Suzanne, illus. Number Slumber. 2016. (ENG.). 40p. (J). (gr. -1-k). 16.95 *(978-1-62979-557-7(7))* Boyds Mills Pr.

Blueraven, Solaris. Mr. Sun & the Halloween Ball. 2010. 20p. 13.99 *(978-1-4520-0431-0(5))* AuthorHouse.

Bockemeier, Karen. Patty's Paper Place, 1 vol. 2010. 18p. 24.95 *(978-1-4489-4577-1(1))* PublishAmerica, Inc.

Bohannon, Erin. Crabby & Shoofly. 2011. 32p. pap. 21.99 *(978-1-4628-8088-1(6))* Xlibris Corp.

Bolander, Sharon Miller. I Wish That I Could Fly. 2011. 36p. pap. 24.95 *(978-1-4560-8058-7(X))* America Star Bks.

Bolden, Tonya. Beautiful Moon: A Child's Prayer. Velasquez, Eric, illus. 2014. (ENG.). 32p. (J). (gr. k-2). 16.95 *(978-1-4197-0792-6(2),* Abrams Bks. for Young Readers) Abrams, Inc.

Bolton, Violet. Heidi & Huber the Adventures Begin. 2011. (Illus.). 60p. pap. *(978-1-908447-90-6(7))* Grosvenor Hse. Publishing Ltd.

Bongiovanni, Debbie. It's All about Magic or Is It?, 1 vol. 2009. 55p. pap. 16.95 *(978-1-61546-875-1(7))* America Star Bks.

Bonnet, Rosalinde. Very First Words Bedtime. 2011. (Very First Words Board Book Ser.). 12p. (J). ring bd. 6.99 *(978-0-7945-3118-8(0),* Usborne) EDC Publishing.

Bonnett-Rampersaud, Louise. Bubble & Squeak, 1 vol. Banta, Susan, illus. 2006. (ENG.). 24p. (J). (gr. -1-2). 14.99 *(978-0-7614-5310-9(5))* Marshall Cavendish Corp.

Book Company Staff. Little Treasures. Francour, Kathleen, illus. 2003. (Stationery Ser.). (J). 14.95 *(978-1-74047-311-8(6))* Book Co. Publishing Pty, Ltd., The AUS. Dist: Penton Overseas, Inc.

Boos, Marcela. Oh No, It's Bedtime! 2009. 23p. (J). pap. 11.95 *(978-1-4327-3338-4(9))* Outskirts Pr., Inc.

Bostrom, Kathleen Long. Good Night, God! Lyon, Tammie, illus. 2014. 20p. (J). bds. 6.99 *(978-0-8249-1940-5(8),* Ideal Pubns.) Worthy Publishing.

Bourgeois, Paulette. La Manta de Franklin. Varela, Alejandra López, tr. Clark, Brenda, illus.Tr. of Franklin's Blanket. (SPA.). (J). (gr. k-2). pap. 5.95 *(978-1-880507-98-8(6),* LC30178); ring bd. 10.95 *(978-1-880507-99-5(4),* LC30179) Lectorum Pubns., Inc.

Boussarhane, Ericka. Sam & the Boogie Man. 2009. 28p. pap. 14.99 *(978-1-4389-3107-4(7))* AuthorHouse.

Bowman, Crystal. Jake's Brave Night, 1 vol. Maizel, Karen, illus. 2007. (I Can Read! / the Jake Ser.). (ENG.). 32p. (J). (gr. -1-3). pap. 3.99 *(978-0-310-71456-9(7))* Zonderkidz.

Boyd, Benjamin. The Adventures of Kid Humpty Dumpty. 2009. 60p. pap. 19.50 *(978-1-60693-265-0(9),* Eloquent Bks.) Strategic Book Publishing & Rights Agency (SBPRA).

Boynton, Sandra. The Going to Bed Book. Boynton, Sandra, illus. (ENG., Illus.). (J). 2006. 14p. bds. 12.95 *(978-1-4169-2794-5(8))* 30th anniv. ed. 2012. 18p. (gr. -1-3). bds. 7.99 *(978-1-4424-5409-5(1))* Little Simon. (Little Simon).

—Pajama Time! (Lap Edition) 2011. (ENG., Illus.). 20p. (J). (gr. k — 1). bds. 11.95 *(978-0-7611-6617-7(3),* 16617) Workman Publishing Co., Inc.

Boza, Eduardo Robles. Mi Amigo Se Hace Pipi... (My Friends Wets His Bed) (SPA.). (J). 4.95 *(978-968-419-812-8(4))* Grijalbo, Editorial MEX. Dist: AIMS International Bks., Inc.

Bradbury, Ray. Switch on the Night. Dillon, Leo & Dillon, Diane, illus. 2004. (ENG.). 40p. (J). (gr. -1-2). reprint ed. pap. 7.99 *(978-0-553-11244-3(9),* Dragonfly Bks.) Random Hse. Children's Bks.

Bradford, William. Jeremy Mcbright Was Afraid of the Night. 2006. (Illus.). 36p. (J). lib. bdg. 13.95 *(978-0-9672585-2-2(9))* CyPress Pubns.

Bradley, Timothy J. Teddy Bear, Teddy Bear, Say Good Night, 1 vol. 2009. (Early Childhood Themes Ser.). (ENG., Illus.). 16p. (J). (gr. -1-2). pap. 6.99 *(978-1-4333-1471-1(1))* Teacher Created Materials, Inc.

Branford, Henrietta. Six Chicks. Elfezzani, Thierry, illus. 2004. (ENG.). 32p. (J). (gr. k-k). pap. 8.99 *(978-0-00-664767-6(7),* HarperCollins Children's Bks.) HarperCollins Pubs. Ltd. GBR. Dist: Independent Pubs. Group.

Braun, Sebastien. Back to Bed, Ed!, 1 vol. Braun, Sebastien, illus. (Illus.). 32p. (J). (gr. -1-3). 2014. (ENG.). pap. 7.95 *(978-1-56145-775-5(2))* 2010. 15.95 *(978-1-56145-518-8(0))* Peachtree Pubs.

—One Sleepy Night. 2013. (Padded Board Books Ser.). (ENG.). 20p. (J). bds. 8.95 *(978-1-58925-619-4(0))* Tiger Tales Pubns.

Bridwell, Norman. Clifford y la Hora de Dormir. 2003. (Clifford Ser.).Tr. of Clifford's Bedtime. (SPA & ENG., Illus.). 7p. (J). (— 1). 4.99 *(978-0-439-54568-6(4),* Scholastic en Espanol) Scholastic, Inc.

—Clifford's Bedtime Story. Bridwell, Norman, illus. 2013. (Clifford Ser.). (ENG., Illus.). 20p. (J). (gr. -1-k). bds. 8.99 *(978-0-545-49577-6(6))* Scholastic, Inc.

Bringsvaerd, Tor Age. When Two Say Goodnight. Soli, Tina, illus. 2009. (When Two Ser.). 36p. (J). (gr. -1-1). 14.95 *(978-0-9815761-3-8(3))* Mackenzie Smiles, LLC.

Brooks, Felicity. Time for Bed, Max & Millie. 2011. (Toddler Bks). 24p. (J). ring bd. 7.99 *(978-0-7945-3068-6(0),* Usborne) EDC Publishing.

Brooks, Walt. Walter's Pet Bee. 2011. 36p. pap. 16.86 *(978-1-4634-4919-3(4))* AuthorHouse.

Brown, Margaret Wise. A Baby's Gift: Goodnight Moon & the Runaway Bunny, 2 vols. Hurd, Clement, illus. 2014. 70p. (J). (gr. -1 — 1). pap. 15.99 *(978-0-694-01638-9(1),* HarperFestival) HarperCollins Pubs.

—Boa Noite Lua. pap. 19.95 *(978-85-336-0713-2(X))* Livraria Martins Editora BRA. Dist: Distribooks, Inc.

—Bonsoir Lune.Tr. of Goodnight Moon. (FRE.). (J). pap. 21.95 *(978-2-211-01028-3(8))* Archimede Editions FRA. Dist: Distribooks, Inc.

—Buenas Noches Conejito. 2006. (Illus.). 24p. (J). (gr. -1-k). 12.95 *(978-1-882077-63-2(6))* Sweetwater Pr.

—Buenas Noches, Luna. 2006.Tr. of Goodnight Moon. (SPA.). (J). (gr. -1-2). lib. bdg. 18.40 *(978-0-613-09961-5(3),* Turtleback) Turtleback Bks.

—Buenas Noches Oso. 2006. (Illus.). 24p. (J). (gr. -1-k). 12.95 *(978-1-882077-61-8(X))* Sweetwater Pr.

—Good Day, Good Night. Long, Loren, illus. 2017. 40p. (J). (gr. -1-3). 18.99 ***(978-0-06-238310-5(8))*** HarperCollins Pubs.

—Goodnight Moon. Hurd, Clement, illus. (J). (gr. -1 — 1). 2012. (ENG.). 8p. pap. 14.99 *(978-0-06-076224-7(1),* HarperFestival) 2007. (ENG.). 32p. pap. 24.99 *(978-0-06-111977-4(6),* HarperFestival) 2005. 32p. lib. bdg. 18.89 *(978-0-06-077586-5(6))* 60th anniv. ed. 2007. (ENG.). 34p. bds. 8.99 *(978-0-694-00361-7(1),* HarperFestival) 60th anniv. ed. 2007. (ENG.). 32p. 18.99 *(978-0-06-077585-8(8))* 60th anniv. ed. 2007. (ENG.). 32p. pap. 8.99 *(978-0-06-443017-3(0))* HarperCollins Pubs.

—Goodnight Moon. 2007. (J). (gr. -1-2). lib. bdg. 18.40 *(978-0-8085-9386-7(2),* Turtleback) Turtleback Bks.

—Goodnight Moon. Hurd, Clement, illus. (J). pap. 32.75 incl. audio. (gr. -1-3). 24.95 incl. audio Weston Woods Studios, Inc.

—Goodnight Moon 123: A Counting Book. Hurd, Clement, illus. (J). 2013. (ENG.). 30p. (gr. -1-k). bds. 9.99 *(978-0-06-224405-5(1),* HarperFestival) 2007. (ENG.). 32p. (gr. -1-k). 16.99 *(978-0-06-112593-5(8))* 2007. 32p. (gr. -1-k). lib. bdg. 17.89 *(978-0-06-112594-2(6))* 2007. *(978-1-4287-4853-8(9))* HarperCollins Pubs.

—Goodnight Moon 123 Lap Edition. Hurd, Clement, illus. 2008. (ENG.). 30p. (J). (gr. -1 — 1). bds. 12.99 *(978-0-06-166755-8(2),* HarperFestival) HarperCollins Pubs.

—Goodnight Moon 123/Buenas Noches, Luna 123: A Counting Book/un Libro para Contar. Hurd, Clement, illus. 2007. (ENG & SPA.). 32p. (J). (gr. -1-k). 16.99 *(978-0-06-117325-7(8),* Rayo) HarperCollins Pubs.

—Goodnight Moon Board Book & Bunny. Hurd, Clement, illus. 2005. (ENG.). 34p. (J). (gr. -1 — 1). bds. 16.99 *(978-0-06-076027-4(3),* HarperFestival) HarperCollins Pubs.

—Goodnight Moon Cloth Book Box. Hurd, Clement, illus. 2012. (ENG.). 8p. (J). (gr. -1 — 1). pap. 14.99 *(978-0-06-223589-3(3),* HarperFestival) HarperCollins Pubs.

—Sleepy ABC. Katz, Karen, illus. 2009. (ENG.). 40p. (J). (gr. -1-3). 16.99 *(978-0-06-128863-0(2))* HarperCollins Pubs.

—Sleepy ABC Board Book. Katz, Karen, illus. 2016. 32p. (J). (gr. -1 — 1). bds. 7.99 *(978-0-06-233793-1(9),* HarperFestival) HarperCollins Pubs.

—Wish upon a Dream. Cooke, Charlotte, illus. 2014. (ENG.). 24p. (J). (gr. -1-3). 7.99 *(978-1-4723-4531-8(2))* Parragon, Inc.

Brueggeman, Karen & Paddock, Briana. Fruzzle's Mystery Talent: A Bed Time Fantasy Story for Children Ages 3-10. Brueggeman, Bryan, illus. 2013. 48p. pap. 10.99 *(978-0-9892565-0-6(2))* Dolphins Publishing.

Brunell, Heather. Bedtime Monster. Adamson, Bonnie, illus. 2010. (ENG.). 32p. (J). (gr. -1-12). lib. bdg. 16.95 *(978-1-934960-03-5(9),* Raven Tree Pr.,Csi) Continental Sales, Inc.

—Bedtime Monster/A Dormir, Monstruito! Del Risco, Eida & de la Vega, Eida, trs. 2010. (ENG & SPA., Illus.). 32p. (J). (gr. -1-3). pap. 7.95 *(978-1-932748-81-9(4),* Raven Tree Pr.,Csi) Continental Sales, Inc.

—Bedtime Monster/A Dormir, Monstruito! de la Vega, Eida, tr. Adamson, Bonnie, illus. 2010. (ENG & SPA.). 32p. (J). (gr. -1-3). lib. bdg. 16.95 *(978-1-932748-80-2(6),* Raven Tree Pr.,Csi) Continental Sales, Inc.

Bryan, Jennifer Liu. The Different Dragon. Hosler, Danamarie, illus. 2006. (J). pap. 12.95 *(978-0-9674468-6-8(4))* Two Lives Publishing.

Buchholz, Quint. Duerme Bien, Pequeño Oso. 2nd ed. 2003. (Rosa y Manzana Ser.). (SPA., Illus.). 208p. 15.16 *(978-84-89804-10-4(9))* Lóguez Ediciones ESP. Dist: Lectorum Pubns., Inc.

Bullard, Lisa. Not Enough Beds! A Christmas Alphabet Book. Oeltjenbruns, Joni, illus. 2004. (Picture Bks.). 32p. (J). (gr. -1-3). 15.95 *(978-1-57505-356-1(X),* Carolrhoda Bks.); per. 6.95 *(978-1-57505-797-2(2))* Lerner Publishing Group.

Buller, Jon & Schade, Susan. I Love You, Good Night. Pons, Bernadette, illus. 2006. (ENG.). 28p. (J). (gr. -1 — 1). bds. 7.99 *(978-0-689-86212-0(1),* Little Simon) Little Simon.

—I Love You, Good Night: Lap Edition. Pons, Bernadette, illus. 2013. (ENG.). 28p. (J). (gr. -1 — 1). bds. 12.99 *(978-1-4424-8539-6(6),* Little Simon) Little Simon.

Bunting, Eve. No Nap. Meddaugh, Susan, illus. 2014. (ENG.). 32p. (J). (— 1). audio compact disk 10.99 *(978-0-544-33917-0(7),* HMH Books For Young Readers) Houghton Mifflin Harcourt Publishing Co.

Burgess, Sushila. Jasmine's Unicorn. 2010. 115p. pap. 18.95 *(978-1-4452-5662-7(2))* Lulu Pr., Inc.

Burgess, Thornton W. The Adventures of Danny Meadow Mouse. 2009. (gr. 4-7). 108p. 22.95 *(978-1-60664-649-6(4));* 104p. pap. 9.95 *(978-1-60664-274-0(X))* Rodgers, Alan Bks.

Burk, Rachelle. Don't Turn the Page! Downing, Julie, illus. 2014. (ENG.). 32p. (J). (gr. -1-3). 16.95 *(978-1-939547-06-4(7))* Creston Bks.

Burlingham, Abi. All Grown Up. Everitt-Stewart, Andy, illus. 2009. (Stories to Grow with Ser.). 24p. (J). (gr. -1-2). 22.60 *(978-1-60754-469-2(5));* pap. 8.15 *(978-1-60754-470-8(9))* Windmill Bks.

Burnett, Melissa. Even Pirates Need Their Sleep. 2010. 32p. (J). pap. 15.00 *(978-1-4490-7092-2(2))* AuthorHouse.

Burri, Hillary Hayden. Bedtime Safari. 2004. *(978-0-9758785-0-7(6))* Haydenburri Lane.

Butler, John. Bedtime in the Jungle. Butler, John, illus. 2009. (Illus.). 32p. (J). (gr. -1-1). 16.95 *(978-1-56145-486-0(9))* Peachtree Pubs.

—Can You Growl Like a Bear? Butler, John, illus. (Illus.). (J). 2012. 20p. bds. 6.95 *(978-1-56145-667-3(5))* 2007. (ENG., 32p. 15.95 *(978-1-56145-396-2(X),* Peachtree Junior) Peachtree Pubs.

—Hush, Little Ones. Butler, John, illus. 2003. (Illus.). 24p. (J). (gr. k-k). bds. 6.95 *(978-1-56145-297-2(1))* Peachtree Pubs.

Butterworth, MyLinda. The Monster Run. Day, Linda S., ed. Mercer, Matthew, illus. l.t. ed. 2004. 32p. (J). (gr. -1-3). 14.95 *(978-1-890905-23-1(2),* Writers Collective, The) Day to Day Enterprises.

Callahan, Michael P. Daddy Daddy, It's Time for Bed! 2009. 24p. pap. 12.99 *(978-1-4389-1288-2(9))* AuthorHouse.

Calle, Juan & Valentino, Serena. Good Dream, Bad Dream: The World's Legendary Heroes Save the Night! 2014. (ENG & SPA., Illus.). 36p. (J). (gr. -1-3). 15.95 *(978-1-59702-103-6(2))* Immedium.

Callen, Sharon. Safari Camp, 1 vol. rev. ed. 2013. (Fiction Readers Ser.). (ENG., Illus.). 20p. (J). (gr. 1-1). pap. 4.99 *(978-1-4333-5494-6(2));* pap. 15.96 *(978-1-4807-1150-1(0))* Shell Educational Publishing.

Camacho, Celi C. Bedtime for Meaghan. 2008. 33p. pap. 24.95 *(978-1-60563-527-9(8))* America Star Bks.

Captain, Cliff. Fables by the Sea, 2 vols. 2005. 145p. (J). Vol. 1. pap. *(978-0-9766401-0-3(4))* Vol. 2. pap. *(978-0-9766401-1-0(2))* Aenor Trust, The.

Capucilli, Alyssa Satin. Biscuit. Schories, Pat, illus. 2017. (My First I Can Read Ser.). 32p. (J). (gr. -1-3). 9.99 *(978-0-06-257276-9(8))* HarperCollins Pubs.

—Biscuit's Pet & Play Bedtime: A Touch & Feel Book. Schories, Pat, illus. 2017. (Biscuit Ser.). 12p. (J). (gr. -1 — 1). bds. 7.99 *(978-0-06-249039-1(7),* HarperFestival) HarperCollins Pubs.

Caracappa, Michael. Storybook: From Age Three to Young Teenager. 2012. 84p. 19.95 *(978-1-4626-6773-4(2))* America Star Bks.

Carlson, Melody. Goodnight, Angels, 1 vol. Allsopp, Sophie, illus. 2011. (ENG.). 32p. (J). 15.99 *(978-0-310-71687-7(X))* Zonderkidz.

Carre, Lilli. Tippy & the Night Parade. Carre, Lilli, illus. 2014. (ENG., Illus.). 32p. (J). (gr. -1-3). 12.95 *(978-1-935179-57-3(8))* TOON Books / RAW Junior, LLC.

Carter, Anne Laurel. Night Boy, 1 vol. Pelletier, Ninon, illus. 2012. (ENG.). 32p. (J). (gr. -1-3). 19.95 *(978-1-55469-402-0(7))* Orca Bk. Pubs. USA.

Carter, David A. Bedtime Bugs. Carter, David A., illus. 2010. (David Carter's Bugs Ser.). (ENG., Illus.). 18p. (J). (gr. -1-2). 12.99 *(978-1-4169-9960-7(4),* Little Simon) Little Simon.

Carter, Erin. Welcome Back Sun. 2012. 30p. pap. 9.99 *(978-1-935711-15-5(6))* Peak City Publishing, LLC.

Carter, Larry. Tommie's Bad Dream. 2013. 28p. pap. 24.95 *(978-1-4626-9668-0(6))* America Star Bks.

Casey, Dawn. A Lullaby for Little One. Fuge, Charles, illus. 2015. (ENG.). 32p. (J). (-k). 12.99 *(978-0-7636-7608-7(X),* Nosy Crow) Candlewick Pr.

Castle, Elizabeth. Because I Love You More Than All the Stars in Heaven. 2008. 21p. pap. 24.95 *(978-1-4241-9395-0(8))* America Star Bks.

Castro, Edmund Lee. Crystal & Her Flying Adventure. 2010. 44p. 16.99 *(978-1-4490-6867-7(7))* AuthorHouse.

Cavaliere, Katrina. Mom! There's a Monster under My Bed! 2008. 24p. per. 24.95 *(978-1-60441-066-2(3))* America Star Bks.

Chaisson, Kristen. Dreamland. 2013. 28p. pap. 24.95 *(978-1-63000-664-8(5))* America Star Bks.

Chapman, Jason. Who's That Snoring? A Pull-the-Tab Bedtime Book. Chapman, Jason, illus. 2010. (ENG., Illus.). 12p. (J). (gr. -1-1). bds. 9.99 *(978-1-4169-8937-0(4),* Little Simon) Little Simon.

Chast, Roz. Too Busy Marco. Chast, Roz, illus. 2010. (ENG., Illus.). 32p. (J). (gr. -1-3). 16.99 *(978-1-4169-8474-0(7),* Atheneum Bks. for Young Readers) Simon & Schuster Children's Publishing.

Child, Lauren. I Am Not Sleepy & I Will Not Go to Bed. 2004. (J). (gr. k-3). spiral bd. *(978-0-616-11105-5(3));* spiral bd. *(978-0-616-11104-8(5))* Canadian National Institute for the Blind/Institut National Canadien pour les Aveugles.

—I Am Not Sleepy & I Will Not Go to Bed. Child, Lauren, illus. (Charlie & Lola Ser.). (ENG., Illus.). (J). (gr. -1-2). 2008. 16p. 19.99 *(978-0-7636-4098-9(0))* 2005. 32p. reprint ed. pap. 8.99 *(978-0-7636-2970-0(7))* Candlewick Pr.

Childress, Story. Blue Moon Cheese. 2008. 28p. pap. 24.95 *(978-1-60610-174-2(9))* America Star Bks.

—The Old Codger, 1 vol. 2009. 23p. pap. 19.95 *(978-1-4489-2511-7(8))* PublishAmerica, Inc.

Chima, Ahiru & Misu, Max. Ellenā__- Ellen meets Frog King - 2005. 32p. pap. 14.99 *(978-1-4116-4050-1(0))* Lulu Pr., Inc.

Choldenko, Gennifer. Putting the Monkeys to Bed. Davis, Jack E., illus. 2015. (ENG.). 32p. (J). (gr. -1-k). 16.99 *(978-0-399-24623-4(1),* G.P. Putnam's Sons Books for Young Readers) Penguin Young Readers Group.

Christelow, Eileen. Five Little Monkeys Jumping on the Bed Lap Board Book. 2008. (Five Little Monkeys Story Ser.). (ENG., Illus.). 30p. (J). (gr. -1 — 1). bds. 12.99 *(978-0-547-13176-4(3))* Houghton Mifflin Harcourt Publishing Co.

—Five Little Monkeys Play Hide & Seek. 2010. (Five Little Monkeys Story Ser.). (ENG., Illus.). 40p. (J). (gr. -1-3). pap. 6.99 *(978-0-547-33787-6(6))* Houghton Mifflin Harcourt Publishing Co.

—Five Little Monkeys Reading in Bed. 2011. (Five Little Monkeys Story Ser.). (ENG., Illus.). 40p. (J). (gr. -1-3). 16.99 *(978-0-547-38610-2(9))* Houghton Mifflin Harcourt Publishing Co.

—Jumping on the Bed. 2017. (Five Little Monkeys Story Ser.). (ENG., Illus.). 30p. (J). (gr. -1 — 1). bds. 8.99 *(978-0-547-51075-0(6),* HMH Books For Young Readers) Houghton Mifflin Harcourt Publishing Co.

Christen, Thiel. Night & Day. 2003. (Illus.). 14p. (J). 4.95 *(978-1-59466-010-8(7),* Little Ones) Port Town Publishing.

Christensen-Hall, Nancy. Good Night, Little Kitten. Hockerman, Dennis, illus. 2004. (My First Reader Ser.). (ENG.). 32p. (J). (gr. k-1). pap. 3.95 *(978-0-516-24628-4(3),* Children's Pr.) Scholastic Library Publishing.

Church, Caroline Jayne. Goodnight, I Love You. Church, Caroline Jayne, illus. 2012. (ENG., Illus.). 20p. (J). (gr. -1-k). bds. 8.99 *(978-0-545-39215-0(2),* Cartwheel Bks.) Scholastic, Inc.

Clairmont, Patsy. Sleep Sweet, My Little One, 1 vol. Johannes, Shelley, illus. 2014. (ENG.). 24p. (J). bds. 12.99 *(978-1-4003-2401-9(7))* Nelson, Thomas Inc.

Clark, Matthew. SongrrrLines: A Beastie Bedtime Dreaming, & Coloring Book. 2005. 26p. (J). pap. 8.95 net. *(978-1-59975-106-1(2))* Independent Pub.

Clayton, Dallas. An Awesome Book of Love! Clayton, Dallas, illus. 2012. (Awesome Book Ser.). (ENG., Illus.). 56p. (J). (gr. -1-3). 16.99 *(978-0-06-211666-6(5))* HarperCollins Pubs.

Coats, Vivian. His Special Love. 2009. 32p. pap. 12.99 *(978-1-4490-1915-0(3))* AuthorHouse.

Cochran, Jean M. On a Dark, Dark Night. Morris, Jennifer E., illus. 2009. (ENG.). 32p. (J). (gr. k-2). 16.95 *(978-1-935025-00-9(7))* Pleasant St. Pr.

Colby, Rebecca. Motor Goose. Kaminsky, Jef, illus. 2017. (ENG.). 32p. (J). 16.99 *(978-1-250-10193-8(X),* 9781250101938) Feiwel & Friends.

Cole, Rachael. City Moon. Gomez, Blanca, illus. 2017. (ENG.). 40p. (J). (gr. -1-2). 17.99 ***(978-0-553-49707-6(3));*** lib. bdg. 20.99 ***(978-0-553-49708-3(1))*** Random Hse. Children's Bks. (Schwartz & Wade Bks.).

Conan, Sally Anne. Sleepy Time Blessings. Rutten, Nicole, illus. 2009. (ENG.). 12p. (J). (gr. -1). 8.00 *(978-0-8028-5350-9(1))* Eerdmans, William B. Publishing Co.

Cooley, Judy. I Love You More. (Illus.). (gr. -1-k). 2007. 32p. bds. 9.95 *(978-1-59038-758-0(9))* 2005. 29p. (J). 19.99 *(978-1-59038-432-9(6))* Shadow Mountain Publishing. (Shadow Mountain).

Coombs, Kate. Goodnight Mr. Darcy Board Book, 1 vol. Arnold, Alli, illus. 2015. (ENG.). 22p. (J). bds. 9.99 *(978-1-4236-4177-3(9))* Gibbs Smith, Publisher.

Coombs, Kate & Austen, Jane. Goodnight Mr. Darcy: A Babylit Parody, 1 vol. 2014. (ENG., Illus.). 32p. (J). 16.99 *(978-1-4236-3670-0(8))* Gibbs Smith, Publisher.

Coppage, Merry Ann. Periwinkle Island. Venema, Lisa J. & Garland, Lynn Rockwell, illus. 2006. 86p. (J). (gr. -1-3). per. 36.99 *(978-1-4259-1931-3(6))* AuthorHouse.

Costales, Amy. Hello Night/Hola Noche. McDonald, Mercedes, illus. 2007. (ENG, SPA & MUL.). 24p. (J). (gr. -1 — 1). 14.95 *(978-0-87358-927-7(0))* Cooper Square Publishing Llc.

Cousins, Lucy. Sweet Dreams, Maisy. Cousins, Lucy, illus. 2009. (Maisy Ser.). (ENG., Illus.). 32p. (J). (gr. -1-2). bds. 6.99 *(978-0-7636-4532-8(X))* Candlewick Pr.

Cowley, Joy. The Bedtime Train. Odone, Jamison, illus. 2008. (ENG.). 32p. (J). (gr. k-2). 16.95 *(978-1-59078-493-8(6),* Front Street) Boyds Mills Pr.

—Big Bear & Little Bear: Cold Feet. Lam, Amy, illus. 2013. (ENG.). 8p. pap. *(978-1-927186-27-5(7),* Joy Cowley Club) Flying Start Bks.

Cox, Judy. Sheep Won't Sleep: Counting by 2s, 5s, And 10s. Cuneo, Nina, illus. 2017. (ENG.). 32p. (J). 16.95 ***(978-0-8234-3701-6(9))*** Holiday Hse., Inc.

Cox, Phil Roxbee & Cartwright, S. Sam Sheep Can't Sleep. 2004. (Phonics Board Bks.). (ENG.). 1p. (J). bds. 4.99 *(978-0-7945-0060-3(9),* Usborne) EDC Publishing.

Cox, Roy. And They Fell Fast Asleep. McCall, Anthony, illus. 2012. 48p. pap. 15.95 *(978-1-61493-045-7(7))* Peppertree Pr., The.

Craig, Lindsey. Farmyard Beat. Brown, Marc, illus. 2012. (ENG.). 32p. (J). (gr. k-k). bds. 6.99 *(978-0-307-93082-8(3),* Knopf Bks. for Young Readers) Random Hse. Children's Bks.

Cratzius, Barbara & Thonissen, Uta. Good Night, Sleep Tight! 2004. (Illus.). 16p. (J). bds. 5.99 *(978-1-59384-040-2(3))* Parklane Publishing.

Crimi, Carolyn. Where's My Mummy? Manders, John, illus. (ENG.). 32p. (J). (gr. -1-3). 2009. 7.99 *(978-0-7636-4337-9(8))* 2008. 15.99 *(978-0-7636-3196-3(5))* Candlewick Pr.

Crow, Kristyn. Bedtime at the Swamp. Pamintuan, Macky, illus. 2008. (ENG.). 32p. (J). (gr. -1-1). 16.99 *(978-0-06-083951-2(1))* HarperCollins Pubs.

Crow, Nosy. Bunny Boo Has Lost Her Teddy: A Tiny Tab Book. 2014. (Tiny Tab Ser.). (ENG.). 8p. (J). (— 1). bds. 7.99 *(978-0-7636-7274-4(2),* Nosy Crow) Candlewick Pr.

—Pip & Posy: the Bedtime Frog. Scheffler, Axel, illus. 2014. (Pip & Posy Ser.). (ENG.). 32p. (J). (-k). 12.99 *(978-0-7636-7068-9(5),* Nosy Crow) Candlewick Pr.

Crow, Sara. Even Superheroes Have to Sleep. Record, Adam, illus. 2017. (ENG.). 32p. (J). (-k). 16.99 *(978-0-399-55806-1(3),* Doubleday Bks. for Young Readers) Random Hse. Children's Bks.

Crowe, Caroline. Pirates in Pajamas. Knight, Tim, illus. 2015. (ENG.). 32p. (J). (gr. -1-3). 16.99 *(978-1-58925-190-8(3))* Tiger Tales.

Cummiskey, Kristen Marie. Bedtime Is Fun. 2011. 24p. (gr. -1 — 1). pap. 12.74 *(978-1-4567-5193-7(X))* AuthorHouse.

Curtis, Tony. The Gnomes of Genom. 2009. 196p. pap. 15.99 *(978-1-4389-5789-0(0))* AuthorHouse.

Czajak, Paul. Monster Needs His Sleep. Grieb, Wendy, illus. 2014. (Monster & Me Ser.). (ENG.). 32p. (J). (-k). 16.95 *(978-1-938063-26-8(0),* Mighty Media Kids) Mighty Media Pr.

DaCosta, Barbara. Nighttime Ninja. 2012. (ENG., Illus.). 32p. (J). (gr. -1-3). 16.99 *(978-0-316-20384-5(X))* Little, Brown Bks. for Young Readers.

Daddo, Andrew. Goodnight, Me. Quay, Emma, illus. 2007. (ENG.). 32p. (J). (gr. -1-k). 14.99 *(978-1-59990-153-4(6),* 9781599901534, Bloomsbury USA Childrens) Bloomsbury Publishing USA.

Daddy, The Bigg. Bed Time Stories to Grandchildren. 2011. 236p. 29.99 *(978-1-4568-4334-2(6))* Xlibris Corp.

Dahl, Michael. Bedtime for Batman. Beavers, Ethen, illus. 2016. (DC Super Heroes Ser.). (ENG.). 32p. (gr. -1-2). 15.95 *(978-1-62370-732-3(3));* lib. bdg. 22.65 *(978-1-5158-0652-3(9))* Stone Arch Bks. (DC Super Heroes).

—Big Bed for Giraffe. Vidal, Oriol, illus. 2015. (Hello Genius Ser.). (ENG.). 20p. (gr. 1-2). bds. 7.99 *(978-1-4795-5791-2(9))* Picture Window Bks.

—Goodnight Baseball. Forshay, Christina, illus. 2013. (Sports Illustrated Kids Bedtime Bks.). (ENG.). 32p. (gr. -1-2). pap. 6.95 *(978-1-4795-4975-7(4))* Capstone Press of Coughlan Cos.

—Goodnight Baseball, 1 vol. Forshay, Christina E., illus. 2013. (Sports Illustrated Kids Bedtime Bks.). (ENG.). 32p. (gr. -1-2). 14.95 *(978-1-62370-000-3(0))* Capstone Press of Coughlan Cos.

—Goodnight Baseball, 1 vol. Forshay, Christina, illus. 2013. (Sports Illustrated Kids Bedtime Bks.). (ENG.). 32p. (gr. -1-2). lib. bdg. 22.60 *(978-1-4048-7979-9(X))* Capstone Press of Coughlan Cos.

—Goodnight Hockey. Forshay, Christina, illus. 2015. (Sports Illustrated Kids Bedtime Bks.). (ENG.). 32p. (gr. -1-2). lib. bdg. 22.60 *(978-1-4795-6526-9(1))* Capstone Press of Coughlan Cos.

—No More Pacifier, Duck. Vidal, Oriol, illus. 2015. (Hello Genius Ser.). (ENG.). 20p. (gr. 1-2). bds. 7.99 *(978-1-4795-5793-6(5))* Picture Window Bks.

—Story Time for Lamb, 1 vol. Vidal, Oriol, illus. 2011. (Hello Genius Ser.). (ENG.). 20p. (gr. 1-2). bds. 7.99 *(978-1-4048-6495-5(4))* Picture Window Bks.

Dale, Penny. Ten in the Bed. Dale, Penny, illus. 2007. (ENG., Illus.). 24p. (J). (— 1). bds. 5.99 *(978-0-7636-3514-5(6))* Candlewick Pr.

Damson, D. A. Dory & Her Long Bedtime Story. 2011. 28p. (gr. 1-2). pap. 13.54 *(978-1-4269-5865-6(X))* Trafford Publishing.

Daniels, Linda. A Friend Called Glen. 2011. 28p. pap. 16.09 *(978-1-4269-4848-0(4))* Trafford Publishing.

Danis, Naomi. Splish-Splash, into the Bath! Kreloff, Elliot, illus. 2007. 16p. (J). *(978-1-59354-609-0(2))* Handprint Bks.

Danna, Minnie. Miss Poppy & Red Jeans: Adventure to Willie Willie's Garden. Danna Sr., Gerald, illus. 2012. 66p. pap. 12.95 *(978-0-9852608-0-4(7))* Flower Publishing.

Dargento, Beverly. Spot the Dot. 2008. 16p. pap. 9.49 *(978-1-4389-2287-4(6))* AuthorHouse.

Darnell, Cynthia. Cameron Asks, What If... 2009. 18p. pap. 24.95 *(978-1-60836-836-5(X))* America Star Bks.

Davey, Owen. Night Knight. Davey, Owen, illus. 2012. (ENG., Illus.). 32p. (J). (gr. k-k). 15.99 *(978-0-7636-5838-0(3),* Templar) Candlewick Pr.

Davies, Becky. Bedtime Blessing. Macnaughton, Tina, illus. 2016. (ENG.). 24p. (J). (gr. -1-k). bds. 8.99 *(978-1-58925-205-9(5))* Tiger Tales.

Davis, Beneta. My Covers. 2008. 24p. pap. 24.95 *(978-1-60441-584-1(3))* America Star Bks.

Davis, Buddy. Whale of a Story: Adventures on the High Seas. 2003. 40p. (J). 14.99 *(978-0-89051-390-3(2))* Master Bks.

Davis, Catherine Jennings & Thompson, Traci Shirley. Goodnight Cavaliers. 2013. (J). 17.95 *(978-1-62086-038-0(4))* Mascot Bks., Inc.

Davis, Heather. Lam & the Pickle-Eating Bear. 2008. 24p. pap. 24.95 *(978-1-60474-332-6(8))* America Star Bks.

Davis, Lowrey. Papa's Storybook. 2008. 116p. 19.99 *(978-1-60791-100-5(0));* pap. 11.99 *(978-1-60791-099-2(3))* Salem Author Services.

DaySpring & Jensen, Bonnie Rickner. Really Woolly 5-Minute Bedtime Treasury, 1 vol. 2016. (Really Woolly Ser.). (ENG., Illus.). 192p. (J). 12.99 *(978-0-7180-8451-6(9))* Nelson, Thomas Inc.

de Monfreid, Dorothée. Shhh! I'm Sleeping. de Monfreid, Dorothée, illus. 2016. (ENG., Illus.). 24p. (gr. -1-1). 12.99 *(978-1-927271-95-7(9))* Gecko Pr. NZL. Dist: Lerner Publishing Group.

Dean, James & Dean, Kimberly. Pete the Cat & the Bedtime Blues. Dean, James, illus. 2015. (Pete the Cat Ser.). (Illus.). 40p. (J). (gr. -1-3). (ENG.). 17.99 *(978-0-06-230430-8(5));* lib. bdg. 18.89 *(978-0-06-230431-5(3))* HarperCollins Pubs.

Dean, Ramsey. Riding on a Beam of Light: Albert Einstein. Hamdan, Noah, illus. 2013. 48p. pap. 10.48 *(978-0-9893372-1-2(9))* Ramsey Dean, Inc.

DeCarmelo, Marie. A Little Christmas Story. 2008. 40p. pap. 18.95 *(978-0-557-02844-3(2))* Lulu Pr., Inc.

Degen, Bruce. I Said, Bed! Degen, Bruce, illus. (I Like to Read(r) Ser.). (ENG., Illus.). 24p. (J). (gr. -1-2). 2015. 6.99 *(978-0-8234-3311-7(0))* 2014. 14.95 *(978-0-8234-2938-7(5))* Holiday Hse., Inc.

DeJohnette-Harvin, Yvonne. Bed Time Blues. 2003. pap. 14.00 *(978-0-8059-6014-3(7))* Dorrance Publishing Co., Inc.

Del George, Dana. The Queen of Fire & the King of Ice. 2009. 24p. 12.50 *(978-0-578-00730-4(4))* Del George, Dana.

Delacroix, Sibylle. Blanche Hates the Night. Morelli, Christelle, tr. from FRE. 2016. (ENG., Illus.). 32p. (J). (gr. -1-2). 16.95 *(978-1-77147-158-9(1),* Owlkids) Owlkids Bks. Inc. CAN. Dist: Publishers Group West (PGW).

Denton, P. J. Keeping Secrets. Denos, Julia, illus. 4th ed. 2008. (Sleepover Squad Ser.: 4). (ENG.). 96p. (J). (gr. 1-4). pap. 4.99 *(978-1-4169-2801-0(4),* Aladdin) Simon & Schuster Children's Publishing.

DePrisco, Dorothea. Lullaby & Good Night: Music & Lights. 2006. (ENG., Illus.). 12p. (gr. -1-k). 12.95 *(978-1-58117-450-2(0),* Intervisual/Piggy Toes) Bendon, Inc.

Dessen, Maci. Bedtime. 2016. (It's Time Ser.). 24p. (gr. 1-1). pap. 8.25 *(978-1-4994-2277-1(6),* PowerKids Pr.) Rosen Publishing Group, Inc., The.

Dewdney, Anna. Llama Llama Nighty-Night. 2012. (Llama Llama Ser.). (ENG., Illus.). 14p. (J). bds. 5.99 *(978-0-670-01327-2(7),* Viking Books for Young Readers) Penguin Young Readers Group.

A B

—Llama Llama Red Pajama. Dewdney, Anna, illus. (Llama Llama Ser.). (ENG., Illus.). 40p. (J). (gr. -1-k). 2014. 25.00 (978-0-451-46990-8(9)) 2005. 17.99 (978-0-670-05983-6(8)) Penguin Young Readers Group. (Viking Books for Young Readers).

—Llama Llama Red Pajama, 6 vols., Pack. gif. ed. 2014. (ENG.). (J). 107.94 (978-0-451-47544-2(5), Viking Books for Young Readers) Penguin Young Readers Group.

—Llama Llama Red Pajama. (978-0-439-90665-4(2)); 2006. lp (978-0-439-90679-1(2)) Scholastic, Inc.

Dickens, Charles. A Christmas Carol. 2005. 92p. (Orig.). (gr. 4-6). per. 6.95 (978-1-933652-47-4(0)) Bed Bks.

Diffenderfer, David W. The Adventures of Boo & Fred. 2010. 58p. pap. 9.99 (978-1-60911-966-9(5), Eloquent Bks.) Strategic Book Publishing & Rights Agency (SBPRA).

Disney. Disney Frozen: Time for Bed, Olaf! 2016. (ENG.). 12p. (J). (gr. -1-k). bds. 12.99 (978-0-7944-3754-1(0)) Studio Fun International.

Disney Baby Staff & Disney Book Group Staff. Cozy Baby. Disney Storybook Artists Staff, illus. 2010. (ENG.). 6p. (J). (gr. -1 — 1). 7.99 (978-1-4231-2827-4(3)) Disney Pr.

Disney Book Group. Bedtime Favorites (3rd Edition) 2016. (Storybook Collection). (ENG.). 304p. (J). (gr. -1-k). 16.99 (978-1-4847-3238-0(3)) Disney Pr.

Disney Book Group Staff. Disney Bedtime Favorites. Disney Storybook Artists Staff & Disney Book Group Staff, illus. 2012. (Storybook Collection). (ENG.). 304p. (J). (gr. -1 — 1). 15.99 (978-1-4231-6034-2(7)) Disney Pr.

Disney Press Staff & Disney Book Group Staff. Thumper's Furry Friends. 2010. (Touch-And-feel Book Ser.). (ENG.). 12p. (J). (gr. -1-k). bds. 6.99 (978-1-4231-1840-4(5)) Disney Pr.

Disney's Read to Me Treasury - Bedtime. 2011. 400p. (978-1-4231-2394-1(8)) Disney Pr.

Docherty, Helen. The Snatchabook. Docherty, Helen, illus. 2013. (ENG., Illus.). 32p. (J). (-2). 16.99 (978-1-4022-9082-4(9), 9781402290824, Sourcebooks Jabberwocky) Sourcebooks, Inc.

Donald, Diana. My Special Angel: A Bedtime Story. Polito, Mike, illus. 2005. 33p. (J). (gr. -1-3). incl. audio compact disk (978-1-894290-01-2(1)) Heart of the Matter Publishing.

Dorling Kindersley Publishing Staff. Baby Night-Night. 2016. (ENG., Illus.). 14p. (J). (— 1). bds. 5.99 (978-1-4654-4389-2(4), DK Children) Dorling Kindersley Publishing, Inc.

—Bedtime. 2008. (Baby Touch & Feel Ser.). (ENG.). 14p. (J). (gr. -1 — 1). bds. 5.99 (978-0-7566-4511-3(5), DK Children) Dorling Kindersley Publishing, Inc.

Downing, Sue. Look, Look! Baby Animal Friends. 2016. (ENG., Illus.). 10p. (J). bds. 7.99 (978-1-61963-832-7(0), 9781619638327, Bloomsbury USA Childrens) Bloomsbury Publishing USA.

Doyle, Malachy. The Snuggle Sandwich. Millward, Gwen, illus. 2013. (ENG.). 32p. (J). (gr. -1-k). pap. 9.99 (978-1-84939-420-8(2)) Andersen Pr. GBR. Dist: Independent Pubs. Group.

Doyle, Teresa J. The Dream Box: Big Dreams for Little Sleepers. 2008. 84p. pap. 26.95 (978-1-4343-9086-8(1)) AuthorHouse.

Dragonwagon, Crescent. All the Awake Animals Are Almost Asleep. McPhail, David, illus. 2012. (ENG.). 40p. (J). (gr. -1-3). 16.99 (978-0-316-07045-4(9)) Little Brown & Co.

—All the Awake Animals Are Almost Asleep. McPhail, David, illus. 2016. (ENG.). 30p. (J). (gr. -1 — 1). bds. 7.99 (978-0-316-33627-7(0)) Little, Brown Bks. for Young Readers.

Dromgoole, Glenn. Good Night Little Texan. Clack, Barbra, illus. 2012. (ENG.). 24p. (J). (gr. k-2). 15.95 (978-1-936474-10-3(7), 9781936474103) Bright Sky Pr.

Dubrule, Jackie. Miranda, God & the Park. Swope, Brenda, illus. 2011. 32p. pap. 24.95 (978-1-4560-0966-3(4)) America Star Bks.

Dunbar, Joyce. Tell Me Something Happy Before I Go to Sleep. Gliori, Debi, illus. 2013. (ENG.). 24p. (J). (— 1). bds. 11.99 (978-0-547-94059-5(9)) Houghton Mifflin Harcourt Publishing Co.

Dunbar, Polly. Goodnight, Tiptoe. Dunbar, Polly, illus. 2009. (Tilly & Friends Ser.). (ENG., Illus.). 32p. (J). (gr. -1-2). 12.99 (978-0-7636-4328-7(9)) Candlewick Pr.

Durand, Hallie. Mitchell's License. Fucile, Tony, illus. 2011. (ENG.). 40p. (J). (gr. -1-2). 15.99 (978-0-7636-4496-3(X)) Candlewick Pr.

Durango, Julia. Angels Watching over Me. Kleven, Elisa, illus. 2007. (ENG.). 32p. (J). (gr. -1-3). 18.99 (978-0-689-86252-6(0), Simon & Schuster Bks. For Young Readers) Simon & Schuster Bks. For Young Readers.

Durango, Julia & Trupiano, Katie Belle. Dream Away. Goldstrom, Robert, illus. 2011. (ENG.). 32p. (J). (gr. -1-3). 16.99 (978-1-4169-8702-4(9), Simon & Schuster Bks. For Young Readers) Simon & Schuster Bks. For Young Readers.

Durant, Alan. Billy Monster's Daymare. Collins, Ross, illus. 2008. 32p. (J). (gr. -1-2). pap. 6.95 (978-1-58925-412-1(0)) Tiger Tales.

Dwyer, Mindy. Just Close Your Eyes. 2005. (J). (978-0-88240-592-6(6)); pap. (978-0-88240-593-3(4)) Graphic Arts Ctr. Publishing Co. (Alaska Northwest Bks.).

Dyan, Penelope. The Warrior Mouse of Forest Hollow. Quinn, Courtney, illus. 2008. 108p. 17.95 (978-1-935118-00-8(5)) Bellissima Publishing, LLC.

Dycus, Warren. Monyum Bay - Time Travel. 2010. 24p. 13.99 (978-0-557-45202-6(3)) Lulu Pr., Inc.

Dyer, Heather. The Girl with the Broken Wing. Bailey, Peter, illus. 2005. 147p. (J). (978-1-4156-3468-4(8)) Scholastic, Inc.

Ebbeler, Jeffrey. Click! 2015. (ENG., Illus.). 32p. (J). (gr. -1-1). 16.95 (978-0-8234-3295-0(5)) Holiday Hse., Inc.

Ebel, Sherry. Cassie's Magic Doors. 2008. 28p. pap. 15.99 (978-1-4363-2970-5(1)) Xlibris Corp.

Eberle, Melissa. Fricka the Flying Frog. 2009. 20p. pap. 11.59 (978-1-4389-7514-6(7)) AuthorHouse.

Ed. Fat Man, Fat Man. 2009. 24p. pap. 12.99 (978-1-4389-6168-2(5)) AuthorHouse.

Edvall, Lilian. The Rabbit Who Didn't Want to Go to Sleep. Dyssegaard, Elisabeth Kallick, tr. from SWE. Gimbergsson, Sara, illus. 2004. 32p. (J). 15.00 (978-91-29-66001-2(7)) R & S Bks. SWE. Dist: Macmillan.

Edwards, Gareth. Never Ask a Dinosaur to Dinner. Parker-Rees, Guy, illus. 2015. (ENG.). 32p. (J). (gr. -1-k). 17.99 (978-0-545-81296-2(8), Scholastic Pr.) Scholastic, Inc.

Edwards, Helen L. Clara's Imagination. Doggett, Al, illus. 2005. 19.95 (978-0-9765414-0-0(8)) Bad Publishing.

Eggleton, Jill. Big Bill's Bed. Matijasevich, Astrid, illus. 2003. (Rigby Sails Early Ser.). (ENG.). 16p. (gr. 1-2). pap. 6.95 (978-0-7578-8731-4(7)) Houghton Mifflin Harcourt Publishing Co.

Egielski, Richard. The Sleepless Little Vampire. 2011. (J). pap. (978-0-545-14598-5(8), Levine, Arthur A. Bks.) Scholastic, Inc.

Ekster, Carol Gordon. Before I Sleep I Say Thank You. Rojas, Mary, illus. 2015. (J). 14.95 (978-0-8198-1225-4(0)) Pauline Bks. & Media.

Ells, Marcia Louise. Glips, Snodagers & Wallywogs. Ells, Marcia Louise, illus. l.t. ed. 2006. (Illus.). 44p. (J). 6.99 (978-0-9777359-0-7(7)) Marcia's Menagerie.

Eltoukhy, G.N. 12 Enchanted Kindles for Bedtime Lullabies: Don't Live in Darkness Sorry for Failed Life , You Must Try the Unwritten. 2012. 56p. pap. 24.40 (978-1-4669-2242-6(7)) Trafford Publishing.

Engelbreit, Mary. Nursery Tales: A Treasury of Children's Classics. Engelbreit, Mary, illus. 2008. (ENG., Illus.). 136p. (J). (gr. 4-7). 19.99 (978-0-06-073168-7(0)) HarperCollins Pubs.

England, Brooke. Guardian Fairies. 2006. 17p. 12.00 (978-1-4116-7923-8(7)) Lulu Pr., Inc.

Engledow, Dave. The Little Girl Who Didn't Want to Go to Bed. Engledow, Dave, illus. 2017. (Illus.). 40p. (J). (gr. -1-3). 17.99 **(978-0-06-242537-9(4))** HarperCollins Pubs.

Enriquez, Lucy Rivas. Dj's Lullaby: A Mother's Love Song. 2013. (ENG.). 26p. (J). pap. 12.95 (978-1-4787-1148-3(5)) Outskirts Pr., Inc.

Ering, Timothy Basil. The Almost Fearless Hamilton Squidlegger. Ering, Timothy Basil, illus. 2014. (ENG., Illus.). 48p. (J). (gr. -1-2). 16.99 (978-0-7636-2357-9(1)) Candlewick Pr.

Fabrizio, T. L. Natalie Bean. 2011. 28p. pap. 24.95 (978-1-4626-0645-0(8)) America Star Bks.

Faith, Susan. Purple Puppy. Offner, Naomi, illus. 2005. 32p. (J). 19.95 (978-0-9707793-0-4(5)) Purple People, Inc.

Farrell, Darren. Thank You, Octopus. 2014. (ENG.). 40p. (J). (gr. -1-k). 16.99 (978-0-8037-3438-8(7), Dial Bks) Penguin Young Readers Group.

Feder, Joel A. Kokomo Superhero. 2011. 32p. pap. 14.99 (978-1-4634-4748-9(5)) AuthorHouse.

—Kokomo's Halloween Adventure. 2012. 32p. pap. 15.99 (978-1-4685-7331-2(4)) AuthorHouse.

—The Legend of Sidney Snowflake. 2009. 24p. pap. 14.99 (978-1-4490-0828-4(3)) AuthorHouse.

Feiffer, Kate. No Go Sleep! Feiffer, Jules, illus. 2012. (ENG.). 32p. (J). (gr. -1-2). 16.99 (978-1-4424-1683-3(1), Simon & Schuster/Paula Wiseman Bks.) Simon & Schuster/Paula Wiseman Bks.

Fenton, Joe. What's under the Bed? Fenton, Joe, illus. 2008. (ENG., Illus.). 32p. (J). (gr. -1-2). 15.99 (978-1-4169-4943-5(7), Simon & Schuster Bks. For Young Readers) Simon & Schuster Bks. For Young Readers.

Fernandes, Eugenie. Waves in the Bathtub. 2015. (ENG., Illus.). 32p. (J). (gr. -1-k). 16.99 (978-1-63220-429-5(0), Sky Pony Pr.) Skyhorse Publishing Co., Inc.

Ferreri, Della Ross. Huggle Wuggle Bedtime Snuggle. 2008. (J). 14.95 (978-0-87358-937-6(8)) Northland Publishing.

Ferri, Francesca, illus. Good Night, Teddy. 2003. (ENG.). 8p. (J). 15.99 (978-0-7641-2595-9(8)) Barron's Educational Series, Inc.

Fiford, Tanya. Children under the Bed. 2009. (Illus.). 20p. pap. 12.49 (978-1-4490-0558-0(6)) AuthorHouse.

Fiona Fox Staff & Giles, Sophie. 365 Bedtime Stories. 2013. (ENG., Illus.). 224p. (J). 24.95 (978-1-84135-614-3(X)) Award Pubns. Ltd. GBR. Dist: Parkwest Pubns., Inc.

Fisher, Rusty. Littlest Vampire's Story, 1 vol. 2014. (Story Time for Little Monsters Ser.). (ENG., Illus.). 24p. (J). (gr. -1-4). lib. bdg. 27.07 (978-1-62402-020-9(8), Looking Glass Library) Magic Wagon.

—Littlest Werewolf's Story, 1 vol. 2014. (Story Time for Little Monsters Ser.). (ENG.). 24p. (J). (gr. -1-4). lib. bdg. 27.07 (978-1-62402-021-6(6), Looking Glass Library) Magic Wagon.

—Littlest Witch's Story, 1 vol. 2014. (Story Time for Little Monsters Ser.). (ENG., Illus.). 24p. (J). (gr. -1-4). lib. bdg. 27.07 (978-1-62402-022-3(4), Looking Glass Library) Magic Wagon.

—Littlest Zombie's Story, 1 vol. 2014. (Story Time for Little Monsters Ser.). (ENG.). 24p. (J). (gr. -1-4). lib. bdg. 27.07 (978-1-62402-023-0(2), Looking Glass Library) Magic Wagon.

Fisk, Cindy. Hooga Booga Presents the Little Pumpkin. Fisk, David, illus. 2013. 28p. pap. 11.95 (978-1-938743-02-3(4)) Reimann Bks.

—Melvin Pickles. Fisk, David, illus. 2013. 26p. pap. 11.95 (978-1-938743-03-0(2)) Reimann Bks.

Fleming, Candace. Go Sleep in Your Own Bed. Nichols, Lori, illus. 2017. (ENG.). 40p. (J). (gr. -1-2). 17.99 (978-0-375-86648-7(5), Schwartz & Wade Bks.) Random Hse. Children's Bks.

Fleming, Denise. Sleepy, Oh So Sleepy. Fleming, Denise, illus. 2010. (ENG., Illus.). 32p. (J). (gr. -1-k). 16.99 (978-0-8050-8126-8(7), 9780805081268, Holt, Henry & Co. Bks. For Young Readers) Holt, Henry & Co.

Foreman, Michael. I Love You, Too! Foreman, Michael, illus. 2014. (ENG., Illus.). 32p. (J). (gr. -1-3). 16.95 (978-1-4677-3451-6(9)) Lerner Publishing Group.

Forgas, Christine. After Dark. Forgas-Davis, Mellssa, illus. 2004. 17p. (J). (gr. 1-6). pap. (978-1-930200-27-2(7)) Martell Publishing Co.

Forssén Ehrlin, Carl-Johan. El Conejito Que Quiere Dormirse: Una Nueva Forma de Hacer Que los Niños Se Duerman. 2015. (SPA.). 32p. (J). (gr. -1-2). 9.95 (978-1-941999-59-2(X)) Beascoa, Ediciones S.A. ESP. Dist: Two Rivers Distribution.

—The Little Elephant Who Wants to Fall Asleep: A New Way of Getting Children to Sleep. Hanson, Sydney, illus. 2016. (ENG.). 40p. (J). (gr. -1-2). 16.99 (978-0-399-55423-0(8), Crown Books For Young Readers) Random Hse. Children's Bks.

—The Rabbit Who Wants to Fall Asleep: A New Way of Getting Children to Sleep. Maununen, Irina, illus. 2015. (ENG.). 32p. (J). (gr. -1-2). 15.99 (978-0-399-55413-1(0), Crown Books For Young Readers) Random Hse. Children's Bks.

Fox, Mem. Baby Bedtime. 2014. (ENG., Illus.). 32p. (J). (gr. -1-3). 17.99 (978-1-4814-2097-6(6), Beach Lane Bks.) Beach Lane Bks.

—Good Night, Sleep Tight. Horacek, Judy, illus. 2013. (ENG.). 32p. (J). (gr. -1-k). 16.99 (978-0-545-53370-6(8), Orchard Bks.) Scholastic, Inc.

—Tell Me about Your Day Today. Stringer, Lauren, illus. 2012. (ENG.). 40p. (J). (gr. -1-3). 17.99 (978-1-4169-9006-2(2), Beach Lane Bks.) Beach Lane Bks.

—This & That. Horacek, Judy, illus. 2017. (ENG.). 32p. (J). (gr. -1-k). 17.99 (978-1-338-03780-7(3), Scholastic Pr.) Scholastic, Inc.

—Time for Bed. braille ed. 2004. (Illus.). (J). (gr. 1). spiral bd., bds. (978-0-616-01863-7(0)) Canadian National Institute for the Blind/Institut National Canadien pour les Aveugles.

—Time for Bed. Dyer, Jane, illus. 2010. (ENG.). 28p. (J). (gr. k — 1). bds. 8.99 (978-0-547-40856-9(0)) Houghton Mifflin Harcourt Publishing Co.

—Time for Bed: Lap-Sized Board Book. Dyer, Jane, illus. 2005. (ENG.). 28p. (J). (gr. k — 1). bds. 12.99 (978-0-15-205349-9(2)) Houghton Mifflin Harcourt Publishing Co.

—Time for Bed (Es Hora de Dormir) Dyer, Jane, illus. 2012. (ENG & SPA.). 28p. (J). (gr. k — 1). bds. 6.99 (978-0-547-71907-8(8)) Houghton Mifflin Harcourt Publishing Co.

Fox, Sabrina. Who Can Help Me Sleep? Rothan, Ann, illus. 2004. 32p. (gr. -1-3). 16.95 (978-1-885394-36-1(5)) Amber Lotus Publishing.

Frank, Church & Barnas, Aloura. The Epic Adventures of Whiz Grass & Poot Berry. 2011. 164p. (gr. -1). 22.99 (978-1-4634-4525-6(3)); pap. 11.99 (978-1-4634-4524-9(5)) AuthorHouse.

Fraser, Mary Ann. Pet Shop Lullaby. Fraser, Mary Ann, illus. 2009. (ENG., Illus.). 32p. (J). (gr. -1-1). 16.95 (978-1-59078-618-5(1)) Boyds Mills Pr.

Frazier, Craig. There Is a Monkey in My Drawers! 2003. (Illus.). 24p. (J). (gr. -1-k). 14.95 (978-1-932026-10-8(X)) Graphis, U.S., Inc.

Frederick, Heather Vogel. Hide-and-Squeak. Payne, C. F., illus. 2011. (ENG.). 32p. (J). (gr. -1-1). 16.99 (978-0-689-85570-2(2), Simon & Schuster Bks. For Young Readers) Simon & Schuster Bks. For Young Readers.

Fredrickson, Lane. Monster Trouble. Robertson, Michael, illus. 2015. (ENG.). 32p. (J). (gr. -1-2). 14.95 (978-1-4549-1345-0(2)) Sterling Publishing Co., Inc.

Freedman, Claire. Good Night, Sleep Tight! Tyger, Rory, illus. 2007. 32p. (J). (gr. -1-1). pap. 6.95 (978-1-58925-405-3(8)) Tiger Tales.

—Goodnight, Sleep Tight! Tyger, Rory, illus. 2013. (ENG.). 32p. (J). (gr. -1). pap. 3.99 (978-1-58925-440-4(6)) Tiger Tales.

—Night-Night, Emily! Massey, Jane, illus. 2005. 32p. (J). 6.95 (978-1-58925-390-2(6)) Tiger Tales.

—Night-Night, Emily! Massey, Jane, tr. Massey, Jane, illus. 2003. 32p. (J). (gr. -1-1). tchr. ed. 15.95 (978-1-58925-032-1(X)) Tiger Tales.

Friden, Chris. Bathtime with Bubbles. Zapater Oliva, Carlos & Depew, Robert, illus. 2008. (J). (978-0-9801849-2-1(4)) Haydenburri Lane.

—Bedtime Safari. 2008. (Illus.). 27p. (J). bds. 14.99 (978-0-9758785-4-5(9)) Haydenburri Lane.

—Bedtime Safari. Otoshi, Kathryn & Ciccarelli, Gary, illus. 2007. (J). (978-0-9758785-3-8(0)) Haydenburri Lane.

—Pajamatime with P.J. Zapater Oliva, Carlos & Glazier, Garth, illus. 2008. (J). (978-0-9801849-5-2(9)); (978-0-9758785-9-0(X)) Haydenburri Lane.

—Sleepytime with Rory. 2008. (Illus.). 27p. (J). bds. 14.99 (978-0-9758785-5-2(7)) Haydenburri Lane.

—Sleepytime with Rory. Zapater Oliva, Carlos & Glazier, Garth, illus. 2008. (J). (978-0-9801849-1-4(6)) Haydenburri Lane.

—Toothtime with Chomper. 2008. (Illus.). 27p. (J). bds. 14.99 (978-0-9758785-7-6(3)) Haydenburri Lane.

—Toothtime with Chomper. Rodríguez Braojos, Alberto et al, illus. 2008. (J). (978-0-9801849-3-8(2)) Haydenburri Lane.

Friden, Chris & Rodríguez Braojos, Alberto. Storytime with Paige. Jaraiz, David, illus. 2008. (J). (978-0-9801849-4-5(0)); (978-0-9758785-8-3(1)) Haydenburri Lane.

Froeb, Lori C. Elmo's Bedtime Countdown. 2016. (ENG.). 12p. (J). (gr. -1-k). bds. 10.99 (978-0-7944-3587-5(4), Reader's Digest Children's Bks.) Studio Fun International.

Fruchter, Jason, illus. Daniel's First Sleepover. 2015. (Daniel Tiger's Neighborhood Ser.). (ENG.). 24p. (J). (gr. -1-2). pap. 3.99 (978-1-4814-2893-4(4), Simon Spotlight) Simon Spotlight.

Fujikawa, Gyo, illus. Sleepy Time. 2011. (ENG.). 20p. (J). (gr. k-k). bds. 5.95 (978-1-4027-6820-0(6)) Sterling Publishing Co., Inc.

Funkhouser, Patricia A. Dripps -. A Little Star's Dream. 2010. 104p. pap. 15.99 (978-1-4535-3762-6(7)) Xlibris Corp.

Gabriel, Andrea. My Favorite Bear. 2014. 32p. pap. 8.00 (978-1-61003-310-7(8)) Center for the Collaborative Classroom.

—My Favorite Bear. Gabriel, Andrea, illus. 2004. (ENG., Illus.). 32p. (J). (-k). pap. 7.95 (978-1-58089-039-7(3)) Charlesbridge Publishing, Inc.

Galindo, Claudia. It's Bedtime, Cucuy!/A la Cama, Cucuy. Pluecker, John, tr. from ENG. Coombs, Jonathan, illus. 2008. (SPA & ENG.). 32p. (J). (gr. -1-2). 16.95 (978-1-55885-491-8(6), Piñata Books) Arte Publico Pr.

Galvin, Laura Gates. Winnie the Pooh Bedtime ABCs. 2008. (ENG.). 20p. (J). (gr. -1-3). 9.99 (978-1-59069-656-9(5)) Studio Mouse LLC.

Gamble, Adam. Buenas Noches, California. Kelly, Cooper, illus. 2012. (Buenas Noches Ser.). (SPA & ENG.). 24p. (J). (gr. k — 1). bds. 9.95 (978-1-60219-070-2(4)) Good Night Bks.

—Buenas Noches, Estados Unidos. Chan, Suwin, illus. 2012. (Buenas Noches Ser.). (SPA & ENG.). 28p. (J). (gr. k — 1). bds. 9.95 (978-1-60219-069-6(0)) Good Night Bks.

—Buenas Noches, Nueva York. Veno, Joe & Jasper, Mark, illus. 2013. (Buenas Noches Ser.). (SPA & ENG.). 24p. (J). (— 1). bds. 9.95 (978-1-60219-091-7(7)) Good Night Bks.

—Good Night Arizona. Veno, Joe & Hansen, Red, illus. 2008. (Good Night Our World Ser.). (ENG.). 20p. (J). (gr. k — 1). bds. 9.95 (978-1-60219-000-9(3)) Good Night Bks.

—Good Night California. Kelly, Cooper, illus. 2008. (Good Night Our World Ser.). (ENG.). 26p. (J). (gr. k — 1). bds. 9.95 (978-1-60219-021-4(6)) Good Night Bks.

—Good Night Country Store. Rosen, Anne & Jasper, Mark, illus. 2010. (Good Night Our World Ser.). (ENG.). 20p. (J). (gr. k — 1). bds. 9.95 (978-1-60219-044-3(5)) Good Night Bks.

—Good Night Georgia. Rosen, Anne & Veno, Joe, illus. 2009. (Good Night Our World Ser.). (ENG.). 20p. (J). (gr. k — 1). bds. 9.95 (978-1-60219-032-0(1)) Good Night Bks.

—Good Night Michigan. Rosen, Anne, illus. 2011. (Good Night Our World Ser.). (ENG.). 20p. (J). (gr. k — 1). bds. 9.95 (978-1-60219-054-2(2)) Good Night Bks.

—Good Night Minnesota. Veno, Joe, illus. 2009. (Good Night Our World Ser.). (ENG.). 20p. (J). (gr. k — 1). bds. 9.95 (978-1-60219-034-4(8)) Good Night Bks.

—Good Night New Hampshire. Rosen, Anne, illus. 2009. (Good Night Our World Ser.). (ENG.). 20p. (J). (gr. k — 1). bds. 9.95 (978-1-60219-037-5(2)) Good Night Bks.

—Good Night North Carolina. Rosen, Anne, illus. 2009. (Good Night Our World Ser.). (ENG.). 20p. (J). (gr. k — 1). bds. 9.95 (978-1-60219-033-7(X)) Good Night Bks.

—Good Night North Pole. Jasper, Mark, illus. 2012. (Good Night Our World Ser.). (ENG.). 20p. (J). (gr. k — 1). bds. 9.95 (978-1-60219-071-9(2), 1350772) Good Night Bks.

—Good Night Tennessee. Veno, Joe, illus. 2007. (Good Night Our World Ser.). (ENG.). 20p. (J). (gr. k — 1). bds. 9.95 (978-1-60219-019-1(4)) Good Night Bks.

—Good Night Texas. Veno, Joe & Kelly, Cooper, illus. 2nd ed. 2011. (Good Night Our World Ser.). (ENG.). 20p. (J). (gr. k — 1). bds. 9.95 (978-1-60219-053-5(4)) Good Night Bks.

—Good Night World. Kelly, Cooper, illus. 2009. (Good Night Our World Ser.). (ENG.). 28p. (J). (gr. k — 1). bds. 9.95 (978-1-60219-030-6(5)) Good Night Bks.

Gamble, Adam & Adams, David J. Good Night Canada. Kelly, Cooper, illus. 2010. (Good Night Our World Ser.). (ENG.). 28p. (J). (gr. k — 1). bds. 9.95 (978-1-60219-038-2(0)) Good Night Bks.

Gamble, Adam & Jasper, Mark. Buenas Noches, Florida. 2013. (Buenas Noches Ser.). (SPA & ENG., Illus.). 20p. (J). (— 1). bds. 9.95 (978-1-60219-092-4(5)) Good Night Bks.

—Buenas Noches, Texas. 2013. (Buenas Noches Ser.). (SPA & ENG., Illus.). 20p. (J). (— 1). bds. 9.95 (978-1-60219-093-1(3)) Good Night Bks.

—Good Night Books. Chan, Suwin, illus. 2017. (Good Night Our World Ser.). (ENG.). 20p. (J). (— 1). bds. 9.95 **(978-1-60219-470-0(X))** Good Night Bks.

—Good Night Central Park. Palmer, Ruth, illus. 2013. (Good Night Our World Ser.). (ENG.). 20p. (J). (— 1). bds. 9.95 (978-1-60219-082-5(8)) Good Night Bks.

—Good Night Daddy. Kelly, Cooper, illus. 2015. (Good Night Our World Ser.). (ENG.). 20p. (J). (— 1). bds. 9.95 (978-1-60219-229-4(4)) Good Night Bks.

—Good Night Dump Truck. Kelly, Cooper, illus. 2014. (Good Night Our World Ser.). (ENG.). 26p. (J). (— 1). bds. 9.95 (978-1-60219-189-1(1)) Good Night Bks.

—Good Night Florida. Veno, Joe & Hansen, Red, illus. 2nd ed. 2010. (Good Night Our World Ser.). (ENG.). 20p. (J). (gr. k — 1). bds. 9.95 (978-1-60219-045-0(3)) Good Night Bks.

—Good Night Maryland. Veno, Joe et al, illus. 2011. (Good Night Our World Ser.). (ENG.). 20p. (J). (gr. k — 1). bds. 9.95 (978-1-60219-046-7(1)) Good Night Bks.

—Good Night Mermaids. Chan, Suwin, illus. 2015. (Good Night Our World Ser.). (ENG.). 20p. (J). (— 1). bds. 9.95 (978-1-60219-226-3(X)) Good Night Bks.

—Good Night Mississippi. Veno, Joe, illus. 2015. (Good Night Our World Ser.). (ENG.). 20p. (J). (— 1). bds. 9.95 (978-1-60219-221-8(9)) Good Night Bks.

—Good Night Nevada. Rosen, Anne & Veno, Joe, illus. 2012. (Good Night Our World Ser.). (ENG.). 20p. (J). (gr. k — 1). bds. 9.95 (978-1-60219-060-3(7)) Good Night Bks.

—Good Night Pittsburgh. Palmer, Ruth, illus. 2012. (Good Night Our World Ser.). (ENG.). 20p. (J). (gr. k — 1). bds. 9.95 (978-1-60219-073-3(9)) Good Night Bks.

—Good Night Race Cars. Veno, Joe, illus. 2015. (Good Night Our World Ser.). (ENG.). 20p. (J). (— 1). bds. 9.95 (978-1-60219-228-7(6), 1396132) Good Night Bks.

—Good Night Toronto. Veno, Joe & Kelly, Cooper, illus. 2011. (Good Night Our World Ser.). (ENG.). 20p. (J). (gr. k — 1). bds. 9.95 (978-1-60219-048-1(8)) Good Night Bks.

—Good Night Utah. Rosen, Anne & Hart, Jason, illus. 2012. (Good Night Our World Ser.). (ENG.). 20p. (J). (gr. k — 1). bds. 9.95 (978-1-60219-059-7(3)) Good Night Bks.

—Good Night Washington State. Veno, Joe & Kelly, Cooper, illus. 2012. (Good Night Our World Ser.). (ENG.). 20p. (J). (gr. k — 1). bds. 9.95 (978-1-60219-072-6(0)) Good Night Bks.

Gamble, Adam & Kelly, Cooper. Good Night Farm. Kelly, Cooper, illus. 2009. (Good Night Our World Ser.). (ENG., Illus.). 28p. (J). (gr. k — 1). bds. 9.95 (978-1-60219-029-0(1)) Good Night Bks.

Gamble, Adam & Mackey, Bill. Good Night Colorado. Rosen, Anne, illus. 2012. (Good Night Our World Ser.). (ENG.). 20p. (J). (gr. k — 1). bds. 9.95 (978-1-60219-055-9(0)) Good Night Bks.

Gamble, Adam, et al. Good Night New Orleans. Kelly, Cooper, illus. 2012. (Good Night Our World Ser.). (ENG.). 20p. (J). (gr. k — 1). bds. 9.95 (978-1-60219-061-0(5)) Good Night Bks.

Garfein, Stanley Joe. Tales of the Temple Mice. 2006. (Illus.). 92p. (J). 14.95 (978-0-9787422-0-1(6)) Garfein, Stanley.

Garis, Howard R. Bed Time Stories: Uncle Wiggily's Adventures. Wisa, Louis, illus. 2007. 140p. per. (978-1-4065-2773-5(4)) Dodo Pr.

Garis, Howard Roger. Bed Time Stories. 2007. 140p. per. (978-1-4065-2760-5(2)); 152p. per. (978-1-4065-2761-2(0)); 132p. per. (978-1-4065-2762-9(9)); 148p. per. (978-1-4065-2769-8(6)) Dodo Pr.

—The Curlytops on Star Island. 2005. 26.95 (978-1-4218-1467-4(6)); 192p. pap. 11.95

(978-1-4218-1567-1(2)) 1st World Publishing, Inc. (1st World Library - Literary Society).

—The Curlytops on Star Island. 2004. reprint ed. pap. 1.99 (978-1-4192-5843-5(5)) Kessinger Publishing, LLC.

Garza, Xavier, illus. The Great & Mighty Nikko. 2015. (ENG.). 32p. (J). pap. 7.95 (978-1-935955-83-2(7)); (gr. -1-4). 16.95 (978-1-935955-82-5(9)) Cinco Puntos Pr.

Gates, Mysti. Noises in the Night. 2009. 52p. pap. 22.99 (978-1-4389-4359-6(8)) AuthorHouse.

Gay, Marie-Louise. Estela, Princesa de la Noche. 2nd ed. 2006.Tr. of Stella Princess of the Sky. (SPA., Illus.). 32p. (J). (gr. 1-2). 10.99 (978-980-257-304-2(3), EK33231) Ekare, Ediciones VEN. Dist: Lectorum Pubns., Inc.

Gehring, Lisa B. Emily Grace & the What Ifs: A Story for Children about Nighttime Fears. Flath, Regina, illus. 2016. 32p. (J). (978-1-4338-2106-6(0), Magination Pr.) American Psychological Assn.

Geiger, Lorraine Lynch. A Wild & Woolly Night. Vargo, Sharon, illus. 2007. (J). (gr. -1-3). 15.95 (978-1-891795-25-1(2)) RGU Group, The.

Geis, Patricia. Let's Go to Sleep! Folch, Sergio, illus. 2009. (Good Habits with Coco & Tula Ser.). 16p. (J). (gr. -1-k). bds. 11.40 (978-1-60754-408-1(3)) Windmill Bks.

Geist, Christina. Buddy's Bedtime Battery. Bowers, Tim, illus. 2016. (ENG.). 40p. (J). (gr. -1-2). lib. bdg. 19.99 (978-0-375-97468-7(7), Random Hse. Bks. for Young Readers) Random Hse. Children's Bks.

Gentry, Jennifer Mills. Maria's Bedtime. 2012. 24p. pap. 24.95 (978-1-4626-7816-7(5)) America Star Bks.

George, Megan & M George. If I Were... 2016. (ENG., Illus.). 24p. (J). 15.95 (978-1-61984-496-4(6)) Price World Publishing.

Gerber, Carole. Tuck-In Time. Pearson, Tracey Campbell, illus. 2014. (ENG.). 40p. (J). (gr. -1 — 1). 16.99 (978-0-374-37860-8(6), 9780374378608, Farrar, Straus & Giroux (BYR)) Farrar, Straus & Giroux.

Gerver, Jane E. Good Night. Flint, Gillian, illus. 2015. (ENG.). 14p. (J). (— 1). bds. 4.99 (978-1-62979-415-0(5), Highlights) Boyds Mills Pr.

Gesser, Bernadette. The Adventures of Rocky, Croaker & Spot. Mavronis, Michelle, illus. 2008. 20p. pap. 24.95 (978-1-60703-178-9(7)) America Star Bks.

Getz, Jeanine Behr. Think Green! Nightingale, Jenny, illus. 2008. (ENG.). 32p. (J). 15.50 (978-0-9797362-0-9(X)) Kids Think Big LLC.

Geurds, Patricia. Bedtime for Percy. 2009. 36p. pap. 16.00 (978-1-4389-5581-0(2)) AuthorHouse.

Geyer, Kim. Go to Sleep, Monty! Geyer, Kim, illus. 2015. (ENG., Illus.). 32p. (J). (gr. -1-3). 17.99 (978-1-4677-9311-7(6)) Lerner Publishing Group.

Giles, Mike, illus. Sleep & Dream of Happy Things. 2009. (Yo Gabba Gabba! Ser.). (ENG.). 26p. (J). (gr. -1 — 1). bds. 5.99 (978-1-4169-7823-7(2), Simon Spotlight) Simon Spotlight.

Gliori, Debi. Goodnight World. Gliori, Debi, illus. 2017. (ENG., Illus.). 32p. (J). 16.99 (978-1-68119-363-2(9), 9781681193632, Bloomsbury USA Childrens) Bloomsbury Publishing USA.

Glowacki, Helen. God's Plan of Salvation. 2013. 152p. pap. 17.50 (978-0-9893807-4-4(2)) Glowacki, Helen.

Godwin, Laura & Buck, Nola. A Christmas Goodnight. Wright, Sarah Jane, illus. 2011. (ENG.). 24p. (J). (gr. -1-k). 12.99 (978-0-06-166491-5(X), Tegen, Katherine Bks) HarperCollins Pubs.

Golda, Kata. Stories for Bedtime: A Keepsake Pocket & Tales to Cherish. 2011. (ENG.). 7p. (J). (gr. -1 — 1). 14.99 (978-0-8118-7498-4(2)) Chronicle Bks. LLC.

Golden Books. Peeps in Pajamas (Peeps) Golden Books & Posner-Sanchez, Andrea, illus. 2017. (Little Golden Book Ser.). (ENG.). 24p. (J). (-k). 4.99 (978-1-5247-1907-4(2), Golden Bks.) Random Hse. Children's Bks.

Golden Books Staff. Sleepytime Tales. 2006. (Little Golden Book Treasury Ser.). (ENG., Illus.). 224p. (J). (gr. -1-2). 12.99 (978-0-375-83848-4(1), Golden Bks.) Random Hse. Children's Bks.

Golden Books Staff & Man-Kong, Mary. Barbie Bedtime Story Collection (Barbie) 2014. (ENG., Illus.). 320p. (J). (gr. -1-2). 15.99 (978-0-385-38784-2(9), Random Hse. Bks. for Young Readers) Random Hse. Children's Bks.

Golden, Robert Charles. Eve. Happel, Sally, illus. 2012. 32p. 24.95 (978-1-4626-7621-7(9)) America Star Bks.

Goldhawk, Emma. Snuggle Bunny. Lambert, Jonathan, illus. 2015. (Snuggle Puppet Ser.). (ENG.). 10p. (J). bds. 14.95 (978-1-62686-327-9(X), Silver Dolphin Bks.) Readerlink Distribution Services, LLC.

Gollub, Matthew. Ten Oni Drummers. Stone, Kazuko G., illus. 2017. (J). (978-1-889910-51-2(1)) Tortuga Pr.

Goodnight Football, 1 vol. 2014. (Sports Illustrated Kids Bedtime Bks.). (ENG., Illus.). 32p. (gr. -1-2). lib. bdg. 22.60 (978-1-4795-5177-4(5)) Capstone Press of Coughlan Cos.

Goodnight, I Wish You Goodnight. (Illus.). (J). (978-1-930948-82-2(4)) Apple Pie Pubs.

Goodwin, John. The Lion Book of Five-Minute Bedtime Stories. Waterhouse, Stephen, illus. 2010. (ENG.). 48p. (J). (gr. k-2). 16.99 (978-0-7459-6143-9(6)) Lion Hudson PLC GBR. Dist: Independent Pubs. Group.

Graff, Lisa. It Is Not Time for Sleeping. Castillo, Lauren, illus. 2016. (ENG.). 40p. (J). (gr. -1-3). 16.99 (978-0-544-31930-1(3), Clarion Bks.) Houghton Mifflin Harcourt Trade & Reference Pubs.

Graham, Bob. How to Heal a Broken Wing. Graham, Bob, illus. 2008. (ENG., Illus.). 40p. (J). (gr. -1-2). 16.99 (978-0-7636-3903-7(6)) Candlewick Pr.

Graham, Bob. How to Heal a Broken Wing. Graham, Bob, illus. 2017. (ENG., Illus.). 40p. (J). (gr. -1-2). 7.99 **(978-0-7636-9841-6(5))** Candlewick Pr.

Graham, Crystal L. My Little Teddy Bear: Has Anybody Seen... . 2010. 16p. 8.49 (978-1-4520-0425-9(0)) AuthorHouse.

Grandpa Peeps. The Squire & the White Dragon. 2011. 24p. 11.95 (978-1-4567-1872-5(X)) AuthorHouse.

Granger, Trudi. Always There Bear. Llewhellin, Gareth, illus. 2015. (ENG.). 32p. (J). (-k). 16.99 (978-1-63220-434-9(7), Sky Pony Pr.) Skyhorse Publishing Co., Inc.

Grant, Holly & Campbell, K. G. Wee Sister Strange. 2017. (ENG.). 40p. (J). (gr. -1-3). 17.99 **(978-0-553-50879-6(2),** Schwartz & Wade Bks.) Random Hse. Children's Bks.

Graves, Jennifer. Ava's Awful Fright! 2009. 28p. pap. 15.99 (978-1-4415-0482-1(6)) Xlibris Corp.

Graves, Sue. Night, Night. 2009. (ENG., Illus.). 24p. (J). pap. (978-0-7787-3898-5(1)); lib. bdg. (978-0-7787-3867-1(1)) Crabtree Publishing Co.

Gravett, Emily. Again! Gravett, Emily, illus. 2013. (ENG., Illus.). 32p. (J). (gr. -1-3). 17.99 (978-1-4424-5231-2(5), Simon & Schuster Bks. For Young Readers) Simon & Schuster Bks. For Young Readers.

Gray, Rita. When the World Is Dreaming. Pak, Kenard, illus. 2016. (ENG.). 32p. (J). (gr. -1-3). 17.99 (978-0-544-58262-0(4), HMH Books For Young Readers) Houghton Mifflin Harcourt Publishing Co.

Grayson, Barry/Scott. Twisted Yarns: Bedtime Stories for Hip Kids. 2007. (Illus.). 40p. (J). pap. (978-0-9774357-1-5(7)) Grayson, Kate.

Greenacres, Levi. Mommy's New Tattoo: A Bedtime Story for People, 1 vol. 2013. (ENG., Illus.). 32p. 16.99 (978-0-7643-4389-6(0), 9780764343896) Schiffer Publishing, Ltd.

Greenway, Bethany. Waikiki Lullaby. America, illus. 2009. (ENG.). 20p. (J). (gr. -1-1). bds. 7.95 (978-1-933067-30-8(6)) Beachhouse Publishing, LLC.

Gribel, Christiane & Orlando. No Voy a Dormir/I Am Not Going to Sleep. Gribel, Christiane & Orlando, illus. 2009. (ENG & SPA., Illus.). 40p. (J). (gr. -1-1). pap. 7.99 (978-1-933032-51-1(0)) Lectorum Pubns., Inc.

Guiffre, William A. The Wrong Side of the Bed. Baron, Cheri Ann, illus. 2003. 36p. (J). (gr. -1-3). lib. bdg. 17.95 (978-1-931650-20-5(9)) Bks. for Children Publishing.

Guy, Ginger Foglesong. Go Back to Bed! Bernardin, James, illus. 2006. (ENG.). 32p. (J). (gr. k-3). 16.95 (978-1-57505-750-7(6), Carolrhoda Bks.) Lerner Publishing Group.

Gwent (Wales), Staff Development Unit Staff & Acen Staff, contrib. by. Nos Da, Arthur. 2005. (WEL., Illus.). 8p. pap. (978-1-874049-31-9(9)) Acen Limited.

Haave, Meghan. Christopher's Bedtime Story. Rittmueller, Jeanne, illus. 2012. 32p. (J). pap. 9.95 (978-1-59530-459-9(2)) Hallmark Card, Inc.

Hacohen, Dean. Tuck Me In! Scharschmidt, Sherry, illus. 2010. (ENG.). 40p. (J). (gr. -1 — 1). 9.99 (978-0-7636-4728-5(4)) Candlewick Pr.

Hadfield, Chris. The Darkest Dark. Fan, Eric et al, illus. 2016. (ENG.). 48p. (J). (gr. -1-3). 17.99 (978-0-316-39472-7(6)) Little, Brown Bks. for Young Readers.

Haft, Sheryl. I Love You, Blankie. Massey, Jane, illus. 2015. (ENG.). 22p. (J). (gr. -1 — 1). bds. 8.99 (978-0-316-28356-4(8)) Little, Brown Bks. for Young Readers.

Halfmann, Janet. Good Night, Little Sea Otter, 1 vol. Williams, Wish, illus. (ENG.). (J). 2012. 24p. 15.95 (978-1-59572-277-5(7)) 2010. 32p. (gr. -1-3). pap. 5.95 (978-1-59572-254-6(8)) Star Bright Bks., Inc.

—Good Night, Little Sea Otter (Burmese Karen/English), 1 vol. Williams, Wish, illus. 2012. (KAR & ENG.). 24p. (J). 5.95 (978-1-59572-371-0(4)) Star Bright Bks., Inc.

—Good Night, Little Sea Otter (Burmese/English), 1 vol. Williams, Wish, illus. 2012. (ENG.). 24p. (J). pap. 5.95 (978-1-59572-370-3(6)) Star Bright Bks., Inc.

—Good Night, Little Sea Otter (Hmong/English), 1 vol. Williams, Wish, illus. 2012. (ENG.). 24p. (J). pap. 5.95 (978-1-59572-365-9(X)) Star Bright Bks., Inc.

—Good Night, Little Sea Otter (Portuguese/English), 1 vol. Williams, Wish, illus. 2012. (ENG.). 24p. (J). pap. 5.95 (978-1-59572-359-8(5)) Star Bright Bks., Inc.

—Good Night, Little Sea Otter (Spanish/English), 1 vol. Williams, Wish, illus. 2012. (ENG.). 32p. (J). pap. 5.95 (978-1-59572-347-5(1)) Star Bright Bks., Inc.

Hall, Rohan. The Little Boy. 2005. (Illus.). 34p. (J). spiral bd. 14.95 (978-0-9729187-7-0(9)) Foundation For Cosmetic Surgery, The.

Hamilton, Martha, et al. Noodlehead Nightmares. Arnold, Tedd, illus. 2017. (ENG.). 48p. (J). (gr. 1-5). pap. 6.99 (978-0-8234-3768-9(X)) Holiday Hse., Inc.

Hang Around Bedtime Stories. (Bedtime Stories Ser.). 6p. (J). bds. (978-2-89393-981-0(3)); bds. (978-2-89393-983-4(X)) Phidal Publishing, Inc./Editions Phidal, Inc.

Hannigan, Paula. Hugs for You. Brown, Heather, illus. 2012. (ENG.). 10p. (J). (-k). bds. 7.99 (978-1-4494-2192-2(X)) Andrews McMeel Publishing.

Hanson, Warren. Sea of Sleep. LaMarche, Jim, illus. 2010. (ENG.). 32p. (J). (gr. -1-3). 16.99 (978-0-439-69735-4(2), Scholastic Pr.) Scholastic, Inc.

Hapka, Catherine, pseud. Disney Sofia the First - Sweet Dreams, Sofia! Cardona, Jose, illus. 2015. (ENG.). 12p. (J). (gr. -1-k). 12.99 (978-0-7944-3383-3(9)) Studio Fun International.

Hapka, Catherine, pseud & Disney Book Group Staff. Sweet Dreams, Roo. Disney Storybook Art Team, illus. 2012. (ENG.). 24p. (J). (gr. -1-k). bds. 6.99 (978-1-4231-4843-2(6)) Disney Pr.

Harby, Melanie. All Aboard for Dreamland! Valério, Geraldo, illus. 2012. (ENG.). 32p. (J). (gr. -1-k). 16.99 (978-1-4424-3091-4(5), Simon & Schuster Bks. For Young Readers) Simon & Schuster Bks. For Young Readers.

harkins, charles. Naptime Adventures of Luksi the Turtle. 2010. 174p. pap. 20.96 (978-0-557-28695-9(6)) Lulu Pr., Inc.

Harris, Angela. Night Light. 2008. 28p. pap. 12.95 (978-1-4389-1971-3(9)) AuthorHouse.

Harris, Brian. Joe's Bedtime Stories for Boys & Girls. 2009. (Illus.). 240p. pap. 16.99 (978-1-4389-7600-6(3)) AuthorHouse.

Harris, Robie H. Maybe a Bear Ate It! Emberley, Michael, illus. 2008. (ENG.). 40p. (J). (gr. -1-k). 16.99 (978-0-439-92961-5(X), Orchard Bks.) Scholastic, Inc.

Harris, Sally M. Rainbow Nights. Grady, Kit, illus. 2009. 20p. pap. 9.95 (978-1-61633-002-6(3)) Guardian Angel Publishing, Inc.

Harry Hamster & his Bedtime. 2004. (Play Pals Ser.). (Illus.). 12p. (J). bds. (978-1-84229-645-5(0)) Top That! Publishing PLC.

Harshbarger, D. The Treasures of Dawn. 2011. 44p. pap. 19.99 (978-1-4634-1585-3(0)) AuthorHouse.

Hartman, Bob. The Lion Storyteller Bedtime Book. Nagy, Krisztina Kállai, illus. 2015. (ENG.). 128p. (J). (gr. k-2). pap. 16.99 (978-0-7459-6494-2(X)) Lion Hudson PLC GBR. Dist: Independent Pubs. Group.

Hartman, Bob & Nagy, Krisztina Kallai. The Lion Storyteller Bedtime Book. 2010. (ENG., Illus.). 128p. (J). (gr. k-2). 19.99 (978-0-7459-6094-4(4)) Lion Hudson PLC GBR. Dist: Independent Pubs. Group.

Hassett, Ann. Goodnight Bob. Hassett, John, illus. 2016. (ENG.). 32p. (J). (gr. -1-3). 16.99 (978-0-8075-3003-0(4)) Whitman, Albert & Co.

Hawley, Greg. Don't Let the Bedbugs Bite. Regan, Dana, illus. 2004. (J). (978-0-9657612-7-7(4)) Paddle Wheel Publishing.

Hawthorn, Phillip. Usborne Stories for Bedtime. Tyler, Jenny, ed. Cartwright, Stephen, illus. 2007. (Stories for Bedtime Ser.). 190p. (J). (gr. -1-3). 19.99 (978-0-7945-1970-4(9), Usborne) EDC Publishing.

Hayes, Geoffrey. Benny & Penny in Lights Out! Hayes, Geoffrey, illus. 2012. (Benny & Penny Ser.). (ENG., Illus.). 32p. (J). (gr. -1-3). 12.95 (978-1-935179-20-7(9)) TOON Books / RAW Junior, LLC.

—A Night-Light for Bunny. Date not set. 32p. (J). (gr. -1-3). pap. 5.99 (978-0-06-443728-8(0)) HarperCollins Pubs.

—A Night-Light for Bunny. Hayes, Geoffrey, illus. 2004. (Illus.). 32p. (J). (gr. -1-3). 14.99 (978-0-06-029163-1(X)) HarperCollins Pubs.

—Patrick Eats His Peas & Other Stories. Hayes, Geoffrey, illus. 2013. (ENG., Illus.). 32p. (J). (gr. -1-3). 12.95 (978-1-935179-34-4(9)) TOON Books / RAW Junior, LLC.

Helquist, Brett. Bedtime for Bear. Helquist, Brett, illus. 2010. (ENG., Illus.). 32p. (J). (gr. -1-2). 16.99 (978-0-06-050205-8(3)) HarperCollins Pubs.

Henig, Sherry. Goodbye to Bedtime Fears: A Children's Book. 2011. (ENG., Illus.). 42p. pap. 7.95 (978-0-9777203-3-0(0)) Brenner Publishing, LLC.

Henry, Jed. Good Night, Mouse! Henry, Jed, illus. 2013. (ENG., Illus.). 32p. (J). (gr. -1-3). 16.99 (978-0-547-98156-7(2)) Houghton Mifflin Harcourt Publishing Co.

Henry, Sandy. A Child's Bedtime Companion. Pavlova, Vera, illus. 2005. 26p. (J). (gr. -1-2). per. 12.95 (978-1-929039-31-9(X)) Ambassador Bks., Inc.

Herbert, Marcus P. Bertie at Bedtime. 2010. (KOR., Illus.). (J). (978-89-527-5776-0(9)) Sigongsa Co., Ltd.

Hest, Amy. Un Beso de Buenas Noches. Rubio, Esther, tr. Jeram, Anita, illus. (SPA.). (J). 16.00 (978-1-930332-04-1(1), LC3294) Lectorum Pubns., Inc.

—Kiss Good Night. Jeram, Anita, illus. (Sam Bks.). (ENG.). (J). (gr. k-12). 2006. 32p. pap. 4.99 (978-0-7636-2114-8(5)) 2004. 30p. bds. 6.99 (978-0-7636-2094-3(7)) Candlewick Pr.

—Kiss Good Night: Book & Toy Gift Set. Jeram, Anita, illus. gif. ed. 2004. (Sam Bks.). (ENG.). 30p. (J). (gr. k-12). bds. 15.99 (978-0-7636-2524-5(8)) Candlewick Pr.

—Kiss Good Night Lap-Size Board Book. Jeram, Anita, illus. 2014. (Sam Bks.). (ENG.). 32p. (J). (— 1). bds. 12.99 (978-0-7636-4748-3(9)) Candlewick Pr.

Hetzer, Michael. Footprints on the Ceiling: Your Child's Footprint Completes the Story. Clayton, Kim, illus. 2nd ed. 2005. 32p. (J). 18.95 (978-0-9728222-2-0(4)) Webster Henrietta Publishing.

Higgs, Carolyn. The Little Knight, 1 vol. 2009. 20p. pap. 24.95 (978-1-61546-095-3(0)) America Star Bks.

Hill, Eric. Good Night, Spot. Hill, Eric, illus. 2004. (Spot Ser.). (ENG., Illus.). 16p. (J). (gr. -1 — 1). bds. 4.99 (978-0-399-24319-6(4), Warne) Penguin Young Readers Group.

Hillert, Margaret. Es Hora de Ir a la Cama, Querido Dragón. Fernandez, Queta, tr. from ENG. Schimmell, David, illus. 2014. (BeginningtoRead Ser.).Tr. of It's Bedtime, Dear Dragon. (ENG & SPA.). 32p. (J). (-2). lib. bdg. 22.60 (978-1-59953-612-5(9)) Norwood Hse. Pr.

—It's Bedtime Dear Dragon. Schimmell, David, illus. 2012. (BeginningtoRead Ser.). 32p. (J). (-2). lib. bdg. 22.60 (978-1-59953-503-6(3)) Norwood Hse. Pr.

Hirsch, Jennifer & Sisson, Stéphanie Roth. The Bitty Twins' Bedtime Story. 2007. (Illus.). (J). (978-1-59369-324-4(9)) American Girl Publishing, Inc.

Hodges, Lynn & Buchanan, Sue. I Love You This Much, 1 vol. Bendall-Brunello, John, illus. 2010. (ENG.). 36p. (J). pap. 6.99 (978-0-310-72265-6(9)) Zonderkidz.

Hodges, Lynn, et al. I Love You This Much, 1 vol. Bendall-Brunello, John, illus. 2005. (Songs of Gods Love Ser.). (ENG.). 16p. (J). (gr. -1). bds. 6.99 (978-0-310-70961-9(X)) Zonderkidz.

Hodgkins, Fran. If You Were My Baby: A Wildlife Lullaby. Bryant, Laura J., illus. (Simply Nature Book Ser.). (J). (gr. -1 — 1). 2007. 26p. bds. 7.95 (978-1-58469-090-0(9)) 2005. 32p. pap. 8.95 (978-1-58469-075-7(5)) 2005. (ENG.). 32p. 16.95 (978-1-58469-074-0(7)) Dawn Pubns.

Hodgson, Mona Gansberg. Bedtime in the Southwest. Graef, Renee, illus. 2004. (ENG.). 32p. (J). (gr. -1-k). 14.95 (978-0-87358-871-3(1)) Cooper Square Publishing Llc.

Holland, Dwayne K. Princess Laura & the Magic Waterfall. 2010. 42p. pap. 15.50 (978-1-60860-744-0(5), Strategic Bk. Publishing) Strategic Book Publishing & Rights Agency (SBPRA).

Holub, Joan. Bed, Bats, & Beyond. Gallagher-Cole, Mernie, illus. (Darby Creek Exceptional Titles Ser.). 64p. (J). 2010. (ENG.). (gr. 1-3). pap. 6.95 (978-0-7613-6451-1(X)) 2008. (gr. -1-1). 14.95 (978-1-58196-077-8(8), Darby Creek) Lerner Publishing Group.

Hood, Karen Jean Matsko. Goodnight, I Wish You Goodnight, Vol. 1. Whispering Pine Press International, Inc. Staff, ed. Hatakeyama, Hiroshi, illus. 2014. (Hood Picture Book Ser.). (ENG.). 44p. (J). 24.95 (978-1-930948-97-6(2)) Whispering Pine Pr. International, Inc.

—Goodnight, I Wish You Goodnight, Bilingual English & Icelandic, Vol. 1. Whispering Pine Press International, ed. Hatakeyama, Hiroshi, illus. 2015. (Hood Picture Book Ser.). (ENG & ICE.). 60p. (J). 94.99 (978-1-930948-83-9(2)) Whispering Pine Pr. International, Inc.

Horácek, Petr. Time for Bed. Horácek, Petr, illus. 2014. (ENG., Illus.). 16p. (J). (— 1). bds. 7.99 (978-0-7636-6779-5(X)) Candlewick Pr.

Horne-Ingram, Gloria. Yonna Bonna & the Big Book. 2012. 16p. pap. 12.68 (978-1-4669-3406-1(9)) Trafford Publishing.

Horvath, Polly. The Trolls. unabr. ed. 2004. 144p. (J). (gr. 3-7). pap. 29.00 incl. audio (978-0-8072-8372-1(X), Listening Library) Random Hse. Audio Publishing Group.

Howatt, Sandra J. Sleepyheads. Wan, Joyce, illus. 2014. (ENG.). 32p. (J). (gr. -1-3). 17.99 (978-1-4424-2266-7(1), Beach Lane Bks.) Beach Lane Bks.

Howland, Naomi. The Princess Says Goodnight. Small, David, illus. 2010. 32p. (J). (gr. -1-2). (ENG.). 16.99 (978-0-06-145525-4(3)); lib. bdg. 17.89 (978-0-06-145526-1(1)) HarperCollins Pubs.

Huisingh, Rosemary. Vocabulary Stories for Toddlers: Getting Ready for Bed. 2012. (Illus.). 10p. (978-0-7606-1345-0(1)) LinguiSystems, Inc.

Hulme, John & Wexler, Michael. The Lost Train of Thought. Bk. 3. 2009. (Seems Ser.). (ENG., Illus.). 304p. (YA). (gr. 3-6). 16.99 (978-1-59990-131-2(5), 9781599901312, Bloomsbury USA Childrens) Bloomsbury Publishing USA.

Hunter, Anne. Cricket Song. 2016. (ENG., Illus.). 32p. (J). (gr. -1-3). 16.99 (978-0-544-58259-0(4), HMH Books For Young Readers) Houghton Mifflin Harcourt Publishing Co.

Hunter, Julius K. Absurd Alphabedtime Stories. Bauman, Todd, illus. 2nd rev. l.t. ed. 2004. 32p. (J). 16.95 (978-0-9761422-0-1(1)) J.K.H. Enterprises.

Hurst, Rich. The Goodnight Thing. Sprague, Lois Rosio, illus. 2006. 25p. (J). (gr. 4-7). 10.99 (978-0-9763770-1-6(2)) Red Door Pr.

Hyde, Margaret E. Mo Smells Sweet Dreams: A Scentsational Journey. Chaudhary, Aman, illus. 2012. (Mo's Nose Ser.). (ENG.). 24p. (J). (-k). 17.95 (978-0-9816255-8-4(4)) Mo's Nose, LLC.

ImageBooks Staff. Little Owl Finger Puppet Book. 2011. (Little Finger Puppet Board Bks.). (ENG.). 12p. (J). (gr. -1 — 1). bds. 6.99 (978-1-4521-0221-4(X)) Chronicle Bks. LLC.

Imai, Ayano. The 108th Sheep. Imai, Ayano, illus. 2007. (Illus.). 32p. (gr. -1-2). 15.95 (978-1-58925-063-5(X)) Tiger Tales.

Imbody, Amy E. & Imbody, Amy. Snug as a Bug, 1 vol. Gordon, Mike, illus. 2008. (I Can Read! Ser.). (ENG.). 32p. (J). (gr. -1-1). pap. 3.99 (978-0-310-71575-7(X)) Zonderkidz.

In My Bed: Individual Title, 6 Packs. (Literatura 2000 Ser.). (gr. k-1). 28.00 (978-0-7635-0007-8(0)) Rigby Education.

In My Room: Individual Title Six-Packs. (Literatura 2000 Ser.). (gr. k-1). 28.00 (978-0-7635-0032-0(1)) Rigby Education.

Inkpen, Mick. Is It Bedtime Wibbly Pig? 2010. (ENG., Illus.). 32p. (J). (gr. -1-k). pap. 10.99 (978-0-340-99750-5(8), Hodder Children's Books) Hachette Children's Group GBR. Dist: Hachette Bk. Group.

—Kipper. (ENG & FRE., Illus.). 32p. (J). (978-1-85430-330-1(9), 93450); (978-1-85430-333-2(3), 93451) Little Tiger Pr. Group.

—Lullabyhullaballoo! Inkpen, Mick, illus. 2007. (ENG., Illus.). 32p. (gr. 13-17). pap. 10.99 (978-0-340-93108-0(6)) Hodder & Stoughton GBR. Dist: Hachette Bk. Group.

Isadora, Rachel. I Just Want to Say Good Night. Isadora, Rachel, illus. 2017. (ENG., Illus.). 32p. (J). (-k). 17.99 (978-0-399-17384-4(6), Nancy Paulsen Books) Penguin Young Readers Group.

—Mr. Moon. Date not set. (J). 15.99 (978-0-06-029821-0(9)); lib. bdg. 16.89 (978-0-06-029822-7(7)) HarperCollins Pubs.

Ives, Penny. Rabbit Pie. Ives, Penny, illus. 2012. (Child's Play Library). (ENG., Illus.). 22p. (J). (gr. 1-1). bds. (978-1-84643-513-3(7)) Child's Play International Ltd.

—Rabbit Pie. 2010. (Child's Play Library). (ENG., Illus.). 32p. (J). (gr. 1-1). pap. (978-1-84643-353-5(3)) Child's Play International Ltd.

Jackson, Richard. All Ears, All Eyes. Tillotson, Katherine, illus. 2017. (ENG.). 40p. (J). (gr. -1-3). 17.99 (978-1-4814-1571-2(9)) Simon & Schuster Children's Publishing.

Jadoul, Emile. Good Night, Chickie. 2010. (ENG.). 26p. (J). (gr. -1-k). 14.00 (978-0-8028-5378-3(1), Eerdmans Bks For Young Readers) Eerdmans, William B. Publishing Co.

Jam, Teddy. Night Cars, 1 vol. Beddows, Eric, illus. 2006. (ENG.). 32p. (J). (gr. k — 1). bds. 11.95 (978-0-88899-748-7(5)) Groundwood Bks. CAN. Dist: Publishers Group West (PGW).

James, Carol Ann. Baby's Sleepy Time Adventure. 2008. 19p. pap. 24.95 (978-1-60563-500-2(6)) America Star Bks.

Jane, Johnson. Are You Ready for Bed? Gaby, Hansen, illus. 2010. (ENG.). 24p. (J). bds. 8.95 (978-1-58925-806-8(1)) Tiger Tales.

Janik, Dan. Sourdough Scott's Bedtime Fairy Tales from Alaska. 2005. (Illus.). (J). 12.95 (978-1-59433-031-5(X)) Publication Consultants.

Janni, Rebecca. Jammy Dance, 1 vol. Dockray, Tracy, illus. 2012. (ENG.). 40p. (J). (gr. -1-1). 16.99 (978-0-374-33680-6(6), 9780374336806, Farrar, Straus & Giroux (BYR)) Farrar, Straus & Giroux.

Jasper, Mark. Good Night Charleston. Kelly, Cooper, illus. 2007. (Good Night Our World Ser.). (ENG.). 20p. (J). (gr. k — 1). bds. 9.95 (978-1-60219-022-1(4)) Good Night Bks.

—Good Night Florida Keys. Rosen, Anne, illus. 2008. (Good Night Our World Ser.). (ENG.). 20p. (J). (gr. k — 1). bds. 9.95 (978-1-60219-020-7(8)) Good Night Bks.

—Good Night Israel. Rosen, Anne, illus. 2010. (Good Night Our World Ser.). (ENG.). 24p. (J). (gr. k — 1). bds. 9.95 (978-1-60219-043-6(7)) Good Night Bks.

Jasper, Mark & Kelly, Cooper. Good Night Ocean. Veno, Joe & Kelly, Cooper, illus. 2009. (Good Night Our World Ser.). (ENG.). 20p. (J). (gr. k — 1). bds. 9.95 (978-1-60219-036-8(4)) Good Night Bks.

Jeffers, Dawn. Beautiful Moon. Leick, Bonnie, illus. 2010. (ENG.). 32p. (J). (gr. -1-3). pap. 7.95 (978-1-934960-06-6(3), Raven Tree Pr.,Csi) Continental Sales, Inc.

Jennings, Sharon. Sleep Tight, Mrs. Ming. 2004. (Illus.). (J). (gr. -1-3). spiral bd. (978-0-616-01683-1(2)) Canadian National Institute for the Blind/Institut National Canadien pour les Aveugles.

Jewel. That's What I'd Do. Bates, Amy June, illus. 2012. (ENG.). 32p. (J). (gr. -1-k). 17.99 (978-1-4424-5813-0(5), Simon & Schuster/Paula Wiseman Bks.) Simon & Schuster/Paula Wiseman Bks.

Jin, Susie Lee, illus. It's Bedtime for Little Monkeys. 2010. (ENG.). 5p. (J). bds. 5.99 (978-0-7369-2832-8(4)) Harvest Hse. Pubs.

John, Jory. Goodnight Already! Davies, Benji, illus. 2014. (ENG.). 32p. (J). (gr. -1-3). 17.99 (978-0-06-228620-8(X)) HarperCollins Pubs.

Johnson, Andi. Little Molly Yo-Yo. 2004. (Illus.). 16p. 9.00 (978-1-84161-114-3(X)) Ravette Publishing, Ltd. GBR. Dist: Parkwest Pubns., Inc.

Johnson, Jane. Are You Ready for Bed? Hansen, Gaby, illus. (J). 2017. (ENG.). 28p. (gr. -1-k). bds. 7.99

(978-1-68010-513-1(2)) 2004. 32p. tchr. ed. 14.95 *(978-1-58925-017-8(6))* Tiger Tales.

Johnson, Jane. Little Bunny's Bedtime. Hansen, Gaby, illus. 2006. Orig. Title: Are You Ready for Bed? 16p. (J). bds. 6.95 *(978-1-58925-773-3(1))* Tiger Tales.

Johnson, Vickey L. The Monster Mix-Up. 2003. (Illus.). (J). pap. 9.00 *(978-0-8059-6125-6(9))* Dorrance Publishing Co., Inc.

Johnston, Jan. Cruiser & the Night Noises. Eugenia, Maria, illus. 2009. (ENG.). 20p. 12.99 *(978-1-934706-51-0(5))* Blue Apple Bks.

Jolley, Mike. I'll See You in the Morning. Moriuchi, Mique, illus. 2008. (ENG.). (J). (gr. -1 — 1). bds. 6.99 *(978-0-8118-6543-2(6))* Chronicle Bks. LLC.

Jones, Anna, illus. Goodnight, Mouse: A Peek-A-Boo Adventure. 2012. (J). *(978-1-4351-4387-6(6))* Barnes & Noble, Inc.

Jones, Frankie. Bedtime: Trace the Trails with Your Finger to Get to Bed! Galloway, Fhiona, illus. 2016. (ENG.). 10p. (J). (gr. -1 — 1). bds. 7.99 *(978-1-4998-0267-2(6))* Little Bee Books Inc.

Jonsberg, Barry. Dreamrider. 2009. (ENG.). 256p. (YA). (gr. 9). pap. 8.99 *(978-0-375-84458-4(9)*, Knopf Bks. for Young Readers) Random Hse. Children's Bks.

Jugran, Jan. Goodnight Faces: A Book of Masks. Larranaga, Ana Martin, illus. 2007. (ENG.). 12p. (J). (gr. -1 — 1). bds. 6.99 *(978-1-58476-672-8(7)*, IKIDS) Innovative Kids.

Kaldor, Connie & Campagne, Carmen. Lullaby Berceuse: A Warm Prairie Night. Deines, Brian, illus. 2006. (ENG & FRE.). 40p. (J). (gr. -1-2). 16.95 *(978-2-923163-22-2(2))* La Montagne Secrete CAN. Dist: Independent Pubs. Group.

Kalman, Maira. Hey Willy, See the Pyramids. 2017. (ENG., Illus.). 48p. (J). (gr. k-3). 18.95 ***(978-1-68137-168-9(5)***, NYR Children's Collection) New York Review of Bks., Inc., The.

Kanevsky, Polly. Sleepy Boy. Anderson, Stephanie, illus. 2006. (ENG.). 32p. (J). (gr. -1-k). 16.99 *(978-0-689-86735-4(2)*, Atheneum/Richard Jackson Bks.) Simon & Schuster Children's Publishing.

Karlin, Ann Bell. Eight Bedtime Stories for Jewish Children. Mazo, Chaim, ed. 2012. 64p. pap. 11.95 *(978-1-936778-67-6(X))* Mazo Pubs.

Katz, Alan. Stalling. Smith, Elwood H., illus. 2010. (ENG.). 40p. (J). (gr. -1-2). 16.99 *(978-1-4169-5567-2(4)*, McElderry, Margaret K. Bks.) McElderry, Margaret K. Bks.

Katz, Karen. Beddy-Bye, Baby. Katz, Karen, illus. 2009. (ENG., Illus.). 12p. (J). (gr. -1 — 1). bds. 7.99 *(978-1-4169-8048-3(2)*, Little Simon) Little Simon.

Kay, Devora. The Sleep Sheep Story. 2012. (ENG.). pap. *(978-1-4675-4640-9(2))* Independent Pub.

Kayler, Ralph. The Tea Party in the Tree Tops. 2009. 48p. pap. 19.49 *(978-1-4389-8000-3(0))* AuthorHouse.

Keast, Ellen Frances. A Snowy Week. 2010. 16p. pap. 9.99 *(978-1-60911-647-7(X)*, Eloquent Bks.) Strategic Book Publishing & Rights Agency (SBPRA).

Kelly, Cooper, et al. Good Night Christmas. 2015. (Good Night Our World Ser.). (ENG., Illus.). 20p. (J). (— 1). bds. 9.95 *(978-1-60219-197-6(2))* Good Night Bks.

Kelly, Mij. A Bed of Your Own. McQuillan, Mary, illus. 2011. 32p. (J). (gr. -1-1). pap. 8.99 *(978-0-7641-4768-5(4))* Barron's Educational Series, Inc.

—Lion's Lullaby. Clifton-Brown, Holly, illus. 2016. (ENG.). 32p. (J). (gr. -1 — 1). 16.99 *(978-1-4847-2526-9(3))* Disney Pr.

Kennedy, Linda. I Love You More... 2010. 17p. (J). pap. 13.95 *(978-1-4327-5196-8(4))* Outskirts Pr., Inc.

Kenney, Cindy. Where Is God When I'm Scared?, 1 vol. 2004. (Big Idea Bks.). (ENG., Illus.). 22p. (J). 4.99 *(978-0-310-70784-4(6))* Zonderkidz.

Kemahan, J. C. & Kemahan, C. Tom, Dot & Talking Mouse & Other Bedtime Stories. 2007. (Illus.). 48p. per. *(978-1-4065-1897-9(2))* Dodo Pr.

Kerr, Valerie. The Adventures of Selwyn & Robert. 2012. 64p. pap. 10.43 *(978-1-4669-5998-9(3))* Trafford Publishing.

Ketteman, Helen. Goodnight, Little Monster, 0 vols. Leick, Bonnie, illus. 2010. (ENG.). 32p. (J). (gr. -1-3). 16.99 *(978-0-7614-5683-4(X)*, 9780761456834, Amazon Children's Publishing) Amazon Publishing.

Keyser, William. Once upon A Night. Barnes, Trisha, illus. 2011. (J). pap. 8.99 *(978-0-9827531-1-8(X))* River Canyon Pr.

Killion, Bette. Little Lek Longtail Learns to Sleep. Vidal, Beatriz, illus. 2016. (ENG.). 28p. (J). (gr. k-3). 17.95 *(978-1-937786-63-2(3)*, Wisdom Tales) World Wisdom, Inc.

Kim, Cecil. I Can't Sleep: Imagination - Bedtime. Cowley, Joy, ed. Bisaillon, Josee, illus. 2015. (Step up - Creative Thinking Ser.). (ENG.). 32p. (gr. -1-2). 7.99 *(978-1-925246-65-0(5))*; 26.65 *(978-1-925246-13-1(2))*; 26.65 *(978-1-925246-39-1(6))* ChoiceMaker Pty. Ltd., The AUS. (Big and SMALL). Dist: Lerner Publishing Group.

—I Can't Sleep: Imagination - Bedtime. Cowley, Joy, ed. Bisaillon, Josée, illus. 2015. (Step up - Creative Thinking Ser.). (ENG.). 32p. (J). (gr. -1-2). 26.65 *(978-1-925186-41-3(5))* Lerner Publishing Group.

Kirk, David. Bedtime Story. 2006. (Illus.). 32p. (J). *(978-0-448-44514-4(X))* Penguin Publishing Group.

Kirkup, Mary. More Tales of Granny Grunt. 2012. (Illus.). 32p. (-18). pap. 19.76 *(978-1-4490-9161-3(X))* AuthorHouse.

Kissell, Casey. Awaiting Your Arrival. 2013. 20p. pap. 24.95 *(978-1-62709-188-6(2))* America Star Bks.

Kitchens, Jennifer. Who Made the Stars? A Collection of Bedtime Stories. 2005. 57p. per. *(978-1-59196-978-5(6))* Instant Pub.

Kittle, Sharon K. & Kittle, Sharon K. The Really Read Book. 2013. 24p. pap. 12.95 *(978-1-61493-234-5(4))* Peppertree Pr., The.

Kleinberg, Naomi. B Is for Bedtime! (Sesame Street) Brannon, Tom, illus. 2017. (Nifty Lift-And-Look Ser.). (ENG.). 12p. (J). (— 1). bds. 6.99 *(978-0-399-55812-2(8)*, Random Hse. Bks. for Young Readers) Random Hse. Children's Bks.

Kleinberg, Naomi. Naptime/Cuddlies (Sesame Street) Moroney, Christopher, illus. 2017. (ENG.). 24p. (J). (— 1). bds. 8.99 ***(978-1-5247-1636-3(7)***, Random Hse. Bks. for Young Readers) Random Hse. Children's Bks.

Kloske, Geoffrey. Once upon a Time, the End: Asleep in 60 Seconds. 2007. (Illus.). 27p. (J). 16.00 *(978-1-4223-6591-5(3))* DIANE Publishing Co.

—Once upon a Time, the End: Asleep in 60 Seconds. Blitt, Barry, illus. 2005. (ENG.). 40p. (J). (gr. -1-3). 18.99 *(978-0-689-86619-7(4)*, Atheneum Bks. for Young Readers) Simon & Schuster Children's Publishing.

Knapman, Timothy. Dinosaurs Don't Have Bedtimes! Dyson, Nikki, illus. 2016. (ENG.). 32p. (J). (gr. -1-2). 15.99 *(978-0-7636-8927-8(0))* Candlewick Pr.

Knibbs, Carl. The Tickly Ogre. 2010. 32p. pap. 21.50 *(978-1-4452-8655-6(6))* Lulu Pr., Inc.

Knotts, Reigan. The Book. 2013. 24p. pap. 10.95 *(978-1-4525-8354-9(4)*, Balboa Pr.) Author Solutions, Inc.

Koksal, Erin. Bedtime for Abbie. 2010. 23p. (J). pap. 11.95 *(978-1-4327-5693-2(1))* Outskirts Pr., Inc.

Koller, Jackie French. No Such Thing. Lewin, Betsy, illus. 2012. (ENG.). 32p. (J). (gr. k-2). pap. 7.95 *(978-1-59078-911-7(3))* Boyds Mills Pr.

Kramer, Andrew. Pajama Pirates. Lammle, Leslie, illus. 2010. (ENG.). 40p. (J). (gr. k-3). 16.99 *(978-0-06-125194-8(1))* HarperCollins Pubs.

Krensky, Stephen. Fraidy Cats. Lewin, Betsy, illus. 2015. (Scholastic Reader, Level 2 Ser.). (ENG.). 32p. (J). (gr. -1-3). pap. 3.99 *(978-0-545-79966-9(X)*, Cartwheel Bks.) Scholastic, Inc.

Krilanovich, Nadia. Moon Child. Sayles, Elizabeth, illus. 2010. (ENG.). 32p. (J). (gr. -1-2). 15.99 *(978-1-58246-325-4(5)*, Tricycle Pr.) Random Hse. Children's Bks.

Krosoczka, Jarrett J. Good Night, Monkey Boy. Krosoczka, Jarrett J., illus. (ENG., Illus.). (J). 2013. 32p. (-k). bds. 6.99 *(978-0-449-81323-2(1)*, Knopf Bks. for Young Readers) 2003. 40p. (gr. -1-2). pap. 7.99 *(978-0-440-41798-9(8)*, Dragonfly Bks.) Random Hse. Children's Bks.

Kruse, Anne. Takota's Dream. 2010. pap. 16.99 *(978-0-578-05291-5(1))* Sisterhaus Publishing.

Kuenzler, Lou. Magical Animals at Bedtime: Tales of Guidance & Inspiration for You to Read with Your Child - To Comfort & Enlighten. Weale, Andrew, illus. 2013. (ENG.). 144p. (J). (gr. -1-3). pap. 16.95 *(978-1-78028-513-9(2)*, Watkins Publishing) Watkins Media Limited GBR. Dist: Penguin Random Hse. LLC.

Kurty, G. Thomas the Treemaker: a Short Story about a Tall Tale. 2007. (ENG.). 76p. per. 19.95 *(978-1-4241-6219-2(X))* America Star Bks.

Kyrja. Rupert's Tales: A Book of Bedtime Stories, 1 vol. Osborn, Tonia Bennington, illus. 2014. (ENG.). 64p. (J). (gr. 5-8). 19.99 *(978-0-7643-4694-1(6)*, 9780764346941) Schiffer Publishing, Ltd.

La Coccinella. Little Star. 2014. (Look & See! Ser.). (ENG., Illus.). 24p. (J). (gr. -1 — 1). bds. 6.95 *(978-1-4549-0599-8(9))* Sterling Publishing Co., Inc.

LaBrant, Kenneth R. Uncle Kenny's Crazy Bedtime Stories. 2008. 73p. pap. 19.95 *(978-1-60563-602-3(9))* America Star Bks.

Ladybird Five-Minute Stories. 2017. (ENG., Illus.). 108p. (J). (gr. k-4). 14.99 ***(978-0-241-24242-1(8))*** Penguin Bks., Ltd. GBR. Dist: Independent Pubs. Group.

Lake Press Ltd. Fun at Home. 2016. (Little Grabbers Ser.). (ENG., Illus.). 6p. (J). (gr. -1 — 1). bds. 5.99 *(978-0-7641-6835-2(5))* Barron's Educational Series, Inc.

Laky, Esther. Just Fairy Tales. 2010. 95p. pap. 11.80 *(978-0-557-01926-7(5))* Lulu Pr., Inc.

Landry, Leo. Space Boy. Landry, Leo, illus. 2007. (ENG., Illus.). 32p. (J). (gr. -1-3). 16.99 *(978-0-618-60568-2(1))* Houghton Mifflin Harcourt Publishing Co.

Lane, Arnetta L. The Nine Steps of Bedtime. 2013. 28p. pap. 24.95 *(978-1-4626-8828-9(4))* America Star Bks.

Lane, Jessica E. Fletcher: The Quickest Chicken Catcher. 2009. 52p. pap. 31.99 *(978-1-4415-3461-3(X))* Xlibris Corp.

—The Secret of the Swans. 2009. 52p. pap. 31.99 *(978-1-4415-5517-5(X))* Xlibris Corp.

Larsen, Mylisa. How to Put Your Parents to Bed. Cole, Babette, illus. 2016. 32p. (J). (gr. -1-3). 17.99 *(978-0-06-232064-3(5))* HarperCollins Pubs.

Leblond, Michaël. New York in Pajamarama. Bertrand, Frederique, illus. 2013. (ENG.). 32p. (J). (gr. -1-2). 15.99 *(978-1-907912-23-8(1))* Phoenix Yard Bks. GBR. Dist: Independent Pubs. Group.

Lee, Nancy. Hoover's Summer Tale. 2004. (J). spiral bd. 8.95 *(978-0-9748087-6-5(8))* Journey Pubns., LLC.

Lee, Silver Ann. Amazing Bedtime Stories. 2010. 32p. pap. 19.99 *(978-1-4490-6094-7(3))* AuthorHouse.

Lehti, Kauko. Beautiful Animal Stories for Good Children. 2009. 44p. pap. 18.00 *(978-1-60693-872-0(X)*, Strategic Bk. Publishing) Strategic Book Publishing & Rights Agency (SBPRA).

Leigh, Susan K. God I Need to Talk to you About Bedtime. 2011. 16p. pap. 1.19 *(978-0-7586-2658-5(4))* Concordia Publishing Hse.

Lemaster, Kevin. Corn for Tomorrow: A Story from Glengary. Lemaster, Michael, illus. 2009. 28p. pap. 13.99 *(978-1-4343-8548-2(5))* AuthorHouse.

Lester, Helen & Munsinger, Lynn. Boris & the Worrisome Wakies. Lester, Helen & Munsinger, Lynn, illus. 2017. (ENG., Illus.). 32p. (J). (gr. -1-3). 16.99 *(978-0-544-64094-8(2)*, HMH Books For Young Readers) Houghton Mifflin Harcourt Publishing Co.

Leuck, Laura. Goodnight, Baby Monster. Date not set. 32p. (J). (gr. -1-1). pap. 4.99 *(978-0-06-443723-3(X))* HarperCollins Pubs.

Levin, Freddie. Goodnight Stained Glass Coloring Book. 2009. (Dover Stained Glass Coloring Book Ser.). (ENG., Illus.). 32p. (J). (gr. -1-2). pap. 6.99 *(978-0-486-47293-5(0))* Dover Pubns., Inc.

Lewis, Rose A. Sweet Dreams. Corace, Jen, illus. 2012. (ENG.). 32p. (J). (gr. -1-k). 16.95 *(978-1-4197-0189-4(4)*, Abrams Bks. for Young Readers) Abrams, Inc.

Leysen, An. The Princess Who Could Not Sleep. 2012. (ENG.). 30p. (J). (gr. -1-k). 15.95 *(978-1-60537-132-0(7))* Cobblestone Publishing Co.

Lignell, Kirk. Listen to the Raindrops: Featuring the Storm Song. Lignell, Brent, illus. 2007. 32p. (J). (gr. -1-3). 17.95 *(978-1-932399-15-8(1))* Huron River Pr.

Lisle, Chris. Bedtime Stories for Girls. 2011. 32p. pap. 13.10 *(978-1-257-04108-4(8))* Lulu Pr., Inc.

Listening with Zachary. (J). pap. 13.75 *(978-0-8136-4655-8(3))* Modern Curriculum Pr.

Little Dolphin & Friends. (Flocked Soft-to-Touch Board Ser.). 5p. bds. *(978-1-4054-9503-5(0))* Parragon, Inc.

Little Elephant & Friends. (Flocked Soft-to-Touch Board Ser.). 5p. bds. *(978-1-4054-9445-8(X))* Parragon, Inc.

Little Monkey & Friends. (Flocked Soft-to-Touch Board Ser.). 5p. bds. *(978-1-4054-9504-2(9))* Parragon, Inc.

Little Penguin & Friends. (Flocked Soft-to-Touch Board Ser.). 5p. bds. *(978-1-4054-9446-5(8))* Parragon, Inc.

Litwin, Eric. The Nuts: Bedtime at the Nut House. Magoon, Scott, illus. 2014. (ENG.). 32p. (J). (gr. -1-3). 18.00 *(978-0-316-32244-7(X))* Little, Brown Bks. for Young Readers.

Lloyd, Alicia. When the Monsters Are Quiet. Rottinger, Amy, illus. 2013. 26p. pap. 11.95 *(978-1-61244-219-8(6))* Halo Publishing International.

Lloyd-Jones, Sally. Time to Say Goodnight. Chapman, Jane, illus. 2006. (ENG.). 32p. (J). (gr. -1-2). 15.99 *(978-0-06-054328-0(0))* HarperCollins Pubs.

Logue, Mary. Sleep Like a Tiger. Zagarenski, Pamela, illus. 2012. (ENG.). 40p. (J). (gr. -1-3). 17.99 *(978-0-547-64102-7(8))* Houghton Mifflin Harcourt Publishing Co.

Long, Ethan. Good Night! 2015. (Animal Sounds Ser.). (ENG., Illus.). 20p. (J). (gr. -1 — 1). bds. 7.95 *(978-1-4197-1366-8(3))* Abrams, Inc.

Long, Greg & Edmundson, Chris. Yeti, Turn Out the Light! Kirwan, Wednesday, illus. 2013. (ENG.). 36p. (J). (gr. -1-k). 12.99 *(978-1-4521-1158-2(8))* Chronicle Bks. LLC.

Long, Heather & Long, Ethan. Max & Milo Go to Sleep! Long, Ethan, illus. 2013. (ENG., Illus.). 32p. (J). (gr. -1-3). 14.99 *(978-1-4424-5143-8(2)*, Aladdin) Simon & Schuster Children's Publishing.

Long, Samantha Gail. Don't Let the Bedbugs Bite, 1 vol. Byers, Bradley, illus. 2010. 24p. 24.95 *(978-1-4512-8681-6(3))* PublishAmerica, Inc.

Longo, Kaitlin. The Secret in Olivia's Garden. 2012. 36p. pap. 20.99 *(978-1-4685-5222-5(8))* AuthorHouse.

Lopilato, Elizabeth H. Marshmello Mountain. 2011. 32p. pap. 12.80 *(978-1-4634-2957-7(6))* AuthorHouse.

Lotz, Dana R. Kids' Tales. 2008. 85p. pap. 19.95 *(978-1-60672-179-7(8))* America Star Bks.

Love, Makada H. Harold's Adventures. Holt, Lindsey, illus. 2008. 92p. pap. 10.99 *(978-1-4343-6875-1(0))* AuthorHouse.

Loye, David. Grandfather's Garden: Bedtime Stories for Little & Big Folk. 2008. (J). pap. 18.95 *(978-0-9795257-7-3(2))* Benjamin Franklin Pr.

Luscier, Kim. Steven Learns about Temper Tantrums, 1 vol. 2009. 48p. pap. 16.95 *(978-1-60749-692-2(5))* America Star Bks.

Lynch, F. Michael. I Don't Want to Share a Bedroom. 2010. 38p. pap. 14.50 *(978-1-60911-313-1(6)*, Eloquent Bks.) Strategic Book Publishing & Rights Agency (SBPRA).

Lynch, Kendra. Sweet Dreams Little. 2011. 24p. pap. 12.74 *(978-1-4520-8295-0(2))* AuthorHouse.

Lyon, George Ella. Sleepsong. Catalanotto, Peter, illus. 2008. (ENG.). 40p. (J). (gr. -1-k). 16.99 *(978-0-689-86973-0(8)*, Atheneum/Richard Jackson Bks.) Simon & Schuster Children's Publishing.

Lyons, P. J. God Is Watching over You, 1 vol. Warnes, Tim, illus. 2016. (ENG.). 16p. (J). bds. 9.99 *(978-0-310-74881-6(X))* Zonderkidz.

MacDonald, George. The Day Boy & the Night Girl. 2008. 128p. 23.95 *(978-1-60664-922-0(1))*; pap. 10.95 *(978-1-60664-042-5(9))* Aegypan.

Mack, Jeff. Hush Little Polar Bear. Mack, Jeff, illus. (ENG., Illus.). (J). (gr. -1-1). 2013. 36p. bds. 7.99 *(978-1-59643-945-0(9)*, 9781596439450) 2008. 40p. 17.99 *(978-1-59643-368-7(X)*, 9781596433687) Roaring Brook Pr.

—Playtime? Mack, Jeff, illus. 2016. (ENG., Illus.). 32p. (J). (-k). 16.99 *(978-0-399-17598-5(9)*, Philomel Bks.) Penguin Young Readers Group.

Mackall, Dandi Daley. Bed Time Blessings. Kucharik, Elena, illus. 2012. (Little Blessings Ser.). (ENG.). 32p. (J). pap. 3.99 *(978-1-4143-7528-1(X))* Tyndale Hse. Pubs.

Mackall, Deborah. What Happens When I'm Asleep? Mackall, Debbie, illus. 2008. (ENG.). 32p. (J). (gr. -1-k). 15.95 *(978-0-9762273-1-1(2))* Dimensions in Media, Inc.

MacLachlan, Marie. Granny Grotbag's Bedtime Stories. 2010. 20p. pap. 8.49 *(978-1-4490-1519-0(0))* AuthorHouse.

MacLachlan, Patricia. The Moon's Almost Here. dePaola, Tomie, illus. 2016. (ENG.). 32p. (J). (gr. -1-3). 17.99 *(978-1-4814-2062-4(3)*, McElderry, Margaret K. Bks.) McElderry, Margaret K. Bks.

MacLelland, Edith Bennett. Grandma Tell Me a Story. 2011. 264p. 24.59 *(978-1-4634-1386-6(6))*; pap. 14.03 *(978-1-4634-1384-2(X))* AuthorHouse.

Madame M. Eerie Little Bedtime Stories. 2006. (ENG.). 132p. (J). 12.99 *(978-0-9777972-0-2(1))* Blue Tie Publishing.

Madden, Gloria. Grandmother's Bedtime Stories. 2005. 57p. pap. 16.95 *(978-1-4137-6489-5(4))* America Star Bks.

—Grandmothers Bedtime Stories: Book 5. 2008. 144p. pap. 11.99 *(978-1-4343-9515-3(4))* AuthorHouse.

Maggiore, Lisa. Ava the Monster Slayer. Felten, Ross, illus. 2015. (ENG.). 32p. (J). (gr. -1-k). 16.99 *(978-1-63450-151-4(9)*, Sky Pony Pr.) Skyhorse Publishing Co., Inc.

Magical Bedtime Stories. 2012. (ENG.). 128p. (J). 9.95 *(978-1-84837-866-7(1))* Arcturus Publishing GBR. Dist: Bookmasters Distribution.

Magsamen, Sandra. Bedtime Bunny. 2009. (Board Books with Plush Toy Ser.). (ENG., Illus.). 20p. (J). (gr. -1 — 1). bds. 7.99 *(978-0-316-00390-2(5))* Little, Brown Bks. for Young Readers.

—Go to Sleepy, Little Sheepy. 2015. (ENG., Illus.). 10p. (J). (gr. -1 — 1). bds. 7.99 *(978-0-316-25515-8(7))* Little, Brown Bks. for Young Readers.

Maillis, Nicole. How Did I Get Here? Safar, Lina, illus. 2011. 4p. (J). 7.95 *(978-1-60131-086-6(2))* Big Tent Bks.

Mammola-Koravos, Beth A. Good Night God, Love Olivia. Bebirian, Helena, illus. l.t. ed. 2006. 32p. (J). (gr. -1-1). 15.95 *(978-1-59879-110-5(9))* Lifevest Publishing, Inc.

Manceau, Édouard, illus. Tickle Monster. 2015. (ENG.). 32p. (J). (gr. -1-k). 14.95 *(978-1-4197-1731-4(6))* Abrams, Inc.

Manning, Maurie J. Kitchen Dance. Manning, Maurie J., illus. 2008. (ENG., Illus.). 32p. (J). (gr. -1-3). 17.99 *(978-0-618-99110-5(7))* Houghton Mifflin Harcourt Publishing Co.

Mansbach, Adam. Seriously, Just Go to Sleep. Cortés, Ricardo, illus. 2012. (ENG.). 36p. (gr. k-5). 15.95 *(978-1-61775-078-6(6))* Akashic Bks.

Marchon, Benoit. Good Night! Bravi, Soledad, illus. 2013. (ENG.). 40p. (J). (gr. k — 1). bds. 7.99 *(978-0-547-89314-3(0))* Houghton Mifflin Harcourt Publishing Co.

Margulies, Julianna & Margulies, Paul. Three Magic Balloons. Shaffer, Grant, illus. 2016. (ENG.). 40p. (J). (gr. -1-2). 17.99 *(978-1-101-93523-1(5)*, Random Hse. Bks. for Young Readers) Random Hse. Children's Bks.

Markes, Julie. Shhhhh! Everybody's Sleeping. Parkins, David, illus. 32p. (J). (gr. -1-1). 2005. lib. bdg. 16.89 *(978-0-06-053791-3(4))* 2004. (ENG.). 16.99 *(978-0-06-053790-6(6))* HarperCollins Pubs.

Marlow, Layn. Hurry up & Slow Down. 2009. (ENG., Illus.). 32p. (J). (gr. -1-3). 16.95 *(978-0-8234-2178-7(3))* Holiday Hse., Inc.

Marsh, Richard Phillip. Mattress People Go to Bear Park. 2009. 44p. pap. 10.95 *(978-1-935125-39-6(7))* Robertson Publishing.

Martin, Bill, Jr. & Sampson, Michael. Kitty Cat, Kitty Cat, Are You Going to Sleep?, 0 vols. Bryant, Laura J., illus. 2011. (ENG.). 24p. (J). (gr. -1-3). 15.99 *(978-0-7614-5946-0(4)*, 9780761459460, Amazon Children's Publishing) Amazon Publishing.

Martin, Emily Winfield. Dream Animals: A Bedtime Journey. (ENG., Illus.). (J). 2015. 34p. (— 1). bds. 8.99 *(978-0-553-52190-0(X))* 2013. 32p. (gr. -1-k). 17.99 *(978-0-449-81080-4(1))* 2013. 32p. (gr. -1-k). lib. bdg. 20.99 *(978-0-375-97149-5(1))* Random Hse. Children's Bks. (Random Hse. Bks. for Young Readers).

Martin, W. Lyon. Watchers. 2008. (Illus.). 32p. (J). (gr. -1-1). lib. bdg. 16.95 *(978-0-9796834-5-9(9)*, Magical Child Bks.) Shades of White.

Martinez, Lisa Bolivar, et al. Good Night Miami. 2011. (Good Night Our World Ser.). (ENG.). 20p. (J). (gr. k — 1). bds. 9.95 *(978-1-60219-051-1(8))* Good Night Bks.

Marts, Doreen Mulryan, illus. Even Monsters Say Good Night. 2015. (ENG.). 32p. (gr. -1-2). 14.95 *(978-1-62370-256-4(9))* Capstone Young Readers of Coughlan Cos.

Mary Barr. The Ditch Dog the Hedge Cat. 2009. 108p. 20.95 *(978-1-4401-5560-4(7))* iUniverse, Inc.

Mason, Margaret. Inside All, 1 vol. Welch, Holly, illus. 2008. (ENG.). 32p. (J). (gr. -1-2). 16.95 *(978-1-58469-111-2(5))*; pap. 8.95 *(978-1-58469-112-9(3))* Dawn Pubns.

Matheson, Christie. Touch the Brightest Star. Matheson, Christie, illus. (Illus.). (J). (gr. -1-3). 2017. 42p. bds. 7.99 *(978-0-06-227448-9(1))* 2015. (ENG., 40p. 15.99 *(978-0-06-227447-2(3))* HarperCollins Pubs. (Greenwillow Bks.).

Matsuda, Christine. Goodnight Little One: Bedtime Around the World. Ishida, Jui, illus. 2008. (J). 15.95 *(978-0-87358-925-3(4)*, Rising Moon Bks. for Young Readers) Northland Publishing.

Mattei, Francesca. Caraselle. 2010. 36p. pap. *(978-1-4269-3219-9(7))* Trafford Publishing (UK) Ltd.

Mayer, Mercer. Bedtime Stories - Little Critter. Mayer, Mercer, illus. 2013. (Little Critter Ser.). (ENG., Illus.). 144p. (J). (gr. -1-3). pap. 11.99 *(978-0-06-223640-1(7)*, HarperFestival) HarperCollins Pubs.

Mayhew, James. Starlight Sailor. Morris, Jackie, illus. (ENG.). 24p. (J). 2013. (gr. -1-1). 14.99 *(978-1-84686-936-5(6))* 2012. pap. 6.99 *(978-1-84686-750-7(9))* 2009. (gr. -1-3). 16.99 *(978-1-84686-185-7(3))* Barefoot Bks., Inc.

Mcauliffe, Timothy & McAuliffe, John Jobin. Snappy the Fox & Other Sleep Time Stories. 2008. 64p. pap. 18.95 *(978-1-4327-1934-0(3))* Outskirts Pr., Inc.

McBratney, Sam. Guess How Much I Love You. Jeram, Anita, illus. 2005. 34p. (J). bds. 19.95 *(978-0-9769313-1-7(1))* BrailleInk.

—Guess How Much I Love You. Jeram, Anita, illus. (Guess How Much I Love You Ser.). (J). 2014. (ENG.). 30p. (gr. k-4). 9.99 *(978-0-7636-7446-5(X))* 2011. (ENG.). 16p. (gr. -1-2). 19.99 *(978-0-7636-5378-1(0))* 2011. (ENG.). (gr. -1-k). bds. 9.99 *(978-0-7636-4976-0(7))* 2006. 32p. (gr. -1-3). 15.99 *(978-0-7636-3503-9(0))* Candlewick Pr.

—Guess How Much I Love You 20th Anniversary Edition. Jeram, Anita, illus. 2014. (Guess How Much I Love You Ser.). (ENG.). 40p. (J). (gr. k-12). 16.99 *(978-0-7636-7448-9(6))* Candlewick Pr.

McCabe, Gusty. The Most Important Critter in the Whole Wide World: Why the Coyote Howls at Night. 2013. 40p. pap. 19.57 *(978-1-4669-8759-3(6))* Trafford Publishing.

McCanna, Tim. Bitty Bot. Carpenter, Tad, illus. 2016. (Bitty Bot Ser.). (ENG.). 32p. (J). (gr. -1-3). 16.99 *(978-1-4814-4929-8(X)*, Simon & Schuster Bks. For Young Readers) Simon & Schuster Bks. For Young Readers.

McCarthy, Dan & Rosen, Anne. Good Night Oregon. Veno, Joe, illus. 2010. (Good Night Our World Ser.). (ENG.). 20p. (J). (gr. k — 1). bds. 9.95 *(978-1-60219-041-2(0))* Good Night Bks.

McCarty, Peter. Bunny Dreams. McCarty, Peter, illus. 2016. (ENG., Illus.). 40p. (J). 16.99 *(978-0-8050-9687-3(6)*, 9780805096873, Holt, Henry & Co. Bks. For Young Readers) Holt, Henry & Co.

McClure, Nikki. Awake to Nap. 2006. (ENG., Illus.). 32p. (J). (gr. k — 1). 9.95 *(978-1-57061-507-8(1)*, Little Bigfoot) Sasquatch Bks.

McCue, Lisa, illus. Time for Bed! A Cozy Counting Bedtime Book. 2015. (ENG.). 20p. (J). (gr. -1 — 1). bds. 12.99 *(978-0-7944-3337-6(5))* Reader's Digest Assn., Inc., The.

McCue, Lisa & Falken, L. C. Snuggle Bunnies. McCue, Lisa, illus. 2003. (Boardbooks - Board Book Ser.). (ENG., Illus.). 11p. (J). (gr. -1 — 1). bds. 6.99 *(978-0-7944-0040-8(X)*, Reader's Digest Children's Bks.) Studio Fun International.

McCullough, Angela. Night Nite. 2008. 24p. pap. 10.00 *(978-1-934925-10-2(1)*, Eloquent Bks.) Strategic Book Publishing & Rights Agency (SBPRA).

McDonnell, Patrick. Thank You & Good Night. 2015. (ENG., Illus.). 40p. (J). (gr. -1-3). 15.99 *(978-0-316-33801-1(X))* Little Brown & Co.

Mcdoogle, Farrah. Olivia Says Good Night. 2016. (Olivia 8x8 Ser.). lib. bdg. 13.55 *(978-0-606-39244-0(0))* Turtleback Bks.

McElroy, Jean. Night-Night, Sleepyhead. Ramljak, Marijan, illus. 2010. (ENG.). 12p. (J). (gr. -1 — 1). 4.99 *(978-1-4424-0902-6(9)*, Little Simon) Little Simon.

McGrath, Craig. The Chocolate Cake Goes to the Gas Station. 2012. 24p. pap. 14.99 *(978-1-4567-6933-8(2))* AuthorHouse.

McJarrow, Shandy. The Adventures of Papilio the Butterfly. 2009. 112p. 20.95 *(978-1-4401-3850-8(8))*; pap. 10.95 *(978-1-4401-3840-9(0))* iUniverse, Inc.

McKee, Brett. The Tickle Ghost. McKee, David, illus. 2011. (ENG.). 32p. (J). (gr. k-2). 19.99 *(978-1-84939-246-4(3))* Andersen Pr. GBR. Dist: Independent Pubs. Group.

McKellar, Danica. Goodnight, Numbers! Padrón, Alicia, illus. 2017. (ENG.). 40p. (J). (-k). 16.99 *(978-1-101-93378-7(X)*, Crown Books For Young Readers) Random Hse. Children's Bks.

McKelvain Kite, Karen. I Had a Dream. 2009. (Illus.). 40p. pap. 18.49 *(978-1-4490-3539-6(6))* AuthorHouse.

McMullan, Kate. Mamas' Kisses. Nyeu, Tao, illus. 2017. (ENG.). 40p. (J). (-k). 16.99 *(978-0-525-42832-9(1)*, Dial Bks) Penguin Young Readers Group.

McPike, Elizabeth. Little Sleepyhead. Barton, Patrice, illus. 2015. (ENG.). 26p. (J). (— 1). 16.99 *(978-0-399-16240-4(2)*, G.P. Putnam's Sons Books for Young Readers) Penguin Young Readers Group.

Meadows, Michelle. Piggies in Pajamas. Hoyt, Ard, illus. 2013. (ENG.). 32p. (J). (gr. -1-2). 15.99 *(978-1-4169-4982-4(8)*, Simon & Schuster Bks. For Young Readers) Simon & Schuster Bks. For Young Readers.

Mele, Leo. Closet Creeps: A Bedtime Mystery. Demmers, Justina, illus. 2011. 20p. pap. 24.95 *(978-1-4560-9002-9(X))* America Star Bks.

Melling, David. Hugless Douglas & the Big Sleepover. 2013. (ENG., Illus.). 32p. (J). *(978-1-58925-116-8(4))* Tiger Tales.

Meng, Cece. Bedtime Is Canceled. Neyret, Aurélie, illus. 2016. (ENG.). 32p. (J). (gr. -1-3). 7.99 *(978-0-544-66837-9(5)*, HMH Books For Young Readers) Houghton Mifflin Harcourt Publishing Co.

—Bedtime Is Canceled. Neyret, Aurélie, illus. 2012. (ENG.). 32p. (J). (gr. -1-3). 16.99 *(978-0-547-63668-9(7))* Houghton Mifflin Harcourt Publishing Co.

Merritt, Kate, illus. Indestructibles: Baby Night-Night. 2014. (Indestructibles Ser.). (ENG.). 12p. (J). pap. 5.95 *(978-0-7611-8182-8(2)*, 18182) Workman Publishing Co., Inc.

Meserve, Jessica. Bedtime Without Arthur. Meserve, Jessica, illus. 2010. (ENG., Illus.). 32p. (J). (gr. -1-3). 16.95 *(978-0-7613-5497-0(2))* Lerner Publishing Group.

Messer, Claire. Grumpy Pants. Messer, Claire, illus. 2016. (ENG., Illus.). 32p. (J). (gr. -1-3). 16.99 *(978-0-8075-3075-7(1))* Whitman, Albert & Co.

Meyer, Julia & Tabler, Marie. One Pea. Tabler, Marie, illus. 2013. (Illus.). 36p. 14.95 *(978-1-62314-139-4(7))* ePub Bud.

Meyers, Susan. Rock-A-Bye Room. Bates, Amy June, illus. 2013. (ENG.). 32p. (J). (gr. -1-k). 17.95 *(978-1-4197-0537-3(7)*, Abrams Bks. for Young Readers) Abrams, Inc.

Meyers, Susan & Fox, Mem. Sweet Stories for Baby Gift Set. Frazee, Marla et al, illus. 2015. (ENG.). 128p. (J). (— 1). 16.99 *(978-0-544-53121-5(3)*, HMH Books For Young Readers) Houghton Mifflin Harcourt Publishing Co.

Michalak, Jamie. Fairy Goodnight Kisses. Watanabe, Kaori, illus. 2008. 24p. (J). (gr. 4-7). bds. 7.95 *(978-1-58925-841-9(X))* Tiger Tales.

Michel, Gay. UNA VEZ MAS. (SPA., Illus.). 32p. (J). 7.16 *(978-84-95150-32-5(8))* Corimbo, Editorial S.L. ESP. Dist: Lectorum Pubns., Inc.

Might Be Giants Staff, et al. Bed, Bed, Bed. Ozama, Marcel & Dzama, Marcel, illus. 2003. (ENG.). 48p. (gr. -1-5). 16.95 *(978-0-7432-5024-5(9))* Simon & Schuster.

Miley, Berry. Christmas Village Chronicles & Other Short Stories. 2005. 63p. pap. 8.95 *(978-1-4116-2617-1(6))* Lulu Pr., Inc.

Miller-Gill, Angela. There Are No Blankets on the Moon. Kellem-Kellner, Blynda, illus. 2004. 32p. (J). 16.00 *(978-0-9716442-2-9(5))* Jackson Publishing.

Miller, Michael Paul. Kid Tales. 2008. 103p. pap. 16.95 *(978-1-4357-0183-0(6))* Lulu Pr., Inc.

Miot, Ray. Alexis the Wizard Rabbit: Pascale & Alain Adventures. 2009. 36p. pap. 17.99 *(978-1-4389-3440-2(8))* AuthorHouse.

Mitchard, Jacquelyn. Baby Bat's Lullaby. Noonan, Julia, illus. 2004. 32p. (J). (gr. -1-1). lib. bdg. 16.89 *(978-0-06-050761-9(6))* HarperCollins Pubs.

Mitchell, Melanie, illus. Good Morning. 2008. (ENG.). 10p. (J). bds. 5.95 *(978-1-58117-708-4(9)*, Intervisual/Piggy Toes) Bendon, Inc.

—Good Morning, Good Night! A Touch & Feel Bedtime Book. 2006. 12p. (J). (gr. -1-k). 12.95 *(978-1-58117-461-8(6)*, Intervisual/Piggy Toes) Bendon, Inc.

—Good Morning, Good Night Bilingual: Buenos Dias! Buenas Noches! 2005. (ENG & SPA.). 12p. (J). 9.95 *(978-1-58117-389-5(X)*, Intervisual/Piggy Toes) Bendon, Inc.

—Good Night. 2008. (ENG.). 6p. (J). bds. 5.95 *(978-1-58117-709-1(7)*, Intervisual/Piggy Toes) Bendon, Inc.

Mitton, Tony. Snowy Bear. Brown, Alison, illus. (ENG.). (J). 2016. 26p. bds. 7.99 *(978-1-68119-084-6(2)*, 9781681190846) 2015. 32p. (gr. -1-1). 16.99 *(978-1-61963-905-8(X)*, 9781619639058) Bloomsbury Publishing USA. (Bloomsbury USA Childrens).

Miyakoshi, Akiko. The Way Home in the Night. Miyakoshi, Akiko, illus. 2017. (ENG., Illus.). 32p. (J). (gr. -1-2). 16.95 *(978-1-77138-663-0(0))* Kids Can Pr., Ltd. CAN. Dist: Hachette Bk. Group.

Mola, Astrid & Khakdan, Wahed. The Good-Night Kiss. 2004. (Illus.). 32p. (J). 10.99 *(978-1-59384-046-4(2))* Parklane Publishing.

Molina, Violet S. & Molina, Ruben. Animals Can Do Nothing. 2012. 20p. pap. 24.95 *(978-1-4626-7728-3(2))* America Star Bks.

Moneer, Simi. Once upon a Time: Part (1) 2012. (Illus.). 92p. pap. 35.08 *(978-1-4685-0353-1(7))* AuthorHouse.

Mongredien, Sue. Harry & the Monster. East, Nick, illus. 2013. (ENG.). 32p. (J). (gr. -1-k). 14.99 *(978-1-58925-146-5(6))* Tiger Tales.

—Tigers Love to Say Goodnight. Braun, Sebastien, illus. 2008. (ENG.). 32p. (J). (gr. k-2). pap. 9.99 *(978-1-84362-547-6(4))* Hodder & Stoughton GBR. Dist: Hachette Bk. Group.

Mora, Pat. Sweet Dreams/Dulces Suenos. Suarez, Maribel, illus. 2008. (My Family: Mi Familia Ser.). (SPA & ENG.). 24p. (J). (gr. -1-1). 12.99 *(978-0-06-085041-8(8)*, Rayo) HarperCollins Pubs.

Morel, John Henry. Odd Events Happen All Around Me. 2009. 96p. pap. 29.00 *(978-1-935436-28-7(7))* Rodaian Pr.

Morgan, Mary. Sleep Tight, Little Mouse. Morgan, Mary, illus. 2015. (ENG., Illus.). 32p. (J). (gr. -1-2). bds. 6.99 *(978-0-553-49829-5(0)*, Knopf Bks. for Young Readers) Random Hse. Children's Bks.

Morgan, Robert. Bob Tales. Banton, Amy Renee, illus. 2003. 216p. (J). pap. 15.00 *(978-1-888562-06-4(4))* booksonnet.com.

Moroney, Trace. Bedtime: The Baxter Bear Collection. Moroney, Trace, illus. 2008. (Baxter Bear Collection). (Illus.). 10p. (gr. -1-1). bds. 5.99 *(978-1-86463-176-0(7))* Gardner Pubns.

—Things I Love about Bedtime. Moroney, Trace, illus. 2012. (ENG., Illus.). 16p. (J). (gr. -1-k). bds. 8.99 *(978-0-545-29016-6(3)*, Cartwheel Bks.) Scholastic, Inc.

Morris, Richard & Morris, Winifred. What If the Shark Wears Tennis Shoes? 2007. (ENG.). 36p. (J). (gr. k-3). 11.99 *(978-1-4169-6726-2(5)*, Simon & Schuster/Paula Wiseman Bks.) Simon & Schuster/Paula Wiseman Bks.

Morrissey, Dean. Ship of Dreams. 2016. (ENG., Illus.). 40p. (J). (gr. -1-2). 17.95 *(978-1-63226-051-2(4)*, Prospecta Pr.) Easton Studio Pr., LLC.

Morrissey, Dean & Krensky, Stephen. The Crimson Comet. Morrissey, Dean, illus. 2006. (Illus.). 32p. (J). (gr. k-4). 17.89 *(978-0-06-008070-9(1))* HarperCollins Pubs.

Moulton, Mark Kimball & Chalmers, Josh. Change the World Before Bedtime, 1 vol. Good, Karen, illus. 2012. (ENG.). 32p. (J). 16.99 *(978-0-7643-4238-7(X)*, 9780764342387) Schiffer Publishing, Ltd.

Mr. Cheesehead Goes for a Ride... 2nd rev. ed. 2005. (Illus.). 32p. (J). 12.99 *(978-0-9764463-1-6(6))* Vertigo Publishing.

Munsch, Robert. Get Out of Bed! 2004. (Illus.). (J). (gr. k-3). spiral bd. *(978-0-616-04557-2(3))*; spiral bd. *(978-0-616-03049-3(5))* Canadian National Institute for the Blind/Institut National Canadien pour les Aveugles.

—Mortimer. Canetti, Yanitzia, tr. from ENG. Martchenko, Michael, illus. 2007. (Munsch for Kids Ser.). (SPA & ENG.). 24p. (J). (gr. -1-2). pap. 7.95 *(978-1-55451-109-9(7)*, 9781554511099) Annick Pr., Ltd. CAN. Dist: Publishers Group West (PGW).

Munson, Kayla, illus. Night Night. 2013. (ENG.). 34p. (J). pap. 12.95 ***(978-0-9821956-3-5(X))*** Fleur De Lis Publishing, LLC.

Murguia, Bethanie Deeney. The Too-Scary Story. 2017. (ENG., Illus.). 40p. (J). (gr. -1-k). 16.99 *(978-0-545-73242-0(5))* Scholastic, Inc.

Murphy, Mary. Good Night Like This. Murphy, Mary, illus. 2016. (ENG., Illus.). 32p. (J). (gr. -1-k). 12.99 *(978-0-7636-7970-5(4))* Candlewick Pr.

Musgrave, Susan. Dreams Are More Real Than Bathtubs. braille ed. 2004. (Illus.). (J). (gr. k-3). spiral bd. *(978-0-616-01748-7(0))* Canadian National Institute for the Blind/Institut National Canadien pour les Aveugles.

My First Book of Bedtime Stories. 2003. (J). 8.99 *(978-1-59384-013-6(6))* Parklane Publishing.

Nash, Margaret. My Big, New Bed. Blake, Beccy, illus. 2008. (Tadpoles Ser.). (ENG.). 24p. (J). (gr. -1-2). lib. bdg. *(978-0-7787-3859-6(0))*; pap. *(978-0-7787-3890-9(6))* Crabtree Publishing Co.

Nemmers, Lee. No Monsters Here! A Bedtime Shadow Book. Zschock, Martha Day, illus. 2015. (ENG.). 7p. (J). 12.99 *(978-1-4413-1833-6(X)*, 9781441318336) Peter Pauper Pr. Inc.

Nethaway, Misty. I Know My Mommy Loves Me. 2008. 17p. pap. 24.95 *(978-1-60672-475-0(4))* America Star Bks.

Neuls, Lillian. It's Okay to Talk to God. L'Eplattenier, Michelle, illus. 2008. 12p. pap. 24.95 *(978-1-60703-855-9(2))* America Star Bks.

Nicely, Adam. Bedtime for Tad. 2009. (ENG., Illus.). 28p. (J). (gr. k — 1). bds. 7.95 *(978-1-894965-84-2(1))* Simply Read Bks. CAN. Dist: Ingram Publisher Services.

Nickelodeon. SpongeBob SquarePants: Goodnight Lagoon. 2014. (ENG.). 32p. (J). (-3). 15.99 *(978-1-4926-1669-6(9)*, Sourcebooks Jabberwocky) Sourcebooks, Inc.

Night Night Baby. 2005. (J). bds. 6.99 *(978-0-9753127-2-8(3))* Family Bks. at Home.

No Longer Will I Hide the Stranger in My Bed. 2003. (YA). per. 15.95 *(978-0-9740081-0-3(9))* RAPHA, Inc.

Nolan, Allia Zobel. When God Tucks in the Day. Chung, Chi, illus. 2005. 16p. (J). 12.99 *(978-0-8254-5524-7(3))* Kregel Pubns.

Noll, Amanda. Hey, That's My Monster! McWilliam, Howard, illus. 2016. (ENG.). 32p. (J). (gr. k-2). 17.95 *(978-1-936261-37-6(5))* Flashlight Pr.

—I Need My Monster. McWilliam, Howard, illus. 2009. (I Need My Monster Ser.). (ENG.). 32p. (J). (gr. k-3). 16.95 *(978-0-9799746-2-5(3))* Flashlight Pr.

Norton, Tamra. Bearubs & Flutterberries. 2008. (Bearubs Ser.). pap. 3.99 *(978-0-9796008-1-4(2))* Lindsley, David Studio.

—Bearubs Clydes New Job. 2008. (Bearubs Ser.). 32p. pap. 3.99 *(978-0-9796008-2-1(0))* Lindsley, David Studio.

—Meet Bearubs. 2008. (Bearubs Ser.). 32p. pap. 3.99 *(978-0-9796008-0-7(4))* Lindsley, David Studio.

Noruziaan, Bahman. The Lonely Snake: Stories of Inspector Rabbit. 2013. 20p. pap. 13.77 *(978-1-4669-8678-7(6))* Trafford Publishing.

Novotny-Hunter, Jana. My Tail's Not Tired. Bowles, Paula, illus. 2017. (Child's Play Library). (ENG.). 32p. (J). ***(978-1-84643-985-8(X))***; pap. ***(978-1-84643-986-5(8))*** Child's Play International Ltd.

Numeroff, Laura Joffe & Munsinger, Lynn. Nighty-Night, Cooper. Munsinger, Lynn, illus. 2013. (ENG., Illus.). 32p. (J). (gr. -1-3). 16.99 *(978-0-547-40205-5(8))* Houghton Mifflin Harcourt Publishing Co.

O'Connor, Jane. Every Day Is Earth Day. 2010. (Fancy Nancy - I Can Read! Ser.). (J). lib. bdg. 13.55 *(978-0-606-12294-8(X)*, Turtleback) Turtleback Bks.

—Fancy Nancy & the Late, Late, Late Night. Glasser, Robin Preiss, illus. 2010. (Fancy Nancy Ser.). (ENG.). 24p. (J). (gr. -1-3). pap. 3.99 *(978-0-06-170377-5(X)*, HarperFestival) HarperCollins Pubs.

—Fancy Nancy & the Late, Late Night. 2010. (Fancy Nancy Picture Bks.). (J). lib. bdg. 13.55 *(978-0-606-12312-9(1)*, Turtleback) Turtleback Bks.

Odgers, Sally. Good Night, Truck. McKenzie, Heath, illus. 2016. (ENG.). 32p. (J). 16.99 *(978-1-250-07019-7(8)*, 9781250070197) Feiwel & Friends.

O'Leary, Sara. When You Were Small. Morstad, Julie, illus. 2006. (ENG.). 32p. (J). (gr. -1-3). 16.95 *(978-1-894965-36-1(1))* Simply Read Bks. CAN. Dist: Ingram Publisher Services.

Olson, Julie, illus. Already Asleep. 2006. (ENG.). 32p. (J). (gr. -1-3). 12.95 *(978-0-9766805-6-7(4))* Keene Publishing.

Olvera, Jillann. Christian's Lullaby. 2006. 29p. pap. 24.95 *(978-1-4241-1909-7(X))* PublishAmerica, Inc.

Oppenheim, Joanne F. The Prince's Bedtime. Latimer, Miriam, illus. (ENG.). 32p. (J). (gr. -1-3). 2007. pap. 7.99 *(978-1-84686-106-2(3))* 2006. 16.99 *(978-1-84148-597-3(7))* Barefoot Bks., Inc.

Oppenheim, Joanne F. & Barefoot Books Staff. El Principe No Duerme. Latimer, Miriam, illus. 2014. (SPA.). 32p. (J). (gr. -1-1). pap. 7.99 *(978-1-78285-077-9(5))* Barefoot Bks., Inc.

Oppenheim, Joanne F. & Latimer, Miriam. The Prince's Bedtime. Latimer, Miriam, illus. 2007. (ENG., Illus.). 32p. (J). (gr. -1-2). 9.99 *(978-1-84686-096-6(2))* Barefoot Bks., Inc.

O'Shea, Pauleen. Buddy's Bedtime. Dohanish, Jason, illus. 2007. 32p. (J). 14.95 *(978-0-9778063-0-0(8))* Idlehour Entertainment.

Ouyessad, Myriam. The Magical Tree: A Children's Book Inspired by Gustav Klimt, 1 vol. 2016. (ENG., Illus.). 32p. (J). (gr. -1-3). 14.95 *(978-3-7913-7214-3(9))* Prestel Verlag GmbH & Co KG. DEU. Dist: Penguin Random Hse. LLC.

Overton, Lou Ann. Thank You, Moon. 2013. 24p. pap. 12.45 *(978-1-4908-0030-1(1)*, WestBow Pr.) Author Solutions, Inc.

Owings, Jeff. Tiny Todd: Swooped Away. 2009. 20p. pap. 10.49 *(978-1-4490-1214-4(0))* AuthorHouse.

—Tiny Todd: Tiny Todd's First Pet. 2009. 20p. pap. 10.49 *(978-1-4490-1216-8(7))* AuthorHouse.

Palatini, Margie. Tub-Boo-Boo. 2004. (Illus.). (J). (gr. k-3). spiral bd. *(978-0-616-11132-1(0))*; spiral bd. *(978-0-616-11133-8(9))* Canadian National Institute for the Blind/Institut National Canadien pour les Aveugles.

Palleschi, Sarah. Did I Really Dream Last Night? 2009. 48p. pap. 16.25 *(978-1-60693-814-0(2)*, Eloquent Bks.) Strategic Book Publishing & Rights Agency (SBPRA).

Palu, P. J. Who Loves You the Most of All? 2015. (ENG., Illus.). 38p. (J). pap. 9.99 *(978-1-63047-422-5(3))* Morgan James Publishing.

PAN Macmillan UK, P. A. N. Macmillan & Books, Campbell. Bedtime Stories. Rinaldo, Luana, illus. 2015. (ENG.). 12p. (J). bds. 11.99 ***(978-1-4472-7704-0(X))*** Pan Macmillan GBR. Dist: Independent Pubs. Group.

Pandell, Karen, et al. Good Night Book. 2007. (Curious George Ser.). (ENG., Illus.). 14p. (J). (gr. k — 1). bds. 7.99 *(978-0-618-77711-2(3))* Houghton Mifflin Harcourt Publishing Co.

Paniagua, Kelly. Bedtime for Sarah Sullivan. Warrick, Jessica, illus. 2012. 36p. (J). 13.95 *(978-1-60131-119-1(2))*; pap. 10.95 *(978-1-60131-120-7(6))* Big Tent Bks. (Castlebridge Bks.).

Panton, Constance. Danielli Brambelli: The Terrible Sleeper. 2012. 16p. pap. 15.99 *(978-1-4772-4965-9(6))* AuthorHouse.

Pappas, Diane H. & Covey, Richard D. Why I Need My Sleep. Estrada, Ric, illus. 2007. (J). pap. *(978-0-545-01427-4(1))* Scholastic, Inc.

Parenteau, Shirley. Bears in Beds. Walker, David, illus. 2012. (ENG.). 32p. (J). (gr. k-k). 15.99 *(978-0-7636-5338-5(1))* Candlewick Pr.

Parker, Amy. Night Night, Daddy, 1 vol. 2016. (Night Night Ser.). (ENG., Illus.). 20p. (J). bds. 9.99 *(978-0-7180-4230-1(1))* Nelson, Thomas Inc.

—Night Night, Farm, 1 vol. Allyn, Virginia, illus. 2016. (Night Night Ser.). (ENG.). 20p. (J). bds. 8.99 *(978-0-7180-8831-6(X))* Nelson, Thomas Inc.

—Night Night, Mommy, 1 vol. 2016. (Night Night Ser.). (ENG., Illus.). 20p. (J). bds. 9.99 *(978-0-7180-4246-2(8))* Nelson, Thomas Inc.

—A Night Night Prayer, 1 vol. Pedler, Caroline, illus. (Night Night Ser.). (ENG.). (J). 2015. 24p. pap. 3.99 *(978-0-7180-3652-2(2))* 2014. 20p. bds. 9.99 *(978-1-4003-2431-6(9))* Nelson, Thomas Inc.

Parker, Amy. Tiny Blessings: for Bedtime (large Trim) Walsh, Sarah, illus. 2017. (ENG.). 10p. (J). (gr. -1 — 1). bds. 9.95 ***(978-0-7624-6210-0(8)***, Running Pr.) Running Pr. Bk. Pubs.

Parrish, Emma. Little Owl Says Goodnight. 2016. (Slide-And-Seek Ser.). (ENG., Illus.). 10p. (J). (gr. -1-k). bds. 8.99 *(978-1-4998-0406-5(7))* Little Bee Books Inc.

Parry, Rosanne. Daddy's Home! Leonard, David, illus. 2009. (ENG.). 20p. (J). bds. 6.99 *(978-0-8249-1823-1(1)*, Ideal Pubns.) Worthy Publishing.

Pasquali, Elena. The Lion Little Book of Bedtime Stories. Smee, Nicola, illus. 2014. (ENG.). 96p. (J). (gr. -1-k). 9.99 *(978-0-7459-6459-1(1))* Lion Hudson PLC GBR. Dist: Independent Pubs. Group.

—Safely Through the Night. Kolanovic, Dubravka, illus. 2008. (ENG.). 32p. (J). (gr. k — 1). pap. 9.95 *(978-0-7459-6047-0(2))* Lion Hudson PLC GBR. Dist: Independent Pubs. Group.

—Safely Through the Night. Kolanovic, Dubravka, illus. 2008. (ENG.). 32p. (J). (gr. k-k). 16.95 *(978-0-7459-6048-7(0))* Lion Hudson PLC GBR. Dist: Independent Pubs. Group.

—Two-Minute Bedtime Stories. Smee, Nicola, illus. 2010. (Two-Minute Stories Ser.). (ENG.). 48p. (J). (gr. -1-k). 12.99 *(978-0-7459-6079-1(0))* Lion Hudson PLC GBR. Dist: Independent Pubs. Group.

Patricelli, Leslie. Nighty-Night. Patricelli, Leslie, illus. 2017. (Leslie Patricelli Board Bks.). (ENG., Illus.). 26p. (J). (— 1). bds. 6.99 *(978-0-7636-7932-3(1))* Candlewick Pr.

—The Patterson Puppies & the Midnight Monster Party. Patricelli, Leslie, illus. 2010. (ENG., Illus.). 32p. (J). (gr. -1-k). 14.99 *(978-0-7636-3243-4(0))* Candlewick Pr.

Paul, Ann Whitford. Hasta Manana, Monito. (SPA.). (J). 8.95 *(978-958-04-7073-1(1))* Norma S.A. COL. Dist: Distribuidora Norma, Inc.

—Snail's Good Night. Litzinger, Rosanne, illus. 2008. (Holiday House Readers: Level 1 Ser.). (ENG.). 32p. (J). (gr. -1-3). 14.95 *(978-0-8234-1912-8(6))* Holiday Hse., Inc.

Paul, Cinco & Daurio, Ken. Sleepy Kittens. Guillon, Eric, illus. 2010. (Despicable Me Ser.). (ENG.). 10p. (J). (gr. -1 — 1). bds. 8.99 *(978-0-316-08381-2(X)*, L,B Kids) Hachette Bk. Group.

Paul Frank Industries. Only in Dreams. 2011. (ENG., Illus.). 24p. (J). (gr. -1 — 1). bds. 6.99 *(978-0-8118-7867-8(8))* Chronicle Bks. LLC.

Paul, Miranda. 10 Little Ninjas. Wragg, Nate, illus. 2016. (ENG.). 32p. (J). (-k). 14.99 *(978-0-553-53497-9(1)*, Knopf Bks. for Young Readers) Random Hse. Children's Bks.

Pea, M. J. The adventures of Benje & Sammy: Probably the naughtiest dogs in the World. 2011. (Illus.). 72p. (gr. -1). pap. 24.83 *(978-1-4567-7812-5(9))* AuthorHouse.

Peacock-Williams, Carol A. & Williams, Christy Jo. Benny the Beetle, 1 vol. Peacock, Bessie Merle, illus. 2010. 28p. 24.95 *(978-1-4489-8373-5(8))* PublishAmerica, Inc.

Pearle, Ida. The Moon Is Going to Addy's House. 2015. (ENG., Illus.). 32p. (J). (gr. -1-k). 17.99 *(978-0-8037-4054-9(9)*, Dial Bks) Penguin Young Readers Group.

Peaty, Mary Alice. The Girl Who Lived on the Moon. 2008. 44p. pap. 26.95 *(978-0-557-02225-0(8))* Lulu Pr., Inc.

Peck, C. L. A Midnight Song. 2013. (Illus.). 56p. pap. 14.95 *(978-1-4575-2343-4(4))* Dog Ear Publishing, LLC.

Peck, Jan. Way up High in a Tall Green Tree. Petrone, Valeria, illus. 2005. (ENG.). 32p. (J). (gr. -1-3). 18.99 *(978-1-4169-0071-9(3)*, Simon & Schuster Bks. For Young Readers) Simon & Schuster Bks. For Young Readers.

Penner, Lucille Recht. Apaguen las Luces! Smath, Jerry, illus. 2007. (Math Matters (Kane Press Spanish) Ser.). 32p. (J). (gr. -1-3). pap. 5.95 *(978-1-57565-241-2(2))* Kane Press, Inc.

Perlman, Willa. Good Night, World. Fisher, Carolyn, illus. 2011. (ENG.). 40p. (J). (gr. -1-k). 16.99 *(978-1-4424-0197-6(4)*, Beach Lane Bks.) Beach Lane Bks.

Pilkey, Dav. Big Dog & Little Dog Going for a Walk (Reader) 2015. (Green Light Readers Level 1 Ser.). (ENG., Illus.). 24p. (J). (gr. -1-3). pap. 3.99 *(978-0-544-43071-6(9)*, HMH Books For Young Readers) Houghton Mifflin Harcourt Publishing Co.

—Big Dog & Little Dog (Reader) 2015. (Green Light Readers Level 1 Ser.). (ENG., Illus.). 24p. (J). (gr. -1-3). pap. 3.99 *(978-0-544-43069-3(7)*, HMH Books For Young Readers) Houghton Mifflin Harcourt Publishing Co.

Piper, Noël. Most of All, Jesus Loves You! Anderson, Debby, illus. 2004. 24p. (J). 11.99 *(978-1-58134-630-5(1))* Crossway.

Pirnot, Karen Hutchins. Keeper of the Lullabies, a Book for Grandmothers Who Cherish the World of Children. Pirnot, Karen Hutchins, illus. 2007. (Illus.). 36p. per. 12.95 *(978-1-934246-90-0(5))* Peppertree Pr., The.

Pizzoli, Greg. Good Night Owl. Pizzoli, Greg, illus. 2016. (ENG., Illus.). 48p. (J). (gr. -1-k). 16.99 *(978-1-4847-1275-7(7))* Disney Pr.

Plourde, Lynn. Wild Child. 2003. 18.40 *(978-0-613-69321-9(3)*, Turtleback) Turtleback Bks.

Plourde, Lynn & Couch, Greg. Wild Child. 2003. (ENG., Illus.). 32p. (J). (gr. -1-3). 7.99 *(978-0-689-86349-3(7)*, Aladdin) Simon & Schuster Children's Publishing.

Porter, Pamela. Yellow Moon, Apple Moon, 1 vol. James, Matt, illus. 2008. (ENG.). 32p. (J). (gr. k — 1). 17.95 *(978-0-88899-809-5(0))* Groundwood Bks. CAN. Dist: Publishers Group West (PGW).

Posner-Sanchez, Andrea. Sleepy Time with Aurora (Disney Princess) RH Disney Staff & DiCicco, Sue, illus. 2015. (Board Book Ser.). (ENG.). 24p. (J). (— 1). bds. 6.99 *(978-0-7364-3311-2(2)*, RH/Disney) Random Hse. Children's Bks.

Potter, George. The Wisemen of Bountiful. Harmon, Glenn, illus. 2005. per. 11.99 *(978-1-55517-814-7(6))* Cedar Fort, Inc./CFI Distribution.

Potter, Giselle. Tell Me What to Dream About. 2015. (ENG., Illus.). 40p. (J). (gr. -1-2). 17.99 *(978-0-385-37423-1(2)*, Schwartz & Wade Bks.) Random Hse. Children's Bks.

Potter, Tina M. The Horse Story. 2005. 36p. (J). pap. 9.65 *(978-1-4116-5761-8(6))* Lulu Pr., Inc.

Potter, Tony, des. Goodnight, Little Leprechaun. 2003. (Illus.). 12p. pap. 10.95 *(978-0-7171-3612-4(4))* M.H. Gill & Co. U. C. IRL. Dist: Dufour Editions, Inc.

Price, Mathew. Cachorro. Goldman, Judy, tr. Kemp, Moira, illus. 2010. (SPA & ENG.). 10p. bds. 5.99 *(978-1-935021-64-3(8))* Price, Mathew Ltd.

Priddy, Roger. Bedtime Lullaby. 2013. (Baby Boxsets Ser.). (ENG.). 32p. (J). (gr. -1-1). 14.99 *(978-0-312-51564-5(2)*, 9780312515645, Priddy Bks.) St. Martin's Pr.

—Little Friends: Sleepy Time. 2014. (Little Friends Ser.). (ENG.). 6p. (J). (gr. -1 — 1). 9.99 *(978-0-312-51681-9(9)*, 9780312516819, Priddy Bks.) St. Martin's Pr.

Publications International Ltd. Staff, creator. Read-along Bedtime Stories. 2005. (Illus.). 37p. (J). (gr. 3-7). 12.98 *(978-1-4127-3501-8(7)*, 7248000) Publications International, Ltd.

—Treasury of Bedtime Stories. 2007. (Padded Treasuries 6x6 Ser.). (Illus.). 318p. (J). (gr. -1-3). 9.98 *(978-1-4127-7433-8(0))* Publications International, Ltd.

Publications International Ltd. Staff, ed. A Baby Is Born. 2011. 22p. (J). bds. 6.98 *(978-1-4508-1865-0(X))* Phoenix International Publications, Inc.

—Bedtime Stories. 2010. (J). bds. 12.98 *(978-0-7853-7921-8(5))* Phoenix International Publications, Inc.

—Good Night, Little Bear: A Sleepy Time Tale. 2010. (J). bds. 7.98 *(978-1-60553-435-0(8))* Phoenix International Publications, Inc.

—Jake & the Neverland Pirates: What Do You See? Pop up Book & Flashlight Set. 2013. 8p. (J). (gr. k-4). bds. 10.99 *(978-1-4508-6836-5(3)*, 2baa77ff-d973-4d57-acdb-676cb1d56b2d) Phoenix International Publications, Inc.

—Lights & Music. 2008. 160p. (J). bds. 17.98 *(978-1-4127-8500-6(6)*, PIL Kids) Publications International, Ltd.

—Mickey Mouse Clubhouse - Who's Not Sleepy? 2011. 12p. (J). bds. *(978-1-4508-0398-4(9))* Publications International, Ltd.

—Record a Story Elmo'S Bedtime Wish. 2011. 20p. 19.98 *(978-1-4508-1876-6(5))* Phoenix International Publications, Inc.

—Sesame Street: Good Night Stories. 2010. 40p. (J). bds. 14.98 *(978-1-60553-861-7(2))* Phoenix International Publications, Inc.

—Who's Not Sleepy? 2010. 18p. (J). bds. 10.98 *(978-1-60553-463-3(3),* PIL Kids) Publications International, Ltd.

—5-Minute Good Night Stories. 2004. (Illus.). 320p. 15.98 *(978-0-7853-7661-3(5),* 3934402) Phoenix International Publications, Inc.

Pulford, Elizabeth. Finding Monkey Moon. Wilkinson, Kate, illus. 2015. (ENG.). 32p. (J). (gr. -1-2). 15.99 *(978-0-7636-6777-1(3))* Candlewick Pr.

Pumphrey, W. Jerome. Creepy Things Are Scaring Me! (Illus.). 32p. (J). (gr. -1-3). 5.99 *(978-0-06-443680-9(2))* HarperCollins Pubs.

Quay, Emma. Good Night, Sleep Tight: A Book about Bedtime. Walker, Anna, illus. 2011. (ENG.). 24p. (J). (gr. -1 — 1). bds. 5.99 *(978-0-8037-3581-1(2),* Dial Bks) Penguin Young Readers Group.

Quintart, Natalie. Mama Bear. Blanchart, Stephanie, illus. 2005. (Tiger Tales Ser.). 32p. (J). (gr. -1-2). 6.95 *(978-1-58925-394-0(9))* Tiger Tales.

Raab, Brigitte. Mama, I Can't Sleep. Olten, Manuela, illus. 2012. (ENG.). 32p. (J). (gr. -1-k). 16.95 *(978-1-61608-965-8(2),* 608965, Sky Pony Pr.) Skyhorse Publishing Co., Inc.

Rae, Philippa. Count the Sheep to Sleep. Röhr, Stéphanie, illus. 2012. (ENG.). 28p. (J). (gr. -1-k). 12.95 *(978-1-61608-660-2(2),* 608660, Sky Pony Pr.) Skyhorse Publishing Co., Inc.

Raitman, Ira. Amanda's Bunny. 2010. 16p. 8.99 *(978-1-4520-2021-1(3))* AuthorHouse.

Ramadier, Cédric. Shhh! This Book Is Sleeping. Bourgeau, Vincent, illus. 2016. (ENG.). 20p. (J). (gr. -1 — 1). bds. 8.99 *(978-0-553-53875-5(6),* Random Hse. Bks. for Young Readers) Random Hse. Children's Bks.

Ramius, Edward. Yawnywawnys. 2009. 28p. pap. 14.95 *(978-1-4389-3066-4(6))* AuthorHouse.

Ramos, Mario. A La Cama, Monstruito! (SPA.). 32p. (J). 16.95 *(978-84-8470-007-4(0))* Corimbo, Editorial S.L. ESP. Dist: Lectorum Pubns., Inc., Distribooks, Inc.

Randall, Ronne. Before I Go to Sleep. Kerins, Tony, illus. 2010. (Picture Books Ser.). (J). (gr. -1-k). bds. *(978-1-4075-8756-1(0))* Parragon, Inc.

Rando, Licia. The Warmest Place of All. Jewett, Anne, illus. 2009. (ENG.). 32p. (J). (gr. -1-k). 16.95 *(978-0-9792035-8-9(9))* Pleasant St. Pr.

Random House Staff. Good Night, Dora! (Dora the Explorer) Hall, Susan, illus. 2013. (Pictureback(R) Ser.). (ENG.). 16p. (J). (gr. -1-2). 4.99 *(978-0-449-81781-0(4),* Random Hse. Bks. for Young Readers) Random Hse. Children's Bks.

Rasheed, Winona. Smiles & Frowns Through Animal Town's Storybook. 2008. 55p. pap. 13.70 *(978-1-4357-4617-6(1))* Lulu Pr., Inc.

Rathmann, Peggy. 10 Minutes till Bedtime. 2004. (ENG., Illus.). 48p. (J). (gr. -1-k). pap. 7.99 *(978-0-14-240024-1(6),* Puffin Books) Penguin Young Readers Group.

—10 Minutos Antes de Dormir. 2004. (SPA.). 46p. (J). (gr. k-18). pap. 6.99 *(978-980-257-276-2(4))* Ekare, Ediciones VEN. Dist: Lectorum Pubns., Inc.

Ray, Christie Jones & Ray, Christie Jones. Eliza Will Not Be Afraid. 2012. (Illus.). 24p. pap. 12.00 *(978-0-9853223-7-3(3))* Rose Water Cottage Pr.

Ray, Mary Lyn. Go to Sleep, Little Farm. Neal, Christopher Silas, illus. (ENG.). (J). 2015. 38p. (— 1). bds. 8.99 *(978-0-544-57916-3(X))* 2014. 40p. (gr. -1-3). 16.99 *(978-0-544-15014-0(7))* Houghton Mifflin Harcourt Publishing Co. (HMH Books For Young Readers).

—Goodnight, Good Dog. Malone, Rebecca, illus. 2015. (ENG.). 32p. (J). (gr. -1-3). 16.99 *(978-0-544-28612-2(X),* HMH Books For Young Readers) Houghton Mifflin Harcourt Publishing Co.

Reade, Maisie. Let's Go to Sleep: A Story with Five Steps to Ease Your Child to Sleep. Huliska-Beith, Laura, illus. 2016. (Read Me to Sleep Ser.). (ENG.). 32p. (J). (gr. -1-3). 14.99 *(978-0-316-35655-8(7))* Little, Brown Bks. for Young Readers.

Reader's Digest Staff & Gold, Gina. Night, Night, Elmo! 2013. (Guess Who Ser.). (ENG.). 10p. (J). (gr. -1-k). 10.99 *(978-0-7944-2798-6(7))* Reader's Digest Assn., Inc., The.

Reed, Len. Monsters at My Bed. 2011. 16p. (gr. 1-2). pap. 8.49 *(978-1-4567-6786-0(0))* AuthorHouse.

Reed, Tracey. Isaiah Has the Bedtime Blues. 2009. 20p. pap. 12.99 *(978-1-4389-4886-7(7))* AuthorHouse.

Reeve, Rosie. Lullaby Moon. Reeve, Rosie, illus. 2010. (ENG., Illus.). 20p. (J). (gr. k — 1). bds. 8.99 *(978-0-545-21146-8(8),* Cartwheel Bks.) Scholastic, Inc.

Regordosa, Adria. Dustrats. 2017. (ENG., Illus.). 32p. (J). (gr. -1-2). 16.99 *(978-1-57687-821-7(X),* powerHouse Bks.) powerHouse Cultural Entertainment, Inc.

Reichert, Amy. While Mama Had a Quick Little Chat. Boiger, Alexandra, illus. 2005. (ENG.). 40p. (J). (gr. -1-2). 16.99 *(978-0-689-85170-4(7),* Atheneum/Richard Jackson Bks.) Simon & Schuster Children's Publishing.

REID, D. H. Fantasies & Dreams. 2008. 208p. pap. 18.95 *(978-0-557-01592-4(8))* Lulu Pr., Inc.

Rescek, Sanja, illus. A Bedtime Prayer. 2013. (ENG.). 24p. (gr. -1). bds. 8.95 *(978-1-58925-606-4(9))* Tiger Tales.

Rex, Michael. Goodnight Goon: A Petrifying Parody. Rex, Michael, illus. 2012. (ENG., Illus.). 30p. (J). (gr. -1 — 1). bds. 6.99 *(978-0-399-26011-7(0),* G.P. Putnam's Sons Books for Young Readers) Penguin Publishing Group.

—Goodnight Goon: A Petrifying Parody. Rex, Michael, illus. 2008. (ENG., Illus.). 32p. (J). (gr. -1-k). 15.99 *(978-0-399-24534-3(0),* G.P. Putnam's Sons Books for Young Readers) Penguin Young Readers Group.

Rey, H. A. Awake-Asleep Cloth Book & Door Hanger. 2010. (Curious Baby Curious George Ser.). (ENG., Illus.). 4p. (J). (gr. -1 — 1). 8.99 *(978-0-547-23897-5(5))* Houghton Mifflin Harcourt Publishing Co.

—Music Play. 2009. (Curious Baby Curious George Ser.). (ENG., Illus.). 10p. (J). (gr. -1 — 1). bds. 8.99 *(978-0-547-23876-0(2))* Houghton Mifflin Harcourt Publishing Co.

—My Curious Dreamer. Set. gif. ed. 2010. (Curious Baby Curious George Ser.). (ENG., Illus.). 10p. (J). (gr. k — 1). 14.99 *(978-0-547-24308-5(1))* Houghton Mifflin Harcourt Publishing Co.

—Sweet Dreams, Curious George. 2013. (Curious George Ser.). (ENG., Illus.). 24p. (J). (gr. -1-3). 9.99 *(978-0-544-03880-6(0))* Houghton Mifflin Harcourt Publishing Co.

Rey, H. A. & Houghton Mifflin Company Editors. Sweet Dreams 5-Minute Bedtime Stories. 2014. (5-Minute Stories Ser.). (ENG., Illus.). 232p. (J). (gr. -1-3). 12.99 *(978-0-544-30178-8(1),* HMH Books For Young Readers) Houghton Mifflin Harcourt Publishing Co.

Reynolds, Luke. Bedtime Blast-Off! Yamada, Mike, illus. 2016. (ENG.). 40p. (J). (gr. -1-1). 16.99 *(978-0-545-77855-8(7),* Orchard Bks.) Scholastic, Inc.

Rhodes, Shayla. I Know Who I Am. 2012. 30p. pap. 15.00 *(978-0-9705008-7-8(4))* J & J Publishing Co.

Ricci, Christine. Buenas Noches, Dora! Cuento Para Levantar la Tapita. Hall, Susan, illus. 2004. (Dora the Explorer Ser.).Tr. of Good Night, Dora! (SPA.). 16p. (J). pap. 5.99 *(978-0-689-86648-7(8),* Libros Para Ninos) Libros Para Ninos.

Richard Bellingham Edd. The Fables of Boris: Invitations to Meaningful Conversations. 2009. 280p. 27.95 *(978-1-4401-6247-3(6));* pap. 17.95 *(978-1-4401-6245-9(X))* iUniverse, Inc.

Richmond, Marianne. Bedtime Blessings. 2016. (ENG.). 40p. (J). 9.99 *(978-1-4926-4182-7(0),* 9781492641827, Sourcebooks Jabberwocky) Sourcebooks, Inc.

—The Night Night Book. Richmond, Marianne, illus. 2011. (Marianne Richmond Ser.: 0). (ENG., Illus.). 24p. (J). (gr. -1-3). bds. 7.95 *(978-1-934082-90-4(2),* Sourcebooks Jabberwocky) Sourcebooks, Inc.

Rickards, Lynne. Jack's Bed. Beardshaw, Rosalind, illus. 2006. (Green Bananas Ser.). (ENG.). 48p. (J). (gr. -1-k). *(978-0-7787-1044-8(0))* Crabtree Publishing Co.

Rinker, Sherri Duskey. Silly Wonderful You. McDonnell, Patrick, illus. 2016. 40p. (J). (gr. -1-3). 17.99 *(978-0-06-227105-1(9))* HarperCollins Pubs.

Rivas, H. J. Word Sag: A Bedtime Story. 2012. 24p. pap. 15.99 *(978-1-4691-5661-3(X))* Xlibris Corp.

Roache, Marjorie D. Night Flights. 2012. 24p. pap. 15.99 *(978-1-4772-2565-3(X))* AuthorHouse.

Roash, Riki. Mom, I Can Sleep in My Bed Tonight! 2013. 24p. pap. 24.95 *(978-1-4626-8255-3(3))* America Star Bks.

Robbins, Heather Roan. Talulla Bear's Bedtime Book: A Sleepytime Tale. 2016. (ENG., Illus.). 32p. (J). (gr. 8-2). 14.95 *(978-1-78249-379-2(4),* 1782493794, CICO Books) Ryland Peters & Small GBR. Dist: WIPRO.

Roberts, Daniel. The Good Night Book: A Book of Animal Sounds. 2009. 36p. pap. 16.99 *(978-1-4389-8278-6(X))* AuthorHouse.

Roberts, Phyllis. Teeny Tiny Star. 2007. (Illus.). 30p. (J). lib. bdg. 19.95 *(978-1-933732-40-4(7))* Big Ransom Studio.

Robertson, Jean. Bedtime Battles. Dufalla, Anita, illus. 2011. (ENG.). 24p. (gr. k-1). pap. 8.95 *(978-1-61236-006-5(8))* Rourke Educational Media.

Robinson, Michelle. Goodnight Digger: The Perfect Bedtime Book! 2015. (Goodnight Ser.). (ENG., Illus.). 32p. (J). (gr. -1 — 1). pap. 7.99 *(978-1-4380-0661-1(6))* Barron's Educational Series, Inc.

—Goodnight Pirate: The Perfect Bedtime Book! 2015. (Goodnight Ser.). (ENG., Illus.). 32p. (J). (gr. -1 — 1). pap. 7.99 *(978-1-4380-0662-8(4))* Barron's Educational Series, Inc.

—Goodnight Princess: The Perfect Bedtime Book! 2015. (Goodnight Ser.). (ENG., Illus.). 32p. (J). (gr. -1 — 1). pap. 7.99 *(978-1-4380-0663-5(2))* Barron's Educational Series, Inc.

—Goodnight Tractor: The Perfect Bedtime Book! 2015. (Goodnight Ser.). (ENG., Illus.). 32p. (J). (gr. -1 — 1). pap. 7.99 *(978-1-4380-0664-2(0))* Barron's Educational Series, Inc.

Root, Phyllis. Ten Sleepy Sheep. Gaber, Susan, illus. 2009. (ENG.). 12p. (J). (-k). bds. 7.99 *(978-0-7636-4142-9(1))* Candlewick Pr.

Roques, Dominique. Sleep Tight, Anna Banana! Dormal, Alexis, illus. 2014. (Anna Banana Ser.). (ENG.). 28p. (J). (gr. -1-2). 15.99 *(978-1-62672-019-0(3),* 9781626720190, First Second Bks.) Roaring Brook Pr.

Roscoe, Lily. The Night Parade. Walker, David, illus. 2014. (ENG.). 32p. (J). (— 1). 16.99 *(978-0-545-39623-3(9),* Orchard Bks.) Scholastic, Inc.

Rose, Deborah Lee. Someone's Sleepy. Andreasen, Dan, illus. 2013. (ENG.). 32p. (J). (gr. -1-k). 16.95 *(978-1-4197-0539-7(3),* Abrams Bks. for Young Readers) Abrams, Inc.

Rosenbaum, Andria Warmflash & Gill, Deirdre. Trains Don't Sleep. Rosenbaum, Andria Warmflash & Gill, Deirdre, illus. 2017. (ENG., Illus.). 40p. (J). (gr. -1-3). 16.99 *(978-0-544-38074-5(6),* HMH Books For Young Readers) Houghton Mifflin Harcourt Publishing Co.

Rosenthal, Amy Krouse. Bedtime for Mommy. Pham, LeUyen, illus. 2010. (ENG.). 32p. (J). (gr. -1-k). 16.99 *(978-1-59990-341-5(5),* 9781599903415, Bloomsbury USA Childrens) Bloomsbury Publishing USA.

—Little Pea; Little Hoot; Little Oink. 3 vols., Set. Corace, Jen, illus. 2009. (ENG.). 80p. (J). (gr. -1 — 1). bds. 19.99 *(978-0-8118-7054-2(5))* Chronicle Bks. LLC.

Ross, Tony. Hora de Dormir. 2006. (Little Princess Ser.).Tr. of Bedtime. (SPA.). (J). (gr. -1-k). bds. 7.95 *(978-968-19-1488-2(0),* AT33282) Lectorum Pubns., Inc.

—I Want a Bedtime Story! Ross, Tony, illus. 2016. (ENG., Illus.). 32p. (J). (gr. -1-3). 17.99 *(978-1-5124-1629-9(0))* Andersen Pr. GBR. Dist: Lerner Publishing Group.

—I Want My Light On! Ross, Tony, illus. 2010. (Andersen Press Picture Bks). (ENG., Illus.). 32p. (J). (gr. -1-3). 16.95 *(978-0-7613-6443-6(9))* Lerner Publishing Group.

Roth, Carol. Five Little Ducklings Go to Bed. Julian, Sean, illus. 2014. (ENG.). 32p. (J). (gr. k-3). 17.95 *(978-0-7358-4128-4(4))* North-South Bks., Inc.

—Who Will Tuck Me in Tonight? Gorbachev, Valeri, illus. 2006. (Cheshire Studio Book Ser.). (ENG.). 32p. (J). (gr. -1-1). 6.95 *(978-0-7358-1976-4(9))* North-South Bks., Inc.

Roth, Carol & Julian, Sean. Five Little Ducklings Go to Bed. 2013. (Illus.). 32p. (J). pap. *(978-0-7358-4153-6(5))* North-South Bks., Inc.

Roth-Fisch, Marla. The Last Bedtime Story: That We Read Each Night. 2013. (ENG.). 32p. (J). pap. 9.95 *(978-1-935567-43-1(8),* 9781935567431) Sensory Resources.

Rothchild, Erik. The Garden Adventures: The Mishaps of Martha & Matilda. Hief, Gina, illus. 2013. 44p. *(978-0-9883568-5-6(6))* Inkwell Books LLC.

Rothstein, Gloria L. Sheep Asleep. Date not set. 224p. (J). (gr. -1-1). pap. 4.99 *(978-0-06-443717-2(5))* HarperCollins Pubs.

Rowe, Ben. Can an Alligator Drive a Nail with His Tail? 2008. 18p. pap. 24.95 *(978-1-60610-625-9(2))* America Star Bks.

Rowe, Papa. Itchy Lee & Itchy Dee Mcgee. Wilkins, Kevan & Mason, Shannon, eds. Shortell, Stephen, illus. 2006. (J). 15.99 *(978-0-9778858-0-0(1))* WowZee Works Inc.

Roy, Philip. Mouse Tales. Torrey Balsara, Andrea, illus. 2014. (ENG.). 32p. pap. 9.95 *(978-1-55380-262-4(4))* Ronsdale Pr. CAN. Dist: SPD-Small Pr. Distribution.

Rummel, Verna. Time for Bed. 2008. 12p. pap. 24.95 *(978-1-60563-573-6(1))* America Star Bks.

Runnells, Treesha. Ten Wishing Stars: A Countdown to Bedtime Book. Dillard, Sarah, illus. 2006. (ENG.). 22p. (J). 9.95 *(978-1-58117-187-7(0),* Intervisual/Piggy Toes) Bendon, Inc.

Rusackas, Francesca. Daddy All Day Long. Burris, Priscilla, tr. Burris, Priscilla, illus. 2004. 32p. (J). (gr. -1-k). lib. bdg. 13.89 *(978-0-06-050285-0(1))* HarperCollins Pubs.

Rusling, Annette. No Time for Bed! Edgson, Alison, illus. 2014. (ENG.). 18p. (J). (gr. -1-k). 12.99 *(978-1-58925-529-6(1))* Tiger Tales.

Russo, Marisabina. The Bunnies Are Not in Their Beds. 2013. lib. bdg. 18.40 *(978-0-606-26964-3(9),* Turtleback) Turtleback Bks.

Rylant, Cynthia. Brownie & Pearl Hit the Hay. Biggs, Brian, illus. 2011. (Brownie & Pearl Ser.). (ENG.). 24p. (J). (gr. -1-k). 13.99 *(978-1-4169-8635-5(9),* Beach Lane Bks.) Beach Lane Bks.

—Brownie & Pearl Hit the Hay. Biggs, Brian, illus. 2013. (Brownie & Pearl Ser.). (ENG.). 24p. (J). (gr. -1-k). 16.99 *(978-1-4424-8742-0(9));* pap. 3.99 *(978-1-4424-8741-3(0))* Simon Spotlight. (Simon Spotlight).

—Henry & Mudge Ready-To-Read Value Pack #2: Henry & Mudge & the Long Weekend; Henry & Mudge & the Bedtime Thumps; Henry & Mudge & the Big Sleepover; Henry & Mudge & the Funny Lunch; Henry & Mudge & the Great Grandpas; Henry & Mudge & the Tall Tree House. Stevenson, Suçie, illus. 2013. (Henry & Mudge Ser.). (ENG.). 240p. (J). (gr. k-2). pap. 15.96 *(978-1-4424-9441-1(7),* Simon Spotlight) Simon Spotlight.

Saleff, Olga. Baba's Bedtime Stories. 2011. 64p. (gr. -1). pap. 25.48 *(978-1-4567-6247-6(8))* AuthorHouse.

Saltzberg, Barney. Chengdu Could Not, Would Not, Fall Asleep. Saltzberg, Barney, illus. (Chengdu Ser.). (ENG., Illus.). (J). (gr. -1-k). 2017. 32p. bds. 6.99 ***(978-1-4847-7565-3(1))*** 2014. 48p. 16.99 *(978-1-4231-6721-1(X))* Hyperion Bks. for Children.

Salyer, Jennifer Marie. My Shadow. Salyer, Adam Ernest, illus. 2011. 32p. pap. *(978-1-77067-642-8(2))* FriesenPress.

Sanroman, Susana. Senora Reganona: A Mexican Bedtime Story. Domi, illus. 2006. 20p. (J). (gr. k-4). reprint ed. 15.00 *(978-1-4223-5466-7(0))* DIANE Publishing Co.

Santiago, Brianna A. Why Is the Moon Following Us? 2008. 16p. pap. 24.95 *(978-1-60474-944-1(X))* America Star Bks.

Santomero, Angela C. Daniel's First Sleepover. 2015. (Daniel Tiger's Neighborhood 8X8 Ser.). lib. bdg. 13.55 *(978-0-606-36315-0(7))* Turtleback Bks.

—Goodnight, Daniel Tiger. Style Guide Staff, illus. 2014. (Daniel Tiger's Neighborhood Ser.). (ENG.). 26p. (J). (gr. -1-2). 12.99 *(978-1-4814-0048-0(7),* Simon Spotlight) Simon Spotlight.

—Goodnight, Daniel Tiger. 2014. (Daniel Tiger's Neighborhood 8X8 Ser.). lib. bdg. 13.55 *(978-0-606-36113-2(8))* Turtleback Bks.

Sanzo, Stephen. Cranky Pants. Whitlock, Matt, illus. 2008. (ENG.). 32p. (J). 16.95 *(978-0-9759627-0-1(1))* Cranky Pants Publishing, LLC.

Sargant, Pam. Mother's Survival Kit. 2007. 68p. pap. 34.50 *(978-1-4303-2786-8(3))* Lulu Pr., Inc.

Sartell, Debra. Time for Bed, Baby Ted. Chorao, Kay, illus. 2010. (ENG.). 32p. (J). (gr. -1). 16.95 *(978-0-8234-1968-5(1))* Holiday Hse., Inc.

Sassi, Laura. Goodnight, Ark. 1 vol. Chapman, Jane, illus. 2014. (ENG.). 32p. (J). 16.99 *(978-0-310-73784-1(2))* Zonderkidz.

Saudo, Coralie. My Dad Is Big & Strong, But... A Bedtime Story. Di Giacomo, Kris, illus. 2012. (ENG.). 32p. (J). (gr. -1-2). 16.95 *(978-1-59270-122-3(1))* Enchanted Lion Bks., LLC.

Sauer, Abe. Goodnight Loon. Davauer, Nathaniel, illus. 2014. (ENG.). 28p. (J). 9.95 *(978-0-8166-9703-8(5))* Univ. of Minnesota Pr.

Sauer, Cat. Flip Flop & Hoot. Jankowski, Daniel, illus. l.t. ed. 2006. (Brown Bag Bedtime Bks.: 1). 35p. (J). (gr. -1-2). 16.95 incl. audio compact disk *(978-0-9704460-6-0(3))* Writer's Ink. Studios, Inc.

—A Possum in the Roses. Jankowski, Daniel, illus. l.t. ed. 2006. (Brown Bag Bedtime Bks.: 1). 27p. (J). (gr. -1-2). 16.95 incl. audio compact disk *(978-0-9704460-7-7(1))* Writer's Ink. Studios, Inc.

—What's a Jaybird to Do? Jankowski, Dan, illus. l.t. ed. 2003. (Brown Bag Bedtime Bks.: 1). 31p. (YA). spiral bd. 16.95 *(978-0-9704460-8-4(X))* Writer's Ink. Studios, Inc.

Saunders, Helen. Good Night Little Man. Groshelle, Dave, illus. 2006. (J). *(978-0-9763143-4-9(7))* Happy Heart Kids Publishing.

Sauro, Joan. Does God Ever Sleep? 2005. (ENG., Illus.). 32p. (J). (gr. -1-3). 8.99 *(978-1-59473-110-5(1),* 9781594731105, Skylight Paths Publishing) LongHill Partners, Inc.

Sayres, Brianna Caplan. Where Do Diggers Sleep at Night? Slade, Christian, illus. (ENG.). (J). (-k). 2014. 26p. bds. 7.99 *(978-0-385-37415-6(1))* 2012. 32p. 16.99 *(978-0-375-86848-1(8))* Random Hse. Children's Bks. (Random Hse. Bks. for Young Readers).

—Where Do Jet Planes Sleep at Night? Slade, Christian, illus. 2017. (ENG.). 32p. (J). (gr. -1-2). 16.99 *(978-0-399-55448-3(3));* lib. bdg. 19.99 ***(978-0-399-55449-0(1))*** Random Hse. Children's Bks. (Random Hse. Bks. for Young Readers).

Sayres, Brianna Caplan. Where Do Steam Trains Sleep at Night? Slade, Christian, illus. (ENG.). (J). (gr. -1 — 1). 2017. 26p. bds. 7.99 ***(978-0-553-52100-9(4))*** 2016. 32p. 19.99 *(978-0-375-97471-7(7))* Random Hse. Children's Bks. (Random Hse. Bks. for Young Readers).

Scand, Sandra. Time for Bed Little Red. Sanderson, Sean, illus. 2009. 20p. pap. 10.00 *(978-1-934925-36-2(5),* Eloquent Bks.) Strategic Book Publishing & Rights Agency (SBPRA).

Scarry, Richard. Richard Scarry's Busytown Treasury. 2016. (ENG., Illus.). 176p. (J). (gr. -1-2). 12.99 *(978-0-553-53899-1(3),* Random Hse. Bks. for Young Readers) Random Hse. Children's Bks.

Schaefer, Carole Lexa. Down in the Woods at Sleepytime. Cabban, Vanessa, illus. 2004. (ENG.). 24p. (J). (— 1). bds. 8.99 *(978-0-7636-2566-5(3))* Candlewick Pr.

Schneider, Dianna. Rocky Ford Stories: Sleepytime at Rocky Ford. 2012. 42p. pap. 17.45 *(978-1-4525-5310-8(6))* Balboa Pr.

Schneider, Josh. Bedtime Monsters. 2013. (ENG., Illus.). 32p. (J). (gr. -1-3). 16.99 *(978-0-544-00270-8(9))* Houghton Mifflin Harcourt Publishing Co.

—Everybody Sleeps (but Not Fred) 2015. (ENG., Illus.). 32p. (J). (gr. -1-3). 16.99 *(978-0-544-33924-8(X))* Houghton Mifflin Harcourt Publishing Co.

Scholastic Editors. Bedtime for Peppa. 2015. (Peppa Pig 8X8 Ser.). (Illus.). (J). lib. bdg. 13.55 *(978-0-606-37768-3(9))* Turtleback Bks.

Scholastic, Inc. Staff. Bedtime for Peppa. Eone, illus. 2015. (Peppa Pig Ser.). (ENG.). 24p. (J). (gr. -1-k). pap. 3.99 *(978-0-545-84231-0(X))* Scholastic, Inc.

—Peppa's First Sleepover. Eone, François René, illus. 2014. (Peppa Pig Ser.). (ENG.). 24p. (J). (gr. -1-k). pap. 3.99 *(978-0-545-69093-5(5))* Scholastic, Inc.

Schott, George. Half Emm. 2012. 24p. pap. 15.99 *(978-1-4771-5104-4(4))* Xlibris Corp.

Schrader, Missy Wolgemuth & Schrader, Missy W. Hooray! I Obeyed!. 1 vol. Nuffer, Bruce, ed. 2008. (ENG., Illus.). 12p. (J). (gr. -1). bds. 3.99 *(978-0-310-71396-8(X))* Zondervan.

Schultz, Aronka. A Dinosaur on the Loose. 2010. 32p. pap. 12.99 *(978-1-4520-4400-2(7))* AuthorHouse.

Scillian, Devin. Cosmo's Moon. Braught, Mark, illus. 2003. (ENG.). 40p. (J). (gr. 1-4). 15.95 *(978-1-58536-123-6(2),* 201986) Sleeping Bear Pr.

Scoggins, Terry. Electric Ellie & Lightning Lucy: Firefly Friends Forever. 2008. 16p. pap. 8.99 *(978-1-4389-1254-7(4))* AuthorHouse.

Scotton, Rob. Russell the Sheep. Scotton, Rob, illus. (ENG., Illus.). (J). (gr. -1-3). 2015. 32p. pap. 5.99 *(978-0-06-239243-5(3),* HarperFestival) 2011. 32p. pap. 6.99 *(978-0-06-059850-1(6))* 2007. 16p. 9.99 *(978-0-06-128434-2(3))* 2005. 32p. 17.99 *(978-0-06-059848-8(4))* HarperCollins Pubs.

Seelen, Christopher. Daddy Is That the Best You Got? Moen, Tyler, illus. 2005. 36p. (J). pap. 8.99 *(978-0-9776385-0-5(2),* Cotton Candy Pr.) Unveiled Media, LLC.

Sesame Workshop. All Tucked in on Sesame Street! 2014. (Sesame Street Scribbles Ser.: 0). (ENG., Illus.). 32p. (J). (-3). 10.99 *(978-1-4022-9725-0(4),* Sourcebooks Jabberwocky) Sourcebooks, Inc.

Seuss, Dr. Dr. Seuss's Sleep Softly Book. 2012. (Dr. Seuss Nursery Collection). (ENG., Illus.). 12p. (J). (gr. k — 1). 11.99 *(978-0-375-87003-3(2),* Random Hse. Bks. for Young Readers) Random Hse. Children's Bks.

shapouri, naiyer. Sweet Dreams Buggy. 2009. 32p. pap. 13.60 *(978-0-557-04866-3(4))* Lulu Pr., Inc.

Sharmat, Mitchell. Berkley, the Terrible Sleeper. Kurilla, Renée, illus. 2015. (Ready-To-Reads Ser.). (ENG.). 32p. (J). (gr. k-2). pap. 3.99 *(978-1-4814-3832-2(8),* Simon Spotlight) Simon Spotlight.

Shaw, Nancy. Sheep Go to Sleep. Apple, Margot, illus. 2015. (ENG.). 32p. (J). (gr. -1-3). 16.99 *(978-0-544-30989-0(8),* HMH Books For Young Readers) Houghton Mifflin Harcourt Publishing Co.

Shaw, Nancy E. Sheep Go to Sleep (board Book) Apple, Margot, illus. 2016. (Sheep in a Jeep Ser.). (ENG.). 30p. (J). (gr. -1-3). bds. 7.99 *(978-0-544-64053-5(5),* HMH Books For Young Readers) Houghton Mifflin Harcourt Publishing Co.

Shaw, Stephanie. Bedtime in the Meadow. Watkins, Laura, illus. 2013. (ENG.). 20p. (gr. -1). bds. 8.95 *(978-1-58925-628-6(X))* Tiger Tales.

—By the Light of the Moon. Harry, Rebecca, illus. 2016. (ENG.). 22p. (J). (gr. -1-k). bds. 8.99 *(978-1-58925-221-9(7))* Tiger Tales.

—Lullaby Farm. Harry, Rebecca, illus. 2017. (ENG.). 22p. (J). (gr. -1-k). bds. 8.99 ***(978-1-68010-512-4(4))*** Tiger Tales.

Shaw, Stephanie. Under the Sleepy Stars. Harry, Rebecca, illus. 2015. (ENG.). 22p. (J). (gr. -1-3). bds. 8.99 *(978-1-58925-204-2(7))* Tiger Tales.

Shea, Bob. Dinosaur vs. Bedtime. Shea, Bob, illus. (Dinosaur vs. Book Ser.). (ENG., Illus.). (J). (gr. -1-k). 2011. 30p. bds. 6.99 *(978-1-4231-3788-7(4))* 2008. 40p. 16.99 *(978-1-4231-1335-5(7))* Hyperion Pr.

—Race You to Bed. Shea, Bob, illus. 2010. (ENG., Illus.). 40p. (J). (gr. -1-2). 16.99 *(978-0-06-170417-8(2),* Tegen, Katherine Bks) HarperCollins Pubs.

Sheehan, Nikki. Goodnight, Boy. 2017. (ENG.). 252p. (gr. 7-13). pap. 12.99 ***(978-1-78607-210-8(6))*** Oneworld Pubns. GBR. Dist: Publishers Group West (PGW).

Shields, Gillian. When the World Is Ready for Bed. Currey, Anna, illus. (ENG.). (J). (gr. -1 — 1). 2010. 26p. bds. 7.99 *(978-1-59990-533-4(7),* 9781599905334) 2009. 32p. 14.99 *(978-1-59990-339-2(3),* 9781599903392) Bloomsbury Publishing USA. (Bloomsbury USA Childrens).

Shoopman, Jim. Zachary Hamm in the Land of Eggs. 2012. 82p. pap. 14.95 *(978-0-9846558-1-6(6))* Taylor and Seale Publishing, LLC.

Shores, Lloyd. The Adventures of Mr. Ant. 2013. 28p. pap. 13.95 *(978-1-4497-9747-8(4),* WestBow Pr.) Author Solutions, Inc.

Shoshan, Beth. Little Rabbit Waits for the Moon. Peel, Stephanie, illus. 2013. (J). *(978-1-4351-4802-4(9))* Barnes & Noble, Inc.

Siegel, Terri. Goodnight Princess Scharazad. 2005. (J). lib. bdg. 19.95 *(978-0-9754728-5-9(2))* Big Ransom Studio.

Sierra, Judy. Sleepy Little Alphabet: A Bedtime Story from Alphabet Town. Sweet, Melissa, illus. 2009. (ENG.). 40p. (J). (gr. -1 — 1). 16.99 *(978-0-375-84002-9(8),* Knopf Bks. for Young Readers) Random Hse. Children's Bks.

—The Sleepy Little Alphabet: A Bedtime Story from Alphabet Town. Sweet, Melissa, illus. 2014. (ENG.). 34p. (J). (— 1).

bds. 6.99 *(978-0-385-75400-2(0)*, Knopf Bks. for Young Readers) Random Hse. Children's Bks.

Silver Dolphin. Sleepyhead. Chang, Flora, illus. 2017. (ENG.). 10p. (J). bds. 7.99 *(978-1-62686-874-8(3)*, Silver Dolphin Bks.) Readerlink Distribution Services, LLC.

Simon, Francesca. Hello, Moon! Cort, Ben, illus. 2014. (ENG.). 32p. (J). (gr. -1-k). 16.99 *(978-0-545-64795-3(9)*, Orchard Bks.) Scholastic, Inc.

Sims, Lesley. Illustrated Classics for Girls. Mason, Conrad, illus. 2009. (Illustrated Stories Ser.). 384p. (YA). (gr. 3-18). 19.99 *(978-0-7945-2419-7(2)*, Usborne) EDC Publishing.

Singhose, Rose. Granny's giggles book Three. 2010. 33p. pap. 16.95 *(978-0-557-59768-0(4))* Lulu Pr., Inc.

Sitomer, Alan Lawrence. Daddy's Zigzagging Bedtime Story. Carter, Abby, illus. 2014. (ENG.). 20p. (J). (gr. -1-k). 16.99 *(978-1-4231-8420-1(3))* Hyperion Bks. for Children.

Slegers, Liesbet. Sleeping. 2010. (Clavis Toddler: Daily Life Ser.). (ENG.). 12p. (J). (gr. k — 1). bds. 5.95 *(978-1-60537-068-2(1))* Cobblestone Publishing Co.

Small, Lily. Daisy the Deer. 2017. (Fairy Animals of Misty Wood Ser.). (ENG., Illus.). 144p. (J). pap. 5.99 *(978-1-62779-738-2(6)*, 9781627797382, Holt, Henry & Co. Bks. For Young Readers) Holt, Henry & Co.

Smallfield, Jane. The Bedtime Treasury of Real Fairy Tales. Smallfield, Graeme, illus. 2005. 96p. 17.95 *(978-0-689-03923-2(9)*, Milk & Cookies) ibooks, Inc.

Smart Kidz Media Studios Staff, ed. It's Bedtime! 2011. 16p. 7.99 *(978-1-891100-78-9(5)*, Smart Kids) Penton Overseas, Inc.

Smiley, Jane. Twenty Yawns, 0 vols. Castillo, Lauren, illus. 2016. (ENG.). 32p. (J). (gr. -1-2). 17.99 *(978-1-4778-2635-5(1)*, 9781477826355, Two Lions) Amazon Publishing.

Smith, Jane. Starlight Starbright. 2006. (ENG.). 12p. 12.95 *(978-1-58117-495-3(0)*, Intervisual/Piggy Toes) Bendon, Inc.

Smith, Lori Joy. The Goodnight Book. 2014. (ENG., Illus.). 24p. (J). (gr. -1-k). 12.95 *(978-1-927018-42-2(0)*, 9781927018422) Simply Read Bks. CAN. Dist: Ingram Publisher Services.

Smith, Michael. My Ducky Buddy. Oliva, Octavio, illus. 2011. 23p. (J). *(978-0-9821675-4-0(7))* East West Discovery Pr.

Smith, Michael & Wang, Emily. My Ducky Buddy. Oliva, Octavio, illus. 2011. (CHI & ENG.). 23p. (J). *(978-0-9821675-7-1(1))* East West Discovery Pr.

Smith, Shoham. An after Bedtime Story. Tsarfati, Einat, illus. 2016. (ENG.). 48p. (J). (gr. k-2). 16.95 *(978-1-4197-1873-1(8)*, Abrams Bks. for Young Readers) Abrams, Inc.

Smucker, Anna. Outside the Window. Schuett, Stacey, illus. 2005. 32p. (J). reprint ed. per. 7.95 *(978-1-891852-40-4(X))* Quarrier Pr.

Snyder, Betsy E. Sweet Dreams Lullaby. 2012. (ENG., Illus.). 32p. (J). (— 1). bds. 6.99 *(978-0-307-98060-1(X)*, Random Hse. Bks. for Young Readers) Random Hse. Children's Bks.

Snyder, Donna. Rose & Rosey. 2008. 16p. pap. 24.95 *(978-1-60441-618-3(1))* America Star Bks.

Sobel, June. The Goodnight Train. Huliska-Beith, Laura, illus. 2006. (ENG.). 32p. (J). (gr. -1-3). 16.99 *(978-0-15-205436-6(7))* Houghton Mifflin Harcourt Publishing Co.

Sobel, June. The Goodnight Train (lap Board Book) Huliska-Beith, Laura, illus. 2017. (ENG.). 30p. (J). (— 1). bds. 12.99 ***(978-1-328-76438-6(9)***, HMH Books For Young Readers) Houghton Mifflin Harcourt Publishing Co.

Sperring, Mark. Max & the Won't Go to Bed Show. Warburton, Sarah, illus. 2014. (ENG.). 32p. (J). (gr. -1-k). 16.99 *(978-0-545-70822-7(2)*, Scholastic Pr.) Scholastic, Inc.

Spinelli, Eileen. When Papa Comes Home Tonight. McPhail, David, illus. 2009. (ENG.). 32p. (J). (gr. -1-k). 16.99 *(978-1-4169-1028-2(X)*, Simon & Schuster Bks. For Young Readers) Simon & Schuster Bks. For Young Readers.

Spinner, Stephanie. It's a Miracle! A Hanukkah Storybook. McElmurry, Jill, illus. 2007. (ENG.). 48p. (J). (gr. -1-3). 6.99 *(978-1-4169-5001-1(X)*, Aladdin) Simon & Schuster Children's Publishing.

Spooner, F. M. Granny Spooner's Christian Bedtime Stories. 2010. (Illus.). 104p. pap. 11.74 *(978-1-4251-1390-2(7))* Trafford Publishing.

Srinivasan, Divya. Little Owl's Day. Srinivasan, Divya, illus. 2014. (ENG., Illus.). 32p. (J). (gr. -1-k). 16.99 *(978-0-670-01650-1(0)*, Viking Books for Young Readers) Penguin Young Readers Group.

Stacey, Tom. The First Dog to Be Somebody's Best Friend: A Likely Story in Two Bits & a Decide. Landels, Angela, illus. 2007. (ENG.). 46p. 15.95 *(978-1-905299-34-8(6)*, Stacey International) Stacey Publishing GBR. Dist: Casemate Pubs. & Bk. Distributors, LLC.

Stack, David Martin. Good Morning Captain. 2009. 58p. pap. 10.99 *(978-0-557-06575-2(5))* Lulu Pr., Inc.

Stadler, Kristina. Frog on my Head. Stader, Kristina & Stroede, Paul, illus. 2011. 24p. (J). lib. bdg. 11.95 *(978-1-59598-138-7(1)*, Goblin Fern Pr.) HenschelHAUS Publishing.

Stalder, Päivi. My Wish Tonight. Wolferman, Iris, illus. 2010. (ENG.). 32p. (J). (gr. -1-3). 12.95 *(978-0-7358-2331-0(6))* North-South Bks., Inc.

Stanek, Robert, pseud. The Bugville Critters Visit Dad & Mom at Work. 2007. (ENG.). (J). 28p. per. 9.99 *(978-1-57545-144-2(1))*; (Illus.). 52p. per. 19.95 *(978-1-57545-121-3(2)*, Reagent Pr. Bks. for Young Readers) RP Media.

Staniszewski, Anna. Power down, Little Robot. Zeltner, Tim, illus. 2015. (ENG.). 32p. (J). (gr. -1-1). 16.99 *(978-1-62779-125-0(6)*, 9781627791250, Holt, Henry & Co. Bks. For Young Readers) Holt, Henry & Co.

Stein, David Ezra. Interrupting Chicken. Stein, David Ezra, illus. (ENG., Illus.). 40p. (J). (gr. -1-3). 2016. 7.99 *(978-0-7636-8903-2(3))* 2010. 16.99 *(978-0-7636-4168-9(5))* Candlewick Pr.

—Interrupting Chicken. (J). 1.25 *(978-1-4498-6832-1(0))*; 2011. 37.75 *(978-1-4498-6828-4(2))*; 2011. 39.75 *(978-1-4498-6829-1(0))*; 2011. 37.75 *(978-1-4498-6831-4(2))* Recorded Bks., Inc.

—Interrupting Chicken. Stein, David Ezra, illus. 2016. (ENG., Illus.). 40p. (J). (gr. -1-3). 18.40 *(978-0-606-39099-6(5))* Turtleback Bks.

—Tad & Dad. Stein, David Ezra, illus. 2015. (ENG., Illus.). 40p. (J). (gr. -1-k). 16.99 *(978-0-399-25671-4(7)*, Nancy Paulsen Books) Penguin Young Readers Group.

Sterling Children's, Sterling, ed. Sleepy Kitty. 2015. (ENG., Illus.). 22p. (J). (— 1). bds. 6.95 *(978-1-4549-1464-8(5))* Sterling Publishing Co., Inc.

—Sleepy Puppy. 2015. (ENG., Illus.). 22p. (J). (— 1). bds. 6.95 *(978-1-4549-1465-5(3))* Sterling Publishing Co., Inc.

Sternberg, Julie. Bedtime at Bessie & Lil's. Gudeon, Adam, illus. 2015. (ENG.). 32p. (J). (gr. -1-2). 16.95 *(978-1-59078-934-6(2))* Boyds Mills Pr.

Stiegemeyer, Julie. Seven Little Bunnies, 0 vols. Bryant, Laura J., illus. 2010. (ENG.). 24p. (J). (gr. -1-3). 15.99 *(978-0-7614-5600-1(7)*, 9780761456001, Amazon Children's Publishing) Amazon Publishing.

Stierle, Cynthia. Diego in the Dark: Being Brave at Night. Maher, Alex, illus. 2008. (Go, Diego, Go! Ser.). (ENG.). 16p. (J). (gr. -1-2). pap. 6.99 *(978-1-4169-5935-9(1)*, Simon Spotlight/Nickelodeon) Simon Spotlight/Nickelodeon.

Stiller, Catrina. Curtis Gets Ready to Dream: A Bedtime Story to Guide Your Child to Sleep. Ritchey, Jessica, illus. 2017. (ENG.). 38p. (J). pap. 9.95 *(978-1-68350-102-2(0))* Morgan James Publishing.

Stills, Caroline & Stills-Blott, Sarcia. The House of 12 Bunnies. Rossell, Judith, illus. 2012. (ENG.). 24p. (J). 16.95 *(978-0-8234-2422-1(7))* Holiday Hse., Inc.

Stories Of The Bible. Bedtime Bear Bible Stories. 2011. 52p. pap. 27.99 *(978-1-4634-4275-0(0))* AuthorHouse.

Strasser, Stephanie. Pink Peanut Butter. 2010. 28p. 12.49 *(978-1-4490-8383-0(8))* AuthorHouse.

Stromberg, Ronica. The Time-for-Bed Angel. Stephenson, Kristina, illus. 2010. (ENG.). 32p. (J). (gr. -1-k). pap. 9.99 *(978-0-7459-6066-1(9))* Lion Hudson PLC GBR. Dist: Independent Pubs. Group.

Strong, Abigail. Troggins Tales. 2010. 60p. pap. 34.95 *(978-1-4457-1581-0(3))* Lulu Pr., Inc.

Strong, Belinda. Hold & Touch Bedtime. 2015. (Hold & Touch Ser.). (ENG., Illus.). (J). bds. *(978-1-74363-413-4(7))* Hinkler Bks. Pty, Ltd.

Sully, Katherine. Night-Night Canada. Poole, Helen, illus. 2017. (ENG.). 20p. (J). (-1). bds. 9.99 *(978-1-4926-4769-0(1)*, 9781492647690, Sourcebooks Jabberwocky) Sourcebooks, Inc.

—Night-Night Maryland. Poole, Helen, illus. 2017. (ENG.). 20p. (J). (-1). bds. 9.99 *(978-1-4926-4768-3(3)*, 9781492647683, Sourcebooks Jabberwocky) Sourcebooks, Inc.

—Night-Night San Francisco. Poole, Helen, illus. 2017. (ENG.). 20p. (J). (-1). bds. 9.99 *(978-1-4926-4765-2(9)*, 9781492647652, Sourcebooks Jabberwocky) Sourcebooks, Inc.

—Night-Night Virginia. Poole, Helen, illus. 2017. (ENG.). 20p. (J). (-1). bds. 9.99 *(978-1-4926-4767-6(5)*, 9781492647676, Sourcebooks Jabberwocky) Sourcebooks, Inc.

—Night-Night Washington. Poole, Helen, illus. 2017. (ENG.). 20p. (J). (-1). bds. 9.99 *(978-1-4926-4766-9(7)*, 9781492647669, Sourcebooks Jabberwocky) Sourcebooks, Inc.

—Where, Oh Where Is Huggle Buggle Bear? Samuel, Janet, illus. 2013. (J). *(978-1-4351-4776-8(6))* Barnes & Noble, Inc.

Sutcliffe, Mandy. Hop along Boo, Time for Bed. 2016. (ENG., Illus.). 40p. (J). (gr. -1-2). 17.99 *(978-0-399-54947-2(1)*, Random Hse. Bks. for Young Readers) Random Hse. Children's Bks.

Sutton, Joe. Wanda & the Oblahlahs. 2011. (ENG., Illus.). 24p. (J). 19.95 *(978-1-936474-11-0(5)*, 9f8eb10d-b421-4222-af62-15e42efdae23) Bright Sky Pr.

Sweeney, Monica & Yelvington, Lauren. Can You Yawn Like a Fawn? Watkins, Laura, illus. 2016. (ENG.). 32p. (J). 15.99 *(978-1-250-10416-8(5)*, 9781250104168) St. Martin's Pr.

Sweet Dreams, Pout-Pout Fish. 2015. (Pout-Pout Fish Mini Adventure Ser.). (ENG., Illus.). 12p. (J). (gr. -1 — 1). bds. 5.99 *(978-0-374-38010-6(4)*, 9780374380106, Farrar, Straus & Giroux (BYR)) Farrar, Straus & Giroux.

Swenson, Jamie A. Boom! Boom! Boom! Walker, David, illus. 2013. (ENG.). 32p. (J). (gr. -1-1). 16.99 *(978-0-374-30868-1(3)*, 9780374308681, Farrar, Straus & Giroux (BYR)) Farrar, Straus & Giroux.

Swinburne, Stephen R. Safe in a Storm. Bell, Jennifer, illus. 2016. (J). *(978-0-545-66987-0(1))*; (ENG.). 32p. (gr. -1-k). 10.99 *(978-0-545-86792-4(4))* Scholastic, Inc.

Sykes, Julie. I Don't Want to Go to Bed! Warnes, Tim, illus. 2013. (ENG.). 32p. (J). *(978-1-58925-148-9(2))* Tiger Tales.

Symes, Sally. Yawn. Sharratt, Nick, illus. 2011. (ENG.). 24p. (J). (gr. -1-2). bds. 7.99 *(978-0-7636-5725-3(5))* Candlewick Pr.

Szarka, Balazs. European Folk Tales. 2009. 60p. pap. 22.00 *(978-1-60860-432-6(2)*, Eloquent Bks.) Strategic Book Publishing & Rights Agency (SBPRA).

Szekeres, Cyndy. Buenas Noches, Rapo. 2005. (Collection Ternura Bedtime Stories Ser.).Tr. of Good Night, Little Fox. (SPA.). (J). (gr. k-2). pap. 4.95 *(978-950-11-0574-2(1))* Sigmar ARG. Dist: Iaconi, Mariuccia Bk. Imports.

—A Comer! 2005. (Collection Ternura Bedtime Stories Ser.).Tr. of Time to Eat! (SPA.). (J). (gr. k-2). pap. 4.95 *(978-950-11-0576-6(8))* Sigmar ARG. Dist: Iaconi, Mariuccia Bk. Imports.

—Las Cuentas Osito. 2005. (Collection Ternura Bedtime Stories Ser.).Tr. of Little Bear Counts. (SPA.). (J). (gr. k-2). pap. 4.95 *(978-950-11-0634-3(9))* Sigmar ARG. Dist: Iaconi, Mariuccia Bk. Imports.

—Un Dia Muy Especial. 2005. (Collection Ternura Bedtime Stories Ser.).Tr. of Very Special Day. (SPA.). (J). (gr. k-2). pap. 4.95 *(978-950-11-0632-9(2))* Sigmar ARG. Dist: Iaconi, Mariuccia Bk. Imports.

—El Juego de Las Escondidas. 2005. (Collection Ternura Bedtime Stories Ser.).Tr. of Hide & Go Seek. (SPA.). (J). (gr. k-2). pap. 4.95 *(978-950-11-0577-3(6))* Sigmar ARG. Dist: Iaconi, Mariuccia Bk. Imports.

—La Mudanza de la Ratita. 2005. (Collection Ternura Bedtime Stories Ser.).Tr. of Little Mouse Moves. (SPA.). (J). (gr. k-2). pap. 4.95 *(978-950-11-0635-0(7))* Sigmar ARG. Dist: Iaconi, Mariuccia Bk. Imports.

—Nada Que Hacer. 2005. (Collection Ternura Bedtime Stories Ser.).Tr. of Nothing To Do. (SPA.). (J). (gr. k-2). pap. 4.95 *(978-950-11-0573-5(3))* Sigmar ARG. Dist: Iaconi, Mariuccia Bk. Imports.

—El Perrito Perdido. 2005. (Collection Ternura Bedtime Stories Ser.). (SPA.). (J). (gr. k-2). pap. 4.95 *(978-950-11-0633-6(0))* Sigmar ARG. Dist: Iaconi, Mariuccia Bk. Imports.

Tafuri, Nancy. All Kinds of Kisses. 2012. (ENG., Illus.). 32p. (J). (gr. -1-1). 16.99 *(978-0-316-12235-1(1))* Little Brown & Co.

Tangerine Designs Ltd. Cuddle up Teddy: A Soft & Snuggly Pillow Book. 2014. (Sleepy Cuddle Pillow Bks.). (ENG.). 8p. (J). (gr. -1 — 1). 11.99 *(978-1-4380-0439-6(7))* Barron's Educational Series, Inc.

Taplin, Sam. Baby's Bedtime Storybook CV. 2011. (Baby Board Bks). 10p. (J). ring bd. 17.99 *(978-0-7945-3096-9(6)*, Usborne) EDC Publishing.

—Little Stories for Bedtime. Chiara, Francesca De, illus. 2010. (Bedtime Stories Ser.). 12p. (J). bds. 12.99 *(978-0-7945-2673-3(X)*, Usborne) EDC Publishing.

—Night-Night Stories. 2009. (Bedtime Board Books (with Bedtime Rhymes) Ser.). 12p. (J). bds. 12.99 *(978-0-7945-2364-0(1)*, Usborne) EDC Publishing.

Taylor, Sean. The World Champion of Staying Awake. Liao, Jimmy, illus. 2011. (ENG.). 32p. (J). (gr. -1-2). 15.99 *(978-0-7636-4957-9(0))* Candlewick Pr.

Teckentrup, Britta. Before I Wake Up..., 1 vol. 2016. (ENG., Illus.). 56p. (J). (gr. -1-3). 14.95 *(978-3-7913-7246-4(7))* Prestel Verlag GmbH & Co KG. DEU. Dist: Penguin Random Hse. LLC.

Thalia. Chupie: The Binky That Returned Home. Larranaga, Ana Martin, illus. 2013. (ENG.). 32p. (J). (gr. -1 — 1). 16.99 *(978-0-451-41605-6(8)*, Celebra Young Readers) Penguin Publishing Group.

Thayer, Kristi. Pajama Knights. Willis, Caleb, illus. 2010. 24p. pap. 11.50 *(978-1-60860-669-6(4)*, Strategic Bk. Publishing) Strategic Book Publishing & Rights Agency (SBPRA).

Thomas, Jan. Let's Sing a Lullaby with the Brave Cowboy. Thomas, Jan, illus. 2012. (ENG., Illus.). 40p. (J). (gr. -1-3). 12.99 *(978-1-4424-4276-4(X)*, Beach Lane Bks.) Beach Lane Bks.

Thomas Nelson Publishing Staff & Hall, Hannah. God Bless You & Good Night, 1 vol. 2013. (God Bless Book Ser.). (ENG.). 20p. (J). bds. 9.99 *(978-1-4003-2294-7(4))* Nelson, Thomas Inc.

Thompson, Lauren. Little Quack's Bedtime. Anderson, Derek, illus. 2005. (ENG.). 32p. (J). (gr. -1-3). 17.99 *(978-0-689-86894-8(4)*, Simon & Schuster Bks. For Young Readers) Simon & Schuster Bks. For Young Readers.

Thompson, Lauren & Anderson, Derek. Little Quack's Bedtime. 2009. (Classic Board Bks.). (ENG., Illus.). 34p. (J). (gr. -1-k). bds. 7.99 *(978-1-4169-6873-3(3)*, Little Simon) Little Simon.

Thomson, Sarah L. Imagine a Night. Gonsalves, Rob, illus. 2003. (Imagine A... Ser.). (ENG.). 40p. (J). (gr. -1-3). 19.99 *(978-0-689-85218-3(5)*, Atheneum Bks. for Young Readers) Simon & Schuster Children's Publishing.

Tibo, Gilles. Noches de Papel. (Barril Sin Fondo Ser.). (SPA.). (J). (gr. 3-5). pap. *(978-968-6465-32-7(4))* Casa de Estudios de Literatura y Talleres Artisticos Amaquemecan A.C. MEX. Dist: Lectorum Pubns., Inc.

Tiger Tales, ed. Goodnight Baby! Ward, Sarah, illus. 2016. (To Baby with Love Ser.). (ENG.). 10p. (J). (gr. -1 — 1). bds. 9.99 *(978-1-58925-211-0(X))* Tiger Tales.

Tiger Tales Staff. Five Minute Bedtime Stories. 2014. (ENG.). 292p. (J). (gr. -1-3). 14.99 *(978-1-58925-507-4(0))* Tiger Tales.

Tiger Tales, Tiger, ed. My First Bedtime Prayers. Jones, Anna, illus. 2017. (ENG.). 38p. (J). (gr. -1-k). bds. 9.99 ***(978-1-68010-520-9(5))*** Tiger Tales.

—Ten in the Bed. Guile, Gill, illus. 2017. (ENG.). 22p. (J). (gr. -1-k). bds. 8.99 ***(978-1-68010-518-6(3))*** Tiger Tales.

—Twinkle, Twinkle, Little Baby. Ward, Sarah, illus. 2017. (To Baby with Love Ser.). (ENG.). 12p. (J). (gr. -1 — 1). bds. 9.99 ***(978-1-68010-515-5(9))*** Tiger Tales.

Tillman, Nancy & Metaxas, Eric. It's Time to Sleep, My Love. Tillman, Nancy, illus. (ENG., Illus.). (J). 2011. 34p. (— 1). bds. 7.99 *(978-0-312-67336-9(1)*, 9780312673369) 2008. 32p. (gr. -1 — 1). 16.95 *(978-0-312-38371-8(1)*, 9780312383718) Feiwel & Friends.

Timbaland & Myers, Christopher. Nighttime Symphony. Myers, Christopher, illus. 2014. (ENG., Illus.). 32p. (J). 16.99 *(978-1-4424-1208-8(9)*, Atheneum Bks. for Young Readers) Simon & Schuster Children's Publishing.

Toms, K. 10 Little Penguins. 2009. (Kate Toms Ser.). 26p. bds. 7.99 *(978-1-84610-980-5(9))* Make Believe Ideas GBR. Dist: Nelson, Thomas Inc.

—10 Little Penguins Mini Book & Plush. 2009. 26p. pap. *(978-1-84879-065-0(1))* Make Believe Ideas.

Torrel, Wendy. GUARDIAN of DREAMS (1st Edition) Klingbeil, Kendall, illus. I.t. ed. 2004. 32p. (J). 14.95 *(978-0-9746890-0-5(9))*; pap. 10.95 *(978-0-9746890-1-2(7))* White Tulip Publishing.

Tracy, Joe. Arnie the Imagination Boy. 2011. 24p. pap. 15.99 *(978-1-4568-9135-0(9))* Xlibris Corp.

Train, Mary. Time for the Fair. Hayes, Karel, illus. 2005. (ENG.). 28p. (J). (gr. k-17). 15.95 *(978-0-89272-694-3(6))* Down East Bks.

Trapani, Iza. Gabe & Goon. Trapani, Iza, illus. 2016. (ENG., Illus.). 32p. (J). (gr. -1-1). lib. bdg. 16.95 *(978-1-58089-640-5(5))* Charlesbridge Publishing, Inc.

Trasler, Janee. Bedtime for Chickies. Trasler, Janee, illus. 2014. (Chickies Ser.). (ENG., Illus.). 24p. (J). (gr. -1 — 1). bds. 8.99 *(978-0-06-227468-7(6)*, HarperFestival) HarperCollins Pubs.

Tresh, Doreene. Elephants, Aren't They Great? 2003. (Illus.). 28p. (J). per. 9.95 *(978-1-59405-028-2(7))* New Age World Publishing.

Trotter, Bob. Up the Wooden Hill: Bedtime Stories for Little Ones. Edgar, Barrie, illus. 2011. 98p. pap. 17.99 *(978-1-60976-139-4(1)*, Eloquent Bks.) Strategic Book Publishing & Rights Agency (SBPRA).

Turnbull, Elizabeth. Bonnwit Kabrit. Vaganos, Erin, illus. 2013. 36p. 17.95 *(978-1-61153-073-5(3))* Light Messages Publishing.

Tyler, Shirley. Nite Nite Bedtime, 1 vol. 2009. 15p. pap. 24.95 *(978-1-61546-966-6(4))* PublishAmerica, Inc.

Tyson, Leigh Ann. Good Night, Little Dragons. 2012. (Little Golden Book Ser.). (ENG., Illus.). 24p. (J). (gr. k-k). 4.99 *(978-0-307-92957-0(4)*, Golden Bks.) Random Hse. Children's Bks.

Under the Bed: Individual Title-Six Packs. (Chiquilibros Ser.). (gr. k-1). 23.00 *(978-0-7635-0449-6(1))* Rigby Education.

Underwood, Deborah. Good Night, Baddies. Kangas, Juli, illus. 2016. (ENG.). 32p. (J). (gr. -1-3). 17.99 *(978-1-4814-0984-1(0)*, Beach Lane Bks.) Beach Lane Bks.

—Part-Time Princess. Evans, Cambria, illus. 2013. (ENG.). 40p. (J). (gr. -1-k). 16.99 *(978-1-4231-2485-6(5))* Hyperion Pr.

Valenzuela, Anabelle. The Day an Angel Ran into My Room. Latham, Sarah, illus. 2012. 56p. 30.50 *(978-1-61897-794-6(6)*, Strategic Bk. Publishing) Strategic Book Publishing & Rights Agency (SBPRA).

Van Fleet, Mara. Mama's Pajamas. Van Fleet, Mara, illus. 2017. (ENG., Illus.). 12p. (J). (gr. -1 — 1). 15.99 *(978-1-4814-7975-2(X)*, Simon & Schuster Bks. For Young Readers) Simon & Schuster Bks. For Young Readers.

van Genechten, Guido. No Ghost under My Bed. 2010. (ENG.). 30p. (J). (gr. -1-k). 17.95 *(978-1-60537-069-9(X))* Cobblestone Publishing Co.

Vega, Denise. If Your Monster Won't Go to Bed. OHora, Zachariah, illus. 2017. (ENG.). 40p. (J). (gr. -1-2). 17.99 *(978-0-553-49655-0(7)*, Knopf Bks. for Young Readers) Random Hse. Children's Bks.

Venning, Edward W. The Truck & a Boy: The Truck with a big Heart. 2007. 48p. (YA). per. 15.95 *(978-1-4327-0738-5(8))* Outskirts Pr., Inc.

Vere, Ed. Bedtime for Monsters. Vere, Ed, illus. 2012. (ENG., Illus.). 32p. (J). (gr. -1-k). 14.99 *(978-0-8050-9509-8(8)*, 9780805095098, Holt, Henry & Co. Bks. For Young Readers) Holt, Henry & Co.

—Max at Night. 2016. (Max Ser.: 2). (ENG.). 32p. (J). (-2). 16.99 *(978-1-4926-3296-2(1)*, 9781492632962, Sourcebooks Jabberwocky) Sourcebooks, Inc.

Villaloz, ChiChi & Etheridge, Katy. Do Dogs Vote? Villaloz, ChiChi & Etheridge, Katy, illus. 2008. (Illus.). 32p. (J). lib. bdg. 24.95 *(978-0-9722180-0-9(9))* Malamute Pr.

Villarreal, Carlos C. The Light Beneath the Shadow: Sharing God's Love with Your Child as You Read Together: A Bedtime Story Intended to Awaken Your Parental Christian Spirit. 2006. 48p. pap. 16.95 *(978-1-4241-1247-0(8))* PublishAmerica, Inc.

Villarreal, Jennifer. The Monster under My Bed. 2008. 20p. pap. 13.50 *(978-1-4389-0371-2(5))* AuthorHouse.

Villasenor, Victor. Goodnight, Papito Dios/Buenos Noches, Papito Dios. Villarroel, Carolina, tr. Ramirez, Jose, illus. 2007. (SPA & ENG.). 32p. (J). (gr. -1-2). 16.95 *(978-1-55885-467-3(3)*, Piñata Books) Arte Publico Pr.

Vogel, Michael. Good Night, Baby Flurry Heart. 2016. (ENG., Illus.). 40p. (J). (gr. -1-3). 15.99 *(978-0-316-38962-4(5))* Little, Brown Bks. for Young Readers.

Vogel, Vin. Bedtime for Yeti. 2016. (ENG., Illus.). 32p. (J). (-k). 16.99 *(978-1-101-99431-3(2)*, Dial Bks) Penguin Young Readers Group.

Votrubec, Shaman. Boo. 2016. (ENG., Illus.). 52p. (J). pap. 32.25 *(978-1-5144-4525-9(5))* Xlibris Corp.

Vrba, Christina. Good Night Connecticut. Rosen, Anne, illus. 2009. (Good Night Our World Ser.). (ENG.). 20p. (J). (gr. k — 1). bds. 9.95 *(978-1-60219-035-1(6))* Good Night Bks.

Vuillamy, Clara. The Bear with Sticky Paws Won't Go to Bed. Vuillamy, Clara, illus. 2010. (ENG., Illus.). 32p. (J). (gr. -1-2). 15.95 *(978-1-58925-087-1(7))* Tiger Tales.

Waber, Bernard. Ira Sleeps Over, 1 vol. 2008. (Read along Book & CD Ser.). (ENG., Illus.). 48p. (J). (gr. -1-3). audio compact disk 10.99 *(978-0-618-85282-6(4))* Houghton Mifflin Harcourt Publishing Co.

Waddell, Martin. Can't You Sleep, Little Bear?: Candlewick Storybook Animations. Firth, Barbara, illus. 2008. (Candlewick Storybook Animations Ser.). (ENG.). 32p. (J). (gr. k-k). 14.99 *(978-0-7636-3537-4(5))* Candlewick Pr.

Wahl, Jan. Elf Night. Weevers, Peter, illus. 2005. (Picture Bks.). 32p. (gr. k-2). 15.25 *(978-1-57505-512-1(0))* Lerner Publishing Group.

Walker, Anna. Alfie's Lost Sharkie. 2016. (ENG., Illus.). 24p. (J). (gr. -1-3). 14.99 *(978-0-544-58656-7(5))* Houghton Mifflin Harcourt Publishing Co.

Wang, Dorothea DePrisco & Imperato, Teresa. All the Ways I Love You. Downing, Julie, illus. 2005. (ENG.). 10p. (J). bds. 8.95 *(978-1-58117-190-7(0)*, Intervisual/Piggy Toes) Bendon, Inc.

Wang, Dorthea Deprisco. Five Minutes until Bed. Vaux, Patricia, illus. 2012. (ENG.). 14p. (J). (-k). bds. 5.99 *(978-1-4494-2244-8(6))* Andrews McMeel Publishing.

Ward-Showers, Latanya. Could It Be a Monster in the Attic? 2013. 24p. pap. 17.99 *(978-1-4817-0542-4(3))* AuthorHouse.

Warner, Rex. Men & Gods: Myths & Legends of the Ancient Greeks. Gorey, Edward, illus. 2008. (New York Review Books Classics). (ENG.). 288p. 17.95 *(978-1-59017-263-6(9)*, NYRB Classics) New York Review of Bks., Inc., The.

Warnes, Tim. Can't You Sleep, Dotty? Warnes, Tim, illus. 2003. (Illus.). 32p. (J). pap. 5.95 *(978-1-58925-376-6(0))* Tiger Tales.

—Can't You Sleep, Little Puppy? Warnes, Tim, illus. 2014. (My First Storybook Ser.). (ENG., Illus.). 32p. (J). (gr. -1). 6.99 *(978-1-58925-508-1(9))* Tiger Tales.

Warnes, Tim, illus. Sweet Dreams, Little Bear. 2013. (ENG.). 18p. (gr. -1). bds. 8.95 *(978-1-58925-604-0(2))* Tiger Tales.

Warnes, Tim, et al. My Little Box of Bedtime Stories: Can't You Sleep, Puppy?/Time to Sleep, Little Bear!/What Are You Doing in My Bed?/Sleep Tight, Giner Kitten/Good Night, Emily!/Don't Be Afraid, Little Ones. Pedler, Caroline & Massey, Jane, illus. 2013. (ENG.). (J). (gr. -1-1). pap. 8.95 *(978-1-58925-442-8(2))* Tiger Tales.

Washer, Mark Gregory. Blue Bonnie Butterfly: Tale of Two Tails. 2013. 36p. pap. 18.41 *(978-1-4669-8434-9(1))* Trafford Publishing.

Washington. Jack the Boogey Is My Real Name: The Truth about the Boogeyman. 2014. (ENG.). (J). 18.93 *(978-0-9960916-0-2(2))* Bedford Hse. Bks.

Watkins, Fred L. Sue, Mary & Charles, 1 vol. 2009. 127p. pap. 19.95 *(978-1-60749-110-1(9))* America Star Bks.

Watt, Fiona. Go to Sleep Little Baby. Watt, Fiona, illus. 2009. (Baby Board Books w/CD Ser.). (Illus.). 12p. (J). (gr. -1). bds. 15.99 *(978-0-7945-1936-0(9)*, Usborne) EDC Publishing.

—Sleepy Baby. MacKinnon, Catherine-Anne, illus. 2006. (Snuggletime Board Bks.). 10p. (J). (gr. -1). bds., bds. 8.99 (978-0-7945-1071-8(X), Usborne) EDC Publishing.

Watt, Fiona & Wells, Rachel. Baby's Bedtime. 2004. (Baby's World Ser.). (ENG., Illus.). 1p. (J). (gr. -1-18). pap. 4.95 (978-0-7460-3374-6(5)) EDC Publishing.

Watters, Mark. Bedtime Snories for Children, Volume One. 2005. 48p. (J). pap. 13.50 (978-1-4116-4995-8(8)) Lulu Pr., Inc.

Wattley, Jason J. Anthology of Chaconia Creations. 2011. 24p. pap. 15.99 (978-1-4568-7683-8(X)) Xlibris Corp.

Watts, Frances. Goodnight, Mice! Watson, Judy, illus. 2017. 24p. bds. 6.99 (978-0-7333-3530-3(6)) ABC Bks. AUS. Dist: HarperCollins Pubs.

Weeks, Sarah. Counting Ovejas. Diaz, David, illus. 2006. (ENG & SPA.). 40p. (J). (gr. -1-2). 18.99 (978-0-689-86750-7(6), Atheneum Bks. for Young Readers) Simon & Schuster Children's Publishing.

Weel, Rosalinda. Dream Clouds: Float Away with Seven Enchanting Children's Stories for Relaxation & Bedtime. 2012. 60p. pap. 23.99 (978-1-4525-5860-8(4)) Balboa Pr.

Weinstone, David. All My Friends Are Fast Asleep. Le Huche, Magali, illus. 2017. (ENG.). 40p. (J). 17.99 **(978-0-374-30535-2(8)**, 9780374305352, Farrar, Straus & Giroux (BYR)) Farrar, Straus & Giroux.

Wells, R. W. Black Mountain Express: A Smoky Mountain Bedtime Tale. 2007. 53p. pap. 16.95 (978-1-60441-396-0(4)) America Star Bks.

Wells, Rosemary. Max & Ruby's Bedtime Book. (Max & Ruby Ser.). (ENG., (J). (gr. -1-k). 2015. Illus.). 42p. 8.99 (978-0-14-751746-3(X), Puffin Books) 2010. 48p. 17.99 (978-0-670-01141-4(X), Viking Books for Young Readers) Penguin Young Readers Group.

Wensink, Patrick. Go Go Gorillas: A Romping Bedtime Tale. Wragg, Nate, illus. 2017. 32p. (J). (gr. -1-3). 17.99 **(978-0-06-238118-7(0))** HarperCollins Pubs.

Weston Woods Staff, creator. Goodnight Moon. 2011. 18.95 (978-0-439-72684-9(0)); 29.95 (978-0-439-73472-1(X)); 38.75 (978-0-439-72686-3(7)) Weston Woods Studios, Inc.

Wetterwald, Florence. Night-Night, Wooly (a Blabla Book) Wetterwald, Florence, illus. 2016. (ENG., Illus.). 24p. (J). (— 1). bds. 7.99 (978-0-553-52051-4(2), Random Hse. Bks. for Young Readers) Random Hse. Children's Bks.

Whitlock, Bonnie. Momma Yeti & the Terribly Tiresome Goodnight. 2009. 40p. pap. 18.49 (978-1-4389-5147-8(7)) AuthorHouse.

Whybrow, Ian. The Bedtime Bear. Scheffler, Axel, illus. 2016. (ENG.). 12p. (J). (gr. -1-2). pap. 9.99 (978-1-5098-0695-9(4)) Pan Macmillan GBR. Dist: Independent Pubs. Group.

—Bedtime Bear. Scheffler, Axel, illus. 4th ed. 2004. (ENG.). 12p. (J). (gr. -1-k). pap. 13.99 (978-1-4050-4993-1(6)) Pan Macmillan GBR. Dist: Independent Pubs. Group.

—The Noisy Way to Bed. Beeke, Tiphanie, tr. Beeke, Tiphanie, illus. 2004. (J). (978-0-439-55690-3(2), Levine, Arthur A. Bks.) Scholastic, Inc.

Wide Awake Jake. (Picture Books Ser.). 24p. 7.33 (978-1-4054-9539-4(1)) Parragon, Inc.

Wilcox, Jean A. Winston's New Camelot. 2011. 24p. pap. 24.95 (978-1-4560-5277-5(2)) America Star Bks.

Wild, Margaret. Nighty Night!, 1 vol. Argent, Kerry, illus. 2014. (ENG.). 32p. (J). (gr. -1-1). 7.95 (978-1-56145-812-7(0)) Peachtree Pubs.

Wiley, Jean. Sweet Dreams for Sydney: A Book to Help Dissipate Nightmares, 1 vol. Green, Burt, illus. 2009. 25p. pap. 24.95 (978-1-60703-602-7(0)) America Star Bks.

Willems, Mo. Don't Let the Pigeon Stay Up Late! Willems, Mo, illus. 2006. (Pigeon Ser.). (ENG., Illus.). 40p. (J). (gr. -1-k). 16.99 (978-0-7868-3746-5(2)) Hyperion Pr.

—Don't Let the Pigeon Stay Up Late! 2011. (J). (gr. -1-2). 29.95 (978-0-545-32735-0(0)); pap. 18.95 incl. audio compact disk (978-0-545-32791-6(1));Set. pap. 38.75 incl. audio compact disk (978-0-545-32792-3(X)) Weston Woods Studios, Inc.

—Time to Sleep, Sheep the Sheep! Willems, Mo, illus. 2010. (Illus.). 32p. (J). (gr. -1-3). (ENG.). 10.99 (978-0-06-172847-1(0)); lib. bdg. 14.89 (978-0-06-172848-8(9)) HarperCollins Pubs.

Williamgoldenpen. Quacker's Bedtime Stories. 2006. 49p. pap. 16.95 (978-1-4241-2236-3(8)) PublishAmerica, Inc.

—Quacker's Bedtime Stories... Continued. 2007. (ENG.). 68p. per. 19.95 (978-1-4241-7448-5(1)) America Star Bks.

Williams, Billie. Angela's Bedtime Adventures, 1 vol. 2009. 31p. pap. 24.95 (978-1-60749-112-5(5)) America Star Bks.

Williams, C. B. Walkers. 2012. 118p. pap. 6.95 (978-0-9881814-0-3(1)) BRYN WILLIAMS LLC.

Williams, Emma Louise. Harry the Hedgehog Loses His Favorite Sock. 2012. 20p. pap. 7.99 (978-1-939076-00-7(5)) Wiggles, Piggy.

Williams, Kristen. Sheepy Sue & the Bedtime Blues. 2012. 28p. pap. 12.95 (978-1-105-48819-1(5)) Lulu.com GBR. Dist: Lulu Pr., Inc.

Williams, Tim & Williams, Tony. Timmy's Bedtime: A Monster Bear Tale. 2011. 28p. pap. 12.50 (978-1-61204-171-1(X), Eloquent Bks.) Strategic Book Publishing & Rights Agency (SBPRA).

Williams, Vera B. Home at Last. Raschka, Chris, illus. 2016. 40p. (J). (gr. -1-3). 17.99 (978-0-06-134973-7(9), Greenwillow Bks.) HarperCollins Pubs.

Wilson, Karma. Mama, Why? Mendez, Simon, illus. 2011. (ENG.). 40p. (J). (gr. -1-2). 16.99 (978-1-4169-4205-4(X), McElderry, Margaret K. Bks.) McElderry, Margaret K. Bks.

—Sleepyhead. Segal, John, illus. 2012. (Classic Board Bks.). (ENG.). 32p. (J). (gr. -1 — 1). bds. 7.99 (978-1-4424-3433-2(3), Little Simon) Little Simon.

—Sleepyhead. Segal, John, illus. 2006. (ENG.). 32p. (J). (gr. -1-2). 16.99 (978-1-4169-1241-5(X), McElderry, Margaret K. Bks.) McElderry, Margaret K. Bks.

Wilson, Porcia D. My Pink Friend: A Rhyming Love Story. 2012. 44p. pap. 18.99 (978-1-4685-6852-3(3)) AuthorHouse.

Wilt, Gerri Ann, et al. My Little One: A Mother's Lullaby. Sargent, Shannon Marie, illus. 2008. (J). (978-0-87839-299-5(8)) North Star Pr. of St. Cloud.

Wisnewski, Andrea. Little Red Riding Hood. 2006. (ENG., Illus.). 32p. (J). (gr. 3-7). 18.95 (978-1-56792-303-2(8)) Godine, David R. Pub.

Witkowski, Teri. Bitty Bunny's Bedtime. Ackley, Peggy Jo, illus. 2004. (J). (978-1-58485-921-5(0)) American Girl Publishing, Inc.

—Time for Bed, Bitty Bunch. Ackley, Peggy Jo, illus. 2008. (J). (978-1-59369-380-0(X)) American Girl Publishing, Inc.

Wolfe, Carolyn. The Bedtime of the Sky & Other Sleepy-Bye Stories. Mathis, Leslie, illus. 2010. 32p. pap. 11.25 (978-1-935105-57-2(4)) Avid Readers Publishing Group.

Won, Brian. Hooray for Today! 2016. (ENG., Illus.). 40p. (J). (gr. -1-3). 16.99 (978-0-544-74803-3(4), HMH Books For Young Readers) Houghton Mifflin Harcourt Publishing Co.

Wood, Audrey. The Napping House. Wood, Don, illus. 2005. (ENG.). 16p. (J). (gr. k — 1). bds. 11.99 (978-0-15-205620-9(3)) Houghton Mifflin Harcourt Publishing Co.

Wood, Audrey & Wood, Don. Piggies. 2016. (ENG., Illus.). 30p. (J). (— 1). bds. 7.99 (978-0-544-79114-5(2), HMH Books For Young Readers) Houghton Mifflin Harcourt Publishing Co.

Woodall, Karen. Listen to the Stars. 2013. (ENG.). 34p. (J). 18.95 (978-1-4787-1446-0(8)) Outskirts Pr., Inc.

Woolf, Julia. Jack's Room. 2009. (Rookie Preschool Ser.). (ENG.). 24p. (J). (gr. -1). 23.00 (978-0-531-24400-5(8)); pap. 6.95 (978-0-531-24575-0(6)) Scholastic Library Publishing. (Children's Pr.).

Wright, Cavin. Bedtime Tales. 2010. 320p. 28.50 (978-1-60911-124-3(9), Eloquent Bks.) Strategic Book Publishing & Rights Agency (SBPRA).

Wu, Mike. Ellie in Concert. Wu, Mike, illus. 2017. (ENG., Illus.). 40p. (J). (gr. -1-k). 16.99 (978-1-4847-1238-2(2)) Hyperion Bks. for Children.

Yarrow, Peter. Day Is Done. Sweet, Melissa, illus. (ENG.). 24p. (J). (— 1). 2014. bds. 7.95 (978-1-4549-1147-0(6)) 2009. 16.95 (978-1-4027-4806-6(X)) Sterling Publishing Co., Inc.

Yates, Louise. Dog Loves Counting. 2013. (ENG.). 32p. (J). (gr. -1-3). 17.99 (978-0-449-81342-3(8), Knopf Bks. for Young Readers) Random Hse. Children's Bks.

Yolen, Jane. Creepy Monsters, Sleepy Monsters. Murphy, Kelly, illus. 2013. (ENG.). 32p. (J). (gr. -1-2). 5.99 (978-0-7636-6283-7(6)) Candlewick Pr.

—How Do Dinosaurs Go to Sleep? Teague, Mark, illus. 2016. (How Do Dinosaurs... ? Ser.). (ENG.). 12p. (J). (— 1). bds. 6.99 (978-0-545-94120-4(2), Blue Sky Pr., The) Scholastic, Inc.

—How Do Dinosaurs Say Good Night? Teague, Mark, illus. 2008. (How Do Dinosaurs... Ser.). (ENG.). (J). (gr. -1-3). 9.99 (978-0-545-09319-4(8)) Scholastic, Inc.

Yolen, Jane & Stemple, Heidi E. Y. Sleep, Black Bear, Sleep. Dyer, Brooke, illus. 2007. 32p. (J). (gr. -1-1). (ENG.). 15.99 (978-0-06-081560-8(4)); lib. bdg. 16.89 (978-0-06-081561-5(2)) HarperCollins Pubs.

—You Nest Here with Me. Sweet, Melissa, illus. 2015. (ENG.). 40p. (J). (gr. -1-3). 16.95 (978-1-59078-923-0(7)) Boyds Mills Pr.

Yoon, Salina. Stormy Night. (ENG., Illus.). (J). 2016. 32p. bds. 7.99 (978-1-68119-165-2(2), 9781681191652) 2015. 40p. (gr. -1-1). 14.99 (978-0-8027-3780-9(3), 9780802737809) Bloomsbury Publishing USA. (Bloomsbury USA Childrens).

Young, Ed. Mighty Moby. 2017. (ENG., Illus.). 40p. (J). (gr. -1-3). 17.99 (978-0-316-29936-7(7)) Little Brown & Co.

Young, Katharine Anne. Grandmother Moon & Roy G Biv: A Colorful Bedtime Story for All Ages. EXPLORE the AMAZING SECRETS of COLOR. 2009. 72p. pap. 23.49 (978-1-4389-7844-4(8)) AuthorHouse.

Youngberg, Yvette M. The Tooting Squirrel. 2009. (Illus.). 20p. pap. 10.95 (978-1-4389-1967-6(0)) AuthorHouse.

Yoyo Books Staff. Bedtime: Learning Words Series. 2004. 12p. bds. (978-90-5843-607-8(1)) YoYo Bks.

Yuly, Toni. Cat Nap. 2017. (ENG., Illus.). 32p. (J). bds. 7.99 (978-1-250-11261-3(3), 9781250112613) Feiwel & Friends.

Yutkins, Ellen A. Jack's Big Surprise. 2011. 20p. pap. (978-1-4269-9464-7(8)) Trafford Publishing (UK) Ltd.

Zafra, Jose. Historias de Sergio. (SPA.). 160p. (J). (978-84-216-2870-6(4), BU6937) Bruño, Editorial ESP. Dist: Lectorum Pubns., Inc.

Zemeckis, Robert, et al. The Polar Express Movie Shadowbook: An Interactive Shadow-Casting Bedtime Story. Van Allsburg, Chris, illus. 2006. 12p. (J). (gr. 4-18). reprint ed. 13.00 (978-1-4223-5172-7(6)) DIANE Publishing Co.

Zenz, Aaron. Monsters Go Night-Night. 2016. (ENG., Illus.). 32p. (J). (gr. -1-k). 12.95 (978-1-4197-1653-9(0), Abrams Appleseed) Abrams, Inc.

Zoboli, Giovanna. The Big Book of Slumber. Mulazzani, Simona, illus. 2014. (ENG.). 26p. (J). 16.00 (978-0-8028-5439-1(7), Eerdmans Bks For Young Readers) Eerdmans, William B. Publishing Co.

BEE

see Bees

BEES

see also Honey

Albright, Rosie. Bee Detectives. 2012. (Animal Detectives Ser.). (ENG., Illus.). 24p. (J). (gr. k-3). pap. 8.25 (978-1-4488-6260-3(4)); lib. bdg. 22.60 (978-1-4488-6150-7(0)) Rosen Publishing Group, Inc., The. (PowerKids Pr.).

—Bee Detectives: Abejas Detectives. Alamán, Eduardo, tr. from ENG. 2012. (Animal Detectives / Detectives Del Reino Animal Ser.). (SPA & ENG., Illus.). 24p. (J). (gr. k-3). lib. bdg. 22.60 (978-1-4488-6717-2(7), PowerKids Pr.) Rosen Publishing Group, Inc., The.

Allen, Judy. Are You a Bee? 2014. 17.00 (978-1-63419-644-4(9)) Perfection Learning Corp.

—Are You a Bee? Allen, Judy & Humphries, Tudor, illus. 2004. (Backyard Bks.). (ENG.). 32p. (J). (gr. k-3). pap. 6.99 (978-0-7534-5804-4(7), 9780753458044, Kingfisher) Roaring Brook Pr.

Amstutz, Lisa J. Honey Bees. 2017. (Little Critters Ser.). (ENG.). 24p. (gr. k-1). lib. bdg. 21.99 **(978-1-5157-7823-3(1))** Capstone Press of Coughlan Cos.

Ang, Karen. Inside the Bee's Hive. 2013. (Science Slam: Snug As a Bug-Where Bugs Live Ser.). 24p. (J). (gr. -1-3). lib. bdg. 23.93 (978-1-61772-905-8(1)) Bearport Publishing Co., Inc.

Ashley, Susan. Bees. (Incredible World of Insects Ser.). (Illus.). 24p. 2011. (J). (gr. 1-3). pap. 8.15 (978-1-4339-4577-9(0)) 2011. (J). (gr. 1-3). lib. bdg. 22.60 (978-1-4339-4575-5(4)) 2004. (gr. k-3). lib. bdg. 22.00 (978-0-8368-4051-3(8), Weekly Reader Leveled Readers) 2004. (YA). (gr. k-3). pap. 8.15 (978-0-8368-4058-2(5), Weekly Reader Leveled Readers) Stevens, Gareth Publishing LLLP.

Bailey, Diane. Pollination Problems: The Battle to Save Bees & Other Vital Animals. 2017. (J). **(978-1-4222-3876-9(8))** Mason Crest.

Ballivián, José Manuel Palazuelos. Abelhas Nativas Sem Ferrão: Myg Pe. 2nd ed. 2011. (POR., Illus.). 128p. pap. **(978-85-7843-056-6(5))** Editora Oikos Ltda.

Barton, Bethany. Give Bees a Chance. Barton, Bethany, illus. 2017. (ENG., Illus.). 40p. (J). (gr. -1-3). 16.99 (978-0-670-01694-5(2), Viking Books for Young Readers) Penguin Young Readers Group.

Bates, Matt. Inside Beehives. 2015. (Inside Animal Homes Ser.). (ENG.). 24p. (J). (gr. 2-3). 23.60 (978-1-4994-0920-8(6), PowerKids Pr.) Rosen Publishing Group, Inc., The.

Bates, Matthew. Colmenas (Inside Beehives) 2015. (Las Casas de Los Animales (Inside Animal Homes) Ser.). (ENG & SPA.). 24p. (J). (gr. 2-3). 23.60 (978-1-4994-0606-1(1), PowerKids Pr.) Rosen Publishing Group, Inc., The.

The Beekeeper, 6 Packs. (Literatura 2000 Ser.). (gr. 2-3). 33.00 (978-0-7635-0161-7(1)) Rigby Education.

Berger, Melvin & Berger, Gilda. Bees. 2011. (Illus.). 16p. (J). pap. (978-0-545-24448-0(X)) Scholastic, Inc.

Black, Nessa. Bees. 2017. (Spot Creepy Crawlies Ser.). (ENG.). 16p. (gr. k-3). 17.95 **(978-1-68151-105-4(3))** Amicus Publishing.

Blobaum, Cindy. Explore Honey Bees! With 25 Great Projects. Stone, Bryan, illus. 2015. (Explore Your World Ser.). (ENG.). 96p. (gr. 1-5). 19.95 (978-1-61930-286-0(1)) Open City Bks.

Buchmann, Stephen. Honey Bees: Letters from the Hive. 2011. (ENG.). 228p. (J). (gr. 5-7). pap. 8.99 (978-0-385-73771-5(8), Ember) Random Hse. Children's Bks.

Burns, Loree Griffin. The Hive Detectives. 2013. (Scientists in the Field Ser.). (Illus.). 69p. lib. bdg. 20.85 (978-0-606-31671-2(X), Turtleback) Turtleback Bks.

—The Hive Detectives: Chronicle of a Honey Bee Catastrophe. Harasimowicz, Ellen, illus. (Scientists in the Field Ser.). (ENG.). 80p. (J). (gr. 5-7). 2013. pap. 9.99 (978-0-544-00326-2(8)) 2010. 18.99 (978-0-547-15231-8(0)) Houghton Mifflin Harcourt Publishing Co.

Cardenas, Ernesto A. A Bee Is an Insect. 2009. 23.95 (978-1-60698-032-3(7)); pap. 4.95 (978-1-60698-030-9(0)) Milo Educational Bks. & Resources.

Carr, Aaron. Bumblebees. 2014. (J). (978-1-4896-1034-8(0)) Weigl Pubs., Inc.

Caviezel, Giovanni, illus. Little Bee. 2014. (Mini-Creatures Ser.). (ENG.). 8p. (J). (gr. -1 — 1). bds. 4.99 (978-0-7641-6713-3(8)) Barron's Educational Series, Inc.

Chrustowski, Rick. Bee Dance. Chrustowski, Rick, illus. 2015. (ENG., Illus.). 32p. (J). (gr. -1-3). 17.99 (978-0-8050-9919-5(0), 9780805099195, Holt, Henry & Co. Bks. For Young Readers) Holt, Henry & Co.

¿Como Hacen Miel las Abejas? (Coleccion Primeros Pasos en la Ciencia). (SPA., Illus.). (J). (gr. 1-3). pap. (978-950-724-691-3(6), LMA8232) Lumen ARG. Dist: Lectorum Pubns., Inc.

Cooper, Jason. Honeybee. 2003. (Life Cycles II Ser.). (Illus.). 24p. (J). lib. bdg. 27.07 (978-1-58952-705-8(4)) Rourke Educational Media.

Cunningham, Kevin. Bees & Flowers. 2016. (21st Century Junior Library: Better Together Ser.). (ENG., Illus.). 24p. (J). (gr. 2-5). 27.07 (978-1-63471-083-1(5), 208411) Cherry Lake Publishing.

Dawson, Emily C. How Bees Make Honey. 2010. (Our Animal World Ser.). 24p. (J). 25.65 (978-1-60753-012-1(0)) Amicus Publishing.

Dawson, Robert. Bees. 2009. (Wild Reads Ser.). (ENG., Illus.). 32p. (YA). (gr. k). pap. 4.95 (978-0-19-911924-0(4)) Oxford Univ. Pr., Inc.

Diary of a Honeybee: Individual Title Six-Packs. (Literatura 2000 Ser.). (gr. 2-3). 33.00 (978-0-7635-0164-8(6)) Rigby Education.

Dibble, Traci. Bees & Wasps. 2015. (1G Bugs Ser.). (ENG., Illus.). 24p. (J). pap. 5.99 (978-1-63437-095-0(3)) American Reading Co.

Dickmann, Nancy. A Bee's Life, 1 vol. 2010. (Watch It Grow Ser.). (ENG., Illus.). 24p. (gr. -1-1). pap. 6.29 (978-1-4329-4146-8(1), Acorn) Heinemann-Raintree.

—La Vida de la Abeja, 1 vol. 2011. (¡Mira Cómo Crece! Ser.). 24p. (gr. -1-1). (SPA & ENG.). 22.65 (978-1-4329-5270-9(6)); (ENG & SPA.). pap. 6.29 (978-1-4329-5282-2(X)) Heinemann-Raintree. (Bellota).

Dorling Kindersley Publishing Staff & Unstead, Sue. DK Readers L2: Amazing Bees. 2016. (DK Readers Ser.). (ENG., Illus.). 48p. (J). (gr. k-2). 14.99 (978-1-4654-4603-9(6)); pap. 3.99 (978-1-4654-4604-6(4)) Dorling Kindersley Publishing, Inc. (DK Children).

Enslow, Brian. Counting Bees 1-2-3. 2011. (All about Counting Bugs 1-2-3 Ser.). (Illus.). 24p. (J). (gr. -1-18). pap. 7.95 (978-1-59845-247-1(9), Enslow Elementary) Enslow Pubs., Inc.

Esbaum, Jill. Honey Bees. 2017. (Explore My World Ser.). (ENG., Illus.). 32p. (J). (gr. -1-2). pap. 4.99 (978-1-4263-2713-1(7), National Geographic Children's Bks.) National Geographic Society.

Felix, Rebecca. What Do Bees Do in Summer? 2014. (21st Century Basic Skills Library: Let's Look at Summer Ser.). (ENG., Illus.). 24p. (J). (gr. k-3). pap. 12.79 (978-1-63137-646-7(2), 205188) Cherry Lake Publishing.

Franks, Katie. Bees up Close. (Nature up Close Ser.). 24p. 2009. (gr. k-1). 42.50 (978-1-61514-825-7(6)) 2008. (Illus.). (J). (gr. -1-3). lib. bdg. 22.60 (978-1-4042-4137-4(X)) Rosen Publishing Group, Inc., The. (PowerKids Pr.).

—Bees up Close / Las Abejas. 2009. (Nature up Close / la naturaleza de cerca Ser.). (ENG & SPA.). 24p. (gr. k-1). 42.50 (978-1-61514-831-8(0), Editorial Buenas Letras) Rosen Publishing Group, Inc., The.

—Bees up Close/Las Abejas. Sanz, Pilar, tr. from ENG. 2008. (Nature up Close / la Naturaleza de Cerca Ser.). (Illus.). 24p. (J). (gr. 4-7). lib. bdg. 22.60 (978-1-4042-7676-5(9), Editorial Buenas Letras) Rosen Publishing Group, Inc., The.

Frisch, Aaron. Bees. 2014. 24p. (J). (978-1-60818-456-9(0)) Creative Co., The.

—Seedlings: Bees. 2015. (Seedlings Ser.). (ENG., Illus.). 24p. (J). (gr. -1-1). pap. 7.99 (978-1-62832-038-1(9), Creative Paperbacks) Creative Co., The.

Gallagher, Debbie. Bees. 2011. (Mighty Minibeasts Ser.). 32p. (gr. 2). 28.50 (978-1-60870-543-6(9)) Marshall Cavendish Corp.

Galvin, Laura Gates. Bumblebee at Apple Tree Lane. Kest, Kristin, illus. 2005. (Smithsonian's Backyard Ser.). (ENG.). 32p. (J). (gr. -1-2). pap. 6.95 (978-1-931465-41-0(X), S5019) Soundprints.

—Bumblebee at Apple Tree Lane. Kest, Kristin, illus. 2005. (Smithsonian's Backyard Ser.: Vol. 19). (ENG.). 32p. (J). (gr. -1-2). 15.95 (978-1-56899-820-6(1), B5019) Soundprints.

Ganeri, Anita & Johnson, Jinny. What's It Like to Be... Bee? Sanzi, Desiderio, illus. 2011. (What's It Like to Be... ? Ser.). 24p. (J). (gr. -1-k). 25.65 (978-1-60753-184-5(4)) Amicus Publishing.

Ghione, Yvette & Gagnon, Celeste, creators. This Is Daniel Cook Making Honey. 2007. (This Is Daniel Cook Ser.). (ENG., Illus.). 24p. (J). (gr. -1-1). 4.95 (978-1-55453-086-1(5)) Kids Can Pr., Ltd. CAN. Dist: Hachette Bk. Group.

Gibbons, Gail. Honey Makers. 2014. 17.00 (978-1-63419-706-9(2)) Perfection Learning Corp.

Gillespie, Katie. Bees. 2017. (Illus.). 24p. (J). **(978-1-4896-4499-2(7)**, AV2 by Weigl) Weigl Pubs., Inc.

Glaser, Linda. Brilliant Bees. 2003. (Illus.). 32p. (J). (gr. k-3). pap. 8.95 (978-0-7613-1943-6(3), Millbrook Pr.) Lerner Publishing Group.

—Brilliant Bees. Holland, Gay W., illus. 2003. 32p. lib. bdg. 22.90 (978-0-7613-2670-0(7), Millbrook Pr.) Lerner Publishing Group.

Goldish, Meish. Killer Bees. 2008. (No Backbone! Ser.). (Illus.). 24p. (J). (gr. k-3). lib. bdg. 21.28 (978-1-59716-581-5(6)) Bearport Publishing Co., Inc.

Green, Emily K. Bumblebees. 2006. (World of Insects Ser.). (ENG., Illus.). 24p. (J). (gr. k-3). lib. bdg. 25.95 (978-1-60014-009-9(2)) Bellwether Media.

Greve, Tom. Buzzing Bugs. 2008. (My First Science Discovery Library). (Illus.). 24p. (J). (gr. k-2). 21.35 (978-1-60472-766-1(7)) Rourke Educational Media.

Hamilton, Sue. Swarmed by Bees, 1 vol. 2010. (Close Encounters of the Wild Kind Ser.). (ENG.). 32p. (YA). (gr. 4-7). 27.07 (978-1-60453-933-2(X)) ABDO Publishing Co.

Hansen, Grace. Bees, 1 vol. 2014. (Insects Ser.). (ENG., Illus.). 24p. (J). (gr. -1-3). lib. bdg. 28.50 (978-1-62970-037-3(1), 1374863) ABDO Publishing Co.

Hansen, Grace, et al. Abejas. 2015. (Insectos Ser.). (SPA., Illus.). 24p. (gr. k-1). pap. 7.95 (978-1-4966-0471-2(7)) Capstone Classroom.

Hanson-Harding, Alexandra. Beekeeping. 2013. (Urban Gardening & Farming for Teens Ser.). 64p. (YA). (gr. 7-12). 33.25 (978-1-4777-1778-3(1)) Rosen Publishing Group, Inc., The.

Hartley, Karen & Macro, Chris. Bee. 2016. (Bug Bks.). (ENG.). 32p. pap. 8.29 (978-1-4846-3872-9(7), Heinemann First Library) Heinemann-Raintree.

Haworth, Katie. Little Honey Bee. Ormes, Jane, illus. 2016. (ENG.). 14p. (J). (gr. -1-2). bds. 14.99 (978-0-7636-8531-7(3), Big Picture Press) Candlewick Pr.

Heiligman, Deborah. Honeybees. 2017. (Jump into Science Ser.). (ENG., Illus.). 32p. (J). (gr. -1-3). pap. 7.99 **(978-1-4263-2835-0(4)**, National Geographic Children's Bks.) National Geographic Society.

—Honeybees. Golembe, Carla, illus. 2007. (Jump into Science Ser.). (ENG.). 32p. (J). (gr. -1-3). per. 6.95 (978-1-4263-0157-5(X), National Geographic Children's Bks.) National Geographic Society.

Heiligman, Deborah. Jump into Science: Honeybees. 2017. (Jump into Science Ser.). (ENG.). 32p. (J). (gr. -1-3). lib. bdg. 17.90 **(978-1-4263-2836-7(2)**, National Geographic Children's Bks.) National Geographic Society.

Herrington, Lisa M. It's a Good Thing There Are Bees. 2014. (Rookie Read-About(r) Science — It's a Good Thing... Ser.). (ENG.). 32p. (J). pap. 5.95 (978-0-531-22831-9(2)); lib. bdg. 25.00 (978-0-531-22359-8(0)) Scholastic Library Publishing.

Hileman, Jane. Honey Bee. 2015. (2G Bugs Ser.). (ENG., Illus.). 28p. (J). pap. 5.99 (978-1-63437-116-2(X)) American Reading Co.

Hodge, Deborah. Bees. Mulock, Julian, illus. 2004. (Denver Museum of Nature & Science Bks.). (ENG.). 32p. (J). (gr. k-3). 5.95 (978-1-55337-656-9(0)) Kids Can Pr., Ltd. CAN. Dist: Hachette Bk. Group.

Honey Bees, Vol. 4. 2005. (Bugs, Bugs, Bugs Ser.). (YA). (gr. k-3). 118.80 (978-0-7368-4206-8(3), Pebble Bks.) Capstone Press of Coughlan Cos.

Honeybee. 2003. (J). 36.95 (978-0-8136-9266-1(0)); 38.95 (978-0-8136-4151-5(9)) Modern Curriculum Pr.

Houghton, Gillian. Abejas: Por dentro y por fuera (Bees: Inside & Out) 2009. (Explora la Naturaleza (Getting into Nature) Ser.). (SPA.). 32p. (gr. 3-4). 47.90 (978-1-61512-333-9(4), Editorial Buenas Letras) Rosen Publishing Group, Inc., The.

—Bee. 2004. (Getting into Nature Ser.). (Illus.). 32p. (YA). (gr. 3-6). lib. bdg. 25.25 (978-0-8239-4204-6(X)) Rosen Publishing Group, Inc., The.

—Bees: Inside & Out. 2009. (Getting into Nature Ser.). 32p. (gr. 3-4). 47.90 (978-1-61512-720-7(8), PowerKids Pr.) Rosen Publishing Group, Inc., The.

Howard, Fran. Bumble Bees [Scholastic]. 2010. (Bugs, Bugs, Bugs! Ser.). 24p. pap. 0.52 (978-1-4296-5055-7(9), Pebble Plus) Capstone Press of Coughlan Cos.

Huber, Raymond. Flight of the Honey Bee. Lovelock, Brian, illus. (Read & Wonder Ser.). (ENG.). 32p. (J). (gr. -1-2). 2015. 6.99 (978-0-7636-7648-3(9)) 2013. 16.99 (978-0-7636-6760-3(9)) Candlewick Pr.

—Flight of the Honey Bee. 2015. (Read & Wonder Ser.). lib. bdg. 17.20 (978-0-606-37324-1(1)) Turtleback Bks.

Hudak, Heather C. Bees. 2008. (Backyard Animals Ser.). (Illus.). 24p. (J). (gr. 4-7). lib. bdg. 24.45 (978-1-60596-003-6(9)) Weigl Pubs., Inc.

Hudak, Heather C., ed. Bees. 2008. (Backyard Animals Ser.). (Illus.). 24p. (J). (gr. 4-7). pap. 8.95 (978-1-60596-009-8(8)) Weigl Pubs., Inc.

Ingram, Kevin. Bee. 2017. (Up Close & Scary Ser.). (Illus.). 32p. (gr. 2-5). 31.35 **(978-1-911242-04-8(0))** Book Hse. GBR. Dist: Black Rabbit Bks.

Ipcizade, Catherine. B Is for Bees: ABCs of Endangered Insects. 2016. (E for Endangered Ser.). (ENG., Illus.). 32p. (gr. 1-2). lib. bdg. 27.32 *(978-1-4914-8035-9(1)*, Aplus Bks.) Capstone Press of Coughlan Cos.
James, Joyce. Bees. 2008. (Nature's Children Ser.). (Illus.). 52p. *(978-0-7172-6217-5(0))* Grolier, Ltd.
Jango-Cohen, Judith. Bees. 2006. (Animals Animals Ser.). (Illus.). 48p. (gr. 3-7). lib. bdg. 29.93 *(978-0-7614-2235-8(8)*, Benchmark Bks.) Marshall Cavendish Corp.
Kaemmerlen, Cathy. The Buzz on Honeybees, 1 vol. Coates, Kathy, illus. 2012. (ENG.). 32p. (J). (gr. k-3). 16.99 *(978-1-4556-1457-8(2))* Pelican Publishing Co., Inc.
Kalman, Bobbie. Les Abeilles. Briere, Marie-Josee, tr. from ENG. 2006. (Petit Monde Vivant Ser.). (FRE., Illus.). 32p. (J). (gr. -1-3). pap. 9.95 *(978-2-89579-079-2(5))* Bayard Canada Livres CAN. Dist: Crabtree Publishing Co.
—The Life Cycle of a Honeybee. (ENG.). 32p. (J). 2007. *(978-0-7787-7701-4(4))* 2005. (Illus.). (gr. 1-4). *(978-0-7787-7691-8(3))* 2003. (Illus.). pap. *(978-0-7787-0694-6(X))* Crabtree Publishing Co.
Kenney, Karen Latchana. Buzz with the Bees, 1 vol. Hedicker, Lisa, illus. 2010. (Bug's World Ser.). (ENG.). 32p. 28.50 *(978-1-60270-784-9(7)*, Looking Glass Library- Nonfiction) Magic Wagon.
Kim, Soo-hyeon. What Does the Bee See? Observation - Parts & Whole. Cowley, Joy, ed. Jo, Eun-hwa, illus. 2015. (Step up - Creative Thinking Ser.). (ENG.). 32p. (J). (gr. -1-2). 26.65 *(978-1-925186-36-9(9))* Lerner Publishing Group.
Lalley, Kristine. Busy Bees. 2008. (Rosen Real Readers: Upper Emergent Ser.). (ENG., Illus.). 12p. (gr. 1-2). pap. 5.90 *(978-0-8239-8132-8(0))* Rosen Publishing Group, Inc., The.
Landau, Elaine. Killer Bees. 2003. (Fearsome, Scary, & Creepy Animals Ser.). (Illus.). 48p. (J). (gr. 1-4). lib. bdg. 23.93 *(978-0-7660-2061-0(4))* Enslow Pubs., Inc.
Lawrence, Ellen. What Lily Gets from Bee: And Other Pollination Facts. 2012. (Science Slam: Plant-Ology Ser.). 24p. (J). (gr. -1-3). lib. bdg. 23.93 *(978-1-61772-587-6(0))* Bearport Publishing Co., Inc.
Leaf, Christina. Honeybees. 2017. (Insects up Close Ser.). (ENG., Illus.). 24p. (J). (gr. k-3). lib. bdg. 25.95 ***(978-1-62617-666-9(3)***, Blastoff! Readers) Bellwether Media.
Linde, Barbara M. The Life Cycle of a Honeybee. 2011. (Nature's Life Cycles Ser.). (Illus.). 24p. (J). (gr. 2-5). pap. 8.15 *(978-1-4339-4676-9(9))*; lib. bdg. 22.60 *(978-1-4339-4675-2(0))* Stevens, Gareth Publishing LLLP. (Gareth Stevens Learning Library).
Lockwood, Sophie. Bees. 2007. (World of Insects Ser.). (ENG., Illus.). 40p. (J). (gr. 3-6). 31.36 *(978-1-59296-818-3(X)*, 200971) Child's World, Inc., The.
Machajewski, Sarah. Killer Bees. 2015. (Things That Sting Ser.). (ENG., Illus.). 24p. (J). (gr. 2-3). lib. bdg. 22.60 *(978-1-4824-1706-7(5))* Stevens, Gareth Publishing LLLP.
Macken, JoAnn Early. Take a Closer Look at Bees. 2016. (Core Content Science — Take a Closer Look Ser.). (ENG., Illus.). 40p. (J). (gr. 2-4). lib. bdg. 26.65 *(978-1-63440-052-7(6))* Red Chair Pr.
Maclaine, James. Bees & Wasps. 2013. (Beginner's Nature Ser.). 32p. (J). ring bd. 4.99 *(978-0-7945-3360-1(4)*, Usborne) EDC Publishing.
Mahoney, Emily Jankowski. Killer Bees. 2016. (Animal Invaders: Destroying Native Habitats Ser.). 00024p. (J). pap. 8.15 *(978-1-4824-5660-8(5))* Stevens, Gareth Publishing LLLP.
Markle, Sandra. The Case of the Vanishing Honeybees: A Scientific Mystery. 2013. 48p. pap. 29.27 *(978-1-4677-1700-7(2))* Lerner Publishing Group.
Markovics, Joyce. The Honey Bee's Hive: A Thriving City. 2009. (Spectacular Animal Towns Ser.). (Illus.). 32p. (J). (gr. 2-7). lib. bdg. 25.27 *(978-1-59716-867-0(X))* Bearport Publishing Co., Inc.
Marsico, Katie. Honey Bee. 2015. (21st Century Junior Library: Creepy Crawly Critters Ser.). (ENG.). 24p. (J). (gr. k-3). 27.07 *(978-1-63362-591-4(5)*, 206548) Cherry Lake Publishing.
Martin, Justin McCory. Busy Honeybees. 2008. (Illus.). 24p. (J). *(978-0-545-00738-2(0))* Scholastic, Inc.
McNeil, Niki, et al. HOCPP 1127 Bees. 2006. spiral bd. *(978-1-60308-127-6(5))* In the Hands of a Child.
Meachen Rau, Dana. Adivina Quién Pica. 2008. (Adivina Quién Ser.). (SPA.). 32p. (gr. k-2). lib. bdg. 15.95 *(978-0-7614-3460-3(7)*, Benchmark Bks.) Marshall Cavendish Corp.
—Buzz, Bee, Buzz! 2007. (Go, Critter, Go! Ser.). (SPA & ENG., Illus.). 24p. (gr. k-1). lib. bdg. 15.95 *(978-0-7614-2648-6(5)*, Benchmark Bks.) Marshall Cavendish Corp.
—Buzz, Bee, Buzz!/Zumba Abeja, Zumba! 2007. (Go, Critter, Go!/¡Vamos Criaturita, Vamos! Ser.). (SPA & ENG., Illus.). 24p. (gr. k-1). lib. bdg. 15.95 *(978-0-7614-2813-8(5)*, Benchmark Bks.) Marshall Cavendish Corp.
—Zumba Abeja, Zumba! 2007. (¡Vamos Criaturita, Vamos! Ser.). (SPA & ENG., Illus.). 24p. (gr. k-1). lib. bdg. 15.95 *(978-0-7614-2789-6(9)*, Benchmark Bks.) Marshall Cavendish Corp.
Miller, Dave. Birds, Bugs, & Bees. 2006. (ENG., Illus.). (J). 3.00 *(978-0-932859-90-7(9))* Apologetics Pr., Inc.
Milton, Joyce. Honeybees. Mueller, Peter R. & Mueller, Pete, illus. 2003. (Penguin Young Readers, Level 3 Ser.). (ENG.). 48p. (J). (gr. 1-3). pap. 3.99 *(978-0-448-42846-8(6)*, Penguin Young Readers) Penguin Young Readers Group.
Morgan, Sally. Bees. 2008. (Down on the Farm (N.Y.) Ser.). (ENG.). 24p. (J). pap. *(978-0-7787-4049-0(8))* Crabtree Publishing Co.
—Bees. 2007. (QEB Down on the Farm Ser.). (Illus.). 24p. (J). (gr. -1-3). lib. bdg. 15.95 *(978-1-59566-386-3(X))* QEB Publishing Inc.
—Bees & Wasps. 2006. (Animal Lives (QEB Publishing) Ser.). (Illus.). 32p. (J). (gr. 4-7). lib. bdg. 19.95 *(978-1-59566-202-6(2))* QEB Publishing Inc.
Morgan, Sally & Teacher Created Resources Staff. Bees & Wasps. 2007. (Animal Lives (QEB Publishing) Ser.). (ENG., Illus.). 32p. (gr. 2-9). pap. 7.99 *(978-1-4206-8112-3(5))* Teacher Created Resources, Inc.
Mortensen, Lori. In the Trees, Honey Bees. Arbo, Cris, illus. 2009. 32p. (J). (gr. -1-5). 16.95 *(978-1-58469-114-3(X))*; (ENG.). pap. 8.95 *(978-1-58469-115-0(8))* Dawn Pubns.
Murray, Julie. Bees, 1 vol. (Big Buddy Bks.). (ENG.). 2010. 32p. (J). (gr. 2-5). 28.50 *(978-1-61613-482-2(8))* 2007. 24p. (gr. -1-3). 25.65 *(978-1-59928-703-4(X)*, Buddy Bks.) 2003. 24p. (J). (gr. 1-4). 25.65 *(978-1-57765-717-0(9))* ABDO Publishing Co.
Nagelhout, Ryan. We Need Honeybees. 2015. (Creatures We Can't Live Without Ser.). (ENG.). 24p. (J). (gr. 3-4). 23.60 *(978-1-4994-1039-6(5)*, PowerKids Pr.) Rosen Publishing Group, Inc., The.
National Geographic Kids Staff & Marsh, Laura. Bees. 2016. (Readers Ser.). (ENG., Illus.). 32p. (J). (gr. k-3). pap. 3.99 *(978-1-4263-2281-5(X)*, National Geographic Children's Bks.) National Geographic Society.
Nelson, Robin. From Flower to Honey. (Start to Finish, Second Series: Nature's Cycles Ser.). 24p. (gr. k-3). 2012. (ENG.). pap. 39.62 *(978-0-7613-9292-7(0))* 2012. (ENG.). pap. 6.95 *(978-0-7613-8574-5(6))* 2012. (ENG.). lib. bdg. 23.93 *(978-0-7613-6563-1(X))* 2003. (Illus.). (J). lib. bdg. 18.60 *(978-0-8225-0717-8(X))* Lerner Publishing Group.
Neye, Emily. Honeybees. Leonard, Tom, illus. 2016. (Step into Reading Ser.). (ENG.). 32p. (J). (gr. -1-1). pap. 3.99 *(978-0-307-26217-2(0)*, Random Hse. Bks. for Young Readers) Random Hse. Children's Bks.
Owings, Lisa. From Egg to Honeybee. 2016. (Start to Finish, Second Ser.). (ENG., Illus.). 24p. (J). (gr. k-3). 23.99 *(978-1-5124-0908-6(1))* Lerner Publishing Group.
—Killer Bees. 2013. (Nature's Deadliest Ser.). (ENG., Illus.). 24p. (J). (gr. 3-8). lib. bdg. 25.95 *(978-1-60014-880-4(8)*, Pilot Bks.) Bellwether Media.
Pattrick, Steve. Bees & Honey: KinderFacts Individual Title Six-Packs. (Kinderstarters Ser.). 8p. (gr. -1-1). 21.00 *(978-0-7635-8740-6(0))* Rigby Education.
Pearson, Scott. Africanized Honeybees. 2017. (Invasive Species Takeover Ser.). (ENG., Illus.). 32p. (J). (gr. 3-7). 31.35 ***(978-1-68072-012-9(0))*** Black Rabbit Bks.
Pugliano-Martin, Carol. Discover the Life Cycle of Bees. 2006. (English Explorers Ser.). (J). pap. *(978-1-4108-6471-0(5))* Benchmark Education Co.
—The Life Cycle of Bees. 2006. (English Explorers Ser.). (J). pap. *(978-1-4108-6468-0(5))* Benchmark Education Co.
Rajczak, Kristen. I'm Allergic to Bees. 2014. (I'm Allergic Ser.). (Illus.). 24p. (J). (gr. 1-3). 22.60 *(978-1-4824-0787-7(6))* Stevens, Gareth Publishing LLLP.
Rau, Dana Meachen. Guess Who Stings/Adivina Quién Pica. 2007. (Guess Who/Adivina Quién Ser.). (SPA & ENG.). 32p. (gr. k-2). 15.95 *(978-0-7614-3485-6(2))* Marshall Cavendish Corp.
Raum, Elizabeth. Bees Build Beehives. Romina Martí, illus. 2017. (Animal Builders Ser.). (ENG.). 24p. (J). (gr. 1-4). 20.95 ***(978-1-68151-169-6(X)***, Amicus Illustrated) Amicus Publishing.
—Los Castores y Sus Madrigueras (Beavers Build Lodges) Romina Martí, illus. 2017. (Animal Builders Ser.). (ENG & SPA.). 24p. (J). (gr. 1-4). 20.95 ***(978-1-68151-279-2(3)***, Amicus Illustrated) Amicus Publishing.
Read, Tracy C. Exploring the World of Bees. 2011. (Exploring the World Of Ser.). (ENG., Illus.). 24p. (J). (gr. 3-7). 16.95 *(978-1-55407-882-0(2)*, 9781554078820); pap. 6.95 *(978-1-55407-955-1(1)*, 9781554079551) Firefly Bks., Ltd.
Rice, Dona Herweck. A Bee's Life, 1 vol. 2nd rev. ed. 2013. (Nonfiction Readers Ser.). (ENG., Illus.). 20p. (J). (gr. 1-1). pap. 19.96 *(978-1-4807-1021-4(0))* Shell Educational Publishing.
—A Bee's Life, 1 vol. 2nd rev. ed. 2011. (Nonfiction Readers Ser.). (ENG.). 20p. (J). (gr. 1-1). pap. 4.99 *(978-1-4333-3588-4(3))* Teacher Created Materials, Inc.
—La Vida de una Abeja, 1 vol. 2nd rev. ed. 2012. (Nonfiction Readers Ser.). (SPA.). 20p. (J). (gr. 1-1). pap. 4.99 *(978-1-4333-4421-3(1))* Teacher Created Materials, Inc.
Riggs, Kate. Bee. 2015. (J). pap. *(978-1-62832-259-0(4)*, Creative Paperbacks) 2012. 32p. (gr. 3-8). 19.95 *(978-1-60818-214-5(2)*, Creative Education) Creative Co., The.
—Grow with Me: Bee. 2013. (Grow with Me Ser.). (ENG.). 32p. (J). (gr. 1-3). pap. 9.99 *(978-0-89812-767-6(X)*, Creative Paperbacks) Creative Co., The.
Riley, Joelle. Buzzing Bumblebees. 2003. (Pull Ahead Books-Animals Ser.). (ENG., Illus.). 32p. (gr. k-3). lib. bdg. 22.60 *(978-0-8225-4668-9(X))* Lerner Publishing Group.
Rissman, Rebecca. Bees, 1 vol. 2012. (Creepy Critters Ser.). (ENG.). 24p. (gr. -1-k). pap. 9.95 *(978-1-4109-4815-1(3))*; lib. bdg. 25.32 *(978-1-4109-4802-1(1))* Heinemann-Raintree.
Rockwell, Anne F. & Rockwell. Honey in a Hive. Schindler, S. D., illus. 2005. (Let's-Read-And-Find-Out Science 2 Ser.). (ENG.). 40p. (J). (gr. k-4). pap. 5.99 *(978-0-06-445204-5(2))* HarperCollins Pubs.
Rockwood, Leigh. Tell Me the Difference Between a Bee & a Wasp. 2013. (How Are They Different? Ser.). (ENG., Illus.). 24p. (J). (gr. k-5). pap. 8.25 *(978-1-4488-9736-0(X))*; lib. bdg. 22.60 *(978-1-4488-9639-4(8))* Rosen Publishing Group, Inc., The. (PowerKids Pr.).
Rollason, Jane. Killer Bees Level 2 Elementary/Lower-intermediate American English. 2010. (ENG., Illus.). 64p. pap. 12.00 *(978-0-521-14896-2(0))* Cambridge Univ. Pr.
Roza, Greg. Sting! The Scorpion & Other Animals That Sting. 2011. (Armed & Dangerous Ser.). (Illus.). 24p. (J). pap. 8.25 *(978-1-4488-2680-3(2)*, PowerKids Pr.); (gr. 1-4). 22.60 *(978-1-4488-2548-6(2))* Rosen Publishing Group, Inc., The.
Salzmann, Mary Elizabeth. Busy Bumblebees, 1 vol. 2012. (Bug Bks.). (ENG.). 24p. (J). (gr. k-3). lib. bdg. 24.21 *(978-1-61783-189-8(1)*, SandCastle) ABDO Publishing Co.
Sayre, April Pulley. The Bumblebee Queen. Wynne, Patricia J., illus. 2006. (ENG.). 32p. (J). (gr. -1-3). pap. 7.95 *(978-1-57091-363-1(3))* Charlesbridge Publishing, Inc.
—The Bumblebee Queen. Wynne, Patricia J., illus. 2006. (gr. -1-3). lib. bdg. 17.95 *(978-0-7569-6968-4(9))* Perfection Learning Corp.
Schaub, Michelle. Honeybees Help Flowers. 2006. (Early Explorers Ser.). (J). pap. *(978-1-4108-6122-1(8))* Benchmark Education Co.
Scheunemann, Pam. Bees Buzz!, 1 vol. 2009. (Animal Sounds Set 1 Ser.). (ENG., Illus.). 24p. (J). (gr. k-3). lib. bdg. 24.21 *(978-1-60453-567-9(9)*, SandCastle) ABDO Publishing Co.
Schuh, Mari. Honeybees. 2013. (ENG., Illus.). 24p. (J). lib. bdg. 25.65 *(978-1-62031-051-9(1))* Jump! Inc.
Sexton, Colleen. Honey Bees. 2007. (World of Insects Ser.). (ENG., Illus.). 24p. (J). (gr. k-3). lib. bdg. 25.95 *(978-1-60014-052-5(1))* Bellwether Media.
—The Life Cycle of a Bee. 2010. (Life Cycles Ser.). (ENG., Illus.). 24p. (J). (gr. k-3). lib. bdg. 25.95 *(978-1-60014-305-2(9)*, Blastoff! Readers) Bellwether Media.
Silverman, Buffy. Can You Tell a Bee from a Wasp? 2011. (Lightning Bolt Books (tm) — Animal Look-Alikes Ser.). (ENG.). 32p. (gr. k-2). pap. 7.95 *(978-0-7613-7843-3(X))*; (Illus.). lib. bdg. 26.60 *(978-0-7613-6730-7(6))* Lerner Publishing Group.
Slade, Suzanne. Bees. (Under the Microscope: Backyard Bugs Ser.). 24p. 2009. (gr. 2-3). 42.50 *(978-1-60854-612-1(8)*, PowerKids Pr.) 2007. (Illus.). (J). (gr. -1-3). lib. bdg. 22.60 *(978-1-4042-3822-0(0))* Rosen Publishing Group, Inc., The.
—What If There Were No Bees? A Book about the Grassland Ecosystem, 1 vol. Schwartz, Carol, illus. 2010. (Food Chain Reactions Ser.). (ENG.). 24p. (gr. 2-4). pap. 9.95 *(978-1-4048-6394-1(X))* Picture Window Bks.
Socha, Piotr. Bees: A Honeyed History. 2017. (ENG., Illus.). 80p. (J). (gr. 1-4). 24.95 *(978-1-4197-2615-6(3)*, Abrams Bks. for Young Readers) Abrams, Inc.
Somervill, Barbara. Africanized Honey Bee. 2008. (21st Century Skills Library: Animal Invaders Ser.). (ENG.). 32p. (gr. 4-8). lib. bdg. 28.50 *(978-1-60279-117-6(1)*, 200090) Cherry Lake Publishing.
Spilsbury, Louise. How Bees Make Honey. 2011. (Big Picture: Food Ser.). (ENG.). 24p. (gr. 1-2). pap. 41.70 *(978-1-4296-6728-9(1)*, First Facts) Capstone Press of Coughlan Cos.
Starosta, Paul. The Bee: Friend of the Flowers. 2005. (Animal Close-Ups Ser.). (Illus.). 28p. (J). (gr. -1-3). per. 6.95 *(978-1-57091-629-8(2))* Charlesbridge Publishing, Inc.
Stewart, Melissa. How Do Bees Make Honey? 2008. (Tell Me Why, Tell Me How Ser.). (Illus.). 32p. (gr. 3-18). lib. bdg. 29.93 *(978-0-7614-2923-4(9)*, Benchmark Bks.) Marshall Cavendish Corp.
—Zoom in on Bees. 2014. (Zoom in on Insects! Ser.). 24p. (J). 22.60 *(978-0-7660-4210-0(3))*; (ENG.). pap. 7.95 *(978-1-4644-0363-7(5)*, Enslow Elementary) Enslow Pubs., Inc.
Stone, Omar. Bumblebees. 2016. (Dig Deep! Bugs That Live Underground Ser.). 24p. (J). (gr. 3-3). pap. 8.25 *(978-1-4994-2046-3(3)*, PowerKids Pr.) Rosen Publishing Group, Inc., The.
Sullivan, Martha. If You Love Honey. Morrison, Cathy, illus. 2015. (ENG.). 32p. (J). (gr. k-4). 16.95 *(978-1-58469-533-2(1))* Dawn Pubns.
Sundance/Newbridge LLC Staff. Busy As a Bee. 2007. (Early Science Ser.). (gr. k-3). 18.95 *(978-1-4007-6594-2(3))*; pap. 6.10 *(978-1-4007-6590-4(0))* Sundance/Newbridge Educational Publishing.
Szymanski, Jennifer. Buzz, Bee! 2017. (Readers Ser.). (ENG., Illus.). 24p. (J). (-k). pap. 3.99 *(978-1-4263-2780-3(3)*, National Geographic Children's Bks.) National Geographic Society.
Tagliaferro, Linda. Bees & Their Hives [Scholastic]. 2010. (Animal Homes Ser.). 24p. pap. 0.49 *(978-1-4296-5797-6(9)*, Pebble Plus) Capstone Press of Coughlan Cos.
Thomson, Ruth. A Bee's Life Cycle. 2010. (Let's Look at Life Cycles Ser.). 24p. (J). (ENG.). pap. 8.25 *(978-1-61532-220-6(5)*, PowerKids Pr.); lib. bdg., E-Book 42.50 *(978-1-4488-0354-5(3))*; (Illus.). lib. bdg. 22.60 *(978-1-61532-216-9(7)*, PowerKids Pr.) Rosen Publishing Group, Inc., The.
—The Life Cycle of a Honeybee. 2007. (Learning about Life Cycles Ser.). (Illus.). 24p. (J). (gr. 4-7). lib. bdg. 22.60 *(978-1-4042-3713-1(5)*, PowerKids Pr.) Rosen Publishing Group, Inc., The.
Time for Kids Editors. Bees! 2005. (Time for Kids Ser.). (ENG., Illus.). 32p. (J). (gr. 1-3). pap. 3.99 *(978-0-06-057642-4(1))* HarperCollins Pubs.
Tourville, Amanda Doering. Buzzing Bees: Discovering Odd Numbers, 1 vol. Holm, Sharon Lane, illus. 2008. (Count the Critters Ser.). (ENG.). 24p. (J). (gr. k-3). 27.07 *(978-1-60270-262-2(4))* Magic Wagon.
Troupe, Thomas Kingsley. Do Bees Poop? Learning about Living & Nonliving Things with the Garbage Gang, 1 vol. Toye, Derek, illus. 2014. (Garbage Gang's Super Science Questions Ser.). (ENG.). 24p. (gr. k-2). lib. bdg. 26.65 *(978-1-4795-5477-5(4))* Picture Window Bks.
Van Dyck, Sara. Bumblebees. 2005. (Early Bird Nature Bks.). (ENG., Illus.). 48p. (gr. 2-5). lib. bdg. 26.60 *(978-0-8225-2498-4(8))* Lerner Publishing Group.
Watts, Barrie. Bee. 2004. (Watch It Grow Ser.). (J). (gr. k-3). lib. bdg. 27.10 *(978-1-58340-502-4(X))* Black Rabbit Bks.
Weber, Valerie J. Por Qué Algunos Animales Viven en Colmenas. 2008. (Donde viven los animales (Where Animals Live) Ser.). (SPA.). 24p. (gr. 1-4). pap. 8.15 *(978-0-8368-8816-4(2)*, Weekly Reader Leveled Readers) Stevens, Gareth Publishing LLLP.
—Por Que Algunos Animales Viven en Colmenas. 2008. (Donde viven los animales (Where Animals Live) Ser.). (SPA., Illus.). 24p. (gr. 1-4). lib. bdg. 22.00 *(978-0-8368-8809-6(X)*, Weekly Reader Leveled Readers) Stevens, Gareth Publishing LLLP.
—Why Animals Live in Hives. 2008. (Where Animals Live Ser.). 24p. (gr. 1-4). pap. 8.15 *(978-0-8368-8802-7(2))*; (Illus.). lib. bdg. 22.00 *(978-0-8368-8795-2(6))* Stevens, Gareth Publishing LLLP. (Weekly Reader Leveled Readers).
Wilcox, Merrie-Ellen. What's the Buzz? Keeping Bees in Flight, 1 vol. 2015. (Orca Footprints Ser.). (ENG., Illus.). 48p. (J). (gr. 3-7). 19.95 *(978-1-4598-0960-4(2))* Orca Bk. Pubs. USA.
Wilson, CeCe. Bees, Bees, Bees. 2015. (Rosen REAL Readers: STEM & STEAM Collection). (ENG.). 12p. (gr. 1-2). pap. 6.33 *(978-1-4994-9747-2(4)*, Rosen Classroom) Rosen Publishing Group, Inc., The.
Wimmer, Teresa. Bees. 2006. (My First Look at Insects Ser.). (Illus.). 24p. (J). (gr. k-2). lib. bdg. 15.95 *(978-1-58341-454-5(1)*, Creative Education) Creative Co., The.
Woodward, John. Bee. 2010. (Garden Minibeasts up Close Ser.). 32p. (gr. 2-4). 30.00 *(978-1-60413-901-3(3)*, Chelsea Clubhouse) Facts On File, Inc.
Woolf, Alex. You Wouldn't Want to Live Without Bees! 2016. (You Wouldn't Want to Live Without Ser.). lib. bdg. 20.80 *(978-0-606-38715-6(3))* Turtleback Bks.
Worthington, Niles. A Bee's Nest. 2016. (Animal Builders Ser.). 24p. (J). pap. 8.22 *(978-1-5026-2082-8(0))* Cavendish Square Publishing.

BEES—FICTION

Adepetun, Simon. The Bee Hive. 2016. (ENG.). 179p. (J). pap. 11.95 *(978-1-78612-220-9(0)*, f5677bc3-6033-4a3a-8542-87c2c4d9ff4d) Austin, Stan AUS. Dist: Bookmasters Distribution.
Al-Ghani, K. I. Bertie Bumble Bee: Troubled by the Letter "B", 1 vol. Al-Ghani, Haitham, illus. 2012. (ENG.). 44p. (J). 16.99 *(978-0-7643-3993-6(1)*, 9780764339936) Schiffer Publishing, Ltd.
Alemayehu, Tsehay. Bee-Come! A Collection of Short Stories. 2012. 58p. pap. 20.95 *(978-1-4525-4816-6(1))* Balboa Pr.
Alexander, Heather. Junior Groovies - Bugs! 2010. (ENG., Illus.). 10p. (J). (gr. -1-1). 15.99 *(978-1-60169-019-7(3))* Innovative Kids.
Anthony, Rachel. The Magic Bee. 2010. 32p. pap. 13.99 *(978-1-4490-8054-9(5))* AuthorHouse.
Appleton-Smith, Laura. Queen Bee Needs to Be Free. Neel, Preston, illus. 2005. (Book to Remember Ser.). (ENG.). 35p. pap. 8.95 *(978-1-929262-43-4(4)*, Books To Remember) Flyleaf Publishing.
Armstrong, Gregory D. The Day Buddy Flew. 2013. 42p. (J). 21.99 *(978-0-578-12191-8(3))* Armstrong, Greg.
—Don't Laugh at Me. 2013. 32p. 21.99 *(978-0-578-12368-4(1))* Armstrong, Greg.
The Baker Street Bunch & the Missing Honeybees Mystery. 2005. (J). per. *(978-0-9754241-5-5(7))* MiMar Publishing.
Banner, Angela. Ant & Bee. 2014. (Ant & Bee Ser.: 1). (ENG., Illus.). 112p. (Orig.). (J). (gr. -1-k). 7.99 *(978-1-4052-6671-0(6))* Egmont Bks., Ltd. GBR. Dist: Independent Pubs. Group.
—Ant & Bee & Kind Dog. 2014. (Ant & Bee Ser.). (ENG., Illus.). 112p. (J). (gr. -1-k). 7.99 *(978-1-4052-7075-5(6))* Egmont Bks., Ltd. GBR. Dist: Independent Pubs. Group.
—Ant & Bee & the ABC. 2014. (Ant & Bee Ser.). (ENG., Illus.). 96p. (J). (gr. -1-k). 7.99 *(978-1-4052-7074-8(8))* Egmont Bks., Ltd. GBR. Dist: Independent Pubs. Group.
—Ant & Bee & the Doctor. 2014. (Ant & Bee Ser.). (ENG., Illus.). 88p. (J). (gr. -1-k). 7.99 *(978-1-4052-7073-1(X))* Egmont Bks., Ltd. GBR. Dist: Independent Pubs. Group.
—Ant & Bee & the Rainbow. 2014. (Ant & Bee Ser.). (ENG., Illus.). 96p. (J). (gr. -1-k). 7.99 *(978-1-4052-6674-1(0))* Egmont Bks., Ltd. GBR. Dist: Independent Pubs. Group.
—Ant & Bee Count 123. 2015. (Ant & Bee Ser.). (ENG., Illus.). 96p. (J). (gr. -1-k). 7.99 *(978-1-4052-7513-2(8))* Egmont Bks., Ltd. GBR. Dist: Independent Pubs. Group.
—Ant & Bee Go Shopping. 2015. (Ant & Bee Ser.). (ENG., Illus.). 84p. (J). (gr. -1-k). 7.99 *(978-1-4052-7514-9(6))* Egmont Bks., Ltd. GBR. Dist: Independent Pubs. Group.
—Ant & Bee Time. 2015. (Ant & Bee Ser.). (ENG., Illus.). 96p. (J). (gr. -1-k). 7.99 *(978-1-4052-7516-3(2))* Egmont Bks., Ltd. GBR. Dist: Independent Pubs. Group.
—Around the World with Ant & Bee. 2014. (Ant & Bee Ser.). (ENG., Illus.). 96p. (J). (gr. -1-k). 7.99 *(978-1-4052-6676-5(7))* Egmont Bks., Ltd. GBR. Dist: Independent Pubs. Group.
—Happy Birthday with Ant & Bee. 2014. (Ant & Bee Ser.). (ENG., Illus.). 96p. (J). (gr. -1-k). 7.99 *(978-1-4052-6675-8(9))* Egmont Bks., Ltd. GBR. Dist: Independent Pubs. Group.
—More & More Ant & Bee. 2014. (Ant & Bee Ser.: 3). (ENG., Illus.). 112p. (J). (gr. -1-k). 7.99 *(978-1-4052-6673-4(2))* Egmont Bks., Ltd. GBR. Dist: Independent Pubs. Group.
—More Ant & Bee. 2014. (Ant & Bee Ser.: 2). (ENG., Illus.). 112p. (J). (gr. -1-k). 7.99 *(978-1-4052-6672-7(4))* Egmont Bks., Ltd. GBR. Dist: Independent Pubs. Group.
Barcita, Pamela, illus. Ruby Lee the Bumble Bee Promotional Coloring Book. 2005. 16p. (J). 4.95 *(978-0-9754342-3-9(3))* Bumble Bee Publishing.
Basha, Irena Canaj. The Birthday Party, It Was Saturday... 2013. 16p. pap. 24.95 *(978-1-62709-182-4(3))* America Star Bks.
Bea's Own Good: Evaluation Guide. 2006. (J). *(978-1-55942-401-1(X))* Witcher Productions.
Beatty, Susi. Angie the Ant & the Bumblebee Tree. 2006. (Illus.). 30p. (J). 19.95 *(978-0-9773653-0-2(1))* Susi B. Marketing, Inc.
Belavilas, Charlotte. Walter, the Carpenter Bee. 2007. pap. 9.00 *(978-0-8059-8504-7(2))* Dorrance Publishing Co., Inc.
Bell, Cece. Bee-Wigged. Bell, Cece, illus. 2017. (ENG., Illus.). 40p. (J). (gr. -1-3). 6.99 *(978-0-7636-9312-1(X))* Candlewick Pr.
Bellisario, Gina. Queen of the Spelling Bee. Von Innerebner, Jessika, illus. 2016. (Ellie Ultra Ser.). (ENG.). 128p. (gr. 2-3). lib. bdg. 25.99 *(978-1-4965-3141-4(8))* Stone Arch Bks.
Bergen, Lara. Buzzy Bee Plays Hide & Seek. 2010. 12p. (J). (gr. -1). 9.95 *(978-1-60747-720-4(3)*, Pickwick Pr.) Phoenix Bks., Inc.
Berner, Beth E. & Riggs, Jenna. Follow That Bee. 2006. (ENG., Illus.). 10p. (J). (gr. -1-k). bds. 9.95 *(978-1-58117-447-2(0)*, Intervisual/Piggy Toes) Bendon, Inc.
Blakemore, Megan Frazer. The Friendship Riddle. (ENG.). 2016. 384p. (J). pap. 7.99 *(978-1-68119-019-8(2)*, 9781681190198) 2015. 368p. (YA). (gr. 3-6). 16.99 *(978-1-61963-630-9(1)*, 9781619636309) Bloomsbury Publishing USA. (Bloomsbury USA Childrens).
Bland, Nick. The Very Hungry Bear. 2013. (Illus.). (J). pap. ***(978-0-545-52290-8(0))*** Scholastic, Inc.
Bloom, C. P. The Monkey & the Bee. Raymundo, Peter, illus. 2015. (Monkey Goes Bananas Ser.). (ENG.). 40p. (J). (gr. -1-2). 14.95 *(978-1-4197-0886-2(4)*, Abrams Bks. for Young Readers) Abrams, Inc.
Bonnell, Kris. A Flower for a Bee. 2006. (J). pap. 3.95 *(978-1-933727-23-3(3))* Reading Reading Bks., LLC.
Boynton, Cara. Sam's Secret World. 2006. (ENG.). 48p. per. 16.95 *(978-1-4241-4529-4(5))* PublishAmerica, Inc.
Bradley, Timothy. Hive Mind, Bk. 1. rev. ed. 2013. (Sci Hi Ser.). (ENG., Illus.). 152p. (J). (gr. 3-6). lib. bdg. 26.96 *(978-1-4807-2612-3(5))* Teacher Created Materials, Inc.
Brandt-Taylor, Diane. The Bunny, the Bear, the Bug & the Bee. Brandt, Michael, illus. 2005. (J). cd-rom 9.88 *(978-0-9773236-0-9(9))* TaySysCo Publishing.
Brennan-Nelson, Denise. Buzzy the Bumblebee. Monroe, Michael Glenn, illus. 2003. (ENG.). 32p. (J). (gr. k-6). pap. 6.95 *(978-1-58536-166-3(6))* Sleeping Bear Pr.

A
B

Brightwood, Laura. Bee Is for Bold. Pifer, Kimberly, ed. Brightwood, Laura, illus. 2012. (Illus.). (J). *(978-1-934409-40-4(5))* 3-C Institute for Social Development.

—Buzz off, Bee! Pifer, Kimberly, ed. Brightwood, Laura, illus. 2012. (Illus.). (J). *(978-1-934409-45-9(6))* 3-C Institute for Social Development.

Brooks, Donna. The Golden Spindle. 2010. 112p. pap. 30.00 *(978-1-60860-852-2(2),* Eloquent Bks.) Strategic Book Publishing & Rights Agency (SBPRA).

—The Magic Amphor. 2009. 100p. pap. 30.00 *(978-1-60693-027-4(3),* Eloquent Bks.) Strategic Book Publishing & Rights Agency (SBPRA).

Brooks, Walt. Walter's Pet Bee. 2011. 36p. pap. 16.86 *(978-1-4634-4919-3(4))* AuthorHouse.

Brosnan, Paris. Billy Bee - Sugarplums & Honey. 2017. (ENG., Illus.). 27p. (J). pap. 13.95 ***(978-1-78710-075-6(8),*** 4d1efa56-0d47-487a-bc8e-b11fdf88ec5d) Austin, Stan AUS. Dist: Bookmasters Distribution.

Brown, J. A. Busy Bee. Knight, Paula, illus. 2003. (Funny Faces Ser.). 10p. (J). bds. 3.95 *(978-1-58925-715-3(4))* Tiger Tales.

Buchmann, Stephen & Cohn, Diana. The Bee Tree. 2012. (ENG., Illus.). 40p. (J). (gr. 1-6). pap. 8.95 *(978-1-935955-14-6(4))* Cinco Puntos Pr.

Buckbee, Johnny. The Adventures of Bumble Bee. 2010. 24p. pap. 12.99 *(978-1-4490-6935-3(5))* AuthorHouse.

Burslem, Diana & Freeman, Diana. Bee Alarm! Webb, Philip, illus. 2013. (ENG.). 24p. (gr. 3-3). pap. *(978-1-77654-020-4(4),* Red Rocket Readers) Flying Start Bks.

Burton M.Sc., Kathryn Mac. Diarmid. Haley Honeybee: Finds the Magic Rose. Cox, Glendyne Dewhurst, illus. 2013. 50p. pap. *(978-0-9917941-0-2(9))* Burton, K. Publishing.

Cain, Janan. Roonie B. Moonie: Lost & Alone. 2007. (Illus.). 32p. (J). (gr. -1-3). 15.95 *(978-0-9740190-8-6(9))* Illumination Arts Publishing Co., Inc.

Callen, Sharon. My Life as a Bee, 1 vol. rev. ed. 2013. (Fiction Readers Ser.). (ENG., Illus.). 20p. (J). (gr. 1-1). pap. 4.99 *(978-1-4333-5483-0(7));* pap. 15.96 *(978-1-4807-1139-6(X))* Shell Educational Publishing.

Cammuso, Frank. The Misadventures of Salem Hyde: Spelling Trouble. 2013. (Misadventures of Salem Hyde Ser.: 1). (J). lib. bdg. 17.15 *(978-0-606-33440-2(8),* Turtleback) Turtleback Bks.

Carter, David A. Bugs at the Beach. Carter, David A., illus. 2016. (David Carter's Bugs Ser.). (ENG., Illus.). 24p. (J). (gr. -1-1). pap. 3.99 *(978-1-4814-4050-9(0),* Simon Spotlight) Simon Spotlight.

—Busy Bug Builds a Fort. Carter, David A., illus. 2016. (David Carter's Bugs Ser.). (ENG., Illus.). 24p. (J). (gr. -1-1). pap. 3.99 *(978-1-4814-4047-9(0),* Simon Spotlight) Simon Spotlight.

—A Snowy Day in Bugland! Carter, David A., illus. 2012. (David Carter's Bugs Ser.). (ENG., Illus.). 24p. (J). (gr. -1-1). 15.99 *(978-1-4424-3895-8(9));* pap. 3.99 *(978-1-4424-3894-1(0))* Simon Spotlight. (Simon Spotlight).

Ceballos, Jacalyn Martin. Little Bee the Size of a Pe. O'Connor, Marcy & O'Connor, Bailey, illus. 2011. 28p. pap. 24.95 *(978-1-4626-3005-9(7))* America Star Bks.

Cecil, Randy. Horsefly & Honeybee. Cecil, Randy, illus. 2012. (ENG., Illus.). 32p. (J). (gr. -1-3). 16.99 *(978-0-8050-9300-1(1),* 9780805093001, Holt, Henry & Co. Bks. For Young Readers) Holt, Henry & Co.

Cervantes, Gerard. Hilda Bee's Special Home. 2012. 48p. pap. 17.45 *(978-1-4497-3140-3(6),* WestBow Pr.) Author Solutions, Inc.

Chenette, Roseanne V. Shellaby Willowbee. 2008. 13p. pap. 24.95 *(978-1-60672-137-7(2))* America Star Bks.

Cheng, Andrea. When the Bees Fly Home, 1 vol. McFadden, Joline, illus. 2005. (ENG.). 32p. (J). (gr. 3-6). 16.95 *(978-0-88448-238-3(3))* Tilbury Hse. Pubs.

Chronicle Books Staff & ImageBooks Staff. Little Bee. van der Put, Klaartje, illus. 2006. (Little Finger Puppet Board Bks.: FING). (ENG.). 12p. (J). (gr. -1-7). bds. 6.99 *(978-0-8118-5236-4(9))* Chronicle Bks. LLC.

Cleveland, Nicole K. Ode to a Fly. 2007. 56p. per. 16.95 *(978-1-4241-7977-0(7))* America Star Bks.

Coccia, Mina. Mother Nature & Mz Bee. 2012. 36p. pap. 14.95 *(978-1-4575-0709-0(9))* Dog Ear Publishing, LLC.

Cohn, Diana & Buchmann, Stephen. The Bee Tree. Mirocha, Paul, illus. 2007. (ENG.). 40p. (J). (gr. 4-6). 17.95 *(978-0-938317-98-2(9))* Cinco Puntos Pr.

Coulton, Mia. Danny's Rocket. Coulton, Mia, photos by. 2009. (ENG., Illus.). pap. 5.35 *(978-1-933624-40-2(X))* Maryruth Bks., Inc.

Craft, James, illus. Five Little Honeybees. 2009. (ENG.). 12p. 5.95 *(978-1-58117-907-1(3),* Intervisual/Piggy Toes) Bendon, Inc.

Crawford, Tracie. Bart the Blue Bee. 2012. 40p. pap. 19.57 *(978-1-4669-4026-0(3))* Trafford Publishing.

Crownberry, Ethan. Bobby Bumble's Afraid to Fly. 2012. 92p. pap. 8.95 *(978-1-300-00801-9(6))* Lulu Pr., Inc.

Cueva, Susana & Shibaja, Calixto. Lita the Hardworking Worm/Lita la Trabajadora. 2012. (ENG & SPA.). 26p. pap. 9.99 *(978-0-9883927-1-7(2))* Carsume.

Dalton, Matthew. The Next Steve Erwin, 1 vol. Cavanaugh, Stacy, illus. 2009. 16p. pap. 24.95 *(978-1-60836-635-4(9))* America Star Bks.

Davies, Rocky. Harvey Happy Bee. 2005. (Bee Attitude Board Books). (Illus.). (J). *(978-1-59156-775-2(0))* Covenant Communications.

Davis, Danielle. Zinnia & the Bees. Horton, Laura K., illus. 2017. (Middle-Grade Novels Ser.). (ENG.). 240p. (gr. 4-7). lib. bdg. 26.65 ***(978-1-4965-4661-6(X))*** Stone Arch Bks.

Davis, Michael Dale. Bumperly Bumper Bee. 2007. (Illus.). 20p. (J). 15.95 *(978-0-9791785-0-4(9))* Luna Publishing.

de Vries, Maggie. Big City Bees, 1 vol. Benoit, Renné, illus. 2013. (ENG.). 48p. (J). (gr. k-3). 17.95 *(978-1-55365-906-8(6))* Greystone Books Ltd. CAN. Dist: Publishers Group West (PGW).

DeLand, M. Maitland. Busy Bees at Work & Play. 2010. (Illus.). 32p. (J). 14.95 *(978-1-60832-028-8(6),* Greenleaf Book Group Pr.) Greenleaf Book Group.

—Busy Bees on Broadway. Martin, Lyn, illus. 2011. 32p. 15.95 *(978-1-60832-063-9(4))* Greenleaf Book Group.

El diario de mis Abejas: Individual Title, 6 packs. (Literatura 2000 Ser.). (SPA.). (gr. 2-3). 33.00 *(978-0-7635-1647-5(3))* Rigby Education.

Dicello, Bob. Juni B. Small, Jan, illus. 2013. 36p. 25.95 *(978-1-61493-157-7(7))* Peppertree Pr., The.

Domogala, Sophia Z. Buzzin' with Kindness. 2012. 24p. pap. 15.99 *(978-1-4797-5023-8(9))* Xlibris Corp.

Donovan, Kyle, Sr. CurBee Races the NasBee 500: The Do'Bees. 2008. (Illus.). 28p. (J). pap. 9.99 *(978-0-9767670-5-3(8))* WannaBees Media LLC.

Donovan, Kyle. HoniBee Loses Her Voice: The Do'Bees. 2007. (J). 15.95 net. *(978-0-9767670-3-9(1))* WannaBees Media LLC.

—Introducing the Do'Bees. 2008. (J). 15.95 net. *(978-0-9767670-1-5(5))* WannaBees Media LLC.

Donovan, Kyle, Sr. Introducing the Do'Bees: The Do'Bees. 2008. (Illus.). 28p. (J). pap. 9.99 *(978-0-9767670-6-0(6))* WannaBees Media LLC.

Doty, Sara. You Are Special Little Bee. Dawley, Sarah, illus. 2009. 16p. pap. 10.99 *(978-1-4389-7040-0(4))* AuthorHouse.

Dyan, Penelope. Mikey & Me & the Bees, the Continuing Story of a Girl & Her Dog. Dyan, Penelope, illus. 2010. (Illus.). 48p. pap. 14.95 *(978-1-935118-90-9(0))* Bellissima Publishing, LLC.

—Olympic Gold — Because Everyone Loves a Winner! Dyan, Penelope, illus. 2008. (Illus.). 44p. pap. 11.95 *(978-1-935118-20-6(X))* Bellissima Publishing, LLC.

Dyas, Mecca. Busy Bee Who Me? 2012. (ENG.). (J). pap. *(978-1-4675-3874-9(4))* Independent Pub.

Edwards, Jamee-Marie. But I Am a Cat! 2013. 44p. pap. 20.00 *(978-1-4772-8231-1(9))* AuthorHouse.

Elise, Christy. Beez Take Flight. 2012. 56p. pap. 24.99 *(978-1-4685-6265-1(7))* AuthorHouse.

Esberger, Trudi. The Boy Who Lost His Bumble. Esberger, Trudi, illus. 2015. (Child's Play Library). (ENG., Illus.). 32p. (J). *(978-1-84643-662-8(1))* Child's Play International Ltd.

Fairchild, Simone. Queen Bee's Midnight Caper, 3 vols. Key, Pamela Marie, illus. 2006. 33p. (J). (gr. -1-3). per. 17.95 *(978-0-9771971-4-9(X))* Brass Frog Bookworks.

Farahay, Michael L. The Butterfly, The Bee & The Spider. Farahay, Naomi E., ed. 2007. 80p. pap. 36.95 *(978-1-4303-2623-6(9))* Lulu Pr., Inc.

Feldman, Karen. Glorious Wings. 2011. 36p. pap. 24.95 *(978-1-4560-8352-6(X))* America Star Bks.

Ferry, Ann. Dollop the Cloud & Dee the Bee. Swope, Brenda, illus. 2012. 28p. pap. 24.95 *(978-1-4626-7433-6(X))* America Star Bks.

Fogwill, Joyce Graham. Bubs the Bumblebee & Her Most Unfortunate Fortunate Adventure. 2009. 24p. pap. 12.99 *(978-1-4490-5042-9(5))* AuthorHouse.

—Bubs the Bumblebee & the Spider's Web. 2012. (ENG.). 24p. (J). pap. 12.95 *(978-1-4327-9586-3(4))* Outskirts Pr., Inc.

Follett, Ross C. Beebear 2. Sievers, Lee, illus. 2013. (ENG.). 52p. (J). (gr. -1-3). 15.95 *(978-0-9881748-0-1(4),* Oddlnt Media) Greenwood Hill Pr.

Ford, Ron. Buzz Gets Lost. 2006. (Neighborhood Readers Ser.). (ENG.). 16p. (gr. 1-3). pap. 6.50 *(978-1-4042-7014-5(0),* Rosen Classroom) Rosen Publishing Group, Inc., The.

Formento, Alison. These Bees Count! Snow, Sarah, illus. 2012. (These Things Count! Ser.). (ENG.). 32p. (J). (gr. -1-3). 16.99 *(978-0-8075-7868-1(1))* Whitman, Albert & Co.

Francis-Bala, Sundari. Olly Jolly Says - Count Your Blessings. 2012. 32p. pap. *(978-1-77097-466-1(0))* FriesenPress.

Friday, Kisha. Three Fuzzy Little Bees. 2012. 34p. 24.95 *(978-1-4626-4735-4(9))* America Star Bks.

Galjanic, Lisa. When Bees Win. Hope, Michelle, illus. 2007. (J). 9.95 *(978-1-933532-04-2(1))* LSG Pubns.

—When Series 6 Volume Set, 6, 6. 2007. (Illus.). 100p. (J). 34.95 *(978-1-933532-06-6(8))* LSG Pubns.

Garza, Lois Ann. Lellie the Different Elephant. Martinez-Neal, Juana, illus. 2011. 36p. pap. 11.95 *(978-1-60047-592-4(2))* Wasteland Pr.

Gherasim, Gabriel & Gherasim, Louise. The Story of the Queen Bee & Children's Corner, 1 vol. 2010. 20p. pap. 24.95 *(978-1-4489-7140-4(3))* PublishAmerica, Inc.

Gibbon, Rebecca, illus. The Bee Who Spoke: The Wonderful World of Belle & the Bee. 2014. (ENG.). 32p. (J). (gr. k-2). 14.95 *(978-0-500-65027-1(6),* 565027) Thames & Hudson.

Giordano, Paula J. The Honey Bees Going to a New School. 2012. 30p. 29.99 *(978-1-61996-501-0(1));* pap. 19.99 *(978-1-61996-500-3(3))* Salem Author Services.

Glaeser, Patricia Heinz. A New Day for Foal. 2007. 40p. per. 24.95 *(978-1-4241-8342-5(1))* America Star Bks.

Goodrich, C. C. Barnabee: At the Picnic. 2009. (Illus.). 32p. pap. 13.99 *(978-1-4389-8388-2(3))* AuthorHouse.

—Barnabee: Goes Shopping. 2009. (Illus.). 32p. pap. 13.99 *(978-1-4389-9728-5(0))* AuthorHouse.

—Barnabee: Goes to Work. 2009. (Illus.). 32p. pap. 13.99 *(978-1-4389-8461-2(8))* AuthorHouse.

—Barnabee: In the Beehive. 2009. (Illus.). 24p. pap. 12.99 *(978-1-4389-7560-3(0))* AuthorHouse.

—Barnabee: In the Meadow. 2009. (Illus.). 32p. pap. 12.99 *(978-1-4389-8389-9(1))* AuthorHouse.

—Barnabee: Meets New Friends. 2009. (Illus.). 24p. pap. 12.99 *(978-1-4389-8390-5(5))* AuthorHouse.

Gray, Hetty. A Bee on Your Face! 2004. (Illus.). (J). *(978-0-9712571-3-9(2))* Sugar Creek Publishing.

Groves. Bee & the Sea, Bk. 9. Date not set. (Illus.). 32p. (J). pap. 129.15 *(978-0-582-18770-2(2))* Addison-Wesley Longman, Ltd. GBR. Dist: Trans-Atlantic Pubns., Inc.

Gudino Kieffer, E. Giraluna (Moonflower) (J). 22.50 *(978-950-04-1280-3(2))* Emecé Editores S.A. ARG. Dist: AIMS International Bks., Inc.

Gummelt, Donna & Melchiorre, Dondino. Don't Get My Honey.... HONEY. Wall, Randy Hugh, ed. Varela, Juan D., tr. Varela, Juan D., illus. 2006. (SPA.). 34p. (J). 14.95 *(978-0-9764798-5-7(0))* Story Store Collection Publishing.

Hansen, Roland. The Story of a Butterfly Called Bee. 2010. 32p. pap. 9.96 *(978-0-9843426-2-4(1))* G Publishing LLC.

Heinrich, Tyson. Where Is My Honey? 2012. 36p. pap. 15.95 *(978-1-4675-2641-8(X))* Heinrich, Tyson Chul.

Hendricks, Brenda K. What's Better Than That, Seren Dippity? Hendricks, Brenda K., illus. 2013. (Illus.). 32p. pap. 9.99 *(978-0-9826582-4-6(9))* Two Small Fish Pubns.

—What's the Buzz, Bumbly Bee? Hendricks, Brenda K., illus. 2013. (Illus.). 30p. pap. 9.99 *(978-0-9826582-3-9(0))* Two Small Fish Pubns.

Hive Enterprise Staff, contrib. by. Spring Bee. 2016. (Illus.). (J). ***(978-1-4844-7010-7(9),*** Grosset & Dunlap) Penguin Publishing Group.

Hofmeister, Alan, et al. The Bee. (Reading for All Learners Ser.). (Illus.). (J). pap. *(978-1-56861-124-2(2))* Swift Learning Resources.

Horowitz, Ruth. Are We Still Friends? Gomez, Blanca, illus. 2017. (ENG.). 40p. (J). (gr. -1-3). 16.99 *(978-0-545-64521-8(2),* Scholastic Pr.) Scholastic, Inc.

Hurth, Barbi. The Butterfly & the Bee. Meyer, Chloe, illus. 2008. 32p. pap. 24.95 *(978-1-60610-226-8(5))* America Star Bks.

Hutchinson, Wanda Phillips. The Bee Man. 2009. 24p. pap. 14.49 *(978-1-4490-3596-9(5))* AuthorHouse.

Inches, Alison. Diego's Buzzing Bee Adventure. Zalme, Ron, illus. 2008. (Go, Diego, Go! Ser.: 7). (ENG.). 24p. (J). (gr. -1-1). pap. 3.99 *(978-1-4169-4776-9(0),* Simon Spotlight/Nickelodeon) Simon Spotlight/Nickelodeon.

Introducing the WanaBees (not Published) 2005. (J). 15.95 *(978-0-9767670-0-8(7))* WannaBees Media LLC.

Jackson, Dessi. The Saint & His Bees. Brandenburg, Claire, illus. 2013. 28p. pap. 9.99 *(978-1-62395-487-1(8))* Xist Publishing.

Jacobs, John. I Wanna Be. 2006. (Illus.). 144p. 9.95 *(978-0-9774659-6-5(9))* Cameo Pubns., LLC.

Jay, Alison. Bee & Me. Jay, Alison, illus. 2017. (ENG., Illus.). 32p. (J). (-k). 15.99 *(978-0-7636-9010-6(4))* Candlewick Pr.

Joven, C. C. Baseball Buzz. Shems, Ed, illus. 2017. (Sports Illustrated Kids Starting Line Readers Ser.). (ENG.). 32p. (gr. -1-1). pap. 3.95 *(978-1-4965-4259-5(2))* Capstone Press of Coughlan Cos.

Kelley, Gerald. Please Please the Bees. Kelley, Gerald, illus. 2017. (ENG., Illus.). 32p. (J). (gr. -1-3). 16.99 ***(978-0-8075-5183-7(X))*** Whitman, Albert & Co.

Kelly, Mij. I Hate Everyone. Palmer, Ruth, illus. 2003. 32p. (YA). *(978-1-85602-362-7(1),* Pavilion Children's Books) Pavilion Bks.

Kessler, Cristina. The Best Beekeeper of Lalibela: A Tale from Africa. Jenkins, Leonard, illus. 2006. (ENG.). 32p. (J). (gr. -1-3). 16.95 *(978-0-8234-1858-9(8))* Holiday Hse., Inc.

Kiernan, Tim. Liams Luck & Finnegans Fortune. 2009. (ENG.). 144p. pap. 10.95 *(978-1-933916-48-4(6),* Ferne Pr.) Nelson Publishing & Marketing.

Kline, Trish & Donev, Mary. Where Can Lost Bee Be? KA Reader 6. 2007. (Illus.). 32p. (J). per. 20.00 *(978-0-9717234-9-8(4))* Ghost Hunter Productions.

Koontz, Robin. Run... It's a Bee! Koontz, Robin, illus. 2012. (ENG., Illus.). 24p. (gr. 2-3). pap. 8.95 *(978-1-61810-333-8(4))* Rourke Educational Media.

Krebs, Laurie & Cis, Valeria. The Beeman. Cis, Valeria, illus. 2008. (ENG., Illus.). 40p. (J). (gr. -1-3). 16.99 *(978-1-84686-146-8(2))* Barefoot Bks., Inc.

Krings, Antoon. Mireille L Abeille. (FRE.). pap. 18.95 *(978-2-07-058440-6(2))* Gallimard, Editions FRA. Dist: Distribooks, Inc.

Krulik, Nancy. Attack of the Tighty Whities! Blecha, Aaron, illus. 2012. (George Brown, Class Clown Ser.: 7). (ENG.). 128p. (J). (gr. 2-4). pap. 4.99 *(978-0-448-45575-4(7),* Grosset & Dunlap) Penguin Young Readers Group.

Lawson-Williams, BerNadette. Blossom Bee's Golf Adventures. 2008. 76p. pap. 24.95 *(978-1-4327-0874-0(0))* Outskirts Pr., Inc.

Lee, Lori K. Bonnie the Honeybee & the Case of the Butterfly Blues. 2011. (ENG., Illus.). 30p. (J). 12.95 *(978-0-9828689-6-6(0),* BQB Publishing) Boutique of Quality Books Publishing Co., Inc.

Leone, Dee. Bizz & Buzz Make Honey Buns. Maritie, illus. 2014. (Penguin Core Concepts Ser.). (ENG.). 32p. (J). (gr. -1-k). 3.99 *(978-0-448-47927-9(3),* Grosset & Dunlap) Penguin Young Readers Group.

Litchmore, Michael. The MB Force: Heroes at the Best! 2007. 56p. pap. 9.00 *(978-0-8059-7399-0(0))* Dorrance Publishing Co., Inc.

Litzenberger, Mona. Humble the Bumblebee. 2013. 24p. pap. 9.99 *(978-0-9894748-0-1(1))* Mindstir Media.

Lobel, Arnold. Sopa de Ratón. 2003. (SPA., Illus.). 62p. (gr. 1-3). pap. 10.99 *(978-980-257-286-1(1))* Ekare, Ediciones VEN. Dist: Lectorum Pubns., Inc.

Loveridge, Pamela. Buzzy Bee. 2012. 24p. pap. 28.03 *(978-1-4797-4802-0(1))* Xlibris Corp.

Lowvorn, Ann R. Chocolate Puddles. Reece, James A., illus. 2010. 36p. pap. 15.49 *(978-1-4520-5158-1(5))* AuthorHouse.

Lucado, Max & Schmidt, Troy. Buzby, the Misbehaving Bee. 2005. 32p. (J). pap. 3.99 *(978-1-4003-0666-4(3))* Nelson, Thomas Inc.

Luddy, Karon. Spelldown: The Big-Time Dreams of a Small-Town Word Whiz. 2008. (Mix Ser.). (ENG.). 224p. (J). (gr. 4-8). pap. 10.99 *(978-1-4169-5452-1(X),* Simon & Schuster/Paula Wiseman Bks.) Simon & Schuster/Paula Wiseman Bks.

Lurie, Craig. Butterflies, Ladybugs, & Bumble Bees & the wonderful world this could Be .... 2011. 36p. (gr. -1). pap. 14.95 *(978-1-4567-6300-8(8))* AuthorHouse.

Lyon, David. Flight of the Buzby Bee. Lyon, David, illus. 2005. (Illus.). 32p. (J). 16.95 *(978-0-9741328-0-8(2))* Lyon, Ernest Media Productions.

Mack, Jeff. Hippo & Rabbit in Brave Like Me. Mack, Jeff, illus. 2011. (Scholastic Reader Level 1 Ser.). (ENG., Illus.). 32p. (J). (gr. -1-2). pap. 3.99 *(978-0-545-28360-1(4),* Cartwheel Bks.) Scholastic, Inc.

MacKey, Esther L. Little Bear & Honey Bee. Mackey, Kaitlin L., illus. 2012. 28p. 14.95 *(978-1-937260-10-1(0))* Sleepytown Pr.

Matheson, Dawn. Ruby Lee the Bumble Bee: A Bee of Possibility. Barcita, Pamela, illus. 2006. 40p. (J). (gr. -1-3). lib. bdg. *(978-0-9754342-6-0(8))* Bumble Bee Publishing.

—Ruby Lee the Bumble Bee: A Bee's Bit of Wisdom. Barcita, Pamela, illus. 2005. 34p. (J). (gr. -1-3). 17.95 *(978-0-9754342-1-5(7))* Bumble Bee Publishing.

—Ruby Lee the Bumble Bee: A Bee's Bit of Wisdom. Cindy, Huffman, ed. Barcita, Pamela, illus. 2004. 40p. (J). 17.95 *(978-0-9754342-0-8(9))* Bumble Bee Publishing.

—Ruby Lee the Bumble Bee Critter Count Search & Find Game. Huffman, Cindy, ed. Barcita, Pamela, illus. 2005. 6p. (J). 4.95 *(978-0-9754342-4-6(1))* Bumble Bee Publishing.

McCreadie, Sandi. Thistle Fables. 2013. 64p. pap. 23.99 *(978-1-4808-0313-8(8))* Archway Publishing.

McCue, Gil. Buzzy the Honey Bee. 2009. 36p. pap. 14.95 *(978-1-4269-1933-6(6))* Trafford Publishing.

McDonald, Megan. Ant & Honey Bee: A Pair of Friends at Halloween. Karas, G. Brian, illus. 2013. (Candlewick Sparks Ser.). (ENG.). 48p. (J). (gr. k-4). pap. 3.99 *(978-0-7636-6864-8(8))* Candlewick Pr.

—Ant & Honey Bee: A Pair of Friends in Winter. Karas, G. Brian, illus. (Candlewick Sparks Ser.). (ENG.). 64p. (J). (gr. k-4). 2014. pap. 3.99 *(978-0-7636-6862-4(1))* 2013. 14.99 *(978-0-7636-5712-3(3))* Candlewick Pr.

McGuiness, Elle J. & Brown, Heather. Bee & Me: A Mini-Motion Book. 2010. (ENG., Illus.). 12p. (J). 9.99 *(978-0-7407-9362-2(4))* Andrews McMeel Publishing.

McGuinness, Elle J. Bee & Me. 2014. (ENG.). 14p. (J). (gr. -1-k). bds. 5.99 *(978-1-4494-4371-9(0))* Andrews McMeel Publishing.

—Bee & Me. Brown, Heather, illus. 2008. (ENG.). 28p. (J). (gr. -1). 16.99 *(978-0-7407-7734-9(3))* Andrews McMeel Publishing.

McKinley, Robin. Chalice. 2010. (ENG.). 288p. (YA). (gr. 7-18). 8.99 *(978-0-14-241720-1(3),* Firebird) Penguin Young Readers Group.

McMahan, Gregg. Christmas Honey. 2012. (ENG.). pap. 10.00 *(978-1-4675-5319-3(0))* Independent Pub.

McMahon, Bea Prior. The Queen & I. Green, Jackie Fourcade, illus. 2013. (ENG.). 54p. (YA). pap. 19.95 *(978-1-4327-4522-6(0))* Outskirts Pr., Inc.

McMahon, Bea Prior & Green, Jackie Fourcade. The Queen & I. 2013. (ENG.). 54p. (YA). 22.95 *(978-1-4787-1568-9(5))* Outskirts Pr., Inc.

McOmber, Rachel B., ed. McOmber Phonics Storybooks: Me & the Bee. rev. ed. (Illus.). (J). *(978-0-944991-46-6(7))* Swift Learning Resources.

Menard, James. The Bees & the Bears. Menard, John C., illus. 2008. 36p. pap. 16.99 *(978-1-4389-2150-1(0))* AuthorHouse.

Merchant, Eryn. My Little Bumblebee. 2013. 28p. pap. 24.95 *(978-1-63000-675-4(0))* America Star Bks.

Meyerhoff, Jenny. Sweet Peas & Honeybees. 2016. (Friendship Garden Ser.: 4). lib. bdg. 16.00 *(978-0-606-38978-5(4))* Turtleback Bks.

Milgrim, David. See Pip Point. Milgrim, David, illus. 2016. (Adventures of Otto Ser.). (ENG., Illus.). 32p. (J). (gr. -1-k). pap. 3.99 *(978-1-4814-6784-1(0),* Simon Spotlight) Simon Spotlight.

Miller, Liza. BusyBugz Adventures: Izzi Goes Missing. Bolton, Bill, illus. 2013. (BusyBugz Adventures Ser.). (ENG.). 16p. (J). (gr. -1). 12.95 *(978-1-60710-714-9(7),* Silver Dolphin Bks.) Readerlink Distribution Services, LLC.

Milligan, Joe. I Bee the Bee, 1 vol. Raymond, Alejandro, illus. 2016. (ENG.). 32p. (J). 9.95 *(978-1-4556-2201-6(X))* Pelican Publishing Co., Inc.

Millsap, Ella. A Portrait of a Church in Stone: The Keeper of the Honeybees. 2013. 62p. (J). pap. 12.00 *(978-0-9891960-3-1(8))* Professional Publishing Hse. LLC.

Morales, Melita. Jam & Honey. Bryant, Laura J., illus. 2011. (ENG.). 32p. (J). (gr. -1-2). 15.99 *(978-1-58246-299-8(2),* Tricycle Pr.) Random Hse. Children's Bks.

Morgan, Bernard. The Beekeeper. Emecz, Steve, ed. Parekh, Rikin, illus. 2007. 28p. per. *(978-1-904312-26-0(8))* MX Publishing, Ltd.

Morgan, Bernard P. Pszczelarz. Juraszek, Barbara, tr. Parekh, Rikin, illus. 2008. 28p. pap. *(978-1-904312-44-4(6))* MX Publishing, Ltd.

Murphy, Christine Faye. Nature Doesn't Scare Me Bees. 2011. 40p. pap. 24.95 *(978-1-4560-9966-4(3))* America Star Bks.

Nargi, Lela. The Honeybee Man. Brooker, Krysten, illus. 2011. (ENG.). 40p. (J). (gr. -1-3). 17.99 *(978-0-375-84980-0(7),* Schwartz & Wade Bks.) Random Hse. Children's Bks.

Niddrie, June. E. B. & the Bees. 2010. 32p. pap. 16.10 *(978-0-557-31873-5(4))* Lulu Pr., Inc.

Oelschlager, Vanita. Let Me Bee. Blackwood, Kristin, illus. 2008. (ENG.). 42p. (J). (gr. -1-3). 17.95 *(978-0-9800162-1-5(5))* VanitaBooks.

Ofanansky, Allison. What's the Buzz? Honey for a Sweet New Year. Alpern, Eliyahu, photos by. 2014. (ENG., Illus.). 32p. (J). (gr. -1-5). 8.95 *(978-1-4677-5706-5(3),* Kar-Ben Publishing) Lerner Publishing Group.

—What's the Buzz? Honey for a Sweet New Year. Alpern, Eliyahu, illus. Alpern, Eliyahu, photos by. 2011. (High Holidays Ser.). (J). (gr. -1-k). lib. bdg. 15.95 *(978-0-7613-5640-0(1))* Lerner Publishing Group.

Palmer, Barbara E. Recoverbee Says Learn with Me. 2011. 28p. pap. 24.95 *(978-1-4560-4983-6(6))* America Star Bks.

Pando, Nancy J. I Don't Want to Go to School: Helping Children Cope with Separation Anxiety. Voerg, Kathy, illus. 2005. (Let's Talk Ser.). (ENG.). 48p. (J). (gr. -1-1). per. 9.95 *(978-0-88282-254-9(3))* New Horizon Pr. Pubs., Inc.

Parker, Emma & Renaud, Marguerite. The Honey Bee Race. 2010. (Illus.). 16p. pap. *(978-1-877561-78-8(9))* First Edition Ltd.

Payne, C. C. Something to Sing About. 2008. (ENG.). 167p. (J). (gr. 4-7). pap. 8.50 *(978-0-8028-5344-8(7))* Eerdmans, William B. Publishing Co.

Payne, M. E. Buzz the Bee in Bee Smart. 2012. 36p. pap. 24.95 *(978-1-4626-7749-8(5))* America Star Bks.

Peschke, Marci. Spelling Queen, 1 vol. Mourning, Tuesday, illus. 2012. (Kylie Jean Ser.). (ENG.). 112p. (gr. 2-3). pap. 5.95 *(978-1-4048-7212-7(4));* lib. bdg. 22.65 *(978-1-4048-6801-4(1))* Picture Window Bks. (Kylie Jean).

Pin, Isabel. Bumblebee Blues. James, J. Alison, tr. from GER. 2003. (Illus.). 32p. (J). (gr. k-3). 15.95 *(978-0-7358-1813-2(4));* lib. bdg. 16.50 *(978-0-7358-1814-9(2))* North-South Bks., Inc. (Michael Neugebauer Bks.).

Pitman, Sandra. 10 Busy Bumble Bees, 1 vol. Sizemore, Carmen, illus. 2009. 20p. pap. 24.95 *(978-1-60749-683-0(6))* America Star Bks.

Pratt, Sally. The Adventures of Bernie the Bee in Sally's Garden. 2013. 46p. pap. 21.99 *(978-1-4772-9759-9(6))* AuthorHouse.

Price, Mary Ellizabeth. Wallbaby Bumblebees. 2004. (Illus.). 40p. (J). per. 15.75 (978-0-9715402-2-4(5), 410-707-6686) Bamhardt & Ashe Publishing, Inc.

Priddy, Roger. Fuzzy Bee & Friends. 2015. (Touch & Feel Cloth Bks.). (ENG.). 6p. (J). (gr. -1 — 1). 12.99 (978-0-312-51891-2(9), 9780312518912, Priddy Bks.) St. Martin's Pr.

Purkapile, Susan & Peck, Amy. Mumbles the Bumble Bee: The Bee Who Couldn't Buzz. Ducommun, Barbara, illus. 2008. (J). (978-1-930596-87-0(1)) Amherst Pr.

Quiroga, Horacio. The Lazy Bee. Leal, Mireya Fonseca, ed. Porras, Javier Fernando, illus. 2003. (Library of Tale Ser.). (SPA.). 12p. (J). (gr. -1-7). pap. (978-958-30-0988-4(1)) Panamericana Editorial.

Rees, Susan. The First Adventure of Baby Bee. 2011. 36p. pap. 16.86 (978-1-4567-9434-7(5)) AuthorHouse.

Rey, H. A. Curious George a Home for Honeybees (CGTV Early Reader) 2014. (Curious George Ser.). (ENG., Illus.). 24p. (J). (gr. -1-3). 12.99 (978-0-544-23777-3(3), HMH Books For Young Readers) Houghton Mifflin Harcourt Publishing Co.

Ring, Susan. Honeybees: An Amazing Insect Discovery BK. 2009. (ENG.). 12p. 5.95 (978-1-58117-910-1(3), Intervisual/Piggy Toes) Bendon, Inc.

Rojas, Oscar. Un Dia, Una Abeja. (SPA.). pap. 8.95 (978-950-07-1986-5(X)) Editorial Sudamericana S.A. ARG. Dist: Distribooks, Inc.

Rollason, Jane. Killer Bees. 2009. (ENG.). 64p. pap. 12.00 (978-84-8323-503-4(X)) Cambridge Univ. Pr.

Roode, Daniel. Little Bea. Roode, Daniel, illus. 2011. (ENG., Illus.). 32p. (J). (gr. -1-3). 12.99 (978-0-06-199392-3(1), Greenwillow Bks.) HarperCollins Pubs.

—Little Bea & the Snowy Day. Roode, Daniel, illus. 2011. (ENG., Illus.). 32p. (J). (gr. -1-k). 12.99 (978-0-06-199395-4(6), Greenwillow Bks.) HarperCollins Pubs.

Rose, Deborah Lee. The Spelling Bee Before Recess. Armstrong-Ellis, Carey F., illus. 2013. (ENG.). 32p. (J). (gr. 1-4). 16.95 (978-1-4197-0847-3(3), Abrams Bks. for Young Readers) Abrams, Inc.

Rosen, Michael. Bilal's Brilliant Bee. Ross, Tony, illus. 2016. (ENG.). 96p. (J). (gr. k-2). pap. 10.99 (978-1-78344-395-6(2)) Andersen Pr. GBR. Dist: Independent Pubs. Group.

Rouseau, Jasmine. Bizzy Bee Goes to School. 2012. 32p. pap. 19.99 (978-1-4685-4884-6(0)) AuthorHouse.

Rubin, Susan Ellen & Rubin, Judith. Bee Yourself: The Story of Bernard the Bee. 2010. (ENG.). 20p. pap. 10.49 (978-1-4490-6143-2(5)) AuthorHouse.

Russell, Pamela L. R. Bee Careful! My Big Kid Safety Manual. 2012. 20p. pap. 17.99 (978-1-4685-9831-5(7)) AuthorHouse.

Ruzzier, Sergio. Bear & Bee. Ruzzier, Sergio, illus. 2013. (Bear & Bee Ser.). (ENG., Illus.). 48p. (J). (gr. -1-k). 14.99 (978-1-4231-5957-5(8)) Hyperion Pr.

—Too Busy. Ruzzier, Sergio, illus. 2014. (Bear & Bee Ser.). (ENG., Illus.). 48p. (J). (gr. -1-k). 14.99 (978-1-4231-5961-2(6)) Disney Pr.

Santillo, LuAnn. Bee. Santillo, LuAnn, ed. 2003. (Half-Pint Kids Readers Ser.). (Illus.). 7p. (J). (gr. -1-1). pap. (978-1-59256-108-7(X)) Half-Pint Kids, Inc.

Satterfield, April. Leah Bug & Her Flying Friends. Guthrie, Lewis, illus. 2011. 20p. pap. 24.95 (978-1-4560-8422-6(4)) America Star Bks.

Sauers, Charlotte. The Bee in Bonnie Bondelle's Bow. Jasuna, Aija, illus. 2008. (J). 16.95 (978-1-60131-014-9(5)) Big Tent Bks.

Scaletta, Kurtis. Rooting for Rafael Rosales. 2017. (ENG.). 288p. (J). (gr. 3-7). 16.99 **(978-0-8075-6742-5(6))** Whitman, Albert & Co.

Schaub, Michelle. The Bee Puzzle. 2006. (Early Explorers Ser.). (J). pap. (978-1-4108-6123-8(6)) Benchmark Education Co.

Scheunemann, Pam. Spelling Bee, 1 vol. 2007. (Critter Chronicles Ser.). (ENG., Illus.). 24p. (J). (gr. k-3). lib. bdg. 24.21 (978-1-59928-472-9(3), SandCastle) ABDO Publishing Co.

Schreiber, Hannah & Hartsock, Conner. One in a Buzzillion. Foster, Jack, illus. 2011. 16p. pap. 9.95 (978-1-61633-154-2(2)) Guardian Angel Publishing, Inc.

Schulz, Lori. Papa's Plan for Buddy Bee. 2012. 40p. pap. 13.95 (978-1-4497-3652-1(1), WestBow Pr.) Author Solutions, Inc.

Sharpless, Rick. Bees: Trouble on the Throne. 2011. 32p. pap. 16.49 (978-1-4634-4250-7(5)) AuthorHouse.

Shultz, Charles M. & Katschke, Judy. It's Time for School, Charlie Brown, 1 vol. Lo Bianco, Nick, illus. 2011. (Peanuts Ready-To-Reads Ser.). (ENG.). 32p. (gr. -1-2). lib. bdg. 24.21 (978-1-59961-802-9(8)) Spotlight.

Siegel, Rv. A Bee Called Kangaroo. 2005. 81p. pap. 9.16 (978-1-4116-2890-8(X)) Lulu Pr., Inc.

Sloan, William. Of Bees & Bats of Crocodiles & Cats. 2009. 73p. pap. 14.95 (978-1-4092-9470-2(6)) Lulu Pr., Inc.

Small, Lily. Mia the Mouse. 2015. (Fairy Animals of Misty Wood Ser.: 4). (ENG., Illus.). 144p. (J). (gr. k-3). pap. 5.99 (978-1-62779-144-1(2), 9781627791441, Holt, Henry & Co. Bks. For Young Readers) Holt, Henry & Co.

Smith, Michelle. Duck in the Hedge: Jeremy & the Big Pond. 2011. (Illus.). 36p. pap. 15.66 (978-1-4567-8818-6(3)) AuthorHouse.

Smith, Timothy R. The Work Bees Go on Strike. 2006. (Buck Wilder's Adventure Ser.: 2). (Illus.). 80p. (J). (gr. -1-3). per. (978-1-934133-06-4(X), Mackinac Island Press, Inc.) Charlesbridge Publishing, Inc.

Sommer, Carl. It's Not Fair! Budwine, Greg, illus. (J). 2014. pap. (978-1-57537-955-5(4)) 2003. (ENG.). 48p. 9.95 (978-1-57537-021-7(2)) 2003. (ENG.). 48p. lib. bdg. 16.95 (978-1-57537-070-5(0)) 2003. (ENG.). 48p. (gr. k-4). lib. bdg. 23.95 incl. audio compact disk (978-1-57537-720-9(9)) 2003. (ENG.). 48p. (gr. 1-4). 16.95 incl. audio compact disk (978-1-57537-520-5(6)) Advance Publishing, Inc.

—It's Not Fair! 2003. (Another Sommer-Time Story Ser.). (Illus.). 48p. (J). 16.95 incl. audio (978-1-57537-569-4(9)) Advance Publishing, Inc.

—It's Not Fair!(No Es Justo) ! Budwine, Greg, illus. 2009. (Another Sommer-Time Story Bilingual Ser.). (SPA & ENG.). 48p. (J). lib. bdg. 16.95 (978-1-57537-155-9(3)) Advance Publishing, Inc.

—The Revolt. Budwine, Greg, illus. 2009. (Quest for Success Ser.). (ENG.). 56p. (YA). pap. 4.95 (978-1-57537-283-9(5)); lib. bdg. 12.95 (978-1-57537-258-7(4)) Advance Publishing, Inc.

—The Revolt(La Revuelta) Budwine, Greg, illus. 2009. (Quest for Success Bilingual Ser.). (SPA & ENG.). 104p. (YA). lib. bdg. 14.95 (978-1-57537-232-7(0)) Advance Publishing, Inc.

Sommer, Carl, narrated by. It's Not Fair! 2003. (Another Sommer-Time Story Ser.). (Illus.). 48p. (J). (gr. k-4). lib. bdg. 23.95 incl. audio (978-1-57537-770-4(5)) Advance Publishing, Inc.

Sonnebom, Scott. Attack of the Zom-Bees! Esparza, Andres et al, illus. 2013. (Tiger Moth Ser.). (ENG.). 48p. (gr. 1-3). pap. 6.19 (978-1-4342-3871-9(7)) Stone Arch Bks.

—Tiger Moth: Attack of the Zom-Bees!, 1 vol. Esparza, Andres, illus. 2013. (Tiger Moth Ser.). (ENG.). 48p. (gr. 1-3). lib. bdg. 23.99 (978-1-4342-3283-0(2)) Stone Arch Bks.

Spelling Bee. 2003. (J). per. (978-1-57657-954-1(9)) Paradise Pr., Inc.

Stanek, Robert, pseud. The Bugville Critters Go on Vacation. 2008. (ENG., Illus.). (J). 32p. per. 9.95 (978-1-57545-148-0(4)); 52p. per. 19.95 (978-1-57545-125-1(5)) RP Media.

—The Bugville Critters Make New Friends: Buster Bee's School Days #2. 2008. (ENG., Illus.). 60p. (J). per. 18.95 (978-1-57545-168-8(9)) RP Media.

—The Bugville Critters Play Their First Big Game. 2008. (ENG., Illus.). (J). 32p. per. 9.95 (978-1-57545-149-7(2)); 52p. per. 16.95 (978-1-57545-127-5(1)) RP Media.

—The Bugville Critters Rush to the Hospital. 2008. (ENG., Illus.). (J). 32p. per. 9.95 (978-1-57545-150-3(6)); 52p. per. 19.95 (978-1-57545-126-8(3)) RP Media.

—The Bugville Critters Too Much Sweets: Buster Bee's School Days #1. 2008. (ENG., Illus.). 60p. (J). per. 18.95 (978-1-57545-167-1(0)) RP Media.

—The Bugville Critters Vacation Surprise: Buster Bee's School Days #3. 2008. (ENG., Illus.). 68p. (J). per. 18.95 (978-1-57545-172-5(7)) RP Media.

—Buster Bee's Adventures with Letters & Words. (ENG., Illus.). (J). 2008. 52p. per. 19.95 (978-1-57545-169-5(7)) 2007. 28p. pap. 9.99 (978-1-57545-156-5(5)) RP Media.

—Go to School. 2008. (ENG., Illus.). 28p. (J). pap. 5.29 (978-1-57545-188-6(3)) RP Media.

—Have a Sleepover. 2008. (ENG., Illus.). 28p. (J). pap. 5.29 (978-1-57545-189-3(1)) RP Media.

—Play Their First Big Game. 2008. (ENG., Illus.). 32p. (J). pap. 5.59 (978-1-57545-193-0(X)) RP Media.

—Robert Stanek's Bugville Critters Storybook Treasury. 2008. (ENG., Illus.). 132p. (J). per. 24.95 (978-1-57545-171-8(9)) RP Media.

—Robert Stanek's Bugville Critters Storybook Treasury Volume 2 (the Bugville Critters Storybook Collection, Volume 2), 4 vols., Vol. 2. 2008. (ENG., Illus.). 124p. (J). per. 24.95 (978-1-57545-173-2(5)) RP Media.

—Rush to the Hospital. 2008. (ENG., Illus.). 32p. (J). pap. 5.59 (978-1-57545-192-3(1)) RP Media.

—Visit Dad & Mom at Work. 2008. (ENG., Illus.). 28p. (J). pap. 5.29 (978-1-57545-187-9(5)) RP Media.

Steve, Smallman. Very Greedy Bee. Jack, Tickle, illus. 2010. (ENG.). 32p. (J). pap. 7.95 (978-1-58925-422-0(8)) Tiger Tales.

Stewart, Bob. Baily Bumble Bee. 2009. 32p. pap. 14.49 (978-1-4389-7254-1(7)) AuthorHouse.

Stine, R. L. The Great Smelling Bee. Park, Trip, illus. 2008. (Rotten School Ser.: 2). (ENG.). 128p. (J). (gr. 3-7). pap. 5.99 (978-0-06-078591-8(8)) HarperCollins Pubs.

—Mutacion Fatal. 2003. (SPA.). pap. (978-0-590-01798-5(5)) Scholastic GBR. Dist: Lectorum Pubns., Inc.

Stockton, Frank Richard. The Bee-Man of Orn. Lynch, P. J., illus. 2006. 44p. (J). (gr. k-4). reprint ed. 18.00 (978-1-4223-5505-3(5)) DIANE Publishing Co.

—The Bee-Man of Orn. Sendak, Maurice, illus. 2005. (Sendak Reissues Ser.). (ENG.). 56p. (J). (gr. -1-18). 15.95 (978-0-06-029729-9(8)) HarperCollins Pubs.

—The Bee-Man of Orn. 2007. (Notable American Authors Ser.). reprint ed. lthr. 79.00 (978-0-7812-8927-6(0)) Reprint Services Corp.

—The Bee-Man of Orn & Other Fanciful Tales. 2005. 124p. per. 10.95 (978-1-59818-695-6(7)) Aegypan.

Story, Rita. The Belly Garden. Galluzzo, Madeline, illus. 2008. 23p. pap. 24.95 (978-1-60610-035-6(1)) America Star Bks.

Studio Mouse Staff. Pooh & Piglet. 2008. (ENG., Illus.). 36p. (J). (gr. -1). 7.99 (978-1-59069-419-0(8)) Studio Mouse LLC.

Suddard, Lisa. Money Grows with Bees. Cabrillo, Cinthya, illus. 2009. 24p. pap. 14.95 (978-1-4251-8673-9(4)) Trafford Publishing.

Swan Publishing Inc. The Brave Little Bee. 2012. 28p. pap. 16.09 (978-1-4669-1541-1(2)) Trafford Publishing.

Sypolt, Carl W. Adventures of David the Honeybee. 2003. 51p. pap. 9.95 (978-0-7414-1526-4(7)) Infinity Publishing.

Taylor, Laura. The Bee-Attitudes: Bee-Atrice the Bumblebee Becomes a Humble Bee. 2017. (ENG.). 32p. (J). 14.99 **(978-1-62998-578-7(3)**, Creation Hse.) Charisma Media.

Thomas, Debbie. Class Act. 2015. (ENG.). 224p. (J). pap. 13.00 (978-1-78117-262-9(5)) Mercier Pr., Ltd., The IRL. Dist: Dufour Editions, Inc.

Tillworth, Mary. Busy as a Bee! Moroney, Christopher, illus. 2012. (Write-On/Wipe-off Activity Book Ser.). (ENG.). 12p. (J). (gr. k — 1). bds. 9.99 (978-0-307-93011-8(4), Golden Bks.) Random Hse. Children's Bks.

Tireman, Loyd. Dumbee. Douglass, Ralph, illus. 2015. (Mesaland Ser.). (ENG.). 48p. (J). 12.95 (978-0-8263-5607-9(9)) Univ. of New Mexico Pr.

To Fly on a Bee. 2006. (J). (978-0-9763798-1-2(3)) Lion's Crest Pr.

Tobin, Paul. How to Outsmart a Billion Robot Bees. Lafontaine, Thierry & Abey, Katie, illus. 2017. (ENG.). 320p. (J). 16.99 (978-1-61963-897-6(5), 9781619638976, Bloomsbury USA Childrens) Bloomsbury Publishing USA.

Unsworth, Anne. Just Be, Little Bee. 2008. (Illus.). 68p. pap. (978-1-84748-331-7(3)) Athena Pr.

Valder, Margret. Henry the Honey Bee. Valder, Justin, illus. 2010. 24p. pap. 11.50 (978-1-60860-537-8(X), Eloquent Bks.) Strategic Book Publishing & Rights Agency (SBPRA).

Wait for Me, Bumblebee. 2004. (J). (978-0-9767179-7-3(2)) ABC Development, Inc.

Walsleben, Edda Brigitte. The Little Bee Who Would Be Queen. 2012. 224p. 45.00 (978-1-937911-33-1(0)); pap. 33.00 (978-1-937911-32-4(2)) Heavenly Realm Publishing.

WannaBees Media LLC, creator. HoniBee Loses Her Voice (paperback) The Do'Bees. 2007. (Illus.). 28p. (J). pap. 9.99 (978-0-9767670-4-6(X)) WannaBees Media LLC.

Warren, Jill. Bizzy Bee & the Flowers. 2012. (ENG.). 31p. (J). pap. 16.95 (978-1-4327-8239-9(8)) Outskirts Pr., Inc.

Watkins, Samuel R. Ant-Bee Kingdom. 2011. 12p. (gr. -1). pap. 12.68 (978-1-4269-5272-2(4)) Trafford Publishing.

Webster, Christy. Thomas & the Buzzy Bees. 2017. (Thomas & Friends Step into Reading Ser.). lib. bdg. 14.75 **(978-0-606-39861-9(9))** Turtleback Bks.

Webster, Christy. Thomas & the Buzzy Bees (Thomas & Friends) 2017. (Step into Reading Ser.). (ENG., Illus.). 24p. (J). (gr. -1-1). pap. 4.99 (978-0-399-55770-5(9), Random Hse. Bks. for Young Readers) Random Hse. Children's Bks.

Wishinsky, Frieda. A Bee in Your Ear. Laliberte, Louise-Andree, illus. 2004. 64p. (J). lib. bdg. 20.00 (978-1-4242-1255-2(3)) Fitzgerald Bks.

Written By Susan J. Perry; Illustrated B. Snuckle-Bee & Snuckle-Bun: The Bee-Attitudes. Dedering, Victoria, illus. 2011. 32p. pap. 24.95 (978-1-4560-8787-6(8)) America Star Bks.

Yoon, Salina. Peek-a-Love. Yoon, Salina, illus. 2010. (ENG., Illus.). 14p. (J). (gr. -1 — 1). 6.99 (978-1-4424-0655-1(0), Little Simon) Little Simon.

Yusuf. Butterfly & Bumble Bee: Adventure in Yellow Stone National Park. 2010. 16p. 8.49 (978-1-4520-4022-6(2)) AuthorHouse.

BEETHOVEN, LUDWIG VAN, 1770-1827

Bauer, Helen. Beethoven for Kids: His Life & Music with 21 Activities. 2011. (For Kids Ser.). (ENG., Illus.). 144p. (J). (gr. 4). pap. 16.95 (978-1-56976-711-5(4)) Chicago Review Pr., Inc.

Carew-Miller, Anna. Ludwig Van Beethoven: Great Composer. (Illus.). 32p. (J). 2013. (People of Importance Ser.: 21). (gr. 4-18). 19.95 (978-1-4222-2849-4(5)) 2004. (Great Names Ser.). (gr. 3-18). lib. bdg. 19.95 (978-1-59084-148-8(4)) Mason Crest.

Fandel, Jennifer. Beethoven's Fifth Symphony. 2006. (What in the World? Ser.). (Illus.). 48p. (J). (gr. 4-7). lib. bdg. 21.95 (978-1-58341-429-3(0), Creative Education) Creative Co., The.

January, Brendan. Ludwig Van Beethoven: Musical Genius. 2004. (Book Report Biographies Ser.). (ENG., Illus.). 111p. (J). 30.50 (978-0-531-11909-9(2), Watts, Franklin) Scholastic Library Publishing.

Josephson, Judith Pinkerton. Bold Composer: A Story about Ludwig Van Beethoven. Kiwak, Barbara, illus. 2007. (Creative Minds Biographies Ser.). (ENG.). 64p. (gr. 4-8). lib. bdg. 22.60 (978-0-8225-5987-0(0)) Lerner Publishing Group.

Kaufmann, Helen L. The Story of Beethoven. Meadowcroft, Enid Lamonte, ed. Kredel, Fritz, illus. 2011. 192p. 42.95 (978-1-258-10000-1(2)) Literary Licensing, LLC.

LUDWIG VAN BEETHOVEN. 2007. (Descubrimos a Los Músicos Ser.). (ENG., Illus.). 24p. (J). (gr. 2-4). 14.95 (978-84-7864-959-4(X)) Combel Editorial, S.A. ESP. Dist: Independent Pubs. Group.

Machajewski, Sarah. Musical Genius: Ludwig Van Beethoven. 2013. (InfoMax Readers Ser.). (ENG.). 24p. (J). (gr. 2-3). pap. 49.50 (978-1-4777-2438-5(9)); (Illus.). pap. 8.25 (978-1-4777-2437-8(0)) Rosen Publishing Group, Inc., The. (Rosen Classroom).

Mapua, Jeff. Ludwig Van Beethoven: Classical Composer of Passion & Power. 2015. (Britannica Beginner Bios Ser.). (ENG.). 32p. (J). 23.45 (978-1-62275-931-6(1), Britannica Educational Publishing) Rosen Publishing Group, Inc., The.

—Ludwig Van Beethoven: Composer of the Classical & Romantic Eras. 2015. (Britannica Beginner Bios Ser.). (ENG.). 32p. (J). (gr. 2-3). 46.90 (978-1-62275-933-0(8), Britannica Educational Publishing) Rosen Publishing Group, Inc., The.

Martin, Russell & Nibley, Lydia. The Mysteries of Beethoven's Hair. 2014. (ENG., Illus.). 128p. (J). (gr. 5). pap. 7.95 (978-1-57091-715-8(9)) Charlesbridge Publishing, Inc.

Mattern, Joanne. Ludwig Van Beethoven: A Revolutionary Composer. 2017. (Rookie Biographies(tm) Ser.). (ENG., Illus.). 32p. (J). lib. bdg. 25.00 (978-0-531-22289-8(6), Children's Pr.) Scholastic Library Publishing.

Myers, Carrie Mieko. What If You'd Met Beethoven? 2004. (Illus.). 16p. (J). (978-0-439-69713-2(1)) Scholastic, Inc.

Summerer, Eric Michael. Ludwig van Beethoven. 2009. (Primary Source Library of Famous Composers Ser.). 32p. (gr. 4-4). 42.50 (978-1-60854-112-6(6), PowerKids Pr.) Rosen Publishing Group, Inc., The.

Turner, Barrie Carson. Beethoven. 2003. (Famous Childhoods Ser.). (Illus.). (J). lib. bdg. 24.25 (978-1-59389-112-1(1)) Chrysalis Education.

Venezia, Mike. Ludwig Van Beethoven (Revised Edition) 2017. (Getting to Know the World's Greatest Composers Ser.). (ENG., Illus.). 40p. (J). lib. bdg. 29.00 (978-0-531-22059-7(1), Children's Pr.) Scholastic Library Publishing.

Viegas, Jennifer. Beethoven's World. 2009. (Music Throughout History Ser.). 64p. (gr. 5-6). 58.50 (978-1-61514-682-6(2), Rosen Reference) Rosen Publishing Group, Inc., The.

Walcker, Yann. Ludwig Van Beethoven, 1 vol. Voake, Charlotte, illus. 2012. (First Discovery Music Ser.). (ENG.). 28p. (J). (gr. 2-6). pap. 19.99 (978-1-85103-310-2(6)) Moonlight Publishing, Ltd. GBR. Dist: Independent Pubs. Group.

White, Stephanie. Ludwig Van Beethoven: Famous Composer. 2013. (Rosen Readers Ser.). (ENG.). 24p. (J). (gr. 2-3). pap. 49.50 (978-1-4777-2291-6(2)); pap. 8.25 (978-1-4777-2290-9(4)) Rosen Publishing Group, Inc., The. (Rosen Classroom).

BEETLES

Aloian, Molly & Kalman, Bobbie. El Ciclo de Vida del Escarabajo. 2006. (Libro de Bobbie Kalman Ser.). (SPA., Illus.). 32p. (J). (gr. 3-7). pap. (978-0-7787-8715-0(X)); lib. bdg. (978-0-7787-8669-6(2)) Crabtree Publishing Co.

—The Life Cycle of a Beetle. 2003. (Life Cycle Ser.). (ENG., Illus.). 32p. (J). pap. (978-0-7787-0692-2(3)); lib. bdg. (978-0-7787-0662-5(1)) Crabtree Publishing Co.

Aloian, Molly, et al. Les Coleopteres. 2006. (Petit Monde Vivant Ser.). (FRE., Illus.). 32p. (J). (gr. k-6). pap. 9.95 (978-2-89579-101-0(5)) Bayard Canada Livres CAN. Dist: Crabtree Publishing Co.

Aston, Dianna Hutts. A Beetle is shy. Long, Sylvia, illus. 2016. (ENG.). 40p. (J). (gr. k-3). 16.99 (978-1-4521-2712-5(3)) Chronicle Bks. LLC.

Berne, Emma Carlson. Dung Beetles: Stronger Than Ten Men! 2013. (Animal Superpowers Ser.). (ENG., Illus.). 24p. (J). (gr. k-5). pap. 8.25 (978-1-4777-0837-8(5), PowerKids Pr.) Rosen Publishing Group, Inc., The.

Berne, Emma Carlson & Carlson Berne, Emma. Dung Beetles. 2013. 24p. (J). (gr. k-5). 22.60 (978-1-4777-0748-7(4), PowerKids Pr.) Rosen Publishing Group, Inc., The.

Black, Nessa. Beetles. 2017. (Spot Creepy Crawlies Ser.). (ENG.). 16p. (gr. k-3). 17.95 **(978-1-68151-106-1(1))** Amicus Publishing.

Bodden, Valerie. Beetles. 2013. (Illus.). 24p. (J). 25.65 (978-1-60818-231-2(2), Creative Education) Creative Co., The.

—Creepy Creatures: Beetles. 2013. (Creepy Creatures Ser.). (ENG., Illus.). 24p. (J). (gr. 1-3). pap. 8.99 (978-0-89812-794-2(7), Creative Paperbacks) Creative Co., The.

Burns, Loree Griffin. Beetle Busters: A Rogue Insect & the People Who Track It. Harasimowicz, Ellen, illus. Harasimowicz, Ellen, photos by. 2014. (Scientists in the Field Ser.). (ENG.). 64p. (J). (gr. 5-7). 18.99 (978-0-547-79267-5(0), HMH Books For Young Readers) Houghton Mifflin Harcourt Publishing Co.

Carlson Berne, Emma. Dung Beetles: Stronger Than Ten Men! 2013. (Animal Superpowers Ser.). 24p. (J). (gr. k-5). pap. 49.50 (978-1-4777-0838-5(3), PowerKids Pr.) Rosen Publishing Group, Inc., The.

Chiger, Arielle. 20 Fun Facts about Beetles. 2013. (Fun Fact File: Bugs! Ser.). (Illus.). 32p. (J). (gr. 2-5). pap. 10.50 (978-1-4339-8226-2(9)); lib. bdg. 25.25 (978-1-4339-8225-5(0)) Stevens, Gareth Publishing LLLP.

Goliath Beetles. 2014. (Giant Animals Ser.). 48p. (J). (gr. 4-6). lib. bdg. 31.36 (978-1-62712-966-4(9)) Cavendish Square Publishing.

Hamilton, S. L. Beetles. 2014. (Xtreme Insects Ser.). (ENG.). 32p. (gr. 3-9). lib. bdg. 27.07 (978-1-62403-688-0(0), Abdo & Daughters) ABDO Publishing Co.

Hansen, Grace. Beetles, 1 vol. 2014. (Insects Ser.). (ENG.). 24p. (J). (gr. 4-8). lib. bdg. 28.50 (978-1-62970-038-0(X)) ABDO Publishing Co.

Hansen, Grace, et al. Escarabajos. 2015. (Insectos Ser.). (SPA., Illus.). 24p. (J). (gr. k-1). pap. 7.95 (978-1-4966-0473-6(3)) Capstone Classroom.

Helget, Nicole. Beetles. 2007. (Bugbooks Ser.). (Illus.). 24p. (J). (gr. -1-3). lib. bdg. 24.25 (978-1-58341-539-9(4), Creative Education) Creative Co., The.

Hipp, Andrew. Dung Beetles. (Really Wild Life of Animals Ser.). 24p. 2009. (gr. 3-4). 42.50 (978-1-60854-190-4(8)) 2003. (Illus.). (J). lib. bdg. 22.60 (978-0-8239-6238-9(5)) Rosen Publishing Group, Inc., The. (PowerKids Pr.).

Hulcr, Jiri & Cognato, Anthony Ignatius. Xyleborini of New Guinea, a Taxonomic Monograph (Coleoptera: Curculionidae: Scolytinae) 2013. (Illus.). 172p. (978-0-9776209-7-5(2)) Entomological Society of America.

Ipcizade, Catherine. Breathtaking Beetles. 2017. (Bugs Are Beautiful! Ser.). (ENG., Illus.). 32p. (gr. 1-2). lib. bdg. 27.32 (978-1-5157-4497-9(3), Aplus Bks.) Capstone Press of Coughlan Cos.

Jenkins, Steve. The Beetle Book. Jenkins, Steve, illus. 2012. (ENG., Illus.). 40p. (J). (gr. -1-3). 17.99 (978-0-547-68084-2(8)) Houghton Mifflin Harcourt Publishing Co.

Lockwood, Sophie. Beetles. 2007. (World of Insects Ser.). (ENG., Illus.). 40p. (J). (gr. 3-6). 31.36 (978-1-59296-819-0(8), 200972) Child's World, Inc., The.

Long, Erin. Ground Beetles. 2016. (Dig Deep! Bugs That Live Underground Ser.). 24p. (J). (gr. 3-3). pap. 8.25 (978-1-4994-2054-8(4), PowerKids Pr.) Rosen Publishing Group, Inc., The.

Markle, Sandra. Diving Beetles. 2008. pap. 52.95 (978-1-57505-981-5(9)) Lerner Publishing Group.

—Diving Beetles: Underwater Insect Predators. 2008. (Insect World Ser.). (Illus.). 48p. (J). (gr. 4-7). lib. bdg. 27.93 (978-0-8225-7295-4(8), Lerner Pubns.) Lerner Publishing Group.

Marsico, Katie. A Ladybug Larva Grows Up. Marsico, Katie, illus. 2007. (Scholastic News Nonfiction Readers Ser.). (ENG., Illus.). 24p. (J). (gr. 1-2). 22.00 (978-0-531-17478-4(6)) Scholastic Library Publishing.

McKinnon, Elaine. The Life Cycle of a Beetle. 2015. (Watch Them Grow! Ser.). (ENG.). 24p. (J). (gr. 1-1). pap. 8.25 (978-1-4994-0660-3(6), PowerKids Pr.) Rosen Publishing Group, Inc., The.

Michele, Tracey. Bugs & Beetles. 2011. (Learn-Abouts Ser.). (Illus.). 16p. (J). pap. 7.95 (978-1-59920-611-0(0)) Black Rabbit Bks.

Packard, Mary. Goliath Beetle: One of the World's Heaviest Insects. 2007. (SuperSized! Ser.). (Illus.). 24p. (J). (gr. k-3). lib. bdg. 21.28 (978-1-59716-388-0(0), 1265933) Bearport Publishing Co., Inc.

Pallotta, Jerry. The Beetle Alphabet Book. Biedrzycki, David, illus. 2004. (ENG.). 32p. (J). (gr. -1-3). 17.95 (978-1-57091-551-2(2)) Charlesbridge Publishing, Inc.

—The Beetle Alphabet Book. Biedrzycki, David, tr. Biedrzycki, David, illus. 2004. (ENG.). 32p. (J). (gr. -1-3). pap. 7.95 (978-1-57091-552-9(0)) Charlesbridge Publishing, Inc.

Petrie, Kristin. Beetles, 1 vol. 2009. (Bugs! Ser.). (ENG.). 32p. (gr. 3-6). 27.07 (978-1-60453-063-6(4), Checkerboard Library) ABDO Publishing Co.

Polinsky, Paige V. Rhinoceros Beetle: Heavyweight Champion. 2016. (ENG., Illus.). 24p. (978-1-68078-150-2(2)) ABDO Publishing Co.

Reher, Matt. All about Beetles. 2015. (2G Bugs Ser.). (ENG., Illus.). 32p. (J). pap. 5.99 (978-1-63437-098-1(8)) American Reading Co.

—The Book of Beetles. 2016. (1G Bugs Ser.). (ENG., Illus.). 32p. (J). pap. 5.99 **(978-1-63437-583-2(1))** American Reading Co.

A B

Reher, Matt. Can You See the Beetle? 2015. (1G Bugs Ser.). (ENG., Illus.). 24p. (J). pap. 5.99 (978-1-63437-088-2(0)) American Reading Co.

Rissman, Rebecca. Beetles, 1 vol. 2012. (Creepy Critters Ser.). (ENG., Illus.). 24p. (gr. -1-k). lib. bdg. 25.32 (978-1-4109-4803-8(X)) Heinemann-Raintree.

Roza, Greg. Beastly Beetles. 2011. (World of Bugs Ser.). (Illus.). 24p. (gr. k-2). 69.20 (978-1-4339-6142-7(3)); (J). (gr. -1-2). lib. bdg. 22.60 (978-1-4339-4599-1(1)); (J). (gr. k-2). pap. 8.15 (978-1-4339-4600-4(9)) Stevens, Gareth Publishing LLLP.

Schuh, Mari. Beetles. 2013. (ENG., Illus.). 24p. (J). lib. bdg. 25.65 (978-1-62031-052-6(X)) Jump! Inc.

Squire, Ann O. Beetles. 2003. (True Bks.). (ENG., Illus.). 48p. (J). 25.00 (978-0-516-22658-3(4), Children's Pr.) Scholastic Library Publishing.

Taylor, Trace. Beetles. 2008. (2G Bugs Ser.). (ENG.). 12p. (J). (gr. k-2). pap. 5.99 (978-1-59301-851-1(7)) American Reading Co.

Taylor, Trace & Sánchez, Lucía M. Escarabajos: Beetles. 2011. (2G - Bichos Ser.). (SPA.). 12p. (J). (gr. k-2). pap. 6.99 (978-1-61541-422-2(3)) American Reading Co.

Taylor, Trace & Sanchez, Lucia M. Escarabajos (Beetles) 2011. (poder de 100 - Bichos Ser.). (SPA.). 12p. pap. 33.92 (978-1-61541-423-9(1)) American Reading Co.

Trueit, Trudi Strain. Beetles. 2013. 32p. (J). (gr. 6-9). 28.50 (978-1-60870-241-1(3)); pap. 10.58 (978-1-62712-027-2(0)) Cavendish Square Publishing.

—Beetles. 2009. (Benchmark Rebus Ser.). 24p. (gr. k-1). 15.95 (978-0-7614-3962-2(5)) Marshall Cavendish Corp.

Turnbaugh, Kay. Mountain Pine Beetle. Brooks, David, illus. 2011. (Pruett Ser.). (ENG.). 48p. (J). pap. 14.95 (978-0-87108-958-8(0)) Pruett Publishing Co.

Watts, Barrie. Beetles. (Illus.). 32p. (YA). (gr. 2-18). lib. bdg. 27.10 (978-1-932889-16-1(7)) Sea-To-Sea Pubns.

Woodward, John. Beetle. 2010. (Garden Minibeasts up Close Ser.). 32p. (gr. 2-4). 30.00 (978-1-60413-897-9(1), Chelsea Clubhouse) Facts On File, Inc.

Zabludoff, Marc. Beetles. 2007. (Animalways Ser.). (Illus.). 104p. (gr. 6-3). lib. bdg. 24.95 (978-0-7614-2532-8(2), Benchmark Bks.) Marshall Cavendish Corp.

BEHAVIOR

see also Christian Life; Courage; Courtesy; Ethics; Etiquette; Friendship; Interpersonal Relations; Love; Patriotism; Self-Control; Self-Culture; Social Adjustment; Spiritual Life; Truthfulness and Falsehood

Abramovitz, Melissa. Understanding Addiction. 2017. (Understanding Psychology Ser.). (ENG.). 80p. (YA). (gr. 5-12). **(978-1-68282-271-5(0))** ReferencePoint Pr., Inc.

Adams, Rodney & Adams, Eunice. Oooooooo, You Said A Bad Wooord! How A Group of Young People Outgrew 'Adult' Language. 2010. 45p. pap. 11.95 (978-1-4327-4252-2(3)) Outskirts Pr., Inc.

Amos, Janine. Don't Do That! How Not to Act. 2009. (Best Behavior Ser.). (Illus.). 32p. (J). (gr. -1-2). pap. 10.55 (978-1-60754-052-6(5)) Windmill Bks.

Amos, Janine & Spenceley, Annabel. Don't Do That! How Not to Act. 2009. (Best Behavior Ser.). (Illus.). 32p. (J). (gr. -1-2). lib. bdg. 22.60 (978-1-60754-030-4(4)) Windmill Bks.

—Don't Say That! Let's Talk Nicely. 2009. (Best Behavior Ser.). (Illus.). 32p. (J). (gr. -1-2). pap. 10.55 (978-1-60754-054-0(1)); lib. bdg. 22.60 (978-1-60754-031-1(2)) Windmill Bks.

—Go Away! What Not to Say. 2009. (Best Behavior Ser.). (Illus.). 32p. (J). (gr. -1-2). pap. 10.55 (978-1-60754-044-1(4)); lib. bdg. 22.60 (978-1-60754-026-7(6)) Windmill Bks.

—It Won't Work! Let's Try Again. 2009. (Best Behavior Ser.). (Illus.). 32p. (J). (gr. -1-2). pap. 10.55 (978-1-60754-046-5(0)); lib. bdg. 22.60 (978-1-60754-027-4(4)) Windmill Bks.

—It's Mine! Let's Try to Share. 2009. (Best Behavior Ser.). (Illus.). 32p. (J). (gr. -1-2). pap. 10.55 (978-1-60754-048-9(7)); lib. bdg. 22.60 (978-1-60754-028-1(2)) Windmill Bks.

—Move Over! Learning to Share Our Space. 2009. (Best Behavior Ser.). (Illus.). 32p. (J). (gr. -1-2). pap. 10.55 (978-1-60754-050-2(9)); lib. bdg. 22.60 (978-1-60754-029-8(0)) Windmill Bks.

Anderson, David A. What You Can See, You Can Be! Jones, Don, illus. 2003. 48p. (gr. 3-8). 13.95 (978-0-87516-603-2(2), Devorss Pubns.) DeVorss & Co.

ARISE Foundation & Benson, Susan. Life Skills Curriculum: ARISE Work in Progress, Book 4. 2011. (Work in Progress Ser.). (Illus.). 102p. (J). pap., wbk. ed. 12.95 (978-1-58614-021-2(3)) Arise Foundation.

Atkinson, Tina Louise. Shape Up. 2012. 20p. pap. 13.77 (978-1-4669-3293-7(7)) Trafford Publishing.

Berry, Joy. Being Patient. 2009. (ENG.). 40p. (J). (gr. -1-k). pap. 7.95 (978-1-60577-212-7(7)) Berry, Joy Enterprises.

—Help Me Be Good about Being Bossy. 2009. (Help Me Be Good Ser.). 32p. pap. 7.95 (978-1-60577-126-7(0)) Berry, Joy Enterprises.

—Help Me Be Good about Gossiping. 2009. (Help Me Be Good Ser.). 32p. pap. 7.95 (978-1-60577-120-5(1)) Berry, Joy Enterprises.

—Help Me Be Good about Tattling. 2009. (ENG.). 40p. (J). (gr. k-2). pap. 7.95 (978-1-60577-119-9(8)) Berry, Joy Enterprises.

—Help Me Be Good Disobeying. Bartholomew, illus. 2010. (Help Me Be Good Ser.). (ENG.). 32p. (J). (gr. -1-2). pap. 4.99 (978-1-60577-137-3(6)) Berry, Joy Enterprises.

—Help Me Be Good Fighting. Bartholomew, illus. 2010. (Help Me Be Good Ser.). (ENG.). 32p. (J). (gr. -1-2). pap. 4.99 (978-1-60577-135-9(X)) Berry, Joy Enterprises.

—Let's Talk about Being Patient. Smith, Maggie, illus. 2010. (Let's Talk About Ser.). (ENG.). 32p. (J). (gr. -1-k). pap. 4.99 (978-1-60577-209-7(7)) Berry, Joy Enterprises.

—Let's Talk about Needing Attention. Smith, Maggie, illus. 2010. (Let's Talk About Ser.). (ENG.). 32p. (J). (gr. -1-k). pap. 4.99 (978-1-60577-222-6(4)) Berry, Joy Enterprises.

Berry, Joy Wilt. A Children's Book about Disobeying. 2005. (Illus.). (J). (978-0-7172-8593-8(6)) Scholastic, Inc.

Criswell, Patti Kelley. What Would You Do? Quizzes about Real-Life Problems. Chobanian, Elizabeth, ed. Bendell, Norm, illus. 2004. (ENG.). 64p. (J). (gr. 3-18). pap. 8.95 (978-1-58485-874-4(5)) American Girl Publishing, Inc.

Dromgoole, Glenn. What Puppies Teach Us: Life's Lessons Learned from Our Little Friends. 2003. (Illus.). 32p. tchr. ed. 12.95 (978-1-57223-684-4(1), 6841) Willow Creek Pr., Inc.

Finn, Carrie. Manners on the Playground, 1 vol. Lensch, Chris, illus. 2007. (Way to Be!: Manners Ser.). (ENG.). 24p. (gr. -1-2). per. 7.95 (978-1-4048-3559-7(8)) Picture Window Bks.

Frost, Shelley. I See Kindness Everywhere. 2009. (Illus.). 28p. pap. 12.99 (978-1-4490-0415-6(6)) AuthorHouse.

Gordon, Sharon. We Are Kind. 2007. (J). pap. 6.99 (978-0-7614-3270-8(1)) Marshall Cavendish Corp.

Greenwald, Zee. Loving Kindness: Stories of Chessed from Our Sages. 2008. 48p. 17.99 (978-1-59826-267-4(X)) Feldheim Pubs.

Gulotta, Charles. Learn This! Stuff You Need to Know, & Mistakes You Need to Stop Making, Before You Step Foot into High School. 3rd rev. ed. 2005. (Illus.). 64p. (YA). (978-0-9653263-5-3(7)) Mostly Bright Ideas.

Huebner, Dawn. What to Do When Bad Habits Take Hold: A Kid's Guide to Overcoming Nail Biting & More. Matthews, Bonnie, illus. 2008. 88p. (J). (gr. 6-12). pap. 15.95 (978-1-4338-0383-3(6), Magination Pr.) American Psychological Assn.

Jensen, Hay R. Home with Honor Vol. 1: A Vietnam P.O.W. Tells How to Conquer Adversity Through Courage, Honor & Faith. (Illus.). 171p. (Orig.). (YA). pap. 14.95 (978-1-877898-15-0(5)) P.O.W. (Pubns. of Worth).

Johnston, Marianne. Dealing with Teasing / Qué hacer con las Burlas. 2009. (Conflict Resolution Library / Biblioteca solución de conflictos Ser.). (ENG & SPA.). 24p. (gr. 2-3). 42.50 (978-1-60853-417-3(0), Editorial Buenas Letras) Rosen Publishing Group, Inc., The.

Joy, Berry. Help Me Good about Being Messy. 2009. 32p. 7.95 (978-1-60577-112-0(0)) Berry, Joy Enterprises.

Leigh, Susan K. God, I Need to Talk to You About Bad Manners. 2005. (J). 1.19 (978-0-7586-0813-0(6)) Concordia Publishing Hse.

—God, I Need to Talk to You about Bad Words. Clark, Bill, illus. 2005. 16p. (J). pap. 1.19 (978-0-7586-0793-5(8)) Concordia Publishing Hse.

Lewis, Barbara A. What Do You Stand For? For Teens: A Guide to Building Character. Espeland, Pamela, ed. 2005. (ENG., Illus.). 288p. (YA). (gr. 5-9). pap. 19.99 (978-1-57542-029-5(5)) Free Spirit Publishing, Inc.

Libal, Autumn. Runaway Train: Youth with Emotional Disturbance. 2003. (Youth with Special Needs Ser.). (Illus.). 127p. (YA). (gr. 7). pap. 14.95 (978-1-4222-0429-0(4)) Mason Crest.

Loggia, Wendy & Roberts, Christa. Employee Handbook. 2014. (Regular Show Ser.). (ENG.). 80p. (J). (gr. 3-7). 6.99 (978-0-8431-7743-5(8), Price Stern Sloan) Penguin Young Readers Group.

Lynette, Rachel. How to Deal with Secrets. 2009. (Let's Work It Out Ser.). (Illus.). 24p. (J). (gr. 2-5). lib. bdg. 22.60 (978-1-4042-4519-8(7)) Rosen Publishing Group, Inc., The.

Mandino, Og. Og Mandino's Great Trilogy: The Greatest Salesman in the World, the Greatest Secret in the World & the Greatest Miracle in the World. 2008. 420p. (J). (978-0-8119-0428-5(8)) Lifetime Bks.

Martin, Dawn. Fast Girls Finish Last: A Girl's Guide to Becoming a Virgin with Attitude! 2nd rev. ed. 2006. (Illus.). 248p. (YA). (gr. 7-13). per. 19.95 (978-0-9668718-0-7(4)) 20/20 Publishing.

Martin, Donald R. "Rick". God Created You: A Guide to Temperament Therapy. 2004. 232p. per. 19.95 (978-0-9726996-2-4(7), GCY) Cook Communication.

Mastering Life Starter Kit Plus. (YA). (gr. 7-12). 39.95 (978-1-928726-01-2(1)) Positive Productions.

Meiners, Cheri J. Be Polite & Kind. 2003. (Learning to Get Along(r) Ser.). (ENG., Illus.). 40p. (J). (gr. -1-3). pap. 10.95 (978-1-57542-151-3(8)) Free Spirit Publishing, Inc.

—Try & Stick with It. Johnson, Meredith, illus. 2004. (Learning to Get Along(r) Ser.). (ENG.). 40p. (J). (gr. -1-3). pap. 10.95 (978-1-57542-159-9(3)) Free Spirit Publishing, Inc.

Morgan, Nicola. Blame My Brain. 2007. (Illus.). 192p. (YA). pap. (978-1-4063-1116-7(2)) Walker Bks., Ltd.

Post, Peggy & Senning, Cindy Post. The Guide to Good Manners for Kids. Björkman, Steve, illus. 2006. 144p. (J). (gr. 4-8). reprint ed. 16.00 (978-1-4223-5621-0(3)) DIANE Publishing Co.

Powell, Jillian. Self-Harm & Suicide. 2008. (Emotional Health Issues Ser.). (Illus.). 48p. (YA). (gr. 7-12). lib. bdg. 31.00 (978-0-8368-9202-4(X)) Stevens, Gareth Publishing LLLP.

Rondeau, Amanda. Justice. 2003. (United We Stand Ser.). (ENG., Illus.). 24p. (J). (gr. k-3). lib. bdg. 24.21 (978-1-57765-879-5(5), SandCastle) ABDO Publishing Co.

Rondina, Catherine. Gossip: Deal with It Before Word Gets Around, 1 vol. Workman, Dan, illus. 2004. (Lorimer Deal with It Ser.). (ENG.). 32p. (J). (gr. 4-8). pap. 12.95 (978-1-55028-821-6(0), 9781550288216) Lorimer, James & Co., Ltd., Pubs. CAN. Dist: Orca Bk. Pubs. USA.

Rorick, William. Society. 2008. 60p. pap. 17.95 (978-1-4327-2481-8(9)) Outskirts Pr., Inc.

Salzmann, Mary Elizabeth. I Am Caring. 2003. (Building Character Ser.). (ENG., Illus.). 24p. (J). (gr. k-3). lib. bdg. 24.21 (978-1-57765-827-6(2), SandCastle) ABDO Publishing Co.

—I Am Respectful. 2003. (Building Character Ser.). (ENG., Illus.). 24p. (J). (gr. k-3). lib. bdg. 24.21 (978-1-57765-829-0(9), SandCastle) ABDO Publishing Co.

Senning, Cindy Post & Post, Emily. Emily Post's the Guide to Good Manners for Kids. Björkman, Steve, illus. 2004. (ENG.). 144p. (J). (gr. 3-7). 16.99 (978-0-06-057196-2(9)) HarperCollins Pubs.

Seto, Alex. What Do You See? Touch My Nose, It Feels Funny. 2006. (Illus.). 14p. bds. (978-0-9734496-4-8(0)) ADVAN Pr., Inc.

Soske, Becky. Just the Way He Wanted Me to Be. Haisch, Joshua, illus. 2007. 32p. (J). (gr. -1-3). per. 11.99 (978-1-59879-339-0(X)) Lifevest Publishing, Inc.

Sprague, Jeff & Golly, Annemieke. Best Behavior: Building Positive Behavior Support in Schools. 2004. (Illus.). 254p. 89.49 (978-1-59318-071-3(3), 230BEST) Cambium Education, Inc.

Sprick, Randall S. The Solution Book. (Solution Book Ser.). (gr. k-8). 99.90 (978-0-07-568978-2(2)) SRA/McGraw-Hill.

Teen Issues, 26 bks., Set. (Illus.). (YA). (gr. 6-12). lib. bdg. 344.10 (978-0-89490-887-3(1)) Enslow Pubs., Inc.

Trainer, Chaim. Shalom Secrets: How to Live in Peace with Friends & Family, A Children's Guide. 2005. (YID., Illus.). 121p. (J). (gr. 4-7). pap. 13.95 (978-1-930640-06-1(4)) Inner Learning.

Verdick, Elizabeth. Feet Are Not for Kicking. Heinlen, Marieka, illus. 2004. (Best Behavior Ser.). (ENG.). 24p. (J). 7.95 (978-1-57542-158-2(5)) Free Spirit Publishing, Inc.

—Sharing Time. Heinlen, Marieka, illus. 2009. (Toddler Tools Ser.). (ENG.). 24p. (J). (gr. -1). 7.95 (978-1-57542-314-2(6)) Free Spirit Publishing, Inc.

—Tails Are Not for Pulling. Heinlen, Marieka, illus. 2005. (Best Behavior Ser.: Bk. 3). (ENG.). 24p. (J). (gr. 3-7). 7.95 (978-1-57542-180-3(1)) Free Spirit Publishing, Inc.

—Teeth Are Not for Biting. Heinlen, Marieka, illus. 2003. (Best Behavior Ser.). (ENG.). 24p. (J). 7.95 (978-1-57542-128-5(3)) Free Spirit Publishing, Inc.

—Words Are Not for Hurting. Heinlen, Marieka, illus. 2004. (Best Behavior Ser.). (ENG.). 24p. (J). 7.95 (978-1-57542-155-1(0)) Free Spirit Publishing, Inc.

Willker, Joshua D. G. Everything You Need to Know about Sports Gambling. 2005. (Need to Know Library). (Illus.). 64p. (YA). (gr. 7-12). lib. bdg. 31.95 (978-0-8239-3229-0(X), NTSPGA) Rosen Publishing Group, Inc., The.

Winkler, Kathleen. Bullying: How to Deal with Taunting, Teasing, & Tormenting. 2005. (Issues in Focus Today Ser.). (Illus.). 104p. (J). (gr. 6-13). lib. bdg. 33.27 (978-0-7660-2355-0(9)) Enslow Pubs., Inc.

Wrazen, Nicholas. Don't Talk to Strangers. 2008. (Real Readers - Upper Emergent Ser.). (ENG., Illus.). 12p. (gr. 1-2). pap. 5.90 (978-0-8239-8192-2(4)) Rosen Publishing Group, Inc., The.

Yomtov, Nelson. The Grimy, Gross Unusual History of the Toilet, 1 vol. 2011. (Unusual Histories Ser.). (ENG.). 48p. (gr. 3-4). lib. bdg. 31.99 (978-1-4296-5489-0(9)) Capstone Press of Coughlan Cos.

BEHAVIOR—FICTION

Adams, Jennifer. Edgar & the Tattle-Tale Heart, 1 vol. Stucki, Ron, illus. 2014. (ENG.). 32p. (J). 16.99 (978-1-4236-3766-0(6)) Gibbs Smith, Publisher.

Adventures in Flatfrost. 2014. (Kingdom of Wrenly Ser.: 5). (ENG., Illus.). 128p. (J). (gr. k-4). pap. 5.99 (978-1-4814-1388-6(0), Little Simon) Little Simon.

Al-Araimi, Saif & Al-Rawahi, Thuria. Smart Parents Meet Mr Motivation (V2) 2010. 85p. pap. 16.40 (978-0-557-20544-8(1)) Lulu Pr., Inc.

Alberto, Daisy. No Rules for Rex! Smath, Jerry, illus. 2005. (Social Studies Connects). 32p. (J). pap. 5.95 (978-1-57565-146-0(7)) Kane Press, Inc.

Allard, Harry. Miss Nelson Is Missing!, 1 vol. Marshall, James, illus. 2007. (Read along Book & CD Ser.). (ENG.). 32p. (J). (gr. -1-3). audio compact disk 10.99 (978-0-618-85281-9(6)) Houghton Mifflin Harcourt Publishing Co.

Allen, Debbie. Dancing in the Wings. Nelson, Kadir, illus. 2003. (J). (gr. -1-3). 14.65 (978-0-7569-7022-2(9)) Perfection Learning Corp.

Allen-Wilson, Regina. Bobo & the Pooch. 2013. 26p. pap. 12.00 (978-1-4575-2084-6(2)) Dog Ear Publishing, LLC.

Aloha Potter! Evaluation Guide: Evaluation Guide. 2006. (J). (978-1-55942-397-7(8)) Witcher Productions.

Andersen, Hans Christian & Starbright Foundation Staff. The Emperor's New Clothes. Burton, Virginia Lee, illus. 2004. (ENG.). 48p. (J). (gr. -1-3). pap. 6.95 (978-0-618-34420-8(9)) Houghton Mifflin Harcourt Publishing Co.

Anderson, Jessica. Case of the Sabotaged Spaghetti. 2015. (ENG.). 64p. (gr. 3-6). 29.95 (978-1-63430-384-2(9)) Rourke Educational Media.

Anderson, Peggy Perry. Out to Lunch. 2015. (Green Light Readers Level 1 Ser.). (ENG., Illus.). 32p. (J). (gr. 1-4). pap. 3.99 (978-0-544-52858-1(1), HMH Books For Young Readers) Houghton Mifflin Harcourt Publishing Co.

Antony, Steve. Betty Goes Bananas. 2014. (ENG., Illus.). 32p. (J). (-k). 16.99 (978-0-553-50761-4(3), Schwartz & Wade Bks.) Random Hse. Children's Bks.

Applegate, Katherine. Never Swim in Applesauce. 2016. (Roscoe Riley Rules Ser.: 4). (J). lib. bdg. 14.75 (978-0-606-38737-8(4)) Turtleback Bks.

Armstrong, Ashley Sage-Taylor. The Adventures of Starlight & Sunny: Building a Dream , How to Focus & Make Your Dreams Come to Life, with Positive Conscious Morals. Picture Boo. 2013. 52p. pap. (978-1-927863-04-6(X)) Armstrong, Ashley.

Arnold, Tedd. No Jumping on the Bed! 25th anniv. ed. 2012. (ENG., Illus.). 32p. (J). (gr. -1-1). 16.99 (978-0-8037-3563-7(4), Dial Bks) Penguin Young Readers Group.

Ashman, Linda. Samantha on a Roll. Davenier, Christine, illus. 2011. (ENG.). 40p. (J). (gr. -1-4). 17.99 (978-0-374-36399-4(4), 9780374363994, Farrar, Straus & Giroux (BYR)) Farrar, Straus & Giroux.

Atherton, Isabel. The Bad Easter Bunny. Röhr, Stéphanie, illus. 2013. (ENG.). 32p. (J). (gr. -1-k). 12.95 (978-1-62087-500-1(4), 620500, Sky Pony Pr.) Skyhorse Publishing Co., Inc.

Atkins, Catherine. Alt Ed. 2004. (ENG.). 208p. (YA). (gr. 7-12). reprint ed. 6.99 (978-0-14-240235-1(4), Speak) Penguin Young Readers Group.

Atwood, Margaret. Up in the Tree, 1 vol. 2010. (ENG., Illus.). 32p. (J). (gr. k-k). 19.95 (978-1-55498-080-2(1)) Groundwood Bks. CAN. Dist: Publishers Group West (PGW).

Auch, Mary Jane. Poultrygeist. Jane, Mary & Auch, Herm, illus. 2004. (ENG.). 32p. (J). (gr. k-3). reprint ed. 6.95 (978-0-8234-1876-3(6)) Holiday Hse., Inc.

Avi. The Fighting Ground. 152p. (J). pap. 4.95 (978-0-8072-1378-0(0), Listening Library) Random Hse. Audio Publishing Group.

Aylesworth, Jim. Naughty Little Monkeys. Cole, Henry, illus. 2006. (ENG.). 32p. (J). (gr. -1-2). reprint ed. 6.99 (978-0-14-240562-8(0), Puffin Books) Penguin Young Readers Group.

Banks, Lynne Reid. Angela & Diabola. 163p. (J). (gr. 4-6). pap. 4.50 (978-0-8072-1515-9(5), Listening Library) Random Hse. Audio Publishing Group.

Banning, Gail. Out on a Limb. 2008. (ENG.). 256p. (YA). (gr. 6-9). (978-1-55470-012-7(4)) Me to We.

Barba, Ale. Time Out! Barba, Ale, illus. 2017. (ENG., Illus.). 32p. (J). (gr. -1-2). 16.99 **(978-0-399-16304-3(2)**, Philomel Bks.) Penguin Young Readers Group.

Barbaresi, Nina, illus. The Tale of Tom Kitten: A Story about Good Behavior. 2006. (J). 6.99 (978-1-59939-002-4(7)) Cornerstone Pr.

Bardhan-Quallen, Sudipta. Tyrannosaurus Wrecks! OHora, Zachariah, illus. 2014. (ENG.). 32p. (J). (gr. k-2). 14.95 (978-1-4197-1035-3(4), Abrams Bks. for Young Readers) Abrams, Inc.

Barnaby, Hannah Rodgers. Bad Guy. Yamada, Mike, illus. 2017. (ENG.). 32p. (J). (gr. -1-3). 17.99 (978-1-4814-6010-1(2), Simon & Schuster Bks. For Young Readers) Simon & Schuster Bks. For Young Readers.

Barnett, Mac. Billy Twitters & His Blue Whale Problem. Rex, Adam, illus. 2009. (ENG.). 48p. (J). (gr. -1-2). 16.99 (978-0-7868-4958-1(4)) Hyperion Pr.

Barrows, Annie. Bound to Be Bad. 2009. (Ivy & Bean Ser.: 5). (J). lib. bdg. 16.00 (978-0-606-14473-5(0), Turtleback) Turtleback Bks.

—Ivy + Bean Bound to Be Bad. Blackall, Sophie, illus. (Ivy & Bean Ser.: IVYB). (ENG.). (J). (gr. 1-5). 2009. 128p. pap. 5.99 (978-0-8118-6857-0(5)) 2008. 124p. 14.99 (978-0-8118-6265-3(8)) Chronicle Bks. LLC.

—Ivy + Bean Take Care of the Babysitter. Blackall, Sophie, illus. (Ivy & Bean Ser.: IVYB). (ENG.). 2008. 128p. (J). (gr. 1-5). pap. 5.99 (978-0-8118-6584-5(3)) 2007. pap., tchr. ed. (978-0-8118-8667-3(0)) Chronicle Bks. LLC.

Barrows, Annie & Blackall, Sophie. Ivy + Bean Bound to Be Bad, 1 vol. 2011. (Ivy & Bean Ser.). (ENG., Illus.). 128p. (J). (gr. 1-4). 24.21 (978-1-59961-932-3(6)) Spotlight.

—Ivy + Bean Take Care of the Babysitter, 1 vol. 2011. (Ivy & Bean Ser.). (ENG., Illus.). 128p. (J). (gr. 1-4). 24.21 (978-1-59961-931-6(8)) Spotlight.

Basye, Dale E. Where the Bad Kids Go. Dob, Bob, illus. 2009. (Heck Ser.). (ENG.). 304p. (J). (gr. 3-7). 6.99 (978-0-375-84076-0(1), Yearling) Random Hse. Children's Bks.

—Wise Acres: the Seventh Circle of Heck. Dob, Bob, illus. 2013. (Heck Ser.). (ENG.). 448p. (J). (gr. 4-7). 16.99 (978-0-307-98185-1(1), Random Hse. Bks. for Young Readers) Random Hse. Children's Bks.

Bauer, Marion Dane. On My Honor. 90p. (J). (gr. 5-6). pap. 4.50 (978-0-8072-1455-8(8), Listening Library) Random Hse. Audio Publishing Group.

—On My Honor. 90p. (YA). 22.25 (978-0-8446-7324-0(2)) Smith, Peter Pub., Inc.

Beck, Carolyn. Richard Was a Picker, 1 vol. Hodson, Ben, illus. 2010. (ENG.). 32p. (J). (gr. -1-3). 19.95 (978-1-55469-088-6(9)) Orca Bk. Pubs. USA.

Becker, Bonny. The Magical Ms. Plum. Portnoy, Amy, illus. 2011. (ENG.). 112p. (J). (gr. 1-4). 6.99 (978-0-375-84760-8(X), Yearling) Random Hse. Children's Bks.

Bee, Clair. Clutch Hitter. (J). 17.95 (978-0-8488-1246-1(8)) Amereon Ltd.

Beil, Karen Magnuson. Mooove Over! A Book about Counting by Twos. Meisel, Paul, tr. Meisel, Paul, illus. 2004. (ENG.). 32p. (J). (gr. k-3). tchr. ed. 16.95 (978-0-8234-1736-0(0)) Holiday Hse., Inc.

Bellingham, Brenda. Lilly in the Middle, 1 vol. Owen, Elizabeth, illus. 2003. (Formac First Novels Ser.: 25). (ENG.). 64p. (J). (gr. 1-5). 4.95 (978-0-88780-589-9(2), 9780887805899); 14.95 (978-0-88780-590-5(6), 9780887805905) Formac Publishing Co., Ltd. CAN. Dist: Casemate Pubs. & Bk. Distributors, LLC.

—Lilly Makes a Friend. MacDonald, Clarke, illus. 2004. 62p. (J). lib. bdg. 12.00 (978-1-4242-1221-7(9)) Fitzgerald Bks.

Benavides, Desiree. Little Henry's Adventures: Henry's Trip to the Supermarket. 2008. 24p. pap. 24.95 (978-1-60563-011-3(X)) America Star Bks.

Bennett, Kelly. Your Daddy Was Just Like You. Walker, David, illus. 2010. (ENG.). 32p. (J). (gr. -1-k). 16.99 (978-0-399-25258-7(4), G.P. Putnam's Sons Books for Young Readers) Penguin Young Readers Group.

Berenstain, Stan & Berenstain, Jan. The Berenstain Bears & the Blame Game. 2004. (Berenstain Bears First Time Bks.). (Illus.). (J). (gr. k-3). spiral bd. (978-0-616-14559-3(4)); spiral bd. (978-0-616-14560-9(8)) Canadian National Institute for the Blind/Institut National Canadien pour les Aveugles.

Berger, Samantha. Crankenstein. Santat, Dan, illus. 2013. (ENG.). 40p. (J). (gr. -1-3). 16.99 (978-0-316-12656-4(X)) Little Brown & Co.

—Crankenstein. Santat, Dan, illus. 2014. (ENG.). 24p. (J). (gr. -1 — 1). bds. 8.99 (978-0-316-28232-1(4)) Little, Brown Bks. for Young Readers.

Berry, Joy. Being Helpful. 2009. (ENG.). 40p. (J). (gr. -1-k). pap. 7.95 (978-1-60577-218-9(6)) Berry, Joy Enterprises.

—Feeling Angry. 2009. (ENG.). 40p. (J). (gr. -1-k). pap. 7.95 (978-1-60577-208-0(9)) Berry, Joy Enterprises.

—Needing Attention. 2009. (ENG.). 40p. (J). (gr. -1-k). pap. 7.95 (978-1-60577-217-2(8)) Berry, Joy Enterprises.

Berry, Julie & Gardner, Sally Faye. The Rat Brain Fiasco. 2010. (Splurch Academy Ser.: 1). (ENG.). 208p. (J). (gr. 3-7). pap. 6.99 (978-0-448-45359-0(2), Grosset & Dunlap) Penguin Young Readers Group.

Bertrand, Diane Gonzales. The F Factor. 2010. 256p. (YA). (gr. 6-18). pap. 12.95 (978-1-55885-598-4(X), Piñata Books) Arte Publico Pr.

Big Bad Bully. 2006. (ENG.). 32p. (J). pap. 12.99 (978-0-9758709-1-4(2)) Send The Light Distribution LLC.

Bingham, Kelly. Circle, Square, Moose. Zelinsky, Paul O., illus. 2014. (ENG.). 48p. (J). (gr. -1-3). 17.99 (978-0-06-229003-8(7), Greenwillow Bks.) HarperCollins Pubs.

—Z Is for Moose. Zelinsky, Paul O., illus. 2012. 32p. (J). (gr. -1-2). (ENG.). 16.99 (978-0-06-079984-7(6)); lib. bdg. 17.89 (978-0-06-079985-4(4)) HarperCollins Pubs. (Greenwillow Bks.).

Birchall, Mark. Rabbit's Wooly Sweater. Birchall, Mark, illus. 2003. (Picture Bks.). (Illus.). 32p. (J). (gr. -1-3). 15.95 (978-1-57505-465-0(5), Carolrhoda Bks.) Lerner Publishing Group.

Birdsall, Jeanne. My Favorite Pets. Bliss, Harry, illus. 2016. (ENG.). 40p. (J). (gr. -1-2). 16.99 (978-0-385-75570-2(8), Knopf Bks. for Young Readers) Random Hse. Children's Bks.

Bishop, Helena Edwards. Simon & the Money Tree. 2012. (Illus.). 40p. pap. 18.95 (978-1-4709-9783-0(5)) Lulu Pr., Inc.

Black, Holly. Kith. Naifeh, Ted, illus. 2010. (Good Neighbors Ser.: 2). (ENG.). 128p. (J). (gr. 3-7). pap. 12.99 (978-0-439-85566-2(7), Graphix) Scholastic, Inc.

Blake, Adriana L. Benjamin Bear's Naughtiest Night Ever! 2011. 60p. pap. 24.00 (978-1-4567-5252-1(9)) AuthorHouse.

Blazek, Frank. Phil & His Fabulous Feathers, 1 vol. Thomas, Wes, illus. 2005. (ENG.). 32p. (J). (gr. k-3). 16.99 (978-1-58980-280-3(2)) Pelican Publishing Co., Inc.

Bledsoe, Amanda. Chores, S'mores!, 1 vol. Perry, Jodi, ed. 2009. 28p. pap. 24.95 (978-1-60703-605-0(3)) PublishAmerica, Inc.

—Chores S'mores, 1 vol. 2010. 26p. 24.95 (978-1-4512-1507-6(X)) PublishAmerica, Inc.

Bloom, Becky. Leo & Lester. Biet, Pascal, illus. 2003. (J). 32p. 15.95 (978-1-59034-582-5(7)); 33p. pap. (978-1-59034-583-2(5)) Mondo Publishing.

Blume, Judy. Otherwise Known as Sheila the Great. 2004. (ENG.). 160p. (J). (gr. 3-7). 7.99 (978-0-425-19380-8(2), Berkley) Penguin Publishing Group.

—Superfudge. 2007. (Fudge Bks.: 3).Tr. of Superfudge. lib. bdg. 18.40 (978-1-4177-8843-9(7), Turtleback) Turtleback Bks.

Blyton, Enid. The Naughtiest Girl Again. (Illus.). 176p. (J). mass mkt. 6.95 (978-0-09-915911-7(2)) Random Hse. GBR. Dist: Trafalgar Square Publishing.

Bochynek, Halina. A Beagle's Tale. 2008. 152p. pap. 14.99 (978-1-4389-1960-7(3)) AuthorHouse.

Bolger, Kevin. Sir Fartsalot Hunts the Booger. Gilpin, Stephen, illus. 2009. (ENG.). 224p. (J). (gr. 3-7). 7.99 (978-1-59514-284-9(3), Razorbill) Penguin Young Readers Group.

Bonacci, Ross. Show & Tell with Rossi & Lucy: A Daytime Story. 2012. 40p. pap. 13.95 (978-1-4525-0456-8(3)) Balboa Pr.

Bottner, Barbara. Priscilla Gorilla. Emberley, Michael, illus. 2017. (ENG.). 40p. (J). (gr. -1-2). 17.99 (978-1-4814-5897-9(3), Atheneum/Caitlyn Dlouhy Books) Simon & Schuster Children's Publishing.

Bottner, Barbara & Kruglik, Gerald. Wallace's Lists. Landstrom, Olof, illus. 2011. (J). (gr. 1-3). 29.95 (978-0-545-04275-8(5)) Weston Woods Studios, Inc.

Bove, C. M. Sebastian's Secret Excuses to Avoid Cleaning His Room: (Do Not Let Adults Read This Book!!!) 2012. 52p. pap. 8.95 (978-1-4697-7925-6(0)) iUniverse, Inc.

Bowdish, Lynea. How to Be Nice — & Other Lessons I Didn't Learn. Gray, Leslie, illus. 2006. 47p. (J). pap. (978-1-59336-726-8(0)) Mondo Publishing.

Bowe, Julie. My Best Frenemy. 2011. (Friends for Keeps Ser.). (ENG.). 256p. (J). (gr. 3-7). 6.99 (978-0-14-241880-2(3), Puffin Books) Penguin Young Readers Group.

Bracken, Beth. The Little Bully, 1 vol. Bell, Jennifer A., illus. 2012. (Little Boost Ser.). (ENG.). 32p. (gr. k-3). lib. bdg. 23.99 (978-1-4048-6795-6(3), Little Boost) Picture Window Bks.

—Terrible, Awful, Horrible Manners!, 1 vol. Watson, Richard, illus. 2011. (Little Boost Ser.). (ENG.). 32p. (gr. k-3). lib. bdg. 23.99 (978-1-4048-6653-9(1), Little Boost) Picture Window Bks.

—Terrible, Awful, Horrible Manners, 1 vol. Watson, Richard, illus. 2012. (Little Boost Ser.). (ENG.). 32p. (gr. k-3). 7.95 (978-1-4048-7419-0(4), Little Boost) Picture Window Bks.

Bramwell, Wendie & Normand, Bridgid. Rhymitis. Kim, Julie J., tr. Kim, Julie J., illus. 2003. 32p. (J). pap. (978-0-9741388-8-6(6)) Committee for Children.

Bramwell, Wendie, et al. The Friendship Alphabet. Ziegler, Michael, illus. Ziegler, Michael, photos by. 2003. 32p. (J). pap. (978-0-9741388-3-1(5)) Committee for Children.

Brancaccio, Terry. Time Out for Gio! 2011. 24p. pap. 15.99 (978-1-4628-7624-2(2)) Xlibris Corp.

Breese, K. Ryer. Future Imperfect. 2011. (ENG.). 320p. (YA). (gr. 8-18). pap. 22.99 (978-0-312-64151-1(6), 9780312641511, St. Martin's Griffin) St. Martin's Pr.

Brennan-Nelson, Denise. He's Been a Monster All Day. Moore, Cyd, illus. 2013. (ENG.). 32p. (J). (gr. -1-1). 14.99 (978-1-58536-827-3(X), 202363) Sleeping Bear Pr.

Brett, Jan. Home for Christmas. Brett, Jan, illus. 2011. (ENG., Illus.). 32p. (J). (gr. -1-k). 17.99 (978-0-399-25653-0(9), G.P. Putnam's Sons Books for Young Readers) Penguin Young Readers Group.

Britton, Faith. If You'D Only Believe. 2009. 24p. pap. 12.99 (978-1-4490-1741-5(X)) AuthorHouse.

Brown, Leslie. Not Yet. 2008. 32p. pap. 12.99 (978-1-4389-3218-7(9)) AuthorHouse.

Brown, Marc. Arthur & the Popularity Test. (Arthur Chapter Bks.: Bk. 12). 58p. (J). (gr. 3-6). pap. 3.95 (978-0-8072-1308-7(X)); 2004. (gr. 2-4). pap. 17.00 incl. audio (978-0-8072-0413-9(7), FTR204SP) Random Hse. Audio Publishing Group. (Listening Library).

Brown, Monica & Ventura, Gabriela Baeza. Clara & the Curandera / Clara y la Curandera. Muraida, Thelma, illus. 2011. (J). 16.95 (978-1-55885-700-1(1), Piñata Books) Arte Publico Pr.

Bruel, Nick. Bad Kitty. Bruel, Nick, illus. 2nd ed. 2007. (Bad Kitty Ser.). (ENG., Illus.). 40p. (J). (gr. -1-3). 17.99 (978-1-59643-299-4(3), 9781596432994) Roaring Brook Pr.

—Bad Kitty Takes a Test. 2017. (Bad Kitty Ser.). (ENG., Illus.). 144p. (J). 13.99 (978-1-62672-589-8(6), 9781626725898) Roaring Brook Pr.

Bruins, David. The Legend of Ninja Cowboy Bear. Leung, Hilary, illus. 2009. (Ninja Cowboy Bear Ser.). (ENG.). 32p. (J). (gr. -1-2). 16.95 (978-1-55453-486-9(0)) Kids Can Pr., Ltd. CAN. Dist: Hachette Bk. Group.

Brun-Cosme, Nadine. With Dad, It's Like That. Huche, Magali Le, illus. 2016. (ENG.). 24p. (J). (gr. -1-3). 16.99 (978-0-8075-8731-7(1)) Whitman, Albert & Co.

Bryan, Ashley. Can't Scare Me! Bryan, Ashley, illus. 2013. (ENG., Illus.). 40p. (J). (gr. -1-3). 16.99 (978-1-4424-7657-8(5), Atheneum Bks. for Young Readers) Simon & Schuster Children's Publishing.

Bryan, Sabrina & DeVillers, Julia. Princess of Gossip. 2008. (ENG.). 384p. pap. 23.99 (978-1-4165-7065-3(9), MTV Bks.) MTV Books.

Bryan, Sean. The Juggling Pug. Murphy, Tom, illus. 2011. (ENG.). 32p. (J). (gr. -1-k). 12.95 (978-1-61608-329-8(8), 608329, Sky Pony Pr.) Skyhorse Publishing Co., Inc.

Buckley, Michael. The Unusual Suspects. 2007. (Sisters Grimm Ser.: 2). (J). lib. bdg. 18.40 (978-1-4178-0732-1(6), Turtleback) Turtleback Bks.

Budic, Hannah Purdy. Ebenezer Flea & the Right Thing to Do, 1 vol. Rosendahl, Melissa M., illus. 2008. (ENG.). 30p. 24.95 (978-1-60441-750-0(1)) America Star Bks.

Bulla, Clyde Robert & Bulla. Shoeshine Girl. Grant, Leigh & Burke, Jim, illus. 2004. (Rise & Shine Ser.). (ENG.). 96p. (J). (gr. 2-5). reprint ed. pap. 4.99 (978-0-06-440228-6(2)) HarperCollins Pubs.

Burns, Ellen Flanagan. Nobody's Perfect: A Story for Children about Perfectionism. Villnave, Erica Pelton, illus. 2008. 48p. (J). (gr. 3-7). 14.95 (978-1-4338-0379-6(8)); pap. 9.95 (978-1-4338-0380-2(1)) American Psychological Assn. (Magination Pr.).

Burns, T. R. The Bad Apple. 2012. (Merits of Mischief Ser.: 1). (ENG.). 352p. (J). (gr. 3-7). 16.99 (978-1-4424-4029-6(5), Aladdin) Simon & Schuster Children's Publishing.

—A World of Trouble. (Merits of Mischief Ser.: 2). (ENG., Illus.). (J). (gr. 3-7). 2014. 400p. pap. 7.99 (978-1-4424-4033-3(3)) 2013. 384p. 16.99 (978-1-4424-4032-6(5)) Simon & Schuster Children's Publishing. (Aladdin).

Buzzeo, Toni. No T. Rex in the Library. Yoshikawa, Sachiko, illus. 2010. (ENG.). 32p. (J). (gr. -1-3). 17.99 (978-1-4169-3927-6(X), McElderry, Margaret K. Bks.) McElderry, Margaret K. Bks.

Byrne, Richard. The Really, Really, Really Big Dinosaur. 2012. (ENG.). 32p. (J). (978-1-58925-123-6(7)) Tiger Tales.

Cabot, Meg. Moving Day. 2009. (Allie Finkle's Rules for Girls Ser.: Bk. 1). (ENG.). 256p. (J). (gr. 3-7). 6.99 (978-0-545-04041-9(8), Scholastic Paperbacks) Scholastic, Inc.

—Moving Day. 2009. (Allie Finkle's Rules for Girls Ser.: 1). lib. bdg. 17.20 (978-0-606-06818-5(X), Turtleback) Turtleback Bks.

—Stage Fright. 2010. (Allie Finkle's Rules for Girls Ser.: 4). (ENG.). 240p. (J). (gr. 3-7). 6.99 (978-0-545-04046-4(9)) Scholastic, Inc.

Carlson, Melody. Charlene's Grumpy Day: A Scoozie Tale about Patience. Fincher, Kathryn Andrews, illus. Date not set. 32p. (J). 9.99 (978-0-7369-0734-7(3)) Harvest Hse. Pubs.

—Forgive Others. Reagan, Susan Joy, illus. 2004. (Just Like Jesus Said Ser.). 32p. (J). (gr. -1-5). 12.99 (978-0-8054-2385-3(0)) B&H Publishing Group.

—Grover Tells a Whopper: A Scoozie Tale about Honesty. Fincher, Kathryn Andrews, illus. Date not set. 32p. (J). 9.99 (978-0-7369-0733-0(5)) Harvest Hse. Pubs.

Carlson, Nancy. Sit Still! Carlson, Nancy, illus. 2012. (Nancy Carlson Picture Bks). (Illus.). 32p. (J). (gr. k-2). (ENG.). 9.95 (978-0-7613-8946-0(6)); 56.72 (978-0-7613-9301-6(3)) Lerner Publishing Group. (Carolrhoda Bks.).

Castillo, Lauren. The Troublemaker. 2014. (ENG., Illus.). 48p. (J). (gr. -1-3). 16.99 (978-0-547-72991-6(X)) Houghton Mifflin Harcourt Publishing Co.

Cederborg, Else. The Naughty Peteyboy, Sonya & the Magic Word. 2011. (Illus.). 28p. pap. 13.78 (978-1-4567-7671-8(1)) AuthorHouse.

Chaltas, Thalia. Because I Am Furniture. 2010. (ENG.). 368p. (YA). (gr. 7-18). 8.99 (978-0-14-241510-8(3), Speak) Penguin Young Readers Group.

Chambers, Mark, illus. Zach & Lucy & the Museum of Natural Wonders. 2016. (Zach & Lucy Ser.). (ENG.). 40p. (J). (gr. 1-3). pap. 3.99 (978-1-4814-3935-0(9), Simon Spotlight) Simon Spotlight.

—Zach & Lucy & the Yoga Zoo. 2016. (Zach & Lucy Ser.). (ENG.). 40p. (J). (gr. 1-3). pap. 3.99 (978-1-4814-3938-1(3), Simon Spotlight) Simon Spotlight.

Changed Behavior! Individual Title Six-Packs. (Bookweb Ser.). 32p. (gr. 6-18). 34.00 (978-0-7578-0892-0(1)) Rigby Education.

Chapman, Jared. Steve, Raised by Wolves. 2015. (ENG., Illus.). 40p. (J). (gr. -1-3). 17.00 (978-0-316-25390-1(1)) Little Brown & Co.

Charlie Bumpers vs. the Squeaking Skull, 1 vol. 2014. (Charlie Bumpers Ser.). (ENG., Illus.). (J). (gr. 2-4). 10p. 16.95 (978-1-56145-809-7(0)); 160p. 13.95 (978-1-56145-808-0(2)) Peachtree Pubs.

Charrier, Lisa. Oh My, Oh No! Domergue, Agnes, illus. 2014. (ENG.). 32p. (-k). 15.95 (978-0-7624-5409-9(1), Running Pr. Kids) Running Pr. Bk. Pubs.

Chartrand, Lili. Taming Horrible Harry. Ouriou, Susan, tr. from FRE. Rogé, illus. 2006. (ENG.). 32p. (J). (gr. -1-3). 16.95 (978-0-88776-772-2(9), Tundra Bks.) Tundra Bks. CAN. Dist: Penguin Random Hse. LLC.

Chichester Clark, Emma. Love Is My Favorite Thing. Chichester Clark, Emma, illus. 2015. (ENG., Illus.). 32p. (J). (gr. -1-k). 16.99 (978-0-399-17503-9(2), Nancy Paulsen Books) Penguin Young Readers Group.

Childrens Press Staff, ed. Messy Bessey. 2005. (Rookie Reader Ser.). (ENG.). 96p. (J). (gr. -1-2). pap. 9.95 (978-0-516-25328-2(X), Children's Pr.) Scholastic Library Publishing.

Chorao, Kay. Bad Boy, Good Boy. 2013. (ENG., Illus.). 32p. (J). (gr. k-2). 17.95 (978-1-4197-0520-5(2), Abrams Bks. for Young Readers) Abrams, Inc.

Christelow, Eileen. Five Little Monkeys Reading in Bed. 2011. (Five Little Monkeys Story Ser.). (ENG., Illus.). 40p. (J). (gr. -1-3). 16.99 (978-0-547-38610-2(9)) Houghton Mifflin Harcourt Publishing Co.

—Five Little Monkeys Trick-Or-Treat. 2013. (Five Little Monkeys Story Ser.). (ENG., Illus.). 40p. (J). (gr. -1-3). 16.99 (978-0-547-85893-7(0)) Houghton Mifflin Harcourt Publishing Co.

Christopher, Matt. Center Court Sting. 2005. (Sports Classics II Ser.). 140p. (J). lib. bdg. 15.00 (978-1-59054-749-6(7)) Fitzgerald Bks.

—Center Court Sting. l.t. ed. 2007. (New Matt Christopher Sports Library). 160p. (J). (gr. 4-6). lib. bdg. 26.60 (978-1-59953-106-9(2)) Norwood Hse. Pr.

—Hot Shot. 2010. (ENG.). 128p. (J). (gr. 3-7). pap. 5.99 (978-0-316-04482-0(2)) Little, Brown Bks. for Young Readers.

Citra, Becky. Whiteout, 1 vol. 2009. (Orca Young Readers Ser.). (ENG.). 112p. (J). (gr. 3-6). pap. 7.95 (978-1-55469-083-1(8)) Orca Bk. Pubs. USA.

Clark, Anthony & Whybrow, Ian. Little Wolf's Book of Badness. 2008. (ENG.). 96p. (J). pap. 18.95 (978-1-84002-823-2(8)) Oberon Bks., Ltd. GBR. Dist: Consortium Bk. Sales & Distribution.

Clements, Andrew. No Talking. 2014. (ENG.). 160p. (J). (gr. 3-7). 11.24 (978-1-63245-298-6(7)) Lectorum Pubns., Inc.

—No Talking. (J). 2008. 78.75 (978-1-4361-5835-0(4)) 2007. 54.75 (978-1-4281-5418-6(3)) 2007. 209.75 (978-1-4281-5419-3(1)) 2007. 1.25 (978-1-4281-5415-5(9)) 2007. 51.75 (978-1-4281-5424-7(8)) 2007. (SPA.). 54.75 (978-1-4281-5422-3(1)) 2007. 52.75 (978-1-4281-5420-9(5)) Recorded Bks., Inc.

—No Talking. Elliott, Mark, illus. (ENG.). 160p. (J). (gr. 3-7). 2009. pap. 7.99 (978-1-4169-0984-2(2)) 2007. 18.99 (978-1-4169-0983-5(4)) Simon & Schuster Children's Publishing. (Atheneum Bks. for Young Readers).

—No Talking. Elliott, Mark, illus. l.t. ed. 2007. (Literacy Bridge Middle Reader Ser.). 155p. (J). (gr. 3-7). 23.95 (978-1-4104-0294-3(0)) Thorndike Pr.

—No Talking. 2009. (CHI., Illus.). 180p. (J). pap. 14.95 (978-7-5309-5645-8(0)) Tianjin Education Pr.

—No Talking. 2009. lib. bdg. 18.40 (978-0-606-14508-4(7), Turtleback) Turtleback Bks.

—Sin Hablar. 2009.Tr. of No Talking. (SPA.). 156p. (gr. 4-6). pap. 10.99 (978-84-441-4100-8(3)) Everest Editora ESP. Dist: Lectorum Pubns., Inc.

—Troublemaker. Elliott, Mark, illus. (ENG.). (J). (gr. 3-7). 2013. 176p. pap. 7.99 (978-1-4169-4932-9(1)) 2011. 160p. lib. bdg. 16.99 (978-1-4169-4930-5(5)) Simon & Schuster Children's Publishing. (Atheneum Bks. for Young Readers).

Clyde, Addie Mae. Charlie the Chair. 2006. (J). per. 10.95 (978-1-59872-694-7(3)) Instant Pub.

Cocca-Leffler, Maryann. Princess Kim & Too Much Truth. 2012. (J). 34.28 (978-1-61913-121-7(8)) Weigl Pubs., Inc.

—Princess Kim & Too Much Truth. Cocca-Leffler, Maryann, illus. 2011. (ENG., Illus.). 32p. (J). (gr. 1-3). 16.99 (978-0-8075-6618-3(7)) Whitman, Albert & Co.

Cohen, Miriam. Liar, Liar, Pants on Fire!, 1 vol. Himler, Ronald, illus. 2008. (ENG.). 32p. (J). (gr. -1-3). 15.95 (978-1-59572-077-1(4)); pap. 5.95 (978-1-59572-078-8(2)) Star Bright Bks., Inc.

Cole, Babette. Princess Smartypants. 2004. (J). (gr. k-2). spiral bd. (978-0-616-01620-6(4)); spiral bd. (978-0-616-01619-0(0)) Canadian National Institute for the Blind/Institut National Canadien pour les Aveugles.

Cole, Henry. Eddie the Bully. 2016. (ENG.). 40p. (J). (gr. -1-3). 17.99 (978-1-4998-0181-1(5)) Little Bee Books Inc.

Conover, Chris. The Lion's Share. 2004. (J). (gr. k-3). spiral bd. (978-0-616-07222-6(8)); spiral bd. (978-0-616-07223-3(6)) Canadian National Institute for the Blind/Institut National Canadien pour les Aveugles.

Cook, Julia. A Bad Case of Tattle Tongue. DuFalla, Anita, illus. 2008. 32p. (J). (gr. -1). pap. 9.95 (978-1-931636-86-5(9)) National Ctr. For Youth Issues.

—But That Rule Doesn't Apply to Me. DuFalla, Anita, illus. 2016. (Responsible Me! Ser.: Vol. 3). (ENG.). 32p. (J). pap. 10.95 (978-1-934490-98-3(9)) Boys Town Pr.

—Decibella & Her 6-Inch Voice. DuFalla, Anita, illus. 2014. (ENG.). 32p. (J). pap. 10.95 (978-1-934490-58-7(X)) Boys Town Pr.

—I Can't Believe You Said That! De Weerd, Kelsey, illus. 2014. (ENG.). 32p. (J). pap. 10.95 (978-1-934490-67-9(9)) Boys Town Pr.

—Technology Tail: A Digital Footprint Story. DuFalla, Anita, illus. 2017. (ENG.). 32p. (J). (gr. 1-6). pap. 10.95 **(978-1-944882-13-6(8))** Boys Town Pr.

Cook, Julia. Well, I Can Top That! Dufalla, Anita, illus. 2014. (ENG.). 32p. (J). pap. 10.95 (978-1-934490-57-0(1)) Boys Town Pr.

Corderoy, Tracey. No! Warnes, Tim, illus. 2015. (ENG.). 28p. (J). (gr. -1-2). bds. 7.99 (978-1-58925-208-0(X)) Tiger Tales.

Coven, Wanda. Heidi Heckelbeck & the Christmas Surprise. Burris, Priscilla, illus. 2013. (Heidi Heckelbeck Ser.: 9). (ENG.). 128p. (J). (gr. k-2). 16.99 (978-1-4424-8125-1(0)); pap. 4.99 (978-1-4424-8124-4(2)) Little Simon. (Little Simon).

—Heidi Heckelbeck & the Christmas Surprise. 2013. (Heidi Heckelbeck Ser.: 9). lib. bdg. 14.75 (978-0-606-32325-3(2), Turtleback) Turtleback Bks.

—Heidi Heckelbeck in Disguise. Burris, Priscilla, illus. 2012. (Heidi Heckelbeck Ser.: 4). (ENG.). 128p. (J). (gr. k-2). 16.99 (978-1-4424-4169-9(0)); pap. 5.99 (978-1-4424-4168-2(2)) Little Simon. (Little Simon).

Cox, Judy. Puppy Power. Björkman, Steve, illus. (ENG.). 96p. (J). 2009. (gr. 2-4). pap. 6.95 (978-0-8234-2210-4(0)) 2008. (gr. -1-3). 15.95 (978-0-8234-2073-5(6)) Holiday Hse., Inc.

Craver, Marcella Marino. Joey Daring, Caring, & Curious. Lew-Vriethoff, Joanne, illus. 2014. (J). (978-1-4338-1652-9(0)); pap. (978-1-4338-1653-6(9)) American Psychological Assn. (Magination Pr.).

Crum, Shutta. Dozens of Cousins. Catrow, David, illus. 2013. (ENG.). 32p. (J). (gr. -1-3). 16.99 (978-0-618-15874-4(X)) Houghton Mifflin Harcourt Publishing Co.

Crutcher, Chris. Staying Fat for Sarah Byrnes. 2003. (ENG.). 304p. (YA). (gr. 8). pap. 9.99 (978-0-06-009489-8(3), Greenwillow Bks.) HarperCollins Pubs.

Cullen, Lynn. Dear Mr. Washington. Carpenter, Nancy, illus. 2015. (ENG.). 32p. (J). (gr. k-3). 16.99 (978-0-8037-3038-0(1), Dial Bks) Penguin Young Readers Group.

Curtiss, Dominique. Where Do I Come From? Hill, Rowland, tr. Fiala, Émilie, illus. 2013. 42p. pap. (978-2-89687-245-9(0)) chouetteditions.com.

Cutler, Henry T. King Mork. 2011. 48p. (gr. -1). pap. 12.95 (978-1-4678-7320-8(9)) AuthorHouse.

Cuyler, Margery. Bullies Never Win. Howard, Arthur, illus. 2009. (ENG.). 32p. (J). (gr. k-3). 17.99 (978-0-689-86187-1(7), Simon & Schuster Bks. For Young Readers) Simon & Schuster Bks. For Young Readers.

—Kindness Is Cooler, Mrs. Ruler. Yoshikawa, Sachiko, illus. 2007. (ENG.). 48p. (J). (gr. k-5). 17.99 (978-0-689-87344-7(1), Simon & Schuster Bks. For Young Readers) Simon & Schuster Bks. For Young Readers.

—Please Say Please! Penguin's Guide to Manners. Hillenbrand, Will, illus. 2005. (J). (978-0-439-67874-2(9)) Scholastic, Inc.

Dahl, Michael. Little Dinos Don't Bite, 1 vol. Record, Adam, illus. 2013. (Little Dinos Ser.). (ENG.). 20p. (gr. -1-k). bds. 7.99 (978-1-4048-7536-4(0)) Picture Window Bks.

—Little Dinos Don't Hit, 1 vol. Record, Adam, illus. 2013. (Little Dinos Ser.). (ENG.). 20p. (gr. -1-k). bds. 7.99 (978-1-4048-7533-3(6)) Picture Window Bks.

—Little Dinos Don't Push, 1 vol. Record, Adam, illus. 2013. (Little Dinos Ser.). (ENG.). 20p. (gr. -1-k). bds. 7.99 (978-1-4048-7534-0(4)) Picture Window Bks.

—Little Dinos Don't Yell, 1 vol. Record, Adam, illus. 2013. (Little Dinos Ser.). (ENG.). 20p. (gr. -1-k). bds. 7.99 (978-1-4048-7912-6(9)) Picture Window Bks.

Dahl, Roald. Charlie & the Chocolate Factory. movie tie-in ed. Date not set. 174p. (J). 19.95 (978-0-8488-2241-5(2)) Amereon Ltd.

—Charlie & the Chocolate Factory. 2009. 9.00 (978-0-88483-905-7(2), Everbind) Marco Bk. Co.

—Charlie & the Chocolate Factory. Brunetti, Ivan & Schindelman, Joseph, illus. 2011. (Penguin Classics Deluxe Edition Ser.). (ENG.). 176p. (gr. 5). 16.00 (978-0-14-310633-3(3), Penguin Classics) Penguin Publishing Group.

—Charlie & the Chocolate Factory. Blake, Quentin, illus. 2007. 17.00 (978-0-7569-8213-3(8)) Penguin Publishing Group.

—Charlie & the Chocolate Factory. Blake, Quentin, illus. (ENG.). (J). (gr. 3-7). 2011. 160p. 15.99 (978-0-14-241821-5(8)) 2007. 192p. 7.99 (978-0-14-241031-8(4)) 2004. 176p. pap. 7.99 (978-0-14-240108-8(0)) Penguin Young Readers Group. (Puffin Books).

—Charlie & the Chocolate Factory. Blake, Quentin, illus. 40th anniv. movie tie-in ed. 2014. (ENG.). 160p. (J). (gr. k-4). 27.99 (978-0-375-83197-3(5), Knopf Bks. for Young Readers) Random Hse. Children's Bks.

—Charlie & the Chocolate Factory. 2008. (J). 1.25 (978-1-4193-5983-5(5)) Recorded Bks., Inc.

—Charlie & the Chocolate Factory. 2007. 18.40 (978-1-4177-8609-1(4)) 2004. 18.40 (978-1-4177-0487-3(X)) Turtleback Bks. (Turtleback).

Daniel, Claire. A Winning Attitude. Winborn, Marsha, illus. 2007. 14p. pap. 4.75 (978-0-15-377381-5(2)) Harcourt Schl. Pubs.

Danziger, Paula. The Cat Ate My Gymsuit. 2004. (Puffin Modern Classics Ser.). (ENG.). 160p. (J). (gr. 3-7). pap. 5.99 (978-0-14-240250-4(8), Puffin Books) Penguin Young Readers Group.

—The Cat Ate My Gymsuit. 128p. (J). (gr. 3-5). pap. 3.99 (978-0-8072-1368-1(3), Listening Library) Random Hse. Audio Publishing Group.

—Second Grade Rules, Amber Brown. Ross, Tony, illus. 2005. (Amber Brown Ser.). 48p. (gr. k-2). 14.00 (978-0-7569-5521-2(1)) Perfection Learning Corp.

Dave & Matt. Yuck's Fart Club. Baines, Nigel, illus. 2013. (Yuck Ser.). (ENG.). 112p. (J). (gr. 2-5). pap. 6.99 (978-1-4424-8152-7(8), Simon & Schuster/Paula Wiseman Bks.) Simon & Schuster/Paula Wiseman Bks.

Davies, Gill. I Won't Do That Today: A Story of Stubbornness. O'Neill, Rachael, illus. 2009. (Let's Grow Together Ser.). 32p. (J). (gr. -1-2). pap. 10.55 (978-1-60754-765-5(1)); lib. bdg. 22.60 (978-1-60754-758-7(9)) Windmill Bks.

Davies, Jacqueline. The Lemonade Crime. 2011. (Lemonade War Ser.: 2). (ENG., Illus.). 160p. (J). (gr. 2-5). 15.99 (978-0-547-27967-1(1)) Houghton Mifflin Harcourt Publishing Co.

—The Lemonade Crime. 2012. (Lemonade War Ser.: 2). lib. bdg. 18.40 (978-0-606-24518-0(9), Turtleback) Turtleback Bks.

Davis, Heather. Never Cry Werewolf. 2010. (ENG.). 224p. (YA). (gr. 8). pap. 9.99 (978-0-06-134925-6(9), HarperTeen) HarperCollins Pubs.

Davis, Katie. The Curse of Addy Mcmahon. 2008. (ENG., Illus.). 288p. (J). (gr. 5-9). 16.99 (978-0-06-128711-4(3), Greenwillow Bks.) HarperCollins Pubs.

—The Curse of Addy McMahon. 2008. (Illus.). 288p. (J). (gr. 5-9). lib. bdg. 17.89 (978-0-06-128712-1(1), Greenwillow Bks.) HarperCollins Pubs.

Degen, Bruce. Snow Joke. 2014. 24p. pap. (978-0-8234-3223-3(8)) Holiday Hse., Inc.

Demers, Dominique. Today, Maybe, 1 vol. Grimard, Gabrielle, illus. 2011. (ENG.). 32p. (J). (gr. -1-3). 19.95 (978-1-55469-400-6(0)) Orca Bk. Pubs. USA.

DePalma, Mary Newell. Uh-Oh! 2011. (ENG., Illus.). 32p. (YA). 14.00 (978-0-8028-5372-1(2)) Eerdmans, William B. Publishing Co.

dePaola, Tomie. Trouble in the Barkers' Class. dePaola, Tomie, illus. 2006. (Barker Twins Ser.). (ENG., Illus.). 32p. (J). (gr. -1-3). reprint ed. pap. 6.99 (978-0-14-240585-7(X), Puffin Books) Penguin Young Readers Group.

Derrick, David G., Jr. Animals Don't, So I Won't! 2012. (ENG., Illus.). 36p. (J). (gr. -1-3). 15.95 (978-1-59702-029-9(X)) Immedium.

Derubertis, Barbara. Frances Frog's Forever Friend. 2010. pap. 45.32 (978-0-7613-6508-2(7)) Kane Press, Inc.

deRubertis, Barbara. Frances Frog's Forever Friend. Alley, R. W., illus. 2010. (Animal Antics A to Z Ser.). 32p. (J). (gr. -1-3). (ENG.). pap. 7.95 (978-1-57565-310-5(9)); lib. bdg. 22.60 (978-1-57565-317-4(6)) Kane Press, Inc.

Derubertis, Barbara. Tessa Tiger's Temper Tantrums. Alley, R. W., illus. 2011. (Animal Antics A to Z Set III Ser.). pap. 45.32 (978-0-7613-8429-8(4)) Kane Press, Inc.

deRubertis, Barbara. Tessa Tiger's Temper Tantrums. Alley, R. W., illus. 2011. (Animal Antics A to Z Ser.). 32p. (J). pap. 7.95 (978-1-57565-345-7(1)); lib. bdg. 22.60 (978-1-57565-353-2(2)) Kane Press, Inc.

deRubertis, Barbara & DeRubertis, Barbara. Frances Frog's Forever Friend. Alley, R. W., illus. 2012. (Animal Antics A to Z Ser.). 32p. (J). (gr. 2 — 1). cd-rom 7.95 (978-1-57565-399-0(0)) Kane Press, Inc.

—Tessa Tiger's Temper Tantrums. Alley, R. W., illus. 2012. (Animal Antics A to Z Ser.). 32p. (J). (gr. 2 — 1). cd-rom 7.95 (978-1-57565-413-3(X)) Kane Press, Inc.

Deuker, Carl. Night Hoops. 2009. (ENG.). 224p. (YA). (gr. 7). pap. 8.99 (978-0-547-24891-2(1)) Houghton Mifflin Harcourt Publishing Co.

—Night Hoops. 2009. 250p. (gr. 7-12). lib. bdg. 19.65 (978-0-613-61919-6(6), Turtleback) Turtleback Bks.

Diesen, Deborah. Picture Day Perfection. Santat, Dan, illus. 2013. (ENG.). 32p. (J). (gr. k-2). 17.95 *(978-1-4197-0844-2(9),* Abrams Bks. for Young Readers) Abrams, Inc.

Diggins, Matthew. Andrew & the Secret Gallery. Diggins, Matthew, illus. 2007. (Illus.). 30p. (J). (gr. 1-5). 15.95 *(978-1-60108-016-5(6))* Red Cygnet Pr.

Diggle, David Mark. Malana: Learns When Enough Is Enough. Preuss, Sarah Louise, illus. 2011. 24p. (J). pap. *(978-0-9871658-7-9(9))* Diggle de Doo Productions Pty, Ltd.

Dipucchio, Kelly. Dragon Was Terrible. Pizzoli, Greg, illus. 2016. (ENG.). 40p. (J). 16.99 *(978-0-374-30049-4(6),* 9780374300494, Farrar, Straus & Giroux (BYR)) Farrar, Straus & Giroux.

Dobell, Darcy. The Oyster Who Looked at the Sky. 2008. (ENG., Illus.). 32p. 16.95 *(978-0-88982-250-4(6))* Oolichan Bks. CAN. Dist: Univ. of Toronto Pr.

Donaldson, Julia & Walker, Sholto. The Pot of Gold. 2006. (Collins Big Cat Ser.). (ENG., Illus.). 24p. (J). (gr. 2-2). pap. 7.99 *(978-0-00-718696-9(7))* HarperCollins Pubs. Ltd. GBR. Dist: Independent Pubs. Group.

Donnelly, Jennifer. Humble Pie. Gammell, Stephen, illus. 2007. (ENG.). 32p. (J). (gr. -1-2). 13.99 *(978-1-4169-6751-4(6),* Aladdin) Simon & Schuster Children's Publishing.

Douthwaite, Wendy. The Orange Pony. 2003. (ENG., Illus.). 96p. (J). (gr. 2-7). mass mkt. 6.99 *(978-0-330-33631-4(2),* Pan) Pan Macmillan GBR. Dist: Trafalgar Square Publishing.

Dowd, Tara. No More Boogers Book. 2009. 16p. 11.50 *(978-0-615-26122-5(1))* Pick It Publishing.

Dower, Laura. Sunny & the Secret Passage. 2013. (Palace Puppies Ser.: 4). (J). lib. bdg. 14.75 *(978-0-606-35108-9(6),* Turtleback) Turtleback Bks.

Duffy, Carol Ann. The Gift. Ryan, Rob, illus. 2009. 32p. (J). *(978-1-84686-354-7(6))* Barefoot Bks., Inc.

Duffy, Carol Ann & Ryan, Rob. The Gift. Ryan, Rob, illus. 2010. (ENG., Illus.). 32p. (J). (gr. 3-18). 16.99 *(978-1-84686-355-4(4))* Barefoot Bks., Inc.

Durant, Alan. Little Miss Muffet's Big Scare. Heming, Leah-Ellen, illus. 2012. (ENG.). 32p. (J). *(978-0-7787-8030-4(9));* pap. *(978-0-7787-8041-0(4))* Crabtree Publishing Co.

Dyan, Penelope. Frugal Frannie — and the Big Room Cleaning Day. Dyan, Penelope, illus. 2009. (Illus.). 44p. pap. 11.95 *(978-1-935118-47-3(1))* Bellissima Publishing, LLC.

—Tammy's Left Shoe — -As Opposed to Her Right. Dyan, Penelope, illus. 2008. (Illus.). 44p. pap. 11.95 *(978-1-935118-41-1(2))* Bellissima Publishing, LLC.

Eareckson Tada, Joni. I'll Be with You Always. Nelson, Craig, illus. 2004. 32p. (gr. 8-12). 14.99 *(978-1-58134-000-6(1))* Crossway.

Eaton, Maxwell, III. The Flying Beaver Brothers & the Fishy Business. 2012. (Flying Beaver Brothers Ser.). (ENG.). 96p. (J). (gr. 1-4). pap. 7.99 *(978-0-375-86448-3(2),* Knopf Bks. for Young Readers) Random Hse. Children's Bks.

—Two Dumb Ducks. 2010. (ENG.). 32p. (J). (gr. -1-2). 12.99 *(978-0-375-84576-5(3),* Knopf Bks. for Young Readers) Random Hse. Children's Bks.

Ebel, Sherry. Cassie's Magic Doors. 2008. 28p. pap. 15.99 *(978-1-4363-2970-5(1))* Xlibris Corp.

Edwards, Pamela Duncan. The Grumpy Morning. 2004. (Illus.). (J). (gr. k-18). spiral bd. *(978-0-616-03030-1(4));* spiral bd. *(978-0-616-04552-7(2))* Canadian National Institute for the Blind/Institut National Canadien pour les Aveugles.

—Why the Stomach Growls. Taylor, Bridget Starr, illus. 2006. (ENG.). 32p. (J). (gr. k-6). 15.95 *(978-1-58536-298-1(0))* Sleeping Bear Pr.

Ehrmantraut, Brenda. I Want One Too! Short, Robbie, illus. 2003. (J). lib. bdg. 16.95 *(978-0-9729833-1-0(7));* per. 9.95 *(978-0-9729833-0-3(9))* Bubble Gum Pr.

Elliott, David. Finn Throws a Fit! Ering, Timothy Basil, illus. (ENG.). 32p. (J). 2011. (gr. k-k). pap. 6.99 *(978-0-7636-5604-1(6))* 2009. (gr. -1-k). 16.99 *(978-0-7636-2356-2(3))* Candlewick Pr.

Elliott, Laura Malone. Hunter's Best Friend at School. Munsinger, Lynn, illus. 2005. (gr. -1-2). 17.00 *(978-0-7569-5786-5(9))* Perfection Learning Corp.

Emmett, Jonathan. The Santa Trap, 1 vol. Bernatene, Poly, illus. 2012. (ENG.). 32p. (J). 15.95 *(978-1-56145-670-3(5))* Peachtree Pubs.

English, Karen. Nikki & Deja: Substitute Trouble. Freeman, Laura, illus. 2014. (ENG.). 112p. (J). (gr. 1-4). pap. 5.99 *(978-0-544-22388-2(8),* HMH Books For Young Readers) Houghton Mifflin Harcourt Publishing Co.

Ernst, Lisa Campbell. Sylvia Jean, the Drama Queen. 2005. (ENG., Illus.). 32p. (J). (gr. -1-3). 16.99 *(978-0-525-46962-9(1),* Dutton Books for Young Readers) Penguin Young Readers Group.

Esham, Barbaraa. Mrs. Gorski, I Think I Have the Wiggle Fidgets. Gordon, Mike, illus. 2008. (ENG, SPA & FRE.). 32p. (J). (gr. k-18). 16.95 *(978-1-60336-469-0(2),* Adventures of Everyday Geniuses, The) Mainstream Connections Publishing.

Falconer, Ian. Olivia. 2004. (Olivia Ser.). (J). (gr. k-3). (FRE., Illus.). spiral bd. *(978-0-616-14599-9(3));* spiral bd. *(978-0-616-07232-5(5));* spiral bd. *(978-0-616-07233-2(3))* Canadian National Institute for the Blind/Institut National Canadien pour les Aveugles.

—Olivia. 2009. (Los Especiales de A la Orilla del Viento Ser.). (SPA.). 32p. (J). 13.99 *(978-968-16-6346-9(2))* Fondo de Cultura Económcia.

—Olivia. Mlawer, Teresa, tr. 2004. (Olivia Ser.). (SPA., Illus.). (J). (gr. k-2). 16.00 *(978-1-930332-20-1(3),* LC5675) Lectorum Pubns., Inc.

Falconer, Ian & Simon & Schuster Audio Firm Staff. The Olivia Collection: Olivia; Olivia Saves the Circus; Olivia... & the Missing Toy; Olivia Forms a Band; Olivia Helps with Christmas; Olivia Goes to Venice; Olivia & the Fairy Princesses. Falconer, Ian, illus. 2012. (ENG., Illus.). 322p. (J). (gr. -1-2). 128.99 *(978-1-4424-8299-9(0),* Atheneum Bks. for Young Readers) Simon & Schuster Children's Publishing.

Farrell, Darren. Stop Following Me, Moon! 2016. (ENG., Illus.). 40p. (J). (-k). 17.99 *(978-0-8037-4159-1(6),* Dial Bks) Penguin Young Readers Group.

Feiffer, Jules. I'm Not Bobby! Feiffer, Jules, illus. 2006. (Illus.). 28p. (J). (gr. k-4). reprint ed. 16.00 *(978-0-7567-9853-6(1))* DIANE Publishing Co.

Feldman, Jody. The Seventh Level. (ENG.). (J). (gr. 5). 2011. 320p. pap. 6.99 *(978-0-06-195107-7(2))* 2010. 304p. 16.99 *(978-0-06-195105-3(6))* HarperCollins Pubs. (Greenwillow Bks.).

Ferguson, Suzanne P. Ferris Give Thanks. Date not set. (Illus.). 12p. (J). (gr. -1-k). *(978-0-9658745-0-2(8))* Ferguson, Suzanne Pamela.

Fernandes, Eugenie. A Difficult Day. (FRE.). (J). pap. 5.99 *(978-0-590-71827-1(4))* Scholastic, Inc.

Ferrell, Sean. The Snurtch. Santoso, Charles, illus. 2016. (ENG.). 40p. (J). (gr. -1-3). 17.99 *(978-1-4814-5656-2(3))* Simon & Schuster Children's Publishing.

FitzGerald, Helen. Deviant. 2014. (ENG.). (YA). (gr. 9). pap. 9.99 *(978-1-61695-419-2(1),* Soho Teen) Soho Pr., Inc.

Fleming, Candace. The Fabled Fifth Graders of Aesop Elementary School. 2012. (Aesop Elementary School Ser.). (ENG.). 176p. (J). (gr. 2-5). 7.99 *(978-0-375-87187-0(X),* Yearling) Random Hse. Children's Bks.

—The Fabled Fourth Graders of Aesop Elementary School. 2009. (Aesop Elementary School Ser.). (ENG.). 192p. (J). (gr. 2-5). 6.99 *(978-0-440-42229-7(9),* Yearling) Random Hse. Children's Bks.

Fleming, David. Saturday Boy. 2013. (ENG.). 272p. (J). (gr. 5). 16.99 *(978-0-670-78551-3(2),* Viking Books for Young Readers) Penguin Young Readers Group.

Flinn, Alex. Breathing Underwater. unabr. ed. 2004. (Young Adult Cassette Librariestm Ser.). 272p. (J). (gr. 7-18). pap. 36.00 incl. audio *(978-0-8072-0992-9(9),* S YA 346 SP, Listening Library) Random Hse. Audio Publishing Group.

Floca, Brian. The Frightful Story of Harry Walfish. Floca, Brian, illus. 2004. (Illus.). 26p. (J). (gr. k-4). reprint ed. pap. *(978-0-7567-7852-1(2))* DIANE Publishing Co.

Folgueira, Rodrigo. Bob the Dog. Bernatene, Poly, illus. 2014. (J). *(978-1-4351-5774-3(5))* Barnes & Noble, Inc.

Fontes, Justine & Jordan, Charles. Daniel el Descortés. Jordan, Charles, illus. 2011. (Rookie Ready to Learn Español Ser.). (SPA., Illus.). 40p. (J). pap. 5.95 *(978-0-531-26790-5(3));* lib. bdg. 23.00 *(978-0-531-26122-4(0))* Scholastic Library Publishing. (Children's Pr.).

Ford, Bernette G. Hurry Up! Kindert, Jennifer C., illus. 2004. (Just for You Ser.). (ENG.). 32p. (gr. k-1). pap. 3.99 *(978-0-439-56849-4(8),* Teaching Resources) Scholastic, Inc.

Ford, Ron. What Do You See? 2006. (Neighborhood Readers Ser.). (ENG.). 12p. (gr. 1-3). pap. 5.90 *(978-1-4042-6831-9(6),* Rosen Classroom) Rosen Publishing Group, Inc., The.

Foutz, Andrea. Friendships & Smiles. 2008. 18p. pap. 24.95 *(978-1-60610-175-9(7))* America Star Bks.

Fox, Mem. Harriet, You'll Drive Me Wild! 2004. (Illus.). (J). (gr. k-3). spiral bd. *(978-0-616-07236-3(8));* spiral bd. *(978-0-616-07237-0(6))* Canadian National Institute for the Blind/Institut National Canadien pour les Aveugles.

—Harriet, You'll Drive Me Wild! Frazee, Marla, illus. 2003. (ENG.). 32p. (J). (gr. -1-3). pap. 7.99 *(978-0-15-204598-2(8))* Houghton Mifflin Harcourt Publishing Co.

Frank, Hannah. If I Had Three Wishes. 2008. 56p. pap. 23.99 *(978-1-4343-7529-2(3))* AuthorHouse.

Freeman, Don. Quiet! There's a Canary in the Library. 2009. (ENG.). 48p. (J). (gr. -1-k). pap. 7.99 *(978-0-14-241452-1(2),* Puffin Books) Penguin Young Readers Group.

Friedman, Laurie. Back-to-School Rules. Murfin, Teresa, illus. 2011. (Carolrhoda Picture Books Ser.). (ENG.). 32p. (J). (gr. k-3). lib. bdg. 16.95 *(978-0-7613-6070-4(0))* Lerner Publishing Group.

—Mallory's Super Sleepover. Kalis, Jennifer, illus. (Mallory Ser.: 16). (ENG.). 160p. (J). (gr. 2-5). 2012. pap. 5.95 *(978-1-4677-0209-6(9))*No. 16. 2011. 15.95 *(978-0-8225-8887-0(0))* Lerner Publishing Group. (Darby Creek).

—Step Fourth, Mallory! Kalis, Jennifer, illus. (Mallory Ser.: 10). (ENG.). 176p. (J). (gr. 2-5). 2009. pap. 5.95 *(978-1-58013-842-0(X),* First Avenue Editions) 2008. 15.95 *(978-0-8225-8881-8(1),* Carolrhoda Bks.) Lerner Publishing Group.

Gaffney, Linda. My Daddy Does GOOD Things, Too! Dabney, Undra & Goettling, Nickalas, illus. 2006. 55p. per. 10.99 *(978-0-9787501-0-7(1))* Gaffney, Linda.

Galindo, Claudia. It's Bedtime, Cucuy!/A la Cama, Cucuy. Pluecker, John, tr. from ENG. Coombs, Jonathan, illus. 2008. (SPA & ENG.). 32p. (J). (gr. -1-2). 16.95 *(978-1-55885-491-8(6),* Piñata Books) Arte Publico Pr.

Gall, Chris. Revenge of the Dinotrux. 2012. (Dinotrux Ser.: 2). (ENG., Illus.). 32p. (J). (gr. -1-3). 16.99 *(978-0-316-13288-6(8))* Little Brown & Co.

—Substitute Creacher. 2011. (ENG., Illus.). 40p. (J). (gr. -1-3). 16.99 *(978-0-316-08915-9(X))* Little, Brown Bks. for Young Readers.

Gantos, Jack. Dead End in Norvelt. 2011. (Norvelt Ser.: 1). (ENG., Illus.). 352p. (J). (gr. 5-9). 15.99 *(978-0-374-37993-3(9),* 9780374379933, Farrar, Straus & Giroux (BYR)) Farrar, Straus & Giroux.

—Dead End in Norvelt. 2013. (Norvelt Ser.: 1). (ENG., Illus.). 384p. (J). (gr. 5-9). pap. 8.99 *(978-1-250-01023-0(3),* 9781250010230) Square Fish.

—Dead End in Norvelt. 2013. (J). lib. bdg. 18.40 *(978-0-606-31901-0(8),* Turtleback) Turtleback Bks.

—The Follower. 2015. (ENG.). 224p. (YA). (gr. 7-10). 17.99 *(978-0-374-37995-7(5),* 9780374379957, Farrar, Straus & Giroux (BYR)) Farrar, Straus & Giroux.

Garza, Xavier & Villarroel, Carolina. Zulema & the Witch Owl/Zulema y la Bruja Lechuza. Garza, Xavier, illus. 2009. (SPA & ENG., Illus.). 32p. (J). (gr. -1-4). 16.95 *(978-1-55885-515-1(7),* Piñata Books) Arte Publico Pr.

Gassman, Julie. Crabby Pants, 1 vol. Watson, Richard, illus. 2012. (Little Boost Ser.). (ENG.). 32p. (gr. k-3). 7.95 *(978-1-4048-7416-9(X),* Little Boost) Picture Window Bks.

Gassman, Julie A. Crabby Pants, 1 vol. Watson, Richard, illus. 2010. (Little Boost Ser.). (ENG.). 32p. (gr. k-3). lib. bdg. 23.99 *(978-1-4048-6165-7(3),* Little Boost) Picture Window Bks.

—Lucille Gets Jealous, 1 vol. Cooke, Charlotte, illus. 2012. (Little Boost Ser.). (ENG.). 32p. (gr. k-3). lib. bdg. 23.99 *(978-1-4048-6797-0(X),* Little Boost) Picture Window Bks.

—You Get What You Get, 1 vol. Horne, Sarah, illus. 2012. (Little Boost Ser.). (ENG.). 32p. (gr. k-3). lib. bdg. 23.99 *(978-1-4048-6794-9(5),* Little Boost) Picture Window Bks.

Gaydos, Nora. Now I'm Growing! Hands Are Not for Hurting. Gutierrez, Akemi, illus. 2012. (ENG.). 30p. (J). (gr. -1-17). 8.99 *(978-1-60169-222-1(6))* Innovative Kids.

Geldart, Thomas. Emilie the Peacemaker. 2004. reprint ed. pap. 15.95 *(978-1-4191-1769-5(6));* pap. 1.99 *(978-1-4192-1769-2(0))* Kessinger Publishing, LLC.

Gene, Barbara. Lamar Montgomery & the Freaky Faces Club. 2006. (J). per. 14.95 *(978-1-889743-50-9(X))* Robbie Dean Pr.

Genhart, Michael. Cake & I Scream! ... Being Bossy Isn't Sweet. Mack, Steve, illus. 2017. (J). **(978-1-4338-2759-4(X),** Magination Pr.) American Psychological Assn.

Gerovasiliou, Oreanthy. Yuri the Lion: Three Stories. 2010. (Illus.). 48p. pap. 13.00 *(978-1-60888-069-0(9))* Nimble Bks. LLC.

Gifaldi, David. Toby Scudder, King of the School. 2005. (ENG.). 208p. (J). (gr. 5-7). pap. 12.95 *(978-0-618-55158-3(1))* Houghton Mifflin Harcourt Publishing Co.

Gifford, Peggy. Moxy Maxwell Does Not Love Writing Thank-You Notes. Fisher, Valorie, illus. 2009. (Moxy Maxwell Ser.). (ENG.). 192p. (J). (gr. 2-5). 6.99 *(978-0-375-84343-3(4),* Yearling) Random Hse. Children's Bks.

Gilbert, Paul T. Bertram & His Funny Animals. Rousseff, Minnie H., illus. 2016. (ENG.). 140p. (J). 24.95 *(978-0-7649-7372-7(X),* POMEGRANATE KIDS) Pomegranate Communications, Inc.

Gillis, Jennifer Blizin. What Do You Say? Losa, Ann, illus. 2006. (Reader's Clubhouse Level 2 Reader Ser.). (ENG.). 24p. (J). (gr. 1-4). pap. 3.99 *(978-0-7641-3298-8(9))* Barron's Educational Series, Inc.

Gilpin, Esther. How the Bear Got Its Hair. 2008. 24p. pap. 12.99 *(978-1-4389-1584-5(5))* AuthorHouse.

Gilson, Jamie. My Teacher Is an Idiom. Tilley, Debbie, illus. 2015. (ENG.). 144p. (J). (gr. 1-4). 16.99 *(978-0-544-05680-0(9))* Houghton Mifflin Harcourt Publishing Co.

Going, K. L. King of the Screwups. 2010. (ENG., Illus.). 320p. (YA). (gr. 7). pap. 9.99 *(978-0-547-33166-9(5))* Houghton Mifflin Harcourt Publishing Co.

Goscinny, René. Nicholas on Vacation. Bell, Anthea, tr. Sempé, Jean-Jacques, illus. 2013. (ENG.). 136p. (J). (gr. 1-4). pap. 9.95 *(978-0-7148-6224-8(X))* Phaidon Pr., Inc.

Gownley, Jim. Amelia & the Other Side of Yuletide: #4, 1 vol. Gownley, Jim, illus. 2011. (Amelia Rules! Ser.). (ENG., Illus.). 36p. 24.21 *(978-1-59961-790-9(0))* Spotlight.

Graves, Annie. A Dog's Breakfast. McElhinney, Glenn, illus. 2015. (Nightmare Club Ser.: 1). (ENG.). 64p. (J). (gr. 2-5). pap. 6.99 *(978-1-4677-6042-3(0));* lib. bdg. 25.32 *(978-1-4677-4350-1(X))* Lerner Publishing Group.

Graves, Sue. Crabby Gabby. Guicciardini, Desideria, illus. 2008. (Tadpoles Ser.). (ENG.). 24p. (J). (gr. -1-3). pap. *(978-0-7787-3883-1(3))* Crabtree Publishing Co.

Gray, Kes. Nelly, the Monster Sitter. Hanson, Stephen, illus. 2009. (ENG.). 272p. (J). (gr. 3-7). 8.99 *(978-1-59514-259-7(2),* Razorbill) Penguin Young Readers Group.

Greenberg, Nicki. The Naughtiest Reindeer. Greenberg, Nicki, illus. 2014. (ENG., Illus.). 32p. (J). (gr. -1-k). 14.99 *(978-1-74331-304-6(7))* Allen & Unwin AUS. Dist: Independent Pubs. Group.

Greene, Stephanie. Princess Posey & the Tiny Treasure. Sisson, Stéphanie Roth, illus. 2013. (Princess Posey, First Grader Ser.: 5). (ENG.). 96p. (J). (gr. k-3). pap. 5.99 *(978-0-14-242415-5(3),* Puffin Books) Penguin Young Readers Group.

Griffin, Kitty & Combs, Kathy. Stinker & the Onion Princess. Manders, John, illus. 2005. (J). *(978-0-8037-2976-6(6),* Dial) Penguin Publishing Group.

Gross, Carmen. Ryan Elias Finds: The Truth Behind Lying. Dixon, Nehemiah F., illus. 2008. 27p. pap. 24.95 *(978-1-60474-945-8(8))* America Star Bks.

Groves. Snatch & Grab. Date not set. (Illus.). 32p. (J). pap. 129.15 *(978-0-582-18303-2(0))* Addison-Wesley Longman, Ltd. GBR. Dist: Trans-Atlantic Pubns., Inc.

Guest, Elissa Haden. Bella's Rules. Halpin, Abigail, illus. 2013. (ENG.). 32p. (J). (gr. -1-k). 16.99 *(978-0-8037-3393-0(3),* Dial Bks) Penguin Young Readers Group.

—Harriet's Had Enough! Meisel, Paul, illus. 2009. (ENG.). 32p. (J). (gr. -1-2). 15.99 *(978-0-7636-3454-4(9))* Candlewick Pr.

Gutman, Anne. Lisa's Baby Sister. Hallensleben, Georg, illus. 2012. (ENG.). 32p. (J). (gr. k-3). pap. 6.99 *(978-0-449-81012-5(7),* Dragonfly Bks.) Random Hse. Children's Bks.

Haddix, Margaret Peterson. Say What? 2004. 91p. (J). lib. bdg. 15.00 *(978-1-4242-0915-6(3))* Fitzgerald Bks.

—Say What? Bernardin, James, illus. 2005. 91p. (J). 11.65 *(978-0-7569-5465-9(7))* Perfection Learning Corp.

—Say What? Bernardin, James, illus. 2005. (ENG.). 96p. (J). (gr. 1-5). pap. 5.99 *(978-0-689-86256-4(3),* Simon & Schuster Bks. For Young Readers) Simon & Schuster Bks. For Young Readers.

Hahn, Mary Downing. All the Lovely Bad Ones. 2009. (ENG.). 192p. (J). (gr. 2-5). pap. 7.99 *(978-0-547-24878-3(4))* Houghton Mifflin Harcourt Publishing Co.

—As Ever, Gordy. 2011. (ENG.). 192p. (J). (gr. 5-7). pap. 7.99 *(978-0-547-54955-2(5))* Houghton Mifflin Harcourt Publishing Co.

Hale, Bruce. Big Bad Baby. Breen, Steve, illus. 2014. (ENG.). 32p. (J). (gr. -1-k). 17.99 *(978-0-8037-3585-9(5),* Dial Bks) Penguin Young Readers Group.

—Clark the Shark. Francis, Guy, illus. 2013. (Clark the Shark Ser.). (ENG.). 32p. (J). (gr. -1-3). 17.99 *(978-0-06-219226-4(4))* HarperCollins Pubs.

Hale, Dean. Scapegoat: The Story of a Goat Named Oat & a Chewed-Up Coat. Slack, Michael, illus. 2011. (ENG.). 32p. (J). (gr. -1-3). 16.99 *(978-1-59990-468-9(3),* 9781599904689, Bloomsbury USA Childrens) Bloomsbury Publishing USA.

Hall, Kirsten & Flaxma, Jessica. Who Says? 2004. (My First Reader Ser.). (ENG.). 32p. (J). (gr. k-1). pap. 3.95 *(978-0-516-24642-0(9),* Children's Pr.) Scholastic Library Publishing.

Hall, Michael. Perfect Square. Hall, Michael, illus. 2011. (ENG., Illus.). 40p. (J). (gr. -1-k). 16.99 *(978-0-06-191513-0(0),* Greenwillow Bks.) HarperCollins Pubs.

Hallinan, P. K. Heartprints. (J). 24p. 7.95 *(978-0-8249-5358-4(4));* (ENG., Illus.). 22p. pap. 5.95 *(978-0-8249-5450-5(5))* Worthy Publishing. (Ideal Pubns.).

—Let's Learn All We Can! (ENG., Illus.). (J). 24p. pap. 6.55 *(978-0-8249-5449-9(1));* 2004. 48p. pap. 9.95 *(978-0-8249-5491-8(2))* Worthy Publishing. (Ideal Pubns.).

—A Rainbow of Friends. 2005. (ENG., Illus.). 32p. (J). (gr. -1-3). 4.35 *(978-0-8249-5519-9(6),* Ideal Pubns.) Worthy Publishing.

Hamilton, Tim. The Big Fib. Hamilton, Tim, illus. 2014. (I Like to Read(r) Ser.). (ENG., Illus.). 24p. (J). (gr. -1-3). 14.95 *(978-0-8234-2939-4(3))* Holiday Hse., Inc.

Hamlyn, Jean. Clumsy Daisy: Meet Clumsy Daisy & her Family. 2009. (Illus.). 40p. pap. 18.49 *(978-1-4490-1780-4(0))* AuthorHouse.

—Clumsy Daisy Goes to School. 2009. (Illus.). 36p. pap. 16.99 *(978-1-4490-3517-4(5))* AuthorHouse.

Handy, Libby & Newnham, Jack. Boss for a Week.Tr. of C'Est Moi Qui Mene. (FRE., Illus.). (J). 13.99 incl. audio *(978-0-590-73908-5(5))* Scholastic, Inc.

Hanny, Diane. Wispy Willy. Baskey, Kim, illus. 2011. 24p. pap. 12.00 *(978-1-4520-9975-0(8))* AuthorHouse.

Hanson, Anders. Monkey Business, 1 vol. Chawla, Neena, illus. 2006. (Animal Tales Ser.). 24p. (J). (gr. k-3). (ENG.). lib. bdg. 24.21 *(978-1-59679-951-6(X),* SandCastle); pap. 48.42 *(978-1-59679-952-3(8))* ABDO Publishing Co.

Hargreaves, Adam. Little Miss Princess. 2011. (Mr. Men & Little Miss Ser.). (ENG.). 32p. (J). (gr. -1-2). mass mkt. 4.99 *(978-0-8431-9834-8(6),* Price Stern Sloan) Penguin Young Readers Group.

Hargreaves, Roger. Little Miss Tidy. 2009. (Mr. Men & Little Miss Ser.). (ENG.). 32p. (J). (gr. -1-2). mass mkt. 4.99 *(978-0-8431-3501-5(8),* Price Stern Sloan) Penguin Young Readers Group.

—Mr. Fussy. 2010. (Mr. Men & Little Miss Ser.). (ENG.). 32p. (J). (gr. -1-2). mass mkt. 4.99 *(978-0-8431-9957-4(1),* Price Stern Sloan) Penguin Young Readers Group.

—Mr. Muddle. 2010. (Mr. Men & Little Miss Ser.). (ENG.). 32p. (J). (gr. -1-2). mass mkt. 3.99 *(978-0-8431-9958-1(X),* Price Stern Sloan) Penguin Young Readers Group.

Harley, Bill. Charlie Bumpers vs. the Really Nice Gnome, 1 vol. Gustavson, Adam, illus. (Charlie Bumpers Ser.). (ENG.). 160p. (J). (gr. 2-4). 2015. pap. 6.95 *(978-1-56145-831-8(7))* 2014. 13.95 *(978-1-56145-740-3(X))* Peachtree Pubs.

—Charlie Bumpers vs. the Squeaking Skull, 1 vol. Gustavson, Adam, illus. 2015. (Charlie Bumpers Ser.). (ENG.). 176p. (J). (gr. 2-4). pap. 6.95 *(978-1-56145-888-2(0))* Peachtree Pubs.

—Charlie Bumpers vs. the Teacher of the Year, 1 vol. Gustavson, Adam, illus. 2014. (Charlie Bumpers Ser.). (ENG.). 160p. (J). pap. 6.95 *(978-1-56145-824-0(4))* Peachtree Pubs.

—Dear Santa: The Letters of James B. Dobbins. Alley, R. W., illus. 2005. 32p. (J). (ENG.). 15.99 *(978-0-06-623778-7(5));* lib. bdg. 16.89 *(978-0-06-623779-4(3))* HarperCollins Pubs.

Harner, Ron. Cool It Frida! Surrey, Michael, illus. 2008. 40p. pap. 11.95 *(978-1-59858-654-1(8))* Dog Ear Publishing, LLC.

Harold, Gwyneth. Bad Girls in School. 2007. (ENG.). 148p. (YA). (gr. 8-12). per. 17.44 *(978-0-435-21517-0(5),* 21517) Heinemann.

Harris, Amber. Wisteria Jane. Hoyt, Ard, illus. 2015. (Wisteria Jane Book Ser.). (ENG.). 32p. (J). (gr. -1-3). 16.95 *(978-1-60554-411-3(6))* Redleaf Pr.

Hart, J. Tristan. The Adventures of Friendly & Barnackel: Book 2. 2011. 36p. pap. 15.14 *(978-1-4567-6284-1(2))* AuthorHouse.

Hartnett, Sonya. Sadie & Ratz. James, Ann, illus. 2012. (ENG.). 64p. (J). (gr. k-3). 14.99 *(978-0-7636-5315-6(2))* Candlewick Pr.

Harvey, Matt. Shopping with Dad. Latimer, Miriam, illus. 2008. (ENG.). 32p. (J). (gr. -1-3). 16.99 *(978-1-84686-172-7(1))* Barefoot Bks., Inc.

Haughton, Chris. Oh No, George! Haughton, Chris, illus. (ENG., Illus.). 32p. (J). 2015. (-k). bds. 7.99 *(978-0-7636-7652-0(7))* 2012. (gr. -1-k). 16.99 *(978-0-7636-5546-4(5))* Candlewick Pr.

Hawley, Richard And Elizabeth. There's a Monster in My Nose. Hawley, R. Spencer, illus. 2009. 36p. pap. 24.95 *(978-1-61546-177-6(9))* America Star Bks.

Haworth, Katie. Terrible Tim! Hughes, Laura, illus. 2016. (ENG.). 32p. (J). (gr. -1-3). 16.99 *(978-1-4998-0137-8(8))* Little Bee Books Inc.

Heeney, Bronwyn. A Dragon Called Wilbur: How a Fire-Breathing Dragon Made Friends. Fekete, Lucy, illus. 2012. 40p. pap. 16.97 *(978-1-61204-803-1(X),* Strategic Bk. Publishing) Strategic Book Publishing & Rights Agency (SBPRA).

Helakoski, Leslie. Woolbur. Harper, Lee, illus. 2008. (ENG.). 32p. (J). (gr. -1-3). 17.99 *(978-0-06-084726-5(3))* HarperCollins Pubs.

—Woolbur. 2008. (J). (gr. -1-2). 29.95 incl. audio *(978-0-8045-6971-2(1))* Spoken Arts, Inc.

Heller, Alyson. Time for T-Ball. Björkman, Steve, illus. 2010. (After-School Sports Club Ser.). (ENG.). 32p. (J). (gr. -1-1). pap. 3.99 *(978-1-4169-9412-1(2),* Simon Spotlight) Simon Spotlight.

Hemingway, Edward. Field Guide to the Grumpasaurus. 2016. (ENG., Illus.). 32p. (J). (gr. -1-3). 16.99 *(978-0-544-54665-3(2))* Houghton Mifflin Harcourt Publishing Co.

Henig, Sherry. Sara Makes Her Mother Proud & Learns Good Behavior: A Children's Book. 2nd ed. 2006. per. 6.95 *(978-0-9777203-2-3(2))* Brenner Publishing, LLC.

Henkes, Kevin. Lilly's Purple Plastic Purse. braille ed. 2004. (J). (gr. k-3). spiral bd. *(978-0-616-01673-2(5))* Canadian National Institute for the Blind/Institut National Canadien pour les Aveugles.

—Waiting. Henkes, Kevin, illus. 2015. (Illus.). 32p. (J). (gr. -1-3). (ENG.). 17.99 *(978-0-06-236843-0(5),* Collins Design); lib. bdg. 18.89 *(978-0-06-236844-7(3),* Greenwillow Bks.) HarperCollins Pubs.

Henrietta: Not Everybody Wears Horseshoes. 2004. (Illus.). 32p. (J). 6.99 *(978-0-9744520-1-2(7))* Glitter Creek, Inc.

Heos, Bridget. Mustache Baby. Ang, Joy, illus. 2016. (ENG.). 36p. (J). (— 1). bds. 7.99 *(978-0-544-78984-5(9),* HMH Books For Young Readers) Houghton Mifflin Harcourt Publishing Co.

—Mustache Baby. Ang, Joy, illus. 2013. (Mustache Baby Ser.). (ENG.). 40p. (J). (gr. -1-3). 17.99 *(978-0-547-77357-5(9),* Clarion Bks.) Houghton Mifflin Harcourt Trade & Reference Pubs.

Herold, Mariette. Luvable Lucind: Jacob & the Bullies. 2011. 40p. pap. 17.99 *(978-1-4520-2356-4(5))* AuthorHouse.

Herz, Henry, et al. When You Give an Imp a Penny, 1 vol. Larson, Abigail, illus. 2016. (ENG.). 32p. (J). (gr. k-3). 16.99 *(978-1-4556-2144-6(7))* Pelican Publishing Co., Inc.

Hoban, Russell. A Birthday for Frances. Hoban, Lillian, illus. 2012. (I Can Read Level 2 Ser.). (ENG.). 48p. (J). (gr. k-3). 16.99 *(978-0-06-083795-2(0))* HarperCollins Pubs.

—A Birthday for Frances. 2012. (I Can Read! Level 2 Ser.). (J). lib. bdg. 13.55 *(978-0-606-26850-9(2),* Turtleback) Turtleback Bks.

Hofmeister, Alan, et al. The Bad Men. (Reading for All Learners Ser.). (Illus.). (J). pap. *(978-1-56861-117-4(X))* Swift Learning Resources.

—See Me. (Reading for All Learners Ser.). (Illus.). (J). pap. *(978-1-56861-076-4(9))* Swift Learning Resources.

—Sid & the Mess. (Reading for All Learners Ser.). (Illus.). (J). pap. *(978-1-56861-090-0(4))* Swift Learning Resources.

Hopkinson, Deborah. A Letter to My Teacher. Carpenter, Nancy, illus. 2017. (ENG.). 40p. (J). (gr. -1-3). 17.99 *(978-0-375-86845-0(3),* Schwartz & Wade Bks.) Random Hse. Children's Bks.

Horse, Harry. Little Rabbit Goes to School. Horse, Harry, illus. (Little Rabbit Ser.). (Illus.). 32p. (J). 2011. (gr. -1-1). pap. 7.95 *(978-1-56145-574-4(1))* 2004. (ENG., (gr. k-1). 15.95 *(978-1-56145-320-7(X))* Peachtree Pubs.

Hosford, Kate. How the Queen Found the Perfect Cup of Tea. Swiatkowska, Gabi, illus. 2017. (Carolrhoda Picture Bks.). (ENG.). 40p. (gr. k-3). (J). 9.99 ***(978-1-5124-3273-2(3));*** (J). 38.65 ***(978-1-5124-3272-5(5));*** 38.65 ***(978-1-4677-9563-0(1))*** Lerner Publishing Group. (Carolrhoda Bks.).

Hosford, Kate. The Perfect Cup of Tea. Swiatkowska, Gabi, illus. 2017. (ENG.). 40p. (gr. k-3). 18.99 *(978-1-4677-3904-7(9))* Lerner Publishing Group.

Hubler, Marsha. Summer Camp Adventure, 1 vol. 2009. (Keystone Stables Ser.). (ENG.). 128p. (J). pap. 7.99 *(978-0-310-71795-9(7))* Zonderkidz.

—Whispering Hope, 1 vol., Bk. 7. 2010. (Keystone Stables Ser.). (ENG.). 144p. (J). pap. 7.99 *(978-0-310-71691-4(8))* Zonderkidz.

Hulst, W. G. van de & Hulst, Willem G. van de, illus. The Basket. 2014. (J). *(978-1-928136-04-0(4))* Inheritance Pubns.

—Bruno the Bear. 2014. (J). *(978-1-928136-03-3(6))* Inheritance Pubns.

—Kittens, Kittens Everywhere. 2014. (J). *(978-1-928136-20-0(6))* Inheritance Pubns.

—The Little Wooden Shoe. 2014. (J). *(978-1-928136-01-9(X))* Inheritance Pubns.

—The Pig under the Pew. 2014. (J). *(978-1-928136-10-1(9))* Inheritance Pubns.

—The Rockity Rowboat. 2014. (J). *(978-1-928136-18-7(4))* Inheritance Pubns.

—The Secret Hiding Place. 2014. (J). *(978-1-928136-16-3(8))* Inheritance Pubns.

—Three Foolish Sisters. 2014. (J). *(978-1-928136-15-6(X))* Inheritance Pubns.

—Through the Thunderstorm. 2014. (J). *(978-1-928136-02-6(8))* Inheritance Pubns.

—The Woods Beyond the Wall. 2017. (J). *(978-1-928136-08-8(7))* Inheritance Pubns.

Human, Deborah. Pinky Promise. 2009. 40p. (J). pap. 11.99 *(978-0-9818374-0-6(9))* Writing Bench LLC., The.

Hunt, Lynda Mullaly. COMO PEZ EN EL ÁRBOL: UNA NOVELA SOBRE LA DISLEXIA. 2016. (SPA.). 240p. (J). (gr. 4). pap. 13.95 *(978-84-15594-69-7(0),* Nube De Tinta) Penguin Random House Grupo Editorial ESP. Dist: Two Rivers Distribution.

—Fish in a Tree. (ENG.). (J). (gr. 5). 2017. 304p. 8.99 *(978-0-14-242642-5(3),* Puffin Books) 2015. 288p. 16.99 *(978-0-399-16259-6(3),* Nancy Paulsen Books) Penguin Young Readers Group.

—Fish in a Tree. 2017. lib. bdg. 19.65 ***(978-0-606-39991-3(7))*** Turtleback Bks.

Hunter, T. H. Car Key Elves. Gavrilovskiy, Olga, illus. 2008. 32p. (J). 16.95 *(978-0-9788085-1-8(7))* Tetoca Pr.

Jacobs, Sherry. "Bobby the Bully" 2012. 32p. pap. 21.99 *(978-1-4797-1069-0(5))* Xlibris Corp.

Jacobson, Jennifer Richard. Andy Shane & the Queen of Egypt. Carter, Abby, illus. 2009. (Andy Shane Ser.: 3). (ENG.). 64p. (J). (gr. k-3). 4.99 *(978-0-7636-4404-8(8))* Candlewick Pr.

—Andy Shane & the Queen of Egypt. 2009. (Andy Shane Ser.: 3). lib. bdg. 14.75 *(978-0-606-06592-4(X),* Turtleback) Turtleback Bks.

—Andy Shane & the Very Bossy Dolores Starbuckle. Carter, Abby, illus. 2006. (Andy Shane Ser.: 1). (ENG.). 64p. (J). (gr. k-3). 4.99 *(978-0-7636-3044-7(6))* Candlewick Pr.

—Andy Shane & the Very Bossy Dolores Starbuckle. Carter, Abby, illus. 2008. (Andy Shane Ser.). (J). (gr. -1-3). 25.95 incl. audio *(978-1-4301-0321-9(3));* pap. 16.95 incl. audio *(978-1-4301-0320-2(5))* Live Oak Media.

Jarman, Julia. Little Bad Riding Hood. 2014. (ENG., Illus.). 32p. (J). *(978-0-7787-0442-3(4));* pap. *(978-0-7787-0450-8(5))* Crabtree Publishing Co.

Javernick, Ellen. What If Everybody Did That?, 0 vols. Madden, Colleen M., illus. 2010. (ENG.). 32p. (J). (gr. -1-2). 12.99 *(978-0-7614-5686-5(4),* 9780761456865, Amazon Children's Publishing) Amazon Publishing.

Jennings, Carol E. Marshall & Satchmo. 2008. 40p. pap. 21.32 *(978-1-4363-7117-9(1))* Xlibris Corp.

Jennings, Terry Catasús. Vivian & the Legend of the Hoodoos. Saroff, Phyllis, illus. 2017. (ENG & SPA.). 32p. (J). (gr. k-3). 17.95 *(978-1-62855-957-6(8))* Arbordale Publishing.

—Viviana y la Leyenda de Los Hoodoos. Saroff, Phyllis, illus. 2017. (SPA.). 32p. (J). (gr. k-3). pap. 9.95 *(978-1-62855-959-0(4))* Arbordale Publishing.

Jensen, Patricia. The Mess. 2004. (My First Reader Ser.). (ENG., Illus.). 32p. (J). (gr. k-1). pap. 3.95 *(978-0-516-24634-5(8),* Children's Pr.) Scholastic Library Publishing.

John, Jory. The Bad Seed. Oswald, Pete, illus. 2017. 40p. (J). (gr. -1-3). 17.99 ***(978-0-06-246776-8(X))*** HarperCollins Pubs.

Jones, Andrea. The Spitting Twins. Kulka, Joe, illus. 2004. 32p. (J). *(978-1-58394-095-2(2),* Frog Ltd.) North Atlantic Bks.

Jones, Christianne C. Dani el Dinosaurio, 1 vol. Lozano, Clara, tr. from ENG. Epstein, Len, illus. 2006. (Read-It! Readers en Español: Story Collection). (SPA.). 24p. (gr. -1-3). lib. bdg. 21.32 *(978-1-4048-2706-6(4),* Easy Readers) Picture Window Bks.

—Lacey Walker, Nonstop Talker, 1 vol. Watson, Richard, illus. 2012. (Little Boost Ser.). (ENG.). 32p. (gr. k-3). lib. bdg. 23.99 *(978-1-4048-6796-3(1),* Little Boost) Picture Window Bks.

Jones, Julie. The Problem at Pepperpine Zoo. Jones, Julie, illus. l.t. ed. 2004. (Illus.). 24p. (J). pap. 7.95 *(978-0-9745553-0-0(4))* Greenwood Street Publishing. GSP.

Jones, Patrick. Always Faithful. 2015. (ENG.). 112p. (YA). (gr. 6-12). lib. bdg. 27.99 *(978-1-4677-8052-0(9));* 7.99 *(978-1-4677-9014-7(1))* Lerner Publishing Group. (Darby Creek).

Joosse, Barbara M. Please Is a Good Word to Say. Plecas, Jennifer, illus. 2007. (J). *(978-1-4287-4649-7(8),* Philomel) Penguin Publishing Group.

Judge, Lita. Good Morning to Me! Judge, Lita, illus. 2015. (ENG., Illus.). 40p. (J). (gr. -1-3). 17.99 *(978-1-4814-0369-6(9))* Simon & Schuster Children's Publishing.

Kabat, Vicki Marsh. Will You Still Love Me? 2012. 28p. pap. 13.99 *(978-1-4624-0346-2(8),* Inspiring Voices) Author Solutions, Inc.

Kaplan, Bruce Eric. Meaniehead. Kaplan, Bruce Eric, illus. 2014. (ENG., Illus.). 40p. (J). (gr. -1-3). 17.99 *(978-1-4424-8542-6(6),* Simon & Schuster Bks. For Young Readers) Simon & Schuster Bks. For Young Readers.

Kaplan, Debbie. Davie Learns a Lesson about Karma. 2012. (Illus.). (J). pap. *(978-1-57043-348-1(8))* Eckankar.

Kaplan, Michael B. Betty Bunny Didn't Do It. Jorisch, Stéphane, illus. 2013. (Betty Bunny Ser.). (ENG.). 32p. (J). (gr. -1-k). 16.99 *(978-0-8037-3858-4(7),* Dial Bks) Penguin Young Readers Group.

—Betty Bunny Loves Chocolate Cake. Jorisch, Stéphane, illus. 2011. (Betty Bunny Ser.). (ENG.). 36p. (J). (gr. -1-k). 17.99 *(978-0-8037-3407-4(7),* Dial Bks) Penguin Young Readers Group.

—Betty Bunny Wants Everything. Jorisch, Stéphane, illus. 2012. (Betty Bunny Ser.). (ENG.). 32p. (J). (gr. -1-k). 17.99 *(978-0-8037-3408-1(5),* Dial Bks) Penguin Young Readers Group.

Katz, Alan. The Day the Mustache Came Back. Easler, Kris, illus. 2016. (Mustache Ser.: 2). (ENG.). 224p. (J). 13.99 *(978-1-61963-560-9(7),* 9781619635609, Bloomsbury USA Childrens) Bloomsbury Publishing USA.

—The Day the Mustache Took Over. Easler, Kris, illus. (Mustache Ser.: 1). (ENG.). 208p. 2016. (J). pap. 6.99 *(978-1-68119-148-5(2),* 9781681191485) 2015. (YA). (gr. 2-4). 13.99 *(978-1-61963-558-6(5),* 9781619635586) Bloomsbury Publishing USA. (Bloomsbury USA Childrens).

—Ricky Vargas: The Funniest Kid in the World. Curtis, Stacy, illus. 2011. (J). pap. *(978-0-545-24583-8(4),* Cartwheel Bks.) Scholastic, Inc.

Katz, Karen. No Hitting! 2011. (ENG.). 24p. (J). (gr. -1-k). mass mkt. 4.99 *(978-0-448-45596-9(X),* Grosset & Dunlap) Penguin Young Readers Group.

Keene, Carolyn. Pool Party Puzzler. Francis, Peter, illus. 2015. (Nancy Drew Clue Book Ser.: 1). (ENG.). 96p. (J). (gr. 1-4). 16.99 *(978-1-4814-3896-4(4),* Aladdin) Simon & Schuster Children's Publishing.

Kelley, Marty. The Messiest Desk. 2009. (J). *(978-1-55933-319-1(7))* Zino Pr. Children's Bks.

Kellogg, Steven. Pinkerton, Behave! 2014. (ENG., Illus.). 32p. (J). (gr. -1-3). 17.99 *(978-0-8037-4130-0(8),* Dial Bks) Penguin Young Readers Group.

Kelly, Bernadette & Ward, Krista. Naughty Norton, 1 vol. Alger, Liz, illus. 2009. (Pony Tales Ser.). (ENG.). 56p. (gr. 2-2). lib. bdg. 21.32 *(978-1-4048-5504-5(1),* Chapter Readers) Picture Window Bks.

—Norton Saves the Day, 1 vol. Alger, Liz, illus. 2009. (Pony Tales Ser.). (ENG.). 56p. (gr. 2-2). lib. bdg. 21.32 *(978-1-4048-5505-2(X),* Chapter Readers) Picture Window Bks.

—Norton's First Show, 1 vol. Alger, Liz, illus. 2009. (Pony Tales Ser.). (ENG.). 56p. (gr. 2-2). lib. bdg. 21.32 *(978-1-4048-5506-9(8),* Chapter Readers) Picture Window Bks.

Kelly, Katy. Melonhead & the Big Stink. 2011. (Melonhead Ser.). (ENG.). 224p. (J). (gr. 3-7). 6.99 *(978-0-375-84527-7(5),* Yearling) Random Hse. Children's Bks.

—Melonhead & the Undercover Operation. Johnson, Gillian, illus. 2012. (Melonhead Ser.). (ENG.). 256p. (J). (gr. 3-7). 7.99 *(978-0-375-84528-4(3),* Yearling) Random Hse. Children's Bks.

—Melonhead & the Vegalicious Disaster. Johnson, Gillian, illus. 2013. (Melonhead Ser.). (ENG.). 224p. (J). (gr. 3-7). 6.99 *(978-0-307-92969-3(8),* Yearling) Random Hse. Children's Bks.

Kelly, Keith. Peace Comes to Ajani. Kelly, Keith, illus. 2009. (Illus.). 56p. (J). pap. 9.95 *(978-0-932112-59-0(5))* Carolina Wren Pr.

Kelso, Mary Jean. Andy & Spirit Go to the Fair. Snider, K. C., illus. 2008. 24p. pap. 10.95 *(978-1-935137-03-0(4))* Guardian Angel Publishing, Inc.

Kim, HoJeong. Kanga & Anger. Kim, SookKyeong, illus. rev. ed. 2014. (MySELF Bookshelf Ser.). (ENG.). 32p. (J). (gr. k-2). pap. 11.94 *(978-1-60357-652-9(5));* lib. bdg. 25.27 *(978-1-59953-643-9(9))* Norwood Hse. Pr.

King-smith, Dick. Lady Lollipop. Barton, Jill, illus. 2003. (ENG.). 128p. (J). (gr. 2-5). pap. 7.99 *(978-0-7636-2181-0(1))* Candlewick Pr.

Kinney, Jeff. Cabin Fever. 2011. (Diary of a Wimpy Kid Ser.). (ENG., Illus.). 224p. (J). (gr. 3-7). 13.95 *(978-1-4197-0223-5(8),* Amulet Bks.) Abrams, Inc.

—Cabin Fever, 2 vols. 2011. (Diary of a Wimpy Kid Ser.: 6). (J). 46.75 *(978-1-4640-2148-0(1));* 44.75 *(978-1-4640-2152-7(X));* *(978-1-4640-2149-7(X));* 1.25 *(978-1-4640-4524-0(0));* 44.75 *(978-1-4640-2151-0(1))* Recorded Bks., Inc.

—Cabin Fever. 2011. (Diary of a Wimpy Kid Ser.: 6). (J). lib. bdg. 25.70 *(978-0-606-23667-6(8),* Turtleback) Turtleback Bks.

—The Third Wheel. 2012. (ENG.). (J). (gr. 3-7). pap. 8.49 *(978-1-4197-0729-2(9))* Abrams, Inc.

Klein, Abby. The Pumpkin Elf Mystery. McKinley, John, illus. 2007. (Ready, Freddy! Ser.: Bk. 11). 95p. (J). (gr. -1-3). 11.65 *(978-0-7569-8301-7(0))* Perfection Learning Corp.

Klein, Adria F. Hank Hammer & the Puppy, 1 vol. Rowland, Andrew, illus. 2012. (Tool School Ser.). (ENG.). 32p. (gr. 1-3). pap. 6.25 *(978-1-4342-4233-4(1));* lib. bdg. 22.65 *(978-1-4342-4020-0(7))* Stone Arch Bks.

Kline, Suzy. Horrible Harry & the June Box. Wummer, Amy, illus. 2012. (Horrible Harry Ser.). (ENG.). 80p. (J). (gr. 2-4). pap. 4.99 *(978-0-14-242185-7(5),* Puffin Books) Penguin Young Readers Group.

—Horrible Harry & the Scarlet Scissors. Wummer, Amy, illus. 2012. (Horrible Harry Ser.). (ENG.). 80p. (J). (gr. 2-4). 14.99 *(978-0-670-01306-7(4),* Viking Books for Young Readers) Penguin Young Readers Group.

—Horrible Harry & the Stolen Cookie. Wummer, Amy, illus. 2013. (Horrible Harry Ser.: 29). (ENG.). 80p. (J). (gr. 2-4). 14.99 *(978-0-670-01425-5(7),* Viking Books for Young Readers) Penguin Young Readers Group.

—Horrible Harry Goes Cuckoo. Wummer, Amy, illus. 2011. (Horrible Harry Ser.). (ENG.). 80p. (J). (gr. 2-4). 4.99 *(978-0-14-241876-5(5),* Puffin Books) Penguin Young Readers Group.

Kline, Suzy & Wells, Rosemary. Horrible Harry & the Birthday Girl. Wummer, Amy, illus. 2016. (Horrible Harry Ser.: 34). (ENG.). 80p. (J). (gr. 2-5). bds. 14.99 *(978-0-451-47331-8(0),* Viking Books for Young Readers) Penguin Young Readers Group.

—Horrible Harry & the Top-Secret Hideout. Wummer, Amy, illus. 2015. (Horrible Harry Ser.: 33). (ENG.). 80p. (J). (gr. 1-3). bds. 14.99 *(978-0-451-47329-5(9),* Viking Books for Young Readers) Penguin Young Readers Group.

—Horrible Harry & the Wedding Spies. Wummer, Amy, illus. 2015. (Horrible Harry Ser.: 32). (ENG.). 80p. (J). (gr. 2-5). bds. 14.99 *(978-0-670-01552-8(0),* Viking Books for Young Readers) Penguin Young Readers Group.

Klise, Kate. Little Rabbit & the Meanest Mother on Earth. Klise, M. Sarah, illus. (ENG.). 32p. (J). (gr. -1-3). 2015. 6.99 *(978-0-544-45611-2(4),* HMH Books For Young Readers) 2010. 17.99 *(978-0-15-206201-9(7))* Houghton Mifflin Harcourt Publishing Co.

—Pop Goes the Circus! Klise, M. Sarah, illus. 2015. (Three-Ring Rascals Ser.: 4). (ENG.). 144p. (J). (gr. 2-5). 15.95 *(978-1-61620-464-8(8))* Algonquin Bks. of Chapel Hill.

Knight, Hilary & Knight, Steve. Nina in That Makes Me Mad! 2011. (ENG., Illus.). 32p. (J). (gr. -1-3). 12.95 *(978-1-935179-10-8(1))* TOON Books / RAW Junior, LLC.

Kochan, Vera. What If Your Best Friend Were Blue?, 0 vols. Garófoli, Viviana, illus. 2011. (ENG.). 24p. (J). (gr. -1-2). 12.99 *(978-0-7614-5897-5(2),* 9780761458975, Amazon Children's Publishing) Amazon Publishing.

Koehler, Fred. How to Cheer up Dad. 2014. (ENG.). 32p. (J). (gr. -1-k). 16.99 *(978-0-8037-3922-2(2),* Dial Bks) Penguin Young Readers Group.

Korman, Gordon. Ungifted. 288p. (J). (gr. 5). 2014. pap. 7.99 *(978-0-06-174267-5(8))* 2012. 16.99 *(978-0-06-174266-8(X))* 2012. lib. bdg. 17.89 *(978-0-06-174268-2(6))* HarperCollins Pubs.

Koss, Amy Goldman. The Cheat. 2004. (ENG.). 176p. (YA). (gr. 7-7). 5.99 *(978-0-14-240128-6(5),* Speak) Penguin Young Readers Group.

Krasnesky, Thad. I Always, Always Get My Way. Parkins, David, illus. 2009. (ENG.). 32p. (J). (gr. k-2). 16.95 *(978-0-9799746-4-9(X))* Flashlight Pr.

Kraus, Jeanne R. Annie's Plan: Taking Charge of Schoolwork & Homework. Beyl, Charles, illus. 2006. 48p. (J). (gr. 2-5). 14.95 *(978-1-59147-481-4(7));* pap. 9.95 *(978-1-59147-482-1(5))* American Psychological Assn. (Magination Pr.).

Kroll, Virginia. Good Neighbor Nicholas: A Concept Book. Cote, Nancy, illus. 2006. (Way I Act Bks.: Vol. 5). (ENG.). 24p. (J). (gr. 1-3). lib. bdg. 15.99 *(978-0-8075-2998-0(2))* Whitman, Albert & Co.

Kropp, Paul. I Didn't Do It! Doherty, Catherine, illus. 72p. pap. *(978-1-897039-23-6(9))* High Interest Publishing (HIP).

Krosoczka, Jarrett J. Good Night, Monkey Boy. Krosoczka, Jarrett J., illus. 2003. (ENG., Illus.). 40p. (J). (gr. -1-2). pap. 7.99 *(978-0-440-41798-9(8),* Dragonfly Bks.) Random Hse. Children's Bks.

Krulik, Nancy. Attack of the Tighty Whities! Blecha, Aaron, illus. 2012. (George Brown, Class Clown Ser.: 7). (ENG.). 128p. (J). (gr. 2-4). pap. 4.99 *(978-0-448-45575-4(7),* Grosset & Dunlap) Penguin Young Readers Group.

—Attack of the Tighty Whities! 2012. (George Brown, Class Clown Ser.: 7). lib. bdg. 14.75 *(978-0-606-23651-5(1),* Turtleback) Turtleback Bks.

—Dance Your Pants Off!, No. 9. Blecha, Aaron, illus. 2013. (George Brown, Class Clown Ser.: 9). (ENG.). 128p. (J). (gr. 2-4). pap. 5.99 *(978-0-448-45679-9(6),* Grosset & Dunlap) Penguin Young Readers Group.

—Dance Your Pants Off! 2013. (George Brown, Class Clown Ser.: 9). lib. bdg. 14.75 *(978-0-606-29802-5(9),* Turtleback) Turtleback Bks.

—Eww! What's on My Shoe? 2013. (George Brown, Class Clown Ser.: 11). lib. bdg. 14.75 *(978-0-606-32126-6(8),* Turtleback) Turtleback Bks.

—Hey! Who Stole the Toilet?, 8 vols. Blecha, Aaron, illus. 2012. (George Brown, Class Clown Ser.: 8). (ENG.). 128p. (J). (gr. 2-4). pap. 5.99 *(978-0-448-45576-1(5),* Grosset & Dunlap) Penguin Young Readers Group.

—Hey! Who Stole the Toilet? 2012. (George Brown, Class Clown Ser.: 8). lib. bdg. 14.75 *(978-0-606-26075-6(7),* Turtleback) Turtleback Bks.

—I Hate Rules! John and Wendy Staff, illus. 2006. (Katie Kazoo, Switcheroo Ser.: 5). (ENG.). 80p. (J). (gr. 2-4). pap. 4.99 *(978-0-448-43100-0(9),* Grosset & Dunlap) Penguin Young Readers Group.

—No Bones about It. John and Wendy Staff, illus. 12th ed. 2004. (Katie Kazoo, Switcheroo Ser.: 12). (ENG.). 80p. (J). (gr. 2-4). pap. 3.99 *(978-0-448-43358-5(3),* Grosset & Dunlap) Penguin Young Readers Group.

—No Messin' with My Lesson. John and Wendy Staff, illus. 11th ed. 2004. (Katie Kazoo, Switcheroo Ser.: 11). (ENG.). 80p. (J). (gr. 2-4). pap. 4.99 *(978-0-448-43357-8(5),* Grosset & Dunlap) Penguin Young Readers Group.

—Super Burp!, No. 1. Blecha, Aaron, illus. 2010. (George Brown, Class Clown Ser.: 1). (ENG.). 128p. (J). (gr. 2-4). pap. 5.99 *(978-0-448-45367-5(3),* Grosset & Dunlap) Penguin Young Readers Group.

—Trouble Magnet. Blecha, Aaron, illus. 2010. (George Brown, Class Clown Ser.: 2). (ENG.). 128p. (J). (gr. 2-4). pap. 5.99 *(978-0-448-45368-2(1),* Grosset & Dunlap) Penguin Young Readers Group.

—The Twelve Burps of Christmas. Blecha, Aaron, illus. 2012. (George Brown, Class Clown Ser.: No. 1). (ENG.). 192p. (J). (gr. 2-4). pap. 5.99 *(978-0-448-45680-5(X),* Grosset & Dunlap) Penguin Young Readers Group.

—The Twelve Burps of Christmas. 2012. (George Brown, Class Clown Ser.: No. 1). lib. bdg. 16.00 *(978-0-606-26652-9(6),* Turtleback) Turtleback Bks.

—Wet & Wild! #5, 5 vols. Blecha, Aaron, illus. 2011. (George Brown, Class Clown Ser.: 5). (ENG.). 128p. (J). (gr. 2-4). pap. 4.99 *(978-0-448-45570-9(6),* Grosset & Dunlap) Penguin Young Readers Group.

—What's Black & White & Stinks All Over? Blecha, Aaron, illus. 2011. (George Brown, Class Clown Ser.: 4). (ENG.). 128p. (J). (gr. 2-4). pap. 5.99 *(978-0-448-45370-5(3),* Grosset & Dunlap) Penguin Young Readers Group.

—World's Worst Wedgie. Blecha, Aaron, illus. 2010. (George Brown, Class Clown Ser.: 3). (ENG.). 128p. (J). (gr. 2-4). pap. 5.99 *(978-0-448-45369-9(X),* Grosset & Dunlap) Penguin Young Readers Group.

Kumin, Maxine. Oh, Harry! Moser, Barry, illus. 2011. (ENG.). 32p. (J). (gr. -1-3). 16.99 *(978-1-59643-439-4(2),* 9781596434394) Roaring Brook Pr.

Kyi, Tanya Lloyd. Truth, 1 vol. 2003. (Orca Soundings Ser.). (ENG.). 128p. (YA). (gr. 8-12). pap. 9.95 *(978-1-55143-265-6(X))* Orca Bk. Pubs. USA.

Landy, Adrienne. Rudy the Shy Car. Seivwright, Leonard, illus. 2009. 48p. pap. 13.75 *(978-1-935125-43-3(5))* Robertson Publishing.

Lane, Nathan & Elliott, Devlin. Naughty Mabel. Krall, Dan, illus. 2015. (Naughty Mabel Ser.). (ENG.). 48p. (J). (gr. -1-3). 17.99 *(978-1-4814-3022-7(X),* Simon & Schuster Bks. For Young Readers) Simon & Schuster Bks. For Young Readers.

—Naughty Mabel Sees It All. Krall, Dan, illus. 2016. (Naughty Mabel Ser.). (ENG.). 48p. (J). (gr. -1-3). 17.99 *(978-1-4814-3024-1(6),* Simon & Schuster Bks. For Young Readers) Simon & Schuster Bks. For Young Readers.

LaRochelle, David. Moo! Wohnoutka, Mike, illus. (ENG.). (J). (gr. -1-3). 2014. 32p. bds. 7.99 *(978-0-8027-3802-8(8),* 9780802738028) 2013. 40p. 16.99 *(978-0-8027-3409-9(X),* 9780802734099) Bloomsbury Publishing USA. (Bloomsbury USA Childrens).

Larson, Hope. Mercury. Larson, Hope, illus. 2010. (ENG., Illus.). 240p. (YA). (gr. 7-18). 19.99 *(978-1-4169-3585-8(1));* pap. 15.99 *(978-1-4169-3588-9(6))* Simon & Schuster Children's Publishing. (Atheneum Bks. for Young Readers).

Latimer, Miriam. Emily's Tiger. 2008. (ENG., Illus.). 32p. (J). (gr. -1-3). 16.99 *(978-1-84686-138-3(1))* Barefoot Bks., Inc.

Latimor, Miriam. Emily's Tiger. Latimor, Miriam, illus. 2011. (ENG., Illus.). 32p. (J). (gr. -1-2). 7.99 *(978-1-84686-594-7(8))* Barefoot Bks., Inc.

Laubach, Melody. Words & Thoughts. 2008. 28p. pap. 17.95 *(978-1-4327-2596-9(3))* Outskirts Pr., Inc.

Lavigne, Guy. L' Obsession de Jerome Delisle. 2003. (Roman Plus Ser.). (FRE., Illus.). 160p. (YA). (gr. 8-18). pap. *(978-2-89021-190-2(8))* Diffusion du livre Mirabel (DLM).

Lawson, Jessica. The Actual & Truthful Adventures of Becky Thatcher. Bruno, Iacopo, illus. 2014. (ENG.). 224p. (J). (gr. 3-7). 16.99 *(978-1-4814-0150-0(5),* Simon & Schuster Bks. For Young Readers) Simon & Schuster Bks. For Young Readers.

Lawson, Polly. Sam Luckless. (Illus.). 32p. (J). pap. 14.95 *(978-0-86315-126-2(4),* 1470) Floris Bks. GBR. Dist: SteinerBooks, Inc.

Lay, Kathryn. Josh's Halloween Pumpkin, 1 vol. Bratun, Katy, illus. 2008. (ENG.). 32p. (J). (gr. k-3). 16.99 *(978-1-58980-595-8(X))* Pelican Publishing Co., Inc.

Leannah, Michael. Most People: (are Good People), 1 vol. Morris, Jennifer E., illus. 2017. (ENG.). 32p. (gr. -1-2). 16.95 *(978-0-88448-554-4(4),* 884554) Tilbury Hse. Pubs.

Lemieux, Jean. Toby & the Mysterious Creature. Cummins, Sarah, tr. from FRE. Casson, Sophie, illus. 2008. (Formac First Novels Ser.). (ENG.). 64p. (J). (gr. 2-5). 14.95 *(978-0-88780-761-9(5),* 9780887807619) Formac Publishing Co., Ltd. CAN. Dist: Casemate Pubs. & Bk. Distributors, LLC.

Lemieux, Jean & Casson, Sophie. Toby & the Mysterious Creature, 1 vol. Cummins, Sarah, tr. from FRE. Casson, Sophie, illus. 2008. (Formac First Novels Ser.). (ENG., Illus.). 64p. (J). (gr. 2-5). 5.95 *(978-0-88780-759-6(3),* 9780887807596) Formac Publishing Co., Ltd. CAN. Dist: Casemate Pubs. & Bk. Distributors, LLC.

Lester, Helen. Hurty Feelings. Munsinger, Lynn, illus. 2007. (ENG.). 32p. (J). (gr. -1-3). 7.99 *(978-0-618-84062-5(1))* Houghton Mifflin Harcourt Publishing Co.

—Hurty Feelings. Munsinger, Lynn, illus. 2014. (Laugh-Along Lessons Ser.). (ENG.). 32p. (J). (gr. -1-3). 8.99 *(978-0-544-10622-2(9))* Houghton Mifflin Harcourt Publishing Co.

—Me First. Munsinger, Lynn, illus. 2013. (Laugh-Along Lessons Ser.). (ENG.). 32p. (J). (gr. -1-3). 8.99 *(978-0-544-00321-7(7))* Houghton Mifflin Harcourt Publishing Co.

—Tacky the Penguin. Munsinger, Lynn, illus. (Tacky the Penguin Ser.). (ENG.). 32p. (J). (gr. -1-3). 2008. bds. 7.99 *(978-0-547-13344-7(8))* 2006. audio compact disk 10.99 *(978-0-618-73754-3(5))* Houghton Mifflin Harcourt Publishing Co.

Levins, Sandra. Bumblebee Bike. Keay, Claire, illus. 2014. (J). *(978-1-4338-1645-1(8));* 32p. pap. *(978-1-4338-1646-8(6))* American Psychological Assn. (Magination Pr.).

Liz, Pichon. Three Horrid Little Pigs. Liz, Pichon, illus. 2010. (ENG., Illus.). 32p. (J). pap. 7.95 *(978-1-58925-423-7(6))* Tiger Tales.

A
B

Lobel, Anita. Playful Pigs from A to Z. 2015. (ENG., Illus.). 40p. (J). (gr. -1-2). lib. bdg. 19.99 (978-0-553-50833-8(4), Knopf Bks. for Young Readers) Random Hse. Children's Bks.

Loftis, Chris & Lowenthal, Gary T. I Want It Now: Helping Children Deal with Frustration & Disappointment. Moore, Darryl, illus. 2003. (Let's Talk Ser.). (ENG.). 48p. (J). pap. 12.95 (978-0-88282-237-2(3), Small Horizons) New Horizon Pr. Pubs., Inc.

Londner, Renee. The Missing Letters: A Dreidel Story. Bodnaruk, Iryna, illus. 2017. (ENG.). 32p. (J). (gr. -1-3). 17.99 (978-1-4677-8933-2(X), Kar-Ben Publishing) Lerner Publishing Group.

London, Jonathan. Froggy Goes to Grandma's. 2017. (Froggy Ser.). (ENG., Illus.). 32p. (J). (-k). 16.99 (978-1-101-99964-6(0), Viking Books for Young Readers) Penguin Young Readers Group.

—Froggy Goes to Hawaii. Remkiewicz, Frank, illus. 2012. (Froggy Ser.). (ENG.). 32p. (J). (gr. -1-k). pap. 6.99 (978-0-14-242119-2(7), Puffin Books) Penguin Young Readers Group.

—Froggy Goes to Hawaii. 2012. (Froggy Ser.). lib. bdg. 17.20 (978-0-606-26083-1(8), Turtleback) Turtleback Bks.

—Froggy Goes to the Library. Remkiewicz, Frank, illus. 2016. (Froggy Ser.). (ENG.). 32p. (J). (gr. -1-k). 16.99 (978-0-670-01573-3(3), Viking Books for Young Readers) Penguin Young Readers Group.

Louis, Sachar. There's a Boy in the Girls' Bathroom. 2014. (ENG.). 208p. (J). (gr. 7-12). 11.24 (978-1-63245-256-6(1)) Lectorum Pubns., Inc.

Lowrey, Chris. Wonec Adventures: The Gift of Giving. 2008. 26p. pap. 24.95 (978-1-60563-622-1(3)) America Star Bks.

Lowrey, Janette Sebring. The Poky Little Puppy. Tenggren, Gustaf, illus. 2007. (Little Golden Book Ser.). (ENG.). 26p. (J). (gr. k — 1). bds. 4.99 (978-0-375-83925-2(9), Golden Bks.) Random Hse. Children's Bks.

Ludwig, Trudy. Confessions of a Former Bully. Adams, Beth, illus. (ENG.). 48p. (J). 2012. (gr. 3-7). pap. 7.99 (978-0-307-93113-9(7), Dragonfly Bks.) 2010. (gr. 1-4). 15.99 (978-1-58246-309-4(3), Tricycle Pr.) Random Hse. Children's Bks.

—Confessions of a Former Bully. 2012. lib. bdg. 18.40 (978-0-606-26382-5(9), Turtleback) Turtleback Bks.

—Sorry! Manning, Maurie J., illus. 2006. (ENG.). 32p. (J). (gr. 1-4). 15.99 (978-1-58246-173-1(2), Tricycle Pr.) Random Hse. Children's Bks.

—Too Perfect. Fields, Lisa, illus. 2009. (ENG.). 32p. (J). (gr. 1-4). 15.99 (978-1-58246-258-5(5), Tricycle Pr.) Random Hse. Children's Bks.

—Trouble Talk. Prevost, Mikela, illus. 2008. (ENG.). 32p. (J). (gr. 1-4). 15.99 (978-1-58246-240-0(2), Tricycle Pr.) Random Hse. Children's Bks.

MacDonald, Alan. Fleas!, 1 vol. Roberts, David, illus. 2013. (Dirty Bertie Ser.). (ENG.). 112p. (gr. 1-3). pap. 4.95 (978-1-4342-4822-0(4)); lib. bdg. 25.32 (978-1-4342-4618-9(3)) Stone Arch Bks.

—Worms!, 1 vol. Roberts, David, illus. 2013. (Dirty Bertie Ser.). (ENG.). 112p. (gr. 1-3). pap. 4.95 (978-1-4342-4823-7(2)); lib. bdg. 25.32 (978-1-4342-4619-6(1)) Stone Arch Bks.

MacDonald, Alan & Roberts, David. Dirty Bertie. 2013. (Dirty Bertie Ser.). (ENG.). 112p. (gr. 1-3). 101.28 (978-1-4342-4849-7(6)); 50.64 (978-1-4342-4850-3(X)) Stone Arch Bks.

MacDonald, Betty Bard. Happy Birthday, Mrs. Piggle-Wiggle. Boiger, Alexandra, illus. 2007. (Mrs. Piggle-Wiggle Ser.). 193p. (J). (gr. 3-7). lib. bdg. 16.89 (978-0-06-072813-7(2)) HarperCollins Pubs.

—Hello, Mrs. Piggle-Wiggle. Knight, Hilary & Boiger, Alexandra, illus. 2007. (ENG.). 176p. (J). (gr. 3-7). 16.99 (978-0-397-31715-8(8)); pap. 5.99 (978-0-06-440149-4(9)) HarperCollins Pubs.

—Mrs. Piggle-Wiggle. Knight, Hilary & Boiger, Alexandra, illus. rev. ed. 2007. (ENG.). 144p. (J). (gr. 3-7). 16.99 (978-0-397-31712-7(3)) HarperCollins Pubs.

—Mrs. Piggle-Wiggle. Boiger, Alexandra, illus. rev. ed. 2007. (Trophy Bk.). (ENG.). 144p. (J). (gr. 3-7). pap. 5.99 (978-0-06-440148-7(0)) HarperCollins Pubs.

Mack, Jeff. Clueless Mcgee. Mack, Jeff, illus. 2012. (Clueless Mcgee Ser.: 1). (ENG., Illus.). 240p. (J). (gr. 3-7). 12.99 (978-0-399-25749-0(7), Philomel Bks.) Penguin Young Readers Group.

—Clueless McGee & the Inflatable Pants, Bk. 2. Mack, Jeff, illus. 2013. (Clueless Mcgee Ser.: 2). (ENG., Illus.). 256p. (J). (gr. 3-7). 12.99 (978-0-399-25750-6(0), Philomel Bks.) Penguin Young Readers Group.

—Clueless Mcgee Gets Famous. Mack, Jeff, illus. 2014. (Clueless Mcgee Ser.: 3). (ENG., Illus.). 288p. (J). (gr. 3-7). 12.99 (978-0-399-25751-3(9), Philomel Bks.) Penguin Young Readers Group.

Mackall, Dandi Daley. Gift Horse. 2003. (Winnie the Horse Gentler Ser.: 6). (ENG., Illus.). 224p. (J). mass mkt. 5.99 (978-0-8423-5547-6(2)) Tyndale Hse. Pubs.

MacRae, Tom. The Opposite, 1 vol. Odriozola, Elena, illus. 2006. (ENG.). 32p. (J). (gr. k-3). 15.95 (978-1-56145-371-9(4)) Peachtree Pubs.

Maddox, Jake. Skateboard Save, 1 vol. Tiffany, Sean, illus. 2008. (Jake Maddox Sports Stories Ser.). (ENG.). 72p. (gr. 2-3). pap. 5.95 (978-1-4342-0871-2(0)) Stone Arch Bks.

—Soccer Spirit. Mourning, Tuesday, illus. 2008. (Jake Maddox Girl Sports Stories Ser.). (ENG.). 72p. (gr. 2-3). 25.32 (978-1-4342-0780-7(3)) Stone Arch Bks.

—Takedown. Tiffany, Sean, illus. 2008. (Jake Maddox Sports Stories Ser.). (ENG.). 72p. (gr. 2-3). 25.32 (978-1-4342-0774-6(9)); pap. 5.95 (978-1-4342-0870-5(2)) Stone Arch Bks.

Madonna, pseud. Good-Bye, Grace?, No. 2. Fulvimari, Jeffrey, illus. 2007. (English Roses Ser.: 2). (ENG.). 144p. (J). (gr. 3-7). 10.99 (978-0-14-240883-4(2), Puffin Books) Penguin Young Readers Group.

Malloy, Brian. Twelve Long Months. 2010. (ENG.). 320p. (J). (gr. 7). 9.99 (978-0-439-87763-3(6), Scholastic Paperbacks) Scholastic, Inc.

Manchego, Chelo. The Want Monsters. 2017. (ENG.). 32p. (J). (gr. -1-1). 16.95 (978-1-61180-365-5(9)) Shambhala Pubns., Inc.

Manning, Jane. Millie Fierce. Manning, Jane, illus. 2012. (Millie Fierce Ser.). (ENG., Illus.). 32p. (J). (gr. -1-2). 16.99 (978-0-399-25642-4(3), Philomel Bks.) Penguin Young Readers Group.

—Millie Fierce Sleeps Out. Manning, Jane, illus. 2014. (Millie Fierce Ser.). (ENG., Illus.). 32p. (J). (gr. -1-2). 16.99 (978-0-399-16093-6(0), Philomel Bks.) Penguin Young Readers Group.

Mannion, Mary. Roaring Rory. Fitzgerald, Brian, illus. 2010. 68p. pap. (978-1-907276-63-7(7)) Lapwing Pubns.

Manushkin, Fran. Boss of the World, 1 vol. Lyon, Tammie, illus. 2009. (Katie Woo Ser.). (ENG.). 32p. (gr. k-2). 21.32 (978-1-4048-5493-2(2)) Picture Window Bks.

Manushkin, Fran & Lyon, Tammie. La Jefa Del Mundo, 1 vol. Lyon, Tammie, illus. 2012. (Katie Woo en Español Ser.). (SPA., Illus.). 32p. (gr. k-2). pap. 6.95 (978-1-4048-7679-8(0)); lib. bdg. 21.32 (978-1-4048-7523-4(9)) Picture Window Bks.

Marsh, Laura F. Big Enough. 2009. (Mama Mirabelle Ser.). (ENG., Illus.). 24p. (J). (gr. -1-2). lib. bdg. 11.90 (978-1-4263-0433-0(1), National Geographic Children's Bks.) National Geographic Society.

Martin, Ann M. & Parnell, Annie. Missy Piggle-Wiggle & the Whatever Cure. Hatke, Ben, illus. 2016. (Missy Piggle-Wiggle Ser.). (ENG.). 256p. (J). 16.99 (978-1-250-07169-9(0), 9781250071699) Feiwel & Friends.

—Missy Piggle-Wiggle & the Whatever Cure. Hatke, Ben, illus. 2017. (Missy Piggle-Wiggle Ser.). (ENG.). 272p. (J). pap. 7.99 (**978-1-250-12953-6(2)**, 9781250129536) Square Fish.

—Missy Piggle-Wiggle & the Whatever Cure. 2017. (Missy Piggle-Wiggle Ser.). (J). lib. bdg. 18.40 (**978-0-606-40585-0(2)**) Turtleback Bks.

—Missy Piggle-Wiggle & the Won't-Walk-The-Dog Cure. Hatke, Ben, illus. 2017. (Missy Piggle-Wiggle Ser.). (ENG.). 240p. (J). 16.99 (**978-1-250-07170-5(4)**, 9781250071705) Feiwel & Friends.

Martin, Steve & Chast, Roz. The Alphabet from A to Y with Bonus Letter Z! 2007. (ENG., Illus.). 64p. (J). (gr. k-k). 17.95 (978-0-385-51662-4(2), Flying Dolphin Pr.) Knopf Doubleday Publishing Group.

Matt & Dave. Yuck's Big Booger Challenge. Baines, Nigel, illus. 2013. (Yuck Ser.). (ENG.). 112p. (J). (gr. 2-5). 15.99 (978-1-4424-8311-8(3)); pap. 4.99 (978-1-4424-8312-5(1)) Simon & Schuster/Paula Wiseman Bks. (Simon & Schuster/Paula Wiseman Bks.).

—Yuck's Pet Worm. Baines, Nigel, illus. 2013. (Yuck Ser.). (ENG.). 112p. (J). (gr. 2-5). 15.99 (978-1-4424-8150-3(1)); pap. 6.99 (978-1-4424-8149-7(8)) Simon & Schuster/Paula Wiseman Bks. (Simon & Schuster/Paula Wiseman Bks.).

—Yuck's Robotic Butt Blast. Baines, Nigel, illus. 2013. (Yuck Ser.). (ENG.). 112p. (J). (gr. 2-5). pap. 4.99 (978-1-4424-8309-5(1), Simon & Schuster/Paula Wiseman Bks.) Simon & Schuster/Paula Wiseman Bks.

Matthews, Morgan & Sinden, David. Yuck's Robotic Butt Blast. Baines, Nigel, illus. 2013. (Yuck Ser.). (ENG.). 112p. (J). (gr. 2-5). 15.99 (978-1-4424-8308-8(3), Simon & Schuster/Paula Wiseman Bks.) Simon & Schuster/Paula Wiseman Bks.

Mayer, Mercer. Bedtime Stories - Little Critter. Mayer, Mercer, illus. 2013. (Little Critter Ser.). (ENG., Illus.). 144p. (J). (gr. -1-3). pap. 11.99 (978-0-06-223640-1(7), HarperFestival) HarperCollins Pubs.

McBratney, Sam. I'm Sorry. Eachus, Jennifer, illus. 2006. (ENG.). 32p. (J). (gr. -1-2). pap. 6.99 (978-0-06-079927-4(7)) HarperCollins Pubs.

McClements, George. Night of the Veggie Monster. McClements, George, illus. 2008. (ENG., Illus.). 32p. (J). (gr. -1-1). 16.99 (978-1-59990-061-2(0), 9781599900612, Bloomsbury USA Childrens) Bloomsbury Publishing USA.

McCloud, Carol. As-Tu Rempli un Seau Aujourd'hui? Un Guide du Bonheur Quotidien Pour Enfants. Messing, David, illus. 2012. (ENG & FRE.). 32p. (J). pap. 9.95 (978-1-933916-92-7(3), Ferne Pr.) Nelson Publishing & Marketing.

—Has Llenado una Cubeta Hoy? Una Guia Diaria de Felicidades para Nios. Messing, David, illus. 2012. (ENG & SPA.). 32p. (J). (gr. -1-4). pap. 9.95 (978-1-933916-91-0(5)) Bucket Fillers, Inc.

McCormick, Scott. It's Go Time! Lazzell, R. H., illus. 2014. (Mr. Pants Ser.: 1). (ENG.). 128p. (J). (gr. 1-3). 14.99 (978-0-8037-4007-5(7), Dial Bks) Penguin Young Readers Group.

Mccormick, Scott. It's Go Time! Lazzell, R. H., illus. 2015. (Mr. Pants Ser.: 1). (ENG.). 128p. (J). (gr. 1-3). 7.99 (978-0-14-751710-4(9), Puffin Books) Penguin Young Readers Group.

McCormick, Scott. Slacks, Camera, Action! Lazzell, R. H., illus. 2015. (Mr. Pants Ser.: 2). (ENG.). 128p. (J). (gr. k-3). 14.99 (978-0-8037-4009-9(3), Dial Bks) Penguin Young Readers Group.

Mccormick, Scott. Slacks, Camera, Action! Lazzell, R. H., illus. 2015. (Mr. Pants Ser.: 2). (ENG.). 128p. (J). (gr. k-3). 7.99 (978-0-14-751711-1(7), Puffin Books) Penguin Young Readers Group.

McDaniel, Becky Bring. Katie Did It. Holt, Richard, illus. rev. ed. 2003. (Rookie Reader Español Ser.). (ENG.). (J). (gr. k-2). pap. 4.95 (978-0-516-27832-2(0), Children's Pr.) Scholastic Library Publishing.

McDaniel, Lurlene. No Time to Cry. 2003. (Dawn Rochelle Ser.: No. 4). (ENG., Illus.). 160p. (YA). (gr. 7-12). reprint ed. pap. 4.99 (978-1-58196-006-8(9)) Lerner Publishing Group.

McDonald, Megan. Hen Hears Gossip. Kim, Joung Un, illus. 2008. 32p. (J). (gr. -1-k). lib. bdg. 17.89 (978-0-06-113877-5(0)); (ENG.). 17.99 (978-0-06-113876-8(2)) HarperCollins Pubs. (Greenwillow Bks.).

McDonnell, Patrick. The Monsters' Monster. 2012. (ENG., Illus.). 40p. (J). (gr. -1-3). 17.00 (978-0-316-04547-6(0)) Little Brown & Co.

McElligott, Matthew. The Lion's Share. McElligott, Matthew, illus. 2012. (ENG., Illus.). 40p. (J). (gr. k-8). pap. 8.99 (978-0-8027-2360-4(8), 9780802723604, Bloomsbury USA Childrens) Bloomsbury Publishing USA.

—The Lion's Share: A Tale of Halving Cake & Eating It, Too. McElligott, Matthew, illus. 2009. (ENG., Illus.). 32p. (J). (gr. k-3). 16.99 (978-0-8027-9768-1(7), 9780802797681, Bloomsbury USA Childrens) Bloomsbury Publishing USA.

McGuinness-Kelly, Tracy-Lee. Bad Cat. McGuinness-Kelly, Tracy-Lee, illus. 2006. (Illus.). 29p. (J). (gr. k-4). reprint ed. 16.00 (978-0-7567-9823-9(X)) DIANE Publishing Co.

McHenry, E. B. Poodlena. 2004. (Illus.). (J). (978-1-58234-962-6(2)) Bloomsbury Publishing USA.

—Poodlena. McHenry, E. B., illus. 2004. (ENG., Illus.). 32p. (J). (gr. -1-3). 16.95 (978-1-58234-824-7(3), 9781582348247, Bloomsbury USA Childrens) Bloomsbury Publishing USA.

McKissack, Patricia C. & McKissack, Fredrick L. Messy Bessey Vol. 2: Messy Bessey's Closet; Messy Bessey's Family Reunion; Messy Bessey's Garden. Regan, Dana, illus. 2008. (Rookie Reader Ser.). (ENG.). 96p. (J). (gr. k-2). pap. 9.95 (978-0-516-25301-5(8), Children's Pr.) Scholastic Library Publishing.

McManis, Margaret. The Wild Texas Stampede!, 1 vol. Dupree, Bruce, illus. 2008. (ENG.). 32p. (J). (gr. 1-3). 16.99 (978-1-58980-568-2(2)) Pelican Publishing Co., Inc.

McNamara, Margaret. Secret Santa. Gordon, Mike, illus. 2012. (Robin Hill School Ser.). (ENG.). 32p. (J). (gr. -1-1). 15.99 (978-1-4424-3649-7(2)); pap. 3.99 (978-1-4424-3648-0(4)) Simon Spotlight. (Simon Spotlight).

McPhail, David. Bad Dog. 2014. (I Like to Read(r) Ser.). (ENG.). 24p. (J). (gr. -1-3). 14.95 (978-0-8234-2852-6(4)) Holiday Hse., Inc.

McPhail, David & McPhail, David. Bad Dog. 2015. (I Like to Read(r) Ser.). (ENG.). 24p. (J). (gr. -1-3). 6.99 (978-0-8234-3298-1(X)) Holiday Hse., Inc.

Meachen Rau, Dana. My Special Space. Kim, Julie J., illus. 2003. (Rookie Readers Ser.). 32p. (J). 19.50 (978-0-516-22881-5(1), Children's Pr.) Scholastic Library Publishing.

Mean Margaret. 2014. (ENG., Illus.). 176p. (J). (gr. 2-7). 16.99 (978-1-4814-1014-4(8), Atheneum Bks. for Young Readers) Simon & Schuster Children's Publishing.

Medlyn, Lynda Lee & Staudenmier, Kelley Anne. The Best Belcher. Parish, Shannon, illus. 2008. (ENG.). 32p. (J). (gr. k-2). lib. bdg. (978-0-9793738-0-0(8)) Window Box Pr. LLC.

Meens, Estelle, illus. Boss No More. 2014. (J). (978-1-4338-1641-3(5), Magination Pr.) American Psychological Assn.

Merrick, Laurie K. Mama, Don't! Eremeyev, Margarita, illus. 2008. 20p. per. 24.95 (978-1-4241-9868-9(2)) America Star Bks.

Metzger, Steve. Five Spooky Ghosts Playing Tricks at School. Harrald-Pilz, Marilee, illus. 2005. (J). (978-0-439-80381-6(0)) Scholastic, Inc.

Mikkelsen, Jon. Skateboard Buddy. Lueth, Nathan, illus. 2008. (We Are Heroes Ser.). (ENG.). 40p. (gr. 2-3). lib. bdg. 23.99 (978-1-4342-0788-3(9), Keystone Bks.) Stone Arch Bks.

Miles, Brenda & Sweet, Susan D. King Calm: Mindful Gorilla in the City. Langdo, Bryan, illus. 2016. (J). (978-1-4338-2272-8(5), Magination Pr.) American Psychological Assn.

Miller, Jayna. Too Much Trick or Treat. Thatch, Nancy, ed. Miller, Jayna, illus. 2005. (Illus.). 29p. (J). per. 19.95 (978-0-933849-83-9(4)) landmark Hse., Ltd.

Mitchell, Laurence. Friends & Forgiving! Character Tales. 2009. 24p. pap. 12.00 (978-1-4389-5423-3(9)) AuthorHouse.

—Patty Liz & Kindness: Character Tales. 2009. 24p. pap. 12.00 (978-1-4389-5408-0(5)) AuthorHouse.

Mochizuki, Chiemi. The Promise. Randle, Walt R., ed. Mochizuki, Chiemi, illus. 2003. (Illus.). 38p. (J). (gr. 3-6). 16.99 (978-0-9720691-0-6(0)) Berkeley Major Publishing.

Moncure, Jane Belk. Rabbits' Habits: A Book about Good Habits. DeSantis, Susan, illus. 2013. (Magic Castle Readers Ser.). (ENG.). 32p. (J). (gr. -1-2). 25.64 (978-1-62323-569-7(3), 206304) Child's World, Inc., The.

—What Do You Do with a Grumpy Kangaroo? A Book about Feelings. Gallagher-Cole, Memie, illus. 2013. (Magic Castle Readers Ser.). (ENG.). 32p. (J). (gr. -1-2). 25.64 (978-1-62323-589-5(8), 206324) Child's World, Inc., The.

—What Do You Say When a Monkey Acts This Way? A Book about Manners. Gallagher-Cole, Memie, illus. 2013. (Magic Castle Readers Ser.). (ENG.). 32p. (J). (gr. -1-2). 25.64 (978-1-62323-590-1(1), 206325) Child's World, Inc., The.

Mondalto, Diane. Have You Ever Wished. 2009. 32p. pap. 12.99 (978-1-4389-4865-2(4)) AuthorHouse.

Monroe, Chris. Sneaky Sheep. Monroe, Chris, illus. 2010. (Carolrhoda Picture Bks.). (ENG., Illus.). 32p. (J). (gr. -1-3). lib. bdg. 16.95 (978-0-7613-5615-8(0)) Lerner Publishing Group.

Morgan, Matthew, et al. Yuck's Fart Club. Baines, Nigel, illus. 2013. (Yuck Ser.). (ENG.). 112p. (J). (gr. 2-5). 15.99 (978-1-4424-8153-4(6), Simon & Schuster/Paula Wiseman Bks.) Simon & Schuster/Paula Wiseman Bks.

Morgan, Todd. Why the Long Face: A Book about Thumb Sucking. 2013. 36p. pap. 16.95 (978-1-4575-1877-5(5)) Dog Ear Publishing, LLC.

Morrison, Denis. Gumball. 2010. 32p. pap. 7.19 (978-0-557-33389-9(X)) Lulu Pr., Inc.

Moss, Deborah. Shelley, the Hyperactive Turtle. Schwartz, Carol, illus. 2nd ed. 2006. (ENG.). 20p. (J). (gr. -1-2). pap. (978-1-890627-75-1(5)) Woodbine Hse.

Moss, Marissa. Amelia's Boredom Survival Guide. Moss, Marissa, illus. 2006. (Amelia Ser.). (ENG., Illus.). 64p. (J). (gr. 2-5). 12.99 (978-1-4169-0916-3(8), Simon & Schuster/Paula Wiseman Bks.) Simon & Schuster/Paula Wiseman Bks.

Most, Bernard & National Geographic Learning Staff. The Very Boastful Kangaroo. 2010. (Rise & Shine Ser.). (ENG., Illus.). 24p. (C). (gr. -1-3). pap. 6.95 (978-0-15-204840-2(5)) National Geographic School Publishing, Inc.

Mullarkey, Lisa. TJ Zaps the Freeze Out: Stopping the Silent Treatment #3, 1 vol. LaCoste, Gary, illus. 2012. (TJ Trapper, Bully Zapper Ser.). (ENG.). 80p. (J). (gr. 2-5). lib. bdg. 27.07 (978-1-61641-907-3(5), Calico Chapter Bks) Magic Wagon.

Murphy, Jim. Revenge of the Green Banana. 2017. (ENG.). 224p. (J). (gr. 5-7). 16.99 (978-0-544-78677-6(7), Clarion Bks.) Houghton Mifflin Harcourt Trade & Reference Pubs.

Murray, Carol. Hurry Up! Garbot, Dave, illus. 2003. (Rookie Readers Ser.). (ENG.). 32p. (J). 19.50 (978-0-516-22585-2(5), Children's Pr.) Scholastic Library Publishing.

Nannestad, Katrina. When Mischief Came to Town. 2016. (ENG.). 192p. (J). (gr. 5-7). 16.99 (978-0-544-53432-2(8), HMH Books For Young Readers) Houghton Mifflin Harcourt Publishing Co.

Neri, G. Chess Rumble. Watson, Jesse Joshua, illus. 2007. (ENG.). 64p. (J). (gr. 3-7). 18.95 (978-1-58430-279-7(8)) Lee & Low Bks., Inc.

Nesbitt, Kenn. The Ultimate Top Secret Guide to Taking over the World. Long, Ethan, illus. 2011. (ENG.). 208p. (J). (gr. 4-8). pap. 10.99 (978-1-4022-3834-5(7), Sourcebooks Jabberwocky) Sourcebooks, Inc.

Neubeck, Jon. The Quest. 2009. 47p. pap. 23.10 (978-0-557-07108-1(9)) Lulu Pr., Inc.

North, Laura. Cinderella's Big Foot. 2014. (ENG., Illus.). 32p. (J). (978-0-7787-0440-9(8)); pap. (978-0-7787-0448-5(3)) Crabtree Publishing Co.

Oates, Joyce Carol. Big Mouth & Ugly Girl. 2003. (ENG.). 288p. (YA). (gr. 8). pap. 8.99 (978-0-06-447347-7(3), HarperTeen) HarperCollins Pubs.

—Naughty Cherie! Graham, Mark, illus. 2008. 32p. (J). (gr. -1-3). lib. bdg. 17.89 (978-0-06-074359-8(X)) HarperCollins Pubs.

O'Boyle, Laurel. Froggy & Bug, 1 vol. 2010. 28p. pap. 24.95 (978-1-4489-7068-1(7)) PublishAmerica, Inc.

O'Connor, Edwin. Benjy: A Ferocious Fairy Tale. O'Neill, Catharine, illus. 2006. 96p. (J). reprint ed. pap. 12.00 (978-1-4223-5421-6(0)) DIANE Publishing Co.

Oeslchlager, Vanita. Big Blue. Blackwood, Kristin, illus. 2008. (ENG.). 32p. (J). (gr. -1-3). 17.95 (978-0-9800162-5-3(8)) VanitaBooks.

Offill, Jenny. 17 Things I'm Not Allowed to Do Anymore. Carpenter, Nancy, illus. 2011. (ENG.). 32p. (J). (gr. -1-3). pap. 7.99 (978-0-375-86601-2(9), Dragonfly Bks.) Random Hse. Children's Bks.

OHora, Zachariah. No Fits, Nilson! OHora, Zachariah, illus. 2013. (ENG., Illus.). 32p. (J). (gr. -1-k). 16.99 (978-0-8037-3852-2(8), Dial Bks) Penguin Young Readers Group.

Olsen EdS, Marci. Lessons to Live by: Character Building Books for School-Age Children. 2008. 52p. pap. 24.95 (978-1-60474-501-6(0)) America Star Bks.

Once upon a Time Spanish Version-the Boy Who Cried Wolf. 2005. (J). (978-1-57022-557-4(5)) ECS Learning Systems, Inc.

Palatini, Margie. Goldie & the Three Hares. Davis, Jack E., illus. 2011. (ENG.). 32p. (J). (gr. -1-2). 16.99 (978-0-06-125314-0(6), Tegen, Katherine Bks) HarperCollins Pubs.

Park, Barbara. Junie B. Jones Is Not a Crook. unabr. ed. 2004. (Junie B. Jones Ser.: No. 9). 67p. (J). (gr. k-3). pap. 17.00 incl. audio (978-0-8072-0530-3(3), Listening Library) Random Hse. Audio Publishing Group.

Parker, David. I'm in Charge of Me! Walker, Sylvia, illus. 2004. (Best Me I Can Be Ser.). (978-0-439-62810-5(5)) Scholastic, Inc.

Parker, Emma. The Naughty Puppy. 2010. (Illus.). pap. (978-1-877547-89-8(1)) First Edition Ltd.

Parr, Todd & Pickthall M.M. Staff. Do's & Don'ts. 2004. (ENG., Illus.). 24p. (J). (gr. -1 — 1). bds. 7.99 (978-0-316-90808-5(8)) Little, Brown Bks. for Young Readers.

Patterson, James. The Worst Years of My Life. 2014. lthr. 79.00 (978-1-62715-524-3(4)) Leatherbound Bestsellers.

—The Worst Years of My Life. 2012. 18.00 (978-1-61383-331-5(8)) Perfection Learning Corp.

Patterson, James & Grabenstein, Chris. Jacky Ha-Ha. Kerascoët, illus. 2016. (ENG.). 384p. (J). (gr. 3-7). 13.99 (978-0-316-26249-1(8), Jimmy Patterson) Little Brown & Co.

—Jacky Ha-Ha. 2017. (Jacky Ha-Ha Ser.). (J). lib. bdg. 18.40 (**978-0-606-40732-8(4)**) Turtleback Bks.

Patterson, James & Grabenstein, Chris. Pottymouth & Stoopid. Gilpin, Stephen, illus. 2017. (ENG.). 336p. (J). (gr. 3-7). 13.99 (978-0-316-34963-5(1)) Little Brown & Co.

Patterson, James & Papademetriou, Lisa. Big Fat Liar. Swaab, Neil, illus. 2014. (Middle School Ser.: Bk. 3). (ENG.). 304p. (J). (gr. 3-7). 13.99 (978-0-316-32203-4(2), Jimmy Patterson) Little Brown & Co.

Patterson, James & Tebbetts, Chris. The Worst Years of My Life. Park, Laura, illus. (Middle School Ser.: Bk. 1). (ENG.). (J). (gr. 3-7). 2014. 320p. 13.99 (978-0-316-32202-7(4), Jimmy Patterson) 2013. pap. 0.01 (978-0-316-25251-5(4)) 2012. 336p. pap. 8.00 (978-0-316-10169-1(9), Jimmy Patterson) Little Brown & Co.

—The Worst Years of My Life. Park, Laura, illus. 2012. (Middle School Ser.: 1). (J). lib. bdg. 18.45 (978-0-606-26164-7(8), Turtleback) Turtleback Bks.

Paul, Ann Whitford. Hasta Manana, Monito. (SPA.). (J). 8.95 (978-958-04-7073-1(1)) Norma S.A. COL. Dist: Distribuidora Norma, Inc.

Paul, Ruth. Bad Dog Flash. 2014. (ENG., Illus.). 32p. (J). (-2). 15.99 (978-1-4926-0153-1(5), 9781492601531, Sourcebooks Jabberwocky) Sourcebooks, Inc.

—Go Home Flash. 2015. (ENG., Illus.). 32p. (J). (-2). 15.99 (978-1-4926-1523-1(4), 9781492615231) Sourcebooks, Inc.

Pearce, Clemency. Frangoline & the Midnight Dream. Elliott, Rebecca, illus. 2011. (ENG.). 32p. (J). (gr. -1-k). 16.99 (978-0-545-31426-8(7), Chicken Hse., The) Scholastic, Inc.

Peine, Jan Muir. Giving Me Away. 2007. (Illus.). 25p. (J). pap. 6.99 (978-0-9754575-7-3(8)) Ashway Pr.

Peirce, Lincoln. Big Nate — Genius Mode. 2013. (Big Nate Graphic Novels Ser.). (J). lib. bdg. 20.85 (978-0-606-31802-0(X), Turtleback) Turtleback Bks.

—Big Nate — In a Class by Himself. Peirce, Lincoln, illus. 2015. (Big Nate Ser.: 1). (ENG., Illus.). 224p. (J). (gr. 3-7). pap. 6.99 (978-0-06-228359-7(6)) HarperCollins Pubs.

—Big Nate — In a Class by Himself. 2010. pap. (978-0-06-199287-2(9)) HarperCollins Pubs.

—Big Nate — In a Class by Himself. 2015. (Big Nate Ser.: 1). (J). lib. bdg. 17.20 (978-0-606-36505-5(2)) Turtleback Bks.

—Big Nate Lives It Up. Peirce, Lincoln, illus. 2015. (Big Nate Ser.: 7). (Illus.). 224p. (J). (gr. 3-7). lib. bdg. 13.89 (978-0-06-211109-8(4)) HarperCollins Pubs.

—Big Nate Strikes Again. Peirce, Lincoln, illus. 2010. (Big Nate Ser.: 2). (Illus.). 224p. (J). (gr. 3-7). (ENG.). 12.99 (978-0-06-194436-9(X)); lib. bdg. 14.89 (978-0-06-194437-6(8)) HarperCollins Pubs.

—Big Nate's Greatest Hits. 2015. (ENG., Illus.). 376p. (J). pap. 12.99 (978-1-4494-6489-9(0)) Andrews McMeel Publishing.

—In a Class by Himself. Peirce, Lincoln, illus. (Big Nate Ser.: 1). (Illus.). (J). (gr. 3-7). 2010. (ENG.). 224p. 12.99 (978-0-06-194434-5(3)) 2010. 224p. lib. bdg. 14.89 (978-0-06-194435-2(1)) 2012. (ENG., 240p. 12.99 (978-0-06-220773-9(3)) HarperCollins Pubs.

—Nate el Grande Ataca de Nuevo. 2015.Tr. of Big Nate Strikes Again. (SPA.). 216p. (J). (gr. 3-5). 17.99 *(978-1-933032-79-5(0))* Lectorum Pubns., Inc.

—Welcome to My World. 2015. (Big Nate Graphic Novels Ser.). lib. bdg. 20.85 *(978-0-606-37391-3(8))* Turtleback Bks.

Peirce, Lincoln, illus. Big Nate Flips Out. 2013. 216p. (J). *(978-0-06-224637-0(2))* Harper & Row Ltd.

Perelman, Helen. Magic Hearts. Waters, Erica-Jane, illus. 2011. (Candy Fairies Ser.: 5). (ENG.). 128p. (J). (gr. 2-5). pap. 5.99 *(978-1-4424-0823-4(5)*, Aladdin) Simon & Schuster Children's Publishing.

—Magic Hearts. Waters, Erica-Jane, illus. 2013. (Candy Fairies Ser.: 5). (ENG.). 128p. (J). (gr. 2-5). 15.99 *(978-1-4424-6494-0(1)*, Simon & Schuster/Paula Wiseman Bks.) Simon & Schuster/Paula Wiseman Bks.

Peschke, Marci. Summer Camp Queen, 1 vol. Mourning, Tuesday, illus. 2013. (Kylie Jean Ser.). (ENG.). 112p. (gr. 2-3). lib. bdg. 22.65 *(978-1-4048-7583-8(2)*, Kylie Jean) Picture Window Bks.

Philippou, Stefanie. Sammy Learns to Say I Am Sorry. 2011. 28p. pap. 21.99 *(978-1-4653-6352-7(1))* Xlibris Corp.

Phillips, Dee. Joyride, 1 vol. unabr. ed. 2011. (Right Now! Ser.). (ENG., Illus.). 45p. (YA). (gr. 9-12). pap. 8.95 *(978-1-61651-251-4(2))* Saddleback Educational Publishing, Inc.

Pierce, Seth J. Camporee of Doom. 2009. (J). pap. 12.99 *(978-0-8163-2364-7(X))* Pacific Pr. Publishing Assn.

—The Day the School Blew Up. 2009. (J). pap. 12.99 *(978-0-8163-2329-6(1))* Pacific Pr. Publishing Assn.

Pierson, Clara Dillingham. Among the Farmyard People. Gordon, F. C., illus. 2008. 176p. pap. 8.95 *(978-1-59915-281-3(9))* Yesterday's Classics.

Pitchford, Dean. Nickel Bay Nick. 2014. (ENG.). 272p. (J). (gr. 3-7). pap. 7.99 *(978-0-14-751227-7(1)*, Puffin Books) Penguin Young Readers Group.

Popsicle, Patty. Crack-a-Doodle Horse Tales: A Tale about Biting. 2011. 24p. (gr. -1). pap. 12.99 *(978-1-4343-5157-9(2))* AuthorHouse.

—Crack-a-doodle Horse Tales: A Tale about Pinching. 2011. 24p. (gr. -1). pap. 12.99 *(978-1-4389-4289-6(3))* AuthorHouse.

—Crack-a-doodle Horse Tales: A Tale about Pulling Hair. 2011. 24p. (gr. -1). pap. 12.99 *(978-1-4520-6096-5(7))* AuthorHouse.

Porter, Jen. I Am Brave. Saunders, Katie, illus. 2016. (ENG.). 16p. (J). (-3). bds. 7.99 *(978-1-4926-4165-0(0)*, 9781492641650, Sourcebooks Jabberwocky) Sourcebooks, Inc.

—I Am Good. Saunders, Katie, illus. 2016. (ENG.). 16p. (J). (-3). bds. 7.99 *(978-1-4926-4167-4(7)*, 9781492641674, Sourcebooks Jabberwocky) Sourcebooks, Inc.

Portis, Antoinette. Wait. 2015. (ENG., Illus.). 32p. (J). (gr. -1-2). 16.99 *(978-1-59643-921-4(1)*, 9781596439214) Roaring Brook Pr.

Posner, Tina. Rabbit Tricks. Corbett, Liza, illus. 2006. 8p. (J). pap. *(978-0-439-73513-1(0))* Scholastic, Inc.

Potter, Beatrix. The Tale of Jemima Puddle-Duck: A Sound Story Book. (Illus.). 12p. 4.95 *(978-1-58989-274-3(7))* Thurman Hse., LLC.

Poydar, Nancy. Bunny Business. 2003. (ENG., Illus.). 32p. (J). (gr. k-3). tchr. ed. 16.95 *(978-0-8234-1771-1(9))* Holiday Hse., Inc.

Pulver, Robin. Persuading Miss Doover. Sisson, Stéphanie Roth, illus. 2015. (J). *(978-0-8234-3426-8(5))* Holiday Hse., Inc.

Raichert, Lance, illus. Treasury of Values for Children. 2012. 159p. (J). *(978-1-4508-3729-3(8))* Phoenix International Publications, Inc.

Rainey. The Greatest Gift. 2004. (Illus.). (J). *(978-0-9666199-3-5(5))* DreamDog Pr.

Rankin, Laura. Ruthie & the (Not So) Teeny Tiny Lie. Rankin, Laura, illus. 2007. (ENG., Illus.). 32p. (J). (gr. -1-3). 17.99 *(978-1-59990-010-0(6)*, 9781599900100, Bloomsbury USA Childrens) Bloomsbury Publishing USA.

Ransom, Jeanie Franz. What Do Parents Do? (When You're Not Home), 1 vol. Moore, Cyd, illus. 2007. (ENG.). 32p. (J). (gr. k-3). 16.95 *(978-1-56145-409-9(5))* Peachtree Pubs.

Rao, Lisa. Don't Bite Your Friends! 2009. (Yo Gabba Gabba! Ser.). (ENG.). 10p. (J). (gr. -1-2). 8.99 *(978-1-4169-9014-7(3)*, Simon Spotlight) Simon Spotlight.

Rathmann, Peggy. Ruby the Copycat. 2006. (ENG., Illus.). 32p. (J). (gr. -1-3). per. 6.99 *(978-0-439-47228-9(8)*, Teaching Resources) Scholastic, Inc.

Ravel, Maurice, et al. The Boy & the Spell. Riglietti, Serena, illus. 2007. (Musical Stories Ser.). (ENG.). 36p. (J). (gr. 2-4). 16.95 *(978-0-9646010-4-8(4))* Pumpkin Hse., Ltd.

Redman, Mary. The Wishing Tree. Rodriguez, Christina, illus. 2008. (ENG.). 32p. (J). 15.95 *(978-1-934617-02-1(4)*, Elva Resa) Elva Resa Publishing, LLC.

Redmond, E. S. The Unruly Queen. Redmond, E. S., illus. 2012. (ENG., Illus.). 32p. (J). (gr. -1-2). 15.99 *(978-0-7636-3445-2(X))* Candlewick Pr.

Rees, Susan A. P. The Pine Cone Wishing Tree. 2008. (Illus.). 20p. pap. 10.49 *(978-1-4343-7155-3(7))* AuthorHouse.

Reiss, Kathryn. A Bundle of Trouble: A Rebecca Mystery. Giovine, Sergio, illus. 2011. (ENG.). 192p. (YA). (gr. 4-18). pap. 6.95 *(978-1-59369-754-9(6))* American Girl Publishing, Inc.

—Dreadful Sorry. 2004. (ENG.). 352p. (YA). (gr. 7-12). pap. 21.95 *(978-0-15-205087-0(6))* Houghton Mifflin Harcourt Publishing Co.

Reiss, Mike & Reiss, Mike. The Boy Who Wouldn't Share. Catrow, David, illus. 2008. (ENG.). 32p. (J). (gr. 1-3). 16.99 *(978-0-06-059132-8(3))* HarperCollins Pubs.

Rex, Michael. The End of the World. Rex, Michael, illus. 2013. (Icky Ricky Ser.: 2). (ENG., Illus.). 128p. (J). (gr. 1-4). 4.99 *(978-0-307-93169-6(2)*, Random Hse. Bks. for Young Readers) Random Hse. Children's Bks.

—The Hole to China. 2014. (Icky Ricky Ser.: 4). (ENG., Illus.). 128p. (J). (gr. 1-4). 4.99 *(978-0-385-37556-6(5)*, Random Hse. Bks. for Young Readers) Random Hse. Children's Bks.

—Icky Ricky #3: the Dead Disco Raccoon. Rex, Michael, illus. 2014. (Icky Ricky Ser.: 3). (ENG., Illus.). 128p. (J). (gr. 1-4). 4.99 *(978-0-307-93171-9(4)*, Random Hse. Bks. for Young Readers) Random Hse. Children's Bks.

—Icky Ricky #6: the Backpack Aquarium. 2015. (Icky Ricky Ser.: 6). (ENG., Illus.). 128p. (J). (gr. 1-4). 4.99 *(978-0-385-37562-7(X)*, Random Hse. Bks. for Young Readers) Random Hse. Children's Bks.

—Toilet Paper Mummy. Rex, Michael, illus. 2013. (Icky Ricky Ser.: 1). (ENG., Illus.). 128p. (J). (gr. 1-4). pap. 4.99 *(978-0-307-93167-2(6)*, Random Hse. Bks. for Young Readers) Random Hse. Children's Bks.

—The Two-Dollar Dirt Shirt. 2015. (Icky Ricky Ser.: 5). (ENG., Illus.). 128p. (J). (gr. 1-4). pap. 4.99 *(978-0-385-37559-7(X)*, Random Hse. Bks. for Young Readers) Random Hse. Children's Bks.

Reynolds, Peter H. The Best Kid in the World: A SugarLoaf Book. Reynolds, Peter H., illus. 2012. (ENG., Illus.). 48p. (J). (gr. -1-2). pap. 22.99 *(978-1-4424-7178-8(6)*, Atheneum Bks. for Young Readers) Simon & Schuster Children's Publishing.

RH Disney Staff & Winkelman, Barbara Gaines. Pinocchio's Nose Grows. 2013. (Step into Reading Ser.). (ENG., Illus.). 32p. (J). (gr. -1-1). lib. bdg. 12.99 *(978-0-7364-8001-7(3)*, RH/Disney) Random Hse. Children's Bks.

Ribke, Simone T. I'll Do It Later. White, Lee, illus. (Rookie Ready to Learn Ser.). (J). 2011. 40p. (gr. -1-k). pap. 5.95 *(978-0-531-26710-3(5))* 2011. 40p. (gr. -1-k). lib. bdg. 23.00 *(978-0-531-26528-4(5))* 2005. (ENG.). 32p. (gr. k-2). lib. bdg. 19.50 *(978-0-516-24861-5(8))* Scholastic Library Publishing. (Children's Pr.).

Rice, David L. Because Brian Hugged His Mother. 2004. (Sharing Nature with Children Book Ser.). (Illus.). 32p. (YA). (gr. -1-3). 16.95 *(978-1-883220-90-7(4))* Dawn Pubns.

—Because Brian Hugged His Mother, 1 vol. Thompson, K. Dyble, illus. 2004. (Sharing Nature with Children Book Ser.). (ENG.). 32p. (YA). (gr. -1-3). pap. 7.95 *(978-1-883220-89-1(0))* Dawn Pubns.

Richard, Laurent. Clowns & Dragons! Gauvin, Edward, tr. from FRE. Ryser, Nicolas, illus. 2014. (Tao, the Little Samurai Ser.: 3). (ENG.). 56p. (J). (gr. 2-5). lib. bdg. 29.27 *(978-1-4677-2096-0(8)*, Graphic Universe™) Lerner Publishing Group.

—Ninjas & Knock Outs! Gauvin, Edward, tr. from FRE. Ryser, Nicolas, illus. 2014. (Tao, the Little Samurai Ser.: 2). (ENG.). 64p. (J). (gr. 2-5). lib. bdg. 29.27 *(978-1-4677-3272-7(9)*, Graphic Universe™) Lerner Publishing Group.

—Pranks & Attacks! Gauvin, Edward, tr. from FRE. Ryser, Nicolas, illus. 2014. (Tao, the Little Samurai Ser.: 1). (ENG.). 64p. (J). (gr. 2-5). lib. bdg. 29.27 *(978-1-4677-2095-3(X)*, Graphic Universe™) Lerner Publishing Group.

Richmond, Marianne. Friendly Floppy Fishie, What Do Wish For? 2009. (Beginner Boards Ser.). (ENG., Illus.). 14p. (gr. -1-k). bds. 7.95 *(978-1-934082-52-2(X)*, Marianne Richmond Studios, Inc.) Sourcebooks, Inc.

Rissi, Anica Mrose. Anna, Banana, & the Friendship Split. Park, Meg, illus. 2015. (Anna, Banana Ser.: 1). (ENG.). 128p. (J). (gr. 1-5). 16.99 *(978-1-4814-1605-4(7)*, Simon & Schuster Bks. For Young Readers) Simon & Schuster Bks. For Young Readers.

—Anna, Banana, & the Monkey in the Middle. Park, Meg, illus. 2015. (Anna, Banana Ser.: 2). (ENG.). 128p. (J). (gr. 1-5). 15.99 *(978-1-4814-1608-5(1)*, Simon & Schuster Bks. For Young Readers) Simon & Schuster Bks. For Young Readers.

Ritz, Lee F. The Sun & the Wind. Hale, Randy, illus. 2013. 62p. 23.99 *(978-1-940840-00-0(7))* Ritz, Lee Pubns.

Rivas, Spelile & Plascencia, Amira. No Time for Monsters/No Hay Tiempo para Monstruos. Cervantes, Valeria, illus. 2010. (SPA & ENG.). 32p. (J). (gr. -1-3). 16.95 *(978-1-55885-445-1(2))* Arte Publico Pr.

Robbins, Trina. The Drained Brains Caper. Page, Tyler, illus. 2010. (Chicagoland Detective Agency Ser.: 1). (ENG.). 64p. (gr. 4-8). pap. 6.95 *(978-0-7613-5635-6(5)*, Graphic Universe™); lib. bdg. 29.27 *(978-0-7613-4601-2(5))* Lerner Publishing Group.

Robert, Bulla Clyde & Bulla. Shoeshine Girl. 2014. (Trophy Chapter Bks). (ENG.). 96p. (J). (gr. 2-5). 9.24 *(978-1-63245-292-4(8))* Lectorum Pubns., Inc.

Roberts, Justin. The Smallest Girl in the Smallest Grade. Robinson, Christian, illus. 2014. (ENG.). 32p. (J). (gr. -1-k). 16.99 *(978-0-399-25743-8(8)*, G.P. Putnam's Sons Books for Young Readers) Penguin Young Readers Group.

Robinson, Barbara. The Best Christmas Pageant Ever. Cornell, Laura, illus. 2011. (ENG.). 40p. (J). (gr. -1-3). 16.99 *(978-0-06-089074-2(6))* HarperCollins Pubs.

—The Best Christmas Pageant Ever. 2005. (ENG., Illus.). 128p. (J). (gr. 3-7). pap. 5.99 *(978-0-06-440275-0(4))* HarperCollins Pubs.

—The Best Christmas Pageant Ever. 2009. 8.32 *(978-0-7848-1246-4(2)*, Everbind) Marco Bk. Co.

—The Best Christmas Pageant Ever. 2005. (Illus.). 108p. (gr. 3-7). 16.00 *(978-0-7569-6531-0(4))* Perfection Learning Corp.

—The Best Christmas Pageant Ever. 2005. (J). 16.00 *(978-0-88103-998-6(5)*, Turtleback) Turtleback Bks.

Robinson, Mark. Vile: A Cautionary Tale for Little Monsters. Horne, Sarah, illus. 2011. (ENG.). 32p. (J). (gr. k-2). 14.99 *(978-0-7459-6254-2(8))* Lion Hudson PLC GBR. Dist: Independent Pubs. Group.

Rockwell, Thomas. How to Fight a Girl. 112p. (J). (gr. 3-5). pap. 3.99 *(978-0-8072-1452-7(3)*, Listening Library) Random Hse. Audio Publishing Group.

Rose, Hayley. The Do's & Don'ts. 2013. 38p. 16.50 *(978-1-939625-38-0(6))* Inkwell Books LLC.

Rosenberg, Madelyn. How to Behave at a Dog Show. Ross, Heather, illus. 2015. (ENG.). 32p. (J). (gr. -1-3). 17.99 *(978-0-06-227927-9(0))* HarperCollins Pubs.

—How to Behave at a Tea Party. Ross, Heather, illus. 2014. (ENG.). 32p. (J). (gr. -1-3). 17.99 *(978-0-06-227926-2(2)*, Tegen, Katherine Bks) HarperCollins Pubs.

Rosenthal, Marc. Phooey! Rosenthal, Marc, illus. 2007. (Illus.). 40p. (J). (gr. -1-3). lib. bdg. 17.89 *(978-0-06-075249-1(1)*, Cotler, Joanna Books) HarperCollins Pubs.

Rosoff, Meg. Meet Wild Boars. Blackall, Sophie, illus. 2008. (Wild Boars Ser.). (ENG.). 40p. (J). (gr. k-3). pap. 7.99 *(978-0-312-37963-6(3)*, 9780312379636) Square Fish.

Ross, Tony. Don't Do That! Ross, Tony, illus. 2011. (ENG., Illus.). 32p. (J). (gr. k — 1). pap. 12.99 *(978-1-84270-936-8(4))* Andersen Pr. GBR. Dist: Independent Pubs. Group.

—Oscar Got the Blame. Date not set. (ENG., Illus.). 24p. (J). pap. 21.44 *(978-0-05-004405-6(2))* Addison-Wesley Longman, Inc.

—Oscar Got the Blame. 2004. (ENG., Illus.). 32p. (J). (-k). pap. 10.99 *(978-1-84270-359-5(5))* Andersen Pr. GBR. Dist: Independent Pubs. Group.

—Super Dooper Jezebel. (ENG., Illus.). 32p. (J). pap. 9.99 *(978-1-84270-096-9(0))* Andersen Pr. GBR. Dist: Trafalgar Square Publishing.

Rouss, Sylvia A. No Rules for Michael. Simon, Susan, illus. 2004. (ENG.). 24p. (J). (gr. -1-1). pap. 6.95 *(978-1-58013-044-8(5)*, Kar-Ben Publishing) Lerner Publishing Group.

Ryan, Pam Muñoz. Tony Baloney. Fotheringham, Edwin, illus. 2011. (ENG.). 40p. (J). (gr. -1-k). 17.99 *(978-0-545-23135-0(3)*, Scholastic Pr.) Scholastic, Inc.

—Tony Baloney: Buddy Trouble. Fotheringham, Edwin, illus. 2014. (ENG.). 40p. (J). (gr. k-2). 6.99 *(978-0-545-48169-4(4)*, Scholastic Pr.) Scholastic, Inc.

—Tony Baloney: Buddy Trouble. Fotheringham, Ed, illus. 2013. 38p. (J). pap. *(978-0-545-48170-0(8))* Scholastic, Inc.

—Tony Baloney: School Rules. Fotheringham, Edwin, illus. (J). (gr. k-2). 2013. (ENG.). 40p. 6.99 *(978-0-545-48166-3(X))* 2012. pap. *(978-0-545-48167-0(8))* Scholastic, Inc.

Rylant, Cynthia. Brownie & Pearl Make Good. Biggs, Brian, illus. 2012. (Brownie & Pearl Ser.). (ENG.). 24p. (J). (gr. -1-k). 13.99 *(978-1-4169-8636-2(7)*, Beach Lane Bks.) Beach Lane Bks.

Said, Taunya D. Smart Alec- Alex: The 5th Grade Schedule Change. 2009. 53p. (YA). pap. 10.95 *(978-1-4327-4187-7(X))* Outskirts Pr., Inc.

Sanders, Cecilia. The Tale of the Perfect Whitetails. 2008. 36p. pap. 17.98 *(978-1-4389-0644-7(7))* AuthorHouse.

Sauer, Tammi. I Love Cake! Starring Rabbit, Porcupine, & Moose. Rozelaar, Angie, illus. 2016. 40p. (J). (gr. -1-3). 17.99 *(978-0-06-227894-4(0)*, Tegen, Katherine Bks) HarperCollins Pubs.

Savannah. Silly Sally Sometime. Seay, Christina, illus. 2007. 188p. per. 24.95 *(978-1-60441-451-6(0))* America Star Bks.

Sawyer-Aitch, Anne. Nalah & the Pink Tiger. Sawyer-Aitch, Anne, illus. 2013. (ENG., Illus.). 40p. pap. 13.95 *(978-1-938063-00-8(7)*, Mighty Media Kids) Mighty Media Pr.

Sazaklis, John. The Ferret Fiasco. Robinson, Lee, illus. 2016. (Billy Burger, Model Citizen Ser.). (ENG.). 96p. (gr. 2-3). lib. bdg. 22.65 *(978-1-4965-2589-5(2))* Stone Arch Bks.

—Recess Is Ruined. Robinson, Lee, illus. 2016. (Billy Burger, Model Citizen Ser.). (ENG.). 96p. (gr. 2-3). lib. bdg. 22.65 *(978-1-4965-2588-8(4))* Stone Arch Bks.

Scarry, Richard. Richard Scarry's Pig Will & Pig Won't. Scarry, Richard, illus. 2014. (Pictureback(R) Ser.). (ENG., Illus.). 24p. (J). (gr. -1-2). 4.99 *(978-0-385-38337-0(1)*, Random Hse. Bks. for Young Readers) Random Hse. Children's Bks.

Schaefer, Lola. One Special Day. Meserve, Jessica, illus. 2012. (Story for Big Brothers & Sisters Ser.). (ENG.). 40p. (J). (gr. -1-k). 16.99 *(978-1-4231-3760-3(4))* Hyperion Pr.

Schmid, Paul. Petunia Goes Wild. Schmid, Paul, illus. 2012. (ENG., Illus.). 40p. (J). (gr. -1-2). 12.99 *(978-0-06-196334-6(8))* HarperCollins Pubs.

Schneider, David. Dillan Mcmillan, Please Eat Your Peas. Shelly, Jeff, Sr., illus. 2016. (ENG.). 36p. (J). 16.95 *(978-0-9744446-4-2(2))* All About Kids Publishing.

Scholastic, Inc. Staff, et al. Don't Hit Me! Grier, Gary, illus. 2004. (Just for You Ser.). (ENG.). 32p. (gr. k-1). pap. 3.99 *(978-0-439-56860-9(9)*, Teaching Resources) Scholastic, Inc.

Schulz, Heidi. Giraffes Ruin Everything. Robertson, Chris, illus. 2016. (ENG.). 40p. (J). 16.99 *(978-1-61963-475-6(9)*, 9781619634756, Bloomsbury USA Childrens) Bloomsbury Publishing USA.

Schwiebert, Pat & DeKlyen, Chuck. Tear Soup: A Recipe for Healing after Loss. Bills, Taylor, illus. 2nd rev. l.t. ed. 2004. (ENG.). 56p. (gr. -1-12). reprint ed. 19.95 *(978-0-9615197-6-6(2)*, 798) Grief Watch.

Scieszka, Jon. Welcome to Trucktown! Shannon, David et al, illus. 2010. (Jon Scieszka's Trucktown Ser.). (ENG.). 40p. (J). (gr. -1-3). pap. 3.99 *(978-1-4424-1271-2(2)*, Simon & Schuster Bks. For Young Readers) Simon & Schuster Bks. For Young Readers.

Scotton, Rob. Merry Christmas, Splat. Scotton, Rob, illus. (Splat the Cat Ser.). (ENG., Illus.). 40p. (J). (gr. -1-2). 2013. 9.99 *(978-0-06-212450-0(1))* 2009. 16.99 *(978-0-06-083160-8(X))* HarperCollins Pubs.

Scraper, Katherine. The Boy Who Cried Wolf: An Aesop's Fable. 2006. (J). pap. *(978-1-4108-6166-5(X))* Benchmark Education Co.

Sendak, Maurice & LaFleur, Richard A. Ubi Fera Sunt: Fabula Ed Picturae. 2015. (LAT.). (J). pap. 24.00 *(978-0-86516-831-2(8))* Bolchazy-Carducci Pubs.

Seuling, Barbara. Robert Goes to Camp. Brewer, Paul, illus. 2007. (Robert Bks.). (ENG.). 160p. (J). (gr. k-4). 16.95 *(978-0-8126-2753-4(9))* Cricket Bks.

Seuss, Dr. El Gato con Sombrero Viene de Nuevo! Canetti, Yanitzia, tr. from ENG. 2004.Tr. of Cat in the Hat Comes Back. (SPA., Illus.). 63p. (gr. -1-1). 8.99 *(978-1-930332-43-0(2))* Lectorum Pubns., Inc.

—How the Grinch Stole Christmas! Jonaitis, Alice, ed. Seuss, Dr., illus. deluxe ed. 2014. (Classic Seuss Ser.). (ENG., Illus.). 64p. (J). (gr. k-4). 25.99 *(978-0-679-89153-6(6)*, Random Hse. Bks. for Young Readers) Random Hse. Children's Bks.

Seven, John & Christy, Jana. A Rule Is to Break: A Child's Guide to Anarchy. 2012. (Wee Rebel Ser.). (ENG., Illus.). 44p. (gr. -1). bds. 14.95 *(978-1-933149-25-7(6))* Manic D Pr.

Sham And Geri Mahabir. Freddie Learns Responsibility. 2009. 24p. pap. 13.99 *(978-1-4389-5573-5(1))* AuthorHouse.

Shannon, David. It's Christmas, David! Shannon, David, illus. 2010. (ENG., Illus.). 32p. (J). (gr. -1-3). 17.99 *(978-0-545-14311-0(X)*, Blue Sky Pr., The) Scholastic, Inc.

—Oh, David! A Diaper David Book. Shannon, David, illus. 2005. (Oh, David! Ser.). (ENG., Illus.). 12p. (J). (gr. -1-k). bds. 6.99 *(978-0-439-68881-9(7)*, Blue Sky Pr., The) Scholastic, Inc.

Sharkey-Wilmot. The Mysterious Golden Horse. 2007. 168p. 22.95 *(978-0-595-69325-2(3))*; per. 12.95 *(978-0-595-45162-3(4))* iUniverse, Inc.

Sharp, Euan. Diggedy Dozer in Treetop Troubles. 2008. 34p. 15.95 *(978-1-4357-0982-9(9))* Lulu Pr., Inc.

Shaw, Mary. Brady Brady & the Twirlin' Torpedo, 11 vols. Temple, Chuck, illus. l.t. ed. 2004. 32p. (J). per. *(978-0-9735557-2-1(6))* Brady Brady, Inc.

Shepard, Sara. Wicked. 5th ed. 2008. (Pretty Little Liars Ser.: 5). (ENG.). 320p. (YA). (gr. 9). 17.99 *(978-0-06-156607-3(1)*, HarperTeen) HarperCollins Pubs.

Shireen, Nadia. Good Little Wolf. 2011. (ENG.). 32p. (J). (gr. -1-2). 16.99 *(978-0-375-86904-4(2)*, Knopf Bks. for Young Readers) Random Hse. Children's Bks.

Shore, Diane Z. How to Drive Your Sister Crazy. Rankin, Laura, illus. 2012. (I Can Read! Level 2 Ser.). (J). lib. bdg. 13.55 *(978-0-606-26869-1(3)*, Turtleback) Turtleback Bks.

Short, Robbie, illus. I Want One Too! 2003. 32p. (J). lib. bdg. 12.95 *(978-0-9729833-2-7(5))* Bubble Gum Pr.

Shubert Sees the Best. 2004. (J). 9.00 *(978-1-889609-23-2(4))* Loving Guidance, Inc.

Sileo, Frank J. Sally Sore Loser: A Story about Winning & Losing. Pillo, Cary, illus. 2012. (J). 14.95 *(978-1-4338-1189-0(8))*; pap. 9.95 *(978-1-4338-1190-6(1))* American Psychological Assn. (Magination Pr.).

Silverstein, Shel. The Giving Tree. (Illus.). 95.94 *(978-0-06-056897-9(6))* HarperCollins Pubs.

—The Giving Tree. Silverstein, Shel, illus. anniv. ed. 2014. (ENG., Illus.). 64p. (J). (gr. -1-3). 19.99 *(978-0-06-058675-1(3))* HarperCollins Pubs.

Simard, Danielle. Little Word Catcher, 1 vol. Côté, Geneviève & Second Story Press Staff, illus. 2008. (ENG.). 32p. (J). (gr. 1-3). 14.95 *(978-1-897187-44-9(0))* Second Story Pr. CAN. Dist: Orca Bk. Pubs. USA.

Simeton, Julia. Mom, Why Can't I Catch Up? 2009. 20p. pap. 12.95 *(978-1-4389-7620-4(8))* AuthorHouse.

Simon, Francesca. Horrid Henry. Ross, Tony, illus. 2009. (Horrid Henry Ser.: 0). (ENG.). 112p. (J). (gr. 2-5). pap. 6.99 *(978-1-4022-1775-3(7)*, 9781402217753, Sourcebooks Jabberwocky) Sourcebooks, Inc.

—Horrid Henry, 1 vol. Ross, Tony, illus. 2012. (Horrid Henry Ser.). (ENG.). 112p. (J). (gr. 2-5). lib. bdg. 24.21 *(978-1-59961-185-3(6))* Spotlight.

—Horrid Henry. 2009. (Horrid Henry Ser.). lib. bdg. 17.20 *(978-0-606-06765-2(5)*, Turtleback) Turtleback Bks.

—Horrid Henry & the Abominable Snowman, 1 vol. Ross, Tony, illus. 2012. (Horrid Henry Ser.). (ENG.). 112p. (J). (gr. 2-5). lib. bdg. 24.21 *(978-1-59961-186-0(4))* Spotlight.

—Horrid Henry & the Mummy's Curse. Ross, Tony, illus. 2009. (Horrid Henry Ser.: 0). (ENG.). 112p. (J). (gr. 2-5). pap. 6.99 *(978-1-4022-1776-0(5)*, 9781402217760, Sourcebooks Jabberwocky) Sourcebooks, Inc.

—Horrid Henry & the Mummy's Curse. 2009. (Horrid Henry Ser.). lib. bdg. 17.20 *(978-0-606-06805-5(8)*, Turtleback) Turtleback Bks.

—Horrid Henry & the Scary Sitter. Ross, Tony, illus. 2009. (Horrid Henry Ser.: 0). (ENG.). 112p. (J). (gr. 2-5). pap. 6.99 *(978-1-4022-1781-4(1)*, 9781402217814, Sourcebooks Jabberwocky) Sourcebooks, Inc.

—Horrid Henry & the Scary Sitter, 1 vol. Ross, Tony, illus. 2012. (Horrid Henry Ser.). (ENG.). 112p. (J). (gr. 2-5). lib. bdg. 24.21 *(978-1-59961-188-4(0))* Spotlight.

—Horrid Henry & the Soccer Fiend. Ross, Tony, illus. 2009. (Horrid Henry Ser.: 0). (ENG.). 112p. (J). (gr. 2-5). pap. 6.99 *(978-1-4022-1778-4(1)*, Sourcebooks Jabberwocky) Sourcebooks, Inc.

—Horrid Henry & the Soccer Fiend, 1 vol. Ross, Tony, illus. 2012. (Horrid Henry Ser.). (ENG.). 112p. (J). (gr. 2-5). lib. bdg. 24.21 *(978-1-59961-189-1(9))* Spotlight.

—Horrid Henry & the Soccer Fiend. 2009. (Horrid Henry Ser.). lib. bdg. 17.20 *(978-0-606-06798-0(1)*, Turtleback) Turtleback Bks.

—Horrid Henry Robs the Bank. Ross, Tony, illus. 2013. (Horrid Henry Ser.: 0). (ENG.). 112p. (J). (gr. 2-5). pap. 6.99 *(978-1-4022-7995-9(7)*, 9781402279959, Sourcebooks Jabberwocky) Sourcebooks, Inc.

—Horrid Henry Rocks, 1 vol. Ross, Tony, illus. 2012. (Horrid Henry Ser.). (ENG.). 112p. (J). (gr. 2-5). lib. bdg. 24.21 *(978-1-59961-190-7(2))* Spotlight.

—The Mega-Mean Time Machine. Ross, Tony, illus. 2009. (Horrid Henry Ser.: 0). (ENG.). 112p. (J). (gr. 2-5). pap. 6.99 *(978-1-4022-1780-7(3)*, 9781402217807, Sourcebooks Jabberwocky) Sourcebooks, Inc.

—The Mega-Mean Time Machine, 1 vol. Ross, Tony, illus. 2012. (Horrid Henry Ser.). (ENG.). 112p. (J). (gr. 2-5). lib. bdg. 24.21 *(978-1-59961-187-7(2))* Spotlight.

—The Mega-Mean Time Machine. 2009. (Horrid Henry Ser.). lib. bdg. 17.20 *(978-0-606-06776-8(0)*, Turtleback) Turtleback Bks.

—Stinkbomb. Ross, Tony, illus. 2009. (Horrid Henry Ser.: 0). (ENG.). 112p. (J). (gr. 2-5). pap. 6.99 *(978-1-4022-1779-1(X)*, 9781402217791, Sourcebooks Jabberwocky) Sourcebooks, Inc.

—Stinkbomb. 2009. (Horrid Henry Ser.). lib. bdg. 17.20 *(978-0-606-06795-9(7)*, Turtleback) Turtleback Bks.

—Tricks the Tooth Fairy. Ross, Tony, illus. 2009. (Horrid Henry Ser.: 0). (ENG.). 112p. (J). (gr. 2-5). pap. 6.99 *(978-1-4022-2275-7(0)*, 9781402222757, Sourcebooks Jabberwocky) Sourcebooks, Inc.

—Tricks the Tooth Fairy, 1 vol. Ross, Tony, illus. 2012. (Horrid Henry Ser.). (ENG.). 112p. (J). (gr. 2-5). lib. bdg. 24.21 *(978-1-59961-191-4(0))* Spotlight.

—Tricks the Tooth Fairy. 2009. (Horrid Henry Ser.). lib. bdg. 17.20 *(978-0-606-06769-0(8)*, Turtleback) Turtleback Bks.

—Underpants. Ross, Tony, illus. 2009. 112p. (J). (gr. 2-5). (Horrid Henry Ser.: 0). (ENG.). pap. 6.99 *(978-1-4022-3825-3(8))*; pap. 4.99 *(978-1-4022-1777-7(3))* Sourcebooks, Inc. (Sourcebooks Jabberwocky).

—Underpants. 2009. (Horrid Henry Ser.). lib. bdg. 17.20 *(978-0-606-06766-9(3)*, Turtleback) Turtleback Bks.

—Wakes the Dead. Ross, Tony, illus. 2011. (Horrid Henry Ser.: 0). (ENG.). 112p. (J). (gr. 2-5). pap. 4.99 *(978-1-4022-5934-0(4)*, Sourcebooks Jabberwocky) Sourcebooks, Inc.

—Wakes the Dead, 1 vol. Ross, Tony, illus. 2012. (Horrid Henry Ser.). (ENG.). 112p. (J). (gr. 2-5). lib. bdg. 24.21 *(978-1-59961-192-1(9))* Spotlight.

Simpson, Dorothy. A Lesson for Janie. Date not set. 190p. (J). 20.95 *(978-0-8488-2617-8(5))* Amereon Ltd.

—Matter of Pride. Date not set. 192p. (J). 20.95 *(978-0-8488-2619-2(1))* Amereon Ltd.

Simpson, Martha Seif. The Dreidel That Wouldn't Spin: A Toyshop Tale of Hanukkah. Bernhard, Durga Yael, illus. 2014. (ENG.). 32p. (J). (gr. -1-2). 16.95 *(978-1-937786-28-1(5)*, Wisdom Tales) World Wisdom, Inc.

Singlehurst, Naomi. Grandpa, What's That Sound in the Middle of the Night? Ellen Koski, Rachel, ed. Jamieson, Victoria, illus. 2008. (ENG.). 32p. (J). (gr. k-2). 14.95 (978-1-930650-24-4(8)) mTrellis Publishing, Inc.

Siomades, Lorianne. Katy Did It! 2009. (ENG., Illus.). 32p. (J). (gr. -1-k). 16.95 (978-1-59078-602-4(5)) Boyds Mills Pr.

Smith, Adam. Other People's Shoes. 2008. 36p. pap. 18.50 (978-1-60693-383-1(3), Eloquent Bks.) Strategic Book Publishing & Rights Agency (SBPRA).

Smith, Bryan. What Were You Thinking? Learning to Control Your Impulses. Griffin, Lisa, illus. 2016. (ENG.). 32p. (J). pap. 10.95 (978-1-934490-96-9(2)) Boys Town Pr.

Smith, Ronn, adapted by. Nothing but the Truth. 104p. (YA). 6.25 (978-1-58342-084-3(3), N51) Dramatic Publishing Co.

Smith, S. Hey Silly Cat! Dont Tease the Dog! 2010. (Illus.). 32p. (J). 17.99 (978-0-9842632-9-5(2)) Scandora.

Snodgrass, Lady Cecily. The Really Rotten Princess & the Cupcake Catastrophe. Lester, Mike, illus. 2013. (Really Rotten Princess Ser.). (ENG.). 32p. (J). (gr. k-2). 16.99 (978-1-4424-8974-5(X)); pap. 3.99 (978-1-4424-8973-8(1)) Simon Spotlight. (Simon Spotlight).

Sommer, Carl. Hopeless to Hopeful. Vignolo, Enrique, illus. 2009. (Quest for Success Ser.). (ENG.). 56p. (YA). pap. 4.95 (978-1-57537-278-5(9)); lib. bdg. 12.95 (978-1-57537-253-2(3)) Advance Publishing, Inc.

—Mayor for a Day. Westbrook, Dick, illus. 2014. (J). pap. (978-1-57537-959-3(7)) Advance Publishing, Inc.

—Mayor for a Day: Alcalde Por un Dia. Westbrook, Dick, illus. 2009. (Another Sommer-Time Story Bilingual Ser.). (SPA & ENG.). 48p. (J). lib. bdg. 16.95 (978-1-57537-159-7(6)) Advance Publishing, Inc.

—Miserable Millie. Vignolo, Enrique, illus. (J). 2014. pap. (978-1-57537-960-9(0)) 2007. (ENG.). 48p. 16.95 incl. audio compact disk (978-1-57537-521-2(4)) 2007. (ENG.). 48p. (gr. -1-3). 9.95 (978-1-57537-022-4(0)) 2007. (ENG.). 48p. (gr. -1-3). lib. bdg. 16.95 (978-1-57537-071-2(9)) Advance Publishing, Inc.

—Miserable Millie(La Pobrecita Mili) Vignolo, Enrique, illus. 2009. (Another Sommer-Time Story Bilingual Ser.). (SPA & ENG.). 48p. (J). lib. bdg. 16.95 (978-1-57537-160-3(X)) Advance Publishing, Inc.

—No Longer a Dilly Dally, 1 bk. 2003. (Another Sommer-Time Story Ser.). (Illus.). 48p. (J). 16.95 incl. audio (978-1-57537-550-2(8)) Advance Publishing, Inc.

—No Longer a Dilly Dally, 11 vols. James, Kennon, illus. 2003. (Another Sommer-Time Story Ser.). (ENG.). 48p. (J). (gr. 1-4). 16.95 incl. audio compact disk (978-1-57537-501-4(X)) Advance Publishing, Inc.

—Proud Rooster & Little Hen. Budwine, Greg, illus. 2014. (J). pap. (978-1-57537-964-7(3)) Advance Publishing, Inc.

—Proud Rooster & Little Hen(Gallito Orgulloso y Gallinita) Budwine, Greg, illus. 2009. (Another Sommer-Time Story Bilingual Ser.). (SPA & ENG.). 48p. (J). 16.95 (978-1-57537-164-1(2)) Advance Publishing, Inc.

—The Rebel. Vignolo, Enrique, illus. 2009. (Quest for Success Ser.). (ENG.). 56p. (YA). pap. 4.95 (978-1-57537-282-2(7)); lib. bdg. 12.95 (978-1-57537-257-0(6)) Advance Publishing, Inc.

—The Rebel(El Rebelde) Vignolo, Enrique, illus. 2009. (Quest for Success Bilingual Ser.). (ENG & SPA.). 104p. (YA). lib. bdg. 14.95 (978-1-57537-231-0(2)) Advance Publishing, Inc.

—The Revolt. Budwine, Greg, illus. 2009. (Quest for Success Ser.). (ENG.). 56p. (YA). pap. 4.95 (978-1-57537-283-9(5)); lib. bdg. 12.95 (978-1-57537-258-7(4)) Advance Publishing, Inc.

—The Runaway(La Escapada) Vignolo, Enrique, illus. 2009. (Quest for Success Bilingual Ser.). (SPA & ENG.). 104p. (YA). lib. bdg. 14.95 (978-1-57537-234-1(7)) Advance Publishing, Inc.

—Spike the Rebel! Vignolo, Enrique, illus. (J). 2014. pap. (978-1-57537-967-8(8)) 2007. (ENG.). 48p. (gr. -1-3). lib. bdg. 16.95 (978-1-57537-072-9(7)) 2007. (ENG.). 48p. 16.95 incl. audio compact disk (978-1-57537-522-9(2)) 2007. (ENG.). 48p. 23.95 incl. audio compact disk (978-1-57537-722-3(5)) 2007. (ENG.). 48p. (gr. -1-3). lib. bdg. 9.95 (978-1-57537-023-1(9)) Advance Publishing, Inc.

—Spike the Rebel!(pua, el Rebelde!) Vignolo, Enrique, illus. 2009. (Another Sommer-Time Story Bilingual Ser.). (SPA & ENG.). 48p. (J). lib. bdg. 16.95 (978-1-57537-167-2(7)) Advance Publishing, Inc.

—Tied up in Knots. Budwine, Greg, illus. 2003. (Another Sommer-Time Story Ser.). (ENG.). 48p. (J). 16.95 incl. audio compact disk (978-1-57537-503-8(6)) Advance Publishing, Inc.

—Tied up in Knots. 2003. (Another Sommer-Time Story Ser.). (Illus.). 48p. (J). (gr. 1-4). 16.95 incl. audio (978-1-57537-552-6(4)) Advance Publishing, Inc.

—Tied up in Knots(Enredados) Budwine, Greg, illus. 2009. (Another Sommer-Time Story Bilingual Ser.). (SPA & ENG.). 48p. (J). lib. bdg. 16.95 (978-1-57537-169-6(3)) Advance Publishing, Inc.

Sonnenblick, Jordan. Zen & the Art of Faking It. 2010. (ENG.). 272p. (J). (gr. 7-12). 9.99 (978-0-439-83709-5(X), Scholastic Paperbacks) Scholastic, Inc.

Spinelli, Jerry. Tooter Pepperday. 2004. (Stepping Stone Book Ser.). (ENG., Illus.). 96p. (J). (gr. 1-4). 3.99 (978-0-679-84702-1(2), Random Hse. Bks. for Young Readers) Random Hse. Children's Bks.

Spring, Debbie. Breathing Soccer, 1 vol. 2008. (ENG.). 208p. (J). (gr. 4-8). pap. 10.95 (978-1-897235-42-3(9)) Thistledown Pr., Ltd. CAN. Dist: Univ. of Toronto Pr.

Spurr, Elizabeth. Monsters, Mind Your Manners! Scales, Simon, illus. 2012. (J). 34.28 (978-1-61913-124-8(2)) Weigl Pubs., Inc.

Stadler, Alexander. Trash Crisis on Earth, No. 1. 2009. (Julian Rodriguez Ser.: 1). (ENG.). 128p. (J). (gr. 2-5). 5.99 (978-0-439-91970-8(3), Scholastic Paperbacks) Scholastic, Inc.

Stanek, Robert, pseud. Break Their Bad Habits. deluxe ed. 2009. (Bugville Critters Ser.: No. 9). (Illus.). 24p. 9.99 (978-1-57545-213-5(8), Reagent Pr. Bks. for Young Readers) RP Media.

—Break Their Bad Habits: (the Bugville Critters, Lass's Adventures Series #2) 2009. (Bugville Critters Ser.: No. 9). (Illus.). 52p. (J). pap. 14.95 (978-1-57545-205-0(7), Reagent Pr. Bks. for Young Readers) RP Media.

—The Bugville Critters So Many Lessons to Learn. 2009. (Illus.). 68p. (J). pap. 18.95 (978-1-57545-237-1(5), Reagent Pr. Bks. for Young Readers) RP Media.

—Have a Backyard Picnic. 2009. (Bugville Critters Ser.: No. 14). (ENG., Illus.). 52p. (J). 14.95 (978-1-57545-210-4(3), Reagent Pr. Bks. for Young Readers) RP Media.

—Have a Bad Day. 2009. (Bugville Critters Ser.: No. 11). (ENG., Illus.). 52p. (J). 14.95 (978-1-57545-207-4(3), Reagent Pr. Bks. for Young Readers) RP Media.

—Visit City Hall. 2009. (Bugville Critters Ser.: No. 12). (ENG., Illus.). 52p. (J). 14.95 (978-1-57545-208-1(1), Reagent Pr. Bks. for Young Readers) RP Media.

Steig, William. Spinky Sulks. Steig, William, illus. 2011. (ENG., Illus.). 32p. (J). (gr. -1-3). pap. 7.99 (978-0-312-67246-1(2), 9780312672461) Square Fish.

Stern, A. J. Check, Please!, 3 vols. Marts, Doreen Mulryan, illus. 2010. (Frankly, Frannie Ser.: 3). (ENG.). 128p. (J). (gr. 1-3). pap. 5.99 (978-0-448-45352-1(5), Grosset & Dunlap) Penguin Young Readers Group.

—Doggy Day Care, 2 vols. Marts, Doreen Mulryan, illus. 2010. (Frankly, Frannie Ser.: 2). (ENG.). 128p. (J). (gr. 1-3). pap. 4.99 (978-0-448-45350-7(9), Grosset & Dunlap) Penguin Young Readers Group.

—Fashion Frenzy. Marts, Doreen Mulryan, illus. 2011. (Frankly, Frannie Ser.: 6). (ENG.). 128p. (J). (gr. 1-3). pap. 5.99 (978-0-448-45544-0(7), Grosset & Dunlap) Penguin Young Readers Group.

—Frankly, Frannie, 1 vol. Marts, Doreen Mulryan, illus. 2010. (Frankly, Frannie Ser.: 1). (ENG.). 128p. (J). (gr. 1-3). pap. 5.99 (978-0-448-45348-4(7), Grosset & Dunlap) Penguin Young Readers Group.

—Frankly, Frannie: Books 1-3. Marts, Doreen Mulryan, illus. 2014. (Frankly, Frannie Ser.). (ENG.). 384p. (J). (gr. 1-3). 8.99 (978-0-448-48461-7(7), Grosset & Dunlap) Penguin Young Readers Group.

—Funny Business, 4 vols. Marts, Doreen Mulryan, illus. 2011. (Frankly, Frannie Ser.: 4). (ENG.). 128p. (J). (gr. 1-3). pap. 5.99 (978-0-448-45540-2(4), Grosset & Dunlap) Penguin Young Readers Group.

—Miss Fortune, 7 vols. Marts, Doreen Mulryan, illus. 2012. (Frankly, Frannie Ser.: 7). (ENG.). 128p. (J). (gr. 1-3). pap. 5.99 (978-0-448-45748-2(2), Grosset & Dunlap) Penguin Young Readers Group.

—Principal for the Day. Marts, Doreen Mulryan, illus. 2011. (Frankly, Frannie Ser.: 5). (ENG.). 128p. (J). (gr. 1-3). pap. 5.99 (978-0-448-45542-6(0), Grosset & Dunlap) Penguin Young Readers Group.

—Rocking Out! Marts, Doreen Mulryan, illus. 2012. (Frankly, Frannie Ser.: 8). (ENG.). 128p. (J). (gr. 1-3). 12.99 (978-0-448-45751-2(2)); pap. 4.99 (978-0-448-45750-5(4)) Penguin Young Readers Group. (Grosset & Dunlap).

Steve, Smallman. Very Greedy Bee. Jack, Tickle, illus. 2010. (ENG.). 32p. (J). pap. 7.95 (978-1-58925-422-0(8)) Tiger Tales.

Stevenson, Peggy. Meet the Spencers & the Smart Knots. 2009. 48p. pap. 16.95 (978-1-60813-517-2(9)) America Star Bks.

Stewart, Colina. Wild Flower. 2004. (Illus.). 56p. (J). (gr. 3-8). 5.95 (978-1-57197-235-4(8)) Pentland Pr., Inc.

Stewart, H. E. Walrus's Gift, 1 vol. 2011. (ENG.). 32p. (J). (gr. -1-3). 18.00 (978-0-9693852-7-1(7)) Tudor Hse. GBR. Dist: Orca Bk. Pubs. USA.

Stewart, Kymberly M. Play It Again, Rachel. 2003. 74p. (J). pap. 10.95 (978-0-9740653-0-4(7)) Neema's Children Literature Assn., Inc.

Stine, R. L. The Heinie Prize. Park, Trip, illus. 2006. (Rotten School Ser.: No. 6). 128p. (J). pap. 4.99 (978-0-06-078816-2(X), Harper Trophy) HarperCollins Pubs.

—The Heinie Prize, 1 vol. Park, Trip, illus. 2011. (Rotten School Ser.: No. 6). (ENG.). 128p. (gr. 2-5). 24.21 (978-1-59961-830-2(3)) Spotlight.

Stott, Ann. Always. Phelan, Matt, illus. 2008. (ENG.). 32p. (J). (gr. k-k). 15.99 (978-0-7636-3232-8(5)) Candlewick Pr.

Stout, Shawn K. Penelope Crumb Never Forgets. Docampo, Valeria, illus. 2013. (Penelope Crumb Ser.: 2). (ENG.). 208p. (J). (gr. 2-5). pap. 5.99 (978-0-14-751009-9(0), Puffin Books) Penguin Young Readers Group.

Studio Mouse, creator. Get Your Grouchies Out! A Vocabulary of Feelings. rev. ed. 2007. (ENG., Illus.). (J). 12.99 (978-1-59069-610-1(7)) Studio Mouse LLC.

Suen, Anastasia. Cutting in Line Isn't Fair!, 1 vol. Ebbeler, Jeffrey, illus. 2007. (Main Street School - Kids with Character Ser.). (ENG.). 32p. (gr. -1-4). 28.50 (978-1-60270-029-1(X), Looking Glass Library) ABDO Publishing Co.

—A Good Team: A Cooperation Story, 1 vol. Ebbeler, Jeffrey, illus. 2008. (Main Street School - Kids with Character Ser.). (ENG.). 32p. (gr. -1-4). 28.50 (978-1-60270-272-1(1), Looking Glass Library) ABDO Publishing Co.

—Show Some Respect, 1 vol. Ebbeler, Jeffrey, illus. 2007. (Main Street School - Kids with Character Ser.). (ENG.). 32p. (gr. -1-4). 28.50 (978-1-60270-033-8(8), Looking Glass Library) ABDO Publishing Co.

Surplice, Holly. About a Bear. Surplice, Holly, illus. 2012. (ENG., Illus.). 32p. (J). (978-1-58925-112-0(1)) Tiger Tales.

Swain, Heather. Selfish Elf Wish. 2010. (ENG.). 208p. (YA). (gr. 7-18). 8.99 (978-0-14-241674-7(6), Speak) Penguin Young Readers Group.

Swallow, Gerry. Blue in the Face: A Story of Risk, Rhyme, & Rebellion. Fabretti, Valerio, illus. (Magnificent Tales of Misadventure Ser.). (ENG.). (J). 2017. 336p. pap. 7.99 (978-1-61963-489-3(9), 9781619634893) 2016. 320p. 16.99 (978-1-61963-487-9(2), 9781619634879) Bloomsbury Publishing USA. (Bloomsbury USA Childrens).

—Long Live the Queen: A Blue in the Face Novel. Fabretti, Valerio, illus. 2017. (Magnificent Tales of Misadventure Ser.). (ENG.). 288p. (J). 16.99 (978-1-61963-490-9(2), 9781619634909, Bloomsbury USA Childrens) Bloomsbury Publishing USA.

Talley, Linda. Aloha Potter! - hardcover Book. Chase, Andra, illus. 2004. 30p. (J). (978-1-55942-200-0(9)) Witcher Productions.

Tayler, Sandra. Hold on to Your Horses. Call, Angela, illus. 2008. 32p. (J). per. 15.00 (978-0-9779074-8-9(1)) Tayler Corp., The.

Tayleur, Karen. Forgetting to Remember. Gamble, Penel, illus. 2004. iv, 36p. (J). pap. (978-0-7608-6746-4(1)) Sundance/Newbridge Educational Publishing.

Taylor, Dorothea. There's a Dragon in My Closet. Palmer, Charly, illus. 2017. (Denene Millner Bks.). (ENG.). 32p. (J). (gr. -1-3). 17.95 **(978-1-57284-227-4(X))** Agate Publishing, Inc.

Taylor, Sean. Mojo & Weeza & the New Hat: Band 04/Blue. Mosedale, Julian, illus. 2007. (Collins Big Cat Ser.). (ENG.). 16p. (J). (gr. -1-1). pap. 5.99 (978-0-00-718662-4(2)) HarperCollins Pubs. Ltd. GBR. Dist: Independent Pubs. Group.

Taylor, Thomas. The Loudest Roar. 2003. (Illus.). (J). pap. (978-0-439-50131-6(8), Levine, Arthur A. Bks.) Scholastic, Inc.

Tharp, Tim. The Spectacular Now. 2013. (ENG.). 304p. (YA). (gr. 9). pap. 9.99 (978-0-385-75430-9(2), Ember) Random Hse. Children's Bks.

That's the Way It Crumbles, Cookie. (Full House Ser.). 96p. (J). (gr. 4-6). pap. 2.95 (978-0-938753-77-3(0), PP5) Parachute Publishing, LLC.

The Duda Family. The Adventures of Newo: Newo & Emma Visit Their Furry Friends. 2008. 28p. pap. 12.49 (978-1-4343-9766-9(1)) AuthorHouse.

Thomassie, Tynia. Feliciana Meets d'Loup Garou: A Cajun Tall Tale, 1 vol. Smith, Cat Bowman, illus. 2005. (ENG.). 32p. (J). (gr. k-3). 16.99 (978-1-58980-287-2(X)) Pelican Publishing Co., Inc.

Thoughts Staff. Lucky Clayman's Story. 2005. 16p. 9.99 (978-1-4116-2217-3(0)) Lulu Pr., Inc.

Thurber, Ginny. My Nanny Comes Today. 2009. 16p. pap. 10.95 (978-1-60693-386-2(8), Eloquent Bks.) Strategic Book Publishing & Rights Agency (SBPRA).

Tice, Kimberly & Litvack, Venita. Lou Knows What to Do: Supermarket. Kerry, Andre, illus. 2017. (Lou Knows What to Do Ser.: 1). (ENG.). 32p. (J). (gr. -1-6). pap. 10.95 **(978-1-944882-14-3(6))** Boys Town Pr.

Tillman, Nancy. Tumford the Terrible. Tillman, Nancy, illus. 2011. (Tumford Ser.). (ENG., Illus.). 32p. (J). (gr. -1-1). 16.99 (978-0-312-36840-1(2), 9780312368401) Feiwel & Friends.

Tireman, Loyd. Dumbee. Douglass, Ralph, illus. 2015. (Mesaland Ser.). (ENG.). 48p. (J). 12.95 (978-0-8263-5607-9(9)) Univ. of New Mexico Pr.

Tolar, Kathy. I Must Be from Another Planet. 2009. 20p. pap. 12.99 (978-1-4389-9378-2(1)) AuthorHouse.

Torrey, Richard. Because. Torrey, Richard, illus. 2011. (ENG., Illus.). 40p. (J). (gr. -1-3). 16.99 (978-0-06-156173-3(8)) HarperCollins Pubs.

—Why? Torrey, Richard, illus. 2010. (ENG., Illus.). 40p. (J). (gr. -1-3). 16.99 (978-0-06-156170-2(3)) HarperCollins Pubs.

Trish Lynch Marquis. Pesty Neighbor. 2009. 28p. pap. 14.99 (978-1-4389-9011-8(1)) AuthorHouse.

Trouble in the Barkers' Class. 2005. (J). 29.95 incl. audio compact disk (978-0-8045-4134-3(5)); 27.95 incl. audio (978-0-8045-6935-4(5)) Spoken Arts, Inc.

Truckey, Don. The Adventures of Caraway Kim... Right Wing. 2008. (ENG.). 256p. (J). pap. 10.95 (978-1-897235-43-0(7)) Thistledown Pr., Ltd. CAN. Dist: Univ. of Toronto Pr.

Trueit, Trudi. No Girls Allowed (Dogs Okay) Paillot, Jim, illus. 2010. (Secrets of a Lab Rat Ser.). (ENG.). 144p. (J). (gr. 3-7). pap. 5.99 (978-1-4169-6111-6(9), Aladdin) Simon & Schuster Children's Publishing.

—No Girls Allowed (Dogs Okay) Paillot, Jim, illus. 2009. (Secrets of a Lab Rat Ser.). (ENG.). 128p. (J). (gr. 3-7). 14.99 (978-1-4169-7592-2(6), Simon & Schuster/Paula Wiseman Bks.) Simon & Schuster/Paula Wiseman Bks.

Tulloch, Scott. Willy's Mum. 2008. (Illus.). 32p. pap. (978-1-86950-682-7(0)) HarperCollins Pubs. Australia.

Tuma, Refe & Tuma, Susan. What the Dinosaurs Did Last Night: A Very Messy Adventure. 2015. (What the Dinosaurs Did Ser.: 1). (ENG., Illus.). 40p. (J). (gr. -1-1). 17.00 (978-0-316-33562-1(2)) Little Brown & Co.

Twain, Mark, pseud. Tom Sawyer. 2008. (Bring the Classics to Life Ser.). (Illus.). 72p. (gr. 2-12). pap., act. bk. ed. 10.95 (978-0-931334-29-0(2), EDCTR-202B) EDCON Publishing Group.

Tyburski, Kimberly. Pesty Boy. 2011. 24p. pap. 15.99 (978-1-4628-9302-7(3)) Xlibris Corp.

Tym, Kate. Be Nice. 2008. (Manners Ser.). (Illus.). 24p. (J). (gr. -1-1). lib. bdg. 16.95 (978-1-59566-590-4(0)) QEB Publishing Inc.

Tyrrell, Melissa. Pinocchio. McMullen, Nigel, illus. 2005. (Fairytale Friends Ser.: Vol. 7). 12p. (J). (gr. -1-k). bds. 5.95 (978-1-58117-151-8(X), Intervisual/Piggy Toes) Bendon, Inc.

Ure, Jean. Babycakes. 2006. 164p. per. (978-1-904529-27-9(5), Back to Front) Solidus.

Valentine, Madeline. The Bad Birthday Idea. 2013. (ENG., Illus.). 40p. (J). (gr. -1-2). 17.99 (978-0-449-81331-7(2), Knopf Bks. for Young Readers) Random Hse. Children's Bks.

Van Draanen, Wendelin. Confessions of a Serial Kisser. 2009. (ENG.). 304p. (YA). (gr. 7-18). pap. 9.99 (978-0-375-84249-8(7), Ember) Random Hse. Children's Bks.

Vande Velde, Vivian. Three Good Deeds. 2007. (ENG., Illus.). 160p. (J). (gr. 5-7). pap. 7.99 (978-0-15-205455-7(3)) Houghton Mifflin Harcourt Publishing Co.

Vandever, Daniel W. Fall in Line, Holden. Frank, LaFrenda, ed. Vandever, Daniel W., illus. 2017. (Illus.). 32p. (J). **(978-1-893354-50-0(4))** Salina Bookshelf Inc.

Viorst, Judith. Alexander, Who's Trying His Best to Be the Best Boy Ever. 2014. (ENG., Illus.). 40p. (J). (gr. -1-3). 17.99 (978-1-4814-2353-3(3), Atheneum Bks. for Young Readers) Simon & Schuster Children's Publishing.

—Lulu & the Brontosaurus. Smith, Lane, illus. (ENG.). 128p. (J). (gr. 1-5). 2012. pap. 7.99 (978-1-4169-9962-1(0)) 2010. 17.99 (978-1-4169-9961-4(2)) Simon & Schuster Children's Publishing. (Atheneum Bks. for Young Readers).

—Lulu & the Brontosaurus. 2012. (Lulu Ser.: 1). lib. bdg. 18.40 (978-0-606-23676-8(7), Turtleback) Turtleback Bks.

—Lulu's Mysterious Mission. Smith, Lane, illus. 2015. (ENG.). 192p. (J). (gr. 1-5). pap. 7.99 (978-1-4424-9747-4(5)) Simon & Schuster Children's Publishing.

Wallace, Rich. The Ball Hogs, No. 1. Holder, Jimmy, illus. 2011. (Kickers Ser.: Bk. 1). (ENG.). 128p. (J). (gr. 1-4). 5.99 (978-0-375-85092-9(9), Yearling) Random Hse. Children's Bks.

Wallen-Nichols, Missy. The Be Good Fairy. Ballard, Ben, illus. 2013. (ENG.). 32p. (J). 16.95 (978-0-9853523-0-1(2)) Mawco, Inc.

—The Be Good Fairy Journal. 2013. (ENG.). 31p. (J). spiral bd. 7.95 (978-0-9853523-4-9(5)) Mawco, Inc.

Wang, Margaret C. When I Grow Up: A Touch & Feel Book. Gévry, Claudine, illus. 2005. (ENG.). 12p. (J). bds. 10.95 (978-1-58117-423-6(3), Intervisual/Piggy Toes) Bendon, Inc.

Wardlaw, Lee. 101 Ways to Bug Your Parents. 2005. (ENG.). 208p. (J). (gr. 5-3). pap. 6.99 (978-0-14-240340-2(7), Puffin Books) Penguin Young Readers Group.

—101 Ways to Bug Your Teacher. 2005. (ENG.). 256p. (J). (gr. 3-7). pap. 6.99 (978-0-14-240331-0(8), Puffin Books) Penguin Young Readers Group.

Warner, Sally. The Dragon Slayer! Biggs, Brian, illus. 2013. (EllRay Jakes Ser.: 4). (ENG.). 144p. (J). (gr. 1-3). 14.99 (978-0-670-78497-4(4), Viking Books for Young Readers) Penguin Young Readers Group.

—Ellray Jakes Is a Rock Star! 2012. (EllRay Jakes Ser.: 2). lib. bdg. 16.00 (978-0-606-23633-1(3), Turtleback) Turtleback Bks.

—EllRay Jakes Is Magic. Biggs, Brian, illus. 2014. (EllRay Jakes Ser.: 6). (ENG.). (J). (gr. 1-3). 160p. 14.99 (978-0-670-78500-1(8), Viking Books for Young Readers); 176p. pap. 5.99 (978-0-14-242360-8(2), Puffin Books) Penguin Young Readers Group.

—Ellray Jakes Is Magic. 2014. (EllRay Jakes Ser.: 6). lib. bdg. 16.00 (978-0-606-34215-5(X), Turtleback) Turtleback Bks.

—EllRay Jakes Is Not a Chicken! 2012. (EllRay Jakes Ser.: 1). lib. bdg. 16.00 (978-0-606-23632-4(5), Turtleback) Turtleback Bks.

—EllRay Jakes the Dragon Slayer. 2013. (EllRay Jakes Ser.: 4). lib. bdg. 16.00 (978-0-606-32136-5(5), Turtleback) Turtleback Bks.

—Ellray Jakes the Dragon Slayer, No. 4. Biggs, Brian, illus. 2013. (EllRay Jakes Ser.: 4). (ENG.). 144p. (J). (gr. 1-3). pap. 5.99 (978-0-14-242358-5(0), Puffin Books) Penguin Young Readers Group.

—EllRay Jakes Walks the Plank! 2013. (EllRay Jakes Ser.: 3). lib. bdg. 16.00 (978-0-606-30188-6(7), Turtleback) Turtleback Bks.

—Walks the Plank! Harper, Jamie, illus. (EllRay Jakes Ser.: 3). (ENG.). 128p. (J). (gr. 1-3). 2013. pap. 5.99 (978-0-14-242409-4(9), Puffin Books) 2012. 14.99 (978-0-670-06306-2(1), Viking Books for Young Readers) Penguin Young Readers Group.

Warnes, Tim. No! Warnes, Tim, illus. 2013. (ENG., Illus.). 32p. (J). 14.99 (978-1-58925-150-2(4)) Tiger Tales Pubns.

Wasson, Dave. The Big Ideas of Buster Bickles. Wasson, Dave, illus. 2015. (ENG., Illus.). 40p. (J). (gr. -1-3). 17.99 (978-0-06-229178-3(5)) HarperCollins Pubs.

Weaver, Will. Checkered Flag Cheater. 2010. (Motor Novels Ser.: 3). (ENG.). 208p. (YA). (gr. 7-12). 19.99 (978-0-374-35062-8(0), 9780374350628, Farrar, Straus & Giroux (BYR)) Farrar, Straus & Giroux.

Weck, Peter. Lima Bear's Halloween. DiSalvo, Len, illus. 2012. (Lima Bear Stories Ser.). 40p. (J). 15.95 (978-1-933872-16-2(0)) Lima Bear Pr LLC, The.

Weeks, Sarah. If I Were a Lion. Solomon, Heather M., illus. 2004. (ENG.). 40p. (J). (gr. -1-3). 17.99 (978-0-689-84836-0(6), Atheneum Bks. for Young Readers) Simon & Schuster Children's Publishing.

Weiss, Ellen. The Taming of Lola: A Shrew Story. Smath, Jerry, illus. 2010. (ENG.). 32p. (J). (gr. k-2). 15.95 (978-0-8109-4066-6(3), Abrams Bks. for Young Readers) Abrams, Inc.

Wells, Rosemary. Hands Off, Harry! Wells, Rosemary, illus. 2011. (ENG., Illus.). 40p. (J). (gr. -1-1). 14.99 (978-0-06-192112-4(2), Tegen, Katherine Bks) HarperCollins Pubs.

—Julieta, Estate Quieta! (SPA.). 43p. (J). 5.50 (978-84-372-1523-5(4)) Santillana USA Publishing Co., Inc.

—Noisy Nora. Wells, Rosemary, illus. 2007. (Illus.). 28p. (gr. -1-2). 17.00 (978-0-7569-7870-9(X)) Perfection Learning Corp.

—Sophie's Terrible Twos. Wells, Rosemary, illus. 2014. (ENG., Illus.). 32p. (J). (gr. -1-k). 16.99 (978-0-670-78512-4(1), Viking Books for Young Readers) Penguin Young Readers Group.

—Time-Out for Sophie. Wells, Rosemary, illus. 2013. (ENG., Illus.). 32p. (J). (gr. -1-k). 15.99 (978-0-670-78511-7(3), Viking Books for Young Readers) Penguin Young Readers Group.

Wenger, Brahm & Green, Alan. Dewey Doo-It Feeds a Friend. Gillmore, Jean, illus. 2004. (J). (978-0-9745143-0-7(6)) RandallFraser Publishing.

Weston, Carrie. If a Chicken Stayed for Supper. Fatus, Sophie, illus. 2007. (ENG.). 32p. (J). (gr. -1-3). 16.95 (978-0-8234-2067-4(1)) Holiday Hse., Inc.

Weston Woods Staff, creator. How Do Dinosaurs Go to School? 2011. 38.75 (978-0-545-19712-0(0)) Weston Woods Studios, Inc.

—Miss Nelson Is Missing. 2011. 18.95 (978-0-439-72847-8(9)); 38.75 (978-0-439-72853-9(3)); 29.95 (978-0-439-73499-8(1)) Weston Woods Studios, Inc.

Wheeler, Lisa. Old Cricket. Goembel, Ponder, illus. 2006. 28p. (gr. -1-1). 18.00 (978-0-7569-6795-6(3)) Perfection Learning Corp.

—Old Cricket. Goembel, Ponder, illus. (ENG.). 32p. (J). (gr. -1-1). 2003. 18.99 (978-0-689-84510-9(3), Atheneum/Richard Jackson Bks.) 2006. reprint ed. 7.99 (978-1-4169-1855-4(8), Atheneum Bks. for Young Readers) Simon & Schuster Children's Publishing.

Whybrow, Ian. Little Wolf's Book of Badness. Ross, Tony, illus. 2005. (Middle Grade Fiction Ser.). 132p. (gr. 3-6). 14.95 (978-1-57505-410-0(8)) Lerner Publishing Group.

—Lobito Aprende a Ser Malo. Azaola, Miguel, tr. from ENG. Ross, Tony, illus. 2007. (Ediciones Lerner Single Titles Ser.). (SPA.). 136p. (J). (gr. 3-6). per. 6.95 (978-0-8225-8644-9(4), Ediciones Lerner) Lerner Publishing Group.

Whybrow, Ian & Ross, Tony. Badness for Beginners: A Little Wolf & Smellybreff Adventure. 2005. (Illus.). 32p. (J). (gr. -1-3). 16.95 (978-1-57505-861-0(8), Carolrhoda Bks.) Lerner Publishing Group.

Wight, Eric. Frankie Pickle & the Closet of Doom. Wight, Eric, illus. 2009. (Frankie Pickle Ser.). (ENG., Illus.). 96p. (J). (gr. 2-5). 9.99 (978-1-4169-6484-1(3), Simon & Schuster Bks. For Young Readers) Simon & Schuster Bks. For Young Readers.

Willey, Margaret. The 3 Bears & Goldilocks. Solomon, Heather M., illus. 2008. (ENG.). 32p. (J). (gr. -1-3). 17.99 *(978-1-4169-2494-4(9),* Atheneum Bks. for Young Readers) Simon & Schuster Children's Publishing.

Williams, Bonnie. Meet Teddy Rex! Gordon, John, illus. 2012. (Dino School Ser.). (ENG.). 24p. (J). (gr. -1-1). 15.99 *(978-1-4424-4996-1(9));* pap. 3.99 *(978-1-4424-4995-4(0))* Simon Spotlight. (Simon Spotlight).

—Say Cheese, Teddy Rex! Gordon, John, illus. 2016. (Dino School Ser.). (J). (ENG.). 24p. (gr. -1-1). pap. 3.99 *(978-1-4814-6609-7(7));* ***(978-1-5182-1896-5(2))*** Simon Spotlight. (Simon Spotlight).

Williams, Heather. Nellie Oleson Meets Laura Ingalls. 2007. (Little House Ser.). 234p. (J). (gr. 3-7). lib. bdg. 16.89 *(978-0-06-124249-6(7))* HarperCollins Pubs.

Williams, Karen Lynn. One Thing I'm Good At. Date not set. (J). (gr. 3-7). pap. 4.99 *(978-0-380-73276-0(9))* HarperCollins Pubs.

Williams, Sam. I'm the Boss. Dufalla, Anita, illus. 2012. (ENG.). 24p. (gr. k-1). pap. 8.95 *(978-1-61810-297-3(4))* Rourke Educational Media.

Willis, Jeanne. Be Gentle, Python! Birchall, Mark, illus. 2005. (Picture Bks.). 28p. (J). (gr. k-2). 7.95 *(978-1-57505-508-4(2))* Lerner Publishing Group.

—Be Quiet, Parrot! Birchall, Mark, illus. 2005. (Picture Bks.). 32p. (J). (gr. k-2). 7.25 *(978-1-57505-492-6(2))* Lerner Publishing Group.

—No Biting, Puma! Birchall, Mark, illus. 2005. (Picture Bks.). 28p. (J). (gr. k-2). 7.25 *(978-1-57505-509-1(0))* Lerner Publishing Group.

—That's Not Funny! Reynolds, Adrian, illus. 2010. (Andersen Press Picture Bks). (ENG.). 32p. (J). (gr. -1-3). 16.95 *(978-0-7613-6445-0(5))* Lerner Publishing Group.

Wilson, Liesl-Yvette. A Balloon & a Bear. 2009. 48p. pap. 20.90 *(978-0-9559752-4-0(7))* Tallulah & Bear GBR. Dist: Lulu Pr., Inc.

Wishinsky, Frieda. You're Mean, Lily Jean! Denton, Kady MacDonald, illus. 2011. (ENG.). 32p. (J). (gr. -1-3). 16.99 *(978-0-8075-9476-6(8))* Whitman, Albert & Co.

Wolff, Virginia Euwer. Make Lemonade. unabr. ed. 2004. (Make Lemonade Trilogy: No. 1). 200p. (J). (gr. 7-18). pap. 36.00 incl. audio *(978-0-8072-0793-2(4),* S YA 348 SP, Listening Library) Random Hse. Audio Publishing Group.

Wood, Audrey. The Princess & the Dragon. 2003. (Child's Play Library). (ENG., Illus.). 10p. (J). *(978-0-85953-717-9(X))* Child's Play International Ltd.

—Silly Sally. braille ed. 2004. (J). (gr. 1). spiral bd., bds. *(978-0-616-01864-4(9))* Canadian National Institute for the Blind/Institut National Canadien pour les Aveugles.

Woodruff, Liza. Emerson Barks. Woodruff, Liza, illus. 2016. (ENG., Illus.). 32p. (J). 16.99 *(978-1-62779-167-0(1),* 9781627791670, Holt, Henry & Co. Bks. For Young Readers) Holt, Henry & Co.

Woods, Cindy Smith. Once Inside A Storybook... Good Morals in Short Stories to Encourage Correct Behavior in the Little Ones in Your Life. 2006. 59p. pap. 16.95 *(978-1-4241-2905-8(2))* America Star Bks.

Wright, Pauline. Why Did My Dad Go to War? 2008. 48p. pap. 19.49 *(978-1-4343-4677-3(3))* AuthorHouse.

Wurge, B. B. Squiggle. 2009. (LeapKids Ser.). (ENG., Illus.). 152p. (J). (gr. 2-7). pap. 9.95 *(978-0-9815148-9-5(8))* Leapfrog Pr.

Wynne-Jones, Tim. Last Piece of Sky. (J). pap. 5.99 *(978-0-88899-181-2(9))* Groundwood Bks. CAN. Dist: Publishers Group West (PGW).

Yagmin, Daniel, Jr., illus. Norton B. Nice. 2009. (J). *(978-1-60108-018-9(2))* Red Cygnet Pr.

Yarlett, Emma, illus. Nibbles: The Book Monster. 2016. (J). *(978-1-61067-467-6(7))* Kane Miller.

The Year We Sailed the Sun. 2015. (ENG., Illus.). 432p. (J). (gr. 3-7). 17.99 *(978-0-689-85827-7(2),* Atheneum/Richard Jackson Bks.) Simon & Schuster Children's Publishing.

Yeoman, John. The Wild Washerwomen. Blake, Quentin, illus. 2009. (Andersen Press Picture Bks). (ENG.). 32p. (J). (gr. k-3). 16.95 *(978-0-7613-5152-8(3))* Lerner Publishing Group.

Yolen, Jane. Como Dicen Estoy Enojado los Dinosaurios? Teague, Mark, illus. 2014. (SPA.). 40p. (J). (gr. -1-k). pap. 6.99 *(978-0-545-62780-1(X),* Scholastic en Espanol) Scholastic, Inc.

—How Do Dinosaurs Go to School? Teague, Mark, illus. 2007. (How Do Dinosaurs... Ser.). (ENG.). 40p. (J). (gr. -1-k). 16.99 *(978-0-439-02081-7(6))* Scholastic, Inc.

—How Do Dinosaurs Go to School? Teague, Mark, illus. 2011. (J). (gr. -1-3). 29.95 *(978-0-545-19700-7(7));* 18.95 *(978-0-545-19707-6(4))* Weston Woods Studios, Inc.

—How Do Dinosaurs Play with Their Friends? Teague, Mark, illus. 2006. (How Do Dinosaurs... Ser.). (ENG.). 12p. (J). (gr. -1-k). bds. 6.99 *(978-0-439-85654-6(X),* Blue Sky Pr., The) Scholastic, Inc.

—How Do Dinosaurs Say Good Night? Teague, Mark, illus. 2008. (How Do Dinosaurs... Ser.). (ENG.). (J). (gr. -1-3). 9.99 *(978-0-545-09319-4(8))* Scholastic, Inc.

—How Do Dinosaurs Say Happy Birthday? Teague, Mark, illus. 2011. (How Do Dinosaurs... Ser.). (ENG.). 12p. (J). (gr. -1-k). bds. 6.99 *(978-0-545-15353-9(0),* Blue Sky Pr., The) Scholastic, Inc.

—How Do Dinosaurs Say Happy Chanukah? Teague, Mark, illus. 2012. (How Do Dinosaurs... ? Ser.). (ENG.). 40p. (J). (— 1). 16.99 *(978-0-545-41677-1(9),* Blue Sky Pr., The) Scholastic, Inc.

—How Do Dinosaurs Say I'm Mad? Teague, Mark, illus. 2013. (How Do Dinosaurs... ? Ser.). (ENG.). 40p. (J). (gr. -1-k). 16.99 *(978-0-545-14315-8(2),* Blue Sky Pr., The) Scholastic, Inc.

—How Do Dinosaurs Say Merry Christmas? Teague, Mark, illus. 2012. (How Do Dinosaurs... ? Ser.). (ENG.). 40p. (J). (gr. -1-k). 16.99 *(978-0-545-41678-8(7),* Blue Sky Pr., The) Scholastic, Inc.

Zafar, Nuzhat. Free Like a Bird. 2009. (Illus.). 28p. pap. 13.99 *(978-1-4389-7312-8(8))* AuthorHouse.

Zail, Suzy. Dependable Dan. Stewart, Chantal, illus. 2004. iv, 36p. (J). pap. *(978-0-7608-6747-1(X))* Sundance/Newbridge Educational Publishing.

BEHAVIOR PROBLEMS IN CHILDREN

see Problem Children

BEIJING (CHINA)

Barber, Nicola. Beijing. 2004. (Great Cities of the World Ser.). (Illus.). 48p. (gr. 5-12). lib. bdg. 31.00 *(978-0-8368-5028-4(9),* Gareth Stevens Secondary Library) Stevens, Gareth Publishing LLLP.

Furstinger, Nancy. Beijing, 1 vol. 2005. (Cities Set 1 Ser.). (ENG., Illus.). 32p. (gr. k-6). 27.07 *(978-1-59197-853-4(X),* Checkerboard Library) ABDO Publishing Co.

Hodge, Susie. The Forbidden City. 2005. (Places in History Ser.). (Illus.). 48p. (gr. 5-12). pap. 14.05 *(978-0-8368-5817-4(4));* lib. bdg. 31.00 *(978-0-8368-5810-5(7))* Stevens, Gareth Publishing LLLP. (World Almanac Library).

Knox, Barbara. Forbidden City: China's Imperial Palace. 2006. (Castles, Palaces, & Tombs Ser.). (Illus.). 32p. (J). (gr. 2-5). lib. bdg. 25.27 *(978-1-59716-070-4(9),* 1251394) Bearport Publishing Co., Inc.

Kwong-Chiu, Chiu. In the Forbidden City. Steinhardt, Nancy S., ed. Wang, Ben, tr. 2014. (ENG., Illus.). 52p. (J). (gr. 4-6). 19.95 *(978-0-9893776-0-7(1))* China Institute Gallery, China Institute in America.

Mason Crest. Beijing, Vol. 8. 2016. (Major World Cities Ser.: Vol. 8). (ENG., Illus.). 48p. (J). (gr. 5-8). 20.95 *(978-1-4222-3539-3(4))* Mason Crest.

Matthews, Sheelagh. Beijing National Stadium. 2009. (Structural Wonders Ser.). (Illus.). 32p. (J). (gr. 4-6). 9.95 *(978-1-60596-141-5(8));* lib. bdg. 26.00 *(978-1-60596-140-8(X))* Weigl Pubs., Inc.

Morley, Jacqueline. Be in the Forbidden City! A Sheltered Life You'd Rather Avoid. Antram, David, illus. 2008. (You Wouldn't Want to Ser.). (ENG.). 32p. (J). (gr. 4-7). 29.00 *(978-0-531-18749-4(7),* Children's Pr.) Scholastic Library Publishing.

Pellegrini, Nancy. Beijing. Cooper, Adrian, photos by. 2007. (Global Cities Ser.). (Illus.). 61p. (gr. 5-8). lib. bdg. 30.00 *(978-0-7910-8848-7(0),* Chelsea Hse.) Facts On File, Inc.

BELACQUA, LYRA (FICTITIOUS CHARACTER)—FICTION

Pullman, Philip. The Amber Spyglass. unabr. ed. 2004. (His Dark Materials Ser.: Bk. 3). 465p. (YA). (gr. 7-18). pap. 63.00 incl. audio *(978-0-8072-1593-7(7),* S YA 169 SP, Listening Library) Random Hse. Audio Publishing Group.

—The Amber Spyglass. 2003. (His Dark Materials Ser.: 3). (ENG.). (J). (gr. 5-12). 480p. mass mkt. 8.99 *(978-0-440-23815-7(3),* Laurel Leaf); (Illus.). 560p. pap. 8.99 *(978-0-440-41856-6(9),* Yearling) Random Hse. Children's Bks.

—The Golden Compass. 2003. (His Dark Materials Ser.: 1). (ENG.). 368p. (J). (gr. 5-12). mass mkt. 8.99 *(978-0-440-23813-3(7),* Laurel Leaf) Random Hse. Children's Bks.

—His Dark Materials: The Golden Compass - The Subtle Knife - The Amber Spyglass, 3 vols. (His Dark Materials Ser.). (ENG.). (J). (gr. 5-12). 2007. 1312p. 60.00 *(978-0-375-84238-2(1),* Knopf Bks. for Young Readers) 2003. mass mkt., mass mkt., mass mkt. 26.97 *(978-0-440-23860-7(9),* Laurel Leaf) Random Hse. Children's Bks.

—His Dark Materials: The Golden Compass, the Subtle Knife, the Amber Spyglass. 2011. (Everyman's Library Contemporary Classics Ser.). (ENG.). 1144p. 35.00 *(978-0-307-95783-2(7),* Everyman's Library) Knopf Doubleday Publishing Group.

—His Dark Materials Set: The Golden Compass - The Subtle Knife - The Amber Spyglass, 3 vols. 2003. (His Dark Materials Ser.: Bks. 1-3). (ENG.). 560p. (J). (gr. 5). 26.97 *(978-0-440-41951-8(4),* Yearling) Random Hse. Children's Bks.

—Once upon a Time in the North. 2008. (His Dark Materials Ser.). (ENG., Illus.). 112p. *(978-0-385-61432-0(2))* Fickling, David Bks.

—The Subtle Knife, Vol. 2. unabr. ed. 2004. (His Dark Materials Ser.: Bk. 2). 326p. (J). (gr. 7-18). pap. 58.00 incl. audio *(978-0-8072-0567-9(2),* S YA 136 SP, Listening Library) Random Hse. Audio Publishing Group.

—The Subtle Knife, Bk. 2. 2003. (His Dark Materials Ser.: 2). (ENG.). 304p. (J). (gr. 5-12). mass mkt. 8.99 *(978-0-440-23814-0(5),* Laurel Leaf) Random Hse. Children's Bks.

BELDEN, TRIXIE (FICTITIOUS CHARACTER)—FICTION

Campbell, Julie. The Secret of the Mansion. Stevens, Mary, illus. 2003. (Trixie Belden Ser.: No. 1). (ENG.). 272p. (J). (gr. 3-7). 6.99 *(978-0-375-82412-8(X),* Random Hse. Bks. for Young Readers) Random Hse. Children's Bks.

BELGIAN CONGO

see Congo (Democratic Republic)

BELGIUM

Deem, James M. The Prisoners of Breendonk: Personal Histories from a World War II Concentration Camp. 2015. (ENG., Illus.). 352p. (YA). (gr. 9). 18.99 *(978-0-544-09664-6(9),* HMH Books For Young Readers) Houghton Mifflin Harcourt Publishing Co.

Owings, Lisa. Belgium. 2012. (Exploring Countries Ser.). (ENG., Illus.). 32p. (J). (gr. 3-7). lib. bdg. 26.95 *(978-1-60014-761-6(5),* Blastoff! Readers) Bellwether Media.

Pateman, Robert & Elliott, Mark. Belgium. 2nd rev. ed. 2006. (Cultures of the World Ser.). (Illus.). 144p. (J). (gr. 6-7). lib. bdg. 42.79 *(978-0-7614-2059-0(2),* Benchmark Bks.) Marshall Cavendish Corp.

Pateman, Robert, et al. Belgium. 2016. (Cultures of the World (r) Ser.). (ENG.). 144p. (J). (gr. 5-5). lib. bdg. 47.07 *(978-1-5026-1835-1(4))* Cavendish Square Publishing.

Walker, Ida. Belgium. 2007. (European Union Ser.). (Illus.). 88p. (YA). (gr. 3-7). lib. bdg. 21.95 *(978-1-4222-0040-7(X),* 1247982) Mason Crest.

Walker, Ida & Indovino, Shaina C. Belgium. Bruton, John, ed. 2012. (Major European Union Nations Ser.). 64p. (J). (gr. 7). 22.95 *(978-1-4222-2233-1(0))* Mason Crest.

Walker, Ida & Indovino, Shaina Carmel. Belgium. 2012. (J). pap. *(978-1-4222-2264-5(0))* Mason Crest.

Wingfield, George. Belgium. 2008. (Modern World Nations Ser.). 120p. (gr. 6-12). 35.00 *(978-0-7910-9670-3(X),* Chelsea Hse.) Facts On File, Inc.

Wingfield, George & Gritzner, Charles F. Belgium. 2nd rev. ed. 2011. (Modern World Nations Ser.). (gr. 6-12). 35.00 *(978-1-61753-044-9(1),* Chelsea Hse.) Facts On File, Inc.

Wood, Alix. Anthony Van Dyck, 1 vol. 2015. (ENG., Illus.). 32p. (J). pap. 10.00 *(978-1-4777-5398-9(2),* Windmill Bks.) Rosen Publishing Group, Inc., The.

World Book, Inc. Staff, contrib. by. Christmas in Belgium. 2004. (Christmas Around the World from World Book Ser.). (Illus.). 1760p. (gr. 2-8). 24.95 *(978-0-7166-0864-6(2),* 20114) World Bk., Inc.

BELGIUM—FICTION

Bemelmans, Ludwig. The Golden Basket. 2016. (ENG., Illus.). 96p. (J). (gr. 1-5). pap. 9.99 *(978-0-486-80717-1(7))* Dover Pubns., Inc.

Brandeis, Madeline. Little Philippe of Belgium. 2005. reprint ed. pap. 22.95 *(978-1-4179-3302-0(X))* Kessinger Publishing, LLC.

Coster, Charles. Flemish Legends. 2005. pap. 15.50 *(978-1-59605-351-9(8),* Cosimo Classics) Cosimo, Inc.

Deary, Terry. The War Game. 2014. (World War I Tales Ser.). (ENG., Illus.). 64p. (J). pap. 9.99 *(978-1-4081-9174-3(1),* 9781408191743, Bloomsbury USA Childrens) Bloomsbury Publishing USA.

Doyle, Marissa. Courtship & Curses. 2013. (ENG.). 368p. (YA). (gr. 9-13). pap. 10.99 *(978-1-250-02744-3(6))* Square Fish.

Farenhorst, Christine. A Cup of Cold Water: The Compassion of Nurse Edith Cavell. 2007. 222p. (J). (gr. 3-7). per. 11.99 *(978-1-59638-026-4(8))* P & R Publishing.

Fiske, James. The Belgians to the Front. 2007. (ENG.). 120p. pap. 18.99 *(978-1-4264-8476-6(3));* 126p. pap. 19.99 *(978-1-4264-8253-3(1))* Creative Media Partners, LLC.

Goscinny, René. Asterix in Belgium. Uderzo, Albert, illus. 2005. (ENG.). 48p. pap. 12.99 *(978-0-7528-6650-5(8),* Orion) Orion Publishing Group, Ltd. GBR. Dist: Hachette Bk. Group.

Hergé. The Shooting Star. 2012. (Adventures of Tintin: Young Readers Edition Ser.). (ENG., Illus.). 96p. (J). (gr. 3-7). pap. 8.99 *(978-0-316-19875-2(7))* Little, Brown Bks. for Young Readers.

Ouida. A Dog of Flanders. 2011. (Dover Children's Thrift Classics Ser.). (ENG., Illus.). 80p. (J). (gr. 3-8). reprint ed. pap. 4.00 *(978-0-486-27087-6(4))* Dover Pubns., Inc.

Perkins, Lucy Fitch. The Belgian Twins. 2004. reprint ed. pap. 15.95 *(978-1-4191-5388-4(9));* pap. 1.99 *(978-1-4192-5388-1(3))* Kessinger Publishing, LLC.

Weyn, Suzanne. Water Song: A Retelling of the Frog Prince. 2012. (Once upon a Time Ser.). (ENG.). 208p. (YA). (gr. 9). pap. 10.99 *(978-1-4424-6052-2(0),* Simon Pulse) Simon Pulse.

BELIEF AND DOUBT

Custom Curricul Staff. Can I Know What to Believe? 2004. (Custom Curriculum Ser.). 256p. pap., pap. 19.99 *(978-0-7814-4089-9(0),* 0781440890) Cook, David C.

Hamod, Rania. I Am Lovable. 2012. 52p. pap. 20.95 *(978-1-4525-5838-7(8))* Balboa Pr.

Nelson, Robin. Am I a Good Friend? A Book about Trustworthiness. 2014. (Show Your Character Ser.). (ENG., Illus.). 32p. (gr. 1-3). pap. 8.95 *(978-1-4677-2386-2(X))* Lerner Publishing Group.

BELL, ALEXANDER GRAHAM, 1847-1922

Auch, Allison. Electrifying Personalities & Personalidades Electrizantes: 6 English, 6 Spanish Adaptations. 2011. (ENG & SPA.). (J). 97.00 net. *(978-1-4108-5713-2(1))* Benchmark Education Co.

Bader, Bonnie. Who Was Alexander Graham Bell? Groff, David, illus. 2013. (Who Was? Ser.). (ENG.). 112p. (J). (gr. 3-7). 5.99 *(978-0-448-46460-2(8),* Grosset & Dunlap) Penguin Young Readers Group.

—Who Was Alexander Graham Bell? 2013. (Who Was... ? Ser.). lib. bdg. 16.00 *(978-0-606-32132-7(2),* Turtleback) Turtleback Bks.

Bankston, John. Alexander Graham Bell & the Story of the Telephone. 2004. (Uncharted, Unexplored, & Unexplained Ser.). (Illus.). 48p. (J). (gr. 4-8). lib. bdg. 29.95 *(978-1-58415-243-9(5))* Mitchell Lane Pubs., Inc.

Biehn, Mike. Alexander Graham Bell: Famous Inventor. 2012. (Beginning Biographies Ser.). (ENG., Illus.). 24p. (J). (gr. 1-3). 22.60 *(978-1-4488-8603-6(1),* PowerKids Pr.) Rosen Publishing Group, Inc., The.

Brown, Natalie. Who Was Alexander Graham Bell? 2012. (InfoMax Readers Ser.). (ENG., Illus.). 24p. (J). (gr. 1-2). pap. 8.25 *(978-1-4488-9085-9(3),* Rosen Classroom) Rosen Publishing Group, Inc., The.

Cefrey, Holly. The Inventions of Alexander Graham Bell: The Telephone. (19th Century American Inventors Ser.). 24p. 2009. (gr. 2-3). 42.50 *(978-1-60854-949-8(6))* 2003. (Illus.). (J). lib. bdg. 22.60 *(978-0-8239-6441-3(8))* Rosen Publishing Group, Inc., The. (PowerKids Pr.).

Chambers, Catherine. Alexander Graham Bell, 1 vol. 2014. (Science Biographies Ser.). (ENG.). 32p. (gr. 2-4). lib. bdg. 30.65 *(978-1-4109-6238-6(5),* Raintree Perspectives) Heinemann-Raintree.

Crompton, Samuel Willard. Alexander Graham Bell & the Telephone: The Invention That Changed Communication. 2008. (Milestones in American History Ser.). (Illus.). 120p. (J). (gr. 7-12). 35.00 *(978-1-60413-004-1(0))* Facts On File, Inc.

Davis, Lynn. Alexander Graham Bell, 1 vol. 2016. (ENG.). 24p. (J). *(978-1-62403-721-4(6))* ABDO Publishing Co.

Feinstein, Stephen. Alexander Graham Bell: The Genius Behind the Phone. 2008. (Inventors Who Changed the World Ser.). (Illus.). 128p. (J). (gr. 6-18). lib. bdg. 34.60 *(978-1-59845-055-2(7),* MyReportLinks.com Bks.) Enslow Pubs., Inc.

Fraser, Mary Ann. Alexander Graham Bell Answers the Call. Fraser, Mary Ann, illus. 2017. (ENG., Illus.). 32p. (J). (gr. 1-4). lib. bdg. 16.99 *(978-1-58089-721-1(5))* Charlesbridge Publishing, Inc.

Garmon, Anita. Alexander Graham Bell Invents. 2007. (History Chapters Ser.). (ENG., Illus.). 48p. (J). (gr. 1-4). lib. bdg. 17.90 *(978-1-4263-0189-6(8),* National Geographic Children's Bks.) National Geographic Society.

Haven, Kendall F. Alexander Graham Bell: Inventor & Visionary. 2003. (Great Life Stories: Inventors & Scientists Ser.). (Illus.). 128p. (J). 30.50 *(978-0-531-12314-0(6),* Watts, Franklin) Scholastic Library Publishing.

James, Emily. Alexander Graham Bell. 2017. (Great Scientists & Inventors Ser.). (ENG.). 24p. (gr. k-1). lib. bdg. 26.65 *(978-1-5157-3883-1(3),* Pebble Plus) Capstone Press of Coughlan Cos.

Klingel, Cynthia Fitterer & Klingel, Cynthia. Alexander Graham Bell: Inventor. 2003. (Our People Ser.). (ENG., Illus.). 32p. (J). (gr. 3-6). 29.93 *(978-1-56766-367-9(2),* 200625) Child's World, Inc., The.

Kramer, Barbara. Alexander Graham Bell. 2015. (Readers Bios Ser.). (ENG.). 32p. (J). (gr. k-3). pap. 3.99 *(978-1-4263-1935-8(5),* National Geographic Children's Bks.) National Geographic Society.

Kulling, Monica. Listen Up! Alexander Graham Bell's Talking Machine. Walz, Richard, illus. 2007. (Step into Reading Ser.). (ENG.). 48p. (J). (gr. k-3). per. 3.99 *(978-0-375-83115-7(0),* Random Hse. Bks. for Young Readers) Random Hse. Children's Bks.

Kuskowski, Alex. Super Simple Telephone Projects: Inspiring & Educational Science Activities, 1 vol. 2016. (ENG., Illus.). 32p. (J). *(978-1-62403-733-7(X))* ABDO Publishing Co.

Lin, Yoming S. Alexander Graham Bell & the Telephone. 2012. (Eureka! Ser.). (Illus.). 24p. (J). (gr. 3-6). lib. bdg. 22.60 *(978-1-4488-5034-1(7))* Rosen Publishing Group, Inc., The.

MacLeod, Elizabeth. Alexander Graham Bell. Krystoforski, Andrej, illus. 2007. (ENG.). 32p. (J). (gr. 1-3). 3.95 *(978-1-55453-002-1(4));* 14.95 *(978-1-55453-001-4(6))* Kids Can Pr., Ltd. CAN. Dist: Hachette Bk. Group.

Mara, Wil. Alexander Graham Bell. 2003. (Rookie Biographies Ser.). (ENG., Illus.). 32p. (J). (gr. 1-2). pap. 4.95 *(978-0-516-27340-2(X),* Children's Pr.) Scholastic Library Publishing.

Marsh, Carole. Alexander Graham Bell. 2003. 12p. (gr. k-4). 2.95 *(978-0-635-02354-4(7))* Gallopade International.

Martin, Justin. Easy Reader Biographies: Alexander Graham Bell: A Famous Inventor. 2007. (ENG.). 16p. pap. 2.99 *(978-0-439-77415-4(2),* Teaching Resources) Scholastic, Inc.

Matthews, Tom L. Always Inventing: A Photobiography of Alexander Graham Bell. 2006. (Photobiographies Ser.). (ENG., Illus.). 64p. (J). (gr. 5-7). per. 7.95 *(978-0-7922-5932-9(7),* National Geographic Children's Bks.) National Geographic Society.

Matthews, Tom L. & National Geographic Kids Staff. Always Inventing: A Photobiography of Alexander Graham Bell. 2015. (Photobiographies Ser.). (ENG.). 64p. (J). (gr. 5). pap. 7.99 *(978-1-4263-2217-4(8),* National Geographic Children's Bks.) National Geographic Society.

McPherson, Stephanie Sammartino. Alexander Graham Bell. 2008. pap. 52.95 *(978-0-8225-9385-0(8))* Lerner Publishing Group.

—Alexander Graham Bell. Butler, Tad, illus. 2007. (History Maker Biographies Ser.). (ENG.). 48p. (gr. 3-6). lib. bdg. 27.93 *(978-0-8225-7606-8(6),* Lerner Pubns.) Lerner Publishing Group.

Mills, Nathan & Biehn, Mike. Alexander Graham Bell: Famous Inventor. 2012. (Rosen Readers Ser.). (ENG., Illus.). 24p. (J). (gr. 1-2). pap. 8.25 *(978-1-4488-8872-6(7),* Rosen Classroom) Rosen Publishing Group, Inc., The.

Rivera, Sheila. Alexander Graham Bell: A Life of Helpfulness. 2007. (Pull Ahead Bks.). (Illus.). 32p. (J). (gr. 3-7). lib. bdg. 22.60 *(978-0-8225-6463-8(7),* Lerner Pubns.) Lerner Publishing Group.

Saddleback Educational Publishing Staff, ed. Alexander Graham Bell, 1 vol. unabr. ed. 2008. (Graphic Biographies Ser.). (ENG., Illus.). 25p. (YA). (gr. 9-12). pap. 7.95 *(978-1-59905-213-7(X))* Saddleback Educational Publishing, Inc.

Schaefer, Lola M. Alexander Graham Bell. 2016. (First Biographies - Scientists & Inventors Ser.). (ENG.). 24p. (gr. k-1). pap. 6.29 *(978-1-5157-5965-2(2),* Pebble Bks.) Capstone Press of Coughlan Cos.

Schuman, Michael. Alexander Graham Bell: Scientist & Inventor. 2015. (Legendary American Biographies Ser.). 96p. (J). (gr. 6-12). 27.94 *(978-0-7660-6430-0(1))* Enslow Pubs., Inc.

Schuman, Michael A. Alexander Graham Bell: Scientist & Inventor. 2015. (Legendary American Biographies Ser.). 96p. (J). (gr. 6-12). pap. 10.95 *(978-0-7660-6431-7(X))* Enslow Pubs., Inc.

Spilsbury, Louise. Alexander Graham Bell & the Telephone, 01 vols., 1. 2016. (Inventions That Changed the World Ser.). (ENG.). 32p. (J). pap. 10.00 *(978-1-5081-4623-0(3),* PowerKids Pr.) Rosen Publishing Group, Inc., The.

Time for Kids Editors. Alexander Graham Bell: Inventor of the Telephone. 2006. (Time for Kids Ser.). (ENG., Illus.). 48p. (J). (gr. 2-4). pap. 3.99 *(978-0-06-057618-9(9))* HarperCollins Pubs.

Venezia, Mike. Alexander Graham Bell: Setting the Tone for Communication. Venezia, Mike, illus. (Getting to Know the World's Greatest Inventors & Scientists Ser.). (ENG., Illus.). 32p. (J). 2009. (gr. 3-4). pap. 6.95 *(978-0-531-22207-2(1),* Children's Pr.) 2008. (gr. 2-5). 28.00 *(978-0-531-14976-8(5))* Scholastic Library Publishing.

BELLS

Holden, Pam. Ringing Bells. 2015. (ENG., Illus.). 16p. (-1). pap. *(978-1-77654-083-9(2),* Red Rocket Readers) Flying Start Bks.

BEN-GURION, DAVID, 1886-1973

World Book, Inc Staff, contrib. by. Golda Meir: With Profiles of David Ben-Gurion & Yitzhak Rabin. 2006. (Biographical Connections Ser.). (Illus.). 112p. (J). *(978-0-7166-1829-4(X))* World Bk., Inc.

BENCH, JOHNNY, 1947-

Jamow, Jesse. Johnny Bench. 2009. (Baseball Hall of Famers Ser.). 112p. (gr. 5-8). 63.90 *(978-1-61511-511-2(0),* Rosen Reference) Rosen Publishing Group, Inc., The.

BENEDICT, SAINT, ABBOT OF MONTE CASSINO

Krenner, Digna. The Twin Who Ran Away: Life of St. Benedict. 2011. 40p. 35.95 *(978-1-258-08842-2(8))* Literary Licensing, LLC.

BENEFICIAL INSECTS

Aloian, Molly. How Are Insects Helpful? 2013. (ENG., Illus.). 24p. (J). *(978-0-7787-1269-5(9));* pap. *(978-0-7787-1281-7(8))* Crabtree Publishing Co.

Gagne, Tammy. Working Animals of the World. 2015. (All about Animals Ser.). (ENG.). 24p. (gr. 1-2). pap. 6.95 *(978-1-4914-2238-0(6))* Capstone Press of Coughlan Cos.

Korrow, Chris. The Organic Bug Book. Korrow, Chris, illus. 2013. (ENG., Illus.). 44p. (J). pap. 11.95 *(978-1-58420-145-8(2),* Lindisfarne Bks.) SteinerBooks, Inc.

Weir, Kirsten. Bugs That Help. 2008. (Bug Alert! Ser.). 32p. (gr. 3-18). lib. bdg. 28.50 *(978-0-7614-3192-3(6),* Benchmark Bks.) Marshall Cavendish Corp.

BENNET, ELIZABETH (FICTITIOUS CHARACTER)—FICTION

Austen, Jane. Pride & Prejudice. Kronheimer, Ann, illus. 2013. (Jane Austen Ser.). (ENG.). 64p. pap. 6.95 *(978-1-906230-06-7(4))* Real Reads Ltd. GBR. Dist: Casemate Pubs. & Bk. Distributors, LLC.

Williams, Marcia. Lizzy Bennet's Diary: Inspired by Jane Austen's Pride & Prejudice. Williams, Marcia, illus. 2014. (ENG., Illus.). 112p. (J). (gr. 3-7). 16.99 *(978-0-7636-7030-6(8))* Candlewick Pr.

BENT, WILLIAM, 1809-1869

Beckwith, Cheryl. William Bent: Frontiersman. 2011. (ENG & SPA., Illus.). 60p. (J). pap. 8.95 *(978-0-86541-117-3(4))* Filter Pr., LLC.

BEOWULF

Barkow, Henriette. Beowulf: An Anglo-Saxon Epic. Down, Alan, illus. 2003. (J). (CHI & ENG.). 30p. pap. 12.95 *(978-1-84444-025-2(7));* (BEN & ENG.). 30p. pap. 12.95 *(978-1-84444-024-5(9));* (URD & ENG.). 32p. pap. 12.95 *(978-1-84444-034-4(6))* Mantra Lingua GBR. Dist: Chinasprout, Inc.

Down, Alan, illus. Beowulf: An Anglo-Saxon Epic. 2004. (J). 32p. pap. *(978-1-84444-023-8(0));* 32p. pap. *(978-1-84444-022-1(2));* 30p. pap. *(978-1-84444-026-9(5));* 30p. pap. *(978-1-84444-028-3(1));* 30p. pap. *(978-1-84444-029-0(X));* 30p. pap. *(978-1-84444-030-6(3));* 32p. pap. *(978-1-84444-031-3(1));* 30p. pap. *(978-1-84444-032-0(X));* (TUR & ENG.). 30p. pap. *(978-1-84444-033-7(8));* 30p. pap. *(978-1-84444-109-9(1));* 30p. pap. *(978-1-84444-110-5(5));* (SER & ENG.). 30p. pap. *(978-1-84444-112-9(1));* 30p. pap. *(978-1-84444-113-6(X));* (CZE & ENG.). 30p. pap. *(978-1-84444-114-3(8));* 30p. pap. *(978-1-84444-027-6(3))* Mantra Lingua.

Morpurgo, Michael. Beowulf. Foreman, Michael, illus. 2015. (ENG.). 160p. (J). (gr. 3-7). pap. 6.99 *(978-0-7636-7297-3(1))* Candlewick Pr.

BERENSTAIN BEARS (FICTITIOUS CHARACTERS)—FICTION

Berenstain, Jan. The Berenstain Bears Christmas Fun Sticker & Activity Book, 1 vol. Berenstain, Mike, illus. 2016. (Berenstain Bears/Living Lights Ser.). (ENG.). 32p. (J). pap. 6.99 *(978-0-310-75384-1(8))* Zonderkidz.

—The Berenstain Bears Easter Fun Sticker & Activity Book, 1 vol. Berenstain, Mike, illus. 2017. (Berenstain Bears/Living Lights Ser.). (ENG.). 32p. (J). pap. 6.99 *(978-0-310-75381-0(3))* Zonderkidz.

—The Berenstain Bears Hugs & Kisses Sticker & Activity Book, 1 vol. Berenstain, Mike, illus. 2016. (Berenstain Bears/Living Lights Ser.). (ENG.). 32p. (J). pap. 6.99 *(978-0-310-75382-7(1))* Zonderkidz.

Berenstain, Jan & Berenstain, Mike. All Aboard! Berenstain, Jan & Berenstain, Mike, illus. 2010. (I Can Read Level 1 Ser.). (ENG., Illus.). 32p. (J). (gr. k-3). 16.99 *(978-0-06-168971-0(8))* HarperCollins Pubs.

—The Berenstain Bears - All Aboard! Berenstain, Jan & Berenstain, Mike, illus. 2010. (I Can Read Level 1 Ser.). (ENG., Illus.). 32p. (J). (gr. k-3). pap. 3.99 *(978-0-06-057418-5(6))* HarperCollins Pubs.

—The Berenstain Bears - We Love Trucks! Berenstain, Jan & Berenstain, Mike, illus. 2013. (I Can Read Level 1 Ser.). (ENG., Illus.). 32p. (J). (gr. -1-3). pap. 3.99 *(978-0-06-207535-2(7))* HarperCollins Pubs.

—The Berenstain Bears & Mama for Mayor! Berenstain, Jan & Berenstain, Mike, illus. 2012. (I Can Read Level 1 Ser.). (ENG., Illus.). 32p. (J). (gr. k-3). 16.99 *(978-0-06-207528-4(4));* pap. 3.99 *(978-0-06-207527-7(6))* HarperCollins Pubs.

—The Berenstain Bears & the Tooth Fairy. Berenstain, Jan & Berenstain, Mike, illus. 2012. (Berenstain Bears Ser.). (ENG., Illus.). 24p. (J). (gr. -1-3). pap. 3.99 *(978-0-06-207549-9(7),* HarperFestival) HarperCollins Pubs.

—The Berenstain Bears & the Tooth Fairy. 2012. (Berenstain Bears Ser.). (J). lib. bdg. 13.55 *(978-0-606-26844-8(8),* Turtleback) Turtleback Bks.

—The Berenstain Bears at the Aquarium. Berenstain, Jan & Berenstain, Mike, illus. 2012. (I Can Read Level 1 Ser.). (ENG., Illus.). 32p. (J). (gr. k-3). 16.99 *(978-0-06-207525-3(X));* pap. 3.99 *(978-0-06-207524-6(1))* HarperCollins Pubs.

—The Berenstain Bears at the Aquarium. 2012. (Berenstain Bears: I Can Read! Ser.). (J). lib. bdg. 13.55 *(978-0-606-23594-5(9),* Turtleback) Turtleback Bks.

—The Berenstain Bears' Caring & Sharing Treasury, 1 vol. 2016. (Berenstain Bears/Living Lights Ser.). (ENG.). 160p. (J). 10.99 *(978-0-310-75358-2(9))* Zonderkidz.

—The Berenstain Bears' Dinosaur Dig. Berenstain, Jan & Berenstain, Mike, illus. 2012. (Berenstain Bears Ser.). (ENG., Illus.). 24p. (J). (gr. -1-3). pap. 3.99 *(978-0-06-207548-2(9),* HarperFestival) HarperCollins Pubs.

—The Berenstain Bears' Dinosaur Dig. 2012. (Berenstain Bears Ser.). (J). lib. bdg. 13.55 *(978-0-606-26290-3(3),* Turtleback) Turtleback Bks.

—The Berenstain Bears Friendship Blessings Collection, 1 vol. 2017. (Berenstain Bears/Living Lights Ser.). (ENG.). 160p. (J). 10.99 *(978-0-310-75338-4(4))* Zonderkidz.

—The Berenstain Bears Get Ready for School. Berenstain, Jan & Berenstain, Mike, illus. 2015. (Berenstain Bears Ser.). (ENG., Illus.). 16p. (J). (gr. -1-1). pap. 6.99 *(978-0-06-207552-9(7),* HarperFestival) HarperCollins Pubs.

—The Berenstain Bears Go Green. 2013. (Berenstain Bears Ser.). (Illus.). (J). lib. bdg. 13.55 *(978-0-606-27142-4(2),* Turtleback) Turtleback Bks.

—The Berenstain Bears' Old-Fashioned Christmas. Berenstain, Jan & Berenstain, Mike, illus. 2012. (Berenstain Bears Ser.). (ENG., Illus.). 32p. (J). (gr. -1-3). 12.99 *(978-0-06-057443-7(7))* HarperCollins Pubs.

—The Berenstain Bears Spring Storybook Collection. Berenstain, Mike, illus. 2017. (Berenstain Bears Ser.). (Illus.). 192p. (J). (gr. -1-3). 11.99 *(978-0-06-243458-6(6))* HarperCollins Pubs.

—The Berenstain Bears Storybook Bible, 1 vol. 2013. (Berenstain Bears/Living Lights Ser.). (ENG., Illus.). 256p. (J). 16.99 *(978-0-310-72721-7(9))* Zonderkidz.

—The Berenstain Bears Take-Along Storybook Set. Berenstain, Mike, illus. 2016. (Berenstain Bears Ser.). (Illus.). 120p. (J). (gr. -1-3). pap. 11.99 *(978-0-06-241155-6(1),* HarperFestival) HarperCollins Pubs.

—We Love Our Dad! 2013. (Berenstain Bears Ser.). (J). lib. bdg. 13.55 *(978-0-606-31785-6(6),* Turtleback) Turtleback Bks.

—We Love Our Mom! Berenstain, Jan & Berenstain, Mike, illus. 2012. (Berenstain Bears Ser.). (ENG., Illus.). 24p. (J). (gr. -1-3). pap. 3.99 *(978-0-06-207547-5(0),* HarperFestival) HarperCollins Pubs.

—We Love Our Mom! 2012. (Berenstain Bears Ser.). (J). lib. bdg. 13.55 *(978-0-606-23578-5(7),* Turtleback) Turtleback Bks.

Berenstain, Jan & Berenstain, Stan. The Berenstain Bears: All in the Family. 2012. (ENG., Illus.). 192p. (J). (gr. -1-2). 10.99 *(978-0-307-93068-2(8),* Random Hse. Bks. for Young Readers) Random Hse. Children's Bks.

—The Berenstain Bears' New Pup. Berenstain, Jan, illus. 2017. (I Can Read Level 1 Ser.). (Illus.). 40p. (J). (gr. -1-3). 9.99 *(978-0-06-257272-1(5))* HarperCollins Pubs.

Berenstain, Jan, et al. The Berenstain Bears Lose a Friend. Berenstain, Jan et al, illus. 2007. (Berenstain Bears Ser.). (ENG.). 32p. (J). (gr. -1-2). pap. 3.99 *(978-0-06-057389-8(9),* HarperFestival) HarperCollins Pubs.

—The Berenstain Bears' New Kitten. Berenstain, Jan et al, illus. 2007. (I Can Read Level 1 Ser.). (ENG.). 32p. (J). (gr. k-3). 16.99 *(978-0-06-058356-9(8));* pap. 3.99 *(978-0-06-058357-6(6))* HarperCollins Pubs.

—The Berenstain Bears Save Christmas. Berenstain, Mike, illus. 2003. (Berenstain Bears Ser.). (ENG.). 48p. (J). (gr. -1-3). 14.99 *(978-0-06-052670-2(X),* HarperFestival) HarperCollins Pubs.

Berenstain, Mike. The Berenstain Bears: Gone Fishin'! Berenstain, Mike, illus. 2014. (I Can Read Level 1 Ser.). (ENG., Illus.). 32p. (J). (gr. -1-3). pap. 3.99 *(978-0-06-207559-8(4))* HarperCollins Pubs.

—The Berenstain Bears - Gone Fishin'! Berenstain, Mike, illus. 2014. (I Can Read Level 1 Ser.). (ENG., Illus.). 32p. (J). (gr. -1-3). 16.99 *(978-0-06-207560-4(8))* HarperCollins Pubs.

—The Berenstain Bears Around the World. Berenstain, Mike, illus. 2016. (I Can Read Level 1 Ser.). (Illus.). 32p. (J). (gr. -1-3). pap. 3.99 *(978-0-06-235023-7(4))* HarperCollins Pubs.

—The Berenstain Bears Bless Our Gramps & Gran, 1 vol. 2017. (Berenstain Bears/Living Lights Ser.). (ENG.). 24p. (J). pap. 3.99 ***(978-0-310-74844-1(5))*** Zonderkidz.

—The Berenstain Bears Bless Our Pets, 1 vol. 2017. (Berenstain Bears/Living Lights Ser.). (ENG.). 24p. (J). pap. 3.99 *(978-0-310-74882-3(8))* Zonderkidz.

—The Berenstain Bears' Easter Parade. Berenstain, Mike, illus. 2014. (Berenstain Bears Ser.). (ENG., Illus.). 24p. (J). (gr. -1-3). pap. 3.99 *(978-0-06-207554-3(3),* HarperFestival) HarperCollins Pubs.

—The Berenstain Bears' Easter Sunday, 1 vol. 2016. (Berenstain Bears/Living Lights Ser.). (ENG.). 24p. (J). pap. 3.99 *(978-0-310-74902-8(6))* Zonderkidz.

—The Berenstain Bears' Graduation Day. Berenstain, Mike, illus. 2014. (Berenstain Bears Ser.). (ENG., Illus.). 24p. (J). (gr. -1-3). pap. 3.99 *(978-0-06-207555-0(1),* HarperFestival) HarperCollins Pubs.

—The Berenstain Bears' Lemonade Stand. Berenstain, Mike, illus. 2014. (I Can Read Level 1 Ser.). (ENG., Illus.). 32p. (J). (gr. -1-3). 16.99 *(978-0-06-207545-1(4));* pap. 3.99 *(978-0-06-207544-4(6))* HarperCollins Pubs.

—The Berenstain Bears Mother's Day Blessings, 1 vol. 2016. (Berenstain Bears/Living Lights Ser.). (ENG., Illus.). 24p. (J). pap. 3.99 *(978-0-310-74869-4(0))* Zonderkidz.

—The Berenstain Bears' Pirate Adventure. Berenstain, Mike, illus. 2016. (Berenstain Bears Ser.). (Illus.). 24p. (J). (gr. -1-3). pap. 3.99 *(978-0-06-235021-3(8),* HarperFestival) HarperCollins Pubs.

—The Berenstain Bears Play Football! 2017. (Berenstain Bears — I Can Read Ser.). lib. bdg. 13.55 ***(978-0-606-40068-8(0))*** Turtleback Bks.

—The Berenstain Bears School Time Blessings, 1 vol. 2016. (Berenstain Bears/Living Lights Ser.). (ENG.). 24p. (J). pap. 3.99 *(978-0-310-74842-7(9))* Zonderkidz.

—The Berenstain Bears' Show-And-Tell. Berenstain, Mike, illus. 2017. (Berenstain Bears Ser.). (Illus.). 24p. (J). (gr. -1-3). pap. 3.99 *(978-0-06-235031-2(5),* HarperFestival) HarperCollins Pubs.

—The Berenstain Bears' Show-And-tell. 2017. (Berenstain Bears Ser.). lib. bdg. 13.55 ***(978-0-606-40060-2(5))*** Turtleback Bks.

—The Berenstain Bears Take Off! Berenstain, Mike, illus. 2016. (I Can Read Level 1 Ser.). (Illus.). 32p. (J). (gr. -1-3). pap. 3.99 *(978-0-06-235018-3(8))* HarperCollins Pubs.

—The Berenstain Bears under the Sea. 2016. (Illus.). (J). ***(978-1-5182-2637-3(X))*** Baker & Taylor, CATS.

—The Berenstain Bears under the Sea. Berenstain, Mike, illus. 2016. (Berenstain Bears Ser.). (Illus.). 24p. (J). (gr. -1-3). pap. 3.99 *(978-0-06-235011-4(0),* HarperFestival) HarperCollins Pubs.

—The Berenstain Bears Visit the Firehouse. Berenstain, Mike, illus. 2016. (Berenstain Bears Ser.). (Illus.). 24p. (J). (gr. -1-3). pap. 3.99 *(978-0-06-235016-9(1),* HarperFestival) HarperCollins Pubs.

—The Berenstain Bears Visit the Firehouse. 2016. (Berenstain Bears Ser.). (J). lib. bdg. 13.55 *(978-0-606-38771-2(4))* Turtleback Bks.

—The Berenstain Bears: We Love Baseball! Berenstain, Mike, illus. 2017. (I Can Read Level 1 Ser.). (Illus.). 32p. (J). (gr. -1-3). pap. 3.99 *(978-0-06-235028-2(5))* HarperCollins Pubs.

—The Berenstain Bears: We Love Soccer! Berenstain, Mike, illus. 2016. (I Can Read Level 1 Ser.). (ENG., Illus.). 32p. (J). (gr. -1-3). pap. 3.99 *(978-0-06-235013-8(7))* HarperCollins Pubs.

—The Berenstain Bears: We Love the Library. Berenstain, Mike, illus. 2017. (Berenstain Bears Ser.). (Illus.). 24p. (J). (gr. -1-3). pap. 3.99 ***(978-0-06-235036-7(6),*** HarperFestival) HarperCollins Pubs.

—The Berenstain Bears: When I Grow Up. Berenstain, Mike, illus. 2015. (Berenstain Bears Ser.). (ENG., Illus.). 24p. (J). (gr. -1-3). pap. 3.99 *(978-0-06-235005-3(6),* HarperFestival) HarperCollins Pubs.

—Berenstain Bears/Living Lights: The Berenstain Bears' Harvest Festival, 1 vol. 2015. (Berenstain Bears/Living Lights Ser.). (ENG., Illus.). 24p. (J). pap. 3.99 *(978-0-310-74865-6(8))* Zonderkidz.

—Hospital Friends. Berenstain, Mike, illus. 2015. (Berenstain Bears Ser.). (ENG., Illus.). 24p. (J). (gr. -1-3). pap. 3.99 *(978-0-06-207541-3(1),* HarperFestival) HarperCollins Pubs.

—Hospital Friends. 2015. (Berenstain Bears Ser.). (J). lib. bdg. 13.55 *(978-0-606-36932-9(5))* Turtleback Bks.

—Mother's Day Blessings. 2016. (Illus.). (J). ***(978-1-4844-6294-2(7))*** Zonderkidz.

—Valentine Love Bug. Berenstain, Mike, illus. 2014. (Berenstain Bears Ser.). (ENG., Illus.). 24p. (J). (gr. -1-3). pap. 6.99 *(978-0-06-207562-8(4))* HarperCollins Pubs.

—When I Grow Up. 2015. (Berenstain Bears Ser.). (J). lib. bdg. 13.55 *(978-0-606-37606-8(2))* Turtleback Bks.

Berenstain, Mike, illus. The Berenstain Bears' Holiday Cookbook: Cub-Friendly Cooking with an Adult, 1 vol. 2016. (Berenstain Bears/Living Lights Ser.). (ENG.). 96p. (J). 12.99 *(978-0-310-75399-5(6))* Zonderkidz.

Berenstain, Mike, et al. The Berenstain Bears(r) Visit the Firehouse. 2016. (Illus.). (J). ***(978-1-5182-1125-6(9))*** Baker & Taylor, CATS.

Berenstain, Stan & Berenstain, Jan. The Berenstain Bears & the Baby Chipmunk. Berenstain, Stan & Berenstain, Jan, illus. 2005. (I Can Read Level 1 Ser.). (ENG., Illus.). 32p. (J). (gr. k-3). pap. 3.99 *(978-0-06-058413-9(0))* HarperCollins Pubs.

—The Berenstain Bears & the Bad Dream. 2004. (Berenstain Bears First Time Bks.). (J). (gr. -1-2). spiral bd. *(978-0-616-01556-8(9));* spiral bd. *(978-0-616-01555-1(0))* Canadian National Institute for the Blind/Institut National Canadien pour les Aveugles.

—The Berenstain Bears & the Blame Game. 2004. (Berenstain Bears First Time Bks.). (Illus.). (J). (gr. k-3). spiral bd. *(978-0-616-14559-3(4));* spiral bd. *(978-0-616-14560-9(8))* Canadian National Institute for the Blind/Institut National Canadien pour les Aveugles.

—The Berenstain Bears & the Papa's Day Surprise. 2003. (First Time Books(R) Ser.). (ENG., Illus.). 32p. (J). (gr. -1-2). pap. 4.99 *(978-0-375-81129-6(X),* Random Hse. Bks. for Young Readers) Random Hse. Children's Bks.

—The Berenstain Bears(r) & the Talent Show. 2014. (ENG.). 32p. (J). (-3). 9.99 *(978-1-4022-9095-4(0),* Sourcebooks Jabberwocky) Sourcebooks, Inc.

—The Berenstain Bears & the Trouble with Chores. Berenstain, Jan, illus. 2005. (Berenstain Bears Ser.). (ENG., Illus.). 32p. (J). (gr. -1-3). pap. 3.99 *(978-0-06-057382-9(1),* HarperFestival) HarperCollins Pubs.

—The Berenstain Bears & the Wishing Star. Berenstain, Stan & Berenstain, Jan, illus. 2005. (I Can Read Level 1 Ser.). (ENG., Illus.). 32p. (J). (gr. k-3). pap. 3.99 *(978-0-06-058347-7(9))* HarperCollins Pubs.

—The Berenstain Bears' Bedtime Battle. Berenstain, Stan & Berenstain, Jan, illus. 2004. (Berenstain Bears Ser.). (ENG., Illus.). 32p. (J). (gr. -1-3). pap. 3.99 *(978-0-06-057381-2(3),* HarperFestival) HarperCollins Pubs.

—The Berenstain Bears Clean House. 2005. (Berenstain Bears Ser.). (Illus.). 32p. (J). (gr. k-3). 16.99 *(978-0-06-058334-7(7))* HarperCollins Pubs.

—The Berenstain Bears Clean House. Berenstain, Stan & Berenstain, Jan, illus. 2004. (I Can Read Level 1 Ser.). (ENG., Illus.). 32p. (J). (gr. k-3). pap. 3.99 *(978-0-06-058335-4(5))* HarperCollins Pubs.

—The Berenstain Bears Go to School. deluxe ed. 2016. (First Time Books(R) Ser.). (ENG., Illus.). 32p. (J). (gr. -1-2). pap. 6.99 *(978-0-399-55589-3(7),* Random Hse. Bks. for Young Readers) Random Hse. Children's Bks.

—The Berenstain Bears Meet Santa Bear (Deluxe Edition) 2016. (First Time Books(R) Ser.). (ENG., Illus.). 32p. (J). (gr. -1-2). pap. 6.99 *(978-0-399-55767-5(9),* Random Hse. Bks. for Young Readers) Random Hse. Children's Bks.

—The Berenstain Bears Merry Christmas. 2013. (Illus.). (J). *(978-0-375-97296-6(X))* Random Hse., Inc.

—The Berenstain Bears New Pup. Berenstain, Jan, illus. 2005. (I Can Read Level 1 Ser.). (ENG., Illus.). 32p. (J). (gr. k-3). pap. 3.99 *(978-0-06-058344-6(4))* HarperCollins Pubs.

—The Berenstain Bears Out West. Berenstain, Stan & Berenstain, Jan, illus. 2006. (I Can Read Level 1 Ser.). (ENG., Illus.). 32p. (J). (gr. k-3). pap. 3.99 *(978-0-06-058354-5(1))* HarperCollins Pubs.

—The Berenstain Bears' Sleepover, 7 vols., Date not set. (Early Childhood First Bks.). (Illus.). (J). (gr. -1-2). lib. bdg. 97.65 *(978-1-56674-942-8(5))* Forest Hse. Publishing Co., Inc.

—The Berenstain Bears' Trouble with Pets. Berenstain, Stan & Berenstain, Jan, illus. 2012. (Berenstain First Time Chapter Bks.). (ENG., Illus.). 32p. (J). (gr. -1-3). pap. 3.99 *(978-0-679-80848-0(5),* Random Hse. Bks. for Young Readers) Random Hse. Children's Bks.

—The Big Book of Berenstain Bears Stories. 2016. (ENG., Illus.). 304p. (J). (gr. -1-2). 16.99 *(978-0-399-55597-8(8),* Random Hse. Bks. for Young Readers) Random Hse. Children's Bks.

—Los Osos Berenstain y Demasiada Fiesta. 2004.Tr. of Berenstain Bears & Too Much Birthday. (SPA., Illus.). (J). (gr. k-3). spiral bd. *(978-0-616-14610-1(8))* Canadian National Institute for the Blind/Institut National Canadien pour les Aveugles.

Berenstain, Stan, et al. The Berenstain Bears 5-Minute Inspirational Stories: Read-Along Classics, 1 vol. 2017. (Berenstain Bears/Living Lights Ser.). (ENG.). 192p. (J). 12.99 *(978-0-310-76080-1(1))* Zonderkidz.

—The Berenstain Bears & the Trouble with Commercials. Berenstain, Stan et al, illus. 2007. (Berenstain Bears Ser.). (ENG.). 32p. (J). (gr. -1-2). pap. 3.99 *(978-0-06-057387-4(2),* HarperFestival) HarperCollins Pubs.

—The Berenstain Bears Go Back to School. Berenstain, Mike, illus. 2005. (Berenstain Bears Ser.). (ENG.). 32p. (J). (gr. -1-3). 15.99 *(978-0-06-052673-3(4),* HarperFestival) HarperCollins Pubs.

—The Berenstain Bears God Shows the Way, 1 vol. Berenstain, Stan & Berenstain, Jan, illus. 2014. (I Can Read! / Berenstain Bears / Living Lights Ser.). (ENG.). 96p. (J). 9.99 *(978-0-310-74211-1(0))* Zonderkidz.

—The Berenstain Bears Learn to Share, 1 vol. 2010. (Berenstain Bears/Living Lights Ser.). (ENG.). 40p. (J). (gr. -1-2). 6.99 *(978-0-310-71939-7(9))* Zonderkidz.

—The Berenstain Bears Save Christmas. Berenstain, Stan et al, illus. 2003. (Berenstain Bears Ser.). (J). (gr. k-3). 129.90 *(978-0-06-056995-2(6))* HarperCollins Pubs.

—The Berenstain Bears Sister Bear & the Golden Rule, 1 vol. 2017. (I Can Read! / Berenstain Bears / Living Lights Ser.). (ENG.). 32p. (J). pap. 3.99 *(978-0-310-76018-4(6))* Zonderkidz.

—The Berenstain Bears Storybook Treasury. Berenstain, Stan & Berenstain, Jan, illus. 2012. (Berenstain Bears Ser.). (ENG.). 192p. (J). 11.99 *(978-0-06-212014-4(X))* HarperCollins Pubs.

Running Press Staff. Berenstain Bears Light-Up Tree House. 2016. (Miniature Editions Ser.). (ENG., Illus.). 32p. pap. 12.95 *(978-0-7624-6083-0(0),* Running Pr. Miniature Editions) Running Pr. Bk. Pubs.

Schorr, Bill & Smith, Ralph. Tucker Grizzwell's Worst Week Ever. 2017. (ENG.). 248p. (J). pap. 9.99 *(978-1-4494-6910-8(8))* Andrews McMeel Publishing.

BERGH, HENRY, 1811-1888

Furstinger, Nancy. Mercy: The Incredible Story of Henry Bergh, Founder of the ASPCA & Friend to Animals. Desjardins, Vincent, illus. 2016. (ENG.). 192p. (J). (gr. 5-7). 16.99 *(978-0-544-65031-2(X),* HMH Books For Young Readers) Houghton Mifflin Harcourt Publishing Co.

BERLIN, IRVING, 1888-1989

Furstinger, Nancy. Say It with Music: The Story of Irving Berlin. 2003. (Modern Music Masters Ser.). (Illus.). 128p. (gr. 6-12). 28.95 *(978-1-931798-12-9(5))* Reynolds, Morgan Inc.

BERLIN (GERMANY)

Candlewick Press Staff. Berlin: a 3D Keepsake Cityscape. McMenemy, Sarah, illus. 2014. (Panorama Pops Ser.). (ENG.). 30p. (J). (gr. k-4). 8.99 *(978-0-7636-6472-5(3))* Candlewick Pr.

Doeden, Matt. The Berlin Wall: An Interactive Modern History Adventure, 1 vol. 2014. (You Choose: Modern History Ser.). (ENG.). 112p. (gr. 3-4). 31.99 *(978-1-4914-0354-9(3),* You Choose Bks.) Capstone Press of Coughlan Cos.

Dunn, Joeming. The Fall of the Berlin Wall, 1 vol. 2008. (Graphic History Ser.). (ENG., Illus.). 32p. 28.50 *(978-1-60270-182-3(2),* Graphic Planet- Nonfiction) ABDO Publishing Co.

Garner, Simon. Berlin. Hunt, Miguel, photos by. 2007. (Global Cities Ser.). (Illus.). 61p. (gr. 5-8). lib. bdg. 30.00 *(978-0-7910-8846-3(4),* Chelsea Hse.) Facts On File, Inc.

Mason Crest. Berlin, Vol. 8. 2016. (Major World Cities Ser.: Vol. 8). (ENG., Illus.). 48p. (J). (gr. 5-8). 20.95 *(978-1-4222-3540-9(8))* Mason Crest.

Tunnell, Michael O. Candy Bomber: The Story of the Berlin Airlift's Chocolate Pilot. 2010. (ENG., Illus.). 120p. (J). (gr. 4-7). pap. 9.95 *(978-1-58089-337-4(6))* Charlesbridge Publishing, Inc.

BERLIN (GERMANY)—FICTION

Avery, Ben & Rogers, Bud. Berlin Breakout, 1 vol. Gaudiamo, Adi Darda, illus. 2008. (Z Graphic Novels / TimeFlyz Ser.). (ENG.). 160p. (J). (gr. 4-7). pap. 6.99 *(978-0-310-71363-0(3))* Zondervan.

Dowswell, Paul. The Auslander. 2011. (ENG.). 304p. (YA). 17.99 *(978-1-59990-633-1(3),* 9781599906331, Bloomsbury USA Childrens) Bloomsbury Publishing USA.

Halcoop, Ursula Lily. Journey. 2012. 160p. pap. 12.50 *(978-1-61204-959-5(1),* Strategic Bk. Publishing) Strategic Book Publishing & Rights Agency (SBPRA).

Harlow, Joan Hiatt. The Watcher. 2015. (ENG.). 304p. (J). (gr. 3-7). pap. 6.99 *(978-1-4424-2912-3(7),* McElderry, Margaret K. Bks.) McElderry, Margaret K. Bks.

Herrndorf, Wolfgang. Why We Took the Car. Mohr, Tim, tr. from GER. 2014. (ENG.). 256p. (J). (gr. 9). 17.99 *(978-0-545-48180-9(5),* Levine, Arthur A. Bks.) Scholastic, Inc.

—You, Me, & a Russian Jeep. 2013. (YA). pap. *(978-0-545-48181-6(3),* Levine, Arthur A. Bks.) Scholastic, Inc.

Kästner, Erich. Dot & Anton. Bell, Anthea, tr. from GER. 2015. (ENG., Illus.). 160p. (YA). (gr. 4-7). pap. 13.95 *(978-1-78269-057-3(3),* Pushkin Press) Steerforth Pr.

Nesbet, Anne. Cloud & Wallfish. 2016. (ENG.). 400p. (J). (gr. 5-9). 16.99 *(978-0-7636-8803-5(7))* Candlewick Pr.

Nielsen, Jennifer A. A Night Divided. 2015. (ENG., Illus.). 336p. (J). (gr. 3-7). 16.99 *(978-0-545-68242-8(8),* Scholastic Pr.) Scholastic, Inc.

O'Dea, Michael, Rory and Cavanaugh & Benchmark Education Co. Staff. The Wall. 2014. (Text Connections Ser.). (J). (gr. 5). *(978-1-4900-1387-9(3))* Benchmark Education Co.

Parry, Rosanne. Second Fiddle. 2012. (ENG.). 240p. (J). (gr. 3-7). 6.99 *(978-0-375-86166-6(1),* Yearling) Random Hse. Children's Bks.

Rahlens, Holly-Jane. Prince William, Maximilian Minsky, & Me. 2007. (ENG.). 320p. (YA). (gr. 7-11). per. 7.99 *(978-0-7636-3299-1(6))* Candlewick Pr.

Schroeder, Niels Olaf. Berlin Brain Odyssee - a trip into the Brain. 2010. 32p. pap. 18.50 *(978-1-4452-3979-8(5))* Lulu Pr., Inc.

Sharenow, Robert. The Berlin Boxing Club. 2012. (ENG.). 432p. (YA). (gr. 8). pap. 9.99 *(978-0-06-157970-7(X),* HarperTeen) HarperCollins Pubs.

—The Berlin Boxing Club. 2012. (YA). lib. bdg. 20.85 *(978-0-606-26871-4(5),* Turtleback) Turtleback Bks.

Smith, Molly. Border Breakdown: The Fall of the Berlin Wall. Opie, David, illus. 2010. (ENG.). 32p. (J). (gr. 1-6). 9.95 *(978-1-60727-126-0(5));* 19.95 *(978-1-60727-125-3(7));* 16.95 *(978-1-60727-123-9(0));* pap. 6.95 *(978-1-60727-124-6(9))* Soundprints.

Steinhöfel, Andreas & Wright, Chantal. The Spaghetti Detectives. 2011. (ENG.). 176p. (J). (gr. 3-7). 16.99 *(978-0-545-28975-7(0),* Chicken Hse., The) Scholastic, Inc.

Terrell, Brandon. Valor & Victory. Max, Iman, illus. 2016. (Time Machine Magazine Ser.). (ENG.). 128p. (gr. 3-4). lib. bdg. 22.65 *(978-1-4965-2594-9(9))* Capstone Press of Coughlan Cos.

Wallace, Kim. Erik & Isabelle Senior Year at Foresthill High. 2008. (Foresthill High Ser.). 220p. (YA). (gr. 8-12). per. 12.00 *(978-0-9755848-3-5(9))* Foglight Pr.

BERLIN WALL, BERLIN, GERMANY, 1961-1989

Doeden, Matt. The Berlin Wall: An Interactive Modern History Adventure, 1 vol. 2014. (You Choose: Modern History Ser.). (ENG.). 112p. (gr. 3-4). 31.99 *(978-1-4914-0354-9(3)*, You Choose Bks.) Capstone Press of Coughlan Cos.

Downey, Glen. Escape from East Berlin. Lingas, Leo, illus. 2007. 48p. (J). lib. bdg. 23.08 *(978-1-4242-1635-2(4))* Fitzgerald Bks.

Dunn, Joeming. The Fall of the Berlin Wall, 1 vol. 2008. (Graphic History Ser.). (ENG., Illus.). 32p. 28.50 *(978-1-60270-182-3(2)*, Graphic Planet- Nonfiction) ABDO Publishing Co.

Schwartz, Simon. The Other Side of the Wall. Watkinson, Laura, tr. from GER. 2015. (ENG., Illus.). 112p. (J). (gr. 7-12). pap. 9.99 *(978-1-4677-6028-7(5)*, Graphic Universe™) Lerner Publishing Group.

Smith, Molly. Border Breakdown: The Fall of the Berlin Wall. Opie, David, illus. 2009. 32p. (J). (gr. 1-6). (ENG.). 17.95 *(978-1-60727-112-3(5))*; 17.95 incl. audio *(978-1-60727-102-4(8))*; pap. 9.95 incl. audio *(978-1-60727-103-1(6))* Soundprints.

Tracy, Kathleen. The Fall of the Berlin Wall. 2005. (Monumental Milestones Ser.). (Illus.). 48p. (YA). (gr. 4-7). lib. bdg. 29.95 *(978-1-58415-405-1(5))* Mitchell Lane Pubs., Inc.

Williams, Brian. The Fall of the Berlin Wall. 2003. (Dates with History Ser.). 45p. (J). lib. bdg. 28.50 *(978-1-58340-409-6(0))* Black Rabbit Bks.

BERLIN WALL, BERLIN, GERMANY, 1961-1989—FICTION

Cole, Tom Clohosy. Wall. Cole, Tom Clohosy, illus. 2014. (ENG., Illus.). 32p. (J). (gr. -1-3). 16.99 *(978-0-7636-7560-8(1)*, Templar) Candlewick Pr.

Nielsen, Jennifer A. A Night Divided. 2015. (ENG., Illus.). 336p. (J). (gr. 3-7). 16.99 *(978-0-545-68242-8(8)*, Scholastic Pr.) Scholastic, Inc.

Schneider, Peter. Der Mauerspringer. (GER.). pap. 18.95 *(978-3-499-13532-3(9))* Rowohlt Taschenbuch Verlag GmbH DEU. Dist: Distribooks, Inc.

Smith, Molly. Border Breakdown: The Fall of the Berlin Wall. 2011. (ENG.). (J). 9.95 *(978-1-60727-113-0(3))* Soundprints.

BERLIOZ, HECTOR, 1803-1869

Whiting, Jim. The Life & Times of Hector Berlioz. 2004. (Masters of Music Ser.). (Illus.). 48p. (gr. 4-8). lib. bdg. 20.95 *(978-1-58415-259-0(1))* Mitchell Lane Pubs., Inc.

BERMUDA ISLANDS

Orr, Tamra. Bermuda. 2008. (Cultures of the World Ser.). (Illus.). 144p. (gr. 6-18). lib. bdg. 42.79 *(978-0-7614-3115-2(2)*, Benchmark Bks.) Marshall Cavendish Corp.

BERMUDA ISLANDS—FICTION

Dillsworth-Swift, Tammy. The Bermuda Triangle & the Lost Island. 2009. 182p. pap. 16.53 *(978-0-557-14503-4(1))* Lulu Pr., Inc.

Lamphere-Slaughter, Sharyn. Droopy Drawers & the Peg Leg Pirate. 2009. 24p. pap. 12.99 *(978-1-4490-6055-8(2))* AuthorHouse.

Litwin, Mike. Lost in Bermooda. Litwin, Mike, illus. 2014. (Welcome to Bermooda! Ser.: Book 1). (ENG., Illus.). 144p. (J). (gr. 1-5). 14.99 *(978-0-8075-8718-8(4))* Whitman, Albert & Co.

Round, J. The Catcher. 2008. 168p. pap. 14.95 *(978-1-4092-0372-8(7))* Lulu Pr., Inc.

Walker, Kathryn. Unsolved! 2008. (J). (gr. 4-7). *(978-0-7787-4140-4(0))* Crabtree Publishing Co.

BERMUDA TRIANGLE

Bingham, Jane. The Bermuda Triangle, 1 vol. 2013. (Solving Mysteries with Science Ser.). (ENG., Illus.). 48p. (gr. 5-5). pap. 9.95 *(978-1-4109-4991-2(5))* Heinemann-Raintree.

Coddington, Andrew. The Bermuda Triangle, Stonehenge, & Unexplained Places. 2017. (J). ***(978-1-5026-2843-5(0))*** Cavendish Square Publishing.

Dalgleish, Sharon. It's a Mystery. 2003. (Real Deal Ser.). (Illus.). 32p. (J). pap. *(978-0-7608-6692-4(9))* Sundance/Newbridge Educational Publishing.

DeMolay, Jack. The Bermuda Triangle: The Disappearance of Flight 19. (Jr. Graphic Mysteries Ser.). (ENG.). 24p. 2009. (J). (gr. 2-3). 47.90 *(978-1-61513-846-3(3)*, PowerKids Pr.) 2007. (Illus.). (J). (gr. 2-5). lib. bdg. 25.25 *(978-1-4042-3404-8(7))* 2007. (Illus.). (gr. 3-8). pap. 10.60 *(978-1-4042-2157-4(3)*, PowerKids Pr.) Rosen Publishing Group, Inc., The.

—El Triángulo de las Bermudas: La Desaparicion del Vuelo 19. Obregón, José María, tr. 2008. (Historietas Juveniles: Misterios (Jr. Graphic Mysteries) Ser.). (SPA., Illus.). 24p. (J). (gr. 2-5). lib. bdg. 25.25 *(978-1-4358-2535-2(7))* Rosen Publishing Group, Inc., The.

—El Triángulo de las Bermudas: La desaparición del vuelo 19 (the Bermuda Triangle:the Disappearance of Flight 19) 2009. (Historietas Juveniles: Misterios (Jr. Graphic Mysteries) Ser.). (SPA.). 24p. (gr. 2-3). 47.90 *(978-1-61513-348-2(8)*, Editorial Buenas Letras) Rosen Publishing Group, Inc., The.

Hamilton, Sue. Bermuda Triangle, 1 vol. 2007. (Unsolved Mysteries Ser.). (ENG.). 32p. (J). (gr. 3-7). lib. bdg. 27.07 *(978-1-59928-834-5(6)*, Abdo & Daughter) ABDO Publishing Co.

Karst, Ken. Bermuda Triangle. 2014. (J). *(978-1-60818-401-9(3)*, Creative Education) Creative Co., The.

—Bermuda Triangle. 2015. (Enduring Mysteries Ser.). lib. bdg. 23.30 *(978-0-606-36992-3(9))* Turtleback Bks.

—Enduring Mysteries: Bermuda Triangle. 2015. (Enduring Mysteries Ser.). (ENG.). 48p. (J). (gr. 5-8). pap. 12.00 *(978-1-62832-072-5(9)*, Creative Paperbacks) Creative Co., The.

Lassieur, Allison. Is the Bermuda Triangle Real? 2015. (Unexplained: What's the Evidence? Ser.). (ENG.). 32p. (J). (gr. 2-4). 19.95 *(978-1-60753-803-5(2))* Amicus Publishing.

Levete, Sarah. The Bermuda Triangle & Other Danger Zones. 2016. (Mystery Hunters Ser.). 00048p. (J). pap. 14.05 ***(978-1-4824-6000-1(9))*** Stevens, Gareth Publishing LLLP.

Nobleman, Marc Tyler, et al. Rescue in the Bermuda Triangle: An Isabel Soto Investigation. 2010. (Graphic Expeditions Ser.). (ENG., Illus.). 32p. (gr. 3-4). pap. 47.70 *(978-1-4296-5713-6(8))*; lib. bdg. 30.65 *(978-1-4296-4770-0(1))* Capstone Press of Coughlan Cos. (Graphic Library).

Noll, Elizabeth. The Bermuda Triangle. 2017. (Strange ... but True? Ser.). (ENG.). 32p. (gr. 3-7). 31.35 ***(978-1-68072-021-1(X))*** Black Rabbit Bks.

Richard, Orlin. The Bermuda Triangle. 2015. (Unsolved Mysteries Ser.). (ENG.). 24p. (J). (gr. 1-4). 28.50 *(978-1-63407-070-6(4)*, 208908) Child's World, Inc., The.

Rudolph, Aaron. Mystery of the Bermuda Triangle. 2013. (Unexplained Mysteries Ser.). (ENG.). 24p. (gr. 1-2). 25.32 *(978-1-4765-3098-7(X)*, First Facts) Capstone Press of Coughlan Cos.

—The Unsolved Mystery of the Bermuda Triangle. 2013. (Unexplained Mysteries Ser.). (ENG.). 24p. (gr. 1-2). pap. 7.95 *(978-1-4765-3443-5(8)*, First Facts) Capstone Press of Coughlan Cos.

Stewart, Gail B. The Bermuda Triangle. 2008. (Mysterious & Unknown Ser.). (YA). (gr. 7-12). 25.95 *(978-1-60152-056-2(5))* ReferencePoint Pr., Inc.

Stone, Adam. The Bermuda Triangle. (Illus.). 24p. (J). 2011. *(978-0-531-26400-3(9))* 2010. (ENG., (gr. 3-7). lib. bdg. 25.95 *(978-1-60014-497-4(7)*, Torque Bks.) Bellwether Media.

Walker, Kathryn. Mysteries of the Bermuda Triangle. 2008. (ENG., Illus.). 32p. (J). (gr. 3-7). pap. *(978-0-7787-4157-2(5))*; lib. bdg. *(978-0-7787-4144-2(3))* Crabtree Publishing Co.

West, David. The Bermuda Triangle: Strange Happenings at Sea. 2009. (Graphic Mysteries Ser.). (ENG.). 48p. (YA). (gr. 5-5). 58.50 *(978-1-61512-968-3(5)*, Rosen Reference) Rosen Publishing Group, Inc., The.

—The Bermuda Triangle: Strange Happenings at Sea. Lacey, Mike, illus. 2006. (Graphic Mysteries Ser.). (ENG.). 48p. (gr. 5-8). pap. 14.05 *(978-1-4042-0806-3(2))*; (YA). lib. bdg. 31.95 *(978-1-4042-0795-0(3))* Rosen Publishing Group, Inc., The.

Whiting, Jim. The Bermuda Triangle. 2006. (Natural Disasters Ser.). (Illus.). 32p. (J). (gr. 1-4). lib. bdg. 25.70 *(978-1-58415-497-6(7))* Mitchell Lane Pubs., Inc.

World Book, Inc Staff, contrib. by. The Bermuda Triangle & Other Mysteries of the Deep. 2015. (Illus.). 48p. (J). *(978-0-7166-2672-5(1))* World Bk., Inc.

Zuchora-Walske, Christine. The Bermuda Triangle, 1 vol. 2012. (Unsolved Mysteries (el) Ser.). (ENG.). 112p. (J). (gr. 6-12). lib. bdg. 35.64 *(978-1-61783-298-7(7)*, Essential Library) ABDO Publishing Co.

BERNADETTE, SAINT, 1844-1879

Maraval-Hutin, Sophie. Bernadette: The Girl from Lourdes. 2010. 36p. 14.99 *(978-1-58617-510-8(6))* Ignatius Pr.

Morse, Letitia M. Yellow Roses on Her Feet. 2008. (J). pap. *(978-0-9815075-0-7(6))* Bienna Bks.

BERNSTEIN, LEONARD, 1918-1990

Ewen, David. Leonard Bernstein: A Biography for Young People. 2011. 190p. 42.95 *(978-1-258-09380-8(4))* Literary Licensing, LLC.

Lazo, Caroline Evensen. Leonard Bernstein: In Love with Music. 128p. (J). (gr. 6-18). 18.95 *(978-1-58013-105-6(0)*, Kar-Ben Publishing) Lerner Publishing Group.

Reef, Catherine. Leonard Bernstein & American Music. 2012. (Modern Music Masters Ser.). (gr. 7-12). 27.95 *(978-1-59935-125-4(0))* Reynolds, Morgan Inc.

Rubin, Susan Goldman. Music Was IT: Young Leonard Bernstein. 2015. (ENG., Illus.). 192p. (J). (gr. 4-7). pap. 12.95 *(978-1-58089-345-9(7))* Charlesbridge Publishing, Inc.

Venezia, Mike. Leonard Bernstein (Revised Edition) 2017. (Getting to Know the World's Greatest Composers Ser.). (ENG.). 40p. (J). pap. 7.95 ***(978-0-531-23034-3(1))***; lib. bdg. 29.00 ***(978-0-531-22656-8(5))*** Scholastic Library Publishing. (Children's Pr.).

BERRIES

Lee, Jackie. Cranberry. 2015. (See It Grow Ser.). (ENG., Illus.). 24p. (J). (gr. -1-3). lib. bdg. 23.93 *(978-1-62724-841-9(2))* Bearport Publishing Co., Inc.

Pallotta, Jerry & Newton, Joy. The Very Berry Counting Book. 2017. (ENG., Illus.). 10p. (J). (— 1). bds. 6.99 *(978-1-58089-784-6(3))* Charlesbridge Publishing, Inc.

Schuh, Mari. Blueberries Grow on a Bush, 1 vol. 2011. (How Fruits & Vegetables Grow Ser.). (ENG., 24p. (gr. k-1). Illus.). pap. 6.29 *(978-1-4296-6183-6(6))*; pap. 35.70 *(978-1-4296-6184-3(4))* Capstone Press of Coughlan Cos. (Pebble Bks.).

Schuh, Mari C. Blueberries Grow on a Bush, 1 vol. 2010. (How Fruits & Vegetables Grow Ser.). (ENG.). 24p. (gr. k-1). lib. bdg. 21.99 *(978-1-4296-5282-7(9)*, Pebble Bks.) Capstone Press of Coughlan Cos.

BERRY, MARTHA, 1866-1942

Hally, Ashleigh. Martha Berry. 2012. (Illus.). 24p. (J). *(978-1-935884-73-6(5))*; pap. *(978-1-935884-79-8(4))* State Standards Publishing, LLC.

BEST BOOKS

Allyn, Pam. Pam Allyn's Best Books for Boys: How to Engage Boys in Reading in Ways That Will Change Their Lives. 2011. (ENG.). 176p. (gr. k-8). pap. 21.99 *(978-0-545-20455-2(0)*, Teaching Resources) Scholastic, Inc.

Buckley, William F., Jr. The National Review Treasury of Classic Children's Literature, Vol. II. 2004. 528p. (J). 29.95 *(978-0-9627841-7-0(6))* ISI Bks.

Buckley, William F., Jr., selected by. The National Review Treasury of Classic Children's Literature. 2003. 523p. (J). 29.95 *(978-0-9627841-5-6(X))* National Review, Inc.

Schulze, Bianca. 101 Books to Read Before You Grow Up. 2017. (101 Ser.). (ENG., Illus.). 144p. (J). (gr. 3-5). lib. bdg. 33.32 ***(978-1-942875-17-8(7)***, Walter Foster Jr) Quarto Publishing Group USA.

Schulze, Bianca. 101 Books to Read Before You Grow Up: The Must-Read Book List for Kids. 2016. (101 Series for Kids Ser.). (ENG., Illus.). 144p. (J). (gr. 3-7). pap. 12.95 *(978-1-63322-169-7(5)*, Walter Foster Jr) Quarto Publishing Group USA.

Spiero, Simon. The Delights of Reading: Written for My Grandchildren. 2012. 368p. 32.95 *(978-1-84624-668-5(7))* Book Guild, Ltd. GBR. Dist: Trans-Atlantic Pubns., Inc.

BETHUNE, MARY MCLEOD, 1875-1955

Broadwater, Andrea. Mary McLeod Bethune: Educator & Activist. 2003. (African-American Biographies Ser.). (Illus.). 112p. (YA). (gr. 6-12). lib. bdg. 26.60 *(978-0-7660-1771-9(0))* Enslow Pubs., Inc.

Dare to Be. . . Mary McLeod Bethune Children's Book. 2003. 3.99 *(978-0-915960-55-2(9))* Ebon Research Systems Publishing, LLC.

Domblewski, Carol. Citizens Who Made a Difference: Set Of 6. 2011. (Navigators Ser.). (J). pap. 44.00 net. *(978-1-4108-5097-3(8))* Benchmark Education Co.

Evento, Susan. Mary McLeod Bethune. 2004. (Rookie Biographies Ser.). (ENG.). 32p. (J). (gr. 1-2). pap. 4.95 *(978-0-516-25830-0(3)*, Children's Pr.) Scholastic Library Publishing.

Hanson, Joyce A. Mary McLeod Bethune & Black Women's Political Activism. 2003. (ENG., Illus.). 264p. (C). (gr. 13-17). 45.00 *(978-0-8262-1451-5(7))* Univ. of Missouri Pr.

Jones, Amy Robin. Mary McLeod Bethune. 2009. (Journey to Freedom Ser.). (ENG., Illus.). 32p. (J). (gr. 4-7). 29.93 *(978-1-60253-129-1(3)*, 200395) Child's World, Inc., The.

McKissack, Patricia C. & McKissack, Fredrick L. Mary McLeod Bethune: Woman of Courage. 2013. (Famous African Americans Ser.). (Illus.). 24p. (J). (gr. k-18). 22.60 *(978-0-7660-4103-5(4))* Enslow Pubs., Inc.

Schwartz, Heather E. Mary McLeod Bethune: Education & Equality. 2016. (Primary Source Readers Ser.). 32p. (J). (gr. 4-4). pap. 8.99 *(978-1-4938-3545-4(9))* Teacher Created Materials, Inc.

Somervill, Barbara A. Mary McLeod Bethune: African-American Educator. 2003. (Our People Ser.). (ENG., Illus.). 32p. (J). (gr. 3-6). 29.93 *(978-1-59296-008-6(1)*, 200647) Child's World, Inc., The.

Sterling, Kristin. Mary Mcleod Bethune. 2008. pap. 40.95 *(978-0-8225-9474-1(9))* Lerner Publishing Group.

—Mary Mcleod Bethune: A Life of Resourcefulness. 2008. (Pull Ahead Books-Biographies Ser.). (ENG.). 32p. (gr. k-3). pap. 7.95 *(978-0-8225-8621-0(5))*; (Illus.). lib. bdg. 22.60 *(978-0-8225-8588-6(X)*, Lerner Pubns.) Lerner Publishing Group.

BEVERAGES

Albrecht, John, Jr. Chocolate Milk Likes Me. Ashby, Chris, illus. 2006. 16p. (J). pap. 8.99 *(978-0-9778586-3-7(4)*, CRP004); pap. 8.99 *(978-0-9778586-2-0(6)*, CRP0003) Crooked River Pr. (Blue Jay Bks.).

Bodden, Valerie. The Story of Coca-Cola. 2011. (ENG., Illus.). 48p. (J). (gr. 5-17). pap. *(978-1-897563-00-7(0))* Saunders Bk. Co.

Cornell, Kari. Slurpable Smoothies & Drinks. Cohen, Brie, photos by. 2013. (You're the Chef Ser.). (ENG., Illus.). 32p. (gr. 3-5). lib. bdg. 26.60 *(978-0-7613-6639-3(3)*, Millbrook Pr.) Lerner Publishing Group.

Cunningham, Kevin. Colas. 2007. (21st Century Skills Library: Global Products Ser.). (ENG., Illus.). 32p. (gr. 4-8). lib. bdg. 28.50 *(978-1-60279-025-4(6)*, 200024) Cherry Lake Publishing.

Furgang, Adam. Carbonated Beverages: The Incredibly Disgusting Story. 2011. (Incredibly Disgusting Food Ser.). (Illus.). 48p. (YA). pap. 11.75 *(978-1-4488-2282-9(3)*, Rosen Reference); (gr. 5-9). lib. bdg. 29.25 *(978-1-4488-1266-0(6))* Rosen Publishing Group, Inc., The.

Jacobson, Ryan. Orange Juice. 2016. (J). *(978-1-4896-4535-7(7))* Weigl Pubs., Inc.

Kuskowski, Alex. Cool Dips & Drinks, 1 vol. 2014. (Cool Home Cooking Ser.). (ENG.). 32p. (gr. 3-6). 28.50 *(978-1-62403-501-2(9))* ABDO Publishing Co.

LaPenta, Marilyn. Way Cool Drinks. 2011. (Yummy Tummy Recipes Ser.). 24p. (J). (gr. 1-4). lib. bdg. 22.61 *(978-1-61772-163-2(8))* Bearport Publishing Co., Inc.

Lynette, Rachel. Soda Pop. 2016. (J). *(978-1-4896-4543-2(8))* Weigl Pubs., Inc.

—Soda Pop Before the Store. McGeehan, Dan, illus. 2012. (Before the Store Ser.). (ENG.). 32p. (J). (gr. 2-5). lib. bdg. 29.93 *(978-1-60973-682-8(6)*, 201257) Child's World, Inc., The.

Martineau, Susan & James, Hel. All Kinds of Drinks. 2012. (Healthy Eating Ser.). (Illus.). 32p. (gr. 2-6). pap. 8.95 *(978-1-59920-241-9(7))* Black Rabbit Bks.

McClellan, Marilyn. The Big Deal about Alcohol: What Teens Need to Know about Drinking. 2004. (Issues in Focus Ser.). (Illus.). 128p. (J). lib. bdg. 27.94 *(978-0-7660-2163-1(7))* Enslow Pubs., Inc.

Rosenberg, Pam. How Did That Get to My Table? Orange Juice. 2009. (Community Connections: How Did That Get to My Table? Ser.). (ENG.). 24p. (gr. 2-5). lib. bdg. 25.64 *(978-1-60279-468-9(5)*, 200265) Cherry Lake Publishing.

Rybolt, Thomas R. Soda Pop Science Projects: Experiments with Carbonated Soft Drinks. 2004. (Science Fair Success Ser.). (Illus.). 104p. (J). lib. bdg. 27.94 *(978-0-7660-2089-4(4))* Enslow Pubs., Inc.

Sullivan, Jaclyn. What's in Your Soda? 2012. (What's in Your Fast Food Ser.). (ENG., Illus.). 24p. (J). (gr. 2-5). pap. 8.25 *(978-1-4488-6379-2(1)*, PowerKids Pr.); lib. bdg. 22.60 *(978-1-4488-6210-8(8))* Rosen Publishing Group, Inc., The.

The Sweet Story of Hot Chocolate! 2014. (History of Fun Stuff Ser.). (ENG., Illus.). 48p. (J). (gr. 1-3). pap. 3.99 *(978-1-4814-2052-5(6)*, Simon Spotlight) Simon Spotlight.

Trumbauer, Lisa. The Story of Orange Juice, 6 vols., Set. 2005. (Yellow Umbrella Fluent Level Ser.). (ENG., Illus.). 16p. (gr. k-1). pap. 35.70 *(978-0-7368-5304-0(9)*, Yellow Umbrella Bks.) Capstone Press of Coughlan Cos.

Winters, Jaime. Get into Smoothies. 2017. (Get-Into-It Guides). (ENG., Illus.). 32p. (J). (gr. 3-6). ***(978-0-7787-3403-1(X))***; pap. ***(978-0-7787-3407-9(2))*** Crabtree Publishing Co.

BIAFRA

see Nigeria

BIBLE

Adams, Linda. Make & Learn Bible Toys. 2004. (Illus.). 96p. (J). (gr. -1-k). pap. 11.95 *(978-1-885358-39-4(3)*, RB36722) Rainbow Pubs. & Legacy Pr.

Allen, Joey. The Scripture: Big Thoughts for Little Thinkers. 2005. (Illus.). 32p. (J). 5.99 *(978-0-89221-615-4(8))* New Leaf Pub. Group.

Alpha Omega Publishing Staff. Bible. 2004. (Illus.). (gr. 2). tchr. ed., stu. ed. 47.95 *(978-0-86717-003-0(4)*, BIB0215, Lifepac) Alpha Omega Pubns., Inc.

Altomare, Deborah. God Gives. 2012. (ENG.). 27p. (J). pap. 21.95 *(978-1-4787-1906-9(0))*; pap. 13.95 *(978-1-4787-1911-3(7))* Outskirts Pr., Inc.

American Bible Society Staff. Read & Learn Bible. Duendes Del Sur Staff, illus. 2005. (ENG.). 544p. (J). (gr. -1-3). 14.99 *(978-0-439-65126-4(3))* Scholastic, Inc.

Amery, Heather. The Old Testament, Children's New Testament. 2004. (Children's Bibles Ser.). (ENG., Illus.). 1p. (J). (gr. -1-4). 8.95 *(978-0-7945-0028-3(5)*, Usborne) EDC Publishing.

Amery, Heather, ed. La Biblia para Ninos. Edwards, Linda, illus. 2004.Tr. of Children's Bible. (SPA.). 144p. (J). (gr. -1-4). 19.95 *(978-0-7460-3674-7(4))* EDC Publishing.

Amiot, Karine-Marie, et al. The Catholic Bible for Children. Bienfait, Andree, illus. 2011. (ENG.). 239p. (J). (gr. -1-3). pap. 14.99 *(978-1-58617-659-4(5))* Ignatius Pr.

The Answer Book for Kids: 25 Questions on Dinosaurs & the Flood of Noah. 2008. 60p. (J). pap. 7.99 *(978-0-89051-527-3(1))* Master Bks.

The B-I-B-L-E Online Children Song. 2.00 *(978-0-687-07975-9(6))* Abingdon Pr.

B&H Editorial Staff, ed. Read to Me Bible for Kids. 2004. (Illus.). 1864p. 19.99 *(978-1-55819-844-9(X))* B&H Publishing Group.

B&H Kids Editorial Staff. The Activity Bible. 2015. (ENG.). 228p. (J). (gr. -1-2). pap. 12.99 *(978-1-4336-8634-4(1)*, B&H Kids) B&H Publishing Group.

Barfield, Maggie. The Little Bible Storybook, 1 vol. Carpenter, Mark et al, illus. 2009. 48p. (J). bds. 9.99 *(978-0-8254-7409-5(4)*, Candle Bks.) Lion Hudson PLC GBR. Dist: Kregel Pubns.

Bauman, Lester. God's Redeemed Family — the Church: Bible 8 Tests. 2004. (Story of God's Chosen Family Ser.). 24p. (gr. 8-18). 1.55 *(978-0-7399-0433-6(7)*, 17811) Rod & Staff Pubs., Inc.

Bays, Patricia. What Is the Bible? (Anglican Learning Centres Ser.). pap. 15.95 *(978-1-55126-317-5(3)*, 1597) Forward Movement Pubns.

Bergt, Carolyn. What Does This Mean? Mitter, Kathryn, illus. 16p. (gr. -1-k). 20.00 *(978-0-570-05545-7(8)*, 54-0077) Concordia Publishing Hse.

Berman, Melanie & Grishaver, Joel Lurie. My Weekly Sidrah. 2007. (Illus.). 192p. (J). (gr. k-3). pap. 14.95 *(978-1-891662-96-6(1))* Torah Aura Productions.

Berndt, Clarence & Rathmann, Rodney L. A Bible History: In the Words of Holy Scripture: With Illustrations, Maps, & Notes. 2003. (Illus.). 480p. stu. ed. 19.75 *(978-0-7586-0288-6(X))* Concordia Publishing Hse.

Bible. 2004. (Switched on Schoolhouse Ser.). (YA). (gr. 7). cd-rom 69.95 *(978-0-7403-0586-3(7))*; (YA). (gr. 8). cd-rom 69.95 *(978-0-7403-0592-4(1))*; (Illus.). (gr. 10). tchr. ed., stu. ed. 47.95 *(978-0-86717-209-6(6)*, BIB1015, Lifepac); (Illus.). (gr. 12). tchr. ed., stu. ed. 47.95 *(978-1-58095-635-2(1)*, BIB1215, Lifepac); (Illus.). (gr. 3). tchr. ed., stu. ed. 47.95 *(978-0-86717-672-8(5)*, BIB0315, Lifepac); (Illus.). (J). (gr. 4). tchr. ed., stu. ed. 47.95 *(978-0-86717-007-8(7)*, BIB0415, Lifepac); (Illus.). (J). (gr. 6). tchr. ed., stu. ed. 47.95 *(978-0-86717-011-5(5)*, BIB0615, Lifepac); (Illus.). (YA). (gr. 8). tchr. ed., stu. ed. 47.95 *(978-0-86717-015-3(8)*, BIB0815, Lifepac); (Illus.). (YA). (gr. 9). tchr. ed., stu. ed. 47.95 *(978-0-86717-017-7(4)*, BIB0915, Lifepac);Complete Set. (gr. 7). 47.95 *(978-1-58095-620-8(3)*, BIB0715, Lifepac);Set. (Illus.). (gr. 11-12). tchr. ed., stu. ed. 47.95 *(978-1-58095-632-1(7)*, BIB1115, Lifepac) Alpha Omega Pubns., Inc.

Bible. 2004. (ENG., Illus.). 1152p. lthr. 39.95 *(978-0-00-718952-6(4)*, Collins) HarperCollins Pubs.

Bible: Student Testing Kit. 2004. (Illus.). (J). (gr. 1-8). stu. ed. 5.00 *(978-0-7403-0041-7(5)*, BD001) Alpha Omega Pubns., Inc.

Bible ABCs Coloring & Activity Book. 2003. (J). *(978-0-9720888-2-4(2))* Three Angels Broadcasting Network.

Bible Activities for Kids. 2004. pap. 1.50 *(978-0-87162-937-1(2))* Warner Pr., Inc.

Bible Discovery: Puppets. (Illus.). 64p. (J). (gr. 1-6). pap. 9.95 *(978-0-937282-97-7(9))* Rainbow Pubs. & Legacy Pr.

Bible Games Company Staff. Bible Scramble. 2004. 17.99 *(978-0-8280-1000-9(5))* Review & Herald Publishing Assn.

Bible KJV Child Burgundy O-Wrap. 2004. (Illus.). 826p. im. lthr. 12.99 *(978-1-55819-758-9(3))* B&H Publishing Group.

Bible KJV Child Pastel Blush O-Wrap. 2004. (Illus.). 826p. im. lthr. 12.99 *(978-1-55819-760-2(5))* B&H Publishing Group.

Bible KJV Childrens Rainbow Gift. 2005. 672p. (J). 14.99 *(978-0-529-12116-5(6))* Nelson, Thomas Inc.

Bible Values. (Bulletin Board Jumbo Cutouts Ser.). (Illus.). 96p. (J). 9.99 *(978-0-7847-0552-0(6)*, 02589) Standard Publishing.

Bible Visuals International Staff, compiled by. Future of the Church Vol. 32: New Testament. 2006. (Illus.). (J). pap. *(978-1-932381-58-0(9)*, 1032) Bible Visuals International, Inc.

Biblia para los Mas Jovenes, Vol. 6.Tr. of Bible for Teenagers. (SPA.). 264p. (YA). 33.48 *(978-84-305-9777-2(8))* Susaeta Ediciones, S.A. ESP. Dist: AIMS International Bks., Inc.

Bloom, Harold, ed. The Bible. 2nd rev. ed. 2006. (Bloom's Modern Critical Views Ser.). 307p. (C). (gr. 9). lib. bdg. 45.00 *(978-0-7910-8137-2(0)*, Chelsea Hse.) Facts On File, Inc.

Boddam-Whetham, Jo & Mitchell, Alison. Beginning with God: Book 1: Exploring the Bible with Your Child, 3 vols. 2010. (Beginning with God Ser.). (Illus.). 80p. (J). pap. *(978-1-906334-98-7(6))* Good Bk. Co.

The Boy with Loaves & Fish. 14p. (J). bds. 7.99 *(978-0-7847-1406-5(1))* Standard Publishing.

Brighter Minds, creator. Classic Bible Stories: Noah's Ark. gif. ed. 2005. (Illus.). 32p. (J). cd-rom 9.99 *(978-1-57791-142-5(3))* Brighter Minds Children's Publishing.

Brighter Minds & Brighter Minds, creators. Birth of Jesus. gif. ed. 2005. (Classic Bible Stories Ser.). (Illus.). 32p. (J). (gr. -1-3). cd-rom 9.99 *(978-1-57791-141-8(5))* Brighter Minds Children's Publishing.

Broadman and Holman Publishers Staff, ed. Read to Me Bible for Kids. 2013. (ENG.). 276p. (J). 19.99 *(978-1-4336-8058-8(0)*, B&H Kids) B&H Publishing Group.

Brost, Corey. Gospel Connections for Teens: Reflections for Sunday Mass, Cycle C. 2006. 129p. (YA). (gr. 8-12). per. 6.25 *(978-0-88489-641-8(2))* St. Mary's Pr. of MN.

Brother Andrew, et al. God's Smuggler. Foley, Tim, illus. 2017. (ENG.). 224p. (J). pap. 9.99 *(978-0-8007-9805-5(8))* Chosen Bks.

Brown, Alan. The Bible & Christianity. 2003. 30p. (J). lib. bdg. 16.95 *(978-1-58340-243-6(8))* Black Rabbit Bks.

Butcher, Sam, illus. Precious Moments: Small Hands Bible with Lavender Bible Cover. 2003. 12.84 *(978-0-7180-0570-2(8))* Nelson, Thomas Inc.

—Precious Moments: Small Hands Bible with Pink Bible Cover. 2003. 12.84 *(978-0-7180-0576-4(7))* Nelson, Thomas Inc.

Cariello, Sergio, illus. Action Bible Media Kit. 2015. (ENG.). cd-rom 49.99 *(978-1-4347-0950-9(7))* Cook, David C.

Cassel, Katrina. The Christian Girl's Guide to the Bible. 2004. (Illus.). 192p. (J). pap. 9.99 *(978-1-58411-044-6(9))*, Legacy Pr.) Rainbow Pubs. & Legacy Pr.

—Promises for God's Princesses. 2014. (ENG.). 224p. (J). 9.99 *(978-1-4143-9660-6(0))* Tyndale Hse. Pubs.

Children's Presentation Bible. 2004. (Illus.). 826p. (J). im. lthr. 12.99 *(978-1-55819-761-9(3))* B&H Publishing Group.

Ciancio, Billie, compiled by. Best Bible Crafts II. 2003. (Illus.). 52p. pap. 12.99 *(978-0-930184-02-5(5))* Clapper Publishing Co.

Clay, Brittney. A B C the Way God Sees You & Me! 2011. 48p. pap. 17.45 *(978-1-4497-2449-8(3))*, WestBow Pr.) Author Solutions, Inc.

Coloring Book of Bible Verses. 2004. pap. 2.50 *(978-0-9618608-4-4(7))* Lynn's Bookshelf.

Cox, Carolyn, illus. My Very Own Bible. 2010. (ENG.). 160p. (J). (gr. 2-4). 7.99 *(978-0-7459-4991-8(6))* Lion Hudson PLC GBR. Dist: Independent Pubs. Group.

Crane, Cheryl L. Pressing on When the Pressure's On: A Bible Study Workbook on Perseverance for Ages 6-12. 2009. 112p. pap. 10.95 *(978-1-4401-5830-8(4))* iUniverse, Inc.

Craughwell, Thomas J. The Bible. 2007. (Catholic Cardlinks Ser.). 48p. 11.95 *(978-1-59276-215-6(8))* Our Sunday Visitor, Publishing Div.

Cronin, Gaynell. Celebrating the Gospels: A Guide for Parents & Teachers: Activities & Prayers for the Sunday Cycles of A, B, & C. 2003. (Illus.). 176p. pap. 16.95 *(978-0-7648-0935-4(0)*, 33022) Liguori Pubns.

Cross, John R. The Lamb: PowerPoint Booklet. Mastin, Ian, illus. 2007. (J). spiral bd. *(978-1-890082-62-8(7))* GoodSeed International.

Crossway Bibles Staff, creator. Children's Bible. 2005. (Illus.). 1632p. (J). (gr. 4-7). per. 26.99 *(978-1-58134-747-0(2)*, Crossway Bibles) Crossway.

Currie, Robin. La Biblia para los Bebes el Padre Nuestro: The Lord's Prayer. 2003. (Bbi Ser.). (SPA., Illus.). 14p. bds. 4.99 *(978-0-7814-3615-1(X)*, 078143615X) Cook, David C.

Custom Curricul Staff. Do I Know What the Bible Says? 2004. (Custom Curriculum Ser.). (ENG.). 256p. pap. 21.99 *(978-0-7814-4086-8(6)*, 0781440866) Cook, David C.

Daughters of St Paul. Stations of Cross Col & Act Bk. 24p. pap. 1.25 *(978-0-8198-7065-0(X)*, 332-362) Pauline Bks. & Media.

David C. Cook Publishing Company Staff & Cook, David C. Ooze & Awes in God's Creations, 1 vol. 2009. (Bible Funstuff Ser.). (ENG.). 112p. (J). pap. 19.99 *(978-1-4347-6720-2(5))* Cook, David C.

Davis, Mary. Five-Minute Sunday School Activities: Exploring the Bible. 2004. (Illus.). 96p. (J). pap. 11.95 *(978-1-58411-048-4(1))* Rainbow Pubs. & Legacy Pr.

—Instant Bible Lessons for Toddlers: God Blesses Me. 2004. (Illus.). 96p. (J). pap. 11.95 *(978-1-58411-038-5(4))* Rainbow Pubs. & Legacy Pr.

—Instant Bible Lessons for Toddlers: God Takes Care of Me. 2004. (Illus.). 96p. (J). pap. 11.95 *(978-1-58411-039-2(2))* Rainbow Pubs. & Legacy Pr.

—Instant Bible Lessons for Toddlers: Growing up for God. 2004. (Illus.). 96p. (J). pap. 11.95 *(978-1-58411-037-8(6))* Rainbow Pubs. & Legacy Pr.

—Instant Bible Lessons for Toddlers: Jesus Is My Friend. 2004. (Illus.). 96p. (J). pap. 11.95 *(978-1-58411-036-1(8))* Rainbow Pubs. & Legacy Pr.

Davis, Mary J. My Answer Journal: What Kids Wonder about God & the Bible. 2004. (Journals Just for Kids Ser.). (Illus.). 136p. (J). (gr. 4-7). pap. 9.99 *(978-1-885358-72-1(5)*, Legacy Pr.) Rainbow Pubs. & Legacy Pr.

—My Bible Journal: A Journey Through the Word for Kids. 2004. (Journals Just for Kids Ser.). (Illus.). 152p. (J). (gr. 4-7). pap. 9.99 *(978-1-885358-70-7(9)*, Legacy Pr.) Rainbow Pubs. & Legacy Pr.

—My Wisdom Journal: A Discovering of Proverbs for Kids. 2004. (Journals Just for Kids Ser.). (Illus.). 160p. (J). (gr. 4-7). pap. 9.99 *(978-1-885358-73-8(3)*, Legacy Pr.) Rainbow Pubs. & Legacy Pr.

Dayspring Staff. Holy Bible, 1 vol. 2008. (Really Woolly Ser.). (ENG., Illus.). 1152p. (gr. -1-2). im. lthr. 19.99 *(978-1-4003-1223-8(X))* Nelson, Thomas Inc.

Delval, Marie-Hélène. Animals of the Bible. Fronty, Aurélia, illus. 2010. (ENG.). 88p. (J). (gr. -1-3). 16.50 *(978-0-8028-5376-9(5)*, Eerdmans Bks For Young Readers) Eerdmans, William B. Publishing Co.

DeYoung, Kevin. The Biggest Story ABC. Clark, Don, illus. 2017. 32p. (J). bds. 12.99 ***(978-1-4335-5818-4(1))*** Crossway.

Dinosaurs & the Bible. 2003. (BUL.). (YA). 0.75 *(978-1-893345-11-9(4))* Answers in Genesis Ministries.

Dorling Kindersley Publishing Staff. My Little Picture Bible. Mayo, Diana, illus. 2008. (ENG.). 80p. (J). (gr. -1 — 1). 7.99 *(978-0-7566-3997-6(2)*, DK Children) Dorling Kindersley Publishing, Inc.

Dorling Kindersley Publishing Staff & Hastings, Selina. The Children's Illustrated Bible. 2005. (ENG.). 320p. (J). (gr. 5-12). 12.99 *(978-0-7566-0935-1(6)*, DK Children) Dorling Kindersley Publishing, Inc.

Dowley, Tim. Would You Like to Know the Bible?, 1 vol. Reeves, Eira, illus. 2015. (ENG.). 28p. (J). pap. 2.99 *(978-1-78128-104-8(1)*, Candle Bks.) Lion Hudson PLC GBR. Dist: Kregel Pubns.

Dowley, Tim, et al. The Complete Collection, 1 vol. Reeves, Eira, illus. 2017. (ENG.). 168p. (J). pap. 12.99 *(978-1-78128-327-1(3)*, Candle Bks.) Lion Hudson PLC GBR. Dist: Kregel Pubns.

Eadie, John. Lectures on the Bible to the Young. 2005. pap. 15.99 *(978-1-59925-015-1(2))* Solid Ground Christian Bks.

Eder, Enelle. Create & Take Bible Crafts: Animals of the Bible. 2004. (Create & Take Bible Crafts). (Illus.). 96p. (J). pap. 11.95 *(978-1-58411-004-0(X))* Rainbow Pubs. & Legacy Pr.

—Create & Take Bible Crafts: Exploring Nature. 2004. (Create & Take Bible Crafts). 96p. (J). (gr. k-6). pap. 11.95 *(978-1-58411-005-7(8))* Rainbow Pubs. & Legacy Pr.

—Create & Take Bible Crafts: Parables & Miracles. 2004. (Create & Take Bible Crafts). (Illus.). 96p. (J). pap. 11.95 *(978-1-58411-007-1(4))* Rainbow Pubs. & Legacy Pr.

—Create & Take Bible Crafts: Special Days. 2004. 96p. (J). (gr. k-6). pap. 11.95 *(978-1-58411-008-8(2))* Rainbow Pubs. & Legacy Pr.

Edgren, David. The Lamb Scroll. 2010. (J). pap. 11.99 *(978-0-8163-2375-3(5))* Pacific Pr. Publishing Assn.

Education and More Staff. Tri-Puzzles for Genesis, Pt. 1. 2004. 152p. per. 7.99 *(978-0-9755809-0-5(6))* Education and More, Inc.

Elkins, Stephen. Bible Blessings. Colton, Ellie, illus. 2003. (Lulla-Bible Series for Little Ones). 32p. (J). 9.99 incl. audio compact disk *(978-0-8054-2761-5(9))* B&H Publishing Group.

—Bible Promises. Colton, Ellie, illus. 2003. (Lulla-Bible Series for Little Ones). 32p. (J). 9.99 incl. audio compact disk *(978-0-8054-2756-1(2))* B&H Publishing Group.

—First Steps in the Bible: A Child's Walk with God Begins Here! 2006. (First Steps Ser.). (Illus.). 32p. (J). (gr. -1-k). 9.99 incl. audio compact disk *(978-0-8054-2672-4(8))* B&H Publishing Group.

—My LullaBible A to Z Promise Book. Colton, Ellie, illus. 2007. 36p. (J). (gr. -1). bds. 14.99 incl. audio compact disk *(978-0-8054-2657-1(4))* B&H Publishing Group.

—The Word & Song Bible. O'Connor, Tim, illus. 2004. 448p. (J). (gr. -1-5). 19.99 *(978-0-8054-1689-3(7))* B&H Publishing Group.

—The Word & Song Songbook Vol. 1: The Old Testament. 2004. (Illus.). 64p. (J). 12.99 incl. audio *(978-0-8054-1694-7(3))* B&H Publishing Group.

Ellis, Gwen. My Little Learner Bible. 2005. 525p. (J). 14.99 *(978-1-4003-0582-7(9))* Nelson, Thomas Inc.

Emmerson, Janice. Your Every Day Read & Pray Bible for Kids. 2016. (Complete Illustrated Children's Bible Library). (ENG.). 384p. (J). 26.99 *(978-0-7369-6683-2(8))* Harvest Hse. Pubs.

Eslinger, Sara. Quick Learn: Meaningful Symbols & Imagery That Makes Bible Verse Learning Easy & Fun. 2008. (Illus.). 150p. spiral bd. 17.95 *(978-1-57258-457-0(2))* TEACH Services, Inc.

EvangeCube Children Bible Study Leader's Guide. 2005. (J). 6.00 *(978-1-933383-46-0(1))* E3 Resources.

Evans, Gwydion, et al. Gemau Gwirion! 2005. (WEL.). 114p. pap. *(978-1-85994-035-8(8))* Cyhoeddiadau'r Gair.

Exodus, Be Redeemed & Delivered. 2004. (YA). spiral bd. 14.00 *(978-0-9729477-2-5(8))* Morningstar Christian Chapel.

Favorite Bible Verses. 2006. 28p. (J). pap. 3.49 *(978-0-7847-1021-0(X)*, 22085) Standard Publishing.

Fawcett, Cheryl & Newman, Robert C. Kids' Questions about the Bible & Creation. 2003. 64p. pap. *(978-1-59402-082-7(5))* Regular Baptist Pr.

Feldick, Les. Questions & Answers from the Bible. 2004. 364p. 12.00 *(978-1-885344-99-1(6))* Feldick, Les Ministries.

Ferguson, Sinclair B. The Plan: How God Got the World Ready for Jesus. Ruta, Angelo, illus. 2009. (Colour Bks.). (ENG.). 40p. (J). 9.99 *(978-1-84550-451-9(8)*, 9781845504519) Christian Focus Pubns. GBR. Dist: Bookmasters Distribution.

Finding Your Way Through the Bible. 2007. (Illus.). 175p. (gr. -1-3). per. 7.99 *(978-0-687-64547-3(6))* Abingdon Pr.

Fisher, Martha, et al. Children of the New Testament. 2005. (Bible Stories for Young Readers Ser.). (Illus.). 39p. (J). (gr. 2). pap. 3.05 *(978-0-7399-2372-6(2))* Rod & Staff Pubs., Inc.

Fiske, Dwight. Without Music. 2005. reprint ed. pap. 22.95 *(978-1-4191-7126-0(7))* Kessinger Publishing, LLC.

Foce, Natalia, tr. from ENG. Jesus el Milagroso. Anderson, Jeff, illus. l.t. ed. 2009. Orig. Title: Jesus the Miracle Worker. (SPA & ENG.). 24p. (J). 3.49 *(978-1-932789-28-7(6))* Editorial Sendas Antiguas, LLC.

—Jesus Maestro. Anderson, Jeff, illus. l.t. ed. 2009. Orig. Title: Jesus the Teacher. (SPA & ENG.). 24p. (J). 3.49 *(978-1-932789-26-3(X))* Editorial Sendas Antiguas, LLC.

—Jesus Niño. Anderson, Jeff, illus. l.t. ed. 2009. Orig. Title: Jesus the Child. (SPA & ENG.). 24p. (J). 3.49 *(978-1-932789-24-9(3))* Editorial Sendas Antiguas, LLC.

Forlini, Victoria, ed. Bible Big Color & Activity Book with Stickers. 2005. (ENG.). 64p. (J). pap. 2.99 *(978-0-696-22824-7(6))* Meredith Bks.

—Bible Ultimate Color & Activity Book with Paints. 2005. (ENG.). 32p. (J). pap. 2.99 *(978-0-696-22823-0(8))* Meredith Bks.

Freeman, Aaron & Rosenzweig, Sharon. The Comic Torah: Reimagining the Good Book. 2010. (Illus.). 128p. (J). 36.00 *(978-1-934730-53-9(X))* Yehuda, Ben Pr.

—The Comic Torah: Reimagining the Very Good Book. Rosenzweig, Sharon, illus. 2010. (ENG., Illus.). 128p. (J). pap. 19.95 *(978-1-934730-54-6(8))* Yehuda, Ben Pr.

Freeman, Kaye. Bible Covenants. 2005. 79p. (YA). pap. 7.99 *(978-0-9703069-6-8(2))* Train-Up A Child, LLC.

Fryar, Jane L., ed. My Christmas Bible. 2004. (J). 0.99 *(978-0-9747923-1-6(4))* C T A, Inc.

—My Christmas Bible: King James Version. 2004. (J). 0.99 *(978-0-9747923-3-0(0))* C T A, Inc.

Genell, Jacqueline. Books of the Bible: Memory Book. 2008. (Illus.). 100p. (J). pap. 10.00 *(978-0-9787631-5-2(7))* Higher Power Publishing.

George, Elizabeth. A Girl's Guide to Discovering Her Bible. 2015. (ENG.). 144p. (J). pap. 10.99 *(978-0-7369-6256-8(5))* Harvest Hse. Pubs.

George, Jim. A Boy's Guide to Discovering His Bible. 2015. (ENG.). 144p. (J). pap. 10.99 *(978-0-7369-6254-4(9))* Harvest Hse. Pubs.

Glaspey, Terry & Kerr, Kathleen. Bible Basics for Kids: An Awesome Adventure Through God's Word. 2014. (ENG.). 112p. (J). pap. 8.99 *(978-0-7369-5820-2(7))* Harvest Hse. Pubs.

Goodings, Christina. My Big Bright Bible Board Book. Barker, Stephen, illus. 2014. (ENG.). 10p. (J). (— 1). bds. 9.99 *(978-0-7459-6525-3(3))* Lion Hudson PLC GBR. Dist: Independent Pubs. Group.

Gospel Light Publications Staff & Kennelly, Colleen. Big Book of Bible Puzzles. Mejia, Roger, illus. 2015. (Big Bks.). (ENG.). 216p. (J). (gr. 3-6). pap. 19.99 *(978-0-8307-2542-7(3))* Gospel Light Pubns.

Graves, Sue. What Is the Bible? 2003. (Illus.). 62p. (J). 12.95 *(978-0-8198-8306-3(9)*, 332-414) Pauline Bks. & Media.

Gray, Charlotte. Traveling Through the Bible with Bible Folks. Henderson, Liz, illus. (J). spiral bd. 14.99 *(978-0-89098-265-5(1))* Twentieth Century Christian Bks.

Greendyk, William, tr. Los DOS Osos. l.t. ed. 2004. (SPA.). 152p. (J). pap. 5.99 *(978-1-932789-02-7(2)*, R009N) Editorial Sendas Antiguas, LLC.

—La Hierba Mala. l.t. ed. 2004.Tr. of Hierba Mala. (SPA.). 156p. (J). pap. 5.99 *(978-1-932789-01-0(4)*, X002N) Editorial Sendas Antiguas, LLC.

—Los Niños de la Biblia. l.t. ed. 2004. (SPA.). 94p. (J). pap. 3.99 *(978-1-932789-03-4(0)*, X003N) Editorial Sendas Antiguas, LLC.

—Primeras Impresiones de Dios. l.t. ed. 2004.Tr. of Primeras Impresiones de Dios. (SPA.). 94p. (J). pap. 3.99 *(978-1-932789-04-1(9)*, W001N) Editorial Sendas Antiguas, LLC.

Griswood, John, ed. La Biblia Juvenil Ilustrada. Sanz Falcon, Maria Teresa, tr. from ENG. D'Ottavi, Francesca, illus. 2006. (SPA.). 320p. (J). (gr. -1-3). 24.95 *(978-1-58087-088-7(0)*, 0278) Stampley, C. D. Enterprises, Inc.

Groce, Mandy. What Is the Gospel? 2012. (ENG., Illus.). 16p. (J). 4.99 *(978-1-84550-820-3(3)*, c3e60a86-e33f-47b6-a9ee-cf8f1addc552) Christian Focus Pubns. GBR. Dist: Bookmasters Distribution.

Guetov, Dimitar D., des. Bulgarian Orthodox Bible: (Pravoslavna Biblia) 2nd ed. 2004. (BUL.). 820p. per. 24.99 *(978-0-9753970-0-8(1))* Capricorn Publishing.

Gunderson, Vivian D. The Bible Is the Best Book. Why? Mowery, Linda Williams & Murphy, Emmy Lou, illus. 36p. (J). (gr. 4-8). pap., wbk. ed. 2.00 *(978-0-915374-00-7(5))* Rapids Christian Pr., Inc.

The Hail Mary. Date not set. bds. 3.95 *(978-0-88271-561-2(5)*, 12011) Regina Pr., Malhame & Co.

Ham, Ken. The Answer Book for Kids: 25 Questions on Creation & the Fall. 2008. 60p. (J). pap. 7.99 *(978-0-89051-526-6(3))* Master Bks.

—The Answers Book for Kids, Volume 3: 22 Questions from Kids on God & the Bible. 2009. (Answers Book for Kids Ser.). (Illus.). 48p. (J). (gr. 4-7). 7.99 *(978-0-89051-525-9(5))* Master Bks.

—My Creation Bible: Teaching Kids to Trust the Bible from the Very First Verse. Taylor, Jonathan, illus. 2006. 12p. (gr. -1-1). bds. 11.99 incl. audio compact disk *(978-0-89051-462-7(3))* Master Bks.

Hastings, Selina. Children's Illustrated Bible. Thomas, Eric, illus. 3rd ed. 2004. (ENG.). 320p. (J). (gr. 5-12). 24.99 *(978-0-7566-0261-1(0)*, DK Children) Dorling Kindersley Publishing, Inc.

Hitzges, Norm. Princess Bible, 1 vol. St. Angelo, Ron, photos by. 2007. (Compact Kids Ser.). (ENG., Illus.). 1152p. pap. 24.99 *(978-1-4003-0987-0(5))* Nelson, Thomas Inc.

Intermediate Bible Class: Winter, 2006/2007. 2006. (YA). pap. *(978-1-59843-039-4(4))* Incorporated Trustees of the Gospel Worker Society, The.

Intermediate Bible Class Vol. 3: Summer 2006. 2006. (YA). pap. *(978-1-59843-037-0(8))* Incorporated Trustees of the Gospel Worker Society, The.

Intermediate Bible Class Vol. 4: Fall 2006. 2006. (YA). pap. *(978-1-59843-038-7(6))* Incorporated Trustees of the Gospel Worker Society, The.

Jackman, Tammy. My Wondrous Words for Children. 2010. 32p. pap. 23.96 *(978-0-557-61840-8(1))* Lulu Pr., Inc.

James, Steven. Believe It! Bible Basics That Won't Break Your Brain. Lee, Jared, illus. 2006. 76p. (YA). pap. 11.99 *(978-0-7847-1393-8(6)*, 42171) Standard Publishing.

Jesus Company Bible Time Grade. 2004. (gr. 6-18). tchr. ed. 15.99 *(978-0-570-00685-5(6))*; stu. ed. 10.50 *(978-0-570-00684-8(8))* Concordia Publishing Hse.

Jim, Madsen, et al. NIV Adventure Bible, 1 vol. 2008. (Adventure Bible Ser.). (ENG., Illus.). 1472p. (J). 27.99 *(978-0-310-71543-6(1))* Zondervan.

John, Hatchard. Hedge of Thorns. 2004. 12.00 *(978-1-58474-011-7(6))* Cornerstone Family Ministries/Lamplighter Publishing.

Julio, Susan & Schooler, Cindy. Interactive Bible Bulletin Boards: Winter. 2004. 128p. (J). pap. 13.95 *(978-1-885358-33-2(4)*, RB36712) Rainbow Pubs. & Legacy Pr.

Jung, Scott. Verdades bíblicas eternas (Timeless Bible Truths) 2011. 32p. pap. 6.99 *(978-0-7586-2680-6(0))* Concordia Publishing Hse.

Junior Bible Class: Winter 2006. 2006. (J). pap. *(978-1-59843-031-8(9))* Incorporated Trustees of the Gospel Worker Society, The.

Junior Bible Class Vol. 2: Spring 2006. 2006. (J). pap. *(978-1-59843-028-8(9))* Incorporated Trustees of the Gospel Worker Society, The.

Junior Bible Class Vol. 3: Summer 2006. 2006. (J). pap. *(978-1-59843-029-5(7))* Incorporated Trustees of the Gospel Worker Society, The.

Junior Bible Class Vol. 4: Fall 2006. 2006. (J). pap. *(978-1-59843-030-1(0))* Incorporated Trustees of the Gospel Worker Society, The.

Keels, Steve. NLT TruthQuest Inductive Student Bible. 2004. (TruthQuest Family Ser.). (Illus.). 1506p. 19.99 *(978-1-55819-929-3(2))* B&H Publishing Group.

Keels, Steve, et al. Truth Quest Inductive Student Bible. 2004. (TruthQuest Family Ser.). (Illus.). 1506p. 19.99 *(978-1-55819-848-7(2))* B&H Publishing Group.

Kuhn, Pamela J. Bible Crafts on a Shoestring Budget: Boxes & Containers. 2004. 96p. (J). pap. 11.95 *(978-1-58411-000-2(7))* Rainbow Pubs. & Legacy Pr.

—Bible Crafts on a Shoestring Budget: Craft Sticks & Clothespins. 2004. 96p. (J). pap. 11.95 *(978-1-58411-001-9(5))* Rainbow Pubs. & Legacy Pr.

—Bible Crafts on a Shoestring Budget: Paper Plates & Cups. 2004. 96p. (J). pap. 11.95 *(978-1-58411-002-6(3))* Rainbow Pubs. & Legacy Pr.

—Bible Crafts on a Shoestring Budget: Paper Sacks & Cardboard Tubes. 2004. 96p. (J). pap. 11.95 *(978-1-58411-003-3(1))* Rainbow Pubs. & Legacy Pr.

Lale, Tim. We Can Trust the Bible: Helping Children Understand Where the Bible Came From. 2011. (Illus.). 80p. (J). pap. *(978-0-8163-2500-9(6))* Pacific Pr. Publishing Assn.

Larsen, Carolyn. Telling the Truth: A Book about Lying. O'Connor, Tim, illus. 2016. (Growing God's Kids Ser.). (ENG.). 32p. (J). pap. 4.99 *(978-0-8010-0926-6(X))* Baker Bks.

—What Does the Bible Say about That? Incrocci, Rick, illus. 2009. 352p. (J). (gr. 3-7). pap. 19.99 *(978-1-4335-0213-2(5))* Crossway.

LaTreill, Donna. The Vinedresser: Two Keys to Reaping the Best Harvest from Your Spiritual & Physical Vineyards. 2004. 64p. per. 19.95 *(978-0-9718838-1-9(5))* Wordwright Communications.

LeSourd, Nancy & Zondervan Staff. Early Reader's Bible: A Bible to Read All by Yourself!, 1 vol. ltd. ed. 2008. (ENG.). 256p. (J). pap. 9.99 *(978-0-310-71804-8(X))* Zonderkidz.

Lifepac Bible, Complete Set. 2004. (gr. 5). 47.95 *(978-1-58095-614-7(9)*, BIB0515, Lifepac) Alpha Omega Pubns., Inc.

Lifetrak Bible Studies for Older Youth. (J). 2005. (gr. 10-12). 29.95 *(978-0-633-19487-1(5))* 2005. (gr. 10-12). 29.95 *(978-0-633-19488-8(3))* 2004. 29.95 *(978-0-633-19484-0(0))* 2004. (gr. 9-12). 29.95 *(978-0-633-19390-4(9))* 2004. (gr. 9-12). 29.95 *(978-0-633-09046-3(8))* 2004. (gr. 9-12). 29.95 *(978-0-633-09045-6(X))* 2003. (gr. 9-12). 29.95 *(978-0-633-09044-9(1))* 2003. (gr. 10-12). 29.95 *(978-0-633-09026-5(3))* 2003. (gr. 10-12). 29.95 *(978-0-633-02209-9(8))* 2003. (gr. 10-12). 29.95 *(978-0-633-02208-2(X))* LifeWay Christian Resources.

Lifetrak Bible Studies for Younger Youth. (J). (gr. 7-9). 2005. 29.95 *(978-0-633-19485-7(9))* 2005. 29.95 *(978-0-633-19486-4(7))* 2004. 29.95 *(978-0-633-19489-5(1))* 2004. 29.95 *(978-0-633-19483-3(2))* 2004. 29.95 *(978-0-633-09294-8(0))* 2004. 29.95 *(978-0-633-09293-1(2))* 2003. 29.95 *(978-0-633-09292-4(4))* 2003. 29.95 *(978-0-633-09047-0(6))* 2003. 29.95 *(978-0-633-02213-6(6))* 2003. 29.95 *(978-0-633-02212-9(8))* LifeWay Christian Resources.

Lingo, Susan L. Preschool Bible Message Make-n-Takes: 50 Fun Crafts with Lively Messages for Preschoolers. 2003. 112p. (J). pap. 16.99 *(978-0-7847-1429-4(0)*, 02523) Standard Publishing.

Little KidsTime 1: Bible Story Pictures. 2004. 104p. 19.99 *(978-0-8307-2773-5(6)*, Gospel Light) Gospel Light Pubns.

Livingstone Corporation, Livingstone & Hudson, Christopher D. NIV, Revolution Bible, Hardcover: The Bible for Teen Guys, 1 vol. 2017. (ENG.). 1728p. (YA). 34.99 ***(978-0-310-07998-9(5))*** Zondervan.

—NIV, Revolution Bible, Imitation Leather, Blue: The Bible for Teen Guys, 1 vol. 2017. (ENG.). 1728p. (YA). im. lthr. 49.99 ***(978-0-310-07999-6(3))*** Zondervan.

—NIV, Revolution Bible, Imitation Leather, Gray/Navy: The Bible for Teen Guys, 1 vol. 2017. (ENG.). 1728p. (YA). im. lthr. 49.99 ***(978-0-310-08000-8(2))*** Zondervan.

—NIV, True Images Bible, Hardcover: The Bible for Teen Girls, 1 vol. 2017. (ENG.). 1760p. (YA). 34.99 ***(978-0-310-08003-9(7))*** Zondervan.

—NIV, True Images Bible, Imitation Leather, Blue/Gold: The Bible for Teen Girls, 1 vol. 2017. (ENG.). 1760p. (YA). im. lthr. 49.99 ***(978-0-310-08004-6(5))*** Zondervan.

—NIV, True Images Bible, Imitation Leather, Pink: The Bible for Teen Girls, 1 vol. 2017. (ENG.). 1760p. (YA). im. lthr. 49.99 ***(978-0-310-08005-3(3))*** Zondervan.

Lovasik, Lawrence G. St. Joseph Catholic Children's Bible. (Illus.). 96p. (J). 6.50 *(978-0-89942-144-5(X)*, 145/122, Resurrection Pr.) Catholic Bk. Publishing Corp.

Lumsden, Colin, illus. Apostles. 2003. (Bible Colour & Learn Ser.). 32p. pap. 2.50 *(978-1-903087-51-0(1))* DayOne Pubns. GBR. Dist: Send The Light Distribution LLC.

—Hebrews Men of Faith. 2003. (Bible Colour & Learn Ser.). 32p. pap. 2.50 *(978-1-903087-52-7(X))* DayOne Pubns. GBR. Dist: Send The Light Distribution LLC.

MacKenzie, Carine. Colour the Bible: Romans-2Thessalonians. 2008. (Bible Art Ser.). (ENG.). 16p. (J). pap., act. bk. ed. 1.99 *(978-1-85792-765-8(6)*, b708e0eb-808e-45e7-a211-9c686cb6fb8a) Christian Focus Pubns. GBR. Dist: Bookmasters Distribution.

—Colour the Bible Bk. 3: Hosea-Malachi. 2008. (Bible Art Ser.). (ENG.). 16p. (J). pap., act. bk. ed. 1.99 *(978-1-85792-763-4(X)*, 70a53dae-b5fa-4bde-9de2-74ed9816d955) Christian Focus Pubns. GBR. Dist: Bookmasters Distribution.

Mackenzie, Carine. My First Book of Bible Promises. 2013. (My First Bks.). (ENG., Illus.). 64p. (J). (gr. -1-3). pap. 3.99 *(978-1-84550-039-9(3)*, 0b7d33be-1c67-4a86-8e10-6b96745df604) Christian Focus Pubns. GBR. Dist: Bookmasters Distribution.

MacKenzie, Carine. Noah: Rescue Plan. Apps, Fred, illus. 2013. (Bible Wise Ser.). (ENG.). 32p. (J). (gr. 1-5). pap. 3.99 *(978-1-85792-466-4(5)*, 9781857924664) Christian Focus Pubns. GBR. Dist: Bookmasters Distribution.

MacLean, Colin and Moira, illus. Baby's First Bible. 2016. (ENG.). 20p. (J). (gr. -1 — 1). bds. 9.99 *(978-0-7944-3849-4(0))* Studio Fun International.

—Baby's First Bible: A CarryAlong Treasury. 2016. (Carry along Treasury Ser.: 1). (ENG.). 20p. (J). (gr. -1 — 1). bds. 14.99 *(978-0-7944-3835-7(0)*, Reader's Digest Children's Bks.) Studio Fun International.

Maltese, Donna K. Know Your Bible for Kids Collection: 399 Need-To-Know People, Places, & Ideas from God's Word. 2016. (ENG., Illus.). 512p. (J). pap. 14.99 *(978-1-63409-410-8(7)*, Barbour Bks.) Barbour Publishing, Inc.

McCann, Carol. 12 Apple Trees. 2010. 28p. 13.95 *(978-1-4497-0273-1(2)*, WestBow Pr.) Author Solutions, Inc.

McCarthy, Michael. The Story of Daniel in the Lions' Den. Ferri, Giuliano, illus. 2003. 32p. (J). (gr. 1-3). 16.99 *(978-1-84148-209-5(9))* Barefoot Bks., Inc.

McDowell, Josh & Johnson, Kevin. The Great Treasure Quest. Jones, Buck, illus. 2006. 103p. (J). (gr. 3-7). per. 10.99 *(978-1-932587-85-2(3))* Practical Christianity Foundation.

Mega Bible Activity Book, 1 vol. 2016. (ENG.). 128p. (J). pap. 9.99 *(978-1-78128-294-6(3)*, Candle Bks.) Lion Hudson PLC GBR. Dist: Kregel Pubns.

Mi Dios es Creador (My God Is Creator) Quarter 1, Level 1. (Caminando con Jesus (Walking with Jesus) Series A).

(SPA.). (J). (gr. -1-k). stu. ed. 3.50 *(978-0-570-05107-7(X),* 16-1811) Concordia Publishing Hse.

Mi Dios es Grande (My God Is Big) Quarter 3, Level 1. (Caminando con Jesus (Walking with Jesus) Series A). (SPA.). (J). (gr. -1-k). stu. ed. 3.50 *(978-0-570-05109-1(6),* 16-1813) Concordia Publishing Hse.

Mi Pequena Biblia Ilustrada.Tr. of My Little Picture Bible. (SPA., Illus.). (J). 5.99 *(978-1-55513-536-2(6),* 498755) Editorial Unilit.

Miley, Dan. The 50 Word Bible. 2013. (Illus.). (J). *(978-1-58411-144-3(5))* Legacy Pr.

Miller, Janet. Cut, Color & Paste: Bible Workers. 2004. 96p. (J). (gr. -1-2). 11.95 *(978-1-885358-82-0(2))* Rainbow Pubs. & Legacy Pr.

Millerm, April. The Holy Book. 2011. 74p. pap. 19.95 *(978-1-4560-9856-8(X))* America Star Bks.

Minges, Barbara. Investigator's Notebook: Faith for Life2 Course Seven Student Book. Janssen, Patricia E., ed. 2nd ed. 2003. Orig. Title: Faith for Life Course Seven. (YA). stu. ed., spiral bd. 14.99 *(978-0-9727146-2-4(6))* LOGOS System Assocs.

Mitchell, Alison. Check It Out: Bible Discovery for Children. 2010. (XTB Ser.). 96p. (J). pap. *(978-1-904889-12-0(3))* Good Bk. Co.

—Christmas Unpacked: Bible Discovery for Children & Families. 2010. (XTB Ser.). 41p. (J). pap. *(978-1-873166-88-8(5))* Good Bk. Co.

—End to End: Bible Discovery for Children. 2010. (XTB Ser.). 76p. (J). pap. *(978-1-904889-16-8(6))* Good Bk. Co.

Moore, Karen. Dear God, Let's Talk about YOU. Wummer, Amy, illus. 2006. 128p. (J). pap. 8.99 *(978-0-7847-1247-4(6),* 42174) Standard Publishing.

Moore, Leslie. Hey Dude, Know Your Scripture-Oye Chico, Conoce Tu Biblia: Find the Hidden Crosses-Encuentra Las Cruces Escondidas. 2012. 36p. pap. 15.99 *(978-1-4497-7071-6(1),* WestBow Pr.) Author Solutions, Inc.

More Time for Bible Puzzles & Games. (Illus.). 32p. (YA). (gr. 5-18). pap. 2.25 *(978-0-87162-664-6(0),* E9706) Warner Pr., Inc.

Mortensen, Carl Anker. Gruff Ar Antur Yn y Beibl. Davies, Aled, tr. from ENG. Montero, Jose Perez, illus. 2005. (WEL.). 66p. *(978-1-85994-503-2(1))* Cyhoeddiadau'r Gair.

Mouser, William E. & Mouser, Barbara K. Five Aspects of Masculinity for Young Men: A Biblical Theology of Manhood, 1. 2003. (YA). pap. *(978-1-929656-10-3(6))* International Council for Gender Studies.

My Bible Words. 2006. 16p. (J). pap. 1.99 *(978-0-7847-1388-4(X),* 22126) Standard Publishing.

My First Picture Bible. Date not set. (J). 8.95 *(978-0-88271-532-2(1),* 10520) Regina Pr., Malhame & Co.

Nappa, Jon. God's Got an Answer for That: Using Your Bible to Solve Everyday Problems. 2015. (ENG., Illus.). 96p. (J). pap. 12.99 *(978-0-7369-5985-8(8))* Harvest Hse. Pubs.

National Geographic Kids Staff. 1,000 Facts about the Bible. 2015. (ENG., Illus.). 96p. (J). (gr. 3-7). 14.99 *(978-1-4263-1865-8(0),* National Geographic Children's Bks.) National Geographic Society.

Neely, Keith. The Illustrated Bible: Joshua / Judges / Ruth. 2007. 128p. (J). pap. 6.99 *(978-1-4003-1105-7(5))* Nelson, Thomas Inc.

The New Testament for Children. Date not set. (J). 2.50 *(978-0-88271-043-3(5));* 2.50 *(978-0-88271-153-9(9))* Regina Pr., Malhame & Co.

Nichols, Roy & Corley, Monte. Bible Discovery: Ideas. (Bible Discovery Ser.). (Illus.). 64p. (J). (gr. 1-6). pap. 9.95 *(978-0-937282-98-4(7))* Rainbow Pubs. & Legacy Pr.

Ninos y Mujeres en la Biblia (Children & Women in the Bible) Quarter 2, Level 2. (Caminando con Jesus (Walking with Jesus) Series A). (SPA.). (J). (gr. 1-2). stu. ed. 3.50 *(978-0-570-05133-6(9),* 16-2812) Concordia Publishing Hse.

Una Nueva Vida (A New Life) Quarter 3, Level 2. (Caminando con Jesus (Walking with Jesus) Series B). (SPA.). (J). (gr. 1-2). stu. ed. 3.50 *(978-0-570-05137-4(1),* 16-2913) Concordia Publishing Hse.

O'Keefe, Kathy Della Torre. Child's Guide to the Beatitudes. 2011. (Illus.). 32p. (J). *(978-0-8091-6756-2(5))* Paulist Pr.

Orme, Robert. Biblical Literacy. 2017. (ENG.). 80p. (J). (gr. 6-9). pap. 29.99 **(978-0-00-822767-8(5))** HarperCollins Pubs. Ltd. GBR. Dist: Independent Pubs. Group.

Osborne, Rick, et al. Weird & Gross Bible Stuff, 1 vol. Carpenter, Anthony, illus. 2003. (2:52 Ser.). (ENG.). 112p. (J). pap. 7.99 *(978-0-310-70484-3(7))* Zonderkidz.

The Our Father. Date not set. bds. 3.95 *(978-0-88271-562-9(3),* 12012) Regina Pr., Malhame & Co.

Palmer, Peggy. Bible Discovery: Games. (Bible Discovery Ser.). (Illus.). 64p. (J). (gr. 1-6). pap. 9.95 *(978-0-937282-95-3(2))* Rainbow Pubs. & Legacy Pr.

Parry, Alan. The Bible Made Easy: A Pop-Up, Pull-Out, Interactive Bible Adventure. Parry, Linda, illus. (J). 14.99 *(978-1-85608-399-7(3))* Hunt, John Publishing Ltd. GBR. Dist: O. M. Literature.

Payne-Krzyzanowski, Anna, et al. 52 More Crafts: For the Church Year. Kyle, Margaret, illus. 2008. (ENG.). 64p. pap. 16.95 *(978-1-55145-570-9(6))* Wood Lake Publishing, Inc. CAN. Dist: Westminster John Knox Pr.

Peterson, Eugene H., tr. My First Message: A Devotional Bible for Kids. Corley, Rob & Bancroft, Tom, illus. 2007. (ENG.). 384p. (J). 19.99 *(978-1-57683-448-0(4))* Tyndale Hse. Pubs.

Petrie, H. D., photos by. All God's Creatures; Jesus Loves Me. 2005. (Illus.). 32p. (J). spiral bd. *(978-0-9774115-0-4(8))* AGC Outreach Ministry.

Precious Moments New Testament Small Hands Catholic Edition: Precious Moments for Little Girls! 2004. (Illus.). 706p. (J). 15.99 *(978-0-7180-0632-7(1))* Nelson, Thomas Inc.

Prestofillipo, Mary Nazarene, tr. The Bible for Little Ones. Flamini, Lorella, illus. 2004. 38p. (J). 9.95 *(978-0-8198-1166-0(1),* 332-029) Pauline Bks. & Media.

Primary Bible Learner: Fall 2006. 2006. (J). pap. *(978-1-59843-014-1(9))* Incorporated Trustees of the Gospel Worker Society, The.

Primary Bible Learner: Spring 2006, Vol. 2. 2006. (J). pap. *(978-1-59843-012-7(2))* Incorporated Trustees of the Gospel Worker Society, The.

Primary Bible Learner: Summer 2006, Vol. 3. 2006. (J). pap. *(978-1-59843-013-4(0))* Incorporated Trustees of the Gospel Worker Society, The.

Primary Bible Learner: Winter, 2006/2007. 2006. (J). pap. *(978-1-59843-015-8(7))* Incorporated Trustees of the Gospel Worker Society, The.

Primetime Take Home Papers. 2004. pap. 2.99 *(978-0-8307-3043-8(5))* Gospel Light Pubns.

Proclaiming Christ (KJV) Around the Corner & Around the World. (J). 139.99 incl. audio *(978-1-55976-232-8(2))* CEF Pr.

Ragel-Dial, Tasha. Say What?, a Photo Book of Inspirational Bible Verses for Kids - Featuring the Photography of Tasha Ragel-Dial. Ragel-Dial, Tasha, photos by. 2013. (Illus.). 24p. 22.95 *(978-1-61493-215-4(8))* Peppertree Pr., The.

Rainbow Publishers Staff. Learning Adventures! Winter. 2004. (Learning Adventures! Ser.). (Illus.). 64p. (J). pap. 9.95 *(978-1-885358-12-7(1),* RB36312) Rainbow Pubs. & Legacy Pr.

Remembering God's Awesome Acts. 2005. stu. ed. 20.00 *(978-1-931292-50-4(7));* Vol. 1 (set) 35.00 *(978-1-931292-52-8(3))* Eagle's Wings Educational Materials.

Reminders of Faith. Boy Scripture Theme. gif. ed. 2004. 7p. pap. 8.99 *(978-0-9763691-1-0(7))* Reminders Of Faith, Inc.

—Girl Scripture Theme Pack. gif. ed. 2004. 7p. pap. 8.99 *(978-0-9763691-2-7(5))* Reminders Of Faith, Inc.

—Mom Scripture Theme Pack. gif. ed. 2004. 7p. pap. 8.99 *(978-0-9763691-0-3(9))* Reminders Of Faith, Inc.

Rhodes, Karen. Numeros en la Biblia. 2004. (SPA., Illus.). 16p. (J). pap. 1.89 *(978-1-59317-062-2(9))* Warner Pr., Inc.

Richards, Lawrence O. NIV Adventure Bible, Imitation Leather, Gray, Full Color Interior, 1 vol. 2017. (Adventure Bible Ser.). (ENG.). 1488p. (J). im. lthr. 34.99 **(978-0-310-75916-4(1))** Zonderkidz.

—NIV Adventure Bible, Imitation Leather, Zebra Print, Full Color Interior, 1 vol. 2017. (Adventure Bible Ser.). (ENG.). 1488p. (J). im. lthr. 34.99 **(978-0-310-75915-7(3))** Zonderkidz.

Richards, Lawrence O. & Richards, Sue. NIV Teen Study Bible, 1 vol. 2008. (ENG.). 1664p. (YA). pap. 22.99 *(978-0-310-71680-8(2))* Zondervan.

—Teen Study Bible, 1 vol. 2008. (ENG.). 1664p. (YA). lthr. 39.99 *(978-0-310-71682-2(9));* lthr. 39.99 *(978-0-310-71681-5(0))* Zondervan.

Rock Solid Tween Leader's Guide Winter 2009-2010. 2009. (Efs Ser.). 6.50 *(978-0-687-46663-4(6))* Abingdon Pr.

Rodgers, Barbara. Bible Outreach Activities: Ages 4-5. 2004. (Illus.). 96p. pap. 11.95 *(978-1-58411-040-8(6))* Rainbow Pubs. & Legacy Pr.

—Bible Outreach Activities: Grades 1-2. 2004. (Illus.). 96p. pap. 11.95 *(978-1-58411-041-5(4))* Rainbow Pubs. & Legacy Pr.

—Bible Outreach Activities: Grades 3-4. 2004. (Illus.). 96p. pap. 11.95 *(978-1-58411-042-2(2))* Rainbow Pubs. & Legacy Pr.

Ropes, Mary. Mary Jones & Her Bible. 2015. (Classic Stories Ser.). (ENG., Illus.). 160p. (J). mass mkt. 8.99 *(978-1-85792-568-5(8),* 4b75ec3c-e772-45f7-ae18-ddb859292ed5) Christian Focus Pubns. GBR. Dist: Bookmasters Distribution.

Rowland, Wilmer. How to Get to Heaven. 2016. (Illus.). (J). *(978-0-7577-5074-8(5))* Word Aflame Pr.

Ruckman, Kathleen. God's Amazing Book. Davies, Lauretta, illus. 2007. (ENG.). 28p. (J). (gr. -1-2). 10.99 *(978-1-59317-201-5(X))* Warner Pr., Inc.

Sanders, Nancy I. The Bible Explorer's Guide: 1,000 Amazing Facts & Photos, 1 vol. 2017. (ENG., Illus.). 80p. (J). 14.99 *(978-0-310-75810-5(6))* Zonderkidz.

Sasso, Sandy Eisenberg. Adam & Eve's New Day. Rothenberg, Joani Keller, illus. 2006. (ENG.). 24p. (gr. -1). bds. 7.99 *(978-1-59473-205-8(1),* 9781594732058, Skylight Paths Publishing) LongHill Partners, Inc.

Schmertz Navarro, Christine, ed. Student Activity Workbook for Breakthrough! the Bible for Young Catholics: An Introduction to People of Faith. 2006. (YA). pap. 11.50 *(978-0-88489-938-9(1))* St. Mary's Pr. of MN.

—Student Activity Workbook for Breakthrough! the Bible for Young Catholics: Getting to Know Jesus. 2007. (Illus.). 32p. pap. 8.50 *(978-0-88489-978-5(0))* St. Mary's Pr. of MN.

Schmidt, Troy. Bible Trivia, Jokes, & Fun Facts for Kids. 2017. (ENG.). 176p. (J). pap. 9.99 *(978-0-7642-1846-0(8))* Bethany Hse. Pubs.

Schneider, Elaine. 52 Children's Moments: A Treasure for Every Week of the Year. 2003. (ENG.). (YA). pap. *(978-0-7443-0720-7(1))* SynergEbks.

Schuller, Robert H. Dr. Robert Schuller's Children's Daily Devotional Bible: With Positive Thoughts for Each Day. 2005. 432p. (J). 16.99 *(978-1-4003-0597-1(7))* Nelson, Thomas Inc.

Schuster-Grossman, Margaret. God's Greatest Miracle. 2012. (Illus.). 32p. pap. 14.51 *(978-1-4669-0446-0(1))* Trafford Publishing.

Senker, Cath. Everyday Life in the Bible Lands. 2005. (Uncovering History Ser.). (Illus.). 46p. (J). (gr. 6-9). lib. bdg. 29.95 *(978-1-58340-711-0(1))* Black Rabbit Bks.

Sewell, Elisabeth. Bible Activity Book. 2010. (ENG., Illus.). 38p. (J). pap. 8.00 *(978-0-7152-0907-3(8))* Saint Andrew Pr., Ltd. GBR. Dist: Westminster John Knox Pr.

Singer-Towns, Brian, ed. The Catholic Youth Bible. gif. ed. 2003. 1772p. (J). lthr. 47.95 *(978-0-88489-797-2(4))* St. Mary's Pr. of MN.

—Catholic Youth Bible: Pray It, Study It, Live It. rev. ed. 2003. (Illus.). 1576p. (YA). (gr. 7-12). 37.95 *(978-0-88489-667-8(6));* pap. 27.95 *(978-0-88489-489-6(4))* St. Mary's Pr. of MN.

Skelton, Stephen. The Lucy Show Bible Study, Vol. 3. 2005. (ENG., Illus.). 40p. pap., stu. ed. 7.99 *(978-0-9765142-3-7(0))* Entertainment Ministry, The.

Smith, Brendan Powell. The Brick Bible for Kids: The Complete Set. 2015. (ENG., Illus.). 192p. (J). (gr. -1-k). 29.99 *(978-1-63450-208-5(6),* Sky Pony Pr.) Skyhorse Publishing Co., Inc.

Soles, Henry, ed. The NEW Children of Color Holy Bible Hardcover Edition. Carter, Fred et al, illus. 2014. 880p. (gr. 2-18). 24.99 *(978-0-9638127-0-4(X))* Urban Spirit!

Sollee, Anne. Scripture Scrapbook for Children. 2012. (Illus.). 32p. pap. 16.99 *(978-1-4624-0424-7(3),* Inspiring Voices) Author Solutions, Inc.

Spanish House Inc. Staff. Sp Little Bible Reader. 2003. 14.99 *(978-0-7899-0214-6(1))* Editorial Unilit.

Spirit Press, creator. The Ultimate Bible Fun Book. 2005. (ENG., Illus.). 400p. (J). (gr. -1-3). pap. 5.99 *(978-1-4037-1230-1(1),* Spirit Pr.) Bendon, Inc.

Springer, Susan K. A Child Can Hear God's Voice. 2011. 24p. pap. 11.32 *(978-1-4567-4785-5(1))* AuthorHouse.

Standke, Linda. Play & Learn Bible Games: 16 Reproducible Games to Help Children Grow in Their Faith. 2003. 160p. (J). per. 12.99 *(978-0-88724-873-3(X))* Carson-Dellosa Publishing, LLC.

Stanley, Charles. The Spirit-Filled Life: Discover the Joy of Surrendering to the Holy Spirit. l.t. ed. 2014. (ENG.). 304p. (gr. 12). E-Book *(978-0-529-10168-6(8),* HG50BG-I) Nelson, Thomas Inc.

Stern, Marie Simchow, illus. Favorite Psalms for Children. 2011. 40p. pap. 35.95 *(978-1-258-07228-5(9))* Literary Licensing, LLC.

Stevenson, Jennifer. Little Hands Story Bible. 16p. (J). pap., act. bk. ed. 1.50 *(978-1-85792-431-2(2));* Vol. 2. pap., act. bk. ed. 1.50 *(978-1-85792-432-9(0));* Vol. 3. pap., act. bk. ed. 1.50 *(978-1-85792-433-6(9));* Vol. 4. pap., act. bk. ed. 1.50 *(978-1-85792-434-3(7))* Christian Focus Pubns. GBR. Dist: Riverside.

Strauss, Ed. Seriously Sick Bible Stuff, 1 vol. Haya, Erwin, illus. 2007. (2:52 Ser.). (ENG.). 128p. (J). (gr. 3-7). pap. 7.99 *(978-0-310-71310-4(2))* Zonderkidz.

Strickler, LeeDell. Super Simple Bible Lessons: 60 Ready-to-Use Bible Activities for Ages 3-5. 2005. 128p. (J). pap. 16.99 *(978-0-687-49770-6(1))* Abingdon Pr.

—Super Simple Bible Lessons: 60 Ready-to-Use Bible Activities for Ages 6-8. 2005. 128p. (J). pap. 16.99 *(978-0-687-49780-5(9))* Abingdon Pr.

Strobel, Lee & Suggs, Rob. The Case for Christ for Kids, 1 vol. enl. rev. expurg. ed. 2010. (Case for... Series for Kids Ser.). (ENG., Illus.). 144p. (J). pap. 7.99 *(978-0-310-71990-8(9))* Zonderkidz.

Taylor, Kenneth N. The New Bible in Pictures for Little Eyes. Spenceley, Annabel, illus. gif. ed. 2004. (Leading Young Hearts & Minds to God Ser.). (ENG.). 384p. (J). 24.99 *(978-0-8024-3078-6(3))* Moody Pubs.

—The Picture Bible for Little People. 2004. (ENG., Illus.). 256p. (J). 14.99 *(978-0-8423-8734-7(X))* Tyndale Hse. Pubs.

Thomas, Isaiah, creator. Curious Hieroglyphick Bible. 2005. (ENG., Illus.). 144p. (J). (gr. 4-7). 9.95 *(978-1-55709-958-7(8))* Applewood Bks.

Thomas-Logan, Sharon. The Miracles of Jesus Christ. 2009. 24p. pap. 12.99 *(978-1-4389-4615-3(5))* AuthorHouse.

Thomas Nelson Publishing Staff. Brave Girls - Better Than Perfect: A 90-Day Devotional for Brave Girls Like You!, 1 vol. 2015. (ENG., Illus.). 144p. (J). pap. 7.99 *(978-0-7180-3052-0(4))* Nelson, Thomas Inc.

—Holy Bible, 1 vol. 2007. (Compact Kids Ser.). (ENG.). 1152p. (gr. 2-6). pap. 19.99 *(978-1-4003-1036-4(9));* pap. 19.99 *(978-1-4003-1035-7(0))* Nelson, Thomas Inc.

—Just for Me Bible, 1 vol. 2015. (ENG.). 40p. (J). bds. 9.99 *(978-0-7180-3373-6(6))* Nelson, Thomas Inc.

—Solomon Says Bible Trivia: Anything Goes: Test Your Bible Knowledge in this Wacky Game Show! 2008. cd-rom 24.95 *(978-0-9754280-9-2(8))* Nelson, Thomas Inc.

—Solomon Says Bible Trivia for Kids: Amazing Animals: Learn about Animals of the Bible. 2008. cd-rom 24.95 *(978-1-4003-1336-5(8))* Nelson, Thomas Inc.

Thomas Nelson Publishing Staff, creator. Compact Kids Bible: Glitter Wings, 1 vol. 2008. (Compact Kids Ser.). (ENG., Illus.). 1152p. (gr. 2-6). 24.99 *(978-1-4003-1119-4(5))* Nelson, Thomas Inc.

—Holy Bible, 1 vol. 2008. (Really Woolly Ser.). (ENG., Illus.). 1152p. (gr. -1-2). im. lthr. 19.99 *(978-1-4003-1222-1(1))* Nelson, Thomas Inc.

Thomas Nelson Publishing Staff & Nelson Bibles Staff. Baby's First Bible, 1 vol. 2008. (ENG.). 1088p. 19.99 *(978-1-4185-3429-5(3))* Nelson, Thomas Inc.

Time for Bible Puzzles & Games. (Illus.). 32p. (YA). (gr. 5-18). pap. 2.25 *(978-0-87162-662-2(4),* E9705) Warner Pr., Inc.

Tricia Lowenfield design. S Is for Shepherd. 2004. (Illus.). 32p. (J). per. 19.99 incl. audio compact disk *(978-0-9747367-0-9(8))* Pumpkins Pansies Bunnies & Bears.

Twin Sisters(r) Staff. Bible Songs Workbook/CD Set. 2008. 96p. 10.99 *(978-1-57583-897-7(4))* Twin Sisters IP, LLC.

Twin Sisters(r) Staff & Thompson, Kim Mitzo. My First Old Testament Bible Stories. 2011. (J). (gr. k-1). audio compact disk 14.99 *(978-1-59922-764-1(9))* Twin Sisters IP, LLC.

Tyndale House Publishers Staff, ed. The One Year Bible for Kids. 2004. (ENG.). 496p. (J). per. 14.99 *(978-0-8423-8517-6(7),* Tyndale Kids) Tyndale Hse. Pubs.

Under the Baobab Tree: Claiming Roots, Kindling Hope, Spreading God's Love. 15.00 *(978-0-687-09994-8(3))* Abingdon Pr.

Vander Klipp, Michael. God Made the World, 1 vol. 2008. (God Made... Ser.). 14p. (J). bds. 3.99 *(978-0-8254-3914-8(0))* Kregel Pubns.

Vineyard Church of Columbus. Little Son Catchers Leader's Guide: Pre-school curriculum Fall Quarter, Year One. 2007. pap. 19.99 *(978-0-9786394-6-4(4))* Ampelon Publishing, LLC.

Walsh, Sheila. I Am Loved, 1 vol. 2010. (ENG.). 352p. 16.99 *(978-1-4003-1475-1(5))* Nelson, Thomas Inc.

Warner Press, creator. Itty-Bitty Bible Activity Book, Easter Edition. 2007. (Itty-Bitty Ser.). (Illus.). 48p. (J). (gr. -1-3). pap. 8.94 *(978-1-59317-016-5(5))* Warner Pr., Inc.

Washington, Linda & Dall, Jeanette. Favorite Bible Children: Ages 2 & 3. 2004. (Illus.). 96p. (J). pap. 11.95 *(978-1-885358-75-2(X))* Rainbow Pubs. & Legacy Pr.

Watson, Richard Jesse. Psalm 23, 1 vol. 2015. (ENG., Illus.). 24p. (J). bds. 7.99 *(978-0-310-73640-0(4))* Zonderkidz.

Wean, Sarah. Teach Them to Your Children: An Alphabet of Biblical Poems, Verses, & Stories. Sanford, Lori Hood, illus. 2006. 56p. (J). 17.00 *(978-0-9787559-5-9(2))* Vision Forum, Inc., The.

Welborn, Amy, ed. Prove It! The Catholic Teen Bible. 2004. 1,600p. (YA). per. 14.95 *(978-1-59276-078-7(3))* Our Sunday Visitor, Publishing Div.

White Stone Books Staff. The Bible Almanac for Kids: A Journey of Discovery into the Wild, Incredible, & Mysterious Facts & Trival of the Bible! 2004. (Illus.). 256p. (J). (gr. 3-6). pap. 12.99 *(978-1-59379-018-9(X))* White Stone Bks.

Wilger, Jennifer Root. Wiggle Worms Learn the Psalms. 2003. (Godprints Bible Funstuff Ser.). 112p. pap., pap. 16.99 *(978-0-7814-3960-2(4),* 0781439604) Cook, David C.

Williams, Sandra. God Knows Me: Pslam 139 for Little Hearts. Williams, Sandra, illus. 2007. (Illus.). 24p. (J). 8.95 *(978-0-9789310-2-5(5))* Hardnett Publishing.

Willoughby, R. A. Guia de la Biblia para Ninos.Tr. of Children's Guide to the Bible. (SPA.). (J). 12.99 *(978-0-7899-0418-8(7),* 498029) Editorial Unilit.

Woodruff, Lisa. The ABC's of the Bible: A Companion to My First Study Bible. 2006. (ENG., Illus.). 196p. pap. 19.99 *(978-1-4185-0626-1(5))* Nelson, Thomas Inc.

Workman Publishing Co., Inc. Bible Brain Quest(r) for Kids: Over 500 Questions & Answers about the Old & New Testaments. 2017. (ENG.). 160p. (J). pap. 10.99 *(978-0-7369-6882-9(2))* Harvest Hse. Pubs.

World Famous Bible Trivia. (Illus.). 16p. (J). pap. 1.50 *(978-0-87162-837-4(6),* E4510) Warner Pr., Inc.

Ybanez, Adelita. Heavenly Seed. 2011. 16p. pap. 8.32 *(978-1-4634-1530-3(3))* AuthorHouse.

Youth Specialties Staff. Biblia G3 de Crecimiento Juvenil NVI, 1 vol. 2005. (Especialidades Juveniles Ser.). (SPA.). 1728p. (YA). lthr. 39.99 *(978-0-8297-4480-4(0));* lthr. 39.99 *(978-0-8297-4481-1(9))* Vida Pubs.

Zona Biblica en el Desierto Preschool Kit Wrap. 2007. *(978-0-687-64773-6(8))* Abingdon Pr.

Zonderkidz Editors. Precious Princess Bible, 1 vol. 2012. (ENG.). 1152p. (J). 14.99 *(978-0-310-73194-8(1))* Zonderkidz.

Zondervan. Faithgirlz Journal: My Doodles, Dreams, & Devotions, 1 vol. 2016. (Faithgirlz Ser.). (ENG.). 208p. (J). pap. 9.99 *(978-0-310-75372-8(4))* Zonderkidz.

—NIV Kids' Visual Study Bible, Hardcover, Full Color Interior: Explore the Story of the Bible — -People, Places, & History, 1 vol. 2017. (ENG.). 1952p. (J). 32.99 **(978-0-310-75860-0(2))** Zonderkidz.

—NIV Kids' Visual Study Bible, Imitation Leather, Bronze, Full Color Interior: Explore the Story of the Bible — -People, Places, & History, 1 vol. 2017. (ENG.). 1952p. (J). im. lthr. 44.99 **(978-0-310-75846-4(7))** Zonderkidz.

—NIV Kids' Visual Study Bible, Imitation Leather, Teal, Full Color Interior: Explore the Story of the Bible — -People, Places, & History, 1 vol. 2017. (ENG.). 1952p. (J). im. lthr. 44.99 **(978-0-310-75842-6(4))** Zonderkidz.

Zondervan Staff. The Beginner's Bible: Timeless Children's Stories, 1 vol. Pulley, Kelly, illus. rev. ed. 2005. (Beginner's Bible Ser.). (ENG.). 512p. (J). 16.99 *(978-0-310-70962-6(8))* Zonderkidz.

—Beginners Bible Super Duper Mighty Jumbo Coloring Book, 1 vol. 2012. (Beginner's Bible Ser.). (ENG.). 384p. (J). pap. 6.99 *(978-0-310-72498-8(6))* Zonderkidz.

—David & God's Giant Victory: Biblical Values, 1 vol. Jones, Dennis, illus. 2010. (I Can Read! / Dennis Jones Ser.). (ENG.). 32p. (J). (gr. -1-2). pap. 3.99 *(978-0-310-71879-6(1))* Zonderkidz.

—Plush - Backpack Bible, 1 vol. rev. ed. 2014. (ENG.). 1152p. (J). 24.99 *(978-0-310-74522-8(5))* Zonderkidz.

—Santa Biblia Palabritas de Vida: La Nueva Biblia de Estudio de los Niños de Hispanoamérica, 1 vol. 2003. (SPA.). 1216p. (J). 27.99 *(978-0-8297-3620-5(4))* Vida Pubs.

Zondervan Staff, creator. Revolution, 1 vol. rev. ed. 2007. (ENG., Illus.). 1664p. (YA). lthr. 44.99 *(978-0-310-93665-7(9))* Zondervan.

—Revolution: The Bible for Teen Guys, 1 vol. rev. ed. 2007. (ENG., Illus.). 1664p. (YA). (gr. 8-11). 29.99 *(978-0-310-93663-3(2))* Zondervan.

BIBLE—ANIMALS

see Bible—Natural History

BIBLE—ANTIQUITIES

Tubb, Jonathan. DK Eyewitness Books: Bible Lands. 2016. (DK Eyewitness Bks.). (ENG., Illus.). 64p. (J). (gr. 3-7). pap. 9.99 *(978-1-4654-4010-5(0),* 1405880, DK Children) Dorling Kindersley Publishing, Inc.

BIBLE—BIOGRAPHY

see also Apostles; Christian Biography; Prophets; Women in the Bible

Bible Games Company Staff. Bible Characters Card Game. 2004. 9.99 *(978-0-8280-1320-8(9))* Review & Herald Publishing Assn.

Boyd, Annalisa. Special Agents of Christ: A Prayer Book for Young Orthodox Saints. 2012. (ENG., Illus.). 96p. (J). pap. 10.95 *(978-1-936270-55-2(2))* Ancient Faith Publishing.

Bringing Bible Characters to Life. (Illus.). 48p. (J). (gr. 1-7). pap. 5.95 *(978-0-87162-634-9(9),* E4604) Warner Pr., Inc.

Butler, David. Bible Ites: An Illustrated Guide to the People in the Holy Bible. Jeppesen, Ryan, illus. 2015. 107p. (J). 19.99 *(978-1-62972-108-8(5))* Deseret Bk. Co.

Christian Focus Publications (CFP) Staff & Russell, Dorothy. Men of Courage: A Study of Elijah & Elisha. 2011. (Geared for Growth Ser.). (ENG.). 64p. pap. 5.99 *(978-1-85792-913-3(6),* 9781857929133, Christian Focus) Christian Focus Pubns. GBR. Dist: Bookmasters Distribution.

Collins, Chris. Abc People of the Bible. DeBroeck, Sarah, illus. 2011. 44p. pap. 24.95 *(978-1-4560-2820-6(0))* America Star Bks.

David, Juliet. Learn & Play: Chalkboard Activities. Prole, Helen, illus. 2007. (Candle Bible for Toddlers Ser.). 12p. (J). (gr. -1-k). bds. 11.99 *(978-0-8254-7331-9(4),* Candle Bks.) Lion Hudson PLC GBR. Dist: Kregel Pubns.

Dickison, Forrest, illus. The Sword of Abram. 2013. (J). *(978-1-59128-046-0(X))* Canon Pr.

Dorn, Owen A. Ruth: A Love Story. 2003. (God's People Ser.). (Illus.). pap. 6.99 *(978-0-8100-1348-3(7))* Northwestern Publishing Hse.

Frank, Penny. Adam & Eve. (Illus.). 24p. pap. 2.99 *(978-0-7459-4102-8(8),* Lion Books) Lion Hudson PLC GBR. Dist: Trafalgar Square Publishing.

Gallaudet, Thomas H. Scripture Biography for the Young: The History of Josiah. 2009. 112p. pap. 12.00 *(978-1-59925-142-4(6))* Solid Ground Christian Bks.

—Scripture Biography for the Young: Vol. 1 - Adam to Jacob. 2009. 212p. pap. 18.00 *(978-1-59925-233-9(3))* Solid Ground Christian Bks.

—Scripture Biography for the Young: Vol. 2 - Joseph. 2009. 220p. pap. 18.00 *(978-1-59925-234-6(1))* Solid Ground Christian Bks.

—Scripture Biography for the Young: Vol. 3 - Moses Part 1. 2009. 224p. pap. 18.00 *(978-1-59925-235-3(X))* Solid Ground Christian Bks.

—Scripture Biography for the Young: Vol. 4 - Moses Part 2. 2009. 276p. pap. 20.00 *(978-1-59925-236-0(8))* Solid Ground Christian Bks.

—Scripture Biography for the Young: Vol. 5 - Joshua & Judges. 2009. 298p. pap. 22.00 *(978-1-59925-237-7(6))* Solid Ground Christian Bks.

Heroes en la Biblia: Quarter 3, Level 2. (Caminando con Jesus (Walking with Jesus) Series A).Tr. of Heroes in the Bible. (SPA.). (J). (gr. 1-2). stu. ed. 3.50 *(978-0-570-05134-3(7),* 16-2813) Concordia Publishing Hse.

Hodges, George. Saints & Heroes to the End of the Middle Ages (Yesterday's Classics) 2006. (Illus.). 188p. (J). per. 9.95 *(978-1-59915-093-2(X))* Yesterday's Classics.

Hudson, Christopher. Bible Tell Me - Who: Lessons from Amazing People of the Bible. 2013. (ENG.). 192p. (gr. k-17). 19.95 *(978-1-61893-098-9(2))* Time Inc. Bks.

Jeffs, Stephanie. A Giant, a Crown & an Open Air Bus. 2003. (SnapShots Ser.). (Illus.). 128p. 5.99 *(978-1-85999-452-8(0))* Scripture Union GBR. Dist: Gabriel Resources.

—People Jesus Met. Tulip, Jenny, illus. 2004. (My First Find Out about Book Ser.). 24p. (gr. -1-18). pap. 3.95 *(978-0-8294-1731-9(1))* Loyola Pr.

Koralek, Jenny. The Moses Basket. Baynes, Pauline, illus. 2004. 32p. (J). 16.00 *(978-0-8028-5251-9(3))* Eerdmans, William B. Publishing Co.

Loesch, Joe. Joshua - Victory Through God: As Told by God's Animals. Cox, Brian T., illus. 2006. 56p. (J). 13.50 incl. audio compact disk *(978-1-932332-62-9(6))* Toy Box Productions.

MacKenzie, Carine. Bible Heroes Gideon. 2005. (Bible Art Ser.). (ENG.). 16p. (J). act. bk. ed. 1.99 *(978-1-84550-090-0(3),* c413bdb8-6ed2-450e-92b3-3dfe97e1313e) Christian Focus Pubns. GBR. Dist: Bookmasters Distribution.

MacKenzie, Carine & Apps, Fred. Miriam: Big Sister's Secret. 2009. (Bible Wise Ser.). (ENG., Illus.). 32p. (J). (gr. -1-3). pap. 3.99 *(978-1-85792-098-7(8),* 5c922e8e-64aa-4448-8aac-442f14be789b) Christian Focus Pubns. GBR. Dist: Bookmasters Distribution.

Martin, Peter. Bible People Factfile. Buckingham, Matt, illus. 2014. (ENG.). 48p. (J). (gr. 2-4). 14.99 *(978-0-7459-6388-4(9))* Lion Hudson PLC GBR. Dist: Independent Pubs. Group.

McAllister, Margaret. Women of the Bible. Massari, Alida, illus. 2013. (ENG.). 48p. (J). 16.99 *(978-1-61261-372-7(1))* Paraclete Pr., Inc.

McKinney, Donna & Herrmann, Angela. Undercover Heroes of the Bible: Ages 2 & 3. 2004. 96p. (J). pap. 11.95 *(978-1-58411-009-5(0))* Rainbow Pubs. & Legacy Pr.

—Undercover Heroes of the Bible: Ages 4 & 5. 2004. 96p. (J). pap. 11.95 *(978-1-58411-010-1(4))* Rainbow Pubs. & Legacy Pr.

—Undercover Heroes of the Bible: Grades 1 & 2. 2004. 96p. (J). (gr. 1-2). pap. 11.95 *(978-1-58411-011-8(2))* Rainbow Pubs. & Legacy Pr.

—Undercover Heroes of the Bible: Grades 3 & 4. 2004. 96p. (J). (gr. 3-4). pap. 11.95 *(978-1-58411-012-5(0))* Rainbow Pubs. & Legacy Pr.

—Undercover Heroes of the Bible: Grades 5 & 6. 2004. 96p. (J). (gr. 5-6). pap. 11.95 *(978-1-58411-013-2(9))* Rainbow Pubs. & Legacy Pr.

My Very Own Bulletin. (Bulletin Bks.). (Illus.). (J). (gr. k-3). pap. 14.95 *(978-0-87162-857-2(0),* U8607) Warner Pr., Inc.

People You Should Know: Set 2. 2016. (People You Should Know Ser.). 184p. (gr. 8-8). 181.25 *(978-1-5081-0220-5(1),* Britannica Educational Publishing) Rosen Publishing Group, Inc., The.

Philip & the Ethiopian. (Illus.). (gr. 1-4). 3.00 *(978-0-570-05526-6(1),* 54-1036) Concordia Publishing Hse.

Priddy, Roger & Priddy Books Staff. The Story of Moses. 2012. (ENG., Illus.). 12p. (J). (gr. -1 — 1). bds. 4.95 *(978-0-312-51455-6(7),* 9780312514556, Priddy Bks.) St. Martin's Pr.

Prime, Derek. Gofors & Gumps. 2005. (Illus.). 160p. 14.00 *(978-1-903087-97-8(X))* DayOne Pubns. GBR. Dist: Send The Light Distribution LLC.

Rottmann, Erik. Timothy Joins Paul. Snyder, Joel, illus. 2005. (ENG.). 16p. (J). 1.99 *(978-0-7586-0506-1(4))* Concordia Publishing Hse.

Sampson Activity Book. Date not set. stu. ed. 1.49 *(978-0-88271-234-5(9),* 1750) Regina Pr., Malhame & Co.

Sanders, Karen Nordberg. Ruth & Naomi. Rooney, Ronnie, illus. 2007. 16p. (J). (gr. k-4). 1.99 *(978-0-7586-1283-0(4))* Concordia Publishing Hse.

Sasso, Sandy Eisenberg. Adam & Eve's First Sunset: God's New Day. Rothenberg, Joani Keller, illus. 2003. (ENG.). 32p. (gr. -1-3). 17.99 *(978-1-58023-177-0(2),* 9781580231770, Jewish Lights Publishing) LongHill Partners, Inc.

Tyner, Stuart. The Meanest Man in the Army: And Other Stories of Grace. 2014. (ENG.). (J). pap. 12.99 *(978-0-8280-2729-8(3))* Review & Herald Publishing Assn.

Zondervan Staff. Wacky Bible Blockheads, 1 vol. 2014. (It's a Fact Ser.). (ENG.). 160p. (J). pap. 9.99 *(978-0-310-74419-1(9))* Zonderkidz.

—Wacky Bible Gross Outs, 1 vol. 2014. (It's a Fact Ser.). (ENG.). 176p. (J). pap. 9.99 *(978-0-310-74424-5(5))* Zonderkidz.

BIBLE—BIRDS

see Bible—Natural History

BIBLE—BOTANY

see Bible—Natural History

BIBLE—COMMENTARIES

Africa/French/Benin Book of Hope: Revised Childrren's Edition. 2003. (J). 1.00 net. *(978-1-931940-49-8(5))* OneHope.

Africa/Portuguese/Portugal Book of Hope. rev. ed. 2003. (J). 1.00 net. *(978-1-931940-48-1(7))* OneHope.

Africa/Portuguese/Portugal Book of Hope: International Pictorial Edition. 2003. (J). 1.00 net. *(978-1-931940-47-4(9))* OneHope.

Allen, Joey. The Gospel: Big Thoughts for Little Thinkers. 2005. (Illus.). 32p. (J). 5.99 *(978-0-89221-617-8(4))* New Leaf Pub. Group.

—The Mission: Big Thoughts for Little Thinkers. 2005. (Illus.). 32p. (J). 5.99 *(978-0-89221-616-1(6))* New Leaf Pub. Group.

—The Trinity: Big Thoughts for Little Thinkers. 2005. (Illus.). 32p. (J). 5.99 *(978-0-89221-614-7(X))* New Leaf Pub. Group.

Arabic Book of Hope. 2003. (J). tchr. ed. 1.00 net. *(978-1-931940-92-4(4))* OneHope.

Arabic Book of Hope: Early Elementary Edition. 2003. (J). 1.00 net. *(978-1-931940-93-1(2))* OneHope.

Arabic Book of Hope: Revised International Pictorial Edition. 2003. (J). 1.00 net. *(978-1-931940-91-7(6))* OneHope.

Bauman, Lester. Exploring the Epistles of John. 2004. (Exploring the Bible Ser.). 77p. 4.80 *(978-0-7399-2307-8(2),* 2219) Rod & Staff Pubs., Inc.

Beginnings II - Jesus, My Shepherd - Answer Key: New Testament Lessons for Young Readers. 2004. (Beginnings II Ser.). 28p. (J). 6.99 *(978-1-889015-90-3(3))* Explorer's Bible Study.

Bible Visuals International Staff, comment. Conduct of the Church Vol. 24: New Testament. 2006. (Illus.). (J). pap. *(978-1-932381-53-5(8),* 1024) Bible Visuals International, Inc.

—A Kingdom Forever Vol. 23: Old Testament. 2006. (Illus.). (J). pap. *(978-1-932381-83-2(X),* 2023) Bible Visuals International, Inc.

—Law & Grace Volume 27: New Testament. 2006. (Illus.). (J). pap. *(978-1-932381-55-9(4),* 1027) Bible Visuals International, Inc.

—The Word of God Vol. 16: Old Testament. 2006. (Illus.). (J). pap. *(978-1-932381-76-4(7),* 2016) Bible Visuals International, Inc.

Bible Visuals International Staff, compiled by. Christ Is God the Son Vol. 34: New Testament. 2006. (Illus.). (J). pap. *(978-1-932381-59-7(7),* 1034) Bible Visuals International, Inc.

—Christ, the Head of the Church Vol. 31: New Testament. 2006. (Illus.). (J). pap. *(978-1-932381-57-3(0),* 1031) Bible Visuals International, Inc.

—Christian Growth Vol. 40: New Testament. 2006. (Illus.). (J). pap. *(978-1-932381-64-1(3),* 1040) Bible Visuals International, Inc.

—Condemnation Vol. 19: New Testament. 2006. (Illus.). (J). pap. *(978-1-932381-49-8(X),* 1019) Bible Visuals International, Inc.

—Conversion Volume 17: New Testament. 2006. (Illus.). (J). pap. *(978-1-932381-47-4(3),* 1017) Bible Visuals International, Inc.

—Disobedience Vol.20: Old Testament. 2006. (Illus.). (J). pap. *(978-1-932381-80-1(5),* 2020) Bible Visuals International, Inc.

—Eternal Salvation: New Testament Volume 35. 2006. (Illus.). (J). pap. *(978-1-932381-60-3(0),* 1035) Bible Visuals International, Inc.

—Forgiveness: New Testament Volume 10. 2006. (Illus.). (J). pap. *(978-1-932381-40-5(6),* 1010) Bible Visuals International, Inc.

—The Holy Spirit Vol. 14: New Testament. 2006. (J). pap. *(978-1-932381-44-3(9),* 1014) Bible Visuals International, Inc.

—Human Suffering (Job) Vol. 29: Old Testament. 2006. (Illus.). (J). pap. *(978-1-932381-88-7(0),* 2029) Bible Visuals International, Inc.

—Israel Vol. 22: New Testament. 2006. (Illus.). (J). pap. *(978-1-932381-51-1(1),* 1022) Bible Visuals International, Inc.

—Jehovah Vol. 30: Old Testament. 2006. (Illus.). (J). pap. *(978-1-932381-89-4(9),* 2030) Bible Visuals International, Inc.

—Justification. 2006. (Illus.). (J). pap. *(978-1-932381-24-5(4))* Bible Visuals International, Inc.

—Law & Faith Volume 26: New Testament. 2006. (Illus.). (J). pap. *(978-1-932381-54-2(6),* 1026) Bible Visuals International, Inc.

—Law & Liberty Volume 28: New Testament. 2006. (Illus.). (J). pap. *(978-1-932381-56-6(2),* 1028) Bible Visuals International, Inc.

—The Lord-He Is God Vol. 25: Old Testament. 2006. (Illus.). (J). pap. *(978-1-932381-85-6(6),* 2025) Bible Visuals International, Inc.

—The Lordship of Christ Volume 07: New Testament. 2006. (Illus.). (J). pap. *(978-1-932381-37-5(6),* 1007) Bible Visuals International, Inc.

—The New Covenant Vol. 37: New Testament. 2006. (Illus.). (J). pap. *(978-1-932381-62-7(7),* 1037) Bible Visuals International, Inc.

—The Providence of God Vol. 8: Old Testament. 2006. (Illus.). (J). pap. *(978-1-932381-71-9(6),* 2008) Bible Visuals International, Inc.

—Rebellion Vol. 18: Old Testament. 2006. (Illus.). (J). pap. *(978-1-932381-78-8(3),* 2018) Bible Visuals International, Inc.

—Sanctification Vol. 21: New Testament. 2006. (Illus.). (J). pap. *(978-1-932381-50-4(3),* 1021) Bible Visuals International, Inc.

—Servants of God Vol. 25: New Testament. 2006. (Illus.). (J). pap. *(978-1-932381-25-2(2),* 1025) Bible Visuals International, Inc.

—Service Vol. 18: New Testament. 2006. (Illus.). (J). pap. *(978-1-932381-48-1(1),* 1018) Bible Visuals International, Inc.

—Suffering Vol. 16: New Testament. 2006. (Illus.). (J). pap. *(978-1-932381-46-7(5),* 1016) Bible Visuals International, Inc.

—Tests of True Faith Vol.39: New Testament. 2006. (Illus.). (J). pap. *(978-1-932381-63-4(5),* 1039) Bible Visuals International, Inc.

—Wisdom Vol. 31: Old Testament. 2006. (Illus.). (J). pap. *(978-1-932381-90-0(2),* 2031) Bible Visuals International, Inc.

Blanks, Andy, et al. 31 Verses - Identity: Every Teenager Should Know. 2008. 76p. (YA). pap. 4.99 *(978-1-935040-07-1(3))* NavPress Publishing Group.

Blitz, Shmuel. [ha-Tehilim Ha-Rishon]: ArtScroll Children's Tehillim. Katz, Tova, illus. 2008. (Artscroll Youth Ser.). 96p. (J). *(978-1-4226-0751-0(8))* Mesorah Pubns., Ltd.

—Megilat Ester: The ArtScroll Children's Megillah. Katz, Tova, illus. 2003. (ArtScroll Ser.). (ENG & HEB.). 79p. (J). 16.99 *(978-1-57819-708-8(2),* MCHH); pap. 10.99 *(978-1-57819-709-5(0),* MCHP) Mesorah Pubns., Ltd.

—[Megilat Rut]: The Artscroll Children's Book of Ruth. Katz, Tova, illus. 2005. (ArtScroll Youth Ser.). 48p. (J). *(978-1-57819-069-0(X))*; pap. *(978-1-57819-070-6(3))* Mesorah Pubns., Ltd.

—[Sefer Yonah]: The Artscroll Children's Book of Jonah. Katz, Tova, illus. 2006. 48p. (J). *(978-1-4226-0130-3(7))*; pap. *(978-1-4226-0131-0(5))* Mesorah Pubns., Ltd.

Blumenthal, Scott. The Explorer's Bible/By Scott E. Blumenthal. 2006. (Illus.). *(978-0-87441-792-0(9))*; *(978-0-87441-793-7(7))* Behrman Hse., Inc.

Brazil/Portuguese Book of Hope: International Graphic Edition. 2003. (J). 1.00 net. *(978-1-931940-68-9(1))* OneHope.

Brazil/Portuguese Book of Hope: Revised International Pictorial Edition. 2003. (J). 1.00 net. *(978-1-931940-67-2(3))* OneHope.

Brost, Corey. Gospel Connections for Teens: Reflections for Sunday Mass - Cycle B. 2006. 129p. (YA). (gr. 8-12). pap. 6.25 *(978-0-88489-848-1(2))* St. Mary's Pr. of MN.

Buevara, Isaias, illus. Revelation: A Visual Journey. 2005. 96p. per. 41.99 *(978-0-9763800-3-0(X),* 10) Orison Pubs.

Carlsen, Derek. Faith & Courage Commentary on Acts. 2004. 544p. per. 12.95 *(978-1-930367-98-2(8),* CLP80091) Christian Liberty Pr.

Charles, Boyd. What God Has Always Wanted. 2006. 30p. 14.99 *(978-1-57229-920-7(7))* FamilyLife.

Chinese Book of Hope: Early Elementary Edition (Simplified Characters) 2003. (J). 1.00 net. *(978-1-931940-87-0(8))* OneHope.

Chinese Book of Hope: Early Elementary Edition (Traditional Characters) 2003. (J). 1.00 net. *(978-1-931940-86-3(X))* OneHope.

Chinese Book of Hope: Revised International Pictorial Edition -d (Simplified) 2003. (J). 1.00 net. *(978-1-931940-82-5(7))* OneHope.

Chinese Book of Hope: Revised International Pictorial Edition -d (Traditional) 2003. (J). 1.00 net. *(978-1-931940-84-9(3))* OneHope.

Cohen, Ron. Bible Survey for High School — Student Workbook, 2 vols. 2005. 149p. (YA). spiral bd., wbk. ed. *(978-0-9767618-1-5(5))* Jew-El Pr. Co.

—Bible Survey for High School — Study Guide, 2 vols. 2005. (Illus.). 187p. (YA). stu. ed., spiral bd. *(978-0-9767618-0-8(7))* Jew-El Pr. Co.

Connect Booklet. 2003. 47p. (YA). pap. 1.49 *(978-1-59312-053-5(2))* North American Mission Board, SBC.

Cuba/Spanish Book of Hope: (Spanish) Revised International Graphic Edition. 2003. (J). 1.00 net. *(978-1-931940-98-6(3))* OneHope.

David C. Cook Publishing Company Staff, creator. Game-a-Thon. 2008. (Bible Funstuff Ser.). (ENG., Illus.). 112p. (YA). (gr. 4-5). pap. 19.99 *(978-1-4347-6857-5(0))* Cook, David C.

Davis, Mary. Five-Minute Sunday School Activities: Jesus' Miracles & Messages. 2004. (Illus.). 96p. (J). pap. 11.95 *(978-1-58411-049-1(X))* Rainbow Pubs. & Legacy Pr.

De Graaf, A. M. La Torre de Babel. (Divertidas Historias Biblicas para Ninos Ser.).Tr. of Tower of Babel. (SPA.). (J). 3.49 *(978-0-7899-0525-3(6),* 496642) Editorial Unilit.

Dill, Melanie, et al. 31 Verses - The Bible: Every Teenager Should Know. 2008. 76p. (YA). pap. 4.99 *(978-1-935040-02-6(2))* NavPress Publishing Group.

Discovery - in the Beginning - Answer Key: Genesis. 2003. (Bible Discovery Ser.). 43p. (J). 6.99 *(978-1-889015-32-3(6))* Explorer's Bible Study.

English Book of Hope: Affect Destiny Book. 2003. (YA). 1.00 net. *(978-1-931940-75-7(4))* OneHope.

English Book of Hope: HopeXtreme. 2003. 48p. (J). 1.00 net. *(978-1-931940-71-9(1))* OneHope.

English Book of Hope: Resource Guide. 2003. (YA). 1.00 net. *(978-1-931940-74-0(6))* OneHope.

English Book of Hope: Revised International Graphic Edition. 2003. (J). 1.00 net. *(978-1-931940-76-4(2))* OneHope.

English Book of Hope: The Life & Teachings of Jesus of Nazareth. 2003. per. 1.00 net. *(978-1-931940-77-1(0))* OneHope.

English/Botswana Book of Hope: Revised International Pictorial Edition. 2003. (J). 1.00 net. *(978-1-931940-44-3(4))* OneHope.

English/Oceania Book of Hope. rev. ed. 2003. (J). 1.00 net. *(978-1-931940-58-0(4))* OneHope.

English/Oceania Book of Hope: Revised International Pictorial Edition. 2003. (J). 1.00 net. *(978-1-931940-52-8(5))* OneHope.

English/Philippines Book of Hope: Revised International Pictorial Edition. 2003. (J). 1.00 net. *(978-1-931940-51-1(7))* OneHope.

France Book of Hope: All They Want Is the Truth. 2003. (J). 1.00 net. *(978-1-931940-41-2(X))* OneHope.

France Book of Hope: Graphic Edition. 2003. (J). 1.00 net. *(978-1-931940-42-9(8))* OneHope.

France/French Book of Hope. 2003. (J). tchr. ed. 1.00 net. *(978-1-931940-50-4(9))* OneHope.

France/French Book of Hope: Early Elementary Edition. 2003. (J). 1.00 net. *(978-1-931940-45-0(2))* OneHope.

France/French Book of Hope: Then Seeds of Spiritual Lineage. 2003. (J). 1.00 net. *(978-1-931940-62-7(2))* OneHope.

Ganz, Nancy. Numbers: A Commentary for Children. 2006. (Herein Is Love Ser.). 222p. per. 13.00 *(978-0-9767582-2-8(9))* Shepherd Pr. Inc.

Gordon Brown, Doris. Jesus Brought Lazarus Back to Life. 2003. 5.95 *(978-1-59427-023-9(6))* Aglob Publishing.

Greiner, Ruth B. The Crucifixion Part 1 ... the Road to the Cross Pt. I, Vol. 11: New Testament Volume 11 Life of Christ Part 11. Mayer, Melody & Olson, Ed, illus. 2011. 36p. (J). pap. *(978-1-932381-41-2(4),* 1011) Bible Visuals International, Inc.

—The Crucifixion Part 2 Christ Sacrifice Our Salvation Pt. 2, Vol. 12: New Testament Volume 12 Life of Christ Part 12. Mayer, Melody & Olson, Ed, illus. 2011. 36p. (J). pap. *(978-1-932381-42-9(2),* 1012) Bible Visuals International, Inc.

—The Resurrection of Christ Vol. 14: Death Conquered! NT Volume 13 Life of Christ Part 13. Hertzler, Frances H., illus. 2012. 36p. (J). pap. *(978-1-932381-43-6(0),* 1013) Bible Visuals International, Inc.

Habecker, Marilyn P. Christian Joy: New Testament Volume 30. Hertzler, Frances H.., illus. 2014. 36p. (J). pap. *(978-1-932381-27-6(9),* 1030) Bible Visuals International, Inc.

Halper, Sharon. To Learn Is to Do: A Tikkun Olam Road Map. Koffsky, Ann D., illus. 2004. vi, 56p. (gr. 4-6). pap. 11.95 *(978-0-8074-0729-5(1),* 123935) URJ Pr.

Hash, John A. The Best of Bible Pathway 2004. exp. ed. 2003. (Illus.). pap. 14.95 *(978-1-879595-37-8(0))* Bible Pathway Ministries.

Hausa New Testament. 2004.Tr. of Sabon Alkawali. (HAU.). (YA). pap. 1.50 *(978-1-882536-67-2(3))* Bible League.

Hershey, Katherine. The Tabernacle, Part 2 a Picture of the Lord Jesus Vol. 10, Pt. 2: Old Testament Volume 10 Exodus Part 5. Willoughby, Yuko, illus. 2013. (ENG.). 32p. (J). pap. *(978-1-932381-73-3(2),* 2010) Bible Visuals International, Inc.

La Historicas de Exodo (The Story of Exodus) (SPA.). (J). 1.59 *(978-0-7899-0549-9(3),* 490535) Editorial Unilit.

Hooten, Emily & Student Life Staff. 31 Verses - Here & Now: Every Teenager Should Know. 2008. 80p. (YA). pap. 4.99 *(978-1-935040-08-8(1))* NavPress Publishing Group.

India/English Book of Hope. 2003. 1.00 net. *(978-1-931940-38-2(X))* OneHope.

India/English Book of Hope: Revised Children's Edition. rev. ed. 2003. (J). 1.00 net. *(978-1-931940-36-8(3))* OneHope.

India/English Book of Hope: Revised International Pictorial Edition. rev. ed. 2003. (Illus.). (J). 1.00 net. *(978-1-931940-37-5(1))* OneHope.

India/Gujarathi Book of Hope. 2003. 1.00 net. *(978-1-931940-32-0(0))*; (J). 1.00 net. *(978-1-931940-30-6(4))*; (Illus.). 1.00 net. *(978-1-931940-31-3(2))* OneHope.

India/Kannada Book of Hope. 2003. 1.00 net. *(978-1-931940-25-2(8))*; (J). 1.00 net. *(978-1-931940-23-8(1))* OneHope.

India/Khasi Book of Hope. rev. ed. 2003. (J). 1.00 net. *(978-1-931940-27-6(4))* OneHope.

India/Malayalam Book of Hope. 2003. 1.00 net. *(978-1-931940-22-1(3))*; (J). 1.00 net. *(978-1-931940-20-7(7))*; (Illus.). 1.00 net. *(978-1-931940-21-4(5))* OneHope.

India/Marathi Book of Hope. 2003. 1.00 net. *(978-1-931940-16-0(9))* OneHope.

India/Punjabi Book of Hope. rev. ed. 2003. (J). 1.00 net. *(978-1-931940-33-7(9))* OneHope.

India/Tamil Book of Hope. 2003. 1.00 net. *(978-1-931940-19-1(3))*; (J). 1.00 net. *(978-1-931940-17-7(7))*; (Illus.). 1.00 net. *(978-1-931940-18-4(5))* OneHope.

Indonesia/Bahasa Book of Hope. 2003. (J). 1.00 net. *(978-1-931940-53-5(3))* OneHope.

Indonesia/Bahasa Book of Hope: Early Elementary Edition. 2003. (J). 1.00 net. *(978-1-931940-60-3(6))* OneHope.

Indonesian Book of Hope. 2003. (J). tchr. ed. 1.00 net. *(978-1-931940-80-1(0))* OneHope.

Jablon, Shmuel. The Student's Pesach Haggadah. 2008. 56p. per. 9.95 *(978-965-7344-45-3(X))* Mazo Pubs.

Japanese/Japan Book of Hope: Early Elementary Edition. 2003. (J). 1.00 net. *(978-1-931940-69-6(X))* OneHope.

Japan/Japanese Book of Hope. 2003. (J). tchr. ed. 1.00 net. *(978-1-931940-73-3(8))* OneHope.

Jesus Company: Bible Time. 30p. (gr. 4-18). stu. ed. 10.50 *(978-0-570-00672-5(4),* 22-2775) Concordia Publishing Hse.

Jesus Company: Bible Time, Grade 5. 30p. (gr. 5-18). stu. ed. 10.50 *(978-0-570-00678-7(3),* 7.99) Concordia Publishing Hse.

Jojean. Twilight in the Vineyard. 2007. 464p. per. 18.95 *(978-1-4327-0653-1(5))* Outskirts Pr., Inc.

Kanzlemar, Joseph. Biblical Creation Authenticated. 2006. (Illus.). 159p. *(978-0-9797786-1-2(1))* Bible Based Studies.

—Biblical Creation Authenticated - Youth Edition. abr. ed. 2007. 18p. (YA). *(978-0-9797786-4-3(6))* Bible Based Studies.

Kimbrough, Lawrence. Bible Promises for Kids. 2003. (ENG.). 128p. pap. 3.99 *(978-0-8054-2740-0(6),* B&H Bks.) B&H Publishing Group.

Kizer, Andy. To the Overcomers. 2003. (YA). per. 10.00 *(978-0-9725894-0-6(6))* Riddle Creek Publishing.

Kuhn, Pamela J. More Instant Bible Lessons: Jesus' Disciples. 2004. 96p. (J). pap. 11.95 *(978-1-58411-017-0(1))* Rainbow Pubs. & Legacy Pr.

—More Instant Bible Lessons: Walking with Jesus. 2004. 96p. (J). pap. 11.95 *(978-1-58411-016-3(3))* Rainbow Pubs. & Legacy Pr.

—More Instant Bible Lessons: Wisdom from God's Word. 2004. 96p. (J). pap. 11.95 *(978-1-58411-018-7(X))* Rainbow Pubs. & Legacy Pr.

Lyster, R. Iona. Believers in Christ Volume 29: New Testament Volume 29 Ephesians: God's Workmanship. Willoughby, Yuko, illus. 2011. (ENG.). 36p. (J). pap. *(978-1-932381-26-9(0),* 1029) Bible Visuals International, Inc.

Madagascar/Malagasy Book of Hope. rev. ed. 2003. (J). 1.00 net. *(978-1-931940-43-6(6))* OneHope.

Madagascar/Malagasy Book of Hope: International Pictorial Edition. 2003. (J). 1.00 net. *(978-1-931940-70-2(3))* OneHope.

Maoz, Baruch. A Prophet on the Run. 2009. 88p. pap. 14.99 *(978-0-9820731-8-6(6))* Audubon Pr. & Christian Bk. Service.

Marchon, Benoît & Rosa, Jean-Pierre. Descubrir la Biblia. Truong, Marcelino, illus. (SPA.). 50p. (J). (gr. 3-5). 7.96 *(978-84-263-3188-5(2))* Vives, Luis Editorial (Edelvives) ESP. Dist: Lectorum Pubns., Inc.

Martin, Harold. Brethren New Testament Commentary - 1 & 2 Timothy & Titus. 2004. (ENG.). 15.00 *(978-0-9745027-3-1(1))* Brethren Revival Fellowship.

Martin, Harold S. Brethren New Testament Commentary - 2 Corinthians. 2006. (ENG.). 224p. 12.00 *(978-0-9745027-8-6(2))* Brethren Revival Fellowship.

McKenzie, Marni Shideler & Bridges, Nancy S. Quest - Faith at Work: Romans, Galatians, & James. Murtha, Dee, ed. 2004. (Bible Quest Ser.). 231p. (YA). stu. ed., per., wbk. ed. 21.99 *(978-1-889015-91-0(1))* Explorer's Bible Study.

Neal, Sharon, ed. Great Is Thy Faithfulness. 2009. (ENG., Illus.). (J). pap. *(978-1-932381-94-8(5)*, 6180) Bible Visuals International, Inc.

Palmer, Edward G. Book of Edward Christian Mythology, 4 vols., Set. l.t. ed. 2005. (Illus.). 1306p. per. 123.80 *(978-0-9768833-4-0(1)*, 0976883341) JVED Publishing.

—Book of Edward Christian Mythology: Itching Christian Ears, 4 vols., Vol. 3. l.t. ed. 2005. (Illus.). 616p. per. 39.95 *(978-0-9768833-2-6(5)*, 0976883325) JVED Publishing.

—Book of Edward Christian Mythology Vol. II: God Does Not Change, 4 vols. l.t. ed. 2005. (Illus.). 356p. per. 27.95 *(978-0-9768833-1-9(7)*, 0976883317) JVED Publishing.

—Book of Edward Christian Mythology Vol. IV: Appendixes Reference, 4 vols. l.t. ed. 2005. (Illus.). 208p. per. 27.95 *(978-0-9768833-3-3(3)*, 0976883333) JVED Publishing.

Pattyn, Denny & Flecker, Katie. SRT 434 for Small Groups. 2005. (YA). ldr.'s hndbk. ed. 59.95 *(978-0-9771248-0-0(0))* SRT Publishing.

—SRT 434 Leaders Guide. 2005. (YA). 9.95 *(978-0-9771248-3-1(5))* SRT Publishing.

Peipgrass, Arlene. Nature of Man: Old Testament Volume 03 Genesis Part 3. Henkel, Vernon, illus. 2014. 36p. (J). pap. *(978-1-932381-68-9(6)*, 2003) Bible Visuals International, Inc.

Philippines/Cebuano Book of Hope: Early Elementary Edition. 2003. (J). 1.00 net. *(978-1-931940-55-9(X))* OneHope.

Philippines/Ilocano Book of Hope: Early Elementary Edition. 2003. (J). 1.00 net. *(978-1-931940-56-6(8))* OneHope.

Philippines/Tagalog Book of Hope: Early Elementary Edition. 2003. (J). 1.00 net. *(978-1-931940-54-2(1))* OneHope.

Piepgrass, Arlene. Election Chosen by God Vol. 06: Old Testament Volume 6 Exodus Part 1. Henkel, Vernon, illus. 2013. 36p. (J). pap. *(978-1-932381-32-0(5)*, 2006) Bible Visuals International, Inc.

—In the Beginning Volume 01: Creation & Man's Fall Old Testament Volume 1 Genesis Part 1. Henkel, Vernon, illus. 2013. 36p. (J). pap. *(978-1-932381-66-5(X)*, 2001) Bible Visuals International, Inc.

—Joseph, a Picture of the Lord Jesus Christ, Part 2 Pt. 2, Vol. 5: Old Testament Volume 05 Genesis Part 5. Henkel, Vernon, illus. 2015. 36p. (J). pap. *(978-1-932381-70-2(8)*, 2005) Bible Visuals International, Inc.

—Redemption Set Free from Sin Vol. 07: Old Testament Volume 07 Exodus Part 2. Henkel, Vernon, illus. 2012. 40p. (J). pap. *(978-1-932381-33-7(3)*, 2007) Bible Visuals International, Inc.

Piepgrass, Arlene & Hershey, Katherine. The Tabernacle, Part 1 a Picture of the Lord Jesus Vol. 09, Pt. 1: Old Testament Volume 9 Exodus Part 4. Willoughby, Yuko, illus. 2013. (ENG.). 36p. (J). pap. *(978-1-932381-72-6(4)*, 2009) Bible Visuals International, Inc.

Poland/Polish Book of Hope: Early Elementary Edition. 2003. (J). 1.00 net. *(978-1-931940-59-7(2))* OneHope.

Portuguese Book of Hope: Then Seeds of Spiritual Lineage. 2003. (J). 1.00 net. *(978-1-931940-63-4(0))* OneHope.

Portuguese/Portugal Book of Hope. 2003. (J). tchr. ed. 1.00 net. *(978-1-931940-46-7(0))* OneHope.

Providing Hope Latin America: Providing Hope Latin America Child Care Life Stories (Donor Book) 2003. (J). 1.00 net. *(978-1-931940-90-0(8))* OneHope.

Quest - Faith at Work - Answer Key: Romans, Galatians, & James. 2004. (Quest Ser.). 25p. (YA). 6.99 *(978-1-889015-92-7(X))* Explorer's Bible Study.

Rich, J. Milton. Heavenly Fathers Plan of Salvation Coloring Book. Knaupp, Andrew & Koford, Adam, illus. 2003. 108p. (J). per. 7.95 *(978-0-9726670-2-9(4))* Rich Publishing.

Romania Book of Hope. 2003. (J). tchr. ed. 1.00 net. *(978-1-931940-95-5(9))* OneHope.

Romania Book of Hope: Early Elementary Edition. 2003. (J). 1.00 net. *(978-1-931940-94-8(0))* OneHope.

Romania Book of Hope: Revised Children's Edition. 2003. (J). 1.00 net. *(978-1-931940-96-2(7))* OneHope.

Romania Book of Hope: Revised International Pictorial Edition. 2003. (J). 1.00 net. *(978-1-931940-99-3(1))* OneHope.

Romania/Romanian Book of Hope: International Pictorial Edition. 2003. (J). 1.00 net. *(978-1-931940-57-3(6))* OneHope.

Rossel, Seymour. Torah Portion-by-Portion. 2007. (Illus.). 368p. (J). pap. 15.95 *(978-1-891662-94-2(5))* Torah Aura Productions.

Russell, Patricia Constance. Beginnings II - Jesus, My Shepherd: New Testament Lessons for Young Readers. Murtha, Dee M., ed. 2004. (Beginnings II Ser.). 301p. (J). stu. ed., spiral bd., wbk. ed. 23.99 *(978-1-889015-89-7(X))* Explorer's Bible Study.

Russia Book of Hope: HopeXtreme. 2003. 48p. (J). 1.00 net. *(978-1-931940-79-5(7))* OneHope.

Russia/Russia Book of Hope: Teen Challenge. 2003. (J). 1.00 net. *(978-1-931940-88-7(6))* OneHope.

Russia/Russian Book of Hope. 2003. (J). 1.00 net. *(978-1-931940-89-4(4))* OneHope.

Russia/Russian Book of Hope: Revised International Pictorial Edition. 2003. (J). 1.00 net. *(978-1-931940-85-6(1))* OneHope.

Skelton, Stephen. The Lucy Show Bible Study, Vol. 2. 2005. (ENG., Illus.). 40p. pap., stu. ed. 7.99 *(978-0-9765142-1-3(4))* Entertainment Ministry, The.

Smart, Dominic. 40 Days with Jesus: A Journey Through Mark's Gospel. 2006. (Daily Readings Ser.). (ENG., Illus.). 144p. (J). per. 10.99 *(978-1-84550-193-8(4)*, 4ae05e0c-fa9c-48fd-8b6d-360a73b461fc) Christian Focus Pubns. GBR. Dist: Bookmasters Distribution.

South Africa/ English Book of Hope: Revised International Pictorial Edition. 2003. (J). 1.00 net. *(978-1-931940-83-2(5))* OneHope.

Spanish Book of Hope: (Cuba/Spanish) Revised International Pictorial Edition. 2003. (J). 1.00 net. *(978-1-931940-97-9(5))* OneHope.

Spanish Book of Hope: Teen Challenge. 2003. (J). 1.00 net. *(978-1-931940-64-1(9))* OneHope.

Spanish Book of Hope: Then Seeds of Spiritual Lineage. 2003. (J). 1.00 net. *(978-1-931940-61-0(4))* OneHope.

Spanish (New Lenguaje Sencillo) Book of Hope. rev. ed. 2003. (J). 1.00 net. *(978-1-931940-72-6(X))* OneHope.

St. John, Patricia. Missing the Way: How Israel Missed God's Rest. 2004. (RUM.). 42p. 3.50 *(978-1-932774-60-3(2))* Christian, Harvey Pubs. Inc.

Strauss, Ed. Big Bad Bible Giants, 1 vol. Carpenter, Anthony, illus. 2005. (2:52 Ser.). (ENG.). 112p. (J). pap. 7.99 *(978-0-310-70869-8(9))* Zonderkidz.

Student Life Staff. 31 Verses - Following: Every Teenager Should Know. 2009. 80p. (YA). pap. 4.99 *(978-1-935040-75-0(8))* NavPress Publishing Group.

—31 Versus - Inhabit: Every Teenager Should Know. 2009. 76p. (YA). pap. 4.99 *(978-1-935040-78-1(2))* NavPress Publishing Group.

Student Life Staff & Navigators Staff, The. 31 Verses - Community: Every Teenager Should Know. 2009. 80p. (YA). pap. 4.99 *(978-1-935040-16-3(2))* NavPress Publishing Group.

—31 Verses - Reverb: Every Teenager Should Know. 2009. 76p. (YA). pap. 4.99 *(978-1-935040-15-6(4))* NavPress Publishing Group.

Suriname/Dutch Book of Hope. 2003. 1.00 net. *(978-1-931940-39-9(8))*; (Illus.). 1.00 net. *(978-1-931940-40-5(1))* OneHope.

Where Did Cain Get His Wife? 2003. (BUL.). (YA). 0.75 *(978-1-893345-12-6(2))* Answers in Genesis Ministries.

100 Prophecies (Unlaminated) 2003. (YA). pap. 9.99 *(978-0-9744451-2-0(6))* Ascension Pr.

2003 Devotional Book of Hope: Devotional. 2003. (YA). per. 1.00 net. *(978-1-931940-66-5(5))* OneHope.

BIBLE—DICTIONARIES

Atkinson, Peter. The Lion Encyclopedia of the Bible. 2014. (ENG., Illus.). 128p. (J). (gr. 4-7). pap. 16.99 *(978-0-7459-6286-3(6))* Lion Hudson PLC GBR. Dist: Independent Pubs. Group.

BIBLE—DRAMA

see Bible As Literature; Bible Plays

BIBLE—FESTIVALS

see Fasts and Feasts

BIBLE—FICTION

see Bible—History of Biblical Events—Fiction

BIBLE—FLOWERS

see Bible—Natural History

BIBLE—GARDENS

see Bible—Natural History

BIBLE—GEOGRAPHY

Bible Maps & Charts for Kids. (Illus.). (gr. 1-6). 16.99 *(978-0-7847-1023-4(6))* Standard Publishing.

Bible Maps for Children: Effectives & Missions Programs. (J). pap. 10.00 *(978-0-8307-1502-2(9))* Gospel Light Pubns.

Concordia Publishing House, creator. Exploring God's Word with Maps. 2014. (ENG., Illus.). 40p. (J). (gr. 4-7). pap. 8.99 *(978-0-7586-4707-8(7))* Concordia Publishing Hse.

Dowley, Tim & David, Juliet. Candle Pop-Up Bible Atlas, 1 vol. Nicholls, Paul, illus. 2014. (ENG.). 16p. (J). bds. 16.99 *(978-1-78128-100-0(9)*, Candle Bks.) Lion Hudson PLC GBR. Dist: Kregel Pubns.

Feiler, Bruce. Walking the Bible: An Illustrated Journey for Kids Through the Greatest Stories Ever Told. Meret, Sasha, tr. Meret, Sasha, illus. 2004. 112p. (J). (gr. 2-7). 16.99 *(978-0-06-051117-3(6))* HarperCollins Pubs.

Martin, Peter. A Time-Travel Guide to the Land of Jesus: Explore the World of the New Testament. 2017. (ENG., Illus.). 64p. (J). (gr. 2-6). 16.99 *(978-0-7459-6589-5(X))* Lion Hudson PLC GBR. Dist: Independent Pubs. Group.

Olson, Marc. The World Jesus Knew: A Curious Kid's Guide to Life in First-Century Palestine. Maybank, Jem, illus. 2017. (ENG.). 64p. (J). (gr. 4-6). 19.99 ***(978-1-5064-2500-9(3)***, Sparkhouse Family) Augsburg Fortress, Pubs.

Snow, Philip. Places of the Bible. Snow, Philip, illus. 2005. (Bible Discover & Colour Ser.). (Illus.). 32p. (J). (gr. -1-7). 4.00 *(978-1-903087-90-9(2))* DayOne Pubns. GBR. Dist: Send The Light Distribution LLC.

BIBLE—HISTORY

Here are entered works on the origin, authorship and composition of the Bible as a book. Works dealing with historical events as described in the Bible are entered under Bible—History of Biblical Events.

Doney, Meryl. How the Bible Came to Us: The Story of the Book That Changed the World. 2003. (Illus.). 48p. (J). (gr. 3-7). pap., pap. 10.99 *(978-0-7459-2098-6(5)*, 0745920985) Cook, David C.

FBS Historias Biblicas Para Preescolares Alumnos. 1.40 *(978-0-7673-4674-0(2))* LifeWay Christian Resources.

Herzog, Joyce. History in His Hands, Volume 1: Study Guide. 2004. (YA). 10.00 *(978-1-887225-14-4(5))* Herzog, Joyce.

Lowry-Manning, Lil. Color God Love: A Bible Study Designed to Excite Children Ages 6-12. 2006. (J). (gr. 1-7). per. 11.95 *(978-1-56167-951-5(8))* American Literary Pr.

Searley, Kevin. Hello, God. 2010. 40p. pap. 23.99 *(978-1-4520-6611-0(6))* AuthorHouse.

Taylor, Kenneth N. La Nueva Biblia en Cuadros para Niños, 1 vol. 2003.Tr. of New Bible in Pictures for Little Eyes. (SPA.). 384p. (J). 16.99 *(978-0-8254-1709-2(0)*, Editorial Portavoz) Kregel Pubns.

BIBLE—HISTORY OF BIBLICAL EVENTS

Cavins, Emily & Christmyer, Sarah. Great Adventure Kids Chart. 2008. (Illus.). pap. 4.95 *(978-1-934217-63-4(8))* Ascension Pr.

Evenson, Wallace. Bible Dates - From Adam to Christ. 2003. 121p. (Orig.). (YA). pap. 7.95 *(978-0-9666834-1-7(2))* Evenson, Laurel.

Foce, Natalia, tr. from ENG. Daniel, el Príncipe que Oraba Apps, Fred, illus. l.t. ed. 2009. (SPA & ENG.). 32p. (J). 3.49 *(978-1-932789-19-5(7))* Editorial Sendas Antiguas, LLC.

—La Historia de Pablo — Viajes de Aventura, 1. Apps, Fred, illus. l.t. ed. 2009. Orig. Title: Journeys of Adventure — the Story of Paul. (SPA & ENG.). 32p. (J). 3.49 *(978-1-932789-23-2(5))* Editorial Sendas Antiguas, LLC.

—Jesus Narrador. Anderson, Jeff, illus. l.t. ed. 2009. Orig. Title: Jesus the Storyteller. (SPA & ENG.). 24p. (J). 3.49 *(978-1-932789-25-6(1))* Editorial Sendas Antiguas, LLC.

—Jesus Salvador. Anderson, Jeff, illus. l.t. ed. 2009. Orig. Title: Jesus the Saviour. (SPA & ENG.). 24p. (J). 3.49 *(978-1-932789-29-4(4))* Editorial Sendas Antiguas, LLC.

—Jesus Sanador. Anderson, Jeff, illus. l.t. ed. 2009. Orig. Title: Jesus the Healer. (SPA & ENG.). 24p. (J). 3.49 *(978-1-932789-27-0(8))* Editorial Sendas Antiguas, LLC.

—El Nacimiento de Jesús: El Niño Prometido, 1. Apps, Fred, illus. l.t. ed. 2009. Orig. Title: The Birth of Jesus — the Promised Child. (SPA & ENG.). 32p. (J). 3.49 *(978-1-932789-20-1(0))* Editorial Sendas Antiguas, LLC.

—La Resurrección: Jesús Está Vivo, 1. Apps, Fred, illus. l.t. ed. 2009. Orig. Title: The Resurrection — Jesus Is Alive. (SPA & ENG.). 32p. (J). 3.49 *(978-1-932789-21-8(9))* Editorial Sendas Antiguas, LLC.

—Samuel, el Niño que Escuchaba. Apps, Fred, illus. l.t. ed. 2009. (SPA & ENG.). 32p. (J). 3.49 *(978-1-932789-17-1(0))* Editorial Sendas Antiguas, LLC.

—Saúl — el Milagro en el Camino, 1. Apps, Fred, illus. l.t. ed. 2009. Orig. Title: Saul — the Miracle on the Road. (SPA & ENG.). 32p. (J). 3.49 *(978-1-932789-22-5(7))* Editorial Sendas Antiguas, LLC.

Hovland, Stephenie. Lydia Believes. Dorenkamp Repa, Michelle, illus. 2014. (Arch Bks.). (ENG.). 16p. (J). (gr. k-4). pap. 2.49 *(978-0-7586-4607-1(0))* Concordia Publishing Hse.

Howat, Irene. 100 Fascinating Bible Facts. 2009. (ENG., Illus.). 176p. pap. 8.99 *(978-1-84550-476-2(3))* Christian Focus Pubns. GBR. Dist: Send The Light Distribution LLC.

MacKenzie, Carine. The Jesus Files. 2005. (ENG., Illus.). 120p. (J). (gr. -1-3). 15.99 *(978-1-84550-040-5(7)*, c73eadbd-917b-485a-9f9f-332952c498fd) Christian Focus Pubns. GBR. Dist: Bookmasters Distribution.

Ward, Elaine M. Old Testament Women. 2003. (ENG., Illus.). 32p. (J). (gr. 3-9). 18.95 *(978-1-59270-011-0(X))* Enchanted Lion Bks., LLC.

Yonge, Charlotte M. The Chosen People: A Compendium of Sacred & Church History for School-Children. 2007. (ENG.). 202p. pap. 20.99 *(978-1-4264-2274-4(1))*; 214p. pap. 22.99 *(978-1-4264-2309-3(8))* Creative Media Partners, LLC.

Zobel-Nolan, Allia. Lift-the-Flap Nativity. Moroney, Trace, illus. 2015. (Lift-The Flap Ser.). (ENG.). 20p. (J). (gr. -1-k). 10.99 *(978-0-7944-3527-1(0)*, Reader's Digest Children's Bks.) Studio Fun International.

BIBLE—HISTORY OF BIBLICAL EVENTS—FICTION

Basaluzzo, Constanza & Stanford, Elisa. The Baby Bible 1,2,3, 1 vol. 2009. (Baby Bible Ser.). (ENG.). 48p. (J). bds. 12.99 *(978-1-4347-6540-6(7))* Cook, David C.

Bateman, Jordan. Dunamis Heroes: Issue #1: the Lost Kingdom. Save, Ken, illus. 2007. 120p. (J). per. *(978-0-9781953-0-4(2))* Dunamis Media.

Baynes, Pauline. El Príncipe Caspian. 2003. (SPA.). pap. *(978-956-13-1670-6(6)*, AB7202) Bello, Andres CHL. Dist: Lectorum Pubns., Inc.

Black, Chuck. Kingdom's Reign, 4 bks. Black, Andrea & Black, Brittney, eds. Johnson, Marcella, illus. 2004. 160p. (YA). per. 9.95 *(978-0-9679240-3-8(0))* Perfect Praise Publishing.

Bledsoe, Amanda. Chores, S'mores!, 1 vol. Perry, Jodi, ed. 2009. 28p. pap. 24.95 *(978-1-60703-605-0(3))* PublishAmerica, Inc.

Booth, Bradley. Escape from Egypt. 2009. (J). pap. 11.99 *(978-0-8163-2305-0(4))* Pacific Pr. Publishing Assn.

—Esther: A Star Is Born. 2009. (J). pap. 12.99 *(978-0-8163-2359-3(3))* Pacific Pr. Publishing Assn.

—Miracles of the Mantle. 2011. (J). pap. 12.99 *(978-0-8163-2453-8(0))* Pacific Pr. Publishing Assn.

—Noah: The Chosen One. 2009. (J). 19.99 *(978-0-8163-2344-9(5))* Pacific Pr. Publishing Assn.

—Noah: The End of the World. 2010. (J). pap. 19.99 *(978-0-8163-2407-1(7))* Pacific Pr. Publishing Assn.

—Prince of Dreams. 2008. (J). pap. 10.99 *(978-0-8163-2253-4(8))* Pacific Pr. Publishing Assn.

—Shepherd Warrior. 2007. 127p. (J). *(978-0-8163-2161-2(2))* Pacific Pr. Pubns.

Broughton, Pamela & Watson, Jane Werner. Miracles of Jesus. Smath, Jerry, illus. 2009. (Little Golden Book Ser.). (ENG.). 24p. (J). (gr. -1-2). 4.99 *(978-0-375-85623-5(4)*, Golden Inspirational) Random Hse. Children's Bks.

Burnett, Mark & Downey, Roma. A Story of God & All of Us Young Readers Edition. 2013. (ENG., Illus.). 224p. (J). (gr. 3-17). pap. 7.99 *(978-0-316-24383-4(3))* Little, Brown Bks. for Young Readers.

Burns, Joanne. Ollie Oyster's Ouch. 2005. 21p. 8.99 *(978-1-4116-5337-5(8))* Lulu Pr., Inc.

Burton, Wade T. Tell Me the Old, Old Story... in a New Way. 2010. 32p. pap. 16.95 *(978-1-4497-0387-5(9)*, WestBow Pr.) Author Solutions, Inc.

Cahill, Bear. We're Brothers & Sisters. Collier, Kevin Scott, illus. 2008. 20p. pap. 9.95 *(978-1-933090-70-2(7))* Guardian Angel Publishing, Inc.

Cohen, Deborah Bodin. Nachshon, Who Was Afraid to Swim: A Passover Story. Jago, illus. 2008. (Passover Ser.). (ENG.). 32p. (J). (gr. -1-3). 17.95 *(978-0-8225-8764-4(5)*, Kar-Ben Publishing) Lerner Publishing Group.

—Papa Jethro. Dippold, Jane, illus. 2007. (Jewish Identity Ser.). (ENG.). 32p. (J). (gr. -1-1). per. 7.95 *(978-1-58013-252-7(9)*, Kar-Ben Publishing) Lerner Publishing Group.

Colvin, Adele. The Donkey of Tarsus: His Tales about the Apostle Paul, 1 vol. Carmichael, Peyton, illus. 2010. (Donkey Tales Ser.). (ENG.). 32p. (J). (gr. k-3). 16.99 *(978-1-58980-780-8(4))* Pelican Publishing Co., Inc.

Currie, Robin. The Baby Bible ABCs, 1 vol. Basaluzzo, Constanza, illus. 2009. (Baby Bible Ser.). (ENG.). 48p. (J). bds. 12.99 *(978-1-4347-6542-0(3))* Cook, David C.

—The Baby Bible Animals, 1 vol. Basaluzzo, Constanza, illus. 2009. (Baby Bible Ser.). (ENG.). 48p. (J). bds. 12.99 *(978-1-4347-6541-3(5))* Cook, David C.

David C. Cook Publishing Company Staff & Currie, Robin. The Baby Bible Sing & Pray. Busaluzzo, Constanza, illus. 2008. (Baby Bible Ser.). (ENG.). 46p. (J). bds. 12.99 *(978-0-7814-4893-2(X))* Cook, David C.

Doyle, Christopher. Amazing Tales & Strange Stories of the Bible. 2009. 64p. (J). (gr. -1). 14.99 *(978-0-7586-1785-9(2))* Concordia Publishing Hse.

Edgren, David. The Serpent Scroll. 2009. (J). 11.99 *(978-0-8163-2330-2(5))* Pacific Pr. Publishing Assn.

Eedle, Arthur. Full Cycle. 2008. 175p. pap. 21.50 *(978-1-4092-1402-1(8))* Lulu Pr., Inc.

Ferguson, Sinclair B. Big Book of Bible Truths 2. Apps, Fred, illus. 2008. (ENG.). 64p. (J). pap. 14.99 *(978-1-84550-372-7(4)*, 9781845503727) Christian Focus Pubns. GBR. Dist: Bookmasters Distribution.

Fox, Ruth M. The Bible, in Story, from the Beginning. 2012. 156p. pap. 53.99 *(978-1-4497-7351-9(6)*, WestBow Pr.) Author Solutions, Inc.

Gadot, A. S. Tower of Babel. Rebora, Cecilia, illus. 2010. 32p. (J). (gr. k-4). lib. bdg. 17.95 *(978-0-8225-9917-3(1)*, Kar-Ben Publishing) Lerner Publishing Group.

Garrelts, Christopher. Squarey Head Tells a Lie. Mayabb, Darrell, ed. 2003. (Adventures of Squarey Head Ser.: Bk. 1). (Illus.). 30p. (J). (gr. k-6). 4.95 *(978-0-9742003-0-9(1))* Squarey Head, Inc.

Gormally, Eleanor. St Paul: The Man with the Letters. 2010. (ENG., Illus.). 32p. (J). pap. 16.95 *(978-1-84730-177-2(0))* Veritas Pubns. IRL. Dist: Dufour Editions, Inc.

Guess, Catherine Ritch. Kipper Finds a Home: A White Squirrel Parable Volume 1. Pace, Christine, illus. 2005. (ENG.). 32p. (J). (gr. -1-7). pap. 13.95 *(978-1-933341-00-2(9))* CRM.

Hardman, Christy. Against the Giant. 2008. 267p. (gr. 3-7). pap. 16.99 *(978-1-59955-117-3(9))* Cedar Fort, Inc./CFI Distribution.

Herskowitz, Benjie. David & Goliath with a Twist. 2013. 34p. pap. *(978-965-550-195-7(7))* Contento De Semrik.

Holter, Bjarden. The Man on My Back: Jesus & His Four-Legged Helpers. 2013. 28p. pap. 13.54 *(978-1-4907-0536-1(8))* Trafford Publishing.

Hyman, Frieda Clark. Victory on the Walls: A Story of Nehemiah. 2005. (Living History Library). 182p. (YA). (gr. 4-7). pap. 12.95 *(978-1-883937-96-6(5))* Bethlehem Bks.

Jakobitz, Marilee. Martha Lu & the Whobegots. 2008. 32p. pap. 24.95 *(978-1-60441-482-0(0))* America Star Bks.

Johnston, Annie. Mary Ware, the Little Colonel's Chum, 1 vol. Barry, Etheldred B., illus. 2005. (Little Colonel Ser.). (ENG.). 336p. (YA). (gr. 3-6). pap. 19.95 *(978-1-56554-813-8(2))* Pelican Publishing Co., Inc.

Kenney, Rebecca. Where I Belong. 2008. (J). 8.99 *(978-1-59166-873-2(5))* BJU Pr.

Kimmel, Eric A. Scarlett & Sam: Escape from Egypt. Stevanovic, Ivica, illus. 2015. (ENG.). 168p. (J). (gr. 1-3). lib. bdg. 15.95 *(978-1-4677-3850-7(6)*, Kar-Ben Publishing) Lerner Publishing Group.

Lester, Julius. Pharaoh's Daughter: A Novel of Ancient Egypt. 2009. (ENG., Illus.). 192p. (J). (gr. 7). pap. 6.99 *(978-0-15-206662-8(4))* Houghton Mifflin Harcourt Publishing Co.

Lovett, Vienna. Mission from God. 2013. 256p. *(978-1-77069-833-8(7))* Word Alive Pr.

Lundy, Charlotte. Thank You, God. Waldrep, Evelyn L., ed. James, Margaret Ray, illus. 2004. 32p. (J). (gr. k-3). 15.95 *(978-0-9670280-9-5(4))* Bay Light Publishing.

MacKenzie, Carine. Little Hands Story Bible. Cosco, Raffaella, illus. rev. ed. 2009. (ENG.). 144p. (J). (gr. -1-3). 10.99 *(978-1-84550-435-9(6)*, 9781845504359) Christian Focus Pubns. GBR. Dist: Bookmasters Distribution.

Martin, Gary & Zondervan Bibles Staff. The Sword of Revenge, 1 vol. Rogers, Bud, ed. Cariello, Sergio, illus. 2009. (Z Graphic Novels / Son of Samson Ser.). (ENG.). 160p. (J). pap. 6.99 *(978-0-310-71285-5(8))* Zondervan.

Martin, Gary & Zondervan Staff. The Heroes of God, 1 vol. Cariello, Sergio, illus. 2009. (Z Graphic Novels / Son of Samson Ser.). (ENG.). 160p. (J). pap. 6.99 *(978-0-310-71284-8(X))* Zondervan.

Martin, Gary, et al. The Maiden of Thunder, 1 vol. Cariello, Sergio & Lanphear, Dave, illus. 2008. (Z Graphic Novels / Son of Samson Ser.). (ENG.). 160p. (J). (gr. 4-7). pap. 6.99 *(978-0-310-71281-7(5))* Zondervan.

McCaughrean, Geraldine. Not the End of the World. 2005. 256p. (YA). (gr. 5-8). (ENG.). 16.99 *(978-0-06-076030-4(3))*; lib. bdg. 17.89 *(978-0-06-076031-1(1))* HarperCollins Pubs. (HarperTeen).

Meek, Carol. Believer Boy's Power. 2007. 32p. (J). pap. 9.00 *(978-0-8059-7249-8(8))* Dorrance Publishing Co., Inc.

Merritt, Virginia. A Ram for Isaac. 2009. (J). *(978-1-59166-983-8(9))* BJU Pr.

Miklowitz, Gloria D. Masada: The Last Fortress. 2004. 198p. (YA). (gr. 4-7). 16.00 *(978-0-8028-5165-9(7))* Eerdmans, William B. Publishing Co.

Miller, Christopher & Miller, Allan. The Legend of Ten-Gallon Sam & the Perilous Mine, 2 bks., Bk.2. Miller, Christopher & Miller, Allan, illus. 2007. (Heroes of Promise Ser.). (ENG., Illus.). 32p. (J). (gr. -1-5). 12.99 *(978-1-59317-225-1(7))* Warner Pr., Inc.

Miller, Mike S. Confession, 1 vol. Ninaltowski, Eric, illus. 2008. (Z Graphic Novels / Hand of the Morning Star Ser.). (ENG.). 160p. (YA). (gr. 8-11). pap. 6.99 *(978-0-310-71371-5(4))* Zondervan.

Morgan-Cole, Trudy J. Esther: Courage to Stand. 2010. 144p. (J). pap. 12.99 *(978-0-8280-2430-3(8))* Review & Herald Publishing Assn.

Napoli, Donna Jo. Song of the Magdalene. 2004. (ENG., Illus.). 256p. (YA). (gr. 7). pap. 12.99 *(978-0-689-87396-6(4)*, Simon Pulse) Simon Pulse.

Pearson, Mary Rose. Bible Town Detectives. 2003. 96p. (J). pap. 9.99 *(978-0-8054-3923-6(4))* B&H Publishing Group.

Publications International Ltd. Staff, ed. Lights & Music Treasury. 2010. 160p. (J). bds. 16.98 *(978-1-4127-7911-1(1))* Phoenix International Publications, Inc.

Quansah, Carol-Ann. The Garden. 2010. 40p. pap. 22.65 *(978-1-4535-1345-3(0))* Xlibris Corp.

Ray, Christie Jones & Ray, Christie Jones. Eliza Will Not Be Afraid. 2012. (Illus.). 24p. pap. 12.00 *(978-0-9853223-7-3(3))* Rose Water Cottage Pr.

Reed, Lynn. Shannon's Search for the Lost Ark. 2010. 52p. pap. 22.99 *(978-1-4490-0392-0(3))* AuthorHouse.

Ricchi, Brenda. The Grandchildren's Bible Journeys - the Creation Story. 2010. 35p. pap. 17.00 *(978-0-557-14903-2(7))* Lulu Pr., Inc.

Schall, Jane. Jump at the Sun Bible Classics David & Goliath. Roos, Maryn, illus. 2007. (ENG.). (J). (gr. -1-2). pap. 3.50 *(978-0-7868-5517-9(7)*, Jump at the Sun) Hyperion Bks. for Children.

—Jump at the Sun Bible Classics Jonah & the Whale. Roos, Maryn, illus. 2007. (ENG.). (J). (gr. -1-2). pap. 3.50 (978-0-7868-5518-6(5), Jump at the Sun) Hyperion Bks. for Children.

Scripture Teachers: Solomon & Friends Learn about Being Wonderfully Made. 2003. pap. (978-0-9712894-3-7(3)) Lighthouse Christian Products Co.

Scripture Teachers: Solomon & Friends Learn about Forgiveness. 2003. pap. (978-0-9712894-1-3(7)) Lighthouse Christian Products Co.

Scripture Teachers: Solomon & Friends Learn about Prayer. 2003. pap. (978-0-9712894-0-6(9)) Lighthouse Christian Products Co.

Scripture Teachers: Solomon & Friends Learn about Trusting God. 2003. pap. (978-0-9712894-2-0(5)) Lighthouse Christian Products Co.

Snyder, Laurel. The Longest Night: A Passover Story. Chien, Catia, illus. 2013. (ENG.). 40p. (J). (gr. -1-3). 17.99 (978-0-375-86942-6(5), Schwartz & Wade Bks.) Random Hse. Children's Bks.

Speer, Laura Y. The Good Ground Seeds. 2008. 20p. pap. 10.95 (978-1-4343-7576-6(5)) AuthorHouse.

Terbay, Susan Handle. Jeremiah & the Man, 6 vols., Vol. 1. Mariants, tr. Children-Oln, illus. 2007. 43p. (J). (gr. 1-6). pap. (978-0-9628309-8-3(4)) Marianist Pr.

Thomas Nelson Publishing Staff. The Pirates Who Don't Do Anything - Veggietales Movie: Squawk-Along Songs & Games. 2008. (Adventures in Odyssey Activity Pack Ser.). 48p. (J). pap. 12.99 (978-1-4003-1235-1(3)) Nelson, Thomas Inc.

—The Pirates Who Don't Do Anything: A VeggieTales Movie: Rowboat Bible Stories. 2008. 64p. (J). pap. 17.99 (978-1-4003-1232-0(9)) Nelson, Thomas Inc.

—The Pirates Who Don't Do Anything: A VeggieTales Movie: Spyglass Bible Theater Guide. 2008. 64p. (J). pap. 12.99 (978-1-4003-1227-6(2)) Nelson, Thomas Inc.

Trachtman, Joseph, illus. & narrated by. Kosher Tales: Not So Grim Stories for Children. Trachtman, Joseph, narrated by. 2007.Tr. of Kosher Tales. (ENG & YID.). 86p. (J). pap. 25.00 (978-0-9795170-0-6(1)) Trachtman, Joseph.

Travis, Lucille. Timna. 2009. (ENG.). 168p. (J). (gr. 3-9). pap. 9.99 (978-0-8361-9484-5(5)) Herald Pr.

Wallace, Lew. Ben-Hur. (SPA., Illus.). (YA). 11.95 (978-84-7281-099-0(2), AF1099) Auriga, Ediciones S.A. ESP. Dist: Continental Bk. Co., Inc.

Wiedeman, Connie. Grandma, Do Angels Have Wings?, 1 vol. Gaston, Sierra, illus. 2010. 40p. 24.95 (978-1-4512-1054-5(X)) PublishAmerica, Inc.

Wilkinson, Simon. Noah's Ark Black & White Visual Development Book for Babies. 2008. 34p. pap. 17.95 (978-1-4092-4702-9(3)) Lulu Pr., Inc.

Youd, Pauline. I Wonder . . . Books: Pack 1, 6 bks. Garvin, Elaine, illus. Incl. Why Did Sarah Laugh? pap. 1.50 (978-0-8198-8275-2(5)); Why Was Daniel Scared? pap. 1.50 (978-0-8198-8282-0(8)); Why Was David Brave? pap. 1.50 (978-0-8198-8280-6(1)); Why Was Pharoah Puzzled? pap. 1.50 (978-0-8198-8278-3(X)); Why Was the Shepherd Glad? pap. 1.50 (978-0-8198-8276-9(3)); Pack 1. Why Did Nehemiah Work So Hard? pap. 1.50 (978-0-8198-8279-0(8)); 16p. (J). (gr. 2-4). 1996. (Illus.). 7.95 (978-0-8198-3675-5(3)) Pauline Bks. & Media.

—I Wonder . . . Books: Pack 2, 6 bks. Garvin, Elaine, illus. Incl. Why Was Andrew Surprised? pap. 1.50 (978-0-8198-8285-1(2)); Why Was Deborah Mad? pap. 1.50 (978-0-8198-8286-8(0)); Why Was Gideon Worried? pap. 2.95 (978-0-8198-8283-7(6)); Why Was Jeremiah Sad? pap. 2.95 (978-0-8198-8277-6(1)); Why Was Mary Embarrassed? pap. 1.50 (978-0-8198-8284-4(4)); Pack 2. Why Did Elijah Hide? pap. 1.50 (978-0-8198-8287-5(9)); 16p. (J). (gr. 2-4). 1996. (Illus.). 7.95 (978-0-8198-3676-2(1)) Pauline Bks. & Media.

Zondervan Staff. The Story for Kids: Later Elementary Curriculum - 31 Lessons, 1 vol. 2011. (Story Ser.). (ENG.). cd-rom 34.99 (978-0-310-71922-9(4)) Zonderkidz.

BIBLE—INTERPRETATION

see Bible—Commentaries

BIBLE—INTRODUCTIONS

see Bible—Study

BIBLE—LANGUAGE, STYLE

see Bible As Literature

BIBLE—LITERARY CHARACTER

see Bible As Literature

BIBLE—MAPS

see Bible—Geography

BIBLE—NATURAL HISTORY

Animals of the Bible. (Illus.). 16p. (J). pap. 1.50 (978-0-87162-874-9(0), E6035) Warner Pr., Inc.

Coburn, Claudia. Did the Aardvarks Say "No Ark"? Hoard, Angela, illus. 2004. 32p. (J). (978-0-9759343-1-9(7)) Purfect Promises.

Currie, Robin. Baby Bible Animals. 2003. (Baby Bible Ser.). (Illus.). 48p. (J). bds. 12.99 (978-0-7814-3865-0(9), 0781438659) Cook, David C.

Dowley, Tim. Bible Animal Stencil Book, 1 vol. 2008. 6p. (J). bds. 11.99 (978-0-8254-7365-4(9), Candle Bks.) Lion Hudson PLC GBR. Dist: Kregel Pubns.

Hahn, Samuel J. Stories Told under the Sycamore Tree: Bible Plant Object Lessons. Patton, Scott, tr. Patton, Scott, illus. 2003. 191p. (J). pap. 19.95 (978-0-7880-1972-2(4)) CSS Publishing Co.

Johnson, Nancy Pelander. 44 Animals of the Bible. Hight, Lloyd R., illus. 2014. (ENG.). 44p. (J). (gr. -1-3). 9.99 (978-0-89051-843-4(2)) Master Bks.

Nolan, Allia Zobel. Touch & Feel Bible Animal Friends. Steele-Morgan, Alex, illus. 2004. (Touch & Feel Ser.). 12p. (J). bds. 10.99 (978-0-8254-5512-4(X)) Kregel Pubns.

Smith, Laurie Chance. Snapshots: Nature Stories in the Bible. 2012. 128p. (J). pap. 19.99 (978-0-8280-2689-5(0)) Review & Herald Publishing Assn.

Snow, Philip. Animals of the Bible. Snow, Philip, illus. 2005. (Bible Discover & Colour Ser.). (Illus.). 32p. (J). (gr. -1-7). 4.00 (978-1-903087-88-6(0)) DayOne Pubns. GBR. Dist: Send The Light Distribution LLC.

—Birds of the Bible. Snow, Philip, illus. 2005. (Bible Discover & Colour Ser.). (Illus.). 32p. (J). (gr. -1-7). 4.00 (978-1-903087-89-3(9)) DayOne Pubns. GBR. Dist: Send The Light Distribution LLC.

—Plants of the Bible. Snow, Philip, illus. 2005. (Bible Discover & Colour Ser.). (Illus.). 32p. (J). (gr. -1-7). 4.00 (978-1-903087-91-6(0)) DayOne Pubns. GBR. Dist: Send The Light Distribution LLC.

BIBLE—NEW TESTAMENT

Arthur, Kay & Arndt, Janna. Bible Prophecy for Kids: Revelation 1-7. 2006. (ENG., Illus.). 160p. (J). (gr. -1). per. 11.99 (978-0-7369-1527-4(3)) Harvest Hse. Pubs.

Bible Visuals International Staff, compiled by. Priesthood of Christ Vol. 36: New Testament. 2005. (Illus.). (J). pap. (978-1-932381-61-0(9), 1036) Bible Visuals International, Inc.

Brost, Corey. Gospel Connections for Teens: Reflections for Sunday Mass, Cycle A. 2007. 129p. per. 6.25 (978-0-88489-643-2(9)) St. Mary's Pr. of MN.

Calaway, Bernie L. & Ledford, Jan Roadarmel. Operation Revelation: A Teen's Script to Earth's Final Curtain. 2006. 195p. pap. 24.95 (978-1-4241-1657-7(0)) America Star Bks.

DeVries, Mike, et al. Acts: Face of the Fire. 2003. (No Limits Discipleship Ser.). (ENG.). 120p. (gr. 3-7). per. 12.99 (978-0-8341-5006-5(9), 083-415-0069) Beacon Hill Pr. of Kansas City.

Greiner, Ruth B. Christ & the Church Vol. 42: New Testament Volume 42 Revelation Part 1. Olson, Ed, illus. 2010. 36p. (J). pap. (978-1-932381-29-0(5), 1042) Bible Visuals International, Inc.

—Faith Volume 5: New Testament. Hertzler, Frances H.. et al, illus. 2004. 36p. (J). pap. (978-1-932381-36-8(8)) Bible Visuals International, Inc.

—Repentance Vol. 6: New Testament Volume 6, Life of Christ, Part 6. 2006. (Illus.). 40p. (J). pap. (978-1-932381-04-7(X), 1006) Bible Visuals International, Inc.

—The Saviour Vol. 3: New Testament Volume 3: the Life of Christ Part 3: Everybody Needs Jesus. Hertzler, Frances H.. et al, illus. 2004. (ENG.). 36p. (J). pap. (978-1-932381-02-3(3), 1003) Bible Visuals International, Inc.

Greiner, Ruth B., et al. Eternity Vol. 45: New Testament , Revelation Part 4: the Lord Reigns Forever. Henkel, Vernon et al, illus. 2005. 36p. (J). pap. (978-1-932381-31-3(7), 1045) Bible Visuals International, Inc.

—GOD His Son, His Book, His Home: New Testament Introductory Volume. Hertzler, Frances H.. & Olson, Ed, illus. 2004. 32p. (J). pap. (978-1-932381-35-1(X), 1000) Bible Visuals International, Inc.

—Sin Vol. 4: New Testament Volume 4, Life of Christ, Part 4. Hertzler, Frances H.. et al, illus. 2005. 36p. (J). pap. (978-1-932381-23-8(6), 1004) Bible Visuals International, Inc.

Hardy, Janet Norris. The Four in One: The Four Gospels from the King James Version Merged into a Single Narrative. 2003. 235p. (gr. 1-12). pap. 16.95 (978-0-9743567-0-9(0)) CSE Publishing.

Harman, Debbie G. Jesus Said- 2004. (Illus.). 17.95 (978-1-59156-091-3(8)) Covenant Communications, Inc.

Hertzler, Frances B. & Ober, Jonathan, illus. The Eternal God Vol. 1: New Testament. 2004. 36p. (J). pap. (978-1-932381-03-0(1), 1001) Bible Visuals International, Inc.

Holman Csb Student New Testament. 2003. (J). (gr. 7-12). 1.50 (978-0-633-09343-3(2)) LifeWay Christian Resources.

Kiefer, Velma, et al. Fellowship, Enjoying God Vol. 41: New Testament Volume 41: 1, 2 & 3 John & Jude. Henkel, Vernon et al, illus. 2004. (ENG.). 36p. (J). pap. (978-1-932381-00-9(7), 1041) Bible Visuals International, Inc.

King, Wanda Fulbright. Fundamentals: Living it Out Study of Book of James, Oldr Child Bk. (J). (gr. 1-6). (978-0-633-05792-3(4)) LifeWay Christian Resources.

—Fundamentals: Living it Out Study of Book of James, Yngr Child Bk. (J). (gr. 1-6). (978-0-633-05793-0(2)) LifeWay Christian Resources.

Lingo, Susan L. Who's Who Object Talks That Teach about the New Testament. 2003. (ENG.). 48p. (J). (gr. k-6). pap. 7.99 (978-0-7847-1312-9(X), 42010, B&H Kids) B&H Publishing Group.

Lyster, R. Iona, et al. The Inspiration of the Scriptures: New Testament Volume 33: 1 & 2 Timothy, Titus, Philemon. Hertzler, Frances & Olson, Ed, illus. 2004. 34p. (J). pap. (978-1-932381-05-4(8), 1033) Bible Visuals International, Inc.

Martin, Harold S. Brethren New Testament Commentary - James & Jude. 2003. (ENG.). 10.00 (978-0-9745027-1-7(5)) Brethren Revival Fellowship.

Martin, Harold S., comment. Brethren New Testament Commentary - Colossians & Philemon. 2003. (ENG.). 10.00 (978-0-9745027-0-0(7)) Brethren Revival Fellowship.

Mooney, Belinda. Itty-Bitty Book: New Testament. 2006. (J). pap. 1.49 (978-1-59317-167-4(6)) Warner Pr., Inc.

Neeley, Deta Petersen & Neeley, Nathan Glen. Paul of Tarsus, V2: A Child's Story of the New Testament. 2011. 152p. 41.95 (978-1-258-07519-4(9)) Literary Licensing, LLC.

Perrotta, Kevin & Darring, Gerald. John 11-21: My Peace I Give You. Perrotta, Kevin, ed. 2004. (Six Weeks with the Bible for Catholic Teens Ser.). (ENG.). 96p. (gr. 8-12). pap. 7.95 (978-0-8294-2084-5(3)) Loyola Pr.

—Luke: The Good News of God's Mercy. Perrotta, Kevin, ed. 2004. (Six Weeks with the Bible for Catholic Teens Ser.). (ENG.). 96p. (gr. 8-12). pap. 7.95 (978-0-8294-2052-4(5)) Loyola Pr.

—Revelation: God's Gift of Hope. Perrotta, Kevin, ed. 2004. (Six Weeks with the Bible for Catholic Teens Ser.). (ENG.). 96p. (gr. 8-12). pap. 7.95 (978-0-8294-2049-4(5)) Loyola Pr.

Reymond, Robert L. Paul, Missionary Theologian: A Survey of His Missionary Labours & Theology. 2006. (ENG., Illus.). 640p. 29.99 (978-1-85792-497-8(5), 4f6c4fe5-c6c9-413f-b275-d3a21f0ca0b0, Mentor) Christian Focus Pubns. GBR. Dist: Bookmasters Distribution.

Ross, Melanie H. & Guymon-King. Primary Partners: New Testament. 2004. cd-rom 12.95 (978-1-59156-165-1(5)) Covenant Communications, Inc.

Route 52 Staff & Jackson, Carol A. Follow Jesus: 52 Bible Lessons from the Life of Christ for Ages 6-8. 2004. (Route 52(tm) Ser.). (ENG.). 320p. (J). pap. 32.99 (978-0-7847-1328-0(6), 42077) Standard Publishing.

Rowland, Wil. Wise & Silly. 2011. (Illus.). (J). (978-1-56722-857-1(7)) Word Aflame Pr.

Standard Publishing Staff. Grow up in Christ: 52 Bible Lessons from the New Testament for Ages 8-12. 2003. (Route 52(tm) Ser.). (ENG., Illus.). 320p. (J). (gr. 4-7). per. 32.99 (978-0-7847-1628-1(5)) Standard Publishing.

Taylor, Damon J. Aprende de las Emociones con la Biblia. 2004. (Mis Calcetines Ser.). (SPA., Illus.). 24p. 5.99 (978-0-8254-0775-8(3), Editorial Portavoz) Kregel Pubns.

Tilley, Steve, et al. Airlock. 2004. (Illus.). 80p. pap. (978-1-84427-050-7(5)) Scripture Union.

—Airlock: Becoming. 2004. (Illus.). 80p. pap. (978-1-84427-048-4(3)) Scripture Union.

Yaconelli, Mike. Devotion: A Raw-Truth Journal on Following Jesus, 1 vol. 2004. (Invert Ser.). (ENG., Illus.). 80p. (YA). pap. 10.99 (978-0-310-25559-8(7)) Zondervan.

BIBLE—OLD TESTAMENT

Award, Anna. Moses in the Bulrushes: See the Picture & Say the Word. 2012. (ENG., Illus.). 24p. (J). pap. 6.50 (978-1-84135-602-0(6)) Award Pubns. Ltd. GBR. Dist: Parkwest Pubns., Inc.

Beck, William F. Bible Stories in Pictures. Rogers, Ruth W. et al, illus. 2nd ed. 2003.Tr. of Bible Stories in Pictures. (ALB, SPA & SWE.). 376p. pap. 10.65 (978-1-931891-08-0(7)) Multi-Language Pubns.

Beginnings II - God's Promises - Answer Key: Old Testament Lessons for Young Readers. 2005. (Beginnings II Ser.). 32p. (J). spiral bd. 6.99 (978-1-889015-03-3(2)) Explorer's Bible Study.

Bible Visuals International Staff, compiled by. Discovering God's Ways Vol. 17: Old Testament. 2005. (Illus.). (J). pap. (978-1-932381-77-1(5), 2017) Bible Visuals International, Inc.

—God Is Sovereign Vol. 27: Old Testament. 2006. (Illus.). (J). pap. (978-1-932381-87-0(2), 2027) Bible Visuals International, Inc.

—Godliness Vol. 23: Old Testament. 2006. (Illus.). (J). pap. (978-1-932381-81-8(3), 2021) Bible Visuals International, Inc.

—Godly/Ungodly Living Vol. 26: Old Testament. 2006. (Illus.). (J). pap. (978-1-932381-86-3(4), 2026) Bible Visuals International, Inc.

—God's Chosen People: Old Testament Volume 12. 2005. (Illus.). (J). pap. (978-1-932381-74-0(0), 2012) Bible Visuals International, Inc.

—God's Faithfulness Vol. 15: Old Testament. 2005. (Illus.). (J). pap. (978-1-932381-34-4(1), 2015) Bible Visuals International, Inc.

—God's King Vol. 22: Old Testament. 2006. (Illus.). (J). pap. (978-1-932381-82-5(1), 2022) Bible Visuals International, Inc.

—The Grace of God Volume 19: Old Testament. 2005. (Illus.). (J). pap. (978-1-932381-79-5(1), 2019) Bible Visuals International, Inc.

Blumenthal, Scott. The Explorer's Bible/By Scott E. Blumenthal. 2006. (Illus.). (978-0-87441-793-7(7)) Behrman Hse., Inc.

Bower, Gary. The Hurry-Up Exit from Egypt. Chotiner, Barbara, illus. 2017. (Faith That God Built Book Ser.). (ENG.). 32p. (J). 14.99 (978-1-4964-1745-9(3)) Tyndale Hse. Pubs.

Busch, Melinda Kay. The Fiery Furnace. Koehler, Ed, illus. 2004. (Arch Bks.). 16p. (J). (gr. k-4). 1.99 (978-0-7586-0479-8(3)) Concordia Publishing Hse.

Daly, Jude. To Everything There Is a Season. Daly, Jude, illus. 2006. (Illus.). 32p. (Orig.). (J). (gr. -1-3). 16.00 (978-0-8028-5286-1(6), Eerdmans Bks For Young Readers) Eerdmans, William B. Publishing Co.

Donaher, D. F. & Bibleco. Biblemania: The Old Testament Magazine. 2003. (Illus.). (YA). pap. 8.95 (978-0-9746058-0-7(8)) Bibleco, Inc.

Ehrlich, Amy. With a Mighty Hand: The Story in the Torah. Nevins, Daniel, illus. 2013. (ENG.). 224p. (J). (gr. k-12). 29.99 (978-0-7636-4395-9(5)) Candlewick Pr.

Eisenberg, Ann & Schanzer, Rosalyn. Bible Heroes I Can Be. 2004. (Illus.). 20p. (J). (gr. -1-18). 6.95 (978-1-58013-124-7(7), Kar-Ben Publishing) Lerner Publishing Group.

Feiler, Bruce. Walking the Bible: An Illustrated Journey for Kids Through the Greatest Stories Ever Told. Meret, Sasha, tr. Meret, Sasha, illus. 2004. 112p. (J). (gr. 2-7). 16.99 (978-0-06-051117-3(6)) HarperCollins Pubs.

French, Fiona. Paradise: With Words from the King James Bible. 2004. (ENG., Illus.). 32p. (J). (gr. -1-3). (978-1-84507-007-6(0)) ReiseArt Buchhandlung GmbH.

Ham, Ken & Ham, Mally. A Is for Adam: The Gospel from Genesis. 2011. (Illus.). 77p. (J). spiral bd. 16.99 (978-0-89051-625-6(1)) Master Bks.

James, M. R. Old Testament Legends: Being Stories Out of Some of the Less Known Apocryphal Books of the Old Testament 1913. 2007. 120p. per. 10.95 (978-1-60312-073-9(4)); 22.95 (978-1-60312-978-7(2)) Aegypan.

JBible Visuals International, compiled by. God's Discipline Vol. 13: Old Testament. 2005. (Illus.). (J). pap. (978-1-932381-75-7(9), 2013) Bible Visuals International, Inc.

Kendall, R. T. Between the Times: Malachi: God's Last Prophet of the Old Testament. 2010. (ENG.). 208p. pap. 12.99 (978-1-85792-792-4(3), bf4d90e6-d439-4e58-93f9-ed6e19bc1571, Christian Focus) Christian Focus Pubns. GBR. Dist: Bookmasters Distribution.

Lersch, Jean. Scrapbook: Faith for Life2 Course Three. Janssen, Patricia E., ed. 2nd ed. 2003. (J). stu. ed., spiral bd. 14.99 (978-0-9727146-4-8(2)) LOGOS System Assocs.

The Life & Accomplishments of the Prophet Shmuel: Based on Sefer Shmuel. 2008. (ENG & HEB., Illus.). 36p. (J). 20.00 (978-0-615-19548-3(2)) Keszler, E.

Lingo, Susan L. Who's Who Object Talks That Teach about the Old Testament. 2003. (ENG.). 48p. (J). (gr. k-6). pap. 7.99 (978-0-7847-1311-2(1), 42009, B&H Kids) B&H Publishing Group.

Lottridge, Celia Barker. Stories from Adam & Eve to Ezekiel, 1 vol. Clement, Gary, illus. 2004. (ENG.). 144p. (J). 24.95 (978-0-88899-490-5(7)) Groundwood Bks. CAN. Dist: Publishers Group West (PGW).

MacKenzie, Carine. Wise Words to Follow: Words of wisdom from the book of Proverbs. 2009. (ENG., Illus.). 24p. (J). 7.99 (978-1-84550-430-4(5), df4c3c1d-0da3-460b-89a2-d274e5f6e2d0) Christian Focus Pubns. GBR. Dist: Bookmasters Distribution.

—Wise Words to Obey: Words of wisdom from the book of Proverbs. 2009. (ENG., Illus.). 24p. (J). 7.99 (978-1-84550-431-1(3), f9c1af98-7597-4d79-9bcc-9589b7d1ddd8) Christian Focus Pubns. GBR. Dist: Bookmasters Distribution.

—Wise Words to Trust: Words of wisdom from the book of Proverbs. 2009. (ENG., Illus.). 24p. (J). 7.99 (978-1-84550-432-8(1), 208c0c67-fced-4e86-9b47-ac39af3768a5) Christian Focus Pubns. GBR. Dist: Bookmasters Distribution.

Martin, Mildred A. Wisdom & the Millers: Proverbs for Children. Burkholder, Edith, illus. 2009. 159p. (J). (978-1-884377-15-0(7)); pap. (978-1-884377-14-3(9)) Green Pastures Pr.

Mooney, Belinda. Itty-Bitty Book: Old Testament. 2006. (J). pap. 1.49 (978-1-59317-166-7(8)) Warner Pr., Inc.

Paluch, Beily. I am a Torah: A Playful Action Rhyme. Argoff, Patti, illus. 2004. 12p. (J). bds. 5.95 (978-1-929628-18-6(8)) Hachai Publishing.

—I Am a Torah: A Playful Action Rhyme. Agroff, Patti, illus. 2014. 12p. (J). bds. 6.95 (978-1-929628-84-1(6)) Hachai Publishing.

Perrotta, Kevin & Darring, Gerald. Exodus: God to the Rescue. Perrotta, Kevin, ed. 2004. (Six Weeks with the Bible for Catholic Teens Ser.). (ENG.). 96p. (gr. 9-12). pap. 7.95 (978-0-8294-2051-7(7)) Loyola Pr.

—God Makes a Start. Perrotta, Kevin, ed. 2004. (Six Weeks with the Bible for Catholic Teens Ser.). (ENG.). 96p. (gr. 8-12). pap. 7.95 (978-0-8294-2050-0(9)) Loyola Pr.

Perry, Marilyn. The Adventures of David: The Story of a Shepherd Who Became King, 4 bklts. 2003. (ENG., Illus.). 208p. (J). (gr. 10-10). pap., pap. 69.95 (978-1-55145-483-2(1)) Wood Lake Publishing, Inc. CAN. Dist: Westminster John Knox Pr.

Piepgrass, Arlene. Death, the Wages of Sin Vol. 14: Old Testament Volume 14, Numbers Part 2. Brubaker, Audrey et al, eds. 2009. (ENG., Illus.). 36p. (J). pap. (978-1-932381-07-8(4), 2014) Bible Visuals International, Inc.

—Joseph, a Picture of the Lord Jesus Christ Part 1 Pt. 1, Vol. 4: Old Testament Volume 04 Genesis Part 4. Henkel, Vernon, illus. 2015. 36p. (J). pap. (978-1-932381-69-6(4), 2004) Bible Visuals International, Inc.

Piepgrass, Arlene S. Sacrifice Vol. 11: Old Testament Volume 11, Leviticus Part 1: the Way to God. Neal, Sharon, ed. 2009. (ENG., Illus.). 36p. (J). pap. (978-1-932381-06-1(6), 2011) Bible Visuals International, Inc.

Regina Press Staff. Old Testament for Children. (J). (gr. -1-3). 1.95 (978-0-88271-044-0(3)) Regina Pr., Malhame & Co.

Russell, Patricia Constance. Beginnings II - God's Promises: Old Testament Lessons for Young Readers. Murtha, Dee M., ed. 2005. (Beginnings II Ser.). 301p. (J). stu. ed., spiral bd., wbk. ed. 23.99 (978-1-889015-01-9(6)) Explorer's Bible Study.

Sanders, Nancy I. The Fall into Sin: Genesis 2-3 for Children. Van Severen, Joe, illus. 2004. (Arch Bks.). (ENG.). 16p. (J). 1.99 (978-0-7586-0618-1(4)) Concordia Publishing Hse.

Steinkühler, Martina. The First Good Shepherd: Psalm 23 for Children. Holzmann, Angela, illus. 2015. (ENG.). 28p. 12.95 (978-0-8091-6774-6(3)) Paulist Pr.

BIBLE—OLD TESTAMENT—BIOGRAPHY

Barberet, Denise-Renée. Samson. (Money at its Best: Millionaires of the Old Testament Ser.). 112p. (YA). (gr. 7-12). 2009. 24.95 (978-1-4222-0475-7(8)) 2007. pap. 14.95 (978-1-4222-0850-2(8)) Mason Crest.

Davis, Cameron Christine. Job. 2007. (Money at its Best: Millionaires of the Old Testament Ser.). 112p. (YA). (gr. 7-18). pap. 14.95 (978-1-4222-0846-5(X)) Mason Crest.

—Job: A Biography of Job. 2009. (Money at its Best: Millionaires of the Old Testament Ser.). 112p. (YA). (gr. 7-12). 24.95 (978-1-4222-0471-9(5)) Mason Crest.

Frank, Penny. La Nueva Familia de Rut.Tr. of Ruth's New Family. (SPA.). (J). 1.99 (978-1-56063-785-1(4), 490315) Editorial Unilit.

Hoak, Benjamin T. Jacob. (Money at its Best: Millionaires of the Old Testament Ser.). 112p. (YA). (gr. 7-12). 2009. 24.95 (978-1-4222-0470-2(7)) 2007. pap. 14.95 (978-1-4222-0845-8(1)) Mason Crest.

Neff, Merlin L. Conquering Heroes. 2008. (J). (978-0-8163-2265-7(1)) Pacific Pr. Pubns.

Paden, Cheryl A. Daniel. 2007. (Money at its Best: Millionaires of the Old Testament Ser.). 112p. (YA). (gr. 7-18). pap. 14.95 (978-1-4222-0842-7(7)) Mason Crest.

—The Life of Daniel. 2009. (Money at its Best: Millionaires of the Old Testament Ser.). 112p. (YA). (gr. 7-12). 24.95 (978-1-4222-0467-2(7)) Mason Crest.

Pennington, Jack & Tank, Daniel, illus. Joseph. 2004. 87p. (J). pap. (978-0-8280-1855-5(3)) Review & Herald Publishing Assn.

Sanders, Nancy I. King David, 1 vol. 2014. (Get to Know Ser.). (ENG.). 128p. (J). pap. 7.99 (978-0-310-74475-7(X)) Zonderkidz.

Vitale, Raoul & Tank, Daniel, illus. Adam & Eve. 2005. (Family Bible Story Ser.). 93p. (J). pap. (978-0-8280-1851-7(0)) Review & Herald Publishing Assn.

Warner Press Kids, creator. Queen Esther. 2008. (Illus.). 16p. (J). (gr. -1-2). pap. 11.34 (978-1-59317-220-6(6)) Warner Pr., Inc.

White, John, Jr. & Tank, Daniel, illus. Abraham. 2004. (Family Bible Story Ser.). 109p. (J). pap. (978-0-8280-1857-9(X)) Review & Herald Publishing Assn.

Woodruff, Stephen B. Esther. (Money at its Best: Millionaires of the Old Testament Ser.). 112p. (YA). (gr. 7-12). 2009. 24.95 (978-1-4222-0469-6(3)) 2007. pap. 14.95 (978-1-4222-0844-1(3)) Mason Crest.

Zediker, Rose Ross. Wealth in Biblical Times. (Money at its Best: Millionaires of the Old Testament Ser.). 112p. (YA). (gr. 7-12). 2009. 24.95 (978-1-4222-0477-1(4)) 2007. pap. 14.95 (978-1-4222-0852-6(4)) Mason Crest.

Zondervan Staff. Queen Esther Helps God's People, 1 vol. Pulley, Kelly, illus. 2008. (I Can Read! / the Beginner's Bible

Ser.). (ENG.). 32p. (J). pap. 3.99 *(978-0-310-71815-4(5))* Zonderkidz.

BIBLE—OLD TESTAMENT—PSALMS

Bluedorn, Johannah, illus. The Lord Builds the House: The 127th Psalm. 2004. 32p. (J). 10.00 *(978-0-9743616-1-1(5))* Trivium Pursuit.

Delval, Marie-Hélène. Psalms for Young Children. Arno, illus. 2008. (ENG.). 88p. (J). (gr. -1-3). 16.50 *(978-0-8028-5322-6(6)*, Eerdmans Bks For Young Readers) Eerdmans, William B. Publishing Co.

Group Publishing Staff, contrib. by. Kids' Travel Guide to the 23rd Psalm. 2009. (ENG.). 114p. (gr. k-5). pap. 19.99 *(978-0-7644-4005-2(5))* Group Publishing, Inc.

Hunt, Susan. Sammy & His Shepherd. Godbey, Corey, illus. 2008. (J). *(978-1-56769-109-2(9))* Reformation Pubs.

Land of Milk & Honey, 2 vols. 2008. (LMH Ser.). (Illus.). (J). Bk. 5. bds. 6.99 *(978-0-7814-4529-0(9))*Bk. 6. bds. 6.99 *(978-0-7814-4530-6(2))* Cook, David C.

Legacy Press Staff & Davis, Mary J. My Praise Journal: A Celebration of Psalms for Kids. 2004. (Journals Just for Kids Ser.). (Illus.). 144p. (J). (gr. 4-7). pap. 9.99 *(978-1-885358-71-4(7)*, Legacy Pr.) Rainbow Pubs. & Legacy Pr.

Moreland, Melanie, illus. Psalm 148: Let all Heaven & Earth Praise the Lord! 2006. 32p. (J). *(978-0-9779194-0-6(4)*, Psalms for Kidz) Little Sprout Publishing Hse.

—Psalm 23: The Lord Is my Shepherd. I am His Lamb. 2007. 32p. (J). 10.00 *(978-0-9779194-1-3(2)*, Psalms for Kidz) Little Sprout Publishing Hse.

Ruth, Peggy Joyce. My Own Psalm 91 Book: German. 2009. (J). pap. *(978-1-61584-658-0(1))* Independent Pub.

—My Own Psalm 91 Book: Russian. 2009. (J). pap. *(978-1-61584-656-6(5))* Independent Pub.

—My Own Psalm 91 Book: Ukraainian. 2009. (J). pap. *(978-1-61584-657-3(3))* Independent Pub.

—My Own Psalm 91 Book: Vietnamese English. 2009. (J). pap. *(978-1-61584-655-9(7))* Independent Pub.

—My Own Psalm 92 Book: Simplified Chinese-English. 2009. (J). pap. *(978-1-61584-654-2(9))* Independent Pub.

Thompson, Patricia. Psalms 23: A Child's Story. 2005. (J). 12.95 *(978-0-9776780-0-6(8))* G Publishing LLC.

Vander Klipp, Michael. God Made Food, 1 vol. 2008. (God Made... Ser.). 14p. (J). bds. 3.99 *(978-0-8254-3913-1(2))* Kregel Pubns.

—God Made My Body, 1 vol. 2008. (God Made... Ser.). 14p. (J). bds. 3.99 *(978-0-8254-3912-4(4))* Kregel Pubns.

Wilson, Anne. The Lord Is My Shepherd. Wilson, Anne, illus. 2004. (Illus.). 32p. 16.00 *(978-0-8028-5250-2(5))* Eerdmans, William B. Publishing Co.

Wilson, Karma. I Will Rejoice: Celebrating Psalm 118. Bates, Amy June, illus. 2007. (ENG.). 32p. (J). (gr. -1-3). 14.99 *(978-0-310-71117-9(7))* Zonderkidz.

BIBLE—PARABLES

see Jesus Christ—Parables

BIBLE—PICTORIAL WORKS

Anglin, Dawnice. God's Creation Bible Coloring Book: Bible Coloring Book. 2007. (Illus.). 24p. (J). per. 6.99 *(978-0-9801320-0-7(2))* Basic Black Publishing.

Carson-Dellosa Publishing Staff. Hidden Pictures, Grades PK - 1. 2010. (Home Workbooks Ser.). (ENG.). 64p. (gr. -1-1). pap. 4.49 *(978-1-60418-770-0(0))* Carson-Dellosa Publishing, LLC.

Daly, Jude. To Everything There Is a Season. Daly, Jude, illus. 2006. (Illus.). 32p. (Orig.). (J). (gr. -1-3). 16.00 *(978-0-8028-5286-1(6)*, Eerdmans Bks For Young Readers) Eerdmans, William B. Publishing Co.

Lindvall, Ella K. The Bible in Pictures for Toddlers. Langton, Roger, illus. adapted ed. 2003. (ENG.). 144p. (J). 9.99 *(978-0-8024-3058-8(9))* Moody Pubs.

—La Biblia en Cuadros para Niños Pequeños, 1 vol. 2004. (SPA.). 144p. (J). 10.99 *(978-0-8254-1710-8(4)*, Editorial Portavoz) Kregel Pubns.

The Lord Is My Shepherd, 1 vol. 2014. (ENG., Illus.). 32p. (J). 9.99 *(978-1-78128-143-7(2)*, Candle Bks.) Lion Hudson PLC GBR. Dist: Kregel Pubns.

Widmer, Becky. Bible Awareness Series, 6 vols. Christian, Heather, illus. Date not set. (J). (gr. -1-18). 9.95 *(978-1-888537-00-0(0))* Publisher Plus.

BIBLE—PLANTS

see Bible—Natural History

BIBLE—STUDY

Abingdon Press, creator. One Room Sunday School: Resource Kit. 2008. (Illus.). (J). pap. 56.00 incl. audio compact disk *(978-0-687-03629-5(1))* Abingdon Pr.

Aguinaco, Carmen F. Amigos de Jesús 2009: A Bilingual Catechetical Program. un Programa Catequético BilingüE. Advent 2008 - November 2009. Petersen, William, illus. 2008.Tr. of Friends of Jesus 2009. (ENG & SPA.). 408p. (J). pap. 99.00 *(978-0-89570-503-7(6))* Claretian Pubns.

Armor of God: With Sticker. 2006. (Illus.). 28p. (J). (gr. -1-2). pap. 3.49 *(978-0-7847-1251-1(4)*, 22084) Standard Publishing.

Arthur, Kay & Arndt, Janna. Becoming God's Champion: 2 Timothy. 2009. (ENG., Illus.). 176p. (J). pap. 11.99 *(978-0-7369-2594-5(5))* Harvest Hse. Pubs.

—Fast-Forward to the Future: Daniel 7-12. 2008. (ENG., Illus.). 192p. (J). per. 11.99 *(978-0-7369-2285-2(7))* Harvest Hse. Pubs.

—God, What's Your Name? 2003. (ENG., Illus.). 192p. (J). pap., wbk. ed. 11.99 *(978-0-7369-1161-0(8))* Harvest Hse. Pubs.

—How to Study Your Bible for Kids. (Discover-4-Yourself for Kids Ser.). 185p. (J). 2006. pap. 9.99 *(978-1-888655-29-2(1))* 2005. pap. 9.99 *(978-1-888655-77-3(1))* Precept Ministries.

Arthur, Kay, et al. How to Study Your Bible for Teens. 2004. 176p. (YA). pap. 9.99 *(978-0-7369-0965-5(6))* Harvest Hse. Pubs.

—Wrong Way, Jonah! Jonah. 2010. (ENG.). 128p. (J). pap. 10.99 *(978-0-7369-2819-9(7))* Harvest Hse. Pubs.

B&H Editorial Staff, ed. Read to Me Bible for Kids. 2004. (Illus.). 1864p. 19.99 *(978-1-55819-844-9(X))* B&H Publishing Group.

Babler, Susan E. Look It up-In the Bible, Book 2: Animals, Gardens, & Trees. 2008. 139p. spiral bd. 16.95 *(978-0-7880-2500-6(7))* CSS Publishing Co.

Balzora, Renaud & Balzora, Lulrick. Fondation: Doctrines Bibliques en 52 Leçons. 2004. (FRE.). 198p. (YA). per. 15.00 *(978-1-58432-189-7(X))* Educa Vision Inc.

Barton, David Charles, creator. Decision for Christ Study of the Bible. 2004. 154p. pap. 3.95 *(978-0-9759426-3-5(8))* Barton, D.C. Publishing.

Bergren, Lisa T. The Good Book for Kids: How the Bible's Big Ideas Relate to YOU. 2017. (ENG.). 416p. (J). pap. 12.99 *(978-1-4347-1024-6(6))* Cook, David C.

Bible. 2004. (Illus.). (gr. 1). tchr. ed., stu. ed. 67.95 *(978-0-86717-671-1(7)*, BIB0115, Lifepac) Alpha Omega Pubns., Inc.

Bible: Student Testing Kit. 2004. (Illus.). (YA). (gr. 7-12). pap., stu. ed. 5.00 *(978-0-7403-0042-4(3)*, BD002) Alpha Omega Pubns., Inc.

Bible Characters & Bulletin Boards. (Illus.). 48p. (J). (gr. 1-7). pap. 5.95 *(978-0-87162-632-5(2)*, E4605) Warner Pr., Inc.

Bible KJV Childrens. 2004. (Illus.). 826p. (J). pap. 16.99 *(978-1-55819-757-2(5))* B&H Publishing Group.

Bible Skills, Drills, & Thrills Activity Bk Gr 1,3 Green Cycle. 2004. (J). 5.95 *(978-0-633-19425-3(5))* LifeWay Christian Resources.

Bible Zone in the Wilderness Older Elementary Kit Wrap. 2007. *(978-0-687-64793-4(2))* Abingdon Pr.

Bible Zone in the Wilderness Younger Elementary Kit Wrap. 2007. *(978-0-687-64783-5(5))* Abingdon Pr.

Big Idea, Inc. VeggieTales Kids' Worship! Getting to Know God: For Children's Church or Large-Group Programming, 0 vols. 2009. (J). 129.99 *(978-1-4003-1353-2(8))* Nelson, Thomas Inc.

—VeggieTales Kids' Worship! Unit 2 - Wild Bible Adventures: For Children's Church or Large-Group Programming, 0 vols. 2009. (J). 129.99 *(978-1-4003-1444-7(5))* Nelson, Thomas Inc.

BJU Staff. Bible Truths Stu Materials Gk5. 2004. pap. 13.50 *(978-1-59166-238-9(9))* BJU Pr.

Blundell, Thalia, et al. On the Way for 11-14's, Bk. 1. 2010. (On the Way (11-14's) Ser.). (ENG.). 96p. (J). pap. 17.99 *(978-1-85792-704-7(4)*, 9781857927047) Christian Focus Pubns. GBR. Dist: Bookmasters Distribution.

Blundell, Trevor, et al. Beginning with the Bible: A Child's First Lessons in Knowing God. 2007. (On the Way (2-3's) Ser.). (ENG., Illus.). 96p. (J). pap. 17.99 *(978-1-85792-224-0(7)*, 9781857922240) Christian Focus Pubns. GBR. Dist: Bookmasters Distribution.

—On the Way, Bk. 3. 2008. (On the Way (11-14's) Ser.). (ENG.). 88p. (J). pap. 17.99 *(978-1-85792-706-1(0)*, 9781857927061) Christian Focus Pubns. GBR. Dist: Bookmasters Distribution.

—On the Way for 11 - 14's, Vol. 2. 2006. (On the Way (11-14's) Ser.). (ENG.). 96p. (J). pap. 17.99 *(978-1-85792-705-4(2)*, 9781857927054) Christian Focus Pubns. GBR. Dist: Bookmasters Distribution.

Broadman and Holman Publishers Staff. Kindergarten. 2004. (Learning Activities from the Bible Ser.). (Illus.). (gr. -1-2). act. bk. ed. 15.99 incl. cd-rom *(978-0-8054-0983-3(1))* B&H Publishing Group.

—Learning Activities from the Bible Series. 2004. (Learning Activities from the Bible Ser.). (Illus.). (gr. -1-2). act. bk. ed. 15.99 incl. cd-rom *(978-0-8054-0984-0(X))*; act. bk. ed. 15.99 incl. cd-rom *(978-0-8054-0985-7(8))* B&H Publishing Group.

—Preschool. 2004. (Learning Activities from the Bible Ser.). (Illus.). (gr. -1-2). act. bk. ed. 15.99 incl. cd-rom *(978-0-8054-0982-6(3))* B&H Publishing Group.

Bunyan, John. El Sacrificio Aceptable. Greendyk, William, tr. from ENG. 2003.Tr. of Acceptable Sacrifice. (SPA.). 102p. (J). pap. *(978-1-932789-05-8(7))* Editorial Sendas Antiguas, LLC.

Burns, Jim & Devries, Mike. Instant Bible Studies. 176p. 19.99 *(978-0-8307-2919-7(4)*, Gospel Light) Gospel Light Pubns.

Burton, Frances. Rainy Day Fun. 2011. 72p. (gr. 4-6). pap. 11.99 *(978-1-4567-6720-4(8))* AuthorHouse.

Canaday, Matt & Canaday, Cindi. Book of Mormon Circle a Word, Bk. 2. Griffin, Grace, ed. 51p. (Orig.). (YA). pap., stu. ed. 2.95 *(978-1-56998-000-2(4))* Cluster Storm Publishing.

Childress, Gavin & Dooley, Audrey. Reading Your Bible: A Starter's Guide. Wild, Gill, illus. 2005. 101p. (J). (gr. -1-7). per. 9.00 *(978-1-903087-41-1(4))* DayOne Pubns. GBR. Dist: Send The Light Distribution LLC.

Choosing Kindness. 2003. (Illus.). 94p. (J). (gr. k-5). pap. 7.99 *(978-0-9703069-3-7(8))* Train-Up A Child, LLC.

Choosing Self-Control. 2004. (Illus.). 94p. (J). (gr. k-5). pap. 7.99 *(978-0-9703069-4-4(6))* Train-Up A Child, LLC.

Christian Literature International Staff & Barbour Publishing Staff. The Barbour Children's Bible. 2014. (ENG.). 944p. (J). 19.99 *(978-1-63058-659-1(5))* Barbour Publishing, Inc.

Collison, Shauna. Heavenites Angels to Zebras Board Book with Audio CD. Nelson, Christine, illus. 2007. 26p. (J). 15.95 *(978-0-9792510-0-9(1))* Revelation Products LLC.

Cook, David C. Publishing Staff & Harmon, Jeannie. God's Promise to Abraham. 2003. (Pencil Fun Bks.: Vol. 10). 16p. (J). (gr. -1-3). pap. 9.90 *(978-1-55513-126-5(3)*, 1555131263) Cook, David C.

Cripe, Daniel Earl. The Other Side of Jordan: A Study in the Book of Hebrews. (New Testament Ser.). (Illus.). (J). 36.00 *(978-1-890875-13-8(9))*; pap. 42.00 *(978-1-890875-14-5(7))* Jordan Publishing Hse.

Custom Spanish Curriculum January Year 3 - Elementary. 2005. 96p. pap. 14.95 *(978-0-7814-4047-9(5)*, 0781440475) Cook, David C.

Custom Spanish Curriculum January Year 3 - Middle School. 2005. 96p. pap. 14.95 *(978-0-7814-4053-0(X)*, 078144053X) Cook, David C.

Custom Spanish Curriculum January Year 3 - Preschool. 2005. 96p. pap. 14.95 *(978-0-7814-4041-7(6)*, 0781440416) Cook, David C.

Custom Spanish Curriculum July Year 3 - Elementary. 2005. 96p. pap. 14.95 *(978-0-7814-4048-6(3)*, 0781440483) Cook, David C.

Custom Spanish Curriculum July Year 3 - Middle School. 2005. 96p. pap. 14.95 *(978-0-7814-4054-7(8)*, 0781440548) Cook, David C.

Custom Spanish Curriculum July Year 3 - Preschool. 2005. 96p. pap. 14.95 *(978-0-7814-4042-4(4)*, 0781440424) Cook, David C.

David C. Cook Publishing Company Staff, creator. Action! Cool Theater. 2008. (Bible Fun Stuff for Middle School Ser.). (Illus.). 112p. (J). (gr. 6-8). pap. 16.99 *(978-1-4347-6856-8(2))* Cook, David C.

David C. Cook Publishing Company Staff & Cook, David C. Dive In! Fun Faith Builders, 1 vol. 2009. (Easy-Prep Lessons Ser.). (ENG.). 112p. pap. 19.99 *(978-1-4347-6693-9(4))* Cook, David C.

Deep Blue One Room Sunday School Leader's Guide Winter 2016-17: Ages 3-12. 2016. (Deep Blue Ser.). 96p. pap. 15.99 *(978-1-5018-1692-5(6))* Abingdon Pr.

Derr, Louise Barrett. Experiencing Bible Science. 2007. 128p. per. 16.95 *(978-1-59919-025-9(7))* Elim Publishing.

Donner, Candie. Apologia Worldview: Assembled: Who Am I Lapbook. Kinney, Cyndi, ed. 2013. (J). pap. 35.99 *(978-1-61625-527-5(7))* Knowledge Box Central.

—Apologia Worldview: Who Am I Lapbook. Kinney, Cyndi, ed. 2013. (J). pap. 25.99 *(978-1-61625-525-1(0))*; cd-rom 19.99 *(978-1-61625-524-4(2))* Knowledge Box Central.

Dowley, Tim. Pop-Up Bible Adventures. Moseley, Dudley, illus. 2005. 12p. (J). (gr. k-2). bds. 11.99 *(978-0-8254-7298-5(9)*, Candle Bks.) Lion Hudson PLC GBR. Dist: Kregel Pubns.

Downs, Downs. Explore Bible People: 52 Bible Lessons for Ages 4-6. 2003. (Route 52(tm) Ser.). (ENG.). 320p. (J). pap. 32.99 *(978-0-7847-1323-5(5)*, 42072) Standard Publishing.

Drion, Donna. Stop & Look at God's Word. 2008. (Stop & Look Ser.). (Illus.). 32p. (J). (gr. -1-3). *(978-1-84625-134-4(6))* DayOne Pubns.

Fawcett, Cheryl & Newman, Robert C. Kids' Questions about Sin & Salvation. 2003. (Illus.). 61p. pap. *(978-1-59402-083-4(3))* Regular Baptist Pr.

Fischer, Carl. Together in Jesus: First Reconciliation Certificate. 2004. (Together in Jesus Ser.). (Illus.). (J). pap. 9.95 *(978-0-937997-75-8(7)*, 912110) Pflaum Publishing Group.

Friedl, Natalie. Help Me Pray Today. 2008. (Illus.). 32p. (J). *(978-0-9797429-1-0(9))* Halo Publishing International.

Frierson, Natasha. Teaching the Abc's W/ the Bible. 2012. 32p. pap. 17.99 *(978-1-4685-5043-6(8))* AuthorHouse.

Gospel Light Publications Staff. The Big Book of Bible Story Activity Pages: Help Kids Play, Listen & Talk Through the Bible. 2015. (Big Bks.). (ENG.). 224p. (J). (gr. -1-k). pap. 29.99 *(978-0-8307-5102-0(5))* Gospel Light Pubns.

Group Publishing Staff, creator. Bible Memory Buddy Care Cards. 2011. (Bible Memory Buddy Bks.). (Illus.). (J). (gr. -1-3). pap. 5.99 *(978-0-7644-6960-2(6))* Group Publishing, Inc.

Gundersen, Bev. Grow Through the Bible: 52 Bible Lessons from Genesis to Revelation for Ages 8-12. 2003. (Route 52(tm) Ser.). (ENG.). 320p. (J). pap. 32.99 *(978-0-7847-1325-9(1)*, 42074) Standard Publishing.

Gurvis, Laura K. Learn & Do Bible Book. Ben-Moshe, Jana, illus. 64p. (J). (gr. k-2). pap. 4.95 *(978-0-87441-530-8(6))* Behrman Hse., Inc.

Hamilton, Anna Housel. The Poor Little Slave Girl. 2011. (Illus.). 20p. pap. 12.45 *(978-1-4497-2338-5(1)*, WestBow Pr.) Author Solutions, Inc.

Hammah, Aisha. The Image Game. Stubblefield, Linda, ed. Hammah, Aisha, illus. 2013. (Illus.). 192p. pap. *(978-0-9810759-3-8(2))*; pap. *(978-0-9810759-8-3(3))* WTL International.

Hanks, Scott. Take Heed to Thyself for Teens. 2007. (YA). spiral bd. 7.00 *(978-0-9799518-6-2(0))* Hanks, Scott.

HealthTeacher. HealthTeacher: K-1. 2006. (Illus.). 334p. lib. bdg. 99.95 *(978-0-9785578-5-0(9))* HealthTeacher.

Hunnicutt, M. E. Giants of Wonder. 2012. 28p. pap. 24.95 *(978-1-4626-7284-4(1))* America Star Bks.

International Inductive Study Bible. 2006. (YA). pap. *(978-1-888655-67-4(4))* Precept Ministries.

Jeremiah, David. Airship Genesis Kids Study Bible, 1 vol. 2016. (ENG., Illus.). 1504p. (J). 29.99 *(978-0-7180-8688-6(0))* Nelson, Thomas Inc.

Jones, Dennis, illus. Read with Me Bible for Little Ones, 1 vol. 2016. (ENG.). 32p. (J). bds. 9.99 *(978-0-310-75386-5(4))* Zonderkidz.

Jones, Karen A. Light Pole Books: Reading Series, Vol. 2. 2009. (J). spiral bd. 24.95 *(978-1-59879-748-0(4))* Lifevest Publishing, Inc.

Jordan, Bernice C. Who Is Jesus Christ? - Textbook: Footsteps of Faith New Testament Volume 1, Vol. 1. 2008. (Footsteps of Faith Ser.). 148p. (J). (gr. 3-9). pap. 14.99 *(978-0-86508-035-5(6))* BCM International Inc.

Keels, Steve, ed. TruthQuest Inductive Student Bible. 2004. (TruthQuest Family Ser.). (Illus.). 1506p. lthr. 44.99 *(978-1-55819-849-4(0))* B&H Publishing Group.

Kenney, Cindy. God's World & Me: Boz's Big Book of Bible Fun. 2007. (Boz the Bear Ser.). (Illus.). 235p. (J). (gr. -1-3). pap. 14.99 *(978-0-7814-4544-3(2))* Cook, David C.

Kidzfirst. Bible Studies for Children: Acts (KOREAN) 2012. 120p. pap. 5.98 *(978-1-56344-736-5(3))* Casa Nazarena de Publicacions.

Kiplagat, Linet. Bible Abc: My Memory Verse Book. 2011. 32p. pap. 13.95 *(978-1-4497-1930-2(9)*, WestBow Pr.) Author Solutions, Inc.

Kohlenberger, John R., III, et al. Truth Quest Inductive Student Bible. 2004. (TruthQuest Family Ser.). (Illus.). 1506p. lthr. 44.99 *(978-1-55819-843-2(1))* B&H Publishing Group.

Lane, Leena. The Kids Bible. Chapman, Gillian, illus. 2003. 64p. (J). 10.49 *(978-0-7586-0561-0(7))* Concordia Publishing Hse.

Lane, Leena & Boshof, Penny. My Little Yellow Book: First Steps in Bible Reading. 2004. 64p. 4.99 *(978-1-85999-693-5(0))* Scripture Union GBR. Dist: Gabriel Resources.

Larsen, Claire A. God's Great Covenant, Old Testament 1. 2009. (ENG.). 238p. (J). (gr. 2-5). pap. 22.95 *(978-1-60051-071-7(X))* Classical Academic Pr.

—God's Great Covenant, Old Testament 2: A Bible Course for Children. 2009. (ENG.). 238p. (J). (gr. 2-5). pap. 22.95 *(978-1-60051-049-6(3))* Classical Academic Pr.

Last Trump Gathering Bible Studies, Vol. 1. 2004. (YA). per. 10.95 *(978-0-9760159-0-1(0))* Rogers, Al M. Jr.

Lepley, Lynne. Scrumptious Scriptures. 2004. 96p. (J). (gr. 1-5). pap. 11.95 *(978-1-885358-47-9(4)*, RB36822) Rainbow Pubs. & Legacy Pr.

Lewis, Carole. Pressing on to the Prize. 2004. (First Place Bible Studies). 224p. pap. 19.99 *(978-0-8307-2926-5(7)*, Gospel Light) Gospel Light Pubns.

Lewolt, Bruce. Bible by Heart: The Ultimate Bible Study & Memorization System. 2004. (Illus.). 39p. cd-rom 69.95 *(978-0-9741604-6-7(6))* BrainX, Inc.

Liening, Cathy. B. I. B. L. E. Be Involved Bible Learners Everyone: A Children's Bible Study. 2008. 63p. per. 12.95 *(978-0-7880-2504-4(X))* CSS Publishing Co.

Lloyd, Janet E. Joy & Wonder in All God's Works: Year B. Date not set. 132p. (Orig.). (J). pap. 14.95 *(978-0-9646362-6-2(3))* Via Media, Pr.

MacArthur, John. The Gospel According to the Apostles, 1 vol. Butcher, Sam, illus. 2005. (ENG.). 288p. pap. 15.99 *(978-0-7852-7180-2(5))* Nelson, Thomas Inc.

Madder, Tracey. The Story Travelers Bible. Crecelius, Tim, illus. 2017. (ENG.). 368p. (J). 16.99 *(978-1-4964-0915-7(9)*, Tyndale Kids) Tyndale Hse. Pubs.

Maltese, Donna K. Know Your Bible for Kids: What Is That? My First Bible Reference for Ages 5-8. 2014. (ENG., Illus.). 128p. (J). pap. 4.99 *(978-1-62836-868-0(3)*, Barbour Bks.) Barbour Publishing, Inc.

Mayfield, Jacqueline V. Step over into Wealth: A Step-By-Step System to Help You Manage Your Current Income. 2008. 100p. pap. 9.95 *(978-1-882185-00-9(5))* Cornerstone Publishing, Inc.

McCallen, A. J. Praise! Songs & Poems from the Bible Retold for Children. 2013. (Illus.). 96p. *(978-0-00-599621-8(X))* Callender Pr.

Meade, Starr. The Most Important Thing You'll Ever Study: A Survey of the Bible. 2010. 1024p. pap. 60.00 *(978-1-4335-1182-0(7))* Crossway.

Miller, Kathy Collard. The un-Devotional for Teens. 164p. pap. 10.99 *(978-0-8307-3510-5(0)*, Gospel Light) Gospel Light Pubns.

Misal 2005 Para Ninos: Tengo una Cita. 2005. (SPA.). 272p. pap. 6.50 *(978-0-8146-4137-8(7))* Liturgical Pr.

Mitzo Thompson, Kim, et al. I Thank God for You Read & Sing-Along Storybook, 1 vol. 2017. (ENG.). 16p. (J). (-5). 9.99 ***(978-1-68322-200-2(8))*** Barbour Publishing, Inc.

Montero, José Pérez, illus. Bible Sleuth: New Testament. 2017. (Bible Sleuth Ser.). (ENG.). 32p. 12.99 *(978-1-4964-2243-9(0)*, Tyndale Kids) Tyndale Hse. Pubs.

—Bible Sleuth: Old Testament. 2017. (Bible Sleuth Ser.). (ENG.). 32p. 12.99 *(978-1-4964-2244-6(9)*, Tyndale Kids) Tyndale Hse. Pubs.

Murray, David. Exploring the Bible: A Bible Reading Plan for Kids. Reifsnyder, Scotty, illus. 2017. 224p. 14.99 ***(978-1-4335-5686-9(3))*** Crossway.

My Bible. 2006. 16p. (J). pap. 1.99 *(978-0-7847-1454-6(1)*, 22133) Standard Publishing.

Napier, Angi. Bible Baby: Shapes. 2012. 28p. 24.95 *(978-1-4626-5633-2(1))* America Star Bks.

Nappa, Mike. When Pigs Fly: A Bible Memory Buddy Book. Harrington, David, illus. 2012. (ENG.). 32p. (J). (-3). 9.99 *(978-0-7644-8189-5(4))* Group Publishing, Inc.

Neely, J. Crucifixion - Countdown to a Promise. 2004. (Daily Bible Study Ser.). 500p. per. 39.95 *(978-1-893968-40-0(5))* Neely, Judy.

—Daily Bible Study Charts & Graphs. 2004. (Daily Bible Study Ser.). 40p. per. 9.95 *(978-1-893968-34-9(0))* Neely, Judy.

No-Miss Lessons for Preteen Kids, Vol. 2. 2004. pap. 16.99 *(978-0-7644-2290-4(1)*, Flagship Church Resources) Group Publishing, Inc.

Noonan, Robert, et al. Three Weavers Plus Companion: A Father's Guide to Guarding His Daughter's Purity. 2004. 120p. pap. 13.95 *(978-0-9700273-5-1(4))* Pumpkin Seed Pr.

Older Elementary KidKit. 2003. (Godprints Curriculum Ser.). (Illus.). 8.99 *(978-0-7814-3680-9(X)*, 2043) Cook, David C.

One Room Sunday School Fall: Resource Kit. (Illus.). 56.00 *(978-0-687-03622-6(4))* Abingdon Pr.

One Room Sunday School Leader's Guide (Spring 2010) 2009. 12.50 *(978-1-4267-0141-2(1))* Abingdon Pr.

One Room Sunday School Winter: Resource Kit. (Illus.). 52.00 *(978-0-687-03619-6(4))* Abingdon Pr.

Partner, Daniel. Bible Devotions for Bedtime. 2004. (Bedtime Bible Stories Ser.). (ENG.). 256p. (J). pap. 5.99 *(978-1-59310-358-3(1)*, Barbour Bks.) Barbour Publishing, Inc.

Perrotta, Kevin & Darring, Gerald. Exodus: God to the Rescue. Perrotta, Kevin, ed. 2004. (Six Weeks with the Bible for Catholic Teens Ser.). (ENG.). 96p. (gr. 9-12). pap. 7.95 *(978-0-8294-2051-7(7))* Loyola Pr.

—God Makes a Start. Perrotta, Kevin, ed. 2004. (Six Weeks with the Bible for Catholic Teens Ser.). (ENG.). 96p. (gr. 8-12). pap. 7.95 *(978-0-8294-2050-0(9))* Loyola Pr.

—John 1-10: I Am the Bread of Life. Perrotta, Kevin, ed. 2004. (Six Weeks with the Bible for Catholic Teens Ser.). (ENG.). 96p. (gr. 8-12). pap. 7.95 *(978-0-8294-2083-8(5))* Loyola Pr.

—John 11-21: My Peace I Give You. Perrotta, Kevin, ed. 2004. (Six Weeks with the Bible for Catholic Teens Ser.). (ENG.). 96p. (gr. 8-12). pap. 7.95 *(978-0-8294-2084-5(3))* Loyola Pr.

—Luke: The Good News of God's Mercy. Perrotta, Kevin, ed. 2004. (Six Weeks with the Bible for Catholic Teens Ser.). (ENG.). 96p. (gr. 8-12). pap. 7.95 *(978-0-8294-2052-4(5))* Loyola Pr.

—Revelation: God's Gift of Hope. Perrotta, Kevin, ed. 2004. (Six Weeks with the Bible for Catholic Teens Ser.). (ENG.). 96p. (gr. 8-12). pap. 7.95 *(978-0-8294-2049-4(5))* Loyola Pr.

Rainbow Publishers Staff. Coloring Plus Activities: God's Promises. 2004. (Illus.). 64p. (J). (gr. -1-3). pap. 9.95 *(978-0-937282-49-6(9)*, RB37165) Rainbow Pubs. & Legacy Pr.

Rhodes, David & Norris, Chad. Broken: When Life Falls Apart. 2005. (Following God Ser.). 168p. pap. *(978-0-89957-738-8(5))* AMG Pubs.

Richards, Lawrence O. The Gospel of Mark, 1 vol. 2010. (ENG.). (J). 31p. pap. 1.99 *(978-0-310-72019-5(2))*; 32p. pap., pap. 47.76 *(978-0-310-72020-1(6))* Zonderkidz.

Richards, Lawrence O. & Zondervan Staff. King James Version Kids Study Bible, 1 vol. 2014. (ENG.). 1600p. (J). im. lthr. 29.99 *(978-0-310-74775-8(9))* Zonderkidz.

Rodgers, Barbara. Bible Activities in a Snap: Holidays. 2004. 96p. (J). (gr. -1-3). pap. 9.95 *(978-1-885358-44-8(X)*, RB36813) Rainbow Pubs. & Legacy Pr.

Rose, Shirley. Let's Discover the Bible, Vol. 1. Yerkes, Lane, illus. 64p. (J). (gr. k-2). pap. 4.75 *(978-0-87441-538-4(1))* Behrman Hse., Inc.

Russell, Patricia C. Discovery - in the Beginning: Genesis. 2003. (Bible Discovery Ser.). 220p. (J). stu. ed., per., wbk. ed. 21.99 *(978-1-889015-31-6(8))* Explorer's Bible Study.
Ryken, Philip Graham. Ecclesiastes (Redesign) Why Everything Matters. 2014. (Preaching the Word Ser.). 320p. 32.99 *(978-1-4335-4888-8(7))* Crossway.
Sabio & Prudente. Numeros, Conceptos y Figuras Geometricas. 2004. (Sabio Y Prudente Ser.). (SPA.). 64p. (J). No. 1. 4.99 *(978-0-8254-0997-4(7))* Vol. 3. (Illus.). 4.99 *(978-0-8254-0999-8(3))* Kregel Pubns. (Editorial Portavoz).
Scherm, Deedra. The ABC Bible Verse Book. Dreyer, Laura, illus. 2007. (ENG.). 26p. (J). (gr. -1-3). bds. 8.99 *(978-1-934789-04-9(6))* Lemon Vision Productions.
School of the Bible for Kids: The Blood of Jesus. 2005. ring bd. 74.95 *(978-0-9767647-4-8(1))* Kids in Ministry International.
Scripture to Grow On: Lesson Plans for the Children in your Home. 2nd rev. ed. 2008. (Illus.). 136p. (J). spiral bd. 10.99 *(978-0-9746361-1-5(8))* Heavenly C. Publishing.
Seifert, Sheila & Naylor, Beth. Getting to Know God. 2006. (Dsj Ser.). (Illus.). 116p. pap., per. 19.99 *(978-0-7814-4322-7(9)*, 0781443229) Cook, David C.
Sheffield, Bill. The Beginnings under Attack. 2003. 192p. per. 10.99 *(978-0-9728899-3-3(0))* 21st Century Pr.
Shepherd, Good. Our Almighty God: A Bible Study. 2008. 48p. pap. 13.49 *(978-1-4389-1850-1(X))* AuthorHouse.
Standard Publishing Staff. Discover God's Love: 52 Bible Lessons for Ages 3 & 4. 2003. (Route 52(tm) Ser.). (ENG.). 320p. (J). pap. 32.99 *(978-0-7847-1322-8(7)*, 42071) Standard Publishing.
—Follow the Bible: 52 Bible Lessons for Beginning Readers Ages 6-8. 2003. (Route 52(tm) Ser.). (ENG.). 320p. (J). pap. 32.99 *(978-0-7847-1324-2(3)*, 42073) Standard Publishing.
Steinbock, Steven E. The Gift of Wisdom: The Books of Prophets & Writings. Mantell, Ahuva & Sperling, S. David, illus. 2004. (J). (gr. 4-6). pap. 13.95 *(978-0-8074-0752-3(6)*, 123944) URJ Pr.
Steve, Crain, Larry. The Bible Fun Book No. 1. 2013. 96p. pap. 13.95 *(978-1-4908-1563-3(5)*, WestBow Pr.) Author Solutions, Inc.
Strauss, Ed. Know Your Bible for Kids: Noah's Ark: My First Bible Reference for 5-8 Year Olds. 2015. (ENG., Illus.). 128p. (J). pap. 4.99 *(978-1-63058-913-4(6)*, Barbour Bks.) Barbour Publishing, Inc.
Sumner, Tracy M. & Landreth, Jane. Big Bible Guide: Kids' Guide to Creation & Bible Animals: Fun & Fascinating Bible Reference for Kids Ages 8-12. 2014. (ENG., Illus.). 320p. (J). pap. 14.99 *(978-1-62416-868-0(X)*, Barbour Bks.) Barbour Publishing, Inc.
Tnt Ministries Staff. On the Way 11 - 14's, Vol. 4. 2003. (On the Way (11-14's) Ser.). (ENG.). 96p. (J). pap. 17.99 *(978-1-85792-707-8(9)*, 9781857927078) Christian Focus Pubns. GBR. Dist: Bookmasters Distribution.
TNT Resource Material Staff. On the Way, 11-14yr, Vol. 5. 2010. (On the Way (11-14's) Ser.). (ENG.). 96p. (J). pap. 17.99 *(978-1-85792-708-5(7)*, 9781857927085) Christian Focus Pubns. GBR. Dist: Bookmasters Distribution.
—On the Way for 11 - 14's, Vol. 6. 2003. (On the Way (11-14's) Ser.). (ENG.). 96p. (J). pap. 17.99 *(978-1-85792-709-2(5)*, 9781857927092) Christian Focus Pubns. GBR. Dist: Bookmasters Distribution.
Todd, Richard E. Baptism: A Bible Study Wordbook for Kids. 2009. (Children's Wordbooks Ser.). (ENG., Illus.). 32p. (gr. 4-7). pap. 5.99 *(978-1-60066-194-5(7))* WingSpread Publishers.
—Church: A Bible Study Wordbook for Kids. 2009. (Children's Wordbooks Ser.). (ENG., Illus.). 32p. (gr. 4-7). pap. 5.99 *(978-1-60066-196-9(3))* WingSpread Publishers.
—Communion: A Bible Study Wordbook for Kids. 2009. (Children's Wordbooks Ser.). (ENG., Illus.). 32p. (gr. 4-7). pap. 5.99 *(978-1-60066-195-2(5))* WingSpread Publishers.
—Giving: A Bible Study Wordbook for Kids. 2009. (Children's Wordbooks Ser.). (ENG., Illus.). 32p. (gr. 4-7). pap. 5.99 *(978-1-60066-197-6(1))* WingSpread Publishers.
Together in Jesus: Spanish First Reconciliation Certificate. 2004. (Together in Jesus Ser.). (Illus.). 1p. (J). pap. 9.95 *(978-0-89837-244-1(5)*, 952110) Pflaum Publishing Group.
Twork, Carol Camp, des. Scripture Notebook. 2003. 48p. (YA). 3.99 *(978-0-9707979-4-0(X))* Contemplation Corner Pr.
VBS Ready, Set, Gold! 2003. (J). *(978-0-8100-1537-1(4))*; (J). stu. ed. *(978-0-8100-1518-0(8))*; (J). cd-rom *(978-0-8100-1534-0(X))*;Level 1. (J). tchr. ed. *(978-0-8100-1522-7(6))*;Level 1. (J). stu. ed. *(978-0-8100-1517-3(X))*;Level 2. (J). tchr. ed. *(978-0-8100-1523-4(4))*;Level 3. (YA). tchr. ed. *(978-0-8100-1524-1(2))* Northwestern Publishing Hse.
Vbs Ready, Set, Gold!, Level 3. 2003. (J). stu. ed. *(978-0-8100-1519-7(6))* Northwestern Publishing Hse.
VBS Ready, Set, Gold! 2003. (J). Level 4. tchr. ed. *(978-0-8100-1525-8(0))*Level 4. stu. ed. *(978-0-8100-1520-3(X))*Level 5. tchr. ed. *(978-0-8100-1526-5(9))*Level 5. stu. ed. *(978-0-8100-1521-0(8))* Northwestern Publishing Hse.
VBS Ready, Set, Gold! Craft Book. 2003. (J). *(978-0-8100-1527-2(7))* Northwestern Publishing Hse.
VBS Ready, Set, Gold! Planning Guide. 2003. (J). *(978-0-8100-1535-7(8))* Northwestern Publishing Hse.
Walters, David. The Gifts of the Spirit, 6 vols. Ellis, Jessica, illus. 2005. 64p. (J). pap. 8.95 *(978-1-888081-68-8(6))* Good News Fellowship Ministries.
Washington, Linda. Home & Back. 2004. (Illus.). 96p. (J). (gr. 1-2). pap. 11.95 *(978-1-885358-50-9(4)*, RB36842); (gr. 3-4). pap. 11.95 *(978-1-885358-51-6(2)*, RB36843); (gr. 5-6). pap. 11.95 *(978-1-885358-52-3(0)*, RB36844) Rainbow Pubs. & Legacy Pr.
Washington, Linda & Dall, Jeanette. Home & Back: Bible Activities. 2004. 96p. (J). (gr. -1-k). pap. 11.95 *(978-1-885358-63-9(6)*, RB36841) Rainbow Pubs. & Legacy Pr.
Wells, Jan. Philemon - an Inductive Bible Study. 2004. 49p. per. *(978-1-932934-13-7(8))* Sunergos Bible Studies.
Wilkes, C. Gene. Jesus on Leadership: Discovering the Secrets of Servant Leadership from the Life of Christ. 2016. (ENG., Illus.). 272p. pap. 14.99 *(978-0-8423-1863-1(1))* Tyndale Hse. Pubs.
Willoughby, Robert. Children's Guide to the Bible. Morris, Tony, illus. 2003. 128p. 9.99 *(978-1-85999-072-8(X))* Scripture Union GBR. Dist: Gabriel Resources.
Wilson, Jacqui. Little Johnny's Faith Adventures: Our Beginnings. 2010. 68p. pap. 9.95 *(978-1-4497-0790-3(4)*, WestBow Pr.) Author Solutions, Inc.
Woell, Tamara. A-Z Teacher Manual, Simon Peter School Scripture Study. 2008. (J). pap. 15.99 *(978-0-9777430-1-8(2))* Simon Peter Pr., Inc.
Woodhouse, John. 1 Samuel (Redesign) Looking for a Leader. 2014. (Preaching the Word Ser.). 672p. 37.99 *(978-1-4335-4884-0(4))* Crossway.
Wright, Christine. My Little Green Book: First Steps in Bible Reading. 2004. 64p. 4.99 *(978-1-85999-696-6(5))* Scripture Union GBR. Dist: Gabriel Resources.
Wright, Lacie. Covenant for Kids! Student Workbook. 2008. 60p. pap. 9.95 *(978-0-615-20658-5(1))* Wright, Lacie.
Younger Elementary KidKit. 2003. (Godprints Curriculum Ser.). 8.99 *(978-0-7814-3672-4(9)*, 2023) Cook, David C.
Zondervan Staff. Adventure Bible for Early Readers, 1 vol. rev. ed. 2014. (Adventure Bible Ser.). (ENG.). 1584p. (J). 31.99 *(978-0-310-72746-0(4))*; (Illus.). 29.99 *(978-0-310-72742-2(1))* Zonderkidz.
—First Communion Bible, 1 vol. 2004. (ENG.). 416p. (J). im. lthr. 12.99 *(978-0-310-70831-5(1))* Zonderkidz.
—NIRV Backpack Bible , 1 vol. rev. ed. 2014. (ENG.). 1152p. (J). im. lthr. 22.99 *(978-0-310-74408-5(3))* Zonderkidz.
—Nirv Precious Princess Bible, 1 vol. rev. ed. 2014. (ENG.). 1152p. (J). im. lthr. 24.99 *(978-0-310-74367-5(2))* Zonderkidz.

BIBLE—THEOLOGY

see Theology

BIBLE—USE

Center for Learning Network Staff. Faith: Minicourse. 2005. (Religion Ser.). 81p. (YA). spiral bd. 12.95 *(978-1-56077-796-0(6))* Center for Learning, The.

BIBLE—ZOOLOGY

see Bible—Natural History

BIBLE AS LITERATURE

see also Religious Literature

David C. Cook Publishing Company Staff, creator. Classy, Flashy Bible Dramas. 2008. (Bible Fun Stuff for Tweens Ser.). (Illus.). 112p. (J). (gr. 4-5). pap. 16.99 *(978-1-4347-6858-2(9))* Cook, David C.
Hahne, Michelle. Song School Greek. 2009. (ENG.). (J). (gr. 3-7). pap. 24.95 incl. cd-rom *(978-1-60051-044-1(2))* Classical Academic Pr.

BIBLE CLASSES

see Bible—Study

BIBLE GAMES AND PUZZLES

ABC Poster Book. 2004. (J). pap. 12.99 *(978-1-59317-080-6(7))* Warner Pr., Inc.
Adams, Anne. See It/Say It Bible Storybook. Incrocci, Rick, illus. 2006. 191p. 12.99 *(978-0-7814-4403-3(9))* Cook, David C.
Awesome Bible Activity Book, 1 vol. 2016. (ENG.). 128p. (J). pap. 9.99 *(978-1-78128-295-3(1)*, Candle Bks.) Lion Hudson PLC GBR. Dist: Kregel Pubns.
B&H Kids Editorial Staff. 100+ Little Bible Words (padded Board Book) 2017. (Little Words Matter(tm) Ser.). (ENG., Illus.). 38p. (J). (gr. -1 — 1). bds. 12.99 *(978-1-4336-4923-3(3)*, B&H Kids) B&H Publishing Group.
Berthel, Alice H. Power Puzzles: John. 2007. (J). per. 12.95 *(978-1-59352-193-6(6))* Christian Services Publishing.
—Power Puzzles: Luke. 2007. (J). per. 12.95 *(978-1-59352-192-9(8))* Christian Services Publishing.
—Power Puzzles: Mark. 2007. (J). per. 12.95 *(978-1-59352-191-2(X))* Christian Services Publishing.
—Power Puzzles: Matthew. 2006. (J). per. 12.95 *(978-1-59352-174-5(X))* Christian Services Publishing.
Best-Loved Bible Stories: Book & Giant Floor Puzzle, 1 vol. 2009. 10p. (J). 17.99 *(978-0-8254-5548-3(0))* Kregel Pubns.
Books, Atkins. Holy Bible Word Search Puzzles Unscramble the Answers. 2011. 218p. pap. 19.99 *(978-1-4568-4324-3(9))* Xlibris Corp.
Boston, Vicki, et al. Wiggles & Squiggles: 60 Bible-Based Classroom Games & Activities. 2007. (CPH Teaching Resource Ser.). (ENG., Illus.). 64p. pap. 10.99 *(978-0-7586-1347-9(4))* Concordia Publishing Hse.
Bowman, Crystal & McKinley, Teri. Adam & Eve's 1-2-3s. Flowers, Luke, illus. 2017. (Our Daily Bread for Little Hearts Ser.). (ENG.). 18p. (J). (— 1). bds. 9.99 *(978-1-62707-600-5(X))* Discovery Hse. Pubs.
Bowman, Crystal & McKinley, Teri. Our Daily Bread for Kids Bible Quizzes & Games: 20 Quizzes & 60 Games for Kids. 2017. (Our Daily Bread for Kids Ser.). (ENG.). 160p. (gr. 1-5). pap. 9.99 ***(978-1-62707-670-8(0))*** Discovery Hse. Pubs.
Brierley, Jane. Life of Jesus Puzzle Book. Lebedev, Aleksandr, illus. 2006. (Play & Learn Puzzle Bks.). (J). 12.95 *(978-0-88271-854-5(1))* Regina Pr., Malhame & Co.
Brown, Jenny. 100 Active Bible Games for Children. 2006. (ENG.). 224p. per. 12.99 *(978-1-84291-129-7(5))* Kingsway Pubns. GBR. Dist: Send The Light Distribution LLC.
Burchett, Author Walter, BA. Christian children's crossword puzzles/circle the words/fill in the Blanks. 2008. 96p. pap. 15.95 *(978-0-557-02507-7(9))* Lulu Pr., Inc.
—Christian children's fill in the Blank. 2008. 33p. pap. 6.95 *(978-0-557-02506-0(0))* Lulu Pr., Inc.
—Christian crossword puzzles for Children. 2008. 36p. pap. 6.95 *(978-0-557-02504-6(4))* Lulu Pr., Inc.
Candle Books, creator. Carry along Bible Activities. 2006. 24p. (J). (gr. -1-3). pap. 11.99 *(978-0-8254-7310-4(1)*, Candle Bks.) Lion Hudson PLC GBR. Dist: Kregel Pubns.
Carson-Dellosa Publishing Staff. Dot-to-Dot Bible Pictures: Make Personal Connections to God's Word! 2004. (Fun Faith-Builders Ser.). (ENG.). 32p. (gr. -1-k). pap. 4.99 *(978-0-88724-219-9(7)*, CD-2040) Carson-Dellosa Publishing, LLC.
Carson-Dellosa Publishing Staff, compiled by. Dot-to-Dot Bible Pictures, Grades 1-3: Make Personal Connections to God's Word! 2004. (Fun Faith-Builders Ser.). (ENG.). 32p. (gr. 1-3). pap. 4.99 *(978-0-88724-220-5(0)*, CD-2041) Carson-Dellosa Publishing, LLC.
Cavins, Emily. Great Adventure Kids Coloring Book: Bible Story Coloring Book. McCook, Eileen, illus. 2008. (Great Adventures: Kids Ser.). 48p. pap. 7.95 *(978-1-934217-64-1(6))* Ascension Pr.
Christian Art Gifts, creator. The Miracles of Jesus Puzzle Bible. 2008. (Illus.). 10p. (J). (gr. -1-3). bds. *(978-1-86920-787-8(4))* Christian Art Pubs.
—My Little Puzzle Bible. 2008. (Illus.). 10p. (J). (gr. -1-3). bds. *(978-1-86920-786-1(6))* Christian Art Pubs.
Coleman, William L. How, Why, When, Where: A Treasure Chest of Wonderful Bible Facts, Stories, Games! Walles, Dwight, illus. 2011. (J). pap. *(978-0-89191-717-5(9))* Cook, David C.
Concordia Publishing House, creator. Exploring God's Word with Puzzles: Grades 3-8. 2014. (ENG., Illus.). 39p. (J). (gr. 4-7). pap. 8.99 *(978-0-7586-4708-5(5))* Concordia Publishing Hse.
Copenhagen Publishing Company, prod. Jesus Calms the Storm. 2015. (Carry Me Puzzle Bks.). (ENG.). 8p. (J). bds. 11.99 *(978-1-4964-1089-4(0))* Tyndale Hse. Pubs.
—Jesus Heals a Lame Man. 2015. (Carry Me Puzzle Bks.). (ENG.). 8p. (J). bds. 11.99 *(978-1-4964-1088-7(2))* Tyndale Hse. Pubs.
—Jonah & the Big Fish. 2015. (Carry Me Puzzle Bks.). (ENG.). 8p. (J). bds. 11.99 *(978-1-4964-1086-3(6))* Tyndale Hse. Pubs.
—Noah's Amazing Ark. 2015. (Carry Me Puzzle Bks.). (ENG.). 8p. (J). bds. 11.99 *(978-1-4964-1087-0(4))* Tyndale Hse. Pubs.
Created By the Master Bible Puzzles Ages 8 & Up. 2006. (YA). per. *(978-1-59872-337-3(5))* Instant Pub.
David C. Cook Publishing Company Staff. Asteroid Alley Games Guide. 2007. (Vacation Bible School Ser.). 48p. (J). (gr. 3-12). pap. 6.99 *(978-1-4347-9960-9(3))* Cook, David C.
David C. Cook Publishing Company Staff, creator. Full Tilt Wacky Games. 2008. (Bible Fun Stuff for Middle School Ser.). (Illus.). 112p. (J). (gr. 6-8). pap. 19.99 *(978-1-4347-6855-1(4))* Cook, David C.
—Score with Scripture Games. 2008. (Bible Fun Stuff for K-1 Ser.). (Illus.). 112p. (J). (gr. k-1). pap. 19.99 *(978-1-4347-6861-2(9))* Cook, David C.
Deep Blue Toddlers & Twos Class Stuff Winter 2016-17. 2016. (Deep Blue Ser.). 24p. pap. 22.99 *(978-1-63088-678-3(5))* Abingdon Pr.
Dowley, Tim. Bible Kings & Queens, 1 vol. 2016. (Activity Fun Ser.). (ENG.). 64p. (J). pap. 4.99 *(978-1-78128-259-5(5)*, Candle Bks.) Lion Hudson PLC GBR. Dist: Kregel Pubns.
Dowley, Tim & Ruta, Angelo. The Story of Jesus, 1 vol. 2016. (Activity Fun Ser.). (ENG.). 64p. (J). pap. 4.99 *(978-1-78128-248-9(X)*, Candle Bks.) Lion Hudson PLC GBR. Dist: Kregel Pubns.
Dyan, Penelope. I Am There! Dyan, Penelope, illus. 2011. (Illus.). 34p. pap. 11.95 *(978-1-935630-98-2(9))* Bellissima Publishing, LLC.
Eden, David. The Potter's Wheel Story & Activity Book. Eden, David, illus. 2011. (ENG., Illus.). 48p. (J). pap. 16.95 *(978-0-9841658-6-5(X)*, Ignition Pr.) Publishing Services @ Thomson-Shore.
Elkins, Stephen. The Ultimate Travel Time Bible. Conaway, Jim, illus. 2007. 170p. (J). (gr. -1-3). 14.99 incl. audio compact disk *(978-0-8054-2647-2(7))* B&H Publishing Group.
Fogle, Robin. Bible Story Hidden Pictures: Coloring & Activity Book. Johnson, Paul, illus. 2006. 16p. (J). (gr. 1-5). 1.79 *(978-1-59317-160-5(9))* Warner Pr., Inc.
—Bible Story Hidden Pictures: Coloring & Activity Book. Denman, Michael, illus. 2006. (J). (gr. 1-5). 1.79 *(978-1-59317-161-2(7))* Warner Pr., Inc.
—Itty-bitty Bible Activity Book, Love. 2007. (Illus.). 48p. (J). pap. 1.49 *(978-1-59317-213-8(3))* Warner Pr., Inc.
—Itty-bitty Bible Activity Book, the Legend of the Candy Cane. 2007. (Illus.). 48p. (J). pap. 1.49 *(978-1-59317-212-1(5))* Warner Pr., Inc.
Gospel Light Publications Staff. Really Big Book of Bible Games: More Than 250 Fun Games for Ages 6 to 12. 2006. (Big Bks.). (ENG., Illus.). 208p. (J). 39.99 *(978-0-8307-4272-1(7))* Gospel Light Pubns.
Houts, Amy. God's People & Me: Boz's Big Book of Bible Fun. Davidson, Leigh, ed. 2008. (Boz the Big Green Bear Next Door Ser.). (Illus.). 235p. (J). (gr. -1). pap. 14.99 *(978-1-4347-9947-0(6))* Cook, David C.
Itt-bitty Bible, No. 5. 2005. (J). pap. 1.49 *(978-1-59317-068-4(8))* Warner Pr., Inc.
Itty-Bitty Bible Activity Book. 2005. (J). pap. 2.50 *(978-1-59317-013-4(0))* Warner Pr., Inc.
Itty-Bitty Bible Activity Book: Christmas Edition. 2005. (J). pap. *(978-1-59317-015-8(7))* Warner Pr., Inc.
Itty-Bitty Bible No. 4: Jesus/Child. 2005. (J). pap. 2.10 *(978-1-59317-014-1(9))* Warner Pr., Inc.
Keffer, Lois & Keffer, Lindy. Bible Brain Benders. 2006. (Illus.). 79p. (J). (gr. 4-7). per. 6.99 *(978-0-7814-4350-0(4)*, 0781443504) Cook, David C.
Lebedev, Aleksandr, illus. Bible Stories. 2006. (Play & Learn Puzzle Bks.). 12p. (J). 12.95 *(978-0-88271-385-4(X))* Regina Pr., Malhame & Co.
Lucey, Marcia T., ed. Catholic Corner: Puzzles & Activities: Year C, Ages 5-7. Radtke, Becky, illus. 2007. 67p. pap. 14.95 incl. cd-rom *(978-1-58459-362-1(8))* World Library Pubns.
MacKenzie, Carine. Glorifying God: Obedient Lives from the Bible. 2013. (ENG., Illus.). 96p. (J). pap. 7.99 *(978-1-78191-124-2(X)*, 404a70e4-6acf-4784-85be-df8caceea0fa) Christian Focus Pubns. GBR. Dist: Bookmasters Distribution.
MacKenzie, Catherine. Jesus Christ the Best King of All. 2010. (Colour Bks.). (ENG., Illus.). 64p. (J). 6.99 *(978-1-84550-568-4(9)*, 9781845505684) Christian Focus Pubns. GBR. Dist: Bookmasters Distribution.
MacLean, Ruth. The Happy Harvest: A Puzzle Book about Ruth. rev. ed. 2008. (Puzzle Ser.). (ENG.). 24p. (J). 4.99 *(978-1-84550-405-2(4)*, 940a47e5-80f8-4841-9210-d657fd18414c) Christian Focus Pubns. GBR. Dist: Bookmasters Distribution.
—The Man Who Ran: A Puzzle Book about Jonah. rev. ed. 2009. (Puzzle Ser.). (ENG., Illus.). 24p. (J). 4.99 *(978-1-84550-496-0(8)*, 9781845504960) Christian Focus Pubns. GBR. Dist: Bookmasters Distribution.
—The Shepherd King: A Puzzle Book about David. rev. ed. 2009. (Puzzle Ser.). (ENG., Illus.). 24p. (J). 4.99 *(978-1-84550-498-4(4)*, c4a1705c-30c9-4390-96f6-fa425d40387e) Christian Focus Pubns. GBR. Dist: Bookmasters Distribution.
Martin, Peter. The Lion Picture Puzzle Bible. Epstein, Len, illus. 2016. (ENG.). 32p. (J). (gr. k-2). 12.99 *(978-0-7459-6545-1(8))* Lion Hudson PLC GBR. Dist: Independent Pubs. Group.
Miller, Steve & Miller, Becky. 101 Awesome Bible Puzzles for Kids. 2015. (Take Me Through the Bible Ser.). (ENG.). 112p. (J). pap. 7.99 *(978-0-7369-6402-9(9))* Harvest Hse. Pubs.
Mitchell, Alison. Easter Unscrambled: Bible Discovery for Children & Families. 2010. 41p. (J). pap. *(978-1-873166-89-5(3))* Good Bk. Co.
Mitzo Thompson, Kim, et al. Amazing Bible Story MAZES. 2017. (I'm Learning the Bible Activity Book Ser.). (ENG.). 48p. (J). pap. 4.99 ***(978-1-68322-193-7(1))*** Barbour Publishing, Inc.
—Bible ABCs Fun Activity Book. 2017. (ENG.). 32p. (J). pap. 4.99 ***(978-1-68322-194-4(X))*** Barbour Publishing, Inc.
Molski, Carol. Bible Puzzlers. Koehler, Ed, illus. 2007. (CPH Teaching Resource Ser.). (ENG.). 63p. (J). (gr. 4-7). per. 10.99 *(978-0-7586-1332-5(6))* Concordia Publishing Hse.
Mooney, Belinda. Itty-Bitty Book: New Testament. 2006. (J). pap. 1.49 *(978-1-59317-167-4(6))* Warner Pr., Inc.
—Itty-Bitty Book: Old Testament. 2006. (J). pap. 1.49 *(978-1-59317-166-7(8))* Warner Pr., Inc.
Moses: God's Man of the Hour — Activity Book. 2005. pap. 1.69 *(978-1-59317-109-4(9))* Warner Pr., Inc.
Preston, Rhoda & Stickler, LeeDell. Abingdon's Books of the Bible Games. 2006. (Illus.). 64p. per. 10.99 *(978-0-687-49480-4(X))* Abingdon Pr.
Rainbow Publishers Staff. Bible Trivia & Truths: Bible Potuzzles. 2006. (J). pap. 11.95 *(978-1-58411-051-4(1))* Rainbow Pubs. & Legacy Pr.
Schlegel, William. Miracle Puzzlers. Moran, Edna, illus. 2009. 64p. pap. 10.99 *(978-0-7586-1605-0(8))* Concordia Publishing Hse.
Schlegl, William. Bible Alphabet Puzzles. 2006. (Illus.). 64p. pap. 10.99 *(978-0-7586-1300-4(8))* Concordia Publishing Hse.
Seifert, Sheila & Naylor, Beth. Stepping up, Stepping Out. 2008. (DSJ Ser.). (Illus.). 112p. (J). (gr. 1-6). pap. 16.99 *(978-0-7814-4562-7(0))* Cook, David C.
Sewell, Elisabeth. Bible Activity Book. 2010. (ENG., Illus.). 38p. (J). pap. 8.00 *(978-0-7152-0907-3(8))* Saint Andrew Pr., Ltd. GBR. Dist: Westminster John Knox Pr.
Spear, Kevin. Itty-bitty Bible Activity Book, Easter. 2007. (Illus.). 48p. (J). pap. 1.49 *(978-1-59317-196-4(X))* Warner Pr., Inc.
Spear, Kevin, des. Favorite Bible Stories Puzzle Book. 2009. (Illus.). 48p. (J). (gr. 1-5). pap. 4.50 *(978-1-59317-353-1(9))* Warner Pr., Inc.
Star Chasers. 2006. (J). pap. 1.79 *(978-1-59317-170-4(6))* Warner Pr., Inc.
Stone, Julia. I Spy Bible: A Picture Puzzle Bible for the Very Young. Meredith, Samantha, illus. 2015. (ENG.). 24p. (J). (gr. -1-k). bds. 9.99 *(978-0-7459-6555-0(5))* Lion Hudson PLC GBR. Dist: Independent Pubs. Group.
Sturtz, Maria. Coloring Book in the Bible. 2004. 32p. (J). 1.79 *(978-0-7586-0106-3(9))* Concordia Publishing Hse.
Thomas Nelson, Thomas. Big Fun Bible Puzzle Book, 1 vol. 2015. (ENG.). 448p. pap. 14.99 *(978-0-7180-4178-6(X))* Nelson, Thomas Inc.
Van Leeuwen, Wendy. Itty-bitty Bible Activity Book, God's Big Christmas Plan. 2007. (Illus.). 48p. (J). pap. 1.49 *(978-1-59317-211-4(7))* Warner Pr., Inc.
VN Industries, Inc. Editorial Staff, ed. 5 Angels - A Jigsaw Puzzle Book: With Inspirational Messages from the Bible. 2005. (Illus.). 12p. bds. 19.95 *(978-1-882330-71-3(4))* Magni Co., The.
Warner Press, creator. Itty-Bitty Bible Activity Book: The First Collection. 2007. (Itty-Bitty Ser.). (ENG., Illus.). 192p. (J). (gr. -1-3). per. 4.99 *(978-1-59317-114-8(5))* Warner Pr., Inc.
—Itty-Bitty Bible Activity Book of Trivia & Cartoons!, pkg. of 6. 2007. (Itty-Bitty Ser.). (Illus.). 48p. (J). pap. 5.99 *(978-1-59317-069-1(6))* Warner Pr., Inc.
Wegener, Bill, illus. & des. The Bible Game - New Testament: The Bible Game - New Testament. Wegener, Bill, des. 2004. (YA). bds. 34.95 *(978-0-9753620-1-3(1))* IMAGINEX, LLC.
—The Bible Game - Old Testament: The Bible Game - Old Testament. Wegener, Bill, des. 2004. (YA). bds. 34.95 *(978-0-9753620-0-6(3)*, Bible Game) IMAGINEX, LLC.
Williams, Carla. Big Puzzles for Little Hands: People Who Obeyed God. 2004. (Illus.). 96p. (J). (gr. -1-2). pap. 11.95 *(978-1-885358-48-6(2))* Rainbow Pubs. & Legacy Pr.
Williamson, Karen. My Little Bible Memory Game, 1 vol. Enright, Amanda, illus. 2014. (ENG.). 40p. (J). 9.99 *(978-1-85985-986-5(0)*, Candle Bks.) Lion Hudson PLC GBR. Dist: Kregel Pubns.
Woodman, Ros. The Beautiful Bride: A Puzzle Book about Rebecca. rev. ed. 2008. (Puzzle Ser.). (ENG.). 24p. (J). 4.99 *(978-1-84550-402-1(X)*, 6dee0292-282e-4dcb-be0a-847794844203) Christian Focus Pubns. GBR. Dist: Bookmasters Distribution.
—Bible Detectives Quiz Book: Noughts & Crosses. 2005. (ENG., Illus.). 64p. (J). pap. 7.99 *(978-1-84550-081-8(4)*, 6ad8c029-b110-4e1a-9ec5-0911d60cd7f3) Christian Focus Pubns. GBR. Dist: Bookmasters Distribution.
—Exodus: Fun Bible Studies Using Puzzles & Stories. Wheeler, Ron, illus. 2005. (Activity Ser.). (ENG.). 64p. (J). (gr. 4-7). pap., act. bk. ed. 7.99 *(978-1-84550-067-2(9)*, 870539af-e943-4634-8ae9-d6317cc1f975) Christian Focus Pubns. GBR. Dist: Bookmasters Distribution.
—Fun Bible Studies Using Puzzles & Stories. Wheeler, Ron, illus. 2006. (ENG.). 64p. (J). pap. 7.99 *(978-1-84550-223-2(X)*, 9781845502232) Christian Focus Pubns. GBR. Dist: Bookmasters Distribution.
—Genesis: Fun Bible Studies Using Puzzles & Stories. Wheeler, Ron, illus. 2005. (Activity Ser.). (ENG.). 64p. (J). (gr. 4-7). pap., act. bk. ed. 7.99 *(978-1-84550-066-5(0)*, 02dba325-10fb-4c5c-8053-5f5a317c8b08) Christian Focus Pubns. GBR. Dist: Bookmasters Distribution.
—The Great Celebration: A Puzzle Book about Hezekiah. rev. ed. 2008. (Puzzle Ser.). (ENG.). 24p. (J). 4.99 *(978-1-84550-403-8(8)*, 5fdc83c5-dfb7-462d-aaa0-4a3833eba38b) Christian Focus Pubns. GBR. Dist: Bookmasters Distribution.
—The Wise King: A Puzzle Book about Solomon. rev. ed. 2008. (Puzzle Ser.). (ENG.). 24p. (J). 4.99

(978-1-84550-404-5(6), bde9e1c9-e7ee-4d1c-98a1-0b3c87149528) Christian Focus Pubns. GBR. Dist: Bookmasters Distribution.

Workman Publishing Co., Inc. Bible Brain Quest(r) for Kids: Over 500 Questions & Answers about the Old & New Testaments. 2017. (ENG.). 160p. (J). pap. 10.99 *(978-0-7369-6882-9(2))* Harvest Hse. Pubs.

World Library Publications, creator. Catholic Corner Puzzles & Activities: Year C. 2007. (Catholic Corner Ser.). (Illus.). 67p. (J). (gr. 2-5). pap. 14.95 incl. cd-rom *(978-1-58459-363-8(6))* World Library Pubns.

Zondervan. The Story Trading Cards: for Elementary & Preschool: Grades 3 & Up, 1 vol. 2016. (Story Ser.). (ENG.). 33p. (J). 5.99 *(978-0-310-08695-6(7))* Zonderkidz.

104 Bible Puzzles for Tweens. 2008. 144p. pap. 18.00 *(978-0-687-65056-9(9))* Abingdon Pr.

BIBLE PLAYS

Cartwright, Teryl, et al. The Humongous Book of Bible Skits for Children's Ministry. 2005. (ENG., Illus.). 208p. pap. 29.99 *(978-0-7644-3083-1(1))* Group Publishing, Inc.

David C. Cook Publishing Company Staff, creator. Pretty Quick & Easy Bible Dramas. 2008. (Bible Fun Stuff for 2nd-3rd Grades Ser.). (Illus.). 112p. (J). (gr. 2-3). pap. 19.99 *(978-1-4347-6860-5(0))* Cook, David C.

Freeman, Kim. Bible Plays for Kids: A Visual Look at the Bible! 2003. 68p. (J). pap. 14.95 *(978-0-9725827-0-4(3))* Amazing Drama Anointed Voices Original Music.

Goodwin, Debbie Salter. Quick Start Drama for Kids: Christmas: No Rehearsal Bible Skits for Classroom or Performance. 2007. (Lillenas Drama Ser.). (ENG.). 40p. pap. 19.99 *(978-0-8341-7561-7(4),* 0834175614) Lillenas Publishing Co.

Neilands, Lynda. 50 Bible Dramas for Children: For Use in Church, Clubs, & School. 2006. (ENG., Illus.). 287p. per. 13.99 *(978-1-84291-253-9(4))* Kingsway Pubns. GBR. Dist: Send The Light Distribution LLC.

Ransom, Nick. Instant Bible Dramas: Easy Skits for Elementary Kids. 2016. 120p. pap. 19.99 *(978-1-5018-2110-3(5))* Abingdon Pr.

Tinsley, Sarah V. Instant Bible Plays, Just Add Kids! 2008. 264p. pap. 24.95 *(978-1-4357-1672-8(8))* Lulu Pr., Inc.

Twork, Carol Camp. "I Want to Be Jesus" Over 150 Easy-to-Use Gospel Plays for Children. 2003. 176p. tchr. ed. 17.95 *(978-0-87793-691-6(9))* Ave Maria Pr.

Wendt, Harry. The Divine Drama - Our Narrative. 4th rev. ed. 2004. (Illus.). 174p. per. 11.95 net. *(978-1-891245-10-7(4),* 4872) Crossways International.

—The Divine Drama - the Biblical Narrative. 4th ed. 2004. (Illus.). 176p. per. 12.95 net. *(978-1-891245-09-1(0),* 4871) Crossways International.

Williams, Guy. The Burning Fiery Furnace: Shadrach, Meshach, & Abednego. 2003. (More for Teens Ser.). 24p. (Orig.). (YA). (gr. 6-12). pap. 5.00 *(978-0-88734-413-8(5))* Players Pr., Inc.

—Joseph & His Brothers. 2003. 24p. (J). (gr. 4-12). pap. 5.00 *(978-0-88734-882-2(3))* Players Pr., Inc.

BIBLE PUZZLES

see Bible Games and Puzzles

BIBLE STORIES

ABCs of the Bible Coloring Book. (Illus.). 16p. (J). pap. 1.50 *(978-0-87162-873-2(2),* E6036) Warner Pr., Inc.

Abingdon. PowerXpress David the Boy Disciple. 2.95 incl. cd-rom *(978-0-687-00191-0(9))* Abingdon Pr.

—PowerXpress David the King Disciple. 2.95 incl. cd-rom *(978-0-687-00211-5(7))* Abingdon Pr.

Abraham, Ken. Jesus Loves Me Bible Storybook & Devotional Combo. 2003. (Illus.). 672p. (J). 24.99 *(978-1-4003-0185-0(8))* Nelson, Thomas Inc.

ABS Staff. Bible Now: 101 Amazing Storie. 2004. pap. 14.99 *(978-1-58516-646-6(4))* American Bible Society.

Adams, Anne. See It/Say It Bible Storybook. Incrocci, Rick, illus. 2006. 191p. 12.99 *(978-0-7814-4403-3(9))* Cook, David C.

Adams, Georgia & Utton, Peter. Cuentame la Biblia.Tr. of Bible Storybook. (SPA.). 96p. (J). (gr. k-3). 17.56 *(978-84-480-1120-8(1))* Timun Mas, Editorial S.A. ESP. Dist: Lectorum Pubns., Inc.

The Adventures of Moses. 2003. (Rub & See Activity Bks.). (Illus.). 24p. (J). 2.99 *(978-0-8254-7260-2(1))* Kregel Pubns.

Alex, Ben. Great Bible Stories. 2010. (ENG., Illus.). 37p. (gr. k-5). pap. 5.95 *(978-87-7247-026-9(7))* Scandinavia Publishing Hse. DNK. Dist: Destiny Image Pubs.

—Great Bible Stories: For Children Age 5 & Up. Scandinavia Publishing House Staff, ed. 2010. (ENG.). 37p. (gr. k-5). 8.95 *(978-87-7247-025-2(9))* Scandinavia Publishing Hse. DNK. Dist: Destiny Image Pubs.

Alexander, Pat. Lion First Bible. Baxter, Leon, illus. 2015. (ENG.). 480p. (J). (gr. k-2). 14.99 *(978-0-7459-6103-3(7))* Lion Hudson PLC GBR. Dist: Independent Pubs. Group.

Alexander, Pat & Box, Su. The Lion First Bible & Prayers, 2 vols. Baxter, Leon, illus. 2016. (ENG.). 608p. (J). (gr. k-3). 16.99 *(978-0-7459-6493-5(1))* Lion Hudson PLC GBR. Dist: Independent Pubs. Group.

Alexander, Pat & Rock, Lois. The Lion Children's Bible: The World's Greatest Story Retold for Every Child. Cox, Carolyn, illus. 2nd ed. 2012. (ENG.). 256p. (J). (gr. 2-7). 12.99 *(978-0-7459-1939-3(1))* Lion Hudson PLC GBR. Dist: Independent Pubs. Group.

All about Me: Bible Story: God Made People. (Scripture Bites Ser.). (Illus.). (J). 7.99 *(978-0-7847-9018-2(3),* 00711) Standard Publishing.

Allen, Jan. Now I Know the Story of Samson. l.t. ed. 2006. (Illus.). 40p. (J). *(978-0-9765514-1-6(1))* Light Bugs Publishing.

Allison, Teresa J. Bobble Stories: The Humbobble's Lost Hum. Allison, Charles T., illus. 2013. 48p. pap. 12.99 *(978-0-9887612-1-6(1))* Tawnsy Publishing.

Alsbrooks, Stephanie. Cow Moooves Through the Books of the Bible: Genesis. Burg, Donna, illus. 2004. (J). bds. 9.99 *(978-1-4183-0002-9(0))* Christ Inspired, Inc.

—Cow Moooves Through the Books of the Bible: Job. Burg, Donna, illus. 2004. (J). bds. 9.99 *(978-1-4183-0006-7(3))* Christ Inspired, Inc.

—Cow Moooves Through the Books of the Bible - Exodus. Burg, Donna, illus. 2004. (J). bds. 9.99 *(978-1-4183-0007-4(1))* Christ Inspired, Inc.

—Cow Moooves Through the Books of the Bible - Joshua. Burg, Donna, illus. 2004. (J). bds. 9.99 *(978-1-4183-0017-3(9))* Christ Inspired, Inc.

American Bible Society Staff. The Amazing Bible Factbook for Kids. 2008. (ENG., Illus.). 256p. (YA). (gr. 7-17). pap. 13.99 *(978-1-60320-778-2(3),* Liberty St.) Time Inc. Bks.

—American Bible Society Favorite Bible Stories & Amazing Facts. 2011. (ENG., Illus.). 224p. (gr. 3-17). 19.95 *(978-1-60320-175-9(0))* Time Inc. Bks.

—American Bible Society Favorite Bible Stories & Amazing Facts. 2011. (ENG., Illus.). 224p. (gr. 3-17). pap. 12.99 *(978-1-60320-900-7(X))* Time Inc. Bks.

American Bible Society Staff, ed. My First Read & Learn Bible. 2006. (ENG., Illus.). 40p. (J). (gr. -1-k). bds. 9.99 *(978-0-439-65128-8(X))* Scholastic, Inc.

Amery, H. Bible Stories Jigsaw Book. 2004. 20p. (J). 14.95 *(978-0-7945-0558-5(9))* EDC Publishing.

—Joseph & the Amazing Coat. 2004. (Bible Tales Readers Ser.). (SPA., Illus.). 16p. (J). lib. bdg. 12.95 *(978-1-58086-540-1(2))* EDC Publishing.

—Moses in the Bulrushes. 2004. (Bible Tales Readers Ser.). (SPA., Illus.). 16p. (J). lib. bdg. 12.95 *(978-1-58086-541-8(0))* EDC Publishing.

Amery, Heather. Bible Stories. Young, Norman, illus. gif. ed. 2004. (Bible Tales Readers Ser.). (ENG.). 1p. (J). (gr. -1-3). 24.95 *(978-0-7460-4145-1(4))* EDC Publishing.

—Book of Bible Stories with CD (Combined Volume) rev. ed. 2007. (Bible Tales Readers Ser.). 200p. (J). 24.99 *(978-0-7945-1659-8(9),* Usborne) EDC Publishing.

—Illustrated Children's Bible Stories. 2015. (Illustrated Children's Bible Stories Ser.). (ENG.). 192p. (J). 29.99 *(978-0-7945-2138-7(X),* Usborne) EDC Publishing.

—Mini Children's Bible. 2011. 144p. pap. 8.99 *(978-0-7945-2802-7(3),* Usborne) EDC Publishing.

Amery, Heather & Temporin, Elena. Family Bible. 2004. (Illus.). 192p. (J). 19.95 *(978-0-7945-0333-8(0),* Usborne) EDC Publishing.

Amooti. Grandma Yarumia Fireside Stories: Bible Stories for Children. 2012. (Illus.). 74p. pap. 15.99 *(978-1-4771-1885-6(3))* Xlibris Corp.

Andersen, Hans Christian. Hans Christian Andersen: Illustrated Fairy Tales, Vol. 2. 2004. (ENG., Illus.). 416p. (J). (gr. -1-3). *(978-87-7247-271-3(5))* Scandinavia Publishing Hse.

Anderson, Jeff, et al. The Lion Comic Book Hero Bible. 2015. (ENG., Illus.). 192p. 19.95 *(978-0-7459-5617-6(3))* Lion Hudson PLC GBR. Dist: Independent Pubs. Group.

Anderson, Linda A., et al. Big Big God: 13 Amazing Lessons Where Preschoolers Experience God, 28 vols. 2007. (ENG., Illus.). 112p. (J). (gr. -1 — 1). pap. 29.99 incl. audio compact disk *(978-0-7644-3602-4(3))* Group Publishing, Inc.

Andrews, Jackie. 100 Bible Stories for Children. Biro, Val, illus. 2012. (ENG.). 208p. (J). 21.50 *(978-1-84135-105-6(9))* Award Pubns. Ltd. GBR. Dist: Parkwest Pubns., Inc.

Animals Big & Small: Bible Story: Noah's Big Boat. (Scripture Bites Ser.). (Illus.). (J). 7.99 *(978-0-7847-9006-9(X),* 00703) Standard Publishing.

Anthony, Michelle. The Big God Story, 1 vol. Godbey, Cory, illus. 2010. (ENG.). 36p. (J). 12.99 *(978-1-4347-6454-6(0))* Cook, David C.

Aranda, Omar, illus. Once upon a Time Storybook Bible, 1 vol. 2017. (ENG.). 144p. (J). 16.99 *(978-0-310-75792-4(4))* Zonderkidz.

Arch Books Staff. Noahs 2 by 2 Adventures Spanis. 2004. (SPA.). 24p. (J). 2.49 *(978-0-570-08320-7(6))* Concordia Publishing Hse.

—Spanish David & Goliat. 2004. (SPA.). 24p. (J). 2.49 *(978-0-570-08322-1(2))* Concordia Publishing Hse.

—Spanish down Thru the Roof. 2004. (SPA.). 24p. (J). 2.49 *(978-0-570-08323-8(0))* Concordia Publishing Hse.

—Spanish Moses Dry Feet. 2004. (SPA.). 24p. (J). 2.49 *(978-0-570-08321-4(4))* Concordia Publishing Hse.

Archbold, Tim & Rock, Lois. The Good Bad Guy & Other Peculiar Parables. 2004. (ENG., Illus.). 64p. (J). (gr. 2-4). pap. 6.99 *(978-0-7459-4695-5(X))* Lion Hudson PLC GBR. Dist: Independent Pubs. Group.

Armadillo Publishing Staff. Baby's Bible Stories: The Birth of Jesus. Lewis, Jan, illus. 2015. (ENG.). 24p. pap. 6.99 *(978-1-86147-484-1(9),* Armadillo) Anness Publishing GBR. Dist: National Bk. Network.

Arthur, Kay & Arndt, Janna. You're a Brave Man, Daniel! 2007. (ENG., Illus.). 160p. (J). (gr. 4-7). per. 11.99 *(978-0-7369-0147-5(7))* Harvest Hse. Pubs.

Aston, Al. Gifts for a King. Hutchinson, Joy, illus. 2005. 16p. pap. 2.00 *(978-1-84427-179-5(X))* Scripture Union GBR. Dist: Send The Light Distribution LLC.

Award, Anna. Moses in the Bulrushes: See the Picture & Say the Word. 2012. (ENG., Illus.). 24p. (J). pap. 6.50 *(978-1-84135-602-0(6))* Award Pubns. Ltd. GBR. Dist: Parkwest Pubns., Inc.

—The Story of Jesus. 2012. (ENG., Illus.). 24p. (J). pap. 6.50 *(978-1-84135-604-4(2))* Award Pubns. Ltd. GBR. Dist: Parkwest Pubns., Inc.

Awesome Retail - Samson's Super Strength. 2004. pap. 13.99 *(978-1-929296-96-5(7))* Grizzly Adams Productions, Inc.

Aydin, Robert, tr. Syriac Bible for Children. 2007. (SYR.). (J). 48.00 *(978-1-59333-749-0(3))* Gorgias Pr., LLC.

B&H Editorial Staff. The Big Picture Interactive Bible Storybook, Hardcover (Case Of 12) Connecting Christ Throughout God's Story. 2014. (Gospel Project Ser.). (ENG., Illus.). 320p. (J). (gr. 1-5). 100.00 *(978-1-4336-8665-8(1),* B&H Kids) B&H Publishing Group.

B&H Editorial Staff, ed. The Big Picture Interactive Bible Stories in 5 Minutes: Connecting Christ Throughout God's Story. McPherson, Heath, illus. 2014. (Gospel Project Ser.). (ENG.). 192p. (J). (gr. -1-3). 15.99 *(978-1-4336-8472-2(1),* B&H Kids) B&H Publishing Group.

B&H Kids Editorial Staff. Bible Stories for Courageous Boys (padded Cover) 2017. (ENG.). 304p. (J). (gr. 1-4). 12.99 *(978-1-4336-4834-2(2),* B&H Kids) B&H Publishing Group.

—Bible Stories for Courageous Girls (padded Cover) 2017. (ENG.). 304p. (J). (gr. 1-4). 12.99 *(978-1-4336-4835-9(0),* B&H Kids) B&H Publishing Group.

—Brave Queen Esther/David & the Giant Flip-Over Book. McPherson, Heath, illus. 2016. (Big Picture Interactive / the Gospel Project Ser.). (ENG.). 32p. (J). (gr. -1-3). pap. 3.99 *(978-1-4336-4329-3(4),* B&H Kids) B&H Publishing Group.

—It's All about Jesus Bible Storybook: 100 Bible Stories. McPherson, Heath, illus. 2016. (Big Picture Interactive / the Gospel Project Ser.). (ENG.). 320p. (J). (gr. k-5). 16.99 *(978-1-4336-9165-2(5),* B&H Kids) B&H Publishing Group.

—Jesus' Miracles/Finding the Lost, Flip-Over Book. McPherson, Heath, illus. 2016. (Big Picture Interactive / the Gospel Project Ser.). (ENG.). 32p. (J). (gr. -1-3). pap. 3.99 *(978-1-4336-4332-3(4),* B&H Kids) B&H Publishing Group.

—Mighty Miracles/Joseph the Dreamer Flip-Over Book. McPherson, Heath, illus. 2016. (Big Picture Interactive / the Gospel Project Ser.). (ENG.). 32p. (J). (gr. -1-3). pap. 3.99 *(978-1-4336-4330-9(8),* B&H Kids) B&H Publishing Group.

—Putting on the Full Armor of God: A Battle Plan Based on Ephesians 6. 2016. (Bibleman Ser.). (ENG., Illus.). 24p. (J). (gr. -1-2). pap. 5.99 *(978-1-4336-4577-8(7),* B&H Kids) B&H Publishing Group.

—50 Bedtime Bible Stories. 2015. (ENG.). 96p. (J). (gr. -1-3). 14.99 *(978-1-4336-8661-0(9),* B&H Kids) B&H Publishing Group.

B&H Kids Editorial Staff, ed. Little Words Matter Bible Storybook (padded Board Book) Conger, Holli, illus. 2015. (Little Words Matter(tm) Ser.). (ENG.). 38p. (J). (gr. -1 — 1). bds. 9.99 *(978-1-4336-8643-6(0),* B&H Kids) B&H Publishing Group.

B&H Kids Editorial Staff & McPherson, Heath. The Birth of a King/Jesus Saves His People Flip-Over Book. 2016. (Big Picture Interactive / the Gospel Project Ser.). (ENG.). 32p. (J). (gr. -1-3). pap. 3.99 *(978-1-4336-4333-0(2),* B&H Kids) B&H Publishing Group.

Baby Blessings Staff. Bathtime Bible Stories. 2006. 8p. 10.99 *(978-0-7847-1502-4(5),* 04153) Standard Publishing.

Baden, Robert. Jesus Returns to Heaven. Hackett, Michael, illus. rev. ed. 2004. (ENG.). 16p. (J). 1.99 *(978-0-7586-0407-1(6))* Concordia Publishing Hse.

Bader, Joanne. Abraham, Sarah, & Isaac. 2011. 16p. pap. 2.49 *(978-0-7586-2580-9(4))* Concordia Publishing Hse.

—God Provides Victory Through Gideon. Giliewe, Unada, illus. 2004. (Arch Bks.). 16p. (J). 1.99 *(978-0-7586-0673-0(7))* Concordia Publishing Hse.

—Jesus resucita a una nina (Jesus Wakes the Little Girl) 2011. 16p. pap. 2.49 *(978-0-7586-3066-7(2))* Concordia Publishing Hse.

—Moses & the Long Walk. von der Sterre, Johanna, illus. 2006. 16p. (J). 1.99 *(978-0-7586-0874-1(8))* Concordia Publishing Hse.

Baer, Sam. Illustrated Bible Stories. 2015. (Illustrated Stories Ser.). (ENG.). 368p. (J). (gr. k-5). 19.99 *(978-0-7945-3417-2(1),* Usborne) EDC Publishing.

Bagley, Val Chadwick & Mullins, Amy. My Favorite Stories from the Bible. 2006. (Illus.). 28p. (J). *(978-1-59811-173-6(6))* Covenant Communications.

Baker, Marvin G. Matthew's Story: Based on the Gospel of Matthew. 2004. 191p. per. 9.95 *(978-0-9729256-2-4(7),* Tweener Pr.) Baker Trittin Pr.

Baker, Tommy. Santa Claus, the Fourth Wise Man. 2012. (ENG.). 25p. (J). pap. 18.95 *(978-1-4327-9774-4(3))* Outskirts Pr., Inc.

Balika, Susan S. Jesus Is My Special Friend. Bolling, Vickey, illus. 2013. (Happy Day Ser.). (ENG.). 16p. (J). pap. 2.49 *(978-1-4143-9294-3(X))* Tyndale Hse. Pubs.

Ball, Ann & Will, Julianne M. Catholic Bible Stories for Children. Davidson, Kevin, illus. 2006. 208p. (J). (gr. -1-3). 19.95 *(978-1-59276-243-9(3))* Our Sunday Visitor, Publishing Div.

—Catholic Bible Stories for Children: 1st Communion Edition. Davidson, Kevin, illus. 2006. 208p. (J). (gr. -1-3). 19.95 *(978-1-59276-221-7(2))* Our Sunday Visitor, Publishing Div.

Ball, Liz, illus. Bible Stories: Find-the-Picture Puzzles. 2004. (Find-the-Picture Puzzle Ser.: 1). 24p. (J). pap. 2.95 *(978-0-8198-1163-9(7),* 332-026) Pauline Bks. & Media.

Banks, Celia. Jacob's Promise: A Story about Faith. Unalp, Janet & Perry, Matt, illus. 2006. 32p. 14.99 *(978-0-9764460-6-4(5))* HonorNet.

Barfield, Maggie. The Big Bible Storybook: 188 Bible Stories to Enjoy Together, 1 vol. Carpenter, Mark And Anna, illus. 2009. 256p. (J). 18.99 *(978-0-8254-7424-8(8),* Candle Bks.) Lion Hudson PLC GBR. Dist: Kregel Pubns.

—Welcome the Baby Jesus. 2004. 32p. (J). 6.99 *(978-0-7586-0249-7(9))* Concordia Publishing Hse.

Batchelor, Mary & Boshoff, Penny. My First Bedtime Bible. 2005. (Illus.). 256p. (J). (gr. -1-2). *(978-1-84610-026-0(7))* Make Believe Ideas.

Baxter, Nicola & Langton, Roger. Children's Stories from the Bible: A Collection of over 20 Tales from the Old & New Testament, Retold for Younger Readers. Langton, Roger, illus. 2013. (ENG., Illus.). 80p. (J). (gr. 5-12). pap. 9.99 *(978-1-84322-982-7(X),* Armadillo) Anness Publishing GBR. Dist: National Bk. Network.

Beck, William F. Bible Stories in Pictures. Rogers, Ruth W. et al, illus. 2nd ed. 2003.Tr. of Bible Stories in Pictures. (ALB, SPA & SWE.). 376p. pap. 10.65 *(978-1-931891-08-0(7))* Multi-Language Pubns.

—Histori Biblike Me Llustrime: Nga Krijimi Ne Kishen e Hershme. Rogers, Ruth W. et al, illus. 2003.Tr. of Bible Stories in Pictures. (ALB, SPA & SWE.). 374p. (J). pap. 10.65 *(978-1-931891-07-3(9),* 38-7378) Multi-Language Pubns.

Bell, Bill. Noah: The Incredible Voyager. Bell, Bill, illus. 2004. (Illus.). 48p. (J). (gr. -1-3). per. 14.99 *(978-0-88092-801-4(8))* Royal Fireworks Publishing Co.

Benjamin-Farren, Joan. Shuli & Me: From Slavery to Freedom A Storybook Omer Calendar. Benjamin-Farren, Joan, illus. 2006. (Illus.). (J). 19.95 *(978-0-9788802-0-0(X))* Black Jasmine.

Bennett, Marian. God Made Kittens. Marlin, Kathryn, illus. 2014. (Happy Day Ser.). (ENG.). 16p. (J). pap. 2.49 *(978-1-4143-9479-4(9))* Tyndale Hse. Pubs.

Bennett, William J. El libro de la familia y el Hogar para Niños. Alonso Blanco, Maria Victoria, tr. 2007. (SPA., Illus.). 112p. (J). 18.95 *(978-84-666-1662-1(4))* Ediciones B ESP. Dist: Spanish Pubs., LLC.

Benton, James. The Case Files of Herman Ootix, B. I. Faith for Life2 Course Five Student Book. Janssen, Patricia E., ed. 2nd ed. 2003. (J). stu. ed., spiral bd. 14.99 *(978-0-9727146-6-2(9))* LOGOS System Assocs.

Berenstain, Jan & Berenstain, Mike. Berenstain Bears - Storybook Bible for Little Ones, 1 vol. 2015. (Berenstain Bears/Living Lights Ser.). (ENG., Illus.). 30p. (J). bds. 9.99 *(978-0-310-74941-7(7))* Zonderkidz.

—The Berenstain Bears Storybook Bible, 1 vol. 2013. (Berenstain Bears/Living Lights Ser.). (ENG., Illus.). 256p. (J). 16.99 *(978-0-310-72721-7(9))* Zonderkidz.

Best-Loved Bible Stories: Book & Giant Floor Puzzle, 1 vol. 2009. 10p. (J). 17.99 *(978-0-8254-5548-3(0))* Kregel Pubns.

Betzer, Dan. Dan & Louie Vol. 2: The Greatest Stories Ever Told. enl. ed. 2005. (J). 89.00 incl. audio compact disk *(978-1-933497-01-3(7))* Robison Gamble Creative.

Beveridge, Amy. God Always Cares. Marlin, Kathryn & Julien, Terry, illus. 2014. (Happy Day Ser.). (ENG.). 16p. (J). pap. 2.49 *(978-1-4143-9417-6(9))* Tyndale Hse. Pubs.

Bianchi, Andrew. 10 Rulz. 2005. (Illus.). 128p. pap. *(978-1-84427-053-8(X))* Scripture Union.

Bible Stories. 2003. (Illus.). 256p. (J). 11.95 *(978-0-7525-8974-9(1))* Parragon, Inc.

Bible Stories for the Little Ones from the Creation to Moses. 2006. 340p. per. 23.99 *(978-1-4255-3445-5(7))* Michigan Publishing.

Bible Time Line. 11.99 *(978-0-7847-1004-3(X))* Standard Publishing.

Bible Visuals International Staff, compiled by. Rainbow Garden. 2005. (Illus.). (J). pap. *(978-1-932381-15-3(5),* 5500) Bible Visuals International, Inc.

—Until the Letter Came. 2004. (Illus.). (J). cd-rom *(978-1-933206-45-5(4))* Bible Visuals International, Inc.

Bible Zone in the Wilderness Older Elementary Kit Wrap. 2007. *(978-0-687-64793-4(2))* Abingdon Pr.

Bible Zone in the Wilderness Younger Elementary Kit Wrap. 2007. *(978-0-687-64783-5(5))* Abingdon Pr.

La Biblia Católica para Niños. 2014. (SPA.). (J). (gr. 1-4). pap. 27.95 *(978-1-59982-675-2(5))* St. Mary's Pr. of MN.

Biggs-Scribner, Stephanie, comment. Children of the Bible. 2005. (KOR.). 184p. (YA). pap. *(978-1-890569-91-4(7),* WD/GBGM Bks.) General Board of Global Ministries, The United Methodist Church.

The Birth of Samson. 2007. (J). mass mkt. *(978-0-9769722-0-4(4))* Leslie, Beverly J.

The Blue Jackal. 2004. bds. 7.99 *(978-0-8254-7283-1(0))* Kregel Pubns.

Bluedorn, Johannah, illus. Bless the Lord: The 103rd Psalm. 2005. 32p. (J). 13.00 *(978-1-933228-02-0(4),* 3000) Trivium Pursuit.

Blundell, T & TNT Ministries Staff. On the Way for 9 - 11's, Vol. 2. 2004. (On the Way (9-11's) Ser.). (ENG., Illus.). 96p. (J). pap. 17.99 *(978-1-85792-552-4(1),* 9781857925524) Christian Focus Pubns. GBR. Dist: Bookmasters Distribution.

Blundell, T & TNT Resource Material Staff. On the Way for 9 - 11's, Vol. 3. 2014. (On the Way (9-11's) Ser.). (ENG.). 88p. (J). pap. 17.99 *(978-1-85792-553-1(X),* 9781857925531) Christian Focus Pubns. GBR. Dist: Bookmasters Distribution.

Blundell, Thalia, et al. On the Way for 9 - 11's, Bk. 4. 2006. (On the Way (9-11's) Ser.). (ENG.). 96p. (J). pap. 17.99 *(978-1-85792-554-8(8),* 9781857925548) Christian Focus Pubns. GBR. Dist: Bookmasters Distribution.

Blundell, Trevor & Tnt. Psalms, in the Beginning-God, New Beginnings from John's Gospel, Christmas Prophecies Fulfilled, Bk. 1. 2011. (On the Way (9-11's) Ser.). (ENG.). 88p. (J). pap. 17.99 *(978-1-85792-551-7(3),* 9781857925517) Christian Focus Pubns. GBR. Dist: Bookmasters Distribution.

Blundell, Trevor, et al. David & Solomon, Bk. 9. 2008. (On the Way (3-9's) Ser.). (ENG.). 88p. (J). pap. 17.99 *(978-1-85792-404-6(5),* 9781857924046) Christian Focus Pubns. GBR. Dist: Bookmasters Distribution.

—Ferrari, 1947-1957, Bk. 10. 2008. (On the Way (3-9's) Ser.). (ENG.). 96p. (J). pap. 17.99 *(978-1-85792-405-3(3),* 9781857924053) Christian Focus Pubns. GBR. Dist: Bookmasters Distribution.

—Joseph, Job & Moses, Bk. 4. 2012. (On the Way (3-9's) Ser.). (ENG., Illus.). 84p. (J). pap. 17.99 *(978-1-85792-324-7(3),* 9781857923247) Christian Focus Pubns. GBR. Dist: Bookmasters Distribution.

—On the Way for 3 - 9's. 2014. (On the Way (3-9's) Ser.). (ENG.). (J). 100p. pap. 17.99 *(978-1-85792-320-9(0),* 9781857923209); (Illus.). 84p. pap. 17.99 *(978-1-85792-325-4(1),* 9781857923254) Christian Focus Pubns. GBR. Dist: Bookmasters Distribution.

—On the Way for 3 - 9's: Creation, Abraham & Jacob. 2014. (On the Way (3-9's) Ser.). (ENG., Illus.). 96p. (J). pap. 17.99 *(978-1-85792-301-8(4),* 9781857923018) Christian Focus Pubns. GBR. Dist: Bookmasters Distribution.

—On the Way for 3 - 9's Vol. 2: The Christmas Story & Miracles of Jesus. 2006. (On the Way (3-9's) Ser.). (ENG.). 96p. (J). pap. 17.99 *(978-1-85792-319-3(7),* 9781857923193) Christian Focus Pubns. GBR. Dist: Bookmasters Distribution.

Blyton, Enid. Moses in the Bulrushes: See the Picture & Say the Word. 2012. (ENG.). 24p. (J). pap. 9.95 *(978-1-84135-747-8(2))* Award Pubns. Ltd. GBR. Dist: Parkwest Pubns., Inc.

—Stories Jesus Told. 2012. (ENG.). 24p. (J). pap. 9.95 *(978-1-84135-745-4(6))* Award Pubns. Ltd. GBR. Dist: Parkwest Pubns., Inc.

Bohnet, Eric. The Christmas Promise. 2009. (Arch Bks.). 16p. (J). (gr. k-4). pap. 2.49 *(978-0-7586-1614-2(7))* Concordia Publishing Hse.

—From Adam to Easter. Dorenkamp, Michelle, illus. 2014. (Arch Bks.). (ENG.). 16p. (J). pap. 2.49 *(978-0-7586-4602-6(X))* Concordia Publishing Hse.

Bohnet, Eric C. Arch Books: The Centurion at the Cross. Murphy, Terri, illus. 2007. (Arch Bks.). (J). 1.99 *(978-0-7586-1260-1(5))* Concordia Publishing Hse.

Bolam, Emily, illus. My First Picture Bible. 2017. (ENG.). 224p. (J). (gr. -1-k). 16.99 *(978-0-7459-6551-2(2))* Lion Hudson PLC GBR. Dist: Independent Pubs. Group.

Bollen, Christine. Frogs by the Dozen. Matyschenko, Tanya, illus. l.t. ed. 2006. 24p. (J). per. 9.99 *(978-1-59879-115-0(X))* Lifevest Publishing, Inc.

Boon, Fiona. My Bible Sticker Backpack, 1 vol. 2013. (ENG.). 56p. (J). pap. 7.99 *(978-1-4003-2355-5(X))* Nelson, Thomas Inc.

Borlasca, Hector, illus. It's Too Crowded in Here! And Other Jewish Folktales. 2010. 64p. (J). pap. 7.95 (978-0-87441-850-7(X)) Behrman Hse., Inc.

Bosch, Hermann. Bedtime Bible Stories for Catholic Children: Loving Jesus through His Word. 2011. 204p. (J). pap. 19.95 (978-1-934185-39-1(6)) Biblio Resource Pubns., Inc.

Bostrom, Kathleen. Stories from the Bible. Mirtalipova, Dinara, illus. 2016. (ENG.). 128p. (J). 19.99 (978-1-84780-833-2(6), Frances Lincoln Children's Bks.) Quarto Publishing Group UK GBR. Dist: Littlehampton Bk Services, Ltd.

—Stories from the Bible. Mirtalipova, Dinara, illus. 2016. (ENG.). 128p. (J). (gr. 1-4). 19.99 (978-1-84780-891-2(3), Frances Lincoln Children's Bks.) Quarto Publishing Group UK GBR. Dist: Hachette Bk. Group.

Bostrom, Kathleen Long. Easter Stories & Prayers. Kucharik, Elena, illus. 2015. (Little Blessings Ser.). (ENG.). 144p. (J). 7.99 (978-1-4964-0280-6(4)) Tyndale Hse. Pubs.

Bowman, Crystal & McKinley, Teri. M Is for Manger. Keay, Claire, illus. 2015. (ENG.). 64p. (J). 7.99 (978-1-4964-0195-3(6)) Tyndale Hse. Pubs.

Bowman, Crystal, et al. My Read & Rhyme Bible Storybook. Engel, Christiane, illus. 2009. (ENG.). 368p. (J). (gr. -1-2). 17.99 (978-1-4143-2016-8(7), Tyndale Kids) Tyndale Hse. Pubs.

Boyd, Charles F. What God Has Always Wanted: The Bible's Big Idea from Genesis Through Revelation. Davis, Dennis, illus. 2006. 22p. (J). (gr. -1-3). (978-1-57229-725-8(5)) FamilyLife.

Brand, Ruth. Joseph. Pennington, Jack & Tank, Daniel, illus. 2004. 87p. (J). 19.99 (978-0-8280-1854-8(5), 104-522) Review & Herald Publishing Assn.

Brand, Ruth R. Adam & Eve. Vitale, Raoul & Tank, Daniel, illus. 2005. (Family Bible Story Ser.). 95p. (J). (gr. -1-7). per. 19.99 (978-0-8280-1850-0(2)) Review & Herald Publishing Assn.

Brand, Ruth Redding. Jacob, Vol. 101-180. 2005. (Family Bible Story Ser.). (Illus.). 127p. (J). 19.99 (978-0-8280-1852-4(9)) Review & Herald Publishing Assn.

Breems, Beau. The Promise. Breems, Beau, illus. 2006. (Illus.). (YA). 10.00 (978-0-9768680-9-5(1)); 20.00 (978-0-9768680-8-8(3)) Burning Bush Creation.

Breems, Beau A. La Gran Historia: The Illustrated Gospel from Creation to Resurrection. Breems, Beau A., illus. 2005.Tr. of His Story. (SPA., Illus.). (J). 10.99 (978-0-9768680-5-7(9)); 50p. 19.95 (978-0-9768680-1-9(6), 1000); 50p. per. 14.95 (978-0-9768680-3-3(2), 3000) Burning Bush Creation.

—His Story: The Illustrated Gospel from Creation to Resurrection. Breems, Beau A., illus. l.t. ed. 2005.Tr. of Gran Historia. (Illus.). 50p. (J). 19.95 (978-0-9768680-0-2(8), 0-9768680-0-8) Burning Bush Creation.

Breems, Beau Alan. His Story: The Illustrated Gospel from Creation to Resurrection. Breems, Beau Alan, illus. 2005. (Illus.). (J). per. 14.95 (978-0-9768680-2-6(4)) Burning Bush Creation.

Britt, Stephanie M. My Little Bible, 1 vol. 2005. (ENG.). 96p. 6.99 (978-1-4003-0647-3(7)) Nelson, Thomas Inc.

Brooks, F. & Litchfield, J. Nativity Lift-the-Flap. 2004. (First Stories Ser.). 24p. (J). 10.95 (978-0-7945-0529-5(5)) EDC Publishing.

Brown, Edna. Fig Leaves & Skin Tunics. 2007. 84p. per. 9.99 (978-1-60477-120-6(8)) Salem Author Services.

Brown, Toni Sorenson, photos by. Heroes of the Bible. 2004. (Illus.). 32p. (J). 17.95 (978-1-59156-097-5(7)) Covenant Communications, Inc.

Bruno, Bonnie & Reinsma, Carol. The Young Reader's Bible. 2016. (ENG.). 448p. (J). (gr. k-3). 16.99 (978-1-4336-9214-7(7), B&H Kids) B&H Publishing Group.

Buck, Deanna Draper. My First Scripture Stories. Harston, Jerry, illus. 2014. (J). pap. 14.99 (978-1-60907-948-2(5)) Deseret Bk. Co.

Budensiek, Joy. Jesus My Very Best Friend: Chinese/English. 2005. (CHI.). (J). 2.95 (978-0-9749168-7-3(0)) FEA Ministries.

—Jesus My Very Best Friend: Russian/English. 2005. (RUS.). (J). per. 2.95 (978-0-9749168-5-9(4)) FEA Ministries.

Burchett, Author Walter, BA. Christian children's questions & answers abraham & keturah to israel & rachel Volume 2. 2009. 32p. pap. 14.28 (978-0-557-08256-8(0)) Lulu Pr., Inc.

Burgdorf, Larry. The Mystery of the Moving Hand. Koehler, Ed, illus. 2014. (Arch Bks.). (ENG.). 16p. (J). pap. 2.49 (978-0-7586-4603-3(8)) Concordia Publishing Hse.

—El prudente y el insensato (The Wise & Foolish Builders) 2011. 16p. pap. 2.49 (978-0-7586-3069-8(7)) Concordia Publishing Hse.

Burghoffer, Michael. My First Bible Storybook. 2011. 384p. 12.99 (978-0-7586-2729-2(7)) Concordia Publishing Hse.

—My First Bible Storybook (Bilingual - English & Spanish) 2011. 384p. 14.99 (978-0-7586-2723-0(8)) Concordia Publishing Hse.

Burroughs, Chrysti & Burroughs, Scott. The Super Short, Amazing Story of David & Goliath. Burroughs, Scott, illus. 2005. (Illus.). 32p. (J). (gr. -1-3). 10.99 (978-0-8254-2412-0(7)) Kregel Pubns.

Butcher, Sam, illus. Precious Moments: Storybook Bible & Girl Prayer Pal Set. 2003. 14.60 (978-0-7180-0569-6(4)) Nelson, Thomas Inc.

Butterfield, Moira. Bible Stories Creativity Book. 2013. (Creativity Bks.). (ENG.). 80p. (J). (gr. 1-6). pap. 12.99 (978-1-4380-0319-1(6)) Barron's Educational Series, Inc.

Byous, Shawn. 7 Days of Awesome: A Creation Tale, 1 vol. Jack, Colin, illus. 2016. (ENG.). 40p. (J). 16.99 (978-0-310-74349-1(4)) Zonderkidz.

La Caida de Jerico. 2004. 15.95 (978-1-56814-617-1(5)) CCC of America.

Candle Bible for Little Ones, 1 vol. 2014. (ENG., Illus.). 72p. (J). pap. 6.99 (978-1-78128-141-3(6), Candle Bks.) Lion Hudson PLC GBR. Dist: Kregel Pubns.

Candle Books, creator. Carry along Bible Activities. 2006. 24p. (J). (gr. -1-3). pap. 11.99 (978-0-8254-7310-4(1), Candle Bks.) Lion Hudson PLC GBR. Dist: Kregel Pubns.

Carpenter, Anne. The Animals Tell: Bible Stories As Told by the Animals That Were There. 2011. (Illus.). 80p. pap. 9.95 (978-1-60047-573-3(6)) Wasteland Pr.

Carr, Jon & Carr, Debra. Jeremy the Giraffe. 2004. 6.00 (978-1-59089-723-2(4)) Creflo Dollar Ministries Pubns.

Carson-Dellosa Publishing Staff. Hidden Pictures, Grades PK - 1. 2010. (Home Workbooks Ser.). (ENG.). 64p. (J). (gr. -1-1). pap. 4.49 (978-1-60418-770-0(0)) Carson-Dellosa Publishing, LLC.

Carson-Dellosa Publishing Staff, compiled by. ABCs of the Bible, Grades PK - K: Coloring Fun from A to Z. 2004. (Fun Faith-Builders Ser.). (ENG.). 32p. (gr. -1-k). pap. 4.99 (978-0-88724-214-4(6), CD-2028) Carson-Dellosa Publishing, LLC.

Carvin, Rose-Mae. Doming the Popsicle Boy: A Story of the Philippines. Hertzler, Frances H., illus. 2010. (ENG.). 68p. (J). spiral bd. (978-1-932381-11-5(2), 5100) Bible Visuals International, Inc.

—Ly Huy's Escape: A Story of Vietnam. Neal, Sharon & Mayer, Kristin, eds. Olson, Ed & Willoughby, Yuko, illus. 2010. (ENG.). 40p. (J). spiral bd. (978-1-932381-13-9(9), 5275) Bible Visuals International, Inc.

Cassilly, Barbara. Numbers from the Bible. 2007. 16p. per. 24.95 (978-1-4241-8876-5(8)) America Star Bks.

Charlie Church Mouse Bible Adventures! Early Elementary. 2003. (J). cd-rom 19.98 (978-0-9714753-1-1(8)) LifeLine Studios, Inc.

Choi, Young-Jin. Jesus Feeds Everybody! 2007.Tr. of Jesus' Breadbasket. (Illus.). 26p. bds. 5.95 (978-0-8198-3987-9(6)) Pauline Bks. & Media.

—Mary's Big Surprise. 2007.Tr. of Mary, Crying & Laughing. (Illus.). 26p. (J). (gr. -1-k). bds. 5.95 (978-0-8198-4853-6(0)) Pauline Bks. & Media.

—Where Are You, Little Lamb? 2007. (Illus.). 26p. bds. 5.95 (978-0-8198-8316-2(6)) Pauline Bks. & Media.

Christian Art Gifts, creator. My Little Puzzle Bible. 2008. (Illus.). 10p. (J). (gr. -1-3). bds. (978-1-86920-786-1(6)) Christian Art Pubs.

Christian Focus Publications (CFP) Staff & MacKenzie, Carine. Joseph: God's Dreamer. Apps, Fred, illus. 2012. (Bible Wise Ser.). (ENG.). 32p. (J). (gr. k-3). pap. 3.99 (978-1-85792-343-8(X), 17e3b960-7681-44e7-8d32-8a68a5d4c3ce) Christian Focus Pubns. GBR. Dist: Bookmasters Distribution.

Christian Focus Publications (CFP) Staff & Scrimshire, Hazel. The Little Rich Man. 2005. (Shaped Board Bks.). (ENG., Illus.). 8p. (J). (gr. -1-k). bds. 3.99 (978-1-85792-345-2(6), 9781857923452, Christian Focus) Christian Focus Pubns. GBR. Dist: Bookmasters Distribution.

—Safe at Sea. 2007. (Shaped Board Bks.). (ENG., Illus.). 8p. (J). (gr. -1-k). bds. 3.99 (978-1-85792-346-9(4), 35992134-a399-435a-aa12-751a0aacdc0a, Christian Focus) Christian Focus Pubns. GBR. Dist: Bookmasters Distribution.

Cjs Closet. 2004. cd-rom, audio compact disk 24.95 (978-0-9707201-0-8(6)) Kay Productions LLC.

Clark, Marian. Benji's Sicarii Sword. 2007. 156p. per. 13.99 (978-1-60266-022-9(0)) Salem Author Services.

Clayden, Julie. Noah. Jolliffe, Angela, illus. 2005. (First Word Heroes Ser.). (ENG.). 12p. (J). (gr. 3-5). bds. 7.99 (978-1-904637-11-0(6), 1904637116) Authentic Media GBR. Dist: EMI CMG Distribution.

Clayden, Julie & Joliffe, Angela. Martha. 2006. (First Word Heroes Ser.). (ENG., Illus.). 14p. bds. 7.99 (978-1-904637-23-3(X), 190463723X) Authentic Media GBR. Dist: EMI CMG Distribution.

Claypoole, Joann. The Gardener's Helpers. 2015. (ENG.). 106p. (J). pap. 14.95 (978-1-63047-532-1(7)) Morgan James Publishing.

Colson, Charles. Fundamentals: Creation vs. Evolution, Real Story Teach Pack. (J). (gr. 4-6). (978-0-633-05790-9(8)) LifeWay Christian Resources.

Comley, Kathryn. Follow God. Lane, Ranae, illus. 2004. (J). bds. 9.99 (978-1-4183-0009-8(8)) Christ Inspired, Inc.

—God Made My Hands. Wacker, Ranae, illus. 2004. (J). bds. 9.99 (978-1-4183-0005-0(5)) Christ Inspired, Inc.

—Know & Remember all These Things. Lane, Ranae, illus. 2004. (J). bds. (978-1-4183-0011-1(X)) Christ Inspired, Inc.

Concordia Publishing Staff, ed. One Hundred Bible Stories. 2005. (Illus.). 208p. (J). 12.99 (978-0-7586-0857-4(8)) Concordia Publishing Hse.

Concordia Publishing House. My Great Big Coloring Bible with Activities. 2015. (ENG.). 192p. (J). pap. 5.99 (978-0-7586-5221-8(6)) Concordia Publishing Hse.

Cook, David C., 3rd. Mary & Martha. 2008. (Pencil Fun Bks). 16p. (J). pap. 9.90 (978-1-4347-6816-2(3)) Cook, David C.

Copenhagen Publishing Company, prod. The Shepherd & the Sheep. 2015. (ENG.). 10p. (J). 4.99 (978-1-4964-0465-7(3), Tyndale Kids) Tyndale Hse. Pubs.

—When Jesus Was Born. 2015. (ENG.). 10p. (J). 4.99 (978-1-4964-0464-0(5), Tyndale Kids) Tyndale Hse. Pubs.

Cosmic City Blast off! Preschool Guide. 2007. (Vacation Bible School Ser.). 112p. (J). (gr. 3-5). pap. 9.99 (978-1-4347-9963-0(8)) Cook, David C.

Cox, Carolyn, illus. My Very Own Bible Gift. 2011. (ENG.). 160p. (J). (gr. 2-4). 9.99 (978-0-7459-6125-5(8)) Lion Hudson PLC GBR. Dist: Independent Pubs. Group.

Cox, Steve. Seek & You Shall Find. 2011. 24p. 14.99 (978-0-7586-2728-5(9)) Concordia Publishing Hse.

Craig, J. Ann, intro. Children of the Bible: Twelve Stories of Children. 2005. 72p. (YA). pap. (978-1-890569-89-1(5), WD/GBGM Bks.) General Board of Global Ministries, The United Methodist Church.

Crandall, Janet. In a Manger. 2006. per. (978-1-59872-604-6(8)) Instant Pub.

Crane, Cheryl L. Facing Lions, Giants & Other Big Dudes: A Bible Study Workbook on Courage for Ages 6-12. 2008. 112p. pap. 17.95 (978-1-4401-0609-5(6)) iUniverse, Inc.

Creation: A Bible Storybook in Color. (Illus.). 16p. (J). pap. 1.50 (978-0-87162-962-3(3), E4911) Warner Pr., Inc.

Crump, Fred, Jr. Three Kings & a Star. Crump, Fred, Jr., illus. 2010. (Illus.). 40p. (J). (gr. -1-3). 12.95 (978-1-932715-52-1(5)) UMI (Urban Ministries, Inc.).

Currie, Robin. Baby Bible 123. 2005. (Baby Bible Ser.). (Illus.). 48p. (J). bds. 12.99 (978-0-7814-3906-0(X), 078143906X) Cook, David C.

—Baby Bible ABC. 2004. (Baby Bible Ser.). (Illus.). 48p. (J). bds. 12.99 (978-0-7814-3907-7(8), 0781439078) Cook, David C.

—The Baby Bible Storybook for Boys. Busaluzzo, Constanza, illus. 2008. (Baby Bible Ser.). (ENG.). 46p. (J). bds. 12.99 (978-0-7814-3501-7(3)) Cook, David C.

—La Biblia Para los Bebes. 2003. (Baby Bible Ser.). (SPA., Illus.). 48p. bds. 10.99 (978-0-7814-3613-7(3), 0781436133) Cook, David C.

Cutrera, Melissa. God's Great Plan. Sample, Matthew II, illus. 2013. 28p. (J). (978-1-936908-83-7(2)); (978-1-936908-82-0(4)); (978-1-936908-81-3(6)) Shepherd Pr. Inc.

Dailey, Joanna. The Catholic Children's Bible Activity Booklet. 2013. (ENG.). (J). (gr. 1-4). spiral bd. 29.95 (978-1-59982-181-8(8)) St. Mary's Pr. of MN.

—The Catholic Children's Bible Leader Guide. 2013. (ENG.). (J). (gr. 1-4). spiral bd. 34.95 (978-1-59982-042-2(0)) St. Mary's Pr. of MN.

Dalmatian Press Staff. Adam & Eve. 2004. (ENG., Illus.). 24p. (J). 2.99 (978-1-4037-0967-7(X), Spirit Pr.) Bendon, Inc.

—The Birth of a Savior. 2004. (ENG., Illus.). 24p. (J). 2.99 (978-1-4037-0970-7(X), Spirit Pr.) Bendon, Inc.

—God's Creation. Mendenhall, Cheryl, illus. 2004. (ENG.). 24p. (J). 2.99 (978-1-4037-0962-2(9), Spirit Pr.) Bendon, Inc.

—My Favorite Bible Storybook for Early Readers. 2003. (ENG., Illus.). 528p. (J). 14.99 (978-1-4037-0286-9(1), Spirit Pr.) Bendon, Inc.

—Noah's Ark. 2004. (ENG., Illus.). 24p. (J). 2.99 (978-1-4037-0968-4(8), Spirit Pr.) Bendon, Inc.

—VeggieTale Champs of the Bible. 2005. (Big Idea's Veggie Tales Ser.). (ENG., Illus.). 80p. (J). pap. 2.99 (978-1-4037-1177-9(1), Spirit Pr.) Bendon, Inc.

Daniel & the Lions' Den. (Bible Friends plus Book Ser.). (Illus.). 10p. (J). (gr. -1-k). 6.99 (978-0-8254-7210-7(5)) Kregel Pubns.

Daniel & the Lion's Den: A Bible Story to Color. (Illus.). 16p. (J). pap. 1.50 (978-0-87162-831-2(7), E6020) Warner Pr., Inc.

Daniels, M. K. Nursery Rhymes & Bible Stories with Eli the Bear. 2012. 24p. pap. 10.95 (978-1-4497-7175-1(0), WestBow Pr.) Author Solutions, Inc.

Daniewicz, Mark. When Jesus Was A Kid. 2004. 14.95 (978-0-9709575-2-8(1)) Singing River Pubns.

David C. Cook Publishing Company Staff. Blast off! Preschool Student Book. 2007. (Vacation Bible School Ser.). 24p. (J). (gr. 3-5). pap. 2.99 (978-1-4347-9956-2(5)) Cook, David C.

—Bread or Stone, 10, Pack. 2008. (Pencil Fun Bks.). (ENG.). 16p. (J). pap. 9.90 (978-1-4347-6823-0(6)) Cook, David C.

—Cosmic City Elementary Student Book. 2007. (Vacation Bible School Ser.). 24p. (J). (gr. 6-12). pap. 2.99 (978-1-4347-9955-5(7)) Cook, David C.

—Jesus & Me: BOZ's Big Book of Bible Fun. 2008. (Boz the Bear Ser.). 236p. (J). pap. 14.99 (978-1-4347-6789-9(2)) Cook, David C.

—Jesus Feeds 5000. 2008. (Pencil Fun Bks). 16p. (J). pap. 9.90 (978-0-7814-4900-7(6)) Cook, David C.

—Jonah & the Big Fish. 2003. (My Jesus Pocket Bks.). (Illus.). 32p. (J). pap., pap. 8.90 (978-1-55513-015-2(1), 155513015I) Cook, David C.

—Lazarus Lives, 10, Pack. 2008. (Pencil Fun Bks). 16p. (J). pap. 9.90 (978-1-4347-6820-9(1)) Cook, David C.

—Outer Limits Mission Log Upper Elementary Student Book. 2007. (Vacation Bible School Ser.). 24p. (YA). (gr. 9-12). pap. 2.99 (978-1-4347-9954-8(9)) Cook, David C.

—Ring, Robe & Shoes, 10, Pack. 2008. (Pencil Fun Bks). 16p. (J). pap. 9.90 (978-1-4347-6822-3(8)) Cook, David C.

—Scripture Pictures - Miracles & Parables of Jesus. 2005. 106p. 29.99 (978-0-7814-4201-5(X), 078144201X) Cook, David C.

David C. Cook Publishing Company Staff & Currie, Robin. The Baby Bible Sing & Pray. Busaluzzo, Constanza, illus. 2008. (Baby Bible Ser.). (ENG.). 46p. (J). bds. 12.99 (978-0-7814-4893-2(X)) Cook, David C.

—The Baby Bible Storybook for Girls. Busaluzzo, Constanza, illus. 2008. (Baby Bible Ser.). (ENG.). 46p. (J). bds. 12.99 (978-1-4347-6783-7(3)) Cook, David C.

—Stories about Jesus. Busaluzzo, Constanza, illus. 2008. (Baby Bible Ser.). (ENG.). 46p. (J). bds. 12.99 (978-0-7814-4889-5(1)) Cook, David C.

David, Juliet. All Aboard with Noah: Pop-Up, 1 vol. Canuso, Julie & Canuso, Jackie, illus. 2016. (ENG.). 12p. (J). 14.99 (978-1-78128-249-6(8), Candle Bks.) Lion Hudson PLC GBR. Dist: Kregel Pubns.

—Bible Animals Story Collection, 1 vol. Smallman, Steve, illus. 2016. (ENG.). 136p. (J). pap. 9.99 (978-1-78128-286-1(2), Candle Bks.) Lion Hudson PLC GBR. Dist: Kregel Pubns.

—Bible Journey Storybook, 1 vol. Abbott, Simon, illus. 2016. (ENG.). 24p. (J). 19.99 (978-1-78128-148-2(3), Candle Bks.) Lion Hudson PLC GBR. Dist: Kregel Pubns.

—Bible Stories Painting Book, 1 vol., Bk. 3. Abbott, Simon, illus. 2014. (ENG.). 24p. (J). 7.99 (978-1-85985-995-7(X), Candle Bks.) Lion Hudson PLC GBR. Dist: Kregel Pubns.

—Candle Bible for Kids Board Book, 1 vol. Parry, Jo, illus. 2014. (ENG.). 42p. (J). bds. 9.99 (978-1-78128-101-7(7), Candle Bks.) Lion Hudson PLC GBR. Dist: Kregel Pubns.

—Candle Bible for Toddlers, 1 vol. Prole, Helen, illus. 2006. (Candle Bible for Toddlers Ser.). 400p. (J). (gr. -1-k). 15.99 (978-0-8254-7311-1(X), Candle Bks.) Lion Hudson PLC GBR. Dist: Kregel Pubns.

—Candle Bible for Toddlers, 1 vol. Prole, Helen, illus. 2015. (ENG.). 400p. (J). 19.99 (978-1-78128-201-4(3), Candle Bks.) Lion Hudson PLC GBR. Dist: Kregel Pubns.

—Candle Bible for Toddlers Carry along Bible Fun. Prole, Helen, illus. 2007. (Candle Bible for Toddlers Ser.). (J). pap. 12.99 (978-0-8254-7336-4(5), Candle Bks.) Lion Hudson PLC GBR. Dist: Kregel Pubns.

—Candle Day by Day Bible, 1 vol. Heyes, Jane, illus. 2014. (ENG.). 400p. (J). 16.99 (978-1-85985-824-0(4), Candle Bks.) Lion Hudson PLC GBR. Dist: Kregel Pubns.

—The Christmas Story, 1 vol. Ellis, Elina, illus. 2016. (ENG.). 24p. (J). 8.99 (978-1-78128-282-3(X), Candle Bks.) Lion Hudson PLC GBR. Dist: Kregel Pubns.

—Magnetic Adventures - My First Bible Stories, 1 vol. Prole, Helen, illus. 2015. (Candle Bible for Toddlers Ser.). (ENG.). 12p. (J). 16.99 (978-1-78128-225-0(0), Candle Bks.) Lion Hudson PLC GBR. Dist: Kregel Pubns.

—Magnetic Adventures - Noah & His Big Boat, 1 vol. Prole, Helen, illus. 2015. (Candle Bible for Toddlers Ser.). (ENG.). 12p. (J). 16.99 (978-1-78128-227-4(7), Candle Bks.) Lion Hudson PLC GBR. Dist: Kregel Pubns.

—My Little Blessings Bible, 1 vol. Butterly, Mikki, illus. 2015. 224p. (J). 14.99 (978-1-78128-193-2(9), Candle Bks.) Lion Hudson PLC GBR. Dist: Kregel Pubns.

—My Little Picture Bible, 1 vol. Ellis, Elina, illus. 2015. (ENG.). 160p. (J). 9.99 (978-1-78128-176-5(9), Candle Bks.) Lion Hudson PLC GBR. Dist: Kregel Pubns.

—My Little Promise Bible, 1 vol. Barnard, Lucy, illus. 2016. (ENG.). 96p. (J). pap. 9.99 (978-1-78128-257-1(9), Candle Bks.) Lion Hudson PLC GBR. Dist: Kregel Pubns.

—My Toddler Bible, 1 vol. Embleton-Hall, Chris, illus. 2016. (ENG.). 224p. (J). 12.99 (978-1-78128-241-0(2), Candle Bks.) Lion Hudson PLC GBR. Dist: Kregel Pubns.

—My Very First Christmas Story, 1 vol. Siewert, Pauline, illus. 2015. 14p. (J). 7.99 (978-1-78128-231-1(5), Candle Bks.) Lion Hudson PLC GBR. Dist: Kregel Pubns.

—Paraclete Bible for Toddlers. Prole, Helen, illus. 2016. (ENG.). 400p. 17.99 (978-1-61261-759-6(X)) Paraclete Pr., Inc.

—Puddle Pen Bible Stories, 1 vol. Martin, Stuart, illus. 2010. (Candle Puddle Pen Ser.). 10p. (J). (gr. -1). bds. 12.99 (978-0-8254-7394-4(2), Candle Bks.) Lion Hudson PLC GBR. Dist: Kregel Pubns.

—The Very First Christmas, 1 vol. Prole, Helen, illus. 2007. (Candle Bible for Toddlers Ser.). 24p. (J). (gr. -1-k). act. bk. ed. 6.99 (978-0-8254-7353-1(5), Candle Bks.) Lion Hudson PLC GBR. Dist: Kregel Pubns.

David, Juliet & Ayliffe, Alex. My Very First Bible & Prayers, 1 vol. Prole, Helen, illus. 2014. (Candle Bible for Toddlers Ser.). (ENG.). 64p. (J). 9.99 (978-1-78128-152-9(1), Candle Bks.) Lion Hudson PLC GBR. Dist: Kregel Pubns.

David, Juliet & Freedman, Claire. Candle Bible & Prayers for Kids, 1 vol. Parry, Jo, illus. 2016. (ENG.). 528p. (J). 24.99 (978-1-78128-274-8(9), Candle Bks.) Lion Hudson PLC GBR. Dist: Kregel Pubns.

David, Juliet & Williamson, Karen. Bible Stories, 1 vol. Wood, Hannah, illus. 2016. (ENG.). 102p. (J). 7.99 (978-1-78128-305-9(2), Candle Bks.) Lion Hudson PLC GBR. Dist: Kregel Pubns.

Davidson, Alice Joyce. My Take-Along Bible. Mazille, Capucine, illus. 2004. 20p. (J). bds. 9.99 (978-0-89221-577-5(1)) New Leaf Pub. Group.

Davies, Rhona. The One Year Children's Bible. Piwowarski, Marcin, illus. 2007. (ENG.). 352p. (J). (gr. 1-5). 19.99 (978-1-4143-1499-0(X)) Tyndale Hse. Pubs.

—Page-A-Day Children's Bible. Piwowarski, Marcin, illus. 2016. 381p. (J). pap. (978-0-8198-6032-3(8)) Pauline Bks. & Media.

Davis, Kim P., compiled by. My Life, His Mission: A Six Week Challenge to Change the World! True Stories from Students Living on the Edge, 1 vol. 2006. (ENG.). 176p. (gr. 8-12). pap. 14.99 (978-1-59145-488-5(3)) Nelson, Thomas Inc.

Davis, Mary J. Five-Minute Sunday School Activities for Preschoolers: Bible Adventures. Galey, Chuck, illus. 2005. 96p. (J). pap. 11.95 (978-1-58411-046-0(5)) Rainbow Pubs. & Legacy Pr.

De Graaf, Anne. The Little Children's Bible Storybook. Montero, Jose Perez, illus. 2003. 448p. (978-87-7247-132-7(8)) Scandinavia Publishing Hse.

De Sturtz, Mari. Living for Jesus. 2004. (ENG & SPA.). 32p. 1.99 (978-0-7586-0295-4(2)) Concordia Publishing Hse.

de Sturtz, Maria Ester H. Milagros en la Biblia. Fernandez, Lucia, illus. 2007. (Manos a la Obra Ser.). 32p. (J). (gr. -1-4). per. 7.99 (978-0-7586-1458-2(6)) Concordia Publishing Hse.

de Sturtz, Marie Ester H. Por Las Aguas De la Biblia (God & Water in the Bible) 2011. 32p. pap. 1.99 (978-0-7586-2677-6(0)) Concordia Publishing Hse.

—Por Las Aguas De La Biblia (God & Water in the Bible) - Bilingual. 2011. 32p. pap. 1.99 (978-0-7586-2679-0(7)) Concordia Publishing Hse.

—Reyes y Profetas (Kings & Prophets) 2011. 32p. pap. 1.99 (978-0-7586-2676-9(2)) Concordia Publishing Hse.

—Reyes y profetas (Kings & Prophets) - Bilingual. 2011. 32p. pap. 1.99 (978-0-7586-2678-3(9)) Concordia Publishing Hse.

Deep Blue Toddlers & Twos Bible Story Picture Cards Winter 2016-17. 2016. (Deep Blue Ser.). 32p. pap. 5.99 (978-1-63088-677-6(7)) Abingdon Pr.

Deep Blue Toddlers & Twos Leader's Guide Winter 2016-17. 2016. (Deep Blue Ser.). 44p. pap. 8.59 (978-1-63088-676-9(9)) Abingdon Pr.

Delval, Marie-Hélène. The Bible for Young Children. Götting, Jean-Claude, illus. 2010. (ENG.). 96p. (J). (gr. -1-3). 16.50 (978-0-8028-5383-7(8), Eerdmans Bks For Young Readers) Eerdmans, William B. Publishing Co.

Denham, Joyce. The Hard to Swallow Tale of Jonah & the Whale. Hall, Amanda, illus. 2015. (ENG.). 32p. (J). (gr. -1-3). pap. 8.99 (978-0-7459-6584-0(9)) Lion Hudson PLC GBR. Dist: Independent Pubs. Group.

Dennis, Trevor. The Book of Books: The Bible Retold. 2009. (ENG., Illus.). 480p. (J). (gr. 6-7). 22.99 (978-0-7459-5372-4(7)) Lion Hudson PLC GBR. Dist: Independent Pubs. Group.

Derr, Louise Barrett. Experiencing Bible Science: An Activity Book for Children. 2013. 128p. (J). pap. 16.95 (978-1-4908-0993-9(7), WestBow Pr.) Author Solutions, Inc.

DeVries, Catherine. Adventure Bible for Little Ones, 1 vol. 2015. (Adventure Bible Ser.). (ENG.). 40p. (J). bds. 9.99 (978-0-310-75366-7(X)) Zonderkidz.

—Adventure Bible Storybook, 1 vol. Madsen, Jim, illus. 2009. (Adventure Bible Ser.). (ENG.). 288p. (J). 16.99 (978-0-310-71637-2(3)) Zonderkidz.

DeYoung, Kevin. The Biggest Story: How the Snake Crusher Brings Us Back to the Garden. Clark, Don, illus. 2015. 132p. 17.99 (978-1-4335-4244-2(7)) Crossway.

DeYoung, Kevin. The Biggest Story ABC. Clark, Don, illus. 2017. 32p. (J). bds. 12.99 **(978-1-4335-5818-4(1))** Crossway.

Dickson, Bill, illus. David & Goliath. 2013. (Happy Day Ser.). (ENG.). 16p. (J). pap. 2.49 (978-1-4143-9324-7(5)) Tyndale Hse. Pubs.

Dietrich, Julie & Fernández, Cecilia. El niño Moisés (Tiny Baby Moses) - Bilingual. 2011. 16p. pap. 2.99 (978-0-7586-3074-2(3)) Concordia Publishing Hse.

Ditchfield, Christin. Bible Heroes. Cook, Ande, illus. 2004. (Little Golden Book Ser.). (ENG.). 24p. (J). (gr. -1-2). 4.99 (978-0-375-82816-4(8), Golden Bks.) Random Hse. Children's Bks.

—Bible Stories of Boys & Girls. Smath, Jerry, illus. 2010. (Little Golden Book Ser.). (ENG.). 24p. (J). (gr. -1-2). 4.99

(978-0-375-85461-3(4), Golden Bks.) Random Hse. Children's Bks.

Dodd, Sarah J. Lion Picture Bible. Ligi, Raffaella, illus. gif. ed. 2017. (ENG.). 384p. (J). (gr. k-2). 24.99 (978-0-7459-7627-3(1)) Lion Hudson PLC GBR. Dist: Independent Pubs. Group.

Dodd, Sarah J. & Ligi, Raffaella. The Lion Picture Bible. 2015. (ENG., Illus.). 384p. (J). (gr. k-2). 16.99 (978-0-7459-6303-7(X)) Lion Hudson PLC GBR. Dist: Independent Pubs. Group.

Doherty, Berlie. The Oxford Book of Bible Stories. Cockcroft, Jason, illus. 2014. (ENG.). 272p. 24.95 (978-0-19-278214-4(2)) Oxford Univ. Pr., Inc.

Doherty, Gillian, ed. First Stories from the Bible. Field, Mandy & Pearson, Maria, illus. 2007. (Bible Tales Readers Ser.). 143p. (J). (gr. -1-k). 17.99 (978-0-7945-1668-0(8), Usborne) EDC Publishing.

Domingo, Roger. Eye Openers & Show Stoppers in the Bible. 2003. 128p. (YA). pap. 9.95 (978-0-9668541-2-1(8)) Turnstyle.

Donaghy, Thomas J. My Golden Children's Bible. 2008. (Illus.). 40p. (J). (gr. -1). bds. 8.95 (978-0-89942-483-5(X)) Catholic Bk. Publishing Corp.

—New Catholic Children's Bible. 2006. (Illus.). 214p. (J). (gr. -1). 11.95 (978-0-89942-644-0(1)) Catholic Bk. Publishing Corp.

Dorling Kindersley Publishing Staff. A First Bible Story Book & a First Book of Prayers. 2017. (ENG.). 160p. (J). (gr. k-3). 15.99 (978-1-4654-5898-8(0), DK Children) Dorling Kindersley Publishing, Inc.

Dowley, Tim. Changing Picture Bible Stories, 1 vol. Martin, Stuart, illus. 2004. 14p. (J). 11.99 (978-0-8254-7279-4(2), Candle Bks.) Lion Hudson PLC GBR. Dist: Kregel Pubns.

—Great Bible Stories, 1 vol. 2016. (Activity Fun Ser.). (ENG.). 64p. (J). pap. 4.99 (978-1-78128-260-1(9), Candle Bks.) Lion Hudson PLC GBR. Dist: Kregel Pubns.

—More Great Bible Stories, 1 vol. 2017. (Activity Fun Ser.). (ENG.). 64p. (J). pap. 4.99 **(978-1-78128-334-9(6)**, Candle Bks.) Lion Hudson PLC GBR. Dist: Kregel Pubns.

—My First Story of Christmas. Langton, Roger, illus. 2004. (My First Story Ser.). (ENG.). 24p. (J). 7.99 (978-0-8024-1758-9(2)) Moody Pubs.

—Paul's Travels, 1 vol. 2010. (Candle Discovery Ser.). (Illus.). 28p. (J). (gr. 2-7). 14.99 (978-0-8254-7383-8(7), Candle Bks.) Lion Hudson PLC GBR. Dist: Kregel Pubns.

—Pop-Up Bible Adventures, 2. Moseley, Dudley, illus. 2007. 12p. (J). (gr. k-2). 11.99 (978-0-8254-7328-9(4), Candle Bks.) Lion Hudson PLC GBR. Dist: Kregel Pubns.

Dowley, Tim. Stories Jesus Told, 1 vol. 2017. (Activity Fun Ser.). (ENG.). 64p. (J). pap. 4.99 **(978-1-78128-330-1(3)**, Candle Bks.) Lion Hudson PLC GBR. Dist: Kregel Pubns.

Dowley, Tim & Reeves, Eira. Bible Storybook, 1 vol. 2016. (ENG., Illus.). 128p. (J). 9.99 (978-1-78128-264-9(1), Candle Bks.) Lion Hudson PLC GBR. Dist: Kregel Pubns.

Ede, Lara. Bible Stories for Boys. 2011. 26p. bds. 6.99 (978-1-84879-994-3(2)) Make Believe Ideas GBR. Dist: Nelson, Thomas Inc.

—Bible Stories for Girls. 2011. 26p. bds. 6.99 (978-1-84879-995-0(0)) Make Believe Ideas GBR. Dist: Nelson, Thomas Inc.

Edgren, David. The Kingdom Scroll. 2011. (J). pap. 11.99 (978-0-8163-2483-5(2)) Pacific Pr. Publishing Assn.

Edwards, Josh. Bible Stories Gone Crazy!, 1 vol. Migliardo, Emiliano, illus. 2015. (ENG.). 24p. (J). 10.99 (978-1-78128-190-1(4), Candle Bks.) Lion Hudson PLC GBR. Dist: Kregel Pubns.

—My Big Story Bible, 1 vol. Tappin, Christine, illus. 2015. (ENG.). 80p. (J). 10.99 (978-1-78128-203-8(X), Candle Bks.) Lion Hudson PLC GBR. Dist: Kregel Pubns.

Egermeier, Elsie. Egermeier's ABC Bible Storybook: Favorite Stories Adapted for Young Children. Rhodes, Karen, ed. Nikiel, Laura Gibbons, illus. 2007. (ENG.). 56p. (J). (gr. -1-5). 14.99 incl. audio compact disk (978-1-59317-198-8(6)) Warner Pr., Inc.

Egermeier, Elsie E. Egermeier's ABC Bible Storybook: Favorite Stories Adapted for Young Children. Rhodes, Karen, ed. Nikiel, Laura Gibbons, illus. 2006. (ENG.). 56p. (gr. -1-k). 12.99 (978-1-59317-156-8(0)) Warner Pr., Inc.

Elkins, Stephen. My Sing-Along Bible: 50 Easy-Read Stories + 50 Fun Bible Songs. Reagan, Susan, illus. 2015. (ENG.). 96p. (J). 12.99 (978-1-4964-0543-2(9)) Tyndale Hse. Pubs.

—Read 'n' See DVD Bible, 1 vol. O'Connor, Tim, illus. 2006. (ENG.). 176p. (gr. -1-3). 19.99 (978-1-59145-486-1(7)) Nelson, Thomas Inc.

—Snuggle Time Devotions That End with a Hug! Jones, Mark, illus. 2015. (Share-A-Hug! Ser.). (ENG.). 168p. (J). 14.99 (978-1-4143-9948-5(0)) Tyndale Hse. Pubs.

—Tell Me about the Bible. 2014. (Train 'Em Up Ser.). (ENG.). 24p. (J). pap. 4.99 (978-1-4143-9677-4(5)) Tyndale Hse. Pubs.

—The Ultimate Travel Time Bible. Conaway, Jim, illus. 2007. 170p. (J). (gr. -1-3). 14.99 incl. audio compact disk (978-0-8054-2647-2(7)) B&H Publishing Group.

—5-Minute Bible: 100 Stories & Songs, 1 vol. 2017. (ENG., Illus.). 208p. (J). 12.99 **(978-0-7180-9764-6(5))** Nelson, Thomas Inc.

—100 Bible Stories 100 Bible Songs, 1 vol. 2005. (ENG., Illus.). 208p. (gr. -1-3). 19.99 (978-1-59145-239-3(2)) Nelson, Thomas Inc.

—100 Ways to Know God Loves Me, 100 Songs to Love Him Back, 1 vol. 2008. (ENG., Illus.). 208p. 19.99 (978-1-4003-1157-6(8)) Nelson, Thomas Inc.

Ellis, Gwen. Bible Adventures. Cox, Steve, illus. 2006. 20p. (J). (gr. -1-k). bds. 9.49 (978-0-7586-1130-7(7)) Concordia Publishing Hse.

—I Can Learn Bible Stories. Regan, Dana, illus. 2006. 10p. (J). spiral bd. 10.99 (978-0-8254-5530-8(8)) Kregel Pubns.

—Read & Share, 1 vol., Vol. 1. 2010. (ENG., Illus.). 208p. 19.99 (978-1-4003-1613-7(8)) Nelson, Thomas Inc.

—Read & Share Bible: More Than 200 Best-Loved Bible Stories, 1 vol. Smallman, Steve, illus. 2007. (Read & Share (Tommy Nelson) Ser.). (ENG.). 440p. (gr. k-3). 16.99 (978-1-4003-0853-8(4)) Nelson, Thomas Inc.

—Read & Share Toddler Bible, 1 vol. 2009. (ENG.). 192p. (J). 14.99 (978-1-4003-1464-5(X)) Nelson, Thomas Inc.

Emmerson-Hicks, J. The Jesus Bible for Kids. 2016. (ENG.). 256p. (J). 19.99 (978-0-7369-6721-1(4)) Harvest Hse. Pubs.

Engelbrecht, Edward A. & Pawlitz, Gail E., eds. The Christmas Story: Drawn Directly from the Bible. 2011. (Illus.). 32p. (J). 13.99 (978-0-7586-1908-2(1)) Concordia Publishing Hse.

Erickson, Jenny. My Favorite Bible. 2003. 112p. (J). pap., act. bk. ed. 14.95 (978-1-58595-268-7(0)) Twenty-Third Pubns./Bayard.

Family Time Bible Stories: Devotions & Interactive Bible Stories for Preschoolers. 2004. (Here's What's Inside the Bright Beginnings Kit Ser.). (Illus.). 224p. 14.99 (978-0-8307-3247-0(0), Regal Bks.) Gospel Light Pubns.

Fenwick, Nellie. Gracie & God's Great Ten: How One Girl Learned to Make Good Choices. 2012. 118p. (-18). pap. 17.99 (978-0-9827627-8-3(X)) Port Hole Pubns.

Finbarr, Desmond. The Big Book of Bible Fish Tales. Gévry, Claudine, illus. 2003. 10p. (J). bds. 8.99 (978-0-8254-5514-8(6)) Kregel Pubns.

Fisher, Martha. ABC Book of Bible People. 2004. (Bible Stories for Young Readers Ser.). (Illus.). 88p. (gr. -1-5). 3.85 (978-0-7399-2331-3(5), 2717) Rod & Staff Pubs., Inc.

—Bible Numbers. 2003. (Bible Stories for Young Readers Ser.). (Illus.). 48p. (gr. -1-5). 3.05 (978-0-7399-2329-0(3), 2715) Rod & Staff Pubs., Inc.

—Bible Time. 2005. (Bible Stories for Young Readers Ser.). (Illus.). 40p. (gr. -1-5). 3.05 (978-0-7399-2332-0(3), 2719) Rod & Staff Pubs., Inc.

—Dictionary of Bible Animals. 2004. (Bible Stories for Young Readers Ser.). (Illus.). 45p. (gr. -1-5). 3.05 (978-0-7399-2330-6(7), 2716) Rod & Staff Pubs., Inc.

Flegal, Daphna & Sky, Brittany. Deep Blue Bible Storybook. 2016. 21.99 (978-1-5018-1501-0(6)) Abingdon Pr.

Fletcher, Betty & Harvest House Publishers Staff. My Very Own Bible. Police, Lou, illus. 2008. (ENG.). 96p. (J). (gr. -1-3). 6.99 (978-0-7369-2153-4(2)) Harvest Hse. Pubs.

Fletcher, Sarah. La Historia de Jesus (My Stories about Jesus) Historias del Nuevo Testamento. (SPA., Illus.). 32p. (gr. -1-3). 1.95 (978-0-570-09970-3(6), 16-6013) Concordia Publishing Hse.

Fogg, Paul, illus. He Leads Me. 2008. 24p. pap. 9.95 (978-0-9814878-1-6(5)) Little Hands Bk. Co., LLC.

Fogle, Robin. David & Golaith Coloring Book. 2007. (Illus.). 16p. (J). pap. 1.89 (978-1-59317-205-3(2)) Warner Pr., Inc.

—The Legend of the Candy Cane. 2006. (J). pap. 1.79 (978-1-59317-158-2(7)) Warner Pr., Inc.

—My Favorite Bible Stories Color-by-number. 2007. (Illus.). 16p. (J). pap. 1.89 (978-1-59317-208-4(7)) Warner Pr., Inc.

—The Shepherd Boy's Christmas. 2005. (J). pap. 1.79 (978-1-59317-105-6(6)) Warner Pr., Inc.

Frank, Penny. Jesus the Teacher. 2nd rev. ed. (ENG., Illus.). 24p. pap. 2.99 (978-0-7459-4117-2(6), Lion Books) Lion Hudson PLC GBR. Dist: Trafalgar Square Publishing.

—When Zacchaeus Met Jesus. Morris, Tony, illus. 2004. (Lion Story Bible Ser.). (ENG.). 24p. (J). (gr. k-2). pap. 30.00 (978-0-7459-4925-3(8), Lion Books) Lion Hudson PLC GBR. Dist: Independent Pubs. Group.

Frazee, Randy. Believe Storybook: Think, Act, Be Like Jesus, 1 vol. Adams, Steve, illus. 2015. (ENG.). 256p. (J). 19.99 (978-0-310-74590-7(X)) Zonderkidz.

Friends & Heroes Activity & Coloring Book. 2008. (Friends & Heroes Ser.). (J). pap. (978-1-4143-2157-8(0), Tyndale Entertainment) Tyndale Hse. Pubs.

Fritz, C. S. Good Night Tales: A Family Treasury of Read-Aloud Stories. Fritz, C. S., illus. 2017. (ENG.). 176p. (J). 19.99 **(978-1-63146-556-7(2))** NavPress Publishing Group.

Froeb, Lori C., ed. My First Bedtime Bible Stories. Jones, Anna, illus. 2015. (ENG.). 10p. (J). (gr. -1-k). bds. 8.99 (978-0-7944-3474-8(6)) Studio Fun International.

Frothingham, Octavius Brooks. Stories of the Patriarchs. 2006. pap. 26.95 (978-1-4286-0972-3(5)) Kessinger Publishing, LLC.

Fun with Colors: Bible Story: Joseph's Colorful Coat. (Scripture Bites Ser.). (Illus.). (J). 7.99 (978-0-7847-9014-4(0), 00707) Standard Publishing.

Gallaudet, Thomas. The Child's Book on the Fall of Man. 2005. pap. 10.99 (978-1-932474-76-3(5)) Solid Ground Christian Bks.

Garris, Norma, illus. The Story of Christmas. 2013. (Happy Day Ser.). (ENG.). 16p. (J). pap. 2.49 (978-1-4143-9524-1(8)) Tyndale Hse. Pubs.

Garwin, Elaine & Youd, Pauline. The Wonder Bible Storybook: 12 Little Stories for Little People. Scandinavia Publishing House Staff, ed. 2011. (ENG., Illus.). 191p. (gr. k-5). 9.95 (978-87-7247-280-5(4)) Scandinavia Publishing Hse. DNK. Dist: Destiny Image Pubs.

Gemmen, Heather. Learn-to-Read Bible. Wilber, Peggy M., ed. 2003. (Rocket Readers Ser.). (Illus.). 448p. (J). (gr. 1-2). 16.99 (978-0-7814-3975-6(2), 0781439752) Cook, David C.

Giampa, Linda. Journey Through the Bible. 2004. 64p. (gr. -1-3). 10.99 (978-0-7586-0248-0(0)) Concordia Publishing Hse.

Gibbons, Erin, ed. The Whirl Story Bible: Lively Bible Stories to Inspire Faith. Keller, Matthew M., illus. 2015. (ENG.). 416p. (J). (gr. -1-5). 22.99 (978-1-5064-0000-6(0), Sparkhouse Family) Augsburg Fortress, Pubs.

Gigante, Carol. The First Family: And Their Struggle to Survive. 2013. 70p. pap. 10.95 (978-1-4796-0180-6(2)) TEACH Services, Inc.

Gilmour, Richard. Bible History. 2009. 120.00 (978-1-60724-278-9(8)) Gorgias Pr., LLC.

Glaser, Rebecca. The Holy Moly Story Bible: Exploring God's Awesome Word. Ferenc, Bill, illus. 2015. (ENG.). 352p. (J). (gr. k-3). 22.99 (978-1-4514-9988-9(4), Sparkhouse Family) Augsburg Fortress, Pubs.

—Jesus Feeds 5,000 & Other Bible Stories. Ferenc, Bill, illus. 2015. (Holy Moly Bible Storybooks Ser.). (ENG.). 32p. (J). (gr. k-3). 12.99 (978-1-5064-0252-9(6), Sparkhouse Family) Augsburg Fortress, Pubs.

Glavich, Mary Kathleen. Student Pack of Bible Stories. 2004. (978-0-8294-1040-2(6)) Loyola Pr.

Godfrey, Jan. My Baptism Bible Catholic Edition. Grudina, Paola Bertolina, illus. 2012. 144p. (J). 16.95 (978-0-8198-4907-6(3)) Pauline Bks. & Media.

—My Sleepytime Bible. Doherty, Paula, illus. 2015. (ENG.). 96p. (J). 14.99 (978-1-4143-9868-6(9)) Tyndale Hse. Pubs.

Godfrey, Jan & Grudina, Paola Bertolini. My Story Bible: 66 Favorite Stories. 2009. (ENG.). 144p. (J). (gr. -1-1). 12.99 (978-1-4143-2671-9(8), Tyndale Kids) Tyndale Hse. Pubs.

Godfrey, Jan, et al. Mi Biblia para la Hora de Dormir. Doherty, Paula, illus. 2015. (SPA.). 96p. (J). 14.99 (978-1-4143-9874-7(3)) Tyndale Hse. Pubs.

Goldin, Barbara Diamond, et al. The 40 Greatest Jewish Stories Ever Told, 4 vols., Set. Allon, Jeffrey, illus. 2005. 192p. (J). (gr. 1-4). 49.95 (978-0-943706-89-4(0), Devora Publishing) Simcha Media Group.

The Good Samaritan. 2014. (Illus.). 24p. (J). (978-1-84898-934-4(2), TickTock Books) Octopus Publishing Group.

Goodings, Christina. Bible & Prayers for Teddy & Me. Samuel, Janet, illus. 2014. (ENG.). 64p. (J). (gr. -1-k). 12.99 (978-0-7459-6452-2(4)) Lion Hudson PLC GBR. Dist: Independent Pubs. Group.

—Bible Stories for Girls. Bursi, Simona, illus. 2014. (ENG.). 48p. (J). (gr. k-4). 14.99 (978-0-7459-6371-6(4)) Lion Hudson PLC GBR. Dist: Independent Pubs. Group.

—Lift-the-Flap Christmas Stories. Hudson, Annabel, illus. 2010. (ENG.). 16p. (J). (gr. -1-k). 12.99 (978-0-7459-6203-0(3)) Lion Hudson PLC GBR. Dist: Independent Pubs. Group.

—The Lion Easy-Read Bible, 1 vol. Smith, Jamie, illus. 2017. (ENG.). 320p. (J). 16.99 **(978-0-7459-6553-6(9)**, Lion Children's) Lion Hudson PLC GBR. Dist: Kregel Pubns.

—Lost Sheep Story. Carletti, Emanuela, illus. 2015. (ENG.). 16p. (J). (gr. -1-k). pap. 6.99 (978-0-7459-6571-0(7)) Lion Hudson PLC GBR. Dist: Independent Pubs. Group.

—My Little Bible Board Book. Mitchell, Melanie, illus. 2015. (ENG.). 40p. (J). (— 1). 9.99 (978-0-7459-6046-3(4)) Lion Hudson PLC GBR. Dist: Independent Pubs. Group.

—My Look & Point Bible. Hudson, Annabel, illus. 2012. (ENG.). 224p. (J). (gr. -1-k). 16.99 (978-0-7459-6206-1(8)) Lion Hudson PLC GBR. Dist: Independent Pubs. Group.

Goodings, Christina & Hudson, Annabel. Bible Stories. 2009. (ENG., Illus.). 24p. (J). (gr. -1-k). 12.95 (978-0-7459-6091-3(X)) Lion Hudson PLC GBR. Dist: Independent Pubs. Group.

—My Look & Point Noah. 2014. (ENG., Illus.). 16p. (J). (gr. -1-k). 6.99 (978-0-7459-6395-2(1)) Lion Hudson PLC GBR. Dist: Independent Pubs. Group.

Goodrich, Donna. My Rhyme-Time Bible for Little Ones. 2016. (ENG., Illus.). 64p. (J). 14.99 (978-0-7369-5549-2(6)) Harvest Hse. Pubs.

Goodwin, John. The Lion Book of Five-Minute Christmas Stories. Johnson, Richard, illus. 2008. (ENG.). 48p. (J). (gr. k-2). 16.95 (978-0-7459-4943-7(6)) Lion Hudson PLC GBR. Dist: Independent Pubs. Group.

Gordon Brown, Doris. Lazarus; the Talk of the Town. 2003. 9.99 (978-0-9708560-0-5(8)) Aglob Publishing.

The Gospel for Kids a Character Book: God's Good News of Eternal Life. 2004. (Illus.). 115p. (J). per. 7.00 (978-0-9778494-1-3(4)) Huseby, Kirby.

Gospel Light Publications Staff. Bible Story Art Activities. 2003. (Big Bks.). (ENG.). 216p. (J). (gr. -1-k). pap. 19.99 (978-0-8307-3308-8(6)) Gospel Light Pubns.

—The Big Book of Bible Story Activity Pages: Help Kids Play, Listen & Talk Through the Bible. 2015. (Big Bks.). (ENG.). 224p. (J). (gr. -1-k). pap. 29.99 (978-0-8307-5102-0(5)) Gospel Light Pubns.

—God's Story for Me: 104 Favorite Bible Stories for Children. 2009. (ENG.). 528p. (J). (gr. -1-1). 16.99 (978-0-8307-4812-9(1)) Gospel Light Pubns.

—I Love to Look! 2008. (ENG.). 12p. (J). pap. 5.99 (978-0-8307-4670-5(6)) Gospel Light Pubns.

Gospel Light Publications Staff, creator. The Best Gift: Forgiveness: A Read-to-Me Bible Story Coloring Book about Jesus & the Paralyzed Man. 2007. (Illus.). 12p. (J). (gr. -1-3). 1.49 (978-0-8307-4428-2(2), Gospel Light) Gospel Light Pubns.

Graham, Billy. God's Good News Bible Storybook, 1 vol. 2015. (ENG., Illus.). 176p. (J). 19.99 (978-0-7180-0630-3(5)) Nelson, Thomas Inc.

Grant, Myrna. Ivan & the American Journey. 140p. (YA). mass mkt. 5.99 (978-1-85792-621-7(8), Christian Focus) Christian Focus Pubns. GBR. Dist: Riverside.

—Ivan & the Hidden Bible. 122p. (YA). mass mkt. 5.99 (978-1-85792-623-1(4), Christian Focus) Christian Focus Pubns. GBR. Dist: Riverside.

Gray, Charlotte. Bible Folks Shape Books. Henderson, Liz, illus. 2003. (J). spiral bd. 14.99 (978-0-89098-267-9(8)) Twentieth Century Christian Bks.

—My Bible Box in Color. Henderson, Liz, illus. 2003. (J). spiral bd. 24.99 (978-0-89098-266-2(X)) Twentieth Century Christian Bks.

Green Egg Media. Power Bible 2: Moses, Leader of the Israelites. 2011. (ENG., Illus.). (J). pap. 14.99 (978-1-937212-01-8(7)) Green Egg Media, Inc.

—Power Bible 5: The Kingdom Becomes Divided. 2011. (ENG., Illus.). (J). pap. 14.99 (978-1-937212-04-9(1)) Green Egg Media, Inc.

—Power Bible 6: Destruction & a Promise. 2011. (ENG., Illus.). (J). pap. 14.99 (978-1-937212-05-6(X)) Green Egg Media, Inc.

Green, Janice D. The Creation. 2011. (Illus.). 24p. 14.99 (978-0-9836808-0-2(9)) Honeycomb Adventures Pr., LLC.

Greene, Rhonda Gowler. Noah & the Mighty Ark, 1 vol. Spengler, Margaret L., illus. 2014. (ENG.). 32p. (J). 9.99 (978-0-310-73217-4(4)) Zonderkidz.

Groenboom, Roger, et al. King Jesus. (Walk with Me Ser.). (gr. k-8). 12.95 (978-1-59255-174-3(2), 017110) Faith Alive Christian Resources.

—Rough Waves? Jesus Saves!, Vol. 2. (Walk with Me Ser.). (gr. k-8). 24.95 (978-1-59255-177-4(7), 017220) Faith Alive Christian Resources.

—Sharable Parables. (Walk with Me Ser.). (gr. k-8). 24.95 (978-1-59255-176-7(9), 017210) Faith Alive Christian Resources.

Grosche, Erwin. Jonah & the Whale. Teich, Karsten, illus. 2016. (ENG.). 28p. (J). (gr. k-3). 12.99 (978-1-5064-0882-8(6), Sparkhouse Family) Augsburg Fortress, Pubs.

Gross, Arthur. A Child's Garden of Bible Stories. Barr, Marilyn, illus. 2005. 144p. (J). 10.49 (978-0-7586-0858-1(6)) Concordia Publishing Hse.

Group Publishing & Tyndale, prods. My First Hands-On Bible. 2015. (ENG.). 416p. (J). im. lthr. 19.99 (978-1-4964-0644-6(3)) Tyndale Hse. Pubs.

Hagan, Scott. Big Bad Bible Bullies. Horne, Doug, illus. 2005. 24p. (J). (gr. -1-3). 9.99 (978-1-59185-604-7(3)) Charisma Media.

—Los Buscapleitos de la Biblia. Horne, Doug, illus. 2005. 22p. (J). (gr. 1-3). 8.99 (978-1-59185-482-1(2), Charisma Kids) Charisma Media.

Haley, Barbara. The Singing Soldiers: And Other Bible Stories You've Gotta Hear. Apps, Fred, illus. 2007. (ENG.). 112p. (J). mass mkt. 7.99 (978-1-84550-249-2(3), 4c6404c2-c55b-4486-a056-134aadbc4aa3) Christian Focus Pubns. GBR. Dist: Bookmasters Distribution.

Halliday, M. A Ladder, a BBQ & a Pillar of Salt. 2003. (Bible Bites Ser.). (Illus.). 128p. 5.99 (978-1-85999-367-5(2)) Scripture Union GBR. Dist: Gabriel Resources.

Halliday, Marc & Potter, Ian. A Red Sea, a Burning Bush & a Plague of Frogs. 2003. (Bible Bites Ser.). (Illus.). 128p. 5.99 (978-1-85999-365-1(6)) Scripture Union GBR. Dist: Gabriel Resources.

—A Tent Peg, a Jawbone & a Sheepskin Rug. 2003. (Bible Bites Ser.). (Illus.). 128p. 5.99 (978-1-85999-294-4(3)) Scripture Union GBR. Dist: Gabriel Resources.

Harrast, Tracy L. My Learn to Read Bible: Stories in Words & Pictures, 1 vol. Schneider, Christine M., illus. 2013. (ENG.). 240p. (J). 19.99 (978-0-310-72740-8(5)) Zonderkidz.

Harthan, Jan. The B-I-B-L-E Vol. 3: Paraphrase of Proverbs & Romans for Children. 2009. 302p. pap. 18.99 (978-1-61579-019-7(5)) Salem Author Services.

Hartman, Bob. The Lion Storyteller Bible, 4 vols. Kallai Nagy, Krisztina, illus. 2014. (ENG.). 160p. (J). (gr. k-2). 22.99 (978-0-7459-6433-1(8)) Lion Hudson PLC GBR. Dist: Independent Pubs. Group.

—More Bible Tales. 2013. (ENG., Illus.). 96p. (J). (gr. 2-4). 8.99 (978-0-7459-6435-5(4)) Lion Hudson PLC GBR. Dist: Independent Pubs. Group.

Harvest House Publishers. Jesus the Miracle Worker. 2015. (ENG.). 32p. (J). 9.99 (978-0-7369-6323-7(5)) Harvest Hse. Pubs.

Harvest House Publishers & Emmerson-Hicks, J. The Complete Illustrated Children's Bible. 2014. (ENG.). 608p. (J). 24.99 (978-0-7369-6213-1(1)) Harvest Hse. Pubs.

—The Illustrated Bible for Little Ones. 2015. (A+ Ser.). (ENG.). 272p. (J). 22.99 (978-0-7369-6552-1(1)) Harvest Hse. Pubs.

Hascall, Glenn. My Big Book of Bible Heroes for Kids: Stories of 50 Weird, Wild, Wonderful People from God's Word. 2015. (ENG., Illus.). 160p. (J). pap. 14.99 (978-1-63409-315-6(1)) Barbour Publishing, Inc.

Hatfield, Tyrel & Hatfield, Justin. Fix Your Eyes on Jesus. Hatfield, Lisa & Hatfield, Kari, eds. Hatfield, Tyrel, illus. 2006. (Illus.). (J). cd-rom 99.00 (978-0-9766703-1-5(3)) Little Acorn LLC.

—The Mystery of Christ. Hatfield, Lisa & Hatfield, Kari, eds. Hatfield, Tyrel, illus. 2006. (Illus.). (J). cd-rom 99.00 (978-0-9766703-2-2(1)) Little Acorn LLC.

Haus, Cari Hoyt. A Brand-New World. 2006. (Illus.). 111p. (J). pap. (978-0-8280-1868-5(5)) Review & Herald Publishing Assn.

—God Makes a Promise. 2006. (Illus.). 95p. (J). pap. (978-0-8280-1893-7(6)) Review & Herald Publishing Assn.

Hawksley, Gerald. Amazing Journey of Noah & His Incredible Ark. 2004. 20p. pap. 11.99 (978-0-8254-7275-6(X)) Kregel Pubns.

Haws, Dona. Angels Foretold of Baby Jesus. 2017. (ENG.). (J). (gr. k-3). 14.99 **(978-1-4621-1987-5(5))** Cedar Fort, Inc./CFI Distribution.

Hayford, Jack W. The Acts Bible Story Book: What Kids Want to Know about the Holy Spirit. 2005. (Illus.). 60p. (J). 11.99 (978-1-59185-211-7(0), Charisma Kids) Charisma Media.

—Jack Hayford Presenta Hechos una Historia de la Biblia. Foote, Dan, illus. 2005. 60p. (J). (gr. -1-5). 9.99 (978-1-59185-487-6(3), Charisma Kids) Charisma Media.

Heart Of Dakota. Little Hands to Heaven. 2004. pap. 29.99 (978-0-9747695-4-7(1)) Ebed Pr.

Helms, Selah & Thompson, Susan. Small Talks on Big Questions Vol. 2: A Historical Companion to the Children's Catechism, 2 vols. Whitney, Caffy, illus. 2003. 192p. 26.99 (978-1-894400-05-3(4)) Joshua Pr., Inc. CAN. Dist: Gabriel Resources.

Hendrickson Publishers, creator. The Explorer Bible. 2006. (Illus.). 190p. (J). (gr. -1-3). pap. 12.95 (978-1-59856-042-8(5)) Hendrickson Pubs. Marketing, LLC.

Henley, Claire. Baby Jesus & the Noisy Stable. 2009. (All Join In Ser.). (ENG., Illus.). 16p. (J). (gr. k — 1). bds. 6.99 (978-0-7459-6068-5(5)) Lion Hudson PLC GBR. Dist: Independent Pubs. Group.

—Lost Sheep & the Scary Day. 2009. (All Join In Ser.). (ENG.). 16p. (J). (gr. k — 1). bds. 6.95 (978-0-7459-6070-8(7)) Lion Hudson PLC GBR. Dist: Independent Pubs. Group.

—Noah & the Flood. 2009. (All Join In Ser.). (ENG.). 16p. (J). (gr. k — 1). bds. 6.99 (978-0-7459-6071-5(5)) Lion Hudson PLC GBR. Dist: Independent Pubs. Group.

Henley, K. P. La Historia de Dios (God's Story) (SPA.). (J). (978-0-7899-0628-1(7), 497542) Editorial Unilit.

Henley, Karyn. Day by Day Begin-to-Read Bible. Sapulich, Joseph, illus. 2007. (ENG.). 448p. (J). (gr. -1-2). 14.99 (978-1-4143-0934-7(1)) Tyndale Hse. Pubs.

—Exploring God's World Through Simple Science: Bible Story Activities for Ages 2 To 5. 2006. (J). tchr. ed., per. 19.99 (978-1-933803-03-6(7), EG1) Child Sensitive Communication, LLC.

—God Made Land, Sea, & Sky. (Children's Ministry Folders). (Illus.). 8p. (gr. -1-k). 2.99 (978-0-7847-0652-7(2), 42202) Standard Publishing.

—Jesus Is My Friend. (Children's Ministry Folders). (Illus.). 8p. (gr. -1-k). 2.99 (978-0-7847-0672-5(7), 42222) Standard Publishing.

—Jesus Made People Well. (Children's Ministry Folders). (Illus.). 8p. (gr. -1-k). 2.99 (978-0-7847-0671-8(9), 42221) Standard Publishing.

—Story Telling: Bible Class Activities for Ages 2 To5. 2006. 186p. (J). tchr. ed., per. 19.99 (978-1-933803-05-0(3), STRY1) Child Sensitive Communication, LLC.

Hester, Carla. Sunday School Sarah: A Book of Children's Bible Stories. 2012. 142p. 29.99 (978-1-4797-1899-3(8)); pap. 19.99 (978-1-4797-1898-6(X)) Xlibris Corp.

Hetherington, Debra Thorpe, ed. The Spark Story Bible: Spark a Journey Through God's Word. Grosshauser, Peter, illus. 2015. (ENG.). 456p. (J). (gr. -1-2). 22.99

(978-1-4514-9978-0(7), Sparkhouse Family) Augsburg Fortress, Pubs.

Heyes, Jane, illus. Candle Day by Day Bible, 1 vol. 2016. (ENG.). 368p. (J). spiral bd. 16.99 *(978-1-78128-281-6(1),* Candle Bks.) Lion Hudson PLC GBR. Dist: Kregel Pubns.

El Hijo Prodigo. (SPA.). (J). *(978-0-89265-493-2(7))* Randall Hse. Pubns.

Hinkle, Cynthia A. The Thankful Leper: The Story of the Ten Lepers: Luke 17:11-19 & 2 Kings 5:1-15 for Children. Collier-Morales, Roberta, illus. 2006. (Arch Bks.). (J). 2.49 *(978-0-7586-1284-7(2))* Concordia Publishing Hse.

Hoeksema, Gertrude. Come, Ye Children: A Bible Storybook for Young Children. Steenholdt, Jeff, illus. 3rd ed. 2010. (ENG.). 599p. (J). reprint ed. 47.95 *(978-0-916206-27-7(0))* Reformed Free Publishing Assn.

Holder, Jennifer. Abraham Trusts God. Julien, Terry, illus. 2015. (Faith That Sticks Bks.). (ENG.). 24p. (J). pap. 3.99 *(978-1-4964-0320-9(7))* Tyndale Hse. Pubs.

—Daniel & His Faithful Friends. Julien, Terry, illus. 2014. (Faith That Sticks Bks.). (ENG.). 27p. (J). pap. 3.99 *(978-1-4143-9827-3(1))* Tyndale Hse. Pubs.

—God Made You Special. Nobens, C. A., illus. 2014. (Faith That Sticks Bks.). (ENG.). 28p. (J). pap. 3.99 *(978-1-4964-0086-4(0))* Tyndale Hse. Pubs.

Hollingsworth, Mary. My Bible Journey Supersaver. 2004. 360p. 11.88 *(978-0-529-11810-3(6))* Nelson, Thomas Inc.

Holmes, Andy. Bible for Me: 12 Favorite Stories, 1 vol. Voltz, Ralph, illus. 2003. (ENG.). 48p. 9.99 *(978-1-4003-0234-5(X))* Nelson, Thomas Inc.

—Mi Biblia Pijama. O'Connor, Tim, illus. 2008. (SPA & ENG.). 33p. (J). (gr. -1). bds. 13.99 *(978-1-4143-1979-7(7),* Tyndale Espanol) Tyndale Hse. Pubs.

—My Great Big God: 20 Bible Stories to Build a Great Big Faith, 1 vol. Miguens, Marta Alvarez, illus. 2017. (ENG.). 40p. (J). bds. 9.99 ***(978-0-7180-9737-0(8))*** Nelson, Thomas Inc.

Holmes, Andy. My Princess Bible. Eliseev, Sergey, illus. 2010. (ENG.). 66p. (J). bds. 12.99 *(978-1-4143-3324-3(2))* Tyndale Hse. Pubs.

Holmes, Andy & Voltz, Ralph. Biblia para Mi, 1 vol. 2004.Tr. of Bible for Me. (SPA., Illus.). 48p. 12.99 *(978-0-88113-785-9(5))* Grupo Nelson.

Honea, Helen. Shedding the Light: Stories from the Bible. 2009. 124p. 21.49 *(978-1-4389-4259-9(1));* pap. 12.95 *(978-1-4389-4260-5(5))* AuthorHouse.

Hoop, Cathy C. PowerXpress Easter: Peter's Story Unit. 2004. (PowerXpress Ser.). 129.95 *(978-0-687-07336-8(7))* Abingdon Pr.

HOP, LLC. Hooked on Bible Stories. deluxe ed. 2006. 99.99 *(978-1-933863-00-9(5))* HOP, LLC.

—Hooked on Bible Stories NT Stories. 2006. 24.99 *(978-1-931020-98-5(1))* HOP, LLC.

—Hooked on Bible Stories Old Testament Stories. 2006. 24.99 *(978-1-931020-97-8(3))* HOP, LLC.

—Hooked on Bible Stories Premium Edition. 2006. 64.99 *(978-1-931020-99-2(X))* HOP, LLC.

—Hooked on Phonics Beginning Reading with Bible Stories. 2006. 29.99 *(978-1-931020-80-0(9))* HOP, LLC.

Horlacher, Bill & Horlacher, Kathy. I'm Glad I'm Your Mother. Johnson, Meredith, illus. 2013. (Happy Day Ser.). (ENG.). 16p. (J). pap. 2.49 *(978-1-4143-9292-9(3))* Tyndale Hse. Pubs.

Horlacher, Kathy & Horlacher, Bill. I'm Glad I'm Your Grandma. Johnson, Meredith, illus. 2014. (Happy Day Ser.). (ENG.). 16p. (J). pap. 2.49 *(978-1-4143-9408-4(X))* Tyndale Hse. Pubs.

Hovland, Stephenie. Isaac Blesses Jacob & Esau. 2011. 16p. pap. 2.49 *(978-0-7586-2744-5(0))* Concordia Publishing Hse.

Howie, Vicky & MacLean, Moira. Cnoc, Cnoc! Pwy Sy 'Na? Llyfr Fflapiau Stori'r Nadolig. Wyn, Delyth, tr. from ENG. 2005. (WEL., Illus.). 16p. *(978-1-85994-498-1(1))* Cyhoeddiadau'r Gair.

Hudson, Angus. Historias Favoritas de la Biblia (Favorite Bible Stories) (Serie Uniendo los Puntos - Dot to Dot Ser.). (SPA.). (J). Bk. 1. 1.89 *(978-1-56063-966-4(0),* 497757)Bk. 2. 1.89 *(978-1-56063-967-1(9),* 497758) Editorial Unilit.

Hughes, Greg. The Shapes & Colors Bible. Hughes, Greg, illus. 2004. (Illus.). 80p. (J). 7.99 *(978-0-9741091-3-8(4),* 7002) smart Life Ministries, Inc., The.

Humbert, Ellen. Bible Crafts on a Shoestring Budget. 2004. (Illus.). 64p. (J). (gr. 1-2). pap. 9.95 *(978-0-937282-10-6(3),* RB36128) Rainbow Pubs. & Legacy Pr.

Hummell, Victoria R. A. Friends of Jesus: Stories & Activities for Chrldren, Parents, & Teachers. 2003. (J). pap. 9.95 net. *(978-0-7648-1101-2(0))* Liguori Pubns.

Hunt, Johnny. My Bible Adventure Through God's Word: 52 Bible Stories for Kids, 1 vol. 2017. (ENG.). 352p. (J). 16.99 *(978-0-7180-9215-3(5))* Nelson, Thomas Inc.

Hyatt, Greg. Moises y la serpiente de bronce (Moses & the Bronze Snake) 2011. 16p. pap. 2.49 *(978-0-7586-3067-4(0))* Concordia Publishing Hse.

A Is for Adam: An Alphabet Book of Bible Heroes. 2017. (ENG.). (J). (gr. -1-1). 14.99 ***(978-1-4621-2024-6(5))*** Cedar Fort, Inc./CFI Distribution.

Jackson, Dave, et al. Hero Tales Vol. 1: A Family Treasury of True Stories from the Lives of Christian Heroes. 2005. (ENG., Illus.). 192p. (J). (gr. 4-7). pap. 14.99 *(978-0-7642-0078-6(X))* Bethany Hse. Pubs.

Jaeger, Elizabeth. The Pentecost Story. Hill, Dave, illus. 2014. (Arch Bks.). (ENG.). 16p. (J). pap. 2.49 *(978-0-7586-4604-0(6))* Concordia Publishing Hse.

A Jailer Is Set Free. 2014. (Happy Day Ser.). (ENG., Illus.). 16p. (J). pap. 2.49 *(978-1-4143-9412-1(8))* Tyndale Hse. Pubs.

James, Bethan. My Toddler Bible. Sgouros, Yorgos, illus. 2008. (ENG.). 36p. (J). (gr. -1-k). 12.99 *(978-1-4143-2013-7(2))* Tyndale Hse. Pubs.

James, Elizabeth. The Kids of Castle Grace. 2011. 48p. pap. 21.99 *(978-1-4535-8055-4(7));* pap. 21.99 *(978-1-4568-6212-1(X))* Xlibris Corp.

Jander, Martha Streufert. The Easter Gift. 2008. (Arch Bks.). 16p. (J). (gr. k-4). pap. 1.99 *(978-0-7586-1450-6(0))* Concordia Publishing Hse.

JANISCH.HEINZ. Stories from the Bible. 2016. (ENG., Illus.). 144p. 26.00 *(978-0-7358-4244-1(2))* North-South Bks., Inc.

Jeffs, Stephanie. Bywyd Iesu. Wyn, Delyth, tr. from ENG. Tulip, Jenny, illus. 2005. (WEL.). 94p. *(978-1-85994-496-7(5))* Cyhoeddiadau'r Gair.

—Jacob: Wrestler with God. 2003. (SnapShots Ser.). (Illus.). 96p. 5.99 *(978-1-85999-444-3(X))* Scripture Union GBR. Dist: Gabriel Resources.

—Joshua: Warrior for God. 2003. (SnapShots Ser.). (Illus.). 96p. 5.99 *(978-1-85999-451-1(2))* Scripture Union GBR. Dist: Gabriel Resources.

—Peter: Fisherman for God. 2003. (SnapShots Ser.). (Illus.). 96p. 5.99 *(978-1-85999-453-5(9))* Scripture Union GBR. Dist: Gabriel Resources.

Jesus Calms the Storm: Thematic Unit: Weather. (Scripture Bites Ser.). (J). (gr. -1). pap. 1.99 *(978-0-7847-9073-1(6))* Standard Publishing.

Jesus Heals Ten Lepers. (Illus.). (J). (gr. 1-4). 3.00 *(978-0-570-05523-5(7),* 54-1033) Concordia Publishing Hse.

Jesus Is a Friend to Zacchaeus. (Illus.). (J). (gr. 1-4). 3.00 *(978-0-570-05522-8(9),* 54-1032) Concordia Publishing Hse.

Jesus Loves the Little Children: Thematic Unit: Self-Esteem/Feelings. (Scripture Bites Ser.). (J). (gr. -1). pap. 1.99 *(978-0-7847-9093-9(0))* Standard Publishing.

Jesus Miracles. 2004. (gr. 3-4). pap. 6.95 *(978-0-382-30784-3(4))* Cobblestone Publishing Co.

Jesus, Name Above All Names: Thematic Unit: Our Names. (Scripture Bites Ser.). (J). (gr. -1). 1.99 *(978-0-7847-9071-7(X))* Standard Publishing.

Jesus Teaches about Forgiveness- the Prodigal Son: Thematic Unit: Our Families. (Scripture Bites Ser.). (J). (gr. -1). pap. 1.99 *(978-0-7847-9087-8(6))* Standard Publishing.

Jesus Teaches about the Lost Coin: Thematic Unit: Money. (Scripture Bites Ser.). (J). (gr. -1). pap. 1.99 *(978-0-7847-9077-9(9))* Standard Publishing.

Jesus Teaches about the Lost Coin, Preschool: Thematic Unit: Money. (Scripture Bites Ser.). (J). pap., tchr. ed. 5.99 *(978-0-7847-9076-2(0))* Standard Publishing.

Jesus Teaches about the Lost Sheep. (Scripture Bites Ser.). (J). (gr. -1). pap. 1.99 *(978-0-7847-9083-0(3))* Standard Publishing.

Jesus Tells of the Wise & Foolish Builders: Thematic Unit: Building Things. (Scripture Bites Ser.). (J). (gr. -1). pap. 1.99 *(978-0-7847-9075-5(2))* Standard Publishing.

Jesus Tells us to Help Others-the Good Samaritan: Thematic Unit: Friendship. (Scripture Bites Ser.). (J). (gr. -1). pap. 1.99 *(978-0-7847-9099-1(X))* Standard Publishing.

Jesus Tells Us to Share the Good News: Thematic Unit: Children of the World. (Scripture Bites Ser.). (J). (gr. -1). pap. 1.99 *(978-0-7847-9081-6(7))* Standard Publishing.

Jesus Travels to Egypt: Thematic Unit: Transportation, "Moving Things" (Scripture Bites Ser.). (J). (gr. -1). pap. 1.99 *(978-0-7847-9095-3(7))* Standard Publishing.

Johnson, Dwayne & Piper, Sophie. The Lion Read & Know Bible. Lewis, Anthony, illus. 2009. (ENG.). 384p. (J). (gr. k-2). 17.95 *(978-0-7459-4996-3(7))* Lion Hudson PLC GBR. Dist: Independent Pubs. Group.

Johnson, Linda & Hodges, Quae. 21st Century Parables: A Child's Book. 2006. 48p. pap. 14.95 *(978-1-60145-071-5(0))* Booklocker.com, Inc.

Johnson, Richard, illus. The Lion Book of Five-Minute Bible Stories. 2013. (ENG.). 96p. (J). (gr. k-2). pap. 10.99 *(978-0-7459-4984-0(3))* Lion Hudson PLC GBR. Dist: Independent Pubs. Group.

Johnson, Roland. Jeremya Jones: A King's Kid. 2012. 120p. (gr. -1). 28.95 *(978-1-4497-3813-6(3));* pap. 11.95 *(978-1-4497-3814-3(1))* Author Solutions, Inc. (WestBow Pr.).

Jonah & the Big Fish. 2003. (J). per. *(978-1-57657-981-7(6))* Paradise Pr., Inc.

Jones, Anna, illus. My First Bible Stories. 2016. (ENG.). 38p. (J). (gr. -1-k). bds. 9.99 *(978-1-58925-222-6(5))* Tiger Tales.

Jones, Sally Lloyd. Lift-the-Flap Bible. Moroney, Tracey, illus. 2011. (Lift-The-Flap Ser.). (ENG.). 20p. (J). (gr. -1-k). bds. 10.99 *(978-0-7944-2278-3(0),* Reader's Digest Children's Bks.) Studio Fun International.

Joseph Bible Sticker Book. 2003. (Illus.). 16p. (J). 2.98 *(978-1-4054-1556-9(8))* Parragon, Inc.

Joslin, Mary. The Lion Day-by-Day Bible. Hall, Amanda, illus. 2008. (ENG.). 384p. (J). (gr. 2-4). 19.95 *(978-0-7459-6132-3(0))* Lion Hudson PLC GBR. Dist: Independent Pubs. Group.

Jung, Scott. Verdades biblicas eternas (Timeless Bible Truths) - Bilingual. 2011. 64p. pap. 7.99 *(978-0-7586-2681-3(9))* Concordia Publishing Hse.

Juravel, Rabbi. Parsha with Rabbi Juravel: Shemos. Toron, Eli, illus. 2006. (J). 27.95 *(978-1-60091-002-9(5))* Israel Bookshop Pubns.

Kampia, Judy. God's Great Book: A Complete Collection of Bible Stories & Activities for All Ages. 2007. 596p. 36.99 *(978-1-4257-4890-6(2))* Xlibris Corp.

Kennedy, Dana & Wilson, Etta. Children's Bible Stories. Dolce, Ellen, illus. 2009. 160p. (J). (gr. -1). 16.99 *(978-0-7586-1634-0(1))* Concordia Publishing Hse.

Kennedy, Nancy B. Make It, Shake It, Mix It Up: 44 Bible Stories Brought to Life with Science. Cannell, Jon, illus. 2008. 61p. pap. 10.99 *(978-0-7586-1334-9(2))* Concordia Publishing Hse.

Kennedy, Pamela & Brady, Anne Kennedy. Five-Minute Bible Devotions for Children: Stories from the New Testament. Wummer, Amy, illus. 2012. 48p. (J). spiral bd. 15.99 *(978-0-8249-5644-8(3),* Ideal Pubns.) Worthy Publishing.

Kenney, Cindy. Veggietales Bible Storybook, 1 vol. 2006. (Big Idea Bks.). (ENG., Illus.). 256p. (J). (gr. -1-3). 16.99 *(978-0-310-71008-0(1))* Zonderkidz.

Kile, Joan. God's Fig Tree. Ragland, Teresa, illus. 2005. 32p. (J). pap. 7.95 *(978-1-57736-345-3(0))* Providence Hse Pubs.

—God's Fruit Tree. Ragland, Teresa, illus. 2005. (Musty the Mustard Seed Ser.). 28p. (J). (gr. -1-4). per. 7.95 *(978-1-57736-344-6(2))* Providence Hse Pubs.

—God's Mustard Seed: Volume 1, Vol. 1. Ragland, Teresa, illus. 2005. (Musty the Mustard Seed Ser.). 32p. (J). (gr. -1-3). per. 11.95 *(978-1-57736-342-2(6))* Providence Hse Pubs.

—God's Protecting Angels. Ragland, Teresa, illus. 2005. (Musty the Mustard Seed Ser.). 28p. (J). (gr. -1-4). per. 7.95 *(978-1-57736-346-0(9))* Providence Hse Pubs.

—God's Rugged Cross. Ragland, Teresa, illus. 2005. (Musty the Mustard Seed Ser.). 32p. (Orig.). (J). (gr. -1-3). per. 4.95 *(978-1-57736-343-9(4))* Providence Hse Pubs.

Kimmel, Eric A. The Brass Serpent. Miller, Joanna, illus. 2005. 32p. (J). 14.95 *(978-1-930143-41-8(9),* 3419); pap. 9.95 *(978-1-930143-42-5(7),* 3427) Simcha Media Group. (Devora Publishing).

Kingfisher. My Pocket Bible Stories Slipcase. 2016. (ENG., Illus.). (J). 13.99 *(978-0-7534-7303-0(8),* 9780753473030, Kingfisher) Roaring Brook Pr.

Kleyn, Diana. Taking Root: Conversion Stories for Children. 2006. (ENG.). 190p. (J). pap. 8.00 *(978-1-60178-001-0(X))* Reformation Heritage Bks.

Knecht, F. J. Child's Bible History. Schumacher, Philip, tr. 2009. (ENG., Illus.). 95p. (gr. 6-6). reprint ed. pap. 12.95 *(978-0-89555-005-7(9))* TAN Bks.

Knowlton, Laurie Lazzaro, et al. Catholic Book of Bible Stories, 1 vol. Ettlinger, Doris, illus. 2004. (ENG.). 224p. (J). 16.99 *(978-0-310-70505-5(3))* Zonderkidz.

Kondeatis, Christos. Scenes from the Life of Jesus Christ: A Three-Dimensional Bible Storybook. Kondeatis, Christos, illus. 2006. (Illus.). 10p. (J). (gr. k-4). reprint ed. 20.00 *(978-0-7567-9826-0(4))* DIANE Publishing Co.

Konzen, Lisa M. Good News for Naaman. Snyder, Joel, illus. 2004. (ENG.). 16p. (J). 1.99 *(978-0-570-07573-8(4))* Concordia Publishing Hse.

Kovacs, Victoria. Elijah/John the Baptist Flip-Over Book. Ryley, David, illus. 2016. (Little Bible Heroes(tm) Ser.). (ENG.). 32p. (J). (gr. k-2). pap. 3.99 *(978-1-4336-4324-8(3),* B&H Kids) B&H Publishing Group.

—Heroes of Babylon/Ruth Flip-Over Book. Ryley, David, illus. 2016. (Little Bible Heroes(tm) Ser.). (ENG.). 32p. (J). (gr. k-2). pap. 3.99 *(978-1-4336-4325-5(1),* B&H Kids) B&H Publishing Group.

—Joshua/Rahab Flip-Over Book. Ryley, David, illus. 2015. (Little Bible Heroes(tm) Ser.). (ENG.). 32p. (J). (gr. k-2). pap. 3.99 *(978-1-4336-8716-7(X),* B&H Kids) B&H Publishing Group.

—Little Bible Heroes Storybook (padded) Krome, Mike & Ryley, David, illus. 2016. (Little Bible Heroes(tm) Ser.). (ENG.). 264p. (J). 14.99 *(978-1-4336-9230-7(9),* B&H Kids) B&H Publishing Group.

—The Little Giver/Zacchaeus Flip-Over Book. Ryley, David, illus. 2016. (Little Bible Heroes(tm) Ser.). (ENG.). 32p. (J). (gr. k-2). pap. 3.99 *(978-1-4336-4326-2(X),* B&H Kids) B&H Publishing Group.

Kucharik, E. NT y Salmos Pequenas Bendiciones. 2003. (Little Hearts Ser.).Tr. of Little Blessings NT & Psalms. 16.99 *(978-0-7899-1118-6(3))* Editorial Unilit.

Kuck, Anna. Seven Holy Sleepers: Amazing Saints. 2012. 38p. pap. 15.95 *(978-1-4497-7065-5(7),* WestBow Pr.) Author Solutions, Inc.

Lafferty, Jill C. Devociones para Niños Chispita. Grosshauser, Peter, illus. 2016. (SPA.). (J). *(978-1-5064-2101-8(6))* Augsburg Fortress, Pubs.

—Spark Story Bible Devotions for Kids. Grosshauser, Peter, illus. 2016. (ENG.). 216p. (J). (gr. -1-3). 14.99 *(978-1-5064-1766-0(3))* Augsburg Fortress, Pubs.

Lafferty, Jill C., ed. The First Christmas: A Spark Story Bible Play & Learn Book. Grosshauser, Peter, illus. 2016. (ENG.). 64p. (J). (gr. -1-3). 9.99 *(978-1-5064-1763-9(9),* Sparkhouse Family) Augsburg Fortress, Pubs.

—The Life of Jesus: A Spark Story Bible Play & Learn Book. Grosshauser, Peter, illus. 2016. (ENG.). 80p. (J). (gr. -1-3). 9.99 *(978-1-5064-1764-6(7),* Sparkhouse Family) Augsburg Fortress, Pubs.

Lafond, Pascale. The Story of Jesus. Flowerpot Press, ed. 2012. (Illus.). 32p. (J). *(978-1-77093-387-3(5))* Flowerpot Children's Pr. Inc.

—The Story of Moses. Flowerpot Press, ed. 2012. (Illus.). 32p. (J). *(978-1-77093-388-0(3))* Flowerpot Children's Pr. Inc.

—The Story of Noah. Flowerpot Press, ed. 2012. (Illus.). 32p. (J). *(978-1-77093-386-6(7))* Flowerpot Children's Pr. Inc.

Lane, Leena. Christmas Fun: My First Bible Activity BK. Bishop, Roma, illus. 2004. 32p. pap. 6.95 *(978-1-59325-043-0(6))* Word Among Us Pr.

—Friends of God: My First Bible Activity BK. Bishop, Roma, illus. 2004. 32p. pap. 6.95 *(978-1-59325-042-3(8))* Word Among Us Pr.

—My First Bible. Chapman, Gillian, illus. 2005. 252p. (J). (gr. -1). 13.49 *(978-0-7586-0910-6(8))* Concordia Publishing Hse.

Larcombe, Jennifer Rees. Lost in Jerusalem! Björkman, Steve, illus. 2004. (Best Bible Stories Ser.). 24p. (gr. -1-3). pap. 2.99 *(978-1-58134-150-8(4))* Crossway.

—The Walls That Fell down Flat. Björkman, Steve, illus. 2004. (Best Bible Stories Ser.). 24p. (gr. -1-3). pap. 2.99 *(978-1-58134-151-5(2))* Crossway.

Larkin, Jean, ed. Sacred Stories: A Child's Bible Book. 2005. (Illus.). 32p. (J). pap. 3.95 *(978-1-933178-21-9(3),* 3510) Pflaum Publishing Group.

Larsen, Carolyn. Bible Stories for Tiny Tots. Incrocci, Rick, illus. 2008. 35p. (J). bds. *(978-1-86920-241-5(4))* Christian Art Pubs.

—Little Angels Bible Storybook. Incrocci, Rick, illus. 2012. (ENG.). 432p. (J). 16.99 *(978-1-4143-7022-4(9))* Tyndale Hse. Pubs.

—Little Boys Bible Storybook for Fathers & Sons. Turk, Caron, illus. rev. ed. 2014. (ENG.). 288p. (J). 14.99 *(978-0-8010-1548-9(0))* Baker Bks.

—Little Girls Bible Storybook for Fathers & Daughters. Turk, Caron, illus. rev. ed. 2014. (ENG.). 288p. (J). 14.99 *(978-0-8010-1549-6(9))* Baker Bks.

—My 123 Bible Storybook. Turk, Caron, illus. 2008. (My Bible Storybooks Ser.). 30p. (J). (gr. -1-3). bds. *(978-1-86920-925-4(7))* Christian Art Pubs.

—My ABC Bible Storybook. Turk, Caron, illus. 2008. (My Bible Storybooks Ser.). 30p. (J). (gr. -1-3). bds. *(978-1-86920-926-1(5))* Christian Art Pubs.

—Stories about Jesus for Little Ones. Incrocci, Rick, illus. 2008. 35p. (gr. -1-k). bds. *(978-1-86920-173-9(6))* Christian Art Pubs.

—101 Bible Stories for Toddlers. 2008. (Illus.). 415p. (J). (gr. -1). *(978-1-86920-927-8(3))* Christian Art Pubs.

Larson, Beverly. Toca y Siente las Historias de la Biblia. Pineda, Nancy, tr. Dillard, Sarah, illus. 2003. (Touch & Feel Ser.). (SPA.). (J). (gr. -1-k). bds. 8.99 *(978-0-7899-1088-2(8))* Editorial Unilit.

Lathbury, Mary A. Child's Story of the Bible. 2011. 260p. pap. 16.99 *(978-1-61203-236-8(2))* Bottom of the Hill Publishing.

Lawson, Michael S. Grandpa Mike Talks about God. 2007. (ENG., Illus.). 112p. (J). (gr. -1-2). pap. 12.99 *(978-1-84550-250-8(7),* 45f2618a-2b73-472b-b400-ad6436e5c5d1) Christian Focus Pubns. GBR. Dist: Bookmasters Distribution.

Lebedev, Aleksandr, illus. Bible Stories. 2006. (Play & Learn Puzzle Bks.). 12p. (J). 12.95 *(978-0-88271-385-4(X))* Regina Pr., Malhame & Co.

Lee, Hye-Seong, illus. The Call of Samuel: From 1 Samuel 3:1-10. 2003. 29p. (J). 13.50 *(978-0-9659164-9-3(9))* Fountain Publishing.

Lessa, Charlotte F. My Bible Storybook. 2003. 455p. (J). 18.99 *(978-0-8280-1792-3(1))* Review & Herald Publishing Assn.

Lewis, Jan, illus. My First Bible Stories: Adam & Eve, Noah's Ark, Moses, Joseph, David & Goliath, Jesus. 2016. (ENG.). 48p. (J). (gr. -1-12). bds. 9.99 *(978-1-86147-737-8(6),* Armadillo) Anness Publishing GBR. Dist: National Bk. Network.

Lillis, Sonya. God's Kids: Being a Light in a Dark World. I.t. ed. 2006. 36p. (J). per. 9.95 *(978-0-9786580-6-9(X))* Christian Voice Publishing, A.

—God's Kids: Great Bit Thoughts for Young Minds. I.t. ed. 2006. 36p. (J). per. 9.95 *(978-0-9786580-7-6(8))* Christian Voice Publishing, A.

—God's Kids: Growing up Holy in an Unholy World, book 1. I.t. ed. 2006. (Illus.). (J). per. 9.95 *(978-0-9786580-5-2(1))* Christian Voice Publishing, A.

Lindvall, Ella K. La Biblia en Cuadros para Niños Pequeños, 1 vol. 2004. (SPA.). 144p. (J). 10.99 *(978-0-8254-1710-8(4),* Editorial Portavoz) Kregel Pubns.

Lingo, Susan L. Hope Finders. Barr, Marilynn G. & Jeffery, Megan E., illus. 2006. (Power Builders Curriculum Ser.). 128p. (J). (gr. 1-5). 15.99 *(978-0-7847-1235-1(2),* 42118) Standard Publishing.

—Joy Builders. Barr, Marilynn G. & Jeffery, Megan E., illus. 2006. (Power Builders Curriculum Ser.). 128p. (J). (gr. 1-5). 15.99 *(978-0-7847-1234-4(4),* 42117) Standard Publishing.

—Peace Makers. Barr, Marilynn G. & Jeffery, Megan E., illus. 2006. (Power Builders Curriculum Ser.). 128p. (J). (gr. 1-5). 15.99 *(978-0-7847-1233-7(6),* 42116) Standard Publishing.

—Power Boosters. Barr, Marilynn G. & Jeffery, Megan E., illus. 2006. (Power Builders Curriculum Ser.). 128p. (J). (gr. 1-5). 15.99 *(978-0-7847-1232-0(8),* 42115) Standard Publishing.

The Lion Little Book of Bible Stories. 2015. (ENG., Illus.). 96p. (J). (gr. -1-k). 9.99 *(978-0-7459-6489-8(3))* Lion Hudson PLC GBR. Dist: Independent Pubs. Group.

The Lion Nursery Bible. gif. ed. 2014. (ENG., Illus.). 192p. (J). (gr. -1 — 1). 19.99 *(978-0-7459-6547-5(4))* Lion Hudson PLC GBR. Dist: Independent Pubs. Group.

Lipara, Laura. Gramma Shares Her Faith: Cain & Abel. 2006. per. 7.95 *(978-0-9791757-1-8(2))* Oak Manor Publishing, Inc.

Lipari, Laura. Gramma Shares Her Faith: Adam & Eve. 2006. 64p. (J). per. 6.95 *(978-0-9747361-4-3(7))* Oak Manor Publishing, Inc.

Little Books of the Bible Stories of Jesus. (J). 14.95 *(978-0-8249-5464-2(5),* Ideal Pubns.) Worthy Publishing.

Lloyd-Jones, Sally. Baby's Hug-a-Bible. Gévry, Claudine, illus. 2010. (ENG.). 24p. (J). (gr. -1 — 1). bds. 15.99 *(978-0-06-156621-9(7),* HarperFestival) HarperCollins Pubs.

—The Jesus Storybook Bible: Every Story Whispers His Name, 1 vol. Jago, illus. (ENG.). 352p. (J). (gr. -1-3). 2007. 17.99 *(978-0-310-70825-4(7))* 2009. 24.99 *(978-0-310-71878-9(3))* Zonderkidz.

—The Jesus Storybook Bible Deluxe Edition, 1 vol. 2014. (ENG.). (J). 24.99 *(978-0-310-74884-7(4))* Zonderkidz.

—My Promise Rainbow: And the Story of Noah's Ark. 2006. (Illus.). 14p. (YA). bds. 10.99 *(978-0-7847-1357-0(X),* 04018) Standard Publishing.

—The Story of God's Love for You, 1 vol. Jago, illus. 2015. (ENG.). 208p. (YA). 14.99 *(978-0-310-73602-8(1))* Zondervan.

—Tiny Bear's Bible, 1 vol. Oleynikov, Igor, illus. 2015. (ENG.). 22p. (J). bds. 15.99 *(978-0-310-74787-1(2))* Zonderkidz.

—Tiny Bear's Bible, 1 vol. Oleynikov, Igor, illus. (Furry Bible Stories Ser.). (ENG.). 22p. (J). (gr. -1-k). 2009. pap. 14.99 *(978-0-310-71818-5(X))* 2007. 14.99 *(978-0-310-71082-0(0))* Zonderkidz.

Lockwood, Barbara. Bible Crafts on a Shoestring Budget. 2004. (Illus.). 64p. (J). (gr. -1-k). pap. 9.95 *(978-0-937282-09-0(X),* RB36127) Rainbow Pubs. & Legacy Pr.

Look & Find Activity Books. 2004. (Illus.). 24p. (J). 2.99 *(978-0-8254-7262-6(8));* Vol. 2. 2.99 *(978-0-8254-7263-3(6))* Kregel Pubns.

The Lost Son. 2003. (Illus.). 12p. (J). bds. 6.99 *(978-0-8254-5506-3(5))* Kregel Pubns.

Louis, Margareth Belledent. When I Make It to Heaven. 2011. 40p. pap. 18.46 *(978-1-4520-8563-0(3))* AuthorHouse.

Lucado, Max. The Christmas Story for Children, 1 vol. 2014. (ENG.). 32p. (J). pap. 6.99 *(978-0-310-73598-4(X))* Zonderkidz.

Lucado, Max, et al. The Story for Children: A Storybook Bible. Bianchi, Fausto, illus. 2011. 287p. (J). *(978-0-310-73211-2(5))* Zonderkidz.

—The Story for Children Bible, 1 vol. rev. ed. 2015. (Story Ser.). (ENG.). 2048p. (J). 27.99 *(978-0-310-74405-4(9))* Zonderkidz.

Lumsden, Colin, illus. John the Baptist. 2003. (Bible Colour & Learn Ser.). 32p. pap. 2.50 *(978-1-903087-44-2(9))* DayOne Pubns. GBR. Dist: Send The Light Distribution LLC.

—Miracles of Jesus. 2003. (Bible Colour & Learn Ser.). 32p. pap. 2.50 *(978-1-903087-48-0(1))* DayOne Pubns. GBR. Dist: Send The Light Distribution LLC.

—Parables of Jesus. 2003. (Bible Colour & Learn Ser.). 32p. pap. 2.50 *(978-1-903087-47-3(3))* DayOne Pubns. GBR. Dist: Send The Light Distribution LLC.

—People in the Life of Jesus. 2003. (Bible Colour & Learn Ser.). 32p. pap. 2.50 *(978-1-903087-49-7(X))* DayOne Pubns. GBR. Dist: Send The Light Distribution LLC.

—People in the Life of Paul. 2003. (Bible Colour & Learn Ser.). 32p. pap. 2.50 *(978-1-903087-50-3(3))* DayOne Pubns. GBR. Dist: Send The Light Distribution LLC.

—Story of Mary. 2003. (Bible Colour & Learn Ser.). 32p. pap. 2.50 (978-1-903087-43-5(0)) DayOne Pubns. GBR. Dist: Send The Light Distribution LLC.

—Story of Paul. 2003. (Bible Colour & Learn Ser.). 32p. pap. 2.50 (978-1-903087-46-6(5)) DayOne Pubns. GBR. Dist: Send The Light Distribution LLC.

—Story of Peter. 2003. (Bible Colour & Learn Ser.). 32p. pap. 2.50 (978-1-903087-45-9(7)) DayOne Pubns. GBR. Dist: Send The Light Distribution LLC.

Lynch, Fred D., et al. My Changes, 1 vol. 2008. (Middle School Survival Ser.). (ENG.). 192p. (YA). pap. 9.99 (978-0-310-27883-2(X)) Zondervan.

Maas, Alice E. Baby Jesus Visits the Temple. Miyake, Yoshi, illus. 2004. (ENG.). 16p. (J). 1.99 (978-0-570-07575-2(0)) Concordia Publishing Hse.

Mackall, Dandi Daley. Wow! The Good News in Four Words. Tempest, Annabel, illus. 2017. (ENG.). 32p. 14.99 (**978-1-4964-1814-2(X)**, Tyndale Kids) Tyndale Hse. Pubs.

MacKenzie, Carine. Barnabas: The Encourager. Apps, Fred, illus. 2007. (Bible Wise Ser.). (ENG.). 32p. (J). (gr. -1-3). pap. 3.99 (978-1-84550-290-4(6), 7a13aecd-9660-45e8-af17-7585c244cb87) Christian Focus Pubns. GBR. Dist: Bookmasters Distribution.

—The Beautiful Garden. 2013. (Bible Art Ser.). (ENG.). 16p. (J). pap., act. bk. ed. 1.99 (978-1-85792-829-7(6), 5043f2cc-49b8-4822-8376-bbbaae134323, Christian Focus) Christian Focus Pubns. GBR. Dist: Bookmasters Distribution.

—Bible Heroes - Noah. 2013. (Bible Art Ser.). (ENG.). 16p. (J). pap., act. bk. ed. 1.99 (978-1-85792-823-5(7), 68bc0ad9-0c11-4662-b243-81a7a41e4b52) Christian Focus Pubns. GBR. Dist: Bookmasters Distribution.

—Bible Heroes Peter. 2003. (Bible Art Ser.). (ENG.). 16p. (J). pap., act. bk. ed. 1.99 (978-1-85792-826-6(1), dbea3229-6423-4a2f-ae08-1b09081b7a52, Christian Focus) Christian Focus Pubns. GBR. Dist: Bookmasters Distribution.

—Christian Focus Story Bible. 2014. (ENG., Illus.). 160p. (J). 15.99 (978-1-84550-494-6(1), f5b322b4-c250-4f43-b5f4-0f659e90d85d) Christian Focus Pubns. GBR. Dist: Bookmasters Distribution.

—Daniel: The Praying Prince. Apps, Fred, illus. 2012. (Bible Wise Ser.). (ENG.). 32p. (J). (gr. -1-3). pap. 3.99 (978-1-85792-155-7(0), 38602c9c-ebf6-473c-a658-9fa0f61b5a9c) Christian Focus Pubns. GBR. Dist: Bookmasters Distribution.

—Hannah: The Mother Who Prayer. McLaren, Duncan, illus. 2013. (Bible Time Ser.). (ENG.). 32p. (J). (gr. -1-2). pap. 3.99 (978-1-84550-163-1(2), 42f83b3d-91f5-4654-9c10-9ee2c9829c4b) Christian Focus Pubns. GBR. Dist: Bookmasters Distribution.

—How to Handle Your Life. 2008. (ENG., Illus.). 208p. (J). pap. 8.99 (978-1-85792-520-3(3), d6d0285b-5832-414a-9151-f1c7642cc75f) Christian Focus Pubns. GBR. Dist: Bookmasters Distribution.

—Jesus the Child. 2013. (Bible Alive Ser.). (ENG., Illus.). 24p. (J). pap. 3.99 (978-1-85792-749-8(4), 1fce3eeb-8372-41af-b4e9-047875bee78d) Christian Focus Pubns. GBR. Dist: Bookmasters Distribution.

—Jesus the Healer. 2014. (Bible Alive Ser.). (ENG., Illus.). 24p. (J). pap. 3.99 (978-1-85792-751-1(6), 7f228c8a-463e-408c-bae7-fc6c0efd7f85) Christian Focus Pubns. GBR. Dist: Bookmasters Distribution.

Mackenzie, Carine. Jesus the Miracle Worker. 2009. (Bible Alive Ser.). (ENG., Illus.). 24p. (J). pap. 3.99 (978-1-85792-752-8(4), e0bc0f71-b64b-4e38-a818-401b8dfb4023) Christian Focus Pubns. GBR. Dist: Bookmasters Distribution.

—Jesus the Saviour. 2013. (Bible Alive Ser.). (ENG., Illus.). 24p. (J). pap. 3.99 (978-1-85792-754-2(0), 3df828b3-877c-4486-8edd-08b73410fcfc) Christian Focus Pubns. GBR. Dist: Bookmasters Distribution.

—Jesus the Storyteller. 2009. (Bible Alive Ser.). (ENG., Illus.). 24p. (J). pap. 3.99 (978-1-85792-750-4(8), a8c14907-428b-4330-aedd-3f105d49f259) Christian Focus Pubns. GBR. Dist: Bookmasters Distribution.

—Jesus the Teacher. 2009. (Bible Alive Ser.). (ENG., Illus.). 24p. (J). pap. 3.99 (978-1-85792-753-5(2), 9781857927535) Christian Focus Pubns. GBR. Dist: Bookmasters Distribution.

MacKenzie, Carine. Jonah & the Big Fish. Apps, Fred, illus. 2015. (Famous Bible Stories (Board Books) Ser.). (ENG.). 12p. (J). (gr. -1-k). bds. 3.99 (978-1-84550-087-0(3), 91bb3c92-5ace-4b9c-ac25-a975065da3b9, Christian Focus) Christian Focus Pubns. GBR. Dist: Bookmasters Distribution.

—Little Hands Story Bible. Cosco, Raffaella, illus. rev. ed. 2009. (ENG.). 144p. (J). (gr. -1-3). 10.99 (978-1-84550-435-9(6), 9781845504359) Christian Focus Pubns. GBR. Dist: Bookmasters Distribution.

—The Long Journey. 2010. (Bible Art Ser.). (ENG.). 16p. (J). pap., act. bk. ed. 1.99 (978-1-85792-832-7(6), b08d043b-fad4-43ca-b0cc-d60aac951311, Christian Focus) Christian Focus Pubns. GBR. Dist: Bookmasters Distribution.

—Mary - Bible Heroes. 2013. (Bible Art Ser.). (ENG.). 16p. (J). pap., act. bk. ed. 1.99 (978-1-85792-828-0(8), 4b90cc51-2f0f-48b9-b374-403691fd0ae7) Christian Focus Pubns. GBR. Dist: Bookmasters Distribution.

Mackenzie, Carine. Moses: God's Leader. 2013. (Bible Time Ser.). (ENG.). 32p. (J). pap. 3.99 (978-1-84550-381-9(3), dd4bb926-7d6d-4143-9766-5b10686d2926) Christian Focus Pubns. GBR. Dist: Bookmasters Distribution.

—Moses the Child: Kept by God. Kennedy, Graham, illus. 2008. (Bible Alive Ser.). (ENG.). 24p. (J). 3.99 (978-1-84550-330-7(9), 156cef3d-f530-4fe2-b8ac-a56d9fd08ef1) Christian Focus Pubns. GBR. Dist: Bookmasters Distribution.

MacKenzie, Carine. Moses the Leader: Used by God. Kennedy, Graham, illus. 2008. (Bible Alive Ser.). (ENG.). 24p. (J). 3.99 (978-1-84550-332-1(5), e4e8286f-94a0-4e13-9832-038525bb82a2) Christian Focus Pubns. GBR. Dist: Bookmasters Distribution.

Mackenzie, Carine. Moses the Traveller: Guided by God. Kennedy, Graham, illus. 2008. (Bible Alive Ser.). (ENG.). 24p. (J). 3.99 (978-1-84550-333-8(3), be99525d-a728-4d19-be2a-89c99cdb04f2) Christian Focus Pubns. GBR. Dist: Bookmasters Distribution.

—My Bible Story Book. Apps, Fred, illus. 2013. (Colour Bks.). (ENG.). 160p. (J). (gr. -1-3). 10.99 (978-1-84550-129-7(2), e950d413-3449-4cb3-b389-13c318e63134) Christian Focus Pubns. GBR. Dist: Bookmasters Distribution.

MacKenzie, Carine. My First Book about Jesus. 2014. (My First Bks.). (ENG., Illus.). 64p. (J). pap. 3.99 (978-1-84550-463-2(1), bec911fb-f239-4a45-9b23-a38b1eaf171a) Christian Focus Pubns. GBR. Dist: Bookmasters Distribution.

Mackenzie, Carine. Paul: God's Traveller. 2014. (Bible Time Ser.). (ENG.). 32p. (J). pap. 3.99 (978-1-84550-382-6(1), d5fece0b-02c0-4ac4-a606-15b5d31ce48d) Christian Focus Pubns. GBR. Dist: Bookmasters Distribution.

MacKenzie, Carine. Peter: The Apostle. McLaren, Duncan, illus. 2014. (Bible Time Ser.). (ENG.). 32p. (J). (gr. -1-2). pap. 3.99 (978-1-84550-170-9(5), d221e48d-3015-44b8-b919-078a770c5b42) Christian Focus Pubns. GBR. Dist: Bookmasters Distribution.

Mackenzie, Carine. Rebekah: The Mother of Twins. McLaren, Duncan, illus. 2012. (Bible Time Ser.). (ENG.). 32p. (J). (gr. -1-2). pap. 3.99 (978-1-84550-172-3(1), b1353d62-4998-4e7b-b65b-f625dabff4e3) Christian Focus Pubns. GBR. Dist: Bookmasters Distribution.

MacKenzie, Carine. Ruth: The Harvest Girl. McLaren, Duncan, illus. 2012. (Bible Time Ser.). (ENG.). 32p. (J). (gr. -1-2). pap. 3.99 (978-1-84550-173-0(X), 3811ae37-6768-4f8e-99ee-b432698842f5) Christian Focus Pubns. GBR. Dist: Bookmasters Distribution.

—Samuel's Surprise. Apps, Fred, illus. 2015. (Famous Bible Stories (Board Books) Ser.). (ENG.). 12p. (J). (gr. -1-k). bds. 3.99 (978-1-84550-088-7(1), e8de870e-b09d-47e1-b16f-bdac12918449, Christian Focus) Christian Focus Pubns. GBR. Dist: Bookmasters Distribution.

—Sarah & Abraham: The Wonderful Promise. Apps, Fred, illus. 2013. (Bible Wise Ser.). (ENG.). 32p. (J). (gr. 4-7). pap. 3.99 (978-1-85792-156-4(9), 9781857921564) Christian Focus Pubns. GBR. Dist: Bookmasters Distribution.

—Simon Peter: The Disciple. McLaren, Duncan, illus. 2014. (Bible Time Ser.). (ENG.). 32p. (J). (gr. -1-2). pap. 3.99 (978-1-84550-174-7(8), 94df319e-616b-45c1-83d7-cccf99eb3192) Christian Focus Pubns. GBR. Dist: Bookmasters Distribution.

MacKenzie, Carine & Apps, Fred. Paul: Journeys of Adventure. 2014. (Bible Wise Ser.). (ENG., Illus.). 32p. (J). (gr. 1-5). pap. 3.99 (978-1-85792-465-7(7), d957aef6-dfe1-4ae6-bbcc-7d40f21f7b94) Christian Focus Pubns. GBR. Dist: Bookmasters Distribution.

Mackenzie, Carine & Gair, Cyhoeddiadau'r. Actau. Taylor, Jane, illus. 2005. (WEL.). 16p. pap. (978-1-85994-271-0(7)) Cyhoeddiadau'r Gair.

—Hosea - Malachi. Taylor, Jane, illus. 2005. (WEL.). 16p. pap. (978-1-85994-272-7(5)) Cyhoeddiadau'r Gair.

—6 1 Timotheus - Datguddiad. Taylor, Jane, illus. 2005. (WEL.). 16p. pap. (978-1-85994-269-7(5)) Cyhoeddiadau'r Gair.

Mackenzie, Carine, et al. Beibl y Bobl Bach: 69 o Storiau. 2005. (WEL., Illus.). 144p. pap. (978-1-85049-183-5(6), Gwasg y Bwthyn) Gwasg Pantycelyn.

MacKenzie, Catherine. Jesus Rose from the Dead - The Evidence. 2010. (ENG., Illus.). 96p. (J). 7.99 (978-1-84550-537-0(9), c1967fb3-066c-446d-84ee-1bc9c8837321) Christian Focus Pubns. GBR. Dist: Bookmasters Distribution.

—My Bible ABC. 2011. (Activity Ser.). (ENG.). 64p. (J). pap. 7.99 (978-1-85792-605-7(6), 41760fc3-486e-4c7e-b3f0-5514b6030f51) Christian Focus Pubns. GBR. Dist: Bookmasters Distribution.

MacKenzie, Erin. Promise Comics - Issue 1. Nummela, Pam, ed. Halbleib, Michael, illus. 2017. (ENG.). (J). pap. 1.49 (**978-0-7586-5742-8(0)**) Concordia Publishing Hse.

MacLean, G. Helen of the Glen. Date not set. (Flamingo Ser.). 3.99 (978-0-906731-80-2(1)) Christian Focus Pubns. GBR. Dist: Spring Arbor Distributors, Inc.

MacMaster, Eve B., contrib. by. Children's Illustrated Bible. 2007. (ENG., Illus.). 498p. (J). (gr. 3). pap. 22.99 (978-0-8361-9344-2(X)) Herald Pr.

Magarino, Aurel. La Evangelizando Por Medio De. 2004. (SPA.). 91p. 4.95 (978-0-570-05185-5(1)) Concordia Publishing Hse.

Mahany, Patricia Shely. Baby Moses in a Basket. Grant, Margriet, illus. 2013. (Happy Day Ser.). (ENG.). 16p. (J). pap. 2.49 (978-1-4143-9297-4(4)) Tyndale Hse. Pubs.

Make Believe Ideas, Ltd. Shiny, Touchy, Smelly Creation. 2007. (Illus.). 12p. (J). (gr. -1). 9.97 (978-1-59145-553-0(7)) Nelson, Thomas Inc.

Mandhardt, Laurie. Life of Jesus. 2005. (J). pap. 10.00 (978-1-931018-28-9(6)) Emmaus Road Publishing.

Martin, Gary. 50 Classic Bible Stories. 2008. (J). pap. 19.95 (978-0-9797863-8-9(X)) Lighthouse Publishing.

Martin, Oscar, Jr., creator. David & Goliath l.t. ed. 2003. (Illus.). 25p. (J). E-Book 19.95 incl. cd-rom (978-0-9748416-3-2(3)) Build Your Story.

Martin, Peter. Bible Stories for Boys. Bursi, Simona, illus. 2014. (ENG.). 48p. (J). (gr. k-4). 14.99 (978-0-7459-6370-9(6)) Lion Hudson PLC GBR. Dist: Independent Pubs. Group.

Mazali, Gustavo, illus. Read & Play Baby Bible, 1 vol. 2016. (ENG.). 46p. (J). bds. 9.99 (978-0-310-75780-1(0)) Zonderkidz.

McAllister, Margaret. Forgotten Bible Stories. Massari, Alida, illus. 2016. (ENG.). 48p. (J). (gr. 2-4). 17.99 (978-0-7459-6520-8(2)) Lion Hudson PLC GBR. Dist: Independent Pubs. Group.

McCardell, Ken. BibleRhymes' Creation. Chirco, Antonella, illus. 2007. (BibleRhymes Ser.). 32p. (J). 17.95 (978-0-9790605-0-2(8), BibleRhymes) BibleRhymes Publishing, L.L.C.

—BibleRhymes' Noah & the Ark, bk. 2. Chirco, Antonella, illus. 2007. (BibleRhymes Ser.: 2). 28p. (J). 17.95 (978-0-9790605-1-9(6), BibleRhymes) BibleRhymes Publishing, L.L.C.

McCaughrean, Geraldine & Dubravka, Kolanovic. The Nativity Story. Williams, Sophy, illus. 2009. (ENG.). 48p. (J). (gr. 2-4). 14.95 (978-0-7459-6092-0(8)) Lion Hudson PLC GBR. Dist: Independent Pubs. Group.

McKinley, Teri & Bowman, Crystal. M Is for Manger. Keay, Claire, illus. 2016. (ENG.). 32p. (J). bds. 6.99 (978-1-4964-2004-6(7), Tyndale Kids) Tyndale Hse. Pubs.

McKinney, Nancy Kruschke, compiled by. A Bible Story Collection: For Kids, by Kids. 2006. (J). 12.95 (978-0-9721964-1-3(2)) Action Organizing.

Meade, Starr. Grandpa's Box: Retelling the Biblical Story of Redemption. Van Patter, Bruce, illus. 2005. 286p. (J). (gr. 3-7). per. 13.99 (978-0-87552-866-3(X)) P & R Publishing.

—Mighty Acts of God: A Family Bible Story Book. O'Connor, Tim, illus. 2010. 288p. (J). 24.99 (978-1-4335-0604-8(1)) Crossway.

Means, Arloa L. Read-Rhyme-Remember: A Poetic Overview of the Book of Genesis. 2013. 74p. pap. 11.00 (978-1-60860-814-0(X), Strategic Bk. Publishing) Strategic Book Publishing & Rights Agency (SBPRA).

Mellen, Wynette. What Do You See? Rasmussen, Jennifer, illus. 2012. 42p. (J). pap. 9.95 (978-0-9839957-4-6(5)) Freundship Pr., LLC.

Mendenhall, Cheryl, illus. Moses Baby in the Bulrushes. 2004. (ENG.). 24p. (J). 2.99 (978-1-4037-0963-9(7), Spirit Pr.) Bendon, Inc.

—Moses Parting the Red Sea. 2004. (ENG.). 24p. (J). 2.99 (978-1-4037-0964-6(5), Spirit Pr.) Bendon, Inc.

Metts, Wallis C., et al. Children's Book of the Bible. 2005. (Illus.). 320p. (J). 15.98 (978-0-7853-7808-2(1), 3922102) Phoenix International Publications, Inc.

Mikelsons, Emily Samantha Ruth. Snowflakes Aren't Scared Because... 2013. (Illus.). 32p. pap. 13.95 (978-1-4908-0328-9(9), WestBow Pr.) Author Solutions, Inc.

Miko, Christopher & Romines, Garrett. The Unofficial Holy Bible for Minecrafters: A Children's Guide to the Old Testament. 2016. (ENG.). 330p. (J). (gr. k). pap. 19.99 (978-1-5107-0225-7(3), Sky Pony Pr.) Skyhorse Publishing Co., Inc.

Miles, David, illus. Brave Queen Esther, 1 vol. 2015. (I Can Read! / Adventure Bible Ser.). (ENG.). 32p. (J). pap. 3.99 (978-0-310-74666-9(3)) Zonderkidz.

—Facing the Blazing Furnace, 1 vol. 2015. (I Can Read! / Adventure Bible Ser.). (ENG.). 32p. (J). pap. 3.99 (978-0-310-75093-2(8)) Zonderkidz.

—Great Stories of the Bible, 1 vol. 2016. (I Can Read! / Adventure Bible Ser.). (ENG.). 192p. (J). 11.99 (978-0-310-75099-4(7)) Zonderkidz.

—Heroes of the Bible Treasury, 1 vol. 2016. (I Can Read! / Adventure Bible Ser.). (ENG.). 192p. (J). 11.99 (978-0-310-75096-3(2)) Zonderkidz.

—Paul Meets Jesus, 1 vol. 2016. (I Can Read! / Adventure Bible Ser.). (ENG.). 32p. (J). pap. 3.99 (978-0-310-75076-5(8)) Zonderkidz.

Miller, Christopher & Miller, Allan. The Legend of Gid the Kid & the Black Bean Bandits, 2 bks., Bk.1. Miller, Christopher & Miller, Allan, illus. 2007. (Heroes of Promise Ser.). (ENG., Illus.). 32p. (J). (gr. 1-5). 12.99 (978-1-59317-202-2(8)) Warner Pr., Inc.

Miller, Claire. El hijo pródigo (The Prodigal Son) - Bilingual. 2011. 16p. pap. 2.49 (978-0-7586-3070-4(0)) Concordia Publishing Hse.

—The Ten Commandments. Miyake, Yoshi, illus. 2004. (Arch Bks.). 16p. (J). 1.99 (978-0-7586-0672-3(9)) Concordia Publishing Hse.

Miller, Ura. 101 Favorite Stories from the Bible. 2007. (Illus.). 215p. (J). (gr. 4-7). 14.99 (978-1-885270-47-4(X)) New Leaf Pub. Group.

Mitzo Thompson, Kim, et al. Amazing Bible Story MAZES. 2017. (I'm Learning the Bible Activity Book Ser.). (ENG.). 48p. (J). pap. 4.99 (**978-1-68322-193-7(1)**) Barbour Publishing, Inc.

—I Can Do All Things: Sing-A-Scripture Series with Music CD. 2017. (ENG.). 16p. (J). (-5). bds. 9.99 (**978-1-68322-196-8(6)**) Barbour Publishing, Inc.

—I Thank God for You Read & Sing-Along Storybook, 1 vol. 2017. (ENG.). 16p. (J). (-5). 9.99 (**978-1-68322-200-2(8)**) Barbour Publishing, Inc.

Monchamp, Genny. Historias de la Biblia para Los Pequenitos. Stott, Apryll, illus. 2014.Tr. of Bible Stories for Little Ones. (SPA.). (J). 16.95 (978-0-8198-3443-0(2)) Pauline Bks. & Media.

Monroe, Colleen. A Is for Ark: Noah's Journey. Monroe, Michael Glenn, illus. 2004. 38p. (gr. -1-1). pap. 17.95 (978-0-9754942-0-2(1)) Storytime Pr., Inc.

Montero, Jose Perez, illus. Seek & Find in the Bible. 2003. 64p. incl. cd-rom (978-87-7247-305-5(3)) Scandinavia Publishing Hse.

Moody, Dwight Lyman. Children's Stories. 2014. (Classic Stories Ser.). (ENG.). 192p. (J). mass mkt. 8.99 (978-1-85792-640-8(4), de4db7e8-46a5-44a3-863d-df44cd719acd) Christian Focus Pubns. GBR. Dist: Bookmasters Distribution.

Moore, Carol Lynn. Dare U 2 Open This Book: 90 Ways to Rock Your Faith, 1 vol. 2014. (ENG.). 192p. (J). pap. 9.99 (978-0-310-74297-5(8)) Zonderkidz.

Morrill, Madge Haines. Angel Stories of the Bible. 2011. 136p. 40.95 (978-1-258-01514-5(5)) Literary Licensing, LLC.

Morris, Neil & Morris, Ting. The Illustrated Bible. McRae Books Staff, ed. D'Ottavi, Francesca, illus. 2008. (ENG.). 320p. (J). (gr. -1). 24.95 (978-88-88166-34-6(3)) McRae Bks. Srl ITA. Dist: Independent Pubs. Group.

Moses & the Princess. 14p. (J). bds. 7.99 (978-0-7847-1403-4(7)) Standard Publishing.

Mrowiec, Katia. The Most Beautiful Images from the Bible: Sharing the Stories with Children. Pillot, édéric, illus. 2012. 48p. 19.95 (978-0-8091-6766-1(2)) Paulist Pr.

My Bible Book. 2006. pap. 9.99 (978-0-8341-2267-3(7)) Nazarene Publishing Hse.

My First Bible. 384p. (978-1-4054-9478-6(6)) Parragon, Inc.

My Very Own Activity Pages: Summer 2004. 2004. (J). pap. 1.79 (978-1-59317-067-7(X)) Warner Pr., Inc.

Nellis, Glenys. Girls' Love Letters from God: Bible Stories for a Girl's Heart, 1 vol. 2017. (Love Letters from God Ser.). (ENG., Illus.). 32p. (J). 16.99 (978-0-310-75328-5(7)) Zonderkidz.

Nellist, Glenys. Christmas Love Letters from God: Bible Stories, 1 vol. Clowes, Rachel, illus. 2016. (Love Letters from God Ser.). (ENG.). 32p. (J). 16.99 (978-0-310-74824-3(0)) Zonderkidz.

—Little Love Letters from God: Bible Stories, 1 vol. Allsopp, Sophie, illus. 2015. (Love Letters from God Ser.). (ENG.). 18p. (J). bds. 9.99 (978-0-310-75047-5(4)) Zonderkidz.

—Love Letters from God: Bible Stories, 1 vol. Allsopp, Sophie, illus. 2014. (Love Letters from God Ser.). (ENG.). 40p. (J). 16.99 (978-0-310-73384-3(7)) Zonderkidz.

Nelson, Kristin. King Josiah & God's Book. 2008. (Arch Bks.). 16p. (J). (gr. k-4). pap. 1.99 (978-0-7586-1453-7(5)) Concordia Publishing Hse.

Noah's Ark Fun Book. (Illus.). 16p. (J). pap. 1.50 (978-0-87162-977-7(1), E4982) Warner Pr., Inc.

Noahs Incredible Voyage. 2004. pap. 13.99 (978-1-929296-91-0(6)) Grizzly Adams Productions, Inc.

Nolan, Allia Zobel. Angels in the Bible Storybook, 1 vol. Massari, Alida, illus. 2016. (ENG.). 224p. (J). 16.99 (978-0-310-74365-1(6)) Zonderkidz.

—My Bible Story Collection. Moroney, Trace, illus. 2004. 96p. (J). 14.99 (978-0-8254-5515-5(4)) Kregel Pubns.

—Touch & Feel Bible Animal Friends. Steele-Morgan, Alex, illus. 2004. (Touch & Feel Ser.). 12p. (J). bds. 10.99 (978-0-8254-5512-4(X)) Kregel Pubns.

Numbers/Counting: Bible Story: God's Ten Special Rules. (Scripture Bites Ser.). (Illus.). (J). (gr. -1). 7.99 (978-0-7847-9004-5(3), 00701) Standard Publishing.

Oghenekaro, Elsie Ovhe. The Speaking Donkey & other Bible Stories. 2011. (Illus.). 40p. (gr. 1-2). pap. 18.68 (978-1-4567-7930-6(3)) AuthorHouse.

Olesen, Cecilie. My First Handy Bible. Mazali, Gustavo, illus. 2006. (ENG.). 64p. (gr. -1-k). bds. 12.99 (978-1-59052-608-8(2), Multnomah) Doubleday Religious Publishing Group, The.

Oliver, Jimothy, illus. Read-Along Bible Stories. 2015. (ENG.). 96p. (J). (gr. -1-k). 14.99 (978-0-7459-6544-4(X)) Lion Hudson PLC GBR. Dist: Independent Pubs. Group.

Olshine, David. The Revelation Epic Vol. 2: Preparing Youth Groups for the Earth's Final Days. 2006. (Empowered Bible Studies). 64p. ldr.'s training gde. ed. 12.99 (978-0-7847-1301-3(4), 23334) Standard Publishing.

One Hundred Bible Stories. rev. ed. 2004. 128p. (gr. 3-6). per., act. bk. ed. 8.99 (978-0-7586-0691-4(5)) Concordia Publishing Hse.

Osborne, Mary Pope & Boyce, Natalie Pope. The Random House Book of Bible Stories. Welply, Michael, illus. 2015. (Random House Book Of ... Ser.). (ENG.). 176p. (J). (gr. k-3). lib. bdg. 27.99 (978-0-375-97425-0(3), Random Hse. Bks. for Young Readers) Random Hse. Children's Bks.

Osborne, Rick & Strauss, Ed. Angels & Demons, 1 vol. 2004. (2:52 Ser.). (ENG., Illus.). 112p. (J). pap. 7.99 (978-0-310-70775-2(7)) Zonderkidz.

Paddock, Susan Star. I Want to Be a Christian: The Story of Blessed Kateri Tekakwitha. Jaurequi, Leticia & Gomez, Elisa, trs. Matheny, Jean Sherlock, illus. 2004. (J). (978-0-9747571-8-6(7)) Catholic World Mission.

Page, Nick & Page, Claire. The Good Samaritan. Loy, Nikki, illus. 2006. (Read with Me (Make Believe Ideas) Ser.). 31p. (J). (gr. k-2). (978-1-84610-174-8(3)) Make Believe Ideas.

—The Runaway Son. Baker, Sara, illus. 2006. (Read with Me Ser.). 31p. (J). (gr. k-2). (978-1-84610-176-2(X)) Make Believe Ideas.

Page, Nick & Claire. Noah & the Ark. 2006. (Read with Me (Make Believe Ideas) Ser.). (Illus.). 32p. (J). (gr. k-2). (978-1-84610-168-7(9)) Make Believe Ideas.

Page, Nick And Claire. Giant Sticker Activity Bible Stories. 2006. (Giant Sticker Bks.). (Illus.). 144p. (J). (gr. -1-3). pap. (978-1-84610-304-9(5)) Make Believe Ideas.

Palonen, Jukka & Conrad, Tim. The Game Plan: A Kids' Musical about God's Master Plan for Each of Us. 2009. (ENG.). 96p. pap. 7.99 (978-0-8341-7742-0(0), 9780834177420) Lillenas Publishing Co.

Parable Venture Partners Staff. Ethan's Parables: Ethan & Goliath & Ethan & His Jacket of Many Colors. 2003. 32p. cd-rom 14.95 (978-0-9728501-0-0(4)) Parable Venture Partners, LLC.

Parker, Amy. Five-Minute Bedtime Bible Stories. Carzon, Walter, illus. 2015. (ENG.). 192p. (J). (gr. -1-3). bds. 12.99 (978-0-545-79960-7(0), Little Shepherd) Scholastic, Inc.

Parker, Laurie. A for Angels: A Bible Alphabet. 2010. (Illus.). 56p. (J). 18.50 (978-1-934193-48-8(8)) Quail Ridge Pr., Inc.

Parker, Victoria. The Children's Bible: Stories from the Old & New Testaments, Specially Written for the Younger Reader, with over 1600 Beautiful Illustrations, 8 vols. 2012. (ENG., Illus.). 184p. (J). (gr. -1-12). pap. 20.00 (978-1-84322-799-1(1), Armadillo) Anness Publishing GBR. Dist: National Bk. Network.

—The Children's Illustrated Bible: Classic Old & New Testament Stories Retold for the Young Reader, with Context Facts, Notes & Features. 2014. (ENG., Illus.). 512p. (J). (gr. -1 — 1). 30.00 (978-1-84322-887-5(4), Armadillo) Anness Publishing GBR. Dist: National Bk. Network.

Parker, Victoria, retold by. Children's Illustrated Bible: The Most Famous & Treasured Passages from the Old & New Testaments, Simply Told & Brought to Life with 1500 Classic Illustrations & Context Notes. 2017. (ENG., Illus.). 512p. (J). (gr. 1-11). 35.00 (**978-1-86147-837-5(2)**, Armadillo) Anness Publishing GBR. Dist: National Bk. Network.

—The Children's Illustrated Bible Stories from the Old & New Testaments: All the Best-Loved Tales from the Bible in Two Volumes, 2 vols. 2014. (ENG., Illus.). 512p. (J). (gr. k-8). 29.99 (978-1-84322-997-1(8), Armadillo) Anness Publishing GBR. Dist: National Bk. Network.

—100 Bible Stories. 2012. (Illus.). 512p. (J). (978-1-4351-3813-1(9)) Barnes & Noble, Inc.

Parry, Alan. The Bible Made Easy: A Pop-Up, Pull-Out, Interactive Bible Adventure. Parry, Linda, illus. (J). 14.99 (978-1-85608-399-7(3)) Hunt, John Publishing Ltd. GBR. Dist: O. M. Literature.

Parry, Alan & Parry, Linda. The Herald Angels. 2003. (Illus.). 16p. 9.99 (978-1-85608-253-2(9)) Hunt, John Publishing Ltd. GBR. Dist: Send The Light Distribution LLC.

Parry, Linda. Bible Story Time with Mr. Bear, 5 vols. 2006. (Illus.). 12p. (J). bds. 11.99 (978-0-7847-1467-6(3), 04387) Standard Publishing.

—Prayer Time with Mr. Bear, 5 vols. 2006. (Illus.). 12p. (J). bds. 11.99 (978-0-7847-1468-3(1), 04388) Standard Publishing.

Parry, Linda & Parry, Alan. Baby Jesus: A Touch & Feel Book. 2003. (Illus.). 14p. 6.99 (978-1-85608-220-4(2)) Hunt, John Publishing Ltd. GBR. Dist: Send The Light Distribution LLC.

A
B

—Bear's First Bible. 2003. (Illus.). 16p. 9.99 (978-1-903019-85-6(0)) Hunt, John Publishing Ltd. GBR. Dist: Send The Light Distribution LLC.

—Follow the Star. 2003. (Illus.). 16p. 12.99 (978-1-85608-147-4(8)) Hunt, John Publishing Ltd. GBR. Dist: Send The Light Distribution LLC.

Pasquali, Elena. The Lion Nursery Bible. Lamont, Priscilla, illus. 2014. (ENG.). 192p. (J). (gr. -1 — 1). 14.99 (978-0-7459-6399-0(4)) Lion Hudson PLC GBR. Dist: Independent Pubs. Group.

Pawlitz, Gail E. & Engelbrecht, Edward A., eds. Moses, Gods Chosen Leader: Drawn directly from the Bible. 2011. (Illus.). 32p. (J). pap. 6.99 (978-0-7586-1909-9(X)) Concordia Publishing Hse.

Paydos, Michael. The Everything(r) Bible Stories Book: Timeless Favorites from the Old & New Testaments. 2003. (Everything Ser.). (ENG., Illus.). 304p. (J). pap. 14.95 (978-1-58062-547-0(9)) Adams Media Corp.

Pelfrey, Wanda B. Bible Crafts on a Shoestring Budget. 2004. (Illus.). 64p. (J). (gr. -1 — 1). pap. 9.95 (978-0-937282-08-3(1), RB36126) Rainbow Pubs. & Legacy Pr.

Pencil Fun Book: Jesus Is Born. 2007. (Pencil Fun Books Ser.). 16p. (J). (gr. 3-7). 9.90 (978-0-7814-4520-7(5)) Cook, David C.

Philip & the Ethiopian. (Illus.). (gr. 1-4). 3.00 (978-0-570-05526-6(1), 54-1036) Concordia Publishing Hse.

Pinchbeck, Neil, illus. Crash, Bang, Yell! 16p. (J). (978-1-85792-366-7(9)) Christian Focus Pubns. GBR. Dist: Riverside.

—The Praying Man. 16p. (J). (978-1-85792-363-6(4)) Christian Focus Pubns. GBR. Dist: Riverside.

—Rescue on the Road. 16p. (J). (978-1-85792-365-0(0)) Christian Focus Pubns. GBR. Dist: Riverside.

—There's a Hole in My Roof! 16p. (J). (978-1-85792-361-2(8)) Christian Focus Pubns. GBR. Dist: Riverside.

Pingry, Patricia A. The Story of Joshua. Pulley, Kelly, illus. 2012. (Little Bible Bks). 22p. (J). bds. 6.99 (978-0-8249-1871-2(1), Ideal Pubns.) Worthy Publishing.

—The Story of the Lord's Prayer. Garvin, Elaine, illus. 2005. (ENG.). 26p. (J). (gr. -1-k). 9.95 (978-0-8249-6637-9(6), Ideal Pubns.) Worthy Publishing.

—The Story of the Ten Commandments. Venturi-Pickett, Stacy, illus. 2006. (ENG.). 26p. (J). (gr. -1-3). bds. 10.95 (978-0-8249-6656-0(2), Ideal Pubns.) Worthy Publishing.

Piper, Sophie. Baby's First Bible. Maddocks, Maria, illus. 2014. (ENG.). 40p. (J). (— 1). bds. 9.99 (978-0-7459-6411-9(7)) Lion Hudson PLC GBR. Dist: Independent Pubs. Group.

—The Christmas Story. Spenceley, Annabel, illus. 2017. (ENG.). 32p. (J). (gr. -1-k). 7.99 **(978-0-7459-6519-2(9))** Lion Hudson PLC GBR. Dist: Independent Pubs. Group.

—Jesus Is Born. Gilbert, Anne Yvonne, illus. 2016. (ENG.). 32p. (J). (gr. -1-3). 16.99 (978-1-68099-187-1(6), Good Bks.) Skyhorse Publishing Co., Inc.

—The Lion Read & Know Bible. Lewis, Anthony, illus. 2016. (ENG.). 384p. (J). (gr. k-2). 14.99 (978-0-7459-7639-6(5)) Lion Hudson PLC GBR. Dist: Independent Pubs. Group.

—My Bible Story Book. Kolanovic, Dubravka, illus. 2016. (ENG.). 64p. (J). (gr. -1-k). 9.99 (978-0-7459-6595-6(4)) Lion Hudson PLC GBR. Dist: Independent Pubs. Group.

Pirotta, Saviour. Children's Stories from the Bible. Gilbert, Anne Yvonne & Andrew, Ian, illus. 2009. (ENG.). 304p. (J). (gr. k-12). 19.99 (978-0-7636-4551-9(6), Templar) Candlewick Pr.

Plante, Patty. Early Bird Baby Bible Curriculum. 2nd ed. 2003. 59p. ring bd. (978-1-889723-06-8(1)) Family Harvest Church.

Plenty to Spare. (Illus.). 16p. (J). (978-1-85792-362-9(6)) Christian Focus Pubns. GBR. Dist: Riverside.

Pomeroy, John. A Little Child Shall Lead Them. Pomeroy, John, illus. 2005. (Illus.). 24p. (J). 9.99 (978-1-59185-632-0(9), Charisma Kids) Charisma Media.

Pope, Amy. Moving Day. George, John, 3rd, illus. 2004. (J). bds. 9.99 (978-1-4183-0010-4(1)) Christ Inspired, Inc.

Powell Smith, Brendan. Baby Moses: The Brick Bible for Kids. 2016. (Brick Bible for Kids Ser.). (ENG., Illus.). 32p. (J). (gr. -1-k). 12.99 (978-1-5107-1266-9(6), Sky Pony Pr.) Skyhorse Publishing Co., Inc.

PowerXpress Easter: Peter's Story Disciple Disc. 2.95 incl. cd-rom (978-0-687-00219-1(2)) Abingdon Pr.

PowerXpress Follow the Star Unit: Bible Experience Station. 2006. 129.95 (978-0-687-04090-2(6)) Abingdon Pr.

PowerXpress Good Samaritan Disciple. 2.95 incl. cd-rom (978-0-687-00179-8(X)) Abingdon Pr.

PowerXpress into the Bible Jesus at the Synagogue. 9.95 incl. audio compact disk (978-0-687-04181-7(3)) Abingdon Pr.

PowerXpress into the Bible Who Is Jesus. 9.95 incl. audio compact disk (978-0-687-04191-6(0)) Abingdon Pr.

PowerXpress Paul Disciple. 2.95 incl. cd-rom (978-0-687-00229-0(X)) Abingdon Pr.

PowerXpress Proverbs. 9.95 incl. audio compact disk (978-0-687-04063-6(9)) Abingdon Pr.

PowerXpress the Sower Unit. 99.00 (978-0-687-04031-5(0)) Abingdon Pr.

PowerXpress Washing Feet Disciple. 2.95 incl. cd-rom (978-0-687-00189-7(7)) Abingdon Pr.

Preschool KidKit. 2003. (Godprints Curriculum Ser.). (Illus.). 8.99 (978-0-7814-3664-9(8), 2013) Cook, David C.

Preston, Rhoda. Rock-a-Bye Toddlers & Two Leader's Guide (2009 - 2010) 2009. (Rockabye Ser.). 24.00 (978-0-687-65534-2(X)) Abingdon Pr.

Price, Olivia. Bible Stories: A Touch & Feel Book. Mitchell, Melanie, illus. 2008. (ENG.). 12p. (J). (gr. -1). 12.95 (978-1-58117-802-9(6), Intervisual/Piggy Toes) Bendon, Inc.

Priddy, Roger. Bible Stories. 2011. (ENG., Illus.). 30p. (J). (gr. -1-1). bds. 12.95 (978-0-312-51089-3(6), 9780312510893, Priddy Bks.) St. Martin's Pr.

—My Favorite Bible Stories. 2015. (Bible Stories Ser.). (ENG.). 16p. (J). (gr. -1-1). 9.99 (978-0-312-51786-1(6), 9780312517861, Priddy Bks.) St. Martin's Pr.

Primetime Starter Pack. 2004. pap. 44.99 (978-0-8307-3025-4(7)) Gospel Light Pubns.

Prole, Helen, illus. The Story of Christmas, 1 vol. 2016. (Candle Bible for Toddlers Ser.). (ENG.). 26p. (J). pap. 6.99 (978-1-78128-309-7(5), Candle Bks.) Lion Hudson PLC GBR. Dist: Kregel Pubns.

Publications International Ltd. Staff. Gilded Treasury Bible Stories. 2006. 320p. (J). 14.98 (978-1-4127-6337-0(1)) Phoenix International Publications, Inc.

Publications International Ltd. Staff, ed. Mi Premera Biblioteca Cuentos. 2004. (ESP.). 72p. 10.98 (978-0-7853-9727-4(2)) Publications International, Ltd.

Pulley, Kelly. Beginner's Bible Collector's Edition, 1 vol. 2014. (Beginner's Bible Ser.). (ENG.). 512p. (J). 14.99 (978-0-310-74736-9(8)) Zonderkidz.

—Treasury of Bible Stories: Rhythmical Rhymes of Biblical Times ISBN: 0-7814-0917-9 ISBN13: 9780781409179 Markets: USA Lang. 2014. (Magnificent Tales Ser.). (ENG., Illus.). 352p. (J). 19.99 (978-0-7814-0917-9(9)) Cook, David C.

Pulley, Kelly, illus. The Beginner's Bible: Timeless Children's Stories. 2014. (Beginner's Bible (Zonderkidz) Ser.). (ENG.). (gr. -1-k). 16.97 (978-0-310-72924-2(6)) Zondervan.

The Quest for Seven Castles. 2006. (J). per. 7.99 (978-0-9785523-1-2(8)) Cross & Crown Publishing.

Racklin-Siegel, Carol, illus. Noah's Ark. 2003. 32p. (J). per. 10.95 (978-0-939144-42-6(5)) EKS Publishing Co.

Rathmann, Rodney L. & Bergt, Carolyn, eds. Family Time: A Collection of 98 Bible Stories & Devotions. 2014. (ENG., Illus.). 208p. (J). (gr. -1-3). 24.99 (978-0-7586-4346-9(2)) Concordia Publishing Hse.

Rayburn, Cathy & Stone, Elaine Murray. Angels in the Bible. 2006. (Illus.). 76p. (J). (gr. 3-7). per. 7.95 (978-0-8091-6729-6(8), 6729-8) Paulist Pr.

Reader's Digest Staff. Baby's First Bible. MacLean, Colin & MacLean, Moira, illus. 2009. (ENG.). 20p. (J). (gr. -1 — 1). bds. 14.99 (978-0-7944-1942-4(9), Reader's Digest Children's Bks.) Studio Fun International.

Redford, Marjorie & Nystrom, Jennifer. Gideon, Blow Your Horn! Dickson, Bill, illus. 2015. (Faith That Sticks Bks.). (ENG.). 24p. (J). pap. 3.99 (978-1-4964-0313-1(4)) Tyndale Hse. Pubs.

Reisch, J. A. Mi Primera Biblia. Rimmington, Natasha, illus. 2016. (SPA.). (J). (978-1-5064-2103-2(2)) Augsburg Fortress, Pubs.

Resplandece: Historias de la Biblia para Niños. 2014. (SPA & ENG., Illus.). 317p. (J). (978-0-8361-9896-6(4)) Herald Pr.

Reynolds, Annette. First COLL of Bible Stories & Stickers: Daniel, Jonah, Jesus & Other Stories. MacLean, Moira, illus. 2004. 16p. pap. 8.95 (978-1-59325-045-4(2)) Word Among Us Pr.

—First COLL of Bible Stories & Stickers: Noahn, Samson, Jesus & Other Stories. MacLean, Moira, illus. 2004. 16p. pap. 8.95 (978-1-59325-044-7(4)) Word Among Us Pr.

Rhodes, Karen. God's Word Then & Now Activity Book. 2007. (Illus.). 16p. (J). pap. 1.89 (978-1-59317-207-7(9)) Warner Pr., Inc.

—7 Sensational Stories. 2005. (J). pap. 1.79 (978-1-59317-084-4(X)) Warner Pr., Inc.

Richards, Lawrence O. King James Version Kids Study Bible, 1 vol. 2013. (ENG.). 1600p. (J). 24.99 (978-0-310-74616-4(7)) Zonderkidz.

Richards, Virginia Helen & Halpin, D. Thomas, illus. My Christmas Picture Book. 2005. 14p. (J). 4.95 (978-0-8198-4829-1(8), 332-220) Pauline Bks. & Media.

Richardson, Jill. Hobbits, You, & the Spiritual World of Middle-Earth. 2013. 114p. pap. 11.95 (978-1-938499-91-3(3)) Lighthouse Publishing of the Carolinas.

Rise & Shine! the Early Church: 12 Instant Bible Lessons for Kids. 2006. (Pick up 'n' Do Ser.). (Illus.). 126p. pap., per. 19.99 (978-0-7814-4376-0(8), 0781443768) Cook, David C.

Robison Gamble Creative, photos by & des. Dan & Louie Vol. 1: The Greatest Stories Ever Told, Robison Gamble Creative, des. deluxe ed. 2005. (Illus.). (J). 89.95 incl. audio compact disk (978-1-933497-00-6(9)) Robison Gamble Creative.

Roche, Maite. The Bible for Little Ones. 2010. 36p. 12.99 (978-1-58617-508-5(4)) Ignatius Pr.

Rock, Lois. Bible & Me. Massari, Alida, illus. 2016. (ENG.). 128p. (J). (gr. k-3). 14.99 (978-0-7459-6495-9(8)) Lion Hudson PLC GBR. Dist: Independent Pubs. Group.

—The First Christmas. Allsopp, Sophie, illus. 2008. (ENG.). 32p. (J). (gr. k-2). 12.95 (978-0-7459-4956-7(8)) Lion Hudson PLC GBR. Dist: Independent Pubs. Group.

—In the Beginning - Bible Stories for Little Hands. Bolam, Emily, illus. 2014. (Bible Stories for Little Hands Ser.). (ENG.). 8p. (J). (gr. -1 — 1). bds. 8.99 (978-0-7459-6449-2(4)) Lion Hudson PLC GBR. Dist: Independent Pubs. Group.

—Jesus Is Born: A Spot-the-Difference Jigsaw Book. Bolam, Emily, illus. 2014. (Bible Stories for Little Hands Ser.). (ENG.). 8p. (J). (gr. -1 — 1). bds. 8.99 (978-0-7459-6450-8(8)) Lion Hudson PLC GBR. Dist: Independent Pubs. Group.

—The Lion Bible to Keep for Ever. Allsopp, Sophie, illus. (ENG.). 320p. (J). (gr. 2-4). 2016. 17.99 (978-0-7459-7635-8(2)) 2015. 19.99 (978-0-7459-6487-4(7)) Lion Hudson PLC GBR. Dist: Independent Pubs. Group.

—The Lion Illustrated Bible for Children. Balit, Christina, illus. 2007. (ENG.). 224p. (J). (gr. -1-4). 17.99 (978-0-7459-4936-9(3)) Lion Hudson PLC GBR. Dist: Independent Pubs. Group.

—A Little Life of Jesus - To Read & Treasure. Langton, Roger W., illus. 2nd ed. 2015. (ENG.). 352p. (J). (gr. -1-k). pap. 8.99 (978-0-7459-6567-3(9)) Lion Hudson PLC GBR. Dist: Independent Pubs. Group.

—Look Inside Bible Times. Lewis, Anthony, illus. 2016. (ENG.). 64p. (J). (gr. k-2). 16.99 (978-0-7459-7614-3(X)) Lion Hudson PLC GBR. Dist: Independent Pubs. Group.

—The Lost Sheep & Other Bible Stories for Little Hands. Bolam, Emily, illus. 2014. (Bible Stories for Little Hands Ser.). (ENG.). 8p. (J). (gr. -1 — 1). bds. 8.99 (978-0-7459-6451-5(6)) Lion Hudson PLC GBR. Dist: Independent Pubs. Group.

—My Very First Bible & Prayers, 2 vols. Ayliffe, Alex, illus. 2013. (My Very First Ser.). (ENG.). 416p. (J). (gr. -1-k). 12.99 (978-0-7459-6186-6(X)) Lion Hudson PLC GBR. Dist: Independent Pubs. Group.

—My Very First Bible Stories Bumper Sticker Book. Ayliffe, Alex, illus. 2014. (My Very First Sticker Bks.). (ENG.). 96p. (J). (gr. -1-k). 13.99 (978-0-7459-6410-2(9)) Lion Hudson PLC GBR. Dist: Independent Pubs. Group.

—Tiny Tots Bible. Widdowson, Kay, illus. 2014. (Tiny Tots Ser.). (ENG.). 128p. (J). (gr. -1-k). 12.99 (978-0-7459-6383-9(8)) Lion Hudson PLC GBR. Dist: Independent Pubs. Group.

—Viaje Por la Biblia. Pimentel, Alejandro, tr. Rowland, Andrew, illus. 2011. (SPA.). 47p. (J). (gr. 4-7). 13.50 (978-1-55883-030-1(8)) Libros Desafio.

Rock, Lois & David, Juliet. My Very First Bible Stories, 1 vol. Siewert, Pauline, illus. 2015. 14p. (J). 7.99 (978-1-78128-232-8(3), Candle Bks.) Lion Hudson PLC GBR. Dist: Kregel Pubns.

Rock, Lois & Piper, Sophie. Daniel & the Lions. Corke, Estelle, illus. 2009. (Bible Story Time Ser.). (ENG.). 32p. (J). (gr. -1-k). 5.95 (978-0-7459-4866-9(9)) Lion Hudson PLC GBR. Dist: Independent Pubs. Group.

Rock, Lois, et al. Beibl y Plant Lleiaf. 2005. (WEL., Illus.). 230p. (978-1-85994-514-8(7)) Cyhoeddiadau'r Gair.

Rock Solid Preschool Bible Storybook Winter 2009-2010. 2009. 5.20 (978-0-687-65817-6(9), Cokesbury) Abingdon Pr.

Romines, Garrett & Miko, Christopher. The Unofficial Holy Bible for Minecrafters: A Children's Guide to the Old & New Testament. 2015. (ENG.). 288p. (J). (gr. k-8). pap. 19.99 (978-1-63220-730-2(3), Sky Pony Pr.) Skyhorse Publishing Co., Inc.

Rose, Drew, illus. God's Heroes. 2005. (Bible Activity Bks.). 94p. (J). (gr. -1-3). 2.99 (978-0-7814-4313-5(X), 078144313X) Cook, David C.

—God's Son, Jesus. 2005. (Bible Activity Bks.). 94p. (J). (gr. -1-3). 2.99 (978-0-7814-4314-2(8), 0781443148) Cook, David C.

—God's World. 2005. (Bible Activity Bks.). 94p. (J). (gr. -1-3). 2.99 (978-0-7814-4312-8(1), 0781443121) Cook, David C.

Ross, Graham. Bible-Story Doodles: Favorite Scenes to Complete & Create. Running Press Staff, ed. 2014. (ENG., Illus.). 160p. (J). (gr. -1-17). pap. 12.95 (978-0-7624-5217-0(X), Running Pr. Kids) Running Pr. Bk. Pubs.

Ross, Marrianne & Ross, Marianne. Bible Detectives - Samuel. 2010. (ENG., Illus.). 64p. (J). 7.99 (978-1-84550-569-1(7), 7f0348b6-e05f-4460-a1da-23b7540e5da1) Christian Focus Pubns. GBR. Dist: Bookmasters Distribution.

Rottmann, Eric. Rahab's Red Thread. 2009. (Arch Bks.). 16p. (J). (gr. k-4). pap. 2.49 (978-0-7586-1617-3(1)) Concordia Publishing Hse.

Rottmann, Erik. Deborah Saves the Day. Marchesi, Stephen, illus. 2008. (Arch Bks.). 16p. (J). (gr. k-4). pap. 1.99 (978-0-7586-1457-5(8)) Concordia Publishing Hse.

Rottmann, Erik J. Jesús alimenta a la multitud (A Meal for Many) - Bilingual. 2011. 16p. pap. 2.99 (978-0-7586-3073-5(5)) Concordia Publishing Hse.

Rowlands, Avril. The Rainbow's End & Other Tales from the Ark. Moran, Rosslyn, illus. 128p. (J). pap. 6.95 (978-0-7459-4073-1(0), Lion Books) Lion Hudson PLC GBR. Dist: Trafalgar Square Publishing.

Rutherford, Peter, illus. Noah's Ark. 2015. (ENG.). 24p. bds. 6.99 (978-1-86147-644-9(2), Armadillo) Anness Publishing GBR. Dist: National Bk. Network.

Ryan, G. William. The Little Donkey: A Palm Sunday/Easter Story for All Ages. 2014. pap. (978-1-4600-0253-7(9)) Essence Publishing.

Samson meets Delilah. 2007. (J). mass mkt. (978-0-9769722-3-5(9)) Leslie, Beverly J.

Samson meets his Wife. 2007. (J). mass mkt. (978-0-9769722-1-1(2)) Leslie, Beverly J.

Samson's destruction of the Philistines. 2007. (J). mass mkt. (978-0-9769722-2-8(0)) Leslie, Beverly J.

Sanders, Nancy I. Bible Crafts on a Shoestring Budget. 2004. (Illus.). 64p. (J). (gr. 3-4). pap. 9.95 (978-0-937282-11-3(1), RB36129) Rainbow Pubs. & Legacy Pr.

—Bible Favorites. Wood, Hannah, illus. 2015. (One Sentence Storybooks Ser.). (ENG.). 120p. (J). pap. 15.99 (978-1-58997-799-0(8)) Focus on the Family Publishing.

—The Fall into Sin: Genesis 2-3 for Children. Van Severen, Joe, illus. 2004. (Arch Bks.). (ENG.). 16p. (J). 1.99 (978-0-7586-0618-1(4)) Concordia Publishing Hse.

Sattgast, L. J. The Rhyme Bible Storybook for Little Ones, 1 vol. Cleyet-Merle, Laurence, illus. rev. ed. 2015. (ENG.). 40p. (J). bds. 9.99 (978-0-310-75363-6(5)) Zonderkidz.

Scarff, Ruth. The Floating Zoo. Combs, Paul, illus. 2003. 21p. (J). pap. (978-0-87398-289-4(4)) Sword of the Lord Pubs.

Schmidt, Troy. The Donkey & Jesus. Jones, Cory, illus. 2015. (Their Side of the Story Ser.). (ENG.). 32p. (J). (gr. -1-3). pap. 3.99 (978-1-4336-8719-8(4), B&H Kids) B&H Publishing Group.

—The Donkey Tells His Side of the Story: Hey God, I'm Sorry to Be Stubborn, but I Just Don't Like Anyone Riding on My Back! Jones, Cory, illus. 2014. (ENG.). 32p. (gr. -1-3). 9.99 (978-1-4336-8309-1(1), B&H Kids) B&H Publishing Group.

—The Lion Tells His Side of the Story: Hey God, I'm Starving in This Den So Why Won't You Let Me Eat This Guy Named Daniel?! Jones, Cory, illus. 2014. (ENG.). 32p. (gr. -1-3). 9.99 (978-1-4336-8310-7(5), B&H Kids) B&H Publishing Group.

—The Raven & Noah's Ark. Jones, Cory, illus. 2015. (Their Side of the Story Ser.). (ENG.). 32p. (J). (gr. -1-3). pap. 3.99 (978-1-4336-8722-8(4), B&H Kids) B&H Publishing Group.

Schmitt, Betsy & Sokolava, Valerie. The Promise of Abraham. 2006. (Illus.). 36p. 15.99 (978-0-7847-1823-0(7)) Standard Publishing.

Schmitthenner, Sam. Between the Lines of the Bible. 2008. 120p. pap. 13.95 (978-1-931475-36-5(9)) Quiet Waters Pubns.

Scholastic, Inc. Staff. Mi Primera Biblia. 2015. (ENG & SPA.). 147p. (J). (gr. -1-k). bds. 9.99 (978-0-545-05656-4(X), Scholastic en Espanol) Scholastic, Inc.

Scholastic, Inc. Staff & American Bible Society Staff. Lee y Aprende: La Biblia. 2007. (SPA.). 544p. (J). (gr. -1-3). 14.99 (978-0-545-00339-1(3), Scholastic en Espanol) Scholastic, Inc.

Scrimshire, Hazel. Big Crash. 2005. (Shaped Board Bks.). (ENG., Illus.). 8p. (J). (gr. -1-k). bds. 3.99 (978-1-85792-085-7(6), 7135c229-921e-450e-96c9-d1a972dafc2a, Christian Focus) Christian Focus Pubns. GBR. Dist: Bookmasters Distribution.

Seifert, Sheila, et al. Lead the Way, Jesus. 2008. (DSJ Ser.). (Illus.). 112p. (J). (gr. 1-6). pap. 16.99 (978-0-7814-4560-3(4)) Cook, David C.

Send a Baby. (Hear Me Read Classroom Sets Ser.). 32.00 (978-0-570-07170-9(4)) Concordia Publishing Hse.

Sessoms, Bob. Buscar Arriba para Alcanzar Alrededor: Guia para Lideres. 2005. (SPA., Illus.). 312p. 39.99 (978-1-4158-2115-2(1)) LifeWay Christian Resources.

Setzer, Lee Ann. I Am a Child of God. Harmon, Glenn, illus. 2007. (Tiny Talks Ser.). 74p. (J). per. 7.99 (978-1-59955-076-3(8)) Cedar Fort, Inc./CFI Distribution.

Sewell, Christina, et al. Legends of the Christ Child. 2003. (ENG., Illus.). 80p. (C). pap. 13.50 (978-0-7188-3026-7(1)) Lutherworth Pr., The GBR. Dist: Casemate Academic.

Sharpe, Jean Ann, ed. The Saving Name of God the Son. 2009. (Illus.). 22p. (J). bds. 9.95 (978-1-932350-30-2(6)) Bethlehem Bks.

Shea, George Beverly. Grandpa's Sleepy-Time Bible Stories with George Beverly Shea. 2004. (J). (978-0-8423-8137-6(6)) Tyndale Hse. Pubs.

Shearer, Amelia. God Made Seasons. Marlin, Kathryn, illus. 2014. (Happy Day Ser.). (ENG.). 16p. (J). pap. 2.49 (978-1-4143-9481-7(0)) Tyndale Hse. Pubs.

—God's Armor for Me. Burroughs, Scott, illus. 2014. (Happy Day Ser.). (ENG.). 16p. (J). pap. 2.49 (978-1-4143-9480-0(2)) Tyndale Hse. Pubs.

Shenton, Tim. Readings from James: Trials + Faith + Riches + Prayer. 2005. (Daily Readings From Ser.). (Illus.). 68p. (J). pap. 6.50 (978-1-903087-61-9(9)) DayOne Pubns. GBR. Dist: Send The Light Distribution LLC.

Shirley Dobson Bible Story Coloring Book Sampler Merchandiser. 129.00 (978-0-8307-2753-7(1), Gospel Light) Gospel Light Pubns.

Shirley Dobson Bible Story Coloring Book Sampler Merchandiser: 55 Unit Mini-Merch. 70.95 (978-0-8307-3024-7(9), Gospel Light) Gospel Light Pubns.

Silverthorne, Sandy. Wild & Wacky Bible Adventures for Kids. 2014. (ENG.). 144p. (J). pap. 8.99 (978-0-7369-5673-4(5)) Harvest Hse. Pubs.

Simeon, S. & Golden Books Staff. The Little Golden Bible Storybook. Sexton, Brenton, illus. 2005. (Padded Board Book Ser.). (ENG.). 36p. (J). (gr. -1 — 1). bds. 6.99 (978-0-375-83549-0(0), Golden Inspirational) Random Hse. Children's Bks.

Simon, Mary. Ay Que Lio. 2004. (SPA.). 32p. (J). 2.75 (978-0-570-05187-9(8)) Concordia Publishing Hse.

—Oh Oh. 2004. (SPA.). 32p. (J). 2.75 (978-0-570-05186-2(X)) Concordia Publishing Hse.

Simon, Mary Mans. Fishes & Loaves: Read & Learn the Bible. 2005. (ENG., Illus.). 24p. (J). pap. 2.99 (978-1-4037-1162-5(3), Spirit Pr.) Bendon, Inc.

—The Good Samaritan: Read & Learn the Bible. 2005. (ENG., Illus.). 24p. (J). pap. 2.99 (978-1-4037-1159-5(3), Spirit Pr.) Bendon, Inc.

—Jesus Blesses the Children: Read & Learn the Bible. 2005. (ENG., Illus.). 24p. (J). pap. 2.99 (978-1-4037-1155-7(0), Spirit Pr.) Bendon, Inc.

—Jesus Fills the Nets: Read & Learn the Bible. 2005. (ENG., Illus.). 24p. (J). pap. 2.99 (978-1-4037-1163-2(1), Spirit Pr.) Bendon, Inc.

—Noah's Ark: Read & Learn the Bible. 2005. (ENG., Illus.). 24p. (J). pap. 2.99 (978-1-4037-1157-1(7), Spirit Pr.) Bendon, Inc.

—See What God Made! Read & Learn the Bible. 2005. (ENG., Illus.). 24p. (J). pap. 2.99 (978-1-4037-1160-1(7), Spirit Pr.) Bendon, Inc.

—Too Tall, Too Small: Read & Learn the Bible. 2005. (ENG., Illus.). 24p. (J). pap. 2.99 (978-1-4037-1156-4(9), Spirit Pr.) Bendon, Inc.

Simon, Mary Manz. Build A Tower. 2004. (Mary Manz Simon/Stick-with-Me Bible Stories Ser.). 16p. (J). pap. 4.99 (978-0-88724-755-2(5), CD-2059) Carson-Dellosa Publishing, LLC.

—Koala Does His Best. Harris, Phyllis & Clearwater, Linda, illus. 2006. (First Virtuestm for Toddlers Ser.). 20p. (J). 5.99 (978-0-7847-1578-9(5), 04072) Standard Publishing.

—Set of eight Books. (Hear Me Read Level 2 Ser.). (J). 34.99 (978-0-570-05096-4(0)) Concordia Publishing Hse.

—Sit Down. (Hear Me Read Classroom Sets Ser.). 32.00 (978-0-570-05098-8(7)) Concordia Publishing Hse.

—Where Is Jesus? (Hear Me Read Classroom Sets Ser.). 32.00 (978-0-570-05460-3(5)) Concordia Publishing Hse.

—The Young Learner's Bible Storybook: 52 Stories with Activities for Family Fun & Learning. Harper, Piers, illus. 2006. (First Virtues for Toddlers Ser.). 336p. (J). (gr. -1-2). 17.99 (978-0-7847-1277-1(8), 04010) Standard Publishing.

Simpson, Roberta. Nana's Bible Stories. Mitchell, Susan, illus. 2007. (ENG.). 96p. (J). (gr. -1-3). 16.99 (978-1-4003-1187-3(X)) Nelson, Thomas Inc.

Skevington, Andrea. The Bible Story Retold in Twelve Chapters. 2016. (ENG., Illus.). 224p. 17.95 (978-0-7459-7664-8(6)) Lion Hudson PLC GBR. Dist: Independent Pubs. Group.

Skipworth, Kelly & Fernández, Cecilia. Los doce disipulos (The Twelve Ordinary Men) 2011. 16p. pap. 2.49 (978-0-7586-3068-1(9)) Concordia Publishing Hse.

Smart Kids Publishing Staff. Jonah & the Whale: A Story about Responsibility. Sharp, Chris, illus. 2006. (I Can Read the Bible Ser.). (ENG.). 12p. (J). (gr. -1-3). 14.95 (978-0-8249-6661-4(9), Ideal Pubns.) Worthy Publishing.

Smith, Angie. For Such a Time As This: Stories of Women from the Bible, Retold for Girls. Brookshire, Breezy, illus. 2014. (ENG.). 256p. (gr. 1-5). 14.99 (978-1-4336-8046-5(7), B&H Kids) B&H Publishing Group.

Smith, Brendan Powell. The Complete Brick Bible for Kids: Six Classic Bible Stories. 2015. (ENG., Illus.). 192p. (J). (gr. -1-k). 15.99 (978-1-63450-209-2(4), Sky Pony Pr.) Skyhorse Publishing Co., Inc.

—Joseph & the Colorful Coat: The Brick Bible for Kids. 2015. (Brick Bible for Kids Ser.). (ENG., Illus.). 32p. (J). (gr. -1-k). 12.99 (978-1-63220-409-7(6), Sky Pony Pr.) Skyhorse Publishing Co., Inc.

Smith, Judah & Smith, Chelsea. I Will Follow Jesus Bible Storybook, 1 vol. 2016. (ENG., Illus.). 208p. (J). 16.99 (978-0-7180-3386-6(8)) Nelson, Thomas Inc.

Smith, Laurie Chance. Snapshots: Nature Stories in the Bible. 2012. 128p. (J). pap. 19.99 (978-0-8280-2689-5(0)) Review & Herald Publishing Assn.

Smith, Martina. La Historia de la Creacion: Un Relato de la Biblia Chispita. Grosshauser, Peter & Temple, Ed, illus.

2016. (SPA.). (J). (978-1-5064-2100-1(8)) Augsburg Fortress, Pubs.

Snow, Philip. Places of the Bible. Snow, Philip, illus. 2005. (Bible Discover & Colour Ser.). (Illus.). 32p. (J). (gr. -1-7). 4.00 (978-1-903087-90-9(2)) DayOne Pubns. GBR. Dist: Send The Light Distribution LLC.

Snyder, Jennifer. Grandad's Book. Bruner, Tammy, illus. 2004. (J). bds. 9.99 (978-1-4183-0015-9(2)) Christ Inspired, Inc.

Spear, Kevin. David & the Giant. 2005. (Illus.). (J). pap. 1.79 (978-1-59317-087-5(4)) Warner Pr., Inc.

—My Very Own Activity Pages: Spring 2004. 2004. (Illus.). (J). pap. 1.79 (978-1-59317-077-6(7)) Warner Pr., Inc.

Spear, Kevin, des. Favorite Bible Stories Puzzle Book. 2009. (Illus.). 48p. (J). (gr. 1-5). pap. 4.50 (978-1-59317-353-1(9)) Warner Pr., Inc.

St. John, Patricia. Until the Letter Came. Brownlie, Ian D., illus. 2004. 44p. (J). pap. (978-1-932381-14-6(7), 5580) Bible Visuals International, Inc.

Standard Publishing Staff. Bible Stories to Color & Tell, Ages 3-6. Grossmann, Dan, illus. 2016. (ENG.). 240p. (J). (gr. -1-3). per. 16.99 (978-0-7847-1779-0(6), 02493) Standard Publishing.

—Bible Stories to Color & Tell, Ages 6-8. Ebert, Len, illus. 2016. (ENG.). 240p. (J). per. 16.99 (978-0-7847-1348-8(0), 02492) Standard Publishing.

—20 Bible Stories Every Child Should Know. 2004. (Heritage Builders Ser.). (Illus.). 92p. (J). 19.99 incl. audio compact disk (978-0-7847-1586-4(6), 04091) Standard Publishing.

Standke, Linda. Hidden Pictures, Grades 1 - 3: Explore Hidden Treasures in God's Word. 2003. (Fun Faith-Builders Ser.). (ENG.). 32p. (gr. 1-3). pap. 4.99 (978-0-88724-911-2(6)) Carson-Dellosa Publishing, LLC.

—Hidden Pictures, Grades 4 - 6: Explore Hidden Treasures in God's Word. 2003. (Fun Faith-Builders Ser.). (ENG.). 32p. (gr. 4-6). pap. 4.99 (978-0-88724-912-9(4)) Carson-Dellosa Publishing, LLC.

—Hidden Pictures, Grades Pk - K: Explore Hidden Treasures in God's Word. 2003. (Fun Faith-Builders Ser.). (ENG.). 32p. (gr. -1-k). pap. 4.99 (978-0-88724-910-5(8)) Carson-Dellosa Publishing, LLC.

Stanley, Mandy, illus. Baby Blessings Baby's Bible. 2005. 6p. (YA). (gr. -1 — 1). 15.99 (978-0-7847-1739-4(7), 04382) Standard Publishing.

Stearns, Richard. God's Love for You Bible Storybook, 1 vol. 2013. (ENG.). 272p. (J). 19.99 (978-1-4003-2187-2(5)) Nelson, Thomas Inc.

Steedman, Amy. The Nursery Book of Bible Stories. 2008. (Illus.). 260p. pap. 11.95 (978-1-59915-268-4(1)) Yesterday's Classics.

—The Read-Aloud Book of Bible Stories. 2010. Orig. Title: The Nursery Book of Bible Stories. (J). pap. 14.95 (978-1-933184-71-5(X)) Sophia Institute Pr.

Stiegemeyer, Julie. Jesus Teaches Us Not to Worry. 2011. 16p. pap. 2.49 (978-0-7586-2581-6(2)) Concordia Publishing Hse.

—Stephen Stands Strong. Myers, Glenn, illus. 2004. (ENG.). 16p. (J). 1.99 (978-0-570-07576-9(9)) Concordia Publishing Hse.

Stockstill. Jesus Nacio en Belen. 2004. (SPA.). 20p. bds. 4.99 (978-0-7586-0261-9(8)) Concordia Publishing Hse.

Stockstill, Gloria McQueen. Basket in the River. Girouard, Patrick, illus. 2004. 20p. (J). bds. 5.49 (978-0-7586-0052-3(6)) Concordia Publishing Hse.

Stoddard, Jeffery. Pete & Pillar: A Story of Friendship Based on John 15:13: the Big Rain. Stoddard, Jeffery, illus. 2007. (Pete & Pillar Ser.). (ENG., Illus.). 32p. (J). (gr. -1-2). 12.99 (978-1-59317-203-9(6)) Warner Pr., Inc.

Stohs, Anita Reith. Praise God with Paper Cups: 45 Easy Bible Crafts; Grades 1-5. Koehler, Ed, illus. 2005. (CPH Teaching Resource Ser.). 64p. pap. 10.99 (978-0-7586-0842-0(X)) Concordia Publishing Hse.

Stone, Julia. I Spy Bible: A Picture Puzzle Bible for the Very Young. Meredith, Samantha, illus. 2015. (ENG.). 24p. (J). (gr. -1-k). bds. 9.99 (978-0-7459-6555-0(5)) Lion Hudson PLC GBR. Dist: Independent Pubs. Group.

Stories about David. (Pict-O-Graph Ser.). (Illus.). (J). 10.99 (978-0-7847-1038-8(4), 02238) Standard Publishing.

Stortz, Diane. I Can Praise God! 2014. (Happy Day Ser.). (ENG.). 16p. (J). pap. 2.49 (978-1-4143-9466-4(7)) Tyndale Hse. Pubs.

—Sweetest Story Bible for Toddlers, 1 vol. Bailey, Sheila, illus. 2014. (ENG.). 32p. (J). bds. 9.99 (978-0-310-74630-0(2)) Zonderkidz.

—Words to Dream On: Bedtime Bible Stories & Prayers, 1 vol. Feyer, Diane Le, illus. 2015. (ENG.). 224p. (J). 14.99 (978-0-529-11101-2(2)) Nelson, Thomas Inc.

Stortz, Diane & Thomas Nelson & Sons Staff. Say & Pray Bible, 1 vol. 2015. (ENG.). 40p. (J). bds. 9.99 (978-0-7180-3657-7(3)) Nelson, Thomas Inc.

Stortz, Diane M. Sweetest Story Bible: Sweet Thoughts & Sweet Words for Little Girls, 1 vol. Bailey, Sheila, illus. 2010. (ENG.). 224p. (J). 16.99 (978-0-310-71673-0(X)) Zonderkidz.

Stowell, Charlotte, illus. God's Wonderful World, 3 vols. 2003. 20p. (J). bds. 6.99 (978-0-8254-7269-5(5), Candle Bks.) Lion Hudson PLC GBR. Dist: Kregel Pubns.

Stowell, Gordon. Libro de Actividades Biblicas (Bible Story Activities) (SPA.). (J). No. 1. 1.89 (978-1-56063-761-5(7), 497741)No. 2. 1.89 (978-1-56063-791-2(9), 497742)No. 3. 1.89 (978-1-56063-792-9(7), 497743)No. 4. 1.89 (978-1-56063-793-6(5), 497744) Editorial Unilit.

—Y Ddihangfa Anhygoel! Llyfr Drysfa Beiblaidd. Davies, Aled, ed. Wyn, Delyth, tr. Richardson-Jones, Tessa, illus. 2005. (WEL.). 12p. (978-1-85994-469-1(8)) Cyhoeddiadau'r Gair.

Streit, Jakob. We Will Build a Temple: The Path of Israel from King Solomon to John the Baptist. Mitchell, David, ed. Samson, Donald, tr. 2004. Orig. Title: Lasst Uns Den Tempel Bauen. (ENG.). (J). per. 15.00 (978-1-888365-55-9(2)) Waldorf Publications.

Suggs, Rob. Comic Book Bible. 2009. (ENG.). 264p. (J). pap. 5.99 (978-1-60260-685-2(4), Barbour Bks.) Barbour Publishing, Inc.

The Sword, the Ring, & the Parchment. 2006. (J). per. 7.99 (978-0-9785523-0-5(X)) Cross & Crown Publishing.

Syswerda, Jean E. My Bedtime Story Bible for Little Ones, 1 vol. Howarth, Daniel, illus. 2016. (ENG.). 32p. (J). bds. 9.99 (978-0-310-75330-8(9)) Zonderkidz.

Takac, Esther. Genesis-the Book with Seventy Faces: A Guide for the Family. Pignataro, Anna, illus. 2008. 241p. (J). (gr. 3-9). 24.95 (978-1-932687-92-7(0), Pitspopany Pr.) Simcha Media Group.

Tanner, Martha. And God Said. 2011. 28p. pap. 13.75 (978-1-4567-3691-0(4)) AuthorHouse.

Taylor, Jane & MacKenzie, Carine. Jesus: The Promised Child. 2015. (Bible Wise Ser.). (ENG., Illus.). 32p. (J). (gr. -1-k). pap. 4.50 (978-1-85792-297-4(2), 9781857922974, CF4Kids) Christian Focus Pubns. GBR. Dist: Bookmasters Distribution.

—Saul: The Miracle on the Road. Apps, Fred, illus. 2015. (Bible Wise Ser.). (ENG.). 32p. (J). (gr. -1-k). pap. 3.99 (978-1-85792-296-7(4), ce4aba24-01b4-4e04-bdd8-77048ba4b872) Christian Focus Pubns. GBR. Dist: Bookmasters Distribution.

Taylor, Jon, illus. Tower of Babel. 2007. 24p. (J). (gr. 4-7). 14.99 (978-0-89051-487-0(9)) Master Bks.

Taylor, Kenneth N. Classic Bible Storybook. 2009. (ENG.). 288p. (J). 14.99 (978-1-4143-0769-5(1)) Tyndale Hse. Pubs.

—Family-Time Bible in Pictures. 2007. (ENG., Illus.). 320p. (J). (gr. -1-1). 12.99 (978-1-4143-1577-5(5)) Tyndale Hse. Pubs.

—Jesus in Pictures for Little Eyes. Spenceley, Annabel, illus. 2003. (ENG.). 128p. (J). (gr. k-3). 9.99 (978-0-8024-3059-5(7)) Moody Pubs.

—The New Bible in Pictures for Little Eyes. Spenceley, Annabel, illus. gif. ed. 2004. (Leading Young Hearts & Minds to God Ser.). (ENG.). 384p. (J). 24.99 (978-0-8024-3078-6(3)) Moody Pubs.

Taylor, Mark A. Breakfast with Jesus. 2014. (Happy Day Ser.). (ENG.). 16p. (J). pap. 2.49 (978-1-4143-9484-8(5)) Tyndale Hse. Pubs.

Tebbs, Victoria. My Best Ever Bible! Cosgrove, Lee, illus. 2016. (ENG.). 160p. (J). (gr. -1-k). 12.99 (978-1-68099-186-4(8), Good Bks.) Skyhorse Publishing Co., Inc.

Tebbs, Victoria & Goodings, Christina. The Lost Sheep Story. Mitchell, Melanie, illus. 2009. (See & Say! Ser.). (ENG.). 20p. (J). (gr. k — 1). 6.95 (978-0-7459-6087-6(1)) Lion Hudson PLC GBR. Dist: Independent Pubs. Group.

Teixeira, Lucas. Mi Pequeña Biblia Hispana. 2014. (ENG & SPA.). (J). (978-0-7648-2445-6(7)) Liguori Pubns.

Ten Cate, Marijke. God's Word for Me: Favorite Bible Stories from the International Children's Bible, 1 vol. 2014. (ENG., Illus.). 192p. (J). 14.99 (978-0-529-10402-1(4)) Nelson, Thomas Inc.

Thank You, God. 2014. (Happy Day Ser.). (ENG., Illus.). 16p. (J). pap. 2.49 (978-1-4143-9413-8(6)) Tyndale Hse. Pubs.

Thomas Nelson. Babytown Bible Stories. 2015. (ENG., Illus.). 22p. (gr. -1). bds. (978-1-78393-869-8(2)) Make Believe Ideas.

—Look & Tell Bible Stories. 2016. (ENG.). 24p. (gr. -1). bds. (978-1-78598-624-6(4)) Make Believe Ideas.

—My Pretty Pink Bible Purse. 2014. (ENG.). 24p. (J). 9.99 (978-0-529-12408-1(4)) Nelson, Thomas Inc.

Thomas Nelson Publishing Staff. Brave Girls Bible Stories, 1 vol. 2014. (ENG.). 224p. (J). 16.99 (978-0-529-10898-2(4)) Nelson, Thomas Inc.

—My Big Book of Catholic Bible Stories, 1 vol. 2014. (ENG.). 432p. (J). 19.99 (978-0-7180-1195-6(3)) Nelson, Thomas Inc.

—My Rainbow Promise Bible, 1 vol. 2015. (ENG.). 1152p. 19.99 (978-0-7180-2243-3(2)) Nelson, Thomas Inc.

—Read Me a Bible Story 365, 1 vol. 2015. (ENG., Illus.). 224p. (J). 14.99 (978-0-7180-3383-5(3)) Nelson, Thomas Inc.

Thomas Nelson Publishing Staff & Hall, Hannah. God Bless You & Good Night, 1 vol. 2013. (God Bless Book Ser.). (ENG.). 20p. (J). bds. 9.99 (978-1-4003-2294-7(4)) Nelson, Thomas Inc.

Thomas Nelson, Thomas. Big Look Bible Book: Make Believe Ideas, 1 vol. 2017. (ENG.). 20p. (J). bds. 9.99 **(978-0-7180-7488-3(2))** Make Believe Ideas GBR. Dist: Nelson, Thomas Inc.

—Look & Tell Bible, 1 vol. 2016. (ENG., Illus.). 24p. (J). bds. 9.99 (978-0-7180-8558-2(2)) Nelson, Thomas Inc.

—My Give Thanks Bible, 1 vol. Masse, Josée, illus. 2015. (ENG.). 32p. (J). bds. 9.99 (978-0-310-74942-4(5)) Zonderkidz.

—My Jesus Bible: With Handle, 1 vol. 2017. (ENG.). 40p. (J). bds. 9.99 (978-0-7180-9188-0(4)) Nelson, Thomas Inc.

—My Lift-The-Flap Bible Stories, 1 vol. 2017. (ENG.). 20p. (J). bds. 9.99 (978-0-7180-9428-7(X)) Nelson, Thomas Inc.

—My Little Bible, 1 vol. Le Feyer, Diane, illus. 2016. (ENG.). 96p. (J). 6.99 (978-0-7180-4018-5(X)) Nelson, Thomas Inc.

—Starter Bible, 1 vol. 2016. (ENG.). 40p. (J). bds. 9.99 (978-0-7180-9005-0(5)) Nelson, Thomas Inc.

—5-Minute Nighttime Bible Stories, 1 vol. 2016. (ENG.). 208p. (J). 12.99 (978-0-7180-8452-3(7)) Nelson, Thomas Inc.

Thomas, Sylvia A. The Disciples of Jesus. 2012. 24p. pap. 17.99 (978-1-61904-668-9(7)) Salem Author Services.

—Moses & the Exodus from Egypt. 2012. 34p. pap. 19.99 (978-1-61904-669-6(5)) Salem Author Services.

Thompson, Kim Mitzo. Bible Stories. 2011. (J). (gr. k-1). audio compact disk 4.99 (978-1-59922-873-0(4)) Twin Sisters IP, LLC.

Thompson, Sharon. Bible Story Puppets & Poems. 2004. (J). per. 12.99 (978-1-59441-007-9(0), CD-204001) Carson-Dellosa Publishing, LLC.

Thoms, Susan Collins. Jonah & the Big Fish. Stoop, Naoko, illus. 2016. (ENG.). 22p. (J). (— 1). bds. 6.95 (978-1-4549-1493-8(9), 1402423) Sterling Publishing Co., Inc.

Thor, Cook Jean. Jesus Calms the Storm. 2004. (Illus.). 16p. (J). 1.99 (978-0-7586-0637-2(0)) Concordia Publishing Hse.

Tiger, Tales, ed. My Little Book of Bible Stories. Scott, Lindsay, illus. 2016. (ENG.). 32p. (J). (gr. -1-2). mass mkt. 3.99 (978-1-58925-487-9(2)) Tiger Tales.

Tiny Tots Christmas. 2015. (Tiny Tots Ser.). (ENG., Illus.). 32p. (J). (gr. -1 — 1). 8.99 (978-0-7459-6455-3(9)) Lion Hudson PLC GBR. Dist: Independent Pubs. Group.

Tnt. Gospel Parables, the Easter Story & Parables on the Second Coming. 2014. (On the Way (3-9's) Ser.). (ENG.). 100p. (J). pap. 17.99 (978-1-85792-403-9(7), 9781857924039) Christian Focus Pubns. GBR. Dist: Bookmasters Distribution.

TNT Ministries Staff. On the Way for 9 - 11's, Vol. 6. 2008. (On the Way (9-11's) Ser.). (ENG.). 80p. (J). pap. 17.99 (978-1-85792-556-2(4), 9781857925562) Christian Focus Pubns. GBR. Dist: Bookmasters Distribution.

Too Tall, Too Small. (Hear Me Read Classroom Sets Ser.). 32.00 (978-0-570-07171-6(2)) Concordia Publishing Hse.

Touched by Him: Bible Story Coloring Book. 2006. (ENG, CHI & RUS.). (J). 1.99 (978-0-9777446-0-2(4)) Childrens Bible Society.

Toulmin, Sarah. Baby's Little Bible. Stephenson, Kristina, illus. gif. ed. 2011. (ENG.). 160p. (J). (gr. k — 1). 13.99 (978-0-7459-6038-8(3)) Lion Hudson PLC GBR. Dist: Independent Pubs. Group.

—Baby's Little Bible & Prayers, 2 vols. Stephenson, Kristina, illus. 2011. (ENG.). 224p. (J). (gr. k — 1). pap. 19.99 (978-0-7459-6039-5(1)) Lion Hudson PLC GBR. Dist: Independent Pubs. Group.

—Baby's Tiny Bible & Prayers, 2 vols., Set. Stephenson, Kristina, illus. 2013. (ENG.). 224p. (J). (— 1). 14.99 (978-0-7459-6205-4(X)) Lion Hudson PLC GBR. Dist: Independent Pubs. Group.

Truitt, Gloria. Jesus bendice a los ninos (Jesus Blesses the Children)- Bilingual. Fernández, Cecilia, ed. 2011. 16p. pap. 2.99 (978-0-7586-3071-1(9)) Concordia Publishing Hse.

Tuck, Mildred. A Child's Book of Miracles & Wonders. Moroney, Tracey, illus. 2006. 28p. (J). (gr. -1-3). 15.99 (978-0-7847-1437-9(1), 04076) Standard Publishing.

Tulloch, Fiona, ed. The Children's Bible: Illustrated Stories from the Old & New Testament. 2008. (Illus.). 208p. (J). 12.99 (978-1-84193-852-3(1)) A Cappella Bks.

Tutu, Desmond. Children of God Storybook Bible, 1 vol. 2010. (ENG.). 128p. (J). (gr. -1-2). 18.99 (978-0-310-71912-0(7)) Zondervan.

—Let There Be Light, 1 vol. Tillman, Nancy, illus. 2014. (ENG.). 30p. (J). bds. 7.99 (978-0-310-73396-6(0)) Zonderkidz.

Twin Sisters(r), et al. Fun Bible Story Rhymes for Kids. 2017. (Let's Share a Story Ser.). (ENG.). 16p. (J). bds. 9.99 (978-1-68322-074-9(9)) Barbour Publishing, Inc.

—I Can Read Bible Stories. 2016. (I Can Read Ser.). (ENG.). 32p. (J). pap. 4.99 (978-1-63409-771-0(8)) Barbour Publishing, Inc.

Twin Sisters(r) Staff, prod. Bible Stories: Songs That Teach. 2006. (J). per. 10.99 (978-1-57583-822-9(2)) Twin Sisters IP, LLC.

Twin Sisters(r) Staff, et al. Bible Fun: Color & Trace. 2016. (ENG.). 64p. (J). pap. 6.99 (978-1-63409-092-6(6)) Barbour Publishing, Inc.

—Bible Fun: Cut & Glue. 2016. (I'm Learning the Bible Activity Book Ser.). (ENG.). 64p. pap. 6.99 (978-1-63409-387-3(9)) Barbour Publishing, Inc.

—Happy Birthday, Jesus: A Sing-Along Storybook. 2015. (ENG., Illus.). 14p. (J). (-5). 9.99 (978-1-63409-025-4(X)) Barbour Publishing, Inc.

—My First Bible Stories for Boys with CD. 2015. (ENG., Illus.). 24p. (J). (-k). 12.99 (978-1-63409-094-0(2)) Barbour Publishing, Inc.

—My First Bible Stories for Girls with CD. 2015. (ENG., Illus.). 24p. (J). (-k). 12.99 (978-1-63409-095-7(0)) Barbour Publishing, Inc.

Tyler, M. Ramifications in Genesis 1-3. 2013. 186p. (gr. 10-12). 30.95 (978-1-4497-9526-9(9)); pap. 13.95 (978-1-4497-9524-5(2)) Author Solutions, Inc. (WestBow Pr.).

Tyndale, prod. Biblia para Exploradores: Nuevo Testamento. 2017. Orig. Title: Bible Sleuth: New Testament. (SPA & ENG.). 32p. 9.99 (978-1-4964-2246-0(5)) Tyndale Hse. Pubs.

—Big Bible Fun Color & Learn, Vol. 1. 2014. (Happy Day Ser.). (ENG.). 96p. (J). pap. 2.49 (978-1-4143-9500-5(0)) Tyndale Hse. Pubs.

—The Gigantic Coloring Book of Bible Stories. 2014. (ENG.). 384p. (J). pap. 5.99 (978-1-4143-9498-5(5)) Tyndale Hse. Pubs.

Tyndale & Group Publishing, prods. My First Hands-On Bible. 2015. (ENG.). 416p. (J). pap. 12.99 (978-1-4964-0643-9(5)) Tyndale Hse. Pubs.

Tyner, Stuart. The Meanest Man in the Army: And Other Stories of Grace. 2014. (ENG.). (J). pap. 12.99 (978-0-8280-2729-8(3)) Review & Herald Publishing Assn.

Ulmer, Louise. The Bible That Wouldn't Burn: William Tyndale's New Testament. Ulmer, Louise, illus. 3rd ed. 2005. Orig. Title: The Bible That Wouldn't Burn: How the Tyndale English Version of the New Testament Came About. (Illus.). 34p. (YA). per., act. bk. ed. 8.95 (978-0-941367-24-0(X)) Peach Blossom Pubns.

Vacation Bible School - Look & Do Stories. 2004. (Vacation Bible School Ser.). (Illus.). 64p. (J). 9.95 (978-1-885358-02-8(4)) Rainbow Pubs. & Legacy Pr.

Van Der Veer, Andrew. Bible Lessons for Juniors, Book 1: Creation Through Moses. 2007. 88p. (J). 6.00 (978-1-60178-012-6(5)) Reformation Heritage Bks.

—Bible Lessons for Juniors, Book 2: Kings & Prophets. 2007. 88p. (J). 6.00 (978-1-60178-013-3(3)) Reformation Heritage Bks.

Van der Veer, Andrew. Bible Lessons for Juniors, Book 3: The Life of Christ. 2007. (ENG.). 88p. (J). 6.00 (978-1-60178-014-0(1)) Reformation Heritage Bks.

Van Der Veer, Andrew. Bible Lessons for Juniors, Book 4: The Early Church. 2007. 88p. (J). 6.00 (978-1-60178-015-7(X)) Reformation Heritage Bks.

VanBibber, Jodi. CD: An Early Childhood Learning Program designed especially for One-Year-Olds. 2005. cd-rom 34.95 (978-0-9755818-3-4(X)) Sunny Hollow Pr.

—CD: An Early Childhood Learning Program designed especially for two & three year olds. It's educational & easy to do. but best of all, it's fun!: Bible Story Concepts for 2s And 3s. 2005. cd-rom 34.95 (978-0-9755818-2-7(1)) Sunny Hollow Pr.

—CD-Bible Story Concepts for 4s And 5s: An Early Childhood Learning Program designed especially for four & five year olds. It's educational & easy to do. but best of all, it's Fun! 2005. cd-rom 34.95 (978-0-9755818-4-1(8)) Sunny Hollow Pr.

Veggie Tales Cast. Veggietales Lots of Fun Color. rev. ed. 2004. (ENG., Illus.). 400p. (J). pap. 5.99 (978-1-4037-0538-9(0), Spirit Pr.) Bendon, Inc.

Vineyard Church of Columbus. Great Big Holy Bible: Fall Quarter, Year One. Campbell, Karen, illus. 2007. (J). ring bd. 19.99 (978-0-9786394-7-1(2)) Ampelon Publishing, LLC.

Vivas, Julie. The Nativity. 2006. (ENG., Illus.). 36p. (J). (gr. -1-3). pap. 7.99 (978-0-15-206085-5(5)) Houghton Mifflin Harcourt Publishing Co.

Walker, John, illus. The Story of Christmas: The Birth of Jesus. 2008. (ENG.). 24p. (J). (gr. 2). 19.95 (978-1-58117-793-0(3), Intervisual/Piggy Toes) Bendon, Inc.

Walker, Joni. Jesus Rose on Easter Morn Span. 2004. (SPA.). 20p. bds. 4.99 (978-0-7586-0322-7(3)) Concordia Publishing Hse.

—Tell Me What God Made. Walker, Joni, illus. 2007. (Illus.). 20p. (J). (gr. -1-3). bds. 6.49 (978-0-7586-1247-2(8)) Concordia Publishing Hse.

Walls, Steven. The Ark Endeavor. 2005. 55p. pap. 16.95 (978-1-4137-9566-0(8)) America Star Bks.

Walsh, Sheila. The Bible Is My Best Friend Bible Storybook. 2017. (Bible Is My Best Friend Ser.). (ENG.). 304p. (J). (gr. -1-3). 16.99 (978-1-4336-8803-4(4), B&H Kids) B&H Publishing Group.

—Goodnight Warrior: Bedtime Bible Stories, Devotions, & Prayers, 1 vol. 2008. (God's Mighty Warrior Ser.). (ENG., Illus.). 336p. 16.99 (978-1-4003-1298-6(1)) Nelson, Thomas Inc.

—Sweet Dreams Princess: God's Little Princess Bedtime Bible Stories, Devotions, & Prayers, 1 vol. 2008. (ENG.). 336p. 17.99 (978-1-4003-1297-9(3)) Nelson, Thomas Inc.

Warner Press, creator. Bible Sports Heroes: Great Lessons You Can Learn from God's Favorite Athletes Activity Book. 2008. (J). (gr. -1-3). pap. 11.34 (978-1-59317-325-8(3)) Warner Pr., Inc.

—My Favorite Bible Stories Coloring Book. 2009. (Illus.). (gr. -1-2). 4.50 (978-1-59317-352-4(0)) Warner Pr., Inc.

Warner Press Kids, creator. Jesus Is Born: Coloring Book. 2008. 16p. (J). (gr. -1-3). pap. 11.34 (978-1-59317-322-7(9)) Warner Pr., Inc.

Water, Mark. The Pilgrim Book of Bible Stories. Shimon, Diana, illus. 2003. 320p. (J). 22.50 (978-0-8298-1487-3(6)) Pilgrim Pr., The/United Church Pr.

Watts, Murray. The Bible for Children. Cann, Helen, illus. 2014. (ENG.). 352p. (J). (gr. 2-6). 17.95 (978-0-7459-4046-5(3)) Lion Hudson PLC GBR. Dist: Independent Pubs. Group.

Webber, Jerry. The Game: None. 2007. 52p. per. 9.95 (978-1-4327-0911-2(9)) Outskirts Pr., Inc.

Wee Ones' Bible Stories. 2004. reprint ed. pap. 15.95 (978-1-4191-9335-4(X)); pap. 1.99 (978-1-4192-9335-1(4)) Kessinger Publishing, LLC.

Weiss, Sam. Jesus Plays the Catskills. 2004. 96p. per. 11.95 (978-0-9754699-0-3(8)) Gross, H. H.

Weitzel, Karen E. John & Betty Stam: Missionary Martyrs to China. Ober, Jonathan & Willoughby, Yuko, illus. 2008. (ENG.). 52p. (J). pap. (978-1-932381-12-2(0), 5190) Bible Visuals International, Inc.

Welborn, Amy. Loyola Kids Book of Bible Stories: 60 Scripture Stories Every Catholic Child Should Know. 2017. (ENG.). 200p. (J). (gr. 2-8). 19.95 **(978-0-8294-4539-8(0))** Loyola Pr.

What Next? (Hear Me Read Classroom Sets Ser.). 32.00 (978-0-570-07173-0(9)) Concordia Publishing Hse.

Wheat, Charlotte. That Bodacious, God-Trustin' Prophet, Elijah! From the down-home Bible Stories Series. 2010. (Illus.). 27p. (J). pap. 12.95 (978-1-4327-5997-1(3)) Outskirts Pr., Inc.

Widenhouse, Kathy. The Un-Bunny Book. 2004. (Illus.). 168p. (J). pap. 14.99 (978-1-58411-028-6(7), Legacy Pr.) Rainbow Pubs. & Legacy Pr.

Wile, Mary Lee. Season of Angels. Stossel, Sage, illus. 2013. (978-0-88028-367-0(X)) Forward Movement Pubns.

Wilkeshuis, Cornelius. The Gift for the Child. Verstegen, Jeska, illus. (ENG.). 28p. (J). 16.95 (978-0-86315-349-5(6)) Floris Bks. GBR. Dist: SteinerBooks, Inc.

Wilkin, Wendy. Bible Stories for Children. Cloke, Rene, illus. 2012. (ENG.). 32p. (J). 9.95 (978-0-86163-797-3(6)) Award Pubns. Ltd. GBR. Dist: Parkwest Pubns., Inc.

Wilkinson, Bruce. My 100 Best-Loved Bible Stories. 2005. (Illus.). 216p. (J). (gr. -1-3). 12.99 (978-1-59185-866-9(6)) Charisma Media.

Williamson, Karen. Adam & Eve, 1 vol. Conner, Sarah, illus. 2017. (Candle Little Lambs Ser.). (ENG.). 24p. (J). pap. 2.99 **(978-1-78128-324-0(9)**, Candle Bks.) Lion Hudson PLC GBR. Dist: Kregel Pubns.

—Baby Jesus, 1 vol. Conner, Sarah, illus. 2015. (Candle Little Lambs Ser.). (ENG.). 24p. (J). pap. 2.99 (978-1-78128-188-8(2), Candle Bks.) Lion Hudson PLC GBR. Dist: Kregel Pubns.

—Bible Sliders, 1 vol. Selbert, Kathryn, illus. 2015. (ENG.). 10p. (J). bds. 9.99 (978-1-78128-224-3(2), Candle Bks.) Lion Hudson PLC GBR. Dist: Kregel Pubns.

—The Christmas Story, 1 vol. Barnard, Lucy, illus. 2016. (Bible Mini-Pops Ser.). (ENG.). 10p. (J). 9.99 (978-1-78128-284-7(6), Candle Bks.) Lion Hudson PLC GBR. Dist: Kregel Pubns.

—Daniel & the Lions, 1 vol. Conner, Sarah, illus. 2015. (Candle Little Lambs Ser.). (ENG.). 24p. (J). pap. 2.99 (978-1-78128-162-8(9), Candle Bks.) Lion Hudson PLC GBR. Dist: Kregel Pubns.

—David & Goliath, 1 vol. Conner, Sarah, illus. 2015. (Candle Little Lambs Ser.). (ENG.). 24p. (J). pap. 2.99 (978-1-78128-160-4(2), Candle Bks.) Lion Hudson PLC GBR. Dist: Kregel Pubns.

—The Good Samaritan, 1 vol. Conner, Sarah, illus. 2017. (Candle Little Lambs Ser.). (ENG.). 24p. (J). pap. 2.99 **(978-1-78128-323-3(0)**, Candle Bks.) Lion Hudson PLC GBR. Dist: Kregel Pubns.

—Joseph, 1 vol. Conner, Sarah, illus. 2016. (Candle Little Lambs Ser.). (ENG.). 24p. (J). pap. 2.99 (978-1-78128-278-6(1), Candle Bks.) Lion Hudson PLC GBR. Dist: Kregel Pubns.

—Lift the Flap Bible, 1 vol. Anglicas, Louise, illus. 2014. (ENG.). 16p. (J). bds. 12.99 (978-1-78128-130-7(0), Candle Bks.) Lion Hudson PLC GBR. Dist: Kregel Pubns.

—Lost Sheep & Other Stories, 1 vol. Barnard, Lucy, illus. 2015. (Bible Mini-Pops Ser.). (ENG.). 10p. (J). bds. 9.99 (978-1-78128-150-5(5), Candle Bks.) Lion Hudson PLC GBR. Dist: Kregel Pubns.

—Mary & Martha, 1 vol. Conner, Sarah, illus. 2016. (Candle Little Lambs Ser.). (ENG.). 24p. (J). pap. 2.99 (978-1-78128-279-3(X), Candle Bks.) Lion Hudson PLC GBR. Dist: Kregel Pubns.

—More Bible Sliders, 1 vol. Selbert, Kathryn, illus. 2016. (Candle Tiny Tots Ser.). (ENG.). 10p. (J). bds. 9.99 *(978-1-78128-273-1(0),* Candle Bks.) Lion Hudson PLC GBR. Dist: Kregel Pubns.

—My First Bible Stories, 1 vol. Allen, Marie, illus. 2014. (ENG.). 108p. (J). spiral bd. 7.99 *(978-1-85985-994-0(1),* Candle Bks.) Lion Hudson PLC GBR. Dist: Kregel Pubns.

—Noah & Other Stories, 1 vol. Barnard, Lucy, illus. 2015. (Bible Mini-Pops Ser.). (ENG.). 10p. (J). 9.99 *(978-1-78128-149-9(1),* Candle Bks.) Lion Hudson PLC GBR. Dist: Kregel Pubns.

—Noah & the Animals, 1 vol. Hanton, Sophie, illus. 2014. (Candle Tiny Tots Ser.). (ENG.). 16p. (J). 11.99 *(978-1-78128-110-9(6),* Candle Bks.) Lion Hudson PLC GBR. Dist: Kregel Pubns.

—Play-Time Noah, 1 vol. Anglicas, Louise, illus. 2014. (ENG.). 8p. (J). bds. 9.99 *(978-1-78128-111-6(4),* Candle Bks.) Lion Hudson PLC GBR. Dist: Kregel Pubns.

—The Prodigal Son, 1 vol. Conner, Sarah, illus. 2017. (Candle Little Lambs Ser.). (ENG.). 24p. (J). pap. 2.99 ***(978-1-78128-325-7(7),*** Candle Bks.) Lion Hudson PLC GBR. Dist: Kregel Pubns.

—Samuel, 1 vol. Conner, Sarah, illus. 2017. (Candle Little Lambs Ser.). (ENG.). 24p. (J). pap. 2.99 ***(978-1-78128-326-4(5),*** Candle Bks.) Lion Hudson PLC GBR. Dist: Kregel Pubns.

—The Wise Men's Story, 1 vol. Barnard, Lucy, illus. 2016. (Bible Mini-Pops Ser.). (ENG.). 10p. (J). 9.99 *(978-1-78128-283-0(8),* Candle Bks.) Lion Hudson PLC GBR. Dist: Kregel Pubns.

—Zacchaeus, 1 vol. Conner, Sarah, illus. 2016. (Candle Little Lambs Ser.). (ENG.). 24p. (J). pap. 2.99 *(978-1-78128-277-9(3),* Candle Bks.) Lion Hudson PLC GBR. Dist: Kregel Pubns.

Willoughby, R. Peter Puts His Foot in It! Buckley, Joel, illus. 2004. 64p. pap. *(978-1-85999-765-9(1))* Scripture Union.

—Peter Strides Out. Buckley, Joel, illus. 2004. 64p. pap. *(978-1-84427-022-4(X))* Scripture Union.

Wilson, N. D. In the Time of Noah. 2007. (Old Stories Ser.). (ENG., Illus.). 32p. (J). (gr. 3-7). 14.00 *(978-1-59128-045-3(1))* Canon Pr.

Wines, Richard. Five Stones. 2007. 116p. per. 12.95 *(978-1-60264-122-8(6))* Virtualbookworm.com Publishing, Inc.

Winkler, Jude. Biblia Ilustrada para Ninos. Todo Color, illus. 2007. 172p. (J). (gr. -1-3). 12.99 *(978-0-89942-636-5(0))* Catholic Bk. Publishing Corp.

Wolf, Kathryn Nider & Robbins, Heather P. Make a Joyful Noise! Music, Movement, & Creative Play to Teach Bible Stories: Preschool - Grade 1. 2007. (ENG., Illus.). 96p. per. 21.99 *(978-0-9789056-8-2(7))* New Day Publishing, Inc.

Woodman, Ros. Luke - Bible Detectives. 2006. (Activity Ser.). (ENG.). 64p. (J). pap., act. bk. ed. 7.99 *(978-1-85792-758-0(3),* 0fc7b655-ce64-46eb-ab02-47ccd3e9556b) Christian Focus Pubns. GBR. Dist: Bookmasters Distribution.

Woodward, Antonia. The Extra Special Baby: The Story of the Christmas Promise. 2017. (ENG., Illus.). 32p. (J). (gr. -1-k). 14.99 ***(978-0-7459-7699-0(9))*** Lion Hudson PLC GBR. Dist: Independent Pubs. Group.

Word Among Us Editorial Staff. 42 Bible Stories for Little Ones: From Creation to Pentecost. Round, Graham, illus. 2008. 96p. pap. 13.95 *(978-1-59325-138-3(6))* Word Among Us Pr.

Word of Life Press, creator. Manga Bible Story. 2006. (JPN., Illus.). 879p. (J). (gr. 4-7). 78.00 *(978-4-264-01798-1(X))* Word of Life Press Ministries JPN. Dist: Send The Light Distribution LLC.

Wright, Melissa & Curelli, Augusta. My Bible: The Story of God's Love. Curreli, Augusta, illus. 2004. 236p. (J). 24.95 *(978-0-8198-4834-5(4),* 332-223) Pauline Bks. & Media.

Wright, Sally Ann. Bible Adventures & Activities. Maclean, Moira, illus. 2012. 144p. (J). pap. 11.95 *(978-0-8198-1199-8(8))* Pauline Bks. & Media.

—The Look & See Bible. MacLean, Moira, illus. 2006. (Children's Bibles & Bible Story Collections). 94p. (J). (gr. -1-3). 12.95 *(978-0-8091-6735-7(2),* 6735-2) Paulist Pr.

—Mix & Match Bible. 2011. 32p. 12.99 *(978-0-7586-2796-4(3))* Concordia Publishing Hse.

—What Did the Fishermen Catch? And Other Questions. Grudina, Paola Bertolini, illus. 2006. 32p. (J). (gr. -1). 10.95 *(978-0-8091-6732-6(8),* 6732-8) Paulist Pr.

—Who Built the Ark? And Other Questions. Grudina, Paola Bertolini, illus. 2006. 32p. (J). (gr. -1-3). 10.95 *(978-0-8091-6730-2(1),* 6730-1) Paulist Pr.

Wright, Sally Ann & Wright, Lesley. My Keepsake Bible. Ayres, Honor, illus. 2015. (ENG.). 144p. (J). 14.99 *(978-1-4143-9867-9(0))* Tyndale Hse. Pubs.

Young, Norman, illus. The Story of Jesus for Young Children. 2005. (Usborne Bible Tales Ser.). 98p. (J). (gr. -1-k). 14.99 incl. audio compact disk *(978-0-7945-0831-9(6),* Usborne) EDC Publishing.

Young, Sarah. Jesus Calling Bible Storybook Deluxe Edition, 1 vol. 2015. (ENG.). 256p. (J). 24.99 *(978-0-7180-2163-4(0))* Nelson, Thomas Inc.

—Jesus Calling for Little Ones, 1 vol. Woodward, Antonia, illus. 2015. (ENG.). 26p. (J). bds. 7.99 *(978-0-7180-3384-2(1))* Nelson, Thomas Inc.

—Jesus Calling My First Bible Storybook, 1 vol. 2016. (ENG., Illus.). 40p. (J). bds. 9.99 *(978-0-7180-7605-4(2))* Nelson, Thomas Inc.

Zobel-Nolan, Allia. Catholic Baby's Bedtime Bible Stories. Stevenson, Peter, illus. 2006. (First Bible Collection). (gr. -1-k). bds. 15.95 *(978-0-88271-067-9(2))* Regina Pr., Malhame & Co.

—Ninos en la Biblia. 2003.Tr. of Children of the Bible. bds. 8.99 *(978-0-7899-1069-9(6))* Editorial Unilit.

—La Primera Biblia del Bebe. 2003. (First Bible Collection). (ENG & SPA., Illus.). 20p. (J). bds. 12.99 *(978-0-7944-0139-9(2))* Reader's Digest Assn., Inc., The.

Zona Biblica en la Casa de Dios Preschool Leader's Guide. 2007. 180p. 19.99 *(978-0-687-64660-9(X))* Abingdon Pr.

Zona Biblica en la Casa de Dios Younger Elementary Leader's Guide. 2007. 178p. 19.99 *(978-0-687-64670-8(7))* Abingdon Pr.

Zondervan. The Beginner's Bible: Timeless Children's Stories, 1 vol. 2016. (Beginner's Bible Ser.). (ENG.). 512p. (J). 16.99 *(978-0-310-75013-0(X))* Zonderkidz.

—The Beginner's Bible Activity Book, 1 vol. 2017. (Beginner's Bible Ser.). (ENG.). 64p. (J). pap. 4.99 *(978-0-310-75979-9(X))* Zonderkidz.

—The Beginner's Bible Carry-Along Treasury, 1 vol. 2017. (Beginner's Bible Ser.). (ENG.). 160p. (J). 12.99 *(978-0-310-76030-6(5))* Zonderkidz.

—The Beginner's Bible Coloring Book, 1 vol. 2017. (Beginner's Bible Ser.). (ENG.). 64p. (J). pap. 4.99 *(978-0-310-75955-3(2))* Zonderkidz.

—The Beginner's Bible for Little Ones, 1 vol. 2017. (Beginner's Bible Ser.). (ENG., Illus.). 32p. (J). bds. 9.99 *(978-0-310-75536-4(0))* Zonderkidz.

—The Beginner's Bible Stories about Jesus, 1 vol. 2016. (Beginner's Bible Ser.). (ENG.). 22p. (J). bds. 9.99 *(978-0-310-75610-1(3))* Zonderkidz.

Zondervan Staff. Adventure Bible for Early Readers, 1 vol. rev. ed. 2014. (Adventure Bible Ser.). (ENG.). 1584p. (J). 31.99 *(978-0-310-72746-0(4));* (Illus.). 29.99 *(978-0-310-72742-2(1))* Zonderkidz.

—All Aboard the Ark, 1 vol. 2016. (ENG., Illus.). 24p. (J). bds. 6.99 *(978-0-310-75377-3(5))* Zonderkidz.

—Beginner's Bible(r), 1 vol. rev. ed. 2012. (Beginner's Bible Ser.). (ENG.). 512p. (J). 26.98 *(978-0-310-71857-4(0))* Zonderkidz.

—Beginner's Bible Collector's Edition: Timeless Children's Stories, 1 vol. Pulley, Kelly, illus. 2014. (Beginner's Bible Ser.). (ENG.). 512p. (J). 39.99 *(978-0-310-74734-5(1))* Zonderkidz.

—The Beginner's Bible Curriculum Kit: 30 Timeless Lessons for Preschoolers, 1 vol. 2014. (ENG.). (J). pap. 129.99 *(978-0-310-82013-0(8))* Zondervan.

—The Beginner's Bible Stories about Jesus, 1 vol. Pulley, Kelly, illus. 2015. (Beginner's Bible Ser.). (ENG.). 22p. (J). bds. 9.99 *(978-0-310-74740-6(6))* Zonderkidz.

—Beginner's Bible with Bible Cover Pack 2015, 1 vol. 2015. (Beginner's Bible Ser.). (ENG.). 512p. (J). 26.98 *(978-0-310-75226-4(4))* Zonderkidz.

—A Father's Love, 1 vol. Miles, David, illus. 2014. (I Can Read! / Adventure Bible Ser.). (ENG.). 32p. (J). pap. 3.99 *(978-0-310-73240-2(9))* Zonderkidz.

—God's Great Creation, 1 vol. Miles, David, illus. 2014. (I Can Read! / Adventure Bible Ser.). (ENG.). 32p. (J). pap. 3.99 *(978-0-310-73238-9(7))* Zondervan.

—The Lost Son: Based on Luke 15:11-32, 1 vol. Pulley, Kelly, illus. 2009. (I Can Read! / the Beginner's Bible Ser.). (ENG.). 32p. (J). pap. 3.99 *(978-0-310-71781-2(7))* Zonderkidz.

—Miracles of Jesus, 1 vol. Miles, David, illus. 2014. (I Can Read! / Adventure Bible Ser.). (ENG.). 32p. (J). pap. 3.99 *(978-0-310-73242-6(5))* Zonderkidz.

—Moses Leads the People, 1 vol. Miles, David, illus. 2014. (I Can Read! / Adventure Bible Ser.). (ENG.). 32p. (J). pap. 3.99 *(978-0-310-73236-5(0))* Zondervan.

—Queen Esther Helps God's People (La Reina Ester Ayuda Al Pueblo de Dios), 1 vol. 2009. (I Can Read! / the Beginner's Bible / ¡Yo Sé Leer! Ser.). (ENG.). 32p. (J). pap. 3.99 *(978-0-310-71888-8(0))* Zonderkidz.

—Wacky Bible Blockheads, 1 vol. 2014. (It's a Fact Ser.). (ENG.). 160p. (J). pap. 9.99 *(978-0-310-74419-1(9))* Zonderkidz.

—Wacky Bible Gross Outs, 1 vol. 2014. (It's a Fact Ser.). (ENG.). 176p. (J). pap. 9.99 *(978-0-310-74424-5(5))* Zonderkidz.

Zondervan Staff & Lyons, P. J. Little Chick's Bible, 1 vol. Mitchell, Melanie, illus. 2015. (ENG.). 16p. (J). bds. 15.99 *(978-0-310-74780-2(5))* Zonderkidz.

365 Bible Activities for Kids: A Bible Story & Actitivity for Each Day of the Year, 1 vol. 2003. (Illus.). 366p. (J). spiral bd. 12.99 *(978-0-8254-7273-2(3),* Candle Bks.) Lion Hudson PLC GBR. Dist: Kregel Pubns.

BIBLE STORIES—N.T.

Amery, H. New Testament. 2004. (Children's Bibles Ser.). 72p. (J). 15.95 *(978-0-7945-0048-1(X),* Usborne) EDC Publishing.

Amoss, Berthe. Draw Yourself into a Starlit Journey. 2003. 32p. (J). spiral bd. 12.95 *(978-1-59325-004-1(5))* Word Among Us Pr.

Aquilina, Michael, III. St. Jude: A Friend in Hard Times. Neely, Keith, illus. 2004. 76p. (J). 14.95 *(978-0-8198-7075-9(7),* 332-371) Pauline Bks. & Media.

B&H Editorial Staff, ed. The Big Picture Interactive Bible Stories for Toddlers, from the New Testament: Connecting Christ Throughout God's Story. McPherson, Heath, illus. 2014. (Gospel Project Ser.). (ENG.). 44p. (J). (— 1). bds. 9.99 *(978-1-4336-8429-6(2),* B&H Kids) B&H Publishing Group.

—Look & Find Bible: New Testament Stories. Guile, Gill, illus. 2015. (Look & Find Ser.). (ENG.). 24p. (J). (gr. -1-3). 12.99 *(978-1-4336-8598-9(1),* B&H Kids) B&H Publishing Group.

B&H Kids Editorial Staff. The Gospel Story. 2015. (Big Picture Interactive / the Gospel Project Ser.). (ENG.). 32p. (J). (gr. 1-5). pap. 1.99 *(978-1-4336-8662-7(7),* B&H Kids) B&H Publishing Group.

—Look & Find Bible Stories: Christmas. Guile, Gill, illus. 2015. (Look & Find Ser.). (ENG.). 20p. (J). (gr. -1-3). 12.99 *(978-1-4336-8786-0(0),* B&H Kids) B&H Publishing Group.

Bader, Joanne. Jesus Heals the Centurion's Servant. 2010. (Arch Bks.). (Illus.). 16p. (J). (gr. k-4). pap. 2.49 *(978-0-7586-1864-1(6))* Concordia Publishing Hse.

—Jesus Wakes the Little Girl. 2009. (Arch Bks.). 16p. (J). (gr. k-4). pap. 2.49 *(978-0-7586-1615-9(5))* Concordia Publishing Hse.

—The Widow's Offering. 2008. (Arch Bks.). 16p. (J). (gr. k-4). pap. 1.99 *(978-0-7586-1451-3(9))* Concordia Publishing Hse.

Baker, Marvin G. Luke's Story: Based on the Gospel of Luke. 2005. 160p. pap. 9.95 *(978-0-9752880-8-5(3))* Baker Trittin Pr.

Benson, Lyn. Who Were the Magi. Joshua, Benson Benson Joshua, illus. 2007. 56p. pap. 23.99 *(978-0-615-13524-3(2))* Benson, Lyn.

Berendes, Mary. The Good Samaritan. Johnson, Pamela & Squier, Robert, illus. 2011. (Parables Ser.). (ENG.). 24p. (J). (gr. k-3). lib. bdg. 28.50 *(978-1-60954-391-4(2),* 201186) Child's World, Inc., The.

—The Lost Sheep. Squier, Robert, illus. 2011. (Parables Ser.). (ENG.). 24p. (J). (gr. k-3). lib. bdg. 28.50 *(978-1-60954-392-1(0),* 201187) Child's World, Inc., The.

Bergt, Carolyn. A Child's Garden of Bible Stories Workbooks: New Testament Workbook. 80p. (gr. 1-3). wbk. ed. 9.95 *(978-0-7586-0474-3(2))* Concordia Publishing Hse.

Bishop, Jennie. The Garden Wall: A Story of Love Based on I Corinthians 13. Stoddard, Jeff, illus. 2006. (ENG.). 32p. (J). (gr. 2-7). 12.99 *(978-1-59317-168-1(4))* Warner Pr., Inc.

Bower, Gary. The Frightening Philippi Jail. Chotiner, Barbara, illus. 2017. (Faith That God Built Book Ser.). (ENG.). 32p. 14.99 *(978-1-4964-1750-3(X))* Tyndale Hse. Pubs.

Buck, Deanna. My First NT Stories Reprint. 2009. 36p. pap. 8.95 *(978-1-60641-111-7(X))* Deseret Bk. Co.

Burgdorf, Larry. Paul's Great Basket Caper. 2009. (Arch Bks.). 16p. (J). (gr. k-4). pap. 2.49 *(978-0-7586-1616-6(3))* Concordia Publishing Hse.

Busch, Melinda Kay. Jesus & the Woman at the Well. Clark, Bill, illus. 2005. (Arch Bks.). (ENG.). 16p. (J). 1.99 *(978-0-7586-0675-4(3))* Concordia Publishing Hse.

Butterworth, Nick. The House on the Rock. Inkpen, Mick, illus. 2008. (ENG.). 32p. pap. *(978-1-85985-749-6(3),* Candle Bks.) Lion Hudson PLC.

Carolyn, Berg. Jesus Walks Away. Paris, Pat, illus. 2003. (Arch Bks.). 16p. (J). 2.49 *(978-0-7586-0504-7(8))* Concordia Publishing Hse.

Carruth, Jane. More Bible Stories for Children. Cloke, Rene, illus. 2012. (ENG.). 32p. (J). 9.95 *(978-0-86163-770-6(4))* Award Pubns. Ltd. GBR. Dist: Parkwest Pubns., Inc.

Choi, Young-Jin & Kim, Jung-cho. A Walk on the Waves. 2007. (Illus.). 26p. bds. 5.95 *(978-0-8198-8315-5(8))* Pauline Bks. & Media.

Christian Focus Publications (CFP) Staff & Scrimshire, Hazel. The Special Baby. 2010. (Shaped Board Bks.). (ENG., Illus.). 10p. (J). (gr. -1-k). bds. 3.99 *(978-1-85792-464-0(9),* 9781857924640, Christian Focus) Christian Focus Pubns. GBR. Dist: Bookmasters Distribution.

Clark, Lisa. The Song of Christmas. Dyrud, Chris Wold, illus. 2014. (Arch Bks.). (ENG.). 16p. (J). (gr. k-4). pap. 2.49 *(978-0-7586-4605-7(4))* Concordia Publishing Hse.

Clark, Paul. The Good Wagon. Preston, Graham, illus. 2012. (J). lthr. *(978-1-921633-88-1(3),* Even Before Publishing) Wombat Bks.

David C. Cook Publishing Company Staff. Pencil Fun Book: Jesus Is Alive. 2007. (Pencil Fun Books Ser.). 16p. (J). (gr. 3-7). 9.90 *(978-0-7814-4521-4(3))* Cook, David C.

—Pencil Fun Book: Joeseph Saves His Family. 2007. (Pencil Fun Books Ser.). 16p. (J). (gr. 3-7). 9.90 *(978-0-7814-4522-1(1))* Cook, David C.

David, Juliet. The Shepherds, 1 vol. Wood, Hannah, illus. 2009. (Christmas Trio Ser.). 18p. (J). bds. 4.99 *(978-0-8254-7406-4(X),* Candle Bks.) Lion Hudson PLC GBR. Dist: Kregel Pubns.

—The Story of Jesus, 1 vol. Prole, Helen, illus. 2016. (Candle Bible for Toddlers Ser.). (ENG.). 26p. (J). pap. 6.99 *(978-1-78128-310-3(9),* Candle Bks.) Lion Hudson PLC GBR. Dist: Kregel Pubns.

dePaola, Tomie. The Miracles of Jesus. 2008. (ENG., Illus.). 32p. (J). (gr. -1-3). pap. 7.99 *(978-0-14-241068-4(3),* Puffin Books) Penguin Young Readers Group.

Derico, Laura Ring. Jesus Lives! the Easter Story. Krum, Ronda, illus. 2014. (Happy Day Ser.). (ENG.). 16p. (J). pap. 2.49 *(978-1-4143-9415-2(2))* Tyndale Hse. Pubs.

Dillon, Sally Pierson. Champions of the King: The Story of the Apostles. 2004. (Pathfinder Junior Book Club Ser.). (Illus.). 231p. (J). pap. 10.99 *(978-0-8280-1704-6(2),* 030-970) Review & Herald Publishing Assn.

Dobson, Shirley. Jesus Takes Care of Me Coloring Book: A Read-to-Me Bible Story Coloring Book about Jesus' Feeding 5,000 People. 2004. 1.49 *(978-0-8307-3540-2(2),* Gospel Light) Gospel Light Pubns.

Dodd, Sarah J. Christmas Stories for Little Angels. Kolanovic, Dubravka, illus. 2010. (Little Angels Ser.). (ENG.). 32p. (J). (gr. -1-k). 12.99 *(978-0-7459-6917-6(8))* Lion Hudson PLC GBR. Dist: Independent Pubs. Group.

Dodd, Sarah J. & Stone, Julia. The Christmas Story for Little Angels. Kolanovic, Dubravka, illus. 2016. (Little Angels Ser.). (ENG.). 32p. (J). (gr. -1-k). 7.99 *(978-0-7459-7610-5(7))* Lion Hudson PLC GBR. Dist: Independent Pubs. Group.

Dreyer, Nicole E. The Lost Coin. Collier-Morales, Roberta, illus. 2006. 16p. (J). 1.99 *(978-0-7586-0873-4(X))* Concordia Publishing Hse.

—Peter's Easter Story. Motoyama, Keiko, illus. 2004. (Arch Bks.). (ENG.). 16p. (J). 1.99 *(978-0-7586-0477-4(7))* Concordia Publishing Hse.

Dyson, Janet. Illustrated Children's Stories from the New Testament: All the Classic Bible Stories Retold with More Than 700 Beautiful Illustrations, Maps & Photographs. 2015. (ENG., Illus.). 256p. pap. 13.99 *(978-1-86147-458-2(X),* Armadillo) Anness Publishing GBR. Dist: National Bk. Network.

Ewald, Thomas C. New Testament Take-Home Bible Stories, Grades Preschool - 2: Easy-to-Make, Reproducible Mini-Books That Children Can Make & Keep. 2003. (ENG.). 128p. (gr. -1-4). pap. 12.99 *(978-0-88724-872-6(1))* Carson-Dellosa Publishing, LLC.

Ferguson, Sinclair B. Big Book of Bible Truths, Vol. 1. Apps, Fred, illus. 2012. (ENG.). 64p. (J). pap. 14.99 *(978-1-84550-371-0(6),* df9d28c0-46d4-40ea-9ab5-380c71e316dc) Christian Focus Pubns. GBR. Dist: Bookmasters Distribution.

Five Small Loaves & Two Small Fish. 2014. (Happy Day Ser.). (ENG., Illus.). 16p. (J). pap. 2.49 *(978-1-4143-9519-7(1))* Tyndale Hse. Pubs.

Follow That Star. (Hear Me Read Classroom Sets Ser.). 32.00 *(978-0-570-07172-3(0))* Concordia Publishing Hse.

Foster, Charles. Story of the Gospel. 2004. reprint ed. pap. 33.95 *(978-1-4191-1372-7(0))* Kessinger Publishing, LLC.

Frank, Penny. The Story of the Good Samaritan. rev. ed. (ENG., Illus.). 24p. pap. 2.99 *(978-0-7459-4119-6(2),* Lion Books) Lion Hudson PLC GBR. Dist: Trafalgar Square Publishing.

Frank, Penny & Allsopp, Sophie. The First Christmas. 2nd rev. ed. (ENG., Illus.). 24p. pap. 2.99 *(978-0-7459-4115-8(X),* Lion Books) Lion Hudson PLC GBR. Dist: Trafalgar Square Publishing.

—The First Easter. 2nd rev. ed. (ENG., Illus.). 24p. pap. 2.99 *(978-0-7459-4123-3(0),* Lion Books) Lion Hudson PLC GBR. Dist: Trafalgar Square Publishing.

Fryar, Jane L. Jesus Enters Jerusalem. Dorenkamp, Michelle, illus. 2004. (ENG.). 16p. (J). 1.99 *(978-0-7586-0641-9(9))* Concordia Publishing Hse.

Glaser, Rebecca. The Good Samaritan & Other Bible Stories. Ferenc, Bill, illus. 2015. (Holy Moly Bible Storybooks Ser.). (ENG.). 32p. (J). (gr. k-3). 12.99 *(978-1-5064-0251-2(8),* Sparkhouse Family) Augsburg Fortress, Pubs.

—The Holy Moly Christmas Story. Ferenc, Bill, illus. 2015. (Holy Moly Bible Storybooks Ser.). (ENG.). 32p. (J). (gr. k-3). 12.99 *(978-1-5064-0257-4(7),* Sparkhouse Family) Augsburg Fortress, Pubs.

—The Holy Moly Easter Story. Ferenc, Bill, illus. 2016. (Holy Moly Bible Storybooks Ser.). (ENG.). 32p. (J). (gr. k-3). 12.99 *(978-1-5064-0256-7(9),* Sparkhouse Family) Augsburg Fortress, Pubs.

—Saul Meets Jesus & Other Bible Stories. Ferenc, Bill, illus. 2016. (Holy Moly Bible Storybooks Ser.). (ENG.). 32p. (J). (gr. k-3). 12.99 *(978-1-5064-0255-0(0),* Sparkhouse Family) Augsburg Fortress, Pubs.

Goodings, Christina. Looking High & Low for One Lost Sheep. Ayliffe, Alex, illus. 2003. 32p. (J). pap. 9.99 *(978-0-7459-4524-8(4),* Lion Books) Lion Hudson PLC GBR. Dist: Trafalgar Square Publishing.

Goodwin, John. The Lion Book of Five-Minute Christmas Stories. Johnson, Richard A., illus. 2014. (ENG.). 48p. (J). (gr. k-2). pap. 12.99 *(978-0-7459-6926-8(7))* Lion Hudson PLC GBR. Dist: Independent Pubs. Group.

Gross, Arthur William. A Child's Garden of Bible Stories: The Classic Edition. 2004. (Illus.). 144p. (J). (gr. k-3). 8.99 *(978-0-570-07163-1(1))* Concordia Publishing Hse.

Hartman, Bob. Stories from the Stable. Hudson, Brett, illus. 2010. (ENG.). 128p. (J). (gr. k-2). pap. 6.99 *(978-0-7459-6109-5(6))* Lion Hudson PLC GBR. Dist: Independent Pubs. Group.

Hartman, Bob & Abel, Simone. Who Frightened the Fishermen? (Illus.). 48p. pap. 6.99 *(978-0-7459-4987-1(8))* Lion Hudson PLC GBR. Dist: Trafalgar Square Publishing.

Hartman, Sara. Mary Magdalene's Easter Story. Koehler, Ed, illus. 2005. (ENG.). 16p. (J). 1.99 *(978-0-7586-0722-5(9))* Concordia Publishing Hse.

—The Ten Plagues. Murphy, Terri, illus. 2006. 16p. (J). 1.99 *(978-0-7586-0875-8(6))* Concordia Publishing Hse.

Henley, Karyn. Jesus Is Alive! Easter. (Children's Ministry Folders). (Illus.). 8p. (gr. -1-k). 2.99 *(978-0-7847-0669-5(7),* 42219) Standard Publishing.

Heyer, Carol. The First Easter. 2nd ed. 2015. (Illus.). 32p. (J). pap. *(978-0-8249-1955-9(6),* Ideal Pubns.) Worthy Publishing.

Hill, Dave, illus. Jesus' Beach Breakfast - Arch Books. 2017. (Arch Books Ser.). (ENG.). (J). pap. 2.99 ***(978-0-7586-5737-4(4))*** Concordia Publishing Hse.

Hinkle, Cynthia. Star of Wonder. van der Sterre, Johanna, illus. 2005. (Arch Bks.). (ENG.). 16p. (J). 1.99 *(978-0-7586-0724-9(5))* Concordia Publishing Hse.

Hoffa, Darlene. Bible Stories about Jesus. 2004. (Illus.). 96p. (J). (gr. -1-k). pap. 11.95 *(978-0-937282-05-2(7),* RB36112); (gr. 1-2). pap. 11.95 *(978-0-937282-06-9(5),* RB36113); (gr. 3-4). pap. 11.95 *(978-0-937282-07-6(3),* RB36114) Rainbow Pubs. & Legacy Pr.

Holder, Jennifer. Peter Said Yes! 2014. (Happy Day Ser.). (ENG.). 16p. (J). pap. 2.49 *(978-1-4143-9525-8(6),* Happy Day) Tyndale Hse. Pubs.

Hook, Richard & Hook, Frances, illus. Jesus the Friend of Children. 6th ed. 2006. (David C Cook Read to Me Bible Stories Ser.). 112p. (J). (gr. 3-7). 14.99 *(978-0-7814-4390-6(3))* Cook, David C.

HOP, LLC. Hooked on Bible Stories NT Stories. 2006. 24.99 *(978-1-931020-98-5(1))* HOP, LLC.

Hovland, Stephenie. Lydia Believes. Dorenkamp Repa, Michelle, illus. 2014. (Arch Bks.). (ENG.). 16p. (J). (gr. k-4). pap. 2.49 *(978-0-7586-4607-1(0))* Concordia Publishing Hse.

Humble-Jackson, Sally. The Miracle Maker: The Greatest Story Ever Told. (Illus.). 48p. (J). pap. *(978-0-340-74958-6(X))* Hodder & Stoughton.

Intermediate/Bible Fun New Testament Coloring Book. 2006. (J). 14.99 *(978-1-59317-147-6(1))* Warner Pr., Inc.

James, Ben, illus. Los Tres Reyes Magos, the Three Wise Men. 2006. (J). bds. *(978-0-9786863-2-1(2))* ITRON Publishing.

Jesus Is Alive: Thematic Unit: Easter/Spring/New Life. (Scripture Bites Ser.). (J). (gr. -1). pap. 1.99 *(978-0-7847-9091-5(4))* Standard Publishing.

Johnson, Alice. Believe & You're There (4 vol. Set), 4 vols. 2009. pap. 24.99 *(978-1-60641-186-5(1))* Deseret Bk. Co.

Kieffer, Jean-Francois, et al. The Illustrated Gospel for Children. 2010. (Illus.). 107p. (J). *(978-1-936260-11-9(5))* Ignatius Pr.

Kovacs, Victoria. Peter/Paul Flip-Over Book. Ryley, David, illus. 2016. (Little Bible Heroes(tm) Ser.). (ENG.). 32p. (J). (gr. k-2). pap. 3.99 *(978-1-4336-4327-9(8),* B&H Kids) B&H Publishing Group.

Kramer, Janice. The Christmas Baby. Rooney, Ronnie, illus. 2008. (Arch Bks.). 16p. (J). (gr. k-4). pap. 1.99 *(978-0-7586-1454-4(3))* Concordia Publishing Hse.

Kueker, Donald, illus. The Easter Story According to Matthew. 2007. 32p. (J). per. 7.49 *(978-0-7586-1008-9(4))* Concordia Publishing Hse.

Larsen, Carolyn. Teachings of Jesus. 2012. (Standard Bible Storybook Ser.). (ENG., Illus.). 32p. (J). 7.99 *(978-0-7847-3565-7(4))* Standard Publishing.

Lashbrook, Marilyn. Out on a Limb. Britt, Stephanie McFetridge, illus. 2012. 32p. (J). pap. 8.00 *(978-1-935014-37-9(4))* Hutchings, John Pubs.

Lebarre, Erika, illus. Jesus Visits Mary & Martha - Arch Books. 2017. (ENG.). (J). pap. 2.99 ***(978-0-7586-5738-1(2))*** Concordia Publishing Hse.

Lindvall, Ella K. Read-Aloud Bible Stories, Vol. 5. 2015. (ENG.). 160p. (J). 15.99 *(978-0-8024-1264-5(5))* Moody Pubs.

Littleton, Mark. Stories Jesus Told. Moroney, Trace, illus. 2004. 20p. (J). bds. 10.99 *(978-0-8254-5519-3(7))* Kregel Pubns.

Lloyd-Jones, Sally. Biblia para Niños - Historias de Jesús: Cada historia susurra Su Nombre, 1 vol. 2008. (SPA.). 352p. (J). 17.99 *(978-0-8297-5606-7(X))* Vida Pubs.

—Found: Psalm 23, 1 vol. Jago, illus. 2017. (ENG.). 20p. (J). bds. 9.99 *(978-0-310-75750-4(9))* Zonderkidz.

Mackall, Dandi Daley. Zacchaeus & Jesus. Manuzak, Lisa, illus. 2016. (Flipside Stories Ser.). (ENG.). 48p. (J). 14.99 *(978-1-4964-1119-8(6))* Tyndale Hse. Pubs.

Mackenzie, Carine. Martha & Mary: Friends of Jesus. McLaren, Duncan, illus. 2014. (Bible Time Ser.). (ENG.). 32p. (J). (gr. -1-2). pap. 3.99 *(978-1-84550-167-9(5),* 71bfc45e-76c2-452a-846a-4937c26352a8) Christian Focus Pubns. GBR. Dist: Bookmasters Distribution.

MacKenzie, Carine. Mary: Mother of Jesus. McLaren, Duncan, illus. 2012. (Bible Time Ser.). (ENG.). 32p. (J). (gr. -1-2). pap. 3.99 *(978-1-84550-168-6(3),* 9781845501686) Christian Focus Pubns. GBR. Dist: Bookmasters Distribution.

—Peter: The Fisherman. McLaren, Duncan, illus. 2014. (Bible Time Ser.). (ENG.). 32p. (J). (gr. -1-2). pap. 3.99 *(978-1-84550-171-6(3),* df59357e-a2a3-4d70-96e4-8ff92835271b) Christian Focus Pubns. GBR. Dist: Bookmasters Distribution.

MacKenzie, Catherine. Jesus Christ the Best King of All. 2010. (Colour Bks.). (ENG., Illus.). 64p. (J). 6.99 *(978-1-84550-568-4(9),* 9781845505684) Christian Focus Pubns. GBR. Dist: Bookmasters Distribution.

Maier, Paul L. The Very First Christmas. 32p. (J). 9.99 *(978-0-570-07186-0(0))* Concordia Publishing Hse.

—The Very First Christmas. Ordaz, Francisco, illus. 2004. 20p. (J). (gr. -1-k). bds. 7.49 *(978-0-7586-0689-1(3))* Concordia Publishing Hse.

Miko, Christopher & Romines, Garrett. Unofficial Holy Bible for Minecrafters: A Children's Guide to the New Testament. 2016. (ENG.). 316p. (J). (gr. k). pap. 19.99 *(978-1-5107-0182-3(6))* Skyhorse Publishing Co., Inc.

Milbourne, Anna & Roberti, Alessandra. The Story of the Nativity. 2010. (Illus.). (J). 10.99 *(978-0-7945-2552-1(0),* Usborne) EDC Publishing.

Miller, Claire. The Parable of the Lost Sheep. van der Sterre, Johanna, illus. 2008. (Arch Bks.). 16p. (J). (gr. k-4). pap. 1.99 *(978-0-7586-1455-1(1))* Concordia Publishing Hse.

Mitzo Thompson, Kim, et al. I Can Read New Testament Bible Stories. 2017. (I Can Read Ser.). (ENG.). 32p. (J). pap. 4.99 ***(978-1-68322-197-5(4))*** Barbour Publishing, Inc.

Moore, Alan & Tavner, Gill. Judas Iscariot. Donnelly, Karen, illus. 2014. (New Testament Ser.). (ENG.). 64p. pap. 6.95 *(978-1-906230-28-9(5))* Real Reads Ltd. GBR. Dist: Casemate Pubs. & Bk. Distributors, LLC.

—Mary Magdalene. Donnelly, Karen, illus. 2014. (New Testament Ser.). (ENG.). 64p. pap. 6.95 *(978-1-906230-27-2(7))* Real Reads Ltd. GBR. Dist: Casemate Pubs. & Bk. Distributors, LLC.

Mother Stories from the New Testament (a. 2006. pap. 87.99 *(978-1-4219-7133-9(X))* IndyPublish.com.

Neeley, Deta Petersen & Neeley, Nathan Glen. Paul of Tarsus, V2: A Child's Story of the New Testament. 2011. 152p. 41.95 *(978-1-258-07519-4(9))* Literary Licensing, LLC.

Neff, LaVonne. The Jesus Book: 40 Bible Stories. Goffe, Toni, illus. 2004. (Life of Christ for Children Ser.). 84p. (gr. -1-k). 9.95 *(978-0-8294-1373-1(1))* Loyola Pr.

Ness, Shirley Fillmore. Mom's New Testament Bible Stories: Heroes & Scoundrels. 2013. 72p. pap. 12.95 *(978-1-4817-0816-6(3))* AuthorHouse.

Parker, Victoria & Dyson, Janet. The New Testament: All the Classic Bible Stories Retold with More Than 700 Beautiful Illustrations, Maps & Photographs. 2009. (ENG., Illus.). 256p. (J). (gr. 4-7). pap. 24.99 *(978-1-84476-604-8(7))* Anness Publishing GBR. Dist: National Bk. Network.

Piantedosi, John J. The Gospel for Children. Cioffi, Ben, illus. 2011. (J). pap. *(978-1-56548-370-5(7))* New City Community Pr.

Pingry, Patricia A. The Story of Jesus. Pulley, Kelly, illus. 2011. (Little Bible Bks). 22p. (J). (gr. -1-k). bds. 6.99 *(978-0-8249-1854-5(1),* Ideal Pubns.) Worthy Publishing.

—The Story of Loaves & Fishes. Venturi-Pickett, Stacy, illus. 2003. 26p. (J). bds. 6.95 *(978-0-8249-6518-1(3),* Ideal Pubns.) Worthy Publishing.

—Treasury of New Testament Heroes. 2005. (ENG., Illus.). 192p. (J). 8.97 *(978-0-8249-5494-9(7),* Ideal Pubns.) Worthy Publishing.

Pulley, Kelly, illus. The Very First Christmas, 1 vol. 2008. (Beginner's Bible Ser.). (ENG.). 32p. (J). pap. 47.76 *(978-0-310-71816-1(3))* Zonderkidz.

Qui, Joseph, illus. The Baby King - Arch Books. 2017. (ENG.). (J). pap. 2.99 ***(978-0-7586-5736-7(6))*** Concordia Publishing Hse.

Rabbit. Parables That Jesus Told. (J). pap. 19.95 *(978-0-689-80229-4(3),* Simon & Schuster Bks. For Young Readers) Simon & Schuster Bks. For Young Readers.

Rock, Lois. Tiny Tots Easter. Widdowson, Kay, illus. 2016. (Tiny Tots Ser.). (ENG.). 32p. (J). (gr. -1 — 1). 7.99 *(978-0-7459-6456-0(7))* Lion Hudson PLC GBR. Dist: Independent Pubs. Group.

Rottmann, Eric. Fruit of the Spirit. 2010. (Arch Bks.). 16p. (J). (gr. k-4). pap. 2.49 *(978-0-7586-1860-3(3))* Concordia Publishing Hse.

Rottmann, Erik. The Easter Victory. Billin-Frye, Paige, illus. 2006. (Arch Bks.). (ENG.). 16p. (J). (gr. -1-3). 2.49 *(978-0-7586-0869-7(1))* Concordia Publishing Hse.

—Jesus, My Good Shepherd. Miyake, Yoski, illus. 2005. (ENG.). 16p. (J). 1.99 *(978-0-7586-0725-6(3))* Concordia Publishing Hse.

—Timothy Joins Paul. Snyder, Joel, illus. 2005. (ENG.). 16p. (J). 1.99 *(978-0-7586-0506-1(4))* Concordia Publishing Hse.

Rucinski, Sandra. The Story of Jesus According to Tobin. 2009. 32p. pap. 14.50 *(978-1-60860-372-5(5),* Eloquent Bks.) Strategic Book Publishing & Rights Agency (SBPRA).

Schkade, Jonathan. Get up, Lazarus! Dorenkamp, Michelle, illus. 2004. (Arch Bks.). (ENG.). 16p. (J). 1.99 *(978-0-7586-0480-4(7))* Concordia Publishing Hse.

—Nicodemus & Jesus. Miyake, Yoshi, illus. 2014. (Arch Bks.). (ENG.). 16p. (J). (gr. k-4). pap. 2.49 *(978-0-7586-4606-4(2))* Concordia Publishing Hse.

Skevington, Andrea. The Story of Jesus. Ruta, Angelo, illus. 2008. (ENG.). 128p. (J). (gr. 2-4). pap. 16.95 *(978-0-7459-6121-7(5))* Lion Hudson PLC GBR. Dist: Independent Pubs. Group.

Skipworth, Kelly. Twelve Ordinary Men. 2009. (Illus.). 16p. (J). (gr. k-4). pap. 2.49 *(978-0-7586-1611-1(2))* Concordia Publishing Hse.

Smith, Brendan Powell. The Brick Bible, Set. 2013. (ENG., Illus.). 576p. 29.95 *(978-1-62636-177-5(0),* 263177) Skyhorse Publishing Co., Inc.

Smith, Cyncie. The Joyful Shepherd. 2004. (Illus.). 32p. (J). 9.99 *(978-1-56309-484-2(3))* New Hope Pubs.

Smouse, Phil. Born Again! 2004. 64p. (J). pap. 4.97 *(978-1-59310-099-5(X))* Barbour Publishing, Inc.

Strong, Cynda. The Resurrection. 2010. (Arch Bks.). 16p. (J). (gr. k-4). pap. 2.49 *(978-0-7586-1859-7(X))* Concordia Publishing Hse.

Teresa, Olive. The Story of the Good Samaritan. 2005. (Illus.). 16p. (J). 1.99 *(978-0-7586-0863-5(2))* Concordia Publishing Hse.

The Concerned Group, prod. See Baby Jesus. I.t. ed. 2012. (Illus.). 8p. (gr. 5). pap. 3.99 *(978-1-58938-004-2(5))* Concerned Communications.

Thompson, Kathy. Lessons from the Vine Second Grade Spring Quarter. Fahringer, Sarah, illus. 2012. 170p. pap. 35.00 *(978-1-935014-31-7(5),* Lessons From The Vine) Hutchings, John Pubs.

Twin Sisters(r) Staff, et al. My First New Testament Bible Stories. 2010. (J). (gr. k-2). bds. 12.99 *(978-1-59922-614-9(6))* Twin Sisters IP, LLC.

White, Angel. The Seed in My Pocket. 2009. 32p. pap. *(978-1-55452-391-7(5),* Guardian Bks.) Essence Publishing.

Widmer, Becky. Bible Awareness Series, 6 vols. Christian, Heather, illus. Date not set. (J). (gr. -1-18). 9.95 *(978-1-888537-00-0(0))* Publisher Plus.

Wildsmith, Brian. The Easter Story. Wildsmith, Brian, illus. 2004. (Illus.). 24p. (gr. -1-7). 18.00 *(978-0-8028-5189-5(4))* Eerdmans, William B. Publishing Co.

Williamson, Karen. Paul, 1 vol. Conner, Sarah, illus. 2016. (Candle Little Lambs Ser.). (ENG.). 24p. (J). pap. 2.99 *(978-1-78128-276-2(5),* Candle Bks.) Lion Hudson PLC GBR. Dist: Kregel Pubns.

Willoughby, R. Peter Goes Feet First! Buckley, Joel, illus. 2004. 64p. pap. *(978-1-85999-766-6(X))* Scripture Union.

Word Search: New Testament. (Illus.). 32p. (YA). (gr. 5-18). pap. 2.25 *(978-0-87162-497-0(4),* E4801) Warner Pr., Inc.

Zacchaeus: Physically Small but Spiritually Tall! (Illus.). 16p. (J). pap. 1.50 *(978-0-87162-871-8(6),* E6038) Warner Pr., Inc.

Zondervan Staff. The First Easter Ever, 1 vol. Jones, Dennis, illus. 2015. (ENG.). 32p. (J). pap. 1.99 *(978-0-310-74084-1(3))* Zonderkidz.

—The Very First Easter, 1 vol. Pulley, Kelly, illus. 2009. (Beginner's Bible Ser.). (ENG.). 32p. (J). pap. 1.99 *(978-0-310-71827-7(9));* pap. 47.76 *(978-0-310-71817-8(1))* Zonderkidz.

BIBLE STORIES—O.T.

Abraham. (Divertidas Historias Biblicas para Ninos Ser.). (SPA.). (J). 3.49 *(978-0-7899-0600-7(7),* 496647) Editorial Unilit.

Amery, H. Jonah & the Whale. 2004. (Bible Tales Readers Ser.). 16p. (J). lib. bdg. 12.95 *(978-1-58086-632-3(8),* Usborne); (Illus.). pap. 4.95 *(978-0-7945-0414-4(0))* EDC Publishing.

—Joseph & the Amazing Coat. 2004. (Bible Tales Readers Ser.). (SPA., Illus.). 16p. (J). pap. 4.95 *(978-0-7945-0417-5(5))* EDC Publishing.

—Moses in the Bulrushes. 2004. (Bible Tales Readers Ser.). (SPA., Illus.). 16p. (J). pap. 4.95 *(978-0-7945-0415-1(9))* EDC Publishing.

—Noah's Ark. rev. ed. 2004. (Bible Tales Readers Ser.). (Illus.). 16p. (J). lib. bdg. 12.95 *(978-1-58086-542-5(9))* EDC Publishing.

Amery, Heather. The Old Testament: A Collection of Bible Stories. 2004. (Children's Bible Ser.). (ENG., Illus.). 1p. (J). (gr. -1-3). 15.95 *(978-0-7460-3457-6(1))* EDC Publishing.

Arthur, Kay & Arndt, Janna. Abraham - God's Brave Explorer: Genesis 11-25. 2003. (ENG.). 208p. (J). pap., wbk. ed. 11.99 *(978-0-7369-0936-5(2),* 6909362) Harvest Hse. Pubs.

Audia, John P. The Creation Story: In Words & Sign Language. Spohn, David, illus. 2007. (ENG.). 16p. (gr. 3-7). 9.95 *(978-0-8146-3174-4(6))* Liturgical Pr.

B&H Editorial Staff, ed. Look & Find Bible: Old Testament Stories. Guile, Gill, illus. 2015. (Look & Find Ser.). (ENG.). 24p. (J). (gr. -1-3). 12.99 *(978-1-4336-8597-2(3),* B&H Kids) B&H Publishing Group.

Balsley, Tilda. Let My People Go! Richard, Ilene, illus. 2008. (ENG.). 32p. (J). (gr. k-3). per. 7.95 *(978-0-8225-7241-1(9),* Kar-Ben Publishing) Lerner Publishing Group.

—Oh No, Jonah! Silver, Jago, illus. 2012. (Bible Ser.). (ENG.). 32p. (J). (gr. k-4). lib. bdg. 17.95 *(978-0-7613-5139-9(6),* Kar-Ben Publishing) Lerner Publishing Group.

Balsley, Tilda & Blasley, Tilda. The Queen Who Saved Her People. Richard, Ilene, illus. 2011. (ENG.). 32p. (J). (gr. 3-5). pap. 7.95 *(978-0-7613-5093-4(4),* Kar-Ben Publishing) Lerner Publishing Group.

Balsley, Tilda & Jago. Oh No, Jonah! 2012. (Bible Ser.). (ENG., Illus.). 32p. (J). (gr. k-4). 7.95 *(978-0-7613-5140-5(X),* Kar-Ben Publishing) Lerner Publishing Group.

Barker, Stephen, illus. Noah's Ark. 2016. (ENG.). 12p. (J). (-k). bds. 9.99 *(978-1-62686-814-4(X),* Silver Dolphin Bks.) Readerlink Distribution Services, LLC.

Bergt, Carolyn. A Child's Garden of Bible Stories Workbooks: Old Testament Workbook. 80p. (gr. 1-3). wbk. ed. 9.95 *(978-0-7586-0473-6(4))* Concordia Publishing Hse.

Blyton, Enid. Noah & the Ark: See the Picture & Say the Word. 2012. (ENG.). 24p. (J). pap. 9.95 *(978-1-84135-746-1(4))* Award Pubns. Ltd. GBR. Dist: Parkwest Pubns., Inc.

Borlasca, Hector, illus. It's Too Crowded in Here! And Other Jewish Folktales. 2010. 64p. (J). pap. 7.95 *(978-0-87441-850-7(X))* Behrman Hse., Inc.

Bower, Gary. The Beautiful Garden of Eden. Chotiner, Barbara, illus. 2017. (Faith That God Built Book Ser.). (ENG.). 32p. (J). 14.99 *(978-1-4964-1743-5(7),* Tyndale Kids) Tyndale Hse. Pubs.

—A Patch on the Peak of Ararat. Chotiner, Barbara, illus. 2017. (Faith That God Built Book Ser.). (ENG.). 32p. (J). 14.99 *(978-1-4964-1744-2(5),* Tyndale Kids) Tyndale Hse. Pubs.

Bowman, Crystal. Joshua Crosses the Jordan, 1 vol. Sokolova, Valerie, illus. 2011. (I Can Read! / Bible Stories Ser.). (ENG.). 32p. (J). (gr. -1-2). pap. 3.99 *(978-0-310-72156-7(3))* Zonderkidz.

Bowman, Crystal & McKinley, Teri. A Is for Ark. Flowers, Luke, illus. 2017. (Our Daily Bread for Little Hearts Ser.). (ENG.). 18p. (J). (— 1). bds. 9.99 *(978-1-62707-599-2(2))* Discovery Hse. Pubs.

Brown, Laaren & Dorling Kindersley Publishing Staff. The Children's Illustrated Jewish Bible. Thomas, Eric, illus. 2007. (ENG.). 192p. (J). (gr. k-3). 19.99 *(978-0-7566-2665-5(X),* DK Children) Dorling Kindersley Publishing, Inc.

Burchett, Author Walter, BA. Christian children's questions & answers moses Volume 4. 2009. 32p. pap. 14.28 *(978-0-557-08123-3(8))* Lulu Pr., Inc.

Burgdorf, Larry. Daniel & the Lions. 2010. (Arch Bks.). (Illus.). 16p. (J). (gr. k-4). pap. 2.49 *(978-0-7586-1857-3(3))* Concordia Publishing Hse.

—How Enemies Became Friends. 2009. (Illus.). 16p. (J). (gr. k-4). pap. 2.49 *(978-0-7586-1612-8(0))* Concordia Publishing Hse.

—Jonah, The Runaway Prophet. 2011. 16p. pap. 2.49 *(978-0-7586-2582-3(0))* Concordia Publishing Hse.

Burkum, Rachel. Matthew's Bible Stories: Esther Is Brave. Keller, Matt, illus. 2011. 52p. (J). 10.00 *(978-1-59799-083-7(3))* Deaf Missions.

Burston, Chaim & Naiditch, Dov. Babel. Lumer, Marc, illus. 2016. (J). *(978-1-68115-514-2(1))* Behrman Hse., Inc.

Caduto, Michael J. In the Beginning: The Story of Genesis & Earth Activities for Children. 2004. 48p. 16.95 *(978-0-8091-6717-3(4),* 6717-4) Paulist Pr.

Caring for My Books: Bible Story: My Bible, God's Special Book. (Scripture Bites Ser.). (Illus.). (J). 7.99 *(978-0-7847-9025-0(6),* 00715) Standard Publishing.

Carlson, Melody. Noah & the Incredible Flood, 5 vols. Francisco, Wendy, illus. 2003. (Bible Adventure Club Ser.). 36p. wbk. ed. 19.99 incl. audio, cd-rom *(978-1-58134-336-6(1))* Crossway.

Collins Thoms, Susan. Noah's Ark. Stoop, Naoko, illus. 2013. (ENG.). 22p. (J). (— 1). bds. 6.95 *(978-1-4027-8549-8(6))* Sterling Publishing Co., Inc.

Coloring Book/Intermediate/Bible Fun Old Testament. 2006. (J). 14.99 *(978-1-59317-146-9(3))* Warner Pr., Inc.

Cousins, Lucy. Noah's Ark. Cousins, Lucy, illus. 2004. (ENG., Illus.). 22p. (J). (gr. k-k). bds. 6.99 *(978-0-7636-2446-0(2))* Candlewick Pr.

CrossStaff Publishing, creator. The Ten Commandments Movie Coloring Book: Part 1. 2007. (Epic Stories of the Bible Ser.). (Illus.). 32p. (J). (gr. -1-3). 5.99 *(978-0-9743876-1-1(4))* CrossStaff Publishing.

Dalmatian Press Staff. David & Goliath. 2004. (ENG., Illus.). 24p. (J). 2.99 *(978-1-4037-0971-4(8),* Spirit Pr.) Bendon, Inc.

—Jonah & the Big Fish. 2004. (ENG.). 24p. (J). 2.99 *(978-1-4037-0969-1(6),* Spirit Pr.) Bendon, Inc.

Dalmatian Press Staff, ed. Daniel in the Lion's Den. 2004. (ENG., Illus.). 24p. (J). 2.99 *(978-1-4037-0965-3(3),* Spirit Pr.) Bendon, Inc.

David & Goliath. 2003. (J). per. *(978-1-57657-980-0(8))* Paradise Pr., Inc.

David & Goliath: A Bible Story to Color. (Illus.). 16p. (J). pap. 1.50 *(978-0-87162-825-1(2),* E6018) Warner Pr., Inc.

David & Goliath Bible Sticker Book. 2003. (Illus.). 16p. (J). 2.98 *(978-1-4054-1554-5(1))* Parragon, Inc.

David C. Cook Publishing Company Staff. Daniel in the Lion's Den. 2003. (My Jesus Pocket Bks.). (Illus.). 32p. (J). pap., pap. 8.90 *(978-1-55513-136-4(0),* 1555131360) Cook, David C.

—Noah & the Floating Zoo. 2003. (My Jesus Pocket Bks.). (Illus.). 32p. (J). pap., pap. 8.90 *(978-1-55513-130-2(1),* 1555131301) Cook, David C.

—Pencil Fun Book: Noah Builds an Ark. 2007. (Pencil Fun Books Ser.). 16p. (J). (gr. 3-7). 9.90 *(978-0-7814-4523-8(X))* Cook, David C.

—Scripture Pictures - Journey through the Old Testament. 2004. 176p. 29.99 *(978-0-7814-4074-5(2),* 0781440742) Cook, David C.

David, Juliet. Daniel & the Lions' Den, 1 vol. Denham, Gemma, illus. 2009. (Candle Playbook Ser.). 18p. (J). bds. 7.99 *(978-0-8254-7385-2(3),* Candle Bks.) Lion Hudson PLC GBR. Dist: Kregel Pubns.

David, R. Noahs Ark. 2010. 12p. *(978-965-91286-1-7(4))* Sifrei Bet Shearim Ltd.

David, R., illus. Joseph & His Brothers. 2010. 12p. *(978-965-91286-0-0(6))* Sifrei Bet Shearim Ltd.

De Graaf, A. M. Dios Crea al Mundo. (Divertidas Historias Biblicas para Ninos Ser.).Tr. of God Makes the World. (SPA.). (J). 3.49 *(978-0-7899-0523-9(X),* 496640) Editorial Unilit.

DeVries, Catherine & Zondervan Staff. All Aboard with Noah!, 1 vol. Pulley, Kelly, illus. 2009. (Beginner's Bible Ser.). (ENG.). 12p. (J). bds. 7.99 *(978-0-310-71726-3(4))* Zonderkidz.

DeVries, Mike & Murphy, Troy. Exodus: The Sacred Journey. 2003. (No Limits Ser.). (ENG.). 112p. (gr. 3-7). per. 12.99 *(978-0-8341-5005-8(0),* 083-415-0050) Beacon Hill Pr. of Kansas City.

Doherty, Berlie. The Oxford Book of Bible Stories. Cockcroft, Jason, illus. 2014. (ENG.). 272p. pap. 18.95 *(978-0-19-278210-6(X))* Oxford Univ. Pr., Inc.

Domeij, Scoti & Kuhn, Pamela J. Favorite Bible Heroes: Grades 1&2. Galey, Chuck, illus. 2005. 96p. (J). (gr. 1-2). pap. 11.95 *(978-0-937282-24-3(3),* RB36198) Rainbow Pubs. & Legacy Pr.

Donaher, D F. & Bibleco. Daniel & the Lions. 2004. (Illus.). (J). bds. *(978-0-9746058-2-1(4),* Biblemania) Bibleco, Inc.

Dorn, Owen A. Ruth: A Love Story. 2003. (God's People Ser.). (Illus.). pap. 6.99 *(978-0-8100-1348-3(7))* Northwestern Publishing Hse.

Dowley, Tim. Noah's Ark Pop-Up. Martin, Stuart, illus. 2007. 6p. (J). bds. 14.99 *(978-0-8254-7330-2(6),* Candle Bks.) Lion Hudson PLC GBR. Dist: Kregel Pubns.

Downer, Maggie, illus. Noah: My First Storybook. 2016. (ENG.). 48p. (J). (gr. -1-12). bds. 9.99 *(978-1-86147-776-7(7),* Armadillo) Anness Publishing GBR. Dist: National Bk. Network.

Dudley, Becki. Remarkable Rescue: Saved on Noah's Ark. 2016. (ENG.). 12p. (J). bds. 7.99 *(978-0-89051-976-9(5))* Master Bks.

Dyson, Janet. Illustrated Children's Stories from the Old Testament: All the Classic Bible Stories Retold with More Than 700 Beautiful Illustrations, Maps & Photographs. 2014. (ENG., Illus.). 256p. pap. 13.99 *(978-1-86147-471-1(7),* Armadillo) Anness Publishing GBR. Dist: National Bk. Network.

Eder, Enelle. Create & Take Bible Crafts: Old Testament Heroes. 2004. 96p. (J). (gr. k-6). pap. 11.95 *(978-1-58411-006-4(6))* Rainbow Pubs. & Legacy Pr.

Ewald, Thomas C. Old Testament Take-Home Bible Stories, Grades Pk - 2: Easy-to-Make, Reproducible Mini-Books That Children Can Make & Keep. 2003. (ENG.). 128p. (gr. -1-2). pap. 12.99 *(978-0-88724-871-9(3))* Carson-Dellosa Publishing, LLC.

Fish-Ocean Life: Bible Story: Jonah & the Big Fish. (Scripture Bites Ser.). (Illus.). (J). 7.99 *(978-0-7847-9009-0(4),* 00706) Standard Publishing.

Frank, Penny. David & Goliath. Morris, Tony, illus. 2nd rev. ed. (ENG.). 24p. pap. 2.99 *(978-0-7459-4111-0(7),* Lion Books) Lion Hudson PLC GBR. Dist: Trafalgar Square Publishing.

—Let My People Go! 2nd rev. ed. (ENG., Illus.). 24p. pap. 2.99 *(978-0-7459-4108-0(7),* Lion Books) Lion Hudson PLC GBR. Dist: Trafalgar Square Publishing.

—La Nueva Familia de Rut.Tr. of Ruth's New Family. (SPA.). (J). 1.99 *(978-1-56063-785-1(4),* 490315) Editorial Unilit.

—The Princess & the Baby. 2nd rev. ed. (ENG., Illus.). 24p. pap. 2.99 *(978-0-7459-4107-3(9),* Lion Books) Lion Hudson PLC GBR. Dist: Trafalgar Square Publishing.

Freedom/Flag/God/Country: Bible Story: God Frees His People. (Scripture Bites Ser.). (Illus.). (J). 7.99 *(978-0-7847-9015-1(9),* 00708) Standard Publishing.

Froeb, Lori C. God's Creation, 1 vol. Rinaldo, Luana, illus. 2008. 12p. (J). bds. 7.99 *(978-0-8254-5545-2(6))* Kregel Pubns.

Fry & Hooper. Little Books of the Bible Stories from the Old Testament. 2004. (J). 14.95 *(978-0-8249-5445-1(9),* Ideal Pubns.) Worthy Publishing.

Gadot, A. S. Tower of Babel. Rébora, Cecilia, illus. 2010. (Adult & Young Adult Bks.). (ENG.). 32p. (J). (gr. k-3). pap. 7.95 *(978-0-8225-9952-4(X),* Kar-Ben Publishing) Lerner Publishing Group.

Gay, Susana. Jonah & the Big Fish. 2017. (Illus.). 16p. (J). ***(978-0-8249-1666-4(2))*** Worthy Publishing.

Goldsack, Gaby. Little Lion & Daniel: A Finger Puppet Play & Read Story. 2003. (Snuffleheads Ser.). (Illus.). 14p. (J). 7.99 *(978-0-8254-7268-8(7))* Kregel Pubns.

Goldsack, Gaby & Dawson, Peter. Noah's Ark: My Little Bible Book. Lawson, Peter, illus. 2003. 12p. (J). bds. 10.99 *(978-0-8254-7266-4(0),* Candle Bks.) Lion Hudson PLC GBR. Dist: Kregel Pubns.

Gould, Robert. Father & Son Read-Aloud Old Testament Stories. Gurin, Lara, illus. 2010. (Father & Son Read-Aloud Stories Ser.). (ENG.). 60p. (J). (gr. -1-k). 14.95 *(978-1-929945-73-3(6))* Big Guy Bks., Inc.

Green, John. Old Testament Scenes Stained Glass Coloring Book. 2009. (Dover Stained Glass Coloring Book Ser.). (ENG., Illus.). 32p. (gr. 3-5). pap. 6.99 *(978-0-486-46763-4(5))* Dover Pubns., Inc.

Groffman, Simcha. Simcha's Kinder Torah: Torah Stories & Thoughts on the Weekly Parasha. 2003. (Illus.). 320p. 19.95 *(978-1-58330-658-1(7))* Feldheim Pubs.

Haidle, Helen & Haidle, David. Creation Story for Children. Haidle, Helen & Haidle, David, illus. 2009. (Illus.). 32p. (J). 14.99 *(978-0-89051-565-5(4))* Master Bks.

Ham, Ken. A Special Door. Looney, Bill, illus. 2016. (ENG.). 24p. (J). 14.99 *(978-0-89051-977-6(3))* Master Bks.

Hansen, Janis. Creation: God's Wonderful Gift, 5 vols. Fransisco, Wendy, illus. 2003. (Bible Adventure Club Ser.). 36p. wbk. ed. 19.99 incl. audio, cd-rom *(978-1-58134-292-5(6))* Crossway.

—David & His Giant Battle, 5 vols. Francisco, Wendy, illus. 2003. (Bible Adventure Club Ser.). 36p. wbk. ed. 19.99 incl. audio, cd-rom *(978-1-58134-321-2(3))* Crossway.

—Jonah & His Amazing Voyage, 5 vols. Francisco, Wendy, illus. 2003. (Bible Adventure Club Ser.). 36p. wbk. ed. 19.99 incl. audio, cd-rom *(978-1-58134-326-7(4))* Crossway.

Hartman, Bob. Noah's Big Boat. Samuel, Janet, illus. 2007. (ENG.). 32p. (J). (gr. -1-k). pap. 9.95 *(978-0-7459-4995-6(9))* Lion Hudson PLC GBR. Dist: Independent Pubs. Group.

Henley, Claire. Jonah & the Big Fish. 2009. (All Join In Ser.). (ENG.). 16p. (J). (gr. k — 1). bds. 6.99 *(978-0-7459-6075-3(8))* Lion Hudson PLC GBR. Dist: Independent Pubs. Group.

Hodges, George. Castle of Zion. 2006. pap. 26.95 *(978-1-4286-3420-6(7))* Kessinger Publishing, LLC.

—The Garden of Eden: Stories from the Fir. 2006. (Illus.). pap. 26.95 *(978-1-4254-9577-0(X))* Kessinger Publishing, LLC.

HOP, LLC. Hooked on Bible Stories Old Testament Stories. 2006. 24.99 *(978-1-931020-97-8(3))* HOP, LLC.

Hyatt, Greg. Moses & the Bronze Snake. 2008. (Arch Bks.). (Illus.). 16p. (J). (gr. k-4). pap. 1.99 *(978-0-7586-1456-8(X))* Concordia Publishing Hse.

Incrocci, Rick, illus. Psalms for Toddlers. 2012. 32p. (J). pap. 12.00 *(978-1-935014-43-0(9))* Hutchings, John Pubs.

Insects/Bugs/Small Creatures: Bible Story: God Made All Creatures - Great & Small. (Scripture Bites Ser.). (Illus.). (J). (gr. -1). 7.99 *(978-0-7847-9005-2(1),* 00702) Standard Publishing.

Jensen, Rebecca Ridges & Jensen, Daniel Loran. The Creation-From the Book of Moses. 2007. (Illus.). 32p. (J). 15.99 *(978-1-55517-894-9(4))* Cedar Fort, Inc./CFI Distribution.

Jesus Feeds the Five Thousand: Thematic Unit: Nutrition. (Scripture Bites Ser.). (J). (gr. -1). pap. 1.99 *(978-0-7847-9079-3(5))* Standard Publishing.

Jesus' Friends Follow Him: Thematic Unit: Friendship. (Scripture Bites Ser.). (J). (gr. -1). pap. 5.99 *(978-0-7847-9096-0(5));* pap. 1.99 *(978-0-7847-9097-7(3))* Standard Publishing.

Jesus Grows Up to Do His Father's Work: Thematic Unit: Community Helpers. (Scripture Bites Ser.). (J). (gr. -1). pap. 1.99 *(978-0-7847-9089-2(2))* Standard Publishing.

Johnson, Alice W. Believe & You're There: When David Slew Goliath, Vol. 9. 2010. (Illus.). 96p. (J). pap. 6.99 *(978-1-60641-816-1(5))* Deseret Bk. Co.

—Believe & You're There: When Esther Saved, Vol. 8. 2010. (Illus.). 96p. (J). pap. 6.99 *(978-1-60641-815-4(7))* Deseret Bk. Co.

Jonah. (J). bds. 5.95 *(978-0-87162-984-5(4))* Warner Pr., Inc.

Jonah Bible Sticker Book. 2003. (Illus.). 16p. (J). 2.98 *(978-1-4054-1555-2(X))* Parragon, Inc.

AB

Joseph & His Coat of Many Colors. 2003. (J). per. *(978-1-57657-982-4(4))* Paradise Pr., Inc.
Jules, Jacqueline. Benjamin & the Silver Goblet. Ugliano, Natascia, illus. 2009. (Bible Ser.). (ENG.). 32p. (J). (gr. k-4). 17.95 *(978-0-8225-8757-6(2),* Kar-Ben Publishing) Lerner Publishing Group.
—Sarah Laughs. Ugliano, Natascia, illus. 2008. (Bible Ser.). 32p. (J). (gr. k-4). lib. bdg. 17.95 *(978-0-8225-7216-9(8));* (ENG.). per. 9.95 *(978-0-8225-9934-0(1))* Lerner Publishing Group. (Kar-Ben Publishing).
Jules, Jacqueline & Hechtkopf, Jacqueline. Miriam in the Desert. Ugliano, Natascia, illus. 2010. (Bible Ser.). (ENG.). 32p. (J). (gr. k-3). 17.95 *(978-0-7613-4494-0(2));* pap. 8.95 *(978-0-7613-4496-4(9))* Lerner Publishing Group. (Kar-Ben Publishing).
Juravel, Rabbi. Parsha with Rabbi Juravel: Bereishis. Toron, Eli, illus. 2005. (J). 26.95 *(978-1-931681-83-4(X))* Israel Bookshop Pubns.
Kennedy, Pamela & Brady, Anne Kennedy. Five-Minute Bible Devotions for Children: Stories from the Old Testament. Wummer, Amy, illus. 2012. 48p. (J). spiral bd. 15.99 *(978-0-8249-5638-7(9),* Ideal Pubns.) Worthy Publishing.
Killian, Rick & Yaxley, Trevor. The Making of the Ten Commandments. 2008. (Illus.). 120p. 16.99 *(978-0-9743876-8-0(1))* CrossStaff Publishing.
Kimmel, Eric A. The Story of Esther. Weber, Jill, illus. 2011. (ENG.). 32p. (J). (gr. -1-3). 16.95 *(978-0-8234-2223-4(2))* Holiday Hse., Inc.
Kneen, Maggie. Two by Two: The Story of Noah & the Ark. 2008. (ENG., Illus.). 12p. (J). *(978-1-55168-324-9(5))* Fenn, H. B. & Co., Ltd.
Knudsen, Michelle. Noah's Ark. Santoro, Christopher, illus. 2016. (Lift-The-Flap Ser.). (ENG.). 14p. (J). (gr. -1 — 1). bds. 6.99 *(978-0-553-53537-2(4),* Random Hse. Bks. for Young Readers) Random Hse. Children's Bks.
Koralek, Jenny. The Moses Basket. Baynes, Pauline, illus. 2004. 32p. (J). 16.00 *(978-0-8028-5251-9(3))* Eerdmans, William B. Publishing Co.
Kovacs, Victoria. Samuel/the Little Maid Flip-Over Book. Krome, Mike, illus. 2015. (Little Bible Heroes(tm) Ser.). (ENG.). 32p. (J). (gr. k-2). pap. 3.99 *(978-1-4336-8718-1(6),* B&H Kids) B&H Publishing Group.
Laff, Becky. Joseph the Dreamer. Laff, Becky, illus. 2016. (ENG., Illus.). 48p. (J). (gr. k-4). 17.99 *(978-1-4677-7845-9(1),* Blackbirch Pr., Inc.) Lerner Publishing Group.
Lafferty, Jill C., ed. Old Testament Adventures: A Spark Story Bible Play & Learn Book. Grosshauser, Peter, illus. 2016. (ENG.). 80p. (J). (gr. -1-3). 9.99 *(978-1-5064-1765-3(5),* Sparkhouse Family) Augsburg Fortress, Pubs.
Larcombe, Jennifer Rees. The Terrible Giant. Björkman, Steve, illus. 2004. (Best Bible Stories Ser.). 24p. (gr. -1-3). 2.99 *(978-1-58134-054-9(0))* Crossway.
Larsen, Carolyn. Egypt to the Promised Land. 2012. (Standard Bible Storybook Ser.). (ENG., Illus.). 32p. (J). 7.99 *(978-0-7847-3564-0(6))* Standard Publishing.
Lashbrook, Marilyn. God, Please Send Fire. Sharp, Chris, illus. 2012. 32p. (J). pap. 8.00 *(978-1-935014-42-3(0))* Hutchings, John Pubs.
—I May Be Little. Britt, Stephanie McFetridge, illus. 2012. 32p. (J). pap. 8.00 *(978-1-935014-41-6(2))* Hutchings, John Pubs.
—Who Needs a Boat? Britt, Stephanie McFetridge, illus. 2012. 32p. (J). pap. 8.00 *(978-1-935014-39-3(0))* Hutchings, John Pubs.
Lee, Young Shin & Rogers, Buddy. Fights, Flights, & the Chosen Ones, 1 vol. Burner, Brett & Earls, J. S., eds. Hwang, Jung Sun, illus. 2008. (Z Graphic Novels / Manga Bible Ser.). (ENG.). 160p. (J). (gr. 4-7). pap. 6.99 *(978-0-310-71289-3(0))* Zondervan.
Lehman-Wilzig, Tami. Green Bible Stories for Children. Bernhard, Durga Yael, illus. 2011. (Bible Ser.). (ENG.). 48p. (J). (gr. 3-5). pap. 7.95 *(978-0-7613-5136-8(1),* Kar-Ben Publishing) Lerner Publishing Group.
—Green Bible Stories for Children. Bernhard, Durga, illus. 2011. (Bible Ser.). (ENG.). 48p. (J). (gr. 3-5). lib. bdg. 17.95 *(978-0-7613-5135-1(3),* Kar-Ben Publishing) Lerner Publishing Group.
—Tasty Bible Stories: A Menu of Tales & Matching Recipes. Kahn, Katherine Janus, illus. 2003. (ENG.). 64p. (J). (gr. 3-5). pap. 10.95 *(978-1-58013-080-6(1),* Kar-Ben Publishing) Lerner Publishing Group.
Lehmann, Charles. God Made It for You! The Story of Creation. Kemly, Kathleen, illus. 2007. 32p. (J). (gr. -1-3). 14.99 *(978-0-7586-1287-8(7))* Concordia Publishing Hse.
Lottridge, Celia Barker. Stories from Adam & Eve to Ezekiel, 1 vol. Clement, Gary, illus. 2004. (ENG.). 144p. (J). 24.95 *(978-0-88899-490-5(7))* Groundwood Bks. CAN. Dist: Publishers Group West (PGW).
Ludy, Mark. Noah: A Wordless Picture Book. 2014. (ENG., Illus.). 64p. (J). 19.95 *(978-0-87486-639-1(1))* Plough Publishing Hse.
Mackall, Dandi Daley. Jonah & the Fish. Marlin, Lissy, illus. 2016. (Flipside Stories Ser.). (ENG.). 48p. (J). 14.99 *(978-1-4964-1120-4(X))* Tyndale Hse. Pubs.
MacKenzie, Carine. Bible Heroes Elijah. 2005. (Bible Art Ser.). (ENG.). 16p. (J). act. bk. ed. 1.99 *(978-1-84550-089-4(X),* 7336c626-8c11-4b07-8c54-3f395d9c105e) Christian Focus Pubns. GBR. Dist: Bookmasters Distribution.
—Bible Heroes Gideon. 2005. (Bible Art Ser.). (ENG.). 16p. (J). act. bk. ed. 1.99 *(978-1-84550-090-0(3),* c413bdb8-6ed2-450e-92b3-3dfe97e1313e) Christian Focus Pubns. GBR. Dist: Bookmasters Distribution.
—Bible Heroes Joseph. 2005. (Bible Art Ser.). (ENG.). 16p. (J). act. bk. ed. 1.99 *(978-1-84550-091-7(1),* 75cca856-6fd6-454b-a66f-ffec2e980d5d) Christian Focus Pubns. GBR. Dist: Bookmasters Distribution.
—Bible Heroes Ruth. 2013. (Bible Art Ser.). (ENG.). 16p. (J). act. bk. ed. 1.99 *(978-1-84550-092-4(X),* 1dddfc7c-5d21-456d-9725-776cca86c003) Christian Focus Pubns. GBR. Dist: Bookmasters Distribution.
—Gideon: Soldier of God. McLaren, Duncan, illus. 2014. (Bible Time Ser.). (ENG.). 32p. (J). (gr. -1-2). pap. 3.99 *(978-1-84550-196-9(9),* 22ac2a20-0b2a-400f-9d67-de54ce3bd1b3) Christian Focus Pubns. GBR. Dist: Bookmasters Distribution.
Mackenzie, Carine. Jonah: The Runaway Preacher. McLaren, Duncan, illus. 2013. (Bible Time Ser.). (ENG.). 32p. (J). (gr. -1-2). pap. 3.99 *(978-1-84550-165-5(9),* 95a31c43-f5e1-4925-9bde-d4dcdcad6fea) Christian Focus Pubns. GBR. Dist: Bookmasters Distribution.
—Jonathan: The Faithful Friend. Apps, Fred, illus. 2007. (Bible Wise Ser.). (ENG.). 32p. (J). (gr. -1-2). 3.99 *(978-1-84550-289-8(2),* b8e20eae-3f28-43e7-b1a4-6f744d81f802) Christian Focus Pubns. GBR. Dist: Bookmasters Distribution.
—Joshua: The Brave Leader. McLaren, Duncan, illus. 2012. (Bible Time Ser.). (ENG.). 32p. (J). (gr. -1-2). pap. 3.99 *(978-1-84550-166-2(7),* e6a48189-9df6-43cf-8264-6ef9b35f7d53) Christian Focus Pubns. GBR. Dist: Bookmasters Distribution.
—Moses the Shepherd: Chosen by God. Kennedy, Graham, illus. 2008. (Bible Alive Ser.). (ENG.). 24p. (J). 3.99 *(978-1-84550-331-4(7),* 018499d7-3c39-4c05-b67c-092fea1603a3) Christian Focus Pubns. GBR. Dist: Bookmasters Distribution.
MacKenzie, Carine. Naaman: The Soldier. Apps, Fred, illus. 2015. (Famous Bible Stories (Board Books) Ser.). (ENG.). 12p. (J). (gr. -1-k). bds. 3.99 *(978-1-84550-085-6(7),* 9e95fa53-f8d4-4c5b-9669-013193ed60d9, Christian Focus) Christian Focus Pubns. GBR. Dist: Bookmasters Distribution.
Mackenzie, Carine. Ruth's Journey. Apps, Fred, illus. 2015. (Famous Bible Stories (Board Books) Ser.). (ENG.). 12p. (J). (gr. -1-k). bds. 3.99 *(978-1-84550-086-3(5),* b0ee13f3-ba02-4e72-a971-8c6d4381502a, Christian Focus) Christian Focus Pubns. GBR. Dist: Bookmasters Distribution.
Mackenzie, Carine & Ross, Neil M. Nehemiah: Builder for God. McLaren, Duncan, illus. 2014. (Bible Time Ser.). (ENG.). 32p. (J). (gr. -1-2). pap. 3.99 *(978-1-84550-169-3(1),* 284cd8f6-9c32-462e-8703-7499eb87adcf) Christian Focus Pubns. GBR. Dist: Bookmasters Distribution.
MacLean, Ruth. The Man Who Ran: A Puzzle Book about Jonah. rev. ed. 2009. (Puzzle Ser.). (ENG., Illus.). 24p. (J). 4.99 *(978-1-84550-496-0(8),* 9781845504960) Christian Focus Pubns. GBR. Dist: Bookmasters Distribution.
—The Shepherd King: A Puzzle Book about David. rev. ed. 2009. (Puzzle Ser.). (ENG., Illus.). 24p. (J). 4.99 *(978-1-84550-498-4(4),* c4a1705c-30c9-4390-96f6-fa425d40387e) Christian Focus Pubns. GBR. Dist: Bookmasters Distribution.
Maier, Paul. The Real Story of the Flood. Barrett, Robert, illus. 2008. 32p. (J). (gr. 4-7). 16.99 *(978-0-7586-1267-0(2))* Concordia Publishing Hse.
Maier, Paul L. The Real Story of the Exodus. Taylor, Gerad, illus. 2009. 32p. (J). (gr. -1-3). 16.99 *(978-0-7586-1268-7(0))* Concordia Publishing Hse.
Martin, Jr., Bill & Sampson, Michael. Noah, Noah, What Do You See?, 1 vol. 2017. (ENG., Illus.). 30p. (J). bds. 7.99 *(978-0-7180-8949-8(9))* Nelson, Thomas Inc.
McCombs, Margi. Noah's Ark. Fox, Lisa, illus. 2014. (ENG.). 10p. (J). (gr. -1-k). bds. 7.99 *(978-0-545-60557-1(1),* Little Shepherd) Scholastic, Inc.
Melania, Mother. Baby Moses. Gillis, Bonnie, illus. 2008. (Old Testament Stories for Children Ser.). (ENG.). 28p. (gr. -1-3). pap. 8.95 *(978-1-888212-97-6(7))* Ancient Faith Publishing.
—Jonah's Journey to the Deep. Gillis, Bonnie, illus. 2009. (Old Testament Stories for Children Ser.). (ENG.). 28p. (J). pap. 8.95 *(978-1-888212-59-4(4))* Ancient Faith Publishing.
Mendenhall, Cheryl, illus. Joseph & His Coat of Many Colors. 2004. (ENG.). 24p. (J). 2.99 *(978-1-4037-0966-0(1),* Spirit Pr.) Bendon, Inc.
Metaxas, Eric, ed. Khalil & the Big Gulp. 2003. (Illus.). 16p. (J). 6.99 *(978-0-310-70471-3(5))* Zondervan.
Miles, David, illus. Elijah, God's Mighty Prophet, 1 vol. 2016. (I Can Read! / Adventure Bible Ser.). (ENG.). 32p. (J). pap. 3.99 *(978-0-310-75081-9(4))* Zonderkidz.
—Joseph the Dreamer. 2015. 32p. (J). *(978-1-5182-0994-9(7))* Zonderkidz.
Mitzo Thompson, Kim, et al. Rise & Shine: Sing-A-Story Book with CD. 2017. (Let's Share a Story Ser.). (ENG.). 16p. (J). (-5). bds. 9.99 ***(978-1-68322-199-9(0))*** Barbour Publishing, Inc.
Mortimer, F. L. Precept upon Precept. 192p. (J). pap. 7.99 *(978-1-85792-587-6(4))* Christian Focus Pubns. GBR. Dist: Riverside.
My Five Senses: Bible Story: Young Samuel Listens to God's Voice. (Scripture Bites Ser.). (Illus.). (J). 7.99 *(978-0-7847-9022-9(1),* 00713) Standard Publishing.
Naha, Ed. The Ten Commandments Movie Storybook. 2007. (Epic Stories of the Bible Ser.). (Illus.). 77p. (J). (gr. -1-3). 14.99 *(978-0-9743876-4-2(9))* CrossStaff Publishing.
Neff, Merlin L. Conquering Heroes. 2008. (J). *(978-0-8163-2265-7(1))* Pacific Pr. Pubns.
Nilsen, Lenie. The Elephant & the Dove. 2013. (Illus.). 42p. (J). 18.99 *(978-1-940473-04-8(7))* Stonebridge Pubns.
Noah & the Ark. 2004. 5.95 *(978-1-57264-240-9(8))* Parsons Technology.
Noah & the Ark. Date not set. (J). 8.95 *(978-0-88271-533-9(X),* 10521) Regina Pr., Malhame & Co.
Noah's Ark: A Bible Story to Color. (Illus.). 16p. (J). pap. 1.50 *(978-0-87162-823-7(6),* E6017) Warner Pr., Inc.
Nolan, Allia Zobel. The Story of Noah's Ark. Moroney, Trace, illus. 2006. 24p. (J). pap. 3.99 *(978-0-8254-5532-2(4))* Kregel Pubns.
Okrant, Mark. Judson's Island. 2006. per. 10.95 *(978-0-9791757-2-5(0))* Oak Manor Publishing, Inc.
Oren, Miriam & Schram, Peninnah. A Tree in the Garden: A New Vision. Whyte, Alice, illus. 2004. vii, 55p. pap. *(978-0-9752958-0-9(2))* Nora Hse.
Parry, Alan & Parry, Linda. Look for the Rainbow: Look Through the Telescope, Lift the Flaps, Work the Puzzles, See the Pop-Ups, & Enjoy Hours of Fun with Noah. 2003. (Illus.). 14p. 12.99 *(978-1-85608-212-9(1))* Hunt, John Publishing Ltd. GBR. Dist: Send The Light Distribution LLC.
Pasquali, Elena. Two-Minute Bible Stories. Smee, Nicola, illus. 2009. (Two-Minute Stories Ser.). (ENG.). 44p. (J). (gr. -1-k). 12.99 *(978-0-7459-6053-1(7),* Lion Children's) Lion Hudson PLC GBR. Dist: Independent Pubs. Group.
Pearson, Mary R. & Kuhn, Pamela J. Favorite Bible Heroes: Grades 3&4. Galey, Chuck, illus. 2005. 96p. (J). (gr. 3-4). pap. 11.95 *(978-0-937282-25-0(1),* RB36199) Rainbow Pubs. & Legacy Pr.
Pelfrey, Wanda B. & Kuhn, Pamela J. Favorite Bible Heroes: Ages 2&3. Galey, Chuck, illus. 2005. 96p. (J). pap. 11.95 *(978-0-937282-22-9(7),* RB36196) Rainbow Pubs. & Legacy Pr.
Pennington, Jack & Tank, Daniel, illus. Joseph. 2004. 87p. (J). pap. *(978-0-8280-1855-5(3))* Review & Herald Publishing Assn.
Perseghetti, Jackie & Perseghetti, Jonie. Faith Factor OT: Thru-the-Bible Devotions. 2007. (ENG., Illus.). 384p. (YA). (gr. 3-7). per. 16.99 *(978-0-7814-4458-3(6))* Cook, David C.
Petach, Heidi. Daniel & the Lions. Dickson, Bill, illus. 2013. (Happy Day Ser.). (ENG.). 16p. (J). pap. 2.49 *(978-1-4143-9298-1(2))* Tyndale Hse. Pubs.
Pingry, Patricia A. Bible Story Cards: The Story of Noah. 2006. (ENG., Illus.). 10p. 7.95 *(978-0-8249-1703-6(0),* Ideal Pubns.) Worthy Publishing.
—David & Goliath: A Story about Trusting in God: Based on 1 Samuel 17:1/50. Munger, Nancy, illus. 2005. (Children of the Bible Ser.). (ENG.). 23p. (J). bds. 6.95 *(978-0-8249-6570-9(1),* Ideal Pubns.) Worthy Publishing.
—Jonah & the Fish: Based on Jonah 1-3:3. Venturi-Pickett, Stacy, illus. 2005. (Stories from the Bible Ser.). (ENG.). 26p. (J). (gr. -1-k). bds. 6.95 *(978-0-8249-6626-3(0),* Ideal Pubns.) Worthy Publishing.
—Joseph & the Dream: Based on Genesis 37/46:7. Spence, Jim, illus. 2005. (Stories from the Bible Ser.). (ENG.). 26p. (J). (gr. -1-k). bds. 6.95 *(978-0-8249-6625-6(2),* Ideal Pubns.) Worthy Publishing.
—The Story of Adam & Eve. Thornburgh, Rebecca, illus. 2003. (ENG.). 24p. (J). bds. 6.95 *(978-0-8249-4229-8(9),* Ideal Pubns.) Worthy Publishing.
—The Story of David. Pulley, Kelly, illus. 2012. (J). *(978-0-8249-1886-6(X),* Ideal Pubns.) Worthy Publishing.
—The Story of Noah. Venturi-Pickett, Stacy, illus. 2007. (ENG.). 32p. (J). (gr. -1-3). per. 3.99 *(978-0-8249-5569-4(2),* Ideal Pubns.) Worthy Publishing.
—Treasury of Old Testament Heroes. 2005. (Illus.). 192p. (J). 8.97 *(978-0-8249-4258-8(2),* Ideal Pubns.) Worthy Publishing.
Pingry, Patricia A. & Venturi-Pickett, Stacy, trs. The Story of Creation. Venturi-Pickett, Stacy, illus. 2003. (Illus.). 26p. (J). bds. 7.95 *(978-0-8249-6504-4(3),* Ideal Pubns.) Worthy Publishing.
Pinkney, Jerry. Noah's Ark. 2004. (J). (gr. k-3). 29.95 *(978-1-55592-533-8(2))* Weston Woods Studios, Inc.
Precious Moments, Precious. Precious Moments: My Noah's Ark Storybook, 1 vol. 2016. (ENG., Illus.). 32p. (J). bds. 9.99 *(978-0-7180-3244-9(6))* Nelson, Thomas Inc.
Priddy, Roger & Priddy Books Staff. Adam & Eve. 2012. (ENG., Illus.). 10p. (J). (gr. -1 — 1). bds. 4.95 *(978-0-312-51454-9(9),* 9780312514549, Priddy Bks.) St. Martin's Pr.
—Noah's Ark. 2012. (ENG., Illus.). 10p. (J). (gr. -1 — 1). bds. 4.95 *(978-0-312-51456-3(5),* 9780312514563, Priddy Bks.) St. Martin's Pr.
—The Story of Moses. 2012. (ENG., Illus.). 12p. (J). (gr. -1 — 1). bds. 4.95 *(978-0-312-51455-6(7),* 9780312514556, Priddy Bks.) St. Martin's Pr.
Prole, Helen, illus. The Story of Noah, 1 vol. 2016. (Candle Bible for Toddlers Ser.). (ENG.). 26p. (J). pap. 6.99 *(978-1-78128-308-0(7),* Candle Bks.) Lion Hudson PLC GBR. Dist: Kregel Pubns.
Pulley, Kelly. Jonah & the Big Fish, 1 vol. 2007. (I Can Read! / the Beginner's Bible Ser.). (ENG., Illus.). 32p. (J). (gr. -1-1). pap. 3.99 *(978-0-310-71459-0(1))* Zonderkidz.
Puppet Prod. Puppet Production - Old Testament Programs (Russian) Life Publishers International Staff, tr. from ENG. 2003. Orig. Title: The Children's Programming Collection. (RUS.). 88p. (J). *(978-0-7361-0332-9(5))* Life Pubs. International.
Rabbit. Ruth in Canaan. 2005. (J). 10.95 *(978-0-689-80232-4(3),* Simon & Schuster Bks. For Young Readers) Simon & Schuster Bks. For Young Readers.
Racklin-Siegel, Alison, illus. Jacob's Travels. 2005. (ENG & HEB.). 32p. (J). per. 10.95 *(978-0-939144-53-2(0))* EKS Publishing Co.
Racklin-Siegel, Carol, illus. Lech Lecha: The Story of Abraham & Rebecca. 2004. (HEB & ENG.). 32p. (J). per. 10.95 *(978-0-939144-49-5(2))* EKS Publishing Co.
Ray, Jane. Adam & Eve & the Garden of Eden. Ray, Jane, illus. 2005. (Illus.). 32p. (J). 17.00 *(978-0-8028-5278-6(5))* Eerdmans, William B. Publishing Co.
—Adam & Eve & the Garden of Eden. 2006. (Illus.). 32p. (J). pap. *(978-1-903919-07-1(X),* Eden Project Books) Transworld Publishers Ltd.
Rice, Tim & Webber, Andrew Lloyd. Joseph & the Amazing Technicolor Dreamcoat. Blake, Quentin, illus. 2012. (ENG.). 48p. (J). (gr. 2-4). 16.99 *(978-1-84365-103-1(3),* Pavilion Children's Books) Pavilion Bks. GBR. Dist: Independent Pubs. Group.
The Roach Approach, Noah's Journey of Faith: Read along. 2003. (J). audio compact disk 12.99 *(978-0-9742997-1-6(5))* Wacky World Studios LLC.
Rock, Lois. The First Rainbow. Allsopp, Sophie, illus. 2010. (ENG.). 28p. (J). (gr. k-2). 12.99 *(978-0-7459-6055-5(3))* Lion Hudson PLC GBR. Dist: Independent Pubs. Group.
—Look Inside Noah's Ark. Coloji, Livia, illus. 2016. (ENG.). 6p. (J). (gr. k-2). bds. 12.99 *(978-0-7459-7612-9(3))* Lion Hudson PLC GBR. Dist: Independent Pubs. Group.
Ruth. 14p. (J). bds. 7.99 *(978-0-7847-1404-1(5))* Standard Publishing.
Sanders, Nancy I. & Kuhn, Pamela J. Favorite Bible Heroes: Ages 4&5. Galey, Chuck, illus. 2005. 96p. (J). (gr. -1-k). pap. 11.95 *(978-0-937282-23-6(5),* RB36197) Rainbow Pubs. & Legacy Pr.
Sasso, Sandy Eisenberg. Adam & Eve's First Sunset: God's New Day. Rothenberg, Joani Keller, illus. 2003. (ENG.). 32p. (gr. -1-3). 17.99 *(978-1-58023-177-0(2),* 9781580231770, Jewish Lights Publishing) LongHill Partners, Inc.
Scherm, Deedra. The Whale & Jonah: A Story of Obedience & Forgiveness. Dreyer, Laura, illus. 2007. (ENG.). 20p. 7.99 *(978-1-934789-00-1(3))* Lemon Vision Productions.
Schmidt, Troy. The Frog & the Plagues. Jones, Cory, illus. 2015. (Their Side of the Story Ser.). (ENG.). 32p. (J). (gr. -1-3). pap. 3.99 *(978-1-4336-8720-4(8),* B&H Kids) B&H Publishing Group.
Schur, Maxine Rose. The Story of Ruth. Connelly, Gwen, illus. 2005. 32p. (J). (gr. 2-4). lib. bdg. 16.95 *(978-1-58013-114-8(X));* (ENG.). (gr. 1-3). per. 9.95 *(978-1-58013-130-8(1))* Lerner Publishing Group. (Kar-Ben Publishing).
Schwarz, Jacob David & Gamoran, Emanuel, eds. Into the Promised Land: The Bible Story in Bible Words, Book 3. 2012. 180p. 42.95 *(978-1-258-25231-1(7));* pap. 27.95 *(978-1-258-25495-7(6))* Literary Licensing, LLC.
Shapes & Sizes: Bible Story: Solomon Builds God's House. (Scripture Bites Ser.). (Illus.). (J). 7.99 *(978-0-7847-9024-3(8),* 00714) Standard Publishing.
Shaw, Luci. The Genesis of It All. Miao, Huai-Kuang, Sr. & Miao, Huai-Kuang, illus. 2006. 32p. (J). (gr. -1-3). 17.95 *(978-1-55725-480-1(X))* Paraclete Pr., Inc.
Simon, Mary Manz. David & Goliath: Read & Learn the Bible. 2005. (ENG., Illus.). 24p. (J). pap. 2.99 *(978-1-4037-1161-8(5),* Spirit Pr.) Bendon, Inc.
—Jonah & the Big Fish: Read & Learn the Bible. 2005. (ENG., Illus.). 24p. (J). pap. 2.99 *(978-1-4037-1158-8(5),* Spirit Pr.) Bendon, Inc.
Smart Kids Publishing Staff. David & Goliath: A Story about Courage. Sharp, Chris, illus. 2006. (I Can Read the Bible Ser.). (ENG.). 12p. (J). (gr. -1-3). 14.95 *(978-0-8249-6659-1(7),* Ideal Pubns.) Worthy Publishing.
—Noah's Ark Story of Being Thankful. 2007. (ENG.). 16p. (J). 19.99 *(978-0-8249-6703-1(8),* Ideal Pubns.) Worthy Publishing.
Smart Kids Publishing Staff, creator. Adam & Eve: A Story about Making the Right Choices. 2006. (I Can Read the Bible Ser.). (ENG., Illus.). 12p. (J). (gr. -1-3). 14.95 *(978-0-8249-6660-7(0),* Ideal Pubns.) Worthy Publishing.
—Noah & the Ark: A Story about Being Thankful. 2005. (I Can Read the Bible Ser.). (Illus.). 12p. (J). (gr. -1-3). 19.95 *(978-0-8249-6658-4(9),* Ideal Pubns.) Worthy Publishing.
Smith, Brendan Powell. The Brick Bible, Set. 2013. (ENG., Illus.). 576p. 29.95 *(978-1-62636-177-5(0),* 263177) Skyhorse Publishing Co., Inc.
Smith, Martina. The Story of King David: A Spark Bible Story. Grosshauser, Peter, illus. 2016. (Spark Bible Stories Ser.). (ENG.). 32p. (J). (gr. -1-2). 12.99 *(978-1-5064-0226-0(7),* Sparkhouse Family) Augsburg Fortress, Pubs.
Smouse, Phil. The Lord Is My Shepherd. 2004. (Illus.). 64p. (J). pap. 4.97 *(978-1-59310-102-2(3))* Barbour Publishing, Inc.
Stories about Daniel. (Old Testament Pict-O-Graph Ser.). (J). 10.99 *(978-0-7847-1040-1(6))* Standard Publishing.
Susan, Hammond. The Lord Calls Samuel. Swisher, Elizabeth, illus. 2005. (Arch Bks.). 16p. (J). 1.99 *(978-0-7586-0639-6(7))* Concordia Publishing Hse.
Thanksgiving: Bible Story: Give Thanks to the Lord. (Scripture Bites Ser.). (Illus.). (J). 7.99 *(978-0-7847-9019-9(1),* 00712) Standard Publishing.
Turgeon, Stephanie, illus. Noah's Ark. 2007. 16p. (J). (gr. -1-3). *(978-2-7641-0340-1(9))* Tormont Pubns.
Twin Sisters(r) Staff. Old Testament Handlebox-4 books. 2009. 12.99 *(978-1-59922-112-0(8))* Twin Sisters IP, LLC.
Twin Sisters(r) Staff, et al. My First Old Testament Bible Stories. 2010. (J). (gr. k-2). bds. 12.99 *(978-1-59922-613-2(8))* Twin Sisters IP, LLC.
van Rijswijk, Cor. David & Goliath. Visser, Rino, illus. 2003. 43p. (J). *(978-1-894666-23-7(2))* Inheritance Pubns.
—Gideon Blows the Trumpet. Visser, Rino, illus. 2003. 43p. (J). *(978-1-894666-22-0(4))* Inheritance Pubns.
Vitale, Raoul & Tank, Daniel, illus. Adam & Eve. 2005. (Family Bible Story Ser.). 93p. (J). pap. *(978-0-8280-1851-7(0))* Review & Herald Publishing Assn.
Warner Press Kids, creator. Queen Esther. 2008. (Illus.). 16p. (J). (gr. -1-2). pap. 11.34 *(978-1-59317-220-6(6))* Warner Pr., Inc.
Watling, James, illus. Jehoshaphat: 2 Chronicles 20:1-30. 2005. (Little Learner Bible Story Books). 16p. (J). pap. 2.29 *(978-0-7586-0945-8(0))* Concordia Publishing Hse.
White, John, Jr. & Tank, Daniel, illus. Abraham. 2004. (Family Bible Story Ser.). 109p. (J). pap. *(978-0-8280-1857-9(X))* Review & Herald Publishing Assn.
Williamson, Karen. Noah, 1 vol. Embleton-Hall, Chris, illus. 2015. (Candle Tabs Ser.). (ENG.). 12p. (J). bds. 7.99 *(978-1-78128-156-7(4),* Candle Bks.) Lion Hudson PLC GBR. Dist: Kregel Pubns.
Wilson, N. D. The Dragon & the Garden. 2007. (Old Stories Ser.). (Illus.). 28p. (J). (gr. 3-7). 14.00 *(978-1-59128-044-6(3))* Canon Pr.
Winch, John. Two by Two. 2004. (ENG., Illus.). 32p. (J). (gr. k-3). tchr. ed. 16.95 *(978-0-8234-1840-4(5))* Holiday Hse., Inc.
Winkler, Jude. Noah & the Flood. 2004. (Illus.). (J). *(978-0-89942-718-8(9))* Catholic Bk. Publishing Corp.
Wolf, Gita, adapted by. The Enduring Ark. 2013. (ENG., Illus.). 34p. (J). (gr. k). 21.95 *(978-93-80340-18-0(4))* Tara Books Agency IND. Dist: Publishers Group West (PGW).
Wood, Nancy. Mr. & Mrs. God in the Creation Kitchen. Ering, Timothy Basil, illus. 2006. (ENG.). 32p. (J). (gr. k-4). 16.99 *(978-0-7636-1258-0(8))* Candlewick Pr.
Woodman, Ros. Exodus: Fun Bible Studies Using Puzzles & Stories. Wheeler, Ron, illus. 2005. (Activity Ser.). (ENG.). 64p. (J). (gr. 4-7). pap., act. bk. ed. 7.99 *(978-1-84550-067-2(9),* 870539af-e943-4634-8ae9-d6317cc1f975) Christian Focus Pubns. GBR. Dist: Bookmasters Distribution.
—Genesis: Fun Bible Studies Using Puzzles & Stories. Wheeler, Ron, illus. 2005. (Activity Ser.). (ENG.). 64p. (J). (gr. 4-7). pap., act. bk. ed. 7.99 *(978-1-84550-066-5(0),* 02dba325-10fb-4c5c-8053-5f5a317c8b08) Christian Focus Pubns. GBR. Dist: Bookmasters Distribution.
Word Search: Old Testament. (Illus.). 32p. (YA). (gr. 5-18). pap. 2.25 *(978-0-87162-496-3(6),* E4800) Warner Pr., Inc.
Zinjiba-Nyakutya, Peshie. From Adam to Noah in Coloring Pages: Genesis 1 To 9. Chitombo, Patience, illus. 2012. 64p. pap. 12.50 *(978-1-61897-769-4(5),* Strategic Bk. Publishing) Strategic Book Publishing & Rights Agency (SBPRA).
Zondervan, A. Ruth & Naomi, 1 vol. Miles, David, illus. 2015. (I Can Read! / Adventure Bible Ser.). (ENG.). 32p. (J). pap. 3.99 *(978-0-310-74650-8(7))* Zonderkidz.
Zondervan Bibles Staff. Moses & the King, 1 vol. Pulley, Kelly, illus. 2009. (I Can Read! / the Beginner's Bible Ser.). (ENG.). 32p. (J). pap. 3.99 *(978-0-310-71800-0(7))* Zonderkidz.

—Noah's Voyage, 1 vol. Miles, David, illus. 2015. (I Can Read! / Adventure Bible Ser.). (ENG.). 32p. (J). pap. 3.99 *(978-0-310-74683-6(3))* Zonderkidz.

Zondervan Staff. Adam & Eve in the Garden, 1 vol. Pulley, Kelly, illus. 2008. (I Can Read! / the Beginner's Bible Ser.). (ENG.). 32p. (J). (gr. -1-1). pap. 3.99 *(978-0-310-71552-8(0))* Zonderkidz.

—Daniel & the Lions, 1 vol. Pulley, Kelly, illus. 2008. (I Can Read! / the Beginner's Bible Ser.). (ENG.). 32p. (J). (gr. -1-1). pap. 3.99 *(978-0-310-71551-1(2))* Zonderkidz.

—Queen Esther Helps God's People, 1 vol. Pulley, Kelly, illus. 2008. (I Can Read! / the Beginner's Bible Ser.). (ENG.). 32p. (J). pap. 3.99 *(978-0-310-71815-4(5))* Zonderkidz.

BIBLE STUDY

see Bible—Study

BIBLICAL ARCHEOLOGY

see Bible—Antiquities

BIBLIOGRAPHY—BEST BOOKS

see Best Books

BIBLIOGRAPHY—REFERENCE BOOKS

see Reference Books

BICYCLE RACING—FICTION

Ciencin, Scott & Maese, Fares. BMX Blitz, 1 vol. Aburto, Jesus & Esparza, Andres, illus. 2011. (Sports Illustrated Kids Graphic Novels Ser.). (ENG.). 56p. (gr. 2-3). pap. 7.19 *(978-1-4342-3071-3(6))* Stone Arch Bks.

—BMX Blitz, 1 vol. Esparza, Andres & Aburto, Jesus, illus. 2011. (Sports Illustrated Kids Graphic Novels Ser.). (ENG.). 56p. (gr. 2-3). lib. bdg. 26.65 *(978-1-4342-2222-0(5))* Stone Arch Bks.

Dow, Suzanne. The Bike Race. 2006. (Neighborhood Readers Ser.). (ENG., Illus.). 12p. (gr. 1-3). pap. 5.90 *(978-1-4042-7018-3(3)*, Rosen Classroom) Rosen Publishing Group, Inc., The.

Jakubowski, Michele. Tour of Trouble. Pinelli, Amerigo, illus. 2017. (Sleuths of Somerville Ser.). (ENG.). 144p. (gr. 4-6). pap. 6.95 *(978-1-4965-3180-3(9))* Stone Arch Bks.

Keene, Carolyn. A Race Against Time. 2nd ed. 2004. (Nancy Drew (All New) Girl Detective Ser.: 2). (ENG.). 160p. (J). (gr. 3-7). pap. 6.99 *(978-0-689-86567-1(8)*, Aladdin) Simon & Schuster Children's Publishing.

—Trails of Treachery. 2008. (Nancy Drew: Girl Detective Ser.). 136p. (gr. 3-7). 15.00 *(978-0-7569-8295-9(2))* Perfection Learning Corp.

Maddox, Jake. BMX Challenge, 1 vol. Tiffany, Sean, illus. 2011. (Jake Maddox Sports Stories Ser.). (ENG.). 72p. (gr. 2-3). pap. 5.95 *(978-1-4342-3423-0(1))* Stone Arch Bks.

—Cycling Champion, 1 vol. Garcia, Eduardo, illus. 2012. (Jake Maddox Sports Stories Ser.). (ENG.). 72p. (gr. 2-3). pap. 5.95 *(978-1-4342-3904-4(7))*; lib. bdg. 25.32 *(978-1-4342-3290-8(5))* Stone Arch Bks.

—El Tramposo de BMX, 1 vol. Heck, Claudia M., tr. from ENG. Tiffany, Sean, illus. 2012. (Jake Maddox en Español Ser.). (SPA.). 72p. (gr. 2-3). 25.32 *(978-1-4342-3817-7(2))* Stone Arch Bks.

Rains, Deborah Jane. Racing with Randy. 2011. 24p. pap. 24.95 *(978-1-4489-4409-5(0))* America Star Bks.

Rodman, Sean. Dead Run, 1 vol. 2012. (Orca Soundings Ser.). (ENG.). 128p. (YA). (gr. 8-12). pap. 9.95 *(978-1-4598-0244-5(6))*; lib. bdg. 16.95 *(978-1-4598-0245-2(4))* Orca Bk. Pubs. USA.

Sherman, M. Zachary. Unchained, Vol. 4. Majado, Caio & Emery, Thomas J., illus. 2011. (Tony Hawk's 900 Revolution Ser.). (ENG.). 128p. (gr. 3-4). pap. 7.19 *(978-1-4342-3454-4(1))*; lib. bdg. 26.65 *(978-1-4342-3215-1(8))* Stone Arch Bks. (Tony Hawk's 900 Revolution).

Stilton, Geronimo. The Race Across America. 2009. (Geronimo Stilton Ser.: 37). lib. bdg. 18.40 *(978-0-606-00228-8(6)*, Turtleback) Turtleback Bks.

Stinson, Kathy. The Great Bike Race, 1 vol. 2005. (Lorimer Streetlights Ser.). (ENG.). 104p. (J). (gr. 2-5). 7.95 *(978-1-55028-890-2(3)*, 9781550288902) Lorimer, James & Co., Ltd., Pubs. CAN. Dist: Casemate Pubs. & Bk. Distributors, LLC.

Stone, Jeff. Five Ancestors Out of the Ashes #2: Lion. 2014. (Five Ancestors Out of the Ashes Ser.). (ENG.). 256p. (J). (gr. 4-7). 6.99 *(978-0-375-87099-6(7)*, Yearling) Random Hse. Children's Bks.

—Five Ancestors Out of the Ashes #3: Jackal. 2014. (Five Ancestors Out of the Ashes Ser.). (ENG.). 192p. (J). (gr. 4-7). 16.99 *(978-0-375-87020-0(2)*, Random Hse. Bks. for Young Readers) Random Hse. Children's Bks.

—Lion. 2013. (Five Ancestors Out of the Ashes Ser.). (ENG.). 240p. (J). (gr. 4-7). 16.99 *(978-0-375-87019-4(9)*, Random Hse. Bks. for Young Readers) Random Hse. Children's Bks.

Street, Emily June. The Velocipede Races. 2016. (Bikes in Space Ser.). (ENG., Illus.). 256p. (J). (gr. 7). pap. 9.95 *(978-1-62106-058-1(6)*, Elly Blue Publishing) Microcosm Publishing.

Suen, Anastasia & Maddox, Jake. BMX Bully, 1 vol. Tiffany, Sean, illus. 2006. (Jake Maddox Sports Stories Ser.). (ENG.). 72p. (gr. 2-3). pap. 5.95 *(978-1-59889-236-9(3))*; lib. bdg. 25.32 *(978-1-59889-059-4(X))* Stone Arch Bks.

Waters, Rod. Eric's Big Day: A Bicycle Race Unlike Any Other. 2014. (ENG., Illus.). 28p. (gr. k-3). 14.95 *(978-1-937715-23-6(X)*, 9781937715236) VeloPress.

White, Naja Learns to Ride. Hyatt, Sean & McGrath, Michael, illus. 2011. 32p. pap. 24.95 *(978-1-4489-8369-8(X))* America Star Bks.

BICYCLES AND BICYCLING

see also Motorcycles

Alexander, Rod. BMX Racing: A Step-by-Step Guide. 2005. (Illus.). 64p. (J). (gr. 4-8). reprint ed. 10.00 *(978-0-7567-9571-9(0))* DIANE Publishing Co.

Amstutz, Lisa J. All Kinds of Bikes: Off-Road to Easy-Riders, 1 vol. 2014. (Spokes Ser.). (ENG.). 24p. (gr. k-1). lib. bdg. 26.65 *(978-1-4765-3967-6(7)*, Pebble Plus) Capstone Press of Coughlan Cos.

—Bicycle Basics: Let It Roll!, 1 vol. 2014. (Spokes Ser.). (ENG.). 24p. (gr. k-1). lib. bdg. 26.65 *(978-1-4765-3964-5(2)*, Pebble Plus) Capstone Press of Coughlan Cos.

—Bike Safety: A Crash Course, 1 vol. 2014. (Spokes Ser.). (ENG.). 24p. (gr. k-1). lib. bdg. 26.65 *(978-1-4765-3965-2(0)*, Pebble Plus) Capstone Press of Coughlan Cos.

—Simple Bike Maintenance: Time for a Tune-Up!, 1 vol. 2014. (Spokes Ser.). (ENG.). 24p. (gr. k-1). lib. bdg. 26.65 *(978-1-4765-3966-9(9)*, Pebble Plus) Capstone Press of Coughlan Cos.

—Spokes, 1 vol. 2014. (Spokes Ser.). (ENG.). 24p. (gr. k-1). lib. bdg. 106.60 *(978-1-4765-7928-3(8)*, Pebble Plus) Capstone Press of Coughlan Cos.

Anderson, A. J. BMX Biking. 2012. (Adrenaline Rush Ser.). (Illus.). 32p. (J). (gr. 4-7). lib. bdg. 31.35 *(978-1-59920-681-3(1))* Black Rabbit Bks.

Bailey, Diane. Mountain Biking, Vol. 10. 2016. (Great Outdoors! Ser.). (Illus.). 48p. (J). (gr. 5). 20.95 *(978-1-4222-3572-0(6))* Mason Crest.

Beyer, Mark. Bicicletas Del Pasado. 2004. (Transporte Ayer y Hoy (Transportation Through the Ages) Ser.). (SPA & ENG., Illus.). 24p. (J). (gr. 2-4). lib. bdg. 22.60 *(978-0-8239-6853-4(7))* Rosen Publishing Group, Inc., The.

—Bicicletas del pasado (Bicycles of the Past) 2009. (transporte ayer y hoy (Transportation Through the Ages) Ser.). (SPA.). 24p. (gr. 1-2). 42.50 *(978-1-61512-254-7(0)*, Editorial Buenas Letras) Rosen Publishing Group, Inc., The.

—Bicycles of the Past. 2009. (Transportation Through the Ages Ser.). 24p. (gr. 1-1). 42.50 *(978-1-60854-586-5(5)*, PowerKids Pr.) Rosen Publishing Group, Inc., The.

Bidder, Jane. Inventions We Use to Go Places. 2006. (Everyday Inventions Ser.). (Illus.). 32p. (gr. 1-4). lib. bdg. 26.00 *(978-0-8368-6901-9(X)*, Gareth Stevens Learning Library) Stevens, Gareth Publishing LLLP.

Blaine, Victor. My Bike, 1 vol. 2015. (ENG.). 24p. (J). lib. bdg. 23.60 *(978-1-4994-0250-6(3)*, PowerKids Pr.) Rosen Publishing Group, Inc., The.

Blomquist, Christopher. BMX in the X Games. 2009. (Kid's Guide to the X Games Ser.). 24p. (gr. 3-3). 42.50 *(978-1-61511-207-4(3)*, PowerKids Pr.) Rosen Publishing Group, Inc., The.

Bloomquist, Christopher. BMX in the X Games. 2003. (Kid's Guide to the X Games Ser.). (Illus.). 24p. (J). lib. bdg. 22.60 *(978-0-8239-6298-3(9)*, PowerKids Pr.) Rosen Publishing Group, Inc., The.

Bodden, Valerie. Bicycling. 2007. (Active Sports Ser.). (Illus.). 24p. (J). (gr. -1-3). lib. bdg. 24.25 *(978-1-58341-467-5(3)*, Creative Education) Creative Co., The.

Bow, James. Cycling Science. 2008. (Sports Science Ser.). (ENG., Illus.). 32p. (J). (gr. 4-6). pap. *(978-0-7787-4552-5(X))*; lib. bdg. *(978-0-7787-4535-8(X))* Crabtree Publishing Co.

Brill, Marlene Targ. Marshall Major Taylor: World Champion Bicyclist, 1899-1901. 2007. (Trailblazer Biographies Ser.). (ENG., Illus.). 112p. (gr. 5-9). lib. bdg. 31.93 *(978-0-8225-6610-6(9)*, Twenty-First Century Bks.) Lerner Publishing Group.

Buckley, Annie. Be a Better Biker. 2006. (Reading Rocks! Ser.). (ENG., Illus.). 32p. (J). (gr. 2-5). 28.50 *(978-1-59296-741-4(8)*, 200728) Child's World, Inc., The.

Butterfield, Moira & Jewitt, Kath. Kids' Cycling Handbook: Cycling Tips, Tricks, Facts & Know-How. 2016. (ENG., Illus.). 40p. (J). (gr. 2-6). spiral bd. 11.95 *(978-1-78312-169-4(6))* Carlton Kids GBR. Dist: Sterling Publishing Co., Inc.

Cain, Patrick G. BMX Street. 2013. (Extreme Summer Sports Zone Ser.). (ENG., Illus.). 32p. (gr. 4-8). lib. bdg. 26.60 *(978-1-4677-0751-0(1)*, Lerner Pubns.) Lerner Publishing Group.

Carleton, Kate. What Happens to Your Body When You Cycle. 2009. (How & Why of Exercise Ser.). (Illus.). 48p. (YA). (gr. 5-9). 29.25 *(978-1-4358-5308-9(3))* Rosen Publishing Group, Inc., The.

Carr, Aaron. Bmx. 2012. (Cool Sports (Av2) Ser.). (ENG., Illus.). 24p. (J). (gr. -1-3). lib. bdg. 27.13 *(978-1-61913-510-9(8)*, AV2 by Weigl) Weigl Pubs., Inc.

—BMX. 2013. *(978-1-62127-627-2(9))* Weigl Pubs., Inc.

—BMX with Code. 2012. (Cool Sports (Av2) Ser.). (ENG., Illus.). 24p. (J). (gr. k-2). pap. 12.95 *(978-1-61913-516-1(7)*, AV2 by Weigl) Weigl Pubs., Inc.

Challen, Paul C. Bicycle Racing, 1 vol. 2015. (ENG., Illus.). 32p. (J). lib. bdg. 26.25 *(978-1-4994-0162-2(0)*, PowerKids Pr.) Rosen Publishing Group, Inc., The.

Champion, Neil. Wild Biking: Off-Road Mountain Biking. 2013. (Illus.). 32p. (J). lib. bdg. *(978-1-59920-811-4(3))* Black Rabbit Bks.

Clark, Willow. Bikes on the Move. 2010. (Transportation Station Ser.). 24p. (J). (ENG.). pap. 8.25 *(978-1-4358-9756-4(0))*; (Illus.). (gr. 2-5). lib. bdg. 22.60 *(978-1-4358-9334-4(4))* Rosen Publishing Group, Inc., The. (PowerKids Pr.).

Cline-Ransome, Lesa. Major Taylor, Champion Cyclist. Ransome, James E., illus. 2004. (ENG.). 40p. (J). (gr. 1-5). 18.99 *(978-0-689-83159-1(5)*, Atheneum Bks. for Young Readers) Simon & Schuster Children's Publishing.

Cohn, Jessica. BMX. 2013. (Incredibly Insane Sports Ser.). (Illus.). 48p. (J). (gr. 4-6). pap. 14.05 *(978-1-4339-8823-3(2))*; lib. bdg. 31.95 *(978-1-4339-8822-6(4))* Stevens, Gareth Publishing LLLP.

—Road Cycling. 2013. (Incredibly Insane Sports Ser.). (Illus.). 48p. (J). (gr. 4-6). 31.95 *(978-1-4339-8834-9(8))*; pap. 14.05 *(978-1-4339-8835-6(6))* Stevens, Gareth Publishing LLLP. (Gareth Stevens Learning Library).

Cole, Steve & Takitin, Sarah. Kids' Easy Bike Care: Tune-Ups, Tools & Quick Fixes. 2008. (ENG., Illus.). 64p. (J). pap. 8.95 *(978-1-885593-86-3(4)*, Ideal Pubns.) Worthy Publishing.

Crossingham, John & Bishop, Amanda. Extreme BMX. 2003. (Extreme Sports - No Limits Ser.). (ENG., Illus.). 32p. (J). (gr. 3). pap. *(978-0-7787-1712-6(7))*; lib. bdg. *(978-0-7787-1666-2(X))* Crabtree Publishing Co.

Crossingham, John & Rouse, Bonna. Le Cyclisme. 2011. (Sans Limites (No Limits!) Ser.: No. 19). (FRE., Illus.). 32p. (J). pap. 11.95 *(978-2-89579-367-0(0))* Bayard Canada Livres CAN. Dist: Crabtree Publishing Co.

Currie, Stephen. Cycling. Greenhaven Press Editors, ed. 2014. (Science Behind Sports Ser.). (ENG., Illus.). 128p. (gr. 7-10). lib. bdg. 39.40 *(978-1-4205-0819-2(9)*, Lucent Bks.) Cengage Gale.

D'Arcy, Sean. Freestyle BMX Tricks: Flatland & Air. 2010. (ENG., Illus.). 128p. pap. 14.95 *(978-1-55407-818-9(0)*, 9781554078189) Firefly Bks., Ltd.

David, Jack. BMX Racing. 2007. (Action Sports Ser.). (ENG., Illus.). 24p. (J). (gr. 3-7). lib. bdg. 25.95 *(978-1-60014-122-5(6))* Bellwether Media.

—Dirt Bikes. 2008. (Cool Rides Ser.). (ENG., Illus.). 24p. (J). (gr. 3-7). lib. bdg. 25.95 *(978-1-60014-147-8(1))* Bellwether Media.

Dayton, Connor. Tricks with Bikes. 2007. (Motorcycles: Made for Speed Ser.). (Illus.). 24p. (J). (gr. 2-5). lib. bdg. 22.60 *(978-1-4042-3657-8(0))* Rosen Publishing Group, Inc., The.

De Medeiros, Michael. Mountain Biking. (J). 2013. *(978-1-62127-358-5(X))* 2013. pap. *(978-1-62127-364-6(4))* 2007. (Illus.). 24p. (gr. 4-7). lib. bdg. 24.45 *(978-1-59036-665-3(4))* 2007. (Illus.). 24p. (gr. 4-7). per. 8.95 *(978-1-59036-666-0(2))* Weigl Pubs., Inc.

DeGraaf, Rob L. Fat Tire Favorites: South Florida off-Road Bicycling. DeGraaf, Rob L. & DeGraaf, Rebecca L., eds. DeGraaf, Rebecca L., photos by. 2003. Orig. Title: Guide to South Florida off-Road Bicycling. (Illus.). 111p. per. 12.95 *(978-0-9678385-2-6(5))* DeGraaf Publishing.

Donovan, Sandy. Cool BMX Racing Facts, 1 vol. (Cool Sports Facts Ser.). (ENG., 24p. (gr. k-1). 2011. Illus.). pap. 7.29 *(978-1-4296-6204-8(2))* 2011. pap. 41.70 *(978-1-4296-6372-4(3))* 2010. lib. bdg. 26.65 *(978-1-4296-5304-6(3))* Capstone Press of Coughlan Cos. (Pebble Plus).

Drummond, Allan. Pedal Power. 2017. (ENG., Illus.). 40p. (J). 17.99 *(978-0-374-30527-7(7)*, 9780374305277, Farrar, Straus & Giroux (BYR)) Farrar, Straus & Giroux.

Eck, Kristin. Bicycle Stunt Riding: Check It Out. 2009. (Extreme Sports Ser.). 24p. (gr. 1-1). 42.50 *(978-1-61512-455-8(1)*, PowerKids Pr.) Rosen Publishing Group, Inc., The.

Elish, Dan. Extreme Mountain Biking. 2011. (Sports on the Edge Ser.). (Illus.). 48p. (J). (gr. 6). 29.93 *(978-1-60870-228-2(6))* Marshall Cavendish Corp.

Endres, Hollie. Mountain Biking. 2007. (Action Sports Ser.). (ENG., Illus.). 24p. (J). (gr. 3-7). lib. bdg. 25.95 *(978-1-60014-126-3(9))* Bellwether Media.

Friddle-Ponder, Alma. Bicycle Unit Study Part 1. 2007. (Illus.). spiral bd. 14.95 *(978-1-934627-08-2(9))* Fish Head Pubns., LLC.

—Bicycle Unit Study Part 1 Reading Enhanced Edition. 2007. (Illus.). spiral bd. 14.95 *(978-1-934627-13-6(5))* Fish Head Pubns., LLC.

—Bicycle Unit Study Part 2. 2007. (Illus.). spiral bd. 14.95 *(978-1-934627-09-9(7))* Fish Head Pubns., LLC.

—Bicycle Unit Study Parts 1 & 2 Comprehensive Edition. 2007. (Illus.). 86p. spiral bd. 19.95 *(978-1-934627-07-5(0))* Fish Head Pubns., LLC.

Gardner, Robert. Bicycle Science Fair Projects. 2015. (Prize-Winning Science Fair Projects Ser.). (ENG.). 128p. (J). (gr. 7-7). lib. bdg. 37.27 *(978-0-7660-7016-5(6))* Enslow Pubs., Inc.

—Bicycle Science Projects: Physics on Wheels. 2004. (Science Fair Success Ser.). (Illus.). 112p. (J). lib. bdg. 27.94 *(978-0-7660-1630-9(7))* Enslow Pubs., Inc.

Gibbons, Gail. Bicycle Book. Gibbons, Gail, illus. 2016. (ENG., Illus.). 32p. (J). (gr. k-3). 7.99 *(978-0-8234-1408-6(6))* Holiday Hse., Inc.

Gifford, Clive. Cycling. 2011. (ENG., Illus.). 32p. (J). pap. 10.95 *(978-1-77092-037-8(4))* Saunders Bk. Co. CAN. Dist: RiverStream Publishing.

Gilbert, Grant. Tour de France. (J). 2013. *(978-1-62127-369-1(5))* 2013. pap. *(978-1-62127-374-5(1))* 2007. (Illus.). 32p. (gr. 4-7). lib. bdg. 26.00 *(978-1-59036-693-6(X))* 2007. (Illus.). 32p. (gr. 4-7). per. 9.95 *(978-1-59036-694-3(8))* Weigl Pubs., Inc.

Graham, Ian. Cars & Bikes. 2008. (QEB Machines at Work Ser.). (Illus.). 36p. (YA). (gr. 4-7). 19.95 *(978-1-59566-317-7(7))* QEB Publishing Inc.

—The Science of a Bicycle: The Science of Forces. 2009. (Science of... Ser.). 32p. (YA). (gr. 3-6). lib. bdg. 26.00 *(978-1-4339-0040-2(8))* Stevens, Gareth Publishing LLLP.

Greathouse, Lisa. Bicicletas y Tablas, 1 vol. rev. ed. 2010. (Science Readers: a Closer Look Ser.). (SPA., Illus.). 32p. (J). (gr. 2-3). pap. 8.99 *(978-1-4333-2146-7(7))* Shell Educational Publishing.

Green, Robert. Bicycles. 2007. (21st Century Skills Library: Global Products Ser.). (ENG., Illus.). 32p. (gr. 4-8). lib. bdg. 28.50 *(978-1-60279-024-7(8)*, 200021) Cherry Lake Publishing.

Guillain, Charlotte. Ciclismo, 1 vol. 2010. (Deporte y Mi Cuerpo Ser.).Tr. of Cycling. (SPA.). 24p. (gr. k-2). 23.32 *(978-1-4329-4346-2(4))*; pap. 6.79 *(978-1-4329-4352-3(9))* Heinemann-Raintree.

Hamilton, Robert M. On a Bike. 2012. (Going Places Ser.). (ENG., Illus.). 24p. (J). (gr. k-2). pap. 8.15 *(978-1-4339-6267-7(5))*; lib. bdg. 22.60 *(978-1-4339-6265-3(9))* Stevens, Gareth Publishing LLLP.

Hamilton, S. L. Biking. 2010. (Xtreme Sports Ser.). 32p. (gr. 3-9). 27.07 *(978-1-61613-002-2(4)*, A&D Xtreme) ABDO Publishing Co.

—Tour de France. 2013. (Xtreme Races Ser.). 32p. (J). (gr. 3-9). lib. bdg. 27.07 *(978-1-61783-697-8(4)*, Abdo & Daughters) ABDO Publishing Co.

Head, Honor. Being Safe on a Bike. 2016. (ENG., Illus.). 24p. (J). (gr. k-2). 16.99 *(978-1-4451-4427-6(1)*, Franklin Watts) Hachette Children's Group GBR. Dist: Hachette Bk. Group.

Heller, D. M. Let's Make a Bike with Everyday Materials. 2006. (Let's Do Arts & Crafts Ser.). (Illus.). 24p. (J). lib. bdg. 22.60 *(978-1-4042-3064-4(5))* Rosen Publishing Group, Inc., The.

Heos, Bridget. Be Safe on Your Bike. Baroncelli, Silvia, illus. 2015. (Be Safe! Ser.). 24p. (J). 25.65 *(978-1-60753-443-3(6))* Amicus Publishing.

Herrington, Lisa M. Bicycle Safety. 2012. (Rookie Read-About Safety Ser.). (ENG., Illus.). 32p. (J). pap. 5.95 *(978-0-531-29270-9(3))*; lib. bdg. 23.00 *(978-0-531-28968-6(0))* Scholastic Library Publishing.

Hinman, Bonnie. Extreme Cycling with Dale Holmes. 2006. (Extreme Sports Ser.). (Illus.). 32p. (J). (gr. 1-4). lib. bdg. 25.70 *(978-1-58415-487-7(X))* Mitchell Lane Pubs., Inc.

Hudak, Heather C. BMX. 2015. (Illus.). 32p. (J). *(978-1-5105-0000-6(6))* SmartBook Media, Inc.

—BMX. 2015. (J). *(978-1-4896-4289-9(7))* Weigl Pubs., Inc.

Job, Chris. BMX. 2003. (Extreme Sports Ser.). (ENG., Illus.). 32p. (gr. 3-6). lib. bdg. 22.60 *(978-0-8225-1243-1(2))* Lerner Publishing Group.

Johanson, Sarah Margaret. Caillou: The Bike Lesson. Sevigny, Eric, illus. 2017. (Read with Caillou Ser.). (ENG.). 32p. (J). (gr. -1-1). 3.99 *(978-2-89718-366-0(7))* Caillouet, Gerry.

Kelley, K. C. Mountain Biking. 2003. (Extreme Sports Ser.). (Illus.). 24p. (gr. 2-5). lib. bdg. 23.00 *(978-0-8368-3723-0(1)*, Gareth Stevens Learning Library) Stevens, Gareth Publishing LLLP.

—Stunt Bicycle Riding. 2003. (Extreme Sports Ser.). (Illus.). 24p. (J). (gr. 2-5). lib. bdg. 23.00 *(978-0-8368-3726-1(6)*, Gareth Stevens Learning Library) Stevens, Gareth Publishing LLLP.

Kelly, Maoliosa. My Bike Ride: Band 02A/Red A. Roberts, Ley Honor, illus. 2006. (Collins Big Cat Ser.). (ENG.). 16p. (J). (gr. -1-k). pap. 5.99 *(978-0-00-718661-7(4))* HarperCollins Pubs. Ltd. GBR. Dist: Independent Pubs. Group.

King, Andy. Mountain Biking. rev. ed. 2005. (Play-by-Play Ser.). (Illus.). 80p. (J). (gr. 4-8). pap. 7.95 *(978-0-8225-9879-4(5))* Lerner Publishing Group.

Labrecque, Ellen. Amazing Bike Tricks, 1 vol. 2013. (Try This at Home! Ser.). (ENG.). 32p. (gr. 1-2). pap. 8.29 *(978-1-4109-5008-6(5))*; lib. bdg. 29.99 *(978-1-4109-5001-7(8))* Heinemann-Raintree. (Read Me!).

Labrecque, Ellen C. BMX Racers. 2010. (Kid Racers Ser.). (Illus.). 48p. (J). (gr. 5-9). 25.27 *(978-0-7660-3484-6(4))* Enslow Pubs., Inc.

Lakin, Patricia. Bicycles. 2017. (Made by Hand Ser.: 2). (ENG., Illus.). 32p. (J). (gr. 3-7). 17.99 *(978-1-4814-7896-0(6)*, Simon & Schuster/Paula Wiseman Bks.) Simon & Schuster/Paula Wiseman Bks.

Laval, Anne-Marie. Mountain Biking. 2012. (Adrenaline Rush Ser.). (Illus.). 32p. (gr. 4-7). lib. bdg. 31.35 *(978-1-59920-684-4(6))* Black Rabbit Bks.

Lupo, Tamar. BMX: X Games. 2008. (Extreme Ser.). (Illus.). 32p. (J). (gr. 4-6). lib. bdg. 26.00 *(978-1-59036-910-4(6))* Weigl Pubs., Inc.

Lupo, Tamar & Hudak, Heather C. BMX: X Games. 2008. (Extreme Ser.). (Illus.). 32p. (J). (gr. 4-6). pap. 9.95 *(978-1-59036-911-1(4))* Weigl Pubs., Inc.

Lynette, Rachel. Bicycles. 2016. (J). *(978-1-4896-4527-2(6))* Weigl Pubs., Inc.

—Bicycles Before the Store. McGeehan, Dan, illus. 2012. (Before the Store Ser.). (ENG.). 32p. (J). (gr. 2-5). lib. bdg. 29.93 *(978-1-60973-676-7(1)*, 201248) Child's World, Inc., The.

MacAulay, Kelley & Kalman, Bobbie. Extreme Mountain Biking. 2006. (Extreme Sports No Limits! Ser.). (ENG., Illus.). 32p. (J). (gr. 3-7). lib. bdg. *(978-0-7787-1678-5(3))* Crabtree Publishing Co.

Mahaney, Ian F. Dave Mirra: Bicycle Stunt Champ. 2005. (Extreme Sports Biographies Ser.). (Illus.). 24p. (J). (gr. 2-5). 22.60 *(978-1-4042-2744-6(X))* Rosen Publishing Group, Inc., The.

Mara, Wil. Extreme BMX. 2011. (Sports on the Edge Ser.). (Illus.). 48p. (J). (gr. 6). 29.93 *(978-1-60870-227-5(8))* Marshall Cavendish GBR. Dist: Marshall Cavendish Corp.

—What Should I Do? On My Bike. 2011. (Community Connections: What Should I Do? Ser.). (ENG.). 24p. (gr. 2-5). lib. bdg. 25.64 *(978-1-61080-055-6(9)*, 201052) Cherry Lake Publishing.

Maskell, Hazel. Cycling IR. 2015. (Discovery Adventures Ser.). (ENG.). 80p. (J). (gr. k-5). pap. 8.99 *(978-0-7945-3459-2(7)*, Usborne) EDC Publishing.

Mason, Paul. Cycling. 2016. (Sports Skills Ser.). (ENG., Illus.). 32p. (J). (gr. 4-6). 16.99 *(978-1-4451-4134-3(5)*, Franklin Watts) Hachette Children's Group GBR. Dist: Hachette Bk. Group.

—Mountain Biking. 2016. (Get Outdoors Ser.). (ENG., Illus.). 32p. (J). (gr. 4-6). pap. 11.99 *(978-0-7502-8895-8(7)*, Wayland) Hachette Children's Group GBR. Dist: Hachette Bk. Group.

—Mountain Biking. (To the Limit Ser.). (Illus.). 32p. (J). 2012. (ENG.). (gr. 5-8). pap. 10.00 *(978-1-4488-7064-6(X))* 2012. (ENG., (gr. 5-8). lib. bdg. 25.25 *(978-1-4488-7028-8(3))* 2011. (gr. 4-6). lib. bdg. 25.25 *(978-1-4488-3296-5(9))* Rosen Publishing Group, Inc., The. (PowerKids Pr.).

McClellan, Ray. BMX Freestyle. 2008. (Action Sports Ser.). (ENG., Illus.). 24p. (J). (gr. 3-7). lib. bdg. 25.95 *(978-1-60014-138-6(2))* Bellwether Media.

—Downhill BMX. 2008. (Action Sports Ser.). (ENG., Illus.). 24p. (J). (gr. 3-7). lib. bdg. 25.95 *(978-1-60014-139-3(0))* Bellwether Media.

Michele, Tracey. Riding a Bike. 2011. (Learn-Abouts Ser.). (Illus.). 16p. (J). pap. 7.95 *(978-1-59920-626-4(9))* Black Rabbit Bks.

Mugford, Simon. Essential BMX. 2004. (Twenty4Sevens Ser.). (Illus.). 48p. (J). pap. *(978-0-439-68104-9(9))* Scholastic, Inc.

Mulder, Michelle. Pedal It! How Bicycles Are Changing the World, 1 vol. (Orca Footprints Ser.). (ENG., Illus.). 48p. (J). (gr. 3-7). 2016. pap. 12.95 *(978-1-4598-1215-4(8))* 2013. 19.95 *(978-1-4598-0219-3(5))* Orca Bk. Pubs. USA.

Nagle, Jeanne. Extreme Biking. 2015. (Sports to the Extreme Ser.). (ENG., Illus.). 48p. (J). (gr. 5-6). 30.25 *(978-1-4994-3565-8(7)*, Rosen Central) Rosen Publishing Group, Inc., The.

Nelson, Robin. From Steel to Bicycle. 2014. (Start to Finish: Sports Gear Ser.). (Illus.). 24p. (gr. k-3). (J). lib. bdg. 23.93 *(978-1-4677-3892-7(1)*, Lerner Pubns.); pap. 6.95 *(978-1-4677-4563-5(4))* Lerner Publishing Group.

Nix, Harvey. Learning to Ride with the Bits. 2007. 30p. 16.95 *(978-0-944353-24-0(X))*; pap. 10.95 *(978-0-944353-25-7(8))* Rivendell Bk. Factory.

Omoth, Tyler. First Source to BMX Racing: Rules, Equipment, & Key Riding Tips. 2017. (First Sports Source Ser.). (ENG.). 24p. (gr. 1-2). lib. bdg. 25.32 ***(978-1-5157-8782-2(6)***, First Facts) Capstone Press of Coughlan Cos.

Omoth, Tyler. Stunning Motorcycle Stunts. 2015. (Wild Stunts Ser.). (ENG., Illus.). 32p. (gr. 3-4). lib. bdg. 27.99 *(978-1-4914-4255-5(7))* Capstone Press of Coughlan Cos.

Oregon Center for Applied Science, creator. Bike Smart. 2006. (J). cd-rom 19.95 *(978-1-933898-09-4(7))* Oregon Ctr. for Applied Science, Inc.

Osborne, Ian. Mountain Biking. (Extreme Sports Ser.). (Illus.). 32p. (J). (gr. 3-6). 2004. lib. bdg. 22.60 *(978-0-8225-1245-5(9))* 2003. pap. 6.95 *(978-0-8225-1195-3(9))* Lerner Publishing Group.

Parker, Ian. Ride On: Bikes & Riders Who Rule. 2007. (Steck-Vaughn BOLDPRINT Anthologies Ser.). (ENG., Illus.). 48p. (gr. 6-9). pap. 16.90 *(978-1-4190-4026-9(X))* Houghton Mifflin Harcourt Publishing Co.

Parker, Steve. Cars Trucks & Bikes. 2010. (How It Works Ser.). (Illus.). 40p. (J). (gr. 3-18). lib. bdg. 19.95 (978-1-4222-1792-4(2), 1317905) Mason Crest.
Pease, Pamela. Pop-up Tour de France: The World's Greatest Bike Race. 2009. (ENG., Illus.). 20p. (J). (gr. 4). 36.00 (978-0-9669433-7-5(6)) Paintbox Pr.
Peppas, Lynn. Bicycles: Pedal Power. 2011. (ENG.). 32p. (J). lib. bdg. (978-0-7787-2725-5(4)); (Vehicles on the Move Ser.: No. 11). pap. (978-0-7787-2732-3(7)) Crabtree Publishing Co.
Petrie, Kristin. Bicycles, 1 vol. 2009. (Everyday Inventions Ser.). (ENG., Illus.). 32p. (gr. 3-6). 27.07 (978-1-60453-084-1(7), Checkerboard Library) ABDO Publishing Co.
Petty, Kate. Bicycles, 4 vols. 2006. (World Show-And-Tell Ser.). (ENG., Illus.). 32p. (J). (gr. -1-1). 14.95 (978-1-58728-529-5(0)); pap. 8.95 (978-1-58728-530-1(4)) Cooper Square Publishing Llc.
Petty, Kate & Quarto Generic Staff. Bicycles. 2013. (Around the World Ser.). (ENG., Illus.). 32p. (J). (gr. -1-1). pap. 8.99 (978-1-84507-554-5(4), Frances Lincoln) Quarto Publishing Group UK GBR. Dist: Hachette Bk. Group.
Pohl, Kathleen. What Happens at a Bike Shop? 2006. (Where People Work Ser.). (Illus.). 24p. (gr. -1-3). lib. bdg. 22.00 (978-0-8368-6885-2(4), Weekly Reader Leveled Readers) Stevens, Gareth Publishing LLLP.
—What Happens at a Bike Shop? (¿Qué pasa en una tienda de Bicicletas?) 2006. (Where People Work/Dónde Trabaja la Gente? Ser.). (ENG & SPA., Illus.). 24p. (gr. -1-3). pap. 8.15 (978-0-8368-7393-1(9), Weekly Reader Leveled Readers) Stevens, Gareth Publishing LLLP.
—What Happens at a Bike Shop?/Que Pasa en una Tienda de Bicicletas? 2006. (Where People Work/Dónde Trabaja la Gente? Ser.). (SPA & ENG., Illus.). 24p. (J). (gr. -1-3). lib. bdg. 22.00 (978-0-8368-7386-3(6), Weekly Reader Leveled Readers) Stevens, Gareth Publishing LLLP.
Polydoros, Lori. BMX Greats, 1 vol. 2011. (Best of the Best Ser.). (ENG.). 32p. (gr. 1-2). pap. 8.10 (978-1-4296-7243-6(9)); 26.65 (978-1-4296-6501-8(7)); pap. 47.70 (978-1-4296-7244-3(7)) Capstone Press of Coughlan Cos. (Blazers).
Rafael, Janis. Playing It Safe with Mr. See-More Safety Vol. 2: Let's Learn about Bicycle Safety. Walsh, Jennifer, illus. Date not set. 24p. (J). (gr. -1-8). (978-0-9655604-1-2(4)) Safeworld Publishing Co.
Rapparlie, Leslie & Wurdinger, Scott. Mountain Biking. 2006. (Adventure Sports Ser.). (Illus.). 48p. (YA). (gr. 5-9). lib. bdg. 21.95 (978-1-58341-396-8(0)) Creative Co., The.
RIGBY. How Bicycles Work: Second Grade Big Books. 2003. (Rigby on Our Way to English Ser.). (ENG.). 24p. (gr. 2-2). pap. 50.70 (978-0-7578-1425-9(5)) Rigby Education.
Rigby Education Staff. Learning to Ride a Bicycle. (Illus.). 8p. (J). bds. 3.95 (978-0-7635-6496-4(6), 764966C99) Rigby Education.
Ringstad, Arnold. Biking. 2014. (Great Outdoors Ser.). (ENG.). 24p. (J). (gr. 2-5). 28.50 (978-1-62687-326-1(7), 207166) Child's World, Inc., The.
Robinson, Laura. Cyclist BikeList: The Book for Every Rider. Pérez, Ramón K., illus. 2010. (ENG.). 64p. (J). (gr. 4-7). pap. 17.95 (978-0-88776-784-5(2), Tundra Bks.) Tundra Bks. CAN. Dist: Penguin Random Hse. LLC.
Rosenberg, Aaron. Mountain Biking. 2005. (Rad Sports: Techniques & Tricks Ser.). (Illus.). 48p. (YA). (gr. 5-8). lib. bdg. 29.25 (978-0-8239-3845-2(X)) Rosen Publishing Group, Inc., The.
—Mountain Biking: Techniques & Tricks. 2009. (Rad Sports: Techniques & Tricks Ser.). 48p. (gr. 5-8). 53.00 (978-1-60851-935-4(X), Rosen Reference) Rosen Publishing Group, Inc., The.
Savage, Jeff. Dave Mirra. 2007. (Amazing Athletes Ser.). (ENG., Illus.). 32p. (J). (gr. 2-5). 25.26 (978-0-8225-6593-2(5)) Lerner Publishing Group.
Saviola, Joseph A. The Tour de France: Solving Addition Problems Involving Renaming. 2009. (PowerMath Ser.). (ENG., Illus.). 24p. (gr. 3-4). pap. 8.25 (978-0-8239-8851-8(1), PowerKids Pr.) Rosen Publishing Group, Inc., The.
—The Tour de France: Solving Addition Problems Using Regrouping. (PowerMath: Intermediate Ser.). 24p. 2009. (gr. 3-4). 45.00 (978-1-60851-386-4(6)) 2004. (Illus.). (J). lib. bdg. 22.50 (978-0-8239-8963-8(1)) Rosen Publishing Group, Inc., The. (PowerKids Pr.).
Seed, Andy. On the Track. 2017. (ENG., Illus.). 32p. (J). pap. 7.99 (**978-0-00-820875-2(1)**) HarperCollins Pubs. Ltd. GBR. Dist: Independent Pubs. Group.
Sévigny, Eric, illus. As Good as New. 2012. (Ecology Club Ser.). (ENG.). 24p. (J). (gr. -1-1). pap. 5.99 (978-2-89450-832-9(8)) Caillouet, Gerry.
—Caillou - Training Wheels. 2010. (Clubhouse Ser.). (ENG.). 24p. (J). (gr. -1-1). pap. 3.99 (978-2-89450-746-9(1)) Caillouet, Gerry.
Shea, Therese. All about Bicycles. 2016. (Let's Find Out! Ser.). 32p. (J). (gr. 3-2). lib. bdg. 24.45 (978-1-68048-439-7(7)) Rosen Publishing Group, Inc., The.
Slade, Suzanne. The Science of Bicycle Racing, 1 vol. 2014. (Science of Speed Ser.). (ENG.). 48p. (gr. 3-4). lib. bdg. 31.99 (978-1-4765-3909-6(X)) Capstone Press of Coughlan Cos.
Speight, Peter. Wally the Whale Says: To Be Safe on a Bike. 2015. (ENG., Illus.). 18p. (J). pap. (978-1-78222-438-9(6)) Paragon Publishing, Rothersthorpe.
Teitelbaum, Michael. Mountain Biking. 2007. (21st Century Skills Library: Healthy for Life Ser.). (ENG.). 32p. (gr. 4-8). lib. bdg. 28.50 (978-1-60279-016-2(7), 200030) Cherry Lake Publishing.
Thomas, Isabel. Freestyle BMX. 2011. (On the Radar: Sports Ser.). (ENG., Illus.). 32p. (J). (gr. 4-8). lib. bdg. 26.60 (978-0-7613-7764-1(6)) Lerner Publishing Group.
Tieck, Sarah. Biking, 1 vol. 2013. (Move Your Body Ser.). (ENG., Illus.). 32p. (J). (gr. 2-5). 27.07 (978-1-61783-560-5(9)) ABDO Publishing Co.
Travis, Tim & Travis, Cindie. The Road That Has No End: How We Traded in Our Ordinary Lives for an Around the World Bicycle Adventure. 2004. (Illus.). 313p. (J). pap. 21.95 (978-0-9754427-0-8(8)) Down The Road Publishing.
Turnbull, Stephanie. Mountain Biking. 2016. (Adventure Sports Ser.). 24p. (gr. 2-6). 28.50 (978-1-62588-385-8(4), Smart Apple Media) Black Rabbit Bks.
Turner, Cherie. Marathon Cycling. 2009. (Ultra Sports Ser.). 64p. (gr. 5-8). 58.50 (978-1-60854-607-7(1), Rosen Reference) Rosen Publishing Group, Inc., The.
VanVoorst, Jenny Fretland. Bicycles. 2016. (Early Physics Fun). 24p. (J). (gr. 2-5). lib. bdg. 25.65 (978-1-62031-314-5(6), Pogo) Jump! Inc.
Walton, Ruth. Let's Ride a Bike. 2013. (Let's Find Out Ser.). (Illus.). 32p. (J). (gr. k-5). 28.50 (978-1-59771-385-6(6)) Sea-To-Sea Pubns.
Ward, Nathan. Salida Singletrack: Mountain Biking in Colorado's Upper Arkansas Valley. 1972nd ed. 2004. (Illus.). 110p. per. 14.95 (978-0-9748814-0-9(6)) Ice Mountain Publishing.
Wayne, Melody & Hayhurst, Chris. Bike Trekking, 01 vols., 1. 2016. (Outdoor Life Ser.). (ENG., Illus.). 64p. (J). 32.95 (978-1-4994-6235-7(2), Rosen Young Adult) Rosen Publishing Group, Inc., The.
Wingate, Brian. BMX Bicycle Racing. 2005. (Rad Sports: Techniques & Tricks Ser.). (Illus.). 48p. (YA). (gr. 5-8). lib. bdg. 29.25 (978-0-8239-3843-8(3)) Rosen Publishing Group, Inc., The.
—BMX Bicycle Racing: Techniques & Tricks. 2009. (Rad Sports: Techniques & Tricks Ser.). 48p. (gr. 5-8). 53.00 (978-1-60851-932-3(5), Rosen Reference) Rosen Publishing Group, Inc., The.

BICYCLES AND BICYCLING—FICTION

Al Mansour, Haifaa. The Green Bicycle. 2015. (ENG.). 352p. (J). (gr. 5). 16.99 (978-0-525-42806-0(2), Dial Bks) Penguin Young Readers Group.
Arena, Felice & Kettle, Phil. Bike Daredevils. Cox, David, illus. 2004. (J). pap. (978-1-59336-371-0(0)) Mondo Publishing.
Barbot, Daniel. Rosaura en Bicicleta. Fuenmayor, Morella, illus. 2005. (SPA.). 23p. (J). (gr. -1-2). reprint ed. pap. 14.00 (978-0-7567-8947-3(8)) DIANE Publishing Co.
Barchers, Suzanne I. Twice as Nice: Long Vowel Storybooks, 1 vol. 2011. (Targeted Phonics Ser.). (ENG.). 16p. (J). (gr. k-2). pap. 5.99 (978-1-4333-2909-8(3)) Teacher Created Materials, Inc.
Barton, Byron. My Bike. Barton, Byron, illus. 2015. (ENG., Illus.). 40p. (J). (gr. -1-3). 16.99 (978-0-06-233699-6(1), Collins Design) HarperCollins Pubs.
—My Bike Board Book. Barton, Byron, illus. 2016. (Illus.). 40p. (J). (gr. -1-3). bds. 7.99 (978-0-06-233701-6(7), Greenwillow Bks.) HarperCollins Pubs.
—My Bike Lap Book. Barton, Byron, illus. 2016. (Illus.). 40p. (J). (gr. -1-3). pap. 12.99 (978-0-06-233702-3(5), Greenwillow Bks.) HarperCollins Pubs.
Best, Cari. Sally Jean, the Bicycle Queen. Davenier, Christine, illus. 2006. (ENG.). 32p. (J). (gr. -1-3). 17.99 (978-0-374-36386-4(2), 9780374363864, Farrar, Straus & Giroux (BYR)) Farrar, Straus & Giroux.
Biggs, Brian. Henry on Wheels. Biggs, Brian & Abbott, Simon, illus. 2013. (My First I Can Read Ser.). (ENG.). 32p. (J). (gr. -1-3). 16.99 (978-0-06-195823-6(9)) HarperCollins Pubs.
The Bike Parade: Individual Title Six-Packs. (Literatura 2000 Ser.). (gr. k-1). 28.00 (978-0-7635-0024-5(0)) Rigby Education.
Blackford, Andy. Bill's Bike. 2011. (Tadpoles Ser.: No. 29). (ENG., Illus.). 24p. (J). (gr. k-3). pap. (978-0-7787-0586-4(2)) Crabtree Publishing Co.
Blackstone, Stella. Bear on a Bike / Ours À Vélo. Harter, Debbie, illus. 2017. (ENG & FRE.). 32p. (J). (gr. -1-1). pap. 6.99 (**978-1-78285-328-2(6)**) Barefoot Bks., Inc.
Blackstone, Stella. Oso en Bicicleta. Sarfatti, Esther, tr. Harter, Debbie, illus. 2003. (Bear Ser.). (SPA.). 32p. (J). pap. 6.99 (978-1-84148-775-5(9)) Barefoot Bks., Inc.
Bowen, Carl & Fuentes, Benny. BMX Breakthrough, 1 vol. Sandoval, Gerardo, illus. 2011. (Sports Illustrated Kids Graphic Novels Ser.). (ENG.). 56p. (gr. 2-3). pap. 7.19 (978-1-4342-3401-8(0)); lib. bdg. 26.65 (978-1-4342-2240-4(3)) Stone Arch Bks.
Bradbury, Jennifer. Shift. (ENG., Illus.). (YA). (gr. 7). 2012. 272p. pap. 10.99 (978-1-4424-0852-4(9)) 2008. 256p. 17.99 (978-1-4169-4732-5(9)) Simon & Schuster Children's Publishing. (Atheneum Bks. for Young Readers).
Braver, Vanita. Madison's Patriotic Project, 1 vol. DiRocco, Carl, illus. 2007. (ENG.). 32p. (J). 14.95 (978-1-59572-110-5(X)) Star Bright Bks., Inc.
Burleigh, Robert. Messenger, Messenger. Root, Barry, illus. 2011. (ENG.). 32p. (J). (gr. -1-3). pap. 16.99 (978-1-4424-5335-7(4), Atheneum Bks. for Young Readers) Simon & Schuster Children's Publishing.
Carbonell, Oliver. Peter Learns to Ride His Bicycle. 2011. 28p. (gr. 1-2). 12.99 (978-1-4520-8626-2(5)) AuthorHouse.
Christie, Douglas, Jr. Dougie Learns to Ride. 2009. 32p. pap. 12.99 (978-0-9794827-5-5(5)) Infinite Love Publishing.
Christopher, Matt. Wild Ride. Koelsch, Michael, illus. 7th ed. 2005. (ENG.). 64p. (J). (gr. 1-4). pap. 13.99 (978-0-316-76263-2(6)) Little, Brown Bks. for Young Readers.
Connor, Leslie. Crunch. 2012. (ENG.). 336p. (J). (gr. 5). pap. 6.99 (978-0-06-169234-5(4), Tegen, Katherine Bks) HarperCollins Pubs.
Costain, Meredith. Kids for Hire. Dale, Rae, illus. 2004. iv, 36p. (J). pap. (978-0-7608-6748-8(8)) Sundance/Newbridge Educational Publishing.
Crow, Melinda Melton. Little Lizard's New Bike, 1 vol. Rowland, Andrew, illus. 2010. (Little Lizards Ser.). (ENG.). 32p. (gr. -1-1). lib. bdg. 22.65 (978-1-4342-2008-0(7)) Stone Arch Bks.
—Little Lizard's New Bike. Rowland, Andrew & Rowlands, Andy, illus. 2010. (Little Lizards Ser.). (ENG.). 32p. (gr. -1-1). pap. 6.25 (978-1-4342-2792-8(8)) Stone Arch Bks.
Davies, Matt. Ben Rides On. 2013. (ENG., Illus.). 32p. (J). (gr. -1-2). 17.99 (978-1-59643-794-4(4), 9781596437944) Roaring Brook Pr.
Dean, James. Go, Pete, Go. 2016. (Pete the Cat (HarperCollins) Ser.). (J). lib. bdg. 14.75 (978-0-606-38759-0(5)) Turtleback Bks.
El desfile de Bicicletas, 6 Pack. (Literatura 2000 Ser.). (SPA.). (gr. k-1). 28.00 (978-0-7635-1016-9(5)) Rigby Education.
Dixon, Franklin W. The Bicycle Thief. Burroughs, Scott, illus. 2011. (Hardy Boys: the Secret Files Ser.: 6). (ENG.). 96p. (J). (gr. 1-4). pap. 5.99 (978-1-4169-9396-4(7), Aladdin) Simon & Schuster Children's Publishing.
Docherty, Thomas. To the Beach. Docherty, Thomas, illus. 2009. (ENG., Illus.). 40p. (J). (gr. -1-2). 15.99 (978-0-7636-4429-1(3), Templar) Candlewick Pr.
Dow, Suzanne. The Bike Race. 2006. (Neighborhood Readers Ser.). (ENG., Illus.). 12p. (gr. 1-3). pap. 5.90 (978-1-4042-7018-3(3), Rosen Classroom) Rosen Publishing Group, Inc., The.
Duck on a Bike. 2017. 59.95 (**978-1-338-18702-1(3)**) Scholastic, Inc.
Dunn, Dennis L. Johnny Bear. 2012. 24p. pap. 24.95 (978-1-62709-421-4(0)) America Star Bks.
Eriksson, Eva E. A Crash Course for Molly. Dyssegaard, Elisabeth Kallick, tr. from SWE. 2005. (Illus.). 32p. (J). 16.00 (978-91-29-66156-9(0)) R & S Bks. SWE. Dist: Macmillan.
Feutl, Rita. The Bike Thief, 1 vol. 2014. (Orca Soundings Ser.). (ENG.). 136p. (YA). (gr. 8-12). pap. 9.95 (978-1-4598-0569-9(0)) Orca Bk. Pubs. USA.
Gentry, Marley. Chase Learns to Ride. 2010. 24p. 14.99 (978-1-4490-4640-8(1)) AuthorHouse.
Gumnut, I. B. Daniel's Pushbike. 2012. 24p. pap. 12.45 (978-1-4525-0463-6(6)) Balboa Pr.
Harley, Bill. The Amazing Flight of Darius Frobisher, 1 vol. 2006. (ENG., Illus.). 160p. (J). (gr. 3-7). 14.95 (978-1-56145-381-8(1)) Peachtree Pubs.
Hillenbrand, Will. Off We Go! A Bear & Mole Story. 2013. (Bear & Mole Ser.). (ENG., Illus.). 32p. (J). (gr. -1-1). 16.95 (978-0-8234-2520-4(7)) Holiday Hse., Inc.
Hoffman, Mary Ann. The Missing Wheel. 2006. (Neighborhood Readers Ser.). (ENG.). 8p. (gr. -1-3). pap. 5.15 (978-1-4042-5668-2(7), Rosen Classroom) Rosen Publishing Group, Inc., The.
Horowitz, Dave. Little Big Horse. 2014. (Scholastic Reader Level 1 Ser.). lib. bdg. 13.55 (978-0-606-35375-5(5)) Turtleback Bks.
Howe, James. Houndsley & Catina Plink & Plunk. Gay, Marie-Louise, illus. 2013. (Candlewick Sparks Ser.). (ENG.). 48p. (J). (gr. k-4). pap. 3.99 (978-0-7636-6640-8(8)) Candlewick Pr.
—Plink & Plunk. Gay, Marie-Louise, illus. 2009. (Houndsley & Catina Ser.). (ENG.). 48p. (J). (gr. k-4). 15.99 (978-0-7636-3385-1(2)) Candlewick Pr.
Hutchins, Hazel. The Great Bike Rescue, 1 vol. 2013. (Orca Young Readers Ser.). (ENG.). 112p. (J). (gr. 3-6). pap. 7.95 (978-1-4598-0478-4(3)) Orca Bk. Pubs. USA.
Isabella, Jude. The Red Bicycle: The Extraordinary Story of One Ordinary Bicycle. Shin, Simone, illus. 2015. (CitizenKid Ser.). (ENG.). 32p. (J). (gr. 3-7). 18.95 (978-1-77138-023-2(3)) Kids Can Pr., Ltd. CAN. Dist: Hachette Bk. Group.
Jacobson, Jennifer Richard. Andy Shane, Hero at Last. Carter, Abby, illus. 2011. (Andy Shane Ser.: 6). (ENG.). 64p. (J). (gr. k-3). pap. 4.99 (978-0-7636-5293-7(8)) Candlewick Pr.
—Hero at Last. Carter, Abby, illus. 2010. (Andy Shane Ser.: 6). (ENG.). 64p. (J). (gr. k-3). 14.99 (978-0-7636-3600-5(2)) Candlewick Pr.
Jakubowski, Michele. The Big Bike. Waters, Erica-Jane, illus. 2015. (Perfectly Poppy Ser.). (ENG.). 32p. (J). (gr. k-2). 22.65 (978-1-4795-5801-8(X)) Picture Window Bks.
—Tour of Trouble. Pinelli, Amerigo, illus. 2016. (Sleuths of Somerville Ser.). (ENG.). 144p. (gr. 4-6). lib. bdg. 25.99 (978-1-4965-3176-6(0)) Stone Arch Bks.
Janni, Rebecca. Every Cowgirl Loves a Rodeo. Avril, Lynne, illus. 2012. (Every Cowgirl Ser.). (ENG.). 32p. (J). (gr. -1-k). 16.99 (978-0-8037-3734-1(3), Dial Bks) Penguin Young Readers Group.
—Spin. Ermos, George, illus. 2017. (Penguin Core Concepts Ser.). (ENG.). 32p. (J). (-k). pap. 3.99 (978-0-448-48948-3(1), Grosset & Dunlap) Penguin Young Readers Group.
Johnston, Annie Fell. The Quilt That Jack Built; and, How He W. 2006. (Illus.). pap. (978-1-4065-1126-0(9)) Dodo Pr.
Keene, Carolyn. Secret at Mystic Lake. 2014. (Nancy Drew Diaries: 6). (ENG., Illus.). 160p. (J). (gr. 3-7). pap. 6.99 (978-1-4814-0012-1(6), Aladdin) Simon & Schuster Children's Publishing.
Kertell, Lynn Maslen. I Can Ride! 2012. (BOB Books: Scholastic Readers Level 1 Ser.: 5). lib. bdg. 13.55 (978-0-606-26535-5(X), Turtleback) Turtleback Bks.
Larsen, Ramonita. Yes, I Can Do It/Sí, lo Puedo Hacer. Larsen, Ramonita, illus. l.t. ed. 2006. (Illus.). 18p. (J). per. 10.99 (978-1-59879-292-8(X)) Lifevest Publishing, Inc.
Lawrie, Robin. First among Losers. 2003. (Chain Gang Ser.). (Illus.). 32p. (YA). pap. (978-0-237-52562-0(3)) Evans Brothers, Ltd.
—Gone Green. 2003. (Chain Gang Ser.). (Illus.). 32p. (YA). pap. (978-0-237-52563-7(1)) Evans Brothers, Ltd.
—Paintball Panic. 2003. (Chain Gang Ser.). (Illus.). 32p. (YA). pap. (978-0-237-52559-0(3)) Evans Brothers, Ltd.
—Radar Riders. 2003. (Chain Gang Ser.). (Illus.). 32p. (YA). pap. (978-0-237-52560-6(7)) Evans Brothers, Ltd.
Lawrie, Robin & Lawrie, Chris, illus. Chain Reaction. 32p. pap. (978-0-237-52110-3(5)) Evans Brothers, Ltd.
—Fear 3.1. 32p. (J). pap. (978-0-237-52107-3(5)) Evans Brothers, Ltd.
—Muddy Mayhem. 32p. (J). pap. (978-0-237-52105-9(9)) Evans Brothers, Ltd.
Levins, Sandra. Bumblebee Bike. Keay, Claire, illus. 2014. (J). (978-1-4338-1645-1(8)); 32p. pap. (978-1-4338-1646-8(6)) American Psychological Assn. (Magination Pr.).
Liu, Cynthea. Bike on, Bear! Litten, Kristyna, illus. 2015. (ENG.). 32p. (J). (gr. -1-2). 17.99 (978-1-4814-0506-5(3), Aladdin) Simon & Schuster Children's Publishing.
London, Jonathan & Remkiewicz, Frank. Froggy Rides a Bike. Remkiewicz, Frank & Remkiewicz, F., illus. 2008. (Froggy Ser.). (ENG.). 32p. (J). (gr. -1-k). pap. 6.99 (978-0-14-241067-7(5), Puffin Books) Penguin Young Readers Group.
Maddox, Jake. Mountain Bike Hero, 1 vol. Tiffany, Sean, illus. 2011. (Jake Maddox Sports Stories Ser.). (ENG.). 72p. (gr. 2-3). lib. bdg. 25.32 (978-1-4342-2536-8(4)) Stone Arch Bks.
Magenta, Emma. Orlando on a Thursday. Magenta, Emma, illus. 2010. (ENG., Illus.). 32p. (J). (gr. -1-2). 15.99 (978-0-7636-4560-1(5)) Candlewick Pr.
Mantell, Paul & Christopher, Matt. Mountain Bike Mania. l.t. ed. 2007. (New Matt Christopher Sports Library). 160p. (J). (gr. 4-6). lib. bdg. 26.60 (978-1-59953-108-3(9)) Norwood Hse. Pr.
McDonald, Kirsten. The Wobbly Wheels, 1 vol. Meza, Erika, illus. 2016. (ENG.). 32p. (J). (978-1-62402-144-2(1)) Magic Wagon.
McDonough, Yona Zeldis. The Bicycle Spy. 2016. (ENG.). 208p. (J). (gr. 3-7). 16.99 (978-0-545-85095-7(9), Scholastic Pr.) Scholastic, Inc.
McMahon, P. J. Mystery of the Swimming Gorilla. Manders, John, illus. 2004. 106p. (J). lib. bdg. 15.38 (978-1-4242-0401-4(1)) Fitzgerald Bks.
McOmber, Rachel B., ed. McOmber Phonics Storybooks: Pete's Bike Ride. rev. ed. (Illus.). (J). (978-0-944991-40-4(8)) Swift Learning Resources.
Mike's Bike: Set D Individual Title Six-Packs. (Supersonic Phonics Ser.). (gr. k-3). 29.00 (978-0-7635-0549-3(8)) Rigby Education.
Mikkelsen, Jon. Race for Home. Lueth, Nathan, illus. 2008. (We Are Heroes Ser.). (ENG.). 40p. (gr. 2-3). lib. bdg. 23.99 (978-1-4342-0786-9(2), Keystone Bks.) Stone Arch Bks.
Milford, Kate. The Boneshaker. Offermann, Andrea, illus. 2011. (ENG.). 384p. (J). (gr. 5-7). pap. 7.99 (978-0-547-55004-6(9)) Houghton Mifflin Harcourt Publishing Co.
Monroe, Chris. Bug on a Bike. Monroe, Chris, illus. 2014. (ENG., Illus.). 32p. (J). (gr. -1-2). 16.95 (978-1-4677-2154-7(9), Carolrhoda Bks.) Lerner Publishing Group.
Mortensen, Lori. Bree's Bike Jump, 1 vol. Sullivan, Mary, illus. 2009. (My First Graphic Novel Ser.). (ENG.). 32p. (gr. k-2). 24.65 (978-1-4342-1620-5(9), My First Graphic Novel) Stone Arch Bks.
—Cowpoke Clyde Rides the Range. Austin, Michael Allen, illus. 2016. (ENG.). 32p. (J). (gr. -1-3). 16.99 (978-0-544-37030-2(9)) Houghton Mifflin Harcourt Publishing Co.
Noll, Tom. The Bicycle Fence. Fall, Brandon & Nishio, Kimiyo, illus. 2014. (Trash to Treasure Ser.: 1). (ENG.). 32p. (J). lib. bdg. 17.99 (978-1-939377-50-0(1)) Green Kids Pr., LLC.
O'Neal-Thorpe, Rochelle. Gabe & the Bike: Riding the Minuteman Trail. O'Neal-Thorpe, Rochelle, illus. 2010. (Illus.). 30p. (J). pap. 12.95 (978-0-9823906-8-9(8)) Wiggles Pr.
—Gabe & the Park & his Big Toy Box: The Adventures of Gabe Series. O'Neal-Thorpe, Rochelle, illus. 2010. (Illus.). 38p. (J). pap. 10.95 (978-0-9823906-9-6(6)) Wiggles Pr.
Pett, Mark. The Girl & the Bicycle. Pett, Mark, illus. 2014. (ENG., Illus.). 40p. (J). 17.99 (978-1-4424-8319-4(9), Simon & Schuster Bks. For Young Readers) Simon & Schuster Bks. For Young Readers.
Pinder, Eric. I'd Rather Be Riding My Bike. Cardinal, John, illus. l.t. ed. 2013. 42p. (gr. k-1). pap. 10.95 (978-1-62253-401-2(8)) Evolved Publishing.
Potter, Noel Gyro. Plan B, 1 vol. Cannon, Joseph, illus. 2010. (Adventures of Marshall & Art Set 2 Ser.). (ENG.). 32p. (gr. -1-4). 28.50 (978-1-60270-736-8(7), Looking Glass Library) ABDO Publishing Co.
Pulley, Kelly. The Cycling Wangdoos. Pulley, Kelly, illus. 2011. (Illus.). 32p. (J). (gr. -1-3). 16.95 (978-0-9820812-1-1(9), Frog Legs Ink) Gauthier Pubns. Inc.
—The Cycling Wangdoos, 1 vol. 2017. (ENG.). 32p. (J). 16.99 (**978-0-7643-5406-9(X)**, 9780764354069) Schiffer Publishing, Ltd.
Rand, Johnathan. Freddie Fernortner #1 the Fantastic Flying Bicycle. 2005. 89p. (J). pap. 4.99 (978-1-893699-78-6(1)) AudioCraft Publishing, Inc.
Ransome, James E. New Red Bike! 2011. (ENG., Illus.). 32p. (J). (gr. -1-3). 16.95 (978-0-8234-2226-5(7)) Holiday Hse., Inc.
Raschka, Chris. Everyone Can Learn to Ride a Bicycle. Raschka, Chris, illus. 2013. (ENG., Illus.). 32p. (J). (gr. -1-3). 16.99 (978-0-375-87007-1(5), Schwartz & Wade Bks.) Random Hse. Children's Bks.
Ready to Ride: Individual Title, 6 packs. (gr. -1-2). 27.00 (978-0-7635-9470-1(9)) Rigby Education.
Rey, H. A. & Rey, Margret. Curious George Rides a Bike, 1 vol. 2006. (Curious George Ser.). (ENG., Illus.). 48p. (J). (gr. -1-3). audio compact disk 10.99 (978-0-618-68946-0(X)) Houghton Mifflin Harcourt Publishing Co.
Roberts, Daniel. Harrison & His Dinosaur Robot & the Super-Fast Race Car. 2009. (Illus.). 32p. pap. 14.95 (978-1-4389-2847-0(5)) AuthorHouse.
Rylant, Cynthia. Poppleton in Spring. Teague, Mark, illus. 2009. (Scholastic Reader Level 3 Ser.). (ENG.). 48p. (J). (gr. -1-3). pap. 3.99 (978-0-545-07867-2(9), Cartwheel Bks.) Scholastic, Inc.
Sachar, Louis. Super Fast, Out of Control. Record, Adam, illus. 2015. (Marvin Redpost Ser.: 7). (ENG.). 96p. (J). (gr. 1-4). lib. bdg. 12.99 (978-0-553-53545-7(5), Random Hse. Bks. for Young Readers) Random Hse. Children's Bks.
Santillo, LuAnn. Rose. Santillo, LuAnn, ed. 2003. (Half-Pint Kids Readers Ser.). (Illus.). 7p. (J). (gr. -1-1). pap. 1.00 (978-1-59256-101-8(2)) Half-Pint Kids, Inc.
Scotto, Michael. Builda the Re-Bicycler. Gabriel, Evette, illus. 2009. (J). (978-1-935193-22-7(8)) National Network of Digital Schls.
Sempé, Jean-Jacques & Bell, Anthea. Raoul Taburin Keeps a Secret. 2010. (ENG., Illus.). 96p. (gr. 7-17). 29.95 (978-0-7148-4979-9(0)) Phaidon Pr., Inc.
Seuling, Barbara. Robert & the Happy Endings. Brewer, Paul, illus. 2007. (Robert Bks.). (ENG.). 160p. (J). (gr. 1-4). 16.95 (978-0-8126-2748-0(2)) Cricket Bks.
Spinelli, Eileen. A Big Boy Now. Lloyd, Megan, illus. 2012. (ENG.). 32p. (J). (gr. -1-3). 16.99 (978-0-06-008673-2(4)) HarperCollins Pubs.
Stanley, George Edward. The Case of the Dirty Clue. Murdocca, Sal, illus. 2005. (Ready-for-Chapters Ser.). (J). lib. bdg. 15.00 (978-1-59054-898-1(1)) Fitzgerald Bks.
Steiner, Michaela & Steiner II, Michael. Mike Lost His Bike. 2012. 32p. pap. 19.99 (978-1-4772-7602-0(5)) AuthorHouse.
Stilton, Geronimo. The Race Across America. 2009. (Geronimo Stilton Ser.: 37). (ENG.). 128p. (J). (gr. 2-5). pap. 7.99 (978-0-545-02137-1(5), Scholastic Paperbacks) Scholastic, Inc.
Stone, Jeff. Lion. 2013. (Five Ancestors Out of the Ashes Ser.). (ENG.). 240p. (J). (gr. 4-7). 16.99 (978-0-375-87019-4(9),

Random Hse. Bks. for Young Readers) Random Hse. Children's Bks.

Viva, Frank. Along a Long Road. 2011. (ENG., Illus.). 40p. (J). (gr. -1-3). 18.99 *(978-0-316-12925-1(9))* Little, Brown Bks. for Young Readers.

Wells, H. G. The Wheels of Chance: a Bicycling Idyll. 2005. pap. *(978-1-4065-0235-0(9))* Dodo Pr.

Weston Woods Staff, creator. Duck on a Bike. 2011. 18.95 *(978-0-545-19704-5(X))*; 29.95 *(978-0-545-19698-7(1))*; 38.75 *(978-0-545-19709-0(0))* Weston Woods Studios, Inc.

Williams, Walter. The Bicycle Garden. 2013. 40p. pap. 6.99 *(978-0-9890698-0-9(X))* Fernwood & Hedges Bks.

BIGOTRY

see Toleration

BILINGUAL BOOKS

Blaine, Victor. Mi Trineo / My Sled, 1 vol. 2015. (¡Mírame, Ahí Voy! / Watch Me Go! Ser.). (ENG & SPA.). 24p. (J). 23.60 *(978-1-4994-0284-1(8),* PowerKids Pr.) Rosen Publishing Group, Inc., The.

Buddhist Text Translation Society Staff, contrib. by. Standards for Students: Instructions in Virtue from the Chinese Heritage = [Di Zi Gui]. 2003. (ENG & CHI., Illus.). 41p. (J). *(978-0-88139-489-4(0))* Buddhist Text Translation Society.

Karapetian, Marjam. Bilingual Content Dictionary: English to Armenian. 2004. (ARM & ENG.). 9.95 *(978-0-9767958-4-1(1))*; 4.95 *(978-0-9767958-2-7(5))*; 4.95 *(978-0-9767958-3-4(3))*; 13.95 *(978-0-9767958-6-5(8))*; 15.95 *(978-0-9767958-7-2(6))* Wizdomlnc.

—Bilingual Content Dictionary: English to Armenian: Social Studies - American History Through 1776. 2004. (ARM & ENG.). 14.95 *(978-0-9767958-5-8(X))* Wizdomlnc.

—Bilingual Content Dictionary: English to Korean. 2004. (KOR & ENG.). 13.95 *(978-0-9767958-0-3(9))*; 4.95 *(978-0-9764829-6-3(7))*; 4.95 *(978-0-9764829-7-0(5))*; 9.95 *(978-0-9764829-8-7(3))*; 15.95 *(978-0-9767958-1-0(7))* Wizdomlnc.

—Bilingual Content Dictionary: English to Korean: Social Studies - American History Through 1776. 2004. (KOR & ENG.). 14.95 *(978-0-9764829-9-4(1))* Wizdomlnc.

—Bilingual Content Dictionary: English to Mandarin Chinese. 2004. (CHI & ENG.). 4.95 *(978-0-9768053-0-4(8))*; 15.95 *(978-0-9768053-5-9(9))*; 4.95 *(978-0-9768053-1-1(6))*; 13.95 *(978-0-9768053-4-2(0))*; 9.95 *(978-0-9768053-2-8(4))* Wizdomlnc.

—Bilingual Content Dictionary: English to Mandarin Chinese: Social Studies - American History Through 1776. 2004. (CHI & ENG.). 14.95 *(978-0-9768053-3-5(2))* Wizdomlnc.

Luton, Susan. Bilingual Beginning Skills, Grades PreK-1. 2009. (Bilingual Beginning Skills Ser.). (Illus.). 96p. (J). (gr. -1-3). pap. 14.99 *(978-1-4190-9929-8(9))* Steck-Vaughn.

Shin, Sun Yung. Cooper's Lesson. Cogan, Kim & Paek, Min, trs. from ENG. Cogan, Kim, illus. 2004. (ENG & KOR.). 32p. (J). 16.95 *(978-0-89239-193-6(6))* Lee & Low Bks., Inc.

A to EZ Handbook for Bilingual Teachers: Staff Development Guide: Bilingual. (Staff Development Ser.). (gr. 1-5). *(978-0-02-178068-6(4))* Macmillan/McGraw-Hill Schl. Div.

Tran, Truong. Going Home, Coming Home. Phong, Ann, illus. 2003.Tr. of Ve Nha Tham Que Hu'o'Ng. (ENG & VIE.). 32p. (J). 16.95 *(978-0-89239-179-0(0))* Lee & Low Bks., Inc.

BILINGUAL BOOKS—FRENCH-ENGLISH

Irwin-Ayotte, Tracy. Bilingual Songs: English-French. 2003. 48p. (J). pap. 14.95 incl. audio *(978-1-894262-77-4(8),* JMP F24K) Jordan Music Productions, Inc.

—Bilingual Songs Vol. 1: English-French. 2003. 48p. (J). pap. 14.95 incl. audio *(978-1-894262-72-9(7),* JMP F23K) Jordan Music Productions, Inc.

BILINGUAL BOOKS—SPANISH-ENGLISH

Abbrederis, Christoph & McLellen, Christoph Elizabeth, illus. Sleeping Beauty. 2003. (Bilingual Fairy Tales Ser.: BILI).Tr. of Bella Durmiente. (ENG & SPA.). 32p. (J). (gr. -1-7). pap. 6.99 *(978-0-8118-3913-6(3))* Chronicle Bks. LLC.

Alexander, Linda. Collection 1 Bilingual. 2003. (SPA.). (J). cd-rom *(978-0-9714299-4-9(4))* I Save A Tree.

Allen, Nancy Kelly. On the Banks of the Amazon/en las orillas del Amazonas. de la Vega, Eida, tr. Driessen, Elizabeth, illus. 2003.Tr. of En las orillas del Amazonas. (SPA & ENG.). 32p. (J). (gr. -1-3). 16.95 *(978-0-9720192-7-9(8),* 626999, Raven Tree Pr.,Csi) Continental Sales, Inc.

Ancona, George. Mi Musica. 2006. (Somos Latinos (We Are Latinos) Ser.).Tr. of My Music. (SPA., Illus.). 32p. (J). (gr. 1-3). per. 8.95 *(978-0-516-25494-4(4),* Children's Pr.) Scholastic Library Publishing.

—Mis Comidas - My Foods. 2005. (Somos Latinos (We Are Latinos) Ser.). (ENG & SPA., Illus.). 32p. (J). (gr. 1-3). lib. bdg. 21.00 *(978-0-516-25292-6(5),* Children's Pr.) Scholastic Library Publishing.

—Mis Juegos/My Games. 2005. (Somos Latinos (We Are Latinos) Ser.). (ENG & SPA., Illus.). 32p. (J). (gr. 1-3). lib. bdg. 21.00 *(978-0-516-25293-3(3),* Children's Pr.) Scholastic Library Publishing.

Andersen, Hans Christian. The Little Mermaid. Capdevila, Francesc, illus. 2003. (Bilingual Fairy Tales Ser.: BILI).Tr. of Sirenita. (ENG & SPA.). 32p. (J). (gr. -1-7). pap. 6.99 *(978-0-8118-3911-2(7))* Chronicle Bks. LLC.

Argueta, Jorge. Xochitl & the Flowers (Xochitl, la Nina de Las Flores) Angel, Carl, illus. 2003.Tr. of Xochitl, la Nina de Las Flores. (ENG & SPA.). 32p. (J). 16.95 *(978-0-89239-181-3(2))* Lee & Low Bks., Inc.

Armas, Teresa. Remembering Grandma / Recordando a Abuela. Ventura, Gabriela Baeza, tr. from ENG. Rodriguez Howard, Pauline, illus. 2003. (ENG & SPA.). 32p. (J). 16.95 *(978-1-55885-344-7(8),* Piñata Books) Arte Publico Pr.

Beaton, Clare, illus. Toys: Los Juguetes. 2003. (Bilingual First Books/English-Spanish Ser.). (ENG & SPA.). 24p. (J). pap. 4.95 *(978-0-7641-2611-6(3))* Barron's Educational Series, Inc.

Beinstein, Phoebe. Dora. Mangano, Tom, illus. 2003. (Dora the Explorer Ser.). (ENG & SPA.). 12p. (J). bds. 7.99 *(978-0-689-85484-2(6),* Simon Spotlight/Nickelodeon) Simon Spotlight/Nickelodeon.

Benatar, Raquel. Isabel Allende: Memories for a Story: Isabel Allende: Recuerdos para un Cuento. Petersen, Patricia, tr. Molinari, Fernando, illus. 2003. (SPA & ENG.). 32p. 16.95 *(978-1-55885-379-9(0),* Piñata Books) Arte Publico Pr.

Benatar, Raquel & Torrecilla, Pablo. Isabel Allende: Recuerdos para un Cuento. Petersen, Patricia, tr. Benatar, Raquel & Torrecilla, Pablo, illus. 2004. (ENG & SPA., Illus.). (J). 14.95 *(978-1-56492-341-7(X),* Piñata Books) Arte Publico Pr.

Brammer, Ethriam Cash. My Tata's Guitar / la guitarra de mi Tata. Lechon, Daniel, illus. (ENG & SPA.). 32p. (J). 16.95 *(978-1-55885-369-0(3),* Piñata Books) Arte Publico Pr.

Byrd, Lee Merrill. Treasure on Gold Street/El Tesoro de la Calle D'Oro: A Neighborhood Story in Spanish & English. Castro L., Antonio, illus. 2003. (ENG & SPA.). 40p. (J). (gr. 4-6). 16.95 *(978-0-938317-75-3(X))* Cinco Puntos Pr.

Cobb, Annie & Jones, Davy. Ruedas! Jones, Davy, illus. 2003. (Road to Reading Ser.). (Illus.). (J). lib. bdg. 11.99 *(978-0-375-91500-0(1),* Golden Bks.) Random Hse. Children's Bks.

Crane Johnson, Amy. A Home for Pearl Squirrel: Una casa para la ardilla Perla, 4 vols. de la Vega, Eida, tr. Mommaerts, Robb, illus. rev. ed. 2004. (Solomon Raven Ser.: 1).Tr. of casa para la ardilla Perla. (SPA & ENG.). 32p. (J). (gr. 4-7). 16.95 *(978-0-9724973-4-3(X),* 626999, Raven Tree Pr.,Csi) Continental Sales, Inc.

Danziger, Paula. Ámbar en Cuarto y Sin Su Amigo, Level 3.7. Ross, Tony, illus. 2003.Tr. of Amber Brown Goes Fourth. (SPA.). 136p. (J). (gr. 3-5). pap. 10.95 *(978-84-204-4412-3(X),* SAN412X) Ediciones Alfaguara ESP. Dist: Santillana USA Publishing Co., Inc.

De Capua, Sarah. Como Nos Orientamos? 2005. (Rookie Reader Español Ser.). (SPA., Illus.). 32p. (J). (gr. k-2). lib. bdg. 19.50 *(978-0-516-24442-6(6),* Children's Pr.) Scholastic Library Publishing.

Delacre, Lulu, illus. & compiled by. Arrorro Mi Nino: Latino Lullabies & Gentle Games, 1 vol. Delacre, Lulu, compiled by. 2004. (ENG & SPA.). 32p. (J). 16.95 *(978-1-58430-159-2(7))* Lee & Low Bks., Inc.

Dole, Mayra L. Toca, Chavi, Toca! Tonel, illus. 2003.Tr. of Drum, Chavi, Drum! (ENG & SPA.). 32p. (J). 16.95 *(978-0-89239-186-8(3))* Lee & Low Bks., Inc.

Drew, Alejandrina. Abra Cadabra, Patas de Cabra: A Spanish, English Story for Young Readers. Satcher, David & Ford, Richard, trs. Mora, Mauricio, illus. 41p. (J). pap. 15.95 *(978-1-57168-505-6(7))* Eakin Pr.

Evan-Moor. Spanish / English Read & Understand, Grade 1. 2005. (SPA & ENG.). 304p. (J). (gr. 1-18). pap. 29.99 *(978-1-55799-999-3(6),* EMC 5307) Evan-Moor Educational Pubs.

—Spanish / English Read & Understand, Grade 2. 2005. (SPA & ENG.). 304p. (J). (gr. 2-18). pap. 29.99 *(978-1-59673-000-7(5),* EMC 5308) Evan-Moor Educational Pubs.

—Spanish / English Read & Understand, Grade 3. 2005. (SPA & ENG.). 304p. (J). (gr. 3-18). pap. 29.99 *(978-1-59673-001-4(3),* EMC 5309) Evan-Moor Educational Pubs.

Ferré, Rosario. El Medio Pollito. 2003. (SPA., Illus.). 32p. (J). (gr. 3-5). pap. 7.95 *(978-968-19-0299-5(8))* Aguilar, Altea, Taurus, Alfaguara, S.A. de C.V MEX. Dist: Santillana USA Publishing Co., Inc.

Flor Ada, Alma. Gathering the Sun. (ENG & SPA.). (J). (gr. k-2). 12.95 net. *(978-1-58186-202-7(4),* DSP8805) Del Sol Publishing.

Gershator, David & Gershator, Phillis. Bread Is for Eating. Shaw-Smith, Emma, illus. 2003. (ENG & SPA.). 25p. (J). (gr. k-4). reprint ed. 16.00 *(978-0-7567-9033-2(6))* DIANE Publishing Co.

Gomi, Taro. My Friends/Mis Amigos. 2006. (ENG & SPA., Illus.). 40p. (J). (gr. -1-7). pap. 6.99 *(978-0-8118-5204-3(0))* Chronicle Bks. LLC.

Hallinan, P. K. How Do I Love You/Como Te Amo. 2008. (SPA & ENG., Illus.). 30p. (J). pap. 4.35 *(978-0-8249-5471-0(8),* Ideal Pubns.) Worthy Publishing.

Heling, Kathryn & Hembrook, Deborah. I Wish I Had Freckles Like Abby/Quisiera Tener Pecas Como Abby. Adamson, Bonnie, illus. 2007. (SPA & ENG.). 32p. (J). (gr. -1-3). pap. 7.95 *(978-0-9770906-6-2(3),* Raven Tree Pr.,Csi) Continental Sales, Inc.

Heling, Kathryn, et al. I Wish I Had Freckles Like Abby/Quisiera Tener Pecas Como Abby. de La Vega, Eida, tr. Adamson, Bonnie, illus. 2007. (I Wish Ser.). (SPA & ENG.). 32p. (J). (gr. -1-3). 16.95 *(978-0-9724973-8-1(2),* 626999, Raven Tree Pr.,Csi) Continental Sales, Inc.

Herrera, Juan Felipe & Herrera, Juan. La Supermina del Cilantro. Robledo Tapia, Honorio, illus. 2003.Tr. of Super Cilantro Girl. (ENG & SPA.). 32p. (J). 16.95 *(978-0-89239-187-5(1))* Lee & Low Bks., Inc.

Holland, Gini. I Live in a Town/Vivo en un Pueblo. Coffey, Colleen & Carrillo, Consuelo, trs. 2004. (Weekly Reader Early Learning Library). (SPA & ENG., Illus.). 24p. (gr. k-3). pap. 8.15 *(978-0-8368-4138-1(7))*; lib. bdg. 22.00 *(978-0-8368-4131-2(X))* Stevens, Gareth Publishing LLLP. (Weekly Reader Leveled Readers).

—I Live in the City/Vivo en la Ciudad. Coffey, Colleen & Carrillo, Consuelo, trs. 2004. (Weekly Reader Early Learning Library). (SPA & ENG., Illus.). 24p. (gr. k-3). lib. bdg. 22.00 *(978-0-8368-4126-8(3),* Weekly Reader Leveled Readers) Stevens, Gareth Publishing LLLP.

—I Live in the Country/Vivo en el Campo. Coffey, Colleen & Carrillo, Consuelo, trs. 2004. (Weekly Reader Early Learning Library). (SPA & ENG., Illus.). 24p. (gr. k-3). lib. bdg. 22.00 *(978-0-8368-4127-5(1),* Weekly Reader Leveled Readers) Stevens, Gareth Publishing LLLP.

—I Live in the Desert/Vivo en el Desierto. Coffey, Colleen & Carrillo, Consuelo, trs. 2004. (Weekly Reader Early Learning Library). (ENG & SPA., Illus.). 24p. (gr. k-3). pap. 8.15 *(978-0-8368-4135-0(2))*; lib. bdg. 22.00 *(978-0-8368-4128-2(X))* Stevens, Gareth Publishing LLLP. (Weekly Reader Leveled Readers).

—I Live in the Mountains/Vivo en las Montañas. Coffey, Colleen & Carrillo, Consuelo, trs. 2004. (Weekly Reader Early Learning Library). (ENG & SPA., Illus.). 24p. (gr. k-3). lib. bdg. 22.00 *(978-0-8368-4129-9(8),* Weekly Reader Leveled Readers) Stevens, Gareth Publishing LLLP.

—I Live near the Ocean/Vivo cerca del Mar. Coffey, Colleen & Carrillo, Consuelo, trs. 2004. (Weekly Reader Early Learning Library). (ENG & SPA., Illus.). 24p. (gr. k-3). pap. 8.15 *(978-0-8368-4137-4(9))*; lib. bdg. 22.00 *(978-0-8368-4130-5(1))* Stevens, Gareth Publishing LLLP. (Weekly Reader Leveled Readers).

Howell, Theresa. A Is for Airplane. Brooks, David, illus. 2003. (SPA, ENG & MUL.). 28p. (J). (gr. -1-k). bds. 6.95 *(978-0-87358-831-7(2))* Cooper Square Publishing Llc.

Huggins-Cooper, Lynn. Alien Invaders (Invasores Extraterrestres) de La Vega, Eida, tr. Leick, Bonnie, illus. 2005. (SPA & ENG.). 32p. (J). (gr. 4-7). 7.95 *(978-0-9741992-7-6(3),* 626999, Raven Tree Pr.,Csi) Continental Sales, Inc.

—Alien Invaders/Invasores Extraterrestres. de la Vega, Eida, tr. from ENG. Leick, Bonnie, illus. 2005.Tr. of Invasores Extraterrestres. (SPA & ENG.). 32p. (J). (gr. 4-7). 16.95 *(978-0-9724973-9-8(0),* 626999, Raven Tree Pr.,Csi) Continental Sales, Inc.

Jeffers, Dawn. Vegetable Dreams/Huerto Sonado. de La Vega, Eida, tr. Schneider, Claude, illus. 2006. (SPA & ENG.). 32p. (J). (gr. -1-3). 16.95 *(978-0-9741992-9-0(X),* 626999, Raven Tree Pr.,Csi) Continental Sales, Inc.

Jiménez, Juan Ramón. Platero & I/Platero y Yo: A Dual-Language Book. Appelbaum, Stanley, ed. Appelbaum, Stanley, tr. from SPA. 2004. (Dover Dual Language Spanish Ser.). (ENG & SPA.). 192p. pap. 12.95 *(978-0-486-43565-7(2))* Dover Pubns., Inc.

Johnson, Amy Crane. Mason Moves Away/Mason se Muda: A Solomon Raven Story: un cuento del cuervo Salomon, 4 vols. de la Vega, Eida, tr. Mommaerts, Robb, illus. 2004. (Solomon Raven Ser.: 4).Tr. of Mason se Muda. (SPA & ENG.). 32p. (J). (gr. -1-3). 16.95 *(978-0-9720192-3-1(5),* 626999, Raven Tree Pr.,Csi) Continental Sales, Inc.

Laínez, René Colato. Waiting for Papá/Esperando a Papá. Accardo, Anthony, illus.Tr. of Esperando a Papa. (ENG & SPA.). 32p. (gr. 1-3). 16.95 *(978-1-55885-403-1(7),* Piñata Books) Arte Publico Pr.

Lowell, Susan. The Tortoise & the Jackrabbit: La Tortuga y la Liebre. Harris, Jim, illus. 2004. (New Bilingual Picture Book Ser.). (ENG, SPA & MUL.). 32p. (J). (gr. -1-3). pap. 7.95 *(978-0-87358-869-0(X))* Cooper Square Publishing Llc.

Luenn, Nancy. A Gift for Abuelita/Un Regalo para Abuelita: Celebrating the Day of the Dead/En Celebration del Dia de los Muertos. Chapman, Robert, illus. 2004.Tr. of Un Regalo para Abuelita: En Celebration del Dia de los Muertos. (ENG, SPA & MUL.). 32p. (J). (gr. k-3). 15.95 *(978-0-87358-688-7(3))* Cooper Square Publishing Llc.

Marcos, Subcomandante. The Story of Colors (La Historia de los Colores) A Bilingual Folktale from the Jungles of Chiapas. Din, Anne Bar, tr. Dominguez, Domitila, illus. 2003. (ENG & SPA.). 40p. (J). (gr. 4-6). pap. 8.95 *(978-0-938317-71-5(7))* Cinco Puntos Pr.

McGrath, Liz & Quick, Barbara. Even More/Todavía Más. de la Vega, Eida, tr. from ENG. McGrath, Liz, illus. 2004.Tr. of Todavía Más. (SPA & ENG., Illus.). 32p. (J). (gr. -1-3). 16.95 *(978-0-9720192-8-6(6),* 626999, Raven Tree Pr.,Csi) Continental Sales, Inc.

Mora, Pat. The Desert Is My Mother/el Desierto Es Mi Madre. Lechon, Daniel, illus. 97th ed. 2008. (SPA & ENG.). 32p. (J). (gr. -1-2). pap. 7.95 *(978-1-55885-158-0(5),* Piñata Books) Arte Publico Pr.

Mycek-Wodecki, Anna. Minutka: The Bilingual Dog & Friends. Mycek-Wodecki, Anna, illus. 2009. (Minutka Ser.). (SPA & ENG., Illus.). 48p. (J). (gr. k — 1). 9.95 *(978-1-84059-527-7(2))* Milet Publishing.

Perez, Amada Irma & Children's Book Press Staff. Nana, Que Sorpresa! Gonzalez, Maya Christina, illus. 2007.Tr. of Nana's Big Surprise. (ENG & SPA.). 32p. (J). (gr. k-2). lib. bdg. 16.95 *(978-0-89239-190-5(1))* Lee & Low Bks., Inc.

Pingry, Patricia A. & Urbano, Aide. One Baby Jesus/Un Nino Dios. Edelson, Wendy, illus. 2003. (ENG & SPA.). 30p. (J). pap. 3.95 *(978-0-8249-5472-7(6),* Ideal Pubns.) Worthy Publishing.

Polette, Keith. Isabel & the Hungry Coyote/Isabel y el Coyote Hambriento. Raven Tree Press Staff, ed. Szegedy, Esther, illus. 2004.Tr. of Isabel y el coyote Hambriento. (SPA & ENG.). 32p. (J). (gr. -1-3). 16.95 *(978-0-9724973-0-5(7),* 626999, Raven Tree Pr.) Continental Sales, Inc.

Read & Color Book Series. Date not set. (Illus.). (J). (gr. -1-5). pap. *(978-0-86545-223-7(7))* Spizzirri Pr., Inc.

Rockhill, Dennis. Meadow Dance. 2007. (Wonderlands Ser.).Tr. of Danza de la Pradera. (ENG., Illus.). 32p. (J). (gr. -1-3). 16.95 *(978-0-9741992-5-2(7),* Raven Tree Pr.,Csi) Continental Sales, Inc.

—Polar Slumber/Sueño Polar. Raven Tree Press Staff, ed. de la Vega, Eida, tr. Rockhill, Dennis, illus. 2004.Tr. of Sueño Polar. (SPA & ENG., Illus.). 32p. (J). (gr. -1-3). 16.95 *(978-0-9724973-1-2(5),* 1234791, Raven Tree Pr.,Csi) Continental Sales, Inc.

Rosa-Mendoza, Gladys. My Family & I. Cifuentes, Carolina, ed. Snider, Jackie, illus. 2004. (English-Spanish Foundations Ser.: Vol. 4).Tr. of Mi Familia y Yo. (ENG & SPA.). 20p. (J). (gr. -1-4). bds. 6.95 *(978-0-9679748-4-2(4))* Me+Mi Publishing.

—Opposites. Cifuentes, Carolina, ed. McGeehan, Dan, illus. 2004. (English-Spanish Foundations Ser.: Vol. 5).Tr. of Opuestos. (ENG & SPA.). 20p. (J). (gr. -1-4). bds. 6.95 *(978-0-9679748-6-6(0))* Me+Mi Publishing.

—The Weather. Cifuentes, Carolina, ed. Hullinger, C. D., illus. 2004. (English-Spanish Foundations Ser.: Vol. 6). Orig. Title: El Tiempo. (ENG & SPA.). 20p. (J). (gr. -1-4). bds. 6.95 *(978-0-9679748-5-9(2))* Me+Mi Publishing.

—What Time Is It? Cifuentes, Carolina, ed. 2004. (English-Spanish Foundations Ser.: Vol. 7).Tr. of Que Hora Es? (ENG & SPA., Illus.). 20p. (J). (gr. -1-4). bds. 6.95 *(978-0-9679748-9-7(5))* Me+Mi Publishing.

Sáenz, Benjamin Alire. A Gift from Papa Diego: Un Regalo de Papa Diego. Garcia, Geronimo, illus. 2008. (Little Diego Book Ser.). (ENG & SPA.). 40p. (J). pap. 10.95 *(978-0-938317-33-3(4))* Cinco Puntos Pr.

School Zone Publishing Company Staff. Bilingual ABC Dot to Dots. 2007. (ENG.). 64p. (J). pap. 3.99 *(978-1-58947-972-2(6))* School Zone Publishing Co.

—Bilingual Manuscript Writing K-2. 2007. (ENG.). 64p. (J). (gr. k-1). pap. 3.99 *(978-1-58947-961-6(0))* School Zone Publishing Co.

—Los Sonidos para Empezar Beginning Sounds. 2007. (ENG.). 64p. (J). pap. 2.69 *(978-1-58947-974-6(2))* School Zone Publishing Co.

—Lowercase Alphabet. 2007. (ENG.). 64p. (J). pap., wbk. ed. 2.69 *(978-1-58947-970-8(X))* School Zone Publishing Co.

Shah, Idries. The Farmer's Wife/la Esposa Del Granjero. Santiago, Rose Mary, illus. 2003. (SPA & ENG.). (J). 18.00 *(978-1-883536-33-6(2),* FAWI2, Hoopoe Bks.) I S H K.

—The Lion Who Saw Himself in the Water/el Leon Que Se Vio en el Agua. Rodriguez, Ingrid, illus. 2003. (SPA & ENG.). (J). 6.95 *(978-1-883536-32-9(4),* LIWS4); 18.00 *(978-1-883536-31-2(6),* LIWS3) I S H K. (Hoopoe Bks.).

Stewart, Mark & Kennedy, Mike. Latino Baseball's Finest Fielders/Las Mas Destacados Guantes del Beisbol Latino. Kalmanovitz, Manuel, tr. from ENG. 2003. (En Fuego Ser.). (ENG & SPA., Illus.). 48p. (J). (gr. 5-18). pap. 9.95 *(978-0-7613-1749-4(X))* Lerner Publishing Group.

Vogel, Elizabeth. Taking Care of My Hair: El Cuidado de Tu Cabello. 2004. (Limpieza y Salud Todo el Dia Ser.). (SPA & ENG., Illus.). 24p. (J). lib. bdg. 18.75 *(978-0-8239-6611-0(9),* Editorial Buenas Letras) Rosen Publishing Group, Inc., The.

Von Zumbusch, Amelie. Cheetahs/Guepardos. Sanz, Pilar, tr. from ENG. 2007. (Safari Animals / Animales de Safari Ser.). (SPA & ENG., Illus.). 24p. (J). (gr. k-3). lib. bdg. 22.60 *(978-1-4042-7604-8(1))* Rosen Publishing Group, Inc., The.

Wilson, Natashya. Bears: Osos. Beullens, Nathalie, tr. 2004. (My World of Animals Ser.). (ENG & SPA., Illus.). 24p. (J). (gr. k-1). lib. bdg. 16.00 *(978-1-4042-7518-8(5),* PowerKids Pr.) Rosen Publishing Group, Inc., The.

BILL OF RIGHTS (UNITED STATES)

see Constitutional Amendments—United States

BILLBOARDS

see Signs and Signboards

BILLIARDS

Givens, R. The Eight Ball Bible: A Guide to Bar Table Play. Givens, R, illus. 2004. (Illus.). 288p. (YA). per. 29.95 *(978-0-9747273-7-0(7),* 415-776-1596) 8-Ball Express, Inc.

BILLS OF CREDIT

see Credit; Paper Money

BILLS OF FARE

see Menus

BILLY, THE KID

Billy the Kid. 2010. (Legends of the Wild West Ser.). (Illus.). 104p. (gr. 6-12). 35.00 *(978-1-60413-596-1(4),* Chelsea Hse.) Facts On File, Inc.

Green, Carl R. & Sanford, William R. Billy the Kid. rev. ed. 2008. (Outlaws & Lawmen of the Wild West, Revised Edition Ser.). (Illus.). 48p. (J). (gr. 5-18). lib. bdg. 25.27 *(978-0-7660-3173-9(X))* Enslow Pubs., Inc.

Healy, Nick. Billy the Kid. 2005. (Legends of the West (Creative Education) Ser.). (Illus.). 48p. (J). (gr. 5-9). lib. bdg. 21.95 *(978-1-58341-335-7(9),* Creative Education) Creative Co., The.

Hefner, Bobby E. The Trial of Billy the Kid. (Illus.). 95p. (YA). *(978-1-886709-08-9(4))* Outlaw Pubns.

Landau, Elaine. Billy the Kid: Wild West Outlaw. 2004. (Best of the West Biographies Ser.). (Illus.). 48p. (J). lib. bdg. 25.27 *(978-0-7660-2207-2(2))* Enslow Pubs., Inc.

Thompson, Paul B. Billy the Kid: It Was a Game of Two & I Got There First. 2010. (Americans—the Spirit of a Nation Ser.). (Illus.). 128p. (J). lib. bdg. 33.27 *(978-0-7660-3480-8(1))* Enslow Pubs., Inc.

BIMETALLISM

see Gold; Silver

BINARY SYSTEM (MATHEMATICS)

Kook, Ima. Binary Numbers: Learning to Count with 0's And 1's. 2008. (Illus.). 28p. (J). pap. 12.00 *(978-1-892298-26-3(0))* Abique Pub.

Rooney, Anne. Alan Turing & His Binary Computer Code. 2012. (Miracle Makers Ser.). (ENG., Illus.). 48p. (YA). (gr. 5-8). 27.95 *(978-1-4488-6037-1(7),* Rosen Reference) Rosen Publishing Group, Inc., The.

BINDERGARTEN, MISS (FICTITIOUS CHARACTER)—FICTION

Slate, Joseph. Miss Bindergarten Stays Home from Kindergarten. Wolff, Ashley, illus. 2004. (ENG.). 48p. (J). (gr. -1-k). reprint ed. pap. 6.99 *(978-0-14-230127-2(2),* Puffin Books) Penguin Young Readers Group.

—Miss Bindergarten Takes a Field Trip with Kindergarten. Wolff, Ashley, illus. 2004. (ENG.). 40p. (J). (gr. -1-k). pap. 6.99 *(978-0-14-240139-2(0),* Puffin Books) Penguin Young Readers Group.

BINDING OF BOOKS

see Bookbinding

BINGHAM, HIRAM, 1875-1956

Hiram Bingham & the Dream of Gold. 2014. (ENG.). 192p. (J). (gr. 3-7). pap. 13.95 *(978-1-59077-350-5(0))* Evans, M. & Co., Inc.

BIOCHEMISTRY

see also Metabolism; Molecular Biology

Canavan, Thomas. Growth & Development: Cells & DNA. 2015. (How Your Body Works). (ENG.). 32p. (J). (gr. 4-4). pap. 10.00 *(978-1-4994-1228-4(2),* PowerKids Pr.) Rosen Publishing Group, Inc., The.

Clark, Julie. The 10 Most Essential Chemical Messengers in the Body. 2008. 14.99 *(978-1-55448-541-3(X))* Scholastic Library Publishing.

Eaton, Louise & Rogers, Kara. Examining Biochemical Reactions. 2017. (J). lib. bdg. ***(978-1-5383-0006-0(0))*** Rosen Publishing Group, Inc., The.

Holt, Rinehart and Winston Staff. Holt Chemistry Chptr.20: Biological Chemistry. 4th ed. Date not set. pap. 11.20 *(978-0-03-068146-2(4))* Holt McDougal.

Hunter, Rebecca. Living Organisms. 2010. (CC: 21st Century Science Ser.). 112p. (gr. 6-12). 42.80 *(978-1-933834-74-0(9))* Brown Bear Bks.

Kennington, Tammy. The Protein Group. 2013. (Healthy Eating with Myplate Ser.). (ENG.). 24p. (J). (gr. 1-4). 28.50 *(978-1-62323-605-2(3),* 206407) Child's World, Inc., The.

Kwarta, James. Decomposers. 2009. (Science Kaleidoscope Ser.). 32p. (gr. 4-4). 47.90 *(978-1-60853-035-9(3),* PowerKids Pr.) Rosen Publishing Group, Inc., The.

Laberge, Monique. Biochemistry. 2008. (Essential Chemistry Ser.). (Illus.). 112p. (YA). (gr. 7-12). 35.00 *(978-0-7910-9693-2(9))* Facts On File, Inc.

Lappi, Megan. Decomposers. (J). 2016. ***(978-1-4896-5776-3(2))*** 2011. (gr. 4-6). pap. 12.95 *(978-1-61690-718-1(5),* AV2 by Weigl) 2011. (Illus.). 24p. (gr. 2-5). 27.13 *(978-1-61690-712-9(6))* Weigl Pubs., Inc.

A B

Lindeen, Mary. Investigating the Carbon Cycle. 2015. (ENG., Illus.). 40p. (J). (gr. 3-5). 29.32 *(978-1-4677-8060-5(X)*, Lerner Pubns.) Lerner Publishing Group.

Martin, Bobi. The Nitrogen Cycle. 2017. (J). ***(978-1-5383-0027-5(3))*** Rosen Publishing Group, Inc., The.

McLaughlin, Marc, et al. How Cells Send, Receive, & Process Information, 1 vol. 2015. (ENG.). 64p. (YA). 31.70 *(978-1-62275-800-5(5)*, Britannica Educational Publishing) Rosen Publishing Group, Inc., The.

Peterson, Judy Monroe. Making Good Choices about Biodegradability. 2009. (J). 77.70 *(978-1-4358-5609-7(0)*, Rosen Reference); (ENG.). 64p. (YA). pap. 12.95 *(978-1-4358-5608-0(2)*, Rosen Reference); (Illus.). 64p. (YA). (gr. 5-9). lib. bdg. 31.95 *(978-1-4358-5313-3(X))* Rosen Publishing Group, Inc., The.

Roza, Greg. Decomposers. 2009. (Real Life Readers Ser.). 32p. (gr. 4-5). pap. 10.00 *(978-1-4358-0145-5(8)*, Rosen Classroom); (J). lib. bdg. 25.25 *(978-1-4358-2981-7(6)*, PowerKids Pr.) Rosen Publishing Group, Inc., The.

Wanjie, Anne, ed. The Basics of Biochemistry. 2013. (Core Concepts Ser.). 96p. (YA). (gr. 7-12). 34.60 *(978-1-4777-2707-2(8))* Rosen Publishing Group, Inc., The.

BIODIVERSITY

Here are entered works on the totality of the variety of living organisms, the genetic differences among them, and the communities and ecosystems in which they occur.

Berlatsky, Noah. Biodiversity. Greenhaven Press Editors, ed. 2013. (Global Viewpoints Ser.). (ENG., Illus.). 224p. (gr. 10-12). pap. 31.70 *(978-0-7377-6905-0(X))*; lib. bdg. 46.20 *(978-0-7377-6904-3(1))* Cengage Gale. (Greenhaven Pr., Inc.).

Booth, Edison. Animals & Their Environments. 2016. (Spotlight on Ecology & Life Science Ser.). 00024p. (J). (gr. 4-6). 26.25 *(978-1-4994-2558-1(9))*; pap. 10.00 *(978-1-4994-2556-7(2))* Rosen Publishing Group, Inc., The. (PowerKids Pr.).

Faguy, Peter & Boleyn-Fitzgerald, Miriam. Biodiversity. 2011. (Contemporary Issues in Science Ser.). (Illus.). 176p. (C). (gr. 9-12). 35.00 *(978-0-8160-6207-2(2))* Facts On File, Inc.

Flounders, Anne. Friends in the Wild. 2014. (Our Green Earth Ser.). (Illus.). 32p. (gr. 2-4). pap. 8.95 *(978-1-939656-29-2(X))* Red Chair Pr.

Gerdes, Louise. Biodiversity. 2010. (At Issue Ser.). (J). 34.45 *(978-0-7377-4677-8(7))*; pap. 24.45 *(978-0-7377-4678-5(5))* Cengage Gale. (Greenhaven Pr., Inc.).

Goldstein, Natalie & Lockwood, Julie L. Biodiversity. 2nd rev. ed. 2011. (Global Issues Ser.). (Illus.). 362p. (C). (gr. 9). 45.00 *(978-0-8160-8242-1(1))* Facts On File, Inc.

Green Technology Set, 8-Volumes. 2009. (Green Technology Ser.). (C). (gr. 9). 320.00 *(978-0-8160-8278-0(2))* Facts On File, Inc.

Holt, Rinehart and Winston Staff. Environmental Science Chptr. 10: Biodiversity. 4th ed. Date not set. pap. 11.20 *(978-0-03-068069-4(7))* Holt McDougal.

Is Diversity Worth Pursuing? 2011. (At Issue Ser.). 128p. pap. 22.50 *(978-0-7377-4427-9(8)*, Greenhaven Pr., Inc.) Cengage Gale.

Kortemeier, Todd & Smibert, Angie. Saving Endangered Species. 2016. (Science Frontiers Ser.). (ENG., Illus.). 32p. (J). pap. 9.95 *(978-1-63235-396-2(2))* Pr. Room Editions LLC.

Mason, Adrienne. Planet Ark: Preserving Earth's Biodiversity. Thompson, Margot, illus. 2013. (CitizenKid Ser.). (ENG.). 32p. (J). (gr. 3-7). 18.95 *(978-1-55453-753-2(3))* Kids Can Pr., Ltd. CAN. Dist: Hachette Bk. Group.

McDougal-Littell Publishing Staff. Diversity of Living Things. 2004. (McDougal Littell Middle School Science Ser.). (ENG., Illus.). 80p. (gr. 6-8). lib. bdg. 21.80 *(978-0-618-33434-6(3)*, 2-01021) Great Source Education Group, Inc.

Miller, Debra A. Biodiversity. (Current Controversies Ser.). (ENG.). 2012. 224p. (gr. 10-12). pap. 32.00 *(978-0-7377-6222-8(5))* 2008. (Illus.). 196p. (YA). (gr. 7-12). pap. 28.45 *(978-0-7377-3953-4(3))* Cengage Gale. (Greenhaven Pr., Inc.).

Miller, Debra A., ed. Biodiversity. (Current Controversies Ser.). (ENG.). 2012. 240p. (J). (gr. 10-12). lib. bdg. 40.95 *(978-0-7377-6221-1(7))* 2008. (Illus.). 196p. (YA). (gr. 7-12). pap. 40.95 *(978-0-7377-3952-7(5))* Cengage Gale. (Greenhaven Pr., Inc.).

Pyers, Greg. Biodiversity of Woodlands. 2010. (Biodiversity Ser.). 32p. (gr. 4-18). 28.50 *(978-1-60870-074-5(7))* Marshall Cavendish Corp.

Redlin, Janice L. Saving the Natural World. 2006. (Understanding Global Issues Ser.). (Illus.). 56p. per. 11.95 *(978-1-59036-510-6(0)*, 1266440) Weigl Pubs., Inc.

Rice, Stanley A. Encyclopedia of Biodiversity. 3rd rev. ed. 2012. (Science Encyclopedia Ser.). (Illus.). 616p. (C). (gr. 9). 95.00 *(978-0-8160-7726-7(6))* Facts On File, Inc.

Richardson, Gillian. Ecosystems. 2016. (J). ***(978-1-5105-2235-0(2))*** SmartBook Media, Inc.

Strauss, Rochelle. Tree of Life: The Incredible Biodiversity of Life on Earth. Thompson, Margot, illus. 2013. (CitizenKid Ser.). (ENG.). 40p. (J). (gr. 3-7). pap. 12.95 *(978-1-55453-961-1(7))* Kids Can Pr., Ltd. CAN. Dist: Hachette Bk. Group.

Worth, Richard & Benchmark Education Co., LLC. Adaptation & Biodiversity. 2013. (PRIME Ser.). (J). (gr. 6-8). pap. *(978-1-4509-9469-5(5))* Benchmark Education Co.

BIOENERGETICS

Klepeis, Alicia. Warm-Blooded & Cold-Blooded Animals Explained. 2016. (Distinctions in Nature Ser.). 32p. (J). pap. 10.58 *(978-1-5026-2181-8(9))* Cavendish Square Publishing.

Morgan, Philip. Getting Energy. 2010. (How Your Body Works). 32p. (YA). (gr. 4-7). 28.50 *(978-1-60753-053-4(8))* Amicus Publishing.

—Getting Energy. 2012. (Illus.). 32p. (gr. 4-7). pap. 8.95 *(978-1-926722-63-4(9))* Saunders Bk. Co. CAN. Dist: RiverStream Publishing.

Rose, Simon. Resource Conservation. 2016. (Illus.). 24p. (J). *(978-1-5105-0936-8(4))* SmartBook Media, Inc.

Stoyles, Pennie & Pentland, Peter. Life on Earth. 2011. (Energy in Action Ser.). (Illus.). 32p. (J). (gr. 4). 28.50 *(978-1-60870-565-8(X))* Marshall Cavendish Corp.

BIOGEOGRAPHY

see Animal Distribution; Plant Distribution

BIOGRAPHY

see also Autobiographies; Christian Biography; Heraldry; Naval Biography; Portraits

also names of classes of persons (e.g. Artists; Authors; Musicians; etc.); names of countries, cities, etc. and special subjects with the subdivision Biography (e.g. United States—Biography; African Americans—Biography; Religions—Biography; Women—Biography; etc.) and names of persons for biographies of individuals

Abbey, Cherie, ed. 2010 Annual Cumulation. 2010. (Biography Today General Ser.). 576p. lib. bdg. 73.00 *(978-0-7808-1063-1(5))* Omnigraphics, Inc.

—2012 3-Issue Subscription. 2012. (Biography Today General Ser.). 576p. pap. 66.00 *(978-0-7808-1251-2(4))* Omnigraphics, Inc.

—2012 3-Issue Subscription + 2012 Annual Cumulation. 2012. (Biography Today General Ser.). (J). pap. 110.00 *(978-0-7808-1252-9(2))* Omnigraphics, Inc.

—2012 Annual Cumulation. 2012. (Biography Today General Ser.). 576p. lib. bdg. 73.00 *(978-0-7808-1256-7(5))* Omnigraphics, Inc.

—2012 Issue 1. 2012. (Biography Today General Ser.). 192p. pap. 23.00 *(978-0-7808-1253-6(0))* Omnigraphics, Inc.

—2012 Issue 2. 2012. (Biography Today General Ser.). 194p. pap. 23.00 *(978-0-7808-1254-3(9))* Omnigraphics, Inc.

—2012 Issue 3. 2012. (Biography Today General Ser.). 192p. pap. 23.00 *(978-0-7808-1255-0(7))* Omnigraphics, Inc.

Abbey, Cherie D., ed. Annual Cumulation 2008. 2008. (Biography Today General Ser.). 525p. 73.00 *(978-0-7808-1021-1(X))* Omnigraphics, Inc.

—Biography Today: Profiles of People of Interest to Young Readers. 2003. (Biography Today Subject Ser.: Vol. 8). 200p. lib. bdg. 44.00 *(978-0-7808-0637-5(9))* Omnigraphics, Inc.

—Biography Today, Annual Cumulation 2003: Profiles of People of Interest to Young Readers. 2003. (Biography Today General Ser.). 554p. lib. bdg. 73.00 *(978-0-7808-0642-9(5))* Omnigraphics, Inc.

—Biography Today Annual Cumulation 2004: Profiles of People of Interest to Young Readers. 2004. (Biography Today General Ser.). 560p. lib. bdg. 73.00 *(978-0-7808-0686-3(7))* Omnigraphics, Inc.

—Biography Today Annual Cumulation 2006: Profiles of People of Interest to Young Readers. 2007. (Biography Today General Ser.). 524p. (gr. 14-18). lib. bdg. 73.00 *(978-0-7808-0815-7(0))* Omnigraphics, Inc.

ABDO. Newsmakers, 1 vol. 2014. (Newsmakers Ser.: 8). (ENG.). 48p. (gr. 3-6). lib. bdg. 262.32 *(978-1-62403-639-2(2))* ABDO Publishing Co.

Abdo Publishing. Beginner Biographies Set 2, 1 vol. 2013. (Beginner Biographies Set 2 Ser.: 6). (ENG.). 32p. (J). (gr. -1-4). lib. bdg. 171.00 *(978-1-61641-935-6(0)*, Looking Glass Library) Magic Wagon.

—Big Buddy Biographies Set 9, 1 vol. 2013. (Big Buddy Biographies Set 9 Ser.: 8). (ENG.). 32p. (J). (gr. 2-5). lib. bdg. 228.00 *(978-1-61783-746-3(6)*, Big Buddy Bks.) ABDO Publishing Co.

ABDO Publishing Company Staff. Essential Critiques Set 4, 1 vol. 2013. (Essential Critiques Set 4 Ser.: 8). (ENG.). 112p. (J). (gr. 6-12). lib. bdg. 285.12 *(978-1-61783-641-1(9)*, Essential Library) ABDO Publishing Co.

—Essential Lives. 2007. (Essential Lives Set 1 Ser.: 8). (ENG.). (J). (gr. 6-12). lib. bdg. 285.12 *(978-1-59928-838-3(9)*, Essential Library) ABDO Publishing Co.

Ahlers, Lena C. Sons Known to Fame. 2005. pap. 28.95 *(978-1-4191-1208-9(2))* Kessinger Publishing, LLC.

Another Great Achiever Biographies Read-along Series, 4 vols. 2003. (Another Great Achiever Ser.). (Illus.). (J). lib. bdg. 95.80 incl. audio *(978-1-57537-794-0(2))*; lib. bdg. 95.80 incl. audio compact disk *(978-1-57537-744-5(6))* Advance Publishing, Inc.

Autobiography & Biography (Gr. PreK-5) 2003. (J). *(978-1-58232-017-5(9))* ECS Learning Systems, Inc.

Bailey, Ellen. Katya's Gold: What Will Her Dreams Cost? 2008. (ENG.). 123p. (J). (gr. 4-9). pap. 10.99 *(978-0-8280-2335-1(2))* Review & Herald Publishing Assn.

Barancik, Sue. Guide to Collective Biographies for Children & Young Adults. 2004. (ENG.). 456p. pap. 72.00 *(978-0-8108-5033-0(8))* Scarecrow Pr., Inc.

Benchmark Education Company, LLC Staff, compiled by. Biography Strands Set. 2005. spiral bd. 350.00 *(978-1-4108-5563-3(5))* Benchmark Education Co.

—Career/Biography Strands Set. 2005. spiral bd. 720.00 *(978-1-4108-5460-5(4))* Benchmark Education Co.

—People Who Changed Our World: Theme Set. 2006. (J). 173.00 *(978-1-4108-7116-9(9))* Benchmark Education Co.

Benjamin, Lisa & Benchmark Education Co. Staff. Rising above - Profiles in Greatness. 2014. (Text Connections Ser.). (J). (gr. 5). *(978-1-4900-1385-5(7))* Benchmark Education Co.

Billings, Henry, et al. In the Spotlight, Vol. 1. 2005. (Jt Hi-Lo Non-fiction Ser.). (ENG., Illus.). 112p. (gr. 6-12). per. 24.60 *(978-0-07-874318-4(4)*, 0078743184) McGraw-Hill Cos., The.

Biographical Connections, 8 vols. 2006. 896p. (gr. 8-12). 299.00 *(978-0-7166-1821-8(4)*, 20188) World Bk., Inc.

Biographies. 2016. (Biographies Ser.). (ENG.). 24p. lib. bdg. 133.25 *(978-1-5158-0757-5(6))* Picture Window Bks.

Biography from Ancient Civilizations: Legends, Folklore, & Stories of Ancient Worlds, 28 vols., Set. Incl. Life & Times of Aristotle. Whiting, Jim. (Illus.). 48p. (gr. 3-7). 2006. lib. bdg. 29.95 *(978-1-58415-508-9(6))*; Life & Times of Cicero. Tracy, Kathleen. (Illus.). 48p. (gr. 4-8). 2006. lib. bdg. 29.95 *(978-1-58415-510-2(8))*; Life & Times of Herodotus. Whiting, Jim. (Illus.). 48p. (gr. 3-7). 2006. lib. bdg. 29.95 *(978-1-58415-509-6(4))*; Life & Times of Hippocrates. Whiting, Jim. (Illus.). 48p. (gr. 3-7). 2006. lib. bdg. 29.95 *(978-1-58415-512-6(4)*, 1259600); Life & Times of King Arthur: The Evolution of the Legend. Harkins, Susan & Harkins, William H. (Illus.). 48p. (gr. 3-7). 2006. lib. bdg. 29.95 *(978-1-58415-513-3(2))*; Life & Times of Nostradamus. Roberts, Russell. (Illus.). 48p. (gr. 4-8). 2007. lib. bdg. 29.95 *(978-1-58415-544-7(2))*; Life & Times of Plato. Whiting, Jim. (Illus.). 48p. (gr. 3-7). 2006. lib. bdg. 29.95 *(978-1-58415-507-2(8)*, 1259591); Life & Times of Pythagoras. Harkins, Susan Sales & Harkins, William H. (Illus.). 48p. (gr. 4-8). 2007. lib. bdg. 29.95 *(978-1-58415-545-4(0))*; Set. (gr. 4-8). 2005. lib. bdg. *(978-1-58415-407-5(1))*; (J). (Biography from Ancient Civilizations Ser.). 2007. Set lib. bdg. 838.60 *(978-1-58415-546-1(9))* Mitchell Lane Pubs., Inc.

A Blue Banner Biography Series, 15 bks. 2004. (YA). 254.25 *(978-1-58415-236-1(2))* Mitchell Lane Pubs., Inc.

Bragg, Georgia. How They Croaked: The Awful Ends of the Awfully Famous. O'Malley, Kevin, illus. 2012. (ENG.). 192p. (J). (gr. 5-14). pap. 9.99 *(978-0-8027-2794-7(8)*, 9780802727947, Bloomsbury USA Childrens) Bloomsbury Publishing USA.

Breakout Biographies: Set 1. 2017. (Breakout Biographies Ser.). 32p. (gr. 9-10). 157.50 ***(978-1-5081-6078-6(3))***; pap. 60.00 ***(978-1-5081-6079-3(1))*** Rosen Publishing Group, Inc., The. (PowerKids Pr.).

Britannica Beginner Bios: Set 2. 2015. (Britannica Beginner Bios Ser.). (ENG.). 32p. (J). (gr. 2-3). 281.40 *(978-1-68048-194-5(0)*, Britannica Educational Publishing) Rosen Publishing Group, Inc., The.

Britannica Learning Library Staff. Remarkable People in History. 2003. (Illus.). 64p. 14.95 *(978-1-59339-039-6(4))* Encyclopaedia Britannica, Inc.

Brooks, E. S. Historic Boys: Their Endeavors, Their Achievements & Their Times. 2003. (Illus.). 259p. (YA). 26.95 *(978-0-918736-55-0(2)*, Castle Keep Pr.) Rock, James A. & Co. Pubs.

—Historic Girls. 2013. 140p. pap. *(978-3-95507-936-9(8))* DOGMA. in Europäischer Hochschulverlag GmbH & Co. KG.

Capstone Press. Star Biographies, 1 vol. 2010. (Star Biographies Ser.). (ENG.). 32p. lib. bdg. 266.50 *(978-1-4296-5910-9(6)*, Snap Bks.) Capstone Press of Coughlan Cos.

Capua, Sarah De. LIfe Skills Biographics. 2007. 48p. lib. bdg. 251.40 *(978-1-60279-110-7(4)*, 200037) Cherry Lake Publishing.

Celebrity Activists, 6 vols., Set. Incl. Al Gore & Global Warming. Harmon, Daniel E. lib. bdg. 34.60 *(978-1-4042-1761-4(4))*; Angelina Jolie: Goodwill Ambassador for the United Nations. La Bella, Laura. lib. bdg. 33.25 *(978-1-4042-1762-1(2))*; Bono: Fighting World Hunger & Poverty. Kamberg, Mary-Lane. lib. bdg. 34.60 *(978-1-4042-1760-7(6))*; George Clooney & the Crisis in Darfur. Orr, Tamra. lib. bdg. 34.60 *(978-1-4042-1763-8(0))*; Leonardo DiCaprio: Environmental Champion. Furgang, Kathy & Furgang, Adam. lib. bdg. 34.60 *(978-1-4042-1764-5(9))*; Michael J. Fox: Parkinson's Disease Research Advocate. Payment, Simone. lib. bdg. 34.60 *(978-1-4042-1765-2(7)*, 1284495); (Illus.). 112p. (YA). (gr. 7-12). 2008. 2008. Set lib. bdg. 199.50 *(978-1-4042-1883-3(1))* Rosen Publishing Group, Inc., The.

Chin-Lee, Cynthia. Akira to Zoltan: Twenty-Six Men Who Changed the World. Halsey, Megan & Addy, Sean, illus. 2006. (ENG.). 32p. (J). (gr. 3-7). lib. bdg. 15.95 *(978-1-57091-579-6(2))* Charlesbridge Publishing, Inc.

Classic Storytellers, 16 vols., Set. Incl. Beverly Cleary. Griskey, Michele. (gr. 4-7). 2006. lib. bdg. 29.95 *(978-1-58415-457-0(8)*, 1259543); E. B. White. Murcia, Rebecca Thatcher. (gr. 4-8). 2004. lib. bdg. 29.95 *(978-1-58415-273-6(7))*; Edgar Allan Poe. Whiting, Jim. (gr. 4-8). 2005. lib. bdg. 29.95 *(978-1-58415-373-3(3))*; Ernest Hemingway. Whiting, Jim. (gr. 6-8). 2005. lib. bdg. 29.95 *(978-1-58415-376-4(8))*; F. Scott Fitzgerald. Bankston, John. (gr. 4-8). 2004. lib. bdg. 29.95 *(978-1-58415-249-1(4))*; Harriet Beecher Stowe. Griskey, Michele. (gr. 4-8). 2005. lib. bdg. 29.95 *(978-1-58415-375-7(X))*; Jack London. Bankston, John. (gr. 4-8). 2004. lib. bdg. 29.95 *(978-1-58415-263-7(X))*; Jacqueline Woodson. Hinton, Kaa Vonia. (gr. 4-8). 2007. lib. bdg. 29.95 *(978-1-58415-533-1(7))*; John Steinbeck. Tracy, Kathleen. (gr. 4-8). 2004. lib. bdg. 29.95 *(978-1-58415-271-2(0))*; Judy Blume. Tracy, Kathleen. (gr. 4-8). 2005. lib. bdg. 29.95 *(978-1-58415-377-1(6))*; Katherine Paterson. Kjelle, Marylou. (gr. 4-8). 2004. lib. bdg. 29.95 *(978-1-58415-268-2(0))*; Mark Twain. Sherman, Josepha. (gr. 4-8). 2005. lib. bdg. 29.95 *(978-1-58415-374-0(1))*; Mildred Taylor. Mangal, Melina. (gr. 4-8). 2004. lib. bdg. 29.95 *(978-1-58415-311-5(3))*; Nathaniel Hawthorne. Roberts, Russell. (gr. 3-7). 2006. lib. bdg. 29.95 *(978-1-58415-454-9(3)*, 1259541); Ray Bradbury. Griskey, Michele. (gr. 3-7). 2006. lib. bdg. 29.95 *(978-1-58415-455-6(1)*, 1259542); Stephen Crane. Kepnes, Caroline. (gr. 4-8). 2004. lib. bdg. 29.95 *(978-1-58415-272-9(9))*; (Illus.). 48p. (J). 2007. Set lib. bdg. 479.20 *(978-1-58415-536-2(1))* Mitchell Lane Pubs., Inc.

Collective Biographies, 43 bks., Set. (Illus.). (YA). (gr. 6-12). lib. bdg. 838.00 *(978-0-89490-570-4(8))* Enslow Pubs., Inc.

Contemporary Biographies, 16 bks., Set. Incl. Barbara Jordan. Patrick-Wexler, Diane. 1996. lib. bdg. 17.98 *(978-0-8172-3976-3(6))*; Edward James Olmos. Carrillo, Louis. 1997. lib. bdg. 17.98 *(978-0-8172-3989-3(8))*; John Lucas. Simmons, Alex. 1996. lib. bdg. 17.98 *(978-0-8172-3978-7(2))*; Ladonna Harris. Schwartz, Michael. 1997. lib. bdg. 17.98 *(978-0-8172-3995-4(2))*; Luis Rodriguez. Schwartz, Michael. 1997. lib. bdg. 17.98 *(978-0-8172-3990-9(1))*; Maya Lin. Ling, Bettina. 1997. lib. bdg. 17.98 *(978-0-8172-3992-3(8))*; Michael Dorris. Weil, Ann. 1997. lib. bdg. 17.98 *(978-0-8172-3994-7(4))*; Nely Galan. Rodriguez, Janel. 1997. lib. bdg. 17.98 *(978-0-8172-3991-6(X))*; Seiji Ozawa. Tan, Sheri. 1997. lib. bdg. 17.98 *(978-0-8172-3993-0(6))*; Toni Morrison. Patrick-Wexler, Diane. 1997. lib. bdg. 17.98 *(978-0-8172-3987-9(1))*; Wynton Marsalis. Ellis, Veronica Freeman. 1997. lib. bdg. 17.98 *(978-0-8172-3986-6(X))*; 48p. (J). (gr. 3-8). (Illus.). Set lib. bdg. 287.68 *(978-0-7398-4110-5(6))* Heinemann-Raintree.

Davidson, Margaret. Louis Braille. Compere, Janet, illus. (FRE.). 80p. (J). pap. 5.99 *(978-0-590-71110-4(5))* Scholastic, Inc.

Davis, Kenneth C. Don't Know Much about George Washington. Shepperson, Rob, illus. 2003. (Don't Know Much About Ser.). 128p. (J). (gr. 3). pap. 4.99 *(978-0-06-442124-9(4))* HarperCollins Pubs.

—Don't Know Much about Thomas Jefferson. Shepperson, Rob, illus. 2005. (Don't Know Much About Ser.). 128p. (J). (gr. 2-5). pap. 4.99 *(978-0-06-442128-7(7))* HarperCollins Pubs.

Dorling Kindersley Publishing Staff & Gilliland, Ben. 100 People Who Made History. 2012. (ENG.). 128p. (J). (gr. 2-5). 16.99 *(978-0-7566-9003-8(X)*, DK Children) Dorling Kindersley Publishing, Inc.

Douglas, Bettye. Portrait of a People: The Bettye Douglas Forum, Inc. Multicultural Resource Book. Douglas, Bettye, ed. Douglas, Ana & Douglas, Garbrielle, illus. 222p. (YA). (gr. 5-13). 100.00 *(978-0-9703183-1-2(6))* Douglas, Bettye Forum, Inc., The.

DuMont, Brianna. Fantastic Fugitives: Criminals, Cutthroats, & Slaves Who Changed History (While on the Run!) Straker, Bethany, illus. 2016. (Changed History Ser.). (ENG.). 192p. (J). (gr. 3-7). 16.99 *(978-1-63220-412-7(6)*, Sky Pony Pr.) Skyhorse Publishing Co., Inc.

Edgar, John. Footprints of Famous Men Biography for. 2006. (Illus.). 404p. per. *(978-1-4067-9701-5(4)*, Hesperides Pr.) Read Bks.

Edgar, Kathleen J., et al. Compassion. 2003. (J). *(978-1-59203-055-2(6))* Learning Challenge, Inc.

—Courage. 2003. (J). *(978-1-59203-056-9(4))* Learning Challenge, Inc.

—Determination. 2003. (J). *(978-1-59203-057-6(2))* Learning Challenge, Inc.

—Imagination. 2003. (J). *(978-1-59203-058-3(0))* Learning Challenge, Inc.

—Responsibility. 2003. (J). *(978-1-59203-059-0(9))* Learning Challenge, Inc.

—Vision. 2003. (J). *(978-1-59203-060-6(2))* Learning Challenge, Inc.

Eggleton, Jill. Living to Tell the Tale. 2007. (Connectors Ser.). (gr. 2-5). pap. *(978-1-877453-15-1(3))* Global Education Systems Ltd.

Famous Lives, 4 vols., Set. Incl. Barack Obama: President for Change. Hicks, Peter. lib. bdg. 26.50 *(978-1-4488-3287-3(X))*; J. K. Rowling: Creator of Harry Potter. Senker, Cath. lib. bdg. 26.50 *(978-1-4488-3288-0(8))*; Lance Armstrong - Racing Hero. Hicks, Peter. lib. bdg. 26.50 *(978-1-4488-3289-7(6))*; Simon Cowell: Global Music Mogul. Foy, Debbie. lib. bdg. 26.50 *(978-1-4488-3290-3(X))*; (YA). (gr. 3-6). (Famous Lives Ser.). (Illus.). 32p. 2011. Set lib. bdg. 101.00 *(978-1-4488-3311-5(6)*, PowerKids Pr.) Rosen Publishing Group, Inc., The.

First Biographies, Set. 2005. (First Biographies Ser.). (YA). (gr. k-3). 267.30 *(978-0-7368-4195-5(4))*; Vol. 2. 267.30 *(978-0-7368-4196-2(2))* Capstone Press of Coughlan Cos. (Pebble Bks.).

First Biographies, 9 bks., Set. Incl. Bill Clinton. Holland, Gini. Rees, Gary, illus. 1997. lib. bdg. 25.69 *(978-0-8172-4450-7(6))*; Booker T. Washington. Gleiter, Jan & Thompson, Kathleen. 1995. lib. bdg. 25.69 *(978-0-8114-8454-1(8))*; Diego Rivera. Holland, Gini. Rees, Gary, illus. 1997. lib. bdg. 25.69 *(978-0-8172-4453-8(0))*; Johnny Appleseed. Holland, Gini. 1997. lib. bdg. 25.69 *(978-0-8172-4452-1(2))*; Nelson Mandela. Holland, Gini. White, Mike, illus. 1997. lib. bdg. 25.69 *(978-0-8172-4454-5(9))*; P. T. Barnum. Wright, David K. White, Mike, illus. 1997. lib. bdg. 25.69 *(978-0-8172-4456-9(5))*; Rosa Parks. Holland, Gini. Price, David, illus. 1997. lib. bdg. 25.69 *(978-0-8172-4451-4(4))*; Sandra Day O'Connor. Holland, Gini. Roberts, Mark, illus. 1997. lib. bdg. 25.69 *(978-0-8172-4455-2(7))*; Wilma Mankiller. Holland, Gini. Crompton, Paul H., illus. 1997. lib. bdg. 25.69 *(978-0-8172-4457-6(3))*; 32p. (J). (gr. 1-4). Set lib. bdg. 231.21 *(978-0-7398-4111-2(4))* Heinemann-Raintree.

First Biographies (Set 1) 2010. (First Biographies Ser.). 24p. pap. 59.50 *(978-1-4296-5038-0(9)*, Pebble Bks.) Capstone Press of Coughlan Cos.

First Biographies (Set 2) 2010. (First Biographies Ser.). 24p. pap. 59.50 *(978-1-4296-5039-7(7)*, Pebble Bks.) Capstone Press of Coughlan Cos.

Flor Ada, Alma & Campoy, F. Isabel, contrib. by. Caminos. (Literature Collection of Puertas Al Sol Ser.). (SPA.). 48p. (J). (gr. k-6). pap. 16.95 *(978-1-59437-710-5(3))* Santillana USA Publishing Co., Inc.

Frank, Ana. The Diary of a Anne Frank. 241p. (J). (gr. 4-6). pap. 4.99 *(978-0-8072-1363-6(2)*, Listening Library) Random Hse. Audio Publishing Group.

Galens, Judy, et al. UXL Newsmakers. 2004. (J). *(978-0-7876-9195-0(X))*; *(978-0-7876-9190-5(9))*; *(978-0-7876-9191-2(7))*; *(978-0-7876-9194-3(1))* Cengage Gale. (UXL).

Ganeri, Anita. The Top Ten Leaders That Changed the World. 2009. (J). 60.00 *(978-1-4358-9166-1(X)*, PowerKids Pr.); (ENG., Illus.). 32p. (J). pap. 10.00 *(978-1-4358-9165-4(1)*, PowerKids Pr.); (Illus.). 32p. (YA). (gr. 3-6). 26.50 *(978-1-4358-9164-7(3))* Rosen Publishing Group, Inc., The.

Gateway Biographies, 12 vols., Set. Incl. Al Gore: Fighting for a Greener Planet. Stefoff, Rebecca. 2008. 26.60 *(978-1-57505-948-8(7))*; Alberto Gonzales: Attorney General. McElroy, Lisa Tucker. (Illus.). (J). 2006. lib. bdg. 23.93 *(978-0-8225-3418-1(5))*; Barack Obama: President for a New Era. Brill, Marlene Targ. 2009. 26.60 *(978-1-57505-950-1(9))*; Condoleezza Rice. Wade, Mary Dodson. (Illus.). 2005. lib. bdg. 26.60 *(978-0-7613-9550-8(4))*; Green Day: Keeping Their Edge. Doeden, Matt. (Illus.). 2006. lib. bdg. 26.60 *(978-0-8225-6390-7(8)*, Lerner Pubns.); John G. Roberts, Jr.: Chief Justice. McElroy, Lisa Tucker. (Illus.). 2006. lib. bdg. 26.60 *(978-0-8225-6389-1(4)*, Lerner Pubns.); Michael Jackson: Ultimate Music Legend. Krohn, Katherine E. (Illus.). 2010. lib. bdg. 26.60 *(978-0-7613-5762-9(9)*, Lerner Pubns.); Michelle Obama: From Chicago's South Side to the White House. Brill, Marlene Targ. (Illus.). 2009. 26.60 *(978-0-7613-5033-0(0))*; Nancy Pelosi: First Woman Speaker of the House. McElroy, Lisa Tucker. (Illus.). 2007. lib. bdg. 26.60 *(978-0-8225-8685-2(1)*, Lerner Pubns.); Sonia Sotomayor: First Hispanic U. S. Supreme Court Justice. McElroy, Lisa Tucker. 2010. lib. bdg. 26.60 *(978-0-7613-5861-9(7))*; Ted Kennedy: A Remarkable Life in the Senate. McElroy, Lisa Tucker. 2009. 26.60 *(978-0-7613-4457-5(8))*; Tyra Banks: From Supermodel to Role Model. Hill, Anne E. 2009. 26.60 *(978-1-57505-949-5(5))*; 48p. (gr. 4-8). 2010. Set lib. bdg. 319.20 *(978-0-8225-8069-0(1))* Lerner Publishing Group.

Gilbert, Ariadne. More Than Conquerors. 2008. 436p. 51.95 *(978-1-4366-1530-3(5))*; 440p. per. 36.95 *(978-0-548-81262-4(4))* Kessinger Publishing, LLC.

Gomez, Rebecca & ABDO Publishing Company Staff. First Biographies, 6 vols., Set III. 2003. (First Biographies Set 3 Ser.). (Illus.). (gr. k-4). 162.42 (978-1-57765-943-3(0), Buddy Bks.) ABDO Publishing Co.

Goodrich, Samuel G. (Samuel Griswold). Famous Men of Ancient Times: By the Author of Peter Parley's Tales. 2006. 320p. per. 23.99 (978-1-4255-3140-9(7)) Michigan Publishing.

Haaren, John. Famous Men of Modern Times. 2008. 140p. pap. 12.95 (978-1-60459-526-0(4)) Wilder Pubns., Corp.

Haaren, John H. John H Haaren's Complete Famous Men Series. 2008. 424p. pap. 19.99 (978-1-60459-527-7(2)) Wilder Pubns., Corp.

Hamilton Wright Mabie. Heroes Every Child Should Know. 2010. (CAM.). 256p. pap. 16.95 (978-1-4385-3611-8(9), Book Jungle) Standard Pubns., Inc.

Hanes, Sharon M., et al. Cold War: Biographies, 2.0. 2003. (Cold War Reference Library). (Illus.). (J). (ENG.). 474p. 191.00 (978-0-7876-7663-6(2)); xxxv, 473p. (978-0-7876-7664-3(0)); xxxv, 473p. (978-0-7876-7665-0(9)) Cengage Gale. (UXL).

Hansen, Grace. History Maker Biographies. 2014. (History Maker Biographies Ser.: 6). (ENG.). 24p. (J). (gr. 2-4). lib. bdg. 171.00 (978-1-62970-700-6(7)) ABDO Publishing Co.

Hearst, Michael. Extraordinary People. Scamihorn, Aaron, illus. 2015. (ENG.). 112p. (J). (gr. 3-7). 16.99 (978-1-4521-2709-5(3)) Chronicle Bks. LLC.

Heinemann Profiles, 20 bks. (Illus.). (J). (gr. 4-6). Set 1-3. lib. bdg. 484.40 (978-1-58810-184-6(3))Set 2. lib. bdg. 145.32 (978-1-57572-295-5(X)) Heinemann-Raintree.

Hopper, Missy. Peggy Sue & the Pepper Patch. Bowden, Cecelia, illus. 2010. 32p. (J). (978-1-57736-430-6(9)) Providence Hse Pubs.

Humphrey, Sandra McLeod. They Stood Alone! 25 Men & Women Who Made a Difference. 2011. (ENG.). 176p. (J). (gr. 3-7). pap. 14.00 (978-1-61614-485-2(8)) Prometheus Bks., Pubs.

Influential Lives: Set 1. 2017. (Influential Lives Ser.). 128p. (gr. 7-8). lib. bdg. 223.62 (978-0-7660-8571-8(6)) Enslow Pubs., Inc.

Internet Biographies: Set 2. 2013. (Internet Biographies Ser.). 128p. (YA). (gr. 7-12). 276.80 (978-1-4488-9539-7(1)) Rosen Publishing Group, Inc., The.

Internet Biographies: Sets 1 - 2. 2013. (Internet Biographies Ser.). 128p. (YA). (gr. 7-12). 553.60 (978-1-4777-0618-3(6)) Rosen Publishing Group, Inc., The.

Junior Biographies: Set 1. 2016. (Junior Biographies Ser.). 24p. (J). lib. bdg. 135.60 (978-0-7660-8386-8(1)) Enslow Pubs., Inc.

Junior Biographies: Set 2. 2017. (Junior Biographies Ser.). 24p. (gr. 3-4). pap. 56.10 (978-0-7660-8811-5(1)); lib. bdg. 135.60 (978-0-7660-8594-7(5)) Enslow Pubs., Inc.

K/H (Pathways). Pathways: Grade 6 Dr. Rabbit Trade Book. rev. ed. 2011. (ENG.). 30p. pap. 11.00 (978-0-7575-4840-6(7)) Kendall Hunt Publishing Co.

Lawrence, Sandra. Murder & Mayhem. 2016. (Hideous History Ser.). (ENG., Illus.). 64p. (J). (gr. 5-9). 11.99 (978-1-4998-0082-1(7)) Little Bee Books Inc.

LernerClassroom Editors, ed. Pull Ahead Biographies: Classroom Set. 2008. pap. 40.95 (978-0-8225-9189-4(8)) Lerner Publishing Group.

—Pull Ahead Biographies: Complete set IV. 2008. pap. 244.95 (978-1-58013-279-4(0)) Lerner Publishing Group.

—Pull Ahead Biographies Set Iv Classroom Set Plus Character Cards. 2008. 51.95 (978-1-58013-781-2(4)) Lerner Publishing Group.

—Pull Ahead Biographies Set Iv Complete Set Plus Character Cards. 2008. 255.95 (978-1-58013-751-5(2)) Lerner Publishing Group.

Lesinski, Jeanne M. Bill Gates. (Biography Ser.). (Illus.). 112p. (gr. 6-12). 2005. lib. bdg. 27.93 (978-0-8225-4949-9(2)) 2003. (J). pap. 7.95 (978-0-8225-9689-9(X)) Lerner Publishing Group.

The Library of American Lives & Times, 12 vols., Set 3. 2005. (Illus.). (gr. 4-8). lib. bdg. 383.40 (978-0-8239-6657-8(7)) Rosen Publishing Group, Inc., The.

The Library of Author Biographies, 6 Bks, Set 4. 2004. (J). 159.00 (978-1-4042-0368-6(0)) Rosen Publishing, Inc.

Lucan, Dawn. Memories of my Childhood. 2010. 72p. pap. 7.95 (978-0-557-48269-6(0)); 80p. pap. 18.95 (978-0-557-48050-0(7)) Lulu Pr., Inc.

Lucke, Deb. The Book of Time Outs: A Mostly True History of the World's Biggest Troublemakers. Lucke, Deb, illus. 2008. (ENG., Illus.). 32p. (J). (gr. 1-4). 15.99 (978-1-4169-2829-4(4), Simon & Schuster Bks. For Young Readers) Simon & Schuster Bks. For Young Readers.

Mabie, H. W., ed. Heroes Every Child Should Know (Yesterday's Classics) 2006. 396p. (J). per. 13.95 (978-1-59915-097-0(2)) Yesterday's Classics.

Mabie, Hamilton Wright. Heroes Every Child Should Know. 2005. 31.95 (978-1-4218-0941-0(9)); 368p. pap. 15.95 (978-1-59540-641-5(7)) 1st World Publishing, Inc. (1st World Library - Literary Society).

—Heroes Every Child Should Know. 2008. 260p. 25.99 (978-0-554-31301-6(4)) 2008. 260p. 28.99 (978-0-554-21998-1(0)) 2006. 268p. pap. 21.99 (978-1-4264-1392-6(0)) 2006. (ENG.). 258p. pap. 23.99 (978-1-4264-1445-9(5)) Creative Media Partners, LLC.

—Heroes Every Child Should Know. 2009. 194p. pap. 15.37 (978-1-4589-5375-9(0)) General Bks. LLC.

—Heroes Every Child Should Know. 2004. reprint ed. pap. 26.95 (978-1-4191-2360-3(2)); pap. 1.99 (978-1-4192-2360-0(7)) Kessinger Publishing, LLC.

Mabie, Hamilton Wright, ed. Heroes Every Child Should Know. 2007. 260p. per. (978-1-4065-2954-8(0)) Dodo Pr.

Mahmout, Ulfet & Thompson, Alan. My Life Story. 2004. (Illus.). 34p. (J). (978-1-85269-885-0(3)) Mantra Lingua.

Manzanero, Paula K. & dePaola, Tomie. Who Is (Your Name Here)? The Story of My Life. Harrison, Nancy, illus. 2015. (Who Was? Ser.). (ENG.). 112p. (J). (gr. 3-7). 8.99 (978-0-448-48715-1(2), Grosset & Dunlap) Penguin Young Readers Group.

McCabe, Matthew. 12 Political Leaders Who Changed the World. 2015. (Change Makers Ser.). (ENG., Illus.). 32p. (J). (gr. 3-5). (978-1-63235-148-7(X), 12-Story Library) Pr. Room Editions LLC.

Melbo, Irving Robert. Our Americ: A Textbook for Elementary School History & Social Studies. 2011. 414p. 54.95 (978-1-258-07894-2(5)) Literary Licensing, LLC.

Mitchell Lane Publishers Inc. Staff. Blue Banner Biographies, 67 vols. 2007. (Blue Banner Biography Ser.). (J). lib. bdg. 1747.60 (978-1-58415-621-5(X)) Mitchell Lane Pubs., Inc.

—A Robbie Reader-Contemporary Biographies, 25 vols., Set. 2007. (Robbie Reader Ser.). (J). (gr. 1-4). lib. bdg. 642.50 (978-1-58415-597-3(3)) Mitchell Lane Pubs., Inc.

Mooney, Brian. Great Leaders. 2012. (Great People in History Ser.). (ENG., Illus.). 128p. (YA). (gr. 8-12). lib. bdg. 34.60 (978-1-4777-0403-5(5)) Rosen Publishing Group, Inc., The.

Multicultural Junior Biographies, 5 bks., Set. (Illus.). (YA). (gr. 4-10). lib. bdg. 104.75 (978-0-89490-661-9(5)) Enslow Pubs., Inc.

Murcia, Rebecca Thatcher. Ronaldinho. 2007. (No Hands Allowed Ser.). (Illus.). 32p. (J). (gr. 2-4). lib. bdg. 25.70 (978-1-58415-600-0(7)) Mitchell Lane Pubs., Inc.

My First Biographies, 6 bks., Set. 2006. (J). (gr. 1-3). 34.95 (978-0-8225-5694-7(4)) Lerner Publishing Group.

National Geographic Kids Staff & Esbaum, Jill. Little Kids First Big Book of Who - National Geographic Kids. 2015. (National Geographic Little Kids First Big Bks.). (ENG., Illus.). 128p. (J). (gr. -1-3). 14.99 (978-1-4263-1917-4(7), National Geographic Children's Bks.) National Geographic Society.

O'Brien, Tony & Sullivan, Michael P. Afghan Dreams: Young Voices of Afghanistan. O'Brien, Tony, photos by. 2008. (ENG., Illus.). 80p. (J). (gr. 2-10). 19.99 (978-1-59990-287-6(7), 9781599902876, Bloomsbury USA Childrens) Bloomsbury Publishing USA.

Oceanak, Karla. All Me, All the Time: The Authorized Art-O-Biography Of... Spanjer, Kendra, illus. 2012. (Aldo Zelnick Comic Novel Ser.). (ENG.). 80p. (J). (gr. 3-7). pap. 7.95 (978-1-934649-20-6(1)) Bailiwick Pr.

Omnigraphics, creator. Biography Today: Profiles of People of Interest to Young Readers. 2005. (Biography Today General Ser.). (Illus.). 504p. 73.00 (978-0-7808-0692-4(1)) Omnigraphics, Inc.

On My Own Biographies Set, Vol. 2. 2004. (Illus.). lib. bdg. 7.95 (978-0-8225-3385-6(5)) Lerner Publishing Group.

Osborne, Mary Pope & Boyce, Natalie Pope. Heroes for All Times. 2014. (Magic Tree House Fact Tracker Ser.: 28). lib. bdg. 16.00 (978-0-606-35197-3(3)) Turtleback Bks.

—Heroes for All Times: A Nonfiction Companion High Time for Heroes. Murdocca, Sal, illus. 2014. (Magic Tree House - Fact Tracker Ser.: 28). (ENG.). 128p. (J). (gr. 2-5). 6.99 (978-0-375-87027-9(X), Random Hse. Bks. for Young Readers) Random Hse. Children's Bks.

Parham, Jerrill. Boundary Breakers: Remarkable People. 2007. (Shockwave: History & Politics Ser.). (ENG., Illus.). 36p. (J). (gr. 4-8). 25.00 (978-0-531-17752-5(1), Children's Pr.) Scholastic Library Publishing.

Pebble Books: First Biographies. 2005. (YA). (gr. k-3). 653.40 (978-0-7368-4218-1(7), Pebble Bks.) Capstone Press of Coughlan Cos.

Peterson, Susan Lynn. Legends of the Martial Arts Masters. 2003. (ENG., Illus.). 120p. (J). (gr. 4-8). pap. 9.95 (978-0-8048-3518-3(7)) Tuttle Publishing.

Pinkney, Andrea Davis. Peace Warriors. 2013. (Profiles Ser.: 6). (ENG.). 144p. (J). (gr. 5-9). pap. 6.99 (978-0-545-51857-4(1), Scholastic Paperbacks) Scholastic, Inc.

Powell, Marie. Unsolved! 2015. (ENG., Illus.). 32p. (J). (978-0-7787-8073-1(2)) Crabtree Publishing Co.

Randy's Corner: Day by Day With, 4 vols., Set. Incl. Day by Day with Beyonce. Marvis, Barbara. (J). lib. bdg. 25.70 (978-1-58415-859-2(X)); Day by Day with Lebron James. Marvis, Barbara. (YA). lib. bdg. 25.70 (978-1-58415-858-5(1)); Day by Day with Miley Cyrus. Leavitt, Amie Jane. (J). lib. bdg. 25.70 (978-1-58415-856-1(5)); Day by Day with Taylor Swift. Reusser, Kayleen. (J). lib. bdg. 25.70 (978-1-58415-857-8(3)); 32p. (gr. -1-2). (Illus.). 2010. Set lib. bdg. 102.80 (978-1-58415-860-8(3)) Mitchell Lane Pubs., Inc.

Real Bios (Set Of 4) 2014. (Real Bios Ser.). (J). lib. bdg. 116.00 (978-0-531-24354-1(0)) Scholastic Library Publishing.

Richard, Orlin. 12 Scientists Who Changed the World. 2016. (Change Makers Ser.). (ENG., Illus.). 32p. (J). (gr. 3-6). 19.95 (978-1-63235-149-4(8), 12-Story Library) Pr. Room Editions LLC.

Ripley's Believe It Or Not! Staff. Amazing People. 2013. (Ripley's Believe It or Not! Enter If You Dare Ser.: 8). 36p. (J). (gr. 4-18). 19.95 (978-1-4222-2770-1(7)) Mason Crest.

A Robbie Reader: Contemporary Biographies, 18 bks., Set. Incl. Alex Rodriquez: Professional Baseball Player. Kjelle, Marylou Morano. (gr. 4-8). 2005. lib. bdg. 25.70 (978-1-58415-394-8(6)); Brittany Murphy. Kjelle, Marylou Morano. (gr. 2-5). 2006. lib. bdg. 25.70 (978-1-58415-520-1(5)); Charles Schulz. Marvis, Barbara J. (gr. 1-4). 2004. lib. bdg. 25.70 (978-1-58415-289-7(3)); Dakota Fanning. Mattern, Joanne. (gr. 2-5). 2006. lib. bdg. 25.70 (978-1-58415-519-5(1)); Dale Earnhardt, Jr. Sherman, Josepha. (gr. 1-4). 2005. lib. bdg. 25.70 (978-1-58415-360-3(1)); Donovan Mcnabb. Mattern, Joanne. (gr. 1-4). 2004. lib. bdg. 25.70 (978-1-58415-294-1(X)); Dr. Seuss. Adil, Janeen R. (gr. 1-4). 2004. lib. bdg. 25.70 (978-1-58415-288-0(5)); Hilary Duff. Kjelle, Marylou Morano. (gr. 1-4). 2004. lib. bdg. 25.70 (978-1-58415-295-8(8)); Jamie Lynn Spears. Adams, Michelle Medlock. (gr. 4-8). 2005. lib. bdg. 25.70 (978-1-58415-395-5(4)); Jesse Mccartney. Kjelle, Marylou Morano. (gr. 2-5). 2006. lib. bdg. 25.70 (978-1-58415-500-3(0)); Johnny Gruelle & the Story of Raggedy Ann & Andy. Sherman, Josepha. (gr. 1-4). 2005. lib. bdg. 25.70 (978-1-58415-359-7(8)); LeBron James. Mattern, Joanne. (gr. 1-4). 2004. lib. bdg. 25.70 (978-1-58415-293-4(1)); Mia Hamm. Zarzycki, Daryl. (gr. 1-4). 2004. lib. bdg. 25.70 (978-1-58415-286-6(9)); Shaquille O'Neal: Basketball Superstar. Sherman, Josepha. (gr. 1-4). 2005. lib. bdg. 25.70 (978-1-58415-361-0(X)); Story of Harley-Davidson. Sherman, Josepha. (gr. 2-5). 2005. lib. bdg. 25.70 (978-1-58415-358-0(X), 1244893); Syd Hoff. Sherman, Josepha. (gr. 1-4). 2005. lib. bdg. 25.70 (978-1-58415-357-3(1)); Tiki Barber: Star NY Giants Running Back. Mattern, Joanne. (gr. 2-5). 2006. lib. bdg. 25.70 (978-1-58415-522-5(1)); Tony Hawk. Kjelle, Marylou Morano. (gr. 1-4). 2004. lib. bdg. 25.70 (978-1-58415-285-9(0)); (Illus.). 32p. (J). 2007. 305.10 (978-1-58415-299-6(0)) Mitchell Lane Pubs., Inc.

Rogers/Logsdon, Deborah J. Without Closure, 1 vol. 2010. 48p. pap. 16.95 (978-1-4489-8595-1(1)) America Star Bks.

Rookie Biographies(r) (Fall 2014 Set 4) 2014. (Rookie Biographies(r) Ser.). (J). (978-0-531-24358-9(3)) Scholastic Library Publishing.

Rosen Publishing Staff. Britannica Beginner Bios, 1 vol. 2015. (Britannica Beginner Bios Ser.). (ENG.). 32p. (J). 140.70 (978-1-62275-701-5(7), Britannica Educational Publishing) Rosen Publishing Group, Inc., The.

—Original Thinkers, 1 vol. 2015. (Original Thinkers Ser.). (ENG.). 192p. (YA). 245.70 (978-1-4777-8152-4(8), Rosen Young Adult) Rosen Publishing Group, Inc., The.

Schlesinger, Arthur M., Jr., ed. Major World Leaders. (Illus.). (gr. 6-12). lib. bdg. (978-0-7910-8055-9(2), Chelsea Hse.) Facts On File, Inc.

Scholastic, Inc. Staff. Easy Reader Biographies: 12 Biographies That Help Students Learn to Read & Comprehend Key Features of Nonfiction. Blood, Danielle, ed. 2007. (ENG.). (-2). 79.99 (978-0-439-77410-9(1), Teaching Resources) Scholastic, Inc.

Scholastic, Inc. Staff, contrib. by. Short Plays for Building Fluency: Famous Americans - 22 Reproducible Plays That Build Fluency, Vocabulary, & Comprehension. 2008. (Short Plays for Building Fluency Ser.). (ENG.). 200p. pap. 19.99 (978-0-545-07216-8(6), Teaching Resources) Scholastic, Inc.

Schuman, Michael A. Rihanna: Music Megastar. 2011. (Hot Celebrity Biographies Ser.). (Illus.). 48p. (J). (gr. 5-9). lib. bdg. 25.27 (978-0-7660-3871-4(8)) Enslow Pubs., Inc.

Schwartz, Heather E. & Meinking, Mary. Star Biographies. 2016. (Star Biographies Ser.). (ENG.). 32p. (gr. 3-4). lib. bdg. 139.95 (978-1-5157-4033-9(1), Snap Bks.) Capstone Press of Coughlan Cos.

Signature Lives, 16 vols. 2006. 112p. (YA). (gr. 5-7). 489.60 (978-0-7565-1893-6(8)) Compass Point Bks.

Star Biographies Fall 2010, 1 vol. 2010. (Star Biographies Ser.). (ENG.). 32p. (gr. 3-4). lib. bdg. 54.64 (978-1-4296-4763-2(9), Snap Bks.) Capstone Press of Coughlan Cos.

Star Files, 6 bks., Set 1. 2004. 179.57 (978-1-4109-1091-2(1)) Harcourt Schl. Pubs.

Teacher Created Materials Staff, ed. Biographies II U. S. & World Leaders: Themed Classroom Readers- 2007. (Themed Reader Sets Ser.). pap. 815.99 (978-1-4333-0161-2(X)) Teacher Created Materials, Inc.

Thomas, Paul. Revolutionaries. (History Makers Ser.). (Illus.). 48p. lib. bdg. 28.50 (978-1-931983-41-9(0)) Chrysalis Education.

Tieck, Sarah. First Biographies, 6 vols., Set 6. Incl. Barack Obama. 27.07 (978-1-60453-985-1(2)); Eleanor Roosevelt. (Illus.). 27.07 (978-1-60453-986-8(0)); Hillary Rodham Clinton. 27.07 (978-1-60453-983-7(6)); J. K. Rowling. 27.07 (978-1-60453-987-5(9)); Mark Twain. 27.07 (978-1-60453-988-2(7)); Walt Disney. (Illus.). 27.07 (978-1-60453-984-4(4)); (J). (gr. 1-4). (First Biographies Set 6 Ser.). 32p. 2010. 162.42 (978-1-60453-982-0(8), Buddy Bks.) ABDO Publishing Co.

Time-Life Books Editors. Famous Faces of the 20th Century: What Makes a Leader? (Illus.). (J). pap. 17.95 (978-0-7835-5079-4(0)) Time-Life Education, Inc.

Trailblazers Biographies. 2004. (Illus.). lib. bdg. 7.95 (978-0-8225-3361-0(8)); lib. bdg. 7.95 (978-0-8225-5224-6(8)); Vol. 1. lib. bdg. 7.95 (978-0-8225-4402-9(4)) Lerner Publishing Group.

Turner, Tracey. Daring, Deadly, Brilliant, Brave: History's Toughest People. Lenman, Jamie, illus. 2012. 110p. (J). (978-1-4351-4760-7(X)) Barnes & Noble, Inc.

Uhlig, Elizabeth. Memoir Writing & Illustrating for Children. 2003. 58p. (J). per. 15.95 (978-0-9677047-2-2(3)) Marble Hse. Editions.

UXL Newsmakers, 4 vols. 2004. (ENG.). 800p. (J). 337.00 (978-0-7876-9189-9(5), UXL) Cengage Gale.

Vickers, Rebecca. Every Person Has a History, 1 vol. 2014. (Everything Has a History Ser.). (ENG., Illus.). 64p. (gr. 7-8). pap. 10.95 (978-1-4329-9589-8(8)); lib. bdg. 35.99 (978-1-4329-9584-3(7)) Heinemann-Raintree.

Wade, Mary H. The Light-Bringers. 2006. (ENG.). 264p. per. 27.95 (978-1-4286-2450-4(3)) Kessinger Publishing, LLC.

Walker, Rebecca, frwd. It's up to Me: Stories of Choices, Predicaments & Decisions by San Francisco Youth. 2003. (Illus.). 232p. (J). per. 15.00 (978-0-9710606-2-3(2)) Streetside Stories, Inc.

Wallace, Archer. Men Who Played the Game. 2003. 127p. 89.00 (978-0-7950-5139-5(5)) New Library Press LLC.

Watts, Franklin. Beating Odds. 2009. pap. 8.95 (978-0-531-22599-8(2)) Scholastic Library Publishing.

Weber, Terri Smith. Bios for Kids: Library Set, Series 1. 2003. (J). lib. bdg. (978-1-932724-17-2(6), Bios for Kids) Panda Publishing, L.L.C.

—Bios for Kids: Series Set 1. 2003. (J). pap. (978-1-932724-15-8(X), Bios for Kids) Panda Publishing, L.L.C.

—Bios for Kids: Series Set, Series 1. 2003. (J). lib. bdg. (978-1-932724-16-5(8), Bios for Kids) Panda Publishing, L.L.C.

What's So Great About...?, 25 bks., Set. Incl. Amelia Earhart. Leavitt, Amie Jane. (J). (gr. 2-4). 2007. lib. bdg. 25.70 (978-1-58415-576-8(0)); Anne Frank. Whiting, Jim. (YA). (gr. 2-4). 2007. lib. bdg. 25.70 (978-1-58415-581-2(7)); Annie Oakley. Whiting, Jim. (J). (gr. 2-4). 2006. lib. bdg. 25.70 (978-1-58415-477-8(2)); Christopher Columbus. Leavitt, Amie Jane. (J). (gr. 2-4). 2007. lib. bdg. 25.70 (978-1-58415-578-2(7)); Daniel Boone. Roberts, Russell. (J). (gr. 2-4). 2006. lib. bdg. 25.70 (978-1-58415-475-4(6)); Davy Crockett. Roberts, Russell. (J). (gr. 2-4). 2006. lib. bdg. 25.70 (978-1-58415-476-1(4)); Donner Party. Harkins, Susan Sales & Harkins, William H. (J). (gr. 2-4). 2008. lib. bdg. 25.70 (978-1-58415-669-7(4)); Elizabeth Blackwell. Leavitt, Amie Jane. (J). (gr. 1-5). 2007. lib. bdg. 25.70 (978-1-58415-579-9(5)); Ferdinand Magellan. Whiting, Jim. (J). (gr. 2-4). 2006. lib. bdg. 25.70 (978-1-58415-480-8(2)); Francis Scott Key. Kjelle, Marylou Morano. (YA). (gr. 2-4). 2006. lib. bdg. 25.70 (978-1-58415-474-7(8)); Galileo. Whiting, Jim. (YA). (gr. 2-4). 2007. lib. bdg. 25.70 (978-1-58415-575-1(2)); George Washington Carver. Leavitt, Amie Jane. (YA). (gr. 2-4). 2007. lib. bdg. 25.70 (978-1-58415-580-5(9)); Harriet Tubman. Leavitt, Amie Jane. (J). (gr. 2-4). 2007. lib. bdg. 25.70 (978-1-58415-577-5(9)); Helen Keller. Leavitt, Amie Jane. (J). (gr. 2-4). 2007. lib. bdg. 25.70 (978-1-58415-583-6(3)); Henry Hudson. Smalley, Carol Parenzan. (J). (gr. 2-4). 2006. lib. bdg. 25.70 (978-1-58415-479-2(9)); Jacques Cartier. Kjelle, Marylou Morano. (YA). (gr. 2-4). 2006. lib. bdg. 25.70 (978-1-58415-481-5(0)); Johnny Appleseed. Zarzycki, Daryl Davis. (YA). (gr. 2-4). 2007. lib. bdg. 25.70 (978-1-58415-483-9(7)); King Tut. Harkins, Susan Sales & Harkins, William H. (YA). (gr. 2-4). 2008. lib. bdg. 25.70 (978-1-58415-681-9(3)); Lewis & Clark. Smalley, Carol Parenzan. (YA). (gr. 2-4). 2008. lib. bdg. 25.70 (978-1-58415-725-0(9)); Martin Luther King, Jr. Hinton, KaaVonia. (YA). (gr. 2-4). 2008. lib. bdg. 25.70 (978-1-58415-724-3(0)); Pochantas. Harkins, Susan Sales & Harkins, William H. (J). (gr. 2-4). 2008. lib. bdg. 25.70 (978-1-58415-682-6(1)); Robert Fulton. Whiting, Jim. (J). (gr. 2-4). 2006. lib. bdg. 25.70 (978-1-58415-478-5(0)); Rosa Parks. Whiting, Jim. (YA). (gr. 2-4). 2007. lib. bdg. 25.70 (978-1-58415-573-7(6)); Sam Houston. Harkins, Susan Sales & Harkins, William H. (J). (gr. 2-4). 2006. lib. bdg. 25.70 (978-1-58415-482-2(9)); (Illus.). 32p. 2009. Set lib. bdg. 642.50 (978-1-58415-683-3(X)) Mitchell Lane Pubs., Inc.

Yomtov, Nel. How to Write a Memoir. Petelinsek, Kathleen, illus. 2013. (Explorer Junior Library: How to Write Ser.). (ENG.). 24p. (J). (gr. 1-4). 25.64 (978-1-62431-188-8(1), 203076); pap. 12.79 (978-1-62431-320-2(5), 203078) Cherry Lake Publishing.

Zalben, Jane Breskin. Paths to Peace: People Who Changed the World. 2006. (ENG., Illus.). 48p. (J). (gr. 3-7). 18.99 (978-0-525-47734-1(9), Dutton Books for Young Readers) Penguin Young Readers Group.

Zelz, Abigail. Pass the Pandowdy, Please: Chewing on History with Famous Folks & Their Fabulous Foods, 1 vol. Zelz, Eric, illus. 2016. (ENG.). 40p. (gr. 2-6). 17.95 (978-0-88448-468-4(8), 884468) Tilbury Hse. Pubs.

BIOGRAPHY—DICTIONARIES

Britannica Beginner Bios: Set 2. 2015. (Britannica Beginner Bios Ser.). (ENG.). 32p. (J). (gr. 2-3). pap., pap., pap. 464.40 (978-1-68048-141-9(X), Britannica Educational Publishing) Rosen Publishing Group, Inc., The.

Dungworth, Richard, et al. The Usborne Book of Famous Lives. 2004. (Famous Lives Ser.). (Illus.). 245p. (J). (gr. 5-18). lib. bdg. 32.95 (978-0-88110-998-6(3)) EDC Publishing.

Encyclopaedia Britannica, Inc. Staff, compiled by. My First Britannica: People in History. 2008. (gr. 7-12). (978-1-59339-404-2(7)) Encyclopaedia Britannica, Inc.

Gale, ed. Encyclopedia of World Biography 1999 Supplement. 2nd ed. 2012. (Encyclopedia of World Biography Ser.: 32). (ENG., Illus.). (J). lib. bdg. 249.00 (978-1-4144-8084-8(9)) Cengage Gale.

Gale Research Inc Staff, contrib. by. Encyclopedia of World Biography: Supplement. 2nd rev. ed. 2008. (Encyclopedia of World Biography Ser.). (ENG., Illus.). 592p. (J). 249.00 (978-1-4144-3366-0(2)) Cengage Gale.

Gall, Timothy. The Lincoln Library of Shapers of Society: 101 Men & Woman Who Shaped the World. 2008. 228.00 (978-0-912168-23-4(4)) Lincoln Library Pr., Inc., The.

History Makers. 2003. 320p. 5.98 (978-1-4054-0325-2(X)) Parragon, Inc.

McCormick, Lisa Wade. Biographies, 6 bks., Set. Incl. Christopher Columbus. (Illus.). 24p. (J). (gr. 1-2). 2005. lib. bdg. 22.00 (978-0-516-24938-4(X)); (Scholastic News Nonfiction Readers Ser.). 2005. 108.00 o.p. (978-0-516-25392-3(1), Children's Pr.) Scholastic Library Publishing.

Nettleton, Pamela Hill. Biographies, 6 bks. Yesh, Jeff, illus. Incl. Pocahontas: Peacemaker & Friend to the Colonists. 26.65 (978-1-4048-0187-5(1)); Sally Ride: Astronaut, Scientist, Teacher. Nichols, Garry, illus. 26.65 (978-1-4048-0189-9(8)); (gr. k-3). (Biographies Ser.). (ENG.). 24p. 2003. 159.90 o.p. (978-1-4048-0183-7(9)) Picture Window Bks.

Shea, Therese. Britannica Beginner BIOS: Set 2. 2015. (Britannica Beginner Bios Ser.). (ENG.). 32p. (J). (gr. 2-3). 140.70 (978-1-68048-137-2(1), Britannica Educational Publishing) Rosen Publishing Group, Inc., The.

UXL Newsmakers. 2005. (UXL Newsmakers Ser.). (ENG.). Vol. 5. 336p. 96.00 (978-1-4144-0156-0(6)) Vol. 6. 320p. 96.00 (978-1-4144-0157-7(4)) Vol. 56. 400p. 173.00 (978-1-4144-0155-3(8)) Cengage Gale. (UXL).

Yenne, Bill. 100 Men Who Shaped World History. 2015. (ENG., Illus.). 100p. pap. 7.95 (978-0-912517-05-6(0)) Bluewood Bks.

BIOGRAPHY AS A LITERARY FORM

Bodden, Valerie. Nonfiction - Writing for Fact & Argument: Truthful Biographies. 2010. (Nonfiction Ser.). 48p. (YA). (gr. 5-18). 23.95 (978-1-58341-932-8(2), Creative Education) Creative Co., The.

—Truthful Biographies. 2011. (Nonfiction Writing Ser.). (ENG., Illus.). 48p. (J). (gr. 4-7). pap. 9.99 (978-0-89812-548-1(0), Creative Education) Creative Co., The.

Jones, Molly. 12 Great Tips on Writing True Stories. 2017. (Great Tips on Writing Ser.). (ENG., Illus.). 32p. (J). (gr. 3-6). 21.95 (978-1-63235-280-4(X)) Pr. Room Editions LLC.

Kalman, Bobbie. I Can Write a Book about My Life. 2012. (ENG.). 32p. (J). (978-0-7787-7993-3(9)); pap. (978-0-7787-8002-1(3)) Crabtree Publishing Co.

Minden, Cecilia & Roth, Kate. How to Write a Biography. 2012. (Explorer Junior Library: Language Arts Explorer Junior Ser.). (ENG.). 24p. (gr. 1-4). 25.64 (978-1-61080-491-2(0), 202101); pap. 12.79 (978-1-61080-665-7(4), 202275) Cherry Lake Publishing.

Vickers, Rebecca. Every Person Has a History, 1 vol. 2014. (Everything Has a History Ser.). (ENG., Illus.). 64p. (gr. 7-8). pap. 10.95 (978-1-4329-9589-8(8)); lib. bdg. 35.99 (978-1-4329-9584-3(7)) Heinemann-Raintree.

BIOLOGICAL CHEMISTRY

see Biochemistry

BIOLOGICAL DIVERSITY

see Biodiversity

BIOLOGY

see also Adaptation (Biology); Anatomy; Biodiversity; Cells; Embryology; Evolution; Freshwater Biology; Genetics; Life (Biology); Marine Biology; Microbiology; Natural History; Physiology; Reproduction; Sex; Zoology

Abramovitz, Melissa. Amazing Feats of Biological Engineering, 1 vol. 2014. (Great Achievements in Engineering Ser.). (ENG.). 112p. (J). (gr. 6-12). lib. bdg. 35.64 *(978-1-62403-426-8(8)*, Essential Library) ABDO Publishing Co.

Ace Academics, ed. Biology: A Whole Course in a Box! 2007. (Exambusters Ser.). 384p. (gr. 7-18). 12.95 *(978-1-881374-94-7(7)*, Exambusters) Ace Academics, Inc.

Allott, Andrew & Mindorff, David. Biology, 2014, Pack. 2014. (IB Diploma Program Ser.). (ENG., Illus.). 1p. 82.00 *(978-0-19-830774-7(8))* Oxford Univ. Pr., Inc.

American Museum of Natural History. Camouflage. 2016. (Science for Toddlers Ser.). (ENG., Illus.). 18p. (J). (gr. -1). bds. 7.95 *(978-1-4549-2079-3(3))* Sterling Publishing Co., Inc.

Amery, Heather. What's Biology All About? 2009. (Young Scientist Ser.). 96p. (YA). (gr. 6-18). pap. 10.99 *(978-0-7945-2115-8(0)*, Usborne) EDC Publishing.

Amstutz, Lisa. Tigers on the Hunt. 2017. (Searchlight Books (tm) — Predators Ser.). (ENG.). (J). (gr. 3-5). pap. 9.99 ***(978-1-5124-5613-4(6))***; (Illus.). lib. bdg. 30.65 ***(978-1-5124-3400-2(0))*** Lerner Publishing Group.

Amstutz, Lisa J. Discover Cryobiology. 2016. (Searchlight Books (tm) — What's Cool about Science? Ser.). (ENG., Illus.). 40p. (J). (gr. 3-5). 30.65 *(978-1-5124-0807-2(7))* Lerner Publishing Group.

Anemone, Robert L. Race Biology & Culture: A Reader. 2nd rev. ed. 2011. (ENG.). 166p. spiral bd. 89.25 *(978-0-7575-8887-7(5))* Kendall Hunt Publishing Co.

Animal Camouflage [Scholastic]. 2010. (Hidden in Nature Ser.). pap. 2.08 *(978-1-4296-5050-2(8)*, Pebble Plus) Capstone Press of Coughlan Cos.

Arbuthnott, Gill. Your Guide to Life on Earth. Mones, Marc, illus. 2016. (ENG.). 64p. (J). lib. bdg. *(978-0-7787-2243-4(0))* Crabtree Publishing Co.

Armentrout, David & Armentrout, Patricia. Crafty Critters. 2008. (Illus.). 32p. (J). 28.50 *(978-1-60472-302-1(5))* Rourke Educational Media.

Bailey, Diane. Black Achievement in Science: Biology, Vol. 10. Pouson, Mel, ed. 2016. (Black Achievement in Science Ser.: Vol. 10). (ENG., Illus.). 64p. (J). (gr. 7-12). 23.95 *(978-1-4222-3555-3(6))* Mason Crest.

Basher, Simon. Basher Science: Extreme Biology. Basher, Simon, illus. 2013. (Basher Science Ser.). (ENG., Illus.). 64p. (J). (gr. 5-9). pap. 7.99 *(978-0-7534-7050-3(0)*, 9780753470503, Kingfisher) Roaring Brook Pr.

Batten, Mary. Aliens from Earth: When Animals & Plants Invade Other Ecosystems, 1 vol. Doyle, Beverly, illus. (ENG.). (J). (gr. 3-7). 2003. 32p. 15.95 *(978-1-56145-236-1(X))* 2016. 36p. 16.95 *(978-1-56145-900-1(3))* Peachtree Pubs.

Belback, Elsie. Masters of Disguise: Animal Mimicry. 2014. (ENG.). 24p. (gr. k-3). 28.50 *(978-1-62717-636-1(5))* Rourke Educational Media.

Benchmark Education Company, LLC Staff, compiled by. Biology: Theme Set. 2006. (J). 226.00 *(978-1-4108-7148-0(7))* Benchmark Education Co.

—Science Theme: Life Science. 2005. spiral bd. 220.00 *(978-1-4108-5318-9(7))* Benchmark Education Co.

—Structures of Life. 2006. spiral bd. 1060.00 *(978-1-4108-6790-2(0))* Benchmark Education Co.

Berger, Melvin & Berger, Gilda. Seres Vivos: Living Things. 2006. (ENG & SPA., Illus.). *(978-0-439-82867-3(8))* Scholastic, Inc.

Biggs, Alton, et al. Biology: The Dynamics of Life. 2003. (Illus.). 1190p. (gr. 6-12). stu. ed. *(978-0-07-829900-1(4))* Glencoe/McGraw-Hill.

Biologie Kompaktwissen-Testfragen: 5. bis 10. Klasse. 4th ed. (Duden-Schuelerduden Ser.). (GER.). 540p. (YA). *(978-3-411-05424-4(7))* Bibliographisches Institut & F. A. Brockhaus AG DEU. Dist: International Bk. Import Service, Inc.

Biology. 3rd rev. ed. 2011. (Careers in Focus Ser.). (Illus.). 216p. (gr. 6-12). 32.95 *(978-0-8160-8030-4(5)*, Ferguson Publishing Co.) Facts On File, Inc.

Braun, Eric. Gertrude & Reginald the Monsters Talk about Living & Nonliving, 1 vol. Bernardini, Cristian, illus. 2012. (In the Science Lab Ser.). (ENG.). 24p. (gr. 2-3). pap. 9.95 *(978-1-4048-7237-0(X))*; lib. bdg. 26.65 *(978-1-4048-7146-5(2))* Picture Window Bks.

Brian, Williams. Los Seres Vivos. (SPA.). 96p. (YA). (gr. 5-8). 18.36 *(978-84-241-1995-9(9))* Everest Editora ESP. Dist: Lectorum Pubns., Inc.

Bright, Michael. The Future of Life on Earth, 1 vol. 2012. (Web of Life Ser.). (ENG., Illus.). 48p. (gr. 6-10). lib. bdg. 34.65 *(978-1-4109-4399-6(2)*, Raintree Freestyle) Heinemann-Raintree.

Brown, Carron. Secrets of Animal Camouflage. Robins, Wesley, illus. 2016. (ENG.). 36p. (J). 12.99 *(978-1-61067-466-9(9))* Kane Miller.

Broyles, Janell. Chemical Biological Incident Response Force. 2009. (Inside Special Operations Ser.). 64p. (gr. 6-6). 58.50 *(978-1-61513-551-6(0)*, Rosen Reference) Rosen Publishing Group, Inc., The.

Buellis, Linda. Life Cycles. 2016. (Spotlight on Ecology & Life Science Ser.). 00024p. (J). (gr. 4-6). 26.25 *(978-1-4994-2577-2(5))*; pap. 10.00 *(978-1-4994-2574-1(0))* Rosen Publishing Group, Inc., The. (PowerKids Pr.).

Burnie, David, et al. Deadly Creatures: A Thrilling Adventure with Nature's Fiercest Hunters. 2016. (Navigators Ser.). (ENG., Illus.). 80p. (J). 15.99 *(978-0-7534-7240-8(6)*, 9780753472408, Kingfisher) Roaring Brook Pr.

Canetti, Yanitzia. La Adaptación, ¡qué Sensación! 2010. (SPA.). (J). *(978-1-59835-167-5(2))* Cambridge BrickHouse, Inc.

—Amazing Adaptations! 2010. (J). *(978-1-59835-191-0(5))* Cambridge BrickHouse, Inc.

Carr, Aaron. Plants. 2013. lib. bdg. 20.00 *(978-1-62127-492-6(6))* Weigl Pubs., Inc.

Charlesworth, Liza, ed. Life Cycles: Exciting Nonfiction Books That Build Kids' Vocabularies. 2007. (Science Vocabulary Readers Ser.). (ENG.). (gr. 1-3). 79.99 *(978-0-545-01597-4(9)*, Teaching Resources) Scholastic, Inc.

Cientificos! 7: Ciencias Biologicas. (SPA.). (J). 55.00 *(978-958-04-6346-7(8))* Norma S.A. COL. Dist: Distribuidora Norma, Inc.

Clark Sawyer, J. Animal Colors: What They Mean. 2014. (Little Bits: Colors Tell a Story Ser.). (ENG.). 24p. (J). (gr. -1-3). lib. bdg. 23.93 *(978-1-62724-321-6(6))* Bearport Publishing Co., Inc.

—Los Colores de la Selva Tropical: Hermosos y Brillantes. 2014. (Los Colores Cuentan una Historia Ser.). (SPA.). 24p. (J). (gr. -1-3). lib. bdg. 23.93 *(978-1-62724-468-8(9))* Bearport Publishing Co., Inc.

—Los Colores de Los Animales: Qué Significan. 2014. (Los Colores Cuentan una Historia Ser.). (SPA., Illus.). 24p. (J). (gr. -1-3). lib. bdg. 23.93 *(978-1-62724-463-3(8))* Bearport Publishing Co., Inc.

—Rain Forest Colors: Bright & Beautiful. 2014. (Little Bits: Colors Tell a Story Ser.). (ENG.). 24p. (J). (gr. -1-3). lib. bdg. 23.93 *(978-1-62724-326-1(7))* Bearport Publishing Co., Inc.

Claybourne, Anna. Living Things. 2017. (Mind Webs Ser.). (ENG., Illus.). 32p. (J). (gr. 4-6). pap. 11.99 *(978-0-7502-8960-3(0)*, Wayland) Hachette Children's Group GBR. Dist: Hachette Bk. Group.

Cohn, Jessica. Parasite Collector. 2010. (Benchmark Rockets: Dirty & Dangerous Jobs Ser.). 32p. (J). (gr. 3-6). 28.50 *(978-1-60870-175-9(1))* Marshall Cavendish Corp.

Coldiron, Deborah. Coral, 1 vol. 2007. (Underwater World Ser.). (ENG.). 32p. (gr. 3-7). 27.07 *(978-1-59928-811-6(7)*, Buddy Bks.) ABDO Publishing Co.

Conklin, Wendy. Life Cycles, 1 vol. 2015. (Science Readers: Content & Literacy Ser.). (ENG., Illus.). 32p. (gr. 3-3). pap. 8.99 *(978-1-4807-4637-4(1))* Teacher Created Materials, Inc.

Contemporary Discourse in the Field of Biology, 6 bks., Set. 2006. (YA). lib. bdg. 183.60 *(978-1-4042-0629-8(9))* Rosen Publishing Group, Inc., The.

Cook, Diane. Charles Darwin: British Naturalist. 2013. (People of Importance Ser.: 21). (Illus.). 32p. (J). (gr. 4-18). 19.95 *(978-1-4222-2844-9(4))* Mason Crest.

Cooke, Andy & Martin, Jean. Spectrum Biology Class. 2004. (Spectrum Key Stage 3 Science Ser.). (ENG., Illus.). 176p. pap. 15.00 *(978-0-521-54921-9(3))* Cambridge Univ. Pr.

Cooper, Jason. Camouflage & Disguise. 2006. (Let's Look at Animals Discovery Library). (Illus.). 24p. (J). (gr. 3-7). lib. bdg. 22.79 *(978-1-60044-170-7(X))* Rourke Educational Media.

—Camuflaje y Disfraz. 2007. (ENG & ENM., Illus.). 24p. (J). lib. bdg. 22.79 *(978-1-60044-268-1(4))* Rourke Educational Media.

Coupe, Robert. Predators & Prey: Battle for Survival. 2014. (Discovery Education: Animals Ser.). 32p. (J). (gr. 3-6). 26.25 *(978-1-4777-6956-0(0))*; pap. 10.00 *(978-1-4777-6957-7(9))* Rosen Publishing Group, Inc., The. (PowerKids Pr.).

Crabtree Publishing Company Staff. A Class of Their Own, 6 vols., Set. 2010. (ENG.). 48p. (J). (gr. 5-8). pap. *(978-0-7787-5385-8(9))*; lib. bdg. *(978-0-7787-5371-1(9))* Crabtree Publishing Co.

Cunningham, Kevin. Clownfish & Sea Anemones. 2016. (21st Century Junior Library: Better Together Ser.). (ENG., Illus.). 24p. (J). (gr. 2-5). 27.07 *(978-1-63471-085-5(1)*, 208419) Cherry Lake Publishing.

—Goby Fish & Pistol Shrimp. 2016. (21st Century Junior Library: Better Together Ser.). (ENG., Illus.). 24p. (J). (gr. 2-5). 27.07 *(978-1-63471-084-8(3)*, 208415) Cherry Lake Publishing.

—Honeyguide Birds & Ratels. 2016. (21st Century Junior Library: Better Together Ser.). (ENG., Illus.). 24p. (J). (gr. 2-5). 27.07 *(978-1-63471-086-2(X)*, 208423) Cherry Lake Publishing.

—Sea Turtles & Yellow Tang Fish. 2016. (21st Century Junior Library: Better Together Ser.). (ENG., Illus.). 24p. (J). (gr. 2-5). 27.07 *(978-1-63471-088-6(6)*, 208431) Cherry Lake Publishing.

—Zebras & Ostriches. 2016. (21st Century Junior Library: Better Together Ser.). (ENG.). 24p. (J). (gr. 2-5). 27.07 *(978-1-63471-082-4(7)*, 208407) Cherry Lake Publishing.

De la Bédoyère, Camilla. Fry to Sea Horse. 2011. (LifeCycles Ser.). (ENG.). 24p. (J). (gr. -1-k). lib. bdg. 15.99 *(978-1-60992-049-4(X))* QEB Publishing Inc.

—Snakelet to Snake. 2011. (LifeCycles Ser.). (ENG.). 24p. (J). (gr. -1-k). lib. bdg. 15.99 *(978-1-60992-046-3(5))* QEB Publishing Inc.

—Strongest & Weakest. 2010. (Animal Opposites Ser.). (ENG., Illus.). 32p. (J). (gr. -1-3). pap. 5.95 *(978-1-55407-823-3(7)*, 9781554078233) Firefly Bks., Ltd.

Diagram Group Staff. Biology: An Illustrated Guide to Science. 2006. (Science Visual Resources Ser.). (Illus.). 208p. (gr. 6-12). 49.50 *(978-0-8160-6162-4(9))* Facts On File, Inc.

Dickmann, Nancy. ¡Mira Cómo Crece!, 11 vols., Set. Incl. Vida de la Abeja. pap. 6.29 *(978-1-4329-5282-2(X))*; Vida de la Manzana. (Illus.). pap. 6.29 *(978-1-4329-5286-0(2))*; Vida de la Mariposa. (Illus.). pap. 6.29 *(978-1-4329-5283-9(8))*; Vida de la Rana. pap. 6.29 *(978-1-4329-5285-3(4))*; Vida de la Tortuga. pap. 6.29 *(978-1-4329-5292-1(7))*; Vida del Frijol. (Illus.). pap. 6.29 *(978-1-4329-5287-7(0))*; Vida del Girasol. pap. 6.29 *(978-1-4329-5289-1(7))*; Vida del Perro. pap. 6.29 *(978-1-4329-5290-7(0))*; Vida del Pingüino. (Illus.). pap. 6.29 *(978-1-4329-5291-4(9))*; Vida del Pollo. (Illus.). pap. 6.29 *(978-1-4329-5284-6(6))*; Vida del Roble. pap. 6.29 *(978-1-4329-5288-4(9))*; (gr. -1-1). (¡Mira Cómo Crece! Ser.). (SPA.). 24p. 2011. Set pap. 69.19 *(978-1-4329-5293-8(5))*; Set lib. bdg. 203.85 *(978-1-4329-5281-5(1))* Heinemann-Raintree. (Bellota).

Ebersole, Rene. Gorilla Mountain: The Story of Wildlife Biologist Amy Vedder. 2006. (ENG., Illus.). 128p. (gr. 7-9). per. 19.95 *(978-0-309-09551-8(4)*, Joseph Henry Pr.) National Academies Pr.

Ebner, Aviva. Health Science Experiments. 2011. (Experiments for Future Scientists Ser.). (Illus.). 160p. (gr. 5-8). 35.00 *(978-1-60413-853-5(X))* Facts On File, Inc.

Eck, Kristin. Hide-and-Seek Animals. 2004. (Hide-And-Seek Books). (Illus.). (J). lib. bdg. 21.25 *(978-1-4042-2702-6(4)*, PowerKids Pr.) Rosen Publishing Group, Inc., The.

—Hide & Seek Animals. 2009. (Tough Toddler Bks.). 16p. (gr. k-k). 42.50 *(978-1-60854-568-1(7)*, PowerKids Pr.) Rosen Publishing Group, Inc., The.

Ehlert, Lois. Lots of Spots. Ehlert, Lois, illus. 2010. (ENG., Illus.). 40p. (J). (gr. -1-3). 17.99 *(978-1-4424-0289-8(X)*, Beach Lane Bks.) Beach Lane Bks.

Enderle, Dotti. Storytime Discoveries: Biological Science. 2003. (Illus.). 64p. (J). pap. 9.95 *(978-1-57310-411-1(6)*, 1200740) Teaching & Learning Co.

Evolution Series, 7 cass.; set. 2004. (gr. 7-18). 99.95 incl. VHS *(978-1-57807-641-3(2)*, WG1158) WGBH Boston Video.

Extreme Biology. 2015. (Extreme Biology Ser.). (ENG.). 48p. (J). (gr. 4-4). 191.70 *(978-1-4824-2254-2(9))* Stevens, Gareth Publishing LLLP.

Favor, Lesli J. Eukaryotic & Prokaryotic Cell Structures: Understanding Cells with & Without a Nucleus. 2004. (Library of Cells Ser.). (Illus.). 48p. (YA). lib. bdg. 29.25 *(978-1-4042-0323-5(0))* Rosen Publishing Group, Inc., The.

Franchino, Vicky. Animal Camouflage. 2015. (True Book — Amazing Animals Ser.). (ENG., Illus.). 48p. (J). pap. 6.95 *(978-0-531-21585-2(7)*, Children's Pr.) Scholastic Library Publishing.

Friedman, Michael & Friedman, Brett. Cell Communication: Understanding How Information Is Stored & Used in Cells. 2004. (Library of Cells Ser.). (Illus.). 48p. (YA). lib. bdg. 29.25 *(978-1-4042-0319-8(2))* Rosen Publishing Group, Inc., The.

Friel, John P., et al, eds. Exploring the World of Aquatic Life, 6 vols., Set. 2008. (Exploring the World of Aquatic Life Ser.). (Illus.). 480p. (gr. 5-8). 210.00 *(978-1-60413-255-7(8)*, Chelsea Hse.) Facts On File, Inc.

Gaff, Jackie. Looking at Growing Up: How Do People Change? 2008. (Looking at Science: How Things Change Ser.). (Illus.). 32p. (J). (gr. 3-7). lib. bdg. 23.94 *(978-0-7660-3090-9(3)*, Enslow Elementary) Enslow Pubs., Inc.

Gagne, Tammy. Lions: Built for the Hunt. 2016. (Predator Profiles Ser.). (ENG., Illus.). 24p. (J). (gr. 1-2). lib. bdg. 25.32 *(978-1-4914-8260-5(5))* Capstone Press of Coughlan Cos.

—Piranhas: Built for the Hunt. 2016. (Predator Profiles Ser.). (ENG., Illus.). 24p. (J). (gr. 1-2). lib. bdg. 25.32 *(978-1-4914-8840-9(9))* Capstone Press of Coughlan Cos.

Gardner, Robert. Desert Experiments: 11 Science Experiments in One Hour or Less. 2014. (Last Minute Science Projects with Biomes Ser.). (Illus.). 48p. (YA). (gr. 5-12). pap. 8.95 *(978-0-7660-5918-4(9)*, Enslow Elementary) Enslow Pubs., Inc.

Glencoe McGraw-Hill Staff. Glencoe Life Science, Reinforcement. 2004. (Life Science Ser.). (ENG., Illus.). 96p. (gr. 6-8). pap., stu. ed., pupil's gde. ed. 8.20 *(978-0-07-867127-2(2)*, 0078671272) McGraw-Hill Higher Education.

Gray, Susan H. Bears Hibernate. 2015. (Tell Me Why Library). (ENG., Illus.). 24p. (J). (gr. 2-5). pap. 12.79 *(978-1-63362-029-2(8)*, 205873) Cherry Lake Publishing.

Green, Dan & Basher, Simon. Biology: Life as We Know It! Basher, Simon, illus. 2008. (Basher Science Ser.). (ENG., Illus.). 128p. (J). (gr. 5-9). pap. 8.99 *(978-0-7534-6253-9(2)*, 9780753462539, Kingfisher) Roaring Brook Pr.

Grolier Educational Staff, contrib. by. Biology Matters!, 10 vols. 2004. (Illus.). (J). 389.00 *(978-0-7172-5979-3(X)*, Grolier) Scholastic Library Publishing.

Guillain, Charlotte. Life Cycles. 2016. (Investigate! Ser.). (ENG.). 32p. (gr. -1-2). pap. 7.99 *(978-1-4846-3565-0(5)*, NA-h) Heinemann-Raintree.

Haakonsen, Jens. Lynx Chase, Hares Dash. 2017. (Hunter & Hunted: Animal Survival Ser.). 24p. (J). (gr. 7-8). 23.60 ***(978-1-5081-5664-2(6)***, PowerKids Pr.) Rosen Publishing Group, Inc., The.

Hantula, Richard. Plants & Animals. 2006. (Real World Science Ser.). (Illus.). 32p. (gr. 2-6). lib. bdg. 26.00 *(978-0-8368-6308-6(9)*, Gareth Stevens Learning Library) Stevens, Gareth Publishing LLLP.

Harmon, Daniel E. Chemical & Biological Weapons: Agents of War & Terror. 2009. (Science & Society Ser.). 64p. (gr. 5-6). 58.50 *(978-1-60853-007-6(8))* Rosen Publishing Group, Inc., The.

Hawley, Ella. Exploring the Classification of Living Things. 2012. (Let's Explore Life Science Ser.). (ENG., Illus.). 24p. (J). (gr. 3-6). pap. 8.25 *(978-1-4488-6302-0(3))*; lib. bdg. 22.60 *(978-1-4488-6172-9(1))* Rosen Publishing Group, Inc., The. (PowerKids Pr.).

Hibbert, Clare. Our Busy Lives. Raga, Sylvia, illus. 2011. (Busy Times Ser.). (ENG.). 24p. (J). 19.99 *(978-0-237-54266-5(8))* Evans Brothers, Ltd. GBR. Dist: Independent Pubs. Group.

Hicks, Kelli. Let's Classify Organisms. 2012. (ENG.). 24p. (gr. 3-4). pap. 8.95 *(978-1-61810-231-7(1))* Rourke Educational Media.

Higgins, Nadia. Life Science Through Infographics. Waananen, Lisa, illus. 2013. (Super Science Infographics Ser.). (ENG.). 32p. (gr. 3-5). pap. 8.95 *(978-1-4677-1592-8(1))* Lerner Publishing Group.

Hollar, Sherman. A Closer Look at Biology, Microbiology, & the Cell. 2011. (J). lib. bdg. 31.70 *(978-1-61530-514-8(9))* Rosen Publishing Group, Inc., The.

Holt, Rinehart and Winston Staff. Biology. 4th ed. 2003. trans. 301.81 *(978-0-03-069919-1(3))*; (SPA., Illus.). pap., stu. ed. 15.46 *(978-0-03-069987-0(8))* Holt McDougal.

—Biology: Chapter Resource Package. 6th ed. 2006. pap. 415.60 *(978-0-03-041317-9(6))* Harcourt Schl. Pubs.

—Holt Biology 2004. 2004. (Holt Biology Ser.). (ENG.). 1168p. (gr. 9-9). stu. ed. 114.60 *(978-0-03-066473-1(X))* Houghton Mifflin Harcourt Publishing Co.

—Holt Biology 2004: Texas Edition. 2004. (J). stu. ed. 83.93 *(978-0-03-068264-3(9))* Holt McDougal.

—Holt Science & Technology: Life Science. 5th ed. 2004. tchr. ed. 128.80 *(978-0-03-066477-9(2))* Holt McDougal.

—Holt Science & Technology: Life Science: Enhanced Online Edition. 4th ed. 2004. 17.26 *(978-0-03-037149-3(X))* Holt McDougal.

—Holt Science & Technology: Life Science: Reading & Comprehension Guide. 5th ed. 2004. (Holt Science & Technology Ser.). (Illus.). pap. 17.13 *(978-0-03-036061-9(7))* Holt McDougal.

—Holt Science & Technology: Life Science: Special Needs Workbook. 5th ed. 2004. (Holt Science & Technology Ser.). pap., wbk. ed. 17.13 *(978-0-03-036053-4(6))* Holt McDougal.

—Holt Science & Technology: Life Science Study Guide. 5th ed. 2004. (Holt Science & Technology Ser.). (Illus.). pap., stu. ed. 17.13 *(978-0-03-030158-2(0))* Holt McDougal.

—Holt Science & Technology Chapter 1: Life Science: The World of Life Science. 5th ed. 2004. (Illus.). pap. 12.86 *(978-0-03-030163-6(7))* Holt McDougal.

—Holt Science & Technology Chapter 2: Life Science: It's Alive!! or Is It? 5th ed. 2004. (Illus.). pap. 12.86 *(978-0-03-030166-7(1))* Holt McDougal.

—Holt Science & Technology Chapter 7: Life Science: Evolution & Living. 5th ed. 2004. (Illus.). pap. 12.86 *(978-0-03-030191-9(2))* Holt McDougal.

—Holt Science & Technology Chapter 9: Life Science: Classification. 5th ed. 2004. (Illus.). pap. 12.86 *(978-0-03-030201-5(3))* Holt McDougal.

—Modern Biology. 6th ed. 2006. tchr. ed. 114.60 *(978-0-03-073542-4(4))*; pap., stu. ed. 21.80 *(978-0-03-036718-2(2))* Harcourt Schl. Pubs.

—Modern Biology. 6th ed. Date not set. 83.93 *(978-0-03-065178-6(6))* Holt McDougal.

—Taks Practice Exams Biology. 4th ed. 2003. (YA). (gr. 10-11). pap. 14.00 *(978-0-03-074082-4(7))* Holt McDougal.

Hyde, Natalie. What Is Germ Theory? 2010. (Shaping Modern Science Ser.). (ENG.). 64p. (J). (gr. 5-8). lib. bdg. *(978-0-7787-7201-9(2))* Crabtree Publishing Co.

Ipcar, Dahlov. Animal Hide & Seek, 1 vol. 2013. (ENG., Illus.). 32p. (J). 17.95 *(978-1-934031-80-3(1)*, d6d51255-f6fd-4100-9abb-cbebfc8ccecf) Islandport Pr., Inc.

Iyer, Rani. Endangered Rain Forests: Investigating Rain Forests in Crisis. 2015. (Endangered Earth Ser.). (ENG.). 32p. (gr. 3-4). lib. bdg. 27.32 *(978-1-4914-2039-3(1))* Capstone Press of Coughlan Cos.

Jackson, Ellen B. The Tree of Life: The Wonders of Evolution. Wiley, Judeanne Winter, illus. 2004. (ENG.). 41p. (J). (gr. -1-3). pap. 14.99 *(978-1-59102-240-4(1))* Prometheus Bks., Pubs.

Jennings, Terry. Camouflage. 2004. (QEB Start Talking Ser.). (Illus.). 24p. (J). lib. bdg. 15.95 *(978-1-59566-001-5(1))* QEB Publishing Inc.

Jepson, Maud. Illustrated Biology, 2 pts., Pt. 2: Animals. (Illus.). (YA). (gr. 8-12). 6.95 *(978-0-7195-0734-2(0))* Transatlantic Arts, Inc.

Johnson, Jinny. Animal Planet Atlas of Animals. 2013. 128p. pap. 35.93 *(978-1-4677-1691-8(X))* Lerner Publishing Group.

Johnson, Rebecca L. Masters of Disguise: Amazing Animal Tricksters. 2016. (ENG., Illus.). 48p. (J). (gr. 4-8). 31.99 *(978-1-5124-0087-8(4))*; 47.99 *(978-1-5124-0105-9(6))* Lerner Publishing Group. (Millbrook Pr.).

—Microquests: Classroom Set. 2008. pap. 43.95 *(978-0-8225-9113-9(8))* Lerner Publishing Group.

—Microquests: Complete Set. 2008. pap. 263.95 *(978-0-8225-9377-5(7))* Lerner Publishing Group.

Johnson, Steve. Holt Biology: Enhanced Online Edition. 4th ed. 2004. 17.26 *(978-0-03-037153-0(8))* 6th ed. Date not set. stu. ed. 83.93 *(978-0-03-074066-4(5))* Holt McDougal.

—Holt Biology: Online Edition Upgrade. 4th ed. 2004. 7.93 *(978-0-03-037216-2(X))* Holt McDougal.

Jones, Mary & Jones, Geoff. CSEC Biology: A Foundation Course. 4th ed. 2009. (ENG.). 416p. pap. 30.75 *(978-0-521-70114-3(7))* Cambridge Univ. Pr.

Jones, Phillip. Kingdoms of Life. 2011. (Science Foundations Ser.). (Illus.). 128p. (gr. 6-12). 35.00 *(978-1-60413-340-0(6)*, Chelsea Hse.) Facts On File, Inc.

Kalman, Bobbie. Camouflage Changing to Hide. 2005. (Nature's Changes Ser.). (ENG., Illus.). 32p. (J). (gr. 1-5). pap. *(978-0-7787-2306-6(2))* Crabtree Publishing Co.

—¿Cómo Se Esconden los Animales? 2010. (SPA., Illus.). 24p. (J). pap. *(978-0-7787-8592-7(0))*; lib. bdg. *(978-0-7787-8566-8(1))* Crabtree Publishing Co.

—How Do Baby Animals Learn? 2012. (ENG., Illus.). 24p. (J). *(978-0-7787-4077-3(3))*; pap. *(978-0-7787-4082-7(X))* Crabtree Publishing Co.

—I Can Write a Book about Butterflies. 2012. (ENG.). 32p. (J). *(978-0-7787-7987-2(4))*; pap. *(978-0-7787-7996-4(3))* Crabtree Publishing Co.

—¿Qué Es el Ciclo de Vida? 2005. (Ciencia de los Seres Vivos Ser.). (SPA., Illus.). 32p. (J). lib. bdg. *(978-0-7787-8754-9(0))* Crabtree Publishing Co.

—¿Qué Son Las Estructuras Naturales? 2009. (SPA.). 24p. (J). *(978-0-7787-8701-3(X))*; pap. *(978-0-7787-8740-2(0))* Crabtree Publishing Co.

—¿Qué Son los Seres Vivos? 2005. (Ciencia de los Seres Vivos Ser.). (SPA., Illus.). 32p. (J). (gr. 3-4). pap. *(978-0-7787-8806-5(7))*; lib. bdg. *(978-0-7787-8760-0(5))* Crabtree Publishing Co.

—What Are Nature's Copycats? 2012. (ENG.). 32p. (J). *(978-0-7787-2771-2(8))*; pap. *(978-0-7787-2776-7(9))* Crabtree Publishing Co.

—What Are Opposites in Nature? 2010. (Looking at Nature Ser.). (ENG.). 24p. (J). (gr. -1-2). pap. *(978-0-7787-3346-1(7))*; lib. bdg. *(978-0-7787-3326-3(2))* Crabtree Publishing Co.

—What Is Symmetry in Nature? 2010. (Looking at Nature Ser.). (ENG., Illus.). 24p. (J). (gr. -1-2). pap. *(978-0-7787-3347-8(5))*; lib. bdg. *(978-0-7787-3327-0(0))* Crabtree Publishing Co.

—Yo soy un ser Vivo. 2008. (SPA.). 24p. (J). lib. bdg. *(978-0-7787-8679-5(X))* Crabtree Publishing Co.

—Yo soy un Ser Vivo. 2008.Tr. of I am a Living Thing. (SPA.). 24p. (J). pap. *(978-0-7787-8688-7(9))* Crabtree Publishing Co.

Katherine Cullen, PH D & Cullen, Katherine E. Biology: The People Behind the Science. 2005. (Pioneers in Science Ser.). (Illus.). 170p. (gr. 6-12). 29.95 *(978-0-8160-5461-9(4))* Facts On File, Inc.

Kato, Sharleen L. Lifespan Development. 2013. (ENG.). 128p. pap., wbk. ed. 21.28 *(978-1-61960-236-6(9))*; 460p. (gr. 9-12). 93.28 *(978-1-61960-231-1(8))* Goodheart-Willcox Pub.

Kawa, Katie. My First Trip to the Aquarium. 2012. (My First Adventures Ser.). (Illus.). 24p. (gr. k-2). 69.20 *(978-1-4339-8047-3(9))*; (J). pap. 8.15 *(978-1-4339-7301-7(4))*; (J). lib. bdg. 22.60 *(978-1-4339-7300-0(6))* Stevens, Gareth Publishing LLLP.

—My First Trip to the Aquarium: Mi Primera Visita Al Acuario. 2012. (My First Adventures / Mis primeras aventuras Ser.). (SPA & ENG., Illus.). 24p. (J). (gr. k-2). lib. bdg. 22.60 *(978-1-4339-7372-7(3))* Stevens, Gareth Publishing LLLP.

Keller, R W. Biology Level I Laboratory Workbook. 2005. (Real Science-4-Kids Ser.). (Illus.). 53p. (J). (gr. 3-7). per. 14.95 *(978-0-9749149-3-0(2))* Gravitas Pubns., Inc.

—Biology Pre-Level 1. 2008. (Real Science-4-Kids Ser.). (Illus.). 70p. pap. 21.95 *(978-0-9799459-1-5(7))* Gravitas Pubns., Inc.

Keller, Rebecca W. Biology Level I. l.t. ed. 2005. (Real Science-4-Kids Ser.). (Illus.). 66p. (J). (gr. 3-6). 24.95 *(978-0-9749149-2-3(4))* Gravitas Pubns., Inc.

—Real Science-4-Kids PreLevel I Biology Student Textbook. 2008. 27.95 *(978-0-9799459-0-8(9))* Gravitas Pubns., Inc.

A Kid's Guide to the Classification of Living Things. (Illus.). (J). (gr. k-5). 127.50 *(978-0-8239-7257-9(7))* Rosen Publishing Group, Inc., The.

Klepeis, Alicia. Orcas on the Hunt. 2017. (Searchlight Books (tm) — Predators Ser.). (ENG.). (J). (gr. 3-5). pap. 9.99 ***(978-1-5124-5609-7(8))***; (Illus.). lib. bdg. 30.65 ***(978-1-5124-3398-2(5))*** Lerner Publishing Group.

Kummer, Patricia K. The Great Barrier Reef. 2008. (Nature's Wonders Ser.). 96p. (gr. 6-18). lib. bdg. 35.64 *(978-0-7614-2852-7(6)*, Benchmark Bks.) Marshall Cavendish Corp.

Kyi, Tanya Lloyd. 50 Body Questions: A Book That Spills Its Guts. Kinnaird, Ross, illus. 2014. (50 Questions Ser.). (ENG.). 108p. (J). (gr. 4-6). 22.95 *(978-1-55451-613-1(7)*, 9781554516131); 2nd ed. pap. 14.95 *(978-1-55451-612-4(9)*, 9781554516124) Annick Pr., Ltd. CAN. Dist: Publishers Group West (PGW).

Landon, Melissa, ed. Biology: Understanding Living Matter. 2014. (Study of Science Ser.). 160p. (YA). (gr. 7-12). 35.25 *(978-1-62275-409-0(3))* Rosen Publishing Group, Inc., The.

Lanier, Wendy. Life Cycles. 2006. (KidHaven Science Library). (ENG., Illus.). 48p. (J). (gr. 4-8). lib. bdg. 27.50 *(978-0-7377-2073-0(5)*, Greenhaven Pr., Inc.) Cengage Gale.

Latham, Donna. Backyard Biology: Investigate Habitats Outside Your Door with 25 Projects. Hetland, Beth, illus. 2013. (Build It Yourself Ser.). (ENG.). 128p. (J). (gr. 3-7). 21.95 *(978-1-61930-152-8(0))*; pap. 15.95 *(978-1-61930-151-1(2))* Open City Bks.

Lawrence, Ellen. Dirt. 2013. (Science Slam: FUN-Damental Experiments Ser.). 24p. (J). (gr. -1-3). lib. bdg. 23.93 *(978-1-61772-737-5(7))* Bearport Publishing Co., Inc.

—A Periodical Cicada's Life. 2016. (Animal Diaries). (ENG.). 24p. (J). (gr. -1-3). lib. bdg. 17.95 *(978-1-944102-47-0(7))* Bearport Publishing Co., Inc.

Leckie and Leckie, Leckie and, et al. Secondary Biology: S1 to National 4 Student Book: Billy Dixon, Graham Moffat & Leckie & Leckie. 2017. (ENG.). 300p. (J). (gr. 6). pap. 23.99 ***(978-0-00-820451-8(9))*** HarperCollins Pubs. Ltd. GBR. Dist: Independent Pubs. Group.

Lehman, Julie. Kyle in His Compost Pile: The Story of a Red Wiggler. 2010. 28p. pap. 14.99 *(978-1-4490-9112-5(1))* AuthorHouse.

LernerClassroom Editors. Life Cycles Teaching Guide. 2009. pap. 7.95 *(978-0-8225-5171-3(3))* Lerner Publishing Group.

LernerClassroom Editors, ed. Microquests. 2008. pap. 7.95 *(978-0-8225-9223-5(1))* Lerner Publishing Group.

Lewis, Mark J. Classification of Living Organisms. 2010. (Understanding Genetics Ser.). (ENG., Illus.). 80p. (YA). lib. bdg. 33.25 *(978-1-4358-9535-5(5))* Rosen Publishing Group, Inc., The.

Life, Module A. 2003. (Scott Foresman Science Ser.). (gr. 3-18). suppl. ed. 15.50 *(978-0-328-03435-2(5))*; (gr. 4-18). suppl. ed. 15.50 *(978-0-328-03439-0(8))*; (gr. 6-18). suppl. ed. 16.00 *(978-0-328-03447-5(9))* Addison-Wesley Educational Pubs., Inc.

Life Science Student Text: Grade 7. 2004. 32.00 *(978-0-89084-884-5(X))* BJU Pr.

Lift-The-Flap First Questions & Answers How Do I See? 2017. (Lift-The-Flap First Questions & Answers Ser.). (ENG.). (J). bds. 14.99 ***(978-0-7945-3939-9(4)***, Usborne) EDC Publishing.

Lindsey, Cameron. The 10 Best Animal Camouflages. 2008. 14.99 *(978-1-55448-492-8(8))* Scholastic Library Publishing.

Living in a Biome. 2005. (Earth & Outer Space Ser.). (YA). (gr. k-3). 237.60 *(978-0-7368-4213-6(6)*, Pebble Bks.) Capstone Press of Coughlan Cos.

Living Processes, 6 vols., Set. Incl. Adaptation & Survival. Spilsbury, Richard. (gr. 5-8). lib. bdg. 29.25 *(978-1-61532-343-2(0))*; Animal Variation & Classification. Spilsbury, Richard. (gr. 5-8). lib. bdg. 29.25 *(978-1-61532-344-9(9))*; Cells & Cell Function. Ballard, Carol. (gr. 5-8). lib. bdg. 29.25 *(978-1-61532-342-5(2)*, 1306852); Food Webs. Ballard, Carol. (gr. 5-8). lib. bdg. 29.25 *(978-1-61532-340-1(6))*; Life Cycles. Spilsbury, Richard. (gr. 8-10). lib. bdg. 29.25 *(978-1-61532-341-8(4))*; Plant Variation & Classification. Ballard, Carol. (gr. 5-8). lib. bdg. 29.25 *(978-1-61532-345-6(7))*; (YA). (Illus.). 48p. 2010. Set lib. bdg. 159.00 *(978-1-61532-385-2(6)*, Rosen Reference) Rosen Publishing Group, Inc., The.

Loewer, Peter & Jenkins, Jean. Pond Water Zoo: An Introduction to Microscopic Life. 2016. (ENG.). 96p. (J). (gr. 3-7). pap. 13.99 *(978-1-4814-8811-2(2)*, Atheneum Bks. for Young Readers) Simon & Schuster Children's Publishing.

Loh-Hagan, Virginia. Top 10 - Partnerships. 2017. (Wild Wicked Wonderful Ser.). (ENG., Illus.). 32p. (J). (gr. 4-8). 29.93 *(978-1-63472-139-4(X)*, 209128, 45th Parallel Press) Cherry Lake Publishing.

Lourie, Peter. Whaling Season: A Year in the Life of an Arctic Whale Scientist. 2015. (Scientists in the Field Ser.). (ENG., Illus.). 80p. (J). (gr. 5-7). pap. 9.99 *(978-0-544-58241-5(1)*, HMH Books For Young Readers) Houghton Mifflin Harcourt Publishing Co.

Lowery, Lawrence F. Looking for Animals. 2015. (I Wonder Why Ser.). (ENG., Illus.). 36p. (J). (gr. k-3). pap. 11.95 *(978-1-941316-27-6(1))* National Science Teachers Assn.

Loxton, Daniel. Evolution. Loxton, Daniel, illus. 2010. (ENG., Illus.). 56p. (J). (gr. 3-8). 18.95 *(978-1-55453-430-2(5))* Kids Can Pr., Ltd. CAN. Dist: Hachette Bk. Group.

Lunis, Natalie. Green Tree Frogs: Colorful Hiders. 2010. (Disappearing Acts Ser.). (Illus.). 24p. (J). (gr. k-3). lib. bdg. 22.61 *(978-1-936087-44-0(8))* Bearport Publishing Co., Inc.

—Katydids: Leaf Look-Alikes. 2010. (Disappearing Acts Ser.). (Illus.). 24p. (J). (gr. k-3). lib. bdg. 22.61 *(978-1-936087-40-2(5))* Bearport Publishing Co., Inc.

—See-Through Animals. 2011. (Animals with Super Powers Ser.). 24p. (YA). (gr. 2-5). lib. bdg. 22.61 *(978-1-61772-120-5(4))* Bearport Publishing Co., Inc.

MacKay, Jennifer. Forensic Biology. 2009. (Crime Scene Investigations Ser.). (ENG., Illus.). 128p. (gr. 7-10). lib. bdg. 40.40 *(978-1-4205-0108-7(9)*, LML02109-245419, Lucent Bks.) Cengage Gale.

Madison, Amelia. Predators of Europe & Africa. 2015. (World's Scariest Predators Ser.). (ENG.). 32p. (J). (gr. 3-3). 28.50 *(978-1-5026-0179-7(6))* Cavendish Square Publishing.

Marsico, Katie. Scholastic News Nonfiction Readers: Life Cycles, 6 bks., Set. Incl. Baby Lobster Grows Up. Marsico, Katie, illus. 22.00 *(978-0-531-17475-3(1))*; Kangaroo Joey Grows Up. 22.00 *(978-0-531-17476-0(X))*; Komodo Dragon Hatchling Grows Up. 22.00 *(978-0-531-17477-7(8))*; Ladybug Larva Grows Up. Marsico, Katie, illus. 22.00 *(978-0-531-17478-4(6))*; Manatee Calf Grows Up. 22.00 *(978-0-531-17479-1(4))*; Peachick Grows Up. Marsico, Katie, illus. 22.00 *(978-0-531-17480-7(8))*; 24p. (J). (gr. 1-2). 2007. 114.00 o.p. *(978-0-531-12606-6(4)*, Children's Pr.) Scholastic Library Publishing.

Massey, Kay. Where Do Animals Hide? Canals, Sonia, illus. 2009. (Little Green Footprints Ser.). 12p. (J). (gr. -1-k). bds. 11.40 *(978-1-60754-696-2(5))* Windmill Bks.

Mauk, Susan & Stettler, Linda. Taxonomy Trail. 2004. (Illus.). (J). (gr. 2-5). 42.00 *(978-1-57336-396-9(0)*, I1125) Interaction Pubs., Inc.

McDougal-Littell Publishing Staff. Life over Time, Grade 6-8. 2004. (McDougal Littell Middle School Science Ser.). (ENG.). 80p. (gr. 6-8). 21.80 *(978-0-618-33436-0(X)*, 2-01023) Great Source Education Group, Inc.

—Modules: Life Science; Human Biology. 2004. (McDougal Littell Middle School Science Ser.). (ENG.). 64p. (gr. 6-8). 21.80 *(978-0-618-33431-5(9)*, 2-01019) Great Source Education Group, Inc.

—Modules: Physical Science. 2004. (McDougal Littell Science Ser.). (ENG.). 56p. (gr. 6-8). pap., lab manual ed. 15.30 *(978-0-618-43730-6(4)*, 2-01223) Great Source Education Group, Inc.

McGraw-Hill Education Staff. Biology: The Dynamics of Life. 2003. (Biology Dynamics of Life Ser.). (ENG., Illus.). 288p. (gr. 9-12). stu. ed., per., lab manual ed. 13.08 *(978-0-07-860228-3(9)*, 0078602289) McGraw-Hill Higher Education.

McGraw-Hill Staff. Biology: The Dynamics of Life. 2nd ed. 2003. (Biology Dynamics of Life Ser.). (ENG.). 192p. (gr. 9-12). pap., stu. ed. 12.28 *(978-0-07-860232-0(7)*, 0078602327) McGraw-Hill Higher Education.

—Biology: The Dynamics of Life Online: MHLN Stand Alone Version. 2003. (Biology Dynamics of Life Ser.). (ENG.). (gr. 9-12). stu. ed. 119.36 *(978-0-07-861529-0(1)*, 0078615291) Glencoe/McGraw-Hill.

McGraw-Hill Staff, creator. Glencoe Science Probeware for Biology Lab Manual. 2003. (ENG., Illus.). 41p. (C). (gr. 6-12). pap., stu. ed., lab manual ed. 8.72 *(978-0-07-860226-9(2)*, 0078602262) Glencoe/McGraw-Hill.

Meinking, Mary. Crocodile vs. Wildebeest, 1 vol. 2011. (Predator vs. Prey Ser.). (ENG., Illus.). 32p. (gr. 1-2). 29.99 *(978-1-4109-3935-7(9))*; pap. 8.29 *(978-1-4109-3944-9(8))* Heinemann-Raintree. (Read Me!).

—Lion vs. Gazelle, 1 vol. 2011. (Predator vs. Prey Ser.). (ENG., Illus.). 32p. (gr. 1-2). 29.99 *(978-1-4109-3934-0(0))*; pap. 8.29 *(978-1-4109-3943-2(X))* Heinemann-Raintree. (Read Me!).

—Owl vs. Mouse, 1 vol. 2011. (Predator vs. Prey Ser.). (ENG., Illus.). 32p. (gr. 1-2). 29.99 *(978-1-4109-3936-4(7))*; pap. 8.29 *(978-1-4109-3945-6(6))* Heinemann-Raintree. (Read Me!).

—Polar Bear vs. Seal, 1 vol. 2011. (Predator vs. Prey Ser.). (ENG., Illus.). 32p. (gr. 1-2). pap. 8.29 *(978-1-4109-3948-7(0)*, Read Me!) Heinemann-Raintree.

—Shark vs. Penguin, 1 vol. 2011. (Predator vs. Prey Ser.). (ENG.). 32p. (gr. 1-2). pap. 8.29 *(978-1-4109-3946-3(4)*, Read Me!) Heinemann-Raintree.

—Tarantula vs. Bird, 1 vol. 2011. (Predator vs. Prey Ser.). (ENG., Illus.). 32p. (gr. 1-2). pap. 8.29 *(978-1-4109-3947-0(2)*, Read Me!) Heinemann-Raintree.

—Wolf vs. Elk, 1 vol. 2011. (Predator vs. Prey Ser.). (ENG., Illus.). 32p. (gr. 1-2). pap. 8.29 *(978-1-4109-3950-0(2)*, Read Me!) Heinemann-Raintree.

Meredith, Sue. El GRAN LIBRO DELAWARE LOS GENES y el ADN - INTERNET LINKED. 2005. (SPA.). 64p. (J). pap. 11.95 *(978-0-7460-6748-2(8)*, Usborne) EDC Publishing.

Metz, Lorijo. What Can We Do about Invasive Species? 2009. (Protecting Our Planet Ser.). (Illus.). 24p. (J). pap. 8.25 *(978-1-4358-2487-4(3)*, PowerKids Pr.) Rosen Publishing Group, Inc., The.

Mitchell, Susan K. Animal Body-Part Regenerators: Growing New Heads, Tails, & Legs. 2008. (Amazing Animal Defenses Ser.). (Illus.). 48p. (J). (gr. 5-9). lib. bdg. 25.27 *(978-0-7660-3295-8(7))* Enslow Pubs., Inc.

—Animal Mimics: Look-Alikes & Copycats. 2008. (Amazing Animal Defenses Ser.). (Illus.). 48p. (J). (gr. 5-9). lib. bdg. 25.27 *(978-0-7660-3293-4(0))* Enslow Pubs., Inc.

—Animals with Crafty Camouflage: Hiding in Plain Sight. 2008. (Amazing Animal Defenses Ser.). (Illus.). 48p. (J). (gr. 5-9). lib. bdg. 25.27 *(978-0-7660-3291-0(4))* Enslow Pubs., Inc.

Moore Niver, Heather. A Trip Through a Coral Reef. 2015. (Fantastic Science Journeys Ser.). (ENG., Illus.). 32p. (J). (gr. 2-3). pap. 10.50 *(978-1-4824-2002-9(3))* Stevens, Gareth Publishing LLLP.

Morgan, Jennifer. Mammals Who Morph: The Universe Tells Our Evolution Story: Book 3. Andersen, Dana Lynne, illus. 2006. (Sharing Nature with Children Book Ser.). 48p. (J). (gr. 3-7). 19.95 *(978-1-58469-084-9(4))*; pap. 9.95 *(978-1-58469-085-6(2))* Dawn Pubns.

Nagle, Jeanne. How Do Animals Hunt & Feed? 2015. (Let's Find Out! Animal Life Ser.). (ENG., Illus.). 32p. (J). (gr. 2-3). 23.45 *(978-1-68048-015-3(4)*, Britannica Educational Publishing) Rosen Publishing Group, Inc., The.

Nichols, Catherine. Emerald Boas: Rain Forest Undercover. 2010. (Disappearing Acts Ser.). (Illus.). 24p. (J). (gr. k-3). lib. bdg. 22.61 *(978-1-936087-41-9(3))* Bearport Publishing Co., Inc.

Oachs, Emily Rose. Emerald Tree Boas. 2014. (Amazing Snakes! Ser.). (ENG., Illus.). 24p. (J). (gr. 3-7). lib. bdg. 25.95 *(978-1-62617-092-6(4)*, Epic Bks.) Bellwether Media.

O'Daly, Anne, ed. Encyclopedia of Life Sciences, 13 vols. 2nd ed. 2003. (Illus.). 1,800p. 657.07 *(978-0-7614-7442-5(0)*, Marshall Cavendish Reference Bks.) Marshall Cavendish Corp.

Oliver, Narelle. Twilight Hunt, 1 vol. Oliver, Narelle, illus. 2007. (Seek-and-Find Bks.). (ENG., Illus.). 32p. (J). (gr. k-3). 16.95 *(978-1-59572-107-5(X))* Star Bright Bks., Inc.

O'Mara, Kennon. Camouflage: Survival in the Wild. 2009. (Real Life Readers Ser.). 32p. (gr. 4-5). pap. 10.00 *(978-1-4358-0153-0(9)*, Rosen Classroom); 32p. (gr. 4-4). 47.90 *(978-1-60853-034-2(5)*, PowerKids Pr.); (J). lib. bdg. 25.25 *(978-1-4358-2985-5(9)*, PowerKids Pr.) Rosen Publishing Group, Inc., The.

Owings, Lisa. From Egg to Ladybug. 2016. (Start to Finish, Second Ser.). (ENG., Illus.). 24p. (J). (gr. k-3). 23.99 *(978-1-5124-0910-9(3))* Lerner Publishing Group.

Oxlade, Chris. Growth, 1 vol. 2012. (Science Behind Ser.). (ENG., Illus.). 32p. (gr. 3-3). pap. 8.29 *(978-1-4109-4501-3(4))*; lib. bdg. 30.65 *(978-1-4109-4490-0(5))* Heinemann-Raintree. (Raintree Perspectives).

Palmer, Bill. What Causes Sexual Orientation? Genetics, Biology, Psychology. 2009. (Gallup's Guide to Modern Gay, Lesbian, & Transgender Lifestyle Ser.). 64p. (YA). (gr. 7-18). pap. 9.95 *(978-1-4222-1876-1(7))*; lib. bdg. 22.95 *(978-1-4222-1757-3(4))* Mason Crest.

Parker, Steve. In Vitro Fertilization. 2007. (Cutting Edge Medicine Ser.). (Illus.). 64p. (gr. 6-12). lib. bdg. 34.00 *(978-0-8368-7866-0(3)*, Gareth Stevens Secondary Library) Stevens, Gareth Publishing LLLP.

Parks, Deborah A. Nature's Machines: The Story of Biomechanist Mimi Koehl. 2006. (ENG., Illus.). 128p. (gr. 7-9). per. 19.95 *(978-0-309-09559-4(X)*, Joseph Henry Pr.) National Academies Pr.

Peterson, Megan Cooley. The Best Camouflaged Animals. 2012. (Extreme Animals Ser.). (ENG.). 24p. (gr. k-1). pap. 41.70 *(978-1-4296-8340-1(6)*, Pebble Plus) Capstone Press of Coughlan Cos.

Peterson, Megan Cooley & Rustad, Martha E. H. The Best Camouflaged Animals, 1 vol. 2012. (Extreme Animals Ser.). (ENG.). 24p. (gr. k-1). pap. 7.29 *(978-1-4296-7902-2(6))*; lib. bdg. 26.65 *(978-1-4296-7599-4(3))* Capstone Press of Coughlan Cos. (Pebble Plus).

—Coral Reefs, 1 vol. 2013. (Little Scientist Ser.). (ENG., Illus.). 32p. (gr. 1-2). 27.99 *(978-1-4765-0247-2(1))*; pap. 6.95 *(978-1-4765-3547-0(7))* Capstone Press of Coughlan Cos.

¿Por Que la Gente Es Diferente? (Coleccion Primeros Pasos en la Ciencia). (SPA., Illus.). (J). (gr. 1-3). pap. *(978-950-724-396-7(8)*, LMA8225) Lumen ARG. Dist: Lectorum Pubns., Inc.

QEB Start Reading & Talking National Book Stores Edition: Camouflage. 2006. (J). per. *(978-1-59566-251-4(0))* QEB Publishing Inc.

Raab & Kiefe, Raab. Exploring Living Systems: Life Science. (YA). (gr. 6-12). 38.95 *(978-1-55675-802-7(2))* Globe Fearon Educational Publishing.

Rabe, Tish. High? Low? Where Did It Go? All about Animal Camouflage. Ruiz, Aristides, illus. 2016. (Cat in the Hat's Learning Library). (ENG.). 48p. (J). (gr. k-3). lib. bdg. 13.99 *(978-0-375-97169-3(6)*, Random Hse. Bks. for Young Readers) Random Hse. Children's Bks.

Racanelli, Marie. Animal Mimics. 2010. (Crazy Nature Ser.). (Illus.). 24p. (J). pap. 8.25 *(978-1-4358-9856-1(7)*, PowerKids Pr.); (YA). (gr. 1-4). lib. bdg. 22.60 *(978-1-4358-9382-5(4))* Rosen Publishing Group, Inc., The.

—Camouflaged Creatures. 2010. (Illus.). 24p. (J). 49.50 *(978-1-4358-9859-2(1)*, PowerKids Pr.); (J). pap. 8.25 *(978-1-4358-9858-5(3)*, PowerKids Pr.); (YA). (gr. 1-4). lib. bdg. 22.60 *(978-1-4358-9383-2(2))* Rosen Publishing Group, Inc., The.

Rafferty, John P. Biomes & Ecosystems. 2011. (Living Earth Ser.). (Illus.). 240p. (YA). (gr. 9-12). lib. bdg. 51.70 *(978-1-61530-302-1(2))* Rosen Publishing Group, Inc., The.

Rake, Jody S. Kings of the Oceans. 2017. (Animal Rulers Ser.). (ENG.). 24p. (gr. 1-2). lib. bdg. 25.32 ***(978-1-5157-8066-3(X)***, First Facts) Capstone Press of Coughlan Cos.

Rake, Matthew. The Dawn of Planet Earth. Minister, Peter, illus. 2015. (Prehistoric Field Guides). (ENG.). 32p. (J). (gr. 3-6). 26.65 *(978-1-4677-6348-6(9))*, Lerner Pubns.) Lerner Publishing Group.

Redmond, Stephanie L. Christian Kids Explore Biology. Taylor, David W., illus. 2007. (Christian Kids Explore Ser.). 291p. per. 34.95 *(978-1-892427-05-2(2))* Bright Ideas! Educational Resources.

Regan, Lisa. Biology Is Wild. 2016. (Amazing World of Science & Math Ser.). 48p. (gr. 5-5). pap. 14.05 *(978-1-4824-4994-5(3))* Stevens, Gareth Publishing LLLP.

Reilly, Kathleen M. Explore Life Cycles! 25 Great Projects, Activities, Experiments. Stone, Bryan, illus. 2011. (Explore Your World Ser.). (ENG.). 96p. (J). (gr. k-4). pap. 12.95 *(978-1-934670-80-4(4))* Open City Bks.

Reis, Ronald A. Eugenie Clark: Marine Biologist. 2005. (Ferguson Career Biographies Ser.). (Illus.). 128p. (gr. 6-12). 25.00 *(978-0-8160-5883-9(0)*, Ferguson Publishing Co.) Facts On File, Inc.

Rice, Dona. Growing Up, 1 vol. rev. ed. 2014. (Science Readers: Content & Literacy Ser.). (ENG., Illus.). 24p. (gr. k-k). pap. 8.99 *(978-1-4807-4524-7(3))* Teacher Created Materials, Inc.

—Growth & Change, 1 vol. rev. ed. 2014. (Science Readers: Content & Literacy Ser.). (ENG., Illus.). 24p. (gr. 1-1). pap. 8.99 *(978-1-4807-4562-9(6))* Teacher Created Materials, Inc.

Riehecky, Janet. Camouflage & Mimicry: Animal Weapons & Defenses, 1 vol. 2012. (Animal Weapons & Defenses Ser.). (ENG.). 32p. (gr. 1-2). 26.65 *(978-1-4296-6508-7(4))*; pap. 8.10 *(978-1-4296-8007-3(5))*; pap. 47.70 *(978-1-4296-8499-6(2))* Capstone Press of Coughlan Cos. (Blazers).

Riley, Peter. Lifecycles. 2016. (Ways into Science Ser.). (ENG., Illus.). 32p. (J). (gr. k-2). pap. 11.99 *(978-1-4451-3483-3(7)*, Franklin Watts) Hachette Children's Group GBR. Dist: Hachette Bk. Group.

Riley, Peter D. Checkpoint Biology. 2005. (Illus.). 240p. pap. 47.50 *(978-0-7195-8067-3(6))* Hodder Education Group GBR. Dist: Trans-Atlantic Pubns., Inc.

Rittner, Don & McCabe, Timothy Lee. Encyclopedia of Biology. 2004. (Facts on File Science Library). (Illus.). 416p. (C). (gr. 9). 85.00 *(978-0-8160-4859-5(2))* Facts On File, Inc.

Rodríguez, Ana María. The Secret of the Deceiving Striped Lizard... & More! 2017. (Animal Secrets Revealed! Ser.). 48p. (J). (gr. 4-4). lib. bdg. 27.93 ***(978-0-7660-8625-8(9))*** Enslow Pubs., Inc.

Romano, Amy & Baum, Margaux. Germ Warfare. 2016. (Germs: Disease Causing Organisms Ser.). 48p. (J). (gr. 5-5). pap. 11.75 *(978-1-4777-8844-8(1)*, Rosen Reference) Rosen Publishing Group, Inc., The.

Rose, Elizabeth. Classification. 2006. (Life Science Library). (Illus.). 24p. (YA). (gr. 3-6). 22.60 *(978-1-4042-2818-4(7))* Rosen Publishing Group, Inc., The.

—Classification of Living & Nonliving Things. 2009. (Life Science Library). 24p. (gr. 3-4). 42.50 *(978-1-60854-000-6(6)*, PowerKids Pr.) Rosen Publishing Group, Inc., The.

Rose, Simon. Coral Reefs. 2014. (Illus.). 32p. (J). *(978-1-62127-484-1(5))* Weigl Pubs., Inc.

—Estuaries. 2014. (Illus.). 32p. (J). *(978-1-62127-485-8(3))* Weigl Pubs., Inc.

—Resource Conservation. 2015. (Illus.). 24p. (J). *(978-1-4896-3683-6(8))* Weigl Pubs., Inc.

Ross, Michael Elsohn. Re-Cycles. Moore, Gustav, illus. 2003. (Cycles Ser.). (ENG.). 32p. (gr. 2-4). pap. 7.95 *(978-0-7613-1949-8(2)*, First Avenue Editions) Lerner Publishing Group.

Royston, Angela. Looking at Life Cycles: How Do Plants & Animals Change? 2008. (Looking at Science: How Things Change Ser.). (Illus.). 32p. (J). (gr. 3-7). lib. bdg. 23.94 *(978-0-7660-3091-6(1)*, Enslow Elementary) Enslow Pubs., Inc.

Rustad, Martha E. H. Animal Camouflage in the Desert [Scholastic]. 2010. (Hidden in Nature Ser.). pap. 0.52 *(978-1-4296-5046-5(X)*, Pebble Plus) Capstone Press of Coughlan Cos.

—Animal Camouflage in the Forest [Scholastic]. 2010. (Hidden in Nature Ser.). pap. 0.52 *(978-1-4296-5047-2(8)*, Pebble Plus) Capstone Press of Coughlan Cos.

—Animal Camouflage in the Snow [Scholastic]. 2010. (Hidden in Nature Ser.). pap. 0.52 *(978-1-4296-5049-6(4)*, Pebble Plus) Capstone Press of Coughlan Cos.

—Do Trees Get Hungry? Noticing Plant & Animal Traits. Moran, Mike, illus. 2015. (ENG.). 24p. (gr. k-2). lib. bdg. 25.32 *(978-1-4677-8559-4(8)*, Millbrook Pr.) Lerner Publishing Group.

Ryan, Lawrie, et al. Biology. 2003. (Illus.). 80p. pap. *(978-0-7487-6799-1(1))* Nelson Thornes Ltd.

Salas, Laura Purdie. From Beginning to End: A Song about Life Cycles, 1 vol. Garofoli, Viviana, illus. 2009. (Science Songs Ser.). (ENG.). 24p. (gr. 1-3). lib. bdg. 26.65 *(978-1-4048-5293-8(X))* Picture Window Bks.

Salzmann, Mary Elizabeth. What Has Spots?, 1 vol. 2007. (Creature Features Ser.). (ENG., Illus.). 24p. (gr. -1-3). 25.65 *(978-1-59928-872-7(9)*, Super SandCastle) ABDO Publishing Co.

—What Has Stripes?, 1 vol. 2007. (Creature Features Ser.). (ENG., Illus.). 24p. (gr. -1-3). 25.65 *(978-1-59928-873-4(7)*, Super SandCastle) ABDO Publishing Co.

Sarquis, Mickey. Squishy, Squashy Sponges: Early Childhood Science Guide for Teachers. 2003. (ENG.). (J). 16.95 *(978-1-883822-36-1(X))* Terrific Science Pr.

Schaefer, Lola M. Lifetime: The Amazing Numbers in Animal Lives. Neal, Christopher Silas, illus. 2013. (ENG.). 40p. (J). (gr. -1-3). 17.99 *(978-1-4521-0714-1(9))* Chronicle Bks. LLC.

Schitt, Christine. Perfectly Hidden: The Animal Kingdom's Fascinating Camouflage. Brandt, Chris, tr. from GER. 2013. (ENG., Illus.). 80p. (J). (gr. 2-7). 16.95 *(978-1-62087-115-7(7)*, 620115, Sky Pony Pr.) Skyhorse Publishing Co., Inc.

Schwartz, David M. & Schy, Yael. Where Else in the Wild? Kuhn, Dwight, illus. Kuhn, Dwight, photos by. 2009. (ENG.). 50p. (J). (gr. -1-2). 16.99 *(978-1-58246-283-7(6)*, Tricycle Pr.) Random Hse. Children's Bks.

—Where in the Wild? Camouflaged Creatures Concealed... & Revealed. Kuhn, Dwight, photos by. 2011. (ENG., Illus.). 44p. (J). (gr. -1-2). pap. 8.99 *(978-1-58246-399-5(9)*, Tricycle Pr.) Random Hse. Children's Bks.

Seeger, Laura Vaccaro. First the Egg. Seeger, Laura Vaccaro, illus. 2007. (ENG., Illus.). 32p. (J). (gr. -1-1). 15.99 *(978-1-59643-272-7(1)*, 9781596432727) Roaring Brook Pr.

Seidensticker, John & Lumpkin, Susan. Predators. 2008. (Insiders Ser.). Orig. Title: Thinning the Predators. (ENG., Illus.). 64p. (J). (gr. 3-7). 17.99 *(978-1-4169-3863-7(X)*, Simon & Schuster Bks. For Young Readers) Simon & Schuster Bks. For Young Readers.

Serafini, Frank. Looking Closely Across the Desert. Serafini, Frank, illus. 2008. (Looking Closely Ser.). (ENG., Illus.). 40p. (J). (gr. -1-2). 16.95 *(978-1-55453-211-7(6))* Kids Can Pr., Ltd. CAN. Dist: Hachette Bk. Group.

Shea, John M. Gross Things about Your Body. 2012. (That's Gross! Ser.). (Illus.). 24p. (J). (gr. 2-5). pap. 8.15 *(978-1-4339-7112-9(7))*; lib. bdg. 22.60 *(978-1-4339-7111-2(9))* Stevens, Gareth Publishing LLLP.

Silverstein, Alvin, et al. Growth & Development. 2007. (Science Concepts, Second Ser.). (Illus.). 112p. (YA). (gr. 5-9). lib. bdg. 31.93 *(978-0-8225-6057-9(7))* Lerner Publishing Group.

Slade, Suzanne. The Elements Common to Most Living Organisms. 2007. (Library of Physical Sciences). (ENG., Illus.). 24p. (gr. 4-8). pap. 7.05 *(978-1-4042-2171-0(9)*, PowerKids Pr.) Rosen Publishing Group, Inc., The.

—Elements in Living Organisms. (Library of Physical Science Ser.). 24p. 2009. (gr. 4-4). 42.50 *(978-1-60853-782-2(X))* 2006. (Illus.). (J). (gr. 3-7). lib. bdg. 21.25 *(978-1-4042-3424-6(1))* Rosen Publishing Group, Inc., The. (PowerKids Pr.).

—The Four Seasons. (Cycles in Nature Ser.). (gr. 3-3). 2009. 24p. 42.50 *(978-1-61512-111-3(0))* 2007. 28p. pap. 21.25 *(978-1-4358-3827-7(0))* Rosen Publishing Group, Inc., The. (PowerKids Pr.).

—What Do You Know about Life Cycles? 2009. (20 Questions: Science Ser.). 24p. (gr. 2-3). 42.50 *(978-1-60854-964-1(X)*, PowerKids Pr.) Rosen Publishing Group, Inc., The.

Smith, Sian. Life Cycles, 1 vol. 2011. (ENG.). 24p. (gr. -1-1). pap. 9.95 *(978-1-4329-5496-3(2))*; 25.99

(978-1-4329-5351-5(6)) Heinemann-Raintree. (Acorn Read-Aloud).

Snedden, Robert. Variation in Living Things, 1 vol. 2012. (Web of Life Ser.). (ENG., Illus.). 48p. (gr. 3-3). pap. 9.49 *(978-1-4109-4434-4(4)*, Raintree Freestyle Express); (gr. 3-3). lib. bdg. 34.65 *(978-1-4109-4427-6(1)*, Raintree Freestyle Express); (gr. 6-10). lib. bdg. 34.65 *(978-1-4109-4400-9(X)*, Raintree Freestyle) Heinemann-Raintree.

Spilsbury, Louise. Coastal Treasure Hunter. 2010. (ENG.). 32p. (J). *(978-0-7787-9907-8(7))* Crabtree Publishing Co.

Spilsbury, Richard. Cells, Tissues, & Organs. 2016. (Human Machine Ser.). (ENG.). 32p. pap. 8.29 *(978-1-4846-4015-9(2)*, Heinemann InfoSearch) Heinemann-Raintree.

—Life Cycles. 2010. (Living Processes Ser.). (Illus.). 48p. (J). pap. 11.75 *(978-1-61532-350-0(3))*; (YA). (gr. 8-10). lib. bdg. 29.25 *(978-1-61532-341-8(4))* Rosen Publishing Group, Inc., The. (Rosen Reference).

Staley, Erin. What Is Animal Camouflage? 2015. (Let's Find Out! Animal Life Ser.). (ENG.). 32p. (J). 23.45 *(978-1-68048-000-9(6)*, Britannica Educational Publishing) Rosen Publishing Group, Inc., The.

Steffora, Tracey. Animal Math: Comparing & Measuring, 1 vol. 2014. (Animal Math Ser.). (ENG.). 32p. (gr. -1-1). 29.99 *(978-1-4846-0062-7(2)*, NA-h) Heinemann-Raintree.

—Comparing with Cats, 1 vol. 2013. (Animal Math Ser.). (ENG.). 24p. (gr. -1-1). 22.65 *(978-1-4329-7559-3(5))*; pap. 6.95 *(978-1-4329-7566-1(8))* Heinemann-Raintree. (NA-h).

Stefoff, Rebecca. The Conifer Division. 2008. (Family Trees Ser.). 96p. (gr. 6-18). lib. bdg. 34.21 *(978-0-7614-3077-3(6)*, Benchmark Bks.) Marshall Cavendish Corp.

—Family Trees - Group 3, 5 bks., Set. Incl. Arachnid Class. (YA). lib. bdg. 34.21 *(978-0-7614-3075-9(X))*; Conifer Division. lib. bdg. 34.21 *(978-0-7614-3077-3(6))*; Moneran Kingdom. lib. bdg. 34.21 *(978-0-7614-3076-6(8))*; Rodent Order. lib. bdg. 34.21 *(978-0-7614-3073-5(3))*; Sea Mammals. lib. bdg. 34.21 *(978-0-7614-3072-8(5))*; 96p. (gr. 6-18). 2008. Set lib. bdg. 171.07 *(978-0-7614-3070-4(9)*, Benchmark Bks.) Marshall Cavendish Corp.

Stephens, Catherine. Classification Clues. 2007. (Nonfiction Reading & Writing Workshops Ser.). (ENG., Illus.). 32p. (J). pap. 17.95 *(978-0-7922-4576-6(8))* CENGAGE Learning.

Stephens, Catherine & National Geographic Learning Staff. Life Cycles. 2006. (Nonfiction Reading & Writing Workshops Ser.). (ENG., Illus.). 32p. (J). pap. 17.95 *(978-0-7922-4579-7(2))* CENGAGE Learning.

Stevenson, Emma. Hide-and-Seek Science: Animal Camouflage. Stevenson, Emma, illus. 2014. (ENG., Illus.). 32p. (J). (gr. 1-5). 7.99 *(978-0-8234-3187-8(8))* Holiday Hse., Inc.

—Hide-and-Seek Science: Animal Camouflage. 2013. (ENG., Illus.). 32p. (J). 16.95 *(978-0-8234-2293-7(3))* Holiday Hse., Inc.

Stewart, Melissa. Classification of Life. 2007. (Great Ideas of Science Ser.). (Illus.). 80p. (YA). (gr. 9-12). lib. bdg. 27.93 *(978-0-8225-6604-5(4))* Twenty First Century Bks.

—National Geographic Readers: Predator Face-Off. 2017. (Readers Ser.). (ENG., Illus.). 32p. (J). (gr. -1-1). lib. bdg. 13.90 ***(978-1-4263-2812-1(5)***, National Geographic Children's Bks.) National Geographic Society.

—Predator Face-Off. 2017. (Readers Ser.). (ENG., Illus.). 32p. (J). (gr. -1-1). pap. 3.99 ***(978-1-4263-2811-4(7)***, National Geographic Children's Bks.) National Geographic Society.

Stewart, Melissa. Tell Me Why, Tell Me How - Group 2, 6 bks., Set. Incl. How Do Bats Fly in the Dark? lib. bdg. 29.93 *(978-0-7614-2924-1(7))*; How Do Bees Make Honey? lib. bdg. 29.93 *(978-0-7614-2923-4(9))*; How Do Chameleons Change Color? lib. bdg. 29.93 *(978-0-7614-2922-7(0))*; How Do Spiders Make Webs? lib. bdg. 29.93 *(978-0-7614-2920-3(4))*; Why Do We See Rainbows? lib. bdg. 29.93 *(978-0-7614-2919-7(0))*; Why Does the Moon Change Shape? (YA). lib. bdg. 29.93 *(978-0-7614-2921-0(2))*; (Illus.). 32p. (gr. 3-18). 2008. Set lib. bdg. 179.57 *(978-0-7614-2918-0(2)*, Benchmark Bks.) Marshall Cavendish Corp.

Stockdale, Susan. Spectacular Spots, 1 vol. Stockdale, Susan, illus. 2015. (ENG & SPA., Illus.). 32p. (J). (gr. 1-1). 15.95 *(978-1-56145-817-2(1))* Peachtree Pubs.

—Spectacular Spots / Magnificas Manchas, 1 vol. Stockdale, Susan, illus. rev. ed. 2017. (ENG & SPA., Illus.). 32p. (J). (gr. -1-1). pap. 8.95 *(978-1-56145-978-0(X))* Peachtree Pubs.

—Stripes of All Types, 1 vol. Stockdale, Susan, illus. 2013. (About Habitats Ser.). (ENG., Illus.). 32p. (J). (gr. -1-1). 16.95 *(978-1-56145-695-6(0))* Peachtree Pubs.

—Stripes of All Types / Rayas de Todas Las Tallas, 1 vol. Stockdale, Susan, illus. 2014. (SPA & ENG., Illus.). 32p. (J). (gr. -1-1). pap. 8.95 *(978-1-56145-793-9(0))* Peachtree Pubs.

Stockland, Patricia M. Stripes, Spots, or Diamonds: A Book about Animal Patterns. Ouren, Todd, illus. 2005. (Animal Wise Ser.). (ENG.). 24p. (gr. k-2). 26.65 *(978-1-4048-0934-5(1))* Picture Window Bks.

Stockley, Corinne. Illustrated Dictionary of Biology. Rogers, Kirsteen, ed. Chen, Kuo Kang & Smith, Guy, illus. 2007. (Illustrated Dictionaries Ser.). 128p. (J). (gr. 4-7). pap. 12.99 *(978-0-7945-1559-1(2)*, Usborne) EDC Publishing.

Strauss, Rochelle. Tree of Life: The Incredible Biodiversity of Life on Earth. Thompson, Margot, illus. 2013. (CitizenKid Ser.). (ENG.). 40p. (J). (gr. 3-7). pap. 12.95 *(978-1-55453-961-1(7))* Kids Can Pr., Ltd. CAN. Dist: Hachette Bk. Group.

Suen, Anastasia. Toco Toucans: Bright Enough to Disappear. 2010. (Disappearing Acts Ser.). (Illus.). 24p. (J). (gr. k-3). lib. bdg. 22.61 *(978-1-936087-45-7(6))* Bearport Publishing Co., Inc.

Sundance/Newbridge LLC Staff. Animals in Hiding. 2007. (Early Science Ser.). (gr. k-3). 18.95 *(978-1-4007-6350-4(9))*; pap. 6.10 *(978-1-4007-6346-7(0))* Sundance/Newbridge Educational Publishing.

Trout, Laura. POGIL Activities for High School Biology. 2012. spiral bd. 49.95 *(978-1-933709-35-2(9))* Flinn Scientific, Inc.

Underwood, Deborah. Hiding in Deserts, 1 vol. 2010. (Creature Camouflage Ser.). (ENG.). 32p. (gr. 1-3). 27.32 *(978-1-4329-4021-8(X))*; pap. 8.29 *(978-1-4329-4030-0(9))* Heinemann-Raintree. (Heinemann First Library).

—Hiding in Forests, 1 vol. 2010. (Creature Camouflage Ser.). (ENG.). 32p. (gr. 1-3). 27.32 *(978-1-4329-4022-5(8)*, Heinemann First Library) Heinemann-Raintree.

—Hiding in Grasslands, 1 vol. 2010. (Creature Camouflage Ser.). (ENG.). 32p. (gr. 1-3). 27.32 *(978-1-4329-4024-9(4))*; pap. 8.29 *(978-1-4329-4033-1(3))* Heinemann-Raintree. (Heinemann First Library).

—Hiding in Mountains, 1 vol. 2010. (Creature Camouflage Ser.). (ENG.). 32p. (gr. 1-3). 27.32 *(978-1-4329-4023-2(6))*; pap. 8.29 *(978-1-4329-4032-4(5))* Heinemann-Raintree. (Heinemann First Library).

—Hiding in Oceans, 1 vol. 2010. (Creature Camouflage Ser.). (ENG., Illus.). 32p. (gr. 1-3). 27.32 *(978-1-4329-4020-1(1))*; pap. 8.29 *(978-1-4329-4029-4(5))* Heinemann-Raintree. (Heinemann First Library).

—Hiding in Rain Forests, 1 vol. 2010. (Creature Camouflage Ser.). (ENG.). 32p. (gr. 1-3). pap. 8.29 *(978-1-4329-4035-5(X)*, Heinemann First Library) Heinemann-Raintree.

—Hiding in the Polar Regions, 1 vol. 2010. (Creature Camouflage Ser.). (ENG., Illus.). 32p. (gr. 1-3). 27.32 *(978-1-4329-4027-0(9))*; pap. 8.29 *(978-1-4329-4036-2(8))* Heinemann-Raintree. (Heinemann First Library).

—Hiding in Wetlands, 1 vol. 2010. (Creature Camouflage Ser.). (ENG., Illus.). 32p. (gr. 1-3). pap. 8.29 *(978-1-4329-4034-8(1)*, Heinemann First Library) Heinemann-Raintree.

Unwin, Mike. Why Do Tigers Have Stripes? Morton, Robert, illus. 2006. (Usborne Starting Point Science Ser.). 22p. (J). (gr. 1). lib. bdg. 12.99 *(978-1-58086-939-3(4)*, Usborne) EDC Publishing.

VanCleave, Janice. Janice VanCleave's Science Around the World: Activities on Biomes from Pole to Pole. 2004. (ENG., Illus.). 128p. (gr. 3-7). pap. 14.95 *(978-0-471-20547-0(8)*, Wiley) Wiley, John & Sons, Inc.

Vogel, Julia. City Food Chains, 1 vol. Adams, Hazel, illus. 2010. (Fascinating Food Chains Ser.). (ENG.). 32p. 28.50 *(978-1-60270-791-7(X)*, Looking Glass Library- Nonfiction) Magic Wagon.

Wadsworth, Pamela. Pethau Byw Ar Waith. 2005. (WEL., Illus.). 24p. pap. *(978-1-85596-233-0(0))* Dref Wen.

Waldron, Melanie, et al. Essential Life Science. 2013. (Essential Life Science Ser.). (ENG.). 48p. (gr. 4-6). lib. bdg. 133.28 *(978-1-4329-7809-9(8)*, Heinemann InfoSearch) Heinemann-Raintree.

Walker, Robert. What Is the Theory of Evolution? 2010. (Shaping Modern Science Ser.). (ENG.). 64p. (J). (gr. 5-8). pap. *(978-0-7787-7205-7(5))* Crabtree Publishing Co.

Wallace, Holly. Life Cycles. (Life Processes Ser.). 32p. pap. 7.50 *(978-1-4034-4075-4(1))* Heinemann-Raintree.

Walters, Peter. The Hungriest Mouth in the Sea, 1 vol. 2015. (ENG., Illus.). 32p. (J). (gr. k-3). pap. 9.95 *(978-1-62855-636-0(6))* Arbordale Publishing.

Wanjie, Anne, ed. The Basics of Animal Systems. 2013. (Core Concepts Ser.). (ENG., Illus.). 96p. (YA). (gr. 7-12). lib. bdg. 34.60 *(978-1-4777-0556-8(2)*, Rosen Classroom) Rosen Publishing Group, Inc., The.

—The Basics of Biology. 2013. (Core Concepts Ser.). (ENG., Illus.). 96p. (YA). (gr. 7-12). lib. bdg. 34.60 *(978-1-4777-0554-4(6))* Rosen Publishing Group, Inc., The.

—The Basics of the Human Body. 2013. (Core Concepts Ser.). (ENG., Illus.). 96p. (YA). (gr. 7-12). lib. bdg. 34.60 *(978-1-4777-0555-1(4))* Rosen Publishing Group, Inc., The.

Weber, Belinda. Discover Science: Animal Disguises. (Discover Science Ser.). (ENG.). (J). 2017. pap. 7.99 ***(978-0-7534-7434-1(4)***, 9780753474341) 2011. (Illus.). 56p. pap. 7.99 *(978-0-7534-6719-0(4)*, 9780753467190) Roaring Brook Pr. (Kingfisher).

Wile, Jay L. & Durnell, Marilyn F. Exploring Creation with Biology, 2 Bks., Set. 2nd ed. 2005. 85.00 *(978-1-932012-57-6(5))* Apologia Educational Ministries, Inc.

Winner, Cherie. Cryobiology. 2005. (Cool Science Ser.). (ENG., Illus.). 48p. (J). (gr. 4-8). lib. bdg. 27.93 *(978-0-8225-2907-1(6)*, Lerner Pubns.) Lerner Publishing Group.

Wood, Alix. Animal Camouflage. 2012. (Wow! Wildlife Ser.). (ENG., Illus.). 24p. (J). (gr. k-5). pap. 8.25 *(978-1-4488-8166-6(8))*; lib. bdg. 22.60 *(978-1-4488-8097-3(1))* Windmill Bks.

World Book, Inc Staff, contrib. by. Encyclopedia of Human Beings, 2 vols. 2014. (Illus.). (J). *(978-0-7166-7520-4(X))* World Bk., Inc.

—Plant & Animal Adaptations. 2014. (Illus.). 32p. (J). *(978-0-7166-2826-2(0))* World Bk., Inc.

Yaw, Valerie. Color-Changing Animals. 2011. (Animals with Super Powers Ser.). 24p. (YA). (gr. 2-5). lib. bdg. 22.61 *(978-1-61772-122-9(0))* Bearport Publishing Co., Inc.

BIOLOGY—ECOLOGY

see Ecology

BIOLOGY, ECONOMIC

see Botany, Economic; Zoology, Economic

BIOLOGY—EXPERIMENTS

Benbow, Ann & Mably, Colin. Sensational Human Body Science Projects. LaBaff, Tom, illus. 2009. (Real Life Science Experiments Ser.). 48p. (J). (gr. 2-5). lib. bdg. 25.27 *(978-0-7660-3149-4(7))* Enslow Pubs., Inc.

Cook, Trevor. Experiments with Plants & Other Living Things. 2009. (Science Lab Ser.). (J). (ENG., Illus.). 32p. (gr. 4-6). pap. 10.00 *(978-1-4358-3219-0(1)*, 1291701); lib. bdg. 26.50 *(978-1-4358-2806-3(2))* Rosen Publishing Group, Inc., The. (PowerKids Pr.).

Gardner, Robert. Genetics & Evolution Science Fair Projects: Using Skeletons, Cereal, Earthworms, & More. 2005. (Biology! Best Science Projects Ser.). (Illus.). 128p. (J). (gr. 6-13). lib. bdg. 27.94 *(978-0-7660-1175-5(5))* Enslow Pubs., Inc.

Gardner, Robert & Conklin, Joshua. Experiments for Future Biologists. 2016. (Experiments for Future STEM Professionals Ser.). 128p. (J). 37.27 *(978-0-7660-8198-7(2))* Enslow Pubs., Inc.

Hawkins, Jay. It's Alive! The Science of Plants & Living Things. 2013. (Big Bang Science Experiments Ser.). (ENG., Illus.). 32p. (J). (gr. 3-6). 26.50 *(978-1-4777-0322-9(5))*; pap. 11.75 *(978-1-4777-0365-6(9))* Windmill Bks.

Holt, Rinehart and Winston Staff. Biology: Practice & Experimental Labs. 4th ed. 2003. (Illus.). pap., lab manual ed. 17.20 *(978-0-03-074078-7(9))* Holt McDougal.

—Biology: Quick Data & Math. 4th ed. 2003. (Holt Biology Ser.). (ENG., Illus.). 136p. (gr. 9-9). pap., lab manual ed. 22.45 *(978-0-03-074079-4(7))* Houghton Mifflin Harcourt Publishing Co.

Latham, Donna. Backyard Biology: Investigate Habitats Outside Your Door with 25 Projects. Hetland, Beth, illus. 2013. (Build It Yourself Ser.). (ENG.). 128p. (J). (gr. 3-7). 21.95 *(978-1-61930-152-8(0))*; pap. 15.95 *(978-1-61930-151-1(2))* Open City Bks.

Loeschnig, L. V. Experimentos Sencillos de Geologia y Biologia. 2004. (Juego de la Ciencia Ser.). (SPA.). 128p. (gr. 5-8). *(978-84-95456-60-1(5)*, 87804) Ediciones Oniro S.A.

Marsico, Katie. Life Cycles. 2016. (J). *(978-1-4896-5280-5(9))* Weigl Pubs., Inc.

—Step-by-Step Experiments with Life Cycles. Ostrom, Bob, illus. 2012. (Step-By-Step Experiments Ser.). (ENG.). 32p. (J). (gr. 1-4). lib. bdg. 29.93 *(978-1-60973-587-6(0)*, 201232) Child's World, Inc., The.

Rainis, Kenneth G. Cell & Microbe Science Fair Projects. rev. exp. ed. 2010. (Biology Science Projects Using the Scientific Method Ser.). (Illus.). 160p. (J). (gr. 5-18). 35.94 *(978-0-7660-3420-4(8))* Enslow Pubs., Inc.

VanCleave, Janice. More of Janice VanCleave's Wild, Wacky, & Weird Biology Experiments. 2016. (Janice VanCleave's Wild, Wacky, & Weird Science Experiments Ser.). 00064p. (J). (gr. 5-5). pap. 12.95 *(978-1-4994-6541-9(6)*, Rosen Young Adult) Rosen Publishing Group, Inc., The.

—Step-by-Step Science Experiments in Biology. 2012. (Janice VanCleave's First-Place Science Fair Projects Ser.). (ENG., Illus.). 80p. (J). (gr. 5-8). 33.25 *(978-1-4488-6982-4(X))*; pap. 14.15 *(978-1-4488-8463-6(2))* Rosen Publishing Group, Inc., The. (Rosen Reference).

VanCleave, Janice Pratt. Even More of Janice Vancleave's Wild, Wacky, & Weird Biology Experiments. 2017. (Janice VanCleave's Wild, Wacky, & Weird Science Experiments Ser.). 64p. (J). (gr. 10-10). 77.70 ***(978-1-4994-6679-9(X)***, Rosen Central) Rosen Publishing Group, Inc., The.

—Janice Vancleave's Wild, Wacky, & Weird Biology Experiments. 2016. (Janice VanCleave's Wild, Wacky, & Weird Science Experiments Ser.). 64p. (J). (gr. 5-5). pap. 12.95 *(978-1-4777-8965-0(0)*, Rosen Reference) Rosen Publishing Group, Inc., The.

VanCleave, Janice Pratt. Many More of Janice VanCleave's Wild, Wacky, & Weird Biology Experiments. 2017. (J). ***(978-1-4994-3943-4(1))***; pap. ***(978-1-4994-3944-1(X))*** Rosen Publishing Group, Inc., The.

BIOLOGY—HISTORY

Haugen, Peter. Biology: Decade by Decade. Cannon, William J., ed. 2007. (Twentieth-Century Science Ser.). (Illus.). 352p. (gr. 6-12). 49.50 *(978-0-8160-5530-2(0))* Facts On File, Inc.

Snedden, Robert. The Scientists Behind Living Things, 1 vol. 2011. (Sci-Hi: Scientists Ser.). (ENG.). 48p. (gr. 4-4). pap. 9.95 *(978-1-4109-4054-4(3))*; lib. bdg. 33.32 *(978-1-4109-4047-6(0))* Heinemann-Raintree. (Sci-Hi).

BIOLOGY, MARINE

see Marine Biology

BIOLOGY, MOLECULAR

see Molecular Biology

BIOLOGY—STUDY AND TEACHING

Holt, Rinehart and Winston Staff. Biology. 4th ed. 2004. (Holt Biology Ser.). (ENG., Illus.). 1040p. (gr. 9-12). pap., pupil's gde. ed. 24.30 *(978-0-03-069982-5(7))* Houghton Mifflin Harcourt Publishing Co.

Lew, Kristi. Cool Biology Activities for Girls, 1 vol. 2012. (Girls Science Club Ser.). (ENG.). 32p. (gr. 3-4). pap. 8.19 *(978-1-4296-8019-6(9))*; pap. 47.70 *(978-1-4296-8517-7(4))*; lib. bdg. 27.99 *(978-1-4296-7676-2(0))* Capstone Press of Coughlan Cos. (Snap Bks.).

Melville, Johnathan, et al. Investigating Biology through Inquiry. 2012. spiral bd. 48.00 *(978-1-929075-88-1(X))* Vernier Software & Technology.

Porterfield, Jason. Looking at How Species Compete Within Environments with Graphic Organizers. 2009. (Using Graphic Organizers to Study the Living Environment Ser.). 48p. (gr. 6-6). 53.00 *(978-1-60854-711-1(6)*, Rosen Reference) Rosen Publishing Group, Inc., The.

Roza, Greg. Looking at Differences Between Living & Nonliving Things with Graphic Organizers. 2009. (Using Graphic Organizers to Study the Living Environment Ser.). 48p. (gr. 6-6). 53.00 *(978-1-60854-707-4(8)*, Rosen Reference) Rosen Publishing Group, Inc., The.

—Looking at the Differences Between Living & Nonliving Things with Graphic Organizers. 2005. (Using Graphic Organizers to Study the Living Environment Ser.). (Illus.). 48p. (YA). (gr. 5-9). 29.25 *(978-1-4042-0611-3(6))* Rosen Publishing Group, Inc., The.

Sutton, Pam. Apologia Exploring Creation with Biology 2nd Ed INTERACTIVE Lapbook Journal. Kinney, Cyndi, ed. 2013. (YA). cd-rom 38.99 *(978-1-61625-549-7(8))* Knowledge Box Central.

BIOLOGY—VOCATIONAL GUIDANCE

Levin, Daniel T. & Hammer, David. Becoming a Responsive Science Teacher: Focusing on Student Thinking in Secondary Science. 2012. (ENG.). 270p. (J). pap. *(978-1-936959-05-1(4))* National Science Teachers Assn.

Payment, Simone. Biologists at Work. 2017. (Scientists at Work Ser.). 32p. (J). (gr. 6-8). pap. 12.90 ***(978-1-68048-749-7(3)***, Britannica Educational Publishing) Rosen Publishing Group, Inc., The.

BIOLUMINESCENCE

Collard, Sneed B., III. In the Deep Sea. 2005. (Science Adventures Ser.). (Illus.). 44p. (YA). (gr. 3-6). lib. bdg. 29.93 *(978-0-7614-1952-5(7))* Marshall Cavendish Corp.

Howell, Sara. Fireflies, 1 vol. 2015. (ENG.). 24p. (J). lib. bdg. 23.60 *(978-1-4994-0114-1(0)*, PowerKids Pr.) Rosen Publishing Group, Inc., The.

—Lantern Fish, 1 vol. 2015. (ENG., Illus.). 24p. (J). lib. bdg. 23.60 *(978-1-4994-0147-9(7)*, PowerKids Pr.) Rosen Publishing Group, Inc., The.

Lunis, Natalie. Glow-in-the-Dark Animals. 2011. (Animals with Super Powers Ser.). 24p. (YA). (gr. 2-5). lib. bdg. 22.61 *(978-1-61772-119-9(0))* Bearport Publishing Co., Inc.

Yomtov, Nel. From African Plant to Vaccine Preservation. 2014. (21st Century Skills Innovation Library: Innovations from Nature Ser.). (ENG., Illus.). 32p. (J). (gr. 4-8). 28.50 *(978-1-62431-753-8(7)*, 203280); pap. 14.21 *(978-1-62431-759-0(6)*, 203281) Cherry Lake Publishing.

BIONICS

see also Artificial Intelligence

Azizi, Kamran. Leggo of the String... 2011. (Illus.). 32p. (gr. -1). pap. 19.48 *(978-1-4567-7282-6(1))* AuthorHouse.

Bethea, Nikole Brooks. Discover Bionics. 2016. (Searchlight Books (tm) — What's Cool about Science? Ser.). (ENG., Illus.). 40p. (J). (gr. 3-5). 30.65 *(978-1-5124-0804-1(2))* Lerner Publishing Group.

Cobb, Allan B. The Bionic Human. (Library of Future Medicine Ser.). 64p. 2009. (gr. 5-5). 58.50 *(978-1-60853-631-3(9))* 2005. (Illus.). (YA). (gr. 7-12). lib. bdg. 31.95 *(978-0-8239-3670-0(8))* Rosen Publishing Group, Inc., The.

Jango-Cohen, Judith. Bionics. 2006. (Cool Science Ser.). (ENG., Illus.). 48p. (J). (gr. 4-8). lib. bdg. 27.93 *(978-0-8225-5937-5(4)*, Lerner Pubns.) Lerner Publishing Group.

Kopp, Megan. Bionic Bodies. 2017. (Illus.). 32p. (J). ***(978-0-7787-3584-7(2))*** Crabtree Publishing Co.

Woog, Adam. The Bionic Hand. 2009. (Great Idea Ser.). (Illus.). 48p. (J). (gr. 4-6). lib. bdg. 26.60 *(978-1-59953-341-4(3))* Norwood Hse. Pr.

BIOTECHNOLOGY

see also Genetic Engineering

Bio Related Technology. 4th rev. ed. 2004. 48p. stu. ed., wbk. ed. *(978-0-86657-509-6(X))* Lab-Volt Systems, Inc.

Bio Related Technology TCG. 5th rev. ed. 2004. 75p. pap. *(978-0-86657-508-9(1))* Lab-Volt Systems, Inc.

Burgan, Michael. Genetic Engineering: Science, Technology, & Engineering. 2016. (Calling All Innovators: a Career for You Ser.). (ENG., Illus.). 64p. (J). lib. bdg. 32.00 *(978-0-531-23001-5(5)*, Children's Pr.) Scholastic Library Publishing.

Dowdy, Penny. Animal Cells. 2009. (Let's Relate to Genetics Ser.). (ENG.). 48p. (J). (gr. 5-8). lib. bdg. *(978-0-7787-4947-9(9))*; (gr. 6-9). pap. *(978-0-7787-4964-6(9))* Crabtree Publishing Co.

Freedman, Jeri. Genetically Modified Food: How Biotechnology Is Changing What We Eat. 2009. (Science & Society Ser.). 64p. (gr. 5-6). 58.50 *(978-1-60853-008-3(6))*; (Illus.). (YA). (gr. 7-12). lib. bdg. 31.95 *(978-1-4358-5025-5(4))* Rosen Publishing Group, Inc., The.

Fridell, Ron. Genetic Engineering. 2005. (Cool Science Ser.). (Illus.). 48p. (J). (gr. 3-7). lib. bdg. 26.60 *(978-0-8225-2633-9(6)*, Lerner Pubns.) Lerner Publishing Group.

Hall, Linley Erin. Careers in Biotechnology. (Cutting-Edge Careers Ser.). 64p. 2009. (gr. 7-7). 55.90 *(978-1-61512-099-4(8))* 2007. (Illus.). (J). (gr. 3-7). lib. bdg. 31.95 *(978-1-4042-0954-1(9)*, 1267025) Rosen Publishing Group, Inc., The.

Hopkins, William G. Plant Biotechnology. 2006. (Green World Ser.). (Illus.). 143p. (gr. 6-12). lib. bdg. 37.50 *(978-0-7910-8964-4(9)*, Chelsea Hse.) Facts On File, Inc.

Lachner, Elizabeth. Bioengineering. 2015. (Biotechnology Revolution Ser.). (ENG., Illus.). 128p. (J). (gr. 10-10). 38.75 *(978-1-62275-580-6(4)*, Britannica Educational Publishing) Rosen Publishing Group, Inc., The.

Lerner, K. Lee & Lerner, Brenda Wilmoth. Biotechnology: Changing Life Through Science. 2007. (J). *(978-1-4144-0154-6(X))*; (Illus.). *(978-1-4144-0152-2(3))*; (Illus.). *(978-1-4144-0153-9(1))* Cengage Gale.

McGraw-Hill Staff, creator. Forensics & Biotechnology Lab Manual. 2003. (ENG., Illus.). 46p. (C). (gr. 6-12). pap., stu. ed., lab manual ed. 8.72 *(978-0-07-860224-5(6)*, 0078602246) Glencoe/McGraw-Hill.

Minton, Eric. Powering up a Career in Biotechnology. 2015. (Preparing for Tomorrow's Careers Ser.). (ENG.). 80p. (J). (gr. 7-8). 34.25 *(978-1-4994-6091-9(0)*, Rosen Young Adult) Rosen Publishing Group, Inc., The.

Naff, Clayton Farris. Designer Babies. 2012. (At Issue Ser.). (ENG.). 128p. (gr. 10-12). pap. 27.80 *(978-0-7377-6164-1(4))*; lib. bdg. 39.40 *(978-0-7377-6163-4(6))* Cengage Gale. (Greenhaven Pr., Inc.).

Rice, Earle. Biosecurity: Preventing Biological Warfare. 2016. (Military Engineering in Action Ser.). (Illus.). 48p. (J). (gr. 6-5). pap. 11.70 *(978-0-7660-7541-2(9))* Enslow Pubs., Inc.

Rooney, Anne. Genetic Engineering & Developments in Biotechnology. 2016. (Engineering in Action Ser.). (ENG., Illus.). 32p. (J). (gr. 5-8). *(978-0-7787-7538-6(0))* Crabtree Publishing Co.

Scientific American Staff. Extreme Engineering. 2009. (Scientific American Cutting-Edge Science Ser.). 120p. (gr. 9-9). 63.90 *(978-1-60853-075-5(2))* Rosen Publishing Group, Inc., The.

Seiple, Todd & Seiple, Samantha. Mutants, Clones, & Killer Corn: Unlocking the Secrets of Biotechnology. 2005. (Discovery! Ser.). (ENG., Illus.). 112p. (gr. 6-12). lib. bdg. 31.93 *(978-0-8225-4860-7(7))* Lerner Publishing Group.

Sterngass, Jon. Reproductive Technology. 2011. (Controversy! 3 Ser.). 112p. (J). (gr. 7). 37.07 *(978-1-60870-494-1(7))* Marshall Cavendish GBR. Dist: Marshall Cavendish Corp.

Swanson, Jennifer A. The Wonderful World of Wearable Devices, 1 vol. 2015. (ENG.). 48p. (YA). 30.25 *(978-1-4777-7938-5(8)*, Rosen Reference) Rosen Publishing Group, Inc., The.

Szumski, Bonnie. Careers in Biotechnology. 2013. (Exploring Careers). (ENG., Illus.). 80p. (J). lib. bdg. *(978-1-60152-702-8(0))* ReferencePoint Pr., Inc.

Ternay, Andrew. The Language of Nightmares. 2003. per. 15.95 *(978-0-9619806-4-1(8))* Simpler Life Pr.

BIPLANES

see Airplanes

BIRD HOUSES

see Birdhouses

BIRD-SONG

see Birdsongs

BIRD WATCHING

see Birds

A
B

BIRDHOUSES

Hord, Colleen. How to Build a Bird House. 2015. (ENG.). 24p. (gr. k-3). 28.50 *(978-1-63430-354-5(7))* Rourke Educational Media.

King, Emiliya. Building a Birdhouse: Step by Step. 2017. (Computer Science for the Real World Ser.). 16p. (gr. 7-8). pap. 7.95 ***(978-1-5383-5230-4(3)***, Rosen Classroom) Rosen Publishing Group, Inc., The.

Miller, Mirella S. Build a Birdhouse. Stewart, Roger, illus. 2016. (Earth-Friendly Projects Ser.). (ENG.). 24p. (J). (gr. 2-5). 28.50 *(978-1-5038-0783-9(5)*, 210619) Child's World, Inc., The.

Schwarz, Renee. Birdhouses. Schwarz, Renee, illus. 2005. (Kids Can Do It Ser.). (ENG., Illus.). 40p. (J). (gr. 3-7). 6.95 *(978-1-55337-550-0(5))* Kids Can Pr., Ltd. CAN. Dist: Hachette Bk. Group.

BIRDHOUSES—FICTION

Allen, Kenny. Bird Builds a House. 2006. (Neighborhood Readers Ser.). (ENG.). 8p. (gr. -1-3). pap. 5.15 *(978-1-4042-6690-2(9)*, Rosen Classroom) Rosen Publishing Group, Inc., The.

Allen, Mitchell. Ben's Birdhouse: Step by Step. 2017. (Computer Science for the Real World Ser.). 16p. (gr. 7-8). pap. 7.95 ***(978-1-5383-5206-9(0)***, Rosen Classroom) Rosen Publishing Group, Inc., The.

Bickel, Chris. The Nest Seekers. 2012. 38p. pap. *(978-1-105-60858-2(1))* Lulu.com.

Eastman, P. D. My Nest Is Best. 2005. (Bright & Early Playtime Bks.). (ENG., Illus.). 16p. (J). (gr. k-k). 8.99 *(978-0-375-83267-3(X)*, Random Hse. Bks. for Young Readers) Random Hse. Children's Bks.

Greve, Meg. The Birdhouse That Jack Built. Poole, Helen, illus. 2012. (ENG.). 24p. (J). (gr. k-1). pap. 8.95 *(978-1-61810-300-0(8))* Rourke Educational Media.

Hanning, Jacob. There Is a Bird at My Window. 2012. 24p. pap. 24.95 *(978-1-4626-7607-1(3))* America Star Bks.

Klein, Adria F. Hank Hammer, 1 vol. Rowland, Andrew, illus. 2011. (Tool School Ser.). (ENG.). 32p. (gr. 1-2). pap. 6.25 *(978-1-4342-3385-1(5))*; lib. bdg. 22.65 *(978-1-4342-3043-0(0))* Stone Arch Bks.

Marinaro, Stacy. Mr. Robin's Ridiculous Birdhouse. 2008. 42p. pap. 8.95 *(978-1-4357-5316-7(X))* Lulu Pr., Inc.

Springer, T. S. Tyler Builds a Birdhouse. 2012. 28p. pap. 24.95 *(978-1-4626-9972-8(3))* America Star Bks.

Sturges, Philemon. I Love Tools! Halpern, Shari, illus. 2006. 24p. (J). (gr. -1-1). 14.89 *(978-0-06-009288-7(2))* HarperCollins Pubs.

Yoon, Salina, illus. Pretend & Play: Toolbox. 2013. (Pretend & Play Ser.). (ENG.). 12p. (J). (gr. -1). bds. 12.95 *(978-1-60710-636-4(1)*, Silver Dolphin Bks.) Readerlink Distribution Services, LLC.

BIRDS

see also Birds of Prey; Game and Game Birds; State Birds; Water Birds

About Raptors: A Guide for Children: a Guide for Children, 1 vol. 2014. (About... Ser.). (ENG., Illus.). 48p. (J). (gr. -1-2). 7.95 *(978-1-56145-811-0(2))* Peachtree Pubs.

Ackland, Nick. What Noise Does an Owl Make? Bee, Bella, illus. 2016. (What Noise Does A.... Ser.). (ENG.). 10p. (J). (gr. -1 — 1). bds. 6.99 *(978-0-7641-6845-1(2))* Barron's Educational Series, Inc.

Aigner-Clark, Julie. Aves. 2004. (Baby Einstein Ser.).Tr. of Birds. (SPA., Illus.). 20p. (J). bds. *(978-970-718-154-0(0)*, Silver Dolphin en Español) Advanced Marketing, S. de R. L. de C. V.

Aiken, Zora. Finding Birds in the Chesapeake Marsh: A Child's First Look, 1 vol. Aiken, David, illus. 2009. (ENG.). 30p. (J). 11.95 *(978-0-87033-533-4(2)*, 9780870335334, Cornell Maritime Pr./Tidewater Pubs.) Schiffer Publishing, Ltd.

Alden, Peter C. & Peterson, Roger Tory. Birds. Peterson, Roger Tory, ed. Sill, John, illus. 2nd ed. 2013. (Peterson Field Guide Color-In Bks.). (ENG.). 64p. (J). 8.95 *(978-0-544-02692-6(6))* Houghton Mifflin Harcourt Publishing Co.

Alderfer, Jonathan. National Geographic Kids Bird Guide of North America: The Best Birding Book for Kids from National Geographic's Bird Experts. 2013. (ENG.). 176p. (J). (gr. 2-4). pap. 15.95 *(978-1-4263-1094-2(3))*; lib. bdg. 23.90 *(978-1-4263-1095-9(1))* National Geographic Society. (National Geographic Children's Bks.).

Alderfer, Jonathan & Beer, Julie. Birds. 2016. (ENG., Illus.). 160p. (J). (gr. 3-7). pap. 12.99 *(978-1-4263-2299-0(2)*, National Geographic Children's Bks.) National Geographic Society.

Alexander, Florence & Alexander, Stanley. Come with Me & See... Birds of the World. l.t. ed. 2003. (Illus.). 32p. (J). 7.99 net. *(978-0-915960-95-8(8))* Ebon Research Systems Publishing, LLC.

American Museum of Natural History. ABC Birds. 2016. (AMNH ABC Board Bks.). (ENG., Illus.). 18p. (J). (gr. -1-k). bds. 7.95 *(978-1-4549-1986-5(8))* Sterling Publishing Co., Inc.

Amstutz, Lisa J. Backyard Birds. 2015. (Backyard Birds Ser.). (ENG.). 24p. (gr. k-1). 106.60 *(978-1-4914-6927-9(7)*, Pebble Plus) Capstone Press of Coughlan Cos.

—Cardinals. 2015. (Backyard Birds Ser.). (ENG., Illus.). 24p. (gr. k-1). lib. bdg. 26.65 *(978-1-4914-6107-5(1))* Capstone Press of Coughlan Cos.

—Goldfinches. 2015. (Backyard Birds Ser.). (ENG., Illus.). 24p. (gr. k-1). lib. bdg. 26.65 *(978-1-4914-6108-2(X))* Capstone Press of Coughlan Cos.

—Mourning Doves. 2016. (Backyard Birds Ser.). (ENG., Illus.). 24p. (gr. k-1). lib. bdg. 26.65 *(978-1-4914-8514-9(0)*, Pebble Plus) Capstone Press of Coughlan Cos.

—Robins. 2015. (Backyard Birds Ser.). (ENG., Illus.). 24p. (gr. k-1). lib. bdg. 26.65 *(978-1-4914-6110-5(1))* Capstone Press of Coughlan Cos.

Andrews, Alexa. At the Beach. Keimig, Candice, illus. 2013. (Penguin Young Readers, Level 1 Ser.). (ENG.). 32p. (J). (gr. k-1). 14.99 *(978-0-448-46570-8(1))*; pap. 3.99 *(978-0-448-46471-8(3))* Penguin Young Readers Group. (Penguin Young Readers).

Appleby, Alex. I See a Bird. 2013. (In My Backyard Ser.). (Illus.). 24p. (J). (gr. k-2). pap. 8.15 *(978-1-4339-8540-9(3))*; lib. bdg. 22.60 *(978-1-4339-8539-3(X))* Stevens, Gareth Publishing LLLP.

—I See a Bird: Puedo Ver un Pájaro. 2013. (In My Backyard / en Mi Jardín Ser.). (SPA & ENG., Illus.). 24p. (J). (gr. k-2). lib. bdg. 22.60 *(978-1-4339-8790-8(2))* Stevens, Gareth Publishing LLLP.

Archer, Reese. Birds from Head to Tail. 2016. (Animals from Head to Tail Ser.). 24p. (J). (gr. k-k). lib. bdg. 22.60 *(978-1-4824-4535-0(2))* Stevens, Gareth Publishing LLLP.

Armentrout, David & Armentrout, Patricia. Animals That Fly & Birds That Don't. 2008. (Illus.). 32p. (J). 28.50 *(978-1-60472-300-7(9))* Rourke Educational Media.

Arnim, Aife. A Bird Watcher's Guide to Mourning Doves. 2017. (Backyard Bird Watchers Ser.). 32p. (J). (gr. 2-3). pap. 10.50 ***(978-1-5382-0323-1(5))*** Stevens, Gareth Publishing LLLP.

Arnold, Quinn M. Flamingos. 2017. (J). ***(978-1-60818-867-3(1)***, Creative Education) Creative Co., The.

—Seedlings: Flamingos. 2017. (Seedlings Ser.). (ENG.). 24p. (J). (gr. -1-1). pap. 7.99 ***(978-1-62832-482-2(1)***, Creative Paperbacks) Creative Co., The.

Atkinson, Linda. The Amazing Chickens at Cliff House. Baker, David, illus. 2011. 28p. pap. 24.95 *(978-1-4560-7744-0(9))* America Star Bks.

Automobile Association (Great Britain) Staff. AA the Garden Bird Kit. 2005. (Illus.). n/ap. 25.00 *(978-0-7495-4178-1(4))* Automobile Assn. GBR. Dist: Trafalgar Square Publishing.

AZ Books Staff. Feathered Singers. Tulup, Natalia, ed. 2012. (How We Speak Ser.). (ENG.). 12p. (J). (gr. -1-k). bds. 10.95 *(978-1-61889-096-2(4))* AZ Bks. LLC.

—Sparrow's Yard. Potapenko, Olga, ed. 2012. (Talking Plush Animals Ser.). (ENG.). 10p. (J). (gr. -1-k). bds. 10.95 *(978-1-61889-114-3(6))* AZ Bks. LLC.

Babcock, Charles A. Bird Day How to Prepare for It. 2004. reprint ed. pap. 15.95 *(978-1-4179-1820-1(9))* Kessinger Publishing, LLC.

Backyard Bird Watchers: Set 2. 2017. (Backyard Bird Watchers Ser.). 32p. (gr. 2-3). pap. 63.00 ***(978-1-5382-0223-4(9))***; lib. bdg. 151.50 ***(978-1-5382-0221-0(2))*** Stevens, Gareth Publishing LLLP.

Backyard Birds. 36p. (J). (gr. 1-5). pap. *(978-1-882210-05-3(0))* Action Publishing, Inc.

Barlowe, Dot. The Birdwatcher's Coloring Book. 2012. (Dover Nature Coloring Book Ser.). (ENG.). 32p. (gr. 3-5). pap. 3.99 *(978-0-486-48794-6(6))* Dover Pubns., Inc.

Barnard, Edward S. Birds. 2010. (Amazing Animals Ser.). (ENG.). 48p. (J). (gr. 2-6). pap. 10.50 *(978-1-4339-4008-8(6))*; lib. bdg. 28.00 *(978-1-4339-4007-1(8))* Stevens, Gareth Publishing LLLP. (Gareth Stevens Learning Library).

—Birds. 2007. (J). *(978-1-59939-131-1(7)*, Reader's Digest Young Families, Inc.) Studio Fun International.

Barry, Frances. Little Eggs, Baby Birds. 2010. (J). *(978-0-7636-4260-0(6))* Candlewick Pr.

Bauld, Jane Scoggins & Waldrip, Gayle. Feathered Friends of Texas. 2003. (J). pap. 7.95 *(978-1-57168-771-5(8)*, Eakin Pr.) Eakin Pr.

Beaumont, Holly. Why Do Owls & Other Birds Have Feathers? 2015. (Animal Body Coverings Ser.). (ENG., Illus.). 24p. (gr. 1-3). pap. 6.99 *(978-1-4846-2538-5(2)*, Heinemann Read & Learn) Heinemann-Raintree.

Berendt, John. My Baby Blue Jays. 2011. (ENG.). 32p. (J). (gr. k-3). 16.99 *(978-0-670-01290-9(4)*, Viking Books for Young Readers) Penguin Young Readers Group.

Berger, Melvin & Berger, Gilda. Egg to Robin. 2004. (Illus.). (J). *(978-0-439-57485-3(4))* Scholastic, Inc.

Berrie, Christine, illus. Bird Bingo. 2012. (ENG.). 160p. (gr. 1-17). bds. 29.95 *(978-1-85669-917-4(X))* King, Laurence Publishing GBR. Dist: Hachette Bk. Group.

Beveridge, Dorothy. Birding in Belize with Colours. Beveridge, Jim, photos by. 2013. (Illus.). 32p. pap. *(978-976-8142-55-9(3))* Producciones de la Hamaca.

A Bird Can Fly. (Lexile Levels Ser.). 7.98 *(978-1-56334-685-9(0))* CENGAGE Learning.

The Bird Lady, 6 Pack. (Story Steps Ser.). (gr. k-2). 32.00 *(978-0-7635-9849-5(6))* Rigby Education.

Bird Talk. 2005. (Book Treks Ser.). (J). (gr. 3-18). stu. ed. 34.95 *(978-0-673-62846-6(9))* Celebration Pr.

Bird-Watcher: Level O, 6 vols. (Wonder Worldtm Ser.). 48p. 39.95 *(978-0-7802-2946-4(0))* Wright Group/McGraw-Hill.

Bird Watchers: Level L, 6 vols. 128p. (gr. 2-3). 40.50 *(978-0-7699-1031-4(9))* Shortland Pubns. (U. S. A.) Inc.

Bjorklund, Ruth. Migratory & Resident Birds Explained. 2016. (Distinctions in Nature Ser.). 32p. (J). pap. 10.58 *(978-1-5026-2169-6(X))* Cavendish Square Publishing.

Black, Ted, et al. Birds of Michigan, 1 vol. rev. ed. 2003. (ENG., Illus.). 360p. (gr. 4). pap. 24.95 *(978-1-55105-336-3(5)*, 1551053365) Lone Pine Publishing USA.

Blanchan, Neltje. Birds That Every Child Should Know. 2006. pap. 31.95 *(978-1-4286-2047-6(8))* Kessinger Publishing, LLC.

Bodden, Valerie. Birds. 2009. (My First Look at: Pets Ser.). (J). (gr. 1-5). 24.25 *(978-1-58341-721-8(4)*, Creative Education) Creative Co., The.

Boone, Mary. Sue Bird. 2011. (Robbie Reader Ser.). (Illus.). 32p. (J). (gr. 2-5). lib. bdg. 25.70 *(978-1-61228-062-2(5))* Mitchell Lane Pubs., Inc.

Boothroyd, Jennifer. Endangered & Extinct Birds. 2014. (Lightning Bolt Books Animals in Danger Ser.). (ENG., Illus.). 32p. (gr. k-2). lib. bdg. 26.60 *(978-1-4677-1330-6(9)*, Lerner Pubns.) Lerner Publishing Group.

—Feathers. 2011. (First Step Nonfiction / Body Coverings Ser.). pap. 33.92 *(978-0-7613-8607-0(6))*; (ENG.). 24p. pap. 6.95 *(978-0-7613-7827-3(8))* Lerner Publishing Group.

Borgert-Spaniol, Megan. Flamingos. 2014. (Animal Safari Ser.). (ENG.). 24p. (J). (gr. k-3). lib. bdg. 25.95 *(978-1-60014-966-5(9)*, Blastoff! Readers) Bellwether Media.

Borgert-Spaniol, Megan. Northern Cardinals. 2017. (North American Animals Ser.). (ENG., Illus.). 24p. (J). (gr. k-3). lib. bdg. 25.95 ***(978-1-62617-640-9(X)***, Blastoff! Readers) Bellwether Media.

Bouler, Olivia. Olivia's Birds: Saving the Gulf. 2011. (ENG., Illus.). 32p. (J). (gr. -1-4). 14.95 *(978-1-4027-8665-5(4))* Sterling Publishing Co., Inc.

Bozzo, Linda. Amazing Beaks. 2008. (Creature Features Ser.). (Illus.). 24p. (J). (gr. 3-7). lib. bdg. 22.60 *(978-1-4042-4169-5(8)*, PowerKids Pr.) Rosen Publishing Group, Inc., The.

—Mi Primer Pajarito. 2008. (My First Pet Bilingual Library from the American Humane Association Ser.).Tr. of My First Bird. (ENG & SPA., Illus.). 32p. (J). (gr. 1-3). lib. bdg. 23.94 *(978-0-7660-3034-3(2))* Enslow Pubs., Inc.

—My First Bird. 2007. (My First Pet Library from the American Humane Association Ser.). (Illus.). 32p. (J). (gr. 1-2). lib. bdg. 23.94 *(978-0-7660-2749-7(X)*, Enslow Elementary) Enslow Pubs., Inc.

Bradford, Nell. Little Cheep-Chirp. 2010. 28p. 13.59 *(978-1-4520-9022-1(X))* AuthorHouse.

Bredeson, Carmen. Weird Birds. 2009. (I Like Weird Animals! Ser.). (Illus.). 24p. (J). (gr. 1-3). lib. bdg. 22.60 *(978-0-7660-3124-1(1))* Enslow Pubs., Inc.

Bredeson, Carmen & Cousins, Lindsey. Can You Find These Birds? 2012. (All about Nature Ser.). 24p. (J). (gr. -1-1). (Illus.). pap. 7.95 *(978-1-4644-0072-8(5)*, Enslow Elementary); 22.60 *(978-0-7660-3977-3(3))* Enslow Pubs., Inc.

Bronson, Wilfrid S., illus. Starlings. 2008. 84p. (J). pap. 18.95 *(978-0-86534-649-9(6))* Sunstone Pr.

Brooks, Felicity. Find the Bird. 2008. (Find-its' Board Bks). 12p. (J). bds. 6.99 *(978-0-7945-1806-6(0)*, Usborne) EDC Publishing.

Buckley, Annie. The World's Most Beautiful Birds. 2007. (Reading Rocks! Ser.). (ENG., Illus.). 32p. (J). (gr. 2-5). 28.50 *(978-1-59296-864-0(3)*, 200751) Child's World, Inc., The.

Buckley, Arabella B. Birds of the Air. 2008. (Illus.). 84p. pap. 11.95 *(978-1-59915-274-5(6))* Yesterday's Classics.

Bugler, Matt. My First Encylopedia of Birds: A First Encyclopedia with Supersize Pictures. 2016. (ENG.). 24p. pap. 7.99 *(978-1-86147-821-4(6)*, Armadillo) Anness Publishing GBR. Dist: National Bk. Network.

Burch, Lynda S. I SEE Seaside Birds! Burch, Lynda S. & Roberts, MarySue, photos by. 2004. (Illus.). 52p. (J). E-Book 9.95 incl. cd-rom *(978-1-933090-05-4(7))* Guardian Angel Publishing, Inc.

Burch, Lynda S. & Roberts, MarySue, photos by. I SEE Seaside Birds! 2006. (Illus.). 32p. (J). 16.99 *(978-1-933090-16-0(2))* Guardian Angel Publishing, Inc.

Burgess, Thornton W. The Burgess Bird Book for Children. (J). 24.95 *(978-0-8488-0404-6(X))* Amereon Ltd.

—The Burgess Bird Book for Children. Fuertes, Louis Agassiz, illus. 2008. 168p. (gr. -1-7). pap. 7.99 *(978-1-4209-3052-8(4))* Digireads.com Publishing.

—The Burgess Bird Book for Children. 2007. 216p. (gr. -1-7). per. *(978-1-4065-5326-0(3))* Dodo Pr.

—The Burgess Bird Book for Children. Fuertes, Louis Agassiz, illus. 2003. (Dover Children's Classics Ser.). (ENG.). 272p. (J). (gr. 3-8). pap. 11.95 *(978-0-486-42840-6(0))* Dover Pubns., Inc.

—The Burgess Bird Book for Children. 2004. reprint ed. pap. 1.99 *(978-1-4192-5556-4(6))*; pap. 22.95 *(978-1-4191-5556-7(3))* Kessinger Publishing, LLC.

—The Burgess Bird Book for Children (Yesterday's Classics) Fuertes, Louis Agassiz, illus. 2006. (J). per. 13.95 *(978-1-59915-170-0(7))* Yesterday's Classics.

Burnie, David. Bird. 2008. (DK Eyewitness Bks.). (ENG., Illus.). 72p. (J). (gr. 3-7). 16.99 *(978-0-7566-3768-2(6)*, DK Children) Dorling Kindersley Publishing, Inc.

Cain, Marie Mowery. Flying Colors. 2013. (Big Books, Blue Ser.). (ENG & SPA., Illus.). 16p. pap. 33.00 *(978-1-59246-019-9(4))* Big Books, by George!

—More & Less. 2013. (Big Books, Blue Ser.). (ENG & SPA., Illus.). 16p. pap. 33.00 *(978-1-59246-009-0(7))* Big Books, by George!

Calasso, Roberto & Parks, Tim. Ka, the Story of Garuda: Based on the English Translation by Tim Parks of the Italian Original by Roberto Calasso. Basu, Suddhasattwa, illus. 2004. (J). *(978-81-89020-04-0(8))* Katha.

Calderwood, Damon & Waite, Donald E. More Baby Birds in the Wild, 1 vol. 2016. (Kids' Own Nature Book Ser.). (ENG., Illus.). 48p. (J). (gr. k-1). pap. 6.95 ***(978-1-77203-119-5(4))*** Heritage Hse. CAN. Dist: Orca Bk. Pubs. USA.

Calhoun, Kelly. Poised & Pink: Flamingo. 2015. (Guess What Ser.). (ENG., Illus.). 24p. (J). (gr. k-2). pap. 12.79 *(978-1-63362-715-4(2)*, 206689) Cherry Lake Publishing.

Calmenson, Stephanie. Look! Birds! Pinillos, Puy, illus. 2016. (Look! Ser.). (ENG.). 24p. (J). (gr. -1-1). 7.99 *(978-1-4998-0114-9(9))* Little Bee Books Inc.

Caputo, Christine A. Birds. 2012. (Illus.). 32p. (J). *(978-0-545-46702-5(0))* Scholastic, Inc.

Carney, Elizabeth. Angry Birds Playground - Atlas: A Global Geographic Adventure! 2013. (ENG.). 128p. (J). (gr. -1-3). lib. bdg. 21.90 *(978-1-4263-1401-8(9))*, National Geographic Children's Bks.) National Geographic Society.

Carney, Elizabeth & National Geographic Kids Staff. Atlas: A Global Geographic Adventure. 2013. (ENG., Illus.). 128p. (J). (gr. -1-3). 14.95 *(978-1-4263-1400-1(0)*, National Geographic Children's Bks.) National Geographic Society.

Carper, Virginia. Animal Teachings Volume Two: Birds, 3 vol. 2005. (Illus.). mass mkt. 20.00 *(978-0-9788858-1-6(3))* Animal Teachers Enterprises.

Carr, Aaron. Bird. 2011. (J). 27.13 *(978-1-61690-919-2(6))* Weigl Pubs., Inc.

—El Pájaro. 2012. (SPA.). (J). *(978-1-61913-180-4(3))* Weigl Pubs., Inc.

Carrington, Edith. History of the Robins & Keepers Trave. 2006. 216p. per. *(978-1-4067-0221-7(8)*, Hesperides Pr.) Read Bks.

Cate, Annette LeBlanc. Look Up! Bird-Watching in Your Own Backyard. Cate, Annette LeBlanc, illus. 2013. (ENG., Illus.). 64p. (J). (gr. 3-7). 15.99 *(978-0-7636-4561-8(3))* Candlewick Pr.

Catt, Thessaly. Migrating with the Arctic Tern. 2011. (Animal Journeys Ser.). (Illus.). 24p. (J). (gr. 1-4). lib. bdg. 22.60 *(978-1-4488-2542-4(3))*; (gr. 2-4). pap. 8.25 *(978-1-4488-2668-1(3)*, PowerKids Pr.) Rosen Publishing Group, Inc., The.

Chandler, David. Animal Fact Files Birds, Vol. 3. 2005. (Animals, Animals, Animals Ser.). (YA). (gr. k-3). 118.80 *(978-0-7368-4209-9(8)*, Pebble Bks.) Capstone Press of Coughlan Cos.

Chandler, David & Flegg, Jim. Birds. 2004. (Collins Gem Ser.). (ENG., Illus.). 256p. pap. 9.95 *(978-0-00-717860-5(3))* HarperCollins Pubs. Ltd. GBR. Dist: Independent Pubs. Group.

Choiniere, Joseph & Golding, Claire Mowbray. What's That Bird? Getting to Know the Birds Around You, Coast to Coast. Robins, James, illus. Vezo, Tom, photos by. 2005. (ENG.). 128p. (J). (gr. 3-8). pap. 14.95 *(978-1-58017-554-8(6)*, 67554) Storey Publishing, LLC.

Clark Sawyer, J. Barn Swallows. 2014. (Little Bits: in Winter, Where Do They Go? Ser.). (ENG.). 24p. (J). (gr. -1-3). lib. bdg. 23.93 *(978-1-62724-314-8(3))* Bearport Publishing Co., Inc.

—Las Golondrinas Comunes. 2014. (¿a dónde Van en Invierno? Ser.). (SPA.). 24p. (J). (gr. -1-3). lib. bdg. 23.93 *(978-1-62724-456-5(5))* Bearport Publishing Co., Inc.

Cleary, Brian P. Sparrow, Eagle, Penguin, & Seagull: What Is a Bird? Goneau, Martin, illus. 2012. (Animal Groups Are CATegorical (tm) Ser.). (ENG.). 32p. (gr. k-3). (J). lib. bdg. 26.60 *(978-0-7613-6207-4(X))*; pap. 7.95 *(978-1-4677-0340-6(0))* Lerner Publishing Group. (Millbrook Pr.).

Cohen, Jessie, photos by. Flamingo Grows Up. 2005. (Let's Go to the Zoo! Ser.). (ENG., Illus.). 16p. (J). (gr. -1-k). 5.95 *(978-1-56899-974-6(7)*, B9009) Soundprints.

Coleman, Miriam. Skua Seabirds Eat Vomit!, 1 vol., 1. 2014. (Disgusting Animal Dinners Ser.). (ENG.). 24p. (J). (gr. k-5). 23.60 *(978-1-4777-2882-6(1)*, PowerKids Pr.) Rosen Publishing Group, Inc., The.

Collard, Sneed B., III. Fire Birds. 2015. (Illus.). 48p. (J). *(978-0-9844460-7-0(9))* Bucking Horse Bks.

Collinson, Clare. British Birds. 2017. (Nature in Your Neighbourhood Ser.). (ENG., Illus.). 32p. (J). (gr. 2-4). 17.99 *(978-1-4451-3635-6(X)*, Franklin Watts) Hachette Children's Group GBR. Dist: Hachette Bk. Group.

¿Como Vuela un Pajaro? (Coleccion Primeros Pasos en la Ciencia). (SPA., Illus.). (J). (gr. 1-3). pap. *(978-950-724-219-9(8)*, LMA8223) Lumen ARG. Dist: Lectorum Pubns., Inc.

Cooper, Ross Gordon. African Birds, 1 vol. 2010. 18p. pap. 24.95 *(978-1-60749-183-5(4))* PublishAmerica, Inc.

Cooper, Sharon Katz. A Is for Albatross: ABCs of Endangered Birds. 2016. (E for Endangered Ser.). (ENG., Illus.). 32p. (gr. 1-2). lib. bdg. 27.32 *(978-1-4914-8032-8(7)*, Aplus Bks.) Capstone Press of Coughlan Cos.

Corcorane, Ann. Animals Everywhere, 1 vol. 2011. (Wonder Readers Emergent Level Ser.). (ENG.). 32p. (gr. -1-1). pap. 5.99 *(978-1-4296-7861-2(5)*, Wonder Readers) Capstone Press of Coughlan Cos.

—A Zoo Full of Birds. 2011. (Wonder Readers Emergent Level Ser.). (ENG.). (gr. -1-1). 16p. pap. 35.94 *(978-1-4296-8063-9(6))*; 32p. pap. 5.99 *(978-1-4296-7857-5(7))* Capstone Press of Coughlan Cos. (Wonder Readers).

Corley, Nikolett. Zendoodle Coloring: Birds & Butterflies: Delicate Beauties to Color & Display. 2017. (ENG., Illus.). 128p. pap. 13.99 *(978-1-250-12823-2(4)*, 9781250128232, St. Martin's Griffin) St. Martin's Pr.

Cosneau, Olivia. Birds of the World: My Nature Sticker Activity Book. 2017. (ENG.). 24p. (J). (gr. k-3). pap. 7.99 *(978-1-61689-566-2(7))* Princeton Architectural Pr.

Coues, Elliott. Citizen Bird Scenes from Bird-Life in Plain English for Beginners. 2010. 196p. pap. 19.99 *(978-1-153-59594-0(X))* General Bks. LLC.

Coues, Elliott & Wright, Mabel Osgood. Citizen Bird: Scenes from Bird-Life in Plain English for Beginners. 2010. 458p. pap. 36.75 *(978-1-146-26596-6(4))* 2010. 456p. pap. 36.75 *(978-1-143-11658-2(5))* 2009. (ENG.). 445p. 41.99 *(978-1-117-67007-2(4))* 2009. (ENG.). 445p. pap. 35.75 *(978-1-117-67008-9(2))* 2009. 442p. 41.99 *(978-1-113-65651-3(4))* 2009. 442p. 34.99 *(978-1-113-65648-3(4))* 2009. 442p. pap. 35.75 *(978-1-113-65645-2(X))* 2009. 442p. pap. 36.75 *(978-1-113-65647-6(6))* Creative Media Partners, LLC.

—Citizen Bird: Scenes from Bird-Life in Plain English for Beginners. 2009. (ENG.). 445p. pap. 26.99 *(978-1-117-67009-6(0)*, BiblioLife) Creative Media Partners, LLC.

Crick, Sharon. Maggie. 2014. 48p. pap. 11.39 *(978-1-4828-9456-1(4))* Partridge Pub.

Cruce, Lana. Caring for Your Pet Bird. 2005. (ENG., Illus.). 20p. (J). (gr. 3-3). pap. 5.97 net. *(978-0-328-13401-4(5)*, Scott Foresman) Pearson Schl.

Cullis, Megan. Birds to Color. Cooper, Jenny, illus. 2012. (Coloring Bks). 32p. (J). pap. 5.99 *(978-0-7945-3285-7(3)*, Usborne) EDC Publishing.

Cummins, Judi, creator. Flying Free Again. 2005. (Illus.). 34p. (J). per. *(978-0-9760377-2-9(6))* Cummins, Judi.

Danielson, Ethan. Inside Bird Nests. 2015. (Inside Animal Homes Ser.). (ENG., Illus.). 24p. (J). (gr. 2-3). pap. 8.25 *(978-1-4994-0874-4(9)*, PowerKids Pr.) Rosen Publishing Group, Inc., The.

Davies, Nicola. Discover Science: Birds. 2017. (Discover Science Ser.). (ENG.). 56p. pap. 7.99 *(978-0-7534-7332-0(1)*, 9780753473320, Kingfisher) Roaring Brook Pr.

Dawson, Emily C. Birds & Trees. 2010. (Our Animal World Ser.). 24p. (J). 25.65 *(978-1-60753-010-7(4))* Amicus Publishing.

De La Bedoyere C. Why Why Why Cant Penguins Fly. 2008. 32p. pap. *(978-1-84810-000-8(0))* Miles Kelly Publishing, Ltd.

De la Bédoyère, Camilla. Why Why Why... Can't Penguins Fly? 2010. (Why Why Why Ser.). 32p. (J). (gr. 1-3). lib. bdg. 18.95 *(978-1-4222-1573-9(3))* Mason Crest.

Dell, Pamela. Birds. 2017. (My First Animal Kingdom Encyclopedias Ser.). (ENG., Illus.). 32p. (gr. 1-2). lib. bdg. 27.32 *(978-1-5157-3927-2(9)*, Aplus Bks.) Capstone Press of Coughlan Cos.

Deneux, Xavier. TouchThinkLearn: Fly! 2017. (ENG., Illus.). 14p. (J). bds. 17.99 *(978-1-4521-5922-5(X))* Chronicle Bks. LLC.

DePrisco, Dorothea. Bluebird's Nest. Parry, Jo, illus. 2006. (ENG.). 16p. (J). 9.95 *(978-1-58117-390-1(3)*, Intervisual/Piggy Toes) Bendon, Inc.

Dittrich, Tina & Morrison, Kathryn. Stellaluna: An Study of Birds & Bats. 2005. pap. 10.95 *(978-1-931334-85-3(4))* Pieces of Learning.

Doherty, Gillian. Aves. 2004.Tr. of Birds. (SPA., Illus.). 64p. (J). pap. 8.95 *(978-0-7460-4514-5(X))*; lib. bdg. 16.95 *(978-1-58086-347-6(7))* EDC Publishing.

—Birds. 2004. (Discovery Program Ser.). (SPA & ENG., Illus.). (J). (gr. 2-18). 1p. pap. 8.95 *(978-0-7460-3738-6(4))*; 64p. lib. bdg. 16.95 *(978-1-58086-334-6(5))* EDC Publishing.

—Birds: Internet -Linked. 2009. (Discovery Nature Ser Ser.). 64p. (YA). (gr. 3-18). 8.99 (978-0-7945-2244-5(0), Usborne) EDC Publishing.
Dorling Kindersley Publishing Staff. Birds. 2017. (ENG., Illus.). 64p. (J). (gr. 1-3). 9.99 (978-1-4654-5757-8(7), DK Children) Dorling Kindersley Publishing, Inc.
—Everything You Need to Know about Birds. 2016. (Everything You Need to Know Ser.). (ENG., Illus.). 80p. (J). (gr. 2-5). 15.99 (978-1-4654-4388-5(6), DK Children) Dorling Kindersley Publishing, Inc.
—Eyewitness Explorer: Bird Watcher. 2015. (ENG., Illus.). 72p. (J). (gr. 3-7). pap. 9.99 (978-1-4654-3502-6(6), DK Children) Dorling Kindersley Publishing, Inc.
Dubois, Philippe J. Birds of the World: 365 Days. 2011. (365 Ser.). (ENG., Illus.). 744p. 29.95 (978-0-8109-9613-7(8)) Abrams, Inc.
Dunn, Mary R. Ospreys. 2015. (Birds of Prey Ser.). (ENG.). 24p. (gr. k-1). pap. 6.95 (978-1-4914-2309-7(9), Pebble Plus) Capstone Press of Coughlan Cos.
Dunning, Joan. Seabird in the Forest: The Mystery of the Marbled Murrelet. Dunning, Joan, illus. 2011. (ENG., Illus.). 32p. (J). (gr. k-4). 17.95 (978-1-59078-715-1(3)) Boyds Mills Pr.
Durand, Stephane & Poyet, Guillaume. Winged Migration: The Junior Edition. Wharry, David, tr. 2006. (Illus.). 46p. (J). (gr. k-4). reprint ed. 20.00 (978-0-7567-9996-0(1)) DIANE Publishing Co.
Eco-Force: Series One: Birds of North America. 2005. (J). 11.99 (978-1-933232-00-3(5)) Terra Denuo, Inc.
Elliott, David. On the Wing. Stadtlander, Becca, illus. 2014. (ENG.). 32p. (J). (gr. -1-2). 16.99 (978-0-7636-5324-8(1)) Candlewick Pr.
Elora, Grace. A Bird Watcher's Guide to Orioles. 2017. (Backyard Bird Watchers Ser.). 32p. (J). (gr. 2-3). pap. 10.50 **(978-1-5382-0327-9(8))** Stevens, Gareth Publishing LLLP.
—A Bird Watcher's Guide to Wrens. 2017. (Backyard Bird Watchers Ser.). 32p. (J). (gr. 2-3). pap. 10.50 **(978-1-5382-0349-1(9))** Stevens, Gareth Publishing LLLP.
Encyclopaedia Britannica, Inc. Staff, compiled by. Britannica Illustrated Science Library: Birds, 16 vols. 2008. (Illus.). (J). 29.95 (978-1-59339-385-4(7)) Encyclopaedia Britannica, Inc.
—My First Britannica: Birds, Insects, Reptiles, & Aquatic Life. 2008. (gr. 7-12). (978-1-59339-411-0(X)) Encyclopaedia Britannica, Inc.
Encyclopedia Britannica Staff, creator. Birds. 2011. (Britannica Illustrated Science Library Ser.). 104p. (J). 37.44 (978-1-61535-465-8(4)) Encyclopaedia Britannica, Inc.
Endangered Birds: Level P, 6 vols. (Wonder Worldtm Ser.). 48p. 39.95 (978-0-7802-7077-0(0)) Wright Group/McGraw-Hill.
Ervin, C. H. Hummingbird,Hummingbird. 2012. 20p. pap. 13.77 (978-1-4669-5912-5(6)) Trafford Publishing.
Esbaum, Jill & National Geographic Kids Staff. Angry Birds Playground: Animals: An Around-The-World Habitat Adventure. 2016. (ENG.). 128p. (J). (gr. -1-3). pap. 9.99 (978-1-4263-2457-4(X), National Geographic Children's Bks.) National Geographic Society.
Esten, Sidney R. Bird Stamps of All Countries, with a Natural History of Each Bird. Cox, William Drought, ed. 2011. 62p. 36.95 (978-1-258-07239-1(4)) Literary Licensing, LLC.
Evans, Marilyn Grohoske. Spit & Sticks: A Chimney Swift Story. Gsell, Nicole, illus. 2015. (ENG.). 32p. (J). (gr. -1-2). lib. bdg. 16.95 (978-1-58089-588-0(3)) Charlesbridge Publishing, Inc.
Feathered Friends. (My Animal Library). (Illus.). 10p. (J). (978-2-7643-0153-1(7)) Phidal Publishing, Inc./Editions Phidal, Inc.
Feathers: Level M, 6 vols. 128p. (gr. 2-3). 41.95 (978-0-7699-1021-5(1)) Shortland Pubns. (U. S. A.) Inc.
Feathers & Flight: 6 Each of 1 Student Book, 6 vols. (Sunshinetm Science Ser.). 24p. (gr. 1-2). 41.95 (978-0-7802-1395-1(5)) Wright Group/McGraw-Hill.
Feathers & Flight: Big Book. (Sunshinetm Science Ser.). 24p. (gr. 1-2). 37.50 (978-0-7802-1396-8(3)) Wright Group/McGraw-Hill.
Feathers & Flight: Level O, 6 vols. (Explorers Ser.). 32p. (gr. 3-6). 44.95 (978-0-7699-0597-6(8)) Shortland Pubns. (U. S. A.) Inc.
Fletcher, Patricia. Why Are Ostriches So Big? And Other Curious Bird Adaptations. 2017. (Odd Adaptations Ser.). 32p. (J). (gr. 3-4). pap. 63.00 **(978-1-5382-0367-5(7))** Stevens, Gareth Publishing LLLP.
Formato, Vicki. Jayson: The True Story of a 20 Year Old Blue Jay. 2004. (Illus.). 264p. 24.95 (978-0-9760072-0-3(7)) CEM Ventures, Ltd.
Fretland VanVoorst, Jenny. Birds in Spring. 2015. (Illus.). 24p. (J). lib. bdg. (978-1-62031-235-3(2)) Jump! Inc.
Friskey, Margaret. The True Book of Birds We Know. Pistorius, Anna, illus. 2011. 48p. pap. 35.95 (978-1-258-09819-3(9)) Literary Licensing, LLC.
Furstinger, Nancy. 12 Birds Back From the Brink. 2015. (ENG., Illus.). 32p. (J). pap. 9.95 (978-1-63235-061-9(0)) RiverStream Publishing.
—12 Birds Back from the Brink. 2014. (ENG., Illus.). 32p. (J). (978-1-63235-001-5(7)) Pr. Room Editions LLC.
Gaines, Alison. Invasive Plants & Birds. 2016. (Invasive Species Ser.). (Illus.). 48p. (J). (gr. 4-4). 31.36 (978-1-5026-1834-4(6)) Cavendish Square Publishing.
Galvin, Laura Gates. If I Were a Bird. 2014. (Illus.). (J). (978-1-58865-787-9(6)) Kidsbooks, LLC.
Gardeski, Christina Mia. Pet Birds: Questions & Answers. 2016. (Pet Questions & Answers Ser.). (ENG., Illus.). 24p. (gr. k-1). lib. bdg. 26.65 (978-1-5157-0354-9(1), Pebble Plus) Capstone Press of Coughlan Cos.
George, Jean Craighead. Winter Moon. 2003. (J). (gr. 3-7). 20.75 (978-0-8446-7244-1(0)) Smith, Peter Pub., Inc.
Gibbs, Edward. I Spy in the Sky. Gibbs, Edward, illus. 2014. (ENG., Illus.). 32p. (J). (-k). 14.99 (978-0-7636-6840-2(0), Templar) Candlewick Pr.
Gibbs, Maddie. Flamingos. 2011. (Safari Animals Ser.). (Illus.). 24p. (J). 22.60 (978-1-4488-3184-5(9)); pap. 8.25 (978-1-4488-3185-2(7)) Rosen Publishing Group, Inc., The. (PowerKids Pr.).
—Flamingos: Flamencos. 2011. (Safari Animals / Animales de Safari Ser.). (SPA & ENG., Illus.). 24p. (J). (gr. -1-2). lib. bdg. 22.60 (978-1-4488-3213-2(6)) Rosen Publishing Group, Inc., The.
Gilbert, Sara. Ice Age Mega Beasts: Monster Birds (Teratorns) 2017. (Ice Age Mega Beasts Ser.). (ENG.). 24p. (J). (gr. 1-3). pap. 8.99 **(978-1-62832-376-4(0)**, Creative Paperbacks) Creative Co., The.
Gilbert, Sara. Monster Birds. 2017. (J). (978-1-60818-768-3(3), Creative Education) Creative Co., The.
Gingold, Janet. My Adventure as a Birder: Advanced My Adventure. 2007. 44p. (J). pap. 8.99 (978-1-59092-406-8(1)) Blue Forge Pr.
Gire, Anna Marie Petrarca. Sal: A Tale of Many Feathers. 2013. 100p. pap. 9.00 (978-1-937958-18-3(3)) Red Engine Pr.
Gish, Melissa. Falcons. 2015. (Illus.). 46p. (J). (978-1-60818-566-5(4), Creative Education) Creative Co., The.
—Flamingos. 2014. 46p. (978-1-60818-416-3(1), Creative Education) Creative Co., The.
—Living Wild: Flamingos. 2015. (Living Wild Ser.). (ENG.). 48p. (J). (gr. 5-8). pap. 12.00 (978-1-62832-002-2(8), Creative Paperbacks) Creative Co., The.
Godkin, Celia. Skydiver: Saving the Fastest Bird in the World. Godkin, Celia, illus. 2015. (ENG., Illus.). 32p. (J). (gr. 1-3). pap. 8.95 (978-1-927485-89-7(4)) Pajama Pr. CAN. Dist: Ingram Publisher Services.
Goldsworthy, Steve. Birds. 2016. (J). (978-1-5105-1110-1(5)) SmartBook Media, Inc.
Goodbody, Slim & Burstein, John. Birds. McGinnis, Ben, illus. 2008. (Slim Goodbody's Inside Guide to Pets Ser.). 32p. (gr. 2-6). lib. bdg. 26.00 (978-0-8368-8953-6(3), Gareth Stevens Learning Library) Stevens, Gareth Publishing LLLP.
Grack, David. Birds of the Northwoods. 2007. (Color & Learn Ser.). (ENG., Illus.). 64p. (J). (gr. 3-4). per., act. bk. ed. 7.95 (978-1-59193-166-9(5)) Adventure Pubns.
Graubart, Norman D. Mi Pjaro / My Bird. Green, Christina, tr. from ENG. 2014. (¡Las Mascotas Son Geniales! / Pets Are Awesome! Ser.). (SPA & BYN.). 24p. (J). (gr. k-2). 23.60 (978-1-4777-3310-3(8), PowerKids Pr.) Rosen Publishing Group, Inc., The.
—My Bird, 1 vol., 1. 2014. (Pets Are Awesome! Ser.). (ENG.). 24p. (J). (gr. k-2). 23.60 (978-1-4777-2867-3(8), PowerKids Pr.) Rosen Publishing Group, Inc., The.
Gray, Susan H. Hornbill. 2015. (21st Century Skills Library: Exploring Our Rainforests Ser.). (ENG., Illus.). 32p. (J). (gr. 3-6). 29.93 (978-1-63188-975-2(3), 205812) Cherry Lake Publishing.
—The Life Cycle of Birds, 1 vol. 2011. (Life Cycles Ser.). (ENG.). 48p. (gr. 3-5). pap. 9.95 (978-1-4329-4986-0(1)); 33.32 (978-1-4329-4979-2(9)) Heinemann-Raintree. (Heinemann InfoSearch).
Gray, Susan H. & Somervill, Barbara A. Bald Eagle. 2009. (21st Century Skills Library: Road to Recovery Ser.). (ENG.). 32p. (gr. 4-8). lib. bdg. 28.50 (978-1-60279-317-0(4), 200213) Cherry Lake Publishing.
—California Condor. 2009. (21st Century Skills Library: Road to Recovery Ser.). (ENG.). 32p. (gr. 4-8). lib. bdg. 28.50 (978-1-60279-318-7(2), 200214) Cherry Lake Publishing.
Green Android, creator. Birds: Pocket Books. 2016. (Illus.). 128p. (J). pap. 4.99 (978-1-61067-385-3(9)) Kane Miller.
Green, Jen. Find Out about Birds: With 16 Projects & More Than 250 Pictures. 2013. (ENG., Illus.). 64p. 9.99 (978-1-84322-967-4(6)) Anness Publishing GBR. Dist: National Bk. Network.
Grogan, Patrick, illus. Birding for Children. 2007. 44p. (J). 19.95 (978-0-615-15948-5(6)) Minton, Art.
Grzimek, Bernhard & McDade, Melissa C. Birds, 5.0, Vol. 5. 2004. (Grzimek's Student Animal Life Resource Ser.). (ENG., Illus.). 1000p. (J). 458.00 (978-0-7876-9235-3(2), UXL) Cengage Gale.
—Grzimek's Student Animal Life Resource, 5 vols. 2004. (Illus.). (J). (978-0-7876-9237-7(9)); (978-0-7876-9236-0(0)); (978-0-7876-9240-7(9)); (978-0-7876-9239-1(5)); (978-0-7876-9238-4(7)) Cengage Gale. (UXL).
Guiberson, Brenda Z. Feathered Dinosaurs. Low, William & Cobalt Illustrations Studio Staff, illus. 2016. (ENG.). 40p. (J). 17.99 (978-0-8050-9828-0(3), 9780805098280, Holt, Henry & Co. Bks. For Young Readers) Holt, Henry & Co.
Guidone, Julie. Toucans & Other Birds. 2009. (Animals That Live in the Rain Forest Ser.). 24p. (gr. -1-3). (J). lib. bdg. 22.60 (978-1-4339-0028-0(9)); pap. 8.15 (978-1-4339-0110-2(2)) Stevens, Gareth Publishing LLLP. (Weekly Reader Leveled Readers).
—Toucans & Other Birds; Tucanes y otras Aves. 2009. (Animals That Live in the Rain Forest/Animales de la selva Ser.). (SPA & ENG.). 24p. (J). (gr. -1-3). pap. 8.15 (978-1-4339-0117-1(X)); lib. bdg. 22.60 (978-1-4339-0067-9(X)) Stevens, Gareth Publishing LLLP. (Weekly Reader Leveled Readers).
Haig-Brown, Roderick. Alison's Fishing Birds. McDougald, Sheryl, illus. 2017. (ENG.). 48p. 21.95 **(978-1-987915-19-8(4))** Caitlin Pr., Inc. CAN. Dist: Midpoint Trade Bks., Inc.
Hall, Kirsten. Great Bustard: The World's Heaviest Flying Bird. 2007. (SuperSized! Ser.). (Illus.). 24p. (J). (gr. k-3). lib. bdg. 21.28 (978-1-59716-390-3(2), 1265935) Bearport Publishing Co., Inc.
Hamilton, Lynn. Bird. 2008. (My Pet Ser.). (Illus.). 32p. (J). (gr. 3-5). pap. 9.95 (978-1-59036-901-2(7)); lib. bdg. 26.00 (978-1-59036-900-5(9)) Weigl Pubs., Inc.
—Caring for Your Bird. 2003. (Caring for Your Pet Ser.). (Illus.). 32p. (J). (gr. -1-3). lib. bdg. 26.00 (978-1-59036-037-8(0)) Weigl Pubs., Inc.
Hamilton, Lynn A. Caring for Your Bird. Marshall, Diana & Nault, Jennifer, eds. 2003. (Caring for Your Pet Ser.). (Illus.). 32p. (J). pap. 9.95 (978-1-59036-067-5(2)) Weigl Pubs., Inc.
Haney, Johannah. Small Birds. 2009. (Great Pets 3 Ser.). 48p. (gr. 3). 29.93 (978-0-7614-4150-2(6)) Marshall Cavendish Corp.
Harasymiw, Mark. A Bird Watcher's Guide to Chickadees. 2016. (Backyard Bird Watchers Ser.). (ENG., Illus.). 32p. (J). (gr. 2-3). pap. 10.50 (978-1-4824-3879-6(8)) Stevens, Gareth Publishing LLLP.
Harkins, Susan Sales & Harkins, William H. Threat to the Whooping Crane. 2008. (On the Verge of Extinction Ser.). (Illus.). 32p. (J). (gr. 2-5). lib. bdg. 25.70 (978-1-58415-685-7(6)) Mitchell Lane Pubs., Inc.
Harper, Charley, illus. Charley Harper's Sticky Birds: An Animal Sticker Kit. 2013. (ENG.). (J). 19.95 (978-0-7649-6467-1(4)) Pomegranate Communications, Inc.
Harris, Tim, ed. Birds. 2011. (FAYFT: Endangered Animals Ser.). 64p. (gr. 4-10). lib. bdg. 39.95 (978-1-936333-31-8(7)) Brown Bear Bks.
Harrison, George H. Bird Watching for Kids. 2015. (ENG., Illus.). 72p. (J). 14.95 (978-1-62343-850-0(0)) Willow Creek Pr., Inc.
Hayes, Amy. An Egg Becomes a Robin. 2016. (Transformations in Nature Ser.). (ENG., Illus.). 24p. (J). (gr. 1-1). pap. 8.22 (978-1-5026-0810-9(3)) Cavendish Square Publishing.
Hengel, Katherine. Cool Birds & Bugs: Great Things to Do in the Great Outdoors, 1 vol. 2016. (ENG., Illus.). 32p. (J). (978-1-62403-694-1(5)) ABDO Publishing Co.
Henkes, Kevin. Birds Board Book. Dronzek, Laura, illus. 2017. 32p. (J). (gr. -1 — 1). bds. 7.99 (978-0-06-257305-6(5), Greenwillow Bks.) HarperCollins Pubs.
Heos, Bridget & Powell, Marie. Do You Really Want a Bird? Longhi, Katya, illus. 2013. (Do You Really Want a Pet? Ser.). (ENG.). 24p. (gr. 1-4). 27.10 (978-1-60753-205-7(0)) Amicus Publishing.
Herkert, Barbara, illus. Birds in Your Backyard. 2004. (Sharing Nature with Children Book Ser.). 36p. (J). pap. 8.95 (978-1-58469-025-2(9)); 17.95 (978-1-58469-026-9(7)) Dawn Pubns.
Hewett, Joan. A Flamingo Chick Grows Up. Hewett, Richard, photos by. (Baby Animals Ser.). (Illus.). 32p. 2005. (gr. k-3). lib. bdg. 21.27 (978-1-57505-164-2(8)) 2003. (J). (gr. -1-2). pap. 6.95 (978-0-8225-0090-2(6), Lerner Pubns.) Lerner Publishing Group.
Himmelman, John. Noisy Bird Sing-Along, 1 vol. Himmelman, John, illus. 2015. (ENG., Illus.). 32p. (J). (gr. -1-4). pap. 8.95 (978-1-58469-514-1(5)) Dawn Pubns.
Hirsch, Rebecca E. Birds vs. Blades? Offshore Wind Power & the Race to Protect Seabirds. 2016. (ENG., Illus.). 48p. (gr. 4-6). 33.32 (978-1-4677-9520-3(8)); 50.65 (978-1-5124-1111-9(6)) Lerner Publishing Group. (Millbrook Pr.).
Holden, Pam. Learn about Birds. 2015. (ENG., Illus.). 16p. (-1). pap. (978-1-77654-080-8(8), Red Rocket Readers) Flying Start Bks.
Holt, Jane E. In Madera Canyon. 2009. pap. 15.95 (978-1-60494-002-2(6)) Wheatmark, Inc.
Holt, Rinehart and Winston Staff. Holt Science & Technology Chapter 17: Life Science: Birds & Mammals. 5th ed. 2004. (Illus.). pap. 12.86 (978-0-03-030226-8(9)) Holt McDougal.
Holub, Joan. Why Do Birds Sing? DiVito, Anna, illus. 2004. (Penguin Young Readers, Level 3 Ser.). (ENG.). 48p. (J). (gr. 1-3). mass mkt. 3.99 (978-0-14-240106-4(4), Penguin Young Readers) Penguin Young Readers Group.
—Why Do Birds Sing? DiVito, Anna, illus. 2004. (Easy-to-Read Ser.). 47p. 14.00 (978-0-7569-3114-8(2)) Perfection Learning Corp.
Honders, Christine. Bloodsucking Birds. 2016. (Real-Life Vampires Ser.). (ENG., Illus.). 24p. (J). (gr. 2-3). pap. 8.15 (978-1-4824-3939-7(5)) Stevens, Gareth Publishing LLLP.
Honey, Elizabeth. Ten Blue Wrens & What a Lot of Wattle! An Absolutely Australian Counting Book. Honey, Elizabeth, illus. (ENG., Illus.). 32p. (J). (gr. -1-3). 2016. pap. 10.99 (978-1-76029-051-1(3)) 2012. 19.99 (978-1-74237-787-2(4)) Allen & Unwin AUS. Dist: Independent Pubs. Group.
Hoose, Phillip. Moonbird: A Year on the Wind with the Great Survivor B95, 1 vol. 2012. (ENG., Illus.). 160p. (J). (gr. 4-8). 21.99 (978-0-374-30468-3(8), 9780374304683, Farrar, Straus & Giroux (BYR)) Farrar, Straus & Giroux.
Houle, Donna Lee. The Eastern Bluebird: A Guide for Young Birdwatchers. Chambliss, Matthew et al, photos by. 2011. (Illus.). 60p. (J). pap. 7.95 (978-0-9846397-1-7(3), PitziGil Pr.) PitziGil Pubns.
How Birds Live: Big Book. (Sunshinetm Science Ser.). 24p. (gr. 1-2). 37.50 (978-0-7802-1399-9(8)) Wright Group/McGraw-Hill.
Howell, Catherine. My First Pocket Guide to Backyard Wilderness. Emmett, Jennifer, ed. 2003. (National Geographic My First Pocket Guides). (ENG.). 80p. (J). (gr. 1-4). pap. 5.95 (978-0-7922-6927-4(6), National Geographic Children's Bks.) National Geographic Society.
Hudak, Heather C. Birds. 2005. (Animal Facts Ser.). (Illus.). 24p. (J). (gr. 2-3). per. 8.95 (978-1-59036-242-6(X)); (gr. 4-7). lib. bdg. 24.45 (978-1-59036-203-7(9)) Weigl Pubs., Inc.
Hughes, Catherine D. Little Kids First Big Book Collector's Set: Birds & Bugs. 2017. (ENG., Illus.). 288p. (J). (gr. -1-3). 25.00 **(978-1-4263-2948-7(2)**, National Geographic Children's Bks.) National Geographic Society.
—Little Kids First Big Book of Birds. 2016. (National Geographic Little Kids First Big Bks.). (ENG., Illus.). 128p. (J). (gr. -1-3). lib. bdg. 24.90 (978-1-4263-2433-8(2), National Geographic Children's Bks.) National Geographic Society.
—National Geographic Little Kids First Big Book of Birds. 2016. (National Geographic Little Kids First Big Bks.). (ENG., Illus.). 128p. (J). (gr. -1-3). 14.99 (978-1-4263-2432-1(4), National Geographic Children's Bks.) National Geographic Society.
Hughes, Mónica. Flying Giants. 2007. (I Love Reading Ser.). (Illus.). 24p. (J). (gr. -1-2). lib. bdg. 19.96 (978-1-59716-541-9(7)) Bearport Publishing Co., Inc.
Hunt, Jilly. A Rookery of Penguins: And Other Bird Groups, 1 vol. 2012. (Animals in Groups Ser.). (ENG.). 48p. (gr. 4-6). pap. 9.95 (978-1-4329-6491-7(7)); lib. bdg. 33.32 (978-1-4329-6484-9(4)) Heinemann-Raintree. (Heinemann InfoSearch).
Hutchcraft, Steve. B Is for Bufflehead: Flying Through the ABC's with Fun Feathered Friends. Hutchcraft, Steve, photos by. 2009. (Illus.). 80p. (J). (gr. -1-4). 19.95 (978-0-9824925-0-5(2)) PhotoHutch.
Hyman, Jeremy. Bird Brains: The Wild & Wacky World of Birds. Levesque, Haude, illus. 2017. (ENG.). 80p. (J). (gr. 3-7). 14.95 (978-1-63322-153-6(9), Moondance) Quarto Publishing Group USA.
Imbriaco, Alison. The California Condor: Help Save This Endangered Species! 2007. (Saving Endangered Species Ser.). (Illus.). 128p. (J). (gr. 4-7). lib. bdg. 34.60 (978-1-59845-043-9(3), MyReportLinks.com Bks.) Enslow Pubs., Inc.
Inserra, Rose. Birds. 2010. (Weird, Wild, & Wonderful Ser.). 24p. (J). (gr. 2-5). lib. bdg. 22.00 (978-1-4339-3580-0(5), Gareth Stevens Learning Library) Stevens, Gareth Publishing LLLP.
Jackson, Demi. Name That Bird! 2016. (Guess That Animal! Ser.). (Illus.). 24p. (J). (gr. 2-1). lib. bdg. 22.60 (978-1-4824-4742-2(8)) Stevens, Gareth Publishing LLLP.
Jackson, Tom. Gulls. 2008. (Nature's Children Ser.). (Illus.). 52p. (J). (978-0-7172-6256-4(1)) Grolier, Ltd.
—Parrots & Rainforest Birds: Macaws, Hummingbirds, Flamingos, Toucans & Other Exotic Species, All Shown in More Than 180 Pictures: 2014. (ENG., Illus.). 64p. (J). (gr. -1-3). 12.99 (978-1-86147-329-5(X), Armadillo) Anness Publishing GBR. Dist: National Bk. Network.
Jacobs, Pat. Why Do Birds Have Feathers? And Other Questions about Evolution & Classification. 2016. (Wildlife Wonders Ser.). 00032p. (J). (gr. 3-3). pap. 10.00 (978-1-4994-3205-3(4), PowerKids Pr.) Rosen Publishing Group, Inc., The.
Janssen, Robert B. & Tessen, Daryl D. Birds of Minnesota & Wisconsin, 1 vol. rev. ed. 2003. (ENG., Illus.). 376p. (gr. 4). pap. 24.95 (978-1-55105-324-0(1), 1551053241) Lone Pine Publishing USA.
Jeffrey, Gary. Firebirds. Cappoli, Sara, illus. 2012. (Graphic Mythical Creatures Ser.). (ENG.). 24p. (J). (gr. 3-5). pap. 8.15 (978-1-4339-6757-3(X)); lib. bdg. 23.95 (978-1-4339-6755-9(3)) Stevens, Gareth Publishing LLLP. (Gareth Stevens Learning Library).
Jeffrey, Laura S. Birds: How to Choose & Care for a Bird. 2004. (American Humane Pet Care Library). (Illus.). 48p. (J). (gr. 3-4). lib. bdg. 25.27 (978-0-7660-2515-8(2)) Enslow Pubs., Inc.
—Choosing a Bird: How to Choose & Care for a Bird. 2013. (American Humane Association Pet Care Ser.). 48p. (J). (gr. 3-18). lib. bdg. 25.27 (978-0-7660-4078-6(X)); pap. 8.95 (978-1-4644-0213-5(2), Enslow Elementary) Enslow Pubs., Inc.
Jenkins, Meghan. The 10 Most Amazing Birds. 2008. (J). 14.99 (978-1-55448-532-1(0)) Scholastic Library Publishing.
Johnson, Jinny. Birds. 2004. (Mosaic of Magical Information Ser.). (Illus.). 48p. (YA). (gr. 3-18). lib. bdg. 19.95 (978-1-59084-447-2(5)) Mason Crest.
—Birds. 2008. (1000 Things You Should Know about Ser.). (Illus.). 61p. (J). pap. (978-1-84236-632-5(7)) Miles Kelly Publishing, Ltd.
—1000 Things You Should Know about Birds. 2004. (1000 Things You Should Know about Ser.). (Illus.). 64p. (YA). (gr. 5-18). lib. bdg. 19.95 (978-1-59084-462-5(9)) Mason Crest.
Jordan, Apple. Guess Who Soars. 2nd rev. ed. 2011. (Bookworms 2nd Edition: Guess Who Ser.). (Illus.). 24p. (J). (gr. k-2). 21.36 (978-1-60870-429-3(7)) Marshall Cavendish Corp.
Jordan, Christopher. Baseball Animals. 2014. (Major League Baseball: First Base Bks.). (ENG., Illus.). 24p. (gr. -1-2). 12.99 (978-1-77049-474-9(X), Fenn-Tundra) Tundra Bks. CAN. Dist: Penguin Random Hse. LLC.
Julivert, Maria Angeles. Birds. 2009. (ENG., Illus.). 64p. (J). (gr. 3-8). 16.95 (978-1-59270-058-5(6)) Enchanted Lion Bks., LLC.
Kalman, Bobbie. Baby Birds. 2008. (It's Fun to Learn about Baby Animals Ser.). (ENG., Illus.). 24p. (J). (gr. 3-7). pap. (978-0-7787-3969-2(4)); lib. bdg. (978-0-7787-3950-0(3)) Crabtree Publishing Co.
—Les Oiseaux. 2004. (Petit Monde Vivant Ser.). (FRE., Illus.). 32p. (J). pap. 9.95 (978-2-89579-013-6(2)) Bayard Canada Livres CAN. Dist: Crabtree Publishing Co.
—Les Oiseaux. 2012. (FRE.). 32p. (J). pap. 9.95 (978-2-89579-475-2(8)) Bayard Canada CAN. Dist: Crabtree Publishing Co.
Kalman, Bobbie & Smithyman, Kathryn. La Vie des Oiseaux. Briere, Marie-Josee, tr. from ENG. 2006. (Petit Monde Vivant Ser.). (FRE., Illus.). 32p. (J). (gr. -1-3). pap. 10.95 (978-2-89579-078-5(7)) Bayard Canada Livres CAN. Dist: Crabtree Publishing Co.
Kaplan, Osman. Animal Wonders of the Sky. Kalender, Oznur, illus. 2009. (Amazing Animals Ser.). (ENG.). 56p. (J). (gr. 2-4). 9.95 (978-1-59784-201-3(X)) Tughra Bks.
Kaspar, Anna. What's a Bird? 2012. (All about Animals Ser.). (ENG., Illus.). 24p. (J). (gr. k-3). pap. 8.25 (978-1-4488-6230-6(2)); lib. bdg. 22.60 (978-1-4488-6136-1(5)) Rosen Publishing Group, Inc., The. (PowerKids Pr.).
—What's a Bird? Qué Es un Ave? 2012. (All about Animals / Todo sobre los animales Ser.). (SPA & ENG., Illus.). 24p. (J). (gr. k-3). lib. bdg. 22.60 (978-1-4488-6702-8(9), PowerKids Pr.) Rosen Publishing Group, Inc., The.
Kenyon, Linda. Rainforest Bird Rescue: Changing the Future for Endangered Wildlife. 2006. (Firefly Animal Rescue Ser.). (ENG., Illus.). 64p. (J). (gr. 5-12). 19.95 (978-1-55407-153-1(4), 9781554071531); pap. 9.95 (978-1-55407-152-4(6), 9781554071524) Firefly Bks., Ltd.
Kessler, Colleen. A Project Guide to Reptiles & Birds. 2010. (Life Science Projects for Kids Ser.). (Illus.). 48p. (J). (gr. 4-8). lib. bdg. 29.95 (978-1-58415-874-5(3)) Mitchell Lane Pubs., Inc.
Khan, Sarah. Birds Lift-the-Flap. Scott, Peter, illus. 2004. (Luxury Lift-the-Flap Ser.). 16p. (J). (gr. 1-18). 11.95 (978-0-7945-0714-5(X), Usborne) EDC Publishing.
Kirby, Pamela F. What Bluebirds Do. Kirby, Pamela F., photos by. 2013. (ENG., Illus.). 48p. (J). (gr. k-2). pap. 6.95 (978-1-62091-593-6(6)) Boyds Mills Pr.
—What Bluebirds Do. 2009. (ENG., Illus.). 48p. (J). (gr. k-2). 18.95 (978-1-59078-614-7(9)) Boyds Mills Pr.
Koystal, K. M. Aves. 2008. (Descubre la Naturaleza Ser.). (Illus.). 60p. (J). (gr. 4-7). 12.95 (978-1-58087-126-6(7)) Stampley, C. D. Enterprises, Inc.
Kurki, Kim & National Wildlife Federation Staff. National Wildlife Federation's World of Birds: A Beginner's Guide. 2014. (ENG., Illus.). 80p. (J). (gr. -1-17). 15.95 (978-1-57912-969-9(2), 81969, Black Dog & Leventhal Pubs. Inc.) Hachette Bks.
Kurtz, John. FLIP OUTS — Bird Bash: Color Your Own Cartoon! 2015. (ENG., Illus.). 64p. (J). (gr. k-3). pap. 1.99 (978-0-486-79485-3(7)) Dover Pubns., Inc.
—Kooky Birds Coloring Book. 2015. (ENG., Illus.). 32p. (J). (gr. -1-5). pap. 3.99 (978-0-486-78812-8(1)) Dover Pubns., Inc.
Lang, Elliott. Peafowls, Peacocks & Peahens Including Facts & Information about Blue, White, Indian & Green Peacocks

Breeding, Owning, Keeping & Raising Pe. 2012. 140p. pap. *(978-0-9566269-9-8(8))* IMB Publishing.

Lappi, Megan. Birds. 2004. (Prehistoric Life Ser.). (Illus.). 32p. (J). (gr. -1-3). per. 9.95 *(978-1-59036-170-2(9))*; lib. bdg. 24.45 *(978-1-59036-111-5(3))* Weigl Pubs., Inc.

Lawrence, Ellen. A Bird's Life. 2012. (Science Slam: Animal Diaries-Life Cycles Ser.). 24p. (J). (gr. -1-3). lib. bdg. 23.93 *(978-1-61772-595-1(1))* Bearport Publishing Co., Inc.

—A Tiny Beak & Spiky Feathers (Cockatiel) 2015. (Whose Little Baby Are You? Ser.). (ENG.). 24p. (J). (gr. -1-3). lib. bdg. 23.93 *(978-1-910549-24-7(X))* Bearport Publishing Co., Inc.

—Wood Duck. 2016. (Swamp Things: Animal Life in a Wetland Ser.). (ENG.). 24p. (J). (gr. -1-3). 17.95 *(978-1-944102-50-0(7))* Bearport Publishing Co., Inc.

Laws, John Muir. Sierra Birds: A Hiker's Guide. 2004. (Illus.). 64p. pap. 9.95 *(978-1-890771-78-2(3))* Heyday.

Lease, Janice M. Rudy the Roadrunner. Lease, Janice m, illus. 2009. 48p. pap. 19.95 *(978-0-9800762-3-3(4))* Cinnamon Ridge Publishing.

Lee, Fran. Backyard Birding for Kids, 1 vol. Lee, Fran, illus. 2005. (ENG., Illus.). 64p. (J). pap. 9.99 *(978-1-58685-411-9(9))* Gibbs Smith, Publisher.

Legg, Gerald. Birds of Prey. Hersey, Bob, illus. 2004. (Scary Creatures Ser.). (ENG.). 32p. (J). (gr. 2-4). pap. 6.95 *(978-0-531-16747-2(X),* Watts, Franklin) Scholastic Library Publishing.

Leighton, Christina. Roadrunners. 2017. (North American Animals Ser.). (ENG., Illus.). 24p. (J). (gr. k-3). lib. bdg. 25.95 *(978-1-62617-568-6(3),* Blastoff! Readers) Bellwether Media.

Lessem, Dino Don. Flying Giants of Dinosaur Time. Bindon, John, illus. 2005. (Meet the Dinosaurs Ser.). 32p. (J). (gr. 2-5). pap. 6.95 *(978-0-8225-2622-3(0))* Lerner Publishing Group.

Lessem, Don. Flying Giants of Dinosaur Time. Bindon, John, illus. 2005. (Meet the Dinosaurs Ser.). 32p. (J). (gr. 3-7). lib. bdg. 23.93 *(978-0-8225-1424-4(9))* Lerner Publishing Group.

Levine, Susan Sachs. Packard Takes Flight: A Bird's-Eye View of Columbus, Ohio. Burchwell, Erin McCauley, illus. 2010. (ENG.). 32p. 17.99 *(978-1-60949-051-5(7),* History Pr., The) Arcadia Publishing.

Levy, Janey. Really Strange Birds. 2016. (Really Strange Adaptations Ser.). 00032p. (J). (gr. 5-5). pap. 10.00 *(978-1-4994-2739-4(5),* PowerKids Pr.) Rosen Publishing Group, Inc., The.

Lewis, Clare. Bird Body Parts. 2015. (Animal Body Parts Ser.). (ENG., Illus.). 24p. (J). (gr. k-2). 23.32 *(978-1-4846-2553-8(6))* Heinemann-Raintree.

Lluch, Alex A. I Like to Learn Colors: Curious Penguin. 2011. (ENG.). 32p. (J). (gr. -1-k). bds. 4.95 *(978-1-934386-02-6(2))* WS Publishing.

Lockwood, Mark W. Learn About... Texas Birds. Ivy, Elena T., illus. 2007. (ENG.). 52p. (J). (gr. 1-7). pap. 10.95 *(978-0-292-71685-8(0))* Univ. of Texas Pr.

London, Jonathan. Flamingo Sunset, 0 vols. Rodanas, Kristina, illus. 2013. (ENG.). 33p. (J). (gr. k-3). pap. 9.99 *(978-1-4778-1674-5(7),* 9781477816745, Amazon Children's Publishing) Amazon Publishing.

Love, Donna. Awesome Ospreys: Fishing Birds of the World, 1 vol. Turley, Joyce Mihran, illus. rev. ed. 2005. (ENG.). 64p. (J). (gr. 3-7). pap. 12.00 *(978-0-87842-512-9(8),* 341) Mountain Pr. Publishing Co., Inc.

Macken, JoAnn Early. The Life Cycle of a Flamingo. 2006. (Things with Wings Ser.). (Illus.). 24p. (J). (gr. k-3). pap. 8.15 *(978-0-8368-6369-5(5))*; lib. bdg. 22.00 *(978-0-8368-6382-6(8))* Stevens, Gareth Publishing LLLP. (Weekly Reader Leveled Readers).

Mara, Wil. Cardinals. 2014. (Backyard Safari Ser.). 32p. (J). (gr. 3-5). 28.50 *(978-1-62712-822-3(0))* Cavendish Square Publishing.

Marsico, Katie. A Peachick Grows Up. Marsico, Katie, illus. 2007. (Scholastic News Nonfiction Readers Ser.). (ENG., Illus.). 24p. (J). (gr. 1-2). 22.00 *(978-0-531-17480-7(8))* Scholastic Library Publishing.

Martin, Isabel. Birds: A Question & Answer Book, 1 vol. 2014. (Animal Kingdom Questions & Answers Ser.). (ENG.). 24p. (gr. k-1). 26.65 *(978-1-4914-0561-1(9))*; (Illus.). pap. 6.95 *(978-1-4914-0629-8(1))* Capstone Press of Coughlan Cos. (Pebble Plus).

Martin, Kathy. Animals, Birds & the Alphabets. 2011. 32p. 14.39 *(978-1-4567-3302-5(8))* AuthorHouse.

Marzollo, Jean. Pierre the Penguin. Regan, Laura, illus. 2010. (ENG.). 32p. (J). (gr. -1-2). 15.95 *(978-1-58536-485-5(1))* Sleeping Bear Pr.

Massie, Elizabeth. A Look at Birds. 2016. (Spring Forward Ser.). (J). (gr. 1). *(978-1-4900-9393-2(1))* Benchmark Education Co.

Mataya, Marybeth. Are You My Bird?, 1 vol. Williams, Matthew, illus. 2008. (Are You My Pet? Ser.). (ENG.). 32p. (J). (gr. 1-4). 28.50 *(978-1-60270-241-7(1))* Magic Wagon.

McAneney, Caitlin. North American Birds: Represent & Solve Problems Involving Multiplication. 2014. (Rosen Common Core Math Readers Ser.). 24p. (J). (gr. 3-4). (ENG.). pap. 49.50 *(978-1-4777-4972-2(1),* Rosen Classroom); (ENG., Illus.). pap. 8.25 *(978-1-4777-4971-5(3),* PowerKids Pr.); (Illus.). lib. bdg. 23.60 *(978-1-4777-6445-9(3),* PowerKids Pr.) Rosen Publishing Group, Inc., The.

McCarthy, Cecilia Pinto. Flamingos. 2011. (Colorful World of Animals Ser.). (ENG.). 24p. (gr. k-1). lib. bdg. 26.65 *(978-1-4296-6048-8(1),* Pebble Plus) Capstone Press of Coughlan Cos.

McCarthy, Meghan. City Hawk: The Story of Pale Male. McCarthy, Meghan, illus. 2007. (ENG., Illus.). 40p. (J). (gr. -1-3). 17.99 *(978-1-4169-3359-5(X),* Simon & Schuster/Paula Wiseman Bks.) Simon & Schuster/Paula Wiseman Bks.

McDonald, Jill. Hello, World! Birds. 2017. (ENG., Illus.). 26p. (J). (— 1). bds. 7.99 *(978-0-553-52107-8(1),* Doubleday Bks. for Young Readers) Random Hse. Children's Bks.

McFadzean, Lesley. Birds: Flying High. 2014. (Discovery Education: Animals Ser.). 32p. (J). (gr. 3-6). 26.25 *(978-1-4777-6930-0(7))*; pap. 60.00 *(978-1-4777-6931-7(5))* Rosen Publishing Group, Inc., The. (PowerKids Pr.).

McGehee, Claudia. Where Do Birds Live? 2010. (Bur Oak Book Ser.). (Illus.). 32p. (gr. -1-3). 17.95 *(978-1-58729-919-3(4))* Univ. of Iowa Pr.

McGraw-Hill, Wright. Purl & the Bird, 6 vols. (Fast Track Reading Ser.). 24p. (gr. 4-8). 40.95 *(978-0-322-05982-5(8))* Wright Group/McGraw-Hill.

McNeil, Niki, et al. HOCPP 1129 Birds. 2006. spiral bd. 15.50 *(978-1-60308-129-0(1))* In the Hands of a Child.

Mead, Wendy. Kids Top 10 Pet Birds. 2015. (American Humane Association Top 10 Pets for Kids Ser.). 48p. (J). (gr. 3-4). 25.27 *(978-0-7660-6625-0(8))*; pap. 8.95 *(978-0-7660-6626-7(6),* Enslow Elementary) Enslow Pubs., Inc.

—Top 10 Birds for Kids. 2008. (Top Pets for Kids with American Humane Ser.). (Illus.). 48p. (J). (gr. 2-5). lib. bdg. 25.27 *(978-0-7660-3072-5(5))* Enslow Pubs., Inc.

Meehan, Sara. Bird Fossils. 2016. (Fossil Files Ser.). 00032p. (J). (gr. 5-5). 26.25 *(978-1-4994-2861-2(8),* PowerKids Pr.) Rosen Publishing Group, Inc., The.

Mehing, Carl. Prehistoric Creatures of the Sea & Skies. 2009. (Discovering Dinosaurs Ser.). (Illus.). 48p. (YA). (gr. 2-6). pap. 12.85 *(978-1-60754-781-5(3))*; (gr. 4-7). 29.25 *(978-1-60754-773-0(2))* Windmill Bks.

Meinking, Mary. Tarantula vs. Bird, 1 vol. 2011. (Predator vs. Prey Ser.). (ENG., Illus.). 32p. (J). (gr. 1-2). pap. 8.29 *(978-1-4109-3947-0(2,* Read Me!) Heinemann-Raintree.

Meister, Cari. Birds. 2014. (Illus.). 24p. (J). lib. bdg. 25.65 *(978-1-62031-120-2(8),* Bullfrog Bks.) Jump! Inc.

Mertz, Leslie A., et al. Grzimeks Student Animal Life Resource, 20.0. 2004. (Grzimek's Student Animal Life Resource Ser.). (ENG., Illus.). 5000p. (J). 1657.00 *(978-0-7876-9402-9(9),* UXL) Cengage Gale.

Mettler, René. Birds. Mettler, René, illus. 2012. (My First Discoveries Ser.: 15). (ENG., Illus.). 38p. (J). (gr. -1-k). spiral bd. 12.99 *(978-1-85103-397-3(1))* Moonlight Publishing, Ltd. GBR. Dist: Independent Pubs. Group.

Mettler, Ren'e, et al. El Pajaro. (Coleccion Mundo Maravilloso). (SPA., Illus.). 40p. (J). (gr. 2-4). *(978-84-348-3726-3(9),* SM5470) SM Ediciones.

Meyer, Therese. The Little Ballerina & Her Friends the Swans. 2004. (Illus.). 52p. *(978-0-9750325-0-3(X))* Baby Swan.

Milbourne, Anna. In the Nest. 2005. (First Discovery Ser.). 24p. (J). 9.95 *(978-0-7945-0735-0(2),* Usborne) EDC Publishing.

Miles, Lisa. Origami Birds & Butterflies. 2013. (Amazing Origami Ser.). 32p. (J). (gr. 2-5). pap. 10.50 *(978-1-4339-9645-0(6))*; pap. 63.00 *(978-1-4339-9646-7(4))*; (ENG., Illus.). lib. bdg. 26.60 *(978-1-4339-9644-3(8))* Stevens, Gareth Publishing LLLP.

Miller, Dave. Birds, Bugs, & Bees. 2006. (ENG., Illus.). (J). 3.00 *(978-0-932859-90-7(9))* Apologetics Pr., Inc.

Miller, Debbie S. Flight of the Golden Plover: The Amazing Migration Between Hawaii & Alaska. Van Zyle, Daniel, illus. 2011. (ENG.). 32p. pap. 11.95 *(978-1-60223-151-1(6))* Univ. of Alaska Pr.

Miniature Birds, 1 vol. 2014. (Mini Animal Marvels Ser.). (ENG., Illus.). 24p. (J). (gr. -1-3). 24.21 *(978-1-62403-064-2(5))* ABDO Publishing Co.

Mitchell, Susan K. Biggest vs. Smallest Things with Wings. 2010. (Biggest vs. Smallest Animals Ser.). (Illus.). 24p. (J). 22.60 *(978-0-7660-3578-2(6),* Enslow Elementary) Enslow Pubs., Inc.

Mohr, Janet & Howard, Adeline. Backyard Bird Book for Kids. 2010. (Illus.). 74p. (J). pap. *(978-0-615-33660-2(4))* Devonshire Bks.

Monroe, Guy. A Bird's Day at Yaquina Head. Monroe, Karol, ed. Golding, J. C., illus. 2003. 52p. 7.95 *(978-0-9742443-0-3(9))* Monroe, Guy.

Montgomery, Sy. Snowball: The Dancing Cockatoo. Oksner, Judith, illus. 2013. (ENG.). 64p. (J). pap. 15.00 *(978-0-87233-156-3(3))* Bauhan Publishing LLC.

Morey, Allan. Birds. 2015. (Animal Kingdom Ser.). (Illus.). 32p. (J). 28.50 *(978-1-60753-472-3(X))* Amicus Publishing.

Morgan, Sally. Birds. 2012. (Pets Plus Ser.). (Illus.). 32p. (gr. 3-6). lib. bdg. 31.35 *(978-1-59920-697-4(8))* Black Rabbit Bks.

Murray, Julie. Birds, 1 vol. 2015. (ENG., Illus.). 24p. (J). 27.07 *(978-1-62970-898-0(4),* 1391168) ABDO Publishing Co.

Niven, Felicia Lowenstein. Learning to Care for a Bird. 2010. (Beginning Pet Care with American Humane Ser.). 48p. (J). 25.27 *(978-0-7660-3192-0(6),* Enslow Elementary) Enslow Pubs., Inc.

O'Donnell, Kerri. Aves: Dinosaurios de nuestros días (Birds: Modern-Day Dinosaurs) 2009. (Reading Room Collection: Spanish Ser.). (SPA.). 24p. (gr. 3-4). 42.50 *(978-1-60854-176-8(2),* Editorial Buenas Letras) Rosen Publishing Group, Inc., The.

—Birds: Modern-Day Dinosaurs. (Reading Room Collection 2 Ser.). 24p. (gr. 3-4). 2009. 42.50 *(978-1-60851-960-6(0),* PowerKids Pr.) 2003. (ENG.). 43.95 *(978-0-8239-8732-0(9))* Rosen Publishing Group, Inc., The.

O'Hare, Ted. Birds. 2005. (What Is an Animal? (Discovery Library) Ser.). (Illus.). 24p. (J). (gr. 1-4). per. 5.45 *(978-1-59515-730-0(1))* Rourke Educational Media.

Olson, Gillia M. Stickler on Stilts. 2010. (Zoo Animal Mysteries Ser.). (ENG.). 24p. (gr. k-1). lib. bdg. 26.65 *(978-1-4296-4500-3(8),* Pebble Plus) Capstone Press of Coughlan Cos.

One Bird Sat on the Fence: Level B, 6 vols. (Wonder Worldtm Ser.). 16p. 24.95 *(978-0-7802-1044-8(1))* Wright Group/McGraw-Hill.

O'Shaughnessy, Ruth. Owls after Dark. 2015. (Animals of the Night Ser.). (ENG., Illus.). 32p. (J). (gr. 3-4). 25.27 *(978-0-7660-6760-8(2))* Enslow Pubs., Inc.

Ouilette, K. T. Valliere-Denis. Two Birds in a Box. Du Houx, E. M. Cornell, illus. 2006. 59p. (J). per. 6.95 *(978-1-882190-55-3(6))* Polar Bear & Co.

Parker, Janice. Birds. 2007. (Life Science (Weigl Hardcover) Ser.). (Illus.). 32p. (J). (gr. 4-7). lib. bdg. 26.00 *(978-1-59036-703-2(0))*; per. 9.95 *(978-1-59036-704-9(9))* Weigl Pubs., Inc.

Patent, Dorothy Hinshaw. Brown Pelicans. 2005. (Early Bird Nature Bks.). (Illus.). (gr. 2-4). lib. bdg. 25.26 *(978-0-8225-2417-5(1))* Lerner Publishing Group.

—The Call of the Osprey. Muñoz, William, illus. Muñoz, William, photos by. 2015. (Scientists in the Field Ser.). (ENG.). 80p. (J). (gr. 5-7). 18.99 *(978-0-544-23268-6(2),* HMH Books For Young Readers) Houghton Mifflin Harcourt Publishing Co.

Patterson, Virginia Sharpe. Dickey Downy: The Autobiography of a Bird. 2007. 106p. pap. 10.99 *(978-1-4346-2478-9(1))*; 116p. pap. 11.99 *(978-1-4346-2479-6(X))* Creative Media Partners, LLC.

Pearce, Q. L. James Quadrino: Wildlife Protector. 2006. (Young Heroes Ser.). (ENG., Illus.). 48p. (J). (gr. 3-7). lib. bdg. 28.75 *(978-0-7377-3612-0(7),* Kidhaven) Cengage Gale.

Person, Stephen. Roseate Spoonbill: Pretty in Pink. 2012. (America's Hidden Animal Treasures Ser.). 32p. (J). (gr. 2-7). lib. bdg. 26.60 *(978-1-61772-570-8(6))* Bearport Publishing Co., Inc.

Petek-Markic, Zdenka. Birds. 2012. 52p. pap. 19.97 *(978-1-61897-694-9(X),* Strategic Bk. Publishing) Strategic Book Publishing & Rights Agency (SBPRA).

Peters, Elisa. It's a Bird! 2009. (Everyday Wonders Ser.). 24p. (gr. 1-1). 42.50 *(978-1-61512-321-6(0))*; (J). lib. bdg. 22.60 *(978-1-4042-4461-0(1))* Rosen Publishing Group, Inc., The. (PowerKids Pr.).

—It's a Bird! Es un Ave! 2009. (Everyday Wonders / Maravillas de Todos Los días Ser.). (SPA & ENG., Illus.). 24p. lib. bdg. 22.60 *(978-1-4358-2526-0(8),* PowerKids Pr.) Rosen Publishing Group, Inc., The.

—It's a Bird! / ¡Es un Ave! 2009. (Everyday Wonders / Maravillas de todos los días Ser.). (ENG & SPA.). 24p. (gr. 1-1). 42.50 *(978-1-61512-327-8(X),* Editorial Buenas Letras) Rosen Publishing Group, Inc., The.

Pingry, Patricia A. Baby Flamingo. Sharp, Chris, illus. 2004. (San Diego Zoo Animal Library: Vol. 8). (ENG.). 26p. (J). bds. 6.95 *(978-0-8249-6557-0(4),* Ideal Pubns.) Worthy Publishing.

Pinnington, Andrea. The Little Book of Backyard Bird Songs. 2016. (ENG., Illus.). 26p. (J). (gr. k-4). 19.95 *(978-1-77085-744-5(3),* 9781770857445) Firefly Bks., Ltd.

Pixton, Kaaren. Flutter! Fly! Hey Baby! Look at These Things with Wings. 2009. (Indestructibles Ser.). (ENG., Illus.). 12p. (J). (gr. k-1). pap. 5.95 *(978-0-7611-5697-0(6),* 15697) Workman Publishing Co., Inc.

Ponka, Katherine. A Bird Watcher's Guide to Blue Jays. 2016. (Backyard Bird Watchers Ser.). (ENG., Illus.). 32p. (J). (gr. 2-3). pap. 10.50 *(978-1-4824-3836-9(4))* Stevens, Gareth Publishing LLLP.

Pruett, Mary, illus. Color the Western Birds. 2010. (Pruett Ser.). (ENG.). 32p. (J). pap. 4.99 *(978-0-87108-957-1(2))* Pruett Publishing Co.

Raptors: Talons & Talents, 6 vols. (Book2WebTM Ser.). (gr. 4-8). 36.50 *(978-0-322-02974-3(0))* Wright Group/McGraw-Hill.

Raum, Elizabeth. Birds Build Nests. Romina Martí, illus. 2017. (Animal Builders Ser.). (ENG.). 24p. (J). (gr. 1-4). 20.95 ***(978-1-68151-170-2(3),*** Amicus Illustrated) Amicus Publishing.

—Las Abejas y Sus Colmenas (Bees Build Beehives) Romina Martí, illus. 2017. (Animal Builders Ser.). (ENG & SPA.). 24p. (J). (gr. 1-4). 20.95 ***(978-1-68151-280-8(7),*** Amicus Illustrated) Amicus Publishing.

Reilly, Pauline & Rolland, Will. Lyrebird. (Picture Roo Bks.). (Illus.). 32p. (J). pap. *(978-0-86417-615-8(5),* Kangaroo Pr.) Simon & Schuster Australia.

Rice, Dona Herweck. Cosas con Alas, 1 vol. 2nd rev. ed. 2012. (Nonfiction Readers Ser.). (SPA.). 20p. (J). (gr. 1-1). pap. 4.99 *(978-1-4333-4422-0(X))* Teacher Created Materials, Inc.

—Things with Wings, 1 vol. 2nd rev. ed. 2011. (Nonfiction Readers Ser.). (ENG.). 20p. (J). (gr. 1-1). pap. 4.99 *(978-1-4333-3589-1(1))* Teacher Created Materials, Inc.

Richardson, Adele D., et al. Birds. 2012. (Birds Ser.). (ENG.). 24p. (gr. 1-2). lib. bdg. 151.92 *(978-1-4296-9155-0(7),* First Facts) Capstone Press of Coughlan Cos.

Richardson, Joy. Birds. 2005. (Variety of Life Ser.). (Illus.). 32p. (gr. 1-4). lib. bdg. 26.00 *(978-0-8368-4502-0(1),* Gareth Stevens Learning Library) Stevens, Gareth Publishing LLLP.

Rigby Education Staff. Using a Beak. (Sails Literacy Ser.). (Illus.). 16p. (gr. 2-3). 27.00 *(978-0-7635-9959-1(X),* 699599C99) Rigby Education.

Riggs, Kate. Amazing Animals: Flamingos. 2015. (Amazing Animals Ser.). (ENG.). 24p. (J). (gr. 2-5). pap. 8.99 *(978-1-62832-088-6(5),* Creative Paperbacks) Creative Co., The.

—Counting on Birds. Van der Linde, Jori, illus. 2017. (ENG.). 14p. (J). (gr. -1 — 1). bds. 8.99 *(978-1-56846-300-1(6),* Creative Education) Creative Co., The.

—Flamingos. 2015. (J). *(978-1-60818-488-0(9),* Creative Education) Creative Co., The.

River Lake Press. An Osprey Summer. 2010. (Illus.). 32p. (J). 17.95 *(978-0-615-36951-8(0))* River Lake Pr.

Robertson, Joyce. Meet the Magpie. 2010. 24p. pap. 16.49 *(978-1-4490-8791-3(4))* AuthorHouse.

Rockwell, Lizzy. A Bird Is a Bird. Rockwell, Lizzy, illus. 2015. (ENG., Illus.). 32p. (J). (gr. -1-2). 16.95 *(978-0-8234-3042-0(1))* Holiday Hse., Inc.

Rodriguez, Ana María. The Secret of the Bird's Smart Brain... & More! 2017. (Animal Secrets Revealed! Ser.). 48p. (J). (gr. 4-4). lib. bdg. 27.93 ***(978-0-7660-8623-4(2))*** Enslow Pubs., Inc.

Rodriguez, Ana Maria. Secret of the Puking Penguins ... & More! 2008. (Animal Secrets Revealed! Ser.). (Illus.). 48p. (J). (gr. 5-9). lib. bdg. 25.27 *(978-0-7660-2955-2(7))* Enslow Pubs., Inc.

Rohan, Rebecca. A Bird Watcher's Guide to Robins. 2016. (Backyard Bird Watchers Ser.). (ENG., Illus.). 32p. (J). (gr. 2-3). pap. 10.50 *(978-1-4824-3907-6(7))* Stevens, Gareth Publishing LLLP.

Rohrer, Martha. Birds, Birds, Birds. 2004. (Illus.). 32p. (gr. -1-5). 1.70 *(978-0-7399-2349-8(8),* 2951) Rod & Staff Pubs., Inc.

Romeu, Emma. The Flamingo's Legs. Vigil, Luis Gerardo Sanchez & Broeck, Fabricio Vanden, illus. 2004. (Colección Animales de América / Animals of the Americas Ser.). (SPA.). 32p. (gr. 3-5). pap. 11.95 *(978-1-59437-846-1(0))* Santillana USA Publishing Co., Inc.

Royston, Angela. Birds. (Illus.). 32p. (YA). (gr. 2-18). lib. bdg. 27.10 *(978-1-932333-34-3(7))* Chrysalis Education.

—Birds. 2015. (Animal Classifications Ser.). (ENG., Illus.). 32p. (gr. 1-3). 27.32 *(978-1-4846-0750-3(3),* Heinemann First Library) Heinemann-Raintree.

Rupp, Kristina. I See You, Bird! 2015. (1-3Y Animals Ser.). (ENG., Illus.). 20p. (J). pap. 5.99 *(978-1-63437-147-6(X))* American Reading Co.

Russo, Monica. Birdology: 30 Activities & Observations for Exploring the World of Birds. Byron, Kevin, photos by. 2015. (Young Naturalists Ser.). (ENG., Illus.). 128p. (J). (gr. 2-4). pap. 15.95 *(978-1-61374-949-4(X))* Chicago Review Pr., Inc.

Rustad, Martha E. H. Zebras & Oxpeckers Work Together. 2011. (Animals Working Together Ser.). (ENG.). 24p. (gr. k-1). pap. 41.70 *(978-1-4296-6369-4(3),* Pebble Plus) Capstone Press of Coughlan Cos.

Ryder, Joanne. Wild Birds. Kwas, Susan Estelle, illus. 2003. 40p. (J). (gr. -1-2). 16.99 *(978-0-06-027738-3(6))* HarperCollins Pubs.

Salzmann, Mary Elizabeth. Accordion to Zeppelin: Inventions from A to Z, 1 vol. 2008. (Let's Look A to Z Ser.). (ENG., Illus.). 32p. (gr. k-4). 27.07 *(978-1-60453-008-7(1),* Super SandCastle) ABDO Publishing Co.

—Albatross to Zebra Finch: Birds from A to Z, 1 vol. 2008. (Let's Look A to Z Ser.). (ENG., Illus.). 32p. (gr. k-4). 27.07 *(978-1-60453-009-4(X),* Super SandCastle) ABDO Publishing Co.

—Brilliant Birds, 1 vol. 2007. (Perfect Pets Ser.). (ENG., Illus.). 24p. (J). (gr. k-3). lib. bdg. 24.21 *(978-1-59928-744-7(7),* SandCastle) ABDO Publishing Co.

—What Has Wings?, 1 vol. 2007. (Creature Features Ser.). (ENG., Illus.). 24p. (J). (gr. -1-3). lib. bdg. 25.65 *(978-1-59928-876-5(1),* Super SandCastle) ABDO Publishing Co.

Sams, Carl R., II & Stoick, Jean. Happy Bird Day! Sams, Carl R., II & Stoick, Jean, photos by. 2012. (ENG., Illus.). 14p. (J). bds. 7.95 *(978-0-9827625-2-3(6))* Sams, II, Carl R. Photography, Inc.

Samson, Tess. See the Birds. 2010. (Sight Word Readers Ser.). (J). 3.49 *(978-1-60719-620-4(4))* Newmark Learning LLC.

Sanchez, Claudia. Cuidador de Pajaros (Bird Trainer & Other Legends) (SPA.). (J). 14.95 *(978-950-02-8449-3(9))* El Ateneo ARG. Dist: AIMS International Bks., Inc.

Sancton, Sylvaine. Some Birds ..., 1 vol. Sancton, Sylvaine, photos by. 2013. (ENG., Illus.). 40p. (J). (gr. k-3). pap. 14.99 *(978-1-4556-1863-7(2))* Pelican Publishing Co., Inc.

Savage, Stephen. Focus on Birds. 2011. (Animal Watch Ser.). 32p. (J). (gr. 3-6). lib. bdg. 26.60 *(978-1-4339-5981-3(X))* Stevens, Gareth Publishing LLLP.

Saxena, Shalini. A Bird Watcher's Guide to Goldfinches. 2016. (Backyard Bird Watchers Ser.). (ENG., Illus.). 32p. (J). (gr. 2-3). pap. 10.50 *(978-1-4824-3903-8(4))* Stevens, Gareth Publishing LLLP.

Sayre, April Pulley. Bird, Bird, Bird! A Chirping Chant. Locke, Gary, illus. 2007. (American City Ser.). (ENG.). 32p. (J). (gr. k-3). 16.95 *(978-1-55971-978-0(8))* Cooper Square Publishing Llc.

Scholastic, Inc. Staff, contrib. by. Bird Babies. 2016. (Rookie Toddler(tm) Ser.). (ENG., Illus.). 12p. (J). bds. 6.95 *(978-0-531-22696-4(4),* Children's Pr.) Scholastic Library Publishing.

Schuetz, Kari. Birds. 2012. (Animal Classes Ser.). (ENG., Illus.). 24p. (J). (gr. k-3). lib. bdg. 25.95 *(978-1-60014-772-2(0),* Blastoff! Readers) Bellwether Media.

Schuh, Mari. The World's Biggest Birds. 2015. (Illus.). 24p. (J). lib. bdg. 17.95 *(978-1-62031-206-3(9))* Jump! Inc.

Schwarz, Renee. Birdfeeders. Schwarz, Renee, illus. 2005. (Kids Can Do It Ser.). (ENG., Illus.). 40p. (J). (gr. 3-7). 6.95 *(978-1-55337-700-9(1))* Kids Can Pr., Ltd. CAN. Dist: Hachette Bk. Group.

Seal, Daisy, selected by. Exotic Birds: Color by Numbers. 2016. (Hobbies & Craft Ser.). (ENG., Illus.). 128p. pap. 15.99 *(978-1-78664-042-0(2),* 9781786640420) Flame Tree Publishing GBR. Dist: Bookmasters Distribution.

Senker, Cath. Birds, 01 vols., 1. 2016. (Adventures in Nature Ser.). (ENG.). 32p. (J). pap. 10.00 *(978-1-5081-4575-2(X),* PowerKids Pr.) Rosen Publishing Group, Inc., The.

Shaw, Frank. Birds of the United States & Canada. 2004. (World Book's Science & Nature Guides Ser.). (Illus.). 80p. (J). *(978-0-7166-4210-7(7))* World Bk., Inc.

Shea, Nicole. Creepy Birds. 2012. (Nature's Creepiest Creatures Ser.). (ENG.). 24p. (J). (gr. 2-5). pap. 8.15 *(978-1-4339-6487-9(2))*; lib. bdg. 22.60 *(978-1-4339-6485-5(6))* Stevens, Gareth Publishing LLLP. (Gareth Stevens Learning Library).

Shea, Therese. Saving the Endangered American Bald Eagle, 01 vols., 1. 2016. (Conservation of Endangered Species Ser.). (ENG., Illus.). 32p. (J). pap. 12.90 *(978-1-5081-0053-9(5),* Britannica Educational Publishing) Rosen Publishing Group, Inc., The.

Sherk, Beth Larson. The Three Sisters. 2012. (Illus.). 35p. (J). 14.95 *(978-1-62086-091-5(0))* Mascot Bks., Inc.

Sill, Cathryn. About Birds: A Guide for Children, 1 vol. Sill, John, illus. 2nd rev. ed. 2013. (About ... Ser.). (ENG.). 40p. (J). (gr. -1-2). 7.95 *(978-1-56145-699-4(3))*; 16.95 *(978-1-56145-688-8(8))* Peachtree Pubs.

—About Birds: A Guide for Children / Sobre Los Pajaros: una Guia para Niños, 1 vol. Sill, John, illus. 2014. (About Ser.). (SPA & ENG.). 40p. (J). (gr. -1-2). pap. 8.95 *(978-1-56145-783-0(3))* Peachtree Pubs.

Sill, Cathryn P. About Birds: A Guide for Children. Sill, John, illus. 2014. (ENG.). (J). *(978-1-56145-799-1(X))* Peachtree Pubs.

Silverman, Buffy. Birds. (Illus.). (J). (gr. 2-4). pap., wbk. ed. 4.99 *(978-0-88743-965-0(9))* School Zone Publishing Co.

—Do You Know about Birds? 2009. (Lightning Bolt Books — Meet the Animal Groups Ser.). (ENG., Illus.). 32p. (gr. k-2). pap. 7.95 *(978-1-58013-857-4(8))*; lib. bdg. 26.60 *(978-0-8225-7541-2(8),* Lerner Pubns.) Lerner Publishing Group.

—¿Sabes Algo Sobre Aves? (Do You Know about Birds?) 2012. (Libros Rayo — Conoce Los Grupos de Animales (Lightning Bolt Books — Meet the Animal Groups) Ser.). (Illus.). 32p. (gr. k-2). (ENG & SPA.). pap. 7.95 *(978-0-7613-9366-5(8))*; (SPA., lib. bdg. 26.60 *(978-0-7613-9334-4(X))* Lerner Publishing Group. (Ediciones Lerner).

Silverstein, Alvin, et al. Beautiful Birds. 2003. (What a Pet! Ser.). (Illus.). 48p. (gr. 5-8). lib. bdg. 23.90 *(978-0-7613-2513-0(1),* Millbrook Pr.) Lerner Publishing Group.

Singer, Beth & Benchmark Education Co., LLC Staff. Red Bird Chirps. 2015. (BuildUp Ser.). (J). (gr. 1). *(978-1-4900-0736-6(9))* Benchmark Education Co.

Sjonger, Rebecca & Kalman, Bobbie. Aves de Todo Tipo. 2005. (?Qui Tipo de Animal Es? Ser.). (SPA., Illus.). 32p. (J). (gr. 3-7). pap. *(978-0-7787-8870-6(9))*; lib. bdg. *(978-0-7787-8834-8(2))* Crabtree Publishing Co.

Smythe, Katie. Robins Lay Eggs. 2015. (Rosen REAL Readers: STEM & STEAM Collection). (ENG.). 8p. pap. 5.46 *(978-1-4994-9727-4(X)*, Rosen Classroom) Rosen Publishing Group, Inc., The.

Snedden, Robert. Birds. (Living Things Ser.). (Illus.). 32p. 2009. (J). (gr. -1-3). pap. 7.95 *(978-1-59920-193-1(3))* 2007. (YA). (gr. 3-6). lib. bdg. 28.50 *(978-1-59920-076-7(7))* Black Rabbit Bks.

Soffer, Ruth. Amazing Birds. 2006. (Dover Nature Coloring Book Ser.). (ENG., Illus.). 32p. (gr. 3-8). 4.99 *(978-0-486-44796-4(0))* Dover Pubns., Inc.

—Birds Alphabet Coloring Book. 2005. (Dover Nature Coloring Book Ser.). (ENG., Illus.). 32p. (J). (gr. -1-5). 3.99 *(978-0-486-44035-4(4))* Dover Pubns., Inc.

—Birds in Flight Coloring Book. 2013. (ENG.). 32p. (gr. 3-12). pap. 3.99 *(978-0-486-49735-8(6))* Dover Pubns., Inc.

Soundprints, creator. Flamingo Grows Up. 2011. (Let's Go to the Zoo! Ser.). (ENG., Illus.). 16p. (gr. -1). 5.95 *(978-1-60727-453-7(1))* Soundprints.

Spilsbury, Louise. Kori Bustard, 1 vol. 2011. (Day in the Life: Grassland Animals Ser.). (ENG., Illus.). 24p. (gr. k-2). 23.32 *(978-1-4329-4733-0(8)*, Heinemann Read & Learn) Heinemann-Raintree.

—Superstar Birds. 2014. (Nature's Got Talent Ser.). (Illus.). 32p. (J). (gr. k-5). lib. bdg. 26.25 *(978-1-4777-7060-3(7)*, PowerKids Pr.) Rosen Publishing Group, Inc., The.

Spizzirri, Linda, ed. Prehistoric Birds. Spizzirri, Peter M., illus. 32p. (J). (gr. 1-8). pap. 4.98 incl. audio *(978-0-86545-023-3(4))* Spizzirri Pr., Inc.

Squire, Ann O. Birds. 2013. (True Book(tm), a — Animal Kingdom Ser.). (ENG.). 48p. (J). 31.00 *(978-0-531-21751-1(5))*; pap. 6.95 *(978-0-531-22336-9(1))* Scholastic Library Publishing.

Staunton, Joseph. Dinosaurs in the Sky. 2010. (Discover the Dinosaurs Ser.). 32p. (J). (gr. 2-5). 28.50 *(978-1-60753-108-1(9))* Amicus Publishing.

Staunton, Joseph & Hynson, Colin. Dinosaurs in the Sky. 2011. (Inside Crime Ser.). 48p. (YA). (gr. 5-9). lib. bdg. 34.25 *(978-1-59920-394-2(4))* Black Rabbit Bks.

Stefoff, Rebecca. The Bird Class. 2007. (Family Trees Ser.). (Illus.). 96p. (gr. 6-7). lib. bdg. 34.21 *(978-0-7614-2693-6(0)*, Benchmark Bks.) Marshall Cavendish Corp.

Sterling Publishing Company Staff & Ward, Adam, contrib. by. Birds. 2004. (Pocket Factfiles Ser.). (Illus.). 256p. (J). 4.98 *(978-1-4027-1848-9(9))* Sterling Publishing Co., Inc.

Sterry, Paul & Read, Rob. Collins Life-Size Birds: the Only Guide to Show British Birds at Their Actual Size. 2016. (ENG., Illus.). 448p. 44.99 *(978-0-00-821873-7(0)*, Collins) HarperCollins Pubs. Ltd. GBR. Dist: HarperCollins Pubs.

Stewart, Melissa. A Place for Birds (revised Edition), 1 vol. Bond, Higgins, illus. rev. ed. 2015. (Place For... Ser.). (ENG.). 32p. (gr. 1-5). 16.95 *(978-1-56145-839-4(2))* Peachtree Pubs.

Stockdale, Susan. Bring on the Birds, 1 vol. Stockdale, Susan, illus. (ENG., Illus.). (J). (gr. -1 — 1). 2013. 22p. bds. 6.95 *(978-1-56145-692-5(6))* 2011. 32p. 16.95 *(978-1-56145-560-7(1))* Peachtree Pubs.

Stoltman, Joan. My First Bird. 2017. (Let's Get a Pet! Ser.). 24p. (J). (gr. 1-2). pap. 8.15 ***(978-1-4824-6437-5(3))*** Stevens, Gareth Publishing LLLP.

Stone, Tanya Lee. Peacocks. 2003. (Wild Wild World Ser.). 24p. (YA). 24.94 *(978-1-56711-818-6(6)*, Blackbirch Pr., Inc.) Cengage Gale.

Sturm, Jeanne. Restoring Wetlands. 2009. (ENG., Illus.). 48p. (gr. 4-8). pap. 10.95 *(978-1-60694-527-8(0))* Rourke Educational Media.

Sundance/Newbridge LLC Staff. Birds, Birds, Birds. 2004. (Reading PowerWorks Ser.). (gr. 1-3). 37.50 *(978-0-7608-9783-6(2))*; pap. 6.10 *(978-0-7608-9784-3(0))* Sundance/Newbridge Educational Publishing.

Taylor, Roger. Atlas Visual de las Aves. (Colección Atlas Visual). (SPA., Illus.). 324p. (YA). (gr. 5-8). *(978-84-216-2575-0(6)*, BU1497) Bruño, Editorial ESP. Dist: Lectorum Pubns., Inc.

Tekiela, Stan. C Is for Cardinal, 1 vol. 2016. (ENG., Illus.). 64p. (J). (-k). 8.95 *(978-1-59193-533-9(4))* Adventure Pubns.

Thomas, Isabel. Beaky's Guide to Caring for Your Bird, 1 vol. Peterson, Rick, illus. 2014. (Pets' Guides). (ENG.). 32p. (gr. 1-3). pap. 8.29 *(978-1-4846-0266-9(8))*; 27.32 *(978-1-4846-0259-1(5))* Heinemann-Raintree. (Heinemann First Library).

—Brilliant Birds, 1 vol. 2012. (Extreme Animals Ser.). (ENG.). 32p. (gr. 1-3). pap. 8.29 *(978-1-4109-4684-3(3))*; lib. bdg. 29.99 *(978-1-4109-4678-2(9))* Heinemann-Raintree. (Read Me!).

Thompson, Bill, III. The Young Birder's Guide to Birds of Eastern North America. 2008. (Illus.). 256p. (J). pap. *(978-0-7534-6108-2(0))* Houghton Mifflin Harcourt Publishing Co.

Thompson III, Bill. The Young Birder's Guide to Birds of North America. 2012. (Peterson Field Guides). (ENG., Illus.). 368p. pap. 15.95 *(978-0-547-44021-7(9))* Houghton Mifflin Harcourt Publishing Co.

Thomson, Sarah L. & Plant, Andrew. Ancient Animals: Terror Bird. 2013. (ENG., Illus.). 32p. (J). (gr. 1-4). 12.95 *(978-1-58089-398-5(8))* Charlesbridge Publishing, Inc.

Thornhill, Jan. The Tragic Tale of the Great Auk, 1 vol. 2016. (ENG., Illus.). 44p. (J). (gr. 2-6). 18.95 *(978-1-55498-865-5(9))* Groundwood Bks. CAN. Dist: Publishers Group West (PGW).

Those Birds! Level M, 6 vols. 128p. (gr. 2-3). 49.95 *(978-0-7699-1020-8(3))* Shortland Pubns. (U. S. A.) Inc.

Thurnherr, Paige. Hunting with Bald Eagles. 2012. (Animal Attack! Ser.). (Illus.). 24p. (J). (gr. 2-5). pap. 8.15 *(978-1-4339-7064-1(3))*; lib. bdg. 26.60 *(978-1-4339-7063-4(5))* Stevens, Gareth Publishing LLLP.

Tildes, Phyllis Limbacher. Baby's First Book of Birds & Colors. Tildes, Phyllis Limbacher, illus. 2017. (ENG., Illus.). 18p. (J). (— 1). bds. 7.99 *(978-1-58089-742-6(8))* Charlesbridge Publishing, Inc.

Toliver, Marilyn. Marcellus Really Wants a Pet. 2012. 28p. pap. 16.09 *(978-1-4669-0090-5(3))* Trafford Publishing.

Top That Publishing Staff, ed. Birds of Paradise. 2005. (Illus.). 24p. *(978-1-84510-534-1(6))* Top That! Publishing PLC.

—Birds of World. 2004. (Know How Know Why Ser.). (Illus.). 48p. (J). pap. *(978-1-84510-075-9(1))* Top That! Publishing PLC.

—Wacky Hen. 2004. (Wacky Animals Ser.). (Illus.). 10p. (J). pap. *(978-1-84510-091-9(3))* Top That! Publishing PLC.

Torrey, Bradford. Everyday Birds. reprint ed. pap. 125.00 *(978-1-4047-9776-5(9))* Classic Textbooks.

—Everyday Birds. 2013. (Notable American Authors). reprint ed. lthr. 79.00 *(978-0-7812-9776-9(1))* Reprint Services Corp.

Towsley, Nanette. Little Birds of a Feather: The Fantastic Adventures of Steve & Timmy. 2011. 48p. pap. 16.25 *(978-1-4575-0638-3(6))* Dog Ear Publishing, LLC.

Troupe, Thomas Kingsley. Wild Weather: Science Adventures with Sonny the Origami Bird, 1 vol. Christoph, Jamey, illus. 2014. (Origami Science Adventures Ser.). (ENG.). 24p. (gr. 3-4). lib. bdg. 27.32 *(978-1-4795-2188-3(4))* Picture Window Bks.

Trueit, Trudi Strain. Birds. 2011. (Backyard Safari Ser.). 32p. (gr. 3). 28.50 *(978-1-60870-242-8(1))* Marshall Cavendish Corp.

Underwood, Deborah. Colorful Peacocks. 2006. (Pull Ahead Books-Animals Ser.). (ENG., Illus.). 32p. (gr. k-3). per. 7.95 *(978-0-8225-6507-9(2)*, First Avenue Editions) Lerner Publishing Group.

Vail, Grace. A Bird Watcher's Guide to Sparrows. 2016. (Backyard Bird Watchers Ser.). (ENG., Illus.). 32p. (J). (gr. 2-3). pap. 10.50 *(978-1-4824-3911-3(5))* Stevens, Gareth Publishing LLLP.

VanDerwater, Amy Ludwig. Every Day Birds. Metrano, Dylan, illus. 2016. (ENG.). 32p. (J). (gr. -1-k). 17.99 *(978-0-545-69980-8(0)*, Orchard Bks.) Scholastic, Inc.

Veitch, Catherine. Bird Babies, 1 vol. 2013. (Animal Babies Ser.). (ENG.). 24p. (gr. -1-1). 22.65 *(978-1-4329-7492-3(0))*; pap. 35.94 *(978-1-4329-8424-3(1))*; pap. 6.95 *(978-1-4329-8417-5(9))* Heinemann-Raintree. (Acorn).

Wallis, Ginger. Finch Discoveries: An Inspiring Tale of Adaptation to a Changing Environment. Dodson, Bert, illus. 2013. 34p. pap. 12.95 *(978-0-9847662-2-2(7))* Dancing Journey Pr.

Waxman, Laura Hamilton. California Condors: Wide-Winged Soaring Birds. 2016. (Comparing Animal Traits Ser.). (ENG., Illus.). 32p. (J). (gr. 2-4). 26.65 *(978-1-4677-9512-8(7)*, Lerner Pubns.) Lerner Publishing Group.

Wechsler, Doug. Ospreys. 2009. (Really Wild Life of Animals Ser.). 24p. (gr. 3-4). 42.50 *(978-1-60854-202-4(5)*, PowerKids Pr.) Rosen Publishing Group, Inc., The.

—Really Wild Life of Birds of Prey, 2 vols., set. (Illus.). 80.70 *(978-0-8239-7077-3(9))* Rosen Publishing Group, Inc., The.

West, David. Terror Bird. Poluzzi, Alessandro, illus. 2017. (Graphic Prehistoric Animals Ser.). 32p. (gr. 3-7). lib. bdg. 31.35 *(978-1-62588-413-8(3))* Black Rabbit Bks.

West, Keith R. & West, Jonathan. Birds. 2006. (Illus.). 48p. (J). lib. bdg. 29.95 *(978-1-60044-258-2(7))* Rourke Educational Media.

Westerskov, Kim, photos by. Albatrosses. 2004. (Illus.). 32p. (J). pap. *(978-0-7685-2117-7(3))* Dominie Pr., Inc.

Wicker, Jan Lee. Those Funny Flamingos. Weaver, Steve, illus. 2004. (Those Amazing Animals Ser.). (ENG.). 55p. (J). pap. 9.95 *(978-1-56164-295-3(9))* Pineapple Pr., Inc.

Williams, Brenda. Amazing Birds. 2008. (Amazing Life Cycles Ser.). (Illus.). 32p. (gr. 2-6). lib. bdg. 26.00 *(978-0-8368-8894-2(4)*, Gareth Stevens Learning Library) Stevens, Gareth Publishing LLLP.

Williams, Zella. Quetzals & Other Latin American Birds: Quetzales y Otras Aves de Latino América. 2009. (Animals of Latin America / Animales de Latinoamérica Ser.). (SPA & ENG., Illus.). 24p. (J). lib. bdg. 22.60 *(978-1-4042-8126-4(6))*; pap. 8.25 *(978-1-4358-3380-7(5))* Rosen Publishing Group, Inc., The. (PowerKids Pr.).

Willson, Mary. The Singer in the Stream: A Story of American Dippers. Hocker, Katherine, illus. 2015. (ENG.). 32p. (J). (gr. k-3). 14.95 *(978-1-930238-56-5(8))* Yosemite Assn.

Wilson, Bill & Fallon, Katie. Look, See the Bird! Carter, Leigh Anne, illus. 2017. (ENG.). 32p. (J). (gr. -1-2). 12.50 ***(978-1-57826-687-6(4)***, Hatherleigh Pr.) Hatherleigh Co., Ltd., The.

Winner, Cherie. Everything Bird: What Kids Really Want to Know about Birds. 2007. (Kids Faqs Ser.). (ENG., Illus.). 64p. (J). (gr. 3-6). 10.95 *(978-1-55971-962-9(1)*, 1267598); pap. 8.95 *(978-1-55971-963-6(X)*, 1267598) Cooper Square Publishing Llc.

Words about Birds. 12p. (J). *(978-2-7643-0192-0(8))* Phidal Publishing, Inc./Editions Phidal, Inc.

World Book, Inc. Staff, contrib. by. All about Birds: A Supplement to Childcraft — The How & Why Library. 2005. (Illus.). 208p. (gr. 2-6). 24.95 *(978-0-7166-0613-0(5))* World Bk., Inc.

World Book, Inc Staff, contrib. by. Birdlike Dinosaurs: Small Theropods & Prehistoric Birds. 2012. (J). *(978-0-7166-0368-9(3))* World Bk., Inc.

—Birds. 2009. (J). *(978-0-7166-0403-7(5))* World Bk., Inc.

World Book, Inc. Staff, contrib. by. Storks & Other Large Wading Birds. 2005. (World Book's Animals of the World Ser.). (Illus.). 64p. (J). *(978-0-7166-1267-4(4))* World Bk., Inc.

Wright, Mabel Osgood. Citizen Bird. 2009. 384p. 31.99 *(978-0-559-09867-3(7))*; 29.99 *(978-0-559-09880-2(4))*; pap. 32.75 *(978-0-559-09876-5(6))*; pap. 33.75 *(978-0-559-09870-3(7))* Creative Media Partners, LLC.

—Citizen Bird. 2008. (Illus.). pap. *(978-1-84830-922-7(8)*, Wildhern Pr.) Echo Library.

—Citizen Bird. 2009. 234p. pap. 19.99 *(978-1-4588-2043-3(2))* General Bks. LLC.

—Citizen Bird Scenes from Bird-Life in Plain English for Beginners. 2011. 400p. pap. *(978-3-8424-5125-4(3))* Tredition GmbH.

Wright, Mabel Osgood, creator. Citizen Bird: Scenes from Bird-Life in Plain English for Beginners. 2012. 456p. pap. *(978-1-290-54080-3(2))* HardPr.

—Citizen Bird: Scenes from Bird-life in Plain English for Beginners. 2010. 452p. pap. 36.75 *(978-1-171-97029-3(3))* Creative Media Partners, LLC.

Wright, Mabel Osgood & Coues, Elliott. Citizen Bird: Scenes from Bird-Life in Plain English for Beginners. Fuertes, Louis Agassiz, illus. 2009. 386p. pap. *(978-1-4099-8625-6(X))* Dodo Pr.

—Citizen Bird: Scenes from bird-life in plain English for Beginners. 2010. (ENG.). 450p. pap. 36.75 *(978-1-176-55166-4(3))* Creative Media Partners, LLC.

—Citizen Bird: Scenes from Bird Life in Plain English for Beginners (1897) Fuertes, Louis Agassiz, illus. 2010. 446p. 41.56 *(978-1-164-42138-2(7))* 2010. 446p. pap. 29.56 *(978-1-164-13374-2(8))* 2008. 444p. 51.95 *(978-1-4366-1564-8(X))* 2008. (ENG.). 448p. per. 36.95 *(978-0-548-81704-9(9))* Kessinger Publishing, LLC.

—Citizen Bird Scenes from Bird-Life in Plain English for Beginners. 2011. 456p. pap. 36.75 *(978-1-175-46461-3(9))* Creative Media Partners, LLC.

Wright, Mabel Osgood, et al. Citizen Bird: Scenes from bird-life in plain English for Beginners. 2010. (ENG.). 454p. pap. 36.75 *(978-1-171-57653-2(6))* Creative Media Partners, LLC.

Yolen, Jane. Birds of a Feather. Stemple, Jason, photos by. 2011. (ENG., Illus.). 32p. (J). (gr. 4-6). 17.95 *(978-1-59078-830-1(3)*, Wordsong) Boyds Mills Pr.

Zondervan Staff. Our Feathered Friends, 1 vol. 2011. (I Can Read! / Made by God Ser.). (ENG.). 32p. (J). (gr. -1-2). pap. 3.99 *(978-0-310-72184-0(9))* Zonderkidz.

BIRDS, AQUATIC

see Water Birds

BIRDS—EGGS

Birds & Eggs Sets: 1 Each of 3 Big Books. (Sunshinetm Science Ser.). (gr. 1-2). 111.50 *(978-0-7802-1393-7(9))* Wright Group/McGraw-Hill.

Birds & Eggs Sets: 1 Each of 3 Student Books. (Sunshinetm Science Ser.). (gr. 1-2). 20.95 *(978-0-7802-1746-1(2))* Wright Group/McGraw-Hill.

Eggs & Baby Birds, 6 vols. (Sunshinetm Science Ser.). 24p. (gr. 1-2). 37.50 *(978-0-7802-1392-0(0))*; 41.95 *(978-0-7802-1391-3(2))* Wright Group/McGraw-Hill.

Munro, Roxie. Hatch!, 0 vols. Munro, Roxie, illus. 2011. (ENG., Illus.). 40p. (J). (gr. k-6). 17.99 *(978-0-7614-5882-1(4)*, 9780761458821, Amazon Children's Publishing) Amazon Publishing.

Sauter, Cynthia M. The Birds Nest Outside My Bedroom Window. 2011. 28p. pap. 14.99 *(978-1-4520-9957-6(X))* AuthorHouse.

BIRDS—FICTION

Abbott Orloff, Chrissy. Lady Humming Fly's Lesson on Staying Safe. 2009. 80p. pap. 28.99 *(978-1-4389-9938-8(0))* AuthorHouse.

Adeney, Anne. Two Hungry Birds. O'Kif, illus. 2008. (Reading Corner Ser.). (ENG.). 24p. (J). (gr. k-2). pap. 6.99 *(978-0-7496-7693-3(0)*, Franklin Watts) Hachette Children's Group GBR. Dist: Hachette Bk. Group.

Adie, Alasdair. The Moca-do-poo Bird. 2011. (ENG., Illus.). 80p. (J). pap. 9.95 *(978-0-7552-0680-3(0))* Authors OnLine, Ltd. GBR. Dist: Printondemand-worldwide.com.

Aesop. The Fox & the Crane. 2012. (J). 29.99 *(978-1-61913-109-5(9))* Weigl Pubs., Inc.

Aina, Olaiya. The Boy, the Dove, & the Hawk. 2010. 20p. pap. 13.80 *(978-1-4269-3298-4(7))* Trafford Publishing.

Akkari, Hélène. Saving Kanki the Antelope. 2010. 20p. 11.49 *(978-1-4520-9156-3(0))* AuthorHouse.

Allen, Kenny. Bird Builds a House. 2006. (Neighborhood Readers Ser.). (ENG.). 8p. (gr. -1-3). pap. 5.15 *(978-1-4042-6690-2(9)*, Rosen Classroom) Rosen Publishing Group, Inc., The.

Alvarez, Juan Ramón. Maximiliano el Nino Que Hablaba con Las Chuparrosas. 2012. (ENG.). pap. 5.00 *(978-1-4675-4391-0(8))* Independent Pub.

Amani, Alexander. The Guardians. 2010. 148p. 24.95 *(978-1-4490-8572-8(5))*; pap. 16.99 *(978-1-4490-8571-1(7))* AuthorHouse.

Amo, Montserrat del. Montes, Pájaros y Amigos. 2007. (SPA.). 104p. (gr. 5-8). pap. 13.99 *(978-84-207-2788-2(1)*, GS6293) Grupo Anaya, S.A. ESP. Dist: Lectorum Pubns., Inc.

Ana, Moh. Kookaburra Tales: Shy Not, My Friend. 2013. 16p. pap. 17.03 *(978-1-4669-3193-0(0))* Trafford Publishing.

Anaya, Rudolfo. The First Tortilla: A Bilingual Story. Lamadrid, Enrique R., tr. Córdova, Amy, illus. 2012. (ENG & SPA.). 32p. (J). pap. 16.95 *(978-0-8263-4215-7(9))* Univ. of New Mexico Pr.

Anaya, Rudolfo A. & Anaya, Rudolfo. The First Tortilla: A Bilingual Story. Lamadrid, Enrique R., tr. from ENG. Córdova, Amy, illus. 2007. (SPA & ENG.). 32p. (J). (gr. 4-7). 16.95 *(978-0-8263-4214-0(0))* Univ. of New Mexico Pr.

Andersen, Hans Christian. The Nightingale. Oleynikov, Igor, illus. 2007.Tr. of Nattergalen. (ENG.). 40p. (J). (gr. k). lib. bdg. 16.50 *(978-1-933327-31-0(6))*; (gr. 1). 15.95 *(978-1-933327-30-3(8))* Purple Bear Bks., Inc.

—El Ruisenor.Tr. of Nightingale. (SPA.). 32p. (J). (gr. 2-3). 12.95 *(978-84-233-1567-3(3))* Ediciones Destino ESP. Dist: Planeta Publishing Corp.

Anderson, David. Charlie Sparrow & the Secret of Flight. Anderson, David, illus. 2013. (Illus.). 98p. pap. *(978-0-9918003-2-2(X))* Underdog Bks.

Anderson, Derek. Blue Burt & Wiggles. Anderson, Derek, illus. 2014.Tr. of Signed in American Sign Language. (ENG., Illus.). 32p. (J). (gr. -1-3). 16.99 *(978-1-4814-1933-8(1))*, Simon & Schuster Bks. For Young Readers) Simon & Schuster Bks. For Young Readers.

Anderson, Mary. My Small Backyard: Birds! 2012. 28p. pap. 17.32 *(978-1-4771-5951-4(7))* Xlibris Corp.

Aqkay. Jungle Olympics-800 Metres Sprint. 2013. 36p. pap. 24.95 *(978-1-62709-117-6(3))* America Star Bks.

Araten, Michel. Honey the Hummingbird. 2004. 57p. per. 13.08 *(978-1-4116-1805-3(X))* Lulu Pr., Inc.

El Arco Iris y Los Pajaros (The Rainbow & the Birds), Big Book. (Superbks./Superlibros). (J). (gr. k-1). 21.95 *(978-0-88272-456-0(8))* Santillana USA Publishing Co., Inc.

Armstrong, Jeannette C. Dancing with the Cranes. Hall, Ron, illus. 2nd rev. ed. 2009. (ENG.). 24p. pap. 10.95 *(978-1-894778-70-1(7))* Theytus Bks., Ltd. CAN. Dist: Univ. of Toronto Pr.

Aryal, Aimee. Hello Cocky! Graybill, Joni, illus. 2004. 24p. (J). 19.95 *(978-1-932888-07-2(1))* Mascot Bks., Inc.

Asch, Frank. Moonbear's Bargain. Asch, Frank, illus. 2014. (Moonbear Ser.). (ENG., Illus.). 32p. (J). (gr. -1-3). 17.99 *(978-1-4424-9436-7(0)*, Aladdin) Simon & Schuster Children's Publishing.

—Moonbear's Pet. Asch, Frank, illus. 2014. (Moonbear Ser.). (ENG., Illus.). 32p. (J). (gr. -1-3). 17.99 *(978-1-4424-9430-5(1)*, Simon & Schuster/Paula Wiseman Bks.) Simon & Schuster/Paula Wiseman Bks.

—Moonbear's Sunrise. Asch, Frank, illus. 2014. (Moonbear Ser.). (ENG., Illus.). 32p. (J). (gr. -1-3). 16.99 *(978-1-4424-6647-0(2)*, Aladdin) Simon & Schuster Children's Publishing.

Aschermann, Kurt. Bj & the Amazing Doctor Directions. 2008. 172p. pap. 11.99 *(978-1-4343-7708-1(3))* AuthorHouse.

Ash. The Thrush's Song. 2011. 20p. pap. 24.95 *(978-1-4626-3720-1(5))* America Star Bks.

Ashrafizadeh, Maedeh. The Life of a Lovebird. 2012. 36p. pap. 21.99 *(978-1-4691-7911-7(3))* Xlibris Corp.

Atwater-Rhodes, Amelia. Falcondance. 2007. (Kiesha'ra Ser.: Bk. 3). (ENG.). 208p. (YA). (gr. 7-12). per. 7.99 *(978-0-440-23885-0(4)*, Delacorte Pr.) Random Hse. Children's Bks.

—Wolfcry. 2008. (Kiesha'ra Ser.: Bk. 4). (ENG.). 208p. (YA). (gr. 9-12). pap. 7.99 *(978-0-440-23886-7(2)*, Delacorte Pr.) Random Hse. Children's Bks.

Baby Lauren & Theodore, Paperback. 2007. (J). pap. 9.95 *(978-0-9779643-0-7(2))* Healing Tree Arts.

Baguley, Elizabeth. A Long Way from Home. Chapman, Jane, illus. 2008. 32p. (J). (gr. 4-7). 15.95 *(978-1-58925-074-1(5))* Tiger Tales.

Baia, Edward. The Flying Fox & the Cockatoo. Mape, Michael, illus. 2013. 22p. pap. *(978-9980-86-507-6(5))* University of Papua New Guinea Press.

Baker, Keith. Just How Long Can a Long String Be? 2009. (J). pap. *(978-0-545-08662-2(0)*, Levine, Arthur A. Bks.) Scholastic, Inc.

Baldini-Chavez, Cecilia. The Silver-Golden Feather Secreted at el Dorado, 1 vol. 2009. 92p. pap. 19.95 *(978-1-60813-664-3(7))* America Star Bks.

Banks, Kate. Dillon Dillon. 2005. 149p. (gr. 3-7). 18.00 *(978-0-7569-5767-4(2))* Perfection Learning Corp.

Barbari, Nader. Eddy the Elephant. 2010. 32p. pap. 13.99 *(978-1-4490-9430-0(9))* AuthorHouse.

Barland, Dj. The Little Ray's Big Rescue. 2013. 40p. pap. 15.99 *(978-1-4808-0284-1(0))* Archway Publishing.

Barnes, Kenneth Edward. A Children's Story Collection. 2011. 216p. (gr. -1). pap. 15.95 *(978-1-4634-2863-1(4))*; (gr. 1-2). 24.59 *(978-1-4634-2864-8(2))* AuthorHouse.

Barnett, Mac. Telephone. Corace, Jen, illus. 2014. (ENG.). 40p. (J). (gr. -1-3). 16.99 *(978-1-4521-1023-3(9))* Chronicle Bks. LLC.

Barsy, Kalman. Los Tres Naufragos. Perez-Moliere, Mamie, illus. 2004. (Orange Ser.). (SPA.). 40p. (J). (gr. 3-5). pap. 5.95 *(978-1-57581-469-8(2))* Santillana USA Publishing Co., Inc.

Barton, Chris. That's Not Bunny! Jack, Colin, illus. 2016. (ENG.). 32p. (J). (gr. -1-k). 16.99 *(978-1-4231-9086-8(6))* Disney Pr.

Barton, Suzanne. The Sleepy Songbird. 2016. (ENG., Illus.). 32p. (J). 16.99 *(978-0-8027-3648-2(3)*, 9780802736482, Bloomsbury USA Childrens) Bloomsbury Publishing USA.

Bass, Joy Wine. The Flamingephants: Story, Songs, & Illustrations. 2011. 96p. 24.99 *(978-1-4568-8553-3(7))*; pap. 15.99 *(978-1-4568-8552-6(9))* Xlibris Corp.

Bauer, Joan. Backwater. rev. ed. 2005. (ENG.). 192p. (YA). (gr. 7-12). pap. 7.99 *(978-0-14-240434-8(9)*, Speak) Penguin Young Readers Group.

—Backwater. 2005. 185p. 18.00 *(978-0-7569-5779-7(6))* Perfection Learning Corp.

Bauer, Marion Dane. The Longest Night. Lewin, Ted, illus. 2009. (ENG.). 40p. (J). (gr. -1-3). 17.95 *(978-0-8234-2054-4(X))* Holiday Hse., Inc.

Baum, L. Frank. Twinkle & Chubbins. 2011. 106p. pap. 9.95 *(978-1-60664-470-6(X))* Rodgers, Alan Bks.

Baum, L. Frank & Bancroft, Laura. Policeman Bluejay. 2009. 116p. pap. 9.95 *(978-1-60664-382-2(7))* Rodgers, Alan Bks.

Baumgartner, Edward Louis. Wabash Boy. 2011. 236p. (gr. 4-6). pap. 16.26 *(978-1-4269-7615-5(1))* Trafford Publishing.

Beal, Scott, ed. The Chameleon Toothbrush: New Stories from the Neutral Zone. 2008. (Illus.). 100p. (YA). per. 12.00 *(978-0-9779289-4-1(2))* 826michigan.

Beaudry, Len. Luther the Looney Bird: In Luther's First Walk. 2010. 12p. 8.49 *(978-1-4520-0358-0(0))* AuthorHouse.

Beck, Barbara. Bill Every Cloud Has a Silver Lining. 2012. 108p. pap. 19.95 *(978-1-4626-9718-2(6))* America Star Bks.

Beck, Dewey. A Ledge, a Pie, & Hazel the Fly. 2012. 28p. pap. 19.99 *(978-1-4772-9154-2(7))* AuthorHouse.

Bednark, Sara & Ung, Bunheang. Wally's Bedroom Aviary. 2008. 32p. 14.95 *(978-0-615-18545-3(2))* Bednark, Sara.

Bee, Nanny. William. 2012. 52p. (-18). pap. 16.95 *(978-1-4626-9765-6(8))* America Star Bks.

Begum, Dilara. Mama Bird & Her Baby. Balogh, Jared, illus. 2011. 28p. pap. 24.95 *(978-1-4560-6924-7(1))* America Star Bks.

Beighey, Carole La Flamme. The Waddodles of Hollow Lake: Ruffed Grouse Courtship Ceremony. 2010. 284p. (gr. 4-7). 25.99 *(978-1-4490-7766-2(8))* AuthorHouse.

Bell, Lucy J. Uri & the Busy Day. Garton, Michael, illus. 2017. (J). 12.99 ***(978-1-5064-1787-5(6)***, Sparkhouse Family) Augsburg Fortress, Pubs.

Belonie, Shannon. Oliver Andrew Ostrich: My Full Name. 2008. 12p. pap. 8.74 *(978-1-4343-5849-3(6))* AuthorHouse.

—Teaching an Ostrich to Fly. 2008. 16p. pap. 8.74 *(978-1-4343-5519-5(5))* AuthorHouse.

Bentley, Dawn. Welcome Back, Puffin! Stover, Beth, illus. 2003. (Soundprints' Read-and-Discover Ser.). (ENG.). 32p. (J). (gr. -1-k). 12.95 *(978-1-59249-010-3(7)*, PS2064); pap. 3.95 *(978-1-59249-009-7(3)*, S2014) Soundprints.

Beranek, Malinda. Rocky, the Country Squirrel. 2008. 12p. pap. 24.95 *(978-1-60563-018-2(7))* America Star Bks.

Berger, Carin. Forever Friends. Berger, Carin, illus. 2010. (ENG., Illus.). 40p. (J). (gr. -1-1). 16.99 *(978-0-06-191528-4(9)*, Greenwillow Bks.) HarperCollins Pubs.

Berglund, Andrea Lloyd. A Good Little Horse: Thunder's Morning Stroll. 2009. 36p. (J). pap. 19.95 *(978-1-4327-3822-8(4))* Outskirts Pr., Inc.

Berkes, Marianne. Marsh Morning. Noreika, Robert, illus. 2011. (ENG.). 32p. (J). (gr. k-3). pap. 6.95 (978-0-7613-7462-6(0), Millbrook Pr.) Lerner Publishing Group.

Berry, Lynne. What Floats in a Moat? Cordell, Matthew, illus. 2013. (ENG.). 48p. (J). (gr. k-4). 17.99 (978-1-4169-9763-4(6), Simon & Schuster Bks. For Young Readers) Simon & Schuster Bks. For Young Readers.

Bevis, Mary. Bird on My Hand (hardcover) Making Friends with Chickadees, 1 vol. Powell, Consie, illus. 2014. (ENG.). 32p. (J). (gr. 1-2). 17.95 (978-0-9883508-9-2(0)) Raven Productions, Inc.

—Bird on My Hand (softcover) Making Friends with Chickadees. Powell, Consie, illus. 2014. (ENG.). 32p. (J). (gr. 1-2). pap. 9.95 (978-0-9883508-8-5(2)) Raven Productions, Inc.

Bianchi, John. Bird at School. 2016. (1-3Y Bird, Bunny & Bear Ser.). (ENG., Illus.). 16p. (J). pap. 5.99 (978-1-63437-438-5(X)) American Reading Co.

Bianchi, John, illus. Where Is Here? 2013. (1G Bird, Bunny, & Bear Ser.). (ENG.). 12p. (J). pap. 5.99 (978-1-61406-592-0(6)) American Reading Co.

Biddle, Steve & Biddle, Megumi. The Crane's Gift. 2003. (ENG.). 32p. pap. 7.33 (978-0-582-46143-7(X)) Pearson ESL.

Billingsley, Victoria. Happy Hoppy's Orchestra & Other Stories. 2010. 44p. 16.99 (978-1-4520-6753-7(8)) AuthorHouse.

Birch, Vanessa Giancamilli. Seagull by the Shore: The Story of a Herring Gull. Langford, Alton, illus. 2010. (Smithsonian Oceanic Collection). (ENG.). 32p. (J). (gr. -1-3). 16.95 (978-1-60727-089-8(7)); pap. 6.95 (978-1-60727-090-4(0)) Soundprints.

Bird, Linda. Charlie Bird: The Best Bird Ever. 2007. 32p. per. 12.95 (978-1-4327-0489-6(3)) Outskirts Pr., Inc.

Bird Song: The Little Stories of Manoosh & Baloosh. 2003. (J). mass mkt. (978-1-932233-02-5(4)) Aurora Libris Corp.

Birkenstock, Michelle M. Harry the Caterpillar. 2010. 20p. pap. 10.95 (978-1-60911-250-9(4), Eloquent Bks.) Strategic Book Publishing & Rights Agency (SBPRA).

Blacklidge, Barbara. Lucky: My Story. 2010. 24p. (J). pap. 12.95 (978-1-934449-64-6(4)) Legacy Publishing Services, Inc.

Blake, Quentin. Loveykins. Blake, Quentin, illus. 2003. (Illus.). 32p. (J). (gr. k-3). 15.95 (978-1-56145-282-8(3)) Peachtree Pubs.

Bloom, Deborah R. The Bird Who Could Fly. 2006. pap. 7.50 (978-1-59971-075-4(7)) Aardvark Global Publishing.

Blunt, Patricia. George the Jackdaw. 2005. (Illus.). 52p. pap. (978-1-84401-540-5(8)) Athena Pr.

Blyton, Enid. Magic Snow Bird: And Other Stories. Hamilton, Dorothy, illus. 2013. (ENG.). 192p. (J). 9.95 (978-1-84135-420-0(1)) Award Pubns. Ltd. GBR. Dist: Parkwest Pubns., Inc.

Bogue, Gary. There's a Hummingbird in My Backyard. Todd, Chuck, illus. 2010. 40p. (J). (gr. -1-3). 15.95 (978-1-59714-131-4(3)) Heyday.

Boiger, Alexandra. Max & Marla. Boiger, Alexandra, illus. 2015. (ENG., Illus.). 32p. (J). (-k). 17.99 (978-0-399-17504-6(0), G.P. Putnam's Sons Books for Young Readers) Penguin Young Readers Group.

Bolton, Robin. Sunny Goes Out to Play. 2011. 28p. pap. 12.03 (978-1-4634-2530-2(9)) AuthorHouse.

Bonazzo, Jennifer. Wings of Peace. 2013. 28p. pap. 24.95 (978-1-4626-9079-4(3)) America Star Bks.

Bonwill, Ann. I Am Not a Copycat! Rickerty, Simon, illus. 2013. (ENG.). 32p. (J). (gr. -1-1). 15.99 (978-1-4424-8053-7(X)) Simon & Schuster Children's Publishing.

Booty, Don V. Brave Little Starling. 2012. (ENG.). 24p. (J). pap. 19.95 (978-1-4327-9017-2(X)) Outskirts Pr., Inc.

Boudreau, Hélène. Keep Out!, 1 vol. Lucas, Diane, illus. 2010. (ENG.). 80p. (J). (gr. 1-4). pap. 8.95 (978-1-55109-753-4(2)) Nimbus Publishing, Ltd. CAN. Dist: Orca Bk. Pubs. USA.

Boutros, Gladys. Bubba & the Sweet Pea: US English Edition. Balogh, Andras, illus. 2012. 86p. (J). pap. (978-0-9873334-1-4(0)) Enlife Pty, Limited.

Bowlby, Linda S. The Rock Garden. Helms, Dana, illus. 2008. 29p. (J). (gr. -1-3). pap. 9.95 (978-0-9779993-4-7(3)) Red Earth Publishing.

Bowser, D. M. The Enchanting Tales of Lilith. 2011. 54p. pap. 16.95 (978-1-4560-9570-3(6)) America Star Bks.

Boyer, Cécile, illus. Woof Meow Tweet-Tweet. 2011. (ENG.). 48p. (J). (gr. -1). 15.95 (978-1-934734-60-5(8)) Seven Footer Pr.

Branch, Beverly, illus. The Nightingale. 2006. (J). 6.99 (978-1-59939-020-8(5)) Cornerstone Pr.

Branson, Terri. Pete, the Peacock, Goes to Town. 2007. (ENG., Illus.). 22p. (J). 14.99 (978-0-9794660-8-3(3)) Dragonfly Publishing, Inc.

—Pete, the Peacock, Goes to Town. Taylor, Chet, illus. l.t. ed. 2005. 22p. (J). lib. bdg. 24.95 (978-0-9765786-1-1(1)) Dragonfly Publishing, Inc.

Brantley, Meg. Love Family Adventures. 2009. 116p. pap. 11.99 (978-1-60791-786-1(6)) Salem Author Services.

Breen, Steve. Woodpecker Wants Waffles. Breen, Steve, illus. 2016. (Illus.). 32p. (J). (gr. -1-3). 17.99 (978-0-06-234257-7(6)) HarperCollins Pubs.

Brice, Gary. The Birds, Their Carols Raise. 2017. (ENG.). 140p. pap. 14.00 **(978-1-62288-162-8(1))** Austin, Stephen F. State Univ. Pr.

Brodzinsky, Anne Braff. The Mulberry Bird: An Adoption Story. 2012. (ENG., Illus.). 48p. 14.95 (978-1-84905-933-6(0), 1852) Kingsley, Jessica Pubs. GBR. Dist: Macmillan Distribution Ltd.

Brouwer, Sigmund. Justine Mckeen & the Bird Nerd, 1 vol. Whamond, Dave, illus. 2013. (Orca Echoes Ser.). (ENG.). 64p. (J). (gr. 2-3). pap. 6.95 (978-1-4598-0394-7(9)) Orca Bk. Pubs. USA.

Brower, Sandra Shane. Princess Zoe & the Mer-Bird. Steele, Andrea M., illus. 2013. 46p. pap. 10.95 (978-1-936688-77-7(8), Compass Flower Pr.) AKA:yoLa.

Brown, Margaret Wise. The Dead Bird. Date not set. 32p. (J). pap. 5.99 (978-0-06-443668-7(3)); lib. bdg. 16.89 (978-0-06-028932-4(5)) HarperCollins Pubs.

—The Dead Bird. Robinson, Christian, illus. 2016. 32p. (J). (gr. -1-3). 17.99 (978-0-06-028931-7(7)) HarperCollins Pubs.

—North, South, East, West. Pizzoli, Greg, illus. 2017. 40p. (J). (gr. -1-3). 17.99 (978-0-06-026278-5(8)) HarperCollins Pubs.

Brown, Peter. Flight of the Dodo. 2010. (ENG., Illus.). 32p. (J). (gr. -1-3). pap. 7.99 (978-0-316-08339-3(9)) Little, Brown Bks. for Young Readers.

Browne, A. SunBirds: #3 Great Lengths. 2003. 112p. pap. 9.95 (978-0-595-26709-5(2), Writers Club Pr.) iUniverse, Inc.

Bruel, Nick. Little Red Bird. Bruel, Nick, illus. 2008. (ENG., Illus.). 32p. (J). (gr. -1-1). 17.99 (978-1-59643-339-7(6), 9781596433397) Roaring Brook Pr.

Buchanan, Jane. Seed Magic, 1 vol. Riley-Webb, Charlotte, illus. 2012. (ENG.). 32p. (J). 16.95 (978-1-56145-622-2(5)) Peachtree Pubs.

Buchholz, Erwin. Born under a Star, 1 vol. Legg, Barbara, illus. 2009. 44p. pap. 24.95 (978-1-61546-130-1(2)) America Star Bks.

Buggs, Michael A. Tabard. Buggs, Michael A., illus. (Illus.). 64p. (Orig.). (J). (gr. 2-6). pap. 15.00 (978-0-9657723-0-3(6)) Mogul Comics.

Bunting, Eve. Rudi's Pond. Himler, Ronald, illus. 2004. (ENG.). 32p. (J). (gr. -1-3). pap. 6.99 (978-0-618-48604-5(6)) Houghton Mifflin Harcourt Publishing Co.

Bunting, Sarah Clare. Why Are You So Lazy Owl? 2012. 16p. pap. 12.50 (978-1-4709-4837-5(0)) Lulu Pr., Inc.

Burgess, Thornton W. Adventures of Bob White. Cady, Harrison, illus. 2011. (Dover Children's Thrift Classics Ser.). (ENG.). 96p. (J). (gr. k-3). pap. 3.00 (978-0-486-48109-8(3)) Dover Pubns., Inc.

—The Adventures of Mr. Mocker. Cady, Harrison, illus. 2011. (Dover Children's Thrift Classics Ser.). (ENG.). 96p. (J). (gr. k-3). pap. 3.00 (978-0-486-48101-2(8)) Dover Pubns., Inc.

—The Adventures of Mr Mocker. 2007. 108p. per. 9.95 (978-1-60312-296-2(6)); (gr. 4-7). 22.95 (978-1-60312-714-1(3)) Aegypan.

—The Adventures of Mr Mocker. 2011. 108p. 23.95 (978-1-4638-9565-5(8)) Rodgers, Alan Bks.

—The Adventures of Sammy Jay. (J). 15.95 (978-0-8488-0381-0(7)) Amereon Ltd.

—Tommy & the Wishing-Stone. Cady, Harrison, illus. 2012. (Dover Children's Thrift Classics Ser.). (ENG.). 240p. (J). (gr. k-3). pap. 4.00 (978-0-486-48105-0(0)) Dover Pubns., Inc.

Burgwyn, Diana. Despin: The Adventures of a Motherless Puffin, a Lonely Great Auk & a Pack of Ferocious White Rats. 2012. (ENG.). 262p. (J). pap. 9.99 (978-1-938135-56-9(3)) Telemachus Pr., LLC.

Burke, Merrilee. Dreamcatcher Garden: A Sacred Journey. 2012. 108p. (gr. 4-6). 28.99 (978-1-4525-5786-1(1)); pap. 8.99 (978-1-4525-5784-7(5)) Balboa Pr.

Burke, Zoe. Charley Harper's Count the Birds. Harper, Charley, illus. 2015. (ENG.). 24p. (J). bds. 10.95 (978-0-7649-7246-1(4), POMEGRANATE KIDS) Pomegranate Communications, Inc.

Burks, James. Bird & Squirrel on Fire. 2017. (Bird & Squirrel Ser.). (ENG.). 192p. (J). (gr. 2-5). 18.99 (978-0-545-80429-5(9), Graphix) Scholastic, Inc.

—Bird & Squirrel on Ice. 2014. (Bird & Squirrel Ser.). (ENG.). 128p. (J). (gr. 2-5). pap. 8.99 (978-0-545-56318-5(6), Graphix) Scholastic, Inc.

—Bird & Squirrel on the Edge! 2015. (Bird & Squirrel Ser.). (ENG., Illus.). 144p. (J). (gr. 2-5). 18.99 (978-0-545-80425-7(6), Graphix) Scholastic, Inc.

—Bird & Squirrel on the Run! 2012. (Bird & Squirrel Ser.). (ENG., Illus.). 128p. (J). (gr. 2-5). pap. 8.99 (978-0-545-31283-7(3), Graphix) Scholastic, Inc.

—Bird & Squirrel on the Run! 2012. (Bird Squirrel Ser.). (Illus.). 125p. (J). lib. bdg. 19.65 (978-0-606-26211-8(3), Turtleback) Turtleback Bks.

Burton, Lynne. Little Ladybird Lost. 2011. (Illus.). 16p. (gr. 1-2). pap. 8.43 (978-1-4567-7960-3(5)) AuthorHouse.

Byers, Letha. Tesa, the Adopted Cow-bird. 2007. pap. 9.00 (978-0-8059-8438-5(0)) Dorrance Publishing Co., Inc.

Bynum, Jeff. Blinky. 2008. 24p. pap. 10.49 (978-1-4389-2331-4(7)) AuthorHouse.

Calfee, Pat. Issy Books Set 3, 10 books. Gee, Isybilla, illus. 2013. 120p. (J). pap. 39.95 (978-1-938406-15-7(X), Compass) Raphel Marketing, Inc.

Candoli, Georgia. Dear Baldy. 2013. 68p. pap. 7.99 (978-1-939288-37-0(1)) Wyatt-MacKenzie Publishing.

Cannon, Janell. Stellaluna. 2017. (ENG., Illus.). 48p. (J). (978-0-544-87435-0(8)) Harcourt.

—Stellaluna. 2007. (ENG., Illus.). 42p. (J). (gr. -1-3). bds. 7.99 (978-0-15-206287-3(4)) Houghton Mifflin Harcourt Publishing Co.

Captain Quake & Boss Bird: 3-in-1 Package. (Sails Literacy Ser.). 24p. (gr. 2-18). 57.00 (978-0-7578-6834-4(7)) Rigby Education.

Captain Quake & Boss Bird: Big Book Only. (Sails Literacy Ser.). 24p. (gr. 2-18). 27.00 (978-0-7578-6822-1(3)) Rigby Education.

Carbone, Courtney. Angry Birds Joke Book. 2016. (Angry Birds Ser.). 144p. (J). (gr. 3-7). pap. 5.99 (978-0-06-246407-1(8), HarperFestival) HarperCollins Pubs.

Casey & the Nest. 2005. (Georgie Giraffe Chapter Ser.). (J). 7.67 (978-1-932570-47-2(0)) Pioneer Valley Bks.

Caso, George R. The Mission. Caso, George R., illus. 2003. (Illus.). 16p. (J). (gr. -1-6). pap. 4.95 (978-0-9719290-1-2(7)) Caso, George R.

Cat in the Hen House: KinderConcepts Individual Title Six-Packs. (Kinderstarters Ser.). 8p. (gr. -1-1). 21.00 (978-0-7635-8728-4(1)) Rigby Education.

Catmull, Katherine. Summer & Bird. 2014. (ENG.). 352p. (J). (gr. 5). pap. 8.99 (978-0-14-242505-3(2), Puffin Books) Penguin Young Readers Group.

Cazet, Denys. Elvis the Rooster & the Magic Words, 4 bks., Set. unabr. ed. 2006. (Readalongs for Beginning Readers Ser.). (J). (gr. -1-3). pap. 31.95 incl. audio compact disk (978-1-59519-693-4(5)); (Illus.). pap. 29.95 incl. audio (978-1-59519-692-7(7)) Live Oak Media.

Cebulski, Megan Elizabeth. The Brave Little Butterfly. 2008. 32p. pap. 24.95 (978-1-60474-739-3(0)) America Star Bks.

Cecelia And Andrew Davis. A Budgie Tale: Rascal Meets Emmit. 2009. 12p. pap. 8.49 (978-1-4389-3304-7(5)) AuthorHouse.

Cerasi, Chris. Angry Birds ICR #2. 2016. (I Can Read Level 2 Ser.). 32p. (J). (gr. -1-3). pap. 3.99 (978-0-06-245334-1(3)) HarperCollins Pubs.

—Angry Birds Junior Novel. 2016. (Angry Birds Ser.). (ENG., Illus.). 144p. (J). (gr. 3-7). pap. 5.99 (978-0-06-245336-5(X), HarperFestival) HarperCollins Pubs.

—The Angry Birds Movie: The Junior Novel. 2016. (J). lib. bdg. 16.00 (978-0-606-38190-1(2)) Turtleback Bks.

Cerasi, Christopher. Angry Birds Guidebook. 2016. (Angry Birds Ser.). 160p. (J). (gr. 3-7). pap. 7.99 (978-0-06-245342-6(4), HarperFestival) HarperCollins Pubs.

—Angry Birds ICR #1. 2016. (I Can Read Level 2 Ser.). 32p. (J). (gr. -1-3). pap. 3.99 (978-0-06-245332-7(7)) HarperCollins Pubs.

—Meet the Angry Birds. 2016. (I Can Read! Level 2 Ser.). (J). lib. bdg. 13.55 (978-0-606-38187-1(2)) Turtleback Bks.

Chambers, Melinda. We Are Whoooo We Are. Spiker, Sue Ann, illus. 2006. 32p. (J). 16.95 (978-0-929915-46-3(1)) Headline Bks., Inc.

Chand, Emlyn. Davey the Detective: A Bird Brain Book. Shaw, Sarah, illus. l.t. ed. 2012. (ENG.). 42p. (gr. k-1). pap. 10.95 (978-1-62253-119-6(1)); 21.95 (978-1-62253-107-3(8)) Evolved Publishing.

—Honey the Hero: A Bird Brain Book. Shaw, Sarah, illus. ed. 2012. (ENG.). 44p. (gr. k-1). (J). 21.95 (978-1-62253-106-6(X)); pap. 10.95 (978-1-62253-118-9(3)) Evolved Publishing.

—Izzy the Inventor: A Bird Brain Book. Giffin, Noelle, illus. l.t. ed. 2013. 7. (ENG.). 56p. (gr. k-3). 21.95 (978-1-62253-123-3(X)); pap. 10.95 (978-1-62253-122-6(1)) Evolved Publishing.

—Larry the Lonely: A Bird Brain Book. Giffin, Noelle, illus. l.t. ed. 2013. 9. (ENG.). 62p. (gr. k-3). pap. 10.95 (978-1-62253-128-8(0)) Evolved Publishing.

—Ricky the Runt: A Bird Brain Book. Giffin, Noelle, illus. l.t. ed. 2013. 8. (ENG.). 52p. (gr. k-3). pap. 10.95 (978-1-62253-125-7(6)) Evolved Publishing.

—Vicky Finds a Valentine: Bird Brain Books. Giffin, Noelle, illus. ed. 2013. (ENG.). 50p. (gr. k-1). pap. 10.95 (978-1-62253-116-5(7)); 21.95 (978-1-62253-117-2(5)) Evolved Publishing.

Chandler, Tony. The Journey. 2013. 242p. pap. (978-1-77115-091-0(2)) Double Dragon ebooks.

Charles, Faustin. The Selfish Crocodile Book of Words. Terry, Michael, illus. 2012. (Selfish Crocodile Ser.). (ENG.). 12p. (J). (gr. -1-k). bds. 10.99 (978-1-4088-1452-9(8), 9781408814529, Bloomsbury USA Childrens) Bloomsbury Publishing USA.

Charvet, Lilian. Princess Dilly & the Kingdom of Pily: Book 1. 2010. 40p. pap. 20.99 (978-1-4490-8330-4(7)) AuthorHouse.

Chast, Roz. Marco Goes to School. Chast, Roz, illus. 2012. (ENG., Illus.). 32p. (J). (gr. -1-3). 16.99 (978-1-4169-8475-7(5), Atheneum Bks. for Young Readers) Simon & Schuster Children's Publishing.

—Too Busy Marco. Chast, Roz, illus. 2010. (ENG., Illus.). 32p. (J). (gr. -1-3). 16.99 (978-1-4169-8474-0(7), Atheneum Bks. for Young Readers) Simon & Schuster Children's Publishing.

Cheetham, Natasha. The Princess of the Sky. 2011. (Illus.). 24p. pap. 14.09 (978-1-4567-7482-0(4)) AuthorHouse.

Childs, Barbara. Sammy & the Cow Bird. 2009. 48p. pap. 21.99 (978-1-4389-8025-6(6)) AuthorHouse.

Chrismer, Melanie. Chachalaca Chiquita, 1 vol. Harrington, David, illus. 2012. (ENG.). 32p. (J). (gr. k-3). 16.99 (978-1-4556-1704-3(0)) Pelican Publishing Co., Inc.

—Phoebe Clappsaddle for Sheriff, 1 vol. Roeder, Virginia M., illus. 2003. (ENG.). 32p. (J). (gr. k-3). 16.99 (978-1-58980-127-1(X)) Pelican Publishing Co., Inc.

Claypoole, Joann. The Gardener's Helpers. 2015. (ENG.). 106p. (J). pap. 14.95 (978-1-63047-532-1(7)) Morgan James Publishing.

Clendenin, Arlene M. & Clendenin, Bernard S. The Adventures of the Yellow Beak Bird & the Flying Cats: Yellow Beak Bird & the Flying Cats. 2013. 48p. pap. 11.99 (978-0-9897662-1-0(7)) Clendenin Fine Art Concepts.

Cofer, Judith Ortiz. If I Could Fly. 2011. (ENG.). 208p. (YA). (gr. 7-12). 24.99 (978-0-374-33517-5(6), 9780374335175, Farrar, Straus & Giroux (BYR)) Farrar, Straus & Giroux.

Cohen, Leah. The Magic Pond: How a Small Flock of Birds Brought Life & Cheer to a Lonely Pond. 2010. 36p. 15.49 (978-1-4520-1082-3(X)) AuthorHouse.

Cohn, Diana. Crane Boy. 2015. (ENG., Illus.). 40p. (J). (gr. 2-5). 17.95 (978-1-941026-16-8(8)) Cinco Puntos Pr.

Collins, Diana Sue. Elfin, the Elf. 2011. 44p. pap. 24.95 (978-1-4560-8493-6(3)) America Star Bks.

Conkling, Neil & Philip, Hilda. A Bird's Way of Singing. Date not set. (J). 12.95 (978-0-8050-4795-0(6), Holt, Henry & Co. Bks. For Young Readers) Holt, Henry & Co.

Conway, Jill Ker, et al. El Flamingo Felipe. Millis, Lokken, illus. 2009. (SPA & ENG.). 32p. (J). (gr. -1-3). pap. 9.95 (978-1-55591-714-2(3)) Fulcrum Publishing.

Cook, Sherry & Johnson, Martin. Underwater Utley, 26. Kuhn, Jesse, illus. l.t. ed. 2006. (Quirkles — Exploring Phonics through Science Ser.: 21). 32p. (J). 7.99 (978-1-933815-20-6(5), Quirkles, The) Creative 3, LLC.

Cosby, Bill. Friends of a Feather: One of Life's Little Fables. Cosby, Erika, illus. 2003. (ENG.). 64p. (gr. k-3). 16.95 (978-0-06-009147-7(9)) HarperCollins Pubs.

Cote, Nancy, illus. Watch the Birdie! 2016. (ENG.). 32p. (J). (gr. -1-k). 16.99 (978-1-63450-202-3(7), Sky Pony Pr.) Skyhorse Publishing Co., Inc.

Cousins, Lucy. Hooray for Birds! 2017. (ENG.). 40p. (J). (-k). 15.99 (978-0-7636-9265-0(4)) Candlewick Pr.

—Peck, Peck, Peck. Cousins, Lucy, illus. 2013. (ENG., Illus.). 32p. (J). (-k). 15.99 (978-0-7636-6621-7(1)) Candlewick Pr.

Coverly, Dave. Night of the Living Shadows. 2016. (Speed Bump & Slingshot Misadventure Ser.). (ENG., Illus.). 128p. (J). 13.99 (978-0-8050-8887-8(3), 9780805088878, Holt, Henry & Co. Bks. For Young Readers) Holt, Henry & Co.

—Night of the Living Worms: A Speed Bump & Slingshot Misadventure. Coverly, Dave, illus. 2015. (Speed Bump & Slingshot Misadventure Ser.). (ENG., Illus.). 128p. (J). (gr. 2-5). 13.99 (978-0-8050-8886-1(5), 9780805088861, Holt, Henry & Co. Bks. For Young Readers) Holt, Henry & Co.

Creech, Sharon. Chasing Redbird. Burckhardt, Marc, illus. 2012. (ENG.). 272p. (J). (gr. 4-18). pap. 6.99 (978-0-06-440696-3(2)) HarperCollins Pubs.

Creevy, Anne. Lets Go Birding, You & Me. 2006. (J). pap. (978-0-9785108-0-0(1)) ABC Bks.

Creighton, Patricia L. Chirpie the Blue Jay: A True Story. 2008. 13p. pap. 24.95 (978-1-60610-291-6(5)) America Star Bks.

Croggon, Alison. The Crow: Book Three of Pellinor. 2017. (Pellinor Ser.). (ENG.). 528p. (J). (gr. 7). pap. 9.99 (978-0-7636-9445-6(2)) Candlewick Pr.

Crow, Kristyn. Hello, Hippo! Goodbye, Bird! Bernatene, Poly, illus. 2016. (ENG.). 32p. (J). (gr. -1-2). 15.99 (978-0-553-50990-8(X), Knopf Bks. for Young Readers) Random Hse. Children's Bks.

Crowne, Alyssa. Green Princess Saves the Day. Alder, Charlotte, illus. 2010. (J). (Perfectly Princess Ser.: 3). (ENG.). 80p. (gr. 2-5). 4.99 (978-0-545-20848-2(3), Scholastic Paperbacks); 71p. (978-0-545-23414-6(X)) Scholastic, Inc.

Cuckoo Clock of Doom. 2003. (J). 84.00 (978-0-590-22756-8(4)) Scholastic, Inc.

Cuddehe, Judy Link. The Heron Chronicles. Cuddehe, Judy Link, illus. 2013. (Illus.). 54p. pap. 13.00 (978-0-9836659-6-0(6)) Found Link.

Cumberland, Dale. Angel Trap. 2012. 166p. (-18). 22.95 (978-1-4759-5601-6(0)); pap. 12.95 (978-1-4759-5599-6(5)) iUniverse, Inc.

Curtis, Jennifer Keats. Osprey Adventure, 1 vol. Ramsey, Marcy Dunn, illus. 2009. (ENG.). 30p. (gr. 3-7). 13.95 (978-0-87033-593-8(6), 9780870335938, Cornell Maritime Pr./Tidewater Pubs.) Schiffer Publishing, Ltd.

Dahl, Roald & Fitt, Matthew. The Eejits. Blake, Quentin, illus. 2006. (ENG.). 96p. (J). (gr. 1-7). pap. 7.99 **(978-1-84502-097-2(9))** Black and White Publishing Ltd. GBR. Dist: Independent Pubs. Group.

Dale, Jay. I Can See It Too!, 1 vol. Gulliver, Amanda, illus. 2012. (Wonder Words Ser.). (ENG.). 32p. (gr. k-2). pap. 5.99 (978-1-4296-8896-3(3), Engage Literacy) Capstone Press of Coughlan Cos.

—Up & Down, 1 vol. Bailey, Martin, illus. 2012. (Engage Literacy Magenta Ser.). (ENG.). 32p. (gr. k-2). pap. 5.99 (978-1-4296-8878-9(5), Engage Literacy) Capstone Press of Coughlan Cos.

Damjan, Mischa. The False Flamingoes. Steadman, Ralph, illus. 32p. (J). (gr. -1-3). 13.95 (978-0-87592-016-0(0)) Scroll Pr., Inc.

Dans, Peter E. Perry's Baltimore Adventure: A Bird's-Eye View of Charm City. Harrell, Kim, illus. 2003. 30p. (J). 11.95 (978-0-87033-540-2(5), Cornell Maritime Pr./Tidewater Pubs.) Schiffer Publishing, Ltd.

Darlene, Cannon. Dollygal, Peacock, & the Serpent. Mathis, Leslie, illus. 2011. 108p. pap. 19.95 (978-1-61286-001-5(X)) Avid Readers Publishing Group.

Davis, Cecelia And Andrew. A Budgie Tale: Emmit Goes to the Vet. 2009. 12p. pap. 8.49 (978-1-4389-3303-0(7)) AuthorHouse.

Davis, Helen J. Good Times with Gregory: Birds: Rescuing a Baby Bird. Davis, Robyn L., illus. 2008. (Good Times with Gregory Ser.). 54p. (J). (gr. -1-4). 12.95 (978-1-935122-10-4(X)) K&B Products.

Day, Kathleen. The Sweet Song of Rainbow Bird. 2012. 32p. pap. 14.75 (978-1-4669-3555-6(3)) Trafford Publishing.

Ddlewis. Adventurers. 2008. 76p. pap. 24.99 (978-1-4343-6769-3(X)) AuthorHouse.

de Brunhoff, Laurent. Babar dans l'Ile aux Oiseaux.Tr. of Babar in the Jungle. (FRE., Illus.). (J). pap. 16.95 (978-2-211-09806-9(1)) Archimede Editions FRA. Dist: Distribooks, Inc.

—Babar dans l'Ile aux Oiseaux. (Babar Ser.).Tr. of Babar in the Jungle. (FRE., Illus.). 29p. (J). (gr. -1-3). 15.95 (978-0-7859-0681-0(9), F2002) French & European Pubns., Inc.

de Mariscal, Blanca Lopez. The Harvest Birds: Los Pajaros de la Cosecha. Flores, Enrique, illus. 2014. (ENG & SPA.). 32p. (J). (gr. 1-18). pap. 9.95 (978-0-89239-169-1(3), Children's Book Press) Lee & Low Bks., Inc.

Decary, Marie. Adam et le Raton Dessinateur. Beshwathy, Steve, illus. 2004. (Premier Roman Ser.). (FRE.). 64p. (J). (gr. 1-4). pap. (978-2-89021-643-3(8)) Diffusion du livre Mirabel (DLM).

—Adam's Tropical Adventure. Beshwaty, Steve, illus. 2005. 54p. (J). lib. bdg. 12.00 (978-1-4242-1202-6(2)) Fitzgerald Bks.

Del Rizzo, Suzanne. My Beautiful Birds. Del Rizzo, Suzane, illus. 2017. (ENG.). 32p. (J). (gr. 1-3). 17.95 (978-1-77278-010-9(3)) Pajama Pr. CAN. Dist: Ingram Publisher Services.

Demi, illus. The Conference of the Birds. 2012. (ENG.). 44p. (J). (gr. -1-3). 19.95 (978-1-937786-02-1(1)) World Wisdom, Inc.

dePaola, Tomie. The Birds of Bethlehem. dePaola, Tomie, illus. 2012. (ENG., Illus.). 40p. (J). (gr. -1-k). 16.99 (978-0-399-25780-3(2), Nancy Paulsen Books) Penguin Young Readers Group.

—Days of the Blackbird: A Tale of Northern Italy. dePaola, Tomie, illus. 2005. (Illus.). (J). 13.65 (978-0-7569-5888-6(1)) Perfection Learning Corp.

DePrisco, Dorothea. Bluebird's Nest. Parry, Jo, illus. 2006. (ENG.). 14p. (gr. -1-k). 5.95 (978-1-58117-504-2(3), Intervisual/Piggy Toes) Bendon, Inc.

deRubertis, Barbara. Nina Nandu's Nervous Noggin. Alley, R. W., illus. 2011. (Animal Antics A to Z Ser.). 32p. (J). pap. 45.32 (978-0-7613-7660-6(7)); (ENG.). lib. bdg. 22.60 (978-1-57565-335-8(4)); (gr. -1-3). pap. 7.95 (978-1-57565-326-6(5)) Kane Press, Inc.

deRubertis, Barbara & DeRubertis, Barbara. Nina Nandu's Nervous Noggin. Alley, R. W., illus. 2012. (Animal Antics A to Z Ser.). 32p. (J). (gr. 2 — 1). cd-rom 7.95 (978-1-57565-407-2(5)) Kane Press, Inc.

Deuchars, Marion. Bob the Artist. 2016. (ENG., Illus.). 32p. (J). (gr. -1-k). 15.95 (978-1-78067-767-5(7)) King, Laurence Publishing GBR. Dist: Hachette Bk. Group.

DeVos, Janie. How High Can You Fly? Rejent, Renee, illus. l.t. ed. 2005. 32p. 16.95 (978-0-9663276-2-5(4)) Red Engine Pr.

Dharma Publishing Staff. The Proud Peacock: A Story about Humility. 3rd ed. 2013. (ENG.). 36p. (gr. -1-7). pap. 8.95 (978-0-89800-494-6(2)) Dharma Publishing.

—Three Wise Birds: A Story about Wisdom & Leadership. 3rd ed. 2013. (ENG.). 36p. (gr. -1-7). pap. 8.95 (978-0-89800-521-9(3)) Dharma Publishing.

—The Value of Friends: A Story about Helping Friends in Need. 2nd ed. 2015. (ENG.). 36p. (gr. -1-7). pap. 8.95 (978-0-89800-493-9(4)) Dharma Publishing.

Dickens, Frank. Fly Away Peter. 2017. (ENG., Illus.). 32p. (J). (gr. k-2). pap. 9.99 **(978-1-84365-321-9(4)**, Pavilion) Pavilion Bks. GBR. Dist: Independent Pubs. Group.

Dickman, Jacqueline Rosett. God's Little Lake: Max & Me, 1 vol. 2009. 48p. pap. 16.95 (978-1-61582-523-3(1)) America Star Bks.

Dickson, Vivian. To Be a Bird. Grandelis, Leiah, illus. 2013. 24p. pap. (978-0-9873438-2-6(3)) Link Spots.

Dilley, Kristi. Squiggy the Squirrel Meets Wallis the Woodpecker. Dilley, Kristi, illus. 2013. (Illus.). 28p. pap. 9.99 (978-1-937165-47-5(7)) Orange Hat Publishing.

Dinardo, Jeff. Bunny & Bird Are Best Friends: Making New Friends. Ho, Jannie, illus. 2014. (Funny Bone Readers: Being a Friend Ser.). 24p. (gr. -1-1). pap. 4.99 (978-1-939656-02-5(8)) Red Chair Pr.

Disney Book Group Staff. Sheriff Callie's Wild West Peck's Trail Mix Mix-Up. Disney Storybook Art Team, illus. 2015. (World of Reading Ser.). (ENG.). 32p. (J). (gr. -1-k). pap. 3.99 (978-1-4847-1566-6(7)) Disney Pr.

Dixon, Tiffany. Everyone Is Special. 2008. 16p. per. 24.95 (978-1-60441-231-4(3)) America Star Bks.

Domm, Kristin Bieber. Atlantic Puffin: Little Brother of the North, 1 vol. Domm, Jeffrey C., illus. 2007. (ENG.). 32p. (J). (gr. -1-2). pap. 8.95 (978-1-55109-518-9(1)) Nimbus Publishing, Ltd. CAN. Dist: Orca Bk. Pubs. USA.

Doss, Jessi. Percy the Uncolorful Peacock, 1 vol. 2010. 18p. 24.95 (978-1-4489-3882-7(1)) PublishAmerica, Inc.

Dubuc, Marianne, creator. The Lion & the Bird. 2014. (ENG., Illus.). 64p. (J). (gr. -1). 17.95 (978-1-59270-151-3(5)) Enchanted Lion Bks., LLC.

Dudley, Blanche R. Siggy's Parade: Helping Kids with Disabilities Find Their Strengths. 2014. (ENG., Illus.). 48p. (J). (gr. -1-2). 9.95 (978-0-88282-469-7(4)) New Horizon Pr. Pubs., Inc.

Duncan, Daniel. South. 2017. (ENG., Illus.). 40p. (J). (gr. k-2). 17.95 (978-1-4197-2299-8(9), Abrams Bks. for Young Readers) Abrams, Inc.

Dunn, Matthew. Day One. 2007. 192p. (YA). per. 15.00 (978-0-9794908-0-4(4)) Onondaga Hill Publishing.

Dunn, Paul. The Why Bird. 2004. (Illus.). 35p. (J). (gr. -1-7). per. 11.95 (978-1-59405-056-5(2), N2Print) New Age World Publishing.

Dunphy, Madeleine. The Peregrine's Journey: A Story of Migration. Kest, Kristin, illus. 2008. (ENG.). 32p. (J). (gr. k-4). per. 9.95 (978-0-9777539-2-5(1)) Web of Life Children's Bks.

Durant, Alan & Lucas, Kath. Bird Flies South. 2005. (Illus.). 32p. (J). lib. bdg. 9.00 (978-1-4242-0888-3(2)) Fitzgerald Bks.

Dureke, Jottn O. Z - the Goodluck Bird. Dureke, Jottn O., tr. 2004. (Illus.). 44p. (YA). pap. 6.95 (978-0-9701144-1-9(9)) Jahs Publishing Group.

Duvall, Deborah L. Rabbit Goes to Kansas. Jacob, Murv, illus. 2007. (ENG.). 32p. (J). (gr. 1-18). 16.95 (978-0-8263-4181-5(0)) Univ. of New Mexico Pr.

Dyan, Penelope. The Christmas Flamingo. Dyan, Penelope, illus. 2013. (Illus.). 34p. pap. 11.95 (978-1-61477-121-0(9)) Bellissima Publishing, LLC.

Dyas, Amy. The Robins of St Lawrence Church. 2009. 128p. pap. 29.96 (978-0-9786567-8-2(4)) Parson Place Pr., LLC.

Eastman, P. D. Are You My Mother? 2015. (Big Bright & Early Board Book Ser.). (ENG., Illus.). 24p. (J). (— 1). bds. 6.99 (978-0-553-49680-2(8), Random Hse. Bks. for Young Readers) Random Hse. Children's Bks.

—Are You My Mother?/¿Eres Tú Mi Mamá? 2016. (ENG & SPA., Illus.). 72p. (J). (gr. 1-4). 16.99 (978-0-553-53990-5(6), Random Hse. Bks. for Young Readers) Random Hse. Children's Bks.

—¿Eres Tú Mi Mamá? (Are You My Mother?) 2016. (Beginner Books(R) Ser.). (ENG & SPA., Illus.). 72p. (J). (gr. 1-4). 9.99 (978-0-553-53989-9(2), Random Hse. Bks. for Young Readers) Random Hse. Children's Bks.

—El Mejor Nido. Mlawer, Teresa, tr. from ENG. 2005.Tr. of Best Nest. (SPA., Illus.). 64p. (J). (gr. k-2). 9.99 (978-1-930332-84-3(X), LC33270) Lectorum Pubns., Inc.

Eaton, Maxwell, III. Birds vs. Bunnies. 2013. (Flying Beaver Brothers Ser.). (ENG., Illus.). 96p. (J). (gr. 1-4). pap. 7.99 (978-0-449-81022-4(4), Knopf Bks. for Young Readers) Random Hse. Children's Bks.

—Birds vs. Bunnies. 2013. (Flying Beaver Brothers Ser.: 4). lib. bdg. 18.40 (978-0-606-32234-8(5), Turtleback) Turtleback Bks.

—Two Dumb Ducks. 2010. (ENG.). 32p. (J). (gr. -1-2). 12.99 (978-0-375-84576-5(3), Knopf Bks. for Young Readers) Random Hse. Children's Bks.

Eggleton, Jill. A Bird Is a Bird. Chambers, Brent, illus. 2003. (Rigby Sails Early Ser.). (ENG.). 16p. (gr. 1-2). pap. 6.95 (978-0-7578-8662-1(0)) Houghton Mifflin Harcourt Publishing Co.

Egmont UK, Egmont. Angry Birds Downloaded. 2015. (ENG., Illus.). 48p. (J). (gr. k). pap. 9.99 (978-1-4052-7712-9(2)) Egmont Bks., Ltd. GBR. Dist: Independent Pubs. Group.

Ehrlich, Esther. Nest. 2016. (ENG.). 336p. (J). (gr. 5). pap. 7.99 (978-0-385-38610-4(9), Yearling) Random Hse. Children's Bks.

Eischen, Michael. The Clever Pheasant. Peterson, Mark, ed. 2005. (Illus.). (J). 16.95 (978-0-9765621-0-8(3)) Small Waters Publishing.

Eliopulos, Nick & Random House Staff. DC Super Friends: Flying High. Wallace, Loston et al, illus. 2008. (Step into Reading Ser.). (ENG.). 32p. (J). (gr. -1-1). pap. 3.99 (978-0-375-85208-4(5), Random Hse. Bks. for Young Readers) Random Hse. Children's Bks.

Ellefson, D. R. Willie Woolly Wiggle Worm. 2011. 20p. pap. 24.95 (978-1-4626-2624-3(6)) America Star Bks.

Elliott, David. And Here's to You! Cecil, Randy, illus. (ENG.). 32p. (J). (gr. -1-2). 2009. pap. 6.99 (978-0-7636-4126-9(X)) 2004. 15.99 (978-0-7636-1427-0(0)) Candlewick Pr.

Ellsworth, Mark R. Boids of a Feather, 1 vol. 2010. 34p. 24.95 (978-1-4489-5142-0(9)) PublishAmerica, Inc.

—Capped for Courage. 2008. 20p. pap. 24.95 (978-1-60474-095-0(7)) America Star Bks.

Emmendorfer, Marianne. The Feather Collection. 2013. 24p. pap. 15.99 (978-1-4797-6699-4(2)) Xlibris Corp.

Empson, Jo. Little Home Bird. Empson, Jo, illus. 2016. (Child's Play Library). (ENG., Illus.). 36p. (J). (978-1-84643-889-9(6)) Child's Play International Ltd.

Ende, Michael. Norberto Nucagorda, Level 5.5. Wittenberg, Stella, illus. 2003. (SPA.). 32p. (J). (gr. 3-5). pap. 8.95 (978-84-204-3719-4(0), AF1328) Santillana USA Publishing Co., Inc.

Engebretson, Monica fall. Lucky: Based on a true Story. 2008. (Illus.). 36p. (J). pap. 15.00 (978-0-615-19395-3(1)) Avian Welfare Coalition, Inc.

Engelbreit, Mary. Queen of Easter. Engelbreit, Mary, illus. 2009. (Ann Estelle Stories Ser.). (ENG., Illus.). 32p. (J). (gr. -1-3). pap. 6.99 (978-0-06-008186-7(4)) HarperCollins Pubs.

Ericson, Nora. Dill & Bizzy: An Odd Duck & a Strange Bird. Ericson, Lisa, illus. 2016. 40p. (J). (gr. -1-3). 17.99 (978-0-06-230452-0(6)) HarperCollins Pubs.

Esbaum, Jill. Tom's Tweet. Stone, Kyle M. & Santat, Dan, illus. 2011. (ENG.). 32p. (J). (gr. -1-2). 16.99 (978-0-375-85171-1(2), Knopf Bks. for Young Readers) Random Hse. Children's Bks.

Falwell, Cathryn. The Nesting Quilt, 1 vol. 2015. (ENG., Illus.). 32p. (gr. -1-3). 16.95 (978-0-88448-418-9(1), 884418) Tilbury Hse. Pubs.

Fan, Nancy Y. Sword Quest. Rioux, Jo-Anne, illus. 2008. (Swordbird Ser.). 176p. (J). (gr. 3-7). 15.99 (978-0-06-124335-6(3)) HarperCollins Pubs.

Fan, Nancy Yi. Sword Mountain. 2012. (Swordbird Ser.: 3). (ENG., Illus.). 336p. (J). (gr. 3-7). 16.99 (978-0-06-165108-3(7)) HarperCollins Pubs.

—Sword Quest. Rioux, Jo-Anne, illus. 2008. (Swordbird Ser.). 288p. (J). (gr. 3-7). lib. bdg. 16.89 (978-0-06-124336-3(1)) HarperCollins Pubs.

—Swordbird. 2008. (J). 54.99 (978-1-60514-800-7(8)) Findaway World, LLC.

—Swordbird. Zug, Mark, illus. 2007. (Swordbird Ser.). (J). (gr. 3-7). 219p. 15.99 (978-0-06-113099-1(0), HarperCollins); 217p. lib. bdg. 16.89 (978-0-06-113100-4(8)) HarperCollins Pubs.

Faye, Charlet. The Chilling Adventures of Marshall McCaw. 2004. (Illus.). 60p. (J). 18.95 (978-0-9655222-1-2(0)) FayeHouse. Pr. International.

Fenske, Jonathan. Woodward & Mctwee. Fenske, Jonathan, illus. 2014. (Penguin Young Readers, Level 2 Ser.). (ENG., Illus.). 32p. (J). (gr. 1-2). pap. 3.99 (978-0-448-47991-0(5), Penguin Young Readers) Penguin Young Readers Group.

Fenstermacher, Mary Wisham. Pablo Visits the Ocean. 2011. 60p. pap. 23.88 (978-1-4634-6035-8(X)) AuthorHouse.

Filmer, Mary, et al. Farmer Frank: Educational Fire Safety, Poetry & Story Colouring Book. 2010. 50p. pap. 9.99 (978-1-60911-721-4(2), Eloquent Bks.) Strategic Book Publishing & Rights Agency (SBPRA).

Finch, Mary & Messing, Debra. The Little Red Hen. Slater, Kate, illus. 2013. (ENG.). 32p. (J). pap. 7.99 (978-1-78285-041-0(4)); (gr. -1-2). 9.99 (978-1-84686-751-4(7)); (gr. -1-2). 16.99 (978-1-84686-575-6(1)) Barefoot Bks., Inc.

Finch, Mary & Slater, Kate. La Gallinita Roja. Slater, Kate, illus. 2013. (SPA., Illus.). 32p. (J). pap. 7.99 (978-1-84686-753-8(3)) Barefoot Bks., Inc.

Fish, Mister, illus. Snerfy Cat Meets Prancy Finch. Fish, Mister, . 2007. 80p. (J). 14.99 (978-0-9794753-0-6(9)) Children's Classic Book Pubs.

Fitzgerald, J. Rupert, the Sturdy Oak Tree: Who thought he was a little better than the other Trees. 2010. 16p. (J). pap. 14.95 (978-1-4327-5734-2(2)) Outskirts Pr., Inc.

Flanagan, Artie & Licari, Peter J. The Birth of Buzzard Baby, 1 vol. 2009. (ENG.). 31p. 24.95 (978-1-60836-706-1(1)) America Star Bks.

Fletcher, Susan. Falcon in the Glass. (ENG., Illus.). (J). (gr. 5-9). 2014. 336p. pap. 9.99 (978-1-4424-2991-8(7)) 2013. 320p. 16.99 (978-1-4424-2990-1(9)) McElderry, Margaret K. Bks. (McElderry, Margaret K. Bks.).

Flock Watch: Individual Title Six-Packs. (Story Steps Ser.). (gr. k-2). 32.00 (978-0-7635-9799-3(6)) Rigby Education.

Flor Ada, Alma & Campoy, F. Isabel. On the Wings of the Condor. Davalos, Felipe et al, illus. (Gateways to the Sun). 48p. (J). (gr. k-6). pap. 13.95 (978-1-58105-964-9(7)) Santillana USA Publishing Co., Inc.

Foley, Greg. Purple Little Bird. Foley, Greg, illus. 2011. (ENG., Illus.). 32p. (J). (gr. -1-2). 14.99 (978-0-06-200828-2(5)) HarperCollins Pubs.

Folgueira, Rodrigo. Bob the Dog. Bernatene, Poly, illus. 2014. (J). (978-1-4351-5774-3(5)) Barnes & Noble, Inc.

Ford, Emily. Ten Little Bluebirds. Julian, Russell, illus. 2016. (ENG.). 22p. (J). (gr. -1-k). bds. 10.99 (978-0-545-79441-1(2), Cartwheel Bks.) Scholastic, Inc.

Ford, Jessie. My Birdie Puzzle Book. 2012. (ENG., Illus.). 8p. (J). (gr. -1-k). 6.95 (978-1-4197-0206-8(8), Abrams Appleseed) Abrams, Inc.

Forward, Valerie. Bird Land. 2012. 24p. pap. 14.00 (978-1-4691-5373-5(4)) Xlibris Corp.

Fourie, Amanda. Daddy Bird's Lousy Night. 2013. 20p. pap. 15.29 (978-1-4669-9145-3(3)) Trafford Publishing.

Franco, Betsy & Franco-Feeney, Betsy. Birdsongs. Jenkins, Steve, illus. 2007. (ENG.). 40p. (J). (gr. -1-3). 17.99 (978-0-689-87777-3(3), McElderry, Margaret K. Bks.) McElderry, Margaret K. Bks.

Freed, Kira. Saving Squirt. Zolotic, Aleksander, illus. 2017. (Text Connections Guided Close Reading Ser.). (J). (gr. 2). (978-1-4900-1834-8(4)) Benchmark Education Co.

Freedman, Deborah. Shy. 2016. (ENG., Illus.). 40p. (J). (-k). 17.99 (978-0-451-47496-4(1), Viking Books for Young Readers) Penguin Young Readers Group.

French, Jackie. Josephine Wants to Dance. Whatley, Bruce, illus. 2008. 32p. (J). pap. (978-0-207-20080-9(7)) HarperCollins Pubs. Australia.

Frith, Nicholas John. Hector & Hummingbird. Frith, Nicholas John, illus. 2016. (ENG., Illus.). 32p. (J). (gr. -1-3). 17.99 (978-0-545-85701-7(5)) Scholastic, Inc.

—Hello, Mr. Dodo! 2017. (ENG.). 32p. (J). (gr. -1-3). 17.99 (978-1-338-08939-4(0)) Scholastic, Inc.

Fuenmayor, Morella & popular, Tradición. Estaba la Pajara Pinta. 2011. (SPA.). 14p. (J). (gr. -1-k). pap. 8.99 (978-980-257-026-3(5)) Ekare, Ediciones VEN. Dist: Lectorum Pubns., Inc.

Fuertes, Gloria. Cuentos de Animales: La Pata Mete la Pata. 2003. (SPA.). 246p. (978-84-305-7806-1(4), SU5196) Susaeta Ediciones, S.A. ESP. Dist: Lectorum Pubns., Inc.

Funk, Lynda. The Snake, the Humming Bird & Me. 2013. 44p. pap. 19.99 (978-1-4685-3329-3(0)) AuthorHouse.

Galvin, Laura Gates. When Will I Fly? 2006. (ENG., Illus.). 28p. (J). (gr. -1-3). pap. 2.99 (978-1-59249-551-1(6)) Soundprints.

Garner, Albert. The Adventures of Dimi. 2013. (ENG.). 48p. (J). 24.95 (978-1-4787-1677-8(0)) Outskirts Pr., Inc.

Gay, Romney. Bonny's Wish. 2011. 36p. pap. 35.95 (978-1-258-06495-2(2)) Literary Licensing, LLC.

George, Jean Craighead. Luck: The Story of a Sandhill Crane. Minor, Wendell, illus. 2006. (Outdoor Adventures Ser.). 32p. (J). (gr. -1-3). (ENG.). 16.99 (978-0-06-008201-7(1), Geringer, Laura Book); 18.89 (978-0-06-008202-4(X)) HarperCollins Pubs.

—Luck: The Story of a Sandhill Crane. Minor, Wendell, illus. 2008. (J). (gr. k-4). 28.95 incl. audio compact disk (978-1-4301-0332-5(9)) Live Oak Media.

Geringswald, Rita T. Benny: The bird who was too lazy to Fly. 2004. (Illus.). 12p. (J). 5.95 (978-0-9797566-0-3(X)) R & D Publishing of Lakeland, Florida.

Geshell, Carmen. Mele da Mynah's Noisy 'Ohana. Pagay, Jeff, illus. 2004. 24p. 10.95 (978-1-57306-225-1(1)) Bess Pr., Inc.

Gidwitz, Adam. The Grimm Conclusion. Santat, Dan, illus. 2014. (ENG.). 384p. (J). (gr. 5). pap. 7.99 (978-0-14-242736-1(5), Puffin Books) Penguin Young Readers Group.

Gifford, Dorinda. Harriet the Ferret, 1 vol. Luevano, Raul, illus. 2009. 20p. pap. 24.95 (978-1-59129-405-4(3)) America Star Bks.

Gingold, Janet. Finch Goes Wild. 2007. 280p. (YA). pap. 14.99 (978-1-59092-365-6(5)) Blue Forge Pr.

Girel, Stephane, illus. A Bird in Winter: A Children's Book Inspired by Pieter Breugel. 2011. (ENG.). 32p. (J). (gr. -1-3). 14.95 (978-3-7913-7080-4(4)) Prestel Verlag GmbH & Co KG. DEU. Dist: Penguin Random Hse. LLC.

Glitterpony, Jessica Noelle. The Warkak & Snoozle. 2013. 42p. pap. 9.87 (978-1-939896-16-2(9)) Levity Pr.

Glover, Emma M. Benjamin Jay Was a Bully. Snider, K. C., illus. 2012. 16p. pap. 9.95 (978-1-61633-327-0(8)) Guardian Angel Publishing, Inc.

Godfrey, Jan. Who Made the Morning? Ayres, Honor, illus. 2008. (ENG.). 28p. (J). (gr. -1-3). 9.99 (978-0-9798247-0-8(2)) New Day Publishing, Inc.

Gogarty, Brian. Shamrock Sean & the Bird's Nest. Burchartz, Roxanne, illus. 2007. (ENG.). 12p. (J). pap. 7.95 (978-0-86278-969-5(9)) O'Brien Pr., Ltd., The IRL. Dist: Dufour Editions, Inc.

Goldberg, Mara J. Issavich's Unruly Nest. 2009. 20p. pap. 12.49 (978-1-4343-7992-4(2)) AuthorHouse.

The Golden Bird. rev. ed. 2006. 152p. 26.95 (978-1-4218-2343-0(8)); pap. 11.95 (978-1-4218-2443-7(4)) 1st World Publishing, Inc. (1st World Library - Literary Society).

Golden Books. Marshall to the Rescue! (Paw Patrol) Golden Books & Jackson, Mike, illus. 2016. (Big Golden Book Ser.). (ENG.). 32p. (J). (gr. -1-2). 9.99 (978-1-101-93847-8(1), Golden Bks.) Random Hse. Children's Bks.

Golden Books & Dwight, Revena. The Together Book. Bradfield, Roger, illus. 2017. (Little Golden Book Ser.). (ENG.). 24p. (J). (-k). 4.99 **(978-1-5247-1978-4(1)**, Golden Bks.) Random Hse. Children's Bks.

Golden, Robert Charles. Pee Wee: The Blackcapped Chickadee. 2013. 36p. pap. 24.95 (978-1-62709-101-5(7)) America Star Bks.

Gorey, Edward. The Osbick Bird. 2012. 32p. (J). 12.95 (978-0-7649-6335-3(X)) Pomegranate Communications, Inc.

Gorin, Leslie. Bertie Wings It! A Brave Bird Learns to Fly. Kearney, Brendan, illus. 2016. (ENG.). 40p. (J). (gr. -1). 14.95 (978-1-4549-1573-7(0)) Sterling Publishing Co., Inc.

Gracia, Amy A. Arby the Singing Cockatoo: Arby Finds His Voice. 2011. 24p. pap. 15.99 (978-1-4568-9723-9(3)) Xlibris Corp.

Grant, Jacob. Little Bird's Bad Word. 2015. (ENG., Illus.). 32p. (J). (gr. -1-2). 16.99 (978-1-250-05149-3(5), 9781250051493) Feiwel & Friends.

Gravett, Emily. The Odd Egg. Gravett, Emily, illus. 2009. (ENG., Illus.). 32p. (J). (gr. -1-3). 16.99 (978-1-4169-6872-6(5), Simon & Schuster Bks. For Young Readers) Simon & Schuster Bks. For Young Readers.

The Great Bird Adventure. 2003. (J). lib. bdg. (978-0-9725485-1-9(3)) Waterfall Ridge.

Green, Poppy. A Surprise Visitor. Bell, Jennifer A., illus. 2016. (Adventures of Sophie Mouse Ser.: 8). (ENG.). 128p. (J). (gr. k-4). pap. 5.99 (978-1-4814-6698-1(4), Little Simon) Little Simon.

Greenslade, David & Rushton, Rhian Wyn. Gloria A'r Berllan Bupur. 2005. (WEL., Illus.). 36p. pap. (978-0-86243-415-1(7)) Y Lolfa.

Grein, Josh. Petunia Bobbin & the Baby Robin: A Christmas Adventure. 2012. 48p. (-18). 28.95 (978-1-4582-0614-5(9)); pap. 20.95 (978-1-4582-0615-2(7)) Author Solutions, Inc. (Abbott Pr.).

Griffiths, Marlene. Crafty Crane of Potpourri Pond. 2004. 40p. pap. 17.00 (978-0-8059-5928-4(9)) Dorrance Publishing Co., Inc.

Grimm, Kristi. Mommy, Tell Me a Story about a Plane, 2nd Edition. Grimm, Dave, illus. 2nd ed. 2013. 36p. pap. 13.99 (978-0-9855699-8-3(0)) Richer Life, LLC.

Grobler, Piet. Little Bird's ABC. Grobler, Piet, illus. 2005. (ENG., Illus.). 52p. (J). (gr. -1-3). 8.95 (978-1-932425-52-9(7), Lemniscaat) Boyds Mills Pr.

Guess, Roberta J. Two Wings, 1 vol. 2010. 16p. pap. 24.95 (978-1-4489-5608-1(0)) PublishAmerica, Inc.

H & T Imaginations Unlimited, Inc. Home Run Derby with Professor Woodpecker. 2009. 12p. pap. 8.49 (978-1-4389-5926-9(5)) AuthorHouse.

—Toy Trains with Professor Woodpecker. 2009. 12p. pap. 8.49 (978-1-4389-5927-6(3)) AuthorHouse.

—Vegetable Gardening with Professor Woodpecker. 2009. 16p. pap. 8.49 (978-1-4389-5402-8(6)) AuthorHouse.

Haas, Irene. Bess & Bella. Haas, Irene, illus. 2006. (ENG., Illus.). 32p. (J). (gr. -1-2). 17.99 (978-1-4169-0013-9(6), McElderry, Margaret K. Bks.) McElderry, Margaret K. Bks.

Hadley Clark, Harriett. Cheep-Cheep! The Little Bird Who Said His Name. 2013. (ENG.). 20.00 (978-1-939710-06-2(5)) Orange Frazer Pr.

Hall, Mike. Chirpi. 2012. 24p. pap. 15.99 (978-1-4691-4955-4(9)) Xlibris Corp.

Hamilton, Matthew. Bobby's Dove. Sosebee, Cheryl, illus. 2005. (J). bds. 9.99 (978-1-4183-0061-6(6)) Christ Inspired, Inc.

Handelsman, Valerie. Birdies' Seaside Gym. Jasmin, Lynn, illus. 2005. (ENG.). 32p. (J). 7.95 (978-0-9748884-2-2(7)) Little Thoughts For Little Ones Publishing, Inc.

Hano, Patricia. Tyler Meets the Moon. 2010. 28p. pap. 11.99 (978-1-60911-189-2(3), Eloquent Bks.) Strategic Book Publishing & Rights Agency (SBPRA).

Hansen, Alli. Huevos Rancheros. 2008. 32p. pap. 24.95 (978-1-60672-993-9(4)) PublishAmerica, Inc.

Hapka, Catherine, pseud. Blu & Friends. 2011. (I Can Read Level 2 Ser.). (ENG.). 32p. (J). (gr. k-3). pap. 3.99 (978-0-06-201487-0(0), HarperFestival) HarperCollins Pubs.

—One Big Blue Family. 2014. (I Can Read! Level 2 Ser.). (J). lib. bdg. 13.55 (978-0-606-35063-1(2), Turtleback) Turtleback Bks.

—Rio 2: Vacation in the Wild. 2014. (I Can Read Level 2 Ser.). (ENG.). 32p. (J). (gr. -1-3). pap. 3.99 (978-0-06-228499-0(1)) HarperCollins Pubs.

—Vacation in the Wild. 2014. (I Can Read! Level 2 Ser.). (J). lib. bdg. 13.55 (978-0-606-35064-8(0), Turtleback) Turtleback Bks.

Harper, Charley. Charley Harper's a Partridge in a Pear Tree. 2014. (ENG., Illus.). 28p. 9.95 (978-0-7649-6851-8(3)) Pomegranate Communications, Inc.

Harper, Jamie. Miss Mingo & the Fire Drill. Harper, Jamie, illus. 2012. (ENG., Illus.). 40p. (J). (gr. -1-3). pap. 6.99 (978-0-7636-6086-4(8)) Candlewick Pr.

—Miss Mingo Weathers the Storm. Harper, Jamie, illus. (ENG., Illus.). 40p. (J). (gr. -1-3). 2017. 6.99 **(978-0-7636-9514-9(9))** 2012. 15.99 (978-0-7636-4931-9(7)) Candlewick Pr.

Harris, Rae Ann & Weintraub, David. Sereena's Secret. Craft, Danna, illus. 2005. (ENG & YID.). 40p. (J). 16.95 (978-1-932687-41-5(6)); pap. 9.95 (978-1-932687-42-2(4)) Simcha Media Group. (Devora Publishing).

Hart, J. Tristan. The Adventures of Friendly & Barnackel: Book 4 Jaybird the BlueJay. 2010. 32p. 12.99 (978-1-4490-8919-1(4)) AuthorHouse.

Hart, Melissa. Avenging the Owl. 2016. (ENG.). 224p. (J). (gr. 5-8). 15.99 (978-1-63450-147-7(0), Sky Pony Pr.) Skyhorse Publishing Co., Inc.

Hart-Plaugher, Teresa. Little Bird & the Wind. Swope, Brenda, illus. 2011. 28p. pap. 24.95 (978-1-4512-9102-5(7)) America Star Bks.

Harvey, Gwendolyn Fowlkes. The Backyard Plum Tree. 2009. (J). pap. (978-1-61623-481-2(4)) Independent Pub.

Hasselbring, Janet. What Do You See, Mrs Night Heron? De Vries, Bruce, illus. 2010. 32p. pap. 12.95 (978-1-936343-03-4(7)) Peppertree Pr., The.

Haugaard, Erik. Prince Boghole. 2013. (ENG., Illus.). 32p. (J). (gr. -1-3). 16.99 (978-1-4814-2167-6(0), Simon & Schuster Bks. For Young Readers) Simon & Schuster Bks. For Young Readers.

Haughton, Chris. Shh! We Have a Plan. Haughton, Chris, illus. (ENG., Illus.). 40p. (J). 2015. (-k). bds. 8.99 (978-0-7636-7977-4(1)) 2014. (gr. -1-2). 16.99 (978-0-7636-7293-5(9)) Candlewick Pr.

Hayes, Arvid. A Little Bird Saves a Little Boy's Life. 2010. 16p. 8.49 (978-1-4389-9255-6(6)) AuthorHouse.

Hayes, Joe. Pajaro Verde. Castro L., Antonio, illus. 2005. (ENG & SPA.). 40p. (J). (gr. 4-6). pap. 8.95 (978-0-938317-90-6(3)) Cinco Puntos Pr.

Hayton, Althea. Two Little Birds. Schlitt, RaRa, illus. 2012. 38p. pap. (978-0-9557808-1-3(0)) Wren Pubns.

Heine, Helme. Ricardo. Heine, Helme, illus. 2003. (la Orilla Del Viento Ser.). (SPA., Illus.). 40p. (J). (gr. -1-7). per. 7.50 (978-968-16-6422-0(1), 152) Fondo de Cultura Economica USA.

Henkes, Kevin. Birds. Dronzek, Laura, illus. 2009. 32p. (J). (gr. -1-k). (ENG.). 17.99 (978-0-06-136304-7(9)); lib. bdg. 18.89 (978-0-06-136305-4(7)) HarperCollins Pubs. (Greenwillow Bks.).

Henry, Judy. Woodland Stories for Our Grandchildren. 2013. 40p. pap. 19.99 (978-1-4669-7752-5(3)) Trafford Publishing.

Heppermann, Christine & Koertge, Ronald. Sadie's Story. Marcero, Deborah, illus. 2015. (Backyard Witch Ser.: 1). (ENG.). 176p. (J). (gr. 3-7). 16.99 (978-0-06-233838-9(2), Greenwillow Bks.) HarperCollins Pubs.

Herman Horatio Hornblower III. 2005. (YA). per. 5.00 (978-1-59872-239-0(5)) Instant Pub.

Herrera, Alberto. Músik: A Delightfully Harmonic Tale of the Origin of Music. 2012. 26p. 25.95 (978-1-4327-8807-0(8)) Outskirts Pr., Inc.

Herrera, Juan Felipe. Calling the Doves. Simmons, Elly, illus. 2014.Tr. of Canto De Las Palomos. (ENG & SPA.). 32p. (J). (gr. 1-18). pap. 9.95 (978-0-89239-166-0(9)) Lee & Low Bks., Inc.

Herrera, Juan Felipe & Cuevas, Ernesto, illus. Featherless. 2013.Tr. of Desplumado. (SPA & ENG.). 32p. (J). pap. 8.95 (978-0-89239-303-9(3)) Lee & Low Bks., Inc.

Hillenbrand, Will. Kite Day: A Bear & Mole Story. Hillenbrand, Will, illus. (ENG., Illus.). 32p. (J). 2013. pap. 6.99 (978-0-8234-2758-1(7)) 2012. 16.95 (978-0-8234-1603-5(8)) Holiday Hse., Inc.

Hillman, Iris H. Back Yard Critters: Things That Go Bump in the Night. 2010. 28p. 16.09 (978-1-4269-4264-8(8)) Trafford Publishing.

Hills, Tad. Drop It, Rocket! 2014. (ENG., Illus.). 32p. (J). (gr. 1-4). 12.99 (978-0-385-37247-3(7), Schwartz & Wade Bks.) Random Hse. Children's Bks.

—How Rocket Learned to Read. Hills, Tad, illus. 2010. (ENG., Illus.). 40p. (J). (gr. -1-2). 17.99 (978-0-375-85899-4(7), Schwartz & Wade Bks.) Random Hse. Children's Bks.

—Rocket Writes a Story. Hills, Tad, illus. 2012. (ENG., Illus.). 40p. (J). (gr. -1-3). 17.99 (978-0-375-87086-6(5), Schwartz & Wade Bks.) Random Hse. Children's Bks.

—Rocket's Learning Box, 2 vols. Hills, Tad, illus. 2012. (ENG., Illus.). 40p. (J). (gr. -1-3). 35.98 (978-0-307-98235-3(1), Schwartz & Wade Bks.) Random Hse. Children's Bks.

Hitchcock, Jan Hoag. Rosie's Flight. 2011. 36p. pap. 24.95 (978-1-4560-8889-7(0)) America Star Bks.

Hodgkinson, Jo. The Talent Show. Hodgkinson, Jo, illus. 2011. (ENG., Illus.). 32p. (J). (gr. -1-3). 16.95 (978-0-7613-7487-9(6)) Lerner Publishing Group.

Hoffman, Judy. The Art of Flying: A Novel. Graegin, Stephanie, illus. 2014. (ENG.). 320p. (J). (gr. 3-7). pap. 7.99 *(978-1-4231-5907-0(1))* Hyperion Bks. for Children.

Hoffpauir, J. R. Wibeau Flies! 2013. 26p. pap. 14.95 *(978-1-62838-118-4(3))* Page Publishing Inc.

Hogan li, Haywood. The Horse, the Dog, & the Bird. 2012. 24p. pap. 16.95 *(978-1-4685-7633-7(X))* AuthorHouse.

Hohl, Richard. The Prairie: A Novelette. 2006. (Illus.). 67p. pap. 12.50 *(978-1-4120-9073-5(3))* Trafford Publishing.

Holub, Joan & Williams, Suzanne. Apollo & the Battle of the Birds. Phillips, Craig, illus. 2014. (Heroes in Training Ser.: 6). (ENG.). 128p. (J). (gr. 1-4). pap. 5.99 *(978-1-4424-8845-8(X),* Aladdin) Simon & Schuster Children's Publishing.

—Apollo & the Battle of the Birds. Phillips, Craig, illus. 2014. (Heroes in Training Ser.: 6). (ENG.). 128p. (J). (gr. 1-4). 16.99 *(978-1-4424-8846-5(8),* Simon & Schuster/Paula Wiseman Bks.) Simon & Schuster/Paula Wiseman Bks.

—Apollo & the Battle of the Birds. 2014. (Heroes in Training Ser.: 6). lib. bdg. 16.00 *(978-0-606-35442-4(5))* Turtleback Bks.

Honsaker, Arthur J. Heart of a Dove: Believe. 2013. 48p. (gr. 2-4). pap. 8.95 *(978-1-4759-7566-6(X))* iUniverse, Inc.

Hooper, Carrie Lynn. Harley & the Hummingbird. 2011. 24p. pap. 11.32 *(978-1-4634-4686-4(1))* AuthorHouse.

Hopkins, Lee Bennett. Mother Goose Around the World. Fehlau, Dagmar et al, illus. 2005. (Lee Bennett Hopkins Mother Goose Ser.). (YA). (gr. -1-1). suppl. ed. 57.00 *(978-0-8215-0494-9(0))* Sadlier, William H. Inc.

Horácek, Petr. Puffin Peter. Horácek, Petr, illus. 2013. (ENG., Illus.). 40p. (J). (gr. -1-2). 16.99 *(978-0-7636-6572-2(X))* Candlewick Pr.

Horstmann, Deborah McFillin. Sylvester the One-Legged Seagull. Buehrle, Jacquelyn, illus. 2012. 28p. 24.95 *(978-1-4560-2308-9(X))* America Star Bks.

Horton, Eleanor. Blue Birds at Willow Bridge. 2011. 24p. (gr. -1). pap. 12.99 *(978-1-4567-3075-8(4))* AuthorHouse.

Howard, Annie Louise. Who's That Voice in the Woods, 1 vol. 2010. 30p. 24.95 *(978-1-4512-2133-6(9))* PublishAmerica, Inc.

Hudson, Phillip. Saying Goodbye, Sam's Love Story. Cook, Jennifer, ed. 2008. (SPA.). 19.95 *(978-0-615-19269-7(6));* 26p. 19.95 *(978-0-615-19154-6(1))* West Coast Learning Development Center.

Hurwitz, Johanna. Ethan Out & about Big Book: Brand New Readers. Floca, Brian, illus. 2010. (Brand New Readers Ser.). (ENG.). 48p. (J). (gr. -1-3). pap. 24.99 *(978-0-7636-4811-4(6))* Candlewick Pr.

Hyman, Jack G. Breakfast with the Birds. 2013. 216p. pap. 15.99 *(978-1-4525-8453-9(2),* Balboa Pr.) Author Solutions, Inc.

I Love Birds. 2004. (Illus.). 26p. (J). lib. bdg. 12.95 *(978-0-9748165-0-0(7))* Jayjil Publishing Co.

Ianieri, Tom. Polar Pals. 2011. 28p. pap. 15.99 *(978-1-4628-5403-5(6))* Xlibris Corp.

Idle, Molly, illus. Flora & the Flamingo. 2013. (ENG.). 44p. (J). (gr. -1-1). 17.99 *(978-1-4521-1006-6(9))* Chronicle Bks. LLC.

Inkpen, Mick. Rollo & Ruff & the Little Fluffy Bird. Inkpen, Mick, illus. 2011. (ENG., Illus.). 32p. (J). (gr. k-2). pap. 9.99 *(978-0-340-98959-3(9))* Hodder & Stoughton GBR. Dist: Hachette Bk. Group.

Ipcar, Dahlov. Bright Barnyard. 2015. (ENG., Illus.). 40p. (J). (gr. -1-5). 17.95 *(978-1-60893-326-6(1))* Down East Bks.

Ishii, Momoko. El Gorrion de la Lengua Cortada. Akaba, Suekichi, illus.Tr. of Tongue-Cut Sparrow. (SPA.). 40p. (J). (gr. 3-18). 14.95 *(978-980-257-073-7(7))* Ekare, Ediciones VEN. Dist: Kane Miller.

Italia, John. The Birds of the Harbor. Caravela, Elena, illus. 2006. (ENG.). 32p. (J). (gr. -1-3). 15.95 *(978-0-9726614-7-8(6))* Shenanigan Bks.

Ives, Bob. The Three Ants & Mother Bird. Deskov, Vladimir, ed. Fairy, Meg, illus. 2004. 40p. (J). *(978-1-920832-06-3(8))* Four Heads Publishing Group Pty, Ltd.

Jack, Lizzie. The Little Loony Tales: Hatched. Bonnell, B. T., illus. 2011. 34p. 19.95 *(978-1-4575-0665-9(3));* pap. 14.95 *(978-1-4575-0520-1(7))* Dog Ear Publishing, LLC.

Jackson, Sarah. Preep of Old Washington Square: A Collection of East Texas Tales. Jenkins, Delores, illus. l.t. ed. 2005. 48p. (J). 16.95 *(978-1-931823-25-8(1))* Halcyon Pr., Ltd.

Jacob, C. W. The Tipperary Bird. 2009. (Illus.). 40p. pap. 18.99 *(978-1-4389-5212-3(0))* AuthorHouse.

Jacques, Brian. Loamhedge. Elliot, David, illus. 2005. (Redwall Ser.). (ENG.). 432p. (J). (gr. 5-5). 8.99 *(978-0-14-240377-8(6),* Firebird) Penguin Young Readers Group.

Jacques, Suzanne. Pee-Wee, 1 vol. 2010. 18p. pap. 24.95 *(978-1-4489-8577-7(3))* PublishAmerica, Inc.

Jaimungal, Richard Neal. The Hungry Bird & the Lonely Fish. 2011. 16p. pap. 11.32 *(978-1-4634-3136-5(8))* AuthorHouse.

James, Ann. Bird & Bear. James, Ann, illus. 2015. (ENG., Illus.). 40p. (J). (gr. -1-2). 16.99 *(978-1-4998-0037-1(1))* Little Bee Books Inc.

James, Shilah & James, Michael. Little Land Adventures - Little Bird. Castles, Heather, illus. 2010. 24p. pap. *(978-1-926635-33-0(7))* Adlibbed, Ltd.

James, Simon. George Flies South. 2011. (ENG., Illus.). 40p. (J). (gr. -1-2). 16.99 *(978-0-7636-5724-6(7))* Candlewick Pr.

Janski, Beverly. A Little Birdie Told Me. 2012. 48p. pap. 14.95 *(978-1-4497-5263-7(2),* WestBow Pr.) Author Solutions, Inc.

Jarkins, Sheila. Adv Marco Flamingo Under Sea. Jarkins, Sheila, illus. 2010. (ENG., Illus.). 32p. (J). (gr. -1-12). pap. 7.95 *(978-1-934960-69-1(1),* Raven Tree Pr.,Csi) Continental Sales, Inc.

—The Adventures of Marco Flamingo in the Jungle. Jarkins, Sheila, illus. 2012. (Illus.). 32p. (J). 1.99 *(978-1-936299-31-7(3),* Raven Tree Pr.) Delta Systems Company, Inc.

—Marco Flamingo Under the Sea. 2009. (Rip Squeak Ser.). (ENG.). 32p. (J). (gr. -1-3). 16.95 *(978-1-934960-68-4(3),* Raven Tree Pr.,Csi) Continental Sales, Inc.

—Marco Flamingo under the Sea/Las Aventuras Submarinas de Marco Flamenco. 2009. (ENG & SPA.). 32p. (J). (gr. -1-3). 16.95 *(978-1-934960-66-0(7),* Raven Tree Pr.,Csi) Continental Sales, Inc.

Jasnoch, Dorothy. Frankie the Bunny: Helping the Birds. Korzeniowski, Samson O., ed. Jasnoch, Dorothy, illus. 2013. (Illus.). 28p. 17.99 *(978-1-937752-20-0(8))* Owl About Bks. Pub., Inc.

—Frankie the Bunny Helping the Birds. Korzeniowski, Samson, ed. Jasnoch, Dorothy, illus. 2012. (ENG., Illus.). 28p. pap. 12.99 *(978-1-937752-05-7(4))* Owl About Bks. Pub., Inc.

Jay, Pamela. Little Jaybird & the Prince of Light. 2008. 52p. pap. 20.49 *(978-1-4389-3055-8(0))* AuthorHouse.

Jazynka, Kitson. Boys Camp: Nate's Story. Orback, Craig, illus. 2015. (ENG.). 144p. (J). (gr. 1-5). pap. 9.95 *(978-1-62914-806-9(7),* Sky Pony Pr.) Skyhorse Publishing Co., Inc.

Jean-Baptiste, Marie V. Goodnight & Seeyoutomorrow. 2013. 28p. pap. 24.95 *(978-1-4626-9551-5(5))* America Star Bks.

Jenkins, Amanda. How the Turtle Cracked its Shell: A Tale from Guatemala. 2006. (J). pap. *(978-1-4108-6171-9(6))* Benchmark Education Co.

Jewell, Sandra. Paula Peacock Discovers She Is Unique. 2005. per. *(978-0-8059-9613-5(3))* Dorrance Publishing Co., Inc.

Jiang, Ji-Li. Lotus & Feather. Downing, Julie, illus. 2016. (ENG.). 40p. (J). (gr. -1-k). 17.99 *(978-1-4231-2754-3(4))* Disney Pr.

Joe, Anna Rose. The Common Snipe. Afcan, Paschal, ed. Afcan, Paschal, tr. Chikoyak, Andrew J., illus. 2004. (J). pap. 7.50 *(978-1-58084-224-2(0))* Lower Kuskokwim Schl. District.

Johnson, Joy. Harry the Woodpecker's Search for a Home. Johnson, Craig, illus. 2013. 28p. (J). pap. 9.95 *(978-0-9785191-7-9(5))* Orange Spot Publishing.

Johnson, Myrna. Let's Take a Hike. 2013. (ENG., Illus.). 32p. (gr. -1-1). pap. 13.95 *(978-1-936205-79-0(3))* Austin, Stephen F. State Univ. Pr.

Jones, Angela. The Bird Lady. Newell, Brian, illus. 2009. 16p. pap. 7.31 *(978-1-4251-8612-8(2))* Trafford Publishing.

Jones, Bryan. Go Hokies Go: An Interactive Book Featuring Virginia Tech University. Bowman, Hootie, illus. 2012. 1. 12p. 19.95 *(978-0-9836211-0-2(1))* Collegiate Kids Bks., LLC.

Jones, Julie Brangers. Can I Fly? 2010. 12p. 9.88 *(978-1-4520-1198-1(2))* AuthorHouse.

Jones, Nicholas. Pandora's Feather. 2017. (ENG., Illus.). 20p. (J). pap. 14.95 ***(978-1-78554-790-4(9),*** de3aac81-0dee-412b-83d2-c5f05b43b521) Austin, Stan AUS. Dist: Bookmasters Distribution.

Jones, Nicky. Toby Fletcher's Fly-Away Tree. 2013. 182p. pap. *(978-1-78299-798-6(9))* FeedARead.com.

Josiah, Iris. Tiny Bird. 2012. (Illus.). 28p. (J). pap. *(978-0-9572728-4-2(7))* Tiny Island Pr.

Joyce, Melanie. Fly, Freddy, Fly. Seal, Julia, illus. 2014. (J). *(978-1-4351-5806-1(7))* Barnes & Noble, Inc.

Jules, Jacqueline. Feathers for Peacock. Cann, Helen, illus. 2016. (ENG.). 28p. (J). (gr. -1-3). 16.95 *(978-1-937786-53-3(6),* Wisdom Tales) World Wisdom, Inc.

Jupin, David Perez, illus. Love. 2013. 20p. pap. 11.95 *(978-1-937504-67-0(0))* Worthy Shorts.

K. B. Kendricks. Travis Taylor & the Dragon Quest. 2010. 344p. 29.95 *(978-1-4502-0261-9(6))* iUniverse, Inc.

Kamon. Hooty & the Magic Power. Krit, Joey, illus. 2011. 36p. pap. 14.39 *(978-1-4634-1042-1(5))* AuthorHouse.

Kann, Victoria. Pinkalicious & the Pink Parakeet. Kann, Victoria, illus. 2015. (I Can Read Level 1 Ser.). (ENG., Illus.). 32p. (J). (gr. -1-3). 16.99 *(978-0-06-224596-0(1))* HarperCollins Pubs.

Kasza, Keiko. A Mother for Choco. 2003. (ENG.). 30p. (J). (gr. -1 — 1). bds. 7.99 *(978-0-399-24191-8(4),* G.P. Putnam's Sons Books for Young Readers) Penguin Young Readers Group.

Kay, Susan. Raspus. VonRecht, illus. 2009. 16p. pap. 8.99 *(978-1-4389-8380-6(8))* AuthorHouse.

Keats, Ezra Jack. Jennie's Hat. Keats, Ezra Jack, illus. 2003. (ENG., Illus.). 40p. (J). (gr. -1-2). 6.99 *(978-0-14-250035-4(6),* Puffin Books) Penguin Young Readers Group.

—Jennie's Hat. 2003. (gr. k-3). 17.20 *(978-0-613-61710-9(X),* Turtleback) Turtleback Bks.

Keithly, Bryan. Timmy Wren. 2009. 24p. pap. 11.49 *(978-1-4389-4094-6(7))* AuthorHouse.

Keller, Holly. Sophie's Window. Keller, Holly, illus. 2005. (Illus.). 32p. (J). 16.89 *(978-0-06-056283-0(8))* HarperCollins Pubs.

Kelso, Mary Jean. Birds in the Flower Basket. Hammond, Julie, illus. 2012. 26p. 19.95 *(978-1-61633-343-0(X))* Guardian Angel Publishing, Inc.

Kelso, Mary Jean & Hammond, Julie. Birds in the Flower Basket. 2012. 26p. pap. 11.95 *(978-1-61633-344-7(8))* Guardian Angel Publishing, Inc.

Kerr, Cora. Love Lessons on Bird Beach. 2010. 88p. pap. 26.50 *(978-1-60860-713-6(5),* Strategic Bk. Publishing) Strategic Book Publishing & Rights Agency (SBPRA).

Kessler, Cristina. Hope Is Here! Castillo, Marcos, illus. 2013. 27p. (J). *(978-1-934370-43-8(6))* Editorial Campana.

Kiki & the Cuckoo: Evaluation Guide. 2006. (J). *(978-1-55942-412-7(5))* Witcher Productions.

Killion, Bette. Little Lek Longtail Learns to Sleep. Vidal, Beatriz, illus. 2016. (ENG.). 28p. (J). (gr. k-3). 17.95 *(978-1-937786-63-2(3),* Wisdom Tales) World Wisdom, Inc.

Kimble, Maggie T. Peep Learns to Sing. 2004. 21p. pap. 24.95 *(978-1-4137-2005-1(6))* PublishAmerica, Inc.

Kimmel, Eric A. Little Red Rosie. Gutiérrez, Mónica, illus. 2016. (J). *(978-1-68115-518-0(4))* Behrman Hse., Inc.

King, Bart. The Drake Equation. 2017. (ENG.). 320p. (J). (gr. 3-7). pap. 7.99 ***(978-1-4847-2554-2(9))*** Hyperion Bks. for Children.

The King's Ring: KinderReaders Individual Title Six-Packs. (Kinderstarters Ser.). 8p. (gr. -1-1). 21.00 *(978-0-7635-8656-0(0))* Rigby Education.

Klco, Gene. Loon Chick's First Flight. Klco, Gene, photos by. 2015. (ENG., Illus.). 36p. (J). (gr. 1-2). pap. 17.95 *(978-1-933272-51-1(1))* Thunder Bay Pr.

Klein, Abby. The King of Show-and-Tell. McKinley, John, illus. 2004. (Ready, Freddy! Ser.: 2). (ENG.). 96p. (J). (gr. -1-3). 5.99 *(978-0-439-55598-2(1),* Blue Sky Pr., The) Scholastic, Inc.

Kleine, Rg. Oiseau. 2008. 32p. pap. 21.99 *(978-1-4257-9245-9(6))* Xlibris Corp.

Kline, Suzy. Horrible Harry Goes Cuckoo. Wummer, Amy, illus. 2011. (Horrible Harry Ser.). (ENG.). 80p. (J). (gr. 2-4). 4.99 *(978-0-14-241876-5(5),* Puffin Books) Penguin Young Readers Group.

Knesek, Marian. Sage & the Peacock. Buehrle, Jackie, illus. 2011. 28p. pap. 24.95 *(978-1-4512-2211-1(4))* America Star Bks.

Knight, Betty. Sailwind the Seabird. Aton, Barbara, illus. 2005. (J). per. 19.95 *(978-1-59858-017-4(5))* Dog Ear Publishing, LLC.

Kohara, Kazuno. Here Comes Jack Frost. Kohara, Kazuno, illus. 2011. (ENG., Illus.). 32p. (J). (gr. -1-1). pap. 7.99 *(978-0-312-60446-2(7),* 9780312604462) Square Fish.

Kohl, T. Michelle. The Magical Adventures of Bailey Boo the Cockatoo: When the Family's Away, the Parrots Will Play! 2012. 24p. pap. 24.95 *(978-1-4626-6215-9(3))* America Star Bks.

Kono, Erin Eitter. Caterina & the Perfect Party. 2013. (ENG., Illus.). 32p. (J). (gr. -1-k). 16.99 *(978-0-8037-3902-4(8),* Dial Bks) Penguin Young Readers Group.

Korth, Melanie. The Hummingbird: Learns Compassion. 2009. 20p. (gr. -1 — 1). 10.49 *(978-1-4490-3774-1(7))* AuthorHouse.

—The Roadrunner: Finds a Friend. 2009. 20p. pap. 10.49 *(978-1-4389-7540-5(6))* AuthorHouse.

—The Songbirds. 2012. 20p. pap. 17.99 *(978-1-4772-3758-8(5))* AuthorHouse.

Kousky, Vern. Blue Songbird. 2017. (ENG., Illus.). 40p. (J). (gr. -1-3). 16.99 *(978-0-7624-6066-3(0),* Running Pr.) Running Pr. Bk. Pubs.

Krauss, Ruth. The Happy Egg. Johnson, Crockett, illus. 2016. 40p. (J). (gr. -1-3). 14.99 *(978-0-06-243031-1(9))* HarperCollins Pubs.

Krebs, Laurie. We're Sailing to Galapagos: A Week in the Pacific. Restelli, Grazia, illus. 2007. (ENG.). 32p. (J). (gr. k-1). pap. 8.99 *(978-1-84686-102-4(0))* Barefoot Bks., Inc.

Kreloff, Elliot. Please Don't Make Me Fly! A Growing-Up Story of Self-Confidence. Kreloff, Elliot, illus. 2017. (Growing Up Ser.). (ENG., Illus.). 32p. (gr. -1-1). lib. bdg. 19.99 ***(978-1-63440-179-1(4));*** 30.65 ***(978-1-63440-183-8(2))*** Red Chair Pr.

Kretzmann, Jane. Eddie & Harry. Ditewig, Diann, illus. 2014. 48p. (J). *(978-0-9846739-3-3(8))* Cornerstone Pr. Chicago.

Krise, Carrie. Even Little Ones Are in God's Care. 2008. 16p. per. 24.95 *(978-1-4241-9902-0(6))* America Star Bks.

Krohn, Kathryn T. Sarah's Most Perfect Day. Sage, Trina, illus. 2007. 24p. (J). 13.99 *(978-1-59879-325-3(X),* Lifevest) Lifevest Publishing, Inc.

Kurrus, Jeff. Have You Seen Mary? 2014. (ENG., Illus.). 44p. (YA). pap. 9.95 *(978-0-9916389-0-1(5))* Forsberg, Michael Photography.

Lachenmeyer, Nathaniel. The Origami Master. Sogabe, Aki, illus. 2008. (ENG.). 32p. (J). (gr. 2-3). 16.99 *(978-0-8075-6134-8(7))* Whitman, Albert & Co.

LaFevers, R. L. Flight of the Phoenix Bk. 1. Murphy, Kelly, illus. 2010. (Nathaniel Fludd, Beastologist Ser.: 1). (ENG.). 144p. (J). (gr. 1-4). pap. 5.99 *(978-0-547-40845-3(5))* Houghton Mifflin Harcourt Publishing Co.

Laing, Amy Wilson. Ginger Helps Spikey. 2011. (Illus.). 28p. pap. 15.99 *(978-1-4568-5912-1(9))* Xlibris Corp.

Lambert, Cheryl A. The Bird That Couldn't Sing. 2012. 24p. pap. 15.99 *(978-1-4797-2327-0(4))* Xlibris Corp.

Laminack, Lester L. Three Hens & a Peacock, 1 vol. Cole, Henry, illus. 2011. (ENG.). 32p. (J). (gr. -1-3). 15.95 *(978-1-56145-564-5(4))* Peachtree Pubs.

Lane, Dakota. The Orpheus Obsession. 2008. (ENG., Illus.). 288p. (YA). (gr. 9). pap. 8.99 *(978-0-06-074175-4(9),* HarperTeen) HarperCollins Pubs.

Lange, Jessica. It's about a Little Bird. 2013. (ENG., Illus.). 40p. (J). (-3). 16.99 *(978-1-4022-8526-4(4),* 9781402285264, Sourcebooks Jabberwocky) Sourcebooks, Inc.

Langton, Jane. The Fledgling. unabr. ed. 2004. 192p. (J). (gr. 4-7). pap. 36.00 incl. audio *(978-0-8072-8779-8(2),* YA265SP, Listening Library) Random Hse. Audio Publishing Group.

Lansky, Bruce. Early Birdy Gets the Worm. Wummer, Amy, illus. 2010. 10p. (J). bds. 6.99 *(978-1-4169-9316-2(9))* Meadowbrook Pr.

Lasky, Kathryn. To Be a King. 2006. (Guardians of Ga'hoole Ser.: 11). (ENG.). 224p. (J). (gr. 3-7). 6.99 *(978-0-439-79570-8(2),* Scholastic Paperbacks) Scholastic, Inc.

Law, Felicia. Florence the Flamingo: A Tale of Pride. Messina, Lilli, illus. 2010. (Animal Fair Values Ser.). (ENG.). 32p. (J). (gr. -1-3). pap. 10.55 *(978-1-60754-907-9(7));* lib. bdg. 22.60 *(978-1-60754-901-7(8))* Windmill Bks.

Lawson, Barbara. An Ugly Black Bird, 1 vol. Lafarge, Kelly, illus. 2009. 35p. pap. 24.95 *(978-1-61546-656-6(8))* America Star Bks.

Leatham, Alan D. Four Cats, Five Monkeys, Absurd Birds & Other Fanciful Stuff. 2006. 108p. pap. 19.95 *(978-1-4241-0692-9(3))* America Star Bks.

Lee, Jonathan. So I Could Fly Free. 2008. (ENG., Illus.). 32p. (J). *(978-1-85345-434-9(6))* Crusade for World Revival.

Lee, Margaret. The Adventures of Sebastian the Helpful Seagull. 2012. (Illus.). 72p. pap. 41.99 *(978-1-4771-0672-3(3))* Xlibris Corp.

Leedy, Nancy. Leah's Pet Bird Beba. 2012. (ENG.). (J). pap. 4.99 *(978-1-4675-2532-9(4))* Independent Pub.

Lehman-Wilzig, Tami. Stork's Landing. Shuttlewood, Anna, illus. 2014. (ENG.). 32p. (J). (gr. -1-2). 17.95 *(978-1-4677-1395-5(3),* Kar-Ben Publishing) Lerner Publishing Group.

Leopold, Nikia Speliakos Clark. Adam's Crayons. Nemett, Barry & Nemett, Laini, illus. 2011. (J). *(978-0-9817519-1-7(1))* Galileo Pr.

Levine, Rhoda. Arthur. Aison, Everett, illus. 2015. (ENG.). 48p. (J). (gr. -1-2). 15.95 *(978-1-59017-935-2(8),* NYR Children's Collection) New York Review of Bks., Inc., The.

Levine, Susan Sachs. Harriett's Homecoming: A High-Flying Tour of Cincinnati. Burchwell, Erin, illus. 2012. (ENG.). 32p. (J). (gr. -1-3). 19.95 *(978-1-933197-97-5(8))* Orange Frazer Pr.

Lewis, Gill. Wild Wings. Onoda, Yuta, illus. (ENG.). 304p. (J). (gr. 3-7). 2012. pap. 7.99 *(978-1-4424-1446-4(4))* 2011. 18.99 *(978-1-4424-1445-7(6))* Simon & Schuster Children's Publishing. (Atheneum Bks. for Young Readers).

Lewis, Judith. Not Like Any Bird I've Ever Heard. 2011. 24p. pap. 24.95 *(978-1-4626-2730-1(7))* America Star Bks.

Lionni, Leo. Inch by Inch. (ENG.). 32p. (J). (gr. -1-2). 2012. bds. 7.99 *(978-0-307-93125-2(0))* 2010. 16.99 *(978-0-375-85764-5(8))* Random Hse. Children's Bks. (Knopf Bks. for Young Readers).

—Inch by Inch. Lionni, Leo, illus. unabr. ed. 2006. (Illus.). (J). (gr. -1-1). 18.95 *(978-0-439-90585-5(0),* WPCD699) Weston Woods Studios, Inc.

—Nicolas, Where Have You Been? 2010. (ENG., Illus.). 32p. (J). (gr. -1-2). pap. 6.99 *(978-0-375-85549-8(1),* Dragonfly Bks.) Random Hse. Children's Bks.

—Tico & the Golden Wings. 2007. (ENG., Illus.). 32p. (J). (gr. -1-2). 16.99 *(978-0-394-81749-1(4),* Knopf Bks. for Young Readers) Random Hse. Children's Bks.

Lister, Tresina. Itty Bitty Birdie. Greengaard, Alex, illus. 2006. 20p. (J). per. 12.95 *(978-0-9791171-0-7(0))* Lister, Tresina.

Little Red Hen. 2005. (J). bds. 3.99 *(978-1-933200-14-9(6))* Family Bks. at Home.

Loftin, Nikki. Nightingale's Nest. (ENG.). (J). (gr. 3-7). 2015. 272p. pap. 8.99 *(978-1-59514-623-6(7))* 2014. 256p. 16.99 *(978-1-59514-546-8(X))* Penguin Young Readers Group. (Razorbill).

Lois, Lowry. Gooney Bird & All Her Charms. Thomas, Middy, illus. 2015. (Gooney Bird Greene Ser.). (ENG.). 160p. (J). (gr. 1-4). pap. 5.99 *(978-0-544-45596-2(7),* HMH Books For Young Readers) Houghton Mifflin Harcourt Publishing Co.

Long, Ethan. Up, Tall & High! Long, Ethan, illus. 2012. (ENG., Illus.). 40p. (J). (gr. -1-2). 15.99 *(978-0-399-25611-0(3),* G.P. Putnam's Sons Books for Young Readers) Penguin Young Readers Group.

Long, Jan. Azule & the White Hummingbird: The Birth of the White Hummingbird. 2014. (ENG., Illus.). 84p. (J). pap. 9.95 *(978-1-63047-171-2(2))* Morgan James Publishing.

Lopez, Maria Lorena. The Bird's Party, Birds in the Tropical Dry Forest. 2009. 28p. pap. 13.00 *(978-1-60860-156-1(0),* Eloquent Bks.) Strategic Book Publishing & Rights Agency (SBPRA).

Lorraine, Nancy. Tatty, the Lonely Monarch. Herron, Dorothy, illus. 2013. 48p. pap. 17.50 *(978-0-9893063-8-6(0))* ProsePress.

Lougheed, Cordelia. Tales of the Magpie. 2008. 36p. pap. 22.95 *(978-1-4327-2032-2(5))* Outskirts Pr., Inc.

Louie, Therese On & Wang, Suling. Raymond's Perfect Present, 1 vol. 2015. (ENG.). 32p. (J). pap. 9.95 *(978-1-62014-229-5(5))* Lee & Low Bks., Inc.

Lucas, David. The Robot & the Bluebird. Lucas, David, illus. 2008. (ENG., Illus.). 32p. (J). (gr. -1-3). 19.99 *(978-0-374-36330-7(7),* 9780374363307, Farrar, Straus & Giroux (BYR)) Farrar, Straus & Giroux.

Lunianski, Stephanie. Luke's Perfect Day. 2003. 48p. (J). pap. 8.95 *(978-0-595-28286-9(5))* iUniverse, Inc.

Luz Uribe, Maria. El Primer Pajaro de Piko-Niko. (SPA.). 32p. (J). 12.95 *(978-84-261-2307-7(4),* JV0593) Juventud, Editorial ESP. Dist: AIMS International Bks., Inc., Lectorum Pubns., Inc.

Macduff, J. R. The Story of a Dewdrop. 2007. (Illus.). 48p. per. *(978-1-4065-2965-4(6))* Dodo Pr.

MacHado, Ana Maria. Pimienta en la Cebecita. (Torre de Papel Ser.). (SPA., Illus.). (J). 7.95 *(978-958-04-5049-8(8),* NR3067) Norma S.A. COL. Dist: Distribuidora Norma, Inc., Lectorum Pubns., Inc.

Mackall, Deborah. Be Still! The Story of a Little Bird & How He Found His Purpose. Mackall, Deborah, illus. 2nd ed. 2008. (ENG., Illus.). 32p. (J). (gr. -1-k). 15.95 *(978-0-9762273-3-5(9))* Dimensions in Media, Inc.

MacKenzie, C. A. The Search for a Golden Eagle. 2013. (Illus.). 48p. pap. 10.95 *(978-0-7552-0712-1(2))* Authors OnLine, Ltd. GBR. Dist: Printondemand-worldwide.com.

Madormo, John V. The Homemade Stuffing Caper, Bk. 1. 2013. (Charlie Collier, Snoop for Hire Ser.: 1). (ENG.). 272p. (J). (gr. 5). pap. 7.99 *(978-0-14-242380-6(7),* Puffin Books) Penguin Young Readers Group.

Mafera, Sandra. Cloud of Dauphin Island. 2009. 28p. pap. 12.49 *(978-1-4389-5159-1(0))* AuthorHouse.

Magden, Loretta. The Treetop Bird Family. Barringer, J. M., illus. 2007. 28p. (J). 15.95 *(978-0-9788771-0-1(1))* Level Green Bks.

Maher, Liam. Golden Daffodils. Movshina, Marina, illus. 2010. 20p. pap. 10.95 *(978-1-61633-073-6(2))* Guardian Angel Publishing, Inc.

Malaspina, Ann. Guinea Fowl & Rabbit Get Justice: An African Folktale. Wendland, Paula, illus. 2013. (Folktales from Around the World Ser.). (ENG.). 24p. (J). (gr. k-3). 28.50 *(978-1-62323-614-4(2),* 206381) Child's World, Inc., The.

Malbrough, Mike. Marigold Bakes a Cake. Malbrough, Mike, illus. 2017. (ENG., Illus.). 40p. (J). (gr. -1-2). 17.99 ***(978-1-5247-3738-2(0),*** Philomel Bks.) Penguin Young Readers Group.

Malnor, Carol & Fuller, Sandy F. The BLUES Go Birding Across America, 1 vol. Schroeder, Louise, illus. 2010. (ENG.). 36p. (J). (gr. k-4). pap. 8.95 *(978-1-58469-125-9(5))* Dawn Pubns.

—The BLUES Go Extreme Birding, 1 vol. Schroeder, Louise, illus. 2011. (ENG.). 36p. (J). (gr. k-4). 16.95 *(978-1-58469-133-4(6));* pap. 8.95 *(978-1-58469-134-1(4))* Dawn Pubns.

Malnor, Carol L. & Fuller, Sandy F. The BLUES Go Birding Across America, 1 vol. Schroeder, Louise, illus. 2010. (ENG.). 36p. (J). (gr. k-4). 16.95 *(978-1-58469-124-2(7))* Dawn Pubns.

—The BLUES Go Birding at Wild America's Shores, 1 vol. Schroeder, Louise, illus. 2010. (ENG.). 36p. (J). 16.95 *(978-1-58469-131-0(X));* pap. 8.95 *(978-1-58469-132-7(8))* Dawn Pubns.

Manley, Curtis. The Crane Girl: A Japanese Folktale. Wang, Lin, illus. 2017. (ENG.). 40p. (J). 18.95 *(978-1-885008-57-2(0))* Lee & Low Bks., Inc.

Mannone, Christine. Flowers for Pudding Street. Carolan, Christine, illus. 2009. (ENG.). 32p. (J). 15.95 *(978-1-934860-02-1(6))* Shenanigan Bks.

Manuel Reeves, Emily. Fiona Flamingo Has Lost Her Pink. 2013. 20p. pap. 10.00 *(978-0-9821506-1-0(X))* Reeves, Emily.

Markarian, Marianne. The Pesky Bird Wasielewski, Margaret M., illus. l.t. ed. 2005. 32p. (J). 16.00 *(978-0-9767377-0-4(1))* Pomegranate Publishing.

Marley, Bob & Marley, Cedella. Every Little Thing: Based on the Song 'Three Little Birds' by Bob Marley.

Brantley-Newton, Vanessa, illus. 2012. (ENG.). 32p. (J). (gr. -1-1). 16.99 *(978-1-4521-0697-7(5))* Chronicle Bks. LLC.

Marlin, Peggy. Wackydoodle. 2009. 20p. pap. 12.49 *(978-1-4389-7573-3(2))* AuthorHouse.

Marmon, Carol. When Mommy Bird Comes to Visit. 2007. 32p. (J). pap. 8.00 *(978-0-8059-7079-1(7))* Dorrance Publishing Co., Inc.

Marmon, Jim. Alexander Barnaby Meadowlark. 2007. 132p. per. 19.95 *(978-1-4241-7662-5(X))* America Star Bks.

Martin, Julie E. Freedom & Love. 2010. 28p. 17.99 *(978-1-4520-0646-8(6))* AuthorHouse.

Marvin, Susan. Birthday Dreamz. 2011. 36p. (gr. -1). pap. 15.99 *(978-1-4567-4173-0(X))* AuthorHouse.

Mason, Janeen. The Gift of the Magpie, 1 vol. Mason, Janeen, illus. 2011. (ENG., Illus.). 32p. (J). (gr. k-3). 16.99 *(978-1-58980-861-4(4))* Pelican Publishing Co., Inc.

Massie, Diane Redfield. The Baby Beebee Bird. Kellogg, Steven, illus. 2003. (ENG.). 32p. (J). (gr. -1-1). pap. 6.99 *(978-0-06-051784-7(0))* HarperCollins Pubs.

Masterson, Hoss. Owl Ball. Alves, Josh, illus. 2017. (Animal All-Stars Ser.). (ENG.). 56p. (gr. 1-3). lib. bdg. 25.32 *(978-1-4965-4309-7(2))* Stone Arch Bks.

Mathieu, Joe, et al. Big Bird's Big Book: Counting Colors Country City Opposites Playing. Mathieu, Joe, illus. 2009. (Sesame Street Ser.). (ENG., Illus.). 14p. (J). (gr. k — 1). bds. 45.00 *(978-0-394-89128-6(7),* Random Hse. Bks. for Young Readers) Random Hse. Children's Bks.

Mayer, Mercer. Little Critter: Just a Baby Bird. Mayer, Mercer, illus. 2016. (My First I Can Read Ser.). (Illus.). 32p. (J). (gr. -1-3). pap. 3.99 *(978-0-06-147821-5(0))* HarperCollins Pubs.

Mazur, Cathy. Stanley Seagull. Gedrich, Colleen, illus. 2011. 32p. (J). 16.95 *(978-0-9837418-1-7(6));* pap. 7.95 *(978-0-9837418-0-0(8))* Tribute Bks.

McBride, Peter & McBride, Judith. Bug & Budgie. 2013. 32p. *(978-1-4602-2343-7(8))* FriesenPress.

McClure, Brian D. The Birds & the Frogs. Plumlee, Buddy, illus. 2009. (Brian D. Mcclure Childrens Book Collection). 37p. (J). (gr. -1-3). 16.95 *(978-1-933426-13-6(6))* Universal Flag Publishing.

McClure, Kim. Edgar the Seagull who was Afraid to Fly. 2009. 34p. pap. 16.70 *(978-0-557-05920-1(8))* Lulu Pr., Inc.

McCorkle, Brent & Parker, Amy. Firebird: He Lived for the Sunsine. Corley, Rob & Vollmer, Chuck, illus. 2014. (ENG.). 32p. (J). (gr. -1-3). 9.99 *(978-1-4336-8467-8(5),* B&H Kids) B&H Publishing Group.

McDonnell, Patrick & Mystery Writers of America Staff. South. 2008. (ENG., Illus.). 48p. (gr. -1-3). 16.99 *(978-0-316-00509-8(6))* Little Brown & Co.

McDowell, Pamela. Ospreys in Danger, 1 vol. Charko, Kasia, illus. 2014. (Orca Echoes Ser.). (ENG.). 64p. (J). (gr. 2-3). pap. 6.95 *(978-1-4598-0283-4(7))* Orca Bk. Pubs. USA.

McGraw, Penny Underwood. Jay's Vacation, 1 vol. 2009. 37p. pap. 24.95 *(978-1-61582-313-0(1))* America Star Bks.

McGreal, Sue. Jimmy Fox's Great Pet Adventure. 2013. 68p. pap. *(978-1-78299-607-1(9))* FeedARead.com.

McHeffey, Adam. Rudy & Claude Splash into Art, 0 vols. 2014. (ENG., Illus.). 32p. (J). (gr. -1-2). 16.99 *(978-1-4778-4777-0(4),* 9781477847770, Amazon Children's Publishing) Amazon Publishing.

McKee, David. Elmer & the Big Bird. McKee, David, illus. 2012. (Andersen Press Picture Bks). (ENG., Illus.). 32p. (J). (gr. -1-3). 16.95 *(978-1-4677-0319-2(2))* Lerner Publishing Group.

McLaren, Meg. Pigeon P. I. 2017. (ENG., Illus.). 40p. (J). (gr. -1-3). 16.99 ***(978-1-328-71561-6(2),*** Clarion Bks.) Houghton Mifflin Harcourt Trade & Reference Pubs.

McPhail, David. Boy, Bird, & Dog. McPhail, David, illus. (I Like to Read(r) Ser.). (ENG., Illus.). 24p. (J). (gr. -1-2). 2012. pap. 6.99 *(978-0-8234-2639-3(4))* 2011. 14.95 *(978-0-8234-2346-0(8))* Holiday Hse., Inc.

—Sick Day. (I Like to Read(r) Ser.). (ENG.). 24p. (J). (gr. -1-3). 2013. pap. 6.99 *(978-0-8234-2910-3(5))* 2012. 14.95 *(978-0-8234-2424-5(3))* Holiday Hse., Inc.

Mcwherter, Barbara. The Wren & the Groundhog. Brandon, Vicky, illus. 2011. 40p. pap. 24.95 *(978-1-4560-5512-7(7))* America Star Bks.

Meade, Holly. If I Never Forever Endeavor. Meade, Holly, illus. 2011. (ENG., Illus.). 32p. (J). (gr. -1-3). 16.99 *(978-0-7636-4071-2(9))* Candlewick Pr.

Meadows, Melissa. What's the Word, Thunderbird? Book A: the Alamo. 2007. (Wishing Well Ser.). (Illus.). 81p. (J). (gr. k-3). per. 4.99 *(978-1-934517-00-0(3))* Firelight Press, Inc.

Meccia, Marc. Wendell Starling: The Story of a Bird Who Was Afraid to Fly. 2012. 24p. pap. 15.99 *(978-1-4797-1778-1(9))* Xlibris Corp.

Meister, Cari. Rio 2 - Off & Flying. 2014. (Rio Ser.). (ENG.). 24p. (J). (gr. -1-3). pap. 3.99 *(978-0-06-228497-6(5),* HarperFestival) HarperCollins Pubs.

—Untamed Talent. 2014. (Rio Ser.). (ENG.). 24p. (J). (gr. -1-3). pap. 3.99 *(978-0-06-228496-9(7),* HarperFestival) HarperCollins Pubs.

Menard, Menard & Menard, Michele. Wood, You Be Real! 2013. 36p. pap. 11.95 *(978-0-9891734-0-7(2))* Four Menards, The.

Meunier, Sylvain. Raffi's Animal Rescue. Cummins, Sarah, tr. from FRE. Eudes-Pascal, Elisabeth, illus. 2007. (ENG.). 64p. (J). (gr. 2-5). *(978-0-88780-742-8(9))* Formac Publishing Co., Ltd.

—Raffi's Animal Rescue, 1 vol. Cummins, Sarah, tr. from FRE. Eudes-Pascal, Elisabeth, illus. 2007. (Formac First Novels Ser.). (ENG.). 64p. (J). (gr. 2-5). 4.95 *(978-0-88780-740-4(2),* 9780887807404) Formac Publishing Co., Ltd. CAN. Dist: Casemate Pubs. & Bk. Distributors, LLC.

Milano, Jacque. Stay-at-Home Hank: The Little Hummingbird That Couldn't Fly. Milano, Jacque, illus. l.t. ed. 2003. (Illus.). 30p. (J). 9.95 *(978-0-9728432-0-1(5))* Milano, Jacque & Assocs.

Milgrim, David. Moo Bird. 2016. (Illus.). 32p. (J). ***(978-1-5182-0400-5(7))*** Scholastic, Inc.

—Moo Bird. Milgrim, David, illus. 2015. (Scholastic Reader, Level 1 Ser.). (ENG., Illus.). 32p. (J). (gr. -1-1). pap. 3.99 *(978-0-545-82502-3(4))* Scholastic, Inc.

Milham, Mary W. Hamilton Lake Bird Population. 2012. 24p. pap. 15.99 *(978-1-4771-1018-8(6))* Xlibris Corp.

Miller, Darcy. Roll. 2017. 224p. (J). (gr. 3-7). 16.99 *(978-0-06-246122-3(2))* HarperCollins Pubs.

Miller, John. Winston & George. Cucco, Giuliano, illus. 2014. (ENG.). 56p. (J). (gr. k-3). 17.95 *(978-1-59270-145-2(0))* Enchanted Lion Bks., LLC.

Miller, Patricia. Tale of Polly Puffin. 2010. 30p. (J). pap. 14.95 *(978-1-4327-5231-6(6))* Outskirts Pr., Inc.

Miller, Toby. The Magic Word. 2011. (Illus.). 24p. pap. 14.09 *(978-1-4567-7793-7(9))* AuthorHouse.

Mitchell, Dawn. A Bird in a Bathing Suit. 2010. 24p. (J). pap. 12.95 *(978-1-4327-5404-4(1))* Outskirts Pr., Inc.

Mitchell, Taylor. Blue Bell. 2012. 28p. pap. 15.99 *(978-1-4797-0292-3(7))* Xlibris Corp.

Mitchell, W. A. Larry & Yuki Go into Business. 2012. 28p. pap. 24.95 *(978-1-4626-9162-3(5))* America Star Bks.

Mitton, Tony & Parker, Ant. Super Submarines. 2014. (Amazing Machines Ser.). (ENG., Illus.). 24p. (J). (gr. -1-k). 4.99 *(978-0-7534-7208-8(2),* 9780753472088, Kingfisher) Roaring Brook Pr.

—Super Submarines. 2014. (Amazing Machines Ser.). (J). lib. bdg. 14.75 *(978-0-606-36133-0(2))* Turtleback Bks.

MJ Illustrations (Group) Staff, contrib. by. Marshall to the Rescue! 2016. (Illus.). (J). ***(978-1-4806-9669-3(2),*** Golden Bks.) Random Hse. Children's Bks.

Mockford, Caroline. What's This? A Seed's Story. Mockford, Caroline, illus. 2007. (ENG., Illus.). 32p. (J). (gr. -1-2). pap. 7.99 *(978-1-84686-071-3(7))* Barefoot Bks., Inc.

Mohler, Marie. Little Bird's Earth Nest. 2008. 32p. 18.95 *(978-1-4357-1711-4(2))* Lulu Pr., Inc.

Molins, Liliana. Bringing Baby Blue Bird Home. 2012. 36p. pap. 24.95 *(978-1-62709-214-2(5))* America Star Bks.

Molloy, Bonnie. Ms Flitter-Flutter. 2009. 24p. pap. 9.00 *(978-1-4269-1587-1(X))* Trafford Publishing.

Moncomble, Gerard & Van den Dries, Sidonie. Half & Half-A Doctor for the Animals. Fortier, Natali & Brenier, Claire, illus. 32p. (J). 2009. 9.95 *(978-1-60115-203-9(5))* 2008. pap. 4.99 *(978-1-60115-204-6(3))* Treasure Bay, Inc.

Montecalvo, Jane. Sammy C-Gull. 2012. 20p. pap. 13.77 *(978-1-4669-5497-7(3))* Trafford Publishing.

Moore, S. D. The Adventures of Pj & Split Pea. Switzer, Bobbi, illus. 2008. 36p. per. 12.95 *(978-1-4327-1288-4(8))* Outskirts Pr., Inc.

Morpurgo, Michael. Colly's Barn. Andrew, Ian, illus. 2nd ed. 2016. (Reading Ladder Ser.). (ENG.). 48p. (J). (gr. k-2). 7.99 *(978-1-4052-8253-6(3))* Egmont Bks., Ltd. GBR. Dist: Independent Pubs. Group.

Moseley, Tabitha. Pearl's Tales a Collection of Children's Stories. 2009. 92p. pap. 17.25 *(978-1-60860-670-2(8),* Strategic Bk. Publishing) Strategic Book Publishing & Rights Agency (SBPRA).

Moster, Jamey S. Fly, Fly Away. 2009. 28p. pap. 13.99 *(978-1-4490-0140-7(8))* AuthorHouse.

Mother Goose & the Children: Take-Home Book. 2005. (Lee Bennett Hopkins Mother Goose Ser.). (YA). (gr. -1-1). 13.50 *(978-0-8215-0561-8(0))* Sadlier, William H. Inc.

Mother Goose Around the World: Take-Home Book. 2005. (Lee Bennett Hopkins Mother Goose Ser.). (YA). (gr. -1-1). 13.50 *(978-0-8215-0564-9(5))* Sadlier, William H. Inc.

Mother Goose Through the Seasons: Take-Home Book. 2005. (Lee Bennett Hopkins Mother Goose Ser.). (YA). (gr. -1-1). 13.50 *(978-0-8215-0563-2(7))* Sadlier, William H. Inc.

Mubiru, Betha. Muzinge the Bird. 2004. (Illus.). 16p. pap. *(978-9970-02-447-6(7))* Fountain Pubs. Ltd. UGA. Dist: Michigan State Univ. Pr.

Muller, Seth. Keepers of the WindClaw Chronicles: The Day of Storms, 3 vols., Vol. 2. Dubay, Tayloe, ed. Whitethorne, Bahe, Jr., illus. 2nd ed. 2010. 224p. (J). pap. 12.95 *(978-1-893354-10-4(5))* Salina Bookshelf Inc.

—Keepers of the WindClaw Chronicles: The Mockingbird's Manual. Tayloe, McConnell Dubay, ed. Whitethorne, Bahe, Jr., illus. 2009. (ENG.). 128p. (J). (gr. 4-7). pap. 12.95 *(978-1-893354-04-3(0))* Salina Bookshelf Inc.

Mulubah, Sr. Denise's Pet Dove. 2009. 36p. pap. 16.99 *(978-1-4389-7536-8(8))* AuthorHouse.

Munroe, Kirk. Flamingo Feather. 2006. 120p. 22.95 *(978-1-59818-510-2(1))* Aegypan.

Murphy, Mary. Utterly Lovely One. 2012. (ENG., Illus.). 32p. (J). (gr. -1-k). 16.99 *(978-0-7636-5267-8(9))* Candlewick Pr.

Murray, Cassie. Olivia, the Olive Bug. 2009. 24p. pap. 15.99 *(978-1-4415-1966-5(1))* Xlibris Corp.

Murray, Lyn. Little Book of Memories. 2011. 100p. pap. 9.99 *(978-1-935105-93-0(0))* Avid Readers Publishing Group.

My Big Book of Beginner Books about Me. 2011. (Beginner Books(R) Ser.). (ENG., Illus.). 208p. (J). (gr. -1-2). 16.99 *(978-0-307-93183-2(8),* Random Hse. Bks. for Young Readers) Random Hse. Children's Bks.

Myrl, Melanie. Why Some Birds Don't Eat Worms. 2011. 16p. 8.99 *(978-1-4490-4092-5(6))* AuthorHouse.

Na, Il Sung. Bird, Balloon, Bear. 2017. (ENG.). 32p. (J). (-k). 17.99 *(978-0-399-55155-0(7),* Knopf Bks. for Young Readers) Random Hse. Children's Bks.

Nancy Elizabeth Bateman. Jason the Brat. 2009. 12p. pap. 8.96 *(978-1-4389-6914-5(7))* AuthorHouse.

Napoli, Donna Jo. Albert. LaMarche, Jim, illus. 2005. (ENG.). 32p. (J). (gr. -1-3). reprint ed. pap. 7.99 *(978-0-15-205249-2(6))* Houghton Mifflin Harcourt Publishing Co.

Nash, Scott. The High-Skies Adventures of Blue Jay the Pirate. Nash, Scott, illus. 2012. (ENG., Illus.). 368p. (J). (gr. 4-7). 17.99 *(978-0-7636-3264-9(3))* Candlewick Pr.

Negroni, Jay. Emerald's Flight, 1 vol. 2008. (ENG.). 29p. pap. 24.95 *(978-1-60672-863-5(6))* America Star Bks.

Neilson, G. G. Beogall's Choice - How a Boy & a Bird Rescue Nature. 2012. 320p. *(978-1-77097-517-0(9));* pap. *(978-1-77097-518-7(7))* FriesenPress.

Nelson, Marilyn. Ostrich & Lark. Artists of the Kuru Art Project in Botswana, San, illus. 2012. (ENG.). 32p. (J). (gr. k-4). 16.95 *(978-1-59078-702-1(1))* Boyds Mills Pr.

Nesbit, E. The Phoenix & the Carpet. 2007. 236p. per. 12.95 *(978-1-4218-3944-8(X),* 1st World Library - Literary Society) 1st World Publishing, Inc.

New York Hall of Science Staff. Charlie & Kiwi: An Evolutionary Adventure. Reynolds, Peter H. & Fable Vision Studios Staff, illus. 2011. (ENG.). 48p. (J). (gr. -1-3). 16.99 *(978-1-4424-2112-7(6),* Atheneum Bks. for Young Readers) Simon & Schuster Children's Publishing.

Nicholai, Rachel, et al. Bird Adventures. Nicholai, Rachel et al, illus. 2006. (Adventure Story Collection Ser.). 28p. (J). (gr. 2-6). pap. 10.00 *(978-1-58084-246-4(1))* Lower Kuskokwim Schl. District.

Niddrie, June. Fly Ladybird, Fly. 2010. 32p. pap. 16.10 *(978-0-557-31862-9(9))* Lulu Pr., Inc.

Niedda, Jeshica. A Bird Name Baby Blue. 2012. 28p. pap. 19.99 *(978-1-4772-7067-7(1))* AuthorHouse.

Nnodim, Paul. The Tortoise & the Birds. Pierotti, Yvonne, illus. 32p. (J). 2012. 24.95 *(978-1-937622-09-1(6))* 2010. 14.95 *(978-0-9825842-9-3(6))* Africana Homestead Legacy Pubs., Inc. (Nefu Bks.).

Nordling, Lee. BirdCatDog. Bosch, Meritxell, illus. 2014. (J). lib. bdg. 25.32 *(978-1-4677-4522-2(7),* Graphic Universe™) Lerner Publishing Group.

—BirdCatDog. 2014. (ENG.). 32p. pap. 6.95 *(978-1-4677-4523-9(5))* Lerner Publishing Group.

O'Connor, George. If I Had a Raptor. O'Connor, George, illus. 2014. (ENG., Illus.). 32p. (J). (gr. -1-2). 15.99 *(978-0-7636-6012-3(4))* Candlewick Pr.

O'Connor, Jane. Super Extraordinaire! Glasser, Robin Preiss, illus. 2009. (Fancy Nancy Ser.). (ENG.). 32p. (J). (gr. -1-2). 12.99 *(978-0-06-168486-9(4))* HarperCollins Pubs.

Odegaard, Sarah. Don Hummer Visits Nana Jane. 2009. 32p. pap. 12.99 *(978-1-4389-6816-2(7))* AuthorHouse.

O'Dell, Kathleen. The Aviary. 2012. (ENG.). 352p. (J). (gr. 3-7). 7.99 *(978-0-375-85226-8(3),* Yearling) Random Hse. Children's Bks.

Oduwole, Ben. The Flying Tortoise. 2009. 182p. pap. 43.50 *(978-1-60693-611-5(5),* Eloquent Bks.) Strategic Book Publishing & Rights Agency (SBPRA).

Oeslchlager, Vanita. Big Blue. Blackwood, Kristin, illus. 2008. (ENG.). 32p. (J). (gr. -1-3). 17.95 *(978-0-9800162-5-3(8))* VanitaBooks.

O'Hagan, William. Anything Else but Me. 2008. 36p. pap. 24.95 *(978-1-60563-701-3(7))* America Star Bks.

O'Leary, Sara & Opal, Paola. Zingy. Morstad, Julie, illus. 2013. (Simply Small Ser.: 10). (ENG.). 24p. (J). (gr. k — 1). bds. 7.95 *(978-1-897476-75-8(2))* Simply Read Bks. CAN. Dist: Ingram Publisher Services.

Oliver, Narelle. The Best Beak in Boonaroo Bay. Oliver, Narelle, illus. (Illus.). 48p. (YA). pap. *(978-0-85091-671-3(2),* Lothian Children's Bks.) Hachette Australia.

O'Loughlin, Erin. The Bluebird Dance. 2013. 44p. pap. 20.45 *(978-1-4908-0670-9(9),* WestBow Pr.) Author Solutions, Inc.

Olsen, La Verne C. If A Peacock Follows You Home: Children's Stories by Grandma. 2007. 52p. pap. 15.99 *(978-1-4257-3087-1(6))* Xlibris Corp.

O'Mara, Robert J. Friends Are Special, 1 vol. 2009. 26p. pap. 24.95 *(978-1-60749-087-6(0))* America Star Bks.

Orbeck, R. My Beautiful Feathers. 2012. 28p. pap. 15.99 *(978-1-4691-8502-6(4))* Xlibris Corp.

Ormondroyd, Edward. David & the Phoenix. 2009. 76p. (gr. 4-7). pap. 4.75 *(978-1-60459-691-5(0))* Wilder Pubns., Corp.

Orrell, Brenda M. Eliza Blackbird. 2010. 256p. pap. 14.49 *(978-1-4520-8359-9(2))* AuthorHouse.

Osborne, M. D. The Rescue of Mr. Goldsmith. l.t. ed. 2005. (Illus.). 40p. (J). 12.95 *(978-0-9762852-1-2(5))* Wooden Shoe Pr.

Oswald, Pete & Thompson, Justin K. Mingo the Flamingo. Oswald, Pete & Thompson, Justin K., illus. 2017. (Illus.). 40p. (J). (gr. -1-3). 17.99 *(978-0-06-239198-8(4))* HarperCollins Pubs.

Ottman, Margaret B. The Lonely Loon. 2012. (ENG.). pap. *(978-1-4675-1800-0(X))* Independent Pub.

Owen, Linda. Robin's Song, 1 vol. 2009. (ENG.). 28p. (J). pap. *(978-1-85345-495-0(8))* Crusade for World Revival.

Page, P. K. Uirapurú: Based on a Brazilian Legend. Bridgeman, Kristi, illus. 2010. (ENG.). 32p. (J). 19.95 *(978-0-88982-264-1(6))* Oolichan Bks. CAN. Dist: Univ. of Toronto Pr.

Palatini, Margie. Gorgonzola: A Very Stinkysaurus. Bowers, Tim, illus. 2008. (ENG.). 32p. (J). (gr. -1-2). 17.99 *(978-0-06-073897-6(9),* Tegen, Katherine Bks) HarperCollins Pubs.

La Paloma y la Hormiga. (SPA.). pap. 5.95 incl. audio compact disk *(978-88-8148-801-8(9))* EMC/Paradigm Publishing.

Pantelides, Sherry. It's Blue Like You! A Story about Loyalty. Perez, Debi, illus. 2007. 32p. (J). 12.99 *(978-0-9771076-1-2(2))* Lacey Productions.

Parish, Herman. Amelia Bedelia Is for the Birds. Avril, Lynne, illus. 2015. (I Can Read Level 1 Ser.). (ENG.). 32p. (J). (gr. -1-3). pap. 3.99 *(978-0-06-233424-4(7),* Greenwillow Bks.) HarperCollins Pubs.

Parker, Amy. A Night Night Prayer, 1 vol. Pedler, Caroline, illus. 2014. (Night Night Ser.). (ENG.). 20p. (J). bds. 9.99 *(978-1-4003-2431-6(9))* Nelson, Thomas Inc.

Parker, Jeff. Super Angry Birds. 2016. lib. bdg. 20.85 *(978-0-606-38024-9(8))* Turtleback Bks.

Patton, Jack. The Poison Frog Assault (Battle Bugs #3) 2015. (Battle Bugs Ser.: 3). (ENG.). 128p. (J). (gr. 2-5). pap. 4.99 *(978-0-545-70744-2(7),* Scholastic Paperbacks) Scholastic, Inc.

Pau Pau. Bird Bandit, 1 vol. 2010. 56p. pap. 16.95 *(978-1-4489-3991-6(7))* America Star Bks.

Payne, Jackson. The Stork & the Birthday Stocking. Williams, Jean, illus. 2009. 24p. pap. 12.00 *(978-1-4389-8146-8(5))* AuthorHouse.

Pearson, Luke, illus. Hilda & the Bird Parade. 2013. (Hildafolk Ser.). (ENG.). 44p. (J). (gr. k). 24.00 *(978-1-909263-06-2(0))* Flying Eye Bks. GBR. Dist: Consortium Bk. Sales & Distribution.

Pedlar, David Stewart. The Emu Who Knew He Could Fly! 2013. 32p. pap. 16.95 *(978-1-4525-7612-1(2),* Balboa Pr.) Author Solutions, Inc.

Penina, M. Dove Builds a Nest: For Young Readers. Kaufman, Yaki, illus. 2012. 22p. 19.75 net. *(978-1-60046-091-3(7))* Yofi Bk. Publishing, Inc.

Perelman, Helen. Bubble Gum Rescue. Waters, Erica-Jane, illus. 2012. (Candy Fairies Ser.: 8). (ENG.). 128p. (J). (gr. 2-5). pap. 5.99 *(978-1-4424-2217-9(3),* Aladdin) Simon & Schuster Children's Publishing.

Perrine, David L. Birdie School Days: The First Day of School. Perry, Margie, illus. 2005. (J). pap. 15.00 *(978-0-8059-6699-2(4))* Dorrance Publishing Co., Inc.

Perry, Andrea. The Bicklebys' Birdbath. Angaramo, Roberta, illus. 2010. (ENG.). 40p. (J). (gr. -1-1). 16.99 *(978-1-4169-0624-7(X),* Atheneum Bks. for Young Readers) Simon & Schuster Children's Publishing.

Peterson, Shelley. Sundancer. Drake, Marybeth, illus. rev. ed. 2007. (ENG.). 264p. (YA). (gr. 7-12). pap. 7.95 *(978-1-55263-842-2(1))* Leaf Storm Pr.

Petreman, Gwen. A Wish for Haidan. 2011. 24p. (gr. -1). 12.56 *(978-1-4269-5739-0(4))* Trafford Publishing.

Pfeiffer, Kathleen. Spartacus Sprout, Please Watch Out! 2011. 32p. pap. 15.99 *(978-1-257-50163-2(1))* Lulu Pr., Inc.

Pham, LeUyen. A Piece of Cake. Pham, LeUyen, illus. 2014. (ENG., Illus.). 40p. (J). (gr. -1-3). 16.99 *(978-0-06-199264-3(X))* HarperCollins Pubs.

Phillips, Dixie & Snider, K. C. Stilts the Stork. 2011. 20p. pap. 10.95 *(978-1-61633-143-6(7))* Guardian Angel Publishing, Inc.

Phillips, Helen. Here Where the Sunbeams Are Green. (ENG.). 304p. (J). (gr. 5). 2013. 7.99 *(978-0-307-93145-0(5),* Yearling) 2012. E-Book *(978-0-307-97487-7(1),* Delacorte Bks. for Young Readers) Random Hse. Children's Bks.

Philpot, Graham, illus. The Emperor & the Nightingale. 2007. (First Reading Level 4 Ser.). 48p. (J). (gr. -1-3). 8.99 *(978-0-7945-1614-7(9),* Usborne) EDC Publishing.

Piantedosi, John J. The Cat That Purred. Maglio-Macullar, Andrea, illus. 2014. (ENG.). (J). pap. 11.95 *(978-1-56548-540-2(8))* New City Press of the Focolare.

Pickering, Lynne. James & the Naughty Seagull. Pickering, Lynne, illus. 2013. (Illus.). 32p. pap. 13.50 *(978-1-62857-333-6(3),* Strategic Bk. Publishing) Strategic Book Publishing & Rights Agency (SBPRA).

Pierce, Christa. Did You Know That I Love You? Pierce, Christa, illus. 2014. (ENG., Illus.). 32p. (J). (gr. -1-3). 17.99 *(978-0-06-229744-0(9))* HarperCollins Pubs.

Pinkwater, Daniel M. Beautiful Yetta: The Yiddish Chicken. Pinkwater, Jill, illus. 2010. (ENG.). 32p. (J). (gr. -1-2). 17.99 *(978-0-312-55824-6(4),* 9780312558246) Feiwel & Friends.

Pixton, Amy, creator. Things with Wings. 2006. (J). *(978-0-9779631-2-6(8))* TyBook.

Plotz, John. Time & the Tapestry. Saroff, Phyllis, illus. 2014. (ENG.). 192p. (YA). (gr. 4-6). 18.50 *(978-1-59373-145-8(0))* Bunker Hill Publishing, Inc.

Polak, Monique. Finding Elmo, 1 vol. 2007. (Orca Currents Ser.). (ENG.). (J). (gr. 5-9). 112p. lib. bdg. 14.95 *(978-1-55143-688-3(4));* 128p. per. 9.95 *(978-1-55143-686-9(8))* Orca Bk. Pubs. USA.

Polette, Nancy. Flying with Mother Goose. 2003. pap. 7.95 *(978-1-931334-19-8(6),* CLC0285) Pieces of Learning.

Popsicle, Patty. Crack-a-doodle Horse Tales: A Tale about Pulling Hair. 2011. 24p. (gr. -1). pap. 12.99 *(978-1-4520-6096-5(7))* AuthorHouse.

Portis, Antoinette. Froodle. Portis, Antoinette, illus. 2014. (ENG., Illus.). 32p. (J). (gr. -1-3). 16.99 *(978-1-59643-922-1(X),* 9781596439221) Roaring Brook Pr.

Powell, Kristen. Flappy & the Big Red Sky. 2006. 17p. (J). 12.00 *(978-1-4116-7756-2(0))* Lulu Pr., Inc.

Prochovnic, Dawn Babb. The Nest Where I Like to Rest: Sign Language for Animals, 1 vol. 2009. (Story Time with Signs & Rhymes Ser.). (ENG., Illus.). 32p. (gr. -1-3). 28.50 *(978-1-60270-670-5(0),* Looking Glass Library) ABDO Publishing Co.

Proffitt, Kim. Coco the Little Red Bird: Massy Returns. 2013. 20p. pap. 24.95 *(978-1-4626-9164-7(1))* America Star Bks.

Publications International Ltd. Staff, ed. Mother Goose. Goodell, Jon & Borgo, Deborah Colvin, illus. 2010. 10p. (J). bds. 12.98 *(978-0-7853-7395-7(0))* Phoenix International Publications, Inc.

—Mother Goose Read a Long Treasury. 2005. 40p. (J). 12.98 *(978-1-4127-3531-5(9),* 7248300) Publications International, Ltd.

Pugliano-Martin, Carol. Ready for Fall! 2006. (Early Explorers Ser.). (J). pap. *(978-1-4108-6103-0(1))* Benchmark Education Co.

—See You in Spring! 2006. (Early Explorers Ser.). (J). pap. *(978-1-4108-6105-4(8))* Benchmark Education Co.

P.Young, Linda. The Adventures of Anna & Andy Hummingbird: Stories 6-10. 2011. 44p. pap. 21.99 *(978-1-4568-8849-7(8))* Xlibris Corp.

Quinn, Spencer, pseud. ARF - A Bowser & Birdie Novel. 2017. (ENG.). 304p. (J). (gr. 3-7). pap. 7.99 ***(978-0-545-64335-1(X),*** Scholastic Pr.) Scholastic, Inc.

Rabe, Tish. Wings & Paws & Fins & Claws. Ruiz, Aristides, illus. 2010. (Deluxe Coloring Book Ser.). (ENG.). 96p. (J). (gr. -1-2). pap. 3.99 *(978-0-375-85928-1(4),* Golden Bks.) Random Hse. Children's Bks.

Rabley, Stephen & Pearson Education Staff. Flying Home. 2nd ed. 2008. (ENG.). 20p. pap. 11.99 *(978-1-4058-6946-1(1))* Pearson Education.

Ramakar, Ram. Little Crow Feather. 2006. (ENG.). 48p. per. 16.95 *(978-1-4241-5134-9(1))* America Star Bks.

Ramoutar, Tagore. I Love Birds! 2012. 36p. pap. *(978-1-907837-44-9(2))* Longshot Ventures, Ltd.

Rana, Tariq. Five Baby Blackbirds: Learn How to Fly. 2011. (Illus.). 24p. (gr. 1-2). pap. 11.74 *(978-1-4567-8131-6(6))* AuthorHouse.

Randolph, Robert. Ben the Flying Cat, 1 vol. Sappington, Ray, illus. 2009. 30p. pap. 24.95 *(978-1-60749-088-3(9))* America Star Bks.

Rankin, Debbie. Butch the Blue Jay. 2010. 36p. pap. 20.00 *(978-1-4490-7809-6(5))* AuthorHouse.

Reasoner, Charles. I'm Just a Bird. 2008. *(978-1-84666-153-2(6))* Top That! Publishing PLC.

—I'm Just a Bird. Reasoner, Charles, illus. 2007. (I'm Just Book Ser.). (Illus.). 12p. (J). (gr. -1). bds. *(978-1-84666-289-8(3),* Tide Mill Pr.) Top That! Publishing PLC.

Reavis, Laura. An Angel to Watch Over. 2008. (ENG., Illus.). 32p. (J). pap. 9.99 *(978-0-9800091-0-1(3))* Stop N Go Fitness.

Reynolds, Aaron. Nerdy Birdy. Davies, Matt, illus. (Nerdy Birdy Ser.). (ENG.). 40p. (J). 2017. 17.99 *(978-1-62672-128-9(9),* 9781626721289) 2015. 16.99 *(978-1-62672-127-2(0),* 9781626721272) Roaring Brook Pr.

Riamliw, J. S. To Fly Out. 2012. 28p. pap. 19.99 *(978-1-4772-9502-1(X))* AuthorHouse.

Rigby Education Staff. Animals Say... (Sails Literacy Ser.). (Illus.). 16p. (gr. 2-3). 27.00 *(978-0-7635-9943-0(3),* 699433C99) Rigby Education.

—Feathered Friends. (Sails Literacy Ser.). (Illus.). 16p. (gr. 1-2). 27.00 *(978-0-7635-9905-8(0),* 699050C99) Rigby Education.

—The Happy House. (Sails Literacy Ser.). (Illus.). 16p. (gr. 1-2). 27.00 (978-0-7635-9908-9(5), 699085C99) Rigby Education.

Rimes, Rebecca. Hippie Hippopotamus. 2011. 24p. (gr. 10-12). pap. 12.74 (978-1-4634-0855-8(2)) AuthorHouse.

Rinaldi, Ann. The Ever-After Bird. 2010. (ENG.). 240p. (J). (gr. 5-7). pap. 8.99 (978-0-547-25854-6(2)) Houghton Mifflin Harcourt Publishing Co.

Roaring Fork Conservancy (Basalt, Colo.) Staff, contrib. by. Dee Dee the Fryingpan River Dipper. 2017. (J). **(978-1-883551-90-2(0)**, Maple Corners Press) Attic Studio Publishing Hse.

Robaard, Jedda. If My Mom Were a Bird. 2015. (ENG., Illus.). 40p. (J). (gr. -1-2). 14.99 (978-1-4998-0021-0(5)) Little Bee Books Inc.

—The Little Bird Who Lost His Song. 2015. (ENG., Illus.). 10p. (J). (gr. -1-k). 7.99 (978-1-4998-0093-7(2)) Little Bee Books Inc.

Roberts, Christa. Rio 2. 2014. (Ramona Ser.). (ENG.). 144p. (J). (gr. 3-7). pap. 5.99 (978-0-06-228504-1(1), HarperFestival) HarperCollins Pubs.

Roberts, Paula Carol. Good Morning Billy. 2011. 32p. pap. 13.95 (978-1-4497-1214-3(2), WestBow Pr.) Author Solutions, Inc.

Robinson, Elda L. Nathanial's Family. 2004. 32p. pap. 18.00 (978-1-4140-4943-4(9)) AuthorHouse.

Rodriguez, AJ. Cycle of Life. 2009. 20p. pap. 12.49 (978-1-4389-5528-5(6)) AuthorHouse.

Rodriguez, Lisa G. The Brave Little Hummingbird. 2012. 24p. 24.95 (978-1-63000-012-7(4)); pap. 24.95 (978-1-4626-9899-8(9)) America Star Bks.

Rohr, Rebecca. Flocks: A Buster Bird Adventure. 2011. pap. 8.95 (978-0-7414-6735-5(6)) Infinity Publishing.

Rooney, Anne. Muffin. Julian, Sean, illus. 2009. (Go! Readers Ser.). 48p. (J). (gr. 2-5). pap. 12.85 (978-1-60754-270-4(6)); lib. bdg. 29.25 (978-1-60754-269-8(2)) Windmill Bks.

Rosasco, Jose Luis. La Mariposa Negra y Otros Cuentos. 2003. (SPA.). pap. (978-956-13-1661-4(7), AB12831) Bello, Andres CHL. Dist: Lectorum Pubns., Inc.

Rosen, Michael J. The Forever Flowers. Danowski, Sonja, illus. 2014. (ENG.). 32p. (J). (gr. 1-3). 18.99 (978-1-56846-273-8(5), Creative Editions) Creative Co., The.

Rosno, Connie. This Is My Lucky Day. 2011. 16p. pap. 9.49 (978-1-4567-5534-8(X)) AuthorHouse.

Ross, Katharine. Twinkle, Twinkle, Little Bug. Cooke, Tom & Brannon, Tom, illus. 2014. (Step into Reading Ser.). (ENG.). 32p. (J). (gr. -1-1). pap. 3.99 (978-0-679-87666-3(9), Random Hse. Bks. for Young Readers) Random Hse. Children's Bks.

Rottgen, Barbara. A Friend Like You. Julian, Sean, illus. 2016. (ENG.). 32p. (J). (gr. -1-2). 16.99 (978-1-68010-031-0(9)) Tiger Tales.

Roy, Alene Adele. The Legend of Dragonfly Pond: Volume One. 2008. 60p. pap. 24.99 (978-1-4343-6824-9(6)) AuthorHouse.

Rubin, Adam. Those Darn Squirrels! Salmieri, Daniel, illus. (ENG.). 32p. (J). (gr. -1-3). 2011. pap. 7.99 (978-0-547-57681-7(1)) 2008. 17.99 (978-0-547-00703-8(5)) Houghton Mifflin Harcourt Publishing Co.

—Those Darn Squirrels & the Cat Next Door. Salmieri, Daniel, illus. 2011. (ENG.). 32p. (J). (gr. -1-3). 17.99 (978-0-547-42922-9(3)) Houghton Mifflin Harcourt Publishing Co.

—Those Darn Squirrels Fly South. Salmieri, Daniel, illus. 2012. (ENG.). 32p. (J). (gr. -1-3). 17.99 (978-0-547-67823-8(1)) Houghton Mifflin Harcourt Publishing Co.

Rutland, J. I Love You No Matter What: A Prince Chirpio Story, 1 vol. 2013. (ENG.). 32p. (J). 9.99 (978-1-4003-2195-7(6)) Nelson, Thomas Inc.

Rylant, Cynthia. Annie & Snowball & the Cozy Nest. Stevenson, Suçie, illus. (Annie & Snowball Ser.: 5). (ENG.). 40p. (J). (gr. k-2). 2010. pap. 3.99 (978-1-4169-3947-4(4)) 2009. 16.99 (978-1-4169-3943-6(1)) Simon Spotlight. (Simon Spotlight).

—Annie & Snowball & the Pink Surprise. Stevenson, Suçie, illus. 2010. (Annie & Snowball Ser.: 4). (ENG.). 40p. (J). (gr. k-2). pap. 3.99 (978-1-4169-1462-4(5), Simon Spotlight) Simon Spotlight.

Saltzberg, Barney. Redbird: Friends Come in Different Sizes. 2015. (ENG., Illus.). 22p. (J). bds. 5.95 (978-0-7611-8190-3(3)) Workman Publishing Co., Inc.

—Redbird: Colors, Colors, Everywhere! 2015. (ENG., Illus.). 22p. (J). bds. 5.95 (978-0-7611-8185-9(7)) Workman Publishing Co., Inc.

Salzmann, Mary Elizabeth. Humming Hummingbird, 1 vol. 2007. (Critter Chronicles Ser.). (ENG., Illus.). 24p. (J). (gr. k-3). lib. bdg. 24.21 (978-1-59928-442-2(1), SandCastle) ABDO Publishing Co.

Sams, Carl R. & Stoick, Jean. Tea with Lady Sapphire. 2011. 48p. 19.95 (978-0-9827625-1-6(8)) Sams, II, Carl R. Photography, Inc.

Sams II, Carl R. & Stoick, Jean, photos by. When Snowflakes Fall. 2009. (ENG., Illus.). 14p. bds. 7.95 (978-0-9770108-9-9(9)) Sams, II, Carl R. Photography, Inc.

Samuels, Linda Nissen. Cuando Elly Fue a la Reserva Ecologica. Samuels, Linda Nissen, illus. 2013. (Illus.). 40p. pap. (978-0-9511751-8-7(1)) Samuels, Linda Y.

—Elly e il Parco Degli Animali. Samuels, Linda Nissen, illus. 2013. (Illus.). 40p. pap. (978-0-9511751-7-0(3)) Samuels, Linda Y.

—When Elly Went to the Animal Park... Samuels, Linda Nissen, illus. 2013. (Illus.). 40p. pap. (978-0-9511751-5-6(7)) Samuels, Linda Y.

Samworth, Kate. Aviary Wonders Inc. Spring Catalog & Instruction Manual. 2014. (ENG., Illus.). 32p. (J). (gr. 5-7). 17.99 (978-0-547-97899-4(5)) Houghton Mifflin Harcourt Publishing Co.

Sandall, Ellie. Copycat Bear! Sandall, Ellie, illus. 2013. (ENG., Illus.). 32p. (J). (gr. -1-k). 14.99 (978-1-58925-120-5(2)) Tiger Tales.

Sands, Maria. Sanjee & Her Delightful Hats. 2008. 20p. pap. 24.95 (978-1-60563-700-6(9)) America Star Bks.

Sanner, Jennifer Jackson, ed. The Three Little Jayhawks. Pearson, Larry Leroy, illus. 2006. 40p. (J). per. 20.00 (978-0-9742918-1-9(1)) Kansas Alumni Assoc.

Sanrio Company, LTD. Hello Kitty Presents the Storybook Collection: Thumbelina. 2017. (Hello Kitty Storybook Ser.). (ENG., Illus.). 32p. (J). (gr. -1-k). pap. 6.95 (978-1-4197-2489-3(4), Abrams Appleseed) Abrams, Inc.

Santilli, Shirley. Trouble in Treeville. Santilli Wolfinger, Lorrie, illus. 2013. 42p. 19.99 (978-0-9910962-0-6(7)) Aperture Pr., LLC.

Santillo, LuAnn. Bluejay. Santillo, LuAnn, ed. 2003. (Half-Pint Kids Readers Ser.). (Illus.). 7p. (J). (gr. -1-1). pap. 1.00 (978-1-59256-110-0(1)) Half-Pint Kids, Inc.

—Flap. Santillo, LuAnn, ed. 2003. (Half-Pint Kids Readers Ser.). (Illus.). 7p. (J). (gr. -1-1). pap. 1.00 (978-1-59256-096-7(2)) Half-Pint Kids, Inc.

Santos, Penelope. Bird & Rabbit. 2015. (Rosen REAL Readers: STEM & STEAM Collection). (ENG.). 8p. pap. 5.46 (978-1-4994-9493-8(9), Rosen Classroom) Rosen Publishing Group, Inc., The.

Santucci, Barbara. Loon Summer. Shine, Andrea, illus. 2004. 32p. (J). (gr. k-3). 16.00 (978-0-8028-5182-6(7)) Eerdmans, William B. Publishing Co.

Sargent, Dave. Bogart Blue Jay: Be Thoughtful, 19, vol. 4. Lenoir, Jane, illus. 2003. (Feather Tales Ser.: 4). 42p. (J). pap. (978-1-56763-726-7(4)) Ozark Publishing.

Sargent, Dave & Sargent, David, Jr. Hummer Hummingbird: Being Small Is Okay, 19. Lenoir, Jane, illus. 2003. (Feather Tales Ser.: 10). (J). 10. 42p. pap. 6.95 (978-1-56763-738-0(8)) Vol. 10. 2nd ed. 24p. lib. bdg. 20.95 (978-1-56763-737-3(X)) Ozark Publishing.

—Kitty Hawk: Stealing, 20 vols., Vol. 11. Lenoir, Jane, illus. 2nd ed. 2003. (Feather Tales Ser.: 11). 42p. (J). lib. bdg. 20.95 (978-1-56763-739-7(6)) Ozark Publishing.

—Pinkie Flamingo: Leaving Home, 20 vols., Vol. 15. Lenoir, Jane, illus. 2nd ed. 2003. (Feather Tales Ser.: 15). 42p. (J). lib. bdg. 20.95 (978-1-56763-747-2(7)) Ozark Publishing.

—Storky Stork: Be Trustworthy, 20 vols., Vol. 18. Lenoir, Jane, illus. 2nd ed. 2003. (Feather Tales Ser.: 18). 42p. (J). lib. bdg. 20.95 (978-1-56763-753-3(1)) Ozark Publishing.

—Tin Wren: Be Nice, 20 vols., Vol. 19. Lenoir, Jane, illus. 2nd ed. 2003. (Feather Tales Ser.: No. 19). 42p. (J). lib. bdg. 20.95 (978-1-56763-755-7(8)) Ozark Publishing.

—Tom Turkey: Don't Bully, 20 vols., Vol. 20. Lenoir, Jane, illus. 2nd ed. 2003. (Feather Tales Ser.: 20). 42p. (J). lib. bdg. 20.95 (978-1-56763-757-1(4)) Ozark Publishing.

Sargent, Dave & Sargent, David M. Bogart Blue Jay: Be Thoughtful, 20 vols., Vol. 4. Lenoir, Jane, illus. 2nd ed. 2003. (Feather Tales Ser.: 3). 42p. (J). lib. bdg. 20.95 (978-1-56763-725-0(6)) Ozark Publishing.

—Buzz Buzzard: Obey the Rules, 19 vols., Vol. 5. Lenoir, Jane, illus. 2003. (Feather Tales Ser.: 5). 42p. (J). pap. 10.95 (978-1-56763-728-1(0)); 2nd ed. lib. bdg. 20.95 (978-1-56763-727-4(2)) Ozark Publishing.

Sargent, Dave & Sargent, David M., Jr. Speedy Roadrunner: Helping Others, 20 vols., Vol. 17. Lenoir, Jane, illus. 2nd ed. 2003. (Feather Tales Ser.: 17). 42p. (J). lib. bdg. 20.95 (978-1-56763-751-9(5)) Ozark Publishing.

Sattler, Jennifer. Sylvie. 2013. (ENG., Illus.). 40p. (J). (gr. -1-2). 7.99 (978-0-449-81072-9(0), Dragonfly Bks.) Random Hse. Children's Bks.

Sattler, Jennifer Gordon. Sylvie. 2009. (ENG., Illus.). 40p. (J). (gr. -1-2). 15.99 (978-0-375-85708-9(7), Random Hse. Bks. for Young Readers) Random Hse. Children's Bks.

Saxby, Claire. Emu. Byrne, Graham, illus. 2015. (ENG.). 32p. (J). (gr. k-3). 16.99 (978-0-7636-7479-3(6)) Candlewick Pr.

Say, Allen. The Boy in the Garden. 2010. (ENG., Illus.). 32p. (J). (gr. -1-3). 17.99 (978-0-547-21410-8(3)) Houghton Mifflin Harcourt Publishing Co.

Scanlon, Liz Garton. Noodle & Lou. Howard, Arthur, illus. 2011. (ENG.). 32p. (J). (gr. -1-1). 15.99 (978-1-4424-0288-1(1), Beach Lane Bks.) Beach Lane Bks.

Scarry, Richard. Lowly Worm Meets the Early Bird. 2013. (Step into Reading Ser.). (ENG., Illus.). 32p. (J). (gr. -1-1). pap. 3.99 (978-0-679-88920-5(5), Random Hse. Bks. for Young Readers) Random Hse. Children's Bks.

Schatzer, Jeffrey L. The Bird in Santa's Beard: How a Christmas Legend Was Forever Changed. 2004. (Illus.). 34p. (J). (978-0-9749554-0-7(X)) Big Belly Bks.

Scheunemann, Pam. Peacock Fan, 1 vol. Chawla, Neena, illus. 2007. (Critter Chronicles Ser.). (ENG.). 24p. (J). (gr. k-3). lib. bdg. 24.21 (978-1-59928-460-6(X), SandCastle) ABDO Publishing Co.

Schulz, Charles. Where Is Woodstock?, 1 vol. 2013. (Peanuts Picture Bks.). (ENG.). 24p. (J). (gr. -1-4). lib. bdg. 24.21 (978-1-61479-033-4(7)) ABDO Publishing Co.

Schurch, Vicky. A Little Songbird Named Annie. 2009. 32p. pap. 14.49 (978-1-4490-2134-4(4)) AuthorHouse.

Schwartz, Ellen. Abby's Birds, 1 vol. Shefrin, Sima Elizabeth, illus. 2007. (ENG.). 32p. (J). (gr. 1-4). 16.95 (978-1-896580-86-9(6)) Tradewind Bks. CAN. Dist: Orca Bk. Pubs. USA.

Schwarz, Evelyn. The Hummingbird Garden. Quinn, Kitty, illus. 2012. (ENG.). 34p. (J). pap. 16.95 (978-1-4327-9815-4(4)) Outskirts Pr., Inc.

The Seagull, 6 Packs. (Story Steps Ser.). (gr. k-2). 20.00 (978-0-7635-9584-5(5)) Rigby Education.

Secuban, Andy S. The Papagayo: Magical Bird of Paradise. 2008. 24p. pap. 12.99 (978-1-4389-0660-7(9)) AuthorHouse.

Sepulveda, Luis. Gaviota y del Gato. 9th ed. 2003. (SPA.). 144p. (978-968-7723-11-2(4), 6020) Tusquests Editores Mexico, S.A. de C.V.

Seuss, Dr. Happy Birthday, Baby! Gerardi, Jan, illus. 2009. (Dr. Seuss Nursery Collection). (ENG.). 12p. (J). (— 1). 11.99 (978-0-375-84621-2(2), Random Hse. Bks. for Young Readers) Random Hse. Children's Bks.

Shackleford, Maudie. An Upside-Down Tale. 2013. 114p. pap. 12.50 (978-1-62212-156-4(2), Strategic Bk. Publishing) Strategic Book Publishing & Rights Agency (SBPRA).

Shah, Indries. The Farmer's Wife/la Esposa Del Granjero. Santiago, Rose Mary, illus. 2003. (SPA & ENG.). (J). 6.95 (978-1-883536-34-3(0), FAWI3, Hoopoe Bks.) I S H K.

Sharp, Stephanie. The Bird That Couldn't. 2008. 44p. per. 24.95 (978-1-4241-8250-3(6)) America Star Bks.

Shats, Marina. Nature Knows (Paperback) 2010. 24p. 21.50 (978-0-557-32587-0(0)) Lulu Pr., Inc.

Sheehan, Peter. Willy Wagtail grows Up. 2010. 32p. pap. 19.99 (978-1-4461-3281-4(1)) Lulu Pr., Inc.

Sheffield, Marilyn. Fizza the Flamingo. Al-Fakhri, Patricia, illus. 2003. 3p. pap. 7.95 (978-1-900988-63-6(1)) Interlink Publishing Group, Inc.

Shelley Ann Boutcher-Caldwell. The Naughty Little Birdie & the Surprise Cake. 2009. 40p. pap. 16.99 (978-1-4389-4896-6(4)) AuthorHouse.

Sheneman, Drew. Nope. 2017. (ENG., Illus.). 40p. (J). (-k). 17.99 (978-1-101-99731-4(1), Viking Books for Young Readers) Penguin Young Readers Group.

Shepard, C. Lori & the Sky of Colors. 2008. 28p. pap. 24.95 (978-1-4241-9094-2(0)) America Star Bks.

Shepperson, Jacqueline. Martins of the Everglades. 2007. (ENG.). 152p. per. 24.95 (978-1-4241-5446-3(4)) America Star Bks.

Sherrell, Deborah. Baby Lauren & Theodore,hardcover. 2007. (Illus.). (J). bds. 17.95 (978-0-9779643-5-2(3)) Healing Tree Arts.

Shi, Charleston. The Quest of the Phoenix: Book Two, Storm of the Kraken. 2010. 180p. pap. 14.95 (978-1-60844-352-9(3)) Dog Ear Publishing, LLC.

Shireen, Nadia. Yeti & the Bird. Shireen, Nadia, illus. 2015. (ENG., Illus.). 32p. (J). (gr. -1-3). 17.99 (978-1-4814-0389-4(3), Atheneum Bks. for Young Readers) Simon & Schuster Children's Publishing.

Silkman, Anne. Country Songbird. Doghouse Press Inc. Staff, ed. (Togetherness Ser.). (Illus.). 200p. (YA). pap. (978-1-885531-34-6(6)) Mess Hall Writers.

Silly Seagull. 2004. (J). per. (978-1-57657-372-3(9)) Paradise Pr., Inc.

Simmons, Jane. Que Valiente Eres, Daisy! (SPA.). 216p. (J). (978-84-488-0950-8(5)) Beascoa, Ediciones S.A. ESP. Dist: Lectorum Pubns., Inc.

Simon, Annette. Mocking Birdies. 2005. (ENG., Illus.). 32p. (J). (gr. -1-3). 16.95 (978-1-894965-29-3(9)) Simply Read Bks. CAN. Dist: Ingram Publisher Services.

Simonson, Lona Marie. Grandma Lucy Feeds the Birds, 1 vol. Herges, Connie, illus. 2009. 44p. pap. 24.95 (978-1-60836-732-0(0)) America Star Bks.

Simpson, Patricia Ann. The Frog, the Birds & the Trout. 2007. (J). per. 24.95 (978-0-9795460-3-7(6)) Creative Bk. Pubs.

Singer, Isaac Bashevis. The Parakeet Named Dreidel. Berkson, Suzanne Raphael, illus. 2015. (J). pap. (978-0-374-30096-8(8)); (ENG.). 32p. 17.99 (978-0-374-30094-4(1), 9780374300944, Farrar, Straus & Giroux (BYR)) Farrar, Straus & Giroux.

Sioux Rose. Cassandra's Tale: Invitation to the Circle. 2010. 200p. pap. 16.95 (978-1-4401-9510-5(2)) iUniverse, Inc.

Sisk, Liza. Clay Birds of Jesus. 2007. 28p. pap. 10.95 (978-1-59526-897-6(9), Llumina Christian Bks.) Aeon Publishing Inc.

Skofield, James. Bear & Bird. Thermes, Jennifer, illus. 2014. (ENG.). 40p. (J). (gr. 1-3). 15.99 (978-1-58536-835-8(0), 203012) Sleeping Bear Pr.

Slack, Michael. Shorty & Clem. Slack, Michael, illus. 2017. (Illus.). 40p. (J). (gr. -1-3). 17.99 (978-0-06-242158-6(1)) HarperCollins Pubs.

Slater, Barbara B. When Wishes Come True. 2009. 165p. (J). 19.95 (978-1-4327-2220-3(4)) Outskirts Pr., Inc.

Sly Fox & the Little Red Hen. 2005. (J). bds. 3.99 (978-1-933200-11-8(1)) Family Bks. at Home.

Smith, Bill O. Chickadees At Night. Murphy, Charles R., illus. 2012. 32p. (978-0-615-56972-7(2)) Smith, Bill O.

Smith, Brooke. Mimi & Maty to the Rescue! Book 3: C. C. the Parakeet Flies the Coop! Arnold, Alli, illus. 2014. (ENG.). 96p. (J). (gr. k-4). 14.95 (978-1-62914-620-1(X), Sky Pony Pr.) Skyhorse Publishing Co., Inc.

Smith, Bruce L. Song of Life. l.t. ed. 2006. (Illus.). 32p. (J). lib. bdg. (978-1-934190-08-1(X)) Ocean Front Bk. Publishing, Inc.

Smith, Duane. Heritage Revealed Series, 3. (J). (gr. 2-9). pap. 13.95 (978-1-886218-00-0(5)) Azimuth Pr.

Smith, Gloria. Annie Elf & Bo Bo Robin. 2012. 24p. 24.95 (978-1-62709-650-8(7)) America Star Bks.

Smith, Ivy. Sully's New Home. 2011. (Illus.). 28p. (J). 19.95 (978-0-9635757-5-3(9)); pap. 11.95 (978-0-9635757-6-0(7)) Red Tail Publishing.

Smith, Michelle. Duck in the Hedge: Jeremy & the Big Pond. 2011. (Illus.). 36p. pap. 15.66 (978-1-4567-8818-6(3)) AuthorHouse.

Smucker, Anna. Outside the Window. Schuett, Stacey, illus. 2005. 32p. (J). reprint ed. per. 7.95 (978-1-891852-40-4(X)) Quarrier Pr.

Snead, Anna. The Bird That Sang the Prettiest Song. 2012. (ENG.). (J). pap. (978-1-4675-3952-4(X)) Independent Pub.

Snicket, Lemony, pseud. 13 Words. Kalman, Maira, illus. (ENG.). 40p. (J). (gr. -1-3). 2014. pap. 6.99 (978-0-06-166467-0(7)) 2010. 16.99 (978-0-06-166465-6(0)) HarperCollins Pubs.

Snider, Brandon T. Dangerous Rescue. 2016. (Transformers 8x8 Ser.). (J). lib. bdg. 13.55 (978-0-606-37515-3(5)) Turtleback Bks.

Spencer, Alison Hill. Bird Color, 1 vol. 2013. (Adventure Boardbook Ser.). (ENG.). 22p. (J). (gr. -1-k). bds. 6.95 (978-1-59193-428-8(1)) Adventure Pubns.

—Bird Count, 1 vol. 2013. (Adventure Boardbook Ser.). (ENG.). 24p. (J). (gr. -1-k). bds. 6.95 (978-1-59193-427-1(3)) Adventure Pubns.

Spink, Matt. Some Birds. 2016. (ENG., Illus.). 32p. (J). (gr. -1-k). 15.95 (978-1-4197-2070-3(8), Abrams Appleseed) Abrams, Inc.

Spremulli, Pam. Letter Birds. 2010. (ENG., Illus.). 40p. (J). (gr. k-4). pap. 14.00 (978-1-935557-56-2(4)) PublishingWorks.

Sprouse, Jackie. Orry & Izzy's Perfect Worm. 2010. 32p. pap. 15.95 (978-0-557-39078-6(8)) Lulu Pr., Inc.

St. Julian, Ska. The Basket of Seeds. Cameron, Eugenia, illus. 2013. 122p. pap. 10.99 (978-0-9899182-0-6(3)) Chris Six Group, The.

St. Pierre, Stephanie. What the Sea Saw, 1 vol. Doyle, Beverly, illus. 2006. (ENG.). 48p. (J). (gr. k-3). 16.95 (978-1-56145-359-7(5)) Peachtree Pubs.

Staake, Bob. Bluebird. Staake, Bob, illus. 2013. (ENG., Illus.). 40p. (J). (gr. -1-3). 17.99 (978-0-375-87037-8(7), Schwartz & Wade Bks.) Random Hse. Children's Bks.

Starr Rose, Caroline. Blue Birds. 2016. lib. bdg. 19.65 (978-0-606-38403-2(0)) Turtleback Bks.

Stasinska, Marta. On the Water's Edge. Fratczak-Rodak, Monika, illus. 2015. (Mommy & Me Bath Bks.). (ENG.). 6p. (J). (gr. -1 — 1). 4.99 (978-1-4380-7591-4(X)) Barron's Educational Series, Inc.

Staton, Debbie. Twiggle. Patzelt, Kasie, illus. 2007. (J). (gr. -1-3). 17.99 (978-1-59879-362-8(4)); 26p. per. 12.99 (978-1-59879-199-0(0)) Lifevest Publishing, Inc.

Stead, Philip C. Hello, My Name Is Ruby. Stead, Philip C., illus. 2013. (ENG., Illus.). 36p. (J). (gr. -1-1). 16.99 (978-1-59643-809-5(6), 9781596438095) Roaring Brook Pr.

—A Home for Bird. Stead, Philip C., illus. 2012. (ENG., Illus.). 32p. (J). (gr. -1-3). 17.99 (978-1-59643-711-1(1), 9781596437111) Roaring Brook Pr.

Stein, Clem. Scotty's Feeder & the Secret Tower. Prouix, Denis, illus. 2011. 40p. 16.99 (978-1-4567-3191-5(2)) AuthorHouse.

Steinlage, Ben. Bird Boy. 2011. 290p. pap. 17.95 (978-1-4327-6667-2(8)) Outskirts Pr., Inc.

Stephens, Sarah. The Angry Birds Movie. Karacan, Tugrul, illus. 2016. (Angry Birds Ser.). 24p. (J). (gr. -1-3). pap. 3.99 (978-0-06-245338-9(6), HarperFestival) HarperCollins Pubs.

—Big Trouble in Bird City. 2016. (J). lib. bdg. 13.55 (978-0-606-38188-8(0)) Turtleback Bks.

—Big Trouble on Bird Island. Karacan, Tugrul, illus. 2016. (Angry Birds Ser.). 24p. (J). (gr. -1-3). pap. 3.99 (978-0-06-245340-2(8), HarperFestival) HarperCollins Pubs.

—Seeing Red. 2016. (J). lib. bdg. 13.55 (978-0-606-38189-5(9)) Turtleback Bks.

Stiegemeyer, Julie. Cheep! Cheep! Baicker-McKee, Carol, illus. 2006. (ENG.). 24p. (J). (gr. k-k). 9.95 (978-1-58234-682-3(8), 9781582346823, Bloomsbury USA Childrens) Bloomsbury Publishing USA.

Stileman, Kali. Roly Poly Egg. 2011. (ENG.). 26p. (J). (gr. -1-k). 12.95 (978-1-58925-852-5(5)) Tiger Tales.

—Snack Time for Confetti. 2013. (ENG., Illus.). 32p. (J). (gr. -1-1). 12.95 (978-1-58925-127-4(X)) Tiger Tales.

Stine, R. L. Calling All Birdbrains. Park, Trip, illus. 2007. (Rotten School Ser.: No. 15). (ENG.). 128p. (J). (gr. 3-7). 6.99 (978-0-06-123275-6(0)) HarperCollins Pubs.

Stoll, Emily. Ookie! Southard, Jan, illus. 2012. 28p. pap. 12.00 (978-1-4575-0859-2(1)) Dog Ear Publishing, LLC.

Story, Rita. The Belly Garden. Galluzzo, Madeline, illus. 2008. 23p. pap. 24.95 (978-1-60610-035-6(1)) America Star Bks.

Stratton-Porter, Gene. Birds of the Limberlost. (J). 35.95 (978-0-8488-1526-4(2)) Amereon Ltd.

Sturdy, Sandy. The Bird Who Wouldn't Sing, 1 vol. 2009. 27p. pap. 24.95 (978-1-60749-010-4(2)) America Star Bks.

Sullivan, Kathryn. Michael & the Elf. Dunningham, Jo, illus. 2nd ed. 2012. 24p. pap. 10.95 (978-1-61633-356-0(1)) Guardian Angel Publishing, Inc.

Suplicki, Mark J. Mirthburdz: The Discovery. 2004. (Illus.). 51p. (J). 19.95 (978-0-9764385-0-2(X), 00B1) Jon'taar Graphxs.

Svoboda, Linda Sue. The Little Brown Bird That Could. 2012. 20p. pap. 24.95 (978-1-4626-8043-6(7)) America Star Bks.

Sweet, George M. The Old Alligator & the Young Bird. 2011. 52p. pap. 19.39 (978-1-4269-5357-6(7)) Trafford Publishing.

Taborn, Debbie. When a Feather Fell. 2012. 32p. pap. 16.99 (978-1-4685-4150-2(1)) AuthorHouse.

Tafuri, Nancy. Whose Chick Are You? Tafuri, Nancy, illus. 2007. (ENG., Illus.). 40p. (J). (gr. -1-k). 16.99 (978-0-06-082514-0(6), Greenwillow Bks.) HarperCollins Pubs.

Tankard, Jeremy. Boo Hoo Bird. Tankard, Jeremy, illus. 2009. (ENG., Illus.). 32p. (J). (gr. -1-k). 16.99 (978-0-545-06570-2(4), Scholastic Pr.) Scholastic, Inc.

—Grumpy Bird. 2016. (ENG.). 30p. (J). (— 1). bds. 6.99 (978-0-545-87182-2(4), Scholastic Pr.) Scholastic, Inc.

—Grumpy Bird. Tankard, Jeremy, illus. 2007. (ENG., Illus.). 32p. (J). (gr. -1-k). 16.99 (978-0-439-85147-3(5), Scholastic Pr.) Scholastic, Inc.

—Hungry Bird. Tankard, Jeremy, illus. 2016. (ENG., Illus.). 32p. (J). (gr. -1-k). 16.99 (978-0-545-86417-6(8), Scholastic Pr.) Scholastic, Inc.

Taravant, Jacques. The Little Wing Giver. Ignatowicz, Nina, tr. from FRE. Sís, Peter, illus. 2004. 30p. (J). (gr. k-4). reprint ed. 15.00 (978-0-7567-7970-2(7)) DIANE Publishing Co.

Tate, Suzanne. Johnny Longlegs: A Tale of Big Birds. Melvin, James, illus. 2005. (Suzanne Tate's Nature Ser.: No. 28). 28p. (J). pap. 4.95 (978-1-878405-50-0(0)) Nags Head Art, Inc.

Taylor, Beverly. The Elusive Puffin. 2011. 24p. pap. 15.99 (978-1-4628-8233-5(1)) Xlibris Corp.

Taylor-Dill, Judith Nell. I Can Fly! 2012. 50p. pap. 19.99 (978-1-4685-5840-1(4)) AuthorHouse.

Teckentrup, Britta. Oskar Loves... 2016. (ENG., Illus.). 32p. (J). (gr. -1-3). 14.95 (978-3-7913-7270-9(X)) Prestel Verlag GmbH & Co KG. DEU. Dist: Penguin Random Hse. LLC.

Tezuka, Osamu. Phoenix, Vol. 7. 2006. (ENG., Illus.). 208p. pap. 15.99 (978-1-4215-0517-6(7)) Viz Media.

Theys, Erchen. Birdie Hop: The True Story. 2011. (Illus.). 28p. 12.19 (978-1-4567-7522-3(7)) AuthorHouse.

Thomas, Jason. The Adventures of Bird & Gator: Best Friends. 2012. 24p. pap. 12.56 (978-1-4669-4973-7(2)) Trafford Publishing.

Thomas, Nancy S. William the Winter Warbler. 2010. 16p. pap. 8.49 (978-1-4490-6467-9(1)) AuthorHouse.

Thomas, Peggy. For the Birds: The Life of Roger Tory Peterson. Jacques, Laura, illus. 2011. (ENG.). 40p. (J). (gr. 3). 16.95 (978-1-59078-764-9(1), Calkins Creek) Boyds Mills Pr.

Tracy, Roseann. Whose Toes Are Those? 2008. 24p. pap. 12.99 (978-1-4343-9291-6(0)) AuthorHouse.

Trawick, Ruth. Jeremy Bird. 2010. 32p. pap. 14.49 (978-1-4490-9946-6(7)) AuthorHouse.

Trimoglie, Mario. The Thorn. 2012. 20p. pap. 24.95 (978-1-4560-0419-4(0)) America Star Bks.

Trujillo, Ron. Bird & the Butterfly. 2011. 36p. pap. 24.95 (978-1-4626-3034-9(0)) America Star Bks.

Tsong, Jing Jing. Counting Birds. 2012. (ENG.). 28p. (J). bds. 8.95 (978-1-58925-638-5(7)) Tiger Tales.

Turnbull, Victoria. Pandora. 2017. (ENG., Illus.). 32p. (J). (gr. -1-3). 16.99 (978-0-544-94733-7(9), Clarion Bks.) Houghton Mifflin Harcourt Trade & Reference Pubs.

Two Little Birds & Other Stories: Individual Title Six-Pack. (Story Steps Ser.). (gr. k-2). 42.00 (978-0-7635-9568-5(3)) Rigby Education.

Typaldos, Melanie. Celeste & the Adorable Kitten. Tayts, Alexandra, illus. 2013. 244p. 14.99 (978-0-9899847-0-6(2)) Capybara Madness.

Ulbrich, Jasper. The Little Owl. 2009. (Illus.). 32p. pap. 16.50 (978-1-60860-047-2(5), Eloquent Bks.) Strategic Book Publishing & Rights Agency (SBPRA).

Ungermann Marshall, Yana. Gilda Gets Wise. Ungermann Marshall, Yana, illus. 2008. (Illus.). 34p. (J). pap. (978-0-9670982-6-5(2)) Yana's Kitchen.

Uslan, Michael E. Chatterbox: The Bird Who Wore Glasses. Gurney, John Steven, illus. 2006. 34p. (J). (978-0-9753843-2-9(5)) Egmont Bks., Ltd.

Van Durme, Leen. Mo & Mac: Socks On! Van Durme, Leen, illus. 2013. (ENG., Illus.). 16p. (J). (— 1). 9.95 (978-1-60537-176-4(9)) Cobblestone Publishing Co.

van Genechten, Guido. The Big Woods Orchestra. 2012. (ENG.). 24p. (J). (gr. -1-k). 17.95 (978-1-60537-113-9(0)) Cobblestone Publishing Co.

Vanover, Rita. Yellow Head the Cockatiel. 2011. 38p. pap. 16.95 (978-1-4626-4493-3(7)) America Star Bks.

Velazquez, Catherine. Dirty Birdie. 2012. 32p. pap. 18.48 (978-0-578-10152-1(1)) Jiovanie.

Vent des Hove, Yaël & Vent des Hove, Yael. Mama, Me Cuentas un Cuento? Vent des Hove, Yaël, illus. 2006. (SPA., Illus.). 32p. (J). (gr. -1-k). 20.99 (978-84-261-3527-8(7)) Lectorum Pubns., Inc.

Ventura, Antonio. Lucas y el Ruisenor. Angela-Lago, illus. 2005. (SPA.). 24p. (J). (gr. 1-3). pap., pap. 6.99 (978-980-257-285-4(3)) Ekare, Ediciones VEN. Dist: Lectorum Pubns., Inc.

Vergo, Franny. Jonathan Ray & His Superhero Pack: Respect. 2012. 42p. pap. 16.50 (978-1-4685-7602-3(X)) AuthorHouse.

Vermeulen, Thomas. Gabangani Guinea Fowl & Huzu the Bird Eating Spider. 2009. 50p. pap. 19.50 (978-1-60693-741-9(3), Eloquent Bks.) Strategic Book Publishing & Rights Agency (SBPRA).

Vernick, Audrey. Unlike Other Monsters. Jack, Colin, illus. 2016. (ENG.). 48p. (J). (gr. -1-k). 16.99 (978-1-4231-9959-5(6)) Disney Pr.

Verrett, Michael. The White Alligator Crown Quatro. 2010. 147p. pap. 13.95 (978-0-557-58121-4(4)) Lulu Pr., Inc.

—The White Alligator (paper Back) 2010. 116p. pap. 17.30 (978-0-557-28042-1(7)) Lulu Pr., Inc.

—The White Alligator (paperback full Color) 2010. 116p. pap. 42.00 (978-0-557-36924-9(X)) Lulu Pr., Inc.

Wall, Suzy. The Dodo's Last Stand. 2005. (J). pap. (978-1-4108-4221-3(5)) Benchmark Education Co.

Wallace, Bill. The Legend of Thunderfoot. 2006. (ENG.). 160p. (J). (gr. 3-7). 15.95 (978-1-4169-0691-9(6), Simon & Schuster/Paula Wiseman Bks.) Simon & Schuster/Paula Wiseman Bks.

Walters, Jack C. Bird Stories & Sightings in Nevada Vol. 1: Loons to Nighthawks 2004. (Illus.). 436p. pap. 38.50 (978-0-9754658-0-6(5)) Walters, Jack C.

Ward, Lindsay. When Blue Met Egg. 2012. (ENG.). 32p. (J). (gr. -1-k). 16.99 (978-0-8037-3718-1(1), Dial Bks) Penguin Young Readers Group.

Ward, Susan. The Red Crayon. 2011. 24p. pap. 10.95 (978-1-60920-029-9(2)) Ajoyin Publishing, Inc.

Wareh, Denny T. Nee Nee the Woodpecker. 2011. 36p. pap. 24.95 (978-1-4560-5680-3(8)) America Star Bks.

—School Bound Nee Nee the Woodpecker. 2011. 36p. pap. 24.95 (978-1-4560-8900-9(5)) America Star Bks.

Waring, Geoff. Oscar & the Bird: A Book about Electricity. Waring, Geoff, illus. 2011. (Start with Science Ser.). (ENG., Illus.). 32p. (J). (gr. -1-3). pap. 6.99 (978-0-7636-5302-6(0)) Candlewick Pr.

Warren, Celia. Bouncing with the Birdie, 8 vols. 2005. (QEB Readers). (Illus.). 24p. (J). (gr. -1-3). lib. bdg. 15.95 (978-1-59566-064-0(X)) QEB Publishing Inc.

Watkins, Greg. A Big Beaked, Big Bellied Bird Named Bill. Watkins, Greg, illus. 2005. (Illus.). 30p. 13.95 (978-0-9761318-1-6(1), 1239651) Cute & Cuddly Productions, Inc.

—A Big Beaked, Big Bellied Bird Named Bill, 1 vol. Watkins, Greg, illus. 2006. (Big Bill & Buddies Ser.). (ENG., Illus.). 32p. (J). (gr. k-3). 16.99 (978-1-58980-441-8(4)) Pelican Publishing Co., Inc.

—Brendon Mouse's Big Idea to Save the Bad Bird Bunch, 1 vol. Watkins, Greg, illus. 2007. (Big Bill & Buddies Ser.). (ENG., Illus.). 32p. (J). (gr. k-3). 16.99 (978-1-58980-449-4(X)) Pelican Publishing Co., Inc.

Watt, Fiona. Tweet Tweet. 2009. (Stroller Bks). 8p. (J). 7.99 (978-0-7945-2497-5(4), Usborne) EDC Publishing.

Watt, Fiona & Wells, Rachel. Hen. 2004. (Illus.). 10p. (J). 10.95 (978-0-7945-0384-0(5), Usborne) EDC Publishing.

Weaver, Anna E. Birds at My Window. 2004. (Illus.). 231p. 9.35 (978-0-7399-2301-6(3), 2138) Rod & Staff Pubs., Inc.

Weston Woods Staff, creator. Inch by Inch. 2011. 38.75 (978-0-439-90543-5(5)) Weston Woods Studios, Inc.

—The Pigeon Finds a Hot Dog. 2011. 38.75 (978-0-545-26298-9(4)) Weston Woods Studios, Inc.

Whaley, John Corey. Where Things Come Back. (ENG., Illus.). (YA). (gr. 9). 2012. 256p. pap. 11.99 (978-1-4424-1334-4(4)) 2011. 240p. 16.99 (978-1-4424-1333-7(6)) Simon & Schuster Children's Publishing. (Atheneum Bks. for Young Readers).

White, Andre'. A Bird Is a Bird, 1 vol. 2009. (ENG.). 24p. 24.95 (978-1-60610-556-6(6)) America Star Bks.

White, Andrea. Windows on the World. 2011. 238p. (J). 18.95 (978-1-60898-105-2(3)); pap. 9.95 (978-1-60898-106-9(1)) namelos llc.

White, Nonie H. D. The Woodpecker Who Suffered from Headaches. White, Nonie H. D., illus. 2006. (Illus.). (J). pap. 14.95 (978-0-9786147-0-6(4)) Westside Studio.

Whitney, Barbara I. Barbara's Quest to Find a Messenger: Journeys I & II. 2009. 40p. pap. 19.49 (978-1-4415-0159-2(2)) Xlibris Corp.

Wiggin, Kate Douglas. The Bird's Christmas Carol. 2008. 88p. (gr. 4-7). pap. 8.95 (978-1-60664-191-0(3)) Aegypan.

—The Birds' Christmas Carol. (J). reprint ed. lib. bdg. 48.00 (978-0-7426-1056-9(X)) Classic Bks.

Wightman, Jillian C. The Adventures of Erin Mctavitt. 2008. 68p. pap. 19.95 (978-1-4327-3164-9(5)) Outskirts Pr., Inc.

Wildsmith, Brian. The Owl & the Woodpecker, 1 vol. Wildsmith, Brian, illus. 2006. (ENG., Illus.). 32p. (J). (gr. -1-3). 16.95 (978-1-59572-043-6(X)) Star Bright Bks., Inc.

Wiley, Pamela. Ethel the Emu. Dewitt, Robin & Dewitt Grush, Patricia, illus. 2007. (ENG.). 32p. (gr. 1-3). pap. 9.95 (978-1-57874-335-3(4), Kaeden Bks.) Kaeden Corp.

—Ethel the Emu (6 Pack) Dewitt, Robin & Grush, Patricia DeWitt, illus. 2007. (ENG.). 32p. (gr. 1-3). pap. (978-1-57874-336-0(2), Kaeden Bks.) Kaeden Corp.

Wilks, Peter. The Foragers. 2006. (ENG., Illus.). 166p. (978-1-905886-07-4(1)) Troubador Publishing Ltd.

Willard, Hugh. The Goodwill Vultures Club. Holjes, Kerry, ed. Eason, D. M., illus. 2013. 122p. pap. 9.99 (978-1-935711-26-1(1)) Peak City Publishing, LLC.

Willems, Mo. Don't Let the Pigeon Drive the Bus! Willems, Mo, illus. 2003. (Pigeon Ser.). (ENG., Illus.). 40p. (J). (gr. -1-k). 16.99 (978-0-7868-1988-1(X)) Hyperion Pr.

—There Is a Bird on Your Head! Willems, Mo, illus. rev. ed. 2007. (Elephant & Piggie Book Ser.). (ENG., Illus.). 64p. (J). (gr. -1-k). 9.99 (978-1-4231-0686-9(5)) Hyperion Pr.

—¡Tienes un Pájaro en la Cabeza! Willems, Mo, illus. 2017. (Elephant & Piggie Book Ser.). (ENG & SPA., Illus.). 64p. (J). (gr. 1-3). 9.99 (978-1-4847-8697-0(1)) Hyperion Bks. for Children.

Willems, Mo, illus. Don't Let the Pigeon Drive the Bus! 2005. 40p. (J). (978-1-84428-013-1(6)) Walker Bks. Australia Pty, Ltd.

Willems, Mo & Harper, Charise Mericle. The Good for Nothing Button! Willems, Mo & Harper, Charise Mericle, illus. 2017. (Elephant & Piggie Like Reading! Ser.). (ENG., Illus.). 64p. (J). (gr. 1-3). 9.99 (978-1-4847-2646-4(4)) Disney Pr.

Williams, Annik. Mr. Mole's Day Off: With Goodnight Little Birdie. 2010. 20p. 15.78 (978-1-4520-3756-1(6)) AuthorHouse.

Williams, Greg. Salty the Sea Gull. 2011. 38p. pap. 19.00 (978-1-60746-205-7(2)) FastPrncil, Inc.

Windhorst, Brenda. Do You Want a Henry Story? 2011. 24p. pap. 15.99 (978-1-4628-8796-5(1)) Xlibris Corp.

Wings, Tanina. The Little Seagull. 2013. 24p. pap. 12.95 (978-1-62516-017-1(8), Strategic Bk. Publishing) Strategic Book Publishing & Rights Agency (SBPRA).

Witrago, Jost. The Wooden Dove. 2007. 16p. per. 24.95 (978-1-4241-9011-9(8)) America Star Bks.

Wofford, Sherry Lynn. Introducing the Adventures of Jerry Giraffe & Feather Bird. 2011. 36p. pap. 16.95 (978-1-4560-3238-8(0)) America Star Bks.

Wright, Velma. Fuzz, an Impatient Chick. 2010. 12p. 12.68 (978-1-4269-3430-8(0)) Trafford Publishing.

Wymer, Tracy Edward. Soar. (ENG., Illus.). 288p. (J). (gr. 3-7). 2017. pap. 7.99 **(978-1-4814-4712-6(2))** 2016. 17.99 (978-1-4814-4711-9(4)) Simon & Schuster Children's Publishing. (Aladdin).

Yasuda, Anita. The Beach Bandit, 1 vol. Harpster, Steve, illus. 2013. (Dino Detectives Ser.). (ENG.). 32p. (gr. 1-2). pap. 5.95 (978-1-4342-4830-5(5)); lib. bdg. 22.65 (978-1-4342-4154-2(8)) Stone Arch Bks.

Yee, Wong Herbert. Fine Feathered Friends. Yee, Wong Herbert, illus. 2011. (Mouse & Mole Story Ser.). (ENG., Illus.). 48p. (J). (gr. 1-4). pap. 3.99 (978-0-547-51977-7(X)) Houghton Mifflin Harcourt Publishing Co.

—Mouse & Mole, Fine Feathered Friends. Yee, Wong Herbert, illus. 2009. (Mouse & Mole Story Ser.). (ENG., Illus.). 48p. (J). (gr. 1-4). 15.00 (978-0-547-15222-6(1)) Houghton Mifflin Harcourt Publishing Co.

Yerger, Susan M. Mighty Little Samuel Seagull. 2013. 20p. pap. 24.95 (978-1-4626-9941-4(3)) America Star Bks.

Yerkes, Jennifer. A Funny Little Bird. 2013. (ENG., Illus.). 48p. (J). (-3). 15.99 (978-1-4022-8013-9(0), 9781402280139, Sourcebooks Jabberwocky) Sourcebooks, Inc.

Yolen, Jane & Stemple, Heidi E. Y. You Nest Here with Me. Sweet, Melissa, illus. 2015. (ENG.). 40p. (J). (gr. -1-3). 16.95 (978-1-59078-923-0(7)) Boyds Mills Pr.

Yoon, Salina. Wings: A Book to Touch & Feel. Yoon, Salina, illus. 2010. (ENG., Illus.). 14p. (J). (gr. -1 — 1). bds. 8.99 (978-1-4169-8958-5(7), Little Simon) Little Simon.

Yost, B. L. Have You Ever Seen a Wild Bird Dance? Perkins, Chelsea, illus. 2008. 16p. pap. 24.95 (978-1-60703-127-7(2)) America Star Bks.

Young, Linda P. The Adventures of Anna & Andy Hummingbird. 2011. 44p. pap. 21.99 (978-1-4568-9568-6(0)) Xlibris Corp.

—The Adventures of Anna & Andy Hummingbird: Anna & Andy Meet the Grandchildren, Book 3 Stories 11, 12 And 13. 2012. 32p. pap. 21.99 (978-1-4797-1637-1(5)) Xlibris Corp.

Yuly, Toni. Early Bird. Yuly, Toni, illus. 2014. (ENG., Illus.). 40p. (J). (— 1). 15.99 (978-1-250-04327-6(1), 9781250043276) Feiwel & Friends.

—The Jelly Bean Tree. Yuly, Toni, illus. 2017. (ENG., Illus.). 40p. (J). 17.99 (978-1-250-09406-3(2), 9781250094063) Feiwel & Friends.

Zaugg, Sandra L. Secret of the Yellow Van: A Book about Dealing with Loss. 2008. (J). pap. 8.99 (978-0-8163-2246-6(5)) Pacific Pr. Publishing Assn.

Zelaya, Carol. Caring for Emily's Family. 2008. (Illus.). 24p. (J). (gr. 2-3). 14.95 (978-0-9796265-1-7(X)) Richlee Publishing.

—Emily Waits for Her Family. Metcalf, Kristin, illus. 2007. (Emily the Chickadee Ser.). 32p. (J). (gr. 2-3). 14.95 (978-0-9796265-0-0(1)) Richlee Publishing.

—Emily's New Home: Emily the Chickadee. 2008. (Illus.). 36p. (J). (gr. 2-3). 14.95 (978-0-9796265-2-4(8)) Richlee Publishing.

Zimmer, Frank. Bird Singing Contest. 2008. 28p. pap. 13.99 (978-1-4343-7971-9(X)) AuthorHouse.

Zubizarreta, Patxi. Paloma, Llegaste Por el Aire. Balzola, Asun, illus. 2003. (SPA.). 24p. (978-84-246-5913-4(9), GL3212) La Galera, S.A. Editorial ESP. Dist: Lectorum Pubns., Inc.

Zubizarreta, Rosalma, et al. The Woman Who Outshone the Sun (la mujer que brillaba aun mas que el Sol) Olivera, Fernando, illus. 2014. (ENG & SPA.). 32p. (J). (gr. -1 — 1). pap. 9.95 (978-0-89239-126-4(X)) Lee & Low Bks., Inc.

Zug, Mark & Fan, Nancy Yi. Swordbird. Zug, Mark, illus. 2008. (Swordbird Ser.: 1). (ENG., Illus.). 256p. (J). (gr. 3-7). pap. 6.99 (978-0-06-113101-1(6)) HarperCollins Pubs.

Zullo, Germano. Little Bird. Albertine, illus. 2012. (ENG.). 72p. (J). (gr. k). 16.95 (978-1-59270-118-6(3)) Enchanted Lion Bks., LLC.

BIRDS—FLIGHT

Arnold, Caroline. Birds: Nature's Magnificent Flying Machines. Wynne, Patricia J., illus. 2003. (ENG.). 32p. (J). (gr. 1-4). pap. 7.95 (978-1-57091-572-7(5)) Charlesbridge Publishing, Inc.

Gregory, Josh. From Birds to... Aircraft. 2012. (21st Century Skills Innovation Library: Innovations from Nature Ser.). (ENG.). 32p. (gr. 4-8). 28.50 (978-1-61080-497-4(X), 202107); pap. 14.21 (978-1-61080-671-8(9), 202281) Cherry Lake Publishing.

Mara, Wil. From Kingfishers to... Bullet Trains. 2012. (21st Century Skills Innovation Library: Innovations from Nature Ser.). (ENG.). 32p. (gr. 4-8). 28.50 (978-1-61080-498-1(8), 202108); pap. 14.21 (978-1-61080-672-5(7), 202282) Cherry Lake Publishing.

Spiro, Ruth & Chan, Irene. Baby Loves Aerospace Engineering! 2016. (Baby Loves Science Ser.). (ENG., Illus.). 20p. (J). (— 1). bds. 8.95 (978-1-58089-541-5(7)) Charlesbridge Publishing, Inc.

Stewart, Melissa. How Do Birds Fly? 2006. (Tell Me Why, Tell Me How Ser.). (Illus.). 32p. (J). (gr. 3-7). lib. bdg. 29.93 (978-0-7614-2110-8(6), Benchmark Bks.) Marshall Cavendish Corp.

BIRDS—HABITS AND BEHAVIOR

Earley, Chris. Weird Birds. 2014. (ENG., Illus.). 64p. (J). (gr. 5-12). pap. 9.95 (978-1-77085-296-9(4), 9781770852969) Firefly Bks., Ltd.

Farndon, John. Remarkable Birds. Portolano, Cristina, illus. 2016. (Animal Bests Ser.). (ENG.). 32p. (J). (gr. 3-6). lib. bdg. 26.65 (978-1-5124-0626-9(0)) Lerner Publishing Group.

Fretland VanVoorst, Jenny. Las Aves en la Primavera. 2015.Tr. of Birds in Spring. (SPA., Illus.). 24p. (J). lib. bdg. (978-1-62031-250-6(6), Bullfrog Bks.) Jump! Inc.

Garland, Michael. Birds Make Nests. 2017. (ENG., Illus.). 32p. (J). (gr. -1-3). 16.95 (978-0-8234-3662-0(4)) Holiday Hse., Inc.

Gray, Rita. Have You Heard the Nesting Bird? Pak, Kenard, illus. 2014. (ENG.). 32p. (J). (gr. -1-3). 16.99 (978-0-544-10580-5(X), HMH Books For Young Readers) Houghton Mifflin Harcourt Publishing Co.

Henshaw, Lorne. Birds in Spring. 2016. (We Love Spring! Ser.). 00024p. (J). pap. 8.15 **(978-1-4824-5477-2(7))** Stevens, Gareth Publishing LLLP.

Heos, Bridget. Birds. Clark, David, illus. 2017. (Just Like Us! Ser.). (ENG.). 32p. (J). (gr. -1-3). 14.99 (978-0-544-57044-3(8), HMH Books For Young Readers) Houghton Mifflin Harcourt Publishing Co.

Hirsch, Rebecca E. Snowy Owls: Stealthy Hunting Birds. 2016. (Comparing Animal Traits Ser.). (ENG., Illus.). 32p. (J). (gr. 2-4). 39.99 (978-1-4677-9628-6(X), Lerner Pubns.) Lerner Publishing Group.

Hoffman, Mary Ann. How Do Penguins Survive the Cold? 2009. (Real Life Readers Ser.). 24p. (gr. 3-4). pap. 8.25 (978-1-4042-8007-6(3), Rosen Classroom) Rosen Publishing Group, Inc., The.

Horning, Sandra. Bizarre Birds (Scholastic Reader, Level 2) 2017. (Scholastic Reader, Level 2 Ser.). (ENG.). 32p. (J). (gr. 1-3). pap. 3.99 (978-1-338-04725-7(6)) Scholastic, Inc.

Kavanagh, James. Birds Nature Activity Book. Leung, Raymond, illus. 2nd ed. 2011. (Nature Activity Book Ser.). (ENG.). 32p. (J). (gr. 4-7). 6.95 (978-1-58355-577-4(3)) Western National Parks Assn.

Rodriguez, Ana Maria. The Secret of the Bird's Smart Brain... & More! 2017. (Animal Secrets Revealed! Ser.). 48p. (J). (gr. 4-4). pap. 11.70 **(978-0-7660-8852-8(9))** Enslow Pubs., Inc.

Roxbee-Cox, Phil. Find the Bird. Cartwright, Stephen, illus. 2004. (Treasury of Farmyard Tales Ser.). (ENG.). 1p. (J). stu. ed., bds. 3.95 (978-0-7460-3820-8(8)) EDC Publishing.

Stewart, Melissa. Bird-Acious. 2013. (Science with Stuff Ser.: 6). (ENG.). 48p. (J). (gr. 1). 11.99 (978-1-935703-90-7(0)) Downtown Bookworks.

—Feathers: Not Just for Flying. Brannen, Sarah S., illus. 2014. (ENG.). 32p. (J). (gr. 1-4). pap. 7.95 (978-1-58089-431-9(3)) Charlesbridge Publishing, Inc.

—A Place for Birds, 1 vol. Bond, Higgins, illus. 2009. (ENG.). 32p. (J). (gr. 1-5). 16.95 (978-1-56145-474-7(5)) Peachtree Pubs.

Tagliaferro, Linda. Birds & Their Nests [Scholastic]. 2010. (Animal Homes Ser.). 24p. pap. 0.49 (978-1-4296-5794-5(4), Pebble Plus) Capstone Press of Coughlan Cos.

BIRDS—MIGRATION

Baker, Jeannie. Circle. Baker, Jeannie, illus. 2016. (ENG., Illus.). 48p. (J). (gr. k-3). 17.99 (978-0-7636-7966-8(6)) Candlewick Pr.

Ball, Jacqueline A. Animales Migratorios: Por Aire. 2007. (En marcha: Migraciones animales (Spanish- on the Move: Animal Migration) Ser.). (SPA.). 24p. (gr. 1-4). pap. 8.15 (978-0-8368-8432-6(9)); (Illus.). lib. bdg. 22.00 (978-0-8368-8427-2(2)) Stevens, Gareth Publishing LLLP. (Weekly Reader Leveled Readers).

—Migrating Animals of the Air. 2007. (On the Move: Animal Migration Ser.). 24p. (gr. 1-4). pap. 8.15 (978-0-8368-8422-7(1)); (Illus.). lib. bdg. 22.00 (978-0-8368-8417-3(5)) Stevens, Gareth Publishing LLLP. (Weekly Reader Leveled Readers).

Benchmark Education Company, compiled by. Bringing Back the Whooping Crane & ¡Vamos a Rescatar a la Grulla Blanca! 2005. (J). 62.00 net. (978-1-4108-4494-1(3)) Benchmark Education Co.

Bronson, Franklin. Why Don't Birds get Lost? Differentiated Studies in Bird Migration: Upper Elementary through Secondary Levels. 2005. (Illus.). 70p. (978-0-910609-49-4(7)) Gifted Education Pr.

Heos, Bridget. Birds. Clark, David, illus. 2017. (Just Like Us! Ser.). (ENG.). 32p. (J). (gr. -1-3). 14.99 (978-0-544-57044-3(8), HMH Books For Young Readers) Houghton Mifflin Harcourt Publishing Co.

Hirsch, Rebecca. Arctic Tern Migration. 2012. (Animal Migrations Ser.). (ENG., Illus.). 32p. (J). (gr. 2-5). lib. bdg. 29.93 (978-1-60973-616-3(8), 201193) Child's World, Inc., The.

Markle, Sandra. The Long, Long Journey: The Godwit's Amazing Migration. Posada, Mia, illus. 2013. (ENG.). 32p. (J). (gr. k-3). lib. bdg. 26.60 (978-0-7613-5623-3(1), Millbrook Pr.) Lerner Publishing Group.

The Migration: Level D, 6 vols. (Wonder Worldtm Ser.). 16p. 24.95 (978-0-7802-4585-3(7)) Wright Group/McGraw-Hill.

Olien, Rebecca. Where Do the Birds Go? A Migration Mystery, 1 vol. McDee, Katie, illus. 2011. (First Graphics: Science Mysteries Ser.). (ENG.). 24p. (gr. 1-2). pap. 6.29 (978-1-4296-7175-0(0)); pap. 35.70 (978-1-4296-7179-8(3)); lib. bdg. 23.99 (978-1-4296-6096-9(1)) Capstone Press of Coughlan Cos.

Thornhill, Jan. Is This Panama? A Migration Story. Kim, Soyeon & Owlkids Books Inc. Staff, illus. 2013. (ENG.). 40p. (J). (gr. k-4). 16.95 (978-1-926973-88-3(7), Owlkids) Owlkids Bks. Inc. CAN. Dist: Publishers Group West (PGW).

Vogel, Carole Garbuny & Leshem, Yossi. The Man Who Flies with Birds. 2009. (Israel Ser.). (ENG., Illus.). 64p. (J). (gr. 5-12). 18.95 (978-0-8225-7643-3(0), Kar-Ben Publishing) Lerner Publishing Group.

Willis, Nancy Carol. Red Knot: A Shorebird's Incredible Journey. 2006. (ENG., Illus.). 32p. (J). (gr. 2-4). 15.95 (978-0-9662761-4-5(0)); pap. 8.95 (978-0-9662761-5-2(9)) Birdsong Bks.

BIRDS—NESTS

Adamson, Heather. Bird Nests. 2010. (Our Animal World Ser.). 24p. (J). 25.65 (978-1-60753-009-1(0)) Amicus Publishing.

Bechard, Clem. Mrs. Robinson Finds a Home. 2008. 24p. per. 24.95 (978-1-4241-9692-0(2)) America Star Bks.

Birds' Nest. 2003. 36.95 (978-0-8136-9272-2(5)); 38.95 (978-0-8136-4185-0(3)) Modern Curriculum Pr.

Birds' Nests: Level L, 6 vols. (Wonder Worldtm Ser.). 16p. 34.95 (978-0-7802-2888-7(X)) Wright Group/McGraw-Hill.

Choi, Eun-gyu. All Kinds of Nests. Cowley, Joy, ed. Kim, Ji-yeon, illus. 2015. (Science Storybooks Ser.). (ENG.). 32p. (J). (gr. k-3). 26.65 (978-1-925233-60-5(X)) Lerner Publishing Group.

Danielson, Ethan. Inside Bird Nests. 2015. (Inside Animal Homes Ser.). (ENG., Illus.). 24p. (J). (gr. 2-3). pap. 8.25 (978-1-4994-0874-4(9), PowerKids Pr.) Rosen Publishing Group, Inc., The.

—Nidos de Aves (Inside Bird Nests) 2015. (Las Casas de Los Animales (Inside Animal Homes) Ser.). (ENG & SPA.). 24p. (J). (gr. 2-3). 23.60 (978-1-4994-0561-3(8), PowerKids Pr.) Rosen Publishing Group, Inc., The.

Dunning, Joan. Seabird in the Forest: The Mystery of the Marbled Murrelet. Dunning, Joan, illus. 2011. (ENG., Illus.). 32p. (J). (gr. k-4). 17.95 (978-1-59078-715-1(3)) Boyds Mills Pr.

Garland, Michael. Birds Make Nests. 2017. (ENG., Illus.). 32p. (J). (gr. -1-3). 16.95 (978-0-8234-3662-0(4)) Holiday Hse., Inc.

Gray, Rita. Have You Heard the Nesting Bird? Pak, Kenard, illus. 2014. (ENG.). 32p. (J). (gr. -1-3). 16.99 (978-0-544-10580-5(X), HMH Books For Young Readers) Houghton Mifflin Harcourt Publishing Co.

Hopkins, Therese. Bird Nests. 2009. (Home Sweet Home Ser.). 24p. (J). (gr. k-2). pap. 8.25 (978-1-4358-3067-7(9), PowerKids Pr.); (gr. 1-1). 42.50 (978-1-61513-396-3(8), PowerKids Pr.); (Illus.). (J). (gr. k-2). lib. bdg. 22.60 (978-1-4358-2693-9(0)) Rosen Publishing Group, Inc., The.

Kelly, Irene. Even an Ostrich Needs a Nest: Where Birds Begin. 2009. (ENG., Illus.). 32p. (J). (gr. -1-3). 16.95 (978-0-8234-2102-2(3)) Holiday Hse., Inc.

The Missing Osprey Nest, 6 vols. (Ragged Island Mysteriestm Ser.). 161p. (gr. 5-7). 42.50 (978-0-322-01646-0(0)) Wright Group/McGraw-Hill.

The Nest: KinderConcepts Individual Title, 6 packs. (Kinderstarters Ser.). 8p. (gr. -1-1). 21.00 (978-0-7635-8727-7(3)) Rigby Education.

Peterson, Megan Cooley & Rustad, Martha E. H. Look Inside a Robin's Nest, 1 vol. 2011. (Look Inside Animal Homes Ser.). (ENG.). 24p. (gr. k-1). 26.65 (978-1-4296-6077-8(5), Pebble Plus) Capstone Press of Coughlan Cos.

Raum, Elizabeth. Las Abejas y Sus Colmenas (Bees Build Beehives) Romina Martí, illus. 2017. (Animal Builders Ser.). (ENG & SPA.). 24p. (J). (gr. 1-4). 20.95 **(978-1-68151-280-8(7)**, Amicus Illustrated) Amicus Publishing.

Riegle, Janet. Piping Plover Summer. Riegle, Janet, illus. 2008. (Illus.). 32p. (J). (gr. 1-2). 18.95 (978-0-9794202-9-0(6)); pap. 12.95 (978-0-9801045-4-7(8)) Raven Productions, Inc.

Roemer, Heidi Bee. Whose Nest Is This? McLennan, Connie, illus. 2009. (ENG.). 32p. (J). (gr. -1-3). 16.95 (978-1-58979-386-6(2)) Taylor Trade Publishing.

Smith, Carrie. Bird Homes: Lap Book. 2009. (My First Reader's Theater Set B Ser.). (J). 28.00 (978-1-4108-8537-1(2)) Benchmark Education Co.

Stradling, Jan. Nests & Shelters: Level H, 6 vols. (First Explorers Ser.). 24p. (gr. 1-2). 29.95 (978-0-7699-1448-0(9)) Shortland Pubns. (U. S. A.) Inc.

Tagliaferro, Linda. Birds & Their Nests [Scholastic]. 2010. (Animal Homes Ser.). 24p. pap. 0.49 (978-1-4296-5794-5(4), Pebble Plus) Capstone Press of Coughlan Cos.

Ward, Jennifer. Mama Built a Little Nest. Jenkins, Steve, illus. 2014. (ENG.). 40p. (J). (gr. -1-3). 17.99 (978-1-4424-2116-5(9), Beach Lane Bks.) Beach Lane Bks.

Weber, Valerie J. Por Qué Algunos Animales Viven en Nidos. 2008. (Donde viven los animales (Where Animals Live) Ser.). (SPA.). 24p. (gr. 1-4). pap. 8.15 (978-0-8368-8817-1(0), Weekly Reader Leveled Readers) Stevens, Gareth Publishing LLLP.

—Por Que Algunos Animales Viven en Nidos. 2008. (Donde viven los animales (Where Animals Live) Ser.). (SPA., Illus.). 24p. (gr. 1-4). lib. bdg. 22.00 (978-0-8368-8810-2(3), Weekly Reader Leveled Readers) Stevens, Gareth Publishing LLLP.

—Why Animals Live in Nests. 2008. (Where Animals Live Ser.). (Illus.). 24p. (gr. 1-4). lib. bdg. 22.00 (978-0-8368-8796-9(4), Weekly Reader Leveled Readers) Stevens, Gareth Publishing LLLP.

—Why Animals Live in Nests. 2008. (Where Animals Live Ser.). 24p. (gr. 1-4). pap. 8.15 (978-0-8368-8803-4(0), Weekly Reader Leveled Readers) Stevens, Gareth Publishing LLLP.

Worthington, Niles. A Bird's Nest. 2016. (Animal Builders Ser.). 24p. (J). lib. bdg. 24.21 (978-1-5026-2080-4(4)) Cavendish Square Publishing.

BIRDS—PICTORIAL WORKS

Calderwood, Damon & Waite, Donald E. Baby Birds in the Wild, 1 vol. 2015. (ENG., Illus.). 48p. (J). (gr. -1-1). pap. 6.95 **(978-1-77203-064-8(3))** Heritage Hse. CAN. Dist: Orca Bk. Pubs. USA.

Earley, Chris G. & McCaw, Robert. Birds A to Z. McCaw, Robert, photos by. 2009. (ENG., Illus.). 32p. (J). (gr. 1-5).

19.95 (978-1-55407-554-6(8), 9781554075546); pap. 7.95 (978-1-55407-500-3(9), 9781554075003) Firefly Bks., Ltd.

Harper, Charley. ABC's. 2013. (ENG., Illus.). 62p. (J). 16.95 (978-1-62326-003-3(5)) AMMO Bks., LLC.

Harper, Charley, illus. Charley Harper's Birds. 2013. (ENG.). (J). 7.95 (978-0-7649-6513-5(1)) Pomegranate Communications, Inc.

Pelletier, Mia. A Children's Guide to Arctic Birds, 1 vol. Christopher, Danny, illus. 2014. (ENG.). 32p. (J). (gr. k-2). 16.95 (978-1-927095-67-6(0)) Inhabit Media Inc. CAN. Dist: Independent Pubs. Group.

Rod and Staff Publishers, Inc Staff, contrib. by. My Little Bird Book. 2012. (Illus.). 24p. (J). pap. (978-0-7399-2439-6(7)) Rod & Staff Pubs., Inc.

Schindel, John. Busy Birdies. Holt, Steven, photos by. 2010. (Busy Book Ser.). (ENG., Illus.). 20p. (J). (gr. -1 — 1). bds. 7.99 (978-1-58246-317-9(4), Tricycle Pr.) Random Hse. Children's Bks.

Schwarzschild, Barbara. Guppy Grebe. 2007. 56p. per. 16.95 (978-1-4327-1246-4(2)) Outskirts Pr., Inc.

Sibbett, Ed JR. & Sibbett, Jr., Ed, Ed. Birds GemGlow Stained Glass Coloring Book. 2010. (Dover Nature Stained Glass Coloring Book Ser.). (ENG., Illus.). 32p. (J). (gr. -1-5). pap. 7.99 (978-0-486-47476-2(3)) Dover Pubns., Inc.

Tait, Leia. Birds. 2008. (U. S. Sites & Symbols Ser.). (Illus.). 48p. (J). (gr. 3-5). pap. 10.95 (978-1-59036-891-6(6)); lib. bdg. 29.05 (978-1-59036-890-9(8)) Weigl Pubs., Inc.

UG, Philippe. Funny Birds. 2013. (ENG., Illus.). 18p. (J). (gr. -1-3). 19.95 (978-3-7913-7147-4(9)) Prestel Verlag GmbH & Co KG. DEU. Dist: Penguin Random Hse. LLC.

Valério, Geraldo. My Book of Birds, 1 vol. 2016. (ENG., Illus.). 60p. (J). (gr. k). 24.95 (978-1-55498-800-6(4)) Groundwood Bks. CAN. Dist: Publishers Group West (PGW).

BIRDS—POETRY

Frost, Helen. Sweep up the Sun. Lieder, Rick, illus. 2015. (ENG.). 32p. (J). (-k). 15.99 (978-0-7636-6904-1(0)) Candlewick Pr.

Gordon, Elizabeth. Bird Children. Ross, M. T., illus. 2011. (ENG.). (J). (gr. -1-3). 14.95 (978-1-55709-083-6(1)) Applewood Bks.

—Bird Children: The Little Playmates of the Flower Children. Ross, M. T., illus. 2008. (ENG.). 96p. (J). (gr. -1-3). pap. 14.95 (978-1-55709-087-4(4)) Applewood Bks.

Nash, Myrna Lee. Spinman, Katydid & Bump: A Spider Vane Collection. Johnson, Sharon, illus. 2003. 48p. (YA). (gr. 4-10). 11.95 (978-0-9724549-0-2(X)) Chapter & Verse Pr.

Rosen, Michael J. The Cuckoo's Haiku: And Other Birding Poems. Fellows, Stan, illus. 2009. (ENG.). 64p. (J). (gr. 1-4). 17.99 (978-0-7636-3049-2(7)) Candlewick Pr.

Ruddell, Deborah. Today at the Bluebird Café: A Branchful of Birds. Rankin, Joan E. & Rankin, Joan, illus. 2007. (ENG.). 32p. (J). (gr. k-5). 17.99 (978-0-689-87153-5(8), McElderry, Margaret K. Bks.) McElderry, Margaret K. Bks.

Sierra, Judy. Antarctic Antics: A Book of Penguin Poems. Aruego, Jose & Dewey, Ariane, illus. 2003. (ENG.). 32p. (J). (gr. -1-3). pap. 6.99 (978-0-15-204602-6(X)) Houghton Mifflin Harcourt Publishing Co.

Spinelli, Eileen. Song for the Whooping Crane. Warnick, Elsa, illus. 2004. 32p. (J). (gr. 3-6). 16.00 (978-0-8028-5172-7(X)) Eerdmans, William B. Publishing Co.

Steffen, Tim. The Big Book of Birds. 2012. (ENG., Illus.). 64p. (J). pap. 9.95 (978-0-9779518-6-4(3)) Cardinal Pr.

Tietjen, Amy. Birds I've Met Through the Alphabet. Fitts, Seth, illus. 2013. 32p. pap. 17.95 (978-1-938230-33-2(7)) Vabella Publishing.

Van Wassenhove, Sue. The Seldom-Ever-Shady Glades. 2008. (ENG., Illus.). 32p. (J). (gr. 3-7). 17.95 (978-1-59078-352-8(2), Wordsong) Boyds Mills Pr.

BIRDS—PROTECTION

Salmansohn, Pete & Kress, Stephen W. Saving Birds: Heroes Around the World, 1 vol. 2005. (ENG., Illus.). 40p. (gr. 3-6). 16.95 (978-0-88448-237-6(5)) Tilbury Hse. Pubs.

BIRDS IN ART

Ames, Lee J. & D'Adamo, Tony. Draw 50 Birds. 2013. (Draw 50 Ser.). lib. bdg. 20.85 (978-0-606-26509-6(0), Turtleback) Turtleback Bks.

—Draw 50 Birds: The Step-By-Step Way to Draw Chickadees, Peacocks, Toucans, Mallards, & Many More of Our Feathered Friends. 2013. (ENG., Illus.). 64p. pap. 9.99 (978-0-8230-8598-9(8), Watson-Guptill) Potter/TenSpeed/Harmony.

Ard, Catherine. Drawing Zentangle Birds. Geddes, Hannah, illus. 2017. (How to Draw Zentangle Art Ser.). 32p. (gr. 3-3). pap. 63.00 **(978-1-5382-0706-2(0))** Stevens, Gareth Publishing LLLP.

Azzità, Emanuele. Origami Birds. 2017. (Exciting Origami Ser.). 48p. (J). (gr. 3-3). pap. 11.70 **(978-0-7660-8759-0(X))** Enslow Pubs., Inc.

Baumbusch, Brigitte. Birds in Art. 2005. (What Makes a Masterpiece? Ser.). (Illus.). 32p. (gr. 1-4). lib. bdg. 23.00 (978-0-8368-4443-6(2), Gareth Stevens Learning Library) Stevens, Gareth Publishing LLLP.

Creative Team at Walter Foster Publishing Staff. Learn to Draw Angry Birds: Learn to Draw All of Your Favorite Angry Birds & Those Bad Piggies! 2012. (Licensed Learn to Draw Ser.). (ENG., Illus.). 64p. (J). (gr. 1-3). pap. 9.95 (978-1-60058-306-3(7), 1600583067) Quarto Publishing Group USA.

—Learn to Draw Angry Birds Drawing Book & Kit: Includes Everything You Need to Draw Your Favorite Angry Birds Characters! 2013. (Licensed Learn to Draw Ser.). (ENG., Illus.). 32p. (J). (gr. 1-17). pap. 19.99 (978-1-60058-373-5(3), 1600583733) Quarto Publishing Group USA.

Cuddy, Robbin. Learn to Draw Birds & Butterflies: Step-By-step Instructions for More Than 25 Winged Creatures. 2016. (Learn to Draw Ser.). (ENG., Illus.). 64p. (J). (gr. 1-3). pap. 8.95 (978-1-63322-064-5(8)) Quarto Publishing Group USA.

Dicker, Katie. You Can Draw Birds! Saunders, Mike, illus. 2013. (Draw Your Pet! Ser.). 32p. (gr. 3-5). 26.60 (978-1-4339-8723-6(6)); pap. 10.50 (978-1-4339-8724-3(4)) Stevens, Gareth Publishing LLLP. (Gareth Stevens Learning Library).

Hardyman, Robyn. Origami Fun: Birds. 2017. (Origami Fun Ser.). (ENG., Illus.). 24p. (YA). (gr. 3-7). lib. bdg. 25.95 **(978-1-62617-708-6(2)**, Express Bks.) Bellwether Media.

Heller, D. M. Let's Make an Owl with Everyday Materials. (Let's Do Arts & Crafts Ser.). 24p. 2009. (gr. 2-2). 42.50 (978-1-61514-201-9(0), PowerKids Pr.) 2006. (Illus.). (J). lib. bdg. 22.60 (978-1-4042-3063-7(7)) Rosen Publishing Group, Inc., The.

Marroquin-Burr, Kristina, illus. Learn to Draw Angry Birds Space. 2014. 64p. (J). (gr. 3-5). 33.27 (978-1-939581-33-4(8)) Quarto Publishing Group USA.

Randolph, Joanne. Let's Draw a Bird with Shapes. Muschinske, Emily, illus. 2005. (Let's Draw with Shapes Ser.). 24p. (J). (gr. k-1). lib. bdg. 22.60 (978-1-4042-2792-7(X), PowerKids Pr.) Rosen Publishing Group, Inc., The.

—Let's Draw a Bird with Shapes: Vamos a Dibujar un Ave Usando Figuras. Muschinske, Emily, illus. 2005. (Let's Draw with Shapes / Vamos a Dibujar con Figuras Ser.). (J). 22.60 (978-1-4042-7555-3(X), PowerKids Pr.) Rosen Publishing Group, Inc., The.

Soffer, Ruth & Coloring Books Staff. Beautiful Birds in Mated Pairs Stained Glass Coloring Book. 2012. (Dover Nature Stained Glass Coloring Book Ser.). (ENG., Illus.). 32p. (gr. 3-5). pap. 7.99 (978-0-486-48680-2(X)) Dover Pubns., Inc.

Visca, Kelley & Visca, Curt. How to Draw Cartoon Birds. 2003. (Kid's Guide to Drawing Ser.). (Illus.). 24p. (J). lib. bdg. 25.25 (978-0-8239-6156-6(7), PowerKids Pr.) Rosen Publishing Group, Inc., The.

Visca, Kelly. How to Draw Cartoon Birds. 2009. (Kid's Guide to Drawing Ser.). 24p. (gr. 3-3). 47.90 (978-1-61511-011-7(9), PowerKids Pr.) Rosen Publishing Group, Inc., The.

BIRDS OF PREY

see also names of birds of prey, e.g. Eagles, etc.

Abbott, Henry. Buzzards, 01 vols., 1. 2016. (Raptors! Ser.). (ENG., Illus.). 24p. (J). pap. 8.25 (978-1-5081-4236-2(X), PowerKids Pr.) Rosen Publishing Group, Inc., The.

Birds of Prey: Level M, 6 vols. 128p. (gr. 2-3). 40.50 (978-0-7699-1030-7(0)) Shortland Pubns. (U. S. A.) Inc.

Burnie, David. Eagles & Birds of Prey. 2016. (DK Eyewitness Bks.). (ENG., Illus.). 72p. (J). (gr. 3-7). pap. 9.99 (978-1-4654-5172-9(2), DK Children) Dorling Kindersley Publishing, Inc.

Chevat, Richie. Ripley's Birds of Prey. 2004. (Illus.). 59p. (J). (978-0-439-63360-4(5)) Scholastic, Inc.

Curtis, Jennifer Keats. Animal Helpers: Raptor Centers, 1 vol. 2015. (Animal Helpers Ser.). (ENG., Illus.). 32p. (J). (gr. 2-5). 17.95 (978-1-62855-447-2(9)) Arbordale Publishing.

De la Bédoyère, Camilla. Birds of Prey. 2010. (Remarkable Man & Beast Ser.). (Illus.). 48p. (J). (gr. 3-18). lib. bdg. 19.95 (978-1-4222-1966-9(6)) Mason Crest.

Donovan, Amy & Shafran, Michael. My First Pocket Guide Birds of Prey. Emmett, Jennifer, ed. 2003. (National Geographic My First Pocket Guides). (ENG.). 80p. (J). (gr. 1-4). pap. 5.95 (978-0-7922-6929-8(2), National Geographic Children's Bks.) National Geographic Society.

Dunn, Mary R. & Hill, Melissa. Birds of Prey. 2015. (Birds of Prey Ser.). (ENG.). 24p. (gr. k-1). lib. bdg. 159.90 (978-1-4914-2580-0(6), Pebble Plus) Capstone Press of Coughlan Cos.

Evert, Laura & Lynch, Wayne. Birds of Prey. 2005. (Our Wild World Ser.). (ENG., Illus.). 192p. (J). (gr. 3-7). 16.95 (978-1-55971-925-4(7)) Cooper Square Publishing Llc.

Hickman, Pamela. Birds of Prey Rescue: Changing the Future for Endangered Wildlife. 2006. (Firefly Animal Rescue Ser.). (ENG., Illus.). 64p. (J). (gr. 5-12). 19.95 (978-1-55407-145-6(3), 9781554071456); pap. 9.95 (978-1-55407-144-9(5), 9781554071449) Firefly Bks., Ltd.

Jennings, Rosemary. Eagles, 01 vols., 1. 2016. (Raptors! Ser.). (ENG., Illus.). 24p. (J). pap. 8.25 (978-1-5081-4240-9(8), PowerKids Pr.) Rosen Publishing Group, Inc., The.

Kerrod, Robin. Birds of Prey: Learn about Eagles, Owls, Falcons, Hawks & Other Powerful Predators of the Air, in 190 Exciting Pictures. 2016. (ENG., Illus.). 64p. 12.99 (978-1-86147-483-4(0), Armadillo) Anness Publishing GBR. Dist: National Bk. Network.

Llewellyn, Claire. Kingfisher Readers L2: Birds of Prey. 2017. (Kingfisher Readers Ser.). (ENG.). 32p. (J). pap. 3.99 (978-0-7534-7342-9(9), 9780753473429, Kingfisher) Roaring Brook Pr.

National Geographic Kids Staff & Hoena, Blake. National Geographic Kids Everything Birds of Prey: Swoop in for Seriously Fierce Photos & Amazing Info. 2015. (National Geographic Kids Everything Ser.). (ENG., Illus.). 64p. (J). (gr. 3-7). pap. 12.99 (978-1-4263-1889-4(8), National Geographic Children's Bks.) National Geographic Society.

Publishers, Hancock House Publishers. Raptors - Birds of Prey Coloring Book. 2005. (Illus.). 24p. (J). pap. 4.95 (978-0-88839-600-6(7)) Hancock Hse. Pubs.

Rafferty, John P. Meat Eaters: Raptors, Sharks, & Crocodiles. 2011. (Britannica Guide to Predators & Prey Ser.). (Illus.). 208p. (YA). (gr. 9-12). lib. bdg. 51.70 (978-1-61530-342-7(1)) Rosen Publishing Group, Inc., The.

Reynolds, Toby & Calver, Paul. Birds of Prey. 2017. (Visual Explorers Ser.). (ENG.). 32p. (J). (gr. 3-7). pap. 6.99 **(978-1-4380-1081-6(8))** Barron's Educational Series, Inc.

Sill, Cathryn. About Raptors: A Guide for Children, 1 vol. Sill, John, illus. 2010. (ENG.). 48p. (J). (gr. -1-2). 16.95 (978-1-56145-536-2(9)) Peachtree Pubs.

BIRDSONGS

Berkes, Marianne. Marsh Morning. Noreika, Robert, illus. 2003. 32p. lib. bdg. 22.90 (978-0-7613-2568-0(9)); (J). 14.95 (978-0-7613-1936-8(0)) Lerner Publishing Group. (Millbrook Pr.).

Gerhard, Ana. Listen to the Birds: An Introduction to Classical Music. Varela, Cecilia, illus. 2013. (ENG.). 48p. (J). (gr. 2-4). 16.95 (978-2-923163-89-5(3)) La Montagne Secrete CAN. Dist: Independent Pubs. Group.

Gray, Rita. Have You Heard the Nesting Bird? Pak, Kenard, illus. 2014. (ENG.). 32p. (J). (gr. -1-3). 16.99 (978-0-544-10580-5(X), HMH Books For Young Readers) Houghton Mifflin Harcourt Publishing Co.

Himmelman, John. Noisy Bird Sing-Along, 1 vol. Himmelman, John, illus. 2015. (ENG., Illus.). 32p. (J). (gr. -1-4). pap. 8.95 (978-1-58469-514-1(5)) Dawn Pubns.

Judge, Lita. Bird Talk: What Birds Are Saying & Why. Judge, Lita, illus. 2012. (ENG., Illus.). 48p. (J). (gr. 1-4). 18.99 (978-1-59643-646-6(8), 9781596436466) Roaring Brook Pr.

Pinnington, Andrea. The Little Book of Backyard Bird Songs. 2016. (ENG., Illus.). 26p. (J). (gr. k-4). 19.95 (978-1-77085-744-5(3), 9781770857445) Firefly Bks., Ltd.

BIRMINGHAM (ALA.)

Levinson, Cynthia Y. We've Got a Job: The 1963 Birmingham Children's March, 1 vol. 2012. (ENG.). 192p. (J). 19.95 (978-1-56145-627-7(6)) Peachtree Pubs.

Tougas, Shelley. Birmingham 1963: How a Photograph Rallied Civil Rights Support, 1 vol. 2011. (Captured History Ser.). (ENG.). 64p. (gr. 5-7). pap. 9.10 (978-0-7565-4446-1(7)); lib. bdg. 34.65 (978-0-7565-4398-3(3)) Compass Point Bks. (CPB Grades 4-8).

BIRTH

see Childbirth

BIRTH CONTROL

see also Abortion

Bailey, Jacqui. The Debate about Birth Control. 2010. (Ethical Debates Ser.). (ENG.). 48p. (YA). lib. bdg. 26.50 (978-1-4488-1429-9(4), Rosen Reference) Rosen Publishing Group, Inc., The.

Birth Control Choices for Teens. 2004. (YA). 4.00 net. (978-1-930996-62-5(4)) Planned Parenthood Federation of America, Inc.

Cox, Vicki. Margaret Sanger. 2004. (Women in Medicine Ser.). (Illus.). 112p. (gr. 6-12). 30.00 (978-0-7910-8030-6(7), Chelsea Hse.) Facts On File, Inc.

Greenhaven Press Editors. Birth Control. 2012. (Issues That Concern You Ser.). (ENG., Illus.). 144p. (gr. 7-10). lib. bdg. 36.95 (978-0-7377-5689-0(6)) Cengage Gale.

Haerens, Margaret. Birth Control. Greenhaven Press Editors & Gale Editors, eds. 2014. (Global Viewpoints Ser.). (ENG., Illus.). 224p. (gr. 7-12). pap. 31.70 (978-0-7377-6436-9(8)); lib. bdg. 46.20 (978-0-7377-6260-0(8)) Cengage Gale. (Greenhaven Pr., Inc.).

Lange, Donna. Contraception & Pregnancy. Forman, Sara & McDonnell, Mary Ann, eds. 2013. (Young Adult's Guide to the Science of Health Ser.). (Illus.). 128p. (J). (gr. 7-18). pap. 14.95 (978-1-4222-3005-3(8)) Mason Crest.

—Contraception & Pregnancy. McDonnell, Mary Ann & Forman, Sara, eds. 2013. (Young Adult's Guide to the Science of Health Ser.: 15). (Illus.). 128p. (J). (gr. 7-18). 24.95 (978-1-4222-2805-0(3)) Mason Crest.

Lew, Kristi. Egg Donation: The Reasons & the Risks. 2009. (J). 77.70 (978-1-4358-5559-5(0)); (ENG.). 64p. (YA). pap. 12.95 (978-1-4358-5558-8(2)); (Illus.). 64p. (YA). (gr. 7-12). lib. bdg. 31.95 (978-1-4358-5276-1(1)) Rosen Publishing Group, Inc., The.

Merino, Noel. Birth Control. Greenhaven Press Editors, ed. 2014. (Teen Rights & Freedoms Ser.). (ENG., Illus.). 176p. (gr. 10-12). lib. bdg. 42.00 (978-0-7377-6994-4(7), Greenhaven Pr., Inc.) Cengage Gale.

Oransky Wittenstein, Vicki. Reproductive Rights: Who Decides? 2016. (ENG., Illus.). 160p. (J). (gr. 7-12). 19.99 (978-1-4677-9237-0(3), Twenty-First Century Bks.) Lerner Publishing Group.

Planned Parenthood Federation of America, Inc. Staff. The Condom. 2003. (YA). pap. 3.00 net. (978-0-934586-80-1(2)) Planned Parenthood Federation of America, Inc.

Vincent, Beverly & Greenberger, Robert. Frequently Asked Questions about Birth Control. 2011. (FAQ: Teen Life Ser.). (ENG.). 64p. (YA). (gr. 7-12). lib. bdg. 31.95 (978-1-4488-5561-2(6)) Rosen Publishing Group, Inc., The.

Waters, Sophie. The Female Reproductive System. (Girls' Health Ser.). 48p. 2009. (gr. 5-6). 53.00 (978-1-61512-732-0(1), Rosen Reference) 2007. (Illus.). (YA). (gr. 7-12). lib. bdg. 29.25 (978-1-4042-1950-2(1)) Rosen Publishing Group, Inc., The.

Wittenstein, Vicki Oransky. Reproductive Rights: Who Decides? 2016. (Nonfiction - Young Adult Ser.). (ENG., Illus.). 160p. (J). (gr. 7-12). 38.65 (978-1-4677-4187-3(6)) Lerner Publishing Group.

BIRTHDAYS

Adamson, Heather. Birthday Parties. 2010. (Special Days Ser.). 24p. (J). 25.65 (978-1-60753-028-2(7)) Amicus Publishing.

Auld, Mary. Celebrating a Birthday. 2011. (My Family & Me Ser.). 24p. lib. bdg. 24.25 (978-1-59771-229-3(9)) Sea-To-Sea Pubns.

Baby's Birthday: Individual Title Six-Packs. (Literatura 2000 Ser.). (gr. k-1). 28.00 (978-0-7635-0021-4(6)) Rigby Education.

Barrance, Reuben & Whatmore, Candice, illus. Birthday. 2008. (Usborne Look & Say Ser.). 12p. (J). (gr. -1-3). bds. 7.99 (978-0-7945-1988-9(1), Usborne) EDC Publishing.

Beringson, Lola. How Can You Lose with a Birthday to Choose? 2012. 24p. pap. 14.93 (978-1-4669-5517-2(1)) Trafford Publishing.

Bickico Enterprises, concept. BabyKids: Birthday Book. 2005. 16p. (J). pap. 2.95 (978-0-9746508-9-0(7)) Bickico Enterprises, Inc.

Birthday Cupcakes. (J). 26.20 (978-0-8136-8432-1(3)); 26.20 (978-0-8136-8431-4(5)); (gr. -1-3). 59.50 (978-0-8136-7984-6(2)) Modern Curriculum Pr.

Birthday in a Bathtub. (J). pap. 13.75 (978-0-8136-3401-2(6)) Modern Curriculum Pr.

Birthday Party Songs. (Early Learning Ser.). (J). incl. audio. 7.98 incl. audio NewSound, LLC.

Bullard, Lisa. Brandon's Birthday Surprise. Saunders, Katie, illus. 2012. (Holidays & Special Days Ser.). 24p. (gr. k-2). (J). pap. 39.62 (978-0-7613-9246-0(7), Millbrook Pr.); (ENG.). pap. 6.95 (978-0-7613-8578-3(9), Millbrook Pr.); (ENG.). lib. bdg. 23.93 (978-0-7613-5085-9(3)) Lerner Publishing Group.

Bye, K. A. I Like Birthdays! Interactive Book about Me. Ridgell, Earl W., Jr., illus. 2008. (ENG.). 30p. (J). (gr. -1-3). 13.95 (978-1-934490-02-0(4)) Boys Town Pr.

Chariot Family Staff. A Very Special Birthday. 2003. (My Jesus Pocket Bks.). 32p. (J). pap., pap. 8.90 (978-1-55513-131-9(X), 155513131X) Cook, David C.

Concordia Publishing House, creator. Happy Birthday: God's Blessings to You! 2007. (Illus.). 22p. (J). (gr. -1-k). bds. 6.49 (978-0-7586-1331-8(8)) Concordia Publishing Hse.

Dale, Jay. The Birthday Party, 1 vol. Robledo, Emilia, illus. 2012. (Engage Literacy Magenta Ser.). (ENG.). 32p. (gr. k-2). pap. 5.99 (978-1-4296-8866-6(1), Engage Literacy) Capstone Press of Coughlan Cos.

—Birthdays Around the World, 1 vol. Zamazing, Cherie, illus. 2012. (Engage Literacy Yellow Ser.). (ENG.). 32p. (gr. k-2). pap. 5.99 (978-1-4296-8966-3(8), Engage Literacy) Capstone Press of Coughlan Cos.

Dorling Kindersley Publishing Staff. Birthday. 2014. (Touch & Feel Ser.). (ENG.). 12p. (J). (gr. -1-k). bds. 6.99 (978-1-4654-1694-0(3), DK Children) Dorling Kindersley Publishing, Inc.

—Happy Birthday! 2013. (Baby Touch & Feel Ser.). (ENG.). 14p. (J). (gr. -1 — 1). bds. 5.99 (978-1-4654-1431-1(2), DK Children) Dorling Kindersley Publishing, Inc.

Dyan, Penelope. Happy Birthday! a Book about Birthdays, Dreams & Wishes. Dyan, Penelope, illus. 2009. (Illus.). 42p. pap. 11.95 (978-1-935118-73-2(0)) Bellissima Publishing, LLC.

Gamblin, Rose Tooley. The Birthday Party. 2007. (J). (978-0-8127-0464-8(9)) Autumn Hse. Publishing Co.

Giulieri, Anne. My Birthday, 1 vol. Kreinberg, Sylvia, photos by. 2012. (Engage Literacy Magenta Ser.). (ENG., Illus.). 32p. (gr. k-2). pap. 5.99 (978-1-4296-8868-0(8), Engage Literacy) Capstone Press of Coughlan Cos.

Happy Birthday!, 4 vols. 2010. (Happy Birthday! Ser.). (ENG.). 24p. (gr. k-1). lib. bdg. 106.60 (978-1-4296-4414-3(1), Pebble Plus) Capstone Press of Coughlan Cos.

Happy Birthday! [Capstone Sole Source]. 2010. (Happy Birthday! Ser.). 24p. lib. bdg. 95.96 (978-1-4296-5863-8(0), Pebble Plus) Capstone Press of Coughlan Cos.

Haworth, Margaret. It's My Birthday. Edwards, Paul, illus. 2003. 31p. (J). (gr. -1-3). pap. 10.00 (978-0-9740313-0-9(5)) Haworth, Margaret.

Hewitt, Sally. Happy Birthday. Cameron, Craig, illus. 2003. 14p. (J). pap. 10.95 (978-1-57145-735-6(6), Silver Dolphin Bks.) Readerlink Distribution Services, LLC.

Hinkler Books, ed. Baby's First Birthday. 2012. (Baby's First Ser.). 24p. (J). bds. 5.99 (978-1-74308-524-0(9)) Hinkler Bks. Pty, Ltd. AUS. Dist: Ideals Pubns.

—Baby's First Numbers. 2012. (Baby's First Ser.). 24p. (J). bds. 5.99 (978-1-74185-532-6(2)) Hinkler Bks. Pty, Ltd. AUS. Dist: Ideals Pubns.

Hogenkamp, S. My Birthday: Learning the IR Sound. 2009. (PowerPhonics Ser.). 24p. (gr. 1-1). 39.90 (978-1-60851-460-1(9), PowerKids Pr.) Rosen Publishing Group, Inc., The.

Holden, Pam. Happy Birthday, 6 pack. Hawley, Kelvin, illus. 2009. (Red Rocket Readers Ser.). (ENG.). 16p. (gr. -1-1). pap. (978-1-877363-03-0(0), Red Rocket Readers) Flying Start Bks.

Jones, Tammy. We Like Birthdays. 2009. (Sight Word Readers Set A Ser.). (J). 3.49 net. (978-1-60719-149-0(0)) Newmark Learning LLC.

Kalman, Bobbie. It Is My Birthday. 2010. (ENG., Illus.). 16p. (J). (gr. k-2). (978-0-7787-9418-9(0)); pap. (978-0-7787-9462-2(8)) Crabtree Publishing Co.

Kelly, Maoliosa. My Party. Lumb, Steve, photos by. 2005. (Collins Big Cat Ser.). (ENG., Illus.). 16p. (J). (gr. -1-k). pap. 5.99 (978-0-00-718533-7(2)) HarperCollins Pubs. Ltd. GBR. Dist: Independent Pubs. Group.

—My Party. 2005. (Big Cat Ser.). (gr. k-2). pap. 6.50 (978-1-60457-020-5(2)) Pacific Learning, Inc.

Lyons, Shelly. If You Were a Question Mark [LTD Commodities]. Gray, Sara, illus. 2010. (Word Fun Ser.). 24p. pap. 3.50 (978-1-4048-6253-1(6), Nonfiction Picture Bks.) Picture Window Bks.

—If You Were a Question Mark [Readers World]. Gray, Sara, illus. 2010. (Word Fun Ser.). 24p. pap. 2.72 (978-1-4048-6705-5(8), Nonfiction Picture Bks.) Picture Window Bks.

McGrath, Barbara Barbieri. The M & M's(r) Brand Birthday Book. Tagel, Peggy, illus. 2004. 12p. (J). (gr. -1-3). bds. 6.95 (978-1-57091-480-5(X)) Charlesbridge Publishing, Inc.

McKay, Sindy. Too Many Cats: Demasiados Gatos. 2010. (SPA., Illus.). 41p. (J). (978-1-60115-039-4(3)) Treasure Bay, Inc.

—We Both Read Bilingual Edition-Too Many Cats/Demasiados Gatos. Johnson, Meredith, illus. 2011. (ENG & SPA.). 44p. (J). pap. 4.99 (978-1-60115-040-0(7)) Treasure Bay, Inc.

McKissick, Katherine. Fun & Games: Planning a Perfect Party: Division (Grade 3) 2017. (Mathematics Readers Ser.). (Illus.). 32p. (gr. 3-3). 8.99 **(978-1-4807-5799-8(3))** Teacher Created Materials, Inc.

Miles, Sandy. Birthday: Words by John Lennon & Paul Mccartney. 2009. 20p. pap. 11.25 (978-1-4389-4951-2(0)) AuthorHouse.

Newman-D'Amico, Fran. Birthday Activity Book. 2006. (Dover Little Activity Bks.). (ENG., Illus.). 64p. (J). (gr. k-3). per., act. bk. ed. 1.99 (978-0-486-44441-3(4)) Dover Pubns., Inc.

Nunn, Daniel. Counting 1 To 10, 1 vol. 2012. (Math Every Day Ser.). (ENG., Illus.). 24p. (gr. -1-k). pap. 9.95 (978-1-4329-5735-3(X)); lib. bdg. 25.99 (978-1-4329-5730-8(9)) Heinemann-Raintree.

Raven, Margot Theis. Happy Birthday to You! The Mystery Behind the Most Famous Song in the World. Soentpiet, Chris K., illus. 2008. (ENG.). 37p. (J). (gr. k-6). 17.95 (978-1-58536-169-4(0)) Sleeping Bear Pr.

Rustad, Martha E. H. Birthdays in Many Cultures. 2016. (Life Around the World Ser.). (ENG.). 24p. (gr. k-1). pap. 7.29 (978-1-5157-4240-1(7), Pebble Plus) Capstone Press of Coughlan Cos.

Ruurs, Margriet. Birthdays Around the World. Barron, Ashley, illus. 2017. (Around the World Ser.). (ENG.). 40p. (J). (gr. -1-2). 18.99 **(978-1-77138-624-1(X))** Kids Can Pr., Ltd. CAN. Dist: Hachette Bk. Group.

Salas, Laura Purdie. C Is for Cake! A Birthday Alphabet. 2010. (Alphabet Fun Ser.). (ENG.). 32p. (gr. 1-2). pap. 47.70 (978-1-4296-5086-1(9)); lib. bdg. 27.32 (978-1-4296-3914-9(8)) Capstone Press of Coughlan Cos. (Aplus Bks.).

Schrock, Cynthia. The Ultimate Gift of a Birthday. 2010. 72p. pap. 9.95 (978-1-936343-17-1(7)) Peppertree Pr., The.

Schuette, Sarah L. Birthday Customs Around the World, 1 vol. 2010. (Happy Birthday! Ser.). (ENG.). 24p. (gr. k-1). lib. bdg. 26.65 (978-1-4296-4001-5(4), Pebble Plus) Capstone Press of Coughlan Cos.

—Birthday Party Games, 1 vol. 2010. (Happy Birthday! Ser.). (ENG.). 24p. (gr. k-1). lib. bdg. 26.65 (978-1-4296-4000-8(6), Pebble Plus) Capstone Press of Coughlan Cos.

Sévigny, Eric, illus. Caillou: The Birthday Party. 2014. (ENG.). 24p. (J). (gr. -1-1). pap. 4.99 *(978-2-89718-122-2(2))* Caillouet, Gerry.

Shaw-Russell, Susan. Under the Sea Party Sticker Activity Book. 2011. (Dover Little Activity Books Stickers Ser.). (ENG., Illus.). 4p. (J). (gr. k-3). 1.99 *(978-0-486-47535-6(2))* Dover Pubns., Inc.

Smith, Paula. Birthdays in Different Places. 2015. (Learning about Our Global Community Ser.). (ENG.). 24p. (J). *(978-0-7787-2011-9(X))* Crabtree Publishing Co.

Speechley, Greta. Birthday Crafts. 2010. (Creative Crafts for Kids Ser.). 32p. (J). (gr. 2-5). lib. bdg. 28.00 *(978-1-4339-3552-7(X))*; (Illus.). pap. 10.50 *(978-1-4339-3553-4(8))* Stevens, Gareth Publishing LLLP. (Gareth Stevens Learning Library).

Tan, Ming, et al. Getting Ready. 2007. (Windows on Literacy Ser.). (ENG., Illus.). 12p. pap. 10.95 *(978-0-7922-8456-7(9))* National Geographic School Publishing, Inc.

Tate, Nikki & Tate-Stratton, Dani. Birthdays: Beyond Cake & Ice Cream. 1 vol. 2017. (Orca Origins Ser.). (ENG., Illus.). 80p. (J). (gr. 3-7). 24.95 *(978-1-4598-1297-0(2))* Orca Bk. Pubs. USA.

Ticktock Media, Ltd. Staff. Birthday Party. 2009. (Busy Tots Ser.). (ENG.). 10p. (J). (gr. -1-k). bds. 6.95 *(978-1-84696-801-3(1)*, TickTock Books) Octopus Publishing Group GBR. Dist: Independent Pubs. Group.

Vallejo-Nagera, Alejandra. Cuando Llegara Mi Cumpleanos? Guerrero, Andres, illus. (SPA.). 29p. (J). (gr. k-1). 8.95 *(978-1-58986-548-8(0))* Santillana USA Publishing Co., Inc.

Walker, Robert. Happy Birthday! 2010. (Celebrations in My World Ser.). (ENG.). 32p. (J). (gr. k-3). pap. *(978-0-7787-4934-9(7))*; lib. bdg. *(978-0-7787-4927-1(4))* Crabtree Publishing Co.

Watson, Stephanie. Plan a Birthday Party. 2014. (Party Time! Ser.). (ENG., Illus.). 32p. (gr. 4-8). lib. bdg. 26.60 *(978-1-4677-3835-4(2)*, Lerner Pubns.) Lerner Publishing Group.

Williams, Colleen Madonna Flood. My Adventure on My Birthday. 2009. 44p. (J). 8.99 *(978-1-59092-553-9(X))* Blue Forge Pr.

BIRTHDAYS—FICTION

Acevedo, Jenny. Ginger's Grand Adventure. 2012. 36p. pap. 24.95 *(978-1-4626-2472-0(3))* America Star Bks.

Adams, Colleen. The Big Day! 2006. (Neighborhood Readers Ser.). (ENG.). 8p. (gr. -1-3). pap. 5.15 *(978-1-4042-5708-5(X)*, Rosen Classroom) Rosen Publishing Group, Inc., The.

Adler, David A. Birthday Mystery. Natti, Susanna, illus. 2005. (Cam Jansen Ser.: 20). (ENG.). 64p. (J). (gr. 2-5). 4.99 *(978-0-14-240354-9(7)*, Puffin Books) Penguin Young Readers Group.

—Bones & the Birthday Mystery, No. 5. Newman, Barbara Johansen, illus. 2009. (Bones Ser.: 5). (ENG.). 32p. (J). (gr. 1-3). mass mkt. 3.99 *(978-0-14-241432-3(8)*, Penguin Young Readers) Penguin Young Readers Group.

—Bones & the Clown Mix-Up Mystery, No. 8. Newman, Barbara Johansen, illus. 2011. (Bones Ser.: 8). (ENG.). 32p. (J). (gr. 1-3). 3.99 *(978-0-14-241825-3(0)*, Penguin Young Readers) Penguin Young Readers Group.

Aikins, Dave, illus. The Birthday Dance Party: Daisy's Fiesta de Quinceañera. 2006. (Dora the Explorer Ser.: 19). (ENG.). 24p. (J). (gr. -1-3). pap. 3.99 *(978-1-4169-1303-0(3)*, Simon Spotlight/Nickelodeon) Simon Spotlight/Nickelodeon.

Alemagna, Beatrice. Bugs in a Blanket. 2009. (ENG.). 42p. (gr. -1-4). 12.95 *(978-0-7148-4970-6(7))* Phaidon Pr., Inc.

Alemagna, Beatrice, creator. The Wonderful Fluffy Little Squishy. 2015. (ENG., Illus.). 48p. (J). (gr. -1-3). 18.95 *(978-1-59270-180-3(9))* Enchanted Lion Bks., LLC.

Allen, Francesca & Brooks, Felicity. Busy Truck. Crisp, Dan, illus. 2007. (Usborne Play Bks.). 10p. (J). (gr. -1-k). bds. 10.99 *(978-0-7945-1453-2(7)*, Usborne) EDC Publishing.

Amatangelo, Sergio Lino. Forever Four, Finally Five. 2008. (Illus.). 32p. (J). pap. 8.00 *(978-0-8059-7680-9(9))* Dorrance Publishing Co., Inc.

Anderson, Airlie, illus. A Very Patchy Flap Book. 2004. 10p. (J). bds. 5.95 *(978-1-58925-702-3(2))* Tiger Tales.

Anderson, Shel. Spoofaloof's Adventures: Rainy Day Fun. Anderson, Shauna, illus. 2008. 52p. pap. 22.50 *(978-1-4389-1689-7(2))* AuthorHouse.

Anderson, T. L. Fifth Street: The Birthday Wish. 2011. 28p. 12.99 *(978-1-4520-9847-0(6))* AuthorHouse.

Andrew-Kollmann, Marcia. Blinky the Magical Elf. Dittus, Jade Moon, illus. 2012. 28p. pap. 24.95 *(978-1-4626-5345-4(6))* America Star Bks.

Anfousse, Ginette. Polo et L'anniversaire. Sarrazin, Marisol, tr. 2003. (Polo Baby Board Bks.). (FRE., Illus.). 16p. (J). (— 1). bds. *(978-2-89021-656-3(X))* Diffusion du livre Mirabel (DLM).

Annie Starks-Johnson, Starks-Johnson & Annie Starks-Johnson. Dottie's Surprise Birthday Party. 2009. 24p. pap. 11.49 *(978-1-4389-4866-9(2))* AuthorHouse.

Arena, Felice & Kettle, Phil. Halloween Gotcha! Gordon, Gus, illus. 2004. (J). pap. *(978-1-59336-373-4(7))* Mondo Publishing.

Armstrong, Kim. Petunia in Manhattan. 2009. 50p. pap. 12.99 *(978-1-935436-97-3(X))* Rodaian Pr.

Asch, Frank. Happy Birthday, Moon. Asch, Frank, illus. 2014. (Moonbear Ser.). (ENG., Illus.). 32p. (J). (gr. -1-3). 7.99 *(978-1-4424-9400-8(X)*, Aladdin) Simon & Schuster Children's Publishing.

Asch, Frank & Asch, Frank. Happy Birthday, Moon. Asch, Frank & Asch, Frank, illus. 2005. (Stories to Go! Ser.). (ENG., Illus.). 32p. (J). 4.99 *(978-1-4169-0307-9(0)*, Simon & Schuster/Paula Wiseman Bks.) Simon & Schuster/Paula Wiseman Bks.

Ashford, Kathy. Spencer's Birthday. 2009. 16p. pap. 24.95 *(978-1-60749-778-3(6))* America Star Bks.

Ashley, Sharon. I Wish I Could See. 2013. 24p. pap. 24.95 *(978-1-4626-9700-7(3))* America Star Bks.

Austin, Cassandra. Born Right Here at Home. 2011. 20p. pap. 9.99 *(978-1-936750-05-4(8))* Yorkshire Publishing Group.

Averbeck, Jim. One Word from Sophia. Ismail, Yasmeen, illus. 2015. (ENG.). 40p. (J). (gr. -1-3). 17.99 *(978-1-4814-0514-0(4))* Simon & Schuster Children's Publishing.

Averill, Esther. Jenny's Birthday Book. Averill, Esther, illus. 2005. (New York Review Children's Collection). (ENG., Illus.). 44p. (J). (gr. -1-2). reprint ed. 15.95 *(978-1-59017-154-7(3)*, NYR Children's Collection) New York Review of Bks., Inc., The.

Avi. Ereth's Birthday. Floca, Brian, illus. 2006. (Poppy Stories Ser.). (ENG.). 224p. (J). (gr. 3-7). pap. 6.99 *(978-0-380-80490-0(5))* HarperCollins Pubs.

Aviation Book Company Staff. Ereth's Birthday. 2006. (Poppy Stories Ser.: 4). (Illus.). viii, 180p. (J). (gr. 3-6). lib. bdg. 17.20 *(978-0-613-44206-0(7)*, Turtleback) Turtleback Bks.

Avraham, Kate Aver. What Will You Be, Sara Mee? O'Brien, Anne Sibley, illus. 2010. (ENG.). 32p. (J). (gr. -1-3). 16.95 *(978-1-58089-210-0(8))*; pap. 7.95 *(978-1-58089-211-7(6))* Charlesbridge Publishing, Inc.

Bach, Annie. Monster Party! 2014. (ENG., Illus.). 32p. (J). (gr. -1-k). 9.95 *(978-1-4549-1051-0(8))* Sterling Publishing Co., Inc.

Bailey's Birthday - Evaluation Guide: Evaluation Guide. 2006. (J). *(978-1-55942-399-1(4))* Witcher Productions.

Baltazar, Franco & Art Baltazar Comic Book Staff. Field Trippin, Vol. 5. 2011. (ENG., Illus.). 160p. (J). (gr. 2-5). pap. 12.99 *(978-1-4012-3173-6(X))* DC Comics.

Baratz-Logsted, Lauren. Zinnia's Zaniness. 2011. (Sisters Eight Ser.: 8). (ENG., Illus.). 128p. (J). (gr. 1-4). pap. 5.99 *(978-0-547-55439-6(7))* Houghton Mifflin Harcourt Publishing Co.

Barn Party: Level M, 6 vols. 128p. (gr. 2-3). 49.95 *(978-0-7699-0983-7(3))* Shortland Pubns. (U. S. A.) Inc.

Barr, Mary. The Trouble with Filly Tucker. 2010. 112p. (gr. 4-6). 20.95 *(978-1-4502-3517-4(4))*; pap. 10.95 *(978-1-4502-3515-0(8))* iUniverse, Inc.

Basha, Irena Canaj. The Birthday Party, It Was Saturday... 2013. 16p. pap. 24.95 *(978-1-62709-182-4(3))* America Star Bks.

Bastianich, Lidia Matticchio. Lidia's Family Kitchen: Nonna's Birthday Surprise. Graef, Renee, illus. 2013. (ENG.). 60p. (J). (gr. -1-17). 16.95 *(978-0-7624-4655-1(2)*, Running Pr. Kids) Running Pr. Bk. Pubs.

Bates, Janet. Seaside Dream. 1 vol. Davis, Lambert, illus. 2016. (ENG.). 32p. (J). pap. 9.95 *(978-1-62014-256-1(2))* Lee & Low Bks., Inc.

Bates, Janet Costa. Seaside Dream. Davis, Lambert, illus. 2013. (ENG.). 32p. (J). (gr. k-5). 17.95 *(978-1-60060-347-1(5))* Lee & Low Bks., Inc.

Baum, L. Frank. The Road to Oz. 2009. (Little Golden Book Ser.). (ENG., Illus.). 24p. (J). (gr. -1-2). 3.99 *(978-0-375-84757-8(X)*, Golden Bks.) Random Hse. Children's Bks.

Beall, Kirsten. Jake & the Big Cake Mistake. Desmond, Hillary, illus. 2011. 36p. pap. 24.95 *(978-1-4626-4524-4(0))* America Star Bks.

Beam, Emily. Tumtum & Nutmeg: Adventures Beyond Nutmouse Hall. 2011. (Tumtum & Nutmeg Ser.: 1). (ENG., Illus.). 512p. (J). (gr. 3-7). pap. 10.00 *(978-0-316-07574-9(4))* Little, Brown Bks. for Young Readers.

—Tumtum & Nutmeg: the Rose Cottage Adventures. Price, Nick, illus. 2013. (Tumtum & Nutmeg Ser.: 2). (ENG.). 416p. (J). (gr. 3-7). pap. 10.99 *(978-0-316-08598-4(7))* Little, Brown Bks. for Young Readers.

Beaty, Andrea. Happy Birthday, Madame Chapeau. Roberts, David, illus. 2014. (ENG.). 32p. (J). (gr. k-2). 16.95 *(978-1-4197-1219-7(5)*, Abrams Bks. for Young Readers) Abrams, Inc.

Beck, Bev. The Birthday Present. DeWeese, Susan, illus. 2011. 40p. pap. 24.95 *(978-1-4560-8398-4(8))* America Star Bks.

Becker, Bonny. A Birthday for Bear. Denton, Kady MacDonald, illus. (Candlewick Sparks Ser.). (ENG.). (J). 2013. 56p. (gr. k-4). pap. 3.99 *(978-0-7636-6861-7(3))* 2012. 48p. (gr. -1-2). 16.99 *(978-0-7636-5823-6(5))* Candlewick Pr.

Bella's Birthday. 2003. (Bella & Rosie Set 1 Ser.). (J). 7.67 *(978-1-932570-09-0(8))* Pioneer Valley Bks.

Benchmark Education Company, LLC Staff, compiled by. Celebrations. 2006. (J). 148.00 *(978-1-4108-7039-1(1))* Benchmark Education Co.

Bennett, David. The Big Surprise. 2004. (Ben & Friends Ser.). (Illus.). 24p. (J). pap. 4.99 *(978-1-85854-692-6(3))* Brimax Books Ltd. GBR. Dist: Byeway Bks.

Benson, Linda Sue. Hey Latrell, 1 vol. Johnson, Bruce, illus. 2009. 48p. pap. 16.95 *(978-1-60813-961-3(1))* America Star Bks.

Bentley, Sue. Party Dreams, 5 vols. Farley, Andrew & Swan, Angela, illus. 2010. (Magic Puppy Ser.: 5). (ENG.). 128p. (J). (gr. 1-3). pap. 5.99 *(978-0-448-45064-3(X)*, Grosset & Dunlap) Penguin Young Readers Group.

Benton, Lynne. Pirate Pete. Chapman, Neil, illus. 2008. (Tadpoles Ser.). (ENG.). 24p. (J). (gr. -1-3). pap. *(978-0-7787-3892-3(2))* Crabtree Publishing Co.

Berenstain, Jan & Berenstain, Mike. Berenstain Bears & the Forgiving Tree, 1 vol. 2011. (Berenstain Bears/Living Lights Ser.). (ENG.). 32p. (J). pap. 3.99 *(978-0-310-72084-3(2))* Zonderkidz.

Berenstain, Stan & Berenstain, Jan. Los Osos Berenstain y Demasiada Fiesta. 2004.Tr. of Berenstain Bears & Too Much Birthday. (SPA., Illus.). (J). (gr. k-3). spiral bd. *(978-0-616-14610-1(8))* Canadian National Institute for the Blind/Institut National Canadien pour les Aveugles.

Bergen, Lara. Diego's Birthday Surprise. Mawhinney, Art, illus. 2008. (Go, Diego, Go! Ser.: 8). (ENG.). 24p. (J). (gr. -1-1). pap. 3.99 *(978-1-4169-5431-6(7)*, Simon Spotlight/Nickelodeon) Simon Spotlight/Nickelodeon.

Bernal, Sandra Marie. I Want a Pand. 2011. 32p. pap. 24.95 *(978-1-4626-2897-1(4))* America Star Bks.

Berrios, Frank. Batman's Birthday Surprise! (DC Super Friends) Random House & Doescher, Erik, illus. 2016. (Pictureback(R) Ser.). (ENG.). 16p. (J). (gr. -1-2). 4.99 *(978-0-553-53983-7(3)*, Random Hse. Bks. for Young Readers) Random Hse. Children's Bks.

Bertrand, Diane Gonzales & Ventura, Gabriela Baeza. A Bean & Cheese Taco Birthday / un Cumpleaños con Tacos de Frijoles con Queso. Trujillo, Robert, illus. 2015. (SPA & ENG.). 32p. (J). (gr. k-3). 17.95 *(978-1-55885-812-1(1))* Arte Publico Pr.

—The Party for Papá Luis/La Fiesta para Papá Luis. Galindo, Alejandro, illus. 2010. (ENG.). 32p. (J). (gr. -1-3). 16.95 *(978-1-55885-532-8(7))* Arte Publico Pr.

The Best Birthday Present: Individual Title Six-Packs. (Literatura 2000 Ser.). (gr. 2-3). 33.00 *(978-0-7635-0216-4(2))* Rigby Education.

Best, Cari. Three Cheers for Catherine the Great! Potter, Giselle, illus. 2003. (Catherine the Great Ser.). (ENG.). 32p. (J). (gr. -1-3). pap. 8.99 *(978-0-374-47551-2(2)*, 9780374475512) Square Fish.

Bianchi, John. Happy Birthday! 2016. (1-3Y Bird, Bunny & Bear Ser.). (ENG., Illus.). 16p. (J). pap. 5.99 ***(978-1-63437-576-4(9))*** American Reading Co.

Bickel, Karla. Surprise Christmas Birthday Party. Bickel, Karla, illus. l.t. ed. 2004. (Illus.). 16p. (J). (gr. -1-6). pap. 5.00 *(978-1-891452-12-3(6)*, 3) Heart Arbor Bks.

Birchall, Mark. Rabbit's Birthday Surprise. Birchall, Mark, illus. 2003. (Illus.). 32p. (J). (gr. -1-3). 15.95 *(978-0-87614-910-2(7)*, Carolrhoda Bks.) Lerner Publishing Group.

Birdsall, Jeanne. The Penderwicks in Spring. 2015. (Penderwicks Ser.). (ENG.). 352p. (J). (gr. 3-7). 16.99 *(978-0-375-87077-4(6)*, Knopf Bks. for Young Readers) Random Hse. Children's Bks.

The Birthday Party. (Early Intervention Levels Ser.). 23.10 *(978-0-7362-0002-8(9))* CENGAGE Learning.

A Birthday Present for Spaceboy. 2003. (Spaceboy Set 1 Ser.). (J). pap. 7.33 *(978-1-932570-03-8(9)*, Pioneer Valley Bks.) Pioneer Valley Bks.

Birthday Vicious. 2014. (Ashley Project Ser.: 3). (ENG., Illus.). 304p. (J). (gr. 4-8). pap. 7.99 *(978-1-4424-9038-3(1)*, Aladdin) Simon & Schuster Children's Publishing.

Blackburn, Sheila M. Stewie Scraps & the Giant Joggers. 2008. 76p. pap. *(978-1-903853-86-3(9))* Brilliant Pubns.

Blackstone, Stella. Bear's Birthday. Harter, Debbie, illus. 2011.Tr. of El Cumpleanos de Oso. (ENG.). 24p. (J). (gr. -1-1). pap. 6.99 *(978-1-84686-515-2(8))*; bds. 7.99 *(978-1-84686-516-9(6))* Barefoot Bks., Inc.

—Bear's Birthday (L'Anniversaire de l'Ours) Harter, Debbie, illus. 2013. (ENG & FRE.). 24p. (J). (gr. k-1). pap. 6.99 *(978-1-84686-944-0(7))* Barefoot Bks., Inc.

—Bear's Birthday/El Cumpleanos de Oso. Harter, Debbie, illus. 2013. (ENG & SPA.). 24p. (J). (gr. k-1). 6.99 *(978-1-84686-943-3(9))* Barefoot Bks., Inc.

Blair, Marcia L. Nana's Birthday Bubbles. 2012. 24p. pap. 24.95 *(978-1-4626-7880-8(7))* America Star Bks.

Blume, Erma Hill. Tattle-Tale Pete. 2012. 28p. pap. 24.95 *(978-1-62709-097-1(5))* America Star Bks.

Blyton, Enid. Birthday Kitten. (Illus.). (J). 95p. pap. 4.95 *(978-0-09-924100-3(5))*; 192p. pap. 5.95 *(978-0-09-977930-8(7))* Random Hse. GBR. Dist: Trafalgar Square Publishing.

Bocanegra, Deborah. Winky Sue's Peppermint Birthday. Buehrle, Jacquelyn, illus. 2012. 26p. 24.95 *(978-1-4560-7282-7(X))* America Star Bks.

Bonnell, Kris. Presents for Mom. 2007. (J). pap. 6.95 *(978-1-933727-61-5(6))* Reading Reading Bks., LLC.

Border, Terry & Mack, Jeff. Happy Birthday, Cupcake! Border, Terry, illus. 2015. (ENG., Illus.). 32p. (J). (gr. k-3). bds. 17.99 *(978-0-399-17160-4(6)*, Philomel Bks.) Penguin Young Readers Group.

Boss, Nicco. Message to Badabu. 2013. 356p. pap. 12.99 *(978-0-9891635-1-4(2))* Nicco Boss, LLC.

Boudreaux, Amanda. A Birthday Breakfast. 2012. 24p. pap. 17.99 *(978-1-62230-383-0(0))* Salem Author Services.

Bouldin, Anthony Roth & Bouldin, Morshica. Tag along with Momo & Jojo: You're It! Series #2. 2012. 16p. pap. 15.99 *(978-1-4772-6797-4(2))* AuthorHouse.

Bourgeois, Paulette & Clark, Brenda. Franklin Snoops. 2003. (Franklin TV Storybook Ser.). (ENG., Illus.). 32p. (J). (gr. -1-3). 4.95 *(978-1-55337-365-0(0))* Kids Can Pr., Ltd. CAN. Dist: Hachette Bk. Group.

Bowe, Julie. Birthday Glamour! 2015. (Victoria Torres, Unfortunately Average Ser.). (ENG.). 160p. (gr. 4-4). lib. bdg. 26.65 *(978-1-4965-0533-0(6))* Stone Arch Bks.

Bowman, Crystal. The Best Thing about My Birthday. 2014. (Happy Day Ser.). (ENG.). 16p. (J). pap. 2.49 *(978-1-4143-9485-5(3))* Tyndale Hse. Pubs.

Bradman, Tony. Dilly & the Birthday Treat. Hellard, Susan, illus. 2016. (Reading Ladder Ser.). (ENG.). 48p. (J). (gr. k-2). 7.99 *(978-1-4052-8210-9(X))* Egmont Bks., Ltd. GBR. Dist: Independent Pubs. Group.

Bradshaw, Dustin W. Counting Candles. 2014. (Illus.). 231p. pap. 15.99 *(978-1-4621-1433-7(4))* Cedar Fort, Inc./CFI Distribution.

Braun, Sebastien. Mayday Mouse. Braun, Sebastien, illus. 2017. (Child's Play Library). (ENG., Illus.). 32p. (J). (gr. k-3). *(978-1-84643-759-5(8))* Child's Play International Ltd.

Brian, Kate, pseud. Sweet 16. 2007. (ENG.). 288p. (YA). (gr. 7-12). pap. 9.99 *(978-1-4169-0033-7(0)*, Simon & Schuster Bks. For Young Readers) Simon & Schuster Bks. For Young Readers.

—Vengeance. 2011. (Private Ser.). (ENG.). 240p. (YA). (gr. 9). pap. 9.99 *(978-1-4169-8473-9(3)*, Simon & Schuster Bks. For Young Readers) Simon & Schuster Bks. For Young Readers.

Bridwell, Norman. Clifford's Birthday Party. Bridwell, Norman, illus. 50th anniv. ed. 2013. (Clifford Ser.). (ENG., Illus.). 32p. (J). (gr. -1-3). pap. 4.99 *(978-0-545-47956-1(8))* Scholastic, Inc.

Bright, Phoebe. Lucky Stars #1: Wish upon a Friend. 2012. (Lucky Stars Ser.). (ENG.). 96p. (J). (gr. 2-5). pap. 5.99 *(978-0-545-41998-7(0)*, Scholastic Paperbacks) Scholastic, Inc.

Broadhurst, Sherree. Bella Finds the Hidden Treasure. 2009. 28p. pap. 12.25 *(978-1-60693-815-7(0)*, Eloquent Bks.) Strategic Book Publishing & Rights Agency (SBPRA).

Brown, Monica. Marisol McDonald & the Clash Bash/Marisol Mcdonald y la Fiesta Sin Igual. Palacios, Sara, illus. 2013. (Marisol Mcdonald Ser.). (ENG & SPA.). 40p. (J). 18.95 *(978-0-89239-273-5(8))* Lee & Low Bks., Inc.

Brown, Ruby. Birthday in a Box: Now I Am 3. Chatterton, Chris, illus. 2016. (ENG.). 20p. (J). (gr. -1 — 1). 19.99 *(978-1-76012-332-1(3))* Hardie Grant Egmont Pty, Ltd. AUS. Dist: Independent Pubs. Group.

—Birthday in a Box: Now I Am 4. Chatterton, Chris, illus. 2016. (ENG.). 20p. (J). (gr. -1 — 1). 19.99 *(978-1-76012-333-8(1))* Hardie Grant Egmont Pty, Ltd. AUS. Dist: Independent Pubs. Group.

—Birthday in a Box: Now I Am 5. Chatterton, Chris, illus. 2016. (ENG.). 20p. (J). (gr. k-k). 19.99 *(978-1-76012-334-5(X))* Hardie Grant Egmont Pty, Ltd. AUS. Dist: Independent Pubs. Group.

Bruel, Nick. Happy Birthday, Bad Kitty. Bruel, Nick, illus. 2009. (Bad Kitty Ser.). (ENG., Illus.). 160p. (J). (gr. 2-5). 15.99 *(978-1-59643-342-7(6)*, 9781596433427) Roaring Brook Pr.

—Happy Birthday, Bad Kitty. Bruel, Nick, illus. 2010. (Bad Kitty Ser.). (ENG., Illus.). 176p. (J). (gr. 2-5). pap. 6.99 *(978-0-312-62902-1(8)*, 9780312629021) Square Fish.

Bruno's Birthday: Individual Title Six-Packs. (Literatura 2000 Ser.). (gr. 1-2). 28.00 *(978-0-7635-0086-3(0))* Rigby Education.

Brust, Beth Wagner. The Great Tulip Trade. Mattheson, Jenny, illus. 2005. (Step into Reading Ser.). 48p. (J). (gr. 1-3). 11.65 *(978-0-7569-5160-3(7))* Perfection Learning Corp.

Bunting, Eve. The Baby Shower. Love, Judy, illus. 2007. (ENG.). 28p. (J). (gr. -1-2). 15.95 *(978-1-58089-139-4(X))* Charlesbridge Publishing, Inc.

—Flower Garden. Hewitt, Kathryn, illus. 2004. 28p. (gr. -1-2). 17.00 *(978-0-7569-4113-0(X))* Perfection Learning Corp.

Burick, Rebecca. Little Daisy Tutu. Burick, Rebecca & Burick Jr., Michael, illus. 2012. 28p. pap. 24.95 *(978-1-4560-6883-7(0))* America Star Bks.

Burke, Patrick J. Getting Your First Allowance. Severino, Philip, illus. 2008. 28p. pap. 24.95 *(978-1-60441-882-8(6))* America Star Bks.

Burkhart, Jessica. Bella's Birthday Unicorn. Ying, Victoria, illus. 2014. (Unicorn Magic Ser.: 1). (ENG.). 144p. (J). (gr. 1-4). 15.99 *(978-1-4814-1105-9(5))*; pap. 5.99 *(978-1-4424-9822-8(6))* Simon & Schuster Children's Publishing. (Aladdin).

—Masquerade. 2012. (Canterwood Crest Ser.: 16). (ENG.). 256p. (J). (gr. 4-7). pap. 7.99 *(978-1-4424-3655-8(7)*, Aladdin) Simon & Schuster Children's Publishing.

—Masquerade. 2012. (Canterwood Crest Ser.: 16). lib. bdg. 18.40 *(978-0-606-26887-5(1)*, Turtleback) Turtleback Bks.

Burroughs, Denise. The Story of the Day You Were Born. 2012. 28p. pap. 16.00 *(978-1-4772-4547-7(2))* AuthorHouse.

Burton, Lynne. Charlotte's Crocodile. 2012. 22p. pap. *(978-1-909395-00-8(5))* Legend Pr.

Butler, Kristi T. A Big Surprise. Paparone, Pamela, illus. 2005. (Green Light Readers Level 1 Ser.). (ENG.). 24p. (J). (gr. -1-3). pap. 3.95 *(978-0-15-205141-9(4))* Houghton Mifflin Harcourt Publishing Co.

Byrd, B. N. My Favorite Toy. 2011. 40p. pap. 21.99 *(978-1-4500-5290-0(8))* Xlibris Corp.

Byrd, Cari Grigsby. Where Did Pop Pop Go? 2013. 24p. pap. 24.95 *(978-1-62709-967-7(0))* America Star Bks.

Cabrera, Jane. One, Two, Buckle My Shoe. 2009. (ENG., Illus.). 32p. (J). (gr. -1-k). 16.95 *(978-0-8234-2230-2(5))* Holiday Hse., Inc.

Cail, Carol. Dibby Witch's Bing Bang Birthday. 2013. 74p. pap. 20.99 *(978-1-60820-908-8(3))* MLR Pr., LLC.

Calford, Farley. The Complete Disaster, Rhonda's Birthday Party. 2009. 86p. pap. 9.95 *(978-1-60860-210-0(9)*, Eloquent Bks.) Strategic Book Publishing & Rights Agency (SBPRA).

Calmenson, Stephanie. Birthday at the Panda Palace. Cushman, Doug, illus. 2007. 32p. (J). (gr. -1-3). 15.99 *(978-0-06-052663-4(7))* HarperCollins Pubs.

Calvani, Mayra. Chocalin! Pylypchuck, Anna, illus. 2009. 24p. pap. 10.95 *(978-1-935137-69-6(7))* Guardian Angel Publishing, Inc.

Calvani, Mayra & Pylypchuk, Anna. Crash! 2008. 24p. pap. 10.95 *(978-1-933090-54-2(5))* Guardian Angel Publishing, Inc.

Camila y Su Fiesta de Cumpleanos. 2003. (SPA.). 62p. (J). (gr. -1-1). *(978-968-5308-79-3(9)*, Silver Dolphin en Español) Advanced Marketing, S. de R. L. de C. V.

Cammuso, Frank. Big Birthday Bash. 2014. (Misadventures of Salem Hyde Ser.). (ENG., Illus.). 96p. (J). (gr. 1-4). 14.95 *(978-1-4197-1025-4(7)*, Amulet Bks.) Abrams, Inc.

Captain Awesome Gets a Hole-In-One. 2014. (Captain Awesome Ser.: 12). (ENG., Illus.). 128p. (J). (gr. k-4). pap. 5.99 *(978-1-4814-1431-9(3)*, Little Simon) Little Simon.

Capucilli, Alyssa Satin. Biscuit's Birthday. Schories, Pat, illus. 2005. (Biscuit Ser.). (ENG.). 24p. (J). (gr. -1-1). pap. 3.99 *(978-0-06-057845-9(9)*, HarperFestival) HarperCollins Pubs.

—This Bear's Birthday. Hussey, Lorna, illus. 2017. (ENG.). 32p. (J). 16.99 *(978-1-62779-701-6(7)*, 9781627797016, Holt, Henry & Co. Bks. For Young Readers) Holt, Henry & Co.

Carbon, Sally & Langer, Justin. I Want to Be a Cricketer. Gollan, Stewart, illus. 2008. 32p. (J). pap. 16.95 *(978-1-921361-24-1(7))* Fremantle Pr. AUS. Dist: Independent Pubs. Group.

Carruthers, Deborah. Olivia's Birthday. Zvonarova, Jenny Desneige, illus. 2011. 20p. (gr. 1-2). 14.99 *(978-1-4269-4967-8(7))* Trafford Publishing.

Casagrande, Jerry. The Birthday Train. 2012. 24p. pap. 14.49 *(978-1-4772-1050-5(4))* AuthorHouse.

Castor, Harriet. The Incredible Present. Young, Norman, illus. 2004. (Usborne Young Reading: Series Two Ser.). 64p. (J). (gr. k-4). 8.99 *(978-0-7945-1785-4(4)*, Usborne) EDC Publishing.

Cazet, Denys. Minnie & Moo & the Haunted Sweater. Cazet, Denys, illus. 2007. (I Can Read Level 3 Ser.). (ENG., Illus.). 48p. (J). (gr. k-3). 16.99 *(978-0-06-073016-1(1))* HarperCollins Pubs.

Celebrate Elmo's Birthday. (J). *(978-0-375-88597-6(8)*, Golden Bks.) Random Hse. Children's Bks.

Chamberlain, Karen, et al. A Feather for the Queen. 2009. 28p. pap. 13.95 *(978-1-4490-3903-5(0))* AuthorHouse.

Chanda, J-P. Happy Birthday, SpongeBob! Martinez, Heather, illus. 2005. (SpongeBob SquarePants Ser.). (ENG.). 24p. (J). pap. 3.99 *(978-0-689-87674-5(2)*, Simon Spotlight/Nickelodeon) Simon Spotlight/Nickelodeon.

Chef Jeff. Do Cows Eat Cake? 2008. 28p. pap. 13.99 *(978-1-4389-0494-8(0))* AuthorHouse.

Chen, Shan-Shan & Goodman, Heidi. Mei-Mei's Lucky Birthday Noodles: A Loving Story of Adoption, Chinese Culture & a Special Birthday Treat. 2014. (ENG., Illus.). 32p. (J). (gr. -1-3). 13.95 *(978-0-8048-4461-1(5))* Tuttle Publishing.

Chima, Ahiru & Misu, Max. Ellenā_- Ellen meets Frog King - 2005. 32p. pap. 14.99 *(978-1-4116-4050-4(0))* Lulu Pr., Inc.

Christelow, Eileen. Cinco Monitos Hacen un Pastel de Cumpleanos. 2014. (Five Little Monkeys Story Ser.).Tr. of Five Little Monkeys Bake a Birthday Cake. (ENG & SPA., Illus.). 30p. (J). (— 1). bds. 7.99 (978-0-544-08899-3(9), HMH Books For Young Readers) Houghton Mifflin Harcourt Publishing Co.

—Five Little Monkeys Bake a Birthday Cake. 2005. (Five Little Monkeys Story Ser.). (ENG., Illus.). 32p. (J). (gr. -1-3). pap. 6.99 (978-0-618-49648-8(3)) Houghton Mifflin Harcourt Publishing Co.

Christianson, Leslie Rose. Malinda Matters: Malinda's Birthday Surprise. 2010. 44p. pap. 16.99 (978-1-4490-6915-5(0)) AuthorHouse.

Ciardi, John. The Wish-Tree. Glanzman, Louis S., illus. 2015. (ENG.). 96p. (J). pap. 9.99 (978-0-486-79618-5(3)) Dover Pubns., Inc.

Ciccone, Tiziana & Linardi, Franca. Lucinda, Queen of Everything. Cannavicci, Luigi A., illus. 2012. 36p. pap. 13.95 (978-1-61897-719-9(9), Strategic Bk. Publishing) Strategic Book Publishing & Rights Agency (SBPRA).

Civardi, Anne. Going to a Party. Watt, Fiona, ed. Cartwright, Stephen, illus. 2007. (Usborne First Experiences Ser.). 16p. (J). (gr. -1-3). pap. 4.99 (978-0-7945-1011-4(6), Usborne) EDC Publishing.

Clancy, Charmaine. My Zombie Dog. 2012. 132p. pap. (978-0-9872863-1-4(5)) Hot Doggy Digital Pr.

Clark, Margaret. Love Charms. 2008. (ENG.). 192p. (J). (gr. 7). pap. 12.95 (978-1-74166-264-1(8)) Random Hse. Australia AUS. Dist: Independent Pubs. Group.

Clarke, Jane. Prince Albert's Birthday. Chatterton, Martin, illus. 2005. 24p. (J). lib. bdg. 23.65 (978-1-59646-748-4(7)) Dingles & Co.

Claus, Nancy. Santa's Prize. Ferchaud, Steve, illus. 2006. (J). (978-0-9746747-5-9(3)) Cypress Bay Publishing.

Coats, Lucy. Captain Beastie's Pirate Party. Mould, Chris, illus. 2014. (ENG.). 32p. (J). (gr. -1-2). 15.99 (978-0-7636-7399-4(4), Nosy Crow) Candlewick Pr.

Cocks, Nancy & Marton, Jirina. Fergie Has a Birthday Party. 2003. (Illus.). 16p. pap. (978-2-89507-301-7(5)) Novalis Publishing.

Coffey, M. Carol. Zoe Lucky: And the Green Gables' Mystery. 2008. 156p. pap. 12.95 (978-1-4327-3190-8(4)) Outskirts Pr., Inc.

Cohen, Jerianne. Max A. Million's Birthday Party. 2008. 193p. pap. 24.95 (978-1-60672-844-4(X)) America Star Bks.

Colfer, Chris. Trollbella Throws a Party: A Tale from the Land of Stories. Dorman, Brandon, illus. 2017. (ENG.). 32p. (J). (gr. -1-3). 17.99 (978-0-316-38340-0(6)) Little Brown & Co.

Colver, Anne. Nobody's Birthday. Bileck, Marvin, illus. 2012. 44p. 35.95 (978-1-258-23347-1(9)); pap. 20.95 (978-1-258-24718-8(6)) Literary Licensing, LLC.

Conlon, Linda L. Not Today. 2011. 32p. 14.39 (978-1-4343-9195-7(7)) AuthorHouse.

Conroy, Christine. Mama Wants a Llam. 2012. 16p. pap. 15.99 (978-1-4772-1605-7(7)) AuthorHouse.

Constantin, Pascale, illus. Little Monster. 2007. (I'm Going to Read(r) Ser.). (ENG.). 28p. (J). (gr. -1-k). pap. 3.95 (978-1-4027-2078-9(5)) Sterling Publishing Co., Inc.

Cook, Tina H. Lindsey & the Yellow Masterpiece. 2011. 36p. pap. 15.99 (978-1-4634-0306-5(2)) AuthorHouse.

Coppola, Denise. Sammy Beagle's Birthday Party. 2005. 15p. (J). 8.03 (978-1-4116-3367-4(9)) Lulu Pr., Inc.

Corderoy, Tracey. More! Warnes, Tim, illus. 2015. (ENG.). 32p. (J). (gr. -1-3). 16.99 (978-1-58925-193-9(8)) Tiger Tales.

Corianne, Strupp. Friends for Keeps. 2013. 124p. (J). pap. 12.99 (978-0-9882940-8-0(7)) Bryson Taylor Publishing.

Cornish, Linda Sowa Young. Pong's Birthday Journey. 2006. (J). pap. 15.00 (978-0-8059-6993-1(4)) Dorrance Publishing Co., Inc.

Cossons, Malcolm & Stevens, Neil. Dot to Dot... 2013. (ENG., Illus.). 32p. (J). (gr. -1-k). 15.95 (978-0-500-65015-8(2), 565015) Thames & Hudson.

Cottrell-Bentley, Lisa M. Wright on Time: Iowa. Bauerle, Tanja, illus. 2013. 164p. pap. 12.99 (978-1-937848-06-4(X)) Do Life Right, Inc.

Cousins, Lucy. Maisy's Birthday Party Sticker Book. Cousins, Lucy, illus. 2015. (Maisy Ser.). (ENG., Illus.). 16p. (J). (gr. -1-2). pap. 7.99 (978-0-7636-7735-0(3)) Candlewick Pr.

Cox, Judy. Happy Birthday, Mrs. Millie!, 0 vols. Mathieu, Joe, illus. 2012. (ENG.). 32p. (J). (gr. k-3). 16.99 (978-0-7614-6126-5(4), 9780761461265, Amazon Children's Publishing) Amazon Publishing.

Crawford, Tammy. Gaby & Her Big Surprise. 2009. 36p. pap. 15.49 (978-1-4389-3323-8(1)) AuthorHouse.

Cregg, R. J. Best Sister Ever. 2017. (Olivia 8x8 Ser.). lib. bdg. 13.55 **(978-0-606-40213-2(6))** Turtleback Bks.

Crow, Melinda Melton. Little Lizard's Big Party, 1 vol. Rowland, Andrew, illus. 2010. (Little Lizards Ser.). (ENG.). 32p. (gr. -1-1). lib. bdg. 22.65 (978-1-4342-2007-3(9)) Stone Arch Bks.

—Little Lizard's Big Party. Rowland, Andrew & Rowlands, Andy, illus. 2010. (Little Lizards Ser.). (ENG.). 32p. (gr. -1-1). pap. 6.25 (978-1-4342-2791-1(X)) Stone Arch Bks.

—Rocky & Daisy & the Birthday Party. Sassin, Eva, illus. 2013. (My Two Dogs Ser.). (ENG.). 32p. (gr. 1-3). pap. 29.70 (978-1-4342-6296-7(0)); (gr. 2-3). lib. bdg. 22.65 (978-1-4342-6011-6(9)) Stone Arch Bks.

Crownberry, Ethan. Johnny Jetpack. 2013. 52p. 17.95 (978-0-9898533-1-6(4)) Jetpack Publishing.

Crowne, Alyssa. Pink Princess Rules the School. Alder, Charlotte, illus. 2009. 80p. (J). pap. (978-0-545-16077-3(4)) Scholastic, Inc.

Crystal, Billy. Grandpa's Little One. Porfirio, Guy, illus. 2006. 40p. (J). (gr. -1-k). lib. bdg. 17.89 (978-0-06-078174-3(2)) HarperCollins Pubs.

Cummings, Priscilla. Beetle Boddiker, 1 vol. Ramsey, Marcy Dunn, illus. 2009. (ENG.). 30p. (J). (gr. k-7). 13.95 (978-0-87033-602-7(9), 9780870336027, Cornell Maritime Pr./Tidewater Pubs.) Schiffer Publishing, Ltd.

Cynthia, Rylant. Henry & Mudge. 2014. (Henry & Mudge Ser.). (ENG.). 40p. (J). (gr. 5-7). 8.24 (978-1-63245-231-3(6)) Lectorum Pubns., Inc.

Czajak, Paul. Monster Needs a Party. Grieb, Wendy, illus. 2015. (Monster & Me Ser.). (ENG.). 32p. (J). (-k). 16.95 (978-1-938063-55-8(4), Mighty Media Kids) Mighty Media Pr.

Daffney. The Birthday Fairy. 2009. 16p. pap. 8.49 (978-1-4490-0095-0(9)) AuthorHouse.

Dale, Jay. Lea's Birthday, 1 vol. Gulliver, Amanda, illus. 2012. (Engage Literacy Yellow Ser.). (ENG.). 32p. (gr. k-2). pap. 5.99 (978-1-4296-8964-9(1), Engage Literacy) Capstone Press of Coughlan Cos.

Dale, Penny. Dinosaur Zoom! Dale, Penny, illus. 2014. (ENG., Illus.). 24p. (J). (-k). bds. 6.99 (978-0-7636-7394-9(3), Nosy Crow) Candlewick Pr.

Dalmatian Press Staff. Fuzzy Ducky's Birthday! 2008. (ENG.). 5p. bds. 4.95 (978-1-58117-725-1(9), Intervisual/Piggy Toes) Bendon, Inc.

Dalton, Annie. Flying High, No. 3. 2003. (Angels Unlimited Ser.). (ENG., Illus.). 144p. (J). pap. 4.99 (978-0-06-008817-0(6)) HarperCollins Pubs.

Daniels, Linda. The Magic Gazebo. 2012. 36p. pap. 18.41 (978-1-4669-6165-4(1)) Trafford Publishing.

Danziger, Paula. It's Justin Time, Amber Brown. Ross, Tony, illus. (Amber Brown Ser.). 9.95 (978-1-59112-294-4(5)) Live Oak Media.

—Justo a Tiempo, Ambar Dorado. Ross, Tony, illus. 2007. (Amber Brown Ser.). (SPA.). 48p. (gr. k-3). per. 8.95 (978-1-59820-595-4(1), Alfaguara) Santillana USA Publishing Co., Inc.

Darsana, Nam Aste. Guppie: God's Unified Perfect Plan Inspiring Everyone. 2011. 40p. pap. 21.99 (978-1-4628-4535-4(5)) Xlibris Corp.

David And Stephanie Williams. The Pajamazon Amazon vs the Goofers Twofers. 2013. 98p. pap. 5.99 (978-0-9910562-0-0(5)) One Million Words, LLC.

David, Jamie. Johann Sebastian Humpbach. David, Jamie, illus. 2009. (Illus.). 167p. pap. 14.95 (978-0-615-31840-0(1)) Chai Yo Maui Pr.

Davis, Brian. Matt's Birthday Blessing. Wheeler, Ron, illus. 2003. (Book of Matt Ser.: Vol. 1). 80p. (J). pap. 4.99 (978-1-59269-056-5(4)) Mcruffy Pr.

Davis, Edith Kunhardt. Pat the Birthday Bunny (Pat the Bunny) 2014. (Touch-And-Feel Ser.). (ENG., Illus.). 18p. (J). (— 1). 9.99 (978-0-375-97395-6(8), Golden Bks.) Random Hse. Children's Bks.

Davis, Martine. There's a Red Hippo at My Door. 2012. 24p. pap. 13.99 (978-1-4772-8070-6(7)) AuthorHouse.

de Brunhoff, Laurent. L' Anniversaire de Babar. (Babar Ser.). (FRE., Illus.). (J). (gr. -1-3). pap. (978-2-01-002551-8(2)) Hachette Groupe Livre.

Defreitas, Henrietta. Henratty Mortimer: Chapter One - Oscar's Birthday. 2010. (Illus.). 48p. pap. 17.49 (978-1-4490-9177-4(6)) AuthorHouse.

deGroat, Diane. Happy Birthday to You, You Belong in a Zoo. deGroat, Diane, illus. 2007. (Gilbert & Friends Ser.). (ENG., Illus.). 32p. (J). (gr. -1-3). pap. 6.99 (978-0-06-001029-4(0)) HarperCollins Pubs.

—Happy Birthday to You, You Belong in a Zoo. deGroat, Diane, illus. 2007. (Gilbert & Friends Ser.). (Illus.). (gr. -1-3). 17.00 (978-0-7569-8108-2(5)) Perfection Learning Corp.

Del Moral, Susana, tr. Sr. Cuadrado. 2005. (Mis figuras Geometricas Ser.). (SPA., Illus.). 6p. (J). (gr. -1-7). (978-970-718-294-3(6), Silver Dolphin en Español) Advanced Marketing, S. de R. L. de C. V.

deRubertis, Barbara. Deena y su centavo de la Suerte. Holub, Joan & Fisher, Cynthia, illus. 2007. (Math Matters Ser.). (SPA.). 32p. (J). (gr. -1-3). pap. 5.95 (978-1-57565-249-8(8)) Kane Press, Inc.

—Deena Y Su Centavo de la Suerte; Deena's Lucky Penny. 2008. pap. 34.95 (978-1-58013-756-0(3)) Kane Press, Inc.

Derubertis, Barbara. Gertie Gorilla's Glorious Gift. 2010. pap. 45.32 (978-0-7613-6509-9(5)) Kane Press, Inc.

deRubertis, Barbara. Gertie Gorilla's Glorious Gift. Alley, R. W., illus. 2010. (Animal Antics A to Z Ser.). 32p. (J). (gr. -1-3). pap. 7.95 (978-1-57565-311-2(7)); lib. bdg. 22.60 (978-1-57565-318-1(4)) Kane Press, Inc.

deRubertis, Barbara & DeRubertis, Barbara. Gertie Gorilla's Glorious Gift. Alley, R. W., illus. 2012. (Animal Antics A to Z Ser.). 32p. (J). (gr. 2 — 1). cd-rom 7.95 (978-1-57565-400-3(8)) Kane Press, Inc.

Desjardins, Dawn. Leopold's Long Awaited Leap Year Birthday. 2008. (Illus.). 32p. (J). 18.95 (978-0-9771495-2-0(8)); per. 10.95 (978-0-9771495-3-7(6)) Artistic Ventures LLC. (Artistic Ventures Publishing).

Desmazieres, Sandra. Emma & Her Friends: A Book about Colors. 2006. (Picture Bks.). (Illus.). 28p. (gr. k-3). lib. bdg. 24.00 (978-0-8368-6997-2(4), Gareth Stevens Learning Library) Stevens, Gareth Publishing LLLP.

—Emma y Sus Amigos: Un Libro Sobre los Colores. 2006. (Picture Bks.). (SPA., Illus.). 28p. (gr. k-3). lib. bdg. 24.00 (978-0-8368-6998-9(2), Gareth Stevens Learning Library) Stevens, Gareth Publishing LLLP.

Dewdney, Anna. Llama Llama - Birthday Party! Dewdney, Anna, illus. 2013. (Llama Llama Ser.). (ENG., Illus.). 16p. (J). (gr. -1-k). 6.99 (978-0-448-45880-9(2), Grosset & Dunlap) Penguin Young Readers Group.

Diaz, Nelbaliz. Laura y Su Caja de Sorpresas. 2007. (SPA.). 48p. 14.95 (978-0-8477-0452-1(1)) Univ. of Puerto Rico Pr.

Dillard, Mary Gregory. Finding Betsyanna. 2006. (ENG.). 48p. per. 16.95 (978-1-4241-5492-0(8)) America Star Bks.

Dipucchio, Kelly. Crafty Chloe. Ross, Heather, illus. 2012. (Crafty Chloe Ser.). (ENG.). 40p. (J). (gr. -1-3). 16.99 (978-1-4424-2123-3(1), Atheneum Bks. for Young Readers) Simon & Schuster Children's Publishing.

Disney Book Group. Elena of Avalor My Best Friend's Birthday. Disney Storybook Art Team, illus. 2017. (ENG.). 24p. (J). (gr. 1-3). pap. 4.99 (978-1-4847-7495-3(7)) Disney Pr.

Disney Princess Staff & Disney Book Group Staff. Ariel: The Birthday Surprise. Cagol, Andrea & Studio Iboix Staff, illus. 2010. (Disney Princess Chapter Book: Series #1 Ser.). (ENG.). 96p. (J). (gr. 1-3). pap. 4.99 (978-1-4231-2971-4(7)) Disney Pr.

Dixon, Linda A. Cupcakes for Cristina! 2010. 16p. 9.99 (978-1-4520-6650-9(7)) AuthorHouse.

Donaldson, Babette. Emma Lea's First Tea Party. Van Dijk, Jerianne, illus. 2007. (ENG.). 32p. (J). 16.95 (978-0-9792612-0-6(1)) Blue Gate Bks.

Dowling, Iris Gray. A Pony for My Birthday. Bouthyette, Valerie, illus. 2012. 36p. pap. 10.99 (978-1-937129-50-7(0)) Faithful Life Pubs.

Down, Reg. The Magic Knot: And other Tangles. 2007. (Illus.). 100p. (J). per. 14.95 (978-0-9794452-0-0(5)) Lightly Pr.

Drinnon, Sheila. Cuddles. 2008. 24p. pap. 24.95 (978-1-60474-857-4(5)) America Star Bks.

Dumble, Carol. R U My Friend? 2011. 20p. pap. 11.99 (978-1-4567-1825-1(8)) AuthorHouse.

Dyan, Penelope. Hooray 4 Five! Dyan, Penelope, illus. 2013. (Illus.). 34p. pap. 11.95 (978-1-61477-103-6(0)) Bellissima Publishing, LLC.

—I Am Three! Dyan, Penelope, illus. 2011. (Illus.). 34p. pap. 11.95 (978-1-935630-97-5(0)) Bellissima Publishing, LLC.

—Today I Am 4! Dyan, Penelope, illus. 2012. (Illus.). 34p. pap. 11.95 (978-1-61477-043-5(3)) Bellissima Publishing, LLC.

—Today I Am Two! I Am Two Years Old Today! Dyan, Penelope, illus. 2010. (Illus.). 34p. pap. 11.95 (978-1-935630-14-2(8)) Bellissima Publishing, LLC.

Easley, Sheila. Abbott Celebrates a Birthday. 2011. 28p. pap. 13.95 (978-1-4634-3208-9(9)) AuthorHouse.

Easley, Terriana. Bubbles & Elle: A Party for Elle. 2011. 28p. pap. 24.95 (978-1-4626-3635-8(7)) America Star Bks.

Edles, Philip. Benny the Penny & the Big Secret. 2012. 52p. (gr. 4-6). 18.22 (978-1-4669-7175-2(4)); pap. 8.22 (978-1-4669-7173-8(8)) Trafford Publishing.

Edwards, Marnie. Pets & Parties. Hodgkinson, Leigh, illus. 2013. (Magical Mix-Ups Ser.). (ENG.). 96p. (J). (gr. 2-5). pap. 6.99 (978-0-7636-6371-1(9), Nosy Crow) Candlewick Pr.

Edwards, Meinir Wyn. Cantre'r Gwaelod. Wade, Gini, illus. 2007. (ENG.). 24p. (J). pap. 4.95 (978-1-84771-021-5(2)) Y Lolfa GBR. Dist: Dufour Editions, Inc.

Elrod, Julie. Splitting Hares. 2008. 36p. pap. 16.50 (978-1-60693-484-5(8), Eloquent Bks.) Strategic Book Publishing & Rights Agency (SBPRA).

Emanuel, Effie Ann. The Penguin Party, 1 vol. 2009. 32p. pap. 24.95 (978-1-60813-544-8(6)) America Star Bks.

English, Karen. Birthday Blues. Freeman, Laura, illus. 2010. (ENG.). 96p. (J). (gr. 1-4). pap. 5.99 (978-0-547-24893-6(8)) Houghton Mifflin Harcourt Publishing Co.

—Nikki & Deja. Freeman, Laura, illus. 2009. (ENG.). 80p. (J). (gr. -1-3). pap. 5.99 (978-0-547-13362-1(6)) Houghton Mifflin Harcourt Publishing Co.

Epstein, Robin. Sleepover Surprise: A Twin-Sational Birthday. 2005. (Groovy Girls Ser.). (ENG., Illus.). 80p. (J). (gr. 2-5). 3.99 (978-0-439-81433-1(2)) Scholastic, Inc.

Eric's Birthday, 6 Pks. (gr. -1-2). 27.00 (978-0-7635-9447-3(4)) Rigby Education.

Erlings, Fridrik. Fish in the Sky. 2012. (ENG., Illus.). 288p. (YA). (gr. 7). 16.99 (978-0-7636-5888-5(X)) Candlewick Pr.

Esbaum, Jill. If a T. Rex Crashes Your Birthday Party. Tolstikova, Daria & Tolstikova, Dasha, illus. 2016. (ENG.). 40p. (J). (gr. -1-2). 14.95 (978-1-4549-1550-8(1)) Sterling Publishing Co., Inc.

Esparza-Vela, Mary. Lucky's Lick. Prouix, Denis, illus. 2013. 16p. pap. 9.95 (978-1-61633-406-2(1)) Guardian Angel Publishing, Inc.

Evans, Pamela. Tina Queen of the Dragons. 2006. 101p. pap. 16.95 (978-1-4241-3356-7(4)) PublishAmerica, Inc.

Evelyn. Lucy the Elephant & Sami the Mouse: The Birthday Party. Conforti, John W., illus. 2004. (J). (978-0-9740115-1-6(7)) WeBeANS Corp.

Evlin, Frances. Ginger Gold. 2004. (J). pap. 12.95 (978-1-59374-119-8(7)) Whiskey Creek Pr., LLC.

Ewart, Francesca, et al. There's a Hamster in My Pocket! Bate, Helen, illus. 2012. (ENG.). 96p. (J). (gr. 3-6). pap. 7.95 (978-1-84780-118-0(8), Frances Lincoln) Quarto Publishing Group UK GBR. Dist: Hachette Bk. Group.

Faundez, Anne. Teddy's Birthday. 2004. (QEB Start Talking Ser.). (Illus.). 24p. (J). lib. bdg. 15.95 (978-1-59566-004-6(6)) QEB Publishing Inc.

Faye Morningstar. Little Dream Athe: The Sand Prince. 2012. 20p. pap. 17.99 (978-1-4772-9540-3(2)) AuthorHouse.

Ferguson, Jamianne. Lost in Past Remembrence. 2010. 265p. pap. 17.25 (978-0-557-52788-5(0)) Lulu Pr., Inc.

Fernandez, Giselle. Gigi & the Birthday Ring. Petersen, Sheli, illus. 2005. (J). (978-1-56492-358-5(4)) Laredo Publishing Co., Inc.

Fernandez, Joyce & Marsh, Laura. Eins und Zwei are One & Two. 2009. 22p. 15.95 (978-0-578-00208-8(6)) My Second Language Publishing, USA.

—Un Is One. 2009. 21p. 15.95 (978-0-615-26238-3(4)) My Second Language Publishing, USA.

—Uno Is One. 2009. 22p. 15.95 (978-0-615-24460-0(2)) My Second Language Publishing, USA.

—Um Is One. 2009. 22p. 15.95 (978-0-557-05629-3(2)) Lulu Pr., Inc.

—Uno y Dos are One & Two. 2008. 22p. pap. 15.95 (978-0-615-26150-8(7)) My Second Language Publishing, USA.

Ferry, Beth. Land Shark. Mantle, Ben, illus. 2015. (ENG.). 36p. (J). (gr. -1-k). 16.99 (978-1-4521-2458-2(2)) Chronicle Bks. LLC.

Figueroa, Juanita Kimberly. Kendra Gives a Birthday Party. 2012. 24p. pap. 24.95 (978-1-4626-6009-4(6)) PublishAmerica, Inc.

Fisch, Sholly & Age, Heroic. Happy Birthday, Superman!, 1 vol. Bone, J., illus. 2014. (DC Super Friends Ser.). (ENG.). 32p. (gr. 1-2). 22.60 (978-1-4342-9222-3(3)) Stone Arch Bks.

Fischer, Kelly. The Moon Throws a Birthday Party. Duckworth, Michelle, illus. 2011. (ENG.). 32p. (J). 19.50 (978-1-58385-237-8(9)) ktf-writers-studio.

Fisher, Doris. Happy Birthday to Whooo? A Baby Animal Riddle Book, 1 vol. Downey, Lisa, illus. 2006. (ENG.). 32p. (J). (gr. -1-3). 15.95 (978-0-9768823-1-2(0)); pap. 8.95 (978-1-934359-06-8(8)) Arbordale Publishing.

Fisher, Dorothy Canfield. Understood Betsy - Illustrated. Williamson, Ada C., illus. 2013. 112p. pap. 3.97 (978-1-60386-582-1(9), Merchant Bks.) Rough Draft Printing.

Fisscher, Tiny. RUBY & the LION. 2008. (ENG.). 48p. (J). (gr. 1-7). 11.95 (978-1-60136-014-4(2)) Audio Holdings, LLC.

Flam, Chanie. Happy Birthday, Vol. 1. (Goldie Gold Board Book Ser.: Vol. 1). (Illus.). (J). (gr. -1-1). bds. 4.95 (978-1-58330-025-1(2)) Feldheim Pubs.

Fleck, Denise. Don't Judge a Book by Its Cover. Chin, Lili, illus. 2013. 24p. pap. 14.99 (978-1-4575-1758-7(2)) Dog Ear Publishing, LLC.

Fleming, Candace. Bulldozer's Big Day. Rohmann, Eric, illus. 2015. (Bulldozer Bks.). (ENG.). 40p. (J). (gr. -1-2). 17.99 (978-1-4814-0097-8(5), Atheneum Bks. for Young Readers) Simon & Schuster Children's Publishing.

—Clever Jack Takes the Cake. Karas, G. Brian, illus. 2010. (ENG.). 40p. (J). (gr. -1-3). 17.99 (978-0-375-84979-4(3), Schwartz & Wade Bks.) Random Hse. Children's Bks.

Fleming, Sean & Ewald, Jenny, eds. To Catch a Mall Thief. 2004. 85p. (YA). pap. 9.95 (978-0-7414-2196-8(8)) Infinity Publishing.

Flor Ada, Alma. Celebrate a Powwow with Sandy Starbright. Alvarez, Maria Jesus, illus. 2007. (Cuentos para Celebrar / Stories to Celebrate Ser.). 30p. (gr. k-6). per. 11.95 (978-1-59820-127-7(1)) Santillana USA Publishing Co., Inc.

—Dear Peter Rabbit. Tryon, Leslie, illus. 2006. (Stories to Go! Ser.). (J). (gr. k-3). 12.65 (978-0-7569-7322-3(8)) Perfection Learning Corp.

Flor Ada, Alma & Campoy, F. Isabel. Happy Birthday, Little Red Riding Hood! (Gateways to the Sun). 32p. (J). (gr. k-6). pap. 13.95 (978-1-58105-961-8(2)) Santillana USA Publishing Co., Inc.

Florence, Tyler. Tyler Makes a Birthday Cake! Frazier, Craig, illus. 2014. (J). lib. bdg. (978-0-06-204761-8(2)) Harper & Row Ltd.

—Tyler Makes a Birthday Cake! Frazier, Craig, illus. 2014. (ENG.). 40p. (J). (gr. -1-3). 17.99 (978-0-06-204760-1(4)) HarperCollins Pubs.

Fogliano, Julie. When's My Birthday? Robinson, Christian, illus. 2017. (ENG.). 40p. (J). 17.99 **(978-1-62672-293-4(5)**, 9781626722934) Roaring Brook Pr.

Fox, Donna L. Salem's Birthday. 2011. 20p. pap. 24.95 (978-1-4560-4103-8(7)) America Star Bks.

Fox, R. J. Stuart & His Incredibly Obnoxious Magical Book: Soccer, 1 vol. 2009. 86p. pap. 19.95 (978-1-4489-9833-3(6)) America Star Bks.

Francis, Anwen. Siani Shetland. 2008. (ENG.). 84p. (J). pap. 9.95 (978-1-905762-62-0(3)) Parthian Bks. GBR. Dist: Independent Pubs. Group.

Freeman, Martha. The Trouble with Twins. Smith, Cat Bowman, illus. 2007. (ENG.). 112p. (J). (gr. 2-6). 16.95 (978-0-8234-2025-4(6)) Holiday Hse., Inc.

Freeman, Mylo. Princess Arabella's Birthday. 2009. (Illus.). 32p. (J). (gr. -1-3). 14.95 (978-0-9815761-7-6(6)) Mackenzie Smiles, LLC.

French, Vivian. Emily Mouse's Birthday Party. Marshall, Mark, illus. 2016. (Early Reader Ser.). (ENG.). 64p. (J). (gr. k-3). 6.99 (978-1-4440-1614-7(8), Orion Children's Bks.) Hachette Children's Group GBR. Dist: Hachette Bk. Group.

Friedman, Laurie. Happy Birthday, Mallory! Schmitz, Tamara, illus. (J). (gr. 2-5). 2006. (Mallory Ser.: 4). (ENG.). 160p. per. 5.95 (978-0-8225-6502-4(1), First Avenue Editions) 2005. 159p. per. 15.95 (978-1-57505-823-8(5), Carolrhoda Bks.) Lerner Publishing Group.

—Mallory's Super Sleepover. Kalis, Jennifer, illus. (Mallory Ser.: 16). (ENG.). 160p. (J). (gr. 2-5). 2012. pap. 5.95 (978-1-4677-0209-6(9))No. 16. 2011. 15.95 (978-0-8225-8887-0(0)) Lerner Publishing Group. (Darby Creek).

Friedman, Laurie B. Birthday Rules. Murfin, Teresa, illus. 2015. (J). (gr. k-3). (ENG.). 32p. lib. bdg. 16.99 (978-0-7613-6071-1(9)); 17.32 (978-1-4677-6177-2(X)) Lerner Publishing Group. (Carolrhoda Bks.).

Friend, Ronda. R. Friend Swallows Her Pride. 2005. (Down on Friendly Acres Ser.: 1). (J). lib. bdg. (978-0-9743627-3-1(5)) Sunflower Seeds Pr.

Froeb, Lori C. & Disney Storybook Artists Staff. Cinderella's Shining Moment. 2012. (Fold-Out Figure Ser.). (ENG., Illus.). 32p. (J). (gr. -1-2). 14.99 (978-0-7944-2547-0(X), Reader's Digest Children's Bks.) Studio Fun International.

Fuchs, Menucha. The Best Gift of All. 2004. (Illus.). 20p. (J). 6.95 (978-1-932443-15-8(0), BGAH) Judaica Pr., Inc., The.

—The Flying Invitation. 2004. (Menucha V'Simcha Ser.). (Illus.). 20p. (J). 6.95 (978-1-932443-07-3(X), FLIH) Judaica Pr., Inc., The.

Fuller, Bob, illus. The Costume Trunk. 2011. (J). (978-1-936169-01-6(0)) Paddywhack Lane LLC.

Gajewski, Lois. Benny, the Stubborn Bubble. 2011. 28p. (gr. 1-2). pap. 12.03 (978-1-4567-4703-9(7)) AuthorHouse.

Garay, Erin. Angel Birthdays. Abbott, Kristin, illus. 2013. (ENG.). 32p. (J). (gr. 2-3). 16.95 (978-1-938301-94-0(3)) Familius LLC.

Garland, Sarah. Eddie's Kitchen. 2014. (ENG., Illus.). 40p. (J). (gr. -1-2). pap. 8.99 (978-1-84780-003-9(3), Frances Lincoln) Quarto Publishing Group UK GBR. Dist: Hachette Bk. Group.

Garratt, Irene Joyce. Happy Birthday: Two in One Stories. 2009. (Illus.). 12p. pap. 8.49 (978-1-4389-4304-6(0)) AuthorHouse.

George R. Cathcart Jr. Ernie's Clever Plan. 2012. 24p. 24.95 (978-1-4626-6795-6(3)) America Star Bks.

Gilman, Phoebe. Jillian Jiggs & the Secret Surprise. 2004. (J). (gr. -1-2). spiral bd. (978-0-616-01655-8(7)) Canadian National Institute for the Blind/Institut National Canadien pour les Aveugles.

Godin, Thelma Lynne. Hula-Hoopin' Queen. Brantley-Newton, Vanessa, illus. 2014. (ENG.). 40p. (J). 18.95 (978-1-60060-846-9(9)) Lee & Low Bks., Inc.

Godwin, Jane & Bell, Davina. Hattie Helps Out. Blackwood, Freya, illus. 2016. (ENG.). 32p. (J). (gr. -1-k). 19.99 **(978-1-74343-543-4(6))** Allen & Unwin AUS. Dist: Independent Pubs. Group.

Golden Books, illus. Nickelodeon Little Golden Book Library (Nickelodeon), 5 vols. 2015. (ENG.). 120p. (J). (-k). 24.95 (978-0-553-50797-3(4), Golden Bks.) Random Hse. Children's Bks.

Golden, Kathleen M. Cleopatra's Big Birthday BBQ. Golden, Kathleen M., illus. 2003. (Illus.). 18p. (J). (gr. -1-k). mass mkt. 14.95 (978-0-9726418-0-7(7)) Happyland Media.

Gomes, Barbara K. Esau at the Big House. 2006. 76p. pap. 19.95 (978-1-4241-2288-2(0)) America Star Bks.

Gonzalez Bertrand, Diane. The Ruiz Street Kids (Los Muchachos de la Calle Ruiz) Ventura, Gabriela Baeza, tr. 2006. (ENG & SPA., Illus.). (J). pap. 9.95 (978-1-55885-321-8(9), Piñata Books) Arte Publico Pr.

Goode, Teresa. Jayhawk Adventures, Jed's Birthday Surprise. Kotrous, Chad, illus. 2006. 27p. (J). (gr. 1-3). pap. 5.95 (978-0-9646898-6-2(3)) Leathers Publishing.

Goodhart, Pippa. Hoppy Birthday, Jo-Jo! Birkett, Georgie, illus. 2005. (Green Bananas Ser.). (ENG.). 48p. (J). lib. bdg. (978-0-7787-1025-7(4)) Crabtree Publishing Co.

Grandpa's Birthday: Individual Title Six-Packs. (Literatura 2000 Ser.). (gr. 2-3). 33.00 *(978-0-7635-0199-0(9))* Rigby Education.

Gray, Kes & Parsons, Garry. Billy's Bucket. 2003. (ENG., Illus.). 32p. (J). 24.95 *(978-0-370-32596-5(6))* Random Hse. GBR. Dist: Random Hse. of Canada.

Green, D. L. Zeke Meeks vs the Big Blah-Rific Birthday, 1 vol. Alves, Josh, illus. 2013. (Zeke Meeks Ser.). (ENG.). 128p. (gr. 2-2). 8.95 *(978-1-4048-8105-1(0))*; lib. bdg. 22.65 *(978-1-4048-7637-8(5))* Picture Window Bks. (Zeke Meeks).

Greene, Stephanie. Happy Birthday, Sophie Hartley. 2011. (ENG.). 128p. (J). (gr. 2-5). pap. 6.99 *(978-0-547-55025-1(1))* Houghton Mifflin Harcourt Publishing Co.

Greig, Allison. Stacey's Adventures. 2006. (Illus.). 64p. pap. *(978-1-84401-035-6(X))* Athena Pr.

Greve, Meg. Birthday Gone Wrong. 2015. (ENG.). 48p. (gr. k-3). 27.07 *(978-1-63430-369-9(5))* Rourke Educational Media.

Grizzard, Sue H. Princess Caylee: An Incredible Birthday Wish Come True. 2009. 44p. pap. 19.95 *(978-1-4490-4001-7(2))* AuthorHouse.

Guest, Elissa Haden. Iris & Walter. Davenier, Christine, illus. 2006. (Iris & Walter Ser.). 43p. (gr. 1-4). 15.95 *(978-0-7569-7008-6(3))* Perfection Learning Corp.

—Iris & Walter & the Birthday Party. Davenier, Christine, illus. 2013. (Green Light Readers Level 3 Ser.). (ENG.). 44p. (J). (gr. 1-4). pap. 3.99 *(978-0-544-10498-3(6))* Houghton Mifflin Harcourt Publishing Co.

Gurtler, Janet. Shyanna's Wish. Wood, Katie, illus. 2015. (Mermaid Kingdom Ser.). (ENG.). 96p. (gr. 3-5). 23.99 *(978-1-4342-9696-2(2))* Stone Arch Bks.

Gutenberg, S. R. Abby Longbotham & the Quilt. 2008. 28p. pap. 24.95 *(978-1-4241-9428-5(8))* America Star Bks.

Hagemann, Bernhard. Charlie Gallina Ciega. (Torre de Papel Ser.). (SPA., Illus.). (J). 7.95 *(978-958-04-5032-0(3))* Norma S.A. COL. Dist: Distribuidora Norma, Inc.

Hall, Kirsten. Birthday Beastie: All about Counting. Luedecke, Bev, illus. 2003. (Beastieville Ser.). 32p. (J). 19.50 *(978-0-516-22891-4(9))*, Children's Pr.) Scholastic Library Publishing.

Hallinan, P. K. Happy Birthday! 2003. (J). (ENG., Illus.). 26p. bds. 7.95 *(978-0-8249-5453-6(X))*; *(978-0-8249-6507-5(8))* Worthy Publishing. (Ideal Pubns.).

Hallwood, Cheri L. The Curious Polka-Dot Present. Rose, Patricia M., illus. 2007. (ENG.). 32p. (J). 16.99 *(978-0-9774422-1-8(7))* Forever Young Pubs.

Hamilton, Elizabeth L. Jeremy Rabbit's Honesty Pie. 2003. (Character Critters Ser.: No. 2). (Illus.). 32p. (J). (gr. -1-3). per. 5.95 *(978-0-9713749-5-9(3)*, Character-in-Action) Quiet Impact, Inc.

Hamilton, Tim. But! Hamilton, Tim, illus. 2014. (ENG., Illus.). 32p. (J). (gr. -1-2). 16.95 *(978-0-8234-3046-8(4))* Holiday Hse., Inc.

Hannam, John-Pierre M., Sr. Uncle Jake's Hat. 2009. 43p. pap. 20.00 *(978-0-557-02568-8(0))* Lulu Pr., Inc.

Hansen, Jeanne. Wow! an Upside down Cake Birthday Party! 2011. 24p. pap. 15.99 *(978-1-4653-6016-8(6))* Xlibris Corp.

Hansen, Tevin. Alexia Versus the Birthday Bear. Hansen, Tevin, illus. 2016. (Illus.). (J). pap. 5.99 *(978-1-941429-37-2(8))* Handersen Publishing.

Hapka, Catherine, pseud. Friends 4 Ever? 2008. (High School Musical Stories from East High Ser.). 124p. (J). (gr. 3-7). 12.65 *(978-0-7569-8820-3(9))* Perfection Learning Corp.

Harbor, Missy. Susan of Bluebonnet Hill, 1 vol. 2009. 28p. pap. 24.95 *(978-1-61546-207-0(4))* America Star Bks.

Hardge, A. Terrence. Bobby's Big Birthday Bash. 2012. (ENG.). 22p. (J). pap. 12.95 *(978-1-4327-9076-9(5))* Outskirts Pr., Inc.

Hardy, Sarah Frances. Puzzled by Pink. 2012. (ENG.). 32p. (J). (gr. -1-k). 16.99 *(978-0-670-01320-3(X)*, Viking Books for Young Readers) Penguin Young Readers Group.

Hargreaves, Adam & Hargreaves, Roger. Little Miss Birthday. Hargreaves, Adam, illus. 2007. (Mr. Men & Little Miss Ser.). (ENG., Illus.). 32p. (J). (gr. -1-2). mass mkt. 4.99 *(978-0-8431-2131-5(9)*, Price Stern Sloan) Penguin Young Readers Group.

—Mr. Birthday. Hargreaves, Adam, illus. 2007. (Mr. Men & Little Miss Ser.). (ENG., Illus.). 32p. (J). (gr. -1-2). mass mkt. 4.99 *(978-0-8431-2130-8(0)*, Price Stern Sloan) Penguin Young Readers Group.

Harper, Charise Mericle. Just Grace & the Super Sleepover. 2014. (Just Grace Ser.: 11). (ENG., Illus.). 208p. (J). (gr. 1-4). 15.99 *(978-0-544-04584-2(X))* Houghton Mifflin Harcourt Publishing Co.

Harris, Patricia. Teddy's Birthday. 2017. (Teddy's Colorful World Ser.). 24p. (gr. 4-6). pap. 8.25 ***(978-1-5383-2159-1(9)***, PowerKids Pr.) Rosen Publishing Group, Inc., The.

Harrison, Hannah E. Bernice Gets Carried Away. 2015. (ENG., Illus.). 32p. (J). (gr. -1-k). 16.99 *(978-0-8037-3916-1(8)*, Dial Bks) Penguin Young Readers Group.

Harrison, Jo. The Jewellery Box Fairies. 2013. (Illus.). 24p. pap. 19.82 *(978-1-4772-5112-6(X))* AuthorHouse.

Hartt-Sussman, Heather. Nana's Summer Surprise. Graham, Georgia, illus. 2013. (ENG.). 32p. (J). (gr. -1-1). 17.95 *(978-1-77049-324-7(7)*, Tundra Bks.) Tundra Bks. CAN. Dist: Penguin Random Hse. LLC.

Harvey, Damian. A Gift for the King. Remphry, Martin, illus. 2005. (Reading Corner Ser.). 24p. (J). (gr. k-3). lib. bdg. 22.80 *(978-1-59771-013-8(X))* Sea-To-Sea Pubns.

Harvey, Jacqueline. Clementine Rose & the Birthday Emergency. 2016. (Clementine Rose Ser.: 10). (ENG.). 160p. (J). (gr. 1-3). 8.99 *(978-0-85798-516-3(7))* Random Hse. Australia AUS. Dist: Independent Pubs. Group.

Hatley, Shannon. The Young Princess & the Brave Knight. 2012. 28p. pap. 24.95 *(978-1-4626-6779-6(1))* America Star Bks.

Hawa, Christine Elias. Joy the Girl How Never Smiled. 2011. 32p. pap. 16.19 *(978-1-4634-3636-0(X))* AuthorHouse.

Hawkins, Elizabeth. Ben's Birthdays. Cemmick, Paul, illus. 2010. (ENG.). 40p. (J). (gr. k-2). pap. 10.99 *(978-1-84853-018-8(8))* Transworld Publishers Ltd. GBR. Dist: Independent Pubs. Group.

Hayward, Jason. Teddy Bear Adventures. 2011. 40p. pap. 24.95 *(978-1-4560-4068-0(5))* America Star Bks.

Hedderwick, Mairi. Katie Morag & the Birthdays. Hedderwick, Mairi, illus. 2005. (Katie Morag Ser.). (ENG., Illus.). 48p. (J). (gr. k-4). per. 14.99 *(978-0-09-946426-6(8)*, Red Fox) Random House Children's Books GBR. Dist: Independent Pubs. Group.

Hedgman, Janis. Party in the Garden. 2009. (Illus.). 52p. pap. *(978-1-84748-514-4(6))* Athena Pr.

Heiss, Renee. Somebody Cares! 2010. 32p. 16.95 *(978-1-4497-0758-3(0)*, WestBow Pr.) Author Solutions, Inc.

Helmer, Marilyn. Sharing Snowy, 1 vol. Charko, Kasia, illus. 2008. (Orca Echoes Ser.). (ENG.). 64p. (J). (gr. 2-3). pap. 6.95 *(978-1-55469-021-3(8))* Orca Bk. Pubs. USA.

Herman, Gail & Studio Iboix Staff. Ariel: The Birthday Surprise, 1 vol. 2012. (Disney Princess Ser.). (ENG., Illus.). 96p. (J). (gr. 2-5). 24.21 *(978-1-59961-877-7(X))* Spotlight.

Hicks, Holly Floyd. Ella's Birthday Wish. 2010. 108p. 20.95 *(978-1-4502-0932-8(7))* iUniverse, Inc.

Hicks, Holly Floyd, ed. Ella's Birthday Wish. 2010. 108p. pap. 10.95 *(978-1-4502-0933-5(5))* iUniverse, Inc.

Higgins, Nadia. Aye, My Eye!, 1 vol. Holder, Jimmy, illus. 2008. (Barnacle Barb & Her Pirate Crew Ser.). (ENG.). 32p. (gr. -1-3). 28.50 *(978-1-60270-090-1(7)*, Looking Glass Library) ABDO Publishing Co.

Higginson, Hadley. Keeker & the Crazy, Upside-Down Birthday. Perrett, Lisa, illus. 2008. (ENG.). 56p. (J). (gr. k-3). pap. 4.99 *(978-0-8118-6256-1(9))* Chronicle Bks. LLC.

Higginson, Sheila Sweeny. Henry Loves Beckett. 2014. (J). lib. bdg. 14.75 *(978-0-606-35907-8(9))* Turtleback Bks.

Higginson, Sheila Sweeny & Disney Book Group Staff. Whose Birthday Is It? Disney Storybook Artists Staff, illus. 2007. (ENG.). 16p. (J). (gr. -1-k). 4.99 *(978-1-4231-0652-4(0))* Disney Pr.

Hill, Eric. Spot Bakes a Cake. Hill, Eric, illus. 2005. (Spot Ser.). (ENG., Illus.). 20p. (J). (gr. k — 1). 6.99 *(978-0-14-240329-7(6)*, Warne) Penguin Young Readers Group.

Hillert, Margaret. The Birthday Car. Girouard, Patrick, illus. 2016. (BeginningtoRead Ser.). (ENG.). 32p. (J). (gr. -1-2). pap. 11.94 *(978-1-60357-936-0(2))*; (gr. k-2). 22.60 *(978-1-59953-795-5(8))* Norwood Hse. Pr.

—Feliz Cumpleaños, Querido Dragón. Pullan, Jack, illus. 2017. (BeginningtoRead Ser.).Tr. of Happy Birthday, Dear Dragon. (ENG & SPA.). 32p. (J). (-2). 22.60 ***(978-1-59953-830-3(X))*** Norwood Hse. Pr.

Hillert, Margaret. Happy Birthday, Dear Dragon. Pullan, Jack, illus. 2016. (BeginningtoRead Ser.). (ENG.). 32p. (J). (-2). lib. bdg. 22.60 *(978-1-59953-767-2(2))*; (gr. 1-2). pap. 11.94 *(978-1-60357-880-6(3))* Norwood Hse. Pr.

Hillyer, Rhonda. Butterfly Magic. Wood, Steve, illus. 2013. 84p. pap. 12.00 *(978-1-62212-306-3(9)*, Strategic Bk. Publishing) Strategic Book Publishing & Rights Agency (SBPRA).

Hoban, Russell. A Birthday for Frances. Hoban, Lillian, illus. 2012. (I Can Read Level 2 Ser.). (ENG.). 48p. (J). (gr. k-3). 16.99 *(978-0-06-083795-2(0))* HarperCollins Pubs.

—A Birthday for Frances. 2012. (I Can Read! Level 2 Ser.). (J). lib. bdg. 13.55 *(978-0-606-26850-9(2)*, Turtleback) Turtleback Bks.

Hobbs, Leigh. Mr Badger & the Big Surprise. l.t. ed. 2012. 120p. (J). pap. 19.99 *(978-1-4596-3343-8(1))* ReadHowYouWant.com, Ltd.

Hock, Dan. The Birthday Bash 2 vols. An Iggy & Igor Mystery (#2) Hock, Dan, illus. l.t. ed. 2004. (Illus.). 51p. (J). per. 4.99 *(978-0-9754046-1-4(X))* Anticipation Pr.

Hoffman, Mary Ann. Happy Birthday, Rita Raccoon! 2006. (Neighborhood Readers Ser.). (ENG.). 16p. (gr. 1-3). pap. 6.50 *(978-1-4042-7140-1(6)*, Rosen Classroom) Rosen Publishing Group, Inc., The.

Holden, Pam. Presents for Grace, 6 pack. Hawley, Kelvin, illus. 2009. (Red Rocket Readers Ser.). (ENG.). 16p. (gr. 2-2). pap. *(978-1-877363-61-0(8)*, Red Rocket Readers) Flying Start Bks.

Holland, Marci. The Birth Day Letter. 2005. 116p. 23.99 *(978-1-4208-2920-4(3))* AuthorHouse.

—The Birth Day Letter: An Alzheimer's Story. 2005. 116p. pap. 14.95 *(978-1-4208-2921-1(1))* AuthorHouse.

Holm, Jennifer L. & Holm, Matthew. Happy Birthday, Babymouse! Holm, Jennifer L. & Holm, Matthew, illus. 2014. (Babymouse Ser.: 18). (ENG., Illus.). 96p. (J). (gr. 2-5). 12.99 *(978-0-375-97097-9(5)*, Random Hse. Bks. for Young Readers) Random Hse. Children's Bks.

—Happy Birthday, Babymouse. Holm, Jennifer L. & Holm, Matthew, illus. 2014. (Babymouse Ser.: 18). (ENG., Illus.). 96p. (J). (gr. 2-5). pap. 6.99 *(978-0-307-93161-0(7)*, Random Hse. Bks. for Young Readers) Random Hse. Children's Bks.

—Happy Birthday, Babymouse. 2014. (Babymouse Ser.: 18). lib. bdg. 17.20 *(978-0-606-35567-4(7))* Turtleback Bks.

Holt, Kimberly Willis. Piper Reed Gets a Job. Davenier, Christine, illus. 2009. (Piper Reed Ser.: 3). (ENG.). 160p. (J). (gr. 3-6). 14.99 *(978-0-8050-8199-2(2)*, 9780805081992, Holt, Henry & Co. Bks. For Young Readers) Holt, Henry & Co.

—Piper Reed, Party Planner. Davenier, Christine, illus. 2011. (Piper Reed Ser.: 3). (ENG.). 176p. (J). (gr. 3-6). pap. 7.99 *(978-0-312-61677-9(5)*, 9780312616779) Square Fish.

Hooks, Gwendolyn. Pets at the Party: A Pet Club Story, 1 vol. Byrne, Mike, illus. 2010. (Pet Club Ser.). (ENG & ABK.). 32p. (gr. 1-2). 22.65 *(978-1-4342-2054-7(0))*; pap. 6.25 *(978-1-4342-2796-6(0))* Stone Arch Bks.

Hope, Rachael. Uncle Birthday. Hope, Mister, illus. 2016. (ENG.). (J). pap. ***(978-1-78222-492-1(0))*** Paragon Publishing, Rothersthorpe.

Horse, Harry. Little Rabbit Lost. Horse, Harry, illus. 2005. (ENG., Illus.). 32p. (J). (gr. k-1). bds. 9.95 *(978-1-56145-345-0(5))* Peachtree Pubs.

Hosford, Kate. Big Birthday. Clifton-Brown, Holly, illus. 2012. (Carolrhoda Picture Bks.). (ENG.). 32p. (J). (gr. k-2). lib. bdg. 16.95 *(978-0-7613-5410-9(7))* Lerner Publishing Group.

Houghton Mifflin Company Staff. Birthday Fun with Curious George. 2005. (J). (gr. -1-k). pap. *(978-0-618-69654-3(7))* Houghton Mifflin Harcourt Trade & Reference Pubs.

Houran, Lori Haskins. Make a Wish, Albert: 3-D Shapes. Melmon, Deborah, illus. 2015. (ENG.). 32p. (J). (gr. -1-1). lib. bdg. 22.60 *(978-1-57565-797-4(X))* Kane Press, Inc.

Howe, James. Creepy-Crawly Birthday. Mack, Jeff, illus. (Bunnicula & Friends Ser.: 6). (ENG.). 48p. (J). (gr. 1-3). 2008. pap. 3.99 *(978-0-689-85753-9(5))* 2007. 16.99 *(978-0-689-85728-7(4))* Simon Spotlight. (Simon Spotlight).

—Houndsley & Catina. Gay, Marie-Louise, illus. 2007. 36p. (J). (gr. k-2). lib. bdg. 12.65 *(978-0-7569-8141-9(7))* Perfection Learning Corp.

—Houndsley & Catina & the Birthday Surprise. Gay, Marie-Louise, illus. 2006. (Houndsley & Catina Ser.: 2). (ENG.). 48p. (J). (gr. k-4). 15.99 *(978-0-7636-2405-7(5))* Candlewick Pr.

—Houndsley & Catina & the Quiet Time. Gay, Marie-Louise, illus. 2013. (Candlewick Sparks Ser.). (ENG.). 48p. (J). (gr. k-4). pap. 3.99 *(978-0-7636-6863-1(X))* Candlewick Pr.

Howell, Julie Ann. Mrs Owl's Nest of Rhymes. LaGrange, Tiffany, illus. 2008. 24p. pap. 12.95 *(978-0-9818683-8-7(X))* Peppertree Pr., The.

Hubbard, Mandy. You Wish. 2010. (ENG.). 304p. (YA). (gr. 7-18). pap. 8.99 *(978-1-59514-292-4(4)*, Razorbill) Penguin Young Readers Group.

Huber, Mike. Evette's Invitation. Cowman, Joseph, illus. 2014. (ENG.). 32p. (gr. -1). 15.95 *(978-1-60554-212-6(1))* Redleaf Pr.

Hudson, Angus. Nacimiento Especial (Special Birthday) (SPA.). (J). 1.69 *(978-0-7899-0535-2(3)*, 498798) Editorial Unilit.

Hudson, Wade. Puddin' Jeffrey & Leah: Happy Birthday Puddin'! Happy Birthday Puddin'! 2009. 16p. 6.95 *(978-1-60349-019-1(1)*, Marimba Bks.) Hudson Publishing Group, The.

Hughes, Shirley. Alfie Gives a Hand. Hughes, Shirley, illus. 2009. (Alfie Ser.). (ENG., Illus.). 32p. (J). (gr. -1-k). pap. 9.99 *(978-1-86230-785-8(7)*, Red Fox) Random House Children's Books GBR. Dist: Independent Pubs. Group.

Hummel, Jim. A Bubble C. 2009. 32p. pap. 14.95 *(978-1-4269-0034-1(1))* Trafford Publishing.

Hunter, Alex. Game Over. Rew, Jen, illus. 2012. 126p. pap. *(978-1-78176-771-9(8))* FeedARead.com.

—Game over - Book Three. 2013. 268p. (J). pap. *(978-1-78299-394-0(0))* FeedARead.com.

Huven, Kim. The Birthday Bears. Padron, Alicia, illus. 2010. 10p. bds. 10.95 *(978-1-60747-774-7(2)*, Pickwick Pr.) Phoenix Bks., Inc.

I Only Like Dogs. 2013. (Illus.). 36p. pap. 9.99 *(978-1-941037-01-0(1))* Gordon Rocket.

Inkpen, Mick. Kipper's Birthday. 2014. (ENG., Illus.). 32p. (J). (gr. -1-k). pap. 10.99 ***(978-1-4449-1817-5(6))*** Hachette Children's Group GBR. Dist: Hachette Bk. Group.

Iriyama, Satoshi. Happy Spring, Chirp! 2015. (Chirp the Chick Ser.). (ENG., Illus.). 32p. (J). (— 1). 8.99 *(978-0-544-36150-8(4)*, HMH Books For Young Readers) Houghton Mifflin Harcourt Publishing Co.

Irwin, Bindi & Kunz, Chris. Trouble at the Zoo. 2011. (Bindi's Wildlife Adventures Ser.: 1). (ENG.). 112p. (gr. 3-6). pap. 5.99 *(978-1-4022-5514-4(4)*, Sourcebooks Jabberwocky) Sourcebooks, Inc.

Iversen, Jeremy. Rush. 2011. (ENG.). 272p. (YA). (gr. 9). pap. 11.99 *(978-1-4424-2400-5(1)*, Simon Pulse) Simon Pulse.

Jackson, Amitra L. Eating Safe with Ace & Mace! 2007. 44p. per. 15.95 *(978-1-4327-1255-6(1))* Outskirts Pr., Inc.

Jacqueline, Thomas. Birthday Picnic. 2010. 24p. pap. 9.99 *(978-0-88144-493-3(6))* Yorkshire Publishing Group.

Janni, Rebecca. Every Cowgirl Needs a Horse. Avril, Lynne, illus. 2010. (Every Cowgirl Ser.). (ENG.). 32p. (J). (gr. -1-k). 16.99 *(978-0-525-42164-1(5)*, Dutton Books for Young Readers) Penguin Young Readers Group.

Jansson, Tove. Moomin & the Birthday Button. Jansson, Tove, illus. 2011. (Moomins Ser.). (ENG., Illus.). 32p. (J). (gr. -1-1). 13.99 *(978-0-374-35050-5(7)*, 9780374350505, Farrar, Straus & Giroux (BYR)) Farrar, Straus & Giroux.

Jarkins, Sheila. The Adventures of Marco Flamingo in the Jungle. Jarkins, Sheila, illus. 2012. (Illus.). 32p. (J). 1.99 *(978-1-936299-31-7(3)*, Raven Tree Pr.) Delta Systems Company, Inc.

Jasnoch, Dorothy. Frankie the Bunny: Wheels of Fortune. Korzeniowski, Samson O., ed. Jasnoch, Dorothy, illus. 2013. (Illus.). 28p. 17.99 *(978-1-937752-17-0(8))* Owl About Bks. Pub., Inc.

Javernick, Ellen. The Birthday Pet, 0 vols. O'Malley, Kevin, illus. 2012. (ENG.). 34p. (J). (gr. k-3). pap. 7.99 *(978-0-7614-6238-5(4)*, 9780761462385, Amazon Children's Publishing) Amazon Publishing.

Jennings, Sharon, et al, adapted by. Franklin Snoops. 2003. (Franklin TV Storybook Ser.). (ENG., Illus.). 32p. (J). (gr. -1-3). 10.95 *(978-1-55337-364-3(2))* Kids Can Pr., Ltd. CAN. Dist: Hachette Bk. Group.

Jiang, Mingyan. Stella Doggy: Book One of Stella's Awesome Adventures. 2011. 88p. (gr. 4-6). 19.95 *(978-1-4620-4610-2(X))*; pap. 9.95 *(978-1-4620-4608-9(8))* iUniverse, Inc.

Jocelyn, Marthe. Hannah & the Seven Dresses. 2006. (Illus.). 23p. (J). (gr. k-4). reprint ed. 15.00 *(978-1-4223-5552-7(7))* DIANE Publishing Co.

Johns, Eric. The Giraffe Tree & Other Tall Stories. 2012. 180p. (-18). pap. 12.95 *(978-1-291-03279-6(7))* Lulu Pr., Inc.

Johnson, Margaret. Gone! Starter/Beginner. 2009. (ENG.). 48p. pap. 11.00 *(978-84-8323-509-6(9))* Cambridge Univ. Pr.

Johnston, Annie Fellows. The Little Colonel's Hero. 2007. (ENG.). 164p. pap. 19.99 *(978-1-4264-8448-3(8))*; 182p. pap. 21.99 *(978-1-4264-8506-0(9))* Creative Media Partners, LLC.

Jones, Christianne C. Dani el Dinosaurio, 1 vol. Lozano, Clara, tr. from ENG. Epstein, Len, illus. 2006. (Read-It! Readers en Español: Story Collection). (SPA.). 24p. (gr. -1-3). lib. bdg. 21.32 *(978-1-4048-2706-6(4)*, Easy Readers) Picture Window Bks.

Jones, Jen. Willow's Boy-Crazy Birthday. Franco, Paula, illus. 2014. (Sleepover Girls Ser.). (ENG.). 128p. (gr. 3-5). lib. bdg. 22.65 *(978-1-4342-9757-0(8))* Stone Arch Bks.

Joy, Christine. The Dream Quest. 2013. 162p. pap. *(978-1-78148-790-7(1))* Grosvenor Hse. Publishing Ltd.

Jules, Jacqueline. Abuela's Birthday. Smith, Kim, illus. 2015. (Sofia Martinez Ser.). (ENG.). 32p. (gr. k-2). lib. bdg. 21.32 *(978-1-4795-5775-2(7)*, Sofia Martinez) Picture Window Bks.

Karen, Frantz. Children's Parables: Earthly Stories with Heavenly Lessons for Children. 2013. 162p. pap. 13.95 *(978-1-4908-1675-3(5)*, WestBow Pr.) Author Solutions, Inc.

Kargman, Jill & Karasyov, Carrie. Bittersweet Sixteen. 2006. (YA). (gr. 7-12). (ENG.). 240p. 15.99 *(978-0-06-077844-6(X))*; 230p. lib. bdg. 16.89 *(978-0-06-077845-3(8))* HarperCollins Pubs.

Kasza, Keiko. My Lucky Birthday. Kasza, Keiko, illus. 2013. (ENG., Illus.). 32p. (J). (gr. -1-k). 16.99 *(978-0-399-25763-6(2)*, G.P. Putnam's Sons Books for Young Readers) Penguin Young Readers Group.

Kathleen, Judith. Attila's Wobbly Birthday Box, 1 vol. 2010. 20p. pap. 24.95 *(978-1-4489-2451-6(0))* PublishAmerica, Inc.

Katz, Karen. Where Is Baby's Birthday Cake? Katz, Karen, illus. 2008. (ENG., Illus.). 14p. (J). (gr. -1 — 1). bds. 6.99 *(978-1-4169-5817-8(7)*, Little Simon) Little Simon.

Kay, L. M. Frederick's Birthday Surprise. 2009. 36p. pap. 24.95 *(978-1-60836-944-7(7))* America Star Bks.

Kay's Birthday: KinderReaders Individual Title Six-Packs. (Kinderstarters Ser.). 8p. (gr. -1-1). 21.00 *(978-0-7635-8651-5(X))* Rigby Education.

Keane, Dave. Who Wants a Tortoise? Campbell, K. G., illus. 2016. (ENG.). 40p. (J). (gr. k-3). 17.99 *(978-0-385-75417-0(5)*, Knopf Bks. for Young Readers) Random Hse. Children's Bks.

Keats, Ezra Jack. A Letter to Amy. 2015. 32p. pap. 7.00 *(978-1-61003-525-5(9))* Center for the Collaborative Classroom.

Keene, Carolyn. Pool Party Puzzler. Francis, Peter, illus. 2015. (Nancy Drew Clue Book Ser.: 1). (ENG.). 96p. (J). (gr. 1-4). 16.99 *(978-1-4814-3896-4(4)*, Aladdin) Simon & Schuster Children's Publishing.

Keithley, Laura Lee. Ellie's Big Day. Holliday, Holly, illus. 2008. 40p. pap. 24.95 *(978-1-60672-474-3(6))* America Star Bks.

Kelley, Gloria. Beverly Babes & Guys: Alicia's Thirtee. 2006. 64p. pap. 16.95 *(978-1-4241-2610-1(X))* PublishAmerica, Inc.

Kennemore, Tim. Alice's Birthday Pig. Spoor, Mike, illus. 2008. 54p. (J). (gr. 2-5). 12.00 *(978-0-8028-5335-6(8))* Eerdmans, William B. Publishing Co.

Kerr, Judith. Mog's ABC. Kerr, Judith, illus. 2005. (ENG., Illus.). 48p. (J). (gr. -1-k). pap. 8.99 *(978-0-00-717131-6(5)*, HarperCollins Children's Bks.) HarperCollins Pubs. Ltd. GBR. Dist: HarperCollins Pubs.

Kertell, Lynn Maslen. Cupcake Surprise! Hendra, Sue, illus. 2012. (Scholastic Reader Level 1 Ser.). (ENG.). 32p. (J). (gr. -1-3). pap. 3.99 *(978-0-545-38269-4(6))* Scholastic, Inc.

—Cupcake Surprise! 2012. (BOB Books: Scholastic Readers Level 1 Ser.). lib. bdg. 13.55 *(978-0-606-23910-3(3)*, Turtleback) Turtleback Bks.

Kessler, Liz. Poppy the Pirate Dog & the Missing Treasure. Phillips, Mike, illus. (Candlewick Sparks Ser.). (ENG.). 64p. (J). (gr. k-4). 2016. pap. 3.99 *(978-0-7636-8772-4(3))* 2015. 14.99 *(978-0-7636-7497-7(4))* Candlewick Pr.

Khan, Hana. Taylor's Birthday Party. Kemble, Mai S., illus. 2008. (J). *(978-1-60108-048-6(4))* Red Cygnet Pr.

Khan, Rukhsana. Big Red Lollipop. Blackall, Sophie, illus. 2010. (ENG.). 40p. (J). (gr. -1-3). 16.99 *(978-0-670-06287-4(1)*, Viking Books for Young Readers) Penguin Young Readers Group.

Kim, YeShil. The Very Best Teacher. Moriuchi, Mique, illus. 2015. (ENG.). 24p. (J). (-3). 12.99 *(978-1-4926-0998-8(6))* Sourcebooks, Inc.

Kingsley, Salome. Two Wishes for Natty's Birthday. 2007. (Illus.). 54p. (J). pap. 15.00 *(978-0-8059-7391-4(5))* Dorrance Publishing Co., Inc.

Kleinberg, Naomi. Elmo's Super-Duper Birthday (Sesame Street) Mathieu, Joe, illus. 2016. (Pictureback(R) Ser.). (ENG.). 24p. (J). (gr. -1-2). pap. 5.99 *(978-0-399-55216-8(2)*, Random Hse. Bks. for Young Readers) Random Hse. Children's Bks.

Kline, Suzy. Horrible Harry & the Triple Revenge. Remkiewicz, Frank, illus. 2008. (Horrible Harry Ser.). (ENG.). 64p. (J). (gr. 2-4). 4.99 *(978-0-14-241081-3(0)*, Puffin Books) Penguin Young Readers Group.

Kline, Suzy & Wells, Rosemary. Horrible Harry & the Birthday Girl. Wummer, Amy, illus. 2016. (Horrible Harry Ser.: 34). (ENG.). 80p. (J). (gr. 2-5). bds. 14.99 *(978-0-451-47331-8(0)*, Viking Books for Young Readers) Penguin Young Readers Group.

Klitzner, Irene & Adams, Peggy. Today Is My Birthday & I Have Nothing to Wear! Lou Who, Carrie, illus. 2011. (ENG.). 48p. (J). 18.95 *(978-0-9846496-0-0(3))* Attitude Pie Publishing.

Koch, Janet Marie. Hallie's Best Birthday. 2008. 48p. pap. 24.95 *(978-1-60610-812-3(3))* America Star Bks.

Kollas, Candace. The Birthday Fairy: A Fairyland Tradition. 2012. 28p. pap. 13.99 *(978-1-4575-1286-5(6))* Dog Ear Publishing, LLC.

Krackow, Eric T. The Lollipop Monster Meets Clem the Klutz, 1 vol. 2013. (ENG., Illus.). 64p. (J). 16.99 *(978-0-7643-4287-5(8)*, 9780764342875) Schiffer Publishing, Ltd.

Krakower, Harold. Sugarland. 2008. 28p. pap. 12.50 *(978-1-934925-12-6(8)*, Eloquent Bks.) Strategic Book Publishing & Rights Agency (SBPRA).

—Sugarland: Volume 2 Trouble in Sugarland. 2009. 28p. pap. 12.50 *(978-1-4490-1880-1(7))* AuthorHouse.

Krise, Gale. It's a Colorful Candy Birthday. 2012. 24p. pap. 24.95 *(978-1-4626-7604-0(9))* America Star Bks.

Kropf, Latifa Berry. Happy Birthday, World: A Rosh Hashanah Celebration. Carlson, Lisa, illus. 2005. (Very First Board Bks.). (ENG.). 12p. (J). (gr. -1 — 1). 5.95 *(978-0-929371-32-0(1)*, Kar-Ben Publishing) Lerner Publishing Group.

Krosoczka, Jarrett J. Annie Was Warned. 2013. (ENG., Illus.). 32p. (J). (gr. -1-2). 7.99 *(978-0-385-75341-8(1)*, Dragonfly Bks.) Random Hse. Children's Bks.

—Annie Was Warned. 2013. lib. bdg. 18.40 *(978-0-606-32188-4(8)*, Turtleback) Turtleback Bks.

Krulik, Nancy. Wet & Wild! #5, 5 vols. Blecha, Aaron, illus. 2011. (George Brown, Class Clown Ser.: 5). (ENG.). 128p. (J). (gr. 2-4). pap. 4.99 *(978-0-448-45570-9(6)*, Grosset & Dunlap) Penguin Young Readers Group.

Kruse, Donald W. Gorilla Soup! 2012. 48p. pap. 12.95 *(978-1-59663-862-4(1)*, Castle Keep Pr.) Rock, James A. & Co. Pubs.

Ku, Grace. When Grace Was. 2009. 24p. pap. 12.99 *(978-1-4389-9945-6(3))* AuthorHouse.

Kuchman, D. S. Krystal Steps: The Journey Begins. 2006. 57p. pap. 16.95 *(978-1-4241-5135-6(X))* America Star Bks.

Lagonegro, Melissa. Mater's Birthday Surprise. 2012. (Cars Step into Reading Ser.). lib. bdg. 13.55 *(978-0-606-23724-6(0)*, Turtleback) Turtleback Bks.

—Mater's Birthday Surprise (Disney/Pixar Cars) Random House Disney Staff, illus. 2012. (Step into Reading Ser.). (ENG.). 32p. (J). (gr. -1-1). pap. 3.99 *(978-0-7364-2858-3(5),* RH/Disney) Random Hse. Children's Bks.

Lammers, Elizabeth A. & McKinney, Dan. Pierre's Stupendous Birthday Bash. Epstein, Gabriela, illus. 2011. 48p. pap. 24.95 *(978-1-4560-4294-3(7))* America Star Bks.

Lamont, Tracey. The Adventures of Speedy & Creedy: The Surprise. 2009. 36p. pap. 16.50 *(978-1-4389-7541-2(4))* AuthorHouse.

Lansky, Bruce. Polar BRRR Delivers. Wummer, Amy, illus. 2010. 10p. (J). bds. 6.99 *(978-1-4169-9318-6(5))* Meadowbrook Pr.

LaRose, Melinda & Disney Book Group Staff. Birthday Bash! Disney Storybook Art Team, illus. 2014. (ENG.). 32p. (J). (gr. -1-k). pap. 4.99 *(978-1-4231-9935-9(9))* Disney Pr.

Lasota, Mary. Kitty Piper, Angel Cat, Book 3, A Surprise for Ashley. 2011. 48p. (gr. 1-2). pap. 11.66 *(978-1-4634-1031-5(X))* AuthorHouse.

Latta, Leslie Jay. Patches' Day Out. 2011. 24p. pap. 24.95 *(978-1-4626-3486-6(9))* PublishAmerica, Inc.

Leavitt, Lindsey. The Birthday Suit. Ford, A. G., illus. 2017. (Commander in Cheese Ser.: 4). (ENG.). 112p. (J). (gr. 2-5). 4.99 *(978-1-101-93121-9(3),* Random Hse. Bks. for Young Readers) Random Hse. Children's Bks.

Leedy, Loreen. Crazy Like a Fox. Leedy, Loreen, illus. 2009. (ENG., Illus.). 32p. (J). (gr. -1-3). 7.99 *(978-0-8234-2248-7(8))* Holiday Hse., Inc.

Leeson, Christine. Just for You! Ellis, Andy, illus. 2008. (Tiger Tales Ser.). 24p. (J). (gr. -1-2). pap. 6.95 *(978-1-58925-408-4(2))* Tiger Tales.

Lenington, Paula. The Forgotten Birthday. Olan, Agnieszka, illus. 2011. 28p. pap. 24.95 *(978-1-4560-2711-7(5))* America Star Bks.

Lepp, Royden. Happy Birthday Barnabas, 1 vol. Lepp, Royden, illus. 2008. (I Can Read! / Barnabas Ser.). (ENG., Illus.). 32p. (J). (gr. -1-1). pap. 3.99 *(978-0-310-71586-3(5))* Zonderkidz.

Lester, Helen & Munsinger, Lynn. Happy Birdday, Tacky! Lester, Helen & Munsinger, Lynn, illus. 2013. (Tacky the Penguin Ser.). (ENG., Illus.). 32p. (J). (gr. -1-3). 16.99 *(978-0-547-91228-8(5))* Houghton Mifflin Harcourt Publishing Co.

Levine, Deborah A. & Riley, JillEllyn. The Icing on the Cake. 2015. (Saturday Cooking Club Ser.: 2). (ENG., Illus.). 304p. (J). (gr. 4-9). 17.99 *(978-1-4424-9942-3(7),* Aladdin) Simon & Schuster Children's Publishing.

—Kitchen Chaos. 2015. (Saturday Cooking Club Ser.: 1). (ENG., Illus.). 336p. (J). (gr. 4-9). pap. 7.99 *(978-1-4424-9940-9(0),* Aladdin) Simon & Schuster Children's Publishing.

Liberts, Jennifer. The Cake Monster. VanTuyle, David, illus. 2015. (Step into Reading Ser.). (ENG.). 24p. (J). (gr. -1-1). 4.99 *(978-0-553-52314-0(7),* Random Hse. Bks. for Young Readers) Random Hse. Children's Bks.

—Happy Birthday, Princess! (Disney Princess) Marrucchi, Elisa, illus. 2016. (Step into Reading Ser.). (ENG.). 24p. (J). (gr. -1-1). pap. 4.99 *(978-0-7364-3664-9(2),* RH/Disney) Random Hse. Children's Bks.

Lieberman, Channah. Happy Birthday to Me! - Boys' Edition. Argoff, Patti, illus. 2006. 32p. (J). 12.95 *(978-1-929628-27-8(7))* Hachai Publishing.

—Happy Birthday to Me! Girls' Edition. Argoff, Patti, illus. 2006. 32p. (J). 12.95 *(978-1-929628-31-5(5))* Hachai Publishing.

Lilienstein, Jennel. Birthday! 2003. 36p. (J). 8.99 *(978-0-9741215-0-5(9))* Stories of My Life, The.

Lin, Grace. Ling & Ting Share a Birthday. (ENG.). 48p. (J). (gr. 1-4). 2014. pap. 4.99 *(978-0-316-18404-5(7))* 2013. (Illus.). 15.00 *(978-0-316-18405-2(5))* Little, Brown Bks. for Young Readers.

—Ling & Ting Share a Birthday. 2014. (Passport to Reading Level 3 Ser.). (J). lib. bdg. 14.75 *(978-0-606-35932-0(X))* Turtleback Bks.

Lindemann, Lindy. A Kicklighter Shadow & Beeples Book: The Beeples' Birthday Bash. 2009. 24p. pap. 12.95 *(978-1-4490-5707-7(1))* AuthorHouse.

Lindgren, Astrid & Vang Nyman, Ingrid. Pippi Fixes Everything. Nunnally, Tiina, tr. from SWE. 2013. (ENG., Illus.). 56p. (J). 14.95 *(978-1-77046-131-4(0),* 9781770461314) Drawn & Quarterly Pubns. CAN. Dist: Macmillan.

Lipe, Riki. Hanging with Yum-Yum & Yuck. 2007. (Illus.). (J). 10.00 *(978-0-9659381-6-7(6))* Hoot N' Cackle Pr.

Little, Jean. The Birthday Girl. Lawrason, June, illus. 2004. 64p. (J). lib. bdg. 20.00 *(978-1-4242-1256-9(1))* Fitzgerald Bks.

Lockhart, Lynne N. & Lockhart, Barbara M. Rambling Raft, 1 vol. Lockhart, Lynne N., illus. 2009. (ENG., Illus.). 30p. (J). (gr. 2-18). 7.95 *(978-0-87033-392-7(5),* 9780870333927, Cornell Maritime Pr./Tidewater Pubs.) Schiffer Publishing, Ltd.

Lodding, Linda Ravin. Wakey, Wakey, Elephant! Robertson, Michael, illus. 2017. (ENG.). 32p. (J). (gr. -1). 16.95 ***(978-1-4549-1999-5(X))*** Sterling Publishing Co., Inc.

Lois, Lowry. The Birthday Ball. Feiffer, Jules, illus. 2011. (ENG.). 192p. (J). (gr. 5-7). pap. 7.99 *(978-0-547-57710-4(9))* Houghton Mifflin Harcourt Publishing Co.

Lokaisingh, Jasmine. The Tales of Mme. Bovarie Vache & Mr. P. Huggins: In Huggsie's Birthday. 2011. 16p. 8.32 *(978-1-4520-4071-4(0))* AuthorHouse.

London, Jonathan. Froggy's Birthday Wish. 2016. (Froggy Ser.). lib. bdg. 17.20 *(978-0-606-38399-8(9))* Turtleback Bks.

London, Jonathan & Wells, Rosemary. Froggy's Birthday Wish. Remkiewicz, Frank, illus. 2015. (Froggy Ser.). (ENG.). 32p. (J). (gr. -1-k). bds. 16.99 *(978-0-670-01572-6(5),* Viking Books for Young Readers) Penguin Young Readers Group.

Long, Ethan. Pig Has a Plan. 2013. (I Like to Read(r) Ser.). (ENG.). 24p. (J). (gr. -1-3). pap. 6.99 *(978-0-8234-2911-0(3))* Holiday Hse., Inc.

Look, Lenore. Henry's First-Moon Birthday. 2004. (Illus.). (J). (gr. k-3). spiral bd. *(978-0-616-07256-1(2))* Canadian National Institute for the Blind/Institut National Canadien pour les Aveugles.

Lootens, Ann. The Birthday Surprise. Faas, Linde, illus. 2013. (Wild Woods Ser.). (ENG.). 32p. (J). (gr. -1-k). 15.95 *(978-1-60537-147-4(5))* Cobblestone Publishing Co.

Lopez, Loretta. Que Suppresa de Cumpleanos! 2004. (SPA.). (J). (gr. k-3). spiral bd. *(978-0-616-07277-6(5))* Canadian National Institute for the Blind/Institut National Canadien pour les Aveugles.

Lopez, Maria Lorena. The Bird's Party, Birds in the Tropical Dry Forest. 2009. 28p. pap. 13.00 *(978-1-60860-156-1(0),* Eloquent Bks.) Strategic Book Publishing & Rights Agency (SBPRA).

Lord, Cynthia. Happy Birthday Hamster. Anderson, Derek, illus. 2011. (ENG.). 40p. (J). (gr. -1-k). 18.99 *(978-0-545-25522-6(8),* Scholastic Pr.) Scholastic, Inc.

Lorenzen, Margaret Brownell. Petunia Patch Pockets & the Golden Locket. Jocelyn, Sawyer & Liza, Behles, illus. 2005. 76p. (J). per. 12.50 *(978-0-9724922-7-0(5))* Authors & Artists Publishers of New York, Inc.

Lorimer, Janet. The Mystery Quilt, 1 vol. unabr. ed. 2010. (Q Reads Ser.). (ENG.). 32p. (YA). (gr. 9-12). pap. 6.95 *(978-1-61651-183-8(4))* Saddleback Educational Publishing, Inc.

Lowrey, Chris. Wonec Adventures: The Gift of Giving. 2008. 26p. pap. 24.95 *(978-1-60563-622-1(3))* America Star Bks.

Luces-Tucker, Max. Bobby & Chrissy: One Gift. 2008. 36p. pap. 17.99 *(978-1-4343-8199-6(4))* AuthorHouse.

Lyle-Soffe, Shari. On the Go with Rooter & Snuffle. Collier, Kevin Scott, illus. 2008. 20p. pap. 9.95 *(978-1-933090-96-2(0))* Guardian Angel Publishing, Inc.

Lynch, Jay. Otto's Backwards Day. Cammuso, Frank, illus. 2013. (ENG.). 32p. (J). (gr. -1-3). 12.95 *(978-1-935179-33-7(0))* TOON Books / RAW Junior, LLC.

Lynn, Tammy. Happy Birthday Puppy: An I See Puppy Book. Stewart, Elaine, ed. Lynn, Tammy, illus. 2006. (Illus.). 12p. (J). bds. 6.99 *(978-0-9774277-0-3(6),* 0-9774277-0-6) I See Puppy, LLP.

MacDonald, Betty Bard & Canham, Anne MacDonald. Happy Birthday, Mrs. Piggle-Wiggle. Boiger, Alexandra, illus. 2008. (ENG.). 208p. (J). (gr. 3-7). pap. 6.99 *(978-0-06-072814-4(0))* HarperCollins Pubs.

Mackall, Dandi Daley. Natalie & the Downside-Up Birthday, 1 vol. Blakeslee, Lys, illus. 2009. (That's Nat! Ser.). (ENG.). 96p. (J). (gr. 1-4). pap. 4.99 *(978-0-310-71569-6(5))* Zonderkidz.

Mackintosh, David. Marshall Armstrong Is New to Our School. 2011. (ENG., Illus.). 32p. (J). (gr. k-2). 17.95 *(978-1-4197-0036-1(7),* Abrams Bks. for Young Readers) Abrams, Inc.

Macmillan, Sue. Bouncy, Pouncy Puppy. Ward, Sarah, illus. 2014. (Cheery Chasers Ser.). (ENG.). 8p. (J). (gr. -1 — 1). bds. 4.99 *(978-0-7641-6698-3(0))* Barron's Educational Series, Inc.

Make Believe Ideas. Flower Friends Poppy's Shapes. 2013. (ENG.). 10p. (J). bds. 6.99 *(978-1-78235-603-5(7))* Make Believe Ideas GBR. Dist: Nelson, Thomas Inc.

Malone, Jen & Nall, Gail. You're Invited. 2015. (ENG., Illus.). 336p. (J). (gr. 4-8). 17.99 *(978-1-4814-3197-2(8),* Aladdin) Simon & Schuster Children's Publishing.

Mandy, Stanley. Bella: The Birthday Party. Mandy, Stanley, illus. 2010. (ENG., Illus.). 32p. (J). (gr. -1-k). 9.95 *(978-1-58925-850-1(9))* Tiger Tales.

Mann, Jennifer K. Two Speckled Eggs. Mann, Jennifer K., illus. 2014. (ENG., Illus.). 32p. (J). (gr. k-3). 14.99 *(978-0-7636-6168-7(6))* Candlewick Pr.

Manushkin, Fran. Katie's Lucky Birthday, 1 vol. Lyon, Tammie, illus. 2011. (Katie Woo Ser.). (ENG.). 32p. (gr. k-2). pap. 5.95 *(978-1-4048-6612-6(4));* lib. bdg. 21.32 *(978-1-4048-6514-3(4))* Picture Window Bks.

Manzak, Bonnie. Lairame's Birthday Surprise. 2011. 28p. pap. 15.99 *(978-1-4568-5815-5(7))* Xlibris Corp.

Marlow, Herb. The Lost Kitten. Head, Pat, illus. 2003. 16p. (J). 19.95 *(978-1-893595-34-7(X))* Four Seasons Bks., Inc.

Marrs, J. Pierce & Marrs, S. Nick. Andy Goes to the Aquarium. 2013. 48p. pap. 14.99 *(978-0-9896681-0-1(X))* 4mPr.

Marshall, Wendy. The O'Clocks: Mr. O'Clock Goes to A Party. 2008. 40p. pap. 18.49 *(978-1-4389-2403-8(8))* AuthorHouse.

Marsoli, Lisa Ann. Harold's Birthday Surprise: Harold & the Purple Crayon. Murawski, Kevin, illus. 2005. 10p. (J). 6.95 *(978-1-58117-261-4(3),* Intervisual/Piggy Toes) Bendon, Inc.

Martin, JoElle. A Bridge in the Forest, Vol. 1. 2008. (ENG.). 224p. (YA). pap. 14.99 *(978-1-59092-372-6(3))* Blue Forge Pr.

—A Promise in the Forest, Vol. 2. 2008. (ENG.). 172p. (YA). pap. 14.99 *(978-1-59092-541-6(6))* Blue Forge Pr.

Martínez, Rafael. El Deseo de Aurelio. Martínez, Enrique, illus. 2006. (la Orilla del Viento Ser.). (SPA.). 48p. (J). (gr. 8-10). pap. *(978-968-16-7988-0(1))* Fondo de Cultura Economica.

Marvin, Susan. Birthday Dreamz. 2011. 36p. (gr. -1). pap. 15.99 *(978-1-4567-4173-0(X))* AuthorHouse.

Mason, Jane B. & Stephens, Sarah Hines. Snowfall Surprise. 2009. (Candy Apple Ser.: 21). (ENG.). 144p. (J). (gr. 3-7). 5.99 *(978-0-545-10067-0(4),* Scholastic Paperbacks) Scholastic, Inc.

Mass, Wendy. Finally. 2011. (ENG.). 304p. (J). (gr. 3-7). pap. 6.99 *(978-0-545-05243-6(2),* Scholastic Paperbacks) Scholastic, Inc.

—The Last Present. 2013. (ENG.). 256p. (J). (gr. 3-7). 16.99 *(978-0-545-31016-1(4),* Scholastic Pr.) Scholastic, Inc.

—Leap Day. 2006. (ENG.). 208p. (YA). (gr. 7-17). per. 10.99 *(978-0-316-05828-5(9))* Little, Brown Bks. for Young Readers.

—11 Birthdays. (ENG.). 272p. (J). (gr. 3-7). 2010. pap. 6.99 *(978-0-545-05240-5(8),* Scholastic Paperbacks) 2009. 17.99 *(978-0-545-05239-9(4),* Scholastic Pr.) Scholastic, Inc.

—11 Birthdays. 2010. (Willow Falls Ser.: 1). lib. bdg. 17.20 *(978-0-606-13990-8(7),* Turtleback) Turtleback Bks.

Matheis, Mickie. Happy Birthday, Strawberry Shortcake. Thomas, Laura, illus. 2015. (Strawberry Shortcake Ser.). (ENG.). 32p. (J). (gr. -1-k). 16.99 *(978-0-448-48748-9(9),* Grosset & Dunlap) Penguin Young Readers Group.

Mathews, Madge. Brandon's Really Big Birthday Surprise. Cook, Laurie, illus. 2008. 24p. (J). 3.99 *(978-0-9796536-0-5(6),* EPI Kid Bks.) EPI Bks.

Matsuura, Richard & Matsuura, Ruth. Birthday Wish. Chao, Linus, illus. (J). 8.95 *(978-1-887916-04-2(0))* Orchid Isle Publishing Co.

Matthews Culp, Dawn. What's up Willie? the Birthday Puppy! 2008. (Illus.). 24p. (J). 28.95 *(978-0-615-22222-6(6))* Sprouting Peanut Pubs.

Maurer, Amy J. A Purple Hippopotamus Pillow & Pink Penguin Sheets. Smith, Rachel, illus. 2006. 52p. (J). 19.99 *(978-1-59879-239-3(3));* per. 15.99 *(978-1-59879-167-9(2))* Lifevest Publishing, Inc.

Mayher, Lauren. The Legend of Darien: A Hero Rises: Book 1. 2008. 423p. (J). per. 12.95 *(978-0-9794545-0-9(6))* Blue Eyed Mayhem Publishing.

McClure, Wendy. The Princess & the Peanut Allergy. Lyon, Tammie, illus. 2012. (J). *(978-1-61913-127-9(7))* Weigl Pubs., Inc.

—The Princess & the Peanut Allergy, 1 vol. Lyon, Tammie, illus. 2009. (ENG.). 32p. (J). (gr. 1-3). 16.99 *(978-0-8075-6623-7(3))* Whitman, Albert & Co.

McCranie, Stephen. Belly Flop! Book 3. McCranie, Stephen, illus. 3rd ed. 2012. (Mal & Chad Ser.: 3). (ENG., Illus.). 240p. (J). (gr. 3-7). pap. 9.99 *(978-0-399-25658-5(X),* Philomel Bks.) Penguin Young Readers Group.

McDaniel Hailey. The Amazing Angelina: And Her Hula Hoop. 2013. 38p. pap. 10.19 *(978-1-62884-794-9(8))* Speedy Publishing LLC.

McDonald, Megan. Mrs. Moody in the Birthday Jinx. Madrid, Erwin, illus. 2016. (Judy Moody & Friends Ser.). (ENG.). 64p. (J). (gr. -1-1). 14.75 *(978-0-606-39092-7(8))* Turtleback Bks.

McDoogle, Farrah. OLIVIA Makes a Charm Bracelet. Osterhold, Jared, illus. 2012. (Olivia TV Tie-In Ser.). (ENG.). 16p. (J). (gr. -1-2). pap. 6.99 *(978-1-4424-4163-7(1),* Simon Spotlight) Simon Spotlight.

McDoogle, Farrah, adapted by. A Party for Brobee! 2010. (Yo Gabba Gabba! Ser.). (ENG.). 14p. (J). (gr. -1-k). bds. 5.99 *(978-1-4169-9934-8(5),* Simon Spotlight) Simon Spotlight.

McGeorge, Constance W. Chestnut, 1 vol. Whyte, Mary, illus. 2004. (ENG.). 32p. (J). 16.95 *(978-1-56145-321-4(8))* Peachtree Pubs.

McGrath, Barbara Barbieri. Birthday Counting. Tagel, Peggy, illus. 2017. (First Celebrations Ser.). (ENG.). 12p. (J). (— 1). bds. 6.99 *(978-1-58089-537-8(9))* Charlesbridge Publishing, Inc.

McKee, David. El Principe Pedro y el oso de Peluche. (SPA.). (J). 7.95 *(978-958-04-6258-3(5))* Norma S.A. COL. Dist: Distribuidora Norma, Inc.

McKee, David, illus. Elmer & the Birthday Quake. 2013. (ENG.). 32p. (J). (gr. -1-3). 16.95 *(978-1-4677-1117-3(9))* Lerner Publishing Group.

McKenna, Jacqueline & Manarino-Leggett, Priscilla. Sourpuss Sue. Manarino, Mark, illus. 2011. 24p. pap. 24.95 *(978-1-4560-8939-9(0))* America Star Bks.

McLaughlin, Lauren. Mitzi Tulane, Preschool Detective, in What's That Smell? Ohi, Debbie Ridpath, illus. 2016. (ENG.). 32p. (J). (-k). 19.99 *(978-0-375-97176-1(9),* Random Hse. Bks. for Young Readers) Random Hse. Children's Bks.

McMullan, Kate. Pearl & Wagner: Three Secrets. 2013. (Penguin Young Readers Level 3 Ser.). lib. bdg. 13.55 *(978-0-606-31708-5(2),* Turtleback) Turtleback Bks.

—Three Secrets. Alley, R. W., illus. 2013. (Pearl & Wagner Ser.: 3). (ENG.). 48p. (J). (gr. 1-3). pap. 3.99 *(978-0-448-46472-5(1),* Penguin Young Readers) Penguin Young Readers Group.

McNamara, Margaret. George Washington's Birthday: A Mostly True Tale. Blitt, Barry, illus. 2012. (ENG.). 40p. (J). (gr. -1-3). 17.99 *(978-0-375-84499-7(6),* Schwartz & Wade Bks.) Random Hse. Children's Bks.

Meadows, Daisy. Belle the Birthday Fairy. 2012. (Rainbow Magic Ser.). (ENG., Illus.). 176p. (J). (gr. 2-5). pap. 6.99 *(978-0-545-27054-0(5),* Scholastic Paperbacks) Scholastic, Inc.

—Belle the Birthday Fairy. 2012. (Rainbow Magic — Special Edition Ser.). lib. bdg. 17.20 *(978-0-606-23726-0(7),* Turtleback) Turtleback Bks.

—The Fairies' Birthday Surprise. 2010. (Scholastic Reader Level 2 Ser.). (ENG.). 32p. (J). (gr. 1-3). pap. 3.99 *(978-0-545-22292-1(3),* Cartwheel Bks.) Scholastic, Inc.

—Nina the Birthday Cake Fairy. 2014. (Sugar & Spice Fairies Ser.: 7). (ENG.). 80p. (J). (gr. 2-5). pap. 4.99 *(978-0-545-60537-3(7),* Scholastic Paperbacks) Scholastic, Inc.

—Rainbow Magic Special Edition: Lila & Myla the Twins Fairies. 2015. (Rainbow Magic Special Edition Ser.). (ENG., Illus.). 176p. (J). (gr. 2-5). pap. 6.99 *(978-0-545-70825-8(7),* Scholastic Paperbacks) Scholastic, Inc.

Meddaugh, Susan. Martha on the Case. 2010. (Martha Speaks Ser.). (ENG., Illus.). 112p. (J). (gr. 1-4). pap. 5.99 *(978-0-547-21055-1(8))* Houghton Mifflin Harcourt Publishing Co.

—Martha Says It with Flowers. 2010. (Martha Speaks Ser.). (ENG., Illus.). 32p. (J). (gr. -1-3). 12.99 *(978-0-547-21058-2(2))* Houghton Mifflin Harcourt Publishing Co.

Meister, Cari. Tiny the Birthday Dog. Davis, Rich, illus. 2013. (Tiny Ser.). (ENG.). 32p. (J). (gr. k-1). 14.99 *(978-0-670-01413-2(3));* pap. 3.99 *(978-0-448-46478-7(0))* Penguin Young Readers Group. (Penguin Young Readers).

—Tiny the Birthday Dog. 2013. (Penguin Young Readers Level 1 Ser.). lib. bdg. 13.55 *(978-0-606-31706-1(6),* Turtleback) Turtleback Bks.

Merer, Laura, illus. Fuzzy Ducky's Birthday: A Touch-and-Feel Pop-up Book. 2005. 10p. (J). 8.95 *(978-1-58117-324-6(5),* Intervisual/Piggy Toes) Bendon, Inc.

Meshon, Aaron. Delivery! Meshon, Aaron, illus. 2017. (ENG., Illus.). 48p. (J). (gr. -1-3). 17.99 *(978-1-4814-4175-9(2))* Simon & Schuster Children's Publishing.

Metzger, Lois & Mazer, Norma Fox. The Year We Missed My Birthday: Eleven Birthday Stories. 2005. (Illus.). 155p. (J). pap. *(978-0-439-73563-6(7))* Scholastic, Inc.

Meyerhoff, Jenny. Project Peep. Chatelain, Eva, illus. 2016. (Friendship Garden Ser.: 3). (ENG.). 144p. (J). (gr. 2-5). pap. 5.99 *(978-1-4814-3913-8(8),* Aladdin) Simon & Schuster Children's Publishing.

Millender, Gwyn. Essie's Birthday Surprise. 2004. (J). 8.95 *(978-0-9727142-0-4(0))* F.R.O.G. the Rock Pubns.

Miller, Lauren. Parallel. 2013. (ENG.). 432p. (YA). (gr. 8). 17.99 *(978-0-06-219977-5(3),* HarperTeen) HarperCollins Pubs.

Miller, Marie. Party Time. 2006. (Neighborhood Readers Ser.). (ENG.). 8p. (gr. -1-3). pap. 5.15 *(978-1-4042-6706-0(9),* Rosen Classroom) Rosen Publishing Group, Inc., The.

Milne, A. A. In Which Everyone Has a Birthday & Gets Two Presents. Shepard, Ernest H., illus. unabr. ed. (Winnie-the-Pooh Ser.). (J). incl. audio *(978-1-57375-015-8(8),* 70134) Audioscope.

Misra, Michelle. Birthday Surprise. Chaffey, Samantha, illus. 2016. (Angel Wings Ser.: 2). (ENG.). 128p. (J). (gr. 1-4). pap. 5.99 *(978-1-4814-5800-9(0),* Aladdin) Simon & Schuster Children's Publishing.

—Birthday Surprise. 2013. (ENG., Illus.). 112p. (J). pap. 5.99 *(978-0-85707-624-3(8))* Simon & Schuster, Ltd. GBR. Dist: Simon & Schuster, Inc.

Mitter, Matt. Grouchy Hugs. Brannon, Tom, illus. 2012. (Hugs Book Ser.). (ENG.). 12p. (J). (gr. -1-k). bds. 10.99 *(978-0-7944-2194-6(6))* Reader's Digest Assn., Inc., The.

Moncure, Jane Belk. Mousekin's Special Day: A Book about Special Days. Gallagher-Cole, Mernie, illus. 2013. (Magic Castle Readers Ser.). (ENG.). 32p. (J). (gr. -1-2). 25.64 *(978-1-62323-586-4(3),* 206321) Child's World, Inc., The.

Monks, Lydia, illus. Mungo Monkey Has a Birthday Party. 2014. (ENG.). 14p. (J). (gr. -1). 12.99 *(978-1-4052-6866-0(2))* Egmont Bks., Ltd. GBR. Dist: Independent Pubs. Group.

Monroe, Chris. Bug on a Bike. Monroe, Chris, illus. 2014. (ENG., Illus.). 32p. (J). (gr. -1-2). 16.95 *(978-1-4677-2154-7(9),* Carolrhoda Bks.) Lerner Publishing Group.

Moodie, Fiona. Noko's Surprise Party. 2008. (ENG., Illus.). 32p. (J). (gr. k-3). 16.95 *(978-1-84507-587-3(0),* Frances Lincoln) Quarto Publishing Group UK GBR. Dist: Hachette Bk. Group.

Moore, Jordan. Queen Serena, 1 vol. rev. ed. 2013. (Fiction Readers Ser.). (ENG., Illus.). 28p. (J). (gr. 3-3). pap. 8.99 *(978-1-4333-5598-1(1))* Shell Educational Publishing.

—Queen Serena. rev. ed. 2013. (Fiction Readers Ser.). (ENG., Illus.). 28p. (gr. 3-3). pap. 19.96 *(978-1-4807-1720-6(7))* Teacher Created Materials, Inc.

Mora, Pat. Una Cesta de Cumpleanos para Tia Abuela. Lang, Cecily, illus. (SPA.). (J). (gr. k-2). pap. 3.16 net. *(978-0-395-78817-2(X),* HMS088) Houghton Mifflin Harcourt Publishing Co.

Morales, Yuyi. Just in Case: A Trickster Tale & Spanish Alphabet Book. Morales, Yuyi, illus. 2008. (ENG., Illus.). 40p. (J). (gr. -1-3). 18.99 *(978-1-59643-329-8(9),* 9781596433298) Roaring Brook Pr.

Moran, Alex. What Day Is It? (¿Qué Día es Hoy?) Campoy, F. Isabel & Flor Ada, Alma, trs. Moreton, Daniel, illus. 2008. (Green Light Readers Level 1 Ser.). (ENG & SPA.). 28p. (J). (gr. -1-3). pap. 3.95 *(978-0-15-206281-1(5))* Houghton Mifflin Harcourt Publishing Co.

Moran, Alex & Trimble, Patti. What Day Is It? Moreton, Daniel, illus. 2003. (Green Light Readers Level 1 Ser.). (ENG.). 24p. (J). (gr. -1-3). pap. 3.95 *(978-0-15-204846-4(4))* Houghton Mifflin Harcourt Publishing Co.

Morris, Paris & Florzak, Douglas. My Twins First Birthday. 2010. (ENG., Illus.). 24p. (J). pap. 12.95 *(978-0-9760095-8-0(7))* New Year Publishing.

Mullarkey, Lisa. Kianna, 1 vol. Franco, Paula, illus. 2016. (Pony Girls Ser.). (ENG.). 112p. (J). (gr. 1-4). 27.07 *(978-1-62402-130-5(1))* Magic Wagon.

Murray, Alison. Fairy Felicity's Moonlight Adventure. Murray, Alison, illus. 2016. (ENG., Illus.). 24p. (J). (gr. -1-2). 15.99 *(978-0-7636-8945-2(9),* Nosy Crow) Candlewick Pr.

Murray, Eva & Hogan, Jamie. Island Birthday, 1 vol. 2015. (ENG., Illus.). 32p. (gr. 1-7). 16.95 *(978-0-88448-425-7(4),* 884425) Tilbury Hse. Pubs.

My Day! 2005. (J). bds. *(978-0-9769910-0-7(4))* Terrific Twins LLC.

Myracle, Lauren. Awesome Blossom. 2013. (Flower Power Ser.). (ENG.). 272p. (J). (gr. 4-8). 17.95 *(978-1-4197-0405-5(2),* Amulet Bks.) Abrams, Inc.

—Awesome Blossom: A Flower Power Book. 2013. (Flower Power Ser.). (ENG.). 272p. (J). (gr. 3-7). pap. 7.95 *(978-1-4197-0791-9(4),* Amulet Bks.) Abrams, Inc.

Nabors, V. L. Mad Craze Middle School; the Case of the Crumpled Balls. 2010. 215p. pap. 16.95 *(978-0-557-44140-2(4))* Lulu Pr., Inc.

Namm, Diane. Pick a Pet. Suarez, Maribel, tr. Suarez, Maribel, illus. 2004. (My First Reader Ser.). (ENG.). 31p. (J). 18.50 *(978-0-516-24417-4(5),* Children's Pr.) Scholastic Library Publishing.

Nathan, Sarah. Jasmine: The Missing Coin, 1 vol. Studio IBOIX, illus. 2012. (Disney Princesses Set 2 Ser.). (ENG.). 96p. (J). (gr. 2-6). lib. bdg. 24.21 *(978-1-59961-182-1(1))* Spotlight.

Naughton, Geraldine. Owl's Birthday. 2010. 20p. 12.68 *(978-1-4269-4481-9(0))* Trafford Publishing.

Nelid, Piper. Happy Birthday, Townville, 01 vols., 1. 2016. (Rosen REAL Readers: Social Studies Nonfiction / Fiction: Family, Community, & the World Ser.). (ENG.). 8p. (J). pap. 5.46 *(978-1-5081-1878-7(7),* Rosen Classroom) Rosen Publishing Group, Inc., The.

Neuschwander, Cindy. Sir Cumference & All the King's Tens. Geehan, Wayne, illus. 2009. (ENG.). 32p. (J). (gr. 3-7). 16.95 *(978-1-57091-727-1(2))* Charlesbridge Publishing, Inc.

Newman, Nanette. Ben's Book. Birkett, Georgie, illus. 2011. (ENG.). 32p. (J). (gr. -1-k). pap. 9.99 *(978-1-84365-193-2(9),* Pavilion Children's Books) Pavilion Bks. GBR. Dist: Independent Pubs. Group.

Nickelodeon Staff. Party Time! 2013. (Spongebob Squarepants Step into Reading Ser.). lib. bdg. 13.55 *(978-0-606-32221-8(3),* Turtleback) Turtleback Bks.

Nielsen, Amy. Victor & the Sun Orb. 2008. 144p. (J). 21.95 *(978-0-595-50307-0(1))* iUniverse, Inc.

Nordqvist, Sven. The Birthday Cake: The Adventures of Pettson & Findus. 2015. (Adventures of Pettson & Findus Ser.). (ENG., Illus.). 32p. (J). 17.95 *(978-0-7358-4203-8(5))* North-South Bks., Inc.

—Pancakes for Findus. Nordqvist, Sven, illus. 2008. (Findus & Pettson Ser.). (ENG., Illus.). 28p. (J). *(978-1-903458-79-2(X))* Hawthorn Pr.

North, Laura. The Boy with the Pudding Touch. Chapman, Neil, illus. 2014. (ENG.). 32p. (J). pap. *(978-0-7787-1364-7(4))* Crabtree Publishing Co.

Nosy Crow Staff. Violet Rose & the Surprise Party. Ho, Jannie, illus. 2016. (ENG.). (J). (gr. -1-3). 8.99 *(978-0-7636-8917-9(3),* Nosy Crow) Candlewick Pr.

Numeroff, Laura Joffe. Happy Birthday, Mouse! Bond, Felicia, illus. 2012. (If You Give... Ser.). (ENG.). 24p. (J). (gr. -1 — 1). bds. 6.99 *(978-0-694-01425-5(7))* HarperCollins Pubs.

Nurse, Lesley D. The Tale of Greedy Reeby. 2013. 82p. pap. 16.99 (978-0-9797699-6-2(5)) Lion Prints Publishing.

O'Brien, Melanie. No More Pacifiers! With Disappearing Pacifiers! Enright, Amanda, illus. 2008. (ENG.). 18p. (J). (gr. -1-k). 10.95 (978-1-58117-684-1(8), Intervisual/Piggy Toes) Bendon, Inc.

Oceanak, Karla. Ignoramus. Spanjer, Kendra, illus. 2013. (Aldo Zelnick Comic Novel Ser.: 9). (ENG.). 160p. (J). (gr. 3-7). 12.95 (978-1-934649-41-1(4)) Bailiwick Pr.

Ochoa, Mary Lou. Andy's Arctic Party. 2009. 20p. pap. 9.14 (978-1-4269-0943-6(8)) Trafford Publishing.

O'Connor, Jane. Bonjour, Butterfly. Glasser, Robin Preiss, illus. (Fancy Nancy Ser.). (ENG.). 32p. (J). (gr. -1-2). 2012. 9.99 (978-0-06-221053-1(X)) 2008. 17.99 (978-0-06-123588-7(1)) HarperCollins Pubs.

—Fancy Nancy: Bonjour, Butterfly. Glasser, Robin Preiss, illus. 2008. (Fancy Nancy Ser.). (J). 203.88 (978-0-06-158245-5(X)) HarperCollins Pubs.

—Puppy Party. 2013. (Fancy Nancy Picture Bks.). (J). lib. bdg. 13.55 (978-0-606-31788-7(0), Turtleback) Turtleback Bks.

Ode, Eric. Bigfoot Does Not Like Birthday Parties. Temairik, Jaime, illus. 2015. (ENG.). 40p. (J). (gr. -1-3). 16.99 (978-1-63217-004-0(3), Little Bigfoot) Sasquatch Bks.

Olding, Lori. The Origami Nun. 2012. 80p. pap. (978-1-908505-74-3(5)) Vamptasy Publishing.

Oliver, Jane. The Birthday Surprise. Raga, Silvia, illus. 2009. (Get Ready (Windmill Books) Ser.). 32p. (J). (gr. k-2). lib. bdg. 22.60 (978-1-60754-257-5(9)) Windmill Bks.

Oneones. Happy Birthday Coco. Oneones, illus. 2006. (ENG., Illus.). 56p. (J). 9.99 (978-1-933605-13-5(8)) Kane Miller.

Osterhold, Jared, illus. Cooks up a Surprise. 2011. (Olivia TV Tie-In Ser.). (ENG.). 24p. (J). (gr. -1-2). pap. 3.99 (978-1-4424-1384-9(0), Simon Spotlight) Simon Spotlight.

Oud, Pauline. Having a Party with Lily & Milo. Oud, Pauline, illus. 2012. (Clavis Toddler: Skills Ser.). (ENG., Illus.). 24p. (J). (— 1). 12.95 (978-1-60537-129-0(7)) Cobblestone Publishing Co.

Owen, Sarah. Sarah the Fairy Princess's Birthday Party. 2009. 32p. pap. 41.50 (978-1-4452-5921-5(4)) Lulu Pr., Inc.

Oxenbury, Helen. La Fiesta de Cumpleanos.Tr. of Birthday Party. (SPA.). 16p. (J). 7.50 (978-84-261-1943-8(3)) Juventud, Editorial ESP. Dist: AIMS International Bks., Inc.

—It's My Birthday. Oxenbury, Helen, illus. 2010. (ENG., Illus.). 24p. (J). (gr. -1-k). bds. 8.99 (978-0-7636-4970-8(8)) Candlewick Pr.

Painter, Grace. The Harry Bear Story. Kacer, Stephen, illus. 2011. 28p. pap. 24.95 (978-1-4626-3327-2(7)) America Star Bks.

Palleschi, Sarah. Did I Really Dream Last Night? 2009. 48p. pap. 16.25 (978-1-60693-814-0(2), Eloquent Bks.) Strategic Book Publishing & Rights Agency (SBPRA).

Paratore, Coleen Murtagh. Catching the Sun. 2010. (J). (978-0-618-45780-9(1)) Houghton Mifflin Harcourt Publishing Co.

Park, Barbara. Junie B. Jones & That Meanie Jim's Birthday, Vol. 6. unabr. ed. 2004. (Junie B. Jones Ser.: No. 6). 85p. (J). (gr. k-3). pap. 17.00 incl. audio (978-0-8072-0642-3(3), Listening Library) Random Hse. Audio Publishing Group.

Park, Barbara & Brunkus, Denise. Junie B. Jones & That Meanie Jim's Birthday. pap. (978-0-439-13075-2(1)) Scholastic, Inc.

Parker, Emma. Birthday Surprise. 2010. (Illus.). pap. (978-1-877547-85-0(9)) First Edition Ltd.

The Party, 6 Packs. (Sails Literacy Ser.). 16p. (gr. k-18). 27.00 (978-0-7635-4414-0(0)) Rigby Education.

The Party Game: Individual Title Six-Packs. (gr. k-1). 23.00 (978-0-7635-8825-0(3)) Rigby Education.

The Party Game: KinderConcepts Individual Title Six-Packs. (Kinderstarters Ser.). 8p. (gr. -1-1). 21.00 (978-0-7635-8723-9(0)) Rigby Education.

Pascual, Dennis Mark. The Adventures of Dj the Butterfly & Friends Series Presents Dj's Birthday Party. 2012. 20p. pap. 10.15 (978-1-105-35838-8(0)) Lulu Pr., Inc.

Patricelli, Leslie. The Birthday Box. Patricelli, Leslie, illus. 2009. (Leslie Patricelli Board Bks.). (ENG., Illus.). 26p. (J). (gr. k — 1). bds. 6.99 (978-0-7636-4449-9(8)) Candlewick Pr.

Patron, Susan. Lucky Breaks. Phelan, Matt, illus. 2009. (ENG.). 192p. (J). (gr. 3-7). 16.99 (978-1-4169-3998-6(9), Atheneum Bks. for Young Readers) Simon & Schuster Children's Publishing.

Payne, Jackson. The Stork & the Birthday Stocking. Williams, Jean, illus. 2009. 24p. pap. 12.00 (978-1-4389-8146-8(5)) AuthorHouse.

Peeler, Penny. The Adventures of Spike & Sally. 2011. 52p. pap. 15.99 (978-1-4568-9981-3(3)) Xlibris Corp.

Perelman, Helen. A Valentine's Surprise. Waters, Erica-Jane, illus. 2011. (Candy Fairies Ser.: 7). (ENG.). 128p. (J). (gr. 2-5). pap. 5.99 (978-1-4424-2215-5(7), Aladdin) Simon & Schuster Children's Publishing.

Peschke, Marci. Party Queen, 1 vol. Mourning, Tuesday, illus. 2013. (Kylie Jean Ser.). (ENG.). 112p. (gr. 2-3). lib. bdg. 22.65 (978-1-4048-7582-1(4), Kylie Jean) Picture Window Bks.

Peyo. Astro Smurf Blasts Off! Peyo, illus. 2013. (Smurfs Classic Ser.). (ENG., Illus.). 24p. (J). (gr. -1-2). pap. 3.99 (978-1-4424-8514-3(0), Simon Spotlight) Simon Spotlight.

Pham, LeUyen. A Piece of Cake. Pham, LeUyen, illus. 2014. (ENG., Illus.). 40p. (J). (gr. -1-3). 16.99 (978-0-06-199264-3(X)) HarperCollins Pubs.

Phillips, Ruby Ann. Dream Birthday, 1 vol. Isik, Semur, illus. 2014. (Krystal Ball Ser.). (ENG.). 112p. (gr. 2-3). 25.32 (978-1-4795-2178-4(7)) Picture Window Bks.

Phillips, Victoria. Why Is There a Raisin in My Meatloaf? 2013. 32p. pap. (978-1-4602-1481-7(1)) FriesenPress.

Pichon, Liz. Everything's Amazing (Sort Of) Pichon, Liz, illus. 2015. (Tom Gates Ser.: 3). (ENG., Illus.). 416p. (J). (gr. 3-7). 12.99 (978-0-7636-7473-1(7)) Candlewick Pr.

Pish, Kathryn & Crider, Darcy R. Bubble Trouble. 2009. 32p. pap. 12.99 (978-1-4389-9208-2(4)) AuthorHouse.

Pitchford, Dean. The Big One-Oh. 2009. (ENG.). 208p. (J). (gr. 3-7). 6.99 (978-0-14-241292-3(9), Puffin Books) Penguin Young Readers Group.

Pokas, Dora. Muriel's Red Sweater. (J). 15.95 (978-0-8118-3771-2(8)) Chronicle Bks. LLC.

Politi, Leo. Juanita. 2009. (ENG., Illus.). 32p. 16.95 (978-0-89236-991-1(4)) Oxford Univ. Pr., Inc.

Porte, Barbara Ann. Harry's Birthday. Abolafia, Yossi, illus. 2003. (I Can Read Bks.). 48p. (J). 15.99 (978-0-06-050355-0(6)); 16.89 (978-0-06-050356-7(4)) HarperCollins Pubs.

Posner-Sanchez, Andrea. Three Royal Birthdays! (Disney Princess) Legramandi, Francesco & Matta, Gabriella, illus. 2015. (Pictureback(R) Ser.). (ENG.). 24p. (J). (gr. -1-2). 5.99 (978-0-7364-3403-4(8), RH/Disney) Random Hse. Children's Bks.

Potts, Elizabeth Ayn. Oh What Fun, You're One! 2011. 28p. pap. 14.99 (978-1-4634-1620-1(2)) AuthorHouse.

Press, J. The Doodles of Sam Dibble. Kline, Michael, illus. 2013. (Doodles of Sam Dibble Ser.: 1). (ENG.). 128p. (J). (gr. 1-3). pap. 4.99 (978-0-448-46107-6(2), Grosset & Dunlap) Penguin Young Readers Group.

—The Doodles of Sam Dibble. 2013. (Doodles of Sam Dibble Ser.: 1). lib. bdg. 14.75 (978-0-606-29777-6(4), Turtleback) Turtleback Bks.

Priddy, Roger. Happy Birthday: A Touch-and-Feel Book. 2014. (Little Friends Ser.). (ENG.). 10p. (J). (gr. -1 — 1). bds. 6.99 (978-0-312-51680-2(0), 9780312516802, Priddy Bks.) St. Martin's Pr.

Pryor, Bonnie. Happy Birthday, Mama. 2013. (ENG.). 24p. (J). (gr. -1-3). 11.99 (978-1-4424-8874-8(3), Atheneum Bks. for Young Readers) Simon & Schuster Children's Publishing.

Publications International Ltd. Staff, ed. Sesame Street Happy Birthday to You. 2013. 12p. (J). bds. 9.98 (978-1-4508-6159-5(8), 0fc64c9f-9454-4eb3-b56f-9c42ccb72c61) Phoenix International Publications, Inc.

Quick, Matthew. Forgive Me, Leonard Peacock. 2014. (ENG.). 304p. (YA). (gr. 10-17). pap. 10.99 (978-0-316-22135-1(X)) Little, Brown Bks. for Young Readers.

Ramsey, Dave. The Big Birthday Surprise: Junior Discovers Giving. Ramsey, Marshall, illus. 2003. 26p. (J). 7.95 (978-0-9726323-2-4(8)) Ramsey Pr.

Ramsey, Grandma. The Surprise Birthday Gift. 2008. 16p. pap. 9.99 (978-1-4259-4459-9(0)) AuthorHouse.

Random House. Barbie Dreamtopia Pictureback (Barbie) 2017. (Pictureback(R) Ser.). (ENG., Illus.). 24p. (J). (gr. -1-2). pap. 4.99 **(978-1-5247-1646-2(4)**, Random Hse. Bks. for Young Readers) Random Hse. Children's Bks.

Random House Staff. Dora's Big Birthday Adventure (Dora the Explorer) Random House Staff, illus. 2013. (Pictureback(R) Ser.). (ENG., Illus.). 24p. (J). (gr. -1-2). pap. 3.99 (978-0-449-81445-1(9), Random Hse. Bks. for Young Readers) Random Hse. Children's Bks.

—Party Time! (SpongeBob SquarePants) Random House Staff & Moore, Harry, illus. 2013. (Step into Reading Ser.). (ENG.). 32p. (J). (gr. -1-1). 3.99 (978-0-449-81875-6(6), Random Hse. Bks. for Young Readers) Random Hse. Children's Bks.

Range, Maureen. A Perfectly Bonkers Birthday. 2009. 52p. pap. 10.49 (978-1-4389-9055-2(3)) AuthorHouse.

Reinke, Beth Bence. Carla's Cloud Catastrophe. Nielson, Ginger, illus. 2011. 28p. pap. 14.99 (978-0-9828346-0-2(8)) 4RV Publishing, LLC.

Reisner, Molly. Dora's Birthday Surprise! Aikins, David, illus. 2010. (Little Golden Book Ser.). (ENG.). 24p. (J). (gr. -1-2). 3.99 (978-0-375-86163-5(7), Golden Bks.) Random Hse. Children's Bks.

Rey, H. A. Curious George Farm to Table (CGTV 8x8) 2016. (Curious George Ser.). (ENG., Illus.). 24p. (J). (gr. -1-3). 12.99 (978-0-544-65220-0(7), HMH Books For Young Readers) Houghton Mifflin Harcourt Publishing Co.

—Happy Birthday, Curious George! 2016. (Curious George Ser.). (ENG., Illus.). 14p. (J). (— 1). bds. 7.99 (978-0-544-75050-0(0), HMH Books For Young Readers) Houghton Mifflin Harcourt Publishing Co.

—Jorge el Curioso y la Pinata. 2009. (Curious George Ser.).Tr. of Curious George Pinata Party. (SPA & ENG., Illus.). 24p. (J). (gr. -1-3). pap. 3.99 (978-0-547-23830-2(4)) Houghton Mifflin Harcourt Publishing Co.

—Pinata Party. 2009. (Curious George Ser.). (ENG., Illus.). 24p. (J). (gr. -1-3). pap. 3.99 (978-0-547-11962-5(3)) Houghton Mifflin Harcourt Publishing Co.

Rey, H. A. & Rey, Margret. Curious George & the Birthday Surprise. Weston, Martha, illus. 2003. (Curious George Ser.). (ENG.). 24p. (J). (gr. -1-3). pap. 4.99 (978-0-618-34687-5(2)) Houghton Mifflin Harcourt Publishing Co.

—Curious George & the Birthday Surprise. 2003. (Curious George 8x8 Ser.). (gr. k-3). lib. bdg. 14.75 (978-0-613-90050-8(2), Turtleback) Turtleback Bks.

RH Disney Staff & Green, Rico. The Best Birthday Ever (Disney Frozen) RH Disney Staff, illus. 2016. (Little Golden Book Ser.). (ENG., Illus.). 24p. (J). (-k). 4.99 (978-0-7364-3619-9(7), Golden/Disney) Random Hse. Children's Bks.

RH Disney Staff & Julius, Jessica. Anna's Birthday Surprise. RH Disney Staff, illus. 2015. (Pictureback(R) Ser.). (ENG., Illus.). 24p. (J). (gr. -1-2). 4.99 (978-0-7364-3439-3(9), RH/Disney) Random Hse. Children's Bks.

Rim, Sujean. Birdie's Big-Girl Dress. 2011. (Birdie Ser.). (ENG., Illus.). 40p. (J). (gr. -1-3). 16.99 (978-0-316-13287-9(X)) Little Brown & Co.

Rippin, Sally. The Best Party Ever. Spartels, Stephanie, illus. 2014. (ENG.). 48p. (J). pap. 4.99 (978-1-61067-261-0(5)) Kane Miller.

—The Birthday Mix-Up. Fukuoka, Aki, illus. 2013. 43p. (J). (978-1-61067-232-0(1)) Kane Miller.

—The Birthday Mix-Up: Billie B. Brown. Fukuoka, Aki, illus. 2014. (ENG.). 48p. (J). pap. 4.99 (978-1-61067-182-8(1)) Kane Miller.

Rivas, Spelile. The Cucuy Stole My Cascarones / el Coco Me Robó Los Cascarones. Baeza Ventura, Gabriela, tr. Cervantes, Valeria, illus. 2013. (SPA & ENG.). 32p. (J). 17.95 (978-1-55885-771-1(0), Piñata Books) Arte Publico Pr.

Roache, Marjorie D. My Hair Is Too Big! 2011. 28p. pap. 15.99 (978-1-4634-0716-2(5)) AuthorHouse.

Roberts, LaDawna. The Haunted Birthday Party. 2007. 48p. per. 16.95 (978-1-4241-8723-2(0)) America Star Bks.

Robertson, Amber. The Runaway Doll. 2009. 20p. pap. 10.49 (978-1-4343-9336-4(4)) AuthorHouse.

Robinson, Ella M. Happy Home Stories. 2005. 137p. per. 6.95 (978-1-57258-313-9(4)) TEACH Services, Inc.

Robinson, Sharon. Under the Same Sun. Ford, A. G., illus. 2014. (ENG.). 40p. (J). (gr. -1-3). 17.99 (978-0-545-16672-0(1), Scholastic Pr.) Scholastic, Inc.

Rockwell, Anne. At the Supermarket. Rockwell, Anne, illus. 2015. (ENG., Illus.). 30p. (J). (gr. -1-k). bds. 7.99 (978-1-62779-315-5(1), 9781627793155, Holt, Henry & Co. Bks. For Young Readers) Holt, Henry & Co.

Roddy-Worsham, Clara. Bear Baby Goes Fishing. 2013. 24p. 24.95 (978-1-63004-070-3(3)) America Star Bks.

—Bear Baby's Birthday Gift. 2013. 24p. 24.95 (978-1-4626-9940-7(5)) America Star Bks.

Rodgers, Ilona. Nanny Musgrove & the New Baby. 2011. (ENG.). 36p. pap. 11.95 (978-1-906768-68-3(4), Stacey International) Stacey Publishing GBR. Dist: Casemate Pubs. & Bk. Distributors, LLC.

Rodman, Mary Ann. A Tree for Emmy, 1 vol. Mai-Wyss, Tatjana, illus. 2009. (ENG.). 32p. (J). (gr. -1-3). 15.95 (978-1-56145-475-4(3)) Peachtree Pubs.

Rodriquez, Ashley. A Mermaid Tale. 2010. 60p. pap. 10.50 (978-0-557-65601-1(X)) Lulu Pr., Inc.

Rogers, Jewels. The Princess & the Puppy. 2011. 28p. pap. 12.50 (978-1-4567-3236-3(6)) AuthorHouse.

Rolston, Steve. One Bad Day. 2003. (ENG., Illus.). 120p. pap. 9.95 (978-1-929998-50-0(3), 9781929998500) Oni Pr., Inc.

Roper, Robert, illus. Happy Birthday, Dora! 2010. (Dora the Explorer Ser.). (ENG.). 14p. (J). (gr. -1-k). bds. 6.99 (978-1-4424-0333-8(0), Simon Spotlight/Nickelodeon) Simon Spotlight/Nickelodeon.

Rosa-Mendoza, Gladys. It's My Birthday!/Es Mi Cumpleanos! Simard, Remy, illus. 2006. (Englishspanish Foundations Ser.). (ENG & SPA.). 20p. (J). (gr. -1-k). bds. 6.95 (978-1-931398-17-6(8)) Me+Mi Publishing.

Rosen, Lucy. Minions: Dracula's Last Birthday. 2015. (Minions 8X8 Ser.). (J). lib. bdg. 16.00 (978-0-606-37223-7(7)) Turtleback Bks.

—Minions: Dracula's Last Birthday. Miller, Ed, illus. 2015. (ENG.). 32p. (J). (gr. -1-3). 7.99 (978-0-316-26693-2(0)) Little, Brown Bks. for Young Readers.

Ross, Tony. I Want Two Birthdays! Ross, Tony, illus. 2010. (ENG., Illus.). 32p. (J). (gr. -1-3). 16.95 (978-0-7613-5495-6(6)) Lerner Publishing Group.

Rouss, Sylvia A. Tali's Jerusalem Scrapbook. Oppenheimer, Nancy, illus. 2003. 32p. (J). (gr. 1-4). 14.95 (978-1-930143-68-5(0)); pap. 9.95 (978-1-930143-69-2(9)) Simcha Media Group. (Pitspopany Pr.).

Rue, Ginger. Aleca Zamm Is Ahead of Her Time. Persico, Zoe, illus. 2017. (Aleca Zamm Ser.: 2). (ENG.). 128p. (J). (gr. 2-5). pap. 6.99 **(978-1-4814-7063-6(9)**, Aladdin) Simon & Schuster Children's Publishing.

Ruiz, Jackson. It's Cool in the Furnace: The first graphic novel by Jackson Ruiz. 2010. 32p. pap. 16.99 (978-1-4520-2634-3(3)) AuthorHouse.

Ryals, Lexi. Liv & Maddie: Double Trouble. 2015. (Liv & Maddie Junior Novel Ser.). (ENG.). 112p. (J). (gr. 3-7). pap. 5.99 (978-1-4847-1694-6(9)) Disney Pr.

Ryan, Pam Muñoz. Mice & Beans. Cepeda, Joe, illus. 2005. (gr. -1-3). lib. bdg. 17.00 (978-0-7569-5089-7(9)) Perfection Learning Corp.

Rylant, Cynthia. Annie & Snowball & the Dress-Up Birthday. Stevenson, Suçie, illus. (Annie & Snowball Ser.: 1). (ENG.). 40p. (J). (gr. k-2). 2008. pap. 3.99 (978-1-4169-1459-4(5)) 2007. 16.99 (978-1-4169-0938-5(9)) Simon Spotlight. (Simon Spotlight).

—Annie & Snowball & the Dress-Up Birthday. 2008. (Annie & Snowball Ready-To-Read Ser.). lib. bdg. 13.55 (978-1-4178-1126-7(9), Turtleback) Turtleback Bks.

—Mr. Putter & Tabby Make a Wish. Howard, Arthur, illus. 2006. (Mr. Putter & Tabby Ser.). (ENG.). 44p. (J). (gr. -1-3). pap. 5.99 (978-0-15-205443-4(X)) Houghton Mifflin Harcourt Publishing Co.

—Mr. Putter & Tabby Make a Wish. Howard, Arthur, illus. 2006. (Mr. Putter & Tabby Ser.). (gr. -1-4). 16.00 (978-0-7569-6892-2(5)) Perfection Learning Corp.

—Mr. Putter & Tabby Smell the Roses. Howard, Arthur, illus. (Mr. Putter & Tabby Ser.: 24). (ENG.). 40p. (J). (gr. 1-4). 2016. pap. 5.99 (978-0-544-80907-9(6)) 2015. 14.99 (978-0-15-206081-7(2)) Houghton Mifflin Harcourt Publishing Co. (HMH Books For Young Readers).

—Poppleton in Winter. Teague, Mark, illus. 2008. 48p. (gr. -1-3). 14.00 (978-0-7569-8910-1(8)) Perfection Learning Corp.

—Poppleton in Winter, Level 3. Teague, Mark, illus. 2008. (Scholastic Reader Level 3 Ser.). (ENG.). 56p. (J). (gr. -1-3). pap. 3.99 (978-0-545-06823-9(1), Cartwheel Bks.) Scholastic, Inc.

Sáenz, Benjamin Alire. A Gift from Papa Diego: Un Regalo de Papa Diego. Garcia, Geronimo, illus. 2008. (Little Diego Book Ser.). (ENG & SPA.). 40p. (J). pap. 10.95 (978-0-938317-33-3(4)) Cinco Puntos Pr.

Saldana, Rene. Dale, Dale, Dale / Hit It, Hit It, Hit It: Una Fiesta de Numeros / a Fiesta of Numbers. Flores, Carolyn Dee, illus. 2014. (ENG & SPA.). (J). 17.95 (978-1-55885-782-7(6), Piñata Books) Arte Publico Pr.

Salzmann, Mary Elizabeth. Leaping Lizards, 1 vol. Chawla, Neena, illus. 2007. (Critter Chronicles Ser.). (ENG.). 24p. (J). (gr. k-3). lib. bdg. 24.21 (978-1-59928-450-7(2), SandCastle) ABDO Publishing Co.

Sammy. 2007. (978-0-9793490-4-1(4)) Dynasty Publishing, Inc.

Sánchez-Korrol, Virginia. A Surprise for Teresita / una Sorpresa para Teresita. Flores, Carolyn Dee, illus. 2016. (ENG & SPA.). 32p. (J). (gr. k-3). 17.95 (978-1-55885-831-2(8), Piñata Books) Arte Publico Pr.

Santa's Birthday. 2005. (J). 5.95 (978-0-9769321-1-6(3)) Steingart, Nathan Publishing.

Santillo, LuAnn. Jake's Big Day. Santillo, LuAnn, ed. 2003. (Half-Pint Kids Readers Ser.). (Illus.). 7p. (J). (gr. -1-1). pap. 1.00 (978-1-59256-104-9(7)) Half-Pint Kids, Inc.

Sauer, Tammi. I Love Cake! Starring Rabbit, Porcupine, & Moose. Rozelaar, Angie, illus. 2016. 40p. (J). (gr. -1-3). 17.99 (978-0-06-227894-4(0), Tegen, Katherine Bks) HarperCollins Pubs.

Saundra Luchs. Wait for the Sunrise. 2010. 172p. pap. 13.95 (978-1-4401-9190-9(5)) iUniverse, Inc.

Saxon, Victoria & RH Disney Staff. Frozen Fever. RH Disney Staff, illus. deluxe ed. 2015. (Junior Novel Ser.). (ENG., Illus.). 96p. (J). (gr. 3-7). 9.99 (978-0-7364-3440-9(2), RH/Disney) Random Hse. Children's Bks.

Scanlon, Liz Garton. Happy Birthday, Bunny! Graegin, Stephanie, illus. 2013. (ENG.). 32p. (J). (gr. -1-3). 16.99 (978-1-4424-0287-4(3), Beach Lane Bks.) Beach Lane Bks.

Scarry, Richard & Farber, Erica. Cake Soup. Scarry, Huck, illus. 2011. (Richard Scarry's Great Big Schoolhouse Ser.). (ENG.). 24p. (J). (gr. -1-k). pap. 3.95 (978-1-4027-7317-4(X)) Sterling Publishing Co., Inc.

Schaefer, Carole Lexa. Monkey & Elephant & a Secret Birthday Surprise. Bernstein, Galia, illus. (Candlewick Sparks Ser.). (ENG.). 48p. (J). (gr. k-4). 2016. pap. 3.99 (978-0-7636-8744-1(8)) 2015. 14.99 (978-0-7636-6131-1(7)) Candlewick Pr.

Schneider, Josh. The Meanest Birthday Girl. (ENG., Illus.). 48p. (J). (gr. 1-4). 2015. pap. 5.99 (978-0-544-45597-9(5), HMH Books For Young Readers) 2013. 14.99 (978-0-547-83814-4(X)) Houghton Mifflin Harcourt Publishing Co.

Schoenherr, Ian. Don't Spill the Beans! Schoenherr, Ian, illus. 2010. (Illus.). 32p. (J). (gr. -1 — 1). (ENG.). 16.99 (978-0-06-172457-2(2)); lib. bdg. 17.89 (978-0-06-172458-9(0)) HarperCollins Pubs. (Greenwillow Bks.).

—Pip & Squeak. Schoenherr, Ian, illus. 2007. (Illus.). 32p. (J). (gr. -1-k). 18.89 (978-0-06-087254-0(3)) HarperCollins Pubs.

Schotter, Roni. Mama, I'll Give You the World. Gallagher, S. Saelig, illus. 2013. (ENG.). 40p. (J). (gr. -1-3). pap. 7.99 (978-0-449-81142-9(5), Dragonfly Bks.) Random Hse. Children's Bks.

Scieszka, Jon & Barnett, Mac. Battle Bunny. Myers, Matthew, illus. 2013. (ENG.). 32p. (J). (gr. k-4). 14.99 (978-1-4424-4673-1(0), Simon & Schuster Bks. For Young Readers) Simon & Schuster Bks. For Young Readers.

Scott, Shirley A. The Adventures of Jack & Dobbie: Doggie Holidays. 2011. 40p. pap. 17.95 (978-1-4567-3426-8(1)) AuthorHouse.

Scotton, Rob. Splat the Cat & the Big Secret. Farley, Rick & Eberz, Robert, illus. 2016. (J). **(978-1-4844-8600-9(5))** Publishers Quality Library Service.

Scraper, Katherine. The Gift-Guessing Kid. 2005. (J). pap. (978-1-4108-4211-4(8)) Benchmark Education Co.

Scrimger, Richard. Bun Bun's Birthday. Johnson, Gillian, illus. 2003. (ENG.). 24p. (J). (gr. -1-2). pap. 6.95 (978-0-88776-637-4(4), Tundra Bks.) Tundra Bks. CAN. Dist: Penguin Random Hse. LLC.

Sendak, Maurice. Bumble-Ardy. Sendak, Maurice, illus. 2011. (ENG., Illus.). 40p. (J). 17.95 (978-0-06-205198-1(9)) HarperCollins Pubs.

Seuss, Dr. Happy Birthday, Baby! Gerardi, Jan, illus. 2009. (Dr. Seuss Nursery Collection). (ENG.). 12p. (J). (— 1). 11.99 (978-0-375-84621-2(2), Random Hse. Bks. for Young Readers) Random Hse. Children's Bks.

—Happy Birthday to Me! by ME, Myself. 2017. (ENG., Illus.). 64p. (J). (gr. -1-2). 16.99 (978-0-553-53719-2(9), Random Hse. Bks. for Young Readers) Random Hse. Children's Bks.

—Happy Birthday to You! 2003. (Mini Pops Ser.). (ENG., Illus.). 12p. (J). (gr. k-4). 8.99 (978-0-375-82311-4(5), Random Hse. Bks. for Young Readers) Random Hse. Children's Bks.

Shawver, Amanda Nicole. Lily's Rag Doll. 2012. 24p. pap. 17.99 (978-1-4772-7459-0(6)) AuthorHouse.

Shea, Lisa. Littlest Pet Shop: a New Attitude: Starring Sunil Nevla. 2017. (ENG.). 144p. (J). (gr. 3-7). pap. 5.99 (978-0-316-39525-0(0)) Little, Brown Bks. for Young Readers.

Shea, Therese. One More Floor! 2006. (Neighborhood Readers Ser.). (ENG.). 16p. (gr. 1-3). pap. 6.50 (978-1-4042-7244-6(5), Rosen Classroom) Rosen Publishing Group, Inc., The.

Sheinmel, Courtney. Broken Birthday. Bell, Jennifer A., illus. 2017. (Stella Batts Ser.). (ENG.). 160p. (J). (gr. 2-3). 9.99 (978-1-58536-921-8(7), 204228) Sleeping Bear Pr.

—Zacktastic. 2015. (Zacktastic Ser.). (ENG.). 272p. (J). (gr. 2-5). 11.99 (978-1-58536-934-8(9), 203947) Sleeping Bear Pr.

Shephard, H. Ferebee. Dad's Birthday Present. 2010. 24p. pap. 15.99 (978-1-4535-3496-0(2)) Xlibris Corp.

Sherman, Linda. Art Fair for Grandma. 2007. (Illus.). 28p. (J). per. 10.00 (978-0-615-16017-7(4)) Sherman, Linda.

Shooter, Sam. The Goat in the Coat. 2012. 24p. pap. 15.99 (978-1-4691-8749-5(3)) Xlibris Corp.

Shughart-Knecht, Kimberly. Princess Kiali & the Purple Box. 2010. 32p. pap. 12.99 (978-1-4490-0913-7(1)) AuthorHouse.

Sigmon-Heck, Christina. The Birthday Wish. 2012. 24p. pap. 24.95 (978-1-4626-6207-4(2)) America Star Bks.

Simpson, Lesley. The Purim Surprise. Church, Peter, illus. 2004. (Purim Ser.). 32p. (J). (gr. -1-3). pap. 6.95 (978-1-58013-090-5(9), Kar-Ben Publishing) Lerner Publishing Group.

Small, Lily. Paddy the Puppy. 2015. (Fairy Animals of Misty Wood Ser.: 3). (ENG., Illus.). 144p. (J). (gr. k-3). pap. 5.99 (978-1-62779-143-4(4), 9781627791434, Holt, Henry & Co. Bks. For Young Readers) Holt, Henry & Co.

Smedstad, Shannon. Tomorrow Is My Birthday. 2009. 24p. pap. 11.99 (978-1-4389-9881-7(3)) AuthorHouse.

Smiley, Jeremy. Chester: Little Turtle, Big Adventure, 1 vol. 2009. 36p. pap. 24.95 (978-1-60703-489-6(1)) America Star Bks.

Smith, Dianne M. Happy Birthday to You! l.t. ed. 2004. 24p. per. (978-1-59196-679-1(5)) Instant Pub.

Smith, Latoya K. My Favorite Trey. 2009. 24p. pap. 11.49 (978-1-4490-4220-2(1)) AuthorHouse.

Smith, Sindy. Charlie the Chipmunk & the Lost Goldmine. Smith, Sindy, illus. 2012. (Illus.). 38p. 29.95 (978-1-4626-9865-3(4)) America Star Bks.

—Charlie the Chipmunk & the Lost Goldmine. 2012. 40p. pap. 24.95 (978-1-4626-8590-5(0)) America Star Bks.

Soderberg, Erin. The Quirks & the Quirkalicious Birthday. Light, Kelly, illus. 2015. (Quirks Ser.). (ENG.). 208p. (YA). (gr. 3-6). 13.99 (978-1-61963-370-4(1), 9781619633704, Bloomsbury USA Childrens) Bloomsbury Publishing USA.

Sola, Lawrence H. Jeremy's Adventures: Miracle on Main Street. 2012. 88p. (978-1-77097-843-0(7)); pap. (978-1-77097-598-9(5)) FriesenPress.

Sommer, A. M. Tucker's Birthday. 2007. 56p. (gr. 2-2). per. 15.99 (978-1-4257-8987-9(0)) Xlibris Corp.

Soto, Gary. Chato & the Party Animals. Guevara, Susan, illus. (Chato Ser.). 28.95 incl. audio compact disk *(978-1-59112-920-2(6))*; 25.95 incl. audio *(978-1-59112-460-3(3))*; 25.95 incl. audio *(978-1-59112-460-3(3))*; pap. 37.95 incl. audio *(978-1-59112-461-0(1))*; pap. 39.95 incl. audio compact disk *(978-1-59112-921-9(4))*; pap. 39.95 incl. audio compact disk *(978-1-59112-921-9(4))* Live Oak Media.

—Chato & the Party Animals. Guevara, Susan, illus. 2004. (Chato Ser.). (ENG.). 32p. (J). (gr. -1-3). reprint ed. pap. 7.99 *(978-0-14-240032-6(7),* Puffin Books) Penguin Young Readers Group.

—Chato & the Party Animals. Guevara, Susan, illus. 2004. (Chato Ser.). (gr. -1-3). 17.00 *(978-0-7569-2921-3(0))* Perfection Learning Corp.

—Chato y los Amigos Pachangueros. Guevara, Susan, illus. 2004.Tr. of Chato & the Party Animals. (SPA & ENG.). 32p. (J). (gr. -1-3). reprint ed. pap. 7.99 *(978-0-14-240033-3(5),* Puffin Books) Penguin Young Readers Group.

Speakman, David. The Adventures of Sierra Rae: The Forgotten Map, 1 vol. 2009. 59p. pap. 16.95 *(978-1-4489-2657-2(2))* PublishAmerica, Inc.

Sperring, Mark. How Many Sleeps 'Til My Birthday? Braun, Sebastien, illus. 2016. (ENG.). 32p. (J). (gr. -1-2). 16.99 *(978-1-68010-009-9(2))* Tiger Tales.

St-Onge, Claire. Caillou: L'anniversaire. (FRE., Illus.). 32p. pap. 11.95 *(978-2-89450-263-1(X))* Éditions Chouette CAN. Dist: Distribooks, Inc.

Standiford, Natalie. Switched at Birthday. 2014. (ENG.). 240p. (J). (gr. 3-7). 16.99 *(978-0-545-34650-4(9),* Scholastic Pr.) Scholastic, Inc.

—Switched at Birthday: a Wish Novel. 2016. (ENG.). 240p. (J). (gr. 3-7). pap. 6.99 *(978-0-545-34653-5(3),* Scholastic Paperbacks) Scholastic, Inc.

Stanton, Karen. Papi's Gift. Moreno, Rene King, illus. 2007. (ENG.). 32p. (J). (gr. 2-4). 16.95 *(978-1-59078-422-8(7))* Boyds Mills Pr.

Starr, Meg. Alicia's Happy Day, 1 vol. Van Wright, Cornelius & Hu, Ying-Hwa, illus. 2003. (ENG.). 32p. (J). pap. 5.95 *(978-1-932065-06-0(7))* Star Bright Bks., Inc.

—Alicia's Happy Day, 1 vol. Hu, Ying-Hwa & Van Wright, Cornelius, illus. 2003. (ENG.). 32p. (J). (gr. -1-3). 15.95 *(978-1-887734-85-1(6))* Star Bright Bks., Inc.

—Alicia's Happy Day (Spanish/English), 1 vol. Fiol, Maria, tr. from ENG. Van Wright, Cornelius & Hu, Ying-Hwa, illus. 2007. (SPA & ENG.). 32p. (J). (gr. k-3). pap. 6.95 *(978-1-59572-116-7(9))* Star Bright Bks., Inc.

—Alicia's Happy Day (Spanish/English), 1 vol. Fiol, Maria, tr. Van Wright, Cornelius & Hu, Ying-Hwa, illus. 2007. (ENG.). 32p. (J). (gr. -1-3). 15.95 *(978-1-59572-115-0(0))* Star Bright Bks., Inc.

—El día más feliz de Alicia, 1 vol. Fiol, Maria A., tr. from ENG. Van Wright, Cornelius & Hu, Ying-Hwa, illus. 2003.Tr. of Alicia's Happy Day. (SPA.). 32p. (J). pap. 5.95 *(978-1-932065-03-9(2))* Star Bright Bks., Inc.

Steiner, Michaela & Steiner II, Michael. Mike Lost His Bike. 2012. 32p. pap. 19.99 *(978-1-4772-7602-0(5))* AuthorHouse.

Stephens, Ann Marie. A Surprise for Ray. Bolan, Michael P., illus. 2003. 47p. (J). per. 11.95 *(978-0-9729285-1-9(0),* 0-9729285-1-0) Kinkachoo Pr., The.

Stewart, Paul. Un Regalo de Cumpleanos. Riddell, Chris, illus. (SPA.). 30p. (J). (gr. k-2). *(978-84-348-6840-3(7),* SM30935) SM Ediciones ESP. Dist: Lectorum Pubns., Inc.

Stine, R. L. The Birthday Party of No Return! 2012. (Goosebumps Hall of Horrors Ser.: 6). (ENG.). 160p. (J). (gr. 3-7). pap. 6.99 *(978-0-545-28938-2(6),* Scholastic Paperbacks) Scholastic, Inc.

—The Birthday Party of No Return. 2012. (Goosebumps HorrorLand: Hall of Horrors Ser.: 6). lib. bdg. 17.20 *(978-0-606-23932-5(4),* Turtleback) Turtleback Bks.

—Fear Street Super Thriller: Party Games & Don't Stay up Late. 2015. (Fear Street Ser.). (ENG.). 592p. (YA). (gr. 7-12). pap. 11.99 *(978-1-250-07693-9(5),* 9781250076939, St. Martin's Griffin) St. Martin's Pr.

—Slappy Birthday to You. 2017. (Goosebumps SlappyWorld Ser.: 1). (ENG.). 160p. (J). (gr. 3-7). pap. 6.99 *(978-1-338-06828-3(8),* Scholastic Paperbacks) Scholastic, Inc.

—Slappy Birthday to You. 2017. (Goosebumps SlappyWorld Ser.: 1). lib. bdg. 17.20 ***(978-0-606-39730-8(2))*** Turtleback Bks.

Stine, R. L. The 13th Warning, 0 vols. unabr. ed. 2012. (ENG.). 76p. (J). (gr. 3-7). pap. 4.99 *(978-1-61218-330-5(1),* 9781612183305, Amazon Children's Publishing) Amazon Publishing.

Stone, Kate. Happy Birthday, Mouse! (ENG.). 16p. (J). 2014. bds. 5.99 *(978-1-4494-4387-0(7))* 2012. (Illus.). bds. 10.99 *(978-1-4494-0838-1(9))* Andrews McMeel Publishing.

Stuart-Russell, C. Playtime with the Animals. 2007. 61p. pap. 19.95 *(978-1-4241-5473-9(1))* America Star Bks.

Studio Mouse Staff. Pooh & Roo. 2008. (ENG., Illus.). 36p. (J). (gr. -1). 7.99 *(978-1-59069-420-6(1))* Studio Mouse LLC.

Suguitan, Jazel A. We're Moving?! Shari Tucker's Wacky World #1. 2010. 124p. 20.95 *(978-1-4502-6874-5(9))*; pap. 10.95 *(978-1-4502-6871-4(4))* iUniverse, Inc.

Summers, Kim. Senor Mundo & Me: A Happy Birthday Story. Mariscal, Javier, illus. 2004. 31p. (J). (gr. k-4). 20.00 *(978-0-7567-7759-3(3))* DIANE Publishing Co.

Surplice, Holly. Guinea Pig Party. Surplice, Holly, illus. 2012. (ENG., Illus.). 32p. (J). (gr. -1-k). 14.99 *(978-0-7636-6269-1(0),* Nosy Crow) Candlewick Pr.

Swain, Cynthia. The Birthday Flowers. 2006. (Early Explorers Ser.). (J). pap. *(978-1-4108-6025-5(6))* Benchmark Education Co.

Swann, Stephen. The Magical TV. 2009. 43p. pap. 21.50 *(978-1-4452-3001-6(1))* Lulu Pr., Inc.

Szymona, Marlene L. My Sister Beth's Pink Birthday. Battuz, Christine, illus. 2014. (J). *(978-1-4338-1654-3(7))*; pap. *(978-1-4338-1655-0(5))* American Psychological Assn. (Magination Pr.).

Tada, Hiroshi. Who's There. Perry, Mia, tr. 2009. 24p. 11.95 *(978-1-74126-350-3(6))* R.I.C. Pubns. AUS. Dist: SCB Distributors.

Tatcheva, Eva. Witch Zelda's Birthday Cake: A Wild & Wicked Pop-up, Pull-the-Tab Book. Tatcheva, Eva, illus. 2004. (Illus.). 12p. (J). (gr. k-3). reprint ed. 18.00 *(978-0-7567-7225-3(7))* DIANE Publishing Co.

Taylor-Butler, Christine. Who Needs Friends? Havice, Susan, illus. 2006. (Rookie Readers Ser.). (ENG.). 32p. (J). (gr. k-2). pap. 4.95 *(978-0-516-24997-1(5),* Children's Pr.) Scholastic Library Publishing.

Taylor, Trace. Happy Birthday Dogtown. 2010. pap. 39.62 *(978-1-61541-139-9(9))* American Reading Co.

Tennapel, Doug. Cardboard. 2012. (ENG., Illus.). 288p. (J). (gr. 4-7). 24.99 *(978-0-545-41872-0(0))*; pap. 12.99 *(978-0-545-41873-7(9))* Scholastic, Inc. (Graphix).

Tessie & Devore, David. Happy Birthday to Me. 2005. (Charisma Kids Ser.). (Illus.). 24p. (J). (gr. k-3). 9.99 *(978-1-59185-207-0(2))* Charisma Media.

Tharlet, Eve. Happy Birthday, Davy Tuff Book. 2011. (ENG., Illus.). 28p. (J). (gr. -1-3). 6.95 *(978-0-7358-4026-3(1))* North-South Bks., Inc.

Thewes Nicolai, Susan. The Thirteenth Butterfly: A Lizzie's Life Novel. 2009. 192p. pap. 14.49 *(978-1-4389-9975-3(5))* AuthorHouse.

Thomas, Frances. Polly's Absolutely Worst Birthday Ever. Gardner, Sally, illus. 2012. (ENG.). 96p. (J). (gr. 2-4). pap. 11.99 *(978-1-4088-2516-7(3),* 9781408825167, Bloomsbury USA Childrens) Bloomsbury Publishing USA.

Thomas, Jan. A Birthday for Cow! 2008. (ENG., Illus.). 40p. (J). (gr. -1-3). 12.95 *(978-0-15-206072-5(3))* Houghton Mifflin Harcourt Publishing Co.

Thomas, Shelley Moore. Happy Birthday, Good Knight. Plecas, Jennifer, illus. 2014. (Penguin Young Readers, Level 3 Ser.). (ENG.). 48p. (J). (gr. 1-3). pap. 3.99 *(978-0-448-46374-2(1),* Penguin Young Readers) Penguin Young Readers Group.

—Happy Birthday, Good Knight. 2014. (Penguin Young Readers Level 3 Ser.). lib. bdg. 13.55 *(978-0-606-35728-9(9))* Turtleback Bks.

Thompson-Swift, Joseph. The Adventures of Primrose Perfect. 2011. 248p. pap. *(978-1-907652-88-2(4))* Grosvenor Hse. Publishing Ltd.

Thomson, Melissa. Keena Ford & the Second-Grade Mix-Up. Morrison, Frank, illus. 2009. (Keena Ford Ser.). (ENG.). 112p. (J). (gr. 1-3). 5.99 *(978-0-14-241396-8(6),* Puffin Books) Penguin Young Readers Group.

Thornton, Amy. Meet Sambam. 2013. 78p. pap. 10.99 *(978-1-59755-312-4(3),* Advantage Childrens) Advantage Bks.

Thorup, Bryce. Two Birthdays. Muller, Daniel, illus. 2005. (J). 18.95 *(978-0-9765964-0-0(7))* Round Tower Pr.

Torrey, Michele. The Case of the Barfy Birthday. Newman, Barbara Johansen, illus. 2009. (Doyle & Fossey, Science Detectives Ser.: 4). (ENG.). 96p. (J). pap. 6.95 *(978-1-4027-4964-3(3))* Sterling Publishing Co., Inc.

Treasure Map. 2008. (Looney Tunes 8*8 Ser.). 24p. pap. *(978-1-4075-2644-7(8))*; pap. *(978-1-4075-2634-8(0))* Parragon, Inc.

Trimble, Marcia. Liberty Cafe Is Open. Hayden, Jennifer, illus. 2006. (J). pap. 895.00 *(978-1-891577-91-8(3))*; 32p. lib. bdg. 15.95 *(978-1-891577-90-1(5))* Images Pr.

Trimble, Patti. What Day Is It? Moreton, Daniel, illus. 2003. (Green Light Readers — Level 1 Ser.). (gr. -1-3). lib. bdg. 13.50 *(978-0-613-66388-5(8),* Turtleback) Turtleback Bks.

Uff, Caroline, reader. Feliz Cumpleanos, Lulu. 2003. (Lovable Lulu Ser.). (SPA.). (J). pap. *(978-970-690-566-6(9))* Planeta Mexicana Editorial S. A. de C. V.

Ugarte, Ane Miren De Rotaeche. A Very Special Tea Party. 2010. 24p. (J). 25.99 *(978-1-4500-5378-5(5))* Xlibris Corp.

Ulrich, Paulina. Flightless Bird. 2011. (ENG.). 424p. pap. 11.99 *(978-1-4565-3438-7(6))* CreateSpace Independent Publishing Platform.

Universal. Mower Minions. Miller, Ed, illus. 2016. (ENG.). 24p. (J). (gr. -1-3). pap. 5.99 *(978-0-316-39297-6(9))* Little, Brown Bks. for Young Readers.

Urish, J. D. The Adventures of Rex Bolton Volume 1. 2010. 60p. pap. 9.98 *(978-0-578-03676-2(2))* Jentmedia.

Valentine, Madeline. The Bad Birthday Idea. 2013. (ENG., Illus.). 40p. (J). (gr. -1-2). 17.99 *(978-0-449-81331-7(2),* Knopf Bks. for Young Readers) Random Hse. Children's Bks.

Van Allsburg, Chris. Probuditi! 2009. 30p. (J). 19.00 *(978-1-4379-6940-5(2))* DIANE Publishing Co.

—Probuditi! 2006. (ENG., Illus.). 32p. (J). (gr. 2-5). 18.95 *(978-0-618-75502-8(0))* Houghton Mifflin Harcourt Publishing Co.

van Genechten, Guido. Ricky's Birthday. 2012. (ENG.). 24p. (J). (gr. -1-k). 16.95 *(978-1-60537-119-1(X))* Cobblestone Publishing Co.

Vassallo, Theresa. Day at the Zoo Sing-along. 2011. 20p. pap. 24.95 *(978-1-4560-6832-5(6))* America Star Bks.

Ventura, Marne. Edgy Estella Aces the Sleepover Party. Trinidad, Leo, illus. 2016. (Worry Warriors Ser.). (ENG.). 96p. (gr. 2-4). lib. bdg. 25.99 *(978-1-4965-3610-5(X))* Stone Arch Bks.

Villanueva, David. Caleb's Birthday Wish. Sanchez, Edmundo, illus. 2006. 40p. (J). (gr. -1-3). per. 17.95 *(978-0-9771971-8-7(2))* Better Be Write Pub., A.

Viorst, Judith. Just in Case. Bluthenthal, Diana Cain, illus. 2006. (ENG.). 40p. (J). (gr. -1-2). 15.95 *(978-0-689-87164-1(3),* Atheneum Bks. for Young Readers) Simon & Schuster Children's Publishing.

—Lulu & the Brontosaurus. Smith, Lane, illus. (ENG.). 128p. (J). (gr. 1-5). 2012. pap. 7.99 *(978-1-4169-9962-1(0))* 2010. 17.99 *(978-1-4169-9961-4(2))* Simon & Schuster Children's Publishing. (Atheneum Bks. for Young Readers).

—Lulu & the Brontosaurus. 2012. (Lulu Ser.: 1). lib. bdg. 18.40 *(978-0-606-23676-8(7),* Turtleback) Turtleback Bks.

Volker, Kerstin. Lilly's Birthday Party. 2003. (Funny Friends Lift-and-Learn Bks.). (Illus.). 14p. (J). 5.99 *(978-1-59384-022-8(5))* Parklane Publishing.

Voskoboinikov, Valery & Linnamagi, Anne. The Icicle. 2007. (POL & ENG., Illus.). 32p. (J). pap. 16.95 *(978-1-60195-100-7(0))* International Step by Step Assn.

Vulliamy, Clara. Muffin & the Birthday Surprise. Vulliamy, Clara, illus. 2012. (ENG., Illus.). 32p. (J). (gr. -1-k). pap. 9.99 *(978-1-4083-1245-2(X))* Hodder & Stoughton GBR. Dist: Hachette Bk. Group.

Waber, Bernard. Lyle, Lyle, Crocodile Storybook Treasury. 2012. (Lyle the Crocodile Ser.). (ENG., Illus.). 192p. (J). (gr. -1-3). 11.99 *(978-0-547-51618-9(5))* Houghton Mifflin Harcourt Publishing Co.

Wagele, Elizabeth. Finding the Birthday Cake: Helping Children Raise Their Self-Esteem. Wagele, Elizabeth, illus. 2007. (ENG., Illus.). 48p. (J). (gr. k-4). per. 8.95 *(978-0-88282-277-8(2))* New Horizon Pr. Pubs., Inc.

Wales, Dirk. Penny House. Kenna, Diane, illus. 2005. 32p. (J). (gr. -1). 16.95 *(978-0-9632459-1-5(0))* Great Plains Pr.

Walker, Anna. I Love Birthdays. Walker, Anna, illus. 2010. (ENG., Illus.). 32p. (J). (gr. -1-1). 9.99 *(978-1-4169-8320-0(1),* Simon & Schuster Bks. For Young Readers) Simon & Schuster Bks. For Young Readers.

Walker, Nan. Follow That Clue! Palmisciano, Diane, illus. 2008. (Social Studies Connects Ser.). 32p. (J). (gr. -1-3). pap. 5.95 *(978-1-57565-274-0(9))* Kane Press, Inc.

—Follow That Clue! Palmisciano, Diane, illus. 2009. (Social Studies Connects (r) Ser.). (ENG.). (gr. k-2). pap. 33.92 *(978-0-7613-4805-4(0))* Lerner Publishing Group.

Wallace Ii, James C. & Wallace, Amanda D. The Emerald Slippers of Oz. 2013. 156p. pap. 14.99 *(978-0-578-12511-4(0))* Scientia Est Vox Pr.

Wallace, Nancy Elizabeth. Tell-A-Bunny, 0 vols. Wallace, Nancy Elizabeth, illus. 2007. (ENG., Illus.). 36p. (J). (gr. -1-1). 7.99 *(978-0-7614-5369-7(5),* 9780761453697, Amazon Children's Publishing) Amazon Publishing.

Warner, Larry. Chocolate Island, 1 vol. 2010. 42p. pap. 24.95 *(978-1-4489-7372-9(4))* PublishAmerica, Inc.

Warnes, Tim. Happy Birthday, Dotty. Warnes, Tim, illus. 2003. (Illus.). 32p. (J). tchr. ed. 15.95 *(978-1-58925-026-0(5))* Tiger Tales.

Watt, Mélanie. Scaredy Squirrel Has a Birthday Party, 0 vols. Watt, Mélanie, illus. (ENG., Illus.). 32p. (J). (gr. -1-3). 2014. pap. 7.95 *(978-1-55453-716-7(9))* 2011. 16.95 *(978-1-55453-468-5(2))* Kids Can Pr., Ltd. CAN. Dist: Hachette Bk. Group.

Watts, Debra G. Carter Car & His Wild & Carazy Birthday. 2011. 40p. pap. 21.99 *(978-1-4628-4864-5(8))* Xlibris Corp.

Watts, Jeri Hanel. Keepers. Marshall, Felicia, illus. 2013. (ENG.). 32p. (J). (gr. -1-5). pap. 9.95 *(978-1-58430-013-7(2))* Lee & Low Bks., Inc.

Weeks, Sarah. Oggie Cooder - Party Animal! 2011. (Oggie Cooder Ser.). (ENG.). 176p. (J). (gr. 2-5). pap. 6.99 *(978-0-439-92796-3(X),* Scholastic Paperbacks) Scholastic, Inc.

Weimer, Heidi R. Happy Birthday to You! 2007. (ENG., Illus.). 14p. (gr. -1-k). bds. 12.99 *(978-0-8249-6699-7(6),* Ideal Pubns.) Worthy Publishing.

Weinberg, Jennifer. Surprise for a Princess. 2003. (Disney Princess Step into Reading Ser.). (gr. -1-2). 13.55 *(978-0-613-73686-2(9),* Turtleback) Turtleback Bks.

Weinberg, Jennifer Liberts. Happy Birthday, Mike! 2014. (Step into Reading Level 2 Ser.). lib. bdg. 13.55 *(978-0-606-36006-7(9))* Turtleback Bks.

—Happy Birthday, Mike! (Disney/Pixar Monsters, Inc.) RH Disney Staff, illus. 2014. (Step into Reading Ser.). (ENG.). 32p. (J). (gr. -1-1). 3.99 *(978-0-7364-3198-9(5),* RH/Disney) Random Hse. Children's Bks.

—Happy Birthday, Princess! 2012. (Disney Princess Step into Reading Ser.). lib. bdg. 13.55 *(978-0-606-23725-3(9),* Turtleback) Turtleback Bks.

Wells, Rosemary. Fiona's Little Lie. Wells, Rosemary, illus. 2016. (Felix & Fiona Ser.). (ENG., Illus.). 32p. (J). (gr. k-3). 14.99 *(978-0-7636-7312-3(9))* Candlewick Pr.

—Max's Birthday. 2004. (Max & Ruby Ser.). (ENG.). 12p. (J). (gr. 1 — 1). bds. 6.99 *(978-0-670-88711-8(0),* Viking Books for Young Readers) Penguin Young Readers Group.

—Sophie's Terrible Twos. Wells, Rosemary, illus. 2014. (ENG., Illus.). 32p. (J). (gr. -1-k). 16.99 *(978-0-670-78512-4(1),* Viking Books for Young Readers) Penguin Young Readers Group.

Weninger, Brigitte. Happy Birthday, Davy! Tharlet, Eve, illus. 2nd rev. ed. 2015. (ENG.). 32p. (J). 15.95 *(978-0-7358-4224-3(8))* North-South Bks., Inc.

West, Tracey. The Birthday Surprise. 2014. (LEGO Friends Ser.: 4). (ENG.). 64p. (J). (gr. 2-5). pap. 4.99 *(978-0-545-60589-2(X))* Scholastic, Inc.

—The Birthday Surprise. 2014. (LEGO Friends Chapter Bks.: 4). lib. bdg. 14.75 *(978-0-606-35408-0(5))* Turtleback Bks.

Weston Woods Staff, creator. Chato & the Party Animals. 2011. 18.95 *(978-0-439-73984-9(5))* 2011. 38.75 *(978-0-439-84581-6(5))* 2004. 29.95 *(978-1-55592-703-5(3))* Weston Woods Studios, Inc.

—Happy Birthday Moon. 2004. 29.95 *(978-1-55592-842-1(0))*; (J). 38.75 *(978-1-55592-822-3(6))*; (J). 18.95 *(978-1-55592-805-6(6))* Weston Woods Studios, Inc.

—Three Cheers for Catherine the Great. 2011. 18.95 *(978-0-439-80506-3(6))* Weston Woods Studios, Inc.

—Three Cheers for Catherine the Great! 2011. 38.75 *(978-0-439-78620-1(7))* Weston Woods Studios, Inc.

When I'm Older, 6 Packs. (Literatura 2000 Ser.). (gr. 1-2). 28.00 *(978-0-7635-0154-9(9))* Rigby Education.

White, Andrea. Radiant Girl. 2008. (ENG.). 256p. (J). (gr. 4-7). 19.95 *(978-1-933979-23-6(2),* 9781933979236) Bright Sky Pr.

White, Jenny. A Surprise for Junior. 2013. 24p. pap. 17.99 *(978-1-4817-0602-5(0))* AuthorHouse.

White, Tim. A Single Heart. 2006. 193p. pap. 24.95 *(978-1-4137-9418-2(1))* PublishAmerica, Inc.

Wilcox, Lucy. Eva the Diva's Fashion Fun Shop: The Birthday Surprise. 2011. 28p. pap. 15.99 *(978-1-4628-6418-8(X))* Xlibris Corp.

Willard, Nancy. The Three Mouths of Little Tom Drum. Hawkes, Kevin, illus. 2015. (ENG.). 48p. (J). (gr. -1-3). 16.99 *(978-0-7636-5476-4(0))* Candlewick Pr.

Williams, Garth. Baby's First Book. Williams, Garth, illus. 2011. (Golden Baby Ser.). (ENG., Illus.). 24p. (J). (— 1). bds. 6.99 *(978-0-375-85905-2(5),* Golden Bks.) Random Hse. Children's Bks.

Williams, Paula. Tom's Wish. Graham, Carl, illus. 2013. 24p. pap. *(978-1-909740-80-8(2))* Legend Pr.

Williams, S. L. Polka-Dot Maddy's Birthday Fun: Colors of the Rainbow. 2008. 36p. pap. 24.95 *(978-1-60672-908-3(X))* America Star Bks.

Willis, Jeanne. Boa's Bad Birthday. Ross, Tony, illus. 2014. (ENG.). 32p. (J). (gr. -1-3). 16.95 *(978-1-4677-3450-9(0))* Lerner Publishing Group.

Wilson, Alexandria M. Happy Birthday Gideon. 2013. 24p. pap. 24.95 *(978-1-62709-808-3(9))* America Star Bks.

Wilson, Angie. Dori's Gift. Teets, Ashley, illus. 2013. (ENG.). 32p. (J). (gr. -1-3). 16.95 *(978-0-938467-85-4(9))* Headline Bks., Inc.

Wilson, Anna. Puppy Party. 1. unabr. ed. 2014. (ENG., Illus.). 256p. (J). (gr. 2-4). pap. 7.99 *(978-0-330-51881-9(X))* Pan Macmillan GBR. Dist: Independent Pubs. Group.

Wilson, Annette. K'Nyah's Big Celebration. 2012. 28p. pap. 24.95 *(978-1-4626-9925-4(1))* America Star Bks.

Wilson, Mary. Mark & the Mega Buffet. 2005. 37p. (J). pap. 15.58 *(978-1-4116-4172-3(8))* Lulu Pr., Inc.

Winfrey, Michelle Whitaker. It's My Birthday. . . Finally! A Leap Year Story. Turley, Joyce M., illus. 2003. 88p. (J). (gr. 3-7). per. 11.95 *(978-0-9727179-0-8(0))* Hobby Hse. Publishing Group.

Winfrey, Michelle/w. It's My Birthday... Finally! A Leap Year Story. 2007. (Illus.). 96p. (J). per. 11.95 *(978-0-9727179-5-3(1))* Hobby Hse. Publishing Group.

Wing, Natasha. The Night Before My Birthday. Wummer, Amy, illus. 2014. (Night Before Ser.). (ENG.). 32p. (J). (gr. -1-k). 4.99 *(978-0-448-48000-8(X),* Grosset & Dunlap) Penguin Young Readers Group.

—The Night Before My Birthday. 2014. (Night Before Ser.). lib. bdg. 14.75 *(978-0-606-34133-2(1),* Turtleback) Turtleback Bks.

Winkler, Henry & Oliver, Lin. Day of the Iguana. 2006. (Hank Zipzer Ser.: No. 3). 154p. (J). (gr. 3-9). 24.21 *(978-1-59961-102-0(3))* Spotlight.

—Fake Snakes & Weird Wizards. Garrett, Scott, illus. 2015. (Here's Hank Ser.: No. 4). (ENG.). 128p. (J). (gr. 1-3). 5.99 *(978-0-448-48252-1(5),* Grosset & Dunlap) Penguin Young Readers Group.

—Who Ordered This Baby? Definitely Not Me! 2007. (Hank Zipzer Ser.: No. 13). (Illus.). 152p. (gr. 4-7). 15.00 *(978-0-7569-8163-1(8))* Perfection Learning Corp.

Witkowski, Teri. Happy Birthday, Bitty Bear! Ackley, Peggy Jo, illus. 2005. (J). *(978-1-58485-959-8(8))* American Girl Publishing, Inc.

Wojtowycz, David, illus. Elephant Joe, Brave Firefighter! 2015. (Step into Reading Ser.). (ENG.). 32p. (J). (gr. -1-1). 12.99 *(978-0-375-97203-4(X),* Random Hse. Bks. for Young Readers) Random Hse. Children's Bks.

Wolf, Elisabeth. Lulu in la la Land. 2013. (Lulu in la la Land Ser.: 1). (ENG.). 272p. (J). (gr. 3-6). pap. 6.99 *(978-1-4022-8504-2(3),* 9781402285042, Sourcebooks Jabberwocky) Sourcebooks, Inc.

Wood, Audrey. The Birthday Queen. Wood, Don, illus. 2013. (ENG.). 32p. (J). (gr. -1-3). 17.99 *(978-0-545-41474-6(1),* Blue Sky Pr., The) Scholastic, Inc.

Woolson, Constance Fenimore. The Old Stone House. 2007. (ENG.). 196p. pap. 19.99 *(978-1-4264-4971-0(2))* Creative Media Partners, LLC.

Wooters, Duane. The Unnamed Manuscript. 2003. 70p. (YA). pap. 8.95 *(978-0-595-29612-5(2))* iUniverse, Inc.

Worley, Roger A. 14 Wishes, 1 vol. 2009. 164p. pap. 24.95 *(978-1-61582-419-9(7))* America Star Bks.

Wright, Betty Ren. The Blizzard. Himler, Ronald, illus. (ENG.). 32p. (J). 2005. pap. 7.95 *(978-0-8234-1981-4(9))* 2003. 17.95 *(978-0-8234-1656-1(9))* Holiday Hse., Inc.

Wright, Maureen. Earth Day, Birthday!, 0 vols. Kim, Violet, illus. 2012. (ENG.). 32p. (J). (gr. k-3). 17.99 *(978-0-7614-6109-8(4),* 9780761461098, Amazon Children's Publishing) Amazon Publishing.

Wuest, Marcia. Twelve Things to Do at Age 12. 2009. (ENG.). 26p. pap. 7.25 *(978-0-521-73733-3(8))* Cambridge Univ. Pr.

Yolen, Jane. How Do Dinosaurs Say Happy Birthday? Teague, Mark, illus. 2011. (How Do Dinosaurs... Ser.). (ENG.). 12p. (J). (gr. -1-k). bds. 6.99 *(978-0-545-15353-9(0),* Blue Sky Pr., The) Scholastic, Inc.

Yorinks, Arthur. Flappy & Scrappy. Ivanov, Olga & Ivanov, Aleksey, illus. 2010. (I Can Read Level 2 Ser.). (ENG.). 48p. (J). (gr. k-3). 16.99 *(978-0-06-205117-2(2))* HarperCollins Pubs.

—Flappy & Scrappy. Ivanov, Aleksey & Ivanov, Olga, illus. 2010. (I Can Read Level 2 Ser.). (ENG.). 48p. (J). (gr. k-3). pap. 3.99 *(978-0-06-205913-0(0))* HarperCollins Pubs.

Young, Elizabeth L. Dozens & Dozens of Cousins & Cousins. Perkins, Ruth, illus. 2012. 30p. 20.95 *(978-1-61633-353-9(7))*; pap. 12.95 *(978-1-61633-352-2(9))* Guardian Angel Publishing, Inc.

Young, Jeanna Stolle & Johnson, Jacqueline Kinney. Princess Joy's Birthday Blessing, 1 vol. Aranda, Omar, illus. 2011. (Princess Parables Ser.). (ENG.). 32p. (J). (gr. -1-2). 14.99 *(978-0-310-71639-6(X))* Zonderkidz.

Your Purrr-Fect Birthday. 2007. (Dragonlarks Ser.). (Illus.). 64p. (J). (gr. k-3). per. 7.99 *(978-1-933390-55-0(7))* Chooseco LLC.

Yutkins, Ellen A. Jack's Big Surprise. 2011. 20p. pap. *(978-1-4269-9464-7(8))* Trafford Publishing (UK) Ltd.

Zann, Tara. Wild Child: Forest's First Birthday Party. Belleza, Rhoda, ed. Widdowson, Dan, illus. 2017. (Wild Child Ser.: 3). (ENG.). 128p. (J). pap. 5.99 *(978-1-250-10389-5(4),* 9781250103895) Imprint IND. Dist: Macmillan.

BIRTHDAYS—POETRY

Greenaway, Kate. Kate Greenaway's Birthday Book. unabr. ed. 2012. (Illus.). 269p. 49.99 *(978-1-4622-8642-3(9))* Repressed Publishing LLC.

Howe, James. Houndsley & Catina & the Birthday Surprise. Gay, Marie-Louise, illus. 2013. (Candlewick Sparks Ser.). (ENG.). 48p. (J). (gr. k-4). pap. 3.99 *(978-0-7636-6639-2(4))* Candlewick Pr.

Kulka, Joe. Wolf's Coming! Kulka, Joe, illus. 2007. (ENG., Illus.). 32p. (J). (gr. -1-3). lib. bdg. 16.95 *(978-1-57505-930-3(4),* Carolrhoda Bks.) Lerner Publishing Group.

BISCUIT (FICTITIOUS CHARACTER: CAPUCILLI)—FICTION

Capucilli, Alyssa Satin. Biscuit. Schories, Pat, illus. 2006. (My First I Can Read Ser.). (ENG.). 32p. (J). (gr. -1 — 1). reprint ed. pap. 3.99 *(978-0-06-444212-1(8))* 10th anniv. ed. 16.99 *(978-0-06-026197-9(8))* HarperCollins Pubs.

—Biscuit. Schories, Pat, illus. 2006. (Biscuit: My First I Can Read! Ser.). 26p. (J). (gr. -1-k). lib. bdg. 13.55 *(978-0-613-37688-4(9),* Turtleback) Turtleback Bks.

—Biscuit: 5-Minute Biscuit Stories. Schories, Pat, illus. 2017. 192p. (J). (gr. -1-3). 12.99 *(978-0-06-256725-3(X))* HarperCollins Pubs.
—Biscuit Gives a Gift. Schories, Pat, illus. 2004. (ENG.). 16p. (J). (gr. -1-3). bds. 4.99 *(978-0-06-009467-6(2),* HarperFestival) HarperCollins Pubs.
—Biscuit Goes to School. Schories, Pat, illus. 2003. (My First I Can Read Ser.). (ENG.). 32p. (J). (gr. -1-3). pap. 3.99 *(978-0-06-443616-8(0))* HarperCollins Pubs.
—Biscuit Goes to School. Schories, Pat, illus. 2003. (Biscuit: My First I Can Read! Ser.). 21p. (J). (gr. -1-3). lib. bdg. 13.55 *(978-0-613-66941-2(X),* Turtleback) Turtleback Bks.
—Biscuit Loves the Library. Schories, Pat, illus. 2014. (My First I Can Read Ser.). (ENG.). 32p. (J). (gr. -1-3). 16.99 *(978-0-06-193507-7(7))*; pap. 3.99 *(978-0-06-193506-0(9))* HarperCollins Pubs.
—Biscuit Plays Ball. Schories, Pat, illus. 2012. (My First I Can Read Ser.). (ENG.). 32p. (J). (gr. -1-2). 16.99 *(978-0-06-193503-9(4))*; pap. 3.99 *(978-0-06-193502-2(6))* HarperCollins Pubs.
—Biscuit Plays Ball. 2012. (Biscuit: My First I Can Read! Ser.). (J). lib. bdg. 13.55 *(978-0-606-23583-9(3),* Turtleback) Turtleback Bks.
—Biscuit Storybook Collection. Schories, Pat, illus. 2004. (Biscuit Ser.). (ENG.). 192p. (J). (gr. -1-3). 11.99 *(978-0-06-075904-9(6),* HarperFestival) HarperCollins Pubs.
—Biscuit Visits the Big City. Schories, Pat, illus. 2006. (My First I Can Read Ser.). (ENG.). 32p. (J). (gr. -1 — 1). 16.99 *(978-0-06-074164-8(3))* HarperCollins Pubs.
—Biscuit Visits the Doctor. Berlin, Rose Mary & Schories, Pat, illus. 2008. (Biscuit Ser.). (ENG.). 24p. (J). (gr. -1-1). pap. 3.99 *(978-0-06-112843-1(0),* HarperFestival) HarperCollins Pubs.
—Biscuit Visits the Pumpkin Patch. Schories, Pat, illus. 2004. (Biscuit Ser.). (ENG.). 16p. (J). (gr. -1-3). bds. 4.99 *(978-0-06-009466-9(4),* HarperFestival) HarperCollins Pubs.
—Biscuit's ABC Adventure. Wenzel, David T. & Schories, Pat, illus. 2008. (Biscuit Ser.). 32p. (J). (gr. -1-2). pap. 3.99 *(978-0-06-112841-7(4),* HarperFestival) HarperCollins Pubs.
—Biscuit's Big Field Trip. Schories, Pat, illus. 2008. (Biscuit Ser.). 32p. (J). pap. 3.99 *(978-0-06-112844-8(9),* HarperFestival) HarperCollins Pubs.
—Biscuit's Day at the Farm. Schories, Pat, illus. 2007. (My First I Can Read Ser.). (ENG.). 32p. (J). (gr. -1 — 1). pap. 3.99 *(978-0-06-074169-3(4))* HarperCollins Pubs.
—Biscuit's First Sleepover. Schories, Pat & Berlin, Rose Mary, illus. 2008. (Biscuit Ser.). (ENG.). 24p. (J). (gr. -1-1). pap. 3.99 *(978-0-06-112842-4(2),* HarperFestival) HarperCollins Pubs.
—Biscuit's First Trip. 2010. (Biscuit 8x8 Ser.). (J). lib. bdg. 13.55 *(978-0-606-10115-8(2),* Turtleback) Turtleback Bks.
—Biscuit's Hanukkah. Schories, Pat & Young, Mary O'Keefe, illus. 2005. (Biscuit Ser.). (ENG.). 16p. (J). (gr. -1-3). bds. 4.99 *(978-0-06-009469-0(9),* HarperFestival) HarperCollins Pubs.
—Biscuit's Pet & Play Bedtime: A Touch & Feel Book. Schories, Pat, illus. 2017. (Biscuit Ser.). 12p. (J). (gr. -1 — 1). bds. 7.99 *(978-0-06-249039-1(7),* HarperFestival) HarperCollins Pubs.
—Biscuit's Pet & Play Easter. Berlin, Rose Mary & Schories, Pat, illus. 2008. (Biscuit Ser.). (ENG.). 12p. (J). (gr. -1 — 1). bds. 7.99 *(978-0-06-112839-4(2),* HarperFestival) HarperCollins Pubs.
—Biscuit's Snowy Day. Schories, Pat & Young, Mary O'Keefe, illus. 2005. (Biscuit Ser.). (ENG.). 16p. (J). (gr. -1-3). bds. 4.99 *(978-0-06-009468-3(0),* HarperFestival) HarperCollins Pubs.
—Meet Biscuit! Schories, Pat, illus. 2005. (Biscuit Ser.). (ENG.). 24p. (J). (gr. -1-1). pap. 3.99 *(978-0-06-057846-6(7),* HarperFestival) HarperCollins Pubs.
Schories, Pat, illus. Biscuit's Fourth of July. 2005. (J). *(978-1-4156-0311-6(1),* HarperFestival) HarperCollins Pubs.
—Biscuit's Graduation Day. 2005. (J). *(978-1-4155-9660-9(3),* HarperFestival) HarperCollins Pubs.

BISMARCK, OTTO, FURST VON, 1815-1898

Heuston, Kimberley. Otto von Bismarck: Iron Chancellor of Germany. (Wicked History Ser.). (ENG., Illus.). 128p. (YA). 2010. (gr. 6-12). pap. 5.95 *(978-0-531-22824-1(X),* Watts, Franklin) 2009. (gr. 5-9). 31.00 *(978-0-531-21278-3(5))* Scholastic Library Publishing.

BISMARCK (BATTLESHIP)

Crompton, Samuel Willard. Sinking of the Bismarck. 2003. (Great Battles Through the Ages Ser.). (Illus.). 112p. (J). (gr. 6-12). 30.00 *(978-0-7910-7438-1(2),* Chelsea Hse.) Facts On File, Inc.

BISON

see also American Bison

Anthony, David. Bison, 01 vols., 1. 2016. (North America's Biggest Beasts Ser.). (ENG., Illus.). 24p. (J). pap. 8.25 *(978-1-5081-4288-1(2),* PowerKids Pr.) Rosen Publishing Group, Inc., The.
Big Bison. 2013. (Great Big Animals Ser.). 24p. (J). (gr. k-2). pap. 48.90 *(978-1-4339-9422-7(4))* Stevens, Gareth Publishing LLLP.
Bodden, Valerie. Amazing Animals: Bison. 2013. (Amazing Animals Ser.). (ENG.). 24p. (J). (gr. 1-3). pap. 8.99 *(978-0-89812-787-4(4),* Creative Paperbacks) Creative Co., The.
—Bison. 2013. (Illus.). 24p. (J). 25.65 *(978-1-60818-085-1(9),* Creative Education) Creative Co., The.
Brodsky, Beverly. Buffalo, 1 vol. 2006. (ENG., Illus.). 32p. (J). (gr. 3-7). *(978-1-55041-587-2(5))* Fitzhenry & Whiteside, Ltd.
Brodsky, Beverly, contrib. by. Buffalo: With Selections from Native American Song-Poems. 2003. (Illus.). 40p. (YA). 18.95 *(978-0-7614-5133-4(1))* Marshall Cavendish Corp.
Caper, William. American Bison: A Scary Prediction. 2007. (America's Animal Comebacks Ser.). (Illus.). 32p. (YA). (gr. 2-5). lib. bdg. 25.27 *(978-1-59716-504-4(2))* Bearport Publishing Co., Inc.
Gish, Melissa. Bison - Living Wild. 2012. (Living Wild Ser.). (ENG., Illus.). 48p. (J). (gr. 4-7). pap. 12.00 *(978-0-89812-669-3(X),* Creative Paperbacks) Creative Co., The.
Hirsch, Rebecca E. Bison: A Winter Journey. 2016. (Illus.). 32p. (J). *(978-1-4896-4511-1(X))* Weigl Pubs., Inc.
Larson, Jennifer S. Mighty Bison. 2006. (Pull Ahead Books-Animals Ser.). (ENG., Illus.). 32p. (gr. k-3). lib. bdg. 22.60 *(978-0-8225-3485-3(1),* Lerner Pubns.) Lerner Publishing Group.
Llanas, Sheila Griffin. Buffaloes, 1 vol. 2013. (Animal Icons Ser.). (ENG.). 32p. (J). (gr. 3-6). lib. bdg. 27.07 *(978-1-61783-569-8(2),* Checkerboard Library) ABDO Publishing Co.
Magby, Meryl. American Bison. 2012. (American Animals Ser.). (ENG., Illus.). 24p. (J). (gr. k-3). lib. bdg. 22.60 *(978-1-4488-6179-8(9))*; pap. 8.25 *(978-1-4488-6317-4(1),* PowerKids Pr.) Rosen Publishing Group, Inc., The.
Nagelhout, Ryan. Big Bison. 2013. (Great Big Animals Ser.). 24p. (J). (gr. k-2). pap. 8.15 *(978-1-4339-9421-0(6))*; (ENG., Illus.). lib. bdg. 22.60 *(978-1-4339-9420-3(8))* Stevens, Gareth Publishing LLLP.
—Big Bison / Grandes Bisontes. 2013. (Great Big Animals / Superanimales Ser.). (SPA.). 24p. (J). (gr. k-2). 22.60 *(978-1-4339-9448-7(8))* Stevens, Gareth Publishing LLLP.
Riggs, Kate & Arnold, Quinn M. Bison. 2017. (Seedlings Ser.). (ENG., Illus.). 24p. (J). (gr. k-2). pap. 7.99 *(978-1-62832-348-1(5),* Creative Paperbacks) Creative Co., The.
Robbins, Ken. Thunder on the Plains: The Story of the American Buffalo. Robbins, Ken, illus. 2009. (ENG., Illus.). 36p. (J). (gr. 2-5). pap. 10.99 *(978-1-4169-9536-4(6),* Atheneum Bks. for Young Readers) Simon & Schuster Children's Publishing.

BISON—FICTION

Bak, Robyn. Lucky Little Bison. 2012. 12p. pap. 15.99 *(978-1-4685-4734-4(8))* AuthorHouse.
Baum, L. Frank. The Enchanted Buffalo. Montileaux, Donald F., illus. 2010. 31p. (J). (gr. 2-5). 14.95 *(978-0-9822749-3-4(9),* South Dakota State Historical Society Pr.) South Dakota State Historical Society Pr.
Berry, R. A. Buddy's Blue Day. 2010. 16p. 10.99 *(978-1-4520-2413-4(8))* AuthorHouse.
Fern, Tracey E. Buffalo Music. Castillo, Lauren, illus. 2008. (ENG.). 32p. (J). (gr. -1-3). 17.99 *(978-0-618-72341-6(2))* Houghton Mifflin Harcourt Publishing Co.
Griffis, Molly. The Buffalo in the Mall. Doner, Kim, illus. 32p. 8.95 *(978-1-57168-635-0(5))* Eakin Pr.
Haukos, Jill. The Autumn Calf. Turley, Joyce Mihran, illus. 2016. (ENG.). 32p. (J). (gr. -1-12). 15.95 *(978-1-63076-237-7(7))* Taylor Trade Publishing.
Lee, Evelyn. Bluestem Horizon: A Story of a Tallgrass Prairie. Brauckmann-Towns, Krista, illus. 2005. (Soundprints' Wild Habitats Ser.). (ENG.). 32p. (J). (gr. 1-4). 8.95 *(978-1-59249-098-1(0))* Soundprints.
—Buffalo Prairie. Brauckmann-Towns, Krista, illus. 2005. (Amazing Animal Adventures Ser.). (ENG.). 36p. (J). (gr. -1-2). 2.95 *(978-1-59249-434-7(X),* S7160); 15.95 *(978-1-59249-432-3(3),* B7110); pap. 6.95 *(978-1-59249-433-0(1),* S7110) Soundprints.
Lubratt, Mark. Buffy Meets the Zoonicorns. Weingartner, Sara, illus. 2015. 32p. (J). 16.95 *(978-1-59298-893-8(8))* Beaver's Pond Pr., Inc.
Meyer, Deanna. Buffalo on the Ridge. 2010. pap. 12.95 *(978-0-7414-6103-2(X))* Infinity Publishing.
Meyer, Kay L. The Adventures of Billie & Annie — Baby Bison. Kirchoff, Arthur, illus. l.t. ed. 2004. 32p. (J). 6.00 *(978-0-9744536-0-6(9),* 9780974453606) Meyer, Tjaden.
Schnell, Robert W. Bonko. Wilkon, Jozef, illus. 28p. (J). (gr. -1-3). 12.95 *(978-0-87592-008-5(X))* Scroll Pr., Inc.
Sisco, Joann Ellen. The Bison of the High Meadow: 1. 2012. 96p. pap. 13.95 *(978-1-4772-5884-2(1))* AuthorHouse.

BLACK AMERICANS

see African Americans

BLACK DEATH

Here are entered works on the outbreak of the plague that swept parts of Asia and Europe in the fourteenth century.

see also Plague

Coping with Catastrophe: The Black Death of the 14th Century. (YA). (gr. 6-9). spiral bd., tchr.'s planning gde. ed. 12.00 *(978-0-382-44466-1(3))* Cobblestone Publishing Co.
Coping with Catastrophe: The Black Death of the 14th Century. (YA). (gr. 6-18). 16.50 *(978-0-8126-7557-3(6))* Cricket Bks.
Cunningham, Kevin. The Bubonic Plague, 1 vol. 2011. (Essential Events Set 6 Ser.). (ENG., Illus.). 112p. (J). (gr. 6-12). lib. bdg. 35.64 *(978-1-61714-762-3(1))* ABDO Publishing Co.
Elliott, Lynne. Medieval Medicine & the Plague. 2005. (Medieval World Ser.). (ENG., Illus.). 32p. (J). (gr. 5-9). lib. bdg. *(978-0-7787-1358-6(X))* Crabtree Publishing Co.
Farndon, John. Plague! Epidemics & Scourges Through the Ages. Dean, Venitia, illus. 2017. (Sickening History of Medicine Ser.). (ENG.). 32p. (J). (gr. 3-6). 26.65 *(978-1-5124-1557-5(X))*; 19.99 ***(978-1-5124-3634-1(8))***; 30.65 ***(978-1-5124-2709-7(8))***; 30.65 ***(978-1-5124-3632-7(1))*** Lerner Publishing Group.
Jeffrey, Gary. The Black Death. 2014. (ENG., Illus.). 48p. (J). *(978-0-7787-0400-3(9))*; pap. *(978-0-7787-0406-5(8))* Crabtree Publishing Co.
Levy, Janey. Plaga: La Peste Negra (Plague: the Black Death) Sarfatti, Esther, tr. from ENG. 2015. (Desastres Ser.). (SPA., Illus.). 32p. (J). (gr. 4-5). lib. bdg. 26.60 *(978-1-4824-3248-0(X))* Stevens, Gareth Publishing LLLP.
Mahoney, Emily & Nardo, Don. The Black Death: Bubonic Plague Attacks Europe. 2017. (World History Ser.). 104p. (YA). (gr. 7-7). lib. bdg. 39.90 ***(978-1-5345-6047-5(5)***, Lucent Pr.) Greenhaven Publishing LLC.
Narayan, Natasha. Black Death & Other Putrid Plagues of London. 2004. (.... of London Ser.). (Illus.). 96p. 8.99 *(978-1-904153-01-6(1))* Watling St., Ltd. GBR. Dist: Independent Pubs. Group.
Peppas, Lynn. Plague! 2013. (ENG.). 48p. (J). *(978-0-7787-1102-5(1))*; pap. *(978-0-7787-1122-3(6))* Crabtree Publishing Co.
Person, Stephen. Bubonic Plague: The Black Death! (Nightmare Plagues Ser.). 32p. (gr. 4-9). 2016. (ENG.). (J). pap. 8.95 *(978-1-944998-69-1(1))* 2010. (YA). lib. bdg. 25.27 *(978-1-936088-03-4(7))* Bearport Publishing Co., Inc.
Slavicek, Louise Chipley. The Black Death. 2008. (Great Historic Disasters Ser.). (Illus.). 128p. (gr. 5-8). 35.00 *(978-0-7910-9649-9(1),* Chelsea Hse.) Facts On File, Inc.

BLACK HAWK, SAUK CHIEF, 1767-1838

Bowes, John P. Black Hawk & the War of 1832: Removal in the North. 2007. (Landmark Events in Native American History Ser.). (Illus.). 131p. (YA). (gr. 9-12). pap. 35.00 *(978-0-7910-9342-9(5))* Facts On File, Inc.
Poulakidas, Georgene. Black Hawk's War. (Primary Sources of American Wars Ser.). 24p. 2009. (gr. 3-4). 42.50 *(978-1-60851-518-9(4),* PowerKids Pr.) 2006. (Illus.). (YA). (gr. 4-7). lib. bdg. 22.60 *(978-1-4042-2682-1(6))* Rosen Publishing Group, Inc., The.

BLACK LITERATURE (AMERICAN)

see American Literature—African American Authors

BLACK MUSLIMS

Aretha, David. A Time for Martyrs: The Life of Malcolm X. 2012. (YA). 28.95 *(978-1-59935-328-9(8))* Reynolds, Morgan Inc.
Burlingame, Jeff. Malcolm X: "I Believe in the Brotherhood of Man, All Men" 2010. (American Rebels Ser.). 160p. (YA). (gr. 7-12). 35.94 *(978-0-7660-3384-9(8))* Enslow Pubs., Inc.
Doeden, Matt. A Marked Man: The Assassination of Malcolm X. 2013. (ENG., Illus.). 88p. (J). (gr. 6-12). lib. bdg. 33.27 *(978-0-7613-5484-0(0),* Twenty-First Century Bks.) Lerner Publishing Group.
Fay, Gail. Malcolm X, 1 vol. 2012. (American Biographies Ser.). (ENG.). 48p. (gr. 4-6). pap. 9.95 *(978-1-4329-6467-2(4),* NA-h) Heinemann-Raintree.
—Malcolm X, 1 vol. Oxford Bible Staff, illus. 2012. (American Biographies Ser.). (ENG.). 48p. (gr. 4-6). lib. bdg. 32.65 *(978-1-4329-6456-6(9),* NA-h) Heinemann-Raintree.
Haley, Alex. The Autobiography of Malcolm X. Bloom, Harold, ed. annot. ed. 2008. (Bloom's Guides). 168p. (C). (gr. 9). 30.00 *(978-0-7910-9832-5(X),* Chelsea Hse.) Facts On File, Inc.
Linde, Barbara M. Malcolm X. 2011. (Civil Rights Crusaders Ser.). 24p. (J). (gr. 2-5). pap. 8.15 *(978-1-4339-5688-1(8),* Gareth Stevens Learning Library); lib. bdg. 22.60 *(978-1-4339-5686-7(1))* Stevens, Gareth Publishing LLLP.
Machajewski, Sarah. Malcolm X in His Own Words. 2014. (Eyewitness to History Ser.). 32p. (J). (gr. 4-6). pap. 63.00 *(978-1-4824-1220-8(9))* Stevens, Gareth Publishing LLLP.
Malcolm X & the Black Pride Movement. 2009. (Lucent Library of Black History Ser.). 128p. (gr. 7-10). 34.80 *(978-1-4205-0123-0(2),* Lucent Bks.) Cengage Gale.
Mancini, Candice. Racism in the Autobiography of Malcolm X. 2008. (Social Issues in Literature Ser.). (ENG., Illus.). 175p. (YA). (gr. 10-12). 28.45 *(978-0-7377-4261-9(5),* LML02109-243175); pap. 40.95 *(978-0-7377-4260-2(7),* LML02109-243171) Cengage Gale. (Greenhaven Pr., Inc.).
Mis, Melody S. Meet Malcolm X. (Civil Rights Leaders Ser.). 24p. (gr. 2-3). 2009. 42.50 *(978-1-61511-853-3(5),* PowerKids Pr.) 2008. (Illus.). (YA). lib. bdg. 22.60 *(978-1-4042-4214-2(7))* Rosen Publishing Group, Inc., The.
Myers, Walter Dean. Malcolm X: A Fire Burning Brightly. 2004. (J). 14.65 *(978-0-7569-3199-5(1))* Perfection Learning Corp.
Robinson, Tom. Malcolm X: Rights Activist & Nation of Islam Leader, 1 vol. 2013. (Essential Lives Set 8 Ser.). (ENG.). 112p. (J). (gr. 6-12). lib. bdg. 35.64 *(978-1-61783-893-4(4),* Essential Library) ABDO Publishing Co.
Shabazz, Ilyasah. Malcolm Little: The Boy Who Grew up to Become Malcolm X. Ford, A. G., illus. 2014. (ENG.). 48p. (J). (gr. 1-5). 17.99 *(978-1-4424-1216-3(X))* Simon & Schuster Children's Publishing.
Vietze, Andrew. The Life & Death of Malcolm X. 2017. (J). ***(978-1-5383-8032-1(3)***, Rosen Young Adult) Rosen Publishing Group, Inc., The.

BLACK POETRY (AMERICAN)

see American Poetry—African American Authors

BLACKBEARD, -1718

see Teach, Edward, -1718

BLACKBOARD DRAWING

see Crayon Drawing

BLACKS

Here are entered works on blacks as an element in the population. Works on black people in countries whose racial composition is predominantly black are assigned headings appropriate for the country as a whole without the use of the heading Blacks. The heading Blacks is assigned to works on such countries only if the work discusses blacks apart from other groups in the country.

Aretha, David. The Middle Passage. 2014. xvi, 585p. (J). *(978-1-59935-408-8(X))* Reynolds, Morgan Inc.
Dingles, Molly. Black as a Bat/Negro como un Murcielago. Velez, Walter, illus. 2003. (Community of Color Ser.). (SPA.). 32p. (J). lib. bdg. 21.65 *(978-1-891997-33-4(5))* Dingles & Co.
Malaspina, Ann. Nelson Mandela: Fighting to Dismantle Apartheid. 2017. (Rebels with a Cause Ser.). 128p. (YA). (gr. 8-8). lib. bdg. 37.27 ***(978-0-7660-8517-6(1))*** Enslow Pubs., Inc.
McConaghy, Lorraine & Bentley, Judy. Free Boy: A True Story of Slave & Master. 2013. (V Ethel Willis White Bks.). (ENG., Illus.). 112p. pap. 18.95 *(978-0-295-99271-6(9))* Univ. of Washington Pr.
Oliver, Patrick M., ed. Turn the Page & You Don't Stop: Sharing Successful Chapters in Our Lives with Youth. 2006. (Illus.). 156p. pap. 12.00 *(978-0-9779499-0-8(7))* Say It Loud! Readers & Writers Series.
Sherman, Jack. Just Zack. 2012. 118p. (gr. 1-1). 29.99 *(978-1-4691-9985-6(8))*; pap. 19.99 *(978-1-4691-9984-9(X))* Xlibris Corp.
Sutherland, Adam. Political Leaders. 2012. (Black History Makers Ser.). (ENG., Illus.). 24p. (J). (gr. 3-8). pap. 8.25 *(978-1-4488-7056-1(9))*; lib. bdg. 22.60 *(978-1-4488-6639-7(1))* Rosen Publishing Group, Inc., The. (PowerKids Pr.).
Taylor, Wanda. Birchtown & the Black Loyalists, 1 vol. 2015. (ENG.). 80p. (J). (gr. 3-6). pap. 15.95 *(978-1-77108-166-5(X))* Nimbus Publishing, Ltd. CAN. Dist: Orca Bk. Pubs. USA.

BLACKS—BIOGRAPHY

Fay, Gail. Malcolm X, 1 vol. 2012. (American Biographies Ser.). (ENG.). 48p. (gr. 4-6). pap. 9.95 *(978-1-4329-6467-2(4),* NA-h) Heinemann-Raintree.
—Malcolm X, 1 vol. Oxford Bible Staff, illus. 2012. (American Biographies Ser.). (ENG.). 48p. (gr. 4-6). lib. bdg. 32.65 *(978-1-4329-6456-6(9),* NA-h) Heinemann-Raintree.
Finlayson, Reggie. Nelson Mandela. pap. 9.95 *(978-0-8225-5743-2(6))* Lerner Publishing Group.
Foy, Debbie. Musicians. 2012. (Black History Makers Ser.). (ENG., Illus.). 24p. (J). (gr. 3-8). pap. 8.25 *(978-1-4488-7052-3(6))*; lib. bdg. 22.60 *(978-1-4488-6637-3(5))* Rosen Publishing Group, Inc., The. (PowerKids Pr.).
Heroes of Black History. 2015. (Heroes of Black History Ser.). (ENG.). 32p. (J). (gr. 3-4). pap., pap., pap. 378.00 *(978-1-4824-3478-1(4))* Stevens, Gareth Publishing LLLP.
Jackson, Dave & Jackson, Neta. Heroes in Black History: True Stories from the Lives of Christian Heroes. 2008. (ENG., Illus.). 192p. (J). (gr. 3-7). pap. 14.99 *(978-0-7642-0556-9(0))* Bethany Hse. Pubs.
Lee, George L. Worldwide Interesting People: 162 History Makers of African Descent, 1 vol. alt. ed. 2012. (ENG., Illus.). 144p. pap. 19.99 *(978-0-7864-6768-6(1),* 5efb588e-8e35-4188-81bd-86ff635cdb1d) McFarland & Co., Inc. Pubs.
Marlowe, Sam. Learning about Dedication from the Life of Frederick Douglass. 2004. (Character Building Book Ser.). (Illus.). 24p. (J). lib. bdg. 22.60 *(978-0-8239-6928-9(2),* PowerKids Pr.) Rosen Publishing Group, Inc., The.
Myers, Walter Dean. Malcolm X: A Fire Burning Brightly. 2004. (J). 14.65 *(978-0-7569-3199-5(1))* Perfection Learning Corp.
Ross, H. K. Black American Women, No. 3. Date not set. (Illus.). 160p. (YA). (gr. 6-12). 11.95 *(978-0-87460-365-1(X))* Lion Bks.

BLACKS—FICTION

Achebe, Chinua. Chike & the River. Rodriguez, Edel, illus. 2011. (ENG.). 96p. (YA). pap. 12.00 *(978-0-307-47386-8(4),* Penguin Books) Penguin Publishing Group.
Anderson, Natalie C. City of Saints & Thieves. 2017. (ENG.). 432p. (YA). (gr. 7). 18.99 *(978-0-399-54758-4(4),* G.P. Putnam's Sons Books for Young Readers) Penguin Young Readers Group.
Baptiste, Tracey. The Jumbies. 2015. (ENG.). 240p. (J). (gr. 3-7). 15.95 *(978-1-61620-414-3(1))* Algonquin Bks. of Chapel Hill.
Baptiste, Tracey. The Rise of the Jumbies. 2017. (Jumbies Ser.). (ENG.). 256p. (J). (gr. 3-7). 16.95 ***(978-1-61620-665-9(9))*** Algonquin Bks. of Chapel Hill.
Beverley, Naidoo. Journey to Jo'Burg: A South African Story. 97th rev. ed. 2014. (ENG.). 96p. (J). (gr. k-4). 10.24 *(978-1-63245-264-1(2))* Lectorum Pubns., Inc.
Bildner, Phil. The Soccer Fence: A Story of Friendship, Hope, & Apartheid in South Africa. Watson, Jesse Joshua, illus. 2014. (ENG.). 40p. (J). (gr. 1-3). 16.99 *(978-0-399-24790-3(4),* G.P. Putnam's Sons Books for Young Readers) Penguin Young Readers Group.
Binch, Caroline. Gregory Cool. 2012. (ENG., Illus.). 32p. (J). (gr. k-3). pap. 8.99 *(978-1-84780-258-3(3),* Frances Lincoln) Quarto Publishing Group UK GBR. Dist: Hachette Bk. Group.
Brown-Wood, Janay. Imani's Moon. Mitchell, Hazell, illus. 2014. (ENG.). 32p. (J). (gr. 1-4). pap. 7.95 *(978-1-934133-58-3(2),* Mackinac Island Press, Inc.) Charlesbridge Publishing, Inc.
Brownworth, Victoria, ed. From Where They Sit: Black Writers Write Black Youth. 2011. (ENG.). 350p. (J). (gr. 6). pap. 16.95 *(978-0-9845318-3-7(1))* Tiny Stachel Pr.
Bryan, Ashley. Can't Scare Me! Bryan, Ashley, illus. 2013. (ENG., Illus.). 40p. (J). (gr. -1-3). 16.99 *(978-1-4424-7657-8(5),* Atheneum Bks. for Young Readers) Simon & Schuster Children's Publishing.
Chamberlain, Mary, et al. Las Crepes de Mama Panya: Un Relato de Kenia. Cairns, Julia, illus. 2016. (SPA.). 40p. (J). (gr. k-5). pap. 8.99 *(978-1-78285-072-4(4))* Barefoot Bks., Inc.
Cobb, Nyelah. True Identity. 2003. 104p. pap. 9.95 *(978-0-595-28227-2(X))* iUniverse, Inc.
Curtis, Christopher Paul. Elijah of Buxton. (ENG.). (J). (gr. 3-7). 2009. 368p. 7.99 *(978-0-439-02345-0(9),* Scholastic Paperbacks) 2007. 352p. 16.99 *(978-0-439-02344-3(0),* Scholastic Pr.) Scholastic, Inc.
—The Madman of Piney Woods. (Illus.). (J). 2016. (ENG.). 384p. (gr. 3-7). pap. 7.99 *(978-0-545-15665-3(3))* 2014. 363p. *(978-0-545-63376-5(1))* 2014. (ENG., 384p. (gr. 3-7). 16.99 *(978-0-545-15664-6(5))* Scholastic, Inc. (Scholastic Pr.).
—The Watsons Go to Birmingham — 1963. 2013. (ENG.). 224p. (J). (gr. 3-7). 7.99 *(978-0-385-38294-6(4),* Yearling) Random Hse. Children's Bks.
Curtis, Christopher Paul & Paul, Curtis Christopher. Elias de Buxton. 2008. (SPA.). 368p. (gr. 6-12). pap. 12.99 *(978-84-441-4101-5(1))* Everest Editora ESP. Dist: Lectorum Pubns., Inc.
Daly, Niki. The Herd Boy. 2012. (ENG., Illus.). 32p. (J). 17.00 *(978-0-8028-5417-9(6),* Eerdmans Bks For Young Readers) Eerdmans, William B. Publishing Co.
Esdaille-Richardson, Eudora. Malcolm & the Money Tree. Williams, Christopher, illus. 2014. 31p. (J). pap. *(978-1-934370-49-0(5))* Editorial Campana.
Farmer, Nancy. The Ear, the Eye & the Arm. 2012. (ENG.). 336p. (J). (gr. 3-7). pap. 7.99 *(978-0-545-35661-9(X),* Scholastic Paperbacks) Scholastic, Inc.
—The Ear, the Eye, & the Arm. 2012. lib. bdg. 18.40 *(978-0-606-23944-8(8),* Turtleback) Turtleback Bks.
Grifalconi, Ann. The Village That Vanished. Nelson, Kadir, illus. 2004. (ENG.). 40p. (J). (gr. k-3). reprint ed. pap. 7.99 *(978-0-14-240190-3(0),* Puffin Books) Penguin Young Readers Group.
Harris, Amber. Black, White & Beautiful. Mamata, Sue, illus. 2007. 25p. pap. 24.95 *(978-1-4241-8932-8(2))* PublishAmerica, Inc.
Henry, Beresford. The Gaulin & the Dove. 2008. 128p. (J). pap. *(978-0-435-89938-7(4))* Pearson Education, Ltd.
Hodge, Merle. For the Life of Laetitia. 2003. 21.25 *(978-0-8446-7246-5(7))* Smith, Peter Pub., Inc.

Hubbell, Patricia & Tate, Don. Black All Around!, 1 vol. 2003. (ENG., Illus.). 32p. (J). pap. 10.95 *(978-1-60060-643-4(1))* Lee & Low Bks., Inc.

Isadora, Rachel. I Just Want to Say Good Night. Isadora, Rachel, illus. 2017. (ENG., Illus.). 32p. (J). (-k). 17.99 *(978-0-399-17384-4(6),* Nancy Paulsen Books) Penguin Young Readers Group.

Kim, JiYu. The Wise Boy. Hwang, YoSeob, illus. 2014. (MySELF Bookshelf Ser.). (ENG.). 32p. (J). (gr. k-2). lib. bdg. 25.27 *(978-1-59953-655-2(2))* Norwood Hse. Pr.

Kim, YeShil. My Best Buddy. Tanco, Miguel, illus. 2014. (MySELF Bookshelf Ser.). (ENG.). 32p. (J). (gr. k-2). lib. bdg. 25.27 *(978-1-59953-658-3(7))* Norwood Hse. Pr.

McCall Smith, Alexander. The Great Cake Mystery: Precious Ramotswe's Very First Case. 2012. (Precious Ramotswe Mysteries for Young Readers Ser.: 1). (ENG.). 96p. (J). (gr. 2-5). 12.99 *(978-0-307-94944-8(3));* (Illus.). pap. 6.99 *(978-0-307-74389-3(6))* Knopf Doubleday Publishing Group. (Anchor).

—The Mystery of the Missing Lion: A Precious Ramotswe Mystery for Young Readers. 2014. (Precious Ramotswe Mysteries for Young Readers Ser.: 3). (ENG., Illus.). 112p. (J). (gr. 2-5). pap. 6.99 *(978-0-8041-7327-8(3),* Anchor) Knopf Doubleday Publishing Group.

McDougal-Littell Publishing Staff. Literature Connections English: I, Juan de Pareja. 2004. (McDougal Littell Literature Connections Ser.). (ENG.). 224p. (gr. 7-7). 16.90 *(978-0-395-77531-8(0),* 2-80100) Great Source Education Group, Inc.

McGee, Ron. Ryan Quinn & the Lion's Claw. Samnee, Chris, illus. 2017. (Ryan Quinn Ser.: 2). 352p. (J). (gr. 3-7). 16.99 ***(978-0-06-242169-2(7))*** HarperCollins Pubs.

McKissack, Patricia C. Never Forgotten. Dillon, Leo & Dillon, Diane, illus. 2011. (ENG.). 48p. (J). (gr. k-12). 18.99 *(978-0-375-84384-6(1),* Schwartz & Wade Bks.) Random Hse. Children's Bks.

Min, SooHyeon. The Drummer Boy. Nille, Peggy, illus. 2014. (MySELF Bookshelf Ser.). (ENG.). 32p. (J). (gr. k-2). lib. bdg. 25.27 *(978-1-59953-661-3(7))* Norwood Hse. Pr.

Mussi, Sarah. The Door of No Return. (ENG.). 400p. (YA). (gr. 7). 2009. pap. 10.99 *(978-1-4169-6825-2(3))* 2008. 17.99 *(978-1-4169-1550-8(8))* McElderry, Margaret K. Bks. (McElderry, Margaret K. Bks.).

The Mystery of the Missing Lion: A Precious Ramotswe Mystery for Young Readers. 2014. (Precious Ramotswe Mysteries for Young Readers Ser.: 3). (ENG., Illus.). 112p. (J). (gr. 2-5). 12.99 *(978-1-101-87202-4(0),* Anchor) Knopf Doubleday Publishing Group.

Naidoo, Beverley. No Turning Back. 2017. (ENG.). 208p. (YA). (gr. 9). pap. 12.99 *(978-0-14-136890-0(X))* Penguin Bks., Ltd. GBR. Dist: Independent Pubs. Group.

—The Other Side of Truth. 2008. 252p. (gr. 5-9). 17.00 *(978-0-7569-8941-5(8))* Perfection Learning Corp.

Nikola-lisa, W. & Nikola-lisa, W. Hallelujah! A Christmas Celebration. Saint James, Synthia, illus. 2009. (ENG.). 36p. (J). (gr. -1-3). 10.99 *(978-1-4424-0224-9(5),* Atheneum Bks. for Young Readers) Simon & Schuster Children's Publishing.

O'Dell, Scott. My Name Is Not Angelica. 2011. (ENG.). 144p. (J). (gr. 2-5). pap. 7.99 *(978-0-547-40630-5(4))* Houghton Mifflin Harcourt Publishing Co.

Odhiambo, Eucabeth. Auma's Long Run. 2017. (ENG.). 304p. (J). (gr. 3-6). 17.99 ***(978-1-5124-2784-4(5),*** Carolrhoda Bks.) Lerner Publishing Group.

Okorafor, Nnedi. Akata Witch. (ENG.). (YA). (gr. 7). 2017. 384p. pap. 10.99 ***(978-0-14-242091-1(3),*** Speak) 2011. 368p. 17.99 *(978-0-670-01196-4(7),* Viking Books for Young Readers) Penguin Young Readers Group.

The Other Side of the Invisible Fence. 2006. (YA). per. 9.95 *(978-0-9787783-8-5(3))* Romain, Trevor Co., The.

Park, Linda Sue. A Long Walk to Water: Based on a True Story. (ENG., 128p. (J). (gr. 5-7). 2011. Illus.). pap. 7.99 *(978-0-547-57731-9(1))* 2010. 17.99 *(978-0-547-25127-1(0))* Houghton Mifflin Harcourt Publishing Co.

—A Long Walk to Water: Based on a True Story. 2009. 8.32 *(978-0-7848-3885-3(2),* Everbind) Marco Bk. Co.

—A Long Walk to Water: Based on a True Story. 2011. 18.00 *(978-1-61383-124-3(2))* Perfection Learning Corp.

—A Long Walk to Water: Based on a True Story. 2011. lib. bdg. 18.40 *(978-0-606-23406-1(3),* Turtleback) Turtleback Bks.

Paul, Curtis Christopher. The Watsons Go to Birmingham 1963. 2014. (ENG.). 224p. (J). (gr. 12-12). 11.24 *(978-1-63245-108-8(5))* Lectorum Pubns., Inc.

Perkyns, Dorothy. Last Days in Africville. 2005. (Illus.). 144p. (YA). pap., tchr. ed. *(978-0-88878-446-9(5),* Sandcastle Bks.) Dundurn.

—Last Days in Africville. 2006. (ENG.). 120p. (J). (gr. 4-7). pap. 10.99 *(978-1-55002-630-6(5),* Dundurn Pr.) Dundurn CAN. Dist: Ingram Publisher Services.

Pinkney, Andrea Davis. The Red Pencil. Evans, Shane W., illus. 2014. (ENG.). 336p. (J). (gr. 4-17). 17.99 *(978-0-316-24780-1(4))* Little, Brown Bks. for Young Readers.

Powers, J. L. This Thing Called the Future. 2011. (FRS & ENG.). 208p. (J). (gr. 7-11). 16.95 *(978-1-933693-95-8(9))* Cinco Puntos Pr.

Prescott, Yolanda. Mama's Pickaninny. 2004. 7.00 *(978-0-9719241-3-0(9))* Chosen Word Publishing.

Rees, Celia. Pirates! The True & Remarkable Adventures of Minerva Sharpe & Nancy Kington, Female Pirates. 2005. (Illus.). 379p. (YA). (gr. 9-12). 16.60 *(978-0-7569-6304-0(4))* Perfection Learning Corp.

Rouss, Sylvia A. Jaekob, the Dreamer. 2015. (Illus.). (J). *(978-1-68115-506-7(0))* Behrman Hse., Inc.

Salkey, Andrew. Riot. 2011. (Caribbean Modern Classics Ser.). (ENG., Illus.). 176p. (J). (gr. 7). pap. 14.95 *(978-1-84523-181-1(3))* Peepal Tree Pr., Ltd. GBR. Dist: Independent Pubs. Group.

Sari. Jeanne-Marie Goes to Market: A Story of the West Indies. 2011. 26p. 35.95 *(978-1-258-10346-0(X))* Literary Licensing, LLC.

Seyforth, Edward L. A Horribly Frightening Deception, 1 vol. 2009. 75p. pap. 19.95 *(978-1-61546-260-5(0))* America Star Bks.

Soriano, Osvaldo. El Negro de Paris. (Torre de Papel Ser.). (SPA.). (J). (gr. 4-18). 8.95 *(978-958-04-3450-4(6))* Norma S.A. COL. Dist: Distribuidora Norma, Inc.

Sorrells, W. A. Nairobi Nightmare. Bancroft, Tom & Corley, Rob, illus. 2007. 144p. (J). *(978-0-9792912-1-0(6))* KidsGive, LLC.

Stiver, Joan. The Door in the Floor: An Underground Railroad Adventure. 2008. 48p. pap. 4.99 *(978-1-4343-2953-0(4))* AuthorHouse.

Stratton, Allan. Chanda's Wars. 2009. (ENG.). 416p. (YA). (gr. 8). pap. 8.99 *(978-0-06-087265-6(9),* HarperTeen) HarperCollins Pubs.

—Chanda's Wars. 2011. 10.36 *(978-0-7848-3486-2(5),* Everbind) Marco Bk. Co.

Sullivan, Tara. The Bitter Side of Sweet. 2016. (ENG.). 320p. (J). (gr. 7). 17.99 *(978-0-399-17307-3(2),* G.P. Putnam's Sons Books for Young Readers) Penguin Young Readers Group.

Taylor, Theodore. The Cay. 2003. (ENG.). 160p. (J). (gr. 5-7). mass mkt. 6.99 *(978-0-440-22912-4(X),* Laurel Leaf) Random Hse. Children's Bks.

—Timothy of the Cay. 2007. (ENG., Illus.). 176p. (J). (gr. 5-7). pap. 6.99 *(978-0-15-206320-7(X))* Houghton Mifflin Harcourt Publishing Co.

Taylor, Theodore & Taylor, Theodore. The Cay. 2003. (gr. 5-8). lib. bdg. 17.20 *(978-0-613-72282-7(5),* Turtleback) Turtleback Bks.

Temple, Frances. Taste of Salt: A Story of Modern Haiti. 2004. (Trophy Bk.). (ENG.). 192p. (YA). (gr. 8-18). pap. 6.99 *(978-0-06-447136-7(5),* HarperTeen) HarperCollins Pubs.

Verde, Susan & Badiel, Georgie. The Water Princess. Reynolds, Peter H., illus. 2016. (ENG.). 40p. (J). (gr. k-3). 17.99 *(978-0-399-17258-8(0),* G.P. Putnam's Sons Books for Young Readers) Penguin Young Readers Group.

Verne, Jules. Dick Sand. Munro, George, tr. 2008. 296p. pap. 15.95 *(978-1-60664-253-5(7))* Rodgers, Alan Bks.

Ward, Rachel. The Chaos. 2011. (Numbers Ser.: 2). (ENG.). 352p. (J). (gr. 9-9). 17.99 *(978-0-545-24269-1(X),* Chicken Hse., The) Scholastic, Inc.

—Infinity: 2012. (Numbers Ser.: 3). (ENG.). 256p. (J). (gr. 9-9). 17.99 *(978-0-545-35092-1(1),* Chicken Hse., The) Scholastic, Inc.

—Numbers. 2010. (Numbers Ser.: 1). (ENG.). 336p. (J). (gr. 7-12). 17.99 *(978-0-545-14299-1(7),* Chicken Hse., The) Scholastic, Inc.

Watson-Doost, Valeria. Issa. 2009. 55p. pap. 9.95 *(978-0-557-03625-7(9))* Lulu Pr., Inc.

Williams, Michael. Diamond Boy. 2014. (Illus.). 384p. (YA). *(978-0-316-32067-2(6))* Little Brown & Co.

—Diamond Boy. 2014. (ENG., Illus.). 400p. (YA). (gr. 7-17). 18.00 *(978-0-316-32069-6(2))* Little, Brown Bks. for Young Readers.

—Now Is the Time for Running. 2013. (ENG.). 240p. (YA). (gr. 7-17). pap. 10.99 *(978-0-316-07788-0(7))* Little, Brown Bks. for Young Readers.

Zephaniah, Benjamin. Gangsta Rap. 2004. (ENG.). 336p. (YA). (gr. 9-13). pap. 8.99 *(978-1-58234-886-5(3),* 9781582348865, Bloomsbury USA Childrens) Bloomsbury Publishing USA.

BLACKS—HISTORY

Barnette, Donald. Is My Skin My Only Sin? Breaking the Color Barrier. 2004. (Illus.). 95p. (YA). pap. 14.95 *(978-0-9747816-0-0(6))* Barnette, Donald.

Dendy, Christina. Underground Railroad: Defining Moments in Canadian History. 2011. (Illus.). 32p. (gr. 5-8). *(978-1-77071-691-9(2))* Weigl Educational Pubs. Ltd.

Lester, Julius. To Be a Slave. Feelings, Tom, illus. 2005. (Puffin Modern Classics Ser.). (ENG.). 176p. (J). (gr. 3-7). 7.99 *(978-0-14-240386-0(5),* Puffin Books) Penguin Young Readers Group.

Meadows, James. Slavery: The Struggle for Freedom. 2009. (Journey to Freedom Ser.). (ENG., Illus.). 32p. (J). (gr. 4-7). 29.93 *(978-1-60253-134-5(X),* 200400) Child's World, Inc., The.

Sadlier, Rosemary. The Kids Book of Black Canadian History. Wang, Qijun, illus. 2010. (Kids Book Of Ser.). (ENG.). 56p. (J). (gr. 3-7). 14.95 *(978-1-55453-587-3(5))* Kids Can Pr., Ltd. CAN. Dist: Hachette Bk. Group.

Warner, Jody Nyasha. Viola Desmond Won't Be Budged, 1 vol. Rudnicki, Richard & Junaid, Bushra, illus. 2010. (ENG.). 32p. (J). (gr. k-4). 18.95 *(978-0-88899-779-1(5))* Groundwood Bks. CAN. Dist: Publishers Group West (PGW).

BLACKS—SOCIAL LIFE AND CUSTOMS

Papi, Liza. Carnavalia! African-Brazilian Folklore & Crafts. Papi, Liza, illus. 2004. (Illus.). 48p. (J). (gr. k-4). reprint ed. 20.00 *(978-0-7567-7760-9(7))* DIANE Publishing Co.

BLACKWELL, ELIZABETH, 1821-1910

Auster, Michael A. They Led the Way. 2005. (Yellow Umbrella Fluent Level Ser.). (ENG.). 16p. (gr. k-1). pap. 35.70 *(978-0-7368-5315-6(4),* Yellow Umbrella Bks.) Capstone Press of Coughlan Cos.

Crayton, Lisa A. Elizabeth Blackwell: Doctor & Advocate for Women in Medicine. 2016. (Heroes of the Women's Suffrage Movement Ser.). (Illus.). 128p. (J). (gr. 6-6). 37.27 *(978-0-7660-7890-1(6))* Enslow Pubs., Inc.

James, Emily. Elizabeth Blackwell. 2017. (Great Scientists & Inventors Ser.). (ENG., Illus.). 24p. (gr. k-1). lib. bdg. 26.65 *(978-1-5157-3882-4(5))* Capstone Press of Coughlan Cos.

Kishel, Ann-Marie. Elizabeth Blackwell: A Life of Diligence. 2007. (Pull Ahead Bks.). (Illus.). 32p. (J). (gr. 3-7). lib. bdg. 22.60 *(978-0-8225-6459-1(9),* Lerner Pubns.) Lerner Publishing Group.

Klobuchar, Lisa. Elizabeth Blackwell: With Profiles of Elizabeth Garrett Anderson & Susan la Flesche Picotte. 2006. (Biographical Connections Ser.). (Illus.). 112p. *(978-0-7166-1826-3(5))* World Bk., Inc.

Leavitt, Amie Jane. Elizabeth Blackwell. 2007. (What's So Great About... ? Ser.). (Illus.). 32p. (J). (gr. 1-5). lib. bdg. 25.70 *(978-1-58415-579-9(5))* Mitchell Lane Pubs., Inc.

Robbins, Trina. Elizabeth Blackwell: America's First Woman Doctor. Martin, Cynthia & Timmons, Anne, illus. 2006. (Graphic Biographies Ser.). (ENG.). 32p. (gr. 3-4). 30.65 *(978-0-7368-6497-8(0));* per. 8.10 *(978-0-7368-9660-3(0))* Capstone Press of Coughlan Cos. (Graphic Library).

Sabin, Francene & Macken, JoAnn Early. Elizabeth Blackwell, the First Woman Doctor. Toulmin-Rothe, Ann, illus. 2007. 53p. (J). *(978-0-439-66044-0(0))* Scholastic, Inc.

Somervill, Barbara A. Elizabeth Blackwell: America's First Female Doctor. 2009. (Life Portraits Ser.). (Illus.). 112p. (YA). (gr. 7-12). lib. bdg. 36.00 *(978-1-4339-0055-6(6))* Stevens, Gareth Publishing LLLP.

Thomas, Isabel. Collins Big Cat - The World's First Women Doctors: Elizabeth Blackwell & Elizabeth Garrett Anderson: Band 16/Sapphire. 2015. (Collins Big Cat Ser.). (ENG., Illus.). 56p. (J). (gr. 4-5). pap. 9.95 *(978-0-00-812789-3(1))* HarperCollins Pubs. Ltd. GBR. Dist: Independent Pubs. Group.

BLAKE, WILLIAM, 1757-1827

Bedard, Michael. William Blake: The Gates of Paradise. 2006. (ENG., Illus.). 200p. (J). (gr. 9). 19.95 *(978-0-88776-763-0(X),* Tundra Bks.) Tundra Bks. CAN. Dist: Penguin Random Hse. LLC.

Bloom, Harold & Harley, Alexis, eds. William Blake. 2008. (Bloom's Classic Critical Views Ser.). 232p. (YA). (gr. 9-12). 45.00 *(978-1-60413-138-3(1))* Facts On File, Inc.

Punter, David, ed. Songs of Innocence & Experience. 2003. (ENG., Illus.). 112p. pap. 20.00 *(978-0-582-78433-8(6))* Pearson Education, Ltd. GBR. Dist: Trans-Atlantic Pubns., Inc.

BLIND

Adams, Colleen. The Courage of Helen Keller. 2009. (Reading Room Collection 2 Ser.). 24p. (gr. 3-4). 42.50 *(978-1-60851-992-7(9),* PowerKids Pr.) Rosen Publishing Group, Inc., The.

Beyer, Mark. Stevie Wonder. 2009. (Rock & Roll Hall of Famers Ser.). 112p. (gr. 5-8). 63.90 *(978-1-60852-475-4(2),* Rosen Reference) Rosen Publishing Group, Inc., The.

Brocker, Susan. Vision Without Sight: Human Capabilities. 2007. (Shockwave: Life Science & Medicine Ser.). (ENG., Illus.). 36p. (J). (gr. 4-6). lib. bdg. 25.00 *(978-0-531-17769-3(6),* Children's Pr.) Scholastic Library Publishing.

Devillier, Christy. Helen Keller, 1 vol. 2004. (First Biographies Set Iv Ser.). (ENG., Illus.). 32p. (gr. k-4). 27.07 *(978-1-59197-514-4(X),* Buddy Bks.) ABDO Publishing Co.

Edison, Erin. Helen Keller, 1 vol. 2014. (Great Women in History Ser.). (ENG.). 24p. (gr. k-1). lib. bdg. 21.99 *(978-1-4765-4217-1(1),* Pebble Bks.) Capstone Press of Coughlan Cos.

Fetty, Margaret. Helen Keller: Break down the Walls! 2006. (Defining Moments Ser.). (Illus.). 32p. (J). (gr. 2-5). lib. bdg. 25.27 *(978-1-59716-271-5(X))* Bearport Publishing Co., Inc.

Jeffrey, Laura S. All about Braille: Reading by Touch. 2004. (Transportation & Communication Ser.). (Illus.). 48p. (J). lib. bdg. 25.27 *(978-0-7660-2184-6(X))* Enslow Pubs., Inc.

Kent, Deborah. What Is Braille? 2012. (Overcoming Barriers Ser.). (Illus.). 48p. (J). (gr. 3-4). pap. 8.95 *(978-1-4644-0155-8(1),* Enslow Elementary) Enslow Pubs., Inc.

—What Is It Like to Be Blind? 2012. (Overcoming Barriers Ser.). 48p. (J). (gr. 3-4). (Illus.). pap. 8.95 *(978-1-4644-0153-4(5));* 25.27 *(978-0-7660-3768-7(1))* Enslow Pubs., Inc. (Enslow Elementary).

Marcovitz, Hal. Blindness. 2008. (Diseases & Disorders (Lucent Books) Ser.). (ENG., Illus.). 104p. (YA). (gr. 7-10). lib. bdg. 34.95 *(978-1-4205-0041-7(4),* LML02109-240028, Lucent Bks.) Cengage Gale.

Mattern, Joanne. Helen Keller. 2015. (Rookie Biographies(r) Ser.). (ENG., Illus.). 32p. (J). pap. 5.95 *(978-0-531-20995-0(4))* Scholastic Library Publishing.

Parker, Vic. I Know Someone with a Visual Impairment, 1 vol. 2011. (Understanding Health Issues Ser.). (ENG.). 32p. (gr. 1-3). 27.32 *(978-1-4329-4562-6(9),* Heinemann First Library) Heinemann-Raintree.

Pruessen, Linda. Saving Eyesight: Adventures of Seva Around the World. 2015. (ENG., Illus.). 64p. (J). (gr. 4-8). 19.95 *(978-1-77085-616-5(1),* 9781770856165); pap. 9.95 *(978-1-77085-615-8(3),* 9781770856158) Firefly Bks., Ltd.

Schaefer, Lola M. Some Kids Are Blind, 1 vol. 2007. (Understanding Differences Ser.). (ENG., Illus.). 24p. (gr. k-1). 21.99 *(978-1-4296-0810-7(2),* Pebble Bks.) Capstone Press of Coughlan Cos.

—Some Kids Are Blind. Saunders-Smith, Gail, ed. rev. ed. 2008. (Understanding Differences Ser.). (ENG., Illus.). 24p. (gr. k-1). pap. 6.29 *(978-1-4296-1774-1(8),* Pebble Bks.) Capstone Press of Coughlan Cos.

Seeing Color It's My Rainbow Too: An Introduction to Color Vision Deficiency. 2003. (J). per. 11.95 *(978-0-9743520-0-8(4))* CVD Publishing.

Souder, Patricia. Blindness & Vision Impairment. Albers, Lisa et al, eds. 2014. (Living with a Special Need Ser.: 16). 128p. (J). (gr. 7-18). 25.95 *(978-1-4222-3030-5(9))* Mason Crest.

Souder, Patti. A Different Way of Seeing: Youth with Blindness & Vision Impairment. 2004. (Youth with Special Needs Ser.). (Illus.). 128p. (YA). 24.95 *(978-1-59084-733-6(4))* Mason Crest.

—A Different Way of Seeing: Youth with Visual Impairments & Blindness. 2003. (Youth with Special Needs Ser.). (Illus.). 127p. (YA). (gr. 7). pap. 14.95 *(978-1-4222-0418-4(9))* Mason Crest.

Stewart, Sheila & Flath, Camden. Seeing with Your Fingers: Kids with Blindness & Visual Impairment. 2010. (Kids with Special Needs Ser.). (Illus.). 48p. (YA). (gr. 7-18). lib. bdg. 19.95 *(978-1-4222-1716-0(7))* Mason Crest.

Sutcliffe, Jane. Helen Keller. Verstraete, Elaine, illus. 2003. (On My Own Biographies Ser.). 48p. (J). (gr. 1-3). 6.95 *(978-0-87614-903-4(4),* Carolrhoda Bks.) Lerner Publishing Group.

Tingle, Tim. Saltypie: A Choctaw Journey from Darkness into Light. Clarkson, Karen, illus. 2010. (ENG.). 40p. (J). (gr. 2-6). 17.95 *(978-1-933693-67-5(3))* Cinco Puntos Pr.

BLIND—BIOGRAPHY

Adler, David A. Helen Keller. Wallner, John, illus. 2006. (ENG.). 32p. (J). (gr. -1-3). 4.95 *(978-0-8234-2042-1(6))* Holiday Hse., Inc.

Barry, Holly M. Helen Keller's Best Friend Belle. Thermes, Jennifer, illus. 2013. (ENG.). 32p. (J). (gr. -1-3). 16.99 *(978-0-8075-3198-3(7))* Whitman, Albert & Co.

Berne, Emma Carlson. What's Your Story, Helen Keller? 2015. (ENG., Illus.). 32p. (J). (gr. k-3). 26.65 *(978-1-4677-7968-5(7))* Lerner Publishing Group.

Beyer, Mark. Stevie Wonder. 2006. (Rock & Roll Hall of Famers Ser.). (Illus.). 112p. (YA). (gr. 5-8). lib. bdg. 34.60 *(978-0-8239-3525-3(6))* Rosen Publishing Group, Inc., The.

Davidson, Margaret. Louis Braille. Compere, Janet, illus. (FRE.). 80p. (J). pap. 5.99 *(978-0-590-71110-4(5))* Scholastic, Inc.

Gillette-Simms, Verdina. My Champion's Eyes: Blind but Not Defeated. 2012. 28p. pap. 7.95 *(978-1-936513-32-1(3))* PearlStone Publishing, Inc.

Hall, Becky. Morris & Buddy: The Story of the First Seeing Eye Dog, 1 vol. Ettlinger, Doris, illus. 2007. (ENG.). 40p. (J). (gr. 2-3). 16.99 *(978-0-8075-5284-1(4))* Whitman, Albert & Co.

Harrah, Madge. Blind Boone: Piano Prodigy. 2004. (Trailblazers Biographies Ser.). (Illus.). 112p. (J). (gr. 5-9). lib. bdg. 30.60 *(978-1-57505-057-7(9))* Lerner Publishing Group.

Hopkinson, Deborah. Annie & Helen. Colón, Raúl, illus. 2012. (ENG.). 48p. (J). (gr. -1-3). 17.99 *(978-0-375-85706-5(0),* Schwartz & Wade Bks.) Random Hse. Children's Bks.

Rubin, Laurie. Do You Dream in Color? Insights from a Girl Without Sight. 2012. (ENG., Illus.). 400p. (J). (gr. 7). pap. 18.95 *(978-1-60980-424-4(4),* Triangle Square) Seven Stories Pr.

Sloate, Susan. Ray Charles: Young Musician. Henderson, Meryl, illus. 2007. (Childhood of Famous Americans Ser.). (ENG.). 176p. (J). (gr. 3-7). pap. 6.99 *(978-1-4169-1437-2(4),* Simon & Schuster/Paula Wiseman Bks.) Simon & Schuster/Paula Wiseman Bks.

Watson, Cindy. Out of Darkness: The Jeff Healey Story. 2010. (ENG., Illus.). 144p. (YA). (gr. k-6). pap. 19.99 *(978-1-55488-706-4(2),* 9781554887064) Dundurn CAN. Dist: Ingram Publisher Services.

BLIND, DOGS FOR THE

see Guide Dogs

BLIND—EDUCATION

Cunningham, Ann Elizabeth. Sadie Can Count: A Multi-sensory Book Cunningham, Ann Elizabeth, illus. l.t. ed. 2006. (Illus.). 16p. (J). bds. 29.95 *(978-0-9770054-8-2(8))* Sensational Bks.

Rappaport, Doreen. Helen's Big World: The Life of Helen Keller. Tavares, Matt, illus. 2012. (Big Words Ser.). (ENG.). 48p. (J). (gr. 1-3). 17.99 *(978-0-7868-0890-8(X))* Hyperion Pr.

Souder, Patti. A Different Way of Seeing: Youth with Blindness & Vision Impairment. 2004. (Youth with Special Needs Ser.). (Illus.). 128p. (YA). 24.95 *(978-1-59084-733-6(4))* Mason Crest.

BLIND—FICTION

Aina, Olaiya. The Boy, the Dove, & the Hawk. 2010. 20p. pap. 13.80 *(978-1-4269-3298-4(7))* Trafford Publishing.

Anderson, Laurie Halse. Teacher's Pet. 2009. (Vet Volunteers Ser.: 7). (ENG.). 160p. (J). (gr. 3-7). 6.99 *(978-0-14-241252-7(X),* Puffin Books) Penguin Young Readers Group.

Auxier, Jonathan. Peter Nimble & His Fantastic Eyes. (ENG.). 400p. (J). (gr. 3-7). 2012. pap. 9.95 *(978-1-4197-0421-5(4))* 2011. 19.95 *(978-1-4197-0025-5(1))* Abrams, Inc. (Amulet Bks.).

Bauer, Marion Dane. The Double-Digit Club. 2004. (ENG.). 126p. (J). (gr. 4-6). tchr. ed. 16.95 *(978-0-8234-1805-3(7))* Holiday Hse., Inc.

Bellingham, Brenda. Lilly Makes a Friend. MacDonald, Clarke, illus. 2004. 62p. (J). lib. bdg. 12.00 *(978-1-4242-1221-7(9))* Fitzgerald Bks.

Best, Cari. My Three Best Friends & Me, Zulay. Brantley-Newton, Vanessa, illus. 2015. (ENG.). 40p. (J). (gr. -1-3). 17.99 *(978-0-374-38819-5(9),* 9780374388195, Farrar, Straus & Giroux (BYR)) Farrar, Straus & Giroux.

Bevins, Rose. Coming to Terms. 2004. (Cover-To-Cover Books). (Illus.). 64p. pap. 9.00 *(978-0-7891-6018-8(8));* 56p. (J). (gr. 1-4). lib. bdg. 16.95 *(978-0-7569-1371-7(3))* Perfection Learning Corp.

Black, Chuck. The Light of the Last, Bk. 3. 2016. (Wars of the Realm Ser.). (ENG.). 368p. (YA). (gr. 7). pap. 11.99 *(978-1-60142-506-5(6),* Multnomah Bks.) Crown Publishing Group.

Bolme, Edward Sarah. Jesus Helps a Blind Man. Gillette, Tim, illus. l.t. ed. 2003. 20p. (J). bds. 6.99 *(978-0-9725546-2-6(9))* CREST Pubns.

Bortner, Lynn A. Color My World. 2010. 28p. pap. 16.95 *(978-1-4269-3327-1(4))* Trafford Publishing.

Bragg, Jane. Teddy Bears Christmas Miracle. 2009. 49p. pap. 18.70 *(978-0-557-22087-8(4))* Lulu Pr., Inc.

Carpenter, Angie. Digewi Deer: The Tale of a Blind Deer. Berner Coble, Lynn, ed. 2013. 82p. (J). pap. 8.99 *(978-0-9846724-3-1(5))* Paws and Claws Publishing, LLC.

Chand, Emlyn. Farsighted. 2012. 260p. pap. 12.95 *(978-0-9839308-3-9(X))* Blue Crown Pr.

Clements, Andrew. Things Not Seen. 2004. (ENG.). 256p. (J). (gr. 5-18). reprint ed. pap. 6.99 *(978-0-14-240076-0(9),* Speak) Penguin Young Readers Group.

—Things Not Seen. 2004. 251p. (gr. 5-9). 17.00 *(978-0-7569-2599-4(1))* Perfection Learning Corp.

—Things Not Seen. 2004. 256p. (J). (gr. 4-7). pap. 38.00 incl. audio *(978-1-4000-9014-3(8),* Listening Library) Random Hse. Audio Publishing Group.

Cole, Barbara. Anna & Natalie, 1 vol. Himler, Ronald, illus. 2007. (ENG.). 32p. (J). 16.95 *(978-1-59572-105-1(3))* Star Bright Bks., Inc.

Cole, Barbara H. Anna & Natalie, 1 vol. Himler, Ronald, illus. 2010. (ENG.). 32p. (J). pap. 6.95 *(978-1-59572-211-9(4))* Star Bright Bks., Inc.

Condra, Estelle. See the Ocean. 7.95 *(978-1-57102-178-6(7),* Ideal Pubns.) Worthy Publishing.

Creech, Sharon. Granny Torrelli Makes Soup. Raschka, Chris, illus. 2012. (ENG.). 160p. (J). (gr. 3-7). reprint ed. pap. 6.99 *(978-0-06-440960-5(0))* HarperCollins Pubs.

—Granny Torrelli Makes Soup. Raschka, Chris, illus. 2004. (Joanna Cotler Bks.). 141p. (gr. 3-7). 17.00 *(978-0-7569-4604-3(2))* Perfection Learning Corp.

Crockett-Blassingame, Linda, illus. See the Ocean. 2006. 32p. (J). 14.95 *(978-0-9778143-0-5(0))* Inclusive Books LLC.

Cummings, Priscilla. Blindsided. (ENG.). (J). (gr. 5-18). 2011. 256p. 7.99 *(978-0-14-241902-1(8),* Puffin Books) 2010. 240p. 16.99 *(978-0-525-42161-0(0),* Dutton Books for Young Readers) Penguin Young Readers Group.

Cummins, Maria S. The Lamplighter. 2011. 308p. pap. 16.99 *(978-1-61203-228-3(1))* Bottom of the Hill Publishing.
Curtis, Marci Lyn. The One Thing. (ENG., Illus.). 336p. (YA). (gr. 7-12). 2017. pap. 9.99 *(978-1-4847-3761-3(X))* 2015. 17.99 *(978-1-4847-0902-3(0))* Hyperion Bks. for Children.
DeWoskin, Rachel. Blind. 2014. (ENG.). 416p. (YA). (gr. 7). 17.99 *(978-0-670-78522-3(9)*, Viking Books for Young Readers) Penguin Young Readers Group.
Dewoskin, Rachel. Blind. 2016. (ENG.). 416p. (YA). (gr. 7). pap. 10.99 *(978-0-14-242455-1(2)*, Speak) Penguin Young Readers Group.
Dorris, Michael. Sees Behind Trees. 104p. (J). (gr. 4-6). pap. 4.95 *(978-0-8072-1516-6(3)*, Listening Library) Random Hse. Audio Publishing Group.
Friedman, Michelle. Close Your Eyes. 2013. (Illus.). 32p. 25.95 *(978-1-4582-1217-7(3)*, Abbott Pr.) Author Solutions, Inc.
Fullwood, Millie. Daddy's Not Afraid of the Dark. 2008. 40p. 17.95 *(978-1-4357-0633-0(1))* Lulu Pr., Inc.
Gantos, Jack. What Would Joey Do? 2004. (Joey Pigza Ser.). 229p. (J). (gr. 5-9). 13.65 *(978-0-7569-2597-0(5))* Perfection Learning Corp.
—What Would Joey Do? 2004. (Joey Pigza Ser.: Bk. 3). 240p. (J). (gr. 5-9). pap. 36.00 incl. audio *(978-1-4000-9020-4(2)*, Listening Library) Random Hse. Audio Publishing Group.
—What Would Joey Do? 2014. (Joey Pigza Ser.: 3). (ENG.). 256p. (J). (gr. 5-9). pap. 7.99 *(978-1-250-06169-0(5)*, 9781250061690) Square Fish.
Gellman, Ellie. Jeremy's Dreidel. Mola, Maria, illus. 2012. (Hanukkah Ser.). 32p. (J). (gr. k-3). (ENG.). lib. bdg. 17.95 *(978-0-7613-7507-4(4))*; (SPA & ENG.). 7.95 *(978-0-7613-7508-1(2))* Lerner Publishing Group. (Kar-Ben Publishing).
Goldin, Barbara Diamond. Cakes & Miracles: A Purim Tale, 0 vols. Zollars, Jaime, illus. 2010. (ENG.). 32p. (J). (gr. k-3). 17.99 *(978-0-7614-5701-5(1)*, 9780761457015, Amazon Children's Publishing) Amazon Publishing.
Goodman, Peggy. Ritzi's Bath. Bunker, Thomas, illus. 2012. 28p. 24.95 *(978-1-4560-4138-0(X))* America Star Bks.
Gutman, Dan. The Million Dollar Putt. 2007. 69p. (J). (gr. 3-7). 13.65 *(978-0-7569-8281-2(2))* Perfection Learning Corp.
Hamil, Nicole. The Magic of Elie. 2009. (Illus.). 36p. pap. 15.49 *(978-1-4389-5545-2(6))* AuthorHouse.
Hammonds, Claudia Muttart. Dreaming in Color. 2004. 232p. 26.45 *(978-1-4184-0355-3(5))* AuthorHouse.
Henry, April. Count All Her Bones. 2017. (Girl, Stolen Ser.). (ENG.). 240p. (YA). 17.99 *(978-1-62779-591-3(X)*, 9781627795913, Holt, Henry & Co. Bks. For Young Readers) Holt, Henry & Co.
—Girl, Stolen. 2010. (Girl, Stolen Ser.). (ENG.). 224p. (YA). (gr. 7-12). 18.99 *(978-0-8050-9005-5(3)*, 9780805090055, Holt, Henry & Co. Bks. For Young Readers) Holt, Henry & Co.
Hubler, Marsha. Leading the Way, 1 vol. 2010. (Keystone Stables Ser.). (ENG.). 128p. (J). pap. 7.99 *(978-0-310-71796-6(5))* Zonderkidz.
Johnson, Judy K. What Is It Like to Be Blind? 2009. 34p. pap. 15.58 *(978-0-557-08477-7(6))* Lulu Pr., Inc.
Keplinger, Kody. Run. (ENG.). 304p. (gr. 9). 2017. (J). pap. 10.99 ***(978-0-545-83114-7(8)**, Scholastic Paperbacks)* 2016. (YA). 17.99 *(978-0-545-83113-0(X)*, Scholastic Pr.) Scholastic, Inc.
Kinsey-Warnock, Natalie. Lumber Camp Library. Bernardin, James, illus. 2003. (ENG.). 96p. (J). (gr. 2-5). pap. 4.99 *(978-0-06-444292-3(6))* HarperCollins Pubs.
Kristie Smith-Armand M.Ed Ctvi. Adventures of Abby Diamond: Out of Sight. 2009. 300p. pap. 18.95 *(978-1-4401-7013-3(4))* iUniverse, Inc.
Kristie Smith-Armand M.Ed Tvi. Adventures of Abby Diamond: Abby Diamond in Teenage Wizard & Secrets in the Attic. 2009. 276p. pap. 17.95 *(978-1-4401-6626-6(9))* iUniverse, Inc.
Lang, Glenna. Looking Out for Sarah. Lang, Glenna, illus. 2003. (ENG., Illus.). 32p. (J). (gr. -1-3). pap. 7.95 *(978-1-57091-607-6(1))* Charlesbridge Publishing, Inc.
Lean, Sarah. A Dog Called Homeless. 2012. (ENG.). 208p. (J). (gr. 3-7). 16.99 *(978-0-06-212220-9(7)*, Tegen, Katherine Bks) HarperCollins Pubs.
Lewis, Joan Lane. See with Me. Hough, Hannah Bliss, illus. 2011. 32p. pap. 24.95 *(978-1-4626-2347-1(6))* America Star Bks.
Lindstrom, Eric. Not If I See You First. 2015. (ENG.). 320p. (YA). (gr. 10-17). 18.00 *(978-0-316-25985-9(3))* Little Brown & Co.
Lupica, Mike. Million-Dollar Throw. 2010. (ENG.). 272p. (J). (gr. 5-18). 7.99 *(978-0-14-241558-0(8)*, Puffin Books) Penguin Young Readers Group.
—Million-Dollar Throw. 2010. (Million Dollar Sports Ser.). lib. bdg. 18.40 *(978-0-606-25316-1(5)*, Turtleback) Turtleback Bks.
Madden, Kerry. Gentle's Holler. 2007. (Maggie Valley Ser.). 237p. (gr. 4-7). 17.00 *(978-0-7569-8090-0(9))* Perfection Learning Corp.
Martin, Rebecca. Eyes for My Heart. 2003. (Illus.). 269p. 10.20 *(978-0-7399-2308-5(0)*, 2231) Rod & Staff Pubs., Inc.
McMurtry, Robby, tr. Song of Moon Pony. 2003. (Illus.). 17.95 *(978-1-57168-740-1(8))* Eakin Pr.
Mead, Richelle. Soundless. l.t. ed. 2016. (ENG.). 352p. 25.99 *(978-1-4104-8817-6(9))* Cengage Gale.
—Soundless. 2015. (ENG.). 272p. (YA). (gr. 7-10). 19.99 *(978-1-59514-763-9(2)*, Razorbill) Penguin Publishing Group.
Mead, Richelle & Loftin, Nikki. Soundless. 2016. (ENG.). 288p. (YA). (gr. 7). 10.99 *(978-1-59514-764-6(0)*, Razorbill) Penguin Young Readers Group.
Miller, Sarah. Miss Spitfire: Reaching Helen Keller. (ENG.). (J). (gr. 5-7). 2010. 256p. pap. 7.99 *(978-1-4424-0851-7(0))* 2007. 240p. 17.99 *(978-1-4169-2542-2(2))* Simon & Schuster Children's Publishing. (Atheneum Bks. for Young Readers).
O'Donnell, Liam. Ginger Leads the Way. Diefendorf, Cathy, illus. (Pet Tales Ser.). (ENG.). 32p. (J). (gr. -1-2). 2005. 2.95 *(978-1-59249-359-3(9)*, 1B024) 2005. 4.95 *(978-1-59249-358-6(0)*, 1B023) 2004. 9.95 *(978-1-59249-360-9(2)*, 1B025) Soundprints.
Petrillo, Genevieve & Lyon, Lea. Keep Your Ear on the Ball, 1 vol. Lyon, Lea07, illus. 2009. (ENG.). 32p. (gr. 2-6). pap. 7.95 *(978-0-88448-324-3(X)*, 884324) Tilbury Hse. Pubs.
—Keep Your Ear on the Ball, 1 vol. Lyon, Lea, illus. 2007. (ENG., Illus.). 32p. (J). (gr. -1-3). 16.95 *(978-0-88448-296-3(0))* Tilbury Hse. Pubs.
Pitts, Constance. Chulita the Blind Cat. 2007. (Illus.). 48p. (J). *(978-0-9652902-2-7(0))* Beevinwood, Inc.
Reynolds, Jason. As Brave As You. (ENG.). 432p. (J). (gr. 5). 2017. pap. 7.99 *(978-1-4814-1591-0(3)*, Atheneum Bks. for Young Readers) 2016. (Illus.). 16.99 *(978-1-4814-1590-3(5)*, Atheneum/Caitlyn Dlouhy Books) Simon & Schuster Children's Publishing.
Richards, Laura Elizabeth Howe. Melody. 2007. 76p. (gr. 4-7). per. *(978-1-4068-3865-7(9))* Echo Library.
Ries, Lori. Aggie Gets Lost. Dormer, Frank W., illus. 2011. (ENG.). 48p. (J). (gr. -1-3). 12.95 *(978-1-57091-633-5(0))* Charlesbridge Publishing, Inc.
Rodanas, Kristina. The Blind Hunter, 1 vol. Rodanas, Kristina, illus. 2003. (ENG., Illus.). 32p. (J). (gr. 1-4). 16.95 *(978-0-7614-5132-7(3))* Marshall Cavendish Corp.
Rue, Nancy N. Lucy Out of Bounds, 1 vol. 2016. (Faithgirlz / a Lucy Novel Ser.). (ENG.). 224p. (J). pap. 7.99 *(978-0-310-75505-0(0))* Zonderkidz.
Sachar, Louis. The Cardturner. 2011. (ENG.). 352p. (YA). (gr. 7). pap. 9.99 *(978-0-385-73663-3(0)*, Ember) Random Hse. Children's Bks.
—The Cardturner. 2011. lib. bdg. 20.85 *(978-0-606-23428-3(4)*, Turtleback) Turtleback Bks.
Sedgwick, Marcus. She Is Not Invisible. 2014. (ENG.). 224p. (YA). (gr. 7). 16.99 *(978-1-59643-801-9(0)*, 9781596438019) Roaring Brook Pr.
—She Is Not Invisible. 2015. (ENG.). 240p. (YA). (gr. 7). pap. 9.99 *(978-1-250-05698-6(5)*, 9781250056986) Square Fish.
Seki, Sunny. Yuko-Chan & the Daruma Doll: The Adventures of a Blind Japanese Girl Who Saves Her Village. 2012. (ENG., Illus.). 32p. (J). (gr. -1-3). 15.95 *(978-4-8053-1187-5(8))* Tuttle Publishing.
Spurling, Wesley. Books for Jacob. 2009. 24p. pap. 14.79 *(978-1-4389-2231-7(0))* AuthorHouse.
Stahler, David, Jr. The Seer. 2008. 320p. (J). pap. 6.99 *(978-0-06-052290-2(9)*, Eos) HarperCollins Pubs.
—Truesight. 2004. (Illus.). (ENG.). 256p. (YA). (gr. 8-18). pap. 8.99 *(978-0-06-052287-2(9)*, HarperTeen); Vol. 1. 192p. (J). (gr. 7-18). lib. bdg. 16.89 *(978-0-06-052286-5(0))* HarperCollins Pubs.
Stevens, Eric & Fuentes, Benny. Skateboard Sonar, 1 vol. Sandoval, Gerardo, illus. 2010. (Sports Illustrated Kids Graphic Novels Ser.). (ENG.). 56p. (gr. 2-3). pap. 7.19 *(978-1-4342-2295-4(0))*; 26.65 *(978-1-4342-1910-7(0))* Stone Arch Bks.
Stockstill, Gloria McQueen. The Blind Man by the Road. Girouard, Patricia L., illus. 2003. (Listen! Look! Ser.). 20p. (J). bds. 5.49 *(978-0-7586-0144-5(1))* Concordia Publishing Hse.
Stokes, K. Lynn. Clouded Visions. 2008. 208p. 24.95 *(978-0-595-51980-4(6))*; pap. 14.95 *(978-0-595-53217-9(9))* iUniverse, Inc.
Sundquist, Josh. Love & First Sight. 2017. (ENG.). 288p. (YA). (gr. 7-17). 17.99 *(978-0-316-30535-8(9))* Little Brown & Co.
Taylor, Theodore. Timothy of the Cay. 2007. (ENG., Illus.). 176p. (J). (gr. 5-7). pap. 6.99 *(978-0-15-206320-7(X))* Houghton Mifflin Harcourt Publishing Co.
Thomas, Leah. Because You'll Never Meet Me. 2015. (ENG.). 352p. (YA). (gr. 9-12). 17.99 *(978-1-61963-590-6(9)*, 9781619635906, Bloomsbury USA Childrens) Bloomsbury Publishing USA.
Tolley, Diane Stringham & Tolley, Diane Stringam. Carving Angels. 2011. 121p. (J). 12.99 *(978-1-59955-944-5(7)*, Bonneville Bks.) Cedar Fort, Inc./CFI Distribution.
Townley, Roderick. Sky. 2010. (ENG.). 272p. (YA). (gr. 7). pap. 12.99 *(978-1-4423-3973-6(X)*, Atheneum Bks. for Young Readers) Simon & Schuster Children's Publishing.
Turner, Rosebud Alford. Through Talen's Eyes: A Visit to Grandma's House. 2012. 26p. (-18). pap. 10.99 *(978-0-9885180-0-1(7))* Mindstir Media.
Vrabel, Beth. A Blind Guide to Normal. 2016. (ENG.). 272p. (J). (gr. 2-7). 16.99 *(978-1-5107-0228-8(8)*, Sky Pony Pr.) Skyhorse Publishing Co., Inc.
—A Blind Guide to Stinkville. (ENG.). (J). (gr. 2-7). 2016. 280p. pap. 7.99 *(978-1-5107-0382-7(9))* 2015. 264p. 16.99 *(978-1-63450-157-6(8))* Skyhorse Publishing Co., Inc. (Sky Pony Pr.).
Walko. Amigos: Friends Forever. 2012. (ENG., Illus.). 28p. (J). (gr. -1-k). 16.95 *(978-1-61608-388-5(3)*, 608388, Sky Pony Pr.) Skyhorse Publishing Co., Inc.
Willard, Elizabeth Kimmel. Mary Ingalls on Her Own. 2007. (Little House Sequel Ser.). (ENG.). 192p. (J). (gr. 3-7). 16.99 *(978-0-06-000905-2(5))* HarperCollins Pubs.

BLIND—REHABILITATION

see Blind—Education

BLOCK PRINTING

see Wood-Engraving

BLOOD

Farndon, John. Stickmen's Guide to Your Beating Heart. Dean, Venitia, illus. 2017. (Stickmen's Guides to Your Awesome Body Ser.). (ENG.). 32p. (J). (gr. 3-6). 26.65 ***(978-1-5124-3215-2(6))*** Lerner Publishing Group.
Furgang, Kathy. My Heart. 2009. (My Body Ser.). 24p. (gr. 3-3). 42.50 *(978-1-61514-689-5(X)*, PowerKids Pr.) Rosen Publishing Group, Inc., The.
Guillain, Charlotte. Nuestra Sangre, 1 vol. 2010. (Nuestros Cuerpos Ser.). (SPA., Illus.). 24p. (gr. -1-1). 22.65 *(978-1-4329-4300-4(6))*; pap. 6.29 *(978-1-4329-4309-7(X))* Heinemann-Raintree. (Bellota).
—Our Blood, 1 vol. 2010. (Our Bodies Ser.). (ENG.). 24p. (gr. -1-1). pap. 6.29 *(978-1-4329-3604-4(2))*; lib. bdg. 22.65 *(978-1-4329-3595-5(X))* Heinemann-Raintree. (Acorn).
Johnson, Rebecca L. Respiration & Circulation. 2007. (Reading Expeditions Ser.). (ENG., Illus.). 32p. (J). pap. 17.95 *(978-0-7922-4586-5(5))* CENGAGE Learning.
Mason, Paul. Your Hardworking Heart & Spectacular Circulatory System. 2015. (Your Brilliant Body! Ser.). (ENG., Illus.). 32p. (J). (gr. 3-7). lib. bdg. *(978-0-7787-2198-7(1))* Crabtree Publishing Co.
Nagelhout, Ryan. The Heart & Blood in Your Body, 1 vol. 2015. (ENG.). 32p. (J). 23.45 *(978-1-62275-640-7(1)*, Britannica Educational Publishing) Rosen Publishing Group, Inc., The.
Newquist, H. P. The Book of Blood: From Legends & Leeches to Vampires & Veins. 2012. (ENG., Illus.). 160p. (J). (gr. 5-7). 18.99 *(978-0-547-31584-3(8))* Houghton Mifflin Harcourt Publishing Co.
Preston, Penny. Controlling the Blood. 2010. (How Your Body Works). 32p. (YA). (gr. 4-7). 28.50 *(978-1-60753-051-0(1))* Amicus Publishing.
—Controlling the Blood. 2012. (Illus.). 32p. (J). (gr. 4-7). pap. 8.95 *(978-1-926722-61-0(2))* Saunders Bk. Co. CAN. Dist: RiverStream Publishing.
Romanek, Trudee. Squirt! The Most Interesting Book You'll Ever Read about Blood. Cowles, Rose, illus. 2006. (Mysterious You Ser.). (ENG.). 40p. (J). (gr. 4-9). 7.95 *(978-1-55337-777-1(X))* Kids Can Pr., Ltd. CAN. Dist: Hachette Bk. Group.
Showers, Paul. A Drop of Blood. Miller, Edward, illus. 2004. (Let's-Read-and-Find-Out Science Ser.). 32p. (J). (gr. k-4). 15.99 *(978-0-06-009108-8(8))*; (ENG.). pap. 5.99 *(978-0-06-009110-1(X)*, Collins); lib. bdg. 16.89 *(978-0-06-009109-5(6))* HarperCollins Pubs.
Stewart, Melissa. Pump It Up! The Secrets of the Heart & Blood. Hamlin, Janet, illus. 2009. (Gross & Goofy Body Ser.). 48p. (gr. 3-4). 29.93 *(978-0-7614-4164-9(6))* Marshall Cavendish Corp.
Stille, Darlene R. Forensic Evidence: Blood. 2008. (ENG., Illus.). 32p. (J). (gr. 6-10). lib. bdg. *(978-0-7787-3815-2(9))* Crabtree Publishing Co.
Winner, Cherie. Circulating Life: Blood Transfusion from Ancient Superstition to Modern Medicine. 2007. (Discovery! Ser.). (ENG., Illus.). 112p. (gr. 6-12). lib. bdg. 31.93 *(978-0-8225-6606-9(0))* Lerner Publishing Group.

BLOOD—CIRCULATION

Ballard, Carol. What Is My Pulse? Blood & Circulation, 1 vol. 2011. (Inside My Body Ser.). (ENG.). 32p. (gr. 3-5). lib. bdg. 30.65 *(978-1-4109-4013-1(6)*, NA-r) Heinemann-Raintree.
Ballen, Karen. A Tour of Your Circulatory System. Jones, Chris B., illus. 2012. (First Graphics: Body Systems Ser.). (ENG.). 24p. (gr. 1-2). pap. 35.70 *(978-1-4296-9323-3(1))*; pap. 6.29 *(978-1-4296-9322-6(3))* Capstone Press of Coughlan Cos.
Bjorklund, Ruth. Circulatory System. 2008. (Amazing Human Body Ser.). 80p. (gr. 5-18). lib. bdg. 34.21 *(978-0-7614-3053-7(9)*, Benchmark Bks.) Marshall Cavendish Corp.
Brett, Flora. Your Circulatory System Works! 2015. (Your Body Systems Ser.). (ENG.). 24p. (gr. 1-2). lib. bdg. 25.32 *(978-1-4914-2063-8(4))* Capstone Press of Coughlan Cos.
Burstein, John. The Amazing Circulatory System: How Does My Heart Work? 2009. (Slim Goodbody's Body Buddies Ser.). (ENG., Illus.). 32p. (J). (gr. 3-5). pap. *(978-0-7787-4431-3(0))*; lib. bdg. *(978-0-7787-4417-7(5))* Crabtree Publishing Co.
Caster, Shannon. Heart. 2010. (Body Works Ser.). (Illus.). 24p. (J). pap. 8.25 *(978-1-4358-9828-8(1)*, PowerKids Pr.); (YA). (gr. 2-5). lib. bdg. 22.60 *(978-1-4358-9370-2(0))* Rosen Publishing Group, Inc., The.
Como Circula la Sangre. (SPA.). 76p. (J). 10.00 *(978-84-342-1467-5(9))* Parramon Ediciones S.A. ESP. Dist: Distribuidora Norma, Inc.
Corcoran, Mary K. The Circulatory Story. Czekaj, Jef, illus. 2010. (ENG.). 44p. (J). (gr. 3-7). pap. 7.95 *(978-1-58089-209-4(4))* Charlesbridge Publishing, Inc.
Donavan, Barbara A. Body Systems: Set of 6: Respiratory & Circulatory. 2011. (Navigators Ser.). (J). 48.00 net. *(978-1-4108-5084-3(6))* Benchmark Education Co.
Elford, Jole Shack. William Harvey & the Mechanics of the Heart. 2005. (Illus.). 141p. (YA). (gr. 6-10). reprint ed. 28.00 *(978-0-7567-9712-6(8))* DIANE Publishing Co.
Gold, John C. The Circulatory & Lymphatic Systems. 2004. (Human Body Library). (Illus.). 48p. (J). lib. bdg. 25.27 *(978-0-7660-2019-1(3))* Enslow Pubs., Inc.
Gold, John Coopersmith. Learning about the Circulatory & Lymphatic Systems. 2013. (Learning about the Human Body Systems Ser.). 48p. (J). (gr. 5-12). pap. 8.95 *(978-1-4644-0234-0(5))*; 25.27 *(978-0-7660-4156-1(5))* Enslow Pubs., Inc.
Gray, Susan H. The Circulatory System. 2014. (Human Body Ser.). (ENG.). 24p. (J). (gr. 2-5). 28.50 *(978-1-62687-334-6(8)*, 207174) Child's World, Inc., The.
Halvorson, Karin. Inside the Blood, 1 vol. 2016. (Super Simple Body Set 2 Ser.). (ENG., Illus.). 32p. (J). (gr. k-4). 27.07 *(978-1-62403-941-6(3))* ABDO Publishing Co.
Holt, Rinehart and Winston Staff. Holt Science & Technology Chapter 23: Life Science: Circulation & Respiration. 5th ed. 2004. (Illus.). pap. 12.86 *(978-0-03-030239-8(0))* Holt McDougal.
Jordan, Apple & Rau, Dana Meachen. My Heart & Blood. 2nd ed. 2013. 24p. (gr. 1-3). 21.36 *(978-1-60870-434-7(3))* Cavendish Square Publishing.
Kingston, Anna & Viegas, Jennifer. The Heart in 3D. 2015. (Human Body In 3D Ser.). (ENG., Illus.). 64p. (J). (gr. 5-6). 32.95 *(978-1-4994-3597-9(5)*, Rosen Central) Rosen Publishing Group, Inc., The.
Kirk, Bill. Circulation Celebration: The Sum of Our Parts Series. Rubie, Eugene, illus. 2010. 24p. pap. 10.95 *(978-1-61633-019-4(8))* Guardian Angel Publishing, Inc.
Leigh, Autumn. The Circulatory System. 2012. (Human Body Ser.). (ENG.). 32p. (J). (gr. 4-6). pap. 10.50 *(978-1-4339-6579-1(8)*, Gareth Stevens Learning Library); lib. bdg. 26.60 *(978-1-4339-6577-7(1))* Stevens, Gareth Publishing LLLP.
Libra, Anna. How Do My Cuts Heal? An Inside Look at the Circulatory System. 2003. (J). *(978-1-58417-003-7(4))*; pap. *(978-1-58417-066-2(2))* Lake Street Pubs.
Manolis, Kay. The Circulatory System. 2009. (Blastoff! Readers Ser.). (ENG., Illus.). 24p. (J). (gr. k-3). 20.00 *(978-0-531-21701-6(9)*, Children's Pr.) Scholastic Library Publishing.
Markle, Sandra. Faulty Hearts: True Survival Stories. 2010. (Powerful Medicine Ser.). (ENG., Illus.). 48p. (J). (gr. 5-8). lib. bdg. 27.93 *(978-0-8225-8699-9(1))* Lerner Publishing Group.
Oleksy, Walter. The Circulatory System. 2009. (Insider's Guide to the Body Ser.). 48p. (gr. 5-8). 53.00 *(978-1-61513-581-3(2)*, Rosen Reference) Rosen Publishing Group, Inc., The.
Orr, Tamra. Super Cool Science Experiments: Circulation. 2009. (Explorer Library: Science Explorer Ser.). (ENG., Illus.). 32p. (gr. 4-8). lib. bdg. 28.50 *(978-1-60279-520-4(7)*, 200304) Cherry Lake Publishing.
Oxlade, Chris. The Circulatory System: Where Do I Get My Energy?, 1 vol. 2014. (Show Me Science Ser.). (ENG., Illus.). 32p. (gr. 3-5). lib. bdg. 30.65 *(978-1-4329-8751-0(8)*, Raintree Perspectives) Heinemann-Raintree.
Randolph, Joanne, ed. Pump It Up: The Heart & Blood. 2017. (Amazing Human Body Ser.). 48p. (J). (gr. 6-6). pap. 11.70 ***(978-0-7660-8985-3(1))*** Enslow Pubs., Inc.
Rau, Dana Meachen. My Heart & Blood. 2013. (Bookworms Fluent — My Body Ser.). 24p. (gr. 1-3). pap. 8.22 *(978-1-62712-034-0(3))* Cavendish Square Publishing.
Rose, Simon. The Cardiovascular System. 2014. (J). *(978-1-4896-1162-8(2))* Weigl Pubs., Inc.
Storad, Conrad J. Circulatory System. 2005. (Illus.). 48p. (YA). pap. 8.95 *(978-0-8225-2518-9(6)*, Lerner Pubns.) Lerner Publishing Group.
—Your Circulatory System. 2012. (Searchlight Books — How Does Your Body Work? Ser.). (ENG., Illus.). 40p. (gr. 3-5). pap. 8.95 *(978-1-58013-959-5(0))*; lib. bdg. 27.93 *(978-0-7613-7447-3(7)*, Lerner Pubns.) Lerner Publishing Group.
Taylor-Butler, Christine. The Circulatory System. 2008. (True Bks.). (ENG.). 48p. (J). (gr. 3-5). pap. 6.95 *(978-0-531-20730-7(7)*, Children's Pr.) Scholastic Library Publishing.
Waldron, Melanie. Your Respiration & Circulation: Understand Them with Numbers, 1 vol. 2014. (Your Body by Numbers Ser.). (ENG.). 48p. (gr. 3-5). lib. bdg. 32.65 *(978-1-4109-5983-6(X))* Heinemann-Raintree.
Whittemore, Susan. The Circulatory System. 2009. (Human Body: How It Works Ser.). 120p. (C). (gr. 9-18). 35.00 *(978-1-60413-376-9(7)*, Chelsea Hse.) Facts On File, Inc.
Wyckoff, Edwin Brit. The African-American Heart Surgery Pioneer: The Genius of Vivien Thomas. 2013. (Genius Inventors & Their Great Ideas Ser.). 48p. (J). (gr. 3-4). pap. 8.95 *(978-1-4644-0210-4(8)*, Enslow Elementary) Enslow Pubs., Inc.
Yount, Lisa. William Harvey: Discoverer of How Blood Circulates. 2008. (Great Minds of Science Ser.). (Illus.). 128p. (J). (gr. 4-10). lib. bdg. 33.27 *(978-0-7660-3010-7(5))* Enslow Pubs., Inc.
—William Harvey: Genius Discoverer of Blood Circulation. 2015. (Genius Scientists & Their Genius Ideas Ser.). 96p. (J). (gr. 5-12). 27.94 *(978-0-7660-6585-7(5))*; pap. 10.95 *(978-0-7660-6586-4(3))* Enslow Pubs., Inc.

BLOOD—DISEASES

Allison, Rose. Everything You Need to Know about Anemia. 2009. (Need to Know Library). 64p. (gr. 5-5). 58.50 *(978-1-60854-053-2(7))* Rosen Publishing Group, Inc., The.
Decker, Janet M., et al. Mononucleosis. 2nd rev. ed. 2008. (Deadly Diseases & Epidemics Ser.). (Illus.). 128p. (C). (gr. 9-18). 34.95 *(978-1-60413-234-2(5)*, Chelsea Hse.) Facts On File, Inc.
Jones, Phill. Sickle Cell Disease. 2008. (Genes & Disease Ser.). 144p. (YA). (gr. 7-12). 35.00 *(978-0-7910-9587-4(8))* Facts On File, Inc.
Ross, Allison J. Everything You Need to Know about Anemia. 2005. (Need to Know Library). (Illus.). 64p. (YA). (gr. 7-12). 31.95 *(978-0-8239-3218-4(4)*, NTANEM) Rosen Publishing Group, Inc., The.
Silverstein, Alvin, et al. The Sickle Cell Anemia Update. 2006. (Disease Update Ser.). (Illus.). 112p. (J). (gr. 4-7). lib. bdg. 33.27 *(978-0-7660-2479-3(2))* Enslow Pubs., Inc.

BLUE (FICTITIOUS CHARACTER)—FICTION

Albee, Sarah. Blue's Checkup. Chernichaw, Ian, illus. 2003. (Blue's Clues Ser.). (ENG.). 24p. (J). pap. 3.99 *(978-0-689-85449-1(8)*, Simon Spotlight/Nickelodeon) Simon Spotlight/Nickelodeon.
—One for Me, One for You: A Book about Sharing. Craig, Karen, illus. 2006. (Blue's Clues Ser.: 20). (ENG.). 24p. (J). (gr. -1-3). pap. 3.99 *(978-1-4169-1300-9(9)*, Simon Spotlight/Nickelodeon) Simon Spotlight/Nickelodeon.

BLUE JAY

Amstutz, Lisa J. Blue Jays. 2016. (Backyard Birds Ser.). (ENG., Illus.). 24p. (gr. k-1). lib. bdg. 26.65 *(978-1-4914-8512-5(4)*, Pebble Plus) Capstone Press of Coughlan Cos.
Ponka, Katherine. A Bird Watcher's Guide to Blue Jays. 2016. (Backyard Bird Watchers Ser.). (ENG., Illus.). 32p. (J). (gr. 2-3). pap. 10.50 *(978-1-4824-3836-9(4))* Stevens, Gareth Publishing LLLP.

BLUE JAY—FICTION

Cronin, Doreen. The Case of the Weird Blue Chicken: The Next Misadventure. 2015. (Chicken Squad Ser.: 2). 35.75 *(978-1-4906-4049-5(5))* Recorded Bks., Inc.
Henson, Tara. The Littlest Blue Jay. 2011. 24p. pap. 15.99 *(978-1-4568-7956-3(1))* Xlibris Corp.
Misty. Tristan, the Youngest Blue Jay. 2012. 24p. 24.95 *(978-1-4626-5184-9(4))* America Star Bks.

BLY, NELLIE, 1867-1922

Bankston, John. Nellie Bly. 2011. (Women of Achievement Ser.). (Illus.). 128p. (gr. 6-12). 35.00 *(978-1-60413-908-2(0)*, Chelsea Hse.) Facts On File, Inc.
Butcher, Nancy. It Can't Be Done, Nellie Bly! A Reporter's Race Around the World, 1 vol. Singh, Jen, illus. 2003. (ENG.). 144p. (J). (gr. 2-5). 12.95 *(978-1-56145-289-7(0))* Peachtree Pubs.
Castaldo, Nancy F. The Race Around the World (Totally True Adventures) Lowe, Wesley, illus. 2015. (Totally True Adventures Ser.). (ENG.). 112p. (J). (gr. 2-5). 4.99 *(978-0-553-52278-5(7)*, Random Hse. Bks. for Young Readers) Random Hse. Children's Bks.
Christensen, Bonnie. The Daring Nellie Bly: America's Star Reporter. 2009. (ENG., Illus.). 32p. (J). (gr. k-3). pap. 7.99 *(978-0-375-85118-6(6)*, Dragonfly Bks.) Random Hse. Children's Bks.
Knudsen, Shannon. Nellie Bly. 2005. (History Maker Bios Ser.). (Illus.). 48p. (J). (gr. 4-7). lib. bdg. 26.60 *(978-0-8225-2943-9(2)*, Lerner Pubns.) Lerner Publishing Group.
Macy, Sue. Bylines: A Photobiography of Nellie Bly. 2009. (Photobiographies Ser.). (ENG., Illus.). 64p. (J). (gr. 5). 19.95 *(978-1-4263-0513-9(3))*; 28.90 *(978-1-4263-0514-6(1))* National Geographic Society. (National Geographic Children's Bks.).

Towsend, Dana. Lonely Orphan Girl: The Story of Nellie Bly. 2005. (Illus.). 32p. (J). *(978-0-7367-2902-4(X))* Zaner-Bloser, Inc.

BOADICEA, QUEEN, -62

Harrison, Paul. Boudicca: Rebelled Against the Romans. 2017. (History VIPs Ser.). (ENG., Illus.). 32p. (J). (gr. 4-6). pap. 12.99 *(978-0-7502-9917-6(7))*, Wayland) Hachette Children's Group GBR. Dist: Hachette Bk. Group.

BOADICIA, QUEEN, -62

see Boadicea, Queen, -62

BOARDING HOUSES

see Hotels, Motels, etc.

BOARDING SCHOOLS

Littlefield, Holly. Children of the Indian Boarding Schools. 2005. (Picture the American Past Ser.). (Illus.). 48p. (J). (gr. 2-5). lib. bdg. 22.60 *(978-1-57505-467-4(1))* Lerner Publishing Group.

Stout, Mary A. Native American Boarding Schools, 1 vol. 2012. (Landmarks of the American Mosaic Ser.). (Illus.). 214p. (C). 64.00 *(978-0-313-38676-3(5))*, A3118C, Greenwood) ABC-CLIO, LLC.

BOARDING SCHOOLS—FICTION

Acosta, Marta. Dark Companion. 2013. (ENG.). 368p. (YA). (gr. 8-12). pap. 10.99 *(978-0-7653-2965-3(4))*, 9780765329653, Tor Teen) Doherty, Tom Assocs., LLC.

Alcott, Louisa May. Jo's Boys. 2005. pap. *(978-1-4065-0107-0(7))* Dodo Pr.

—Jo's Boys. l.t. ed. 2005. 424p. pap. *(978-1-84637-067-0(1))* Echo Library.

—Little Men. l.t. ed. 2005. 564p. pap. *(978-1-84637-068-7(X))* Echo Library.

—Little Men: Life at Plumfield with Jo's Boys. 2013. (Works of Louisa May Alcott). 292p. reprint ed. lthr. 79.00 *(978-0-7812-1629-6(X))* Reprint Services Corp.

Alger, Horatio. Hector's Inheritance: Or, The Boys of Smith Institute. 2006. pap. *(978-1-4065-0708-9(3))* Dodo Pr.

—Hector's Inheritance: Or: the Boys of Smith Institute. 2007. (ENG.). 186p. pap. 19.99 *(978-1-4346-5065-8(0))*; 192p. pap. 21.99 *(978-1-4346-5066-5(9))* Creative Media Partners, LLC.

Alger Jr. Horatio Staff. Hector's Inheritance. rev. ed. 2006. 276p. 28.95 *(978-1-4218-1758-3(6))*; pap. 13.95 *(978-1-4218-1858-0(2))* 1st World Publishing, Inc. (1st World Library - Literary Society).

Allen, C. William. The African Interior Mission. Lee, Xiongpao, illus. 2006. 232p. (J). pap. 20.00 *(978-0-9653308-5-5(0))* Africana Homestead Legacy Pubs., Inc.

Alphin, Elaine Marie. Simon Says. 2005. (ENG.). 264p. (YA). (gr. 9-12). pap. 14.95 *(978-0-15-204678-1(X))* Houghton Mifflin Harcourt Publishing Co.

Anhalt, Ariela. Freefall. 2011. (ENG.). 252p. (YA). (gr. 9). pap. 14.99 *(978-0-547-55216-3(5))* Houghton Mifflin Harcourt Publishing Co.

Arnett, Mindee. The Nightmare Charade. 2015. (Arkwell Academy Ser.: 3). (ENG.). 384p. (YA). (gr. 8-12). 18.99 *(978-0-7653-3335-3(X))*, 9780765333353, Tor Teen) Doherty, Tom Assocs., LLC.

—The Nightmare Dilemma. 2015. (Arkwell Academy Ser.: 2). (ENG.). 400p. (YA). (gr. 8-12). pap. 10.99 *(978-0-7653-3337-7(6))*, 9780765333377, Tor Teen) Doherty, Tom Assocs., LLC.

Baldwin, Kathleen. A School for Unusual Girls: A Stranje House Novel. 2016. (Stranje House Ser.: 1). (ENG.). 352p. (YA). pap. 9.99 *(978-0-7653-7601-5(6))*, 9780765376015, Tor Teen) Doherty, Tom Assocs., LLC.

Beck, Nina. This Book Isn't Fat, It's Fabulous. 2009. (ENG.). 256p. (J). (gr. 9). pap. 8.99 *(978-0-545-01704-6(1))* Scholastic, Inc.

Benson, Amber. Among the Ghosts. Grace, Sina, illus. 2010. (ENG.). 256p. (J). (gr. 3-7). 15.99 *(978-1-4169-9405-3(X))*, Simon & Schuster/Paula Wiseman Bks.) Simon & Schuster/Paula Wiseman Bks.

Bentley, Sue. Classroom Chaos, 2 vols. Swan, Angela & Farley, Andrew, illus. 2008. (Magic Kitten Ser.: 2). (ENG.). 128p. (J). (gr. 1-3). pap. 5.99 *(978-0-448-44999-9(4))*, Grosset & Dunlap) Penguin Young Readers Group.

Berry, Julie. The Scandalous Sisterhood of Prickwillow Place. 2014. (ENG.). 368p. (J). (gr. 5-9). 15.99 *(978-1-59643-956-6(4))*, 9781596439566) Roaring Brook Pr.

Blyton, Enid. St Clare's: 02: the o'Sullivan Twins at St Clare's St Clare's: 02: the o'Sullivan Twin. 2016. (St Clare's Ser.). (ENG., Illus.). 192p. (J). (gr. 4-7). pap. ***(978-1-4449-3000-9(1))*** Hachette Children's Group GBR. Dist: Hachette Bk. Group.

Boie, Kirsten. The Princess Trap. (ENG.). 416p. (J). (gr. 5-9). 2012. pap. 7.99 *(978-0-545-22262-4(1))* 2010. 17.99 *(978-0-545-22261-7(3))* Scholastic, Inc. (Chicken Hse., The).

Bray, Libba. A Great & Terrible Beauty. 2005. (Gemma Doyle Trilogy Ser.: Bk. 1). (ENG.). 432p. (YA). (gr. 7). reprint ed. pap. 9.99 *(978-0-385-73231-4(7))*, Ember) Random Hse. Children's Bks.

—Rebel Angels. 2006. (Gemma Doyle Trilogy Ser.: Bk. 2). (ENG.). 576p. (YA). (gr. 7-12). pap. 10.99 *(978-0-385-73341-0(0))*, Ember) Random Hse. Children's Bks.

—The Sweet Far Thing. 2009. (Gemma Doyle Trilogy Ser.: Bk. 3). (ENG.). 848p. (YA). (gr. 7). pap. 10.99 *(978-0-440-23777-8(7))*, Ember) Random Hse. Children's Bks.

Brazil, Angela. Monitress Merle. 2004. reprint ed. pap. 19.95 *(978-1-4191-3491-3(4))* Kessinger Publishing, LLC.

Brian, Kate. A Private Collection, 4 vols., Set, Vols. 1-4. 2007. (Private Ser.: Nos. 1-4). (ENG.). 1032p. (YA). (gr. 9). pap. 34.99 *(978-1-4169-5818-5(5))*, Simon & Schuster Bks. For Young Readers) Simon & Schuster Bks. For Young Readers.

Brian, Kate, pseud. Ambition. 2008. (Private Ser.: No. 7). (ENG.). 288p. (YA). (gr. 9-18). pap. 12.99 *(978-1-4169-5882-6(7))*, Simon & Schuster Bks. For Young Readers) Simon & Schuster Bks. For Young Readers.

—Beautiful Disaster. 2009. (Privilege Ser.: No. 2). (ENG.). 288p. (YA). (gr. 9-18). pap. 9.99 *(978-1-4169-6760-6(5))*, Simon & Schuster Bks. For Young Readers) Simon & Schuster Bks. For Young Readers.

—The Book of Spells. 2011. (Private Ser.). (ENG.). 320p. (YA). (gr. 9). pap. 9.99 *(978-1-4424-1237-8(2))*, Simon & Schuster Bks. For Young Readers) Simon & Schuster Bks. For Young Readers.

—Last Christmas: The Private Prequel. 2010. (Private Ser.). (ENG.). 288p. (YA). (gr. 9). pap. 9.99 *(978-1-4169-1370-2(X))*, Simon & Schuster Bks. For Young Readers) Simon & Schuster Bks. For Young Readers.

—Ominous. 2011. (Private Ser.). (ENG.). 224p. (YA). (gr. 9-18). pap. 9.99 *(978-1-4169-8472-6(0))*, Simon & Schuster Bks. For Young Readers) Simon & Schuster Bks. For Young Readers.

—Privilege. 2008. (Privilege Ser.: No. 1). (ENG.). 304p. (YA). (gr. 9-18). pap. 9.99 *(978-1-4169-6759-0(1))*, Simon & Schuster Bks. For Young Readers) Simon & Schuster Bks. For Young Readers.

—Scandal. 2010. (Private Ser.: No. 11). (ENG., Illus.). 240p. (YA). (gr. 9-18). pap. 9.99 *(978-1-4169-8470-2(4))*, Simon & Schuster Bks. For Young Readers) Simon & Schuster Bks. For Young Readers.

—Suspicion. 2009. (Private Ser.: No. 10). (ENG.). 224p. (YA). (gr. 9-18). pap. 9.99 *(978-1-4169-5885-7(1))*, Simon & Schuster Bks. For Young Readers) Simon & Schuster Bks. For Young Readers.

—Sweet Deceit. 2010. (Privilege Ser.: Bk. 4). (ENG.). 224p. (YA). (gr. 9-18). pap. 9.99 *(978-1-4169-6762-0(1))*, Simon & Schuster Bks. For Young Readers) Simon & Schuster Bks. For Young Readers.

—Vanished. 2010. (Private Ser.: Bk. 12). (ENG.). 224p. (YA). (gr. 9-18). pap. 9.99 *(978-1-4169-8471-9(2))*, Simon & Schuster Bks. For Young Readers) Simon & Schuster Bks. For Young Readers.

Brissenden, Constance & Loyie, Larry. Goodbye Buffalo Bay, 1 vol. 2008. (ENG.). 160p. pap. 14.95 *(978-1-894778-62-6(6))* Theytus Bks., Ltd. CAN. Dist: Univ. of Toronto Pr.

Brooke, Lauren. All or Nothing. 2007. (Chestnut Hill Ser.: No. 6). 184p. (J). lib. bdg. 15.38 *(978-1-4242-1719-9(9))* Fitzgerald Bks.

—Making Strides. 2005. (Chestnut Hill Ser.: No. 2). 219p. (J). (gr. 4-7). 12.65 *(978-0-7569-6478-8(4))* Perfection Learning Corp.

—The New Class. 2005. (Chestnut Hill Ser.: No. 1). 212p. (J). (gr. 4-7). lib. bdg. 12.65 *(978-0-7569-6479-5(2))* Perfection Learning Corp.

Brown, Jennifer. Pennybaker School Is Headed for Disaster. Kissi, Marta, illus. 2017. (ENG.). 320p. (J). 16.99 *(978-1-68119-174-4(1))*, 9781681191744, Bloomsbury USA Childrens) Bloomsbury Publishing USA.

Bruchac, Joseph. The Dark Pond. Comport, Sally Wern, illus. 2005. 142p. (gr. 5-9). 17.00 *(978-0-7569-5436-9(3))* Perfection Learning Corp.

—Dark Pond. Comport, Sally Wern, illus. 2005. (ENG.). 160p. (J). (gr. 5-18). pap. 6.99 *(978-0-06-052998-7(9))* HarperCollins Pubs.

Burkhart, Jessica. Home Sweet Drama. 2010. (Canterwood Crest Ser.: 8). (ENG.). 240p. (J). (gr. 4-8). pap. 7.99 *(978-1-4169-9040-6(2))*, Aladdin) Simon & Schuster Children's Publishing.

Burnett, Frances Hodgson. A Little Princess. 2008. 156p. 25.95 *(978-1-60664-768-4(7))*; pap. 13.95 *(978-1-60664-141-5(7))* Aegypan.

—A Little Princess. 2008. 212p. (gr. 2-4). 24.99 *(978-0-554-38458-0(2))*; 27.99 *(978-0-554-29155-0(X))* Creative Media Partners, LLC.

—A Little Princess. Aldous, Kate, illus. 2005. 62p. (J). (gr. 4-7). 8.95 *(978-0-7945-1123-4(6))*, Usborne) EDC Publishing.

—A Little Princess. 2012. 212p. pap. 8.99 *(978-1-60796-454-4(6))* Meirovich, Igal.

—A Little Princess. 2012. (ENG., Illus.). 280p. *(978-1-905716-04-3(4))*, Collector's Library, The) Pan Macmillan.

—A Little Princess. 2012. (Puffin Classics Ser.). (ENG., Illus.). 320p. (J). (gr. 5-7). 16.99 *(978-0-14-134171-2(8))*, Puffin Books) Penguin Young Readers Group.

—A Little Princess. Gill, Margery, illus. 2008. (Puffin Classics Ser.). (ENG.). 320p. (J). (gr. 5-7). 5.99 *(978-0-14-132112-7(1))*, Puffin Books) Penguin Young Readers Group.

—A Little Princess. 188p. 2009. pap. 13.95 *(978-1-4385-0876-4(X))* 2008. pap. 13.45 *(978-1-4385-0194-9(3))* Standard Pubns., Inc. (Book Jungle).

—A Little Princess. McKowen, Scott, illus. 2004. (Sterling Unabridged Classics Ser.). (ENG.). 208p. (J). (gr. 5). 9.95 *(978-1-4027-1454-2(8))* Sterling Publishing Co., Inc.

—A Little Princess. Engelbreit, Mary, illus. 2007. (Mary Engelbreit's Classic Library). (ENG.). 304p. (J). (gr. 3-7). 9.99 *(978-0-06-008137-9(6))*, HarperFestival) HarperCollins Pubs.

—A Little Princess. 2012. (Children's Classics Ser.). (ENG.). 186p. pap. 19.99 *(978-1-909438-52-1(9))*, Sovereign) Bollinger, Max GBR. Dist: Lightning Source UK, Ltd.

—A Little Princess. Kliros, Thea, illus. abr. ed. 2012. (Dover Children's Thrift Classics Ser.). (ENG.). 96p. (J). (gr. 3-8). pap. 3.00 *(978-0-486-29171-0(5))* Dover Pubns., Inc.

—A Little Princess: Being the whole story of Sara Crewe now told for T. 2007. 196p. per. 19.99 *(978-1-4346-7028-1(7))*; (ENG.). 210p. per. 22.99 *(978-1-4346-7029-8(5))* Creative Media Partners, LLC.

—A Little Princess: The Story of Sara Crewe. (J). 16.95 *(978-0-8488-1253-9(0))* Amereon Ltd.

—A Little Princess: The Story of Sara Crewe. Warren, Eliza, ed. Marcos, Pablo, illus. 2006. 239p. (YA). reprint ed. 10.00 *(978-0-7567-9835-2(3))* DIANE Publishing Co.

—A Little Princess: The Story of Sara Crewe. 2005. 112p. per. 4.95 *(978-1-4209-2529-6(6))* Digireads.com Publishing.

—A Little Princess: The Story of Sara Crewe. 2006. pap. *(978-1-4065-0559-7(5))* Dodo Pr.

—A Little Princess: The Story of Sara Crewe. l.t. ed. 2005. 376p. pap. *(978-1-84637-117-2(1))* Echo Library.

—A Little Princess: The Story of Sara Crewe. 2004. reprint ed. pap. 1.99 *(978-1-4192-0213-1(8))*; pap. 22.95 *(978-1-4191-0213-4(3))* Kessinger Publishing, LLC.

—A Little Princess: The Story of Sara Crewe. 2006. 204p. (YA). 19.95 *(978-1-934169-20-9(X))*; pap. 7.95 *(978-1-934169-21-6(8))* Norilana Bks.

—A Little Princess: The Story of Sara Crewe. 2005. (Twelve-Point Ser.). lib. bdg. 25.00 *(978-1-58287-320-6(8))*; lib. bdg. 26.00 *(978-1-58287-814-0(5))* North Bks.

—A Little Princess: The Story of Sara Crewe. Rust, Graham, illus. (J). pap. 22.95 *(978-0-590-24079-6(X))* Scholastic, Inc.

—A Little Princess: The Story of Sara Crewe. l.t. ed. 2003. 342p. pap. 10.95 *(978-0-7862-6247-2(8))* Thorndike Pr.

—A Little Princess: With a Discussion of Generosity. Gribbon, Sean & Jael, trs. Gribbon, Sean & Jael, illus. 2003. (Values in Action Illustrated Classics Ser.). (J). *(978-1-59203-050-7(5))* Learning Challenge, Inc.

—Petite Princess. pap. 19.95 *(978-2-07-051994-1(5))* Gallimard, Editions FRA. Dist: Distribooks, Inc.

—Sara Crewe. 2011. 66p. 16.95 *(978-1-4638-9633-1(6))* 2009. 68p. pap. 7.95 *(978-1-60664-388-4(6))* Rodgers, Alan Bks.

—Sara Crewe or What Happened at Miss Minchin's. 2006. (ENG.). 88p. per. 8.95 *(978-1-59462-359-2(7))*, 395, Book Jungle) Standard Pubns., Inc.

—Sara Crewe, or What Happened at Miss Minchin's. 2007. 48p. per. *(978-1-4068-4489-4(6))* Echo Library.

Burns, T. R. The Bad Apple. 2013. (Merits of Mischief Ser.: 1). (ENG.). 368p. (J). (gr. 3-7). pap. 7.99 *(978-1-4424-4030-2(9))*, Aladdin) Simon & Schuster Children's Publishing.

—Watch Your Step. (Merits of Mischief Ser.: 3). (ENG., Illus.). (J). (gr. 3-7). 2015. 464p. pap. 7.99 *(978-1-4424-4036-4(8))* 2014. 480p. 16.99 *(978-1-4424-4035-7(X))* Simon & Schuster Children's Publishing. (Aladdin).

—A World of Trouble. (Merits of Mischief Ser.: 2). (ENG., Illus.). (J). (gr. 3-7). 2014. 400p. pap. 7.99 *(978-1-4424-4033-3(3))* 2013. 384p. 16.99 *(978-1-4424-4032-6(5))* Simon & Schuster Children's Publishing. (Aladdin).

Burton, Jennifer. Princess's Journey. 2003. (Topeka Heights Ser.). (YA). (gr. 9-12). pap. 10.99 *(978-0-9724733-0-9(0))* ALEXZUS Bks.

Cach, Lisa. Wake unto Me. 2011. (ENG.). 320p. (YA). (gr. 7-18). 8.99 *(978-0-14-241436-1(0))*, Speak) Penguin Young Readers Group.

Canales, Viola. The Tequila Worm. 2007. (ENG., Illus.). 208p. (YA). (gr. 7-11). pap. 7.99 *(978-0-375-84089-0(3))*, Lamb, Wendy Bks.) Random Hse. Children's Bks.

Cannon, Chris. Trial by Fire. 2016. (ENG., Illus.). 330p. (J). pap. 16.99 *(978-1-68281-140-5(9))* Entangled Publishing, LLC.

Carriger, Gail. Curtsies & Conspiracies. (Finishing School Ser.: 2). (ENG.). (YA). (gr. 7-17). 2014. 336p. pap. 10.00 *(978-0-316-19020-6(9))* 2013. 320p. 18.00 *(978-0-316-19011-4(X))* Little, Brown Bks. for Young Readers.

—Etiquette & Espionage. 2013. (Finishing School Ser.: 1). (ENG.). 320p. (YA). (gr. 7-17). 18.99 *(978-0-316-19008-4(X))* Little Brown & Co.

—Etiquette & Espionage. 2013. (Finishing School Ser.: 1). (ENG.). 336p. (YA). (gr. 7-17). pap. 10.99 *(978-0-316-19010-7(1))* Little, Brown Bks. for Young Readers.

—Manners & Mutiny. 2015. (Finishing School Ser.: 4). (ENG., Illus.). 336p. (YA). (gr. 7-17). 18.00 *(978-0-316-19028-2(4))* Little, Brown Bks. for Young Readers.

—Manners & Mutiny. 2016. (Finishing School Ser.: 4). (ENG., Illus.). 352p. (YA). (gr. 7-17). pap. 10.99 *(978-0-316-19029-9(2))* Little, Brown Bks. for Young Readers.

—Waistcoats & Weaponry. 2014. (Finishing School Ser.: 3). (ENG.). 304p. (YA). (gr. 7-17). 18.00 *(978-0-316-19027-5(6))* Little Brown & Co.

—Waistcoats & Weaponry. 2015. (Finishing School Ser.: 3). (ENG.). 320p. (YA). (gr. 7-17). pap. 10.00 *(978-0-316-19025-1(X))* Little, Brown Bks. for Young Readers.

Carter, Ally. Only the Good Spy Young. 2016. (Gallagher Girls Ser.: 4). (J). lib. bdg. 20.85 *(978-0-606-38298-4(4))* Turtleback Bks.

Carvell, Marlene. Sweetgrass Basket. 2005. (ENG.). 256p. (J). (gr. 5-6). 16.99 *(978-0-525-47547-7(8))*, Dutton Books for Young Readers) Penguin Young Readers Group.

Caulfield, Annie. Solves Crimes: And So On... 2006. (Katie Milk Ser.). (ENG.). 208p. (J). (gr. 4-7). pap. 9.95 *(978-0-440-86686-2(3))* Transworld Publishers Ltd. GBR. Dist: Independent Pubs. Group.

Cavallaro, Brittany. A Study in Charlotte. 2016. (Charlotte Holmes Novel Ser.: 1). 336p. (YA). (gr. 8). 17.99 *(978-0-06-239890-1(3))*, Tegen, Katherine Bks) HarperCollins Pubs.

Chan, Queenie. The Dreaming Collection. 2010. (ENG., Illus.). 576p. pap. 19.99 *(978-1-4278-1871-3(1))* TOKYOPOP, Inc.

Chapman, Allen. Tom Fairfield's Pluck & Luck. rev. ed. 2006. (ENG.). 184p. 26.95 *(978-1-4218-2018-7(8))*; per. 11.95 *(978-1-4218-2118-4(4))* 1st World Publishing, Inc. (1st World Library - Literary Society).

—Tom Fairfield's Pluck & Luck. 2006. (ENG.). 138p. pap. 18.99 *(978-1-4264-7576-4(4))*; 152p. pap. 21.99 *(978-1-4264-7627-3(2))* Creative Media Partners, LLC.

—Tom Fairfields Pluck & Luck or Working. 2007. pap. *(978-1-4065-1433-9(0))* Dodo Pr.

—Tom Fairfield's Pluck & Luck; or, Working to Clear His Name. 2007. 100p. per. *(978-1-4068-4517-4(5))* Echo Library.

Chapman, Lara. The XYZs of Being Wicked. 2014. (ENG., Illus.). 272p. (J). (gr. 4-8). 17.99 *(978-1-4814-0108-1(4))*, Simon & Schuster/Paula Wiseman Bks.) Simon & Schuster/Paula Wiseman Bks.

Clark, Bridie. Maybe Tonight? 2013. (Snap Decision Ser.: 1). (ENG.). 224p. (YA). (gr. 7). pap. 9.99 *(978-1-59643-816-3(9))* Roaring Brook Pr.

—You Only Live Once. 2014. (Snap Decision Ser.: 2). (ENG.). 224p. (YA). (gr. 7). pap. 9.99 *(978-1-59643-817-0(7))*, 9781596438170) Roaring Brook Pr.

Cleverly, Sophie. The Lost Twin. 2016. (Scarlet & Ivy Ser.: 1). (ENG.). 304p. (J). (gr. 5-8). 16.99 *(978-1-4926-3339-6(9))*, 9781492633396, Sourcebooks Jabberwocky) Sourcebooks, Inc.

Cochran, Molly. Legacy. 2011. (Legacy Ser.). (ENG.). 432p. (YA). (gr. 9). 17.99 *(978-1-4424-1739-7(0))*, Simon & Schuster/Paula Wiseman Bks.) Simon & Schuster/Paula Wiseman Bks.

—Poison. (Legacy Ser.). (ENG., 368p. (YA). (gr. 9). 2014. Illus.). pap. 9.99 *(978-1-4424-5051-6(7))* 2012. 17.99 *(978-1-4424-5050-9(9))* Simon & Schuster/Paula Wiseman Bks. (Simon & Schuster/Paula Wiseman Bks.).

Cook, Eileen. The Education of Hailey Kendrick. 2011. (ENG.). (YA). (gr. 9). 288p. pap. 9.99 *(978-1-4424-1326-9(3))*; 272p. 16.99 *(978-1-4424-1325-2(5))* Simon Pulse. (Simon Pulse).

Cook, Kristi. Eternal. 2013. (ENG., Illus.). 416p. (YA). (gr. 9). 16.99 *(978-1-4424-8532-7(9))*, Simon Pulse) Simon Pulse.

—Haven. (ENG.). (YA). (gr. 9). 2012. 448p. pap. 9.99 *(978-1-4424-0761-9(1))* 2011. 416p. 16.99 *(978-1-4424-0760-2(3))* Simon Pulse. (Simon Pulse).

—Mirage. 2013. (ENG., Illus.). 416p. (YA). (gr. 9). pap. 9.99 *(978-1-4424-4300-6(6))*, Simon Pulse) Simon Pulse.

Coolidge, Susan. What Katy Did at School. 2007. (ENG.). 108p. per. *(978-1-4068-4853-3(0))* Echo Library.

—What Katy Did at School. 2006. (ENG.). 180p. per. 8.95 *(978-1-59462-472-8(0))*, 508, Book Jungle) Standard Pubns., Inc.

—What Katy Did at School. 2004. reprint ed. pap. 20.95 *(978-1-4191-9354-5(6))*; pap. 1.99 *(978-1-4192-9354-2(0))* Kessinger Publishing, LLC.

Creech, Sharon. Bloomability. 2012. (Illus.). 272p. (J). (gr. 3-7). pap. 6.99 *(978-0-06-440823-3(X))* HarperCollins Pubs.

Croall, Marie P. School of Evil. Carruthers, Sandy, illus. 2010. (Twisted Journeys (r) Ser.: 13). (ENG.). 112p. (J). (gr. 4-7). pap. 7.95 *(978-0-8225-9271-6(1))*, Graphic Universe™); lib. bdg. 27.93 *(978-0-8225-9263-1(0))* Lerner Publishing Group.

Davidson, Jenny. The Explosionist. 2008. 464p. (YA). (gr. 7-18). lib. bdg. 18.89 *(978-0-06-123976-2(3))*, HarperTeen) HarperCollins Pubs.

Day, Susie. My Invisible Boyfriend. 2010. (ENG.). 288p. (J). (gr. 7-18). 16.99 *(978-0-545-07354-7(5))*, Scholastic Pr.) Scholastic, Inc.

De Witt, Peter. Toaster Pond. 2006. (ENG.). 248p. (YA). (gr. 7-12). per. 8.95 *(978-1-933255-21-7(8))* DNA Pr.

Deutsch, Stacia. Rotten Apple #1: Mean Ghouls. 2012. (Rotten Apple Ser.). (ENG.). 192p. (J). (gr. 3-7). pap. 5.99 *(978-0-545-39823-7(1))*, Scholastic Paperbacks) Scholastic, Inc.

d'Lacey, Chris. Fire Star. 2008. (Last Dragon Chronicles Ser.: 3). (ENG.). 560p. (J). (gr. 3-7). 8.99 *(978-0-439-90185-7(5))*, Orchard Bks.) Scholastic, Inc.

Dunlap, Susanne. The Academie. 2012. (ENG.). 368p. (YA). 16.99 *(978-1-59990-586-0(8))*, 9781599905860, Bloomsbury USA Childrens) Bloomsbury Publishing USA.

Ehrenhaft, Daniel. Drawing a Blank: Or How I Tried to Solve a Mystery, End a Feud, & Land the Girl of My Dreams. Ristow, Trevor, illus. 2009. (ENG.). 352p. (J). pap. 8.99 *(978-0-06-075254-5(8))*, HarperTeen) HarperCollins Pubs.

Emerson, Alice. Betty Gordon at Boarding School. 2004. reprint ed. pap. 1.99 *(978-1-4192-0976-5(0))*; pap. 20.95 *(978-1-4191-0976-8(6))* Kessinger Publishing, LLC.

Emerson, Alice B. Betty Gordon at Boarding School: The Treasure of Indian Chasm. l.t. ed. 2006. 156p. pap. 24.99 *(978-1-4264-4097-7(9))* Creative Media Partners, LLC.

Farmer, Penelope. Charlotte Sometimes. 2017. (ENG., Illus.). 208p. (gr. 7-9). pap. 9.99 *(978-1-68137-104-7(9))*, NYRB Kids) New York Review of Bks., Inc., The.

García, Cristina. Dreams of Significant Girls. 2011. (ENG.). 256p. (YA). (gr. 9-18). 16.99 *(978-1-4169-7920-3(4))*, Simon & Schuster Bks. For Young Readers) Simon & Schuster Bks. For Young Readers.

Gardam, Jane. Bilgewater. 2016. (ENG.). 208p. pap. 17.00 *(978-1-60945-331-2(X))* Europa Editions, Inc.

Gensler, Sonia. The Revenant. 2013. (ENG.). 354p. (YA). (gr. 7). pap. 9.99 *(978-0-375-86139-0(4))*, Ember) Random Hse. Children's Bks.

Glass, George. Black-Tie Spy. 2013. 94p. (J). pap. *(978-0-545-47271-5(7))* Scholastic, Inc.

Goodman, Carol & Wells, Rosemary. Hawthorn. 2015. (Blythewood Novel Ser.). (ENG.). 416p. (YA). (gr. 7). bds. 17.99 *(978-0-670-78478-3(8))*, Viking Books for Young Readers) Penguin Young Readers Group.

Gratz, Alan. Samurai Shortstop. 2008. (ENG.). 288p. (YA). (gr. 7-18). 7.99 *(978-0-14-241099-8(3))*, Speak) Penguin Young Readers Group.

Grau, Sheila. Dr. Critchlore's School for Minions. Sutphin, Joe, illus. (Dr. Critchlore's School for Minions Ser.). (ENG.). (J). (gr. 3-7). 2016. 304p. pap. 7.95 *(978-1-4197-2029-1(5))* 2015. 288p. 14.95 *(978-1-4197-1370-5(1))* Abrams, Inc. (Amulet Bks.).

Gray, Claudia. Afterlife. 2012. (Evernight Ser.: 4). (ENG.). 384p. (YA). (gr. 8). pap. 9.99 *(978-0-06-128451-9(3))*, HarperTeen) HarperCollins Pubs.

—Evernight. 2009. (Evernight Ser.: 1). (ENG.). 352p. (YA). (gr. 8). pap. 8.99 *(978-0-06-128444-1(0))*, HarperTeen) HarperCollins Pubs.

—Stargazer. (Evernight Ser.: 2). (ENG.). (YA). (gr. 8). 2010. 352p. pap. 8.99 *(978-0-06-128446-5(7))* 2009. 336p. 17.99 *(978-0-06-128440-3(8))* HarperCollins Pubs. (HarperTeen).

Green, John. Looking for Alaska. 2014. (ENG.). 256p. (YA). (gr. 12-12). 14.24 *(978-1-63245-185-9(9))* Lectorum Pubns., Inc.

—Looking for Alaska. 2009. 11.04 *(978-0-7848-1838-1(X))*, Everbind) Marco Bk. Co.

—Looking for Alaska. 2014. *(978-0-525-42728-5(7))*, Dutton Adult) 2006. 20.00 *(978-0-7569-6726-0(0))* Penguin Publishing Group.

—Looking for Alaska. (ENG.). (YA). 2006. 256p. (gr. 9-18). pap. 10.99 *(978-0-14-240251-1(6))*, Speak) 2005. 160p. (gr. 8-12). 18.99 *(978-0-525-47506-4(0))*, Dutton Books for Young Readers) 10th anniv. ed. 2015. 368p. (gr. 9). 19.99 *(978-0-525-42802-2(X))*, Dutton Books for Young Readers) Penguin Young Readers Group.

—Looking for Alaska. l.t. ed. 2016. (ENG.). pap. 13.99 *(978-1-59413-982-6(2))*, Large Print Pr.) Thorndike Pr.

—Looking for Alaska. 2006. 221p. (gr. 7-12). lib. bdg. 20.85 *(978-1-4177-2915-9(5))*, Turtleback) Turtleback Bks.

The Guardians. 2014. (ENG., Illus.). 288p. (J). (gr. 4-8). pap. 7.99 *(978-1-4814-1834-8(3))*, Aladdin) Simon & Schuster Children's Publishing.

Haberdasher, Violet. Knightley Academy. 2011. (ENG.). 512p. (J). (gr. 3-7). pap. 5.99 *(978-1-4169-9144-1(1))*, Aladdin) Simon & Schuster Children's Publishing.

—Knightley Academy. 2010. (ENG.). 480p. (J). (gr. 3-7). 16.99 *(978-1-4169-9143-4(3))*, Simon & Schuster/Paula Wiseman Bks.) Simon & Schuster/Paula Wiseman Bks.

—The Secret Prince. 2011. (ENG.). 512p. (J). (gr. 3-7). 16.99 (978-1-4169-9145-8(X), Simon & Schuster/Paula Wiseman Bks.) Simon & Schuster/Paula Wiseman Bks.
—The Secret Prince: A Knightley Academy Book. 2012. (ENG.). 512p. (J). (gr. 3-7). pap. 7.99 (978-1-4169-9146-5(8), Simon & Schuster/Paula Wiseman Bks.) Simon & Schuster/Paula Wiseman Bks.
Harold, Gwyneth. Bad Girls in School. 2007. (ENG.). 148p. (YA). (gr. 8-12). per. 17.44 (978-0-435-21517-0(5), 21517) Heinemann.
Harrison, Lisi. Alphas. 2009. (Alphas Ser.: 1). (ENG.). 272p. (YA). (gr. 7-17). pap. 9.99 (978-0-316-03579-8(3), Poppy) Little, Brown Bks. for Young Readers.
—Movers & Fakers. 2010. (Alphas Ser.: 2). (ENG.). 240p. (YA). (gr. 7-17). pap. 9.99 (978-0-316-03580-4(7), Poppy) Little, Brown Bks. for Young Readers.
—Top of the Feud Chain. 2011. (Alphas Ser.: 4). (ENG.). 240p. (YA). (gr. 7-17). pap. 9.99 (978-0-316-03582-8(3), Poppy) Little, Brown Bks. for Young Readers.
Harvey, Jacqueline. Alice-Miranda at School. 2012. (ENG.). 272p. (J). (gr. 2-5). 7.99 (978-0-385-73994-8(X), Yearling) Random Hse. Children's Bks.
—Alice-Miranda Takes the Stage. 2013. (ENG.). 304p. (J). (gr. 2-5). 14.99 (978-0-385-74333-4(5), Delacorte Bks. for Young Readers) Random Hse. Children's Bks.
Hawkins, Rachel. Hex Hall, Bk. 1. 2010. (ENG.). 336p. (J). (gr. 7-17). 16.99 (978-1-4231-2130-5(9)) Hyperion Pr.
Henderson, Jason. Vampire Rising. (Alex Van Helsing Ser.: 1). (ENG.). (YA). (gr. 8). 2011. 272p. pap. 8.99 (978-0-06-195100-8(5)) 2010. 256p. 16.99 (978-0-06-195099-5(8)) HarperCollins Pubs. (HarperTeen).
—Voice of the Undead. 2011. (Alex Van Helsing Ser.: 2). (ENG.). 304p. (YA). (gr. 8). 16.99 (978-0-06-195101-5(3), HarperTeen) HarperCollins Pubs.
Hendrickson, David H. Cracking the Ice. 2011. 365p. (YA). (gr. 9-18). 16.95 (978-1-934813-55-3(9)) Westside Bks.
Holder, Nancy. The Screaming Season. 3rd ed. 2011. (Possessions Ser.). (ENG.). 336p. (YA). (gr. 7-18). 9.99 (978-1-59514-333-4(5), Razorbill) Penguin Young Readers Group.
Houston, Julian. New Boy. 2008. (ENG.). 288p. (YA). (gr. 7-12). pap. 7.99 (978-0-618-88405-6(X)) Houghton Mifflin Harcourt Publishing Co.
—New Boy. 2007. 282p. (gr. 7-12). 18.00 (978-0-7569-8139-6(5)) Perfection Learning Corp.
Huang, Charlotte. Going Geek. 2016. (ENG.). 304p. (YA). (gr. 7). 17.99 (978-0-553-53943-1(4), Delacorte Pr.) Random Hse. Children's Bks.
Hutchison, Dot. A Wounded Name. 2013. 320p. 17.95 (978-1-4677-1618-5(9)); (ENG.). (YA). (gr. 7-12). 17.95 (978-1-4677-0887-6(9), Carolrhoda Lab™) Lerner Publishing Group.
Ibbotson, Eva. The Dragonfly Pool. 2009. (ENG.). 384p. (J). (gr. 3-7). 7.99 (978-0-14-241486-6(7), Puffin Books) Penguin Young Readers Group.
—The Dragonfly Pool. 9 vols. 2008. (YA). 122.75 (978-1-4361-5209-9(7)); 120.75 (978-1-4361-5211-2(9)); 90.75 (978-1-4361-5207-5(0)); 1.25 (978-1-4361-5202-0(X)); 256.75 (978-1-4361-5206-8(2)); 92.75 (978-1-4361-5205-1(4)) Recorded Bks., Inc.
Jackson, Gabrielle E. Caps & Capers. 2010. (Illus.). 74p. pap. 14.14 (978-1-153-79856-3(5)) General Bks. LLC.
—Caps & Capers: A Story of Boarding-School Life. Relyea, C. M., illus. 2008. 136p. pap. (978-1-4099-4255-9(4)) Dodo Pr.
Jackson, Gabrielle Emilie Snow. Caps & Capers: A story of boarding-school Life. 2011. 284p. pap. 28.75 (978-1-172-90025-1(6)) Creative Media Partners, LLC.
—Caps & Capers: A Story of Boarding-school Life. 2012. 288p. pap. (978-1-290-08698-1(2)) HardPr.
—Caps & Capers: A Story of Boarding School Life (1901) Relyea, C. M., illus. 284p. 2010. 35.16 (978-1-164-31862-0(4)) 2010. pap. 23.16 (978-1-164-12697-3(0)) 2008. 43.95 (978-1-4366-0917-3(8)) 2008. (ENG.). per. 28.95 (978-0-548-82612-6(9)) Kessinger Publishing, LLC.
—Caps & Capers; a Story of Boarding-School Life. 2010. 72p. pap. 18.84 (978-1-152-81865-1(1)) General Bks. LLC.
Jocelyn, Marthe. What We Hide. (ENG.). 288p. (YA). (gr. 9). 2015. pap. 9.99 (978-0-375-85544-3(0), Ember) 2014. 16.99 (978-0-385-73847-7(1), Lamb, Wendy Bks.) Random Hse. Children's Bks.
Johnson, Maureen. The Madness Underneath. 2013. (Shades of London Ser.: 2). (ENG.). 304p. (YA). (gr. 7). pap. 9.99 (978-0-14-242754-5(3), Speak) Penguin Young Readers Group.
—The Name of the Star. (Shades of London Ser.: 1). (ENG.). (YA). (gr. 7). 2012. 400p. pap. 10.99 (978-0-14-242205-2(3), Speak) 2011. 368p. 16.99 (978-0-399-25660-8(1), G.P. Putnam's Sons Books for Young Readers) Penguin Young Readers Group.
Kazerooni, Abbas. The Boy with Two Lives. 2016. (ENG.). 256p. (YA). (gr. 7). 12.99 (978-1-74331-483-8(3)) Allen & Unwin AUS. Dist: Independent Pubs. Group.
Keeble, Helen. No Angel. 2013. (ENG.). 384p. (YA). (gr. 8). pap. 9.99 (978-0-06-208227-5(2), HarperTeen) HarperCollins Pubs.
Kerr, Esme. The Girl with the Glass Bird. 2015. (ENG.). 272p. (J). (gr. 3-7). 16.99 (978-0-545-69984-6(3)) Scholastic, Inc.
—Mischief at Midnight. 2016. (ENG.). 272p. (J). (gr. 3-7). 16.99 (978-0-545-90403-2(X), Chicken Hse., The) Scholastic, Inc.
Killer Connections. 2010. (Hardy Boys (All New) Undercover Brothers Ser.: 33). (ENG.). 176p. (J). (gr. 3-7). pap. 6.99 (978-1-4169-8696-6(0), Aladdin) Simon & Schuster Children's Publishing.
Kindl, Patrice & Wells, Rosemary. A School for Brides. 2015. (ENG.). 272p. (J). (gr. 7). bds. 17.99 (978-0-670-78608-4(X), Viking Books for Young Readers) Penguin Young Readers Group.
Kingsley, Kate. Everything but the Truth. 2010. (Young, Loaded, & Fabulous Ser.: 2). (ENG.). 304p. (YA). (gr. 9-18). pap. 9.99 (978-1-4169-9400-8(9), Simon Pulse) Simon Pulse.
—Kiss & Break Up. 2011. (Young, Loaded, & Fabulous Ser.: 3). (ENG.). 320p. (YA). (gr. 9-18). pap. 9.99 (978-1-4169-9401-5(7), Simon Pulse) Simon Pulse.
—Pretty on the Outside. 2010. (Young, Loaded, & Fabulous Ser.: 1). (ENG.). 320p. (YA). (gr. 9-18). pap. 9.99 (978-1-4169-9399-5(1), Simon Pulse) Simon Pulse.
Kleinman, Estelle. Bloomability. Friedland, Joyce & Kessler, Rikki, eds. 2009. (Novel-Ties Ser.). (Illus.). 41p. pap. 16.95 (978-0-7675-4276-0(2)) Learning Links Inc.
Knight, Karsten. Wildefire. 2011. (ENG.). 400p. (YA). (gr. 9-18). 16.99 (978-1-4424-2117-2(7), Simon & Schuster Bks. For Young Readers) Simon & Schuster Bks. For Young Readers.
Koponen, Libby. Blow Out the Moon. 2006. (ENG., Illus.). 224p. (gr. 8-17). per. 18.99 (978-0-316-01480-9(X), Tingley, Megan Bks.) Little, Brown Bks. for Young Readers.
Kuenzler, Lou. Princess DisGrace: a Royal Disaster. 2016. (Princess DisGrace Ser.). (ENG., Illus.). 240p. (J). (gr. 3-7). 12.99 (978-0-553-53775-8(X), Random Hse. Bks. for Young Readers) Random Hse. Children's Bks.
Lackey, Mercedes & Edghill, Rosemary. Conspiracies. 2011. (Shadow Grail Ser.: 2). (ENG.). 352p. (YA). (gr. 8-12). pap. 19.99 (978-0-7653-1762-9(1), 9780765317629, Tor Teen) Doherty, Tom Assocs., LLC.
—Legacies, No. 1. 2010. (Shadow Grail Ser.: 1). (ENG.). 320p. (YA). (gr. 8-12). pap. 11.99 (978-0-7653-1761-2(3), Tor Teen) Doherty, Tom Assocs., LLC.
—Shadow Grail #3: Sacrifices. 2013. (Shadow Grail Ser.: 3). (ENG.). 304p. (YA). (gr. 8-12). pap. 14.99 (978-0-7653-1763-6(X), 9780765317636, Tor Teen) Doherty, Tom Assocs., LLC.
Lehman, Barbara. The Secret Box. 2011. (ENG., Illus.). 48p. (J). (gr. -1-3). 16.99 (978-0-547-23868-5(1)) Houghton Mifflin Harcourt Publishing Co.
L'Engle, Madeleine. And Both Were Young. 2011. (ENG.). 272p. (YA). (gr. 7-12). pap. 17.99 (978-0-312-60277-2(4), 9780312602772) Square Fish.
Lloyd-Jones, Emily. The Hearts We Sold. 2017. (ENG.). 400p. (YA). (gr. 10-17). 17.99 **(978-0-316-31459-6(5))** Little Brown & Co.
Lockhart, E. The Disreputable History of Frankie Landau-Banks. 2009. (ENG.). 352p. (J). (gr. 5-9). pap. 9.99 (978-0-7868-3819-6(1)) Hyperion Pr.
—The Disreputable History of Frankie Landau-Banks. l.t. ed. 2009. (ENG.). 502p. (YA). 23.95 (978-1-4104-1439-7(6)) Thorndike Pr.
Lockwood, Cara. Wuthering High: At Boarding School, No One Can Hear Your Scream. 2006. (Bard Academy Ser.: 1). (ENG.). 272p. (gr. 8-12). pap. 17.99 (978-1-4165-2475-5(4), MTV Bks.) MTV Books.
Maizel, Rebecca. Stolen Nights. 2013. (Vampire Queen Ser.: 2). (ENG.). 320p. (YA). (gr. 7-18). pap. 9.99 (978-0-312-64992-0(4), 9780312649920, St. Martin's Griffin) St. Martin's Pr.
Major, Roberta Olsen. The Ice Cream Crone. 2007. (Royal Pains Ser.: 5). (YA). pap. 11.95 (978-1-59705-801-8(7)) Wings ePress, Inc.
Marchetta, Melina. Jellicoe Road. (ENG.). 432p. (YA). (gr. 9). 2010. pap. 9.99 (978-0-06-143185-2(0)) 2008. 17.99 (978-0-06-143183-8(4)) HarperCollins Pubs. (HarperTeen).
Marciniak, Christine. Always Ali. 2015. 258p. (YA). (978-1-61271-279-6(7)) Zumaya Pubns. LLC.
—Honestly, Ali! 2014. (YA). (978-1-61271-249-9(5)) Zumaya Pubns. LLC.
—Reality Ali. 2012. (J). (978-1-61271-075-4(1)); (978-1-61271-076-1(X)); pap. 13.99 (978-1-61271-074-7(3)) Zumaya Pubns. LLC.
Mattel & Deutsch, Stacia. Ever after High: Dragon Games: The Junior Novel. 2016. (ENG.). 144p. (J). (gr. 3-7). pap. 5.99 (978-0-316-30184-8(1)) Little, Brown Bks. for Young Readers.
—Ever after High Entertainment Tie-In: the Deluxe Junior Novel. 2016. (ENG.). 144p. (J). (gr. 3-7). 9.99 (978-0-316-27045-8(8)) Little, Brown Bks. for Young Readers.
Mattel & Green, Margaret. Ever after High. 2016. (ENG., Illus.). 24p. (J). (gr. -1-3). pap. 3.99 (978-0-316-30179-4(5)) Little, Brown Bks. for Young Readers.
—Ever after High Entertainment Tie-In: Reader. 2016. (Passport to Reading Level 3 Ser.). (ENG., Illus.). 32p. (J). (gr. -1-3). pap. 3.99 (978-0-316-30180-0(9)) Little, Brown Bks. for Young Readers.
McCall Smith, Alexander. School Ship Tobermory. 2016. (School Ship Tobermory Ser.). (ENG., Illus.). 224p. (J). (gr. 3-7). 15.99 (978-0-399-55261-8(8), Delacorte Bks. for Young Readers) Random Hse. Children's Bks.
McKay, Hilary. Wishing for Tomorrow: The Sequel to a Little Princess. Maland, Nick, illus. (ENG.). 288p. (J). (gr. 3-7). 2011. pap. 6.99 (978-1-4424-0170-9(2)) 2010. 16.99 (978-1-4424-0169-3(9)) McElderry, Margaret K. Bks. (McElderry, Margaret K. Bks.).
McMullen, Beth. Mrs. Smith's Spy School for Girls. 2017. (Mrs. Smith's Spy School for Girls Ser.: 1). (ENG., Illus.). 304p. (J). (gr. 4-8). 16.99 **(978-1-4814-9020-7(6)**, Aladdin) Simon & Schuster Children's Publishing.
McTiernan, Deborah. Lilly Noble & Actual Magic. 2013. (ENG.). 318p. (YA). pap. 14.99 (978-0-9891807-0-2(0)) Actual Magic Enterprises, LLC.
Mead, Richelle. The Golden Lily. (Bloodlines Ser.: 2). (ENG.). (YA). (gr. 7). 2013. 448p. pap. 10.99 (978-1-59514-602-1(4)) 2012. 432p. 18.99 (978-1-59514-318-1(1)) Penguin Young Readers Group. (Razorbill).
Miller, Lauren. Free to Fall. 2014. (ENG.). 480p. (YA). (gr. 8). 17.99 (978-0-06-219980-5(3), HarperTeen) HarperCollins Pubs.
Miller, Sarah. The Other Girl. 2010. (ENG.). 304p. (YA). (gr. 8). pap. 20.99 (978-0-312-33416-1(8), 9780312334161, St. Martin's Griffin) St. Martin's Pr.
Mitchell, Todd. The Secret to Lying. (ENG., Illus.). 336p. (YA). (gr. 9). 2011. pap. 7.99 (978-0-7636-5620-1(8)) 2010. 17.99 (978-0-7636-4084-2(0)) Candlewick Pr.
Morpurgo, Michael. The War of Jenkins' Ear. 2nd ed. 2017. (ENG.). 192p. (J). (gr. 5-7). pap. 9.99 **(978-1-4052-2672-1(2))** Egmont Bks., Ltd. GBR. Dist: Independent Pubs. Group.
Moss, Alexandra. Lara's Leap of Faith. 2005. (Royal Ballet School Diaries). 138p. (J). 12.65 (978-0-7569-5894-7(6)) Perfection Learning Corp.
Mulligan, Andy. Return to Ribblestrop. 2016. (Ribblestrop Ser.). (ENG., Illus.). 352p. (J). (gr. 3-7). 17.99 (978-1-4424-9907-2(9), Beach Lane Bks.) Beach Lane Bks.
—Ribblestrop. (Ribblestrop Ser.). (ENG., Illus.). (J). (gr. 3-7). 2016. 400p. pap. 7.99 (978-1-4424-9905-8(2)) 2014. 384p. 16.99 (978-1-4424-9904-1(4)) Beach Lane Bks. (Beach Lane Bks.).
—Ribblestrop Forever! 2016. (Ribblestrop Ser.). (ENG., Illus.). 320p. (J). (gr. 3-7). 16.99 (978-1-4424-9910-2(9), Beach Lane Bks.) Beach Lane Bks.
Neill, Chloe. Firespell: A Novel of the Dark Elite. 2010. (Dark Elite Ser.: 1). (ENG.). 256p. (YA). (gr. 9-18). 6.99 (978-0-451-22886-4(3), Berkley) Penguin Publishing Group.
Nurse, Holly. Meridian Brown Goes to School. 2009. (Illus.). 60p. pap. (978-1-84748-535-9(9)) Athena Pr.
O'connell, Tyne. A Royal Match. 2011. (Calypso Chronicles Ser.). (ENG.). 512p. (YA). pap. 9.99 (978-1-59990-751-2(8), 9781599907512, Bloomsbury USA Childrens) Bloomsbury Publishing USA.
O'Connell, Tyne. A Royal Mess. 2011. (Calypso Chronicles Ser.). (ENG.). 512p. (YA). pap. 9.99 (978-1-59990-888-5(3), 9781599908885, Bloomsbury USA Childrens) Bloomsbury Publishing USA.
Ohlin, Nancy. Always, Forever. 2014. (ENG., Illus.). 320p. (YA). (gr. 9). pap. 9.99 (978-1-4424-6487-2(9), Simon Pulse) Simon Pulse.
Orenstein, Denise Gosliner. Unseen Companion. 2003. 368p. (J). 15.99 (978-0-06-052056-4(6)); lib. bdg. 16.89 (978-0-06-052057-1(4)) HarperCollins Pubs.
Orenstein, Denise Gosliner & Orenstein, Denise G. Unseen Companion. 2005. (ENG.). 368p. (YA). (gr. 8). reprint ed. pap. 7.99 (978-0-06-052058-8(2), Tegen, Katherine Bks) HarperCollins Pubs.
Palmer, Pamela. Horse of the Dawn. 2005. 89p. pap. 16.95 (978-1-4137-9545-5(5)) PublishAmerica, Inc.
Park, Louise. New Girl. May, Kyla & Matthews, Melanie, illus. 2015. (Star Girl Ser.). (ENG.). 80p. (gr. 1-4). lib. bdg. 22.65 (978-1-4795-8275-4(1)) Picture Window Bks.
—Odd One Out. May, Kyla & Matthews, Melanie, illus. 2015. (Star Girl Ser.). (ENG.). 80p. (gr. 1-4). lib. bdg. 22.65 (978-1-4795-8276-1(X)) Picture Window Bks.
—Three's a Crowd. May, Kyla & Matthews, Melanie, illus. 2015. (Star Girl Ser.). (ENG.). 80p. (gr. 1-4). lib. bdg. 22.65 (978-1-4795-8278-5(6)) Picture Window Bks.
—Winning Moves. May, Kyla & Matthews, Melanie, illus. 2015. (Star Girl Ser.). (ENG.). 80p. (gr. 1-4). lib. bdg. 22.65 (978-1-4795-8277-8(8)) Picture Window Bks.
Pearson, Mary E. The Miles Between. 2011. (ENG.). 288p. (YA). (gr. 9-12). pap. 15.99 (978-0-312-65926-4(1)) Square Fish.
Perkins, Stephanie. Anna & the French Kiss. 2010. (ENG.). 384p. (YA). (gr. 7-18). 16.99 (978-0-525-42327-0(3), Dutton Books for Young Readers) Penguin Young Readers Group.
—Isla & the Happily Ever After. 2015. (ENG.). 368p. (YA). (gr. 9-12). pap. 10.99 (978-0-14-242627-2(X), Speak) Penguin Publishing Group.
—Isla & the Happily Ever After. 2014. (ENG.). 352p. (YA). (gr. 9). 17.99 (978-0-525-42563-2(2), Dutton Books for Young Readers) Penguin Young Readers Group.
Philpot, Chelsey. Even in Paradise. 2016. 384p. (YA). (gr. 8). pap. 9.99 (978-0-06-229370-1(2)) HarperCollins Pubs.
Pismarov, Vivienne. The Crazy Days of Sam B. 2009. 88p. pap. 10.49 (978-1-4490-3826-7(3)) AuthorHouse.
Primavera, Elise. Making Mistakes on Purpose. 2016. (Ms. Rapscott's Girls Ser.). (ENG., Illus.). 160p. (J). (gr. 3-7). 16.99 (978-0-8037-3824-9(2), Dial Bks) Penguin Young Readers Group.
Ray, Delia. Finding Fortune. 2015. (ENG.). 288p. (J). (gr. 5-7). 16.99 (978-0-374-30065-4(8), 9780374300654, Farrar, Straus & Giroux (BYR)) Farrar, Straus & Giroux.
Raymond, Patrick. Daniel & Esther. 2007. (ENG.). 176p. (J). (gr. 3-7). pap. 9.95 (978-1-4169-6798-9(2), Simon & Schuster/Paula Wiseman Bks.) Simon & Schuster/Paula Wiseman Bks.
Reiss, Kathryn. The Strange Case of Baby H. 2009. (Mysteries Through Time Ser.). 144 - 176p. (YA). (gr. 4-8). 31.95 (978-1-60754-423-4(7)); pap. 15.25 (978-1-60754-424-1(5)) Windmill Bks.
Ryan, Hugh. The Hunt. 2012. 90p. (J). (978-0-545-46306-5(8)) Scholastic, Inc.
—Spy Academy: Mission Twinpossible. 2012. 93p. (J). pap. (978-0-545-37173-5(2)) Scholastic, Inc.
Samarasinghe, Sara. Dalaina. 2007. 352p. pap. 18.95 (978-0-9798997-2-0(9)) iTeenBooks Inc.
Santiago, Chiori. Home to Medicine Mountain. 2014. 18.45 (978-1-63419-705-2(4)) Perfection Learning Corp.
Sarn, Amélie & Trouillot, Virgile. The Argument. 2009. (Groove High Ser.). (Illus.). 112p. (YA). (gr. 5-8). 31.95 (978-1-60754-538-5(1)); pap. 15.25 (978-1-60754-539-2(X)) Windmill Bks.
—The Audition. 2009. (Groove High Ser.). (Illus.). 112p. (YA). (gr. 5-8). 31.95 (978-1-60754-203-2(X), 1293913); pap. 15.25 (978-1-60754-204-9(8), 1293913) Windmill Bks.
—A Day of Surprises. 2009. (Groove High Ser.). (Illus.). 112p. (YA). (gr. 5-8). 31.95 (978-1-60754-209-4(9), 1293912); pap. 15.25 (978-1-60754-210-0(2), 1293912) Windmill Bks.
—Everyone on Stage. 2009. (Groove High Ser.). (Illus.). 112p. (YA). (gr. 5-8). 31.95 (978-1-60754-529-3(2)); pap. 15.25 (978-1-60754-530-9(6)) Windmill Bks.
—The New Girl. 2009. (Groove High Ser.). (Illus.). 112p. (YA). (gr. 5-8). 31.95 (978-1-60754-536-1(5)); pap. 15.25 (978-1-60754-535-4(7)) Windmill Bks.
Selfors, Suzanne. Ever after High: Hero Training: A Destiny Do-Over Diary. 2015. (ENG., Illus.). 160p. (J). (gr. 3-7). 9.99 (978-0-316-40139-5(0)) Little, Brown Bks. for Young Readers.
—Ever after High: Science & Sorcery: a Destiny Do-Over Diary. 2015. (ENG., Illus.). 160p. (J). (gr. 3-7). 9.99 (978-0-316-40133-3(1)) Little, Brown Bks. for Young Readers.
—Next Top Villain. 2015. (School Story Ser.). (ENG., Illus.). 224p. (J). (gr. 3-7). 13.99 (978-0-316-40128-9(5)) Little Brown & Co.
—A Semi-Charming Kind of Life. 2015. (Ever after High Ser.: Bk. 3). 213p. (J). (978-0-316-40135-7(8)) Little Brown & Co.
—A Semi-Charming Kind of Life. 2015. (Ever after High Ser.: Bk. 3). (ENG., Illus.). 224p. (J). (gr. 3-7). 13.99 (978-0-316-40136-4(6)) Little, Brown Bks. for Young Readers.
Shade, Jeff. An Unusual Education. 2010. (J). pap. (978-0-88092-317-0(2)) Royal Fireworks Publishing Co.
Shields, Gillian. Eternal. (Immortal Ser.: 3). (ENG.). (YA). (gr. 8). 2012. 384p. pap. 9.99 (978-0-06-200040-8(3)) 2011. 368p. 16.99 (978-0-06-200039-2(X)) HarperCollins Pubs. (Tegen, Katherine Bks).
—Immortal. 2010. (Immortal Ser.: 1). (ENG.). 384p. (YA). (gr. 8). pap. 8.99 (978-0-06-137583-5(7), Tegen, Katherine Bks) HarperCollins Pubs.
Shulman, Polly. Enthusiasm. 2007. (ENG.). 224p. (YA). (gr. 7-18). pap. 8.99 (978-0-14-240935-0(9), Speak) Penguin Young Readers Group.
Smith, Andrew. Stand-off. Bosma, Sam, illus. 2016. (ENG.). 432p. (YA). (gr. 7). pap. 10.99 (978-1-4814-1830-0(0), Simon & Schuster Bks. For Young Readers) Simon & Schuster Bks. For Young Readers.
—Winger. Bosma, Sam, illus. 2013. (ENG.). 448p. (YA). (gr. 7). 16.99 (978-1-4424-4492-8(4), Simon & Schuster Bks. For Young Readers) Simon & Schuster Bks. For Young Readers.
Smith, Evelyn. Seven Sisters at Queen Anne's. Coller, H., illus. 2013. 162p. pap. (978-1-909423-07-7(6)) Bks. to Treasure.
Snicket, Lemony, pseud. The Austere Academy. Helquist, Brett, illus. 2008. (Series of Unfortunate Events Ser.: Bk. 5). (ENG.). 240p. (J). (gr. 5-18). pap. 6.99 (978-0-06-114634-3(X), Harper Trophy) HarperCollins Pubs.
Spradlin, Michael P. Live & Let Shop. 2005. (Spy Goddess Ser.: Bk. 1). (ENG., Illus.). 224p. (gr. 7-18). 15.99 (978-0-06-059407-7(1)) HarperCollins Pubs.
Spratt, R. A. Friday Barnes, Girl Detective. Gosier, Phil, illus. 2016. (Friday Barnes Mysteries Ser.: Bk. 1). (ENG.). 272p. (J). 13.99 (978-1-62672-297-2(8), 9781626722972) Roaring Brook Pr.
Stephens, Sarah Hines. Lights Out. 2006. (Zoey 101 Ser.). 110p. (J). (978-1-4287-0831-0(6)) Scholastic, Inc.
—Pranks for Nothing! 2006. (Zoey 101 Ser.). 109p. (J). (978-1-4156-5292-3(9)) Scholastic, Inc.
Stevens, Robin. Murder Is Bad Manners. 2015. (Wells & Wong Mystery Ser.). (ENG., Illus.). 320p. (J). (gr. 5). 17.99 (978-1-4814-2212-3(X), Simon & Schuster Bks. For Young Readers) Simon & Schuster Bks. For Young Readers.
Stine, R. L. Battle of the Dum Diddys, 1 vol. Park, Trip, illus. 2011. (Rotten School Ser.: No. 12). (ENG.). 128p. (gr. 2-5). 24.21 (978-1-59961-836-4(2)) Spotlight.
—The Big Blueberry Barf-Off!, 1 vol. Park, Trip, illus. 2011. (Rotten School Ser.: No. 1). (ENG.). 128p. (gr. 2-5). 24.21 (978-1-59961-825-8(7)) Spotlight.
—The Big Blueberry Barf-Off! Park, Trip, illus. 2008. (Rotten School Ser.: 1). (ENG.). 128p. (J). (gr. 3-7). pap. 5.99 (978-0-06-078588-8(8)) HarperCollins Pubs.
—Calling All Birdbrains. Park, Trip, illus. 2007. (Rotten School Ser.: No. 15). (ENG.). 128p. (J). (gr. 3-7). 6.99 (978-0-06-123275-6(0)) HarperCollins Pubs.
—Dudes, the School Is Haunted!, 1 vol. Park, Trip, illus. 2011. (Rotten School Ser.: No. 7). (ENG.). 128p. (gr. 2-5). 24.21 (978-1-59961-831-9(1)) Spotlight.
—Dumb Clucks. Park, Trip, illus. 2008. (Rotten School Ser.: 16). (ENG.). 128p. (J). (gr. 3-7). 6.99 (978-0-06-123278-7(5)) HarperCollins Pubs.
—The Good, the Bad & the Very Slimy. Park, Trip, illus. 2008. (Rotten School Ser.: 3). (ENG.). 128p. (J). (gr. 3-7). pap. 5.99 (978-0-06-078594-9(2)) HarperCollins Pubs.
—The Good, the Bad & the Very Slimy, 1 vol. Park, Trip, illus. 2011. (Rotten School Ser.: No. 3). (ENG.). 128p. (gr. 2-5). 24.21 (978-1-59961-827-2(3)) Spotlight.
—The Great Smelling Bee, 1 vol. Park, Trip, illus. 2011. (Rotten School Ser.: No. 2). (ENG.). 128p. (gr. 2-5). 24.21 (978-1-59961-826-5(5)) Spotlight.
—The Heinie Prize. Park, Trip, illus. 2006. (Rotten School Ser.: No. 6). 128p. (J). pap. 4.99 (978-0-06-078816-2(X), Harper Trophy) HarperCollins Pubs.
—The Heinie Prize, 1 vol. Park, Trip, illus. 2011. (Rotten School Ser.: No. 6). (ENG.). 128p. (gr. 2-5). 24.21 (978-1-59961-830-2(3)) Spotlight.
—Lose, Team, Lose! Park, Trip, illus. 2008. (Rotten School Ser.: 4). (ENG.). 128p. (J). (gr. 3-7). pap. 5.99 (978-0-06-078810-0(0)) HarperCollins Pubs.
—Lose, Team, Lose!, 1 vol. Park, Trip, illus. 2011. (Rotten School Ser.: No. 4). (ENG.). 128p. (gr. 2-5). 24.21 (978-1-59961-828-9(1)) Spotlight.
—Night of the Creepy Things. Park, Trip, illus. (Rotten School Ser.: Bk. 14). 4.99 (978-0-06-123274-9(2)) HarperCollins Pubs.
—Party Poopers. Park, Trip, illus. (Rotten School Ser.: Bk. 9). 4.99 (978-0-06-078826-1(7)) HarperCollins Pubs.
—Party Poopers, 1 vol. Park, Trip, illus. 2011. (Rotten School Ser.: No. 9). (ENG.). 128p. (gr. 2-5). 24.21 (978-1-59961-833-3(8)) Spotlight.
—Punk'd & Skunked, 1 vol. Park, Trip, illus. 2011. (Rotten School Ser.: No. 11). (ENG.). 128p. (gr. 2-5). 24.21 (978-1-59961-835-7(4)) Spotlight.
—Rotten School #12: Battle of the Dum Diddys. Park, Trip, illus. 4.99 (978-0-06-078835-3(6)) HarperCollins Pubs.
—Rotten School #15: Calling All Birdbrains. Park, Trip, illus. 4.99 (978-0-06-123277-0(7)) HarperCollins Pubs.
—Rotten School #16: Dumb Clucks. Park, Trip, illus. 4.99 (978-0-06-123280-0(7)) HarperCollins Pubs.
—The Rottenest Angel. Park, Trip, illus. (Rotten School Ser.: Bk. 10). 4.99 (978-0-06-078829-2(1)) HarperCollins Pubs.
—The Rottenest Angel, 1 vol. Park, Trip, illus. 2011. (Rotten School Ser.: No. 10). (ENG.). 128p. (gr. 2-5). 24.21 (978-1-59961-834-0(6)) Spotlight.
—Shake, Rattle, & Hurl! Park, Trip, illus. 2008. (Rotten School Ser.: 5). (ENG.). 128p. (J). (gr. 3-7). pap. 5.99 (978-0-06-078813-1(5)) HarperCollins Pubs.
—Shake, Rattle, & Hurl!, 1 vol. Park, Trip, illus. 2011. (Rotten School Ser.: No. 5). (ENG.). 128p. (gr. 2-5). 24.21 (978-1-59961-829-6(X)) Spotlight.
—The Teacher from Heck. Park, Trip, illus. 2009. (Rotten School Ser.: No. 8). 128p. (J). pap. 4.99 (978-0-06-078823-0(2), Harper Trophy) HarperCollins Pubs.
—The Teacher from Heck, 1 vol. Park, Trip, illus. 2011. (Rotten School Ser.: No. 8). (ENG.). 128p. (gr. 2-5). 24.21 (978-1-59961-832-6(X)) Spotlight.

—30 Tales to Give You Goosebumps. 2004. 391p. (J). (978-0-7607-5680-5(5)) Scholastic, Inc.
Stone, Sonja. Desert Dark. 2017. (ENG.). 344p. (YA). (gr. 7). pap. 7.99 (978-0-8234-3766-5(3)) Holiday Hse., Inc.
Stout, Katie M. Hello, I Love You: A Novel. 2015. (ENG.). 304p. (YA). (gr. 7-12). 18.99 (978-1-250-05259-9(9), 9781250052599, St. Martin's Griffin) St. Martin's Pr.
Talbot, Sophie. Fabulous Terrible: The Adventures of You. 2011. 280p. (YA). (gr. 7-18). pap. 12.99 (978-1-933390-76-5(X)) Chooseco LLC.
Taylor, Kara. Prep School Confidential. 2013. (Prep School Confidential Novel Ser.: 1). (ENG.). 336p. (YA). (gr. 7). pap. 9.99 (978-1-250-01759-8(9), 9781250017598, St. Martin's Griffin) St. Martin's Pr.
Taylor, Laini. Daughter of Smoke & Bone. 2011. (ENG.). 432p. (YA). (gr. 10-17). 20.00 (978-0-316-13402-6(3)) Little Brown & Co.
—Daughter of Smoke & Bone. 2012. (ENG.). (YA). (gr. 10-17). 448p. pap. 12.99 (978-0-316-13399-9(X)); 624p. pap. 28.99 (978-0-316-22435-2(9)) Little, Brown Bks. for Young Readers.
—Daughter of Smoke & Bone. 2012. (Daughter of Smoke & Bone Ser.: 1). (YA). lib. bdg. 24.50 (978-0-606-26704-5(2), Turtleback) Turtleback Bks.
—Days of Blood & Starlight. 2012. (ENG., (YA). (gr. 10-17). Illus.). 528p. 18.99 (978-0-316-13397-5(3)); 688p. 39.99 (978-0-316-22433-8(2)) Little, Brown Bks. for Young Readers.
Torres, J. The Collected Alison Dare Little Miss Adventures. Bone, J., illus. 2005. (J). (978-1-4156-1359-7(1)) Oni Pr., Inc.
Trigiani, Adriana. Viola in Reel Life. (Viola Ser.: 1). (ENG.). (YA). (gr. 8). 2011. 304p. pap. 8.99 (978-0-06-145104-1(5)) 2009. 288p. 17.99 (978-0-06-145102-7(9)) HarperCollins Pubs. (HarperTeen).
van de Ruit, John. Spud. 2005. 300p. pap. (978-0-14-302484-2(1)) Penguin Publishing Group.
—Spud. 2008. (ENG.). 336p. (YA). (gr. 7-18). 9.99 (978-1-59514-187-3(1), Razorbill) Penguin Young Readers Group.
Van De Ruit, John. Spud - The Madness Continues. 2009. (ENG.). 352p. (YA). (gr. 7-18). 9.99 (978-1-59514-245-0(2), Razorbill) Penguin Young Readers Group.
Vanderpool, Clare. Navigating Early. (ENG.). (J). (gr. 5). 2014. 336p. pap. 7.99 (978-0-307-93065-1(3), Yearling) 2013. 320p. 16.99 (978-0-385-74209-2(6), Delacorte Bks. for Young Readers) 2013. 320p. lib. bdg. 19.99 (978-0-375-99040-3(2), Delacorte Bks. for Young Readers) Random Hse. Children's Bks.
—Navigating Early. 2014. lib. bdg. 18.40 (978-0-606-36420-1(X)) Turtleback Bks.
Vipont, Elfrida. The Lark in the Morn. Freeman, T. R., illus. 2007. 196p. (YA). pap. 12.95 (978-1-932350-22-7(5)) Bethlehem Bks.
Von Meck. My Name Is Vaselinetjie. 2011. 256p. pap. (978-0-624-04658-5(3)) NB Pubs. Ltd.
Wallace, Barbara Brooks. The Perils of Peppermints. 2005. (ENG., Illus.). 272p. (J). (gr. 3-7). pap. 12.99 (978-0-689-85045-5(X), Simon & Schuster/Paula Wiseman Bks.) Simon & Schuster/Paula Wiseman Bks.
Wallace, Jason. Out of Shadows. (ENG., Illus.). 272p. (J). (gr. 10). 2012. pap. 8.95 (978-0-8234-2436-8(7)) 2011. 17.95 (978-0-8234-2342-2(5)) Holiday Hse., Inc.
Webster, Frank V. The Boys of Bellwood School. 2007. 176p. 26.95 (978-1-4218-3232-6(1)); per. 11.95 (978-1-4218-3332-3(8)) 1st World Publishing, Inc. (1st World Library - Literary Society).
Webster, Jean. Just Patty. 2011. 156p. 24.95 (978-1-4638-9965-3(3)); pap. 12.95 (978-1-60664-435-5(1)) Rodgers, Alan Bks.
Weiner, Jennifer. The Littlest Bigfoot. 2017. (Littlest Bigfoot Ser.: 1). (ENG.). 352p. (J). (gr. 3-7). pap. 7.99 **(978-1-4814-7075-9(2)**, Aladdin) Simon & Schuster Children's Publishing.
—The Littlest Bigfoot. Mulvanny, Sara, illus. 2016. (Littlest Bigfoot Ser.: 1). (ENG.). 304p. (J). (gr. 3-7). 16.99 (978-1-4814-7074-2(4), Aladdin) Simon & Schuster Children's Publishing.
—The Littlest Bigfoot. 2017. lib. bdg. 18.40 **(978-0-606-40206-4(3))** Turtleback Bks.
Wells, Helen. Cherry Ames, Boarding School Nurse. 10th ed. 2007. (Cherry Ames Nurse Stories Ser.). 224p. (YA). (gr. 7-12). 14.95 (978-0-8261-0413-7(4)) Springer Publishing Co., Inc.
Wells, Robison. Variant. (Variant Ser.: 1). (ENG.). (YA). (gr. 8). 2012. 400p. pap. 9.99 (978-0-06-202609-5(7)) 2011. 384p. 17.99 (978-0-06-202608-8(9)) HarperCollins Pubs. (HarperTeen).
Werlin, Nancy. Black Mirror. 2003. (ENG.). 256p. (YA). (gr. 7-12). 6.99 (978-0-14-250028-6(3), Puffin Books) Penguin Young Readers Group.
White, Amy Brecount. Forget-Her-Nots. 2010. (ENG.). 384p. (YA). (gr. 8-18). 16.99 (978-0-06-167298-9(X), Greenwillow Bks.) HarperCollins Pubs.
Whitehouse, Howard. The Faceless Fiend: Being the Tale of a Criminal Mastermind, His Masked Minions & a Princess with a Butter Knife, Involving Explosives & a Certain Amount of Pushing & Shoving. Slavin, Bill, illus. 2007. (Mad Misadventures of Emmaline & Rubberbones Ser.). (ENG.). 272p. (J). (gr. 4-7). 7.95 (978-1-55453-180-6(2)) Kids Can Pr., Ltd. CAN. Dist: Hachette Bk. Group.
Whitney, Daisy. The Mockingbirds. 2012. (ENG.). 368p. (YA). (gr. 10-17). pap. 8.99 (978-0-316-09054-4(9)) Little, Brown Bks. for Young Readers.
Wiebe, Joanna. The Wicked Awakening of Anne Merchant. 2015. (V Trilogy Ser.: Bk. 2). (ENG.). 320p. (gr. 7). pap. 12.95 (978-1-940363-29-5(2)) BenBella Bks.
Winfield, Arthur M. Rover Boys in the Land of Luck or Stirri. 2006. pap. 30.95 (978-1-4286-4101-3(7)) Kessinger Publishing, LLC.
Wodehouse, P. G. Mike at Wrykyn. 2013. 189p. reprint ed. lthr. 69.00 (978-0-7426-3265-3(2)) Classic Bks.
Wolf, Joan M. Someone Named Eva. 2009. (ENG., Illus.). 208p. (J). (gr. 5-7). pap. 7.99 (978-0-547-23766-4(9)) Houghton Mifflin Harcourt Publishing Co.
Wolitzer, Meg. Belzhar. 2014. (ENG.). 272p. (YA). (gr. 9). 17.99 (978-0-525-42305-8(2), Dutton Books for Young Readers) Penguin Young Readers Group.
Yolen, Jane. A Plague of Unicorns, 1 vol. 2016. (ENG.). 192p. (J). pap. 7.99 (978-0-310-74611-9(6)) Zonderkidz.
Zamorsky, Tania & Burnett, Frances Hodgson. A Little Princess. Corvino, Lucy, illus. 2005. (Classic Starts(tm) Ser.). (ENG.). 160p. (J). (gr. 2-4). 6.95 (978-1-4027-1275-3(8)) Sterling Publishing Co., Inc.
Ziegesar, Cecily von, creator. Notorious. 2006. (It Girl Ser.: 2). (ENG.). 288p. (YA). (gr. 10-17). per. 9.99 (978-0-316-01186-0(X), Poppy) Little, Brown Bks. for Young Readers.

BOAT RACING

see Motorboat Racing; Rowing

BOATBUILDING

see also Shipbuilding; Yachts and Yachting

Icanberry, Mark. Picnic on a Cloud. Mount, Arthur, illus. 2010. (Look, Learn & Do Ser.). 48p. (J). (gr. -1-3). pap. 7.95 (978-1-893327-02-3(7)) Look, Learn & Do Pubns.

BOATBUILDING—FICTION

Branson, Eve. Sarky Puddleboat. Lowe, Wes, illus. 2011. 44p. (J). 14.99 (978-1-4520-9754-1(2)) AuthorHouse.
Dale, Jay. Let's Make a Boat, 1 vol. Zamazing, Cherie, illus. 2012. (Wonder Words Ser.). (ENG.). 32p. (gr. k-2). pap. 5.99 (978-1-4296-8916-8(1), Engage Literacy) Capstone Press of Coughlan Cos.
Herndon, S. N. Uncle Deek's Boating Adventure. 2012. 46p. 24.95 (978-1-4512-7187-4(5)) America Star Bks.

BOATING

see Boats and Boating

BOATS AND BOATING

see also Boatbuilding; Canoes and Canoeing; Houseboats; Motorboats; Rowing; Sailing; Ships; Steamboats; Submarines (Ships); Yachts and Yachting

Aiken, David & Aiken, Zora. All about Boats: A to Z, 1 vol. Aiken, David, illus. 2012. (ENG., Illus.). 32p. (J). 14.99 (978-0-7643-4184-7(7), 9780764341847) Schiffer Publishing, Ltd.
Anderson, Scoular. Ships, Boats & Things That Float. 2016. (Cambridge Reading Adventures Ser.). (ENG.). 24p. pap. 7.19 (978-1-107-56041-3(1)) Cambridge Univ. Pr.
Ardagh, Philip. A Hole in the Road. (Illus.). 32p. (J). lib. bdg. 24.25 (978-1-931983-02-0(X)) Chrysalis Education.
Bailey, Gerry. Sea Transportation. 2008. (Simply Science Ser.). (Illus.). 32p. (YA). (gr. 3-6). lib. bdg. 26.00 (978-0-8368-9230-7(5)) Stevens, Gareth Publishing LLLP.
Barton, Byron. Boats. Barton, Byron, illus. 2006. (Illus.). 34p. (J). (gr. -1-2). 12.99 (978-0-06-115017-3(7), HarperFestival) HarperCollins Pubs.
Bender, Lionel. Ships & Boats. 2006. (J). (978-1-59389-268-5(3)) Chrysalis Education.
Blount, Rachel. Lifeboat Crew Member. 2017. (Here to Help Ser.). (ENG., Illus.). 24p. (J). (gr. k-2). 16.99 (978-1-4451-4024-7(1), Franklin Watts) Hachette Children's Group GBR. Dist: Hachette Bk. Group.
Boating Safety for Kids. (USPS Learning Guides Ser.). (Illus.). 159p. (J). pap. (978-1-891148-25-5(7)) United States Power Squadrons.
Boating Safety Sidekicks: US Power Squadron Version. 2004. (J). (978-0-9718864-3-8(1)) Within Reach, Inc.
Bodden, Valerie. Kayaking. 2009. (Active Sports Ser.). 24p. (J). (gr. 1-5). lib. bdg. 24.25 (978-1-58341-699-0(4), Creative Education) Creative Co., The.
—Rescue Boats. 2011. (Rescue Vehicles Ser.). 24p. (J). (ENG.). (gr. 1-3). pap. 6.99 (978-0-89812-578-8(2), Creative Paperbacks); (gr. k-2). 16.95 (978-1-60818-007-3(7)) Creative Co., The.
Bornhoft, Simon. High-Speed Boats. 2003. (Need for Speed Ser.). (Illus.). 32p. (J). (gr. 3-6). pap. 7.95 (978-0-8225-9856-5(6)) Lerner Publishing Group.
Broutin, Christian. El Barco. (Coleccion Mundo Maravilloso). (SPA., Illus.). 40p. (J). (gr. 2-4). (978-84-348-3810-9(9), BA9293) SM Ediciones.
Burch, Lynda S. Wicky wacky Things that Go! Boats 1. Burch, Lynda S., photos by. 2004. (Illus.). 28p. (J). E-Book 9.95 incl. cd-rom (978-1-933090-03-0(0)) Guardian Angel Publishing, Inc.
Cache, Dee. ABC's of Boating Terms, 1 vol. 2012. (ENG., Illus.). 32p. (J). pap. 6.99 (978-0-7643-3982-0(6), 9780764339820) Schiffer Publishing, Ltd.
Carrière, Nicholle. Ships & Boats, 1 vol. 2017. (Super Explorers Ser.). (ENG., Illus.). 64p. (J). pap. 6.99 **(978-1-926700-76-2(7)**, 9781926700762) Blue Bike Bks. CAN. Dist: Lone Pine Publishing USA.
Champion, Neil. Wild Water: Canoeing & Kayaking. 2013. (Illus.). 32p. (J). lib. bdg. 28.50 (978-1-59920-812-1(1)) Black Rabbit Bks.
Chan, Arlene. Awakening the Dragon: The Dragon Boat Festival. Zhang, Song Nan, illus. 2007. (ENG.). 24p. (J). (gr. 1-4). pap. 10.95 (978-0-88776-805-7(9), Tundra Bks.) Tundra Bks. CAN. Dist: Penguin Random Hse. LLC.
Chancellor, Deborah. Sea Rescue. 2013. (Emergency Vehicles Ser.). (Illus.). 24p. (gr. k-3). lib. bdg. 28.50 (978-1-59920-891-6(1)) Black Rabbit Bks.
Ciovacco, Justine. All about Small Boats. 2016. (Let's Find Out! Ser.). 32p. (gr. 3-2). lib. bdg. 24.45 (978-1-68048-444-1(3)) Rosen Publishing Group, Inc., The.
Clark, Willow. Boats on the Move. 2010. (Transportation Station Ser.). 24p. (J). (ENG.). pap. 8.25 (978-1-4358-9760-1(9)); (Illus.). (gr. 2-5). lib. bdg. 22.60 (978-1-4358-9336-8(0)) Rosen Publishing Group, Inc., The. (PowerKids Pr.).
Close, Edward. Wheels, Wings, & Motors, 1 vol., 1. 2014. (Discovery Education: How It Works). (ENG.). 32p. (gr. 3-6). 26.25 (978-1-4777-6313-1(9), PowerKids Pr.) Rosen Publishing Group, Inc., The.
Coffin, Rebecca J., et al, eds. Boats: The Work They Do & the Way They Do It. 2011. 28p. 35.95 (978-1-258-06539-3(8)) Literary Licensing, LLC.
Curley, Robert, ed. The Complete History of Ships & Boats: From Sails & Oars to Nuclear-Powered Vessels. 2011. (Transportation & Society Ser.). (ENG.). 192p. (YA). (gr. 10-12). lib. bdg. 38.75 (978-1-61530-670-1(6)) Rosen Publishing Group, Inc., The.
Curry, Peter, illus. Trains, Boats, & Planes. 2016. (ENG.). 12p. (J). (gr. -1 — 1). bds. 4.99 (978-1-4998-0262-7(5)) Little Bee Books Inc.
Davis, Charles. Boating Book for Boys: A Guide to Motor Boating, Sailing, Canoeing & Rowing. 2010. 420p. pap. 19.95 (978-1-4290-4137-9(4)) Applewood Bks.
Dubowski, Mark. Superfast Boats. 2005. (Ultimate Speed Ser.). (Illus.). 32p. (J). (gr. 3-6). lib. bdg. 25.27 (978-1-59716-079-7(2)) Bearport Publishing Co., Inc.
Farndon, John. Stickmen's Guide to Watercraft. Paul de Quay, John, illus. 2016. (Stickmen's Guides to How Everything Works). (ENG.). 32p. (J). (gr. 3-6). 30.65 (978-1-5124-0699-3(6)); 30.65 (978-1-4677-9594-4(1)) Lerner Publishing Group.
Fitzsimmons, Kakie. Bur Bur's Boating ABC's: Learn the Most Amazing Things with the ABCs of Boating! 2007. (Bur Bur & Friends Ser.). (Illus.). (J). (gr. 3-7). lib. bdg. (978-0-9777121-2-0(5)) IGI Pr.
Fortuna, Lois. Rescue Boats. 2016. (To the Rescue! Ser.). (Illus.). 24p. (J). (gr. k-k). 22.60 (978-1-4824-4662-3(6)) Stevens, Gareth Publishing LLLP.
Gamble, Adam & Jasper, Mark. Good Night Boats. Veno, Joe, illus. 2016. (Good Night Our World Ser.). (ENG.). 20p. (J). (— 1). bds. 9.95 (978-1-60219-500-4(5)) Good Night Bks.
Ganeri, Anita. Flip the Flaps: Things That Go! Humphries, Tudor, illus. 2014. (Flip the Flaps Ser.). (ENG.). 32p. (J). (gr. -1-1). pap. 6.99 (978-0-7534-7133-3(7), 9780753471333, Kingfisher) Roaring Brook Pr.
Gilpin, Daniel & Pang, Alex. Rescue Vehicles. 2010. (Machines Close-Up Ser.). 32p. (J). (gr. 4-7). 28.50 (978-1-60870-111-7(5)) Marshall Cavendish Corp.
Hamilton, Robert M. Going Places: On a Boat. 2012. (Going Places Ser.). (ENG.). 24p. (J). (gr. k-2). pap. 8.15 (978-1-4339-6271-4(3)); lib. bdg. 22.60 (978-1-4339-6269-1(1)) Stevens, Gareth Publishing LLLP.
Hanson, Anders. Let's Go by Boat, 1 vol. 2008. (Let's Go Ser.). (ENG., Illus.). 24p. (J). (gr. k-3). lib. bdg. 24.21 (978-1-59928-894-9(X), SandCastle) ABDO Publishing Co.
Harrison, Paul. Superboats. 2015. 32p. (gr. 1-5). lib. bdg. 31.35 (978-1-78404-076-5(2)) Arcturus Publishing GBR. Dist: Black Rabbit Bks.
Hirsch, Judd, reader. Fireboat: The Heroic Adventures of the John J. Harvey. (Illus.). (J). 2006. pap. incl. audio (978-1-59112-985-1(0)) 2004. pap. 39.95 incl. audio compact disk (978-1-59112-989-9(3)) Live Oak Media.
HOP, LLC. Hooked on Boats Super Activity Kit. 2006. (J). (gr. -1). 9.99 (978-1-60143-002-1(7)) HOP, LLC.
Hunt, Jilly & Collins UK Staff. Super Boats. 2016. (ENG.). 32p. (J). (gr. 2-3). pap. 8.95 (978-0-00-816381-5(2)) HarperCollins Pubs. Ltd. GBR. Dist: Independent Pubs. Group.
Ipcizade, Catherine. BIG Boats. 2010. (Big Ser.). (ENG.). 24p. (gr. k-1). lib. bdg. 26.65 (978-1-4296-3993-4(8), Pebble Plus) Capstone Press of Coughlan Cos.
Jankowski, Susan & Library. True Ocean Rescue Stories. 2010. (True Rescue Stories Ser.). 48p. (J). lib. bdg. 22.60 (978-0-7660-3665-9(0)) Enslow Pubs., Inc.
Justice, William E. Kodoku. Rivera, Hanae, illus. 2012. (ENG.). 32p. (J). 16.95 (978-1-59714-173-4(9)) Heyday.
Kalman, Maira. Fireboat: The Heroic Adventures of the John J. Harvey. Kalman, Maira, illus. 2005. (ENG., Illus.). 48p. (J). (gr. -1-3). reprint ed. pap. 6.99 (978-0-14-240362-4(8), Puffin Books) Penguin Young Readers Group.
Kerr, Daisy. Ships. 2015. (Wonderwise Ser.). (Illus.). 32p. (gr. 2-6). 31.35 (978-1-62588-362-9(5)) Black Rabbit Bks.
Kihm, Steve. The Lost Candy Bar. 2004. (J). mass mkt. 6.95 (978-0-9786794-0-8(7)) Lost Candy Bar Pr., LLC.
Klein, Adam G. Boating, 1 vol. 2008. (Outdoor Adventure! Ser.). (ENG.). 32p. (gr. k-6). 27.07 (978-1-59928-956-4(3), Checkerboard Library) ABDO Publishing Co.
Koroknay, Tom. Lyman Boats: America's Lapstake Classic: Legend of the Lakes. 2004. (Illus.). 156p. 3.95 (978-0-9749705-0-9(6)) Koroknay, Thomas.
Let's Look at Boats. 2009. (Let's Go! Ser.). (Illus.). 18p. (J). (gr. -1-k). bds. 12.75 (978-1-60754-417-3(2)) Windmill Bks.
Lindeen, Mary. All about Boats, 1 vol. 2011. (Wonder Readers: Social Studies). (ENG.). (gr. -1-2). 20p. lib. bdg. 22.65 (978-1-4296-8639-6(1)); 32p. pap. 5.99 (978-1-4296-7906-0(9)); 16p. pap. 35.94 (978-1-4296-8065-3(2)) Capstone Press of Coughlan Cos. (Wonder Readers).
Mahaney, Ian F. Extreme Watercraft. 2015. (Extreme Machines Ser.). (ENG.). 32p. (J). (gr. 3-4). pap. 10.00 (978-1-4994-1191-1(X), PowerKids Pr.) Rosen Publishing Group, Inc., The.
McFee, Shane. Whitewater Rafting. 2009. (Living on the Edge Ser.). 24p. (gr. 2-3). 42.50 (978-1-61514-303-0(3), PowerKids Pr.) Rosen Publishing Group, Inc., The.
Mitton, Tony & Parker, Ant. Busy Boats. 2005. (Amazing Machines Ser.). (ENG., Illus.). 24p. (J). (gr. -1-k). 4.99 (978-0-7534-5916-4(7), 9780753459164, Kingfisher) Roaring Brook Pr.
Molzahn, Arlene Bourgeois. Ships & Boats. 2003. (Transportation & Communication Ser.). (Illus.). 48p. (J). (gr. 1-4). lib. bdg. 25.27 (978-0-7660-2025-2(8)) Enslow Pubs., Inc.
Murray, Julie. Barcos. 2015. (Medios de Transporte Ser.). (SPA & ENG., Illus.). 24p. (gr. k-1). pap. 7.95 (978-1-4966-0487-3(3)) Capstone Classroom.
—Boats, 1 vol. 2014. (Transportation Ser.). (ENG.). 24p. (J). (gr. 4-8). lib. bdg. 28.50 (978-1-62970-078-6(9)) ABDO Publishing Co.
Oxlade, Chris. Ships & Boats: Sail; Navigation; Radar; Anchor; Keel. 2015. (ENG., Illus.). 64p. (J). (gr. 3-7). 12.99 (978-1-86147-412-4(1), Armadillo) Anness Publishing GBR. Dist: National Bk. Network.
Oxlade, Chris & Farndon, John. Stickmen's Guide to Watercraft. Pyke, Jerry & Quay, John Paul de, illus. 2016. (Stickmen's Guides to How Everything Works). (ENG.). 32p. (J). (gr. 3-6). lib. bdg. 26.65 (978-1-4677-9362-9(0)) Lerner Publishing Group.
Parker, Steve. On the Sea. 2010. (J). 28.50 (978-1-59920-286-0(7)) Black Rabbit Bks.
Parker, Steven. On Water. 2011. (Future Transport Ser.). (Illus.). 32p. (J). (gr. 4). 28.50 (978-1-60870-780-5(6)) Marshall Cavendish Corp.
Paulsen, Gary. Caught by the Sea: My Life on Boats. 2003. (Illus.). 103p. (gr. 7). 16.00 (978-0-7569-1635-0(6)) Perfection Learning Corp.
—Caught by the Sea: My Life on Boats. 2003. (ENG., Illus.). 112p. (YA). (gr. 7). mass mkt. 5.99 (978-0-440-40716-4(8), Laurel Leaf) Random Hse. Children's Bks.
Peppas, Lynn. Boats on the Water. 2011. (ENG.). 32p. (J). lib. bdg. (978-0-7787-2727-9(0)); (Vehicles on the Move Ser.: No. 13). pap. (978-0-7787-2734-7(3)) Crabtree Publishing Co.
Randolph, Joanne. Coast Guard Boats. 2008. (To the Rescue! Ser.). (Illus.). 24p. (J). (gr. 3-7). lib. bdg. 22.60 (978-1-4042-4152-7(3), PowerKids Pr.) Rosen Publishing Group, Inc., The.
—Coast Guard Boats/Lanchas Guardacostas. Alaman, Eduardo, tr. from ENG. 2008. (To the Rescue! / ¡Al Rescate! Ser.). (Illus.). 24p. (J). (gr. -1-3). lib. bdg. 22.60 (978-1-4042-7671-0(8), Editorial Buenas Letras) Rosen Publishing Group, Inc., The.
Rapparlie, Leslie & Wurdinger, Scott. Kayaking. 2006. (Adventure Sports Ser.). (Illus.). 48p. (J). (gr. 4-7). lib. bdg. 21.95 (978-1-58341-397-5(9), 1262845, Creative Education) Creative Co., The.
Rau, Dana Meachen. Boats. 2009. (Bookworms Ser.). 24p. (gr. k-1). 15.95 (978-0-7614-4076-5(3)) Marshall Cavendish Corp.
—Boats/En Barcos. 2009. (Bookworms Ser.). (SPA & ENG.). 24p. (gr. k-1). lib. bdg. 15.95 (978-0-7614-4765-8(2)) Marshall Cavendish Corp.
Richter, A. Boats that Float: Learning the OA Sound. 2009. (PowerPhonics Ser.). 24p. (gr. 1-1). 39.90 (978-1-60851-435-9(8), PowerKids Pr.) Rosen Publishing Group, Inc., The.
Ridley, Frances. Lost at Sea. 2008. (Crabtree Contact Ser.). (ENG., Illus.). 32p. (J). (gr. 3-7). lib. bdg. (978-0-7787-3809-1(4)) Crabtree Publishing Co.
Riggs, Kate. Rescue Boats. 2015. (Illus.). 24p. (J). (978-1-60818-583-2(4), Creative Education) Creative Co., The.
—Rescue Boats: Seedlings. 2016. (Seedlings Ser.). (ENG.). 24p. (J). (gr. k-2). pap. 7.99 (978-1-62832-188-3(1), Creative Paperbacks) Creative Co., The.
Ring, Susan. Boats, Boats, Boats. 2005. (Yellow Umbrella Fluent Level Ser.). (ENG., Illus.). 16p. (gr. k-1). pap. 35.70 (978-0-7368-5309-5(X), Yellow Umbrella Bks.) Capstone Press of Coughlan Cos.
Ringstad, Arnold. Kayaking. 2014. (Great Outdoors Ser.). (ENG.). 24p. (J). (gr. 2-5). 28.50 (978-1-62687-332-2(1), 207172) Child's World, Inc., The.
Rose, Simon. Fisher. 2014. (Illus.). 24p. (J). (978-1-4896-2986-9(6)) Weigl Pubs., Inc.
Scheff, Matt. Speedboats, 1 vol. 2014. (Speed Machines Ser.). (ENG.). 32p. (gr. 3-6). lib. bdg. 27.07 (978-1-62403-614-9(7), SportsZone) ABDO Publishing Co.
Sciarrino, Stephanie. Multiplication at the Marina: Multiply Within 100. 2014. (Rosen Common Core Math Readers Ser.). 24p. (J). (gr. 3-4). (ENG.). pap. 49.50 (978-1-4777-4951-7(9), Rosen Classroom); (ENG., Illus.). pap. 8.25 (978-1-4777-4950-0(0), PowerKids Pr.); (Illus.). lib. bdg. 23.60 (978-1-4777-6451-0(8), PowerKids Pr.) Rosen Publishing Group, Inc., The.
Scraper, Katherine. You Can Sort Boats. 2006. (Early Explorers Ser.). (J). pap. (978-1-4108-6038-5(8)) Benchmark Education Co.
Shusterman, Danielle. What's on the Little Boat? 2016. (1-3Y Moving on Wheels Ser.). (ENG., Illus.). 16p. (J). pap. 5.99 (978-1-63437-456-9(8)) American Reading Co.
Summers, Alex. Boat. 2017. (Transportation & Me! Ser.). (ENG.). (J). (gr. k-1). 28.51 **(978-1-68342-164-1(7))** Rourke Educational Media.
Sunfish Sailboats Owner's Manual: AMF, Alcort, Pearson, & Vanguard Sailboats. 2004. (Illus.). 37p. (YA). 30.00 (978-0-9760569-0-4(9)) Wilson, Rebecca.
Tatge, Cathy. Boats. 2007. (My First Look at: Vehicles Ser.). (Illus.). 24p. (J). (gr. -1-3). lib. bdg. 24.25 (978-1-58341-526-9(2), Creative Education) Creative Co., The.
Thomas, Serena J. & Draper, Allison Stark. Kayaking, 01 vols., 1. 2016. (Outdoor Life Ser.). (ENG.). 64p. (J). 32.95 (978-1-4994-6233-3(6), Rosen Young Adult) Rosen Publishing Group, Inc., The.
Tiner, John Hudson. Ships & Boats. (Illus.). 32p. 2004. pap. 8.95 (978-0-89812-390-6(9), Creative Paperbacks) 2003. (J). lib. bdg. 18.95 (978-1-58341-257-2(3), Creative Education) Creative Co., The.
Trapani, Iza. Sing along with Iza & Friends: Row Row Row Your Boat. Trapani, Iza, illus. 2004. (Illus.). 32p. (J). pap. 11.95 incl. audio compact disk (978-1-58089-102-8(0)) Charlesbridge Publishing, Inc.
Tripp, Will. Water Adventures. 2005. (Real Deal Ser.). (Illus.). 32p. (J). pap. (978-0-7608-9636-5(4)) Sundance/Newbridge Educational Publishing.
Trombello, William. Trains & Tow Boats. Tangen, Nick, illus. 2013. 34p. pap. (978-0-9842998-1-2(5)) Roxby Media Ltd.
Veitch, Catherine. Big Machines Float!, 1 vol. 2014. (Big Machines Ser.). (ENG.). 24p. (gr. k-1). pap. 3.95 (978-1-4846-0984-2(0)); (Illus.). 23.32 (978-1-4846-0587-5(X)) Heinemann-Raintree. (Heinemann Read & Learn).
Veronica, Nick. Icebreakers. 2016. (Technology Takes on Nature Ser.). 00032p. (J). pap. 10.50 **(978-1-4824-5779-7(2))** Stevens, Gareth Publishing LLLP.
Volke, Gordon. Louis the Lifeboat Activity Sticker Book. Bowler, Colin, illus. 2004. 16p. pap. 6.00 (978-1-84161-120-4(4)) Ravette Publishing, Ltd. GBR. Dist: Parkwest Pubns., Inc.
Walke, Ted, illus. & compiled by. Boating Safety Sidekicks Color a Fish: Freshwater Fish Coloring Book. Walke, Ted, compiled by. 2008. 28p. (J). (978-0-9718864-4-5(X)) Within Reach, Inc.
Yoyo Books, creator. Vroom. 2011. (Baby's First Library). (ENG., Illus.). 38p. (gr. -1-k). bds. (978-90-8622-910-9(7)) YoYo Bks.
Zuehlke, Jeffrey. Tugboats. 2007. (Pull Ahead Books-Mighty Movers Ser.). (ENG., Illus.). 32p. (gr. k-3). pap. 7.95 (978-0-8225-6422-5(X), First Avenue Editions); lib. bdg. 22.60 (978-0-8225-6417-1(3), Lerner Pubns.) Lerner Publishing Group.

BOATS AND BOATING—FICTION

Appleton, Victor. Tom Swift & his Motor-Boat. 2005. 26.95 (978-1-4218-1501-5(X)); 196p. pap. 11.95

(978-1-4218-1600-5(8)); 192p. pap. 11.95 *(978-1-4218-1601-2(6))* 1st World Publishing, Inc. (1st World Library - Literary Society).

—Tom Swift & His Motor-Boat: Or the Rivals of Lake Carlopa. l.t. ed. 2007. (ENG.). 148p. pap. 19.99 *(978-1-4346-1907-5(9))* Creative Media Partners, LLC.

—Tom Swift & His Motor-Cycle, Tom Swift & His Motor-Boat, Tom Swift & His Airship. 2007. 292p. per. 12.99 *(978-1-60459-097-5(1))* Wilder Pubns., Corp.

—Tom Swift & His MotorBoat or the Rival. 2006. pap. *(978-1-4065-0904-5(3))* Dodo Pr.

—Tom Swift & His Submarine Boat. 2004. reprint ed. pap. 20.95 *(978-1-4191-8462-8(8))*; pap. 1.99 *(978-1-4192-8462-5(2))* Kessinger Publishing, LLC.

Arena, Felice & Kettle, Phil. Pirate Ship: By Felice Arena & Phil Kettle: Illustrated by Susy Boyer. Boyer, Susy, illus. 2004. (J). pap. *(978-1-59336-362-8(1))* Mondo Publishing.

Bagley, Jessixa. Boats for Papa. 2015. (ENG., Illus.). 40p. (J). (gr. -1-2). 17.99 *(978-1-62672-039-8(8))*, 9781626720398) Roaring Brook Pr.

Ballantyne, R. M. Saved by the Lifeboat. 2004. reprint ed. pap. 1.99 *(978-1-4192-4624-1(0))*; pap. 15.95 *(978-1-4191-4624-4(6))* Kessinger Publishing, LLC.

Barnum, Vance. Frank & Andy Afloat. 2007. 212p. 27.95 *(978-1-4218-3911-0(3)*, 1st World Library - Literary Society) 1st World Publishing, Inc.

—Frank & Andy Afloat: The Cave on the Island. 2007. (ENG.). 160p. pap. 19.99 *(978-1-4346-3226-5(1))*; 180p. pap. 21.99 *(978-1-4346-3227-2(X))* Creative Media Partners, LLC.

—Frank & Andy Afloat or the Cave on the Island. 2007. 184p. 19.99 *(978-1-4280-7450-7(3))*; per. 13.99 *(978-1-4280-7469-9(4))* IndyPublish.com.

Beauvais, Clémentine. Scam on the Cam. Home, Sarah, illus. 2016. (Sesame Seade Mystery Ser.: 3). (ENG.). 192p. (J). 16.95 *(978-0-8234-3630-9(6))* Holiday Hse., Inc.

Biggs, Brian. Everything Goes - By Sea. Biggs, Brian, illus. 2013. (ENG., Illus.). 56p. (J). (gr. -1-3). 14.99 *(978-0-06-195811-3(5))* HarperCollins Pubs.

Blackstone, Stella. Hip Shapes. Bell, Siobhan, illus. 2012. (ENG.). 24p. (J). (gr. -1-k). 6.99 *(978-1-84686-762-0(2))* Barefoot Bks., Inc.

—Ship Shapes. Bell, Siobhan, illus. (J). 2008. (ENG.). 24p. (gr. -1-k). bds. 7.99 *(978-1-84686-157-4(8))* 2006. 0024p. 15.99 *(978-1-905236-34-3(4))* 2006. *(978-1-4156-6474-2(9))* Barefoot Bks., Inc.

—Ship Shapes. 2012. lib. bdg. 17.20 *(978-0-606-23826-7(3)*, Turtleback) Turtleback Bks.

Blane, Francisco. Row, Row, Row Your Boat. Kelley, Gerald, illus. 2010. (Rising Readers Ser.). (J). 3.49 *(978-1-60719-695-2(6))* Newmark Learning LLC.

Boat. 2004. (J). per. *(978-1-57657-353-2(2))* Paradise Pr., Inc.

Bonnell, Kris. The Little Boat. 2006. (J). pap. 5.95 *(978-1-933727-34-9(9))* Reading Reading Bks., LLC.

Boricchio, Frances. The Adventure of Rodney & Diane. 2012. 26p. pap. 17.99 *(978-1-4685-6445-7(5))* AuthorHouse.

Brezenoff, Steve. Lost Island, 1 vol. Pinelli, Amerigo, illus. 2013. (Ravens Pass Ser.). (ENG.). 96p. (gr. 2-3). lib. bdg. 25.32 *(978-1-4342-4614-1(0))* Stone Arch Bks.

Buell, Janet. Sail Away, Little Boat. Ishida, Jui, illus. 2006. 32p. (J). 15.95 *(978-1-57505-821-4(9)*, Carolrhoda Bks.) Lerner Publishing Group.

Bulion, Leslie. Uncharted Waters, 1 vol. (ENG.). 192p. (J). (gr. 3-7). 2009. pap. 7.95 *(978-1-56145-485-3(0))* 2006. 14.95 *(978-1-56145-365-8(X))* Peachtree Pubs.

Bunting, Eve. Big Bear's Big Boat. Carpenter, Nancy, illus. 2013. (ENG.). 32p. (J). (gr. -1-3). 12.99 *(978-0-618-58537-3(0))* Houghton Mifflin Harcourt Publishing Co.

Burchett, Loni. Bear & Katie in A Riverboat Ride, 4 vols., Vol. 4. 2006. (Illus.). 104p. (J). per. 12.95 *(978-0-9742815-3-7(0))* Black Lab Publishing LLC.

Burleigh, Cyril. The Hilltop Boys on the River. 2005. 172p. pap. 11.95 *(978-1-4218-0427-9(1)*, 1st World Library - Literary Society) 1st World Publishing, Inc.

Burningham, John. Mr. Gumpy's Outing. Date not set. (Illus.). (J). bds. 6.95 *(978-0-8050-7373-7(6)*, Holt, Henry & Co. Bks. For Young Readers) Holt, Henry & Co.

Burroughs, Polly. The Honey Boat, 1 vol. 2008. (ENG., Illus.). 48p. (J). 14.99 *(978-0-7643-3121-3(3)*, 9780764331213) Schiffer Publishing, Ltd.

Carnesi, Mônica. Little Dog Lost: The True Story of a Brave Dog Named Baltic. Carnesi, Mônica, illus. 2012. (ENG., Illus.). 32p. (J). (gr. -1-k). 16.99 *(978-0-399-25666-0(0)*, Nancy Paulsen Books) Penguin Young Readers Group.

Catchpool, Michael. Grandpa's Boat. Williams, Sophy, illus. 2008. (ENG.). 32p. (J). (gr. k-k). 21.95 *(978-1-84270-690-9(X))* Andersen Pr. GBR. Dist: Independent Pubs. Group.

Clark, Katie. Grandma Drove the Lobsterboat, 1 vol. Huntington, Amy, illus. 2012. (ENG.). 32p. (J). (gr. -1-1). 16.95 *(978-1-60893-004-3(1))* Down East Bks.

Cockrum, James L. Short Boat on a Long River. Sansevero, Tony, illus. 2013. 180p. (YA). pap. 14.95 *(978-0-9768586-1-4(4))* Pangloss Publishing.

Collier, Kristen & Collier, Kevin Scott. The Jumbo Shrimp of Dire Straits. 2008. 20p. pap. 9.95 *(978-1-933090-92-4(8))* Guardian Angel Publishing, Inc.

Compton, Peggy. Captain Johnnie, 1 vol. 2008. (ENG.). 32p. 24.95 *(978-1-60441-693-0(9))* America Star Bks.

Cooke, James. Pink Pig in a Boat. 2004. 59p. pap. 16.95 *(978-1-4137-4338-8(2))* America Star Bks.

Cousins, Lucy. Maisy's Sailboat. Cousins, Lucy, illus. 2017. (Maisy Ser.). (ENG., Illus.). 18p. (J). (— 1). bds. 5.99 *(978-0-7636-9405-0(3))* Candlewick Pr.

Crampton, Gertrude. Scuffy the Tugboat. Gergely, Tibor, illus. deluxe ed. Date not set. (J). (gr. -1-2). reprint ed. *(978-1-929566-59-4(X))* Cronies.

—Scuffy the Tugboat: Classic Edition. Gergely, Tibor, illus. Date not set. (J). reprint ed. *(978-1-929566-52-5(2))* Cronies.

Cummings, Priscilla. Red Kayak. 2006. (ENG.). 224p. (J). (gr. 5-18). 7.99 *(978-0-14-240573-4(6)*, Puffin Books) Penguin Young Readers Group.

Cursed by the Wind: A Boy, a Mighty River, a Bittersweet Tragedy. 2006. 115p. per. 15.95 *(978-0-9749058-0-8(1))* Lovstad, Joel Publishing.

Darragh, Jill. Milly Feather. Gamble, Gael, illus. 2013. 64p. pap. *(978-0-473-26560-1(5))* Rangitawa Publishing.

de Sève, Randall. Toy Boat. Long, Loren, illus. (ENG.). (J). (gr. -1 — 1). 2014. 30p. bds. 7.99 *(978-0-399-16797-3(8))* 2007. 40p. 17.99 *(978-0-399-24374-5(7))* Penguin Young Readers Group. (Philomel Bks.).

Declercq, Al, et al. Bernida: A Michigan Sailing Legend. Miles, David, illus. 2014. (ENG.). 32p. (J). (gr. 1-4). 16.99 *(978-1-58536-904-1(7)*, 203553) Sleeping Bear Pr.

DeFelice, Cynthia C. The Missing Manatee. 2008. (ENG.). 192p. (J). (gr. 3-7). pap. 8.99 *(978-0-374-40020-0(2)*, 9780374400200) Square Fish.

Demarest, Chris L. My Blue Boat. 20th ed. 2014. (J). 18.95 *(978-1-930900-76-9(7))* Purple Hse. Pr.

deRubertis, Barbara. Rosie Raccoon's Rock & Roll Raft. Alley, R. W., illus. 2011. (Animal Antics A to Z Ser.). 32p. (J). lib. bdg. 22.60 *(978-1-57565-339-6(7))*; (gr. -1-3). pap. 7.95 *(978-1-57565-330-3(3))* Kane Press, Inc.

Docherty, Thomas. Little Boat. Docherty, Thomas, illus. 2009. (ENG., Illus.). 40p. (J). (gr. -1-2). 15.99 *(978-0-7636-4428-4(5)*, Templar) Candlewick Pr.

—To the Beach. Docherty, Thomas, illus. 2009. (ENG., Illus.). 40p. (J). (gr. -1-2). 15.99 *(978-0-7636-4429-1(3)*, Templar) Candlewick Pr.

Dream Boat: Individual Title Six-Packs. (Action Packs Ser.). 120p. (gr. 3-5). 44.00 *(978-0-7635-8429-0(0))* Rigby Education.

Dubose, Sarah. Uncharted Waters. 2013. 440p. pap. *(978-1-4596-6282-7(2))* ReadHowYouWant.com, Ltd.

Dunbar, Polly. Arthur's Dream Boat. Dunbar, Polly, illus. 2012. (ENG., Illus.). 40p. (J). (gr. -1-k). 15.99 *(978-0-7636-5867-0(7))* Candlewick Pr.

Escalante, Travis. Henry the Little Sailboat & the Happy Harbor. 2013. 28p. 16.99 *(978-0-9911512-5-7(9))* Mindstir Media.

Escott, John & Pearson Longman Staff. Hannah & the Hurricane. 2nd ed. 2009. (ENG., Illus.). 20p. pap. 11.99 *(978-1-4058-6947-6(X))* Pearson Education.

Falk, Elsa. Fire Canoe. Frankenberg, Robert, illus. 2012. 188p. 42.95 *(978-1-258-23680-9(X))*; pap. 27.95 *(978-1-258-24375-3(X))* Literary Licensing, LLC.

Feldman, Thea. Things That Go. 2006. 3p. 5.99 *(978-1-932915-31-0(1))* Sandvik Publishing.

Felix, Monique, creator. Mouse Books: the Boat. 2014. (ENG.). 32p. (J). (gr. -1-k). 12.99 *(978-1-56846-252-3(2)*, Creative Editions) Creative Co., The.

Ferguson, Sarah & Duchess of York Staff. Little Red's Summer Adventure. Williams, Sam, illus. 2006. (ENG.). 40p. (J). (gr. -1-3). 17.99 *(978-0-689-85562-7(1)*, Simon & Schuster/Paula Wiseman Bks.) Simon & Schuster/Paula Wiseman Bks.

Flack, Annie. Mysteries of the Lake. 2009. 92p. pap. 10.49 *(978-1-4389-6264-1(9))* AuthorHouse.

Fuller, Harvey. Tommy & the Island. Fuller, Harvey, illus. 2007. (Illus.). (J). pap. 18.95 *(978-0-9773725-7-7(X))* Flat Hammock Pr.

Furbush, Helen. Lying Awake. McCroskey, Christine, illus. l.t. ed. 2004. 32p. (J). (gr. 1-6). 15.95 *(978-0-9741787-0-7(5)*, 1239134) Harbor Island Bks.

Gaetz, Dayle Campbell. Sea Dog. Meissner, Amy, illus. 2006. 62p. (J). lib. bdg. 20.00 *(978-1-4242-1249-1(9))* Fitzgerald Bks.

—Sea Dog, 1 vol. Meissner, Amy, illus. 2006. (Orca Echoes Ser.). (ENG.). 64p. (J). (gr. 2-3). per. 6.95 *(978-1-55143-406-3(7))* Orca Bk. Pubs. USA.

Gamble, Robin. Samphire Tides. 2012. 112p. pap. *(978-1-909039-38-4(1))* Legend Pr.

Graves, Kassie. Brave Little Sailboat. Graves, Kassie, illus. 2003. (Illus.). 20p. (J). 14.95 *(978-0-9728019-0-4(1))* Bright Eyes Pr.

Hammond, Jo. Home Before Dark, 1 vol. 2005. (ENG.). 144p. (YA). (gr. 7-12). per. 7.95 *(978-1-55143-340-0(0))* Orca Bk. Pubs. USA.

Harnish, Jeannette. The Duck Who Drove a Boat. Harnish, Alexander, illus. 2008. 31p. pap. 24.95 *(978-1-60610-665-5(1))* America Star Bks.

Hart, Alison. Emma's River, 1 vol. Bachem, Paul, illus. 2010. (ENG.). 160p. (J). (gr. 2-5). 12.95 *(978-1-56145-524-9(5)*, Peachtree Junior) Peachtree Pubs.

Hawksley, Gerald, illus. Splashy Dolphin's Boat: Press Out Parts Make a Boat Carrying Splashy Dolphin. 2009. (Toddler Make & Play Ser.). 10p. bds. 6.95 *(978-1-59496-183-0(2))* Teora USA LLC.

Hayes, Geoffrey. The Mystery of the Riverboat Robber. 2016. (Step into Reading Ser.). (ENG., Illus.). 48p. (J). (gr. k-3). lib. bdg. 12.99 *(978-0-375-97470-0(9)*, Random Hse. Bks. for Young Readers) Random Hse. Children's Bks.

Hayes, James. Tuggy the Little Tug Boat. 2012. 24p. pap. 17.99 *(978-1-4772-9075-0(3))* AuthorHouse.

Hearne, Betsy. Seven Brave Women. Andersen, Bethanne, illus. 2006. (gr. -1-3). 17.00 *(978-0-7569-6669-0(8))* Perfection Learning Corp.

Hiaasen, Carl. Flush. 2007. 263p. (gr. 5-9). 19.00 *(978-0-7569-8192-1(1))* Perfection Learning Corp.

—Flush. (ENG.). 272p. (J). (gr. 5-6). 2010. 6.99 *(978-0-375-86125-3(4)*, Yearling) 2007. pap. 8.99 *(978-0-375-84185-9(7)*, Knopf Bks. for Young Readers) Random Hse. Children's Bks.

Hicks, Greg & Foster, Rick. The Martha Is Mine: An Almost True Story. Sheldon, Kristin, illus. 2007. 56p. (J). 16.95 *(978-0-9790709-0-7(2))* Foster, Hicks & Assocs.

Hillert, Margaret. The Yellow Boat. Baird, Roberta, illus. 2016. (BeginningtoRead Ser.). (ENG.). 32p. (J). (gr. -1-2). 22.60 *(978-1-59953-811-2(3))*; pap. 11.94 *(978-1-60357-952-0(4))* Norwood Hse. Pr.

Hoogstad, Alice. BOLDER & BOAT. 2008. (ENG.). 32p. (J). (gr. 1-7). 13.95 *(978-1-60136-015-1(0))* Audio Holdings, LLC.

Horender, Philip M. The Mighty Maximilian: Samuel Clemens's Traveling Companion, 1 vol. Wolek, Guy, illus. 2013. (Maximilian P. Mouse, Time Traveler Ser.). (ENG.). 112p. (J). (gr. 3-6). lib. bdg. 27.07 *(978-1-61641-960-8(1)*, Calico Chapter Bks) Magic Wagon.

Hubbell, Patricia. Boats: Speeding! Sailing! Cruising!, 0 vols. Halsey, Megan & Addy, Sean, illus. 2009. (ENG.). 32p. (J). (gr. -1-1). 17.99 *(978-0-7614-5524-0(8)*, 9780761455240, Amazon Children's Publishing) Amazon Publishing.

The Invisible Boat, 1 vol. 2013. (ENG.). 336p. pap. 18.00 *(978-1-936367-44-3(0))* Waldorf Publications.

Johnson, Gail. Chasing the Sun. 2009. 40p. pap. 17.99 *(978-1-4389-2192-1(6))* AuthorHouse.

Johnson, Maureen. Girl at Sea. 2008. (ENG., Illus.). 336p. (YA). (gr. 8-12). pap. 8.99 *(978-0-06-054146-0(6)*, HarperTeen) HarperCollins Pubs.

Jones, Christianne C. Bella's Boat Surprise, 1 vol. Sullivan, Mary, illus. (My First Graphic Novel Ser.). (ENG.). 32p. (gr. k-2). 2010. pap. 6.25 *(978-1-4342-2287-9(X))* 2009. 24.65 *(978-1-4342-1617-5(9))* Stone Arch Bks. (My First Graphic Novel).

The Journey of the Little Red Boat: A Story from the Coast of Maine, 1. 2003. (Illus.). 29p. (J). bds. 16.95 *(978-0-9740434-0-1(0)*, 255-3716) Smith, George Publishing.

Kelly, David A. The San Francisco Splash. 2013. (Ballpark Mysteries Ser.: Bk. 7). lib. bdg. 14.75 *(978-0-606-31940-9(9)*, Turtleback) Turtleback Bks.

Kennedy, Robert F., Jr. Robert Smalls: The Boat Thief. Faricy, Patrick, illus. 2008. (Robert F. Kennedy, Jr.'s American Heroes Ser.). (ENG.). 48p. (gr. 5-8). 16.99 *(978-1-4231-0802-3(7))* Hyperion Pr.

Kessler, Liz. Poppy the Pirate Dog. Phillips, Mike, illus. 2013. (ENG.). 64p. (J). (gr. k-3). 14.99 *(978-0-7636-6569-2(X))* Candlewick Pr.

Kline, Suzy. Horrible Harry Goes to Sea: Puffine Chapters. Remkiewicz, Frank, illus. 2003. (Horrible Harry Ser.). (ENG.). 64p. (J). (gr. 2-4). 4.99 *(978-0-14-250002-6(X)*, Puffin Books) Penguin Young Readers Group.

—Horrible Harry Goes to Sea: Puffine Chapters. 2003. (Horrible Harry Ser.: 13). (gr. 3-6). lib. bdg. 14.75 *(978-0-613-61629-4(4)*, Turtleback) Turtleback Bks.

Krebs, Laurie. We're Sailing to Galapagos: A Week in the Pacific. Restelli, Grazia, illus. 2007. (ENG.). 32p. (J). (gr. k-1). pap. 8.99 *(978-1-84686-102-4(0))* Barefoot Bks., Inc.

Kwan, James. How It Feels to Be a Boat. 2017. (ENG., Illus.). 40p. (J). (gr. -1-3). 16.99 *(978-0-544-71533-2(0)*, HMH Books For Young Readers) Houghton Mifflin Harcourt Publishing Co.

Lee, Amy Sue. Lou Lou & Lenny's Boat Ride. 2005. (Illus.). 28p. (J). (gr. -1-3). per. 19.99 *(978-1-4208-6447-2(5))* AuthorHouse.

Lemke, Donald. Diver Down, 1 vol. Glass House Graphics Staff, illus. 2011. (Good vs Evil Ser.). (ENG.). 48p. (gr. 1-2). pap. 6.29 *(978-1-4342-3446-9(0)*, Good vs Evil) Stone Arch Bks.

Lemke, Donald B. Diver Down, 1 vol. 2011. (Good vs Evil Ser.). (ENG.). 48p. (gr. 1-2). lib. bdg. 23.99 *(978-1-4342-2092-9(3)*, Good vs Evil) Stone Arch Bks.

Lewis, Anthony, illus. Little Ocean Explorers. 2007. (Little Explorers Ser.). (ENG.). 14p. (J). (gr. 1-1). bds. *(978-1-84643-039-8(9))* Child's Play International Ltd.

Light, John. Making a Splash! 2005. (Illus.). 24p. *(978-1-897968-20-5(5))* Photon Pr.

Lloyd-Jones, Sally. Old MacNoah Had an Ark. Newton, Jill, illus. 2008. (HarperBlessings Ser.). 32p. (J). (gr. -1-2). 17.89 *(978-0-06-055718-8(4))* HarperCollins Pubs.

Lockhart, Lynne N. & Lockhart, Barbara M. Rambling Raft, 1 vol. Lockhart, Lynne N., illus. 2009. (ENG., Illus.). 30p. (J). (gr. 2-18). 7.95 *(978-0-87033-392-7(5)*, 9780870333927, Cornell Maritime Pr./Tidewater Pubs.) Schiffer Publishing, Ltd.

Luciani, Brigitte. What a Team! Gauvin, Edward, tr. from FRE. Tharlet, Eve, illus. 2011. (Mr. Badger & Mrs. Fox Ser.: 3). (ENG.). 32p. (J). (gr. k-3). 25.26 *(978-0-7613-5627-1(4))*; pap. 6.95 *(978-0-7613-5633-2(9)*, Graphic Universe™) Lerner Publishing Group.

Luper, Eric. Jeremy Bender vs. the Cupcake Cadets. 2011. (ENG.). 240p. (J). (gr. 3-7). 16.99 *(978-0-06-201512-9(5))* HarperCollins Pubs.

Lyon, George Ella & Lyon, Benn. Boats Float! Wiggins, Mick, illus. 2015. (ENG.). 40p. (J). (gr. -1-3). 17.99 *(978-1-4814-0380-1(X))* Simon & Schuster Children's Publishing.

Mabee, Andrea. Dory Glory: Building A Boat from Stem to Stern. Mabee, Andrea, photos by. 2005. (Illus.). 67p. (YA). per. 15.95 *(978-0-9630074-1-4(6))* Bass Cove Bks.

Maddox, Tony & Wen, Dref. Ffred Ar y Môr: Cyfres Ffred Ci'r Fferm. 2005. (WEL., Illus.). 32p. pap. *(978-1-85596-666-6(2))* Dref Wen.

Marin, Cheech. Captain Cheech. Ramirez, Orlando L., illus. 2008. 32p. (J). (gr. -1-3). lib. bdg. 17.89 *(978-0-06-113208-7(X))* HarperCollins Pubs.

Maybank, Roger. The Sun Boat: A Fairytale. 2005. 324p. pap. 25.60 *(978-1-4120-6452-1(X))* Trafford Publishing.

Mayer, Mercer. Just an Adventure at Sea. 2017. (Little Critter: I Can Read! Ser.). lib. bdg. 13.55 ***(978-0-606-40062-6(1))*** Turtleback Bks.

—Little Critter: 5-Minute Little Critter Stories. Mayer, Mercer, illus. 2017. (Little Critter Ser.). (Illus.). 192p. (J). (gr. -1-3). 12.99 ***(978-0-06-265525-7(6)***, HarperFestival) HarperCollins Pubs.

Mayer, Mercer. Little Critter: Just an Adventure at Sea. Mayer, Mercer, illus. 2017. (My First I Can Read Ser.). (Illus.). 32p. (J). (gr. -1-3). pap. 3.99 *(978-0-06-243140-0(4))* HarperCollins Pubs.

Mayfield, Sue. The Four Franks. 2005. (Blue Go Bananas Ser.). (ENG., Illus.). 48p. (J). (gr. 1-2). lib. bdg. *(978-0-7787-2629-6(0))* Crabtree Publishing Co.

McCall, Edith. Stories of American Steamboats. Borja, Robert, illus. 2011. 126p. 40.95 *(978-1-258-10111-4(4))* Literary Licensing, LLC.

Miller, Bobbi. Big River's Daughter. 2013. (ENG.). 224p. (J). (gr. 2-7). 16.95 *(978-0-8234-2752-9(8))* Holiday Hse., Inc.

Miyares, Daniel. Float. Miyares, Daniel, illus. 2015. (ENG., Illus.). 48p. (J). (gr. -1-3). 17.99 *(978-1-4814-1524-8(7)*, Simon & Schuster Bks. For Young Readers) Simon & Schuster Bks. For Young Readers.

Moncure, Jane Belk. Nanny Goat's Boat: A Book of Rhyming. Girouard, Patrick, illus. 2013. (Magic Castle Readers Ser.). (ENG.). 32p. (J). (gr. -1-2). 25.64 *(978-1-62323-567-3(7)*, 206301) Child's World, Inc., The.

O'Donnell, Liam. Lucy & the Busy Boat. Hynes, Robert, illus. (Pet Tales Ser.). (ENG.). 32p. (J). (gr. -1-2). 2005. 2.95 *(978-1-59249-296-1(7)*, 1B021) 2004. 4.95 *(978-1-59249-295-4(9)*, 1B019) 2004. 9.95 *(978-1-59249-319-7(X)*, 1B022) Soundprints.

Optic, Oliver, pseud. Little by Little or the Cruise of the Fl. 2005. pap. 27.95 *(978-1-4179-9436-6(3))* Kessinger Publishing, LLC.

—Taken by the Enemy. 2007. 132p. (gr. 4-7). per. *(978-1-4068-4346-0(6))* Echo Library.

—[the Boat Club; or, the Bunkers of Rippleton a Tale for Boys by Oliver Optic, Pseud. 2006. 252p. per. 23.99 *(978-1-4255-2253-7(X))* Michigan Publishing.

Orr, Wendy. Mokie & Bik Go to Sea. Bean, Jonathan, illus. 2010. (ENG.). 80p. (J). (gr. 2-5). 15.99 *(978-0-8050-8174-9(7)*, 9780805081749, Holt, Henry & Co. Bks. For Young Readers) Holt, Henry & Co.

Pallotta, Jerry. Dory Story. Biedrzycki, David, illus. 2006. (ENG.). 32p. (J). (gr. -1-3). pap. 7.95 *(978-0-88106-076-8(3))* Charlesbridge Publishing, Inc.

Pallotta, Jerry, et al. Dory Story. Biedrzycki, David, illus. 2003. (Avenues Ser.). (ENG.). 32p. (C). (gr. -1-3). pap. 27.95 *(978-0-88106-075-1(5))* National Geographic School Publishing, Inc.

Pantin, Yolanda. Splash! Faria, Rosana, illus. 2003. (SPA.). 16p. (J). (gr. -1-1). *(978-980-6437-19-7(5))* Playco Editores, C.A.

Parks, Kathy. The Lifeboat Clique. 2016. 336p. (YA). (gr. 8). 17.99 *(978-0-06-239396-8(0)*, Tegen, Katherine Bks) HarperCollins Pubs.

Phillips, Gina & Cassettari, Noeline. Mighty Tugboats. 2003. (Button Bks.). (Illus.). (J). bds. 12.95 *(978-1-74047-312-5(4))* Book Co. Publishing Pty, Ltd., The AUS. Dist: Penton Overseas, Inc.

Picou, Lin. Best Boat Race Ever! Reasoner, John, illus. 2012. (ENG.). 24p. (gr. 1-2). pap. 8.95 *(978-1-61810-317-8(2))* Rourke Educational Media.

Porta, Bill K. Adventures of Henry the Little Boat. 2011. 24p. (gr. -1). pap. 11.32 *(978-1-4520-4448-4(1))* AuthorHouse.

Preiss, Thomas. The Boat under the Boat: A Story about the Golden Rule. 2nd rev. ed. 2004. (ENG., Illus.). 32p. (J). per. 14.95 *(978-0-9798620-1-4(9))* Peralta Publishing, LLC.

Ransome, Arthur. Great Northern? 2003. (Swallows & Amazons Ser.). (ENG., Illus.). 352p. (J). pap. 14.95 *(978-1-56792-259-2(7))* Godine, David R. Pub.

—Swallows & Amazons. Ransome, Arthur, illus. 2010. (Swallows & Amazons Ser.). (Illus.). 351p. (J). pap. 14.95 *(978-1-56792-420-6(4))* Godine, David R. Pub.

—Swallows & Amazons. 2013. (ENG.). 384p. (gr. 4-13). 22.95 *(978-1-4683-0661-3(8)*, 460661) Overlook Pr., The.

Rathborne, St. George. The House Boat Boys. 2007. 160p. per. *(978-1-4065-4243-1(1))* Dodo Pr.

—The House Boat Boys; or, Drifting down to the Sunny South. 2007. 108p. per. *(978-1-4068-3747-6(4))* Echo Library.

Remole, Arnulf. The Island of Alphebia. 2007. 34p. 24.55 *(978-1-4303-2720-2(0))* Lulu Pr., Inc.

Rey, H. A. & Rey, Margret. Curious George the Boat Show. 2008. (Curious George Ser.). (ENG., Illus.). 24p. (J). (gr. -1-3). pap. 3.99 *(978-0-618-89196-2(X))* Houghton Mifflin Harcourt Publishing Co.

Rigby Education Staff. Row, Row, Row Your Boat. (Illus.). (J). suppl. ed. 20.00 *(978-0-7635-6457-5(5)*, 764575C99) Rigby Education.

Riggs, Sandy. Joe Boat. Barr, Kristin, illus. 2006. (Reader's Clubhouse Level 2 Reader Ser.). (ENG.). 24p. (J). (gr. 1-4). pap. 3.99 *(978-0-7641-3296-4(2))* Barron's Educational Series, Inc.

Robb, R. E. I Learned about Boating from This... 2004. per. 11.99 *(978-0-9716681-5-7(9))* Magic Valley Pubs.

Rocco, John & Primiano, Jay. Swim That Rock. Rocco, John, illus. 2014. (ENG., Illus.). 304p. (YA). (gr. 7). 16.99 *(978-0-7636-6905-8(9))* Candlewick Pr.

Rockity Rock: KinderReaders Individual Title Six-Packs. (Kinderstarters Ser.). 8p. (gr. -1-1). 21.00 *(978-0-7635-8643-0(9))* Rigby Education.

Rosman, Yitz. Jerry Sets Sail. 2013. 40p. pap. 16.46 *(978-1-4669-8202-4(0))* Trafford Publishing.

Roy, Lillian Elizabeth. Polly's Southern Cruise: The Polly Brewster Series. Barbour, H. S., illus. 2011. 294p. 48.95 *(978-1-258-10514-3(4))* Literary Licensing, LLC.

Ryan, John. Pugwash & the Sea Monster. fac. ed. 2009. (ENG., Illus.). 32p. (J). (gr. -1-2). 16.95 *(978-1-84507-888-1(8)*, Frances Lincoln) Quarto Publishing Group UK GBR. Dist: Hachette Bk. Group.

Rylant, Cynthia. Mr. Putter & Tabby Clear the Decks. Howard, Arthur, illus. alt. ed. 2011. (Mr. Putter & Tabby Ser.). (ENG.). 44p. (J). (gr. 1-4). pap. 5.99 *(978-0-547-57695-4(1))* Houghton Mifflin Harcourt Publishing Co.

Salimena, Kathleen Elizabeth. The Royal Yacht. 2008. (Illus.). 24p. (J). (gr. 11-18). 15.95 *(978-0-9798624-0-3(X))* Royal Imprint Pr., Inc.

Santillo, LuAnn. Toad. Santillo, LuAnn, ed. 2003. (Half-Pint Kids Readers Ser.). (Illus.). 7p. (gr. -1-1). pap. 1.00 *(978-1-59256-107-0(1))* Half-Pint Kids, Inc.

Scarry, Richard. Richard Scarry's the Great Steamboat Mystery. 2014. (ENG., Illus.). 34p. (J). (gr. 1-2). 4.95 *(978-1-4549-1010-7(0))* Sterling Publishing Co., Inc.

Segal, John. Alistair & Kip's Great Adventure! Segal, John, illus. 2008. (ENG., Illus.). 32p. (J). (gr. -1-3). 17.99 *(978-1-4169-0280-5(5)*, McElderry, Margaret K. Bks.) McElderry, Margaret K. Bks.

Seitz, Melissa. Stewie Meets New Friends. Accrocco, Anthony, illus. 2012. 26p. pap. 12.95 *(978-1-61244-079-8(7))* Halo Publishing International.

Shelton, Dave. A Boy & a Bear in a Boat. 2013. (ENG.). 304p. (J). (gr. 2-5). 6.99 *(978-0-449-81060-6(7)*, Yearling) Random Hse. Children's Bks.

Shusterman, Danielle. On the Big Boat. 2016. (1-3Y Getting Around Ser.). (ENG., Illus.). 16p. (J). pap. 5.99 *(978-1-63437-487-3(8))* American Reading Co.

Sims, Lesley. Goat in a Boat. 2015. (Phonics Readers (no Flaps) Ser.). (ENG.). 24p. (J). pap. 6.99 *(978-0-7945-3408-0(2)*, Usborne) EDC Publishing.

Singleton, Glynn. Buddy Boy Brooks Takes the Wheel: A Mile Wide Tale from the Mighty Mississippi. Carisse, Carissa, illus. 2007. 32p. (J). (gr. 2-4). 12.95 *(978-1-57072-320-9(6))* Overmountain Pr.

Smith, George. The Journey of the Little Red Boat: A Story from the Coast of Maine. 2nd ed. 2004. (Illus.). 50p. (J). per. 7.99 *(978-0-9740434-1-8(9)*, 255-3716) Smith, George Publishing.

Snell, Roy J. The Blue Envelope. 2009. 112p. 22.95 *(978-1-60664-675-5(3))*; pap. 9.95 *(978-1-60664-304-4(5))* Rodgers, Alan Bks.

Soman, David. Three Bears in a Boat. Soman, David, illus. 2014. (ENG., Illus.). 40p. (J). (gr. -1-k). 17.99 *(978-0-8037-3993-2(1)*, Dial Bks) Penguin Publishing Group.

Starfall Education. Soap Boat. Starfall Education, ed. 2004. (ENG., Illus.). 8p. (J). pap. *(978-1-59577-011-0(9))* Starfall Education.

Starkoff, Vanina. Along the River, 1 vol. Springer, Jane, tr. from POR. Starkoff, Vanina, illus. 2017. (ENG., Illus.). 32p. (J). (gr. -1). 17.95 *(978-1-55498-977-5(9))* Groundwood Bks. CAN. Dist: Publishers Group West (PGW).

Stead, Philip C. Jonathan & the Big Blue Boat. Stead, Philip C., illus. 2011. (ENG., Illus.). 32p. (J). (gr. -1-2). 16.99 *(978-1-59643-562-9(3)*, 9781596435629) Roaring Brook Pr.

Stevenson, Robin. Dead in the Water, 1 vol. 2008. (Orca Sports Ser.). (ENG.). 176p. (YA). (gr. 6-10). pap. 9.95 *(978-1-55143-962-4(X))* Orca Bk. Pubs. USA.

Stiles, Martha Bennett. Sailing to Freedom. 2012. (ENG.). 256p. (J). (gr. 3-7). 16.99 *(978-0-8050-9238-7(2)*, 9780805092387, Holt, Henry & Co. Bks. For Young Readers) Holt, Henry & Co.

—Sailing to Freedom. 2014. (ENG.). 256p. (J). (gr. 3-7). pap. 6.99 *(978-1-250-03991-0(6)*, 9781250039910) Square Fish.

Stuck in the MUD. l.t. ed. 2004. (Illus.). 20p. (J). cd-rom 19.95 *(978-0-9759370-0-6(6))* Brown&Matthews.

Swift, Ginger. Little Blue Boat. Persico, Zoe, illus. 2016. (ENG.). 10p. (J). bds. 0.00 *(978-1-68052-077-4(6))* Cottage Door Pr.

Swinson, Joyce Ann. Noah's Boat. Clark, Casey, illus. 2007. 32p. per. 24.95 *(978-1-4241-9012-6(6))* America Star Bks.

Szymanski, Lois K. Grandfather's Secret, 1 vol. 2010. (ENG., Illus.). 64p. (J). pap. 12.99 *(978-0-7643-3535-8(9)*, 9780764335358) Schiffer Publishing, Ltd.

TenNapel, Doug. Bad Island. 2011. (ENG.). 224p. (J). (gr. 4-7). pap. 10.99 *(978-0-545-31480-0(1)*, Graphix) Scholastic, Inc.

Tetlow, Karin. Harry Goes Rowing. Guze, Tessa, illus. 2013. 32p. pap. 11.95 *(978-0-615-75585-4(2))* Juping Horse Pr.

Thomson, John. A Small Boat at the Bottom of the Sea. 2005. (ENG., Illus.). (J). (gr. 4-7). 152p. 16.95 *(978-1-57131-657-8(4))*; 156p. per. 6.95 *(978-1-57131-656-1(6))* Milkweed Editions.

Tolcser, Sarah. Song of the Current. 2017. (ENG.). 384p. (YA). 17.99 *(978-1-68119-297-0(7)*, 9781681192970, Bloomsbury USA Childrens) Bloomsbury Publishing USA.

Tuzee, John & Tuzee, Diane. Charlie Canoe & Other Boats, Too. Kasun, Mike, illus. 2006. (J). *(978-0-9755348-2-3(3))* Kids Life Pr.

Van Allsburg, Chris. The Wreck of the Zephyr. 2014. 32p. pap. 9.00 *(978-1-61003-222-3(5))* Center for the Collaborative Classroom.

—The Wreck of the Zephyr. 30th anniv. ed. 2013. (ENG., Illus.). 32p. (J). (gr. -1-3). 18.99 *(978-0-544-05005-1(3))* Houghton Mifflin Harcourt Publishing Co.

Vance Barnum. Frank & Andy Afloat. 2007. 212p. per. 12.95 *(978-1-4218-4011-6(1)*, 1st World Library - Literary Society) 1st World Publishing, Inc.

Virján, Emma J. What This Story Needs Is a Pig in a Wig. Virján, Emma J., illus. 2015. (Pig in a Wig Book Ser.). (ENG., Illus.). 40p. (J). (gr. -1-3). 9.99 *(978-0-06-232724-6(0))* HarperCollins Pubs.

Waddell, Martin. Captain Small Pig, 1 vol. Varley, Susan, illus. 2010. (ENG.). 32p. (J). (gr. -1-3). 15.95 *(978-1-56145-519-5(9))* Peachtree Pubs.

Walker, Melissa. Unbreak My Heart. (ENG., (YA). (gr. 7). 2013. Illus.). 256p. pap. 9.99 *(978-1-61963-007-9(9)*, 9781619630079) 2012. 240p. 16.99 *(978-1-59990-528-0(0)*, 9781599905280) Bloomsbury Publishing USA. (Bloomsbury USA Childrens).

Warren, George A. The Banner Boy Scouts on a Tour. 2005. pap. 30.95 *(978-1-885529-38-1(4))* Stevens Publishing.

Waters, Michael. Tommy & his Flying Saucer of Milk. 2009. 32p. 18.95 *(978-1-4092-8450-5(6))* Lulu Pr., Inc.

Winkler, Ashley & Winkler, Michael. One Good Quest Deserves Another: A Crown of Amaranth Story. 2009. 292p. 28.95 *(978-0-595-71039-3(5))*; pap. 18.95 *(978-0-595-47365-6(2))* iUniverse, Inc.

Zimmer, Tracie Vaughn & Vaughn Zimmer, Tracie. The Floating Circus. 2008. (ENG.). 208p. (YA). (gr. 3-7). 16.99 *(978-1-59990-185-5(4)*, 9781599901855, Bloomsbury USA Childrens) Bloomsbury Publishing USA.

BOATS AND BOATING—HISTORY

Beyer, Mark. Barcos Del Pasado. 2004. (Transporte Ayer y Hoy (Transportation Through the Ages) Ser.). (SPA & ENG., Illus.). 24p. (J). (gr. 2-4). lib. bdg. 22.60 *(978-0-8239-6855-8(3))* Rosen Publishing Group, Inc., The.

—Barcos del pasado (Boats of the Past) 2009. (transporte ayer y hoy (Transportation Through the Ages) Ser.). (SPA.). 24p. (gr. 1-2). 42.50 *(978-1-61512-253-0(2)*, Editorial Buenas Letras) Rosen Publishing Group, Inc., The.

—Boats of the Past. 2009. (Transportation Through the Ages Ser.). 24p. (gr. 1-1). 42.50 *(978-1-60854-587-2(3)*, PowerKids Pr.) Rosen Publishing Group, Inc., The.

The Complete History of Ships & Boats: From Sails & Oars to Nuclear-Powered Vessels. 2011. (Transportation & Society Ser.). (ENG.). 192p. (YA). (gr. 10-12). 77.50 *(978-1-61530-770-8(2))* Rosen Publishing Group, Inc., The.

Richardson, Gillian. 10 Ships That Rocked the World. Rosen, Kim, illus. 2015. (World of Tens Ser.). (ENG.). 176p. (J). (gr. 4-7). pap. 14.95 *(978-1-55451-781-7(8)*, 9781554517817) Annick Pr., Ltd. CAN. Dist: Publishers Group West (PGW).

BOB THE BUILDER (FICTITIOUS CHARACTER)—FICTION

Bob the Builder. 2003. (J). (gr. -1-2). spiral bd. 14.99 *(978-1-59319-000-2(X))* LeapFrog Enterprises, Inc.

Forte, Lauren. Bob the Builder: Car Wash Crunch. 2017. (Passport to Reading Level 1 Ser.). (ENG., Illus.). 32p. (J). (gr. -1-3). pap. 4.99 *(978-0-316-54815-1(4))* Little, Brown Bks. for Young Readers.

Forte, Lauren. Bob the Builder: Dino Park. 2017. (ENG., Illus.). 24p. (J). (gr. -1-3). pap. 4.99 ***(978-0-316-54814-4(6))*** Little, Brown Bks. for Young Readers.

Lee, Justus. Bob the Builder. 2016. (ENG., Illus.). 12p. (J). (gr. -1 — 1). bds. 6.99 *(978-0-316-27297-1(3))* Little, Brown Bks. for Young Readers.

—The Things We Love. 2016. (ENG.). 12p. (J). (gr. -1 — 1). bds. 6.99 *(978-0-316-27295-7(7))* Little, Brown Bks. for Young Readers.

Lucci, Cindy. Bob the Builder: Big Book of Words. 2017. (ENG., Illus.). 12p. (J). (gr. -1 — 1). bds. 8.99 *(978-0-316-27299-5(X))* Little, Brown Bks. for Young Readers.

Mattel. Bob the Builder: Alien Mix-Up. 2016. (Passport to Reading Level 1 Ser.). (ENG., Illus.). 32p. (J). (gr. -1-3). pap. 3.99 *(978-0-316-35683-1(2))* Little, Brown Bks. for Young Readers.

—Bob the Builder: All about Scoop! 2016. (ENG.). 10p. (J). (gr. -1-1). bds. 6.99 *(978-0-316-39445-1(9))* Little, Brown Bks. for Young Readers.

—Bob the Builder: Can We Build It? Yes, We Can! 2016. (ENG., Illus.). 24p. (J). (gr. -1-3). pap. 5.99 *(978-0-316-35681-7(6))* Little, Brown Bks. for Young Readers.

—Bob the Builder: Milkshake Madness. 2016. (ENG., Illus.). 24p. (J). (gr. -1-3). 3.99 *(978-0-316-35584-1(4))* Little, Brown Bks. for Young Readers.

—Bob the Builder: Welcome to Spring City! 2016. (ENG., Illus.). 16p. (J). (gr. -1-1). bds. 8.99 *(978-0-316-39449-9(1))* Little, Brown Bks. for Young Readers.

Mattel & Sollinger, Emily. Bob the Builder: Sky-High Scoop. 2016. (ENG.). 20p. (J). (gr. -1-3). 12.99 *(978-0-316-39443-7(2))* Little, Brown Bks. for Young Readers.

Mattel & Tumnus, Hermione. Bob the Builder: All about Lofty. 2017. (ENG., Illus.). 12p. (J). (gr. -1 — 1). bds. 6.99 ***(978-0-316-39907-4(8))*** Little, Brown Bks. for Young Readers.

Milton, Elizabeth. Bob the Builder. 2016. (ENG.). 24p. (J). (gr. -1-3). pap. 3.99 *(978-0-316-27294-0(9))* Little, Brown Bks. for Young Readers.

—Bob the Builder: a Present for Bob. 2016. (ENG., Illus.). 32p. (J). (gr. -1-3). 15.99 *(978-0-316-27293-3(0))* Little, Brown Bks. for Young Readers.

Running Press Staff. Opposites. 2004. (Sticker Math Ser.). (ENG.). 1p. (J). pap., act. bk. ed. 4.95 *(978-0-7945-0042-9(0)*, Usborne) EDC Publishing.

Sollinger, Emily. Bob the Builder. 2016. (Passport to Reading Level 1 Ser.). (ENG.). 32p. (J). (gr. -1-3). pap. 3.99 *(978-0-316-27296-4(5))* Little, Brown Bks. for Young Readers.

BOBBSEY TWINS (FICTITIOUS CHARACTERS)—FICTION

Hope, Laura. The Bobbsey Twins. 2005. pap. 14.95 *(978-1-55742-523-2(X))* Wildside Pr., LLC.

—The Bobbsey Twins at the County Fair. 2005. pap. 14.95 *(978-1-55742-397-9(0))* Wildside Pr., LLC.

—Bobbsey Twins or Merry Days Indoors and. 2006. 18.99 *(978-1-4219-7001-1(5))* IndyPublish.com.

Hope, Laura Lee. Bobbsey Twins. 2006. 25.95 *(978-1-4218-2978-4(9))*; pap. 10.95 *(978-1-4218-3078-0(7))* 1st World Publishing, Inc.

—The Bobbsey Twins at Meadow Brook. 2005. 200p. 27.95 *(978-1-4218-0653-2(3)*, 1st World Library - Literary Society) 1st World Publishing, Inc.

—The Bobbsey Twins at the Seashore. 2005. 26.95 *(978-1-4218-1070-6(0))*; 176p. pap. 11.95 *(978-1-4218-1170-3(7))* 1st World Publishing, Inc. (1st World Library - Literary Society).

—The Bobbsey Twins in a Great City. 2005. 27.95 *(978-1-4218-1482-7(X))*; 204p. pap. 12.95 *(978-1-4218-1582-4(6))* 1st World Publishing, Inc. (1st World Library - Literary Society).

—The Bobbsey Twins in the Country. 2005. 208p. 27.95 *(978-1-4218-0655-6(X)*, 1st World Library - Literary Society) 1st World Publishing, Inc.

—The Bobbsey Twins in the Great West. 2005. 27.95 *(978-1-4218-0365-4(8)*, 1st World Library - Literary Society) 1st World Publishing, Inc.

—The Bobbsey Twins in Washington. 2005. 27.95 *(978-1-4218-0974-8(5)*, 1st World Library - Literary Society) 1st World Publishing, Inc.

—The Bobbsey Twins in.Washington. 2007. 256p. 29.95 *(978-1-4344-8591-5(9))*; per. 17.95 *(978-1-4344-8590-8(0))* Wildside Pr., LLC.

—The Bobbsey Twins on a House Boat. 2005. 204p. pap. 12.95 *(978-1-4218-1167-3(7)*, 1st World Library - Literary Society) 1st World Publishing, Inc.

—The Bobbsey Twins on A House Boat. 2005. 27.95 *(978-1-4218-1067-6(0)*, 1st World Library - Literary Society) 1st World Publishing, Inc.

—Freddie & Flossie. Pyle, Chuck, illus. 2005. 32p. (J). lib. bdg. 15.00 *(978-1-59054-999-5(6))* Fitzgerald Bks.

BODICCA, QUEEN, -62

see Boadicea, Queen, -62

BODY, HUMAN

see Human Body

BODY AND MIND

see Mind and Body

BODY FLUIDS

BourkeKenna. SLIME: THE WONDERFUL WORLD OF MUCUS LOW INTERMEDIATE BOOK WITH ONLINE ACCESS. 2014. (ENG.). 24p. (J). pap. 9.50 *(978-1-107-67343-4(7))* Cambridge Univ. Pr.

Cleary, Brian P. Oils (Just a Bit) to Keep Your Body Fit: What Are Oils? Goneau, Martin, illus. 2010. (Food Is CATegorical Ser.). (ENG.). 32p. (gr. k-3). lib. bdg. 25.26 *(978-1-58013-592-4(7))* Lerner Publishing Group.

Conrad, David. Burps, Boogers, & Other Body Functions, 1 vol. 2011. (Health & Your Body Ser.). (ENG.). 24p. (gr. k-1). pap. 7.29 *(978-1-4296-7125-5(4))*; lib. bdg. 26.65 *(978-1-4296-6808-8(3))* Capstone Press of Coughlan Cos. (Pebble Plus).

Flynn, Wes. What Makes Me Stinky?, Vol. 1. 2014. (My Body Does Strange Stuff! Ser.). (ENG.). 24p. (J). (gr. 1-2). pap. 8.15 *(978-1-4824-0304-6(8))* Stevens, Gareth Publishing LLLP.

James, Lincoln. What Happens When I Sweat? 2013. (My Body Does Strange Stuff! Ser.). (ENG., Illus.). 24p. (J). (gr. 1-3). pap. 8.15 *(978-1-4339-9348-0(1))*; lib. bdg. 22.60 *(978-1-4339-9347-3(3))* Stevens, Gareth Publishing LLLP.

Koontz, Robin Michal. Spits & Squirts: How Animals Squirt to Survive. 2011. (Amazing Animal Skills Ser.). (Illus.). 48p. (J). (gr. 4). 29.93 *(978-0-7614-4909-6(4))* Marshall Cavendish Corp.

Larsen, C. S. Crust & Spray: Gross Stuff in Your Eyes, Ears, Nose, & Throat. Slack, Michael H., illus. 2009. (Gross Body Science Ser.). (ENG.). 48p. (gr. 3-5). lib. bdg. 29.27 *(978-0-8225-8964-8(8))* Lerner Publishing Group.

Murray, Julie. The Body, 1 vol. 2009. (That's Gross!:A Look at Science Ser.). (ENG., Illus.). 32p. (J). (gr. 2-5). 28.50 *(978-1-60453-554-9(7))* ABDO Publishing Co.

Peterson, Judy Monroe. Understanding Cholesterol. 2010. (Healthy Habits Ser.). (Illus.). 64p. (YA). (gr. 5-8). pap. 12.95 *(978-1-4488-0610-2(0))*; lib. bdg. 31.95 *(978-1-4358-9440-2(5))* Rosen Publishing Group, Inc., The. (Rosen Reference).

Rosenberg, Pam. Eew! Icky, Sticky, Gross Stuff in Your Body. Ramos, Beatriz Helena, illus. 2007. (Icky, Sticky, Gross-Out Bks.). (ENG.). 24p. (J). (gr. 3-6). 27.07 *(978-1-59296-894-7(5)*, 200355) Child's World, Inc., The.

Royston, Angela. Why We Need Water & Fiber. 2011. (Science of Nutrition Ser.: No. 6). (ENG., Illus.). 48p. (J). (gr. 5-8). pap. *(978-0-7787-1698-3(8))* Crabtree Publishing Co.

Silverstein, Alvin, et al. Poop Collectors, Armpit Sniffers, & More: The Yucky Jobs Book. Kelley, Gerald, illus. 2010. (Yucky Science Ser.). 48p. (J). 25.27 *(978-0-7660-3316-0(3))* Enslow Pubs., Inc.

Stewart, Melissa. It's Spit-Acular! The Secrets of Saliva. Hamlin, Janet, illus. 2009. (Gross & Goofy Body Ser.). 48p. (gr. 3-4). 29.93 *(978-0-7614-4163-2(8))* Marshall Cavendish Corp.

What Happens When I Sweat? 2013. (My Body Does Strange Stuff! Ser.). 24p. (J). (gr. 1-3). pap. 48.90 *(978-1-4339-9349-7(X))* Stevens, Gareth Publishing LLLP.

BODY TEMPERATURE

Arnold, Caroline. Too Hot? Too Cold? Keeping Body Temperature Just Right. Patterson, Annie, illus. 2013. (ENG.). 32p. (J). (gr. 1-4). pap. 7.95 *(978-1-58089-277-3(9))* Charlesbridge Publishing, Inc.

Felix, Rebecca. Keeping Cool in Summer. 2014. (21st Century Basic Skills Library: Let's Look at Summer Ser.). (ENG.). 24p. (J). (gr. k-3). 22.79 *(978-1-63137-597-2(0)*, 205171) Cherry Lake Publishing.

Gregoire, Maryellen. Staying Warm, 1 vol. 2011. (Wonder Readers Emergent Level Ser.). (ENG.). (gr. -1-1). 32p. pap. 5.99 *(978-1-4296-7872-8(0))*; 16p. pap. 35.94 *(978-1-4296-8159-9(4))* Capstone Press of Coughlan Cos. (Wonder Readers).

Klepeis, Alicia. Warm-Blooded & Cold-Blooded Animals Explained. 2016. (Distinctions in Nature Ser.). 32p. (J). pap. 10.58 *(978-1-5026-2181-8(9))* Cavendish Square Publishing.

BODY WEIGHT CONTROL

see Weight Control

BOER WAR, 1899-1902

see South African War, 1899-1902

BOGS

see Marshes

BOHR, NIELS, 1885-1962

Pasachoff, Naomi E. Niels Bohr: Physicist & Humanitarian. 2003. (Great Minds of Science Ser.). (Illus.). 128p. (J). (gr. 4-10). lib. bdg. 27.94 *(978-0-7660-1997-3(7))* Enslow Pubs., Inc.

Spangenburg, Ray & Moser, Diane Kit. Niels Bohr: Atomic Theorist. 2nd rev. ed. 2008. (Makers of Modern Science Ser.). (Illus.). 141p. (gr. 6-12). 35.00 *(978-0-8160-6178-5(5)*, Chelsea Hse.) Facts On File, Inc.

BOLIVAR, SIMON, 1783-1830

Cruz, Bárbara C. Simón Bolívar: Fighting for Latin American Liberation. 2017. (Rebels with a Cause Ser.). 128p. (J). (gr. 8-8). lib. bdg. 37.27 ***(978-0-7660-8952-5(5))*** Enslow Pubs., Inc.

Simon Bolivar. 2010. (Great Hispanic Heritage Ser.). (Illus.). 120p. (J). (gr. 6-12). 35.00 *(978-1-60413-731-6(2)*, Chelsea Hse.) Facts On File, Inc.

BOLIVIA

DiPiazza, Francesca Davis. Bolivia in Pictures. 2nd ed. 2008. (Visual Geography (Lerner) Ser.). (Illus.). 80p. (YA). (gr. 7-12). lib. bdg. 31.93 *(978-0-8225-8568-8(5))* Twenty First Century Bks.

Gelletly, LeeAnne. Bolivia. (South America Today Ser.). 2009. (Illus.). 64p. (J). (gr. 4-7). 21.95 *(978-1-4222-0632-4(7))* 2007. 63p. (YA). (gr. 7-18). pap. 9.95 *(978-1-4222-0699-7(8))* Mason Crest.

—Bolivia, Vol. 13. Henderson, James D., ed. 2015. (Discovering South America: History, Politics, & Culture Ser.). (Illus.). 64p. (J). (gr. 7). lib. bdg. 22.95 *(978-1-4222-3295-8(6))* Mason Crest.

Gomez, Leticia & Rozario, Paul A. Bolivia. 2004. (Countries of the World Ser.). (Illus.). 96p. (gr. 5-12). lib. bdg. 31.00 *(978-0-8368-3108-5(X))* Stevens, Gareth Publishing LLLP.

Lineback, Mandy & Gritzner, Jason. Bolivia. 2003. (Modern World Nations Ser.). (Illus.). 150p. (gr. 6-12). 35.00 *(978-0-7910-7481-7(1)*, Chelsea Hse.) Facts On File, Inc.

Owings, Lisa. Bolivia. 2014. (Exploring Countries Ser.). (ENG., Illus.). 32p. (J). (gr. 3-7). lib. bdg. 26.95 *(978-1-60014-984-9(7)*, Blastoff! Readers) Bellwether Media.

Pateman, Robert & Cramer, Marcus. Bolivia. 2nd rev. ed. 2006. (Cultures of the World Ser.). (Illus.). 144p. (gr. 6-7). lib. bdg. 42.79 *(978-0-7614-2066-8(5)*, Benchmark Bks.) Marshall Cavendish Corp.

BOLIVIA—FICTION

Crowder, Melanie. An Uninterrupted View of the Sky. 2017. (ENG.). 304p. (YA). (gr. 7). 17.99 *(978-0-399-16900-7(8)*, Philomel Bks.) Penguin Young Readers Group.

Ellis, Deborah. I Am a Taxi, 1 vol. 2008. (ENG.). 208p. (J). (gr. 4-9). pap. 8.95 *(978-0-88899-736-4(1))* Groundwood Bks. CAN. Dist: Publishers Group West (PGW).

—Sacred Leaf, 1 vol. (ENG.). 208p. (J). (gr. 4-9). 2009. pap. 8.95 *(978-0-88899-808-8(2))* 2007. 16.95 *(978-0-88899-751-7(5))* Groundwood Bks. CAN. Dist: Publishers Group West (PGW).

Russel, Mary. Flickertail & Paint, Barnyard Sleuths, 1 vol. 2010. 96p. pap. 19.95 *(978-1-4489-7248-7(5))* America Star Bks.

Sickler, Jonas & Pixton, Kaaren, illus. Old Macdonald Had a Farm: Hey Baby! Look at These Animals on the Farm — in Bolivia! 2011. (Indestructibles Ser.). (ENG.). 12p. (J). (gr. k — 1). pap. 5.95 *(978-0-7611-5922-3(3)*, 15922) Workman Publishing Co., Inc.

Withers, Pam. Andreo's Race. 2015. (ENG., Illus.). 216p. (J). (gr. 7). pap. 12.99 *(978-1-77049-766-5(8)*, Tundra Bks.) Tundra Bks. CAN. Dist: Penguin Random Hse. LLC.

BOLL WEEVIL

Kravetz, Jonathan. Boll Weevils. 2006. (Gross Bugs Ser.). (Illus.). 24p. (J). lib. bdg. 22.60 *(978-1-4042-3041-5(6)*, PowerKids Pr.) Rosen Publishing Group, Inc., The.

BOLSHEVISM

see Communism

BOMBERS

Basmadjian, E. E. The B-2 Spirit. 2009. (U. S. Warplanes Ser.). 48p. (gr. 5-8). 53.00 *(978-1-60854-593-3(8)*, Rosen Reference) Rosen Publishing Group, Inc., The.

Bodden, Valerie. Bombers. 2012. (J). 25.65 *(978-1-60818-125-4(1)*, Creative Education) Creative Co., The.

Casil, Amy Sterling. The B-1 Lancer. (U. S. Warplanes Ser.). 48p. (gr. 5-8). 2009. 53.00 *(978-1-60854-592-6(X)*, Rosen Reference) 2005. (Illus.). (YA). lib. bdg. 29.25 *(978-0-8239-3871-1(9))* Rosen Publishing Group, Inc., The.

Cooke, Tim. Bombers. 2012. (Ultimate Military Machines Ser.). (Illus.). 32p. (gr. 4-7). lib. bdg. 31.35 *(978-1-59920-819-0(9))* Black Rabbit Bks.

Dartford, Mark. Bombers. 2003. (Military Hardware in Action Ser.). (ENG., Illus.). 48p. (gr. 5-9). lib. bdg. 25.26 *(978-0-8225-4705-1(8))* Lerner Publishing Group.

David, Jack. B-1B Lancers. 2009. (Military Machines Ser.). (ENG., Illus.). 24p. (YA). (gr. 3-7). lib. bdg. 25.95 *(978-1-60014-258-1(3))* Bellwether Media.

—B-2 Stealth Bombers. 2007. (Military Machines Ser.). (ENG., Illus.). 24p. (J). (gr. 3-7). lib. bdg. 25.95 *(978-1-60014-103-4(X))* Bellwether Media.

—B-52 Stratofortresses. 2009. (Military Machines Ser.). (ENG., Illus.). 24p. (YA). (gr. 3-7). lib. bdg. 25.95 *(978-1-60014-259-8(1))* Bellwether Media.

—Torque: B-1B Lancers. 2009. (Torque Ser.). 24p. (J). (gr. 3-7). 20.00 *(978-0-531-21736-8(1)*, Children's Pr.) Scholastic Library Publishing.

—Torque: B-52 Stratofortresses. 2009. (Torque Ser.). 24p. (J). (gr. 3-7). 20.00 *(978-0-531-21735-1(3)*, Children's Pr.) Scholastic Library Publishing.

Fitzgerald, Lee. Bomb Squads, 01 vols., 1. 2016. (Careers for Heroes Ser.). (ENG., Illus.). 24p. (J). pap. 8.25 *(978-1-5081-4394-9(3)*, PowerKids Pr.) Rosen Publishing Group, Inc., The.

Greene, Meg. The B-52 Stratofortress. (U. S. Warplanes Ser.). 48p. (gr. 5-8). 2009. 53.00 *(978-1-60854-594-0(6)*, Rosen Reference) 2005. (Illus.). (YA). lib. bdg. 29.25 *(978-0-8239-3872-8(7))* Rosen Publishing Group, Inc., The.

Hamilton, John. B-52 Stratofortress. 2013. (Xtreme Military Aircraft Set 2 Ser.). 32p. (J). (gr. 3-9). lib. bdg. 27.07 *(978-1-61783-687-9(7)*, Abdo & Daughters) ABDO Publishing Co.

In the Air: Bombers. 2013. (Military Experience: in the Air Ser.). (ENG., Illus.). 64p. (YA). (gr. 3-7). 27.45 *(978-1-59935-378-4(4))* Reynolds, Morgan Inc.

Jackson, Robert. 101 Great Bombers. 2010. (101 Greatest Weapons of All Times Ser.). (Illus.). 112p. (YA). (gr. 9-12). lib. bdg. 34.60 *(978-1-4358-3594-8(8))* Rosen Publishing Group, Inc., The.

Mullins, Matt. How Does It Fly? Bomber Plane. 2011. (Community Connections: How Does It Fly? Ser.). (ENG.). 24p. (gr. 2-5). lib. bdg. 25.64 *(978-1-61080-067-9(2)*, 201060) Cherry Lake Publishing.

BOMBS, FLYING

see Guided Missiles

BOMBINGS

Here are entered works on the use of explosive devices for the purposes of political terrorism, protest, etc.

Brimner, Larry Dane. Birmingham Sunday. 2010. (ENG., Illus.). 48p. (J). (gr. 5-18). 17.95 *(978-1-59078-613-0(0)*, Calkins Creek) Boyds Mills Pr.

Brownell, Richard. The Oklahoma City Bombing. 2007. (Crime Scene Investigations Ser.). (ENG., Illus.). 104p. (YA). (gr. 7-12). lib. bdg. 35.45 *(978-1-59018-843-9(8))* Cengage Gale.

Burnett, Betty. The Attack on the U. S. S. Cole in Yemen on October 12, 2000. 2005. (Terrorist Attacks Ser.). (Illus.). 64p. (YA). (gr. 7-12). lib. bdg. 31.95 *(978-0-8239-3860-5(3))* Rosen Publishing Group, Inc., The.

Ferguson, Amanda. The Attack Against the U. S. Embassies in Kenya & Tanzania. 2009. (Terrorist Attacks Ser.). 64p. (gr. 5-5). 58.50 *(978-1-60853-309-1(3))* Rosen Publishing Group, Inc., The.

Giordano, Geraldine. The Oklahoma City Bombing. 2005. (Terrorist Attacks Ser.). (Illus.). 64p. (YA). (gr. 7-12). lib. bdg. 31.95 *(978-0-8239-3655-7(4))* Rosen Publishing Group, Inc., The.

Greenberger, Robert. Suicide Bombers. 2009. (In the News Ser.). 64p. (gr. 6-6). 58.50 *(978-1-61513-490-8(5))* Rosen Publishing Group, Inc., The.

Landau, Elaine. Suicide Bombers: Foot Soldiers of the Terrorist Movement. 2006. (Exceptional Social Studies Titles for Upper Grades). (ENG., Illus.). 120p. (gr. 7-12). lib. bdg. 31.93 *(978-0-7613-3470-5(X))* Lerner Publishing Group.

Paul, Michael. Oklahoma City & Anti-Government Terrorism. 2006. (Terrorism in Today's World Ser.). (Illus.). 48p. (gr. 5-12). pap. 14.05 *(978-0-8368-6565-3(0))*; lib. bdg. 31.00 *(978-0-8368-6558-5(8))* Stevens, Gareth Publishing LLLP. (Gareth Stevens Secondary Library).

Sherrow, Victoria. Homegrown Terror: The Oklahoma City Bombing. 2012. (Disasters — People in Peril Ser.). (Illus.). 48p. (J). (gr. 5-18). lib. bdg. 25.27 *(978-0-7660-4016-8(X))* Enslow Pubs., Inc.

Spencer, Betty. Life Is Fragile: One Girl's Story of the Bath School Disaster. Gallinger, Jared, illus. 2007. 68p. per. 19.95 *(978-1-60441-772-2(2))* America Star Bks.

Stein, R. Conrad. The Oklahoma City National Memorial. 2003. (Cornerstones of Freedom Ser.). (ENG., Illus.). 48p. (YA). (gr. 4-7). 26.00 *(978-0-516-24205-7(9))* Scholastic Library Publishing.

BOMBINGS—FICTION

Davidson, Jenny. The Explosionist. 2008. 464p. (YA). (gr. 7-18). lib. bdg. 18.89 *(978-0-06-123976-2(3))*, HarperTeen) HarperCollins Pubs.

Hayes, Rosemary. Mixing It. 2007. (ENG.). 192p. (J). (gr. 4-7). per. *(978-1-84507-495-1(5))* Rough Guides, Ltd.

Heidell, Valerie. Mirika's Story. 2006. (YA). per. 10.95 *(978-0-9774822-4-5(3))* Crosam Pr.

Levy, Marilyn. Checkpoints. 2009. (ENG.). 256p. (gr. 7). pap. 14.95 *(978-0-8276-0870-2(5))* Jewish Pubn. Society.

Mattingley, Christobel. Maralinga's Long Shadow: Yvonne's Story. 2016. (ENG.). 208p. (YA). (gr. 7). pap. 15.99 *(978-1-76029-017-7(3))* Allen & Unwin AUS. Dist: Independent Pubs. Group.

McKenzie, Sophie. In a Split Second. 2015. (ENG., Illus.). 368p. (YA). (gr. 7). 17.99 *(978-1-4814-1394-7(5))* Simon & Schuster Children's Publishing.

Patterson, Valerie O. Operation Oleander. (ENG.). 192p. (J). (gr. 5-7). 2015. pap. 7.99 *(978-0-544-43935-1(X)*, HMH Books For Young Readers) 2013. 16.99 *(978-0-547-24437-2(1))* Houghton Mifflin Harcourt Publishing Co.

You Came for Me. 2013. (ENG.). 240p. pap. 14.99 *(978-1-60861-221-5(X))* Covenant Communications, Inc.

BONAPARTE, NAPOLEON, 1769-1821

see Napoleon I, Emperor of The French, 1769-1821

BONDS, BARRY, 1964-

Bernstein, Ross. Barry Bonds. 2004. (Sports Heroes & Legends Ser.). (ENG., Illus.). 112p. (gr. 5-12). lib. bdg. 30.60 *(978-0-8225-1791-7(4))* Lerner Publishing Group.

Savage, Jeff. Barry Bonds. 2008. pap. 40.95 *(978-1-58013-717-1(2))* 2004. (ENG., Illus.). 32p. (gr. 2-5). lib. bdg. 25.26 *(978-0-8225-3688-8(9))* 2008. (Illus.). 32p. (J). (gr. 3-7). lib. bdg. 23.93 *(978-1-58013-611-2(7)*, Lerner Pubns.) 2008. (ENG., Illus.). 32p. (gr. 2-5). per. 7.95 *(978-1-58013-612-9(5))* Lerner Publishing Group.

—Barry Bonds: Record Breaker. 2nd rev. ed. 2003. (Sports Achievers Biographies Ser.). (Illus.). 64p. (J). (gr. 4-9). 5.95 *(978-0-8225-0472-6(3)*, Carolrhoda Bks.) Lerner Publishing Group.

BONDS

see also Investments; Stocks

Gagne, Tammy. A Teen Guide to Buying Bonds. 2013. (ENG., Illus.). 48p. (gr. 4-8). lib. bdg. 29.95 *(978-1-61228-424-8(8))* Mitchell Lane Pubs., Inc.

Healy, Aaron. Making the Trade: Stocks, Bonds, & Other Investments. 2011. (Global Marketplace Ser.). (ENG.). 56p. (gr. 6-9). pap. 9.95 *(978-1-4329-5478-9(4)*, NA-h) Heinemann-Raintree.

BONES

Abramovitz, Melissa. Osteoporosis. 2011. (Diseases & Disorders Ser.). (ENG.). 128p. (gr. 10-10). 39.90 *(978-1-4205-0339-5(1)*, Lucent Bks.) Cengage Gale.

Arnold, Caroline. The Skeletal System. 2005. (Early Bird Body Systems Ser.). (Illus.). 48p. (J). (gr. 2-4). lib. bdg. 25.26 *(978-0-8225-5140-9(3))* Lerner Publishing Group.

Baines, Becky. The Bones You Own: A Book about the Human Body. 2009. (ZigZag Ser.). (ENG., Illus.). 32p. (J). (gr. k-3). 16.95 *(978-1-4263-0410-1(2))*; lib. bdg. 25.90 *(978-1-4263-0411-8(0))* National Geographic Society. (National Geographic Children's Bks.).

Ballard, Carol. What Happens to Broken Bones? Bones, 1 vol. 2011. (Inside My Body Ser.). (ENG.). 32p. (gr. 3-5). 30.65 *(978-1-4109-4011-7(X))*; pap. 8.95 *(978-1-4109-4022-3(5))* Heinemann-Raintree. (NA-r).

Beevor, Lucy. Understanding Our Skeleton. 2017. (Brains, Body, Bones! Ser.). (ENG., Illus.). 32p. (gr. 3-5). lib. bdg. 30.65 *(978-1-4109-8578-1(4)*, Raintree Perspectives) Heinemann-Raintree.

Berger, Melvin & Berger, Gilda. Your Bones. 2005. (Illus.). pap. *(978-0-439-77373-7(3))* Scholastic, Inc.

Brett, Flora. Your Skeletal System Works! 2015. (Your Body Systems Ser.). (ENG.). 24p. (gr. 1-2). lib. bdg. 25.32 *(978-1-4914-2068-3(5))* Capstone Press of Coughlan Cos.

Burstein, John. The Mighty Muscular-Skeletal System: How Do My Bones & Muscles Work? 2009. (Slim Goodbody's Body Buddies Ser.). (ENG., Illus.). 32p. (J). (gr. 3-5). pap. *(978-0-7787-4433-7(7))* Crabtree Publishing Co.

Cobb, Vicki. Your Body Battles A Broken Bone. 2009. pap. 40.95 *(978-0-7613-4622-7(8))* Lerner Publishing Group.

—Your Body Battles a Broken Bone. Harris, Andrew, illus. 2009. (Body Battles Ser.). (ENG.). 32p. (gr. 2-5). 25.26 *(978-0-8225-7468-2(3))* Lerner Publishing Group.

DaSilva-Gordon, Maria. Powerful Bones: Keeping Your Skeleton Healthy. 2012. (Healthy Habits Ser.). (ENG., Illus.). 64p. (J). (gr. 5-8). lib. bdg. 31.95 *(978-1-4488-6949-7(8)*, Rosen Reference) Rosen Publishing Group, Inc., The.

Dawson, Emily C. My Bones. Alberini, Teresa, illus. 2015. (Inside My Body Ser.). (ENG.). 24p. (J). (gr. 1-3). 19.95 *(978-1-60753-753-3(2))* Amicus Publishing.

Derkazarian, Susan. You Have Healthy Bones! 2005. (Rookie Read-About Health Ser.). (ENG., Illus.). 32p. (J). (gr. k-2). per. 5.95 *(978-0-516-27919-0(X))*; 20.50 *(978-0-516-25878-2(8))* Scholastic Library Publishing. (Children's Pr.).

Domnauer, Teresa. The Skeletal System. 2003. (Illus.). 24p. (J). lib. bdg. 21.35 *(978-1-58340-311-2(6))* Black Rabbit Bks.

Earhart, Kristin. The Magic School Bus Fixes a Bone. Bracken, Carolyn, illus. 2010. 32p. (J). pap. *(978-0-545-23950-9(8)*, Cartwheel Bks.) Scholastic, Inc.

Farndon, John. Stickmen's Guide to Your Mighty Muscles & Bones. Dean, Venitia, illus. 2017. (Stickmen's Guides to Your Awesome Body Ser.). (ENG.). 32p. (J). (gr. 3-6). 26.65 ***(978-1-5124-3214-5(8))*** Lerner Publishing Group.

Gilbert, Laura. The Skeletal System. 2009. (Insider's Guide to the Body Ser.). 48p. (gr. 5-8). 53.00 *(978-1-61513-586-8(3)*, Rosen Reference) Rosen Publishing Group, Inc., The.

Gold, Susan Dudley. The Musculoskeletal System & the Skin. 2003. (Human Body Library). (Illus.). 48p. (J). (gr. 4-10). lib. bdg. 25.27 *(978-0-7660-2023-8(1))* Enslow Pubs., Inc.

Gregory, Josh. From Woodpeckers to... Helmets. 2012. (21st Century Skills Innovation Library: Innovations from Nature Ser.). (ENG.). 32p. (gr. 4-8). 28.50 *(978-1-61080-495-0(3)*, 202105); pap. 14.21 *(978-1-61080-669-5(7)*, 202279) Cherry Lake Publishing.

Guillain, Charlotte. Nuestros Huesos, 1 vol. 2010. (Nuestros Cuerpos Ser.). (SPA.). 24p. (gr. -1-1). 22.65 *(978-1-4329-4301-1(4))*; pap. 6.29 *(978-1-4329-4310-3(3))* Heinemann-Raintree. (Bellota).

—Our Bones, 1 vol. 2010. (Our Bodies Ser.). (ENG.). 24p. (gr. -1-1). 22.65 *(978-1-4329-3596-2(8))*; pap. 6.29 *(978-1-4329-3605-1(0))* Heinemann-Raintree. (Acorn).

Halvorson, Karin. Inside the Bones, 1 vol. 2016. (Super Simple Body Set 2 Ser.). (ENG., Illus.). 32p. (J). (gr. k-4). 27.07 *(978-1-62403-939-3(1))* ABDO Publishing Co.

Herrington, Lisa M. I Broke My Arm. 2015. (Rookie Read-About(tm) Health Ser.). (ENG., Illus.). 32p. (J). lib. bdg. 25.00 *(978-0-531-21037-6(5))* Scholastic Library Publishing.

Hewitt, Sally. My Bones. 2012. (My Body Ser.). (ENG., Illus.). 24p. (gr. k-4). pap. 7.95 *(978-1-926853-95-6(4))* Saunders Bk. Co. CAN. Dist: RiverStream Publishing.

Jenkins, Steve. Bones: Skeletons & How They Work. Jenkins, Steve, illus. 2010. (ENG., Illus.). 48p. (J). (gr. 2-5). 19.99 *(978-0-545-04651-0(3)*, Scholastic Reference) Scholastic, Inc.

Korb, Rena B. & Weinhaus, Anthony J. My Spine, 1 vol. Simard, Remy, illus. 2010. (My Body Ser.). (ENG.). 32p. (J). (gr. k-3). 28.50 *(978-1-60270-809-9(6))* Magic Wagon.

Landau, Elaine. Broken Bones. 2008. (Head-to-Toe Health Ser.). 32p. (gr. 2-7). lib. bdg. 28.50 *(978-0-7614-2847-3(X)*, Benchmark Bks.) Marshall Cavendish Corp.

Leading Women 2. 2013. (Bookworms Fluent — My Body Ser.). (gr. 1-3). 239.58 *(978-1-62712-000-5(9))* Cavendish Square Publishing.

Levine, Sara C. Bone by Bone: Comparing Animal Skeletons. Spookytooth, T. S., illus. 2013. (ENG.). 32p. (J). (gr. k-4). lib. bdg. 26.60 *(978-0-7613-8464-9(2)*, Millbrook Pr.) Lerner Publishing Group.

Loria, Laura. The Bones in Your Body, 1 vol. 2015. (ENG.). 32p. (J). 23.45 *(978-1-62275-624-7(X)*, Britannica Educational Publishing) Rosen Publishing Group, Inc., The.

Maestro, Betsy. What Is a Skeleton? Date not set. 40p. (J). (gr. -1-1). 15.99 *(978-0-06-029006-1(4))*; pap. 4.99 *(978-0-06-445215-1(8))*; lib. bdg. 16.89 *(978-0-06-029007-8(2))* HarperCollins Pubs.

Malaspina, Ann. Take a Closer Look at Your Bones. 2013. (Take a Closer Look Ser.). (ENG.). 24p. (J). (gr. 2-5). 28.50 *(978-1-62323-552-9(9)*, 206348) Child's World, Inc., The.

Markle, Sandra. Shattered Bones. 2010. (Powerful Medicine Ser.). (ENG.). 48p. (gr. 5-8). lib. bdg. 27.93 *(978-0-8225-8703-3(3))* Lerner Publishing Group.

Meachen Rau, Dana. Huesos y Musculos: Que Hay Dentro de Mi? 2006. (Bookworms Ser.). (SPA & ENG., Illus.). 32p. (gr. 1-2). lib. bdg. 15.95 *(978-0-7614-2401-7(6))* Marshall Cavendish Corp.

—My Bones & Muscles. 2004. (Bookworms Ser.). (ENG & SPA., Illus.). 32p. (gr. 1-2). 15.95 *(978-0-7614-1777-4(X)*, Benchmark Bks.) Marshall Cavendish Corp.

—My Bones & Muscles/Huesos y Musculos. 2006. (Bookworms Ser.). (ENG & SPA., Illus.). 32p. (gr. 1-2). lib. bdg. 15.95 *(978-0-7614-2479-6(2))* Marshall Cavendish Corp.

Nelson, Kristen Rajczak. What If I Break a Bone? 2016. (Benched: Dealing with Sports Injuries Ser.). 24p. (J). (gr. 3-2). 22.60 *(978-1-4824-4885-6(8))* Stevens, Gareth Publishing LLLP.

Ollhoff, Jim. Muscles & Bones. 2012. (J). *(978-1-61783-256-7(1))* ABDO Publishing Co.

Orr, Tamra B. Frequently Asked Questions about Bone Cancer. 2007. (FAQ: Teen Life Ser.). (Illus.). 64p. (YA). (gr. 7-12). lib. bdg. 31.95 *(978-1-4042-1934-2(X))* Rosen Publishing Group, Inc., The.

Ratway, Michael J. & Ratway, Virginia K. Fractured Femur Fable. l.t. ed. 2003. (Illus.). 24p. (J). spiral bd. 10.00 *(978-0-9724698-1-4(8))* Ratway, Michael.

Rau, Dana Meachen. My Bones & Muscles. 2013. (Bookworms Fluent — My Body Ser.). 24p. (gr. 1-3). pap. 8.22 *(978-1-62712-032-6(7))* Cavendish Square Publishing.

Rotner, Shelley. Body Bones. White, David, illus. Rotner, Shelley, photos by. 2014. (ENG.). 32p. (J). (gr. k-5). 16.95 *(978-0-8234-3162-5(2))* Holiday Hse., Inc.

—Body Bones. 2014. pap. *(978-0-8234-3249-3(1))* Holiday Hse., Inc.

Royston, Angela. Cuts, Bruises, & Breaks. 2009. (How's Your Health? Ser.). (J). (gr. 1-4). 28.50 *(978-1-59920-222-8(0))* Black Rabbit Bks.

Silverstein, Alvin, et al. Scoliosis. 2003. (My Health Ser.). (ENG.). 48p. (J). (gr. 3-5). pap. 6.95 *(978-0-531-16639-0(2)*, Watts, Franklin) Scholastic Library Publishing.

Taylor, Lauren & Taylor, Sean. My Strong Bones. 2012. (Inside Me Ser.). (ENG.). 24p. (J). (gr. -1-k). 15.99 *(978-1-60992-311-2(1))* QEB Publishing Inc.

Thames, Susan. Our Skeleton. 2007. (ENG., Illus.). 24p. (gr. k-1). 28.50 *(978-1-60472-113-3(8))* Rourke Educational Media.

Tieck, Sarah. Skeletal System, 1 vol. 2011. (Body Systems Ser.). (ENG., Illus.). 32p. (J). (gr. 2-5). lib. bdg. 27.07 *(978-1-61613-502-7(6))* ABDO Publishing Co.

Treays, Rebecca. Understanding Your Muscles & Bones: Internet-Linked. Fox, Christyan, illus. rev. ed. 2006. (Usborne Science for Beginners Ser.). 32p. (J). (gr. 3-7). per. 7.99 *(978-0-7945-0813-5(8)*, Usborne) EDC Publishing.

Waldron, Melanie. Your Skin & Bones: Understand Them with Numbers, 1 vol. 2014. (Your Body by Numbers Ser.). (ENG.). 48p. (gr. 3-5). lib. bdg. 32.65 *(978-1-4109-5981-2(3))* Heinemann-Raintree.

Walker, Sally M. Written in Bone: Buried Lives of Jamestown & Colonial Maryland. 2009. (Exceptional Social Studies Titles for Intermediate Grades). (ENG., Illus.). 144p. (J). (gr. 5-8). lib. bdg. 22.95 *(978-0-8225-7135-3(8))* Lerner Publishing Group.

BONIFACE, SAINT, ARCHBISHOP OF MAINZ, APPROXIMATELY 675-754

McAdam, Claudia Cangilla. Kristoph & the First Christmas Tree: A Legend of St. Boniface. Hill, David, illus. 2015. (ENG.). 32p. (J). 16.99 *(978-1-61261-630-8(5))* Paraclete Pr., Inc.

BOOK ILLUSTRATION

see Illustration of Books

BOOK INDUSTRIES AND TRADE

see also Bookbinding; Paper Making and Trade; Printing; Publishers and Publishing

D'Cruz, Anna-Marie. Make Your Own Books. 2009. (Do It Yourself Projects! Ser.). (ENG., Illus.). 24p. (J). (gr. 3-5). pap. 9.40 *(978-1-4358-2927-5(1)*, 1291888, PowerKids Pr.) Rosen Publishing Group, Inc., The.

Guillain, Charlotte. Reading & Writing, 1 vol. 2012. (Jobs If You Like... Ser.). (ENG.). 32p. (gr. 1-3). pap. 8.29 *(978-1-4329-6821-2(1))*; lib. bdg. 27.32 *(978-1-4329-6810-6(6))* Heinemann-Raintree. (Heinemann First Library).

Hayward, Linda. I Am a Book. Nicklaus, Carol, illus. (Silly Millies Ser.). 32p. (J). (gr. k-2). 2005. pap. 4.99 *(978-0-7613-1826-2(7)*, First Avenue Editions) 2004. lib. bdg. 17.90 *(978-0-7613-2905-3(6)*, Millbrook Pr.) Lerner Publishing Group.

J.G. Ferguson Publishing Company Staff, contrib. by. Publishing. 3rd rev. ed. 2007. (Careers in Focus Ser.). (Illus.). 192p. (gr. 6-12). 32.95 *(978-0-8160-6572-1(1)*, Ferguson Publishing Co.) Facts On File, Inc.

Kallen, Stuart A. Jeff Bezos & Amazon. 2015. (ENG., Illus.). 80p. (J). lib. bdg. *(978-1-60152-872-8(8))* ReferencePoint Pr., Inc.

Marshall, Pam. De la Idea Al Libro. Translations.com Staff, tr. (De Principio a Fin (Start to Finish) Ser.). 24p. (gr. 3-5). 2007. (SPA., Illus.). per. 5.95 *(978-0-8225-6632-8(X))* 2006. (ENG & SPA.). lib. bdg. 19.93 *(978-0-8225-6495-9(5))* Lerner Publishing Group. (Ediciones Lerner).

—From Idea to Book. 2004. (Start to Finish Ser.). (Illus.). 24p. (J). pap. 5.95 *(978-0-8225-2143-3(1))*; 18.60 *(978-0-8225-1385-8(4)*, Lerner Pubns.) Lerner Publishing Group.

Reeves, Diane Lindsey & Clasen, Lindsey. Career Ideas for Kids Who Like Writing. Bond, Nancy, illus. 2nd rev. ed. 2007. (Career Ideas for Kids Ser.). 208p. (gr. 4-9). 32.95 *(978-0-8160-6555-4(1)*, Ferguson Publishing Co.) Facts On File, Inc.

BOOK LISTS

see Best Books

BOOK REVIEWS

Ayer, Joan. Beyond Good Night, Moon - 75 Reviews of Classic Books for Young Children. 2006. 116p. per. 10.95 *(978-1-59858-240-6(2))* Dog Ear Publishing, LLC.

Owings, Lisa. Share Your Book Report. 2013. (Library Smarts Ser.). (ENG., Illus.). 24p. (gr. -1-2). lib. bdg. 23.93 *(978-1-4677-1504-1(2)*, Lerner Pubns.) Lerner Publishing Group.

BOOK TRADE

see Book Industries and Trade; Publishers and Publishing

BOOKBINDING

Dawson, Willow. Lila & Ecco's Do-It-Yourself Comics Club. Dawson, Willow, illus. 2010. (ENG., Illus.). 112p. (J). (gr. 3-7). 7.95 *(978-1-55453-439-5(9))*; 16.95 *(978-1-55453-438-8(0))* Kids Can Pr., Ltd. CAN. Dist: Hachette Bk. Group.

D'Cruz, Anna-Marie. Make Your Own Books. 2009. (Do It Yourself Projects! Ser.). (ENG., Illus.). 24p. (J). (gr. 3-5). pap. 9.40 *(978-1-4358-2927-5(1)*, 1291888); lib. bdg. 25.25 *(978-1-4358-2855-1(0))* Rosen Publishing Group, Inc., The. (PowerKids Pr.).

Leveson, Sarah. From Tree to Book. 2015. (Collins Big Cat Ser.). (ENG.). 24p. (J). (gr. 2-2). pap. 6.95 *(978-0-00-759111-4(X))* HarperCollins Pubs. Ltd. GBR. Dist: Independent Pubs. Group.

Petelinsek, Kathleen. Learning to Make Books. Petelinsek, Kathleen, illus. 2015. (How-To Library). (ENG., Illus.). 32p. (J). (gr. 3-6). 29.93 *(978-1-63362-372-9(6)*, 206908) Cherry Lake Publishing.

Smith, Keith A. Quick Leather Bindings: Non-Adhesive Binding Volume V. 2003. (Illus.). 320p. (C). pap. 30.00 *(978-0-9637682-9-2(8))* Smith, Keith Bks.

BOOKMOBILES—FICTION

Houston, Gloria M. Miss Dorothy & Her Bookmobile. Lamb, Susan Condie, illus. 2011. (ENG.). 32p. (J). (gr. 1-4). 16.99 *(978-0-06-029155-6(9))* HarperCollins Pubs.

—Miss Dorothy's Bookmobile. Date not set. 32p. (J). (gr. -1-3). pap. 5.99 *(978-0-06-443726-4(4))* HarperCollins Pubs.

Sierra, Judy. Wild about Books. Brown, Marc, tr. Brown, Marc, illus. 2004. (ENG.). 40p. (J). (gr. -1-2). 16.95 *(978-0-375-82538-5(X)*, Knopf Bks. for Young Readers) Random Hse. Children's Bks.

Sorensen. Curious Missie C. 2003. (J). *(978-0-15-204717-7(4))* Harcourt Trade Pubs.

—Curious Missie P. 2003. (J). pap. *(978-0-15-204716-0(6))* Harcourt Trade Pubs.

BOOKS

see also Authors; Best Books; Bilingual Books; Illustration of Books; Libraries; Printing; Publishers and Publishing

also headings beginning with the word Book

Agard, John. Book. Packer, Neil, illus. 2015. (ENG.). 144p. (J). (gr. 5). 15.99 *(978-0-7636-7236-2(X))* Candlewick Pr.

Barnett, Mac. How This Book Was Made: Based on a True Story. Rex, Adam, illus. 2016. (ENG.). 48p. (J). (gr. -1-k). 17.99 *(978-1-4231-5220-0(4))* Disney Pr.

Bolte, Mari. Colorful Creations You Can Make & Share, 1 vol. Franco, Paula, illus. 2014. (Sleepover Girls Crafts Ser.). (ENG.). 32p. (gr. 3-4). 27.99 *(978-1-4914-1734-8(X)*, Snap Bks.) Capstone Press of Coughlan Cos.

Capstone Press. You Choose Books. 2010. (You Choose Bks.). (ENG.). 32p. 950.15 *(978-1-4296-5896-6(7)*, You Choose Bks.) Capstone Press of Coughlan Cos.

D'Cruz, Anna-Marie. Make Your Own Books. 2009. (Do It Yourself Projects! Ser.). (ENG., Illus.). 24p. (J). (gr. 3-5). pap. 9.40 *(978-1-4358-2927-5(1)*, 1291888, PowerKids Pr.) Rosen Publishing Group, Inc., The.

Donovan, Sandy. Karl & Carolina Uncover the Parts of a Book, 1 vol. Mullan, Michael, illus. 2010. (In the Library). (ENG.). 24p. (gr. k-4). lib. bdg. 26.65 *(978-1-4048-5760-5(5))* Picture Window Bks.

—Pingpong Perry Experiences How a Book Is Made, 1 vol. Christoph, James, illus. 2010. (In the Library). (ENG.). 24p. (gr. k-4). lib. bdg. 26.65 *(978-1-4048-5759-9(1))* Picture Window Bks.

Fox, Kathleen. A Book Is Just Like You! All about the Parts of a Book. Wallace, John, illus. 2012. 32p. (J). 17.95 *(978-1-60213-060-9(4)*, Upstart Bks.) Highsmith Inc.

Gaylord, Susan Kapuscinski & Jabbour, Joyce. Make, Draw, & Design Your Own Book. Labat, Yancey C., illus. 2006. 48p. (J). *(978-0-439-81339-6(5))* Scholastic, Inc.

Gifford, Clive. Track & Field. 2008. (Personal Best Ser.). (Illus.). 32p. (YA). (gr. 3-6). lib. bdg. 26.50 *(978-1-4042-4442-9(5))* Rosen Publishing Group, Inc., The.

Hamilton, John. Books, 1 vol. 2005. (Straight to the Source Ser.). (ENG.). 32p. (gr. k-6). 27.07 *(978-1-59197-543-4(3)*, Checkerboard Library) ABDO Publishing Co.

Hayward, Linda. I Am a Book. Nicklaus, Carol, illus. (Silly Millies Ser.). 32p. (J). (gr. k-2). 2005. pap. 4.99 *(978-0-7613-1826-2(7)*, First Avenue Editions) 2004. lib. bdg. 17.90 *(978-0-7613-2905-3(6)*, Millbrook Pr.) Lerner Publishing Group.

Hudson, Amanda. This Is My Book. 2008. (Our Toys Ser.). (Illus.). 16p. (gr. -1-2). (J). lib. bdg. 19.00 *(978-0-8368-9254-3(2))*; pap. 5.30 *(978-0-8368-9353-3(0))* Stevens, Gareth Publishing LLLP. (Weekly Reader Leveled Readers).

Leveson, Sarah. From Tree to Book. 2015. (Collins Big Cat Ser.). (ENG.). 24p. (J). (gr. 2-2). pap. 6.95 *(978-0-00-759111-4(X))* HarperCollins Pubs. Ltd. GBR. Dist: Independent Pubs. Group.

Libros, 6, Pack. (Chiquilibros Ser.). (SPA.). (gr. k-1). 23.00 *(978-0-7635-8599-0(8))* Rigby Education.

Lusted, Marcia Amidon. Banned Books. 2013. (ENG.). 48p. (J). pap. 15.64 *(978-1-61783-781-4(4))* ABDO Publishing Co.

Malam, John. Journey of a Book, 1 vol. 2012. (Journey of A... Ser.). (ENG.). 32p. (gr. 1-3). pap. 8.29 *(978-1-4329-6607-2(3))*; lib. bdg. 27.32 *(978-1-4329-6600-3(6))* Heinemann-Raintree. (Heinemann First Library).

Marshall, Pam. De la Idea Al Libro. Translations.com Staff, tr. (De Principio a Fin (Start to Finish) Ser.). 24p. (gr. 3-5). 2007. (SPA., Illus.). per. 5.95 *(978-0-8225-6632-8(X))* 2006. (ENG & SPA.). lib. bdg. 19.93 *(978-0-8225-6495-9(5))* Lerner Publishing Group. (Ediciones Lerner).

—From Idea to Book. 2004. (Start to Finish Ser.). (Illus.). 24p. (J). pap. 5.95 *(978-0-8225-2143-3(1))*; 18.60 *(978-0-8225-1385-8(4)*, Lerner Pubns.) Lerner Publishing Group.

McCain, Murray. Books! Alcorn, John, illus. 2013. (ENG.). 42p. (J). (gr. -1). 17.95 *(978-1-62326-020-0(5))* AMMO Bks., LLC.

Michele, Angela. Books at the Library: Understanding Addition. 2013. (Rosen Math Readers Ser.). (ENG.). 16p. (J). (gr. k-1). pap. 42.00 *(978-1-4777-1630-4(0))*; (Illus.). pap. 7.00 *(978-1-4777-1629-8(7))* Rosen Publishing Group, Inc., The. (Rosen Classroom).

Otfinoski, Steven. Classic Books. 2009. (Our Freedom to Read Ser.). 144p. (gr. 5-8). 40.00 *(978-1-60413-029-4(6)*, Chelsea Hse.) Facts On File, Inc.

—Coming-of-Age Fiction. 2009. (Freedom to Read Ser.). 144p. (gr. 5-8). 40.00 *(978-1-60413-030-0(X)*, Chelsea Hse.) Facts On File, Inc.

—Our Freedom to Read Set, 4-Volumes. 2009. (Our Freedom to Read Ser.). (gr. 5-8). 160.00 *(978-1-60413-647-0(2)*, Chelsea Hse.) Facts On File, Inc.

Owings, Lisa. Learn about Authors & Illustrators. 2013. (Library Smarts Ser.). (ENG., Illus.). 24p. (gr. -1-2). lib. bdg. 23.93 *(978-1-4677-1502-7(6)*, Lerner Pubns.) Lerner Publishing Group.

Piehl, Janet. Know the Parts of a Book. 2013. (Library Smarts Ser.). (ENG., Illus.). 24p. (gr. -1-2). lib. bdg. 23.93 *(978-1-4677-1501-0(8)*, Lerner Pubns.) Lerner Publishing Group.

Pietromarchi, Sophie Benini. The Book Book. 2007. (ENG., Illus.). 128p. (J). (gr. 5-8). 21.95 *(978-81-86211-24-3(1))* Tara Books Agency IND. Dist: Publishers Group West (PGW).

Prieto, Anita C. B Is for Bookworm: A Library Alphabet. Graef, Renee, illus. 2007. (J). (gr. k-7). 16.10 *(978-0-7569-6657-7(4))* Perfection Learning Corp.

Rossi, Renzo. The Age of the Book. Baldanzi, Alessandro, illus. 2008. (Reading & Writing Ser.). 32p. (gr. 4-7). 28.50 *(978-0-7614-4321-6(5))* Marshall Cavendish Corp.

Rustad, Martha E. H. How Books Are Made, 1 vol. 2013. (Wonderful World of Reading Ser.). (ENG.). 24p. (gr. k-1). lib. bdg. 26.65 *(978-1-62065-095-0(9)*, Pebble Plus) Capstone Press of Coughlan Cos.

—The Parts of a Book, 1 vol. 2013. (Wonderful World of Reading Ser.). (ENG.). 24p. (gr. k-1). lib. bdg. 26.65 *(978-1-62065-094-3(0)*, Pebble Plus) Capstone Press of Coughlan Cos.

StJohn, Amanda. How an e-Book Works. Ostrom, Bob, illus. 2012. (Library Skills Ser.). (ENG.). 24p. (J). (gr. -1-2). 28.50 *(978-1-61473-248-8(5)*, 204950) Child's World, Inc., The.

Turnbull, Stephanie. Diaries & Keepsakes: Style Secrets for Girls. 2014. (Girl Talk Ser.). (ENG., Illus.). 32p. (J). (gr. 4-8). pap. 9.95 *(978-1-77092-202-0(4))* Saunders Bk. Co. CAN. Dist: RiverStream Publishing.

Vasquez, Lidia. Damaged Friends: Sad but true stories about damaged Books. 2010. 28p. pap. 13.99 *(978-1-4520-1548-4(1))* AuthorHouse.

Walton, Ruth. Let's Read a Book: Find Out about Books & How They Are Made. 2013. (Let's Find Out Ser.). (Illus.). 32p. (J). (gr. k-5). 28.50 *(978-1-59771-387-0(2))* Sea-To-Sea Pubns.

Wood, Alix. Book Design. 2017. (Design It! Ser.). 32p. (gr. 3-4). pap. 63.00 ***(978-1-5382-0779-6(6))*** Stevens, Gareth Publishing LLLP.

Woolf, Alex. You Wouldn't Want to Live Without Books! Antram, David, illus. 2014. (You Wouldn't Want to Live Without... Ser.). (ENG.). 32p. (J). lib. bdg. 29.00 *(978-0-531-21220-2(3)*, Watts, Franklin) Scholastic Library Publishing.

You Choose Books Classroom Collection. 2010. (You Choose Bks.). (ENG.). 112p. (gr. 3-4). pap. 1292.79 *(978-1-4296-5124-0(5)*, You Choose Bks.) Capstone Press of Coughlan Cos.

BOOKS—BILINGUAL EDITIONS

see Bilingual Books

AB

BOOKS—FICTION

Alexander, Carol. The Book Thief. Friedland, Joyce & Kessler, Rikki, eds. 2009. (Novel-Ties Ser.). (Illus.). 40p. pap. 16.95 *(978-0-7675-4277-7(0))* Learning Links Inc.

Alexander, Kwame. Booked. 2016. (ENG.). 320p. (J). (gr. 5-7). 16.99 *(978-0-544-57098-6(7)*, HMH Books For Young Readers) Houghton Mifflin Harcourt Publishing Co.

—Booked. 2016. lib. bdg. 29.40 *(978-0-606-37992-2(4))* Turtleback Bks.

—Surf's Up. Miyares, Daniel, illus. 2016. (ENG.). 32p. (J). 17.95 *(978-0-7358-4220-5(5))* North-South Bks., Inc.

Alvis, Cheyenne. Don't Open This Book!! 2012. 32p. pap. 19.99 *(978-1-4634-7458-4(X))* AuthorHouse.

Berg, Brook. What Happened to Marion's Book? Alberg, Nathan, illus. 2003. 48p. (J). (gr. -1-2). per. 16.95 *(978-1-932146-05-9(9)*, Upstart Bks.) Highsmith Inc.

Brookes, Archer. Vampireology: The True History of the Fallen. Holt, Nick, ed. 2010. (Ologies Ser.: 9). (ENG., Illus.). 30p. (YA). (gr. 7-9). 21.99 *(978-0-7636-4914-2(7))* Candlewick Pr.

Buzzeo, Toni. Penelope Popper, Book Doctor. Christy, Jana, illus. 2011. 32p. (J). 17.95 *(978-1-60213-054-8(X)*, Upstart Bks.) Highsmith Inc.

Byrne, Richard. This Book Is Out of Control! 2016. (ENG., Illus.). 32p. (J). 16.99 *(978-1-62779-933-1(8)*, 9781627799331, Holt, Henry & Co. Bks. For Young Readers) Holt, Henry & Co.

Carnavas, Peter. The Children Who Loved Books. Carnavas, Peter, illus. 2013. (ENG., Illus.). 32p. (J). 11.99 *(978-1-61067-145-3(7))* Kane Miller.

Clamp Staff. Cardcaptor Sakura, 4 vols., Bk. 4. Horn, Carl Gustav, ed. 2012. (ENG., Illus.). 592p. pap. 19.99 *(978-1-59582-889-7(3))* Dark Horse Comics.

—Cardcaptor Sakura, 4 vols., Vol. 3. Clamp Staff, illus. 2012. (ENG., Illus.). 600p. pap. 19.99 *(978-1-59582-808-8(7))* Dark Horse Comics.

Claudine Sherels Johnson. Nire Goes to the Color Books Bookstore: Featuring God Is Awesome & Pink Carnation. 2009. 84p. pap. 10.49 *(978-1-4389-5952-8(4))* AuthorHouse.

Colandro, Lucille. There Was an Old Lady Who Swallowed Some Books! Lee, Jared, illus. 2012. (There Was an Old Lady Ser.). lib. bdg. 17.20 *(978-0-606-26208-8(3)*, Turtleback) Turtleback Bks.

Colin, Thompson. How to Live Forever. 2008. 32p. 16.99 *(978-0-681-49757-3(2)*, State Street Pr.) Borders Pr.

Cousins, Lucy. Maisy Goes to the Local Bookstore: A Maisy First Experiences Book. Cousins, Lucy, illus. 2017. (Maisy Ser.). (ENG., Illus.). 32p. (J). (-k). 12.99 *(978-0-7636-9255-1(7))* Candlewick Pr.

Crowley, Cath. Words in Deep Blue. 2017. (ENG.). 288p. (YA). (gr. 9). 17.99 *(978-1-101-93764-8(5))*; lib. bdg. 20.99 *(978-1-101-93765-5(3))* Random Hse. Children's Bks. (Knopf Bks. for Young Readers).

Dale, Anna. Magical Mischief. 2011. (ENG.). 304p. (YA). 16.99 *(978-1-59990-629-4(5)*, 9781599906294, Bloomsbury USA Childrens) Bloomsbury Publishing USA.

Deedy, Carmen Agra. Return of the Library Dragon, 1 vol. White, Michael P., illus. 2012. (ENG.). 32p. (J). 16.95 *(978-1-56145-621-5(7))* Peachtree Pubs.

Donaldson, Julia. Charlie Cook's Favorite Book. Scheffler, Axel, illus. 2008. (ENG.). 32p. (J). (gr. -1-k). pap. 7.99 *(978-0-14-241138-4(8)*, Puffin Books) Penguin Young Readers Group.

Everest, D. D. Archie Greene & the Magician's Secret. 2015. (Archie Greene Ser.: 1). (ENG.). 320p. (J). (gr. 3-7). 16.99 *(978-0-06-231211-2(1))* HarperCollins Pubs.

Fry, Erin. Secrets of the Book, 0 vols. 2014. (ENG.). 304p. (YA). (gr. 7-9). 14.99 *(978-1-4778-4716-9(2)*, 9781477847169, Two Lions) Amazon Publishing.

Gerstein, Sherry. The Great Cake. Bennett, Andy, illus. 2006. 14p. (J). (gr. -1-3). bds. 6.95 *(978-1-57791-260-6(8))* Brighter Minds Children's Publishing.

Global Fund for Children Staff, contrib. by. Global Baby Girls. 2013. (ENG., Illus.). 16p. (J). (— 1). bds. 6.95 *(978-1-58089-439-5(9))* Charlesbridge Publishing, Inc.

Hao, K. T. The Magic Book. Ferri, Giuliano, illus. 2008. (ENG.). 32p. (J). (gr. -1). 16.50 *(978-1-933327-44-0(8))*; 15.95 *(978-1-933327-43-3(X))* Purple Bear Bks., Inc.

Heath, Kay S. Books Are NOT My Favorite Things. 2012. (ENG.). pap. *(978-1-4675-4432-0(9))* Independent Pub.

Higgins, Ryan T. Be Quiet! Higgins, Ryan T., illus. 2017. (ENG., Illus.). 40p. (J). (gr. -1-k). 17.99 *(978-1-4847-3162-8(X))* Hyperion Bks. for Children.

Home-Ingram, Gloria. Yonna Bonna & the Big Book. 2012. 16p. pap. 12.68 *(978-1-4669-3406-1(9))* Trafford Publishing.

Hutton, John. Book: Baby Unplugged. Hutton, John, ed. Kang, Andrea, illus. 2012. (Baby Unplugged Ser.). (ENG.). 14p. (J). (— 1). bds. 7.99 *(978-1-936669-06-6(4))* Blue Manatee Press.

Jarvis, Robin. Dancing Jax. 2012. (ENG., Illus.). 576p. (YA). 8.99 *(978-0-00-745341-2(8)*, HarperCollins Children's Bks.) HarperCollins Pubs. Ltd. GBR. Dist: HarperCollins Pubs.

Jeffers, Oliver. The Incredible Book Eating Boy. Jeffers, Oliver, illus. (ENG., Illus.). 32p. pap. *(978-0-00-718231-2(7)*, HarperCollins Children's Bks.) HarperCollins Pubs. Ltd.

—The Incredible Book Eating Boy. Jeffers, Oliver, illus. 2007. (ENG., Illus.). 32p. (J). (gr. -1-3). 17.99 *(978-0-399-24749-1(1)*, Philomel Bks.) Penguin Young Readers Group.

Knotts, Reigan. The Book. 2013. 24p. pap. 10.95 *(978-1-4525-8354-9(4)*, Balboa Pr.) Author Solutions, Inc.

Lacy, Kendra. The Stone Garden. 2004. 72p. (YA). pap. 8.95 *(978-0-595-30719-7(1))* iUniverse, Inc.

Luker, Penny. The Green Book. 2013. 68p. pap. *(978-0-9559896-3-6(9))* Bindon Bks.

MacKenzie, Emily. Wanted! Ralfy Rabbit, Book Burglar. 2016. (ENG., Illus.). 32p. (J). 16.99 *(978-1-68119-220-8(9)*, 9781681192208, Bloomsbury USA Childrens) Bloomsbury Publishing USA.

Marcotte, Danielle. Mom, Dad, Our Books, & Me. Bisaillon, Josée, illus. 2016. (ENG.). 32p. (J). (gr. -1-3). 16.95 *(978-1-77147-201-2(4)*, Owlkids) Owlkids Bks. Inc. CAN. Dist: Publishers Group West (PGW).

Mazurak, Tena. Harley Hits a Homer. 2010. 24p. pap. 12.99 *(978-1-4490-9977-0(7))* AuthorHouse.

McQuinn, Anna, et al. Lola Reads to Leo: Lola le Lee Al Pequeño Leo. Beardshaw, Rosalind, illus. 2017. (SPA & ENG.). (J). pap. *(978-1-63289-028-3(3))* Charlesbridge Publishing, Inc.

Metcalf, Dan. The Scroll of Alexandria: A Lottie Lipton Adventure. Panagarry, Rachelle, illus. 2017. (Adventures of Lottie Lipton Ser.). (ENG.). 80p. (J). (gr. 2-5). 25.32 ***(978-1-5124-8181-5(5))***; pap. 6.99 ***(978-1-5124-8189-1(0))*** Lerner Publishing Group. (Darby Creek).

Mörchen, Roland. Wir Gehen in Die Bibliothek - A Visit to the Library: Deutsch-Englische Ausgabe. Kiefer, Katja, illus. 2010. (ENG.). 40p. (J). (gr. 3-7). 19.99 *(978-3-487-08843-3(6))* Olms, Georg Verlag AG DEU. Dist: Independent Pubs. Group.

Morris, Richard T. Piggypine. Jarvis, Peter, illus. 2017. (J). *(978-0-525-43000-1(8)*, Dial Bks) Penguin Young Readers Group.

Neumann, A. C. The Drawer's Gift. 2010. 60p. pap. 25.95 *(978-1-935340-62-1(X))* Worthy Shorts.

North, Pearl. Libyrinth. 2010. (Libyrinth Ser.: 1). (ENG.). 336p. (YA). (gr. 7). pap. 22.99 *(978-0-7653-2687-4(6)*, 9780765326874, Tor Teen) Doherty, Tom Assocs., LLC.

Papademetriou, Lisa. A Tale of Highly Unusual Magic. 2015. (ENG.). 320p. (J). (gr. 3-7). 16.99 *(978-0-06-237121-8(5))* HarperCollins Pubs.

Perelman, Helen. Marshmallow Mystery. Waters, Erica-Jane, illus. 2014. (Candy Fairies Ser.: 12). (ENG.). 128p. (J). (gr. 2-5). 15.99 *(978-1-4424-6500-8(X))*; pap. 5.99 *(978-1-4424-5301-2(X))* Simon & Schuster Children's Publishing. (Aladdin).

Perry, John. The Book That Eats People. Fearing, Mark, illus. 2009. (ENG.). 38p. (J). (gr. -1-2). 15.99 *(978-1-58246-268-4(2)*, Tricycle Pr.) Random Hse. Children's Bks.

Pires, Curt. The Fiction. 2016. lib. bdg. 26.95 *(978-0-606-38936-5(9))* Turtleback Bks.

Plourde, Lynn. The Dump Man's Treasures. Owens, Mary Beth, illus. 2008. (ENG.). 32p. (J). (gr. -1-3). 15.95 *(978-0-89272-725-4(X))* Down East Bks.

Pranali. The Secret Storybook. 2013. 64p. pap. 23.95 *(978-1-4828-0147-7(7))* Partridge Pub.

Proimos, James, Jr. Knuckle & Potty Destroy Happy World. Proimos, James, Jr., illus. 2012. (ENG., Illus.). 80p. (J). (gr. 2-5). 12.99 *(978-0-8050-9155-7(6)*, 9780805091557, Holt, Henry & Co. Bks. For Young Readers) Holt, Henry & Co.

Ramadier, Cédric. Shhh! This Book Is Sleeping. Bourgeau, Vincent, illus. 2016. (ENG.). 20p. (J). (gr. -1 — 1). bds. 8.99 *(978-0-553-53875-5(6)*, Random Hse. Bks. for Young Readers) Random Hse. Children's Bks.

Ray, Price V. The Somebody Book. 2004. (Illus.). 32p. (J). per. 9.99 *(978-0-9761844-2-3(7))* South Hadley Publishing.

Rey, H. A. & Rey, Margret. Curious George Goes to a Bookstore. 2014. (Curious George Ser.). (ENG., Illus.). 32p. (J). (gr. -1-3). 13.99 *(978-0-544-32073-4(5)*, HMH Books For Young Readers) Houghton Mifflin Harcourt Publishing Co.

—Librarian for a Day. 2012. (Curious George TV Tie-In Early Reader Ser.). lib. bdg. 13.55 *(978-0-606-26602-4(X)*, Turtleback) Turtleback Bks.

Rhodes, Morgan. A Book of Spirits & Thieves. 2015. (Book of Spirits & Thieves Ser.: 1). (ENG.). 368p. (YA). (gr. 7). 18.99 *(978-1-59514-759-2(4)*, Razorbill) Penguin Young Readers Group.

—The Darkest Magic. 2016. (Book of Spirits & Thieves Ser.: 2). (ENG.). 368p. (YA). (gr. 7). 18.99 *(978-1-59514-761-5(6)*, Razorbill) Penguin Young Readers Group.

Rissman, Rebecca. A Dog's Day, 1 vol. 2014. (ENG.). 32p. (gr. 1-2). 26.65 *(978-1-4109-6173-0(7)*, NA-r) Heinemann-Raintree.

Robertson, Elysia Hill. Tool of Life My Pink School Books. Robertson, Elysia Hill, illus. 2005. (Illus.). 112p. (J). per. 12.95 *(978-0-9764444-3-5(7)*, EJWV-004) E. J. Publishing.

Robins, Eleanor. Library Book Mystery, 1 vol. unabr. ed. 2011. (Carter High Mysteries Ser.). (ENG.). 48p. (YA). (gr. 9-12). 7.95 *(978-1-61651-564-5(3))* Saddleback Educational Publishing, Inc.

Rocheleau, Nicole. Ryan, Me, & the Mysterious Book. 2006. (ENG.). 204p. per. 24.95 *(978-1-4241-3422-9(6))* PublishAmerica, Inc.

Scott, Jeff. Becoming the King: Where's my Father? 2006. 222p. (J). per. 17.95 *(978-0-9787624-0-7(1))* TDO Enterprises.

Shannon, David. Duck & a Book. 2005. (Illus.). (J). pap. *(978-0-439-80288-8(1))* Scholastic, Inc.

Slater, David Michael. Milo & the Monster, 1 vol. Ebbeler, Jeff, illus. 2009. (David Michael Slater Set 2 Ser.). (ENG.). 32p. (gr. -1-4). 28.50 *(978-1-60270-656-9(5)*, Looking Glass Library) ABDO Publishing Co.

Smith, Lane. It's a Book. Smith, Lane, illus. 2010. (ENG., Illus.). 32p. (J). (gr. 1-5). 15.99 *(978-1-59643-606-0(9)*, 9781596436060) Roaring Brook Pr.

StJohn, Amanda. How to Find a Book. Ostrom, Bob, illus. 2012. (Library Skills Ser.). (ENG.). 24p. (J). (gr. -1-2). 28.50 *(978-1-61473-250-1(7)*, 204952) Child's World, Inc., The.

Thomas, Scarlett. Dragon's Green. 2017. (Worldquake Ser.: 1). (ENG., Illus.). 384p. (J). (gr. 4-7). 17.99 ***(978-1-4814-9784-8(7)***, Simon & Schuster Bks. For Young Readers) Simon & Schuster Bks. For Young Readers.

—Dragon's Green. 2017. (J). pap. ***(978-1-4814-9785-5(5)***, Simon & Schuster Bks. For Young Readers) Simon & Schuster Bks. For Young Readers.

Trooboff, Rhoda. A Book for Elie. Radjou, Anna Nazaretz, illus. 2008. (ENG.). 31p. pap. 15.00 *(978-0-9773536-1-3(3))* Univ. of Toledo Pr.

Vaughan, Grace. Annie & the Magic Book. 2012. 30p. pap. 19.99 *(978-1-4772-5498-1(6))* AuthorHouse.

Waisanen, Emily. The Book Monster. Konecny, John, illus. 2012. 24p. pap. 8.99 *(978-1-937165-25-3(6))* Orange Hat Publishing.

Walton, Ann. Something to Do. Hinrichsen, Natalie, illus. 2010. (ENG.). 24p. (J). (gr. k-2). pap. 6.00 *(978-1-77009-706-3(6))* Jacana Media ZAF. Dist: Independent Pubs. Group.

BOOKS—HISTORY

Fern, Ella. Questions & Answers about World History. 2003. 320p. (YA). *(978-0-7525-8227-6(5))* Parragon, Inc.

Krensky, Stephen. Breaking into Print: Before & after the Invention of the Printing Press. Christensen, Bonnie, illus. 2003. 30p. (J). (gr. 3-8). reprint ed. 18.00 *(978-0-7567-6843-0(8))* DIANE Publishing Co.

Olson, Kay Melchisedech. Johann Gutenberg & the Printing Press, 1 vol. Smith, Tod G., illus. 2006. (Inventions & Discovery Ser.). (ENG.). 32p. (gr. 3-4). pap. 8.10 *(978-0-7368-9644-3(9)*, Graphic Library) Capstone Press of Coughlan Cos.

Rumford, James. From the Good Mountain: How Gutenberg Changed the World. Rumford, James, illus. 2012. (ENG., Illus.). 36p. (J). (gr. -1-3). 17.99 *(978-1-59643-542-1(9)*, 9781596435421) Roaring Brook Pr.

World Book, Inc. Staff, contrib. by. Hieroglyphics to Hypertext: A Timeline of the Written Word. 2016. (J). *(978-0-7166-3546-8(1))* World Bk.-Childcraft International.

BOOKS—REVIEWS

see Book Reviews

BOOKS AND READING

see also Book Reviews; Children's Literature; Libraries; Reference Books

Allen, Susan & Lindaman, Jane. Read Anything Good Lately? Enright, Vicky, illus. 32p. 2006. (ENG.). (J). (gr. k-3). per. 6.95 *(978-0-8225-6470-6(X)*, First Avenue Editions) 2003. 22.90 *(978-0-7613-2322-8(8)*, Millbrook Pr.) 2003. (J). (gr. -1-3). 14.95 *(978-0-7613-1889-7(5)*, Millbrook Pr.) Lerner Publishing Group.

April, Elyse. Nos Gusta Leer. rev. ed. 2008. (SPA.). 32p. (J). pap. 10.95 *(978-1-890772-81-9(X))* Hohm Pr.

—We Like to Read: A Picture Book for Pre-Readers & Parents. Thompson, Angie, illus. 2015. (ENG.). 32p. (J). (gr. 3-7). pap. 9.95 *(978-1-890772-80-2(1))* Hohm Pr.

Bacon, Arthur & Bacon, Henry. I Hate Reading: How to Get Through 20 Minutes of Reading a Day Without Really Reading. Hantel, Johanna, illus. 2008. 20p. (J). (gr. -1-3). 17.95 *(978-1-60213-025-8(6)*, Upstart Bks.) Highsmith Inc.

Big Books. (Rosen Real Readers Big Bookstm Ser.). 16p. (J). (gr. 3-4). 264.00 *(978-0-8239-8734-4(5))* Rosen Publishing Group, Inc., The.

Brand New Teen Read. Date not set. (YA). pap. 468.00 *(978-0-590-39632-5(3))* Scholastic, Inc.

Brown, Don. Across a Dark & Wild Sea. 2004. (Illus.). (J). (gr. k-3). spiral bd. *(978-0-616-14616-3(7))* Canadian National Institute for the Blind/Institut National Canadien pour les Aveugles.

Dakers, Diane. American Life & Best Sellers from the Catcher in the Rye to the Hunger Games. 2016. (Pop Culture Ser.). (ENG.). 112p. (J). (gr. 7-7). 39.93 *(978-1-5026-1981-5(4))* Cavendish Square Publishing.

Foster, Thomas C. How to Read Literature: Like a Professor for Kids. 2013. (ENG.). 176p. (J). (gr. 3-7). 16.99 *(978-0-06-220086-0(0))* HarperCollins Pubs.

—How to Read Literature Like a Professor: For Kids. 2013. (ENG.). 176p. (J). (gr. 3-7). pap. 6.99 *(978-0-06-220085-3(2))* HarperCollins Pubs.

Greenhaven Press Editors. Are Books Becoming Extinct? 2012. (At Issue Ser.). (ENG.). 128p. (YA). (gr. 9-12). lib. bdg. 34.45 *(978-0-7377-5546-6(6))* Cengage Gale.

Greenhaven Press Editors & Haugen, David. Are Books Becoming Extinct? 2012. (At Issue Ser.). (ENG.). 128p. (gr. 10-12). pap. 27.80 *(978-0-7377-5547-3(4)*, Greenhaven Pr., Inc.) Cengage Gale.

Harcourt School Publishers Staff. Harcourt Trophies. 3rd ed. 2003. (Harcourt School Publishers Trophies Ser.). (ENG., Illus.). 784p. (gr. 4-4). pupil's gde. ed. 87.50 *(978-0-15-322478-2(9))* Harcourt Schl. Pubs.

—Just for You Level 2-1. 3rd ed. 2003. (Harcourt School Publishers Trophies Ser.). (ENG., Illus.). 464p. (gr. 2-2). stu. ed., pupil's gde. ed. 63.55 *(978-0-15-322474-4(6))* Harcourt Schl. Pubs.

—On Your Mark Level 3-2. 3rd ed. 2003. (Harcourt School Publishers Trophies Ser.). (ENG., Illus.). 464p. (gr. 3-3). stu. ed., pupil's gde. ed. 60.35 *(978-0-15-322477-5(0))* Harcourt Schl. Pubs.

—Time/Kids, Bk. 11. 3rd ed. 2003. (Horizontes (Social Studies) Ser.). (SPA., Illus.). pap. 7.00 *(978-0-15-333802-1(4))* Harcourt Schl. Pubs.

Lusted, Marcia Amidon. Banned Books, 1 vol. 2013. (Hot Topics in Media Ser.). (ENG.). 48p. (J). (gr. 3-6). lib. bdg. 32.79 *(978-1-61783-731-9(8))* ABDO Publishing Co.

Marcovitz, Hal. EBooks. 2013. (Technology 360 Ser.). (ENG., Illus.). 128p. (gr. 7-10). lib. bdg. 39.90 *(978-1-4205-0902-1(0)*, Lucent Bks.) Cengage Gale.

McCain, Murray. Books! Alcorn, John, illus. 2013. (ENG.). 42p. (J). (gr. -1). 17.95 *(978-1-62326-020-0(5))* AMMO Bks., LLC.

McClintock Miller, Shannon. Fiction or Nonfiction? Durst, Kathryn, illus. 2017. (Library Skills Ser.). (ENG.). 24p. (gr. 1-3). 33.99 ***(978-1-68410-025-5(9))*** Cantata Learning.

—Find a Book! Durst, Kathryn, illus. 2017. (Library Skills Ser.). (ENG.). 24p. (gr. 1-3). 33.99 ***(978-1-68410-027-9(5))*** Cantata Learning.

Messner, Kate. How to Read a Story. Siegel, Mark, illus. 2015. (ENG.). 32p. (J). (gr. k-3). 16.99 *(978-1-4521-1233-6(9))* Chronicle Bks. LLC.

Pearl, Sydelle. Books for Children of the World: The Story of Jella Lepman, 1 vol. Iantorno, Danlyn, illus. 2007. (ENG.). 32p. (J). (gr. k-3). 16.99 *(978-1-58980-438-8(4))* Pelican Publishing Co., Inc.

Phipps, Michael. Hi, My Name Is Book. 2011. 28p. pap. 13.99 *(978-1-4567-5285-9(5))* AuthorHouse.

Ridge, Judith. The Book That Made Me: A Collection of Personal Stories. 2017. (ENG.). 256p. (YA). (gr. 9). pap. 9.99 *(978-0-7636-9671-9(4))* Candlewick Pr.

Ridge, Judith, ed. The Book That Made Me. 2017. (ENG.). 256p. (YA). (gr. 9). 17.99 *(978-0-7636-9549-1(1))* Candlewick Pr.

Ross, Val. You Can't Read This: Forbidden Books, Lost Writing, Mistranslations, & Codes. 2006. (ENG., Illus.). 152p. (J). (gr. 5-7). 19.95 *(978-0-88776-732-6(X)*, Tundra Bks.) Tundra Bks. CAN. Dist: Penguin Random Hse. LLC.

Roza, Greg. What Is Fiction?, 1 vol. 2015. (ENG., Illus.). 32p. (J). 23.45 *(978-1-62275-660-5(6)*, Britannica Educational Publishing) Rosen Publishing Group, Inc., The.

Rustad, Martha. Sam Visits the School Library. Golden, Jess, illus. 2017. (Cloverleaf Books (tm) — off to School Ser.). (ENG.). (J). (gr. k-2). pap. 7.99 ***(978-1-5124-5578-6(4))***; lib. bdg. 25.32 ***(978-1-5124-3938-0(X))*** Lerner Publishing Group. (Millbrook Pr.).

Rustad, Martha E. H. Reading Is Everywhere, 1 vol. 2013. (Wonderful World of Reading Ser.). (ENG.). 24p. (gr. k-1). lib. bdg. 26.65 *(978-1-62065-096-7(7)*, Pebble Plus) Capstone Press of Coughlan Cos.

—Wonderful World of Reading. 2013. (Wonderful World of Reading Ser.). (ENG.). 24p. (gr. k-1). lib. bdg. 106.60 *(978-1-62065-097-4(5)*, Pebble Plus) Capstone Press of Coughlan Cos.

Silva, Patricia. Modern Times. Baldanzi, Alessandro, illus. 2008. (Reading & Writing Ser.). 32p. (gr. 4-7). 28.50 *(978-0-7614-4322-3(3)*, Benchmark Bks.) Marshall Cavendish Corp.

Spiero, Simon. The Delights of Reading: Written for My Grandchildren. 2012. 368p. 32.95 *(978-1-84624-668-5(7))* Book Guild, Ltd. GBR. Dist: Trans-Atlantic Pubns., Inc.

Thorne, Randy. Quick & Short Book Reports. (FRE.). (YA). pap. 8.99 *(978-0-590-74468-3(2))* Scholastic, Inc.

Troupe, Thomas Kingsley. Margo & Marky's Adventures in Reading, 1 vol. Vasquez, Natalia, illus. 2010. (In the Library). (ENG.). 24p. (gr. k-4). lib. bdg. 26.65 *(978-1-4048-6291-3(9))* Picture Window Bks.

Wallace, G. G. An Illustrate It Yourself Book. 2013. 64p. (gr. 2-4). pap. 10.43 *(978-1-4669-8703-6(0))* Trafford Publishing.

Walton, Ruth. Let's Read a Book: Find Out about Books & How They Are Made. 2013. (Let's Find Out Ser.). (Illus.). 32p. (J). (gr. k-5). 28.50 *(978-1-59771-387-0(2))* Sea-To-Sea Pubns.

Winter, Jeanette. Biblioburro: A True Story from Colombia. Winter, Jeanette, illus. 2010. (ENG., Illus.). 32p. (J). (gr. 1-4). 17.99 *(978-1-4169-9778-8(4)*, Beach Lane Bks.) Beach Lane Bks.

BOOKS AND READING—FICTION

Abbott, Tony. The Postcard. 2009. (ENG.). 368p. (J). (gr. 3-7). pap. 8.00 *(978-0-316-01173-0(8))* Little Brown & Co.

Abraham, Susan Gonzales & Abraham, Denise Gonzales. Cecilia's Year. (Latino Fiction for Young Adults Ser.). (ENG., Illus.). (J). 2007. 210p. (gr. 4-6). pap. 11.95 *(978-1-933693-02-6(9))* 2004. 160p. (gr. 7-9). 16.95 *(978-0-938317-87-6(3))* Cinco Puntos Pr.

Acampora, Paul. I Kill the Mockingbird. 2014. (ENG.). 176p. (J). (gr. 5-9). 16.99 *(978-1-59643-742-5(1)*, 9781596437425) Roaring Brook Pr.

—I Kill the Mockingbird. 2015. (ENG.). 192p. (J). (gr. 5-9). pap. 7.99 *(978-1-250-06808-8(8)*, 9781250068088) Square Fish.

Alexander, Kwame. The Book Party. 2016. (J). *(978-0-06-230781-1(9))* Harper & Row Ltd.

Alexander, William. A Properly Unhaunted Place. Murphy, Kelly, illus. 2017. (ENG.). 192p. (J). (gr. 3-7). 16.99 ***(978-1-4814-6915-9(0)***, McElderry, Margaret K. Bks.) McElderry, Margaret K. Bks.

Allen, Jonathan. I'm Not Reading! 2013. (Baby Owl Ser.). (ENG., Illus.). 32p. (J). (gr. -1-k). 16.95 *(978-1-907967-44-3(3))* Boxer Bks., Ltd. GBR. Dist: Sterling Publishing Co., Inc.

Asher, Sandy. Chicken Story Time. Fearing, Mark, illus. 2016. (ENG.). 40p. (J). (-k). 17.99 *(978-0-8037-3944-4(3)*, Dial Bks) Penguin Young Readers Group.

Auch, Mary Jane & Auch, Herm. The Buk Buk Buk Festival. 2015. (ENG., Illus.). 32p. (J). (gr. -1-3). 16.95 *(978-0-8234-3201-1(7))* Holiday Hse., Inc.

Auxier, Jonathan. Sophie Quire & the Last Storyguard. (ENG.). 464p. (gr. 3-7). 2017. (J). pap. 8.95 *(978-1-4197-2202-8(6))* 2016. (YA). 18.95 *(978-1-4197-1747-5(2))* Abrams, Inc. (Amulet Bks.).

Avi. Prairie School. Farnsworth, Bill, illus. 2003. (I Can Read Level 4 Ser.). (ENG.). 48p. (J). (gr. 3-4). pap. 3.99 *(978-0-06-051318-4(7))* HarperCollins Pubs.

—Prairie School. Farnsworth, Bill, illus. 2003. (I Can Read Bks.). 47p. (gr. 3-7). 14.00 *(978-0-7569-1452-3(3))* Perfection Learning Corp.

Awalt, Barbe. Don't Touch This Book. 2015. (ENG., Illus.). 28p. (J). (gr. -1-k). pap. 16.99 *(978-1-936744-28-2(7))* LPD Pr.

Banks, Angelica. Finding Serendipity. Lewis, Stevie, illus. 2015. (Tuesday Mcgillycuddy Adventures Ser.). (ENG.). 288p. (J). (gr. 3-7). 16.99 *(978-1-62779-154-0(X)*, 9781627791540, Holt, Henry & Co. Bks. For Young Readers) Holt, Henry & Co.

—Finding Serendipity. Lewis, Stevie, illus. 2016. (Tuesday Mcgillycuddy Adventures Ser.). (ENG.). 304p. (J). pap. 7.99 *(978-1-250-07337-2(5)*, 9781250073372) Square Fish.

—A Week Without Tuesday. Lewis, Stevie, illus. 2016. (Tuesday Mcgillycuddy Adventures Ser.). (ENG.). 384p. (J). 16.99 *(978-1-62779-155-7(8)*, 9781627791557, Holt, Henry & Co. Bks. For Young Readers) Holt, Henry & Co.

Barchers, Suzanne I. What Can I Read?, 1 vol. 2011. (Targeted Phonics Ser.). (ENG., Illus.). 16p. (J). (gr. k-2). pap. 5.99 *(978-1-4333-2917-3(4))* Teacher Created Materials, Inc.

Barnett, Mac. The Case of the Case of Mistaken Identity. Rex, Adam, illus. (Brixton Brothers Ser.: 1). (ENG.). (J). (gr. 3-7). 2010. 208p. pap. 7.99 *(978-1-4169-7816-9(X))* 2009. 192p. 15.99 *(978-1-4169-7815-2(1))* Simon & Schuster Bks. For Young Readers. (Simon & Schuster Bks. For Young Readers).

—Danger Goes Berserk. Myers, Matthew, illus. (Brixton Brothers Ser.: 4). (ENG.). 256p. (J). (gr. 3-7). 2013. pap. 7.99 *(978-1-4424-3978-8(5))* 2012. 17.99 *(978-1-4424-3977-1(7))* Simon & Schuster Bks. For Young Readers. (Simon & Schuster Bks. For Young Readers).

—Mysterious Case of Cases: The Case of the Case of Mistaken Identity - The Ghostwriter Secret - It Happened on a Train - Danger Goes Berserk. Rex, Adam & Myers, Matthew, illus. 2013. (Brixton Brothers Ser.). (ENG.). 1024p. (J). (gr. 3-7). pap. 29.99 *(978-1-4424-9818-1(8)*, Simon & Schuster Bks. For Young Readers) Simon & Schuster Bks. For Young Readers.

Barnhill, Kelly. Iron Hearted Violet. Bruno, Iacopo, illus. 2014. (ENG.). 448p. (J). (gr. 3-7). pap. 7.00 *(978-0-316-05675-5(8))* Little, Brown Bks. for Young Readers.

Bauer, Michael Gerard. Don't Call Me Ishmael. 2007. 255p. (YA). (gr. 9-12). lib. bdg. 17.89 *(978-0-06-134835-8(X)*, HarperTeen) HarperCollins Pubs.

Bell, Juliet. Kepler's Dream. 2013. (ENG.). 256p. (J). (gr. 5). pap. 6.99 *(978-0-14-242648-7(2)*, Puffin Books) Penguin Young Readers Group.

Benton, Jim. The End (Almost) Benton, Jim, illus. 2014. (ENG., Illus.). 40p. (J). (gr. -1-k). 16.99 *(978-0-545-17731-3(6)*, Scholastic Pr.) Scholastic, Inc.

—The End (Almost) 2014. (Illus.). (J). *(978-0-545-67536-9(7),* Scholastic Pr.) Scholastic, Inc.

Berenstain, Stan, et al. Nothing Ever Happens at the South Pole. Berenstain, Jan & Berenstain, Mike, illus. 2012. (ENG.). 40p. (J). (gr. -1-3). 10.99 *(978-0-06-207532-1(2))* HarperCollins Pubs.

Berg, Brook. What Happened to Marion's Book? Alberg, Nathan, illus. 2003. 48p. (J). (gr. -1-2). per. 16.95 *(978-1-932146-05-9(9),* Upstart Bks.) Highsmith Inc.

Berne, Jennifer. Calvin Can't Fly: The Story of a Bookworm Birdie. Bendis, Keith, illus. 2015. (ENG.). 40p. (J). (gr. -1-2). pap. 6.95 *(978-1-4549-1575-1(7))* Sterling Publishing Co., Inc.

—Calvin, Look Out! A Bookworm Birdie Gets Glasses. Bendis, Keith, illus. 2014. (ENG.). 32p. (J). (gr. -1-2). 14.95 *(978-1-4549-0910-1(2))* Sterling Publishing Co., Inc.

Bernheimer, Kate. The Lonely Book. Sheban, Chris, illus. 2012. (ENG.). 40p. (J). (gr. -1-3). 17.99 *(978-0-375-86226-7(9),* Schwartz & Wade Bks.) Random Hse. Children's Bks.

Bernstein, Nina. Magic by the Book, 4 vols. unabr. ed. 2005. (J). 65.75 *(978-1-4193-3607-2(X),* 42048) Recorded Bks., Inc.

Bertram, Debbie & Bloom, Susan. The Best Book to Read. Garland, Michael, illus. 2011. (ENG.). 32p. (J). (gr. -1-2). pap. 7.99 *(978-0-375-87300-3(7),* Dragonfly Bks.) Random Hse. Children's Bks.

Bird, Benjamin. Don't Give This Book a Bowl of Milk!, 1 vol. Pérez, Carmen, illus. 2014. (Tom & Jerry Ser.). (ENG.). 32p. (gr. -1-2). 22.65 *(978-1-4795-5230-6(5))* Picture Window Bks.

—This Book Is Not a Piece of Cheese!, 1 vol. Pérez, Carmen, illus. 2014. (Tom & Jerry Ser.). (ENG.). 32p. (gr. -1-2). 22.65 *(978-1-4795-5231-3(3))* Picture Window Bks.

Blatt, Jane. Books Always Everywhere. 2014. (ENG., Illus.). 32p. (J). (gr. -1-2). 16.99 *(978-0-385-37506-1(9),* Random Hse. Bks. for Young Readers) Random Hse. Children's Bks.

—Books Always Everywhere. Massini, Sarah, illus. 2013. (J). *(978-0-385-37535-1(2))* Random Hse., Inc.

Blue, Rose, et al. Ron's Big Mission. Tate, Don, illus. 2009. (ENG.). 32p. (J). (gr. 1-3). 16.99 *(978-0-525-47849-2(3),* Dutton Books for Young Readers) Penguin Young Readers Group.

The Book with No Pictures. 2014. (ENG.). 48p. (J). (gr. k-3). 17.99 *(978-0-8037-4171-3(5),* Dial Bks) Penguin Publishing Group.

Borden, Louise & Gustavson, Adam. The Day Eddie Met the Author. 2004. (ENG., Illus.). 44p. (J). (gr. 2-5). 7.99 *(978-0-689-86720-0(4),* McElderry, Margaret K. Bks.) McElderry, Margaret K. Bks.

Bottner, Barbara. Miss Brooks Loves Books! (And I Don't) Emberley, Michael, illus. 2010. (ENG.). 32p. (J). (gr. -1-2). 17.99 *(978-0-375-84682-3(4),* Knopf Bks. for Young Readers) Random Hse. Children's Bks.

Bourgeois, Paulette, et al. Franklin's Reading Club. 2003. (Kids Can Read Ser.). (ENG., Illus.). 32p. (J). (gr. 1-2). 3.95 *(978-1-55337-370-4(7));* 14.95 *(978-1-55337-369-8(3))* Kids Can Pr., Ltd. CAN. Dist: Hachette Bk. Group.

Britt, Fanny. Jane, the Fox & Me, 1 vol. Ouriou, Susan & Morelli, Christelle, trs. from FRE. Arsenault, Isabelle, illus. 2013. (ENG.). 104p. (J). (gr. 5). 19.95 *(978-1-55498-360-5(6))* Groundwood Bks. CAN. Dist: Publishers Group West (PGW).

Brown, Marc. D. W.'s Library Card. Brown, Marc, illus. 2003. (ENG., Illus.). 24p. (J). (gr. -1-3). pap. 7.00 *(978-0-316-73820-0(4))* Little, Brown Bks. for Young Readers.

Brown, Marc & Sarfatti, Esther. D. W. y el Carne de Biblioteca. 2004.Tr. of D.W.'s Library Card. (ENG & SPA., Illus.). (J). pap. 6.95 *(978-1-930332-47-8(5))* Lectorum Pubns., Inc.

Brown, Monica. Waiting for the Biblioburro. Parra, John, illus. 2011. (ENG.). 32p. (J). (gr. k-3). 16.99 *(978-1-58246-353-7(0),* Tricycle Pr.) Random Hse. Children's Bks.

Browne, Anthony. Willy's Stories. Browne, Anthony, illus. 2015. (ENG., Illus.). 32p. (J). (gr. k-3). 16.99 *(978-0-7636-7761-9(2))* Candlewick Pr.

Buckley, Michael. The Inside Story. Ferguson, Peter, illus. 2011. (Sisters Grimm Ser.: 8). (ENG.). 288p. (J). (gr. 3-7). pap. 7.95 *(978-0-8109-9726-4(6),* Amulet Bks.) Abrams, Inc.

—The Inside Story, 6 vols. 2010. (Sisters Grimm Ser.: 8). (J). 89.75 *(978-1-4498-1969-9(9));* 72.75 *(978-1-4498-1967-5(2));* 1.25 *(978-1-4498-1973-6(7));* 219.75 *(978-1-4498-1966-8(4));* 87.75 *(978-1-4498-1971-2(0))* Recorded Bks., Inc.

—The Inside Story. 2011. (Sisters Grimm Ser.: 8). (J). lib. bdg. 18.40 *(978-0-606-23818-2(2),* Turtleback) Turtleback Bks.

—The Inside Story Bk. 8, Bk. 8. Ferguson, Peter, illus. 2010. (Sisters Grimm Ser.: Bk. 8). (ENG.). 288p. (J). (gr. 3-7). 16.95 *(978-0-8109-8430-1(X),* Amulet Bks.) Abrams, Inc.

Burfoot, Ella. How to Bake a Book. 2014. (ENG., Illus.). 32p. (J). (-2). 16.99 *(978-1-4926-0651-2(0),* 9781492606512, Sourcebooks Jabberwocky) Sourcebooks, Inc.

Burk, Rachelle. Don't Turn the Page! Downing, Julie, illus. 2014. (ENG.). 32p. (J). (gr. -1-3). 16.95 *(978-1-939547-06-4(7))* Creston Bks.

Burleigh, Robert. I Love Going Through This Book. Yaccarino, Dan, illus. Date not set. 40p. (J). (gr. -1-3). pap. 5.99 *(978-0-06-443647-2(0))* HarperCollins Pubs.

Burt, Marissa. Story's End. 2013. (Storybound Ser.: 2). (ENG.). 368p. (J). (gr. 3-7). 16.99 *(978-0-06-202054-3(4))* HarperCollins Pubs.

Bush, Laura & Hager, Jenna Bush. Read All about It! Brunkus, Denise, illus. 32p. (J). (gr. -1-3). 2010. (ENG.). pap. 6.99 *(978-0-06-156077-4(4))* 2008. (ENG.). 17.99 *(978-0-06-156075-0(8))* 2008. lib. bdg. 18.89 *(978-0-06-156076-7(6))* HarperCollins Pubs.

Buzbee, Lewis. Steinbeck's Ghost. 2010. (ENG.). 368p. (J). (gr. 5-9). pap. 18.99 *(978-0-312-60211-6(1),* 9780312602116) Square Fish.

Byrne, Richard. This Book Just Ate My Dog! Byrne, Richard, illus. 2014. (ENG., Illus.). 32p. (J). (gr. -1). 16.99 *(978-1-62779-071-0(3),* 9781627790710, Holt, Henry & Co. Bks. For Young Readers) Holt, Henry & Co.

—We're in the Wrong Book! Byrne, Richard, illus. 2015. (ENG., Illus.). 32p. (J). (gr. -1-3). 16.99 *(978-1-62779-451-0(4),* 9781627794510, Holt, Henry & Co. Bks. For Young Readers) Holt, Henry & Co.

Campos, Llanos & Campos Martinez, Llanos. The Treasure of Barracuda. Sardà, Júlia, illus. 2016. (ENG.). 156p. (J). (gr. 3-7). 15.95 *(978-1-939775-14-6(0))* March 4th, Inc.

Casale, Karen. Never Let a Ghost Borrow Your Library Book: Book Care Guidelines from the Library Secret Service. Rebora, Cecilia, illus. 2012. 32p. (J). 17.75 *(978-1-60213-061-6(2),* Upstart Bks.) Highsmith Inc.

Casanova, Mary. The Day Dirk Yeller Came to Town. Hoyt, Ard, illus. 2011. (ENG.). 36p. (J). (gr. -1-3). 16.99 *(978-0-374-31742-3(9),* 9780374317423, Farrar, Straus & Giroux (BYR)) Farrar, Straus & Giroux.

Castle, M. E. Fakespeare: Something Stinks in Hamlet. Jennewein, Daniel, illus. 2017. (J). pap. ***(978-1-250-10157-0(3))*** St. Martin's Pr.

—Fakespeare: Starcrossed in Romeo & Juliet. Jennewein, Daniel, illus. 2017. (J). pap. ***(978-1-250-10160-0(3))*** St. Martin's Pr.

—Fakespeare: Something Stinks in Hamlet. Jennewein, Daniel, illus. 2017. (Fakespeare Ser.: 1). (ENG.). 272p. (J). 13.99 *(978-1-250-10159-4(X),* 9781250101594) Imprint IND. Dist: Macmillan.

—Starcrossed in Romeo & Juliet. Jennewein, Daniel, illus. 2017. (Fakespeare Ser.: 2). (ENG.). 304p. (J). 13.99 *(978-1-250-10162-4(X),* 9781250101624) Imprint IND. Dist: Macmillan.

Catalanotto, Peter. Ivan the Terrier. Catalanotto, Peter, illus. 2007. (ENG., Illus.). 32p. (J). (gr. -1-3). 17.99 *(978-1-4169-1247-7(9),* Atheneum/Richard Jackson Bks.) Simon & Schuster Children's Publishing.

Cazet, Denys. Will You Read to Me? Cazet, Denys, illus. 2007. (ENG., Illus.). 32p. (J). (gr. -1-1). 16.99 *(978-1-4169-0935-4(4),* Atheneum/Richard Jackson Bks.) Simon & Schuster Children's Publishing.

Chambers, Aidan. Breaktime. 2008. (ENG.). 192p. (YA). (gr. 9-17). pap. 9.95 *(978-0-8109-7262-9(X),* Amulet Bks.) Abrams, Inc.

Chambliss Bertman, Jennifer. Book Scavenger. 2015. (Book Scavenger Ser.). (ENG., Illus.). 368p. (J). (gr. 4-9). 16.99 *(978-1-62779-115-1(9),* 9781627791151, Holt, Henry & Co. Bks. For Young Readers) Holt, Henry & Co.

—Book Scavenger. 2016. (Book Scavenger Ser.). (ENG.). 368p. (J). pap. 7.99 *(978-1-250-07980-0(2),* 9781250079800) Square Fish.

—The Unbreakable Code. 2017. (Book Scavenger Ser.). (ENG., Illus.). 368p. (J). 16.99 *(978-1-62779-116-8(7),* 9781627791168, Holt, Henry & Co. Bks. For Young Readers) Holt, Henry & Co.

Chee, Traci. The Reader. (Sea of Ink & Gold Ser.: 1). (ENG.). 464p. (YA). (gr. 7). 2017. pap. 10.99 ***(978-0-14-751805-7(9),*** Speak)Bk. 1. 2016. 19.99 *(978-0-399-17677-7(2),* G.P. Putnam's Sons Books for Young Readers) Penguin Young Readers Group.

—The Reader. 2017. (Sea of Ink & Gold Ser.: 1). lib. bdg. 22.10 ***(978-0-606-40001-5(X))*** Turtleback Bks.

Child, Lauren. Beware of the Storybook Wolves. 2004. (Illus.). (J). (gr. k-3). spiral bd. *(978-0-616-14568-5(3))* Canadian National Institute for the Blind/Institut National Canadien pour les Aveugles.

—But Excuse Me That Is My Book. Child, Lauren, illus. 2006. (Charlie & Lola Ser.). (ENG., Illus.). 32p. (J). (gr. -1-3). 16.99 *(978-0-8037-3096-0(9),* Dial Bks) Penguin Young Readers Group.

—Utterly Me, Clarice Bean. Child, Lauren, illus. 2005. (Clarice Bean Ser.). (ENG., Illus.). 208p. (J). (gr. 3-7). reprint ed. pap. 5.99 *(978-0-7636-2788-1(7))* Candlewick Pr.

—Utterly Me, Clarice Bean. Child, Lauren, illus. 2006. (Clarice Bean Ser.). (Illus.). 16.00 *(978-0-7569-6567-9(5))* Perfection Learning Corp.

Christelow, Eileen. Five Little Monkeys Reading in Bed. 2011. (Five Little Monkeys Story Ser.). (ENG., Illus.). 40p. (J). (gr. -1-3). 16.99 *(978-0-547-38610-2(9))* Houghton Mifflin Harcourt Publishing Co.

Clark, Platte F. Bad Unicorn. (Bad Unicorn Trilogy Ser.: 1). (ENG., Illus.). (J). (gr. 3-7). 2014. 448p. pap. 7.99 *(978-1-4424-5013-4(4))* 2013. 432p. 15.99 *(978-1-4424-5012-7(6))* Simon & Schuster Children's Publishing. (Aladdin).

Clarke, Justine & Baysting, Arthur. Gobbledygook Is Eating a Book. 2016. (ENG.). 32p. (J). (gr. -1-2). 13.99 ***(978-0-14-350693-5(5))*** Random Hse. Australia AUS. Dist: Independent Pubs. Group.

Clements, Andrew. The Losers Club. 2017. (ENG.). 240p. (J). (gr. 3-7). 16.99 ***(978-0-399-55755-2(5),*** Random Hse. Bks. for Young Readers) Random Hse. Children's Bks.

Codell, Esmé Raji. Fairly Fairy Tales. Chavarri, Elisa, illus. 2011. (ENG.). 32p. (J). (gr. -1-3). 18.99 *(978-1-4169-9086-4(0),* Aladdin) Simon & Schuster Children's Publishing.

Columbus, Chris & Vizzini, Ned. Battle of the Beasts. Call, Greg, illus. 2015. (House of Secrets Ser.: 2). (ENG.). 480p. (J). (gr. 3-7). pap. 7.99 *(978-0-06-219250-9(7))* HarperCollins Pubs.

—Battle of the Beasts. 2014. (House of Secrets Ser.: 2). (ENG.). 480p. (J). (gr. 3-7). 17.99 *(978-0-06-219249-3(3))* HarperCollins Pubs.

—House of Secrets. 2015. (House of Secrets Ser.: Vol. 1). (KOR.). 580p. (J). *(978-89-491-7127-2(9))* Biryongso Publishing Co.

—House of Secrets. Call, Greg, illus. (House of Secrets Ser.: 1). (J). 2014. (ENG.). 512p. (gr. 3-7). pap. 7.99 *(978-0-06-219247-9(7))* 2013. (ENG.). 496p. (gr. 3-7). 17.99 *(978-0-06-219246-2(9))* 2013. 490p. *(978-0-06-225964-6(4))* HarperCollins Pubs.

—House of Secrets. 2014. (House of Secrets Ser.: 1). (J). lib. bdg. 18.40 *(978-0-606-35070-9(5),* Turtleback) Turtleback Bks.

Cotten, Cynthia. The Book Boat's In. Lessac, Frané, illus. 2013. (ENG.). 32p. (J). (gr. 1-5). 16.95 *(978-0-8234-2521-1(5))* Holiday Hse., Inc.

Cotter, Bill. Don't Push the Button! 2015. (ENG., Illus.). 24p. (J). (-3). bds. 8.99 *(978-1-4926-0763-2(0))* Sourcebooks, Inc.

Couloumbis, Audrey. The Misadventures of Maude March: Or Trouble Rides a Fast Horse. 2007. (Illus.). 295p. (gr. 3-7). 18.00 *(978-0-7569-7770-2(3))* Perfection Learning Corp.

Crimi, Carolyn. Henry & the Buccaneer Bunnies. Manders, John, illus. 2009. (ENG.). 40p. (J). (gr. -1-3). pap. 7.99 *(978-0-7636-4540-3(0))* Candlewick Pr.

—Henry & the Crazed Chicken Pirates. Manders, John, illus. 2010. (ENG.). 40p. (J). (gr. -1-3). pap. 7.99 *(978-0-7636-4999-9(6))* Candlewick Pr.

Cushman, Doug, illus. Dirk Bones & the Mystery of the Missing Books. 2009. (I Can Read Level 1 Ser.). (ENG.). 32p. (J). (gr. -1-3). 16.99 *(978-0-06-073768-9(9))* HarperCollins Pubs.

Dahl, Michael. Blood in the Library, 1 vol. Kendall, Bradford, illus. 2011. (Return to the Library of Doom Ser.). (ENG.). 72p. (gr. 1-3). lib. bdg. 23.99 *(978-1-4342-3228-1(X),* Zone Bks.) Stone Arch Bks.

—The Book That Ate My Brother, 1 vol. Kendall, Bradford, illus. 2010. (Return to the Library of Doom Ser.). (ENG.). 72p. (gr. 1-3). lib. bdg. 23.99 *(978-1-4342-2144-5(X),* Zone Bks.) Stone Arch Bks.

—Cave of the Bookworms, 1 vol. Kendall, Bradford, illus. 2008. (Library of Doom Ser.). (ENG.). 40p. (gr. 1-3). pap. 6.25 *(978-1-4342-0549-0(5));* lib. bdg. 23.99 *(978-1-4342-0489-9(8))* Stone Arch Bks. (Zone Bks.).

—The Creeping Bookends, 1 vol. Kendall, Bradford, illus. 2008. (Library of Doom Ser.). (ENG.). 40p. (gr. 1-3). pap. 6.25 *(978-1-4342-0546-9(0));* lib. bdg. 23.99 *(978-1-4342-0486-8(3))* Stone Arch Bks. (Zone Bks.).

—Death Sentence. Evergreen, Nelson, illus. 2015. (Library of Doom: the Final Chapters Ser.). (ENG.). 40p. (gr. 1-3). 23.99 *(978-1-4342-9678-8(4))* Stone Arch Bks.

—Dictionary of 1,000 Rooms, 1 vol. Kendall, Bradford, illus. 2011. (Return to the Library of Doom Ser.). (ENG.). 72p. (gr. 1-3). lib. bdg. 23.99 *(978-1-4342-3229-8(8),* Zone Bks.) Stone Arch Bks.

—Don't Open It! Kendall, Bradford, illus. 2016. 40p. (J). *(978-1-4747-1054-1(9))* Stone Arch Bks.

—Escape from the Pop-Up Prison. Kendall, Bradford, illus. 2008. (Library of Doom Ser.). (ENG.). 40p. (gr. 1-3). pap. 6.25 *(978-1-4342-0550-6(9));* lib. bdg. 23.99 *(978-1-4342-0490-5(1))* Stone Arch Bks. (Zone Bks.).

—Ghost Writer, 1 vol. Kendall, Bradford, illus. 2011. (Return to the Library of Doom Ser.). (ENG.). 72p. (gr. 1-3). lib. bdg. 23.99 *(978-1-4342-3230-4(1),* Zone Bks.) Stone Arch Bks.

—The Golden Book of Death. Souleiman, Serg, illus. 2008. (Library of Doom Ser.). (ENG.). 40p. (gr. 1-3). lib. bdg. 23.99 *(978-1-4342-0487-5(1));* per. 6.25 *(978-1-4342-0547-6(9))* Stone Arch Bks. (Zone Bks.).

—The Last Word. Kendall, Bradford, illus. 2016. 40p. (J). *(978-1-4747-1055-8(7))* Stone Arch Bks.

—The Lost Page. Evergreen, Nelson, illus. 2015. (Library of Doom: the Final Chapters Ser.). (ENG.). 40p. (gr. 1-3). 23.99 *(978-1-4342-9679-5(2))* Stone Arch Bks.

—Night of the Scrawler. Kendall, Bradford, illus. 2016. 40p. (J). *(978-1-4747-1056-5(5))* Stone Arch Bks.

—Rats on the Page, 1 vol. Kendall, Bradford, illus. 2010. (Return to the Library of Doom Ser.). (ENG.). 72p. (gr. 1-3). lib. bdg. 23.99 *(978-1-4342-2147-6(4),* Zone Bks.) Stone Arch Bks.

—The Sea of Lost Books, 1 vol. Kendall, Bradford, illus. 2010. (Return to the Library of Doom Ser.). (ENG.). 72p. (gr. 1-3). lib. bdg. 23.99 *(978-1-4342-2142-1(3),* Zone Bks.) Stone Arch Bks.

—The Spine Tingler. Evergreen, Nelson, illus. 2015. (Library of Doom: the Final Chapters Ser.). (ENG.). 40p. (gr. 1-3). 23.99 *(978-1-4342-9680-1(6))* Stone Arch Bks.

—Tome Raider. Evergreen, Nelson, illus. 2015. (Library of Doom: the Final Chapters Ser.). (ENG.). 40p. (gr. 1-3). 23.99 *(978-1-4342-9677-1(6))* Stone Arch Bks.

—The Twister Trap, 1 vol. Kendall, Bradford, illus. 2008. (Library of Doom Ser.). (ENG.). 40p. (gr. 1-3). pap. 6.25 *(978-1-4342-0548-3(7));* lib. bdg. 23.99 *(978-1-4342-0488-2(X))* Stone Arch Bks. (Zone Bks.).

—The Vampire Chapter, 1 vol. Kendall, Bradford, illus. 2010. (Return to the Library of Doom Ser.). (ENG.). 72p. (gr. 1-3). 23.99 *(978-1-4342-2143-8(1),* Zone Bks.) Stone Arch Bks.

—The Word Eater, 1 vol. Kendall, Bradford, illus. 2008. (Library of Doom Ser.). (ENG.). 40p. (gr. 1-3). lib. bdg. 23.99 *(978-1-4342-0491-2(X));* per. 6.25 *(978-1-4342-0551-3(7))* Stone Arch Bks. (Zone Bks.).

Dakos, Kalli & DesMarteau, Alicia. Our Principal Promised to Kiss a Pig. DiRocco, Carl, illus. (ENG.). 32p. (J). 2017. (gr. -1-3). pap. 7.99 ***(978-0-8075-6635-0(7))*** 2004. (gr. 2-5). 16.99 *(978-0-8075-6629-9(2))* Whitman, Albert & Co.

Dakota, Heather. Emma's Very Busy Week. Panaccione, Nancy, illus. 2009. 31p. (J). *(978-0-545-17227-1(6))* Scholastic, Inc.

Dalton, Michelle. Fifteenth Summer. 2013. (ENG.). 272p. (YA). (gr. 7). 17.99 *(978-1-4424-7267-9(7));* (Illus.). pap. 10.99 *(978-1-4424-7266-2(9))* Simon Pulse. (Simon Pulse).

de Las Casas, Dianne. There's a Dragon in the Library, 1 vol. Gentry, Marita, illus. 2011. (ENG.). 32p. (J). (gr. k-3). 16.99 *(978-1-58980-844-7(4))* Pelican Publishing Co., Inc.

De Smet, Marian. Anna's Tight Squeeze. Meijer, Marja, illus. 2003. Orig. Title: Op Slot. 32p. (J). pap. 5.95 *(978-1-58925-378-0(7))* Tiger Tales.

Deedy, Carmen Agra. The Library Dragon, 1 vol. White, Michael P., illus. 2012. (ENG.). 32p. (J). 19.95 *(978-1-56145-639-0(X))* Peachtree Pubs.

DeMatteis, J. M. Imaginalis. 2010. (ENG.). 256p. (J). (gr. 3-7). 16.99 *(978-0-06-173286-7(9),* Tegen, Katherine Bks) HarperCollins Pubs.

DePalma, Mary Newell. The Perfect Gift. 2010. (J). pap. *(978-0-545-15403-1(0),* Levine, Arthur A. Bks.) Scholastic, Inc.

Dipucchio, Kelly. Dragon Was Terrible. Pizzoli, Greg, illus. 2016. (ENG.). 40p. (J). 16.99 *(978-0-374-30049-4(6),* 9780374300494, Farrar, Straus & Giroux (BYR)) Farrar, Straus & Giroux.

DiTerlizzi, Tony. Kenny & the Dragon. 2008. (Playaway Children Ser.). (J). (gr. 3-7). 39.99 *(978-1-60640-958-9(1))* Findaway World, LLC.

—Kenny & the Dragon. DiTerlizzi, Tony, illus. (ENG., Illus.). (J). (gr. 3-7). 2012. 176p. pap. 8.99 *(978-1-4424-3651-0(4))* 2008. 160p. 17.99 *(978-1-4169-3977-1(6))* Simon & Schuster Bks. For Young Readers. (Simon & Schuster Bks. For Young Readers).

—Kenny & the Dragon. DiTerlizzi, Tony, illus. 2008. (Illus.). 160p. (J). (gr. 3-7). 15.99 Simon & Schuster Children's Publishing.

Docherty, Helen. The Snatchabook. Docherty, Helen, illus. 2013. (ENG., Illus.). 32p. (J). (-2). 16.99 *(978-1-4022-9082-4(9),* 9781402290824, Sourcebooks Jabberwocky) Sourcebooks, Inc.

—The Storybook Knight. Docherty, Thomas, illus. 2016. (ENG.). 32p. (J). (-4). 16.99 *(978-1-4926-3814-8(5),* 9781492638148, Sourcebooks Jabberwocky) Sourcebooks, Inc.

Donaldson, Julia. The Quick Brown Fox Cub. 2006. (Red Bananas Ser.). (ENG., Illus.). 48p. (J). (gr. -1-3). lib. bdg. *(978-0-7787-1080-6(7))* Crabtree Publishing Co.

Donbavand, Tommy. Blood of the Witch: Book 2, 1 vol. Cartoon Saloon, illus. 2012. (ENG.). 120p. (J). 24.21 *(978-1-59961-993-4(8),* Chapter Bks.) Spotlight.

—Claw of the Werewolf, Bk. 6. Cartoon Saloon Staff, illus. 2010. (Scream Street Ser.: 6). (ENG.). 128p. (J). (gr. 3-7). pap. 5.99 *(978-0-7636-4638-7(5))* Candlewick Pr.

—Claw of the Werewolf: Book 6, 1 vol. Cartoon Saloon, illus. 2012. (ENG.). 120p. (J). 24.21 *(978-1-59961-997-2(0),* Chapter Bks.) Spotlight.

—Fang of the Vampire: Book 1, 1 vol. Cartoon Saloon, illus. 2012. (ENG.). 129p. (J). 24.21 *(978-1-59961-992-7(X),* Chapter Bks.) Spotlight.

Driscoll, Amanda. Duncan the Story Dragon. 2015. (ENG., Illus.). 40p. (J). (gr. -1-2). 16.99 *(978-0-385-75507-8(4),* Knopf Bks. for Young Readers) Random Hse. Children's Bks.

Falatko, Julie. Snappsy the Alligator (Did Not Ask to Be in This Book) Miller, Tim J., illus. 2016. (ENG.). 40p. (J). (gr. -1-3). 16.99 *(978-0-451-46945-8(3),* Viking Books for Young Readers) Penguin Young Readers Group.

Fernandez, Giselle. Gigi & the Birthday Ring. Petersen, Sheli, illus. 2005. (J). *(978-1-56492-358-5(4))* Laredo Publishing Co., Inc.

Fields, Jan. Big City Blues: Back to Wonderland, 1 vol. Altmann, Scott, illus. 2013. (Adventures in Extreme Reading Ser.). (ENG.). 112p. (J). (gr. 3-6). 27.07 *(978-1-61641-923-3(7))* Magic Wagon.

—The Calm Before the Storm: A Night in Sleepy Hollow, 1 vol. Altmann, Scott, illus. 2013. (Adventures in Extreme Reading Ser.). (ENG.). 112p. (J). (gr. 3-6). 27.07 *(978-1-61641-920-2(2))* Magic Wagon.

—Hack Attack: A Trip to Wonderland, 1 vol. Altmann, Scott, illus. 2013. (Adventures in Extreme Reading Ser.). (ENG.). 112p. (J). (gr. 3-6). 27.07 *(978-1-61641-919-6(9))* Magic Wagon.

—Lightning Strikes Twice: Escaping Great Expectations, 1 vol. Altmann, Scott, illus. 2013. (Adventures in Extreme Reading Ser.). (ENG.). 112p. (J). (gr. 3-6). 27.07 *(978-1-61641-922-6(9))* Magic Wagon.

—A Novel Nightmare: The Purloined Story, 1 vol. Altmann, Scott, illus. 2013. (Adventures in Extreme Reading Ser.). (ENG.). 112p. (J). (gr. 3-6). 27.07 *(978-1-61641-924-0(5))* Magic Wagon.

—Trapped in Stormy Seas: Sailing to Treasure Island, 1 vol. Altmann, Scott, illus. 2013. (Adventures in Extreme Reading Ser.). (ENG.). 112p. (J). (gr. 3-6). 27.07 *(978-1-61641-921-9(0))* Magic Wagon.

Finchler, Judy & O'Malley, Kevin. Miss Malarkey Leaves No Reader Behind. O'Malley, Kevin, illus. 2010. (Miss Malarkey Ser.). (ENG., Illus.). 32p. (J). (gr. k-3). pap. 7.99 *(978-0-8027-2098-6(6),* 9780802720986, Bloomsbury USA Childrens) Bloomsbury Publishing USA.

Fitzpatrick, Joe. The Book That I Love to Read. Kurner, Mark, illus. 2012. 32p. (J). *(978-1-77093-145-9(7))* Flowerpot Children's Pr. Inc.

Florian, Douglas. Pig Is Big on Books. Florian, Douglas, illus. 2015. (I Like to Read(r) Ser.). (ENG., Illus.). 24p. (J). (gr. -1-3). 6.99 *(978-0-8234-3424-4(9))* Holiday Hse., Inc.

—Pig Is Big on Books. 2015. (I Like to Read(r) Ser.). (ENG., Illus.). 24p. (J). (gr. -1-3). 14.95 *(978-0-8234-3393-3(5))* Holiday Hse., Inc.

Forsythe, Matthew, illus. Please, Open This Book! 2015. (ENG.). 40p. (J). (gr. -1-3). 17.99 *(978-1-4424-5071-4(1),* Simon & Schuster/Paula Wiseman Bks.) Simon & Schuster/Paula Wiseman Bks.

Forte, Lauren. Olivia Goes to the Library. 2013. (Olivia Ready-To-Read Level 1 Ser.). lib. bdg. 13.55 *(978-0-606-35186-7(8))* Turtleback Bks.

Foster, Travis & Long, Ethan. Give Me Back My Book! 2017. (ENG., Illus.). 56p. (J). (gr. k-3). 16.99 ***(978-1-4521-6040-5(6))*** Chronicle Bks. LLC.

Fox, Diane. The Cat, the Dog, Little Red, the Exploding Eggs, the Wolf, & Grandma. Fox, Christyan, illus. 2014. (ENG.). 32p. (J). (gr. -1-3). 16.99 *(978-0-545-69481-0(7),* Scholastic Pr.) Scholastic, Inc.

Frederick, Heather Vogel. Home for the Holidays. 2012. (Mother-Daughter Book Club Ser.). (ENG.). 384p. (J). (gr. 4-9). pap. 8.99 *(978-1-4424-0686-5(0),* Simon & Schuster Bks. For Young Readers) Simon & Schuster Bks. For Young Readers.

—Mother-Daughter Book Camp. 2016. (Mother-Daughter Book Club Ser.). (ENG., Illus.). 336p. (J). (gr. 5-9). 16.99 *(978-1-4424-7183-2(2),* Simon & Schuster Bks. For Young Readers) Simon & Schuster Bks. For Young Readers.

—The Mother-Daughter Book Club. (Mother-Daughter Book Club Ser.). (ENG.). (J). 2008. 288p. (gr. 4-7). pap. 7.99 *(978-1-4169-7079-8(7))* 2007. (Illus.). 256p. (gr. 5-7). 17.99 *(978-0-689-86412-4(4))* Simon & Schuster Bks. For Young Readers. (Simon & Schuster Bks. For Young Readers).

—Much Ado about Anne. 2009. (Mother-Daughter Book Club Ser.). (ENG., Illus.). 352p. (J). (gr. 4-7). pap. 7.99 *(978-1-4169-8269-2(8),* Simon & Schuster Bks. For Young Readers) Simon & Schuster Bks. For Young Readers.

—Pies & Prejudice. (Mother-Daughter Book Club Ser.). (ENG.). (J). (gr. 4-7). 2011. 400p. pap. 8.99 *(978-1-4424-2019-9(7))* 2010. 384p. 15.99 *(978-1-4169-7431-4(8))* Simon & Schuster Bks. For Young Readers. (Simon & Schuster Bks. For Young Readers).

—Wish You Were Eyre. 2013. (Mother-Daughter Book Club Ser.). (ENG.). 480p. (J). (gr. 4-9). pap. 7.99 *(978-1-4424-3065-5(6),* Simon & Schuster Bks. For Young Readers) Simon & Schuster Bks. For Young Readers.

Freedman, Deborah. Shy. 2016. (ENG., Illus.). 40p. (J). (-k). 17.99 *(978-0-451-47496-4(1),* Viking Books for Young Readers) Penguin Young Readers Group.

—The Story of Fish & Snail. 3rd ed. 2013. (ENG., Illus.). 40p. (J). (gr. -1-k). 16.99 *(978-0-670-78489-9(3)*, Viking Books for Young Readers) Penguin Young Readers Group.
Frueh, Stacy. Jonah Gets into a Good Book. 2007. 52p. per. 16.95 *(978-1-4241-8934-2(9))* America Star Bks.
Funke, Cornelia. Inkdeath. 2010. (Inkheart Trilogy Ser.).Tr. of Tintentod. (ENG.). 704p. (J). (gr. 3-7). 12.99 *(978-0-439-86629-3(4)*, Scholastic Paperbacks) Scholastic, Inc.
—Inkheart. Bell, Anthea, tr. 2005. (Inkheart Trilogy Ser.: Bk. 1).Tr. of Tintenherz. (ENG., Illus.). 576p. (J). (gr. 3-7). pap. 10.99 *(978-0-439-70910-1(5))* Scholastic, Inc.
—Inkheart Trilogy Boxed Set: Inkheart, Inkspell, Inkdeath. 2003. (Inkheart Trilogy: Bks. 1-3). 544p. (J). 60.00 *(978-0-439-61671-3(9)*, Chicken Hse., The) Scholastic, Inc.
—Inkspell. Bell, Anthea, tr. from GER. 2007. (Illus.). 653p. (gr. 3-7). 21.00 *(978-0-7569-7917-1(X))* Perfection Learning Corp.
—Inkspell. Bell, Anthea, tr. 2007. (Inkheart Trilogy Ser.: Bk. 2). (ENG., Illus.). 672p. (J). (gr. 3-7). pap. 10.99 *(978-0-439-55401-5(2)*, Chicken Hse., The) Scholastic, Inc.
—Inkspell. 2007. (Inkheart Trilogy Ser.: 2). lib. bdg. 22.10 *(978-1-4177-7471-5(1)*, Turtleback) Turtleback Bks.
Galbraith, Kathryn O. Sparky & Tidbit. Kelley, Gerald, illus. 2015. (Ready-To-Reads Ser.). (ENG.). 40p. (J). (gr. 1-3). pap. 3.99 *(978-1-4814-0424-2(5)*, Simon Spotlight) Simon Spotlight.
Gamble, Adam & Jasper, Mark. Good Night Books. Chan, Suwin, illus. 2017. (Good Night Our World Ser.). (ENG.). 20p. (J). (— 1). bds. 9.95 **(978-1-60219-470-0(X))** Good Night Bks.
Gangloff, Sylviane, illus. Zoom the Zebra. 2015. (Talking Back Ser.). (ENG.). 36p. (J). (gr. -1-2). 7.95 *(978-0-7892-1246-7(3)*, Abbeville Kids) Abbeville Pr., Inc.
—Zulka the Wolf. 2015. (Talking Back Ser.). (ENG.). 36p. (J). (gr. -1-2). 7.95 *(978-0-7892-1245-0(5)*, Abbeville Kids) Abbeville Pr., Inc.
Garland, Michael. King Puck. Garland, Michael, illus. 2009. (ENG., Illus.). 32p. (J). (gr. -1-3). pap. 6.99 *(978-0-06-084811-8(1))* HarperCollins Pubs.
—Miss Smith & the Haunted Library. 2012. (ENG.). 32p. (J). (gr. -1-2). 6.99 *(978-0-14-242122-2(7)*, Puffin Books) Penguin Young Readers Group.
—Miss Smith & the Haunted Library. Garland, Michael, illus. 2009. (ENG., Illus.). 32p. (J). (gr. -1-2). 16.99 *(978-0-525-42139-9(4)*, Dutton Books for Young Readers) Penguin Young Readers Group.
—Miss Smith Reads Again! 2006. (Illus.). (J). *(978-1-4156-8098-8(1)*, Dutton Juvenile) Penguin Publishing Group.
—Miss Smith Reads Again! Garland, Michael, illus. 2008. (ENG., Illus.). 32p. (J). (gr. -1-2). pap. 6.99 *(978-0-14-241140-7(X)*, Puffin Books) Penguin Young Readers Group.
—Miss Smith's Incredible Storybook. Garland, Michael, illus. (ENG., Illus.). 32p. (J). (gr. -1-2). 2005. pap. 6.99 *(978-0-14-240282-5(6)*, Puffin Books) 2003. 16.99 *(978-0-525-47133-2(2)*, Dutton Books for Young Readers) Penguin Young Readers Group.
—Miss Smith's Incredible Storybook. 2007. 27.95 incl. audio *(978-0-8045-6945-3(2))*; 29.95 incl. audio compact disk *(978-0-8045-4159-6(0))* Spoken Arts, Inc.
Gifford, Peggy. Moxy Maxwell Does Not Love Stuart Little. Fisher, Valorie, photos by. 2008. (Moxy Maxwell Ser.). (ENG., Illus.). 112p. (J). (gr. 2-5). 5.99 *(978-0-440-42230-3(2)*, Yearling) Random Hse. Children's Bks.
Gläser, Mechthild. The Book Jumper. 2017. (ENG.). 384p. (YA). 17.99 *(978-1-250-08666-2(3)*, 9781250086662) Feiwel & Friends.
Gleeson, Libby & Blackwood, Freya. Look, a Book! 2012. (ENG.). 32p. 16.99 *(978-88-89854-89-1(8))* Officina Libraria srl ITA. Dist: National Bk. Network.
Gonzales Betrand, Diane. The Story Circle / el Circulo de Cuentos. Martin, Wendy, illus. 2016. (ENG, MUL & SPA.). 32p. (J). (gr. k-3). 17.95 *(978-1-55885-826-8(1)*, Piñata Books) Arte Publico Pr.
Grabenstein, Chris. Escape from Mr. Lemoncello's Library. (ENG.). (J). (gr. 3-7). 2014. 336p. 7.99 *(978-0-307-93147-4(1)*, Yearling) 2013. 304p. 17.99 *(978-0-375-87089-7(X)*, Random Hse. Bks. for Young Readers) 2013. 304p. lib. bdg. 19.99 *(978-0-375-97089-4(4)*, Random Hse. Bks. for Young Readers) 2017. 336p. 7.99 **(978-0-525-58037-9(9)**, *Yearling)* Random Hse. Children's Bks.
—Escape from Mr. Lemoncello's Library. 2014. lib. bdg. 18.40 *(978-0-606-37114-8(1))* Turtleback Bks.
—The Island of Dr. Libris. 2016. (ENG.). 272p. (J). (gr. 3-7). 7.99 *(978-0-385-38845-0(4)*, Yearling) Random Hse. Children's Bks.
—Mr. Lemoncello's Library Olympics. (ENG., (J). (gr. 3-7). 2017. Illus.). 320p. 7.99 **(978-0-553-51042-3(8)**, *Yearling)* 2016. 288p. 16.99 *(978-0-553-51040-9(1)*, Random Hse. Bks. for Young Readers) 2016. 288p. lib. bdg. 19.99 *(978-0-553-51041-6(X)*, Random Hse. Bks. for Young Readers) Random Hse. Children's Bks.
—Mr. Lemoncello's Library Olympics. 2017. lib. bdg. 18.40 **(978-0-606-39875-6(9))** Turtleback Bks.
Gravett, Emily. Again! Gravett, Emily, illus. 2013. (ENG., Illus.). 32p. (J). (gr. -1-3). 17.99 *(978-1-4424-5231-2(5)*, Simon & Schuster Bks. For Young Readers) Simon & Schuster Bks. For Young Readers.
—Wolves. Gravett, Emily, illus. 2006. (ENG., Illus.). 40p. (J). (gr. k-3). 17.99 *(978-1-4169-1491-4(9)*, Simon & Schuster Bks. For Young Readers) Simon & Schuster Bks. For Young Readers.
Gray, Keith. The Chain. 2013. (ENG.). 80p. (YA). (gr. 6-12). pap. 6.95 *(978-1-78112-173-3(7))*; lib. bdg. 22.60 *(978-1-78112-172-6(9))* Lerner Publishing Group.
Greene, Rhonda Gowler. No Pirates Allowed! Said Library Lou. Ajhar, Brian, illus. 2013. (ENG.). 40p. (J). (gr. 1-3). 15.95 *(978-1-58536-796-2(6)*, 202364) Sleeping Bear Pr.
Greenwald, Tommy. Charlie Joe Jackson's Guide to Not Reading. Coovert, J. P., illus. 2011. (Charlie Joe Jackson Ser.: 1). (ENG.). 224p. (J). (gr. 4-7). 15.99 *(978-1-59643-691-6(3)*, 9781596436916) Roaring Brook Pr.
—Charlie Joe Jackson's Guide to Not Reading. 2012. (Charlie Joe Jackson's Guide Ser.: 1). (J). lib. bdg. 17.20 *(978-0-606-26127-2(3)*, Turtleback) Turtleback Bks.
Griffiths, Andy. The 13-Story Treehouse. Denton, Terry, illus. 2013. (Treehouse Bks.: 1). (ENG.). 256p. (J). (gr. 1-5). 13.99 *(978-1-250-02690-3(3)*, 9781250026903) Feiwel & Friends.
—The 13-Story Treehouse. Denton, Terry, illus. 2015. (Treehouse Bks.: 1). (ENG.). 272p. (J). (gr. 1-5). pap. 6.99 *(978-1-250-07065-4(1)*, 9781250070654) Square Fish.
Griswell, Kim T. Rufus Goes to School. Gorbachev, Valeri, illus. 2013. (ENG.). 32p. (J). (gr. -1-1). 14.95 *(978-1-4549-0416-8(X))* Sterling Publishing Co., Inc.
—Rufus Goes to Sea. Gorbachev, Valeri, illus. 2015. (ENG.). 32p. (J). (gr. -1-1). 14.95 *(978-1-4549-1052-7(6))* Sterling Publishing Co., Inc.
Gutman, Dan. Nightmare at the Book Fair. 2010. (ENG.). 240p. (J). (gr. 3-7). pap. 7.99 *(978-1-4169-2439-5(6)*, Simon & Schuster Bks. For Young Readers) Simon & Schuster Bks. For Young Readers.
Hahn, Mary Downing. Daphne's Book. 2008. (ENG., Illus.). 192p. (J). (gr. 5-7). pap. 7.99 *(978-0-547-01641-2(7))* Houghton Mifflin Harcourt Publishing Co.
Hall, Kirsten. The Jacket. Tolstikova, Dasha, illus. 2014. (ENG.). 48p. (J). (gr. -1-3). 17.95 *(978-1-59270-168-1(X))* Enchanted Lion Bks., LLC.
Hall, Michael. Frankencrayon. Hall, Michael, illus. 2016. (Illus.). 40p. (J). (gr. -1-3). 17.99 *(978-0-06-225211-1(9))*; lib. bdg. 18.89 *(978-0-06-225212-8(7))* HarperCollins Pubs. (Greenwillow Bks.).
Hallinan, P. K. Just Open a Book. (J). 24p. 7.95 *(978-0-8249-5353-9(3))*; (ENG.). 22p. pap. 6.55 *(978-0-8249-5354-6(1))*; 24p. lib. bdg. 11.00 *(978-0-8249-5355-3(X))*; 2004. (ENG., Illus.). 48p. pap. 9.95 *(978-0-8249-5490-1(4))* Worthy Publishing. (Ideal Pubns.).
Hanlon, Abigail & Hanlon, Abby. Dory Dory Black Sheep. 2016. (Dory Fantasmagory Ser.). (ENG., Illus.). 160p. (J). (gr. 1-3). 14.99 *(978-1-101-99426-9(6)*, Dial Bks) Penguin Young Readers Group.
Hardinge, Frances. Fly by Night. 2008. 512p. (J). (gr. 5-9). per. 7.99 *(978-0-06-087630-2(1))* HarperCollins Pubs.
Harper, Charise Mericle. A Big Surprise for Little Card. Raff, Anna, illus. 2016. (ENG.). 40p. (J). (gr. -1-3). 16.99 *(978-0-7636-7485-4(0))* Candlewick Pr.
Harris, Robie H. Maybe a Bear Ate It! Emberley, Michael, illus. 2008. (ENG.). 40p. (J). (gr. -1-k). 16.99 *(978-0-439-92961-5(X)*, Orchard Bks.) Scholastic, Inc.
Haskell, Merrie. Handbook for Dragon Slayers. 2013. (ENG.). 336p. (J). (gr. 3-7). 16.99 *(978-0-06-200816-9(1))* HarperCollins Pubs.
Hautzig, Deborah. Little Witch Learns to Read. Wickstrom, Sylvie K., illus. 2003. (Step into Reading Ser.). (ENG.). 48p. (J). (gr. k-3). pap. 3.99 *(978-0-375-82179-0(1)*, Random Hse. Bks. for Young Readers) Random Hse. Children's Bks.
Hector, Julian. The Gentleman Bug. Hector, Julian, illus. 2010. (ENG., Illus.). 40p. (J). (gr. -1-k). 16.99 *(978-1-4169-9467-1(X)*, Atheneum Bks. for Young Readers) Simon & Schuster Children's Publishing.
Hennessy, B. G. Claire & the Unicorn Happy Ever After. Mitchell, Susan, illus. 2006. (ENG.). 32p. (J). (gr. -1-3). 17.99 *(978-1-4169-0815-9(3)*, Simon & Schuster Bks. For Young Readers) Simon & Schuster Bks. For Young Readers.
Henson, Heather. That Book Woman. Small, David, illus. 2008. (ENG.). 40p. (J). (gr. -1-3). 17.99 *(978-1-4169-0812-8(9)*, Atheneum Bks. for Young Readers) Simon & Schuster Children's Publishing.
—That Book Woman. Small, David, illus. 2011. (J). (gr. 2-4). 29.95 *(978-0-545-23715-4(7))* Weston Woods Studios, Inc.
Hest, Amy. The Reader, 0 vols. Castillo, Lauren, illus. 2012. (ENG.). 32p. (J). (gr. -1-1). 16.99 *(978-0-7614-6184-5(1)*, 9780761461845, Amazon Children's Publishing) Amazon Publishing.
Hillert, Margaret. Dear Dragon Goes to the Library. Schimmell, David, illus. 2008. (BeginningtoRead Ser.). 32p. (J). (gr. k-2). lib. bdg. 22.60 *(978-1-59953-160-1(7))* Norwood Hse. Pr.
—Dear Dragon Goes to the Library (Querido Dragon Va a la Biblioteca) Del Risco, Eida, tr. from ENG. Schimmell, David, illus. 2010. (BeginningtoRead Ser.). (SPA & ENG.). 32p. (J). (gr. k-2). lib. bdg. 22.60 *(978-1-59953-361-2(8))* Norwood Hse. Pr.
—Querido Dragón Va a la Biblioteca/Dear Dragon Goes to the Library. del Risco, Eida, tr. Schimmell, David, illus. 2010. (BeginningtoRead Ser.). 32p. (J). (-2). pap. 11.94 *(978-1-60357-549-2(9))* Norwood Hse. Pr.
Hills, Tad. Rocket Writes a Story. Hills, Tad, illus. 2012. (ENG., Illus.). 40p. (J). (gr. -1-3). 17.99 *(978-0-375-87086-6(5)*, Schwartz & Wade Bks.) Random Hse. Children's Bks.
Hodgkinson, Leigh. A Place to Read. 2017. (ENG., Illus.). 32p. (J). 16.99 *(978-1-68119-323-6(X)*, 9781681193236, Bloomsbury USA Childrens) Bloomsbury Publishing USA.
Holt, K. A. Gnome-A-geddon. Jack, Colin, illus. 2017. (ENG.). 304p. (J). (gr. 3-7). 16.99 **(978-1-4814-7845-8(1)**, *McElderry, Margaret K. Bks.)* McElderry, Margaret K. Bks.
—Gnomeageddon. 2017. (Illus.). 285p. (J). pap. **(978-1-4814-7846-5(X)**, *McElderry, Margaret K. Bks.)* McElderry, Margaret K. Bks.
Hopkins, Lee Bennett. Jumping off Library Shelves. Manning, Jane, illus. 2015. (ENG.). 32p. (J). (gr. k). 17.95 *(978-1-59078-924-7(5)*, 1396014, Wordsong) Boyds Mills Pr.
Hubbell, Patricia. Check It Out! Reading, Finding, Helping. 0 vols. Speir, Nancy, illus. 2011. (ENG.). 32p. (J). (gr. -1-3). 16.99 *(978-0-7614-5803-6(4)*, 9780761458036, Amazon Children's Publishing) Amazon Publishing.
Hutton, John. Book: Baby Unplugged. Hutton, John, ed. Kang, Andrea, illus. 2012. (Baby Unplugged Ser.). (ENG.). 14p. (J). (— 1). bds. 7.99 *(978-1-936669-06-6(4))* Blue Manatee Press.
Inkpen, Mick. This Is My Book. Inkpen, Mick, illus. 2010. (ENG., Illus.). 32p. (J). (gr. -1-k). pap. 8.99 *(978-0-340-98963-0(7))* Hodder & Stoughton GBR. Dist: Hachette Bk. Group.
The Island of Dr. Libris. 2015. (ENG.). 256p. (J). (gr. 3-7). 16.99 *(978-0-385-38844-3(6))*; lib. bdg. 19.99 *(978-0-385-38846-7(2))* Random Hse. Children's Bks. (Random Hse. Bks. for Young Readers).
Ivey, Randall. Jay & the Bounty of Books, 1 vol. Galey, Chuck, illus. 2007. (ENG.). 32p. (J). (gr. k-3). 16.99 *(978-1-58980-372-5(8))* Pelican Publishing Co., Inc.
Jeffers, Oliver & Winston, Sam. A Child of Books. Jeffers, Oliver & Winston, Sam, illus. 2016. (ENG., Illus.). 40p. (J). (gr. k-12). 17.99 *(978-0-7636-9077-9(5))* Candlewick Pr.
Jenkins, Jerry B. & Fabry, Chris. The Book of the King. 2007. (Wormling Ser.: 1). (ENG.). 288p. (J). (gr. 5-9). per. 7.99 *(978-1-4143-0155-6(3))* Tyndale Hse. Pubs.
—El Libro del Rey. 2008. (Lombricero Ser.: 1).Tr. of Book of the King. (SPA.). 304p. (J). pap. 7.99 *(978-1-4143-2216-2(X)*, Tyndale Espanol) Tyndale Hse. Pubs.
Jennings, Sharon, et al. Franklin's Library Book. Gagnon, Céleste, illus. 2005. 32p. (J). *(978-0-439-82297-8(1))* Scholastic, Inc.
Jeram, Anita. I Love My Little Storybook. Jeram, Anita, illus. 2010. (ENG., Illus.). 32p. (J). (-k). 7.99 *(978-0-7636-4806-0(X))* Candlewick Pr.
John, Jory. I Will Chomp You! Shea, Bob, illus. 2015. (ENG.). 40p. (J). (gr. -1-2). 20.99 *(978-0-385-38987-7(6)*, Random Hse. Bks. for Young Readers) Random Hse. Children's Bks.
Jones, Lloyd. Mister Pip. 2010. 256p. 21.85 *(978-0-7569-9114-2(5))* Perfection Learning Corp.
Joyce, William. Billy's Booger. Joyce, William, illus. 2015. (ENG., Illus.). 40p. (J). (gr. -1-3). 17.99 *(978-1-4424-7351-5(7))* Simon & Schuster Children's Publishing.
—The Fantastic Flying Books of Mr. Morris Lessmore. 2006. *(978-0-06-050838-8(8))* HarperCollins Canada, Ltd.
—The Fantastic Flying Books of Mr. Morris Lessmore. Joyce, William & Bluhm, Joe, illus. 2012. (ENG.). 56p. (J). (gr. -1-3). 18.99 *(978-1-4424-5702-7(3)*, Atheneum Bks. for Young Readers) Simon & Schuster Children's Publishing.
Kerrin, Jessica Scott. The Spotted Dog Last Seen, 1 vol. 2013. (ENG.). 196p. (J). 14.95 *(978-1-55498-387-2(8))* Groundwood Bks. CAN. Dist: Publishers Group West (PGW).
Kinsey-Warnock, Natalie. Lumber Camp Library. Bernardin, James, illus. 2003. (ENG.). 96p. (J). (gr. 2-5). pap. 4.99 *(978-0-06-444292-3(6))* HarperCollins Pubs.
Kirk, Daniel. Library Mouse: A World to Explore. 2010. (ENG., Illus.). 32p. (J). (gr. 1-4). 17.95 *(978-0-8109-8968-9(9)*, Abrams Bks. for Young Readers) Abrams, Inc.
Klausmeier, Jesse. Open This Little Book. Lee, Suzy, illus. 2013. (ENG.). 40p. (J). (gr. -1-3). 16.99 *(978-0-8118-6783-2(8))* Chronicle Bks. LLC.
Klein, Adria F. Max Goes to the Library. Gallagher-Cole, Mernie, illus. (Read-It! Readers: the Life of Max Ser.). (ENG.). 24p. (gr. -1-2). 2007. per. 3.95 *(978-1-4048-3062-2(6))* 2005. lib. bdg. 21.32 *(978-1-4048-1182-9(6))* Picture Window Bks. (Easy Readers).
—Max Va a la Biblioteca, 1 vol. Lozano, Clara, tr. Gallagher-Cole, Mernie, illus. 2007. (Read-It! Readers en Español: la Vida de Max Ser.). (SPA.). 24p. (gr. -1-3). per. 3.95 *(978-1-4048-3036-3(7)*, Easy Readers) Picture Window Bks.
Klise, Kate. Over My Dead Body. Klise, M. Sarah, illus. (43 Old Cemetery Road Ser.: Bk. 2). (ENG.). 128p. (J). (gr. 2-5). 2011. pap. 6.99 *(978-0-547-57713-5(3))* 2009. 15.99 *(978-0-15-205734-3(X))* Houghton Mifflin Harcourt Publishing Co.
Knowlton, Laurie. I Know a Librarian Who Chewed on a Word, 1 vol. Leonhard, Herb, illus. 2012. (ENG.). 32p. (J). (gr. k-3). 16.99 *(978-1-58980-892-8(4))* Pelican Publishing Co., Inc.
Kohara, Kazuno. The Midnight Library. Kohara, Kazuno, illus. 2014. (ENG., Illus.). 32p. (J). (gr. -1-1). 16.99 *(978-1-59643-985-6(8)*, 9781596439856) Roaring Brook Pr.
Kozlowsky, M. P. The Dyerville Tales. Thompson, Brian, illus. 2014. (ENG.). 336p. (J). (gr. 3-7). 16.99 *(978-0-06-199871-3(0)*, Waldon Pond Pr.) HarperCollins Pubs.
Krys, Michelle. Hexed. 2014. (ENG.). 384p. (YA). (gr. 7). 17.99 *(978-0-385-74337-2(8)*, Delacorte Pr.) Random Hse. Children's Bks.
Lachenmeyer, Nathaniel. The Boo! Book. Ceccoli, Nicoletta, illus. 2012. (ENG.). 46p. (J). (gr. -1-3). 17.99 *(978-1-4169-3513-1(4)*, Atheneum Bks. for Young Readers) Simon & Schuster Children's Publishing.
Ladd, Debbie. Ethan the Ending Eater. Nakasone, Shaun, illus. 2008. 64p. (J). 17.95 *(978-0-9727615-2-9(7))* Deb on Air Bks.
Lai, Trevor. Piggy. 2016. (ENG., Illus.). 32p. (J). 16.99 *(978-1-68119-065-5(6)*, 9781681190655, Bloomsbury USA Childrens) Bloomsbury Publishing USA.
Lammle, Leslie. Princess Wannabe. Lammle, Leslie, illus. 2014. (ENG., Illus.). 40p. (J). (gr. -1-3). 17.99 *(978-0-06-125197-9(6))* HarperCollins Pubs.
Langlois, Florence. The Extraordinary Gift. Goodman, John, tr. from FRE. Langlois, Florence, illus. 2005. (Illus.). 48p. (J). (gr. -1-2). reprint ed. 15.00 *(978-0-7567-8942-8(7))* DIANE Publishing Co.
Lasky, Kathryn. Spiders on the Case. Gilpin, Stephen, illus. (Deadlies Ser.). (ENG.). 176p. (J). (gr. 2-5). 2012. pap. 5.99 *(978-0-545-11731-9(3))*Bk. 2. 2011. 15.99 *(978-0-545-11682-4(1))* Scholastic, Inc. (Scholastic Pr.).
Lavette, Lavaille. The Adventures of Roopster Roux: That's Not Punny, 1 vol. Nguyen, Duke, ed. Kuon, Vuthy, illus. 2007. (Roupster Roux Ser.: Vol. 5). (ENG.). 32p. (J). (gr. 3-7). 16.95 *(978-1-58980-483-8(X))* Pelican Publishing Co., Inc.
Lê, Minh. Let Me Finish! Roxas, Isabel, illus. 2016. (ENG.). 20p. (J). (gr. -1-k). 16.99 *(978-1-4847-2173-5(X))* Disney Pr.
Lefranc, Karin & Parker, Tyler. I Want to Eat Your Books. 2015. (ENG., Illus.). 32p. (J). (gr. -1-k). 16.99 *(978-1-63450-172-9(1)*, Sky Pony Pr.) Skyhorse Publishing Co., Inc.
Lethem, Mara. The Highest Mountain of Books in the World. Bonilla, Rocio, illus. 2016. (J). *(978-1-4413-1999-9(9))* Peter Pauper Pr. Inc.
Letria, José Jorge. If I Were a Book. Letria, Andre, illus. 2014. (ENG.). 64p. 12.95 *(978-1-4521-2144-4(3))* Chronicle Bks. LLC.
Lies, Brian. Bats at the Library. 2014. (Bat Book Ser.). (ENG., Illus.). 32p. (J). (gr. -1-3). pap. 7.99 *(978-0-544-33920-0(7)*, HMH Books For Young Readers) Houghton Mifflin Harcourt Publishing Co.
—Bats at the Library. Lies, Brian, illus. 2008. (Bat Book Ser.). (ENG., Illus.). 32p. (J). (gr. -1-3). 17.99 *(978-0-618-99923-1(X))* Houghton Mifflin Harcourt Publishing Co.
Luper, Eric. The Haunted Howl. 2016. (Key Hunters Ser.: 3). (ENG., Illus.). 128p. (J). (gr. 2-5). pap. 4.99 *(978-0-545-82211-4(4)*, Scholastic Paperbacks) Scholastic, Inc.
—The Mysterious Moonstone. 2016. (Key Hunters Ser.: 1). (ENG., Illus.). 128p. (J). (gr. 2-5). pap. 4.99 *(978-0-545-82204-6(1))* Scholastic, Inc.
—The Spy's Secret. 2016. (Key Hunters Ser.: 2). (ENG.). 128p. (J). (gr. 2-5). pap. 4.99 *(978-0-545-82206-0(8))* Scholastic, Inc.
—The Titanic Treasure. 2017. (Key Hunters Ser.: 5). (ENG.). 128p. (J). (gr. 2-5). pap. 4.99 **(978-1-338-14926-5(1)**, *Scholastic Paperbacks)* Scholastic, Inc.
—The Titanic Treasure (Key Hunters #5) 2017. (Key Hunters Ser.: 5). (ENG.). 128p. (J). (gr. 2-5). lib. bdg. 16.99 **(978-1-338-14927-2(X)**, *Scholastic Paperbacks)* Scholastic, Inc.
Luper, Eric. The Wizard's War (Key Hunters #4) 2017. (Key Hunters Ser.: 4). (ENG.). 128p. (J). (gr. 2-5). pap. 4.99 *(978-0-545-82213-8(0)*, Scholastic Paperbacks) Scholastic, Inc.
Lytton, Deborah. Ruby Starr. 2017. (Ruby Starr Ser.: 1). (ENG.). 272p. (J). (gr. 3-7). pap. 7.99 **(978-1-4926-4577-1(X)**, *Sourcebooks Jabberwocky)* Sourcebooks, Inc.
Mack, Jeff. Duck in the Fridge, 0 vols. 2014. (ENG.). 40p. (J). (gr. 1-3). 16.99 *(978-1-4778-4776-3(6)*, 9781477847763, Amazon Children's Publishing) Amazon Publishing.
—Look! Mack, Jeff, illus. 2015. (ENG., Illus.). 32p. (J). (gr. -1-k). 16.99 *(978-0-399-16205-3(4)*, Philomel Bks.) Penguin Young Readers Group.
—The Things I Can Do. Mack, Jeff, illus. 2013. (ENG., Illus.). 32p. (J). (gr. -1-1). 16.99 *(978-1-59643-675-6(1)*, 9781596436756) Roaring Brook Pr.
MacLachlan, Patricia. The True Gift. Floca, Brian, illus. 2013. (ENG.). 112p. (J). (gr. 2-6). pap. 6.99 *(978-1-4424-8858-8(1)*, Atheneum Bks. for Young Readers) Simon & Schuster Children's Publishing.
—The True Gift: A Christmas Story. Floca, Brian, illus. 2009. (ENG.). 96p. (J). (gr. 2-6). 14.99 *(978-1-4169-9081-9(X)*, Atheneum Bks. for Young Readers) Simon & Schuster Children's Publishing.
Maclear, Kyo. The Good Little Book. Arbona, Marion, illus. 2015. (ENG.). 40p. (J). (gr. k-4). 16.99 *(978-1-77049-451-0(0)*, Tundra Bks.) Tundra Bks. CAN. Dist: Penguin Random Hse. LLC.
Manley, Curtis. The Summer Nick Taught His Cats to Read. Berube, Kate, illus. 2016. (ENG.). 32p. (J). (gr. -1-3). 17.99 *(978-1-4814-3569-7(8)*, Simon & Schuster Bks. For Young Readers) Simon & Schuster Bks. For Young Readers.
Mantchev, Lisa. Eyes Like Stars. 2010. (Theatre Illuminata Ser.: 1). (ENG.). 384p. (YA). (gr. 7-12). pap. 11.99 *(978-0-312-60866-8(7)*, 9780312608668) Square Fish.
Marshall, Rita. I Hate to Read! Delessert, Etienne, illus. 2013. (ENG.). 32p. (J). (gr. k-17). 16.99 *(978-1-56846-232-5(8)*, Creative Editions) Creative Co., The.
—I Hate to Read! Delessert, Etienne, illus. 2008. (J). (gr. k-3). 27.95 incl. audio *(978-0-8045-6973-6(8))*; 29.95 incl. audio compact disk *(978-0-8045-4198-5(1))* Spoken Arts, Inc.
—I Still Hate to Read! Delessert, Etienne, illus. 2008. (ENG.). 32p. (J). (gr. 1-3). 19.95 *(978-1-56846-174-8(7)*, Creative Editions) Creative Co., The.
Martin, Ann M. The Secret Book Club. 2008. (Main Street Ser.). (Illus.). 212p. (J). (gr. 4-7). 14.65 *(978-0-7569-8823-4(3))* Perfection Learning Corp.
May, Eleanor. Albert Adds Up! Melmon, Deborah, illus. 2014. (Mouse Math (r) Ser.). 32p. (J). (gr. -1-1). 22.60 *(978-1-57565-744-8(9))* Kane Press, Inc.
McDonald, Megan. Stink & the Midnight Zombie Walk. Reynolds, Peter H., illus. 2013. (Stink Ser.: 7). (ENG.). 160p. (J). (gr. 1-4). 12.99 *(978-0-7636-6394-0(8))*; pap. 4.99 *(978-0-7636-6422-0(7))* Candlewick Pr.
—Stink & the Midnight Zombie Walk. 2013. (Stink Ser.: 7). lib. bdg. 14.75 *(978-0-606-31586-9(1)*, Turtleback) Turtleback Bks.
McDonnell, Patrick. A Perfectly Messed-Up Story. 2014. (ENG., Illus.). 40p. (J). (gr. -1-3). 17.99 *(978-0-316-22258-7(5))* Little, Brown Bks. for Young Readers.
McQuinn, Anna. Lola at the Library. Beardshaw, Rosalind, illus. 2006. (ENG.). 32p. (J). (gr. -1-k). 15.95 *(978-1-58089-113-4(6))*; 6.95 *(978-1-58089-142-4(X))* Charlesbridge Publishing, Inc.
—Lola at the Library. Beardshaw, Rosalind, illus. 2007. 22p. (gr. -1). 16.95 *(978-0-7569-7931-7(5))* Perfection Learning Corp.
—Lola le Lee Al Pequeño Leo. Beardshaw, Rosalind, illus. 2013. (SPA & ENG.). 28p. (J). (-k). pap. 7.95 *(978-1-58089-599-6(9))* Charlesbridge Publishing, Inc.
—Lola Loves Stories. Beardshaw, Rosalind, illus. 2010. (ENG.). 28p. (J). (gr. k-3). pap. 6.95 *(978-1-58089-259-9(0))* Charlesbridge Publishing, Inc.
—Lola Reads to Leo. Beardshaw, Rosalind, illus. 2012. (ENG.). 28p. (J). (-k). 15.95 *(978-1-58089-403-6(8))*; pap. 6.95 *(978-1-58089-404-3(6))* Charlesbridge Publishing, Inc.
—Lola Reads to Leo. 2012. pap. 19.95 incl. audio compact disk *(978-0-8045-4236-4(8))* Spoken Arts, Inc.
McQuinn, Anna & Beardshaw, Rosalind. A Lola le Encantan Los Cuentos. Canetti, Yanitzia, tr. from ENG. Beardshaw, Rosalind, illus. 2012. (SPA., Illus.). 28p. (J). (-k). pap. 7.95 *(978-1-58089-444-9(5))* Charlesbridge Publishing, Inc.
Medearis, Angela Shelf. Lucy's Quiet Book. Ernst, Lisa Campbell, illus. 2004. (Green Light Readers Level 2 Ser.). (ENG.). 24p. (J). (gr. -1-3). pap. 3.95 *(978-0-15-205143-3(0))* Houghton Mifflin Harcourt Publishing Co.
—Lucy's Quiet Book. Ernst, Lisa Campbell, illus. 2004. (Green Light Readers Level 2 Ser.). (gr. k-2). 13.95 *(978-0-7569-4310-3(8))* Perfection Learning Corp.
Melling, David. The Ghost Library. Melling, David, illus. 2004. (ENG., Illus.). 32p. (J). (gr. -1-k). 16.99 *(978-0-340-86088-5(X))* Hodder & Stoughton GBR. Dist: Hachette Bk. Group.
Meng, Cece. I Will Not Read This Book. Ang, Joy, illus. 2011. (ENG.). 32p. (J). (gr. -1-3). 16.99 *(978-0-547-04971-7(4))* Houghton Mifflin Harcourt Publishing Co.

Miles, David. The Book. Hoopes, Natalie, illus. 2015. (ENG.). 32p. (J). 16.95 (978-1-939629-65-4(9)) Familius LLC.

Miller, Chris & Miller, Allan. Hunter Brown & the Consuming Fire, 3 bks., Bk.2. 2009. (ENG., Illus.). 352p. (J). pap. 13.99 (978-1-59317-357-9(1)) Warner Pr., Inc.

Miller, Christopher & Miller, Allan. Hunter Brown & the Eye of Ends, 3 bks., Bk.3. 2011. (J). pap. 13.99 (978-1-59317-400-2(4)) Warner Pr., Inc.

Miller, Pat. We're Going on a Book Hunt. Bernard Westcott, Nadine, illus. 2008. (J). (gr. -1). 17.95 (978-1-60213-034-0(5), Upstart Bks.) Highsmith Inc.

Miller, William. Richard Wright y el Carne de Biblioteca. Christie, Gregory R., illus. 2003. (SPA.). (J). 32p. 16.95 (978-1-58430-180-6(5)); pap. 6.95 (978-1-58430-181-3(3)) Lee & Low Bks., Inc.

Mills, Claudia. Kelsey Green, Reading Queen, 1 vol. Shepperson, Rob, illus. 2013. (Franklin School Friends Ser.: 1). (ENG.). 128p. (J). (gr. 2-5). 15.99 (978-0-374-37485-3(6), 9780374374853, Farrar, Straus & Giroux (BYR)) Farrar, Straus & Giroux.

—Kelsey Green, Reading Queen. Shepperson, Rob, illus. 2014. (Franklin School Friends Ser.: 1). (ENG.). 144p. (J). (gr. 2-5). pap. 5.99 (978-1-250-03405-2(1), 9781250034052) Square Fish.

Mone, Gregory. Dangerous Waters: An Adventure on Titanic. 2012. (ENG.). 240p. (J). (gr. 4-7). 16.99 (978-1-59643-673-2(5), 9781596436732) Roaring Brook Pr.

—Dangerous Waters: An Adventure on Titanic. 2013. (ENG.). 256p. (J). (gr. 4-7). pap. 7.99 (978-1-250-01671-3(1), 9781250016713) Square Fish.

Mora, Pat. Book Fiesta! Celebrate Children's Day. López, Rafael, illus. 2009.Tr. of Celebremos el Día de los Niños, el Día de los Libros. (SPA & ENG.). 40p. (J). (gr. -1-1). 17.99 (978-0-06-128877-7(2), Rayo) HarperCollins Pubs.

—Tomas & the Library Lady. Colón, Raúl, illus. 2007. (gr. k-3). 18.00 (978-0-7569-7935-5(8)) Perfection Learning Corp.

—Tomas y la Senora de la Biblioteca. 2004. (SPA., Illus.). (J). (gr. k-3). spiral bd. (978-0-616-03092-9(4)) Canadian National Institute for the Blind/Institut National Canadien pour les Aveugles.

Moreillon, Judi. Read to Me, 1 vol. Teis, Kyra, illus. (J). 2004. (ENG.). 32p. (gr. -1). bds. 6.95 (978-1-59572-014-6(6)) 2003. 24p. 6.95 (978-1-932065-49-7(0), 1-718-784-9112) Star Bright Bks., Inc.

Moriarty, Jaclyn. The Spell Book of Listen Taylor. 2007. (YA). (978-0-439-84679-0(X), Levine, Arthur A. Bks.) Scholastic, Inc.

Morrison, Toni & Morrison, Slade. Please, Louise. Strickland, Shadra, illus. 2014. (ENG.). 32p. (J). (gr. -1-3). 17.99 (978-1-4169-8338-5(4), Simon & Schuster Bks. For Young Readers) Simon & Schuster Bks. For Young Readers.

Moulton, Mark Kimball. Scarecrow Pete & His Suitcase of Dreams. Crouch, Karen Hillard, illus. 2005. (ENG.). 36p. (J). (gr. -1-3). 14.95 (978-0-8249-5151-1(4), Ideal Pubns.) Worthy Publishing.

Muntean, Michaela. Do Not Open This Book. Lemaître, Pascal, illus. 2006. (ENG.). 40p. (J). (gr. -1-3). 17.99 (978-0-439-69839-9(1), Scholastic Pr.) Scholastic, Inc.

Neff, Henry H. The Fiend & the Forge. 2011. (Tapestry Ser.). (ENG., Illus.). 560p. (J). (gr. 3-7). 7.99 (978-0-375-83899-6(6), Yearling) Random Hse. Children's Bks.

—The Second Siege. 2010. (Tapestry Ser.). (ENG., Illus.). 512p. (J). (gr. 3-7). 7.99 (978-0-375-83897-2(X), Yearling) Random Hse. Children's Bks.

Nelson, Vaunda Micheaux. No Crystal Stair: A Documentary Novel of the Life & Work of Lewis Michaux, Harlem Bookseller. Christie, R. Gregory, illus. 2012. (Carolrhoda YA Ser.). (ENG.). 192p. (YA). (gr. 7-12). 17.95 (978-0-7613-6169-5(3), Carolrhoda Lab™) Lerner Publishing Group.

Nomura, Mizuki. Book Girl & the Captive Fool. 2011. (Book Girl Ser.: 3). (ENG., Illus.). 240p. (YA). (gr. 8-17). pap. 13.00 (978-0-316-07693-7(7), Yen Pr.) Orbit.

—Book Girl & the Corrupted Angel. 2012. (Book Girl Ser.: 4). (ENG., Illus.). 240p. (YA). (gr. 8-17). pap. 13.00 (978-0-316-07694-4(5), Yen Pr.) Orbit.

—Book Girl & the Suicidal Mime. 2010. (Book Girl Ser.: 1). (ENG., Illus.). 192p. (YA). (gr. 8-17). pap. 13.00 (978-0-316-07690-6(2), Yen Pr.) Orbit.

—Book Girl & the Undine Who Bore a Moonflower. 2013. (Book Girl Ser.: 6). (ENG., Illus.). 240p. (YA). (gr. 8-17). pap. 11.99 (978-0-316-07696-8(1), Yen Pr.) Orbit.

—Book Girl & the Wayfarer's Lamentation, Vol. 5. 2012. (Book Girl Ser.: 5). (ENG., Illus.). 272p. (YA). (gr. 8-17). pap. 11.99 (978-0-316-07695-1(3), Yen Pr.) Orbit.

Numeroff, Laura Joffe & Evans, Nate. The Jellybeans & the Big Book Bonanza. Munsinger, Lynn, illus. 2010. (ENG.). 32p. (J). (gr. k-2). 17.95 (978-0-8109-8412-7(1), Abrams Bks. for Young Readers) Abrams, Inc.

—The Jellybeans Love to Read. Munsinger, Lynn, illus. 2014. (ENG.). 24p. (J). (gr. -1-k). bds. 7.95 (978-1-4197-1162-6(8), Abrams Appleseed) Abrams, Inc.

O'Connor, Jane. Fancy Nancy: Best Reading Buddies. Glasser, Robin Preiss, illus. 2016. (I Can Read Level 1 Ser.). 32p. (J). (gr. -1-3). pap. 3.99 (978-0-06-237783-8(3)) HarperCollins Pubs.

Ohi, Debbie Ridpath. Where Are My Books? Ohi, Debbie Ridpath, illus. 2015. (ENG., Illus.). 40p. (J). (gr. -1-3). 17.99 (978-1-4424-6741-5(X), Simon & Schuster Bks. For Young Readers) Simon & Schuster Bks. For Young Readers.

OHora, Zachariah. The Not So Quiet Library. 2016. (ENG., Illus.). 40p. (J). (-k). 17.99 (978-0-8037-4140-9(5), Dial Bks) Penguin Young Readers Group.

Oliver, Carmen. Bears Make the Best Reading Buddies. Claude, Jean, illus. 2016. (Fiction Picture Bks.). (ENG.). 32p. (gr. -1-1). lib. bdg. 21.27 (978-1-4795-9181-7(5), Fiction Picture Bks.) Picture Window Bks.

Oppenheim, Joanne F. The Prince's Bedtime. Latimer, Miriam, illus. 2006. (ENG.). 32p. (J). (gr. -1-3). 16.99 (978-1-84148-597-3(7)) Barefoot Bks., Inc.

Oppenheim, Joanne F. & Barefoot Books Staff. El Principe No Duerme. Latimer, Miriam, illus. 2014. (SPA.). 32p. (J). (gr. -1-1). pap. 7.99 (978-1-78285-077-9(5)) Barefoot Bks., Inc.

Oppenheim, Joanne F. & Latimer, Muriam. The Prince's Bedtime. Latimer, Muriam, illus. 2007. (ENG., Illus.). 32p. (J). (gr. -1-2). 9.99 (978-1-84686-096-6(2)) Barefoot Bks., Inc.

Palmer, Robin. Little Miss Red. 2010. (ENG.). 320p. (YA). (gr. 7-18). 9.99 (978-0-14-241123-0(X), Speak) Penguin Young Readers Group.

Parachini, Jodie. This Is a Serious Book. Rieley, Daniel, illus. 2016. 32p. (J). (gr. -1-3). 17.99 (978-0-06-247052-2(3), Greenwillow Bks.) HarperCollins Pubs.

Paratore, Coleen Murtagh. Wish I Might. 2011. (ENG.). 176p. (J). (gr. 5-9). pap. 6.99 (978-0-545-09402-3(X), Scholastic Paperbacks) Scholastic, Inc.

—Wish I Might: From the Life of Willa Havisham. 2010. (ENG.). 176p. (J). (gr. 5-9). 16.99 (978-0-545-09406-1(2), Scholastic Pr.) Scholastic, Inc.

Parish, Herman. Amelia Bedelia's First Library Card. Avril, Lynne, illus. 2013. (Amelia Bedelia Ser.). 32p. (J). (gr. -1-3). (ENG.). 17.99 (978-0-06-209512-1(9)); lib. bdg. 18.89 (978-0-06-209513-8(7)) HarperCollins Pubs. (Greenwillow Bks.).

Parlato, Stephen. The World That Loved Books. (ENG., Illus.). 32p. (J). (gr. -1-3). 2017. 8.99 (978-1-77229-012-7(2)) 2008. 16.95 (978-1-894965-98-9(1)) Simply Read Bks. CAN. Dist: Ingram Publisher Services.

Parr, Todd. Reading Makes You Feel Good. 2009. (ENG., Illus.). 32p. (J). (gr. -1-1). pap. 8.00 (978-0-316-04348-9(6)) Little Brown & Co.

—Reading Makes You Feel Good. 2005. (ENG., Illus.). 32p. (J). (gr. -1-1). 17.99 (978-0-316-16004-9(0)) Little, Brown Bks. for Young Readers.

Patterson, James & Grabenstein, Chris. Laugh Out Loud. Ebbeler, Jeff, illus. 2017. (ENG.). 304p. (J). (gr. 3-7). 13.99 **(978-0-316-43146-0(X)**, Jimmy Patterson) Little Brown & Co.

Paulsen, Gary. Shelf Life: Stories by the Book. 2003. (ENG., Illus.). 192p. (J). (gr. 5-9). 17.99 (978-0-689-84180-4(9), Simon & Schuster Bks. For Young Readers) Simon & Schuster Bks. For Young Readers.

Pavanello, Roberto. The Ghost of Dr. Mold. Zeni, Marco, tr. from ITA. Pisapia, Blasco & Brughera, Pamela, illus. 2012. (Echo & the Bat Pack Ser.). (ENG.). 128p. (gr. 2-3). 25.32 (978-1-4342-3834-4(2), Echo & the Bat Pack) Stone Arch Bks.

Pawagi, Manjusha. The Girl Who Hated Books, 1 vol. Franson, Leanne, illus. 24p. (J). (gr. k-3). 2010. (ENG.). pap. 7.95 (978-1-896764-09-2(6)) 2005. 12.95 (978-1-896764-11-5(8)) Second Story Pr. CAN. Dist: Orca Bk. Pubs. USA.

Pearson, Mary E. I Can Do It All. Shelley, Jeff, illus. 2011. (Rookie Ready to Learn - I Can! Ser.). 32p. (J). (gr. -1-k). lib. bdg. 23.00 (978-0-531-26429-4(7), Children's Pr.) Scholastic Library Publishing.

Pearson, Mary E. & Shelly, Jeff. Puedo Hacer de Todo. Shelly, Jeff, illus. 2011. (Rookie Ready to Learn Español Ser.).Tr. of I Can Do It All. (SPA., Illus.). 40p. (J). pap. 5.95 (978-0-531-26787-5(3)); lib. bdg. 23.00 (978-0-531-26119-4(0)) Scholastic Library Publishing. (Children's Pr.).

Pearson, Tracey Campbell. Elephant's Story. Pearson, Tracey Campbell, illus. 2013. (ENG., Illus.). 40p. (J). (gr. -1-3). 17.99 (978-0-374-39913-9(1), 9780374399139, Farrar, Straus & Giroux (BYR)) Farrar, Straus & Giroux.

Pett, Mark, illus. This Is My Book. 2016. (ENG.). 40p. (J). (gr. -1-2). 17.99 (978-1-101-93790-7(4), Knopf Bks. for Young Readers) Random Hse. Children's Bks.

Picoult, Jodi & van Leer, Samantha. Between the Lines. (ENG., Illus.). 368p. (YA). (gr. 7). 2013. pap. 12.99 (978-1-4516-3581-2(8)) 2012. 19.99 (978-1-4516-3575-1(3)) Atria/Emily Bestler Bks. (Atria/Emily Bestler Bks.).

—Off the Page. Gilbert, Yvonne, illus. 2015. (YA). lib. bdg. (978-0-553-53557-0(9), Delacorte Pr) Random House Publishing Group.

—Off the Page. Gilbert, Yvonne, illus. (ENG.). (YA). (gr. 7). 2016. 368p. pap. 9.99 (978-0-553-53559-4(5), Ember) 2015. 384p. 19.99 (978-0-553-53556-3(0), Delacorte Pr.) Random Hse. Children's Bks.

Plourde, Lynn. Book Fair Day. Wickstrom, Thor, illus. 2006. (J). (978-1-4156-8095-7(7), Dutton Juvenile) Penguin Publishing Group.

Poblocki, Dan. The Nightmarys. 2011. (ENG.). 336p. (J). (gr. 3-7). pap. 7.99 (978-0-375-84257-3(8), Yearling) Random Hse. Children's Bks.

—The Stone Child. 2010. (ENG.). 288p. (J). (gr. 3-7). pap. 7.99 (978-0-375-84255-9(1), Yearling) Random Hse. Children's Bks.

Polacco, Patricia. The Mermaid's Purse. Polacco, Patricia, illus. 2016. (ENG., Illus.). 48p. (J). (gr. k-3). 17.99 (978-0-399-16692-1(0), G.P. Putnam's Sons Books for Young Readers) Penguin Young Readers Group.

Portman, Frank. Andromeda Klein. 2010. (ENG.). 432p. (YA). (gr. 9). pap. 9.99 (978-0-385-73526-1(X), Delacorte Bks. for Young Readers) Random Hse. Children's Bks.

Quick, Matthew. Every Exquisite Thing. 2016. (ENG.). 272p. (YA). (gr. 10-17). 17.99 (978-0-316-37959-5(X)) Little Brown & Co.

—Every Exquisite Thing. 2017. (ENG.). 288p. (YA). (gr. 10-17). pap. 9.99 (978-0-316-37961-8(1)) Little, Brown Bks. for Young Readers.

Rey, H. A. Visits the Library / Jorge el Curioso Va a la Biblioteca. 2011. (Curious George Ser.). (ENG & SPA., Illus.). 24p. (J). (gr. -1-3). pap. 3.99 (978-0-547-55075-6(8)) Houghton Mifflin Harcourt Publishing Co.

Rey, H. A. & Rey, Margret. Curious George Visits the Library. Weston, Martha, illus. 2013. (Curious George Ser.). (ENG.). 24p. (J). (gr. -1-3). pap. 4.99 (978-0-544-11450-0(7)) Houghton Mifflin Harcourt Publishing Co.

Richards, Kitty & Studio IBOIX. Belle: The Mysterious Message, 1 vol. 2012. (Disney Princess Ser.). (ENG., Illus.). 96p. (J). (gr. 2-5). 24.21 (978-1-59961-878-4(8)) Spotlight.

Richemont, Enid. The Big Purple Wonderbook. Waldek, Kelly, illus. 2009. (Go! Readers Ser.). 48p. (J). (gr. 2-5). pap. 12.85 (978-1-60754-279-7(X)); lib. bdg. 29.25 (978-1-60754-278-0(1)) Windmill Bks.

Riley, James. Secret Origins. 2017. (Story Thieves Ser.: 3). (ENG., Illus.). 384p. (J). (gr. 3-7). 17.99 (978-1-4814-6125-2(7), Simon & Schuster/Paula Wiseman Bks.) Simon & Schuster/Paula Wiseman Bks.

—The Stolen Chapters. 2016. (Story Thieves Ser.: 2). (ENG., Illus.). 368p. (J). (gr. 3-7). 17.99 (978-1-4814-0922-3(0), Aladdin) Simon & Schuster Children's Publishing.

—Story Thieves. 2015. (Story Thieves Ser.: 1). (ENG., Illus.). (J). (gr. 3-7). 416p. pap. 7.99 (978-1-4814-0920-9(4)); 400p. 17.99 (978-1-4814-0919-3(0)) Simon & Schuster Children's Publishing. (Aladdin).

—Story Thieves. 2015. (Story Thieves Ser.: Vol. 1). (ENG.). (J). (gr. 3-7). lib. bdg. 18.40 **(978-0-606-39444-4(3))** Turtleback Bks.

Robberecht, Thierry. The Wolf Who Fell Out of a Book, 1 vol. 2017. (ENG.). 24p. (J). 14.99 **(978-1-4236-4797-3(1))** Gibbs Smith, Publisher.

Rock, Zack. A Good Story. Rock, Zack, illus. 2017. (ENG., Illus.). 32p. (J). (gr. 3-5). 17.99 **(978-1-56846-280-6(8)**, Creative Editions) Creative Co., The.

Rockwell, Anne. Library Day. Rockwell, Lizzy, illus. 2016. (My First Experience Book Ser.). (ENG.). 32p. (J). (gr. -1-3). 16.99 (978-1-4814-2731-9(8), Aladdin) Simon & Schuster Children's Publishing.

Ross, Tony. I Want a Bedtime Story! Ross, Tony, illus. 2016. (ENG., Illus.). 32p. (J). (gr. -1-3). 17.99 (978-1-5124-1629-9(0)) Andersen Pr. GBR. Dist: Lerner Publishing Group.

Rue, Nancy N. Motorcycles, Sushi & One Strange Book, 1 vol. 2010. (Real Life Ser.). (ENG.). 224p. (YA). (gr. 8-11). pap. 9.99 (978-0-310-71484-2(2)) Zondervan.

Rupp, Rebecca. After Eli. (ENG.). 256p. (J). (gr. 4-7). 2015. pap. 8.99 (978-0-7636-7674-2(8)) 2012. (Illus.). 15.99 (978-0-7636-5810-6(3)) Candlewick Pr.

Ruzzier, Sergio. This Is Not a Picture Book! 2016. (ENG., Illus.). 40p. (J). (gr. -1-k). 16.99 (978-1-4521-2907-5(X)) Chronicle Bks. LLC.

Rylant, Cynthia. Annie & Snowball & the Book Bugs Club. Stevenson, Suçie, illus. (Annie & Snowball Ser.: 9). (ENG.). 40p. (J). (gr. k-2). 2012. pap. 3.99 (978-1-4169-7201-3(3)) 2011. 16.99 (978-1-4169-7199-3(8)) Simon Spotlight. (Simon Spotlight).

—Annie & Snowball & the Book Bugs Club. 2012. (Annie & Snowball Ready-To-Read Ser.). lib. bdg. 13.55 (978-0-606-23692-8(9), Turtleback) Turtleback Bks.

—Mr. Putter & Tabby Turn the Page. Howard, Arthur, illus. (Mr. Putter & Tabby Ser.). (ENG.). 40p. (J). (gr. 1-4). 2015. pap. 5.99 (978-0-544-58232-3(2)) 2014. 14.99 (978-0-15-206063-3(4)) Houghton Mifflin Harcourt Publishing Co. (HMH Books For Young Readers).

—Mr. Putter & Tabby Turn the Page. 2015. (Mr. Putter & Tabby Ser.). lib. bdg. 16.00 (978-0-606-37453-8(1)) Turtleback Bks.

—Poppleton. Teague, Mark, illus. 2015. 56p. pap. 4.00 (978-1-61003-551-4(8)) Center for the Collaborative Classroom.

Saint-Lot, Katia Novet & Tokunbo, Dimitrea. Amadi's Snowman. 2008. (ENG., Illus.). 32p. (gr. 1-6). 16.95 (978-0-88448-298-7(7), 884298) Tilbury Hse. Pubs.

Saltzberg, Barney. Inside This Book. 2015. (ENG., Illus.). 40p. (J). (gr. -1-1). 15.95 (978-1-4197-1487-0(2)) Abrams, Inc.

Sateren, Shelley Swanson. Max & Zoe at the Library, 1 vol. Sullivan, Mary, illus. 2011. (Max & Zoe Ser.). (ENG.). 32p. (gr. k-2). lib. bdg. 21.32 (978-1-4048-6210-4(2), Max & Zoe) Picture Window Bks.

Sazaklis, John. Recess Is Ruined. Robinson, Lee, illus. 2016. (Billy Burger, Model Citizen Ser.). (ENG.). 96p. (gr. 2-3). lib. bdg. 22.65 (978-1-4965-2588-8(4)) Stone Arch Bks.

Schoenherr, Ian. Read It, Don't Eat It! Schoenherr, Ian, illus. 2009. (Illus.). 32p. (J). (gr. -1 — 1). (ENG.). 17.99 (978-0-06-172455-8(6)); lib. bdg. 18.89 (978-0-06-178034-9(0)) HarperCollins Pubs. (Greenwillow Bks.).

Schumacher, Julie. The Unbearable Book Club for Unsinkable Girls. 2013. (ENG.). 240p. (YA). (gr. 7). pap. 8.99 (978-0-375-85127-8(5), Ember) Random Hse. Children's Bks.

Scieszka, Jon. Summer Reading Is Killing Me! Smith, Lane, illus. 2004. (Time Warp Trio Ser.: 7). (ENG.). 80p. (J). (gr. 2-4). pap. 5.99 (978-0-14-240115-6(3), Puffin Books) Penguin Young Readers Group.

—Summer Reading Is Killing Me! Smith, Lane, illus. 2004. (Time Warp Trio Ser.: No. 7). 73p. (J). (gr. 4-7). 12.65 (978-0-7569-6781-9(3)) Perfection Learning Corp.

—Viking It & Liking It. McCauley, Adam, illus. 2004. (Time Warp Trio Ser.: No. 12). 73p. (gr. 2-6). 15.00 (978-0-7569-2589-5(4)) Perfection Learning Corp.

—Viking It & Liking It. 2004. (Time Warp Trio Ser.: 12). 16.00 (978-1-4176-3613-6(0), Turtleback) Turtleback Bks.

Scollon, Bill. A Goofy Fairy Tale. 2014. (Mickey Mouse 8x8 Ser.). (J). lib. bdg. 14.75 (978-0-606-35900-9(1)) Turtleback Bks.

Service, Pamela F. Escape from Planet Yastol. Gorman, Mike, illus. (Way-Too-Real Aliens Ser.: 1). (ENG.). 112p. (J). (gr. 4-6). 2015. 34.65 (978-1-4677-5960-1(0), Lerner Digital)No. 1. 2011. 15.95 (978-0-7613-7918-8(5), Darby Creek)No. 1. 2011. pap. 5.95 (978-0-7613-7921-8(5), Darby Creek) Lerner Publishing Group.

Sharmat, Marjorie Weinman & Sharmat, Mitchell. Nate the Great & the Hungry Book Club. Wheeler, Jody, illus. 2011. (Nate the Great Ser.: No. 26). (ENG.). 80p. (J). (gr. 1-4). 5.99 (978-0-375-84548-2(8), Yearling) Random Hse. Children's Bks.

Shelton, Jayne C. In Grandma's Arms. Katz, Karen, illus. 2008. (ENG.). 24p. (J). (gr. -1-k). bds. 6.99 (978-0-545-06868-0(1)) Scholastic, Inc.

Sheth, Kashmira. Tiger in My Soup, 1 vol. Ebbeler, Jefferey, illus. 2015. (ENG.). 32p. (J). (gr. -1-3). pap. 7.95 (978-1-56145-890-5(2)) Peachtree Pubs.

—Tiger in My Soup, 1 vol. Ebbeler, Jeffrey, illus. 2013. (ENG.). 32p. (J). (gr. -1-3). 15.95 (978-1-56145-696-3(9)) Peachtree Pubs.

Shields, Gillian. Library Lily. Chessa, Francesca, illus. 2011. (ENG.). 26p. (YA). 16.00 (978-0-8028-5401-8(X)) Eerdmans, William B. Publishing Co.

Shoulders, Michael. Goodnight Baby Bear. Weidner, Teri, illus. 2010. (ENG.). 32p. (J). (gr. -1-k). 15.95 (978-1-58536-471-8(1)) Sleeping Bear Pr.

—Say Daddy! Weidner, Teri, illus. (ENG.). (J). 2013. 26p. (gr. -1-k). 8.99 (978-1-58536-863-1(6), 202383) 2008. 32p. (gr. k-6). 15.95 (978-1-58536-354-4(5)) Sleeping Bear Pr.

Shulman, Polly & Airgood, Ellen. The Poe Annex. 2015. (ENG.). 272p. (J). (gr. 5). 16.99 (978-0-399-16614-3(9), Nancy Paulsen Books) Penguin Young Readers Group.

Sierra, Judy. Born to Read. Brown, Marc, illus. 2008. (ENG.). 40p. (J). (gr. -1-2). 16.99 (978-0-375-84687-8(5), Knopf Bks. for Young Readers) Random Hse. Children's Bks.

—Make Way for Readers. Karas, G. Brian, illus. 2016. (ENG.). 32p. (J). (gr. -1-3). 17.99 (978-1-4814-1851-5(3), Simon & Schuster Bks. For Young Readers) Simon & Schuster Bks. For Young Readers.

—Wild about Books. Brown, Marc, tr. Brown, Marc, illus. 2004. (ENG.). 40p. (J). (gr. -1-2). 16.95 (978-0-375-82538-5(X), Knopf Bks. for Young Readers) Random Hse. Children's Bks.

Silvestro, Annie. Bunny's Book Club. Mai-Wyss, Tatjana, illus. 2017. (ENG.). 40p. (J). (gr. -1-2). 17.99 (978-0-553-53758-1(X), Doubleday Bks. for Young Readers) Random Hse. Children's Bks.

Skelton, Matthew. Endymion Spring. 2008. (ENG.). 416p. (YA). (gr. 7). pap. 9.99 (978-0-385-73456-1(5), Delacorte Bks. for Young Readers) Random Hse. Children's Bks.

Skevington, Andrea. Little Red Riding Hood. Hersey, Bob, illus. 2003. 48p. (J). (978-0-439-57189-0(8)) Scholastic, Inc.

Skye, obert. Lord of the Hat. Skye, obert, illus. 2015. (Creature from My Closet Ser.: 5). (ENG., Illus.). 256p. (J). (gr. 4-7). 13.99 (978-1-62779-162-5(0), 9781627791625, Holt, Henry & Co. Bks. For Young Readers) Holt, Henry & Co.

—Pinocula. Skye, obert, illus. 2013. (Creature from My Closet Ser.: 3). (ENG., Illus.). 256p. (J). (gr. 4-7). 12.99 (978-0-8050-9689-7(2), 9780805096897, Holt, Henry & Co. Bks. For Young Readers) Holt, Henry & Co.

—Potterwookiee. Skye, obert, illus. 2012. (Creature from My Closet Ser.: 2). (ENG., Illus.). 256p. (J). (gr. 4-7). 13.99 (978-0-8050-9451-0(2), 9780805094510, Holt, Henry & Co. Bks. For Young Readers) Holt, Henry & Co.

—Wonkenstein. Skye, obert, illus. 2011. (Creature from My Closet Ser.: 1). (ENG., Illus.). 240p. (J). (gr. 4-7). 12.99 (978-0-8050-9268-4(4), 9780805092684, Holt, Henry & Co. Bks. For Young Readers) Holt, Henry & Co.

—Wonkenstein. Skye, obert, illus. 2015. (Creature from My Closet Ser.: 1). (ENG., Illus.). 256p. (J). (gr. 4-7). pap. 6.99 (978-1-250-01022-3(5), 9781250010223) Square Fish.

Slater, David Michael. The Boy & the Book. Kolar, Bob, illus. 2015. (ENG.). 32p. (J). (-k). lib. bdg. 16.95 (978-1-58089-562-0(X)) Charlesbridge Publishing, Inc.

Smith, Lane. It's a Book. Smith, Lane, illus. 2010. (ENG., Illus.). 32p. (J). (gr. 1-5). 15.99 (978-1-59643-606-0(9), 9781596436060) Roaring Brook Pr.

—It's a Little Book. 2011. (ENG., Illus.). 24p. (J). (— 1). bds. 7.99 (978-1-59643-758-6(8), 9781596437586) Roaring Brook Pr.

Smothers, Ethel Footman & Smothers, Ethel F. Hard-Times Jar. Holyfield, John, illus. 2003. (ENG.). 32p. (J). (gr. k-3). 18.99 (978-0-374-32852-8(8), 9780374328528, Farrar, Straus & Giroux (BYR)) Farrar, Straus & Giroux.

Soffer, Gilad. Duck's Vacation. 2015. (ENG., Illus.). 48p. (J). (gr. -1-k). 17.99 (978-1-250-05647-4(0), 9781250056474) Feiwel & Friends.

Sorenson, Margo. Spaghetti Smiles, 1 vol. Harrington, David, illus. 2014. (ENG.). 32p. (J). (gr. k-3). 16.99 (978-1-4556-1922-1(1)) Pelican Publishing Co., Inc.

Sortland, Bjorn. The Story of the Search for the Story. Elling, Lars, illus. 2003. (Picture Bks.). 40p. (J). (gr. -1-3). 15.95 (978-1-57505-375-2(6), Carolrhoda Bks.) Lerner Publishing Group.

Staake, Bob. The Book of Gold. Staake, Bob, illus. 2017. (ENG., Illus.). 40p. (J). (gr. -1-3). 17.99 (978-0-553-51077-5(0), Schwartz & Wade Bks.) Random Hse. Children's Bks.

—Look! Another Book! 2012. (Look! a Book! Ser.). (ENG., Illus.). 48p. (J). (gr. -1-3). 16.99 (978-0-316-20459-0(5)) Little Brown & Co.

—My Pet Book. 2014. (ENG., Illus.). 40p. (J). (gr. -1-2). lib. bdg. 20.99 (978-0-375-97195-2(5), Random Hse. Bks. for Young Readers) Random Hse. Children's Bks.

Stellings, Caroline. The Contest, 1 vol. 2009. (ENG.). 160p. (J). (gr. 4-7). pap. 9.95 (978-0-9779183-5-5(1), 7th Generation) Book Publishing Co.

Stephens, John. The Black Reckoning. 2015. (Books of Beginning Ser.). (ENG.). 432p. (J). (gr. 3-7). 17.99 (978-0-375-86872-6(0), Knopf Bks. for Young Readers) Random Hse. Children's Bks.

—The Emerald Atlas. (Books of Beginning Ser.). (ENG.). (J). (gr. 3-7). 2012. 448p. 7.99 (978-0-375-87271-6(X), Yearling) 2011. 432p. 17.99 (978-0-375-86870-2(4), Knopf Bks. for Young Readers) Random Hse. Children's Bks.

—The Emerald Atlas. l.t. ed. 2012. (Books of Beginning Ser.). (ENG.). 548p. (J). (gr. 4-7). 23.99 (978-1-4104-4234-5(9)) Thorndike Pr.

—The Fire Chronicle. 2012. (Illus.). 437p. (J). (978-0-449-81015-6(1)) Knopf, Alfred A. Inc.

—The Fire Chronicle. (Books of Beginning Ser.). (ENG.). 448p. (J). (gr. 3-7). 2013. 7.99 (978-0-375-87272-3(8), Yearling) 2012. (Illus.). 17.99 (978-0-375-86871-9(2), Knopf Bks. for Young Readers) Random Hse. Children's Bks.

Stewart, Sarah. The Library. Small, David, illus. pap. 35.95 incl. audio compact disk (978-1-59519-010-9(4)); 2004. (J). (gr. -1-2). 28.95 incl. audio compact disk (978-1-59519-011-6(2)) Live Oak Media.

StJohn, Amanda. How to Check Out a Book. Ostrom, Bob, illus. 2012. (Library Skills Ser.). (ENG.). 24p. (J). (gr. -1-2). 28.50 (978-1-61473-249-5(3), 204951) Child's World, Inc., The.

Stoop, Naoko. Red Knit Cap Girl & the Reading Tree. 2014. (ENG., Illus.). 40p. (J). (gr. -1-3). 17.00 (978-0-316-22886-2(9)) Little, Brown Bks. for Young Readers.

Tashjian, Janet. My Life As a Book. Tashjian, Jake, illus. 2010. (My Life Ser.: 1). (ENG.). 224p. (J). (gr. 4-7). 17.99 (978-0-8050-8903-5(9), 9780805089035, Holt, Henry & Co. Bks. For Young Readers) Holt, Henry & Co.

—My Life As a Book. Tashjian, Jake, illus. 2011. (My Life Ser.: 1). (ENG.). 240p. (J). (gr. 4-7). pap. 7.99 (978-0-312-67289-8(6), 9780312672898) Square Fish.

Thaler, Mike. The Book Fair from the Black Lagoon. Lee, Jared, illus. 2006. pap. (978-0-439-88348-1(2)) Scholastic, Inc.

Time, Nicholas O. Going, Going, Gone. 2016. (In Due Time Ser.: 1). (ENG., Illus.). 160p. (J). (gr. 3-7). pap. 6.99 (978-1-4814-6729-2(8), Simon Spotlight) Simon Spotlight.

—Going, Going, Gone. 2016. (In Due Time Ser.: 1). lib. bdg. 17.20 (978-0-606-38985-3(7)) Turtleback Bks.

Townley, Roderick. The Great Good Thing. unabr. ed. 2004. (Middle Grade Cassette Librariestm Ser.). 176p. (J). (gr. 4-6). pap. 29.00 incl. audio *(978-0-8072-1001-7(3)*, S YA 302 SP, Listening Library) Random Hse. Audio Publishing Group.

Tubb, Kristin O'Donnell. The 13th Sign. 2013. (ENG.). 272p. (J). (gr. 5-9). 16.99 *(978-0-312-58352-1(4)*, 9780312583521) Feiwel & Friends.

—The 13th Sign. 2014. (ENG.). 288p. (J). (gr. 5-9). pap. 9.99 *(978-1-250-05059-5(6)*, 9781250050595) Square Fish.

Van Biesen, Koen & Watkinson, Laura. Roger Is Reading a Book. 2015. (ENG., Illus.). 42p. (J). 16.00 *(978-0-8028-5442-1(7)*, Eerdmans Bks For Young Readers) Eerdmans, William B. Publishing Co.

Van Leeuwen, Jean. Amanda Pig, First Grader. Schweninger, Ann, illus. 2007. (Oliver & Amanda Ser.). 40p. (J). *(978-1-4287-4781-4(8)*, Dial) Penguin Publishing Group.

—Amanda Pig, First Grader. Schweninger, Ann, illus. 2009. (Oliver & Amanda Ser.). (ENG.). 48p. (J). (gr. 1-3). mass mkt. 3.99 *(978-0-14-241276-3(7)*, Penguin Young Readers) Penguin Young Readers Group.

Viehl, Lynn. Dead of Night. 2012. (Youngbloods Ser.: 2). (ENG.). 312p. (YA). pap. 9.95 *(978-0-7387-2646-5(X)*, Flux) North Star Editions.

Wahl, Jan. Cobweb Castle. 2014. (ENG., Illus.). 32p. (J). 14.95 *(978-0-7649-6801-3(7))* Pomegranate Communications, Inc.

Wallace, Nancy K. Claim to Fame, 1 vol. Chronister, Amanda, illus. 2013. (Abby & the Book Bunch Ser.). (ENG.). 80p. (J). (gr. 2-5). 27.07 *(978-1-61641-912-7(1))* Magic Wagon.

—The Haunted Sleepover, 1 vol. Chronister, Amanda, illus. 2013. (Abby & the Book Bunch Ser.). (ENG.). 80p. (J). (gr. 2-5). 27.07 *(978-1-61641-913-4(X))* Magic Wagon.

—Movie Mishaps, 1 vol. Chronister, Amanda, illus. 2013. (Abby & the Book Bunch Ser.). (ENG.). 80p. (J). (gr. 2-5). 27.07 *(978-1-61641-914-1(8))* Magic Wagon.

—The Mystery of the Golden Key, 1 vol. Chronister, Amanda, illus. 2013. (Abby & the Book Bunch Ser.). (ENG.). 80p. (J). (gr. 2-5). 27.07 *(978-1-61641-915-8(6))* Magic Wagon.

—Out to Lunch, 1 vol. Chronister, Amanda, illus. 2013. (Abby & the Book Bunch Ser.). (ENG.). 80p. (J). (gr. 2-5). 27.07 *(978-1-61641-916-5(4))* Magic Wagon.

—Presumed Missing, 1 vol. Chronister, Amanda, illus. 2013. (Abby & the Book Bunch Ser.). (ENG.). 80p. (J). (gr. 2-5). 27.07 *(978-1-61641-917-2(2))* Magic Wagon.

Warner, Michael N. The Titanic Game. Ordaz, Frank, illus. 2007. (ENG.). 208p. (J). pap. 11.95 *(978-0-9744446-2-8(6))* All About Kids Publishing.

Watt, Mélanie. You're Finally Here! Watt, Mélanie, illus. 2011. (Illus.). 40p. (gr. -1-1). 15.99 *(978-1-4231-3486-2(9))* Hyperion Pr.

Weeks, Sarah. Catfish Kate & the Sweet Swamp Band. Smith, Elwood H., illus. 2009. (ENG.). 32p. (J). (gr. -1-3). 17.99 *(978-1-4169-4026-5(X)*, Atheneum Bks. for Young Readers) Simon & Schuster Children's Publishing.

Wells, Rosemary. Read to Your Bunny. Wells, Rosemary, illus. 2003. (ENG., Illus.). 6p. (J). bds. 7.99 *(978-0-439-54337-8(1)*, Cartwheel Bks.) Scholastic, Inc.

Wersba, Barbara. Walter: The Story of a Rat. Diamond, Donna, illus. 2012. (ENG.). 64p. (J). (gr. 4-6). pap. 8.95 *(978-1-59078-948-3(2))* Boyds Mills Pr.

West, Jacqueline. Spellbound, 2 vols. (Books of Elsewhere Ser.: 2). (ENG.). (J). (gr. 5-18). 2012. 320p. pap. 7.99 *(978-0-14-242102-4(2)*, Puffin Books) Vol. 2. 2011. (Illus.). 304p. 16.99 *(978-0-8037-3441-8(7)*, Dial Bks) Penguin Young Readers Group.

Weston Woods Staff, creator. Wild about Books. 2011. 29.95 *(978-0-439-80485-1(X))* Weston Woods Studios, Inc.

Wexler, Django. The Forbidden Library. 2015. (ENG., Illus.). 400p. (J). (gr. 5). 8.99 *(978-0-14-242681-4(4)*, Puffin Books) Penguin Young Readers Group.

—The Mad Apprentice. Jansson, Alexander, illus. 2015. (Forbidden Library). (ENG.). 352p. (J). (gr. 5). 16.99 *(978-0-8037-3976-5(1)*, Kathy Dawson Books) Penguin Young Readers Group.

—The Palace of Glass: The Forbidden Library: Volume 3. 2016. (Forbidden Library). (ENG., Illus.). 368p. (J). (gr. 5). 16.99 *(978-0-8037-3978-9(8)*, Kathy Dawson Books) Penguin Young Readers Group.

Willems, Mo & Campoy, F. Isabel. !Estamos en un Libro! Willems, Mo, illus. 2015. (Elephant & Piggie Book Ser.). (SPA., Illus.). 64p. (J). (gr. 1-3). 9.99 *(978-1-4847-2288-6(4))* Hyperion Bks. for Children.

Willson, Sarah. La Mochila de Dora. Roper, Robert, illus. 2003. (Dora the Explorer Ser.).Tr. of Dora's Backpack. (SPA.). 24p. (J). pap. 3.99 *(978-0-689-86306-6(3)*, Libros Para Ninos) Libros Para Ninos.

Windham, Kathryn Tucker. Ernest's Gift. Hardy, Frank, illus. 2004. (ENG.). 20p. (J). 16.95 *(978-1-58838-149-1(8)*, NewSouth Bks.) NewSouth, Inc.

Won, Brian. Hooray for Books! 2017. (ENG., Illus.). 40p. (J). (gr. -1-3). 16.99 ***(978-0-544-74802-6(6)***, HMH Books For Young Readers) Houghton Mifflin Harcourt Publishing Co.

Yates, Louise. Dog Loves Books. 2010. (ENG., Illus.). 32p. (J). (gr. -1-2). 16.99 *(978-0-375-86449-0(0)*, Knopf Bks. for Young Readers) Random Hse. Children's Bks.

—Dog Loves Counting. 2013. (ENG.). 32p. (J). (gr. -1-3). 17.99 *(978-0-449-81342-3(8)*, Knopf Bks. for Young Readers) Random Hse. Children's Bks.

—Dog Loves Fairy Tales. 2015. (ENG., Illus.). 32p. (J). (-k). 17.99 *(978-0-85755-017-0(9))* Transworld Publishers Ltd. GBR. Dist: Independent Pubs. Group.

Young, Timothy. I Hate Picture Books!, 1 vol. 2013. (ENG., Illus.). 32p. (J). 16.99 *(978-0-7643-4387-2(4)*, 9780764343872) Schiffer Publishing, Ltd.

Zagarenski, Pamela. The Whisper. 2015. (ENG., Illus.). 40p. (J). (gr. -1-3). 17.99 *(978-0-544-41686-4(4)*, HMH Books For Young Readers) Houghton Mifflin Harcourt Publishing Co.

Zusak, Markus. The Book Thief. 2014. (ENG.). 576p. (YA). 17.24 *(978-1-63245-052-4(6))* Lectorum Pubns., Inc.

—The Book Thief. 2009. 12.64 *(978-0-7848-1941-8(6)*, Everbind) Marco Bk. Co.

—The Book Thief. 2008. 552p. (gr. 7-12). 23.00 *(978-0-7569-8440-3(8))* Perfection Learning Corp.

—The Book Thief. (ENG., Illus.). (YA). (gr. 7). 2016. 592p. lib. bdg. 22.99 *(978-0-399-55652-4(4))* 2007. 592p. pap. 12.99 *(978-0-375-84220-7(9))* 2013. 576p. pap. 12.99 *(978-0-385-75472-9(8))* 2016. 592p. 19.99 *(978-1-101-93418-0(2))* Random Hse. Children's Bks. (Knopf Bks. for Young Readers).

—The Book Thief. l.t. ed. 2006. (ENG.). 552p. 23.99 *(978-1-4104-6806-2(2))*; 757p. (YA). (gr. 7-12). 24.95 *(978-0-7862-9021-5(8))* Thorndike Pr.

—The Book Thief. 2008. (ENG., Illus.). 560p. pap. *(978-0-552-77389-8(1)*, Black Swan) Transworld Publishers Ltd.

—The Book Thief. 2007. 552p. lib. bdg. 24.50 *(978-1-4177-9738-7(X))* 2013. lib. bdg. 24.50 *(978-0-606-34656-6(2))* Turtleback Bks. (Turtleback).

—La Ladrona de Libros. 2010. (Vintage Espanol Ser.).Tr. of Book Thief. (SPA.). 544p. (YA). (gr. 7). pap. 12.99 *(978-0-307-47573-2(5)*, Vintage Espanol) Knopf Doubleday Publishing Group.

BOOKS AND READING FOR CHILDREN

see Children—Books and Reading

BOOKS FOR CHILDREN

see Children's Literature

BOONE, DANIEL, 1734-1820

Adler, David A. & Adler, Michael S. A Picture Book of Daniel Boone. Collins, Matt, illus. 2013. (ENG.). 32p. (J). (gr. -1-3). 17.95 *(978-0-8234-2748-2(X))* Holiday Hse., Inc.

Allen, Nancy Kelly. Daniel Boone: Trailblazer, 1 vol. Waites, Joan C., illus. 2005. (ENG.). 32p. (J). (gr. k-3). 16.99 *(978-1-58980-212-4(8))* Pelican Publishing Co., Inc.

Benge, Janet & Benge, Geoff. Heroes of History - Daniel Boone: Frontiersman. 2004. (ENG.). 224p. (YA). pap. 9.99 *(978-1-932096-09-5(4))* Emerald Bks.

Blair, Eric. Daniel Boone, 1 vol. Chambers-Goldberg, Micah, illus. (My First Classic Story Ser.). (ENG.). 32p. (gr. k-3). 2013. pap. 7.10 *(978-1-4795-1859-3(X))* 2011. lib. bdg. 22.65 *(978-1-4048-6578-5(0))* Picture Window Bks. (My First Classic Story).

Brandt, Keith & Macken, JoAnn Early. Daniel Boone: Frontier Explorer. Lawn, John, illus. 2008. 55p. (J). pap. *(978-0-439-02020-6(4))* Scholastic, Inc.

Copeland, Peter F. Daniel Boone Coloring Book. 2006. (Dover History Coloring Book Ser.). (ENG., Illus.). 32p. (J). (gr. 3-5). 3.99 *(978-0-486-44738-4(3))* Dover Pubns., Inc.

Dean, Arlan. The Wilderness Road: From the Shenandoah Valley to the Ohio River. 2003. (Famous American Trails Ser.). (Illus.). 24p. (J). lib. bdg. 22.60 *(978-0-8239-6477-2(9)*, PowerKids Pr.) Rosen Publishing Group, Inc., The.

—The Wilderness Trail: From the Shenandoah Valley to the Ohio River. 2009. (Famous American Trails Ser.). 24p. (gr. 3-3). 42.50 *(978-1-61512-493-0(4)*, PowerKids Pr.) Rosen Publishing Group, Inc., The.

Harness, Cheryl. The Trailblazing Life of Daniel Boone & How Early Americans Took to the Road. 2007. (Cheryl Harness Histories Ser.). (ENG., Illus.). 144p. (J). (gr. 5-9). 16.95 *(978-1-4263-0145-2(6))*; 25.90 *(978-1-4263-0146-9(4))* National Geographic Society. (National Geographic Children's Bks.).

Johnston, Marianne. Daniel Boone. 2009. (American Legends Ser.). 24p. (gr. 3-3). 42.50 *(978-1-61511-380-4(0)*, PowerKids Pr.) Rosen Publishing Group, Inc., The.

Kennedy, Emily. Daniel Boone. 2014. (Illus.). 31p. (J). lib. bdg. *(978-1-62712-280-1(X))* Cavendish Square Publishing.

Kramer, Sydelle. Who Was Daniel Boone? Ulrich, George, illus. 2006. (Who Was? Ser.). (ENG.). 112p. (J). (gr. 3-7). pap. 5.99 *(978-0-448-43902-0(6)*, Grosset & Dunlap) Penguin Young Readers Group.

—Who Was Daniel Boone? Ulrich, George, illus. 2006. (Who Was... ? Ser.). 108p. (gr. 2-6). 15.00 *(978-0-7569-6951-6(4))* Perfection Learning Corp.

Meloche, Renee Taft. Daniel Boone: Bravery on the Frontier. Pollard, Bryan, illus. 2009. (Heroes of History for Young Readers Ser.). 32p. (J). (gr. 1). 8.99 *(978-1-932096-61-3(2))* Emerald Bks.

Nemerson, Roy. Daniel Boone. 2005. (Heroes of America Ser.). 239p. (gr. 3-8). 27.07 *(978-1-59679-256-2(6)*, Abdo & Daughters) ABDO Publishing Co.

Petrie, Kristin. Daniel Boone, 1 vol. 2004. (Explorers Set 1 Ser.). (ENG.). 32p. (gr. k-6). 27.07 *(978-1-59197-592-2(1)*, Checkerboard Library) ABDO Publishing Co.

Ransom, Candice. Daniel Boone. 2005. (History Maker Biographies Ser.). (ENG., Illus.). 48p. (gr. 3-6). lib. bdg. 27.93 *(978-0-8225-2941-5(6)*, Lerner Pubns.) Lerner Publishing Group.

Raum, Elizabeth. Cutting a Path: Daniel Boone & the Cumberland Gap. 2015. (Adventures on the American Frontier Ser.). (ENG., Illus.). 32p. (gr. 3-4). pap. 7.95 *(978-1-4914-4909-7(8))* Capstone Press of Coughlan Cos.

Roberts, Russell. Daniel Boone. 2006. (What's So Great About... ? Ser.). (Illus.). 32p. (J). (gr. 2-4). lib. bdg. 25.70 *(978-1-58415-475-4(6))* Mitchell Lane Pubs., Inc.

Saddleback Educational Publishing Staff, ed. Daniel Boone, 1 vol. unabr. ed. 2008. (Graphic Biographies Ser.). (ENG., Illus.). 25p. (YA). (gr. 9-12). pap. 7.95 *(978-1-59905-219-9(9))* Saddleback Educational Publishing, Inc.

Sanford, William R. & Green, Carl R. Daniel Boone: Courageous Frontiersman. 2012. (Courageous Heroes of the American West Ser.). (Illus.). 48p. (J). pap. 8.95 *(978-1-4644-0085-8(7))*; (gr. 5-18). 22.60 *(978-0-7660-4002-1(X))* Enslow Pubs., Inc.

Smith, Andrea P. Daniel Boone. 2012. (Illus.). 24p. (J). 63.60 *(978-1-4488-5227-7(7))*; pap. 10.60 *(978-1-4488-5226-0(9))*; lib. bdg. 25.25 *(978-1-4488-5194-2(7))* Rosen Publishing Group, Inc., The. (PowerKids Pr.).

Streissguth, Thomas. Daniel Boone. Chantland, Loren, illus. 2003. (On My Own Biographies Ser.). 48p. (J). (gr. 1-3). pap. 5.95 *(978-1-57505-532-9(5))* Lerner Publishing Group.

Zronik, John Paul & Zronik, John. Daniel Boone: Woodsman of Kentucky. 2006. (In the Footsteps of Explorers Ser.). (ENG., Illus.). 32p. (J). (gr. 4-7). pap. *(978-0-7787-2464-3(6)*, 1253442); lib. bdg. *(978-0-7787-2428-5(X)*, 1253442) Crabtree Publishing Co.

BOONE, DANIEL, 1734-1820—FICTION

Lunsford, Russell. Benjamin Nathan Tuggle: Adventurer: Daniel Boone & the Settlement of Boonesborough, Kentucky. 2010. 112p. (gr. 4-6). 20.95 *(978-1-4502-3361-3(9))*; pap. 10.95 *(978-1-4502-3360-6(0))* iUniverse, Inc.

BOOTH, WILLIAM, 1829-1912

Andrew, Edwards & Fleur, Thornton. Footsteps of the Past: William Booth. 2005. (Footsteps of the Past Ser.). pap. 5.00 *(978-1-903087-83-1(X))* DayOne Pubns. GBR. Dist: Send The Light Distribution LLC.

BOOTS

see Shoes

BORDEN, LIZZIE, 1860-1927

Miller, Sarah. The Borden Murders: Lizzie Borden & the Trial of the Century. 2016. (ENG., Illus.). 304p. (J). (gr. 5). 17.99 *(978-0-553-49808-0(8)*, Schwartz & Wade Bks.) Random Hse. Children's Bks.

BORDER LIFE

see Frontier and Pioneer Life

BORGLUM, JOHN GUTZON DE LA MOTHE, 1867-1941

Patrick, Jean L. S. Who Carved the Mountain? The Story of Mount Rushmore. Graef, Renee, illus. 2005. 37p. (J). 16.99 *(978-0-9752617-4-3(6))* Mount Rushmore Bookstores.

BORNEO—FICTION

Burchett, Jan & Vogler, Sara. Rainforest Rescue, 1 vol. Le Feyer, Diane, illus. 2012. (Wild Rescue Ser.). (ENG.). 152p. (gr. 3-6). 9.95 *(978-1-4342-4595-3(0))*; lib. bdg. 25.32 *(978-1-4342-3768-2(0))* Stone Arch Bks.

Lumry, Amanda & Hurwitz, Laura. Operation Orangutan. 2007. (Adventures of Riley (Unnumbered) Ser.). (Illus.). 36p. (J). (gr. -1-3). 15.95 *(978-0-9748411-4-4(5))* Eaglemont Pr.

Smith, Dale. What the Orangutan Told Alice: A Rain Forest Adventure. Smith, Dale & Russon, Anne E., photos by. 2003. (Illus.). 192p. (gr. 6-12). pap. 15.95 *(978-0-9651452-8-2(X))* Deer Creek Publishing.

Youngberg, Norma R. Jungle Thorn. 2010. (Illus.). 132p. reprint ed. per. 11.95 *(978-1-57258-157-9(3)*, 945-6024) TEACH Services, Inc.

BORROWERS (FICTITIOUS CHARACTERS)—FICTION

Norton, Mary. The Borrowers. Krush, Beth & Krush, Joe, illus. 2003. (Borrowers Ser.: 1). (ENG.). 192p. (J). (gr. 2-5). pap. 7.99 *(978-0-15-204737-5(9))* Houghton Mifflin Harcourt Publishing Co.

—The Borrowers Afield. Krush, Beth & Krush, Joe, illus. 50th anniv. ed. 2003. (Borrowers Ser.: 2). (ENG.). 224p. (J). (gr. 2-5). pap. 7.99 *(978-0-15-204732-0(8))* Houghton Mifflin Harcourt Publishing Co.

—The Borrowers Afloat. Krush, Beth & Krush, Joe, illus. 2003. (Borrowers Ser.: 3). (ENG.). 192p. (J). (gr. 2-5). pap. 7.99 *(978-0-15-204733-7(6))* Houghton Mifflin Harcourt Publishing Co.

—The Borrowers Aloft: Plus the Short Tale Poor Stainless. Krush, Beth & Krush, Joe, illus. 50th anniv. ed. 2003. (Borrowers Ser.: 4). (ENG.). 224p. (J). (gr. 2-5). pap. 7.99 *(978-0-15-204734-4(4))* Houghton Mifflin Harcourt Publishing Co.

—The Borrowers Avenged. Krush, Joe et al, illus. 50th anniv. ed. 2003. (Borrowers Ser.: 5). (ENG.). 304p. (J). (gr. 2-5). pap. 7.99 *(978-0-15-204731-3(X))* Houghton Mifflin Harcourt Publishing Co.

Yonebayashi, Hiromasa & Miyazaki, Hayao. The Secret World of Arrietty (Film Comic), Vol. 1. 2012. (ENG., Illus.). 272p. pap. 16.99 *(978-1-4215-4116-7(5))* Viz Media.

—The Secret World of Arrietty (Film Comic), Vol. 2. 2012. (ENG.). 336p. pap. 16.99 *(978-1-4215-4117-4(3))* Viz Media.

—The Secret World of Arrietty Picture Book. 2012. (ENG., Illus.). 144p. (J). 19.99 *(978-1-4215-4115-0(7))* Viz Media.

BOSNIA AND HERCEGOVINA

Cruden, Alex, ed. The Bosnian Conflict. 2012. (Perspectives on Modern World History Ser.). (ENG., Illus.). 224p. (YA). (gr. 9-12). 42.45 *(978-0-7377-5786-6(8))* Cengage Gale.

Englar, Mary. Bosnia-Herzegovina in Pictures. 2006. (Visual Geography Series, Second Ser.). (ENG., Illus.). 80p. (gr. 5-12). lib. bdg. 31.93 *(978-0-8225-2393-2(0))* Lerner Publishing Group.

Halilbegovich, Nadja. My Childhood under Fire: A Sarajevo Diary. 2008. (ENG., Illus.). 120p. (J). (gr. 5-9). pap. 8.95 *(978-1-55453-267-4(1))* Kids Can Pr., Ltd. CAN. Dist: Hachette Bk. Group.

Zuljevic, Vida. I Was Almost Five. 2010. 74p. pap. 13.46 *(978-0-557-17282-5(9))* Lulu Pr., Inc.

BOSNIA AND HERCEGOVINA—FICTION

Farah, Barbara. Parabola O Jednom Mostu. Conway, Tricia, illus. 2006. 44p. (gr. 4-7). per. 14.99 *(978-1-59919-011-2(7))* Elim Publishing.

Linden, Dianne. Peacekeepers. (J). 82p. stu. ed. 9.95 *(978-1-55050-297-8(2))*; 2003. (ENG., Illus.). 208p. (gr. 3-6). pap. 7.95 *(978-1-55050-271-8(9))* Coteau Bks. CAN. Dist: Fitzhenry & Whiteside, Ltd., Orca Bk. Pubs. USA.

—Shimmerdogs, 1 vol. 2008. (ENG.). 176p. (J). pap. 10.95 *(978-1-897235-37-9(2))* Thistledown Pr., Ltd. CAN. Dist: Univ. of Toronto Pr.

McCutcheon, John. Flowers for Sarajevo, 1 vol. Caldwell, Kristy, illus. 2017. (ENG.). 32p. (J). (gr. 2-4). 19.95 *(978-1-56145-943-8(7))* Peachtree Pubs.

The Royal Guard Dragons. 2007. (Illus.). 160p. (YA). per. 14.95 *(978-0-9791733-0-1(2))* Royal Guard Dragon Society, The.

Schraff, Anne. Gingerbread Heart. 2008. 114p. (J). (gr. 4-7). 13.95 *(978-0-7569-8406-9(8))* Perfection Learning Corp.

BOSTON (MASS.)

Adventures in Suburbia Boston 2003. 2003. 365p. (J). per. 19.95 *(978-0-9743319-0-4(2))* Kiwi Media Group, Inc.

Boehm Jerome, Kate. Boston & the State of Massachusetts: Cool Stuff Every Kid Should Know. 2011. (Arcadia Kids Ser.). (ENG., Illus.). 48p. (J). (gr. 3-6). pap. 9.99 *(978-1-4396-0099-3(6))* Arcadia Publishing.

Challen, Paul C. Surviving the Boston Marathon Bombing. 2015. (Surviving Disaster Ser.). (ENG.). 48p. (J). (gr. 5-6). 30.25 *(978-1-4994-3661-7(0)*, Rosen Central) Rosen Publishing Group, Inc., The.

Danis Drouot, Lucile, illus. Boston Monsters: A Search-And-Find Book. 2017. (ENG.). 22p. (J). (gr. -1). bds. 9.99 ***(978-2-924734-05-6(3))*** City Monsters Bks. CAN. Dist: Publishers Group West (PGW).

Furstinger, Nancy. Boston, 1 vol. 2005. (Cities Set 1 Ser.). (ENG., Illus.). 32p. (gr. k-6). 27.07 *(978-1-59197-854-1(8)*, Checkerboard Library) ABDO Publishing Co.

Lodge, Henry Cabot. Boston. 2004. (Illus.). vii, 241p. *(978-1-929154-16-6(X))* Levenger Pr.

Pierce, Charlotte & Schoenthaler, Robin. The Compleat Day Tripper-Greater Boston: Greater Boston's Best Classic & Eclectic Destinations for Kids & Grown-Ups! Pierce, Charlotte, ed. 2008. (Illus.). 100p. (J). per. *(978-0-9776396-1-8(4))* Pierce Pr.

Segal, Robin. ABC in Boston. 2008. (All 'Bout Cities Ser.). (ENG.). 32p. (J). (gr. -1-k). *(978-0-9719697-1-1(X))* Murray Hill Bks., LLC.

Sherman, Patrice. Boston. 2009. (Class Trip Ser.). (Illus.). 48p. (J). (gr. 2-5). lib. bdg. 29.95 *(978-1-58415-806-6(9))* Mitchell Lane Pubs., Inc.

Skewes, John. Larry Loves Boston! 2016. (Larry Gets Lost Ser.). (ENG., Illus.). 20p. (J). (— 1). pap. 9.99 *(978-1-63217-047-7(7)*, Little Bigfoot) Sasquatch Bks.

Vernick, Shirley & La Forest, Courtney. Boston Baby: A Local Baby Book. 2016. (Local Baby Bks.). (ENG., Illus.). 22p. (J). (-k). bds. 8.95 *(978-1-938093-69-2(0))* Duo Pr. LLC.

Weintraub, Aileen. Boston Light: The First Lighthouse in North America. 2003. (Great Lighthouses of North America Ser.). (Illus.). 24p. (YA). (gr. 3-6). 22.60 *(978-0-8239-6170-2(2))* Rosen Publishing Group, Inc., The.

BOSTON (MASS.)—FICTION

Alcott, Louisa May. A Garland for Girls. 2006. 300p. pap. 19.95 *(978-1-59462-405-6(4)*, 441, Book Jungle) Standard Pubns., Inc.

Alger, Horatio. Do & Dare: Or, A Brave Boy's Fight for Fortune. 2006. 182p. pap. 19.99 *(978-1-4264-0880-9(3))*; 170p. pap. 21.99 *(978-1-4264-0861-8(7))* Creative Media Partners, LLC.

—Do & Dare: Or, A Brave Boy's Fight for Fortune. 2006. pap. *(978-1-4065-0701-0(6))* Dodo Pr.

Ayres, Katherine. Under Copp's Hill. 2009. (Mysteries Through Time Ser.). 176p. (YA). (gr. 4-8). 31.95 *(978-1-60754-185-1(8))*; pap. 15.25 *(978-1-60754-186-8(6))* Windmill Bks.

Baggott, Julianna. The Prince of Fenway Park. 2011. (ENG.). 352p. (J). (gr. 3-7). pap. 6.99 *(978-0-06-087244-1(6))* HarperCollins Pubs.

Batson, Priscilla. Big Dig Ducks. 2010. 68p. pap. 23.49 *(978-1-4389-9249-5(1))* AuthorHouse.

Bogart, Mike. Ice Warriors, 1 vol. 2010. 72p. pap. 19.95 *(978-1-4489-3885-8(6))* America Star Bks.

Bradford James Nolan. The Mouse Who Lived in Fenway Park. Jim Connelly, illus. 2009. 36p. pap. 19.99 *(978-1-4389-4491-3(8))* AuthorHouse.

Brodeur, Tom. Regina Silsby's Phantom Militia. 2005. (Illus.). 267p. (J). (gr. 3-7). 7.49 *(978-1-59166-385-0(7))* BJU Pr.

—Regina Silsby's Secret War. 2004. 248p. (J). 7.49 *(978-1-59166-235-8(4))* BJU Pr.

Brown, Jeff. Flat Stanley's Worldwide Adventures #13: the Midnight Ride of Flat Revere. Pamintuan, Macky, illus. 2016. (Flat Stanley's Worldwide Adventures Ser.: 13). 144p. (J). (gr. 1-5). pap. 4.99 *(978-0-06-236603-0(3))* HarperCollins Pubs.

Calkhoven, Laurie. Daniel at the Siege of Boston 1776. 2010. (Boys of Wartime Ser.: 1). (ENG.). 208p. (J). (gr. 4-7). 16.99 *(978-0-525-42144-3(0)*, Dutton Books for Young Readers) Penguin Young Readers Group.

Corriveau, Art. How I Got a Life & a Dog. 2012. (ENG.). 288p. (J). (gr. 3-7). pap. 7.95 *(978-1-4197-0015-6(4)*, Amulet Bks.) Abrams, Inc.

—How I, Nicky Flynn, Finally Got a Life (And a Dog) 2010. (ENG.). 272p. (YA). (gr. 3-7). 16.95 *(978-0-8109-8298-7(6)*, Amulet Bks.) Abrams, Inc.

—13 Hangmen. 2012. (ENG.). 352p. (J). (gr. 3-7). 17.95 *(978-1-4197-0159-7(2)*, Amulet Bks.) Abrams, Inc.

Cronin, Carol Newman. Cape Cod Surprise: Oliver Matches Wits with Hurricane Carol. Cronin, Laurie Ann, illus. 2010. (ENG.). 150p. (J). pap. 9.95 *(978-1-934848-47-0(6))* GemmaMedia.

Cunningham, Sheila S. Willow's Walkabout: A Children's Guide to Boston. Kelleher, Kathie, illus. 2012. (ENG.). 32p. (J). (gr. 1-3). 17.95 *(978-1-59373-096-3(9))* Bunker Hill Publishing, Inc.

Denenberg, Barry. A True Patriot: The Journal of William Thomas Emerson, a Revolutionary War Patriot. 2012. lib. bdg. 17.20 *(978-0-606-26736-6(0)*, Turtleback) Turtleback Bks.

Dionne, Erin. Moxie & the Art of Rule Breaking: A 14-Day Mystery. (ENG.). (J). (gr. 5). 2014. 288p. pap. 6.99 *(978-0-14-242614-2(8)*, Puffin Books) 2013. 256p. 16.99 *(978-0-8037-3871-3(4)*, Dial Bks) Penguin Young Readers Group.

Dorset, Skylar. The Boy with the Hidden Name. 2014. (Otherworld Ser.: 2). (ENG.). 320p. (YA). (gr. 7-12). pap. 9.99 *(978-1-4022-9256-9(2)*, 9781402292569) Sourcebooks, Inc.

Dwyer, Kerry, illus. Rhett's Colorful Campus Tour- Boston University A-Z. 2004. (J). 9.99 *(978-1-933069-03-6(1))* Odd Duck Ink, Inc.

Emerson, Kevin. Carlos Is Gonna Get It. 2008. (J). pap. *(978-0-439-93526-5(1)*, Levine, Arthur A. Bks.) Scholastic, Inc.

Emily Breaks Free - Evaluation Guide. 2006. (J). *(978-1-55942-404-2(4))* Witcher Productions.

Forbes, Esther. Johnny Tremain. 2003. (EMC Masterpiece Series Access Editions). (Illus.). xvi, 308p. (J). 13.99 *(978-0-8219-2408-2(7))* EMC/Paradigm Publishing.

—Johnny Tremain. McCurdy, Michael, illus. l.t. ed. 2005. (ENG.). 440p. (YA). pap. 10.95 *(978-0-7862-7178-8(7))* Thorndike Pr.

Frazier, Angie. The Mastermind Plot. 2012. (ENG.). 240p. (J). (gr. 3-7). 16.99 *(978-0-545-20864-2(5)*, Scholastic Pr.) Scholastic, Inc.

Gamble, Adam. Good Night Boston. Veno, Joe, illus. 2007. (Good Night Our World Ser.). (ENG.). 20p. (J). (gr. k — 1). bds. 9.95 *(978-1-60219-003-0(8))* Good Night Bks.

—Good Night Boston. Veno, Joe, illus. 2005. (J). bds. 9.95 *(978-0-9758502-4-4(5))* On Cape Pubns.

Gill, David Macinnis. Uncanny. 2017. 544p. (YA). (gr. 9). 17.99 ***(978-0-06-229016-8(9)***, Greenwillow Bks.) HarperCollins Pubs.

Gillmore, Inez Haynes. Maida's Little Shop. 2007. (ENG.). 158p. pap. 19.99 *(978-1-4346-1156-7(6))*; 172p. pap. 21.99 *(978-1-4346-1227-4(9))* Creative Media Partners, LLC.

—Maida's Little Shop. 2007. 172p. per. *(978-1-4065-4467-1(1))* Dodo Pr.

Hardman, Ron & Hardman, Jessica. Shadow Fox: Sons of Liberty. Barnecut, Suzanne, ed. Harrigan, Mike, illus. 2010. (Shadow Fox Ser.). 186p. (J). (gr. 4-8). 22.99 (978-0-9819607-1-5(5)) Fox Run Pr., LLC.
—Shadow Fox: Sons of Liberty. Barnecut, Suzanne, ed. Harrigan, Mike, illus. 2010. (Shadow Fox Ser.). 186p. (J). (gr. 4-8). pap. 11.99 (978-0-9819607-0-8(7)) Fox Run Pr., LLC.
—Shadow Fox: Sons of Liberty Teacher's Edition. Barnecutt, Suzanne, ed. Harrigan, Mike, illus. 2010. (Shadow Fox Ser.: 1). 186p. (J). 34.99 (978-0-9819607-2-2(3)) Fox Run Pr., LLC.
Harlow, Joan Hiatt. Joshua's Song. 2003. (ENG., Illus.). 160p. (J). (gr. 3-6). pap. 7.99 (978-0-689-85542-9(7), McElderry, Margaret K. Bks.) McElderry, Margaret K. Bks.
Hawthorne, Nathaniel. Scarlet Letter. 2014. (Differentiated Timeless Classics Ser.). (ENG.). 80p. (YA). (gr. 9-12). 12.95 (978-1-62250-716-0(9)) Saddleback Educational Publishing, Inc.
—The Scarlet Letter - Spotlight Edition. Grudzina, Douglas, ed. 2004. (Illus.). 150p. (YA). per. 5.95 (978-1-58049-550-9(8), PWH5508) Prestwick Hse., Inc.
Hobbs, Valerie. Maggie & Oliver or a Bone of One's Own. Thermes, Jennifer, illus. 2013. (ENG.). 208p. (J). (gr. 3-7). pap. 6.99 (978-1-250-01672-0(X), 9781250016720) Square Fish.
Holm, Jennifer L. Wilderness Days. 2004. (Boston Jane Ser.: No. 2). 240p. (J). (gr. 5-18). 15.99 (978-0-06-029045-0(5)); lib. bdg. 16.89 (978-0-06-029046-7(3)) HarperCollins Pubs.
Horender, Philip M. Patriotic Mouse: Boston Tea Party Participant, 1 vol. Wolek, Guy, illus. 2013. (Maximilian P. Mouse, Time Traveler Ser.). (ENG.). 112p. (J). (gr. 3-6). lib. bdg. 27.07 (978-1-61641-957-8(1), Calico Chapter Bks) Magic Wagon.
Jacobs, Lily. The Littlest Bunny in Boston: An Easter Adventure. 2015. (ENG.). 32p. (J). (-3). 9.99 (978-1-4926-1036-6(4), Sourcebooks Jabberwocky) Sourcebooks, Inc.
James, Eric. Santa's Sleigh Is on Its Way to Boston: A Christmas Adventure. Dunn, Robert, illus. 2016. (ENG.). 32p. (J). (-2). 12.99 (978-1-4926-4319-7(X), 9781492643197, Sourcebooks Jabberwocky) Sourcebooks, Inc.
Jones, Patrick. Returning to Normal. 2015. (J). 104p. 9.99 (978-1-4677-7700-1(5)); (ENG.). 112p. (gr. 6-12). lib. bdg. 27.99 (978-1-4677-5799-7(3)) Lerner Publishing Group.
Kelly, David A. The Fenway Foul-Up. Meyers, Mark, illus. 2011. (Ballpark Mysteries Ser.: Bk. 1). (ENG.). 112p. (J). (gr. 1-4). pap. 4.99 (978-0-375-86703-3(1), Random Hse. Bks. for Young Readers) Random Hse. Children's Bks.
Kluger, Steve. My Most Excellent Year: A Novel of Love, Mary Poppins, & Fenway Park. 2009. (ENG.). 416p. (YA). (gr. 7-18). 9.99 (978-0-14-241343-2(7), Speak) Penguin Young Readers Group.
Lasky, Kathryn. Hannah. 2011. (Daughters of the Sea Ser.: 1). (ENG.). 320p. (J). (gr. 7-7). pap. 9.99 (978-0-545-23803-8(X)) Scholastic, Inc.
—Spiders on the Case. Gilpin, Stephen, illus. (Deadlies Ser.). (ENG.). 176p. (J). (gr. 2-5). 2012. pap. 5.99 (978-0-545-11731-9(3))Bk. 2. 2011. 15.99 (978-0-545-11682-4(1)) Scholastic, Inc. (Scholastic Pr.).
Limbaugh, Rush H., III & Limbaugh, Kathryn Adams. Rush Revere & the American Revolution. 2014. (ENG.). 256p. 19.99 (978-1-4767-8987-3(8), Threshold Editions) Threshold Editions.
—Rush Revere & the American Revolution. Hiers, Christopher, illus. 2014. 244p. (J). pap. (978-1-4767-8989-7(4), Threshold Editions) Threshold Editions.
Lupica, Mike. Last Man Out. (ENG.). (J). (gr. 5). 2017. 272p. 8.99 **(978-0-14-751491-2(6)**, Puffin Books) 2016. 256p. 17.99 (978-0-399-17279-3(3), Philomel Bks.) Penguin Young Readers Group.
Lupica, Mike. Miracle on 49th Street. 2007. (ENG.). 272p. (J). (gr. 5-18). 7.99 (978-0-14-240942-8(1), Puffin Books) Penguin Young Readers Group.
—Miracle on 49th Street. 2007. 246p. (gr. 5-9). 18.00 (978-0-7569-8157-0(3)) Perfection Learning Corp.
Lynch, Chris. Sins of the Fathers. 2006. 232p. (YA). (gr. 9-12). lib. bdg. 17.89 (978-0-06-074038-2(8), HarperTeen) HarperCollins Pubs.
Marsh, Carole. The Mystery at the Boston Marathon. 2003. 160p. (gr. 2-8). 14.95 (978-0-635-01642-3(7), Marsh, Carole Bks.) Gallopade International.
—The Mystery on the Freedom Trail. (Real Kids, Real Places Ser.). (J). 2009. 148p. 18.99 (978-0-635-06988-7(1), Marsh, Carole Mysteries) 2003. 160p. (gr. 2-8). pap. 5.95 (978-0-635-01640-9(0)) Gallopade International.
McCloskey, Robert. Abran Paso a los Patitos. Blanco, Osvaldo, tr. from ENG. 2005.Tr. of Make Way for Ducklings. (SPA., Illus.). 62p. (J). (gr. k-4). reprint ed. 15.00 (978-0-7567-8841-4(2)) DIANE Publishing Co.
—Make Way for Ducklings, 1 vol. (Puffin Storytime Ser.). (ENG.). (J). (gr. -1-2). 2010. 15p. 9.99 (978-0-14-241386-9(0), Puffin Books) 75th anniv. ed. 2016. (Illus.). 68p. 24.99 (978-1-101-99795-6(8), Viking Books for Young Readers) Penguin Young Readers Group.
McDonald, Megan. Judy Moody Declares Independence. Reynolds, Peter H., illus. 2010. (Judy Moody Ser.: 6). (ENG.). 160p. (J). (gr. 1-4). 15.99 (978-0-7636-4852-7(3)); pap. 5.99 (978-0-7636-4851-0(5)) Candlewick Pr.
—Judy Moody Declares Independence. (Judy Moody Ser.: 6). 2010. lib. bdg. 16.00 (978-0-606-12345-7(8)) 2007. 16.00 (978-1-4177-6896-7(7)) Turtleback Bks. (Turtleback).
McGovern, Kate. Rules for 50/50 Chances: If You could Find Out How it All Ends, Would You? 2015. (ENG.). 352p. (YA). (gr. 7). 17.99 (978-0-374-30158-3(1), 9780374301583, Farrar, Straus & Giroux (BYR)) Farrar, Straus & Giroux.
Miceli, Mary Anne. Boston North Shore's Car Wash Squid. 2012. 44p. pap. 20.00 (978-0-578-08747-4(2)) Miceli, Mary Anne.
Millet, Lydia. The Shimmers in the Night. 2012. (Dissenters Ser.). (ENG.). 256p. (J). (gr. 3-7). 16.95 (978-1-931520-78-2(X), Big Mouth Hse.) Small Beer Pr.
Nichols, Lee. Deception. 2010. (Haunting Emma Ser.). (ENG.). 336p. (YA). (gr. 9-12). 16.99 (978-1-59990-308-8(3), 9781599903088); pap. 9.99 (978-1-59990-421-4(7), 9781599904214) Bloomsbury Publishing USA. (Bloomsbury USA Childrens).
Otis, James. Under the Liberty Tree, a Story of the Boston Massacre. 2011. 84p. pap. 9.99 (978-1-61203-273-3(7)) Bottom of the Hill Publishing.
Pennypacker, Sara. Clementine & the Spring Trip. Frazee, Marla, illus. 2013. (ENG.). 160p. (J). (gr. 2-5). 14.99 (978-1-4231-2357-6(3)) Hyperion Pr.
—Clementine & the Spring Trip. 2014. (Clementine Ser.: 6). (J). lib. bdg. 16.00 (978-0-606-32287-4(6), Turtleback) Turtleback Bks.
—Clementine, Friend of the Week. Frazee, Marla, illus. (Clementine Book Ser.). (ENG.). 176p. (J). 2011. (gr. 1-3). pap. 5.99 (978-1-4231-1560-1(0)) 2010. (gr. 2-5). 14.99 (978-1-4231-1355-3(1)) Hyperion Pr.
Philbrick, Nathaniel. Ben's Revolution: Benjamin Russell & the Battle of Bunker Hill. Minor, Wendell, illus. 2017. (ENG.). 64p. (J). (gr. 2-4). 17.99 (978-0-399-16674-7(2), Nancy Paulsen Books) Penguin Young Readers Group.
Rahim, Rahimah. The Trunk. 2012. 64p. pap. (978-1-78176-715-3(7)) FeedARead.com.
Ray, Anna Chapin. Half a Dozen Girls. 2007. 148p. (gr. 4-7). per. (978-1-4068-3752-0(0)) Echo Library.
Reinhardt, Dana. The Things a Brother Knows. 2011. (ENG.). 256p. (YA). (gr. 9). pap. 8.99 (978-0-375-84456-0(2), Ember) Random Hse. Children's Bks.
Remy, Jerry. Hello, Wally! Boston Red Sox. Moore, Danny, illus. 2006. 24p. (J). lib. bdg. 17.95 (978-1-932888-80-5(2)) Mascot Bks., Inc.
Rinaldi, Ann. The Fifth of March: A Story of the Boston Massacre. 2004. (Great Episodes Ser.). (ENG.). 352p. (J). (gr. 5-7). pap. 8.99 (978-0-15-205078-8(7)) Houghton Mifflin Harcourt Publishing Co.
Ritter, John H. Fenway Fever. 2013. (ENG.). 256p. (J). (gr. 5). pap. 7.99 (978-0-14-242491-9(9), Puffin Books) Penguin Young Readers Group.
Schneider, Richard H. The Christmas Pea Coat. Bond, Higgins, illus. 2004. 32p. (J). 14.95 (978-0-8249-5474-1(2), Ideal Pubns.) Worthy Publishing.
Shankman, Ed. The Boston Balloonies. O'Neill, Dave, illus. (Shankman & O'Neill Ser.). (J). (gr. -1-3). 2012. (ENG.). 40p. pap. 12.95 (978-1-933212-66-1(7)) 2008. 36p. 14.95 (978-1-933212-76-0(4)) Applewood Bks. (Commonwealth Editions).
Shea, John & Harmon, Michael B. A Kid from Southie. 2011. 240p. (YA). (gr. 9-18). 16.95 (978-1-934813-53-9(2)) Westside Bks.
Silvano, Wendi. Love Is All Around Boston. Czernichowska, Joanna, illus. 2016. (ENG.). 32p. (J). (-6). 12.99 (978-1-4926-2907-8(3), Sourcebooks Jabberwocky) Sourcebooks, Inc.
Skewes, John & Mullin, Michael. Larry Gets Lost in Boston. Skewes, John, illus. 2013. (Larry Gets Lost Ser.). (ENG., Illus.). 32p. (J). (gr. -1-2). 17.99 (978-1-57061-793-5(7), Little Bigfoot) Sasquatch Bks.
Smith, Sarah. The Other Side of Dark. (ENG.). 320p. (YA). (gr. 7). 2011. Illus.). pap. 11.99 (978-1-4424-0281-2(4)) 2010. 16.99 (978-1-4424-0280-5(6)) Simon & Schuster Children's Publishing. (Atheneum Bks. for Young Readers).
Sones, Sonya. What My Girlfriend Doesn't Know. 2011. 9.68 (978-0-7848-3389-6(3), Everbind) Marco Bk. Co.
—What My Girlfriend Doesn't Know. 2013. (ENG., Illus.). 320p. (YA). (gr. 7). pap. 9.99 (978-1-4424-9384-1(4), Simon & Schuster Bks. For Young Readers) Simon & Schuster Bks. For Young Readers.
Soria, Destiny. Iron Cast. 2016. (ENG.). 384p. (YA). (gr. 8-17). 17.95 (978-1-4197-2192-2(5), Amulet Bks.) Abrams, Inc.
Specter, Baron. Dodging Danger on the Dartmouth, 1 vol., Bk. 1. Evans, Dustin, illus. 2010. (Ghostly Graphic Adventures Ser.). (ENG.). 32p. (J). (gr. 3-6). 28.50 (978-1-60270-770-2(7)) ABDO Publishing Co.
Stossel, Sage. On the Loose in Boston. 2009. (Find the Animals Ser.). (ENG., Illus.). 36p. (J). (gr. k-3). 14.95 (978-1-933212-92-0(6), Commonwealth Editions) Applewood Bks.
Strout, Morgan. Petri's Adventures. 2013. 18p. pap. 8.95 (978-1-4575-2094-5(X)) Dog Ear Publishing, LLC.
Sully, Katherine. Night-Night Boston. Kolanovic, Dubravka & Poole, Helen, illus. 2016. (ENG.). 20p. (J). (-1). bds. 9.99 (978-1-4926-3937-4(0), 9781492639374, Sourcebooks Jabberwocky) Sourcebooks, Inc.
Tegan-Olsen, Sandra, illus. Joey's adventures by the Sea: Jellyfish Everywhere! 2008. 20p. (J). per. 9.95 (978-0-9801527-0-8(4)) Freefox Publishing.
Thompson, Paul B. Liberty's Son: A Spy Story of the American Revolution. 2012. (Historical Fiction Adventures (HFA) Ser.). 160p. (J). pap. 10.95 (978-0-7660-3654-3(5)) Enslow Pubs., Inc.
Tirabassi, Maren C. Footlights & Fairy Dust: Matt & Maria Go to the Theatre. Kramer, Brandie, illus. 2007. (ENG.). 48p. (J). (gr. 2-7). pap. 14.95 (978-1-933002-26-2(3)) PublishingWorks.
Voelkel, Jon & Voelkel, Pamela. Middleworld. 2007. (Jaguar Stones Ser.: Bk. 1). (Illus.). 397p. (gr. 6-9). (978-1-57525-561-3(8)) Smith & Kraus Pubs., Inc.
Webb, Robert N. We Were There at the Boston Tea Party. Ward, E. F., illus. 2013. (ENG.). 192p. (J). (gr. 3-8). pap. 6.99 (978-0-486-49260-5(5)) Dover Pubns., Inc.
Weston Woods Staff, creator. Make Way for Ducklings. 2011. 18.95 (978-0-439-72774-7(X)); 38.75 (978-0-439-72776-1(6)); 29.95 (978-0-439-73489-9(4)) Weston Woods Studios, Inc.
Wilhelm, Kj. Grandma Coocoonutts Goes to Boston. 2009. 28p. pap. 15.99 (978-1-4363-9933-3(5)) Xlibris Corp.
Wilson, Diane Lee. Firehorse. (ENG.). 336p. (YA). (gr. 7). 2010. pap. 8.99 (978-1-4424-0331-4(4)) 2006. (Illus.). 17.99 (978-1-4169-1551-5(6)) McElderry, Margaret K. Bks. (McElderry, Margaret K. Bks.).
Wittenstein, Barry & Ladd, London. Waiting for Pumpsie. 2017. (ENG., Illus.). 32p. (J). (gr. k-3). lib. bdg. 16.99 (978-1-58089-545-3(X)) Charlesbridge Publishing, Inc.
Woodruff, Elvira. George Washington's Spy. (Time Travel Adventures Ser.). (ENG.). 240p. (J). (gr. 3-7). 2012. pap. 6.99 (978-0-545-10488-3(2), Scholastic Paperbacks) 2010. 16.99 (978-0-545-10487-6(4), Scholastic Pr.) Scholastic, Inc.
—George Washington's Spy. 2012. lib. bdg. 17.20 (978-0-606-26216-3(4), Turtleback) Turtleback Bks.
Young, Samantha. The Impossible Vastness of Us. 2017. (ENG.). 368p. 18.99 **(978-0-373-21242-2(9)**, Harlequin Teen) Harlequin Enterprises, Ltd. CAN. Dist: HarperCollins Pubs.

BOSTON (MASS.)—HISTORY

Barter, James. Colonial Boston. 2003. (Travel Guide To Ser.). (ENG., Illus.). 112p. (J). 30.85 (978-1-59018-357-1(6), Lucent Bks.) Cengage Gale.
Birle, Pete. Boston Celtics. 2013. (On the Hardwood Ser.). (ENG., Illus.). 47p. (gr. 3-8). pap. 8.95 (978-1-61570-832-1(4)) Scobre Pr. Corp.
Boston: The Way It Was. 2004. (Wgbh Specials Ser.). 120p. (gr. 7-18). 39.95 incl. VHS (978-1-57807-239-2(5), WG114) WGBH Boston Video.
The Boston Celtics. rev. ed. 2014. (Team Spirit Ser.). (ENG.). 48p. (J). (gr. 3-6). lib. bdg. 29.27 (978-1-59953-630-9(7)) Norwood Hse. Pr.
Burgan, Michael & Hoena, Blake A. The Boston Massacre. Wiacek, Bob et al, illus. 2005. (Graphic History Ser.). (ENG.). 32p. (gr. 3-4). 30.65 (978-0-7368-4368-3(X), Graphic Library) Capstone Press of Coughlan Cos.
Burt, Barbara & Schifini, Alfredo. Colonial Life. 2007. (Avenues Ser.). (ENG., Illus.). 40p. (J). pap. 19.95 (978-0-7922-8678-3(2)) CENGAGE Learning.
Canasi, Brittany. Boston. 2016. (Dropping in On Ser.). (ENG., Illus.). 32p. (gr. 2-4). 32.79 (978-1-68191-408-4(5)) Rourke Educational Media.
Candlewick Press, Candlewick. Boston: Panorama Pops. Trounce, Charlotte, illus. 2016. (Panorama Pops Ser.). (ENG.). 30p. (J). (gr. k-4). 8.99 (978-0-7636-7863-0(5)) Candlewick Pr.
Clinton, Catherine. When Harriet Met Sojourner. Evans, Shane W., illus. 2007. (ENG.). 32p. (J). (gr. k-2). 16.99 (978-0-06-050425-0(0), Tegen, Katherine Bks) HarperCollins Pubs.
Daly, Gael. Hopkinton & the Boston Marathon from, a Tp Z. 2013. 38p. pap. 14.95 (978-0-9910923-0-7(9)) CONVERPAGE.
Draper, Allison Stark. The Start of the American Revolutionary War: Paul Revere Rides at Midnight. 2009. (Headlines from History Ser.). 24p. (gr. 3-3). 42.50 (978-1-61513-247-8(3), PowerKids Pr.) Rosen Publishing Group, Inc., The.
Epstein, Brad M. Boston 101. l.t. ed. 2009. (My First City Ser.). (Illus.). 24p. (J). (gr. -1-k). bds. (978-1-60730-000-7(1), 101 Bk.) Michaelson Entertainment.
Heims, Neil. Reading Johnny Tremain. 2005. (Engaged Reader Ser.). (Illus.). 96p. (gr. 5-8). lib. bdg. 25.00 (978-0-7910-8831-9(6), Chelsea Hse.) Facts On File, Inc.
Kops, Deborah. The Great Molasses Flood. 2015. (ENG.). 112p. (J). (gr. 4-7). pap. 11.95 (978-1-58089-349-7(X)) Charlesbridge Publishing, Inc.
—The Great Molasses Flood: Boston 1919. 2015. lib. bdg. 23.25 (978-0-606-36650-2(4)) Turtleback Bks.
Kravitz, Danny. The Untold Story of Henry Knox: The Man Who Saved Boston. 2015. (What You Didn't Know about the American Revolution Ser.). (ENG., Illus.). 64p. (gr. 4-8). 34.65 (978-0-7565-4972-5(8)) Compass Point Bks.
Malaspina, Ann. Boston Tea Party. 2013. (Foundations of Our Nation EBook Ser.). (ENG., Illus.). 48p. (J). pap. 15.64 (978-1-61783-757-9(1)) ABDO Publishing Co.
Mattern, Joanne. The Freedom Trail. 2015. (ENG.). 32p. (gr. 3-6). 32.79 (978-1-63430-045-2(9)) Rourke Educational Media.
Price, Denise D. Freedom Trail Pop up Book of Boston. 2015. (ENG., Illus.). 17p. (J). 29.99 (978-0-9907781-0-3(X)) White Dharma Ltd.
Sabatino, Chris. City Doodles - Boston. 2013. (ENG., Illus.). 240p. (J). pap. 9.99 (978-1-4236-3207-8(9)) Gibbs Smith, Publisher.
Trumbauer, Lisa. Hopes Fulfilled: The Irish Immigrants in Boston. 2005. (Illus.). 32p. (J). pap. (978-0-7367-2881-2(3)) Zaner-Bloser, Inc.
Winters, Kay. Colonial Voices: Hear Them Speak. Day, Larry, illus. 2008. (ENG.). 32p. (J). (gr. 4-7). 17.99 (978-0-525-47872-0(8), Dutton Books for Young Readers) Penguin Young Readers Group.

BOSTON MASSACRE, 1770

Beier, Anne. Crispus Attucks: Hero of the Boston Massacre / Héroe de la masacre de Boston. 2009. (Famous People in American History/Grandes personajes en la historia de los Estados Unidos Ser.). (ENG & SPA.). 32p. (gr. 2-3). 47.90 (978-1-61512-541-8(8), Editorial Buenas Letras) Rosen Publishing Group, Inc., The.
—Crispus Attucks: Heroe de la masacre de Boston. 2004. (Grandes personajes en la historia de los Estados Unidos Ser.). (SPA.). 32p. (gr. 3-6). pap. 10.00 (978-0-8239-4224-4(4), Rosen Classroom) Rosen Publishing Group, Inc., The.
—Crispus Attucks: Héroe de la masacre de Boston (Crispus Attucks: Hero of the Boston Massacre) 2009. (Grandes personajes en la historia de los Estados Unidos (Famous People in American History) Ser.). (SPA.). 32p. (gr. 2-3). 47.90 (978-1-61512-793-1(3), Editorial Buenas Letras) Rosen Publishing Group, Inc., The.
Benoit, Peter. The Boston Massacre. 2013. (ENG.). 64p. (J). 30.00 (978-0-531-28201-4(5)); pap. 8.95 (978-0-531-27666-2(X)) Scholastic Library Publishing.
Burgan, Michael & Raum, Elizabeth. The Revolutionary War Experience, 1 vol. 2014. (You Choose: History Ser.). (ENG., Illus.). 328p. (gr. 3-4). pap. 14.95 (978-1-4914-1513-9(4), You Choose Bks.) Capstone Press of Coughlan Cos.
Decker, Timothy. For Liberty: The Story of the Boston Massacre. 2009. (ENG.). 40p. (J). (gr. 4-6). 17.95 (978-1-59078-608-6(4), Calkins Creek) Boyds Mills Pr.
Draper, Allison Stark. The Boston Massacre: Five Colonists Killed by British Soldiers. 2009. (Headlines from History Ser.). 24p. (gr. 3-3). 42.50 (978-1-61513-243-0(0), PowerKids Pr.) Rosen Publishing Group, Inc., The.
Fradin, Dennis Brindell. The Boston Massacre. 2008. (Turning Points in U. S. History Ser.). 48p. (gr. 3-18). lib. bdg. 31.36 (978-0-7614-3010-0(5), Benchmark Bks.) Marshall Cavendish Corp.
Jeffrey, Gary. John Adams & the Boston Massacre. 2011. (Graphic Heroes of the American Revolution Ser.). (Illus.). 24p. (J). (gr. 3-6). lib. bdg. 23.95 (978-1-4339-6016-1(8)); pap. 8.15 (978-1-4339-6017-8(6), Gareth Stevens Learning Library) Stevens, Gareth Publishing LLLP.
Kjelle, Marylou Morano. Boston Massacre. 2013. (Foundations of Our Nation EBook Ser.). (ENG.). 48p. (J). pap. 15.64 (978-1-61783-756-2(3)); (gr. 3-6). lib. bdg. 32.79 (978-1-61783-706-7(7)) ABDO Publishing Co.
Mattern, Joanne. The Cost of Freedom: Crispus Attucks & the Boston Massacre. 2009. (Great Moments in American History Ser.). 32p. (gr. 3-3). 47.90 (978-1-61513-153-2(1)) Rosen Publishing Group, Inc., The.
Raum, Elizabeth. The Boston Massacre: An Interactive History Adventure. 2016. (You Choose: History Ser.). (ENG.). 112p. (gr. 3-4). pap. 6.95 (978-1-5157-4261-6(X), You Choose Bks.) Capstone Press of Coughlan Cos.
Rausch, Monica. Crispus Attucks. 2007. (Grandes personajes (Spanish- Great Americans) Ser.). (SPA.). 24p. (gr. 1-4). pap. 8.15 (978-0-8368-7987-2(2), Weekly Reader Leveled Readers) Stevens, Gareth Publishing LLLP.
Rausch, Monica L. Crispus Attucks. 2007. (Grandes personajes (Great Americans) Ser.). (SPA., Illus.). 24p. (gr. 1-4). lib. bdg. 22.00 (978-0-8368-7980-3(5), Weekly Reader Leveled Readers) Stevens, Gareth Publishing LLLP.
Shea, Therese. The Boston Massacre, Vol. 1. 2014. (What You Didn't Know about History Ser.). 24p. (J). (gr. 2-3). (ENG.). 22.60 (978-1-4824-0580-4(6)); pap. 8.15 (978-1-4824-3328-9(1)) Stevens, Gareth Publishing LLLP.
Siddons, Brian. Crispus Attucks & African American Patriots of the American Revolution. 2015. (Spotlight on American History Ser.). (ENG., Illus.). 24p. (J). (gr. 4-6). pap. 10.00 (978-1-4994-1739-5(X), PowerKids Pr.) Rosen Publishing Group, Inc., The.
Taylor, Charlotte. Crispus Attucks: A Hero of the American Revolution. 2016. (Exceptional African Americans Ser.). (ENG., Illus.). 24p. (J). (gr. 3-3). 22.60 (978-0-7660-7187-2(1)); pap. 9.35 (978-0-7660-7185-8(5)) Enslow Pubs., Inc.
Weiss, Lynne. Crispus Attucks & the Boston Massacre. 2013. (Jr. Graphic African American History Ser.). 24p. (J). (gr. 3-6). pap. 63.60 (978-1-4777-1456-0(1)); (ENG., Illus.). pap. 10.60 (978-1-4777-1455-3(3)); (ENG., Illus.). lib. bdg. 25.25 (978-1-4777-1315-0(8)) Rosen Publishing Group, Inc., The. (PowerKids Pr.).

BOSTON RED SOX (BASEBALL TEAM)

Connery-Boyd, Peg. Boston Red Sox. 2016. (Hawk's Nest Activity Bks.: 0). (ENG.). 64p. (J). (gr. k-3). pap., act. bk. ed. 8.99 (978-1-4926-3362-4(3)) Sourcebooks, Inc.
Freedman, Lew. Boston Red Sox, 1 vol. (Inside MLB Ser.). (ENG., 48p. (gr. 3-6). 2011. Illus.). (YA). lib. bdg. 32.79 (978-1-61714-037-2(6)) 2014. lib. bdg. 32.79 (978-1-62403-463-3(2), SportsZone) ABDO Publishing Co.
Frisch, Aaron. Boston Red Sox. 2009. (World Series Champions Ser.). 23p. (J). (gr. 2-3). 24.25 (978-1-58341-694-5(3), Creative Education) Creative Co., The.
Gilbert, Sara. Boston Red Sox. 2013. (Illus.). 24p. (J). 25.65 (978-1-60818-260-2(6), Creative Education) Creative Co., The.
—World Series Champs: Boston Red Sox. 2013. (World Series Champions Ser.). (ENG.). 24p. (J). (gr. 1-3). pap. 7.99 (978-0-89812-811-6(0), Creative Paperbacks) Creative Co., The.
Goodman, Michael E. The Story of the Boston Red Sox. 2011. (J). 35.65 (978-1-60818-034-9(4), Creative Education) Creative Co., The.
Hammer, Max. Superstars of the Boston Red Sox. 2014. (Pro Sports Superstars Ser.). 24p. (J). 27.10 (978-1-60753-591-1(2)) Amicus Publishing.
Hammer, Maxwell. Boston Red Sox: World Series Champions. 2015. (Today's MVPs & Champions Ser.). (ENG.). 24p. (J). (gr. 2-5). 27.07 (978-1-63143-735-9(6), 208570) Child's World, Inc., The.
Kelley, K. C. Boston Red Sox. 2016. (J). **(978-1-4896-5935-4(8)**, AV2 by Weigl) Weigl Pubs., Inc.
Kelly, David A. Babe Ruth & the Baseball Curse. Jessell, Tim, illus. 2009. (Totally True Adventures Ser.). (ENG.). 112p. (J). (gr. 2-5). 4.99 (978-0-375-85603-7(X), Random Hse. Bks. for Young Readers) Random Hse. Children's Bks.
Kennedy, Mike & Stewart, Mark. Meet the Red Sox. 2010. (Smart about Sports Ser.). 24p. (J). (gr. k-3). lib. bdg. 22.60 (978-1-59953-368-1(5)) Norwood Hse. Pr.
MacRae, Sloan. The Boston Red Sox. (Illus.). 24p. (J). 2010. pap. 8.25 (978-1-4358-3392-0(9)) 2009. lib. bdg. 22.60 (978-1-4042-8130-1(4)) Rosen Publishing Group, Inc., The. (PowerKids Pr.).
Sandler, Michael. Baseball: The 2004 Boston Red Sox. 2006. (Upsets & Comebacks Ser.). (Illus.). 32p. (J). (gr. 3-6). lib. bdg. 25.27 (978-1-59716-165-7(9)) Bearport Publishing Co., Inc.
—Manny Ramirez & the Boston Red Sox: 2004 World Series. 2008. (World Series Superstars). (Illus.). 24p. (J). (gr. 1-4). lib. bdg. 22.61 (978-1-59716-628-7(6)) Bearport Publishing Co., Inc.
—Mike Lowell & the Boston Red Sox: 2007 World Series. 2008. (World Series Superstars). (Illus.). 24p. (J). (gr. 1-4). lib. bdg. 22.61 (978-1-59716-739-0(8), 1284374) Bearport Publishing Co., Inc.
Shaughnessy, Dan. The Legend of the Curse of the Bambino. Payne, C. F., illus. 2005. (ENG.). 32p. (J). (gr. k-3). 16.95 (978-0-689-87235-8(6), Simon & Schuster/Paula Wiseman Bks.) Simon & Schuster/Paula Wiseman Bks.
Stewart, Mark. The Boston Red Sox. 2012. (Team Spirit Ser.). 48p. (J). (gr. 3-6). lib. bdg. 29.27 (978-1-59953-475-6(4)) Norwood Hse. Pr.
Tavares, Matt. There Goes Ted Williams: The Greatest Hitter Who Ever Lived. Tavares, Matt, illus. 2015. (Candlewick Biographies Ser.). (ENG., Illus.). 48p. (J). (gr. 1-4). 14.99 (978-0-7636-7655-1(1)) Candlewick Pr.
Wisnia, Saul. Miracle at Fenway: The Inside Story of the Boston Red Sox 2004 Championship Season. 2015. (ENG., Illus.). 320p. pap. 16.99 (978-1-250-06871-2(1), 9781250068712, St. Martin's Griffin) St. Martin's Pr.

BOSTON TEA PARTY, 1773

Benchmark Education Company. The Boston Tea Party (Teacher Guide) 2005. (978-1-4108-4674-7(1)) Benchmark Education Co.
Brannon, Barbara. Discover the Boston Tea Party. 2005. (J). pap. (978-1-4108-5157-4(5)) Benchmark Education Co.
Brennan, Linda Crotta. The Boston Tea Party: A History Perspectives Book. 2013. (Perspectives Library). (ENG., Illus.). 32p. (J). (gr. 4-8). 28.50 (978-1-62431-416-2(3),

202784); pap. 14.21 *(978-1-62431-492-6(9)*, 202786) Cherry Lake Publishing.

Cook, Peter. You Wouldn't Want to Be at the Boston Tea Party! Wharf Water You'd Rather Not Drink. Antram, David, illus. 2013. (ENG.). (J). 32p. 29.00 *(978-0-531-27105-6(6))*; 40p. pap. 9.95 *(978-0-531-23856-1(3))* Scholastic Library Publishing. (Watts, Franklin).

Crompton, Samuel Willard. The Boston Tea Party: Colonists Protest the British Government. 2011. (Milestones in American History Ser.). (Illus.). 122p. (J). (gr. 6-12). 35.00 *(978-1-60413-764-4(9)*, Chelsea Hse.) Facts On File, Inc.

Cunningham, Kevin. The Boston Tea Party. 2012. (Cornerstones of Freedom, Third Ser.). (ENG.). 64p. (J). pap. 8.95 *(978-0-531-28151-2(5))*; lib. bdg. 30.00 *(978-0-531-23051-0(1))* Scholastic Library Publishing.

Doeden, Matt. The Boston Tea Party, 1 vol. Barnett, Charles, III & Hoover, Dave, illus. 2005. (Graphic History Ser.). (ENG.). 32p. (gr. 3-4). per. 8.10 *(978-0-7368-5243-2(3)*, Graphic Library) Capstone Press of Coughlan Cos.

Draper, Allison Stark. The Boston Tea Party: Angry Colonists Dump British Tea. 2009. (Headlines from History Ser.). 24p. (gr. 3-3). 42.50 *(978-1-61513-244-7(9)*, PowerKids Pr.) Rosen Publishing Group, Inc., The.

Espinosa, Rod. The Boston Tea Party, 1 vol. Espinosa, Rod, illus. 2007. (Graphic History Ser.). (ENG., Illus.). 32p. (gr. 3-6). 28.50 *(978-1-60270-075-8(3)*, Graphic Planet-Nonfiction) ABDO Publishing Co.

Fradin, Dennis Brindell. The Boston Tea Party. 2007. (Turning Points in U. S. History Ser.). (J). lib. bdg. 31.36 *(978-0-7614-2035-4(5)*, Benchmark Bks.) Marshall Cavendish Corp.

Freedman, Russell. The Boston Tea Party. Malone, Peter, illus. 2012. (ENG.). 40p. (J). (gr. 1-5). 17.95 *(978-0-8234-2266-1(6))* Holiday Hse., Inc.

Gilman, Sarah. The Boston Tea Party. 2016. (Explore Colonial America Ser.). (Illus.). 48p. (J). (gr. 5-4). 27.93 *(978-0-7660-7872-7(8))* Enslow Pubs., Inc.

Gondosch, Linda. How Did Tea & Taxes Spark a Revolution? And Other Questions about the Boston Tea Party. 2010. (Six Questions of American History Ser.). (ENG.). (gr. 4-6). pap. 56.72 *(978-0-7613-6946-2(5))*; 48p. pap. 9.95 *(978-0-7613-6122-0(7))*; (Illus.). 48p. lib. bdg. 30.60 *(978-1-58013-666-2(4))* Lerner Publishing Group.

Gunderson, Cory. Boston Tea Party, 1 vol. 2004. (American Moments Ser.). (ENG., Illus.). 48p. (gr. 4-8). 27.07 *(978-1-59197-280-8(9)*, Abdo & Daughters) ABDO Publishing Co.

Hull, Mary. Witness the Boston Tea Party in United States History. 2015. (In United States History Ser.). 96p. (J). (gr. 5-12). 27.94 *(978-0-7660-6335-8(6))* Enslow Pubs., Inc.

Hull, Mary E. Witness the Boston Tea Party in United States History. 2015. (In United States History Ser.). 96p. (J). (gr. 5-12). pap. 10.95 *(978-0-7660-6336-5(4))* Enslow Pubs., Inc.

Jeffrey, Gary. Samuel Adams & the Boston Tea Party. 2011. (Graphic Heroes of the American Revolution Ser.). 24p. (J). (gr. 3-6). lib. bdg. 23.95 *(978-1-4339-6022-2(2))*; pap. 8.15 *(978-1-4339-6023-9(0)*, Gareth Stevens Learning Library) Stevens, Gareth Publishing LLLP.

Krull, Kathleen. What Was the Boston Tea Party? Mortimer, Lauren & Bennett, James, illus. 2013. (What Was? Ser.). (ENG.). 112p. (J). (gr. 3-7). pap. 5.99 *(978-0-448-46288-2(5)*, Penguin Workshop) Penguin Young Readers Group.

—What Was the Boston Tea Party? 2013. (What Was... ? Ser.). lib. bdg. 16.00 *(978-0-606-29971-8(8)*, Turtleback) Turtleback Bks.

Landau, Elaine. The Boston Tea Party: Would You Join the Revolution? 2014. (What Would You Do? Ser.). (Illus.). 48p. (J). (gr. 3-4). lib. bdg. 25.27 *(978-0-7660-4223-0(5)*, Enslow Elementary) Enslow Pubs., Inc.

—Witness the Boston Tea Party with Elaine Landau. 2006. (Explore Colonial America with Elaine Landau Ser.). (Illus.). 48p. (J). (gr. 3-7). lib. bdg. 25.27 *(978-0-7660-2553-0(5)*, Enslow Elementary) Enslow Pubs., Inc.

Malaspina, Ann. Boston Tea Party, 1 vol. 2013. (Foundations of Our Nation Ser.). (ENG.). 48p. (J). (gr. 3-6). lib. bdg. 32.79 *(978-1-61783-707-4(5))*; (Illus.). pap. 15.64 *(978-1-61783-757-9(1))* ABDO Publishing Co.

Marciniak, Kristin. 12 Incredible Facts about the Boston Tea Party. 2015. (Turning Points in US History Ser.). (ENG., Illus.). 32p. (J). (gr. 3-5). *(978-1-63235-126-5(9)*, 12-Story Library) Pr. Room Editions LLC.

Moss, Marissa. America's Tea Parties: Not One but Four!: Boston, Charleston, New York, Philadelphia. 2016. (ENG., Illus.). 56p. (J). (gr. 3-7). 19.95 *(978-1-4197-1874-8(6)*, Abrams Bks. for Young Readers) Abrams, Inc.

Roza, Greg. Analyzing the Boston Tea Party: Establishing Cause-and-Effect Relationships. (Critical Thinking in American History Ser.). 48p. 2009. (gr. 5-8). 53.00 *(978-1-61512-088-8(2)*, Rosen Reference) 2005. (Illus.). (J). (gr. k-3). lib. bdg. 29.25 *(978-1-4042-0411-9(3))* Rosen Publishing Group, Inc., The.

Russell, Freedman. The Boston Tea Party. Malone, Peter, illus. 2013. (ENG.). 40p. (J). (gr. 1-5). pap. 7.99 *(978-0-8234-2915-8(6))* Holiday Hse., Inc.

Sutton, Adam J. What Happened at the Boston Tea Party? 2006. (Rosen Publishing Group's Reading Room Collection). (Illus.). 16p. (J). (gr. 3-7). lib. bdg. 17.25 *(978-1-4042-3350-8(4)*, PowerKids Pr.) Rosen Publishing Group, Inc., The.

—What Happened at the Boston Tea Party. 2009. (Reading Room Collection 1 Ser.). 16p. (gr. 2-3). 37.50 *(978-1-60851-951-4(1)*, PowerKids Pr.) Rosen Publishing Group, Inc., The.

Tovar, Alicia. The Boston Tea Party: No Taxation Without Representation. 2015. (Spotlight on American History Ser.). (ENG., Illus.). 24p. (J). (gr. 4-6). 26.25 *(978-1-4994-1726-5(8)*, PowerKids Pr.) Rosen Publishing Group, Inc., The.

Trueit, Trudi Strain. The Boston Tea Party. 2005. (Cornerstones of Freedom Ser.). (ENG., Illus.). 48p. (YA). (gr. 4-7). lib. bdg. 26.00 *(978-0-516-23636-0(9))* Scholastic Library Publishing.

Wachter, Joanne. The Boston Tea Party. 2005. (J). pap. *(978-1-4108-4626-6(1))* Benchmark Education Co.

Walker, Ida. The Boston Tea Party, 1 vol. 2007. (Essential Events Set 1 Ser.). (ENG., Illus.). 112p. (J). (gr. 6-12). lib. bdg. 35.64 *(978-1-59928-849-9(4))* ABDO Publishing Co.

Winters, Kay. Colonial Voices: Hear Them Speak. Day, Larry, illus. 2008. (ENG.). 32p. (J). (gr. 4-7). 17.99 *(978-0-525-47872-0(8)*, Dutton Books for Young Readers) Penguin Young Readers Group.

—Colonial Voices - Hear Them Speak: The Outbreak of the Boston Tea Party Told from Multiple Points-of-View! Day, Larry, illus. 2015. (ENG.). 48p. (J). (gr. 4-7). pap. 8.99 *(978-0-14-751162-1(3)*, Puffin Books) Penguin Young Readers Group.

Yomtov, Nel. Night of Rebellion! Nickolas Flux & the Boston Tea Party, 1 vol. Ginevra, Dante, illus. 2014. (Nickolas Flux History Chronicles Ser.). (ENG.). 32p. (gr. 3-4). lib. bdg. 30.65 *(978-1-4765-3946-1(4)*, Graphic Library) Capstone Press of Coughlan Cos.

BOSTON TEA PARTY, 1773—FICTION

Brodeur, Tom. Regina Silsby's Secret War. 2004. 248p. (J). 7.49 *(978-1-59166-235-8(4))* BJU Pr.

Gunderson, J. Ropes of Revolution: The Boston Tea Party, 1 vol. Schoonover, Brent, illus. 2008. (Historical Fiction Ser.). (ENG.). 56p. (gr. 2-3). pap. 6.25 *(978-1-4342-0492-9(8)*, Graphic Flash) Stone Arch Bks.

Horender, Philip M. Patriotic Mouse: Boston Tea Party Participant, 1 vol. Wolek, Guy, illus. 2013. (Maximilian P. Mouse, Time Traveler Ser.). (ENG.). 112p. (J). (gr. 3-6). lib. bdg. 27.07 *(978-1-61641-957-8(1)*, Calico Chapter Bks) Magic Wagon.

Seabrooke, Brenda. The Chester Town Tea Party, 1 vol. Smith, Nancy C., illus. 2009. (ENG.). 30p. (J). (gr. -1-3). 8.95 *(978-0-87033-422-1(0)*, 9780870334221, Cornell Maritime Pr./Tidewater Pubs.) Schiffer Publishing, Ltd.

Thompson, Paul B. Liberty's Son: A Spy Story of the American Revolution. (Historical Fiction Adventures (HFA) Ser.). 160p. (J). 2012. pap. 10.95 *(978-0-7660-3654-3(5))* 2009. (Illus.). (gr. 3-6). lib. bdg. 29.27 *(978-0-7660-3309-2(0))* Enslow Pubs., Inc.

Webb, Robert N. We Were There at the Boston Tea Party. Ward, E. F., illus. 2013. (ENG.). 192p. (J). (gr. 3-8). pap. 6.99 *(978-0-486-49260-5(5))* Dover Pubns., Inc.

BOTANY

see also Flower Gardening; Flowers; Fruit; Leaves; Plant Anatomy; Plant Ecology; Plant Physiology; Plants; Plants, Fossil; Seeds; Shrubs; Trees; Vegetables

Anders, Mason. Plant Cells. 2017. (Genetics Ser.). (ENG.). 32p. (gr. 3-4). pap. 7.95 ***(978-1-5157-7262-0(4))*** Capstone Press of Coughlan Cos.

Benbow, Ann & Mably, Colin. Lively Plant Science Projects. Labaff, Tom & LaBaff, Tom, illus. 2009. (Real Life Science Experiments Ser.). 48p. (J). (gr. 2-5). lib. bdg. 25.27 *(978-0-7660-3146-3(2))* Enslow Pubs., Inc.

Bishop, Celeste. Plants That Poke. 2016. (Plant Defenses Ser.). (Illus.). 24p. (J). (gr. 3-3). pap. 8.25 *(978-1-4994-2159-0(1)*, PowerKids Pr.) Rosen Publishing Group, Inc., The.

—Why Do Plants Have Stems?, 01 vols., 1. 2016. (Plant Parts Ser.). (ENG., Illus.). 24p. (J). 23.60 *(978-1-4994-1851-4(5)*, PowerKids Pr.) Rosen Publishing Group, Inc., The.

Boothroyd, Jennifer. Self-Pollination. 2015. (First Step Nonfiction - Pollination Ser.). (ENG.). 24p. (gr. k-2). lib. bdg. 23.99 *(978-1-4677-5740-9(3)*, Lerner Pubns.) Lerner Publishing Group.

Bozak, Kristin & Cohen, Judith Love. You Can Be a Woman Botanist. Katz, David Arthur, illus. Date not set. 40p. (J). (gr. 3-6). 13.95 *(978-1-880599-41-9(4))* Cascade Pass, Inc.

Canavan, Thomas. Do Plants Really Eat Insects? Questions & Answers about the Science of Plants. 2013. (Science F. A. Q. Ser.). (Illus.). 32p. (gr. 3-6). 31.35 *(978-1-78212-392-7(X))* Arcturus Publishing GBR. Dist: Black Rabbit Bks.

Castle, Patricia. In the Garden. 2012. (InfoMax Readers Ser.). (ENG., Illus.). 16 pp.p. (J). (gr. k-1). pap. 7.00 *(978-1-4488-8944-0(8)*, Rosen Classroom) Rosen Publishing Group, Inc., The.

Cavell-Clarke, Steffi. Plant Parts. 2017. (Closer Look at Living Things Ser.). 24p. (J). (gr. 2-2). pap. 8.25 ***(978-1-5345-2069-1(4))***; lib. bdg. 24.60 ***(978-1-5345-2070-7(8))*** Greenhaven Publishing LLC. (KidHaven Publishing).

De la Bédoyère, Camilla. Plants. 2013. (Illus.). 40p. (J). *(978-1-4351-5095-9(3))* Barnes & Noble, Inc.

Doudna, Kelly. Super Simple Things to Do with Plants: Fun & Easy Science for Kids, 1 vol. 2011. (Super Simple Science Ser.). (ENG., Illus.). 24p. (J). (gr. k-3). lib. bdg. 25.65 *(978-1-61714-674-9(9))* ABDO Publishing Co.

Elpel, Thomas J. Shanleya's Quest: A Botany Adventure for Kids Ages 9 - 99, 1 vol. Brown, Gloria Dean, illus. 32p. 12.50 *(978-1-892784-16-2(5)*, 1511) HOPS Pr., LLC.

Farndon, John. Stems. 2006. (World of Plants (Blackbirch) Ser.). (ENG., Illus.). 24p. (J). (gr. 2-6). lib. bdg. 26.65 *(978-1-4103-0420-9(5)*, Blackbirch Pr., Inc.) Cengage Gale.

Fox, Frances Margaret. Flowers & Their Travels. Funk, Clotilde Embree, illus. 2011. 230p. 46.95 *(978-1-258-07400-5(1))* Literary Licensing, LLC.

Fulbright, Jeannie. Exploring Creation with Botany. Wile, Jay L., ed. 2004. 35.00 *(978-1-932012-49-1(4))* Apologia Educational Ministries, Inc.

Gardner, Robert. Experimenting with Plants Science Projects. 2013. (Exploring Hands-On Science Projects Ser.). 128p. (J). (gr. 5-18). 27.94 *(978-0-7660-4144-8(1))* Enslow Pubs., Inc.

Gardner, Robert & Perry, Phyllis Jean. Ace Your Plant Science Project: Great Science Fair Ideas. 2009. (Ace Your Biology Science Project Ser.). (Illus.). 104p. (J). (gr. 5-9). lib. bdg. 33.27 *(978-0-7660-3221-7(3))* Enslow Pubs., Inc.

Goldstein, Natalie. Photosynthesis & Other Plant Life Processes. 2012. (YA). 35.00 *(978-1-61753-026-5(3)*, Chelsea Hse.) Facts On File, Inc.

Gottlieb. Plant Life. 2004. (Wonders of Science Ser.). (ENG.). (gr. 7-12). 176p. pap., tchr. ed. 27.70 *(978-0-7398-9186-5(3))*; (Illus.). 144p. pap. 24.55 *(978-0-7398-9180-3(4))* Houghton Mifflin Harcourt Publishing Co.

Gray, Susan H. Super Cool Science Experiments: Plants. 2009. (Explorer Library: Science Explorer Ser.). (ENG., Illus.). 32p. (gr. 4-8). lib. bdg. 28.50 *(978-1-60279-522-8(3)*, 200286) Cherry Lake Publishing.

Green, Jen. Projects with Plants. 2014. (Make & Learn Ser.). (Illus.). 32p. (J). (gr. 3-6). 27.50 *(978-1-4777-7161-7(1)*, PowerKids Pr.) Rosen Publishing Group, Inc., The.

Gumm, Amy L. Let It Grow, Let It Grow, Let It Grow: Hands-on Activities to Explore the Plant Kingdom. 2005. (Illus.). 104p. spiral bd. 14.95 *(978-0-9761724-6-8(1))* NSR Pubns.

Hewitt, Sally. Amazing Plants. 2007. (Amazing Science Ser.). (ENG.). 32p. (J). pap. *(978-0-7787-3628-8(8))* Crabtree Publishing Co.

Hixson, Bryce. Plant Stigmas & Other Botanical Concerns. Hixson, Bryce, illus. 2003. (Illus.). (J). per. 12.95 *(978-1-931801-09-6(6))* Loose In The Lab.

Howell, Laura & Rogers, Kirsteen. World of Plants. 2004. (Internet-Linked Library of Science). (J). (ENG.). 1p. pap. 9.95 *(978-0-7945-0086-3(2)*, Usborne); 64p. lib. bdg. 17.95 *(978-1-58086-379-7(5))* EDC Publishing.

Jones, Alan & Ellis, Jane. My Life As a Plant - Russian: Activity & Coloring Book for Plant Biology. Khvostova, Ekaterina, tr. 2013. 40p. pap. 5.38 *(978-0-943088-53-2(4))* American Society of Plant BIOLOGISTS.

Kalman, Bobbie. ?Que Son Las Plantas? 2005. (Ciencia de los Seres Vivos Ser.). (SPA., Illus.). 32p. (J). (gr. 3-4). lib. bdg. *(978-0-7787-8759-4(1))* Crabtree Publishing Co.

—¿Qué Son Las Plantas? 2005. (Ciencia de los Seres Vivos Ser.). (SPA., Illus.). 32p. (J). (gr. 7-12). pap. *(978-0-7787-8805-8(9))* Crabtree Publishing Co.

Klepeis, Alicia. Fruits & Vegetables Explained. 2016. (Distinctions in Nature Ser.). 32p. (J). (gr. 3-3). 28.50 *(978-1-5026-1744-6(7))* Cavendish Square Publishing.

Lawrence, Ellen. Amazing Plant Bodies: Tiny to Gigantic. 2012. (Science Slam: Plant-Ology Ser.). 24p. (J). (gr. -1-3). lib. bdg. 23.93 *(978-1-61772-592-0(7))* Bearport Publishing Co., Inc.

—Plants. 2016. (FUN-Damental Experiments Ser.). (ENG., Illus.). 24p. (J). (gr. -1-3). 17.95 *(978-1-943553-17-4(3))* Bearport Publishing Co., Inc.

Levy, Janey. Freaky Stories about Plants. 2016. (Freaky True Science Ser.). 32p. (J). (gr. 5-4). pap. 10.50 *(978-1-4824-4831-3(9))* Stevens, Gareth Publishing LLLP.

Long, Erin. Plants & Their Environments. 2016. (Spotlight on Ecology & Life Science Ser.). 00024p. (J). (gr. 4-6). pap. 10.00 *(978-1-4994-2587-1(2)*, PowerKids Pr.) Rosen Publishing Group, Inc., The.

McNeil, Niki, et al. Botany. 2007. (In the Hands of a Child: Custom Designed Project Pack Ser.). (Illus.). 55p. spiral bd. 20.00 *(978-1-60308-116-0(X))* In the Hands of a Child.

Midthun, Joseph. Plant Life Cycles. 2014. (Illus.). 32p. (J). *(978-0-7166-2825-5(2))* World Bk., Inc.

Mitchell, Melanie S. Stems. 2004. (First Step Nonfiction - Parts of Plants Ser.). (ENG., Illus.). 8p. (gr. -1-1). pap. 4.95 *(978-0-8225-3921-6(7)*, Lerner Pubns.) Lerner Publishing Group.

Murphy, Patricia J. Mirando a las Plantas con un Cientifico. 2008. (I Like Science! Bilingual Ser.).Tr. of Looking at Plants with a Scientist. (SPA & ENG., Illus.). 24p. (J). (gr. 1-3). lib. bdg. 22.60 *(978-0-7660-2981-1(6)*, Enslow Elementary) Enslow Pubs., Inc.

—Peeking at Plants with a Scientist. 2004. (I Like Science! Ser.). (Illus.). 24p. (J). lib. bdg. 21.26 *(978-0-7660-2266-9(8))* Enslow Pubs., Inc.

Owen, Ruth. How Do Animals Help Plants Reproduce? 2014. (World of Plants Ser.). 32p. (J). (gr. 2-5). 26.25 *(978-1-4777-7141-9(7)*, PowerKids Pr.) Rosen Publishing Group, Inc., The.

Owings, Lisa. From Seed to Cattail. 2017. (Start to Finish, Second Ser.). (ENG.). (J). (gr. k-3). 24p. 23.99 *(978-1-5124-3443-9(4))*; pap. 6.99 ***(978-1-5124-5625-7(X))*** Lerner Publishing Group.

Plants. 2005. (Plants Ser.). (Illus.). 32p. (gr. 2-4). 138.00 *(978-0-7910-8464-9(7)*, Chelsea Hse.) Facts On File, Inc.

Rake, Jody Sullivan. Roots, Bulbs, & Bacteria: Growths of the Underground. 2015. (Underground Safari Ser.). (ENG., Illus.). 24p. (gr. 1-2). lib. bdg. 25.32 *(978-1-4914-5062-8(2))* Capstone Press of Coughlan Cos.

Rice, William B. Los Pastizales Africanos. 2017. (TIME for Kids en Español - Level 3 Ser.). (SPA & ENG.). 32p. (gr. 3-3). lib. bdg. 31.99 ***(978-1-5157-5177-9(5))*** Capstone Press of Coughlan Cos.

Riley, Peter. All about Plants. 2016. (Ways into Science Ser.). (ENG., Illus.). 32p. (J). (gr. k-2). pap. 11.99 *(978-1-4451-3470-3(5)*, Franklin Watts) Hachette Children's Group GBR. Dist: Hachette Bk. Group.

Rustad, Martha E. H. Plants in Spring, 1 vol. 2012. (All about Spring Ser.). (ENG.). 24p. (gr. k-1). lib. bdg. 26.65 *(978-1-4296-8656-3(1)*, Pebble Plus) Capstone Press of Coughlan Cos.

Selwyn, Josephine. What Do Plants Need? 2014. (Little Books of Answers: Level a Ser.). (Illus.). 16p. (gr. k-2). pap. 7.95 *(978-1-927136-08-9(3))* Three Crows Media NZL. Dist: RiverStream Publishing.

Senker, Cath. Plant Reproduction: How Do You Grow a Giant Pumpkin?, 1 vol. 2014. (Show Me Science Ser.). (ENG.). 32p. (gr. 3-5). lib. bdg. 30.65 *(978-1-4329-8749-7(6)*, Raintree Perspectives) Heinemann-Raintree.

Silverthorne, Elizabeth. Plants. 2009. (21st Century Skills Library: Real World Science Ser.). (ENG.). 32p. (gr. 4-8). lib. bdg. 28.50 *(978-1-60279-461-0(8)*, 200228) Cherry Lake Publishing.

Sterling, Kristin. Exploring Stems. 2011. (First Step Nonfiction / Let's Look at Plants Ser.). pap. 33.92 *(978-0-7613-8618-6(1))*; (ENG.). 24p. pap. 6.95 *(978-0-7613-7836-5(7))*; (ENG.). 24p. lib. bdg. 23.93 *(978-0-7613-5783-4(1))* Lerner Publishing Group.

Teacher Created Materials, creator. Stem Grade 5, 10 bks., Set. 2015. (Teacher Created Materials Ser.). (ENG., Illus.). 32p. (J). (gr. 5-5). spiral bd. 89.90 *(978-1-4938-1446-6(X))* Shell Educational Publishing.

Throp, Claire. All about Stems, 1 vol. 2014. (All about Plants Ser.). (ENG.). 24p. (gr. -1-1). 22.65 *(978-1-4846-0510-3(1)*, Acorn) Heinemann-Raintree.

Time Living Wonders: The Marvels & Mysteries of Life on Earth. 2009. (Time Inc. Home Entertainment Library-Bound Titles Ser.). (ENG.). 128p. (gr. 5-12). 39.93 *(978-0-7613-4229-8(X)*, Twenty-First Century Bks.) Lerner Publishing Group.

Troupe, Thomas Kingsley. Do Plants Have Heads? Learning about Plant Parts with the Garbage Gang. Toye, Derek, illus. 2015. (Garbage Gang's Super Science Questions Ser.). (ENG.). 24p. (gr. k-2). lib. bdg. 26.65 *(978-1-4795-7059-1(1))* Picture Window Bks.

Wadsworth, Pamela. Golwg Gyntaf Ar Bethau Byw. Owen, Ken & Owen, Siân, illus. 2005. (WEL.). 24p. pap. *(978-1-85596-250-7(0))* Dref Wen.

Wakefield, Priscilla. An Introduction to Botany: In a Series of Familiar Letters, with Illustrative Engravings. 2015. (Cambridge Library Collection - Education Ser.). (ENG., Illus.). 222p. pap. 26.99 *(978-1-108-07721-7(8))* Cambridge Univ. Pr.

Waldron, Melanie. Leaves, 1 vol. 2014. (Plant Parts Ser.). (ENG.). 32p. (gr. 2-4). lib. bdg. 30.65 *(978-1-4109-5421-3(8)*, Raintree Perspectives) Heinemann-Raintree.

—Plants, 1 vol. (Essential Life Science Ser.). (ENG.). 48p. (gr. 4-6). 2014. 33.32 *(978-1-4329-7812-9(8))* 2013. pap. 9.95 *(978-1-4329-7843-3(8))* Heinemann-Raintree. (Heinemann InfoSearch).

—Roots, 1 vol. 2014. (Plant Parts Ser.). (ENG., Illus.). 32p. (gr. 2-4). pap. 8.95 *(978-1-4109-6281-2(4))*; lib. bdg. 30.65 *(978-1-4109-5422-0(6))* Heinemann-Raintree. (Raintree Perspectives).

—Seeds & Fruits, 1 vol. 2014. (Plant Parts Ser.). (ENG.). 32p. (gr. 2-4). lib. bdg. 30.65 *(978-1-4109-5423-7(4)*, Raintree Perspectives) Heinemann-Raintree.

—Stems & Trunks, 1 vol. 2014. (Plant Parts Ser.). (ENG.). 32p. (gr. 2-4). lib. bdg. 30.65 *(978-1-4109-5424-4(2)*, Raintree Perspectives) Heinemann-Raintree.

Walker, Maryalice. Entomology & Palynology. Noziglia, Carla Miller & Siegel, Jay A., eds. 2013. (Solving Crimes with Science: Forensics Ser.: 12). (Illus.). 112p. (J). (gr. 7-18). 22.95 *(978-1-4222-2866-1(5))* Mason Crest.

Wanjie, Anne, ed. The Basics of Plant Structures. 2013. (Core Concepts Ser.). (ENG., Illus.). 96p. (YA). (gr. 7-12). lib. bdg. 34.60 *(978-1-4777-0553-7(8))* Rosen Publishing Group, Inc., The.

What a Weird Plant!, 6 vols. (Book2WebTM Ser.). (gr. 4-8). 36.50 *(978-0-322-02980-4(5))* Wright Group/McGraw-Hill.

Willis, Kathy. Botanicum. Scott, Katie, illus. 2017. (Welcome to the Museum Ser.). (ENG.). 112p. (J). (gr. 3-7). 35.00 *(978-0-7636-8923-0(8)*, Big Picture Press) Candlewick Pr.

World Book, Inc Staff, contrib. by. Encyclopedia of Plants. 2013. (J). *(978-0-7166-7522-8(6))* World Bk., Inc.

The World of Plants. 2014. (World of Plants Ser.). 32p. (J). (gr. 2-5). pap. 60.00 *(978-1-4777-7252-2(9)*, PowerKids Pr.) Rosen Publishing Group, Inc., The.

Yapp, R. H. Botany: A Junior Book for Schools. 2013. (ENG., Illus.). 218p. pap. 29.99 *(978-1-107-61954-8(8))* Cambridge Univ. Pr.

BOTANY, AGRICULTURAL

see Botany, Economic

BOTANY—ANATOMY

see Plant Anatomy

BOTANY—ECOLOGY

see Plant Ecology

BOTANY, ECONOMIC

see also Cotton; Grasses; Plant Introduction; Plants, Edible; Weeds

MacAulay, Kelley. How Are Plants Helpful? 2013. (ENG., Illus.). 24p. (J). *(978-0-7787-0002-9(X))*; pap. *(978-0-7787-0018-0(6))* Crabtree Publishing Co.

BOTANY, FOSSIL

see Plants, Fossil

BOTANY, MEDICAL

Colby, Jennifer. Healing Plants. 2014. (21st Century Junior Library: Plants Ser.). (ENG.). 24p. (J). (gr. 2-5). 25.64 *(978-1-63188-037-7(3)*, 205555) Cherry Lake Publishing.

Guttmacher, Joyce. Harvesting Medicine on the Hill. 2005. (ENG., Illus.). 24p. (J). (gr. 5-5). pap. 5.97 net. *(978-0-328-13510-3(0)*, Scott Foresman) Pearson Schl.

Judy, Beth. Medicinal Plants of North America: A Flora Delaterre Coloring Book. 2007. (Illus.). 32p. (J). (gr. 2-7). pap. 12.00 *(978-0-9792302-0-2(9))* Flora Delaterre Productions.

Lawrence, Ellen. Healing Plants. 2015. (Plant-Ology Ser.). (ENG., Illus.). 24p. (J). (gr. -1-3). lib. bdg. 23.93 *(978-1-62724-866-2(8))* Bearport Publishing Co., Inc.

Morgan, Sally. How We Use Plants for Medicine & Health. (How We Use Plants Ser.). (Illus.). 32p. 2009. (ENG.). (gr. 2-5). pap. 10.60 *(978-1-4358-2613-7(2))* 2008. (J). lib. bdg. 26.50 *(978-1-4042-4423-8(9))* Rosen Publishing Group, Inc., The. (PowerKids Pr.).

Rosenberg, Pam. Healing Plants. 2008. (21st Century Junior Library: Plants Ser.). (ENG.). 24p. (gr. 2-5). lib. bdg. 25.64 *(978-1-60279-278-4(X)*, 200184) Cherry Lake Publishing.

BOTANY—PHYSIOLOGY

see Plant Physiology

BOTANY—VOCATIONAL GUIDANCE

Bozak, Kristin & Cohen, Judith Love. You Can Be a Woman Botanist. Katz, David Arthur, illus. Date not set. 40p. (J). (gr. 3-6). pap. 12.95 *(978-1-880599-42-6(2))* Cascade Pass, Inc.

BOTANY OF THE BIBLE

see Bible—Natural History

BOTSWANA

Behnke, Alison. Botswana in Pictures. 2009. (Visual Geography Series, Second Ser.). (ENG.). 80p. (gr. 5-12). 31.93 *(978-1-57505-953-2(3)*, Lerner Pubns.) Lerner Publishing Group.

LeVert, Suzanne. Botswana. 2007. (Cultures of the World Ser.). (Illus.). 144p. (J). (gr. 3-7). lib. bdg. 39.93 *(978-0-7614-2330-0(3)*, Benchmark Bks.) Marshall Cavendish Corp.

Wittman, Kelly. Botswana. Rotberg, Robert I., ed. 2009. (Africa Ser.). (Illus.). 79p. (YA). (gr. 3-7). lib. bdg. 21.95 *(978-1-4222-0087-2(6))* Mason Crest.

Wittmann, Kelly. Botswana. 2012. (J). pap. *(978-1-4222-2221-8(7))* Mason Crest.

—Botswana. Rotberg, Robert I., ed. 2012. (Evolution of Africa's Major Nations Ser.). (Illus.). 80p. (J). (gr. 7). 22.95 *(978-1-4222-2193-8(8))* Mason Crest.

BOTSWANA—FICTION

Jones, Judith. You're from Where Grandma? 2011. 24p. pap. 12.99 *(978-1-4568-8150-4(7))* Xlibris Corp.

Lee, Lacey. Josephine Tea. 2015. (ENG.). 138p. (J). pap. 11.95 *(978-1-84963-903-3(5)*, 35a7e324-8162-4404-b33d-adb7031c9188) Austin, Stan AUS. Dist: Bookmasters Distribution.

McCall Smith, Alexander. The Great Cake Mystery: Precious Ramotswe's Very First Case. 2012. (Precious Ramotswe Mysteries for Young Readers Ser.: 1). (ENG.). 96p. (J). (gr. 2-5). 12.99 *(978-0-307-94944-8(3))*; (Illus.). pap. 6.99 *(978-0-307-74389-3(6))* Knopf Doubleday Publishing Group. (Anchor).

—The Mystery of Meerkat Hill. McIntosh, Iain, illus. 2013. (Precious Ramotswe Mysteries for Young Readers Ser.: 2). (ENG.). 112p. (J). (gr. 2-5). pap. 6.99 *(978-0-345-80446-4(5)*, Anchor) Knopf Doubleday Publishing Group.

—The Mystery of Meerkat Hill: A Precious Ramotswe Mystery for Young Readers. McIntosh, Iain, illus. 2013. (Precious Ramotswe Mysteries for Young Readers Ser.: 2). (ENG.). 112p. (J). (gr. 2-5). 12.99 *(978-0-345-80458-7(9))*; lib. bdg. 13.99 *(978-0-345-80616-1(6))* Knopf Doubleday Publishing Group. (Anchor).

—The Mystery of the Missing Lion: A Precious Ramotswe Mystery for Young Readers. 2014. (Precious Ramotswe Mysteries for Young Readers Ser.: 3). (ENG., Illus.). 112p. (J). (gr. 2-5). pap. 6.99 *(978-0-8041-7327-8(3)*, Anchor) Knopf Doubleday Publishing Group.

—Precious & the Puggies: Precious Ramotswe's Very First Case. Robertson, James, tr. from ENG. 2011. (ENG., Illus.). 96p. pap. 10.95 *(978-1-84502-332-4(3))* Black and White Publishing Ltd. GBR. Dist: Interlink Publishing Group, Inc.

The Mystery of the Missing Lion: A Precious Ramotswe Mystery for Young Readers. 2014. (Precious Ramotswe Mysteries for Young Readers Ser.: 3). (ENG., Illus.). 112p. (J). (gr. 2-5). 12.99 *(978-1-101-87202-4(0)*, Anchor) Knopf Doubleday Publishing Group.

BOTTICELLI, SANDRO, 1447?-1510

Connolly, Sean. Botticelli. 2004. (Lives of the Artists Ser.). (Illus.). 48p. (gr. 5-12). lib. bdg. 31.00 *(978-0-8368-5648-4(1)*, Gareth Stevens Secondary Library) Stevens, Gareth Publishing LLLP.

Mattern, Joanne. Sandro Botticelli, 1 vol. 2005. (Great Artists Set 1 Ser.). (ENG., Illus.). 32p. (gr. k-6). 27.07 *(978-1-59197-839-8(4)*, Checkerboard Library) ABDO Publishing Co.

Venezia, Mike. Sandro Boticelli. Venezia, Mike, illus. rev. ed. 2016. (Getting to Know the World's Greatest Artists Ser.). (ENG., Illus.). 40p. (J). pap. 7.95 *(978-0-531-22086-3(9)*, Children's Pr.) Scholastic Library Publishing.

BOUDICA, QUEEN, -62

see Boadicea, Queen, -62

BOUDICCA, QUEEN, -62

see Boadicea, Queen, -62

BOULDER DAM (ARIZ. AND NEV.)

see Hoover Dam (Ariz. and Nev.)

BOUNTY (SHIP)

Willett, Edward. The Bounty Mutiny: From the Court Case to the Movie. 2009. (Famous Court Cases That Became Movies Ser.). (Illus.). 128p. (J). (gr. 6-18). lib. bdg. 33.27 *(978-0-7660-3128-9(4))* Enslow Pubs., Inc.

BOWED INSTRUMENTS

see Stringed Instruments

BOWIE, JAMES, 1805-1836

Edmondson, J. R. Jim Bowie: Frontier Legend, Alamo Hero. (Library of American Lives & Times Ser.). 112p. 2009. (gr. 5-5). 69.20 *(978-1-60853-488-3(X))* 2005. (Illus.). (YA). (gr. 4-8). lib. bdg. 34.60 *(978-0-8239-5734-7(9))* Rosen Publishing Group, Inc., The.

Smith, Andrea P. Jim Bowie. 2012. (Illus.). 24p. (J). 63.60 *(978-1-4488-5231-4(5))*; pap. 10.60 *(978-1-4488-5230-7(7))*; lib. bdg. 25.25 *(978-1-4488-5196-6(3))* Rosen Publishing Group, Inc., The. (PowerKids Pr.).

BOWLING

Abramovitz, Melissa. Bowling. 2015. (Science Behind Sports Ser.). (ENG., Illus.). 128p. (J). (gr. 7-10). 39.40 *(978-1-4205-1251-9(X)*, Lucent Bks.) Cengage Gale.

Bussiere, Desireé. Bowling by the Numbers, 1 vol. 2013. (Sports by the Numbers Ser.). (ENG.). 24p. (J). (gr. k-3). lib. bdg. 24.21 *(978-1-61783-842-2(X)*, SandCastle) ABDO Publishing Co.

Cruickshank, Don. Bowling. 2013. (J). *(978-1-62127-316-5(4))*; pap. *(978-1-62127-321-9(0))* Weigl Pubs., Inc.

Cruikshank, Don. For the Love of Bowling. 2006. (For the Love of Sports Ser.). 24p. (J). (gr. 3-7). lib. bdg. 24.45 *(978-1-59036-384-3(1))*; (Illus.). per. 8.95 *(978-1-59036-385-0(X))* Weigl Pubs., Inc.

Walker, Niki & Dann, Sarah. Bowling in Action. 2003. (Sports in Action Ser.). (ENG., Illus.). 32p. (J). (gr. 3-4). pap. *(978-0-7787-0355-6(X))* Crabtree Publishing Co.

BOXCAR CHILDREN (FICTITIOUS CHARACTERS)—FICTION

Bloodworth, Mark, illus. The Castle Mystery. 2010. (Boxcar Children Graphic Novels Ser.: 12). (ENG.). 32p. (J). (gr. 1-5). pap. 6.99 *(978-0-8075-1080-3(7))* Whitman, Albert & Co.

Dubisch, Mike, illus. The Haunted Cabin Mystery. 2009. (Boxcar Children Graphic Novels Ser.: 9). (ENG.). 32p. (J). (gr. 1-5). pap. 6.99 *(978-0-8075-3180-8(4))* Whitman, Albert & Co.

—Mike's Mystery, No. 5. 2009. (Boxcar Children Graphic Novels Ser.). (ENG.). 32p. (J). (gr. 2-5). 6.99 *(978-0-8075-2871-6(4))* Whitman, Albert & Co.

—Mystery Ranch. 2009. (Boxcar Children Graphic Novels Ser.: 4). (ENG.). 32p. (J). (gr. 1-5). 6.99 *(978-0-8075-2870-9(6))* Whitman, Albert & Co.

—Tree House Mystery. 2009. (Boxcar Children Graphic Novels Ser.: 8). (ENG.). 32p. (J). (gr. 1-5). pap. 6.99 *(978-0-8075-8088-2(0))* Whitman, Albert & Co.

Dubisch, Mike & Bloodworth, Mark, illus. The Amusement Park Mystery. 2010. (Boxcar Children Graphic Novels Ser.: 10). (ENG.). 32p. (J). (gr. 1-5). pap. 6.99 *(978-0-8075-0321-8(5))* Whitman, Albert & Co.

Jessell, Tim, illus. The Boxcar Children, Set. 2013. (Boxcar Children Mysteries Ser.). (ENG.). 538p. (J). (gr. 1-5). 45.00 *(978-0-8075-0864-0(0))* Whitman, Albert & Co.

—Mystery of the Fallen Treasure. 2013. (Boxcar Children Mysteries Ser.: 132). (ENG.). 128p. (J). (gr. 1-5). 5.99 *(978-0-8075-5506-4(1))*; 15.99 *(978-0-8075-5508-8(8))* Whitman, Albert & Co.

—The Return of the Graveyard Ghost. 2013. (Boxcar Children Mysteries Ser.: 133). (ENG.). 128p. (J). (gr. 1-5). 15.99 *(978-0-8075-6935-1(6))*; 5.99 *(978-0-8075-6936-8(4))* Whitman, Albert & Co.

Papp, Robert, illus. The Amazing Mystery Show. 2010. (Boxcar Children Mysteries Ser.: 123). (ENG.). 128p. (J). (gr. 1-5). pap. 6.99 *(978-0-8075-0315-7(0))*;No. 123. 14.99 *(978-0-8075-0314-0(2))* Whitman, Albert & Co.

—The Box That Watch Found. 2007. (Boxcar Children Mysteries Ser.: 113). (ENG.). 128p. (J). (gr. 1-5). lib. bdg. 14.99 *(978-0-8075-5568-2(1))*; per. 5.99 *(978-0-8075-5569-9(X))* Whitman, Albert & Co.

—The Cupcake Caper. 2010. (Boxcar Children Mysteries Ser.: 125). (ENG.). 128p. (J). (gr. 1-5). 14.99 *(978-0-8075-1373-6(3))*;No. 125. pap. 5.99 *(978-0-8075-1374-3(1))* Whitman, Albert & Co.

—The Ghost in the First Row, Vol. 112. 2007. (Boxcar Children Mysteries Ser.: 112). (ENG.). 128p. (J). (gr. 1-5). per. 5.99 *(978-0-8075-5567-5(3))* Whitman, Albert & Co.

—The Great Detective Race. 2008. (Boxcar Children Mysteries Ser.: 115). (ENG.). 128p. (J). (gr. 1-5). 14.99 *(978-0-8075-5573-6(8))* Whitman, Albert & Co.

—The Great Detective Race. 2008. (Boxcar Children Mysteries Ser.: 115). (ENG.). 128p. (J). (gr. 1-5). pap. 5.99 *(978-0-8075-5574-3(6))* Whitman, Albert & Co.

—The Seattle Puzzle. 2007. (Boxcar Children Mysteries Ser.: 111). (ENG.). 128p. (J). (gr. 1-5). lib. bdg. 14.99 *(978-0-8075-5560-6(6))*; per. 5.99 *(978-0-8075-5561-3(4))* Whitman, Albert & Co.

—The Secret of the Mask. 2007. (Boxcar Children Mysteries Ser.: 110). (ENG.). 128p. (J). (gr. 1-5). lib. bdg. 14.99 *(978-0-8075-5564-4(9))*; per. 5.99 *(978-0-8075-5565-1(7))* Whitman, Albert & Co.

—Spooktacular Special. 2013. (Boxcar Children Mysteries Ser.). (ENG.). 400p. (J). (gr. 1-5). 9.99 *(978-0-8075-7605-2(0))* Whitman, Albert & Co.

—The Spy Game. 2009. (Boxcar Children Mysteries Ser.: 118). (ENG.). 128p. (J). (gr. 1-5). pap. 5.99 *(978-0-8075-7604-5(2))* Whitman, Albert & Co.

—The Spy in the Bleachers. 2010. (Boxcar Children Mysteries Ser.: 122). (ENG.). 128p. (J). (gr. 1-5). 14.99 *(978-0-8075-7606-9(9))*;No. 122. pap. 6.99 *(978-0-8075-7607-6(7))* Whitman, Albert & Co.

Papp, Robert L., illus. The Dog-Gone Mystery. 2009. (Boxcar Children Mysteries Ser.: 119). (ENG.). 128p. (J). (gr. 1-5). pap. 5.99 *(978-0-8075-1657-7(0))* Whitman, Albert & Co.

—The Spy Game. 2009. (Boxcar Children Mysteries Ser.: 118). (ENG.). 128p. (J). (gr. 1-5). 14.99 *(978-0-8075-7603-8(4))* Whitman, Albert & Co.

—Superstar Watch. 2009. (Boxcar Children Mysteries Ser.: 121). (ENG.). 128p. (J). (gr. 1-5). pap. 5.99 *(978-0-8075-7668-7(9))*; lib. bdg. 14.99 *(978-0-8075-7667-0(0))* Whitman, Albert & Co.

—The Vampire Mystery. 2009. (Boxcar Children Mysteries Ser.: 120). (ENG.). 128p. (J). (gr. 1-5). pap. 5.99 *(978-0-8075-8461-3(4))*; lib. bdg. 14.99 *(978-0-8075-8460-6(6))* Whitman, Albert & Co.

Soileau, Hodges, illus. The Great Shark Mystery. 2003. (Boxcar Children Mystery & Activities Specials Ser.: 20). (ENG.). 160p. (J). (gr. 1-5). pap. 6.99 *(978-0-8075-5532-3(0))* Whitman, Albert & Co.

VanArsdale, Anthony, illus. The Sleepy Hollow Mystery. 2015. 111p. (J). ***(978-1-4806-9407-1(X))*** Whitman, Albert & Co.

Warner, Gertrude Chandler. The Boxcar Children. Date not set. (Boxcar Children Ser.: No. 1). (J). (gr. 2-5). lib. bdg. 18.95 *(978-0-8488-1712-1(5))* Amereon Ltd.

—The Boxcar Children. (Boxcar Children Ser.: No. 1). 154p. (J). (gr. 2-5). pap. 3.95 *(978-0-8072-1447-3(7)*, Listening Library) Random Hse. Audio Publishing Group.

—Boxcar Children Graphic Novels, 6 vols., Set 2. Incl. Amusement Park Mystery. Denton, Shannon Eric. Dubisch, Mike, illus. 28.50 *(978-1-60270-718-4(9))*; Castle Mystery. Denton, Shannon Eric. Dubisch, Mike, illus. 28.50 *(978-1-60270-720-7(0))*; Haunted Cabin Mystery. Bloodworth, Mark, illus. 28.50 *(978-1-60270-717-7(0))*; Pizza Mystery. Worley, Rob M. Dubisch, Mike, illus. 28.50 *(978-1-60270-719-1(7))*; Snowbound Mystery. Dubisch, Mike, illus. 28.50 *(978-1-60270-715-3(4))*; Tree House Mystery. Long, Christopher E. Bloodworth, Mark, illus. 28.50 *(978-1-60270-716-0(2))*; (J). (gr. 2-5). (Boxcar Children Graphic Novels Ser.). 32p. 2010. 171.00 *(978-1-60270-714-6(6)*, Graphic Planet- Fiction) ABDO Publishing Co.

—Boxcar Children Graphic Novels, 6 vols., Set 3. Dunn, Ben, illus. Incl. Bk. 13. Woodshed Mystery. Dunn, Joeming. 28.50 *(978-1-61641-121-3(X))*; Bk. 14. Lighthouse Mystery. Dunn, Joeming. 28.50 *(978-1-61641-122-0(8))*; Bk. 15. Mountain Top Mystery. Dunn, Joeming. 28.50 *(978-1-61641-123-7(6))*; Bk. 16. Houseboat Mystery. Dunn, Joeming W., illus. & adapted by. 28.50 *(978-1-61641-124-4(4))*; Bk. 17. Bicycle Mystery. Dunn, Joeming W., illus. & adapted by. 28.50 *(978-1-61641-125-1(2))*; Bk. 18. Mystery in the Sand. Dunn, Joeming. 28.50 *(978-1-61641-126-8(0))*; (J). (gr. 2-5). (Boxcar Children Graphic Novels Ser.). (Illus.). 32p. 2011. 171.00 *(978-1-61641-120-6(1)*, Graphic Planet- Fiction) ABDO Publishing Co.

—The Boxcar Children Guide to Adventure: A How-To for Mystery Solving, Make-It-Yourself Projects, & More. 2014. (Boxcar Children Mysteries Ser.). (ENG.). 144p. (J). (gr. 1-5). 12.99 *(978-0-8075-0905-0(1))* Whitman, Albert & Co.

—The Lighthouse Mystery. (Boxcar Children Ser.: No. 8). 147p. (J). (gr. 2-5). pap. 3.95 *(978-0-8072-1474-9(4)*, Listening Library) Random Hse. Audio Publishing Group.

—Mike's Mystery. (Boxcar Children Ser.: No. 5). 128p. (J). (gr. 2-5). pap. 3.95 *(978-0-8072-1462-6(0)*, Listening Library) Random Hse. Audio Publishing Group.

—Mystery Ranch. (Boxcar Children Ser.: No. 4). 128p. (J). (gr. 2-5). pap. 3.95 *(978-0-8072-1450-3(7)*, Listening Library) Random Hse. Audio Publishing Group.

—Snowbound Mystery. Dubisch, Mike, illus. 2009. (Boxcar Children Graphic Novels Ser.: 7). (ENG.). 32p. (J). (gr. 1-5). pap. 6.99 *(978-0-8075-7515-4(1))* Whitman, Albert & Co.

—The Yellow House Mystery. (Boxcar Children Ser.: No. 3). 191p. (J). (gr. 2-5). pap. 3.95 *(978-0-8072-1449-7(3)*, Listening Library) Random Hse. Audio Publishing Group.

—The Yellow House Mystery, No. 3. Dubisch, Mike, illus. 2009. (Boxcar Children Graphic Novels Ser.). (ENG.). 32p. (J). (gr. 2-5). 6.99 *(978-0-8075-2869-3(2))* Whitman, Albert & Co.

Warner, Gertrude Chandler, creator. The Garden Thief. 2012. (Boxcar Children Mysteries Ser.: 130). (ENG., Illus.). 128p. (J). (gr. 1-5). 5.99 *(978-0-8075-2752-8(1))* Whitman, Albert & Co.

—The Garden Thief. 2012. (Boxcar Children Mysteries Ser.: 130). (ENG., Illus.). 128p. (J). (gr. 1-5). 15.99 *(978-0-8075-2751-1(3))* Whitman, Albert & Co.

—The Ghost at the Drive-In Movie. 2008. (Boxcar Children Mysteries Ser.: 116). (ENG.). 128p. (J). (gr. 1-5). 14.99 *(978-0-8075-5577-4(0))* Whitman, Albert & Co.

—The Ghost-Hunting Special. 2015. (Boxcar Children Mysteries Ser.). (ENG.). 352p. (J). (gr. 1-5). 9.99 *(978-0-8075-2846-4(3))* Whitman, Albert & Co.

—The Haunted Legends Special. 2016. (Boxcar Children Mysteries Ser.). (ENG.). 368p. (J). (gr. 1-5). 9.99 *(978-0-8075-0724-7(5))* Whitman, Albert & Co.

—The Legend of the Irish Castle. 2016. (Boxcar Children Mysteries Ser.: 142). (ENG., Illus.). 128p. (J). (gr. 1-5). 15.99 *(978-0-8075-0705-6(9))* Whitman, Albert & Co.

—The Mystery at the Calgary Stampede. 2015. (Boxcar Children Mysteries Ser.: 140). (ENG.). 128p. (J). (gr. 1-5). 15.99 *(978-0-8075-2840-2(4))* Whitman, Albert & Co.

—The Sleepy Hollow Mystery. 2015. (Boxcar Children Mysteries Ser.: 141). (ENG., Illus.). 128p. (J). (gr. 1-5). 15.99 *(978-0-8075-2843-3(9))* Whitman, Albert & Co.

—The Tattletale Mystery. 2003. (Boxcar Children Mysteries Ser.: 92). (ENG., Illus.). 128p. (J). (gr. 1-5). pap. 5.99 *(978-0-8075-5526-2(6))* Whitman, Albert & Co.

BOXERS (SPORTS)

Ali: An American Champion. 2014. (ENG., Illus.). 96p. (J). (gr. 3-7). 17.99 *(978-1-4814-0141-8(6)*, Simon & Schuster Bks. For Young Readers) Simon & Schuster Bks. For Young Readers.

Apps, Roy. Nicola Adams. King, Chris, illus. 2017. (EDGE - Dream to Win Ser.). (ENG.). 48p. (J). (gr. 2-4). pap. 9.99 *(978-1-4451-4136-7(1)*, Franklin Watts) Hachette Children's Group GBR. Dist: Hachette Bk. Group.

Bolden, Tonya. The Champ. Christie, R. Gregory, illus. 2007. (gr. k-3). 17.00 *(978-0-7569-7940-9(4))* Perfection Learning Corp.

—The Champ: The Story of Muhammad Ali. Christie, R. Gregory, illus. 2007. (ENG.). 40p. (J). (gr. 1-4). pap. 7.99 *(978-0-440-41782-8(1)*, Dragonfly Bks.) Random Hse. Children's Bks.

Brickweg, Jason. Chris Jericho. 2013. (Pro Wrestling Champions Ser.). (ENG., Illus.). 24p. (J). (gr. 3-7). lib. bdg. 25.95 *(978-1-60014-902-3(2)*, Torque Bks.) Bellwether Media.

—Santino Marella. 2013. (Pro Wrestling Champions Ser.). (ENG., Illus.). 24p. (J). (gr. 3-7). lib. bdg. 25.95 *(978-1-60014-904-7(9)*, Torque Bks.) Bellwether Media.

—Zack Ryder. 2013. (Pro Wrestling Champions Ser.). (ENG., Illus.). 24p. (J). (gr. 3-7). lib. bdg. 25.95 *(978-1-60014-905-4(7)*, Torque Bks.) Bellwether Media.

Brignall, Richard. Fearless: The Story of George Chuvalo, Canada's Greatest Boxer, 1 vol. 2009. (Lorimer Recordbooks Ser.). (ENG., Illus.). 160p. (YA). (gr. 7-12). 16.95 *(978-1-55277-436-6(8)*, 9781552774366); 9.95 *(978-1-55277-435-9(X)*, 9781552774359) Lorimer, James & Co., Ltd., Pubs. CAN. Dist: Casemate Pubs. & Bk. Distributors, LLC.

Brown, Jonatha A. Muhammad Ali. 2005. (People We Should Know Ser.). (Illus.). 24p. (J). (gr. 1-4). lib. bdg. 22.00 *(978-0-8368-4743-7(1)*, Weekly Reader Leveled Readers) Stevens, Gareth Publishing LLLP.

Buckley, James, Jr. Muhammad Ali. 2004. (Trailblazers of the Modern World Ser.). (Illus.). 48p. (J). (gr. 5-12). pap. 14.05 *(978-0-8368-5256-1(7))*; lib. bdg. 31.00 *(978-0-8368-5096-3(3))* Stevens, Gareth Publishing LLLP. (Gareth Stevens Secondary Library).

—Who Is Muhammad Ali? Marchesi, Stephen & Harrison, Nancy, illus. 2014. (Who Was? Ser.). (ENG.). 112p. (J). (gr. 3-7). 5.99 *(978-0-448-47955-2(9)*, Grosset & Dunlap) Penguin Young Readers Group.

Buckley, James. Who Is Muhammad Ali? 2014. (Who Was... ? Ser.). lib. bdg. 16.00 *(978-0-606-35696-1(7))* Turtleback Bks.

Burgan, Michael. Muhammad Ali: American Champion, 1 vol. Bascle, Brian, illus. 2008. (Graphic Biographies Ser.). (ENG.). 32p. (gr. 3-4). per. 8.10 *(978-1-4296-1771-0(3)*, Graphic Library) Capstone Press of Coughlan Cos.

De La Hoya, Oscar. Super Oscar. Montejo, Andrea, tr. Kopelke, Lisa, illus. 2012. (ENG & SPA.). 32p. (J). (gr. -1-3). 7.99 *(978-1-4169-0612-4(6)*, Simon & Schuster Bks. For Young Readers) Simon & Schuster Bks. For Young Readers.

De La Hoya, Oscar & Shulman, Mark. Super Oscar. 2012. (SPA & ENG.). lib. bdg. 17.20 *(978-0-606-23671-3(6)*, Turtleback) Turtleback Bks.

De la Peña, Matt. A Nation's Hope: The Story of Boxing Legend Joe Louis. Nelson, Kadir, illus. 2011. (ENG.). 40p. (J). (gr. 1-3). 17.99 *(978-0-8037-3167-7(1)*, Dial Bks) Penguin Young Readers Group.

—A Nation's Hope: The Story of Boxing Legend Joe Louis. 2013. lib. bdg. 19.65 *(978-0-606-34169-1(2)*, Turtleback) Turtleback Bks.

Doeden, Matt. Muhammad Ali: The Greatest. 2017. (Gateway Biographies Ser.). (ENG.). 48p. (J). (gr. 4-8). 12.99 ***(978-1-5124-4433-9(2)***, Lerner Pubns.); 39.99 ***(978-1-5124-4434-6(0)***, Lerner Pubns.); (Illus.). 26.65 *(978-1-5124-4431-5(6))*; 39.99 ***(978-1-5124-4432-2(4)***, Lerner Pubns.) Lerner Publishing Group.

Down, Susan. Muhammad Ali: The Greatest. 2013. (ENG., Illus.). 112p. (J). pap. *(978-0-7787-1043-1(2))* Crabtree Publishing Co.

Down, Susan Brophy. Muhammad Ali: The Greatest. 2013. (ENG., Illus.). 112p. (J). *(978-0-7787-1034-9(3))* Crabtree Publishing Co.

Feinstein, Stephen. Muhammad Ali. 2007. (African-American Heroes Ser.). (Illus.). 24p. (J). (gr. 1-3). lib. bdg. 22.60 *(978-0-7660-2763-3(5)*, Enslow Elementary) Enslow Pubs., Inc.

Fishman, Jon M. Manny Pacquiao. 2016. (Amazing Athletes Ser.). (ENG., Illus.). 32p. (J). (gr. 2-5). 26.65 *(978-1-4677-9387-2(6))* Lerner Publishing Group.

Frederick, Shane. Boxing. 2012. (Illus.). 48p. (J). 35.65 *(978-1-60818-209-1(6)*, Creative Education) Creative Co., The.

Gagne, Tammy. What It's Like to Be Oscar de la Hoya. 2012. (Illus.). 32p. (J). lib. bdg. 25.70 *(978-1-61228-322-7(5))* Mitchell Lane Pubs., Inc.

Gifford, Clive. Amir Khan: Champion Boxer. 2017. (Inspirational Lives Ser.). (ENG., Illus.). 32p. (J). (gr. 4-6). pap. 12.99 ***(978-1-5263-0126-0(1)***, Wayland) Hachette Children's Group GBR. Dist: Hachette Bk. Group.

Golus, Carrie. Muhammad Ali. 2006. (Sports Heroes & Legends Ser.). (ENG., Illus.). 120p. (J). (gr. 5-12). lib. bdg. 30.60 *(978-0-8225-5960-3(9))* Lerner Publishing Group.

Gordon, Nick. Dolph Ziggler. 2012. (Pro Wrestling Champions Ser.). (ENG., Illus.). 24p. (J). (gr. 3-7). lib. bdg. 25.95 *(978-1-60014-783-8(6)*, Torque Bks.) Bellwether Media.

Graham, Tim. Muhammad Ali: Conscientious Objector. 2016. (Game-Changing Athletes Ser.). (ENG., Illus.). 112p. (J). (gr. 9-9). lib. bdg. 42.79 *(978-1-5026-1051-5(5))* Cavendish Square Publishing.

Graubart, Norman D. Laila Ali. 2015. (Exceptional African Americans Ser.). (ENG., Illus.). 24p. (J). (gr. 3-4). 22.60 *(978-0-7660-6656-4(8))* Enslow Pubs., Inc.

Gregory, Josh. Muhammad Ali. 2017. (True Book(tm), A — Biographies Ser.). (ENG., Illus.). 48p. (J). lib. bdg. 31.00 *(978-0-531-22170-9(9)*, Children's Pr.) Scholastic Library Publishing.

Healy, Nick. Muhammad Ali. 2005. (Genius Ser.). (Illus.). 48p. (J). (gr. 5-9). lib. bdg. 21.95 *(978-1-58341-333-3(2)*, Creative Education) Creative Co., The.

Hord, Colleen. Muhammad Ali. 2013. (ENG., Illus.). 24p. (J). (gr. k-3). pap. 8.95 *(978-1-61810-285-0(0))* Rourke Educational Media.

Horn, Geoffrey M. Laila Ali. 2006. (Today's Superstars). (Illus.). 32p. (gr. 5-8). lib. bdg. 31.95 *(978-0-8368-6181-5(7))* Stevens, Gareth Publishing LLLP.

Jordan, Denise M. Muhammad Ali: Meet the Champion. 2003. (Meeting Famous People Ser.). (Illus.). 32p. (J). lib. bdg. 22.60 *(978-0-7660-2272-0(2))* Enslow Pubs., Inc.

Kent, Daniel T. Muhammad Ali & Laila Ali. 2004. (Famous Families Ser.). (Illus.). 48p. (J). lib. bdg. 29.25 *(978-1-4042-0261-0(7))* Rosen Publishing Group, Inc., The.

Kirkpatrick, Rob. Evander Holyfield: Campeón de los Pesos Pesados (Heavyweight Champion) 2009. (Grandes Idolos (Hot Shots) Ser.). (SPA.). 24p. (gr. 1-1). 42.50 *(978-1-61512-736-8(4)*, Editorial Buenas Letras) Rosen Publishing Group, Inc., The.

—Evander Holyfield: Heavyweight Champion / Campeón de los Pesos Pesados. 2009. (Hot Shots/Grandes idolos Ser.). (ENG & SPA.). 24p. (gr. 1-1). 42.50 *(978-1-61513-414-4(X)*, Editorial Buenas Letras) Rosen Publishing Group, Inc., The.

—Oscar de la Hoya: Boxeador de Medalla de Oro (Gold-Medal Boxer) 2009. (Grandes Idolos (Hot Shots) Ser.). (SPA.). 24p. (gr. 1-1). 42.50 *(978-1-61512-738-2(0)*, Editorial Buenas Letras) Rosen Publishing Group, Inc., The.

—Oscar de la Hoya: Gold-Medal Boxer / Boxeador de Medalla de Oro. 2009. (Hot Shots/Grandes idolos Ser.). (ENG & SPA.). 24p. (gr. 1-1). 42.50 *(978-1-61513-416-8(6)*, Editorial Buenas Letras) Rosen Publishing Group, Inc., The.

—Oscar de la Hoya, Gold Medal Boxer/Boxeador de Medalla de Oro. De Leon, Mauricio Velzaquez, tr. 2008. (Reading Power Ser.). (ENG., Illus.). 24p. (gr. 1-6). per. 8.85 *(978-0-8239-6211-2(3))* Rosen Publishing Group, Inc., The.

Latimer, Clay. Muhammad Ali. 2009. (Journey to Freedom Ser.). (ENG., Illus.). 32p. (J). (gr. 4-7). 29.93 *(978-1-60253-132-1(3)*, 200398) Child's World, Inc., The.

Mattern, Joanne. Muhammad Ali: The Greatest. 2017. (Rookie Biographies(tm) Ser.). (ENG., Illus.). 32p. (J). lib. bdg. 25.00 *(978-0-531-22117-4(2)*, Children's Pr.) Scholastic Library Publishing.

Micklos, John. Muhammad Ali: "I Am the Greatest" 2010. (American Rebels Ser.). 160p. (J). (gr. 7-12). 35.94 *(978-0-7660-3381-8(3))* Enslow Pubs., Inc.

Myers, Walter Dean. Muhammad Ali: The People's Champion. Delinois, Alix, illus. 40p. (J). (gr. -1-3). 2016. pap. 6.99 *(978-0-06-443718-9(3)*, Amistad) 2009. (ENG.). 16.99 *(978-0-06-029131-0(1)*, Collins) HarperCollins Pubs.

—Muhammad Ali: The People's Champion. 2016. (J). lib. bdg. 17.20 *(978-0-606-38179-6(1))* Turtleback Bks.

Owens, Thomas. Muhammad Ali: Boxing Champ & Role Model, 1 vol. 2011. (Legendary Athletes Ser.). (ENG., Illus.). 112p. (YA). (gr. 7-12). 34.22 *(978-1-61714-752-4(4)*, 1324107) ABDO Publishing Co.

Peters, Gregory N. Muhammad Ali Boxing Legend, 1 vol. 2014. (Sports & Recreation Ser.). (ENG., Illus.). 48p. (gr. 4-12). 31.99 *(978-1-4765-8439-3(7))* Capstone Press of Coughlan Cos.

Schulman, Arlene. Muhammad Ali. (Just the Facts Biographies Ser.). (Illus.). (J). (gr. 6-12). 2005. 112p. 27.93 *(978-0-8225-2448-9(1))* 2003. 128p. pap. 7.95 *(978-0-8225-9693-6(8)*, Lerner Pubns.) Lerner Publishing Group.

Shange, Ntozake. Float Like a Butterfly. Rodriguez, Edel, illus. 2017. (ENG.). 40p. (J). (gr. -1-3). 17.99 ***(978-1-368-00827-3(5)***, Jump at the Sun) Hyperion Bks. for Children.

Shone, Rob. Muhammad Ali: The Life of a Boxing Hero. Spender, Nick, illus. 2007. (Graphic Nonfiction Biographies Ser.). (ENG.). 48p. (J). (gr. 4-7). lib. bdg. 31.95 *(978-1-4042-0856-8(9))*; (gr. 5-8). pap. 14.05 *(978-1-4042-0919-0(0))* Rosen Publishing Group, Inc., The.

Sjonger, Rebecca. Knockout! How "Little Giant" Tommy Burns Became the World Heavyweight Champion, 1 vol. 2008. (Lorimer Recordbooks Ser.). (ENG., Illus.). 136p. (J). (gr. 2-12). 16.95 *(978-1-55277-004-7(4)*, 9781552770047); (gr. 7-12). 9.95 *(978-1-55277-003-0(6)*, 9781552770030) Lorimer, James & Co., Ltd., Pubs. CAN. Dist: Casemate Pubs. & Bk. Distributors, LLC.

Smith, Charles R., Jr. Black Jack: The Ballad of Jack Johnson. Evans, Shane W., illus. 2010. (ENG.). 40p. (J). (gr. -1-1). 16.99 *(978-1-59643-473-8(2)*, 9781596434738) Roaring Brook Pr.

—Twelve Rounds to Glory: The Story of Muhammad Ali. Collier, Bryan, illus. 2010. (ENG.). 80p. (J). (gr. 5). pap. 10.99 *(978-0-7636-5002-5(1))* Candlewick Pr.

Spray, John. Next Round: A Young Athlete's Journey to Gold. 2016. (ENG., Illus.). 112p. (J). (gr. 5-9). pap. 9.95 *(978-1-77278-001-7(4))* Pajama Pr. CAN. Dist: Ingram Publisher Services.

Stone, Adam. John Cena. 2011. (Pro Wrestling Champions Ser.). (ENG., Illus.). 24p. (J). (gr. 3-7). lib. bdg. 25.95 (978-1-60014-636-7(8), Torque Bks.) Bellwether Media.

Stout, Glenn & Christopher, Matt. Muhammad Ali: Legends in Sports. 2005. (ENG., Illus.). 128p. (J). (gr. 5-8). pap. 15.99 (978-0-316-10843-0(X)) Little, Brown Bks. for Young Readers.

Sullivan, George. Knockout! A Photobiography of Boxer Joe Louis. 2008. (Photobiographies Ser.). (ENG., Illus.). 64p. (J). (gr. 5). 17.95 (978-1-4263-0328-9(9)); lib. bdg. 27.90 (978-1-4263-0329-6(7)) National Geographic Society. (National Geographic Children's Bks.).

Swan, Bill. Real Justice: Jailed for Life for Being Black: The Story of Rubin Hurricane Carter, 1 vol. 2014. (Lorimer Real Justice Ser.). (ENG., Illus.). 144p. (YA). (gr. 8-12). pap. 12.95 (978-1-4594-0665-0(6), 9781459406650) Lorimer, James & Co., Ltd., Pubs. CAN. Dist: Casemate Pubs. & Bk. Distributors, LLC.

Wilmore, Kathy. Muhammad Ali: With a Discussion of Honesty. 2003. (Values in Action Ser.). (J). (978-1-59203-065-1(3)) Learning Challenge, Inc.

Wilson, Hoyt R. Joe Louis: The Brown Bomber. 2005. (Alabama Roots Biography Ser.). (Illus.). 100p. (J). pap. (978-1-59421-013-6(6)) Seacoast Publishing, Inc.

BOXING

De la Peña, Matt. A Nation's Hope: The Story of Boxing Legend Joe Louis. Nelson, Kadir, illus. 2013. (ENG.). 40p. (J). (gr. 1-3). 8.99 (978-0-14-751061-7(9), Puffin Books) Penguin Young Readers Group.

Di Marino, Stefano. A Complete Guide to Kickboxing. 2017. (Mastering Martial Arts Ser.). 128p. (J). (gr. 6-6). lib. bdg. 37.27 **(978-0-7660-8543-5(0))** Enslow Pubs., Inc.

Doeden, Matt. Combat Sports. 2015. (Summer Olympic Sports Ser.). (ENG., Illus.). 32p. (J). (gr. 2-4). 19.95 (978-1-60753-807-3(5)) Amicus Publishing.

Ford, Carin T. Muhammad Ali: I Am the Greatest. 2006. (African-American Biography Library). (Illus.). 128p. (J). (gr. 6-12). lib. bdg. 33.27 (978-0-7660-2460-1(1)) Enslow Pubs., Inc.

Frederick, Shane. Boxing. 2012. (Illus.). 48p. (J). 35.65 (978-1-60818-209-1(6), Creative Education) Creative Co., The.

Gifford, Clive. Kickboxing. 2010. (Combat Sports Ser.). 32p. (J). (gr. 2-5). lib. bdg. 28.50 (978-1-59771-276-7(0)) Sea-To-Sea Pubns.

Graham, Tim. Muhammad Ali: Conscientious Objector. 2016. (Game-Changing Athletes Ser.). (ENG., Illus.). 112p. (J). (gr. 9-9). lib. bdg. 42.79 (978-1-5026-1051-5(5)) Cavendish Square Publishing.

Graubart, Norman D. Laila Ali: Champion Boxer. 2015. (Exceptional African Americans Ser.). (ENG.). 24p. (J). (gr. 3-4). pap. 9.35 (978-0-7660-7130-8(8)) Enslow Pubs., Inc.

Hanzie, Christopher. Punch: All about Boxing Intermediate Book with Online Access, 1 vol. 2014. (ENG., Illus.). 28p. pap. 9.50 (978-1-107-67727-2(0)) Cambridge Univ. Pr.

Mason, Paul. Boxing. 2010. (Combat Sports Ser.). 32p. (J). (gr. 2-5). lib. bdg. 28.50 (978-1-59771-273-6(6)) Sea-To-Sea Pubns.

Page, Jason. Martial Arts, Boxing, & Other Combat Sports: Fencing, Judo, Wrestling, Taekwondo, & a Whole Lot More. 2008. (Olympic Sports Ser.). (ENG., Illus.). 32p. (J). (gr. 3-7). pap. (978-0-7787-4033-9(1)); lib. bdg. (978-0-7787-4016-2(1)) Crabtree Publishing Co.

Polydoros, Lori, et al. The Best of the Best. 2012. (Best of the Best Ser.). (ENG.). 32p. (gr. 1-2). lib. bdg. 53.30 (978-1-4296-9135-2(2), Blazers) Capstone Press of Coughlan Cos.

Smith, Charles R., Jr. Black Jack: The Ballad of Jack Johnson. Evans, Shane W., illus. 2010. (ENG.). 40p. (J). (gr. -1-1). 16.99 (978-1-59643-473-8(2), 9781596434738) Roaring Brook Pr.

Weber, Terri. Oscar de la Hoya. 2004. (J). pap. (978-1-932724-31-8(1)); lib. bdg. (978-1-932724-30-1(3)) Panda Publishing, L.L.C. (Bios for Kids).

BOXING—FICTION

Acheson, A. S. Fighting Words. 2014. (Bareknuckle Ser.). 96p. (YA). (gr. 6-12). lib. bdg. 27.93 (978-1-4677-1461-7(5), Darby Creek) Lerner Publishing Group.

Barchers, Suzanne I. Top That!, 1 vol. 2011. (Targeted Phonics Ser.). (ENG., Illus.). 16p. (J). (gr. k-2). pap. 5.99 (978-1-4333-2414-7(8)) Teacher Created Materials, Inc.

Bott, Paula. Fighting el Fuego. 2013. (Av2 Audio Chapter Bks.). (ENG.). 113p. (J). (gr. 4-7). lib. bdg. 27.13 (978-1-62127-975-4(8), AV2 by Weigl) Weigl Pubs., Inc.

Brouwer, Sigmund. Unleashed, 1 vol. 2015. (Retribution Ser.). (ENG.). 168p. (YA). (gr. 8-12). pap. 9.95 (978-1-4598-0730-3(8)) Orca Bk. Pubs. USA.

Dixon, John. Phoenix Island. 2014. (ENG.). 320p. pap. 11.99 (978-1-4767-3865-9(3), Gallery Bks.) Gallery Bks.

Ellington, Kyseme Ali & Crawford, Bobby. I'mpossible: ChessLife Strategies for Children & Young Adults. 2010. 108p. pap. 32.95 (978-1-4490-6741-0(7)) AuthorHouse.

Friend, Natasha. My Life in Black & White. 2012. (ENG.). 304p. (YA). (gr. 7-18). pap. 8.99 (978-0-670-78494-3(X), Viking Books for Young Readers) Penguin Young Readers Group.

Goodman, Gabriel. Lightning's Run. 2014. (Bareknuckle Ser.). (ENG.). 104p. (YA). (gr. 6-12). pap. 7.95 (978-1-4677-2162-2(X), Darby Creek) Lerner Publishing Group.

Jimenez, Joe. Bloodline. 2016. (ENG.). 128p. (YA). (gr. 8-12). pap. 11.95 (978-1-55885-828-2(8), Piñata Books) Arte Publico Pr.

Jones, Patrick. The Gamble. 2014. (Bareknuckle Ser.). 104p. (YA). (gr. 6-12). lib. bdg. 27.93 (978-1-4677-1462-4(3), Darby Creek) Lerner Publishing Group.

Karr, Kathleen. Boxer. 2004. (ENG.). 176p. (YA). (gr. 7-12). reprint ed. pap. 12.99 (978-0-374-40886-2(6), Sunburst) Farrar, Straus & Giroux.

Lee, Fonda. Zeroboxer. 2015. (ENG.). 360p. (YA). pap. 11.99 (978-0-7387-4338-7(0), Flux) North Star Editions.

Lipsyte, Robert. The Brave. 2003. (Charlotte Zolotow Bk.). (ENG.). 240p. (J). (gr. 8-18). pap. 6.99 (978-0-06-447079-7(2)) HarperCollins Pubs.

—The Contender. 2003. (Trophy Keypoint Bks.). (ENG.). 240p. (YA). (gr. 8-18). pap. 8.99 (978-0-06-447039-1(3), HarperTeen) HarperCollins Pubs.

—The Contender. 2003. (YA). lib. bdg. 19.65 (978-0-88103-014-3(7), Turtleback) Turtleback Bks.

—Warrior Angel. 2004. 183p. (YA). 13.65 (978-0-7569-3102-5(9)) Perfection Learning Corp.

Lynch, Chris. Shadow Boxer. 2013. (ENG.). 176p. (YA). (gr. 7). 16.99 (978-1-4424-5811-6(9), Simon & Schuster Bks. For Young Readers) Simon & Schuster Bks. For Young Readers.

Mary-Todd, Jonathan. The Giant. 2014. (Bareknuckle Ser.). 104p. (YA). (gr. 6-12). lib. bdg. 27.93 (978-1-4677-1457-0(7), Darby Creek) Lerner Publishing Group.

Miller, William. Joe Louis, My Champion. Pate, Rodney S., illus. 2004. (ENG.). 32p. (J). pap. 10.95 (978-1-60060-426-3(9)) Lee & Low Bks., Inc.

—Joe Louis, My Champion, 1 vol. Pate, Rodney, tr. Pate, Rodney, illus. 2004. (ENG.). 32p. (J). 16.95 (978-1-58430-161-5(9)) Lee & Low Bks., Inc.

Nichols, Michael. Beating the Air. 2007. 176p. per. 24.95 (978-1-4241-7795-0(2)) America Star Bks.

Olshan, Matthew. The Mighty Lalouche. Blackall, Sophie, illus. 2013. (ENG.). 40p. (J). (gr. -1-3). 17.99 (978-0-375-86225-0(0), Schwartz & Wade Bks.) Random Hse. Children's Bks.

Parker, Robert B. The Boxer & the Spy. 2009. (ENG.). 240p. (YA). (gr. 9-18). pap. 8.99 (978-0-14-241439-2(5), Puffin Books) Penguin Young Readers Group.

Polak, Monique. Straight Punch, 1 vol. 2014. (ENG.). 256p. (YA). (gr. 8-12). pap. 12.95 (978-1-4598-0391-6(4)) Orca Bk. Pubs. USA.

Robert, Lipsyte. The Contender. 2014. (Trophy Keypoint Bks). (ENG.). 240p. (J). 13.24 (978-1-63245-206-1(5)) Lectorum Pubns., Inc.

Sacks, Nathan. The Big Fix. 2014. (Bareknuckle Ser.). 112p. (YA). (gr. 6-12). lib. bdg. 27.93 (978-1-4677-1459-4(3), Darby Creek) Lerner Publishing Group.

Saldana, Rene. The Whole Sky Full of Stars. 2008. (ENG.). 144p. (YA). (gr. 7-11). mass mkt. 5.99 (978-0-440-23791-4(2), Laurel Leaf) Random Hse. Children's Bks.

Sharenow, Robert. The Berlin Boxing Club. (ENG.). (YA). (gr. 8). 2012. 432p. pap. 9.99 (978-0-06-157970-7(X)) 2011. 416p. 17.99 (978-0-06-157968-4(8)) HarperCollins Pubs. (HarperTeen).

—The Berlin Boxing Club. 2012. (YA). lib. bdg. 20.85 (978-0-606-26871-4(5), Turtleback) Turtleback Bks.

Shea, John & Harmon, Michael B. A Kid from Southie. 2011. 240p. (YA). (gr. 9-18). 16.95 (978-1-934813-53-9(2)) Westside Bks.

Stofko, Michael D. A Visit from the Zoo. 2011. 32p. pap. 12.77 (978-1-4567-2968-4(3)) AuthorHouse.

Stone, Heather Duffy. Fighter's Alley. 2014. (Bareknuckle Ser.). 104p. (YA). (gr. 6-12). lib. bdg. 27.93 (978-1-4677-1460-0(7), Darby Creek) Lerner Publishing Group.

BOXING—HISTORY

History of Boxing: The Joe Louis Story. (Sports Legacy Ser.). (J). (gr. 6-10). 26.60 (978-0-8225-3330-6(8)) Lerner Publishing Group.

BOY SCOUTS

Baden-Powell, Robert. Young Knights of the Empire. 2006. pap. (978-1-4065-0430-9(0)) Dodo Pr.

Rakes, Jerry D. Becoming an Eagle Scout: A Simplified, Step by Step Guideline for the Life Scout?S Eagle Project. 2007. 60p. per. 10.95 (978-1-4327-0360-8(9)) Outskirts Pr., Inc.

BOY SCOUTS—FICTION

Archibald Lee Fletcher. Boy Scouts on a Long Hike: Or to the Rescue in the Black Water Swamps. 2007. (ENG.). 120p. per. 18.99 (978-1-4346-3906-6(1)); 124p. per. 19.99 (978-1-4346-3907-3(X)) Creative Media Partners, LLC.

Bennett, Richard. Everything I Need to Know I Learned in Boy Scouts. 2011. 180p. pap. 15.95 (978-1-4357-6618-1(0)) Lulu Pr., Inc.

Blaine, John. Boy Scouts in Russia. 2006. 25.95 (978-1-4218-2968-5(1)); pap. 10.95 (978-1-4218-3068-1(X)) 1st World Publishing, Inc.

—The Boy Scouts on a Submarine. 2007. 112p. pap. 18.99 (978-1-4346-3960-8(6)) Creative Media Partners, LLC.

—Boy Scouts on A Submarine. 2006. 25.95 (978-1-4218-2969-2(X)); pap. 10.95 (978-1-4218-3069-8(8)) 1st World Publishing, Inc.

—The Boy Scouts on a Submarine. l.t. ed. 2007. 124p. pap. 19.99 (978-1-4346-3961-5(4)) Creative Media Partners, LLC.

Brown, Sam. Herbert: I Am - I Can. 2009. (Illus.). 48p. pap. 10.95 (978-1-4327-4842-5(4)) Outskirts Pr., Inc.

Carter, Herbert. The Boy Scouts' First Camp Fire. 2007. 124p. per. (978-1-4068-4409-2(8)) Echo Library.

—The Boy Scouts' First Camp Fire: Or Scouting with the Silver Fox Patrol. 2007. (ENG.). 176p. pap. 19.99 (978-1-4346-6046-6(X)); 190p. pap. 21.99 (978-1-4346-6047-3(8)) Creative Media Partners, LLC.

—The Boy Scouts on Sturgeon Island. 2007. pap. (978-1-4065-1300-4(8)) Dodo Pr.

—The Boy Scouts on Sturgeon Island. 2004. reprint ed. pap. 21.95 (978-1-4191-5507-9(5)); pap. 1.99 (978-1-4192-5507-6(X)) Kessinger Publishing, LLC.

—The Boy Scouts on Sturgeon Island or Marooned among the Game-Fish Poachers. 2007. 124p. per. (978-1-4068-4410-8(1)) Echo Library.

—The Boy Scouts on the Trail or Scouting. 2005. pap. 27.95 (978-1-885529-56-5(2)) Stevens Publishing.

Davis, Richard. The Boy Scout & Other Stories for Boys. 2005. pap. 30.95 (978-1-885529-45-9(7)) Stevens Publishing.

de Groot, Bob. Clifton Vol. 6: Kidnapping. 2009. (Clifton Ser.: 6). (ENG., Illus.). 48p. (J). (gr. 3-17). pap. 11.95 (978-1-905460-87-8(2)) CineBook GBR. Dist: National Bk. Network.

Douglas, Alan. Afloat: Or Adventures on Watery Trails. 2007. 120p. pap. 18.99 (978-1-4346-6016-9(8)); (ENG.). 134p. pap. 19.99 (978-1-4346-6017-6(6)) Creative Media Partners, LLC.

Drake, Robert L. The Boy Scouts of the Eagle Patrol. 2007. (ENG.). 150p. pap. 18.99 (978-1-4264-5808-8(8)); 80p. pap. 18.99 (978-1-4264-5868-2(1)) Creative Media Partners, LLC.

—The Boy Scouts of the Eagle Patrol. 2004. reprint ed. pap. 1.99 (978-1-4192-5506-9(1)); pap. 21.95 (978-1-4191-5506-2(7)) Kessinger Publishing, LLC.

Durston, George. Boy Scouts' Victory. 2005. pap. 26.95 (978-1-885529-58-9(9)) Stevens Publishing.

Eaton, Walter Pricha. Peanut Cub Reporter: A Boy Scout's Life. 2005. pap. 28.95 (978-1-885529-74-9(0)) Stevens Publishing.

Eaton, Walter Prichard. Boy Scouts in the White Mountains: the Story of a Long Hike. Merrill, Frank T., illus. 2006. (ENG.). 316p. per. 30.95 (978-1-4286-4117-4(3)) Kessinger Publishing, LLC.

Fitzgugh, Percy Keese. Tom Slade with the Boys over There. 2007. (ENG.). 140p. pap. 18.99 (978-1-4264-9511-3(0)); 150p. pap. 19.99 (978-1-4264-9892-3(6)) Creative Media Partners, LLC.

Fitzhugh, Keese Percy. Tom Slade's Double Dare. 2007. 148p. 41.99 (978-1-4280-7506-1(2)); per. 35.99 (978-1-4280-7492-7(9)) IndyPublish.com.

Fitzhugh, Percy. Tom Slade on Mystery Trail. 2006. pap. 12.95 (978-1-55742-910-0(3)) Wildside Pr., LLC.

Fitzhugh, Percy K. Pee Wee Harris on the Trail. 2005. (Illus.). pap. 24.95 (978-1-885529-75-6(9)) Stevens Publishing.

—Roy Blakeley on the Mohawk Trail. 2005. (Illus.). pap. 24.95 (978-1-885529-76-3(7)) Stevens Publishing.

—Tom Slade Boy Scout of the Moving Pictur. 2005. pap. 26.95 (978-1-885529-85-5(6)) Stevens Publishing.

—Tom Slade on Mystery Trail. 2005. (Illus.). pap. 24.95 (978-1-885529-88-6(0)) Stevens Publishing.

—Tom Slade with the Boys over There. 2005. (Illus.). pap. 24.95 (978-1-885529-89-3(9)) Stevens Publishing.

—Tom Slade with the Flying Corps. 2005. (Illus.). pap. 27.95 (978-1-885529-87-9(2)) Stevens Publishing.

—Tom Slade's Double Dare. 2005. (Illus.). pap. 26.95 (978-1-885529-86-2(4)) Stevens Publishing.

Fitzhugh, Percy Keese. Pee-Wee Harris & Roy Blakeley's Adventures in Camp. l.t. ed. 2007. (ENG.). 282p. pap. 23.99 (978-1-4346-1532-9(4)) Creative Media Partners, LLC.

Fletcher, Archibald Lee. Boy Scouts in Northern Wilds. 2006. (ENG.). 124p. pap. 18.99 (978-1-4264-6161-3(5)); 134p. pap. 19.99 (978-1-4264-6216-0(6)) Creative Media Partners, LLC.

George Cary Eggleston. Captain Sam: The Boy Scouts of 1814. 2007. (ENG.). 124p. per. 18.99 (978-1-4346-3940-0(1)); 132p. per. 19.99 (978-1-4346-3941-7(X)) Creative Media Partners, LLC.

Groot, Bob de. Jade Vol. 5. Rodrigue, illus. 2008. (Clifton Ser.: 5). (ENG.). 48p. pap. 11.95 (978-1-905460-52-6(X)) CineBook GBR. Dist: National Bk. Network.

Herbert Carter. The Boy Scouts' First Camp Fire. 2007. 224p. per. 12.95 (978-1-4218-4548-7(2)); 27.95 (978-1-4218-4464-0(8)) 1st World Publishing, Inc. (1st World Library - Literary Society).

Heyliger, William. Jerry Hicks, Explorer. Salg, Bert, illus. 2011. 210p. 44.95 (978-1-258-08964-1(5)) Literary Licensing, LLC.

Nuttbucket, Oliver S., III. A Boy Scout's Handbook of Madcap Tales. Glover, Robert, illus. 2003. 48p. (YA). per. 7.95 (978-0-9741310-0-9(8), 0-9741310-0-8) Lost Scout Pr.

Payson, Howard. The Boy Scouts at the Canadian Border. 2005. pap. 30.95 (978-1-885529-49-7(X)) Stevens Publishing.

—The Boy Scouts at the Panama Canal. 2007. 332p. per. 19.95 (978-1-60466-006-7(6)) Capricorn Hse. Publishing.

—The Boy Scouts at the Panama Canal. 2005. pap. 30.95 (978-1-885529-44-2(9)) Stevens Publishing.

—Boy Scouts' Mountain Camp. 2005. (Illus.). pap. 28.95 (978-1-885529-54-1(6)) Stevens Publishing.

—The Boy Scouts on the Range. 2007. 324p. per. 19.95 (978-1-60466-005-0(8)) Capricorn Hse. Publishing.

—The Boy Scouts under Sealed Orders. 2005. (Illus.). pap. 30.95 (978-1-885529-57-2(0)) Stevens Publishing.

Percy Keese, Fitzhugh. Pee-Wee Harris & Roy Blakeley's Adventures in Camp. 2007. (ENG.). 262p. pap. 21.99 (978-1-4346-1438-4(7)) Creative Media Partners, LLC.

Ralphson, G. Harvey. The Boy Scout Camera Club. 2007. 108p. per. (978-1-4068-3725-4(3)) Echo Library.

—Boy Scouts in a Motor Boat or Adventures. 2005. pap. 26.95 (978-1-885529-50-3(3)) Stevens Publishing.

—Boy Scouts in a Submarine. 2007. 104p. per. (978-1-4068-3726-1(1)) Echo Library.

—Boy Scouts in an Airship. 2007. 104p. per. (978-1-4068-3727-8(X)) Echo Library.

—Boy Scouts in Death Valley. 2005. pap. 27.95 (978-1-885529-51-0(1)) Stevens Publishing.

—Boy Scouts in Mexico. 2007. 112p. (gr. 4-7). per. (978-1-4068-3728-5(8)) Echo Library.

—Boy Scouts in Mexico or on Guard with un. 2005. pap. 27.95 (978-1-885529-52-7(X)) Stevens Publishing.

—Boy Scouts in Mexico,Or on Guard with Uncle Sam. 2003. 136p. pap. 14.99 (978-1-59224-085-2(2)) Wildside Pr., LLC.

—Boy Scouts in Southern Waters. 2007. 158p. pap. 19.99 (978-1-4264-7439-2(3)); 182p. pap. 21.99 (978-1-4264-7516-0(0)) Creative Media Partners, LLC.

—Boy Scouts in Southern Waters. 2007. 128p. (gr. -1-7). per. (978-1-4068-3730-8(X)) Echo Library.

—Boy Scouts in the Philippines. 2007. 112p. per. (978-1-4068-3729-2(6)) Echo Library.

—Boy Scouts in the Philippines: Or the Key to the Treaty Box. 2007. (ENG.). 146p. pap. 18.99 (978-1-4346-3798-7(0)); 164p. pap. 21.99 (978-1-4346-3799-4(9)) Creative Media Partners, LLC.

—Boy Scouts on Motorcycles. 2007. 100p. per. (978-1-4068-3731-5(8)) Echo Library.

—Boy Scouts on the Open Plain. 2005. pap. 27.95 (978-1-885529-55-8(4)) Stevens Publishing.

Salisbury, Graham. Night of the Howling Dogs. 2009. (ENG.). 208p. (YA). (gr. 7-7). mass mkt. 6.99 (978-0-440-23839-3(0), Laurel Leaf) Random Hse. Children's Bks.

Scotton, Rob. Splat the Cat & the Hotshot. Scotton, Rob, illus. 2015. (I Can Read Level 1 Ser.). (ENG., Illus.). 32p. (J). (gr. -1-3). pap. 3.99 (978-0-06-229415-9(6)) HarperCollins Pubs.

Shaler, Robert. Boy Scouts of the Flying Squadron. 2006. pap. (978-1-4068-0464-5(9)) Echo Library.

—Boy Scouts of the Geological Survey. 2006. pap. (978-1-4068-0465-2(7)) Echo Library.

—Boy Scouts on Picket Duty. 2006. pap. (978-1-4068-0466-9(5)) Echo Library.

—The Boy Scouts with the Motion Picture P. 2005. pap. 21.95 (978-1-885529-59-6(7)) Stevens Publishing.

—Boy Scouts with the Motion Picture Playe. 2006. pap. (978-1-4068-0463-8(0)) Echo Library.

Sherman, V. T. The Call of the Beaver Patrol: Or A Break in the Glacier. 2007. (ENG.). 238p. pap. 20.99 (978-1-4346-3570-9(8)) Creative Media Partners, LLC.

—The Call of the Beaver Patrol: Or a Break in the Glacier. l.t. ed. 2007. (ENG.). 270p. pap. 23.99 (978-1-4346-3571-6(6)) Creative Media Partners, LLC.

Victor, Ralph. The Boy Scouts Patrol. rev. ed. 2006. 160p. 26.95 (978-1-4218-1806-1(X)); pap. 11.95 (978-1-4218-1906-8(6)) 1st World Publishing, Inc. (1st World Library - Literary Society).

—The Boy Scouts Patrol. 2007. 84p. per. (978-1-4068-1747-8(3)) Echo Library.

Walden, Walter. Boy Scouts Afloat. 2005. (Illus.). pap. 27.95 (978-1-885529-48-0(1)) Stevens Publishing.

Warren, George A. The Banner Boy Scouts on a Tour. 2005. pap. 30.95 (978-1-885529-38-1(4)) Stevens Publishing.

—Banner Boy Scouts or the Struggle for le. 2005. pap. 30.95 (978-1-885529-42-8(2)) Stevens Publishing.

Warren George A. Staff. The Banner Boy Scouts. rev. ed. 2006. 248p. 27.95 (978-1-4218-1729-3(2)); pap. 12.95 (978-1-4218-1829-0(9)) 1st World Publishing, Inc. (1st World Library - Literary Society).

Webster, Frank V. The Boy Scouts of Lenox: Or the Hike over Big Bear Mountain. 2007. 146p. pap. 18.99 (978-1-4346-4443-5(X)) Creative Media Partners, LLC.

BOY SCOUTS—HANDBOOKS, MANUALS, ETC.

Boy Scouts of America Staff, creator. Boy Scouts of Americ: The Official Handbook for Boys. 2007. 440p. (978-956-291-499-4(2)) Editorial Benei Noaj.

BOYCOTTS

Gitlin, Martin. The 1980 U. S. Olympic Boycott: A History Perspectives Book. 2014. (Perspectives Library). (ENG., Illus.). 32p. (J). (gr. 4-8). 28.50 (978-1-62431-663-0(8), 203216) Cherry Lake Publishing.

Mis, Melody S. Meet Rosa Parks. 2008. (Civil Rights Leaders Ser.). (Illus.). 24p. (YA). (gr. 2-5). lib. bdg. 22.60 (978-1-4042-4210-4(4)) Rosen Publishing Group, Inc., The.

BOYLE, ROBERT, 1627-1691

Allen, John. Robert Boyle. 2005. (Giants of Science Ser.). (gr. 5-7). 24.95 (978-1-4103-0354-7(3), Blackbirch Pr., Inc.) Cengage Gale.

—Robert Boyle: Father of Chemistry. 2005. (Giants of Science Ser.). (ENG., Illus.). 64p. (J). (gr. 3-7). lib. bdg. 28.35 (978-1-56711-887-2(9), Blackbirch Pr., Inc.) Cengage Gale.

Baxter, Roberta. Skeptical Chemist: The Story of Robert Boyle. 2006. (Profiles in Science Ser.). (Illus.). 128p. (gr. 6-12). lib. bdg. 27.95 (978-1-59935-025-7(4)) Reynolds, Morgan Inc.

Burling, Alexis. Robert Boyle. 2017. (Leaders of the Scientific Revolution Ser.). 112p. (gr. 12-13). 37.10 **(978-1-5081-7476-9(8)**, Rosen Young Adult) Rosen Publishing Group, Inc., The.

Gow, Mary. Robert Boyle: Pioneer of Experimental Chemistry. 2005. (Great Minds of Science Ser.). (Illus.). 128p. (J). lib. bdg. 27.94 (978-0-7660-2501-1(2)) Enslow Pubs., Inc.

BOYS

see also Boy Scouts; Youth

Ajmera, Maya. Global Baby Boys. 2014. (ENG., Illus.). 16p. (J). (— 1). bds. 6.95 (978-1-58089-440-1(2)) Charlesbridge Publishing, Inc.

Alagna, Magdalena. Everything You Need to Know about the Dangers of Binge Drinking. 2009. (Need to Know Library). 64p. (gr. 5-5). 58.50 (978-1-60854-091-4(X)) Rosen Publishing Group, Inc., The.

Allyn, Pam. Pam Allyn's Best Books for Boys: How to Engage Boys in Reading in Ways That Will Change Their Lives. 2011. (ENG.). 176p. (gr. k-8). pap. 21.99 (978-0-545-20455-2(0), Teaching Resources) Scholastic, Inc.

Aronson, Marc & Newquist, H. P. For Boys Only: The Biggest, Baddest Book Ever. Headcase Design, illus. 2007. (ENG.). 160p. (J). (gr. 5-8). 16.99 (978-0-312-37706-9(1), 9780312377069) Feiwel & Friends.

Baker, Tim & Hascall, Glenn. 3-Minute Devotions for Boys: 90 Exciting Readings for Men under Construction. 2015. (3-Minute Devotions Ser.). (ENG.). 192p. pap. 4.99 (978-1-63058-678-2(1), Barbour Bks.) Barbour Publishing, Inc.

Barber, Genise. The Tryouts. 2010. 32p. pap. 12.77 (978-1-4520-7630-0(8)) AuthorHouse.

Basen, Ryan. Got Your Back: Dealing with Friends & Enemies, 1 vol. 2010. (Essential Health: a Guy's Guide Ser.). (ENG.). 112p. (J). (gr. 6-12). lib. bdg. 35.64 (978-1-61613-540-9(9)) ABDO Publishing Co.

Beard, Daniel. The American Boy's Handy Book: Turn-of-the-Century Classic of Crafts & Activities. unabr. ed. 2003. (Dover Children's Activity Bks.). (ENG., Illus.). 464p. (J). pap. 12.95 (978-0-486-43138-3(X)) Dover Pubns., Inc.

Beard, Daniel C. American Boy's Handy Book. 2014. (ENG., Illus.). 320p. (J). (gr. -1-3). pap. 12.95 (978-0-8048-4403-1(8)) Tuttle Publishing.

Bishop, Jennie & Henson, Susan. Life Lessons from the Squire & the Scroll: Battle Plans for a Pure Heart. 2006. (Revive Our Hearts Ser.). (ENG., Illus.). 65p. pap. 9.99 (978-0-940110-67-0(9)) Life Action Inc.

Bob Gresh. It's Great to Be a Guy! 2016. (ENG., Illus.). 128p. (J). pap. 11.99 (978-0-7369-6278-0(6)) Harvest Hse. Pubs.

A Boy's Guide to Growing up. 2005. (Illus.). tchr. ed. 22.95 (978-1-55942-210-9(6)) Witcher Productions.

A Boy's Guide to Growing up - Booklet, 10 per packet. 2005. (Illus.). (J). 63.95 (978-1-55942-211-6(4)) Witcher Productions.

Boys to Men: A Christian Teen Survival Guide by Young Men Who Are Survivors. 2007. 165p. (J). (978-0-929540-59-7(X)) Publishing Designs, Inc.

Braun, Eric. The Guys' Guide to Making Every Day More Awesome, 1 vol. 2014. (Guys' Guides). (ENG.). 32p. (gr. 3-4). lib. bdg. 27.99 (978-1-4765-3924-9(3), Edge Bks.) Capstone Press of Coughlan Cos.

—The Guys' Guide to Making Life More Awesome. 2014. (ENG.). 112p. (gr. 3-4). pap. 9.95 (978-1-62370-060-7(4)) Capstone Young Readers of Coughlan Cos.

—The Guys' Guides, 1 vol. 2014. (Guys' Guides). (ENG.). 32p. (gr. 3-4). lib. bdg. 111.96 *(978-1-4765-7924-5(5)*, Edge Bks.) Capstone Press of Coughlan Cos.

Broderick, Kevin Joyce. The JipiJapa Hat. 2007. 124p. per. 12.95 *(978-0-595-45071-8(7))* iUniverse, Inc.

Clark, Travis. A Stressed-Out Guy's Guide: How to Deal. 2014. (ENG.). 64p. (J). (gr. 5-12). 15.95 *(978-1-62293-010-4(X))* Enslow Pubs., Inc.

Clark, Travis & Belfield, Annie. A Guys' Guide to Stress. 2008. (Flip-It-Over Guides to Teen Emotions Ser.). (Illus.). 128p. (J). (gr. 8-13). lib. bdg. 33.27 *(978-0-7660-2857-9(7))* Enslow Pubs., Inc.

Cleary, Beverly. Otis Spofford. Darling, Louis & Dockray, Tracy, illus. 2008. (Cleary Reissue Ser.). (ENG.). 208p. (J). (gr. 3-7). reprint ed. pap. 6.99 *(978-0-380-70919-9(8))* HarperCollins Pubs.

Countryman, Jack & Parker, Amy. God's Promises for Boys, 1 vol. 2010. (ENG.). 128p. (gr. 1-5). 12.99 *(978-1-4003-1592-5(1))* Nelson, Thomas Inc.

Coy, John. For Extreme-Sports Crazy Boys Only. 2015. (ENG., Illus.). 160p. (J). (gr. 2-7). 15.99 *(978-1-250-04944-5(X)*, 9781250049445) Feiwel & Friends.

Dixon, Dallas L. Little Boys Run. Little Boys Play. Williams, Nancy E., ed. Cappoen, Jennifer Tipton, illus. 2013. 44p. (J). pap. 12.98 *(978-1-938526-40-4(6))* Laurus Bks.

Doudna, Kelly. Boys & Girls Around the World, 1 vol. 2004. (Around the World Ser.). (ENG., Illus.). 24p. (J). (gr. k-3). lib. bdg. 24.21 *(978-1-59197-564-9(6)*, SandCastle) ABDO Publishing Co.

Dunham, Kelli. The Boy's Body Book. 4th rev. ed. 2017. (ENG.). 148p. (J). pap. 12.95 ***(978-1-60433-713-6(3)***, Applesauce Pr.) Cider Mill Pr. Bk. Pubs., LLC.

Fallon, Michael. Who Are These People? Coping with Family Dynamics, 1 vol. 2010. (Essential Health: a Guy's Guide Ser.). (ENG., Illus.). 112p. (J). (gr. 6-12). lib. bdg. 35.64 *(978-1-61613-545-4(X))* ABDO Publishing Co.

Finnis, Anne & Bond, Denis. It's a Boy/Girl Thing! The Truth... in Their Own Words. 2003. (ENG., Illus.). 144p. (J). pap. 10.95 *(978-0-09-943212-8(9)*, Red Fox) Random House Children's Books GBR. Dist: Random Hse. of Canada.

Frankel, Alona. Once upon a Potty — Boy. 2014. (Once upon a Potty Ser.). (ENG., Illus.). 24p. (J). (gr. -1 — 1). bds. 6.95 *(978-1-77085-404-8(5)*, 9781770854048) Firefly Bks., Ltd.

—Once upon a Potty - Boy. Frankel, Alona, illus. 2007. (Once upon a Potty Ser.). (ENG., Illus.). 40p. (J). (gr. -1 — 1). 7.95 *(978-1-55407-283-5(2)*, 9781554072835) Firefly Bks., Ltd.

Gallagher, Jim. A Hassled Guy's Guide: How to Deal. 2014. (ENG.). 64p. (J). (gr. 5-12). 15.95 *(978-1-62293-005-0(3))* Enslow Pubs., Inc.

Gallagher, Jim & Kavanaugh, Dorothy. A Guys' Guide to Conflict. 2008. (Flip-It-Over Guides to Teen Emotions Ser.). (Illus.). 128p. (J). (gr. 3-7). lib. bdg. 33.27 *(978-0-7660-2852-4(6))* Enslow Pubs., Inc.

George, Jim. A Boy after God's Own Heart Action Devotional. 2017. (ENG.). 160p. (J). 9.99 *(978-0-7369-6751-8(6))* Harvest Hse. Pubs.

—A Boy's Guide to Discovering His Bible. 2015. (ENG.). 144p. (J). pap. 10.99 *(978-0-7369-6254-4(9))* Harvest Hse. Pubs.

Gravelle, Karen. What's Going on down There? A Boy's Guide to Growing Up. Leighton, Robert, illus. 2017. (ENG.). 144p. (J). pap. 13.99 *(978-1-68119-361-8(2)*, 9781681193618, Bloomsbury USA Childrens) Bloomsbury Publishing USA.

Greven, Alec. How to Talk to Girls. Acedera, Kei, illus. 2008. (ENG.). 48p. (J). (gr. 1-5). 9.99 *(978-0-06-170999-9(9)*, Collins) HarperCollins Pubs.

Hascall, Glenn. Power Prayers for Boys. 2015. (ENG.). 224p. (J). pap. 7.99 *(978-1-63058-858-8(X))* Barbour Publishing, Inc.

Howat, Irene. Ten Boys Who Changed the World. 2015. (Lightkeepers Ser.). (ENG., Illus.). 160p. (J). pap. 8.99 *(978-1-85792-579-1(3)*, 09e3cfcb-1d36-4ad6-88e2-bae1faaf956b) Christian Focus Pubns. GBR. Dist: Bookmasters Distribution.

—Ten Boys Who Made a Difference. 2010. (Lightkeepers Ser.). (ENG.). 160p. (J). pap. 8.99 *(978-1-85792-775-7(3)*, 689d0fc4-ab04-447c-948f-db750a0415ae) Christian Focus Pubns. GBR. Dist: Bookmasters Distribution.

Jones, Molly. 21st-Century Education & Careers: Options & Strategies. 2011. (Young Man's Guide to Contemporary Issues Ser.). (ENG.). 104p. (YA). (gr. 9-12). lib. bdg. 34.60 *(978-1-4488-5526-1(8))* Rosen Publishing Group, Inc., The.

Kelly, Bill. You Ought to Know: A Guy's Guide to Sex. 2005. (Guys' Guides). (Illus.). 48p. (J). (gr. 5-8). lib. bdg. 29.25 *(978-0-8239-3084-5(X)*, GUYOSH) Rosen Publishing Group, Inc., The.

King, Bart & Sabatino, Chris. The Big Book of Boy Stuff, 1 vol. 2014. (ENG., Illus.). 304p. pap. 19.99 *(978-1-4236-3761-5(5))* Gibbs Smith, Publisher.

Larsen, Carolyn. Prayers for Little Boys. Turk, Caron, illus. 2008. (Prayers For... Ser.). 131p. (J). (gr. -1-3). *(978-1-86920-527-0(8))* Christian Art Pubs.

LaVoice, Patricia. Helmets & Hoses, Toes & Noses. 2006. 44p. (J). 10.99 *(978-1-59092-233-0(6))* Blue Forge Pr.

Lazurek, Michelle S. Mommy, Am I Strong? Spinks, Scott, illus. 2015. 25p. (J). pap. *(978-0-8198-4948-9(0))* Pauline Bks. & Media.

Lee, Sungju & McClelland, Susan Elizabeth. Every Falling Star: The True Story of How I Survived & Escaped North Korea. 2016. (ENG.). (J). (gr. 8-17). 336p. 16.95 *(978-1-4197-2132-8(1)*, Amulet Bks.); 320p. pap. 8.95 *(978-1-4197-2381-0(2))* Abrams, Inc.

Lessons in Responsibility for Boys: Level One. 2007. (YA). per. 18.95 *(978-0-9792446-0-5(9))* Messiah Publishing - Pearables.

Lessons in Responsibility for boys Level Two. 2007. (YA). per. 18.95 *(978-0-9792446-1-2(7))* Messiah Publishing - Pearables.

Madaras, Lynda & Madaras, Area. My Body, My Self for Boys. 2nd rev. ed. 2007. (What's Happening to My Body? Ser.). (ENG., Illus.). 128p. (J). (gr. 4-6). pap. 12.99 *(978-1-55704-767-0(7)*, William Morrow Paperbacks) HarperCollins Pubs.

Madaras, Lynda, et al. "What's Happening to My Body?" Book for Boys. 3rd rev. ed. 2007. (What's Happening to My Body? Ser.). (ENG., Illus.). 256p. (gr. 5-7). pap. 15.99 *(978-1-55704-765-6(0)*, William Morrow Paperbacks) HarperCollins Pubs.

—The "What's Happening to My Body?" Book for Boys. 3rd rev. ed. 2007. (What's Happening to My Body? Ser.). (ENG., Illus.). 256p. (gr. 7-9). 24.99 *(978-1-55704-769-4(3)*, Morrow, William & Co.) HarperCollins Pubs.

Mannion, Mary. The Boy & the Fish. Fitzgerald, Brian, illus. 2010. 52p. pap. *(978-1-907276-62-0(9))* Lapwing Pubns.

Marcovitz, Hal. An Angry Guy's Guide: How to Deal. 2014. (Guy's Guide Ser.). (ENG.). 64p. (J). (gr. 5-12). pap. 9.95 *(978-1-62293-000-5(2))* Enslow Pubs., Inc.

—A Jealous Guy's Guide: How to Deal. 2014. (ENG.). 64p. (J). (gr. 5-12). 15.95 *(978-1-62293-015-9(0))* Enslow Pubs., Inc.

—A Lonely Guy's Guide: How to Deal. 2014. (ENG.). 64p. (J). (gr. 5-12). 15.95 *(978-1-62293-025-8(8))* Enslow Pubs., Inc.

Marcovitz, Hal & Snyder, Gail. A Guys' Guide to Anger. 2008. (Flip-It-Over Guides to Teen Emotions Ser.). (Illus.). 128p. (J). (gr. 8-13). lib. bdg. 33.27 *(978-0-7660-2853-1(4))* Enslow Pubs., Inc.

—A Guys' Guide to Jealousy. 2008. (Flip-It-Over Guides to Teen Emotions Ser.). (Illus.). 128p. (J). (gr. k-5). lib. bdg. 33.27 *(978-0-7660-2854-8(2))* Enslow Pubs., Inc.

McCann, Michelle Roehm. Boys Who Rocked the World: Heroes from King Tut to Bruce Lee. Hahn, David, illus. 2012. (ENG.). 256p. (J). (gr. 3-7). 18.99 *(978-1-58270-362-6(0))*; pap. 10.99 *(978-1-58270-331-2(0))* Aladdin/Beyond Words.

Mccann, Michelle Roehm. Boys Who Rocked the World: Heroes from King Tut to Shaun White. 2012. lib. bdg. 22.10 *(978-0-606-26897-4(9)*, Turtleback) Turtleback Bks.

McCarney, Rosemary & Plan International (India) Staff. As a Boy, 1 vol. 2016. (ENG., Illus.). 24p. (J). (gr. 1-5). 18.95 *(978-1-77260-016-2(4))* Second Story Pr. CAN. Dist: Orca Bk. Pubs. USA.

Pfeffer, Wendy. Many Ways to Be a Soldier. Verstraete, Elaine, illus. 2008. (On My Own History Ser.). (ENG.). 48p. (gr. 2-4). lib. bdg. 25.26 *(978-0-8225-7279-4(6)*, Millbrook Pr.) Lerner Publishing Group.

—Many Ways to Be A Soldier. 2009. pap. 40.95 *(978-0-7613-4795-8(X))* Lerner Publishing Group.

Picone, Linda. My Changing Body. 2010. (ENG.). 150p. (J). (gr. 4-7). pap. 9.95 *(978-1-57749-181-1(5))* Taylor Trade Publishing.

Pitt, Steve. Guyness: Body & Soul, 1 vol. Murray, Steven, illus. 2005. (Lorimer Deal with It Ser.). (ENG.). 32p. (J). (gr. 4-6). pap. 12.95 *(978-1-55028-892-6(X)*, 9781550288926) Lorimer, James & Co., Ltd., Pubs. CAN. Dist: Casemate Pubs. & Bk. Distributors, LLC.

Pitt, Steve. Guyness: Deal with It Body & Soul. Murray, Steven, illus. 2017. (Lorimer Deal with It Ser.). (ENG.). 32p. (J). (gr. 4-9). lib. bdg. 22.65 ***(978-1-4594-1187-6(0)***, 9781459411876) Lorimer, James & Co., Ltd., Pubs. CAN. Dist: Casemate Pubs. & Bk. Distributors, LLC.

Plaisted, Caroline. Boy Talk. 2011. (ENG., Illus.). 48p. (J). pap. 11.95 *(978-1-926853-90-1(3))* Saunders Bk. Co. CAN. Dist: RiverStream Publishing.

Roselius, J. Chris. Surviving School: Managing School & Career Paths, 1 vol. 2010. (Essential Health: a Guy's Guide Ser.). (ENG.). 112p. (J). (gr. 6-12). lib. bdg. 35.64 *(978-1-61613-544-7(1))* ABDO Publishing Co.

Scholastic, Inc. Staff & Campbell, Guy. The Boys' Book of Survival: How to Survive Anything, Anywhere. 2009. (Best at Everything Ser.). (ENG., Illus.). 128p. (J). (gr. 3-7). 10.99 *(978-0-545-08536-6(5))* Scholastic, Inc.

Scholastic, Inc. Staff & Norton, Sally. The Girls' Book of Excellence: Even More Ways to Be the Best at Everything. 2009. (Best at Everything Ser.). (ENG.). 128p. (J). (gr. 3-7). 9.99 *(978-0-545-13409-5(9)*, Scholastic Nonfiction) Scholastic, Inc.

Scholastic, Inc. Staff & Oliver, Martin. The Boys' Book of Greatness: Even More Ways to Be the Best at Everything. 2009. (Best at Everything Ser.). (ENG.). 128p. (J). (gr. 3-7). 9.99 *(978-0-545-13408-8(0)*, Scholastic Nonfiction) Scholastic, Inc.

Scollen, C. My Big Book for Boys. 2009. 80p. (J). 12.99 *(978-1-84879-048-3(1))* Make Believe Ideas GBR. Dist: Nelson, Thomas Inc.

Smiley, Bob & Florea, Jesse. Devotions for Super Average Kids 2. 2014. (ENG.). 240p. (J). pap. 12.99 *(978-1-62405-131-9(6))* Tyndale Hse. Pubs.

Spector, Todd. How to Pee: Potty Training for Boys. Chung, Arree, illus. 2015. (ENG.). 40p. (J). (— 1). 12.99 *(978-0-8050-9773-3(2)*, 9780805097733, Holt, Henry & Co. Bks. For Young Readers) Holt, Henry & Co.

St. Stephen's Community House Staff. The Little Black Book for Guys: Guys Talk about Sex. 3rd ed. 2008. (ENG., Illus.). 256p. (YA). (gr. 9-12). pap. 9.95 *(978-1-55037-962-4(3)*, 9781550379624) Annick Pr., Ltd. CAN. Dist: Publishers Group West (PGW).

Strauss, Ed. Bible Freaks & Geeks, 1 vol. Haya, Erwin, illus. 2007. (2:52 Ser.). (ENG.). 128p. (J). (gr. 3-7). pap. 7.99 *(978-0-310-71309-8(9))* Zonderkidz.

—Devotions to Make You Smarter, 1 vol. 2007. (2:52 Ser.). (ENG., Illus.). 192p. (J). (gr. 3-7). pap. 9.99 *(978-0-310-71312-8(9))* Zonderkidz.

—Devotions to Take You Deeper, 1 vol. 2007. (2:52 Ser.). (ENG.). 192p. (J). (gr. 4-7). pap. 9.99 *(978-0-310-71313-5(7))* Zonderkidz.

Twin Sisters(r) Staff, et al. My First Bedtime Prayers for Boys. 2016. (Let's Share a Story Ser.). (Illus.). 14p. (J). bds. 5.99 *(978-1-63409-645-4(2))* Barbour Publishing, Inc.

Vranich, Belisa & Eagleson, Holly. Boys Lie: How Not to Get Played. 2010. (ENG.). 264p. (YA). (gr. 13-18). pap. 12.95 *(978-0-7573-1364-6(7)*, HCI Teens) Health Communications, Inc.

Wiggin, Kate Douglas. The Story of Patsy. 2004. reprint ed. pap. 15.95 *(978-1-4179-2620-6(1))* Kessinger Publishing, LLC.

—The Story of Patsy. 2009. (gr. 4-7). 108p. 22.95 *(978-1-60664-686-1(9))*; 104p. pap. 9.95 *(978-1-60664-316-7(9))* Rodgers, Alan Bks.

Wilkinson, Bruce & Thomas, Mack. A Life God Rewards: Guys Only. ltd. ed. 2006. 96p. bds. 9.99 *(978-1-60142-002-2(1)*, Multnomah) Doubleday Religious Publishing Group, The.

World Book, Inc Staff, contrib. by. Bullied by Boys. 2013. (J). *(978-0-7166-2071-6(5))* World Bk., Inc.

BOYS—EMPLOYMENT

see Child Labor

BOYS—FICTION

Abbott, Hailey. Next Summer. 2005. (Summer Boys Ser.: 2). (ENG.). 240p. (J). (gr. 7-12). pap. 9.99 *(978-0-439-75540-5(9))* Scholastic, Inc.

—Summer Boys. 2004. (Summer Boys Ser.: 1). (ENG.). 224p. (J). (gr. 7). pap. 9.99 *(978-0-439-54020-9(8))* Scholastic, Inc.

—Waking up to Boys. 2007. (ENG.). 256p. (YA). (gr. 9). pap. 8.99 *(978-0-06-082435-8(2)*, HarperTeen) HarperCollins Pubs.

Abbott, Jacob. Rollo at Play. 2008. 124p. (gr. 3-7). 23.95 *(978-1-60664-760-8(1))*; pap. 10.95 *(978-1-60664-132-3(8))* Aegypan.

Abshire, Lisa D. Sam's Magical Day. 2006. 48p. pap. 16.95 *(978-1-4241-1484-9(5))* PublishAmerica, Inc.

Adams, Elizabeth. The Boy Who Cried Wolf. 2012. (ENG., Illus.). 24p. (J). pap. *(978-0-7787-7902-5(5))* Crabtree Publishing Co.

Adderson, Caroline. Bruno for Real, 1 vol. Flook, Helen, illus. 2009. (Orca Echoes Ser.). (ENG.). 64p. (J). (gr. 2-3). pap. 6.95 *(978-1-55469-023-7(4))* Orca Bk. Pubs. USA.

The Adventures of Bug & Roofus: Clean Your Room Roofus. 2008. (Illus.). 32p. (J). 9.95 *(978-0-615-17074-9(9))* Big Bk. Pubns.

Aebersold, Carol V., et al. The Elf on the Shelf - Girl LT: Light Girl. 2012. (ENG.). 32p. (J). lib. bdg. 15.00 net. *(978-0-9769907-3-4(3))* CCA & B, LLC.

Aina, Olaiya. The Boy, the Dove, & the Hawk. 2010. 20p. pap. 13.80 *(978-1-4269-3298-4(7))* Trafford Publishing.

Aker, Don. The Space Between. 2014. 256p. (YA). (gr. 8). pap. 8.99 *(978-0-06-231354-6(1))* HarperCollins Pubs.

Al-Emadi, Hesham. The Savior's Threshold: The Chronicles of Dourren. 2010. 192p. pap. 13.95 *(978-1-4502-1846-7(6))* iUniverse, Inc.

—The Savior's Threshold: The Chronicles of Dourren. 2010. 192p. 23.95 *(978-1-4502-1848-1(2))* iUniverse, Inc.

Alan E. And Lisa J. Laird. Cows Can Be Scary. 2009. 40p. pap. 18.49 *(978-1-4389-8150-5(3))* AuthorHouse.

Alcott, Louisa May. Hombrecitos.Tr. of Little Men. (SPA., Illus.). 160p. (YA). 11.95 *(978-84-7281-168-3(9)*, AF1168) Auriga, Ediciones S.A. ESP. Dist: Continental Bk. Co., Inc.

—Los Muchachos de Jo.Tr. of Jo's Boys. (SPA., Illus.). 160p. (YA). 11.95 *(978-84-7281-055-6(0)*, AF1055) Auriga, Ediciones S.A. ESP. Dist: Continental Bk. Co., Inc.

Alegria, Ciro. Sacha en el Reino de los Arboles. (SPA.). 96p. (YA). (gr. 5-8). *(978-84-204-3693-7(3)*, AF1748) Ediciones Alfaguara ESP. Dist: Lectorum Pubns., Inc.

—Sacha en el Reino de los Arboles. (SPA.). (YA). (gr. 5-8). *(978-956-11-0965-0(4)*, UV6346) Universitaria, Editorial S.A.

Alfaro, Manuel. Griego el Magnifico y la Gotita Verde Golosa Pegajos. Harrington, David, illus. 2007. (SPA.). 36p. per. 15.50 *(978-1-59858-337-3(9))* Dog Ear Publishing, LLC.

Alger, Horatio. Do & Dare: Or, A Brave Boy's Fight for Fortune. reprint ed. pap. 79.00 *(978-1-4047-3563-7(1))* Classic Textbooks.

—The Errand Boy. 2005. 296p. pap. 13.95 *(978-1-4218-0455-2(7)*, 1st World Library - Literary Society) 1st World Publishing, Inc.

—Frank Fowler, the Cash Boy. reprint ed. pap. 79.00 *(978-1-4047-3558-3(5))* Classic Textbooks.

—Frank Fowler, the Cash Boy. 2013. (Works of Horatio Alger Jr.). 254p. reprint ed. lthr. 79.00 *(978-0-7812-3558-7(8))* Reprint Services Corp.

—Joe the Hotel Boy: Or, Winning Out by Pluck. 363p. reprint ed. pap. 79.00 *(978-1-4047-3578-1(X))* Classic Textbooks.

—Paul Prescott's Charge. rev. ed. 2006. (ENG.). 308p. 29.95 *(978-1-4218-2089-7(7)*, 1st World Library - Literary Society) 1st World Publishing, Inc.

Alger Jr. Horatio Staff. Struggling Upward. rev. ed. 2006. 284p. 28.95 *(978-1-4218-1760-6(8))*; pap. 13.95 *(978-1-4218-1860-3(4))* 1st World Publishing, Inc. (1st World Library - Literary Society).

Ali, Raydin. The Mystic Museum. 2010. 64p. pap. 12.00 *(978-1-4269-1138-5(6))* Trafford Publishing.

Alston, Colin. The Invisible Boy. 2009. 32p. pap. 13.75 *(978-1-60860-598-9(1)*, Eloquent Bks.) Strategic Book Publishing & Rights Agency (SBPRA).

Altein, Chani. Hashem Is Truly Everywhere. Rosenfeld, D. L. & Leverton, Yossi, eds. Lumer, Marc, illus. 2011. 28p. (J). 12.95 *(978-1-929628-57-5(9))* Hachai Publishing.

Amnesty International Staff, ed. Free? Stories about Human Rights. 2010. (ENG., Illus.). 224p. (J). (gr. 5-18). pap. 9.99 *(978-0-7636-4926-5(0))* Candlewick Pr.

Anaya, Hector. Cuenta Cuenta. Moreno, Sergio, illus. 2nd rev. ed. 2005. (Castillo de la Lectura Verde Ser.). (SPA & ENG.). 184p. (J). (gr. -1-7). pap. 7.95 *(978-970-20-0135-5(8))* Castillo, Ediciones, S. A. de C. V. MEX. Dist: Macmillan.

Anderson, Alice. Danny Be Good! 2012. 24p. pap. 17.99 *(978-1-4685-6433-4(1))* AuthorHouse.

Anderson, Ashley. My Day with Jesus. 2010. 26p. pap. 7.99 *(978-0-88144-017-1(5)*, Thorncrown Publishing) Yorkshire Publishing Group.

Anderson, Ebony. If I Were Just a Little Taller. Barrett, Noah, illus. 2005. (ENG.). 48p. (J). (gr. -1-3). per. 9.99 *(978-0-9760901-8-2(X))* Morgan James Publishing.

Anderson, Pamela. My New School: Blonde Boy. Lee, Han & Wu, Stacie, illus. 2004. (J). 12.95 *(978-1-932555-05-9(6))* Watch Me Grow Kids.

—My New School: Brunette Boy. Lee, Han & Wu, Stacie, illus. 2004. (J). 12.95 *(978-1-932555-07-3(2))* Watch Me Grow Kids.

Anderson, William. River Boy. Date not set. 32p. (J). (gr. 2-5). pap. 5.99 *(978-0-06-443573-4(3))* HarperCollins Pubs.

—River Boy: The Story of Mark Twain. Andreasen, Dan, illus. 2003. (ENG.). 40p. (J). (gr. 2-5). 17.99 *(978-0-06-028400-8(5))* HarperCollins Pubs.

Andreae, Giles. Billy Bonkers. Sharratt, Nick, illus. 2006. (ENG.). 128p. (J). (gr. -1-12). pap. 7.99 *(978-1-84616-151-3(7))* Hodder & Stoughton GBR. Dist: Hachette Bk. Group.

Anh, Nguyen Nhat. Ticket to Childhood. Naythons, Will, tr. from VIE. 2014. (ENG.). 160p. (gr. 12). 21.95 *(978-1-4683-0959-1(5)*, 460959) Overlook Pr., The.

Anna, Jennifer. Maxwell Dreams of Trains. Blue, Buster, illus. 2009. (ENG.). 88p. (J). 10.99 *(978-1-883573-05-8(X))* Blue Forge Pr.

Annie. The Giving Children. 2012. 28p. pap. 18.65 *(978-1-4653-6578-1(8))* Xlibris Corp.

Anza, Ana Luisa. El Misterio de la Casa Chueca (y el Bulto Color Mugre) The Mystery of the Crooked House. Escobar, Antonio Rocha, illus. rev. ed. 2006. (Castillo de la Lectura Naranja Ser.). (SPA & ENG.). 120p. (J). (gr. 4-7). pap. 7.95 *(978-970-20-0200-0(1))* Castillo, Ediciones, S. A. de C. V. MEX. Dist: Macmillan.

Appleton, Victor. The Alien Probe. (Tom Swift Ser.). (J). (gr. 3-7). 20.95 *(978-0-88411-464-2(3))* Amereon Ltd.

—The City in the Stars. (Tom Swift Ser.). (J). (gr. 3-7). 20.95 *(978-0-88411-463-5(5))* Amereon Ltd.

—The Moving Picture Boys at Panama. 2005. 27.95 *(978-1-4218-1499-5(4))*; 208p. pap. 12.95 *(978-1-4218-1599-2(0))* 1st World Publishing, Inc. (1st World Library - Literary Society).

—The Moving Picture Boys at Panama. 2004. reprint ed. pap. 20.95 *(978-1-4191-7472-8(X))*; pap. 1.99 *(978-1-4192-7472-5(4))* Kessinger Publishing, LLC.

—The Rescue Mission. (Tom Swift Ser.). (J). (gr. 3-7). 20.95 *(978-0-88411-458-1(9))* Amereon Ltd.

—Terror on the Moons of Jupiter. (Tom Swift Ser.). (J). (gr. 3-7). 20.95 *(978-0-88411-460-4(0))* Amereon Ltd.

—Tom Swift & His Electronic Electroscope. (J). (gr. 5-6). 20.95 *(978-0-88411-462-8(7))* Amereon Ltd.

—Tom Swift & His Triphibian Atomicar. (Tom Swift Ser.). (J). (gr. 5-6). 20.95 *(978-0-88411-459-8(7))* Amereon Ltd.

Arai, Kiyoko. Beauty Pop, Vol. 1. 2006. (ENG., Illus.). 208p. pap. 8.99 *(978-1-4215-0575-6(4))* Viz Media.

Archuleta, Robert B. The Boys' Club: Lost & Found. 2007. 52p. per. 16.95 *(978-1-4241-7372-3(8))* America Star Bks.

Arnold, Adolf W. A Boy Without Toys. 2004. (Illus.). 240p. pap. 24.95 *(978-1-57197-157-9(2))* Pentland Pr., Inc.

Arnold, Tedd. Even More Parts. Arnold, Tedd, illus. 2007. (ENG., Illus.). 40p. (J). (gr. -1-3). pap. 7.99 *(978-0-14-240714-1(3)*, Puffin Books) Penguin Young Readers Group.

Arrington, R. Region. Billy Buckins & the Pirates Map, 1 vol. 2010. 64p. pap. 19.95 *(978-1-4512-2087-2(1))* America Star Bks.

—The Voyage of Billy Buckins, 1 vol. Harrington, Linda, illus. 2009. 73p. pap. 19.95 *(978-1-4489-2083-9(3))* America Star Bks.

Asch, Frank. The Earth & I. 2010. (Rise & Shine Ser.). (ENG., Illus.). 32p. (C). (gr. -1-3). pap. 11.95 *(978-0-15-206395-5(1))* National Geographic School Publishing, Inc.

Ashley, Bernard. Johnnie's Blitz. 2005. 218p. (J). (gr. k-17). pap. 6.95 *(978-1-903015-28-5(6))* Barn Owl Bks, London GBR. Dist: Independent Pubs. Group.

Asner, Anne-Marie. Klutzy Boy. Asner, Anne-Marie, illus. l.t. ed. 2007. (Illus.). 32p. (J). (gr. -1-2). per. 6.95 *(978-0-9753629-4-5(1))* Matzah Ball Bks.

—Kvetchy Boy. Asner, Anne-Marie, illus. l.t. ed. 2006. (Illus.). 32p. (J). per. 6.95 *(978-0-9753629-3-8(3))* Matzah Ball Bks.

Austin, Karen D. Jay Jay & the Broken Picture Frame. 2009. 20p. pap. 10.49 *(978-1-4389-9003-3(0))* AuthorHouse.

Avery, Pat McGrath. Tommy's War: A Parent Goes to War, 1. Ray, Eric, illus. 2003. 36p. (J). per. 5.95 *(978-0-9663276-8-7(3))* Red Engine Pr.

Avila, Nelson Moreno. The Boy & the Zoo. 2012. 32p. pap. 16.95 *(978-1-4497-7474-5(1)*, WestBow Pr.) Author Solutions, Inc.

AZ Books Staff. Little Thumb. Zyl, Olga, ed. 2012. (Classic Fairy Tales Ser.). (ENG.). 10p. (J). (gr. -1-k). bds. 9.95 *(978-1-61889-008-5(5))* AZ Bks. LLC.

Babooram, Vima. Poco & His Missing Puppy. Babooram, Aasha, illus. 2012. 24p. pap. *(978-1-4602-0296-8(1))* FriesenPress.

Bach, Sherry. Abundant Christmas, 1 vol. 2009. 48p. pap. 16.95 *(978-1-4489-9120-4(X))* America Star Bks.

Baghdasaryan, Rouzanna. Moush Wants to Get Lost. Yulia, Lushnikova, illus. 2010. (POL & ENG.). 32p. (J). pap. 16.95 *(978-1-60195-103-8(5))* International Step by Step Assn.

Bailey, Kristin. Average Joe. 2006. 56p. per. *(978-1-84667-004-6(7))* Derwent Pr., The.

Bailey, Tressie. Things Sammy Likes to Do. 2009. 37p. pap. 24.10 *(978-0-557-04150-3(3))* Lulu Pr., Inc.

Baker, Monica S. Freestyle, 1 vol. 2010. (ENG., Illus.). 160p. (J). 14.99 *(978-0-7643-3538-9(3)*, 9780764335389) Schiffer Publishing, Ltd.

Baldwin, James. Fifty Famous People. l.t. ed. 2006. (ENG.). 126p. pap. 19.99 *(978-1-4264-1427-5(7))* Creative Media Partners, LLC.

Balian, Lorna. Where in the World Is Henry?, 1 vol. Balian, Lecia & Balian, Lorna, illus. 2005. (ENG.). 32p. (J). (gr. -1-2). *(978-1-59572-035-1(9))* Star Bright Bks., Inc.

Bancroft, Myles. The Trouble with Adam's Heart. Brouillette, Peter, ed. Smith, Richard, illus. 2004. (YA). per. 19.99 *(978-0-9760419-4-8(4))* ThatsMyLife Co.

Bapiraju Gandham. The Wizard of Ants. 2010. 88p. pap. 33.48 *(978-1-4269-1940-4(9))* Trafford Publishing.

Barklem, Jill. Cuento de Otono.Tr. of Autumn Story. (SPA.). 32p. (J). 8.95 *(978-84-233-2620-4(9))* Ediciones Destino ESP. Dist: Planeta Publishing Corp.

Barnes, Bobbie Jo. The Message. 2012. 24p. pap. 24.95 *(978-1-4626-9047-3(5))* America Star Bks.

Barnett, Mac. Sam & Dave Dig a Hole. 2015. (JPN.). (J). *(978-4-7515-2714-6(2))* Asunaro Shobo.

—Sam & Dave Dig a Hole. Klassen, Jon, illus. 2014. (ENG.). 40p. (J). (gr. -1-3). 16.99 *(978-0-7636-6229-5(1))* Candlewick Pr.

—Sam & Dave Dig a Hole. 2014. (CHI.). (J). (gr. -1-3). pap. *(978-986-241-935-9(0))* Common Wealth.

—Sam & Dave Dig a Hole. 2014. (CHI.). 32p. (J). (gr. -1-3). *(978-7-5332-8178-6(0))* Mingtian Chubanshe.

Barr, Bitsy. Zock's Adventures: Just for Boys ... 2010. 40p. pap. 16.99 *(978-1-4490-5880-7(9))* AuthorHouse.

Baum, L. Frank. The Master Key: An Electrical Fairy Tale. 2007. 120p. per. *(978-1-4065-3669-0(5))* Dodo Pr.

Bauman, Boomer. One Star at a Time. 2009. 68p. pap. 20.50 *(978-1-60860-571-2(X)*, Eloquent Bks.) Strategic Book Publishing & Rights Agency (SBPRA).

Baumgartner, Edward Louis. Wabash Boy. 2011. 236p. (gr. 4-6). pap. 16.26 *(978-1-4269-7615-5(1))* Trafford Publishing.

Baxter B. Ballyhoo Rides Again. 2011. 52p. (gr. 1-2). pap. 9.99 *(978-1-4634-3088-7(4))* AuthorHouse.

Beach, Kathy Ann. Helping a Garden Grow, 1 vol. 2010. 20p. pap. 24.95 *(978-1-4489-8836-5(5))* PublishAmerica, Inc.

Beaty, Noel. The Legend of Snowy the Shrew. 2007. 168p. per. (978-0-7552-0295-9(3)) Authors OnLine, Ltd.

Beck, Adrian. Stuff Happens: Dale. 11th ed. 2016. (Stuff Happens Ser.). (ENG.). 96p. (J). (gr. 2-4). 8.99 **(978-0-14-330896-6(3))** Random Hse. Australia AUS. Dist: Independent Pubs. Group.

Bedell, Lorraine Frances. The Christmas Cat Story, 1 vol. 2010. 48p. pap. 16.95 (978-1-4512-0249-6(0)) America Star Bks.

Bednark, Sara & Ung, Bunheang. Wally's Bedroom Aviary. 2008. 32p. 14.95 (978-0-615-18545-3(2)) Bednark, Sara.

Bee, Clair. Clutch Hitter. (J). 17.95 (978-0-8488-1246-1(8)) Amereon Ltd.

Bell, Aaron. Jak's Story. 2010. (ENG., Illus.). 96p. (YA). (gr. 4). pap. 10.99 (978-1-55488-710-1(0)) Dundurn CAN. Dist: Ingram Publisher Services.

Bell, Cheryl. Boy Jesus. 2011. 24p. pap. 10.95 (978-1-4497-1636-3(9), WestBow Pr.) Author Solutions, Inc.

Bell, Holly. Ethan Goes Green. Sidwell, Kathy, illus. 2009. 32p. pap. 12.99 (978-1-4389-0115-2(1)) AuthorHouse.

Bell, Ted. Nick of Time. 2009. (Nick Mciver Adventures Through Time Ser.: 1). (ENG., Illus.). 464p. (J). (gr. 5-9). pap. 8.99 (978-0-312-58143-5(2), 9780312581435) Square Fish.

—The Time Pirate. 2011. (Nick Mciver Adventures Through Time Ser.: 2). (ENG., Illus.). 480p. (J). (gr. 5-9). pap. 10.99 (978-0-312-66549-4(0), 9780312665494) Square Fish.

Bellows, Greg. The Giant. 2011. 24p. pap. 13.50 (978-1-4634-3940-8(7)) AuthorHouse.

Benchmark Education Co., LLC. Look at Me! Big Book. 2014. (Shared Reading Foundations Ser.). (J). (gr. -1). (978-1-4509-9421-7(0)) Benchmark Education Co.

Bender, Carol. Picky Eater, That Peter. 2011. 25p. (J). 24.95 (978-1-4327-7055-6(1)) Outskirts Pr., Inc.

Benjamin, Ruth. Yesterday's Child. Cohen, Deene, illus. (YA). 16.95 (978-1-56062-176-8(1), CFR122H); pap. 13.95 (978-1-56062-177-5(X), CFR122S) C I S Communications, Inc.

Benson, Patty. The Nameless Child. 2012. 36p. pap. 24.95 (978-1-4626-7559-3(X)) America Star Bks.

Benton, Jim. Okay, So Maybe I Do Have Superpowers. Benton, Jim, illus. 2011. (Dear Dumb Diary Ser.: 11). (ENG., Illus.). 160p. (J). (gr. 3-7). pap. 6.99 (978-0-545-11615-2(5), Scholastic Paperbacks) Scholastic, Inc.

Berger, Samantha. Pirate Potty. Cartwright, Amy, illus. 2010. (ENG.). 24p. (J). (gr. -1 — 1). pap. 5.99 (978-0-545-17295-0(0), Cartwheel Bks.) Scholastic, Inc.

Bernal, Sandra Marie. The Wish: Johnny's Story. Merriman, Christi, illus. 2011. 48p. pap. 24.95 (978-1-4560-4934-8(8)) America Star Bks.

Bernstein, Owen. My Turtle & Me. Thompson, Carol, illus. 2012. (ENG.). 10p. (J). (— 1). bds. 9.99 (978-0-545-43387-7(8)) Scholastic, Inc.

Bertrand, Diane Gonzales. My Pal, Victor/Mi Amigo, Victor. de La Vega, Eida, tr. 2008. (ENG., Illus.). 32p. (J). (gr. -1-3). per. 7.95 (978-1-932748-72-7(5), Raven Tree Pr.,Csi) Continental Sales, Inc.

Bezek, Lyn. Daisy: The Cripple Creek Donkey. 2004. (J). pap. 7.95 (978-1-932738-09-4(6)) Western Reflections Publishing Co.

Bickford, Janette. Vern's Vacation. 2012. 16p. pap. 12.68 (978-1-4669-2311-9(3)) Trafford Publishing.

Biemiller, Carl L. The Magic Ball from Mars & Starboy. Voute, Kathleen, illus. 2003. 302p. (J). pap. 19.95 (978-0-918736-09-3(9), Sense of Wonder Pr.) Rock, James A. & Co. Pubs.

Biggs, Pauline. A Wild Ride. Mayne, Michael, illus. 2004. 20p. (J). per. 12.95 (978-0-9760129-0-0(1)) The Publishing Place LLC.

Bigham, Madge A. Little Folks' Land. Ripperton, Lisa M., ed. 2009. 452p. pap. 15.95 (978-1-59915-375-9(0)) Yesterday's Classics.

Billy Ray Pyle's Style. Date not set. 5.95 (978-0-89868-363-9(7)) ARO Publishing Co.

Blair, Eric. The Boy Who Cried Wolf, 1 vol. Silverman, Dianne, illus. 2011. (My First Classic Story Ser.). (ENG.). 24p. (gr. k-3). pap. 7.10 (978-1-4048-7364-3(3), My First Classic Story) Picture Window Bks.

Blair, Eric & Aesop Enterprise Inc. Staff. The Boy Who Cried Wolf: A Retelling of Aesop's Fable, 1 vol. Silverman, Dianne, illus. 2011. (My First Classic Story Ser.). (ENG.). 24p. (gr. k-3). lib. bdg. 22.65 (978-1-4048-6507-5(1), My First Classic Story) Picture Window Bks.

Blane, Francisco. Row, Row, Row Your Boat. Kelley, Gerald, illus. 2010. (Rising Readers Ser.). (J). 3.49 (978-1-60719-695-2(6)) Newmark Learning LLC.

Blanton, Edwin. Together We Can. 2012. 24p. pap. (978-1-105-51042-7(5)) Lulu.com.

Blatchford, Claire H. Nick's Secret. Harden, Laurie, illus. 2003. (Lerner Mysteries Ser.). 168p. (J). (gr. 4-7). 14.95 (978-0-8225-0743-7(9), Lerner Pubns.) Lerner Publishing Group.

Blevins, Wiley. Go, Billy, Go! Being Yourself. Gordon, John, illus. 2015. (ENG.). 24p. (J). (gr. k-2). lib. bdg. 19.99 (978-1-63440-003-9(8)) Red Chair Pr.

—How to Deal with Bullies Superhero-Style: Response to Bullying. Palen, Debbie, illus. 2015. (ENG.). 24p. (gr. k-2). lib. bdg. 19.99 (978-1-63440-009-1(7)) Red Chair Pr.

—Jack & the Bloody Beanstalk. Cox, Steve, illus. 2016. (Scary Tales Retold Ser.). (ENG.). 24p. (gr. k-3). lib. bdg. 23.99 (978-1-63440-099-2(2)) Red Chair Pr.

Bloomberg, Sandi. Michael & the Magic Dinosaur. Collier, Kevin, illus. 2012. 30p. pap. 13.95 (978-1-61244-066-8(5)) Halo Publishing International.

Blythe, Enid. Three Boys & a Circus. (Illus.). 144p. (J). (gr. k-6). pap. 5.95 (978-0-09-987870-4(4)) Random Hse. GBR. Dist: Trafalgar Square Publishing.

Boelts, Maribeth. The PS Brothers. 2011. (ENG.). 144p. (J). (gr. 2-5). pap. 6.99 (978-0-547-57717-3(6)) Houghton Mifflin Harcourt Publishing Co.

Bolander, Sharon Miller. Hiram's Song. 2012. 20p. pap. 24.95 (978-1-4626-6234-0(X)) America Star Bks.

Bolinger, Carolyn Lewis. One More. 2012. 24p. pap. 17.99 (978-1-4685-7478-4(7)) AuthorHouse.

Bond, A. Russel. Scientific American Boy. 2006. pap. 11.95 (978-1-4218-3014-8(0)) 1st World Publishing, Inc.

Bond, Thomas A. Mill Creek Kids. 2009. 132p. pap. 14.99 (978-1-60791-634-5(7)) Salem Author Services.

Bongers, Christine. Henry Hoey Hobson. 2016. (ENG.). 320p. (J). (gr. 4-6). pap. 14.99 (978-1-925324-92-1(3)) Random Hse. Australia AUS. Dist: Independent Pubs. Group.

Booking, Walt. Teddy's Tale. 2006. (Neighborhood Readers Ser.). (ENG.). 12p. (gr. 1-3). pap. 5.90 (978-1-4042-7054-1(X), Rosen Classroom) Rosen Publishing Group, Inc., The.

Boone, Connie. The Lost Zoo. 2004. 24p. (J). 12.95 (978-1-56167-768-9(X)) American Literary Pr.

Borer, Christopher. Patrick & Hatrick, 1 vol. McDonald, Patrick, illus. 2010. 44p. pap. 24.95 (978-1-4489-7978-3(1)) PublishAmerica, Inc.

Bourgeois, Paulette. Franklin Goes to the Hospital. 2004. (Illus.). (J). (gr. -1-2). spiral bd. (978-0-616-04547-3(6)); spiral bd. (978-0-616-03024-0(X)) Canadian National Institute for the Blind/Institut National Canadien pour les Aveugles.

Boussarhane, Ericka. Sam & the Boogie Man. 2009. 28p. pap. 14.99 (978-1-4389-3107-4(7)) AuthorHouse.

Bowlby, Linda S. Future Hope. Helms, Dana, illus. 2008. 298p. (J). (gr. -1-3). pap. 9.95 (978-0-9779993-6-1(X)) Red Earth Publishing.

The Boy Who Went to the North Wind: Individual Title Six-Packs. (Literatura 2000 Ser.). (gr. 2-3). 33.00 (978-0-7635-0217-1(0)) Rigby Education.

Boyd, Lizi. Flashlight. 2014. (ENG., Illus.). 40p. (J). (gr. -1-1). 16.99 (978-1-4521-1894-9(9)) Chronicle Bks. LLC.

Boykin, Antonee. Alex & Tony Learn to Be Gentlemen. 2011. 31p. (J). pap. 13.95 (978-1-4327-5255-2(3)) Outskirts Pr., Inc.

Boza, Eduardo Robles. Mi Amiga Quiere - Grande (My Friend Wants to Be Big) (SPA.). (J). 4.95 (978-968-419-981-1(3)) Grijalbo, Editorial MEX. Dist: AIMS International Bks., Inc.

Bradford, Danette J. Eric & Wrinkles Meet the Bunnyworms. Bunker, Thomas, illus. 2012. 28p. pap. 24.95 (978-1-4560-4261-5(0)) America Star Bks.

Braffet, Mary. No Slippers! 2005. (Illus.). 32p. (J). 10.95 (978-1-56647-730-7(1)) Mutual Publishing LLC.

Brand, Jack. Freddy Tangles - Champ or Chicken? Jellett, Tom, illus. 2017. (Freddy Tangles Ser.: 2). (ENG.). 128p. (J). (gr. 2-5). 7.99 **(978-1-76011-035-2(3))** Allen & Unwin AUS. Dist: Independent Pubs. Group.

Brand, Jack. Freddy Tangles - Legend or Loser? Jellett, Tom, illus. 2017. (Freddy Tangles Ser.: 1). (ENG.). 128p. (J). (gr. 2-5). 7.99 (978-1-76011-034-5(5)) Allen & Unwin AUS. Dist: Independent Pubs. Group.

Brandeis, Madeline. Little Tom of England. 2011. 160p. 41.95 (978-1-258-09313-6(8)) Literary Licensing, LLC.

Branson, Terri. Brother Dragon. Taylor, Chet, illus. 2004. (J). 18.99 (978-0-9755888-5-7(0)) Dragonfly Publishing, Inc.

Braunns, Melissa. Big Bear Cares. 2009. 24p. pap. 11.50 (978-1-60860-636-8(8), Strategic Bk. Publishing) Strategic Book Publishing & Rights Agency (SBPRA).

Breathed, Berkeley. The Bill the Cat Story: A Bloom County Epic. Breathed, Berkeley, illus. 2016. (ENG., Illus.). 40p. (J). (gr. -1-3). 18.99 (978-0-399-54662-4(6), Philomel Bks.) Penguin Young Readers Group.

Brenda Slack, Slack & Brenda Slack. Everybody. 2010. 28p. pap. 13.85 (978-1-4269-0264-2(6)) Trafford Publishing.

Brenner, Martha F. Montones de Problemas. Woodruff, Liza, illus. 2007. (Math Matters en Espanol Ser.). (SPA.). 32p. (J). (gr. 1-3). pap. 5.95 (978-1-57565-252-8(8)) Kane Press, Inc.

Briggs, Raymond. The Puddleman. Briggs, Raymond, illus. 2006. (ENG., Illus.). 32p. (J). (gr. k-2). pap. 16.95 (978-0-09-945642-1(7), Red Fox) Random House Children's Books GBR. Dist: Independent Pubs. Group.

Brignole, Giancarla, tr. El Globo de Pablito. Casagrande, Donata Dal Molin, illus. (Fabulas De Familia Ser.). (SPA.). 32p. (978-970-20-0269-7(9)) Castillo, Ediciones, S. A. de C. V.

Britan, Denise G. Harry Meets Sam. 2011. 24p. pap. 12.99 (978-1-4628-6756-1(1)) Xlibris Corp.

Brockenbrough, Martha. The Game of Love & Death. 2015. (ENG.). 336p. (J). (gr. 7). 17.99 (978-0-545-66834-7(4)) Scholastic, Inc.

Brouwer, Sigmund. Tin Soldier, 1 vol. 2014. (Seven Sequels Ser.). (ENG., Illus.). 272p. (J). (gr. 5-10). pap. 10.95 (978-1-4598-0546-0(1)) Orca Bk. Pubs. USA.

Brown, Alison. Eddie & Dog, 1 vol. 2014. (ENG.). 32p. (gr. -1-2). 14.95 (978-1-62370-114-7(7)) Capstone Young Readers of Coughlan Cos.

Brown, Jeff. Flat Stanley. 2013. (Flat Stanley Ser.: 1). (J). (gr. k-3). lib. bdg. 14.75 (978-0-613-65076-2(X), Turtleback) Turtleback Bks.

—Flat Stanley - His Original Adventure! Nash, Scott & Pamintuan, Macky, illus. 40th anniv. ed. 2013. (Flat Stanley Ser.). (ENG.). 96p. (J). (gr. 1-5). pap. 4.99 (978-0-06-009791-2(4)) HarperCollins Pubs.

—Flat Stanley & the Firehouse. Pamintuan, Macky, illus. 2011. (I Can Read Level 2 Ser.). (ENG.). 32p. (J). (gr. -1-3). 16.99 (978-0-06-143006-0(4)); pap. 3.99 (978-0-06-143009-1(9)) HarperCollins Pubs.

—Flat Stanley Goes Camping. Pamintuan, Macky, illus. 2013. (I Can Read Level 2 Ser.). (ENG.). 32p. (J). (gr. -1-3). 16.99 (978-0-06-143013-8(7)); pap. 3.99 (978-0-06-143015-2(3)) HarperCollins Pubs.

Brown, Skila. Caminar. 2016. (ENG.). 208p. (J). (gr. 5-9). pap. 7.99 (978-0-7636-9094-6(5)) Candlewick Pr.

—Caminar. 2016. (ENG.). 208p. (J). (gr. 5-9). 18.40 (978-0-606-39096-5(0)) Turtleback Bks.

Browning, Frances G. Dillow. Neon Ned. 2009. 20p. pap. 10.95 (978-1-60860-152-3(8), Strategic Bk. Publishing) Strategic Book Publishing & Rights Agency (SBPRA).

Buckeridge, Anthony. Jennings Goes to School. 2009. (Jennings Ser.: 1). (ENG.). 226p. (J). (gr. -1-12). pap. 12.95 (978-0-7551-1368-2(3)) House of Stratus, Inc. GBR. Dist: Gardners Bks. Ltd.

Buckle, J. A. Half My Facebook Friends Are Ferrets, 1 vol. 2014. (ENG.). 224p. (gr. 9-12). 16.95 (978-1-63079-000-4(1)) Switch Pr.

Bulfinch, Thomas. The Boy Inventor. 2013. (Works of Thomas Bulfinch). 425p. reprint ed. lthr. 79.00 (978-0-7812-2164-1(1)) Reprint Services Corp.

Bullock, Rob. Noah Ramsbottom & the Cave Elves. 2009. 48p. pap. 12.25 (978-1-60860-335-0(0), Strategic Bk. Publishing) Strategic Book Publishing & Rights Agency (SBPRA).

Burleigh, Cyril. The Hilltop Boys on the River. 2006. (ENG.). 118p. pap. 18.99 (978-1-4264-6538-3(6)) Creative Media Partners, LLC.

Burris, Andrea. Tater & Tot. 2008. (Tater & Tot Ser.). (ENG.). 32p. (J). (gr. -1-k). 15.95 (978-0-9743294-2-0(8)) A & D Bks.

Burroughs, Scott, illus. Hopping Mad. 2010. (Hardy Boys: the Secret Files Ser.: 4). (ENG.). 96p. (J). (gr. 1-4). pap. 5.99 (978-1-4169-9395-7(9), Aladdin) Simon & Schuster Children's Publishing.

—Lights, Camera ... Zombies! 2013. (Hardy Boys: the Secret Files Ser.: 12). (ENG.). 96p. (J). (gr. 1-4). pap. 4.99 (978-1-4424-5369-2(9), Aladdin) Simon & Schuster Children's Publishing.

Burton, Martin Nelson. Dear Mr. Leprechaun: Letters from My First Friendship. Hansen, Clint, illus. Tanner, Dean, photos by. 2003. (ENG.). 32p. (J). 17.00 (978-0-9666490-0-0(1)) London Town Pr.

Byars, Betsy. La Casa de las Alas.Tr. of House of Wings. (SPA., Illus.). (YA). (gr. 5-8). pap. (978-84-406-0861-1(6), EB3416) Ediciones B ESP. Dist: Lectorum Pubns., Inc.

Caine, Paul. Jake's Journey. 2010. 68p. pap. 10.49 (978-1-4520-0508-9(7)) AuthorHouse.

Cairo, Anna. The Spider in My Shower. 2012. 28p. pap. 16.99 (978-1-4634-8768-3(1)) AuthorHouse.

Calabrese, Linda Lee. It Is What It Is: In a Kid's Mind. 2012. 28p. pap. 24.95 (978-1-4626-5643-1(9)) America Star Bks.

Campbell, Rod. Buster's Bedtime. (Illus.). 12p. (J). (gr. -1-k). bds. (978-1-56021-376-5(0), #223) W.J. Fantasy, Inc.

Campbell, Suzy. My Daddy Is a Soldier, 1 vol. 2009. 19p. pap. 24.95 (978-1-61546-724-2(6)) America Star Bks.

Candy, T. M. & Fisher, W. A. Dear Mister Mayor. 2010. 126p. pap. 15.54 (978-0-557-09733-3(9)) Lulu Pr., Inc.

Caprio-Scalera, Jill. Gramma's 'Jammas. Caprio-Scalera, Jill & Edrington, Greg Q., illus. 2013. 28p. pap. 12.50 (978-1-60976-464-7(1), Strategic Bk. Publishing) Strategic Book Publishing & Rights Agency (SBPRA).

Carlson, J. Kelley. Freeing Golden Eagle. 2007. 140p. 19.95 (978-1-4327-0315-8(3)); per. 10.95 (978-1-4327-0302-8(1)) Outskirts Pr., Inc.

Carlson, Nancy. Loudmouth George & the New Neighbors. 20th anniv. rev. ed. 2003. (Nancy Carlson's Neighborhood Ser.). (ENG., Illus.). 32p. (J). (gr. k-2). pap. 9.95 (978-1-57505-614-2(3)) Lerner Publishing Group.

Carmichael, Jodi. Spaghetti Is Not a Finger Food (and Other Life Lessons) Sarah, Ackerley, illus. 2013. (ENG.). 152p. (J). (gr. 1-5). pap. 6.95 (978-1-939775-03-0(5)) March 4th, Inc.

Carroll, Thomas. The Colony. 2009. 154p. pap. 16.95 (978-0-86534-379-5(9)) Sunstone Pr.

Carter, Herbert. The, Boy Scouts on Sturgeon Island. rev. ed. 2006. (ENG.). 212p. 27.95 (978-1-4218-2084-2(6), 1st World Library - Literary Society) 1st World Publishing, Inc.

Casero, Joseph M. Patxi of the Pyrenees. 2010. pap. 13.95 (978-0-7414-5934-3(5)) Infinity Publishing.

Cassidy, Sara. Seeing Orange, 1 vol. Meissner, Amy, illus. 2012. (Orca Echoes Ser.). (ENG.). 64p. (J). (gr. 2-3). pap. 6.95 (978-1-55469-991-9(6)) Orca Bk. Pubs. USA.

Castlemon, Harry. Go-Ahead; or, the Fisher-Boy's Motto, by Harry Castlemon [Pseud]. 2006. 308p. per. 23.99 (978-1-4255-2946-8(1)) Michigan Publishing.

—The Sportsman's Club among the Trappers. 2005. pap. 28.95 (978-1-4179-5498-8(1)) Kessinger Publishing, LLC.

—Sportsmans Club in the Saddle. 2006. pap. 30.95 (978-1-4286-5231-6(0)) Kessinger Publishing, LLC.

Cat Concert: Individual Title Six-Packs. (Literatura 2000 Ser.). (gr. 2-3). 33.00 (978-0-7635-0163-1(8)) Rigby Education.

Catone, Gina. Homework Time with Charlie. 2011. 20p. pap. 10.99 (978-1-4567-1713-1(8)) AuthorHouse.

Cauvin, Raoul. Cedric Vol. 4: Hot & Cold. Laudec, illus. 2013. (Cedric Ser.: 4). (ENG.). 48p. pap. 11.95 (978-1-84918-158-7(6)) CineBook GBR. Dist: National Bk. Network.

—Dad's Got Class. 2009. (Cedric Ser.: 2). (ENG., Illus.). 48p. (J). (gr. 4-7). pap. 11.95 (978-1-84918-003-0(2)) CineBook GBR. Dist: National Bk. Network.

—What Got into Him?, Vol. Laudec, illus. 2011. (Cedric Ser.: 3). (ENG.). 48p. (gr. 3-17). pap. 11.95 (978-1-84918-081-8(4)) CineBook GBR. Dist: National Bk. Network.

Censullo, Chris. The Boy with the Big Blue Hair. 2013. 30p. (J). 16.99 (978-0-9797868-7-7(8), OddInt Media) Greenwood Hill Pr.

Cerny, Michele. No More Rules! A Boy's Discovery of What Life is Like Without Rules. Cable, Annette, illus. 2013. 32p. (J). (978-0-9860405-0-4(9)) Hat Trick Publishing.

Chacko, Miss Hannah. The Lie. 2009. 372p. pap. 25.50 (978-0-557-06829-6(0)) Lulu Pr., Inc.

Chambers, Aidan. Dying to Know You. 2012. (ENG.). 288p. (YA). (gr. 9-17). 16.95 (978-1-4197-0165-8(7), Amulet Bks.) Abrams, Inc.

Chand, Vimi. The World of Peanut Butter Jelly Boy: Peanut Butter Jelly Boy's Stay in the Hospital, 1 vol. 2010. 44p. 24.95 (978-1-4489-5610-4(2)) PublishAmerica, Inc.

Chapman, Carlene. Jackson Goes to the Beach. 2010. 24p. pap. 11.95 (978-1-4490-9768-4(5)) AuthorHouse.

Charles, Rie. No More Dragons. 2010. (ENG., Illus.). 112p. (J). (gr. 5-7). pap. 9.95 (978-1-926607-12-2(0), Napoleon & Co.) Dundurn CAN. Dist: Ingram Publisher Services.

Chaudhary, Shahida. Sammy's Midnight Hunger. Mikle, Toby, illus. 2012. 38p. pap. 14.50 (978-1-61897-255-2(3), Strategic Bk. Publishing) Strategic Book Publishing & Rights Agency (SBPRA).

Childress, Jamie. Lost Universe. Braun, Chris, illus. 2015. (ENG.). 100p. (J). (gr. 4-7). per. 4.99 (978-1-931882-74-3(6)) Adventures Unlimited Pr.

Chipley, John. The Secret Place: A Boy's Journey into the Woods. 2011. 92p. (gr. 1-1). pap. 13.95 (978-1-4567-4593-6(X)) AuthorHouse.

Chomock, Ruth. Devin's New Bed. 2010. 32p. pap. 12.99 (978-1-4490-3538-9(8)) AuthorHouse.

Choyce, Lesley. Reckless, 1 vol. 2010. (Orca Currents Ser.). (ENG.). (gr. 5-9). 128p. (J). pap. 9.95 (978-1-55469-223-1(7)); 112p. (YA). lib. bdg. 16.95 (978-1-55469-224-8(5)) Orca Bk. Pubs. USA.

Christian, Anna. The Newcomer. 2013. 56p. pap. 6.99 (978-0-9799273-5-5(8)) Dadielte Production.

Christian Mauricio Constante. What a Catch! 2009. 24p. pap. 11.49 (978-1-4389-6423-2(4)) AuthorHouse.

Christopher, Matt. Lacrosse Firestorm. 2008. (ENG.). 144p. (J). (gr. 3-7). pap. 5.99 (978-0-316-01631-5(4)) Little, Brown Bks. for Young Readers.

Church, Caroline Jayne. Here Comes Christmas! Church, Caroline Jayne, illus. 2010. (ENG., Illus.). 14p. (J). (gr. k — 1). bds. 7.99 (978-0-545-11817-0(4), Cartwheel Bks.) Scholastic, Inc.

Ciocca, Donna. Harley & Homer for Hire. 2006. (YA). per. 11.95 (978-0-9747361-9-8(8)) Oak Manor Publishing, Inc.

Cioffi, Dom, illus. Digby & the Lake Monster. l.t. ed. 2006. 36p. (J). per. (978-0-9745931-0-4(9)) Vermont Bookworks.

Clark, Brenda. Spiro Goes West: More Adventures of Spiro the Shooting Star. 2008. 57p. pap. 16.95 (978-1-60474-770-6(6)) America Star Bks.

Clark, Todd. The Ice Cream Kid: Brain Freeze! 2014. (ENG.). 176p. (J). 13.99 (978-1-4494-4424-2(5)) Andrews McMeel Publishing.

Clay Iii, J. Percy. Sampson's Pumpkin Playhouse. 2012. 30p. 24.95 (978-1-4626-7226-4(4)) America Star Bks.

Cleary, Beverly. The Henry & Ribsy Box Set: Henry Huggins, Henry & Ribsy, Ribsy. 2015. (Henry Huggins Ser.). (ENG.). 624p. (J). (gr. 3-7). pap. 18.99 (978-0-06-236063-2(9)) HarperCollins Pubs.

—Henry & the Paper Route. Darling, Louis et al, illus. 2014. (Henry Huggins Ser.: 4). (ENG.). 224p. (J). (gr. 3-7). 16.99 (978-0-688-21380-0(4)); reprint ed. pap. 7.99 (978-0-380-70921-2(X)) HarperCollins Pubs.

—Henry Huggins. Darling, Louis et al, illus. 2014. (Henry Huggins Ser.: 1). (ENG.). 208p. (J). (gr. 3-7). 16.99 (978-0-688-21385-5(5)) HarperCollins Pubs.

—Henry Huggins, 1 vol. Darling, Louis, illus. 2004. (Henry Huggins Ser.: 1). (SPA.). 160p. (J). (gr. 3-7). pap. 7.99 (978-0-06-073600-2(3)) HarperCollins Pubs.

—Henry Huggins. Darling, Louis et al, illus. 50th anniv. ed. 2016. (Henry Huggins Ser.: 1). (ENG.). 208p. (J). (gr. 3-7). pap. 6.99 (978-0-380-70912-0(0)) HarperCollins Pubs.

—Runaway Ralph. Darling, Louis et al, illus. 2014. (Ralph Mouse Ser.: 2). (ENG.). 224p. (J). (gr. 3-7). 16.99 (978-0-688-21701-3(X)) HarperCollins Pubs.

Cleave, Brenda. The Money Tree. 2010. 40p. pap. 18.99 (978-1-4490-7468-5(5)) AuthorHouse.

Clements, Andrew. The Janitor's Boy. 2004. 144p. (J). (gr. 3-7). pap. 29.00 incl. audio (978-0-8072-8360-8(6), Listening Library) Random Hse. Audio Publishing Group.

Clifford, Kathryn & Renn, Chantal. George the Sun Safe Superstar. 2012. (Illus.). 26p. pap. 11.00 (978-1-78035-317-3(0), Fastprint Publishing) Upfront Publishing Ltd. GBR. Dist: Printondemand-worldwide.com.

Cogar, Tubal U., et al. The Journeys of Wobblefoot the Beginning. Cogar, Karen S., ed. O'Connor, Tim, illus. 2003. (J). pap. 17.50 (978-0-9747149-0-5(9)) Wobblefoot Ltd.

Collier, Kevin Scott. Diligence the Dragon Vol. 1: A Prebiblical Fable. l.t. ed. 2005. (Illus.). 22p. (J). E-Book 9.95 incl. cd-rom (978-1-933090-25-2(1)) Guardian Angel Publishing, Inc.

Collins, Billy. Daddy's Little Boy. Date not set. 32p. (J). (gr. -1-3). pap. 5.99 (978-0-06-443687-8(X)) HarperCollins Pubs.

Connolly, John. The Book of Lost Things. 2011. (ENG.). 368p. (J). (gr. 5-9). pap. 7.99 (978-1-4424-2934-5(8), Simon & Schuster Bks. For Young Readers) Simon & Schuster Bks. For Young Readers.

—The Gates. 2009. (ENG.). 304p. 24.00 (978-1-4391-7263-6(3), Beyond Words/Atria Bks.) Atria Bks.

—The Gates. 2011. (Samuel Lord Ser.: 1). (ENG.). 320p. (J). (gr. 5-9). pap. 8.99 (978-1-4424-2933-8(X), Simon & Schuster Bks. For Young Readers) Simon & Schuster Bks. For Young Readers.

Connor, David. Archie & Billy in Monster Cave. 2011. (Illus.). 40p. 18.68 (978-1-4567-7308-3(9)) AuthorHouse.

Connor, Naomi. Rainy Day Blues. 2012. 26p. pap. 15.99 (978-1-4685-7388-6(8)) AuthorHouse.

Cook, Alison Reeger. The Scholar, the Sphinx & the Shades of Nyx. 2013. (Scholar & the Sphinx Ser.: 1). (ENG.). 296p. (YA). pap. (978-1-908483-87-4(3)) Knox Robinson Pubs.

Cook, Jeremy. The Illusion Stick. 2008. 115p. pap. 19.95 (978-1-60474-705-8(6)) America Star Bks.

Cook, Julia. But That Rule Doesn't Apply to Me. DuFalla, Anita, illus. 2016. (Responsible Me! Ser.: Vol. 3). (ENG.). 32p. (J). pap. 10.95 (978-1-934490-98-3(9)) Boys Town Pr.

Coomber, Suzanne. The Magic Sandcastle. 2011. 16p. 8.32 (978-1-4520-9612-4(0)) AuthorHouse.

Corbett, Sue. The Last Newspaper Boy in America. 2010. (ENG.). 208p. (J). (gr. 5-18). 6.99 (978-0-14-241696-9(7), Puffin Books) Penguin Young Readers Group.

Coren, Alan. Arthur & the Purple Panic. 2004. (Illus.). 64p. (978-0-86051-141-0(3), Robson Bks. Ltd.) Pavilion Bks.

—Arthur's Last Stand. 2004. (Illus.). 64p. (978-0-903895-94-1(3), Robson Bks. Ltd.) Pavilion Bks.

Corriveau, Art. How I Got a Life & a Dog. 2012. (ENG.). 288p. (J). (gr. 3-7). pap. 7.95 (978-1-4197-0015-6(4), Amulet Bks.) Abrams, Inc.

Cosgrove, Stephen. Button Breaker. 2016. (Treasure Trolls Ser.). (ENG., Illus.). 32p. (J). (gr. k-4). pap. 7.95 (978-1-941437-79-7(6)) Heritage Builders, LLC.

Cowley, Joy. Little Dan Big Book. 2010. 48.25 (978-1-60559-248-0(X)) Hameray Publishing Group, Inc.

Cox, Kimberley & Wilde, David. If I Were a Dragon. 2011. 20p. (gr. -1). pap. 12.99 (978-1-4567-2236-4(0)) AuthorHouse.

Cox, Stephen Angus. The Dare Boys of 1776. 2004. reprint ed. pap. 1.99 (978-1-4192-5856-5(7)); pap. 15.95 (978-1-4191-5856-8(2)) Kessinger Publishing, LLC.

Cox, Steven. Justin's Very Own Drum. Saavedra, Anthony, illus. 2009. 24p. pap. 24.95 (978-1-60749-553-6(8)) America Star Bks.

Crawford, Clint. The Rag Tag Gang, 1 vol. 2009. 83p. pap. 19.95 (978-1-4489-9697-1(X)) America Star Bks.

Crawford, John. Life in Honeysuckle Valley the Adventur. 2006. pap. 14.95 (978-1-4327-0104-8(5)) Outskirts Pr., Inc.

Crawford, Teresa. I'm Not Stupid! I'm ADHD! 2004. 23p. pap. 24.95 (978-1-4137-3249-8(6)) PublishAmerica, Inc.

Crompton, Richard. More William. 2008. 112p. pap. (978-1-4068-4959-2(6)) Echo Library.

Crompton, Richmal. Just William As Seen on TV. 2003. (ENG., Illus.). 176p. (J). pap. 6.95 (978-0-333-62802-7(0)) Macmillan Pubs., Ltd. GBR. Dist: Trafalgar Square Publishing.

—More William. 2008. 188p. 25.99 (978-0-554-26245-1(2)) 2008. 188p. 22.99 (978-0-554-35548-1(5)) 2007. 168p. pap.

19.99 (978-1-4346-0719-5(4)) 2007. (ENG.). 186p. pap. 21.99 (978-1-4346-0779-9(8)) Creative Media Partners, LLC.

—More William. Henry, Thomas, illus. 2008. 196p. pap. (978-1-4099-4227-6(9)) Dodo Pr.

—More William. 2010. (Illus.). 102p. pap. 19.99 (978-1-4432-2651-6(3)) General Bks. LLC.

—William at War. 2nd rev. ed. (ENG., Illus.). 272p. (J). pap. (978-0-333-63793-7(3), Macmillan Children's Bks.) Pan Macmillan.

Cronn-Mills, Kirstin. Beautiful Music for Ugly Children. 2012. (ENG.). 288p. (YA). pap. 11.99 (978-0-7387-3251-0(6), Flux) North Star Editions.

Crowne, Alyssa. Pink Princess Rules the School. Alder, Charlotte, illus. 2009. 80p. (J). pap. (978-0-545-16077-3(4)) Scholastic, Inc.

Cumberland, Wendy. Inkwelo Mountain: A Child's Adventure in Kwa Zulu, South Africa. 2013. 46p. pap. 10.95 (978-1-62857-135-6(7), Strategic Bk. Publishing) Strategic Book Publishing & Rights Agency (SBPRA).

Curley, Marianne. Key. 2011. (Guardians of Time Ser.). (ENG.). 416p. (YA). (gr. 7). pap. 9.99 (978-1-59990-545-7(0), 9781599905457, Bloomsbury USA Childrens) Bloomsbury Publishing USA.

—Old Magic. 2009. (ENG.). 400p. (YA). (gr. 7-18). pap. 9.99 (978-1-4169-8991-2(9), Simon Pulse) Simon Pulse.

Curry, Kenneth. Chuka & the Drum. 2007. (Illus.). 22p. (J). 10.95 (978-0-9798364-4-2(1)) Curry Brothers Publishing Group.

Curtis, Gavin. The Bat Boy & His Violin. 2004. (Illus.). (J). (gr. k-3). spiral bd. (978-0-616-07254-7(6)) Canadian National Institute for the Blind/Institut National Canadien pour les Aveugles.

Cyr, Liz. Pete-O Burrito & the Lucky Stripes. Cyr, Christopher & Cyr, James, illus. 2012. 28p. 24.95 (978-1-4626-5566-3(1)) America Star Bks.

Dahl, Roald. Charlie y el Gran Ascensor de Cristal. Jacques, Faith, illus. 2003.Tr. of Charlie & the Great Glass Elevator. (SPA.). 164p. (J). (gr. 5-8). pap. 12.95 (978-968-19-0988-8(7)) Santillana USA Publishing Co., Inc.

—CHARLIE Y EL GRAN ASCENSOR DE CRISTAL. 27th ed. 2005. (SPA., Illus.). 208p. (J). (gr. 5-8). pap. 11.95 (978-84-204-6573-9(9), Alfaguara) Santillana USA Publishing Co., Inc.

—Charlie y la Fabrica de Chocolate. Jacques, Faith, illus. 2003.Tr. of Charlie & the Chocolate Factory. (FRE & SPA.). 176p. (J). (gr. 4-7). (978-84-204-4771-1(4), AF0153) Ediciones Alfaguara.

—Charlie y la Fabrica de Chocolate.Tr. of Charlie & the Chocolate Factory. (SPA.). (J). 8.95 (978-968-6026-71-9(1)) Santillana USA Publishing Co., Inc.

—Danny el Campeon del Mundo. Blake, Quentin, illus. 2003.Tr. of Danny the Champion of the World. (SPA.). 200p. (YA). (gr. 5-8). 9.95 (978-84-204-4431-4(6)) Ediciones Alfaguara ESP. Dist: Santillana USA Publishing Co., Inc.

Dail, Ernestine. A Voice in the Night. Gillen, Rosemarie, illus. 2012. 46p. pap. 9.99 (978-1-61286-099-2(0)) Avid Readers Publishing Group.

Dal Santo, Sandy. My Fantasy Forest. 2009. 36p. pap. 15.65 (978-1-4389-6035-7(2)) AuthorHouse.

Daly, Mariah. James Has Diabetes. 2009. 56p. pap. 21.99 (978-1-4389-3188-3(3)) AuthorHouse.

Damiron, Anya. Dreamboy. Pino, Pablo, illus. 2010. (SPA.). 26p. (J). (978-9945-421-42-2(5)) Lucia Stories.

—Nino Inventor. Pino, Pablo, illus. 2010. 26p. (J). (978-9945-00-153-2(1)) Lucia Stories.

Damon, Sidney. Harold the Orange Juice Boy. 40p. (Orig.). (J). (gr. k-4). pap. (978-0-937148-14-3(8)) Wild Horses Publishing Co.

Daniels, Katie C. Danny's Adventure in Afric. 2009. 24p. pap. 12.99 (978-1-4389-3404-4(1)) AuthorHouse.

DANOWSKI, Sonja. Night Cat. 2016. (ENG., Illus.). 48p. 19.95 (978-0-7358-4266-3(3)) North-South Bks., Inc.

Dave, Grandpa. Children's Stories Iii. 2012. 104p. (gr. 2-4). pap. 11.79 (978-1-4669-1829-0(2)) Trafford Publishing.

Dave, Matt. Supercool Snotman, No. 8. Baines, Nigel, illus. (ENG.). 112p. pap. (978-1-84738-288-7(6)) Simon & Schuster, Ltd.

Davenport, Kelly. Do Hotdogs Grow on Trees? 2010. 32p. pap. 17.99 (978-1-4520-6636-3(1)) AuthorHouse.

Davies, Jocelyn. A Beautiful Dark. 2011. (ENG.). 400p. (YA). (gr. 8). 17.99 (978-0-06-199065-6(5), HarperTeen) HarperCollins Pubs.

Davies, Mike. Lousy Thinking: Hitching a Ride on a Schoolboy's Mind. 2012. 162p. pap. (978-1-906954-53-6(4)) Live It Publishing.

Davis, Brian. Matthew & Goliath. Wheeler, Ron, illus. 2003. (Book of Matt Ser.: 3). 80p. (J). pap. 4.99 (978-1-59269-058-9(0)) Mcruffy Pr.

Davis, Raymond Mace. Sinjin & the Mosaic Garden, 1 vol. 2009. 47p. pap. 24.95 (978-1-60836-634-7(0)) America Star Bks.

Davis, Richard. The Boy Scout & Other Stories for Boys. 2005. pap. 30.95 (978-1-885529-45-9(7)) Stevens Publishing.

de Las Casas, Dianne. The Cajun Cornbread Boy, 1 vol. Gentry, Marita, illus. 2008. (ENG.). 32p. (J). (gr. k-3). 16.99 (978-1-58980-224-7(1)) Pelican Publishing Co., Inc.

De Munnik, Hema. Bhole: Adventures of a Young Yogi. 2006. (ENG., Illus.). 352p. (J). (gr. 3-7). per. 18.95 (978-81-88157-37-2(6)) Lotus Pr.

Dean, Lani. One Misty Morning. Cassidy, Al, illus. 2004. 36p. (J). 14.95 (978-0-9645844-9-5(2)) Manor Hse. Publishing Co., Inc.

Debaer-Levoy, Carole. The Story of Candyland. 2007. 40p. per. 13.95 (978-1-59858-328-1(X)) Dog Ear Publishing, LLC.

Decker, Tim. The Punk Ethic. Decker, Tim, illus. 2012. (ENG., Illus.). 188p. (YA). 18.95 (978-1-60898-120-5(7)); pap. 9.95 (978-1-60898-121-2(5)) namelos llc.

Deford, Ted. Po & the Gang: In Two Big Adventures. 2005. 49p. pap. 16.95 (978-1-4137-9068-9(2)) PublishAmerica, Inc.

DeLoach, Kathleen. Le Monde de Daniel: Un livre sur les enfants Handicapés. Best, Cathy, illus. 2005. (FRE.). (J). pap. 15.95 (978-1-933514-01-7(9)) Three Moons Media.

—El Mundo de Daniel: Un libro sobre niños Minusválidos. Best, Cathy, illus. 2005. (SPA.). 20p. (J). pap. 15.95 (978-1-933514-00-0(0)) Three Moons Media.

Demarest, Jeannie. My Best Friend Troubles. 2009. 28p. pap. 21.99 (978-1-4415-3236-7(6)) Xlibris Corp.

DeNivo, Jennifer. Sneaky Sam. 2011. 24p. (gr. 1-2). pap. 12.79 (978-1-4567-5181-4(6)) AuthorHouse.

Denou, Violeta. Teo en la Escuela (Teo at School) (SPA.). 32p. (J). 12.95 (978-84-7176-311-2(7)) Timun Mas, Editorial S.A. ESP. Dist: AIMS International Bks., Inc.

Denucci, Sharon. Ava Goes to Alask: Grammie & the Gecko Series. 2012. 32p. pap. 19.99 (978-1-4685-6157-9(X)) AuthorHouse.

Desrosiers, Sylvie & Franson, Leanne. Je Suis Thomas. 2003. (Premier Roman Ser.). (FRE., Illus.). 64p. (J). (gr. 1-4). pap. (978-2-89021-617-4(9)) Diffusion du livre Mirabel (DLM).

Devorsine, Sally. Now I Know... That We All Have a Jewel Inside Us, Somewhere. 2012. (Now I Know Ser.). (ENG., Illus.). 56p. (J). (gr. -1-3). pap. 15.00 (978-0-9740268-3-1(2)) Chocolate Sauce.

DiCicco, Sue. Superhero Potty Time. 2011. (ENG., Illus.). 14p. (J). (— 1). bds. 7.99 (978-0-375-87201-3(9), Golden Bks.) Random Hse. Children's Bks.

Dickens, Charles. David Copperfield. 2006. (ENG.). 130p. per. 18.95 (978-1-84002-570-5(0)) Consortium Bk. Sales & Distribution.

—David Copperfield. 2008. (Bring the Classics to Life Ser.). (Illus.). 72p. (gr. 4-12). pap., act. bk. ed. 10.95 (978-1-55576-322-0(7), EDCTR-408B) EDCON Publishing Group.

—David Copperfield. 2009. 186p. pap. 19.99 (978-1-4590-4328-2(6)) General Bks. LLC.

—David Copperfield. 2009. (Foundation Classics Ser.). 56p. (J). (gr. 5-9). lib. bdg. 27.95 (978-1-60754-852-2(6)) Windmill Bks.

—David Copperfield. 2006. (Oxford Progressive English Readers Ser.). (ENG., Illus.). 103p. (J). (gr. 4-7). per. (978-0-19-597140-8(X)) Oxford Univ. Pr.

Dickens, Frank. Albert Herbert Hawkins: The Naughtiest Boy in the World. Dickens, Frank, illus. (Illus.). 32p. (J). (gr. -1-3). 12.95 (978-0-87592-000-9(4)) Scroll Pr., Inc.

Diehl, Jean Heilprin. Loon Chase, 1 vol. Freeman, Kathryn S., illus. 2006. (ENG.). 32p. (J). (gr. 1-5). 15.95 (978-0-9764943-8-6(8)) Arbordale Publishing.

Digby Tracks a Catamount. 2008. (Illus.). 36p. (J). per. (978-0-9745931-1-1(7)) Vermont Bookworks.

Dixon, Franklin W. Feeding Frenzy. 20th ed. 2008. (Hardy Boys (All New) Undercover Brothers Ser.: 20). (ENG., Illus.). 160p. (J). (gr. 3-7). pap. 7.99 (978-1-4169-5499-6(6), Aladdin) Simon & Schuster Children's Publishing.

—House Arrest. 23rd ed. 2008. (Hardy Boys (All New) Undercover Brothers Ser.: 23). (ENG., Illus.). 176p. (J). (gr. 3-7). pap. 5.99 (978-1-4169-6171-0(2), Aladdin) Simon & Schuster Children's Publishing.

The Doctor, 2 Pack. (Chiquilibros Ser.). (gr. -1-1). 12.00 (978-0-7635-8544-0(0)) Rigby Education.

Dor, George Vincent. Sit. 2012. (Illus.). 112p. 27.45 (978-1-4678-9732-7(9)); pap. 15.18 (978-1-4678-9731-0(0)) AuthorHouse.

Dorenda W. Madkins. Sammy's Battle with the L-I-E Word. 2011. 48p. pap. 24.95 (978-1-4626-2650-2(5)) America Star Bks.

Douglas-Hobbs, Kathy. Kobe & the Rescue Adventure. 2012. 16p. pap. 15.99 (978-1-4772-0326-2(5)) AuthorHouse.

Doyle, Brian. Spud Sweetgrass, 1 vol. 2nd ed. 2006. (ENG.). 140p. (J). (gr. 2-7). pap. 5.95 (978-0-88899-756-2(6)) Groundwood Bks. CAN. Dist: Publishers Group West (PGW).

Dragland. Simon Jesse's Journey. (J). pap. 2.95 (978-0-88899-025-9(1), Libros Tigrillo) Groundwood Bks. CAN. Dist: Publishers Group West (PGW).

Driscoll, James R. The Brighton Boys with the Flying Corps. 2005. 152p. pap. 11.95 (978-1-59540-820-4(7), 1st World Library - Literary Society) 1st World Publishing, Inc.

Du Jardin, Rosamond. Marcy Catches Up. 2003. (YA). pap. 12.95 (978-1-930009-75-2(5), 800-691-7779) Image Cascade Publishing.

Du Lac, Leo J. Moon Fruit & the Dragons: Santa Claus & the Flying Carpet 3. Washington, Victoria, ed. Baker, David, illus. 2012. 26p. 24.95 (978-1-4560-1037-9(9)) America Star Bks.

Dudney, Emma Mae. The Runaway. 2008. 144p. pap. 9.95 (978-0-9800854-0-2(3)) Authors' Discovery Cooperation, Inc.

Duffy, Tanya. Bonkers. 2011. (Illus.). 28p. pap. 10.35 (978-1-4520-5631-9(5)) AuthorHouse.

Dulemba, Elizabeth O. Soap, Soap, Soap. Dulemba, Elizabeth O., illus. 2010. (ENG., Illus.). 32p. (J). (gr. -1-3). pap. 7.95 (978-1-934960-65-3(9), Raven Tree Pr.,Csi) Continental Sales, Inc.

Duncan, Brenda. Reese - the Dog Who Almost Ruined Christmas. 2012. 24p. pap. 17.99 (978-1-4772-6105-7(2)) AuthorHouse.

Durbin, William. Until the Last Spike: The Journal of Sean Sullivan, a Transcontinental Railroad Worker, Nebraska & Points West 1867. 2013. (My Name Is America Ser.). lib. bdg. 17.20 (978-0-606-32342-0(2), Turtleback) Turtleback Bks.

Durfee, Jody Wind. Hadley-Hadley Benson. 2013. (ENG.). 144p. (J). pap. 11.99 (978-1-62108-151-7(6)) Covenant Communications, Inc.

Dyan, Penelope. Ben's Adventures — -Proof Positive That Boys Will Be Boys. Dyan, Penelope, illus. 2008. (Illus.). 44p. pap. 11.95 (978-1-935118-40-4(4)) Bellissima Publishing, LLC.

—Bubble Trouble — -for Boys Only (r). Dyan, Penelope, illus. 2011. (Illus.). 34p. pap. 11.95 (978-1-935630-92-0(X)) Bellissima Publishing, LLC.

—Pass the Gas! for Boys Only(r). 2011. 34p. pap. 11.95 (978-1-935630-73-9(3)) Bellissima Publishing, LLC.

Dyan, Penelope, creator. For Love of Pete! The Story of the Boy Who Played the Taps on Iwo Jima. 2005. 292p. (YA). per. 15.95 (978-0-9768417-9-1(7)) Bellissima Publishing, LLC.

Dycus, Warren. Monyum Bay - Time Travel. 2010. 24p. 13.99 (978-0-557-45202-6(3)) Lulu Pr., Inc.

Dyer, Jill. The Plant of the Zorks. 2005. 11p. 6.65 (978-1-4116-6641-2(0)) Lulu Pr., Inc.

Eagle Feathers, 6 vols. (Multicultural Programs Ser.). 16p. (gr. 1-6). 31.95 (978-0-7802-8327-5(9)) Wright Group/McGraw-Hill.

Echerique, Alfredo Bryce & Duenas, Ana Maria. Goig. Roederer, Charlotte, illus. (Literary Encounters Ser.). (SPA.). (J). (gr. 3-5). pap. (978-968-494-065-9(3), CI7706) Centro de Informacion y Desarrollo de la Comunicacion y la Literatura MEX. Dist: Lectorum Pubns., Inc.

Echols, Jennifer. The Boys Next Door. 2007. (Romantic Comedies Ser.). (ENG.). 336p. (YA). (gr. 9-12). mass mkt. 6.99 (978-1-4169-1831-8(0), Simon Pulse) Simon Pulse.

Edward, J. P. Bobby & Buddy Friends for Life. Hose, Ryan, illus. 2011. 16p. pap. 24.95 (978-1-4560-7520-0(9)) America Star Bks.

Eggers, Jeanette S. Grandmas Don't Tilt-A-Whirl(r). 2009. 44p. pap. 18.49 (978-1-4490-0546-7(2)) AuthorHouse.

Eichler, Ken. Swift Eagle's Odyssey with the Buffalo. 2007. 59p. pap. 16.95 (978-1-60474-199-5(6)) America Star Bks.

—Swift Eagle's Wagon Train Adventure, 1 vol. 2010. 80p. pap. 19.95 (978-1-4489-4364-7(7)) America Star Bks.

Eliopoulis, Chris, text. Franklin Richards: Son of a Genius Ultimate Collection - Book 1. 2010. (ENG., Illus.). 208p. (J). (gr. -1-17). pap., pap. 19.99 (978-0-7851-4924-8(4)) Marvel Worldwide, Inc.

Eliopulos, Nick. The Book of Shane. 2015. (Spirit Animals Special Edition Ser.). (ENG.). 192p. (J). (gr. 3-7). 12.99 (978-0-545-91098-9(6)) Scholastic, Inc.

Elkington, John. The Pirates of the Gayoso Bayou. 2012. 24p. pap. 15.99 (978-1-4797-3940-0(5)) Xlibris Corp.

Elliott, George. The Boy Who Loved Bananas. Krystoforski, Andrej, illus. 2005. 32p. (J). (gr. -1-2). 15.95 (978-1-55337-744-3(3)) Kids Can Pr., Ltd. CAN. Dist: Hachette Bk. Group.

Ellis, Deborah. The Cat at the Wall, 1 vol. (ENG., Illus.). (J). 2015. 152p. pap. 9.95 (978-1-55498-707-8(5)) 2014. 144p. (gr. 3-7). 16.95 (978-1-55498-491-6(2)) Groundwood Bks. CAN. Dist: Publishers Group West (PGW).

Ellis, Edward Sylvester. Two Boys in Wyoming: A Tale of Adventure (Northwest Series No. 3) 2007. (ENG.). 204p. (J). pap. 20.99 (978-1-4346-3792-5(1)); 228p. pap. 22.99 (978-1-4346-3793-2(X)) Creative Media Partners, LLC.

Ely, Lesley, et al. Cuidando a Louis. 2004. (SPA., Illus.). 28p. (J). (gr. 2-3). 18.99 (978-84-8488-115-5(6)) Serres, Ediciones, S. L. ESP. Dist: Lectorum Pubns., Inc.

Emanuel, Lora. The Puppy Tree, 1 vol. Swope, Brenda, illus. 2009. 30p. pap. 24.95 (978-1-60749-614-4(3)) America Star Bks.

Erickson, Timothy Ronald. Death's Whisper Recoil, 2. Erickson, Timothy Ronald, illus. 2003. (Illus.). (YA). pap. 14.95 (978-1-59492-001-1(X)) Erickson, Tim.

Erlings, Fridrik. Boy on the Edge. 2014. (ENG.). 240p. (YA). (gr. 9). 16.99 (978-0-7636-6680-4(7)) Candlewick Pr.

Esenwa, Anthony. Jaja, King of Opobo. 2009. (Illus.). 24p. pap. 11.49 (978-1-4389-5886-6(2)) AuthorHouse.

Exelby, Kathy. My Dog Harpo: The Biggest Kid I Know. Wall Darby, Colleen, illus. 2007. (J). per. 20.00 (978-1-932583-39-7(4)) digital@batesjackson llc.

Fairchild-Lenyo, Mary. When Winston Wins. Vigil, Cristina, illus. 2007. 36p. per. 14.95 (978-1-59858-405-9(7)) Dog Ear Publishing, LLC.

Fambro, Sonja Grimsley. Santa Spent the Night with Me! 2011. 52p. pap. 25.06 (978-1-4634-4626-0(8)) AuthorHouse.

Fantasia, Kathryn. Pass It On. Flanagan, Jeff, illus. 2009. 28p. pap. 18.65 (978-1-4415-5446-8(7)) Xlibris Corp.

Farley, Colby King. A Warm Familiar Feeling. 2nd ed. 2003. (YA). per. 13.50 (978-0-943864-48-8(8)) Davenport, May Pubs.

Faulconer, Charlotte. The Green Button Wish. 2010. 28p. pap. 12.49 (978-1-4490-8003-7(0)) AuthorHouse.

Feasey, Steve. Wereling. 2010. (Wereling Ser.: 1). (ENG.). 288p. (YA). (gr. 7-18). pap. 9.99 (978-0-312-59612-5(X), 9780312596125) Feiwel & Friends.

Fiford, Tanya. How to Bake Grandm. 2009. (Illus.). 16p. pap. 8.49 (978-1-4389-6352-5(1)) AuthorHouse.

Findlay, Andrew. Roddy & the Magic Mattress. 2005. 54p. pap. 5.61 (978-1-4116-3612-5(0)) Lulu Pr., Inc.

Finkelstein, Chaim. The Burksfield Bike Club, Book 2: Lost & Found. Jennings, R. W., illus. 2007. 224p. (J). 15.95 (978-1-932443-69-1(X), BBC1H) Judaica Pr., Inc., The.

Finley, Leah. The One & Only Mr C. 2009. 82p. pap. 8.95 (978-1-935118-75-6(7)) Bellissima Publishing, LLC.

Firth, Rachel & Sims, Leslie B. Illustrated Classics for Boys. 2010. (Illustrated Stories Ser.). 383p. (J). (gr. 4-7). 19.99 (978-0-7945-2439-5(7), Usborne) EDC Publishing.

Fishman, Cathy Goldberg. Car Wash Kid. Gott, Barry, illus. 2003. (Rookie Reader Skill Set Ser.). (ENG.). (J). (gr. k-2). pap. 4.95 (978-0-516-27811-7(8), Children's Pr.) Scholastic Library Publishing.

Fite, Ramona. A Boy & His God. Monick, Susie, illus. 2012. 36p. 22.50 (978-1-937763-37-4(4)) Published by Westview, Inc.

Fitzpatrick, Huntley. The Boy Most Likely To. 2015. (ENG.). 432p. (YA). (gr. 9). 17.99 (978-0-8037-4142-3(1), Dial Bks) Penguin Young Readers Group.

Fleming, Candace. Clever Jack Takes the Cake. Karas, G. Brian, illus. 2010. (ENG.). 40p. (J). (gr. -1-3). 17.99 (978-0-375-84979-4(3), Schwartz & Wade Bks.) Random Hse. Children's Bks.

Fletcher, Steffi. The Lone Ranger. Dreany, E. Joseph, illus. 2013. (Little Golden Book Ser.). (ENG.). 24p. (J). (-k). 4.99 (978-0-449-81793-3(8), Golden Bks.) Random Hse. Children's Bks.

Flores-Galbis, Enrique. 90 Miles to Havana. 2012. (ENG.). 304p. (J). (gr. 4-7). pap. 7.99 (978-1-250-00559-5(0), 9781250005595) Square Fish.

Flynn, Dave. Nick & the Old Man of the Mountain. 2010. 40p. pap. 18.49 (978-1-4389-9356-0(0)) AuthorHouse.

Flynn, Ian. Mega Man 3: Return of Dr. Wily. Bates, Ben, illus. 2012. (Mega Man Ser.: 3). (ENG.). 112p. (gr. 4-7). pap. 11.99 (978-1-936975-11-2(4), Archie Comics) Archie Comic Pubns., Inc.

—Mega Man 4: Spiritus Ex Machina. 2012. (Mega Man Ser.: 4). (ENG.). 112p. (gr. 4-7). pap. 11.99 (978-1-936975-27-3(0), Archie Comics) Archie Comic Pubns., Inc.

Foley, Sue. Tyrone: A Turtle Tale. Kobak, Carrie, illus. 2010. (ENG.). 32p. (gr. -1-5). 14.95 (978-1-885003-88-1(9)) Reed, Robert D. Pubs.

Fontaine, Renee. Boy in the Hoodie. Margolis, Al, illus. 2012. 34p. (J). 19.95 (978-1-61863-105-3(5)) Bookstand Publishing.

Foreman, Michael. Norman's Ark. Foreman, Michael, illus. 2006. (Tiger Tales Ser.). (Illus.). 24p. (J). (gr. -1-3). pap. 6.95 (978-1-58925-401-5(5)) Tiger Tales.

Forgey, Winchester. Chronicle of the Bent Nail. 2004. (J). per. (978-0-9666572-7-2(6)) Acacia Publishing, Inc.

Forte, Joyce. The Lost Leprechaun, 1 vol. 2010. 32p. pap. 24.95 (978-1-4489-9518-9(3)) PublishAmerica, Inc.

Fosberry, Jennifer. My Name Is Not Alexander. Litwin, Mike, illus. 2011. (ENG.). 32p. (J). (gr. k-3). 16.99 (978-1-4022-5433-8(4), Sourcebooks Jabberwocky) Sourcebooks, Inc.

Fourniea, Stephanie. Are You a Monster When You Eat. 2011. 24p. pap. 12.29 (978-1-4634-2958-4(4)) AuthorHouse.

Fower, C. A. The Bramblefrost Fairies. 2013. 116p. (978-1-909740-40-2(3)); pap. (978-1-909593-96-1(6)) Legend Pr.

Fragoza, Samuel. Josh & the Sock Army. 2012. 24p. pap. 17.99 (978-1-4772-9532-8(1)) AuthorHouse.

Francis-Bala, Sundari. Olly Jolly Says - Count Your Blessings. 2012. 32p. pap. (978-1-77097-466-1(0)) FriesenPress.

Frankowski, Leo A. & Frankowski, Leo. A Boy & His Tank. 2004. (ENG.). 288p. reprint ed. mass mkt. 6.99 (978-0-671-57850-3(2)) Baen Bks.

Friedman, Laurie. McDonald, Super Sitter. Kalis, Jennifer, illus. 2017. (Mallory Ser.: 27). (ENG.). 160p. (gr. 2-5). 31.99 **(978-1-5124-2696-0(2)**, Darby Creek) Lerner Publishing Group.

Friedman, Robin. Nothing. 2008. (ENG.). 240p. (YA). (gr. 8-18). pap. 9.95 (978-0-7387-1304-5(X), Flux) North Star Editions.

Friel, Maeve. Charlie's Story, 1 vol. 2004. (ENG.). 112p. (YA). (gr. 7-9). pap. 6.95 (978-1-56145-315-3(3)) Peachtree Pubs.

From zero to Hero. 2007. (J). bds. 14.95 (978-0-9793882-1-7(X)) Over The Rainbow Bks. Publishing.

Fuqua, Jonathon Scott. King of the Pygmies. 2005. (ENG.). 256p. (YA). (gr. 7-18). 16.99 (978-0-7636-1418-8(1)) Candlewick Pr.

Furraway, Bec. Matthew's Family Moves / Robert's Family Moves. 2011. 30p. pap. 14.50 (978-1-60860-995-6(2), Strategic Bk. Publishing) Strategic Book Publishing & Rights Agency (SBPRA).

Galdone, Paul. The Gingerbread Boy. 2011. (Folk Tale Classics Ser.). (ENG., Illus.). 48p. (J). (gr. -1-3). 8.99 (978-0-547-59940-3(4)) Houghton Mifflin Harcourt Publishing Co.

Garant, Andre J. The Elite Eight. 2011. 120p. (gr. 4-6). pap. 10.99 (978-1-4567-4302-4(3)) AuthorHouse.

Garces Iii, Joseph Louis. Garrett the Firefighter. Abercrombie, Bethaney, illus. 2008. 24p. pap. 12.99 (978-1-59858-716-6(1)) Dog Ear Publishing, LLC.

Garcia, Cindy Booth. Rat-a-Tat-Tat Not That!, 1 vol. 2010. 22p. 24.95 (978-1-4489-7425-2(9)) PublishAmerica, Inc.

Gardner, L. S. From Bobcat to Wolf: The Story of Den Seven, Pack Four. Stevens, illus. 2011. 192p. 42.95 (978-1-258-04225-7(8)) Literary Licensing, LLC.

Gebhart, Ryan. There Will Be Bears. 2016. (ENG.). 224p. (J). (gr. 5). pap. 8.99 (978-0-7636-8765-6(0)) Candlewick Pr.

Gee, Randi. Everybody Has a Cat Named Molly. 2010. 32p. pap. 15.50 (978-0-557-27671-4(3)) Lulu Pr., Inc.

Geldart, Thomas. Emilie the Peacemaker. 2004. reprint ed. pap. 1.99 (978-1-4192-1769-2(0)) Kessinger Publishing, LLC.

Geller, Mark. Raymond. (SPA.). 94p. (YA). (gr. 5-8). (978-84-279-3215-9(4), NG0896) Noguer y Caralt Editores, S. A. ESP. Dist: Lectorum Pubns., Inc.

Gentry, Nancy. Little Blue, Little Gray. Keaggy, Sarah, illus. 2012. 56p. pap. 10.00 (978-0-9846244-9-2(X)) O'More Publishing.

Geraldi, Michele J. The Way to Papou Lake. 2011. 112p. (gr. 2-4). 20.95 (978-1-4620-3134-4(X)); pap. 10.95 (978-1-4620-3133-7(1)) iUniverse, Inc.

Gervay, Susanne. Being Jack. Wilcox, Cathy, illus. 2015. 167p. (J). (978-1-61067-455-3(3)) Kane Miller.

Getting Rid of Harold. 80p. (YA). (gr. 6-12). pap. 10.95 (978-0-8224-3944-8(1)) Globe Fearon Educational Publishing.

Gibbs, Gail L. What about Those Pants? 2012. 24p. pap. 15.99 (978-1-4691-7338-2(7)) Xlibris Corp.

Gibson, B. W. Extra Innings: The Diamond Thieves. 2014. 152p. pap. 14.95 (978-1-4918-5663-5(7)) AuthorHouse.

Gilchrist, J. Into the Land of Nede. 2010. 108p. (gr. 4-6). 20.95 (978-1-4502-5433-5(0)); pap. 10.95 (978-1-4502-5432-8(2)) iUniverse, Inc.

Giles, Doris. Foursome. 2009. 24p. pap. 13.49 (978-1-4389-1203-5(X)) AuthorHouse.

Gill, Raj. A Monkey Ate My Pancakes. 2013. (ENG.). 34p. pap. 10.95 (978-1-927005-28-6(0)) Burman Books, Inc. CAN. Dist: Innovative Logistics.

Gilley, Mel. Sam & the Sad Dinosaur. 2011. 28p. pap. 13.59 (978-1-4567-6751-8(8)) AuthorHouse.

Gillmor, Don. The Christmas Orange. 2004. (Illus.). (J). (gr. k-3). spiral bd. (978-0-616-03035-6(5)) Canadian National Institute for the Blind/Institut National Canadien pour les Aveugles.

Gilman, Dorothy Foster. Ted Gilman. Caley, Isabel W., illus. 2011. 200p. 44.95 (978-1-258-06474-7(X)) Literary Licensing, LLC.

Gipson, Fred. Old Yeller. Date not set. 192p. (J). 20.95 (978-0-8488-2273-6(0)) Amereon Ltd.

—Old Yeller. 2003. (Trophy Bk.). (ENG.). 192p. (J). (gr. 5-18). pap. 6.99 (978-0-06-440382-5(3)) HarperCollins Pubs.

—Old Yeller. 2009. (Perennial Classics Ser.). 132p. (gr. 4-7). 20.85 (978-0-613-85744-4(5), Turtleback) Turtleback Bks.

Gipson, Fred & Polson, Steven. Old Yeller. 2009. (Perennial Classics Ser.). (ENG., Illus.). 144p. (gr. 4-7). pap. 12.99 (978-0-06-093547-4(2), Harper Perennial) HarperCollins Pubs.

Giulieri, Anne. To the Shops, 1 vol. Florian, Mélanie, illus. 2012. (Engage Literacy Magenta Ser.). (ENG.). 32p. (gr. k-2). pap. 5.99 (978-1-4296-8882-6(3), Engage Literacy) Capstone Press of Coughlan Cos.

Golding, William. El Senor de las Moscas.Tr. of Lord of the Flies. (SPA.). 240p. (J). 10.95 (978-84-206-1381-9(9),

AZ9078) Alianza Editorial, S. A. ESP. Dist: Lectorum Pubns., Inc.

Goldman, Lisa Bear. Amadito & Spider Woman. Pena, Amado M., Jr., illus. 2003. 32p. (J). 15.95 *(978-1-885772-30-5(0))* Kiva Publishing, Inc.

Gómez Cerda, Alfredo. Barro de Medellín/ Mud of Medellin. Lopez, Xan, illus. 2010. (SPA.). 146p. (YA). (gr. 5-8). *(978-84-263-6849-2(2))* Vives, Luis Editorial (Edelvives).

Gonyea, Maria. Princess Maria. 2013. 28p. pap. 13.95 *(978-1-4525-8189-7(4),* Balboa Pr.) Author Solutions, Inc.

Gooding-Alber, Karry. Red Shoelace. 1 vol. 2010. 16p. pap. 24.95 *(978-1-4489-6255-6(2))* America Star Bks.

Goodman, George. The Boy They Thought Never Wanted to Work. 2012. 48p. (gr. -1-2). pap. 11.95 *(978-1-4685-5656-8(8))* AuthorHouse.

Goscinny, René. Le Petit Nicolas. Date not set. (FRE & ENG., Illus.). 80p. (J). pap. 46.50 *(978-0-582-36071-6(4))* Addison-Wesley Longman, Ltd. GBR. Dist: Trans-Atlantic Pubns., Inc.

Gott, Ricky. I Wish, I Wish... I Wish to Fish / IT. 2011. (Illus.). 80p. (J). pap. 24.95 *(978-0-9837334-1-6(4))* Digi-Tall Media.

Gower, Catherine & Zhihong, He. Long-Long's New Year. 2005. (ENG., Illus.). 32p. (J). (gr. k-3). 16.95 *(978-0-8048-3666-1(3))* Tuttle Publishing.

Grace, Samantha & Michael. My Little Boy. 2012. 32p. pap. 19.99 *(978-1-4772-0333-0(8))* AuthorHouse.

Graftinvine, D. J. Hobbledehoy: Salvation. 2012. (ENG.). 73p. pap. 12.95 *(978-1-4787-1600-6(2))* Outskirts Pr., Inc.

Grande, Gabrielle. Fluffy's Book. 2013. 24p. (J). pap. 12.99 *(978-1-4808-0067-0(8))*; (Illus.). 22.99 *(978-1-4808-0068-7(6))* Archway Publishing.

Grandma, Sue. Rocky the Rocking Horse. 2010. 24p. 12.99 *(978-1-4520-7333-0(3))* AuthorHouse.

Grant, Vicki. Pigboy. 2007. (Orca Currents Ser.). 101p. (gr. 5). 19.95 *(978-0-7569-8067-2(4))* Perfection Learning Corp.

Graves, Damien. The Deadly Catch. 2008. (Midnight Library). (Illus.). 170p. (J). (gr. 4-7). 13.65 *(978-0-7569-8824-1(1))* Perfection Learning Corp.

Gray, Bianca. Back to School: Adventures of Alex & Joey. 2013. 20p. pap. 17.99 *(978-1-4817-0425-0(7))* AuthorHouse.

Green, Jack. Dusty the Dust Devil. 2011. 70p. pap. 19.95 *(978-1-4560-8507-0(7))* America Star Bks.

—The Microchip Kid. 2011. 52p. pap. 16.95 *(978-1-4560-8494-3(1))* America Star Bks.

Greenburg, Dan. The Shluffmuffin Boy Is History, Bk. 5. Fischer, Scott M., illus. 2006. (Secrets of Dripping Fang Ser.: Bk. 5). (ENG.). 176p. (J). (gr. 2-5). 12.99 *(978-0-15-206035-0(9))* Houghton Mifflin Harcourt Publishing Co.

Greene, Stephanie. Princess Posey & the First-Grade Boys. Sisson, Stéphanie Roth, illus. 2014. (Princess Posey, First Grader Ser.: 8). (ENG.). 96p. (J). (gr. k-3). pap. 5.99 *(978-0-14-242735-4(7),* Puffin Books) Penguin Young Readers Group.

Griffiths, Andy. The Big Fat Cow That Goes Kapow. Denton, Terry, illus. 2010. (ENG.). 144p. (J). (gr. -1-3). pap. 7.99 *(978-0-312-65301-9(8),* 9780312653019) Square Fish.

Grillo, Tine. I'm Not Afraid of That. 2011. (Illus.). 44p. (J). pap. 18.99 *(978-1-59092-761-8(3))* Blue Forge Pr.

Grimes, Charles J. The Boys!, 1 vol. 2010. 186p. pap. 24.95 *(978-1-4489-5736-1(2))* America Star Bks.

Gross, S. D. Freddie. 2007. (Illus.). 22p. (J). per. 12.99 *(978-1-59879-342-0(X))* Lifevest Publishing, Inc.

—Freddie, Fireman Mike. 2007. (Illus.). 24p. (J). (gr. -1-3). per. 12.99 *(978-1-59879-343-7(8))* Lifevest Publishing, Inc.

—Mugallumps. 2007. (Illus.). 32p. (J). per. 13.99 *(978-1-59879-303-1(9))* Lifevest Publishing, Inc.

Grover, Neha Lamba. Shaurya's Adventures. 2010. 43p. pap. 17.40 *(978-0-557-12636-1(3))* Lulu Pr., Inc.

Guarneri, Lauren. Do You Know Who I Am Now? 2011. 36p. pap. 16.86 *(978-1-4670-2618-5(2))* AuthorHouse.

Guettier, Nancy. Jude's Moon. Walsh, Tina, illus. 2014. (ENG.). 32p. (gr. -1-4). pap. 9.95 *(978-1-61448-964-1(5))* Morgan James Publishing.

Gumnut, I. B. Daniel's Pushbike. 2012. 24p. pap. 12.45 *(978-1-4525-0463-6(6))* Balboa Pr.

Gunderson, J. Ropes of Revolution: The Boston Tea Party, 1 vol. Schoonover, Brent, illus. 2008. (Historical Fiction Ser.). (ENG.). 56p. (gr. 2-3). pap. 6.25 *(978-1-4342-0492-9(8),* Graphic Flash) Stone Arch Bks.

Gunderson, Jessica. The Songs of Stones River: A Civil War Novel. 2015. (Civil War Ser.). (ENG., Illus.). 96p. (gr. 4-4). lib. bdg. 26.65 *(978-1-4342-9703-7(9))* Stone Arch Bks.

Gurewitz, Samantha & Polay, Ellyn. Marvin Mogunk & All of His Junk. 2012. (ENG.). 27p. (J). pap. 12.95 *(978-1-4327-9705-8(0))* Outskirts Pr., Inc.

Hahn, Nancy. One Lost Boy. Ayoub, Hamid, illus. 2012. pap. 19.95 *(978-1-4276-5351-2(8))* Aardvark Global Publishing.

Hall, Christina. Can Checkers Come Too? Hall, Lowell, illus. 2011. 36p. pap. 24.95 *(978-1-4560-7753-2(8))* America Star Bks.

Halsey, Jacqueline. Bluenose Adventure. Orchard, Eric, illus. 2013. (ENG.). 32p. (J). (gr. -1-3). 16.95 *(978-1-4595-0280-2(9),* 9781459502802) Formac Publishing Co., Ltd. CAN. Dist: Casemate Pubs. & Bk. Distributors, LLC.

Hamil, Nicole. The Magic of Elie. 2009. (Illus.). 36p. pap. 15.49 *(978-1-4389-5545-2(6))* AuthorHouse.

Hamilton, Patricia Birdsong & Scripts Publishing Staff. What's Up: William Explains Ataxia to His New Friends. l.t. ed. 2005. (Ataxia: A Lifestyle Change). 44p. 18.95 *(978-1-889826-90-5(1))* Scripts Publishing.

Hammer. Willy's Wild Weekend: Friday. 2007. 30p. pap. 24.95 *(978-1-4241-8875-8(X))* America Star Bks.

Hancock, Dennis & Uyen. The Tree House on the Bluff. Hancock, Uyen, illus. 2012. 36p. pap. 24.95 *(978-1-4626-7318-6(X))* America Star Bks.

Hancock, H. Irving. The High School Boys' Canoe Club. rev. ed. 2006. 220p. 27.95 *(978-1-4218-1753-8(5))*; pap. 12.95 *(978-1-4218-1853-5(1))* 1st World Publishing, Inc. (1st World Library - Literary Society).

—The High School Boys' Canoe Club. 2007. 184p. per. *(978-1-4065-1983-9(9))* Dodo Pr.

—The High School Pitcher. rev. ed. 2006. 212p. 27.95 *(978-1-4218-1743-9(8))*; pap. 12.95 *(978-1-4218-1843-6(4))* 1st World Publishing, Inc. (1st World Library - Literary Society).

—The High School Pitcher. 2007. 176p. per. *(978-1-4065-1990-7(1))* Dodo Pr.

Hand, Reuben W. The Thirst for Life, 1 vol. 2010. 52p. pap. 16.95 *(978-1-4489-4897-0(5))* America Star Bks.

Hankins, Larry. Stickboy at the Fair. 2011. 32p. pap. 24.95 *(978-1-4512-2206-7(8))* America Star Bks.

Hanks, Larry R. Stickboy, 1 vol. 2010. 28p. 24.95 *(978-1-4489-5141-3(0))* PublishAmerica, Inc.

Hanna, John Fairbanks. Vincent J Muggs: What If? 2009. 48p. pap. 17.50 *(978-1-60693-874-4(6),* Eloquent Bks.) Strategic Book Publishing & Rights Agency (SBPRA).

Hannigan, Lynne. Sam's Passover. 2004. (ENG., Illus.). 32p. pap. 5.95 *(978-0-7136-4084-7(7),* 93342, A&C Black) Bloomsbury Publishing Plc GBR. Dist: Consortium Bk. Sales & Distribution.

Hansen, MaryAnn Shelley. Sam the Second. 2010. 32p. 14.49 *(978-1-4520-2408-0(1))* AuthorHouse.

Harden, Perry Lee. The Percy Hargrove Stories: It's All Elementary. 2012. 160p. pap. 14.95 *(978-1-4772-2438-0(6))* AuthorHouse.

Harper, Charise Mericle. If Waffles Were Like Boys. Magoon, Scott, illus. 2011. (ENG.). 40p. (J). (gr. -1-1). 14.99 *(978-0-06-177998-5(9))* HarperCollins Pubs.

Harris, Danielle. The Second Chance Sant. 2012. 28p. pap. 24.95 *(978-1-4626-6778-9(3))* America Star Bks.

Harris, Philip. Trever & the Phoenix. 2009. 40p. pap. 16.99 *(978-1-4389-9537-3(7))* AuthorHouse.

Harrison, Patrick Gb. Who says Kist Can't Fight Global Warming. 2009. pap. 16.97 *(978-1-61584-921-5(1))* Independent Pub.

Hartnett, Sonya. Sadie & Ratz. James, Ann, illus. 2013. (ENG.). 64p. (J). (gr. k-3). pap. 5.99 *(978-0-7636-6461-9(8))* Candlewick Pr.

Hashimoto, Meika & Tillworth, Mary. I Am Buzz Lightyear (Disney/Pixar Toy Story) Random House Disney Staff, illus. 2011. (Shaped Board Book Ser.). (ENG.). 12p. (J). (— 1). bds. 4.99 *(978-0-7364-2821-7(6),* Golden/Disney) Random Hse. Children's Bks.

Hastings, Eileen. Rufus & Christopher Series, 3 vols., Set. (Illus.). (J). (gr. 2-4). pap. 23.82 incl. audio *(978-0-87783-234-8(X))*; lib. bdg. 29.95 *(978-0-87783-168-6(8))*; pap. 11.82 *(978-0-87783-169-3(6))* Oddo Publishing, Inc.

Hayes, Arvid. A Little Bird Saves a Little Boy's Life. 2010. 16p. 8.49 *(978-1-4389-9255-6(6))* AuthorHouse.

Hayes, Clair W. The Boy Allies in the Trenches: Midst Shot & Shell along the Aisne. 2007. (ENG.). 180p. pap. 19.99 *(978-1-4346-2323-2(8))* Creative Media Partners, LLC.

Heer, Andrew De. The Story of Kwesi Appiah: The GHANAIAN AMERICAN BOY, for young Readers. 2011. 28p. pap. 15.99 *(978-1-4568-7751-4(8))* Xlibris Corp.

Heidari, Mahdi. Little Red Fire. Taylor, Adam, illus. 2012. 40p. (J). pap. 12.99 *(978-0-9838321-8-8(8))* Higher Ground Pr.

Heide, Florence Parry. A Promise Is a Promise. Auth, Tony, illus. 2007. (ENG.). 40p. (J). (gr. k-4). 15.99 *(978-0-7636-2285-5(0))* Candlewick Pr.

Henderson, Aileen Kilgore. Hard Times for Jake Smith: A Story of the Depression Era. 2004. (Historical Fiction for Young Readers Ser.). (ENG.). 232p. (J). pap. 8.00 *(978-1-57131-649-3(3))* Milkweed Editions.

Hennessy, B. G. The Boy Who Cried Wolf. Kulikov, Boris, illus. 2006. (ENG.). 40p. (J). (gr. -1-3). 17.99 *(978-0-689-87433-8(2),* Simon & Schuster Bks. For Young Readers) Simon & Schuster Bks. For Young Readers.

Henry, Sherrie. Last of the Summer Tomatoes. 2016. (ENG., Illus.). (YA). (gr. 8-12). 24.99 ***(978-1-63533-039-7(4))*** 2013. 246p. pap. 14.99 *(978-1-62380-959-1(2))* Dreamspinner Pr. (Harmony Ink Pr.).

Higdon, Patrick A. Grandpa & My Report, 1 vol. 2009. 48p. pap. 16.95 *(978-1-61582-752-7(8))* PublishAmerica, Inc.

Higesanbon. Mo Mo Mo Mo Monster: Mon Monster. 2011. 56p. pap. 34.95 *(978-1-4327-4149-5(7))* Outskirts Pr., Inc.

Higginson, Sheryl. Dilbert's Pets, 1 vol. 2010. 94p. pap. 19.95 *(978-1-4489-5757-6(5))* America Star Bks.

Higgs, Carolyn. One Village Boy Loses His Friends. 2011. 20p. pap. 24.95 *(978-1-4489-4290-9(X))* America Star Bks.

Hilditch, Kevin M. Kevin & the Smiling Dog. 38p. 2011. pap. 19.99 *(978-1-257-01514-6(1))* 2010. pap. 9.99 *(978-0-557-56904-5(4))* Lulu Pr., Inc.

Hinton, S. E. The Outsiders. 40th anniv. ed. 2007. (ENG.). 192p. (YA). (gr. 7-18). 17.99 *(978-0-670-06251-5(0),* Viking Books for Young Readers) Penguin Young Readers Group.

Hitchcock, Alfred. Misterio de la Calavera Parlante. (Alfred Hitchcock y los Tres Investigadores Ser.). (SPA.). (YA). 8.95 *(978-84-272-4911-0(X),* MO63) Molino, Editorial ESP. Dist: Continental Bk. Co., Inc.

—Misterio de la Cueva de los Lamentos. (Alfred Hitchcock y los Tres Investigadores Ser.). (SPA.). 160p. (YA). 8.95 *(978-84-272-4910-3(1),* MO62) Molino, Editorial ESP. Dist: Continental Bk. Co., Inc.

—Misterio de la Montana del Monstruo. (Alfred Hitchcock y los Tres Investigadores Ser.). (SPA.). (YA). 8.95 *(978-84-272-4920-2(9),* MO72) Molino, Editorial ESP. Dist: Continental Bk. Co., Inc.

—Misterio de Leon Mervioso. (Alfred Hitchcock y los Tres Investigadores Ser.). (SPA.). 192p. (YA). 8.95 *(978-84-272-4916-5(0),* MO68) Molino, Editorial ESP. Dist: Continental Bk. Co., Inc.

—Misterio del Dragon. (Alfred Hitchcock y los Tres Investigadores Ser.). (SPA.). 176p. (YA). 8.95 *(978-84-272-4914-1(4),* MO66) Molino, Editorial ESP. Dist: Continental Bk. Co., Inc.

—Misterio del Gato de Trapo. (Alfred Hitchcock y los Tres Investigadores Ser.). (SPA.). 152p. (YA). 8.95 *(978-84-272-4913-4(6),* MO65) Molino, Editorial ESP. Dist: Continental Bk. Co., Inc.

—Misterio del Lago Fantasma. (Alfred Hitchcock y los Tres Investigadores Ser.). (SPA.). 173p. (YA). 8.95 *(978-84-272-4919-6(5),* MO71) Molino, Editorial ESP. Dist: Continental Bk. Co., Inc.

—Misterio del Testamento Sorprendiente. (Alfred Hitchcock y los Tres Investigadores Ser.). (SPA.). (YA). 8.95 *(978-84-272-4922-6(5),* MO74) Molino, Editorial ESP. Dist: Continental Bk. Co., Inc.

Hitchcock, Fleur. Mayhem & Meteorites. 2016. (Shrunk! Adventure Ser.: 2). (ENG., Illus.). 256p. (J). (gr. 3-7). pap. 9.99 *(978-1-84812-481-3(3))* Bonnier Publishing GBR. Dist: Independent Pubs. Group.

—Shrunk! 2016. (Shrunk! Adventure Ser.: 1). (ENG., Illus.). 256p. (J). (gr. 3-7). pap. 9.99 *(978-1-84812-480-6(5))* Bonnier Publishing GBR. Dist: Independent Pubs. Group.

Hlad, Carole. Daisy's Dance Party: (from the Amanda's Cats Series) 2011. 24p. pap. 15.99 *(978-1-4628-8006-5(1))* Xlibris Corp.

Hobbs, William. Down the Yukon. unabr. ed. 2004. (Middle Grade Cassette Librariestm Ser.). 208p. (J). (gr. 5-9). pap. 36.00 incl. audio *(978-0-8072-0786-4(1),* S YA 310 SP, Listening Library) Random Hse. Audio Publishing Group.

Hodgson, Julie. Juno & the Half -Man. 2010. 42p. pap. 12.95 *(978-1-4461-6589-8(2))* Lulu Pr., Inc.

—Juno & the Windwalker. 2010. 40p. pap. 18.95 *(978-1-4461-4244-8(2))* Lulu Pr., Inc.

Hofmeister, Alan, et al. I See Sam. (Reading for All Learners Ser.). (Illus.). (J). pap. *(978-1-56861-073-3(4))* Swift Learning Resources.

—Sam. (Reading for All Learners Ser.). (Illus.). (J). pap. *(978-1-56861-074-0(2))* Swift Learning Resources.

—Sam Sat. (Reading for All Learners Ser.). (Illus.). (J). pap. *(978-1-56861-083-2(1))* Swift Learning Resources.

—See Sam. (Reading for All Learners Ser.). (Illus.). (J). pap. *(978-1-56861-075-7(0))* Swift Learning Resources.

—Sis. (Reading for All Learners Ser.). (Illus.). (J). pap. *(978-1-56861-082-5(3))* Swift Learning Resources.

Hoke, Jeehyun. Boy & the Little Violet Flower. 2012. (ENG.). (J). pap. 10.99 *(978-1-4675-2921-1(4))* Independent Pub.

Holder, Nancy. On Fire. 2012. (ENG.). 256p. pap. 11.00 *(978-1-4516-7447-7(3),* MTV Bks.) MTV Books.

Holt, Cija. Zwarkowski & the Show & Tell Collection. 2010. 48p. pap. 11.49 *(978-1-4520-4173-5(3))* AuthorHouse.

Holt, Theresa. What If I Wet My Pants. 2011. 28p. pap. 15.99 *(978-1-4628-5319-9(6))* Xlibris Corp.

Honowitz, Stacey. Genius with a Penis, Don't Touch! 2012. 24p. 19.95 *(978-1-4575-1326-8(9))* Dog Ear Publishing, LLC.

Hooks, Bell. Be Boy Buzz. Raschka, Chris, illus. 2016. (ENG.). 32p. (J). (gr. -1 — 1). bds. 7.99 *(978-1-4847-8840-0(0),* Jump at the Sun) Hyperion Bks. for Children.

Hopkins, Cathy. The Princess of Pop. 2012. (Truth or Dare Ser.). (ENG.). 224p. (YA). (gr. 7). pap. 10.99 *(978-1-4424-6057-7(1),* Simon Pulse) Simon Pulse.

Horton, Elizabeth. Pick Me, Pick Me. Kinsley, Sean, illus. 2008. (ENG.). 32p. (J). 16.95 *(978-0-9797460-0-0(0))* Lerue Pr., LLC.

Houtman, Jacqueline. The Reinvention of Edison Thomas. 2012. (ENG.). 192p. (J). (gr. 3-7). pap. 8.95 *(978-1-59078-951-3(2))* Boyds Mills Pr.

Howell, Julie Ann. Mrs Owl's Nest of Rhymes. LaGrange, Tiffany, illus. 2008. 24p. pap. 12.95 *(978-0-9818683-8-7(X))* Peppertree Pr., The.

Howland, Michele. The Flying Boy, 1 vol. 2009. 21p. pap. 19.95 *(978-1-61582-678-0(5))* PublishAmerica, Inc.

Hoyt, Kathleen. Kerloon & Cooley. 2012. 24p. pap. *(978-1-77097-833-1(X))* FriesenPress.

Huddleston, Courtney & Zirkel, Scott. A Bit Haywire. Huddleston, Courtney, illus. 2006. (Illus.). 112p. per. 11.95 *(978-0-9777883-5-4(0))* Viper Comics.

Hudson, Judith. Bayo a Good African Boy. 2009. 28p. (J). pap. 12.95 *(978-1-4327-4067-2(9))* Outskirts Pr., Inc.

Hughes, Shirley. Alfie & the Big Boys. Hughes, Shirley, illus. 2009. (Alfie Ser.). (ENG., Illus.). 32p. (J). (gr. -1-k). pap. 12.99 *(978-0-09-948844-6(2),* Red Fox) Random House Children's Books GBR. Dist: Independent Pubs. Group.

—Alfie's Feet. 2004. (Illus.). 32p. (J). *(978-0-370-32455-5(2),* Red Fox) Random House Children's Books.

Hulme, Lucy V. Passages, 1 bk. Redpath, Dale, illus. 2005. 40p. (J). 7.95 *(978-0-9769854-0-2(3),* 001) Combs-Hulme Publishing.

Hurtado, Ernest R. Freddy the Unfixer. 2011. 28p. (J). pap. 21.99 *(978-1-4568-0995-9(4))* Xlibris Corp.

I Don't Believe It!, 6 Packs. (gr. k-1). 23.00 *(978-0-7635-9056-7(8))* Rigby Education.

I Never Want to go There Again. 2007. per. *(978-1-59916-217-1(2))* Printing Systems.

Ian Pugh. Wolfstorm: The First Danny Piper Adventure. 2010. 388p. pap. 22.95 *(978-1-4269-0238-3(7))* Trafford Publishing.

Ilka, Benjamin Alexander. A Boy & His Shadow. Ilka, Benjamin Alexander, illus. (Illus.). (YA). Pt. 1. 2005. per. 4.95 net. *(978-0-9779504-0-9(9))*Pt. 2. 2006. 3.95 net. *(978-0-9779504-1-6(7))* Hogan Publishing LLC.

I'll Run Away: Individual Title Six-Packs. (gr. -1-2). 23.00 *(978-0-7635-8793-2(1))* Rigby Education.

Ingalls, Laura. Un Granjero de Diez Años. 2004. (Cuatro Vientos Ser.: Vol. 102). (SPA., Illus.). 200p. (gr. 5-8). pap. 12.99 *(978-84-279-3224-1(3),* NG6460) Noguer y Caralt Editores, S. A. ESP. Dist: Lectorum Pubns., Inc.

Ingelow, Jean. Mopsa the Fairy. 2004. reprint ed. pap. 1.99 *(978-1-4192-3510-8(9))* Kessinger Publishing, LLC.

Ingman, Bruce & Ahlberg, Allan. The Runaway Dinner. Ingman, Bruce, illus. 2008. (ENG., Illus.). 40p. (J). (gr. -1-3). pap. 6.99 *(978-0-7636-3893-1(5))* Candlewick Pr.

Inkpen, Mick & Butterworth, Nick. Just Like Jasper! (Illus.). 32p. (J). pap. 11.95 *(978-0-340-52582-1(7))* Hodder & Stoughton GBR. Dist: Trafalgar Square Publishing.

Irwin, Chris. Nightmare of Shadows. 2007. 140p. pap. 18.95 *(978-0-615-15008-6(X))* Irwin, Christine.

Irwin, Esther. White Cloud: A Little Boy's Dream. Puett, Gayle, ed. Roberson, Ron, illus. 2006. 61p. (J). spiral bd. 10.00 *(978-0-9778462-0-7(2))* Irwin, Esther L.

Italia, John. The Birds of the Harbor. Caravela, Elena, illus. 2006. (ENG.). 32p. (J). (gr. -1-3). 15.95 *(978-0-9726614-7-8(6))* Shenanigan Bks.

Izumi, Kaneyoshi. Seiho Boys' High School!, Vol. 3. Izumi, Kaneyoshi, illus. 2010. (ENG., Illus.). 200p. pap. 9.99 *(978-1-4215-3733-7(8))* Viz Media.

Jack R. Wilder. Devil with a Halo. 2009. 256p. pap. 24.95 *(978-1-4251-1283-7(8))* Trafford Publishing.

Jackson, Alisha. Noah's Fire Engine. 2011. 16p. 9.00 *(978-1-4567-2977-6(2))* AuthorHouse.

Jacobs, Joseph. Jack & the Beanstalk. Crane, Walter, illus. 2013. 20p. pap. *(978-1-909115-63-7(0))* Planet, The.

Jacobsen, Laura, illus. The Boy & the North Wind: A Tale from Norway. 2013. (Tales of Honor Ser.). (ENG.). 32p. (J). (gr. 1-4). pap. 8.95 *(978-1-937529-56-7(8))* Red Chair Pr.

Jacobsen, Laura, illus. & retold by. The Boy & the North Wind: A Tale from Norway. Jacobsen, Laura, retold by. 2013. (Tales of Honor (Red Chair Press) Ser.). (ENG.). 32p. (J). (gr. 1-4). lib. bdg. 26.60 *(978-1-937529-72-7(X))* Red Chair Pr.

Jeffers, Stewart. The Collapse of the Crew. 2005. 111p. pap. 19.95 *(978-1-4137-8714-6(2))* PublishAmerica, Inc.

Jempsa, Alice B. Why Does Everything Happen to Me? 2011. 28p. (gr. -1). pap. 13.54 *(978-1-4269-5005-6(5))* Trafford Publishing.

Jenkins, Amanda. The Strong & the Weak Hammurabi's Code, Tomb Robbers! A Story of Ancient Egypt. 2011. (Readers' & Writers' Genre Workshop Ser.). (YA). pap. *(978-1-4509-3020-8(4))* Benchmark Education Co.

Jennings, Linda. Tom's Tail. Warnes, Tim, tr. Warnes, Tim, illus. 2003. 32p. (J). pap. 6.95 *(978-1-58925-383-4(3))* Tiger Tales.

Jennings, Sharon. Sleep Tight, Mrs. Ming. 2004. (Illus.). (J). (gr. -1-3). spiral bd. *(978-0-616-01683-1(2))* Canadian National Institute for the Blind/Institut National Canadien pour les Aveugles.

Jessica Hoel. Adam B Brave. Samantha Nowak, illus. 2009. 20p. pap. 12.49 *(978-1-4389-3240-8(5))* AuthorHouse.

Johnson, Angela. Bird. 2006. (ENG.). 144p. (YA). (gr. 7-18). reprint ed. 6.99 *(978-0-14-240544-4(2),* Puffin Books) Penguin Young Readers Group.

Johnson, Donnie. The Little Flying Boy. 2012. 36p. pap. 17.95 *(978-1-4685-4750-4(X))* AuthorHouse.

Johnson, James A. The Terror & the Talking Stick: Sundown Stories II. 2011. 56p. pap. 8.95 *(978-1-4502-8156-0(7))* iUniverse, Inc.

Johnson, Margaret. Running Wild Level 3 Lower-Intermediate. 2009. (ENG.). 80p. pap. 12.75 *(978-84-8323-501-0(3))* Cambridge Univ. Pr.

Johnson, Terry David. As I Sat on My Grandpa's Knee. 2009. 32p. pap. 16.50 *(978-1-60860-202-5(8),* Eloquent Bks.) Strategic Book Publishing & Rights Agency (SBPRA).

Johnston, William. Limpy. 2003. 356p. pap. 34.95 *(978-1-932080-47-6(3))* Ross & Perry, Inc.

Jones, Debbie Knatt. Maurice ... As Read to the Students in Room D183 & D184. 2013. 150p. pap. 13.95 *(978-1-62516-536-7(6),* Strategic Bk. Publishing) Strategic Book Publishing & Rights Agency (SBPRA).

Jones, Diana Wynne. Enchanted Glass. 2011. 304p. (J). (gr. 3-7). pap. 6.99 *(978-0-06-186685-2(7),* Greenwillow Bks.) HarperCollins Pubs.

Jones, Ralph E. The Adventures of Kele: Boy of the Rock Shelter. 2012. 56p. pap. 24.99 *(978-1-4685-7696-2(8))* AuthorHouse.

Jones, Shelley Lynn. The Story of Corey & Alice. 2005. (J). pap. 8.00 *(978-0-8059-6846-0(6))* Dorrance Publishing Co., Inc.

Jonsberg, Barry. Ironbark. 2010. (ENG.). 210p. (YA). (gr. 8-18). 13.99 *(978-1-74114-955-5(X))* Allen & Unwin AUS. Dist: Independent Pubs. Group.

Jordan, Dana Hall. Clang Went the Cymbals: An Onomatopoeia Alphabet Book. Burma, Willingham, illus. 2008. 32p. (J). 15.99 *(978-0-9798664-0-1(5))* Capture Bks.

Joseph, Doug. The Last Bye: Book Three of the Millennial Teleport Trilogy. 2011. (ENG.). 194p. pap. 9.95 *(978-1-4680-1209-5(6))* CreateSpace Independent Publishing Platform.

Joyce, William. Billy's Booger. Date not set. 32p. (J). (gr. -1-3). pap. 14.99 *(978-0-06-027111-4(6))*; lib. bdg. 15.89 *(978-0-06-027112-1(4))* HarperCollins Pubs.

Jungman, Ann & Quarto Generic Staff. The Most Magnificent Mosque. Fowles, Shelley, illus. 2007. (ENG.). 32p. (J). (gr. 1-4). pap. 8.99 *(978-1-84507-085-4(2),* Frances Lincoln) Quarto Publishing Group UK GBR. Dist: Hachette Bk. Group.

Kaczmarczyk, Kyle J. The Misadventures of Silent Boy - Volume II: the Stupid Strikes Back. 2005. 52p. (YA). pap. 17.99 *(978-1-4116-5231-6(2))* Lulu Pr., Inc.

Kamofonas, Mary Katherine. In the Doghouse. 2013. 24p. pap. *(978-1-77097-510-1(1))* FriesenPress.

Karen & Kary. Little Wizard. 2004. 21p. pap. 24.95 *(978-1-4137-2956-6(8))* PublishAmerica, Inc.

Karst, Patrice. The Smile That Went Around the World (Revised) New Updated Edition. Christy, Jana, illus. 2014. (ENG.). 22p. (J). 15.95 *(978-0-87516-875-3(2),* Devorss Pubns.) DeVorss & Co.

Kasper, Beth. Billy's Secret. 2013. 36p. pap. 16.95 *(978-1-4808-0344-2(8))* Archway Publishing.

Kathleen, Judith. Attila's Wobbly Birthday Box, 1 vol. 2010. 20p. pap. 24.95 *(978-1-4489-2451-6(0))* PublishAmerica, Inc.

Katschke, Judy. Karate Kangaroos (Disney Junior: Doc Mcstuffins) Random House Disney Staff & Martinez, Heather, illus. 2016. (Little Golden Book Ser.). (ENG.). 24p. (J). (gr. -1-k). 4.99 *(978-0-7364-3382-2(1),* Golden/Disney) Random Hse. Children's Bks.

Katz, Karen. My Big Boy Undies. 2012. (ENG.). 14p. (J). (gr. -1-k). bds. 7.99 *(978-0-448-45705-5(9),* Grosset & Dunlap) Penguin Young Readers Group.

Katz, T. Miss L'eau. 2007. 44p. (YA). pap. 14.99 *(978-1-59092-404-4(5))* Blue Forge Pr.

Kean, Edward. Howdy Doody in Funland. Seiden, Art, illus. 2011. 30p. 35.95 *(978-1-258-02315-7(6))* Literary Licensing, LLC.

—Howdy Doody in the Wild West. Seiden, Art, illus. 2011. 34p. 35.95 *(978-1-258-02316-4(4))* Literary Licensing, LLC.

—Howdy Doody's Lucky Trip. McNaught, Harry, illus. 2011. 30p. 35.95 *(978-1-258-02772-8(0))* Literary Licensing, LLC.

Keen, Karl D. They Call Me Chief. 2004. (YA). per. 10.95 *(978-0-9742791-3-8(7))* Litho Tech, LLC.

Keith, David. Hands Across Time. 2010. 129p. pap. 10.98 *(978-0-557-27121-4(5))* Lulu Pr., Inc.

Kellogg, Elijah. The Young Shipbuilders of Elm Island by Rev Elijah Kellogg. 2006. 316p. per. 23.99 *(978-1-4255-3063-1(X))* Michigan Publishing.

Kelly, Matthew. Why Am I Here? A Story about Becoming The-Best-Version-of-Yourself! Mitchell, Hazel, illus. 2009. 60p. (J). 17.99 *(978-0-9841318-0-8(9))* Beacon Publishing.

Kelsey, Linda J. Big Fish. Kelsey-Livin, Barbara, illus. 2012. 28p. pap. 24.95 *(978-1-4626-6887-8(9))* America Star Bks.

Kenny A Portrait of a Prodigy. 2004. per. (978-1-59581-010-6(2)) Brentwood Communications Group.

Kent, Trilby. Medina Hill. 2009. (ENG.). 176p. (YA). (gr. 5-9). 19.95 (978-0-88776-888-0(1), Tundra Bks.) Tundra Bks. CAN. Dist: Penguin Random Hse. LLC.

Keselman, Porter Gabr. Ponete Los Zapatos. (SPA.). pap. 7.95 (978-950-07-2021-2(3)) Editorial Sudamericana S.A. ARG. Dist: Distribooks, Inc.

Khan, Farheen. Ibrahim Khan & the Mystery of the Haunted Lake. 2011. (Ibrahim Khan Ser.). (ENG., Illus.). 64p. (J). (gr. k-5). pap. 7.50 (978-0-86037-423-7(8)) Kube Publishing Ltd. GBR. Dist: Consortium Bk. Sales & Distribution.

—Ibrahim Khan & the Mystery of the Roaring Lion. 2010. (Ibrahim Khan Ser.). (ENG., Illus.). 56p. (J). (gr. 2-6). pap. 6.50 (978-0-86037-467-1(X)) Kube Publishing Ltd. GBR. Dist: Consortium Bk. Sales & Distribution.

Kibuishi, Kazu. Copper. 2010. lib. bdg. 24.50 (978-0-606-14274-8(6), Turtleback) Turtleback Bks.

Kiely, Brendan. The Gospel of Winter. 2014. (ENG., Illus.). 304p. (YA). (gr. 9). 19.99 (978-1-4424-8489-4(6), McElderry, Margaret K. Bks.) McElderry, Margaret K. Bks.

Killian, Brandon. The Seesaw Book. 2011. 20p. 12.90 (978-1-4567-4163-1(2)) AuthorHouse.

Kimmel, Eric A. Medio Pollito: A Spanish Tale, 0 vols. Docampo, Valeria, illus. 2010. (ENG.). 32p. (J). (gr. k-3). 17.99 (978-0-7614-5705-3(4), 9780761457053, Amazon Children's Publishing) Amazon Publishing.

King, Dedie. I See the Sun in Russia. Ossipova, Irina, tr. Inglese, Judith, illus. 2012. (I See the Sun Ser.: 0). (RUS & ENG.). 40p. (J). (gr. 1-2). 12.95 (978-1-935874-08-9(X)) Satya Hse. Pubns.

King, Kimberly. God Is in the Window. Jones, Erik, illus. 2007. 37p. (J). 18.95 (978-0-9771936-6-0(7)) InterWeave Corp.

Kingsley, Kaza. Erec Rex: The Dragon's Eye. Payne, John, ed. Grant, Melvyn, illus. 2006. 360p. (J). 17.99 (978-0-9786555-6-3(7)) Firelight Press, Inc.

Kipling, Rudyard. The Jungle Book. Detmold, Edward J. & Detmold, Maurice, illus. 2010. (Calla Editions Ser.). (ENG.). 192p. 30.00 (978-1-60660-009-2(5)) Dover Pubns., Inc.

—The Jungle Books. 2013. (ENG.). 384p. (gr. 12). mass mkt. 5.95 (978-0-451-41918-7(9), Signet) Penguin Publishing Group.

Kirk, Bill. There's a Beetle in My Bed. Brown, Suzy, illus. 2009. 16p. pap. 9.95 (978-1-61633-005-7(8)) Guardian Angel Publishing, Inc.

Kirkpatrick, Brenna. My Motorcycle & Me: A Trip in the Mountains. 2011. 28p. pap. 14.56 (978-1-4634-0469-7(7)) AuthorHouse.

Kirkpatrick, Taylor. Worthwhile. Lynch, Jason, illus. 2003. 32p. (J). 15.95 (978-0-9725420-0-5(0)) Chapman Pr., LLC.

Kishimoto, Seishi. O-Parts Hunter, Vol. 3. Kishimoto, Seishi, illus. 2007. (O-Parts Hunter Ser.: 3). (ENG., Illus.). 200p. pap. 9.99 (978-1-4215-0857-3(5)) Viz Media.

—O-Parts Hunter, Vol. 2. Kishimoto, Seishi, illus. 2007. (ENG., Illus.). 200p. pap. 9.99 (978-1-4215-0856-6(7)) Viz Media.

Kleber, Dori. More-Igami. Karas, G. Brian, illus. 2016. (ENG.). 40p. (J). (gr. -1-3). 15.99 (978-0-7636-6819-8(2)) Candlewick Pr.

Klein-Higger, Joni. Ten Tzedakah Pennies. Leff, Tova, illus. 2005. 30p. (J). 10.95 (978-1-929628-19-3(6)) Hachai Publishing.

Kline, Suzy. Herbie Jones. 96p. (J). (gr. 3-4). pap. 3.99 (978-0-8072-1269-1(5), Listening Library) Random Hse. Audio Publishing Group.

Knight, Diedre. Beanie's Backyard. 2012. 28p. pap. 12.95 (978-1-62141-812-2(X)) Booklocker.com, Inc.

Knowles, Jo. Living with Jackie Chan. (ENG.). 384p. (YA). (gr. 9). 2015. pap. 8.99 (978-0-7636-7663-6(2)) 2013. 16.99 (978-0-7636-6280-6(1)) Candlewick Pr.

Koch, Edward R. Relay. 2009. 188p. pap. 12.95 (978-1-59858-989-4(X)) Dog Ear Publishing, LLC.

Koenig, Faydra. Two Homes for Daniel. 2013. 30p. pap. 10.95 (978-0-9891471-1-8(8)) Alpine River Pr.

Kohara, Kazuno. Here Comes Jack Frost. Kohara, Kazuno, illus. 2011. (ENG., Illus.). 32p. (J). (gr. -1-1). pap. 7.99 (978-0-312-60446-2(7), 9780312604462) Square Fish.

Kollin, Dani. My Very Own Dreidel: A Pop-up Hanakkah Celebration! Howard, Juliet, illus. 2007. (ENG.). 12p. 10.95 (978-1-58117-592-9(2), Intervisual/Piggy Toes) Bendon, Inc.

Konigbagbe, Olutobi. Joy in the Morning. 2012. (Illus.). 100p. pap. (978-1-908064-14-1(5)) Grace Publishing Group.

Korczak, Janusz. Kaytek the Wizard. Lloyd-Jones, Antonia, tr. from POL. 2012. (ENG.). 272p. (J). (gr. 4-7). 17.95 (978-0-9838685-0-7(6)) Flashlight Pr.

Korr, Mary. Winston the water Dog: Portuguese water dog tales book One. 2009. 40p. pap. 17.49 (978-1-4415-8406-9(4)) Xlibris Corp.

Kowalski, Bernard. Alexis & Ralph the Dragon. Phillips, Dawn, illus. 2009. 32p. pap. 24.95 (978-1-60749-167-5(2)) America Star Bks.

Krauss, Ruth. The Growing Story. Oxenbury, Helen, illus. 2007. (ENG.). 40p. (J). (gr. -1-3). 16.99 (978-0-06-024716-4(9)) HarperCollins Pubs.

Krensky, Stephen. Now I Am Big! Gillingham, Sara, illus. 2012. (Empowerment Ser.). (ENG.). 12p. (J). (gr. -1 — 1). bds. 6.95 (978-1-4197-0416-1(8), Abrams Appleseed) Abrams, Inc.

Kropf, Latifa Berry. Happy Birthday, World: A Rosh Hashanah Celebration. Carlson, Lisa, illus. 2005. (Very First Board Bks.). (ENG.). 12p. (J). (gr. -1 — 1). 5.95 (978-0-929371-32-0(1), Kar-Ben Publishing) Lerner Publishing Group.

Kruse, Donald W. There's a Goof on My Roof. Crank, Donny, illus. 2012. 48p. pap. 12.95 (978-1-59663-855-6(9), Castle Keep Pr.) Rock, James A. & Co. Pubs.

Lamaro, Glenda. Max Goes to Kindy. Ratyna, Linda, illus. 2009. 36p. pap. 16.44 (978-1-4251-8830-6(3)) Trafford Publishing.

Lancett, Peter. Seeing Red. 2008. (Cutting Edge Ser.). (ENG.). 224p. pap. (978-1-84167-696-8(9)) Ransom Publishing Ltd.

Landowne, Youme. Selavi, That Is Life: A Haitian Story of Hope. Landowne, Youme, illus. 2005. (ENG., Illus.). 40p. (J). (gr. k-2). pap. 8.95 (978-0-938317-95-1(4)) Cinco Puntos Pr.

Lang, George. Pixy's Holiday Journey. 2007. (ENG.). 146p. pap. 18.99 (978-1-4264-9501-4(3)); 164p. pap. 21.99 (978-1-4264-9882-4(9)) Creative Media Partners, LLC.

Langworthy, John Luther. The Aeroplane Boys Flight. 2004. reprint ed. pap. 1.99 (978-1-4192-5169-6(4)) Kessinger Publishing, LLC.

Lannen, Jon Jon. The Giraffe That Taught Me How to Laugh. 2010. 28p. pap. 14.99 (978-1-4490-5930-9(9)) AuthorHouse.

Lara, Mike. A Boy & a Horse. 2011. 40p. pap. 21.99 (978-1-4628-8024-9(X)) Xlibris Corp.

Larichev, Andrei Borisovich. The Boy Who was President. Moresco, Jamie, ed. Roberts, Marilyn, illus. 2004. 24p. (J). 9.95 (978-0-9724386-0-5(2), 2002096236) BlueSky Publishing.

Lathan, Betty Jean. Are You Sure That's My Child? 2011. 48p. pap. 31.99 (978-1-4628-5759-3(0)) Xlibris Corp.

Lawhead, Stephen R. The Tale of Jeremy Vole. 2003. (Riverbank Stories Ser.: Bk. 1). (Illus.). 112p. pap. 7.50 (978-0-7459-4675-7(5), Lion Books) Lion Hudson PLC GBR. Dist: Trafalgar Square Publishing.

—The Tale of Timothy Mallard. 2003. (Illus.). 112p. pap. 7.50 (978-0-7459-4676-4(3), Lion Books) Lion Hudson PLC GBR. Dist: Trafalgar Square Publishing.

Lawrence, P. Anthony. Jessie & Fumbling Giant. 2013. 28p. pap. 24.95 (978-1-63000-899-4(0)) America Star Bks.

Le Fanu, J. Sheridan. Madam Crowl's Ghost & the Dead Sexton. 2004. reprint ed. pap. 15.95 (978-1-4191-3188-2(5)); pap. 1.99 (978-1-4192-3188-9(X)) Kessinger Publishing, LLC.

Leblanc, A. J. Donnie the Little Knee Boarder. 2012. 28p. pap. 24.95 (978-1-4626-8313-0(4)) PublishAmerica, Inc.

Leck, James. After Dark. 2016. (ENG.). 256p. (J). (gr. 5-9). 7.95 (978-1-77138-344-8(5)) Kids Can Pr., Ltd. CAN. Dist: Hachette Bk. Group.

Lee, Vanessa Rose. Funny Jimmy. 2011. 28p. pap. 21.00 (978-1-4567-2347-7(2)) AuthorHouse.

Lekich, John. The Prisoner of Snowflake Falls, 1 vol. 2012. (ENG.). 280p. (YA). (gr. 8-12). pap. 12.95 (978-1-55469-978-0(9)) Orca Bk. Pubs. USA.

Leota, Kealaulaokamamo. Zhaka. 2008. (ENG & HAW., Illus.). (J). lib. bdg. (978-0-9773495-9-3(4)) Na Kamalei Koolauloa Early Education Program.

Leseberg, Bambi. Rollo's Rescue. 2012. 128p. pap. 14.95 (978-1-935079-88-0(3)) Lighthouse Publishing of the Carolinas.

Let's Pretend: Individual Title Six-Packs. (gr. -1-2). 23.00 (978-0-7635-9001-7(0)) Rigby Education.

Letscher, Lance. The Perfect Machine. 2010. (ENG., Illus.). 56p. (J). 19.95 (978-0-292-72338-2(5)) Univ. of Texas Pr.

Levy, Carol L. Elphy Grey. 2012. 24p. pap. 17.99 (978-1-4772-6687-8(9)) AuthorHouse.

Lewis, Kelly. Johan & the Dragon. 2011. 44p. pap. 21.99 (978-1-4628-7149-0(6)) Xlibris Corp.

Lewis, Lisa. Tsunaxen's Journey. 2013. (ENG.). 23p. (J). pap. 14.95 (978-1-4787-1979-3(6)) Outskirts Pr., Inc.

Liepelt, Juanita. Blue: The Luckiest Dog in the World. Kasy, Frank, illus. 2008. 48p. 19.95 (978-0-9791317-0-7(7), RealityIsBooks.com, Inc.

Linz, Kathryn. Jim Brandon's Adventures. 2006. (ENG.). 100p. per. 19.95 (978-1-4241-3160-0(X)) America Star Bks.

Lionheart, Amelia. The Dolphin Heptad. 2009. 200p. (gr. 4-6). pap. 14.95 (978-1-4401-8028-6(8)) iUniverse, Inc.

The Little Dutch Boy: 6 Small Books. (gr. k-2). 23.00 (978-0-7635-8509-9(2)) Rigby Education.

The Little Dutch Boy: Big Book. (gr. k-2). 26.00 (978-0-7635-2427-2(1)) Rigby Education.

Little, Judy. Yody & Bippy the Boo: Friends for Life. 2010. 28p. pap. 12.49 (978-1-4389-7145-2(1)) AuthorHouse.

Lloyd, Patricia. I Love Me 2! 2012. 20p. pap. 9.95 (978-0-9771160-5-8(0), Vaughanworks) Vaughanworks Publishing.

Locke, Terry. Spencer Hurley & the Aliens: Book One: the Abduction, Vol. 1. Hucks, Robin, ed. Locke, Terry, illus. 2008. (Spencer Hurley & the Aliens Ser.: 1). (Illus.). 256p. (J). per. 8.99 (978-0-9786940-1-2(5)) Dream Workshop Publishing Co., LLC, The.

Lockley, Belinda. Sometimes I Think of the Fish in the Sea. 2008. 16p. pap. 24.95 (978-1-60474-844-4(3)) America Star Bks.

Loranger, Marc J. Down There. 2012. (ENG.). 277p. pap. 19.95 (978-1-4327-9142-1(7)) Outskirts Pr., Inc.

Lorenz Guest, Donna. The Enchanted Ride. 2009. 32p. pap. 14.99 (978-1-4389-8116-1(3)) AuthorHouse.

Lovegrove, James. The Lord of Fire (Five Lords of Pain Book 5) 2013. (Five Lords of Pain Ser.: 5). (ENG.). 96p. (YA). (gr. 8-12). pap. 7.95 (978-1-78112-262-4(8)) Lerner Publishing Group.

—The Lord of Tears (Five Lords of Pain Book 3) 2013. (Five Lords of Pain Ser.: 3). (ENG.). 96p. (YA). (gr. 8-12). pap. 7.95 (978-1-78112-256-3(3)) Lerner Publishing Group.

—The Lord of the Mountain (Five Lords of Pain Book 1) 2013. (Five Lords of Pain Ser.: 1). (ENG.). 96p. (YA). (gr. 8-12). pap. 7.95 (978-1-78112-250-1(4)) Lerner Publishing Group.

—The Lord of the Typhoon (Five Lords of Pain Book 4) 2013. (Five Lords of Pain Ser.: 4). (ENG.). 96p. (YA). (gr. 8-12). pap. 7.95 (978-1-78112-259-4(8)) Lerner Publishing Group.

Lovett, Tracy M. Buck's Rodeo. Lovett, Tracy M., illus. 2012. (Illus.). 470p. pap. 16.50 (978-0-9819736-6-1(3)) Inclement Pr.

Lubar, David. Punished! (Darby Creek Exceptional Titles Ser.). (ENG.). 96p. (J). (gr. 2-5). 2007. per. 4.99 (978-1-58196-063-1(8)) 2006. 15.95 (978-1-58196-042-6(5)) Lerner Publishing Group. (Darby Creek).

Lucken, Eve M. The Tree, the Crazy Leaf, & Me. 2012. 64p. pap. 20.99 (978-1-4525-5016-9(6)) Balboa Pr.

Lunsford, Gary. Georgia Is on My Mind: A Tale of a Guardian Angel. 2010. 374p. 30.50 (978-1-60911-164-9(8), Eloquent Bks.) Strategic Book Publishing & Rights Agency (SBPRA).

Lutz Ii, William. Prisoner of Castle Windward. 2007. 232p. pap. 14.95 (978-1-4116-9260-2(8)) Lulu Pr., Inc.

Luzio-Poitras, Linda Di. Kitchi's Christmas Wish. 2009. 32p. pap. 12.99 (978-1-4490-2121-4(2)) AuthorHouse.

Lynch, F. Michael. I Don't Want to Share a Bedroom. 2010. 38p. pap. 14.50 (978-1-60911-313-1(6), Eloquent Bks.) Strategic Book Publishing & Rights Agency (SBPRA).

Lyzenga, Antonia Babauta. Happy Island. 2012. 32p. pap. 21.99 (978-1-4797-2037-8(2)) Xlibris Corp.

Mabee, Andrea. Dory Glory: Building A Boat from Stem to Stern. Mabee, Andrea, photos by. 2005. (Illus.). 67p. (YA). per. 15.95 (978-0-9630074-1-4(6)) Bass Cove Bks.

Mabille, Christine. Potato-Kid & the Adventure: Treasures Within, 1 vol. 2009. 76p. pap. 19.95 (978-1-61582-981-1(4)) America Star Bks.

MacDonald, Alysha. Noodles - a Lunchtime Adventure. Swaim, Mike, illus. 2012. 28p. pap. (978-0-9735526-8-3(9)) Cold Rock Publishing.

Mack, Jeff. Hippo & Rabbit in Brave Like Me. Mack, Jeff, illus. 2011. (Scholastic Reader Level 1 Ser.). (ENG., Illus.). 32p. (J). (gr. -1-2). pap. 3.99 (978-0-545-28360-1(4), Cartwheel Bks.) Scholastic, Inc.

Mackinnon, Bernard. The Boy Who Turned Green. 2005. 119p. pap. 19.95 (978-1-4137-7262-3(5)) America Star Bks.

MacLachlan, Patricia. Caleb's Story. 2004. (Sarah, Plain & Tall Ser.: 3). (ENG.). 160p. (J). (gr. 1-5). pap. 5.99 (978-0-06-440590-4(7)) HarperCollins Pubs.

Macy, Tana. Tap Shoes & Horse Shoes. Gardiner, Nancy, illus. 2011. 50p. pap. 18.00 (978-1-60976-086-1(7), Eloquent Bks.) Strategic Book Publishing & Rights Agency (SBPRA).

Maddox, Jake. Lacrosse Laser. Aburtov, Jesus Aburto, illus. 2016. (Jake Maddox Sports Stories Ser.). (ENG.). 72p. (gr. 2-3). lib. bdg. 25.32 (978-1-4965-3051-6(9)) Stone Arch Bks.

Maddox, Nicklas. The Big Tiny Spaceman, 1 vol. 2010. 36p. 24.95 (978-1-4489-7870-0(X)) PublishAmerica, Inc.

Madou, Carol. When Pigs Can Fly! 2011. 40p. pap. 18.99 (978-1-4567-3534-0(9)) AuthorHouse.

Maggs, William Alan. The Jungle Adventures of Henry Littlejohn. 2012. 96p. pap. 11.52 (978-1-4669-1252-6(9)) Trafford Publishing.

Mahy, Margaret. The Magician of Hoad. 2010. (ENG.). 432p. (YA). (gr. 9). pap. 9.99 (978-1-4169-7808-4(9), McElderry, Margaret K. Bks.) McElderry, Margaret K. Bks.

Majumdar, Debu. Viku & the Elephant: A Story from the Forests of India. Wolfe, Lynn, illus. 2011. (ENG.). 54p. (J). pap. 12.99 (978-0-9832227-0-5(3)) Bo-Tree Hse.

Mallett, Joanne A. Sharnus. 2011. 24p. pap. 13.99 (978-1-4634-2969-0(X)) AuthorHouse.

Malone, Cheryl Lawton. Dario & the Whale. Masseva, Bistra, illus. 2016. (ENG.). 32p. (J). (gr. -1-3). 16.99 (978-0-8075-1463-4(2)) Whitman, Albert & Co.

Malone, Peter & Prokofiev, Sergei. Sergei Prokofiev's Peter & the Wolf: With a Fully-Orchestrated & Narrated CD. Malone, Peter, illus. 2004. (ENG., Illus.). 40p. (J). (gr. -1-2). 19.99 (978-0-375-82430-2(8), Knopf Bks. for Young Readers) Random Hse. Children's Bks.

Manushkin, Fran. Pedro & the Shark. Lyon, Tammie, illus. 2017. (Pedro Ser.). (ENG.). 32p. (gr. k-2). lib. bdg. 21.32 (978-1-5158-0873-2(4)) Pedro Pubns. GBR. Dist: Capstone Pub.

—Pirate Pedro. Lyon, Tammie, illus. 2017. (Pedro Ser.). (ENG.). 32p. (gr. k-2). lib. bdg. 21.32 (978-1-5158-0872-5(6)) Pedro Pubns. GBR. Dist: Capstone Pub.

Marciano, John Bemelmans. The Nine Lives of Alexander Baddenfield. Blackall, Sophie, illus. 2014. (ENG.). 144p. (J). (gr. 5). pap. 7.99 (978-0-14-751233-8(6), Puffin Books) Penguin Young Readers Group.

Margolis, Leslie. Boys Are Dogs. 2009. (Annabelle Unleashed Ser.). (ENG.). 224p. (YA). (gr. 3-6). pap. 6.99 (978-1-59990-381-1(4), 9781599903811, Bloomsbury USA Childrens) Bloomsbury Publishing USA.

Marks, Graham. How It Works: Everyone Gets the Angel They Deserve. (ENG.). 240p. (J). pap. 12.99 (978-0-7475-7015-8(9)) Bloomsbury Publishing Plc GBR. Dist: Trafalgar Square Publishing.

Marr, Nikki. Marty Misbehaves. 2008. 40p. pap. 17.99 (978-1-4389-3171-5(9)) AuthorHouse.

Marrell, Mar'ce. Ben & the Carrot Predicament. (Illus.). 48p. (J). pap. 4.95 (978-1-895836-54-7(9)) River Bks. CAN. Dist: Coteau Bks.

Marsh, Carole. The Case of the Crybaby Cowboy. 2006. (3 Amigos Ser.). (Illus.). 54p. (J). (gr. 4-7). 14.95 (978-0-635-06199-7(6)) Gallopade International.

Martín Fernández de Velasco, Miguel. Pabluras. (SPA.). 120p. (YA). (gr. 5-8). (978-84-279-3146-6(8), NG3678) Noguer y Caralt Editores, S. A. ESP. Dist: Lectorum Pubns., Inc.

Martin, Paige. Daniel Keep Dreaming. Price, Ronnalda, ed. Williams, Angela, photos by. 2011. (Illus.). 48p. (J). pap. 15.00 (978-0-578-08272-1(1)) Paige Martin Bks.

Martinez, Victor. Parrot in the Oven. Scott, Steve, illus. rev. ed. 2004. (ENG.). 240p. (YA). (gr. 8-18). pap. 8.99 (978-0-06-447186-2(1), Rayo) HarperCollins Pubs.

Mary E. Gale. Mountain Boy in the City. 2009. 136p. 21.95 (978-1-4401-6771-3(0)); pap. 11.95 (978-1-4401-6773-7(7)) iUniverse, Inc.

Maskell, Philip Mo. King Milo & His Royal Court. 2011. 36p. pap. 19.95 (978-1-4634-1792-5(6)) AuthorHouse.

Mateos, Pilar. Historias de Ninguno. (Barco de Vapor). (SPA.). 120p. (J). (gr. 4-5). (978-84-348-0907-9(9)) SM Ediciones.

Mateos, Pilar & Lucini, Chata. Lucas y Lucas. (Barco de Vapor). (SPA.). 88p. (YA). (gr. 5-8). (978-84-348-1233-8(9)) SM Ediciones.

Mathews, Madge. Brandon's Really Bad, Really Good Day. Cook, Laurie, illus. 2007. (J). 3.99 (978-0-9726075-1-3(X)) EPI Bks.

Mattassi, Ezio. Pepito the Penguin, 1 vol. Mattassi, Ezio, illus. 2009. (Illus.). 15p. pap. 24.95 (978-1-61582-731-2(5)) PublishAmerica, Inc.

Matthews, Caroline. Uncle Orange. 2012. 30p. 24.95 (978-1-4626-6623-2(X)) America Star Bks.

Matthews, Helen. In a Pocket of Time. 2012. 84p. pap. (978-1-78176-789-4(0)) FeedARead.com.

May, E. J. Louis' School Days: A Story for Boys. 2007. (ENG.). 242p. pap. 20.99 (978-1-4346-4563-0(0)); 274p. pap. 23.99 (978-1-4346-4564-7(9)) Creative Media Partners, LLC.

Mayer, Mercer. A Boy, a Dog, & a Frog. Mayer, Mercer, illus. 2003. (Boy, a Dog, & a Frog Ser.). (ENG., Illus.). 32p. (J). (gr. -1-k). 6.99 (978-0-8037-2880-6(8), Dial Bks) Penguin Young Readers Group.

Mayer, Mercer & Mayer, Marianna. A Boy, a Dog, a Frog & a Friend. Mayer, Mercer & Mayer, Marianna, illus. 2003. (Boy, a Dog & a Frog Ser.). (ENG., Illus.). 32p. (J). (gr. -1-k). 6.99 (978-0-8037-2882-0(4), Dial Bks) Penguin Young Readers Group.

Mayo, Jason. Do Witches Make Fishes? 2010. 36p. pap. 16.99 (978-1-4520-6944-9(1)) AuthorHouse.

McBride, Maurice & Wallace, Jessica K. Oliver Vance Pull up Your Pants! Jackson, Anthony B., illus. 2011. 32p. (J). 13.95 (978-1-935802-06-8(2)) Father & Son Publishing.

McClintock, Norah. Bang, 1 vol. 2007. (Orca Soundings Ser.). (ENG.). 112p. (YA). (gr. 8-12). per. 9.95 (978-1-55143-654-8(X)) Orca Bk. Pubs. USA.

McClure, Brian D. The Bubble. 2006. (Illus.). 64p. (J). 14.95 (978-1-933426-05-1(5)) Universal Flag Publishing.

—Who Am I? 2006. (Illus.). 52p. (J). 12.95 (978-1-933426-03-7(9)) Universal Flag Publishing.

McConnell, L'Rain. What If the Rainbow Is a Place: A Magic Rainbow Story. 2010. 76p. 51.99 (978-1-4415-7210-3(4)) Xlibris Corp.

McCormick, Wilfred. Quick Kick: A Bronc Burnett Story. 2011. 192p. 42.95 (978-1-258-10149-7(1)) Literary Licensing, LLC.

—The Three-Two Pitch: A Bronc Burnett Story. 2011. 192p. 42.95 (978-1-258-10008-7(8)) Literary Licensing, LLC.

McDaniel Rockstad, Jean. Eric Jay, Eric Jay, What Are You Gonna Do All Day? 2011. (Illus.). 24p. 16.95 (978-1-60844-941-5(6)) Dog Ear Publishing, LLC.

McDonald, Ann-Eve. The Bad Day. 2004. (J). (978-0-9770158-1-8(5)) BeachWalk Bks. Inc.

McFadden, Jennifer. Rusty My Playful Cat. 2010. 24p. pap. 11.49 (978-1-4490-5101-3(4)) AuthorHouse.

Mcfarland, Jewel. Zach & His Frog. 2010. 16p. 9.95 (978-1-4520-4504-7(6)) AuthorHouse.

McGovern, Ann. Little Wolf. 2011. 48p. (gr. 2-4). pap. 8.95 (978-1-4620-2711-8(3)) iUniverse, Inc.

McGovern, Cammie. Just My Luck. 2016. 240p. (J). (gr. 3-7). 16.99 (978-0-06-233065-9(9)) HarperCollins Pubs.

McIntyre, Sheila Adam. The Cave in the Forest. 2012. pap. 9.95 (978-0-7414-7480-3(8)) Infinity Publishing.

McKee, David. Not Now, Bernard. 35th ed. 2015. (ENG., Illus.). 32p. (J). (gr. -1-k). 24.99 (978-1-78344-298-0(0)) Andersen Pr. GBR. Dist: Independent Pubs. Group.

McMahon, Kara. Everyone Is Different. Giles, Mike & Style Guide Staff, illus. 2010. (Yo Gabba Gabba! Ser.). (ENG.). 24p. (J). (gr. -1-2). 6.99 (978-1-4169-9936-2(1), Simon Spotlight) Simon Spotlight.

McMahon, Susan. Sean O'Grady. 2009. 12p. pap. 9.50 (978-1-4389-5149-2(3)) AuthorHouse.

McMillan, Angelo. The Adventures of W D: The Dreamers Series Vol. 1. 2012. 24p. 24.95 (978-1-4626-5270-9(0)) America Star Bks.

McMillan, Dawn & Kinnaird, Ross. I Need a New Butt! 2014. (ENG.). 32p. (J). (gr. 1-5). pap. 7.99 (978-0-486-78799-2(0)) Dover Pubns., Inc.

McNamee, Kevin. If I Could Be Anything. Movshina, Marina, illus. 2009. 16p. pap. 9.95 (978-1-61633-011-8(2)) Guardian Angel Publishing, Inc.

McOmber, Rachel B., ed. McOmber Phonics Storybooks: Ben in Bed. rev. ed. (Illus.). (J). (978-0-944991-29-9(7)) Swift Learning Resources.

—McOmber Phonics Storybooks: Ben Will Get Well. rev. ed. (Illus.). (J). (978-0-944991-30-5(0)) Swift Learning Resources.

—McOmber Phonics Storybooks: Max. rev. ed. (Illus.). (J). (978-0-944991-01-5(7)) Swift Learning Resources.

—McOmber Phonics Storybooks: Max Is Six. rev. ed. (Illus.). (J). (978-0-944991-43-5(2)) Swift Learning Resources.

—McOmber Phonics Storybooks: Max Ran. rev. ed. (Illus.). (J). (978-0-944991-02-2(5)) Swift Learning Resources.

—McOmber Phonics Storybooks: Max the Grand. rev. ed. (Illus.). (J). (978-0-944991-57-2(2)) Swift Learning Resources.

McVay, Kinsy. Just Line Around. 2009. 52p. pap. 18.50 (978-1-60860-423-4(3), Eloquent Bks.) Strategic Book Publishing & Rights Agency (SBPRA).

Mealue, Monique. Johnny Goes Shopping. 2010. 24p. 12.95 (978-1-4520-0227-9(4)) AuthorHouse.

Meeks, John R. Dugan's Magical Island. 2011. 28p. pap. 12.40 (978-1-4567-3947-8(6)) AuthorHouse.

Meister, Cari. Tiny Goes to the Movies. 2016. (Penguin Young Readers Level 2 Ser.). lib. bdg. 13.55 (978-0-606-38851-1(6)) Turtleback Bks.

Mercado, Nancy E. & Mercado, Nancy, eds. Every Man for Himself: Ten Short Stories about Being a Guy. 2007. (ENG., Illus.). 176p. (YA). (gr. 7-18). 6.99 (978-0-14-240813-1(1), Speak) Penguin Young Readers Group.

Merrick, Sylvia Bach. Me & My Flea Steed, Clyde, at Home on Ralph. Cerda, Edward, illus. 2011. 24p. pap. 24.95 (978-1-60813-938-5(7)) America Star Bks.

Meyer, Brad. A Matchless Age. 2006. 302p. pap. 29.95 (978-1-4241-0523-6(4)) PublishAmerica, Inc.

Meyers, Carly J. J. Michael's Superheroes. Bruner, Garth, illus. 2013. 28p. (J). pap. (978-0-8425-2845-0(8), BYU Creative Works) Brigham Young Univ.

Michaels, Robbie. Caught in the Middle. 2016. (Caught in the ACT Ser.: Vol. 2). (ENG., Illus.). (YA). 24.99 (978-1-63477-951-7(7), Harmony Ink Pr.) Dreamspinner Pr.

Middleton, Leeanne. Sweetest Joy, 1 vol. Boyer, Christine M., illus. 2010. 18p. pap. 24.95 (978-1-4489-8068-0(2)) PublishAmerica, Inc.

Middleton, Shawn. Sam & the Peanut Butter Crackers. 2009. 32p. pap. 12.99 (978-1-4389-3400-6(9)) AuthorHouse.

Milbourne, Anna. In the Castle. Davies, Benji, illus. 2006. (English Heritage Ser.). 24p. (J). (gr. -1-3). 9.99 (978-0-7945-1243-9(7), Usborne) EDC Publishing.

Miller, Daniel, et al. A Miller Cousin Mystery. 2010. 120p. pap. 17.80 (978-0-557-57118-5(9)) Lulu Pr., Inc.

Miller, Darcy. Roll. 2017. 224p. (J). (gr. 3-7). 16.99 (978-0-06-246122-3(2)) HarperCollins Pubs.

Miller, Ray JR. & Miller, Ray. How Kris Became Claus. 2009. (Illus.). 20p. pap. 12.99 (978-1-4389-7474-3(4)) AuthorHouse.

Milligan, Chris & Smith, David. Check Mate! Two Boys Experience the Life & Death Fight for Control of the Hudson Bay Fur Trade. 2013. 192p. (978-1-4602-1041-3(7)); pap. (978-1-4602-1039-0(5)) FriesenPress.

Millman, Selena. Our Dream Project. 2006. 99p. (YA). per. 11.51 (978-1-4243-2352-4(5)) Independent Publisher Services.

Mills-Darlow, Beryl C. My Beach Granny. 2012. 36p. pap. 14.50 (978-1-61897-681-9(8), Strategic Bk. Publishing) Strategic Book Publishing & Rights Agency (SBPRA).

Mills, Robert. Lump of Gump. 2012. 28p. pap. 24.95 (978-1-4626-7489-3(5)) America Star Bks.

Minton, Ross. Baseball, from the Street to the Diamond, 1 vol. 2010. 94p. pap. 19.95 *(978-1-4489-4918-2(1))* America Star Bks.

Miranda, Edward. A Ribbon for Diego. Bohart, Lisa, illus. 2008. 28p. pap. 12.95 *(978-0-9821654-5-4(5))* Peppertree Pr., The.

Mitchard, Jacquelyn & Lewis, Michael S. Eagle Eyes. 2009. (ENG.). 128p. (gr. 4-7). pap. 9.99 *(978-0-9790072-2-4(4))* MAHVL Publishing.

Mochizuki, Ken. El Beisbol Nos Salvo. 2004. (SPA., Illus.). (J). (gr. k-4). spiral bd. *(978-0-616-03090-5(8))* Canadian National Institute for the Blind/Institut National Canadien pour les Aveugles.

Modern Staff. Marcos is Magnificent Big Book, No. 1. (J). 22.95 *(978-0-8136-4829-3(7))* Modern Curriculum Pr.

Monaghan, Joseph. The Boy Who Loved Trees. 2013. (Illus.). 24p. pap. 19.82 *(978-1-4817-8225-8(8))* AuthorHouse.

Monnar, Alexander. Annoying Alex. Pileggi, Steven, illus. 2008. (J). per. 14.99 *(978-0-9768035-9-1(3))* Readers Are Leaders U.S.A., Inc.

Montes, Juan Mari. Diario del Autobus a de la Linea 3. 2006. (SPA., Illus.). 96p. (J). *(978-84-667-5192-6(0))* Grupo Anaya, S.A.

More Than This. 2014. (ENG.). 480p. (YA). (gr. 9). pap. 10.99 *(978-0-7636-7620-9(9))* Candlewick Pr.

Morgan, Charles. Flight of the Solar Ducks. 2009. 219p. pap. 15.01 *(978-0-557-07503-4(3))* Lulu Pr., Inc.

Morgan, Ruth. Big Liam, Little Liam. Archbold, Tim, illus. 2005. (ENG.). 24p. (J). lib. bdg. 23.65 *(978-1-59646-728-6(2))* Dingles & Co.

Morimoto, Sango. Taro & the Magic Pencil. Morimoto, Sango, illus. 2010. (ENG., Illus.). 104p. (J). pap. 7.99 *(978-1-4215-3524-1(6))* Viz Media.

—Taro & the Terror of Eats Street. Morimoto, Sango, illus. 2011. (Adventures of Taro Ser.). (ENG., Illus.). 96p. (J). (gr. 1-4). pap. 7.99 *(978-1-4215-3525-8(4))* Viz Media.

Morris, Lolita. Mike & Me-Sh. 2012. 24p. pap. 14.93 *(978-1-4669-6169-2(4))* Trafford Publishing.

Moseley, Tabitha. Pearl's Tales a Collection of Children's Stories. 2009. 92p. pap. 17.25 *(978-1-60860-670-2(8)*, Strategic Bk. Publishing) Strategic Book Publishing & Rights Agency (SBPRA).

Moskowitz, Ellen. Bandages: 6 Copies, 6 vols. Gedeon, Gloria, illus. 2006. (ENG.). 16p. (gr. k-2). pap. 7.95 *(978-1-879835-71-9(1)*, Kaeden Bks.) Kaeden Corp.

Mostoller, Marcia. Poor William Dill. 2011. 28p. pap. 24.95 *(978-1-4626-0835-5(3))* America Star Bks.

Mowry, Jess. Tyger Tales. 2007. 227p. per. 14.99 *(978-1-59092-358-0(8))* Blue Forge Pr.

Mulligan, Andy. The Boy with Two Heads. 2015. (ENG.). 400p. (J). (gr. 4-6). 12.99 *(978-0-552-57347-4(7))* Transworld Publishers Ltd. GBR. Dist: Independent Pubs. Group.

Murtagh, Ciaran. Megastar. Wesson, Tim, illus. 2016. (Fincredible Diary of Fin Spencer Ser.: 2). (ENG.). 224p. (J). (gr. 4-7). pap. 7.99 *(978-1-84812-447-9(3))* Bonnier Publishing GBR. Dist: Independent Pubs. Group.

Mwangi, Meja. The Mzungu Boy, 1 vol. 2006. (ENG.). 152p. (J). (gr. 4-7). pap. 8.95 *(978-0-88899-664-0(0))* Groundwood Bks. CAN. Dist: Publishers Group West (PGW).

Mysak, Mary. Little Train! Stickley, Kelly, illus. 2004. 16p. (J). 7.50 *(978-0-9762274-0-3(1))* Helping Hands Children's Bks.

Naegele, K. Z. The Chatty Hat. 2011. 36p. pap. 24.95 *(978-1-4626-3652-5(7))* America Star Bks.

Najafi, Imran. Dreams. 2013. 18p. pap. 9.95 *(978-1-62857-238-4(8)*, Strategic Bk. Publishing) Strategic Book Publishing & Rights Agency (SBPRA).

Nash, Arizona. Red Rooster, Green Rooster. 2009. 48p. pap. 16.99 *(978-1-935436-98-0(8))* Rodaian Pr.

Nast, Thomas, illus. The Fat Boy. 2011. (American Antiquarian Society Ser.). (ENG.). 24p. (gr. 1). 24.95 *(978-1-4290-9736-9(1))* Applewood Bks.

Naughton, Bill. Pony Boy. 2012. (ENG.). 256p. (YA). pap. 15.99 *(978-1-4482-0327-7(9)*, 9781448203277, Bloomsbury Reader) Bloomsbury Publishing Plc GBR. Dist: Macmillan.

Nelson, Jan. Signs of Love. Bohart, Lisa, illus. 2009. 24p. pap. 12.95 *(978-1-936051-54-0(0))* Peppertree Pr., The.

Nelson, Suzanne. Cake Pop Crush. 2013. 247p. (J). *(978-0-545-50389-1(2))* Scholastic, Inc.

Nelson, Suzanne. Hot Cocoa Hearts. 2015. 248p. (J). pap. ***(978-0-545-83968-6(8))*** Scholastic, Inc.

Neuhofer, Sheri L. Courageous Warrior. Amory, Deanna & O'Hara, Cynthia, illus. 2010. 28p. pap. 10.95 *(978-0-9787472-7-5(5))* Ajoyin Publishing, Inc.

The Nevergreen. 2003. (J). 15.99 *(978-0-9744565-9-1(4))* Heart-to-Heart Pubns.

Newell, Carol Donsky. Blue Lewis & Sasha the Great. Grisham, Betty, illus. 2005. (J). per. 6.95 *(978-0-9766199-0-1(3))* Cally Pr.

Nguyen, Thao. Consequences: A Chance for Hope. 2012. 60p. pap. 15.99 *(978-1-4691-8794-5(9))* Xlibris Corp.

Nichols, C. D. Kids Courageous. 2010. 66p. pap. 9.99 *(978-1-60911-809-9(X)*, Eloquent Bks.) Strategic Book Publishing & Rights Agency (SBPRA).

Nichols, Walter H. The Measure of a Boy. 2005. (Illus.). pap. 28.95 *(978-1-885529-73-2(2))* Stevens Publishing.

Nickel, Scott. The Boy Who Burped Too Much, 1 vol. Harpster, Steve, illus. 2006. (Graphic Sparks Ser.). (ENG.). 40p. (gr. 1-3). 23.99 *(978-1-59889-037-2(9)*, Graphic Sparks) Stone Arch Bks.

Nielsen, Jennifer A. Elliot & the Pixie Plot. Kendall, Gideon, illus. 2011. (Underworld Chronicles: Bk. 2). (ENG.). 208p. (J). (gr. 3-8). 12.99 *(978-1-4022-4020-1(1)*, Sourcebooks Jabberwocky) Sourcebooks, Inc.

Nieto, Terry. Sun Go Away. 2010. 24p. pap. 15.99 *(978-1-4535-3543-1(8))* Xlibris Corp.

Night, P. J. Together Forever. 2012. (Creepover Ser.: 8). lib. bdg. 16.00 *(978-0-606-26339-9(X)*, Turtleback) Turtleback Bks.

Nilsson, Bo Sigvard. Come on, Brian! A Young Boy's Struggle to Play in an All-Star Hockey Tournament. 2012. 56p. (gr. 4-6). pap. 8.95 *(978-1-4502-9301-3(8))* iUniverse, Inc.

Noble, Trinka Hakes. The Last Brother: A Civil War Tale. Papp, Robert, illus. 2006. (Tales of Young Americans Ser.). (ENG.). 32p. (J). (gr. 3-7). 17.95 *(978-1-58536-253-0(0))* Sleeping Bear Pr.

Norton, Charles. The Perfect Plan & the Four Brother's Pact. 2012. 24p. pap. 15.99 *(978-1-4691-6503-5(1))* Xlibris Corp.

Nunes, Lygia Bojunga. Seis Veces Lucas. (SPA.). (YA). (gr. 5-8). 8.95 *(978-958-04-5050-4(1)*, NR3069) Norma S.A. COL. Dist: Distribuidora Norma, Inc., Lectorum Pubns., Inc.

Nuo, Johnny. Dinh Van Binh: Vietnamese Village Boy. 2006. (Illus.). 176p. per. 15.12 *(978-1-4120-9966-0(8))* Trafford Publishing.

Obiols, Anna. Stegosaurus: the Friendliest Dinosaur. Subi, illus. 2012. (Dinosaur Bks.). (ENG.). 36p. (J). (gr. -1-1). pap. 6.99 *(978-1-4380-0107-4(X))* Barron's Educational Series, Inc.

O'Brien, Richard. Christopher & Joshua Go Fishing. 2012. (Illus.). 38p. pap. 11.00 *(978-1-78035-257-2(3)*, Fastprint Publishing) Upfront Publishing Ltd. GBR. Dist: Printondemand-worldwide.com.

O'Callaghan, G. The Eternals. 2007. 376p. per. *(978-1-84693-055-3(3))* Best Global Publishing Ltd.

—Sorcerers Apprentice. 2007. 244p. per. *(978-1-84693-024-9(3))* Best Global Publishing Ltd.

Oda, Matthew K. The Time MacHine: Mario's Box A Journey into Creativity. 2011. 36p. pap. 24.95 *(978-1-4626-3892-5(9))* America Star Bks.

O'Dowd, Chris & Murphy, Nick V. The Blunder Years. 2015. (Moone Boy Ser.). (ENG., Illus.). 400p. (J). (gr. 4-7). 14.99 *(978-1-250-05707-5(8)*, 9781250057075) Feiwel & Friends.

Oelschlager, Vanita. I Came from the Water: One Haitian Boy's Incredible Tale of Survival. Blanc, Mike, illus. 2012. (ENG.). 40p. (J). (gr. -1-3). 15.95 *(978-0-9832904-4-5(X))* VanitaBooks.

Oelschlager, Vanita & Blanc, Mike. I Came from the Water: One Haitian Boy's Incredible Tale of Survival. 2012. (ENG., Illus.). 40p. (J). (gr. -1-3). pap. 8.95 *(978-0-9832904-5-2(8))* VanitaBooks.

Ofoche, Uzo. Monte & Me. 2012. 20p. pap. 10.95 *(978-1-60911-511-1(2)*, Eloquent Bks.) Strategic Book Publishing & Rights Agency (SBPRA).

O'Hagan, William. Anything Else but Me. 2008. 36p. pap. 24.95 *(978-1-60563-701-3(7))* America Star Bks.

O'Hara, Susan. Tim's First Soccer Game. Barrett, Rebecca, illus. 2012. 38p. pap. 14.97 *(978-1-61897-199-9(9)*, Strategic Bk. Publishing) Strategic Book Publishing & Rights Agency (SBPRA).

On Thin Ice. 2005. per. *(978-0-9772505-2-3(0))* Adibooks.com.

Optic, Oliver, pseud. Northern Lands: Or, Young America in Russia & Prussia; A Story of Travel & Adventure / by William T. Adams (Oliver Optic). 2006. 384p. per. 26.99 *(978-1-4255-4074-6(0))* Michigan Publishing.

—Northern Lands; or, Young America in Russia & Prussia a Story of Travel & Adventure. 2006. 376p. per. 26.99 *(978-1-4255-3923-8(8))* Michigan Publishing.

Orobosa-Ogbeide, Kathryn. The Boy & the Moon. 2012. 12p. pap. 12.68 *(978-1-4669-1894-8(2))* Trafford Publishing.

O'Shea, M.J. Catch My Breath. 2013. 350p. pap. 17.99 *(978-1-62380-870-9(7))* Dreamspinner Pr.

Osmond, Joanne H. A Fishy Adventure. Osmond, Jack, illus. 2013. 152p. pap. 12.99 *(978-1-933334-26-4(6))* Vision Tree, Ltd., The.

Otis, James. A District Messenger Boy & a Necktie Party. 2007. 60p. per. *(978-1-4068-4366-8(0))* Echo Library.

—Toby Tyler: Or Ten Weeks with a Circus. 2013. 178p. pap. 15.00 *(978-0-9831857-8-9(6))* MPR Publishing.

Owens, Connie S. I know I am Special! 2003. pap. 5.99 *(978-1-59317-010-3(6))* Warner Pr., Inc.

Owens, Robert & Owens, Donna. The Misadventures of Our Son Henry. Bollinger, Carol, illus. 2007. 52p. per. 16.95 *(978-1-4241-8721-8(4))* America Star Bks.

Owings, Jeff. Tiny Todd: Swooped Away. 2009. 20p. pap. 10.49 *(978-1-4490-1214-0(4))* AuthorHouse.

—Tiny Todd: Tiny Todd's First Pet. 2009. 20p. pap. 10.49 *(978-1-4490-1216-8(7))* AuthorHouse.

Pacheco, Miguel Angel. La Familia de Mic. Escriva, Ana Lopez, illus. 2003. (SPA.). (J). *(978-970-690-761-5(0))* Planeta Mexicana Editorial S. A. de C. V.

Paley, Rebecca, et al. The Body Book for Boys. 2010. (ENG.). 128p. (J). (gr. 5-9). pap. 8.99 *(978-0-545-23751-2(3)*, Scholastic Paperbacks) Scholastic, Inc.

Park, Barbara. The Graduation of Jake Moon. unabr. ed. 2004. 115p. (J). (gr. 4-7). pap. 29.00 incl. audio *(978-0-8072-8722-4(9)*, Listening Library) Random Hse. Audio Publishing Group.

—Junie B. Jones Loves Handsome Warren. unabr. ed. 2004. (Junie B. Jones Ser.: No. 7). 71p. (J). (gr. k-3). pap. 17.00 incl. audio *(978-0-8072-0643-0(1)*, Listening Library) Random Hse. Audio Publishing Group.

Park, Linda Sue. Forest of Wonders. Madsen, Jim, illus. 2016. (Wing & Claw Ser.: 1). 352p. (J). (gr. 3-7). 16.99 *(978-0-06-232738-3(0))* HarperCollins Pubs.

Parker, C. Brad. Chosen Generation. 2007. 118p. (YA). pap. 12.86 *(978-1-4116-3497-8(7))* Lulu Pr., Inc.

Parrott, Matt. Daniel & the Dark. 2011. 24p. 16.99 *(978-1-4520-8830-3(6))* AuthorHouse.

Partee, Andrea. Jed, the Boy, the Snake & the Window. 2007. 160p. 30.99 *(978-1-4257-6401-2(0))* Xlibris Corp.

Paterson, Katherine. Ame a Jacob. 2003.Tr. of Jacob Have I Loved. (SPA., Illus.). (YA). (gr. 5-8). pap. *(978-84-279-3251-7(0)*, NG31211) Noguer y Caralt Editores, S. A. ESP. Dist: Lectorum Pubns., Inc.

—Marvin One Too Many. Brown, Jane Clark, illus. 2003. (I Can Read Bks.). 48p. (J). (gr. k-3). pap. 3.99 *(978-0-06-444279-4(9))* HarperCollins Pubs.

Paton, Stuart. The Extraordinary Tale of an Ordinary Boy. 2011. (Illus.). 112p. (gr. -1). pap. 12.21 *(978-1-4670-0987-4(3))* AuthorHouse.

Patton, Jack. The Komodo Conflict. 2016. (Battle Bugs Ser.: 6). (ENG.). 128p. (J). (gr. 2-5). pap. 4.99 *(978-0-545-79148-9(0)*, Scholastic Paperbacks) Scholastic, Inc.

—The Snake Fight. 2016. (Battle Bugs Ser.: 8). (ENG.). 128p. (J). (gr. 2-5). pap. 4.99 *(978-0-545-94512-7(7)*, Scholastic Paperbacks) Scholastic, Inc.

Paulits, John. Philip & the Boy Who Said Huh? 2003. (ENG.). 60p. (J). pap. 12.95 *(978-1-878044-72-3(9))* Mayhaven Publishing, Inc.

Paulsen, Gary. Brian's Return. unabr. ed. 2004. (Middle Grade Cassette Librariestm Ser.). 115p. (J). (gr. 5-9). pap. 29.00 incl. audio *(978-0-8072-0658-4(X)*, S YA 292 SP, Listening Library) Random Hse. Audio Publishing Group.

—Harris & Me. 2007. (ENG., Illus.). 176p. (J). (gr. 5-7). pap. 6.99 *(978-0-15-205880-7(X))* Houghton Mifflin Harcourt Publishing Co.

—Harris & Me. 2007. 157p. (gr. 5). 15.95 *(978-0-7569-7810-5(6))* Perfection Learning Corp.

Payne, Raymond. Shelter from the Storm. rev. ed. 2004. 144p. (YA). pap. 9.95 *(978-0-9740552-1-3(2))* Harbourside Pr.

Payne, Richard A. The Banjo & the Telescope. 2008. 44p. per. 24.95 *(978-1-4241-9776-7(7))* America Star Bks.

Peake, Mervyn. Boy in Darkness. (Illus.). 144p. (J). pap. *(978-0-340-67822-0(4))* Hodder & Stoughton.

Pearce, Jonathan. John-Browne's Body & Sole: A Semester of Life. 2nd ed. 2004. (Illus.). 150p. (J). pap. 15.95 *(978-1-59411-053-5(0))* Writers' Collective, The.

Peekhaus, Jennifer. The Little Red House. 2009. 16p. pap. 19.50 *(978-1-4389-1857-0(7))* AuthorHouse.

Pefferly, Lawrence. Larry Tyler & the Planet Buksdahud. 2007. 312p. pap. 16.95 *(978-0-9789969-2-5(5))*; 24.95 *(978-0-9789969-1-8(7))* Tradition Publishing.

Peirce, Lincoln. Big Nate: Mr. Popularity. Peirce, Lincoln, illus. 2014. (Big Nate Ser.). (ENG., Illus.). 224p. (J). (gr. 3-7). pap. 9.99 *(978-0-06-208700-3(2))* HarperCollins Pubs.

—Big Nate — Mr. Popularity. 2014. (Big Nate Graphic Novels Ser.: 4). (J). lib. bdg. 20.85 *(978-0-606-35482-0(4))* Turtleback Bks.

—Big Nate — Welcome to My World. 2015. (Big Nate Ser.: 13). (ENG., Illus.). 176p. (J). pap. 9.99 *(978-1-4494-6226-0(X))* Andrews McMeel Publishing.

—Big Nate - The Crowd Goes Wild! 2014. (Big Nate Graphic Novels Ser.). lib. bdg. 20.85 *(978-0-606-36143-9(X))* Turtleback Bks.

—Big Nate Strikes Again. Peirce, Lincoln, illus. 2015. (Big Nate Ser.: 2). (ENG., Illus.). 224p. (J). (gr. 3-7). pap. 7.99 *(978-0-06-228358-0(8))* HarperCollins Pubs.

—I Can't Take It! 2013. (Big Nate Graphic Novels Ser.). lib. bdg. 20.85 *(978-0-606-32313-0(9)*, Turtleback) Turtleback Bks.

—Thunka, Thunka, Thunka. 2016. (Big Nate Graphic Novels Ser.). lib. bdg. 20.85 *(978-0-606-38234-2(8))* Turtleback Bks.

Penn, Linda M. Clayton's Birding Adventure: A Young Boy Learns the Secret Ways of Birds. 2013. 46p. pap. 10.95 *(978-0-9852488-5-7(8))* Racing to Joy Pr. LLC.

Pennington, Beverly A. Jonathan's Discovery. Pennington, Beverly A., illus. 2006. (Illus.). 29p. (J). (gr. -1-3). pap. 12.95 *(978-1-56167-920-1(8))* American Literary Pr.

Perry, Roseann. When Mama Says No. 2009. 36p. pap. 16.99 *(978-1-4389-1938-6(7))* AuthorHouse.

Peter, Dawn. Mark the Remarkable & Can't Say Can't. 2012. 24p. pap. *(978-1-77067-033-4(5))* FriesenPress.

Petersen, Jeffrey Lee. A Boy a Dog & a Creek. 2013. 102p. pap. *(978-1-78299-794-8(6))* FeedARead.com.

Phelps, Elizabeth Stuart. Gypsy Breynton. 2007. (ENG.). 122p. pap. 18.99 *(978-1-4264-9365-2(7))*; 136p. pap. 19.99 *(978-1-4264-9746-9(6))* Creative Media Partners, LLC.

Phelps, Elizabeth Stuart & Robert Williams Wood. Gypsy's Cousin Joy. l.t. ed. 2007. (ENG.). 160p. pap. 21.99 *(978-1-4264-9775-9(X))* Creative Media Partners, LLC.

Philips, A. If You Believe in Mermaids Don't Tell. 2007. 160p. per. 12.95 *(978-1-59858-359-5(X))* Dog Ear Publishing, LLC.

Phypers, Lisa Marie. My Favorite Little Boy. 2011. 28p. pap. 15.99 *(978-1-4628-6060-9(5))* Xlibris Corp.

Picard, Barbara Leonie. One Is One. 2006. (ENG.). 286p. (J). (gr. 3-7). per. 9.95 *(978-1-58988-027-6(7))* Consortium Bk. Sales & Distribution.

Pichon, Liz. The Brilliant World of Tom Gates: Read It & Go Ha! Ha! Ha! Pichon, Liz, illus. 2014. (Tom Gates Ser.: 1). (ENG., Illus.). 256p. (J). (gr. 3-7). 12.99 *(978-0-7636-7472-4(9))* Candlewick Pr.

Pittar, Gill. Milly & Molly's Monday. Morrell, Cris, illus. 2nd rev. ed. 2003. 27p. *(978-1-877297-06-9(2))* Milly Molly Bks.

Ponto, Kristina. Fissy. 2012. 20p. pap. 24.95 *(978-1-4626-4621-0(2))* America Star Bks.

Poulsen, David A. Last Sam's Cage. rev. ed. 2004. (ENG.). 224p. (YA). pap. 9.95 *(978-1-55263-611-4(9))* Keyhole Pr.

Power, Nicholas D. Puddle's Magical Adventures. 2009. 236p. 24.75 *(978-1-60693-534-7(8)*, Strategic Bk. Publishing) Strategic Book Publishing & Rights Agency (SBPRA).

Prentice-Hall Staff. The Red Pony. 2nd ed. (J). stu. ed. *(978-0-13-717133-0(1))* Prentice Hall (Schl. Div.).

Preston-Gannon, Frann. How to Lose a Lemur. 2014. (ENG., Illus.). 32p. (J). (gr. -1 — 1). 14.95 *(978-1-4549-1131-9(X))* Sterling Publishing Co., Inc.

Price, J. M. Patience, 1 vol. Bullard, Joyce, illus. 2010. 16p. pap. 24.95 *(978-1-4489-6233-4(1))* PublishAmerica, Inc.

Price, Roxanne M. Troy & the Championship Trophy. 2007. 20p. per. 11.95 *(978-1-4327-0613-5(6))* Outskirts Pr., Inc.

Prineas, Sarah. Found. Caparo, Antonio Javier, illus. 2011. (Magic Thief Ser.: 3). (ENG.). 384p. (J). (gr. 5). pap. 7.99 *(978-0-06-137595-8(0))* HarperCollins Pubs.

Project-00. 2003. (J). 15.95 *(978-0-9743843-0-6(5))* Endeavor Publishing.

Pryor, Bonnie. Seth of the Lion People. 2003. 116p. (J). pap. 5.95 *(978-0-9729339-0-2(5))* Kid's Shelf.

Publishing, Racehorse & Twain, Mark. Classics to Color: Adventures of Huckleberry Finn. 2016. (ENG., Illus.). 80p. (J). (gr. 1-6). pap. 8.99 *(978-1-944686-99-4(1)*, Racehorse Publishing) Skyhorse Publishing Co., Inc.

Pulchinski, Erin. Ethan Is Caught Blue Faced! Werrun, Anna, illus. 2013. 32p. pap. *(978-1-4602-2416-8(7))* FriesenPress.

Pullen, Zachary. Friday My Radio Flyer Flew. Pullen, Zachary, illus. 2008. (ENG., Illus.). 32p. (J). (gr. -1-2). 18.99 *(978-1-4169-3983-2(0)*, Simon & Schuster Bks. For Young Readers) Simon & Schuster Bks. For Young Readers.

Quigley, Michael. A Monkey's Riddle. 2013. 24p. pap. 24.95 *(978-1-63000-506-1(1))* America Star Bks.

Raden, Tammy. Lucky Dime. 2011. 24p. 11.32 *(978-1-4567-2137-4(2))* AuthorHouse.

Raleigh, Michael H. Ted & Jimmy, 1 vol. 2010. 99p. pap. 19.95 *(978-1-4489-6225-9(0))* America Star Bks.

The Rambunctious Tommy Tumpike. 2nd ed. 2005. (J). *(978-0-9773760-0-1(1))* Johnson, Anthony.

Random House Staff. Chase Is on the Case! (Paw Patrol) Random House Staff & Petrossi, Fabrizio, illus. 2014. (Step into Reading Ser.). (ENG.). 24p. (J). (gr. -1-1). 3.99 *(978-0-385-38447-6(5)*, Random Hse. Bks. for Young Readers) Random Hse. Children's Bks.

Ransom, Candice. The Life-Saving Adventure of Sam Deal, Shipwreck Rescuer. 2010. pap. 51.02 *(978-0-7613-6918-9(X))* Lerner Publishing Group.

Raphael, Marie. A Boy from Ireland. 2007. (Karen & Michael Braziller Bks.). (ENG.). 224p. (YA). (gr. 8-12). 19.95 *(978-0-89255-331-0(6))* Persea Bks., Inc.

Rate, Kristina. Potato Boy. Formosa, Natasha, illus. 2005. 32p. (J). (gr. -1). per. *(978-0-9549372-0-1(1))* Fastback TV Ltd.

Rawlings, Marjorie Kinnan. The Yearling. Wyeth, N. C., illus. 2013. (Scribner Classics Ser.). (ENG.). 416p. (J). (gr. 5-9). 29.99 *(978-1-4424-8209-8(5)*, Atheneum Bks. for Young Readers) Simon & Schuster Children's Publishing.

Rawls, Wilson. Where the Red Fern Grows. 249p. (YA). (gr. 5-18). pap. 5.99 *(978-0-8072-1467-1(1))*; pap. 5.99 *(978-0-8072-1358-2(6))* Random Hse. Audio Publishing Group. (Listening Library).

—Where the Red Fern Grows. l.t. ed. 2005. 376p. pap. 10.95 *(978-0-7862-7312-6(7)*, Large Print Pr.) Thorndike Pr.

Reed, Jennifer. Hadi's Journey. 2003. 110p. pap. 10.95 *(978-0-595-29375-9(1))* iUniverse, Inc.

Reeves, Pamela. United We Stand, a Story about Two Bullies. LaGrange, Tiffany, illus. 2009. 24p. pap. 12.95 *(978-1-936051-36-6(2))* Peppertree Pr., The.

Reid, Janet. Granny Rags. 2012. 194p. pap. *(978-1-922120-25-0(1)*, IP Kidz) Interactive Pubns. Pty, Ltd.

Reid-Tulloch, Joseph. Manu's Special Day. 2012. 16p. pap. 14.99 *(978-1-4520-9150-1(1))* AuthorHouse.

Reynolds, Carl Stanley. The Turkey Mountain Gang: The Adventures Begin. 2009. 52p. pap. 22.50 *(978-1-4389-7496-5(5))* AuthorHouse.

Richards, Pat. Bardolph Bedivere Wolf Returns. Richards, Charles, illus. 2007. 42p. (J). *(978-0-9790796-4-1(0))* PJR Assocs., Ltd.

Richey, Denise. Four in a Fire. 2011. 28p. (gr. -1). pap. 12.03 *(978-1-4520-6142-9(4))* AuthorHouse.

Richmond, Marianne. Big Boys Go Potty. Richmond, Marianne, illus. 2012. (ENG., Illus.). 32p. (J). 9.99 *(978-1-4022-6659-1(6)*, Sourcebooks Jabberwocky) Sourcebooks, Inc.

Richter, Conrad. The Light in the Forest. 2005. (ENG., Illus.). 176p. *(978-1-85715-515-0(7))* Knopf, Alfred A. Inc.

Ride Like the Wind. 2005. (YA). per. *(978-0-9744448-4-0(7))* McCourtie, Anne.

Riding, Will. Ebenezer's Tale. 2008. (Illus.). 188p. pap. 14.49 *(978-1-4343-9694-5(0))* AuthorHouse.

Ringo. Loss of a Friend. 2009. 24p. pap. 19.95 *(978-1-4389-8680-7(7))* AuthorHouse.

Ripken, Cal. Cal Ripken, Jr. 's All-Stars Squeeze Play. 2015. (Cal Ripken, Jr. 's All Stars Ser.). (ENG.). 224p. (J). (gr. 3-7). pap. 6.99 *(978-1-4231-9465-1(9))* Hyperion Bks. for Children.

Rippin, Sally. The Circus Lesson. Spartels, Stephanie, illus. 2013. 41p. (J). *(978-1-61067-236-8(4))* Kane Miller.

—The Circus Lesson: Hey Jack! Spartels, Stephanie, illus. 2014. (ENG.). 48p. (J). pap. 4.99 *(978-1-61067-186-6(4))* Kane Miller.

—The Crazy Cousins. Spartels, Stephanie, illus. (J). 2013. (ENG.). 48p. pap. 4.99 *(978-1-61067-121-7(X))* 2012. 42p. *(978-1-61067-135-4(X))* Kane Miller.

—The Robot Blues. Spartels, Stephanie, illus. 2014. (ENG.). 48p. (J). pap. 4.99 *(978-1-61067-124-8(4))* Kane Miller.

—The Scary Solo. Spartels, Stephanie, illus. (J). 2013. (ENG.). 48p. pap. 4.99 *(978-1-61067-122-4(8))* 2012. 43p. *(978-1-61067-136-1(8))* Kane Miller.

—The Winning Goal. Spartels, Stephanie, illus. (J). 2013. (ENG.). 48p. pap. 4.99 *(978-1-61067-123-1(6))* 2012. 43p. *(978-1-61067-137-8(6))* Kane Miller.

—The Worry Monsters. Spartels, Stephanie, illus. 2014. (ENG.). 48p. (J). pap. 4.99 *(978-1-61067-126-2(0))* Kane Miller.

—The Worst Sleepover: Hey Jack! Spartels, Stephanie, illus. 2014. (ENG.). 48p. (J). pap. 4.99 *(978-1-61067-185-9(6))* Kane Miller.

Ritsema van Eck, Patricia. The Dreaming of Paradise. 2005. 62p. (J). pap. 24.70 *(978-1-4116-6097-7(8))* Lulu Pr., Inc.

Robert, Lytle. Mr. Blair's Labyrinth. Gayle, Vandercook, illus. 2011. (J). 10.95 *(978-0-9798088-4-5(7))* EDCO Publishing, Inc.

Robertson, Elysia Hill. D. J. 's Sneakers. Robertson, Elysia Hill & Bruce, Cindy, illus. 2005. 104p. (J). per. 12.95 *(978-0-9764444-2-8(9)*, EJWV-003) E. J. Publishing.

Robertson, Keith. Henry Reed, Inc. abr. ed. (J). (gr. 4-7). pap. 15.95 incl. audio *(978-0-670-36801-3(6))* Live Oak Media.

—Henry Reed, Inc., Set. McCloskey, Robert, illus. abr. ed. (J). (gr. 4-7). 24.95 incl. audio *(978-0-670-36800-6(8))* Live Oak Media.

Robins, Eleanor. The Best Week Ever, 1 vol. unabr. ed. 2011. (Carter High Chronicles Ser.). (ENG.). 50p. (YA). (gr. 9-12). pap. 7.95 *(978-1-61651-304-7(7))* Saddleback Educational Publishing, Inc.

—Boy of Their Dreams. 2004. (Carter High Chronicles (High-Interest Readers) Ser.). (Illus.). 48p. (J). per. 3.95 *(978-1-56254-679-3(1)*, SP6791) Saddleback Educational Publishing, Inc.

Robley Blake, Colleen. I Can't Wait till I'm Five. 2006. (J). 9.95 *(978-0-9767342-0-8(6))* Imaajinn This.

Rock, Michelle L. Nighttime Adventures Counting Sheep. Longmore, Nickolai, illus. 2006. 32p. (J). 3.99 net. *(978-0-9771700-1-2(2))* Mystic Arts, LLC.

Rockwell, Thomas. How to Eat Fried Worms. (J). (gr. 3-5). 179p. pap. 4.99 *(978-0-8072-1395-7(0))*; 2004. 116p. pap. 29.00 incl. audio *(978-0-8072-8797-2(0))* Random Hse. Audio Publishing Group. (Listening Library).

Roeder, Mark. This Time Around. 2003. 226p. (YA). pap. 15.95 *(978-0-595-27361-4(0)*, Writers Club Pr.) iUniverse, Inc.

Roger, Marie-Sabine. Of Course They Do! Boys & Girls Can Do Anything. Sol, Anne, photos by. 2014. (ENG., Illus.). 40p. (J). (-k). lib. bdg. 9.95 *(978-1-58089-669-6(3))* Charlesbridge Publishing, Inc.

Rogers, Leslie E. It Is Me. Wilhelm, Doris L., illus. 2011. 24p. pap. 24.95 *(978-1-4626-4596-1(8))* America Star Bks.

Romeu, Emma. Gregorio y el Mar. 2003.Tr. of Gregory & the Sea. (SPA., Illus.). 151p. (J). (gr. 5-8). pap. 15.95 *(978-968-19-0316-9(1))* Santillana USA Publishing Co., Inc.

Romo, Brandyn. Rustlings of an Old Tree. 2012. 28p. pap. 24.95 *(978-1-4626-5581-6(5))* America Star Bks.

Rosado, Jessica E. The Princess. 2012. 26p. 24.95 *(978-1-4512-9466-8(2))* America Star Bks.

Ross, Daisy T. Ty & the Moon. 2012. 80p. pap. 25.25 *(978-1-4772-6950-3(9))* AuthorHouse.

Ross, Dev. We Both Read-Frank & the Tiger. Reinhart, Larry, illus. 2011. 44p. (J). 9.95 *(978-1-60115-259-6(0))* Treasure Bay, Inc.

Ross, Patrick. Joseph & Snowy Joe Blue, 1 vol. Burcham, David, illus. 2009. 25p. pap. 24.95 *(978-1-61582-314-7(X))* PublishAmerica, Inc.

Rossing, Nina. Fjord Blue. 2016. (ENG., Illus.). (YA). 27.99 ***(978-1-63533-016-8(5))***; 256p. (J). pap. 16.99 *(978-1-63476-385-1(8))* Dreamspinner Pr. (Harmony Ink Pr.).

Rothwell, Barbara Yates. The Boy from the Hulks. 2011. 264p. (gr. 4-6). 27.08 *(978-1-4269-9414-2(1))*; pap. 17.08 *(978-1-4269-9415-9(X))* Trafford Publishing.

Rotman, Stuart. Welcome to Trashtown. 2007. 192p. 34.95 *(978-1-4303-2662-5(X))* Lulu Pr., Inc.

Rozen, Beti. Stolen Spirit. Lima, Graca, illus. 2nd ed. 2004. 32p. (gr. 3-7). pap. *(978-0-9642333-1-7(2))* Sem Fronteiras Pr., Ltd.

Rushdie, Salman. Luka & the Fire of Life. 2009. 14.75 *(978-0-7848-3731-3(7),* Everbind) Marco Bk. Co.

—Luka & the Fire of Life. 2011. (ENG.). 240p. (J). (gr. 7). pap. 17.00 *(978-0-679-78347-3(4),* Random Hse. Trade Paperbacks) Random House Publishing Group.

Russell, Joyce. My First Bus Ride to School. 2011. 28p. 12.03 *(978-1-4567-1111-5(3))* AuthorHouse.

Sabatino, N. S. The Tiny Donut with a Big Heart, 1 vol. 2009. 48p. pap. 24.95 *(978-1-60836-132-8(2))* America Star Bks.

Sachar, Louis. There's a Boy in the Girls' Bathroom. 195p. (J). (gr. 4-6). pap. 4.99 *(978-0-8072-1453-4(1),* Listening Library) Random Hse. Audio Publishing Group.

Saddleback Educational Publishing Staff, ed. The Best Week Ever. 2011. (Carter High Chronicles Ser.). (ENG.). 16p. (YA). (gr. 9-12). tchr. ed. 7.95 incl. cd-rom *(978-1-61651-314-6(4))* Saddleback Educational Publishing, Inc.

Sadu, Itah & Condy, Roy. Christopher Changes His Name. (Illus.). 32p. (J). pap. 4.99 *(978-0-590-24624-8(0))* Scholastic, Inc.

Sáenz, Benjamin Alire. He Forgot to Say Goodbye. 2010. (ENG.). 352p. (YA). (gr. 7). pap. 12.99 *(978-1-4169-9434-3(3),* Simon & Schuster Bks. For Young Readers) Simon & Schuster Bks. For Young Readers.

Saffiedine, Amanda. I Don't Understand. 2009. 32p. pap. 12.99 *(978-1-4490-1310-3(4))* AuthorHouse.

Sambrone, Erika Elizabeth. Heavenly Angel Bugs: God Answers Prayers. 2011. 56p. pap. 25.00 *(978-1-4634-6807-1(5))* AuthorHouse.

Samuels, Linda Nissen. Cuando Elly Fue a la Reserva Ecologica. Samuels, Linda Nissen, illus. 2013. (Illus.). 40p. pap. *(978-0-9511751-8-7(1))* Samuels, Linda Y.

Sarah Taylor. The Teddy That Went to Iraq. Baker, David, illus. 2011. 28p. pap. 24.95 *(978-1-4560-8382-3(1))* America Star Bks.

Sargent, Dave, et al. Summer Milky Way: (Blackfeet) Be Compassionate, 20 vols., Vol. 16. Lenoir, Jane, illus. l.t. ed. 2004. (Story Keeper Ser.). 48p. (J). lib. bdg. 23.60 *(978-1-56763-933-9(X))*; pap. 10.95 *(978-1-56763-934-6(8))* Ozark Publishing.

—Tattoos of Honor Vol. 17: (Osage) Be Gentle & Giving, 20 vols. Lenoir, Jane, illus. l.t. ed. 2004. (Story Keeper Ser.: Vol. 17). 42p. (J). pap. 10.95 *(978-1-56763-936-0(4))*; lib. bdg. 23.60 *(978-1-56763-935-3(6))* Ozark Publishing.

—Truth, Power & Freedom Vol. 19: (Sioux) Show Respect, 20 vols., Vol. 19. Lenoir, Jane, illus. l.t. ed. 2004. (Story Keeper Ser.: 19). 42p. (J). pap. 10.95 *(978-1-56763-940-7(2))* Ozark Publishing.

Satera, Diane. The Angel of Wild Springs: Jaiden & the Sacred Stones. 2010. 168p. 23.99 *(978-1-4520-3460-7(5))*; pap. 11.99 *(978-1-4520-3461-4(3))* AuthorHouse.

Savoie, Jacques & Zekina, Daniela. Un Chapeau Qui Tournait Autour de la Terre. 2003. (Illus.). 24p. (J). pap. *(978-2-89021-295-4(5))* Diffusion du livre Mirabel (DLM).

Sayre, Justin & dePaola, Tomie. Husky. 2015. (ENG.). 272p. (YA). (gr. 5). bds. 16.99 *(978-0-448-48413-6(7),* Grosset & Dunlap) Penguin Young Readers Group.

Schaffter, Ehren. Through the Curtain. 2009. 239p. pap. 20.00 *(978-0-557-20001-6(6))* Lulu Pr., Inc.

Schamerhorn, Ronna. Dreamy Navy Boy. 2007. 44p. per. 24.95 *(978-1-4241-8372-2(3))* America Star Bks.

Schmidt, Gary D. Trouble. 2010. (ENG.). 304p. (YA). (gr. 7). pap. 8.99 *(978-0-547-33133-1(9))* Houghton Mifflin Harcourt Publishing Co.

Scholastic, Inc. Staff & Taylor-Butler, Christine. No Boys Allowed! Page, Mark, illus. 2004. (Just for You Ser.). (ENG.). 32p. pap. 3.99 *(978-0-439-56856-2(0),* Teaching Resources) Scholastic, Inc.

Scholl, Jenny. Four Farm Boys: Turkey Times. Casto, Christina, illus. 2010. 36p. (J). pap. 13.95 *(978-1-4327-5886-8(1))* Outskirts Pr., Inc.

Schotter, Roni. The Boy Who Loved Words. Potter, Giselle, illus. 2006. (ENG.). 40p. (J). (gr. -1-3). 17.99 *(978-0-375-83601-5(2),* Schwartz & Wade Bks.) Random Hse. Children's Bks.

Schultz, Aronka. A Dinosaur on the Loose. 2010. 32p. pap. 12.99 *(978-1-4520-4400-2(7))* AuthorHouse.

Scott, Kate. Spies in Disguise: Boy in a Tutu. 2016. (ENG., Illus.). 192p. (J). (gr. 1-5). pap. 7.99 *(978-1-63450-695-3(2),* Sky Pony Pr.) Skyhorse Publishing Co., Inc.

Scott, Kevin. Stevie Wonderboy. 2009. 72p. pap. 11.49 *(978-1-4490-5839-5(6))* AuthorHouse.

Seabag-Montefiore, Mary, retold by. David Copperfield. 2008. (Young Reading Series 3 Gift Books - Famous Lives Ser.). 64p. (J). 8.99 *(978-0-7945-2097-7(9),* Usborne) EDC Publishing.

Sealey, Edmund J. Toast. 2009. 76p. pap. *(978-1-84923-790-1(5))* YouWriteOn.

Seaman, John E. On the Road with Ruben Doyle. 2010. 170p. 29.99 *(978-1-4500-3196-7(X))* Xlibris Corp.

Sebring, Janet And Jordan. Every Child Can Be a Hero. 2012. 36p. pap. 21.95 *(978-1-4685-3031-5(3))* AuthorHouse.

Sebring, Ruthie. Itty's Guinea Pig. 2009. 24p. pap. 24.95 *(978-1-61582-555-4(X))* America Star Bks.

Seidon, Bonnie Bale. The Adventures of Trevor & the Tiger. 2012. 104p. 21.79 *(978-1-4669-4389-6(0))*; pap. 11.79 *(978-1-4669-4391-9(2))* Trafford Publishing.

Sendak, Maurice. La Cocina de Noche. Sendak, Maurice, illus. 2003. (Picture Books Collection). (SPA., Illus.). 40p. (J). (gr. k-3). 10.95 *(978-84-204-4570-0(3))* Ediciones Alfaguara ESP. Dist: Santillana USA Publishing Co., Inc.

Sennell, Joles. Yuyo, Nino No Podia... (Yuyo, Boy Who...) (SPA.). 24p. (J). 12.50 *(978-84-7183-169-9(4))* El Hogar y La Moda, S.A. ESP. Dist: AIMS International Bks., Inc.

Sermons, Faye. No Ordinary Cat. Becket, Nancy, illus. 2009. 40p. pap. 16.99 *(978-1-4389-6242-9(8))* AuthorHouse.

Servi Machlin, Edda. My Puppy Marrano. 2007. (YA). 19.95 *(978-1-878857-13-2(4))* Giro Pr.

Seton, Ernest Thompson. Rolf in the Woods: The Adventures of a Boy Scout with Indian Quonab & Little Dog Skookum. 2013. (ENG., Illus.). 400p. (J). (gr. 6-17). pap. 14.95 *(978-1-62087-386-1(9),* 620386) Skyhorse Publishing Co., Inc.

Seyforth, Edward L. A Horribly Frightening Deception, 1 vol. 2009. 75p. pap. 19.95 *(978-1-61546-260-5(0))* America Star Bks.

Shally, Celeste. Since We're Friends: An Autism Picture Book. Harrington, David, illus. 2007. 32p. (J). (gr. -1-3). per. 8.99 *(978-0-9794713-0-8(3))* Awaken Specialty Pr.

Sharma, Shivan. The Castle, Dragons & a Cricket Ball. 2009. 76p. pap. *(978-1-84549-415-5(6),* Swirl) arima publishing.

Shaw, Alexander William. The Adventures of A Teenage Time Traveller. 2009. 84p. pap., pap. 12.95 *(978-0-9561592-2-9(2))* Hetman Publishing GBR. Dist: Lulu Pr., Inc.

Shepperson, Jacqueline Ruth. The Blue Jay Tales. 2005. 89p. pap. 19.95 *(978-1-4137-3884-1(2))* America Star Bks.

Shepple, Sue Ann. Christopher & Grammy Join the Circus. 2011. 28p. pap. 15.99 *(978-1-4628-6245-0(4))* Xlibris Corp.

Shertzer, Twilene & Eshbach, Karen. No Glass Between: A Boy's Journey with Loving & Then Losing His Baby Brother. 2012. (Illus.). 24p. (J). 16.95 *(978-1-61314-050-5(9),* Innovo Pr.) Innovo Publishing, LLC.

Sherwood-Sitts, Herm. The Secret of Cypress Swamp. 2011. 20p. pap. 24.95 *(978-1-4560-6166-1(6))* America Star Bks.

Shrode, Donna. Fun with Nana: Let's Play. 2011. 28p. (gr. -1). pap. 12.03 *(978-1-4567-4600-1(6))* AuthorHouse.

Shusterman, Neal. Bruiser. 2011. (ENG.). 352p. (YA). (gr. 9). pap. 9.99 *(978-0-06-113410-4(4),* HarperTeen) HarperCollins Pubs.

Shute, Henry. Sequil or Things Whitch Aint Finished in The. 2007. 108p. per. 14.99 *(978-0-9773040-3-5(5))* Wilder Pubns., Corp.

Shute, Henry A. The Real Diary of A Real Boy. 2004. reprint ed. pap. 1.99 *(978-1-4192-7985-0(8))* Kessinger Publishing, LLC.

Shute, Henry Augustus. The Real Diary of a Real Boy. 2011. (Illus.). 74p. pap. 9.99 *(978-1-61279-087-9(9))* Publishing in Motion.

Sierra i Fabra, Jordi. El Nino Que Vivia en las Estrellas. (SPA.). 120p. (YA). (gr. 5-8). 8.95 *(978-84-204-4429-1(4))* Ediciones Alfaguara ESP. Dist: Santillana USA Publishing Co., Inc.

Simon, Francesca. Horrid Henry. 2009. (Horrid Henry Ser.). lib. bdg. 17.20 *(978-0-606-06765-2(5),* Turtleback) Turtleback Bks.

Simpson, Wanda. Jupiter the Space Donkey, 1 vol. 2009. 17p. pap. 24.95 *(978-1-61582-733-6(1))* PublishAmerica, Inc.

Sitner, Nechama. What Did Pinny Do? An Upsherin Story. Leff, Tova, illus. 2013. 36p. (J). 12.95 *(978-1-929628-72-8(2))* Hachai Publishing.

Skye, obert. Pillagy: The Complete Trilogy. 2013. (ENG., Illus.). 712p. (YA). (gr. 6). pap. 17.99 *(978-1-60907-706-8(7),* Shadow Mountain) Shadow Mountain Publishing.

Slater, David Michael. David Michael Slater: Missy Swiss & More - 6 Titles, 6 vols., Set. Incl. Comin' Through. Rooney, Ronnie, illus. 28.50 *(978-1-60270-008-6(7))*; Flour Girl: A Recipe for Disaster. Brooks, S. G., illus. 28.50 *(978-1-60270-009-3(5))*; Missy Swiss. Reibeling, Brandon, illus. 28.50 *(978-1-60270-010-9(9))*; Ned Loses His Head. 28.50 *(978-1-60270-011-6(7))*; Seven Ate Nine. Trover, Zachary, illus. 28.50 *(978-1-60270-012-3(5))*; Sharpest Tool in the Shed. Reibeling, Brandon, illus. 28.50 *(978-1-60270-013-0(3))*; (gr. -1-4). (Missy Swiss & More Ser.). (ENG.). 32p. 2007. 171.00 *(978-1-60270-007-9(9),* Looking Glass Library) ABDO Publishing Co.

Smart Kidz, creator. It's Potty Time for Boys. 2013. (ENG., Illus.). 12p. (J). bds. 12.99 *(978-1-891100-05-5(X),* Smart Kids) Penton Overseas, Inc.

Smedley, Frank E. Frank Fairlegh: Scenes from the Life of a Private Pupil. 2007. (ENG.). 570p. per. 30.99 *(978-1-4346-4557-9(6))*; 640p. per. 45.75 *(978-1-4346-4558-6(4))* Creative Media Partners, LLC.

Smith, Andrew. Passenger. 2012. (ENG.). 480p. (YA). (gr. 9-13). 17.99 *(978-1-250-00487-1(X))* Feiwel & Friends.

Smith, C. Michelle. Skeeter Sneeter Doodlebop. Foreman, A., illus. 2009. 24p. pap. 15.63 *(978-1-934840-54-2(8))* Nimble Bks. LLC.

Smith, Carrie. The Boy Who Cried Wolf: Classic Tales Edition. Kelley, Gerald, illus. 2011. (Classic Tales Ser.). (J). *(978-1-936258-59-8(5))* Benchmark Education Co.

Smith, Emily Wing. The Way He Lived. 2016. (ENG.). 224p. (YA). (gr. 9). 17.99 *(978-0-399-18722-3(7),* Dutton Books for Young Readers) Penguin Young Readers Group.

Smith, Julie. Hearts for the Homeless. 2012. 28p. pap. 19.99 *(978-1-4685-5602-5(9))* AuthorHouse.

Smith, Peggy. The Champ: The Adventures of a Boy & His New Puppy. Told in One-syllable Words for the Barton Reading & Spelling System. 2003. (J). pap. 7.95 *(978-0-9744343-3-9(7),* SA-304) Bright Solutions for Dyslexia, LLC.

Snell, Roy F. Wings for Victory. 2005. pap. 26.95 *(978-1-4191-6999-1(8))* Kessinger Publishing, LLC.

A Soap Story: Individual Title, 6 packs. (gr. -1-2). 27.00 *(978-0-7635-9475-6(X))* Rigby Education.

Sobel, Gerrie. Jacob & His Magical Flying Bears, a Halloween Story. Torres, Dottie, illus. 2009. 32p. pap. 12.95 *(978-1-936051-42-7(7))* Peppertree Pr., The.

Soloman, Debra. Don't Look under the Bridge. 2006. 25p. 21.00 *(978-1-4116-7114-0(7))* Lulu Pr., Inc.

Solomon, Michelle & Pereira, Lavinia. Uh - Oh! Faust, Laurie A., illus. 2009. 24p. pap. 10.96 *(978-1-4251-8950-1(4))* Trafford Publishing.

Sommer, A. M. Tucker's Birthday. 2007. 56p. (gr. 2-2). per. 15.99 *(978-1-4257-8987-9(0))* Xlibris Corp.

Souhami, Jessica & Quarto Generic Staff. The Strongest Boy in the World. 2014. (ENG., Illus.). 32p. (J). (gr. k-3). 17.99 *(978-1-84780-411-2(X),* Frances Lincoln) Quarto Publishing Group UK GBR. Dist: Hachette Bk. Group.

Sparks, Evan. Freddy's Tale. 2006. 44p. pap. 14.88 *(978-1-4116-7427-1(8))* Lulu Pr., Inc.

Spies, Ben. Weirdo. Spies, Robert, illus. 2015. (ENG.). 54p. (J). pap. *(978-0-473-33563-2(8))* Spies Publishing.

Spinelli, Jerry. Milkweed. 2010. (ENG.). 240p. (YA). (gr. 7). pap. 9.99 *(978-0-375-86147-5(5),* Ember) Random Hse. Children's Bks.

Springer, Audrey. Rusty's Gift. Richards, Kris, illus. 2012. 28p. 24.95 *(978-1-4626-6589-1(6))* America Star Bks.

Spurr, Judy. Trapped. 2007. 84p. per. 8.95 *(978-0-595-43915-7(2))* iUniverse, Inc.

Stahl, Matt. Fuzzy Winkerbane: The Boy Who Would Never Change. 2011. 28p. pap. 14.50 *(978-1-4634-0758-2(0))* AuthorHouse.

Standish, Burt L. Frank Merriwell down South. Rudman, Jack, ed. (Frank Merriwell Ser.). (YA). (gr. 9-18). 29.95 *(978-0-8373-9305-6(1))*; 2003. pap. 9.95 *(978-0-8373-9005-5(2),* FM-005) Merriwell, Frank Inc.

—Frank Merriwell in Europe. Rudman, Jack, ed. (Frank Merriwell Ser.). (YA). (gr. 9-18). 29.95 *(978-0-8373-9308-7(6))*; pap. 9.95 *(978-0-8373-9008-6(7),* FM-008) Merriwell, Frank Inc.

—Frank Merriwell's Bravery. Rudman, Jack, ed. (Frank Merriwell Ser.). (YA). (gr. 9-18). 29.95 *(978-0-8373-9306-3(X))*; 2003. pap. 9.95 *(978-0-8373-9006-2(0),* FM-006) Merriwell, Frank Inc.

—Frank Merriwell's Hunting Tour. Rudman, Jack, ed. (Frank Merriwell Ser.). (YA). (gr. 9-18). 29.95 *(978-0-8373-9307-0(8))*; 2003. pap. 9.95 *(978-0-8373-9007-9(9),* FM-007) Merriwell, Frank Inc.

—Frank Merriwell's New Boy. Rudman, Jack, ed. 2003. (Frank Merriwell Ser.). pap. 9.95 *(978-0-8373-9134-2(2))* Merriwell, Frank Inc.

—Frank Merriwell's Sports Afield. Rudman, Jack, ed. (Frank Merriwell Ser.). (YA). (gr. 9-18). 29.95 *(978-0-8373-9310-0(8))*; pap. 9.95 *(978-0-8373-9010-9(9),* FM-010) Merriwell, Frank Inc.

—Frank Merriwell's Trip West. Rudman, Jack, ed. (Frank Merriwell Ser.). (YA). (gr. 9-18). 29.95 *(978-0-8373-9304-9(3))*; pap. 9.95 *(978-0-8373-9004-8(4),* FM-004) Merriwell, Frank Inc.

Star, Eloney. Heavy Duty Trucker. 2007. 28p. (J). per. 7.99 *(978-1-59879-287-4(3))* Lifevest Publishing, Inc.

Stassen, Jean-Philippe. Deogratias. 2006. (Illus.). 96p. (J). pap. *(978-0-330-44467-5(0),* First Second Bks.) Roaring Brook Pr.

Steele, Andrew. The Galaxy Boys & the Sphere. 2008. (ENG.). 285p. (J). (gr. 4-7). pap. *(978-1-85756-687-1(4))* Janus Publishing Co.

Stein, Evaleen. Our Little Norman Cousin of Long Ago. Goss, John, illus. 2007. 112p. per. 8.95 *(978-1-59915-245-5(2))* Yesterday's Classics.

Stevenson, Robert Louis. Kidnapped & Catriona. 2007. (ENG.). 496p. per. *(978-1-84697-033-7(4))* Birlinn, Ltd.

Stevenson, Tysheia E. Jude, 1 vol. 2009. 57p. pap. 12.95 *(978-1-61582-624-7(6))* PublishAmerica, Inc.

Stever, Karen Malloy. Jabin, the Talking Donkey: In Jerusalem. 2012. 24p. pap. 24.95 *(978-1-4626-8285-0(5))* America Star Bks.

Stewart, Samara. Solomon's Smile. 2011. 24p. (gr. -1). pap. 11.32 *(978-1-4567-3734-4(1))* AuthorHouse.

Stine, R. L. Three Faces of Me, 0 vols. unabr. ed. 2012. (ENG.). 86p. (J). (gr. 3-7). pap. 4.99 *(978-1-61218-326-8(3),* 9781612183268, Amazon Children's Publishing) Amazon Publishing.

—You Can't Scare Me! 2010. (Classic Goosebumps Ser.: 17). (ENG.). 160p. (J). (gr. 3-7). pap. 6.99 *(978-0-545-17796-2(0),* Scholastic Paperbacks) Scholastic, Inc.

Stirnkorb, Patricia. All about Me! Regular Version. 2005. (Illus.). 12p. (J). bds. 12.99 *(978-0-9758709-8-3(X),* A.W.A. Gang) Journey Stone Creations, LLC.

—Stranger Danger: The reluctantly written but absolutly necessary book for todays boys & Girls. 2005. (Illus.). 32p. (J). 12.99 *(978-0-9758709-9-0(8))* Journey Stone Creations, LLC.

Stoddard, William O. Dab Kinzer: A Story of a Growing Boy. l.t. ed. 2007. (ENG.). 262p. pap. 23.99 *(978-1-4264-4106-6(1))*; 214p. pap. 20.99 *(978-1-4264-4047-2(2))* Creative Media Partners, LLC.

—Dab Kinzer A Story of A Growing Boy. 2004. reprint ed. pap. 24.95 *(978-1-4191-1488-5(3))*; pap. 1.99 *(978-1-4192-1488-2(8))* Kessinger Publishing, LLC.

Stofko, Michael D. Has Anybody Seen Me? 2009. 24p. pap. 12.99 *(978-1-4389-9032-3(4))* AuthorHouse.

—A Visit from the Zoo. 2011. 32p. pap. 12.77 *(978-1-4567-2968-4(3))* AuthorHouse.

Stratemeyer, Edward. The Mystery at Putnam Hall: Or the School Chums' Strange Discovery. 2007. (ENG.). 186p. pap. 19.99 *(978-1-4346-1186-4(8))*; 204p. pap. 22.99 *(978-1-4346-1257-1(0))* Creative Media Partners, LLC.

—The Rover Boys at School: Or the Cadets of Putnam Hall. 2007. (ENG.). 164p. pap. 19.99 *(978-1-4264-2004-7(8))* Creative Media Partners, LLC.

—The Rover Boys on the Ocean: Or, a Chase for a Fortune. 2007. (ENG.). 158p. pap. 19.99 *(978-1-4264-2766-4(2))*; 170p. pap. 21.99 *(978-1-4264-2804-3(9))* Creative Media Partners, LLC.

Strauss, Ed. Devotions to Make You Stronger, 1 vol. 2007. (2:52 Ser.). (ENG., Illus.). 192p. (J). (gr. 3-7). pap. 9.99 *(978-0-310-71311-1(0))* Zonderkidz.

Strauss, Joanne. Charlie & His Friends. 2011. 30p. pap. 16.95 *(978-1-4626-4401-8(5))* America Star Bks.

Strouss, Jessica & Strouss, Stephen. There's a Dog at My Feet when I Eat. 2010. 36p. 15.49 *(978-1-4269-4342-3(3))* Trafford Publishing.

Strow, Lorie. The Shimmers. 2011. 32p. pap. 21.99 *(978-1-4568-8133-7(7))* Xlibris Corp.

Suhajcik, Andrea. Mommy, I Did Nothing Wrong! 2012. 16p. pap. 15.99 *(978-1-4772-1192-2(6))* AuthorHouse.

Susanne, Gervay & Gervay, Susanne. Being Jack. Wilcox, Cathy, illus. 2016. (ENG.). 192p. (J). pap. 5.99 *(978-1-61067-379-2(4))* Kane Miller.

Sutcliffe, William. Bad Influence. Anderson, Laura Ellen & Busby, Ailie, illus. 2015. (ENG.). 224p. (YA). (gr. 9). pap. 15.99 *(978-1-4088-3653-8(X),* 9781408836538, Bloomsbury USA Childrens) Bloomsbury Publishing USA.

Sutton, Pamelina Jean'e. Bill Bill the Burger Boy. 2012. 24p. pap. 12.00 *(978-1-61286-108-1(3))* Avid Readers Publishing Group.

Sweetser, Kate Dickinson. Boys & girls from Thackeray. l.t. ed. 2007. (ENG.). 264p. pap. 21.99 *(978-1-4264-3943-8(1))* Creative Media Partners, LLC.

Sylvester, Sr. Talking Memories. Morrison, Nancy, illus. 2011. 36p. pap. 24.95 *(978-1-4489-4967-0(X))* America Star Bks.

Taber-Montgomery, Kathy. We Live in a Zoo. 2012. 24p. pap. *(978-1-4602-0028-5(4))* FriesenPress.

Tan, Shaun. The Lost Thing. (Illus.). 32p. pap. *(978-0-7344-0388-9(7),* Lothian Children's Bks.) Hachette Australia.

Tanner-Moore, Margie. What Noah Knows. 2010. 49p. pap. 10.00 *(978-0-557-45753-3(X))* Lulu Pr., Inc.

Tate, Elizabeth Dawn. There's a Storm Brewing Outside. 2009. 24p. pap. 15.50 *(978-1-60693-239-1(X),* Eloquent Bks.) Strategic Book Publishing & Rights Agency (SBPRA).

Tatulli, Mark. Desmond Pucket & the Mountain Full of Monsters. 2014. (Desmond Pucket Ser.: 2). (ENG.). 240p. (J). 13.99 *(978-1-4494-3549-3(1))* Andrews McMeel Publishing.

Tavner, Gill & Dickens, Charles. David Copperfield. Donnelly, Karen, illus. 2009. (Real Reads Ser.). 64p. (J). (gr. 4-8). pap. 13.55 *(978-1-60754-383-1(4))* Windmill Bks.

Temple, Valerie. Mud Witch Boy of Ghost Canyon. 2009. 113p. pap. 10.95 *(978-1-4327-3103-8(3))* Outskirts Pr., Inc.

Tennapel, Doug. Cardboard. 2012. lib. bdg. 24.50 *(978-0-606-26212-5(1),* Turtleback) Turtleback Bks.

Terrell, Brandon. Second Chance Delivery. 2016. (Tartan House Ser.). (ENG., Illus.). 96p. (J). (gr. 5-12). pap. 9.95 *(978-1-63235-205-7(2),* 12-Story Library) Pr. Room Editions LLC.

Tetro, Marc. No Rest for Edwin. 2004. (J). (gr. k-3). spiral bd. *(978-0-616-01789-0(8))* Canadian National Institute for the Blind/Institut National Canadien pour les Aveugles.

Thiele, Colin. Storm Boy. Ingpen, Robert R., illus. 2006. (ENG.). 1p. (J). (gr. -1-3). 7.95 *(978-1-74110-187-4(5))*; 40th anniv. ed. pap. 7.95 *(978-1-86436-804-8(7))* New Holland Pubs. Pty, Ltd. AUS. Dist: Tuttle Publishing.

Thomas, Beth. Jack & the Richmond Bubble. 2012. pap. 11.95 *(978-0-7414-7495-7(6))* Infinity Publishing.

Thomas, Erin. Haze, 1 vol. 2012. (Orca Sports Ser.). (ENG.). 192p. (YA). (gr. 6-10). pap. 9.95 *(978-1-4598-0070-0(2))* Orca Bk. Pubs. USA.

Thompson, Jenean. All in a Day's Play. Thompson, Jenean, illus. l.t. ed. 2005. (Illus.). 40p. (J). 14.95 *(978-1-59879-066-5(8))* Lifevest Publishing, Inc.

Thorsen, Jody & Gates, Jeremy S. The Boy Who Cried Dinosaur. 2012. 24p. pap. 15.99 *(978-1-4771-0990-8(0))* Xlibris Corp.

Tibo, Gilles. Simon et le Petit Cirque. 2004.Tr. of Simon at the Circus. (FRE.). (J). (gr. -1-2). spiral bd. *(978-0-616-01846-0(0))* Canadian National Institute for the Blind/Institut National Canadien pour les Aveugles.

—Simon et les Deguisements. 2004.Tr. of Simon's Disguise. (FRE.). (J). (gr. -1-2). spiral bd. *(978-0-616-01844-6(4))* Canadian National Institute for the Blind/Institut National Canadien pour les Aveugles.

—Simon Makes Music. 2004. (J). (gr. -1-2). spiral bd. *(978-0-616-01793-7(6))*; spiral bd. *(978-0-616-01792-0(8))* Canadian National Institute for the Blind/Institut National Canadien pour les Aveugles.

Timothy, Ering. Frog Belly Rat F & G. 2003. (J). bds. 16.99 *(978-0-7636-2248-0(6))* Candlewick Pr.

Todd, John S. The Goodfellow Boys & the Talking Dinosaur. 2004. (Illus.). 32p. (gr. 3-5). 10.95 *(978-1-57197-190-6(4))* Pentland Pr., Inc.

Tooke, Wes. Lucky: Maris, Mantle, & My Best Summer Ever. 2011. (ENG.). 192p. (J). (gr. 3-7). pap. 6.99 *(978-1-4169-8664-5(2),* Simon & Schuster Bks. For Young Readers) Simon & Schuster Bks. For Young Readers.

Torribio, Penelope. The Magic in You: From vacant lot to community Garden. 2011. 40p. pap. 16.46 *(978-1-4269-5723-9(8))* Trafford Publishing.

Toska, Mary Lou. Ernest's Dream: A Young Boy Wanting to Spend the Summer in the High Alps. 2012. 20p. pap. 24.95 *(978-1-4626-8662-9(1))* America Star Bks.

Tousey, Sanford. Jack Finds Gold. 2011. 44p. 35.95 *(978-1-258-09840-7(7))* Literary Licensing, LLC.

Towne, C. Ross. Old Jack: The very smart Dog. 2011. 16p. 8.32 *(978-1-4567-2178-7(X))* AuthorHouse.

Tracy, Joe. Arnie the Imagination Boy. 2011. 24p. pap. 15.99 *(978-1-4568-9135-0(9))* Xlibris Corp.

Tremblay, Marc. Le Petit Frere du Chaperon Rouge. Fil et al, illus. 2004. (était une Fois Ser.). (FRE.). 24p. (J). (gr. -1). pap. *(978-2-89021-698-3(5))* Diffusion du livre Mirabel (DLM).

Trent, Sandy Chase. Tommy's Amazing Journey: The Cat that Could Fly. 2011. 16p. pap. 24.95 *(978-1-4626-2363-1(8))* America Star Bks.

Trest, Candace D. Zack & Tripp & the Indian Village. 2007. 64p. per. 9.99 *(978-1-60477-526-6(2))* Salem Author Services.

Trottier, Doug. The Crow & His Boy. 2011. 382p. pap. 19.00 *(978-1-60976-469-2(2),* Eloquent Bks.) Strategic Book Publishing & Rights Agency (SBPRA).

Tucker, Jasmin. Robot School. 2010. 28p. 12.49 *(978-1-4520-5011-9(2))* AuthorHouse.

Turcios, Omar. David, Fish & Penguins... 2012. (ENG., Illus.). 36p. (J). (gr. -1-k). *(978-84-15241-94-2(1))* D P & G Military Pubs.

Turner, Jennifer. My Name Is Jake. Bell, Susan, illus. 2012. 32p. (J). 14.99 *(978-1-938032-04-2(7))*; pap. 7.99 *(978-1-938032-05-9(5))* Peaks Pr. LLC.

Tuthill, Louisa C. Hurrah for New England! or the Virginia Boy's Vacation. 2004. reprint ed. pap. 15.95 *(978-1-4191-2504-1(4))*; pap. 1.99 *(978-1-4192-2504-8(9))* Kessinger Publishing, LLC.

Twain, Mark, pseud. The Adventures of Huckleberry Finn. Andreasen, Dan, illus. 2010. (Classic Starts(tm) Ser.). (ENG.). 160p. (J). (gr. 2-4). cd-rom 9.95 *(978-1-4027-7355-6(2))* Sterling Publishing Co., Inc.

—The Adventures of Tom Sawyer. Ingpen, Robert R., illus. 2010. (Sterling Illustrated Classics Ser.). (ENG.). 240p. (J). (gr. 5-18). 19.95 *(978-1-4027-6762-3(5))* Sterling Publishing Co., Inc.
—Las Aventuras de Huckleberry Finn. de Atauri, Ines & de Atauri, Juan Diaz, eds. 2006. (Clasicos Juveniles Ser.).Tr. of Adventures of Huckleberry Finn. (SPA., Illus.). 359p. pap. 17.95 *(978-84-263-5252-1(9))* Vives, Luis Editorial (Edelvives) ESP. Dist: Lectorum Pubns., Inc.
—The Prince & the Pauper. 2006. (Aladdin Classics Ser.). (ENG.). 352p. (J). pap. 7.99 *(978-1-4169-2805-8(7)*, Aladdin) Simon & Schuster Children's Publishing.
—Tom Sawyer. 2005. 264p. 28.95 *(978-1-4218-0768-3(8)*, 1st World Library - Literary Society) 1st World Publishing, Inc.
—Tom Sawyer. 2004. reprint ed. pap. 1.99 *(978-1-4192-5166-5(X))* Kessinger Publishing, LLC.
—Tom Sawyer, 1 vol. Mullarkey, Lisa, illus. 2010. (Calico Illustrated Classics Ser.: No. 1). (ENG.). 112p. (J). (gr. 3-6). 27.07 *(978-1-60270-704-7(9))* Magic Wagon.
—Tom Sawyer. 2009. 196p. (gr. 4-7). pap. 12.99 *(978-1-934941-63-8(8))* Red & Black Pubs.
Tysinger, Dona. The Cheyenne Dragon & the Dragonfly. 2011. 52p. (gr. 4-6). pap. 10.99 *(978-1-4634-3032-0(9))* AuthorHouse.
Ungerer, Tomi. Rufus. Ungerer, Tomi, illus. 2003. (SPA., Illus.). 36p. (J). (gr. k-3). pap. 7.95 *(978-968-19-0746-4(9))* Aguilar, Altea, Taurus, Alfaguara, S.A. de C.V MEX. Dist: Santillana USA Publishing Co., Inc.
Unsworth, Anne. Danny Is Dyslexic. 2011. 68p. (gr. 4-6). pap. 12.10 *(978-1-4567-8417-1(X))* AuthorHouse.
The Unwelcome Visitors. 2004. (ENG., Illus.). 48p. (J). per. *(978-0-9746849-0-1(2))* Littletonhouse Publishing.
Urmston, Kathleen & Evans, Karen. Snowflakes. Kaeden Corp. Staff, ed. Graves, Dennis, illus. 2006. (ENG.). 12p. (gr. k-1). pap. 7.95 *(978-1-879835-01-6(0)*, Kaeden Bks.) Kaeden Corp.
Vail, Rachel. School, Drool, & Other Daily Disasters. Cordell, Matthew, illus. 2011. (Justin Case Ser.: 1). (ENG.). 272p. (J). (gr. 2-4). pap. 7.99 *(978-0-312-56357-8(4)*, 9780312563578) Square Fish.
Valentine, James. Stuff Happens: Luke. 12th ed. 2016. (Stuff Happens Ser.). (ENG.). 96p. (J). (gr. 2-4). 8.99 ***(978-0-14-330897-3(1))*** Random Hse. Australia AUS. Dist: Independent Pubs. Group.
Van Draanen, Wendelin. Swear to Howdy. 2005. (ENG.). 144p. (J). (gr. 3-7). reprint ed. 6.99 *(978-0-440-41943-3(3)*, Yearling) Random Hse. Children's Bks.
Varsell, Linda. A Journey for Rainbows. Curtis, E., illus. 2003. 166p. (YA). per. 6.00 *(978-0-9725479-1-8(6))* Rainbow Communications.
Veremiah, Omari. Paper Boy Two: Over Whelming 0005. Rolling, Beanic, illus. 2004. 74p. (YA). (gr. 7-12). pap. 12.99 *(978-1-929188-10-9(2))* Morton Bks.
Verrett, Michael. It Followed Me Home Can I Keep It? 2010. 35p. pap. 10.00 *(978-0-557-28827-4(4))* Lulu Pr., Inc.
—It Followed Me Home Can I Keep It? (full Color) 2010. 35p. pap. 19.00 *(978-0-557-29796-2(6))* Lulu Pr., Inc.
Viorst, Judith. Just in Case. Bluthenthal, Diana Cain, illus. 2006. (ENG.). 40p. (J). (gr. -1-2). 15.95 *(978-0-689-87164-1(3)*, Atheneum Bks. for Young Readers) Simon & Schuster Children's Publishing.
Vosailagi, Jo, illus. Pentapus. 2006. 120p. per. 12.56 *(978-1-4120-9272-2(8))* Trafford Publishing.
Waines, Frances Drummond. Humpi, the Orphan Camel, 1 vol. 2010. 104p. pap. 19.95 *(978-1-4489-3963-3(1))* America Star Bks.
Wakeman, Daniel. Ben's Big Dig, 1 vol. Van Stralen, Dirk, illus. 2005. (ENG.). 32p. (J). (gr. -1-3). 17.95 *(978-1-55143-384-4(2))* Orca Bk. Pubs. USA.
Waldman, Neil. Al & Teddy. 2013. 48p. 17.95 *(978-0-615-72969-5(X))* Dream Yard Pr.
Walker, Cheryl. The Little Black & White Pony. 2003. 28p. (J). pap. 2.50 *(978-0-9726326-1-4(1))* TechArts International LLC.
Wallace, Ian. Boy of the Deeps, 1 vol. 2005. (ENG., Illus.). 32p. (J). pap. 8.95 *(978-0-88899-660-2(8))* Groundwood Bks. CAN. Dist: Publishers Group West (PGW).
Wallen, Virginia. Sonny & Sammy. 2006. 17.00 *(978-0-8059-9809-2(8))* Dorrance Publishing Co., Inc.
Walter, Chris. Tell Your Dreams to Me. 2008. 32p. pap. 14.95 *(978-1-4389-0162-6(3))* AuthorHouse.
Ward, Stephen J. The GREATEST Togger Story Ever Told - Part 1: Thrifty's Stand. 2010. 66p. pap. 14.95 *(978-1-4461-3060-5(6))* Lulu Pr., Inc.
Warner, Charles Dudley. Being A Boy. 2005. 26.95 *(978-1-4218-0314-2(3))*; 124p. pap. 10.95 *(978-1-4218-0414-9(X))* 1st World Publishing, Inc. (1st World Library - Literary Society).
—Being A Boy. 2004. reprint ed. pap. 1.99 *(978-1-4192-0953-6(1))*; pap. 15.95 *(978-1-4191-0953-9(7))* Kessinger Publishing, LLC.
Warren, Cynthia Marie. The Crazy Untamable, Tamable Tongue: Love with Your Words. 2012. 48p. pap. 20.45 *(978-1-4497-4322-2(6)*, WestBow Pr.) Author Solutions, Inc.
Waterman, Diana. In a While, Kyle. 2012. 24p. pap. 24.95 *(978-1-4626-6672-0(8))* PublishAmerica, Inc.
Waters, Michael. Tommy & his Flying Saucer of Milk. 2009. 32p. 18.95 *(978-1-4092-8450-5(6))* Lulu Pr., Inc.
Watkins, Constance L. Happy Was His Name. 2011. 24p. (gr. 1-2). pap. 11.75 *(978-1-4634-0421-5(2))* AuthorHouse.
Watt, Fiona. That's Not My Baby (Boy) 2010. (Touchy Feely Board Book Ser.). 43p. (J). bds. 8.99 *(978-0-7945-2604-7(7)*, Usborne) EDC Publishing.
Webb-King, Marian. Sweet Dreams Bear Cub: My Life As a Cricket. 2011. 20p. 11.49 *(978-1-4520-0979-7(1))* AuthorHouse.
Weeks, Sarah. Michael. Date not set. 32p. (J). (gr. -1-2). 14.99 *(978-0-06-028231-8(2))*; pap. 4.99 *(978-0-06-443541-3(5))* HarperCollins Pubs.
Wells, R. W. Black Mountain Express: A Smoky Mountain Bedtime Tale. 2007. 53p. pap. 16.95 *(978-1-60441-396-0(4))* America Star Bks.
Welsh, Karen Leis. Frolicking Friends. 2012. (Illus.). 44p. pap. 21.99 *(978-1-4685-6422-8(6))* AuthorHouse.
West, Tracey, adapted by. Robotic Fish Gone Wild! 2005. (Illus.). 30p. (J). pap. *(978-0-439-76833-7(0))* Scholastic, Inc.
Westley, William. Charlie & Crow. 2011. 66p. 24.99 *(978-1-4628-6802-5(9))*; pap. 15.99 *(978-1-4628-6801-8(0))* Xlibris Corp.
Weston Woods Staff, creator. The North Star. 2011. 29.95 *(978-0-545-23796-3(3))* Weston Woods Studios, Inc.
—The Story about Ping. 2011. 29.95 *(978-0-439-73519-3(X))*; 38.75 *(978-0-439-72894-2(0))*; 18.95 *(978-0-439-72893-5(2))* Weston Woods Studios, Inc.
—Too Many Toys! 2011. 29.95 *(978-0-545-37421-7(9))* Weston Woods Studios, Inc.
Westra, Elizabeth. Alexander & the Stallion. Ampel, Kenneth Robert, illus. 2003. (Books for Young Learners). 16p. (J). per. 5.75 net. *(978-1-57274-534-6(7)*, 2721, Bks. for Young Learners) Owen, Richard C. Pubs., Inc.
Wheeler, Jordan. Just a Walk. 2009. (ENG., Illus.). 32p. (J). (gr. -1-k). pap. 8.95 *(978-1-894778-82-4(0))* Theytus Bks., Ltd. CAN. Dist: Univ. of Toronto Pr.
Whipple, Wayne. Radio Boys Cronies. 2004. reprint ed. pap. 1.99 *(978-1-4192-4378-3(0))*; pap. 15.95 *(978-1-4191-4378-6(6))* Kessinger Publishing, LLC.
Whitaker, Kenneth. Hood-Hearted Child, Life as a Nobody: Based on a True Story, 1 vol. 2009. 48p. pap. 16.95 *(978-1-61546-369-5(0))* America Star Bks.
Whitby, Rozene. Luke & Nana, 1 vol. Fowler, Elizabeth, illus. 2010. 16p. pap. 24.95 *(978-1-4489-3826-1(0))* PublishAmerica, Inc.
White, Michelle A. Anthony with an A. 2011. 16p. pap. 9.50 *(978-1-4634-1641-6(5))* AuthorHouse.
White, Ramy Allison. Sunny Boy & His Playmates. 2007. 104p. pap. 18.99 *(978-1-4346-1569-5(3))*; (ENG.). 112p. pap. 19.99 *(978-1-4346-1782-8(3))* Creative Media Partners, LLC.
—Sunny Boy in the Far West. Hastings, Howard L., illus. 2011. 216p. 44.95 *(978-1-258-09942-8(X))* Literary Licensing, LLC.
Whited, Wayne & Burns, Robert David. The Adventures of Orie Alexander - the Story Thief (Paperback Edition) 2010. 70p. pap. 7.95 *(978-0-557-63433-0(4))* Lulu Pr., Inc.
Whybrow, Ian. Boy Racer. 2017. (ENG., Illus.). 64p. (J). (gr. 1-6). pap. 7.99 ***(978-1-4449-3576-9(3))*** Hachette Children's Group GBR. Dist: Hachette Bk. Group.
Whyte, Elana. My Gift: A Book about a Child Who Sees Spirit. 2013. 32p. pap. 13.95 *(978-1-4525-8724-0(8)*, Balboa Pr.) Author Solutions, Inc.
Wiechman, Kathy Cannon. Like a River. 2015. (ENG.). 336p. (J). (gr. 3). 17.95 *(978-1-62979-209-5(8)*, Calkins Creek) Boyds Mills Pr.
Wilkins, Lisa. The Key Seekers. 2005. 68p. pap. 16.95 *(978-1-4137-8681-1(2))* PublishAmerica, Inc.
Willard, Nancy. The Three Mouths of Little Tom Drum. Hawkes, Kevin, illus. 2015. (ENG.). 48p. (J). (gr. -1-3). 16.99 *(978-0-7636-5476-4(0))* Candlewick Pr.
Willems, Ashley. The Boy & the Wind. 2013. 52p. pap. 20.99 *(978-1-4525-8369-3(2)*, Balboa Pr.) Author Solutions, Inc.
William Bradford Pilgrim Boy. 2004. pap. 8.95 *(978-0-01-210122-3(2))* Beautiful Feet Bks.
Williams, C. G., illus. The Incredibly Helpful Helper. 2008. (ENG.). 40p. (J). (gr. -1-k). 14.95 *(978-0-7892-1001-2(0)*, Abbeville Kids) Abbeville Pr., Inc.
Williams, Darnell Denzel. One in a Million. 2013. 32p. pap. 17.25 *(978-1-4669-7913-0(5))* Trafford Publishing.
Williams, Garth. Benjamin's Treasure. Date not set. 32p. (J). (gr. -1-2). pap. 5.99 *(978-0-06-443636-6(5))* HarperCollins Pubs.
Williams, John Joseph. Vak's War. 2013. 102p. (J). pap. *(978-1-78299-323-0(1))* FeedARead.com.
Williams, Joyce Hall & West, Nancy H. Ruffitt versus Do-Well: Let's Play Ball at the Taj Mahal. 2004. 112p. (YA). pap. 11.95 *(978-0-7414-2095-4(3))* Infinity Publishing.
Williams, Justine. Nobody Likes Me: What Am I Doing Wrong? Martinez, Michael, illus. 2013. 20p. pap. 10.95 *(978-1-62212-778-8(1)*, Strategic Bk. Publishing) Strategic Book Publishing & Rights Agency (SBPRA).
Williams, Teri. I Got Bank! What My Granddad Taught Me about Money. 2010. (ENG., Illus.). 88p. (J). pap. 14.95 *(978-0-9827943-7-1(1))* Beckham Pubns. Group, Inc.
Williams, Tova. The Boy Who Did Not Want to Read, 1 vol. Suggs, Aisha, illus. 2010. 36p. pap. 24.95 *(978-1-4489-5705-7(2))* PublishAmerica, Inc.
Willis, Jeanne. El Nino Que Perdio el Ombligo. Ross, Tony, illus. (SPA.). (J). 8.95 *(978-958-04-5632-2(1))* Norma S.A. COL. Dist: Distribuidora Norma, Inc., Lectorum Pubns., Inc.
Wilson, Kevin. Brown Spot. 2006. 60p. (J). pap. 12.00 *(978-1-4116-8059-3(6))* Lulu Pr., Inc.
Wilson, W. Shane. Little Monsters. 2009. 99p. pap. 11.96 *(978-0-557-20687-2(1))* Lulu Pr., Inc.
Winfield, Arthur M. The Rover Boys at School. 2004. reprint ed. pap. 1.99 *(978-1-4192-8115-0(1))* Kessinger Publishing, LLC.
Wiseman, David. Jeremy Visick. 2003. (ENG.). 176p. (J). (gr. 5-7). pap. 11.95 *(978-0-618-34514-4(0))* Houghton Mifflin Harcourt Publishing Co.
Wolf, Sallie. Peter's Trucks. 2013. 26p. 26.95 *(978-1-62352-033-5(9))* IntoPrint Publishing LLC.
Wolfe, Jack & Wolfe, Jennifer. The Tales of Spy Dogs Archie & Hazel. 2011. 44p. pap. 16.59 *(978-1-4567-6244-5(3))* AuthorHouse.
Wonderley, Stanley. A Boy & His Horse. 2012. 19.95 *(978-0-7414-7806-1(4))*; pap. 11.95 *(978-0-7414-7805-4(6))* Infinity Publishing.
Wood, Cary D. Davis & Pop Go Hiking. Turner, Cecilia, illus. 2014. (ENG.). 32p. (J). (gr. -1-4). pap. 14.95 *(978-1-63047-068-5(6))* Morgan James Publishing.
Wood, Deanna Plummer. Whenever Monkeys Move Next Door, 1 volume. 2005. (Illus.). 24p. (J). pap. 8.50 *(978-0-9762935-1-4(X))* Perkins Crawford.
Wood, Fiona. Six Impossible Things. 2016. (ENG.). 304p. (YA). (gr. 7-17). pap. 9.99 *(978-0-316-29941-1(3)*, Poppy) Little, Brown Bks. for Young Readers.
Woodson, Jacqueline. Peace, Locomotion. 2010. (ENG.). 176p. (J). (gr. 5-18). 8.99 *(978-0-14-241512-2(X)*, Puffin Books) Penguin Young Readers Group.
Wright, K. Paige. Steven & Huggey: The story of a boy & his Blankey. 2004. (J). per. 5.95 *(978-1-59196-705-7(8))* Instant Pub.
Written By Dana Wright; Illustrated By S. Crazy Pants. 2011. 20p. pap. 24.95 *(978-1-4626-3469-9(9))* America Star Bks.
Wyman, Dorothy. Kaysell the Dragon Pup. 2011. 28p. pap. 13.54 *(978-1-4269-4802-2(6))* Trafford Publishing.
Wyn, Dafydd. Hunting the Man in the Moon. 2015. (ENG.). 192p. (J). pap. 13.00 *(978-1-84771-833-4(7))* Y Lolfa GBR. Dist: Dufour Editions, Inc.
Yaccarino, Dan. Zorgoochi Intergalactic Pizza: Delivery of Doom. Yaccarino, Dan, illus. 2014. (ENG., Illus.). 336p. (J). (gr. 3-7). 16.99 *(978-1-250-00844-2(1)*, 9781250008442) Feiwel & Friends.
Yeva, Laura. Joshua Cleans Up! Likhovidova, Yekaterina, illus. 2017. (ENG.). 36p. (J). pap. 15.95 ***(978-1-78693-648-6(8)***, ca0be078-05cf-48f2-be1a-3ae50fc62a61) Austin, Stan AUS. Dist: Bookmasters Distribution.
Young, Blaike. The Window of Opportunity. 2013. 64p. pap. 26.52 *(978-1-4907-0764-8(6))* Trafford Publishing.
Zahn, Ellsworth E. Dudley. Zahn, Ellsworth E., illus. 2012. (ENG., Illus.). 44p. (J). (gr. -1-k). 15.95 *(978-0-9637308-1-7(9))* Marion Street Pr., LLC.
Zion, Gene. Harry, el Perrito Sucio. 2003.Tr. of Harry the Dirty Dog. (SPA.). (J). (gr. -1-2). 17.20 *(978-0-7857-2621-0(7)*, Turtleback) Turtleback Bks.

BOYS—POETRY

Attaboy. You Might Be a Monster: And Other Stories I Made Up! 2011. (ENG., Illus.). 36p. (J). (gr. 1-3). 15.95 *(978-1-59702-025-1(7))* Immedium.
Jackson, Robert Bradley. Weekend Mischief. Beech, Mark, illus. 2010. (ENG.). 32p. (J). (gr. 2-4). 17.95 *(978-1-59078-494-5(4)*, Wordsong) Boyds Mills Pr.
Keats, John & Prosek, James. Bird, Butterfly, Eel. Prosek, James, illus. 2009. (ENG., Illus.). 32p. (J). (gr. 1-5). 17.99 *(978-0-689-86829-0(4)*, Simon & Schuster Bks. For Young Readers) Simon & Schuster Bks. For Young Readers.
Raczka, Bob & Reynolds, Peter H. Guyku: A Year of Haiku for Boys. Reynolds, Peter H., illus. 2010. (ENG., Illus.). 48p. (J). (gr. -1-3). 16.99 *(978-0-547-24003-9(1))* Houghton Mifflin Harcourt Publishing Co.

BOYS' CLUBS—FICTION

Rand, Edward A. The Knights of the White Shield: Up-the-Ladder Club Series Round One Play. 2007. 166p. pap. 19.99 *(978-1-4264-8273-1(6))*; (ENG.). 184p. pap. 21.99 *(978-1-4264-8310-3(4))* Creative Media Partners, LLC.
—The Knights of the White Shield; or, up-the-Ladder Club Series, Round One Play. 2007. 120p. per. *(978-1-4068-3739-1(3))* Echo Library.
Walker, E. G. Boys' Club. Graffam, Merle, illus. 2004. (J). (gr. 2-8). pap. 12.95 *(978-0-9716071-5-6(X))* Walker, Esther.

BRADFORD, WILLIAM, 1588-1657

Benge, Janet & Benge, Geoff. William Bradford: Plymouth's Rock. 2016. (ENG., Illus.). 200p. (J). pap. 9.99 *(978-1-62486-092-8(3))* Emerald Bks.
Philbrick, Nathaniel. The Mayflower & the Pilgrims' New World. 2009. (ENG.). 368p. (J). (gr. 5-18). 8.99 *(978-0-14-241458-3(1)*, Puffin Books) Penguin Young Readers Group.
Wagner, Heather Lehr. William Bradford. 2010. (Leaders of the Colonial Era Ser.). 120p. (gr. 5-8). 35.00 *(978-1-60413-743-9(6)*, Chelsea Hse.) Facts On File, Inc.
Whitehurst, Susan. William Bradford & Plymouth: A Colony Grows. 2009. (Library of the Pilgrims Ser.). 24p. (gr. 3-4). 42.50 *(978-1-60853-916-1(4)*, PowerKids Pr.) Rosen Publishing Group, Inc., The.

BRADLEY, BILL, 1943-

Buckley, James, Jr. Bill Bradley. 2009. (Basketball Hall of Famers Ser.). 112p. (gr. 5-8). 63.90 *(978-1-61511-529-7(3)*, Rosen Reference) Rosen Publishing Group, Inc., The.

BRADSTREET, ANNE, 1612?-1672

Hoehne, Marcia. Anne Bradstreet: America's Puritan Poet. 2007. 203p. pap. *(978-1-888105-75-9(5))* Avisson Pr., Inc.

BRADY, MATHEW B., 1823-1896

Armstrong, Jennifer. Photo by Brady: A Picture of the Civil War. 2005. (ENG., Illus.). 160p. (J). (gr. 4-9). 22.99 *(978-0-689-85785-0(3)*, Atheneum Bks. for Young Readers) Simon & Schuster Children's Publishing.
Baxter, Kathleen & McConnell, Robert L., contrib. by. Civil War Witness: Mathew Brady's Photos Reveal the Horrors of War, 1 vol. 2013. (Captured History Ser.). (ENG.). 64p. (gr. 5-7). 34.65 *(978-0-7565-4693-9(1)*, CPB Grades 4-8) Compass Point Bks.
McConnell, Robert L., contrib. by. Civil War Witness: Mathew Brady's Photos Reveal the Horrors of War, 1 vol. 2013. (Captured History Ser.). (ENG.). 64p. (gr. 5-7). pap. 9.10 *(978-0-7565-4699-1(0)*, CPB Grades 4-8) Compass Point Bks.
Murray, Stuart A. P. Mathew Brady: Photographer of Our Nation. 2009. (ENG., Illus.). 83p. (gr. 6-18). lib. bdg. 158.00 *(978-0-7656-8151-5(X)*, Y182957) Routledge.
Nardo, Don. Mathew Brady: The Camera Is the Eye of History. 2008. (Americans—the Spirit of a Nation Ser.). (Illus.). 128p. (J). (gr. 5-6). lib. bdg. 33.27 *(978-0-7660-3023-7(7))* Enslow Pubs., Inc.

BRAHMS, JOHANNES, 1833-1897

Getzinger, Donna & Felsenfeld, Daniel. Johannes Brahms & the Twilight of Romanticism. 2004. (Classical Composers Ser.). (Illus.). 144p. (YA). (gr. 6-12). 26.95 *(978-1-931798-21-1(4))* Reynolds, Morgan Inc.

BRAILLE, LOUIS, 1809-1852

Bryant, Jen. Six Dots: A Story of Young Louis Braille. Kulikov, Boris, illus. 2016. (ENG.). 40p. (J). (gr. -1-3). 17.99 *(978-0-449-81337-9(1)*, Knopf Bks. for Young Readers) Random Hse. Children's Bks.
Davidson, Margaret. Louis Braille. Compere, Janet, illus. (FRE.). 80p. (J). pap. 5.99 *(978-0-590-71110-4(5))* Scholastic, Inc.
Donaldson, Madeline. Louis Braille. 2008. pap. 52.95 *(978-0-8225-9393-5(9))* Lerner Publishing Group.
—Louis Braille. Butler, Tad, illus. 2007. (History Maker Biographies Ser.). 48p. (J). lib. bdg. 26.60 *(978-0-8225-7608-2(2)*, Lerner Pubns.) Lerner Publishing Group.
Frith, Margaret. Who Was Louis Braille? Anderson, Scott & Squier, Robert, illus. 2014. (Who Was? Ser.). (ENG.). 112p. (J). (gr. 3-7). 5.99 *(978-0-448-47903-3(6)*, Grosset & Dunlap) Penguin Young Readers Group.
—Who Was Louis Braille? 2014. (Who Was... ? Ser.). (Illus.). 104p. (J). lib. bdg. 16.00 *(978-0-606-34167-7(6)*, Turtleback) Turtleback Bks.
Jeffrey, Laura S. All about Braille: Reading by Touch. 2004. (Transportation & Communication Ser.). (Illus.). 48p. (J). lib. bdg. 25.27 *(978-0-7660-2184-6(X))* Enslow Pubs., Inc.
Kent, Deborah. What Is Braille? 2012. (Overcoming Barriers Ser.). 48p. (J). (gr. 3-4). 25.27 *(978-0-7660-3770-0(3)*, Enslow Elementary) Enslow Pubs., Inc.
Mellor, C. Michael. Louis Braille: A Touch of Genius. 2006. (Illus.). 144p. (J). 35.00 *(978-0-939173-70-9(0))* National Braille Pr.
O'Connor, Barbara. The World at His Fingertips. 2003. (Creative Minds Biographies Ser.). (Illus.). 64p. (J). (gr. -1-1). pap. 6.95 *(978-1-57505-461-2(2))* Lerner Publishing Group.

BRAIN

see also Dreams; Mind and Body; Nervous System; Psychology; Sleep

Acosta, Jamey & Rice, Dona. Use Your Brain, 1 vol. 2010. (Early Childhood Themes Ser.). (ENG., Illus.). 16p. (J). (gr. -1-2). pap. 19.99 *(978-1-4333-1811-5(3))*; pap. 6.99 *(978-1-4333-1810-8(5))* Shell Educational Publishing.
Andrews, Linda Wasmer. Intelligence. 2004. (Life Balance Ser.). (ENG.). 80p. (YA). (gr. 5-8). pap. 6.95 *(978-0-531-16608-6(2)*, Watts, Franklin) Scholastic Library Publishing.
Aretha, David. Top 10 Worst Injuries in Football. 2016. (Sports Greats Ser.). 48p. (J). pap. 11.70 *(978-0-7660-8300-4(4))* Enslow Pubs., Inc.
Asselin, Kristine Carlson. What You Need to Know about Concussions. 2015. (Focus on Health Ser.). (ENG., Illus.). 32p. (gr. 3-4). pap. 7.95 *(978-1-4914-4902-8(0))* Capstone Press of Coughlan Cos.
Bailey, Diane. Brain Surgeons. (Extreme Careers Ser.). (gr. 5-5). 2009. 64p. 58.50 *(978-1-61512-387-2(3)*, Rosen Reference) 2008. (Illus.). 62p. (YA). lib. bdg. 31.95 *(978-1-4042-1787-4(8))* Rosen Publishing Group, Inc., The.
Ballard, Carol. How Your Brain Works. 2010. (Your Body at Work Ser.). (ENG.). 32p. (YA). (gr. 2-5). lib. bdg. 26.60 *(978-1-4339-4103-0(1))* Stevens, Gareth Publishing LLLP.
Beevor, Lucy. Understanding Our Head. 2017. (Brains, Body, Bones! Ser.). (ENG., Illus.). 32p. (gr. 3-5). lib. bdg. 30.65 *(978-1-4109-8580-4(6)*, Raintree Perspectives) Heinemann-Raintree.
Berger, Melvin & Berger, Gilda. Your Brain. 2005. (Illus.). pap. *(978-0-439-77370-6(9))* Scholastic, Inc.
Birmingham, Maria. Tastes Like Music: 17 Quirks of the Brain & Body. Melnychuk, Monika, illus. 2014. (ENG.). 40p. (J). (gr. 3-7). 17.95 *(978-1-77147-010-0(0)*, Owlkids) Owlkids Bks. Inc. CAN. Dist: Publishers Group West (PGW).
Brett, Flora. Your Nervous System Works! 2015. (Your Body Systems Ser.). (ENG.). 24p. (gr. 1-2). lib. bdg. 25.32 *(978-1-4914-2066-9(9))* Capstone Press of Coughlan Cos.
Brynie, Faith Hickman. 101 Questions Your Brain Has Asked about Itself but Couldn't Answer... until Now. 2007. (101 Questions... Ser.). (Illus.). 176p. (YA). (gr. 7-12). lib. bdg. 30.60 *(978-0-8225-6795-0(4))* Twenty First Century Bks.
Bulging Brains. (YA). (gr. 5-8). pap. *(978-0-439-14976-1(2))* Scholastic GBR. Dist: Lectorum Pubns., Inc.
Burstein, John. The Astounding Nervous System: How Does My Brain Work? 2009. (Slim Goodbody's Body Buddies Ser.). (ENG., Illus.). 32p. (J). (gr. 3-5). pap. *(978-0-7787-4428-3(0))*; lib. bdg. *(978-0-7787-4414-6(0))* Crabtree Publishing Co.
Carlson, Dale. The Teen Brain Book: Who & What Are You? Teasdale, Nancy, ed. Nicklaus, Carol, illus. 2004. (ENG.). 230p. (gr. 7-12). pap. 14.95 *(978-1-884158-29-2(3))* Team Kreskin Productions, LLC.
Caster, Shannon. Brain. 2010. (Body Works Ser.). (Illus.). 24p. (J). pap. 8.25 *(978-1-4358-9824-0(9)*, PowerKids Pr.); (YA). (gr. 2-5). lib. bdg. 22.60 *(978-1-4358-9368-9(9))* Rosen Publishing Group, Inc., The.
El Cerebro. 2003. (Megabites Ser.). (SPA., Illus.). (J). pap. *(978-970-690-689-2(4))* Planeta Mexicana Editorial S. A. de C. V.
Chowdhury, Uttom & Robertson, Mary. Why Do You Do That? A Book about Tourette Syndrome for Children & Young People. Whallett, Liz, illus. 2006. (ENG.). 96p. (J). (gr. 3-11). per. 15.95 *(978-1-84310-395-0(8)*, 1915) Kingsley, Jessica Pubs. GBR. Dist: Macmillan Distribution Ltd.
Chudler, Eric H. Inside Your Brain. 2007. (Brain Works). (Illus.). 124p. (YA). (gr. 5-9). lib. bdg. 32.95 *(978-0-7910-8944-6(4))* Facts On File, Inc.
Chudler, Eric H., ed. Brain Works, 5 vols., Set. 2007. (Brain Works). (gr. 5-8). 164.75 *(978-0-7910-9461-7(8)*, Chelsea Hse.) Facts On File, Inc.
—Gray Matter, 19 vols., Set. 2007. (Gray Matter Ser.). (C). (gr. 9). 665.00 *(978-0-7910-9659-8(9)*, Chelsea Hse.) Facts On File, Inc.
Claybourne, Anna. Mental Development: From Birth to Old Age, 1 vol. 2013. (Your Body for Life Ser.). (ENG., Illus.). 64p. (gr. 7-8). pap. 10.95 *(978-1-4329-7092-5(5))*; lib. bdg. 35.99 *(978-1-4329-7085-7(2))* Heinemann-Raintree.
Cleveland, Don. How Do We Know How the Brain Works. 2005. (Great Scientific Questions & the Scientists Who Answered Them Ser.). (Illus.). 112p. (J). (gr. 7-12). lib. bdg. 34.60 *(978-1-4042-0078-4(9))* Rosen Publishing Group, Inc., The.
Cleveland, Donald. How Do We Know How the Brain Works. 2009. (Great Scientific Questions & the Scientists Who Answered Them Ser.). 112p. (gr. 7-12). 63.90 *(978-1-61513-195-2(7))* Rosen Publishing Group, Inc., The.
Como Funciona el Cerebro. 2003. (Essential Science Ser.). (SPA., Illus.). (J). pap. *(978-970-690-601-4(0))* Planeta Mexicana Editorial S. A. de C. V.
Cook-Cottone, Catherine. The brain owner's manual for Kids: Helping the feeling & thinking parts work Together. 2006. (Illus.). (J). pap. 5.00 *(978-0-9795773-0-7(6))* Growing & Learning Pr.
Cook, Louis J. & Freedman, Jeri. Brain Tumors. 2011. (Understanding Brain Diseases & Disorders Ser.). (ENG.). 64p. (YA). (gr. 7-12). lib. bdg. 31.95 *(978-1-4488-5544-5(6))* Rosen Publishing Group, Inc., The.
Curry, Don L. How Does Your Brain Work? 2004. (Rookie Read-About Health Ser.). (ENG.). 32p. (J). (gr. k-2). pap. 5.95 *(978-0-516-27853-7(3)*, Children's Pr.) Scholastic Library Publishing.

Deak, JoAnn. Your Fantastic, Elastic Brain: Stretch It, Shape It. O'Malley, Judy, ed. Ackerley, Sarah, illus. 2010. (ENG.). 32p. (J). (gr. -1-3). 18.95 (978-0-9829938-0-4(3)) March 4th, Inc.

Deak, JoAnn & Deak, Terrence. The Owner's Manual for Driving Your Adolescent Brain. Harrison, Freya, illus. 2013. (ENG.). 72p. (J). (gr. 3-9). pap. 15.95 (978-1-939775-02-3(7), 9781939775023) March 4th, Inc.

DeSalle, Rob. Brain: A 21st Century Look at a 400 Million Year Old Organ. Wynne, Patricia, illus. 2010. (Wallace & Darwin Ser.: 2). (ENG.). 40p. (gr. 3-7). 18.95 (978-1-59373-085-7(3)) Bunker Hill Publishing, Inc.

Dittmer, Lori. Parkinson's Disease. 2011. (Living with Disease Ser.). (Illus.). 48p. (J). (gr. 5-8). lib. bdg. 34.25 (978-1-60818-076-9(X), Creative Education) Creative Co., The.

Dorling Kindersley Publishing Staff. How to Be a Genius. 2013. (ENG.). 192p. (J). (gr. 5-12). pap. 12.99 (978-1-4654-1424-3(X), DK Children) Dorling Kindersley Publishing, Inc.

Drimmer, Stephanie Warren & Cohen, Julie K. Mastermind: Over 100 Games, Tests, & Puzzles to Unleash Your Inner Genius. 2016. (ENG., Illus.). 176p. (J). (gr. 3-7). pap. 12.99 (978-1-4263-2110-8(4), National Geographic Children's Bks.) National Geographic Society.

Einspruch, Andrew. Brain Works, 1 vol., 1. 2014. (Discovery Education: How It Works). (ENG.). 32p. (gr. 3-6). 26.25 (978-1-4777-6305-6(8), PowerKids Pr.) Rosen Publishing Group, Inc., The.

Esherick, Joan. Brain Injury. Albers, Lisa et al, eds. 2014. (Living with a Special Need Ser.: 16). 128p. (J). (gr. 7-18). 25.95 (978-1-4222-3031-2(7)) Mason Crest.

—The Journey Toward Recovery: Youth with Brain Injury. 2004. (Youth with Special Needs Ser.). (Illus.). 128p. (YA). 24.95 (978-1-59084-734-3(2)) Mason Crest.

Farndon, John. Stickmen's Guide to Your Brilliant Brain. Dean, Venitia, illus. 2017. (Stickmen's Guides to Your Awesome Body Ser.). (ENG.). 32p. (J). (gr. 3-6). 26.65 **(978-1-5124-3213-8(X))** Lerner Publishing Group.

Fitzpatrick, Anne. The Brain. 2003. (Illus.). 24p. (J). lib. bdg. 21.35 (978-1-58340-310-5(8)) Black Rabbit Bks.

Freedman, Jeri. Brain Cancer: Current & Emerging Trends in Detection & Treatment. 2009. (Cancer & Modern Science Ser.). lib. bdg. 31.95 (978-1-4358-5011-8(4)) Rosen Publishing Group, Inc., The.

Frith, Alex & King, Colin. See Inside Your Head. 2008. (Usborne Lift the Flap Bks.). 15p. (J). (gr. 4-7). bds. 12.99 (978-0-7945-1948-3(2), Usborne) EDC Publishing.

Furgang, Kathy. My Brain. 2009. (My Body Ser.). 24p. (gr. 3-3). 42.50 (978-1-61514-686-4(5), PowerKids Pr.) Rosen Publishing Group, Inc., The.

Gillard, Arthur. Stroke. 2012. (Perspectives on Diseases & Disorders Ser.). (ENG., Illus.). 144p. (gr. 10-12). lib. bdg. 44.30 (978-0-7377-6359-1(0), Greenhaven Pr., Inc.) Cengage Gale.

Gillard, Arthur, ed. Traumatic Brain Injury. 2012. (Perspectives on Diseases & Disorders Ser.). (ENG., Illus.). 144p. (gr. 10-12). lib. bdg. 38.95 (978-0-7377-6349-2(3), Greenhaven Pr., Inc.) Cengage Gale.

Goldsmith, Connie. Traumatic Brain Injury: From Concussion to Coma. 2014. (Illus.). 88p. (gr. 6-12). lib. bdg. 34.60 (978-1-4677-1348-1(1), Twenty-First Century Bks.) Lerner Publishing Group.

Green, Dan. The Adventures of Your Brain. Sims, Sean, illus. 2017. (ENG.). 14p. (J). (gr. k). 14.95 **(978-1-4549-2512-5(4))** Sterling Publishing Co., Inc.

Guillain, Charlotte. Nuestros Cerebros, 1 vol. 2010. (Nuestros Cuerpos Ser.). (SPA.). 24p. (gr. -1-1). 22.65 (978-1-4329-4297-7(2)); pap. 6.29 (978-1-4329-4306-6(5)) Heinemann-Raintree. (Bellota).

—Our Brains, 1 vol. 2010. (Our Bodies Ser.). (ENG.). 24p. (gr. -1-1). 22.65 (978-1-4329-3592-4(5)); pap. 6.29 (978-1-4329-3601-3(8)) Heinemann-Raintree. (Acorn).

Halvorson, Karin. Inside the Brain, 1 vol. 2013. (Super Simple Your Body Ser.). (ENG.). 32p. (J). (gr. k-4). 27.07 (978-1-61783-609-1(5)) ABDO Publishing Co.

Heos, Bridget. The Brain in Your Body, 1 vol. 2015. (ENG., Illus.). 32p. (J). 23.45 (978-1-62275-636-0(3), Britannica Educational Publishing) Rosen Publishing Group, Inc., The.

Hewitt, Sally. My Brain. 2012. (My Body Ser.). (ENG., Illus.). 24p. (gr. k-4). pap. 7.95 (978-1-926853-96-3(2)) Saunders Bk. Co. CAN. Dist: RiverStream Publishing.

Human Brain Power, 6 vols. (Book2WebTM Ser.). (gr. 4-8). 36.50 (978-0-322-02975-0(9)) Wright Group/McGraw-Hill.

Jerome, Kate Boehm & National Geographic Learning Staff. Understanding the Brain. 2007. (Nonfiction Reading & Writing Workshops Ser.). (ENG., Illus.). 32p. (J). pap. 17.95 (978-0-7922-8859-6(9)) CENGAGE Learning.

Jordan, Apple & Rau, Dana Meachen. My Brain. 2nd ed. 2013. 24p. (gr. 1-3). 21.36 (978-1-60870-432-3(7)) Cavendish Square Publishing.

Kamberg, Mary-Lane. Sports Concussions. 2011. (Headlines! Ser.). (ENG.). 64p. (YA). lib. bdg. 31.95 (978-1-4488-1289-9(5)) Rosen Publishing Group, Inc., The.

Kirk, Bill. A Brainy Refrain: The Sum of Our Parts Book 4. Ruble, Eugene, illus. 2012. 24p. pap. 10.95 (978-1-61633-231-0(X)) Guardian Angel Publishing, Inc.

Klepeis, Alicia Z. Brain Eaters: Creatures with Zombelike Diets. 2016. (Real-Life Zombies Ser.). (ENG., Illus.). 32p. (gr. 3-4). lib. bdg. 27.99 (978-1-5157-2479-7(4), Edge Bks.) Capstone Press of Coughlan Cos.

Korb, Rena B. & Weinhaus, Anthony J. My Brain, 1 vol. Simard, Remy, illus. 2010. (My Body Ser.). (ENG.). 32p. (J). (gr. k-3). 28.50 (978-1-60270-805-1(3)) Magic Wagon.

Kulman, Randy. Train Your Brain for Success: A Teenager's Guide to Executive Functions. 2012. (ENG., Illus.). 100p. (J). (gr. 7). pap. 17.95 (978-1-886941-76-2(9)) Specialty Pr., Inc.

Kuskowski, Alex. Cool Thinking: Healthy & Fun Ways to Train Your Brain, 1 vol. 2012. (Cool Health & Fitness Ser.). (ENG.). 32p. (J). (gr. 3-6). lib. bdg. 27.07 (978-1-61783-430-1(0), Checkerboard Library) ABDO Publishing Co.

La Pierre, Yvette. Neandertals: A Prehistoric Puzzle. 2008. (Discovery! Ser.). (ENG., Illus.). 112p. (gr. 6-12). lib. bdg. 31.93 (978-0-8225-7524-5(8)) Lerner Publishing Group.

Leardi, Jeannette. The Brain. 2011. (Readers' & Writers' Genre Workshop Ser.). (J). pap. (978-1-4509-3032-1(8)) Benchmark Education Co.

Lennard, Kate. Brains. Gulliksen, Eivind, illus. 2007. (Young Genius Bks.). (ENG.). 32p. (J). (gr. k-3). pap. 6.99 (978-0-7641-3670-2(4)) Barron's Educational Series, Inc.

Libra, Anna. Why Does My Head Hurt? An Inside Look at the Nervous System. 2003. (J). pap. (978-1-58417-065-5(4)); lib. bdg. (978-1-58417-002-0(6)) Lake Street Pubs.

Marcovitz, Hal & Jimerson, Maxine Newman. Brain Trauma. 2009. (Diseases & Disorders Ser.). (ENG., Illus.). 128p. (gr. 7-10). lib. bdg. 39.90 (978-1-4205-0112-4(7), LML02109-245423, Lucent Bks.) Cengage Gale.

Margulies, Philip. Creutzfeldt-Jakob Disease. 2004. (Epidemics Ser.). (Illus.). 64p. (YA). (gr. 7-12). lib. bdg. 31.95 (978-0-8239-4199-5(X)) Rosen Publishing Group, Inc., The.

Margulies, Phillip. Creutzfeldt-Jakob Disease. 2009. (Epidemics Ser.). 64p. (gr. 5-5). 58.50 (978-1-61512-278-3(8)) Rosen Publishing Group, Inc., The.

Markle, Sandra. Battered Brains. 2010. (Powerful Medicine Ser.). (ENG.). 48p. (gr. 5-8). lib. bdg. 27.93 (978-0-8225-8704-0(1)) Lerner Publishing Group.

Mason, Paul. Your Mind-Bending Brain & Networking Nervous System. 2015. (Your Brilliant Body! Ser.). (ENG., Illus.). 32p. (J). (978-0-7787-2199-4(X)) Crabtree Publishing Co.

McClafferty, Carla Killough. Fourth down & Inches: Concussions & Football's Make-or-Break Moment. 2013. (ENG., Illus.). 96p. (gr. 6-12). 20.95 (978-1-4677-1067-1(9), Carolrhoda Bks.) Lerner Publishing Group.

Meachen Rau, Dana. El Cerebro: Que Hay Dentro de Mi? 2006. (Bookworms Ser.). (SPA & ENG., Illus.). 32p. (gr. 1-2). lib. bdg. 15.95 (978-0-7614-2402-4(4)) Marshall Cavendish Corp.

—My Brain/el Cerebro. 2006. (Bookworms Ser.). (SPA & ENG., Illus.). 32p. (gr. 1-2). lib. bdg. 15.95 (978-0-7614-2480-2(6)) Marshall Cavendish Corp.

Meister, Cari. Totally Wacky Facts about the Human Mind. 2016. (Mind Benders Ser.). (ENG., Illus.). 112p. (gr. 1-3). lib. bdg. 23.32 (978-1-4914-8361-9(X)) Capstone Press of Coughlan Cos.

—Totally Wacky Facts about YOU! 2016. (Mind Benders Ser.). (ENG., Illus.). 240p. (gr. 1-3). pap. 7.95 (978-1-4914-8376-3(8)) Capstone Press of Coughlan Cos.

Mooney, Carla. The Brain: Journey Through the Universe Inside Your Head. Casteel, Tom, illus. 2015. (Inquire & Investigate Ser.). (ENG.). 128p. (gr. 6-10). 22.95 (978-1-61930-274-7(8), 1394243) Open City Bks.

Morgan, Nicola. Blame My Brain. 2007. (Illus.). 192p. (YA). pap. (978-1-4063-1116-7(2)) Walker Bks., Ltd.

Nagelhout, Ryan. What If I Get a Concussion? 2016. (Benched: Dealing with Sports Injuries Ser.). 24p. (J). (gr. 3-2). 22.60 (978-1-4824-4888-7(2)) Stevens, Gareth Publishing LLLP.

Nettleton, Pamela Hill. Think, Think, Think: Learning about Your Brain. Shipe, Becky, illus. 2004. (Amazing Body Ser.). (ENG.). 24p. (gr. k-3). per. 8.95 (978-1-4048-0503-3(6)) Picture Window Bks.

O'Brien, Cynthia. Amazing Brain Mysteries. 2015. (ENG., Illus.). 32p. (J). (978-0-7787-8070-0(8)) Crabtree Publishing Co.

Ollhoff, Jim. The Brain. 2012. (J). (978-1-61783-252-9(9)) ABDO Publishing Co.

Owens, Jim. The Survivorship Net: A Parable for the Family, Friends, & Caregivers of People with Cancer. Cass, Bill, illus. 2010. (ENG.). 48p. (gr. 2). 14.95 (978-1-60443-018-9(4)) American Cancer Society, Inc.

Peterson, Judy Monroe. I Have a Concussion, Now What? 2016. (Teen Life 411 Ser.). 00112p. (J). (gr. 7-7). 37.10 (978-1-5081-7196-6(3)) Rosen Publishing Group, Inc., The.

Phillips, Sherre Florence. The Teen Brain. 2007. (Gray Matter Ser.). (Illus.). 130p. (YA). (gr. 9-12). lib. bdg. 35.00 (978-0-7910-9415-0(4)) Facts On File, Inc.

Pimentel, Annette Bay. My Brain. Alberini, Teresa, illus. 2015. (Inside My Body Ser.). (ENG.). 24p. (J). (gr. 1-3). 19.95 (978-1-60753-754-0(0)) Amicus Publishing.

Potts, Francesca. Left Brain, Right Brain: Facts, Trivia, & Quizzes. 2017. (Mind Games Ser.). (ENG., Illus.). (J). (gr. 2-5). lib. bdg. 27.99 **(978-1-5124-3414-9(0))** Lerner Publishing Group.

Quinones-Hinojosa, Alfredo. Video Atlas of Neurosurgery: Contemporary Tumor & Skull Base Surgery. 2016. (ENG., Illus.). 316p. 299.99 (978-0-323-26149-4(3), Elsevier) Elsevier - Health Sciences Div.

Randolph, Joanne, ed. Understanding the Brain. 2017. (Amazing Human Body Ser.). 48p. (J). (gr. 6-6). pap. 11.70 **(978-0-7660-9001-9(9))** Enslow Pubs., Inc.

Rau, Dana Meachen. Freaking Out! The Science of the Teenage Brain, 1 vol. 2011. (Everyday Science Ser.). (ENG.). 64p. (gr. 5-7). pap. 9.10 (978-0-7565-4500-0(5), CPB Grades 4-8) Compass Point Bks.

—My Brain. 2013. (Bookworms Fluent — My Body Ser.). 24p. (gr. 1-3). pap. 8.22 (978-1-62712-033-3(5)) Cavendish Square Publishing.

Ripley Entertainment Staff, contrib. by. Body & Mind. 2010. (Ripley's Believe It or Not Ser.). 36p. (YA). (gr. 3-18). lib. bdg. 19.95 (978-1-4222-1532-6(6)) Mason Crest.

Rissman, Rebecca. Smart Girl: Yoga for Brain Power. 2015. (Yoga for You Ser.). (ENG.). 64p. (gr. 4-5). lib. bdg. 34.65 (978-1-4914-2119-2(3)) Capstone Press of Coughlan Cos.

Rodriguez, Ana Maria. A Day in the Life of the Brain. 2006. (Brain Works). (Illus.). 112p. (YA). (gr. 5-9). 32.95 (978-0-7910-8947-7(9)) Facts On File, Inc.

Romanek, Trudee. Aha! The Most Interesting Book You'll Ever Read about Intelligence. Cowles, Rose, tr. Cowles, Rose, illus. 2004. (Mysterious You Ser.). (ENG.). 40p. (J). (gr. 4-9). 7.95 (978-1-55337-569-2(6)) Kids Can Pr., Ltd. CAN. Dist: Hachette Bk. Group.

Rosen, Marvin. The Brain & Love. 2007. (Brain Works). (Illus.). 104p. (YA). (gr. 5-9). lib. bdg. 32.95 (978-0-7910-8950-7(9)) Facts On File, Inc.

Ross, Veronica. Brain. 2004. (Body Ser.). (Illus.). 32p. (J). (gr. -1-3). lib. bdg. (978-1-59389-163-3(6)) Chrysalis Education.

Shackleton, Caroline. Get Smart: Our Amazing Brain Intermediate Book with Online Access. 2014. (ENG., Illus.). 28p. (J). pap. 9.50 (978-1-107-65063-3(1)) Cambridge Univ. Pr.

Simon, Seymour. The Brain: Our Nervous System. 2006. (ENG., Illus.). 32p. (J). (gr. k-4). pap. 6.99 (978-0-06-087719-4(7), Collins) HarperCollins Pubs.

—The Brain: Our Nervous System. 2006. (Illus.). 30p. (gr. k-4). 17.00 (978-0-7569-6740-6(6)) Perfection Learning Corp.

El Sistema Nervioso, Nuestro Proceso de Datos. (Coleccion Mundo Invisible).Tr. of Nervous System & the Brain. (SPA.). (YA). (gr. 5-8). pap. 8.00 (978-958-04-3226-5(0)) Norma S.A. COL. Dist: Distribuidora Norma, Inc.

Snedden, Robert. Understanding the Brain & the Nervous System. 2010. (Understanding the Human Body Ser.). (Illus.). 48p. (YA). pap. 11.75 (978-1-4358-9691-8(2)); (gr. 5-8). lib. bdg. 29.25 (978-1-4358-9685-7(8)) Rosen Publishing Group, Inc., The. (Rosen Reference).

Spalding, Maddie. 12 Tips to Maintain Brain Health. 2017. (Healthy Living Ser.). (ENG., Illus.). 32p. (J). (gr. 3-6). 21.95 (978-1-63235-368-9(7)) Pr. Room Editions LLC.

Spalding, Maddie & Ventura, Marne. 12 Tips to Maintain Brain Health. 2016. (Healthy Living Ser.). (ENG., Illus.). 32p. (J). pap. 9.95 (978-1-63235-386-3(5)) Pr. Room Editions LLC.

Spilsbury, Louise. The Science of the Brain. 2017. (Flowchart Smart Ser.). 48p. (gr. 4-5). pap. 84.30 **(978-1-5382-0681-2(1))** Stevens, Gareth Publishing LLLP.

Stevens, Noel. In the Never-Never-Converse with an Archangel. 2008. 132p. pap. 13.95 (978-0-595-52727-4(2)) iUniverse, Inc.

Stewart, Sheila. What's Wrong with My Brain? Kids with Brain Injury. 2009. (Kids with Special Needs Ser.). 48p. (YA). (gr. 5-18). pap. 7.95 (978-1-4222-1928-7(3)) Mason Crest.

Stewart, Sheila & Flath, Camden. What's Wrong with My Brain? Kids with Brain Injury. 2010. (Kids with Special Needs Ser.). 48p. (YA). (gr. 5-18). lib. bdg. 19.95 (978-1-4222-1725-2(6)) Mason Crest.

Stimola, Aubrey. Brain Injuries. 2011. (Understanding Brain Diseases & Disorders Ser.). (ENG.). 64p. (YA). (gr. 7-12). lib. bdg. 31.95 (978-1-4488-5543-8(8)) Rosen Publishing Group, Inc., The.

Stoltman, Joan. Gareth's Guide to Becoming a Brain Surgeon. 2017. (Gareth Guides to an Extraordinary Life Ser.). 32p. (J). (gr. 4-5). pap. 63.00 **(978-1-5382-0334-7(0))** Stevens, Gareth Publishing LLLP.

Swanson, Jennifer & National Geographic Kids Staff. Brain Games: The Mind-Blowing Science of Your Amazing Brain. 2015. (ENG., Illus.). 112p. (J). (gr. 3-7). pap. 12.99 (978-1-4263-2070-5(1), National Geographic Children's Bks.) National Geographic Society.

Szpirglas, Jeff. Heads up! Concussion Awareness. 2017. 48p. (J). **(978-0-7787-3508-3(7))** Crabtree Publishing Co.

—Your Brain: Understanding Your Body's Control Center. 2017. 48p. (J). **(978-0-7787-3509-0(5))** Crabtree Publishing Co.

—Your Changing Brain: A Guidebook. 2017. 48p. (J). **(978-0-7787-3499-4(4))** Crabtree Publishing Co.

Treays, Rebecca. Understanding Your Brain. 2004. (Illus.). 32p. pap. (978-0-439-79804-4(3)) Scholastic, Inc.

Viegas, Jennifer. The Revolution in Healing the Brain. (Library of Future Medicine Ser.). 64p. 2009. (gr. 5-5). 58.50 (978-1-60853-633-7(5)) 2005. (Illus.). (YA). (gr. 7-12). lib. bdg. 31.95 (978-0-8239-3668-7(6)) Rosen Publishing Group, Inc., The.

Waldron, Melanie. Your Brain: Understand It with Numbers, 1 vol. 2014. (Your Body by Numbers Ser.). (ENG., Illus.). 48p. (gr. 3-5). pap. 9.95 (978-1-4109-5985-0(6)); lib. bdg. 32.65 (978-1-4109-5980-5(5)) Heinemann-Raintree.

Watt, Fiona. Understanding Your Brain Kid Kit. 2004. (Titles in Spanish Ser.). 96p. (J). lib. bdg. 26.95 (978-1-58086-594-4(1)) EDC Publishing.

Williams, Ben. Look Inside: Your Brain, 1 vol. 2nd rev. ed. 2013. (Nonfiction Readers Ser.). (ENG., Illus.). 28p. (J). (gr. 2-2). pap. 23.96 (978-1-4807-1055-9(5)) Shell Educational Publishing.

—Look Inside - Your Brain, 1 vol. 2nd rev. ed. 2011. (Nonfiction Readers Ser.). (ENG., Illus.). 28p. (J). (gr. 2-2). pap. 6.99 (978-1-4333-3634-8(0)) Teacher Created Materials, Inc.

Wilson, Michael R. Frequently Asked Questions about How the Teen Brain Works. 2009. (FAQ: Teen Life Ser.). (Illus.). 64p. (J). (gr. 5-6). lib. bdg. 31.95 (978-1-4358-5324-9(5)) Rosen Publishing Group, Inc., The.

Winston, Robert. What Goes on in My Head? 2016. (Big Questions Ser.). (ENG., Illus.). 96p. (J). (gr. 3-7). pap. 9.99 (978-1-4654-1747-3(8), DK Children) Dorling Kindersley Publishing, Inc.

Wynne, Patricia J. & Silver, Donald. My First Book about the Brain. 2013. (Dover Children's Science Bks.). (ENG., Illus.). 32p. (J). (gr. 3-8). pap. 3.99 (978-0-486-49084-7(X)) Dover Pubns., Inc.

BRAMBLY HEDGE (IMAGINARY PLACE)—FICTION

Barklem, Jill. Adventures in Brambly Hedge. 2014. (ENG., Illus.). 128p. (J). 29.99 (978-0-00-746145-5(3), HarperCollins Children's Bks.) HarperCollins Pubs. Ltd. GBR. Dist: HarperCollins Pubs.

—Spring Story. Barklem, Jill, illus. 2011. (Brambly Hedge Ser.). (ENG., Illus.). 32p. (J). 9.99 (978-0-00-183922-9(5), HarperCollins Children's Bks.) HarperCollins Pubs. Ltd. GBR. Dist: HarperCollins Pubs.

Barklem, Jill. A Year in Brambly Hedge. Barklem, Jill, illus. 2017. (ENG., Illus.). 128p. (J). 29.99 **(978-0-00-824117-9(1)**, HarperCollins Children's Bks.) HarperCollins Pubs. Ltd. GBR. Dist: HarperCollins Pubs.

BRASS INSTRUMENTS

see Wind Instruments

BRAVERY

see Courage

BRAZIL

Brimson, Samuel. Brazil-East Timor, 8 vols. 2003. (Nations of the World Ser.: Vol. 2). (Illus.). 64p. (gr. 5-12). lib. bdg. 31.00 (978-0-8368-5486-2(1), Gareth Stevens Secondary Library) Stevens, Gareth Publishing LLLP.

Burlingame, Jeff. Soccer Star Kak. 2014. (Goal! Latin Stars of Soccer Ser.). 48p. 14.95 (978-1-62285-230-7(3)) Enslow Pubs., Inc.

—Soccer Star Kaká. 2014. (Goal! Latin Stars of Soccer Ser.). 48p. (J). (gr. 4-9). pap. 8.95 (978-1-62285-231-4(1)) Enslow Pubs., Inc.

Chambers, Catherine. Dilma Rousseff, 1 vol. 2014. (Extraordinary Women Ser.). (ENG.). 48p. (gr. 6-6). pap. 9.95 (978-1-4109-5953-9(8)) Heinemann-Raintree.

Franchino, Vicky. Brazil. 2010. (Explorer Library: Social Studies Explorer Ser.). (ENG.). 48p. (gr. 4-8). lib. bdg. 31.36 (978-1-60279-827-4(3), 200520) Cherry Lake Publishing.

Ganeri, Anita. Brazil: A Benjamin Blog & His Inquisitive Dog Guide, 1 vol. Isik, Semur, illus. 2014. (Country Guides, with Benjamin Blog & His Inquisitive Dog Ser.). (ENG.). 32p. (gr. 1-3). pap. 7.99 (978-1-4109-6674-2(7), Read Me!) Heinemann-Raintree.

Gitlin, Martin. Soccer Star Robinho. 2014. (Goal! Latin Stars of Soccer Ser.). 48p. 14.95 (978-1-62285-216-1(8)) Enslow Pubs., Inc.

Greenbaum, Harry. Brazil. Gritzner, Charles F., ed. 2003. (Modern World Nations Ser.). (Illus.). 150p. (gr. 6-12). lib. bdg. 35.00 (978-0-7910-7240-0(1), Chelsea Hse.) Facts On File, Inc.

—Iceland. 2003. (Modern World Nations Ser.). (Illus.). 150p. (gr. 6-12). 35.00 (978-0-7910-7232-5(0), Chelsea Hse.) Facts On File, Inc.

Holiday, Jane. Exploring Brazil with the Five Themes of Geography. (Library of the Western Hemisphere Ser.). 24p. 2009. (gr. 4-4). 42.50 (978-1-60853-922-2(9), PowerKids Pr.) 2005. (Illus.). (J). 22.60 (978-1-4042-2679-1(6), PowerKids Pr.) 2005. (ENG., Illus.). (gr. 3-8). pap. 8.25 (978-0-8239-4639-6(8)) Rosen Publishing Group, Inc., The.

Jokulsson, Illugi. Neymar. 2015. (World Soccer Legends Ser.). (ENG., Illus.). 64p. (J). (gr. 1). 13.95 (978-0-7892-1227-6(7), Abbeville Kids) Abbeville Pr., Inc.

Klepeis, Alicia. Brazil. 2016. (Exploring World Cultures Ser.). (Illus.). 32p. (J). (gr. 3-3). 28.50 (978-1-5026-1802-3(8)) Cavendish Square Publishing.

Lynch, Annabelle & Green, Jen. Brazil. 2017. (Living In Ser.). (ENG., Illus.). 24p. (J). (gr. k-2). 16.99 (978-1-4451-4874-8(9), Franklin Watts) Hachette Children's Group GBR. Dist: Hachette Bk. Group.

Marshall Cavendish. The Cooking of Brazil. 2nd rev. ed. 2011. (Superchef, Second Edition Ser.). (Illus.). 96p. (J). (gr. 6). 35.64 (978-1-60870-549-8(8)) Marshall Cavendish Corp.

Marshall, David. Brazil. (World Focus Ser.). (Illus.). 32p. (J). (gr. 3-7). pap. 3.99 (978-0-431-07256-2(6)) Oxfam Publishing GBR. Dist: Stylus Publishing, LLC.

McNamara, Margaret. Brazil. 2006. (J). pap. (978-1-4108-6457-4(X)) Benchmark Education Co.

Mis, Melody S. How to Draw Brazil's Sights & Symbols. 2009. (Kid's Guide to Drawing the Countries of the World Ser.). 48p. (gr. 4-4). 53.00 (978-1-61511-108-4(5), PowerKids Pr.) Rosen Publishing Group, Inc., The.

Montgomery, Sy & Bishop, Nic. The Tapir Scientist: Saving South America's Largest Mammal. 2013. (Scientists in the Field Ser.). (ENG., Illus.). 80p. (J). (gr. 5-7). 18.99 (978-0-547-81548-0(4)) Houghton Mifflin Harcourt Publishing Co.

Morrison, Marion. Brazil. 2004. (Country Files Ser.). (Illus.). 32p. (J). (gr. 4-8). lib. bdg. 24.25 (978-1-58340-235-1(7)) Black Rabbit Bks.

Obregón, José María. Brazil: Brasil. 2009. (Great National Soccer Teams / Grandes selecciones del fútbol mundial Ser.). (SPA & ENG.). 24p. pap. 8.25 (978-1-4358-2489-8(X)); (Illus.). lib. bdg. 22.60 (978-1-4042-8085-4(5)) Rosen Publishing Group, Inc., The. (PowerKids Pr.).

Obregon, Jose Maria. Ronaldhino. 2009. (World Soccer Stars / Estrellas del fútbol mundial Ser.). (ENG & SPA.). 24p. (gr. 2-2). 42.50 (978-1-60854-850-7(3), Editorial Buenas Letras) Rosen Publishing Group, Inc., The.

—Ronaldinho. Benson, Megan, tr. 2008. (World Soccer Stars / Estrellas Del Fútbol Mundial Ser.). (SPA., Illus.). 24p. (J). (gr. 2-5). lib. bdg. 22.60 (978-1-4042-7664-2(5)) Rosen Publishing Group, Inc., The.

Papi, Liza. Carnavalia! African-Brazilian Folklore & Crafts. Papi, Liza, illus. 2004. (Illus.). 48p. (J). (gr. k-4). reprint ed. 20.00 (978-0-7567-7760-9(7)) DIANE Publishing Co.

Parker, Edward. Brazil. 2010. (Countries in Our World Ser.). 32p. (YA). (gr. 2-5). lib. bdg. 28.50 (978-1-59920-441-3(X)) Black Rabbit Bks.

Savery, Annabel. Brazil. 2011. (ENG., Illus.). 32p. (J). pap. 10.95 (978-1-77092-021-7(8)) Saunders Bk. Co. CAN. Dist: RiverStream Publishing.

Scoones, Simon. Focus on Brazil. 2006. (World in Focus Ser.). (Illus.). 64p. (gr. 5-12). pap. 14.05 (978-0-8368-6727-5(0)); lib. bdg. 34.00 (978-0-8368-6720-6(3)) Stevens, Gareth Publishing LLLP. (Gareth Stevens Secondary Library).

Teixeira, Thiago Jorge. Neymar. 2012. (Superstars of Soccer ENGLISH Ser.). (ENG., Illus.). 32p. (J). (gr. 4-7). lib. bdg. 19.95 (978-1-4222-2648-3(4)) Mason Crest.

Thomas, Mark. The Itaipu Dam: World's Biggest Dam. 2009. (Record-Breaking Structures Ser.). 24p. (gr. 1-2). 42.50 (978-1-60852-455-6(8), PowerKids Pr.) Rosen Publishing Group, Inc., The.

—The Maracana: World's Largest Soccer Stadium. 2009. (Record-Breaking Structures Ser.). 24p. (gr. 1-2). 42.50 (978-1-60852-456-3(6), PowerKids Pr.) Rosen Publishing Group, Inc., The.

Torres, John Albert. Soccer Star Ronaldinho. 2014. (Goal! Latin Stars of Soccer Ser.). 48p. 14.95 (978-1-62285-223-9(0)) Enslow Pubs., Inc.

Walters, Tara. Brazil. 2008. (True Book(tm), A — Countries Ser.). (ENG., Illus.). 48p. (J). (gr. 3-7). 31.00 (978-0-531-16851-6(4), Children's Pr.) Scholastic Library Publishing.

Wandersman, Aldo. Ronaldo. 2012. (Superstars of Soccer ENGLISH Ser.). (ENG., Illus.). 32p. (J). (gr. 4-7). lib. bdg. 19.95 (978-1-4222-2658-2(1)) Mason Crest.

Weitzman, Elizabeth. Brazil. 2008. pap. 40.95 (978-0-8225-9298-3(3)) 2007. (ENG., Illus.). 48p. (gr. 2-4). lib. bdg. 29.27 (978-0-8225-7127-8(7), Lerner Pubns.) Lerner Publishing Group.

BRAZIL—FICTION

Angel, Ido. Vipo in Brazil: The Crocodile Who Lost His Teeth. 2015. (AV2 Animated Storytime Ser.). (ENG.). (J). lib. bdg. 29.99 (978-1-4896-3896-0(2), AV2 by Weigl) Weigl Pubs., Inc.

Bell, Michele Ashman. Rescue: A Jungle Adventure. 2006. 246p. (J). pap. (978-1-59811-093-7(4)) Covenant Communications.

Carvalho, Marcela. Three Sisters, Three Weddings, & One Dress. 2011. 38p. pap. 24.94 (978-0-557-52962-9(X)) Lulu Pr., Inc.

Crespo, Ana. The Sock Thief. 2016. (Av2 Fiction Readalong 2017 Ser.). (ENG.). (J). (gr. -1-2). 34.28 **(978-1-4896-5329-1(5)**, AV2 by Weigl) Weigl Pubs., Inc.

—The Sock Thief. Gonzales, Nana, illus. 2015. (ENG.). 32p. (J). (gr. -1-3). 16.99 *(978-0-8075-7538-3(0))* Whitman, Albert & Co.

De la Cruz, Melissa. Revelations. 2009. (ENG.). 288p. (J). (gr. 7-17). pap. 8.99 *(978-1-4231-0229-8(0))* Hyperion Pr.

De Laurentiis, Giada, et al. Rio de Janeiro! #5. Gambatesa, Francesca, illus. 2015. (Recipe for Adventure Ser.: 5). (ENG.). 160p. (J). (gr. 2-4). bds. 6.99 *(978-0-448-48204-0(5)*, Grosset & Dunlap) Penguin Young Readers Group.

Garlando, Luigi. ¡Nos Vamos a Brasil! ¡Gol! 2013. (Vintage Espanol Ser.). (SPA.). 144p. (J). (gr. 2-5). pap. 9.95 *(978-0-345-80423-5(6)*, Vintage Espanol) Knopf Doubleday Publishing Group.

Hanson, Ed. Amazon Adventure. 2003. (Barclay Family Adventure Ser.: Bk. 1). 64p. (J). (gr. k-6). per. 3.95 *(978-1-56254-550-5(7)*, SP 5507) Saddleback Educational Publishing, Inc.

Hapka, Catherine, pseud. Blu & Friends. 2011. (I Can Read Level 2 Ser.). (ENG.). 32p. (J). (gr. k-3). pap. 3.99 *(978-0-06-201487-0(0)*, HarperFestival) HarperCollins Pubs.

—Rio - Learning to Fly. 2011. (I Can Read Level 2 Ser.). (ENG.). 32p. (J). (gr. k-3). pap. 3.99 *(978-0-06-201488-7(9)*, HarperFestival) HarperCollins Pubs.

Harper, Benjamin. Greetings from Rio! 2011. (Rio Ser.). (ENG.). 24p. (J). (gr. -1-2). pap. 3.99 *(978-0-06-202266-0(0)*, HarperFestival) HarperCollins Pubs.

Hillyer, Lexa. Rio. 2011. (Rio Ser.). (ENG.). 144p. (J). (gr. 3-7). pap. 5.99 *(978-0-06-202269-1(5)*, HarperFestival) HarperCollins Pubs.

Huelin, Jodi. The Movie Storybook. 2011. (Rio Ser.). (ENG.). 48p. (J). (gr. -1-2). pap. 8.99 *(978-0-06-202270-7(9)*, HarperFestival) HarperCollins Pubs.

Ibbotson, Eva. Journey to the River Sea. 5th unabr. ed. 2008. (ENG.). 304p. (J). (gr. 10-14). 14.95 *(978-0-330-39715-5(X)*, Macmillan) Pan Macmillan GBR. Dist: Trans-Atlantic Pubns., Inc.

—Journey to the River Sea. Hawkes, Kevin, illus. 2003. 298p. (gr. 3-7). 18.00 *(978-0-7569-1552-0(X))* Perfection Learning Corp.

Janesh, Ron. Ariela Aparecida E O Vale Da Neblina Da Cachoeir. Gonçalves da Silva, Fabio, illus. 2012. 56p. pap. 20.50 *(978-1-60976-925-3(2)*, Strategic Bk. Publishing) Strategic Book Publishing & Rights Agency (SBPRA).

Johnson, Alaya Dawn. The Summer Prince. (ENG.). 304p. (J). (gr. 9). 2014. pap. 9.99 *(978-0-545-41780-8(5))* 2013. 17.99 *(978-0-545-41779-2(1))* Scholastic, Inc. (Levine, Arthur A. Bks.).

Korman, Susan. Birds of a Feather. 2011. (Rio Ser.). (ENG.). 24p. (J). (gr. -1-2). pap. 3.99 *(978-0-06-202267-7(9)*, HarperFestival) HarperCollins Pubs.

Lerasle, Magdeleine. Songs from a Journey with a Parrot: Lullabies & Nursery Rhymes from Portugal & Brazil. Fronty, Aurélia, illus. 2013. (POR & ENG.). 52p. (J). (gr. -1-k). 16.95 *(978-2-923163-99-4(0))* La Montagne Secrete CAN. Dist: Independent Pubs. Group.

Lewis, Axel. Rain Forest Rampage, 1 vol. 2014. (Robot Racers Ser.). (ENG.). 160p. (gr. 2-4). 26.65 *(978-1-4342-6571-5(4))* Stone Arch Bks.

Lumry, Amanda & Hurwitz, Laura. Amazon River Rescue. McIntyre, Sarah, illus. 2004. (Adventures of Riley Ser.). 36p. 15.95 *(978-0-9662257-9-2(1))* Eaglemont Pr.

MacHado, Ana Maria. Del Otro Lado Hay Secretos. (SPA.). pap. 11.95 *(978-950-07-2221-6(6))* Editorial Sudamericana S.A. ARG. Dist: Distribooks, Inc.

Machado, Ana Maria. What a Party!, 1 vol. Amado, Elisa, tr. from POR. Moreau, Hélène, illus. 2013. (ENG.). 32p. (J). (gr. -1-2). 18.95 *(978-1-55498-168-7(9))* Groundwood Bks. CAN. Dist: Publishers Group West (PGW).

Monkey Girl Staff. Jays Travels to the U S A. 2012. 20p. pap. 17.99 *(978-1-4685-4778-8(X))* AuthorHouse.

Osorio, Rick. The Great Adventure of Sally Rock & the Secret of Man, 1 vol. 2009. 164p. pap. 24.95 *(978-1-60813-596-7(9))* America Star Bks.

Page, P. K. Uirapurú: Based on a Brazilian Legend. Bridgeman, Kristi, illus. 2010. (ENG.). 32p. (J). 19.95 *(978-0-88982-264-1(6))* Oolichan Bks. CAN. Dist: Univ. of Toronto Pr.

Pedraza, M. Eugenia Rueda. Nico's Voyage. 2013. 32p. pap. *(978-1-4602-2360-4(8))* FriesenPress.

Publications International Ltd. Staff. Look & Find Rio. 2011. 24p. (J). 7.98 *(978-1-4508-1382-2(8))* Publications International, Ltd.

Rabley, Stephen & Pearson Education Staff. Flying Home. 2nd ed. 2008. (ENG.). 20p. pap. 11.99 *(978-1-4058-6946-1(1))* Pearson Education.

Saddleback Educational Publishing Staff, ed. River, 1 vol. unabr. ed. 2011. (Heights Ser.). (ENG.). 49p. (gr. 5-8). pap. 7.95 *(978-1-61651-281-1(4))* Saddleback Educational Publishing, Inc.

Smith, Roland. Mutation. (ENG.). 352p. (J). (gr. 3-7). 2016. (Cryptid Hunters Ser.: 4). pap. 6.99 *(978-0-545-08181-8(5))* 2014. 16.99 *(978-0-545-08180-1(7))* Scholastic, Inc. (Scholastic Pr.).

Stilton, Geronimo. Rumble in the Jungle. 2013. (Geronimo Stilton Ser.: 53). lib. bdg. 18.40 *(978-0-606-31527-2(6)*, Turtleback) Turtleback Bks.

Thompson, Adria. Droves Cove. 2008. 72p. pap. 9.99 *(978-1-60477-653-9(6))* Salem Author Services.

Yeager, Paugh Paugh Tom. The 26th of June. 2008. 34p. pap. 24.95 *(978-1-60563-822-5(6))* America Star Bks.

BRAZIL—HISTORY

Brooks, Susie. Brazil. 2006. (Our Lives, Our World Ser.). (J). *(978-1-59389-286-9(1))* Chrysalis Education.

Coleman-Smith, Charlotte. Spotlight on Brazil - Collins Big Cat. 2015. (Collins Big Cat Ser.). (ENG., Illus.). 32p. (J). (gr. 2-3). pap. 8.95 *(978-0-00-812777-0(8))* HarperCollins Pubs. Ltd. GBR. Dist: Independent Pubs. Group.

Deckker, Zilah & National Geographic Kids Staff. Brazil. 2008. (Countries of the World Ser.). (ENG., Illus.). 64p. (J). (gr. 5). 27.90 *(978-1-4263-0298-5(3)*, National Geographic Children's Bks.) National Geographic Society.

Forest, Christopher. Brazil, 1 vol. 2011. (Countries of the World Set 1 Ser.). (ENG., Illus.). 144p. (J). (gr. 6-12). lib. bdg. 37.07 *(978-1-61783-106-5(9))* ABDO Publishing Co.

Gagne, Tammy. Brazilian Cultures in Perspective. 2014. 64p. (J). (gr. 4-8). 33.95 *(978-1-61228-560-3(0))* Mitchell Lane Pubs., Inc.

—What It's Like to Be Pele. de la Vega, Eida, tr. 2011. (What It's Like to Be... = Que Se Sienta Al Ser... Ser.). (ENG & SPA., Illus.). 32p. (J). (gr. -1-2). lib. bdg. 25.70 *(978-1-58415-993-3(6))* Mitchell Lane Pubs., Inc.

Gitlin, Marty. Brazil. 2017. (Country Profiles Ser.). (ENG., Illus.). 32p. (J). (gr. 3-8). lib. bdg. 26.95 **(978-1-62617-676-8(0)**, Blastoff! Discovery) Bellwether Media.

Goldsworthy, Steve. Brazil. 2013. (J). *(978-1-62127-250-2(8))*; pap. *(978-1-62127-256-4(7))* Weigl Pubs., Inc.

Heinrichs, Ann. Brazil. 2013. (ENG.). 144p. (J). 40.00 *(978-0-531-23675-8(7))* Scholastic Library Publishing.

Kalman, Bobbie. Spotlight on Brazil. 2011. (ENG.). 32p. (J). *(978-0-7787-3461-1(7))*; (Spotlight on My Country Ser.: No. 16). pap. *(978-0-7787-3487-1(0))* Crabtree Publishing Co.

Markovics, Joyce L. Brazil. 2017. (Countries We Come From Ser.). (ENG., Illus.). 32p. (J). (gr. -1-3). 19.95 *(978-1-68402-055-3(7))* Bearport Publishing Co., Inc.

McNamara, Margaret. Discover Brazil. 2006. (J). pap. *(978-1-4108-6460-4(X))* Benchmark Education Co.

Morrison, Marion. Brazil, 1 vol. 2011. (Countries Around the World Ser.). (ENG.). 48p. (J). (gr. 3-6). pap. 9.95 *(978-1-4329-5221-1(8)*, NA-h) Heinemann-Raintree.

Parker, Ed. Discover Brazil. 2010. (Illus.). 32p. (J). 63.60 *(978-1-61532-291-6(4)*, PowerKids Pr.); pap. 10.60 *(978-1-61532-290-9(6)*, PowerKids Pr.); (gr. 3-5). lib. bdg. 26.50 *(978-1-61532-286-2(8))* Rosen Publishing Group, Inc., The.

Parker, Lewis K. Portuguese Colonies in the Americas. 2003. (European Colonies in the Americas Ser.). (Illus.). 24p. (J). lib. bdg. 22.60 *(978-0-8239-6474-1(4)*, PowerKids Pr.) Rosen Publishing Group, Inc., The.

Perkins, Chloe & Silva, Reg. Living in ... Brazil. Woolley, Tom, illus. 2016. (Living In... Ser.). (ENG.). 32p. (J). (gr. k-2). pap. 3.99 *(978-1-4814-5203-8(7))* Simon & Schuster, Inc.

Perritano, John. Brazil, Vol. 12. 2015. (Major Nations in a Global World: Tradition, Culture, & Daily Life Ser.). (Illus.). 64p. (J). (gr. 7). 23.95 *(978-1-4222-3341-2(3))* Mason Crest.

Roholt, Christine VeLure. Foods of Brazil. 2014. (Cook with Me Ser.). (ENG., Illus.). 24p. (J). (gr. 3-7). lib. bdg. 25.95 *(978-1-62617-115-2(7)*; Express Bks.) Bellwether Media.

Savery, Annabel. Brazil. 2014. (My Country Ser.). 24p. (gr. k-3). lib. bdg. 28.50 *(978-1-59920-902-9(0))* Black Rabbit Bks.

Sexton, Colleen. Brazil. 2010. (Exploring Countries Ser.). (ENG., Illus.). 32p. (J). (gr. 3-7). lib. bdg. 26.95 *(978-1-60014-474-5(8)*, Blastoff! Readers) Bellwether Media.

Shields, Charles J. Brazil. (South America Today Ser.). 64p. 2009. (Illus.). (J). (gr. 4-7). 21.95 *(978-1-4222-0633-1(5))* 2007. (YA). (gr. 7-18). pap. 9.95 *(978-1-4222-0700-0(5))* Mason Crest.

—Brazil, Vol. 13. Henderson, James D., ed. 2015. (Discovering South America: History, Politics, & Culture Ser.). (Illus.). 64p. (J). (gr. 7). lib. bdg. 22.95 *(978-1-4222-3296-5(4))* Mason Crest.

Spilsbury, Louise. Brazil. 2015. (Emerging Nations Ser.). (ENG., Illus.). 48p. (J). (gr. 4-9). 37.10 *(978-1-59920-988-3(8))* Black Rabbit Bks.

Tieck, Sarah. Brazil, 1 vol. 2013. (Explore the Countries Ser.). (ENG.). 40p. (J). (gr. 2-5). lib. bdg. 29.93 *(978-1-61783-805-7(5)*, Big Buddy Bks.) ABDO Publishing Co.

Tracy, Kathleen. We Visit Brazil. 2010. (Your Land & My Land Ser.). (Illus.). 64p. (J). (gr. 3-6). lib. bdg. 33.95 *(978-1-58415-887-5(5))* Mitchell Lane Pubs., Inc.

Trusdell, Brian. Pel: Soccer Star & Ambassador, 1 vol. 2014. (Legendary Athletes Set 2 Ser.). (ENG.). 112p. (gr. 5-12). lib. bdg. 34.22 *(978-1-62403-132-8(3)*, SportsZone) ABDO Publishing Co.

Wells, Garrison. Brazilian Jiujitsu: Ground-Fighting Combat. 2012. (Martial Arts Sports Zone Ser.). (ENG., Illus.). 32p. (gr. 4-8). lib. bdg. 26.60 *(978-0-7613-8456-4(1)*, Lerner Pubns.) Lerner Publishing Group.

Whiting, Jim. My Teenage Life in Brazil. 2017. (Custom & Cultures of the World Ser.: Vol. 12). (ENG., Illus.). (YA). (gr. 7-12). 23.95 **(978-1-4222-3901-8(2))** Mason Crest.

BREAD

see also Baking

Benduhn, Tea. Bread & Cereal. 2007. (Find Out about Food Ser.). 24p. (gr. k-3). pap. 8.15 *(978-0-8368-8257-5(1))*; (Illus.). lib. bdg. 22.00 *(978-0-8368-8250-6(4))* Stevens, Gareth Publishing LLLP. (Weekly Reader Leveled Readers).

—Bread & Cereal/Pan y Cereales. 2007. (Find Out about Food/ Conoce la comida Ser.). (SPA & ENG., Illus.). 24p. (gr. k-3). pap. 8.15 *(978-0-8368-8461-6(2))*; lib. bdg. 22.00 *(978-0-8368-8454-8(X))* Stevens, Gareth Publishing LLLP. (Weekly Reader Leveled Readers).

Blake, Susannah. Bread & Pizza. 2009. (Make & Eat Ser.). (ENG., Illus.). 24p. (J). (gr. 3-5). pap. 9.40 *(978-1-4358-2932-9(8)*, PowerKids Pr.) Rosen Publishing Group, Inc., The.

—Bread & Pizza. Crawford, Andy, photos by. 2009. (Make & Eat Ser.). (Illus.). 24p. (J). (gr. 3-5). 25.25 *(978-1-4358-2858-2(5)*, PowerKids Pr.) Rosen Publishing Group, Inc., The.

Cornell, Kari. Marvelous Muffins, Breads, & Pancakes. Cohen, Brie, photos by. 2013. (You're the Chef Ser.). (ENG., Illus.). 32p. (gr. 3-5). lib. bdg. 26.60 *(978-0-7613-6636-2(9)*, Millbrook Pr.) Lerner Publishing Group.

Dilkes, D. H. Bread & Grains. 2011. (All about Good Foods We Eat Ser.). (Illus.). 24p. (J). (gr. -1-18). pap. 7.95 *(978-1-59845-252-5(5)*, Enslow Elementary); (gr. k-3). lib. bdg. 22.60 *(978-0-7660-3923-0(4))* Enslow Pubs., Inc.

Gregory, Helen. Bread Around the World. 2011. (Wonder Readers Early Level Ser.). (ENG.). (gr. -1-1). 16p. pap. 35.94 *(978-1-4296-8073-8(3))*; 32p. pap. 5.99 *(978-1-4296-7798-1(8))* Capstone Press of Coughlan Cos. (Wonder Readers).

Hayes, Amy. Turning Wheat into Bread. 2015. (Step-By-Step Transformations Ser.). (ENG., Illus.). 24p. (J). (gr. 1-1). pap. 8.22 *(978-1-5026-0445-3(0))* Cavendish Square Publishing.

Heos, Bridget. From Wheat to Bread. Coleman, Stephanie Fizer, illus. 2017. (Who Made My Lunch? Ser.). (ENG.). 24p. (gr. 1-4). 20.95 **(978-1-68151-118-4(5))** Amicus Publishing.

Hepker, Sue. This Is the Challah. Wummer, Amy, illus. 2012. (J). *(978-0-87441-522-3(5))*; *(978-0-87441-922-1(0))* Behrman Hse., Inc.

Jules, Jacqueline. Before We Eat: A Thank You Prayer. Iwai, Melissa, illus. 2010. (ENG.). 12p. (J). (gr. -1-1). 5.95 *(978-0-7613-3954-0(X)*, Kar-Ben Publishing) Lerner Publishing Group.

Kuskowski, Alex. Cool Breads & Biscuits, 1 vol. 2014. (Cool Home Cooking Ser.). (ENG.). 32p. (J). (gr. 3-6). 28.50 *(978-1-62403-500-5(0))* ABDO Publishing Co.

Levenson, George. Bread Comes to Life: A Garden of Wheat & a Loaf to Eat. Thaler, Shmuel, photos by. 2008. (ENG., Illus.). 32p. (J). (gr. -1-2). pap. 7.99 *(978-1-58246-273-8(9)*, Tricycle Pr.) Random Hse. Children's Bks.

Lunis, Natalie. Baking Bread. 2011. (Early Connections Ser.). (J). *(978-1-61672-609-6(1))* Benchmark Education Co.

Making Fresh Bread. 2008. 96p. *(978-1-4075-2898-4(X))* Parragon, Inc.

Martineau, Susan & James, Hel. Bread, Rice, & Pasta. 2012. (Healthy Eating Ser.). (Illus.). 32p. (gr. 2-6). pap. 8.95 *(978-1-59920-242-6(5))* Black Rabbit Bks.

Meachen Rau, Dana. Bread. 2008. (What's Cooking? Ser.). 24p. (gr. k-1). lib. bdg. 15.95 *(978-0-7614-2892-3(5)*, Benchmark Bks.) Marshall Cavendish Corp.

—Pan. 2008. (Qué Preparamos Hoy? Ser.). (SPA.). 24p. (gr. k-1). lib. bdg. 15.95 *(978-0-7614-3438-2(0)*, Benchmark Bks.) Marshall Cavendish Corp.

Nolan, Janet. PBandJ Hooray! 2016. (J). *(978-1-4896-3870-0(9))* Weigl Pubs., Inc.

—PB&J Hooray! Your Sandwich's Amazing Journey from Farm to Table. Patton, Julia, illus. 2014. (ENG.). 32p. (J). (gr. -1-3). 16.99 *(978-0-8075-6397-7(8))* Whitman, Albert & Co.

Paulsen, Gary. La Tortilleria. Andujar, Gloria Dearagon, tr. from ENG. Paulsen, Ruth Wright, illus. 2006.Tr. of Tortilla Factory. 27p. (J). (gr. k-4). reprint ed. 16.00 *(978-1-4223-5319-6(2))* DIANE Publishing Co.

Price, Pamela S. Cool Quick Breads: Easy Recipes for Kids to Bake, 1 vol. 2010. (Cool Baking Ser.). (ENG.). 32p. (gr. 3-6). 28.50 *(978-1-60453-779-6(5)*, Checkerboard Library) ABDO Publishing Co.

Rickards, Lynne. Baking Bread Green Band. 2016. (Cambridge Reading Adventures Ser.). (ENG.). 17p. pap. 6.56 *(978-1-316-50327-0(5))* Cambridge Univ. Pr.

Rush, Diana. Where Does Your Bread Come From? 2009. 24p. pap. 12.00 *(978-1-4389-7735-5(2))* AuthorHouse.

Shaffer, Jody Jensen. Bread. 2016. (J). *(978-1-4896-4529-6(2))* Weigl Pubs., Inc.

—Bread Before the Store. McGeehan, Dan, illus. 2012. (Before the Store Ser.). (ENG.). 32p. (J). (gr. 2-5). lib. bdg. 29.93 *(978-1-60973-629-3(X)*, 201250) Child's World, Inc., The.

Snyder, Inez. Welcome Books: Grains to Bread: How Things Are Made. 2005. (How Things Are Made Ser.). (ENG., Illus.). 24p. (J). (gr. -1-2). pap. 4.95 *(978-0-516-25527-9(4)*, Children's Pr.) Scholastic Library Publishing.

Steinwender, Cherry. Bread Is a Simple Food: Teaching Children about Cultures. 2011. 32p. pap. 16.95 *(978-1-4520-8561-6(7))* AuthorHouse.

Taus-Bolstad, Stacy. From Wheat to Bread. 2012. (Start to Finish, Second Series: Food Ser.: No. 2). (ENG., Illus.). 24p. (gr. k-3). pap. 6.95 *(978-1-58013-970-0(1))*; lib. bdg. 23.93 *(978-0-7613-9178-4(9)*, Lerner Pubns.) Lerner Publishing Group.

BREATHING

see Respiration

BREEDING

see Plant Breeding

BRIDAL CUSTOMS

see Marriage Customs and Rites

BRIDGE (GAME)

Levin, David H. Bridge Puzzles for Children Vol. 1: Simple Card Play Problems to Introduce Them to This Wonderful Game. 2004. (Illus.). 128p. (J). pap. 14.95 *(978-0-9638001-2-1(4))* Syllogism Pr.

BRIDGER, JIM, 1804-1881

Maynard, Charles W. Jim Bridger: Frontiersman & Mountain Guide. (Famous Explorers of the American West Ser.). 24p. 2009. (gr. 3-4). 42.50 *(978-1-61512-502-9(7))* 2003. (Illus.). (J). lib. bdg. 22.60 *(978-0-8239-6288-4(1))* Rosen Publishing Group, Inc., The. (PowerKids Pr.).

BRIDGER, JIM, 1804-1881—FICTION

Hollmann, Clide Anne & Plummer, Myrtes Marie. Jim Bridger: King of Scouts. 2011. 166p. 41.95 *(978-1-258-10077-3(0))* Literary Licensing, LLC.

BRIDGES

Aloian, Sam. How a Bridge Is Built. 2016. (Engineering Our World Ser.). (ENG.). 24p. (J). (gr. 2-3). pap. 8.15 *(978-1-4824-3919-9(0))* Stevens, Gareth Publishing LLLP.

Barry, Myles. Examining Bridge Collapses. 2015. (ENG., Illus.). 48p. (J). lib. bdg. 24.95 net. *(978-1-934545-62-1(7))* Oliver Pr., Inc.

Bethea, Nikole Brooks. The Science of a Bridge Collapse. 2014. (21st Century Skills Library: Disaster Science Ser.). (ENG.). 32p. (J). (gr. 4-8). 28.50 *(978-1-63137-623-8(3)*, 205275) Cherry Lake Publishing.

Blake, Kevin. The Golden Gate Bridge. 2016. (American Places: from Vision to Reality Ser.). (ENG.). 32p. (J). (gr. 2-7). 19.95 *(978-1-944102-44-9(2))* Bearport Publishing Co., Inc.

Bridges, Ruby. Ruby Bridges Goes to School: My True Story. 2009. (Scholastic Reader Level 2 Ser.). (ENG.). 32p. (J). (gr. -1-3). pap. 3.99 *(978-0-545-10855-3(1))* Scholastic, Inc.

Briscoe, Diana. Bridge Building: Bridge Designs & How They Work. 2004. (High Five Reading - Purple Ser.). (ENG., Illus.). 64p. (gr. 3-4). per. 9.00 *(978-0-7368-3853-5(8)*, High Five Reading (RBL)) Capstone Press of Coughlan Cos.

Briscoe, Diana C. Bridge Building Set: Bridge Designs & How They Work, 6 vols. 2004. (High Five Reading - Purple Ser.). (ENG.). 64p. (gr. 3-4). pap. 54.00 *(978-0-7368-3871-9(6)*, High Five Reading (RBL)) Capstone Press of Coughlan Cos.

Burns, Kylie. A Bridge Goes Over. 2017. 24p. (J). **(978-0-7787-2907-5(9))** Crabtree Publishing Co.

Chapman, Tony. Buildings, Bridges, & Landmarks: a Complete History. 2016. (ENG., Illus.). 118p. pap. 19.99 *(978-1-62686-556-3(6)*, Thunder Bay Pr.) Readerlink Distribution Services, LLC.

Cornille, Didier. Who Built That? Bridges. Broad, Yolanda Stern, tr. from FRE. 2016. (ENG., Illus.). 96p. (J). (gr. 2-7). 17.95 *(978-1-61689-516-7(0))* Princeton Architectural Pr.

Cortright, Robert S. Bridging the World. Cortright, Robert S., photos by. 2003. (Illus.). 208p. 35.00 *(978-0-9641963-3-9(6))* Bridge Ink.

Donaldson, Madeline. Ruby Bridges. 2009. (History Maker Biographies Ser.). (ENG., Illus.). 48p. (gr. 3-6). 27.93 *(978-0-7613-4220-5(6)*, Lerner Pubns.) Lerner Publishing Group.

Engineering is Elementary Team. Javier Builds a Bridge: A Civil Engineering Story. 2005. (Illus.). 41p. (J). per. *(978-1-933758-01-5(5))* Engineering is Elementary.

Enz, Tammy. Building Bridges. 2017. (Young Engineers Ser.). (ENG., Illus.). 32p. (J). (gr. 1-2). lib. bdg. 27.32 *(978-1-4846-3745-6(3)*, Heinemann First Library) Heinemann-Raintree.

Finger, Brad. 13 Bridges Children Should Know. 2015. (ENG., Illus.). 48p. (J). (gr. 3-7). 14.95 *(978-3-7913-7240-2(8))* Prestel Verlag GmbH & Co KG. DEU. Dist: Penguin Random Hse. LLC.

Franchino, Vicky. How Did They Build That? Bridge. 2009. (Community Connections: How Did They Build That? Ser.). (ENG.). 24p. (gr. 2-5). lib. bdg. 25.64 *(978-1-60279-483-2(9)*, 200254) Cherry Lake Publishing.

Franks, Gary L. Bridges at the Foot of the Rapids: An Illustrated History of Maumee-Perrysburg River Crossings & Construction of the 2002 Fort Meigs Memorial Bridge. 2003. 243p. per. *(978-1-59196-333-2(8))* Instant Pub.

Furgang, Kathy. Building Bridges & Construcción de Puentes: 6 English, 6 Spanish Adaptations. 2011. (ENG & SPA.). (J). 89.00 net. *(978-1-4108-5683-8(6))* Benchmark Education Co.

Graham, Ian. Fabulous Bridges. 2010. (Superstructures Ser.). 32p. (YA). (gr. 4-7). lib. bdg. 28.50 *(978-1-60753-132-6(1))* Amicus Publishing.

—Fabulous Bridges. 2012. (What's in My Food Ser.). 32p. (gr. 1-4). lib. bdg. 27.10 *(978-1-59920-417-8(7))* Black Rabbit Bks.

Hardyman, Robyn. Bridges. 2016. (Engineering Eurekas Ser.). 00032p. (J). (gr. 3-4). pap. 10.00 *(978-1-4994-3089-9(2)*, PowerKids Pr.) Rosen Publishing Group, Inc., The.

Hayes, Amy. Building Bridges & Roads: Civil Engineers, 01 vols., 1. 2016. (Engineers Rule Ser.). (ENG., Illus.). 32p. (J). pap. 11.75 *(978-1-5081-4532-5(6)*, PowerKids Pr.) Rosen Publishing Group, Inc., The.

Hoena, Blake. Building the Golden Gate Bridge: An Interactive Engineering Adventure, 1 vol. 2014. (You Choose: Engineering Marvels Ser.). (ENG., Illus.). 112p. (gr. 3-4). 31.99 *(978-1-4914-0398-3(5)*, You Choose Bks.) Capstone Press of Coughlan Cos.

Hurley, Michael. The World's Most Amazing Bridges, 1 vol. 2011. (Landmark Top Tens Ser.). (ENG.). 32p. (gr. 3-5). pap. 8.29 *(978-1-4109-4249-4(X))*; 30.65 *(978-1-4109-4238-8(4))* Heinemann-Raintree. (Raintree Perspectives).

Isbell, Hannah. Zoom in on Bridges. 2017. (Zoom in on Engineering Ser.). 24p. (J). (gr. 2-2). lib. bdg. 22.60 **(978-0-7660-8724-8(7))** Enslow Pubs., Inc.

Johmann, Carol A. Bridges! Amazing Structures to Design, Build & Test. 2004. (gr. 3-6). 24.45 *(978-0-613-27751-8(1)*, Turtleback) Turtleback Bks.

Latham, Donna. Bridges & Tunnels: Investigate Feats of Engineering with 25 Projects. Vaughn, Jen, illus. 2012. (Build It Yourself Ser.). (ENG.). 128p. (J). (gr. 3-7). 21.95 *(978-1-936749-52-2(1))* Open City Bks.

Loh-Hagan, Virginia. Bridges. 2017. (21st Century Junior Library: Extraordinary Engineering Ser.). (ENG., Illus.). 24p. (J). (gr. 2-5). lib. bdg. 27.07 *(978-1-63472-162-2(4)*, 209220) Cherry Lake Publishing.

Marsico, Katie. Bridges. 2016. (True Book(tm) — Engineering Wonders Ser.). (ENG., Illus.). 48p. (J). pap. 6.95 *(978-0-531-22269-0(1)*, Children's Pr.) Scholastic Library Publishing.

Mattern, Joanne. Bridges. 2015. (ENG.). 48p. (gr. 3-6). 35.64 *(978-1-63430-419-1(5))* Rourke Educational Media.

Maxwell, Yolanda. Famous Bridges of the World: Measuring Length, Weight, & Volume. 2009. (PowerMath: Proficiency Plus Ser.). 32p. (gr. 4-5). 47.90 *(978-1-60851-409-0(9)*, PowerKids Pr.) Rosen Publishing Group, Inc., The.

Maxwell, Yolonda. Famous Bridges of the World: Measuring Length, Weight, & Volume. (PowerMath Ser.). (Illus.). 32p. 2009. (ENG.). (gr. 5-6). pap. 10.00 *(978-1-4042-5137-3(5))* 2005. (J). (gr. 3-6). lib. bdg. 25.25 *(978-1-4042-2937-2(X))* Rosen Publishing Group, Inc., The. (PowerKids Pr.).

Mitchell, Susan K. The Longest Bridges. 2007. (Megastructures Ser.). (Illus.). 32p. (gr. 5-8). lib. bdg. 26.00 *(978-0-8368-8364-0(0))* Stevens, Gareth Publishing LLLP.

Murray, Julie. Golden Gate Bridge, 1 vol. 2003. (Buddy Book Ser.). (ENG., Illus.). 24p. (gr. k-4). 25.65 *(978-1-57765-672-2(5)*, Buddy Bks.) ABDO Publishing Co.

Nelson, Robin. Del Cemento Al Puente. Translations.com Staff, tr. from ENG. 2006. (De Principio a Fin (Start to Finish) Ser.). (SPA., Illus.). 24p. (gr. 3-5). lib. bdg. 19.93 *(978-0-8225-6498-0(X)*, Ediciones Lerner) Lerner Publishing Group.

Pettiford, Rebecca. Bridges. 2015. 24p. (J). lib. bdg. 25.65 *(978-1-62031-211-7(5))* Jump! Inc.

Phillips, Cynthia & Priwer, Shana. Bridges & Spans. 2009. (ENG., Illus.). 112p. (C). (gr. 6-18). lib. bdg. 158.00 *(978-0-7656-8120-1(X)*, Y181468) Routledge.

Ratliff, Thomas. You Wouldn't Want to Work on the Brooklyn Bridge! An Enormous Project That Seemed Impossible. Bergin, Mark, illus. 2009. (You Wouldn't Want to Ser.). (ENG.). 32p. (J). (gr. 3-18). pap. 9.95 *(978-0-531-20519-8(3))* Scholastic Library Publishing.

Ratliff, Tom. You Wouldn't Want to Work on the Brooklyn Bridge! An Enormous Project That Seemed Impossible. Bergin, Mark, illus. 2009. (You Wouldn't Want to Ser.). (ENG.). 32p. (J). (gr. 3-12). 29.00 *(978-0-531-21328-5(5))* Scholastic Library Publishing.

Riggs, Kate. Golden Gate Bridge. 2015. (J). pap. *(978-1-62832-260-6(8)*, Creative Paperbacks) Creative Co., The.

Ringstad, Arnold. The Building of the Golden Gate Bridge. 2017. (Engineering That Made America Ser.). (ENG.). 32p.

A
B

(J). (gr. 3-6). lib. bdg. 28.50 *(978-1-5038-1640-4(0),* 211152) Child's World, Inc., The.

Squire, Ann O. Extreme Bridges. 2014. (ENG.). 48p. (J). lib. bdg. 29.00 *(978-0-531-20745-1(5))* Scholastic Library Publishing.

Stanborough, Rebecca. Golden Gate Bridge. 2016. (Engineering Wonders Ser.). (ENG., Illus.). 32p. (gr. 3-4). lib. bdg. 27.32 *(978-1-4914-8196-7(X),* Fact Finders) Capstone Press of Coughlan Cos.

Stefoff, Rebecca. Building Bridges. 2015. (Great Engineering Ser.). (ENG.). 32p. (J). (gr. 3-4). pap. 10.58 *(978-1-5026-0597-9(X))* Cavendish Square Publishing.

Stine, Megan. Where Is the Brooklyn Bridge? 2016. (Where Is...? Ser.). lib. bdg. 16.00 *(978-0-606-38411-7(1))* Turtleback Bks.

Stine, Megan & dePaola, Tomie. Where Is the Brooklyn Bridge? Hinderliter, John & Groff, David, illus. 2016. (Where Is? Ser.). (ENG.). 112p. (J). (gr. 3-7). 5.99 *(978-0-448-48424-2(2),* Grosset & Dunlap) Penguin Young Readers Group.

Tan, Richard. The Bridges & Tunnels of New York City. 2011. (My Community Ser.). (ENG., Illus.). 12p. (gr. 2-2). pap. 6.95 *(978-1-4488-5717-3(1),* Rosen Classroom) Rosen Publishing Group, Inc., The.

Thomas, Mark. The Akashi-Kaikyo Bridge: World's Longest Bridge. 2009. (Record-Breaking Structures Ser.). 24p. (gr. 1-2). 42.50 *(978-1-60852-453-2(1),* PowerKids Pr.) Rosen Publishing Group, Inc., The.

—El Puente Akashi Kaikyo: El Puente Mas Largo Del Mundo. 2004. (Estructuras extraordinarias (Record-Breaking Structures) Ser.). (SPA & ENG., Illus.). 24p. (J). (gr. 3-6). lib. bdg. 22.60 *(978-0-8239-6866-4(9),* Editorial Buenas Letras) Rosen Publishing Group, Inc., The.

—El puente Akashi Kaikyo: El puente más largo del mundo (the Akashi-Kaikyo Bridge: World's Longest Bridge) 2009. (Estructuras extraordinarias (Record-Breaking Structures) Ser.). (SPA.). 24p. (gr. 1-2). 42.50 *(978-1-61512-311-7(3),* Editorial Buenas Letras) Rosen Publishing Group, Inc., The.

Wolny, Philip. High Risk Construction Work: Life Building Skyscrapers, Bridges, & Tunnels. 2008. (Extreme Careers Ser.). (Illus.). 64p. (YA). (gr. 5-9). lib. bdg. 31.95 *(978-1-4042-1789-8(4))* Rosen Publishing Group, Inc., The.

—High-Risk Construction Work: Life Building Skyscrapers, Bridges, & Tunnels. 2009. (Extreme Careers Ser.). 64p. (gr. 5-5). 58.50 *(978-1-61512-397-1(0),* Rosen Reference) Rosen Publishing Group, Inc., The.

Zaunders, Bo. The Great Bridge-Building Contest. Munro, Roxie, illus. 2006. 30p. (J). (gr. 4-8). reprint ed. 17.00 *(978-1-4223-5239-7(0))* DIANE Publishing Co.

BRIDGES—FICTION

Biggs, Brian. Tinyville Town Gets to Work! 2016. (Tinyville Town Ser.). (ENG., Illus.). 32p. (J). (gr. -1-k). 16.95 *(978-1-4197-2133-5(X),* Abrams Appleseed) Abrams, Inc.

Bunting, Eve. Pop's Bridge. Payne, C. F., illus. 2006. (ENG.). 32p. (J). (gr. -1-3). 17.99 *(978-0-15-204773-3(5))* Houghton Mifflin Harcourt Publishing Co.

Christen, Dennis H. Lundon's Bridge & the Three Keys. 2005. (YA). lib. bdg., act. bk. ed. 24.95 *(978-0-9718151-3-1(5))* 2006. (ENG.). (J). per. 12.95 *(978-0-9718151-2-4(7))* C-It Entertainment Group, LLC.

Curtis, Kelli. Amber & the Fallen Bridge. 2009. 32p. pap. 13.00 *(978-1-60860-631-3(7),* Strategic Bk. Publishing) Strategic Book Publishing & Rights Agency (SBPRA).

Dahms, Theresa V. Pookie & the Rainbow Bridge. 2010. 24p. 11.49 *(978-1-4490-7994-9(6))* AuthorHouse.

Darke, J. A. The Screaming Bridge. Evergreen, Nelson, illus. 2015. (Spine Shivers Ser.). (ENG.). 128p. (gr. 3-4). lib. bdg. 26.65 *(978-1-4965-0219-3(1))* Stone Arch Bks.

Fallenstein, J. Graffiti. 2017. (Midnight Ser.). (ENG.). 88p. (YA). (gr. 6-12). 26.65 *(978-1-5124-2767-7(5));* 12.99 ***(978-1-5124-3489-7(2),*** Darby Creek); 39.99 ***(978-1-5124-2787-5(X),*** Darby Creek); 39.99 ***(978-1-5124-3488-0(4),*** Darby Creek) Lerner Publishing Group.

Gaston, Sharon D. Who's Laughing Now? & Don't Burn Your Bridge. 2009. 48p. pap. 19.50 *(978-1-4389-7832-1(4))* AuthorHouse.

Hajdusiewicz, Babs Bell. The Bridge Is Up! Hefferan, Rob, illus. 2006. (J). pap. 7.99 *(978-0-15-365089-5(3))* Houghton Mifflin Harcourt School Pubs.

Harper, Charise Mericle. Go, Go, Go, Stop! 2014. (ENG.). 32p. (J). (-k). 16.99 *(978-0-375-86924-2(7),* Knopf Bks. for Young Readers) Random Hse. Children's Bks.

Harris, Brooke. London Bridge. Boyer, Lyn, illus. 2010. (Rising Readers Ser.). (J). 3.49 *(978-1-60719-702-7(2))* Newmark Learning LLC.

Jolby, illus. Monsters under Bridges. 2013. (ENG.). 32p. (J). (gr. -1-3). 16.99 *(978-1-57061-856-7(9),* Little Bigfoot) Sasquatch Bks.

Kipling, Rudyard. The Bridge Builders. 2005. pap. *(978-1-4065-0310-4(X))* Dodo Pr.

Marsh, Carole. The Ghost of the Golden Gate Bridge. 2009. (Real Kids, Real Places Ser.). (Illus.). 146p. (J). lib. bdg. 18.99 *(978-0-635-07047-0(2),* Marsh, Carole Mysteries) Gallopade International.

May, Melba L. Old Swinging Bridge. 2011. (ENG., Illus.). 30p. (J). pap. 12.95 *(978-1-4327-7229-1(5))* Outskirts Pr., Inc.

McNeal, Laura. The Incident on the Bridge. 2016. (ENG.). 336p. (YA). (gr. 7). 17.99 *(978-0-375-87079-8(2),* Knopf Bks. for Young Readers) Random Hse. Children's Bks.

Sloan, L. Bridges. 2005. 164p. 22.99 *(978-1-58832-123-7(1));* per. 12.99 *(978-1-58832-122-0(3))* Unlimited Publishing LLC.

Strong, B. L. The Troll & His Bridge. 2011. 26p. pap. 12.00 *(978-1-60911-028-4(5),* Eloquent Bks.) Strategic Book Publishing & Rights Agency (SBPRA).

Weston Woods Staff, creator. Little Red Lighthouse & the Great Gray Bridge. 2011. 38.75 *(978-0-439-72751-8(0));* 18.95 *(978-0-439-72750-1(2));* 29.95 *(978-0-439-73487-5(8))* Weston Woods Studios, Inc.

Whelan, Gloria. Mackinac Bridge: The Story of the Five-Mile Poem. van Frankenhuyzen, Gijsbert, illus. 2006. (Tales of Young Americans Ser.). (ENG.). 32p. (J). 17.95 *(978-1-58536-283-7(2))* Sleeping Bear Pr.

BRIDGMAN, LAURA DEWEY, 1829-1889

Alexander, Sally Hobart & Alexander, Robert. She Touched the World: Laura Bridgman, Deaf-Blind Pioneer. 2008. (ENG., Illus.). 112p. (J). (gr. 5-7). 18.99 *(978-0-618-85299-4(9))* Houghton Mifflin Harcourt Publishing Co.

BRIGANDS AND ROBBERS

see Robbers and Outlaws

BRITAIN, BATTLE OF, GREAT BRITAIN, 1940

Allport, Alan. The Battle of Britain. 2012. 128p. (J). 35.00 *(978-1-60413-920-4(X),* Chelsea Hse.) Facts On File, Inc.

Asso, B. & Bergese, F. Cinebook Recounts: Battle of Britain. movie tie-in ed. 2010. (Cinebook Recounts Ser.). (ENG., Illus.). 48p. pap. 11.95 *(978-1-84918-025-2(3))* CineBook GBR. Dist: National Bk. Network.

Asso, Bernard & Bergèse, Francis. Battle of Britain. 2008. (ENG., Illus.). 48p. pap. 11.95 *(978-1-905460-39-7(2))* CineBook GBR. Dist: National Bk. Network.

Barber, Nicola. Churchill & the Battle of Britain: Days of Decision, 1 vol. 2013. (Days of Decision Ser.). (ENG.). 64p. (gr. 7-8). 35.99 *(978-1-4329-7634-7(6));* pap. 10.95 *(978-1-4329-7641-5(9))* Heinemann-Raintree.

Hunter, Nick & Collins UK Staff. Technology in the Battle of Britain. 2016. (ENG.). 56p. (J). (gr. 5-6). pap. 9.95 *(978-0-00-816400-3(2))* HarperCollins Pubs. Ltd. GBR. Dist: Independent Pubs. Group.

BRITISH COLUMBIA

Dyan, Penelope. VanCouver's Song — - a Kid's Guide to Vancouver, Bc, Canada. Weigand, John, photos by. 2013. (Illus.). 34p. pap. 11.95 *(978-1-61477-104-3(9))* Bellissima Publishing, LLC.

Flatt, Lizann. Life in a Forestry Community. 2009. (Learn about Rural Life Ser.). (ENG., Illus.). 32p. (J). (gr. 3-6). pap. *(978-0-7787-5086-4(8));* lib. bdg. *(978-0-7787-5073-4(6))* Crabtree Publishing Co.

Hanna, Dawn. Best Hikes & Walks of Southwestern British Columbia, 1 vol., Vol. 1. 2nd rev. ed. 2006. (ENG., Illus.). 360p. (gr. 4). per. 21.95 *(978-1-55105-455-1(8),* 1551054558) Lone Pine Publishing USA.

Kupperberg, Paul. The Alaska Highway. 2009. (Building America Ser.). (Illus.). 144p. (gr. 5-8). 35.00 *(978-1-60413-074-4(1),* Chelsea Hse.) Facts On File, Inc.

Read, Nicholas. A Bear's Life, 1 vol. McAllister, Ian, photos by. 2017. (My Great Bear Rainforest Ser.). (ENG., Illus.). 32p. (J). (gr. k-3). 19.95 ***(978-1-4598-1270-3(0))*** Orca Bk. Pubs. USA.

—The Great Bear Sea: Exploring the Marine Life of a Pacific Paradise, 1 vol. McAllister, Ian, photos by. 2013. (ENG., Illus.). 128p. (J). (gr. 3-9). pap. 19.95 *(978-1-4598-0019-9(2))* Orca Bk. Pubs. USA.

—Wolf Island, 1 vol. McAllister, Ian, photos by. 2017. (My Great Bear Rainforest Ser.). (ENG., Illus.). 32p. (J). (gr. k-3). 19.95 *(978-1-4598-1264-2(6))* Orca Bk. Pubs. USA.

Roberts, G. Gregory. S Is for Spirit Bear: A British Columbia Alphabet. Doucet, Bob, illus. rev. ed. 2006. (Discover Canada Province by Province Ser.). (ENG.). 40p. (J). (gr. 3-7). 18.95 *(978-1-58536-291-2(3))* Sleeping Bear Pr.

Stevens, Dave. Weirdly Wonderful a to Z: Exotic, Aquatic Creatures from the West Coast of British Columbia, Canada. Stevens, Dave, illus. 2016. (ENG., Illus.). 32p. (J). *(978-0-9950594-0-5(3))* Treewind Publishing.

Vernon, Caitlyn. Nowhere Else on Earth: Standing Tall for the Great Bear Rainforest, 1 vol. 2011. (ENG., Illus.). 136p. (J). (gr. 4-12). pap. 22.95 *(978-1-55469-303-0(9))* Orca Bk. Pubs. USA.

Vickers, Roy Henry & Budd, Robert. Cloudwalker. Vickers, Roy Henry, illus. 2014. (ENG., Illus.). 40p. (J). 19.95 *(978-1-55017-619-3(6))* Harbour Publishing Co., Ltd. CAN. Dist: Midpoint Trade Bks., Inc.

—Hello Humpback! Vickers, Roy Henry, illus. 2017. (ENG., Illus.). 20p. (J). pap. 9.95 ***(978-1-55017-799-2(0))*** Harbour Publishing Co., Ltd. CAN. Dist: Midpoint Trade Bks., Inc.

Vickers, Roy Henry & Budd, Robert. Raven Brings the Light: A Northwest Coast Legend. Vickers, Roy Henry, illus. 2013. (ENG., Illus.). 40p. (J). 19.95 *(978-1-55017-593-6(9))* Harbour Publishing Co., Ltd. CAN. Dist: Midpoint Trade Bks., Inc.

BRITISH COLUMBIA—FICTION

Adams, David J. Good Night Vancouver. Veno, Joe & Rosen, Anne, illus. 2010. (Good Night Our World Ser.). (ENG.). 20p. (J). (gr. k — 1). bds. 9.95 *(978-1-60219-039-9(9))* Good Night Bks.

Amani, Alexander. The Guardians. 2010. 148p. 24.95 *(978-1-4490-8572-8(5));* pap. 16.99 *(978-1-4490-8571-1(7))* AuthorHouse.

Armstrong, Kelley. The Calling. 2012. (Darkness Rising Ser.: Bk. 2). 336p. pap. *(978-1-907410-47-5(3))* Atom Pr.

—The Calling. (Darkness Rising Ser.: 2). (YA). (gr. 8). 2013. 352p. pap. 9.99 *(978-0-06-179706-4(5))* 2012. 336p. 17.99 *(978-0-06-179705-7(7))* HarperCollins Pubs.

—The Rising. 2013. (Darkness Rising Ser.: 3). 416p. (YA). (gr. 8). 17.99 *(978-0-06-179708-8(1))* HarperCollins Pubs.

Asnong, Jocey, illus. Nuptse & Lhotse Go to the Rockies. rev. ed. 2016. (ENG.). 40p. (J). (gr. k-4). 18.00 *(978-1-77160-152-8(3))* Road West Publishing Co.

Baker, Deirdre. Becca at Sea, 1 vol. 2009. (ENG.). 168p. (J). (gr. 3-7). pap. 8.95 *(978-0-88899-738-8(8))* Groundwood Bks. CAN. Dist: Publishers Group West (PGW).

Cameron, Anne. Dreamspeaker. unabr. ed. 2005. (ENG.). 128p. pap. 9.95 *(978-1-55017-364-2(2))* Harbour Publishing Co., Ltd. CAN. Dist: Midpoint Trade Bks., Inc.

Campbell, Nicola I. Grandpa's Girls, 1 vol. LaFave, Kim, illus. 2011. (ENG & SAL.). 32p. (J). (gr. -1-2). 16.95 *(978-1-55498-084-0(4))* Groundwood Bks. CAN. Dist: Publishers Group West (PGW).

Chamberlain, Penny. Chasing the Mooon, 1 vol. 2007. (ENG.). 252p. (J). (gr. 3-8). per. 8.95 *(978-1-55039-157-2(7))* Sono Nis Pr. CAN. Dist: Orca Bk. Pubs. USA.

Chandler, Ann. Kootenay Silver. 2010. (ENG.). 216p. (YA). (gr. 9). pap. 12.99 *(978-1-55488-755-2(0))* Dundurn CAN. Dist: Ingram Publisher Services.

Charles, Norma. Boxcar Kid. 2008. (ENG.). 120p. (YA). (gr. 6-7). pap. 11.99 *(978-1-55002-755-6(7))* Dundurn CAN. Dist: Ingram Publisher Services.

Charles, Rie. A Hole in My Heart. 2014. (ENG.). 160p. (J). pap. 12.99 *(978-1-4597-1052-8(5),* 9781459710528) Dundurn CAN. Dist: Ingram Publisher Services.

Cormack, Kim. Being. 2011. 26p. pap. 12.00 *(978-1-60911-891-4(X),* Eloquent Bks.) Strategic Book Publishing & Rights Agency (SBPRA).

de Bree, Alexander. Casting Dragon, 1 vol. 2010. 94p. pap. 19.95 *(978-1-4512-8691-5(0))* America Star Bks.

de Vries, Maggie. Tale of a Great White Fish: A Sturgeon Story. Benoit, Renné, illus. 2010. (ENG.). 48p. (J). (gr. k-4). pap. 10.95 *(978-1-55365-303-5(3))* Greystone Books Ltd. CAN. Dist: Publishers Group West (PGW).

Fontaine, Nadine. More Than Anything in the World. 2008. 16p. per. 24.95 *(978-1-4241-9870-2(4))* America Star Bks.

Hart, Christine. Best Laid Plans, 1 vol. 2009. (Lorimer SideStreets Ser.). (ENG.). 152p. (YA). (gr. 9-12). 16.95 *(978-1-55277-447-2(3),* 9781552774472); 9.95 *(978-1-55277-446-5(5),* 9781552774465) Lorimer, James & Co., Ltd., Pubs. CAN. Dist: Casemate Pubs. & Bk. Distributors, LLC.

Heneghan, James. Hit Squad. 2004. (Orca Soundings Ser.). 106p. 19.95 *(978-0-7569-4300-4(0))* Perfection Learning Corp.

Horne, Constance. The Tenth Pupil. 2005. (ENG., Illus.). 160p. (J). (gr. 3-9). pap., tchr. ed. 8.95 *(978-0-921870-86-9(8))* Ronsdale Pr. CAN. Dist: Literary Pr. Group of Canada.

Horvath, Polly. Everything on a Waffle. 2008. (Illus.). 154p. (gr. 5-9). 18.00 *(978-0-7569-8776-3(8))* Perfection Learning Corp.

—Everything on a Waffle. 2008. (ENG., Illus.). 176p. (J). (gr. 5-9). pap. 7.99 *(978-0-312-38004-5(6),* 9780312380045) Square Fish.

—Mr. & Mrs. Bunny: Detectives Extraordinaire! Blackall, Sophie, illus. 2012. (ENG.). 256p. (J). (gr. 3-7). 16.99 *(978-0-375-86755-2(4),* Schwartz & Wade Bks.) Random Hse. Children's Bks.

—The Night Garden. 2017. (ENG.). 304p. (J). 16.99 ***(978-0-374-30452-2(1),*** 9780374304522, Farrar, Straus & Giroux (BYR)) Farrar, Straus & Giroux.

Horvath, Polly. One Year in Coal Harbor. 2014. (ENG.). 224p. (J). (gr. 4-7). 7.99 *(978-0-385-38653-1(2),* Yearling) Random Hse. Children's Bks.

Howard, Cheryl Lynne. Captured by Love: A Wild Horse Story Based on Psalm 139. 2011. 48p. pap. 11.00 *(978-1-4567-1822-0(3))* AuthorHouse.

Howse, Jennifer. Les Ours Esprit: Les Animaux du Canada. Karvonen, Tanjah, tr. from ENG. 2011. (FRE.). 24p. (gr. 3-6). *(978-1-77071-415-1(4))* Weigl Educational Pubs. Ltd.

Johnson, E. Pauline. The Lost Island. Matsoureff, Atanas, illus. 2004. (ENG.). 40p. (J). (gr. -1-3). 16.95 *(978-1-894965-07-1(8))* Simply Read Bks. CAN. Dist: Ingram Publisher Services.

Juby, Susan. Alice MacLeod, Realist at Last. 2005. 320p. (J). (ENG.). 15.99 *(978-0-06-051549-2(X));* lib. bdg. 16.89 *(978-0-06-051550-8(3))* HarperCollins Pubs. (HarperTeen).

—Another Kind of Cowboy. 2007. 344p. (YA). lib. bdg. 6.99 *(978-0-06-076521-7(6),* HarperTeen) HarperCollins Pubs.

—Getting the Girl: A Guide to Private Investigation, Surveillance, & Cookery. 2010. (ENG.). 352p. (YA). (gr. 8). pap. 8.99 *(978-0-06-076528-6(3),* HarperTeen) HarperCollins Pubs.

—Miss Smithers. 2004. (Illus.). 336p. (J). 15.99 *(978-0-06-051546-1(5),* HarperTeen) HarperCollins Pubs.

Kent, Gary. Fishing with Gubby. LaFave, Kim, illus. unabr. ed. 2010. (ENG.). 48p. (J). 19.95 *(978-1-55017-497-7(5))* Harbour Publishing Co., Ltd. CAN. Dist: Midpoint Trade Bks., Inc.

Leavitt, Martine. My Book of Life by Angel. 2014. (ENG.). 272p. (YA). (gr. 9-13). pap. 11.99 *(978-1-250-04003-9(5),* 9781250040039) Square Fish.

Maes, Nicholas. Transmigration. 2013. 296p. pap. *(978-1-4596-6404-3(3))* ReadHowYouWant.com, Ltd.

Many Ways to Be a Soldier. 2009. (On My Own History Ser.). (gr. 2-4). pap. 6.95 *(978-0-8225-9021-7(2),* First Avenue Editions) Lerner Publishing Group.

Manzer, Jenny. Save Me, Kurt Cobain. 2016. (ENG.). 272p. (YA). (gr. 7). 17.99 *(978-0-553-52126-9(8),* Delacorte Pr.) Random Hse. Children's Bks.

Marsh, Charis. I Forgot to Tell You: Ballet School Confidential (Large Print 16pt) 2013. 284p. pap. *(978-1-4596-6320-6(9))* ReadHowYouWant.com, Ltd.

—Love You, Hate You. 2011. (Ballet School Confidential Ser.: 1). (ENG.). 213p. (YA). (gr. 9). pap. 12.99 *(978-1-55488-961-7(8),* 9781554889617) Dundurn CAN. Dist: Ingram Publisher Services.

—You're So Sweet: Ballet School Confidential (Large Print 16pt) 2013. 292p. pap. *(978-1-4596-6408-1(6))* ReadHowYouWant.com, Ltd.

Maycock, Dianne. Lucky's Mountain, 1 vol. 2007. (Orca Young Readers Ser.). (ENG.). 112p. (J). (gr. 3-8). per. 6.95 *(978-1-55143-682-1(5))* Orca Bk. Pubs. USA.

McMurchy-Barber, Gina. Reading the Bones. 2008. (Peggy Henderson Adventure Ser.: 1). (ENG.). 152p. (J). (gr. 6). pap. 11.99 *(978-1-55002-732-7(8),* Sandcastle Bks.) Dundurn CAN. Dist: Ingram Publisher Services.

Nielsen, Susin. Dear George Clooney: Please Marry My Mom. 2012. (ENG., Illus.). 232p. (J). (gr. 5-9). 10.95 *(978-1-77049-295-0(X),* Tundra Bks.) Tundra Bks. CAN. Dist: Penguin Random Hse. LLC.

Olsen, Sylvia. Counting on Hope, 1 vol. 2010. (ENG.). 304p. (YA). (gr. 6-12). pap. 14.95 *(978-1-55039-173-2(9))* Sono Nis Pr. CAN. Dist: Orca Bk. Pubs. USA.

Parr, Garnet A. Mosey. 2012. 60p. pap. 31.99 *(978-1-4691-7928-5(8))* Xlibris Corp.

Pearce, Jacqueline. Flood Warning, 1 vol. Franson, Leanne, illus. 2012. (Orca Echoes Ser.). (ENG.). 64p. (J). (gr. 2-3). pap. 6.95 *(978-1-4598-0068-7(0))* Orca Bk. Pubs. USA.

Roberts, Ken. The Thumb in the Box. 2013. 56p. pap. *(978-1-4596-6500-2(7))* ReadHowYouWant.com, Ltd.

—Thumb on a Diamond, 1 vol. Franson, Leanne, illus. 2007. (ENG.). 128p. (J). (gr. 2-5). pap. 7.95 *(978-0-88899-705-0(1))* Groundwood Bks. CAN. Dist: Publishers Group West (PGW).

—Thumb on a Diamond. 2013. 112p. pap. *(978-1-4596-6492-0(2))* ReadHowYouWant.com, Ltd.

Ross, Jeff. The Drop, 1 vol. 2011. (Orca Sports Ser.). (ENG.). 168p. (YA). (gr. 6-10). pap. 9.95 *(978-1-55469-392-4(6))* Orca Bk. Pubs. USA.

Rykken, John. Bloodwood: The Chronicles of Max Mayhem. 2011. 264p. (gr. 10-12). 26.95 *(978-1-4620-0656-4(6));* pap. 16.95 *(978-1-4620-0657-1(4))* iUniverse, Inc.

Sargeant, Glen. Ghost Ship: A y-Files Mystery. 2012. 128p. pap. 19.95 *(978-1-4626-8020-7(8))* America Star Bks.

Schwartz, Ellen. Heart of a Champion. 2016. (ENG.). 272p. (J). (gr. 4-7). 16.99 *(978-1-77049-880-8(X),* Tundra Bks.) Tundra Bks. CAN. Dist: Penguin Random Hse. LLC.

Shaw, Carol Anne. Hannah & the Spindle Whorl. 2010. (ENG., Illus.). 244p. pap. 10.95 *(978-1-55380-103-0(2))* Ronsdale Pr. CAN. Dist: SPD-Small Pr. Distribution.

Silvano, Wendi. Love Is All Around Vancouver. Czernichowska, Joanna, illus. 2016. (ENG.). 32p. (J). (-6). 12.99 *(978-1-4926-2969-6(3),* Sourcebooks Jabberwocky) Sourcebooks, Inc.

Silvey, Diane. Spirit Quest. 2009. (ENG., Illus.). 64p. (J). (gr. 6). pap. 11.99 *(978-1-55002-831-7(6),* Sandcastle Bks.) Dundurn CAN. Dist: Ingram Publisher Services.

Spalding, Andrea. An Island of My Own. 2008. (ENG., Illus.). 112p. (YA). (gr. 8-12). pap. 11.99 *(978-1-55002-635-1(6),* Sandcastle Bks.) Dundurn CAN. Dist: Ingram Publisher Services.

Stewart, Elizabeth. The Lynching of Louie Sam. 2012. (ENG., Illus.). 288p. (YA). (gr. 6-10). 21.95 *(978-1-55451-439-7(8),* 9781554514397); pap. 12.95 *(978-1-55451-438-0(X),* 9781554514380) Annick Pr., Ltd. CAN. Dist: Publishers Group West (PGW).

Tullson, Diane. Sea Change, 1 vol. 2010. (Orca Soundings Ser.). (ENG.). 128p. (YA). (gr. 8-12). pap. 9.95 *(978-1-55469-332-0(2))* Orca Bk. Pubs. USA.

Walsh, Ann. By the Skin of His Teeth: A Barkerville Mystery. 2006. (Barkerville Mystery Ser.: 3). (ENG.). 168p. (J). (gr. 4-7). pap. 10.99 *(978-1-55002-634-4(8))* Dundurn CAN. Dist: Ingram Publisher Services.

—The Doctor's Apprentice. 2005. 160p. (YA). (gr. 3-8). pap., tchr. ed. 8.95 *(978-0-88878-389-9(2))* Beach Holme Pubs., Ltd. CAN. Dist: Literary Pr. Group of Canada.

—The Doctor's Apprentice: A Barkerville Mystery. 2007. (Barkerville Mystery Ser.: 2). (ENG.). 160p. (J). pap. 9.99 *(978-1-55002-633-7(X),* Sandcastle Bks.) Dundurn CAN. Dist: Ingram Publisher Services.

—The Ghost of Soda Creek. 2009. (ENG.). 176p. (J). pap. 11.99 *(978-1-55002-830-0(8),* Sandcastle Bks.) Dundurn CAN. Dist: Ingram Publisher Services.

—Moses, Me, & Murder: A Barkerville Mystery. 2nd ed. 2013. (Barkerville Mystery Ser.: 1). (ENG., Illus.). 112p. (J). pap. 10.99 *(978-1-4597-0967-6(5))* Dundurn CAN. Dist: Ingram Publisher Services.

—Shabash! 2nd ed. 2008. (ENG.). 112p. (J). (gr. 4-8). pap. 11.99 *(978-1-55002-829-4(4),* Sandcastle Bks.) Dundurn CAN. Dist: Ingram Publisher Services.

Wilson, John. Red Goodwin. 2006. (ENG., Illus.). 170p. (J). per. *(978-1-55380-034-7(6))* Ronsdale Pr.

Winters, Kari-Lynn. On My Walk, 1 vol. Leist, Christina, illus. 2010. (ENG.). 32p. (J). (gr. k-1). 16.95 *(978-1-896580-61-6(0))* Tradewind Bks. CAN. Dist: Orca Bk. Pubs. USA.

Wishinsky, Frieda. A Whale Tale. Griffiths, Dean & Owlkids Books Inc. Staff, illus. 2008. (Canadian Flyer Adventures Ser.: 8). (ENG.). 96p. (J). (gr. 1-4). pap. 7.95 *(978-1-897349-17-5(3),* Maple Tree Pr.) Owlkids Bks. Inc. CAN. Dist: Publishers Group West (PGW).

Woodson, Marion. Charlotte's Vow. 2006. (ENG.). 144p. (J). (gr. 4). pap., tchr. ed. 8.95 *(978-0-88878-413-1(9))* Dundurn CAN. Dist: Ingram Publisher Services.

Wright, L. R. Prized Possessions. 2017. (ENG.). 288p. pap. 14.95 *(978-1-937384-98-2(5))* Felony & Mayhem, LLC.

Yee, Paul. The Bone Collector's Son, 1 vol. 2012. (ENG., Illus.). 175p. (YA). (gr. 6-8). pap. 12.95 *(978-1-896580-50-0(5))* Tradewind Bks. CAN. Dist: Orca Bk. Pubs. USA.

BRITISH EMPIRE

see Great Britain—Colonies

BRITISH GUIANA

see Guyana

BRITISH—UNITED STATES

Alvarez, Pilar. New Jobs, New Opportunities: British Immigrants Arrive in America (1830s-1890s), 01 vols., 1. 2016. (Spotlight on Immigration & Migration Ser.). (ENG., Illus.). 24p. (J). pap. 10.00 *(978-1-5081-4090-0(1),* PowerKids Pr.) Rosen Publishing Group, Inc., The.

Thornton, Jeremy. New Industries, New Jobs: British Immigrants Come to America (1830s-1890s) 2004. (Primary Sources of Immigration & Migration Ser.). (Illus.). 24p. (ENG.). (gr. 4-8). pap. 9.40 *(978-0-8239-8958-4(5),* Rosen Classroom); (J). lib. bdg. 22.60 *(978-0-8239-6832-9(4),* PowerKids Pr.) Rosen Publishing Group, Inc., The.

BRITTANY (FRANCE)—FICTION

LaFevers, Robin. Dark Triumph. (His Fair Assassin Ser.: 2). (ENG.). 400p. (YA). (gr. 9). 2014. pap. 9.99 *(978-0-544-22720-0(4),* HMH Books For Young Readers) 2013. 17.99 *(978-0-547-62838-7(2))* Houghton Mifflin Harcourt Publishing Co.

—Dark Triumph, 10 vols. 2013. (His Fair Assassin Ser.: 2). (YA). *(978-1-4640-2397-2(2))* Recorded Bks., Inc.

—Grave Mercy. 2012. (His Fair Assassin Ser.: 1). (ENG., Illus.). 560p. (YA). (gr. 9). 17.99 *(978-0-547-62834-9(X))* Houghton Mifflin Harcourt Publishing Co.

—Grave Mercy, 10 vols. 2012. (His Fair Assassin Trilogy: Bk. 1). (YA). 132.75 *(978-1-4640-2388-0(3));* 287.75 *(978-1-4640-2386-6(7));* 130.75 *(978-1-4640-2390-3(5));* 130.75 *(978-1-4640-2387-3(5))* Recorded Bks., Inc.

—Mortal Heart. 2014. (His Fair Assassin Ser.: 3). (ENG.). 464p. (YA). (gr. 9). 17.99 *(978-0-547-62840-0(4),* HMH Books For Young Readers) Houghton Mifflin Harcourt Publishing Co.

BROADCASTING

see also Radio Broadcasting; Television Broadcasting

Aaseng, Nathan. Business Builders in Broadcasting. 2005. (Business Builders Ser.: Vol. 8). (Illus.). 160p. (J). (gr. 5-18). lib. bdg. 24.95 *(978-1-881508-83-0(8))* Oliver Pr., Inc.

Radio & Television. 2nd rev. ed. 2007. (What Can I Do Now? Ser.). 176p. (YA). (gr. 7-12). 32.95 *(978-0-8160-6032-0(0))* Facts On File, Inc.

Robinson, Tom. Media Ownership, 1 vol. 2009. (Essential Viewpoints Set 4 Ser.). (ENG., Illus.). 112p. (J). (gr. 6-12). lib. bdg. 35.64 *(978-1-60453-534-1(2))* ABDO Publishing Co.

Sawyer, Sarah. Career Building Through Podcasting. (Digital Career Building Ser.). 64p. 2009. (gr. 6-6). 58.50 *(978-1-61512-170-0(6))* 2007. (Illus.). (YA). (gr. 7-12). lib.

bdg. 31.95 *(978-1-4042-1944-1(7))* Rosen Publishing Group, Inc., The.

BROCK, ISAAC, SIR, 1769-1812

Fryer, Mary Beacock. Bold, Brave, & Born to Lead: Major General Isaac Brock & the Canadas. 2004. (ENG., Illus.). 264p. (YA). pap. 9.99 *(978-1-55002-501-9(5))* Dundurn CAN. Dist: Ingram Publisher Services.

BRONTE, CHARLOTTE, 1816-1855

Bloom, Harold. Charlotte Brontë's Jane Eyre. annot. ed. 2007. (Bloom's Guides). 100p. (YA). (gr. 9-12). lib. bdg. 30.00 *(978-0-7910-9362-7(X))* Facts On File, Inc.

Brontë, Charlotte. Charlotte Brontë's Jane Eyre. Bloom, Harold, ed. 2nd rev. ed. 2006. (Bloom's Modern Critical Interpretations Ser.). 235p. (C). (gr. 9-18). lib. bdg. 45.00 *(978-0-7910-9304-7(2),* Chelsea Hse.) Facts On File, Inc.

Castor, Harriet & Collins UK Staff. Charlotte Bronte. 2016. (ENG.). 80p. (J). (gr. 5-6). pap. 9.95 *(978-0-00-816405-8(3))* HarperCollins Pubs. Ltd. GBR. Dist: Independent Pubs. Group.

Manning, Mick & Granström, Brita. The Brontës: Children of the Moors. 2016. (ENG., Illus.). 48p. (J). (gr. 2-17). 16.99 *(978-1-4451-4731-4(9),* Franklin Watts) Hachette Children's Group GBR. Dist: Hachette Bk. Group.

Pasachoff, Naomi. Reading & Interpreting the Works of the Brontë Sisters. 2017. (Lit Crit Guides). 160p. (J). (gr. 8-8). lib. bdg. 39.93 ***(978-0-7660-8949-5(5))*** Enslow Pubs., Inc.

Pasachoff, Naomi E. A Student's Guide to the Brontë Sisters. 2009. (Understanding Literature Ser.). (Illus.). 160p. (YA). (gr. 9-12). lib. bdg. 29.27 *(978-0-7660-3267-5(1))* Enslow Pubs., Inc.

Reef, Catherine. The Brontë Sisters: The Brief Lives of Charlotte, Emily, & Anne. (ENG., Illus.). 240p. (J). (gr. 5-7). 2015. pap. 9.99 *(978-0-544-45590-0(8),* HMH Books For Young Readers) 2012. 18.99 *(978-0-547-57966-5(7))* Houghton Mifflin Harcourt Publishing Co.

Saddleback Educational Publishing Staff, ed. Jane Eyre. 2011. (Timeless Classics Ser.). (ENG.). 48p. (YA). (gr. 9-12). pupil's gde. ed. 19.95 incl. cd-rom *(978-1-61651-139-5(7))* Saddleback Educational Publishing, Inc.

BRONTE, CHARLOTTE, 1816-1855—FICTION

Frederick, Heather Vogel. Wish You Were Eyre. 2013. (Mother-Daughter Book Club Ser.). (ENG.). 480p. (J). (gr. 4-9). pap. 7.99 *(978-1-4424-3065-5(6),* Simon & Schuster Bks. For Young Readers) Simon & Schuster Bks. For Young Readers.

MacColl, Michaela. Always Emily. (ENG.). (YA). (gr. 7-12). 2015. 304p. pap. 9.99 *(978-1-4521-4130-5(4))* 2014. 282p. 16.99 *(978-1-4521-1174-2(X))* Chronicle Bks. LLC.

BRONTE, EMILY, 1818-1848

Lacey, Saskia. The Prehistoric Masters of Literature: Discover Literary History with a Prehistoric Twist! 2016. (Jurassic Classics Ser.). (ENG., Illus.). 40p. (J). (gr. 2-6). 14.95 *(978-1-63322-098-0(2))* Quarto Publishing Group USA.

Manning, Mick & Granström, Brita. The Brontës: Children of the Moors. 2016. (ENG., Illus.). 48p. (J). (gr. 2-17). 16.99 *(978-1-4451-4731-4(9),* Franklin Watts) Hachette Children's Group GBR. Dist: Hachette Bk. Group.

Pasachoff, Naomi. Reading & Interpreting the Works of the Brontë Sisters. 2017. (Lit Crit Guides). 160p. (J). (gr. 8-8). lib. bdg. 39.93 ***(978-0-7660-8949-5(5))*** Enslow Pubs., Inc.

Pasachoff, Naomi E. A Student's Guide to the Brontë Sisters. 2009. (Understanding Literature Ser.). (Illus.). 160p. (YA). (gr. 9-12). lib. bdg. 29.27 *(978-0-7660-3267-5(1))* Enslow Pubs., Inc.

BRONZE AGE

Butterfield, Moira. Bronze Age. 2017. (Britain in the Past Ser.). (ENG., Illus.). 32p. (J). (gr. 4-6). pap. 12.99 ***(978-1-4451-4059-9(4),*** Franklin Watts) Hachette Children's Group GBR. Dist: Hachette Bk. Group.

Claybourne, Anna & Collins UK Staff. Time-Traveller's Guide to the Bronze Age. 2016. (ENG.). 56p. (J). (gr. 4-5). pap. 9.95 *(978-0-00-816396-9(0))* HarperCollins Pubs. Ltd. GBR. Dist: Independent Pubs. Group.

Green, Jen. The Stone Age & Bronze Age. 2016. (Discover Through Craft Ser.). (ENG., Illus.). 32p. (J). (gr. 1-3). pap. 12.99 *(978-1-4451-3746-9(1),* Franklin Watts) Hachette Children's Group GBR. Dist: Hachette Bk. Group.

Hagler, Gina. The Technology of Ancient India. 2016. (Spotlight on the Rise & Fall of Ancient Civilizations Ser.). 48p. (YA). (gr. 6-6). pap. 11.75 *(978-1-4777-8942-1(1))* Rosen Publishing Group, Inc., The.

Newland, Sonya. Stone, Bronze & Iron Ages. 2017. (Explore! Ser.). (ENG., Illus.). 32p. (J). (gr. 4-6). pap. 12.99 ***(978-0-7502-9736-3(0),*** Wayland) Hachette Children's Group GBR. Dist: Hachette Bk. Group.

BRONZE AGE—FICTION

Mirarchi, Anthony J. The King's Challenge. 2007. (Cristo's Chronicles Ser.). (ENG., Illus.). 224p. (YA). (gr. 4-7). pap. *(978-1-933255-32-3(3))* DNA Pr.

Paver, Michelle. The Burning Shadow. 2015. (Gods & Warriors Ser.: 2). (ENG.). 320p. (J). (gr. 5). 7.99 *(978-0-14-242285-4(1),* Puffin Books) Penguin Young Readers Group.

—Gods & Warriors. (Gods & Warriors Ser.: 1). (ENG.). 336p. (J). (gr. 5). 2013. pap. 8.99 *(978-0-14-242284-7(3))* 2012. E-Book *(978-1-101-59197-0(8))* Penguin Young Readers Group. (Puffin Books).

—Warrior Bronze. 2017. (Gods & Warriors Ser.). (ENG.). 272p. (J). (gr. 3-7). 16.99 *(978-0-8037-3884-3(6),* Dial Bks) Penguin Young Readers Group.

Smith, Icy. Mystery of the Giant Mask of Sanxingdui. Roski, Gayle Garner, illus. 2015. (J). *(978-0-9913454-8-9(7))* East West Discovery Pr.

BROOKLYN (NEW YORK, N.Y.)

Fernandez, Rajiv. Baby to Brooklyn. 2017. (ENG., Illus.). 32p. (J). (— 1). bds. 6.99 *(978-1-57687-785-2(X),* powerHouse Bks.) powerHouse Cultural Entertainment, Inc.

Poluchowicz, Krzysztof. Brooklyn ABC: A Scrapbook of Everyone's Favorite Borough. 2015. (ENG., Illus.). 58p. (J). (gr. 2-5). pap. 14.95 *(978-1-57687-751-7(5),* powerHouse Bks.) powerHouse Cultural Entertainment, Inc.

Zschock, Martha Day. Hello, Brooklyn! 2013. (Hello! Ser.). (ENG., Illus.). 16p. (gr. -1-k). bds. 9.95 *(978-1-938700-20-0(1),* 9781938700200, Commonwealth Editions) Applewood Bks.

BROOKLYN (NEW YORK, N.Y.)—FICTION

Abrahams, Peter. Outlaws of Sherwood Street: Stealing from the Rich. 2013. (ENG.). 320p. (J). (gr. 5). 7.99 *(978-0-14-242438-4(2),* Puffin Books) Penguin Young Readers Group.

Anderson, Josh. Heat on the Street. 2009. (Dream Ser.). (gr. 3-8). pap. 9.95 *(978-1-934713-94-5(5))* Scobre Pr. Corp.

Avi. Catch You Later, Traitor. 2016. (ENG.). 304p. (J). (gr. 3-7). pap. 7.95 *(978-1-61620-587-4(3))* Algonquin Bks. of Chapel Hill.

—Don't You Know There's a War On? 2nd ed. 2003. 208p. (J). pap. *(978-0-439-53096-5(2),* HarperCollins) HarperCollins Pubs.

—Don't You Know There's a War On? 2003. 193p. (gr. 3-7). 18.00 *(978-0-7569-1383-0(7))* Perfection Learning Corp.

Baer, Marianna. The Inconceivable Life of Quinn. 2017. (ENG.). 384p. (YA). 18.95 *(978-1-4197-2302-5(2),* Amulet Bks.) Abrams, Inc.

Blythe, Carolita. Revenge of a Not-So-Pretty Girl. 2013. (ENG.). 336p. (YA). (gr. 7). 19.99 *(978-0-375-99081-6(X),* Delacorte Bks. for Young Readers) Random Hse. Children's Bks.

Bohrer, Maria. Sofia's Stoop Story: 18th Street, Brooklyn: 18th Street, Brooklyn. Fancher, Lou & Johnson, Steve, illus. 2014. 32p. (J). 17.95 *(978-0-9885295-2-6(1))* Blue Marlin Pubns.

Brezenoff, Steve. Brooklyn, Burning. 2011. (Carolrhoda YA Ser.). (ENG.). 208p. (YA). (gr. 9-12). 17.95 *(978-0-7613-7526-5(0),* Carolrhoda Lab™) Lerner Publishing Group.

Christopher, Matt. Fairway Phenom. 2003. (Matt Christopher Sports Bio Bookshelf Ser.). 132p. (J). (gr. 4-7). 12.65 *(978-0-7569-1605-3(4))* Perfection Learning Corp.

Danticat, Edwidge. Behind the Mountains. 2004. (First Person Fiction Ser.). (ENG.). 192p. (J). (gr. 7-10). pap. 6.99 *(978-0-439-37300-5(X),* Orchard Bks.) Scholastic, Inc.

Dee, Barbara. Solving Zoe. 2010. (Mix Ser.). (ENG.). 256p. (J). (gr. 4-8). pap. 7.99 *(978-1-4169-9159-5(X),* Aladdin) Simon & Schuster Children's Publishing.

Estes, Eleanor. The Alley. Ardizzone, Edward, illus. 2003. (ENG.). 288p. (J). (gr. 2-5). pap. 18.95 *(978-0-15-204918-8(5))* Houghton Mifflin Harcourt Publishing Co.

—The Alley. Ardizzone, Edward, illus. 2004. (Odyssey/Harcourt Young Classic Ser.). 283p. 15.95 *(978-0-7569-3475-0(3))* Perfection Learning Corp.

—The Tunnel of Hugsy Goode. Ardizzone, Edward, illus. 2003. (ENG.). 256p. (J). (gr. 2-5). pap. 14.95 *(978-0-15-204916-4(9))* Houghton Mifflin Harcourt Publishing Co.

Farrar, Josh. A Song for Bijou. 2013. (ENG.). 304p. (YA). (gr. 5-8). 16.99 *(978-0-8027-3394-8(8),* 9780802733948, Bloomsbury USA Childrens) Bloomsbury Publishing USA.

Giff, Patricia Reilly. All the Way Home. 2003. (ENG., Illus.). 176p. (J). (gr. 3-7). pap. 7.99 *(978-0-440-41182-6(3),* Yearling) Random Hse. Children's Bks.

—A House of Tailors. 2006. (ENG.). 160p. (J). (gr. 3-7). per. 6.99 *(978-0-440-23800-3(5),* Yearling) Random Hse. Children's Bks.

Gratz, Alan. The Brooklyn Nine. 2010. (ENG.). 320p. (J). (gr. 3-7). 8.99 *(978-0-14-241544-3(8),* Puffin Books) Penguin Young Readers Group.

Greenwald, Lisa. Sweet Treats & Secret Crushes. (ENG.). (YA). (gr. 3-7). 2011. 320p. pap. 7.95 *(978-1-4197-0029-3(4))* 2010. 304p. 16.95 *(978-0-8109-8990-0(5))* Abrams, Inc. (Amulet Bks.).

Griffin, Adele. Loud Awake & Lost. (ENG.). 304p. (YA). (gr. 7). 2015. pap. 9.99 *(978-0-385-75275-6(X),* Ember) 2013. lib. bdg. 19.99 *(978-0-385-75273-2(3),* Knopf Bks. for Young Readers) Random Hse. Children's Bks.

Harris, Loretta. The Inside Struggle. 2007. 30p. (YA). 1.99 *(978-0-9786681-3-6(8))* Triumphant Living Enterprises, Inc.

Hurley, Tonya. Passionaries. 2014. (Blessed Ser.). (ENG., Illus.). 368p. (YA). (gr. 9). 17.99 *(978-1-4424-2954-3(2),* Simon & Schuster Bks. For Young Readers) Simon & Schuster Bks. For Young Readers.

—Precious Blood. Watkins, Abbey, illus. 2013. (Blessed Ser.). (ENG.). 432p. (YA). (gr. 9). pap. 9.99 *(978-1-4424-2952-9(6),* Simon & Schuster Bks. For Young Readers) Simon & Schuster Bks. For Young Readers.

Jenkins, Emily. Dangerous Pumpkins. Bliss, Harry, illus. 2012. (Invisible Inkling Ser.: 2). (ENG.). 160p. (J). (gr. 1-5). 14.99 *(978-0-06-180223-2(9))* HarperCollins Pubs.

—Invisible Inkling. Bliss, Harry, illus. (Invisible Inkling Ser.: 1). (ENG.). (J). (gr. 1-5). 2012. 176p. pap. 5.99 *(978-0-06-180222-5(0))* 2011. 160p. 16.99 *(978-0-06-180220-1(4))* HarperCollins Pubs.

—The Whoopie Pie War. Bliss, Harry, illus. 2013. (Invisible Inkling Ser.: 3). (ENG.). 160p. (J). (gr. 1-5). 14.99 *(978-0-06-180226-3(3))* HarperCollins Pubs.

Jordan, Dream. Bad Boy. 2012. (ENG.). 208p. (YA). (gr. 6-11). pap. 17.99 *(978-0-312-54997-8(0),* 9780312549978, St. Martin's Griffin) St. Martin's Pr.

Kravitz, Danny. Tommy Mcknight & the Great Election. 2016. (Presidential Politics Ser.). (ENG.). 96p. (gr. 3-4). lib. bdg. 26.65 *(978-1-4965-2585-7(X),* Connect) Stone Arch Bks.

—Tommy McKnight & the Great Election. 2016. (J). pap. *(978-1-4965-2752-3(6))* Stone Arch Bks.

Lariviere, Sarah. The Bad Kid. 2016. (ENG., Illus.). 304p. (J). (gr. 3-7). 16.99 *(978-1-4814-3581-9(7),* Simon & Schuster Bks. For Young Readers) Simon & Schuster Bks. For Young Readers.

Laskin, Pamela L. Getting to Know You. 2003. (YA). 16.95 *(978-0-936389-92-9(3))* Tudor Pubs., Inc.

Lord, Bette Bao. In the Year of the Boar & Jackie Robinson. Simont, Marc, illus. 2003. (ENG.). 176p. (J). (gr. 3-7). pap. 6.99 *(978-0-06-440175-3(8))* HarperCollins Pubs.

—In the Year of the Boar & Jackie Robinson. 2009. 8.32 *(978-0-7848-0826-9(0),* Everbind) Marco Bk. Co.

—In the Year of the Boar & Jackie Robinson. (J). 2008. 67.75 *(978-1-4281-8016-1(8))* 2004. 46.75 *(978-1-4025-9147-1(0))* Recorded Bks., Inc.

—In the Year of the Boar & Jackie Robinson. 2003. (J). (gr. 3-6). 16.00 *(978-0-8085-7599-3(6),* Turtleback) Turtleback Bks.

Maldonado, Torrey. Secret Saturdays. 2012. (ENG.). 208p. (YA). (gr. 7-18). 7.99 *(978-0-14-241747-8(5),* Puffin Books) Penguin Young Readers Group.

—Secret Saturdays. 2012. lib. bdg. 18.40 *(978-0-606-23645-4(7),* Turtleback) Turtleback Bks.

Margolis, Leslie. Girl's Best Friend. (Maggie Brooklyn Mystery Ser.). (ENG.). (YA). (gr. 3-12). 2011. 288p. pap. 7.99 *(978-1-59990-690-4(2),* 9781599906904) 2010. 272p. 14.99 *(978-1-59990-525-9(6),* 9781599905259) Bloomsbury Publishing USA. (Bloomsbury USA Childrens).

McCann, Thomas P. "Tom". The Tree Nobody Wanted: A Christmas Story. 2007. 14.95 *(978-0-9797407-0-1(3))* Exeter Pr.

McSween, Michele. Gordon & Li Li Count in Mandarin. Nam, Doan, illus. 2010. 32p. 9.99 *(978-0-9820881-3-5(2))* McWong Ink.

—Gordon & Li Li Learn Animals in Mandarin. Nam, Doan, illus. 2010. 32p. 9.99 *(978-0-9820881-2-8(4))* McWong Ink.

Nemec, Thomas F., creator. Owenopolis: A New Childrens Book, Created by Thomas Nemec-N. Y. C. 2007. (J). lib. bdg. 15.00 *(978-0-9791612-0-9(7))* Goon Dog Publishing.

Park, Linda Sue. Keeping Score. 2010. (ENG.). 224p. (J). (gr. 2-5). pap. 7.99 *(978-0-547-24897-4(0))* Houghton Mifflin Harcourt Publishing Co.

Pinkwater, Daniel M. Beautiful Yetta: The Yiddish Chicken. Pinkwater, Jill, illus. 2010. (ENG.). 32p. (J). (gr. -1-2). 17.99 *(978-0-312-55824-6(4),* 9780312558246) Feiwel & Friends.

Reynolds, Jason. The Boy in the Black Suit. 2015. (ENG., Illus.). 272p. (YA). (gr. 7). 17.99 *(978-1-4424-5950-2(6))* Simon & Schuster Children's Publishing.

—The Boy in the Black Suit. 2016. (ENG.). (J). lib. bdg. 22.10 *(978-0-606-38272-4(0))* Turtleback Bks.

Rush, Ken. The Seltzer Man. 2013. (ENG., Illus.). 32p. (J). (gr. -1-3). 16.99 *(978-1-4814-0149-4(1),* Simon & Schuster Bks. For Young Readers) Simon & Schuster Bks. For Young Readers.

Sayre, Justin & dePaola, Tomie. Husky. 2015. (ENG.). 272p. (YA). (gr. 5). bds. 16.99 *(978-0-448-48413-6(7),* Grosset & Dunlap) Penguin Young Readers Group.

Scieszka, Jon. Spaceheadz. Prigmore, Shane, illus. (Spaceheadz Ser.: 3). (ENG.). (J). (gr. 2-5). 2012. 224p. pap. 7.99 *(978-1-4169-7956-2(5))* 2011. 224p. 15.99 *(978-1-4169-7955-5(7))*Set. 2013. 864p. pap. 23.99 *(978-1-4424-9858-7(7))* Simon & Schuster Bks. For Young Readers. (Simon & Schuster Bks. For Young Readers).

—SPHDZ 4 Life! Prigmore, Shane, illus. 2013. (Spaceheadz Ser.: 4). (ENG.). 192p. (J). (gr. 2-5). pap. 5.99 *(978-1-4169-7958-6(1))*;Bk. 4. 16.99 *(978-1-4169-7957-9(3))* Simon & Schuster Bks. For Young Readers. (Simon & Schuster Bks. For Young Readers).

—SPHDZ Book #1! Prigmore, Shane, illus. 2011. (Spaceheadz Ser.: 1). (ENG.). 192p. (J). (gr. 2-5). pap. 7.99 *(978-1-4424-1986-5(5),* Simon & Schuster Bks. For Young Readers) Simon & Schuster Bks. For Young Readers.

—SPHDZ Book #2! Prigmore, Shane, illus. (Spaceheadz Ser.: 2). (ENG.). (J). (gr. 2-5). 2011. 256p. pap. 7.99 *(978-1-4169-7954-8(9))* 2010. 240p. 14.99 *(978-1-4169-7953-1(0))* Simon & Schuster Bks. For Young Readers. (Simon & Schuster Bks. For Young Readers).

Shalant, Phyllis. When Pirates Came to Brooklyn. 2010. 224p. pap. 14.95 *(978-1-4401-8338-6(4))* iUniverse, Inc.

Sheldon, Dyan. I Conquer Britain. 2007. (ENG., Illus.). 208p. (YA). (gr. 7). 15.99 *(978-0-7636-3300-4(3))* Candlewick Pr.

—Sophie Pitt-Turnbull Discovers America. 2007. (ENG.). 192p. (YA). (gr. 7-12). per. 7.99 *(978-0-7636-3295-3(3))* Candlewick Pr.

Shusterman, Neal. Antsy Does Time. 2010. (ENG.). 256p. (J). (gr. 5-18). pap. 6.99 *(978-0-14-241487-3(5),* Puffin Books) Penguin Young Readers Group.

Smallman, Steve. Santa Is Coming to Brooklyn. Dunn, Robert, illus. 2013. (ENG.). 32p. (J). (-3). 9.99 *(978-1-4022-9003-9(9),* Sourcebooks Jabberwocky) Sourcebooks, Inc.

Stead, Rebecca. Liar & Spy. (ENG.). (J). (gr. 3-7). 2013. 208p. 7.99 *(978-0-375-85087-5(2),* Yearling) 2012. 192p. 15.99 *(978-0-385-73743-2(2),* Lamb, Wendy Bks.) Random Hse. Children's Bks.

Sullivan, Maureen. Custard & Mustard: Carlos in Coney Island. Josephs, Alison, illus. 2009. 32p. 17.95 *(978-0-9820381-1-6(9))* MoJo InkWorks.

The Sweetest Heist in History. 2015. (Randi Rhodes, Ninja Detective Ser.: 2). (ENG., Illus.). 224p. (J). (gr. 3-7). 16.99 *(978-1-4424-7684-4(2),* Simon & Schuster Bks. For Young Readers) Simon & Schuster Bks. For Young Readers.

Trigiani, Adriana. Viola in the Spotlight. 2012. (Viola Ser.: 2). (ENG.). 288p. (YA). (gr. 8). pap. 8.99 *(978-0-06-145107-2(X),* HarperTeen) HarperCollins Pubs.

Tyree, Omar R. 12 Brown Boys. 2008. 196p. (J). (gr. 3-7). pap. 9.95 *(978-1-933491-12-7(4))* Just Us Bks., Inc.

Uhlberg, Myron. Dad, Jackie, & Me, 1 vol. Bootman, Colin, illus. 2010. (ENG.). 32p. (J). pap. 8.95 *(978-1-56145-531-7(8))* Peachtree Pubs.

van Diepen, Allison. Street Pharm. 2013. (ENG., Illus.). 320p. (YA). (gr. 8). pap. 10.99 *(978-1-4424-8166-4(8),* Simon Pulse) Simon Pulse.

Wang, Corrie. The Takedown. 2017. (ENG.). 384p. (YA). (gr. 9-17). 17.99 *(978-1-4847-5742-0(4))* Disney Publishing Worldwide.

Welvaert, Scott R. Grotesque. 2015. (Tartan House Ser.). (ENG.). 96p. (J). (gr. 4-12). *(978-1-63235-163-0(3),* 12-Story Library) Pr. Room Editions LLC.

Williams-Garcia, Rita. P. S. Be Eleven. 2015. (ENG.). 304p. (J). (gr. 3-7). pap. 7.99 *(978-0-06-193864-1(5),* Amistad) HarperCollins Pubs.

Wiseman, Eva. The World Outside. 2014. (ENG., Illus.). 236p. (YA). (gr. 7). 19.99 *(978-0-88776-981-8(0),* Tundra Bks.) Tundra Bks. CAN. Dist: Penguin Random Hse. LLC.

Woodson, Jacqueline. From the Notebooks of Melanin Sun. 2011. 9.68 *(978-0-7848-3512-8(8))* 2009. 7.84 *(978-0-7848-2356-9(1))* Marco Bk. Co. (Everbind).

—From the Notebooks of Melanin Sun. 2010. (ENG.). 176p. (J). (gr. 5-18). 7.99 *(978-0-14-241641-9(X),* Puffin Books) Penguin Young Readers Group.

—From the Notebooks of Melanin Sun. 2003. (Point Ser.). (ENG.). 141p. (YA). (gr. 7). 13.65 *(978-0-7807-7292-2(X))* Perfection Learning Corp.

BROOKLYN BRIDGE (NEW YORK, N.Y.)

Mann, Elizabeth. The Brooklyn Bridge: The Story of the World's Most Famous Bridge & the Remarkable Family That Built It. Witschonke, Alan, illus. 2006. (Wonders of the World Book Ser.). (ENG.). 48p. (J). (gr. 4-8). pap. 12.95 *(978-1-931414-16-6(5),* 9781931414166) Mikaya Pr.

Prentzas, G. S. The Brooklyn Bridge. 2009. (Building America Ser.). (Illus.). 144p. (gr. 5-8). 35.00 *(978-1-60413-073-7(3),* Chelsea Hse.) Facts On File, Inc.

Ratliff, Thomas. You Wouldn't Want to Work on the Brooklyn Bridge! An Enormous Project That Seemed Impossible. Bergin, Mark, illus. 2009. (You Wouldn't Want to Ser.). (ENG.). 32p. (J). (gr. 3-18). pap. 9.95 *(978-0-531-20519-8(3))* Scholastic Library Publishing.

Ratliff, Tom. You Wouldn't Want to Work on the Brooklyn Bridge! An Enormous Project That Seemed Impossible. Bergin, Mark, illus. 2009. (You Wouldn't Want to Ser.). (ENG.). 32p. (J). (gr. 3-12). 29.00 *(978-0-531-21328-5(5))* Scholastic Library Publishing.

Stine, Megan & dePaola, Tomie. Where Is the Brooklyn Bridge? Hinderliter, John & Groff, David, illus. 2016. (Where Is? Ser.). (ENG.). 112p. (J). (gr. 3-7). 5.99 *(978-0-448-48424-2(2),* Grosset & Dunlap) Penguin Young Readers Group.

Tieck, Sarah. Brooklyn Bridge, 1 vol. 2008. (All Aboard America Ser.). (ENG.). 24p. (J). (gr. 1-4). 25.65 *(978-1-59928-934-2(2))* ABDO Publishing Co.

Weiner, Vicki. The Brooklyn Bridge: New York City's Graceful Connection. 2004. (High Interest Bks.). (ENG., Illus.). 48p. (J). (gr. 7-12). pap. 6.95 *(978-0-516-25905-5(9),* Children's Pr.) Scholastic Library Publishing.

BROOKLYN BRIDGE (NEW YORK, N.Y.)—FICTION

Bildner, Phil. Twenty-One Elephants. Pham, LeUyen, illus. 2004. (ENG.). 40p. (J). (gr. -1-3). 17.99 *(978-0-689-87011-8(6),* Simon & Schuster Bks. For Young Readers) Simon & Schuster Bks. For Young Readers.

Giff, Patricia Reilly. Water Street. 2008. (ENG.). 176p. (J). (gr. 3-7). 6.99 *(978-0-440-41921-1(2),* Yearling) Random Hse. Children's Bks.

Hurley, Tonya. Passionaries. 2015. (Blessed Ser.). (ENG., Illus.). 368p. (YA). (gr. 9). pap. 12.99 *(978-1-4424-2955-0(0),* Simon & Schuster Bks. For Young Readers) Simon & Schuster Bks. For Young Readers.

Prince, April Jones. Twenty-One Elephants & Still Standing. Roca, François, illus. 2005. (ENG.). 32p. (J). (gr. -1-3). 17.99 *(978-0-618-44887-6(X))* Houghton Mifflin Harcourt Publishing Co.

Uhlberg, Myron. Flying over Brooklyn, 1 vol. Fitzgerald, Gerald, illus. 2003. (ENG.). 32p. (J). (gr. k-3). pap. 7.95 *(978-1-56145-294-1(7))* Peachtree Pubs.

BROTHERS AND SISTERS

Auld, Mary. Mi hermano (My Brother) Coffey, Colleen & Carrillo, Consuelo, trs. from ENG. 2004. (Conoce la Familia Ser.). (SPA., Illus.). 24p. (gr. k-3). lib. bdg. 22.00 *(978-0-8368-3931-9(5),* Gareth Stevens Learning Library) Stevens, Gareth Publishing LLLP.

—My Brother. 2004. (Meet the Family Ser.). (Illus.). 24p. (J). (gr. k-3). 22.00 *(978-0-8368-3924-1(2),* Gareth Stevens Learning Library) Stevens, Gareth Publishing LLLP.

Barber, Nicola. A New Baby Arrives. 2009. (Big Day! Ser.). 24p. (J). (gr. k-2). (ENG., Illus.). pap. 8.25 *(978-1-4358-2898-8(4),* 1291898); lib. bdg. 22.60 *(978-1-4358-2842-1(9))* Rosen Publishing Group, Inc., The. (PowerKids Pr.).

Barber, Ronde & Barber, Tiki. Go Long! 2008. (Barber Game Time Bks.). (ENG.). 160p. (J). (gr. 3-7). 15.99 *(978-1-4169-3619-0(X),* Simon & Schuster/Paula Wiseman Bks.) Simon & Schuster/Paula Wiseman Bks.

Barber, Tiki & Barber, Ronde. By My Brother's Side. Root, Barry, illus. 2004. (ENG.). 32p. (J). (gr. 1-5). 17.99 *(978-0-689-86559-6(7),* Simon & Schuster/Paula Wiseman Bks.) Simon & Schuster/Paula Wiseman Bks.

—Game Day. Root, Barry, illus. 2005. (ENG.). 32p. (J). (gr. k-5). 17.99 *(978-1-4169-0093-1(4),* Simon & Schuster/Paula Wiseman Bks.) Simon & Schuster/Paula Wiseman Bks.

—Kickoff! 2008. (Barber Game Time Bks.). (ENG.). 176p. (J). (gr. 3-7). pap. 7.99 *(978-1-4169-7080-4(0),* Simon & Schuster/Paula Wiseman Bks.) Simon & Schuster/Paula Wiseman Bks.

—Teammates. Root, Barry, illus. 2006. (ENG.). 32p. (J). (gr. 1-5). 16.95 *(978-1-4169-2489-0(2),* Simon & Schuster/Paula Wiseman Bks.) Simon & Schuster/Paula Wiseman Bks.

Berry, Joy. I Love Brothers & Sisters. Regan, Dana, illus. 2010. (Teach Me About Ser.). (ENG.). 20p. (J). (gr. k — 1). pap. 5.99 *(978-1-60577-002-4(7))* Berry, Joy Enterprises.

Bradex, Melissa A. Little Gregory. Crane, Eddie, illus. 2009. 32p. pap. 14.99 *(978-1-4490-3549-5(3))* AuthorHouse.

Crist, James J. & Verdick, Elizabeth. Siblings: You're Stuck with Each Other, So Stick Together. 2010. (Laugh & Learn(r) Ser.). (ENG., Illus.). 112p. (J). (gr. 3-7). pap. 8.95 *(978-1-57542-336-4(7),* 1301018) Free Spirit Publishing, Inc.

Danzig, Dianne. Babies Don't Eat Pizza: A Big Kids' Book about Baby Brothers & Baby Sisters. Tilley, Debbie, illus. 2009. (ENG.). 32p. (J). (gr. -1-k). 16.99 *(978-0-525-47441-8(2),* Dutton Books for Young Readers) Penguin Young Readers Group.

Dwight, Laura. Brothers & Sisters, 1 vol. (ENG., Illus.). 32p. (J). 2012. pap. 7.95 *(978-1-59572-364-2(1))* 2005. (gr. -1-3). 15.95 *(978-1-887734-80-6(5))* Star Bright Bks., Inc.

Dysinger, Stephen. William. Dysinger, Stephen, illus. 2007. (Illus.). 28p. (J). (gr. -1-3). per. 12.99 *(978-1-59879-297-3(0))* Lifevest Publishing, Inc.

Edwards, Dianna. It's Not Easy Being Patou - Book One. 2004. (J). *(978-0-9767756-1-4(1))* Patou Bks., LLC.

—Meet Patou. 2006. (J). pap. 29.95 *(978-0-9767756-0-7(3))* Patou Bks., LLC.

—When Niki Got Sick, Bk. 2. 2004. (J). *(978-0-9767756-2-1(X))* Patou Bks., LLC.

—Why Can't Everything Just Stay the Same? Book Three. 2004. (J). *(978-0-9767756-3-8(8))* Patou Bks., LLC.

Felix, Erica Lynn. Brother & Sisterly Love. 2011. 24p. pap. 24.95 *(978-1-4560-9726-4(1))* America Star Bks.

Ferguson, Addy. What to Do When Your Brother or Sister Is a Bully. 2014. (Stand up: Bullying Prevention Ser.). 24p. (J). (gr. k-3). pap. 49.50 *(978-1-4777-6621-7(9),* PowerKids Pr.) Rosen Publishing Group, Inc., The.

Feuer, Bonnie. I Hear a Red Crayon: A Child's Perspective of Her Brother's Autism. Boemmels, Kayleigh, illus. l.t. ed. 2015. (ENG.). 36p. (gr. 3-12). 19.95 *(978-0-9825468-9-5(0))* Connecticut Pr., The.

Green, Tim. Football Hero. l.t. ed. 2008. (YA). 23.95 *(978-1-4104-1116-7(8))* Thorndike Pr.

Guillain, Charlotte. A New Brother or Sister, 1 vol. 2011. (Growing Up Ser.). (ENG.). 24p. (gr. k-2). 23.32 *(978-1-4329-4803-0(2),* Heinemann Read & Learn) Heinemann-Raintree.

Hale, Natalie. Oh, Brother! Growing up with a Special Needs Sibling. Sternberg, Kate, tr. Sternberg, Kate, illus. 2004. 48p. (J). 14.95 *(978-1-59147-060-1(9));* pap. 9.95 *(978-1-59147-061-8(7))* American Psychological Assn. (Magination Pr.).

Hancock Ms Lsc, Dionna. Where Did My Half-Brother Come From: Book 1 of the Half-Brother/Step-Brother Children's Series. 2012. 28p. pap. 19.99 *(978-1-4634-1244-9(4))* AuthorHouse.

Harper, Hill. Letters to a Young Sister: DeFINE Your Destiny. 2009. (ENG.). 304p. (gr. 12-18). 17.00 *(978-1-59240-459-9(6),* Avery) Penguin Publishing Group.

Harrison, Anne-Marie. Babies Are Noisy: A Book for Big Brothers & Sisters Including Those on the Autism Spectrum. Byrne, Beth, illus. 2013. (ENG.). 40p. (J). 15.95 *(978-1-84905-459-1(2),* 4085) Kingsley, Jessica Pubs. GBR. Dist: Macmillan Distribution Ltd.

Hashey, Heather. I'm A Big Sister. Hashey, Kim, photos by. 2010. (Illus.). 16p. 8.49 *(978-1-4520-6293-8(5))* AuthorHouse.

Hewitt, Sally. Our New Baby. 2009. (J). 28.50 *(978-1-59920-232-7(8))* Black Rabbit Bks.

Jackson, Aariane R. Can You Hear Me Smiling? A Child Grieves a Sister. 2004. (New Child & Family Press Titles Ser.). (Illus.). 40p. (J). pap. 9.95 *(978-0-87868-835-7(8),* 8358, Child & Family Pr.) Child Welfare League of America, Inc.

Jenner, Caryn. My Brother. 2017. (Family World Ser.). (ENG., Illus.). 24p. (J). (gr. 1-3). pap. 9.99 ***(978-1-4451-5220-2(7),*** Franklin Watts) Hachette Children's Group GBR. Dist: Hachette Bk. Group.

Kane, Darlene. Missing Hannah: Based on a True Story of Sudden Infant Death. 2006. 60p. pap. 26.49 *(978-1-4259-0136-3(0))* AuthorHouse.

King Sprools, Wendy. Brothers Are Forever. 2011. 24p. pap. 7.99 *(978-0-88144-122-2(8))* Yorkshire Publishing Group.

Krohn, Katherine E. Everything You Need to Know about Birth Order. 2005. (Need to Know Library). (Illus.). 64p. (YA). (gr. 7-12). 31.95 *(978-0-8239-3228-3(1),* NTBIOR) Rosen Publishing Group, Inc., The.

Laff, Becky. Joseph the Dreamer. Laff, Becky, illus. 2016. (ENG., Illus.). 48p. (J). (gr. k-4). 17.99 *(978-1-4677-7845-9(1),* Blackbirch Pr., Inc.) Lerner Publishing Group.

Langston-George, Rebecca. The Booth Brothers: Drama, Fame, & the Death of President Lincoln. 2017. (Encounter: Narrative Nonfiction Stories Ser.). (ENG.). 112p. (gr. 3-5). lib. bdg. 30.65 ***(978-1-5157-7338-2(8))*** Encounter Bks.

Loewen, Nancy & Skelley, Paula. Siblings, Curfews, & How to Deal: Questions & Answers about Family Life. Mora, Julissa, illus. 2015. (Girl Talk Ser.). (ENG.). 32p. (gr. 3-4). lib. bdg. 27.99 *(978-1-4914-1858-1(3),* Snap Bks.) Capstone Press of Coughlan Cos.

Mally, Sarah, et al. Making Brothers & Sisters Best Friends: How to Fight the Good Fight at Home. 2006. (ENG., Illus.). 272p. pap. 14.00 *(978-0-9719405-0-5(9))* Tomorrow's Forefathers, Inc.

McCormick, Patricia. Just Add One Chinese Sister (p) 2010. pap. 10.95 *(978-1-59078-772-4(2))* Boyds Mills Pr.

McKeon, Tess. Carried in Our Hearts. 2011. 52p. pap. 16.95 *(978-1-4560-8394-6(5))* America Star Bks.

Meyer, D J. Sibling Slam Book. 2005. (ENG., Illus.). 152p. pap. 15.95 *(978-1-890627-52-2(6))* Woodbine Hse.

Meyer, Donald J. & Vadasy, Patricia. Living with a Brother or Sister with Special Needs: A Book for Sibs. 2nd exp. rev. ed. 2003. (ENG., Illus.). 144p. (C). (gr. -1-18). pap. 24.95 *(978-0-295-97547-4(4))* Univ. of Washington Pr.

Mills, Lois. Three Together: Story of the Wright Brothers & Their Sister. Moyers, William, illus. 2011. 160p. 41.95 *(978-1-258-05968-2(1))* Literary Licensing, LLC.

Mullery Jr., Matthew W. Hanging Out with Happy Crackers, Fingers Baloo & Stinky Magoo: One Sunny Morning. 2008. 25p. pap. 24.95 *(978-1-60672-136-0(4))* America Star Bks.

Pacheco, Amanda J. Designer Genes. 2012. 28p. (-18). pap. 24.95 *(978-1-4626-5371-3(5))* America Star Bks.

Page, Robin. Sisters & Brothers: Sibling Relationships in the Animal World. 2012. lib. bdg. 18.40 *(978-0-606-23994-3(4),* Turtleback) Turtleback Bks.

Poulin, Andree. The Magic Clothesline. Arbona, Marion, illus. 2012. 32p. (J). 14.95 *(978-1-4338-1194-4(4));* pap. 9.95 *(978-1-4338-1195-1(2))* American Psychological Assn. (Magination Pr.).

Powell, Jillian. Baby. 2017. (My New Ser.). (ENG., Illus.). 24p. (J). (gr. k-2). pap. 11.99 *(978-0-7502-9484-3(1),* Wayland) Hachette Children's Group GBR. Dist: Hachette Bk. Group.

Raatma, Lucia. Brothers Are Part of a Family. 2017. (Our Families Ser.). (ENG.). 24p. (gr. k-1). lib. bdg. 21.99 ***(978-1-5157-7461-7(9),*** Pebble Bks.) Capstone Press of Coughlan Cos.

Raden, Tammy. Every Time I Want to Play, Brother & Sister Get in My Way. 2010. 24p. pap. 11.49 *(978-1-4490-5454-0(4))* AuthorHouse.

Rice, Earle. The Life & Times of the Brothers Custer: Galloping to Glory. 2008. (Profiles in American History Ser.). (Illus.). 48p. (J). (gr. 4-8). lib. bdg. 29.95 *(978-1-58415-665-9(1))* Mitchell Lane Pubs., Inc.

Rissman, Rebecca. Brothers & Sisters, 1 vol. 2011. (Families Ser.). (ENG., Illus.). 24p. (gr. -1-1). pap. 6.29 *(978-1-4329-4663-0(3));* lib. bdg. 22.65 *(978-1-4329-4655-5(2))* Heinemann-Raintree. (Acorn).

Rogers, Amy B. I Learn from My Brother & Sister. 2016. (Things I Learn Ser.). (Illus.). 24p. (J). (gr. 1-1). pap. 8.25 *(978-1-4994-2339-6(X),* PowerKids Pr.) Rosen Publishing Group, Inc., The.

Rosenberg, Marsha Sarah. Coping When a Brother or Sister Is Autistic. 2005. (Coping Ser.). (Illus.). 192p. (YA). (gr. 7-12). lib. bdg. 34.60 *(978-0-8239-3194-1(3))* Rosen Publishing Group, Inc., The.

—Everything You Need to Know When a Brother or Sister Is Autistic. 2005. (Need to Know Library). (Illus.). 64p. (YA). (gr. 7-12). lib. bdg. 31.95 *(978-0-8239-3123-1(4),* NTAUTI) Rosen Publishing Group, Inc., The.

Rusch, Elizabeth. Ready, Set... Baby! Leng, Qin, illus. 2017. (ENG.). 32p. (J). (gr. -1-3). 17.99 *(978-0-544-47272-3(1),* HMH Books For Young Readers) Houghton Mifflin Harcourt Publishing Co.

Sanschagrin, Joceline. Caillou: The Broken Castle. Brignaud, Pierre, illus. 2nd ed. 2011. (Clubhouse Ser.). (ENG.). 24p. (J). (gr. -1-k). pap. 3.95 *(978-2-89450-764-3(X))* Caillouet, Gerry.

Schaefer, Lola M. Brothers. Saunders-Smith, Gail, ed. rev. ed. 2008. (Families Ser.). (ENG., Illus.). 24p. (gr. k-1). 21.99 *(978-1-4296-1221-0(5));* per. 6.29 *(978-1-4296-1750-5(0))* Capstone Press of Coughlan Cos. (Pebble Bks.).

Sebastian, Emily. My Brothers & Sisters. 2010. (My Family Ser.). (ENG.). 24p. (J). pap. 8.25 *(978-1-4488-1492-3(8));* lib. bdg. 22.60 *(978-1-4488-1463-3(4))* Rosen Publishing Group, Inc., The. (PowerKids Pr.).

—My Brothers & Sisters: MIS Hermanos. 2010. (My Family / Mi Familia Ser.). (SPA & ENG.). 24p. lib. bdg. 22.60 *(978-1-4488-0718-5(2),* Editorial Buenas Letras) Rosen Publishing Group, Inc., The.

Seidler, Tor & Tor, Seidler. Hermanos Bajo Cero. McCarty, Peter, illus. 2004. (Punto de Encuentro (Editorial Everest) Ser.).Tr. of Brothers Below Zero. (SPA.). 118p. (J). (gr. 5-12). pap., pap. 11.99 *(978-84-241-8076-8(3))* Everest Editora ESP. Dist: Lectorum Pubns., Inc.

Sévigny, Eric, illus. Show & Tell. 2012. (Clubhouse Ser.). (ENG.). 24p. (J). (gr. -1-1). pap. 3.99 *(978-2-89450-946-3(4))* Caillouet, Gerry.

Shanta, N. D. He's My Brother. 2006. 24p. (J). 19.95 *(978-1-58909-380-5(1))* Bookstand Publishing.

Sheldon, Annette. Big Brother Now: A Story about Me & Our New Baby. Maizel, Karen, illus. 2008. 32p. (J). (gr. -1-1). 14.95 *(978-1-4338-0381-9(X));* pap. 9.95 *(978-1-4338-0382-6(8))* American Psychological Assn. (Magination Pr.).

—Big Sister Now: A Story about Me & Our New Baby. Maizel, Karen, illus. 2005. 32p. (J). (gr. -1-1). per. 9.95 *(978-1-59147-244-5(X));* 14.95 *(978-1-59147-243-8(1))* American Psychological Assn. (Magination Pr.).

Skotko, Brian & Levine, Susan P. Fasten Your Seatbelt: A Crash Course on Down Syndrome for Brothers & Sisters. 2008. (ENG.). 192p. (YA). (gr. 4-9). pap. 18.95 *(978-1-890627-86-7(0))* Woodbine Hse.

Smith, Brendan Powell. Joseph & the Colorful Coat: The Brick Bible for Kids. 2015. (Brick Bible for Kids Ser.). (ENG., Illus.). 32p. (J). (gr. -1-k). 12.99 *(978-1-63220-409-7(6),* Sky Pony Pr.) Skyhorse Publishing Co., Inc.

Smith, L. J. Destiny Rising. 2012. (Vampire Diaries: the Hunters Ser.: 3). (ENG.). 400p. (YA). (gr. 9). 17.99 *(978-0-06-201773-4(X),* HarperTeen) HarperCollins Pubs.

Sutherland, Joe. The Broken Egg: A story to help children cope with the loss of a younger Sibling. 2010. (Illus.). 24p. 11.99 *(978-1-4490-8347-2(1))* AuthorHouse.

Telgemeier, Raina. Sisters. 2014. (ENG., Illus.). 208p. (J). (gr. 3-7). 24.99 *(978-0-545-54059-9(3));* pap. 10.99 *(978-0-545-54060-5(7))* Scholastic, Inc. (Graphix).

—Sisters. 2014. lib. bdg. 22.10 *(978-0-606-36038-8(7))* Turtleback Bks.

Vernick, Audrey. Brothers at Bat: The True Story of an Amazing All-Brother Baseball Team. Salerno, Steven, illus. 2012. (ENG.). 40p. (J). (gr. -1-3). 17.99 *(978-0-547-38557-0(9),* Clarion Bks.) Houghton Mifflin Harcourt Trade & Reference Pubs.

Vitterito, Joseph A., 2nd. My Sister Is a Preemie: A Children's Guide to the NICU Experience. Chuzzlewit, Abraham R., illus. 2012. 30p. (J). (-18). pap. 15.99 *(978-0-9882940-9-7(5))* Bryson Taylor Publishing.

Webb, Jessica. A Simple Wish. 2009. 16p. pap. 10.95 *(978-1-4389-7899-4(5))* AuthorHouse.

Winchester, Elizabeth Siris & Siris-Winchester, Elizabeth. Sisters & Brothers: The Ultimate Guide to Understanding Your Siblings & Yourself. 2008. (Scholastic Choices Ser.). (ENG., Illus.). 112p. (J). (gr. 7-12). 27.00 *(978-0-531-13870-0(4),* Children's Pr.) Scholastic Library Publishing.

Yoon, Salina. Duck, Duck, Porcupine! 2016. (Duck, Duck, Porcupine Book Ser.). (ENG., Illus.). 64p. (J). 9.99 *(978-1-61963-723-8(5),* 9781619637238, Bloomsbury USA Childrens) Bloomsbury Publishing USA.

—Duck, Duck, Porcupine! 2017. (J). lib. bdg. 16.00 ***(978-0-606-40593-5(3))*** Turtleback Bks.

BROTHERS AND SISTERS—FICTION

Abbott, Jacob. Aunt Margaret; or, How John True Kept His Resolutions. 2013. 160p. pap. 19.95 *(978-1-4455-2937-0(8))* Research Pr.

Abdo Publishing. Monster on the Loose, 1 vol. 2013. (Monster on the Loose Ser.: 4). (ENG.). 32p. (J). (gr. -1-4). lib. bdg. 114.00 *(978-1-61641-930-1(X),* Looking Glass Library) Magic Wagon.

ABDO Publishing Company Staff. Hank Zipzer: World's Best Underachiever. 2006. (Hank Zipzer Ser.). (ENG.). 150p. (J). (gr. 3-8). 72.63 *(978-1-59961-101-3(5))* Spotlight.

Abdullah, Shaila. A Manual for Marco: Living, Learning, & Laughing with an Autistic Sibling. Tejpar, Iman, illus. 2015. (J). *(978-1-61599-248-5(0))* Loving Healing Pr., Inc.

Aboitiz, Victoria De & Afraz. Mystery of the Breast. 2012. (ENG., Illus.). 32p. (J). (gr. -1-12). pap. 9.99 *(978-1-905177-31-8(3))* Pinter & Martin Ltd. GBR. Dist: National Bk. Network.

Achatz, Eric. The Adventures of Ryan Alexander: The Great Space Chase. 2010. 52p. pap. 23.50 *(978-1-4269-3763-7(6))* Trafford Publishing.

Ackerman, Helen. Casper's Paper Caper. 2013. 36p. pap. 18.41 *(978-1-4669-7448-7(6))* Trafford Publishing.

Adamchuk, Rachelle G. Disappearance: The First Part of Trickery & Honest Deception. 2006. 169p. pap. 16.99 *(978-1-4120-8991-3(3))* Trafford Publishing.

Adam's Creations Publishing. Enchanted Fairyland: A Sphinx & Trevi Adventure. Bishop, Christina, illus. 2007. (ENG.). 30p. (J). 19.95 *(978-0-9785695-0-1(4))* Adam's Creations Publishing, LLC.

Adams, Jennifer. Edgar & the Tattle-Tale Heart, 1 vol. Stucki, Ron, illus. 2014. (ENG.). 32p. (J). 16.99 *(978-1-4236-3766-0(6))* Gibbs Smith, Publisher.

—Edgar & the Tree House of Usher: Inspired by Edgar Allan Poe's the Fall of the House of Usher, 1 vol. Stucki, Ron, illus. 2016. (ENG.). 22p. (J). bds. 9.99 *(978-1-4236-4493-4(X))* Gibbs Smith, Publisher.

—Edgar & the Treehouse of Usher: A BabyLit First Steps Book, 1 vol. Stucki, Ron, illus. 2015. (ENG.). 32p. (J). 16.99 *(978-1-4236-4043-1(8))* Gibbs Smith, Publisher.

Adams, Lisa. The Twelve Days of Christmas in New York City. Adams, Lisa, illus. 2009. (Twelve Days of Christmas in America Ser.). (ENG., Illus.). 40p. (J). (gr. k-3). 12.95 *(978-1-4027-6440-0(5))* Sterling Publishing Co., Inc.

Adams, Sheila Murphy. Beads, Bands, & a Brass Ring. 2011. 28p. pap. 14.95 *(978-1-4567-1550-2(X))* AuthorHouse.

Adderson, Caroline. Jasper John Dooley: Star of the Week. Clanton, Ben, illus. 2014. (Jasper John Dooley Ser.). (ENG.). 128p. (J). (gr. 2-5). pap. 7.95 *(978-1-77138-119-2(1))* Kids Can Pr., Ltd. CAN. Dist: Hachette Bk. Group.

Adler, David A. Andy & Tamika. Hillenbrand, Will, illus. 2005. (Andy Russell Ser.: 2). (ENG.). 144p. (J). (gr. 1-4). pap. 5.99 *(978-0-15-205446-5(4))* Houghton Mifflin Harcourt Publishing Co.

—Andy & Tamika. Hillenbrand, Will, illus. 2005. (Andy Russell Ser.: Bk. 2). 129p. 16.00 *(978-0-7569-4898-6(3))* Perfection Learning Corp.

Agha-Khan, Aliyar. Cyrus & Kaleo Go Rock Hunting. 2012. 32p. pap. 12.99 *(978-1-4634-1567-9(2))* AuthorHouse.

Ahern, Dianne. Break-in at the Basilica: Adventures with Sister Philomena, Special Agent to the Pope. Larson, Katherine, illus. 2006. (J). *(978-0-9679437-8-7(7))* Aunt Dee's Attic, Inc.

Aikins, Dave, illus. Big Sister Dora! 2005. (Dora the Explorer Ser.). (ENG.). 24p. (J). pap. 3.99 *(978-0-689-87846-6(X),* Simon Spotlight/Nickelodeon) Simon Spotlight/Nickelodeon.

Al Shaikh, Latifa. I'm Still Waiting for that Chocolate. 2007. 52p. (YA). per. 8.95 *(978-0-595-42982-0(3))* iUniverse, Inc.

AlaBee. "When Will My Mommy Come?" World & Cross-Cultural Philosophy. 2007. 164p. per. 12.95 *(978-1-59800-231-7(7))* Outskirts Pr., Inc.

Alarid, Carilyn & Markel, Marilyn. Talks All Day Has the Courage to Speak: Mimbres Children Learn Citizenship. Alarid, Carilyn & Markel, Marilyn, illus. 2006. (Illus.). 125p. (J). pap. 16.95 *(978-0-86534-470-9(1))* Sunstone Pr.

Alarid, Carilyn & Markel, Marilyn, illus. Runs Like the Wind Stops in Her Tracks: Mimbres Children Learn about Trustworthiness. 2016. (J). pap. *(978-1-63293-099-6(4))* Sunstone Pr.

Alborozo. And Then... Alborozo, illus. 2016. (Child's Play Library). (ENG., Illus.). 32p. (J). *(978-1-84643-696-3(6));* pap. *(978-1-84643-695-6(8))* Child's Play International Ltd.

Alcock, Deborah. The King's Service: A Story of the Thirty Years' War. 2008. (YA). *(978-1-894666-06-0(2))* Inheritance Pubns.

Alexander, James W. Good - Better - Best: Classic Treatment of a Christian's Duty to the Poor. 2009. 224p. pap. 17.00 *(978-1-59925-143-1(4))* Solid Ground Christian Bks.

Alexander, Kwame. The Crossover. 2014. (ENG.). (J). (gr. 4-7). E-Book 16.99 *(978-1-306-46985-2(6))* Harcourt Trade Pubs.

—The Crossover. 2014. (ENG.). 240p. (J). (gr. 4-7). 16.99 *(978-0-544-10771-7(3),* HMH Books For Young Readers) Houghton Mifflin Harcourt Publishing Co.

—The Crossover. 2014. lib. bdg. 29.40 *(978-0-606-37975-5(4))* Turtleback Bks.

Alexander, William. Goblin Secrets. (ENG., Illus.). (J). (gr. 3-7). 2013. 256p. pap. 7.99 *(978-1-4424-2727-3(2))* 2012. 240p. 16.99 *(978-1-4424-2726-6(4))* McElderry, Margaret K. Bks. (McElderry, Margaret K. Bks.).

Alfonsi, Alice. Freaked Out. 2004. 148p. (J). lib. bdg. 16.92 *(978-1-4242-0687-2(1))* Fitzgerald Bks.

Alley, R. W. Annabelle at the South Pole. 2016. (ENG., Illus.). 32p. (J). (gr. -1-3). 14.99 *(978-0-547-90704-8(4),* Clarion Bks.) Houghton Mifflin Harcourt Trade & Reference Pubs.

—Clark in the Deep Sea. 2016. (ENG., Illus.). 32p. (J). (gr. -1-3). 14.99 *(978-0-547-90692-8(7))* Houghton Mifflin Harcourt Publishing Co.

—Gretchen over the Beach. 2016. (ENG., Illus.). 32p. (J). (gr. -1-3). 14.99 *(978-0-547-90708-6(7))* Houghton Mifflin Harcourt Publishing Co.

—Mitchell on the Moon. 2016. (ENG., Illus.). 32p. (J). (gr. -1-3). 14.99 *(978-0-547-90703-1(6))* Houghton Mifflin Harcourt Publishing Co.

Alley, R. W., illus. Bratty Brothers & Selfish Sisters: All about Sibling Rivalry. 2007. (Elf-Help Books for Kids Ser.). 28p. (J). (gr. -1-3). per. 7.95 *(978-0-87029-404-4(0))* Abbey Pr.

Alward, Diane. Pedals & Promises: An Adventure Devotional for Kids. 2013. 86p. pap. 9.95 *(978-1-4908-0512-2(5),* WestBow Pr.) Author Solutions, Inc.

Amato, Mary. Sniff a Skunk!, Bk. 3. Jenkins, Ward, illus. 2015. (Good Crooks Ser.: Bk. 3). (ENG.). 128p. (gr. 2-4). 14.99 *(978-1-60684-598-1(5),* Darby Creek) Lerner Publishing Group.

Amery, H. & Cartwright, S. The Tournament. 2004. (First Stories Ser.). 16p. (J). pap. 4.95 *(978-0-7945-0520-2(1));* lib. bdg. 12.95 *(978-1-58086-571-5(2))* EDC Publishing.

Andersen, C. B. The Book of Mormon Sleuth Vol. 3: The Hidden Path. 2003. ix, 214p. (J). pap. *(978-1-57008-988-6(4))* Deseret Bk. Co.

Anderson, Laurie Halse. New Beginnings #13, 13 vols. 2012. (Vet Volunteers Ser.: 13). (ENG.). 192p. (J). (gr. 3-7). 6.99 *(978-0-14-241675-4(4),* Puffin Books) Penguin Young Readers Group.

Anderson, Phil. The Thomas Family Values. 2012. 84p. pap. 13.95 *(978-1-4772-2529-5(3))* AuthorHouse.

Andreae, Giles. I Love You, Baby. Dodd, Emma, illus. 2015. (ENG.). 32p. (J). (gr. -1-k). 15.99 *(978-1-4847-2230-5(2))* Disney Publishing Worldwide.

Andrews, Jerome. The Initiation. 2006. 40p. pap. 8.50 *(978-1-4116-9167-4(9))* Lulu Pr., Inc.

Andrews, Julie. The Little Grey Men: A Story for the Young in Heart. Watkins-Pitchford, Denys, illus. 2004. 304p. (J). 17.89 *(978-0-06-055449-1(5),* Julie Andrews Collection) HarperCollins Pubs.

Andros, Camille. Charlotte the Scientist Is Squished. Farley, Brianne, illus. 2017. (ENG.). 40p. (J). (gr. -1-3). 16.99 *(978-0-544-78583-0(5))* Houghton Mifflin Harcourt Publishing Co.

Anholt, Laurence. Hansel & Gretel & the Space Witch. 2016. (Seriously Silly: Scary Fairy Tales Ser.). (ENG., Illus.). 48p. (J). (gr. k-17). pap. 6.99 *(978-1-4083-2960-3(3),* Orchard Bks.) Hachette Children's Group GBR. Dist: Hachette Bk. Group.

Annie S. Swan. Thankful Rest. 2007. 98p. pap. 16.99 *(978-1-4346-1978-5(8));* (ENG.). 102p. pap. 19.99 *(978-1-4346-1888-7(9))* Creative Media Partners, LLC.

Ant Plays Bear. 9.95 *(978-1-59112-166-4(3))* Live Oak Media.

Antieau, Kim. Broken Moon. 2007. (ENG.). 192p. (YA). (gr. 9-12). 16.99 *(978-1-4169-1767-0(5),* McElderry, Margaret K. Bks.) McElderry, Margaret K. Bks.

Appelt, Kathi. Brand-New Baby Blues. Murphy, Kelly, illus. 2009. (ENG.). 32p. (J). (gr. -1-1). 16.99 *(978-0-06-053233-8(5))* HarperCollins Pubs.

Apted, Violet. Tommy & Jacqui: Laughing with Kookaburras. 2011. 32p. pap. 13.00 *(978-1-61204-118-6(3),* Eloquent Bks.) Strategic Book Publishing & Rights Agency (SBPRA).

Aragón, Carla, et al. Dance of the Eggshells: Baile de los Cascarones. Saville, Kathy Dee, illus. 2010. (SPA & ENG.). 32p. (J). (gr. 1). 18.95 *(978-0-8263-4770-1(3))* Univ. of New Mexico Pr.

Arbuthnott, Gill. Chaos Quest, 1 vol. 2004. (Kelpies Ser.). (ENG.). 192p. 10.00 *(978-0-86315-459-1(X))* Floris Bks. GBR. Dist: SteinerBooks, Inc.

Arcos, Carrie. Out of Reach. (ENG., (YA). (gr. 9). 2013. Illus.). 272p. pap. 9.99 *(978-1-4424-4054-8(6))* 2012. 256p. 16.99 *(978-1-4424-4053-1(8))* Simon Pulse. (Simon Pulse).

—There Will Come a Time. 2014. (ENG., Illus.). 320p. (YA). (gr. 9). 17.99 *(978-1-4424-9585-2(5),* Simon Pulse) Simon Pulse.

Aris, Mary. Bartholomew. 2010. 86p. pap. 36.95 *(978-1-4457-8958-3(2));* pap. 36.50 *(978-1-4457-5351-5(0))* Lulu Pr., Inc.

Arnett, Mindee. Avalon. 2014. (Avalon Ser.: 1). (ENG.). 432p. (YA). (gr. 8). 17.99 *(978-0-06-223559-6(1))* HarperCollins Pubs.

—Polaris. 2015. (Avalon Ser.: 2). (ENG.). 432p. (YA). (gr. 8). 17.99 *(978-0-06-223562-6(1))* HarperCollins Pubs.

Asch, Frank. Gravity Buster: Journal #2 of a Cardboard Genius. Asch, Frank, illus. 2007. (Journals of a Cardboard Genius Ser.). (ENG., Illus.). 144p. (J). (gr. 2-5). 5.95 *(978-1-55453-069-4(5))* Kids Can Pr., Ltd. CAN. Dist: Hachette Bk. Group.

—Gravity Buster: Journal 2 of a Cardboard Genius. Asch, Frank, illus. 2007. (Journals of a Cardboard Genius Ser.). (ENG., Illus.). 144p. (J). (gr. 2-5). 15.95 *(978-1-55453-068-7(7))* Kids Can Pr., Ltd. CAN. Dist: Hachette Bk. Group.

—Star Jumper: Journal of a Cardboard Genius. Asch, Frank, illus. 2006. (ENG., Illus.). 128p. (J). (gr. 2-5). 14.95 *(978-1-55337-886-0(5))* Kids Can Pr., Ltd. CAN. Dist: Hachette Bk. Group.

Ashton, Anna. Molly & Ben. 2007. (Illus.). 76p. per. *(978-1-84401-178-0(X))* Athena Pr.

Atkinson, Elizabeth. Lisa's Totally Unforgettable Winter. 2006. (ENG.). 56p. per. 16.95 *(978-1-4241-6249-9(1))* America Star Bks.

Auerbach, Annie. The Grosse Adventures Vol. 3: Trouble at Twilight Cave, 1 vol. Nicholas, Jamar, illus. 2009. (Tokyopop Ser.). (ENG.). 96p. (gr. 2-6). 25.65 *(978-1-59961-562-2(2))* Spotlight.

Auerbach, Annie & Mike, Norton. Grosse Adventures - The Good, the Bad & the Gassy, Vol. 1. 2006. (Illus.). 96p. pap. 4.99 *(978-1-59816-049-9(4))* TOKYOPOP, Inc.

Austin, Jamie Lea-Elizabeth. Reverie. 2012. 312p. 29.95 *(978-1-4626-6734-5(1))* PublishAmerica, Inc.

Authement, Louise. Diaries of the Fifth Grade Miseries. 2013. 68p. pap. 10.95 *(978-1-4327-9996-0(7))* Outskirts Pr., Inc.

Auxier, Jonathan. The Night Gardener. (ENG.). (YA). (gr. 3-7). 2015. 384p. pap. 8.95 *(978-1-4197-1531-0(3))* 2014. 368p. 16.95 *(978-1-4197-1144-2(X))* Abrams, Inc. (Amulet Bks.).

—The Night Gardener. 2015. (J). lib. bdg. 19.60 *(978-0-606-36891-9(4))* Turtleback Bks.

Avi & Vail, Rachel. Never Mind! 2005. (Twin Novels Ser.). 200p. (gr. 5-9). 16.00 *(978-0-7569-5667-7(6))* Perfection Learning Corp.

Avraham, Kate Aver. What Will You Be, Sara Mee? O'Brien, Anne Sibley, illus. 2010. (ENG.). 32p. (J). (gr. -1-3). 16.95 *(978-1-58089-210-0(8));* pap. 7.95 *(978-1-58089-211-7(6))* Charlesbridge Publishing, Inc.

Ayers, Linda. The Time Bridge Travelers & the Time Travel Station, 3 bks., Bk. 3. Ayers, Ryan, illus. l.t. ed. 2007. (Time Bridge Travelers Ser.: 3). 140p. (J). lib. bdg. 16.95 *(978-0-9786302-8-7(9));* per. 7.95 *(978-0-9786302-7-0(0))* Blue Thistle Pr.

Babee says No. 2006. (YA). spiral bd. *(978-1-59872-479-0(7))* Instant Pub.

Bader, Arlys Elaine. The Adventures of Garth & Cloey. 2008. 40p. pap. 16.99 *(978-1-4389-2472-4(0))* AuthorHouse.

Baghdasaryan, Rouzanna. The Dark. Morchiladze, Manana, illus. 2007. 32p. (J). (ARA & ENG.). pap. 12.95 *(978-1-60195-086-4(1));* (POL & ENG.). pap. 12.95 *(978-1-60195-096-3(9))* International Step by Step Assn.

Bahk, Jane. Juna's Jar. Hoshino, Felicia, illus. 2015. (ENG.). 32p. (J). 17.95 *(978-1-60060-853-7(1),* 9781600000000) Lee & Low Bks., Inc.

Bailey, J. L. Children's Gate. 2005. 292p. 21.95 *(978-1-58939-814-6(9))* Virtualbookworm.com Publishing, Inc.

Bailey, Tressie. The Little Box Kittens meet Santa Claus. 2009. 37p. pap. 24.10 *(978-0-557-03198-6(2))* Lulu Pr., Inc.

Bair, Sheila. Rock, Brock, & the Savings Shock. Gott, Barry, illus. 2006. (Rise & Shine Ser.). (ENG.). 32p. (J). (gr. 1-3). 16.99 *(978-0-8075-7094-4(X))* Whitman, Albert & Co.

Ballantyne, R. M. Silver Lake. 2004. reprint ed. pap. 1.99 *(978-1-4192-4729-3(8));* pap. 19.95 *(978-1-4191-4729-6(3))* Kessinger Publishing, LLC.

Ballantyne, Robert Michael. My Doggie & I. 2007. 120p. pap. 18.99 *(978-1-4346-3682-9(8));* (ENG.). 130p. pap. 19.99 *(978-1-4346-3730-7(1))* Creative Media Partners, LLC.

Banash, Jennifer. Silent Alarm. 2015. (ENG.). 336p. (YA). (gr. 7). bds. 17.99 *(978-0-399-25789-6(6),* G.P. Putnam's Sons Books for Young Readers) Penguin Young Readers Group.

Bankert, Lisa. Operation: Oddball. Meyers, Nancy, illus. 2007. 100p. per. 5.99 *(978-0-9795364-0-3(5))* Chowder Bay Bks.

Banks, Jacqueline Turner & Turner Banks, Jacqueline. Egg-Drop Blues. 2003. (ENG.). 128p. (J). (gr. 5-7). pap. 10.95 *(978-0-618-25080-6(8))* Houghton Mifflin Harcourt Publishing Co.

Banks, Kate. Max's Words. 2011. (J). (gr. k-2). 29.95 (978-0-545-04373-1(5)) Weston Woods Studios, Inc.

Banting, Celia. I only said I was telling the Truth. 2006. 240p. (YA). per. 14.99 (978-0-9786648-4-8(1)) Wighita Pr.

Barber, Tiki & Barber, Ronde. End Zone. 2014. (Barber Game Time Bks.). (ENG., Illus.). 192p. (J). (gr. 3-7). pap. 7.99 (978-1-4169-9098-7(4), Simon & Schuster/Paula Wiseman Bks.) Simon & Schuster/Paula Wiseman Bks.

—Red Zone. 2013. (Barber Game Time Bks.). (ENG., Illus.). 176p. (J). (gr. 3-7). pap. 7.99 (978-1-4169-6861-0(X), Simon & Schuster/Paula Wiseman Bks.) Simon & Schuster/Paula Wiseman Bks.

—Wild Card. (Barber Game Time Bks.). (ENG.). 160p. (J). (gr. 3-7). 2012. pap. 7.99 (978-1-4169-6859-7(8)) 2009. 15.99 (978-1-4169-6858-0(X)) Simon & Schuster/Paula Wiseman Bks. (Simon & Schuster/Paula Wiseman Bks.).

Barbo, Maria S. The Rescue Mission. 2016. (Pokémon Ser.: 1). (ENG.). 32p. (J). (gr. -1-3). pap. 3.99 (978-1-338-11290-0(2)) Scholastic, Inc.

Barclay, Eric. Hiding Phil. 2013. (Illus.). (J). (978-0-545-60456-7(7), Scholastic Pr.) Scholastic, Inc.

Bardhan-Quallen, Sudipta. The Worst Twelve Days of Christmas. Wood, Ryan, illus. 2011. (ENG.). 32p. (J). (gr. k-2). 15.95 (978-1-4197-0033-0(2), Abrams Bks. for Young Readers) Abrams, Inc.

Barnaby, Hannah. Some of the Parts. 2016. (ENG.). 304p. (YA). (gr. 7). 17.99 (978-0-553-53963-9(9), Knopf Bks. for Young Readers) Random Hse. Children's Bks.

Barnaby, Hannah Rodgers. Bad Guy. Yamada, Mike, illus. 2017. (ENG.). 32p. (J). (gr. -1-3). 17.99 (978-1-4814-6010-1(2), Simon & Schuster Bks. For Young Readers) Simon & Schuster Bks. For Young Readers.

Barnacott, Anthony Royce. Permanoids of Chilon. 2009. 260p. 27.99 (978-1-4389-3824-0(1)) AuthorHouse.

Barnes, Derrick. Brand New School, Brave New Ruby. Newton, Vanessa Brantley, illus. 2008. (Ruby & the Booker Boys Ser.: 1). (ENG.). 144p. (J). (gr. 2-5). pap. 5.99 (978-0-545-01760-2(2), Scholastic Paperbacks) Scholastic, Inc.

Barnes, Derrick D. Trivia Queen/Supreme. Newton, Vanessa Brantley, illus. 2008. (Ruby & the Booker Boys Ser.: 2). (ENG.). 144p. (J). (gr. 2-5). pap. 5.99 (978-0-545-01761-9(0)) Scholastic, Inc.

Barnett, Mac. Rules of the House. Myers, Matt, illus. 2016. (ENG.). 48p. (J). (gr. -1-k). 17.99 (978-1-4231-8516-1(1)) Disney Publishing Worldwide.

Barnett, Mac & Klassen, Barnett -. Sam y Leo Cavan un Hoyo. 2014.Tr. of Sam & Dave Dig a Hole. (SPA.). 44p. (gr. 1-3). 21.99 (978-84-261-4091-3(2)) Juventud, Editorial ESP. Dist: Lectorum Pubns., Inc.

Baron Cohen, H. V. The Story of Joe & His Magic Snout: An Operetta of Nursery Fairytales for 2 to 10 years Olds. 2009. 106p. pap. 19.27 (978-1-4251-3582-9(X)) Trafford Publishing.

Barrett, Judi. Cloudy with a Chance of Meatballs. Barrett, Ron, illus. 2011. (Classic Board Bks.). (ENG.). 34p. (J). (gr. -1-k). bds. 7.99 (978-1-4424-3023-5(0), Little Simon) Little Simon.

Barrett, Tracy. The Beast of Blackslope. 2011. (Sherlock Files Ser.: 2). (ENG., Illus.). 192p. (J). (gr. 3-7). pap. 7.99 (978-0-312-65918-9(0), 9780312659189) Square Fish.

—The Case That Time Forgot. 2011. (Sherlock Files Ser.: 3). (ENG., Illus.). 176p. (J). (gr. 3-7). pap. 7.99 (978-0-312-56358-5(2), 9780312563585) Square Fish.

—The Missing Heir. 2012. (Sherlock Files Ser.: 4). (ENG., Illus.). 192p. (J). (gr. 3-7). pap. 8.99 (978-1-250-00480-2(2), 9781250004802) Square Fish.

—The Missing Heir. 2012. (Sherlock Files Ser.: 4). (J). lib. bdg. 19.65 (978-0-606-26131-9(1), Turtleback) Turtleback Bks.

—The 100-Year-Old Secret. 2010. (Sherlock Files Ser.: 1). (ENG., Illus.). 176p. (J). (gr. 3-7). pap. 6.99 (978-0-312-60212-3(X), 9780312602123) Square Fish.

Barrowman, John & Barrowman, Carole E. Bone Quill. 2014. (Hollow Earth Ser.). (ENG., Illus.). 304p. (J). (gr. 3-7). pap. 8.99 (978-1-4424-8929-5(4), Aladdin) Simon & Schuster Children's Publishing.

—Book of Beasts. 2016. (Hollow Earth Ser.). (ENG.). 336p. (J). (gr. 3-7). pap. 7.99 (978-1-4814-4231-2(7), Simon & Schuster/Paula Wiseman Bks.) Simon & Schuster/Paula Wiseman Bks.

—Conjuror. 2016. (Orion Chronicles Ser.). (ENG.). 320p. (YA). (gr. 7). 16.99 (978-1-78185-637-6(0)) Head of Zeus GBR. Dist: Independent Pubs. Group.

Barrows, Annie. Ivy + Bean + Me: A Fill-in-the-Blank Book. Blackall, Sophie, illus. 2014. (ENG.). 104p. (J). (gr. 3-9). 10.99 (978-1-4521-3729-2(3)) Chronicle Bks. LLC.

—The Magic Half. 2008. (ENG.). 224p. (YA). (gr. 3-7). 16.99 (978-1-59990-132-9(3), 9781599901329, Bloomsbury USA Childrens) Bloomsbury Publishing USA.

Barrows, Marjorie. Little Duck. Myers, Marie Honre, illus. 2011. 50p. 35.95 (978-1-258-08897-2(5)) Literary Licensing, LLC.

Bartone, Elisa. Peppe the Lamplighter. Lewin, Ted, illus. 2015. 32p. pap. 7.00 (978-1-61003-612-2(3)) Center for the Collaborative Classroom.

Barwin, Steven. Hurricane Heat, 1 vol. 2013. (Orca Sports Ser.). (ENG.). 176p. (YA). (gr. 6-10). pap. 9.95 (978-1-4598-0213-1(6)) Orca Bk. Pubs. USA.

Basir, A. As Told By: Sofie. 2006. 51p. pap. 16.95 (978-1-4241-2030-7(6)) PublishAmerica, Inc.

Bass, Alexis. What's Broken Between Us. 2015. (ENG.). 304p. (YA). (gr. 9). 17.99 (978-0-06-227535-6(6), HarperTeen) HarperCollins Pubs.

Bass, Ruth. Sarah's Daughter. 2007. 389p. (YA). (gr. 8-12). per. 14.95 (978-0-9774053-4-3(6)) North River Pr. Publishing Corp., The.

Basye, Dale E. Blimpo Vol. 3: The Third Circle of Heck. Dob, Bob, illus. 2011. (Heck Ser.). (ENG.). 464p. (J). (gr. 3-7). pap. 7.99 (978-0-375-85677-8(3), Yearling) Random Hse. Children's Bks.

—Fibble. Dob, Bob, illus. 2012. (Heck Ser.). (ENG.). 384p. (J). (gr. 4-7). pap. 6.99 (978-0-375-85679-2(X), Yearling) Random Hse. Children's Bks.

—Precocia: the Sixth Circle of Heck. Dob, Bob, illus. 2013. (Heck Ser.). (ENG.). 432p. (J). (gr. 3-7). 6.99 (978-0-375-86807-8(0), Yearling) Random Hse. Children's Bks.

—Rapacia. Dob, Bob, illus. 2010. (Heck Ser.). (ENG.). 384p. (J). (gr. 3-7). pap. 6.99 (978-0-375-84078-4(8), Yearling) Random Hse. Children's Bks.

—Snivel: the Fifth Circle of Heck. Dob, Bob, illus. 2013. (Heck Ser.). (ENG.). 448p. (J). (gr. 4-7). 8.99 (978-0-375-86806-1(2), Yearling) Random Hse. Children's Bks.

—Where the Bad Kids Go. Dob, Bob, illus. 2009. (Heck Ser.). (ENG.). 304p. (J). (gr. 3-7). 6.99 (978-0-375-84076-0(1), Yearling) Random Hse. Children's Bks.

—Wise Acres: the Seventh Circle of Heck. Dob, Bob, illus. 2013. (Heck Ser.). (ENG.). 448p. (J). (gr. 4-7). 16.99 (978-0-307-98185-1(1), Random Hse. Bks. for Young Readers) Random Hse. Children's Bks.

Bateman, Anya. The Makeover of James Orville Wickenbee. 2007. 262p. (J). pap. (978-1-59038-707-8(4)) Deseret Bk. Co.

Bates, Sonya. Thunder Creek Ranch, 1 vol. Charko, Kasia, illus. 2013. (Orca Echoes Ser.). (ENG.). 64p. (J). (gr. 2-3). pap. 6.95 (978-1-4598-0112-7(1)) Orca Bk. Pubs. USA.

Batterson, Veronica Randolph. Billy's First Dance. 2010. (J). pap. 9.95 (978-0-7414-5913-8(2)) Infinity Publishing.

Baucom, Ian. Through the Skylight. Gerard, Justin, illus. (ENG.). 400p. (J). (gr. 4-8). 2014. pap. 6.99 (978-1-4424-8167-1(6)) 2013. 17.99 (978-1-4169-1777-9(2)) Simon & Schuster Children's Publishing. (Atheneum Bks. for Young Readers).

Baugh, Ayana Sala. Loopiethotamus, the Chihuahua Who Thinks He Is a Hippopotamus Book: His Journey. 2011. 20p. pap. 14.99 (978-1-4634-3437-3(5)) AuthorHouse.

Baum, Lonna. Monty the Menace: Understanding Differences. Messing, Dave, illus. 2012. (ENG.). 32p. (J). 16.95 (978-0-9839373-0-2(3)) Baum & Baum, LLC.

Baumgart, Klaus. Laura's Secret. Waite, Judy, tr. from GER. 2003. (Illus.). 32p. (J). (gr. -1-2). tchr. ed. 16.95 (978-1-58925-031-4(1)) Tiger Tales.

Bayard, Louis. Lucky Strikes. 2016. (ENG., Illus.). 320p. (YA). 16.99 (978-1-62779-390-2(9), 9781627793902, Holt, Henry & Co. Bks. For Young Readers) Holt, Henry & Co.

—Lucky Strikes. 2017. (YA). lib. bdg. 20.85 **(978-0-606-39951-7(8))** Turtleback Bks.

Bean, Raymond. The Curse of Mars. 2016. (Out of This World Ser.). (ENG., Illus.). 112p. (gr. 2-5). lib. bdg. 32.65 (978-1-4965-3615-0(0)) Out of this World GBR. Dist: Capstone Pub.

—First Family in Space. 2016. (Out of This World Ser.). (ENG., Illus.). 112p. (gr. 2-5). lib. bdg. 32.65 (978-1-4965-3617-4(7)) Out of this World GBR. Dist: Capstone Pub.

—Journey to the Moon. 2016. (Out of This World Ser.). (ENG., Illus.). 112p. (gr. 2-5). lib. bdg. 32.65 (978-1-4965-3616-7(9)) Out of this World GBR. Dist: Capstone Pub.

—Trouble on Venus. 2016. (Out of This World Ser.). (ENG., Illus.). 112p. (gr. 2-5). lib. bdg. 32.65 (978-1-4965-3614-3(2)) Out of this World GBR. Dist: Capstone Pub.

Beardslee, Nellie L. The Glenn's of Newberry Hills. 2008. 164p. pap. 24.95 (978-1-60703-471-1(9)) America Star Bks.

Bearn, Emily. Tumtum & Nutmeg: Adventures Beyond Nutmouse Hall. 2011. (Tumtum & Nutmeg Ser.: 1). (ENG., Illus.). 512p. (J). (gr. 3-7). pap. 10.00 (978-0-316-07574-9(4)) Little, Brown Bks. for Young Readers.

—Tumtum & Nutmeg: the Rose Cottage Adventures. Price, Nick, illus. 2013. (Tumtum & Nutmeg Ser.: 2). (ENG.). 416p. (J). (gr. 3-7). pap. 10.99 (978-0-316-08598-4(7)) Little, Brown Bks. for Young Readers.

Beasley, David R. Canoe Trip. Milner, Elizabeth B., illus. 2006. 129p. (YA). per. 15.00 (978-0-915317-21-9(4)) Davus Publishing.

Beaty, Andrea. Attack of the Fluffy Bunnies. 2012. (Fluffy Bunnies Ser.). (ENG.). 192p. (YA). (gr. 2-8). pap. 7.95 (978-1-4197-0519-9(9), Amulet Bks.) Abrams, Inc.

—Fluffy Bunnies 2: The Schnoz of Doom. Santat, Dan, illus. 2015. (Fluffy Bunnies Ser.). (ENG.). 192p. (J). (gr. 3-7). 12.95 (978-1-4197-1051-3(6), Amulet Bks.) Abrams, Inc.

—Secrets of the Cicada Summer. (ENG.). 176p. (gr. 3-7). 2010. (YA). pap. 6.95 (978-0-8109-8419-6(9)) 2008. (J). 16.95 (978-0-8109-9472-0(0)) Abrams, Inc. (Amulet Bks.).

Beaufrand, M. J. Useless Bay. 2016. (ENG.). 240p. (YA). (gr. 8-17). 17.95 (978-1-4197-2138-0(0), Amulet Bks.) Abrams, Inc.

Beauty of the Broken. 2014. (ENG., Illus.). 368p. (YA). (gr. 9). 17.99 (978-1-4814-0709-0(0), Simon Pulse) Simon Pulse.

Beifus, Ruth. Shlavim Classics 2-in-1 Vol.2: Goodbye to Miri's Mess & Half a Cup of Water. 2009. 32p. 14.99 (978-1-59826-330-5(7)) Feldheim Pubs.

Bell, Jennifer. The Crooked Sixpence. Helquist, Brett, illus. 2017. (Uncommoners Ser.: 1). (ENG.). 320p. (J). (gr. 3-7). 16.99 (978-0-553-49843-1(6), Crown Books For Young Readers) Random Hse. Children's Bks.

Bell, Lisa M. E. I Talked to Mom. 2013. 104p. pap. 9.99 (978-1-60820-873-9(7)) MLR Pr., LLC.

Bellingham, Brenda. Lilly Babysits Her Brother, 1 vol. MacDonald, Clarke, illus. 2013. (Formac First Novels Ser.). (ENG.). 60p. (J). (gr. 2-3). 14.95 (978-1-4595-0286-4(8), 9781459502864); pap. 5.95 (978-1-4595-0287-1(6), 9781459502871) Formac Publishing Co., Ltd. CAN. Dist: Casemate Pubs. & Bk. Distributors, LLC.

Bemis, John Claude. The Nine Pound Hammer. 2010. (Clockwork Dark Ser.: Bk. 1). (ENG.). 384p. (J). (gr. 3-7). pap. 7.99 (978-0-375-85565-8(3), Yearling) Random Hse. Children's Bks.

Benedis-Grab, Daphne. Army Brats. 2017. (ENG.). 240p. (J). (gr. 3-7). 17.99 (978-0-545-93205-9(X), Scholastic Pr.) Scholastic, Inc.

Benenfeld, Rikki. I Go to the Dentist. Rosenfeld, Dina & Leverton, Yossi, eds. Bennenfeld, Rikki, illus. 2011. (Toddler Experience Ser.). (ENG.). 32p. (J). 10.95 (978-1-929628-60-5(9)) Hachai Publishing.

—Let's Go Shopping. Benenfeld, Rikki, illus. 2005. (Toddler Experience Ser.). (Illus.). 24p. (J). 10.95 (978-1-929628-20-9(X)) Hachai Publishing.

—Let's Go to the Park. 2015. (ENG., Illus.). 36p. (J). 10.95 (978-1-929628-82-7(X)) Hachai Publishing.

Bennett, Holly. The Bonemender's Oath, 1 vol. 2006. (Bonemender Ser.: 2). (ENG.). 176p. (YA). (gr. 8-12). per. 9.95 (978-1-55143-443-8(1)) Orca Bk. Pubs. USA.

Bennett, Kelly. Vampire Baby. Meisel, Paul, illus. 2013. (ENG.). 32p. (J). (gr. -1-3). 15.99 (978-0-7636-4691-2(1)) Candlewick Pr.

Bentley, Sue. Moonlight Mischief. 2009. (Magic Kitten Ser.: 5). lib. bdg. 14.75 (978-0-606-06016-5(2), Turtleback) Turtleback Bks.

Berenstain, Jan & Berenstain, Mike. The Berenstain Bears & Mama for Mayor! Berenstain, Jan & Berenstain, Mike, illus. 2012. (I Can Read Level 1 Ser.). (ENG., Illus.). 32p. (J). (gr. k-3). 16.99 (978-0-06-207528-4(4)) HarperCollins Pubs.

—The Berenstain Bears & the Shaggy Little Pony. Berenstain, Jan & Berenstain, Mike, illus. 2011. (I Can Read Level 1 Ser.). (ENG., Illus.). 32p. (J). (gr. k-3). 16.99 (978-0-06-168972-7(6)); pap. 3.99 (978-0-06-057419-2(4)) HarperCollins Pubs.

—The Berenstain Bears & the Tooth Fairy. Berenstain, Jan & Berenstain, Mike, illus. 2012. (Berenstain Bears Ser.). (ENG., Illus.). 24p. (J). (gr. -1-3). pap. 3.99 (978-0-06-207549-9(7), HarperFestival) HarperCollins Pubs.

—The Berenstain Bears at the Aquarium. Berenstain, Jan & Berenstain, Mike, illus. 2012. (I Can Read Level 1 Ser.). (ENG., Illus.). 32p. (J). (gr. k-3). 16.99 (978-0-06-207525-3(X)); pap. 3.99 (978-0-06-207524-6(1)) HarperCollins Pubs.

—The Berenstain Bears' Dinosaur Dig. Berenstain, Jan & Berenstain, Mike, illus. 2012. (Berenstain Bears Ser.). (ENG., Illus.). 24p. (J). (gr. -1-3). pap. 3.99 (978-0-06-207548-2(9), HarperFestival) HarperCollins Pubs.

—The Berenstain Bears' Old-Fashioned Christmas. Berenstain, Jan & Berenstain, Mike, illus. 2012. (Berenstain Bears Ser.). (ENG., Illus.). 32p. (J). (gr. -1-3). 12.99 (978-0-06-057443-7(7)) HarperCollins Pubs.

—Sick Days. Berenstain, Jan & Berenstain, Mike, illus. 2009. (Berenstain Bears Ser.). (ENG., Illus.). 32p. (J). (gr. -1-3). pap. 3.99 (978-0-06-057392-8(9), HarperFestival) HarperCollins Pubs.

—We Love Our Mom! Berenstain, Jan & Berenstain, Mike, illus. 2012. (Berenstain Bears Ser.). (ENG., Illus.). 24p. (J). (gr. -1-3). pap. 3.99 (978-0-06-207547-5(0), HarperFestival) HarperCollins Pubs.

—We Love Trucks! Berenstain, Jan & Berenstain, Mike, illus. 2013. (I Can Read Level 1 Ser.). (ENG., Illus.). 32p. (J). (gr. -1-3). 16.99 (978-0-06-207536-9(5)) HarperCollins Pubs.

Berenstain, Mike. The Berenstain Bears & the Biggest Brag, 1 vol. 2014. (Berenstain Bears/Living Lights Ser.). (ENG.). 24p. (J). pap. 3.99 (978-0-310-73479-6(7)) Zonderkidz.

—The Berenstain Bears' Lemonade Stand. Berenstain, Mike, illus. 2014. (I Can Read Level 1 Ser.). (ENG., Illus.). 32p. (J). (gr. -1-3). 16.99 (978-0-06-207545-1(4)); pap. 3.99 (978-0-06-207544-4(6)) HarperCollins Pubs.

—The Berenstain Bears' Lemonade Stand. 2014. (Berenstain Bears: I Can Read! Ser.). (J). lib. bdg. 13.55 (978-0-606-35072-3(1), Turtleback) Turtleback Bks.

Berenstain, Stan & Berenstain, Jan. The Berenstain Bears Meet Santa Bear (Deluxe Edition) 2016. (First Time Books(R) Ser.). (ENG., Illus.). 32p. (J). (gr. -1-2). pap. 6.99 (978-0-399-55767-5(9), Random Hse. Bks. for Young Readers) Random Hse. Children's Bks.

—The Berenstain Bears Play T-Ball. Berenstain, Stan & Berenstain, Jan, illus. Berenstain, Mike, illus. (I Can Read Level 1 Ser.). (ENG.). 32p. (J). (gr. k-3). 2005. 16.99 (978-0-06-058337-8(1)) 2004. pap. 3.99 (978-0-06-058338-5(X)) HarperCollins Pubs.

—The Berenstain Bears Play T-Ball. 2005. (Berenstain Bears Ser.). (Illus.). 32p. (J). 11.65 (978-0-7569-5228-0(X)) Perfection Learning Corp.

Berenstain, Stan, et al. The Berenstain Bears Go Back to School. Berenstain, Mike, illus. 2009. (Berenstain Bears Ser.). (ENG.). 32p. (J). (gr. -1-3). pap. 6.99 (978-0-06-052675-7(0), HarperFestival) HarperCollins Pubs.

—The Berenstain Bears Storybook Treasury. Berenstain, Stan & Berenstain, Jan, illus. 2012. (Berenstain Bears Ser.). (ENG.). 192p. (J). 11.99 (978-0-06-212014-4(X)) HarperCollins Pubs.

—Do Not Fear, God Is Near, 1 vol. 2013. (I Can Read! / Berenstain Bears / Living Lights Ser.). (ENG.). 32p. (J). pap. 3.99 (978-0-310-72511-4(9)) Zonderkidz.

—God Loves You!, 1 vol. 2008. (Berenstain Bears/Living Lights Ser.). (ENG., Illus.). 32p. (J). pap. 3.99 (978-0-310-71250-3(5)) Zonderkidz.

Bergman, Mara. Snip Snap! What's That? Maland, Nick, illus. 2005. (ENG.). 32p. (J). (gr. -1-3). 16.99 (978-0-06-077754-8(0), Greenwillow Bks.) HarperCollins Pubs.

Bergstrom, Sarah. Desert Dwellers Born by Fire: The First Book in the Paintbrush Saga. 2015. (ENG.). 312p. (YA). (gr. 8-17). pap. 12.95 (978-1-78279-587-2(1), Lodestone Bks.) Hunt, John Publishing Ltd. GBR. Dist: National Bk. Network.

Berlin, Eric. The Puzzling World of Winston Breen. 2009. (Puzzling World of Winston Breen Ser.: 1). (ENG.). 224p. (J). (gr. 3-7). pap. 7.99 (978-0-14-241388-3(7), Puffin Books) Penguin Young Readers Group.

Bernard, Norah S. CLIVE & BRIE. 2006. (YA). per. 8.95 (978-0-615-15932-4(X)) HELORO Publishing Group.

Bernstein, Nina. Magic by the Book, 4 vols. unabr. ed. 2005. (J). 65.75 (978-1-4193-3607-2(X), 42048) Recorded Bks., Inc.

Berry, Lynne. Squid Kid the Magnificent. 2015. (ENG., Illus.). 48p. (J). (gr. -1-k). 16.99 (978-1-4231-6119-6(X)) Disney Pr.

Betancourt, Jeanne. Penny & Pepper. Riley, Kellee, illus. 2011. (Scholastic Reader Level 3 Ser.). (ENG.). 48p. (J). (gr. 1-4). pap. 3.99 (978-0-545-11508-7(6), Cartwheel Bks.) Scholastic, Inc.

Bezek, Lyn. Ribbon the Border Collie: From Herder to Healer. 2008. (J). pap. 11.95 (978-1-932738-51-3(7)) Western Reflections Publishing Co.

Bingham, Laura. Älvor. 2009. pap. 17.99 (978-1-59955-272-9(8)) Cedar Fort, Inc./CFI Distribution.

—Wings of Light. 2011. 240p. pap. 15.99 (978-1-59955-492-1(5), Sweetwater Bks.) Cedar Fort, Inc./CFI Distribution.

Binns, B. A. Pull. 2010. 310p. (YA). (gr. 9-18). 16.95 (978-1-934813-43-0(5)) Westside Bks.

Birdsall, Jeanne. Flora's Very Windy Day. Phelan, Matt, illus. 2013. (ENG.). 32p. (J). (gr. -1-3). pap. 6.99 (978-0-547-99485-7(0)) Houghton Mifflin Harcourt Publishing Co.

Birkett, Georgie, illus. Clean It!/¡A Limpiar! 2009. (Helping Hands English/Spanish Edition Ser.). (ENG & SPA.). 24p. (J). (gr. -1-k). pap. (978-1-84643-569-0(2)) Child's Play International Ltd.

Bitner, Pamela. A Brother-Sister Team. Poppen, Alex, illus. 2008. 16p. pap. 24.95 (978-1-60474-583-2(5)) America Star Bks.

Bitterman, Kevin. BD's Big Hit, 1 vol. 2009. (ENG.). 63p. pap. 19.95 (978-1-60836-366-7(X)) America Star Bks.

Black, Holly. White Cat. (Curse Workers Ser.: 1). (ENG.). (YA). (gr. 9). 2011. 336p. pap. 8.99 (978-1-4169-6397-4(9)) 2010. 320p. 17.99 (978-1-4169-6396-7(0)) McElderry, Margaret K. Bks. (McElderry, Margaret K. Bks.).

Black, Holly & DiTerlizzi, Tony. The Field Guide. DiTerlizzi, Tony, illus. (Spiderwick Chronicles Ser.: 1). (ENG., Illus.). (J). 2013. 128p. (gr. 1-5). 17.99 (978-1-4424-8693-5(7)) 2013. 144p. (gr. 1-5). pap. 7.99 (978-1-4424-8692-8(9)) 2008. 128p. (gr. 2-5). 10.99 (978-1-4169-5017-2(6)) Simon & Schuster Bks. For Young Readers. (Simon & Schuster Bks. For Young Readers).

—The Ironwood Tree. DiTerlizzi, Tony, illus. 2013. (Spiderwick Chronicles Ser.: 4). (ENG., Illus.). (J). (gr. 1-5). 128p. 15.99 (978-1-4424-8702-4(X)); 144p. pap. 7.99 (978-1-4424-8701-7(1)) Simon & Schuster Bks. For Young Readers. (Simon & Schuster Bks. For Young Readers).

—Lucinda's Secret. DiTerlizzi, Tony, illus. 2013. (Spiderwick Chronicles Ser.: 3). (ENG., Illus.). (J). (gr. 1-5). 128p. 15.99 (978-1-4424-8700-0(3)); 144p. pap. 7.99 (978-1-4424-8697-3(X)) Simon & Schuster Bks. For Young Readers. (Simon & Schuster Bks. For Young Readers).

—The Seeing Stone. DiTerlizzi, Tony, illus. (Spiderwick Chronicles Ser.: 2). (ENG., Illus.). (J). (gr. 1-5). 2013. 128p. 15.99 (978-1-4424-8695-9(3)) 2013. 144p. pap. 7.99 (978-1-4424-8694-2(5))Bk. 2. 2nd ed. 2003. 128p. 11.99 (978-0-689-85937-3(6), 53409541) Simon & Schuster Bks. For Young Readers. (Simon & Schuster Bks. For Young Readers).

—The Spiderwick. DiTerlizzi, Tony, illus. 2009. (Spiderwick Chronicles Ser.). (ENG., Illus.). 608p. (J). (gr. 3-7). 29.99 (978-1-4169-8685-0(5), Simon & Schuster Bks. For Young Readers) Simon & Schuster Bks. For Young Readers.

—The Spiderwick Chronicles Set: The Field Guide - The Seeing Stone - Lucinda's Secret - The Ironwood Tree - The Wrath of Mulgrath. DiTerlizzi, Tony, illus. 2013. (Spiderwick Chronicles Ser.). (ENG., Illus.). (J). (gr. 1-5). 752p. pap. 39.99 (978-1-4424-8798-7(4)); 672p. 79.99 (978-1-4424-8797-0(6)) Simon & Schuster Bks. For Young Readers. (Simon & Schuster Bks. For Young Readers).

—The Wrath of Mulgarath. DiTerlizzi, Tony, illus. 2013. (Spiderwick Chronicles Ser.: 5). (ENG., Illus.). (J). (gr. 1-5). 160p. 15.99 (978-1-4424-8704-8(6)); 176p. pap. 7.99 (978-1-4424-8703-1(8)) Simon & Schuster Bks. For Young Readers. (Simon & Schuster Bks. For Young Readers).

—The Wrath of Mulgarath. l.t. ed. 2006. (Spiderwick Chronicles: Bk. 5). (Illus.). 183p. (J). (gr. 3-7). 23.95 (978-0-7862-8579-2(6)) Thorndike Pr.

Blackford, Ami. Quest for the Dragon Stone: A Duncan Family Adventure. Blackford, Ami, illus. 2006. (Illus.). 48p. (J). (gr. 3-7). 16.95 (978-1-60108-008-0(5)) Red Cygnet Pr.

—Quest for the Elfin Elixir: A Duncan Family Adventure Book 2. Blackford, Ami, illus. 2007. (Illus.). 79p. (J). (gr. 3-7). 16.95 (978-1-60108-021-9(2)) Red Cygnet Pr.

Blade, Adam. Chasing Evil. (Chronicles of Avantia Ser.). (ENG.). 176p. (J). (gr. 3-7). 2013. pap. 5.99 (978-0-545-36157-6(5), Scholastic Paperbacks) 2012. 15.99 (978-0-545-36158-3(3), Scholastic Pr.) Scholastic, Inc.

—First Hero. 2012. (Chronicles of Avantia Ser.). (ENG.). 176p. (J). (gr. 3-7). 15.99 (978-0-545-36160-6(5), Scholastic Pr.) Scholastic, Inc.

Blake-Garrett, Andrea. Las Aventuras de Izzy y Juju: Gemelos Detectives Investigadores (G. D. I.) 2012. 28p. pap. 19.99 (978-1-4772-2523-3(4)) AuthorHouse.

Blakemore, Megan Frazer. Good & Gone. 2017. 304p. (YA). (gr. 8). 17.99 **(978-0-06-234842-5(6)**, HarperTeen) HarperCollins Pubs.

Blevins, Wiley. Hansel & Gretel & the Haunted Hut. Cox, Steve, illus. 2016. (Scary Tales Retold Ser.). (ENG.). 24p. (gr. k-3). pap. 6.99 (978-1-63440-097-8(6)) Red Chair Pr.

—Hansel & Gretel & the Haunted Hut. Cox, Steve, illus. 2016. (Scary Tales Retold Ser.). (ENG.). 24p. (gr. k-3). lib. bdg. 23.99 (978-1-63440-096-1(8)) Red Chair Pr.

Bliss, Bryan. No Parking at the End Times. 2015. (ENG.). 272p. (YA). (gr. 9). 17.99 (978-0-06-227541-7(0), Greenwillow Bks.) HarperCollins Pubs.

Block, Francesca Lia. Wasteland. 2003. (Illus.). 160p. (J). 16.89 (978-0-06-028645-3(8), Cotler, Joanna Books) HarperCollins Pubs.

Bloodworth, Mark, illus. The Castle Mystery. 2010. (Boxcar Children Graphic Novels Ser.: 12). (ENG.). 32p. (J). (gr. 1-5). pap. 6.99 (978-0-8075-1080-3(7)) Whitman, Albert & Co.

Bloor, Edward. Tangerine. 2007. (ENG.). 320p. (J). (gr. 5-7). 18.00 (978-0-15-201246-5(X)) Houghton Mifflin Harcourt Publishing Co.

Bloss, Josie. Faking Faith. 2011. (ENG.). 240p. (YA). pap. 9.95 (978-0-7387-2757-8(1), Flux) North Star Editions.

Blume, Judy. BFF: Just as Long as We're Together/Here's to You, Rachel Robinson. 2007. (ENG., Illus.). 512p. (J). (gr. 3-7). 18.99 (978-0-385-73407-3(7), Delacorte Bks. for Young Readers) Random Hse. Children's Bks.

—Cool Zone with the Pain & the Great One. Stevenson, James, illus. 2009. (ENG.). 128p. (J). (gr. 3-7). 5.99 (978-0-440-42093-4(8), Yearling) Random Hse. Children's Bks.

—Double Fudge. 2007. (ENG.). 240p. (J). (gr. 3-7). 7.99 (978-0-14-240878-0(6), Puffin Books) Penguin Young Readers Group.

—Double Fudge. 2004. (Fudge Ser.). 160p. (J). (gr. 3-7). pap. 36.00 incl. audio (978-0-8072-2036-8(1), Listening Library) Random Hse. Audio Publishing Group.

—Double Fudge. 2007. (Fudge Bks.: 5). lib. bdg. 18.40 (978-1-4177-8371-7(0), Turtleback) Turtleback Bks.

—Friend or Fiend? With the Pain & the Great One. Stevenson, James, illus. 2010. (ENG.). 128p. (J). (gr. 3-7). 5.99 (978-0-440-42095-8(4), Yearling) Random Hse. Children's Bks.

—Fudge-a-Mania. 2007. (ENG.). 176p. (J). (gr. 3-7). 7.99 *(978-0-14-240877-3(8),* Puffin Books) Penguin Young Readers Group.

—Going, Going, Gone! with the Pain & the Great One. Stevenson, James, illus. 2010. (ENG.). 128p. (J). (gr. 3-7). 5.99 *(978-0-440-42094-1(6),* Yearling) Random Hse. Children's Bks.

—Here's to You, Rachel Robinson. 2010. (ENG.). 208p. (J). (gr. 5). pap. 8.99 *(978-0-385-73987-0(7),* Delacorte Bks. for Young Readers) Random Hse. Children's Bks.

—The One in the Middle Is the Green Kangaroo. Ohi, Debbie Ridpath, illus. 2014. (ENG.). 48p. (J). (gr. 1-5). pap. 5.99 *(978-1-4814-1131-8(4),* Atheneum Bks. for Young Readers) Simon & Schuster Children's Publishing.

—The Pain & the Great One. Ohi, Debbie Ridpath, illus. 2014. (ENG.). 48p. (J). (gr. 1-5). pap. 5.99 *(978-1-4814-1145-5(4),* Atheneum Bks. for Young Readers) Simon & Schuster Children's Publishing.

—Soupy Saturdays with the Pain & the Great One. Stevenson, James, illus. 2009. (ENG.). 128p. (J). (gr. 3-7). 5.99 *(978-0-440-42092-7(X),* Yearling) Random Hse. Children's Bks.

—Superfudge. (Fudge Ser.).Tr. of Superfudge. 166p. (J). (gr. 2-4). pap. 4.99 *(978-0-8072-1457-2(4),* Listening Library) Random Hse. Audio Publishing Group.

—Superfudge. 2007. (Fudge Bks.: 3).Tr. of Superfudge. lib. bdg. 18.40 *(978-1-4177-8843-9(7),* Turtleback) Turtleback Bks.

—Tales of a Fourth Grade Nothing. 2009. 8.32 *(978-0-7848-3046-8(0));* 8.32 *(978-0-7848-0332-5(3))* Marco Bk. Co. (Everbind).

—Tales of a Fourth Grade Nothing. 2007. 17.00 *(978-0-7569-7937-9(4))* 2004. (ENG.). 144p. (J). (gr. 3-7). 7.99 *(978-0-425-19379-2(9),* Berkley) Penguin Publishing Group.

—Tales of a Fourth Grade Nothing. 2007. (ENG.). 160p. (J). (gr. 3-7). 7.99 *(978-0-14-240881-0(6),* Puffin Books) Penguin Young Readers Group.

—Tales of a Fourth Grade Nothing. (Fudge Ser.). 120p. (J). (gr. 3-5). pap. 4.99 *(978-0-8072-1496-1(5),* Listening Library) Random Hse. Audio Publishing Group.

—Tales of a Fourth Grade Nothing. 2003. pap. *(978-0-439-57779-3(9),* Scholastic) Scholastic, Inc.

Blumenthal, Deborah. Don't Let the Peas Touch! Ering, Timothy Basil, illus. 2004. (J). *(978-0-439-29733-2(8),* Levine, Arthur A. Bks.) Scholastic, Inc.

Blumer, J. Michael. The Book of Broken Promises, Vol. 2. 2007. 280p. (YA). pap. 15.99 *(978-1-59092-540-9(8))* Blue Forge Pr.

—The Book of Second Chances, Bk. 1. 2006. (Secret Books of Gabendoor Ser.). 284p. per. 14.99 *(978-1-59092-317-7(0))* Blue Forge Pr.

Bo, Ben. Skullcrack. 2003. (ENG.). 168p. (YA). (gr. 5-12). pap. 6.95 *(978-0-8225-3311-5(1))* Lerner Publishing Group.

Boat, Patty. A Disappointing Homecoming: (A Soldier's Story), 1 vol. 2009. 158p. pap. 24.95 *(978-1-61546-997-0(4))* PublishAmerica, Inc.

Bogart, Jo Ellen. The Big Tree Gang. Griffiths, Dean, illus. 2005. 60p. (J). lib. bdg. 20.00 *(978-1-4242-1251-4(0))* Fitzgerald Bks.

Boggs, Patdee. Island of Angels. 2006. 55p. pap. 16.95 *(978-1-4241-3758-9(6))* PublishAmerica, Inc.

Bohannon, C. S. Spatula Boy: And the Secret of the Mysterious Old House. 2007. 52p. per. 16.95 *(978-1-4241-6956-6(9))* America Star Bks.

Bolden, Tonya. Crossing Ebenezer Creek. 2017. (ENG.). 240p. (YA). 17.99 *(978-1-59990-319-4(9),* 9781599903194, Bloomsbury USA Childrens) Bloomsbury Publishing USA.

Bollback, Anthony G. Capture of the Twin Dragon. 2012. 152p. pap. 8.99 *(978-0-9849359-1-8(6))* Finding the Cause, LLC.

—Hijacked. 2012. 176p. pap. 8.99 *(978-0-9849359-5-6(9))* Finding the Cause, LLC.

—Mystery of the Counterfeit Money. 2012. 170p. (gr. 4-7). pap. 8.99 *(978-0-9849359-2-5(4))* Finding the Cause, LLC.

—Rescue at Cripple Creek. 2012. 178p. pap. 8.99 *(978-0-9849359-3-2(2))* Finding the Cause, LLC.

—Smugglers in Hong Kong. 2012. 156p. pap. 8.99 *(978-0-9849359-0-1(8))* Finding the Cause, LLC.

—The Tiger Shark Strikes Again. 2012. 172p. pap. 8.99 *(978-0-9849359-4-9(0))* Finding the Cause, LLC.

Bollen, Christina. An Angel in My Garden, 1 vol. Matyuschenko, Tanya, illus. 2009. 47p. pap. 24.95 *(978-1-60813-661-2(2))* America Star Bks.

Bond, Juliet C. Sam's Sister. Majewski, Dawn, illus. 2004. (J). 18.00 *(978-0-944934-30-2(7))* Perspectives Pr., Inc.

Boonen, Stefan. Totally Lisa. 2008. (ENG., Illus.). 118p. (J). (gr. 4-7). 15.95 *(978-1-60537-005-7(3))* Clavis Publishing.

Booty, Don V. Brave Little Starling. 2012. (ENG.). 24p. (J). pap. 19.95 *(978-1-4327-9017-2(X))* Outskirts Pr., Inc.

Borden, Louise. Big Brothers Don't Take Naps. Dodd, Emma, illus. 2011. (ENG.). 32p. (J). (gr. -1-3). 17.99 *(978-1-4169-5503-0(8),* McElderry, Margaret K. Bks.) McElderry, Margaret K. Bks.

Boston, Ruth. Super Hero for A Day. 2007. 152p. per. 13.95 *(978-1-4327-1427-7(9))* Outskirts Pr., Inc.

Bourgeois, Paulette. Franklin's Baby Sister. 2004. (Illus.). (J). (gr. k-3). spiral bd. *(978-0-616-07219-6(8));* spiral bd. *(978-0-616-07218-9(X))* Canadian National Institute for the Blind/Institut National Canadien pour les Aveugles.

—Franklin's Baby Sister. Clark, Brenda, illus. (Franklin Ser.). (ENG.). 32p. (J). (gr. -1-3). *(978-1-55074-858-1(0))* Kids Can Pr., Ltd.

Bowen, Anne. When You Visit Grandma & Grandpa. Bogacki, Tomasz, tr. Bogacki, Tomasz, illus. 2004. (Carolrhoda Picture Books Ser.). 32p. (J). (gr. -1-3). 15.95 *(978-1-57505-610-4(0))* Lerner Publishing Group.

Bowler, Tim. Frozen Fire. 2010. (ENG.). 352p. (YA). (gr. 7-18). 8.99 *(978-0-14-241465-1(4),* Speak) Penguin Young Readers Group.

Bowman, Andy. Pokey's Garden. Travis, Stephanie, illus. 26p. (J). (gr. k-5). pap. 6.95 *(978-1-931650-08-3(X));* lib. bdg. 14.95 *(978-1-931650-09-0(8))* Coastal Publishing Carolina, Inc.

Boyce, Frank Cottrell & Boyce, Frank Cottrell. Millions. 2004. (Illus.). 256p. (J). (gr. 3-18). 15.99 *(978-0-06-073330-8(6));* lib. bdg. 16.89 *(978-0-06-073331-5(4))* HarperCollins Pubs.

—Millions, 6. Lenton, Steven, illus. 2nd unabr. ed. 2008. (ENG.). 272p. 15.95 *(978-0-330-45084-3(0),* Macmillan) Pan Macmillan GBR. Dist: Trans-Atlantic Pubns., Inc.

Bracegirdle, P. J. Fiendish Deeds. 2009. (Joy of Spooking Ser.: 1). (ENG.). 224p. (J). (gr. 3-7). pap. 5.99 *(978-1-4169-3417-2(0),* McElderry, Margaret K. Bks.) McElderry, Margaret K. Bks.

Bracken, Beth. Henry Helps with the Baby, 1 vol. Busby, Allie, illus. 2012. (Henry Helps Ser.). (ENG.). 24p. (gr. -1 — 1). pap. 5.95 *(978-1-4048-7672-9(3),* Henry Helps) Picture Window Bks.

Bradford, Michael. Button Hill, 1 vol. 2015. (ENG.). 264p. (J). (gr. 4-7). pap. 9.95 *(978-1-4598-0755-6(3))* Orca Bk. Pubs. USA.

Bradley, Kimberly Brubaker. The War That Saved My Life. (ENG.). (J). (gr. 4-7). 2016. 336p. 8.99 *(978-0-14-751048-8(1),* Puffin Books) 2015. 320p. 17.99 *(978-0-8037-4081-5(6),* Dial Bks) Penguin Young Readers Group.

—The War That Saved My Life. 2016. (J). lib. bdg. 19.65 *(978-0-606-38843-6(5))* Turtleback Bks.

Bradley, Natasha R. & Bradley, Jasmine N. Jessika's Diaries:Life's Not Fair. 2008. 132p. pap. 14.95 *(978-0-615-21079-7(1))* On The Ball Publishing.

Branch, Dianne. Sydney Becomes a Big Sister. 2011. 24p. pap. 11.32 *(978-1-4634-4093-0(6))* AuthorHouse.

Branch, Ken & Tanguay, Dave. Mr. Who? Mr. Atom! 2015. (Billy Batson & the Magic of Shazam! Ser.). (ENG., Illus.). 32p. (gr. 2-3). lib. bdg. 22.60 *(978-1-4342-9656-6(3))* Stone Arch Bks.

Brandeis, Madeline. Mitz & Fritz of Germany. 2011. 164p. 41.95 *(978-1-258-10138-1(6))* Literary Licensing, LLC.

Branson, Terri. Brother Dragon. Taylor, Chet, illus. 2004. (J). 18.99 *(978-0-9755888-5-7(0))* Dragonfly Publishing, Inc.

Braun, Sebastien. Mayday Mouse. Braun, Sebastien, illus. 2017. (Child's Play Library). (ENG., Illus.). 32p. (J). (gr. k-3). *(978-1-84643-759-5(8))* Child's Play International Ltd.

Bray, Pamela. The Day Lonyaie's Life Changed. 2008. 32p. pap. 24.95 *(978-1-60474-859-8(1))* America Star Bks.

Break Away. 64p. (J). (gr. 6-12). pap. *(978-0-8224-2391-1(X))* Globe Fearon Educational Publishing.

Breathed, Berkeley. Edwurd Fudwupper Fibbed Big. Breathed, Berkeley, illus. 2003. (ENG., Illus.). 40p. (J). (gr. 1-4). pap. 8.00 *(978-0-316-14425-4(8))* Little, Brown Bks. for Young Readers.

Brenda Jenkins. Trick or Treat Every Night. 2012. 24p. 24.95 *(978-1-4626-6055-1(X))* America Star Bks.

Brennan-Nelson, Denise. Leopold the Lion. Barshaw, Ruth McNally, illus. 2015. (ENG.). 32p. (J). (gr. 1-3). 16.99 *(978-1-58536-828-0(8),* 203951) Sleeping Bear Pr.

Brennan, Sarah Rees. The Demon's Covenant. 2010. (Demon's Lexicon Trilogy Ser.: 2). (ENG., Illus.). 448p. (YA). (gr. 9-18). 17.99 *(978-1-4169-6381-3(2),* McElderry, Margaret K. Bks.) McElderry, Margaret K. Bks.

—The Demon's Lexicon. 2009. (Demon's Lexicon Trilogy Ser.: 1). (ENG., Illus.). 336p. (YA). (gr. 9-18). 18.99 *(978-1-4169-6379-0(0),* McElderry, Margaret K. Bks.) McElderry, Margaret K. Bks.

Brewer, Heather. The Cemetery Boys. 2015. (ENG.). 288p. (YA). (gr. 8). 17.99 *(978-0-06-230788-0(6),* HarperTeen) HarperCollins Pubs.

—The Cemetery Boys. 2016. 304p. (YA). (gr. 8). pap. 9.99 *(978-0-06-230789-7(4),* HarperTeen) HarperCollins Pubs.

—The Cemetery Boys. 2016. (YA). lib. bdg. 20.85 *(978-0-606-38741-5(2))* Turtleback Bks.

Brezenoff, Steve. The Absolute Value of -1. 2010. (Carolrhoda YA Ser.). (ENG.). 296p. (YA). (gr. 9-12). lib. bdg. 16.95 *(978-0-7613-5417-8(4),* Carolrhoda Bks.) Lerner Publishing Group.

—The Absolute Value Of -1. 2011. (Carolrhoda YA Ser.). (ENG.). 296p. (YA). (gr. 9-12). pap. 9.95 *(978-0-7613-8130-3(9),* Carolrhoda Lab™) Lerner Publishing Group.

Brian, Kate, pseud. Megan Meade's Guide to the McGowan Boys. 2006. (ENG.). 288p. (YA). (gr. 7-12). pap. 9.99 *(978-1-4169-0031-3(4),* Simon & Schuster Bks. For Young Readers) Simon & Schuster Bks. For Young Readers.

—Private. 2009. (Private Ser.: No. 1). (ENG.). 240p. (YA). pap. 9.99 *(978-1-4169-9946-1(9),* Simon & Schuster Bks. For Young Readers) Simon & Schuster Bks. For Young Readers.

Brightwood, Laura, illus. Ka-ulu the Strong. Brightwood, Laura, 2006. (J). *(978-0-9789871-3-8(6))* 3-C Institute for Social Development.

Brink, Carol Ryrie. Caddie Woodlawn. 2006. (ENG., Illus.). 288p. (J). (gr. 3-7). pap. 7.99 *(978-1-4169-4028-9(6),* Aladdin) Simon & Schuster Children's Publishing.

Brisebois, Ro. Sherlock & Elf: The Mystery of the Thicket Behind the Shed. 2008. 100p. pap. 12.99 *(978-1-4343-9987-8(7))* AuthorHouse.

Brodien-Jones, Christine. The Dreamkeepers. 2009. (ENG.). 148p. (YA). (gr. 7). pap. 8.99 *(978-1-4424-0221-8(0),* Simon & Schuster Bks. For Young Readers) Simon & Schuster Bks. For Young Readers.

A Brother's Sin. 2008. 84p. pap. 9.95 *(978-1-934335-21-5(5))* WordWright.biz, Inc.

Brown, Anne Greenwood. Deep Betrayal. 2013. (ENG.). 352p. (YA). (gr. 7). pap. 9.99 *(978-0-385-74204-7(5),* Ember) Random Hse. Children's Bks.

—Lies Beneath. 2013. (ENG.). 320p. (YA). (gr. 7). pap. 8.99 *(978-0-385-74202-3(9),* Ember) Random Hse. Children's Bks.

Brown, Jeff. Invisible Stanley. Nash, Scott & Pamintuan, Macky, illus. 2009. (Flat Stanley Ser.). (ENG.). 112p. (J). (gr. 2-5). pap. 4.99 *(978-0-06-009792-9(2))* HarperCollins Pubs.

—Invisible Stanley. 2009. (Flat Stanley Ser.: 4). (J). (gr. k-3). lib. bdg. 14.75 *(978-0-613-68434-7(6),* Turtleback) Turtleback Bks.

Brown, Jeffrey. Lucy & Andy Neanderthal. 2016. (Lucy & Andy Neanderthal Ser.: 1). (ENG., Illus.). 224p. (J). (gr. 3-7). 12.99 *(978-0-385-38835-1(7),* Crown Books For Young Readers) Random Hse. Children's Bks.

Brown, Jennifer. Perfect Escape. 2012. (ENG.). 368p. (YA). (gr. 7-17). 17.99 *(978-0-316-18557-8(4))* Little, Brown Bks. for Young Readers.

Brown, Linnet. Keep Your Eyes on the Goal. 2013. 48p. pap. *(978-1-4602-1828-0(0))* FriesenPress.

Brown, Marc. Arthur & the Baby. Brown, Marc, illus. 2011. (Classic Arthur Adventure Ser.). (ENG., Illus.). 32p. (J). (gr. -1-3). pap. 7.99 *(978-0-316-12905-3(4))* Little Brown & Co.

—Arthur in New York. 2008. (Step into Reading Ser.). (ENG., Illus.). 24p. (J). (gr. k-3). pap. 3.99 *(978-0-375-82976-5(8),* Random Hse. Bks. for Young Readers) Random Hse. Children's Bks.

—Arthur Turns Green. 2014. (ENG.). 32p. (J). (gr. 1-4). 7.00 *(978-0-316-12923-7(2))* Little Brown & Co.

—Arthur Turns Green. 2014. (Arthur Adventures Ser.). (J). lib. bdg. 17.20 *(978-0-606-34069-4(6),* Turtleback) Turtleback Bks.

—Arthur's Classroom Fib. 2007. (Arthur Step into Reading Ser.). lib. bdg. 13.55 *(978-1-4177-7281-0(6),* Turtleback) Turtleback Bks.

—Arthur's Reading Trick. 2009. (Step into Reading Ser.). (ENG., Illus.). 24p. (J). (gr. k-3). pap. 3.99 *(978-0-375-82977-2(6),* Random Hse. Bks. for Young Readers) Random Hse. Children's Bks.

—Monkey: Not Ready for the Baby. 2016. (ENG., Illus.). 32p. (J). (gr. -1-2). 16.99 *(978-1-101-93327-5(5),* Knopf Bks. for Young Readers) Random Hse. Children's Bks.

Brown, Marc. Monkey: Not Ready for the Baby. 2017. (ENG.). 32p. (J). (gr. -1-2). 5.99 ***(978-0-399-55781-1(4),*** Dragonfly Bks.) Random Hse. Children's Bks.

Brown, Marc & Sarfatti, Esther. D. W. y el Carne de Biblioteca. 2004.Tr. of D.W.'s Library Card. (ENG & SPA., Illus.). (J). pap. 6.95 *(978-1-930332-47-8(5))* Lectorum Pubns., Inc.

Brown, Margery W. Baby Jesus Like My Brother. 2008. (Illus.). 32p. 6.95 *(978-1-60349-000-9(0),* Marimba Bks.) Hudson Publishing Group, The.

Bruce, Mary Grant. Back to Billabong. l.t. ed. 2006. 200p. pap. 21.99 *(978-1-4264-2197-6(4))* Creative Media Partners, LLC.

Bruneau M. D., Denise J. & Bruneau, Denise J. My Baby: Illustrations by MikeMotz. com. 2010. 28p. 13.99 *(978-1-4490-8475-2(3))* AuthorHouse.

Buckley-Archer, Linda. The Time Quake. 2009. (Gideon Trilogy Ser.: 3). (ENG.). 464p. (J). (gr. 5-9). 17.99 *(978-1-4169-1529-4(X),* Simon & Schuster Bks. For Young Readers) Simon & Schuster Bks. For Young Readers.

Buckley, Michael. The Council of Mirrors. Ferguson, Peter, illus. (Sisters Grimm Ser.). (ENG.). 352p. (gr. 3-7). 2013. (YA). pap. 7.95 *(978-1-4197-0538-0(5))* 2012. (J). 16.95 *(978-1-4197-0186-3(X))* Abrams, Inc. (Amulet Bks.).

Buckley, Michael. The Problem Child. 2017. (Sisters Grimm Ser.: 3). (J). lib. bdg. 19.60 ***(978-0-606-39687-5(X))*** Turtleback Bks.

Bucky Badger A Children's Story: Becky Gets a Brother, 4 vols. l.t. ed. 2005. (Illus.). (J). 9.99 *(978-0-9765510-0-3(4))* Badgerland Bks. LLC.

Budreau, Craig. Trail Map: Barton Creek Greenbelt — Loop 360 to Zilker Park. 2006. (J). per. 5.00 *(978-1-932196-26-9(9))* WordWright.biz, Inc.

Bulion, Leslie. Uncharted Waters, 1 vol. (ENG.). 192p. (J). (gr. 3-7). 2009. pap. 7.95 *(978-1-56145-485-3(0))* 2006. 14.95 *(978-1-56145-365-8(X))* Peachtree Pubs.

Bumgarner, Sam. Little Sami's Silly Again, 1 vol. 2009. 32p. pap. 24.95 *(978-1-60813-863-0(1))* America Star Bks.

—Silly Little Sami. 2008. 24p. pap. 24.95 *(978-1-60474-260-2(7))* America Star Bks.

Bunting, Eve. A Sudden Silence. 2007. (ENG., Illus.). 144p. (YA). (gr. 7-12). pap. 7.99 *(978-0-15-205868-5(0))* Houghton Mifflin Harcourt Publishing Co.

—Will It Be a Baby Brother? Spiegel, Beth, illus. 2010. (ENG.). 32p. (J). (gr. -1-1). 16.95 *(978-1-59078-439-6(1))* Boyds Mills Pr.

Burch, Christian. Hit the Road, Manny: A Manny Files Novel. 2008. (ENG.). 240p. (J). (gr. 3-7). 16.99 *(978-1-4169-2812-6(X),* Atheneum Bks. for Young Readers) Simon & Schuster Children's Publishing.

—The Manny Files. 2008. (Mix Ser.). (ENG.). 304p. (J). (gr. 4-8). pap. 14.99 *(978-1-4169-5534-4(8),* Aladdin) Simon & Schuster Children's Publishing.

Burchett, Jan & Vogler, Sara. Avalanche Alert, 1 vol. Le Feyer, Diane, illus. 2012. (Wild Rescue Ser.). (ENG.). 152p. (gr. 3-6). 25.32 *(978-1-4342-3772-9(9))* Stone Arch Bks.

—Desert Danger, 1 vol. Le Feyer, Diane & Kennedy, Sam, illus. 2012. (Wild Rescue Ser.). (ENG.). 152p. (gr. 3-6). lib. bdg. 25.32 *(978-1-4342-3773-6(7))* Stone Arch Bks.

—Earthquake Escape, 1 vol. Le Feyer, Diane, illus. 2012. (Wild Rescue Ser.). (ENG.). 152p. (gr. 3-6). lib. bdg. 25.32 *(978-1-4048-6891-5(7))* Picture Window Bks.

—Ocean S. O. S. Le Feyer, Diane & Kennedy, Sam, illus. 2012. (Wild Rescue Ser.). (ENG.). 152p. (gr. 3-6). lib. bdg. 25.32 *(978-1-4342-3771-2(0))* Stone Arch Bks.

—Poacher Panic, 1 vol. Le Feyer, Diane, illus. 2012. (Wild Rescue Ser.). (ENG.). 152p. (gr. 3-6). 9.95 *(978-1-4342-4593-9(4));* lib. bdg. 25.32 *(978-1-4342-3286-1(7))* Stone Arch Bks.

—Polar Meltdown, 1 vol. Le Feyer, Diane, illus. 2012. (Wild Rescue Ser.). (ENG.). 152p. (gr. 3-6). 9.95 *(978-1-4342-4594-6(2));* lib. bdg. 25.32 *(978-1-4342-3769-9(9))* Stone Arch Bks.

—Rainforest Rescue, 1 vol. Le Feyer, Diane, illus. 2012. (Wild Rescue Ser.). (ENG.). 152p. (gr. 3-6). 9.95 *(978-1-4342-4595-3(0));* lib. bdg. 25.32 *(978-1-4342-3768-2(0))* Stone Arch Bks.

—Safari Survival, 1 vol. Le Feyer, Diane & Kennedy, Sam, illus. 2012. (Wild Rescue Ser.). (ENG.). 152p. (gr. 3-6). lib. bdg. 25.32 *(978-1-4342-3770-5(2))* Stone Arch Bks.

Burg, Ann E. Serafina's Promise. (ENG.). 304p. (J). (gr. 3-7). 2015. pap. 7.99 *(978-0-545-53567-0(0))* 2013. 16.99 *(978-0-545-53564-9(6))* Scholastic, Inc. (Scholastic Pr.).

Burgess, Lisa Maria. Juma & Little Sungura. Gugu, Abdul M., illus. 2013. 32p. 19.95 *(978-1-939604-06-4(0));* pap. 9.99 *(978-1-939604-02-6(8))* Barranca Pr.

—Juma Cooks Chapati. Gugu, Abdul M., illus. 2013. 32p. 19.95 *(978-1-939604-08-8(7));* pap. 9.99 *(978-1-939604-04-0(4))* Barranca Pr.

—Juma on Safari. Gugu, Abdul M., illus. 2013. 32p. 19.95 *(978-1-939604-07-1(9));* pap. 9.99 *(978-1-939604-03-3(6))* Barranca Pr.

Burgess, Thornton W. The Christmas Reindeer. Chase, Rhoda, illus. 2013. (Dover Children's Classics Ser.). (ENG.). 160p. (J). (gr. k-3). pap. 5.99 *(978-0-486-49153-0(6))* Dover Pubns., Inc.

Burgis, Stephanie. Stolen Magic. (Kat, Incorrigible Ser.: 3). (ENG., Illus.). 400p. (YA). (gr. 5-8). 2014. pap. 7.99 *(978-1-4169-9452-7(1))* 2013. 17.99 *(978-1-4169-9451-0(3),* Atheneum Bks. for Young Readers) Simon & Schuster Children's Publishing.

Burks, James. Pigs & a Blanket. Burks, James, illus. 2016. (ENG., Illus.). 32p. (J). (gr. -1 — 1). 16.99 *(978-1-4847-2523-8(9))* Hyperion Bks. for Children.

Burnham, Molly B. Almost an Outlaw. Spencer, Trevor, illus. 2017. (Teddy Mars Ser.: 3). 288p. (J). (gr. 3-7). 16.99 *(978-0-06-227816-6(9),* Tegen, Katherine Bks) HarperCollins Pubs.

—Teddy Mars: Almost a World Record Breaker. Spencer, Trevor, illus. (Teddy Mars Ser.: 1). (J). (gr. 3-7). 2016. 240p. pap. 6.99 *(978-0-06-227811-1(8),* Tegen, Katherine Bks) 2015. (ENG.). 224p. 16.99 *(978-0-06-227810-4(X))* HarperCollins Pubs.

Burningham, John. There's Going to Be a Baby. Oxenbury, Helen, illus. 48p. (J). 2014. (ENG.). (-k). 7.99 *(978-0-7636-7265-2(3))* 2010. *(978-0-7445-4996-6(5))* 2010. (ENG.). (gr. -1-k). 16.99 *(978-0-7636-4907-4(4))* Candlewick Pr.

Burns, Ian. Lissie Pendle. 2006. 196p. pap. 13.04 *(978-1-4116-5491-4(9))* Lulu Pr., Inc.

Burns, Theresa. Queen Emileen. Burns, Theresa, illus. 2013. (Illus.). 36p. 15.50 *(978-1-949224-23-8(6))* Taylor and Seale Publishing, LLC.

Bush, Maureen. The Nexus Ring, 1 vol. 2007. (Veil of Magic Ser.: 1). (ENG.). 136p. (J). (gr. 3-6). per. 6.95 *(978-1-55050-362-3(6))* Coteau Bks. CAN. Dist: Orca Bk. Pubs. USA.

But I Knew Better: Individual Title, 6 pack. (gr. k-1). 23.00 *(978-0-7635-9033-8(9))* Rigby Education.

Butcher, Kristin. Cheat, 1 vol. 2010. (Orca Currents Ser.). (ENG.). 128p. (J). (gr. 5-9). pap. 9.95 *(978-1-55469-274-3(1))* Orca Bk. Pubs. USA.

Butcher, Nicholas. The Hand above the Gate. 2008. 204p. pap. *(978-1-84923-348-4(9))* YouWriteOn.

Byars, Betsy. The Not-Just-Anybody Family. 2008. (Blossom Family Ser.: Bk. 1). (ENG., Illus.). 160p. (J). (gr. -1-7). 8.95 *(978-0-8234-2145-9(7))* Holiday Hse., Inc.

—The Summer of the Swans. 2004. (Puffin Modern Classics Ser.). (ENG.). 144p. (J). (gr. 3-7). pap. 6.99 *(978-0-14-240114-9(5),* Puffin Books) Penguin Young Readers Group.

—The Summer of the Swans. 2008. (Puffin Modern Classics Ser.). (Illus.). 129p. (gr. 4). 16.00 *(978-0-7569-8944-6(2))* Perfection Learning Corp.

Bynum, Janie. The Twelve Days of Christmas in Texas. Bynum, Janie, illus. 2009. (Twelve Days of Christmas in America Ser.). (ENG., Illus.). 40p. (J). (gr. k). 12.95 *(978-1-4027-6350-2(6))* Sterling Publishing Co., Inc.

Byrne, Gayle. Sometimes Just One Is Just Right. Haverfield, Mary, illus. 2013. (ENG.). 32p. (J). (gr. k-k). 15.95 *(978-0-7892-1129-3(7),* Abbeville Kids) Abbeville Pr., Inc.

Caldwell, V. M. Runt: Story of a Boy. 2006. (ENG.). 208p. (J). (gr. 2-8). 16.95 *(978-1-57131-662-2(0));* (gr. 3-7). per. 6.95 *(978-1-57131-661-5(2))* Milkweed Editions.

Callahan, Susan. A New Way. 2012. 20p. pap. 17.99 *(978-1-4772-4507-1(3))* AuthorHouse.

Callahan, Thera S. All Wrapped Up. 2004. (Rookie Reader Español Ser.). (ENG., Illus.). 32p. (J). (gr. k-2). pap. 4.95 *(978-0-516-21949-3(9),* Children's Pr.) Scholastic Library Publishing.

—All Wrapped Up. Gordon, Mike, illus. 2003. (Rookie Readers Ser.). 32p. (J). 19.50 *(978-0-516-22844-0(7),* Children's Pr.) Scholastic Library Publishing.

Calonita, Jen. Summer State of Mind. 2014. (ENG.). 256p. (YA). (gr. 7-17). pap. 10.00 *(978-0-316-09115-2(4),* Poppy) Little, Brown Bks. for Young Readers.

Campagne, Michelle & Gallant, Dany. Fabuleuse Melodie De. 2013. (FRE., Illus.). 44p. (J). (gr. -1-k). 16.95 *(978-2-923163-30-7(3))* La Montagne Secrete CAN. Dist: Independent Pubs. Group.

Candlewick Press, Candlewick. Peppa Pig & the Day at Snowy Mountain. 2014. (Peppa Pig Ser.). (ENG.). 32p. (J). (-k). 12.99 *(978-0-7636-7455-7(9),* Candlewick Entertainment) Candlewick Pr.

Candlewick Press Staff. Peppa Pig & the Lost Christmas List. Ladybird Books Staff, illus. 2012. (Peppa Pig Ser.). (ENG.). 32p. (J). (gr. k-k). 12.99 *(978-0-7636-6276-9(3),* Candlewick Entertainment) Candlewick Pr.

Capucilli, Alyssa Satin. Henry Is a Big Brother. Stott, Dorothy, illus. 2014. (Hannah & Henry Ser.). (ENG.). 32p. (J). (gr. -1-k). 5.99 *(978-0-7641-6749-2(9))* Barron's Educational Series, Inc.

Caputo, Kenneth. The Adventures of Jay & Tay: Our First Karate Class. 2011. 32p. pap. 14.99 *(978-1-4567-1999-9(8))* AuthorHouse.

Caraballo, Samuel. My Big Sister / Mi Hermana Mayor. Muraida, Thelma, illus. 2012. (ENG & SPA.). (J). (gr. 3-8). 16.95 *(978-1-55885-750-6(8),* Piñata Books) Arte Publico Pr.

Carey, Janet Lee. Wenny Has Wings. 2004. (ENG.). 240p. (J). (gr. 3-7). reprint ed. pap. 11.99 *(978-0-689-86759-0(X),* Atheneum Bks. for Young Readers) Simon & Schuster Children's Publishing.

Carlson, Melody. Playing with Fire. 2007. (Secret Life of Samantha Mcgregor Ser.: No. 3). (ENG.). 256p. (YA). (gr. 7-12). per. 12.99 *(978-1-59052-694-1(5),* Multnomah Bks.) Crown Publishing Group.

Carlson, Nancy. Harriet & Walt. rev. ed. 2004. (Carolrhoda Picture Books Ser.). (ENG., Illus.). 32p. (J). (gr. k-2). 15.95 *(978-1-57505-672-2(0));* pap. 6.95 *(978-1-57505-723-1(9))* Lerner Publishing Group.

—I Don't Like to Read! Carlson, Nancy & Carlson, illus. 2009. (ENG.). 32p. (J). (gr. k-2). pap. 6.99 *(978-0-14-241451-4(4),* Puffin Books) Penguin Young Readers Group.

—Louanne Pig in the Perfect Family. 2nd rev. ed. 2004. (Nancy Carlson's Neighborhood Ser.). (ENG., Illus.). 32p. (J). (gr. k-2). 15.95 *(978-1-57505-611-1(9));* pap. 6.95 *(978-1-57505-616-6(X))* Lerner Publishing Group.

—Loudmouth George Earns His Allowance. Carlson, Nancy, illus. 2007. (ENG., Illus.). 32p. (J). (gr. k-2). 15.95 *(978-0-8225-6560-4(9),* Carolrhoda Bks.) Lerner Publishing Group.

Carpenter, Lynette Stutzman. My Brother, the Senator. 2010. 40p. pap. 16.95 (978-1-4497-0629-6(0), WestBow Pr.) Author Solutions, Inc.

Carr, C. Hanna's Way. 2011. (Illus.). 112p. 28.31 (978-1-4567-8179-8(0)); pap. 14.11 (978-1-4567-8178-1(2)) AuthorHouse.

Carroll, Emma. In Darkling Wood. 2017. (ENG.). 240p. (J). (gr. 5). 16.99 (978-0-399-55601-2(X), Delacorte Bks. for Young Readers) Random Hse. Children's Bks.

Carroll, Katie L. Elixir Bound. 2013. 158p. pap. (978-1-77127-465-4(4)) MuseItUp Publishing.

Carter, Ally. Take the Key & Lock Her Up. 2016. (Embassy Row Ser.: 3). (ENG.). 336p. (J). (gr. 7). 17.99 (978-0-545-65495-1(5), Scholastic Pr.) Scholastic, Inc.

Carter, Anne Laurel. Night Boy, 1 vol. Pelletier, Ninon, illus. 2012. (ENG.). 32p. (J). (gr. -1-3). 19.95 (978-1-55469-402-0(7)) Orca Bk. Pubs. USA.

Carter, Dorothy. Wilhe'mina Miles: After the Stork Night. Stevenson, Harvey, illus. 2005. 30p. (J). (gr. k-4). reprint ed. 16.00 (978-0-7567-9421-7(8)) DIANE Publishing Co.

Cartwheel: A Sequel to Double Eagle. 2013. (ENG.). 252p. (YA). 17.00 (978-0-9844460-3-2(6)) Bucking Horse Bks.

Carty, Hilda. Catventure. 2009. (Illus.). 40p. pap. 18.49 (978-1-4389-4659-7(7)) AuthorHouse.

Cascioli, Lucia. Shifters. 2011. 126p. 25.99 (978-1-257-86200-9(6)); pap. 9.99 (978-1-257-86197-2(2)) Lulu Pr., Inc.

Cassell, Jody. Where's Leon? Storybook & Reader's Guide CD-ROM, 1. Kristof Pincheira, Kyra, illus. l.t. ed. 2006. 48p. (J). lib. bdg. 17.95 (978-1-59494-013-2(4)) CPCC Pr.

Cassidy, Anne. Innocent. 2014. (ENG.). 192p. (YA). (gr. 7). pap. 8.99 (978-0-340-88200-9(X)) Hodder & Stoughton GBR. Dist: Hachette Bk. Group.

Castilla, Julia Mercedes. Strange Parents. 2009. 144p. (J). (gr. 6-18). pap. 9.95 (978-1-55885-590-8(4), Piñata Books) Arte Publico Pr.

Castlemon, Harry. Sportsmans Club in the Saddle. 2006. pap. 30.95 (978-1-4286-5231-6(0)) Kessinger Publishing, LLC.

Caterer, Claire M. The Key & the Flame. (ENG.). (J). (gr. 3-7). 2015. 496p. pap. 7.99 (978-1-4424-5742-3(2)) 2013. 480p. 17.99 (978-1-4424-5741-6(4)) McElderry, Margaret K. Bks. (McElderry, Margaret K. Bks.).

Cayen, Alise. Patty Pom-Poms. 2009. 36p. pap. 16.50 (978-1-60693-685-6(9), Strategic Bk. Publishing) Strategic Book Publishing & Rights Agency (SBPRA).

Cento, Nucci. Maverick & Miss Murphy at Rascal's Rescue Ranch. 2009. 48p. pap. 12.50 (978-1-60860-388-6(1), Eloquent Bks.) Strategic Book Publishing & Rights Agency (SBPRA).

Chambers, Mark, illus. Zach & Lucy & the Museum of Natural Wonders. 2016. (Zach & Lucy Ser.). (ENG.). 40p. (J). (gr. 1-3). pap. 3.99 (978-1-4814-3935-0(9), Simon Spotlight) Simon Spotlight.

—Zach & Lucy & the Yoga Zoo. 2016. (Zach & Lucy Ser.). (ENG.). 40p. (J). (gr. 1-3). pap. 3.99 (978-1-4814-3938-1(3), Simon Spotlight) Simon Spotlight.

Chandler, Ann. Kootenay Silver. 2010. (ENG.). 216p. (YA). (gr. 9). pap. 12.99 (978-1-55488-755-2(0)) Dundurn CAN. Dist: Ingram Publisher Services.

Chappas, Bess. Kiki & the Red Shoes. Branam, Sandy, illus. 2007. (J). 17.99 (978-1-60131-012-5(9)) Big Tent Bks.

Charbonneau, Joelle. Dividing Eden. 2017. 336p. (YA). (gr. 8). 17.99 (978-0-06-245384-6(X), HarperTeen) HarperCollins Pubs.

Charles, Norma. Chasing a Star. 2009. (ENG., Illus.). 182p. (YA). (gr. 5-8). pap. (978-1-55380-077-4(X)) Ronsdale Pr.

Chase, Mary. Loretta Mason Potts. Berson, Harold, illus. 2014. (ENG.). 224p. (J). (gr. 3-7). 16.95 (978-1-59017-757-0(6), NYR Children's Collection) New York Review of Bks., Inc., The.

Cheaney, J. B. & Cheaney, Janie. The Middle of Somewhere. 2008. (ENG.). 224p. (J). (gr. 3-7). 7.99 (978-0-440-42165-8(9), Yearling) Random Hse. Children's Bks.

Chew, Ruth. A Matter-of-Fact Magic Book: The Would-Be Witch. 2014. (Matter-Of-Fact Magic Book Ser.). (ENG., Illus.). 144p. (J). (gr. 2-5). 15.99 (978-0-449-81567-0(6), Random Hse. Bks. for Young Readers) Random Hse. Children's Bks.

—No Such Thing as a Witch. 2013. (Matter-Of-Fact Magic Book Ser.). (ENG., Illus.). 128p. (J). (gr. 2-5). 5.99 (978-0-449-81562-5(5)); 15.99 (978-0-449-81559-5(5)) Random Hse. Children's Bks. (Random Hse. Bks. for Young Readers).

Chichester Clark, Emma. Mimi's Book of Opposites. Chichester Clark, Emma, illus. 2004. (Illus.). 24p. (J). 9.95 (978-1-57091-574-1(1)) Charlesbridge Publishing, Inc.

—My Baby Sister. Chichester Clark, Emma, illus. 2009. (Humber & Plum Ser.: 2). (ENG., Illus.). 32p. (J). (gr. -1-k). 9.99 (978-0-00-727324-9(X), HarperCollins Children's Bks.) HarperCollins Pubs. Ltd. GBR. Dist: HarperCollins Pubs.

—Plum & Rabbit & Me, Bk. 3. Chichester Clark, Emma, illus. 2010. (Humber & Plum Ser.: 3). (ENG., Illus.). 32p. (J). (gr. -1-k). pap. 9.99 (978-0-00-727325-6(8), HarperCollins Children's Bks.) HarperCollins Pubs. Ltd. GBR. Dist: HarperCollins Pubs.

Chick, Bryan. The Secret Zoo. 2010. (Secret Zoo Ser.: 1). (ENG.). 304p. (J). (gr. 3-7). 16.99 (978-0-06-198750-2(6), Greenwillow Bks.) HarperCollins Pubs.

Child, Lauren. But Excuse Me That Is My Book. Child, Lauren, illus. 2006. (Charlie & Lola Ser.). (ENG., Illus.). 32p. (J). (gr. -1-3). 16.99 (978-0-8037-3096-0(9), Dial Bks) Penguin Young Readers Group.

—But I Am an Alligator. 2008. (Charlie & Lola Ser.). (ENG.). 24p. (J). (gr. -1-k). mass mkt. 3.99 (978-0-448-44697-4(9), Grosset & Dunlap) Penguin Young Readers Group.

—But I've Used All My Pocket Change. 2012. (Charlie & Lola Ser.). (ENG.). 32p. (J). (gr. -1-k). 16.99 (978-0-8037-3728-0(9), Dial Bks) Penguin Young Readers Group.

—I Absolutely Must Do Coloring Now or Painting or Drawing. Child, Lauren, illus. 2006. (Charlie & Lola Ser.). (ENG., Illus.). 24p. (J). (gr. -1-k). 3.99 (978-0-448-44415-4(1), Grosset & Dunlap) Penguin Young Readers Group.

—I Am Going to Save a Panda! 2010. (Charlie & Lola Ser.). lib. bdg. 13.55 (978-0-606-10628-3(6), Turtleback) Turtleback Bks.

—I Am Too Absolutely Small for School. Child, Lauren, illus. (Charlie & Lola Ser.). (ENG., Illus.). 32p. (J). (gr. -1-2). 2004. 16.99 (978-0-7636-2403-3(9)) 2005. reprint ed. per. 8.99 (978-0-7636-2887-1(5)) Candlewick Pr.

—I Am Too Absolutely Small for School. 2007. (Charlie & Lola (Shang Yi Publishing) Ser.). (CHI., Illus.). (J). (978-957-762-437-6(5)) Hsin Yi Pubns.

—I Am Too Absolutely Small for School. Child, Lauren, illus. 2005. (ENG., Illus.). (J). (gr. -1-1). lib. bdg. 14.65 (978-0-7569-6495-5(4)) Perfection Learning Corp.

—I Can't Stop Hiccuping! 2010. (Charlie & Lola Ser.). lib. bdg. 13.55 (978-0-606-10629-0(4), Turtleback) Turtleback Bks.

—I Completely Must Do Drawing Now & Painting & Coloring. 2007. (Charlie & Lola Ser.). (ENG., Illus.). 24p. (J). (gr. -1-k). 3.99 (978-0-448-44560-1(3), Grosset & Dunlap) Penguin Young Readers Group.

—I Want to Be Much More Bigger Like You. 2008. (Charlie & Lola Ser.). (ENG.). 24p. (J). (gr. -1-k). mass mkt. 3.99 (978-0-448-44867-1(X), Grosset & Dunlap) Penguin Young Readers Group.

—I Will Never Not Ever Eat a Tomato. Child, Lauren, illus. 2003. (Charlie & Lola Ser.). (ENG., Illus.). 32p. (J). (gr. -1-3). reprint ed. 8.99 (978-0-7636-2180-3(3)) Candlewick Pr.

—I Will Never Not Ever Eat a Tomato. 2004. (Charlie & Lola Ser.). (Illus.). (gr. -1-3). 17.00 (978-0-7569-3178-0(9)) Perfection Learning Corp.

—I Will Never Not Ever Eat a Tomato. 2003. (Charlie & Lola Ser.). lib. bdg. 19.65 (978-0-613-69403-2(1), Turtleback) Turtleback Bks.

—I've Won, No I've Won, No I've Won. 2006. (Charlie & Lola Ser.). (ENG., Illus.). 32p. (J). (gr. -1-2). mass mkt. 6.99 (978-0-448-44350-8(3), Grosset & Dunlap) Penguin Young Readers Group.

—My Best, Best Friend. 2011. (Charlie & Lola Ser.). (ENG.). 32p. (J). (gr. -1-k). 16.99 (978-0-8037-3586-6(3), Dial Bks) Penguin Young Readers Group.

—My Wobbly Tooth Must Not Ever Never Fall Out. Child, Lauren, illus. 2006. (Charlie & Lola Ser.). (ENG., Illus.). 32p. (J). (gr. -1-2). mass mkt. 6.99 (978-0-448-44255-6(8), Grosset & Dunlap) Penguin Young Readers Group.

—Sizzles Is Completely Not Here. 2007. (Illus.). 10p. (J). bds. (978-0-14-138337-8(2), Puffin) Penguin Publishing Group.

—Slightly Invisible. Child, Lauren, illus. 2011. (Charlie & Lola Ser.). (ENG., Illus.). 40p. (J). (gr. -1-2). 16.99 (978-0-7636-5347-7(0)) Candlewick Pr.

—You Can Be My Friend. 2007. (Charlie & Lola Ser.). (ENG., Illus.). 24p. (J). (gr. -1-k). mass mkt. 3.99 (978-0-448-44840-4(8), Grosset & Dunlap) Penguin Young Readers Group.

Child, Lauren, et al. Carys Blodyn, Dyma Fi. 2005. (WEL., Illus.). 32p. pap. (978-1-85596-670-3(0)) Dref Wen.

—Fydda i Byth Bythoedd yn Bwyta Tomato. 2005. (WEL., Illus.). 32p. pap. (978-1-85596-668-0(9)) Dref Wen.

Childs, Karin Alfelt. The Balm of Gilead. 2007. 356p. (YA). 15.95 (978-0-9748423-7-0(0)) Fountain Publishing.

Chin, Oliver. Timmy & Tammy's Train of Thought. McPherson, Heath, illus. 2007. (ENG.). 36p. (J). (gr. -1-3). 15.95 (978-1-59702-008-4(7)) Immedium.

Choldenko, Gennifer. Al Capone Does My Homework. 2013. Bk. 3. (ENG.). 224p. (J). (gr. 5). 17.99 (978-0-8037-3472-2(7), Dial Bks) Penguin Publishing Group.

—Al Capone Does My Homework. 2014. (ENG.). 240p. (J). (gr. 5). pap. 7.99 (978-0-14-242522-0(2), Puffin Books) Penguin Young Readers Group.

—Al Capone Does My Homework. 2014. (Tale from Alcatraz (Al Capone) Ser.: 3). lib. bdg. 18.40 (978-0-606-35714-2(9)) Turtleback Bks.

—Al Capone Does My Shirts. (Tales from Alcatraz Ser.). (ENG., Illus.). (J). (gr. 5-18). 2004. 240p. 17.99 (978-0-399-23861-1(1), G.P. Putnam's Sons Books for Young Readers) 2006. 288p. reprint ed. pap. 7.99 (978-0-14-240370-9(9), Puffin Books) Penguin Young Readers Group.

—Al Capone Does My Shirts. 2006. (Illus.). 317p. (J). (gr. 4-7). per. 10.95 (978-0-7862-8927-1(9)) Thorndike Pr.

—Al Capone Shines My Shoes. (ENG.). (J). (gr. 5-18). 2011. 304p. 7.99 (978-0-14-241718-8(1), Puffin Books) 2009. 288p. 17.99 (978-0-8037-3460-9(3), Dial Bks) Penguin Young Readers Group.

—Al Capone Shines My Shoes. 2011. (Tale from Alcatraz (Al Capone) Ser.: 2). lib. bdg. 18.40 (978-0-606-23072-8(6), Turtleback) Turtleback Bks.

—No Passengers Beyond This Point. 2012. (ENG.). 272p. (J). (gr. 5-18). 7.99 (978-0-14-242052-2(2), Puffin Books) Penguin Young Readers Group.

—No Passengers Beyond This Point. 2012. lib. bdg. 17.20 (978-0-606-23637-9(6), Turtleback) Turtleback Bks.

Choldenko, Gennifer, et al. No Passengers Beyond This Point. 2011. (Playaway Children Ser.). (J). 49.99 (978-1-61707-000-6(9)) Findaway World, LLC.

Christopher, Danny. Putuguq & Kublu, 1 vol. Arijanto, Astrid, illus. 2017. (ENG.). 40p. (J). (gr. k-2). pap. 5.95 **(978-1-77227-143-0(8))** Inhabit Media Inc. CAN. Dist: Independent Pubs. Group.

Christopher, Matt. The Great Quarterback Switch. 2008. (New Matt Christopher Sports Library). 144p. (J). (gr. 4-6). lib. bdg. 26.60 (978-1-59953-216-5(6)) Norwood Hse. Pr.

—Lacrosse Face-Off. 2006. (ENG.). 128p. (J). (gr. 3-7). per. 15.99 (978-0-316-79641-5(7)) Little, Brown Bks. for Young Readers.

—Snowboard Showdown. 2005. (Sports Classics IV Ser.). 167p. (J). lib. bdg. 15.00 (978-1-59054-770-0(5)) Fitzgerald Bks.

—Snowboard Showdown. l.t. ed. 2007. (New Matt Christopher Sports Library). 160p. (J). (gr. 4-6). lib. bdg. 26.60 (978-1-59953-109-0(7)) Norwood Hse. Pr.

Chung, Arree. Ninja! Chung, Arree, illus. 2014. (Ninja! Ser.). (ENG., Illus.). 40p. (J). (gr. -1-2). 17.99 (978-0-8050-9911-9(5), 9780805099119, Holt, Henry & Co. Bks. For Young Readers) Holt, Henry & Co.

Church, Alfred J. Three Greek Children. 2008. (Illus.). 160p. pap. 9.95 (978-1-59915-081-9(6)) Yesterday's Classics.

Church, Caroline Jayne. I Am a Big Sister! 2015. (SPA & ENG.). 24p. (J). (gr. -1 — 1). 6.99 (978-0-545-84718-6(4), Scholastic en Espanol) Scholastic, Inc.

—I Am a Big Sister! Church, Caroline Jayne, illus. 2015. (ENG., Illus.). 24p. (J). (gr. -1 — 1). 6.99 (978-0-545-68898-7(1), Cartwheel Bks.) Scholastic, Inc.

Ciraolo, Simona, illus. Whatever Happened to My Sister? 2015. (ENG.). 40p. (J). (gr. k). 17.95 (978-1-909263-52-9(4)) Flying Eye Bks. GBR. Dist: Consortium Bk. Sales & Distribution.

Clark, Catherine. Frozen Rodeo. 2003. (ENG.). 304p. (J). (gr. 8-18). 15.99 (978-0-06-009070-8(7)) HarperCollins Pubs.

Clark, Eleanor. Mary Elizabeth: Welcome to America. 2007. (Eleanor Ser.: Bk. 1). (Illus.). 187p. (J). (gr. 4-7). 14.99 (978-0-9753036-7-2(8)) HonorNet.

Clark, Isabelle. The Enchanted Forest of Hope. 2009. 44p. pap. 18.50 (978-1-4389-7781-2(6)) AuthorHouse.

Clark, Katherine. Seagull Sam. Huntington, Amy, illus. 2007. (ENG.). 32p. (J). (gr. -1-3). 15.95 (978-0-89272-715-5(2)) Down East Bks.

Clarke, Jane. G. E. M. Parsons, Garry, illus. 2008. (ENG.). 32p. (J). (gr. -1-k). pap. 9.95 (978-0-09-948012-9(3), Red Fox) Random House Children's Books GBR. Dist: Independent Pubs. Group.

Clarke, Judith. One Whole & Perfect Day. (ENG.). 2013. 248p. (YA). (gr. 9-12). pap. 9.95 (978-1-62091-025-2(X)) 2007. 250p. (J). (gr. 8-13). 16.95 (978-1-932425-95-6(0), Front Street) Boyds Mills Pr.

Claus, Rimana. I Want That! Moran, Lyn, illus. 2012. 36p. pap. 15.97 (978-1-61897-838-7(1), Strategic Bk. Publishing) Strategic Book Publishing & Rights Agency (SBPRA).

Clayton, Emma. The Whisper. 2012. 309p. (978-0-545-43365-5(7), Chicken Hse., The) Scholastic, Inc.

Cleary, Beverly. Ramona la Chinche. Palacios, Argentina, tr. Darling, Louis, illus. 2006. (Ramona Quimby Spanish Ser.: 2).Tr. of Ramona the Pest. (SPA.). 181p. (J). (gr. 4-7). lib. bdg. 16.00 (978-0-613-00464-0(7), Turtleback) Turtleback Bks.

—Ramona the Pest. (Ramona Quimby Ser.). (J). (gr. 3-5). Random House Publishing Group.

—Two Times the Fun. Taylor, Thomas & Thompson, Carol, illus. 2005. (ENG.). 96p. (J). (gr. -1-2). 16.99 (978-0-06-057921-0(8)) HarperCollins Pubs.

Cleaver, Vera & Cleaver, Bill. Donde Florecen los Lirios. (SPA.). 168p. (YA). (gr. 5-8). (978-84-204-3648-7(8), AF0285) Ediciones Alfaguara ESP. Dist: Lectorum Pubns., Inc.

Clements, Andrew. Troublemaker. Elliott, Mark, illus. 2011. (ENG.). 160p. (J). (gr. 3-7). lib. bdg. 16.99 (978-1-4169-4930-5(5), Atheneum Bks. for Young Readers) Simon & Schuster Children's Publishing.

Clifton, Lutricia. Immortal Max. Sheban, Chris, illus. 2014. (ENG.). 192p. (J). (gr. 3-7). 16.95 (978-0-8234-3041-3(3)) Holiday Hse., Inc.

C.M.M. A Life of Many Forms. 2012. 52p. pap. 16.95 (978-1-62709-318-7(4)) America Star Bks.

Coakley, Lena. Worlds of Ink & Shadow. 2016. (ENG.). 352p. (YA). (gr. 8-17). 17.95 (978-1-4197-1034-6(6), Amulet Bks.) Abrams, Inc.

Cocca-Leffler, Maryann. Theo's Mood: A Book of Feelings. Cocca-Leffler, Maryann, illus. 2013. (ENG., Illus.). 24p. (J). (gr. -1-3). 15.99 (978-0-8075-7778-3(2)) Whitman, Albert & Co.

Codell, Esmé Raji. Vive la Paris. 2006. (ENG.). 224p. (gr. 4-7). 15.99 (978-0-7868-5124-9(4)) Hyperion Pr.

Cody, Matthew. The Peddler's Road. 2015. (Secrets of the Pied Piper Ser.: 1). (ENG., Illus.). 368p. (J). (gr. 3-7). 17.99 (978-0-385-75522-1(8), Knopf Bks. for Young Readers) Random Hse. Children's Bks.

—The Secrets of the Pied Piper 2: the Magician's Key. 2016. (Secrets of the Pied Piper Ser.: 2). (ENG., Illus.). 336p. (J). (gr. 3-7). 17.99 (978-0-385-75526-9(0), Knopf Bks. for Young Readers) Random Hse. Children's Bks.

Coerr, Eleanor. Circus Day in Japan: Bilingual English & Japanese Text. Matsunari, Yumi, tr. 2010. (ENG & JPN., Illus.). 48p. (J). (gr. -1-3). 15.95 (978-4-8053-1059-5(6)) Tuttle Publishing.

Coerr, Eleanor & Matsunari, Yumi. Circus Day in Japan: Bilingual English & Japanese Text. 2016. (ENG & JPN., Illus.). 48p. (J). (gr. -1-3). 9.95 (978-0-8048-4743-8(6)) Tuttle Publishing.

Cohen, Miriam. My Big Brother, 1 vol. Himler, Ronald, illus. 2005. (ENG.). 32p. (J). 15.95 (978-1-59572-007-8(3)); pap. 6.95 (978-1-59572-158-7(4)) Star Bright Bks., Inc.

Coker, Rachel. Chasing Jupiter, 1 vol. 2013. (ENG.). 224p. (YA). 15.99 (978-0-310-73293-8(X)) Zondervan.

Colbert, Brandy. Little & Lion. 2017. (ENG.). 336p. (YA). (gr. 9-17). 17.99 **(978-0-316-34900-0(3))** Little, Brown Bks. for Young Readers.

Cold Moon. 2nd ed. 2014. 180p. pap. 14.99 (978-1-62798-459-1(3), Harmony Ink Pr.) Dreamspinner Pr.

Cole, Joanna. I'm a Big Brother. Kightley, Rosalinda, illus. 2010. (ENG.). 32p. (J). (gr. -1-3). 6.99 (978-0-06-190065-5(6), HarperFestival) HarperCollins Pubs.

—I'm a Big Sister. Kightley, Rosalinda, illus. 2010. (ENG.). 32p. (J). (gr. -1-3). 6.99 (978-0-06-190062-4(1), HarperFestival) HarperCollins Pubs.

—Soy un Hermano Mayor, 1 vol. Kightley, Rosalinda, illus. 2010. (SPA & ENG.). 32p. (J). (gr. -1-k). 6.99 (978-0-06-190066-2(4)) HarperCollins Pubs.

Colfer, Chris. An Author's Odyssey. 2016. (Land of Stories Ser.: 5). (ENG.). (J). (gr. 3-7). 496p. pap. 11.99 (978-0-316-27214-8(0)); (Illus.). 464p. 19.99 (978-0-316-38329-5(5)) Little, Brown Bks. for Young Readers.

—Beyond the Kingdoms. Dorman, Brandon, illus. 2015. (Land of Stories Ser.: Bk. 4). (ENG.). 432p. (J). (gr. 3-7). 19.99 (978-0-316-40689-5(9)) Little, Brown Bks. for Young Readers.

—Beyond the Kingdoms. l.t. ed. 2015. (Land of Stories Ser.: No. 4). (ENG.). 624p. (J). (gr. 3-7). 28.99 (978-0-316-33938-4(5)) Little, Brown Bks. for Young Readers.

—The Curvy Tree. Dorman, Brandon, illus. 2015. (ENG.). 32p. (J). (gr. -1-3). 17.00 (978-0-316-40685-7(6)) Little Brown & Co.

—The Enchantress Returns. (Land of Stories Ser.: 2). (ENG.). (J). (gr. 3-7). 2014. 544p. pap. 9.99 (978-0-316-20155-1(3)) 2013. (Illus.). 528p. 19.99 (978-0-316-20154-4(5)) 2013. 832p. 43.99 (978-0-316-24235-6(7)) Little, Brown Bks. for Young Readers.

—The Enchantress Returns. 2014. (Land of Stories Ser.: 2). (J). lib. bdg. 20.85 (978-0-606-37229-9(6)) Turtleback Bks.

—A Grimm Warning. (Land of Stories Ser.: 3). (ENG.). (J). (gr. 3-7). 2015. 496p. pap. 9.99 (978-0-316-40682-6(1)) 2014. 480p. 19.99 (978-0-316-40681-9(3)) 2014. 768p. 32.99 (978-0-316-40964-3(2)) Little, Brown Bks. for Young Readers.

—A Grimm Warning. 2015. (Land of Stories Ser.: 3). (J). lib. bdg. 20.85 (978-0-606-37230-5(X)) Turtleback Bks.

—The Land of Stories: an Author's Odyssey. 2017. (Land of Stories Ser.: 5). (ENG., Illus.). 464p. (J). (gr. 3-7). pap. 9.99 **(978-0-316-38321-9(X))** Little, Brown Bks. for Young Readers.

Colfer, Chris. The Wishing Spell. 2013. (Land of Stories Ser.: Bk. 1). (ENG.). 464p. (J). (gr. 3-7). pap. 9.99 (978-0-316-20156-8(1)) Little, Brown Bks. for Young Readers.

—The Wishing Spell. Dorman, Brandon, illus. 2012. (Land of Stories Ser.: 1). (ENG.). 448p. (J). (gr. 3-7). 19.99 (978-0-316-20157-5(X)) Little, Brown Bks. for Young Readers.

—The Wishing Spell. l.t. ed. 2013. (Land of Stories Ser.: 1). (ENG.). 672p. (J). (gr. 3-7). pap. 10.00 (978-0-316-24236-3(5)) Little, Brown Bks. for Young Readers.

—The Wishing Spell. 2013. (Land of Stories Ser.: 1). (J). lib. bdg. 20.85 (978-0-606-31746-7(5), Turtleback) Turtleback Bks.

Colfer, Chris & Dorman, Brandon. The Land of Stories the Wishing Spell. 2013. pap. (978-0-545-64793-9(2)) Scholastic, Inc.

Colin, Beatrice & Pinto, Sara. My Invisible Sister. Pinto, Sara, illus. 2011. (ENG., Illus.). 128p. (YA). (gr. 3-6). pap. 6.99 (978-1-59990-678-2(3), 9781599906782, Bloomsbury USA Childrens) Bloomsbury Publishing USA.

Collar, Orpheus & Riordan, Rick. The Throne of Fire. Collar, Orpheus, illus. 2015. (Kane Chronicles Ser.). (ENG., Illus.). 160p. (J). (gr. 5-9). 21.99 (978-1-4847-1490-4(3)) Hyperion Bks. for Children.

Collins, Carleen. Everyone Loves Chocolate. 2009. 60p. pap. 23.99 (978-1-4490-3049-0(1)) AuthorHouse.

Collins, Suzanne. Gregor, Set, Nos. 1-5. 2009. (Underland Chronicles Ser.). (ENG.). (J). (gr. 3-7). pap., pap., pap. 39.95 (978-0-545-16681-2(0)) Scholastic, Inc.

—Gregor & the Code of Claw. 2008. (Underland Chronicles Ser.: 5). (ENG., Illus.). 416p. (J). (gr. 3-7). pap. 7.99 (978-0-439-79144-1(8), Scholastic Paperbacks) Scholastic, Inc.

—Gregor & the Code of Claw. l.t. ed. 2007. (Underland Chronicles: Bk. 5). 413p. (YA). (gr. 8-12). 22.95 (978-0-7862-9696-5(8)) Thorndike Pr.

—Gregor & the Curse of the Warmbloods. 2006. (Underland Chronicles: Bk. 3). 358p. (gr. 4-7). 17.00 (978-0-7569-6766-6(X)) Perfection Learning Corp.

—Gregor & the Curse of the Warmbloods, Bk. 3. 2006. (Underland Chronicles Ser.: 3). (ENG.). 368p. (J). (gr. 3-7). pap. 7.99 (978-0-439-65624-5(9), Scholastic Paperbacks) Scholastic, Inc.

—When Charlie McButton Lost Power. Lester, Mike, illus. 2007. (ENG.). 32p. (J). (gr. -1-3). pap. 6.99 (978-0-14-240857-5(3), Puffin Books) Penguin Young Readers Group.

—When Charlie McButton Lost Power. Lester, Mike, illus. 2009. 32p. 16.00 (978-1-60686-529-3(3)) Perfection Learning Corp.

Columbus, Chris & Vizzini, Ned. Battle of the Beasts. Call, Greg, illus. 2015. (House of Secrets Ser.: 2). (ENG.). 480p. (J). (gr. 3-7). pap. 7.99 (978-0-06-219250-9(7)) HarperCollins Pubs.

—Battle of the Beasts. 2014. (House of Secrets Ser.: 2). (ENG.). 480p. (J). (gr. 3-7). 17.99 (978-0-06-219249-3(3)) HarperCollins Pubs.

—House of Secrets. 2015. (House of Secrets Ser.: Vol. 1). (KOR.). 580p. (J). (978-89-491-7127-2(9)) Biryongso Publishing Co.

—House of Secrets. Call, Greg, illus. (House of Secrets Ser.: 1). (J). 2014. (ENG.). 512p. (gr. 3-7). pap. 7.99 (978-0-06-219247-9(7)) 2013. (ENG.). 496p. (gr. 3-7). 17.99 (978-0-06-219246-2(9)) 2013. 490p. (978-0-06-225964-6(4)) HarperCollins Pubs.

—House of Secrets. 2014. (House of Secrets Ser.: 1). (J). lib. bdg. 18.40 (978-0-606-35070-9(5), Turtleback) Turtleback Bks.

Coman, Carolyn. The Big House. Shepperson, Rob, illus. 2004. (ENG.). 224p. (J). (gr. 4-6). 16.95 (978-1-932425-09-3(8), Lemniscaat) Boyds Mills Pr.

—Sneaking Suspicions. Shepperson, Rob, illus. 2007. (ENG.). 204p. (J). (gr. 4-6). 16.95 (978-1-59078-491-4(X), Front Street) Boyds Mills Pr.

Compestine, Ying. The Story of Kites: Amazing Chinese Inventions. Xuan, YongSheng, illus. 2016. (ENG & CHI.). 40p. (J). (gr. -1-3). 15.95 (978-1-59702-122-7(9)) Immedium.

Condie, Catherine. Whirl of the Wheel. 2010. 107p. pap. 12.95 (978-1-4452-8648-8(3)) Lulu Pr., Inc.

Condon, Bill. Riley & the Treasure. Hopgood, Andrew, illus. 2015. (Legends in Their Own Lunchbox Ser.). (ENG.). 56p. (gr. 2-3). pap. 7.99 (978-1-4966-0258-9(7), Legends in Their Own Lunchbox) Capstone Classroom.

—Riley Versus the Giant Banana. Hopgood, Andrew, illus. 2015. (Legends in Their Own Lunchbox Ser.). (ENG.). 48p. (gr. 1-2). pap. 7.99 (978-1-4966-0246-6(3), Legends in Their Own Lunchbox) Capstone Classroom.

Conklin, Melanie. Counting Thyme. 2016. (ENG.). 320p. (J). (gr. 5). 16.99 (978-0-399-17330-1(7), G.P. Putnam's Sons Books for Young Readers) Penguin Young Readers Group.

Connelly, Neil. The Miracle Stealer. 2010. (ENG.). 240p. (J). (gr. 9-18). 17.99 (978-0-545-13195-7(2), Levine, Arthur A. Bks.) Scholastic, Inc.

Connelly, Neil O. The Miracle Stealer. 2012. (ENG.). 240p. (J). (gr. 9-9). pap. 9.99 (978-0-545-13312-8(2), Levine, Arthur A. Bks.) Scholastic, Inc.

Conner, Sharon Landsberg. The Magnetizing Princess: A children's story that uses some of the most powerful tools available, to get more of what you Want. 2007. 56p. per. 8.95 (978-0-595-44229-4(3)) iUniverse, Inc.

Connolly, MarcyKate. Ravenous. 2016. (Illus.). 416p. (J). (gr. 3-7). 16.99 *(978-0-06-227274-4(8))* HarperCollins Pubs.
Connor, Leslie. Crunch. 2012. (ENG.). 336p. (J). (gr. 5). pap. 6.99 *(978-0-06-169234-5(4))*, Tegen, Katherine Bks) HarperCollins Pubs.
Connor, Patrick M. Tree House. 2011. 312p. pap. 29.95 *(978-1-4560-9578-9(1))* America Star Bks.
Conrique, Samantha. The Pod-Poppers. 2007. (J). pap. 8.00 *(978-0-8059-7200-9(5))* Dorrance Publishing Co., Inc.
Cook, Deena & McIntosh, Cherie. Pinky & Peanut: The Adventure Begins. Scruggs, Trina, illus. 2007. 78p. (J). per. 4.99 *(978-0-9797020-0-6(3))* P & P Publishing LLC.
Cook, Julia. I Want to Be the Only Dog! DuFalla, Anita, illus. 2015. (ENG.). 32p. (J). pap. 10.95 *(978-1-934490-86-0(5))* Boys Town Pr.
Cook, Tina H. Lindsey & the Yellow Masterpiece. 2011. 36p. pap. 15.99 *(978-1-4634-0306-5(2))* AuthorHouse.
Coolidge, Susan. Clover. 2005. (Illus.). 133p. pap. *(978-1-59569-026-5(3))* Mondial.
Coolidge, Susan. What Katy Did. 2013. (ENG., Illus.). 200p. (J). 15.00 *(978-1-84135-843-7(6))* Award Pubns. Ltd. GBR. Dist: Parkwest Pubns., Inc.
—What Katy Did. Ledyard, Addie, illus. 2013. 132p. pap. *(978-1-909735-03-3(5))* Aziloth Bks.
—What Katy Did. 2012. 246p. pap. *(978-1-78139-262-1(5))* Benediction Classics.
—What Katy Did. Hellard, Susan, illus. 2016. (ENG.). 246p. (J). pap. 9.99 ***(978-1-84749-607-2(5)***, 9781847496072, Alma Classics) Bloomsbury Publishing USA.
—What Katy Did. 2017. (ENG., Illus.). (J). (gr. 4-6). pap. 9.90 ***(978-1-366-50696-2(0))*** Blurb, Inc.
—What Katy Did. 2015. (ENG., Illus.). (J). (gr. 2-4). 25.95 ***(978-1-297-62709-5(1))*** 2012. 302p. pap. 29.75 *(978-1-286-07372-8(3))* 2012. 300p. pap. 29.75 *(978-1-286-00091-5(2))* 2011. 290p. (gr. 3-7). pap. 28.75 *(978-1-179-65265-8(7))* 2010. (ENG.). 300p. pap. 29.75 *(978-1-178-00783-1(9))* 2010. (ENG.). 282p. (gr. 3-7). pap. 28.75 *(978-1-177-27477-7(9))* 2010. 302p. pap. 29.75 *(978-1-145-74830-9(9))* 2008. 164p. (gr. 4-7). 22.99 *(978-0-554-37937-1(6))* 2008. 164p. (gr. 4-7). 25.99 *(978-0-554-28634-1(3))* 2007. (ENG.). 144p. pap. 18.99 *(978-1-4346-5943-9(7))* 2007. (ENG.). 160p. pap. 21.99 *(978-1-4346-5944-6(5))* Creative Media Partners, LLC.
—What Katy Did. 2007. (ENG.). 148p. per. *(978-1-4065-1527-5(2))* Dodo Pr.
—What Katy Did. 2006. (Dover Children's Classics Ser.). (ENG., Illus.). 160p. (J). (gr. 3-8). per. 6.95 *(978-0-486-44760-5(X))* Dover Pubns., Inc.
—What Katy Did. 2007. (ENG.). 104p. per. *(978-1-4068-4855-7(7))* Echo Library.
—What Katy Did. 2010. (Illus.). 92p. (gr. 3-7). pap. 19.99 *(978-1-153-74507-9(0))* 2009. 104p. pap. 6.40 *(978-0-217-53637-0(9))* General Bks. LLC.
—What Katy Did. 2010. 132p. pap. *(978-1-4076-5115-6(3))* HardPr.
—What Katy Did. Ledyard, Addie, illus. 284p. 2010. 35.16 *(978-1-163-85079-4(9))* 2010. pap. 23.16 *(978-1-163-77965-1(2))* 2007. 43.95 *(978-0-548-53870-8(0))* 2007. per. 28.95 *(978-0-548-48700-6(6))* Kessinger Publishing, LLC.
—What Katy Did. 2010. (Puffin Classics Ser.). (ENG., Illus.). 240p. (J). (gr. 5-7). pap. 5.99 *(978-0-14-132671-9(9))*, Puffin Books) Penguin Young Readers Group.
—What Katy Did. 2013. (ENG., Illus.). 256p. (J). (gr. 4-7). pap. 12.99 *(978-0-09-957312-8(1))* Random Hse. GBR. Dist: Independent Pubs. Group.
—What Katy Did. 2007. (ENG.). 192p. pap. 12.45 *(978-1-60424-403-8(8))*, Book Jungle) Standard Pubns., Inc.
—What Katy Did. 2011. 162p. (gr. 3-7). pap. *(978-3-8424-6664-7(1))* Tredition GmbH.
—What Katy Did. 2010. 144p. pap. 4.99 *(978-1-61720-100-4(6))* Wilder Pubns., Corp.
Coolidge, Susan & Ledyard, Addie. What Katy Did. 2010. (ENG.). 292p. pap. 28.75 *(978-1-172-34659-2(3))* Creative Media Partners, LLC.
Cooney, Caroline B. A Friend at Midnight. 2008. (ENG.). 192p. (YA). (gr. 7). pap. 8.99 *(978-1-4000-7209-5(3))*, WaterBrook Pr.) Crown Publishing Group.
—A Friend at Midnight. 2008. (ENG.). 192p. (YA). (gr. 7). pap. 8.99 *(978-0-385-73327-4(5))*, Delacorte Bks. for Young Readers) Random Hse. Children's Bks.
—If the Witness Lied. 2010. (ENG.). 224p. (YA). (gr. 7). pap. 8.99 *(978-0-385-73449-3(2))*, Ember) Random Hse. Children's Bks.
—The Terrorist. 2012. (ENG.). 144p. (YA). pap. 6.99 *(978-1-4532-7467-5(7))* Open Road Integrated Media, Inc.
—The Voice on the Radio. 2012. (ENG.). 208p. (YA). (gr. 7). pap. 9.99 *(978-0-385-74240-5(1))*, Ember) Random Hse. Children's Bks.
—The Voice on the Radio. 2012. (Janie Bks.: 3). lib. bdg. 20.85 *(978-0-606-26369-6(1))*, Turtleback) Turtleback Bks.
—Whatever Happened to Janie? 2012. (ENG.). 224p. (YA). (gr. 7). pap. 9.99 *(978-0-385-74239-9(8))*, Ember) Random Hse. Children's Bks.
Cooper, Susan. The Dark Is Rising. 2009. 7.64 *(978-0-7848-2212-8(3))*, Everbind) Marco Bk. Co.
—The Dark Is Rising. 15.85 *(978-0-7569-8464-9(5))* Perfection Learning Corp.
—The Dark Is Rising. (Dark Is Rising Sequence Ser.). 244p. (YA). (gr. 5-18). pap. 4.99 *(978-0-8072-1533-3(3))*, Listening Library) Random Hse. Audio Publishing Group.
—Green Boy. 2003. (ENG., Illus.). 208p. (J). (gr. 4-7). pap. 7.99 *(978-0-689-84760-8(2))*, McElderry, Margaret K. Bks.) McElderry, Margaret K. Bks.
—Over Sea, under Stone. 2013. (Dark Is Rising Sequence Ser.: 1). (ENG., Illus.). 288p. (J). (gr. 3-7). 17.99 *(978-1-4424-9592-0(8))*, McElderry, Margaret K. Bks.) McElderry, Margaret K. Bks.
Corbett, Sue. 12 Again. 2007. (ENG.). 240p. (J). (gr. 5-18). 6.99 *(978-0-14-240729-5(1))*, Puffin Books) Penguin Young Readers Group.
Corlett, William. The Bridge in the Clouds. 2010. (Magician's House Quartet Ser.: 4). (ENG.). 352p. (YA). (gr. 5-8). pap. 15.99 *(978-1-4424-1412-9(X))*, Simon Pulse) Simon Pulse.
—The Door in the Tree. 2010. (Magician's House Quartet Ser.: 2). (ENG.). 304p. (YA). (gr. 5-8). pap. 13.99 *(978-1-4424-1414-3(6))*, Simon Pulse) Simon Pulse.
—The Steps up the Chimney. 2011. (Magician's House Quartet Ser.: 1). (ENG.). 288p. (YA). (gr. 7). pap. 13.99 *(978-1-4424-2935-2(6))*, Simon Pulse) Simon Pulse.
Corso, Erika. The Day You Came. Corso, Erika & Corso, Bertina, illus. 2006. (ENG.). 20p. (J). per. 12.95 *(978-1-59800-242-3(2))* Outskirts Pr., Inc.
Cory, Kim Delmar. Home to Mackinac: The Tale of Young Jack Murphy's Discovery of Loyalty, Family, & Forgiveness. Evans, Laura, illus. 2007. (ENG.). 175p. (J). (gr. 3-7). per. 9.95 *(978-0-911872-87-3(6))* Mackinac State Historic Parks.
—Tending Ben's Garden. 2009. (J). pap. *(978-0-88092-778-9(X))* Royal Fireworks Publishing Co.
Cosgrove, Stephen. Katy Didd Bigg: Standing up for Yourself. Arroyo, Fian, illus. 2004. (J). *(978-1-58804-378-8(9))* P C I Education.
Costa, T. L. Playing Tyler. 2013. (ENG.). 304p. (J). (gr. 9). pap. 9.99 *(978-1-908844-61-3(2))*, Strange Chemistry) Watkins Media Limited GBR. Dist: Penguin Random Hse. LLC.
Costello, David Hyde. Little Pig Joins the Band. Costello, David Hyde, illus. 2014. (ENG., Illus.). 32p. (J). (gr. -1-3). pap. 7.95 *(978-1-58089-265-0(5))* Charlesbridge Publishing, Inc.
—Little Pig Joins the Band. Costello, David Hyde, illus. 2012. (Illus.). 29.95 incl. audio compact disk *(978-1-4301-1139-9(9))* Live Oak Media.
—Little Pig Saves the Ship. Costello, David Hyde, illus. 2017. (ENG., Illus.). 32p. (J). (gr. -1-2). 14.99 *(978-1-58089-715-0(0))* Charlesbridge Publishing, Inc.
Cotler, Steve. Cheesie Mack Is Running Like Crazy! Holgate, Douglas, illus. (Cheesie Mack Ser.). (ENG.). (J). (gr. 3-7). 2014. 256p. pap. 6.99 *(978-0-307-97716-8(1))*, Yearling) 2013. 240p. 15.99 *(978-0-307-97713-7(7))*, Random Hse. Bks. for Young Readers) Random Hse. Children's Bks.
Couloumbis, Audrey & Couloumbis, Akila. War Games. 2011. (ENG.). 240p. (J). (gr. 3-7). pap. 6.99 *(978-0-375-85629-7(3))*, Yearling) Random Hse. Children's Bks.
Cousins, Dave. Waiting for Gonzo. 2015. (ENG.). 288p. (YA). pap. 9.99 *(978-0-7387-4199-4(X))*, Flux) North Star Editions.
Covey, Sean. Sammy & the Pecan Pie. Curtis, Stacy, illus. 2013. (7 Habits of Happy Kids Ser.: 4). (ENG.). 32p. (J). (gr. -1-1). 7.99 *(978-1-4424-7647-9(8))*, Simon & Schuster Bks. For Young Readers) Simon & Schuster Bks. For Young Readers.
Cowen-Fletcher, Jane. It Takes a Village. (J). (gr. 1-2). pap. *(978-0-590-46598-4(8))* Scholastic, Inc.
Cowley, Marjorie. The Golden Bull. 2012. (ENG.). 216p. (J). (gr. 4-7). pap. 8.95 *(978-1-58089-182-0(9))* Charlesbridge Publishing, Inc.
Cowsar, Susan. The Magic Flower. 2013. 58p. pap. 10.99 *(978-1-62697-943-7(X))* Salem Author Services.
Coyle, Carmela Lavigna. Do Princesses Scrape Their Knees? 2006. (ENG., Illus.). 32p. (J). (gr. -1-2). 15.95 *(978-0-87358-909-3(2))* Cooper Square Publishing Llc.
—Do Princesses Scrape Their Knees? Keepsake Sticker Doodle Book. Gordon, Mike & Gordon, Carl, illus. 2014. (ENG.). 96p. (J). (gr. -1-2). 15.95 *(978-1-58979-948-6(8))* Taylor Trade Publishing.
Cozzo, Karole. How to Say I Love You Out Loud. 2015. (ENG.). 240p. (YA). (gr. 7). pap. 9.99 *(978-1-250-06359-5(0))* Feiwel & Friends.
Creech, Sharon. The Castle Corona. Diaz, David, illus. (J). 2013. (ENG.). 352p. (gr. 3-7). pap. 7.99 *(978-0-06-206395-3(2))* 2007. 336p. (gr. 4-7). lib. bdg. 19.89 *(978-0-06-084622-0(4))*, Cotler, Joanna Books) HarperCollins Pubs.
—Ruby Holler. 2012. (ENG.). 288p. (J). (gr. 3-7). pap. 6.99 *(978-0-06-056015-7(0))* HarperCollins Pubs.
—Ruby Holler. 2004. (Joanna Cotler Bks.). 310p. (gr. 3-7). 17.00 *(978-0-7569-1940-5(1))* Perfection Learning Corp.
—Ruby Holler. 2012. (J). (gr. 3-6). 17.20 *(978-0-613-86272-1(4))*, Turtleback) Turtleback Bks.
Croggon, Alison. The Singing: Book Four of Pellinor. 2017. (Pellinor Ser.). (ENG.). 496p. (J). (gr. 7). pap. 9.99 *(978-0-7636-9446-3(0))* Candlewick Pr.
Crompton, Laurie Boyle. Blaze (Or, Love in the Time of Supervillains) 2013. (ENG.). 320p. (YA). (gr. 7-12). pap. 8.99 *(978-1-4022-7343-8(6))* Sourcebooks, Inc.
Crook, M. J. Village on Crooked Hill. 2008. 168p. pap. 11.99 *(978-1-4389-0486-3(X))* AuthorHouse.
Crouch, Cheryl. Troo's Secret Clubhouse, 1 vol. Zimmer, Kevin, illus. 2011. (I Can Read! / Rainforest Friends Ser.). (ENG.). 32p. (J). (gr. -1-2). pap. 3.99 *(978-0-310-71809-3(0))* Zonderkidz.
Crow, Melinda Melton. Little Lizard's New Baby, 1 vol. Rowland, Andrew, illus. 2011. (Little Lizards Ser.). (ENG.). 32p. (gr. -1-1). pap. 6.25 *(978-1-4342-3047-8(3))* Stone Arch Bks.
Crum, Sally. Race to Moonrise Rev. Carlson, Eric S., illus. 2006. 12.95 *(978-1-932738-31-5(2))* Western Reflections Publishing Co.
Crumbaugh, David. The Primrose Kids. 2006. 81p. pap. 16.95 *(978-1-4241-3250-8(9))* PublishAmerica, Inc.
Crump, Fred, Jr. The Brave Toy Soldier. 2007. (Illus.). 32p. (J). 12.95 *(978-1-934056-20-2(0))* UMI (Urban Ministries, Inc.).
Crump Jr., Fred. The Brave Toy Soldier. 2007. (Illus.). 32p. (J). (gr. -1). pap. 9.95 *(978-1-932715-82-8(7))* UMI (Urban Ministries, Inc.).
Cullen, Lynn. Dear Mr. Washington. Carpenter, Nancy, illus. 2015. (ENG.). 32p. (J). (gr. k-3). 16.99 *(978-0-8037-3038-0(1))*, Dial Bks) Penguin Young Readers Group.
Cumberland, Dale. Angel Trap. 2012. 166p. (-18). 22.95 *(978-1-4759-5601-6(0))*; pap. 12.95 *(978-1-4759-5599-6(5))* iUniverse, Inc.
Cummings, Priscilla. Beetle Boddiker, 1 vol. Ramsey, Marcy Dunn, illus. 2009. (ENG.). 30p. (J). (gr. k-7). 13.95 *(978-0-87033-602-7(9))*, 9780870336027, Cornell Maritime Pr./Tidewater Pubs.) Schiffer Publishing, Ltd.
Cumyn, Alan. The Secret Life of Owen Skye. 2nd ed. 2008. (ENG.). 176p. (J). (gr. 3-7). pap. 9.95 *(978-0-88899-867-5(8))* Groundwood Bks. CAN. Dist: Publishers Group West (PGW).
Currie, Colleen & Currie, David. Loving Baby Louie: Hope in the Midst of Grief. Streeter, Talena, illus. 2015. (ENG.). 54p. (J). 24.95 *(978-1-941447-44-4(9))* Emmaus Road Publishing.
Currinder, Michael. Running Full Tilt. 2017. (ENG.). 336p. (YA). (gr. 7). lib. bdg. 17.99 ***(978-1-58089-802-7(5)***, Charlesbridge Teen) Charlesbridge Publishing, Inc.
Curtis, Christopher Paul. The Watsons Go to Birmingham—1963. 2013. (ENG.). 224p. (J). (gr. 3-7). 7.99 *(978-0-385-38294-6(4))*, Yearling) Random Hse. Children's Bks.
—The Watsons Go to Birmingham 1963. 210p. (YA). (gr. 5-18). pap. 5.50 *(978-0-8072-8336-3(3))*; 2004. (J). (gr. 4-18). pap. 38.00 incl. audio *(978-0-8072-8335-6(5))*, YA166SP) Random Hse. Audio Publishing Group. (Listening Library).
Curtis, Christopher Paul & Vega, Eida de la. Los Watson Van a Birmingham - 1963. 2016. (SPA.). 200p. (J). (gr. 5-12). pap. 12.99 ***(978-1-63245-640-3(0))*** Lectorum Pubns., Inc.
Curtis, Jennifer Keats. Baby Owl's Rescue, 1 vol. Jacques, Laura, illus. 2009. (ENG.). 32p. (J). (gr. -1-3). 16.95 *(978-1-934359-95-2(5))*, 9781934359952) Arbordale Publishing.
Curtis, Vanessa & Quarto Generic Staff. The Taming of Lilah May. 2012. (ENG.). 192p. (J). (gr. 7-9). pap. 8.99 *(978-1-84780-149-4(8))*, Frances Lincoln) Quarto Publishing Group UK GBR. Dist: Hachette Bk. Group.
Cusack, Dale. Gwen & the Dragon. 2007. (Illus.). 114p. pap. 9.95 *(978-1-4303-1080-8(4))* Lulu Pr., Inc.
Cushman, Jean, et al. Little Golden Book Mommy Stories. Wilkin, Eloise & Meisel, Paul, illus. 2015. (Little Golden Book Favorites Ser.). (ENG.). 80p. (J). (-k). 6.99 *(978-0-385-39273-0(7))*, Golden Bks.) Random Hse. Children's Bks.
Cussler, Clive. The Adventures of Hotsy Totsy. 2011. (ENG., Illus.). 176p. (J). (gr. 3-7). 6.99 *(978-0-14-241873-4(0))*, Puffin Books) Penguin Young Readers Group.
Cuyler, Margery. Tick Tock Clock. Neubecker, Robert, illus. 2012. (My First I Can Read Ser.). (ENG.). 32p. (J). (gr. -1—1). 16.99 *(978-0-06-136309-2(X))*; pap. 3.99 *(978-0-06-136311-5(1))* HarperCollins Pubs.
Dafydd, Myrddin ap. Brwydr y Brodyr. 2005. (WEL.). 68p. pap. *(978-0-86381-906-3(0))* Gwasg Carreg Gwalch.
Dagg, Stephanie. The Big Brother. Clarke, Alan, illus. 2003. (Pandas Ser.: 24). (ENG.). 64p. (J). pap. 9.95 *(978-0-86278-779-0(3))* O'Brien Pr., Ltd., The IRL. Dist: Dufour Editions, Inc.
Daher, Anita. Two Foot Punch, 1 vol. 2007. (Orca Sports Ser.). (ENG., Illus.). 176p. (YA). (gr. 6-10). per. 9.95 *(978-1-55143-876-4(3))* Orca Bk. Pubs. USA.
Dahl, Khetam. The Mulberry Tree. 2013. 100p. (gr. -1). pap. 11.65 *(978-1-4669-8313-7(2))* Trafford Publishing.
Dahl, Michael. Fangs in the Mirror, 1 vol. Aime, Luigi, illus. 2012. (Dragonborn Ser.). (ENG.). 72p. (gr. 1-3). pap. 7.10 *(978-1-4342-4255-6(2))*; lib. bdg. 23.99 *(978-1-4342-4042-2(8))* Stone Arch Bks.
Dales, Cindy. Autumn's First Easter. 2009. 28p. pap. 12.99 *(978-1-4343-1433-8(2))* AuthorHouse.
Daley, James Ryan. Jesus Jackson. 2014. (ENG.). 278p. (YA). pap. 10.95 *(978-1-929345-06-9(2))* Poisoned Pen Pr.
Dana Kittendorf. Trail of Dreams. 2009. 136p. 21.95 *(978-1-4401-7787-3(2))*; pap. 11.95 *(978-1-4401-7785-9(6))* iUniverse, Inc.
Daniels, J. M. The Secret of the Little Dutch Doll. 2009. 68p. pap. 25.49 *(978-1-4343-9356-2(9))* AuthorHouse.
D'Argenzio, Gertilyn Elinor. What Color Is Your Happiness? 2012. 24p. pap. 15.99 *(978-1-4669-1443-8(2))* Trafford Publishing.
Darrow, Sharon. Trash. 2006. (ENG.). 160p. (YA). (gr. 7-12). 16.99 *(978-0-7636-2624-2(4))* Candlewick Pr.
Dateno, Maria Grace. Braving the Storm, 6 vols., Vol. 2. Cunningham, Paul, illus. 2013. 70p. (J). pap. 5.95 *(978-0-8198-1204-9(8))* Pauline Bks. & Media.
—Courageous Quest. Cunningham, Paul, illus. 2014. 81p. (J). pap. 5.95 *(978-0-8198-1628-3(0))* Pauline Bks. & Media.
—Danger at Sea. Cunningham, Paul, illus. 2013. 80p. (J). pap. 5.95 *(978-0-8198-1891-1(7))* Pauline Bks. & Media.
—Discovery at Dawn. Cunningham, Paul, illus. 2014. (ENG.). 79p. (J). pap. 5.95 *(978-0-8198-1895-9(X))* Pauline Bks. & Media.
—Mystery of the Missing Jars. Cunningham, Paul, illus. 2014. 77p. (J). 5.95 *(978-0-8198-4922-9(7))* Pauline Bks. & Media.
—Shepherds to the Rescue, 6 vols., Vol. 1. Cunningham, Paul, illus. 2013. 71p. (J). pap. 5.95 *(978-0-8198-7251-7(2))* Pauline Bks. & Media.
Daunis, Marcia Prosco. Miller's Ben. 2008. 159p. pap. 24.95 *(978-1-60672-759-1(1))* America Star Bks.
Daviddi, Evelyn. My Sister Makes Me Happy! My Sister Makes Me Mad! 2007. (ENG., Illus.). 32p. (J). (gr. 4-7). 10.95 *(978-1-59687-170-0(9))* IBks., Inc.
Davies, Jacqueline. The Bell Bandit. (Lemonade War Ser.). (ENG., Illus.). 192p. (J). (gr. 2-5). 2013. pap. 7.99 *(978-0-544-02274-4(2))* 2012. 16.99 *(978-0-547-56737-2(5))* Houghton Mifflin Harcourt Publishing Co.
—The Bell Bandit. 2013. (Lemonade War Ser.: 3). lib. bdg. 18.40 *(978-0-606-31669-9(8))*, Turtleback) Turtleback Bks.
—The Candy Smash. (Lemonade War Ser.). (ENG., Illus.). 240p. (J). (gr. 2-5). 2014. pap. 7.99 *(978-0-544-22500-8(7))*, HMH Books For Young Readers) 2013. 15.99 *(978-0-544-02208-9(4))* Houghton Mifflin Harcourt Publishing Co.
—The Lemonade Crime. 2011. (Lemonade War Ser.: 2). (ENG., Illus.). 160p. (J). (gr. 2-5). 15.99 *(978-0-547-27967-1(1))* Houghton Mifflin Harcourt Publishing Co.
—The Lemonade Crime. 2012. (Lemonade War Ser.: 2). lib. bdg. 18.40 *(978-0-606-24518-0(9))*, Turtleback) Turtleback Bks.
—The Lemonade War. (Lemonade War Ser.: 1). (ENG.). 192p. (J). (gr. 2-5). 2009. pap. 7.99 *(978-0-547-23765-7(0))* 2007. (Illus.). 16.99 *(978-0-618-75043-6(6))* Houghton Mifflin Harcourt Publishing Co.
—The Magic Trap. 2014. (Lemonade War Ser.: 5). (ENG., Illus.). 272p. (J). (gr. 2-5). 15.99 *(978-0-544-05289-5(7))*, HMH Books For Young Readers) Houghton Mifflin Harcourt Publishing Co.
Davies, Katie. The Great Cat Conspiracy. Shaw, Hannah, illus. 2012. (Great Critter Capers Ser.). (ENG.). 224p. (J). (gr. 3-7). 12.99 *(978-1-4424-4513-0(0))*, Beach Lane Bks.) Beach Lane Bks.
—The Great Dog Disaster. Shaw, Hannah, illus. 2013. (Great Critter Capers Ser.). (ENG.). 208p. (J). (gr. 3-7). 12.99 *(978-1-4424-4517-8(3))*, Beach Lane Bks.) Beach Lane Bks.
—The Great Hamster Massacre. Shaw, Hannah, illus. 2011. (Great Critter Capers Ser.). (ENG.). 208p. (J). (gr. 3-7). 12.99 *(978-1-4424-2062-5(6))*, Beach Lane Bks.) Beach Lane Bks.
Davies, Stephen. Outlaw. 2011. (ENG.). 304p. (YA). (gr. 7). 16.99 *(978-0-547-39017-8(3))* Houghton Mifflin Harcourt Publishing Co.
Davis, Catherine. Abby & Alex Feel Their Hearts' Little. 2006. 57p. pap. 16.95 *(978-1-4241-4586-7(4))* PublishAmerica, Inc.
Davis, Jacky. The Amazing Adventures of Bumblebee Boy. Soman, David, illus. 2011. (Ladybug Girl Ser.). (ENG.). 40p. (J). (gr. -1-k). 16.99 *(978-0-8037-3418-0(2))*, Dial Bks) Penguin Young Readers Group.
—Ladybug Girl. Soman, David, illus. 2015. (Ladybug Girl Ser.). (ENG.). 40p. (J). (-k). 18.99 *(978-1-101-99433-7(9))*, Dial Bks) Penguin Young Readers Group.
Davis, Jacky & Soman, David. Ladybug Girl. Soman, David, illus. 2008. (Ladybug Girl Ser.). (ENG., Illus.). 40p. (J). (gr. -1-k). 17.99 *(978-0-8037-3195-0(7))*, Dial Bks) Penguin Young Readers Group.
Davis, Jill. The First Rule of Little Brothers. McMenemy, Sarah, illus. 2008. (ENG.). 40p. (J). (gr. -1-2). 16.99 *(978-0-375-84046-3(X))*, Knopf Bks. for Young Readers) Random Hse. Children's Bks.
Davis, Rachel. My Life at Mapleleaf Cabin. 2nd ed. 2004. (YA). per. 10.00 *(978-0-9741176-8-3(4))* Wu Li Turtle Corp.
Davis, Samira And Edwina. Nikko & Sierra's Adventures: I Hate Knuckle Sandwiches. 2011. 24p. pap. 11.32 *(978-1-4634-0408-6(5))* AuthorHouse.
Davis, Tanita S. Happy Families. (ENG.). 240p. (YA). (gr. 7). 2013. pap. 9.99 *(978-0-375-87170-2(5))*, Ember) 2012. 16.99 *(978-0-375-86966-2(2))*, Knopf Bks. for Young Readers) Random Hse. Children's Bks.
—Peas & Carrots. 2016. (ENG.). 288p. (YA). (gr. 7). 17.99 *(978-0-553-51281-6(1))*; lib. bdg. 20.99 *(978-0-553-51282-3(X))* Random Hse. Children's Bks. (Knopf Bks. for Young Readers).
De Graaf, Anne. Son of a Gun. 2012. (ENG.). 125p. (YA). pap. 8.00 *(978-0-8028-5406-3(0))*, Eerdmans Bks For Young Readers) Eerdmans, William B. Publishing Co.
De Haven, Tom. The Orphan's Tent. 2005. (Illus.). 192p. mass mkt. 5.99 *(978-0-7434-9772-5(4))* ibooks, Inc.
De la Cruz, Melissa & Johnston, Michael. Stolen Bk. 2: Heart of Dread. 2014. (Heart of Dread Ser.: 2). (ENG.). 304p. (YA). (gr. 7). 17.99 *(978-0-399-25755-1(1))*, G.P. Putnam's Sons Books for Young Readers) Penguin Young Readers Group.
de la Vega, Eida, tr. from ENG. Estela en el Mercado de Pulgas. Sanchez, Enrique O., illus. 2005. (SPA.). 32p. (J). (gr. -1-k). 16.95 *(978-1-58430-245-2(3))* Lee & Low Bks., Inc.
De Laurentiis, Giada. Hong Kong! #3. Gambatesa, Francesca, illus. 2014. (Recipe for Adventure Ser.: 3). (ENG.). 144p. (J). (gr. 2-5). 6.99 *(978-0-448-46258-5(3))*; 16.99 *(978-0-448-48040-4(9))* Penguin Young Readers Group. (Grosset & Dunlap).
—Paris!, No. 2. Gambatesa, Francesca, illus. 2013. (Recipe for Adventure Ser.: 2). (ENG.). 144p. (J). (gr. 2-5). 6.99 *(978-0-448-46257-8(5))*, Grosset & Dunlap) Penguin Young Readers Group.
—Paris! No. 2. Gambatesa, Francesca, illus. 2013. (Recipe for Adventure Ser.: 2). (ENG.). 144p. (J). (gr. 2-5). 16.99 *(978-0-448-47854-8(4))*, Grosset & Dunlap) Penguin Young Readers Group.
De Laurentiis, Giada, et al. Hawaii! #6. Gambatesa, Francesca, illus. 2015. (Recipe for Adventure Ser.: 6). (ENG.). 160p. (J). (gr. 2-4). bds. 6.99 *(978-0-448-48391-7(2))*, Grosset & Dunlap) Penguin Young Readers Group.
—Rio de Janeiro! #5. Gambatesa, Francesca, illus. 2015. (Recipe for Adventure Ser.: 5). (ENG.). 160p. (J). (gr. 2-4). bds. 6.99 *(978-0-448-48204-0(5))*, Grosset & Dunlap) Penguin Young Readers Group.
Dealey, Erin. Goldie Locks Has Chicken Pox. 2004. (Illus.). (J). (gr. k-3). spiral bd. *(978-0-616-14573-9(X))*; spiral bd. *(978-0-616-14572-2(1))* Canadian National Institute for the Blind/Institut National Canadien pour les Aveugles.
—Goldie Locks Has Chicken Pox. Wakiyama, Hanako, illus. 2005. (ENG.). 40p. (J). (gr. -1-2). reprint ed. 8.99 *(978-0-689-87610-3(6))*, Aladdin) Simon & Schuster Children's Publishing.
Deans, Sis Boulos. Racing the Past. 2005. (ENG.). 160p. (J). (gr. 3-7). reprint ed. 5.99 *(978-0-14-240308-2(3))*, Puffin Books) Penguin Young Readers Group.
Debono, Angelo. The Magic in You. 2011. 36p. pap. 13.95 *(978-1-61204-783-6(1))*, Strategic Bk. Publishing) Strategic Book Publishing & Rights Agency (SBPRA).
Dee, Barbara. Just Another Day in My Insanely Real Life. 2007. (Mix Ser.). (ENG.). 256p. (J). (gr. 4-8). pap. 7.99 *(978-1-4169-4739-4(6))*, Aladdin) Simon & Schuster Children's Publishing.
deGroat, Diane. Trick or Treat, Smell My Feet, 4 bks., Set. 2008. (J). (gr. -1-2). pap. 39.95 incl. audio compact disk *(978-1-4301-0428-5(7))*; pap. 37.95 incl. audio *(978-1-4301-0426-1(0))* Live Oak Media.
Deighton, Jo, adapted by. Codadad & His Brothers: Traditional Stories:The Grocer, the Student & the Elf: The Ugly Duckling. (Scheherezade Presents Ser.: No. 13). (Illus.). 48p. (J). pap. *(978-1-85964-103-3(2))*, Ithaca Pr.) Garnet Publishing, Ltd.
Dekker, James. Scum, 1 vol. 2008. (Orca Soundings Ser.). (ENG.). 112p. (YA). (gr. 8-12). pap. 9.95 *(978-1-55143-924-2(7))* Orca Bk. Pubs. USA.
Dekker, James C. Scum, 1 vol. 2008. (Orca Soundings Ser.). (ENG.). 112p. (YA). (gr. 8-12). 16.95 *(978-1-55143-926-6(3))* Orca Bk. Pubs. USA.
Delacre, Lulu. Rafi & Rosi. 2004. (Illus.). 64p. (J). lib. bdg. 13.85 *(978-1-4242-0596-7(4))* Fitzgerald Bks.
—Rafi & Rosi. Delacre, Lulu, illus. 2005. (I Can Read Bks.). (Illus.). 64p. (J). (gr. k-3). pap. 3.99 *(978-0-06-009897-1(X))*, Rayo) HarperCollins Pubs.
—Rafi & Rosi. Delacre, Lulu, illus. 2016. (Rafi & Rosi Ser.). (ENG., Illus.). 63p. (J). (gr. k-3). pap. 8.95 *(978-0-89239-377-0(7))* Lee & Low Bks., Inc.
—Rafi & Rosi Carnival!, 1 vol. 2016. (Rafi & Rosi Ser.). (ENG., Illus.). 64p. (J). (gr. k-3). pap. 8.95 *(978-0-89239-379-4(3))* Lee & Low Bks., Inc.

—Rafi y Rosi. Delacre, Lulu, illus. 2016. (Rafi & Rosi Ser.).Tr. of Rafi & Rosi. (SPA., Illus.). (J). pap. 8.95 *(978-0-89239-378-7(5))* Lee & Low Bks., Inc.

—Rafi y Rosi ¡Carnaval!, 1 vol. 2016. (Rafi & Rosi Ser.).Tr. of Rafi & Rosi Carnival. (SPA & ENG., Illus.). 64p. (J). pap. 8.95 *(978-0-89239-380-0(7))* Lee & Low Bks., Inc.

Demetrios, Heather. Something Real. 2014. (ENG.). 416p. (YA). (gr. 7). 17.99 *(978-0-8050-9794-8(5),* Holt, Henry & Co. Bks. For Young Readers) Holt, Henry & Co.

Dempsey, Kristy. Superhero Instruction Manual. Fearing, Mark, illus. 2016. (ENG.). 40p. (J). (gr. k-3). 16.99 *(978-0-385-75534-4(1),* Knopf Bks. for Young Readers) Random Hse. Children's Bks.

DeNivo, Jennifer. Sneaky Sam. 2011. 24p. (gr. 1-2). pap. 12.79 *(978-1-4567-5181-4(6))* AuthorHouse.

Dennard, Susan. A Darkness Strange & Lovely. (Something Strange & Deadly Trilogy Ser.: 2). (ENG.). (YA). (gr. 9). 2014. 432p. pap. 9.99 *(978-0-06-208330-2(9))* 2013. 416p. 17.99 *(978-0-06-208329-6(5))* HarperCollins Pubs. (HarperTeen).

—Something Strange & Deadly. (Something Strange & Deadly Trilogy Ser.: 1). (ENG.). (YA). (gr. 9). 2013. 416p. pap. 9.99 *(978-0-06-208327-2(9))* 2012. 400p. 17.99 *(978-0-06-208326-5(0))* HarperCollins Pubs. (HarperTeen).

dePaola, Tomie. Meet the Barkers: Morgan & Moffat Go to School. dePaola, Tomie, illus. 2003. (Barker Twins Ser.). (ENG., Illus.). 32p. (J). (gr. -1-3). 6.99 *(978-0-14-250083-5(6),* Puffin Books) Penguin Young Readers Group.

—Meet the Barkers: Morgan & Moffat Go to School. 2005. (J). (gr. k-3). pap. 17.95 incl. audio *(978-0-8045-6934-7(7),* SAC6934) Spoken Arts, Inc.

Derby, Sally. Kyle's Island. (ENG.). 192p. (J). (gr. 5). 2014. pap. 7.95 *(978-1-58089-317-6(1))* 2010. 16.95 *(978-1-58089-316-9(3))* Charlesbridge Publishing, Inc.

deRubertis, Barbara. Oliver Otter's Own Office. Alley, R. W., illus. 2011. (Animal Antics A to Z Ser.). 32p. (J). pap. 45.32 *(978-0-7613-7661-3(5));* lib. bdg. 22.60 *(978-1-57565-336-5(2));* (gr. -1-3). pap. 7.95 *(978-1-57565-327-3(3))* Kane Press, Inc.

deRubertis, Barbara & DeRubertis, Barbara. Oliver Otter's Own Office. Alley, R. W., illus. 2012. (Animal Antics A to Z Ser.). 32p. (J). (gr. 2 — 1). cd-rom 7.95 *(978-1-57565-408-9(3))* Kane Press, Inc.

Despain, Bree. The Dark Divine. 2009. (ENG.). 384p. (J). (gr. 7-18). 17.99 *(978-1-60684-057-3(6),* Carolrhoda Lab™) Lerner Publishing Group.

Dessen, Sarah. Saint Anything. (ENG.). (YA). (gr. 7). 2016. 448p. pap. 10.99 *(978-0-14-751603-9(X),* Speak) 2015. 432p. 19.99 *(978-0-451-47470-4(8),* Viking Books for Young Readers) Penguin Young Readers Group.

—Saint Anything. 2016. lib. bdg. 22.10 *(978-0-606-38833-7(8))* Turtleback Bks.

DeVillers, Julia & Roy, Jennifer Rozines. Trading Faces. Smith, Alison, illus. 2009. (Mix Ser.). (ENG.). 320p. (J). (gr. 4-8). pap. 7.99 *(978-1-4169-6168-0(2),* Aladdin) Simon & Schuster Children's Publishing.

DiCamillo, Kate. The Magician's Elephant. Tanaka, Yoko, illus. (ENG.). (J). (gr. 3-7). 2015. 224p. pap. 7.99 *(978-0-7636-8088-6(5))* 2009. 208p. 16.99 *(978-0-7636-4410-9(2))* Candlewick Pr.

—The Magician's Elephant. l.t. ed. 2010. (ENG.). 242p. 23.95 *(978-1-4104-2493-8(6))* Thorndike Pr.

—The Magician's Elephant. 2015. lib. bdg. 17.20 *(978-0-606-37891-8(X))* 2011. lib. bdg. 17.20 *(978-0-606-15375-1(6),* Turtleback) Turtleback Bks.

Diehl, Jean Heilprin. Three Little Beavers, 1 vol. Morrison, Cathy, illus. 2012. (ENG.). 32p. (J). (gr. -1-3). 17.95 *(978-1-60718-524-6(5));* pap. 9.95 *(978-1-60718-533-8(4))* Arbordale Publishing.

Dill, Margo L. Finding My Place: One Girl's Strength at Vicksburg. 2012. (ENG.). 202p. (J). pap. 8.95 *(978-1-57249-408-4(5),* White Mane Kids) White Mane Publishing Co., Inc.

Disney Press Staff. School's Out. 2010. 128p. pap. 4.99 *(978-1-4231-2677-5(7))* Disney Pr.

DiTerlizzi, Tony & Black, Holly. The Field Guide. DiTerlizzi, Tony, illus. 2003. (Spiderwick Chronicles Ser.: 1). (ENG., Illus.). 128p. (J). (gr. 1-5). 12.99 *(978-0-689-85936-6(8),* 53409542, Simon & Schuster Bks. For Young Readers) Simon & Schuster Bks. For Young Readers.

—The Ironwood Tree. DiTerlizzi, Tony, illus. 4th ed. 2004. (Spiderwick Chronicles Ser.: 4). (ENG., Illus.). 128p. (J). (gr. 2-6). 10.99 *(978-0-689-85939-7(2),* Simon & Schuster Bks. For Young Readers) Simon & Schuster Bks. For Young Readers.

—The Ironwood Tree. l.t. ed. 2006. (Spiderwick Chronicles: Bk. 4). 90p. (YA). (gr. 2-18). 23.95 *(978-0-7862-8583-9(4))* Thorndike Pr.

—Lucinda's Secret, BK. 3. DiTerlizzi, Tony, illus. 3rd ed. 2003. (Spiderwick Chronicles Ser.: 3). (ENG., Illus.). 128p. (J). (gr. 2-7). 12.99 *(978-0-689-85938-0(4),* Simon & Schuster Bks. For Young Readers) Simon & Schuster Bks. For Young Readers.

—Lucinda's Secret. l.t. ed. 2006. (Spiderwick Chronicles: Bk. 3). (Illus.). 142p. (J). (gr. 4-7). 23.95 *(978-0-7862-8585-3(0))* Thorndike Pr.

—The Nixies Song - A Giant Problem - The Wyrm King Set, Set. DiTerlizzi, Tony, illus. 2009. (Beyond the Spiderwick Chronicles Ser.: Nos. 1-3). (ENG., Illus.). 528p. (J). (gr. 2-5). 33.99 *(978-1-4169-9011-6(9),* Simon & Schuster Bks. For Young Readers) Simon & Schuster Bks. For Young Readers.

DiVito, Anna. Annie Oakley Saves the Day. DiVito, Anna, illus. 2005. (Illus.). 32p. (J). lib. bdg. 15.00 *(978-1-59054-939-1(2))* Fitzgerald Bks.

Dixon, Franklin W. The Bicycle Thief. Burroughs, Scott, illus. 2011. (Hardy Boys: the Secret Files Ser.: 6). (ENG.). 96p. (J). (gr. 1-4). pap. 5.99 *(978-1-4169-9396-4(7),* Aladdin) Simon & Schuster Children's Publishing.

—Burned. 6th ed. 2005. (Hardy Boys (All New) Undercover Brothers Ser.: 6). (ENG., Illus.). 160p. (J). (gr. 3-7). pap. 5.99 *(978-1-4169-0008-5(X),* Aladdin) Simon & Schuster Children's Publishing.

—Deprivation House. 22nd ed. 2008. (Hardy Boys (All New) Undercover Brothers Ser.: 22). (ENG., Illus.). 176p. (J). (gr. 3-7). pap. 5.99 *(978-1-4169-6170-3(4),* Aladdin) Simon & Schuster Children's Publishing.

—Double Down. 26th ed. 2008. (Hardy Boys (All New) Undercover Brothers Ser.: 26). (ENG.). 172p. (J). (gr. 3-7). pap. 5.99 *(978-1-4169-7446-8(6),* Aladdin) Simon & Schuster Children's Publishing.

Dixon, Franklin W. & Walker, Jeff. Typhoon Island, Vol. 180. 2003. (Hardy Boys Ser.: 180). (ENG., Illus.). 160p. (J). (gr. 3-7). pap. 5.99 *(978-0-689-85884-0(1),* Aladdin) Simon & Schuster Children's Publishing.

Dockter, Debra. Deadly Design. 2015. (ENG.). 368p. (YA). (gr. 7). 17.99 *(978-0-399-17105-5(3),* G.P. Putnam's Sons Books for Young Readers) Penguin Young Readers Group.

Dodge, Mary Mapes. Hans Brinker, or the Silver Skates. 2007. 308p. (gr. 3-7). 32.95 *(978-1-4344-9309-5(1));* per. 19.95 *(978-1-4344-9308-8(3))* Wildside Pr., LLC.

—Hans Brinker or the Silver Skates A Story of Life in Holland. Doggett, Allen B., illus. 2004. reprint ed. pap. 34.95 *(978-1-4179-4127-8(8))* Kessinger Publishing, LLC.

—Hans Brinker; or, the Silver Skates (Dod. 2006. pap. *(978-1-4065-0961-8(2))* Dodo Pr.

Doerrfeld, Cori. Maggie & Wendel: Imagine Everything! Doerrfeld, Cori, illus. 2016. (ENG., Illus.). 48p. (J). (gr. -1-3). 17.99 *(978-1-4814-3974-9(X),* Simon & Schuster Bks. For Young Readers) Simon & Schuster Bks. For Young Readers.

—Penny Loves Pink. 2011. (ENG., Illus.). 40p. (J). (gr. -1-3). 15.99 *(978-0-316-05458-4(5))* Little, Brown Bks. for Young Readers.

Dokey, Cameron. The World Above. 2010. (Once upon a Time Ser.). (ENG.). 208p. (YA). (gr. 7-18). pap. 6.99 *(978-1-4424-0337-6(3),* Simon Pulse) Simon Pulse.

Donaldson, Julia. The Giants & the Joneses. Swearingen, Greg, illus. 2008. (ENG.). 224p. (J). (gr. 3-5). pap. 14.99 *(978-0-312-37961-2(7),* 9780312379612) Square Fish.

Donegan, Noel & Donegan, Luz. The Sad Little Violin. 2013. (Magical Mozart & His Musical Ser.). (ENG.). 32p. (J). pap. 8.95 *(978-1-84730-393-6(5))* Veritas Pubns. IRL. Dist: Dufour Editions, Inc.

Donlon, Diane Youngblood. Tippee Tippee Tiptoe. Suhr, James W., illus. 2003. (J). 16.95 *(978-0-9720427-0-3(9))* OLLY Publishing Co.

Donoghue, Emma. The Lotterys Plus One. Hadilaksono, Caroline, illus. 2017. (ENG.). 320p. (J). (gr. 3-7). 17.99 *(978-0-545-92581-5(9))* Scholastic, Inc.

Dooley, Sarah. Free Verse. 2017. lib. bdg. 19.65 ***(978-0-606-39788-9(4))*** Turtleback Bks.

Dorato, A. P. Arthur, Donna, & the Magic Crown of Tiabora. 2006. pap. 24.95 *(978-1-4137-8898-3(X))* PublishAmerica, Inc.

Dorisann. Blasting Ogres. 2012. 108p. (gr. 4-6). 20.95 *(978-1-4759-2900-3(5));* pap. 10.95 *(978-1-4759-2899-0(8))* iUniverse, Inc.

Dorris, Michael. Morning Girl. 2005. 80p. (J). (gr. 3-18). 20.50 *(978-0-8446-7272-4(6),* 3587) Smith, Peter Pub., Inc.

dos Santos, Steven. The Culling. 2013. (Torch Keeper Ser.: 1). (ENG.). 432p. (YA). pap. 9.99 *(978-0-7387-3537-5(X),* Flux) North Star Editions.

Doty, Linda. Hydrangea Hill: A New Home for Amy Manchester. 2008. 182p. pap. 24.95 *(978-1-60610-840-6(9))* America Star Bks.

Double Deception, Bk. 3. 2009. (Hardy Boys (All New) Undercover Brothers Ser.: 27). (ENG.). 176p. (J). (gr. 3-7). pap. 5.99 *(978-1-4169-6766-8(4),* Aladdin) Simon & Schuster Children's Publishing.

Dougherty, John. Stinkbomb & Ketchup-Face & the Badness of Badgers. Ricks, Sam, illus. 2017. (Stinkbomb & Ketchup-Face Ser.). (ENG.). 144p. (J). (gr. 3-7). 15.99 *(978-1-101-99662-1(5),* G.P. Putnam's Sons Books for Young Readers) Penguin Young Readers Group.

Dowd, Siobhan. The London Eye Mystery. 2009. (ENG.). 336p. (J). (gr. 3-7). 7.99 *(978-0-385-75184-1(2),* Yearling) Random Hse. Children's Bks.

—The London Eye Mystery. 2009. lib. bdg. 18.40 *(978-0-606-14413-1(7),* Turtleback) Turtleback Bks.

Downham, Jenny. Unbecoming. (ENG.). 384p. (J). (gr. 9-9). 2017. pap. 9.99 ***(978-1-338-16072-7(9))*** 2016. 17.99 *(978-0-545-90717-0(9))* Scholastic, Inc.

Downham, Jenny. You Against Me. 2012. (ENG.). 416p. (YA). (gr. 9). pap. 9.99 *(978-0-385-75266-4(0),* Ember) Random Hse. Children's Bks.

Doyle, Roddy. Brilliant. Hughes, Emily, illus. 2015. (ENG.). 192p. (J). (gr. 3-7). 16.95 *(978-1-4197-1479-5(1),* Amulet Bks.) Abrams, Inc.

Draper, Polly. Cry Wolff. 2007. 89p. (J). pap. *(978-0-545-02570-6(2))* Scholastic, Inc.

Draper, Sharon M. Forged by Fire. 2013. (Hazelwood High Trilogy Ser.: 2). (ENG., Illus.). 176p. (YA). (gr. 7). pap. 9.99 *(978-1-4424-8914-1(6),* Atheneum Bks. for Young Readers) Simon & Schuster Children's Publishing.

—Forged by Fire. 2013. (Hazelwood High Trilogy Ser.: 2). lib. bdg. 20.85 *(978-0-606-32333-8(3),* Turtleback) Turtleback Bks.

Driscoll, Laura. A Mousy Mess. Melmon, Deborah, illus. 2014. (Mouse Math (r) Ser.). 32p. (J). (gr. -1-1). 22.60 *(978-1-57565-646-5(9))* Kane Press, Inc.

—My Brother, the Knight. Smath, Jerry, illus. 2004. (Social Studies Connects). 32p. (J). (gr. 1-3). pap. 5.95 *(978-1-57565-140-8(8))* Kane Press, Inc.

—Super Specs. Gott, Barry, illus. 2005. (Math Matters Ser.). (ENG.). 32p. (J). (gr. -1-3). pap. 5.95 *(978-1-57565-145-3(9))* Kane Press, Inc.

Driscoll, Roger K. Echo Mccool, Outlaw Through Time. 2011. 190p. pap. *(978-1-908105-26-4(7))* Grosvenor Hse. Publishing Ltd.

Dube, Jasmine. Gratelle au Bois Mordant. 2004. (FRE., Illus.). (J). (gr. -1-3). spiral bd. *(978-0-616-01848-4(7))* Canadian National Institute for the Blind/Institut National Canadien pour les Aveugles.

Dubisch, Mike, illus. The Haunted Cabin Mystery. 2009. (Boxcar Children Graphic Novels Ser.: 9). (ENG.). 32p. (J). (gr. 1-5). pap. 6.99 *(978-0-8075-3180-8(4))* Whitman, Albert & Co.

—The Pizza Mystery. 2010. (Boxcar Children Graphic Novels Ser.: 11). (ENG.). 32p. (J). (gr. 1-5). pap. 6.99 *(978-0-8075-6537-7(7))* Whitman, Albert & Co.

—Tree House Mystery. 2009. (Boxcar Children Graphic Novels Ser.: 8). (ENG.). 32p. (J). (gr. 1-5). pap. 6.99 *(978-0-8075-8088-2(0))* Whitman, Albert & Co.

Dubisch, Mike & Bloodworth, Mark, illus. The Amusement Park Mystery. 2010. (Boxcar Children Graphic Novels Ser.: 10). (ENG.). 32p. (J). (gr. 1-5). pap. 6.99 *(978-0-8075-0321-8(5))* Whitman, Albert & Co.

Dubose, Sarah. Uncharted Waters. 2013. 440p. pap. *(978-1-4596-6282-7(2))* ReadHowYouWant.com, Ltd.

Dubyn, Bj. The Thrilling & Dynamic Adventures of Barbara Ann, Her Kid Brother, Billy, Jr., & Manfred the Magnificent, Their Parrot. 2008. 104p. pap. 15.99 *(978-1-4363-2652-0(4))* Xlibris Corp.

Duggan, Matt. The Royal Woods. 2010. (ENG., Illus.). 244p. (J). (gr. 4-7). pap. *(978-1-55470-060-8(4))* Me to We.

Dumas, Alexandre. The Man in the Iron Mask. Howell, Troy, illus. 2008. (Classic Starts(tm) Ser.). (ENG.). 160p. (J). (gr. 2-4). 6.95 *(978-1-4027-4579-9(6))* Sterling Publishing Co., Inc.

Dumin, Jennifer. Wolfie & Freddie: the New Puppy. 2006. (ENG.). 44p. per. 22.65 *(978-1-4257-0680-7(0))* Xlibris Corp.

Dunbar, Joyce. Tell Me Something Happy Before I Go to Sleep. Gliori, Debi, illus. 2013. (ENG.). 24p. (J). (— 1). bds. 11.99 *(978-0-547-94059-5(9))* Houghton Mifflin Harcourt Publishing Co.

Dungy, Tony & Dungy, Lauren. Go, Jade, Go! Newton, Vanessa Brantley, illus. 2013. (Tony & Lauren Dungy Ready-To-Reads Ser.). (ENG.). 32p. (J). (gr. k-2). 16.99 *(978-1-4424-5467-5(9));* pap. 3.99 *(978-1-4424-5466-8(0))* Simon Spotlight. (Simon Spotlight).

Dunlop, Ed. Escape to Liechtenstein. 2003. (Young Refugees Ser.). 152p. (J). (gr. 3-7). per. 7.49 *(978-1-59166-013-2(0))* BJU Pr.

—The Incredible Rescues. Halverson, Tom, illus. 2003. 166p. (J). (gr. 4-7). 7.49 *(978-1-59166-012-5(2))* BJU Pr.

Dunmore, Helen. Ingo. (gr. 5). 2008. (Ingo Ser.: 1). 336p. (YA). per. 7.99 *(978-0-06-081854-8(9))* 2006. 328p. (J). lib. bdg. 17.89 *(978-0-06-081853-1(0))* HarperCollins Pubs.

—The Tide Knot. 2008. 330p. (J). 5.99 *(978-0-06-081857-9(3));* (Ingo Ser.: 2). (ENG.). 336p. (YA). (gr. 5-8). 16.99 *(978-0-06-081855-5(7))* HarperCollins Pubs.

Dunn, Joeming & Dunn, Ben, illus. Houseboat Mystery. 2011. (Boxcar Children Graphic Novels Ser.: 16). (ENG.). 32p. (J). (gr. 1-5). pap. 6.99 *(978-0-8075-3395-6(5))* Whitman, Albert & Co.

Dunn, Joeming & Warner, Gertrude Chandler. The Lighthouse Mystery, 1 vol., Bk. 14. Dunn, Ben, illus. 2011. (Boxcar Children Graphic Novels Ser.). (ENG.). 32p. (J). (gr. 2-5). 28.50 *(978-1-61641-122-0(8))* ABDO Publishing Co.

—The Woodshed Mystery, 1 vol., Bk. 13. Dunn, Ben, illus. 2011. (Boxcar Children Graphic Novels Ser.). (ENG.). 32p. (J). (gr. 2-5). 28.50 *(978-1-61641-121-3(X))* ABDO Publishing Co.

Dunrea, Olivier. Gemma & Gus. (Gossie & Friends Ser.). (ENG., Illus.). 32p. (J). 2017. (gr. -1-3). pap. 3.99 *(978-0-544-93722-2(8),* HMH Books For Young Readers) 2016. (— 1). bds. 6.99 *(978-0-544-65647-5(4),* HMH Books For Young Readers) 2015. (— 1). lib. bdg. 9.99 *(978-0-547-86851-6(0))* Houghton Mifflin Harcourt Publishing Co.

—Gemma & Gus (reader) 2017. (Gossie & Friends Ser.). (ENG., Illus.). 32p. (J). (gr. -1-3). 12.99 *(978-0-544-93680-5(9),* HMH Books For Young Readers) Houghton Mifflin Harcourt Publishing Co., Inc.

Durand, Hallie. Just Desserts. Davenier, Christine, illus. (ENG.). (J). (gr. 2-5). 2011. 224p. pap. 5.99 *(978-1-4169-6388-2(X))* 2010. 208p. 15.99 *(978-1-4169-6387-5(1))* Simon & Schuster Children's Publishing. (Atheneum Bks. for Young Readers).

—No Room for Dessert. Davenier, Christine, illus. (ENG.). 192p. (J). (gr. 2-5). 2012. pap. 6.99 *(978-1-4424-0361-1(6))* 2011. 15.99 *(978-1-4424-0360-4(8))* Simon & Schuster Children's Publishing. (Atheneum Bks. for Young Readers).

Durfee, Jody Wind. Hadley-Hadley Benson. 2013. (ENG.). 144p. (J). pap. 11.99 *(978-1-62108-151-7(6))* Covenant Communications, Inc.

Durst, Sarah Beth. Roar & Sparkles Go to School. Whitehouse, Ben, illus. 2017. (ENG.). 40p. (J). (gr. -1-1). 16.99 ***(978-0-7624-5986-5(7),*** Running Pr.) Running Pr. Bk. Pubs.

Dwyer, Cynthia. Can You See Me Now? Schuepbach, Lynnette, illus. 2006. 24p. (J). 12.95 *(978-0-9677685-8-8(6))* Grannie Annie Family Story Celebration, The.

Dyer, Heather. The Girl with the Broken Wing. Bailey, Peter, illus. 2005. 147p. (J). *(978-1-4156-3468-4(8))* Scholastic, Inc.

Dyer, Sarah. Princess for a Day: A Clementine & Mungo Story. Dyer, Sarah, illus. (ENG., Illus.). 32p. (J). (gr. -1-k). 2009. pap. 12.95 *(978-0-7475-8891-7(0))* 2007. 22.95 *(978-0-7475-8753-8(1))* Bloomsbury Publishing Plc GBR. Dist: Independent Pubs. Group.

Earhart, Kristin. Buttercup Mystery. Geddes, Serena, illus. 2015. (Marguerite Henry's Misty Inn Ser.: 2). (ENG.). 128p. (J). (gr. 2-5). pap. 5.99 *(978-1-4814-1416-6(X),* Aladdin) Simon & Schuster Children's Publishing.

—Finding Luck. Geddess, Serena, illus. 2016. (Marguerite Henry's Misty Inn Ser.: 4). (ENG.). 128p. (J). (gr. 2-5). pap. 5.99 *(978-1-4814-1422-7(4),* Aladdin) Simon & Schuster Children's Publishing.

—Runaway Pony. Geddess, Serena, illus. 2015. (Marguerite Henry's Misty Inn Ser.: 3). (ENG.). 128p. (J). (gr. 2-5). pap. 5.99 *(978-1-4814-1419-7(4),* Aladdin) Simon & Schuster Children's Publishing.

—Runaway Pony. 2015. (Marguerite Henry's Misty Inn Ser.: 3). lib. bdg. 16.00 *(978-0-606-37835-2(9))* Turtleback Bks.

—Welcome Home! Geddes, Serena, illus. 2015. (Marguerite Henry's Misty Inn Ser.: 1). (ENG.). 128p. (J). (gr. 2-5). 16.99 *(978-1-4814-1414-2(3),* Aladdin) Simon & Schuster Children's Publishing.

—Welcome Home! 2015. (Marguerite Henry's Misty Inn Ser.: 1). lib. bdg. 16.00 *(978-0-606-37126-1(5))* Turtleback Bks.

Earhart, Kristin & Geddes, Serena. Welcome Home!; Buttercup Mystery; Runaway Pony; Finding Luck. 2016. (Marguerite Henry's Misty Inn Ser.). (ENG., Illus.). 512p. (J). (gr. 2-5). pap. 23.99 *(978-1-4814-7012-4(4),* Aladdin) Simon & Schuster Children's Publishing.

Earl, Cheri Pray & Williams, Carol Lynch. Secret in Pennsylvania. 2009. (J). *(978-1-56145-477-8(X),* Peachtree Junior) Peachtree Pubs.

Eastman, Brock D. & Eastman, Brock. Taken. 2011. (Illus.). 315p. (J). pap. *(978-1-59638-245-9(7))* P & R Publishing.

Eaton, Deborah. Canciones de Monstruos. Translations.com Staff, tr. from ENG. Handelman, Dorothy, photos by. 2007. (Lecturas para niños de verdad - Nivel 2 (Real Kids Readers - Level 2) Ser.).Tr. of Monster Songs. (SPA., Illus.). 32p. (gr. k-3). per. 5.95 *(978-0-8225-7803-1(4))* Lerner Publishing Group.

Eaves, Victor Caleb. Vee's the Chapters of Expudict: Book One. 2008. 128p. pap. 12.00 *(978-1-4389-3385-6(1))* AuthorHouse.

Eboch, Chris. The Riverboat Phantom. 2009. (Haunted Ser.). (ENG.). 192p. (J). (gr. 3-7). pap. 5.99 *(978-1-4169-7549-6(7),* Aladdin) Simon & Schuster Children's Publishing.

Eddy, Daniel. Walter's Tours in the East: Walter in Je. 2005. pap. 16.95 *(978-1-59605-437-0(9),* Cosimo Classics) Cosimo, Inc.

Edgren, David. The Serpent Scroll. 2009. (J). 11.99 *(978-0-8163-2330-2(5))* Pacific Pr. Publishing Assn.

Edgren, Elizabeth. Little Tree's Mightiest Deed. Penk, Kathryn, illus. 2009. 36p. pap. 12.95 *(978-1-59858-825-5(7))* Dog Ear Publishing, LLC.

Edgson, Alison & Stockham, Jessica. Hansel & Gretel. Petrlik, Andrea, illus. 2006. (Flip-Up Fairy Tales Ser.). (ENG.). 24p. (J). (gr. 1-2). *(978-1-904550-73-0(8))* Child's Play International Ltd.

Edvall, Lilian. The Rabbit Who Couldn't Find His Daddy. Gimbergsson, Sara, illus. 2006. 32p. (J). (gr. -1-3). 15.00 *(978-91-29-66429-4(2))* R & S Bks. SWE. Dist: Macmillan.

Edwards, Felicity. The Spider King. 2012. 176p. pap. *(978-1-78176-753-5(X))* FeedARead.com.

Edwards, Tanille & Edwards, Latoya. Jordan & Justine's Weekend Adventures Pts. 1-2: Plants. 2007. (SPA.). 32p. (J). (gr. k-3). 12.95 *(978-0-9787302-3-9(2))* Fire Flies Entertainment, LLC.

Eggleston, George Cary. The Big Brother: A Story of Indian War. 2007. (Illus.). 104p. per. *(978-1-4065-2541-0(3))* Dodo Pr.

Ehrmantraut, Brenda. I Want One Too! Short, Robbie, illus. 2003. (J). lib. bdg. 16.95 *(978-0-9729833-1-0(7));* per. 9.95 *(978-0-9729833-0-3(9))* Bubble Gum Pr.

Eisan, Daniel. The Lonely Peach. 2011. (Illus.). 48p. pap. 15.99 *(978-1-4628-5634-3(9))* Xlibris Corp.

Ellery, Amanda. If I Had a Dragon. Ellery, Tom, illus. 2006. (ENG.). 40p. (J). (gr. -1-3). 17.99 *(978-1-4169-0924-8(9),* Simon & Schuster Bks. For Young Readers) Simon & Schuster Bks. For Young Readers.

Elliott, Patricia. The Pale Assassin. 320p. (YA). 2010. (ENG.). (gr. 6-18). pap. 8.95 *(978-0-8234-2312-5(3))* 2009. (gr. 7-18). 17.95 *(978-0-8234-2250-0(X))* Holiday Hse., Inc.

Elliott, Rebecca. Just Because. (ENG., Illus.). (J). (gr. k-2). 2014. 12p. bds. 7.99 *(978-0-7459-6460-7(5))* 2012. 32p. pap. 8.99 *(978-0-7459-6235-1(1))* Lion Hudson PLC GBR. Dist: Independent Pubs. Group.

—Just Because. Elliott, Rebecca, illus. 2011. (ENG., Illus.). 32p. (J). (gr. -1-2). 14.99 *(978-0-7459-6267-2(X))* Lion Hudson PLC GBR. Dist: Independent Pubs. Group.

—Sometimes. Elliott, Rebecca, illus. (ENG., Illus.). 32p. (J). (gr. k-2). 2014. pap. 8.99 *(978-0-7459-6269-6(6))* 2012. 14.99 *(978-0-7459-6297-9(1))* Lion Hudson PLC GBR. Dist: Independent Pubs. Group.

Ellis, Edward Sylvester. Through Forest & Fire. 2005. pap. 14.95 *(978-1-59224-221-4(9))* Wildside Pr., LLC.

Ellis, Sarah. Big Ben. LaFave, Kim, illus. 2004. (J). (gr. -1-1). spiral bd. *(978-0-616-11108-6(8));* spiral bd. *(978-0-616-11109-3(6))* Canadian National Institute for the Blind/Institut National Canadien pour les Aveugles.

Ellison, Elizabeth Stow. Flight. 2008. (ENG.). 192p. (YA). (gr. 3-7). 16.95 *(978-0-8234-2128-2(7))* Holiday Hse., Inc.

Emery, Joanna. Brothers of the Falls. Erickson, David, illus. 2004. (Adventures in America Ser.). (gr. 4). 14.95 *(978-1-893110-37-3(0))* Silver Moon Pr.

Emily, Katelyn. The Treasure-Trove Tales at the Gazebo. 2009. 120p. 18.95 *(978-1-59858-940-5(7));* pap. 8.95 *(978-1-59858-855-2(9))* Dog Ear Publishing, LLC.

Encyclopaedia Britannica, Inc. Staff, compiled by. My Little Foster Sister. 2008. 49.95 *(978-1-59339-666-4(X))* Encyclopaedia Britannica, Inc.

Enderle, Dotti. Book 15: Rock & Roll!, 1 vol. 2014. (Ghost Detectors Set 3 Ser.). (ENG., Illus.). 80p. (J). (gr. 2-5). lib. bdg. 27.07 *(978-1-62402-003-2(8),* Calico Chapter Bks) Magic Wagon.

—Book 17: Grow a Ghost! 2014. (Ghost Detectors Set 3 Ser.). 80p. (J). (gr. 2-5). lib. bdg. 27.07 *(978-1-62402-005-6(4),* Calico Chapter Bks) Magic Wagon.

—Granny Gert & the Bunion Brothers, 1 vol. Kulka, Joe, illus. 2006. (ENG.). 32p. (J). (gr. k-3). 16.99 *(978-1-58980-373-2(6))* Pelican Publishing Co., Inc.

—Grow a Ghost!, 1 vol. McWilliam, Howard, illus. 2016. (ENG.). 80p. (J). *(978-1-62402-100-8(X))* Magic Wagon.

Enderle, Judith Ross & Gordon, Stephanie Jacob. Smile, Principessa! Currni, Serena, illus. 2012. (ENG.). 40p. (J). (gr. -1-1). 16.99 *(978-1-4424-3096-9(6),* McElderry, Margaret K. Bks.) McElderry, Margaret K. Bks.

Engle, Margarita. Forest World. 2017. (ENG., Illus.). 208p. (J). (gr. 5). 16.99 ***(978-1-4814-9057-3(5),*** Atheneum Bks. for Young Readers) Simon & Schuster Children's Publishing.

Enright, Elizabeth. Gone-Away Lake. Krush, Beth & Krush, Joe, illus. 2006. 256p. (J). (gr. 4-8). reprint ed. pap. 6.00 *(978-1-4223-5436-0(9))* DIANE Publishing Co.

—The Saturdays. Enright, Elizabeth, illus. 3rd ed. 2008. (Melendy Quartet Ser.: 1). (ENG., Illus.). 192p. (J). (gr. 3-7). per. 7.99 *(978-0-312-37598-0(0),* 9780312375980) Square Fish.

—Then There Were Five. Enright, Elizabeth, illus. 3rd ed. 2008. (Melendy Quartet Ser.: 3). (ENG., Illus.). 272p. (J). (gr. 3-7). per. 9.99 *(978-0-312-37600-0(6),* 9780312376000) Square Fish.

Enright, Robert D. Rising above the Storm Clouds: What It's Like to Forgive. Finney, Kathryn Kunz, illus. 2004. 32p. (J). 14.95 *(978-1-59147-075-5(7));* pap. 9.95 *(978-1-59147-076-2(5))* American Psychological Assn. (Magination Pr.).

Eone, illus. Peppa's Busy Day Magnet Book (Peppa Pig) 2016. (Peppa Pig Ser.). (ENG.). 10p. (J). (gr. -1-k). 12.99 *(978-0-545-92545-7(2))* Scholastic, Inc.

A
B

Ephron, Amy. The Castle in the Mist. 2017. (ENG.). 192p. (J). (gr. 3-7). 16.99 (978-0-399-54698-3(7), Philomel Bks.) Penguin Young Readers Group.
Erickson, Mary Ellen. Who Jinxed the CG Ranch? 2009. 196p. 24.95 (978-1-4401-4218-5(1)); pap. 14.95 (978-1-4401-4216-1(5)) iUniverse, Inc.
Erlings, Fridrik. Fish in the Sky. 2012. (ENG., Illus.). 288p. (YA). (gr. 7). 16.99 (978-0-7636-5888-5(X)) Candlewick Pr.
Ernst, Lisa Campbell. Snow Surprise. 2008. (Green Light Readers Level 2 Ser.). (ENG., Illus.). 24p. (J). (gr. k-2). pap. 3.95 (978-0-15-206559-1(8)) Houghton Mifflin Harcourt Publishing Co.
Ervin, Randy. Maycroft From 232nd. 2010. 150p. (YA). pap. 10.00 (978-0-578-05732-3(8)) Ervin, Randy.
Esparza- Vela, Mary. You Can't Take the Dinosaur Home. Motz, Mike, illus. 2013. 16p. pap. 9.95 (978-1-61633-364-5(2)) Guardian Angel Publishing, Inc.
Esther Cravens Schwaiger. Not Too Close. Eve Cravens Nawahine, illus. 2009. 16p. pap. 8.49 (978-1-4389-6987-9(2)) AuthorHouse.
Evan, Kelsey L. Starshine. 2013. 102p. pap. 19.95 (978-1-63000-770-6(6)) PublishAmerica, Inc.
Evans, Rose-Marie. The Unexpected Adventure at East Haddam High. 2009. 80p. pap. 10.75 (978-1-60860-182-0(X), Strategic Bk. Publishing) Strategic Book Publishing & Rights Agency (SBPRA).
Eve, Laure. The Graces. 2016. (ENG.). 352p. (YA). (gr. 8-17). 18.95 (978-1-4197-2123-6(2), Amulet Bks.) Abrams, Inc.
Falk, Nick & Flowers, Tony. A Pterodactyl Stole My Homework: Saurus Street 2 (Large Print 16pt) 2013. 98p. pap. (978-1-4596-5772-4(1)) ReadHowYouWant.com, Ltd.
Falwell, Cathryn. Mystery Vine. Falwell, Cathryn, illus. 2009. (Illus.). 32p. (J). lib. bdg. 17.89 (978-0-06-177197-2(X), Greenwillow Bks.) HarperCollins Pubs.
Fangs for the Memories. 2008. (Looney Tunes 8*8 Ser.). 24p. pap. (978-1-4075-2630-0(8)); pap. (978-1-4075-2640-9(5)) Parragon, Inc.
Fantastik, B. Save the Sleepless Slumbernots! Valentine, M. K., illus. 2013. 32p. (978-1-4602-2777-0(8)) FriesenPress.
Fantich, Susanna. A Cat's Tale. 2012. 210p. 33.99 (978-1-4582-0527-8(4)); pap. 15.99 (978-1-4582-0525-4(8)) Author Solutions, Inc. (Abbott Pr.).
Fardell, John. The Day Louis Got Eaten. Fardell, John, illus. 2012. (Andersen Press Picture Bks). (ENG., Illus.). 32p. (J). (gr. -1-3). 16.95 (978-1-4677-0315-4(X)) Lerner Publishing Group.
Farmer, Nancy. The Sea of Trolls. (ENG., Illus.). 480p. 2004. (J). (gr. 5-8). 19.99 (978-0-689-86744-6(1), Atheneum/Richard Jackson Bks.) 2006. (YA). (gr. 9-8). reprint ed. pap. 11.99 (978-0-689-86746-0(8), Atheneum Bks. for Young Readers) Simon & Schuster Children's Publishing.
Farnworth, Michael M. The Sinister Mr. Pickle & the Fickle He Got the Mcwickles Into. 2008. 40p. per. 24.95 (978-1-60441-285-7(2)) America Star Bks.
Farrant, Natasha. After Iris. 2013. (ENG.). 272p. (J). (gr. 5). 16.99 (978-0-8037-3982-6(6), Dial Bks) Penguin Young Readers Group.
Farrell, Bill. Walter's Pond: The True Story of Three Brothers Who Went Fishing for Trouble. Julich, Jenniffer, illus. 2008. 16p. 8.95 (978-0-9797790-0-8(6)) Lower Lane Publishing LLC.
Faulkner, Matt. A Taste of Colored Water. Faulkner, Matt, illus. 2008. (ENG., Illus.). 48p. (J). (gr. 1-3). 17.99 (978-1-4169-1629-1(6), Simon & Schuster Bks. For Young Readers) Simon & Schuster Bks. For Young Readers.
—A Taste of Colored Water. 2008. (YA). 29.95 incl. audio compact disk (978-0-8045-4201-2(5)) Spoken Arts, Inc.
Faust, Jon. Helicopter Harry & the Copter Kids. 2016. (ENG., Illus.). (J). pap. 9.95 **(978-0-692-78184-5(6))** Mother Lode Pr. LLC.
Fearnley, Jan. Billy Tibble Moves Out! Fearnley, Jan, illus. 2006. (Illus.). 29p. (J). (gr. k-4). reprint ed. 16.00 (978-1-4223-5557-2(8)) DIANE Publishing Co.
Feiffer, Kate. But I Wanted a Baby Brother! Goode, Diane, illus. 2010. (ENG.). 32p. (J). (gr. -1-3). 16.99 (978-1-4169-3941-2(5), Simon & Schuster/Paula Wiseman Bks.) Simon & Schuster/Paula Wiseman Bks.
Feldman, Luke & Chin, Amanda. Chaff n' Skaffs: Mai & the Lost Moskivvy. Feldman, Luke, illus. 2009. (ENG., Illus.). 36p. (J). (gr. -1-3). 15.95 (978-1-59702-013-8(3)) Immedium.
Fenner, Carol. Yolonda's Genius. unabr. ed. 2004. 211p. (J). (gr. 4-6). pap. 38.00 incl. audio (978-0-8072-0462-7(5), Listening Library) Random Hse. Audio Publishing Group.
Fenwick, Nellie. Gracie & God's Great Ten: How One Girl Learned to Make Good Choices. 2012. 118p. (-18). pap. 17.99 (978-0-9827627-8-3(X)) Port Hole Pubns.
Ferreri, Della Ross. Star of the Show. Weinstock, Tony, illus. 2009. (ENG.). 36p. (J). (gr. -1-3). 15.95 (978-1-934860-03-8(4)) Shenanigan Bks.
Fields, T. S. Missing in the Mountains. 2008. (ENG.). 108p. (J). (gr. 4-7). pap. 6.95 (978-0-87358-950-5(5)) Cooper Square Publishing Llc.
Finley, Mary Peace. Meadow Lark. 2003. (Santa Fe Trail Trilogy Ser.). (Illus.). 199p. (J). 15.95 (978-0-86541-070-1(4)) Filter Pr., LLC.
Finn, Perdita. Ever after High. 2016. (ENG.). 144p. (J). (gr. 3-7). 9.99 (978-0-316-39394-2(0)) Little, Brown Bks. for Young Readers.
Fiona Fox Staff, ed. The Railway Children. 2012. (ENG., Illus.). 64p. (J). 15.00 (978-1-84135-840-6(1)) Award Pubns. Ltd. GBR. Dist: Parkwest Pubns., Inc.
Fiore, Kelly. Thicker Than Water. 2016. 320p. (YA). (gr. 9). 17.99 (978-0-06-232473-3(X), HarperTeen) HarperCollins Pubs.
Fischel, Ana. The Twelve Quests - Book 4, Rapunzel's Hair. 2009. 158p. pap. (978-1-84923-876-2(6)) YouWriteOn.
—The Twelve Quests - Book 6, the Enchanted Harp. 2009. 158p. pap. (978-1-84923-878-6(2)) YouWriteOn.
Fishbone, Greg. The Penguins of Doom. 2007. (From the Desk of Septina Nash Ser.). (ENG., Illus.). 182p. (J). (gr. 2-7). 13.95 (978-1-933831-03-9(0)) Blooming Tree Pr.
Fisher, Catherine. Darkhenge. 2006. 340p. (YA). (gr. 7-12). 15.99 (978-0-06-078582-6(9)) HarperCollins Pubs.
Fisher, Sam. Scare Scape. 2015. (ENG.). 352p. (J). (gr. 3-7). 12.99 (978-0-545-74497-3(0), Scholastic Pr.) Scholastic, Inc.
—The Midnight Door. 2015. (Scare Scape Ser.: 2). (ENG.). 352p. (J). (gr. 3-7). 12.99 (978-0-545-52163-5(7), Scholastic Pr.) Scholastic, Inc.
Fitzgerald, John. Great Brain. 2006. 20.75 (978-0-8446-7293-9(9)) Smith, Peter Pub., Inc.
Five Children & It. 2013. 58p. pap. 5.60 (978-1-236-72792-3(4)) General Bks. LLC.
Five Children & It. 2010. (CAM.). 142p. pap. 10.95 (978-1-4385-3539-5(2), Book Jungle) Standard Pubns., Inc.
Flammer, JoAnn. The Last Wish. 2007. 80p. pap. 10.00 (978-0-615-16197-6(9)) Flammer, Josephine.
Fleischman, Sid. The 13th Floor: A Ghost Story. Sis, Peter, illus. 2007. (ENG.). 240p. (J). (gr. 3-7). per. 6.99 (978-0-06-134503-6(2), Greenwillow Bks.) HarperCollins Pubs.
Fletcher, Pamela. Who Is Freddy Farlittle? 2011. 40p. pap. 16.99 (978-1-4634-1086-5(7)) AuthorHouse.
Fletcher, Susan. Alphabet of Dreams. 2006. (ENG., Illus.). 304p. (YA). (gr. 7-12). 16.95 (978-0-689-85042-4(5), Atheneum Bks. for Young Readers) Simon & Schuster Children's Publishing.
—Alphabet of Dreams. 2008. (ENG., Illus.). 432p. (YA). (gr. 7-12). mass mkt. 7.99 (978-0-689-85152-0(9), Simon Pulse) Simon Pulse.
Flo & Wendell Explore. 2014. (ENG.). 32p. (J). (gr. -1-k). 17.99 (978-0-8037-3930-7(3), Dial Bks) Penguin Young Readers Group.
Flood, Tony. Jody Richards & the Secret Potion. 2nd ed. 2012. 146p. pap. (978-0-9569682-9-6(5)) My Voice Publishing.
Flor Ada, Alma. Celebrate Christmas & Three Kings Day with Pablo & Carlitos. Torres, Walter, illus. 2006. (Cuentos para Celebrar / Stories to Celebrate Ser.). 30p. (gr. k-6). per. 11.95 (978-1-59820-136-9(0)) Santillana USA Publishing Co., Inc.
—Celebrate Hanukkah with Bubbe's Tales. Hayes, Joe & Franco, Sharon, trs. Epelbaum, Mariano, illus. 2007. (Cuentos para Celebrar / Stories to Celebrate Ser.). 30p. (gr. k-6). per. 11.95 (978-1-59820-134-5(4)) Santillana USA Publishing Co., Inc.
Flynn, M. H. The Shadow City Ghost Hunters Vol. 1: The Mystery of Mapleshade Manor. 2006. 48p. pap. 16.95 (978-1-4241-2002-4(0)) PublishAmerica, Inc.
Forrester, Emma. Uncle Arthur's Art Studio. Nunn, Paul E., illus. 2008. (Spiderwick Chronicles). (ENG.). 48p. (J). (gr. 2-7). 10.99 (978-1-4169-4955-8(0), Simon Scribbles) Simon Scribbles.
Forte, Joseph. At the Window. 2013. 32p. pap. (978-1-4602-2190-7(7)) FriesenPress.
Foster, Stewart. Bubble. 2017. (ENG., Illus.). 352p. (J). (gr. 3-5). 16.99 **(978-1-4814-8742-9(6)**, Simon & Schuster Bks. For Young Readers) Simon & Schuster Bks. For Young Readers.
Fox, Janet. The Charmed Children of Rookskill Castle. 2016. (ENG., Illus.). 400p. (J). (gr. 5). 16.99 (978-0-451-47633-3(6), Viking Books for Young Readers) Penguin Young Readers Group.
Fox, Paula. Gus Cara de Piedra.Tr. of Stone-Faced Boy. (SPA.). 128p. (J). (gr. 3-5). (978-84-279-3450-4(5), NG4694) Noguer y Caralt Editores, S. A. ESP. Dist: Lectorum Pubns., Inc.
Fragasso, Ruth Ann (Reichner). The Little Boy Who Ate Like a Bird. 2011. 16p. (gr. -1). 12.68 (978-1-4269-6287-5(8)) Trafford Publishing.
Francois, Rose Darlie. Little Miss Daring Evelynne. 2009. 47p. pap. 19.10 (978-0-557-07136-4(4)) Lulu Pr., Inc.
Frank, E. R. Wrecked. (ENG., (YA). 2015. Illus.). 336p. (gr. 9). pap. 10.99 (978-1-4814-5137-6(5)) 2007. 256p. (gr. 7-12). pap. 9.99 (978-0-689-87384-3(0)) Simon & Schuster Children's Publishing. (Atheneum Bks. for Young Readers).
Franklin, Kristine L. Dove Song. 2006. (ENG.). 192p. (J). (gr. 5-9). per. 5.99 (978-0-7636-3219-9(8)) Candlewick Pr.
Franklin, Shirley A. Emma's Fantastique Word Play. 2009. 80p. pap. 8.95 (978-1-4401-3824-9(9)) iUniverse, Inc.
Fraser, Mary Ann. Heebie-Jeebie Jamboree. 2011. (ENG.). 32p. (J). (gr. -1-2). 15.95 (978-1-59078-857-8(5)) Boyds Mills Pr.
Fraser, Mary Ann, illus. No Yeti Yet. 2015. (ENG.). 32p. (J). 16.99 (978-1-4413-0855-9(5), 9781441308559) Peter Pauper Pr. Inc.
Fraustino, Lisa Rowe. The Hole in the Wall. 2011. (ENG.). 232p. (J). (gr. 2-8). pap. 8.00 (978-1-57131-698-1(1)) Milkweed Editions.
Frayre, A. R. Shannon Cabbage-Head. 2008. 33p. pap. 14.28 (978-0-557-00442-3(X)) Lulu Pr., Inc.
Frazee, Marla. The Bossier Baby. Frazee, Marla, illus. 2016. (ENG., Illus.). 40p. (J). (gr. -1-3). 17.99 (978-1-4814-7162-6(7), Beach Lane Bks.) Beach Lane Bks.
Frederick, Heather Vogel. Once upon a Toad. (ENG., Illus.). (J). (gr. 5-9). 2013. 288p. pap. 6.99 (978-1-4169-8479-5(8)) 2012. 272p. 16.99 (978-1-4169-8478-8(X)) Simon & Schuster Bks. For Young Readers. (Simon & Schuster Bks. For Young Readers).
French, Jackie. Josephine Wants to Dance. Whatley, Bruce, illus. 2007. (ENG.). 32p. (J). (gr. -1-1). 17.95 (978-0-8109-9431-7(3), Abrams Bks. for Young Readers) Abrams, Inc.
French, Vivian. Mountain Mona: Band 09/Gold. Fisher, Chris, illus. 2006. (Collins Big Cat Ser.). (ENG.). 24p. (J). (gr. 2-2). pap. 7.99 (978-0-00-718700-3(9)) HarperCollins Pubs. Ltd. GBR. Dist: Independent Pubs. Group.
Friedland, Joyce, ed. Cool Zone with Pain & the Great One: Novel-Ties Study Guide. 2011. 29p. pap. 16.95 (978-0-7675-4471-9(4)) Learning Links Inc.
Friedman, Laurie. High Five, Mallory! Kalis, Jennifer, illus. (Mallory Ser.: Vol. 26). (ENG.). 160p. (J). 2017. (gr. 2-5). pap. 5.95 **(978-1-5124-5867-1(8))** 2016. (gr. 3-3). E-Book 11.99 (978-1-5124-0898-0(0), 9781512408980) Lerner Publishing Group. (Darby Creek).
—High Five, Mallory! Kalis, Jennifer, illus. 2016. (Mallory Ser.: 26). (ENG.). 160p. (gr. 2-5). 15.95 (978-1-4677-5030-1(1)) Lerner Publishing Group.
—Mallory Mcdonald, Baby Expert. Kalis, Jennifer, illus. 2015. (Mallory Ser.: Vol. 22). (ENG.). 152p. (J). (gr. 2-5). pap. 5.95 (978-1-4677-0938-5(7), Darby Creek) Lerner Publishing Group.
—Mallory McDonald, Super Snoop. Kalis, Jennifer, illus. (Mallory Ser.: 18). (ENG.). 152p. (J). (gr. 2-5). 2013. pap. 5.95 (978-1-4677-0929-3(8), Darby Creek) 2012. 15.95 (978-0-7613-6073-5(5)) Lerner Publishing Group.
Friedman, Robin. Nothing. 2008. (ENG.). 240p. (YA). (gr. 8-18). pap. 9.95 (978-0-7387-1304-5(X), Flux) North Star Editions.
Friend, Ronda. R. Friend Swallows Her Pride. 2005. (Down on Friendly Acres Ser.: 1). (J). lib. bdg. (978-0-9743627-3-1(5)) Sunflower Seeds Pr.
Friskey, Margaret. Surprise on Wheels. Patton, Lucia, illus. 2004. reprint ed. pap. 15.95 (978-1-4191-1496-0(4)) Kessinger Publishing, LLC.
Frost, Robert Temple. Long Trip Home: Stand up Paddleboard Fantasy. 2013. 82p. pap. 10.95 (978-1-62212-924-9(5), Strategic Bk. Publishing) Strategic Book Publishing & Rights Agency (SBPRA).
Fruchter, Jason, illus. The Baby Is Here! 2015. (Daniel Tiger's Neighborhood Ser.). (ENG.). 24p. (J). (gr. -1-2). pap. 3.99 (978-1-4814-3013-5(0), Simon Spotlight) Simon Spotlight.
Fry, Jason. Edge of the Galaxy. Balmet, Jean-Paul, illus. 2014. (ENG.). 176p. (J). (gr. 3-7). pap. 6.99 (978-1-4847-0485-1(1)) Disney Pr.
—Edge of the Galaxy. 2014. 172p. (J). lib. bdg. 17.20 (978-0-606-36536-9(2)) Turtleback Bks.
—Imperial Justice. 2015. (ENG.). 176p. (J). (gr. 3-7). pap. 6.99 (978-1-4847-1660-1(4), Disney Lucasfilm Press) Disney Publishing Worldwide.
—The Jupiter Pirates: Hunt for the Hydra. 2013. (Jupiter Pirates Ser.: 1). (ENG.). 256p. (J). (gr. 3-7). 16.99 (978-0-06-223020-1(4)) HarperCollins Pubs.
—The Jupiter Pirates: Hunt for the Hydra. 2014. (Jupiter Pirates Ser.: 1). (ENG.). 272p. (J). (gr. 3-7). pap. 6.99 (978-0-06-223021-8(2)) HarperCollins Pubs.
—Servants of the Empire: The Secret Academy. 2015. (ENG.). 192p. (J). (gr. 3-7). pap. 6.99 (978-1-4847-1661-8(2), Disney Lucasfilm Press) Disney Publishing Worldwide.
Fry, Jason. Star Wars Rebels: Edge of the Galaxy. 2014. 172p. (J). **(978-1-4242-6295-3(X)**, Disney Lucasfilm Press) Disney Publishing Worldwide.
Fry, Jason & Weisman, Greg. Servants of the Empire. 2015. 171p. (J). **(978-1-4242-6297-7(6)**, Disney Lucasfilm Press) Disney Publishing Worldwide.
Fuchs-Rice, Dwayne. Shades of Ember. 2008. 456p. pap. 24.95 (978-0-595-53315-2(9)) iUniverse, Inc.
Fuller, Rachel, illus. Look at Me! 2009. (New Baby Ser.). (ENG.). 12p. (J). (gr. -1). bds. (978-1-84643-278-1(2)) Child's Play International Ltd.
—My New Baby. 2009. (New Baby Ser.). (ENG.). 12p. (J). (gr. -1). bds. (978-1-84643-276-7(6)) Child's Play International Ltd.
Funari-Willever, Lisa. Theres A Kid under My Bed (Cj) 2008. 40p. 12.95 (978-0-9760469-4-3(6)) Franklin Mason Pr.
Gaiman, Neil. The Day I Swapped My Dad for Two Goldfish. McKean, Dave, illus. 2004. (ENG.). 64p. (J). (gr. k). 17.99 (978-0-06-058701-7(6)) HarperCollins Pubs.
Gaither, Stefanie. Into the Abyss. 2016. (ENG., Illus.). 352p. (YA). (gr. 7). 18.99 (978-1-4814-4995-3(8), Simon & Schuster Bks. For Young Readers) Simon & Schuster Bks. For Young Readers.
Galante, Cecilia. Stealing Our Way Home. 2017. (ENG.). 304p. (J). (gr. 3-7). 17.99 **(978-1-338-04296-2(3)**, Scholastic Pr.) Scholastic, Inc.
—The World from up Here. (ENG.). 320p. (J). (gr. 3-7). 2017. pap. 6.99 **(978-0-545-84846-6(6))** 2016. 16.99 (978-0-545-84845-9(8), Scholastic Pr.) Scholastic, Inc.
Galaxy X: Book One in the Galaxy X Trilogy, Bk. 1. 2009. (Hardy Boys (All New) Undercover Brothers Ser.: 28). (ENG.). 160p. (J). (gr. 3-7). pap. 5.99 (978-1-4169-7801-5(1), Aladdin) Simon & Schuster Children's Publishing.
Galvin, Laura. I Love My Sister. 2008. (ENG., Illus.). 16p. (J). (gr. -1-k). bds. 6.95 (978-1-59249-867-3(1)) Soundprints.
Galvin, Laura Gates. I Love My Brother. Oughton, Taylor, illus. 2008. (ENG.). 16p. (J). (gr. -1-k). bds. 6.95 (978-1-59249-866-6(3)) Soundprints.
—I Love My Sister. Oughton, Taylor et al, illus. 2011. (I Love My... Ser.). (ENG.). 16p. (J). (gr. -1-k). 6.95 (978-1-60727-311-0(X)) Soundprints.
Ganz, Yaffa. The Adventures of Jeremy & Heddy Levi. Katz, Avi, illus. 2005. 204p. (J). 16.95 (978-1-930143-50-0(8), 3508); pap. 12.95 (978-1-930143-51-7(6), 3516) Simcha Media Group. (Devora Publishing).
Garcia, Maria. Las Aventuras de Connie y Diego. 2004. (ENG & SPA., Illus.). (J). (gr. k-3). spiral bd. (978-0-616-14605-7(1)) Canadian National Institute for the Blind/Institut National Canadien pour les Aveugles.
Garfield, Leon. The Complete Bostock & Harris. 2014. (ENG.). 336p. (J). (gr. 3-7). 17.95 (978-1-59017-783-9(5), NYR Children's Collection) New York Review of Bks., Inc., The.
Garis, Howard R. The Curlytops & Their Playmates. 2009. 120p. 22.95 (978-1-60664-610-6(9)); pap. 10.95 (978-1-60664-342-6(8)) Rodgers, Alan Bks.
—The Curlytops at Silver Lake. 2007. 260p. 29.95 (978-1-4344-9207-4(9)); per. 19.95 (978-1-4344-9113-8(7)) Wildside Pr., LLC.
—The Curlytops on Star Island. 2009. 120p. 22.95 (978-1-60664-611-3(7)); pap. 10.95 (978-1-60664-343-3(6)) Rodgers, Alan Bks.
—The Curlytops on Star Island; or, Camping Out with Grandpa. 2007. 164p. per. (978-1-4065-2764-3(5)) Dodo Pr.
Garis, Howard Roger. The Curlytops at Uncle Franks Ranch. 2005. 192p. pap. 11.95 (978-1-4218-1566-4(4), 1st World Library - Literary Society) 1st World Publishing, Inc.
—Daddy Takes Us Skating. 2007. 56p. per. (978-1-4065-2765-0(3)) Dodo Pr.
—Daddy Takes Us to the Garden. 2007. (Illus.). 132p. per. (978-1-4065-2766-7(1)) Dodo Pr.
Garner, Alan. The Weirdstone of Brisingamen: A Tale of Alderley. 2006. (ENG., Illus.). 288p. (J). (gr. 4-8). pap. 16.95 (978-0-15-205636-0(X)) Houghton Mifflin Harcourt Publishing Co.
Garthwaite, Lynn D. Dirkle Smat Inside Mount Flatbottom. Howarth, Craig, illus. 2006. 48p. (J). pap. 9.95 (978-1-59663-512-8(6), Castle Keep Pr.) Rock, James A. & Co. Pubs.
Gary, Meredith. Sometimes You Get What You Want. Brown, Lisa, illus. 2008. (ENG.). 32p. (J). (gr. -1 — 1). 16.99 (978-0-06-114015-0(5)) HarperCollins Pubs.
Gaskin, Terri. Me & My Brother. 2010. 24p. 11.49 (978-1-4520-5939-6(X)) AuthorHouse.
—Me & My Brother: Coloring Book. 2011. 24p. pap. 11.32 (978-1-4567-6031-1(9)) AuthorHouse.
Gaskins, Terry & Treigle, Jimmy. The Very Big Storm: Created by Terry Gaskins Inspired by Jimmy Treigle. 2009. 28p. pap. 13.99 (978-1-4389-4220-9(6)) AuthorHouse.
Gay, Marie-Louise. Buenos Dias Samuel. 2004.Tr. of Good Morning Sam. (SPA.). (J). (gr. k-18). pap. 7.99 (978-980-257-293-9(4)) Ekare, Ediciones VEN. Dist: Lectorum Pubns., Inc.
—Estela, Princesa de la Noche. 2nd ed. 2006.Tr. of Stella Princess of the Sky. (SPA., Illus.). 32p. (J). (gr. 1-2). 10.99 (978-980-257-304-2(3), EK33231) Ekare, Ediciones VEN. Dist: Lectorum Pubns., Inc.
—Princess Pistachio, 1 vol. Homel, Jacob, tr. from FRE. Gay, Marie-Louise, illus. 2015. Orig. Title: Princesse Pistache. (ENG., Illus.). 48p. (J). (gr. k-3). 10.95 (978-1-927485-69-9(X)) Pajama Pr. CAN. Dist: Ingram Publisher Services.
—Stella - Fairy of the Forest. 2004. (Illus.). (J). (gr. -1-2). spiral bd. (978-0-616-14581-4(0)); spiral bd. (978-0-616-14580-7(2)) Canadian National Institute for the Blind/Institut National Canadien pour les Aveugles.
—Stella - Fairy of the Forest, 1 vol. 2010. (Stella & Sam Ser.). (ENG., Illus.). 32p. (J). (gr. k-k). pap. 7.95 (978-0-88899-993-1(3)) Groundwood Bks. CAN. Dist: Publishers Group West (PGW).
—Stella, Queen of the Snow. 2004. (J). (gr. -1-1). spiral bd. (978-0-616-08493-9(5)) Canadian National Institute for the Blind/Institut National Canadien pour les Aveugles.
—Stella, Star of the Sea, 1 vol. (Stella & Sam Ser.). (ENG., Illus.). 32p. (J). (gr. k-k). 2010. pap. 7.95 (978-0-88899-992-4(5)) 2004. 7.95 (978-0-88899-572-8(5)) Groundwood Bks. CAN. Dist: Publishers Group West (PGW).
Geist, Ken. Who's Who? Cole, Henry, illus. 2012. (ENG.). 28p. (J). (gr. -1 — 1). 16.99 (978-0-312-64437-6(X), 9780312644376) Feiwel & Friends.
Gennifer, Choldenko. Al Capone Does My Shirts. 2014. (ENG.). 240p. (J). (gr. 6-12). 12.24 (978-1-63245-251-1(0)) Lectorum Pubns., Inc.
George, Jean Craighead. Crowbar, the Smartest Bird in the World. Minor, Wendell, illus. 2015. (J). (978-0-06-000257-2(3)) HarperCollins Pubs.
George, Jessica Day. Fridays with the Wizards. (Tuesdays at the Castle Ser.). (ENG.). 2017. 256p. (J). pap. 7.99 (978-1-68119-204-8(7), 9781681192048) 2016. 240p. (YA). 16.99 (978-1-61963-429-9(5), 9781619634299) Bloomsbury Publishing USA. (Bloomsbury USA Childrens).
—Thursdays with the Crown. (Tuesdays at the Castle Ser.). (ENG.). 2017. 240p. (J). pap. 7.99 (978-1-68119-221-5(7), 9781681192215) 2016. 240p. (J). pap. 7.99 (978-1-61963-796-2(0), 9781619637962) 2014. 224p. (YA). (gr. 3-6). 16.99 (978-1-61963-299-8(3), 9781619632998) Bloomsbury Publishing USA. (Bloomsbury USA Childrens).
Gerber, Lisa Ann. Elaina's Sleuthing Days, 1 vol. 2009. 60p. pap. 16.95 (978-1-60749-623-6(2)) PublishAmerica, Inc.
Getzinger, Donna. Special. 2004. 108p. (J). pap. 7.95 (978-0-87714-530-1(X)) i-5 Publishing LLC.
Gewirtz, Adina Rishe. Zebra Forest. (ENG., 208p. (J). (gr. 4-7). 2014. Illus.). pap. 7.99 (978-0-7636-7166-2(5)) 2013. 15.99 (978-0-7636-6041-3(8)) Candlewick Pr.
Gibson, Douglas. Tales of a Fifth-Grade Knight. Tuya, Jez, illus. 2015. (Middle-Grade Novels Ser.). (ENG.). 160p. (gr. 4-7). lib. bdg. 26.65 (978-1-4965-0488-3(7)) Stone Arch Bks.
Gidwitz, Adam. The Grimm Conclusion. 2014. (Grimm Ser.: 3). lib. bdg. 18.40 (978-0-606-36187-3(1)) Turtleback Bks.
—A Tale Dark & Grimm. D'Andrade, Hugh & Santat, Dan, illus. 2011. (ENG.). 288p. (J). (gr. 5-18). 7.99 (978-0-14-241967-0(2), Puffin Books) Penguin Young Readers Group.
—A Tale Dark & Grimm, 4 vols. (J). 55.75 (978-1-4498-6835-2(5)) Recorded Bks., Inc.
—A Tale Dark & Grimm. 2011. (Grimm Ser.: 1). lib. bdg. 18.40 (978-0-606-23144-2(7), Turtleback) Turtleback Bks.
Gidwitz, Adam, et al. A Tale Dark & Grimm. D'Andrade, Hugh, illus. 2010. (ENG.). 272p. (J). (gr. 5-18). 16.99 (978-0-525-42334-8(6), Dutton Books for Young Readers) Penguin Young Readers Group.
Giff, Patricia Reilly. Gingersnap. 2014. (ENG.). 160p. (J). (gr. 3-7). 6.99 (978-0-440-42178-8(0), Yearling) Random Hse. Children's Bks.
—Hunter Moran Digs Deep. Sheban, Chris, illus. 2014. (ENG.). 160p. (J). (gr. 3-7). 16.95 (978-0-8234-3165-6(7)) Holiday Hse., Inc.
—Hunter Moran Hangs Out. (ENG.). 144p. (J). (gr. 3-7). 2014. pap. 6.99 (978-0-8234-3189-2(4)) 2013. (Illus.). 16.95 (978-0-8234-2859-5(1)) Holiday Hse., Inc.
—Hunter Moran Saves the Universe. (ENG.). 128p. (J). (gr. 2-7). 2013. pap. 6.99 (978-0-8234-2917-2(2)) 2012. 16.95 (978-0-8234-1949-4(5)) Holiday Hse., Inc.
—Nory Ryan's Song. 2004. 160p. (J). (gr. 4-7). pap. 36.00 incl. audio (978-0-8072-2093-1(0), Listening Library) Random Hse. Audio Publishing Group.
—The Number One Kid. Bright, Alasdair, illus. 2010. (Zigzag Kids Ser.). (ENG.). 80p. (J). (gr. 1-4). pap. 4.99 (978-0-553-49468-6(6), Yearling) Random Hse. Children's Bks.
—R My Name Is Rachel. 2012. (ENG.). 176p. (J). (gr. 4-7). pap. 6.99 (978-0-440-42176-4(4), Yearling) Random Hse. Children's Bks.
Gifford, Peggy. Moxy Maxwell Does Not Love Writing Thank-You Notes. Fisher, Valorie, illus. 2009. (Moxy Maxwell Ser.). (ENG.). 192p. (J). (gr. 2-5). 6.99 (978-0-375-84343-3(4), Yearling) Random Hse. Children's Bks.
Gill, Timothy. Flip & Fin: Super Sharks to the Rescue! Numberman, Neil, illus. 2016. 32p. (J). (gr. -1-3). 15.99 (978-0-06-224301-0(2), Greenwillow Bks.) HarperCollins Pubs.
Gillam, David. Gingertown. Gilliam, David, illus. 2012. 216p. (J). 29.99 (978-1-60131-122-1(2)) Big Tent Bks.

Giordano, Margaret A. The Bowditchers. 2006. 242p. per. 14.95 *(978-1-59824-406-9(X))* E-BookTime LLC.
Giurco, Diane. The Adventures of Willy & Nilly. 2008. (Illus.). 32p. pap. 14.49 *(978-1-4389-1134-2(3))* AuthorHouse.
Glaser, P. H. Chrystallia & the Source of Light. 2011. (Illus.). 196p. (J). 18.99 *(978-1-60832-232-9(7))* Greenleaf Book Group.
Glewwe, Eleanor. Wildings. 2016. (ENG.). 336p. (J). (gr. 5). 16.99 *(978-0-451-46885-7(6),* Viking Books for Young Readers) Penguin Young Readers Group.
Gloster, Dean. Dessert First. 2016. (ENG.). 304p. (YA). 17.99 *(978-1-4405-9454-0(6),* Simon Pulse) Simon Pulse.
Glyn, Pamela. The green light in the Mountains. 2010. 32p. pap. 23.96 *(978-1-4457-5153-5(4))* Lulu Pr., Inc.
Goebel, Jenny. Fortune Falls. (ENG.). 208p. (J). (gr. 3-7). 2017. pap. 6.99 ***(978-1-338-13470-4(1))*** 2016. 16.99 *(978-0-545-81190-3(2),* Scholastic Pr.) Scholastic, Inc.
Goebel, Jenny. Mission Hurricane. 2016. (39 Clues: Doublecross Ser.: 3). (ENG., Illus.). 192p. (J). (gr. 3-7). 12.99 *(978-0-545-76748-4(2))* Scholastic, Inc.
Goelman, Ari. The Path of Names. 2013. (Illus.). 339p. (J). pap. *(978-0-545-47431-3(0),* Levine, Arthur A. Bks.) Scholastic, Inc.
Golant, Galina & Grant, Lisa. Play Checkers with Me. Golant, Evgenia, illus. 2003. 32p. (J). pap. 6.95 *(978-1-932133-01-1(1))* Writers' Collective, The.
Goldberg, Whoopi. Perfectly Prima, No. 3. Roos, Maryn, illus. 2010. (ENG.). 160p. (J). (gr. 1-17). pap. 4.99 *(978-0-7868-5262-8(3),* Jump at the Sun) Hyperion Bks. for Children.
—Toeshoe Trouble. Roos, Maryn, illus. 2009. (ENG.). 160p. (J). (gr. 1-17). pap. 4.99 *(978-0-7868-5261-1(5),* Jump at the Sun) Hyperion Bks. for Children.
Goldman, Marcia, photos by. Lola & Tattletale Zeke. 2015. (Lola Ser.). (ENG., Illus.). 32p. (J). (gr. -1-3). 16.95 *(978-1-939547-16-3(4))* Creston Bks.
Goldsberry, Booty. Scaredy-Cat, I'm Not. 2007. (ENG., Illus.). 40p. (gr. 4-7). pap. 9.95 *(978-0-9792875-0-3(2))* Goldsberry, Booty.
Gonzalez Bertrand, Diane. The Ruiz Street Kids (Los Muchachos de la Calle Ruiz) Ventura, Gabriela Baeza, tr. 2006. (ENG & SPA., Illus.). (J). pap. 9.95 *(978-1-55885-321-8(9),* Piñata Books) Arte Publico Pr.
Gonzalez, Rafael. Cookie Boy! 2011. 20p. pap. 11.99 *(978-1-4634-0324-9(0))* AuthorHouse.
Goobie, Beth & Fernández, Queta. Ni un Día Más, 1 vol. 2009. (Spanish Soundings Ser.). (SPA.). 112p. (YA). (gr. 8-12). pap. 9.95 *(978-1-55469-137-1(0))* Orca Bk. Pubs. USA.
Good Night, Little Brother: Individual Title Six-Packs. (Literatura 2000 Ser.). (gr. 1-2). 28.00 *(978-0-7635-0090-0(9))* Rigby Education.
Goodhart, Pippa. Ginny's Egg. Brouwer, Aafke, illus. 142p. (J). pap. 7.50 *(978-0-7497-4557-8(6))* Egmont Bks., Ltd. GBR. Dist: Trafalgar Square Publishing.
Gorbachev, Valeri. The Best Cat. Gorbachev, Valeri, illus. 2010. (ENG., Illus.). 32p. (J). (gr. -1-2). 15.99 *(978-0-7636-3675-3(4))* Candlewick Pr.
Gordon, David. The Ugly Truckling. Gordon, David, illus. 2004. (Illus.). 32p. (J). (gr. -1-2). lib. bdg. 16.89 *(978-0-06-054601-4(8),* Geringer, Laura Book) HarperCollins Pubs.
Gordon, Pauline C. The Adventures of the Droplet Twins. 2013. 136p. *(978-1-4602-1343-8(2));* pap. *(978-1-4602-1344-5(0))* FriesenPress.
Gorges, Julie A. Just Call Me Goody-Two-Shoes. 2006. 146p. (YA). per. 9.95 *(978-0-9763274-1-7(4))* I.Form Ink, Publishing.
Gormally, Eleanor. The Little Flower Bulb: Helping Children Bereaved by Suicide. Loki & Splink, illus. 2011. (ENG.). 32p. (J). (gr. -1-3). pap. 21.95 *(978-1-84730-260-1(2))* Veritas Pubns. IRL. Dist: Dufour Editions, Inc.
Gosling, Sharon. The Sapphire Cutlass. 2016. (Diamond Thief Ser.). (ENG.). 336p. (gr. 9-12). 16.95 *(978-1-63079-041-7(9))* Switch Pr.
Gourlay, Candy. Tall Story. 2012. (ENG.). 304p. (J). (gr. 5). 6.99 *(978-0-385-75233-6(4),* Yearling) Random Hse. Children's Bks.
Grab, Daphne. Halftime. 2010. (J). *(978-0-385-73783-8(1)); (978-0-385-90693-7(5))* Random House Publishing Group. (Delacorte Pr).
Grace, Amanda. No One Needs to Know. 2014. (ENG.). 240p. (YA). pap. 9.99 *(978-0-7387-3625-9(2),* Flux) North Star Editions.
Grace, Hannah. The Popcorn MacHine. 2013. 56p. *(978-1-4602-3282-8(8))* FriesenPress.
Grace, Kathleen. The Perfect Pug. 2011. 24p. pap. 24.95 *(978-1-4512-7557-5(9))* America Star Bks.
Graff, Lisa. Lost in the Sun. 2015. (ENG.). 304p. (J). (gr. 5). 16.99 *(978-0-399-16406-4(5),* Philomel Bks.) Penguin Young Readers Group.
Graham, Bob. The Silver Button. Graham, Bob, illus. 2013. (ENG., Illus.). 32p. (J). (gr. -1-1). 16.99 *(978-0-7636-6437-4(5))* Candlewick Pr.
Graham, Richard. Jack y el Monstruo. Varley, Susan, illus. (Cotton Cloud Ser.). (SPA.). 32p. (J). (gr. 1-3). *(978-84-7722-680-2(6))* Timun Mas, Editorial S.A. ESP. Dist: Lectorum Pubns., Inc.
Grahame, Kenneth. The Golden Age. 2006. pap. *(978-1-4068-3332-4(0))* Echo Library.
Grandma Bette. The Excellent Adventures of Max & Madison: Bedtime Stories for Youngsters. 2013. 32p. pap. 16.95 *(978-1-4525-7266-6(6));* 32p. pap. 16.95 *(978-1-4525-7264-2(X));* 36p. pap. 16.95 *(978-1-4525-7270-3(4));* 32p. pap. 16.95 *(978-1-4525-7268-0(2))* Author Solutions, Inc. (Balboa Pr.).
Grandpa Casey. Another Müsh-Mice Adventure: Florida Vacation, 1 vol. Brennan, Lisa, illus. 2009. 45p. pap. 24.95 *(978-1-60813-329-1(X))* America Star Bks.
Grant, Tess. Flying in the Dark. 2013. 186p. pap. 10.99 *(978-1-62237-167-9(4))* Turquoise Morning Pr.
Gratton, Tessa. Blood Magic. 2011. (YA). pap. *(978-0-375-86486-5(5))* Random Hse. Children's Bks.
Graves, Annie. Guinea Pig Killer. McElhinney, Glenn, illus. 2015. (Nightmare Club Ser.: 4). (ENG.). 64p. (J). (gr. 2-5). pap. 6.99 *(978-1-4677-6044-7(7));* lib. bdg. 25.32 *(978-1-4677-4351-8(8))* Lerner Publishing Group.
Graves, Susan Elaine. Lily the Lucky Ducky, 1 vol. 2010. 44p. 24.95 *(978-1-4489-4433-0(3))* PublishAmerica, Inc.
Gray, Grandpa. The Land of the Three Elves Vol. 1: Beginnings. 2012. (ENG.). 317p. pap. 14.95 *(978-1-4327-9551-1(1))* Outskirts Pr., Inc.
Green, D. L. Zeke Meeks vs the Annoying Princess Sing-Along, 1 vol. Alves, Josh, illus. 2014. (Zeke Meeks Ser.). (ENG.). 128p. (gr. 2-2). 22.65 *(978-1-4795-4828-6(6),* Zeke Meeks) Picture Window Bks.
—Zeke Meeks vs the Big Blah-Rific Birthday, 1 vol. Alves, Josh, illus. 2013. (Zeke Meeks Ser.). (ENG.). 128p. (gr. 2-2). 8.95 *(978-1-4048-8105-1(0));* lib. bdg. 22.65 *(978-1-4048-7637-8(5))* Picture Window Bks. (Zeke Meeks).
—Zeke Meeks vs the Crummy Class Play, 1 vol. Alves, Josh, illus. 2014. (Zeke Meeks Ser.). (ENG.). 128p. (gr. 2-2). 22.65 *(978-1-4795-4827-9(8),* Zeke Meeks) Picture Window Bks.
—Zeke Meeks vs the Gruesome Girls, 1 vol. Alves, Josh, illus. 2012. (Zeke Meeks Ser.). (ENG.). 128p. (gr. 2-2). pap. 5.95 *(978-1-4048-7221-9(3));* lib. bdg. 22.65 *(978-1-4048-6805-2(4))* Picture Window Bks. (Zeke Meeks).
—Zeke Meeks vs the Horrendous Halloween, 1 vol. Alves, Josh, illus. 2013. (Zeke Meeks Ser.). (ENG.). 128p. (gr. 2-2). lib. bdg. 22.65 *(978-1-4048-7638-5(3),* Zeke Meeks) Picture Window Bks.
—Zeke Meeks vs the Mother's Day Meltdown. Alves, Josh, illus. 2015. (Zeke Meeks Ser.). (ENG.). 128p. (gr. 2-2). 22.65 *(978-1-4795-2168-5(X),* Zeke Meeks) Picture Window Bks.
—Zeke Meeks vs the No-Fun Fund-Raiser, 1 vol. Alves, Josh, illus. 2013. (Zeke Meeks Ser.). (ENG.). 128p. (gr. 2-2). lib. bdg. 22.65 *(978-1-4048-7640-8(5),* Zeke Meeks) Picture Window Bks.
—Zeke Meeks vs the Stinky Soccer Team. Alves, Josh, illus. 2015. (Zeke Meeks Ser.). (ENG.). 128p. (gr. 2-2). 22.65 *(978-1-4795-5768-4(4),* Zeke Meeks) Picture Window Bks.
—Zeke Meeks vs the Super Stressful Talent Show, 1 vol. Alves, Josh, illus. 2013. (Zeke Meeks Ser.). (ENG.). 128p. (gr. 2-2). 8.95 *(978-1-4048-8106-8(9));* lib. bdg. 22.65 *(978-1-4048-7639-2(1))* Picture Window Bks. (Zeke Meeks).
Green, Lucyna A. M., illus. Love You Little Brother. 2006. (J). *(978-1-58669-185-1(6)); (978-1-58669-186-8(4))* Childcraft Education Corp.
Green, Paige. Family over Everything. 2013. (ENG., Illus.). 224p. pap. 15.99 *(978-1-59309-501-7(5),* Strebor Bks.) Strebor Bks.
Green, Poppy. Looking for Winston. Bell, Jennifer A., illus. 2015. (Adventures of Sophie Mouse Ser.: 4). (ENG.). 128p. (J). (gr. k-4). pap. 5.99 *(978-1-4814-3003-6(3),* Little Simon) Little Simon.
Green, Tim. Deep Zone. 2012. (Football Genius Ser.: 5). (J). lib. bdg. 17.20 *(978-0-606-26854-7(5),* Turtleback) Turtleback Bks.
—Football Hero. (Football Genius Ser.: 2). (ENG.). (J). (gr. 3-7). 2009. 320p. pap. 6.99 *(978-0-06-112276-7(9))* 2008. (Illus.). 304p. 16.99 *(978-0-06-112274-3(2))* HarperCollins Pubs.
—Pinch Hit. 2013. (ENG.). 336p. (J). (gr. 3-7). pap. 6.99 *(978-0-06-201247-0(9))* HarperCollins Pubs.
Greenburg, Dan. Secrets of Dripping Fang: Attack of the Giant Octopus. Fischer, Scott M., illus. 2009. (Secrets of Dripping Fang Ser.). (ENG.). 160p. 25.65 *(978-1-59961-537-0(1))* Spotlight.
—Secrets of Dripping Fang: Fall of the House of Mandible. Fischer, Scott M., illus. 2009. (Secrets of Dripping Fang Ser.). (ENG.). 160p. 25.65 *(978-1-59961-535-6(5))* Spotlight.
—Secrets of Dripping Fang: Please Don't Eat the Children: Book 7: Book 7. Fischer, Scott M., illus. 2009. (Secrets of Dripping Fang Ser.). (ENG.). 160p. 25.65 *(978-1-59961-538-7(X))* Spotlight.
—Secrets of Dripping Fang: The Onts. Fischer, Scott M., illus. 2009. (Secrets of Dripping Fang Ser.). (ENG.). 144p. 25.65 *(978-1-59961-532-5(0))* Spotlight.
—Secrets of Dripping Fang: The Shluffmuffin Boy Is History. Fischer, Scott M., illus. 2009. (Secrets of Dripping Fang Ser.). (ENG.). 176p. 25.65 *(978-1-59961-536-3(3))* Spotlight.
—Secrets of Dripping Fang: The Vampire's Curse: Book 3: Book 3. Fischer, Scott M., illus. 2009. (Secrets of Dripping Fang Ser.). (ENG.). 144p. 25.65 *(978-1-59961-534-9(7))* Spotlight.
—Secrets of Dripping Fang: Treachery & Betrayal at Jolly Days. Fischer, Scott M., illus. 2009. (Secrets of Dripping Fang Ser.). (ENG.). 144p. 25.65 *(978-1-59961-533-2(9))* Spotlight.
—Secrets of Dripping Fang: When Bad Snakes Attack Good Children. Fischer, Scott M., illus. 2009. (Secrets of Dripping Fang Ser.). (ENG.). 144p. 25.65 *(978-1-59961-539-4(8))* Spotlight.
—Secrets of Dripping Fang, Book Seven: Please Don't Eat the Children. Fischer, Scott M., illus. 2007. (Secrets of Dripping Fang Ser.: Bk. 7). (ENG.). 160p. (J). (gr. 2-5). 11.95 *(978-0-15-206047-3(2))* Houghton Mifflin Harcourt Publishing Co.
Greene, Stephanie. Happy Birthday, Sophie Hartley. 2011. (ENG.). 128p. (J). (gr. 2-5). pap. 6.99 *(978-0-547-55025-1(1))* Houghton Mifflin Harcourt Publishing Co.
Greenfield, Eloise. She Come Bringing Me That Little Baby Girl. Steptoe, John, illus. 2014. 32p. pap. 7.00 *(978-1-61003-336-7(1))* Center for the Collaborative Classroom.
Greer, Hannah. The Castle Ivengless: The Velvet Bag Memoirs, Bk. 3. 2009. 145p. pap. 24.95 *(978-1-60749-105-7(2))* America Star Bks.
—The Lighthouse Summer Greer, Tica, illus. 2009. 156p. pap. 24.95 *(978-1-60813-493-9(8))* America Star Bks.
Gresh, Dannah. Danika's Totally Terrible Toss. 2008. (Secret Keeper Girl Fiction Ser.). (ENG.). 112p. pap. 7.99 *(978-0-8024-8702-5(5))* Moody Pubs.
Gresh, Dannah & Mylin, Janet. Just Call Me Kate. 2008. (Secret Keeper Girl Fiction Ser.). (ENG.). 112p. pap. 7.99 *(978-0-8024-8703-2(3))* Moody Pubs.
Greves, Julie, et al. Upside down & Backwards: A Sibling's Journey Through Childhood Cancer. 2014. (Illus.). 112p. (J). *(978-1-4338-1637-6(7),* Magination Pr.) American Psychological Assn.
Griffin, Adele. The Knaveheart's Curse. 2009. (Vampire Island Ser.). (ENG.). 160p. (J). (gr. 3-7). 6.99 *(978-0-14-241407-1(7),* Puffin Books) Penguin Young Readers Group.
Griffin, Bethany. The Fall. 2014. (ENG.). 432p. (YA). (gr. 9). 17.99 *(978-0-06-210785-5(2),* Greenwillow Bks.) HarperCollins Pubs.
Grigsby, Cynthia. Hollow Creek: A Haunted Beginning, 01. 2006. 163p. (J). 14.95 *(978-0-9786840-0-6(1))* Grigsby, Cynthia.
Grime, L. L. The Make up Story. 2007. 36p. 17.50 *(978-1-4357-0585-2(8))* Lulu Pr., Inc.
Grimes, Nikki. The Road to Paris. 2008. 153p. (gr. 3-7). 17.00 *(978-0-7569-8932-3(9))* Perfection Learning Corp.
—Road to Paris. 2008. (ENG.). 160p. (J). (gr. 3-7). 6.99 *(978-0-14-241082-0(9),* Puffin Books) Penguin Young Readers Group.
Grindley, Sally. Hurricane Wills. 2007. (ENG.). 256p. (J). (gr. 4-7). pap. 8.95 *(978-0-7475-9095-8(8))* Bloomsbury Publishing Plc GBR. Dist: Independent Pubs. Group.
Gritton, Steve. ... & Then I... 2007. (Illus.). (J). 17.95 *(978-0-9795361-1-3(1))* Bad Frog Art/SMG Bks.
—The Trouble with Sisters & Robots. 2012. (J). 34.28 *(978-1-61913-150-7(1))* Weigl Pubs., Inc.
Grosset and Dunlap Staff & Child, Lauren. I Slightly Want to Go Home. 2011. (Charlie & Lola Ser.). (ENG.). 24p. (J). (gr. k-3). mass mkt. 3.99 *(978-0-448-45461-0(0),* Grosset & Dunlap) Penguin Young Readers Group.
Grosset and Dunlap Staff & Penguin Young Readers Group Staff. Beach Day! 2011. (Max & Ruby Ser.). (ENG., Illus.). 32p. (J). (gr. 1-2). pap. 3.99 *(978-0-448-45593-8(5),* Penguin Young Readers) Penguin Young Readers Group.
Guest, Elissa Haden. Iris & Walter & Baby Rose. Davenier, Christine, illus. 2012. (Green Light Readers Level 3 Ser.). (ENG.). 44p. (J). (gr. 1-4). pap. 3.99 *(978-0-547-85064-1(6))* Houghton Mifflin Harcourt Publishing Co.
Guevara, Melva Vizcarrondo. My Grandma, My Hero. 2007. 58p. pap. 10.00 *(978-0-8059-7296-2(X))* Dorrance Publishing Co., Inc.
Guiffre, William. The First Gift of Christmas. Baron, Cheri Ann, illus. 2008. 32p. (J). (gr. -1-3). pap. 9.95 *(978-1-931650-33-5(0))* Bks. for Children Publishing.
Gundel, Jean. The Mystery Key at Camp Green Meadow. Robertson, R. H., illus. 2011. (J). pap. 14.95 *(978-1-59571-730-6(7))* Word Association Pubs.
Gutierrez-Haley, Lisa. The New Pet: Adventures of Hayden & Jace. 2011. 20p. pap. 24.95 *(978-1-4626-1872-9(3))* America Star Bks.
—The Wiggly Tooth: Adventures of Hayden & Jace. 2011. 16p. pap. 24.95 *(978-1-4626-1874-3(X))* America Star Bks.
Gutknecht, Allison. Don't Wear Polka-Dot Underwear with White Pants: And Other Lessons I've Learned. Lewis, Stevie, illus. 2013. (ENG.). 160p. (J). (gr. 2-5). pap. 6.99 *(978-1-4424-8392-7(X),* Aladdin) Simon & Schuster Children's Publishing.
—Don't Wear Polka-Dot Underwear with White Pants: And Other Lessons I've Learned. Lewis, Stevie, illus. 2013. (ENG.). 160p. (J). (gr. 2-5). 15.99 *(978-1-4424-8393-4(8),* Simon & Schuster/Paula Wiseman Bks.) Simon & Schuster/Paula Wiseman Bks.
Gutman, Dan. From Texas with Love. 2014. (ENG.). (J). (gr. 3-7). (Genius Files Ser.: 4). 304p. pap. 6.99 *(978-0-06-182775-4(4));* (Genius Files Ser.: Bk. 4). (Illus.). 288p. 16.99 *(978-0-06-182773-0(8))* HarperCollins Pubs.
—From Texas with Love. 2014. (Genius Files Ser.: 4). (J). lib. bdg. 17.20 *(978-0-606-36462-1(5))* Turtleback Bks.
—The Genius Files #4: from Texas with Love. 2014. (Genius Files Ser.: 4). 288p. (J). (gr. 3-7). lib. bdg. 17.89 *(978-0-06-182774-7(6))* HarperCollins Pubs.
—The Genius Files #5: License to Thrill. 2016. (Genius Files Ser.: 5). (Illus.). 272p. (J). (gr. 3-7). pap. 6.99 *(978-0-06-223633-3(4))* HarperCollins Pubs.
—License to Thrill. 2015. (Genius Files Ser.: 5). (ENG.). 272p. (J). (gr. 3-7). 16.99 *(978-0-06-223632-6(6))* HarperCollins Pubs.
—Mission Unstoppable. 2011. (Genius Files Ser.: 1). (ENG.). 304p. (J). (gr. 3-7). pap. 6.99 *(978-0-06-182766-2(5));* (Illus.). 16.99 *(978-0-06-182764-8(9))* HarperCollins Pubs.
—Mission Unstoppable. 2011. (Genius Files Ser.: 1). (J). lib. bdg. 17.20 *(978-0-606-23559-4(0),* Turtleback) Turtleback Bks.
—Never Say Genius. 2012. (Genius Files Ser.: 2). (J). (gr. 3-7). (ENG.). 304p. pap. 6.99 *(978-0-06-182769-3(X));* (ENG.). 288p. 16.99 *(978-0-06-182767-9(3));* 288p. lib. bdg. 17.89 *(978-0-06-182768-6(1))* HarperCollins Pubs.
—Never Say Genius. 2012. (Genius Files Ser.: 2). (J). lib. bdg. 17.20 *(978-0-606-27128-8(7),* Turtleback) Turtleback Bks.
—You Only Die Twice. 2013. (Genius Files Ser.: 3). (J). (gr. 3-7). (ENG.). 320p. pap. 6.99 *(978-0-06-182772-3(X));* (ENG., Illus.). 304p. 16.99 *(978-0-06-182770-9(3));* (Illus.). 304p. lib. bdg. 17.89 *(978-0-06-182771-6(1))* HarperCollins Pubs.
—You Only Die Twice. 2013. (Genius Files Ser.: 3). (J). lib. bdg. 17.20 *(978-0-606-35043-3(8),* Turtleback) Turtleback Bks.
Guy, Ginger Foglesong & Guy, Ginger F. Siesta. Moreno, Rene King, illus. 2005. (ENG & SPA.). 32p. (J). (gr. -1-k). 17.99 *(978-0-06-056061-4(4),* Greenwillow Bks.) HarperCollins Pubs.
—Siesta Board Book. Moreno, Rene King, illus. 2009. (SPA & ENG.). 34p. (J). (gr. -1 — 1). bds. 7.99 *(978-0-06-168884-3(3),* Greenwillow Bks.) HarperCollins Pubs.
Guzman, Raquel. The Adventures of Eliseo & Stefano: My Daddy Can Fly! Guzman, Jacob, illus. 2006. 28p. (J). 16.95 *(978-0-9788332-0-6(1))* Images & Pages.
Haddix, Margaret Peterson. Among the Barons. 2004. (Shadow Children Ser.). 182p. (gr. 3-7). 17.00 *(978-0-7569-3923-6(2))* Perfection Learning Corp.
—Among the Barons. (Shadow Children Ser.: 4). (ENG.). (J). (gr. 3-7). 2003. 192p. 17.99 *(978-0-689-83906-1(5))* 2004. 208p. reprint ed. pap. 7.99 *(978-0-689-83910-8(3))* Simon & Schuster Bks. For Young Readers. (Simon & Schuster Bks. For Young Readers).
—Children of Refuge. 2017. (Children of Exile Ser.: 2). (ENG., Illus.). 272p. (J). (gr. 5). 17.99 ***(978-1-4424-5006-6(1),*** Simon & Schuster Bks. For Young Readers) Simon & Schuster Bks. For Young Readers.
—In over Their Heads. 2017. (Under Their Skin Ser.: 2). (ENG., Illus.). 320p. (J). (gr. 3-7). 16.99 *(978-1-4814-1761-7(4),* Simon & Schuster Bks. For Young Readers) Simon & Schuster Bks. For Young Readers.
—Redeemed. 2015. (Missing Ser.: 8). (ENG.). 416p. (J). (gr. 3-7). 17.99 *(978-1-4424-9756-6(4),* Simon & Schuster Bks. For Young Readers) Simon & Schuster Bks. For Young Readers.
—Redeemed. 2016. (Missing Ser.: 8). lib. bdg. 18.40 *(978-0-606-39234-1(3))* Turtleback Bks.
—Say What? Bernardin, James, illus. 2005. 91p. (J). 11.65 *(978-0-7569-5465-9(7))* Perfection Learning Corp.
—Takeoffs & Landings. 2004. 201p. (gr. 5-9). 17.00 *(978-0-7569-4255-7(1))* Perfection Learning Corp.
—Under Their Skin. 2016. (Under Their Skin Ser.: 1). (ENG.). 320p. (J). (gr. 3-7). 16.99 *(978-1-4814-1758-7(4),* Simon & Schuster Bks. For Young Readers) Simon & Schuster Bks. For Young Readers.
Haesche, Richard Paul, Sr. My Pet Dinosaur. 2007. (ENG.). 60p. (J). 6.99 *(978-0-9800552-0-7(2))* Kreative X-Pressions Pubns.
Hahn, Mary Downing. All the Lovely Bad Ones. 2009. (ENG.). 192p. (J). (gr. 2-5). pap. 7.99 *(978-0-547-24878-3(4))* Houghton Mifflin Harcourt Publishing Co.
—As Ever, Gordy. 2011. (ENG.). 192p. (J). (gr. 5-7). pap. 7.99 *(978-0-547-54955-2(5))* Houghton Mifflin Harcourt Publishing Co.
—Deep & Dark & Dangerous: A Ghost Story. 2007. (ENG.). 192p. (J). (gr. 5-7). 16.99 *(978-0-618-66545-7(5))* Houghton Mifflin Harcourt Publishing Co.
—The Ghost of Crutchfield Hall. (ENG.). 160p. (J). (gr. 5-7). 2011. pap. 6.99 *(978-0-547-57715-9(X))* 2010. 17.00 *(978-0-547-38560-0(9))* Houghton Mifflin Harcourt Publishing Co.
—Hear the Wind Blow. (ENG.). (J). (gr. 5-7). 2017. 288p. pap. 7.99 ***(978-1-328-74092-2(7),*** HMH Books For Young Readers) 2003. (Illus.). 224p. tchr. ed. 17.99 *(978-0-618-18190-2(3))* Houghton Mifflin Harcourt Publishing Co.
Hahn, Mary Downing. The Old Willis Place. 2007. (ENG.). 208p. (J). (gr. 5-7). pap. 7.99 *(978-0-618-89741-4(0))* Houghton Mifflin Harcourt Publishing Co.
Haig, Matt. Samuel Blink & the Forbidden Forest. 2008. (ENG.). 352p. (J). (gr. 3-7). 7.99 *(978-0-14-241191-9(4),* Puffin Books) Penguin Young Readers Group.
—Shadow Forest. 2009. pap. 1.00 *(978-1-4074-4391-1(7))* Recorded Bks., Inc.
Hairston, Kennard Lee. Rosie Bear Plays Baseball. 2009. 48p. pap. 19.49 *(978-1-4389-7343-2(8))* AuthorHouse.
Haislip, Phyllis Hall. Lili's Gift: A Civil War Healer's Story. 2008. (ENG., Illus.). 204p. (J). pap. 8.95 *(978-1-57249-392-6(5),* White Mane Kids) White Mane Publishing Co., Inc.
Hajj, Sharon. Zula Blackburn & the Rising Sun Festival. 2012. 146p. 34.94 *(978-1-105-79464-3(4))* Lulu.com GBR. Dist: Lulu Pr., Inc.
Hale, Bruce. Pirates of Underwhere. Hillman, Shane, illus. (Underwhere Ser.: 2). (J). (gr. 3-7). 2009. (ENG.). 176p. pap. 6.99 *(978-0-06-085129-3(5))* 2008. 164p. lib. bdg. 16.89 *(978-0-06-085128-6(7))* HarperCollins Pubs.
—Prince of Underwhere. Hillman, Shane, illus. 2009. (Underwhere Ser.: 1). (ENG.). 176p. (J). (gr. 3-7). pap. 5.99 *(978-0-06-085126-2(0))* HarperCollins Pubs.
Haley, Jeannette. The Adventures of Zack & Mira. 2013. 116p. pap. 12.95 *(978-0-9891683-0-4(1))* Hidden Manna Pubns.
Hall, C. Aubrey. The Call of Eirian, 0 vols. 2012. (Faelin Chronicles Ser.: 2). (ENG.). 352p. (YA). (gr. 7-11). 17.99 *(978-0-7614-6262-0(7),* 9780761462620, Amazon Children's Publishing) Amazon Publishing.
Hallinan, P. K. My Brother & I. 2008. (ENG., Illus.). 24p. (J). (gr. -1-k). bds. 7.95 *(978-0-8249-5455-0(6),* Ideal Pubns.) Worthy Publishing.
Halpern, Julie. Into the Wild Nerd Yonder. 2011. (ENG.). 272p. (YA). (gr. 8-13). pap. 16.99 *(978-0-312-65307-1(7),* 9780312653071) Square Fish.
Hamburg, Jennifer. Daniel Goes to the Playground. 2015. (Daniel Tiger's Neighborhood 8X8 Ser.). lib. bdg. 13.55 *(978-0-606-38256-4(9))* Turtleback Bks.
Hamilton, Pat. Peaches the Private Eye Poodle: The Missing Muffin Caper. 2008. 32p. pap. 13.50 *(978-1-60693-277-3(2),* Eloquent Bks.) Strategic Book Publishing & Rights Agency (SBPRA).
Hamilton-Sturdy, K. The Tree of Dreams. 2013. 138p. pap. *(978-1-78299-683-5(4))* FeedARead.com.
Hamley, Dennis. The Ghosts Who Waited. 2005. 172p. (gr. -1-7). per. *(978-1-904529-15-6(1),* Back to Front) Solidus.
Han, Jenny. We'll Always Have Summer. 2011. (YA). 1.25 *(978-1-4640-1977-7(0))* Recorded Bks., Inc.
Hanlon, Abby. Dory & the Real True Friend. 2016. (Dory Ser.: 2). lib. bdg. 18.40 *(978-0-606-38846-7(X))* Turtleback Bks.
—Dory Fantasmagory. (Dory Fantasmagory Ser.: 1). (ENG., (J). (gr. 1-3). 2015. Illus.). 176p. 7.99 *(978-0-14-751067-9(8),* Puffin Books) 2014. 160p. 14.99 *(978-0-8037-4088-4(3),* Dial Bks) Penguin Young Readers Group.
—The Real True Friend. 2015. (Dory Fantasmagory Ser.: 2). (ENG., Illus.). 160p. (J). (gr. 1-3). 14.99 *(978-0-525-42866-4(6),* Dial Bks) Penguin Young Readers Group.
Hannan, Peter. Freddy! Deep-Space Food Fighter. Hannan, Peter, illus. 2011. (Freddy! Ser.: 2). (ENG., Illus.). 144p. (J). (gr. 2-6). pap. 5.99 *(978-0-06-128468-7(8))* HarperCollins Pubs.
—Freddy! King of Flurb. Hannan, Peter, illus. 2011. (Freddy! Ser.: 1). (ENG., Illus.). 160p. (J). (gr. 2-6). pap. 5.99 *(978-0-06-128466-3(1))* HarperCollins Pubs.
—Freddy! Locked in Space. Hannan, Peter, illus. 2011. (Freddy! Ser.: 3). (ENG., Illus.). 160p. (J). (gr. 2-6). pap. 5.99 *(978-0-06-128470-0(X))* HarperCollins Pubs.
Hansel et Gretel.Tr. of Hansel & Gretel. (FRE.). 48p. pap. 12.95 incl. audio compact disk *(978-2-89558-055-3(3))* Coffragants CAN. Dist: Penton Overseas, Inc.
Hanson, Anders. Whale Tale, 1 vol. 2007. (Critter Chronicles Ser.). (ENG., Illus.). 24p. (J). (gr. k-3). lib. bdg. 24.21 *(978-1-59928-476-7(6),* SandCastle) ABDO Publishing Co.
Hapka, Cathy, pseud & Titlebaum, Ellen. How Not to Babysit Your Brother. Palen, Debbie, illus. 2005. (Step into Reading Ser.). (ENG.). 48p. (J). (gr. 2-4). pap. 3.99

(978-0-375-82856-0(7), Random Hse. Bks. for Young Readers) Random Hse. Children's Bks.

—How Not to Start Third Grade. Palen, Debbie, illus. 2007. (Step into Reading Ser.). (ENG.). 48p. (J). (gr. 2-4). pap. 3.99 *(978-0-375-83904-7(6)*, Random Hse. Bks. for Young Readers) Random Hse. Children's Bks.

Hardesty, Ann A. Lucy's Trials in the Black Hills. 2009. 104p. pap. 10.99 *(978-1-4490-5368-0(8))* AuthorHouse.

Harel, Moshe. Elf Prince. 2012. (ENG.). 258p. pap. *(978-965-550-089-9(6))* Contento De Semrik.

Hargreaves, Roger. Little Miss Whoops. 2008. (Mr. Men & Little Miss Ser.). (ENG.). 32p. (J). (gr. -1-2). mass mkt. 4.99 *(978-0-8431-3350-9(3)*, Price Stern Sloan) Penguin Young Readers Group.

Harley, Bill. Dirty Joe the Pirate: A True Story. Davis, Jack E., illus. 2008. (ENG.). 32p. (J). (gr. k-3). 17.99 *(978-0-06-623780-0(7))* HarperCollins Pubs.

Harmon, Michael. Skate. 2008. (ENG.). 256p. (YA). (gr. 9). per. 6.99 *(978-0-553-49510-2(0)*, Laurel Leaf) Random Hse. Children's Bks.

Harper, Anita. It's Not Fair. McQuillan, Mary, illus. 2007. (ENG.). 32p. (J). (gr. -1-3). 16.95 *(978-0-8234-2094-0(9))* Holiday Hse., Inc.

Harper, Jamie. Splish Splash, Baby Bundt: A Recipe for Bath Time. Harper, Jamie, illus. 2007. (ENG., Illus.). 24p. (J). (—1). bds. 6.99 *(978-0-7636-3240-3(6))* Candlewick Pr.

Harper, Jessica. Uh-Oh, Cleo. Berkeley, Jon, illus. 2008. (Uh-Oh, Cleo Ser.: 1). (ENG.). 64p. (J). (gr. 1-4). 14.99 *(978-0-399-24671-5(1)*, G.P. Putnam's Sons Books for Young Readers) Penguin Young Readers Group.

Harper, Meg. My Mum & the Green-Eyed Monster. 2006. (My Mum Ser.). (ENG.). 160p. (J). (gr. 4-7). per. 8.99 *(978-0-7459-4993-2(2))* Lion Hudson PLC GBR. Dist: Independent Pubs. Group.

—My Mum & the Gruesome Twosome. 2nd ed. (ENG.). 160p. pap. 9.99 *(978-0-7459-4829-4(4)*, Lion Books) Lion Hudson PLC GBR. Dist: Trafalgar Square Publishing.

Harper, Suzanne. A Mischief of Mermaids. 2013. (Unseen World of Poppy Malone Ser.: 3). (ENG.). 288p. (J). (gr. 3-7). 16.99 *(978-0-06-199613-9(0)*, Greenwillow Bks.) HarperCollins Pubs.

HarperCollins Publishers Ltd. Staff, et al. Origins No. 5. 2010. (Vampire Diaries: Stefan's Diaries: 1). (ENG.). 256p. (YA). (gr. 9-18). pap. 9.99 *(978-0-06-200393-5(3)*, HarperTeen) HarperCollins Pubs.

Harrington, Kim. Clarity. (ENG.). 256p. (J). (gr. 9-9). 2012. pap. 8.99 *(978-0-545-23051-3(9))* 2011. 16.99 *(978-0-545-23050-6(0))* Scholastic, Inc.

Harris, Donna. Ruff Life. 2011. 240p. pap. 17.99 *(978-1-4567-5081-7(X))* AuthorHouse.

Harris, Dorothy Joan. Cameron & Me. 2004. (Illus.). (J). (gr. k-3). spiral bd. *(978-0-616-01667-1(0))*; spiral bd. *(978-0-616-01668-8(9))* Canadian National Institute for the Blind/Institut National Canadien pour les Aveugles.

Harris, Robie H. Mail Harry to the Moon! Emberley, Michael, illus. 2008. (ENG.). 40p. (J). (gr. -1-3). 16.99 *(978-0-316-15376-8(1))* Little, Brown Bks. for Young Readers.

—Who's in My Family? All about Our Families. Westcott, Nadine Bernard, illus. 2012. (Let's Talk about You & Me Ser.). (ENG.). 40p. (J). (gr. -1-2). 15.99 *(978-0-7636-3631-9(2))* Candlewick Pr.

Hartnett, Sonya. Sadie & Ratz. James, Ann, illus. 2012. (ENG.). 64p. (J). (gr. k-3). 14.99 *(978-0-7636-5315-6(2))* Candlewick Pr.

Harvey, Alyxandra. Whisper the Dead. 2014. (Lovegrove Legacy Ser.: Bk. 2). (ENG.). 408p. (YA). (gr. 7). 17.99 *(978-0-8027-3750-2(1)*, 9780802737502, Bloomsbury USA Childrens) Bloomsbury Publishing USA.

Harvey, Gwen. Esperanza Means Hope. Porfirio, Guy, illus. 2010. (J). *(978-0-910037-51-8(5))*; pap. *(978-0-910037-52-5(3))* Arizona Historical Society.

Harwood, Kelsey. Still Alive. 2012. 144p. pap. 9.99 *(978-1-60820-746-6(3))* MLR Pr., LLC.

Hausman, Michelle. Amelia's Eyes. 2010. 32p. pap. 15.95 *(978-0-557-38618-5(7))* Lulu Pr., Inc.

Havill, Juanita. Flower Garden. O'Brien, Anne Sibley, illus. 2015. 32p. pap. 7.00 *(978-1-61003-503-3(8))* Center for the Collaborative Classroom.

—Jamaica Tag-Along, 1 vol. O'Brien, Anne Sibley, illus. 2011. (ENG.). 32p. (J). (gr. -1-3). audio compact disk 10.99 *(978-0-547-48105-0(5))* Houghton Mifflin Harcourt Publishing Co.

Hawes, Adrienne Hill. Moving Danielle. 2008. 22p. pap. 24.95 *(978-1-4241-4977-3(0))* America Star Bks.

Hawkins, Aaron. The Year Money Grew on Trees. 2011. (ENG.). 304p. (J). (gr. 5-7). pap. 6.99 *(978-0-547-57716-6(8))* Houghton Mifflin Harcourt Publishing Co.

Hawkins-Walsh, Elizabeth & Pierson-Solis, Lennard. Katie's Premature Brother = el Hermano Prematuro de Katie. Blake, Anne Catharine, illus. 2006. (J). *(978-1-56123-197-3(5))* Centering Corp.

Hawley, Mabel C. Four Little Blossoms & Their Winter Fun. 2007. (ENG.). 100p. per. 16.99 *(978-1-4346-4265-3(8))*; 116p. per. 19.99 *(978-1-4346-4266-0(6))* Creative Media Partners, LLC.

—Four Little Blossoms & Their Winter Fun. 2007. 108p. per. *(978-1-4065-4372-8(1))* Dodo Pr.

Hawthorn, Libby. Incredibilia. 2017. (ENG.). 40p. (J). (gr. -1-k). 17.99 ***(978-1-76012-525-7(3))*** Little Hare Bks. AUS. Dist: Independent Pubs. Group.

Hayes, Celeste. Cacao & the Jaded Orb: A Sphinx & Trevi Adventure. 2011. (Illus.). 62p. (J). pap. 22.95 *(978-0-9785695-2-5(0))* Adam's Creations Publishing, LLC.

—Enchanted Fairyland: A Sphinx & Trevi Adventure. 2011. (Illus.). 30p. (J). pap. 19.95 *(978-0-9785695-4-9(7))* Adam's Creations Publishing, LLC.

—The Puzzle Box of Nefertiti: A Sphinx & Trevi Adventure. Bishop, Christina, illus. 2011. 42p. (J). pap. 19.95 *(978-0-9785695-3-2(9))* Adam's Creations Publishing, LLC.

Hayes, Christine. The Mothman's Curse. Hindle, James K., illus. 2015. (ENG.). 320p. (J). (gr. 3-7). 15.99 *(978-1-62672-027-5(4)*, 9781626720275) Roaring Brook Pr.

—Mothman's Curse. 2016. (J). lib. bdg. 18.40 *(978-0-606-39560-1(1))* Turtleback Bks.

Hayes, Geoffrey. Benny & Penny in Just Pretend, 1 vol. 2013. (Toon Bks). (ENG.). 36p. (J). (gr. 1-2). lib. bdg. 27.07 *(978-1-61479-148-5(1))* Spotlight.

—Benny & Penny in Just Pretend. Hayes, Geoffrey, illus. 2008. (Benny & Penny Ser.). (ENG., Illus.). 32p. (J). (gr. -1-3). 12.95 *(978-0-9799238-0-7(8))* TOON Books / RAW Junior, LLC.

—Benny & Penny in Just Pretend. 2013. (Toon Books Level 2 Ser.). lib. bdg. 14.75 *(978-0-606-31597-5(7)*, Turtleback) Turtleback Bks.

—Benny & Penny in Lights Out! Hayes, Geoffrey, illus. 2012. (Benny & Penny Ser.). (ENG., Illus.). 32p. (J). (gr. -1-3). 12.95 *(978-1-935179-20-7(9))* TOON Books / RAW Junior, LLC.

—Benny & Penny in Lost & Found. Hayes, Geoffrey, illus. 2013. (Benny & Penny Ser.). (ENG., Illus.). 40p. (J). (gr. -1-3). 12.95 *(978-1-935179-64-1(0))* TOON Books / RAW Junior, LLC.

—Benny & Penny in the Big No-No! Hayes, Geoffrey, illus. 2014. (Benny & Penny Ser.). (ENG., Illus.). 32p. (J). (gr. -1-3). pap. 6.99 *(978-1-935179-35-1(7))* TOON Books / RAW Junior, LLC.

—Benny & Penny in the Big No-No! Mouly, Francoise, ed. Hayes, Geoffrey, illus. 2009. (Benny & Penny Ser.). (ENG., Illus.). 32p. (J). (gr. -1-3). 12.95 *(978-0-9799238-9-0(1))* TOON Books / RAW Junior, LLC.

—Benny & Penny in the Big No-No! 2014. (Toon Books Level 1 Ser.). lib. bdg. 14.75 *(978-0-606-32102-0(0)*, Turtleback) Turtleback Bks.

—Benny & Penny in the Toy Breaker, 1 vol. 2013. (Toon Bks). (ENG.). 36p. (J). (gr. 1-2). lib. bdg. 27.07 *(978-1-61479-149-2(X))* Spotlight.

—Benny & Penny in the Toy Breaker. Mouly, Francoise, ed. Hayes, Geoffrey, illus. 2010. (Benny & Penny Ser.). (ENG., Illus.). 32p. (J). (gr. -1-3). 12.95 *(978-1-935179-07-8(1))* TOON Books / RAW Junior, LLC.

—Benny & Penny in the Toy Breaker. 2013. (Toon Books Level 2 Ser.). lib. bdg. 14.75 *(978-0-606-31598-2(5)*, Turtleback) Turtleback Bks.

—How to Say Goodbye. Hayes, Geoffrey, illus. 2016. (Benny & Penny Ser.). (ENG., Illus.). 32p. (J). (gr. -1-3). 12.95 *(978-1-935179-99-3(3))* TOON Books / RAW Junior, LLC.

Hayes, Geoffrey & Rosenstiehl, Agnes. Toon Books. 2013. (Toon Bks: 10). 36p. (J). (gr. k-3). lib. bdg. 270.70 *(978-1-61479-147-8(3))* Spotlight.

Hayes, Sadie. The Social Code. 2013. (Start-Up Ser.: 1). (ENG., Illus.). 320p. (YA). (gr. 7-12). pap. 9.99 *(978-1-250-03565-3(1)*, 9781250035653, St. Martin's Griffin) St. Martin's Pr.

Hayward, Linda. Monster Bug. Palmisciano, Diane, illus. 2004. 32p. (J). lib. bdg. 20.00 *(978-1-4242-1097-8(6))* Fitzgerald Bks.

—Monster Bug. Palmisciano, Diane, illus. 2004. (Science Solves It Ser.). 32p. (gr. -1-3). 15.00 *(978-0-7569-4313-4(2))* Perfection Learning Corp.

Haywood, Carolyn. Here's a Penny. 2005. (ENG., Illus.). 160p. (J). (gr. 1-4). pap. 6.99 *(978-0-15-205225-6(9))* Houghton Mifflin Harcourt Publishing Co.

Head, Jean. Andrew's Christmas Dream. 2012. 28p. pap. 5.00 *(978-1-937260-19-4(4))* Sleepytown Pr.

Headrick, Julianna. Our New Addition. Baker, David, illus. 2011. 28p. pap. 24.95 *(978-1-4560-0933-5(8))* America Star Bks.

Hearne, Betsy. Wishes, Kisses, & Pigs. 2003. (ENG.). 144p. (J). (gr. 3-7). pap. 6.99 *(978-0-689-86347-9(0)*, Simon & Schuster/Paula Wiseman Bks.) Simon & Schuster/Paula Wiseman Bks.

Heath, Michael. Garlic Bread for Eugene. 2013. (ENG.). 112p. (J). (gr. 4-6). pap. 7.95 *(978-1-9835-0124-1(7))* Turn the Page Publishing.

Heath, Paulette Powell. In the Mist. 2012. 24p. pap. 15.99 *(978-1-4797-4354-4(2))* Xlibris Corp.

Heaton, Mark. Ruth Tells the Truth. 2006. (Neighborhood Readers Ser.). (ENG.). 16p. (gr. 1-3). pap. 6.50 *(978-1-4042-7264-4(X)*, Rosen Classroom) Rosen Publishing Group, Inc., The.

Hegg, Tom & Hanson, Warren. Peef & the Baby Sister. Hegg, Tom & Hanson, Warren, illus. 2006. (ENG., Illus.). 36p. (J). (gr. -1-3). 16.95 *(978-0-931674-67-9(0)*, Waldman House Pr.) TRISTAN Publishing, Inc.

Helidoniotis, Kathy. Horse Mad Heroes. 2007. 272p. (J). *(978-0-7322-8423-7(6))* HarperCollins Pubs. Australia.

—Horse Mad Western. 2008. 272p. *(978-0-7322-8424-4(4))* HarperCollins Pubs. Australia.

Heller, Linda. How Dalia Put a Big Yellow Comforter Inside a Tiny Blue Box: And Other Wonders of Tzedakah. McQueen, Stacey Dressen, illus. 2011. (ENG.). 32p. (J). (gr. -1-2). 16.99 *(978-1-58246-378-0(6)*, Tricycle Pr.) Random Hse. Children's Bks.

Hellman, Charles. Adventures in SportsLand - the Tennis Bully (with accompanying CD) Tiritilli, Robert, illus. 2008. (Adventures in SportsLand: the Bully Ser.). 32p. (J). (gr. -1-3). 19.95 *(978-0-935938-32-6(X))* Stogo, Malcolm Assocs.

Helmer, Marilyn. Sharing Snowy, 1 vol. Charko, Kasia, illus. 2008. (Orca Echoes Ser.). (ENG.). 64p. (J). (gr. 2-3). pap. 6.95 *(978-1-55469-021-3(8))* Orca Bk. Pubs. USA.

Hendershot, Eric. At Season's End. 2012. pap. 13.99 *(978-1-59955-995-7(1))* Cedar Fort, Inc./CFI Distribution.

—A Horse for Christmas. 2012. pap. 8.99 *(978-1-4621-1078-0(9))* Cedar Fort, Inc./CFI Distribution.

Henderson, Leah. One Shadow on the Wall. 2017. (ENG., Illus.). 448p. (J). (gr. 3-7). 16.99 *(978-1-4814-6295-2(4)*, Atheneum Bks. for Young Readers) Simon & Schuster Children's Publishing.

Hendey, Lisa M. The Whisper in the Ruins. Bower, Jenn, illus. 2016. (Chime Travelers Ser.: 3). (ENG.). 128p. (gr. 2-5). pap. 6.99 *(978-1-63253-036-3(8)*, Servant Bks.) Franciscan Media.

Hendry, Frances. Quest for a Queen: The Jackdaw. 2006. pap. *(978-1-905665-05-1(9))* Pollinger In Print.

—Wee Malkie. l.t. ed. 2007. 240p. per. *(978-1-905665-19-8(9))* Pollinger In Print.

Henkes, Kevin. Julius, el Rey de la Casa. 2017.Tr. of Julius, the Baby of the World. (SPA.). (J). pap. ***(978-1-63245-668-7(0))*** Lectorum Pubns., Inc.

Hennessy, Claire. Afterwards. 2005. 188p. (YA). pap. *(978-1-84223-207-1(X))* Poolbeg Pr.

Henry, Marguerite. Misty of Chincoteague. Dennis, Wesley, illus. 2007. 173p. (gr. 3-7). 17.00 *(978-0-7569-8227-0(8))* Perfection Learning Corp.

—Misty of Chincoteague. Dennis, Wesley, illus. 60th ed. 2006. (ENG.). 176p. (J). (gr. 3-7). pap. 7.99 *(978-1-4169-2783-9(2)*, Aladdin) Simon & Schuster Children's Publishing.

Hensley, Nathaniel. The Strange Tale of Hector & Hannah Crowe. 2015. (ENG.). 222p. (J). (gr. 8-18). 13.95 *(978-1-937240-49-3(5))* Casa de Snapdragon LLC.

Herbertson, Lisa. Swimming Along. Kennedy, Catherine, illus. 2011. 26p. pap. 12.00 *(978-1-60976-293-3(2)*, Eloquent Bks.) Strategic Book Publishing & Rights Agency (SBPRA).

Herman, Gail. Buried in the Backyard. Smath, Jerry, illus. 2003. (Science Solves It! Ser.). 32p. (J). pap. 5.95 *(978-1-57565-126-2(2))* Kane Press, Inc.

—The Creeping Tide. Nez, John, illus. 2003. (Science Solves It! Ser.). 32p. (J). pap. 5.95 *(978-1-57565-128-6(9))* Kane Press, Inc.

—Enterrado en el Jardin. Smath, Jerry, illus. 2008. (Science Solves It! en Espanol Ser.). (SPA.). 32p. (J). (gr. -1-3). pap. 5.95 *(978-1-57565-262-7(5))* Kane Press, Inc.

—Enterrado en el Jardin; Buried in the Backyard. 2008. pap. 34.95 *(978-1-58013-768-3(7))* Kane Press, Inc.

Hermes, Patricia. Emma Dilemma & the Two Nannies, 0 vols. Carter, Abby, illus. 2011. (Emma Dilemma Ser.: 2). (ENG.). 126p. (J). (gr. 3-6). pap. 7.99 *(978-0-7614-5835-7(2)*, 9780761458357, Amazon Children's Publishing) Amazon Publishing.

Hernandez, David. Suckerpunch. 2007. (ENG.). 224p. (YA). (gr. 9-18). 17.99 *(978-0-06-117330-1(4)*, HarperTeen) HarperCollins Pubs.

Herron, Carolivia, photos by & told to. Little Georgia & the Apples: A Retelling of Aunt Georgia's First Catalpa Tale Herron, Carolivia, told to. l.t. ed. 2004. (Illus.). 33p. (J). 10.00 *(978-0-9760222-0-6(6)*, Catalpa01) Epicenter Literary Software.

Hershenhorn, Esther. Fancy That. Lloyd, Megan, illus. 2003. (ENG.). 32p. (J). (gr. k-3). tchr. ed. 16.95 *(978-0-8234-1605-9(4))* Holiday Hse., Inc.

Hervey, Cheston & Doane, Darren. Kill the Dragon, Get the Girl. 2017. (J). pap. ***(978-1-59128-188-7(1))*** Canon Pr.

Hicks, Betty. Out of Order. 2007. (ENG.). 176p. (J). (gr. 3-7). pap. 14.99 *(978-0-312-37355-9(4)*, 9780312373559) Square Fish.

Hicks, Deron R. Secrets of Shakespeare's Grave, Bk. 1. Geyer, Mark Edward, illus. 2013. (Shakespeare Mysteries Ser.: 1). (ENG.). 320p. (J). (gr. 2-5). pap. 7.99 *(978-0-544-10504-1(4))* Houghton Mifflin Harcourt Publishing Co.

Hicks, Faith Erin. Friends with Boys. Hicks, Faith Erin, illus. 2012. (ENG., Illus.). 224p. (YA). (gr. 7-11). pap. 16.99 *(978-1-59643-556-8(9)*, 9781596435568, First Second Bks.) Roaring Brook Pr.

Hicks, Kelli. Evan in the Middle. 2015. (ENG.). 48p. (gr. k-3). 27.07 *(978-1-63430-373-6(3))* Rourke Educational Media.

Higgins, Jack & Richards, Justin. Death Run. 2009. (Rich & Jade Ser.: Bk. 2). (ENG.). 288p. (YA). (gr. 7-18). 8.99 *(978-0-14-241475-0(1)*, Speak) Penguin Young Readers Group.

—First Strike. 2011. (Rich & Jade Ser.: Bk. 4). (ENG.). 240p. (YA). (gr. 7-18). 8.99 *(978-0-14-241909-0(5)*, Speak) Penguin Young Readers Group.

—Sharp Shot. 2010. (Rich & Jade Ser.: Bk. 3). (ENG.). 240p. (YA). (gr. 7-18). 8.99 *(978-0-14-241730-0(0)*, Speak) Penguin Young Readers Group.

—Sure Fire. 2008. (Rich & Jade Ser.: Bk. 1). (ENG.). 272p. (YA). (gr. 7-18). 8.99 *(978-0-14-241213-8(9)*, Speak) Penguin Young Readers Group.

Higgins, M. G. Family Fix-It Plan. Taylor, Jo, illus. 2016. (Sibling Split Ser.). (ENG.). 112p. (gr. 2-3). lib. bdg. 25.32 *(978-1-4965-2590-1(6))* Stone Arch Bks.

—The Impossible Wish. Taylor, Jo, illus. 2016. (Sibling Split Ser.). (ENG.). 112p. (gr. 2-3). lib. bdg. 25.32 *(978-1-4965-2593-2(0))* Stone Arch Bks.

—Party of Nine. Taylor, Jo, illus. 2016. (Sibling Split Ser.). (ENG.). 112p. (gr. 2-3). lib. bdg. 25.32 *(978-1-4965-2592-5(2))* Stone Arch Bks.

—Sibling Split, 4 vols. Taylor, Jo, illus. 2016. (Sibling Split Ser.). (ENG.). 112p. (gr. 2-3). lib. bdg. 101.28 *(978-1-4965-2721-9(6))* Stone Arch Bks.

—Trouble in the City. Taylor, Jo, illus. 2016. (Sibling Split Ser.). (ENG.). 112p. (gr. 2-3). lib. bdg. 25.32 *(978-1-4965-2591-8(4))* Stone Arch Bks.

Higgins, Tiffany A. We've Seen Sant. Higgins, Clark L., illus. 2011. 26p. pap. 12.27 *(978-1-61204-267-1(8)*, Eloquent Bks.) Strategic Book Publishing & Rights Agency (SBPRA).

Higginson, Sheila Sweeny. You're Getting a Baby Brother! Williams, Sam, illus. 2012. (ENG.). 24p. (J). (gr. -1-k). bds. 7.99 *(978-1-4424-2021-2(9)*, Little Simon) Little Simon.

—You're Getting a Baby Sister! Williams, Sam, illus. 2012. (ENG.). 24p. (J). (gr. -1-k). bds. 7.99 *(978-1-4424-2050-2(2)*, Little Simon) Little Simon.

Hill, C. J. Echo in Time. 2014. 387p. (YA). *(978-0-06-212395-4(5))* HarperCollins Pubs.

Hill, Genita. My Very Special Brother. McCall, William L., illus. 2007. 40p. per. 24.95 *(978-1-4241-8852-9(0))* America Star Bks.

Hill, Janet Muirhead. Kendall & Kyleah. Leonhard, Herb, illus. 2012. (J). pap. 13.00 *(978-1-937849-05-4(8))* Raven Publishing Inc. of Montana.

Hill, Michelle M. Stanley. 2012. 12p. pap. 15.99 *(978-1-4772-2923-1(X))* AuthorHouse.

Hill, Susanna Leonard. Not yet, Rose. Rutten, Nicole, illus. 2009. (ENG.). 34p. (J). (gr. -1-3). 16.50 *(978-0-8028-5326-4(9)*, Eerdmans Bks For Young Readers) Eerdmans, William B. Publishing Co.

Hilmo, Tess. Cinnamon Moon. 2016. (ENG.). 256p. (J). 16.99 *(978-0-374-30282-5(0)*, 9780374302825, Farrar, Straus & Giroux (BYR)) Farrar, Straus & Giroux.

Hilton, Marilyn. Found Things. (ENG.). 240p. (J). (gr. 4-7). 2015. pap. 7.99 *(978-1-4424-6088-1(1))* 2014. 16.99 *(978-1-4424-6087-4(3))* Simon & Schuster Children's Publishing.

Hilton, N. E. The Spell. 2010. (Illus.). 216p. pap. 15.95 *(978-1-4452-7791-2(3))* Lulu Pr., Inc.

Hilton, Nette. Sprite Downberry. 2008. 288p. *(978-0-7322-8548-7(8))* HarperCollins Pubs. Australia.

Hinton, S. E. Rumble Fish. 2006. 21.50 *(978-0-8446-7283-0(1))* Smith, Peter Pub., Inc.

—Rumble Fish. 2013. lib. bdg. 18.40 *(978-0-606-35120-1(5))* Turtleback Bks.

Hinton, Susan E. & E Hinton, Susan. La Ley de la Calle. 2015. (ENG & SPA., Illus.). 128p. (YA). pap. 13.95 *(978-607-01-2325-2(5)*, Alfaguara) Santillana USA Publishing Co., Inc.

Hirsch, Andy. Varmints. 2016. (J). lib. bdg. 29.40 *(978-0-606-39563-2(6))* Turtleback Bks.

Hirsch, Jeff. The Darkest Path. 2013. (YA). pap. *(978-0-545-51224-4(7)*, Scholastic Pr.) Scholastic, Inc.

Hirst, Daisy. Alphonse, That Is Not OK to Do! Hirst, Daisy, illus. 2016. (ENG., Illus.). 40p. (J). (-k). 15.99 *(978-0-7636-8103-6(2))* Candlewick Pr.

Hoare, Pauline M. My Naughty Brother, David: And Other Stories. 2010. (Illus.). 124p. pap. 33.49 *(978-1-4490-9696-0(4))* AuthorHouse.

Hoban, Russell. Best Friends for Frances. Hoban, Lillian, illus. 2009. (I Can Read Level 2 Ser.). (ENG.). 48p. (J). (gr. k-3). pap. 3.99 *(978-0-06-083803-4(5))* HarperCollins Pubs.

—The Sorely Trying Day. Hoban, Lillian, illus. 2010. (ENG.). 48p. (J). (gr. -1-3). 14.95 *(978-1-59017-343-5(0)*, NYR Children's Collection) New York Review of Bks., Inc., The.

Hobbs, Will. Jackie's Wild Seattle. (ENG.). 208p. (J). (gr. 5-18). 2004. pap. 6.99 *(978-0-380-73311-8(0))* 2003. 19.99 *(978-0-688-17474-3(4))* HarperCollins Pubs.

Hoberman, Mary Ann. The Seven Silly Eaters. Frazee, Marla, illus. 2004. (J). (gr. k-3). spiral bd. *(978-0-616-14576-0(4))* Canadian National Institute for the Blind/Institut National Canadien pour les Aveugles.

Hodge, A. D. Bubbles & Boundaries. 2013. 32p. *(978-1-4602-2858-6(8))* FriesenPress.

Hoena, Blake. Daring, 1 vol. Cano, Fernando, illus. 2014. (Tony Hawk: Live2Skate Ser.). (ENG.). 72p. (gr. 4-5). lib. bdg. 25.32 *(978-1-4342-9139-4(1))* Stone Arch Bks.

Hoena, Blake A. The Big Mistake, 1 vol. Harpster, Steve, illus. 2014. (Eek & Ack Early Chapter Bks.). (ENG.). 32p. (gr. k-2). lib. bdg. 22.65 *(978-1-4342-6408-4(4))* Stone Arch Bks.

Hoffman, Mary. City of Ships. 2010. (Stravaganza Ser.). (ENG.). 368p. (YA). (gr. 7-18). 17.99 *(978-1-59990-491-7(8)*, 9781599904917, Bloomsbury USA Childrens) Bloomsbury Publishing USA.

—Stravaganza: City of Ships. 2012. (Stravaganza Ser.). (ENG.). 384p. (YA). (gr. 7). pap. 9.99 *(978-1-59990-832-8(8)*, 9781599908328, Bloomsbury USA Childrens) Bloomsbury Publishing USA.

Holeman, Linda. Search of the Moon King's Daughter. 2003. (ENG.). 320p. (J). (gr. 5). pap. 10.95 *(978-0-88776-609-1(9)*, Tundra Bks.) Tundra Bks. CAN. Dist: Penguin Random Hse. LLC.

Holland, Amy L. The Adventures of Bubba & Sis: Book One. 2009. 16p. pap. 8.49 *(978-1-4389-5941-2(9))* AuthorHouse.

Holm, Jennifer L. Our Only May Amelia. unabr. ed. 2004. 253p. (J). (gr. 5-9). pap. 36.00 incl. audio *(978-0-8072-8366-0(5)*, YA191SP, Listening Library) Random Hse. Audio Publishing Group.

—Swing It, Sunny. Holm, Matthew, illus. 2017. (Sunny Ser.: 2). (ENG.). 224p. (J). (gr. 3-7). 24.99 ***(978-0-545-74170-5(X))***; pap. 12.99 ***(978-0-545-74172-9(6))*** Scholastic, Inc. (Graphix).

Holm, Jennifer L. The Trouble with May Amelia. Gustavson, Adam, illus. (ENG.). 224p. (J). (gr. 3-7). 2012. pap. 5.99 *(978-1-4169-1374-0(2))* 2011. 15.99 *(978-1-4169-1373-3(4))* Simon & Schuster Children's Publishing. (Atheneum Bks. for Young Readers).

Holman, T. A. Stop It, Tyrone! (Illus.). 42p. (J). (gr. k-4). pap. 7.50 *(978-0-9660617-1-0(3))* PLEO.

Holub, Joan. Bed, Bats, & Beyond. Gallagher-Cole, Mernie, illus. 2010. (Darby Creek Exceptional Titles Ser.). (ENG.). 64p. (J). (gr. 1-3). pap. 6.95 *(978-0-7613-6451-1(X))* Lerner Publishing Group.

Holub, Joan & Williams, Suzanne. Artemis the Loyal. 2013. (Goddess Girls Ser.: 7). (ENG., Illus.). 288p. (J). (gr. 3-7). 16.99 *(978-1-4424-8594-5(9)*, Aladdin) Simon & Schuster Children's Publishing.

Holubitsky, Katherine. Tweaked, 1 vol. 2008. (ENG.). 192p. (YA). (gr. 8-12). pap. 12.95 *(978-1-55143-851-1(8))* Orca Bk. Pubs. USA.

Hood, Ann. Anastasia Romanov: The Last Grand Duchess. Zilber, Denis, illus. 2014. (Treasure Chest Ser.: 10). (ENG.). 240p. (J). (gr. 3-7). 15.99 *(978-0-448-46770-2(4))*;No. 10. 6.99 *(978-0-448-46771-9(2))* Penguin Young Readers Group. (Grosset & Dunlap).

—Clara Barton: Angel of the Battlefield. Kwasney, Karl et al, illus. 2012. (Treasure Chest Ser.: 1). (ENG.). 208p. (J). (gr. 3-7). pap. 6.99 *(978-0-448-45467-2(X)*, Grosset & Dunlap) Penguin Young Readers Group.

—Crazy Horse: Brave Warrior. Altmann, Scott & Zilber, Denis, illus. 2013. (Treasure Chest Ser.: 5). (ENG.). 192p. (J). (gr. 3-7). pap. 6.99 *(978-0-448-45728-4(8)*, Grosset & Dunlap) Penguin Young Readers Group.

—Harry Houdini: Prince of Air. Altmann, Scott & Zilber, Denis, illus. 2012. (Treasure Chest Ser.: 4). (ENG.). 208p. (J). (gr. 3-7). pap. 6.99 *(978-0-448-45470-2(X)*, Grosset & Dunlap) Penguin Young Readers Group.

—Jewel of the East. Kwasny, Karl et al, illus. 2012. (Treasure Chest Ser.: 3). (ENG.). 208p. (J). (gr. 3-7). 15.99 *(978-0-448-45473-3(4))*; pap. 6.99 *(978-0-448-45469-6(6))* Penguin Young Readers Group. (Grosset & Dunlap).

—Prince of Air, No. 4. Altmann, Scott & Zilber, Denis, illus. 2012. (Treasure Chest Ser.: 4). (ENG.). 208p. (J). (gr. 3-7). 15.99 *(978-0-448-45474-0(2)*, Grosset & Dunlap) Penguin Young Readers Group.

—Queen Liliuokalani: Royal Prisoner. Altmann, Scott & Zilber, Denis, illus. 2013. (Treasure Chest Ser.: 6). (ENG.). 176p. (J). (gr. 3-7). 15.99 *(978-0-448-45739-0(3))*; pap. 6.99 *(978-0-448-45729-1(6))* Penguin Young Readers Group. (Grosset & Dunlap).

Hood, Ann & Altmann, Scott. Alexander Hamilton: Little Lion. Kwasney, Karl & Zilber, Denis, illus. 2012. (Treasure Chest Ser.: 2). (ENG.). 224p. (J). (gr. 3-7). pap. 6.99

(978-0-448-45468-9(8), Grosset & Dunlap) Penguin Young Readers Group.

—Angel of the Battlefield. Kwasney, Karl & Zilber, Denis, illus. 2012. (Treasure Chest Ser.: 1). (ENG.). 240p. (J). (gr. 3-7). 15.99 *(978-0-448-45471-9(8),* Grosset & Dunlap) Penguin Young Readers Group.

Hood, Susan. Mission: New Baby. Lundquist, Mary, illus. 2015. (ENG.). 32p. (J). (gr. -1-2). 16.99 *(978-0-385-37672-3(3),* Random Hse. Bks. for Young Readers) Random Hse. Children's Bks.

Hooks, William H. Mr. Big Brother. Duke, Kate, illus. 2015. (ENG.). 34p. (J). pap. 11.95 *(978-1-899694-58-7(7),* ipicturebooks) ibooks, Inc.

Hope, Laura. Bunny Brown & His Sister Sue Giving A. 2006. pap. 14.95 *(978-1-55742-655-0(4))* Wildside Pr., LLC.

Hope, Laura Lee. Bunny Brown & His Sister Sue. 2005. 188p. pap. 11.95 *(978-1-4218-1165-9(0),* 1st World Library - Literary Society) 1st World Publishing, Inc.

—Bunny Brown & his Sister Sue. 2005. 26.95 *(978-1-4218-1065-2(4),* 1st World Library - Literary Society) 1st World Publishing, Inc.

—Bunny Brown & his Sister Sue. 2007. (ENG.). 144p. pap. 18.99 *(978-1-4264-1980-5(5))* Creative Media Partners, LLC.

—Bunny Brown & His Sister Sue. Lt. ed. 2007. (ENG.). 138p. pap. 19.99 *(978-1-4264-2091-7(9))* Creative Media Partners, LLC.

—Bunny Brown & His Sister Sue & Their Shetland Pony. 2007. 204p. 27.95 *(978-1-4218-3282-1(8));* per. 12.95 *(978-1-4218-3382-8(4))* 1st World Publishing, Inc. (1st World Library - Literary Society).

—Bunny Brown & His Sister Sue at Aunt Lu's City Home. 2007. 184p. 25.96 *(978-1-4218-3886-1(9),* 1st World Library - Literary Society) 1st World Publishing, Inc.

—Bunny Brown & His Sister Sue at Camp R. 2006. 26.95 *(978-1-4218-2972-2(X));* pap. 11.95 *(978-1-4218-3072-8(8))* 1st World Publishing, Inc.

—Bunny Brown & His Sister Sue at Christmas Tree Cove. 2007. 176p. 27.95 *(978-1-4218-3887-8(7),* 1st World Library - Literary Society) 1st World Publishing, Inc.

—Bunny Brown & His Sister Sue Giving A. 2006. 26.95 *(978-1-4218-2973-9(8));* pap. 11.95 *(978-1-4218-3073-5(6))* 1st World Publishing, Inc.

—Bunny Brown & His Sister Sue in the Bi. 2006. 26.95 *(978-1-4218-2974-6(6));* pap. 11.95 *(978-1-4218-3074-2(4))* 1st World Publishing, Inc.

—Bunny Brown & His Sister Sue Keeping S. 2006. 26.95 *(978-1-4218-2975-3(4));* pap. 11.95 *(978-1-4218-3075-9(2))* 1st World Publishing, Inc.

—Bunny Brown & His Sister Sue Keeping Store. 2007. (ENG.). 142p. pap. 18.99 *(978-1-4264-5200-0(4))* 2006. 160p. pap. 21.99 *(978-1-4264-5501-8(1))* Creative Media Partners, LLC.

—Bunny Brown & His Sister Sue on an Aut. 2006. 26.95 *(978-1-4218-2976-0(2));* pap. 11.95 *(978-1-4218-3076-6(0))* 1st World Publishing, Inc.

—Bunny Brown & His Sister Sue on Grandpa's Farm. 2007. 192p. 26.95 *(978-1-4218-3283-8(6));* per. 11.95 *(978-1-4218-3383-5(2))* 1st World Publishing, Inc. (1st World Library - Literary Society).

—Bunny Brown & His Sister Sue Playing C. 2006. 26.95 *(978-1-4218-2977-7(0));* pap. 11.95 *(978-1-4218-3077-3(9))* 1st World Publishing, Inc.

—Freddie & Flossie. Pyle, Chuck, illus. 2005. (Bobbsey Twins Ser.). (ENG.). 32p. (J). (gr. -1-k). pap. 3.99 *(978-1-4169-0270-6(8),* Simon Spotlight) Simon Spotlight.

—Freddie & Flossie & Snap. Pyle, Chuck, illus. 2005. (Bobbsey Twins Ser.). (ENG.). 32p. (J). (gr. -1-k). pap. 13.99 *(978-1-4169-0267-6(8),* Simon Spotlight) Simon Spotlight.

—Freddie & Flossie & the Train Ride. Pyle, Chuck, illus. 2005. (Bobbsey Twins Ser.). (ENG.). 32p. (J). (gr. -1-k). pap. 13.99 *(978-1-4169-0269-0(4),* Simon Spotlight) Simon Spotlight.

—Freddie & Flossie at the Beach. Pyle, Chuck, illus. 2005. (Bobbsey Twins Ser.). (ENG.). 32p. (J). (gr. -1-k). pap. 13.99 *(978-1-4169-0268-3(6),* Simon Spotlight) Simon Spotlight.

—Six Little Bunkers at Cowboy Jack's. 2007. 180p. 25.96 *(978-1-4218-3888-5(5),* 1st World Library - Literary Society) 1st World Publishing, Inc.

—Six Little Bunkers at Grandma Bell's. 2005. 26.95 *(978-1-4218-1066-9(2));* 188p. pap. 11.95 *(978-1-4218-1166-6(9))* 1st World Publishing, Inc. (1st World Library - Literary Society).

—Six Little Bunkers at Grandpa Ford's. 2007. 188p. 25.96 *(978-1-4218-3889-2(3),* 1st World Library - Literary Society) 1st World Publishing, Inc.

Hope, Lee Laura. Bunny Brown & His Sister Sue & Their Shetland Pony. 2007. 172p. 41.99 *(978-1-4280-7508-5(9));* per. 35.99 *(978-1-4280-7514-6(3))* IndyPublish.com.

—Six Little Bunkers at Aunt Jo's. 2007. (ENG.). 144p. pap. 18.99 *(978-1-4346-3234-0(2))* Creative Media Partners, LLC.

—Six Little Bunkers at Aunt Jo's. 2007. 164p. 95.99 *(978-1-4280-7622-8(0));* per. 89.99 *(978-1-4280-7620-4(4))* IndyPublish.com.

—Six Little Bunkers at Cowboy Jack's. 2007. (ENG.). 138p. pap. 18.99 *(978-1-4346-3242-5(3));* 156p. pap. 21.99 *(978-1-4346-3243-2(1))* Creative Media Partners, LLC.

Hopkins, Ellen. Fallout. (ENG., (YA). (gr. 9). 2013. Illus.). 720p. pap. 12.99 *(978-1-4424-7180-1(8))* 2010. 672p. 18.99 *(978-1-4169-5009-7(5))* McElderry, Margaret K. Bks. (McElderry, Margaret K. Bks.).

Hopkinson, Nalo. The Chaos. (ENG., 256p. (YA). (gr. 9). 2013. Illus.). pap. 9.99 *(978-1-4424-5926-7(3))* 2012. 16.99 *(978-1-4169-5488-0(0))* McElderry, Margaret K. Bks. (McElderry, Margaret K. Bks.).

Horowitz, Anthony. Nightrise. 2008. (Gatekeepers Ser.: 3). (ENG.). 368p. (J). (gr. 3-7). pap. 8.99 *(978-0-439-68007-3(7),* Scholastic Paperbacks) Scholastic, Inc.

—Public Enemy Number Two. 2004. (Diamond Brothers Ser.). (ENG.). 208p. (J). (gr. 3-7). 16.99 *(978-0-399-24154-3(X),* Philomel Bks.); pap. 6.99 *(978-0-14-240218-4(4),* Puffin Books) Penguin Young Readers Group.

—South by Southeast. 2005. (Diamond Brothers Ser.). (ENG.). 160p. (J). (gr. 3-7). 6.99 *(978-0-14-240374-7(1),* Puffin Books) Penguin Young Readers Group.

—Three of Diamonds. 2005. (Diamond Brothers Ser.). (ENG.). 240p. (J). (gr. 3-7). 6.99 *(978-0-14-240298-6(2),* Puffin Books) Penguin Young Readers Group.

Horse, Harry. Little Rabbit's New Baby, 1 vol. Horse, Harry, illus. (Little Rabbit Ser.). (Illus.). 32p. (J). 2016. (ENG.). (gr. -1-k). pap. 7.95 *(978-1-56145-915-5(1))* 2008. (gr. k-1). 16.95 *(978-1-56145-431-0(1))* Peachtree Pubs.

—Little Rabbit's New Baby / Book & Doll Package. 2008. (Illus.). 32p. (J). (gr. k-1). pap., pap. 22.90 *(978-1-56145-453-2(2))* Peachtree Pubs.

Horvath, Polly. My One Hundred Adventures. 2010. (My One Hundred Adventures Ser.). (ENG., Illus.). 272p. (J). (gr. 3-7). 7.99 *(978-0-375-85526-9(2),* Yearling) Random Hse. Children's Bks.

—The Trolls. 2008. (ENG.). 160p. (J). (gr. 4-7). pap. 7.99 *(978-0-312-38419-7(X),* 9780312384197) Square Fish.

Houghton Mifflin Harcourt Publishing Company Staff. Girl Power 5-Minute Stories. 2015. (5-Minute Stories Ser.). (ENG., Illus.). 224p. (J). (gr. -1-3). 12.99 *(978-0-544-33925-5(8),* HMH Books For Young Readers) Houghton Mifflin Harcourt Publishing Co.

Howland, Ashley. The Homework Goblin. 2013. 24p. pap. 13.97 *(978-1-62516-301-1(0),* Strategic Bk. Publishing) Strategic Book Publishing & Rights Agency (SBPRA).

Howland, Naomi. Latkes, Latkes, Good to Eat Send-A-Story. 2011. (Send a Story Ser.). (ENG., Illus.). 32p. (J). (gr. -1-3). pap. 4.99 *(978-0-547-56690-0(5))* Houghton Mifflin Harcourt Publishing Co.

Hughes, Shirley. Alfie Gets in First. Hughes, Shirley, illus. 2009. (Alfie Ser.). (ENG., Illus.). 32p. (J). (gr. -1-k). pap. 9.99 *(978-1-86230-783-4(0),* Red Fox) Random House Children's Books GBR. Dist: Independent Pubs. Group.

—The Big Alfie & Annie Rose. Hughes, Shirley, illus. 2007. (Alfie Ser.). (ENG., Illus.). 64p. (J). (gr. -1-k). pap. 14.99 *(978-0-09-975030-7(9),* Red Fox) Random House Children's Books GBR. Dist: Independent Pubs. Group.

Hulst, W. G. van de & Hulst, Willem G. van de, illus. The Basket. 2014. (J). *(978-1-928136-04-0(4))* Inheritance Pubns.

—Bruno the Bear. 2014. (J). *(978-1-928136-03-3(6))* Inheritance Pubns.

—Three Foolish Sisters. 2014. (J). *(978-1-928136-15-6(X))* Inheritance Pubns.

—Through the Thunderstorm. 2014. (J). *(978-1-928136-02-6(8))* Inheritance Pubns.

Humphreys, Neil. Secrets of the Swamp. Koon, Cheng Puay, illus. 2014. (ENG.). 72p. pap. 11.90 *(978-981-4484-16-9(4))* Marshall Cavendish International (Asia) Private Ltd. SGP. Dist: National Bk. Network.

Huneke, Amanda. A Monster at School, 1 vol. Wolek, Guy, illus. 2013. (Monster on the Loose Ser.). (ENG.). 32p. (J). (gr. -1-4). 28.50 *(978-1-61641-931-8(8))* Magic Wagon.

—A Monster in the Park, 1 vol. Wolek, Guy, illus. 2013. (Monster on the Loose Ser.). (ENG.). 32p. (J). (gr. -1-4). 28.50 *(978-1-61641-932-5(6))* Magic Wagon.

—A Monster on the Bus, 1 vol. Wolek, Guy, illus. 2013. (Monster on the Loose Ser.). (ENG.). 32p. (J). (gr. -1-4). 28.50 *(978-1-61641-933-2(4))* Magic Wagon.

—A Monster on the Loose, 1 vol. Wolek, Guy, illus. 2013. (Monster on the Loose Ser.). (ENG.). 32p. (J). (gr. -1-4). 28.50 *(978-1-61641-934-9(2))* Magic Wagon.

Hunt, Elizabeth Singer. The Pursuit of the Ivory Poachers: Kenya. Williams, Brian, illus. 2008. (Secret Agent Jack Stalwart Ser.: 6). (ENG.). 144p. (J). (gr. 1-4). pap. 5.99 *(978-1-60286-021-6(1),* Weinstein Bks.) Perseus Bks. Group.

Hunter, Erin. Dark River. (Warriors: Power of Three Ser.: 2). (ENG.). (J). (gr. 3-7). 2015. 368p. pap. 7.99 *(978-0-06-236709-9(9))* 2008. 368p. pap. 6.99 *(978-0-06-089207-4(2))* 2007. (Illus.). 352p. 16.99 *(978-0-06-089205-0(6))* HarperCollins Pubs.

—Eclipse. (Warriors: Power of Three Ser.: 4). (ENG.). (J). (gr. 3-7). 2015. 368p. pap. 7.99 *(978-0-06-236711-2(0))* 2009. 336p. pap. 7.99 *(978-0-06-089213-5(7))* 2008. (Illus.). 336p. 16.99 *(978-0-06-089211-1(0))* HarperCollins Pubs.

—Long Shadows. (Warriors: Power of Three Ser.: 5). (ENG.). (J). (gr. 3-7). 2015. 368p. pap. 7.99 *(978-0-06-236712-9(9))* 2009. 352p. pap. 7.99 *(978-0-06-089216-6(1))* 2008. 336p. 16.99 *(978-0-06-089214-2(5))* HarperCollins Pubs.

—Outcast. (Warriors: Power of Three Ser.: 3). (ENG.). (J). (gr. 3-7). 2015. 368p. pap. 7.99 *(978-0-06-236710-5(2))* 2008. (Illus.). 352p. 16.99 *(978-0-06-089208-1(0))* HarperCollins Pubs.

—The Sight. 2015. (Warriors: Power of Three Ser.: 1). (ENG.). 416p. (J). (gr. 3-7). pap. 7.99 *(978-0-06-236708-2(0))* HarperCollins Pubs.

—Sunrise. (Warriors: Power of Three Ser.: 6). (ENG.). (J). (gr. 3-7). 2010. 368p. pap. 7.99 *(978-0-06-089219-7(6))* 6th ed. 2009. 352p. 16.99 *(978-0-06-089217-3(X))* HarperCollins Pubs.

Hunter, R. C. Moon Kids. 2010. 64p. pap. 11.99 *(978-1-4490-7846-1(X))* AuthorHouse.

Hurwitz, Johanna. Magical Monty. McGrory, Anik, illus. 2013. (Monty Ser.). (ENG.). 112p. (J). (gr. k-4). pap. 5.99 *(978-0-7636-6457-2(X))* Candlewick Pr.

Hutchins, Pat. Titch. 2014. 32p. pap. 7.00 *(978-1-61003-367-1(1))* Center for the Collaborative Classroom.

Huy, Barbara. Llamas Need Pajamas. 2012. 36p. pap. 15.49 *(978-1-4669-5752-7(2))* Trafford Publishing.

Hyde, Catherine Ryan. The Year of My Miraculous Reappearance. 2009. (ENG.). 240p. (YA). (gr. 7). pap. 8.99 *(978-0-375-83261-1(0),* Knopf Bks. for Young Readers) Random Hse. Children's Bks.

I'm a Big Brother! (Big Brother/Sister Ser.). 32p. *(978-1-4054-5023-2(1));* 2008. *(978-1-4075-0857-3(1))* Parragon, Inc.

Imfeld, Robert. Baylor's Guide to the Other Side. 2016. (Beyond Baylor Ser.: 1). (ENG., Illus.). 320p. (J). (gr. 5-9). 16.99 *(978-1-4814-6636-3(4),* Aladdin) Simon & Schuster Children's Publishing.

Inches, Alison. Big Sister Dora! Aikins, Dave, illus. 2005. (Dora the Explorer Ser.: 13). 32p. (J). lib. bdg. 15.00 *(978-1-59054-790-8(X))* Fitzgerald Bks.

—Súper Bebés! Miller, Victoria, illus. 2006. (Dora la Exploradora Ser.). (SPA.). 24p. (J). (gr. -1-3). pap. 3.99 *(978-1-4169-2461-6(2),* Libros Para Ninos) Libros Para Ninos.

Ingram, Fiona. The Secret of the Sacred Scarab. 2008. 272p. (gr. -1 — 1). 27.95 *(978-0-595-71977-8(5));* pap. 17.95 *(978-0-595-45716-8(9))* iUniverse, Inc.

Interiano, Jeffrey. Critters of Forest City. 2006. pap. 10.00 *(978-1-4257-1721-6(7))* Xlibris Corp.

Iserles, Inbali. The Taken. 2015. (Foxcraft Ser.). (ENG., Illus.). 272p. (J). (gr. 3-7). 16.99 *(978-0-545-69081-2(1),* Scholastic Pr.) Scholastic, Inc.

Iserles, Inbali, illus. The Taken. 2015. 252p. (J). pap. ***(978-0-545-91869-5(3),*** Scholastic Pr.) Scholastic, Inc.

Jack, Keats Ezra. Peter's Chair. 2014. (ENG.). 40p. (J). (gr. k-k). 11.24 *(978-1-63245-276-4(6))* Lectorum Pubns., Inc.

Jacobson, Jennifer Richard. Paper Things. 2015. (ENG.). 384p. (J). (gr. 5). 16.99 *(978-0-7636-6323-0(9))* Candlewick Pr.

—Paper Things. 2017. (ENG.). (J). (gr. 5). lib. bdg. 19.65 ***(978-0-606-39841-1(4))*** Turtleback Bks.

Jacques, Karen. Monsters Have My Brother. Cahanes, Erin, illus. 2015. (ENG.). 16.95 *(978-1-59298-863-1(6))* Beaver's Pond Pr., Inc.

Jakubowski, Michele. The Grass Is Always Greener. (Ashley Small & Ashlee Tall Ser.). (ENG., Illus.). 64p. (J). (gr. 1-3). 2017. pap. 4.95 *(978-1-5158-0016-3(4))* 2016. lib. bdg. 20.65 *(978-1-5158-0012-5(1))* Picture Window Bks.

—The Professor's Discovery. Pinelli, Amerigo, illus. 2016. (Sleuths of Somerville Ser.). (ENG.). 144p. (gr. 4-6). lib. bdg. 25.99 *(978-1-4965-3177-3(9))* Stone Arch Bks.

—The Professor's Discovery. Pinelli, Amerigo, illus. 2017. (Sleuths of Somerville Ser.). (ENG.). 144p. (gr. 4-6). pap. 6.95 *(978-1-4965-3181-0(7))* Stone Arch Bks.

—Tour of Trouble. Pinelli, Amerigo, illus. 2016. (Sleuths of Somerville Ser.). (ENG.). 144p. (gr. 4-6). lib. bdg. 25.99 *(978-1-4965-3176-6(0))* Stone Arch Bks.

—Tour of Trouble. Pinelli, Amerigo, illus. 2017. (Sleuths of Somerville Ser.). (ENG.). 144p. (gr. 4-6). pap. 6.95 *(978-1-4965-3180-3(9))* Stone Arch Bks.

Jamal L. Q'Ettelle. Jayden & the Return of the Jalon Warriors. 2010. 120p. pap. 10.95 *(978-1-4502-0288-6(8))* iUniverse, Inc.

James, Richard E., III. Adventures of the Elements Vol. 3: Dangerous Games. Lyle, Maryann, ed. Welch, Chad, illus. 2004. 169p. (YA). (gr. 3-12). pap. 5.95 *(978-0-9675901-2-7(4))* Alchemy Creative, Inc.

Jane, Pamela. Milo & the Flapjack Fiasco! Johnson, Meredith, ed. Johnson, Meredith, tr. 2004. (Illus.). 32p. (J). 13.95 *(978-1-59336-113-6(0));* pap. *(978-1-59336-114-3(9))* Mondo Publishing.

Janni, Rebecca. Jammy Dance, 1 vol. Dockray, Tracy, illus. 2012. (ENG.). 40p. (J). (gr. -1-1). 16.99 *(978-0-374-33680-6(6),* 9780374336806, Farrar, Straus & Giroux (BYR)) Farrar, Straus & Giroux.

Janow, Jody. Eddie's Great Escape. 2010. 44p. pap. 19.99 *(978-1-4520-1764-8(6))* AuthorHouse.

Jaramillo, Ann. La Linea. 2008. (ENG.). 144p. (J). (gr. 5-9). pap. 8.99 *(978-0-312-37354-2(6),* 9780312373542) Square Fish.

Jarrell, Robert. Sunday Afternoon Walk. 2012. 36p. pap. 24.95 *(978-1-4626-6620-1(5))* America Star Bks.

Javier's Sister - A Family's Struggle with Drug Addiction: One Day the Sun Will Shine Again Series. 2005. (J). pap. 16.95 *(978-0-9768827-8-7(7))* Prevention Through Puppetry, Inc.

Jeanmarie, Michele. Curiosity, Curiosity: Lost in an Array. 2008. 74p. pap. 19.95 *(978-1-60610-169-8(2))* America Star Bks.

Jenkins, Amanda. Mutant Bugs. 2005. (J). pap. *(978-1-4108-4219-0(3))* Benchmark Education Co.

Jenkins, Amanda & Benchmark Education Co., LLC. The Secret Life of Wally Smithers. Fagan, Martin, illus. 2014. (Text Connections Ser.). (J). (gr. 3). *(978-1-4509-9656-3(6))* Benchmark Education Co.

Jenkins, Emily. Lemonade in Winter: A Book about Two Kids Counting Money. Karas, G. Brian, illus. 2012. (ENG.). 40p. (J). (gr. -1-2). 16.99 *(978-0-375-85883-3(0),* Schwartz & Wade Bks.) Random Hse. Children's Bks.

Jenkins, Jerry B. & Fabry, Chris. Wind Chill. 2006. (Red Rock Mysteries Ser.: 14). (ENG.). 240p. (YA). (gr. 3-7). per. 6.99 *(978-1-4143-0153-2(7),* Tyndale Kids) Tyndale Hse. Pubs.

Jennings, Sharon. The Bye-Bye Pie. 2004. (Illus.). (J). (gr. k-3). spiral bd. *(978-0-616-01684-8(0))* Canadian National Institute for the Blind/Institut National Canadien pour les Aveugles.

Jessell, Tim. The Boardwalk Mystery. Dunn, Robert, illus. 2013. (Boxcar Children Mysteries Ser.: 131). (ENG.). 144p. (J). (gr. 1-5). 15.99 *(978-0-8075-0802-2(0));* pap. 5.99 *(978-0-8075-0803-9(9))* Whitman, Albert & Co.

—The Mystery of the Stolen Snowboard. 2014. (Boxcar Children Mysteries Ser.: 134). (ENG.). 128p. (J). (gr. 1-5). 15.99 *(978-0-8075-8728-7(1))* Whitman, Albert & Co.

—The Mystery of the Wild West Bandit. 2014. (Boxcar Children Mysteries Ser.: 135). (ENG.). 128p. (J). (gr. 1-5). 15.99 *(978-0-8075-8725-6(7))* Whitman, Albert & Co.

Jessell, Tim, illus. The Boxcar Children, Set. 2013. (Boxcar Children Mysteries Ser.). (ENG.). 538p. (J). (gr. 1-5). 45.00 *(978-0-8075-0864-0(0))* Whitman, Albert & Co.

—Mystery of the Fallen Treasure. 2013. (Boxcar Children Mysteries Ser.: 132). (ENG.). 128p. (J). (gr. 1-5). 15.99 *(978-0-8075-5508-8(8));* 5.99 *(978-0-8075-5506-4(1))* Whitman, Albert & Co.

—The Return of the Graveyard Ghost. 2013. (Boxcar Children Mysteries Ser.: 133). (ENG.). 128p. (J). (gr. 1-5). 5.99 *(978-0-8075-6936-8(4));* 15.99 *(978-0-8075-6935-1(6))* Whitman, Albert & Co.

Johnson, Angela. Looking for Red. 2003. (ENG., Illus.). 128p. (YA). (gr. 7). pap. 6.99 *(978-0-689-86388-2(8),* Simon Pulse) Simon Pulse.

Johnson, C. Homecoming. 2007. (Illus.). 64p. per. 10.00 *(978-1-4251-1358-2(3))* Trafford Publishing.

Johnson, Mo. Noah's Garden: When Someone You Love Is in the Hospital. Josse, Annabelle, illus. 2010. (ENG.). 32p. (J). (gr. -1-2). 15.99 *(978-0-7636-4782-7(9))* Candlewick Pr.

Johnson, Sandi. White Wolf at Dawn. Johnson, Britt, ed. Sturgen, Bobbi, illus. 2014. (ENG.). 30p. (J). (gr. k-5). pap. 12.99 *(978-1-929063-72-7(5),* 171) Moons & Stars Publishing For Children.

Johnson, William C. Little Tree. 2007. pap. 9.00 *(978-0-8059-8486-6(0))* Dorrance Publishing Co., Inc.

Johnston, James D. The Adventures of Lucas & Celi: Lucas Stows Away. 2009. 32p. pap. 12.99 *(978-1-4343-6372-5(4))* AuthorHouse.

Jonell, Lynne. Grasshopper Magic. Dorman, Brandon, illus. (Magical Mix-Ups Ser.: 3). (ENG.). 112p. (J). (gr. 1-4). 2014. pap. 4.99 *(978-0-307-93123-8(4))* 2013. 12.99 *(978-0-375-87084-2(9))* Random Hse. Children's Bks. (Random Hse. Bks. for Young Readers).

—Wild Water Magic. Dorman, Brandon, illus. 2014. (Magical Mix-Ups Ser.: 4). (ENG.). 112p. (J). (gr. 1-4). 12.99 *(978-0-375-87085-9(7),* Random Hse. Bks. for Young Readers) Random Hse. Children's Bks.

Jones, C. B. Gone to the Buzzards. Green, Chris, illus. 2017. (Bog Hollow Boys Ser.). (ENG.). 72p. (gr. 4-5). lib. bdg. 25.32 *(978-1-4965-4058-4(1))* Stone Arch Bks.

Jones, Callie Carol Rodgers. Sweet Potato Pie. 2012. 20p. pap. 17.99 *(978-1-4685-6114-2(6))* AuthorHouse.

Jones, Chris. Cameron Jack & the Key to the Universe. 2010. (Illus.). 136p. pap. 10.99 *(978-1-4490-6547-8(3))* AuthorHouse.

Jones, Destry. What We Like. 2008. 16p. pap. 24.95 *(978-1-60474-364-7(6))* America Star Bks.

Jones, Jen. Willow's Boy-Crazy Birthday. Franco, Paula, illus. 2014. (Sleepover Girls Ser.). (ENG.). 128p. (gr. 3-5). lib. bdg. 22.65 *(978-1-4342-9757-0(8))* Stone Arch Bks.

Jones, Kelly. Mama. Kewley, Ken, illus. 2004. 32p. (J). *(978-0-9745930-0-5(1))* Stunt Publishing.

Jones, Lisa A. The Black Dog. 2008. 20p. pap. 24.95 *(978-1-60474-960-1(1))* America Star Bks.

Jones, Michael. Finding Imagine Nation. 2007. (YA). per. 10.95 *(978-0-9789386-4-2(X))* Lucy Rose Publishing LLC.

Jones, Patrick. Taking Sides. 2015. (J). 97p. 9.99 *(978-1-4677-7703-2(X));* (ENG.). 104p. (gr. 6-12). lib. bdg. 27.99 *(978-1-4677-5800-0(0))* Lerner Publishing Group.

Jonsberg, Barry. Game Theory. 2017. (ENG.). 320p. (YA). (gr. 9). 13.99 ***(978-1-76029-015-3(7))*** Allen & Unwin AUS. Dist: Independent Pubs. Group.

Jordan, Apple. Oh, Brother! 2012. (Disney Princess Step into Reading Ser.). lib. bdg. 13.55 *(978-0-606-26560-7(0),* Turtleback) Turtleback Bks.

Jordan, Apple & Posner-Sanchez, Andrea. Berry's Sweet Surprise. Random House Disney Staff et al, illus. 2016. (Little Golden Book Ser.). (ENG.). 24p. (J). (gr. -1-k). 4.99 *(978-0-7364-3444-7(5),* Golden/Disney) Random Hse. Children's Bks.

Jordan, Brian. I Told You I Can Play! 2008. (Illus.). 32p. 6.95 *(978-1-60349-001-6(9),* Marimba Bks.) Hudson Publishing Group, The.

Jordan, Mark. Courage the Monkey. 2006. (Illus.). 40p. (J). 13.95 *(978-0-9717013-7-3(7))* Decere Publishing.

Joseph, Lynn. Flowers in the Sky. 2013. (ENG.). 240p. (YA). (gr. 8). 17.99 *(978-0-06-029794-7(8),* HarperTeen) HarperCollins Pubs.

Jougla, Frederic. Tricked on Halloween: Rina & Jax's Stories. Jougla, Karina, illus. Lt. ed. 2004. 36p. (J). bds. 14.99 *(978-0-9754287-0-2(5))* Imagery Pr.

Joyce, William. Rolie Polie Olie. Joyce, William, illus. 2017. (World of William Joyce Ser.). (ENG., Illus.). 48p. (J). (gr. -1-2). 17.99 ***(978-1-4814-8957-7(7),*** Atheneum Bks. for Young Readers) Simon & Schuster Children's Publishing.

Judge, Chris. Tin. Judge, Chris, illus. 2014. (ENG., Illus.). 32p. (J). (gr. -1-3). 16.95 *(978-1-4677-5013-4(1))* Lerner Publishing Group.

Judge, Lita. Hoot & Peep. 2016. (Hoot & Peep Ser.). (ENG., Illus.). 40p. (J). (-k). 17.99 *(978-0-525-42837-4(2),* Dial Bks) Penguin Young Readers Group.

Julie Shelton. World of Vampires Part 1: The Huntress. 2006. 49p. pap. 10.00 *(978-1-59926-998-6(8))* Xlibris Corp.

The Jupiter Pirates - Curse of the Iris. 2014. (Jupiter Pirates Ser.: 2). (ENG.). 352p. (J). (gr. 3-7). 16.99 *(978-0-06-223023-2(9))* HarperCollins Pubs.

Kaaberbøl, Lene. Heartbreak Island. 2005. (W. I. T. C. H. Adventures Ser.: Bk. 3). (Illus.). 105p. (J). lib. bdg. 11.00 *(978-1-4242-0786-2(X))* Fitzgerald Bks.

—The Serpent Gift. 3rd ed. 2007. (Shamer Chronicles Ser.: 3). Orig. Title: Slangens Gave. (ENG.). 384p. (J). (gr. 5-9). pap. 22.99 *(978-0-8050-8655-3(2),* 9780805086553, Holt, Henry & Co. Bks. For Young Readers) Holt, Henry & Co.

Kadohata, Cynthia. The Thing about Luck. Kuo, Julia, illus. (ENG.). (J). (gr. 5-9). 2014. 304p. pap. 8.99 *(978-1-4424-7465-9(3),* Atheneum Bks. for Young Readers) 2013. 288p. 16.99 *(978-1-4169-1882-0(5))* Simon & Schuster Children's Publishing.

—The Thing about Luck. 2014. lib. bdg. 18.40 *(978-0-606-35798-2(X))* Turtleback Bks.

Kalman, Maira. Hey Willy, See the Pyramids. 2017. (ENG., Illus.). 48p. (J). (gr. k-3). 18.95 ***(978-1-68137-168-9(5),*** NYR Children's Collection) New York Review of Bks., Inc., The.

Kalz, Jill. I Hate to Read: Belle Pepper. 2004. (Illus.). 32p. (J). pap. 9.95 *(978-0-89812-521-4(9),* Creative Paperbacks) Creative Co., The.

Kann, Victoria. Aqualicious. Kann, Victoria, illus. 2015. (ENG., Illus.). 40p. (J). (gr. -1-3). 17.99 *(978-0-06-233016-1(0))* HarperCollins Pubs.

—Goldilicious. Kann, Victoria, illus. 2009. (Illus.). 40p. (J). (gr. k-3). (ENG.). 17.99 *(978-0-06-124408-7(2));* lib. bdg. 18.89 *(978-0-06-124409-4(0))* HarperCollins Pubs.

—Silverlicious. Kann, Victoria, illus. 2011. (Illus.). 40p. (J). (gr. k-3). (ENG.). 17.99 *(978-0-06-178123-0(1));* lib. bdg. 18.89 *(978-0-06-178124-7(X))* HarperCollins Pubs.

Kaplan, Bruce Eric. Meaniehead. Kaplan, Bruce Eric, illus. 2014. (ENG., Illus.). 40p. (J). (gr. -1-3). 17.99 *(978-1-4424-8542-6(6),* Simon & Schuster Bks. For Young Readers) Simon & Schuster Bks. For Young Readers.

—Monsters Eat Whiny Children. Kaplan, Bruce Eric, illus. 2010. (ENG., Illus.). 40p. (J). (gr. -1-3). 17.99 *(978-1-4169-8689-8(8),* Simon & Schuster Bks. For Young Readers) Simon & Schuster Bks. For Young Readers.

Karr, Kathleen. The Seventh Knot, 1 vol. 2003. (ENG., Illus.). 300p. (J). 15.95 *(978-0-7614-5135-8(8))* Marshall Cavendish Corp.

Karre, Elizabeth. Blind Curve: Acura Integra. 2013. (Turbocharged Ser.). (ENG.). 96p. (YA). (gr. 6-12). pap. 7.95 *(978-1-4677-1477-8(1));* lib. bdg. 27.93 *(978-1-4677-1244-6(2))* Lerner Publishing Group. (Darby Creek).

Katcher, Brian. The Improbable Theory of Ana & Zak. (YA). (gr. 8). 2016. 352p. pap. 9.99 (978-0-06-227278-2(0)) 2015. (ENG.). 336p. 17.99 (978-0-06-227277-5(2)) HarperCollins Pubs. (Tegen, Katherine Bks).

Katz, Karen. Best-Ever Big Brother. 2006. (ENG., Illus.). 14p. (J). (gr. -1-k). 6.99 (978-0-448-43914-3(X), Grosset & Dunlap) Penguin Young Readers Group.

Keane, Claire. Little Big Girl. 2016. (ENG., Illus.). 32p. (J). (-k). 17.99 (978-0-8037-3912-3(5), Dial Bks) Penguin Young Readers Group.

Kear, Nicole C. The Fix-It Friends: Have No Fear! Dockray, Tracy, illus. 2017. (Fix-It Friends Ser.). (ENG.). 144p. (J). 16.99 (978-1-250-11577-5(9), 9781250115775) Imprint IND. Dist: Macmillan.

—The Fix-It Friends: Sticks & Stones. Dockray, Tracy, illus. 2017. (Fix-It Friends Ser.: 2). (ENG.). 144p. (J). pap. 5.99 (978-1-250-08586-3(1), 9781250085863) Imprint IND. Dist: Macmillan.

—The Fix-It Friends: the Show Must Go On. Dockray, Tracy, illus. 2017. (Fix-It Friends Ser.: 3). (ENG.). 160p. (J). pap. 5.99 **(978-1-250-08668-6(X)**, 9781250086686) Imprint IND. Dist: Macmillan.

—The Fix-It Friends: Wish You Were Here. Dockray, Tracy, illus. 2017. (Fix-It Friends Ser.: 4). (ENG.). 160p. (J). pap. 5.99 **(978-1-250-08670-9(1)**, 9781250086709) Imprint IND. Dist: Macmillan.

Keats, Ezra Jack. Peter's Chair. 2015. 40p. pap. 7.00 (978-1-61003-534-7(8)) Center for the Collaborative Classroom.

—Peter's Chair. Keats, Ezra Jack, illus. 2006. (ENG., Illus.). 32p. (J). (gr. -1 — 1). bds. 6.99 (978-0-670-06190-7(5), Viking Books for Young Readers) Penguin Young Readers Group.

—Peter's Chair. (J). (gr. -1-3). pap. 12.95 incl. audio Weston Woods Studios, Inc.

Keeling, Annie E. Andrew Golding A Tale of the Great Plague. 2004. reprint ed. pap. 1.99 (978-1-4192-0694-8(X)); pap. 15.95 (978-1-4191-0694-1(5)) Kessinger Publishing, LLC.

Kehret, Peg. Abduction! 2006. (ENG.). 224p. (J). (gr. 5-18). 6.99 (978-0-14-240617-5(1), Puffin Books) Penguin Young Readers Group.

—Abduction! 2007. 215p. (gr. 3-7). 17.00 (978-0-7569-8282-9(0)) Perfection Learning Corp.

—Escaping the Giant Wave. 2004. (ENG., Illus.). 160p. (J). (gr. 3-7). pap. 7.99 (978-0-689-85273-2(8), Aladdin) Simon & Schuster Children's Publishing.

Kellerman, Faye & Kellerman, Aliza. Prism. (YA). 2010. (ENG.). 288p. (gr. 8). pap. 8.99 (978-0-06-168724-2(3)) 2009. 272p. (gr. 7-18). lib. bdg. 17.89 (978-0-06-168722-8(7), HarperTeen) HarperCollins Pubs.

Kemler, Nancy. Dragon Box: The Key to Magic. 2005. 108p. pap. 19.95 (978-1-4137-8445-9(3)) America Star Bks.

Kenah, Katharine. Scholastic Reader Level 1: the Saturday Triplets #2: the Pumpkin Fair Problem. Lyon, Tammie, illus. 2013. (Scholastic Reader Level 1 Ser.). (ENG.). 32p. (J). (gr. -1-2). pap. 3.99 (978-0-545-48144-1(9)) Scholastic, Inc.

Kennedy Center Staff. Teddy Roosevelt & the Treasure of Ursa Major. Hoyt, Ard, illus. 2011. (ENG.). 128p. (J). (gr. 2-5). pap. 5.99 (978-1-4169-4860-5(0), Simon & Schuster Bks. For Young Readers) Simon & Schuster Bks. For Young Readers.

Kennedy, Pamela. A Sister for Matthew. 2008. (ENG., Illus.). 32p. (J). (gr. -1-3). 8.95 (978-0-8249-5527-4(7), 1256104, Ideal Pubns.) Worthy Publishing.

Kennemore, Tim. Alice's Shooting Star. 2009. 100p. (J). (gr. 2-6). 12.00 (978-0-8028-5337-0(4), Eerdmans Bks For Young Readers) Eerdmans, William B. Publishing Co.

Kent, Jaden. #1: the Cave of Aaaaah! Doom! Bodnaruk, Iryna, illus. 2017. (Ella & Owen Ser.: 1). (ENG.). 112p. (J). (gr. 1-3). pap. 5.99 (978-1-4998-0368-6(0)) Little Bee Books Inc.

—#2: Attack of the Stinky Fish Monster! Bodnaruk, Iryna, illus. 2017. (Ella & Owen Ser.: 2). (ENG.). 112p. (J). (gr. 1-3). pap. 5.99 (978-1-4998-0369-3(9)) Little Bee Books Inc.

Kent, Rose. Rocky Road. 2012. (ENG.). 304p. (J). (gr. 3-7). 7.99 (978-0-375-86345-5(1), Yearling) Random Hse. Children's Bks.

Kerascoët, illus. Paul & Antoinette. 2016. (ENG.). 40p. (J). (gr. -1-3). 17.95 (978-1-59270-196-4(5)) Enchanted Lion Bks., LLC.

Kerr, P. B., pseud. The Day of the Djinn Warriors. 2008. (Children of the Lamp Ser.: 4). (ENG.). 400p. (J). (gr. 3-7). 7.99 (978-0-439-93216-5(5), Scholastic Paperbacks) Scholastic, Inc.

—The Eye of the Forest. 2009. (Children of the Lamp Ser.: 5). (ENG.). 432p. (J). (gr. 3-7). 17.99 (978-0-439-93215-8(7), Orchard Bks.) Scholastic, Inc.

—The Five Fakirs of Faizabad. 2011. (Children of the Lamp Ser.: Vol. 6). (ENG.). 448p. (J). (gr. 3-7). pap. 8.99 (978-0-545-12659-5(2), Scholastic Paperbacks) Scholastic, Inc.

Keyser, Amber J. The Way Back from Broken. 2015. (ENG.). 216p. (YA). (gr. 6-12). 18.99 (978-1-4677-8817-5(1), Carolrhoda Lab™); 18.99 (978-1-4677-7590-8(8)) Lerner Publishing Group.

Kibuishi, Kazu. The Cloud Searchers. (Amulet Ser.: 3). (ENG.). 208p. (J). (gr. 3-7). 2015. 24.99 (978-0-545-20884-0(X)) 2010. pap. 12.99 (978-0-545-20885-7(8)) Scholastic, Inc. (Graphix).

—Escape from Lucien. (Amulet Ser.: 6). (ENG., Illus.). 224p. (J). (gr. 3-7). 2015. 24.99 (978-0-545-84899-2(7)) 2014. pap. 12.99 (978-0-545-43315-0(0)) Scholastic, Inc. (Graphix).

—Firelight. 2016. (Amulet Ser.: 7). (ENG., Illus.). 208p. (J). (gr. 3-7). 24.99 (978-0-545-83966-2(1)); pap. 12.99 (978-0-545-43316-7(9)) Scholastic, Inc. (Graphix).

—Firelight. 2016. (Amulet Ser.: 7). (ENG., Illus.). 224p. (J). (gr. 3-7). lib. bdg. 24.50 (978-0-606-38070-6(1)) Turtleback Bks.

—The Last Council. 2015. (Amulet Ser.: 4). (ENG.). 224p. (J). (gr. 3-7). 24.99 (978-0-545-20886-4(6), Graphix) Scholastic, Inc.

—Prince of the Elves. 2015. (Amulet Ser.: 5). (ENG.). 208p. (J). (gr. 3-7). 24.99 (978-0-545-20888-8(2), Graphix) Scholastic, Inc.

—The Stonekeeper. 2008. (Amulet Ser.: 1). (ENG., Illus.). 192p. (J). (gr. 3-7). 24.99 (978-0-439-84680-6(3)); pap. 12.99 (978-0-439-84681-3(1)) Scholastic, Inc. (Graphix).

—The Stonekeeper's Curse. 2009. (Amulet Ser.: 2). (ENG., Illus.). 224p. (J). (gr. 4-7). 24.99 (978-0-439-84682-0(X), Graphix) Scholastic, Inc.

Kibuishi, Kazu, illus. Firelight. 2016. 197p. (J). (978-1-4806-9909-0(8)) Baker & Taylor, CATS.

Kidd, Ronald. Undercover Kid: The Comic Book King. Sklar, Andy, illus. 2007. (All Aboard Mystery Reader Ser.). (ENG.). 48p. (J). pap. 3.99 (978-0-448-44438-3(0), Grosset & Dunlap) Penguin Publishing Group.

Kidwell, Justina. The Haunted Tree House, the Ghost Town, & the Dark Reaper: The Kent Boys' Adventures, 1 vol. 2009. 48p. pap. 16.95 (978-1-60813-234-8(X)) America Star Bks.

Kimble, Maggie T. Peep Learns to Sing. 2004. 21p. pap. 24.95 (978-1-4137-2005-1(6)) PublishAmerica, Inc.

Kimmel, Elizabeth Cody. ParaNormaN. 2012. (ENG.). (J). (gr. 4-7). 64.99 (978-1-61969-450-7(6)) Findaway World, LLC.

—ParaNorman: A Novel. 2013. (ENG., Illus.). 256p. (J). (gr. 3-7). pap. 6.99 (978-0-316-20987-8(2)) Little, Brown Bks. for Young Readers.

Kimmel, Eric A. Scarlett & Sam: Escape from Egypt. Stevanovic, Ivica, illus. 2015. (J). 6.99 (978-1-4677-6207-6(5)); (ENG.). 168p. (gr. 1-3). lib. bdg. 15.95 (978-1-4677-3850-7(6)) Lerner Publishing Group. (Kar-Ben Publishing).

King, Caro. Seven Sorcerers. 2011. (ENG.). 352p. (J). (gr. 3-7). 15.99 (978-1-4424-2042-7(1), Aladdin) Simon & Schuster Children's Publishing.

—Shadow Spell. 2012. (ENG.). 320p. (J). (gr. 3-7). pap. 6.99 (978-1-4423-3908-8(X), Aladdin) Simon & Schuster Children's Publishing.

—Shadow Spell. 2012. (ENG.). 320p. (J). (gr. 3-7). 15.99 (978-1-4424-2045-8(6), Simon & Schuster/Paula Wiseman Bks.) Simon & Schuster/Paula Wiseman Bks.

King, Caro & Bowater, Charlie. Seven Sorcerers. 2012. (ENG.). 352p. (J). (gr. 3-7). pap. 6.99 (978-1-4424-2043-4(X), Aladdin) Simon & Schuster Children's Publishing.

King, Juaness. The Prodigal's Quest. 2012. 54p. 19.95 (978-1-4626-9042-8(4)) America Star Bks.

King, Lisa. Lurkey the Proud Turkey. 2013. 24p. pap. 24.95 (978-1-63004-113-7(0)) America Star Bks.

Kirby, Jessi. In Honor. (ENG., (YA). (gr. 9). 2013. Illus.). 256p. pap. 9.99 (978-1-4424-1698-7(X)) 2012. 240p. 16.99 (978-1-4424-1697-0(1)) Simon & Schuster Bks. For Young Readers. (Simon & Schuster Bks. For Young Readers).

Kirkham, Teresa. Tattle Tom. 2003. 27p. pap. 12.95 (978-1-4137-0141-8(8)) America Star Bks.

Kirsch, R. A. The Big One: (A Bicycle Tale), 1 vol. 2009. 191p. pap. 24.95 (978-1-60703-341-7(0)) PublishAmerica, Inc.

Kizer, Amber. A Matter of Days. 2016. (ENG.). 288p. (YA). (gr. 7). pap. 9.99 (978-0-385-73974-0(5), Ember) Random Hse. Children's Bks.

—A Matter of Days. 2016. lib. bdg. 20.85 (978-0-606-38875-7(3)) Turtleback Bks.

Kjersgaard, Carly. Muffins' New Beginning. 2009. 20p. pap. 10.95 (978-1-4389-8001-0(9)) AuthorHouse.

Klein, Abby. Camping Catastrophe! McKinley, John, illus. 2008. (Ready, Freddy! Ser.: Bk. 14). 95p. (J). (gr. -1-3). 11.65 (978-0-7569-8837-1(3)) Perfection Learning Corp.

Kleven, Elisa. The Puddle Pail. Kleven, Elisa, illus. 2007. (ENG., Illus.). 32p. (J). (gr. -1-2). pap. 6.99 (978-1-58246-206-6(2), Tricycle Pr.) Random Hse. Children's Bks.

Kline, C. A. & Lauder, M. F. Halloween Night. 2012. 24p. pap. 17.99 (978-1-4772-7417-0(0)) AuthorHouse.

Kling, Kevin. Big Little Mother. Monroe, Chris, illus. 2013. (ENG.). 32p. (J). (gr. -1-3). 17.95 (978-0-87351-911-3(6), Borealis Bk.) Minnesota Historical Society Pr.

Klingensmith, Ryan Lee & Klingensmith, Sherri Ann. Starlight Blue: A New Baby. Rollinger, Marsha, illus. 2012. 32p. pap. 24.95 (978-1-4626-8219-5(7)) America Star Bks.

Knapman, Timothy. Time Now to Dream. Oxenbury, Helen, illus. 2017. (ENG.). 32p. (J). (gr. -1-2). 16.99 (978-0-7636-9078-6(3)) Candlewick Pr.

Knecht, Eileen. Christine's Christmas Crib. 2009. 40p. pap. 18.49 (978-1-4389-2265-2(5)) AuthorHouse.

Knight, Christopher. World Is Black & White. 2008. 459p. (YA). pap. 14.95 (978-1-893699-97-7(8)) AudioCraft Publishing, Inc.

Knowles, Jo. See You at Harry's. 2012. (ENG., Illus.). 310p. (J). (gr. 5). 16.99 (978-0-7636-5407-8(8)) Candlewick Pr.

Knutsson, Catherine. Shadows Cast by Stars. (ENG., Illus.). 464p. (YA). (gr. 7). 2013. pap. 11.99 (978-1-4424-0192-1(3)) 2012. 17.99 (978-1-4424-0191-4(5)) Simon & Schuster Children's Publishing. (Atheneum Bks. for Young Readers).

Koffsky, Ann D. Judah Maccabee Goes to the Doctor. Shipman, Talitha, illus. 2017. (J). **(978-1-68115-522-7(2))** Behrman Hse., Inc.

Koger, Danny K. The Misadventures of Carson & C J Crenshaw: In Search of the Book of Life. 2007. 184p. per. 13.95 (978-0-595-42365-1(5)) iUniverse, Inc.

Kogler, Jennifer. The Otherworldlies. 2008. 400p. (J). lib. bdg. 17.89 (978-0-06-073960-7(6)); (ENG.). (gr. 5-18). 16.99 (978-0-06-073959-1(2)) HarperCollins Pubs. (Eos).

Kogler, Jennifer Anne. The Siren's Cry. 2011. (ENG.). 384p. (YA). (gr. 8). 16.99 (978-0-06-199443-2(X), HarperTeen) HarperCollins Pubs.

Kogler, Jennifer Anne & Kogler, Jennifer A. The Otherworldlies. 2009. (ENG.). 400p. (YA). (gr. 8). pap. 8.99 (978-0-06-073961-4(4), HarperTeen) HarperCollins Pubs.

Kohlhepp, Michael. Within the Hearthstone: Book 1: the Trea. 2006. 127p. pap. 19.95 (978-1-4241-3744-2(6)) PublishAmerica, Inc.

Kohlhepp, Michael G. Within the Hearthstone Book 2: The Fountain of Balance. 2007. (ENG.). 184p. per. 24.95 (978-1-4241-4446-4(9)) PublishAmerica, Inc.

Konigsburg, E. L. Silent to the Bone. unabr. ed. 2004. (Middle Grade Cassette Librariestm Ser.). 272p. (J). (gr. 5-9). pap. 38.00 incl. audio (978-0-8072-8741-5(5), S YA 253 SP, Listening Library) Random Hse. Audio Publishing Group.

—Silent to the Bone. 2004. (ENG.). 272p. (YA). (gr. 7). mass mkt. 7.99 (978-0-689-86715-6(8), Simon Pulse) Simon Pulse.

Kopelke, Lisa. The Younger Brother's Survival Guide. Kopelke, Lisa, illus. 2006. (ENG., Illus.). 32p. (J). (gr. -1-3). 17.99 (978-0-689-86249-6(0), Simon & Schuster Bks. For Young Readers) Simon & Schuster Bks. For Young Readers.

Korman, Gordon. The Abduction, Bk. 1. 2006. (Kidnapped Ser.: 1). (ENG.). (J). (gr. 3-7). audio compact disk 39.95 (978-0-439-89847-8(1)) Scholastic, Inc.

—The Medusa Plot. 2011. (39 Clues: Cahills vs. Vespers Ser.: 1). (ENG., Illus.). 224p. (J). (gr. 3-7). 12.99 (978-0-545-32409-0(2), Scholastic Pr.); 12.99 (978-0-545-29839-1(3)) Scholastic, Inc.

—One False Note. 2009. (39 Clues Ser.: 2). (ENG.). 160p. (J). (gr. 3-7). 12.99 (978-0-545-06042-4(7)); (Illus.). 12.99 (978-0-545-09060-5(1)) Scholastic, Inc.

—Slacker. 2016. (ENG.). 240p. (J). (gr. 3-7). 16.99 (978-0-545-82315-9(3), Scholastic Pr.) Scholastic, Inc.

Korngold, Jamie. Sadie's Lag Ba'Omer Mystery. Fortenberry, Julie, illus. 2014. (Lag Ba'Omer & Shavuot Ser.). (ENG.). 32p. (J). (gr. -1-3). 7.95 (978-0-7613-9048-0(0)); 17.95 (978-0-7613-9047-3(2)) Lerner Publishing Group. (Kar-Ben Publishing).

Korngold, Jamie S. Mazel Tov! It's a Boy: Mazel Tov! It's a Girl. Finkelstein, Jeff, illus. Finkelstein, Jeff, photos by. 2015. (J). (ENG.). 32p. (gr. -1-1). lib. bdg. 17.95 (978-1-4677-1957-5(9)); 6.99 (978-1-4677-6206-9(7)) Lerner Publishing Group. (Kar-Ben Publishing).

Krackow, Eric T. Have an Abominably Good Day, 1 vol. 2010. (ENG., Illus.). 64p. (J). 16.99 (978-0-7643-3496-2(4), 9780764334962) Schiffer Publishing, Ltd.

Kraft, Erik P. Lenny & Mel. Kraft, Erik P., illus. 2012. (Ready-for-Chapters Ser.). (ENG., Illus.). 64p. (J). (gr. 2-5). pap. 6.99 (978-0-689-85891-8(4), Aladdin) Simon & Schuster Children's Publishing.

—Lenny & Mel after-School Confidential. Kraft, Erik P., illus. 2012. (Lenny & Mel Ser.). (ENG., Illus.). 64p. (J). (gr. 2-5). pap. 6.99 (978-1-4424-6314-1(7), Simon & Schuster/Paula Wiseman Bks.) Simon & Schuster/Paula Wiseman Bks.

—Lenny & Mel's Summer Vacation. Kraft, Erik P., illus. 2012. (Ready-For-Chapters Ser.). (ENG., Illus.). 64p. (J). (gr. 2-5). pap. 6.99 (978-0-689-86874-0(X), Simon & Schuster/Paula Wiseman Bks.) Simon & Schuster/Paula Wiseman Bks.

Kranz, Jonathan David. Our Brothers at the Bottom of the Bottom of the Sea. 2015. (ENG.). 240p. (YA). (gr. 9-12). 17.99 (978-1-62779-050-5(0), Holt, Henry & Co. Bks. For Young Readers) Holt, Henry & Co.

Krawitz, Susan. Viva, Rose! 2017. (ENG.). 240p. (J). (gr. 5). 16.95 (978-0-8234-3756-6(6)) Holiday Hse., Inc.

Kreilein, Debra. The Tombstone Treasure Mystery. 2013. 142p. pap. 12.99 (978-1-62509-458-2(2)) Salem Author Services.

Kreller, Susan. You Can't See the Elephants. Gaffney, Elizabeth, tr. from GER. 2015. (ENG.). 192p. (J). (gr. 5-7). 16.99 (978-0-399-17209-0(2), G.P. Putnam's Sons Books for Young Readers) Penguin Young Readers Group.

Krensky, Stephen. We Just Had a Baby. Graux, Amélie, illus. 2016. (ENG.). 32p. (J). (gr. -1-2). 14.95 (978-1-62370-603-6(3)) Capstone Young Readers of Coughlan Cos.

Krishnaswami, Uma. Bringing Asha Home, 1 vol. Akib, Jamel, illus. 2015. (ENG.). 32p. (J). pap. 9.95 (978-1-62014-225-7(2)) Lee & Low Bks., Inc.

—Bringing Asha Home, 1 vol. Jeyaveeran, Ruth & Akib, Jamel, illus. 2006. (ENG.). 32p. (J). (gr. -1-3). 16.95 (978-1-58430-259-9(3)) Lee & Low Bks., Inc.

Kropp, Paul. Against All Odds. Melanson, Matt, illus. 2004. (New Series Canada). 87p. (J). pap. (978-1-897039-06-9(9)) High Interest Publishing (HIP).

Krull, Kathleen. How to Trick or Treat in Outer Space. Brewer, Paul, illus. 2004. (ENG.). 32p. (J). (gr. k-3). tchr. ed. 16.95 (978-0-8234-1844-2(8)) Holiday Hse., Inc.

Kuchman, D. S. Krystal Steps: The Journey Begins. 2006. 57p. pap. 16.95 (978-1-4241-5135-6(X)) America Star Bks.

Kuehn, Stephanie. Complicit. (ENG.). 256p. (YA). 2016. pap. 10.99 (978-1-250-04460-0(X), 9781250044600) 2014. (gr. 8-12). 19.99 (978-1-250-04459-4(6), 9781250044594) St. Martin's Pr. (St. Martin's Griffin).

Kuhlman, Evan. Great Ball of Light. Holmes, Jeremy, illus. 2015. (ENG.). 304p. (J). (gr. 5-9). 16.99 (978-1-4169-6461-2(4)) Simon & Schuster Children's Publishing.

Kuhn, Douglas Wolcik. Uncle Kyle's Magic Kite. Kuhn, Douglas Wolcik, illus. 2012. (Illus.). 28p. pap. 24.95 (978-1-4626-9699-4(6)) America Star Bks.

Kuipers, Alice. The Best-Ever Bookworm Book. Murguia, Bethanie Deeney, illus. 2014. (ENG.). 40p. (J). (gr. -1-3). 17.00 (978-0-316-21200-7(8)) Little, Brown Bks. for Young Readers.

—Violet & Victor Write the Most Fabulous Fairy Tale. 2016. (ENG., Illus.). 40p. (J). (gr. -1-3). 17.00 (978-0-316-21202-1(4)) Little Brown & Co.

Kunkel, Mike. Brother vs. Brother!, 1 vol. Kunkel, Mike, illus. 2014. (Billy Batson & the Magic of Shazam! Ser.). (ENG., Illus.). 32p. (gr. 2-3). 22.60 (978-1-4342-9228-5(2)) Stone Arch Bks.

—Magic Words!, 1 vol. Kunkel, Mike, illus. 2014. (Billy Batson & the Magic of Shazam! Ser.). (ENG., Illus.). 32p. (gr. 2-3). 22.60 (978-1-4342-9209-4(6)) Stone Arch Bks.

—Perilous Peril!, 1 vol. Kunkel, Mike, illus. 2014. (Billy Batson & the Magic of Shazam! Ser.). (ENG., Illus.). 32p. (gr. 2-3). 22.60 (978-1-4342-9227-8(4)) Stone Arch Bks.

—The World's Mightiest Mortal!, 1 vol. Kunkel, Mike, illus. 2014. (Billy Batson & the Magic of Shazam! Ser.). (ENG., Illus.). 32p. (gr. 2-3). 22.60 (978-1-4342-9226-1(6)) Stone Arch Bks.

Kurtz, Jane. In the Small, Small Night. Isadora, Rachel, illus. 2005. (Amistad Ser.). (ENG.). 32p. (J). (gr. k-5). 17.99 (978-0-06-623814-2(5), Greenwillow Bks.) HarperCollins Pubs.

Lachenmeyer, Nathaniel. Eureka! Jack, Colin, illus. 2013. (J). (978-0-8037-3514-9(6), Dial) Penguin Publishing Group.

LaFleur, Suzanne. Listening for Lucca. 2015. (ENG.). 240p. (J). (gr. 4-7). pap. 7.99 (978-0-307-98030-4(8), Yearling) Random Hse. Children's Bks.

Lam, Maple. My Little Sister & Me. Lam, Maple, illus. 2016. (Illus.). 40p. (J). (gr. -1-3). 17.99 (978-0-06-239697-6(8)) HarperCollins Pubs.

LaMarche, Una & Loftin, Nikki. Don't Fail Me Now. 2015. (ENG.). 288p. (YA). (gr. 7). 17.99 (978-1-59514-817-9(5), Razorbill) Penguin Young Readers Group.

Lambert, Roy. Lamb, the Hip Cat Daddy. 2005. per. 13.95 (978-1-58909-253-2(8)) Bookstand Publishing.

Landis, Mary M. Winter Days with the Treelo Triplets. 2012. (Illus.). 218p. (J). (978-0-7399-2447-1(8)) Rod & Staff Pubs., Inc.

Landman, Tanya. I Am Apache. 2008. (ENG., Illus.). 320p. (YA). (gr. 7-18). 17.99 (978-0-7636-3664-7(9)) Candlewick Pr.

Lane, Jessica E. The Secret of the Swans. 2009. 52p. pap. 31.99 (978-1-4415-5517-5(X)) Xlibris Corp.

Langdale, Mark Roland. Professor Doppelganger & the Fantastical Cloud Factory. 2012. 106p. pap. (978-1-78003-267-2(6)) Pen Pr. Pubs., Ltd.

Lansdale, Joe R. All the Earth, Thrown to the Sky. 2012. (ENG.). 252p. (YA). (gr. 7). pap. 8.99 (978-0-385-73932-0(X), Ember) Random Hse. Children's Bks.

Larsen, Andrew. A Squiggly Story. Lowery, Mike, illus. 2016. (ENG.). 32p. (J). (gr. -1-2). 16.95 (978-1-77138-016-4(0)) Kids Can Pr., Ltd. CAN. Dist: Hachette Bk. Group.

Larson, Hope. Compass South. Mock, Rebecca, illus. 2016. (Four Points Ser.: 1). (ENG.). 224p. (J). 17.99 (978-0-374-30043-2(7), 9780374300432, Farrar, Straus & Giroux (BYR)) Farrar, Straus & Giroux.

Laskin, Pamela L. Getting to Know You. 2003. (YA). 16.95 (978-0-936389-92-9(3)) Tudor Pubs., Inc.

Lasky, Kathryn. Broken Song. 2007. (ENG.). 160p. (J). (gr. 5-18). 6.99 (978-0-14-240741-7(0), Puffin Books) Penguin Young Readers Group.

—A Voice in the Wind. 2008. (ENG., Illus.). 272p. (J). (gr. 2-5). pap. 15.95 (978-0-15-205875-3(3)) Houghton Mifflin Harcourt Publishing Co.

Lassiter, Rhiannon. Void: Hex; Shadows; Ghosts. 2011. (ENG.). 688p. (YA). (gr. 7). pap. 9.99 (978-1-4424-2929-1(1), Simon Pulse) Simon Pulse.

Latimer, Alex. Never Follow a Dinosaur, 1 vol. Latimer, Alex, illus. 2016. (ENG., Illus.). 32p. (J). (gr. -1-3). 16.95 (978-1-56145-704-5(3)) Peachtree Pubs.

Laura Lee Hope. Bunny Brown & His Sister Sue at Aunt Lu's City Home. 2007. 184p. per. 11.95 (978-1-4218-3986-8(5), 1st World Library - Literary Society) 1st World Publishing, Inc.

—Bunny Brown & His Sister Sue at Christmas Tree Cove. 2007. 176p. per. 12.95 (978-1-4218-3987-5(3), 1st World Library - Literary Society) 1st World Publishing, Inc.

—Six Little Bunkers at Cowboy Jack's. 2007. 180p. per. 11.95 (978-1-4218-3988-2(1), 1st World Library - Literary Society) 1st World Publishing, Inc.

—Six Little Bunkers at Grandma Bell's. l.t. ed. 2007. (ENG.). 162p. pap. 21.99 (978-1-4264-8193-2(4)) Creative Media Partners, LLC.

—Six Little Bunkers at Grandpa Ford's. 2007. 188p. per. 11.95 (978-1-4218-3989-9(X), 1st World Library - Literary Society) 1st World Publishing, Inc.

Laurie, Victoria. The Curse of Deadman's Forest. 2011. (ENG.). 432p. (J). (gr. 3-7). 8.99 (978-0-440-42259-4(0), Yearling) Random Hse. Children's Bks.

Lauterbach, B. L. Home-Grown Experiences. 2008. 68p. pap. 7.95 (978-1-4327-2620-1(0)) Outskirts Pr., Inc.

Law, Ingrid. Savvy. 2011. 9.68 (978-0-7848-3575-3(6), Everbind) Marco Bk. Co.

—Savvy. (ENG.). (J). (gr. 4-7). 2010. 368p. 7.99 (978-0-14-241433-0(6), Puffin Books) 2008. (Illus.). 352p. 18.99 (978-0-8037-3306-0(2), Dial Bks) Penguin Young Readers Group.

—Savvy. l.t. ed. 2011. (ENG.). 500p. 23.99 (978-1-4104-3530-9(X)) Thorndike Pr.

—Savvy. 2010. lib. bdg. 18.40 (978-0-606-14394-3(7), Turtleback) Turtleback Bks.

Lawlor, Laurie. The Biggest Pest on Eighth Avenue. Fisher, Cynthia, illus. (Holiday House Reader Ser.). (ENG.). 47p. (J). (gr. k-3). tchr. ed. 14.95 (978-0-8234-1321-8(7)) Holiday Hse., Inc.

Lawrence, Antoinette & Lewis, Terry. I Remember. 2011. (ENG.). 29p. (J). pap. 12.95 (978-1-4327-7342-7(9)) Outskirts Pr., Inc.

Lawson, Janet. The Alberts & Me. 2009. (J). (978-0-15-205327-7(1)) Harcourt Trade Pubs.

Lay, Kathryn. The Substitutes: An Up2U Action Adventure, 1 vol. Calo, Marcos, illus. 2015. (ENG.). 80p. (J). (978-1-62402-095-7(X)) Magic Wagon.

Layne, Steven L. Stay with Sister, 1 vol. Hoyt, Ard, illus. 2012. (ENG.). 32p. (J). (gr. k-3). 16.99 (978-1-4556-1523-0(4)) Pelican Publishing Co., Inc.

Lazar, Tara. The Monstore. Burks, James, illus. 2013. (ENG.). 32p. (J). (gr. -1-2). 16.99 (978-1-4424-2017-5(0), Aladdin) Simon & Schuster Children's Publishing.

Leavitt, Lindsey. The Big Move. Ford, A. G., illus. 2016. (Commander in Cheese Ser.: 1). (ENG.). 112p. (J). (gr. 2-5). 4.99 (978-1-101-93112-7(4), Random Hse. Bks. for Young Readers) Random Hse. Children's Bks.

—Have a Mice Flight! Ford, A. G., illus. 2016. (Commander in Cheese Ser.: 3). (ENG.). 112p. (J). (gr. 2-5). 4.99 (978-1-101-93118-9(3), Random Hse. Bks. for Young Readers) Random Hse. Children's Bks.

—Oval Office Escape. Ford, A. G., illus. 2016. (Commander in Cheese Ser.: 2). (ENG.). 112p. (J). (gr. 2-5). 4.99 (978-1-101-93115-8(9), Random Hse. Bks. for Young Readers) Random Hse. Children's Bks.

Lee, J. M. & dePaola, Tomie. Shadows of the Dark Crystal. Froud, Brian & Godbey, Cory, illus. 2016. (Jim Henson's the Dark Crystal Ser.: 1). (ENG.). 272p. (J). (gr. 7). bds. 17.99 (978-0-448-48289-7(4), Grosset & Dunlap) Penguin Young Readers Group.

Lee, Mary Ellen. Danny & Life on Bluff Point: Blizzard of '95 revised Edition. 2009. 160p. (gr. 4-7). pap. 12.95 (978-0-595-53308-4(6)) iUniverse, Inc.

Lemke, Amy J. & Lemke, Donald B. My Little Bro-Bot, 1 vol. Bradley, Jessica, illus. 2013. (Comics Land Ser.). (ENG.). 32p. (gr. k-2). 7.95 (978-1-4342-6285-1(5)); lib. bdg. 25.32 (978-1-4342-4989-0(1)) Stone Arch Bks.

Leno, Katrina. The Lost & Found. 2016. 352p. (J). (gr. 8). 17.99 (978-0-06-223120-8(0), HarperTeen) HarperCollins Pubs.

Leo, Domenic. The Messengers: The Secret of the Orbs. 2007. 324p. per. 19.95 (978-0-595-42668-3(9)) iUniverse, Inc.

Leonard, Marcia. Trae la Pelota, Tito. Handelman, Dorothy, photos by. 2005.Tr. of Get the Ball, Slim. (Illus.). 32p. (J).

(ENG & SPA.). (gr. -1-1). pap. 4.99 *(978-0-8225-3293-4(X))*; (SPA., (gr. 1-1). per. 5.95 *(978-0-8225-3292-7(1)*, Ediciones Lerner) Lerner Publishing Group.

Lerangis, Peter. The Sword Thief. 2009. (39 Clues Ser.: 3). (ENG.). 160p. (J). (gr. 3-7). 12.99 *(978-0-545-06043-1(5)*, Scholastic Pr.); (Illus.). 12.99 *(978-0-545-09059-9(8))* Scholastic, Inc.

Leslie, Emma. Glaucia the Greek Slave: A Tale of Athens in the First Century. Felter & Butterworth & Heath, illus. 2007. 308p. per. 14.95 *(978-1-934671-01-6(0))* Salem Ridge Press LLC.

Lester, Julius. When Dad Killed Mom. 2003. (YA). (gr. 7-12). mass mkt. 6.95 *(978-0-15-524698-0(4)*, Silver Whistle) Harcourt Trade Pubs.

—When Dad Killed Mom. 2003. (ENG.). 216p. (YA). (gr. 7-12). pap. 13.95 *(978-0-15-204698-9(4))* Houghton Mifflin Harcourt Publishing Co.

Lettrick, Robert. The Murk. Disney Storybook Art Team, illus. 2015. (ENG.). 320p. (J). (gr. 5-9). 16.99 *(978-1-4231-8695-3(8))* Hyperion Bks. for Children.

Leuck, Laura. My Beastly Brother. Nash, Scott, illus. 2003. 32p. (J). (gr. -1-1). 16.89 *(978-0-06-029548-6(1))* HarperCollins Pubs.

Levin, Betty. Shoddy Cove. 2003. 208p. (J). (gr. 5-18). 15.99 *(978-0-06-052271-1(2))* HarperCollins Pubs.

Levine, Anna. Jodie's Passover Adventure. Topaz, Ksenia, illus. 2012. (Passover Ser.). (ENG.). 32p. (J). (gr. k-3). pap. 7.95 *(978-0-7613-5642-4(8)*, Kar-Ben Publishing) Lerner Publishing Group.

Levithan, David. Are We There Yet? 2007. (ENG.). 224p. (YA). (gr. 7-12). per. 8.99 *(978-0-375-83956-6(9)*, Knopf Bks. for Young Readers) Random Hse. Children's Bks.

Levitin, Sonia. Junk Man's Daughter. Porfirio, Guy, illus. rev. ed. 2007. (Tales of Young Americans Ser.). (ENG.). 32p. (J). (gr. 3-7). 17.95 *(978-1-58536-315-5(4))* Sleeping Bear Pr.

Lewis, Beverly. In Jesse's Shoes: Appreciating Kids with Special Needs. Nikiel, Laura Gibbons, illus. 2007. (ENG.). 32p. (J). (gr. -1-4). 11.99 *(978-0-7642-0313-8(4))* Bethany Hse. Pubs.

—What Is God Like? Querin, Pamela, illus. 2008. (ENG.). 32p. (J). (gr. -1-3). 14.99 *(978-0-7642-0466-1(1))* Bethany Hse. Pubs.

Lewis, R. C. Spinning Starlight. 2015. (ENG., Illus.). 336p. (YA). (gr. 7-12). 17.99 *(978-1-4231-8515-4(3))* Hyperion Bks. for Children.

Lewis, Richard. The Killing Sea. 2008. (ENG., Illus.). 256p. (YA). (gr. 7-12). mass mkt. 7.99 *(978-1-4169-5372-2(8)*, Simon Pulse) Simon Pulse.

Liberts, Jennifer. Go, Go, Trucks! Yamada, Mike, illus. 2017. (Step into Reading Ser.). (ENG.). 32p. (J). (gr. -1-1). 3.99 ***(978-0-399-54951-9(X))***; lib. bdg. 12.99 ***(978-0-399-54952-6(8))*** Random Hse. Children's Bks. (Random Hse. Bks. for Young Readers).

Lincoln, James. The Rainbow Jars. Smith, Jacqui, illus. 2013. 28p. (J). pap. 14.95 *(978-1-60131-153-5(2)*, Castlebridge Bks.) Big Tent Bks.

Lindenbaum, Pija. Bridget & the Moose Brothers. Board, Kjersti, tr. from SWE. 2004. (Illus.). 32p. (J). 16.00 *(978-91-29-66046-3(7))* R & S Bks. SWE. Dist: Macmillan.

Lindgren, Astrid & Crampton, Patricia. The Red Bird. Tornqvist, Marit, illus. 2005. (J). 5.99 *(978-0-439-62797-9(4)*, Levine, Arthur A. Bks.) Scholastic, Inc.

Lindsay, Maud. Mother Stories. 2005. 25.95 *(978-1-4218-1492-6(7))*; 120p. pap. 10.95 *(978-1-4218-1592-3(3))* 1st World Publishing, Inc. (1st World Library - Literary Society).

Linehan, Jess Golden. Martin Mixed-Up at the Beach. 2011. (ENG., Illus.). 32p. (J). 15.95 *(978-0-615-45705-5(3))* Salty Pond Pubs.

Liparulo, Robert. Gatekeepers, 1 vol. 2009. (Dreamhouse Kings Ser.: 3). (ENG.). 320p. pap. 9.99 *(978-1-59554-729-3(0))* Nelson, Thomas Inc.

—Whirlwind, 1 vol. 2010. (Dreamhouse Kings Ser.: 5). (ENG.). 320p. pap. 9.99 *(978-1-59554-892-4(0))* Nelson, Thomas Inc.

Liphardt, Linda. Secret in the Old Barn. 2008. 116p. pap. 19.95 *(978-1-60703-615-9(0))* America Star Bks.

Lisle, Holly. Ruby Key, Bk. 1. 2008. (ENG.). 384p. (J). *(978-0-545-00013-0(0)*, Orchard Bks.) Scholastic, Inc.

Little, Jean. Emma's Strange Pet. Plecas, Jennifer, illus. (I Can Read Level 3 Ser.). 64p. (J). (gr. k-3). 2004. (ENG.). pap. 3.99 *(978-0-06-444259-6(4))* 2003. 15.99 *(978-0-06-028350-6(5))* HarperCollins Pubs.

Little, Jennifer. My Brother Is Such a Slob! 2013. 24p. pap. 24.95 *(978-1-63000-879-6(6))* America Star Bks.

Littlewood, Kathryn. Bite-Sized Magic: A Bliss Novel. McGuire, Erin, illus. (Bliss Bakery Trilogy Ser.: 3). (ENG.). 432p. (J). (gr. 3-7). 2015. pap. 7.99 *(978-0-06-208427-9(5))* 2014. 16.99 *(978-0-06-208426-2(7))* HarperCollins Pubs. (Tegen, Katherine Bks).

—Bliss. (Bliss Bakery Trilogy Ser.: 1). (ENG.). (J). (gr. 3-7). 2013. 400p. pap. 7.99 *(978-0-06-208424-8(0))* 2012. 384p. 16.99 *(978-0-06-208423-1(2))* HarperCollins Pubs. (Tegen, Katherine Bks).

—A Dash of Magic: A Bliss Novel. McGuire, Erin, illus. 2013. (Bliss Bakery Trilogy Ser.: 2). (ENG.). 368p. (J). (gr. 3-7). 16.99 *(978-0-06-208429-3(1)*, Tegen, Katherine Bks) HarperCollins Pubs.

Llewellyn, Claire. Go Away, Baby!, 1 vol. Lovsin, Polona, illus. 2013. (Start Reading Ser.). (ENG.). 24p. (gr. k-1). pap. 7.95 *(978-1-4765-3183-0(8))*; pap. 41.94 *(978-1-4765-3214-1(1))* Capstone Press of Coughlan Cos.

Lloyd-Jones, Sally. His Royal Highness, King Baby: A Terrible True Story. Roberts, David, illus. 2017. (ENG.). 48p. (J). (gr. -1-3). 16.99 ***(978-0-7636-9793-8(1))*** Candlewick Pr.

Lobe, Mira & Kovács, Cécilie. Hoppelpopp & the Best Bunny. Kaufmann, Angelika, illus. 2015. (ENG.). 32p. (J). (gr. -1-3). 16.95 *(978-0-8234-3287-5(4))* Holiday Hse., Inc.

Loccisano, Rina. Baby Dario Eats His First Carrot. Baker, David, illus. 2012. 48p. pap. 24.95 *(978-1-4560-6100-5(3))* America Star Bks.

Loccisano, Rina Fuda. Little Rina Meets Baby Brother. Prouix, Denis, illus. 2011. 48p. pap. 24.95 *(978-1-4512-6299-5(X))* America Star Bks.

Loewen, Ann E. Fast for My Feet. 2013. 176p. *(978-1-4602-3384-9(0))* FriesenPress.

Lois, Lowry. Anastasia off Her Rocker. 2015. (Anastasia Krupnik Story Ser.). (ENG., Illus.). 160p. (J). (gr. 5-7). pap. 6.99 *(978-0-544-43959-7(7)*, HMH Books For Young Readers) Houghton Mifflin Harcourt Publishing Co.

—The Willoughbys. Lois, Lowry, illus. 2008. (ENG., Illus.). 176p. (J). (gr. 1-4). 17.99 *(978-0-618-97974-5(3))* Houghton Mifflin Harcourt Publishing Co.

—The Willoughbys. 2010. (ENG.). 176p. (J). (gr. 3-7). 6.99 *(978-0-385-73776-0(9)*, Yearling) Random Hse. Children's Bks.

London, C. Alexander. We Are Not Eaten by Yaks. (Accidental Adventure Ser.: 1). (ENG.). (J). (gr. 3-7). 2013. 384p. pap. 7.99 *(978-0-14-242056-0(5)*, Puffin Books) 2011. 224p. 12.99 *(978-0-399-25487-1(0)*, Philomel Bks.) Penguin Young Readers Group.

—We Dine with Cannibals. 2013. (Accidental Adventure Ser.: 2). (ENG.). 384p. (J). (gr. 3-7). pap. 7.99 *(978-0-14-242474-2(9)*, Puffin Books) Penguin Young Readers Group.

London, Jonathan. Froggy's Baby Sister. Remkiewicz, Frank, illus. 2005. (Froggy Ser.). (ENG.). 32p. (J). (gr. -1-k). pap. 6.99 *(978-0-14-240342-6(3)*, Puffin Books) Penguin Young Readers Group.

Long, Christopher E. & Warner, Gertrude Chandler. Tree House Mystery, 1 vol. Bloodworth, Mark, illus. 2010. (Boxcar Children Graphic Novels Ser.). (ENG.). 32p. (J). (gr. 2-5). 28.50 *(978-1-60270-716-0(2))* ABDO Publishing Co.

The Long Legged Turtle. 2013. 44p. pap. 16.99 *(978-1-4808-0460-9(6))* Archway Publishing.

Long, Loren & Bildner, Phil. Blastin' the Blues. Long, Loren, illus. 2011. (Sluggers Ser.: 5). (ENG., Illus.). 448p. (J). (gr. 3-7). pap. 8.99 *(978-1-4169-1891-2(4)*, Simon & Schuster Bks. For Young Readers) Simon & Schuster Bks. For Young Readers.

—Home of the Brave. Long, Loren, illus. (Sluggers Ser.: 6). (ENG., Illus.). 336p. (J). (gr. 3-7). 2011. pap. 8.99 *(978-1-4169-1892-9(2))* 2010. 15.99 *(978-1-4169-1868-4(X))* Simon & Schuster Bks. For Young Readers. (Simon & Schuster Bks. For Young Readers).

—Magic in the Outfield. Long, Loren, illus. 2009. (Sluggers Ser.: 1). (ENG., Illus.). 160p. (J). (gr. 3-7). pap. 8.99 *(978-1-4169-1884-4(1)*, Simon & Schuster Bks. For Young Readers) Simon & Schuster Bks. For Young Readers.

—Water, Water Everywhere. Long, Loren, illus. (Sluggers Ser.: 4). (ENG., Illus.). (J). (gr. 3-7). 2010. 288p. pap. 7.99 *(978-1-4169-1890-5(6))* 2009. 272p. 14.99 *(978-1-4169-1866-0(3))* Simon & Schuster Bks. For Young Readers. (Simon & Schuster Bks. For Young Readers).

Longson, D. M. The Scunner. 2009. 32p. pap. 21.50 *(978-1-4092-6995-3(7))* Lulu Pr., Inc.

Look, Lenore. Alvin Ho: Allergic to Girls, School, & Other Scary Things. Pham, LeUyen, illus. 2009. (Alvin Ho Ser.). (ENG.). 192p. (J). (gr. 1-4). 6.99 *(978-0-375-84930-5(0)*, Yearling) Random Hse. Children's Bks.

—Ruby Lu, Brave & True. Wilsdorf, Anne, illus. 2006. (Ruby Lu Ser.). 105p. (J). (gr. 1-5). 11.65 *(978-0-7569-6553-2(5))* Perfection Learning Corp.

Lopez Dekker, Anna. Everwhere. 2008. 137p. 31.95 *(978-1-4092-0318-6(2))* Lulu Pr., Inc.

Lord, Cynthia. Rules. 2009. 8.44 *(978-0-7848-2921-9(7)*, Everbind) Marco Bk. Co.

—Rules. 2008. (Illus.). 200p. (gr. 4-7). 17.00 *(978-0-7569-8283-6(9))* Perfection Learning Corp.

—Rules. (J). 2008. 77.49 *(978-1-4361-5837-4(0))* 2007. 220.75 *(978-1-4281-5209-0(1))* 2007. 89.75 *(978-1-4281-5212-0(1))* 2007. 87.75 *(978-1-4281-5214-4(8))* 2007. 74.75 *(978-1-4281-5208-3(3))* 2007. (SPA.). 72.75 *(978-1-4281-5210-6(5))* Recorded Bks., Inc.

—Rules. (ENG.). (J). (gr. 3-7). 2008. 224p. pap. 7.99 *(978-0-439-44383-8(0)*, Scholastic Paperbacks) 2006. 208p. 15.99 *(978-0-439-44382-1(2)*, Scholastic Pr.) Scholastic, Inc.

—Rules. rev. l.t. ed. 2007. (Literacy Bridge Middle Reader Ser.). 191p. (J). (gr. 4-7). 23.95 *(978-0-7862-9559-3(7))* Thorndike Pr.

—Rules. 2008. lib. bdg. 17.20 *(978-1-4178-2956-9(7))* Turtleback Bks.

Louise, Zanni. Too Busy Sleeping. 2015. (Illus.). 32p. (J). (— 1). 18.99 *(978-1-74297-962-5(9))* Little Hare Bks. AUS. Dist: Independent Pubs. Group.

Loving, Winifred "Oyoko". My Grandma Loves to Play. 2013. 28p. pap. 16.99 *(978-1-4669-7405-0(2))* Trafford Publishing.

Lowden, Stephanie. Time of the Eagle: A Story of an Ojibwe Winter. 2004. 128p. (J). pap. 12.00 *(978-1-883953-34-8(0))* Great Lakes Literary, LLC.

Lowden, Stephanie Golightly. Time of the Eagle: A Story of an Ojibwe Winter. 2006. 127p. (J). (gr. 3-7). 18.95 *(978-1-883953-38-6(3)*, Blue Horse Books) Great Lakes Literary, LLC.

Lowell, Susan. The Great Grand Canyon Time Train. Shroades, John / W., illus. 2011. 32p. (J). 15.95 *(978-1-933855-63-9(0))* Rio Nuevo Pubs.

Lowry, Brigid. Follow the Blue. 2004. (ENG.). 205p. (J). (gr. 7-18). tchr. ed. 16.95 *(978-0-8234-1827-5(8))* Holiday Hse., Inc.

—Follow the Blue. 2006. (ENG.). 208p. (YA). (gr. 8-12). pap. 18.99 *(978-0-312-34297-5(7)*, 9780312342975, St. Martin's Griffin) St. Martin's Pr.

Lu, Marie. Legend. aut. ltd. collector's ed. 2013. (Legend Trilogy: Bk. 1). (Illus.). 306p. (YA). mass mkt. 100.00 net. *(978-1-934267-38-7(4))* Gauntlet, Inc.

—Legend. 2011. (Legend Trilogy: Bk. 1). (ENG.). (YA). (gr. 8-12). 54.99 *(978-1-61657-044-6(X)*, Penguin AudioBooks) Penguin Publishing Group.

—Legend. (Legend Ser.: 1). (ENG.). (YA). (gr. 7). 2013. 352p. pap. 9.99 *(978-0-14-242207-6(X)*, Speak) 2011. 320p. 17.99 *(978-0-399-25675-2(X)*, G.P. Putnam's Sons Books for Young Readers) Penguin Young Readers Group.

—Legend. l.t. ed. 2012. (Legend Trilogy: Bk. 1). (ENG.). 394p. (J). (gr. 7-12). 23.99 *(978-1-4104-4606-0(9))* Thorndike Pr.

—Legend. (Legend Graphic Novels Ser.: 1). 2015. lib. bdg. 26.95 *(978-0-606-38424-7(3))* 2013. lib. bdg. 20.85 *(978-0-606-31701-6(5)*, Turtleback) Turtleback Bks.

Lubar, David. Curse of the Campfire Weenies: And Other Warped & Creepy Tales. 2008. (Weenies Stories Ser.). (ENG.). 208p. (J). (gr. 4-9). mass mkt. 5.99 *(978-0-7653-5771-7(2)*, 9780765357717, Starscape) Doherty, Tom Assocs., LLC.

—Dinosaur Disaster. Loveridge, Matt, illus. 2013. (Looniverse Ser.: 3). (ENG.). 96p. (J). (gr. 1-3). 15.99 *(978-0-545-49605-6(5))*; pap. 4.99 *(978-0-545-49606-3(3))* Scholastic, Inc.

—Dinosaur Disaster. 2013. (Looniverse Ser.: 3). lib. bdg. 14.75 *(978-0-606-32367-3(8)*, Turtleback) Turtleback Bks.

—The Gloomy Ghost. 2014. (Monsterrific Tales Ser.). (ENG., Illus.). 144p. (J). (gr. 3-7). 15.99 *(978-0-7653-3080-2(6)*, 9780765330802, Starscape) Doherty, Tom Assocs., LLC.

—Sleeping Freshmen Never Lie. 2007. (ENG.). 288p. (YA). (gr. 7-18). 10.99 *(978-0-14-240780-6(1)*, Speak) Penguin Young Readers Group.

Lucado, Max. Itsy Bitsy Christmas: You're Never Too Little for His Love, 1 vol. 2013. (ENG., Illus.). 32p. (J). pap. 9.99 *(978-1-4003-2404-0(1))* Nelson, Thomas Inc.

Luchesi, Dennis. Benji Rabbit. 2013. 24p. pap. 24.95 *(978-1-62709-894-6(1))* America Star Bks.

Luciani, Brigitte. A Hubbub. Gauvin, Edward, tr. from FRE. Tharlet, Eve, illus. 2010. (Mr. Badger & Mrs. Fox Ser.: 2). (ENG.). 32p. (J). (gr. k-3). pap. 6.95 *(978-0-7613-5632-5(0)*, Graphic Universe™)Bk. 2. 25.26 *(978-0-7613-5626-4(6))* Lerner Publishing Group.

—The Meeting. Burrell, Carol, tr. from FRE. Tharlet, Eve, illus. 2010. (Mr. Badger & Mrs. Fox Ser.: 1). (ENG.). 32p. (J). (gr. k-3). lib. bdg. 25.26 *(978-0-7613-5625-7(8))* Lerner Publishing Group.

—The Meeting. Burrell, Carol, tr. from FRE. Tharlet, Eve, illus. 2010. 1. (ENG.). 32p. (C). (gr. k-3). pap. 10.95 *(978-0-7613-5631-8(2))* National Geographic School Publishing, Inc.

—Peace & Quiet. Burrell, Carol, tr. Tharlet, Eve, illus. 2012. (Mr. Badger & Mrs. Fox Ser.: 4). (ENG.). 32p. (J). (gr. k-3). pap. 6.95 *(978-0-8225-9163-4(4))*; lib. bdg. 25.26 *(978-0-7613-8520-2(7))* Lerner Publishing Group. (Graphic Universe™).

—What a Team! Gauvin, Edward, tr. from FRE. Tharlet, Eve, illus. 2011. (Mr. Badger & Mrs. Fox Ser.: 3). (ENG.). 32p. (J). (gr. k-3). 25.26 *(978-0-7613-5627-1(4))* Lerner Publishing Group.

Lunney, Linda Hayward. Monster Bug. Palmisciano, Diane, tr. Palmisciano, Diane, illus. 2004. (Science Solves It! Ser.). 32p. (J). pap. 5.95 *(978-1-57565-135-4(1))* Kane Press, Inc.

Luongo, Jane. Jake's First Word. Kelley, Patrick, illus. 2003. (Books for Young Learners). 16p. (J). 5.75 net. *(978-1-57274-258-1(5)*, 2456, Bks. for Young Learners) Owen, Richard C. Pubs., Inc.

Lupica, Mike. Heat. 2007. (ENG.). 256p. (J). (gr. 5-18). 7.99 *(978-0-14-240757-8(7)*, Puffin Books) Penguin Young Readers Group.

—Heat. 2007. 220p. (gr. 5-9). 18.00 *(978-0-7569-8131-0(X))* Perfection Learning Corp.

—Hot Hand, 1 vol. 2012. (Comeback Kids Ser.). (ENG.). 176p. (J). (gr. 4-8). lib. bdg. 27.07 *(978-1-59961-175-4(9))* Spotlight.

Lupica, Mike. Last Man Out. (ENG.). (J). (gr. 5). 2017. 272p. 8.99 ***(978-0-14-751491-2(6)***, Puffin Books) 2016. 256p. 17.99 *(978-0-399-17279-3(3)*, Philomel Bks.) Penguin Young Readers Group.

Lynch, Chris. Angry Young Man. 2012. (ENG.). 192p. (YA). (gr. 7). pap. 10.99 *(978-1-4424-5419-4(9)*, Simon & Schuster Bks. For Young Readers) Simon & Schuster Bks. For Young Readers.

—The Gravedigger's Cottage. 2004. (ENG.). 208p. (J). (gr. 7-18). 15.99 *(978-0-06-623940-8(0))* HarperCollins Pubs.

—World War II Book 2: Dead in the Water. 2014. (World War II Ser.: 2). (ENG.). 192p. (J). (gr. 5-9). 18.99 *(978-0-545-52298-4(6)*, Scholastic Pr.) Scholastic, Inc.

Lynn, Deidre. Treasure Delight: A Sweet Story about the Joy in Sharing. Morris, Jessica, illus. 2013. 36p. pap. 12.95 *(978-0-9893181-0-5(9))* LoveLight Media.

Lynn, Joseph. Color of My Words. 2014. (ENG.). 144p. (J). (gr. 5-12). 10.24 *(978-1-63245-277-1(4))* Lectorum Pubns., Inc.

Lyons, Maggie. Vin & Dorky Duet. 2012. 94p. pap. 9.95 *(978-1-61244-091-0(6))* Halo Publishing International.

Lyons-Reid, Nashika. My Brother the Superhero. 2008. 28p. pap. 15.99 *(978-1-4363-5941-2(4))* Xlibris Corp.

MacDonald, George. The History of Gutta-Percha Willie. 2006. 116p. per. 9.95 *(978-1-59818-578-2(0))* Aegypan.

—Ranald Bannermans Boyhood. 2006. 168p. per. 13.95 *(978-1-59818-238-5(2))* Aegypan.

MacDonald, Maryann. No Room for Francie. Richards, Virginia Helen, illus. 2010. 64p. (J). (gr. 1-3). pap. 6.95 *(978-0-8198-5168-0(X))* Pauline Bks. & Media.

MacDonald, Tom. Secret of the Tree: Marcus Speer's Ecosentinel. Stieber, Joel, illus. 2009. 300p. pap. 18.95 *(978-0-595-52402-0(8))* iUniverse, Inc.

Mack, Harry. The Treasure Mystery Clues. 2011. 70p. pap. 19.95 *(978-1-4626-2487-4(1))* America Star Bks.

Mack, Paulette. Cookout at Grandma's House: The Adventures of Mielle & Cheeky. 2006. (ENG., Illus.). 24p. per. 10.95 *(978-1-59800-998-9(2))* Outskirts Pr., Inc.

Mackall, Dandi Daley. Natalie Wants a Puppy, 1 vol. Blakeslee, Lys, illus. 2009. (That's Nat! Ser.). (ENG.). 96p. (J). (gr. 1-4). pap. 4.99 *(978-0-310-71571-9(7))* Zonderkidz.

—The Silence of Murder. (ENG.). 336p. (YA). (gr. 9). 2012. pap. 9.99 *(978-0-375-87293-8(0)*, Ember) 2011. 16.99 *(978-0-375-86896-2(8)*, Knopf Bks. for Young Readers) Random Hse. Children's Bks.

—There's a Baby in There!, 0 vols. Whitt, Carlynn, illus. 2012. (ENG.). 32p. (J). (gr. -1-3). 16.99 *(978-0-7614-6191-3(4)*, 9780761461913, Amazon Children's Publishing) Amazon Publishing.

MacKenzie, Carine. El Secreto de la Hermana Mayor, el Maria.Tr. of Big Sister's Secret. (SPA.). (J). 1.99 *(978-1-56063-700-4(5)*, 497731) Editorial Unilit.

MacLachlan, Patricia. The Boxcar Children Beginning. Jessell, Tim, illus. (Boxcar Children Mysteries Ser.). (ENG.). 144p. (J). (gr. 1-5). 2013. 6.99 *(978-0-8075-6617-6(9))* 2012. 16.99 *(978-0-8075-6616-9(0))* Whitman, Albert & Co.

—Fly Away. 2014. (ENG., Illus.). 128p. (J). (gr. 2). 15.99 *(978-1-4424-6008-9(3)*, McElderry, Margaret K. Bks.) McElderry, Margaret K. Bks.

—The True Gift. Floca, Brian, illus. 2013. (ENG.). 112p. (J). (gr. 2-6). pap. 6.99 *(978-1-4424-8858-8(1)*, Atheneum Bks. for Young Readers) Simon & Schuster Children's Publishing.

Maddox, Jake. Cycling Champion, 1 vol. Garcia, Eduardo, illus. 2012. (Jake Maddox Sports Stories Ser.). (ENG.). 72p. (gr. 2-3). pap. 5.95 *(978-1-4342-3904-4(7))*; lib. bdg. 25.32 *(978-1-4342-3290-8(5))* Stone Arch Bks.

Mader, Jan. My Brother Wants to Be Like Me. Palmer, Kate Salley, illus. l.t. ed. 2005. (ENG.). 16p. (gr. k-2). pap. 7.95 *(978-1-879835-27-6(4)*, Kaeden Bks.) Kaeden Corp.

The Madrona Heroes Register: Echoes of the Past. 2013. (Illus.). 344p. pap. 12.43 *(978-0-9899905-4-7(0))* Atelier Mythologie.

Madrzak, Carole. The Arronna Crystal. 2012. 234p. pap. 24.95 *(978-1-4137-9968-2(X))* America Star Bks.

Magnin, Joyce. Jelly Bean Summer. 2017. (ENG.). 272p. (J). (gr. 3-7). 16.99 *(978-1-4926-4672-3(5)*, Sourcebooks Jabberwocky) Sourcebooks, Inc.

Magoon, Kekla. Fire in the Streets. 2013. (ENG., Illus.). 352p. (J). (gr. 5-9). pap. 7.99 *(978-1-4424-2231-5(9)*, Aladdin) Simon & Schuster Children's Publishing.

—The Rock & the River. 2009. (ENG.). 304p. (J). (gr. 5-9). 17.99 *(978-1-4169-7582-3(9)*, Aladdin) Simon & Schuster Children's Publishing.

Magoon, Kekla & Keene, Carolyn. Strangers on a Train. 2013. (Nancy Drew Diaries: 2). (ENG.). 208p. (J). (gr. 3-7). pap. 6.99 *(978-1-4169-9073-4(9)*, Aladdin) Simon & Schuster Children's Publishing.

Maher, Mickle Brandt. Master Stitchum & the Moon. Dousias, Spiro, illus. 2003. (J). 19.99 *(978-1-932188-01-1(0))* Bollix Bks.

Mahmoodian, Maryam. Muslim Teens In: Pitfalls & Pranks. 2008. (YA). per. 10.95 *(978-0-9793577-3-2(X))* Muslim Writers Publishing.

Mahoney, Jerry. My Stupid Stepbrother Ruined Aladdin. Bitskoff, Aleksei, illus. 2017. (J). lib. bdg. ***(978-1-4965-4464-3(1))*** Stone Arch Bks.

—My Stupid Stepbrother Ruined Beauty & the Beast. 2017. (J). lib. bdg. ***(978-1-4965-4465-0(X))*** Stone Arch Bks.

Mahoney, Jerry. My Stupid Stepbrother Ruined Cinderella. 2017. (J). lib. bdg. *(978-1-4965-4466-7(8))* Stone Arch Bks.

Maier, Inger M. Ben's Flying Flowers. Bogade, Maria, illus. 2012. (J). 14.95 *(978-1-4338-1133-3(2))*; pap. 9.95 *(978-1-4338-1132-6(4))* American Psychological Assn. (Magination Pr.).

—When Lizzie Was Afraid: Of Trying New Things. Candon, Jennifer, illus. 2004. 32p. (J). 14.95 *(978-1-59147-170-7(2))*; pap. 9.95 *(978-1-59147-171-4(0))* American Psychological Assn. (Magination Pr.).

Mair, J. Samia. The Great Race to Sycamore Street. 2013. (ENG., Illus.). 196p. (J). (gr. 3-6). pap. 12.99 *(978-1-84774-057-1(X))* Kube Publishing Ltd. GBR. Dist: Consortium Bk. Sales & Distribution.

Malcolm, Jahnna N. Pirate's Revenge. Comport, Sally Wern, illus. 2003. 77p. (J). *(978-1-931020-09-1(4))* HOP, LLC.

Malea. Princess Melia. 2007. 145p. (J). pap. 15.95 *(978-1-58909-367-6(4))* Bookstand Publishing.

Malison, Anna. Through Thick & Thin. 2006. (ENG.). 136p. per. *(978-1-897117-14-9(0))* Gospel Folio Pr.

Maltese, John. I Love You the Most. 2009. 33p. pap. 16.40 *(978-0-557-09465-3(8))* Lulu Pr., Inc.

Mammay, Judith. Knowing Joseph. (ENG., Illus.). 256p. (J). (gr. 2-7). 2009. pap. 8.95 *(978-1-933831-06-0(5))* 2008. 13.95 *(978-1-933831-05-3(7))* Blooming Tree Pr.

Mancusi, Mari. Shattered. (Scorched Ser.: 2). (ENG.). (YA). 2015. 416p. (gr. 8-12). pap. 9.99 *(978-1-4926-0869-1(6))* 2014. 400p. (gr. 7-12). 16.99 *(978-1-4022-8461-8(6)*, 9781402284618) Sourcebooks, Inc.

Mandarino, Gene. What's Autism? 2006. pap. 25.00 *(978-0-9786795-0-7(4))* Charlie's Gift.

Mangum, James A. & Spires, Sidney. The Fairy the Chupacabra & Those Marfa Lights: A West Texas Fable. Mangum, James A., illus. 2008. (Illus.). 32p. (J). 17.95 *(978-0-9798391-5-3(7))* Hardy, John M. Publishing Co.

Manivong, Laura. Escaping the Tiger. 2010. (ENG.). 224p. (J). (gr. 5-18). 15.99 *(978-0-06-166177-8(5))* HarperCollins Pubs.

Mannering, Rose. The Spotty Dotty Daffodil. Straker, Bethany, illus. 2014. (ENG.). 32p. (J). (gr. -1-k). 16.95 *(978-1-62636-346-5(3)*, Sky Pony Pr.) Skyhorse Publishing Co., Inc.

Mansfield, Keith. Star Blaze. 2010. (Johnny Mackintosh,Johnny Mackintosh Trilogy Ser.: 2). (ENG.). 276p. (J). (gr. 4-6). pap. 8.99 *(978-1-84916-126-8(7))* Quercus GBR. Dist: Hachette Bk. Group.

Manushkin, Fran. Big Brothers Are the Best, 1 vol. Richards, Kirsten, illus. 2012. (Fiction Picture Bks.). (ENG.). 24p. (gr. -1 — 1). 6.95 *(978-1-4048-7224-0(8))*; lib. bdg. 22.65 *(978-1-4048-7137-3(3))* Picture Window Bks. (Fiction Picture Bks.).

—Big Sisters Are the Best, 1 vol. Richards, Kirsten, illus. 2012. (Fiction Picture Bks.). (ENG.). 24p. (gr. -1 — 1). 6.95 *(978-1-4048-7225-7(6))*; lib. bdg. 22.65 *(978-1-4048-7138-0(1))* Picture Window Bks. (Fiction Picture Bks.).

Marciniak, Christine. Lights, Camera, Ali! 2013. 232p. pap. 13.99 *(978-1-61271-214-7(2))* Zumaya Pubns. LLC.

Marcionette, Jake. Just Jake: Dog Eat Dog. Villa, Victor Rivas, illus. 2015. (Just Jake Ser.: No. 2). (ENG.). 196p. (J). (gr. 3-7). 11.99 *(978-0-448-46693-4(7)*, Grosset & Dunlap) Penguin Young Readers Group.

Maresca, Beth Anne, illus. Megan Owlet. 2015. (ENG.). 32p. (J). (gr. -1-k). 16.99 *(978-1-63220-404-2(5)*, Sky Pony Pr.) Skyhorse Publishing Co., Inc.

Margaret I. Pascuzzo. Anton Finds a Treasure. Bicking, Judith, illus. 2008. 16p. pap. 12.00 *(978-1-4251-8683-8(1))* Trafford Publishing.

Margolis, Leslie. Girl's Best Friend. (Maggie Brooklyn Mystery Ser.). (ENG.). (YA). (gr. 3-12). 2011. 288p. pap. 7.99 *(978-1-59990-690-4(2)*, 9781599906904) 2010. 272p. 14.99 *(978-1-59990-525-9(6)*, 9781599905259) Bloomsbury Publishing USA. (Bloomsbury USA Childrens).

—The Secrets at the Chocolate Mansion. 2013. (Maggie Brooklyn Mystery Ser.). (ENG.). 256p. (YA). (gr. 3-6). 16.99 *(978-1-61963-036-9(2)*, 9781619630369, Bloomsbury USA Childrens) Bloomsbury Publishing USA.

—Secrets at the Chocolate Mansion. 2014. (Maggie Brooklyn Mystery Ser.). (ENG.). 272p. (YA). (gr. 3-6). pap. 7.99 *(978-1-61963-493-0(7)*, 9781619634930, Bloomsbury USA Childrens) Bloomsbury Publishing USA.

—Vanishing Acts. (Maggie Brooklyn Mystery Ser.). (ENG.). (YA). (gr. 3-6). 2013. 256p. pap. 6.99 *(978-1-59990-981-3(2)*,

A
B

9781599909813) 2012. 240p. 15.99 *(978-1-59990-536-5(1)*, 9781599905365) Bloomsbury Publishing USA. (Bloomsbury USA Childrens).

Marinsky, Jane. Just Perfect. 2012. (Illus.). 32p. (J). (gr. k). 16.95 *(978-1-56792-428-2(X))* Godine, David R. Pub.

Marmon, Jim. Alexander Barnaby Meadowlark. 2007. 132p. per. 19.95 *(978-1-4241-7662-5(X))* America Star Bks.

Marquess, Dana. Night of the Lighted Freedom - A Firefly Fantasy. 2006. (ENG., Illus.). 32p. (J). 19.95 *(978-1-932278-06-4(0))* Mayhaven Publishing, Inc.

Marquis, Michelle. Mikey & the Mysterious Door. 2008. 32p. pap. 14.99 *(978-1-4343-4823-4(7))* AuthorHouse.

Marr, Ella J. The Adventures of Curtis & Grammy. 2006. 57p. pap. 16.95 *(978-1-4241-4743-4(3))* PublishAmerica, Inc.

Marsden, Carolyn. The White Zone. 2012. (Exceptional Reading & Language Arts Titles for Intermediate Grades Ser.). (ENG.). 192p. (J). (gr. 4-8). 17.95 *(978-0-7613-7383-4(7)*, Carolrhoda Bks.) Lerner Publishing Group.

Marsh, Carole. The Behemoth Blizzard Mystery. (Masters of Disasters Ser.). (Illus.). 118p. (J). (gr. 3-5). 2008. per. 5.99 *(978-0-635-06464-6(2))* 2007. 14.95 *(978-0-635-06467-7(7))* Gallopade International.

—The Colonial Caper Mystery at Williamsburg. 2009. (Real Kids, Real Places Ser.). (J). (gr. 2-9). lib. bdg. 18.99 *(978-0-635-06832-3(X))*; (Illus.). 143p. (gr. 4-7). pap. 7.99 *(978-0-635-06826-2(5)*, Marsh, Carole Bks.) Gallopade International.

—The Earthshaking Earthquake Mystery! 2007. (Masters of Disasters Ser.). (Illus.). 118p. (J). (gr. 2-9). per. 5.99 *(978-0-635-06339-7(5))* Gallopade International.

—The Ferocious Forest Fire Mystery. 2008. (Masters of Disasters Ser.). (Illus.). 118p. (J). (gr. 3-5). 14.95 *(978-0-635-06468-4(5))*; per. 5.99 *(978-0-635-06465-3(0))* Gallopade International.

—The Ghost of the Golden Gate Bridge. 2009. (Real Kids, Real Places Ser.). (Illus.). 146p. (J). lib. bdg. 18.99 *(978-0-635-07047-0(2)*, Marsh, Carole Mysteries) Gallopade International.

—The Horrendous Hurricane Mystery. 2007. (Carole Marsh Mysteries Ser.). (Illus.). 118p. (J). (gr. 2-9). per. 7.99 *(978-0-635-06340-3(9))* Gallopade International.

—The Mystery at Fort Thunderbolt. 2007. (Pretty Darn Scary Mysteries Ser.). (Illus.). 113p. (YA). lib. bdg. 18.99 *(978-0-635-07021-0(9)*, Marsh, Carole Mysteries) Gallopade International.

—The Mystery at Mount Vernon. Friedlander, Randolyn, illus. 2010. (Real Kids, Real Places Ser.). 32p. pap. 7.99 *(978-0-635-07444-7(3)*, Marsh, Carole Mysteries) Gallopade International.

—The Mystery at Mount Vernon: Home of America's First President George Washington. 2010. (Real Kids, Real Places Ser.). (Illus.). 158p. (J). 18.99 *(978-0-635-07443-0(5)*, Marsh, Carole Mysteries) Gallopade International.

—The Mystery at Yellowstone National Park. 2010. (Real Kids, Real Places Ser.). (Illus.). 158p. (J). 18.99 *(978-0-635-07437-9(0)*, Marsh, Carole Mysteries) Gallopade International.

—The Mystery in Hawaii. Friedlander, Randolyn, illus. 2010. (Real Kids, Real Places Ser.). 32p. pap. 7.99 *(978-0-635-07447-8(8)*, Marsh, Carole Mysteries) Gallopade International.

—The Mystery in Hawaii: The 50th State. 2010. (Real Kids, Real Places Ser.). (Illus.). 157p. (J). 18.99 *(978-0-635-07446-1(X)*, Marsh, Carole Mysteries) Gallopade International.

—The Mystery in Las Vegas. 2009. (Real Kids, Real Places Ser.). (Illus.). 145p. (J). lib. bdg. 18.99 *(978-0-635-07045-6(6)*, Marsh, Carole Mysteries) Gallopade International.

—The Mystery of the Graveyard of the Atlantic. 2009. (Real Kids, Real Places Ser.). (Illus.). 144p. (J). lib. bdg. 18.99 *(978-0-635-07046-3(4)*, Marsh, Carole Mysteries) Gallopade International.

—The Mystery of the Haunted Ghost Town. 2009. (Real Kids, Real Places Ser.). 144p. (J). 18.99 *(978-0-635-07044-9(8)*, Marsh, Carole Mysteries) Gallopade International.

—The Mystery on the Oregon Trail. 2010. (Real Kids, Real Places Ser.). (Illus.). 158p. (J). 18.99 *(978-0-635-07440-9(0)*, Marsh, Carole Mysteries) Gallopade International.

—The Mystery on the Oregon Trail. Friedlander, Randolyn, illus. 2010. (Real Kids, Real Places Ser.). 32p. pap. 7.99 *(978-0-635-07441-6(9)*, Marsh, Carole Mysteries) Gallopade International.

—The Secret of Eyesocket Island. 2009. (Pretty Darn Scary Mysteries Ser.). (Illus.). 113p. (J). lib. bdg. 18.99 *(978-0-635-07022-7(7)*, Marsh, Carole Mysteries) Gallopade International.

—The Treacherous Tornado Mystery. 2007. (Masters of Disasters Ser.). (Illus.). 118p. (J). (gr. 2-9). 14.95 *(978-0-635-06394-6(8))*; per. 5.99 *(978-0-635-06338-0(7))* Gallopade International.

—The Voracious Volcano Mystery. 2008. (Masters of Disasters Ser.). (Illus.). 118p. (J). (gr. 3-5). 14.95 *(978-0-635-06466-0(9))*; per. 5.99 *(978-0-635-06463-9(4))* Gallopade International.

Marshall, Carly. The Babysitter & Little Mr. Trouble Maker. 2013. 24p. 24.95 *(978-1-63000-616-7(5))*; pap. 24.95 *(978-1-63000-539-9(8))* America Star Bks.

Martens, Kara. The Two Missing Kids. 2008. 80p. pap. 11.49 *(978-1-4343-8696-0(1))* AuthorHouse.

Martín Anguita, Carmen & Carmen, Martin Anguita. El Primer Día de Colegio de David. Cortazar, Alicia Canas, illus. 2008. (SPA.). 32p. (J). 10.99 *(978-84-241-5790-6(7))* Everest Editora ESP. Dist: Lectorum Pubns., Inc.

Martin, Ann M. Ten Good & Bad Things about My Life (So Far) 2012. (ENG.). 272p. (J). (gr. 4-7). 16.99 *(978-0-312-64299-0(7)*, 9780312642990) Feiwel & Friends.

Martin, Brian. The Lost Ring. McDonald, Kim, illus. 2007. 42p. (J). *(978-0-9798059-1-2(0))* Lunchbox Stories Inc.

Martin, C. L. Ducky Goes to the Dentist. 2013. 16p. pap. 24.95 *(978-1-62709-742-0(2))* America Star Bks.

Martin, David. Three Little Bears Play All Day. Gutierrez, Akemi, illus. 2010. (Brand New Readers Ser.). (ENG.). 48p. (J). (gr. -1-3). pap. 5.99 *(978-0-7636-4230-3(4))* Candlewick Pr.

Martin, Gary, et al. The Maiden of Thunder, 1 vol. Cariello, Sergio & Lanphear, Dave, illus. 2008. (Z Graphic Novels / Son of Samson Ser.). (ENG.). 160p. (J). (gr. 4-7). pap. 6.99 *(978-0-310-71281-7(5))* Zondervan.

Martin, Lisa & Martin, Valerie. Anton & Cecil, Book 2: Cats on Track. Murphy, Kelly, illus. 2016. (Anton & Cecil Ser.: 2). (ENG.). 272p. (J). (gr. 3-7). pap. 6.95 *(978-1-61620-638-3(1))* Algonquin Bks. of Chapel Hill.

Maschari, Jennifer. The Remarkable Journey of Charlie Price. 2016. 304p. (J). (gr. 3-7). 16.99 *(978-0-06-238010-4(9))* HarperCollins Pubs.

Masessa, Ed. Wandmaker. 2016. (ENG.). 336p. (J). (gr. 3-7). 12.99 *(978-0-545-86174-8(8)*, Scholastic Pr.) Scholastic, Inc.

Mason, Craig. Turtle Games. Mason, Bergetta, illus. 2003. 32p. (J). 4.99 *(978-0-9729153-0-4(3))* 1 Sleeve Publishing.

Masters, Susan Rowan. Night Journey to Vicksburg. Killcoyne, Hope L., ed. Smith, Duane A., illus. 2003. (Adventures in America Ser.). 74p. (gr. 4). 14.95 *(978-1-893110-30-4(3))* Silver Moon Pr.

Matheson, Shirlee Smith. Gambler's Daughter. 2009. (ENG.). 144p. (YA). pap. 11.99 *(978-1-55002-718-1(2)*, Sandcastle Bks.) Dundurn CAN. Dist: Ingram Publisher Services.

Mathieu, Jennifer. Afterward. 2016. (ENG.). 320p. (YA). 17.99 *(978-1-62672-238-5(2)*, 9781626722385) Roaring Brook Pr.

—Afterward. 2017. (ENG.). 336p. (YA). pap. 9.99 ***(978-1-250-12962-8(1)***, 9781250129628) Square Fish.

—Afterward. 2017. (YA). lib. bdg. 20.85 ***(978-0-606-40590-4(9))*** Turtleback Bks.

Mathieu, Jennifer. Devoted. 2015. (ENG.). 336p. (YA). (gr. 7). 16.99 *(978-1-59643-911-5(4)*, 9781596439115) Roaring Brook Pr.

Matsakis, Cynthia. Sister Sun, Brother Storm. Silver, Jane, illus. 2012. 32p. 24.95 *(978-1-4575-0768-7(4))* Dog Ear Publishing, LLC.

Matt & Dave. Yuck's Pet Worm. Baines, Nigel, illus. 2013. (Yuck Ser.). (ENG.). 112p. (J). (gr. 2-5). 15.99 *(978-1-4424-8150-3(1))*; pap. 6.99 *(978-1-4424-8149-7(8))* Simon & Schuster/Paula Wiseman Bks. (Simon & Schuster/Paula Wiseman Bks.).

—Yuck's Robotic Butt Blast. Baines, Nigel, illus. 2013. (Yuck Ser.). (ENG.). 112p. (J). (gr. 2-5). pap. 4.99 *(978-1-4424-8309-5(1)*, Simon & Schuster/Paula Wiseman Bks.) Simon & Schuster/Paula Wiseman Bks.

Matthews, Morgan & Sinden, David. Yuck's Robotic Butt Blast. Baines, Nigel, illus. 2013. (Yuck Ser.). (ENG.). 112p. (J). (gr. 2-5). 15.99 *(978-1-4424-8308-8(3)*, Simon & Schuster/Paula Wiseman Bks.) Simon & Schuster/Paula Wiseman Bks.

Matthews, Owen. How to Win at High School. 2015. (ENG.). 496p. (YA). (gr. 9). 17.99 *(978-0-06-233686-6(X)*, HarperTeen) HarperCollins Pubs.

Maxwell, John C. Sometimes You Win — Sometimes You Learn for Kids. Björkman, Steve, illus. 2016. (ENG.). 32p. (J). (gr. -1-3). 18.00 *(978-0-316-28408-0(4))* Little Brown & Co.

May, Eleanor. Albert Adds Up! Melmon, Deborah, illus. 2014. (Mouse Math (r) Ser.). 32p. (J). (gr. -1-1). 22.60 *(978-1-57565-744-8(9))* Kane Press, Inc.

—The Great Shape-up. 2008. pap. 34.95 *(978-1-58013-763-8(6))* Kane Press, Inc.

—The Great Shape-up. Gott, Barry, illus. 2007. (Science Solves It! Ser.). 32p. (J). (gr. -1-3). pap. 5.95 *(978-1-57565-248-1(X))* Kane Press, Inc.

—Keesha's Bright Idea. Wummer, Amy, illus. 2008. (Social Studies Connects Ser.). 32p. (J). (gr. -1-3). pap. 5.95 *(978-1-57565-273-3(0))* Kane Press, Inc.

—Keesha's Bright Idea. Wummer, Amy, illus. 2009. (Social Studies Connects (r) Ser.). (ENG.). (gr. 1-3). pap. 33.92 *(978-0-7613-4806-1(9))* Lerner Publishing Group.

Mayer, Mercer. Bedtime Stories - Little Critter. Mayer, Mercer, illus. 2013. (Little Critter Ser.). (ENG., Illus.). 144p. (J). (gr. -1-3). pap. 11.99 *(978-0-06-223640-1(7)*, HarperFestival) HarperCollins Pubs.

—It's Easter, Little Critter! Mayer, Mercer, illus. 2007. (Little Critter Ser.). (ENG., Illus.). 20p. (J). (gr. -1-1). pap. 6.99 *(978-0-06-053974-0(7)*, HarperFestival) HarperCollins Pubs.

—Just a Little Too Little. 2012. (Little Critter Ser.). (Illus.). (J). lib. bdg. 13.55 *(978-0-606-23567-9(1)*, Turtleback) Turtleback Bks.

—Little Critter(r) I Am Sharing. 2012. (Little Critter Ser.). (ENG., Illus.). 24p. (J). (gr. k — 1). bds. 6.95 *(978-1-4027-9747-7(8))* Sterling Publishing Co., Inc.

Mayer, Mercer & Mayer, Gina. The New Potty. 2003. (Look-Look Ser.). (ENG., Illus.). 24p. (J). (-k). pap. 3.99 *(978-0-375-82631-3(9)*, Random Hse. Bks. for Young Readers) Random Hse. Children's Bks.

Mazurick, Shannon K. Gemm: The Treasure Hunt with Griffin. 2012. 32p. pap. 19.99 *(978-1-4772-7740-9(4))* AuthorHouse.

Mbuthia, Waithira. My Sister's Wedding: A Story of Kenya. Karanja, Geoffrey Gacheru, illus. 2005. (Make Friends Around the World Ser.). (ENG.). 32p. (J). (gr. k-3). 19.95 *(978-1-56899-898-5(8)*, BC8006); 15.95 *(978-1-56899-896-1(1)*, B8006) Soundprints.

McAllister, Margaret. 15 Things Not to Do with a Baby. Sterling, Holly, illus. 2015. (15 Things Not to Do Ser.). (ENG.). 32p. (J). (gr. -1-1). 17.99 *(978-1-84780-752-6(6)*, Frances Lincoln Children's Bks.) Quarto Publishing Group UK GBR. Dist: Hachette Bk. Group.

McCall Smith, Alexander. School Ship Tobermory. 2016. (School Ship Tobermory Ser.). (ENG., Illus.). 224p. (J). (gr. 3-7). 15.99 *(978-0-399-55261-8(8)*, Delacorte Bks. for Young Readers) Random Hse. Children's Bks.

McCarthy, Andrew. Just Fly Away. 2017. (ENG.). 272p. (YA). (gr. 9-12). 17.95 *(978-1-61620-629-1(2))* Algonquin Bks. of Chapel Hill.

McCarthy, Cori. You Were Here. 2016. (ENG., Illus.). 400p. (YA). (gr. 8-12). 17.99 *(978-1-4926-1704-4(0)*, 9781492617044) Sourcebooks, Inc.

McCarty, Peter. Chloe. McCarty, Peter, illus. 2012. (Illus.). 40p. (J). (gr. -1-1). (ENG.). 16.99 *(978-0-06-114291-8(3))*; lib. bdg. 17.89 *(978-0-06-114292-5(1))* HarperCollins Pubs.

McClintock, Barbara. Adèle & Simon. McClintock, Barbara, illus. 2006. (Adèle & Simon Ser.). (ENG., Illus.). 40p. (J). (gr. -1-3). 17.99 *(978-0-374-38044-1(9)*, 9780374380441, Farrar, Straus & Giroux (BYR)) Farrar, Straus & Giroux.

—Adèle & Simon in America. McClintock, Barbara, illus. 2008. (Adele & Simon Ser.). (ENG., Illus.). 40p. (J). (gr. -1-3). 18.99 *(978-0-374-39924-5(7)*, 9780374399245, Farrar, Straus & Giroux (BYR)) Farrar, Straus & Giroux.

—Lost & Found: Adèle & Simon in China. 2016. (Adele & Simon Ser.). (ENG., Illus.). 40p. (J). 17.99 *(978-0-374-39923-8(9)*, 9780374399238, Farrar, Straus & Giroux (BYR)) Farrar, Straus & Giroux.

McClure, Beverly Stowe. Listen to the Ghost. 2005. (J). per. 16.95 *(978-1-933353-51-7(1)*, Paladin Timeless) Twilight Times Bks.

McClure, Beverly Stowe. Tumbleweed Christmas. McKenna, Bridgett, illus. 2011. 24p. pap. 13.99 *(978-0-9832740-4-9(5))* 4RV Publishing, LLC.

McClure, Wendy. Wanderville. 2014. (Wanderville Ser.: 1). (ENG.). (J). (gr. 3-7). 240p. pap. 7.99 *(978-1-59514-701-1(2))*; 224p. 16.99 *(978-1-59514-700-4(4))* Penguin Young Readers Group. (Razorbill).

Mccormick, Scott. Camping Catastrophe! Lazzell, R. H., illus. 2016. (Mr. Pants Ser.: 4). (ENG.). 128p. (J). (gr. k-3). 12.99 *(978-0-525-42812-1(7)*, Dial Bks) Penguin Young Readers Group.

McCormick, Scott. It's Go Time! Lazzell, R. H., illus. 2014. (Mr. Pants Ser.: 1). (ENG.). 128p. (J). (gr. 1-3). 14.99 *(978-0-8037-4007-5(7)*, Dial Bks) Penguin Young Readers Group.

Mccormick, Scott. It's Go Time! Lazzell, R. H., illus. 2015. (Mr. Pants Ser.: 1). (ENG.). 128p. (J). (gr. 1-3). 7.99 *(978-0-14-751710-4(9)*, Puffin Books) Penguin Young Readers Group.

McCormick, Scott. Slacks, Camera, Action! Lazzell, R. H., illus. 2015. (Mr. Pants Ser.: 2). (ENG.). 128p. (J). (gr. k-3). 14.99 *(978-0-8037-4009-9(3)*, Dial Bks) Penguin Young Readers Group.

Mccormick, Scott. Slacks, Camera, Action! Lazzell, R. H., illus. 2015. (Mr. Pants Ser.: 2). (ENG.). 128p. (J). (gr. k-3). 7.99 *(978-0-14-751711-1(7)*, Puffin Books) Penguin Young Readers Group.

McCormick, Scott. Trick or Feet! Lazzell, R. H., illus. 2015. (Mr. Pants Ser.: 3). (ENG.). 128p. (J). (gr. k-3). 12.99 *(978-0-525-42811-4(9)*, Dial Bks) Penguin Young Readers Group.

McCullough, Myrina D. Feet. Schafrath, Ty, illus. 2013. 28p. pap. 15.00 *(978-0-9847740-1-2(7))* Systems Group, Inc., The.

McCully, Emily Arnold. Sam & the Big Kids. McCully, Emily Arnold, illus. (I Like to Read(r) Ser.). (ENG., Illus.). 24p. (J). (gr. -1-3). 2014. 6.99 *(978-0-8234-3060-4(X))* 2013. 14.95 *(978-0-8234-2427-6(8))* Holiday Hse., Inc.

McDaniel, Lurlene. Breathless. 2010. (ENG.). 180p. (YA). (gr. 7). mass mkt. 7.99 *(978-0-440-24016-7(6)*, Delacorte Bks. for Young Readers) Random Hse. Children's Bks.

—Raina's Story. 2006. (Angels in Pink Ser.). (ENG.). 208p. (YA). (gr. 7-12). mass mkt. 6.99 *(978-0-440-23866-9(8)*, Laurel Leaf) Random Hse. Children's Bks.

McDine, Donna M. Powder Monkey. Snider, Kc, illus. 2013. 24p. 19.95 *(978-1-61633-384-3(7))*; pap. 10.95 *(978-1-61633-385-0(5))* Guardian Angel Publishing, Inc.

McDonald, Kirsten. The Big Rain, 1 vol. Meza, Erika, illus. 2016. (Carlos & Carmen Ser.). (ENG.). 32p. (J). (gr. k-3). 27.07 *(978-1-62402-137-4(9))* Magic Wagon.

—The Costume Contest. 2016. (Carlos & Carmen Set 3 Ser.). (ENG.). (gr. -1-3). lib. bdg. 27.07 ***(978-1-62402-182-4(4))*** ABDO Publishing Co.

—The Green Surprise, 1 vol. Meza, Erika, illus. 2016. (Carlos & Carmen Ser.). (ENG.). 32p. (J). (gr. k-3). 27.07 *(978-1-62402-138-1(7))* Magic Wagon.

—The Nighttime Noise, 1 vol. Meza, Erika, illus. 2016. (Carlos & Carmen Ser.). (ENG.). 32p. (J). (gr. k-3). 27.07 *(978-1-62402-139-8(5))* Magic Wagon.

—The One-Tire House, 1 vol. Meza, Erika, illus. 2016. (Carlos & Carmen Ser.). (ENG.). 32p. (J). (gr. k-3). 27.07 *(978-1-62402-140-4(9))* Magic Wagon.

—The Perfect Piñatas. 2016. (Carlos & Carmen Set 3 Ser.). (ENG.). (gr. -1-3). lib. bdg. 27.07 ***(978-1-62402-183-1(2))*** ABDO Publishing Co.

—The Pet Show Problem. 2016. (Carlos & Carmen Set 3 Ser.). (ENG., Illus.). (J). (gr. -1-3). lib. bdg. 27.07 ***(978-1-62402-184-8(0))*** ABDO Publishing Co.

—The Sandy Weekend, 1 vol. Meza, Erika, illus. 2016. (ENG.). 32p. (J). 27.07 *(978-1-62402-142-8(5))* Magic Wagon.

—The Sparkly Night. 2016. (Carlos & Carmen Set 3 Ser.). (ENG., Illus.). (J). (gr. -1-3). lib. bdg. 27.07 ***(978-1-62402-185-5(9))*** ABDO Publishing Co.

—Tio Time, 1 vol. Meza, Erika, illus. 2016. (ENG.). 32p. (J). 27.07 *(978-1-62402-143-5(3))* Magic Wagon.

—The Wobbly Wheels, 1 vol. Meza, Erika, illus. 2016. (ENG.). 32p. (J). 27.07 *(978-1-62402-144-2(1))* Magic Wagon.

—The Yummy Mistake. Meza, Erika, illus. 2016. (ENG.). 32p. (J). 27.07 *(978-1-62402-145-9(X))* Magic Wagon.

McDonald, Megan. The Doctor Is In! Reynolds, Peter H., illus. 2010. (Judy Moody Ser.: 5). (ENG.). 176p. (J). (gr. 1-4). 15.99 *(978-0-7636-4862-6(0))*; pap. 5.99 *(978-0-7636-4861-9(2))* Candlewick Pr.

—The Doctor Is In! 2010. (Judy Moody Ser.: 5). lib. bdg. 16.00 *(978-0-606-12343-1(1)*, Turtleback) Turtleback Bks.

—Girl Detective. Reynolds, Peter H., illus. (Judy Moody Ser.: 9). (ENG.). 192p. (J). (gr. 1-4). 2011. pap. 5.99 *(978-0-7636-4349-2(1))*Bk. 9. 2010. 15.99 *(978-0-7636-3450-6(6))* Candlewick Pr.

—The Incredible Shrinking Kid. Reynolds, Peter H., illus. 2013. (Stink Ser.: 1). (ENG.). (J). (gr. 1-4). 112p. 12.99 *(978-0-7636-6388-9(3))*; 128p. pap. 4.99 *(978-0-7636-6426-8(X))* Candlewick Pr.

—Judy Moody & Stink: La Loca, Loca Busqueda del Tesoro. Reynolds, Peter, illus. 2011. (SPA.). 256p. (J). (gr. 2-5). pap. 14.95 *(978-1-61605-137-2(X))* Ediciones Alfaguara ESP. Dist: Two Rivers Distribution.

—Judy Moody & Stink: The Mad, Mad, Mad, Mad Treasure Hunt. Reynolds, Peter H., illus. 2009. (Judy Moody Ser.: No. 2). (ENG.). 128p. (J). (gr. 1-4). 14.99 *(978-0-7636-3962-4(1))* Candlewick Pr.

—Judy Moody & Stink: the Wishbone Wish. Reynolds, Peter H., illus. 2015. (Judy Moody Ser.). (ENG.). 128p. (J). (gr. 1-4). 14.99 *(978-0-7636-7206-5(8))* Candlewick Pr.

—Judy Moody & the Bad Luck Charm. Reynolds, Peter H., illus. 2012. (Judy Moody Ser.: 11). (ENG.). 176p. (J). (gr. 1-4). 15.99 *(978-0-7636-3451-3(4))* Candlewick Pr.

—Judy Moody & the Not Bummer Summer. Reynolds, Peter H., illus. movie tie-in ed. (Judy Moody Ser.: Bk. 10). (ENG.). (J). (gr. 1-4). 2011. 128p. pap. 5.99 *(978-0-7636-5351-4(9))*Bk. 10. 2012. 208p. 15.99 *(978-0-7636-5711-6(5))*Bk. 10. 2012. 208p. pap. 5.99 *(978-0-7636-5710-9(7))* Candlewick Pr.

—Judy Moody & the Not Bummer Summer. 2012. (Judy Moody Ser.: 10). lib. bdg. 16.00 *(978-0-606-23800-7(X)*, Turtleback) Turtleback Bks.

—Judy Moody Gets Famous! Reynolds, Peter H., illus. 2010. (Judy Moody Ser.: 2). (ENG.). 144p. (J). (gr. 1-4). 15.99 *(978-0-7636-4854-1(X))*; pap. 5.99 *(978-0-7636-4853-4(1))* Candlewick Pr.

—Judy Moody Gets Famous! 2010. (Judy Moody Ser.: 2). lib. bdg. 16.00 *(978-0-606-12332-7(6)*, Turtleback) Turtleback Bks.

—Judy Moody Saves the World! Reynolds, Peter H., illus. 2004. (Judy Moody Ser.: Bk. 3). 144p. (J). (gr. 1-5). 13.65 *(978-0-7569-2588-8(6))* Perfection Learning Corp.

—Judy Moody Saves the World! Reynolds, Peter H., illus. 2010. (Judy Moody Ser.: 3). (ENG.). 160p. (J). (gr. 1-4). 15.99 *(978-0-7636-4860-2(4))* Candlewick Pr.

—Judy Moody Saves the World! 2010. (Judy Moody Ser.: 3). lib. bdg. 16.00 *(978-0-606-12340-2(7)*, Turtleback) Turtleback Bks.

—Judy Moody Saves the World!, Bk. 3. Reynolds, Peter H., illus. 2010. (Judy Moody Ser.: 3). (ENG.). 160p. (J). (gr. 1-4). pap. 5.99 *(978-0-7636-4859-6(0))* Candlewick Pr.

—Judy Moody se Vuelve Famosa! Mendoza Garcia, Isabel, tr. Reynolds, Peter H., illus. 2004. (SPA.). 340p. (J). (gr. 3-5). pap. 7.95 *(978-1-59437-817-1(7))* Ediciones Alfaguara ESP. Dist: Two Rivers Distribution.

—The Mad, Mad, Mad, Mad Treasure Hunt. Reynolds, Peter H., illus. 2010. (Judy Moody Ser.: Bk. 2). (ENG.). 128p. (J). (gr. 1-4). pap. 7.99 *(978-0-7636-4351-5(3))* Candlewick Pr.

—The Mad, Mad, Mad, Mad Treasure Hunt. 2010. (Judy Moody & Stink Ser.: 2). lib. bdg. 18.40 *(978-0-606-01311-6(3)*, Turtleback) Turtleback Bks.

—Stink. 2013. (Stink Ser.: 1). lib. bdg. 14.75 *(978-0-606-31587-6(X)*, Turtleback) Turtleback Bks.

—Stink: The Incredible Shrinking Kid. Reynolds, Peter H., illus. 2010. (Stink Ser.: No. 1). 112p. (J). (gr. k-4). 24.21 *(978-1-59961-686-5(6))* Spotlight.

—Stink - The Super-Incredible Collection, Bks. 1-3. Reynolds, Peter H., illus. 2013. (Stink Ser.). (ENG.). 352p. (J). (gr. k-3). pap. 14.97 *(978-0-7636-6831-0(1))* Candlewick Pr.

—Stink, el Increible Niño Menguante. 2008. (SPA.). 272p. (J). (gr. 3-5). pap. 7.95 *(978-1-60396-193-6(3))* Ediciones Alfaguara ESP. Dist: Two Rivers Distribution.

—Stink Moody in Master of Disaster. Madrid, Erwin, illus. 2015. (Judy Moody Ser.: 5). (ENG.). 64p. (J). (gr. -1-1). 12.99 *(978-0-7636-7218-8(1))* Candlewick Pr.

—The Wishbone Wish. Reynolds, Peter H., illus. 2016. (Judy Moody & Stink Ser.: 4). (ENG.). 116p. (J). (gr. 1-4). lib. bdg. 18.40 *(978-0-606-39093-4(6))* Turtleback Bks.

McDonald, Rae A. A Fishing Surprise. Kemly, Kathleen, illus. 2007. (ENG.). 32p. (J). (gr. -1-3). 16.95 *(978-1-55971-977-3(X))* Cooper Square Publishing Llc.

Mcdoogle, Farrah. Olivia Says Good Night. 2016. (Olivia 8x8 Ser.). lib. bdg. 13.55 *(978-0-606-39244-0(0))* Turtleback Bks.

McDowell, Andrew. Beyond the Forest. 2007. 286p. pap. 16.95 *(978-0-7414-4238-3(8))* Infinity Publishing.

McDunn, Rosemary. When Kids Dream & Trucks Fly. 2007. (ENG.). 52p. per. 12.99 *(978-0-9792258-6-4(8))* Bezalel Bks.

McFadden, Deanna. Hansel & Gretel. Graegin, Stephanie, illus. 2012. (Silver Penny Stories Ser.). (ENG.). 48p. (J). (gr. -1-1). 4.95 *(978-1-4027-8335-7(3))* Sterling Publishing Co., Inc.

McFarlane, Brian. The Hockey Book. 11th ed. 2008. (Mitchell Brothers Ser.). (ENG.). 200p. (J). (gr. 3-7). per. *(978-1-55168-312-6(1))* Magma.

—Season of Surprises. 9th ed. 2008. (Mitchell Brothers Ser.). (ENG.). 184p. (J). (gr. 3-7). pap. *(978-1-55168-300-3(8))* Me to We.

McGeorge, Darby Q. Trickster Tre. 2012. 24p. pap. 9.95 *(978-1-4575-0971-1(7))* Dog Ear Publishing, LLC.

McGowan, Keith. The Witch's Curse. Tanaka, Yoko, illus. 2013. (ENG.). 304p. (J). (gr. 4-7). 16.99 *(978-0-8050-9324-7(9)*, 9780805093247, Holt, Henry & Co. Bks. For Young Readers) Holt, Henry & Co.

—The Witch's Guide to Cooking with Children. Tanaka, Yoko, illus. 2011. (ENG.). 192p. (J). (gr. 4-7). pap. 8.99 *(978-0-312-67486-1(4)*, 9780312674861) Square Fish.

McGowan, Maureen. Compliance, 0 vols. 2014. (Dust Chronicles Ser.: 2). (ENG.). 386p. (YA). (gr. 7-12). pap. 9.99 *(978-1-4778-1696-7(8)*, 9781477816967, Skyscape) Amazon Publishing.

—Deviants, 0 vols. 2014. (Dust Chronicles Ser.: 1). (ENG.). 322p. (YA). (gr. 9-12). pap. 9.99 *(978-1-4778-1032-3(3)*, 9781477810323, Skyscape) Amazon Publishing.

—Glory, 0 vols. 2014. (Dust Chronicles Ser.: 3). (ENG.). 326p. (YA). (gr. 9-12). pap. 9.99 *(978-1-4778-4797-8(9)*, 9781477847978, Amazon Children's Publishing) Amazon Publishing.

McGrath, Alister. Chosen Ones, 1 vol. 2010. (Aedyn Chronicles Ser.). (ENG.). 208p. (J). (gr. 4-7). 14.99 *(978-0-310-71812-3(0))* Zondervan.

McGugan, Jim. Bridge 6. 2004. (Illus.). (J). (gr. k-3). spiral bd. *(978-0-616-01721-0(9))* Canadian National Institute for the Blind/Institut National Canadien pour les Aveugles.

McKay, Hilary. Caddy Ever After. (ENG.). 224p. (J). 2007. (gr. 4-8). per. 6.99 *(978-1-4169-0931-6(1))* 2006. (gr. 5-9). 16.99 *(978-1-4169-0930-9(3))* McElderry, Margaret K. Bks. (McElderry, Margaret K. Bks.).

—Caddy's World. (ENG.). (J). (gr. 5-9). 2013. 288p. pap. 6.99 *(978-1-4424-4106-4(2))* 2012. 272p. 16.99 *(978-1-4424-4105-7(4))* McElderry, Margaret K. Bks. (McElderry, Margaret K. Bks.).

—Indigo's Star. 2006. (ENG.). 272p. (J). (gr. 3-7). reprint ed. per. 7.99 *(978-1-4169-1403-7(X)*, McElderry, Margaret K. Bks.) McElderry, Margaret K. Bks.

—Permanent Rose. 2006. (ENG.). 256p. (J). (gr. 3-7). reprint ed. per. 7.99 *(978-1-4169-2804-1(9)*, McElderry, Margaret K. Bks.) McElderry, Margaret K. Bks.

—Saffy's Angel. 2003. (ENG., Illus.). 160p. (J). (gr. 3-7). pap. 7.99 *(978-0-689-84934-3(6)*, McElderry, Margaret K. Bks.) McElderry, Margaret K. Bks.

—Saffy's Angel. 2004. (Casson Family Ser.: Bk. 1). 160p. (J). (gr. 4-7). pap. 36.00 incl. audio *(978-0-8072-2098-6(1),* Listening Library) Random Hse. Audio Publishing Group.

McKernan, Victoria. The Devil's Paintbox. (ENG.). (YA). (gr. 9). 2013. 384p. pap. 9.99 *(978-0-449-81655-4(9),* Ember) 2010. 368p. mass mkt. 8.99 *(978-0-440-23962-8(1),* Laurel Leaf) Random Hse. Children's Bks.

McKernan, Wendy. The Thing I Say I Saw Last Night: A Christmas Story. Bzymek, Izabela, illus. 2011. 32p. (J). *(978-0-9866204-0-9(8));* pap. *(978-0-9866204-1-6(6))* Little Dragon Publishing.

McKinley, Ryan. The Pirate Bride. 2010. 105p. 21.95 *(978-1-4327-5546-1(3));* (Illus.). pap. 14.95 *(978-1-4327-5545-4(5))* Outskirts Pr., Inc.

McKissack, Patricia C. The Home-Run King. 2009. (Scraps of Time Ser.). (ENG.). 112p. (J). (gr. 3-7). 6.99 *(978-0-14-241459-0(X),* Puffin Books) Penguin Young Readers Group.

McKy, Katie. Pumpkin Town! or, Nothing Is Better & Worse Than Pumpkins. Bernasconi, Pablo, illus. 2008. (ENG.). 32p. (J). (gr. -1-3). pap. 7.99 *(978-0-547-18193-6(0))* Houghton Mifflin Harcourt Publishing Co.

McMahan, Stephanie K. The Mystery of the Golden Rings. 2007. 140p. 21.95 *(978-0-595-68451-9(3));* per. 11.95 *(978-0-595-43998-0(5))* iUniverse, Inc.

McManis, Margaret. The Wild Texas Stampede!, 1 vol. Dupree, Bruce, illus. 2008. (ENG.). 32p. (J). (gr. 1-3). 16.99 *(978-1-58980-568-2(2))* Pelican Publishing Co., Inc.

McMann, Lisa. Dragon Captives. 2017. (Unwanteds Quests Ser.: 1). (ENG., Illus.). 432p. (J). (gr. 3-7). 17.99 *(978-1-4814-5681-4(4),* Simon & Schuster/Paula Wiseman Bks.) Simon & Schuster/Paula Wiseman Bks.

—Dragon Captives. 2018. (Unwanteds Quests Ser.: 1). lib. bdg. 18.40 ***(978-0-606-40846-2(0))*** Turtleback Bks.

—Island of Dragons. 2017. (Unwanteds Ser.: 7). (ENG., Illus.). 544p. (J). (gr. 3-7). pap. 8.99 *(978-1-4424-9338-4(0),* Aladdin) Simon & Schuster Children's Publishing.

—Island of Shipwrecks. 2015. (Unwanteds Ser.: 5). (ENG., Illus.). 480p. (J). (gr. 3-7). pap. 8.99 *(978-1-4424-9332-2(1),* Aladdin) Simon & Schuster Children's Publishing.

—Island of Silence. 2013. (Unwanteds Ser.: 2). lib. bdg. 18.40 *(978-0-606-32044-3(X),* Turtleback) Turtleback Bks.

—The Unwanteds, 6 vols. 2011. (Unwanteds Ser.: Bk. 1). (J). 90.75 *(978-1-4618-4113-5(5));* 88.75 *(978-1-4618-4117-3(8));* 245.75 *(978-1-4618-4114-2(3));* 1.25 *(978-1-4640-2489-4(8));* 88.75 *(978-1-4618-4116-6(X))* Recorded Bks., Inc.

—The Unwanteds. (Unwanteds Ser.: 1). (ENG., Illus.). (J). (gr. 3-7). 2012. 416p. pap. 7.99 *(978-1-4424-0769-5(7))* 2011. 400p. 18.99 *(978-1-4424-0768-8(9))* Simon & Schuster Children's Publishing. (Aladdin).

—The Unwanteds. 2012. (Unwanteds Ser.: 1). lib. bdg. 18.40 *(978-0-606-26953-7(3),* Turtleback) Turtleback Bks.

—The Unwanteds Set: The Unwanteds; Island of Silence; Island of Fire. 2013. (Unwanteds Ser.). (ENG.). 1280p. (J). (gr. 3-7). 51.99 *(978-1-4424-9450-3(6),* Aladdin) Simon & Schuster Children's Publishing.

McMillan, Ernest. Psalms of Passion. 2006. 48p. pap. 8.95 *(978-1-59800-224-9(4))* Outskirts Pr., Inc.

McMillion, Gloria. Whirlwinds Whirl Around. 2007. 136p. per. 11.95 *(978-0-595-42248-7(9))* iUniverse, Inc.

McMullin, Perry. Fireflies. 2009. 20p. pap. 14.95 *(978-1-4490-2730-8(X))* AuthorHouse.

McNamara, Margaret. The Three Little Aliens & the Big Bad Robot. Fearing, Mark, illus. 2011. (ENG.). 40p. (J). (gr. -1-3). 16.99 *(978-0-375-86689-0(2),* Schwartz & Wade Bks.) Random Hse. Children's Bks.

McPhail, David. Sisters. McPhail, David, illus. 2003. (ENG., Illus.). 32p. (J). (gr. -1-3). 9.95 *(978-0-15-204659-0(3))* Houghton Mifflin Harcourt Publishing Co.

McQuerry, Maureen Doyle. Time Out of Time. 2015. (Time Out of Time Ser.). (ENG., Illus.). 368p. (J). (gr. 5-9). 16.95 *(978-1-4197-1494-8(5),* Amulet Bks.) Abrams, Inc.

—Time Out of Time: Book One: Beyond the Door. 2015. (Time Out of Time Ser.). (ENG., Illus.). 400p. (J). (gr. 5-9). pap. 7.95 *(978-1-4197-1493-1(7),* Amulet Bks.) Abrams, Inc.

—Time Out of Time: Book Two: the Telling Stone. 2016. (ENG., Illus.). 376p. (J). (gr. 3-7). pap. 8.95 *(978-1-4197-1916-5(5),* Amulet Bks.) Abrams, Inc.

—Time Out of Time Bk. 1: Beyond the Door. 2014. (Time Out of Time Ser.). (ENG., Illus.). 384p. (J). (gr. 3-7). 16.95 *(978-1-4197-1016-2(8),* Amulet Bks.) Abrams, Inc.

McQuinn, Anna. Lola le Lee Al Pequeño Leo. Beardshaw, Rosalind, illus. 2013. (SPA & ENG.). 28p. (J). (-k). pap. 7.95 *(978-1-58089-599-6(9))* Charlesbridge Publishing, Inc.

—Lola Reads to Leo. Beardshaw, Rosalind, illus. 2012. (ENG.). 28p. (J). (-k). 15.95 *(978-1-58089-403-6(8));* pap. 6.95 *(978-1-58089-404-3(6))* Charlesbridge Publishing, Inc.

—Lola Reads to Leo. 2012. pap. 19.95 incl. audio compact disk *(978-0-8045-4236-4(8))* Spoken Arts, Inc.

McQuinn, Anna, et al. Lola Reads to Leo: Lola le Lee Al Pequeño Leo. Beardshaw, Rosalind, illus. 2017. (SPA & ENG.). (J). pap. ***(978-1-63289-028-3(3))*** Charlesbridge Publishing, Inc.

Mead, Alice. Junebug. 2009. (Junebug Ser.). (ENG.). 128p. (J). (gr. 3-7). pap. 7.99 *(978-0-312-56126-0(1),* 9780312561260) Square Fish.

Medearis, Angela Shelf. Lucy's Quiet Book. Ernst, Lisa Campbell, illus. 2004. (Green Light Readers Level 2 Ser.). (ENG.). 24p. (J). (gr. -1-3). pap. 3.95 *(978-0-15-205143-3(0))* Houghton Mifflin Harcourt Publishing Co.

—Lucy's Quiet Book. Ernst, Lisa Campbell, illus. 2004. (Green Light Readers Level 2 Ser.). (gr. k-2). 13.95 *(978-0-7569-4310-3(8))* Perfection Learning Corp.

Meeks, Jane. Finding Home. 2011. 24p. pap. 15.99 *(978-1-4653-6606-1(7))* Xlibris Corp.

Meierhenry, Mark V. & Volk, David. The Mystery of the Maize. Two Bulls, Marty Grant, illus. 2010. (J). *(978-0-9822749-1-0(2),* South Dakota State Historical Society Pr.) South Dakota State Historical Society Pr.

Mejias, John & Mejias, John, illus. The Hungry Brothers. 2009. (ENG.). 32p. (J). (gr. -1-2). 15.95 *(978-0-9798841-1-5(X))* 4N Publishing LLC.

Meloy, Colin. Wildwood. Ellis, Carson, illus. (Wildwood Chronicles Ser.: 1). (ENG.). (J). (gr. 3). 2012. 576p. pap. 9.99 *(978-0-06-202470-1(1))* 2011. 560p. 17.99 *(978-0-06-202468-8(X))* HarperCollins Pubs.

—Wildwood. Ellis, Carson, illus. 2012. (Wildwood Chronicles Ser.: 1). (J). lib. bdg. 20.85 *(978-0-606-26864-6(2),* Turtleback) Turtleback Bks.

Mercer, Sienna. Cry Wolf!, Vol. 1. 2013. (My Brother the Werewolf Ser.: 1). (ENG.). 256p. (J). (gr. 4-6). pap. 9.99 *(978-1-4052-6438-9(1))* Egmont Bks., Ltd. GBR. Dist: Independent Pubs. Group.

—Puppy Love! 2013. (My Brother the Werewolf Ser.: 2). (ENG.). 240p. (J). (gr. 4-6). pap. 8.99 *(978-1-4052-6439-6(X))* Egmont Bks., Ltd. GBR. Dist: Independent Pubs. Group.

—Switched. 2007. (My Sister the Vampire Ser.: 1). (ENG.). 208p. (J). (gr. 3-7). pap. 6.99 *(978-0-06-087113-0(X))* HarperCollins Pubs.

Meroto, Tina. The Tooth Gnashing Witch. 2007. (ENG., Illus.). 48p. (J). 18.95 *(978-84-96788-82-4(2))* OQO, Editora ESP. Dist: Baker & Taylor Bks.

Merry, Lindsay R. Dackshew Dragonfly. 2012. 24p. pap. 17.99 *(978-1-4685-9885-8(6))* AuthorHouse.

Meserve, Jessica. Bedtime Without Arthur. Meserve, Jessica, illus. 2010. (ENG., Illus.). 32p. (J). (gr. -1-3). 16.95 *(978-0-7613-5497-0(2))* Lerner Publishing Group.

Metikosh, Anne. Terra Incognita. 2005. (ENG., Illus.). 144p. (J). (gr. 3-9). pap., tchr. ed. 8.95 *(978-0-921870-76-0(0))* Ronsdale Pr. CAN. Dist: Literary Pr. Group of Canada.

Meunier, Sylvain & Lapierre, Steeve. Graindsel et Bretel. Fil et, Julie, illus. 2004. (était une Fois Ser.). (FRE.). 24p. (J). (gr. -1). pap. 10.95 *(978-2-89021-699-0(3))* Diffusion du livre Mirabel (DLM).

Michaels, Craig. Blackbeard's Treasure. 2008. (J). *(978-0-936389-99-8(0))* Tudor Pubs., Inc.

Michaels, Joanna. Call Me Charly. Specht, Jessica, illus. 2012. 92p. pap. 10.95 *(978-1-61493-102-7(X))* Peppertree Pr., The.

Michaels, Rune. Fix Me. 2011. (ENG., Illus.). 160p. (YA). (gr. 9). 16.99 *(978-1-4169-5772-0(3),* Atheneum Bks. for Young Readers) Simon & Schuster Children's Publishing.

—Genesis Alpha. 2007. (ENG.). 208p. (YA). (gr. 7-12). 23.80 *(978-1-4287-4620-6(X),* Follettbound) Follett School Solutions.

—Genesis Alpha. 2011. (ENG.). 224p. (YA). (gr. 7). pap. 8.99 *(978-1-4169-6500-8(9),* Atheneum Bks. for Young Readers) Simon & Schuster Children's Publishing.

Michels-Gualtieri, Zaydek G. I was Born to Be a Brother. Liegey, Daniel, illus. 2005. (ENG.). 32p. (J). (gr. -1-3). 9.95 incl. lp *(978-1-930775-10-7(5))* Platypus Media, L.L.C.

Mignerey, Mary Buhs. If Dogs Could Talk: & Dogs Can Talk Two. 2007. 56p. per. 16.95 *(978-1-4241-7675-5(1))* America Star Bks.

Miller, Gary R. Taming Chaos: A Parable on Decision Making. 2017. (ENG.). 150p. (YA). pap. 14.95 *(978-1-68350-060-5(1))* Morgan James Publishing.

Miller-Johnston, Renee. Courtney Logan Kennedy Presents Zoe. 2008. 76p. pap. 19.95 *(978-1-60703-558-9(8))* America Star Bks.

Millet, Lydia. Pills & Starships. 2014. (ENG.). 256p. (J). (gr. 7). 22.95 *(978-1-61775-275-9(4),* Black Sheep) Akashic Bks.

Millner, Robert W. The Chicken Coop Gang. 2011. 130p. 29.99 *(978-1-4568-5517-8(4));* pap. 19.99 *(978-1-4568-5516-1(6))* Xlibris Corp.

Mills, Claudia. Write This Down. 2016. (ENG.). 256p. (J). 15.99 *(978-0-374-30164-4(6),* 9780374301644, Farrar, Straus & Giroux (BYR)) Farrar, Straus & Giroux.

Minich, Eric. Digger & the Search for Home. 2006. 48p. pap. 16.95 *(978-1-4241-0321-8(5))* PublishAmerica, Inc.

Miraucourt, Christophe. Pirate Treasure. 2015. (Race Further with Reading Ser.). (ENG., Illus.). 48p. (J). *(978-0-7787-2031-7(4))* Crabtree Publishing Co.

Miyazaki, Hayao. Ponyo Film Comic, Vol. 1. Miyazaki, Hayao, illus. movie tie-in ed. 2009. (ENG., Illus.). 172p. (J). pap. 9.99 *(978-1-4215-3077-2(5))* Viz Media.

—Ponyo Film Comic, Vol. 2. Miyazaki, Hayao, illus. movie tie-in ed. 2009. (ENG., Illus.). 172p. (J). pap. 9.99 *(978-1-4215-3078-9(3))* Viz Media.

—Ponyo Film Comic, Vol. 3. Miyazaki, Hayao, illus. movie tie-in ed. 2009. (ENG., Illus.). 172p. (J). pap. 9.99 *(978-1-4215-3079-6(1))* Viz Media.

—Ponyo Film Comic, Vol. 4. Miyazaki, Hayao, illus. movie tie-in ed. 2009. (ENG., Illus.). 172p. (J). pap. 9.99 *(978-1-4215-3080-2(5))* Viz Media.

Mlawer, Teresa. If I Had a Dragon/Si Yo Tuviera un Dragon. Ellery, Tom & Ellery, Amanda, illus. 2006. (ENG & SPA.). (J). (gr. -1-3). per. 3.99 *(978-1-933032-17-7(0));* 32p. (gr. 5-6). 12.99 *(978-1-933032-16-0(2))* Lectorum Pubns., Inc.

Mlynowski, Sarah. Bad Hair Day. 2014. (Whatever After Ser.: No. 5). (ENG.). 176p. (J). (gr. 3-7). 14.99 *(978-0-545-62728-3(1),* Scholastic Pr.) Scholastic, Inc.

—Beauty Queen. (Whatever After Ser.: 7). (ENG.). 176p. (J). (gr. 3-7). 2016. pap. 5.99 *(978-0-545-74657-1(4))* 2015. 14.99 *(978-0-545-74654-0(X))* Scholastic, Inc. (Scholastic Pr.).

—Cold As Ice. 2015. (Whatever After Ser.: 6). (ENG.). 176p. (J). (gr. 3-7). pap. 5.99 *(978-0-545-62736-8(2),* Scholastic Pr.) Scholastic, Inc.

—Cold as Ice. 2014. (Whatever After Ser.: 6). (ENG.). 176p. (J). (gr. 3-7). 14.99 *(978-0-545-62734-4(6),* Scholastic Pr.) Scholastic, Inc.

—Dream On. (Whatever After Ser.: 4). (ENG.). 176p. (J). (gr. 3-7). 2014. pap. 5.99 *(978-0-545-41572-9(1),* Scholastic Paperbacks) 2013. 14.99 *(978-0-545-41571-2(3),* Scholastic Pr.) Scholastic, Inc.

—Fairest of All. (Whatever After Ser.: 1). (ENG.). 176p. (J). (gr. 3-7). 2013. pap. 5.99 *(978-0-545-48571-5(1))* 2012. 14.99 *(978-0-545-40330-6(8))* Scholastic, Inc. (Scholastic Pr.).

—Genie in a Bottle (Whatever After #9) 2016. (Whatever After Ser.: 9). (ENG.). 176p. (J). (gr. 3-7). 14.99 *(978-0-545-85102-2(5),* Scholastic Pr.) Scholastic, Inc.

—If the Shoe Fits. 2013. 176p. (Whatever After Ser.: 2). (ENG.). (J). (gr. 3-7). pap. 5.99 *(978-0-545-41568-2(3),* Scholastic Pr.); 14.99 *(978-0-545-50465-2(1));* (Whatever After Ser.: 2). (ENG.). (J). (gr. 3-7). 14.99 *(978-0-545-41567-5(5),* Scholastic Pr.) Scholastic, Inc.

—Once upon a Frog. 2015. (Whatever After Ser.: 8). (ENG., Illus.). 176p. (J). (gr. 3-7). 14.99 *(978-0-545-74660-1(4),* Scholastic Pr.) Scholastic, Inc.

—Sink or Swim. 2013. (Whatever After Ser.: No. 3). (J). 165p. *(978-0-545-53316-4(3));*Bk. 3. (ENG.). 176p. (gr. 3-7). 14.99 *(978-0-545-41569-9(1))* Scholastic, Inc. (Scholastic Pr.).

—Sugar & Spice. 2016. (Whatever After Ser.: 10). (ENG.). 176p. (J). (gr. 3-7). 14.99 *(978-0-545-85106-0(8),* Scholastic Pr.) Scholastic, Inc.

Moffett, Elzater. Tenan & Colleen: I Don't Want to Go to Bed. Thibodeaux, Rebecca, illus. 2010. 36p. 15.49 *(978-1-4490-6633-8(X))* AuthorHouse.

—Tenan & Colleen: Who Is Harry? 2011. 36p. pap. 16.86 *(978-1-4567-5378-8(9))* AuthorHouse.

Molesworth & Molesworth, Mary Louisa S. Peterkin. 2009. 128p. 23.95 *(978-1-60664-659-5(1))* Rodgers, Alan Bks.

—Robin Redbreast. 2011. 190p. 26.95 *(978-1-4638-9847-2(9));* pap. 14.95 *(978-1-4638-0123-6(8))* Rodgers, Alan Bks.

—The Tapestry Room. 2008. 116p. 22.95 *(978-1-60664-990-6(6))* Aegypan.

Molesworth, Mary Louisa S. & Molesworth. Grandmother Dear. 2008. 128p. 23.95 *(978-1-60664-726-4(1))* Rodgers, Alan Bks.

—Peterkin. 2009. 128p. pap. 10.95 *(978-1-60664-287-0(1))* Rodgers, Alan Bks.

Molitoris, Cathy. I've Got Music! McConnell, Sarah, illus. 2006. (J). *(978-0-439-88620-8(1))* Scholastic, Inc.

Molk, Laurel. Eeny, Meeny, Miney, Mo, & Flo. Molk, Laurel, illus. 2015. (ENG., Illus.). 32p. (J). (gr. -1-k). 16.99 *(978-0-670-01538-2(5),* Viking Books for Young Readers) Penguin Young Readers Group.

Monette, Roz. Alex & the Enderson Brothers: Book One, bks. 3. 2nd ed. 2013. (ENG., Illus.). 162p. (gr. 7-7). pap. 12.95 *(978-0-9835077-1-0(6))* Cedar Grove Bks.

Monninger, Joseph. Wish. 2012. (ENG.). 204p. (YA). (gr. 7). pap. 8.99 *(978-0-375-86213-7(7),* Ember) Random Hse. Children's Bks.

Monson, Marianne. The Enchanted Tunnel Vol. 3: Journey to Jerusalem. Burr, Dan, illus. 2011. (J). (gr. 3-6). pap. 7.99 *(978-1-60908-068-6(8))* Deseret Bk. Co.

—The Enchanted Tunnel Vol. 4: Wandering in the Wilderness. Burr, Dan, illus. 2011. 85p. (YA). (gr. 3-6). pap. 7.99 *(978-1-60908-069-3(6))* Deseret Bk. Co.

—Escape from Egypt. 2010. (J). *(978-1-60641-670-9(7))* Deseret Bk. Co.

—Pioneer Puzzle. 2010. (J). *(978-1-60641-669-3(3))* Deseret Bk. Co.

Montgomery, L. M. Rainbow Valley. 2007. (ENG.). 234p. pap. 20.99 *(978-1-4346-5245-4(9));* 258p. pap. 23.99 *(978-1-4346-5246-1(7))* Creative Media Partners, LLC.

Moore, Jodi. When a Dragon Moves in Again. McWilliam, Howard, illus. 2015. (When a Dragon Moves In Ser.). (ENG.). 32p. (J). (gr. k-2). 17.95 *(978-1-936261-35-2(9))* Flashlight Pr.

Moore, Judith. Jessica the Furry Baroo. Brown, Karen, illus. 2007. 44p. per. 14.95 *(978-1-59858-364-9(6))* Dog Ear Publishing, LLC.

Moore, Karen. Everybody Counts. Reed, Lisa, illus. 2012. (Roma Downey's Little Angels Ser.). 24p. (J). bds. 7.99 *(978-0-8249-5643-1(5),* Ideal Pubns.) Worthy Publishing.

Moore, Kelly, et al. Amber House. 2013. (Amber House Ser.: 1). (ENG.). 384p. (J). (gr. 7). pap. 9.99 *(978-0-545-43417-1(3),* Levine, Arthur A. Bks.) Scholastic, Inc.

Moore, Margaret & Moore, John Travers. The Three Tripps. Funk, Clotilde Embree, illus. 2011. 158p. 41.95 *(978-1-258-08478-3(3))* Literary Licensing, LLC.

Moore, Stephanie Perry. Enjoying True Peace, 1 vol. 2010. (Yasmin Peace Ser.: 5). (ENG.). 176p. pap. 6.99 *(978-0-8024-8606-6(1),* Lift Every Voice) Moody Pubs.

—Experiencing the Joy, 1 vol. 2009. (Yasmin Peace Ser.: 3). (ENG.). 160p. (gr. 7-10). pap. 7.99 *(978-0-8024-8604-2(5),* Lift Every Voice) Moody Pubs.

Moore, Stephanie Perry & Moody Publishing Staff. Believing in Hope. 2009. (Yasmin Peace Ser.: 2). (ENG.). 176p. (gr. 7-10). pap. 7.99 *(978-0-8024-8603-5(7),* Lift Every Voice) Moody Pubs.

—Finding Your Faith 2009. (Yasmin Peace Ser.: 1). (ENG.). 176p. (gr. 7-10). pap. 7.99 *(978-0-8024-8602-8(9),* Lift Every Voice) Moody Pubs.

Moraja, Melissa Perry. Madison & Ga: Tale of the Messed up Talent Show. 2013. 156p. pap. *(978-0-9898293-1-1(6))* Roxby Media Ltd.

Morales, Yuyi. Niño: Wrestles the World. Morales, Yuyi, illus. 2013. (ENG., Illus.). 40p. (J). (gr. -1-3). 17.99 *(978-1-59643-604-6(2),* 9781596436046) Roaring Brook Pr.

—Rudas: Niño's Horrendous Hermanitas. 2016. (ENG., Illus.). 40p. (J). 17.99 *(978-1-62672-240-8(4),* 9781626722408) Roaring Brook Pr.

Morelli, Licia & Morris, Jennifer. The Lemonade Hurricane: A Story of Mindfulness & Meditation, 1 vol. 2015. (ENG., Illus.). 32p. (gr. -1-3). 17.95 *(978-0-88448-396-0(7),* 884396) Tilbury Hse. Pubs.

Morgan, Melissa J. A Fair to Remember. 2007. (Camp Confidential Ser.: 13). (ENG.). 160p. (J). (gr. 3-7). pap. 4.99 *(978-0-448-44451-2(8),* Grosset & Dunlap) Penguin Young Readers Group.

Morpurgo, Michael. Twist of Gold. 2004. (ENG.). 304p. (J). pap. 8.99 *(978-0-7497-4687-2(4))* Egmont Bks., Ltd. GBR. Dist: Trafalgar Square Publishing.

Morrel Disbrow, Corlyss. Ran's Upside-Down Day. 2012. 20p. pap. 24.95 *(978-1-4626-8368-0(1))* America Star Bks.

Morris, Chad. Cragbridge Hall, Book 2: The Avatar Battle. 2014. (Cragbridge Hall Ser.: 2). (ENG., Illus.). 360p. (J). (gr. 3-9). 17.99 *(978-1-60907-809-6(8),* Shadow Mountain) Shadow Mountain Publishing.

—Cragbridge Hall, Book 3: The Impossible Race. 2015. (Cragbridge Hall Ser.: 3). (ENG., Illus.). 432p. (J). (gr. 3-9). 18.99 *(978-1-60907-979-6(5),* Shadow Mountain) Shadow Mountain Publishing.

Morrissey, Dean & Krensky, Stephen. The Crimson Comet. Morrissey, Dean, illus. 2006. (Illus.). 32p. (J). (gr. k-4). 17.89 *(978-0-06-008070-9(1))* HarperCollins Pubs.

Morse, William A. and & Morse, William A. And Dana Jo. Kurkle Kids: Spirit of America. 2009. 44p. pap. 16.99 *(978-1-4490-1009-6(1))* AuthorHouse.

Mosby, Pamela. I'm So Angry. Brever, Amy, illus. 2013. 28p. pap. 7.99 *(978-0-9886272-4-6(8))* Brothers N Publishing Corp.

Moskowitz, Hannah. Invincible Summer. 2011. (ENG.). 288p. (YA). (gr. 9-18). pap. 9.99 *(978-1-4424-0751-0(4),* Simon Pulse) Simon Pulse.

Moss, Christopher Hawthorne. Beloved Pilgrim. 2nd ed. 2016. (ENG., Illus.). (J). 29.99 ***(978-1-63477-939-5(8))*** 2014. 304p. pap. 17.99 *(978-1-62798-538-3(7))* Dreamspinner Pr. (Harmony Ink Pr.).

Moss, Marissa. Alien Eraser to the Rescue. Moss, Marissa, illus. 2009. (Max Disaster Ser.: No. 1). (ENG., Illus.). 56p. (J). (gr. 3-7). pap. 6.99 *(978-0-7636-4407-9(2))* Candlewick Pr.

Moss, Miriam. Matty Takes Off! Simmons, Jane, illus. 2008. (Matty & Milly Ser.). (ENG.). 32p. (J). (gr. -1-k). 19.95 *(978-1-84270-701-2(9))* Andersen Pr. GBR. Dist: Independent Pubs. Group.

—Matty Takes Off! Simmons, Jane, illus. 2009. (Matty & Milly Ser.). (ENG.). 32p. (J). (gr. k-k). pap. 9.99 *(978-1-84270-758-6(2))* Andersen Pr. GBR. Dist: Independent Pubs. Group.

Movie Menace. 2011. (Hardy Boys (All New) Undercover Brothers Ser.: 37). (ENG.). 176p. (J). (gr. 3-7). pap. 5.99 *(978-1-4424-0258-4(X),* Aladdin) Simon & Schuster Children's Publishing.

Mowll, Joshua. Operation Storm City, Bk. 3. 2009. (Guild of Specialists Ser.). (ENG., Illus.). 288p. (J). (gr. 5). 16.99 *(978-0-7636-4224-2(X))* Candlewick Pr.

Mrozek, Elizabeth. The Fifth Chair. Mrozek, Elizabeth, illus. 2013. (Illus.). 38p. 19.95 *(978-1-935766-80-3(5))* Windy City Pubs.

Muirhead, Maria. My Asthma Book. 2007. 72p. (J). (gr. 1-2). per. 11.95 *(978-0-595-42925-7(4))* iUniverse, Inc.

Mull, Brandon. Fablehaven. 2006. (ENG., Illus.). 351p. (J). lib. bdg. 20.00 *(978-1-4242-4831-5(0))* Fitzgerald Bks.

—Fablehaven. 2009. (SPA.). 306p. (YA). (gr. 5-8). 24.95 *(978-84-9918-033-5(7))* Roca Editorial ESP. Dist: Spanish Pubs., LLC.

—Fablehaven. 2006. (Fablehaven Ser.: 1). (ENG., Illus.). 368p. (J). (gr. 3-7). 19.99 *(978-1-59038-581-4(0),* Shadow Mountain) Shadow Mountain Publishing.

—Fablehaven. Dorman, Brandon, illus. 2007. (Fablehaven Ser.: 1). (ENG.). 384p. (J). (gr. 3-8). pap. 8.99 *(978-1-4169-4720-2(5),* Aladdin) Simon & Schuster Children's Publishing.

—Fablehaven. 2007. (Fablehaven Ser.: 01). lib. bdg. 18.40 *(978-1-4177-9328-0(7),* Turtleback) Turtleback Bks.

—Fablehaven: Las Llaves de la Prision de los Demonios. 2012. (SPA.). 466p. (YA). 24.95 *(978-84-9918-438-8(3))* Roca Editorial ESP. Dist: Spanish Pubs., LLC.

—Fablehaven Vol. 5: The Complete Series Boxed Set. 2010. (Fablehaven Ser.: Bks. 1-3). 99.99 *(978-1-60641-832-1(7),* Shadow Mountain) Shadow Mountain Publishing.

—Fablehaven Collection Set. Dorman, Brandon, illus. 2011. (Fablehaven Ser.). (ENG.). 2512p. (J). (gr. 3-8). pap. 42.99 *(978-1-4424-2977-2(1),* Aladdin) Simon & Schuster Children's Publishing.

—Grip of the Shadow Plague. Dorman, Brandon, illus. 2008. (Fablehaven Ser.: 3). (ENG.). 480p. (J). (gr. 3-7). 19.99 *(978-1-59038-898-3(4),* Shadow Mountain) Shadow Mountain Publishing.

—Keys to the Demon Prison. Dorman, Brandon, illus. 2011. (Fablehaven Ser.: 5). (ENG.). 640p. (J). (gr. 3-8). pap. 8.99 *(978-1-4169-9029-1(1),* Aladdin) Simon & Schuster Children's Publishing.

—Rise of the Evening Star. Dorman, Brandon, illus. 2007. (Fablehaven Ser.: 2). (ENG.). 456p. (J). (gr. 3-7). 19.99 *(978-1-59038-742-9(2),* Shadow Mountain) Shadow Mountain Publishing.

—Rise of the Evening Star. Dorman, Brandon, illus. 2008. (Fablehaven Ser.: 2). (ENG.). 480p. (J). (gr. 3-8). pap. 7.99 *(978-1-4169-5770-6(7),* Aladdin) Simon & Schuster Children's Publishing.

—Secrets of the Dragon Sanctuary. Dorman, Brandon, illus. 2010. (Fablehaven Ser.: 4). (ENG.). 560p. (J). (gr. 3-8). pap. 8.99 *(978-1-4169-9028-4(3),* Aladdin) Simon & Schuster Children's Publishing.

—Secrets of the Dragon Sanctuary. 2010. (Fablehaven Ser.: 4). lib. bdg. 19.65 *(978-0-606-10685-6(5),* Turtleback) Turtleback Bks.

Mullarkey, Lisa & Mullarkey, John. Get Ella to the Apollo, 1 vol. Bernard, Courtney, illus. 2015. (ENG.). 128p. (J). *(978-1-62402-087-2(9))* Magic Wagon.

Mullinax, Jerry. Enoree. 2009. (YA). pap. *(978-0-88092-646-1(5))* Royal Fireworks Publishing Co.

Muñoz, Isabel. Desastre en la Cocina. Mazali, Gustavo, illus. 2012. (Eric & Julieta Ser.). (SPA & ENG.). 24p. (J). (gr. -1-3). pap. 3.99 *(978-0-545-35581-0(8),* Scholastic en Espanol) Scholastic, Inc.

Munoz, Isabel. It's Mine (Es Mío) Mazali, Gustavo, illus. 2006. (Eric & Julieta Ser.). (ENG & SPA.). 24p. (J). (gr. -1-3). pap. 3.99 *(978-0-439-78370-5(4))* Scholastic, Inc.

Muñoz, Isabel. Just Like Mom. Mazali, Gustavo, illus. 2005. 22p. (J). pap. *(978-0-439-78844-1(7))* Scholastic, Inc.

Munoz, Isabel. Where Is Eric? (¿Donde Está Eric?) Mazali, Gustavo, illus. 2006. (Eric & Julieta Ser.). (ENG & SPA.). 24p. (J). (gr. -1-3). pap. 3.99 *(978-0-439-78371-2(2))* Scholastic, Inc.

Murdoch, Patricia. Revelación, 1 vol. 2008. (Spanish Soundings Ser.). (SPA.). 112p. (YA). (gr. 8-12). pap. 9.95 *(978-1-55469-053-4(6))* Orca Bk. Pubs. USA.

Murphy, Emily Bain. The Disappearances. 2017. (ENG.). 400p. (YA). (gr. 7). 17.99 *(978-0-544-87936-2(8),* HMH Books For Young Readers) Houghton Mifflin Harcourt Publishing Co.

Murphy, Patty. When I Grow Up. 2012. 24p. pap. 24.95 *(978-1-4626-6441-2(5))* America Star Bks.

Murray, George. The Tales of Molly Brand & MacNessie. 2008. 70p. pap. 14.95 *(978-1-4092-3724-2(9))* Lulu Pr., Inc.

Muschla, Gary Robert. The Sword & the Cross. 2009. (YA). pap. *(978-0-88092-472-6(1))* Royal Fireworks Publishing Co.

Muscia, Marilena Carrubba. Misses Cowy to the Rescue. 2011. 24p. (gr. -1). 12.99 *(978-1-4567-3582-1(9))* AuthorHouse.

Muth, Jon J. Zen Ghosts. 2010. (ENG.). 40p. (J). (gr. -1-3). 17.99 *(978-0-439-63430-4(X),* Scholastic Pr.) Scholastic, Inc.

—Zen Shorts. 2010. (ENG.). (J). (gr. -1-3). 18.99 *(978-0-545-22760-5(7))* Scholastic, Inc.

—Zen Shorts. Muth, Jon J., illus. 2005. (ENG., Illus.). 40p. (J). (gr. -1-3). 17.99 *(978-0-439-33911-7(1))* Scholastic, Inc.

A
B

—Zen Socks. 2015. (ENG., Illus.). 40p. (J). (gr. -1-3). 17.99 (978-0-545-16669-0(1), Scholastic Pr.) Scholastic, Inc.
—Zen Ties. Muth, Jon J., illus. 2008. (ENG., Illus.). 40p. (J). (gr. -1-3). 17.99 (978-0-439-63425-0(3), Scholastic Pr.) Scholastic, Inc.
My Baby Sister, Annie: Big Book. (Pebble Soup Explorations Ser.). 16p. (gr. -1-18). 31.00 (978-0-7578-1654-3(1)) Rigby Education.
My Baby Sister, Annie: Small Book. (Pebble Soup Explorations Ser.). 16p. (gr. -1-18). 5.00 (978-0-7578-1694-9(0)) Rigby Education.
Myers, Benjamin J. Blood Alchemy. 2010. (ENG.). 384p. (978-1-84255-641-2(X)) Orion Publishing Group, Ltd. GBR. Dist: Hachette Bk. Group.
Myers, Bill. The Chamber of Lies, 1 vol. 2009. (Elijah Project Ser.). (ENG.). 128p. (J). (gr. 4-7). pap. 6.99 (978-0-310-71196-4(7)) Zonderkidz.
—The Enemy Closes In, 1 vol. 2009. (Elijah Project Ser.). (ENG.). 128p. (J). (gr. 4-7). pap. 6.99 (978-0-310-71194-0(0)) Zonderkidz.
Myers, Bill & Riordan, James. On the Run, 1 vol. 2009. (Elijah Project Ser.). (ENG.). 128p. (J). (gr. 4-7). pap. 4.99 (978-0-310-71193-3(2)) Zonderkidz.
Myers, Edward. Climb or Die. 2nd ed. 2016. 154p. (J). pap. (978-1-932727-12-8(4)) Montemayor Pr.
—Solos en la Montaña. 2016. (SPA.). 157p. (J). pap. (978-1-932727-18-0(3)) Montemayor Pr.
Myers, Kate Kae. The Vanishing Game. (ENG.). (YA). (gr. 7). 2014. 384p. pap. 9.99 (978-1-61963-127-4(X), 9781619631274) 2012. 368p. 17.99 (978-1-59990-694-2(5), 9781599906942) Bloomsbury Publishing USA. (Bloomsbury USA Childrens).
Myers, Walter Dean. A Star Is Born. 2012. (Cruisers Ser.: Bk. 3). (J). (978-0-439-91631-8(3)); (ENG.). 176p. (gr. 5-9). 17.99 (978-0-439-91628-8(3)) Scholastic, Inc.
Myracle, Lauren. Friends of a Feather. Henry, Jed, illus. 2015. (Life of Ty Ser.: 3). (ENG.). 144p. (J). (gr. 1-4). 5.99 (978-0-14-242320-2(3), Puffin Books); 12.99 (978-0-525-42288-4(9), Dutton Books for Young Readers) Penguin Young Readers Group.
—The Life of Ty - Non-Random Acts of Kindness. Henry, Jed, illus. 2015. (Life of Ty Ser.: 2). (ENG.). 128p. (J). (gr. 1-4). 5.99 (978-0-14-242319-6(X), Puffin Books) Penguin Young Readers Group.
—Penguin Problems. Henry, Jed, illus. 2013. (Life of Ty Ser.: 1). (ENG.). 128p. (J). (gr. 1-4). 12.99 (978-0-525-42264-8(1), Dutton Books for Young Readers) Penguin Young Readers Group.
—Penguin Problems. 2014. (Life of Ty Ser.: 1). lib. bdg. 16.00 (978-0-606-34213-1(3), Turtleback) Turtleback Bks.
The Mystery of the Lion's Tail. 2014. (Greetings from Somewhere Ser.: 5). (ENG., Illus.). 128p. (J). (gr. -1-4). pap. 5.99 (978-1-4814-1464-7(X), Little Simon) Little Simon.
Mystery on Church Hill. 2013. 196p. (J). pap. 8.99 (978-0-9893414-3-1(7)) MyBoys3 Pr.
Naidoo, Beverley. The Other Side of Truth. 2008. 252p. (gr. 5-9). 17.00 (978-0-7569-8941-5(8)) Perfection Learning Corp.
Napoli, Donna Jo. The Wishing Club: A Story about Fractions. Currey, Anna, illus. rev. ed. 2007. (ENG.). 32p. (J). (gr. 1-4). 17.99 (978-0-8050-7665-3(4), 9780805076653, Holt, Henry & Co. Bks. For Young Readers) Holt, Henry & Co.
Narsimhan, Mahtab. The Silver Anklet. 2009. (Tara Trilogy Ser.: 2). (ENG.). 272p. (YA). (gr. 5-18). pap. 10.99 (978-1-55488-445-2(4), Dundurn Pr.) Dundurn CAN. Dist: Ingram Publisher Services.
—The Third Eye. 2007. (Tara Trilogy Ser.: 1). (ENG.). 240p. (YA). (gr. 5-7). pap. 12.99 (978-1-55002-750-1(6), Boardwalk Bks.) Dundurn CAN. Dist: Ingram Publisher Services.
Nash, Andy. Marcus & His Monkey: For Kids Blessed with Popularity. 2010. (J). (978-0-8127-0452-5(5)) Autumn Hse. Publishing Co.
Natl Children's Book & Literacy Alliance. The Exquisite Corpse Adventure. 2011. (ENG., Illus.). 288p. (J). (gr. 4-7). pap. 7.99 (978-0-7636-5773-4(5)) Candlewick Pr.
Nayeri, Daniel and Dina. Another Faust. 2010. (ENG., Illus.). 400p. (YA). (gr. 9). pap. 8.99 (978-0-7636-4834-3(5)) Candlewick Pr.
Naylor, Phyllis Reynolds. Alice in Blunderland. 2005. 200p. (J). (gr. 2-7). 13.65 (978-0-7569-5075-0(9)) Perfection Learning Corp.
—Alice in Blunderland. 2012. (Alice Ser.). (ENG., Illus.). 240p. (J). (gr. 2-7). pap. 5.99 (978-1-4424-4643-4(9), Atheneum Bks. for Young Readers) Simon & Schuster Children's Publishing.
—Boys in Control. 2005. (Boys Against Girls Ser.: No. 9). 143p. (J). (gr. 4-7). 13.65 (978-0-7569-5094-1(5)) Perfection Learning Corp.
—Boys in Control. 2005. (Boy/Girl Battle Ser.: No. 9). (ENG.). 160p. (J). (gr. 3-7). 6.99 (978-0-440-41681-4(7), Yearling) Random Hse. Children's Bks.
—The Boys Return. l.t. ed. 2003. (Boys Against Girls Ser.: No. 7). 170p. (J). 23.95 (978-0-7862-5822-2(5)) Thorndike Pr.
—Boys Rock! 2007. (Boy/Girl Battle Ser.). (ENG.). 144p. (J). (gr. 3-7). 5.99 (978-0-440-41990-7(5), Yearling) Random Hse. Children's Bks.
—Girls Rule! 2006. (Boy/Girl Battle Ser.: No. 10). (ENG.). 160p. (J). (gr. 3-7). per. 6.99 (978-0-440-41989-1(1), Yearling) Random Hse. Children's Bks.
—The Girls Take Over. 2004. (Boys Against Girls Ser.: No. 8). 146p. (J). (gr. 4-7). 13.65 (978-0-7569-2804-9(4)) Perfection Learning Corp.
—I Like Him, He Likes Her: Alice Alone; Simply Alice; Patiently Alice. 2010. (Alice Ser.). (ENG.). 640p. (YA). (gr. 7). pap. 12.99 (978-1-4424-0978-1(9), Atheneum Bks. for Young Readers) Simon & Schuster Children's Publishing.
—Simply Alice. 2003. (Alice Ser.: 14). (ENG., Illus.). 240p. (YA). (gr. 7). mass mkt. 5.99 (978-0-689-85965-6(1), Simon Pulse) Simon Pulse.
Neale, Jonathan. Lost at Sea. 2004. (ENG.). 112p. (J). (gr. 5-7). reprint ed. pap. 8.95 (978-0-618-43236-3(1)) Houghton Mifflin Harcourt Publishing Co.
Neenan, Colin. Thick. 2006. 126p. (YA). (gr. 7-16). per. 6.95 (978-0-9746481-9-4(1)) Brown Barn Bks.
Neil, Deanna. The Land of Curiosities (Book 2)) Lost in Yellowstone, 1872-1873. 2009. 320p. (J). pap. 12.95 (978-0-9798800-2-5(5)) EcoSeekers, The.
Neilsen, David. Beyond the Doors. 2017. (ENG.). 368p. (J). (gr. 3-7). 16.99 **(978-1-101-93582-8(0)**, Crown Books For Young Readers) Random Hse. Children's Bks.
Nelson, Jandy. I'll Give You the Sun. 2015. (CHI.). 384p. (YA). (gr. 9). pap. (978-986-359-180-1(7)) Ecus Publishing Hse.
—I'll Give You the Sun. 2014. (ENG.). 384p. (YA). (gr. 9). 17.99 (978-0-8037-3496-8(4), Dial Bks) Penguin Publishing Group.
—I'll Give You the Sun. 2015. (ENG.). 400p. (YA). (gr. 9-12). pap. 10.99 (978-0-14-242576-3(1), Speak) Penguin Young Readers Group.
—I'll Give You the Sun. 2015. (ENG.). 400p. (YA). (gr. 9). 21.30 (978-1-68065-512-4(4)) Perfection Learning Corp.
—I'll Give You the Sun. 2015. lib. bdg. 22.10 (978-0-606-37572-6(4)) Turtleback Bks.
Nelson, S. D. The Star People: A Lakota Story. 2003. (ENG., Illus.). 36p. (J). (gr. -1-3). 18.95 (978-0-8109-4584-5(3)) Abrams, Inc.
Nelson, Theresa. Ruby Electric. 2004. 264p. (J). (gr. 5-7). 13.65 (978-0-7569-3530-6(X)) Perfection Learning Corp.
—Ruby Electric. 2004. (ENG.). 272p. (J). (gr. 5-7). reprint ed. pap. 12.99 (978-0-689-87146-7(5), Atheneum Bks. for Young Readers) Simon & Schuster Children's Publishing.
Nesbit, E. Five Children & It. 2007. 192p. per. 12.95 (978-1-4218-3940-0(7)); (gr. 4-7). 27.95 (978-1-4218-3840-3(0)) 1st World Publishing, Inc. (1st World Library - Literary Society).
—Five Children & It. 207p. 20.95 (978-0-8488-2523-2(3)) Amereon Ltd.
—Five Children & It. 2013. 132p. pap. (978-1-908388-99-5(4)) Aziloth Bks.
—Five Children & It. (gr. 4-6). 2011. 428p. pap. 35.75 (978-1-179-45023-0(X)) 2008. 200p. 25.99 (978-0-554-29413-1(3)) 2008. 200p. 22.99 (978-0-554-38716-1(6)) Creative Media Partners, LLC.
—Five Children & It. Millar, H. R., illus. 2007. (ENG.). 178p. pap. 19.99 (978-1-4346-7586-6(6)); 198p. pap. 21.99 (978-1-4346-7587-3(4)) Creative Media Partners, LLC.
—Five Children & It. 2005. 96p. per. 4.95 (978-1-4209-2587-6(3)) Digireads.com Publishing.
—Five Children & It. Millar, H. R., illus. 2007. (ENG.). 204p. per. (978-1-4065-3077-3(8)) Dodo Pr.
—Five Children & It. 2017. (Dover Children's Evergreen Classics Ser.). (ENG., Illus.). 160p. (J). (gr. 3-8). pap. 4.00 (978-0-486-42366-1(2)) Dover Pubns., Inc.
—Five Children & It. 2006. pap. (978-1-4068-3501-4(3)) 2005. 296p. pap. (978-1-84637-200-1(3)) Echo Library.
—Five Children & It. 2010. 98p. pap. 19.99 (978-1-153-62213-4(0)) General Bks. LLC.
—Five Children & It. 2010. 144p. pap. (978-1-4076-4577-3(3)) HardPr.
—Five Children & It. 2010. 152p. pap. 17.56 (978-1-162-66290-9(5)) 2010. 152p. (gr. 3-7). 29.56 (978-1-169-26518-9(9)) 2010. 152p. 36.95 (978-1-161-43155-1(1)) 2004. reprint ed. pap. 21.95 (978-1-4191-1987-3(7)) 2004. reprint ed. pap. 1.99 (978-1-4192-1987-0(1)) Kessinger Publishing, LLC.
—Five Children & It. 2013. (Oxford Children's Classics Ser.). (ENG.). 208p. 9.95 (978-0-19-273343-6(5)) Oxford Univ. Pr., Inc.
—Five Children & It. Hische, Jessica, illus. 2013. (Penguin Drop Caps Ser.). (ENG.). 256p. (gr. 12). 25.00 (978-0-14-312466-5(8), Penguin Books) Penguin Publishing Group.
—Five Children & It. Nesbit, E. & Millar, H. R., illus. 2004. (ENG.). 240p. (gr. 12-18). 14.00 (978-0-14-303915-0(6), Penguin Classics) Penguin Publishing Group.
—Five Children & It. 2008. (Puffin Classics Ser.). (ENG., Illus.). 272p. (J). (gr. 5-7). 5.99 (978-0-14-132161-5(X), Puffin Books) Penguin Young Readers Group.
—Five Children & It. 2013. (ENG., Illus.). 272p. (J). (gr. 4-7). pap. 10.99 (978-0-09-957298-5(2)) Random Hse. GBR. Dist: Independent Pubs. Group.
—Five Children & It. 2005. (J). 1.25 (978-1-4025-4084-4(1)) Recorded Bks., Inc.
—Five Children & It. 2013. 160p. (978-3-8495-1928-5(7)) 2013. 160p. pap. (978-3-8495-0897-5(8)) 2011. 208p. pap. (978-3-8424-8390-3(2)) Tredition GmbH.
—Five Children & It. 2009. 128p. (gr. 4-7). pap. 4.95 (978-1-60459-692-2(9)) Wilder Pubns., Corp.
—Five Children & It. 2005. (ENG.). 29.95 (978-1-55742-510-2(8)); pap. 14.95 (978-1-55742-506-5(X)) Wildside Pr., LLC.
—The House of Arden. 2006. 184p. (gr. 3-7). per. 14.95 (978-1-59818-967-4(0)); 26.95 (978-1-59818-181-4(5)) Aegypan.
—The House of Arden. 2006. (New York Review Children's Collection). (ENG.). 260p. (J). (gr. 4-7). 17.95 (978-1-59017-202-5(7), NYR Children's Collection) New York Review of Bks., Inc., The.
—The Railway Children. 2007. 236p. per. 12.95 (978-1-4218-3945-5(8)); (ENG.). (gr. 4-7). 27.95 (978-1-4218-3845-8(1)) 1st World Publishing, Inc. (1st World Library - Literary Society).
—The Railway Children. 2006. (ENG.). 228p. (gr. 4-7). per. 14.95 (978-1-59818-933-9(6)); 26.95 (978-1-59818-179-1(3)) Aegypan.
—The Railway Children. 2013. 140p. pap. (978-1-908388-94-0(3)) Aziloth Bks.
—The Railway Children. 2008. (J). 8.99 (978-1-59166-924-1(3)) BJU Pr.
—The Railway Children. Brock, C. E., illus. (YA). 14.95 (978-0-8118-4933-3(3)) Chronicle Bks. LLC.
—The Railway Children. 2012. (ENG.). 234p. pap. 14.99 (978-1-4812-4818-1(9)) CreateSpace Independent Publishing Platform.
—The Railway Children. 2008. 204p. (gr. 4-7). 24.99 (978-0-554-36009-6(8)); 27.99 (978-0-554-26706-7(3)) Creative Media Partners, LLC.
—The Railway Children. 2008. (gr. 4-7). pap. 5.99 (978-1-4209-3105-1(9)) Digireads.com Publishing.
—The Railway Children. Brock, C. E., illus. 2008. (ENG.). 248p. per. (978-1-4065-9815-5(1)) Dodo Pr.
—The Railway Children. 2007. (ENG.). 204p. per. (978-1-4065-3083-4(2)) Dodo Pr.
—The Railway Children. 2006. pap. (978-1-4068-3505-2(6)) 2005. 348p. pap. (978-1-84637-205-6(4)) Echo Library.
—The Railway Children. Brock, Charles Edmund, illus. 2012. 232p. pap. (978-1-78201-004-3(1)) Evertype.
—The Railway Children. 2010. (Illus.). 118p. pap. 19.99 (978-1-153-71841-7(3)) General Bks. LLC.
—The Railway Children. Dryhurst, Dinah, tr. Dryhurst, Dinah, illus. 2004. 184p. 18.95 (978-1-56792-261-5(9)) Godine, David R. Pub.
—The Railway Children. 2010. 184p. pap. (978-1-4076-1891-3(1)) HardPr.
—The Railway Children. (J). (978-0-340-71497-3(2)) Hodder & Stoughton.
—The Railway Children. 2010. 194p. 30.36 (978-1-169-28328-2(4)) 2010. 194p. pap. 18.36 (978-1-162-70632-0(5)) 2010. 194p. 37.95 (978-1-161-47496-1(X)) 2004. reprint ed. pap. 1.99 (978-1-4192-7972-0(6)) 2004. reprint ed. pap. 22.95 (978-1-4191-7972-3(1)) Kessinger Publishing, LLC.
—The Railway Children. 2006. (Twelve-Point Ser.). lib. bdg. 25.00 (978-1-58287-399-2(2)); lib. bdg. 26.00 (978-1-58287-890-4(0)) North Bks.
—The Railway Children. 2012. (Oxford Children's Classics Ser.). (ENG.). 240p. 9.95 (978-0-19-275819-4(5)) Oxford Univ. Pr., Inc.
—The Railway Children. unabr. ed. 2004. (Chrysalis Childrens Classics Ser.). (Illus.). 128p. (YA). pap. (978-1-84365-050-8(9), Pavilion Children's Books) Pavilion Bks.
—The Railway Children. 2nd ed. 2008. (ENG., Illus.). 48p. pap. 11.99 (978-1-4058-6964-5(X)) Pearson Education.
—The Railway Children. 2nd ed. 2011. (Puffin Classics Ser.). (ENG., Illus.). 304p. (J). (gr. 5-7). pap. 5.99 (978-0-14-132160-8(1), Puffin Books) Penguin Young Readers Group.
—The Railway Children. (ENG.). (J). (gr. 4-7). 2013. 320p. pap. 10.99 (978-0-09-957299-2(0)) 2012. 290p. 10.99 (978-0-09-957715-7(1)) Random Hse. GBR. Dist: Independent Pubs. Group.
—The Railway Children. 2010. 146p. (gr. 4-7). pap. 8.95 (978-1-61104-337-2(9)) ReadaClassic.com.
—The Railway Children. 2004. (ENG.). 580p. (978-0-9548401-2-9(7)) Shoes & Ships & Sealing Wax Ltd.
—The Railway Children. 2011. 200p. (gr. 4-7). pap. (978-3-8424-4120-0(7)) Tredition GmbH.
—The Railway Children. 2009. 156p. (gr. 4-7). pap. 6.99 (978-1-60459-698-4(8)) Wilder Pubns., Corp.
—Story of the Treasure Seekers. 2006. pap. (978-1-4068-3507-6(2)) Echo Library.
—The Story of the Treasure Seekers. 2009. 128p. (gr. 4-7). pap. 5.50 (978-1-60459-695-3(3)) Wilder Pubns., Corp.
—The Story of the Treasure Seekers: Being the Adventures of the Bastable Children in Search of a Fortune. 2007. (ENG.). 150p. pap. 18.99 (978-1-4346-5163-1(0)); 170p. pap. 21.99 (978-1-4346-5164-8(9)) Creative Media Partners, LLC.
—The Story of the Treasure Seekers: Being the Adventures of the Bastable Children in Search of A Fortune. l.t. ed. 2005. 288p. pap. (978-1-84637-207-0(0)) Echo Library.
Nettrour, Nelani. Nunkey's Adventures Bk. 2: Birth of Reekey. 2006. (Illus.). 74p. (J). pap. 11.95 (978-1-932657-54-8(1)) Third Millennium Pubns.
Neubecker, Robert. Fall Is for School. Neubecker, Robert, illus. 2017. (ENG., Illus.). 32p. (J). (gr. -1-k). 17.99 **(978-1-4847-3254-0(5))** Disney Pr.
Neuschwander, Cindy. Pastry School in Paris: An Adventure in Capacity. Langdo, Bryan, illus. 2009. (ENG.). 32p. (J). (gr. 2-6). 18.99 (978-0-8050-8314-9(6), 9780805083149, Holt, Henry & Co. Bks. For Young Readers) Holt, Henry & Co.
Newman, John. Mimi. 2011. (ENG., Illus.). 192p. (J). (gr. 3-7). 15.99 (978-0-7636-5415-3(9)) Candlewick Pr.
Newman, Nanette. Ben's Book. Birkett, Georgie, illus. 2011. (ENG.). 32p. (J). (gr. -1-k). pap. 9.99 (978-1-84365-193-2(9), Pavilion Children's Books) Pavilion Bks. GBR. Dist: Independent Pubs. Group.
Nickerson, Sara. The Secrets of Blueberries, Brothers, Moose & Me. 2016. (ENG.). 336p. (J). (gr. 5). 8.99 (978-0-14-751179-9(8), Puffin Books) Penguin Young Readers Group.
Nielsen, Susin. Snake, 1 vol. 2006. (Degrassi Junior High Ser.). (ENG.). 184p. (YA). (gr. 5-10). 7.95 (978-1-55028-926-8(8), 9781550289268) Lorimer, James & Co., Ltd., Pubs. CAN. Dist: Casemate Pubs. & Bk. Distributors, LLC.
Nikakhtar, Manijeh. Love & Joy. 2010. 65p. pap. 21.95 (978-1-4327-4394-9(5)) Outskirts Pr., Inc.
Nimmo, Jenny. The Box Boys & the Magic Shell. (Box Boys Ser.). (Illus.). 64p. (J). pap. (978-0-340-73290-8(3)) Hodder & Stoughton.
—The Stones of Ravenglass. 2012. (Chronicles of the Red King Ser.). (ENG.). 272p. (J). (gr. 3-7). 16.99 (978-0-439-84674-5(9), Scholastic Pr.) Scholastic, Inc.
Nitz, Kristin Wolden. Saving the Griffin, 1 vol. Jaeggi, Yoshiko, illus. 2007. (ENG.). 192p. (J). (gr. 3-7). 14.95 (978-1-56145-380-1(3)) Peachtree Pubs.
Nix, Garth. The Ragwitch. 2004. (ENG., Illus.). 400p. (YA). (gr. 8-18). pap. 8.99 (978-0-06-050807-4(8), HarperTeen) HarperCollins Pubs.
Nix, Garth & Williams, Sean. The Magic, Bk. 1. 2012. (Troubletwisters Ser.: 1). (ENG.). 304p. (J). (gr. 3-7). pap. 7.99 (978-0-545-25903-3(7), Scholastic Paperbacks) Scholastic, Inc.
—The Missing. 2014. (Troubletwisters Ser.: 4). (ENG.). 320p. (J). (gr. 3-7). 17.99 (978-0-545-25900-2(2), Scholastic Pr.) Scholastic, Inc.
—The Monster. (Troubletwisters Ser.: 2). (ENG.). 304p. (J). (gr. 3-7). 2013. pap. 6.99 (978-0-545-25904-0(5), Scholastic Paperbacks) 2012. 16.99 (978-0-545-25898-2(7), Scholastic Pr.) Scholastic, Inc.
—The Mystery. (Troubletwisters Ser.: 3). (ENG.). 304p. (J). (gr. 3-7). 2014. pap. 6.99 (978-0-545-25905-7(3), Scholastic Paperbacks) 2013. 16.99 (978-0-545-25899-9(5)) Scholastic, Inc.
—Troubletwisters, Bk. 1. 2011. (Troubletwisters Ser.: 1). (ENG.). 304p. (J). (gr. 3-7). 16.99 (978-0-545-25897-5(9), Scholastic Pr.) Scholastic, Inc.
Noble, Trinka Hakes. The Last Brother: A Civil War Tale. Papp, Robert, illus. 2006. (Tales of Young Americans Ser.). (ENG.). 32p. (J). (gr. 3-7). 17.95 (978-1-58536-253-0(0)) Sleeping Bear Pr.
—The Scarlet Stockings Spy. Papp, Robert, illus. 2004. (Tales of Young Americans Ser.). (ENG.). 48p. (J). (gr. 1-7). 16.95 (978-1-58536-230-1(1)) Sleeping Bear Pr.
Noland, Charles. The Adventures of Drew & Ellie: The Daring Rescue. Moyer, Tom, illus. 2nd ed. 2006. 92p. (J). per. 7.95 (978-0-9789297-2-5(1)) TMD Enterprises.
Nolen, Jerdine. Block Party Surprise. Henninger, Michelle, illus. 2015. 41p. (J). (978-1-4806-8574-1(7)) Harcourt.
—Bradford Street Buddies: Block Party Surprise. Henninger, Michelle, illus. 2015. (Green Light Readers Level 3 Ser.). (ENG.). 48p. (J). (gr. 1-4). pap. 3.99 (978-0-544-35863-8(5), HMH Books For Young Readers) Houghton Mifflin Harcourt Publishing Co.
Noll, Amanda. Hey, That's My Monster! McWilliam, Howard, illus. 2016. (ENG.). 32p. (J). (gr. k-2). 17.95 (978-1-936261-37-6(5)) Flashlight Pr.
Novak, Ali. The Heartbreakers. 2015. (Heartbreak Chronicles Ser.: 1). (ENG.). 336p. (YA). (gr. 6-12). pap. 10.99 (978-1-4926-1256-8(1), 9781492612568) Sourcebooks, Inc.
—My Life with the Walter Boys. 2014. (ENG.). 368p. (YA). (gr. 7-12). pap. 10.99 (978-1-4022-9786-1(6), 9781402297861) Sourcebooks, Inc.
Ntihemuka, Patty Froese. Hyacinth Doesn't Go to Jail: And, Hyacinth Doesn't Miss Christmas. 2009. (J). pap. 10.99 (978-0-8163-2372-2(0)) Pacific Pr. Publishing Assn.
Nugent, Matthew. Nightmares on Goose Rocks Beach in Kennebunkport, Maine: Book 4 of the Goose Rocks Tales. 2003. (Illus.). 204p. (J). per. 14.95 (978-0-9705812-3-5(8)) CBI Pr.
Numeroff, Laura Joffe. Beatrice Doesn't Want To. Munsinger, Lynn, illus. 2008. (ENG.). 32p. (J). (gr. -1-2). pap. 7.99 (978-0-7636-3843-6(9)) Candlewick Pr.
—What Brothers Do Best. Munsinger, Lynn, illus. 2012. (ENG.). 20p. (J). (gr. -1 — 1). bds. 7.99 (978-1-4521-1073-8(5)) Chronicle Bks. LLC.
—What Sisters Do Best. Munsinger, Lynn, illus. 2009. (ENG.). 44p. (J). (gr. -1-2). 15.99 (978-0-8118-6545-6(2)) Chronicle Bks. LLC.
Nyaradi, J. A. Catching Santa. 2006. 140p. pap. 11.95 (978-0-7414-3462-3(8)) Infinity Publishing.
Nytra, David. The Secret of the Stone Frog. Nytra, David, illus. 2012. (Leah & Alan Adventures Ser.). (ENG., Illus.). 80p. (J). (gr. 2-7). 14.95 (978-1-935179-18-4(7)) TOON Books / RAW Junior, LLC.
—Windmill Dragons: A Leah & Alan Adventure - A Toon Graphic. 2015. (Leah & Alan Adventures Ser.). (ENG., Illus.). 120p. (J). (gr. 2). 18.95 (978-1-935179-88-7(8)) TOON Books / RAW Junior, LLC.
O'Brien, Anne Sibley. In the Shadow of the Sun. 2017. (ENG.). 304p. (J). (gr. 3-7). 17.99 **(978-0-545-90574-9(5))** Scholastic, Inc.
O'Connell, Jenny. Plan B. 2006. (ENG.). 288p. pap. 18.99 (978-1-4165-2033-7(3), MTV Bks.) MTV Books.
O'Connor, Barbara. How to Steal a Dog. 2009. (ENG.). 192p. (J). (gr. 3-7). pap. 6.99 (978-0-312-56112-3(1), 9780312561123) Square Fish.
O'Connor, Jane. Fancy Nancy: the Worst Secret Keeper Ever. Glasser, Robin Preiss, illus. 2016. (Fancy Nancy Ser.). 24p. (J). (gr. -1-3). pap. 4.99 (978-0-06-226960-7(7), HarperFestival) HarperCollins Pubs.
O'Coyne, James. Gravelle's Land of Horror. Whispering Pine Press International, Inc. Staff, ed. Baer, Brian, illus. 2007. (ENG.). 120p. (J). per. 9.95 (978-1-59649-604-0(5)) Whispering Pine Pr. International, Inc.
Offill, Jenny. While You Were Napping. Blitt, Barry, illus. 2014. (ENG.). 40p. (J). (gr. -1-3). 16.99 (978-0-375-86572-5(1), Schwartz & Wade Bks.) Random Hse. Children's Bks.
Ogaz, Nancy. Wishing on the Midnight Star: My Asperger Brother. 2003. (ENG.). 144p. (J). pap. 22.95 (978-1-84310-757-6(0), 4318) Kingsley, Jessica Pubs. GBR. Dist: Macmillan Distribution Ltd.
Ogden, Charles. Frost Bites. Carton, Rick, illus. 2008. (Edgar & Ellen Nodyssey Ser.: 2). (ENG.). 192p. (J). (gr. 3-7). 23.99 (978-1-4169-5464-4(3), Simon & Schuster/Paula Wiseman Bks.) Simon & Schuster/Paula Wiseman Bks.
—Hot Air. Carton, Rick, illus. 2008. (Edgar & Ellen Nodyssey Ser.: 1). (ENG.). 192p. (J). (gr. 3-7). 9.99 (978-1-4169-5465-1(1), Aladdin) Simon & Schuster Children's Publishing.
—Nod's Limbs. Carton, Rick, illus. 2007. (Edgar & Ellen Ser.: 6). (ENG.). 224p. (J). (gr. 3-7). 24.99 (978-1-4169-1501-0(X), Simon & Schuster/Paula Wiseman Bks.) Simon & Schuster/Paula Wiseman Bks.
Oh, DaYun. We Are Brothers. Godeassi, Anna, illus. 2014. (MySELF Bookshelf Ser.). (ENG.). 32p. (J). (gr. k-2). pap. 11.94 (978-1-60357-692-5(4)) Norwood Hse. Pr.
O'Hair, Margaret. Twin to Twin. Courtin, Thierry, illus. 2003. (ENG.). 32p. (J). (gr. -1-3). 17.99 (978-0-689-84494-2(8), McElderry, Margaret K. Bks.) McElderry, Margaret K. Bks.
O'Hara, Mo. Jurassic Carp. Jagucki, Marek, illus. 2017. (My Big Fat Zombie Goldfish Ser.: 6). (ENG.). 224p. (J). pap. 6.99 **(978-1-250-10260-7(X)**, 9781250102607) Square Fish.
Ohi, Ruth. Me & My Brother. Ohi, Ruth, illus. 2007. (ENG., Illus.). 24p. (J). (gr. -1-k). 19.95 (978-1-55451-092-4(9), 9781554510924); pap. 6.95 (978-1-55451-091-7(0), 9781554510917) Annick Pr., Ltd. CAN. Dist: Publishers Group West (PGW).
Oldfield, Jenny. Sunny the Hero. (Home Farm Twins Ser.: No. 7). (Illus.). 120p. (J). pap. 7.99 (978-0-340-68990-5(0)) Hodder & Stoughton GBR. Dist: Trafalgar Square Publishing.
Olesen, Demetria Vassiliou. Lambyro. Forcada, Adiela & Giron, Elizabeth, illus. 2011. (ENG.). 32p. (J). 19.00 (978-0-615-47664-3(3)) Elissian Publishing Co.
Oliver, Helen. Ellen's First Swim. 2009. 32p. pap. 16.49 (978-1-4389-9828-2(7)) AuthorHouse.
Oliver, Lauren. The Spindlers. Bruno, Iacopo, illus. (ENG.). (J). (gr. 3-7). 2013. 272p. pap. 8.99 (978-0-06-197809-8(4)) 2012. 256p. 16.99 (978-0-06-197808-1(6)) HarperCollins Pubs.
Oliver, Lin. Attack of the Growling Eyeballs. Gilpin, Stephen, illus. 2009. (Who Shrunk Daniel Funk? Ser.: 1). (ENG.). 160p. (J). (gr. 3-7). pap. 6.99 (978-1-4169-0958-3(3), Simon & Schuster Bks. For Young Readers) Simon & Schuster Bks. For Young Readers.

—Double-Crossed #3. 2013. (Almost Identical Ser.: 3). (ENG.). 224p. (J). (gr. 3-7). pap. 7.99 *(978-0-448-45193-0(X)*, Grosset & Dunlap) Penguin Young Readers Group.

—Revenge of the Itty-Bitty Brothers. Gilpin, Stephen, illus. (Who Shrunk Daniel Funk? Ser.: 3). (ENG.). 176p. (J). (gr. 3-7). 2010. pap. 6.99 *(978-1-4169-0962-0(1))* 2009. 14.99 *(978-1-4169-0961-3(3))* Simon & Schuster Bks. For Young Readers. (Simon & Schuster Bks. For Young Readers).

Oliver, Lin & Baker, Theo. The Shadow Mask, No. 2. 2013. (Sound Bender Ser.: 2). (ENG.). 368p. (J). (gr. 5-9). 16.99 *(978-0-545-19694-9(9)*, Scholastic Pr.) Scholastic, Inc.

OLIVIA Helps the Tooth Fairy. 2015. (Olivia TV Tie-In Ser.). (ENG., Illus.). 24p. (J). (gr. -1-2). pap. 3.99 *(978-1-4814-1906-2(4)*, Simon Spotlight) Simon Spotlight.

Olson, D. A. The Treasure Map. 2011. 36p. pap. 24.95 *(978-1-4626-3655-6(1))* America Star Bks.

Olson, Jennifer Gray. Ninja Bunny: Sister vs. Brother. 2016. (ENG., Illus.). 32p. (J). (gr. -1-2). 16.99 *(978-0-399-55074-4(7)*, Knopf Bks. for Young Readers) Random Hse. Children's Bks.

One Tree Hill, No. 3. (YA). *(978-0-439-71562-1(8))* Scholastic, Inc.

O'Neill, Alexis. Estela en el Mercado de Pulgas. de la Vega, Eida, tr. from ENG. Sanchez, Enrique O., illus. 2005. (SPA.). 32p. (J). (gr. -1-k). pap. 9.95 *(978-1-58430-246-9(1))* Lee & Low Bks., Inc.

O'Neill, Catharine. Annie & Simon. O'Neill, Catharine, illus. 2008. (ENG., Illus.). 64p. (J). (gr. k-4). 15.99 *(978-0-7636-2688-4(0))* Candlewick Pr.

—Annie & Simon: The Sneeze & Other Stories. O'Neill, Catharine, illus. (Candlewick Sparks Ser.). (ENG., Illus.). 64p. (J). (gr. k-4). 2015. pap. 3.99 *(978-0-7636-7788-6(4))* 2013. 15.99 *(978-0-7636-4921-0(X))* Candlewick Pr.

—Annie & Simon: Banana Muffins & Other Stories. O'Neill, Catharine, illus. 2017. (ENG., Illus.). 64p. (J). (gr. k-3). 15.99 *(978-0-7636-7498-4(2))* Candlewick Pr.

Oppel, Kenneth. This Dark Endeavor: The Apprenticeship of Victor Frankenstein. 2011. (Apprenticeship of Victor Frankenstein Ser.: Bk. 1). (ENG.). (YA). (gr. 7-12). 64.99 *(978-1-4558-2316-1(3))* Findaway World, LLC.

Optic, Oliver, pseud. Fighting for the Right. 2007. 136p. per. *(978-1-4068-3635-6(4))* Echo Library.

—Taken by the Enemy. 2007. 132p. (gr. 4-7). per. *(978-1-4068-4346-0(6))* Echo Library.

Oram, Hiawyn. Little Brother & the Cough. Rees, Mary, illus. 32p. (J). (gr. -1-1). *(978-0-7112-0844-5(1))* ReiseArt Buchhandlung GmbH.

Orgill, Roxane & Orgill. Go-Go Baby!, 1 vol. Salerno, Steven, tr. Salerno, Steven, illus. 2004. (ENG.). 32p. (J). 14.95 *(978-0-7614-5157-0(9))* Marshall Cavendish Corp.

Orme, Helen. Brother Bother. 2008. (Siti's Sisters Ser.). (ENG., Illus.). 36p. pap. *(978-1-84167-684-5(5))* Ransom Publishing Ltd.

—Party Time. 2008. (ENG., Illus.). 36p. pap. *(978-1-84167-819-1(8))* Ransom Publishing Ltd.

Ormerod, Jan. The Baby Swap. Joyner, Andrew, illus. 2015. (ENG.). 32p. (J). (gr. -1-1). 16.99 *(978-1-4814-1914-7(5)*, Little Simon) Little Simon.

Orr, Wendy. Mokie & Bik Go to Sea. Bean, Jonathan, illus. 2010. (ENG.). 80p. (J). (gr. 2-5). 15.99 *(978-0-8050-8174-9(7)*, 9780805081749, Holt, Henry & Co. Bks. For Young Readers) Holt, Henry & Co.

—Wanted! - A Guinea Pig Called Henry. Castelao, Patricia, illus. 2012. (Rainbow Street Shelter Ser.: 3). (ENG.). 128p. (J). (gr. 2-5). 15.99 *(978-0-8050-8933-2(0)*, 9780805089332, Holt, Henry & Co. Bks. For Young Readers) Holt, Henry & Co.

Ortiz, Zirzeria. The Queen in Me & My Bumblebee. 2008. 48p. pap. 24.95 *(978-1-60441-045-7(0))* America Star Bks.

O'Ryan, Ray. Operation Twin Trouble. Kraft, Jason, illus. 2015. (Galaxy Zack Ser.: 12). (ENG.). 128p. (J). (gr. k-4). pap. 5.99 *(978-1-4814-4399-9(2)*, Little Simon) Little Simon.

Osborne Hale, Jennifer. Danny Blue! What Did You Do? 2009. 16p. pap. 9.95 *(978-1-4490-1171-0(3))* AuthorHouse.

Osborne, Mary Pope. Abe Lincoln at Last! Murdocca, Sal, illus. 2013. (Magic Tree House Merlin Mission Ser.: 19). (ENG.). 144p. (J). (gr. 2-5). 5.99 *(978-0-375-86797-2(X)*, Random Hse. Bks. for Young Readers) Random Hse. Children's Bks.

—Abe Lincoln at Last! 2013. (Magic Tree House Merlin Missions Ser.: 19). lib. bdg. 16.00 *(978-0-606-35563-6(4))* Turtleback Bks.

—Blizzard of the Blue Moon. Murdocca, Sal, illus. 2007. (Magic Tree House Merlin Mission Ser.: 8). (ENG.). 144p. (J). (gr. 2-5). 5.99 *(978-0-375-83038-9(3)*, Random Hse. Bks. for Young Readers) Random Hse. Children's Bks.

—Carnival at Candlelight. Murdocca, Sal, illus. 2006. (Magic Tree House Merlin Mission Ser.: 5). (ENG.). 144p. (J). (gr. 2-5). 5.99 *(978-0-375-83034-1(0)*, Random Hse. Bks. for Young Readers) Random Hse. Children's Bks.

—Christmas in Camelot. Murdocca, Sal, illus. 2009. (Magic Tree House Merlin Mission Ser.: 1). (ENG.). 144p. (J). (gr. 2-5). 5.99 *(978-0-375-85812-3(1)*, Random Hse. Bks. for Young Readers) Random Hse. Children's Bks.

—Christmas in Camelot. 2009. (Magic Tree House Merlin Missions Ser.: 1). lib. bdg. 16.00 *(978-0-606-06386-9(2)*, Turtleback) Turtleback Bks.

—A Crazy Day with Cobras. Murdocca, Sal, illus. (ENG.). (J). 2012. (Magic Tree House Merlin Missions Ser.: No. 17). 144p. (gr. 1-4). 5.99 *(978-0-375-86795-8(3))* 2011. (Magic Tree House Merlin Mission Ser.: 45). 128p. (gr. 2-5). 12.99 *(978-0-375-86823-8(2))* Random Hse. Children's Bks. (Random Hse. Bks. for Young Readers).

—A Crazy Day with Cobras. 2012. (Magic Tree House Merlin Missions Ser.: 17). lib. bdg. 16.00 *(978-0-606-26997-1(5)*, Turtleback) Turtleback Bks.

—Danger in the Darkest Hour. Murdocca, Sal, illus. 2015. (Stepping Stone Book Ser.: No. 1). (ENG.). 192p. (J). (gr. 2-5). 14.99 *(978-0-553-49772-4(3)*, Random Hse. Bks. for Young Readers) Random Hse. Children's Bks.

—Dark Day in the Deep Sea. 2009. (Magic Tree House Merlin Missions Ser.: 11). lib. bdg. 16.00 *(978-0-606-01778-7(X)*, Turtleback) Turtleback Bks.

—Dogs in the Dead of Night. Murdocca, Sal, illus. 2013. (Magic Tree House (R) Merlin Mission Ser.: 18). (ENG.). 144p. (J). (gr. 2-5). 5.99 *(978-0-375-86796-5(1)*, Random Hse. Bks. for Young Readers) Random Hse. Children's Bks.

—Dogs in the Dead of Night. 2013. (Magic Tree House Merlin Missions Ser.: 18). lib. bdg. 16.00 *(978-0-606-31939-3(5)*, Turtleback) Turtleback Bks.

—Dragon of the Red Dawn. Murdocca, Sal, illus. 2008. (Magic Tree House Merlin Mission Ser.: 9). (ENG.). 144p. (J). (gr. 2-5). 5.99 *(978-0-375-83728-9(0)*, Random Hse. Bks. for Young Readers) Random Hse. Children's Bks.

—Eve of the Emperor Penguin. Murdocca, Sal, illus. 2009. (Magic Tree House Merlin Mission Ser.: No. 12). (ENG.). 144p. (J). (gr. 2-5). 5.99 *(978-0-375-83734-0(5)*, Random Hse. Bks. for Young Readers) Random Hse. Children's Bks.

—A Ghost Tale for Christmas Time. Murdocca, Sal, illus. (Magic Tree House Merlin Mission Ser.: No. 16). (ENG.). (J). (gr. 2-5). 2012. 144p. pap. 5.99 *(978-0-375-85653-2(6))* 2010. 128p. 12.99 *(978-0-375-85652-5(8))* Random Hse. Children's Bks. (Random Hse. Bks. for Young Readers).

—A Ghost Tale for Christmas Time. 2012. (Magic Tree House Merlin Missions Ser.: 16). lib. bdg. 16.00 *(978-0-606-26808-0(1)*, Turtleback) Turtleback Bks.

—A Good Night for Ghosts. 2010. (Magic Tree House Merlin Missions Ser.: No. 14). (Illus.). 157p. (J). pap. *(978-4-8401-3411-8(1))* Fukuinkan Shoten.

—A Good Night for Ghosts. Murdocca, Sal, illus. 2011. (Magic Tree House Merlin Mission Ser.: 14). (ENG.). 144p. (J). (gr. 2-5). 5.99 *(978-0-375-85649-5(8)*, Random Hse. Bks. for Young Readers) Random Hse. Children's Bks.

—High Tide in Hawaii. Murdocca, Sal, illus. 2003. (Magic Tree House (R) Ser.: 28). (ENG.). 96p. (J). (gr. 1-4). pap. 5.99 *(978-0-375-80616-2(4)*, Random Hse. Bks. for Young Readers) Random Hse. Children's Bks.

—High Tide in Hawaii. 2003. (Magic Tree House Ser.: 28). (gr. k-3). lib. bdg. 16.00 *(978-0-613-62386-5(X)*, Turtleback) Turtleback Bks.

—Hurry up, Houdini! 2015. (Magic Tree House Merlin Missions Ser.: 22). lib. bdg. 16.00 *(978-0-606-37718-8(2))* Turtleback Bks.

—Leprechaun in Late Winter. Murdocca, Sal, illus. (Magic Tree House Merlin Mission Ser.: No. 15). (ENG.). 128p. (J). (gr. 2-5). 2012. 5.99 *(978-0-375-85651-8(X))* 2010. 12.99 *(978-0-375-85650-1(1))* Random Hse. Children's Bks. (Random Hse. Bks. for Young Readers).

—Leprechaun in Late Winter. 2012. (Magic Tree House Merlin Missions Ser.: 15). lib. bdg. 16.00 *(978-0-606-23860-1(3)*, Turtleback) Turtleback Bks.

—Monday with a Mad Genius. Murdocca, Sal, illus. (Magic Tree House Merlin Mission Ser.: 10). (ENG.). (J). (gr. 2-5). 2009. 144p. 5.99 *(978-0-375-83730-2(2))* 2007. 128p. 11.99 *(978-0-375-83729-6(9))* Random Hse. Children's Bks. (Random Hse. Bks. for Young Readers).

—Monday with a Mad Genius. 2009. (Magic Tree House Merlin Missions Ser.: 10). lib. bdg. 16.00 *(978-0-606-01777-0(1)*, Turtleback) Turtleback Bks.

—Moonlight on the Magic Flute. Murdocca, Sal, illus. 2010. (Magic Tree House Merlin Mission Ser.: No. 13). (ENG.). 144p. (J). (gr. 2-5). pap. 5.99 *(978-0-375-85647-1(1)*, Random Hse. Bks. for Young Readers) Random Hse. Children's Bks.

—Navidad en Camelot. 2015. (Casa De árbol Ser.: 29). (SPA., Illus.). 144p. (J). (gr. 2-4). pap. 5.99 *(978-1-63245-532-1(3))* Lectorum Pubns., Inc.

—Night of the New Magicians. Murdocca, Sal, illus. 2007. (Magic Tree House Merlin Mission Ser.: 7). (ENG.). 144p. (J). (gr. 2-5). 5.99 *(978-0-375-83036-5(7)*, Random Hse. Bks. for Young Readers) Random Hse. Children's Bks.

—Night of the New Magicians. 2007. (Magic Tree House Merlin Missions Ser.: 7). lib. bdg. 16.00 *(978-1-4177-9108-8(X)*, Turtleback) Turtleback Bks.

—Night of the Ninth Dragon. Murdocca, Sal, illus. 2016. (Magic Tree House Merlin Missions Ser.: No. 27). (ENG.). 144p. (J). (gr. 2-5). 13.99 *(978-0-553-51089-8(4)*, Random Hse. Bks. for Young Readers) Random Hse. Children's Bks.

—A Perfect Time for Pandas. Murdocca, Sal, illus. 2014. (Magic Tree House Merlin Mission Ser.: No. 20). (ENG.). 144p. (J). (gr. 2-5). pap. 5.99 *(978-0-375-86798-9(8)*, Random Hse. Bks. for Young Readers) Random Hse. Children's Bks.

—A Perfect Time for Pandas. 2014. (Magic Tree House Merlin Missions Ser.: 20). lib. bdg. 16.00 *(978-0-606-35564-3(2))* Turtleback Bks.

—Season of the Sandstorms. 2014. (Magic Tree House Merlin Missions Ser.: No. 6). 15.00 *(978-1-63419-681-9(3))* Perfection Learning Corp.

—Season of the Sandstorms. Murdocca, Sal, illus. 2006. (Magic Tree House Merlin Mission Ser.: No. 6). (ENG.). 144p. (J). (gr. 2-5). 5.99 *(978-0-375-83032-7(4)*, Random Hse. Bks. for Young Readers) Random Hse. Children's Bks.

—Shadow of the Shark. 2017. (Magic Tree House Merlin Mission Ser.: 25). (ENG., Illus.). 144p. (J). (gr. 2-5). 5.99 ***(978-0-553-51084-3(3)***, Random Hse. Bks. for Young Readers) Random Hse. Children's Bks.

—Shadow of the Shark. Murdocca, Sal, illus. 2015. (Magic Tree House Merlin Mission Ser.: No. 25). (ENG.). 144p. (J). (gr. 2-5). lib. bdg. 15.99 *(978-0-553-51082-9(7)*, Random Hse. Bks. for Young Readers) Random Hse. Children's Bks.

—Soccer on Sunday. Murdocca, Sal, illus. (Magic Tree House Merlin Missions Ser.: No. 24). (ENG.). (J). (gr. 2-5). 2016. 144p. 5.99 *(978-0-307-98056-4(1))* 2014. 128p. 12.99 *(978-0-307-98053-3(7))* Random Hse. Children's Bks. (Random Hse. Bks. for Young Readers).

—Stallion by Starlight. Murdocca, Sal, illus. (Magic Tree House Merlin Mission Ser.: No. 21). (ENG.). (J). (gr. 2-5). 2014. 144p. pap. 5.99 *(978-0-307-98044-1(8))* 2013. 128p. lib. bdg. 15.99 *(978-0-307-98042-7(1))* Random Hse. Children's Bks. (Random Hse. Bks. for Young Readers).

—Stallion by Starlight. 2014. (Magic Tree House Merlin Missions Ser.: 21). lib. bdg. 16.00 *(978-0-606-36411-9(0))* Turtleback Bks.

—Summer of the Sea Serpent. Murdocca, Sal, illus. 2011. (Magic Tree House Merlin Mission Ser.: No. 3). (ENG.). 144p. (J). (gr. 2-5). 5.99 *(978-0-375-86491-9(1)*, Random Hse. Bks. for Young Readers) Random Hse. Children's Bks.

—El Verano de la Serpiente Marina. 2015. (Casa De árbol Ser.: 31). (SPA., Illus.). 144p. (J). (gr. 2-4). pap. 5.99 *(978-1-63245-534-5(X))* Lectorum Pubns., Inc.

Osborne, Mary Pope & Osborne, Magic Tree. Dark Day in the Deep Sea. Murdocca, Sal, illus. 2009. (Magic Tree House Merlin Mission Ser.: 11). (ENG.). 144p. (J). (gr. 2-5). 5.99 *(978-0-375-83732-6(9)*, Random Hse. Bks. for Young Readers) Random Hse. Children's Bks.

Osborne, Mary Pope & PLC Editors Staff. Carnival at Candlelight. Murdocca, Sal, illus. 2006. (Magic Tree House Merlin Missions Ser.: No. 5). 105p. (gr. 2-6). 15.00 *(978-0-7569-6690-4(6))* Perfection Learning Corp.

Osborne, Mary Pope, et al. Carnaval a Media Luz. Murdocca, Sal, illus. 2016. (SPA.). (J). (gr. 2-4). pap. 5.99 ***(978-1-63245-643-4(5))*** Lectorum Pubns., Inc.

—La Estación de Las Tormentas de Arena. Murdocca, Sal, illus. 2016. (SPA.). (J). (gr. 2-4). pap. 5.99 ***(978-1-63245-644-1(3))*** Lectorum Pubns., Inc.

—Maremoto en Hawái. Murdocca, Sal, illus. 2014. 28. (SPA.). 88p. (J). (gr. 2-4). pap. 5.99 *(978-1-933032-95-5(2))* Lectorum Pubns., Inc.

—La Noche de los Nuevos Magos. Murdocca, Sal, illus. 2016. (SPA.). (J). (gr. 2-4). pap. 5.99 ***(978-1-63245-645-8(1))*** Lectorum Pubns., Inc.

—Tormenta de Nieve en Luna Azul. Murdocca, Sal, illus. 2016. (SPA.). (J). (gr. 2-4). pap. 5.99 ***(978-1-63245-646-5(X))*** Lectorum Pubns., Inc.

O'Shea, M.J. Cold Moon. 2nd ed. 2016. (ENG., Illus.). (J). 24.99 ***(978-1-63477-954-8(1)***, Harmony Ink Pr.) Dreamspinner Pr.

Osterhold, Jared, illus. Olivia & the Babies. 2010. (Olivia TV Tie-In Ser.). (ENG.). 24p. (J). (gr. -1-2). pap. 3.99 *(978-1-4169-9529-6(3)*, Simon Spotlight) Simon Spotlight.

Ostow, Micol. Amity. 2014. (ENG.). 362p. (J). (gr. 9). 18.99 *(978-1-60684-156-3(4)*, Carolrhoda Lab™) Lerner Publishing Group.

O'Sullivan, Deirdre. Cousin Caleigh's Cartoons: And Other Stories, 1 vol. 2009. 97p. pap. 19.95 *(978-1-60836-304-9(X))* America Star Bks.

Oswald, Michael J. 3 Years Apart. 2006. 72p. pap. 11.95 *(978-0-7414-3108-0(4))* Infinity Publishing.

Owens, L. L. The Longest Car Ride Ever. Tolson, Scott, illus. 2004. 28p. *(978-1-57021-032-7(2))* Comprehensive Health Education Foundation.

Pace, Anne Marie. Pigloo. Hussey, Lorna, illus. 2016. (ENG.). 32p. (J). 16.99 *(978-1-62779-202-8(3)*, 9781627792028, Holt, Henry & Co. Bks. For Young Readers) Holt, Henry & Co.

Palmer, Deokie Savie. My Little Baby Sister & I, on a Cold Winter Day. 2007. 38p. 17.95 *(978-1-4303-2061-6(3))* Lulu Pr., Inc.

Palmer, Pamela. Horse of the Dawn. 2005. 89p. pap. 16.95 *(978-1-4137-9545-5(5))* PublishAmerica, Inc.

Panzieri, Lucia & Maccarone, Grace. Little Brother Pumpkin Head. Enria, Samantha, illus. 2016. (ENG.). 32p. (J). 16.95 *(978-0-8234-3537-1(7))* Holiday Hse., Inc.

Papp, Lisa & Noble, Trinka Hakes. The Battles. Papp, Robert, illus. 2013. (American Adventures Ser.). (ENG.). 88p. (J). (gr. 3-6). pap. 9.99 *(978-1-58536-861-7(X)*, 202368) Sleeping Bear Pr.

Papp, Robert, illus. The Amazing Mystery Show. 2010. (Boxcar Children Mysteries Ser.: 123). (ENG.). 128p. (J). (gr. 1-5). pap. 6.99 *(978-0-8075-0315-7(0))*;No. 123. 14.99 *(978-0-8075-0314-0(2))* Whitman, Albert & Co.

—The Clue in the Recycling Bin. 2011. (Boxcar Children Mysteries Ser.: 126). (ENG.). 128p. (J). (gr. 1-5). pap. 6.99 *(978-0-8075-1209-8(5))* Whitman, Albert & Co.

—The Clue in the Recycling Bin. 2011. (Boxcar Children Mysteries Ser.: 126). (ENG.). 128p. (J). (gr. 1-5). lib. bdg. 14.99 *(978-0-8075-1208-1(7))* Whitman, Albert & Co.

—The Creature in Ogopogo Lake. 2006. (Boxcar Children Mysteries Ser.: 108). (ENG.). 128p. (J). (gr. 1-5). per. 6.99 *(978-0-8075-1337-8(7))* Whitman, Albert & Co.

—The Ghost of the Chattering Bones. 2007. (Boxcar Children Ser.). 120p. 15.00 *(978-0-7569-7611-8(1))* Perfection Learning Corp.

—The Ghost of the Chattering Bones. 2005. (Boxcar Children Mysteries Ser.: 102). (ENG.). 128p. (J). (gr. 1-5). pap. 5.99 *(978-0-8075-0874-9(8))* Whitman, Albert & Co.

—The Giant Yo-Yo Mystery. 2006. (Boxcar Children Mysteries Ser.: 107). (ENG.). 128p. (J). (gr. 1-5). per. 5.99 *(978-0-8075-0879-4(9))* Whitman, Albert & Co.

—The Great Detective Race. 2008. (Boxcar Children Mysteries Ser.: 115). (ENG.). 128p. (J). (gr. 1-5). 14.99 *(978-0-8075-5573-6(8))* Whitman, Albert & Co.

—The Great Detective Race. 2008. (Boxcar Children Mysteries Ser.: 115). (ENG.). 128p. (J). (gr. 1-5). pap. 5.99 *(978-0-8075-5574-3(6))* Whitman, Albert & Co.

—The Great Turkey Heist. 2011. (Boxcar Children Mysteries Ser.: 129). (ENG.). (J). (gr. 1-5). 144p. 6.99 *(978-0-8075-3051-1(4))*; 128p. lib. bdg. 14.99 *(978-0-8075-3050-4(6))* Whitman, Albert & Co.

—Monkey Trouble. 2011. (Boxcar Children Mysteries Ser.: 127). (ENG.). 128p. (J). (gr. 1-5). pap. 5.99 *(978-0-8075-5240-7(2))* Whitman, Albert & Co.

—Monkey Trouble. 2011. (Boxcar Children Mysteries Ser.: 127). (ENG.). 128p. (J). (gr. 1-5). lib. bdg. 14.99 *(978-0-8075-5239-1(9))* Whitman, Albert & Co.

—The Rock 'n' Roll Mystery. 2006. (Boxcar Children Mysteries Ser.: 109). (ENG.). 128p. (J). (gr. 1-5). lib. bdg. 14.99 *(978-0-8075-7089-0(3))*; per. 5.99 *(978-0-8075-7090-6(7))* Whitman, Albert & Co.

—The Seattle Puzzle. 2007. (Boxcar Children Mysteries Ser.: 111). (ENG.). 128p. (J). (gr. 1-5). lib. bdg. 14.99 *(978-0-8075-5560-6(6))*; per. 5.99 *(978-0-8075-5561-3(4))* Whitman, Albert & Co.

—Spooktacular Special. 2013. (Boxcar Children Mysteries Ser.). (ENG.). 400p. (J). (gr. 1-5). 9.99 *(978-0-8075-7605-2(0))* Whitman, Albert & Co.

—The Spy in the Bleachers. 2010. (Boxcar Children Mysteries Ser.: 122). (ENG.). 128p. (J). (gr. 1-5). 14.99 *(978-0-8075-7606-9(9))*;No. 122. pap. 6.99 *(978-0-8075-7607-6(7))* Whitman, Albert & Co.

—The Sword of the Silver Knight. 2005. (Boxcar Children Mysteries Ser.: 103). (ENG.). 128p. (J). (gr. 1-5). per. 6.99 *(978-0-8075-0876-3(4))* Whitman, Albert & Co.

—The Vanishing Passenger. 2006. (Boxcar Children Mysteries Ser.: 106). (ENG.). 128p. (J). (gr. 1-5). 14.99 *(978-0-8075-1066-7(1))* Whitman, Albert & Co.

—The Zombie Project. 2011. (Boxcar Children Mysteries Ser.: 128). (ENG.). 128p. (J). (gr. 1-5). 6.99 *(978-0-8075-9493-3(8))*; lib. bdg. 14.99 *(978-0-8075-9492-6(X))* Whitman, Albert & Co.

Papp, Robert L., illus. The Dog-Gone Mystery. 2009. (Boxcar Children Mysteries Ser.: 119). (ENG.). 128p. (J). (gr. 1-5). lib. bdg. 14.99 *(978-0-8075-1658-4(9))* Whitman, Albert & Co.

—The Spy Game. 2009. (Boxcar Children Mysteries Ser.: 118). (ENG.). 128p. (J). (gr. 1-5). 14.99 *(978-0-8075-7603-8(4))* Whitman, Albert & Co.

Paratore, Coleen Murtagh. Wish I Might. 2011. (ENG.). 176p. (J). (gr. 5-9). pap. 6.99 *(978-0-545-09402-3(X)*, Scholastic Paperbacks) Scholastic, Inc.

—Wish I Might: From the Life of Willa Havisham. 2010. (ENG.). 176p. (J). (gr. 5-9). 16.99 *(978-0-545-09406-1(2)*, Scholastic Pr.) Scholastic, Inc.

Paris, Harper. The Mystery Across the Secret Bridge. Calo, Marcos, illus. 2015. (Greetings from Somewhere Ser.: 7). (ENG.). 128p. (J). (gr. k-4). pap. 5.99 *(978-1-4814-2367-0(3)*, Little Simon) Little Simon.

—The Mystery at the Coral Reef. Calo, Marcos, illus. 2015. (Greetings from Somewhere Ser.: 8). (ENG.). 128p. (J). (gr. k-4). pap. 5.99 *(978-1-4814-2370-0(3)*, Little Simon) Little Simon.

—The Mystery in the Forbidden City. Calo, Marcos, illus. 2014. (Greetings from Somewhere Ser.: 4). (ENG.). 128p. (J). (gr. k-2). pap. 5.99 *(978-1-4814-0299-6(4)*, Little Simon) Little Simon.

—The Mystery of the Gold Coin. Calo, Marcos, illus. 2014. (Greetings from Somewhere Ser.: 1). (ENG.). 128p. (J). (gr. k-4). pap. 5.99 *(978-1-4424-9718-4(1)*, Little Simon) Little Simon.

—The Mystery of the Icy Paw Prints. Calo, Marcos, illus. 2015. (Greetings from Somewhere Ser.: 9). (ENG.). 128p. (J). (gr. k-4). pap. 5.99 *(978-1-4814-2373-1(8)*, Little Simon) Little Simon.

—The Mystery of the Mosaic. Calo, Marcos, illus. 2014. (Greetings from Somewhere Ser.: 2). (ENG.). 128p. (J). (gr. k-2). pap. 5.99 *(978-1-4424-9721-4(1)*, Little Simon) Little Simon.

—The Mystery of the Secret Society. Calo, Marcos, illus. 2016. (Greetings from Somewhere Ser.: 10). (ENG.). 128p. (J). (gr. k-4). pap. 5.99 *(978-1-4814-5171-0(5)*, Little Simon) Little Simon.

—The Mystery of the Stolen Painting. Calo, Marcos, illus. 2014. (Greetings from Somewhere Ser.: 3). (ENG.). 128p. (J). (gr. k-2). pap. 5.99 *(978-1-4814-0296-5(X)*, Little Simon) Little Simon.

—The Mystery of the Suspicious Spices. Calo, Marcos, illus. 2014. (Greetings from Somewhere Ser.: 6). (ENG.). 128p. (J). (gr. k-4). pap. 5.99 *(978-1-4814-1467-8(4)*, Little Simon) Little Simon.

Park, Barbara. Junie B. Jones & a Little Monkey Business, Vol. 2. unabr. ed. 2004. (Junie B. Jones Ser.: Vol. 2). 68p. (J). (gr. k-3). pap. 17.00 incl. audio *(978-0-8072-0779-6(9)*, LFTR 238 SP, Listening Library) Random Hse. Audio Publishing Group.

—Mick Harte Was Here. 88p. (J). (gr. 4-6). pap. 4.99 *(978-0-8072-1502-9(3)*, Listening Library) Random Hse. Audio Publishing Group.

Park, Barbara, ed. Mick Harte Was Here. unabr. ed. 2004. (Middle Grade Cassette Librariestm Ser.). 88p. (J). (gr. 3-7). pap. 29.00 incl. audio *(978-0-8072-7797-3(5)*, S YA 922 SP, Listening Library) Random Hse. Audio Publishing Group.

Park, Linda Sue. Trust No One. 2012. (39 Clues: Cahills vs. Vespers Ser.: Bk. 5). (ENG.). 192p. (J). (gr. 3-7). 12.99 *(978-0-545-32415-1(7))* Scholastic, Inc.

Parker, Glenn. The Shutout Girl. 2013. 152p. *(978-1-4602-1816-7(7))*; pap. *(978-1-4602-1817-4(5))* FriesenPress.

Parker, Natalie C. Beware the Wild. 2014. (Beware the Wild Ser.: 1). (ENG.). 336p. (YA). (gr. 8). 17.99 *(978-0-06-224152-8(4)*, HarperTeen) HarperCollins Pubs.

Parramore, Helen. Maudie's Promise: A Girl on the Florida Frontier. 2008. 36p. pap. 20.99 *(978-1-4389-0226-5(3))* AuthorHouse.

Partis, Joanne. Stripe's Naughty Sister. 2003. (Picture Bks.). (Illus.). 32p. (J). (gr. -1-3). 15.95 *(978-0-87614-466-4(0)*, Carolrhoda Bks.) Lerner Publishing Group.

Paterson, Katherine. The Same Stuff As Stars. 2015. (ENG.). 256p. (J). (gr. 5-7). pap. 7.99 *(978-0-544-54030-9(1)*, HMH Books For Young Readers) Houghton Mifflin Harcourt Publishing Co.

—The Same Stuff as Stars. 2004. 270p. (gr. 3-7). 17.00 *(978-0-7569-2801-8(X))* Perfection Learning Corp.

Paton, Doug. Our Plane Is Down. Melanson, Matt, illus. 2004. (New Series Canada). 90p. (J). pap. *(978-1-897039-03-8(4))* High Interest Publishing (HIP).

Patricelli, Leslie. The Patterson Puppies & the Midnight Monster Party. Patricelli, Leslie, illus. 2010. (ENG., Illus.). 32p. (J). (gr. -1-k). 14.99 *(978-0-7636-3243-4(0))* Candlewick Pr.

Patron, Kristine Mary. An Artist? That's Me! 2013. 20p. (J). pap. 6.95 *(978-1-4327-8377-8(7))* Outskirts Pr., Inc.

Patterson, James. The Fire. 2011. (Playaway Children Ser.). (ENG.). (YA). (gr. 8-12). 59.99 *(978-1-61113-385-1(8))* Hachette Audio.

—The Gift. 2010. (Witch & Wizard Ser.: No. 2). (J). 59.99 *(978-1-60941-012-4(2))* Findaway World, LLC.

—The Gift. 2014. lthr. 79.00 *(978-1-62715-523-6(6))* Leatherbound Bestsellers.

—Maximum Ride. 2010. (ENG.). 1392p. (YA). (gr. 5-17). pap., pap. 29.99 *(978-0-316-12825-4(2)*, Jimmy Patterson) Little Brown & Co.

—Witch & Wizard. 2014. lthr. 79.00 *(978-1-62715-529-8(5))* Leatherbound Bestsellers.

—Witch & Wizard. 2010. (Witch & Wizard Ser.: 1). (ENG.). 336p. (YA). (gr. 5-17). pap. 10.00 *(978-0-316-03834-8(2)*, Jimmy Patterson) Little Brown & Co.

—Witch & Wizard. 2010. (Witch & Wizard Ser.: 1). (YA). lib. bdg. 20.85 *(978-0-606-15119-1(2)*, Turtleback) Turtleback Bks.

Patterson, James & Bergen, Julia. Ultimate Showdown. 2014. (Middle School Ser.: 5). (ENG., Illus.). 256p. (J). (gr. 3-7). 13.99 *(978-0-316-32211-9(3)*, Jimmy Patterson) Little Brown & Co.

Patterson, James & Charbonnet, Gabrielle. Witch & Wizard. 2011. (Witch & Wizard Ser.: 1). (ENG.). 368p. mass mkt. 8.00 *(978-0-446-56243-0(2)*, Jimmy Patterson) Little Brown & Co.

—Witch & Wizard. 2011. (Witch & Wizard Ser.: 1). lib. bdg. 18.45 *(978-0-606-26452-5(3)*, Turtleback) Turtleback Bks.

Patterson, James & Dembowski, Jill. The Fire. (Witch & Wizard Ser.: 3). (ENG.). 352p. (YA). 2013. (gr. 7-17). mass mkt. 8.00 *(978-1-4555-2152-4(3))* 2011. (gr. 5-17). 17.99 *(978-0-316-10190-5(7))* Little Brown & Co. (Jimmy Patterson).

—The Fire. 2012. (Witch & Wizard Ser.: 3). (YA). lib. bdg. 20.85 *(978-0-606-26698-7(4)*, Turtleback) Turtleback Bks.

—The Kiss. 2013. (Witch & Wizard Ser.: 4). (YA). lib. bdg. 20.85 *(978-0-606-32281-2(7)*, Turtleback) Turtleback Bks.

Patterson, James & Grabenstein, Chris. Danger down the Nile. Neufeld, Juliana, illus. 2014. (Treasure Hunters Ser.). (ENG.). 480p. (J). (gr. 3-7). 14.99 *(978-0-316-37086-8(X)*, Jimmy Patterson) Little Brown & Co.

—Peril at the Top of the World. Neufeld, Juliana, illus. 2016. (Treasure Hunters Ser.: 4). (ENG.). 384p. (J). (gr. 3-7). 14.99 *(978-0-316-34693-1(4)*, Jimmy Patterson) Little Brown & Co.

—Secret of the Forbidden City. Neufeld, Juliana, illus. 2015. (Treasure Hunters Ser.: 3). (ENG.). 448p. (J). (gr. 3-7). 14.99 *(978-0-316-28480-6(7)*, Jimmy Patterson) Little Brown & Co.

—Treasure Hunters. Neufeld, Juliana, illus. (Treasure Hunters Ser.: 1). (ENG.). 480p. (J). (gr. 3-7). 2015. pap. 8.00 *(978-0-316-20757-7(8))* 2013. 14.99 *(978-0-316-20756-0(X))* Little Brown & Co. (Jimmy Patterson).

—Treasure Hunters. 2015. (Treasure Hunters Ser.: 1). (J). lib. bdg. 18.45 *(978-0-606-37305-0(5))* Turtleback Bks.

Patterson, James & Paetro, Maxine. Confessions: The Paris Mysteries. 2014. (Confessions Ser.). (ENG.). 320p. (YA). (gr. 7-17). 18.00 *(978-0-316-37084-4(3)*, Jimmy Patterson) Little Brown & Co.

—Confessions: The Private School Murders. 2013. 422p. (YA). *(978-0-316-24263-9(2))* Little Brown & Co.

—Confessions of a Murder Suspect. 2014. (Confessions Ser.: 1). (ENG.). 352p. (gr. 7-17). mass mkt. 8.00 *(978-1-4555-4774-6(3)*, Jimmy Patterson) 2013. (ENG.). 400p. (J). (gr. 7-17). pap. 10.00 *(978-0-316-20700-3(4)*, Jimmy Patterson) 2012. (Confessions Ser.: 1). (ENG.). 384p. (YA). (gr. 7-17). 19.99 *(978-0-316-20698-3(9)*, Jimmy Patterson) 2012. 372p. (J). 11.99 *(978-0-316-22641-7(6))* 2012. (Confessions Ser.: 1). (ENG.). 400p. (YA). (gr. 7-17). 31.99 *(978-0-316-22418-5(9)*, Jimmy Patterson) Little Brown & Co.

—Confessions of a Murder Suspect. 2013. (Confessions Ser.: 1). lib. bdg. 20.85 *(978-0-606-32278-2(7)*, Turtleback) Turtleback Bks.

—Confessions: the Murder of an Angel. (Confessions Ser.: 4). (ENG.). 304p. (YA). (gr. 7-17). 2016. pap. 9.99 *(978-0-316-39218-1(9))* 2015. 18.00 *(978-0-316-30102-2(7))* Little Brown & Co. (Jimmy Patterson).

—The Paris Mysteries. l.t. ed. 2014. (Confessions Ser.: 3). (ENG.). 352p. (YA). (gr. 7-17). 30.99 *(978-0-316-40963-6(4)*, Jimmy Patterson) Little Brown & Co.

—The Paris Mysteries. 2015. (Confessions Ser.: 3). (YA). lib. bdg. 20.85 *(978-0-606-37526-9(0))* Turtleback Bks.

—The Private School Murders. 2015. (Confessions Ser.: 2). (ENG.). 400p. mass mkt. 8.00 *(978-1-4555-5946-6(6)*, Jimmy Patterson) Grand Central Publishing.

—The Private School Murders. (Confessions Ser.: 2). (ENG.). (YA). (gr. 7-17). 2014. 448p. pap. 10.00 *(978-0-316-20764-5(0))* 2013. 448p. 18.00 *(978-0-316-20765-2(9))* 2013. 480p. 22.00 *(978-0-316-23992-9(5))* Little Brown & Co. (Jimmy Patterson).

—The Private School Murders. 2014. (Confessions Ser.: 2). (YA). lib. bdg. 20.85 *(978-0-606-35945-0(1))* Turtleback Bks.

Patterson, James & Papademetriou, Lisa. Big Fat Liar. Swaab, Neil, illus. 2014. (Middle School Ser.: Bk. 3). (ENG.). 304p. (J). (gr. 3-7). 13.99 *(978-0-316-32203-4(2)*, Jimmy Patterson) Little Brown & Co.

Patterson, James & Raymond, Emily. The Lost. 2014. (YA). (Witch & Wizard Ser.: 5). (ENG.). 384p. (gr. 7-17). 18.00 *(978-0-316-20770-6(5)*, Jimmy Patterson); 355p. *(978-0-316-24266-0(7))* Little Brown & Co.

Patterson, James & Rust, Ned. The Gift. (Witch & Wizard Ser.: 2). (ENG.). 2012. 352p. mass mkt. 7.99 *(978-0-446-56245-4(9))* 2011. 400p. (gr. 5-17). pap. 9.99 *(978-0-316-03835-5(0))* 2010. 352p. (gr. 5-17). 17.99 *(978-0-316-03625-2(0))* Little Brown & Co. (Jimmy Patterson).

—The Gift. 2012. (Witch & Wizard Ser.: 2). lib. bdg. 18.40 *(978-0-606-26451-8(5)*, Turtleback) Turtleback Bks.

Patterson, James, et al. Treasure Hunters. Neufeld, Juliana, illus. 2013. 451p. (J). *(978-0-316-24262-2(4))* Little Brown & Co.

Paul, Curtis Christopher. The Watsons Go to Birmingham 1963. 2014. (ENG.). 224p. (J). (gr. 12-12). 11.24 *(978-1-63245-108-8(5))* Lectorum Pubns., Inc.

Paulsen, Gary. Harris & Me. 2007. (ENG., Illus.). 176p. (J). (gr. 5-7). pap. 6.99 *(978-0-15-205880-7(X))* Houghton Mifflin Harcourt Publishing Co.

Paulsen, Gary & Paulsen, Jim. Field Trip. 2015. (ENG.). 128p. (J). (gr. 5). 12.99 *(978-0-553-49674-1(3)*, Lamb, Wendy Bks.) Random Hse. Children's Bks.

Paver, Michelle. The Burning Shadow. 2015. (Gods & Warriors Ser.: 2). (ENG.). 320p. (J). (gr. 5). 7.99 *(978-0-14-242285-4(1)*, Puffin Books) Penguin Young Readers Group.

—Warrior Bronze. 2017. (Gods & Warriors Ser.). (ENG.). 272p. (J). (gr. 3-7). 16.99 *(978-0-8037-3884-3(6)*, Dial Bks) Penguin Young Readers Group.

PC Treasures Staff, prod. Hansel & Gretel. 2007. (J). *(978-1-60072-030-7(7))* PC Treasures, Inc.

Peacock, L. A. Panic in Pompeii. Hale, Nathan, illus. 2011. 92p. (J). pap. *(978-0-545-34062-5(4))* Scholastic, Inc.

—Terror at Troy. Hale, Nathan, illus. 2012. 90p. (J). *(978-0-545-34063-2(2))* Scholastic, Inc.

Pearce, Jackson. Sweetly. 2012. (Fairy Tale Retelling Ser.). (ENG.). 336p. (YA). (gr. 10-17). pap. 8.99 *(978-0-316-06866-6(7))* Little, Brown Bks. for Young Readers.

Pearce, Jacqueline. The Truth about Rats (and Dogs). 1 vol. 2006. (ENG.). 160p. (J). (gr. 4-7). per. 7.95 *(978-1-55143-473-5(3))* Orca Bk. Pubs. USA.

Pearson, Ridley. Lock & Key: the Initiation. 2017. (Lock & Key Ser.: 1). 384p. (J). (gr. 3-7). pap. 9.99 ***(978-0-06-239902-1(0))*** HarperCollins Pubs.

Pearson, Yvonne. Sadie Braves the Wilderness. Ritz, Karen, illus. 2017. (ENG.). 32p. (J). (gr. -1-2). 16.95 ***(978-1-68134-038-8(0))*** Minnesota Historical Society Pr.

Peck, Richard. Secrets at Sea. 2012. (ENG.). 272p. (J). (gr. 3-7). pap. 7.99 *(978-0-14-242183-3(9)*, Puffin Books) Penguin Young Readers Group.

—Secrets at Sea. Murphy, Kelly, illus. 2011. (ENG.). 256p. (J). (gr. 3-7). 16.99 *(978-0-8037-3455-5(7)*, Dial Bks) Penguin Young Readers Group.

Peck, Robert Newton. Bro. 2004. (ENG.). 160p. (J). (gr. 7-18). 16.99 *(978-0-06-052974-1(1))* HarperCollins Pubs.

Pedley, Linda J. A Journey of Brothers. 2013. 96p. pap. *(978-0-9878319-7-2(6))* Dream Write Publishing, Ltd.

Peete, Holly Robinson & Peete, Ryan Elizabeth. My Brother Charlie. Evans, Shane W., illus. 2010. (ENG.). 40p. (J). (gr. 2-5). 17.99 *(978-0-545-09466-5(6)*, Scholastic Pr.) Scholastic, Inc.

Pelham, David. Sam's Sandwich. Pelham, David, illus. 2015. (ENG., Illus.). 24p. (J). (gr. -1-2). 9.99 *(978-0-7636-7808-1(2))* Candlewick Pr.

Pellowski, Anne. Stairstep Farm: Anna Rose's Story. Sharpe, Roseanne, illus. 2011. 182p. (J). pap. 12.95 *(978-1-932350-40-1(3))* Bethlehem Bks.

Pennypacker, Sara. Clementine & the Family Meeting. Frazee, Marla, illus. (ENG.). 176p. (J). (gr. 2-5). 2012. pap. 5.99 *(978-1-4231-2436-8(7))* 2011. 14.99 *(978-1-4231-2356-9(5))* Hyperion Pr.

—Clementine & the Family Meeting. 2012. (Clementine Ser.: 5). (J). lib. bdg. 16.00 *(978-0-606-26093-0(5)*, Turtleback) Turtleback Bks.

—Waylon! One Awesome Thing. Frazee, Marla, illus. 2016. (Waylon Ser.). (ENG.). 204p. (J). (gr. 1-3). 15.99 *(978-1-4847-0152-2(6))* Disney Pr.

Peppermint, Aurora. Beneath the Scales. 2016. (ENG., Illus.). (J). 24.99 ***(978-1-63477-940-1(1)***, Harmony Ink Pr.) Dreamspinner Pr.

Percival, Tom. The Magic Looking Glass. 2017. (Little Legends Ser.: 4). (ENG.). 192p. (J). (gr. 2-5). 14.99 ***(978-1-4926-4667-9(9))***; pap. 5.99 ***(978-1-4926-4259-6(2))*** Sourcebooks, Inc. (Sourcebooks Jabberwocky).

Perry, Jolene. The Next Door Boys. 2011. (YA). *(978-1-59955-910-0(2)*, Bonneville Bks.) Cedar Fort, Inc./CFI Distribution.

Perry, Roseann. When Mama Said Yes. 2009. 36p. pap. 16.99 *(978-1-4490-5210-2(X))* AuthorHouse.

—When Mama Says No. 2009. 36p. pap. 16.99 *(978-1-4389-1938-6(7))* AuthorHouse.

Pertzborn, Cindy. How Do We Get to Heaven? 2012. 36p. pap. 16.95 *(978-1-4497-4585-1(7)*, WestBow Pr.) Author Solutions, Inc.

Peschke, Marci. Dancing Queen, 1 vol. Mourning, Tuesday, illus. 2012. (Kylie Jean Ser.). (ENG.). 112p. (gr. 2-3). pap. 5.95 *(978-1-4048-7209-7(4))*; lib. bdg. 22.65 *(978-1-4048-6798-7(8))* Picture Window Bks. (Kylie Jean).

—Football Queen, 1 vol. Mourning, Tuesday, illus. 2012. (Kylie Jean Ser.). (ENG.). 112p. (gr. 2-3). pap. 5.95 *(978-1-4048-7210-3(8))*; lib. bdg. 22.65 *(978-1-4048-6799-4(6))* Picture Window Bks. (Kylie Jean).

Peters, Anna. The Friendly Rubbish Monsters. 2011. 92p. pap. 10.00 *(978-1-60911-878-5(2)*, Eloquent Bks.) Strategic Book Publishing & Rights Agency (SBPRA).

Peters, Julie Anne. Luna. 2006. (ENG.). 256p. (YA). (gr. 10-17). reprint ed. pap. 10.99 *(978-0-316-01127-3(4)*, Tingley, Megan Bks.) Little, Brown Bks. for Young Readers.

Petersen, Alicia. A Sparrow Alone. 2004. 154p. (YA). 8.99 *(978-1-59166-204-4(4))* BJU Pr.

Petersen, P. J. Wild River. 2013. (ENG.). 128p. (J). (gr. 4-7). 6.99 *(978-0-375-84624-3(7)*, Yearling) Random Hse. Children's Bks.

Peterson, Andrew. On the Edge of the Dark Sea of Darkness: Adventure. Peril. Lost Jewels. & the Fearsome Toothy Cows of Skree. 2008. (Wingfeather Saga Ser.). (ENG., Illus.). 304p. pap. 15.99 *(978-1-4000-7384-9(7)*, WaterBrook Pr.) Crown Publishing Group.

Peterson Haddix, Margaret. EL DESAFÍO FINAL: THE 39 CLUES 10. 2013. (SPA.). 304p. (J). pap. 14.99 *(978-84-08-10876-4(X))* Noguer y Caralt Editores, S. A. ESP. Dist: Lectorum Pubns., Inc.

Peterson, John C. Adam Has No Brothers. 2009. 20p. pap. 10.99 *(978-1-4490-3207-4(9))* AuthorHouse.

Peterson, Will. The Gathering. 2010. (Triskellion Ser.: 3). (ENG., Illus.). 384p. (YA). (gr. 9-18). 16.99 *(978-0-7636-4847-3(7))* Candlewick Pr.

—Triskellion. (Triskellion Ser.: 1). (ENG., Illus.). 384p. (YA). (gr. 9). 2009. pap. 8.99 *(978-0-7636-3933-4(8))* 2008. 16.99 *(978-0-7636-3971-6(0))* Candlewick Pr.

Petrlik, Andrea, illus. Hansel & Gretel. 2007. (Flip-Up Fairy Tales Ser.). (ENG.). 24p. (J). (gr. -1-2). audio compact disk *(978-1-84643-090-9(9))* Child's Play International Ltd.

Pez, Alberto. Martes Peludo. Gleich, Jacky, illus. (SPA.). (J). 8.95 *(978-958-04-5092-4(7))* Norma S.A. COL. Dist: Distribuidora Norma, Inc.

Pfeffer, Susan Beth. The Dead & the Gone. 2010. (Life As We Knew It Ser.: 2). (ENG.). 336p. (YA). (gr. 7-12). pap. 8.99 *(978-0-547-25855-3(0))* Houghton Mifflin Harcourt Publishing Co.

—The Dead & the Gone. 2010. (Last Survivors Ser.: 2). 321p. lib. bdg. 19.65 *(978-0-606-14464-3(1)*, Turtleback) Turtleback Bks.

Pflugfelder, Bob & Hockensmith, Steve. Nick & Tesla's Secret Agent Gadget Battle. 2014. (Nick & Tesla Ser.: 3). (ENG., Illus.). 256p. (J). (gr. 4-7). 12.95 *(978-1-59474-676-5(1))* Quirk Bks.

—Nick & Tesla's Special Effects Spectacular: A Mystery with Animatronics, Alien Makeup, Camera Gear, & Other Movie Magic You Can Make Yourself! 2015. (Nick & Tesla Ser.: 5). (ENG.). 256p. (J). (gr. 4-7). 12.95 *(978-1-59474-760-1(1))* Quirk Bks.

Philbrick, Rodman. The Mostly True Adventures of Homer P. Figg. 2009. (ENG.). 224p. (J). (gr. 3-7). 16.99 *(978-0-439-66818-7(2)*, Blue Sky Pr., The) Scholastic, Inc.

Phillips, Leigh Hope. Birthday Wishes. Fountain, John, illus. 2005. (J). pap. *(978-1-933156-10-1(4))*; per. *(978-1-933156-03-3(1))* GSVQ Publishing. (VisionQuest Kids).

Phineas and Ferb. Phineas & Ferb Batter Up! 2010. pap. 5.99 *(978-1-4231-2408-5(1))* Disney Pr.

Pichon, Liz. TOM GATES: EXCUSAS PERFECTAS (Y OTRAS COSILLAS GENIALES) 2013. (SPA.). 346p. (J). pap. 21.99 *(978-84-216-8765-9(4))* Lectorum Pubns., Inc.

Pickett, Lanaya A. Walking with Angels. 2011. 192p. 23.95 *(978-1-4620-2306-6(1))*; pap. 13.95 *(978-1-4620-2307-3(X))* iUniverse, Inc.

Pierpoint, Eric. The Last Ride of Caleb O'Toole. 2013. (ENG.). 304p. (J). (gr. 4-7). pap. 7.99 *(978-1-4022-8171-6(4)*, 9781402281716, Sourcebooks Jabberwocky) Sourcebooks, Inc.

Pike, Kenneth & Stewart, Isaac. Jacob's Journal of Doom: Confessions of an Almost-Deacon. 2012. (J). 14.99 *(978-1-60907-016-8(X))* Deseret Bk. Co.

Pincus, Gregory K. The 14 Fibs of Gregory K. 2013. (J). pap. *(978-0-439-91300-3(4))*; (ENG.). 240p. (gr. 3-7). 17.99 *(978-0-439-91299-0(7))* Scholastic, Inc. (Levine, Arthur A. Bks.).

Pisarik, Michael E. Loonhaunt. 2006. (J). per. 19.95 *(978-1-59872-600-8(5))* Instant Pub.

Platt, Chris. Wind Dancer, 1 vol. 2014. (ENG.). 176p. (J). (gr. 3-6). 15.95 *(978-1-56145-736-6(1))* Peachtree Pubs.

Plitt, Kay. Why Isn't Bobby Like Me, Mom? 2010. 32p. 14.75 *(978-1-4269-4038-5(6))* Trafford Publishing.

Plotkin, Andy. The Black Block Legend. 2007. 64p. per. 19.95 *(978-1-4241-9190-1(4))* America Star Bks.

Pointon, Janet. A Matter of Choice. 2008. 82p. pap. 11.51 *(978-1-4092-3108-0(9))* Lulu Pr., Inc.

Polacco, Patricia. My Rotten Redheaded Older Brother. 2014. 40p. pap. 8.00 *(978-1-61003-358-9(2))* Center for the Collaborative Classroom.

—An Orange for Frankie. Polacco, Patricia, illus. 2004. (ENG., Illus.). 48p. (J). (gr. 1-4). 17.99 *(978-0-399-24302-8(X)*, Philomel Bks.) Penguin Young Readers Group.

—Rotten Richie & the Ultimate Dare. Polacco, Patricia, illus. 2006. (ENG., Illus.). 48p. (J). (gr. k-3). 17.99 *(978-0-399-24531-2(6)*, Philomel Bks.) Penguin Young Readers Group.

Polisner, Gae. The Summer of Letting Go. (ENG.). (YA). (gr. 7-10). 2015. 336p. pap. 9.95 *(978-1-61620-480-8(X))* 2014. 320p. 16.95 *(978-1-61620-256-9(4)*, 73256) Algonquin Bks. of Chapel Hill.

Poole, Richard. Jewel & Thorn. 2007. (Book of Lowmoor Ser.: 1). (ENG., Illus.). 400p. (J). (gr. 7-12). pap. 11.95 *(978-0-689-87290-7(9))* Simon & Schuster, Ltd. GBR. Dist: Simon & Schuster, Inc.

The Portal in the Park: By Cricket Casey, songs & audio book performed by Grandmaseter Melle Mel, features Lady Gaga, Included CD in Book. 2010. (Illus.). 132p. (J). mass mkt. 19.95 *(978-0-9786488-0-0(3))* SCOJO ENTERTAINMENT.

Potter, Ellen. The Kneebone Boy. 2011. (ENG.). 304p. (J). (gr. 4-7). pap. 8.99 *(978-0-312-67432-8(5)*, 9780312674328) Square Fish.

—Piper Green & the Fairy Tree. Leng, Qin, illus. 2015. (Piper Green & the Fairy Tree Ser.). (ENG.). 112p. (J). (gr. 2-4). pap. 5.99 *(978-0-553-49926-1(2)*, Yearling) Random Hse. Children's Bks.

—Slob. 2009. (ENG.). 208p. (J). (gr. 3-7). 16.99 *(978-0-399-24705-7(X)*, Philomel Bks.) Penguin Young Readers Group.

Poulin, Andree. Monkey in the Mud. Eudes-Pascal, Elisabeth, illus. 2009. (Rainy Day Readers Ser.). 32p. (J). (gr. -1-3). pap. 10.55 *(978-1-60754-371-8(0))* Windmill Bks.

Poulin, Andrée. Monkey in the Mud. Eudes-Pascal, Elisabeth, illus. 2009. (Rainy Day Readers Ser.). 32p. (J). (gr. -1-3). 22.60 *(978-1-60754-370-1(2))* Windmill Bks.

Powell, Gregg E. Goobadabers. Lea, Corinne, illus. 2011. 24p. pap. 24.95 *(978-1-4626-0734-1(9))* America Star Bks.

Powell-Tuck, Maudie. Pirates Aren't Afraid of the Dark! Edgson, Alison, illus. 2014. (ENG.). 32p. (J). (gr. -1-3). 16.99 *(978-1-58925-165-6(2))* Tiger Tales.

Power, Molly. Up & down with Lena Larocha. Carter, Barbara, illus. 2013. 169p. pap. 15.00 *(978-0-60571-176-8(4)*, Shires Press) Northshire Pr.

Pranali. The Secret Storybook. 2013. 64p. pap. 23.95 *(978-1-4828-0147-7(7))* Partridge Pub.

Preble, Joy. The Sweet Dead Life. 2014. (ENG., Illus.). 278p. (YA). (gr. 9). pap. 10.99 *(978-1-61695-368-3(3)*, Soho Teen) Soho Pr., Inc.

Preller, James. Swamp Monster. Bruno, Iacopo, illus. 2015. (Scary Tales Ser.: 6). (ENG.). 96p. (J). (gr. 2-5). 15.99 *(978-1-250-04097-8(3)*, 9781250040978) Feiwel & Friends.

Price, Lissa. Starters. (ENG.). (YA). (gr. 7). 2013. 384p. pap. 9.99 *(978-0-385-74248-1(7)*, Ember) 2012. 352p. 17.99 *(978-0-385-74237-5(1)*, Delacorte Pr.) Random Hse. Children's Bks.

Priestley, Chris. Tales of Terror from the Black Ship. Roberts, David, illus. 2008. (Tales of Terror Ser.: 1). (ENG.). 256p. (YA). (gr. 3-6). 12.99 *(978-1-59990-290-6(7)*, 9781599902906, Bloomsbury USA Childrens) Bloomsbury Publishing USA.

P.Young, Linda. The Adventures of Anna & Andy Hummingbird: Stories 6-10. 2011. 44p. pap. 21.99 *(978-1-4568-8849-7(8))* Xlibris Corp.

Qualey, Marsha. Thin Ice. 2007. (YA). *(978-0-9793444-0-4(9))* Quercus Pr.

Quarles, Pamela. Jake & Josh Go Camping. Denison, Susan, illus. 2007. 40p. per. 14.00 *(978-1-59858-407-3(3))* Dog Ear Publishing, LLC.

Quinlan, Nigel. The Weatherman. 2015. (ENG.). 320p. (J). (gr. 4-7). 16.99 *(978-1-62672-033-6(9)*, 9781626720336) Roaring Brook Pr.

Raabe, Emily. Lost Children of the Far Islands. 2014. (ENG.). 288p. (J). (gr. 3-7). 16.99 *(978-0-375-87091-0(1)*, Knopf Bks. for Young Readers) Random Hse. Children's Bks.

Rae, Kimberly. Buying Samir. 2014. (YA). *(978-1-60682-952-3(1))* BJU Pr.

Ragawa, Marimo & Marimo, Ragawa. Baby & Me, Vol. 5. Robertson, Ian, ed. Ragawa, Marimo & Marimo, Ragawa, illus. 2007. (Baby & Me Ser.: 5). (ENG., Illus.). 192p. pap. 8.99 *(978-1-4215-1008-8(1))* Viz Media.

Rainey. School Is Cool. Huggens, Karin, illus. 2004. (J). *(978-0-9666199-9-7(4))* DreamDog Pr.

Ramage, Rosalyn Rikel. The Graveyard: N/a. 2012. 184p. (gr. 4-6). pap. 11.88 *(978-1-4669-5033-7(1))* Trafford Publishing.

—The Windmill. 2013. 182p. (gr. 4-6). pap. 11.66 *(978-1-4907-0909-3(6))* Trafford Publishing.

Ramrattan Smith, Sherry & Smith, Benjamin Eric. Brothers: Best Friends Growing Up. 2010. 28p. pap. 14.95 *(978-1-4490-6339-9(X))* AuthorHouse.

Randolph, Joanne. Rose: A Flower's Story. 2009. (Nature Stories Ser.). (Illus.). 24p. (J). (gr. -1-2). pap. 8.15 *(978-1-60754-102-8(5))*; lib. bdg. 22.60 *(978-1-60754-101-1(7))* Windmill Bks.

Random House Disney Staff. Disney Frozen: Special Edition Junior Novelization (Disney Frozen) Random House Disney Staff, illus. 2014. (Junior Novel Ser.). (ENG., Illus.). 128p. (J). (gr. 3-7). 12.99 *(978-0-7364-3296-2(5)*, RH/Disney) Random Hse. Children's Bks.

Ransom, Marty. Our Father, Our Soldier, Our Hero. 2011. 36p. pap. 24.95 *(978-1-4626-1377-9(2))* America Star Bks.

Ransome, Arthur. Swallowdale. Ransome, Arthur, illus. 2010. (Swallows & Amazons Ser.). (Illus.). 431p. (YA). pap. 14.95 *(978-1-56792-421-3(2))* Godine, David R. Pub.

—Swallowdale. 2014. (ENG., Illus.). 464p. (gr. 4-13). 24.95 *(978-1-4683-0956-0(0)*, 460956) Overlook Pr., The.

Rapp, Adam. Punkzilla. 2010. (ENG., Illus.). 256p. (YA). (gr. 9). pap. 7.99 *(978-0-7636-5297-5(0))* Candlewick Pr.

Rasheed, Winnona. Itchy Scratchy Spots. 2012. 56p. pap. 8.99 *(978-1-60820-727-5(7))* MLR Pr., LLC.

Ratatouille, Oh, Brother! Oh, Hermano! (Disney 8*8's Bilingual Ser.). 24p. pap. *(978-1-4054-9388-8(7))* Parragon, Inc.

Rath, Tom & Reckmeyer, Mary. How Full Is Your Bucket? For Kids. Manning, Maurie J., illus. 2009. (ENG.). 32p. (J). (gr. -1-4). 17.95 *(978-1-59562-027-9(3))* Gallup Pr.

Raynor, Michelle. A Magical World. 2011. 20p. pap. 11.99 *(978-1-257-65025-5(4))* Lulu Pr., Inc.

Reagan, Jean & Pollema-Cahill, Phyllis. Always My Brother, 1 vol. 2009. (ENG., Illus.). 32p. (gr. 2-6). 16.95 *(978-0-88448-313-7(4)*, 884313) Tilbury Hse. Pubs.

Reece, Colleen L. Wilderness Warriors. 2012. 114p. 18.95 *(978-1-61633-309-6(X))*; pap. 8.95 *(978-1-61633-310-2(3))* Guardian Angel Publishing, Inc.

Reed, T. K. Quasar & the Eye of the Serpent. 2009. 136p. 21.95 *(978-1-4401-2753-3(0))*; pap. 11.95 *(978-1-4401-2751-9(4))* iUniverse, Inc.

Rees, Gwyneth. Cosmo & the Secret Spell. 1. Hearn, Samuel, illus. unabr. ed. 2010. (Cosmo Ser.: 3). (ENG.). 208p. (J). (gr. 2-4). pap. 7.99 *(978-0-330-44216-9(3))* Macmillan Pubs., Ltd. GBR. Dist: Independent Pubs. Group.

Reeve, Penny. The Back Leg of a Goat: A Tania Abbey Adventure. Apps, Fred, illus. 2008. (Tania Abbey Adventure Ser.). (ENG.). 96p. (J). pap. 6.99 *(978-1-84550-340-6(6)*, c8e23bb3-9904-4201-971e-e57faa66b8f3) Christian Focus Pubns. GBR. Dist: Bookmasters Distribution.

Reeve, Philip. Starcross: A Stirring Adventure of Spies, Time Travel & Curious Hats. Wyatt, David, illus. 2007. (ENG.). 384p. (YA). (gr. 5-18). 16.95 *(978-1-59990-121-3(8)*, 9781599901213, Bloomsbury USA Childrens) Bloomsbury Publishing USA.

Regan, Dian. Space Boy & His Dog. Neubecker, Robert, illus. 2015. (Space Boy Ser.). (ENG.). 32p. (J). (gr. k-5). 16.95 *(978-1-59078-955-1(5))* Boyds Mills Pr.

—Space Boy & the Space Pirate. Neubecker, Robert, illus. 2016. (Space Boy Ser.). (ENG.). 40p. (J). (gr. k-5). 16.95 *(978-1-59078-956-8(3))* Boyds Mills Pr.

Reid, Karlene & Reid, Mason. Me & My Big Brother. 2012. 32p. pap. 19.99 *(978-1-4685-2765-0(7))* AuthorHouse.

Reiss, Mike & Reiss, Mike. The Boy Who Wouldn't Share. Catrow, David, illus. 2008. (ENG.). 32p. (J). (gr. 1-3). 16.99 *(978-0-06-059132-8(3))* HarperCollins Pubs.

Repkin, Mark. Mommy Breastfeeds My Baby Brother/ Mama Amamanta A Mi Hermanito. Moneysmith, David, illus. 2011.Tr. of Mama Amamanta A Mi Hermanito. 24p. (J). pap. 9.99 *(978-0-9816538-1-5(2))* Istoria Hse.

Respondek, Kelly. Big Sister's Busy Day! 2010. 20p. 10.75 *(978-1-4520-6355-3(9))* AuthorHouse.

Rex, Adam. Cold Cereal. (Cold Cereal Saga Ser.: 1). (ENG.). (J). (gr. 3-7). 2013. 448p. pap. 7.99 *(978-0-06-206003-7(1))* 2012. 432p. 16.99 *(978-0-06-206002-0(3))* HarperCollins Pubs.

—Unlucky Charms. 2013. (Cold Cereal Saga Ser.: 2). (ENG., Illus.). 400p. (J). (gr. 3-7). 16.99 *(978-0-06-206005-1(8))* HarperCollins Pubs.

Reynolds, Jason. As Brave As You. (ENG.). 432p. (J). (gr. 5). 2017. pap. 7.99 *(978-1-4814-1591-0(3)*, Atheneum Bks. for Young Readers) 2016. (Illus.). 16.99 *(978-1-4814-1590-3(5)*, Atheneum/Caitlyn Dlouhy Books) Simon & Schuster Children's Publishing.

—When I Was the Greatest. Frost, Michael, photos by. 2014. (ENG., Illus.). 240p. (YA). (gr. 7). 17.99 *(978-1-4424-5947-2(6)*, Atheneum Bks. for Young Readers) Simon & Schuster Children's Publishing.

Reynolds, Paul A. Sydney & Simon: To the Moon & Beyond! Reynolds, Peter H., illus. 2017. (ENG.). 48p. (J). (gr. 1-4). lib. bdg. 12.99 *(978-1-58089-679-5(0))* Charlesbridge Publishing, Inc.

—Sydney & Simon: Full Steam Ahead! Reynolds, Peter H., illus. 2014. (Sydney & Simon Ser.). (ENG.). 48p. (J). (gr. 1-4). 12.95 *(978-1-58089-675-7(8))* Charlesbridge Publishing, Inc.

Reynolds, Peter H. The Best Kid in the World: A SugarLoaf Book. Reynolds, Peter H., illus. 2012. (ENG., Illus.). 48p. (J). (gr. -1-2). pap. 22.99 *(978-1-4424-7178-8(6)*, Atheneum Bks. for Young Readers) Simon & Schuster Children's Publishing.

Reynolds, Peter H. & Reynolds, Peter. Ish. Reynolds, Peter H. & Reynolds, Peter, illus. 2004. (Creatrilogy Ser.). (ENG., Illus.). 32p. (J). (gr. k-12). 15.00 *(978-0-7636-2344-9(X))* Candlewick Pr.

Ricchi, Brenda. The Grandchildren's Bible Journeys - the Creation Story. 2010. 35p. pap. 17.00 *(978-0-557-14903-2(7))* Lulu Pr., Inc.

Richard Richtmyer. A Bit of Magic: A Novel. 2009. 116p. pap. 10.95 *(978-1-4401-5565-9(8))* iUniverse, Inc.

Richardson, Deborra. Treasures at the Museum. 2011. (Illus.). 64p. (J). pap. 5.99 *(978-0-9824945-1-6(3))* Elevator Group, The.

Richmond, Marianne. Dear Sister: A Message of Love. 2008. (Illus.). 40p. (J). 15.95 *(978-1-934082-46-1(5)*, Marianne Richmond Studios, Inc.) Sourcebooks, Inc.

—You're a Big Brother. 2017. (ENG., Illus.). 32p. (J). (-3). 8.99 *(978-1-4926-5049-2(8)*, 9781492650492, Sourcebooks Jabberwocky) Sourcebooks, Inc.

—You're a Big Sister. 2017. (ENG., Illus.). 32p. (J). (-3). 8.99 *(978-1-4926-5051-5(X)*, 9781492650515, Sourcebooks Jabberwocky) Sourcebooks, Inc.

Riley, Clifford. Operation Trinity. 2012. (39 Clues: the Cahill Files Ser.). (ENG.). 144p. (J). (gr. 3-7). 9.99 *(978-0-545-43143-9(3))* Scholastic, Inc.

—Spymasters. 2013. (39 Clues: the Cahill Files Ser.). (ENG., Illus.). 256p. (J). (gr. 3-7). 12.99 *(978-0-545-56468-7(9))* Scholastic, Inc.

Rinaldi, Ann. Juliet's Moon. 2010. (ENG., Illus.). 256p. (YA). (gr. 7). pap. 14.99 *(978-0-547-25874-4(7))* Houghton Mifflin Harcourt Publishing Co.

—Leigh Ann's Civil War. 2011. (ENG.). 320p. (YA). (gr. 7). pap. 17.99 *(978-0-547-54999-6(7))* Houghton Mifflin Harcourt Publishing Co.

—My Vicksburg. 2011. (ENG.). 160p. (YA). (gr. 7). pap. 11.95 *(978-0-547-55000-8(6))* Houghton Mifflin Harcourt Publishing Co.

Rinehart, J. D. The Lost Realm. 2017. (Crown of Three Ser.: 2). (ENG., Illus.). 512p. (J). (gr. 4-8). pap. 8.99 ***(978-1-4814-2447-9(5)***, Aladdin) Simon & Schuster Children's Publishing.

Riordan, Rick. The Kane Chronicles Box Set. Rocco, John, illus. 2013. (Kane Chronicles Ser.). (ENG.). 1472p. (J). (gr. 3-7). pap. 26.99 *(978-1-4231-9962-5(6))* Hyperion Bks. for Children.

—The Red Pyramid. 2011. (ENG.). 544p. (J). (gr. 5-17). pap. 9.99 *(978-1-4231-1345-4(4))* Disney Publishing Worldwide.

—The Red Pyramid. 2010. (Kane Chronicles Ser.). (ENG.). 528p. (J). (gr. 5-9). 17.99 *(978-1-4231-1338-6(1))* Hyperion Pr.

—The Red Pyramid, Bk. 1. Collar, Orpheus, illus. 2012. (Kane Chronicles Ser.). (ENG.). 192p. (J). (gr. 5-9). pap. 12.99 *(978-1-4231-5069-5(4))* Hyperion Pr.

—The Red Pyramid. 2009. (Kane Chronicles: Bk. 1). 11.04 *(978-0-7848-3733-7(3)*, Everbind) Marco Bk. Co.

—The Red Pyramid. 2012. 20.00 *(978-1-61383-660-6(0))* Perfection Learning Corp.

—The Red Pyramid. 2010. pap. *(978-0-545-40016-9(3))* Scholastic, Inc.

—The Red Pyramid. l.t. ed. 2010. (Kane Chronicles: Bk. 1). (ENG.). 671p. 23.95 *(978-1-4104-2536-2(3))* Thorndike Pr.

—The Red Pyramid. (Kane Chronicles Graphic Novels Ser.: 1). (J). 2012. lib. bdg. 24.50 *(978-0-606-37510-8(4))* 2011. lib. bdg. 20.85 *(978-0-606-39216-7(5))* Turtleback Bks.

—The Serpent's Shadow. (Kane Chronicles Ser.). (ENG.). (gr. 5-17). 2013. 464p. (J). pap. 9.99 *(978-1-4231-4202-7(0))*Bk. 3. 2012. 416p. (YA). 19.99 *(978-1-4231-4057-3(5))* Hyperion Pr.

—The Serpent's Shadow. 2012. 416p. *(978-0-14-133568-1(8)*, Puffin) Penguin Bks., Ltd.

—The Serpent's Shadow. l.t. ed. 2012. (Kane Chronicles: Bk. 3). (ENG.). 521p. (gr. 5-12). 23.99 *(978-1-4104-4789-0(8))* Thorndike Pr.

—The Throne of Fire. 2011. (Kane Chronicles: Bk. 2). 452p. (J). pap. *(978-1-4231-5059-6(7))* Disney Pr.

—The Throne of Fire. 2nd ed. 2012. (ENG.). 464p. (YA). (gr. 5-9). pap. 9.99 *(978-1-4231-6703-7(1))* Hyperion Bks. for Children.

—The Throne of Fire, Bk. 2. (ENG.). 464p. (gr. 5-17). 2012. (YA). pap. 9.99 *(978-1-4231-4201-0(2))* 2011. (J). 18.99 *(978-1-4231-4056-6(7))* Hyperion Pr.

—The Throne of Fire. 2011. (Kane Chronicles: Bk. 2). (ENG., Illus.). 451p. 28.25 *(978-0-85757-231-8(8))*; 2nd ed. 554p. pap. *(978-0-14-133566-7(1))* Penguin Publishing Group. (Puffin).

—The Throne of Fire. l.t. ed. 2011. (Kane Chronicles: Bk. 2). (ENG.). 591p. 23.99 *(978-1-4104-3607-8(1))* Thorndike Pr.

—The Throne of Fire. (Kane Chronicles Graphic Novels Ser.: 2). 2015. lib. bdg. 24.50 *(978-0-606-37509-2(0))* 2012. (YA). lib. bdg. 20.85 *(978-0-606-39217-4(3))* Turtleback Bks.

Rizzo, Cynthia Marie. No No, Cocco. 2008. 49p. pap. 16.95 *(978-1-60563-819-5(6))* America Star Bks.

(Robert Thompson), Pau Pau. Santa's Secret Helpers, 1 vol. 2009. 55p. pap. 16.95 *(978-1-60836-859-4(9))* America Star Bks.

Roberts, Bethany. Double Trouble Groundhog Day. Cauley, Lorinda Bryan, illus. 2011. (ENG.). 40p. (J). (gr. -1-3). pap. 6.99 *(978-0-312-55350-0(1)*, 9780312553500) Square Fish.

Roberts, Willo Davis. Surviving Summer Vacation. 2015. (ENG., Illus.). 208p. (J). (gr. 3-7). pap. 6.99 *(978-1-4814-3718-9(6)*, Aladdin) Simon & Schuster Children's Publishing.

Robertson, Jacob Ryan. Far Away. 2012. 50p. (-18). pap. 15.99 *(978-1-4797-4679-8(7))* Xlibris Corp.

Robins, Eleanor. The Secret Message, 1 vol. unabr. ed. 2011. (Carter High Mysteries Ser.). (ENG.). 48p. (YA). (gr. 9-12). 7.95 *(978-1-61651-568-3(6))* Saddleback Educational Publishing, Inc.

Robinson, Barbara. The Best Christmas Pageant Ever. Cornell, Laura, illus. 2011. (ENG.). 40p. (J). (gr. -1-3). 16.99 *(978-0-06-089074-2(6))* HarperCollins Pubs.

—The Best Christmas Pageant Ever. 2005. (ENG., Illus.). 128p. (J). (gr. 3-7). pap. 5.99 *(978-0-06-440275-0(4))* HarperCollins Pubs.

—The Best Christmas Pageant Ever. 2009. 8.32 *(978-0-7848-1246-4(2)*, Everbind) Marco Bk. Co.

—The Best Christmas Pageant Ever. 2005. (Illus.). 108p. (gr. 3-7). 16.00 *(978-0-7569-6531-0(4))* Perfection Learning Corp.

—The Best Christmas Pageant Ever. 2005. (J). 16.00 *(978-0-88103-998-6(5)*, Turtleback) Turtleback Bks.

—The Best Halloween Ever. 2006. (Illus.). 117p. (J). (gr. 3-7). 13.65 *(978-0-7569-6985-1(9))* Perfection Learning Corp.

Robinson, Craig & Mansbach, Adam. Jake the Fake Keeps It Real. Knight, Keith, illus. 2017. (Jake the Fake Ser.: 1). (ENG.). 144p. (J). (gr. 3-7). 13.99 *(978-0-553-52351-5(1)*, Crown Books For Young Readers) Random Hse. Children's Bks.

Robinson, Gary. Little Brother of War. 2013. (PathFinders Ser.). (ENG.). 113p. (YA). pap. 9.95 *(978-1-939053-02-2(1)*, 7th Generation) Book Publishing Co.

Robinson, Jeanette. Blueberry Bunny. 2012. 32p. pap. 19.99 *(978-1-4685-6410-5(2))* AuthorHouse.

Robley Blake, Colleen. I Can't Wait till I'm Five. 2006. (J). 9.95 *(978-0-9767342-0-8(6))* Imaajinn This.

Rockind, Pat. McGooster & Mcgyman Begin Their Adventures. Wozniak, Patricia A., illus. 2008. 144p. (J). (gr. 4-7). per. 12.95 *(978-0-9792430-1-1(7))* Wing Lane Pr.

Rocklin, Joanne. The Five Lives of Our Cat Zook. (ENG.). 240p. (J). (gr. 3-7). 2013. pap. 7.95 *(978-1-4197-0525-0(3))* 2012. 17.95 *(978-1-4197-0192-4(4))* Abrams, Inc. (Amulet Bks.).

Rockwell, Anne F. & Rockwell. Brendan & Belinda & the Slam Dunk! Meisel, Paul, illus. 2007. (Good Sports Ser.). 40p. (J). (gr. -1-1). 15.99 *(978-0-06-028443-5(9))* HarperCollins Pubs.

Rodda, Emily. The Silver Door. 2013. (Illus.). (J). 278p. pap. *(978-0-545-42993-1(5))*; (ENG., 288p. (gr. 3-7). 16.99 *(978-0-545-42992-4(7))* Scholastic, Inc. (Scholastic Pr.).

—The Third Door. 2013. (J). pap. *(978-0-545-42995-5(1)*, Scholastic Pr.) Scholastic, Inc.

Roddie, Shen. Baby Goes Too. Stojic, Manya, illus. 2003. 32p. (YA). *(978-1-85602-460-0(1)*, Pavilion Children's Books) Pavilion Bks.

Roddy, Lee. Eye of the Hurricane. 2007. (Ladd Family Adventure Ser.: Vol. 9). (Illus.). 161p. (J). (gr. 3-7). per. 7.99 *(978-0-88062-258-5(X))* Mott Media.

Röder, Marlene. In the River Darkness. Reichel, Tammi, tr. 2014. 224p. 18.95 *(978-1-62324-010-3(7))* Enslow Pubs., Inc.

Rodkey, Geoff. The Tapper Twins Go to War (with Each Other) 2015. (Tapper Twins Ser.: 1). (ENG., Illus.). 240p. (J). (gr. 3-7). 13.99 *(978-0-316-29779-0(8))* Little Brown & Co.

—The Tapper Twins Go to War (with Each Other) 2016. (Tapper Twins Ser.: 1). (ENG., Illus.). 240p. (J). (gr. 3-7). pap. 5.99 *(978-0-316-31597-5(4))* Little, Brown Bks. for Young Readers.

—The Tapper Twins Go Viral. 2017. (Tapper Twins Ser.: 4). (ENG., Illus.). 256p. (J). (gr. 3-7). 13.99 *(978-0-316-29784-4(4))* Little Brown & Co.

—The Tapper Twins Run for President. 2016. (Tapper Twins Ser.: 3). (ENG., Illus.). 304p. (J). (gr. 3-7). 13.99 *(978-0-316-29785-1(2))* Little, Brown Bks. for Young Readers.

—The Tapper Twins Tear up New York. 2015. (Tapper Twins Ser.: 2). (ENG., Illus.). 288p. (J). (gr. 3-7). 13.99 *(978-0-316-29783-7(6))* Little Brown & Co.

—The Tapper Twins Tear up New York. 2016. (Tapper Twins Ser.: 2). (ENG., Illus.). 288p. (J). (gr. 3-7). pap. 5.99 *(978-0-316-31601-9(6))* Little, Brown Bks. for Young Readers.

Rogers, Don. The Adventures of Shawn & Jeremy with Sister Nicole & the Hot Air Balloon: Volume Two. 2012. 24p. pap. 24.95 *(978-1-4626-7649-1(9))* America Star Bks.

Roland, Timothy. Monkey Me & the Golden Monkey. Roland, Timothy, illus. 2014. (Monkey Me Ser.: 1). (ENG., Illus.). 96p. (J). (gr. 1-3). pap. 4.99 *(978-0-545-55976-8(6))* Scholastic, Inc.

—Monkey Me & the Golden Monkey. 2014. (Monkey Me Ser.: 1). lib. bdg. 14.75 *(978-0-606-35354-0(2))* Turtleback Bks.

—Monkey Me & the New Neighbor. Roland, Timothy, illus. 2014. (Monkey Me Ser.: 3). (ENG., Illus.). 96p. (J). (gr. 1-3). pap. 4.99 *(978-0-545-55984-3(7))* Scholastic, Inc.

—Monkey Me & the New Neighbor. 2014. (Monkey Me Ser.: 3). lib. bdg. 14.75 *(978-0-606-35360-1(7))* Turtleback Bks.

—Monkey Me & the Pet Show. 2014. (Monkey Me Ser.: 2). (ENG.). 96p. (J). (gr. 1-3). 15.99 *(978-0-545-55981-2(2))* Scholastic, Inc.

—Monkey Me & the Pet Show. 2014. (Monkey Me Ser.: 2). lib. bdg. 14.75 *(978-0-606-35359-5(3))* Turtleback Bks.

—Monkey Me & the School Ghost. 2014. (Monkey Me Ser.: 4). (ENG.). 96p. (J). (gr. 1-3). pap. 4.99 *(978-0-545-55989-8(8))* Scholastic, Inc.

—Monkey Me & the School Ghost. Roland, Timothy, illus. 2014. (Monkey Me Ser.: 4). (ENG., Illus.). 96p. (J). (gr. 1-3). 15.99 *(978-0-545-55990-4(1))* Scholastic, Inc.

—Monkey Me & the School Ghost. 2014. (Illus.). 90p. (J). *(978-1-4844-3840-4(X))* Scholastic, Inc.

—Monkey Me & the School Ghost. 2014. (Monkey Me Ser.: 4). lib. bdg. 14.75 *(978-0-606-36053-1(0))* Turtleback Bks.

—The Pet Show. 2014. (Monkey Me Ser.: 2). (ENG.). 96p. (J). (gr. 1-3). pap. 4.99 *(978-0-545-55980-5(4))* Scholastic, Inc.

Rollins, James. Jake Ransom & the Howling Sphinx. (Jake Ransom Ser.: 2). (ENG.). 384p. (J). (gr. 5). 2012. pap. 7.99 *(978-0-06-147384-5(7))* 2011. 16.99 *(978-0-06-147382-1(0))* HarperCollins Pubs.

—Jake Ransom & the Skull King's Shadow. (Jake Ransom Ser.: 1). (ENG.). (J). (gr. 5). 2010. 432p. pap. 7.99 *(978-0-06-147381-4(2))* 2009. 416p. 16.99 *(978-0-06-147379-1(0))* HarperCollins Pubs.

Romano, Ray. Raymie, Dickie, & the Bean: Why I Love & Hate My Brothers. Locke, Gary, illus. 2007. 30p. (J). 18.00 *(978-1-4223-6806-0(8))* DIANE Publishing Co.

Roop, Peter & Roop, Connie. An Eye for an Eye. 2004. 168p. (J). lib. bdg. 16.92 *(978-1-4242-0772-5(X))* Fitzgerald Bks.

Rorby, Ginny. How to Speak Dolphin. (ENG.). 272p. (J). (gr. 3-7). 2017. pap. 6.99 *(978-0-545-67607-6(X))* 2015. 16.99 *(978-0-545-67605-2(3))* Scholastic, Inc. (Scholastic Pr.).

Rosen, Chaya & Braverman, Rivkie. Our New Special Baby. 2013. *(978-1-59826-960-4(7))* Feldheim Pubs.

Rosen, Lev Ac & Rosen, Ellis J. Woundabout. Rosen, Lev Ac & Rosen, Ellis J., illus. 2015. (ENG., Illus.). 288p. (J). (gr. 3-7). 17.00 *(978-0-316-37078-3(9))* Little Brown & Co.

Rosen, Wendy & End, Jackie. Chicken Fingers, Mac & Cheese... Why Do You Always Have to Say Please? Tuck-Bernstein, Cheryl, illus. 2005. 32p. (J). 14.99 *(978-0-7666-1986-9(9))* Modern Publishing.

Rosenberg, Aaron. Case of the Secret Sauce, Vol. 1. Harrington, David, illus. 2011. (Pete & Penny's Pizza Puzzles Ser.: 1). (ENG.). 64p. (J). (gr. 1-3). pap. 3.99 *(978-0-8431-9928-4(8)*, Price Stern Sloan) Penguin Young Readers Group.

—Case of the Topsy-Turvy Toy. Harrington, David, illus. 2011. (Pete & Penny's Pizza Puzzles Ser.: 2). (ENG.). 64p. (J). (gr. 1-3). pap. 3.99 *(978-0-8431-9929-1(6)*, Price Stern Sloan) Penguin Young Readers Group.

Rosenberg, Madelyn. How to Behave at a Dog Show. Ross, Heather, illus. 2015. (ENG.). 32p. (J). (gr. -1-3). 17.99 *(978-0-06-227927-9(0))* HarperCollins Pubs.

—How to Behave at a Tea Party. Ross, Heather, illus. 2014. (ENG.). 32p. (J). (gr. -1-3). 17.99 *(978-0-06-227926-2(2)*, Tegen, Katherine Bks) HarperCollins Pubs.

—Nanny X. (ENG., Illus.). (J). (gr. 2-5). 2015. 128p. 16.95 *(978-0-8234-3533-3(4))* 2014. 144p. 16.95 *(978-0-8234-3166-3(5))* Holiday Hse., Inc.

Rosenblum, Gregg. City 1. 2015. (Revolution 19 Ser.: 3). (ENG.). 288p. (YA). (gr. 8). 17.99 *(978-0-06-212601-6(6)*, HarperTeen) HarperCollins Pubs.

—Fugitive X. 2014. (Revolution 19 Ser.: 2). (ENG.). 272p. (YA). (gr. 8). 17.99 *(978-0-06-212597-2(4)*, HarperTeen) HarperCollins Pubs.

—Revolution 19. 2013. (Revolution 19 Ser.: 1). (ENG.). 272p. (YA). (gr. 8). 17.99 *(978-0-06-212595-8(8)*, HarperTeen) HarperCollins Pubs.

Rosoff, Meg. Just in Case. 2008. (ENG.). 256p. (gr. 12-18). 14.00 *(978-0-452-28937-6(8)*, Penguin Books) Penguin Publishing Group.

Ross, Sylvia. Lion Singer. Ross, Sylvia, illus. 2005. (Illus.). 33p. (J). (gr. 3-7). 12.95 *(978-1-59714-009-6(0)*, Great Valley Bks.) Heyday.

Ross, Tony & Ross, Tony. I Want a Sister! 2013. (Illus.). 32p. (J). (gr. -1-3). 16.95 *(978-1-4677-2047-2(X))* Andersen Pr. GBR. Dist: Lerner Publishing Group.

Rothchild, Erik. The Garden Adventures: The Mishaps of Martha & Matilda. Hief, Gina, illus. 2013. 44p. *(978-0-9883568-5-6(6))* Inkwell Books LLC.

Rothgery, Laura. My Brother's Heart. 2013. 26p. pap. 13.95 *(978-1-4497-8022-7(9)*, WestBow Pr.) Author Solutions, Inc.

Rothstein, Evelyn. My Great Grandpa Dave. 2007. (J). per. 12.95 *(978-0-9786745-1-9(0))* Marble Hse. Editions.

Rottman, S. L. Shadow of a Doubt, 1 vol. 2005. (ENG.). 224p. (YA). (gr. 7-18). pap. 7.95 *(978-1-56145-354-2(4))* Peachtree Pubs.

Rouss, Sylvia A. Aaron's Bar Mitzvah. Dubois, Liz Goulet, tr. Dubois, Liz Goulet, illus. 2003. (J). 14.95 *(978-0-8246-0447-9(4))* David, Jonathan Pubs., Inc.

Rovetch, Lissa & Rowe, Jeffrey. Gravity Falls Dipper & Mabel & the Curse of the Time Pirates' Treasure! I Don't Know, You Tell Me! Adventure! No New Art Needed et al, illus. 2016. (ENG.). 288p. (J). (gr. 3-7). 12.99 *(978-1-4847-4668-4(6))* Disney Pr.

Rowley, Melissa. The Falcon Shield. 2009. (J). 6.99 *(978-1-60641-103-2(9))* Deseret Bk. Co.

Rowley, M'lin. The Silver Coat. 2009. (Knights of Right Ser.: Bk. 2). 71p. (J). (gr. 1-5). pap. 6.99 *(978-1-60641-104-9(7)*, Shadow Mountain) Shadow Mountain Publishing.

Roy, Kasi. Elizabeth Dreams: And the Christmas House Clock. 2011. 96p. pap. 12.10 *(978-1-4520-1864-5(2))* AuthorHouse.

Roy, Ron. April Adventure. Gurney, John Steven, illus. 2010. (Calendar Mysteries Ser.: 4). (ENG.). 80p. (J). (gr. 1-4). 4.99 *(978-0-375-86116-1(5)*, Random Hse. Bks. for Young Readers) Random Hse. Children's Bks.

—April Adventure. 2010. (Calendar Mysteries Ser.: 4). lib. bdg. 14.75 *(978-0-606-12465-2(9)*, Turtleback) Turtleback Bks.

—August Acrobat. Gurney, John Steven, illus. 2012. (Calendar Mysteries Ser.: 8). (ENG.). 80p. (J). (gr. 1-4). 4.99 *(978-0-375-86886-3(0))*; lib. bdg. 12.99 *(978-0-375-96886-0(5))* Random Hse. Children's Bks. (Random Hse. Bks. for Young Readers).

—August Acrobat. 2012. (Calendar Mysteries Ser.: 8). lib. bdg. 14.75 *(978-0-606-26403-7(5)*, Turtleback) Turtleback Bks.

—February Friend. Gurney, John Steven, illus. 2009. (Calendar Mysteries Ser.: 2). (ENG.). 80p. (J). (gr. 1-4). 4.99 *(978-0-375-85662-4(5)*, Random Hse. Bks. for Young Readers) Random Hse. Children's Bks.

—January Joker. Gurney, John Steven, illus. 2009. (Calendar Mysteries Ser.: 1). (ENG.). 96p. (J). (gr. 1-4). 4.99 *(978-0-375-85661-7(7)*, Random Hse. Bks. for Young Readers) Random Hse. Children's Bks.

—July Jitters. Gurney, John Steven, illus. 2012. (Calendar Mysteries Ser.: 7). (ENG.). 80p. (J). (gr. 1-4). 4.99 *(978-0-375-86882-5(8)*, Random Hse. Bks. for Young Readers) Random Hse. Children's Bks.

—July Jitters. 2012. (Calendar Mysteries Ser.: 7). lib. bdg. 14.75 *(978-0-606-26402-0(7)*, Turtleback) Turtleback Bks.

—June Jam. Gurney, John Steven, illus. 2011. (Calendar Mysteries Ser.: 6). (ENG.). 80p. (J). (gr. 1-4). 4.99 *(978-0-375-86112-3(2)*, Random Hse. Bks. for Young Readers) Random Hse. Children's Bks.

—March Mischief. Gurney, John Steven, illus. 2010. (Calendar Mysteries Ser.: 3). (ENG.). 80p. (J). (gr. 1-4). 4.99 *(978-0-375-85663-1(3)*, Random Hse. Bks. for Young Readers) Random Hse. Children's Bks.

—March Mischief. 2010. (Calendar Mysteries Ser.: 3). lib. bdg. 14.75 *(978-0-606-12460-7(8)*, Turtleback) Turtleback Bks.

—May Magic. Gurney, John Steven, illus. 2011. (Calendar Mysteries Ser.: 5). (ENG.). 80p. (J). (gr. 1-4). 4.99 *(978-0-375-86111-6(4)*, Random Hse. Bks. for Young Readers) Random Hse. Children's Bks.

—October Ogre. Gurney, John Steven, illus. 2013. (Calendar Mysteries Ser.: 10). (ENG.). 80p. (J). (gr. 1-4). 4.99 *(978-0-375-86888-7(7))*; lib. bdg. 12.99 *(978-0-375-96888-4(1))* Random Hse. Children's Bks. (Random Hse. Bks. for Young Readers).

—October Ogre. 2013. (Calendar Mysteries Ser.: 10). lib. bdg. 14.75 *(978-0-606-32232-4(9)*, Turtleback) Turtleback Bks.

—September Sneakers. Gurney, John Steven, illus. 2013. (Calendar Mysteries Ser.: 9). (ENG.). 80p. (J). (gr. 1-4). 4.99 *(978-0-375-86887-0(9)*, Random Hse. Bks. for Young Readers) Random Hse. Children's Bks.

—September Sneakers. 2013. (Calendar Mysteries Ser.: 9). lib. bdg. 14.75 *(978-0-606-32231-7(0)*, Turtleback) Turtleback Bks.

Roy, Ronald. November Night. Gurney, John Steven, illus. 2014. (Calendar Mysteries Ser.: 11). (ENG.). 80p. (J). (gr. 1-4). 4.99 *(978-0-385-37165-0(9)*, Random Hse. Bks. for Young Readers) Random Hse. Children's Bks.

Rozanski, Bonnie. Borderline. 2007. (ENG.). 208p. (YA). (gr. 10). pap. 22.95 *(978-0-88984-293-9(0))* Porcupine's Quill, Inc. CAN. Dist: Univ. of Toronto Pr.

Rubinacci, Mary Ellen. Srepsihw: The Land of Quiet? 2012. 36p. 19.95 *(978-1-4626-5872-5(5))* America Star Bks.

Ruby, Anne. Children of the Sea. Meier, Ty, illus. 2007. (YA). per. *(978-0-9787881-0-0(9))* Seachild.

Ruby, Laura. Bone Gap. 368p. (YA). (gr. 9). 2016. pap. 9.99 *(978-0-06-231762-9(8))* 2015. (ENG.). 17.99 *(978-0-06-231760-5(1))* HarperCollins Pubs.

Ruelle, Karen Gray. April Fool! (ENG., Illus.). 32p. (J). (gr. k-3). 4.95 *(978-0-8234-1780-3(8))* Holiday Hse., Inc.

—Easter Egg Disaster: A Harry & Emily Adventure. Ruelle, Karen Gray, illus. 2003. (Holiday House Readers Ser.). (ENG., Illus.). 32p. (J). (gr. k-3). pap. 4.95 *(978-0-8234-1823-7(5))* Holiday Hse., Inc.

—Easter Egg Disaster: A Harry & Emily Adventure. 2003. (ENG., Illus.). 32p. (J). (gr. k-3). tchr. ed. 14.95 *(978-0-8234-1806-0(5))* Holiday Hse., Inc.

—Just in Time for New Year's! 2004. (ENG., Illus.). 32p. (J). tchr. ed. 14.95 *(978-0-8234-1841-1(3))* Holiday Hse., Inc.

—The Monster in Harry's Backyard. Ruelle, Karen Gray, illus. 2003. (Holiday House Readers Ser.). (ENG., Illus.). 32p. (J). (gr. k-3). 4.95 *(978-0-8234-1783-4(2))* Holiday Hse., Inc.

—Mother's Day Mess. 2003. (ENG., Illus.). 32p. (J). (gr. k-3). tchr. ed. 14.95 *(978-0-8234-1773-5(5))* Holiday Hse., Inc.

—Spookier Than a Ghost. (Holiday House Readers Ser.). (ENG., Illus.). 32p. (J). (gr. k-3). pap. 4.95 *(978-0-8234-1801-5(4))* Holiday Hse., Inc.

—The Thanksgiving Beast Feast. (Holiday House Readers Ser.). (ENG., Illus.). 32p. (J). (gr. k-3). pap. 4.95 *(978-0-8234-1802-2(2))* Holiday Hse., Inc.

—The Thanksgiving Beast Feast Level 2: A Holiday House Reader. Ruelle, Karen Gray, illus. (ENG., Illus.). 32p. (J). (gr. k-3). tchr. ed. 15.95 *(978-0-8234-1511-3(2))* Holiday Hse., Inc.

Ruggieri, J. G. Weather Changes, Mountains Move, & Islands Disappear. 2012. 168p. pap. 15.00 *(978-0-9860300-0-0(7))* Alabaster Bk. Pub.

Ruiz Zafón, Carlos. The Prince of Mist. 2011. (ENG.). 256p. (YA). (gr. 7-17). pap., pap. 10.99 *(978-0-316-04480-6(6))* Little, Brown Bks. for Young Readers.

Ruskin, John. The King of the Golden River. 2004. reprint ed. pap. 1.99 *(978-1-4192-6821-2(X))* Kessinger Publishing, LLC.

—The King of the Golden River. Ghiuselev, Iassen, illus. 2005. (ENG.). 65p. (J). (gr. k). 19.95 *(978-1-894965-15-6(9))* Simply Read Bks. CAN. Dist: Ingram Publisher Services.

Russell, James. The Dragon Riders. Choi, Link, illus. 2017. (Dragon Brothers Ser.: 3). (ENG.). 32p. (J). (-4). 16.99 ***(978-1-4926-4867-3(1)***, Sourcebooks Jabberwocky) Sourcebooks, Inc.

Russo, Marisabina. Peter Is Just a Baby. 2011. (ENG., Illus.). 32p. (J). 16.00 *(978-0-8028-5384-4(6)*, Eerdmans Bks For Young Readers) Eerdmans, William B. Publishing Co.

—The Trouble with Baby. Russo, Marisabina, illus. 2003. (Illus.). 32p. (J). (gr. -1-18). 16.89 *(978-0-06-008925-2(3))* HarperCollins Pubs.

Ruth-Killgore, Chanacee. Alphabet Soup. 2012. 108p. pap. 9.99 *(978-1-936453-13-9(4))* Bezalel Bks.

Ryan, Pam Muñoz. Becoming Naomi Leon. 2005. (ENG.). 272p. (J). (gr. 3-7). reprint ed. per. 7.99 *(978-0-439-26997-1(0)*, Scholastic Paperbacks) Scholastic, Inc.

—Tony Baloney. Fotheringham, Edwin, illus. 2011. (ENG.). 40p. (J). (gr. -1-k). 17.99 *(978-0-545-23135-0(3)*, Scholastic Pr.) Scholastic, Inc.

—Tony Baloney: Buddy Trouble. Fotheringham, Edwin, illus. 2014. (ENG.). 40p. (J). (gr. k-2). 6.99 *(978-0-545-48169-4(4)*, Scholastic Pr.) Scholastic, Inc.

—Tony Baloney: Buddy Trouble. Fotheringham, Ed, illus. 2013. 38p. (J). pap. *(978-0-545-48170-0(8))* Scholastic, Inc.

—Yo, Naomi León. 2005. (SPA.). 272p. (J). (gr. 3-7). pap. 6.99 *(978-0-439-75572-6(7)*, Scholastic en Espanol) Scholastic, Inc.

Ryan, Patrick. Gemini Bites. 2011. (ENG.). 240p. (J). (gr. 7-8). 17.99 *(978-0-545-22128-3(5)*, Scholastic Pr.) Scholastic, Inc.

Sackett, Frances. The Misadventures of the Magician's Dog. 2013. (ENG.). 192p. (J). (gr. 2-7). 16.95 *(978-0-8234-2869-4(9))* Holiday Hse., Inc.

Saedi, Sara. Never Ever. 2016. (ENG.). 320p. (YA). (gr. 7). 17.99 *(978-0-451-47576-3(3)*, Viking Books for Young Readers) Penguin Young Readers Group.

Sage, Angie. Flyte. Zug, Mark, illus. (Septimus Heap Ser.: 2). (ENG.). 544p. (J). (gr. 4-7). 2007. pap. 7.99 *(978-0-06-057736-0(3))* 2006. 17.99 *(978-0-06-057734-6(7))* HarperCollins Pubs. (Tegen, Katherine Bks).

—Flyte. (Septimus Heap Ser.: 2). (J). 2009. 84.49 *(978-1-4361-5831-2(1))* 2008. 1.25 *(978-1-4193-9383-9(9))* 2006. 114.75 *(978-1-4193-9386-0(3))* 2006. 133.75 *(978-1-4193-9390-7(1))* 2006. 282.75 *(978-1-4193-9387-7(1))* 2006. 131.75 *(978-1-4193-9392-1(8))* 2006. 111.75 *(978-1-4193-9388-4(X))* Recorded Bks., Inc.

Salom, Susie. Kyle Finds Her Way. 2016. (ENG.). 256p. (J). (gr. 4-7). 16.99 *(978-0-545-85266-1(8)*, Levine, Arthur A. Bks.) Scholastic, Inc.

Saltzberg, Barney. Inside This Book. 2015. (ENG., Illus.). 40p. (J). (gr. -1-1). 15.95 *(978-1-4197-1487-0(2))* Abrams, Inc.

Same Day, Different Way! 2005. (J). pap. *(978-0-9769910-3-8(9))* Terrific Twins LLC.

Sammel, Rochelle. Tales of Two Mouse Brothers. 2008. 45p. pap. 24.95 *(978-1-4241-9798-9(8))* America Star Bks.

Samuel, Lynette M. Mommy's Hat. Capps, Leigh, illus. 2005. (J). per. *(978-0-9727703-3-0(X))* P.R.A. Publishing.

Sanchez, Helen. The Buddy Boys. 2008. 15p. pap. 24.95 *(978-1-60672-352-4(9))* America Star Bks.

Sanchez, Priscilla. Champ the Boxing Boxer. 2011. 12p. pap. 8.32 *(978-1-4634-7423-2(7))* AuthorHouse.

Sandau, Carol E. Prairie Patchwork. 2012. 88p. (gr. 4-6). pap. 9.95 *(978-1-4759-4807-3(7))* iUniverse, Inc.

Sanders-Wells, Linda. Maggie's Monkeys. Carter, Abby, illus. 2009. (ENG.). 32p. (J). (gr. -1-2). 16.99 *(978-0-7636-3326-4(7))* Candlewick Pr.

Sandford, John, pseud & Cook, Michele. Outrage. 2015. (Singular Menace Ser.: Bk. 2). (ENG.). 336p. (YA). (gr. 9). 18.99 *(978-0-385-75309-8(8)*, Knopf Bks. for Young Readers) Random Hse. Children's Bks.

—Rampage. (Singular Menace Ser.: 3). (ENG.). 336p. (YA). (gr. 9). 2017. pap. 10.99 *(978-0-385-75315-9(2)*, Ember) 2016. 18.99 *(978-0-385-75313-5(6)*, Knopf Bks. for Young Readers) Random Hse. Children's Bks.

—Uncaged. (Singular Menace Ser.: Bk. 1). (ENG.). 416p. (gr. 9). 2015. (YA). pap. 10.99 *(978-0-385-75305-0(5)*, Ember) 2014. (J). 18.99 *(978-0-385-75306-7(3)*, Knopf Bks. for Young Readers) 2014. (YA). lib. bdg. 21.99 *(978-0-385-75307-4(1)*, Knopf Bks. for Young Readers) Random Hse. Children's Bks.

Sam, Amélie & Trouillot, Virgile. The Argument. 2009. (Groove High Ser.). (Illus.). 112p. (YA). (gr. 5-8). 31.95 (978-1-60754-538-5(1)); pap. 15.25 (978-1-60754-539-2(X)) Windmill Bks.

Sarrasin, Alex. The Guardians of Neoegypti: Book One. 2007. 300p. per. 18.95 (978-0-595-45710-6(X)) iUniverse, Inc.

Sarwari, Zohra. The Inheritance: A Journey to China (Book 1) 2013. 148p. pap. (978-1-935948-30-8(X)) Roxby Media Ltd.

Satera, Diane. The Angel of Wild Springs: Jaiden & the Sacred Stones. 2010. 168p. 23.99 (978-1-4520-3460-7(5)); pap. 11.99 (978-1-4520-3461-4(3)) AuthorHouse.

Sateren, Shelley Swanson. Fearless Freddie. Melmon, Deborah, illus. 2015. (Adventures at Hound Hotel Ser.). (ENG.). 72p. (gr. 2-3). lib. bdg. 25.32 (978-1-4795-5898-8(2), Adventures at Hound Hotel) Picture Window Bks.

—Growling Gracie. Melmon, Deborah, illus. 2015. (Adventures at Hound Hotel Ser.). (ENG.). 72p. (gr. 2-3). lib. bdg. 25.32 (978-1-4795-5899-5(0), Adventures at Hound Hotel) Picture Window Bks.

—Homesick Herbie. Melmon, Deborah, illus. 2015. (Adventures at Hound Hotel Ser.). (ENG.). 72p. (gr. 2-3). lib. bdg. 25.32 (978-1-4795-5897-1(4), Adventures at Hound Hotel) Picture Window Bks.

—Mudball Molly. Melmon, Deborah, illus. 2015. (Adventures at Hound Hotel Ser.). (ENG.). 72p. (gr. 2-3). lib. bdg. 25.32 (978-1-4795-5900-8(8), Adventures at Hound Hotel) Picture Window Bks.

Sathre, Vivian. J. B. Wigglebottom & the Parade of Pets: True Ringside Tales, BBQ, & down-Home Recipies. O'Neill, Catharine, illus. 2013. (ENG.). 96p. (J). (gr. 2-5). pap. 13.99 (978-1-4814-2159-1(X), Atheneum Bks. for Young Readers) Simon & Schuster Children's Publishing.

Sattler, Jennifer. Pig Kahuna Pirates! 2014. (Pig Kahuna Ser.). (ENG., Illus.). 32p. (J). (gr. -1-1). 16.99 (978-1-61963-200-4(4), 9781619632004, Bloomsbury USA Childrens) Bloomsbury Publishing USA.

Saunders, Kate. The Curse of the Chocolate Phoenix: A Companion to the Whizz Pop Chocolate Shop. 2015. (ENG.). 272p. (J). (gr. 5). 19.99 (978-0-375-99183-7(2), Delacorte Bks. for Young Readers) Random Hse. Children's Bks.

—The Whizz Pop Chocolate Shop. (ENG.). 304p. (J). (gr. 5). 2014. 7.99 (978-0-385-74302-0(5), Yearling) 2013. 16.99 (978-0-385-74301-3(7), Delacorte Bks. for Young Readers) Random Hse. Children's Bks.

Saunders, Kate & Nesbit, E. Five Children on the Western Front. 2016. (J). (978-0-553-49785-4(5), Delacorte Pr) Random House Publishing Group.

Saunders, Katie. Olive the Alien. 2016. (ENG., Illus.). 32p. (J). (gr. -1-1). 16.99 (978-1-4998-0195-8(5)) Little Bee Books Inc.

Sava, Scott Christian. Magic Carpet. 2010. (Illus.). 110p. (J). pap. 11.99 (978-1-60010-563-0(7)) Idea & Design Works, LLC.

Sawyer, Jacqueline. Little Racer Big Heart. 2012. 28p. pap. 16.95 (978-1-62709-783-3(X)) America Star Bks.

Scaletta, Kurtis. The Tanglewood Terror. 2012. (ENG.). 272p. (J). (gr. 4-7). 7.99 (978-0-375-86542-8(X), Yearling) Random Hse. Children's Bks.

Scampering Through Savannah. 2007. (YA). lib. bdg., act. bk. ed. (978-0-9787589-2-9(7)) ON Words Publishing, LLC.

Schaaf, Ron. Tiger's Quest: Rounding Cape Horn. 2007. (J). (978-0-9787555-0-8(2)) Hickory Tales Publishing.

Schaefer, Lola. One Special Day. Meserve, Jessica, illus. 2012. (Story for Big Brothers & Sisters Ser.). (ENG.). 40p. (J). (gr. -1-k). 16.99 (978-1-4231-3760-3(4)) Hyperion Pr.

Schaefer, Lola M. One Busy Day: A Story for Big Brothers & Sisters. Meserve, Jessica, illus. 2014. (ENG.). 40p. (J). (gr. -1-k). 16.99 (978-1-4231-7112-6(8)) Hyperion Bks. for Children.

Schmitt, Michel-Yves. Snowball Truce! Caut, Vincent, illus. 2013. (Where's Leopold? Ser.: 2). (ENG.). 32p. (J). (gr. 2-4). pap. 6.95 (978-1-4677-1523-2(9), Graphic Universe™) Lerner Publishing Group.

—Your Pajamas Are Showing! Caut, Vincent, illus. 2013. (Where's Leopold? Ser.: 1). (ENG.). 40p. (J). (gr. 2-4). pap. 6.95 (978-1-4677-0871-5(2)); lib. bdg. 25.26 (978-1-4677-0769-5(4)) Lerner Publishing Group. (Graphic Universe™).

Schmitt, Michel-Yves & Burrell, Carol klio. Snowball Truce! Caut, Vincent, illus. 2013. (Where's Leopold? Ser.: 2). (ENG.). 32p. (J). (gr. 2-4). lib. bdg. 25.26 (978-1-4677-0770-1(8), Graphic Universe™) Lerner Publishing Group.

Schneider, Erin L. Summer of Sloane. (ENG.). 304p. (YA). (gr. 9-17). 2017. pap. 9.99 (978-1-4847-2670-9(7)) 2016. (Illus.). 17.99 (978-1-4847-2525-2(5)) Hyperion Bks. for Children.

Schneider, Josh. Kid Amazing vs. the Blob. 2017. (ENG., Illus.). 32p. (J). (gr. -1-3). 16.99 (978-0-544-80125-7(3), Clarion Bks.) Houghton Mifflin Harcourt Trade & Reference Pubs.

Schneider, Mical. Annie Quinn in America. 2003. (Adventures in Time Ser.). (Illus.). 252p. (J). (gr. 4-7). 15.95 (978-1-57505-510-7(4), Carolrhoda Bks.) Lerner Publishing Group.

Schnitzlein, Danny. Trick or Treat on Monster Street, 1 vol. Faulkner, Matt, illus. 2008. (ENG.). 32p. (J). (gr. k-3). 16.95 (978-1-56145-465-5(6)) Peachtree Pubs.

Scholastic, Inc. Staff. Cahills vs Vespers, Pack. 2011. (39 Clues: Cahills vs. Vespers Ser.). (ENG.). 16p. (J). (gr. 3-7). 6.99 (978-0-545-31640-8(5)) Scholastic, Inc.

Scholastic, Inc. Staff, contrib. by. The Story of Peppa Pig. 2013. (Peppa Pig Ser.). (ENG.). 32p. (J). (gr. -1-k). 8.99 (978-0-545-46805-3(1)) Scholastic, Inc.

Scholastic, Inc. Staff & Hooks, Gwendolyn. The Mystery of the Missing Dog. Devard, Nancy, illus. 2004. (Just for You Ser.). (ENG.). 32p. (gr. k-3). pap. 3.99 (978-0-439-56864-7(1), Teaching Resources) Scholastic, Inc.

Scholastic, Inc. Staff & Hudson, Cheryl Willis. What Do You Know? Snow! Walker, Sylvia, illus. 2004. (Just for You Ser.). (ENG.). 32p. pap. 3.99 (978-0-439-56851-7(X), Teaching Resources) Scholastic, Inc.

Scholastic, Inc. Staff & Roberson, Karla. My Shoelaces Are Hard to Tie! Holley, Vanessa, illus. 2004. (Just for You Ser.). (ENG.). 32p. pap. 3.99 (978-0-439-56869-2(2), Teaching Resources) Scholastic, Inc.

Scholastic, Inc. Staff & Watson, Jude. Doublecross - Mission Titanic, Bk. 1. 2015. (39 Clues: Doublecross Ser.: 1). (ENG.). 224p. (J). (gr. 3-7). 12.99 (978-0-545-76719-4(9)) Scholastic, Inc.

Schraff, Anne. Gingerbread Heart. 2008. 114p. (J). (gr. 4-7). 13.95 (978-0-7569-8406-9(8)) Perfection Learning Corp.

—A Song to Sing. 2008. (Passages Ser.). 130p. (YA). (gr. 7-9). lib. bdg. 13.95 (978-0-7569-8384-0(3)) Perfection Learning Corp.

—Under the Mushroom Cloud. 2008. (Passages to Adventure Ser.). 115p. (J). (gr. 4-6). lib. bdg. 13.95 (978-0-7569-8399-4(1)) Perfection Learning Corp.

Schreiber, Ellen. Kissing Coffins. (Vampire Kisses Ser.: No. 2). (ENG.). 2007. 240p. (J). pap., pap. 5.99 (978-0-06-077624-4(2), HarperTeen) 2005. 176p. (YA). (gr. 8-18). 17.99 (978-0-06-077622-0(6), Tegen, Katherine Bks) HarperCollins Pubs.

—Vampire Kisses Boxed Set: Vampire Kisses; Kissing Coffins; Vampireville. 2008. (Vampire Kisses Ser.: Nos. 1-3). (J). pap. 15.99 (978-0-06-169160-7(7), HarperTeen) HarperCollins Pubs.

Schuster, Judith A. No Place to Call Home: Book Two-the Eddie Brewster Adventures. 2008. 196p. pap. 24.95 (978-1-60563-559-0(6)) PublishAmerica, Inc.

Schwab, Victoria. New Beginnings. 2014. (Everyday Angel Ser.: 1). (J). (ENG.). 208p. (gr. 3-7). pap. 6.99 (978-0-545-52846-7(1), Scholastic Paperbacks); 195p. pap. (978-0-545-68443-9(9)) Scholastic, Inc.

Schwalbach, Pamela. The Happiest Day for Simeon & Sula. 2011. 28p. (gr. 4-6). pap. 15.00 (978-1-4567-5062-6(3)) AuthorHouse.

Schwarz, S. L. Treasure at Lure Lake. 2016. (Illus.). 185p. (J). **(978-1-4621-2600-2(6))** Cedar Fort, Inc./CFI Distribution.

Scollon, Bill & Nee, Chris. Engine Nine, Feelin' Fine! 2013. (Illus.). 24p. (J). (978-1-4844-0835-3(7)) Disney Pr.

Scott, Dee Mary. The Adventures of Charles & Camilla Chinchilla. 2012. (Illus.). 46p. pap. 6.99 (978-1-78035-389-0(8), Fastprint Publishing) Upfront Publishing Ltd. GBR. Dist: Printondemand-worldwide.com.

Scott, Eric. Santa & the Cyberspace Plot. 2013. 114p. pap. 7.99 (978-1-78333-397-4(9)) Acorn Bks.

Scott, Michael. The Alchemyst. 2009. (ENG., Illus.). 375p. (gr. 6-10). 19.00 (978-1-60686-514-9(5)) Perfection Learning Corp.

—The Alchemyst. (Secrets of the Immortal Nicholas Flamel Ser.: Bk. 1). (ENG.). 400p. (YA). (gr. 7). 2008. pap. 10.99 (978-0-385-73600-8(2), Ember) 2007. (Illus.). 16.99 (978-0-385-73357-1(7), Delacorte Bks. for Young Readers) Random Hse. Children's Bks.

—The Enchantress. 2012. (Secrets of the Immortal Nicholas Flamel Ser.). (ENG.). 528p. (YA). (gr. 7). 18.99 (978-0-385-73535-3(9), Delacorte Bks. for Young Readers) Random Hse. Children's Bks.

—The Enchantress. 2013. (Secrets of the Immortal Nicholas Flamel Ser.: 6). (ENG.). 528p. (YA). (gr. 7). pap. 10.99 (978-0-385-73536-0(7), Ember) Random Hse. Children's Bks.

—The Enchantress. 2013. (Secrets of the Immortal Nicholas Flamel Ser.: 6). lib. bdg. 22.10 (978-0-606-31947-8(6), Turtleback) Turtleback Bks.

—The Magician. 2009. (Secrets of the Immortal Nicholas Flamel Ser.: Bk. 2). (ENG.). 496p. (YA). (gr. 7). pap. 10.99 (978-0-385-73728-9(9), Ember) Random Hse. Children's Bks.

—The Necromancer. 2011. (Secrets of the Immortal Nicholas Flamel Ser.). (ENG.). 416p. (YA). (gr. 7). pap. 10.99 (978-0-385-73532-2(4), Ember) Random Hse. Children's Bks.

—The Necromancer the Secrets of the Immortal Nicholas Flamel. l.t. ed. 2010. (Secrets of the Immortal Nicholas Flamel Ser.). (ENG.). 492p. 23.99 (978-1-4104-2851-6(6)) Thorndike Pr.

—The Sorceress. (Secrets of the Immortal Nicholas Flamel Ser.: 3). (ENG.). 512p. (YA). (gr. 7-18). 2010. pap. 10.99 (978-0-385-73530-8(8), Ember) 2009. 17.99 (978-0-385-73529-2(4), Delacorte Bks. for Young Readers) Random Hse. Children's Bks.

—The Sorceress. 2010. (Secrets of the Immortal Nicholas Flamel Ser.: 3). lib. bdg. 22.10 (978-0-606-14133-8(2), Turtleback) Turtleback Bks.

—The Sorceress the Secrets of the Immortal Nicholas Flamel. l.t. ed. 2009. (Secrets of the Immortal Nicholas Flamel Ser.). (ENG.). 614p. (YA). 23.95 (978-1-4104-2092-3(2)) Thorndike Pr.

—The Warlock. (Secrets of the Immortal Nicholas Flamel Ser.: 5). (ENG.). 400p. (YA). (gr. 7). 2012. pap. 10.99 (978-0-385-73534-6(0), Ember) 2011. 18.99 (978-0-385-73533-9(2), Delacorte Bks. for Young Readers) Random Hse. Children's Bks.

—The Warlock. 2012. (Secrets of the Immortal Nicholas Flamel Ser.: 5). lib. bdg. 22.10 (978-0-606-26411-2(6), Turtleback) Turtleback Bks.

—The Warlock the Secrets of the Immortal Nicholas Flamel. l.t. ed. 2011. (Secrets of the Immortal Nicholas Flamel Ser.). (ENG.). 486p. 23.99 (978-1-4104-4157-7(1)) Thorndike Pr.

Scott, Victoria. Fire & Flood. 2014. (ENG.). 320p. (J). (gr. 9). 17.99 (978-0-545-53746-9(0), Scholastic Pr.) Scholastic, Inc.

—Salt & Stone. 2015. (ENG.). 320p. (J). (gr. 7). 17.99 (978-0-545-53748-3(7), Scholastic Pr.) Scholastic, Inc.

Sealls, Arthur. The Three Little Heroes: Book One of Kirk, Chelsea, & Samantha's Adventures. 2007. 84p. per. 8.95 (978-0-595-44083-2(5)) iUniverse, Inc.

Searles, Rachel. The Stolen Moon. 2015. (Lost Planet Ser.: 2). (ENG.). 368p. (YA). (gr. 4-9). 15.99 (978-1-250-03880-7(4), 9781250038807) Feiwel & Friends.

Sedgwick, Chantele. Love, Lucas. 2015. (ENG.). 280p. (J). (gr. 6). 16.99 (978-1-63220-417-2(7), Sky Pony Pr.) Skyhorse Publishing Co., Inc.

Sedgwick, Marcus. She Is Not Invisible. 2014. (ENG.). 224p. (YA). (gr. 7). 16.99 (978-1-59643-801-9(0), 9781596438019) Roaring Brook Pr.

—She Is Not Invisible. 2015. (ENG.). 240p. (YA). (gr. 7). pap. 9.99 (978-1-250-05698-6(5), 9781250056986) Square Fish.

Seidler, Tor. The Dulcimer Boy. Selznick, Brian, illus. 2003. 160p. (J). (gr. 3-7). lib. bdg. 16.89 (978-0-06-623610-0(X)) HarperCollins Pubs.

—The Dulcimer Boy. Selznick, Brian, illus. 2004. 153p. (gr. 5-7). 17.00 (978-0-7569-3520-7(2)) Perfection Learning Corp.

Seif, Adam, creator. Tacos, Beans & Rice... the Episodes: From the Beginning. l.t. ed. 2006. (Illus.). 32p. (J). (978-0-9719518-0-8(2)) Doodle Publishing.

Seif, Adam/Jeffrey. Tacos, Beans & Rice Episode 2: Lights, Camera, Action! 2007. (Illus.). 32p. (J). per. 5.00 (978-0-9719518-1-5(0)) Doodle Publishing.

Selfors, Suzanne. Smells Like Dog. 2011. (Smells Like Dog Ser.: 1). (ENG.). 384p. (J). (gr. 3-7). pap. 7.99 (978-0-316-04397-7(4)) Little, Brown Bks. for Young Readers.

Sensenig, Janet Martin. The Missing Bible: And Other Stories. 2003. (Sunbeam Ser.). (Illus.). 160p. (gr. -1-5). 6.40 (978-0-7399-0341-4(1), 2325) Rod & Staff Pubs., Inc.

Service, Pamela F. Escape from Planet Yastol. Gorman, Mike, illus. (Way-Too-Real Aliens Ser.: 1). (ENG.). 112p. (J). (gr. 4-6). 2015. 34.65 (978-1-4677-5960-1(0), Lerner Digital)No. 1. 2011. 15.95 (978-0-7613-7918-8(5), Darby Creek)No. 1. 2011. pap. 5.95 (978-0-7613-7921-8(5), Darby Creek) Lerner Publishing Group.

—The Not-So-Perfect Planet. Gorman, Mike, illus. (Way-Too-Real Aliens Ser.: 2). (ENG.). 120p. (J). (gr. 4-6). 2015. 34.65 (978-1-4677-5961-8(9), Lerner Digital) 2012. 15.95 (978-0-7613-7919-5(3), Darby Creek) 2012. pap. 6.95 (978-0-7613-7923-2(1), Darby Creek) Lerner Publishing Group.

—The Wizards of Wyrd World. Gorman, Mike, illus. (Way-Too-Real Aliens Ser.: 3). (ENG.). 112p. (J). (gr. 4-6). 2015. 34.65 (978-1-4677-5962-5(7), Lerner Digital) 2013. pap. 6.95 (978-0-7613-7922-5(3), Darby Creek) 2012. 15.95 (978-0-7613-7920-1(7)) Lerner Publishing Group.

Seuss, Dr. El Gato con Sombrero Viene de Nuevo! Canetti, Yanitzia, tr. from ENG. 2004.Tr. of Cat in the Hat Comes Back. (SPA., Illus.). 63p. (gr. -1-1). 8.99 (978-1-930332-43-0(2)) Lectorum Pubns., Inc.

Seven, John. The Outlaw of Sherwood Forest, 1 vol. Hans, Stephanie, illus. 2014. (Time-Tripping Faradays Ser.). (ENG.). 192p. (gr. 4-5). lib. bdg. 26.65 (978-1-4342-9174-5(X)) Stone Arch Bks.

Sévigny, Eric, illus. Caillou: Watches Rosie. rev. ed. 2008. (Playtime Ser.). (ENG.). 24p. (J). (gr. -1-1). pap. 4.95 (978-2-89450-635-6(X)) Caillouet, Gerry.

Shakespeare, William. Twelfth Night Paperback Book. 2006. (Shakespeare Classics Ser.). (Illus.). 94p. (J). (gr. 4-7). per. 7.95 (978-1-56254-858-2(1)) Saddleback Educational Publishing, Inc.

—Twelfth Night Study Guide. 2006. (Shakespeare Classics Ser.). (Illus.). 48p. (J). (gr. 4-7). per. 17.95 (978-1-56254-859-9(X)) Saddleback Educational Publishing, Inc.

Sharing: Individual Title Six-Packs. (Literatura 2000 Ser.). (gr. k-1). 28.00 (978-0-7635-0038-2(0)) Rigby Education.

Sharpe, Luke. Billy Sure Kid Entrepreneur & the Haywire Hovercraft. Ross, Graham, illus. 2016. (Billy Sure Kid Entrepreneur Ser.: 7). (ENG.). 160p. (J). (gr. 3-7). pap. 6.99 (978-1-4814-6193-1(1), Simon Spotlight) Simon Spotlight.

Shaw, Dana Alton, III. My Friend Zundel. 2006. per. (978-0-9791091-0-2(8)) Shaw, Dana.

Sheinmel, Courtney. My So-Called Family. 2008. (ENG.). 208p. (J). (gr. 4-7). 15.99 (978-1-4169-5785-0(5), Simon & Schuster Bks. For Young Readers) Simon & Schuster Bks. For Young Readers.

—Twinsanity. Bell, Jennifer A., illus. 2017. (Zacktastic Ser.). (ENG.). 272p. (J). (gr. 2-4). 11.99 **(978-1-58536-936-2(5)**, 204319); pap. 6.99 **(978-1-58536-937-9(3)**, 204333) Sleeping Bear Pr.

Sheinmel, Courtney. Zacktastic. 2015. (Zacktastic Ser.). (ENG.). 272p. (J). (gr. 2-5). 11.99 (978-1-58536-934-8(9), 203947) Sleeping Bear Pr.

Sheridan, Celi. Tolly & Maisie's Ghastly Adventure. 2011. (Illus.). 48p. (gr. -1). pap. 11.95 (978-1-4670-0397-1(2)) AuthorHouse.

Sheriff, Jeanne. Walkabout Kid. 2013. 172p. pap. 12.95 (978-1-4787-2130-7(8)) Outskirts Pr., Inc.

Sherrard, Valerie. Three Million Acres of Flame. 2007. (ENG.). 200p. (YA). pap. 10.99 (978-1-55002-727-3(1), Boardwalk Bks.) Dundurn CAN. Dist: Ingram Publisher Services.

Sherry, Maureen. Walls Within Walls. Stower, Adam, illus. (ENG.). 368p. (J). (gr. 3-7). 2012. pap. 6.99 (978-0-06-176703-6(4)) 2010. 16.99 (978-0-06-176700-5(X)) HarperCollins Pubs. (Tegen, Katherine Bks).

Sheth, Kashmira. Sona & the Wedding Game, 1 vol. Jaeggi, Yoshiko, illus. 2015. (ENG.). 32p. (J). (gr. 1-3). 16.95 (978-1-56145-735-9(3)) Peachtree Pubs.

—Tiger in My Soup, 1 vol. Ebbeler, Jefferey, illus. 2015. (ENG.). 32p. (J). (gr. -1-3). pap. 7.95 (978-1-56145-890-5(2)) Peachtree Pubs.

—Tiger in My Soup, 1 vol. Ebbeler, Jeffrey, illus. 2013. (ENG.). 32p. (J). (gr. -1-3). 15.95 (978-1-56145-696-3(9)) Peachtree Pubs.

Shields, Gillian. The Littlest Bunny. Lovsin, Polona, illus. 2015. 32p. (J). (978-1-4351-5967-9(5)) Barnes & Noble, Inc.

Shinoda, Anna. Learning Not to Drown. 2014. (ENG., Illus.). 352p. (YA). (gr. 9). 17.99 (978-1-4169-9393-3(2), Atheneum Bks. for Young Readers) Simon & Schuster Children's Publishing.

Shook, Karl. The Family Thing. 2004. 166p. (YA). pap. 12.95 (978-0-595-31121-7(0)) iUniverse, Inc.

Shore, Diane Z. How to Drive Your Sister Crazy. Rankin, Laura, illus. 2008. (I Can Read Level 2 Ser.). (ENG.). 48p. (J). (gr. k-3). 16.99 (978-0-06-052762-4(5)) HarperCollins Pubs.

—How to Drive Your Sister Crazy. Rankin, Laura, illus. 2012. (I Can Read! Level 2 Ser.). (J). lib. bdg. 13.55 (978-0-606-26869-1(3), Turtleback) Turtleback Bks.

Short, Robbie, illus. I Want One Too! 2003. 32p. (J). lib. bdg. 12.95 (978-0-9729833-2-7(5)) Bubble Gum Pr.

Shull, Megan. The Swap. 2014. (ENG.). 400p. (J). (gr. 5-9). 16.99 (978-0-06-231169-6(7), Tegen, Katherine Bks) HarperCollins Pubs.

Shultz, Charles M. & Bailer, Darice. Lose the Blanket, Linus!, 1 vol. Lo Bianco, Peter, illus. 2011. (Peanuts Ready-To-Reads Ser.). (ENG.). 32p. (gr. -1-2). lib. bdg. 24.21 (978-1-59961-804-3(4)) Spotlight.

Shusterman, Neal. Bruiser. 2010. (ENG.). 336p. (YA). (gr. 9-18). 17.99 (978-0-06-113408-1(2), HarperTeen) HarperCollins Pubs.

—Full Tilt. 2004. (ENG.). 208p. (YA). (gr. 7). mass mkt. 8.99 (978-0-689-87325-6(5), Simon Pulse) Simon Pulse.

The Siblings Four. 2006. (J). (978-0-9629124-6-7(8)) Floppinfish Publishing Co., Ltd.

Sicks, Linda. Nick's Holiday Celebration. Messing, Dave, illus. 2010. (Importance of Family Ser.). 40p. (J). 18.95 (978-1-936193-05-9(1)) Nick The Cat, LLC.

Sidney, Margaret. Five Little Peppers Abroad. 2008. 212p. (gr. 4-7). 26.95 (978-1-60664-996-1(5)); per. 14.95 (978-1-60312-546-8(9)) Aegypan.

—Five Little Peppers & How They Grew. 2006. (Dover Children's Classics Ser.). (ENG., Illus.). 224p. (J). (gr. 3-5). per. 6.95 (978-0-486-45267-8(0)) Dover Pubns., Inc.

—Five Little Peppers & How They Grew. Andreasen, Dan, illus. 2009. (Classic Starts(tm) Ser.). (ENG.). 160p. (J). (gr. 2-4). 6.95 (978-1-4027-5420-3(5)) Sterling Publishing Co., Inc.

—Polly Pepper's Book. 2011. 316p. 50.95 (978-1-258-10539-6(X)) Literary Licensing, LLC.

Silberman, Shoshana. A Family Haggadah II, Vol. 2. Kahn, Katherine Janus, illus. l.t. ed. 2003. 64p. (J). pap. 6.95 (978-1-58013-014-1(3), Kar-Ben Publishing) Lerner Publishing Group.

Sill, Cathryn. About Mollusks: A Guide for Children, 1 vol. Sill, John, illus. 2008. (About... Ser.). (ENG.). 40p. (J). (gr. k-3). pap. 7.95 (978-1-56145-406-8(0)) Peachtree Pubs.

Silvey, Diane. Time of the Thunderbird. Mantha, John, illus. 2008. (ENG.). 88p. (J). (gr. 6-5). pap. 11.99 (978-1-55002-792-1(1), Sandcastle Bks.) Dundurn CAN. Dist: Ingram Publisher Services.

Simmons, Jane. Daisy & the Egg. 2005. (Daisy Ser.). (Illus.). 36p. (J). (gr. -1-1). (ARA, ENG, VIE, CHI & BEN.). pap. 11.95 (978-1-84059-216-0(8)); (VIE, ENG, CHI, ARA & BEN., pap. 11.95 (978-1-84059-176-7(5)) Milet Publishing.

Simon, Charnan. Me Gusta Ganar! Translations.com Staff, tr. from ENG. Handelman, Dorothy, photos by. 2007. (Lecturas para niños de Verdad - Nivel 1 (Real Kids Readers - Level 1) Ser.).Tr. of I Like to Win! (SPA., Illus.). 32p. (gr. k-2). per. 5.95 (978-0-8225-7801-7(8), Ediciones Lerner) Lerner Publishing Group.

—Me Gusta Ganar; I Like to Win. 2008. pap. 34.95 (978-0-8225-9499-4(4)) Lerner Publishing Group.

—Tressa the Musical Princess. Allen, Joy, illus. 2005. 25p. (J). (978-1-58987-112-0(X)) Kindermusik International.

Simon, Coco. Emma: Sugar & Spice & Everything Nice. 2013. (Cupcake Diaries: 15). lib. bdg. 16.00 (978-0-606-32052-8(0), Turtleback) Turtleback Bks.

—Emma All Stirred Up! (Cupcake Diaries: 7). (ENG., 160p. (J). (gr. 3-7). 2013. Illus.). 17.99 (978-1-4424-8567-9(1)) 2012. pap. 6.99 (978-1-4424-5078-3(9)) Simon Spotlight. (Simon Spotlight).

—Emma All Stirred Up! 2012. (Cupcake Diaries: 7). lib. bdg. 17.20 (978-0-606-26309-2(8), Turtleback) Turtleback Bks.

—Emma Raining Cats & Dogs ... & Cupcakes! 2016. (Cupcake Diaries: 27). (ENG., Illus.). 160p. (J). (gr. 3-7). pap. 6.99 (978-1-4814-5524-4(9), Simon Spotlight) Simon Spotlight.

—Emma Raining Cats & Dogs... & Cupcakes! 2016. (Cupcake Diaries: 27). lib. bdg. 17.20 (978-0-606-38251-9(8)) Turtleback Bks.

Simon, Francesca. Horrid Henry. Ross, Tony, illus. 2009. (Horrid Henry Ser.: 0). (ENG.). 112p. (J). (gr. 2-5). pap. 6.99 (978-1-4022-1775-3(7), 9781402217753, Sourcebooks Jabberwocky) Sourcebooks, Inc.

Simonds, William. Marcus; or, the Boy-Tamer by Walter Aimwell [Pseud]. 2006. 336p. per. 23.99 (978-1-4255-3348-9(5)) Michigan Publishing.

Simons, Paullina. Poppet Gets Two Big Brothers. Thomas, Cassia, illus. 2015. (ENG.). 32p. (J). 17.99 (978-0-00-811041-3(7), HarperCollins Children's Bks.) HarperCollins Pubs. Ltd. GBR. Dist: HarperCollins Pubs.

Simpson, Craig. Resistance. 2007. (ENG., Illus.). 368p. (YA). (gr. 7). pap. 15.99 (978-0-552-55571-5(1)) Transworld Publishers Ltd. GBR. Dist: Independent Pubs. Group.

Singer, Marilyn. I'm Gonna Climb a Mountain in My Patent Leather Shoes. Avril, Lynne, illus. 2014. (ENG.). 40p. (J). (gr. k-2). 16.95 (978-1-4197-0336-2(6), Abrams Bks. for Young Readers) Abrams, Inc.

—Tallulah's Solo. Boiger, Alexandra, illus. 2012. (Tallulah Ser.). (ENG.). 40p. (J). (gr. -1-3). 16.99 (978-0-547-33004-4(9)) Houghton Mifflin Harcourt Publishing Co.

Singleton, Clive. The City through the Clouds. 2006. 208p. pap. 13.99 (978-1-4116-5982-7(1)) Lulu Pr., Inc.

Siobhan, Dowd. The London Eye Mystery. 2014. (ENG.). 336p. (J). (gr. 3-7). 12.24 (978-1-63245-320-4(7)) Lectorum Pubns., Inc.

Siriano, A. M. Nod. 2010. 168p. pap. 14.95 (978-0-557-26127-7(9)) Lulu Pr., Inc.

Sirowy, Alexandra. The Creeping: If You Hunt for Monsters, You'll Find Them. 2015. (ENG., Illus.). 400p. (YA). (gr. 7). 17.99 (978-1-4814-1886-7(6)) Simon & Schuster Children's Publishing.

—The Telling. 2016. (ENG., Illus.). 400p. (YA). (gr. 7). 17.99 (978-1-4814-1889-8(0), Simon & Schuster Bks. For Young Readers) Simon & Schuster Bks. For Young Readers.

Sitomer, Alan Lawrence. Caged Warrior. 2014. (ENG., Illus.). 224p. (YA). (gr. 7-12). 16.99 (978-1-4231-7124-9(1)) Disney Pr.

Skead, Robert A. & Skead, Robert J. Patriots, Redcoats & Spies, 1 vol. 2015. (American Revolutionary War Adventures Ser.). (ENG.). 192p. (J). 14.99 (978-0-310-74841-0(0)) Zonderkidz.

Skinner, Daphne. Henry Lleva la Cuenta. O'Rourke, Page Eastburn, illus. 2007. (Math Matters Ser.). 32p. (J). (gr. -1-3). pap. 5.95 (978-1-57565-250-4(1)) Kane Press, Inc.

—Henry Lleva la Cuenta; Henry Keeps Score. 2008. pap. 34.95 (978-1-58013-757-7(1)) Kane Press, Inc.

Skuse, C. J. Pretty Bad Things. 2011. (ENG.). 256p. (J). (gr. 7-7). 17.99 (978-0-545-28973-3(4), Chicken Hse., The) Scholastic, Inc.

Skye, obert. Witherwood Reform School. Thompson, Keith, illus. 2015. (Witherwood Reform School Ser.: 1). (ENG.). 240p. (J). (gr. 4-7). 16.99 (978-0-8050-9879-2(8), 9780805098792, Holt, Henry & Co. Bks. For Young Readers) Holt, Henry & Co.

Slanina, Anne M. Baby Brother Goes to the Hospital. Agnew, Alicia, illus. 2007. (Adventures of Annie Mouse Ser.: Bk. 2).

28p. (J). 18.99 (978-0-9793379-1-8(7)); per. 9.99 (978-0-9793379-0-1(9)) Annie Mouse Bks.

Smadja, Brigitte. Tarte aux Escargots. pap. 17.95 (978-2-211-03633-7(3)) Archimede Editions FRA. Dist: Distribooks, Inc.

Smiley, Sophie. Team Trouble. Foreman, Michael, illus. 2007. (ENG.). 64p. (J). (gr. 2-4). pap. 9.95 (978-1-84270-684-8(5)) Andersen Pr. GBR. Dist: Independent Pubs. Group.

Smith, Cheryl Jean. The Offering. 2006. (ENG.). 140p. per. 11.95 (978-0-7414-3181-3(5)) Infinity Publishing.

Smith, Cynthia Leitich. Feral Pride. 2015. (ENG.). 304p. (YA). (gr. 9). 17.99 (978-0-7636-5911-0(8)) Candlewick Pr.

Smith, Greg Leitich. Chronal Engine. Henry, Blake, illus. 2013. (ENG.). 192p. (J). (gr. 5-7). pap. 6.99 (978-0-544-02277-5(7)) Houghton Mifflin Harcourt Publishing Co.

Smith, J. Albert. Goosey Green. 2011. 24p. pap. 24.95 (978-1-4626-3392-0(7)) America Star Bks.

Smith, Jada. Touched by an Angel. 2009. 76p. pap. 13.95 (978-1-4251-8552-7(5)) Trafford Publishing.

Smith, Jennifer E. The Storm Makers. Helquist, Brett, illus. 2013. (ENG.). 384p. (J). (gr. 3-7). pap. 8.00 (978-0-316-17959-1(0)) Little, Brown Bks. for Young Readers.

Smith, L. J. The Fury & Dark Reunion, 2 vols. 2007. (Vampire Diaries: Nos. 3-4). (ENG.). 528p. (YA). (gr. 8-12). pap. 9.99 (978-0-06-114098-3(8), HarperTeen) HarperCollins Pubs.

—The Fury & Dark Reunion. 2007. (Vampire Diaries: 3). (YA). lib. bdg. 20.85 (978-0-606-07135-2(0), Turtleback) Turtleback Bks.

—Heart of Valor. 2008. (ENG.). 244p. (YA). pap. 11.99 (978-1-4169-8966-0(8), Simon & Schuster Bks. For Young Readers) Simon & Schuster Bks. For Young Readers.

—Heart of Valor. 2010. (ENG.). 352p. (J). (gr. 3-7). pap. 7.99 (978-1-4169-9841-9(1), Aladdin) Simon & Schuster Children's Publishing.

—Midnight. (Vampire Diaries: the Return Ser.: 3). (ENG.). (YA). (gr. 8). 2012. 592p. pap. 9.99 (978-0-06-172086-4(0)) 2011. 576p. 17.99 (978-0-06-172085-7(2)) HarperCollins Pubs. (HarperTeen).

—Moonsong Vol. 9. 2013. (Vampire Diaries: the Hunters Ser.: 2). (ENG.). 416p. (YA). (gr. 9). pap. 10.99 (978-0-06-201771-0(3), HarperTeen) HarperCollins Pubs.

—The Night of the Solstice. 2010. (ENG.). 352p. (J). (gr. 3-7). pap. 7.99 (978-1-4169-9840-2(3), Aladdin) Simon & Schuster Children's Publishing.

—Nightfall. (Vampire Diaries: the Return Ser.: 1). (ENG.). (YA). (gr. 8). 2010. 608p. pap. 9.99 (978-0-06-172080-2(1)) 2009. 592p. 17.99 (978-0-06-172077-2(1)) HarperCollins Pubs. (HarperTeen).

—Phantom. (Vampire Diaries: the Hunters Ser.: 1). (ENG.). (YA). (gr. 9). 2012. 432p. pap. 9.99 (978-0-06-201769-7(1)) 2011. 416p. 17.99 (978-0-06-201768-0(3)) HarperCollins Pubs. (HarperTeen).

—Shadow Souls. (Vampire Diaries: the Return Ser.: 2). (ENG.). (YA). (gr. 8). 2011. 624p. pap. 9.99 (978-0-06-172083-3(6)) 2010. (Illus.). 608p. 17.99 (978-0-06-172081-9(X)) HarperCollins Pubs. (HarperTeen).

—The Struggle. 2010. (Vampire Diaries: 2). (ENG.). 304p. (YA). (gr. 8). mass mkt. 7.99 (978-0-06-199076-2(0)) HarperCollins Pubs.

Smith, L. J. & Smith, Tom. The Night of the Solstice. 2008. (ENG.). 244p. (YA). pap. 11.99 (978-1-4169-8965-3(X), Simon & Schuster Bks. For Young Readers) Simon & Schuster Bks. For Young Readers.

Smith, L. J. & Williamson, Kevin. The Asylum. 2012. (Vampire Diaries: Stefan's Diaries: 5). (ENG.). 256p. (YA). (gr. 9). pap. 9.99 (978-0-06-211395-5(X), HarperTeen) HarperCollins Pubs.

Smith, Maggie. My Blue Bunny, Bubbit. 2014. (ENG., Illus.). 40p. (J). (gr. -1-3). 16.99 (978-0-547-55861-5(9)) Houghton Mifflin Harcourt Publishing Co.

Smith-Mansell, Dana. The Smith Family's New Puppy: Helping Children Cope with a New Family Member. Voerg, Kathy, illus. 2008. (Let's Talk Ser.). (ENG.). 48p. (J). (gr. -1-4). pap. 8.95 (978-0-88282-327-0(2)) New Horizon Pr. Pubs., Inc.

Smith, R. L. The Journals of Underwich: Book One. 2007. 253p. pap. 27.95 (978-1-60441-490-5(1)) America Star Bks.

Smith, Roland. Cryptid Hunters. 2006. (ENG.). 352p. (J). (gr. 5-17). pap. 6.99 (978-0-7868-5162-1(7)) Hyperion Pr.

—Independence Hall. (I, Q Ser.: Bk. 1). (ENG., 312p. (gr. 5-9). 2009. Illus.). (J). 15.95 (978-1-58536-468-8(1)) 2008. (YA). pap. 8.95 (978-1-58536-325-4(1)) Sleeping Bear Pr.

Smithwick, John W. Drift. 2012. 36p. pap. 13.95 (978-1-61897-972-8(8), Strategic Bk. Publishing) Strategic Book Publishing & Rights Agency (SBPRA).

Smothers, Ethel Footman. Down in the Piney Woods. 2004. 128p. (J). pap. 7.00 (978-0-8028-5248-9(3)) Eerdmans, William B. Publishing Co.

Snicket, Lemony, pseud. The Austere Academy. Helquist, Brett, illus. 2008. (Series of Unfortunate Events Ser.: Bk. 5). (ENG.). 240p. (J). (gr. 5-18). pap. 6.99 (978-0-06-114634-3(X), Harper Trophy) HarperCollins Pubs.

—The Bad Beginning. 2007. (Ser. of Unfortunate Events Ser.: 1). (J). lib. bdg. 17.20 (978-1-4177-8840-8(2), Turtleback) Turtleback Bks.

—The Bad Beginning No. 1: Or, Orphans! Helquist, Brett & Kupperman, Michael, illus. 2007. (Series of Unfortunate Events Ser.: 1). (ENG.). 176p. (J). (gr. 5-9). pap. 7.99 (978-0-06-114630-5(7)) HarperCollins Pubs.

—The Complete Wreck, Bks. 1-13. Helquist, Brett, illus. 2006. (Series of Unfortunate Events Ser.: Bks. 1-13). (J). (gr. 5). 180.00 (978-0-06-111906-4(7)) HarperCollins Pubs.

—The Gloom Looms, Bks. 10-12. Helquist, Brett, illus. 2005. (Series of Unfortunate Events Ser.: Bks. 10-12). (J). (gr. 5). 41.99 (978-0-06-083909-3(0)) HarperCollins Pubs.

—The Grim Grotto. Helquist, Brett & Kupperman, Michael, illus. 2004. (Series of Unfortunate Events Ser.: 11). (ENG.). 352p. (J). (gr. 5-6). 13.99 (978-0-06-441014-4(5)) HarperCollins Pubs.

—The Loathsome Library, Bks. 1-6. Helquist, Brett, illus. 2005. (Series of Unfortunate Events Ser.: Bks. 1-6). (J). (gr. 5). 65.00 (978-0-06-083353-4(X)) HarperCollins Pubs.

—The Miserable Mill, 13 vols. Helquist, Brett, illus. 2008. (Series of Unfortunate Events Ser.: Bk. 4). (ENG.). 208p. (J). (gr. 5-18). pap. 6.99 (978-0-06-114632-9(3), Harper Trophy) HarperCollins Pubs.

—The Reptile Room: Or, Murder! Helquist, Brett & Kupperman, Michael, illus. 2007. (Series of Unfortunate Events Ser.: 2). (ENG.). 192p. (J). (gr. 5-9). pap. 6.99 (978-0-06-114631-2(5)) HarperCollins Pubs.

—The Slippery Slope. Helquist, Brett, illus. 2003. (Series of Unfortunate Events Ser.: Bk. 10). (YA). (gr. 5-18). 197.82 (978-0-06-057743-8(6)); 352p. (J). (gr. 3-6). lib. bdg. 15.89 (978-0-06-029641-4(0)) HarperCollins Pubs.

—The Slippery Slope. Helquist, Brett & Kupperman, Michael, illus. 2003. (Series of Unfortunate Events Ser.: 10). (ENG.). 352p. (J). (gr. 5-6). 13.99 (978-0-06-441013-7(7)) HarperCollins Pubs.

—The Trouble Begins. Helquist, Brett, illus. movie tie-in ed. 2004. (Series of Unfortunate Events Ser.: Bks. 1-3). (J). 35.99 (978-0-06-075773-1(6)) HarperCollins Pubs.

—The Wide Window - Or, Disappearance! Helquist, Brett & Kupperman, Michael, illus. 2007. (Series of Unfortunate Events Ser.: 3). (ENG.). 208p. (J). (gr. 5). pap. 6.99 (978-0-06-114633-6(1)) HarperCollins Pubs.

Snowe, Olivia. Hansen & Gracie, 1 vol. Lamoreaux, Michelle, illus. 2014. (Twicetold Tales Ser.). (ENG.). 128p. (gr. 3-4). pap. 5.95 (978-1-4342-9150-9(2)) Stone Arch Bks.

Snyder, Carol. One up, One Down. Chambliss, Maxie, illus. 2013. (ENG.). 32p. (J). (gr. -1-3). 16.99 (978-1-4814-2144-7(1), Atheneum Bks. for Young Readers) Simon & Schuster Children's Publishing.

Snyder, Laurel. Any Which Wall. Pham, LeUyen, illus. 2010. (ENG.). 256p. (J). (gr. 3-7). pap. 7.99 (978-0-375-85561-0(0), Yearling) Random Hse. Children's Bks.

—Charlie & Mouse. Hughes, Emily, illus. 2017. (Charlie & Mouse Ser.: 1). (ENG.). 48p. (J). 14.99 (978-1-4521-3153-5(8)) Chronicle Bks. LLC.

Snyder, Rebecca. Two Hearts Are Better Than One. 2012. 174p. pap. 19.99 (978-1-4797-5225-6(8)) Xlibris Corp.

Snyder, Zilpha Keatley. The Unseen. 2005. 199p. 16.00 (978-0-7569-5670-7(6)) Perfection Learning Corp.

—William S. & the Great Escape. (ENG.). (J). (gr. 3-7). 2010. 240p. pap. 7.99 (978-1-4169-6764-4(8)) 2009. 224p. 16.99 (978-1-4169-6763-7(X)) Simon & Schuster Children's Publishing. (Atheneum Bks. for Young Readers).

—William's Midsummer Dreams. (ENG., (J). (gr. 3-7). 2012. Illus.). 240p. pap. 6.99 (978-1-4424-1998-8(9)) 2011. 224p. 16.99 (978-1-4424-1997-1(0)) Simon & Schuster Children's Publishing. (Atheneum Bks. for Young Readers).

Soileau, Hodges, illus. The Black Widow Spider Mystery. 2004. (Boxcar Children Special Ser.). 130p. (gr. 2-7). 15.50 (978-0-7569-3266-4(1)) Perfection Learning Corp.

—The Comic Book Mystery. 2003. (Boxcar Children Ser.). 106p. (gr. 4-7). 15.00 (978-0-7569-1611-4(9)) Perfection Learning Corp.

—The Great Shark Mystery. 2003. (Boxcar Children Special Ser.). 130p. (gr. 4-7). 15.50 (978-0-7569-1616-9(X)) Perfection Learning Corp.

—The Mystery at Skeleton Point. 2003. (Boxcar Children Ser.). 120p. (gr. 4-7). 15.00 (978-0-7569-1609-1(7)) Perfection Learning Corp.

Solomons, David. My Brother Is a Superhero. (ENG.). (J). (gr. 3-7). 2017. 320p. 7.99 (978-0-14-751605-3(6), Puffin Books) 2015. 304p. 16.99 (978-0-451-47477-3(5), Viking Books for Young Readers) Penguin Young Readers Group.

—My Brother Is a Superhero. 2017. lib. bdg. 18.40 **(978-0-606-39790-2(6))** Turtleback Bks.

Soman, David. Three Bears in a Boat. Soman, David, illus. 2014. (ENG., Illus.). 40p. (J). (gr. -1-k). 17.99 (978-0-8037-3993-2(1), Dial Bks) Penguin Publishing Group.

Sommer, Carl. You Move You Lose. James, Kennon, illus. 2014. (J). pap. (978-1-57537-972-2(4)) Advance Publishing, Inc.

—You Move You Lose(El Que Se Mueva, Pierde) James, Kennon, illus. 2009. (Another Sommer-Time Story Bilingual Ser.). (SPA & ENG.). 48p. (J). lib. bdg. 16.95 (978-1-57537-172-6(3)) Advance Publishing, Inc.

Sommers, Jackie Lea. Truest. 2015. (ENG.). 384p. (YA). (gr. 8). 17.99 (978-0-06-234825-8(6), Tegen, Katherine Bks) HarperCollins Pubs.

Somper, Justin. Black Heart. 2010. (Vampirates Ser.: 4). (ENG.). 512p. (J). (gr. 3-7). pap. 8.99 (978-0-316-02088-6(5)) Little, Brown Bks. for Young Readers.

—Blood Captain. 2009. (Vampirates Ser.: 3). (ENG.). 592p. (J). (gr. 3-7). pap. 10.99 (978-0-316-02086-2(9)) Little Brown & Co.

—Empire of Night. 2011. (Vampirates Ser.: 5). (ENG.). 512p. (J). (gr. 3-7). pap. 10.99 (978-0-316-03323-7(5)) Little, Brown Bks. for Young Readers.

—Immortal War. 2013. (Vampirates Ser.: 6). (ENG.). 512p. (J). (gr. 3-7). pap. 10.99 (978-0-316-03325-1(1)) Little, Brown Bks. for Young Readers.

—Immortal War. 2013. (Vampirates Ser.: 6). (J). lib. bdg. 22.10 (978-0-606-26696-3(8), Turtleback) Turtleback Bks.

Sonnenblick, Jordan. After Ever After. 2014. (ENG.). 272p. (J). pap. 9.99 (978-0-545-72287-2(X)) Scholastic, Inc.

—Drums, Girls, & Dangerous Pie. 2005. (ENG.). 288p. (J). (gr. 7-12). 18.99 (978-0-439-75519-1(0), Scholastic Pr.) Scholastic, Inc.

—Falling over Sideways. (ENG.). 272p. (J). (gr. 7). 2017. pap. 9.99 **(978-0-545-86325-4(2))** 2016. 17.99 (978-0-545-86324-7(4), Scholastic Pr.) Scholastic, Inc.

Soo, Kean, illus. The Baker's Run. 2015. (March Grand Prix Ser.). (ENG.). 48p. (gr. 1-3). lib. bdg. 33.32 (978-1-4342-9640-5(7)) Capstone Young Readers of Coughlan Cos.

—The Great Desert Rally. 2015. (March Grand Prix Ser.). (ENG.). 48p. (gr. 1-3). lib. bdg. 33.32 (978-1-4342-9641-2(5)) Capstone Young Readers of Coughlan Cos.

—March Grand Prix: The Fast & the Furriest. 2015. (March Grand Prix Ser.). (ENG.). 144p. (gr. 1-3). pap. 14.95 (978-1-62370-171-0(6)) Capstone Young Readers of Coughlan Cos.

Sosna, Marvin. Brandon's Trail. 2006. 220p. per. 13.95 (978-1-58939-875-7(0)) Virtualbookworm.com Publishing, Inc.

Spalding, Andrea & Spalding, David A. E. The Klondike Ring, 1 vol. 2003. (Adventure - Net Ser.). (ENG.). 128p. (J). pap. (978-1-55285-461-7(2)) Whitecap Bks., Ltd.

Spalding, Esta. Knock about with the Fitzgerald-Trouts. Smith, Sydney, illus. 2017. (ENG.). 320p. (J). (gr. 3-7). 16.99 (978-0-316-29860-5(3)) Little, Brown Bks. for Young Readers.

—Look Out for the Fitzgerald-Trouts. Smith, Sydney, illus. 2016. (ENG.). 256p. (J). (gr. 3-7). 16.99 (978-0-316-29858-2(1)) Little, Brown Bks. for Young Readers.

Sparkes, Ali. Alligator Action. Collins, Ross, illus. 2014. (S. W. I. T. C. H. Ser.: 14). (ENG.). 112p. (J). (gr. 2-5). lib. bdg. 27.93 (978-1-4677-2117-2(4), Darby Creek) Lerner Publishing Group.

—Crane Fly Crash. Collins, Ross, illus. 2013. (S. W. I. T. C. H. Ser.: 5). (ENG.). 104p. (J). (gr. 2-5). pap. 7.95 (978-1-4677-0714-5(7), Darby Creek); lib. bdg. 27.93 (978-0-7613-9203-3(3)) Lerner Publishing Group.

—Turtle Terror. Collins, Ross, illus. 2014. (S. W. I. T. C. H. Ser.: 11). (ENG.). 104p. (J). (gr. 2-5). lib. bdg. 27.93 (978-1-4677-2114-1(X), Darby Creek) Lerner Publishing Group.

Spaziante, Patrick, illus. OLIVIA & Her Alien Brother. 2014. (Olivia TV Tie-In Ser.). (ENG.). 24p. (J). (gr. -1-2). pap. 3.99 (978-1-4424-9749-8(1), Simon Spotlight) Simon Spotlight.

Spence, Tom. Tough Day at the Plate. 2004. 39p. (J). (gr. -1-7). per. 5.95 (978-1-59353-241-3(5)) Mountain Valley Publishing, LLC.

Sperring, Mark. Dino-Baby. Lloyd, Sam, illus. 2013. (ENG.). 32p. (J). (gr. -1-1). 14.99 (978-1-61963-151-9(2), 9781619631519); lib. bdg. 15.89 (978-1-61963-152-6(0), 9781619631526) Bloomsbury Publishing USA. (Bloomsbury USA Childrens).

Sperry, John Lamont. Where Is Home? 2006. 136p. pap. 24.95 (978-1-4241-1008-7(4)) PublishAmerica, Inc.

Spinelli, Eileen. Baby Loves You So Much! Wenzel, David, illus. 2008. (ENG.). 40p. (J). (gr. -1-3). 16.99 (978-0-8249-5550-2(1), Ideal Pubns.) Worthy Publishing.

Spinelli, Jerry. Jake & Lily. 2012. 352p. (J). (gr. 3-7). (ENG.). 16.99 (978-0-06-028135-9(9)); lib. bdg. 16.89 (978-0-06-028136-6(7)) HarperCollins Pubs.

—Smiles to Go. 2009. (ENG.). 272p. (J). (gr. 5). pap. 6.99 (978-0-06-447197-8(7)) HarperCollins Pubs.

Spires, Sharlene. The Grandsisters. 2010. 56p. pap. 15.99 (978-1-4535-3004-7(5)) Xlibris Corp.

Spooner, Meagan. Shadowlark. 2013. 327p. pap. 17.95 (978-1-4677-1664-2(2)); (ENG.). 336p. (YA). (gr. 7-12). 17.95 (978-0-7613-8866-1(4), Carolrhoda Lab™) Lerner Publishing Group.

Spratt, R. A. The Adventures of Nanny Piggins. Santat, Dan, illus. 2012. (Nanny Piggins Ser.: 1). (ENG.). 272p. (J). (gr. 3-7). pap. 7.00 (978-0-316-06818-5(7)) Little, Brown Bks. for Young Readers.

—Nanny Piggins & the Runaway Lion. 2014. (Nanny Piggins Ser.: 3). (ENG., Illus.). 320p. (J). (gr. 3-7). 17.00 (978-0-316-25453-3(3)) Little, Brown Bks. for Young Readers.

—Nanny Piggins & the Wicked Plan. 2013. (Nanny Piggins Ser.: 2). (ENG.). 320p. (J). (gr. 3-7). pap. 7.99 (978-0-316-19922-3(2)) Little, Brown Bks. for Young Readers.

Springer, Nancy. The Boy on a Black Horse. 2010. (ENG.). 176p. (YA). (gr. 7). pap. 9.99 (978-1-4424-1353-5(0), Atheneum Bks. for Young Readers) Simon & Schuster Children's Publishing.

—Possessing Jessie. 2010. (ENG.). 128p. (YA). (gr. 7-18). pap. 16.95 (978-0-8234-2259-3(3)) Holiday Hse., Inc.

—Somebody. 2009. (ENG.). 128p. (YA). (gr. 7-18). 16.95 (978-0-8234-2099-5(X)) Holiday Hse., Inc.

Springham, James. Earth-n-Bones: Blue Things. 2006. 54p. pap. 16.95 (978-1-4137-9738-1(5)) America Star Bks.

Springstubb, Tricia. Phoebe & Digger. Newman, Jeff, illus. (ENG.). 32p. (J). (gr. -1-2). 2016. 7.99 (978-0-7636-8894-3(0)) 2013. 16.99 (978-0-7636-5281-4(4)) Candlewick Pr.

Spykman, E. C. Terrible, Horrible Edie. 2010. (ENG.). 232p. (J). (gr. 4-7). 16.95 (978-1-59017-353-4(8), NYR Children's Collection) New York Review of Bks., Inc., The.

St John, Patricia. Other Kitten. 2007. (Illus.). 96p. pap. (978-1-84427-290-7(7)) Scripture Union.

Stanley, Pauline. The Children & the Witches Magic. 2010. (Illus.). 48p. pap. 10.49 (978-1-4490-9544-4(5)) AuthorHouse.

Stanton, Andy. Danny Mcgee Drinks the Sea. Layton, Neal, illus. 2017. (ENG.). 32p. (J). (gr. -1-3). 17.99 **(978-1-5247-1736-0(3))**; lib. bdg. 20.99 **(978-1-5247-1737-7(1))** Random Hse. Children's Bks. (Schwartz & Wade Bks.).

Starlight, Cyandria. Daydreams of a Little Girl. 2012. 18p. pap. 16.95 (978-1-4626-6003-2(7)) America Star Bks.

Starmer, Aaron. The Storyteller. 2016. (Riverman Trilogy Ser.: 3). (ENG.). 336p. (J). 16.99 (978-0-374-36313-0(7), 9780374363130, Farrar, Straus & Giroux (BYR)) Farrar, Straus & Giroux.

Starrenburg, Hasko. The Queen's Orb. 2012. (Illus.). 144p. pap. 8.00 (978-1-4349-8782-2(5), RoseDog Bks.) Dorrance Publishing Co., Inc.

Stead, Judy. The Twelve Days of Christmas in North Carolina. Stead, Judy, illus. 2009. (Twelve Days of Christmas in America Ser.). (ENG., Illus.). 40p. (J). (gr. k). 12.95 (978-1-4027-4467-9(6)) Sterling Publishing Co., Inc.

Stead, Judy, illus. The Twelve Days of Christmas in North Carolina. 2017. (Twelve Days of Christmas in America Ser.). (ENG.). 22p. (J). (— 1). bds. 7.95 **(978-1-4549-2285-8(0))** Sterling Publishing Co., Inc.

Steele, Giselle. The off-Limits Watermelon Patch. 2006. (Illus.). 35p. (J). per. 12.95 (978-0-9769949-0-9(9)) Stuart & Weitz Publishing Group.

Steensland, Mark. Behind the Bookcase. Murphy, Kelly, illus. 2013. (ENG.). 288p. (J). (gr. 3-7). 6.99 (978-0-385-74072-2(7), Yearling) Random Hse. Children's Bks.

Steer, Dugald A. The Dragon Diary, Vol. 2. Carrel, Douglas, illus. 2010. (Ologies Ser.: Vol. 2). (ENG.). 272p. (J). (gr. 4-7). pap. 7.99 (978-0-7636-4514-4(1)) Candlewick Pr.

Stein, Tammar. Kindred. 2012. (ENG.). 276p. (YA). (gr. 7). pap. 8.99 (978-0-375-85349-4(9), Ember) Random Hse. Children's Bks.

Steinkraus, Kyla. Dessert with Daniel Boone. 2016. (Time Hop Sweets Shop Ser.). (ENG.). 32p. (gr. k-3). 25.65 (978-1-68191-373-5(9)) Rourke Educational Media.

—Sundaes with Harriet Tubman. 2016. (Time Hop Sweets Shop Ser.). (ENG.). 32p. (gr. k-3). 25.65 (978-1-68191-371-1(2)) Rourke Educational Media.

Stemke, Kathy. Sh Sh Sh Let the Baby Sleep. Foster, Jack, illus. 2011. 20p. pap. 10.95 (978-1-61633-156-6(9)) Guardian Angel Publishing, Inc.

Stenton, Murray, illus. My Brother Is Special: A Sibling with Cerebral Palsy. 2016. (J). pap. **(978-1-61599-309-3(6))** Loving Healing Pr., Inc.

Stephens, John. The Black Reckoning. 2015. (Books of Beginning Ser.). (ENG.). 432p. (J). (gr. 3-7). 17.99 (978-0-375-86872-6(0), Knopf Bks. for Young Readers) Random Hse. Children's Bks.

—The Emerald Atlas. (Books of Beginning Ser.). (ENG.). (J). (gr. 3-7). 2012. 448p. 7.99 (978-0-375-87271-6(X), Yearling) 2011. 432p. 17.99 (978-0-375-86870-2(4), Knopf Bks. for Young Readers) Random Hse. Children's Bks.

—The Emerald Atlas. l.t. ed. 2012. (Books of Beginning Ser.). (ENG.). 548p. (J). (gr. 4-7). 23.99 (978-1-4104-4234-5(9)) Thorndike Pr.

—The Fire Chronicle. 2012. (Illus.). 437p. (J). (978-0-449-81015-6(1)) Knopf, Alfred A. Inc.

—The Fire Chronicle. (Books of Beginning Ser.). (ENG.). 448p. (J). (gr. 3-7). 2013. 7.99 (978-0-375-87272-3(8), Yearling) 2012. (Illus.). 17.99 (978-0-375-86871-9(2), Knopf Bks. for Young Readers) Random Hse. Children's Bks.

Stevenson, James. Peor Que Willy. (SPA., Illus.). (J). (gr. k-2). pap. (978-84-348-1895-8(7), SM2858) SM Ediciones ESP. Dist: Lectorum Pubns., Inc.

Stevenson, Robin. Ben's Robot, 1 vol. Parkins, David, illus. 2010. (Orca Echoes Ser.). (ENG.). 64p. (J). (gr. 2-3). pap. 6.95 (978-1-55469-153-1(2)) Orca Bk. Pubs. USA.

Stewart, A. W. Rooktime. 2010. 284p. pap. 15.49 (978-1-4520-1460-9(4)) AuthorHouse.

Stiegemeyer, Julie. Under the Baobab Tree, 1 vol. Lewis, E. B., illus. 2012. (ENG.). 32p. (J). 16.99 (978-0-310-72561-9(5)) Zonderkidz.

Stine, Fay. Star Ship Fantasy: The New Frontier of Space. 2008. 52p. pap. 10.95 (978-1-4327-2703-1(6)) Outskirts Pr., Inc.

Stine, R. L. Attack of the Jack (Goosebumps SlappyWorld #2) 2017. (Goosebumps SlappyWorld Ser.: 2). (ENG.). 160p. (J). (gr. 3-7). pap. 6.99 **(978-1-338-06836-8(9)**, Scholastic Paperbacks) Scholastic, Inc.

—Espanto Marino. 2009. (Goosebumps Horrorland Ser.: 2). (SPA.). 160p. (J). (gr. 3-7). pap. 6.99 (978-0-545-15408-6(1), Scholastic en Espanol) Scholastic, Inc.

—The Five Masks of Dr. Scream. 2011. (Goosebumps Hall of Horrors Ser.: 3). (ENG.). 192p. (J). (gr. 3-7). pap. 7.99 (978-0-545-28936-8(X), Scholastic Paperbacks) Scholastic, Inc.

—Here Comes the Shaggedy. 2016. (Goosebumps: Most Wanted Ser.: 9). (ENG., Illus.). 160p. (J). (gr. 3-7). pap. 6.99 (978-0-545-82547-4(4), Scholastic Paperbacks) Scholastic, Inc.

—Here Comes the Shaggedy. 2016. (Goosebumps Most Wanted Ser.: 9). (Illus.). 140p. (J). lib. bdg. 17.20 (978-0-606-38587-9(8)) Turtleback Bks.

—A Night in Terror Tower. 2009. (Goosebumps Ser.: 11). lib. bdg. 17.20 (978-0-606-00240-0(5), Turtleback) Turtleback Bks.

—Welcome to Camp Slither. 2009. (Goosebumps Horrorland Ser.: 9). (ENG.). 160p. (J). (gr. 3-7). 6.99 (978-0-439-91877-0(4), Scholastic Paperbacks) Scholastic, Inc.

Stinson, Kathy. What Happened to Ivy, 1 vol. 2012. (ENG.). 256p. (YA). (gr. 6-9). pap. 11.95 (978-1-926920-81-8(3)) Second Story Pr. CAN. Dist: Orca Bk. Pubs. USA.

Stokes, Phil. Phillip & Dickie. 2004. 384p. (YA). 28.95 (978-0-9744360-0-5(3)) Da Wong Bks.

Stone, Heather Duffy. This Is What I Want to Tell You. 2009. (ENG.). 240p. (YA). (gr. 7-18). pap. 9.95 (978-0-7387-1450-9(X), Flux) North Star Editions.

Stone, Jeff. Tiger. 2006. (Five Ancestors Ser.: Bk. 1). (ENG., Illus.). 208p. (J). (gr. 3-7). reprint ed. 6.99 (978-0-375-83072-3(3), Yearling) Random Hse. Children's Bks.

The Strange & Beautiful Sorrows of Ava Lavender. 2014. 320p. (J). (gr. 9). E-Book 8.99 (978-0-7636-7034-4(0)) Candlewick Pr.

Strasnick, Lauren. Her & Me & You. (ENG.). 208p. (YA). (gr. 9). 2011. pap. 9.99 (978-1-4169-8267-8(1)) 2010. 16.99 (978-1-4169-8266-1(3)) Simon Pulse. (Simon Pulse).

Strasser, Todd. Battle Drift. Phillips, Craig, illus. 2006. (DriftX Ser.: 2). (ENG.). 224p. (YA). (gr. 9-12). pap. 10.99 (978-1-4169-0582-0(0), Simon Pulse) Simon Pulse.

Stratton, Allan. Chanda's Wars. 2009. (ENG.). 416p. (J). mass mkt. 7.99 (978-1-55468-566-0(4), Harper Trophy) HarperCollins Pubs.

Streib, Sally. Octopus Encounter. 2007. (Illus.). 126p. (J). 6.97 (978-0-8163-2210-7(4)) Pacific Pr. Publishing Assn.

Stretton, Hesba. Lost Gip. 2003. (Golden Inheritance Ser.: Vol. 7). (Illus.). 121p. (J). (978-0-921100-93-5(0)) Inheritance Pubns.

Strickland, James R. Lincoln's Lost Papers. 2008. 131p. (J). pap. 11.95 (978-0-7414-4601-5(4)) Infinity Publishing.

Stroud, Jonathan. Buried Fire. 2004. 332p. (J). pap. (978-0-7818-5794-9(5)) Hippocrene Bks., Inc.

Strungis, Elaine. Sammi & Danny Learn about Jupiter. 2012. 32p. pap. 14.50 (978-1-4669-5411-3(6)) Trafford Publishing.

—Sammi & Danny Learn about Mercury. 2012. 28p. pap. 13.55 (978-1-4669-5413-7(2)) Trafford Publishing.

—Sammi & Danny Learn about the Earth. 2012. 32p. pap. 14.50 (978-1-4669-3731-4(9)) Trafford Publishing.

—Sammi & Danny Learn about Uranus. 2012. 32p. pap. 14.50 (978-1-4669-6297-2(6)) Trafford Publishing.

—Sammi & Danny Learn about Venus. 2012. 32p. pap. 14.50 (978-1-4669-3733-8(5)) Trafford Publishing.

Sturges, Philemon. I Love School! Halpern, Shari, illus. 2014. 32p. pap. 7.00 (978-1-61003-329-9(9)) Center for the Collaborative Classroom.

—I Love School! Halpern, Shari, illus. 32p. (J). (gr. -1-1). 2004. lib. bdg. 14.89 (978-0-06-009285-6(8)) 2006. (ENG.). reprint ed. pap. 6.99 (978-0-06-009286-3(6)) HarperCollins Pubs.

Sturgill, Jean A. Bouncing Beaver Discovers God: A Drew's Animals Book. 2007. (ENG.). 30p. pap. 15.99 (978-1-4196-7822-6(1)) CreateSpace Independent Publishing Platform.

Sullivan, Laura L. Under the Green Hill. 2011. (ENG.). 336p. (J). (gr. 4-8). pap. 17.99 (978-0-312-55149-0(5), 9780312551490) Square Fish.

Sullivan, Mary. Dear Blue Sky. 2013. (ENG.). 256p. (J). (gr. 5). pap. 6.99 (978-0-14-242667-8(9), Puffin Books) Penguin Young Readers Group.

Sullivan-Ringe, Laurie. Noise in the Night. Matiuzzo, Nick, illus. 2008. 37p. pap. 24.95 (978-1-60672-476-7(2)) America Star Bks.

Summers, Sherri Pankratz. Humpty Dumpty, Back Together Again? Pankratz, Justin, illus. 2003. 32p. (J). 8.95 (978-0-9742637-1-7(0)) Pankratz Creations.

Susie's Sister Has Food Allergy. 2004. (J). 5.00 (978-1-882541-36-2(7)) Food Allergy & Anaphylaxis Network.

Sutton, Michelle. It's Not about Me. 2012. (Second Glances Ser.). (ENG.). 252p. pap. 12.99 (978-0-9838836-9-2(6)) Sword of the Spirit Publishing.

Suzuma, Tabitha. Forbidden. (ENG.). 464p. (YA). (gr. 11). 2012. pap. 11.99 (978-1-4424-1996-4(2)) 2011. 17.99 (978-1-4424-1995-7(4)) Simon Pulse. (Simon Pulse).

Swanson, Matthew. Babies Ruin Everything. Behr, Robbi, illus. 2016. (ENG.). 40p. (J). 16.99 (978-1-250-08057-8(6), 9781250080578) Imprint IND. Dist: Macmillan.

Swanson, Matthew. The Real McCoys. Behr, Robbi, illus. 2017. (J). pap. **(978-1-250-09853-5(X))** ETT Imprint.

Swanson Sateren, Shelley. Adventures of Hound Hotel. Melmon, Deborah, illus. 2015. (Adventures at Hound Hotel Ser.). (ENG.). 72p. (gr. 2-3). 101.28 (978-1-4795-6291-6(2), Adventures at Hound Hotel) Picture Window Bks.

—Cool Crosby. Melmon, Deborah, illus. 2016. (Adventures at Hound Hotel Ser.). (ENG.). 72p. (gr. 2-3). lib. bdg. 25.32 (978-1-5158-0066-8(0), Adventures at Hound Hotel) Picture Window Bks.

—Drooling Dudley. Melmon, Deborah, illus. 2016. (Adventures at Hound Hotel Ser.). (ENG.). 72p. (gr. 2-3). lib. bdg. 25.32 (978-1-5158-0220-4(5), Adventures at Hound Hotel) Picture Window Bks.

—Mighty Murphy. Melmon, Deborah, illus. 2016. (Adventures at Hound Hotel Ser.). (ENG.). 72p. (gr. 2-3). lib. bdg. 25.32 (978-1-5158-0067-5(9), Adventures at Hound Hotel) Picture Window Bks.

—Stinky Stanley. Melmon, Deborah, illus. 2016. (Adventures at Hound Hotel Ser.). (ENG.). 72p. (gr. 2-3). lib. bdg. 25.32 (978-1-5158-0221-1(3), Adventures at Hound Hotel) Picture Window Bks.

Swenson, Lynn. Rollie & Mollie: Disappearing Act. Baker, David, illus. 2012. 26p. 24.95 (978-1-4626-5277-8(8)) America Star Bks.

Taddonio, Lea. Book 3: First Fight. 2016. (Head over Heels Ser.). (ENG., Illus.). 46p. (J). (gr. 2-8). lib. bdg. 28.50 **(978-1-62402-194-7(8))** ABDO Publishing Co.

Tagert-Paul, Kimberley. God's Ten Promises: Helping Children Understand the Ten Commandments. 2010. (J). 12.99 (978-0-8163-2379-1(8)) Pacific Pr. Publishing Assn.

Tahir, Sabaa. A Torch Against the Night. (Ember in the Ashes Ser.: 2). (ENG.). (YA). (gr. 9). 2017. 480p. pap. 11.99 **(978-1-101-99888-5(1))** 2016. 464p. 19.95 (978-1-101-99887-8(3)) Penguin Young Readers Group. (Razorbill).

—A Torch Against the Night. 2017. (Ember in the Ashes Ser.: 2). lib. bdg. 23.30 **(978-0-606-40085-5(0))** Turtleback Bks.

Taitano, Janice G. The Legend of Lutung. 2006. 260p. pap. 29.00 (978-1-59752-482-7(4), Resource Pubns.(OR)) Wipf & Stock Pubs.

Talarico Msn, Karen M. My Hands. 2008. 36p. pap. 15.75 (978-1-4389-3521-8(8)) AuthorHouse.

Tanaka, Shelley. Nobody Knows, 1 vol. 2012. (ENG.). 144p. (J). (gr. 4). 16.95 (978-1-55498-140-3(9)) Groundwood Bks. CAN. Dist: Publishers Group West (PGW).

Tanguay, Dave. Come Together! Vaughns, Byron, illus. 2015. (Billy Batson & the Magic of Shazam! Ser.). (ENG.). 32p. (gr. 2-3). lib. bdg. 22.60 (978-1-4342-9744-0(6)) Stone Arch Bks.

—Deception Reception! Vaughns, Byron, illus. 2015. (Billy Batson & the Magic of Shazam! Ser.). (ENG.). 32p. (gr. 2-3). lib. bdg. 22.60 (978-1-4342-9742-6(X)) Stone Arch Bks.

—Fire Fire Everywhere! Vaughns, Byron, illus. 2015. (Billy Batson & the Magic of Shazam! Ser.). (ENG.). 32p. (gr. 2-3). lib. bdg. 22.60 (978-1-4342-9745-7(4)) Stone Arch Bks.

—The Legacy of Mr. Banjo! Vaughns, Byron, illus. 2015. (Billy Batson & the Magic of Shazam! Ser.). (ENG.). 32p. (gr. 2-3). lib. bdg. 22.60 (978-1-4342-9746-4(2)) Stone Arch Bks.

Tashjian, Janet. Tru Confessions. 2007. (ENG., Illus.). 176p. (J). (gr. 4-7). per. 15.99 (978-0-312-37273-6(6), 9780312372736) Square Fish.

Taylor, Bonnie Highsmith. Simon Can't Say Hippopotamus. Hornung, Phyllis, tr. Hornung, Phyllis, illus. 2003. 24p. (J). 14.95 (978-1-59336-017-7(7)); pap. (978-1-59336-018-4(5)) Mondo Publishing.

Taylor, C. Brian. Atop the Tree Top: A Christmas Story. Butler, Sharon, illus. 2003. (J). 15.95 (978-0-9747054-0-8(3)) Rilly Silly Bk. Co., The.

Taylor, S. S. The Expeditioners & the Treasure of Drowned Man's Canyon. Roy, Katherine, illus. 2013. (ENG.). 384p. pap. 12.95 (978-1-938073-71-7(1)) McSweeney's Publishing.

Taylor, Theodore & Taylor, Theodore. Ice Drift. 2006. (ENG., Illus.). 240p. (J). (gr. 2-5). pap. 7.99 (978-0-15-205550-9(9)) Houghton Mifflin Harcourt Publishing Co.

Taylor, Thomas. The Pets You Get. Reynolds, Adrian, illus. 2013. 32p. (gr. -1-3). 16.95 (978-1-4677-1143-2(8)) Andersen Pr. GBR. Dist: Lerner Publishing Group.

Taylor, Vincent. Cornbread Has a Bad Habit. 2007. (Illus.). 96p. (J). pap. 4.99 (978-0-9704512-5-5(3)) TriEclipse, Inc.

Teele, Elinor. The Mechanical Mind of John Coggin. 2016. (Illus.). 352p. (J). (gr. 3-7). 16.99 (978-0-06-234510-3(9), Walden Pond Pr.) HarperCollins Pubs.

Teitelbaum, Michael. The Ghost at the Grand Inn. 2015. (Cold Whispers Ser.). (ENG., Illus.). 32p. (J). (gr. 2-6). lib. bdg. 26.60 (978-1-62724-808-2(0)) Bearport Publishing Co., Inc.

Teitelbaum, Michael, adapted by. Skateboard Adventures. 2012. (Wind-Up Toy Ser.). (ENG., Illus.). 48p. (J). (gr. 1). 12.99 (978-0-7944-2470-1(8)) Reader's Digest Assn., Inc., The.

Telgemeier, Raina. Drama. 2012. (ENG., Illus.). 240p. (J). (gr. 5-9). 24.99 (978-0-545-32698-8(2)); pap. 10.99 (978-0-545-32699-5(0)) Scholastic, Inc. (Graphix).

Tellier, Derek. Anderson's Heat. 2016. (What's Your Dream? Ser.). (ENG.). 96p. (gr. 3-4). lib. bdg. 25.32 (978-1-4965-3441-5(7)) Capstone Press of Coughlan Cos.

Terrell, Brandon. Mars for Humanity. Foti, Anthony J., illus. 2015. (Exploring Space & Beyond Ser.). (ENG.). 96p. (gr. 3-4). lib. bdg. 26.65 (978-1-4965-0502-6(6)) Stone Arch Bks.

—Phantom of the Library. Epelbaum, Mariano, illus. 2017. (Snoops, Inc Ser.). (ENG.). 112p. (gr. 4-6). lib. bdg. 26.65 **(978-1-4965-5060-6(9))** Stone Arch Bks.

—Science Fair Sabotage. Epelbaum, Mariano, illus. 2017. (Snoops, Inc Ser.). (ENG.). 112p. (gr. 4-6). lib. bdg. 26.65 (978-1-4965-4347-9(5)) Stone Arch Bks.

—The Vanishing Treasure. Epelbaum, Mariano, illus. 2017. (Snoops, Inc Ser.). (ENG.). 112p. (gr. 4-6). lib. bdg. 26.65 (978-1-4965-4345-5(9)) Stone Arch Bks.

Tesh, Jane & Klein-Higger, Joni. Land of Lost Socks: A Children's Musical. 2013. 24p. pap. 7.95 (978-1-61633-397-3(9)) Guardian Angel Publishing, Inc.

Testa, Maggie. Olivia & Her Alien Brother. 2014. (Olivia 8x8 Ser.). lib. bdg. 13.55 (978-0-606-35199-7(X)) Turtleback Bks.

Tetzlaff, Wendy Jo. A Girl Named Frannie. 2008. 28p. pap. 24.95 (978-1-60703-055-3(1)) America Star Bks.

Tharp, Barbara, et al. Tillena Lou's Day in the Sun. Denk, James, ed. Lewis, T., illus. 2nd ed. 2013. (My World & Me Ser.). (ENG.). 32p. (J). (gr. k-2). pap. (978-1-888997-44-6(3), BioEd) Baylor College of Medicine.

Tharp, Jason. Monsta Doodle, Bk. 1. 2016. (Super Monsta Friends Ser.: 2). (ENG.). 128p. (J). (gr. 2-5). pap. 12.99 (978-0-545-83964-8(5)) Scholastic, Inc.

Tharp, Tim. Badd. 2012. (ENG.). 324p. (YA). (gr. 9). pap. 9.99 (978-0-375-86401-8(6), Ember) Random Hse. Children's Bks.

The Duda Family. The Adventures of Newo: Newo & Emma Visit Their Furry Friends. 2008. 28p. pap. 12.49 (978-1-4343-9766-9(1)) AuthorHouse.

Theriault, Francis. Just Another Ghost Story: A critical thinking Novel. 2007. 68p. (J). per. 8.95 (978-0-595-45258-3(2)) iUniverse, Inc.

Thiel, Annie. Chloe's New Baby Brother. Marjoribanks, Karen & Edwards, William M., illus. 2006. (Playdate Kids Ser.). 32p. (J). (gr. -1-3). 14.95 (978-1-933721-01-9(4)) Playdate Kids Publishing.

Thiel Annie. The Playdate Kids Chloe's New Baby Brother 2ED 2007. 2007. 32p. 12.95 (978-1-933721-28-6(6)); pap. 6.95 (978-1-933721-24-8(3)) Playdate Kids Publishing.

Thomas, Charlie. I Need Glasses. Goldfinger, Jennifer P., illus. 2005. (Rookie Readers Ser.). (ENG.). 32p. (J). (gr. k-2). lib. bdg. 19.50 (978-0-516-24863-9(4), Children's Pr.) Scholastic Library Publishing.

Thomas, Dee. Silly, Silly, Eggleton Egg: Meet the Egg's of Eggville. 2012. 28p. pap. 21.99 (978-1-4771-5325-3(X)) Xlibris Corp.

Thomas, Louis. Hug It Out! 2017. (ENG., Illus.). 40p. (J). 16.99 (978-0-374-30314-3(2), 9780374303143, Farrar, Straus & Giroux (BYR)) Farrar, Straus & Giroux.

Thompson, Aiyana M. Miranda Fishhook: Makes a New Friend. 2010. 24p. 16.00 (978-1-4520-2364-9(6)) AuthorHouse.

Thompson Ii, Roger E. A Sister's Love: A Novel. 2007. 80p. per. 8.95 (978-0-595-44549-3(7)) iUniverse, Inc.

Thompson, Laurie. Be Gentle with Baby, 1 vol. 2010. 24p. 24.95 (978-1-4489-3910-7(0)) PublishAmerica, Inc.

Tiger Tales, ed. & compiled by. Stories for Boys. Tiger Tales, compiled by. 2015. (ENG.). 176p. (J). (gr. -1-3). 12.99 (978-1-58925-535-7(6)) Tiger Tales.

Tilford, Michael. Reemie the Preemie. 2005. 22p. 8.72 (978-1-4116-1394-2(5)) Lulu Pr., Inc.

To Be Perfectly Honest: A Novel Based on an Untrue Story. 2014. (ENG., Illus.). 496p. (YA). (gr. 7). pap. 11.99 (978-0-689-87605-9(X), Simon & Schuster Bks. For Young Readers) Simon & Schuster Bks. For Young Readers.

Tobin, Richard K. Skating on Thick Ice. LeBlanc, Rebecca, ed. Chapman, Jesse, illus. 2013. 122p. (J). pap. 12.00 (978-1-929682-96-0(3)) Biographical Publishing Co.

Todd, Anne. Teddy Powers: The Stone Keepers. 2012. 394p. pap. 13.99 (978-1-938993-00-8(4)) Keogh, Anne.

Tomasi-Dubois, Mary. Danger in the Jeweled City: A Matt & Heather Thriller. 2007. 188p. (YA). per. 15.95 (978-0-9798633-5-6(X)) Robertson Publishing.

Torres, J., et al. Blackfire's Back!, 1 vol. 2014. (Teen Titans GO! Ser.). (ENG., Illus.). 32p. (gr. 2-3). 22.60 (978-1-4342-9215-5(0)) Stone Arch Bks.

Townsend, Una Belle. The Great Elephant Escape, 1 vol. Hechter, Janice, illus. 2012. (ENG.). 32p. (J). (gr. k-3). 16.99 (978-1-4556-1582-7(X)) Pelican Publishing Co., Inc.

Treasure Quest Guide. 2004. pap. 5.99 (978-1-56309-913-7(6)) Woman's Missionary Union.

Trevayne, Emma. Chorus. 2014. (ENG.). 288p. (YA). (gr. 2-17). pap. 9.95 (978-0-7624-4950-7(0), Running Pr. Kids) Running Pr. Bk. Pubs.

Treyes, Jill. Brooke & Brandon Welcome Brandon. 2010. 28p. pap. 12.99 (978-1-4389-1939-3(5)) AuthorHouse.

Triffo, Khaleigh H. Relentless Tears. 2011. 108p. (gr. 10-12). pap. 11.92 (978-1-4269-6288-2(6)) Trafford Publishing.

Trillo, Carlos. Bird. Bobillo, Juan, illus. 2003. 48p. (YA). (gr. 11-18). 12.95 (978-1-931724-22-7(9)) Diamond Select Toys & Collectibles.

Trimble, Tonya. Curiosity, with a Capital S. Enik, Ted, illus. 2011. 144p. (J). pap. 9.95 (978-0-9816453-9-1(9)); 16.95 (978-0-9829421-5-4(X)) Tell Me Pr., LLC.

Trottier, Maxine. Three Songs for Courage. 2008. (ENG.). 328p. (YA). (gr. 9). pap. 10.95 (978-0-88776-831-6(8), Tundra Bks.) Tundra Bks. CAN. Dist: Penguin Random Hse. LLC.

Troupe, Thomas Kingsley. Tornado: a Twisting Tale of Survival. Fagan, Kirbi, illus. 2016. (Survive! Ser.). (ENG.). 56p. (gr. 4-6). lib. bdg. 25.32 (978-1-4965-2556-7(6)) Stone Arch Bks.

Trueit, Trudi. No Girls Allowed (Dogs Okay) Paillot, Jim, illus. 2010. (Secrets of a Lab Rat Ser.). (ENG.). 144p. (J). (gr. 3-7). pap. 5.99 (978-1-4169-6111-6(9), Aladdin) Simon & Schuster Children's Publishing.

—No Girls Allowed (Dogs Okay) Paillot, Jim, illus. 2009. (Secrets of a Lab Rat Ser.). (ENG.). 128p. (J). (gr. 3-7). 14.99 (978-1-4169-7592-2(6), Simon & Schuster/Paula Wiseman Bks.) Simon & Schuster/Paula Wiseman Bks.

Trueit, Trudi Strain. Mom, There's a Dinosaur in Beeson's Lake. Paillot, Jim, illus. 2010. (Secrets of a Lab Rat Ser.). (ENG.). 160p. (J). (gr. 3-7). 14.99 (978-1-4169-7593-9(4), Simon & Schuster/Paula Wiseman Bks.) Simon & Schuster/Paula Wiseman Bks.

Tuck, Justin. Home-Field Advantage. Rodriguez, Leonardo, illus. 2011. (ENG.). 40p. (J). (gr. -1-3). 16.99 (978-1-4424-0369-7(1), Simon & Schuster Bks. For Young Readers) Simon & Schuster Bks. For Young Readers.

Turnbull, Elizabeth J. Janjak & Freda Go to the Iron Market. Turnbull, Wally R., tr. Jones, Mark, illus. 2013. 36p. pap. 12.95 (978-1-61153-062-9(8)) Light Messages Publishing.

Tutor, Margaret. A Make-Do Christmas, 1 vol. 2009. 74p. pap. 19.95 (978-1-4489-0849-3(3)) America Star Bks.

Two Lies & a Spy. 2014. (ENG., Illus.). 272p. (YA). (gr. 9). pap. 11.99 (978-1-4424-8173-2(0), Simon & Schuster Bks. For Young Readers) Simon & Schuster Bks. For Young Readers.

Tyrrell, Melissa. Hansel & Gretel. McMullen, Nigel, illus. 2005. (Fairytale Friends Ser.). 12p. (J). bds. 5.95 (978-1-58117-152-5(8), Intervisual/Piggy Toes) Bendon, Inc.

Umansky, Kaye. Clover Twig & the Perilous Path. Wright, Johanna, illus. 2013. (ENG.). 272p. (J). (gr. 3-7). pap. 7.99 (978-1-250-02727-6(6), 9781250027276) Square Fish.

—Sophie in Charge. Currey, Anna, illus. 2005. 30p. (J). 9.95 (978-1-56148-478-2(4), Good Bks.) Skyhorse Publishing Co., Inc.

Underwood, Kim. The Wonderful World of Sparkle Girl & Doobins. Goldman, Garnet, illus. 2009. 48p. (J). pap. 16.95 (978-0-89587-373-6(7)) Blair, John F. Pub.

Ungerer, Tomi. Fog Island. 2013. (ENG., Illus.). 48p. 16.95 (978-0-7148-6535-5(4)) Phaidon Pr., Inc.

—Fog Island IBook. 2013. (ENG.). 48p. 5.99 (978-0-7148-6777-9(2)) Phaidon Pr., Inc.

Vaid, Raj. The Case of the Holi Chocolate: The Super Sleuth - Mystery #1. 2011. 56p. pap. 9.99 (978-1-4520-6903-6(4)) AuthorHouse.

Vail, Rachel & Avi. Never Mind! 2005. (ENG.). 208p. (J). (gr. 5-18). reprint ed. pap. 6.99 (978-0-06-054316-7(7)) HarperCollins Pubs.

Valente, Shannon. Trucks, Trains & Worm Brains. 2009. 16p. pap. 10.79 (978-1-4389-5411-0(5)) AuthorHouse.

Valentine, Madeline. The Bad Birthday Idea. 2013. (ENG., Illus.). 40p. (J). (gr. -1-2). 17.99 (978-0-449-81331-7(2), Knopf Bks. for Young Readers) Random Hse. Children's Bks.

Van Allsburg, Chris. Probuditi! 2009. 30p. (J). 19.00 (978-1-4379-6940-5(2)) DIANE Publishing Co.

—Probuditi! 2006. (ENG., Illus.). 32p. (J). (gr. 2-5). 18.95 (978-0-618-75502-8(0)) Houghton Mifflin Harcourt Publishing Co.

Van Dyne, Edith. Aunt Jane's Nieces at Millville. 2004. reprint ed. pap. 21.95 (978-1-4191-0823-5(9)); pap. 1.99 (978-1-4192-0823-2(3)) Kessinger Publishing, LLC.

—Aunt Jane's Nieces in Society. 2004. reprint ed. pap. 20.95 (978-1-4191-0824-2(7)); pap. 1.99 (978-1-4192-0824-9(1)) Kessinger Publishing, LLC.

—Aunt Jane's Nieces on Vacation. 2004. reprint ed. pap. 21.95 (978-1-4191-0825-9(5)); pap. 1.99 (978-1-4192-0825-6(X)) Kessinger Publishing, LLC.

—Aunt Jane's Nieces Out West. 2004. reprint ed. pap. 21.95 (978-1-4191-0826-6(3)); pap. 1.99 (978-1-4192-0826-3(8)) Kessinger Publishing, LLC.

Van Leeuwen, Jean. Cabin on Trouble Creek. 2008. (ENG.). 224p. (J). (gr. 3-7). 7.99 (978-0-14-241164-3(7), Puffin Books) Penguin Young Readers Group.

—Five Funny Bunnies: Three Bouncing Tales, 0 vols. Wilsdorf, Anne, illus. 2012. (ENG.). 40p. (J). (gr. -1-3). 17.99 (978-0-7614-6114-2(0), 9780761461142, Amazon Children's Publishing) Amazon Publishing.

Van Stockum, Hilda. A Day on Skates: The Story of a Dutch Picnic. Van Stockum, Hilda, illus. 2007. (Illus.). 40p. (J). (gr. 1). 19.95 (978-1-932350-18-0(7)) Bethlehem Bks.

Van Wright, Cornelius & Hu, Ying-Hwa, illus. I Told You I Can Play! 2006. (ENM.). 32p. (J). 16.95 (978-1-933491-06-6(X)) Just Us Bks., Inc.

Vande Velde, Vivian. There's a Dead Person Following My Sister Around. 2008. (ENG., Illus.). 160p. (J). (gr. 5-7). pap. 11.95 (978-0-15-206467-9(2)) Houghton Mifflin Harcourt Publishing Co.

Venable, Alan. The Man in the Iron Mask. 2007. (Classic Adventures Ser.). pap. 9.95 (978-1-4105-0860-7(9)) Johnston, Don Inc.

—Take Me with You When You Go. Marshall, Laurie, illus. 2008. 112p. (J). 12.95 (978-0-9777082-7-7(6)) One Monkey Bks.

Venkatraman, Padma. Climbing the Stairs. 2010. (ENG., Illus.). 272p. (YA). (gr. 7-18). 9.99 (978-0-14-241490-3(5), Speak) Penguin Young Readers Group.

Ventrillo, James & Ventrillo, Nick. Rick & Bobo: Two Brothers. One a Genius. One Not, 4 vols. Kunardi, Marco, illus. 2009. 332p. (YA). pap. 13.95 (978-0-615-28865-9(0)) Vanir Bks.

Vernick, Audrey. Edgar's Second Word. Burris, Priscilla, illus. 2014. (ENG.). 32p. (J). (gr. -1-3). 16.99 (978-0-547-68462-8(2), Clarion Bks.) Houghton Mifflin Harcourt Trade & Reference Pubs.

Verstraete, Majanka. The Doll Maker: Weirdville. l.t. ed. 2013. 1. (ENG.). 86p. (gr. 2-6). pap. 9.95 (978-1-62253-065-6(9)) Evolved Publishing.

Viehl, Lynn. Dead of Night. 2012. (Youngbloods Ser.: 2). (ENG.). 312p. (YA). pap. 9.95 (978-0-7387-2646-5(X), Flux) North Star Editions.

Vilcoq, Marianne. Espero un Hermanito. (SPA.). 24p. (J). (978-84-8470-013-5(5)) Corimbo, Editorial S.L. ESP. Dist: Lectorum Pubns., Inc.

Voigt, Cynthia. Dicey's Song. 2012. (Tillerman Cycle Ser.: 2). (ENG., Illus.). 256p. (YA). (gr. 7). 19.99 (978-1-4424-5060-8(6)); pap. 9.99 (978-1-4424-2879-9(1)) Simon & Schuster Children's Publishing. (Atheneum Bks. for Young Readers).

—Dicey's Song. 2012. (Tillerman Ser.: 2). lib. bdg. 20.85 (978-0-606-25260-7(6), Turtleback) Turtleback Bks.

—The Tale of Elske. 2015. (Tales of the Kingdom Ser.: 4). (ENG., Illus.). 368p. (YA). (gr. 7). 19.99 (978-1-4814-2189-8(1), Atheneum Bks. for Young Readers) Simon & Schuster Children's Publishing.

Vrettos, Adrienne Maria. Skin. (ENG.). (YA). (gr. 7-12). 2007. 272p. pap. 9.99 (978-1-4169-0656-8(8)) 2006. (Illus.). 240p. 16.95 (978-1-4169-0655-1(X)) McElderry, Margaret K. Bks. (McElderry, Margaret K. Bks.).

Vulliamy, Clara. Martha Bunny Loves School. Vulliamy, Clara, illus. 2013. (ENG., Illus.). 32p. (J). (gr. -1-3). 16.99 (978-0-8075-4976-6(2)) Whitman, Albert & Co.

W. Parents Are Lucky: They Don't Have to Do Chores. 2010. 24p. pap. 12.49 (978-1-4520-7671-3(5)) AuthorHouse.

Waggener, Anna. Grim. 2012. (ENG.). 320p. (J). (gr. 7-7). 17.99 (978-0-545-38480-3(X), Scholastic Pr.) Scholastic, Inc.

Wagner, Lori. Gateway of the Sun. 2007. 120p. pap. 9.95 (978-0-9798627-2-4(8)) Affirming Faith.

Wait, Lea. Stopping to Home. 2003. (ENG.). 160p. (J). (gr. 3-7). pap. 8.99 (978-0-689-83849-1(2), Simon & Schuster/Paula Wiseman Bks.) Simon & Schuster/Paula Wiseman Bks.

—Wintering Well. 2006. (ENG., Illus.). 192p. (J). (gr. 3-7). pap. 6.99 (978-0-689-85647-1(4), McElderry, Margaret K. Bks.) McElderry, Margaret K. Bks.

Waldman, Neil. Al & Teddy. 2013. 48p. 17.95 (978-0-615-72969-5(X)) Dream Yard Pr.

Walker, Courtney King. Chasing Midnight. 2016. 250p. (YA). pap. 16.99 (978-1-4621-1763-5(5)) Cedar Fort, Inc./CFI Distribution.

Walker-Cox, Krysten. Amber's Metal Singlet. 2009. 48p. pap. 12.13 (978-1-60860-316-9(4), Eloquent Bks.) Strategic Book Publishing & Rights Agency (SBPRA).

Walker-Renner, Christa. Santa's Magic. 2009. 20p. pap. 11.00 (978-1-4389-8206-9(2)) AuthorHouse.

Walker, Sharon. Little Rose Grows. 2013. 24p. pap. 15.99 (978-1-4797-6813-4(8)) Xlibris Corp.

Walker, Susan Eileen. Not Enough Time, 1 vol. 2010. 52p. pap. 16.95 (978-1-4489-6198-6(X)) America Star Bks.

Wallace, Barbara Brooks. Secret in St. Something. 2003. (ENG., Illus.). 160p. (J). (gr. 3-7). pap. 9.95 (978-0-689-85601-3(6), Aladdin) Simon & Schuster Children's Publishing.

Wallace, Bill. Snot Stew. McCue, Lisa, illus. 2nd ed. 2008. (ENG.). 96p. (J). (gr. 3-7). pap. 6.99 (978-1-4169-5804-8(5), Aladdin) Simon & Schuster Children's Publishing.

Wallace, Karen. Wendy. 2005. 307p. (gr. 7-12). 17.00 (978-0-7569-5658-5(7)) Perfection Learning Corp.

Wallace, Nancy Elizabeth. Valentine Express, 0 vols. 2008. (ENG., Illus.). 32p. (J). (gr. -1-2). pap. 9.99 (978-0-7614-5447-2(0), 9780761454472, Amazon Children's Publishing) Amazon Publishing.

Wallingford, Stephanie & Rynders, Dawn. A Day at the Lake. Villnave, Erica Pelton, illus. 2013. (ENG.). 32p. (-k). pap. 10.95 (978-1-938063-03-9(1), Mighty Media Kids) Mighty Media Pr.

Walls, Robert D. Tiny's Second-Grade Field Trip. 2010. 40p. 19.99 (978-1-4490-9011-1(7)) AuthorHouse.

Walters, Eric. Walking Home. 2014. (ENG.). 304p. (J). (gr. 5). pap. 10.99 (978-0-385-68157-5(7), Doubleday Canada) Penguin Random House Canada Young Readers CAN. Dist: Penguin Random Hse. LLC.

Walton, Leslye. The Strange & Beautiful Sorrows of Ava Lavender. (ENG.). 320p. (YA). (gr. 9). 2015. pap. 8.99 (978-0-7636-8027-5(3)) 2014. 17.99 (978-0-7636-6566-1(5)) Candlewick Pr.

—The Strange & Beautiful Sorrows of Ava Lavender. 2015. lib. bdg. 19.65 (978-0-606-36879-7(5)) Turtleback Bks.

Ward, Caias. The Only Brother. 2008. (Cutting Edge Ser.). (ENG.). 200p. pap. (978-1-84167-719-4(1)) Ransom Publishing Ltd.

Ward, Greta. Pinkie the Cat Gets a Baby Sister. 2007. (Illus.). 44p. (J). pap. 9.95 (978-0-9798346-0-8(0)) P.M. Publishing.

Ward, Marcia. The Girl Who Found Her Voice. 2013. (ENG.). 276p. pap. 14.99 (978-1-939927-28-6(5)) Telemachus Pr., LLC.

Wargin, Kathy-jo. Mitt & Minn's Illinois Adventure. Holman, Karen Busch, illus. 2007. (Mitt Midwest Ser.: 4). (ENG.). 144p. (J). (gr. k-7). 14.95 (978-1-58726-306-4(8), Mitten Pr.) Ann Arbor Editions LLC.

Waring, Scott C. West's Time MacHine. 2007. 200p. 24.95 (978-0-595-88775-0(9)); per. 14.95 (978-0-595-41887-9(2)) iUniverse, Inc.

Warner, Gertrude Chandler. The Haunted Cabin Mystery, 1 vol. Bloodworth, Mark, illus. 2010. (Boxcar Children Graphic Novels Ser.). (ENG.). 32p. (J). (gr. 2-5). 28.50 (978-1-60270-717-7(0)) ABDO Publishing Co.

—The Mystery of the Grinning Gargoyle. VanArsdale, Anthony, illus. 2014. (Boxcar Children Mysteries Ser.: 137). (ENG.). 128p. (J). (gr. 1-5). pap. 5.99 (978-0-8075-0893-0(4)) Whitman, Albert & Co.

—The Mystery of the Runaway Ghost. Soileau, Hodges, illus. 2004. (Boxcar Children Ser.). 135p. (J). 12.65 (978-0-7569-3264-0(5)) Perfection Learning Corp.

—The Mystery of the Soccer Snitch. VanArsdale, Anthony, illus. 2014. (Boxcar Children Mysteries Ser.: 136). (ENG.). 128p. (J). (gr. 1-5). pap. 5.99 (978-0-8075-0896-1(9)) Whitman, Albert & Co.

—Snowbound Mystery. Dubisch, Mike, illus. 2009. (Boxcar Children Graphic Novels Ser.: 7). (ENG.). 32p. (J). (gr. 1-5). pap. 6.99 (978-0-8075-7515-4(1)) Whitman, Albert & Co.

—Snowbound Mystery, 1 vol. Dubisch, Mike, illus. 2010. (Boxcar Children Graphic Novels Ser.). (ENG.). 32p. (J). (gr. 2-5). 28.50 (978-1-60270-715-3(4)) ABDO Publishing Co.

Warner, Gertrude Chandler, creator. The Creature in Ogopogo Lake. 2006. (Boxcar Children Mysteries Ser.: 108). (ENG., Illus.). 128p. (J). (gr. 1-5). lib. bdg. 14.99 (978-0-8075-1336-1(9)) Whitman, Albert & Co.

—The Garden Thief. 2012. (Boxcar Children Mysteries Ser.: 130). (ENG., Illus.). 128p. (J). (gr. 1-5). 5.99 (978-0-8075-2752-8(1)) Whitman, Albert & Co.

—The Garden Thief. 2012. (Boxcar Children Mysteries Ser.: 130). (ENG., Illus.). 128p. (J). (gr. 1-5). 15.99 (978-0-8075-2751-1(3)) Whitman, Albert & Co.

—The Ghost at the Drive-In Movie. 2008. (Boxcar Children Mysteries Ser.: 116). (ENG.). 128p. (J). (gr. 1-5). 14.99 (978-0-8075-5577-4(0)) Whitman, Albert & Co.

—The Ghost-Hunting Special. 2015. (Boxcar Children Mysteries Ser.). (ENG.). 352p. (J). (gr. 1-5). 9.99 *(978-0-8075-2846-4(3))* Whitman, Albert & Co.
—The Haunted Legends Special. 2016. (Boxcar Children Mysteries Ser.). (ENG.). 368p. (J). (gr. 1-5). 9.99 *(978-0-8075-0724-7(5))* Whitman, Albert & Co.
—The Legend of the Irish Castle. 2016. (Boxcar Children Mysteries Ser.: 142). (ENG., Illus.). 128p. (J). (gr. 1-5). 15.99 *(978-0-8075-0705-6(9))* Whitman, Albert & Co.
—The Mystery of the Missing Pop Idol. 2015. (Boxcar Children Mysteries Ser.: 138). (ENG., Illus.). 128p. (J). (gr. 1-5). 15.99 *(978-0-8075-5605-4(X))* Whitman, Albert & Co.
—The Mystery of the Stolen Dinosaur Bones. 2015. (Boxcar Children Mysteries Ser.: 139). (ENG., Illus.). 128p. (J). (gr. 1-5). 15.99 *(978-0-8075-5608-5(4))* Whitman, Albert & Co.
—The Vanishing Passenger. 2006. (Boxcar Children Mysteries Ser.: 106). (ENG., Illus.). 112p. (J). (gr. 1-5). per. 6.99 *(978-0-8075-1067-4(X))* Whitman, Albert & Co.
Warner, Michael N. The Titanic Game. Ordaz, Frank, illus. 2007. (ENG.). 208p. (J). pap. 11.95 *(978-0-9744446-2-8(6))* All About Kids Publishing.
Wass, Eliza. The Cresswell Plot. 2016. (ENG., Illus.). 268p. (YA). (gr. 9-17). 17.99 *(978-1-4847-3043-0(7))* Hyperion Bks. for Children.
Waters, Tawni. Beauty of the Broken. 2014. 368p. 17.99 *(978-1-4814-1857-7(2))* Simon & Schuster, Inc.
Watson, Jude. A King's Ransom. 2011. (39 Clues: Cahills vs. Vespers Ser.: 2). (ENG.). 192p. (J). (gr. 3-7). 12.99 *(978-0-545-29840-7(7),* Scholastic Pr.);Bk. 2. 12.99 *(978-0-545-32410-6(6))* Scholastic, Inc.
—Loot. (ENG.). 272p. (J). (gr. 3-7). 2015. pap. 6.99 *(978-0-545-46803-9(5),* Scholastic Paperbacks) 2014. 17.99 *(978-0-545-46802-2(7),* Scholastic Pr.) Scholastic, Inc.
—Nowhere to Run. 2013. (39 Clues Ser.: Bk. 1). (ENG., Illus.). 272p. (J). (gr. 3-7). 12.99 *(978-0-545-52137-6(8))* Scholastic, Inc.
—Sting. 2016. (ENG.). 272p. (J). (gr. 3-7). 16.99 *(978-0-545-86346-9(5),* Scholastic Pr.) Scholastic, Inc.
Watson, Michael. Treasure, Trash, & Turtles. 2010. 24p. pap. 11.50 *(978-1-60911-500-5(7),* Eloquent Bks.) Strategic Book Publishing & Rights Agency (SBPRA).
Watts, Frances. The Song of the Winns: the Spies of Gerander. 2013. (ENG., Illus.). 320p. (J). (gr. -1-2). 12.95 *(978-0-7624-4658-2(7),* Running Pr. Kids) Running Pr. Bk. Pubs.
Watts, Irene N. When the Bough Breaks. 2007. (ENG.). 152p. (YA). (gr. 4-7). pap. 9.95 *(978-0-88776-821-7(0),* Tundra Bks.) Tundra Bks. CAN. Dist: Penguin Random Hse. LLC.
Webb, Philip. Six Days. 2011. (ENG.). 352p. (J). (gr. 5-9). 17.99 *(978-0-545-31767-2(3),* Chicken Hse., The) Scholastic, Inc.
Webb, Robert N. We Were There at the Boston Tea Party. Ward, E. F., illus. 2013. (ENG.). 192p. (J). (gr. 3-8). pap. 6.99 *(978-0-486-49260-5(5))* Dover Pubns., Inc.
Webber, Katherine. The Heartbeats of Wing Jones. 2017. (ENG.). 336p. (YA). (gr. 7). 17.99 *(978-0-399-55502-2(1),* Delacorte Pr.) Random Hse. Children's Bks.
Weber, Bob. Oh, Brother! Brat Attack! Stephens, Jay, illus. 2015. (ENG.). 176p. (J). pap. 9.99 *(978-1-4494-7225-2(7))* Andrews McMeel Publishing.
Weber, Jen Funk. Thimbletack's Activity Book. 2008. (Spiderwick Chronicles). (ENG., Illus.). 64p. (J). (gr. 2-7). pap. 4.99 *(978-1-4169-4954-1(2),* Simon Scribbles) Simon Scribbles.
Weeks, Sarah. Sophie Peterman Tells the Truth! Neubecker, Robert, illus. 2009. (ENG.). 32p. (J). (gr. -1-3). 17.99 *(978-1-4169-8686-7(3),* Beach Lane Bks.) Beach Lane Bks.
Wein, Elizabeth. Black Dove, White Raven. 2015. (ENG.). 368p. (YA). (gr. 7-12). 17.99 *(978-1-4231-8310-5(X))* Hyperion Bks. for Children.
Weiner, Ellis. The Templeton Twins Make a Scene: Book 2. Holmes, Jeremy, illus. 2014. (ENG.). 272p. (J). (gr. 3-7). pap. 6.99 *(978-1-4521-2872-6(3))* Chronicle Bks. LLC.
Weinstein, Natalie. Katrina's New Room. Pluum, Ave, illus. 2004. (J). pap. 19.95 *(978-0-9749531-0-6(5))* Images For Presentation.
Weiss, Ellen & Friedman, Mel. The Stinky Giant. Girasole, Alessia, illus. 2012. (Step into Reading Ser.). (ENG.). 48p. (J). (gr. k-3). pap. 3.99 *(978-0-375-86743-9(0),* Random Hse. Bks. for Young Readers) Random Hse. Children's Bks.
—The Stinky Giant. Girasole, Alessia, illus. 2012. (Step into Reading Level 3 Ser.). lib. bdg. 13.55 *(978-0-606-23858-8(1),* Turtleback) Turtleback Bks.
Welch, Leah. Pretty on the Inside. 2007. (J). per. 10.00 *(978-1-59872-779-1(6))* Instant Pub.
Welch, Sheila. Waiting to Forget. 2011. 172p. (J). 18.95 *(978-1-60898-114-4(2))* namelos llc.
Welch, Sheila Kelly. Waiting to Forget. 2011. 172p. (J). pap. 9.95 *(978-1-60898-115-1(0))* namelos llc.
Wells, Carolyn. Marjorie's Maytime. 2007. (ENG.). 196p. per. 11.95 *(978-1-4218-3318-7(2))* 1st World Publishing, Inc.
Wells, Rosemary. Bunny Cakes. Wells, Rosemary, illus. 2014. (Max & Ruby Ser.). (ENG & SPA., Illus.). 32p. (J). (gr. -1-k). 7.99 *(978-0-14-751586-5(6),* Puffin Books) Penguin Young Readers Group.
—Bunny Party. 2003. (Max & Ruby Ser.). (ENG., Illus.). 32p. (J). (gr. -1-k). pap. 6.99 *(978-0-14-250162-7(X),* Puffin Books) Penguin Young Readers Group.
—Max & Ruby Play School. 2003. (All Aboard Reading Ser.). (gr. -1-2). lib. bdg. 13.55 *(978-0-613-64064-0(0),* Turtleback) Turtleback Bks.
—Max & Ruby's Bedtime Book. 2010. (Max & Ruby Ser.). (ENG.). 48p. (J). (gr. -1-k). 17.99 *(978-0-670-01141-4(X),* Viking Books for Young Readers) Penguin Young Readers Group.
—Max & Ruby's Preschool Pranks. 2016. (Max & Ruby Ser.). (ENG., Illus.). 40p. (J). (-k). 17.99 *(978-0-670-78462-2(1),* Viking Books for Young Readers) Penguin Young Readers Group.
—Max & Ruby's Show-and-Tell. 2006. (Max & Ruby Ser.). (ENG., Illus.). 32p. (J). (gr. -1-k). mass mkt. 3.99 *(978-0-448-43952-5(2),* Grosset & Dunlap) Penguin Young Readers Group.
—Max & Ruby's Treasure Hunt. 2012. (Max & Ruby Ser.). (ENG.). 32p. (J). (gr. -1-k). 17.99 *(978-0-670-06317-8(7),* Viking Books for Young Readers) Penguin Young Readers Group.
—Max's ABC. 2006. (Max & Ruby Ser.). (ENG., Illus.). 32p. (J). (gr. -1-k). 16.99 *(978-0-670-06074-0(7),* Viking Books for Young Readers) Penguin Young Readers Group.
—Max's Breakfast. 2004. (Max & Ruby Ser.). (ENG.). 12p. (J). (gr. 1 — 1). bds. 5.99 *(978-0-670-88712-5(9),* Viking Books for Young Readers) Penguin Young Readers Group.
—Max's Bunny Business. 2008. (Max & Ruby Ser.). (ENG., Illus.). 32p. (J). (gr. -1-k). 15.99 *(978-0-670-01105-6(3),* Viking Books for Young Readers) Penguin Young Readers Group.
—Max's Christmas. 2013. (Max & Ruby Ser.). (ENG.). 32p. (J). (gr. -1-k). 8.99 *(978-0-14-750947-5(5),* Puffin Books) Penguin Young Readers Group.
—Max's Christmas. 2013. (Max Ruby Ser.). lib. bdg. 18.40 *(978-0-606-32139-6(X),* Turtleback) Turtleback Bks.
—Ruby's Beauty Shop. Wells, Rosemary, illus. 2004. (Max & Ruby Ser.). (ENG., Illus.). 32p. (J). (gr. -1-k). pap. 6.99 *(978-0-14-240194-1(3),* Puffin Books) Penguin Young Readers Group.
—Ruby's Falling Leaves. 2007. (Max & Ruby Ser.). lib. bdg. 13.55 *(978-1-4177-9651-9(0),* Turtleback) Turtleback Bks.
—Sporty Bunny Tales. 2014. (Max & Ruby Ser.). lib. bdg. 14.75 *(978-0-606-34464-7(0),* Turtleback) Turtleback Bks.
Welvaert, Scott R. The Mosquito King: An Agate & Buck Adventure, 1 vol. Garvey, Brann, illus. (Vortex Bks.). (ENG.). 112p. (gr. 2-3). 2008. pap. 6.95 *(978-1-59889-923-8(6))* 2007. 26.65 *(978-1-59889-857-6(4))* Stone Arch Bks. (Vortex Bks.).
Weninger, Brigitte. Davy Loves the Baby. Tharlet, Eve, illus. 2015. (ENG.). 32p. (J). 15.95 *(978-0-7358-4210-6(8))* North-South Bks., Inc.
Weninger, Brigitte & Tharlet, Eve. Davy Loves His Mommy. 2014. (ENG., Illus.). 32p. (J). (gr. k-3). 15.95 *(978-0-7358-4164-2(0))* North-South Bks., Inc.
Werlin, Nancy. The Rules of Survival. 2008. (ENG.). 304p. (YA). (gr. 7-18). 8.99 *(978-0-14-241071-4(3),* Speak) Penguin Young Readers Group.
West, Kasie. On the Fence. 2014. (ENG.). 304p. (YA). (gr. 8). pap. 9.99 *(978-0-06-223567-1(2),* HarperTeen) HarperCollins Pubs.
West, Steve, reader. Island of Legends. 2014. (Unwanteds Ser.: 4). (ENG., Illus.). 496p. (J). (gr. 3-7). 18.99 *(978-1-4424-9328-5(3),* Aladdin) Simon & Schuster Children's Publishing.
Weston, Anne. My Brother Needs a Boa, 1 vol. Nathan, Cheryl, illus. 2005. (ENG.). 32p. (J). (gr. -1-3). 15.95 *(978-1-932065-96-1(2))* Star Bright Bks., Inc.
Weston Woods Staff, creator. Casi. 2011. (SPA.). 29.95 *(978-0-439-90592-3(3))* Weston Woods Studios, Inc.
—Peter's Chair. 2011. 29.95 *(978-0-439-76006-5(2))* Weston Woods Studios, Inc.
Westover, Steve. Crater Lake: Battle for Wizard Island. 2012. pap. 14.99 *(978-1-59955-960-5(9))* Cedar Fort, Inc./CFI Distribution.
—Return of the Mystic Gray. 2013. 15.99 *(978-1-4621-1187-9(4))* Cedar Fort, Inc./CFI Distribution.
Wewer, Iris. My Wild Sister & Me. 2012. (ENG., Illus.). 32p. (J). pap. 7.95 *(978-0-7358-4064-5(4))* North-South Bks., Inc.
Whelan, Gloria. The Disappeared. 2010. (ENG.). 144p. (YA). (gr. 7-18). 6.99 *(978-0-14-241540-5(5),* Speak) Penguin Young Readers Group.
Whirlwhim. The Baffelgagging Blundernagging Brothers: In Curse of the Bog Frog. 2008. (Illus.). 192p. (YA). 29.95 *(978-0-9800274-0-2(3))* Whirlwhim.
Whitaker, Alecia. The Way Back Home. 2016. (Wildflower Ser.: 3). (ENG.). 336p. (YA). (gr. 7-17). 17.99 *(978-0-316-25144-0(5),* Poppy) Little, Brown Bks. for Young Readers.
White, Amanda. Sand Sister. Morales, Yuyi, illus. 2004. 32p. (J). 16.99 *(978-1-84148-617-8(5))* Barefoot Bks., Inc.
White, J. A. The Thickety: a Path Begins. Offermann, Andrea, illus. 2017. (Thickety Ser.: 4). 512p. (J). (gr. 5). 16.99 *(978-0-06-238139-2(3),* Tegen, Katherine Bks) HarperCollins Pubs.
—Well of Witches. Offermann, Andrea, illus. 2016. (Thickety Ser.: 3). 512p. (J). (gr. 5). 16.99 *(978-0-06-225732-1(3),* Tegen, Katherine Bks) HarperCollins Pubs.
—The Whispering Trees. Offermann, Andrea, illus. 2015. (Thickety Ser.: 2). (ENG.). 528p. (J). (gr. 5). 16.99 *(978-0-06-225729-1(3),* Tegen, Katherine Bks) HarperCollins Pubs.
White, Kathryn. El Hermanito de Ruby. Latimer, Miriam, illus. 2013. (SPA.). 32p. (J). pap. 7.99 *(978-1-78285-026-7(0))* Barefoot Bks., Inc.
—Ruby's Baby Brother. Latimer, Miriam, illus. 2013. (ENG.). 32p. (J). 16.99 *(978-1-84686-864-1(5));* (gr. -1-2). pap. 7.99 *(978-1-84686-950-1(1))* Barefoot Bks., Inc.
White, Tom. Lost in the Texas Desert. 2004. (Illus.). 132p. per. 7.95 *(978-0-9753611-0-8(4))* Arlington Pubns.
Whittemore, Jo. Odd Girl In. 2011. (Mix Ser.). (ENG.). 240p. (J). (gr. 4-8). pap. 6.99 *(978-1-4424-1284-2(4),* Aladdin) Simon & Schuster Children's Publishing.
Whitten, A. J. The Well. 2009. (ENG., Illus.). 336p. (YA). (gr. 7-18). pap. 18.95 *(978-0-547-23229-4(2))* Houghton Mifflin Harcourt Publishing Co.
Whybrow, Ian. Little Wolf's Diary of Daring Deeds. Ross, Tony, illus. (Middle Grade Fiction Ser.). 132p. (gr. 3-6). 2005. 14.95 *(978-1-57505-411-7(6))* 2003. (J). pap. 6.95 *(978-0-87614-536-4(5),* Carolrhoda Bks.) Lerner Publishing Group.
—Malicia para Principiantes: Una Aventura de Lobito y Apestosito. Quintana, Joela, tr. Ross, Tony, illus. 2005. (Libros Ilustrados (Picture Bks.)). (SPA.). 32p. (J). (gr. k-2). 16.95 *(978-0-8225-3211-8(5),* Ediciones Lerner) Lerner Publishing Group.
—That Naughty Meerkat! Parsons, Garry, illus. 2016. (ENG.). 32p. (J). 17.99 *(978-0-00-813945-2(8),* HarperCollins Children's Bks.) HarperCollins Pubs. Ltd. GBR. Dist: HarperCollins Pubs.
Whybrow, Ian & Ross, Tony. Badness for Beginners: A Little Wolf & Smellybreff Adventure. 2005. (Illus.). 32p. (J). (gr. -1-3). 16.95 *(978-1-57505-801-6(8),* Carolrhoda Bks.) Lerner Publishing Group.
Wiesner, David. Hurricane, 1 vol. Wiesner, David, illus. 2008. (Read along Book & CD Ser.). (ENG., Illus.). 32p. (J). (gr. -1-3). 10.99 *(978-0-547-06433-8(0))* Houghton Mifflin Harcourt Publishing Co.
Wiggins, Bethany. Cured. 2015. (ENG.). 320p. (YA). (gr. 7). pap. 9.99 *(978-0-8027-3787-8(0),* 9780802737878, Bloomsbury USA Childrens) Bloomsbury Publishing USA.
Wildavsky, Rachel. The Secret of Rover. Caparo, Antonio, illus. (ENG.). 368p. (J). (gr. 3-7). 2015. pap. 7.95 *(978-1-4197-1968-4(8))* 2011. 17.95 *(978-0-8109-9710-3(X))* Abrams, Inc. (Amulet Bks.).
Wildman, Dale. Nicholas Knows: Big Brother Nicholas Knows It All! Sisung, Peter, illus. 2006. 24p. (J). per. 2.99 *(978-1-59958-005-0(5))* Journey Stone Creations, LLC.
Wiles, Deborah. Countdown. (ENG.). 400p. (J). 2013. (gr. 3-7). pap. 8.99 *(978-0-545-10606-1(0),* Scholastic Paperbacks) 2010. (gr. 4-7). 19.99 *(978-0-545-10605-4(2),* Scholastic Pr.) Scholastic, Inc.
Williams, Alan. Archy the Flying Dolphin & the Vampire's Curse. 2007. pap. 15.38 *(978-1-4251-3151-7(4))* Trafford Publishing.
Williams, Annie Morris. Marianne's Secret Cousins. Oldham, Cindi, illus. 2005. (Family History Adventures for Young Readers Ser.: 2). 240p. (J). per. 10.00 *(978-0-9645272-8-7(6))* Field Stone Pubs.
Williams, Carol Lynch. Waiting. (ENG.). 352p. (YA). (gr. 9). 2013. pap. 9.99 *(978-1-4424-4354-9(5))* 2012. 16.99 *(978-1-4424-4353-2(7))* Simon & Schuster/Paula Wiseman Bks. (Simon & Schuster/Paula Wiseman Bks.).
Williams, Carol Lynch & Earl, Cheri Pray. Wizard of Menlo Park, New Jersey. Oliphant, Manelle, illus. 2014. (Just in Time Ser.). (ENG.). 140p. (J). pap. 9.95 *(978-1-938301-77-3(3))* Familius LLC.
Williams, Maiya. The Golden Hour. 2006. (ENG.). 288p. (J). (gr. 5-10). per. 5.95 *(978-0-8109-9216-0(7))* Abrams, Inc.
Williams, Michael. Now Is the Time for Running. 2013. (ENG.). 240p. (YA). (gr. 7-17). pap. 10.99 *(978-0-316-07788-0(7))* Little, Brown Bks. for Young Readers.
Williams, Suzanne Morgan. Bull Rider. 2009. (ENG.). 256p. (YA). (gr. 7-9). 17.99 *(978-1-4169-6130-7(5),* McElderry, Margaret K. Bks.) McElderry, Margaret K. Bks.
Williams, Tad & Beale, Deborah. The Dragons of Ordinary Farm. Swearingen, Greg, illus. 2009. (ENG.). 416p. (J). (gr. 4-7). 16.99 *(978-0-06-154345-6(4))* HarperCollins Pubs.
Williams, Vera B. Amber Was Brave, Essie Was Smart. Williams, Vera B., illus. 2004. (ENG., Illus.). 72p. (J). (gr. 2-7). reprint ed. pap. 7.99 *(978-0-06-057182-5(9),* Greenwillow Bks.) HarperCollins Pubs.
Willson, Sarah. Do Not Wake Jake. Johnson, Meredith, illus. 2006. (Step-By-Step Readers Ser.). (J). *(978-1-59939-059-8(0),* Reader's Digest Young Families, Inc.) Studio Fun International.
—Pet Peeves! Nez, John A., illus. 2005. (Social Studies Connects). 32p. (J). pap. 5.95 *(978-1-57565-149-1(1))* Kane Press, Inc.
Wilson, Jodi L. When I Grow Up. Anderson, Kari A., illus. 32p. (Orig.). (J). (gr. 1-3). pap. 4.95 *(978-0-9628335-0-2(9))* Wilander Publishing Co.
Wilson, Mark A. The Legend of Crawley Creek. 2008. 104p. pap. 9.95 *(978-1-60693-423-4(6),* Eloquent Bks.) Strategic Book Publishing & Rights Agency (SBPRA).
Wilson, N. D. The Dragon's Tooth. (Ashtown Burials Ser.: Bk. 1). (ENG.). 496p. (J). (gr. 3-7). 2012. 8.99 *(978-0-375-86396-7(6),* Yearling) 2011. 16.99 *(978-0-375-86439-1(3),* Random Hse. Bks. for Young Readers) Random Hse. Children's Bks.
—The Drowned Vault. 2013. (Ashtown Burials Ser.: Bk. 2). (ENG.). 464p. (J). (gr. 3-7). 8.99 *(978-0-375-86397-4(4),* Yearling) Random Hse. Children's Bks.
Wilson, Shelliah. Samuel's Little Brother. 2005. 12p. 9.72 *(978-1-4116-4789-3(0))* Lulu Pr., Inc.
Winkler, Ashley & Winkler, Michael. One Good Quest Deserves Another: A Crown of Amaranth Story. 2009. 292p. 28.95 *(978-0-595-71039-3(5));* pap. 18.95 *(978-0-595-47365-6(2))* iUniverse, Inc.
Winkler, Henry & Oliver, Lin. Day of the Iguana. 2004. (Hank Zipzer Ser.: No. 3). 160p. (J). (gr. 2-6). pap. 29.00 incl. audio *(978-1-4000-9008-2(3),* Listening Library) Random Hse. Audio Publishing Group.
—Day of the Iguana. 2006. (Hank Zipzer Ser.: No. 3). 154p. (J). (gr. 3-9). 24.21 *(978-1-59961-102-0(3))* Spotlight.
—Who Ordered This Baby? Definitely Not Me! 2007. (Hank Zipzer Ser.: No. 13). (Illus.). 152p. (gr. 4-7). 15.00 *(978-0-7569-8163-1(8))* Perfection Learning Corp.
Winter, Ariel S. One of a Kind. Hitch, David, illus. 2012. (ENG.). 32p. (J). (gr. -1-2). 15.99 *(978-1-4424-2016-8(2),* Aladdin) Simon & Schuster Children's Publishing.
Winthrop, Elizabeth. The Red-Hot Rattoons. Lewin, Betsy, illus. 2006. (ENG.). 224p. (J). (gr. 3-6). pap. 16.99 *(978-0-8050-7986-9(6),* 9780805079869, Holt, Henry & Co. Bks. For Young Readers) Holt, Henry & Co.
Wirth, Beverly. Flowers from Seeds: A Garden Parable. 2012. 40p. pap. 16.99 *(978-1-4624-0101-7(5),* Inspiring Voices) Author Solutions, Inc.
Wishinsky, Frieda. Please, Louise!, 1 vol. Gay, Marie-Louise, illus. 2007. (ENG.). 32p. (J). (gr. k-k). 17.95 *(978-0-88899-796-8(5))* Groundwood Bks. CAN. Dist: Publishers Group West (PGW).
Wissinger, Tamera Will. Gone Camping: A Novel in Verse. Cordell, Matthew, illus. 2017. (ENG.). 112p. (J). (gr. 1-4). 15.99 *(978-0-544-63873-0(5),* HMH Books For Young Readers) Houghton Mifflin Harcourt Publishing Co.
Wissinger, Tamera Will & Long, Earlene R. Gone Fishing: A Novel. Cordell, Matthew & Brown, Richard, illus. (ENG.). 128p. (J). 2015. (gr. 5-7). pap. 6.99 *(978-0-544-43931-3(7),* HMH Books For Young Readers) 2013. (gr. 1-4). 15.99 *(978-0-547-82011-8(9))* Houghton Mifflin Harcourt Publishing Co.
Wizards of Waverly Place Insider's Guide. 2009. 128p. pap. 8.99 *(978-1-4231-2473-3(1))* Disney Pr.
Wodehouse, P. G. Mike at Wrykyn. 2013. 189p. reprint ed. lthr. 69.00 *(978-0-7426-3265-3(2))* Classic Bks.
Wolf, Elaine. Camp. 2012. (ENG.). 256p. (YA). (gr. 6-17). 16.95 *(978-1-61608-657-2(2),* 608657, Sky Pony Pr.) Skyhorse Publishing Co., Inc.
Woodrow, Allan. The Pet War. 2015. (ENG.). 272p. (J). (gr. 3-7). pap. 6.99 *(978-0-545-51320-3(0),* Scholastic Paperbacks) Scholastic, Inc.
Woodrum, Margaret. The Christmas Tree Fort. Woodrum, Larry, illus. 2010. 32p. pap. 13.00 *(978-1-60911-329-2(2),* Eloquent Bks.) Strategic Book Publishing & Rights Agency (SBPRA).
Woodson, J. L. The Things I Could Tell You! Malone, Susan Mary et al, eds. collector's ed. 2003. 206p. pap. 14.95 *(978-0-9702699-6-6(X))* Macro Publishing Group.
Woodson, Jacqueline. Miracle's Boys. 2010. (ENG.). 176p. (YA). (gr. 7-18). 8.99 *(978-0-14-241553-5(7),* Speak) Penguin Young Readers Group.
—Peace, Locomotion. (ENG.). (J). 2010. 176p. (gr. 5-18). 8.99 *(978-0-14-241512-2(X),* Puffin Books) 2009. 144p. (gr. 4-7). 15.99 *(978-0-399-24655-5(X),* G.P. Putnam's Sons Books for Young Readers) Penguin Young Readers Group.
Woodward, J. Howland. A Moment in Time. 2006. 55p. pap. 16.95 *(978-1-4241-1334-7(2))* America Star Bks.
Worrell, Maryellen. The Accidental Hero. 2008. 101p. pap. 19.95 *(978-1-60672-145-2(3))* America Star Bks.
Wozniak, Patricia. McGooster & Mcgyman Begin Their Adventures. 2008. (Illus.). 144p. (J). 16.95 *(978-0-9792430-0-4(9))* Wing Lane Pr.
Wrede, Patricia C. Snow White & Rose Red. 2009. (ENG.). 288p. (YA). (gr. 7-18). 8.99 *(978-0-14-241121-6(3),* Firebird) Penguin Young Readers Group.
Wrench, Peter. The Night of the Round Stable. Holland, Ruth, illus. 2012. 174p. pap. *(978-1-908895-49-3(7))* FeedARead.com.
Wunsch, Emma. The Movie Version. 2016. (ENG.). 368p. (YA). (gr. 9-17). 18.95 *(978-1-4197-1900-4(9),* Amulet Bks.) Abrams, Inc.
Yaccarino, Dan. Where the Four Winds Blow. Yaccarino, Dan, illus. 2003. (Illus.). 104p. (J). 17.89 *(978-0-06-623627-8(4),* Cotler, Joanna Books) HarperCollins Pubs.
Yang, Belle. Always Come Home to Me. Yang, Belle, illus. 2007. (ENG., Illus.). 32p. (J). (gr. -1-3). 16.99 *(978-0-7636-2899-4(9))* Candlewick Pr.
Yang, Belle & Williams, Marcia. Archie's War: My Scrapbook of the First World War. Williams, Marcia, illus. 2007. (ENG., Illus.). 48p. (J). (gr. 3-7). 18.99 *(978-0-7636-3532-9(4))* Candlewick Pr.
Yarlett, Emma. Sidney, Stella, & the Moon. Yarlett, Emma, illus. 2013. (ENG., Illus.). 44p. (J). (gr. k-3). 16.99 *(978-0-7636-6623-1(8),* Templar) Candlewick Pr.
Yasuda, Anita. Ghost Sounds, 1 vol. Harpster, Steve, illus. 2013. (Dino Detectives Ser.). (ENG.). 32p. (gr. 1-2). pap. 5.95 *(978-1-4342-4831-2(3));* lib. bdg. 22.65 *(978-1-4342-4152-8(1))* Stone Arch Bks.
—The Missing Trumpet, 1 vol. Harpster, Steve, illus. 2013. (Dino Detectives Ser.). (ENG.). 32p. (gr. 1-2). pap. 5.95 *(978-1-4342-4832-9(1));* lib. bdg. 22.65 *(978-1-4342-4155-9(6))* Stone Arch Bks.
Yates, Alexander. The Winter Place. 2015. (ENG., Illus.). 448p. (YA). (gr. 9). 17.99 *(978-1-4814-1981-9(1))* Simon & Schuster Children's Publishing.
Yavin, T. S. All-Star Season. 2006. 160p. (J). (gr. 3-7). lib. bdg. 15.95 *(978-1-58013-211-4(1),* Kar-Ben Publishing) Lerner Publishing Group.
Yazdani, Aliza. Protection: How far Would you go to Save a Brother? 2012. 84p. pap. 11.11 *(978-1-4669-0895-6(5))* Trafford Publishing.
The Year We Sailed the Sun. 2015. (ENG., Illus.). 432p. (J). (gr. 3-7). 17.99 *(978-0-689-85827-7(2),* Atheneum/Richard Jackson Bks.) Simon & Schuster Children's Publishing.
Yoo, David. The Detention Club. (ENG.). 304p. (J). (gr. 5). 2012. pap. 6.99 *(978-0-06-178380-7(3))* 2011. 16.99 *(978-0-06-178378-4(1))* HarperCollins Pubs.
Yoon, Salina. Penguin & Pumpkin. 2014. (Illus.). (J). *(978-0-8027-3770-0(6))* Walker & Co.
Yorinks, Arthur. Making Scents. Lamb, Braden & Paroline, Shelli, illus. 2017. (ENG.). 112p. (J). 15.99 *(978-1-59643-452-3(X),* 9781596434523, First Second Bks.) Roaring Brook Pr.
Young, Amy. Don't Eat the Baby! 2013. (ENG.). 32p. (J). (gr. -1-k). 16.99 *(978-0-670-78513-1(X),* Viking Books for Young Readers) Penguin Young Readers Group.
Young, Cybèle. A Few Bites, 1 vol. 2012. (ENG., Illus.). 48p. (J). (gr. -1-2). 18.95 *(978-1-55498-295-0(2))* Groundwood Bks. CAN. Dist: Publishers Group West (PGW).
—A Few Blocks, 1 vol. 2011. (ENG., Illus.). 48p. (J). (gr. -1-2). 18.95 *(978-0-88899-995-5(X))* Groundwood Bks. CAN. Dist: Publishers Group West (PGW).
Young, Jessica. Fin-Tastic Fashion. Secheret, Jessica, illus. 2017. (Finley Flowers Ser.). (ENG.). 128p. (gr. 2-3). lib. bdg. 25.32 ***(978-1-4795-9804-5(6),*** Finley Flowers) Picture Window Bks.
—Finley Flowers Collection. Secheret, Jessica, illus. 2016. (Finley Flowers Ser.). (ENG.). 256p. (gr. 2-3). 9.99 *(978-1-4795-9850-2(X),* Finley Flowers) Picture Window Bks.
—Nature Calls. Secheret, Jessica, illus. 2015. (Finley Flowers Ser.). (ENG.). 128p. (gr. 2-3). 8.95 *(978-1-4795-5879-7(6),* Finley Flowers) Picture Window Bks.
—New & Improved. Secheret, Jessica, illus. 2015. (Finley Flowers Ser.). (ENG.). 128p. (gr. 2-3). 8.95 *(978-1-4795-5959-6(8),* Finley Flowers) Picture Window Bks.
—Pet-Rified. Secheret, Jessica, illus. 2017. (Finley Flowers Ser.). (ENG.). 128p. (gr. 2-3). lib. bdg. 25.32 ***(978-1-4795-9805-2(4),*** Finley Flowers) Picture Window Bks.
—Super Spooktacular. Secheret, Jessica, illus. 2017. (Finley Flowers Ser.). (ENG.). 128p. (gr. 2-3). lib. bdg. 25.32 ***(978-1-4795-9807-6(0),*** Finley Flowers) Picture Window Bks.
Young, Judy. Digger & Daisy Go on a Picnic. Sullivan, Dana, illus. 2014. (I Am a Reader: Digger & Daisy Ser.). (ENG.). 32p. (J). (gr. k-1). 9.99 *(978-1-58536-843-5(1),* 203006) Sleeping Bear Pr.
—Digger & Daisy Go to the Doctor. Sullivan, Dana, illus. 2014. (I AM a READER!: Digger & Daisy Ser.). (ENG.). 32p. (J). (gr. k-2). 9.99 *(978-1-58536-845-7(8),* 203674); pap. 4.99 *(978-1-58536-846-4(6),* 203728) Sleeping Bear Pr.
—Digger & Daisy Go to the Zoo. 2013. (ENG.). (J). *(978-1-58536-841-9(5))* Sleeping Bear Pr.
—Digger & Daisy Plant a Garden. Sullivan, Dana, illus. 2016. (I AM a READER: Digger & Daisy Ser.). (ENG.). 32p. (J). (gr. k-2). 9.99 *(978-1-58536-931-7(4),* 204030) Sleeping Bear Pr.
—Digger et Daisy Vont Au Docteur (Digger & Daisy Go to the Doctor) Sullivan, Dana, illus. 2016. (I AM a READER: Digger & Daisy Ser.). (FRE & ENG.). 32p. (J). (gr. k-2). 12.95 *(978-1-62753-949-4(2),* 204172) Sleeping Bear Pr.

—Digger y Daisy Van a la Ciudad (Digger & Daisy Go to the City) Sullivan, Dana, illus. 2016. (I AM a READER: Digger & Daisy Ser.). (SPA & ENG.). 32p. (J). (gr. k-2). 9.99 (978-1-62753-954-8(9), 204177) Sleeping Bear Pr.

—Digger y Daisy Van Al Médico (Digger & Daisy Go to the Doctor) Sullivan, Dana, illus. 2016. (I AM a READER: Digger & Daisy Ser.). (SPA & ENG.). 32p. (J). (gr. k-2). 9.99 (978-1-62753-953-1(0), 204176) Sleeping Bear Pr.

—Digger y Daisy Van Al Zoológico (Digger & Daisy Go to the Zoo) Sullivan, Dana, illus. 2016. (I AM a READER: Digger & Daisy Ser.). (SPA & ENG.). 32p. (J). (gr. k-2). 9.99 (978-1-62753-951-7(4), 204174) Sleeping Bear Pr.

—Digger y Daisy Van de Picnic (Digger & Daisy Go on a Picnic) Sullivan, Dana, illus. 2016. (I AM a READER: Digger & Daisy Ser.). (SPA & ENG.). 32p. (J). (gr. k-2). 9.99 (978-1-62753-952-4(2), 204175) Sleeping Bear Pr.

—Star in a Play. Sullivan, Dana, illus. 2015. (I AM a READER: Digger & Daisy Ser.). (ENG.). 32p. (J). (gr. k-2). 9.99 (978-1-58536-929-4(2), 203950) Sleeping Bear Pr.

Young, Judy & Sullivan, Dana. Digger & Daisy Go to the City. 2015. (I AM a READER!: Digger & Daisy Ser.). (ENG., Illus.). 32p. (J). (gr. k-2). pap. 4.99 (978-1-58536-848-8(2), 203821) Sleeping Bear Pr.

Young, Linda P. The Adventures of Anna & Andy Hummingbird. 2011. 44p. pap. 21.99 (978-1-4568-9568-6(0)) Xlibris Corp.

Young, Moira. Blood Red Road. (Dust Lands Ser.: 1). (ENG.). (YA). (gr. 9). 2012. 480p. pap. 10.99 (978-1-4424-2999-4(2)) 2011. (Illus.). 464p. 17.99 (978-1-4424-2998-7(4)) McElderry, Margaret K. Bks. (McElderry, Margaret K. Bks.).

—Blood Red Road, 9 vols. 2011. (YA). 122.75 (978-1-4618-0629-5(1)); 120.75 (978-1-4618-0630-1(5)); 120.75 (978-1-4618-0633-2(X)); 286.75 (978-1-4618-0634-9(8)); 1.25 (978-1-4640-2632-4(7)) Recorded Bks., Inc.

—Raging Star. (Dust Lands Ser.: 3). (ENG., Illus.). 448p. (YA). (gr. 9). 2015. pap. 10.99 (978-1-4424-3003-7(6)) 2014. 17.99 (978-1-4424-3002-0(8)) McElderry, Margaret K. Bks. (McElderry, Margaret K. Bks.).

—Rebel Heart. (Dust Lands Ser.: 2). (ENG., Illus.). (YA). (gr. 9). 2013. 448p. pap. 11.99 (978-1-4424-3001-3(X)) 2012. 432p. 17.99 (978-1-4424-3000-6(1)) McElderry, Margaret K. Bks. (McElderry, Margaret K. Bks.).

Young, Suzanne. All in Pieces. 2016. (ENG., Illus.). 272p. (YA). (gr. 9). 17.99 (978-1-4814-1883-6(1), Simon Pulse) Simon Pulse.

—Hotel for the Lost. 2016. (ENG., Illus.). 304p. (YA). (gr. 9). pap. 10.99 (978-1-4814-2301-4(0), Simon Pulse) Simon Pulse.

—Hotel Ruby. 2015. (ENG., Illus.). 288p. (YA). (gr. 9). 17.99 (978-1-4814-2300-7(2), Simon Pulse) Simon Pulse.

Young, T. M. My Ten Cents. Victoria Washington and Carla Watts, ed. Cromwell, Danielle, illus. 2013. 24p. pap. 24.95 (978-1-4626-5790-2(7)) America Star Bks.

Zafón, Carlos Ruiz. The Midnight Palace. 2012. (ENG.). 320p. (YA). (gr. 7-17). pap. 10.00 (978-0-316-04474-5(1)) Little, Brown Bks. for Young Readers.

Zamenhof, Robert. The Adventures of Armadillo Baby & Annabelli. Baker, Sara, illus. 2013. 56p. pap. 9.29 (978-0-615-80196-4(X)) RGZ Consulting.

Zarr, Sara. Gem & Dixie. 2017. 288p. (YA). (gr. 9). 17.99 (978-0-06-243459-3(4)) HarperCollins Pubs.

—The Lucy Variations. 2014. (ENG.). 336p. (YA). (gr. 7-17). pap. 10.00 (978-0-316-20500-9(1)) Little, Brown Bks. for Young Readers.

Zaugg, Sandra L. Secret of the Desert Lights: A Story about Following God's Laws. 2009. (J). pap. 9.99 (978-0-8163-2294-7(5)) Pacific Pr. Publishing Assn.

Zeltser, David. Ninja Baby. Goode, Diane, illus. 2015. (ENG.). 32p. (J). (gr. -1-k). 16.99 (978-1-4521-3542-7(8)) Chronicle Bks. LLC.

Zerza, Safoora Z. Sophia V. Is Flower Girl. 2012. 24p. pap. 17.99 (978-1-4685-5136-5(1)) AuthorHouse.

Zimmerman, Andrea & Clemesha, David. Digger Man. Zimmerman, Andrea & Clemesha, David, illus. 2007. (ENG., Illus.). 32p. (J). (gr. -1-k). pap. 7.99 (978-0-8050-8203-6(4), 9780805082036) Square Fish.

Zimmerman, Andrea Griffing & Clemesha, David. Digger Man. Zimmerman, Andrea Griffing & Clemesha, David, illus. rev. ed. 2003. (ENG., Illus.). 32p. (J). (gr. -1-k). 17.95 (978-0-8050-6628-9(4), 9780805066289, Holt, Henry & Co. Bks. For Young Readers) Holt, Henry & Co.

Zimmerman, Diana S. Kandide & the Secret of the Mists. Gadd, Maxine, illus. 2008. (Calabiyau Chronicles Ser.: Bk. 1). 296p. (YA). (gr. 5-18). 17.99 (978-0-9794328-3-5(9));Bk. 1. 289p. (J). (gr. 4-7). pap. 9.99 (978-0-9794328-2-8(0)) Noesis Publishing.

Zindel, Paul. Loch. 2005. 209p. (YA). (gr. 7-12). 13.65 (978-0-7569-6001-8(0)) Perfection Learning Corp.

Zink, Michelle. Promises I Made. 2015. (Lies I Told Ser.: 2). (ENG.). 304p. (YA). (gr. 8). 17.99 (978-0-06-232715-4(1)) HarperCollins Pubs.

Zuppardi, Sam. The Nowhere Box. Zuppardi, Sam, illus. 2013. (ENG., Illus.). 40p. (J). (gr. -1-3). 15.99 (978-0-7636-6367-4(0)) Candlewick Pr.

Zusak, Markus. Underdogs. 2011. (ENG.). 512p. (J). (gr. 7-5). 19.99 (978-0-545-35442-4(0), Levine, Arthur A. Bks.) Scholastic, Inc.

BROWN, AMBER (FICTITIOUS CHARACTER)—FICTION

Danziger, Paula. Ámbar en Cuarto y Sin Su Amigo, Level 3.7. Ross, Tony, illus. 2003.Tr. of Amber Brown Goes Fourth. (SPA.). 136p. (J). (gr. 3-5). pap. 10.95 (978-84-204-4412-3(X), SAN412X) Ediciones Alfaguara ESP. Dist: Santillana USA Publishing Co., Inc.

—Amber Brown Goes Fourth. (Amber Brown Ser.: No. 3). 112p. (J). (gr. 3-6). pap. 3.99 (978-0-8072-1291-2(1), Listening Library) Random Hse. Audio Publishing Group.

—Amber Brown Is Feeling Blue. 2004. (Amber Brown Ser.: No. 7). 131p. (J). (gr. 2-4). pap. 17.00 incl. audio (978-0-8072-2063-4(9), Listening Library) Random Hse. Audio Publishing Group.

—Amber Brown Is Feeling Blue. 2010. (Amber Brown Ser.: 7). (gr. 3-6). lib. bdg. 16.00 (978-0-613-20096-7(9), Turtleback) Turtleback Bks.

—Amber Brown Is Not a Crayon. (Amber Brown Ser.: No. 1). 80p. (J). (gr. 3-6). pap. 3.50 (978-0-8072-1289-9(X), Listening Library) Random Hse. Audio Publishing Group.

—Amber Brown Sees Red. (Amber Brown Ser.: No. 6). 116p. (J). (gr. 3-6). pap. 3.99 (978-0-8072-1294-3(6), Listening Library) Random Hse. Audio Publishing Group.

—Amber Brown Sees Red. 2009. (Amber Brown Ser.: 6). (gr. 3-6). lib. bdg. 16.00 (978-0-613-09442-9(5), Turtleback) Turtleback Bks.

—Amber Brown Wants Extra Credit. (Amber Brown Ser.: No. 4). 120p. (J). (gr. 3-6). pap. 3.99 (978-0-8072-1292-9(X), Listening Library) Random Hse. Audio Publishing Group.

—Forever Amber Brown. (Amber Brown Ser.: No. 5). 101p. (J). (gr. 3-6). pap. 3.99 (978-0-8072-1293-6(8), Listening Library) Random Hse. Audio Publishing Group.

—Get Ready for Second Grade, Amber Brown. 2003. (Young Amber Brown Easy-To-Read Ser.: 3). (gr. k-3). lib. bdg. 13.55 (978-0-613-67547-5(9), Turtleback) Turtleback Bks.

—It's a Fair Day, Amber Brown. Ross, Tony, illus. 2003. pap. 31.95 incl. audio compact disk (978-1-59112-564-8(2)); (J). (gr. -1-2). audio compact disk 28.95 (978-1-59112-565-5(0)) Live Oak Media.

—It's Justin Time, Amber Brown. Ross, Tony, illus. (Amber Brown Ser.). 9.95 (978-1-59112-294-4(5)) Live Oak Media.

—Orange You Glad It's Halloween, Amber Brown?, 4 bks., Set. Ross, Tony, illus. 2007. (Amber Brown Ser.). (J). (gr. 1-3). pap. 29.95 incl. audio (978-1-4301-0080-5(X)) Live Oak Media.

—Orange You Glad It's Halloween, Amber Brown? Ross, Tony, illus. 2007. (Is for Amber Ser.). (ENG.). 48p. (J). (gr. 1-3). 3.99 (978-0-14-240809-4(3), Penguin Young Readers) Penguin Young Readers Group.

—Second Grade Rules, Amber Brown. Ross, Tony, illus. 2005. (Is for Amber Ser.). (ENG.). 48p. (J). (gr. 1-3). mass mkt. 3.99 (978-0-14-240421-8(7), Penguin Young Readers) Penguin Young Readers Group.

—You Can't Eat Your Chicken Pox, Amber Brown. (Amber Brown Ser.: No. 2). 101p. (J). (gr. 3-6). pap. 3.50 (978-0-8072-1290-5(3), Listening Library) Random Hse. Audio Publishing Group.

Danziger, Paula & Mazer, Anne. Is Green with Envy. Ross, Tony, illus. 2004. (Amber Brown Ser.: 9). (ENG.). 160p. (J). (gr. 2-5). pap. 4.99 (978-0-439-07171-0(2), Scholastic Paperbacks) Scholastic, Inc.

BROWN, CHARLIE (FICTITIOUS CHARACTER)—FICTION

Brannon, Tom, illus. What's the Big Idea, Charlie Brown? 2014. (Peanuts Great American Adventure Ser.). (ENG.). 40p. (J). (gr. -1). 16.99 (978-1-62157-257-2(9), Little Patriot Pr.) Regnery Publishing, Inc., An Eagle Publishing Co.

—Where Are You Going, Charlie Brown? 2014. (Peanuts Great American Adventure Ser.). (ENG.). 40p. (J). (gr. -1). 16.99 (978-1-62157-258-9(7), Little Patriot Pr.) Regnery Publishing, Inc., An Eagle Publishing Co.

—Who Cares, Charlie Brown? 2014. (Peanuts Great American Adventure Ser.). (ENG.). 40p. (J). (gr. -1). 16.99 (978-1-62157-259-6(5), Little Patriot Pr.) Regnery Publishing, Inc., An Eagle Publishing Co.

Lundell, Margo. Where's Woodstock? (Peanuts) Schulz, Charles & Ellis, Kim, illus. 2015. (Little Golden Book Ser.). (ENG.). 24p. (J). (gr. -1-1). 4.99 (978-1-101-93517-0(0), Golden Bks.) Random Hse. Children's Bks.

Schulz, Charles. Alles Peanuts. Herbst, Gabriele & Rolle, Ekkehard, trs. from ENG. (Snoopy & die Peanuts Ser.: Vol. 26). (GER., Illus.). 96p. (J). pap. (978-3-8105-1871-2(9)) Kruger, Wolfgang Verlag, GmbH DEU. Dist: International Bk. Import Service, Inc.

—A Charlie Brown Christmas, 1 vol. 2013. (Peanuts Picture Bks.). (ENG., Illus.). 48p. (J). (gr. -1-4). lib. bdg. 24.21 (978-1-61479-029-7(9)) ABDO Publishing Co.

—A Charlie Brown Christmas. Running Press Staff, ed. 2010. (ENG., Illus.). 10p. (J). (gr. -1-3). 22.95 (978-0-7624-4004-7(X)) Running Pr. Bk. Pubs.

—A Charlie Brown Christmas: The Making of a Tradition. 2013. (ENG.). 192p. 19.99 (978-0-06-227214-0(4)) HarperCollins Pubs.

—Charlie Brown Thanksgiving, 1 vol. 2013. (Peanuts Picture Bks.). (ENG.). 24p. (J). (gr. -1-4). lib. bdg. 24.21 (978-1-61479-030-3(2)) ABDO Publishing Co.

—Cowabunga! 2013. (Peanuts Kids Ser.: 1). (ENG., Illus.). 224p. (J). 9.99 (978-1-4494-5079-3(2)) Andrews McMeel Publishing.

—It's the Great Pumpkin, Charlie Brown, 1 vol. 2013. (Peanuts Picture Bks.). (ENG.). 48p. (J). (gr. -1-4). lib. bdg. 24.21 (978-1-61479-032-7(9)) ABDO Publishing Co.

—Peanuts Movie Novelization. 2015. (Peanuts Movie Ser.). (ENG., Illus.). 144p. (J). (gr. 3-7). 17.99 (978-1-4814-6044-6(7)); pap. 6.99 (978-1-4814-4136-0(1)) Simon Spotlight. (Simon Spotlight).

—The Ultimate Box, Set. 2007. (Peanuts(r) Ser.). (ENG., Illus.). 648p. 39.95 (978-1-933662-71-8(9)) Cider Mill Pr. Bk. Pubs., LLC.

Schulz, Charles & Houghton, Shane. Peanuts, Vol. 2. Braddock, Paige, illus. 2013. (Peanuts Ser.). (ENG.). 112p. (J). (gr. 1). pap. 13.99 (978-1-60886-299-3(2)) Boom! Studios.

Schulz, Charles & Pastis, Stephan. Happiness Is a Warm Blanket, Charlie Brown! Scott, Bob, illus. 2011. (Peanuts Ser.). (ENG.). 96p. (gr. 3). pap. 9.99 (978-1-60886-681-6(5)); (J). 19.99 (978-1-60886-682-3(3)) Boom! Studios.

Schulz, Charles & Schulz, Charles M. It's the Great Pumpkin, Charlie Brown: with Sound & Music. 2012. (ENG., Illus.). 48p. (J). (gr. -1-3). 19.95 (978-0-7624-4606-3(4), Running Pr. Kids) Running Pr. Bk. Pubs.

Schulz, Charles M. Be Kind: Peanuts Wisdom to Carry You Through. 2013. (ENG., Illus.). 72p. (J). (gr. -1-17). 7.95 (978-0-7624-4862-3(8), Running Pr. Kids) Running Pr. Bk. Pubs.

—Be My Valentine, Charlie Brown. 2007. (Miniature Editions Ser.). (ENG., Illus.). 128p. (gr. 1-17). 5.95 (978-0-7624-2754-3(X)) Running Pr. Bk. Pubs.

—Be Thankful: Peanuts Wisdom to Carry You Through. 2013. (ENG., Illus.). 72p. (J). (gr. -1-17). 7.95 (978-0-7624-5045-9(2), Running Pr. Kids) Running Pr. Bk. Pubs.

—A Charlie Brown Christmas. deluxe ed. 2003. (Miniature Editions Ser.). (ENG., Illus.). 128p. (gr. 1-17). 5.95 (978-0-7624-1601-1(7)) Running Pr. Bk. Pubs.

—A Charlie Brown Christmas Kit: A Book & Tree. 2007. (Miniature Editions Ser.). (ENG., Illus.). 128p. (gr. 1-17). pap. 9.95 (978-0-7624-3145-8(8)) Running Pr. Bk. Pubs.

—It's the Easter Beagle, Charlie Brown, 1 vol. 2013. (Peanuts Picture Bks.). (ENG.). 48p. (J). (gr. -1-4). lib. bdg. 24.21 (978-1-61479-031-0(0)) ABDO Publishing Co.

—It's the Easter Beagle, Charlie Brown. Scott, Vicki, illus. 2016. (Peanuts Ser.). (ENG.). 32p. (J). (gr. -1). 7.99 (978-1-4814-6159-7(1), Simon Spotlight) Simon Spotlight.

—It's the Easter Beagle, Charlie Brown: with Sound & Music. 2013. (ENG., Illus.). 48p. (J). (gr. -1-17). 19.95 (978-0-7624-4608-7(0), Running Pr. Kids) Running Pr. Bk. Pubs.

—It's the Great Pumpkin, Charlie Brown. 2004. (Miniature Editions Ser.). (ENG., Illus.). 128p. (gr. -1-17). 5.95 (978-0-7624-2033-9(2)) Running Pr. Bk. Pubs.

—Peanuts: Be Friends. 2013. (ENG., Illus.). 72p. (J). (gr. -1-17). 7.95 (978-0-7624-5044-2(4), Running Pr. Kids) Running Pr. Bk. Pubs.

Schulz, Charles M., creator. Be Yourself! 2013. (ENG., Illus.). 40p. (J). (gr. -1-17). 12.95 (978-0-7624-4718-3(4), Running Pr. Kids) Running Pr. Bk. Pubs.

—Peanuts: Be Brave: Peanuts Wisdom to Carry You Through. 2013. (ENG., Illus.). 72p. (J). (gr. -1-17). 7.95 (978-0-7624-4861-6(X), Running Pr. Kids) Running Pr. Bk. Pubs.

Verr, Harry Coe. Let's Fly a Kite, Charlie Brown! (Peanuts) Ellis, Kim & Schulz, Charles, illus. 2015. (Little Golden Book Ser.). (ENG.). 24p. (J). (gr. -1-1). 4.99 (978-1-101-93519-4(7), Golden Bks.) Random Hse. Children's Bks.

BROWN, ENCYCLOPEDIA (FICTITIOUS CHARACTER)—FICTION

Sobol, Donald J. Encyclopedia Brown, 4 vols., Set. Shortall, Leonard W., illus. 2007. (Encyclopedia Brown Ser.). (ENG.). 384p. (J). (gr. 2-18). 19.96 (978-0-14-240985-5(5), Puffin Books) Penguin Young Readers Group.

—Encyclopedia Brown & His Best Cases Ever. 2013. (Encyclopedia Brown Ser.). (ENG.). 160p. (J). (gr. 3-7). pap. 6.99 (978-0-14-750871-3(1), Puffin Books) Penguin Young Readers Group.

—Encyclopedia Brown & the Case of the Dead Eagles. Shortall, Leonard W., illus. 2008. (Encyclopedia Brown Ser.: 12). (ENG.). 96p. (J). (gr. 3-7). 4.99 (978-0-14-241135-3(3), Puffin Books) Penguin Young Readers Group.

—Encyclopedia Brown & the Case of the Jumping Frogs. Papp, Robert, illus. 2005. (Encyclopedia Brown Ser.). 69p. (J). (gr. 3-7). 13.15 (978-0-7569-5100-9(3)) Perfection Learning Corp.

—Encyclopedia Brown & the Case of the Jumping Frogs. 2005. (Encyclopedia Brown Ser.: No. 23). (ENG., Illus.). 80p. (J). (gr. 3-7). 5.99 (978-0-553-48758-9(2), Yearling) Random Hse. Children's Bks.

—Encyclopedia Brown & the Case of the Midnight Visitor. Brandi, Lillian, illus. 2008. (Encyclopedia Brown Ser.: 13). (ENG.). 96p. (J). (gr. 3-7). 4.99 (978-0-14-241106-3(X), Puffin Books) Penguin Young Readers Group.

—Encyclopedia Brown & the Case of the Secret Pitch. Shortall, Leonard W., illus. 2007. (Encyclopedia Brown Ser.: 2). (ENG.). 96p. (J). (gr. 3-7). 4.99 (978-0-14-240889-6(1), Puffin Books) Penguin Young Readers Group.

—Encyclopedia Brown & the Case of the Secret Pitch. 2004. (Encyclopedia Brown Ser.: No. 2). 112p. (J). (gr. 3-7). pap. 17.00 incl. audio (978-0-8072-1985-0(1), Listening Library) Random Hse. Audio Publishing Group.

—Encyclopedia Brown & the Case of the Slippery Salamander. Chang, Warren, illus. 2003. (Encyclopedia Brown Ser.). 87p. (gr. 3-7). 16.00 (978-0-7569-1619-0(4)) Perfection Learning Corp.

—Encyclopedia Brown & the Case of the Soccer Scheme. Bernadin, James, illus. 2013. (Encyclopedia Brown Ser.). (ENG.). 96p. (J). (gr. 3-7). pap. 4.99 (978-0-14-242288-5(6), Puffin Books) Penguin Young Readers Group.

—Encyclopedia Brown, Boy Detective. Shortall, Leonard W., illus. 2007. (Encyclopedia Brown Ser.: 1). (ENG.). 96p. (J). (gr. 3-7). 4.99 (978-0-14-240888-9(3), Puffin Books) Penguin Young Readers Group.

—Encyclopedia Brown, Boy Detective. 2004. (Encyclopedia Brown Ser.: No. 1). 128p. (J). (gr. 3-7). pap. 17.00 incl. audio (978-0-8072-1984-3(3), Listening Library) Random Hse. Audio Publishing Group.

—Encyclopedia Brown Finds the Clues. Shortall, Leonard W., illus. 2007. (Encyclopedia Brown Ser.: 3). (ENG.). 96p. (J). (gr. 3-7). 4.99 (978-0-14-240890-2(5), Puffin Books) Penguin Young Readers Group.

—Encyclopedia Brown Gets His Man. Shortall, Leonard W., illus. 2007. (Encyclopedia Brown Ser.: 4). (ENG.). 96p. (J). (gr. 3-7). 4.99 (978-0-14-240891-9(3), Puffin Books) Penguin Young Readers Group.

—Encyclopedia Brown Lends a Hand. Shortall, Leonard W., illus. 2008. (Encyclopedia Brown Ser.: 11). (ENG.). 96p. (J). (gr. 3-7). 4.99 (978-0-14-241105-6(1), Puffin Books) Penguin Young Readers Group.

—Encyclopedia Brown Saves the Day. Shortall, Leonard W., illus. 2008. (Encyclopedia Brown Ser.: 7). (ENG.). 96p. (J). (gr. 3-7). 4.99 (978-0-14-240921-3(9), Puffin Books) Penguin Young Readers Group.

—Encyclopedia Brown Shows the Way. Shortall, Leonard W., illus. 2008. (Encyclopedia Brown Ser.: 9). (ENG.). 96p. (J). (gr. 3-7). 4.99 (978-0-14-241086-8(1), Puffin Books) Penguin Young Readers Group.

—Encyclopedia Brown Shows the Way. Shortall, Leonard W., illus. 2008. (Encyclopedia Brown Ser.). 96p. (J). (gr. 2-5). 12.65 (978-0-7569-8937-8(X)) Perfection Learning Corp.

—Encyclopedia Brown Solves Them All. Shortall, Leonard W., illus. 2008. (Encyclopedia Brown Ser.: 5). (ENG.). 96p. (J). (gr. 3-7). 4.99 (978-0-14-240920-6(0), Puffin Books) Penguin Young Readers Group.

—Encyclopedia Brown Takes the Case. Shortall, Leonard W., illus. 2008. (Encyclopedia Brown Ser.: 10). (ENG.). 96p. (J). (gr. 3-7). 4.99 (978-0-14-241085-1(3), Puffin Books) Penguin Young Readers Group.

—Encyclopedia Brown Tracks Them Down. Shortall, Leonard W., illus. 2008. (Encyclopedia Brown Ser.: No. 8). (ENG.). 96p. (J). (gr. 3-7). 4.99 (978-0-14-240951-0(0), Puffin Books) Penguin Young Readers Group.

BROWN, JOHN, 1800-1859

Glaser, Jason. John Brown's Raid on Harpers Ferry. Milgrom, Al et al, illus. 2005. (Graphic History Ser.). (ENG.). 32p. (gr. 3-4). 30.65 (978-0-7368-4369-0(8), Graphic Library) Capstone Press of Coughlan Cos.

Horn, Geoffrey Michael. John Brown: Putting Actions above Words. 2009. (Voices for Freedom Ser.). (ENG., Illus.). 64p. (J). (gr. 5-8). pap. (978-0-7787-4839-7(1)); lib. bdg. (978-0-7787-4823-6(5)) Crabtree Publishing Co.

Marrin, Albert. A Volcano Beneath the Snow: John Brown's War Against Slavery. (ENG., Illus.). 256p. (YA). (gr. 7). 2016. pap. 15.99 (978-0-307-98154-7(1), Ember) 2014. 19.99 (978-0-307-98152-3(5), Knopf Bks. for Young Readers) Random Hse. Children's Bks.

The Raid on Harpers Ferry: John Brown's Rebellion. 2010. (Milestones in American History Ser.). (Illus.). 136p. (J). (gr. 6-12). 35.00 (978-1-60413-678-4(2), Chelsea Hse.) Facts On File, Inc.

Schraff, Anne E. John Brown: We Came to Free the Slaves. 2010. (Americans—the Spirit of a Nation Ser.). (Illus.). 128p. (J). lib. bdg. 33.27 (978-0-7660-3355-9(4)) Enslow Pubs., Inc.

Stefoff, Rebecca. John Brown & Armed Resistance to Slavery. 2015. (Primary Sources of the Abolitionist Movement Ser.). (ENG., Illus.). 64p. (J). (gr. 6-6). 34.21 (978-1-5026-0534-4(1)) Cavendish Square Publishing.

Yomtov, Nel. John Brown: Defending the Innocent or Plotting Terror?, 1 vol. 2013. (Perspectives on History Ser.). (ENG.). 32p. (gr. 3-4). 27.32 (978-1-4765-0244-1(7)); pap. 7.95 (978-1-4765-3408-4(X)) Capstone Press of Coughlan Cos. (Fact Finders).

BROWN, JOHN, 1800-1859—FICTION

Barnhart, Aaron. Firebrand. 2015. (ENG., Illus.). 168p. (J). 19.95 (978-0-9669258-6-9(6)) Quindaro Pr.

BROWN, MARGARET WISE, 1910-1952

Ruffin, Frances E. Unsinkable Molly Brown. 2009. (American Legends Ser.). 24p. (gr. 3-3). 42.50 (978-1-61511-377-4(0), PowerKids Pr.) Rosen Publishing Group, Inc., The.

Wheeler, Jill C. Margaret Wise Brown, 1 vol. 2007. (Children's Authors Set 4 Ser.). (ENG., Illus.). 24p. (J). (gr. 2-5). 25.65 (978-1-59679-762-8(2)) ABDO Publishing Co.

BRYANT, WILLIAM CULLEN, 1794-1878

Cody, Sherwin. Four American Poets. 2009. 198p. pap. 14.14 (978-0-217-47860-1(3)) General Bks. LLC.

BUCCANEERS

see also Pirates

Hamilton, Sue L. Henry Morgan, 1 vol. 2007. (Pirates! Ser.). (ENG., Illus.). 32p. (gr. 4-8). 27.07 (978-1-59928-760-7(9), Abdo & Daughters) ABDO Publishing Co.

Smith, Helen. Pirates, Swashbucklers & Buccaneers of London. 2004. (.... of London Ser.). (ENG., Illus.). 96p. pap. 8.99 (978-1-904153-17-7(8)) Watling St., Ltd. GBR. Dist: Trafalgar Square Publishing.

Spooner, J. B. The Little Black Dog Buccaneer. Seeley, Terre Lamb, illus. 2011. (Little Black Dog Ser.). (ENG.). 32p. (J). (gr. -1-k). 16.95 (978-1-61145-000-2(4), 611000, Arcade Publishing) Skyhorse Publishing Co., Inc.

Steele, Philip. The Amazing History of Pirates: See What a Buccaneer's Life Was Really Like, with over 350 Exciting Pictures. 2016. (ENG., Illus.). 64p. 12.99 (978-1-86147-711-8(2), Armadillo) Anness Publishing GBR. Dist: National Bk. Network.

Stockton, Frank Richard. Buccaneers & Pirates. Varian, George & Clinedinst, B. West, illus. 2007. (Dover Maritime Ser.). (ENG.). 368p. per. 12.95 (978-0-486-45425-2(8)) Dover Pubns., Inc.

—Buccaneers & Pirates of Our Coasts. 2008. 232p. 24.99 (978-0-559-13822-5(9)) 2008. 232p. pap. 24.75 (978-0-559-13821-8(0)) 2008. 228p. (gr. 4-7). 27.99 (978-0-554-26260-4(6)) 2008. 228p. (gr. 4-7). 24.99 (978-0-554-35563-4(9)) 2007. (ENG.). 206p. pap. 20.99 (978-1-4346-0736-2(4)) 2007. 224p. pap. 22.99 (978-1-4346-0796-6(8)) Creative Media Partners, LLC.

—Buccaneers & Pirates of Our Coasts. 2007. (ENG., Illus.). 216p. (J). (gr. 4-7). per. (978-1-4065-6187-6(8)) Dodo Pr.

—Buccaneers & Pirates of Our Coasts. Varian, George & Clinedinst, B. West, illus. 2008. 364p. (gr. 4-7). 46.95 (978-1-4369-8234-4(0)); pap. 31.95 (978-1-4367-9391-9(2)) Kessinger Publishing, LLC.

—Buccaneers & Pirates of Our Coasts. 2013. (Notable American Authors Ser.). reprint ed. lthr. 79.00 (978-0-7812-8936-8(X)) Reprint Services Corp.

—Buccaneers & Pirates of Our Coasts. 2005. pap. 30.95 (978-1-885529-90-9(2)) Stevens Publishing.

—Buccaneers & Pirates of Our Coasts. 2005. 35.00 (978-1-55742-497-6(7)); pap. 15.95 (978-1-55742-486-0(1)) Wildside Pr., LLC.

Sullivan, Laura L. Sir Henry Morgan. 2015. (J). lib. bdg. (978-1-62713-308-1(9)) Cavendish Square Publishing.

Teitelbaum, Michael. Pirate Life. 2007. (Reading Rocks! Ser.). (ENG., Illus.). 32p. (J). (gr. 2-5). 28.50 (978-1-59296-859-6(7), 200747) Child's World, Inc., The.

Weintraub, Aileen. Henry Morgan: 17th-Century Buccaneer. 2009. (Library of Pirates Ser.). 24p. (gr. 3-3). 42.50 (978-1-60853-812-6(5), PowerKids Pr.) Rosen Publishing Group, Inc., The.

BUCCANEERS—FICTION

Phillips, Dee. Pirate: The Story of a Buccaneer. 2015. (Yesterday's Voices Ser.). (YA). lib. bdg. 19.60 (978-0-606-36673-1(3)) Turtleback Bks.

Pyle, Howard. Stolen Treasure. 2006. (ENG.). pap. (978-1-4068-3429-1(7)) Echo Library.

Stockton, Frank Richard. Buccaneers & Pirates of Our Coasts. 2006. 168p. (gr. 4-7). per. 13.95 (978-1-59818-872-1(0)); 25.95 (978-1-59818-255-2(2)) Aegypan.

BUCHANAN, JAMES, 1791-1868

Burgan, Michael. James Buchanan. 2010. (Presidents & Their Times 4 Ser.). 96p. (gr. 6). 34.21 (978-0-7614-4810-5(1)) Marshall Cavendish Corp.

Donovan, Sandra. James Buchanan. 2004. (Presidential Leaders Ser.). (Illus.). 112p. (J). (gr. 3-7). lib. bdg. 29.27 (978-0-8225-1399-5(4)) Lerner Publishing Group.

Gunderson, Megan M. James Buchanan, 1 vol. 2009. (United States Presidents Ser.). (ENG., Illus.). 40p. (YA). (gr. 3-6). 27.07 (978-1-60453-442-9(7)) ABDO Publishing Co.

Mis, Melody S. How to Draw the Life & Times of James Buchanan. (Kid's Guide to Drawing the Presidents of the United States of America Ser.). 2009. 32p. (gr. 4-4). 50.50 (978-1-61511-146-6(8), PowerKids Pr.) 2006. (YA). (gr. 2-5). 26.50 (978-1-4042-2992-1(2)) Rosen Publishing Group, Inc., The.

Souter, Gerry & Souter, Janet. James Buchanan. 2008. (Presidents of the U. S. A. Ser.). (ENG., Illus.). 48p. (J). (gr. 3-6). 32.79 (978-1-60253-044-7(0), 200683) Child's World, Inc., The.

Venezia, Mike. James Buchanan: Fifteenth President. Venezia, Mike, illus. 2005. (Getting to Know the U. S. Presidents Ser.). (ENG., Illus.). 32p. (J). (gr. 3-7). lib. bdg. 28.00 (978-0-516-22620-0(7), Children's Pr.) Scholastic Library Publishing.

Wheeler, Jill C. Harriet Lane, 1 vol. 2010. (First Ladies Set 2 Ser.). (ENG., Illus.). 32p. (YA). (gr. 1-4). 27.07 (978-1-60453-631-7(4)) ABDO Publishing Co.

Young, Jeff C. James Buchanan: A MyReportLinks.com Book. 2003. (Presidents Ser.). (Illus.). 48p. (J). (gr. 4-10). lib. bdg. 25.26 (978-0-7660-5101-0(3), MyReportLinks.com Bks.) Enslow Pubs., Inc.

BUDDHA

see Gautama Buddha

BUDDHISM

Carew-Miller, Anna. Buddha. 2004. (Great Names Ser.). (Illus.). 32p. (J). (gr. 3-18). lib. bdg. 19.95 (978-1-59084-137-2(9)) Mason Crest.

Chodzin, Sherab. The Barefoot Book of Buddhist Tales. Cameron, Marie, illus. 2012. (ENG.). 80p. (J). (gr. 1-5). pap. 14.99 (978-1-84686-824-5(6)) Barefoot Bks., Inc.

Conover, Sarah. Kindness: A Treasury of Buddhist Tales & Wisdom. Wahl, Valerie, illus. 2010. (ENG.). 184p. (YA). pap. 19.95 (978-1-55896-568-3(8), Skinner Hse. Bks.) Unitarian Universalist Assn.

Cooper, Alison. Facts about Buddhism. 2010. (World Religions Ser.). (ENG.). 48p. (YA). lib. bdg. 29.25 (978-1-61532-319-7(8), Rosen Reference) Rosen Publishing Group, Inc., The.

Dicker, Katie & De Silva, Nisansa. I Belong to the Buddhist Faith. 2009. (I Belong Ser.). (Illus.). 24p. (J). (ENG.). pap. 8.25 (978-1-4358-8616-2(X), PowerKids Pr.); (gr. 1-4). lib. bdg. 22.60 (978-1-4358-3031-8(8)) Rosen Publishing Group, Inc., The.

Elby, Tristan & McKain, Neil. World Religions: Hinduism, Buddhism & Sikhism. 2017. (ENG.). 120p. (J). (gr. 6-9). pap. 29.99 **(978-0-00-822769-2(1))** HarperCollins Pubs. Ltd. GBR. Dist: Independent Pubs. Group.

Foran, Jill. Buddha Day. 2003. (Celebrating Cultures Ser.). (Illus.). 24p. (J). lib. bdg. 24.45 (978-1-59036-090-3(7)) Weigl Pubs., Inc.

Fossey, Kevin. Buddhism. 2006. (QEB World of Faiths Ser.). (Illus.). 32p. (J). (gr. 3-6). lib. bdg. 27.10 (978-1-59566-212-5(X)) QEB Publishing Inc.

Fu, Zhiying. Handing down the Light: The Biography of Venerable Master Hsing Yun. 2003. (Illus.). 335p. (J). 14.00 (978-1-932293-00-5(0)) Buddha's Light Publications USA Corp.

Ganeri, Anita. Buddhism. 2007. (Atlas of World Faiths/Arcturus Ser.). (Illus.). 48p. (YA). (gr. 7-12). lib. bdg. 32.80 (978-1-59920-058-3(9)) Black Rabbit Bks.

—Buddhism. 2005. (Religions of the World Ser.). (Illus.). 48p. (gr. 5-12). pap. 14.05 (978-0-8368-5871-6(9)); lib. bdg. 31.00 (978-0-8368-5865-5(4)) Stevens, Gareth Publishing LLLP. (Gareth Stevens Secondary Library).

—Buddhist. (Beliefs & Cultures Ser.). (Illus.). 32p. (YA). (gr. 3-6). lib. bdg. 27.10 (978-1-932889-15-4(9)) Sea-To-Sea Pubns.

—Buddhist Festivals Through the Year. 2003. (Year of Festivals Ser.). 30p. (J). lib. bdg. 24.25 (978-1-58340-375-4(2)) Black Rabbit Bks.

—Buddhist Stories. 2014. (Storyteller Ser.). (ENG., Illus.). 32p. (J). (gr. 2-4). pap. 10.99 (978-1-78388-006-5(6)) Tulip Books GBR. Dist: Independent Pubs. Group.

George, Charles, et al. The Dalai Lama. 2009. (People in the News Ser.). (Illus.). 128p. (YA). (gr. 7-12). 33.95 (978-1-4205-0232-9(8)) Cengage Gale.

Gerner, Katy. Buddhism. 2008. (Religions Around the World Ser.). 32p. (gr. 3-18). lib. bdg. 18.56 (978-0-7614-3164-0(0), Benchmark Bks.) Marshall Cavendish Corp.

Gyatso, Geshe Kelsang. The Story of Angulimala: Buddhism for Children Level 1. 2nd ed. 2013. (Buddhism for Children Ser.: 1). (ENG., Illus.). 32p. (J). (gr. k-2). 8.95 (978-1-61606-021-3(2)) Tharpa Pubns. GBR. Dist: Ingram Publisher Services.

—What Is Buddhism? Buddhism for Children Level 3. 2013. (Buddhism for Children Ser.). (ENG., Illus.). 32p. (J). (gr. 4-6). 8.95 (978-1-61606-023-7(9)) Tharpa Pubns. GBR. Dist: Ingram Publisher Services.

—What Is Meditation? Buddhism for Children Level 4. 2013. (Buddhism for Children Ser.). (ENG., Illus.). 32p. (J). (gr. 4-7). 8.95 (978-1-61606-024-4(7)) Tharpa Pubns. GBR. Dist: Ingram Publisher Services.

Hanh, Thich Nhat. The Coconut Monk. Mai, Vo-Dinh, illus. 2005. (ENG.). 40p. (J). (gr. -1-3). pap. 10.95 (978-1-888375-97-8(3), Plum Blossom Bks.) Parallax Pr.

—Is Nothing Something? Kids' Questions & Zen Answers about Life, Death, Family, Friendship, & Everything in Between. McClure, Jessica, illus. 2014. (ENG.). 40p. (J). (gr. -1-3). 16.95 (978-1-937006-65-5(4), Plum Blossom Bks.) Parallax Pr.

—A Pebble for Your Pocket. Ames, Philippe & Hop, Nguyen Thi, illus. rev. ed. 2006. (ENG.). 144p. (J). (gr. 3-7). pap. 12.95 (978-1-935209-45-4(0), Plum Blossom Bks.) Parallax Pr.

Hawker, Frances & Sunantha Phusomsai. Buddhism in Thailand. Campbell, Bruce, photos by. 2009. (ENG., Illus.). 32p. (J). (gr. 3-6). (978-0-7787-5006-2(X)); pap. (978-0-7787-5023-9(X)) Crabtree Publishing Co.

Hazell, Rebecca. The Sweeper: A Buddhist Tale. 2017. (ENG., Illus.). 32p. (gr. k-4). 16.95 **(978-1-61180-438-6(8))** Shambhala Pubns., Inc.

Hellstrom, Travis. My Day with the Dalai Lama: A Coloring Book for All Ages. Hoyle, Leighanna, illus. 2017. (ENG.). 48p. (J). (gr. -1-2). pap. 5.99 (978-1-57826-639-5(4), Hatherleigh Pr.) Hatherleigh Co., Ltd., The.

Hsuan Hua. Dew Drops: Pearls of Wisdom by the Venerable Master Hua = [Zhao Lu: Xuanhuashangren Yi Li Ming Zhu]. 2003. (ENG & CHI., Illus.). 91p. (J). 5.00 (978-0-88139-862-5(4)) Buddhist Text Translation Society.

Ikeda, Daisaku. Soar into the Skies of Hope. 2015. (ENG., Illus.). 224p. (J). pap. 8.95 (978-1-935523-77-2(5)) World Tribune Pr.

Jin Rou. Snow-Covered Peaks: What Are Bodhisattvas Like? 2016. (Illus.). 38p. (J). pap. (978-1-60103-077-1(0)) Buddhist Text Translation Society.

Kolka, Diane & Clarke, Steve. Buddhism. 2012. (Illus.). 72p. pap. 29.50 (978-1-4441-2220-6(7)) Hodder Education Group GBR. Dist: Trans-Atlantic Pubns., Inc.

Komarudin, illus. The Golden Feather: A Jataka Tale: A Story & Coloring Book. 2012. (CHI & ENG.). 30p. (J). (978-1-60103-008-5(8)) Buddhist Text Translation Society.

Koo, Rob, illus. Great Buddhist Stories. 2011. (J). pap. (978-1-935523-22-2(8)) World Tribune Pr.

Linenthal, Peter. Jaya's Golden Necklace: A Silk Road Tale. 2015. (ENG., Illus.). 40p. (J). 16.95 (978-1-61429-232-6(9)) Wisdom Pubns.

The Lost Key of the Buddha: The Immortal Series, Book III. 2003. (Illus.). 350p. per. 19.95 (978-0-9665053-3-7(6), 009) Great AD-Ventures.

Marsico, Katie. Buddhism. 2017. (21st Century Skills Library: Global Citizens: World Religions Ser.). (ENG., Illus.). 32p. (J). (gr. 4-7). lib. bdg. 29.93 (978-1-63472-158-5(6), 209204) Cherry Lake Publishing.

McKain, Neil. Buddhism. 2017. (ENG.). 40p. (J). (gr. 6-9). pap. 11.99 **(978-0-00-822773-9(X))** HarperCollins Pubs. Ltd. GBR. Dist: Independent Pubs. Group.

Nagle, Jeanne. The Dalai Lama. 2014. (Making a Difference: Leaders Who Are Changing the World Ser.). (Illus.). 48p. (J). (gr. 5-8). 25.85 (978-1-62275-440-3(9)) Rosen Publishing Group, Inc., The.

Nagle, Jeanne. The 14th Dalai Lama: Spiritual Leader of Tibetan Buddhists. 2017. (J). **(978-1-5081-7745-6(7))** Rosen Publishing Group, Inc., The.

Quinn, Daniel P. I Am Buddhist. (Religions of the World Ser.). 24p. 2009. (gr. 3-3). 42.50 (978-1-60852-459-4(0)) 2004. (Illus.). (J). (gr. k-5). lib. bdg. 22.60 (978-0-8239-6814-5(6)) Rosen Publishing Group, Inc., The. (PowerKids Pr.).

Rivera, Sheila. The Dalai Lama: A Life of Compassion. 2006. (Pull Ahead Bks.). (Illus.). 32p. (J). (gr. k-3). lib. bdg. 22.60 (978-0-8225-6386-0(X), Lerner Pubns.) Lerner Publishing Group.

—Dalai Lama: A Life of Compassion. 2007. (Pull Ahead Books-Biographies Ser.). (ENG., Illus.). 32p. (gr. k-3). pap. 7.95 (978-0-8225-6435-5(1)) Lerner Publishing Group.

Sakya, Kalden D. The Life of the Great Mahasiddha Virupa. 2011. (ENG., Illus.). 40p. pap. 9.95 (978-1-55939-385-0(8), Snow Lion Publications, Inc,) Shambhala Pubns., Inc.

Senker, Cath. My Buddhist Year. 2007. (Year of Religious Festivals Ser.). (Illus.). 32p. (J). (gr. 1-4). lib. bdg. 25.25 (978-1-4042-3730-8(5)) Rosen Publishing Group, Inc., The.

Seth, Shantum. Siddhartha Gautama: The Life of the Buddha - Based on Original Sources. Mukherjee, Aniruddha, illus. adapted ed. 2014. (ENG.). 64p. pap. 6.95 (978-1-906230-61-6(7)) Real Reads Ltd. GBR. Dist: Casemate Pubs. & Bk. Distributors, LLC.

Shaw, Maura D. Thich Nhat Hanh: Buddhism in Action. Marchesi, Stephen, illus. 2003. (ENG.), 32p. (J). (gr. 1-3). 12.95 (978-1-893361-87-4(X), 9781893361874, Skylight Paths Publishing) LongHill Partners, Inc.

Stewart, Whitney. The 14th Dalai Lama: Spiritual Leader of Tibet. 2005. (Biography Ser.). (Illus.). 112p. (gr. 6-12). pap., lib. bdg. 27.93 (978-0-8225-9691-2(1)) Lerner Publishing Group.

Sullivan, Anne Marie. Dalai Lama: Spiritual Leader. 2004. (Great Names Ser.). (Illus.). 32p. (J). (gr. 3-18). lib. bdg. 19.95 (978-1-59084-151-8(4)) Mason Crest.

—Dalai Lama: Spiritual Leader of Tibet. 2013. (People of Importance Ser.: 21). (Illus.). 32p. (J). (gr. 4-18). 19.95 (978-1-4222-2846-3(0)) Mason Crest.

Thomas, Mark. Buddhism. 2017. (J). **(978-1-4222-3816-5(4))** Mason Crest.

Townshend, Dominique. Shantideva: How to Wake up a Hero. Norbu, Tenzing, illus. 2015. (ENG.). 64p. (J). 22.95 (978-1-61429-058-2(X)) Wisdom Pubns.

Walker, Peggy, illus. My First Book of Buddhist Treasures. 2003. 38p. (J). 8.95 (978-0-915678-81-5(0)) World Tribune Pr.

White, Bender Richardson, et al. Buddhism. 4th rev. ed. 2009. (World Religions Ser.). (Illus.). 144p. (gr. 6-12). 40.00 (978-1-60413-105-5(5), Chelsea Hse.) Facts On File, Inc.

Whitworth, Christy, illus. Come Back, o Tiger! A Jataka Tale. 2012. (978-1-60103-015-3(0)) Buddhist Text Translation Society.

Yun, Hsing, et al. Prescription for the Heart: Between Ignorance & Enlightenment II, 7 vols., Vol. 2. 2003. (Between Ignorance & Enlightenment Ser.: Vol. 2). 131p. pap. 13.00 (978-1-932293-02-9(7)) Buddha's Light Publications USA Corp.

Yung Dong, Venerable & Jacobs, Marjorie. The Short March to Wisdom. Martin, Peter, illus. 2015. 64p. (J). pap. 0.00 (978-1-943211-00-5(0)) Fo Guang Shan International Translation Ctr.

BUDDHISM—FICTION

Alderfer, Lauren. Mindful Monkey, Happy Panda. MacLean, Kerry Lee, illus. 2011. (ENG.). 32p. (J). (gr. -1-3). 16.95 (978-0-86171-683-8(3)) Wisdom Pubns.

Allende, Isabel. Kingdom of the Golden Dragon. 2009. (City of the Beasts Ser.: Bk. 2).Tr. of Reino del Dragón de Oro. (ENG.). 480p. pap. 14.99 (978-0-06-182512-5(3), Harper Perennial) HarperCollins Pubs.

Bowser, Milton, illus. Cartoon Stories from the Teachings of Buddha. l.t. ed. 2003. (Cartoon Ser.). (JPN & SPA.). 72p. (YA). 10.00 (978-0-940178-34-2(6), Buddha 1) Sitare, Ltd.

Coatsworth, Elizabeth. The Cat Who Went to Heaven. 2011. 7.64 (978-0-7848-3455-8(5), Everbind) Marco Bk. Co.

Joo, Mi-hwa. I Am a Little Monk: Thailand. Cowley, Joy, ed. Gahng, Hwa-kyeong, illus. 2015. (Global Kids Storybooks Ser.). (ENG.). 32p. (gr. 1-4). 26.65 (978-1-925246-32-2(9)); 7.99 (978-1-925246-58-2(2)); 26.65 (978-1-925246-06-3(X)) ChoiceMaker Pty. Ltd., The AUS. (Big and SMALL). Dist: Lerner Publishing Group.

—I Am a Little Monk: Thailand. Cowley, Joy, ed. Gahng, Hwa-kyeong, illus. 2015. (Global Kids Storybooks Ser.). (ENG.). 32p. (J). (gr. 1-4). pap. 7.99 (978-1-925233-47-6(2)) Lerner Publishing Group.

Kato, Etsuo. The King Who Saved the Dove. Yasui, Koji, illus. 2014. (J). 8.95 (978-1-935523-68-0(6)) World Tribune Pr.

Koja, Kathe. Buddha Boy. 2004. (ENG.). 128p. (YA). (gr. 7-11). reprint ed. 6.99 (978-0-14-240209-2(5), Speak) Penguin Young Readers Group.

—Buddha Boy. 2004. 117p. (gr. 3-7). 16.00 (978-0-7569-3117-9(7)) Perfection Learning Corp.

Manos, Helen. Samsara Dog. Vivas, Julie, illus. 2007. (ENG.). 40p. (J). (gr. 3-6). 10.99 (978-1-933605-51-7(0)) Kane Miller.

Millhouse, Jackie. The Tiger & the General. Girouard, Patrick, illus. 2007. (J). (978-1-932911-32-9(4)) World Tribune Pr.

Padma, T. V. The Cleverest Thief. 2008. (Story Cove Ser.). (ENG., Illus.). 32p. (J). (gr. -1-3). pap. 4.95 (978-0-87483-882-4(7)) August Hse. Pubs., Inc.

Pandey, Pooja. Little Monk's Buddha. 2015. (ENG.). 100p. pap. 14.95 (978-81-8328-064-8(1)) SCB Distributors.

Sonnenblick, Jordan. Zen & the Art of Faking It. (ENG.). 272p. (J). (gr. 7-12). 2010. 9.99 (978-0-439-83709-5(X), Scholastic Paperbacks) 2007. 16.99 (978-0-439-83707-1(3), Scholastic Pr.) Scholastic, Inc.

Tidwell, Susan. Three Virtuous Brothers: A Story of the Three Acts of Goodness. Tidwell, Susan, illus. 2012. (Illus.). 47p. (J). pap. 9.95 (978-1-932293-63-0(9)) Buddha's Light Publications USA Corp.

Whitfield, Peter. Bruno Dreams of Ice Cream. Bevington, Nancy, illus. 2005. (Zen Tails Ser.). (ENG.). 28p. (J). (gr. k-3). 15.95 (978-1-894965-21-7(3)) Simply Read Bks. CAN. Dist: Ingram Publisher Services.

BUDGERIGARS

Alderton, David. How to Look after Your Budgie: A Practical Guide to Caring for Your Pet, in Step-By-Step Photographs. 2014. (ENG., Illus.). 20p. (J). (gr. k-5). 8.99 (978-1-86147-326-4(5), Armadillo) Anness Publishing GBR. Dist: National Bk. Network.

Kalman, Bobbie. Les Perruches. 2012. (FRE., Illus.). 32p. (J). pap. 9.95 (978-2-89579-438-7(3)) Bayard Canada CAN. Dist: Crabtree Publishing Co.

MacAulay, Kelley & Kalman, Bobbie. Parakeets. 2004. (Pet Care Ser.). (ENG., Illus.). 32p. (J). pap. (978-0-7787-1789-8(5)); lib. bdg. (978-0-7787-1757-7(7)) Crabtree Publishing Co.

Thomas, Isabel. Beaky's Guide to Caring for Your Bird, 1 vol. Peterson, Rick, illus. 2014. (Pets' Guides). (ENG.). 32p. (gr. 1-3). pap. 8.29 (978-1-4846-0266-9(8)); 27.32 (978-1-4846-0259-1(5)) Heinemann-Raintree. (Heinemann First Library).

BUDGERIGARS—FICTION

Wright, Joan M. Flo: A Very Special Budgie. 2010. (ENG., Illus.). 48p. pap. (978-1-84748-792-6(0)) Athena Pr.

BUDGETS, HOUSEHOLD

see Home Economics—Accounting

BUDGETS, PERSONAL

see Finance, Personal

BUFFALO, AMERICAN

see Bison

BUFFALO BILL, 1846-1917

Bair, Diane. Western Legends & Leyendas del Oeste: 6 English, 6 Spanish Adaptations. 2011. (ENG & SPA.). (J). 101.00 net. (978-1-4108-5735-4(2)) Benchmark Education Co.

Buffalo Bill Cody. 2010. (Legends of the Wild West Ser.). (Illus.). 136p. (gr. 6-12). 35.00 (978-1-60413-528-2(X), Chelsea Hse.) Facts On File, Inc.

Davidson, Mary Richmond. Buffalo Bill: Wild West Showman. Savitt, Sam, illus. 2011. 80p. 37.95 (978-1-258-01669-2(9)) Literary Licensing, LLC.

Fleming, Candace. Presenting Buffalo Bill: The Man Who Invented the Wild West. 2016. (ENG., Illus.). 288p. (J). 19.99 (978-1-59643-763-0(4), 9781596437630) Roaring Brook Pr.

Goodman, Michael E. Buffalo Bill. 2005. (Legends of the West (Creative Education) Ser.). (Illus.). 48p. (J). (gr. 5-9). lib. bdg. 21.95 (978-1-58341-336-4(7), Creative Education) Creative Co., The.

Kolars, Frank. The Long Trail: The Story of Buffalo Bill. Micale, Albert, illus. 2011. 190p. 42.95 (978-1-258-05136-5(2)) Literary Licensing, LLC.

Sanford, William R. & Green, Carl R. Buffalo Bill Cody: Courageous Wild West Showman. 2012. (Courageous Heroes of the American West Ser.). (Illus.). 48p. (J). pap. 8.95 (978-1-4644-0090-2(3)); (gr. 5-18). 22.60 (978-0-7660-4007-6(0)) Enslow Pubs., Inc.

Spies, Karen Bornemann. Buffalo Bill Cody: Legend of the Wild West. 2015. (Legendary American Biographies Ser.). 96p. (J). (gr. 6-12). 27.94 (978-0-7660-6450-8(6)); pap. 10.95 (978-0-7660-6451-5(4)) Enslow Pubs., Inc.

Warren, Andrea. The Boy Who Became Buffalo Bill: Growing up Billy Cody in Bleeding Kansas, 0 vols. 2015. (ENG., Illus.). 256p. (J). 19.99 (978-1-4778-2718-5(8), 9781477827185, Two Lions) Amazon Publishing.

BUFFALOES

Here are entered works on buffaloes of the eastern hemisphere. Works on the American buffalo are entered under American bison.

Barnett, Tracy. The Buffalo Soldiers. 2004. (History of the Old West Ser.). (Illus.). 64p. (YA). (gr. 5-18). lib. bdg. 19.95 (978-1-59084-072-6(0)) Mason Crest.

Boddington, Craig. Buffalo! 2010. (ENG.). 248p. 39.95 (978-1-57157-354-4(2)) Safari Pr., Inc.

Borgert-Spaniol, Megan. Cape Buffalo. 2014. (Animal Safari Ser.). (ENG.). 24p. (J). (gr. k-3). lib. bdg. 25.95 (978-1-60014-965-8(0), Blastoff! Readers) Bellwether Media.

Group/McGraw-Hill, Wright. Spider & Buffalo: Level N, 6 vols. (Summer Skies Ser.). 128p. (gr. 3-6). 36.95 (978-0-322-05887-3(2)) Wright Group/McGraw-Hill.

Lawson, Cheri. Chip the Buffalo: Based on a True Story. Lawson, J., illus. Beerntsen, Tammy, photos by. 2006. 32p. (J). lib. bdg. 14.95 (978-1-930580-61-9(4), Luminary Media Group) Pine Orchard, Inc.

Meister, Cari. Do You Really Want to Meet a Cape Buffalo? Fabbri, Daniele, illus. 2015. (Do You Really Want to Meet ... ? Ser.). (ENG.). 24p. (J). (gr. 1-3). 19.95 (978-1-60753-738-0(9)) Amicus Publishing.

Owings, Lisa. The Cape Buffalo. 2012. (Nature's Deadliest Ser.). (ENG., Illus.). 24p. (J). (gr. 3-8). lib. bdg. 25.95 (978-1-60014-741-8(0), Pilot Bks.) Bellwether Media.

—The Cape Buffalo. 2012. (ENG., Illus.). 24p. 23.00 (978-0-531-20880-9(X), Children's Pr.) Scholastic Library Publishing.

Whelan, Piper. Water Buffalo. 2016. (J). **(978-1-4896-5384-0(8))** Weigl Pubs., Inc.

BUFFALOES—FICTION

Derib, et al. Yakari & the White Buffalo. 2007. (Yakari Ser.: 2). (ENG., Illus.). 48p. (J). (gr. 4-7). per. 11.95 (978-1-905460-05-2(8)) CineBook GBR. Dist: National Bk. Network.

Eash, Sara. Adeline. 2011. 28p. pap. 15.99 (978-1-4568-7099-7(8)) Xlibris Corp.

Eichler, Ken. Swift Eagle's Odyssey with the Buffalo. 2007. 59p. pap. 16.95 (978-1-60474-199-5(6)) America Star Bks.

Hankey, Wilbur. Skinny the Bull: As Told to Me by Grandpa. 2009. 16p. pap. 8.49 (978-1-4389-4619-1(8)) AuthorHouse.

Kienzle, Ed. The Last Buffalo. 2013. (ENG.). 214p. (YA). 29.95 (978-1-4787-0802-5(6)); pap. 13.95 (978-1-4787-0944-2(8)) Outskirts Pr., Inc.

Lee, Evelyn. Buffalo Prairie. Brauckmann-Towns, Krista, illus. 2005. (Amazing Animal Adventures Ser.). (ENG.). 36p. (J). (gr. -1-2). 2.95 (978-1-59249-434-7(X), S7160); 15.95 (978-1-59249-432-3(3), B7110); pap. 6.95 (978-1-59249-433-0(1), S7110) Soundprints.

Meyers, Haily & Meyers, Kevin. Gotta Go, Buffalo: The Goodbye Book, 1 vol. 2017. (ENG., Illus.). 20p. (J). 12.99 (978-1-4236-4598-6(7)) Gibbs Smith, Publisher.

Moore, P. B. The Day the Buffalo Ran. 2008. 48p. pap. 16.95 (978-1-60563-461-6(1)) America Star Bks.

Olson, Lute. Hello, Wilbur! De Angel, M., illus. 2007. 24p. (J). lib. bdg. 14.95 (978-1-932888-40-9(3)) Mascot Bks., Inc.

Ross, Patrick. Oliver: The Great Escape. Burcham, David, illus. 2009. 34p. pap. 24.95 (978-1-60749-151-4(6)) America Star Bks.

Santillo, LuAnn. The Big Hunt. Santillo, LuAnn, ed. 2003. (Half-Pint Kids Readers Ser.). (Illus.). 7p. (J). (gr. -1-1). pap. 1.00 (978-1-59256-076-9(8)) Half-Pint Kids, Inc.

Sargent, Dave, et al. A Strand of Wampum Vol. 2: Be Honest, 20 vols. Lenoir, Sue, illus. l.t. ed. 2003. (Story Keeper Ser.: 2). 42p. (J). pap. 10.95 (978-1-56763-906-3(2)) Ozark Publishing.

—A Strand of Wampum Vol. 2: Be Honest, 20 vols. Lenoir, Jane, illus. l.t. ed. 2003. (Story Keeper Ser.: 2). 42p. (J). lib. bdg. 23.60 (978-1-56763-905-6(4)) Ozark Publishing.

Stone, Judith. Billie the Buffalo Goes to Great Sand Dunes National Park. 2009. 24p. pap. 15.95 (978-1-4490-1495-7(X)) AuthorHouse.

—Billie the Buffalo Goes to Town. 2008. 20p. pap. 12.95 (978-1-4389-2877-7(7)) AuthorHouse.

The Tiger's Stripes & the Water Buffalo's Teeth. 2010. 40p. 19.57 (978-1-4269-3110-9(7)) Trafford Publishing.

Vernick, Audrey. Is Your Buffalo Ready for Kindergarten? Jennewein, Daniel, illus. 2010. (ENG.). 32p. (J). (gr. -1-3). 16.99 (978-0-06-176275-8(X)) HarperCollins Pubs.

—Teach Your Buffalo to Play Drums. Jennewein, Daniel, illus. 2011. (ENG.). 32p. (J). (gr. -1-3). 16.99 (978-0-06-176253-6(9)) HarperCollins Pubs.

BUFFY, THE VAMPIRE SLAYER (FICTITIOUS CHARACTER)—FICTION

Beyer, Kirsten. One Thing or Your Mother. 2008. (Buffy the Vampire Slayer Ser.). (ENG.). 240p. (YA). (gr. 8-12). mass mkt. 6.99 (978-1-4169-3632-9(7)) Pocket Books.

Brereton, Dan, et al. Buffy the Vampire Slayer Omnibus, 7 vols., Vol. 1. Golden, Christopher, illus. 2007. (Buffy the Vampire Slayer Ser.). (ENG.). 408p. pap. 24.99 (978-1-59307-784-6(X)) Dark Horse Comics.

Goddard, Drew, et al. No Future for You, 8 vols., Vol. 2. Jeanty, Georges et al, illus. 2008. (Buffy the Vampire Slayer Ser.). (ENG.). 320p. pap. 15.99 (978-1-59307-963-5(X)) Dark Horse Comics.

Golden, Christopher, illus. Omnibus, 7 vols., Vol. 4. 2008. (ENG.). 408p. pap. 24.95 (978-1-59307-968-0(0)) Dark Horse Comics.

Jeanty, Georges, et al. The Core, Vol. 5. Allie, Scott & Hahn, Sierra, eds. 2014. (ENG., Illus.). 168p. pap. 17.99 (978-1-61655-254-1(9)) Dark Horse Comics.

BUGLE—FICTION

Kimpton, Paul & Kimpton, Ann Kaczkowski. Starting Early: A Boy & His Bugle in America During WWII. 2011. (Adventures with Music Ser.: 1). (ENG., Illus.). 204p. (J). (gr. 4-7). pap. 8.95 (978-1-57999-805-9(4)) G I A Pubns., Inc.

BUGS

see Insects

BUGS BUNNY (FICTITIOUS CHARACTER)—FICTION

Carrotblanca. Date not set. (J). 7.98 incl. audio (978-1-57042-320-8(2)) Warner Brothers Records.

Cox, Tracey M. Liddil Gets Her Light. Ruble, Eugene, illus. 2011. 16p. pap. 9.95 (978-1-61633-151-1(8)) Guardian Angel Publishing, Inc.

Granny Vanishes. 2008. (Looney Tunes 8*8 Ser.). 24p. pap. (978-1-4075-2641-6(3)); pap. (978-1-4075-2631-7(6)) Parragon, Inc.

Jewel Robbery. 2008. (Looney Tunes 8*8 Ser.). 24p. pap. (978-1-4075-2632-4(4)); pap. (978-1-4075-2642-3(1)) Parragon, Inc.

BUILDING

see also Architecture; Carpentry; Engineering; Masonry

Adamson, Heather. A Day in the Life of a Construction Worker, 1 vol. 2004. (Community Helpers at Work Ser.). (ENG., Illus.). 24p. (gr. 1-2). 25.32 (978-0-7368-2505-4(3), First Facts) Capstone Press of Coughlan Cos.

Albee, Sarah. Poop Happened! A History of the World from the Bottom Up. Leighton, Robert, illus. 2010. (ENG.). 176p. (YA). (gr. 5-9). pap. 18.99 (978-0-8027-2077-1(3), 9780802720771, Bloomsbury USA Childrens) Bloomsbury Publishing USA.

Anderson, Jenna. How It Happens at the Building Site. Wolfe, Bob & Wolfe, Diane, photos by. 2004. (How It Happens Ser.). (Illus.). 32p. (J). (gr. 2-5). lib. bdg. 19.95 (978-1-881508-95-3(1)) Oliver Pr., Inc.

Anderson, Scoular. Sticks & Bricks & Bits of Stone White Band. 2016. (Cambridge Reading Adventures Ser.). (ENG.). 32p. pap. 7.81 (978-1-107-56056-7(X)) Cambridge Univ. Pr.

Arbogast, Joan Marie. Buildings in Disguise: Architecture That Looks Like Animals, Food, & Other Things. 2010. (ENG.). 48p. (J). (gr. 2-4). pap. 12.95 (978-1-59078-824-0(9), Calkins Creek) Boyds Mills Pr.

Arnold, Quinn M. Seedlings: Construction Workers. 2017. (J). **(978-1-60818-871-0(X)**, Creative Education) Creative Co., The.

Bailey, Gerry. Working Homes. Dreidemy, Joëlle et al, illus. 2013. (ENG.). 32p. (J). (978-0-7787-0290-0(1)) Crabtree Publishing Co.

Baker, Theo. Hard Hat Zone. 2014. (Penguin Core Concepts Ser.). (ENG., Illus.). 32p. (J). (gr. -1-k). 3.99 (978-0-448-47923-1(0), Grosset & Dunlap) Penguin Young Readers Group.

Biard, Philippe. Construir. (Coleccion Mundo Maravilloso). (SPA., Illus.). (J). (gr. 2-4). (978-84-348-5208-2(X), SM8405) SM Ediciones.

Blane, Francisco. Buildings Around Town: Lap Book. 2009. (My First Reader's Theater Set B Ser.). (J). 28.00 (978-1-4108-8538-8(0)) Benchmark Education Co.

Blankenbaker, E. Keith. Construction & Building Technology. 2012. (ENG.). 656p. (gr. 9-12). 93.28 (978-1-60525-810-2(5)) Goodheart-Willcox Pub.

Borth, Teddy. Buildings on the Farm, 1 vol. 2014. (On the Farm Ser.). (ENG.). 24p. (J). (gr. 4-8). lib. bdg. 28.50 (978-1-62970-051-9(7)) ABDO Publishing Co.

Borth, Teddy, et al. Construcciones de la Granja. 2015. (En la Granja Ser.). (SPA., Illus.). 24p. (gr. k-1). pap. 7.95 (978-1-4966-0445-3(8)) Capstone Classroom.

Brasch, Nicolas. Triumphs of Engineering. 2012. (Discovery Education: Technology Ser.). (ENG., Illus.). 32p. (J). (gr. 3-6). 25.25 (978-1-4488-7887-1(X)); pap. 10.00 (978-1-4488-7969-4(8)) Rosen Publishing Group, Inc., The. (PowerKids Pr.).

Bruce, Julia. Conquest! Can You Build a Roman City? Dennis, Peter, illus. 2009. (Step into History Ser.). 32p. (J). (gr. 2-5). lib. bdg. 23.94 (978-0-7660-3478-5(X)) Enslow Pubs., Inc.

Building. (Make it Work Ser.). 42p. (J). (gr. 4-8). pap. (978-1-882210-45-9(X)) Action Publishing, Inc.

Business & Construction. 2010. (Green Careers Ser.). (Illus.). 160p. (C). (gr. 9-18). 32.95 (978-0-8160-8149-3(2), Ferguson Publishing Co.) Facts On File, Inc.

Butterfield, Moira & Greathead, Helen. Superstats - Structures. 2016. (Superstats Ser.). (ENG.). 64p. (J). (gr. 2-4). 11.99 (978-1-4998-0241-2(2)) Little Bee Books Inc.

Byers, Ann. Jobs As Green Builders & Planners. 2010. (Green Careers Ser.). 80p. (YA). (gr. 7-12). E-Book 61.20 (978-1-4488-0131-2(1)) Rosen Publishing Group, Inc., The.

Chambers, Mary & Meinking, Mary. Who Swings the Wrecking Ball? Working on a Construction Site. 2010. (Wild Work Ser.). (ENG.). 32p. (gr. 1-2). 29.99 (978-1-4109-3854-1(9), Read Me!) Heinemann-Raintree.

Chapmann, Helen. Shapes & Scapes. 2007. (Action Numeracy Middle Primary Ser.). 32p. pap. 9.95 (978-0-86431-622-6(4)) ACER Pr. AUS. Dist: ISBS Publisher Services.

Construction. 5th rev. ed. 2010. (Careers in Focus Ser.). (Illus.). 208p. (gr. 6-12). 32.95 (978-0-8160-8018-2(6), Ferguson Publishing Co.) Facts On File, Inc.

Craats, Rennay. Construction. 2016. (J). **(978-1-5105-2233-6(6))** SmartBook Media, Inc.

—Construction. 2008. (Science Q & A Ser.). (Illus.). 48p. (YA). (gr. 5-8). pap. 10.95 (978-1-59036-957-9(2)); lib. bdg. 29.05 (978-1-59036-956-2(4)) Weigl Pubs., Inc.

—Construction Q & A. 2013. (J). (978-1-62127-412-4(8)); pap. (978-1-62127-418-6(7)) Weigl Pubs., Inc.

Crabtree Staff & Solway, Andrew. Civil Engineering & the Science of Structures. 2012. (ENG., Illus.). 32p. (J). pap. (978-0-7787-7501-0(1)) Crabtree Publishing Co.

Dahl, Michael. Un Gran Edificio: Un Libro para Contar Sobre Construcción. Ouren, Todd, illus. 2010. (Apréndete Tus Números/Know Your Numbers Ser.).Tr. of One Big Building - A Counting Book about Construction. (ENG, SPA & MUL.). 24p. (gr. -1-2). lib. bdg. 26.65 (978-1-4048-6294-4(3)) Picture Window Bks.

—One Big Building: A Counting Book about Construction, 1 vol. Ouren, Todd, illus. 2004. (Know Your Numbers Ser.). (ENG.). 24p. (gr. -1-2). per. 8.95 (978-1-4048-1120-1(6)) Picture Window Bks.

Deedrick, Tami. Construction Workers Help, 1 vol. 2014. (Our Community Helpers Ser.). (ENG.). 24p. (gr. k-1). lib. bdg. 21.99 (978-1-4765-3950-8(2), Pebble Bks.) Capstone Press of Coughlan Cos.

Dillon, Patrick. The Story of Buildings: From the Pyramids to the Sydney Opera House & Beyond. Biesty, Stephen, illus. 2014. (ENG.). 96p. (J). (gr. 4-7). 19.99 (978-0-7636-6990-4(3)) Candlewick Pr.

Dorling Kindersley Publishing Staff. My Best Pop-Up Construction Site Book. 2016. (ENG., Illus.). 18p. (J). (-k). bds. 14.99 (978-1-4654-5391-4(1), DK Children) Dorling Kindersley Publishing, Inc.

Ellison, Nora. A Trip to the Construction Site. 2016. (PowerKids Readers: My Community Ser.). 00024p. (J). (gr. k-k). pap. 8.25 (978-1-4994-2780-6(8), PowerKids Pr.) Rosen Publishing Group, Inc., The.

Enz, Tammy. Building Structures & Towers. 2017. (Young Engineers Ser.). (ENG., Illus.). 32p. (gr. 1-2). lib. bdg. 27.32 (978-1-4846-3746-3(1), Heinemann First Library) Heinemann-Raintree.

—Super Cool Construction Activities with Max Axiom. Baez, Marcelo, illus. 2015. (Max Axiom Science & Engineering Activities Ser.). (ENG.). 32p. (gr. 3-4). lib. bdg. 30.65 (978-1-4914-2078-2(2), Graphic Library) Capstone Press of Coughlan Cos.

Friend, Robyn C. & Cohen, Judith Love. A Clean City: The Green Construction Story. 2008. (Illus.). 44p. (J). pap. 7.00 (978-1-880599-84-6(8)) Cascade Pass, Inc.

Friend, Robyn C. & cohen, Judith Love. A Clean City: The Green Construction Story. 2008. (Illus.). 44p. (J). 13.95 (978-1-880599-85-3(6)) Cascade Pass, Inc.

Gerstein, Mordicai. The Man Who Walked Between the Towers. 2007. (J). 18.40 (978-1-4177-7491-3(6), Turtleback) Turtleback Bks.

Ghione, Yvette & Gagnon, Celeste, creators. This Is Daniel Cook at the Construction Site. 2007. (This Is Daniel Cook Ser.). (ENG., Illus.). 24p. (J). (gr. -1-1). 4.95 (978-1-55453-084-7(9)) Kids Can Pr., Ltd. CAN. Dist: Hachette Bk. Group.

Gonzales, Doreen. What Are the 7 Wonders of the Modern World? 2013. (What Are the Seven Wonders of the World? Ser.). 48p. (J). (gr. 4-10). pap. 8.95 (978-1-4644-0231-9(0)); 25.27 (978-0-7660-4152-3(2)) Enslow Pubs., Inc.

Graham, Ian. Megastructures: Tallest, Longest, Biggest, Deepest. 2012. (ENG., Illus.). 128p. (J). (gr. 2-4). 19.95 (978-1-77085-111-5(9), 9781770851115) Firefly Bks., Ltd.

Gregoire, Maryellen. Structures. 2011. (Wonder Readers Early Level Ser.). (ENG.). (gr. -1-1). 16p. pap. 35.94 (978-1-4296-8160-5(8)); 32p. pap. 5.99 (978-1-4296-7835-3(6)) Capstone Press of Coughlan Cos. (Wonder Readers).

Gregory, Josh. Minecraft: Guide to Building. 2017. (21st Century Skills Innovation Library: Unofficial Guides). (ENG., Illus.). 32p. (J). (gr. 4-8). lib. bdg. 29.93 (978-1-63472-195-0(0), 209352) Cherry Lake Publishing.

Greve, Meg. From Empty Lot to Building. 2015. (ENG.). 24p. (gr. k-2). 28.50 (978-1-63430-059-9(9)) Rourke Educational Media.

Griffiths, Rachel. Why Do Bridges Arch? Level 3 Factbook. 2010. (Cambridge Young Readers Ser.). (ENG., Illus.). 16p. pap. 6.00 (978-0-521-13717-1(9)) Cambridge Univ. Pr.

Grossartige Bauwerke. (GER., Illus.). 40p. (978-3-411-08151-6(1)) Bibliographisches Institut & F. A. Brockhaus AG DEU. Dist: i. b. d., Ltd.

Hanson, Anders & Mann, Elissa. Cool Structures: Creative Activities That Make Math & Science Fun for Kids!, 1 vol. 2013. (Cool Art with Math & Science Ser.). (ENG.). 32p. (J). (gr. 3-6). lib. bdg. 28.50 (978-1-61783-825-5(X), Checkerboard Library) ABDO Publishing Co.

Harris, Nicholas. A Year at a Construction Site. 2008. (Time Goes By Ser.). (Illus.). 24p. (J). (gr. k-3). lib. bdg. 22.60 (978-1-58013-549-8(8)) Lerner Publishing Group.

Harrison, Nicholas. A Year at a Construction Site. 2009. (Time Goes By Ser.). (ENG.). (gr. k-3). pap. 39.62 (978-0-7613-4712-5(7)) Lerner Publishing Group.

Haslam, Andrew, et al. Building. (Make It Work! Ser.). (Illus.). 48p. (J). pap. 7.99 (978-0-590-24616-3(X)) Scholastic, Inc.

Hearst, Michael. Curious Constructions: A Peculiar Portfolio of Fifty Fascinating Structures. Johnstone, Matt, illus. 2017. (ENG.). 112p. (J). 19.99 (978-1-4521-4484-9(2)) Chronicle Bks. LLC.

Heos, Bridget. Let's Meet a Construction Worker. Moran, Mike, illus. 2013. (Cloverleaf Books — Community Helpers Ser.). (ENG.). 24p. (gr. k-2). (J). lib. bdg. 23.93 (978-0-7613-9023-7(5)); pap. 6.95 (978-1-4677-0799-2(6)) Lerner Publishing Group. (Millbrook Pr.).

Highlights for Children Editorial Staff, creator. Find It! at the Construction Site. 2016. (Highlights(tm) Find It! Padded Board Bks.). (ENG., Illus.). 14p. (J). (— 1). bds. 8.99 (978-1-62979-705-2(7), Highlights) Boyds Mills Pr.

Holland, Trish. Build It from A to Z. 2010. (J). (978-1-60617-136-3(4)) Teaching Strategies, LLC.

Hudson, Cheryl Willis. Construction Zone. Sobol, Richard, illus. 2017. (ENG.). 32p. (J). (gr. -1-3). 6.99 **(978-0-7636-9344-2(8))** Candlewick Pr.

Ipcizade, Catherine. BIG Buildings. 2010. (Big Ser.). (ENG.). 24p. (gr. k-1). lib. bdg. 26.65 (978-1-4296-3994-1(6), Pebble Plus) Capstone Press of Coughlan Cos.

Isaacson, Philip M. Round Buildings, Square Buildings, & Buildings That Wiggle Like a Fish. 2016. (ENG., Illus.). 128p. (YA). (gr. 7). pap. 15.99 (978-1-101-93320-6(8), Ember) Random Hse. Children's Bks.

Jackson, Tom. Buildings & Structures. 2012. (FAYFT: Invention & Technology Ser.). 64p. (gr. 4-10). lib. bdg. 39.95 (978-1-936333-38-7(4)) Brown Bear Bks.

Jones, Rob Lloyd. See Inside Famous Buildings. Ablett, Barry, illus. 2009. (See Inside Board Bks). 16p. (J). (gr. 2). bds. 13.99 (978-0-7945-2350-3(1), Usborne) EDC Publishing.

Kalman, Bobbie. ¿Qué Son Las Estructuras Naturales? 2009. (SPA.). 24p. (J). (978-0-7787-8701-3(X)); pap. (978-0-7787-8740-2(0)) Crabtree Publishing Co.

Kenah, Katharine. Amazing Creations. 2006. (Extreme Readers: Level 2 Ser.). (Illus.). 32p. (gr. 4-7). 13.95 (978-0-7569-6844-1(5)) Perfection Learning Corp.

Klobuchar, Lisa. How Did They Do That? 2005. (Real Deal Ser.). (Illus.). 32p. (J). pap. (978-0-7608-9633-4(X)) Sundance/Newbridge Educational Publishing.

Knight, Margy Burns. Talking Walls: Discover Your World. O'Brien, Anne Sibley, illus. 2014. (ENG.). 64p. (gr. 2-7). 18.95 (978-0-88448-356-4(8), 884356) Tilbury Hse. Pubs.

Lambert, George J. There's a Barn up Ahead, There's a Barn! 2012. 36p. pap. 24.95 (978-1-4626-6884-7(4)) America Star Bks.

Landau, Elaine. The Statue of Liberty. 2008. (True Bks.). (ENG., Illus.). 48p. (J). (gr. 4-6). pap. 6.95 (978-0-531-14785-6(1), Children's Pr.) Scholastic Library Publishing.

Lassieur, Allison. Building the Empire State Building: An Interactive Engineering Adventure, 1 vol. 2014. (You Choose: Engineering Marvels Ser.). (ENG.). 112p. (gr. 3-4). 31.99 (978-1-4914-0400-3(0), You Choose Bks.) Capstone Press of Coughlan Cos.

Laxton, Laura. The Budding Builder. 2012. (Budding Ser.). (ENG., Illus.). 72p. pap. 9.95 (978-0-87659-381-3(3), Gryphon House Inc) Gryphon Hse., Inc.

Lee, Brian, illus. A Construction Site. 2005. (What's Inside Ser.). (J). (978-0-7607-6570-8(7)) backpackbook.

Litchfield, Jo & Brooks, Felicity. Building Site. 2004. (Chunky Board Bks.). (ENG., Illus.). 6p. (J). bds. 4.95 (978-0-7945-0347-5(0), Usborne) EDC Publishing.

Luxbacher, Irene. 123 I Can Build! Luxbacher, Irene, illus. 2009. (Starting Art Ser.). (ENG., Illus.). 24p. (J). (gr. -1-2). 14.95 (978-1-55453-315-2(5)); pap. 6.95 (978-1-55453-316-9(3)) Kids Can Pr., Ltd. CAN. Dist: Hachette Bk. Group.

Macaulay, David. City: A Story of Roman Planning & Construction. 2012. 21.00 (978-1-61383-577-7(9)) Perfection Learning Corp.

Marsico, Katie. Levels. 2013. (21st Century Junior Library: Basic Tools Ser.). (ENG.). 24p. (J). (gr. 2-5). 25.64 (978-1-62431-172-7(5), 203008); pap. 12.79 (978-1-62431-304-2(3), 203010) Cherry Lake Publishing.

Mason, Adrienne. Build It! Structures, Systems & You. Dávila, Claudia, illus. 2006. (Primary Physical Science Ser.). (ENG.). 32p. (J). (gr. -1-2). 7.95 (978-1-55337-836-5(9)) Kids Can Pr., Ltd. CAN. Dist: Hachette Bk. Group.

Mattern, Joanne. Built to Last. 2011. (ENG., Illus.). 48p. (gr. 4-6). pap. 10.95 (978-1-61741-989-8(3)) Rourke Educational Media.

McGill, Jordan. Buildings: Arabic-English Bilingual Edition. 2016. (Community Helpers Ser.). (ENG.). (J). (gr. -1-3). 29.99 (978-1-61913-901-5(4)) Weigl Pubs., Inc.

—Edificios. 2012. (SPA.). (J). (978-1-61913-208-5(7)) Weigl Pubs., Inc.

Meachen Rau, Dana. Builders. 2007. (Tools We Use Ser.). (Illus.). 31p. (J). (gr. -1-3). lib. bdg. 22.79 (978-0-7614-2656-1(6), Benchmark Bks.) Marshall Cavendish Corp.

—Builders/Los Contructores. 2007. (Tools We Use/Instrumentos de Trabajo Ser.). (SPA & ENG., Illus.). 32p. (gr. k-2). lib. bdg. 15.95 (978-0-7614-2821-3(6), Benchmark Bks.) Marshall Cavendish Corp.

—Los Constructores. 2007. (Instrumentos de Trabajo Ser.). (SPA., Illus.). 32p. (gr. k-2). lib. bdg. 15.95 (978-0-7614-2797-1(X), Benchmark Bks.) Marshall Cavendish Corp.

Meister, Cari. Totally Amazing Facts about Stuff We've Built. 2017. (Mind Benders Ser.). (ENG.). 112p. (gr. 1-3). lib. bdg. 23.32 (978-1-5157-4753-6(0)) Capstone Press of Coughlan Cos.

Michele, Tracey. Old Buildings, New Buildings. 2011. (Learn-Abouts Ser.). (Illus.). 16p. (J). pap. 7.95 (978-1-59920-591-5(2)) Black Rabbit Bks.

Moskal, Greg. Modern Buildings: Identifying Bilateral & Rotational Symmetry & Transformations. 2009. (PowerMath: Proficiency Ser.). 32p. (gr. 4-5). 47.90 (978-1-60851-397-0(1), PowerKids Pr.) Rosen Publishing Group, Inc., The.

Mullins, Matt. How Did They Build That? Stadium. 2009. (Community Connections: How Did They Build That? Ser.). (ENG.). 24p. (gr. 2-5). lib. bdg. 25.64 (978-1-60279-489-4(8), 200259) Cherry Lake Publishing.

Nelson, Robin. Del Cemento Al Puente. Translations.com Staff, tr. from ENG. 2006. (De Principio a Fin (Start to Finish) Ser.). (SPA., Illus.). 24p. (gr. 3-5). lib. bdg. 19.93 (978-0-8225-6498-0(X), Ediciones Lerner) Lerner Publishing Group.

—From Tree to House. 2004. (Start to Finish Ser.). (J). pap. 5.95 (978-0-8225-2147-1(4)) Lerner Publishing Group.

—From Tree to House. Donaldson, Stephen G., photos by. 2004. (Start to Finish Ser.). (Illus.). 24p. (J). (gr. -1-3). lib. bdg. 18.60 (978-0-8225-1392-6(7), Lerner Pubns.) Lerner Publishing Group.

O'Connor, Rachel. Construction Worker. 2004. (Great Jobs Ser.). (ENG., Illus.). 48p. (J). 24.50 (978-0-516-24089-3(7), Children's Pr.) Scholastic Library Publishing.

Oxlade, Chris. Constructions for Towering Intellects. (Illus.). 128p. (J). pap. 8.99 (978-0-340-68994-3(3)) Hodder & Stoughton GBR. Dist: Trafalgar Square Publishing.

Pallotta, Jerry. The Construction Alphabet Book. Bolster, Rob, illus. 2006. (Jerry Pallotta's Alphabet Bks.). (ENG.). 32p. (J). (gr. -1-3). lib. bdg. 17.95 (978-1-57091-437-9(0)); per. 7.95 (978-1-57091-438-6(9)) Charlesbridge Publishing, Inc.

Pallotta, Jerry & Bolster, Rob. The Construction Alphabet. 2017. (ENG., Illus.). 28p. (J). (— 1). bds. 7.99 (978-1-57091-799-8(X)) Charlesbridge Publishing, Inc.

Parker, Janice. The Science of Structures. 2003. (Living Science Ser.). (Illus.). 32p. (J). (gr. 1-3). pap. 9.95 (978-1-930954-26-7(3)) Weigl Pubs., Inc.

Parker, Steve. On the Building Site. 2010. (J). 28.50 (978-1-59920-288-4(3)) Black Rabbit Bks.

Pattrick, Steve. Building: KinderFacts Individual Title Six-Packs. (Kinderstarters Ser.). 8p. (gr. -1-1). 21.00 (978-0-7635-8742-0(7)) Rigby Education.

Petruccio, Steven James. At the Construction Site. 2004. (Dover Coloring Bks.). (ENG., Illus.). 32p. (J). (gr. -1-3). pap. 3.99 (978-0-486-43661-6(6)) Dover Pubns., Inc.

Phidal Publishing Staff, ed. Construction Crew, 3 vols. 2004. (Read & Roll Ser.). (Illus.). 10p. (J). bds. (978-2-7643-0208-8(8)) Phidal Publishing, Inc./Editions Phidal, Inc.

Price, Jane. Underworld: Exploring the Secret World Beneath Your Feet, 0 vols. Hancock, James Gulliver, illus. 2014. (ENG.). 96p. (J). (gr. 3-7). 18.95 (978-1-894786-89-8(0)) Kids Can Pr., Ltd. CAN. Dist: Hachette Bk. Group.

Rau, Dana Meachen. Builders. 2007. (J). pap. 6.99 (978-0-7614-3289-0(2)) Marshall Cavendish Corp.

—Pyramid. 2007. (J). pap. 6.99 (978-0-7614-3302-6(3)) Marshall Cavendish Corp.

Rhatigan, Joe. Get a Job at the Construction Site. 2016. (Bright Futures Press: Get a Job Ser.). (ENG., Illus.). 32p. (J). (gr. 4-6). 29.93 (978-1-63471-904-9(2), 208937) Cherry Lake Publishing.

Richards, Jon & Simkins, Ed. Record-Breaking Building Feats. 2015. (Infographic Top 10s Ser.). (ENG.). 32p. (J). (gr. 4-6). 26.65 (978-1-4677-8594-5(6)) Lerner Publishing Group.

Ritchie, Scot. Look at That Building: A First Book of Structures. Ritchie, Scot, illus. 2011. (ENG., Illus.). 32p. (J). (gr. -1-2). 16.95 (978-1-55453-696-2(0)) Kids Can Pr., Ltd. CAN. Dist: Hachette Bk. Group.

Roeder, Annette. 13 Buildings Children Should Know. 2009. (ENG., Illus.). 48p. (J). (gr. 3-7). 14.95 (978-3-7913-4171-2(5)) Prestel Verlag GmbH & Co KG. DEU. Dist: Penguin Random Hse. LLC.

Rosen, Michael J. Place Hacking: Venturing off Limits. 2015. (Illus.). 72p. (J). (978-1-4677-6311-0(X)) Twenty First Century Bks.

Rosen, Michael J. & Kassoy, Ben. Crazy Buildings. Jones, Doug, illus. 2013. (No Way! Ser.). (ENG.). 32p. (gr. 3-5). lib. bdg. 26.60 (978-0-7613-8986-6(5), Millbrook Pr.) Lerner Publishing Group.

Sandvold, Lynnette Brent. Revolution in Construction. 2009. (It Works! Ser.). 32p. (gr. 3). 28.50 (978-0-7614-4378-0(9)) Marshall Cavendish Corp.

Schuh, Mari. Community Helpers at the Construction Site. 2016. (Community Helpers on the Scene Ser.). (ENG., Illus.). 24p. (gr. k-1). lib. bdg. 21.99 (978-1-5157-2401-8(8), Pebble Bks.) Capstone Press of Coughlan Cos.

Shofner, Melissa Raé. Earthquake-Proof Buildings. 2016. (Technology Takes on Nature Ser.). 00032p. (J). pap. 10.50 (978-1-4824-5767-4(9)) Stevens, Gareth Publishing LLLP.

Solway, Andrew. Buildings & Structures, 1 vol. 2011. (Sci-Hi: Science & Technology Ser.). (ENG.). 48p. (gr. 4-4). pap. 9.95 (978-1-4109-4280-7(5), Sci-Hi) Heinemann-Raintree.

—Civil Engineering & the Science of Structures. 2012. (ENG.). 32p. (J). (978-0-7787-7496-9(1)) Crabtree Publishing Co.

Stamper, Judith Bauer. Buildings, Buildings, Buildings. 2010. (J). (978-1-60617-140-0(2)) Teaching Strategies, LLC.

Stefoff, Rebecca. Soil for Building Materials. 2016. (Science of Soil Ser.). 48p. (J). 31.36 (978-1-5026-2164-1(9)) Cavendish Square Publishing.

Stern, Steven L. Building Green-Scrapers. 2009. (Going Green Ser.). (Illus.). 32p. (YA). (gr. 3-6). lib. bdg. 25.27 (978-1-59716-962-2(5)) Bearport Publishing Co., Inc.

Stiles, David. Forts for Kids. 2011. (ENG., Illus.). 96p. pap. 16.95 (978-0-7627-6453-2(8), Lyons Pr.) Globe Pequot Pr., The.

Stradling, Jan. Buildings for a Purpose: Level K, 6 vols., Vol. 2. (First Explorers Ser.). 24p. (gr. 1-2). 34.95 (978-0-7699-1456-5(X)) Shortland Pubns. (U. S. A.) Inc.

Suen, Anastasia. From Factory to Store. 2015. (ENG.). 24p. (gr. k-2). 28.50 (978-1-63430-060-5(2)) Rourke Educational Media.

Suen, Anastasia & O'Rourke, Ryan. Up! up! up! Skyscraper. 2017. (ENG., Illus.). 32p. (J). (gr. -1-2). lib. bdg. 16.99 (978-1-58089-710-5(X)) Charlesbridge Publishing, Inc.

Sundance/Newbridge LLC Staff. Design It! Build It! 2007. (Early Science Ser.). (gr. k-3). 18.95 (978-1-4007-6603-1(6)); pap. 6.10 (978-1-4007-6599-7(4)) Sundance/Newbridge Educational Publishing.

Taylor, Saranne. Green Homes. Chiacchiera, Moreno & Todd, Michelle, illus. 2014. (ENG.). 32p. (J). (978-0-7787-1452-1(7)) Crabtree Publishing Co.

Verderosa, Laura. In Our Town. 2010. (Sight Word Readers Ser.). (J). 3.49 (978-1-60719-609-9(3)) Newmark Learning LLC.

Way, Steve & Bailey, Gerry. Structures. 2009. (Simply Science Ser.). (Illus.). 32p. (YA). (gr. 3-6). lib. bdg. 26.00 (978-1-4339-0036-5(X)) Stevens, Gareth Publishing LLLP.

Weber, Rebecca. Making a House. 2011. (Early Connections Ser.). (J). (978-1-61672-326-2(2)) Benchmark Education Co.

What Does a Construction Worker Do? 2006. (What Does a Community Helper Do? Ser.). (Illus.). 24p. (J). (gr. -1-3). lib. bdg. 21.26 (978-0-7660-2326-0(5), Enslow Elementary) Enslow Pubs., Inc.

When I Grow Up - Builder. 2016. (When I Grow Up ... Ser.). (ENG., Illus.). 32p. (J). (gr. -1-2). pap. 8.99 **(978-0-7232-9471-9(2))** Penguin Bks., Ltd. GBR. Dist: Independent Pubs. Group.

Whitehouse, Patty. Energia Por Dondequiera / Energy Everywhere. 2006. (Construction Forces Discovery Library). (Illus.). 24p. (J). (gr. k-2). lib. bdg. 22.79 (978-1-60044-274-2(9)) Rourke Educational Media.

Wilkinson, Colin. Using Math in Construction. 2017. (Math You Will Actually Use Ser.). 48p. (J). (gr. 10-10). pap. 11.75 **(978-1-4994-3852-9(4)**, Rosen Central) Rosen Publishing Group, Inc., The.

Wilkinson, Philip & Donati, Paolo. Amazing Buildings. (Illus.). (J). pap. 21.95 (978-0-590-74608-3(1)) Scholastic, Inc.

Winnick, Nick. Green Buildings. 2016. (J). **(978-1-5105-2215-2(8))** SmartBook Media, Inc.

Wolny, Philip. Money-Making Opportunities for Teens Who Are Handy. 2013. (Make Money Now! Ser.). (ENG., Illus.). 80p. (YA). (gr. 7-12). lib. bdg. 33.25 (978-1-4488-9382-9(8), Rosen Classroom) Rosen Publishing Group, Inc., The.

Woods, Mary B. & Woods, Michael. Ancient Construction: From Tents to Towers. 2005. (Ancient Technology Ser.). (Illus.). 96p. (gr. 6-12). 25.26 (978-0-8225-2998-9(X)) Lerner Publishing Group.

Woods, Michael & Woods, Mary B. Ancient Construction Technology: From Pyramids to Fortresses. 2011. (Technology in Ancient Cultures Ser.). (ENG., Illus.). 96p. (J). (gr. 6-12). lib. bdg. 31.93 (978-0-7613-6527-3(3)) Lerner Publishing Group.

Woolf, Alex. Buildings, 1 vol. 2013. (Design & Engineering for STEM Ser.). (ENG., Illus.). 56p. (gr. 6-8). pap. 9.99 (978-1-4329-7034-5(8), NA-h) Heinemann-Raintree.

World Book, Inc. Staff, contrib. by. Adobe Shelters to Steel Skyscrapers: A Timeline of Building. 2016. (J). (978-0-7166-3540-6(2)) World Bk., Inc.

BUILDING—FICTION

Adler, David A. Bones & the Big Yellow Mystery. Newman, Barbara Johansen, illus. 2008. (Puffin Easy-to-Read Ser.). 32p. (gr. k-3). 14.00 (978-0-7569-8914-9(0)) Perfection Learning Corp.

Ashburn, Boni. The Fort That Jack Built. Helquist, Brett, illus. 2013. (ENG.). 32p. (J). (gr. k-2). 18.95 (978-1-4197-0795-7(7), Abrams Bks. for Young Readers) Abrams, Inc.

Avi. The Barn. 2014. (ENG.). 112p. (J). (gr. 3-7). pap. 6.99 (978-0-545-60744-5(2), Scholastic Paperbacks) Scholastic, Inc.

AZ Books Staff. Sam the Builder. Boroda, Janna, ed. 2012. (Little Master Ser.). (ENG.). 10p. (J). (gr. -1-k). bds. 10.95 (978-1-61889-147-1(2)) AZ Bks. LLC.

Barton, Byron. My House. Barton, Byron, illus. 2016. (Illus.). 40p. (J). (gr. -1-3). 16.99 (978-0-06-233703-0(3), Greenwillow Bks.) HarperCollins Pubs.

Bean, Jonathan. Building Our House. Bean, Jonathan, illus. 2013. (ENG., Illus.). 48p. (J). (gr. -1-1). 18.99 (978-0-374-38023-6(6), 9780374380236, Farrar, Straus & Giroux (BYR)) Farrar, Straus & Giroux.

Beaty, Andrea. Iggy Peck, Architect. Roberts, David, illus. 2007. (ENG.). 32p. (J). (gr. k-17). 17.95 (978-0-8109-1106-2(X), Abrams Bks. for Young Readers) Abrams, Inc.

—Iggy Peck, Architect. Roberts, David, illus. 2010. (ENG.). 32p. (J). (gr. k-17). pap. 7.95 (978-0-8109-8928-3(X)) UK Abrams Bks. for Young Readers.

Beil, Karen Magnuson. Jack's House. Wohnoutka, Mike, illus. 2009. (ENG.). 32p. (J). (gr. -1-3). pap. 7.99 (978-0-8234-2242-5(9)) Holiday Hse., Inc.

Blackstone, Stella. Bear at Home (Oso en Casa) Harter, Debbie, illus. 2010. (ENG & SPA.). 24p. (J). (gr. -1-1). pap. 6.99 *(978-1-84686-422-3(4))* Barefoot Bks., Inc.
Boston, Lucy M. The Children of Green Knowe Collection. 2013. (ENG., Illus.). 368p. (J). 12.95 *(978-0-571-30347-2(1))* Faber & Faber, Inc.
Burn, Doris. Andrew Henry's Meadow. Burn, Doris, illus. 2012. (ENG., Illus.). 48p. (J). (gr. 1-4). 16.99 *(978-0-399-25608-0(3),* Philomel Bks.) Penguin Young Readers Group.
Cabot, Meg. Project Princess. 2003. (Princess Diaries: 4.5). (ENG.). 64p. (YA). (gr. 8-18). pap. 6.99 *(978-0-06-057131-3(4),* HarperTeen) HarperCollins Pubs.
Carter, David A. Busy Bug Builds a Fort. Carter, David A., illus. 2016. (David Carter's Bugs Ser.). (ENG., Illus.). 24p. (J). (gr. -1-1). pap. 3.99 *(978-1-4814-4047-9(0),* Simon Spotlight) Simon Spotlight.
Clement, Nathan. Job Site. Clement, Nathan, illus. 2011. (ENG., Illus.). 32p. (J). (gr. -1-1). 16.95 *(978-1-59078-769-4(2))* Boyds Mills Pr.
Clement, Nathan, illus. Job Site. 2015. (ENG.). 32p. (J). (— 1). bds. 7.99 *(978-1-62979-407-5(4))* Boyds Mills Pr.
Cousins, Lucy. Where Does Maisy Live? 2010. 12p. bds. 4.99 *(978-976-3-64668-7(5))* Candlewick Pr.
Cyrus, Kurt. Billions of Bricks. Cyrus, Kurt, illus. 2016. (ENG., Illus.). 32p. (J). 17.99 *(978-1-62779-273-8(2),* 9781627792738, Holt, Henry & Co. Bks. For Young Readers) Holt, Henry & Co.
Dale, Penny. Dinosaur Dig! Dale, Penny, illus. 2012. (ENG., Illus.). 14p. (J). (gr. k-k). bds. 6.99 *(978-0-7636-6270-7(4),* Nosy Crow) Candlewick Pr.
De Fonté, Desiree. Zach: A Story of Obedience. 2012. 36p. pap. 24.95 *(978-1-4626-5114-6(3))* America Star Bks.
Duckworth, Michael. Voodoo Island. Oxford University Press Staff & Bassett, Jennifer, eds. 3rd ed. 2008. (ENG., Illus.). 64p. 10.00 *(978-0-19-479075-8(4))* Oxford Univ. Pr., Inc.
Eldarova, Sofia. Builder Mouse. 2016. (ENG., Illus.). 32p. (J). (gr. -1-3). 16.99 *(978-0-544-35766-2(3),* Clarion Bks.) Houghton Mifflin Harcourt Trade & Reference Pubs.
Evans, Nate & Brown, Stephanie Gwyn. Bang! Boom! Roar! A Busy Crew of Dinosaurs. Santoro, Christopher, illus. 2012. (ENG.). 40p. (J). (gr. -1-2). 15.99 *(978-0-06-087960-0(2))* HarperCollins Pubs.
—Dinosaur ABC. Santoro, Christopher, illus. 2011. (J). lib. bdg. 16.89 *(978-0-06-087962-4(9))* HarperCollins Pubs.
Fleming, Meg. Ready, Set, Build! Jarvis, illus. 2017. (ENG.). 32p. (J). (gr. -1-3). 16.99 *(978-1-4998-0175-0(0))* Little Bee Books Inc.
Fliess, Sue. Let's Build!, 0 vols. 2014. (ENG.). 24p. (J). (gr. -1-3). 14.99 *(978-1-4778-4724-4(3),* 9781477847244, Amazon Children's Publishing) Amazon Publishing.
Fox, Paula. Maurice's Room. Fetz, Ingrid, illus. 2010. (ENG.). 64p. (J). (gr. 2-5). pap. 6.99 *(978-1-4424-1678-9(5),* Simon & Schuster/Paula Wiseman Bks.) Simon & Schuster/Paula Wiseman Bks.
Friskey, Margaret. Surprise on Wheels. Patton, Lucia, illus. 2004. reprint ed. pap. 15.95 *(978-1-4191-1496-0(4))* Kessinger Publishing, LLC.
Fritz, Betty. Bang Bang Bang... Hammers in the Morning. 2010. 16.95 *(978-0-578-05104-8(4))* Kinderhaus Publishing Co.
Fry, Sonali. Bang! Clang! 2005. (Ready-to-Read Ser.). (J). pap. 3.99 *(978-0-689-87419-2(7),* Simon Spotlight) Simon Spotlight.
Gelsey, James & Duendes Del Sur Staff. Scooby-Doo & the Karate Caper, 1 vol. 2011. (Scooby-Doo Mysteries Ser.). (ENG., Illus.). 64p. (J). (gr. 3-6). 24.21 *(978-1-59961-891-3(5))* Spotlight.
Greenberg, David E. The Ugly Brown Pear. 2010. 40p. pap. 12.96 *(978-0-557-28055-1(9))* Lulu Pr., Inc.
Greenwald, Lisa. My Summer of Pink & Green. 2013. (Pink & Green Ser.). (ENG.). 272p. (YA). (gr. 3-7). 17.95 *(978-1-4197-0413-0(3),* Amulet Bks.) Abrams, Inc.
—My Summer of Pink & Green: Pink & Green Book Two. 2014. (Pink & Green Ser.). (ENG.). 288p. (YA). (gr. 3-7). pap. 7.95 *(978-1-4197-0931-9(3),* Amulet Bks.) Abrams, Inc.
Hannigan, Paula. Under Construction. Brown, Heather, illus. 2013. (ENG.). 18p. (J). bds. 5.99 *(978-1-4494-3556-1(4))* Andrews McMeel Publishing.
Hannigan, Paula & Accord Publishing Staff. Under Construction. Brown, Heather, illus. 2012. (ENG.). 12p. (J). bds. 14.99 *(978-1-4494-0498-7(7))* Andrews McMeel Publishing.
Harris, Nicholas. A Year at a Construction Site. 2009. (Time Goes By Ser.). (ENG.). 24p. (gr. k-3). pap. 6.95 *(978-1-58013-795-9(4),* First Avenue Editions) Lerner Publishing Group.
Hatke, Ben. Julia's House for Lost Creatures. Hatke, Ben, illus. 2014. (ENG., Illus.). 40p. (J). (gr. k-3). 17.99 *(978-1-59643-866-8(5),* 9781596438668, First Second Bks.) Roaring Brook Pr.
Hearn, Sam. Busy Builders. Hearn, Sam, illus. 2016. (ENG., Illus.). 16p. (J). (— 1). bds. 10.99 *(978-0-545-79957-7(0),* Cartwheel Bks.) Scholastic, Inc.
Henn, Sophy. Where Bear? Henn, Sophy, illus. 2015. (ENG., Illus.). 32p. (J). (gr. k-3). 16.99 *(978-0-399-17158-1(4),* Philomel Bks.) Penguin Young Readers Group.
Henson, Jim & Martin, Craig. Doozers. 2015. (Illus.). (J). *(978-1-4806-9271-8(9),* Simon Spotlight) Simon Spotlight.
Hill, Isabel. Building Stories, 1 vol. 2011. (ENG., Illus.). 32p. (J). 17.95 *(978-1-59572-279-9(3));* pap. 7.95 *(978-1-59572-280-5(7))* Star Bright Bks., Inc.
Hopkinson, Deborah. Sky Boys: How They Built the Empire State Building. Ransome, James E., illus. 2012. (ENG.). 48p. (J). (gr. -1-3). pap. 7.99 *(978-0-375-86541-1(1),* Dragonfly Bks.) Random Hse. Children's Bks.
—Sky Boys: How They Built the Empire State Building. Ransome, James E., illus. 2012. lib. bdg. 18.40 *(978-0-606-23847-2(6),* Turtleback) Turtleback Bks.
Kittinger, Jo S. The House on Dirty-Third Street, 1 vol. González, Thomas, illus. 2012. (ENG.). 32p. (J). 16.95 *(978-1-56145-619-2(5))* Peachtree Pubs.
Klein, Adria F. Sammy Saw, 1 vol. Rowland, Andrew, illus. 2011. (Tool School Ser.). (ENG.). 32p. (gr. 1-2). pap. 6.25 *(978-1-4342-3387-5(1));* lib. bdg. 22.65 *(978-1-4342-3045-4(7))* Stone Arch Bks.
Lai, Trevor. Tomo Explores the World. Lai, Trevor, illus. 2016. (Tomo's Adventure Journal Ser.). (ENG., Illus.). 40p. (J). 17.99 *(978-1-250-08545-0(4),* 9781250085450) Imprint IND. Dist: Macmillan.
Lancett, Peter. The Dark Glass, 1 vol. unabr. ed. 2010. (Dark Man Ser.). (ENG.). 34p. (YA). (gr. 9-12). pap. 7.95 *(978-1-61651-018-3(8))* Saddleback Educational Publishing, Inc.
Langley, Jan. The Captain & Harry: A Trembling Tail of Thieves. Robinson, Susan, illus. 2006. 30p. (J). (gr. 4-7). pap. 10.95 *(978-1-892384-23-2(X))* Avery Color Studios, Inc.
Liparulo, Robert. Whirlwind, 1 vol. 2010. (Dreamhouse Kings Ser.: 5). (ENG.). 320p. pap. 9.99 *(978-1-59554-892-4(0))* Nelson, Thomas Inc.
London, Jonathan. Froggy Builds a Tree House. 2013. (Froggy Ser.). (ENG.). 32p. (J). (-k). pap. 6.99 *(978-0-14-242533-6(8),* Puffin Books) Penguin Young Readers Group.
—Froggy Builds a Tree House. 2013. (Froggy Ser.). lib. bdg. 17.20 *(978-0-606-30518-1(1),* Turtleback) Turtleback Bks.
Lynch, Casey. Mighty Mike Builds a Ball Field, 1 vol. Lynch, Kelly, illus. 2011. (Mighty Mike Ser.). (ENG.). 32p. (gr. -1-2). 28.50 *(978-1-61641-128-2(7),* Looking Glass Library) ABDO Publishing Co.
—Mighty Mike Builds a Library, 1 vol. Lynch, Kelly, illus. 2011. (Mighty Mike Ser.). (ENG.). 32p. (gr. -1-2). 28.50 *(978-1-61641-129-9(5),* Looking Glass Library) ABDO Publishing Co.
Lynch, Kelly. Mighty Mike Builds a Nature Trail, 1 vol. Lynch, Casey, illus. 2011. (Mighty Mike Ser.). (ENG.). 32p. (gr. -1-2). 28.50 *(978-1-61641-130-5(9),* Looking Glass Library) ABDO Publishing Co.
Lyon, George Ella. You & Me & Home Sweet Home. Anderson, Stephanie, illus. 2009. (ENG.). 48p. (J). (gr. -1-3). 17.99 *(978-0-689-87589-2(4),* Atheneum/Richard Jackson Bks.) Simon & Schuster Children's Publishing.
Martinez, Claudia Guadalupe. Pig Park. 2014. (ENG.). 248p. (J). 15.95 *(978-1-935955-76-4(4))* Cinco Puntos Pr.
Meltzer, Lynn. The Construction Crew. Eko-Burgess, Carrie, illus. 2011. (ENG.). 40p. (J). (gr. -1-k). 15.99 *(978-0-8050-8884-7(9),* 9780805088847, Holt, Henry & Co. Bks. For Young Readers) Holt, Henry & Co.
Monroe, Chris. Monkey with a Tool Belt. Monroe, Chris, illus. 2008. (Carolrhoda Picture Bks.). (ENG., Illus.). 32p. (J). (gr. -1-2). lib. bdg. 16.95 *(978-0-8225-7631-0(7),* Carolrhoda Bks.) Lerner Publishing Group.
Moore, Inga. A House in the Woods. 2011. (ENG., Illus.). 48p. (J). (gr. -1-2). 16.99 *(978-0-7636-5277-7(6))* Candlewick Pr.
Nevius, Carol. Building with Dad, 0 vols. Thomson, Bill, illus. 2012. (ENG.). 32p. (J). (gr. k-3). pap. 9.99 *(978-0-7614-5984-2(7),* 9780761459842, Amazon Children's Publishing) Amazon Publishing.
Parish, Herman. Amelia Bedelia under Construction. Sweat, Lynn, illus. (I Can Read Level 2 Ser.). 64p. (J). (gr. k-3). 2007. (ENG.). pap. 3.99 *(978-0-06-084346-5(2))* 2006. (ENG.). 15.99 *(978-0-06-084344-1(6))* 2006. lib. bdg. 16.89 *(978-0-06-084345-8(4))* HarperCollins Pubs. (Greenwillow Bks.).
—Amelia Bedelia under Construction. Sweat, Lynn, illus. 2007. (I Can Read Bks.). 64p. (gr. k-3). 14.00 *(978-0-7569-8054-2(2))* Perfection Learning Corp.
Parragon Publishing Staff. Busy Day at the Construction Site. (Busy Books Large Ser.). *(978-1-4054-7874-8(8))* Parragon, Inc.
Priddy, Roger. Playtown: Construction. 2015. (Playtown Ser.). (ENG., Illus.). 14p. (J). (gr. -1-k). bds. 9.99 *(978-0-312-51912-4(5),* 9780312519124, Priddy Bks.) St. Martin's Pr.
Randolph, Robert. Their Very Own Bike, 1 vol. 2010. 28p. 24.95 *(978-1-4489-8322-3(3))* PublishAmerica, Inc.
Random House Staff. The Best Doghouse Ever! Random House Staff & Jackson, Mike, illus. 2013. (Step into Reading Ser.). (ENG.). 24p. (J). (gr. -1-1). pap. 3.99 *(978-0-449-81388-1(6),* Random Hse. Bks. for Young Readers) Random Hse. Children's Bks.
Ranson, Erin. Let's Build. Green, Barry, illus. 2007. (Magnetic Story & Play Scene Ser.). (ENG.). 8p. (J). (gr. -1). 9.99 *(978-1-84666-091-7(2))* Top That! Publishing PLC GBR. Dist: Independent Pubs. Group.
Reidy, Jean. Busy Builders, Busy Week! Timmers, Leo, illus. 2016. (ENG.). 32p. (J). 16.99 *(978-1-61963-556-2(9),* 9781619635562, Bloomsbury USA Childrens) Bloomsbury Publishing USA.
Reinhardt, Dana. How to Build a House. 2009. (ENG.). 240p. (YA). (gr. 9-11). pap. 8.99 *(978-0-375-84454-6(6),* Ember) Random Hse. Children's Bks.
Rex, Adam. School's First Day of School. Robinson, Christian, illus. 2016. (ENG.). 40p. (J). (gr. -1-3). 17.99 *(978-1-59643-964-1(5),* 9781596439641) Roaring Brook Pr.
Rey, H. A. Builds a Home. 2011. (Curious George Ser.). (ENG., Illus.). 24p. (J). (gr. -1-3). 6.99 *(978-0-547-59410-1(0))* Houghton Mifflin Harcourt Publishing Co.
Rockliff, Mara. Me & Momma & Big John. Low, William, illus. 2012. (ENG.). 32p. (J). (gr. -1-2). 16.99 *(978-0-7636-4359-1(9))* Candlewick Pr.
Scholastic, Inc. Staff, contrib. by. Build This City! 2010. (LEGO City Ser.). (ENG.). 24p. (J). (gr. -1-3). pap. 3.99 *(978-0-545-17765-8(0))* Scholastic, Inc.
Schwartz, Corey Rosen & Gomez, Rebecca J. What about Moose? Yamaguchi, Keika, illus. 2015. (ENG.). 40p. (J). (gr. -1-3). 17.99 *(978-1-4814-0496-9(2),* Atheneum Bks. for Young Readers) Simon & Schuster Children's Publishing.
Shaw, Natalie, adapted by. Doozers Stick with It. 2015. (Doozers Ser.). (ENG., Illus.). 32p. (J). (gr. -1-1). pap. 3.99 *(978-1-4814-3217-7(6),* Simon Spotlight) Simon Spotlight.
Shea, Therese. One More Floor! 2006. (Neighborhood Readers Ser.). (ENG.). 16p. (gr. 1-3). pap. 6.50 *(978-1-4042-7244-6(5),* Rosen Classroom) Rosen Publishing Group, Inc., The.
Shulman, Lisa. Old MacDonald Had a Woodshop. Wolff, Ashley, illus. 2004. (ENG.). 32p. (J). (gr. -1-k). reprint ed. pap. 6.99 *(978-0-14-240186-6(2),* Puffin Books) Penguin Young Readers Group.
Silverman, Erica. Cowgirl Kate & Cocoa: Horse in the House. Lewin, Betsy, illus. 2010. (Cowgirl Kate & Cocoa Ser.). (ENG.). 44p. (J). (gr. 1-4). pap. 5.99 *(978-0-547-31672-7(0))* Houghton Mifflin Harcourt Publishing Co.
Smith, Joshua T. Frog's Van. 2010. 36p. pap. 15.95 *(978-0-557-72956-2(4))* Lulu Pr., Inc.
Sobel, June. B Is for Bulldozer: A Construction ABC. Iwai, Melissa, illus. 2006. 28p. (gr. -1-k). 17.00 *(978-0-7569-7037-6(7))* Perfection Learning Corp.
—B Is for Bulldozer: A Construction ABC. Iwai, Melissa, illus. 2006. (ENG.). 32p. (J). (gr. -1-3). pap. 7.99 *(978-0-15-205774-9(9))* Houghton Mifflin Harcourt Publishing Co.
Sobel, June & Iwai, Melissa. B Is for Bulldozer: A Construction ABC. Iwai, Melissa, illus. 2013. (ENG., Illus.). 32p. (J). (— 1). bds. 7.99 *(978-0-544-10808-0(6))* Houghton Mifflin Harcourt Publishing Co.
Sorenson, Margo. Ambrose & the Cathedral Dream. Szegedi, Katalin, illus. 2006. (ENG.). 32p. (J). (gr. -1-3). 4.24 *(978-0-8146-3004-4(9))* Liturgical Pr.
Spangler, Lois. The Fort on Fourth Street, 1 vol. Wald, Christina, illus. 2013. (ENG.). 32p. (J). (gr. 1-4). 17.95 *(978-1-60718-620-5(9));* pap. 9.95 *(978-1-60718-632-8(2))* Arbordale Publishing.
Stanley the Builder, 1 vol. 2014. (Stanley Ser.). (ENG., Illus.). 32p. (J). (gr. -1-2). 14.95 *(978-1-56145-801-1(5))* Peachtree Pubs.
Stelten, Gene. A House for Wally & Me. Johnson, Chelsea, illus. 2009. 32p. (J). 13.95 *(978-1-935130-13-0(7))* Grateful Steps.
Stine, R. L. Welcome to Dead House. 2010. (Classic Goosebumps Ser.: 13). (ENG.). 160p. (J). (gr. 3-7). 6.99 *(978-0-545-15888-6(5),* Scholastic Paperbacks) Scholastic, Inc.
Sutton, Sally. Construyendo. Lovelock, Brian, illus. 2015. (ENG & SPA.). 32p. (J). (gr. -1-2). bds. 6.99 *(978-0-7636-7976-7(3))* Candlewick Pr.
Tillworth, Mary. Dump Truck Trouble/Let's Build a Doghouse! (Bubble Guppies) Random House Beginners Books Staff & MJ Illustrations Staff, illus. 2014. (Pictureback(R) Ser.). (ENG.). 32p. (J). (gr. -1-2). 4.99 *(978-0-385-37526-9(3),* Random Hse. Bks. for Young Readers) Random Hse. Children's Bks.
Weinberg, Steven. Fred & the Lumberjack. Weinberg, Steven, illus. 2017. (ENG., Illus.). 40p. (J). (gr. -1-3). 17.99 ***(978-1-4814-2983-2(3),*** McElderry, Margaret K. Bks.) McElderry, Margaret K. Bks.
Widmer, Kirsten & Buxton, Sarah. Workshops That Work! 30 Days of Mini-Lessons That Help Launch & Establish All-Important Routines for an Effective Reading & Writing Workshop. 2004. (ENG.). 160p. pap. 20.99 *(978-0-439-44406-4(3),* Teaching Resources) Scholastic, Inc.

BUILDING—REPAIR AND RECONSTRUCTION

Beyer, Mark. Demolition Experts: Life Blowing Things Up. 2009. (Extreme Careers Ser.). 64p. (gr. 5-5). 58.50 *(978-1-61512-389-6(X),* Rosen Reference) Rosen Publishing Group, Inc., The.
Edison, Erin. Destruction. 2013. (Destruction Ser.). (ENG.). 12p. (gr. k-1). bds. 19.98 *(978-1-4765-3696-5(1),* Pebble Plus) Capstone Press of Coughlan Cos.
Gish, Melissa. A Construction Site. 2003. 24p. (J). lib. bdg. 21.35 *(978-1-58340-323-5(X))* Black Rabbit Bks.
Healy, Nick. The Statue of Liberty. 2003. (J). pap. *(978-1-58417-117-1(0))* Lake Street Pubs.
Troupe, Thomas Kingsley. Destruction. 2013. (Destruction Ser.). (ENG.). 24p. (gr. k-1). lib. bdg. 106.60 *(978-1-4765-3695-8(3),* Pebble Plus) Capstone Press of Coughlan Cos.
Wolny, Philip. Getting a Job in Building Maintenance. 2013. (Job Basics: Getting the Job You Need Ser.). (ENG., Illus.). 80p. (YA). (gr. 9-12). lib. bdg. 33.25 *(978-1-4488-9608-0(8),* Rosen Classroom) Rosen Publishing Group, Inc., The.

BUILDING—VOCATIONAL GUIDANCE

Facts on File, Inc. Staff. Construction. 2010. (New Discovering Careers for Your Future Ser.). (Illus.). 128p. (gr. 4-9). 24.95 *(978-0-8160-8045-8(3),* Ferguson Publishing Co.) Facts On File, Inc.
Guillain, Charlotte. Building Things, 1 vol. 2012. (Jobs If You Like... Ser.). (ENG.). 32p. (gr. 1-3). pap. 8.29 *(978-1-4329-6816-8(5),* Heinemann First Library) Heinemann-Raintree.
Horn, Geoffrey M. Construction Worker. 2008. (Cool Careers Ser.). 32p. (gr. 5-8). pap. 10.50 *(978-0-8368-9325-0(5));* (YA). lib. bdg. 26.00 *(978-0-8368-9192-8(9))* Stevens, Gareth Publishing LLLP.
Leavitt, Amie Jane. The Vo-Tech Track to Success in Architecture & Construction. 2014. (Learning a Trade, Preparing for a Career Ser.). (Illus.). 80p. (J). (gr. 7-12). 34.25 *(978-1-4777-7726-8(1))* Rosen Publishing Group, Inc., The.
Liebman, Dan. I Want to Be a Builder. 2003. (I Want to Be Ser.). (ENG., Illus.). 24p. (J). (gr. -1-2). pap. 3.99 *(978-1-55297-757-6(9),* 9781552977576) Firefly Bks., Ltd.
Liebman, Daniel & Liebman, Dan. I Want to Be a Builder. 2003. (I Want to Be Ser.). (ENG., Illus.). 24p. (J). (gr. -1-2). 14.95 *(978-1-55297-758-3(7),* 9781552977583) Firefly Bks., Ltd.
—Quiero Ser Constructor. 2003. (Quiero Ser.). (SPA., Illus.). 24p. (J). (gr. -1-2). pap. 5.99 *(978-1-55297-762-0(5),* 9781552977620) Firefly Bks., Ltd.
Malam, John. You Wouldn't Want to Be a Skyscraper Builder! 2009. (You Wouldn't Want To Ser.). lib. bdg. 20.80 *(978-0-606-04274-1(1),* Turtleback) Turtleback Bks.
Masters, Nancy Robinson. Heavy Equipment Operator. 2010. (21st Century Skills Library: Cool Careers Ser.). (ENG.). 32p. (gr. 4-8). lib. bdg. 28.50 *(978-1-60279-941-7(5),* 200627) Cherry Lake Publishing.
Mondschein, Kenneth C. Construction & Trades. 2008. (Great Careers with a High School Diploma Ser.). 116p. (C). (gr. 9). 32.95 *(978-0-8160-7043-5(1),* Ferguson Publishing Co.) Facts On File, Inc.
Morgan, Elizabeth. Construction Workers, 01 vols., 1. 2016. (Hands-On Jobs Ser.). (ENG., Illus.). 24p. (J). pap. 8.25 *(978-1-5081-4355-0(2),* PowerKids Pr.) Rosen Publishing Group, Inc., The.
Nijs, Erika de. A Carpenter's Job. 2015. (Community Workers Ser.). (ENG., Illus.). 24p. (J). (gr. 1-1). pap. 8.22 *(978-1-5026-0427-9(2))* Cavendish Square Publishing.
O'Connor, Rachel. Construction Worker. 2004. (Great Jobs Ser.). (ENG., Illus.). 48p. (J). 24.50 *(978-0-516-24089-3(7),* Children's Pr.) Scholastic Library Publishing.
Senker, Cath. Construction Careers. 2010. (In the Workplace Ser.). 48p. (J). 35.65 *(978-1-60753-089-3(9))* Amicus Publishing.
Senker, Cath & Savery, Annabel. Construction Careers. 2011. (Been There! Ser.). (Illus.). 32p. (gr. 3-6). lib. bdg. 31.35 *(978-1-59920-469-7(X))* Black Rabbit Bks.
Somervill, Barbara. Green General Contractor. 2011. (21st Century Skills Library: Cool Careers Ser.). (ENG.). 32p. (gr. 4-8). lib. bdg. 28.50 *(978-1-60279-987-5(3),* 200978) Cherry Lake Publishing.
Wolny, Philip. Getting a Job in Building Maintenance. 2013. (Job Basics: Getting the Job You Need Ser.). (ENG., Illus.). 80p. (YA). (gr. 9-12). lib. bdg. 33.25 *(978-1-4488-9608-0(8),* Rosen Classroom) Rosen Publishing Group, Inc., The.
—High Risk Construction Work: Life Building Skyscrapers, Bridges, & Tunnels. 2008. (Extreme Careers Ser.). (Illus.). 64p. (YA). (gr. 5-9). lib. bdg. 31.95 *(978-1-4042-1789-8(4))* Rosen Publishing Group, Inc., The.
—High-Risk Construction Work: Life Building Skyscrapers, Bridges, & Tunnels. 2009. (Extreme Careers Ser.). 64p. (gr. 5-5). 58.50 *(978-1-61512-397-1(0),* Rosen Reference) Rosen Publishing Group, Inc., The.

BUILDING REPAIR

see Building—Repair and Reconstruction

BUILDINGS—MAINTENANCE AND REPAIR

see Building—Repair and Reconstruction

BUILDINGS—REMODELING

see Building—Repair and Reconstruction

BULGARIA

Goldstein, Margaret J. Bulgaria in Pictures. 2nd ed. 2005. (Visual Geography Series, Second Ser.). (ENG., Illus.). 80p. (gr. 5-12). 31.93 *(978-0-8225-3057-2(0))* Lerner Publishing Group.
Stavreva, Kirilka & Quek, Lynette. Bulgaria. 2nd rev. ed. 2007. (Cultures of the World Ser.). 144p. (gr. 6). lib. bdg. 42.79 *(978-0-7614-2078-1(9),* Benchmark Bks.) Marshall Cavendish Corp.
Stavreva, Kirilka, et al. Bulgaria. 2017. (J). ***(978-1-5026-2609-7(8))*** Cavendish Square Publishing.

BULGARIA—FICTION

Topakian, Patricia E. The Mystery of the Old Brown Suitcase. 2007. (ENG.). 26p. pap. 15.99 *(978-1-4196-2819-1(4))* CreateSpace Independent Publishing Platform.

BULIMIA

see Eating Disorders

BULL RUN, 1ST BATTLE OF, VA., 1861

Gitlin, Martin. The Battle of Bull Run: A History Perspectives Book. 2014. (Perspectives Library). (ENG., Illus.). 32p. (J). (gr. 4-8). pap. 14.21 *(978-1-63137-662-7(4),* 205252) Cherry Lake Publishing.
Hama, Larry. The Battle of First Bull Run: The Civil War Begins. 2009. (Graphic Civil War Battles Ser.). (ENG.). 48p. (YA). (gr. 4-5). 58.50 *(978-1-61512-898-3(0),* Rosen Reference) Rosen Publishing Group, Inc., The.
—The Battle of First Bull Run: The Civil War Begins. Moore, Scott, illus. 2007. (Graphic Battles of the Civil War Ser.). (ENG.). 48p. (YA). (gr. 4-7). lib. bdg. 31.95 *(978-1-4042-0776-9(7))* Rosen Publishing Group, Inc., The.
Lassieur, Allison & Doeden, Matt. The Civil War Experience: An Interactive History Adventure, 1 vol. 2014. (You Choose: History Ser.). (ENG.). 328p. (gr. 3-4). pap. 14.95 *(978-1-4765-0839-9(9),* You Choose Bks.) Capstone Press of Coughlan Cos.
Vierow, Wendy. The Battle of Bull Run. 2004. (Headlines from History Ser.). (Illus.). 24p. (YA). (gr. 2-5). lib. bdg. 22.60 *(978-0-8239-6221-1(0))* Rosen Publishing Group, Inc., The.
—The Battle of Bull Run: Confederate Forces Overwhelm Union Troops. 2009. (Headlines from History Ser.). 24p. (gr. 3-3). 42.50 *(978-1-61513-241-6(4),* PowerKids Pr.) Rosen Publishing Group, Inc., The.

BULL RUN, 1ST BATTLE OF, VA., 1861—FICTION

Altsheler, Joseph A. The Guns of Bull Run: A Story of the Civil War's Eve. 2006. (Civil War Ser.: Vol. 1). 300p. (J). reprint ed. 29.95 *(978-1-4218-1777-4(2));* pap. 14.95 *(978-1-4218-1877-1(9))* 1st World Publishing, Inc. (1st World Library - Literary Society).
—The Guns of Bull Run: A Story of the Civil War's Eve. 2009. 278p. reprint ed. pap. 14.99 *(978-1-60512-409-4(5));* (Civil War Ser.: Vol. 1). (J). 27.99 *(978-1-60512-309-7(9))* Akasha Publishing, LLC. (Akasha Classics).
—The Guns of Bull Run: A Story of the Civil War's Eve. l.t. ed. (Civil War Ser.: Vol. 1). (J). 2007. 272p. per. 23.99 *(978-1-4346-7679-5(X))* 2008. 272p. reprint ed. 28.99 *(978-0-554-29458-2(3))* 2008. 272p. reprint ed. 25.99 *(978-0-554-38761-1(1))* 2007. (ENG.). 238p. reprint ed. per. 20.99 *(978-1-4346-7678-8(1))* Creative Media Partners, LLC.
—The Guns of Bull Run: A Story of the Civil War's Eve. 2006. (Civil War Ser.: Vol. 1). (J). reprint ed. pap. *(978-1-4065-0812-3(8))* Dodo Pr.
—The Guns of Bull Run: A Story of the Civil War's Eve. 2007. (Civil War Ser.: Vol. 1). 176p. (J). reprint ed. per. *(978-1-4068-1678-5(7))* Echo Library.
—The Guns of Bull Run: A Story of the Civil War's Eve. 2010. (Civil War Ser.: Vol. 1). (Illus.). 162p. (J). (gr. 4-7). reprint ed. pap. 19.99 *(978-1-153-70504-2(4))* General Bks. LLC.
—The Guns of Bull Run: A Story of the Civil War's Eve. (Civil War Ser.: Vol. 1). (J). reprint ed. 2010. 238p. (gr. 4-7). 33.56 *(978-1-169-29842-2(7))* 2010. 238p. (gr. 4-7). pap. 21.56 *(978-1-162-69670-6(2))* 2010. 41.95 *(978-1-161-46535-8(9))* 2004. pap. 26.95 *(978-1-4191-6519-1(4))* 2004. pap. 1.99 *(978-1-4192-6519-8(9))* Kessinger Publishing, LLC.
—The Guns of Bull Run: A Story of the Civil War's Eve. 2011. (Civil War Ser.: Vol. 1). 256p. (J). (gr. 4-7). reprint ed. pap. *(978-3-8424-5271-8(3))* Tredition GmbH.
—The Guns of Bull Run: A Story of the Civil War's Eve. 2009. (Civil War Ser.: Vol. 1). (YA). (gr. 4-7). reprint ed. pap. 16.95 *(978-1-933573-82-3(1))* Zeezok Publishing, LLC.
—The Guns of Bull Run (Webster's French Thesaurus Edition) 2008. (Civil War Ser.: Vol. 1). (ENG & FRE.). 306p. reprint ed. pap. 28.95 *(978-0-497-97879-2(2))* Icon Group International, Inc.

AB

—The Guns of Bull Run (Webster's Spanish Thesaurus Edition) 2008. (Civil War Ser.: Vol. 1). (ENG & SPA.). 313p. pap. 28.95 *(978-0-497-99968-1(4))* Icon Group International, Inc.

Hansen, Lynne. Shades of Blue & Gray. 2007. (YA). pap. *(978-1-4114-9674-3(4),* Spark Publishing Group) Sterling Publishing Co., Inc.

Hemphill, Michael & Angleberger, Tom. Stonewall Hinkleman & the Battle of Bull Run. 2014. (ENG.). 192p. (J). (gr. 3-7). pap. 7.99 *(978-0-14-751182-9(8),* Puffin Books) Penguin Young Readers Group.

Riddleburger, Sam & Michael Hemphill. Stonewall Hinkleman & the Battle of Bull Run. 2014. lib. bdg. 18.40 *(978-0-606-35709-8(2))* Turtleback Bks.

BULLDOZERS

Addison, D. R. Bulldozers at Work. 2009. (Big Trucks Ser.). (Illus.). 24p. (J). (gr. k-2). pap. 8.25 *(978-1-4358-3088-2(1));* 24p. (gr. 1-1). 42.50 *(978-1-61511-573-0(0));* (J). 22.60 *(978-1-4358-2702-8(3))* Rosen Publishing Group, Inc., The. (PowerKids Pr.).

Alinas, Marv. Bulldozers. 2014. (Big Machines at Work Ser.). (ENG.). 24p. (J). (gr. -1-2). 25.64 *(978-1-62323-962-6(1),* 206737) Child's World, Inc., The.

Askew, Amanda. Bulldozers. 2010. (Mighty Machines Ser.). (ENG., Illus.). 24p. (J). (gr. -1-2). pap. 5.95 *(978-1-55407-703-8(6),* 9781554077038) Firefly Bks., Ltd.

Bowman, Chris. Bulldozers. 2017. (Mighty Machines in Action Ser.). (ENG., Illus.). 24p. (J). (gr. k-3). lib. bdg. 25.95 *(978-1-62617-601-0(9),* Blastoff! Readers) Bellwether Media.

—Monster Bulldozers. 2014. (Monster Machines Ser.). (ENG., Illus.). 24p. (J). (gr. k-3). lib. bdg. 25.95 *(978-1-62617-053-7(3),* Blastoff! Readers) Bellwether Media.

Brady, Peter. Bulldozers in Action. 2012. (Transportation Zone Ser.). (ENG.). 24p. (gr. 1-2). pap. 41.70 *(978-1-4296-8393-7(7));* lib. bdg. 25.32 *(978-1-4296-7692-2(2))* Capstone Press of Coughlan Cos. (First Facts).

Butterfield, Moira. Bulldozers & Other Construction Machines. Lyon, Chris & Biggin, Gary, illus. 32p. (J). mass mkt. 8.99 *(978-0-590-24556-2(2))* Scholastic, Inc.

Capici, Gaetano. What Does It Do? Bulldozer. 2011. (Community Connections: What Does It Do? Ser.). (ENG.). 24p. (gr. 2-5). lib. bdg. 25.64 *(978-1-60279-972-1(5),* 200966) Cherry Lake Publishing.

Clay, Kathryn. Bulldozers. 2016. (Construction Vehicles at Work Ser.). (ENG.). 24p. (gr. k-1). lib. bdg. 21.99 *(978-1-5157-2529-9(4))* Capstone Press of Coughlan Cos.

Frisch, Aaron. Bulldozers. 2013. 24p. 22.65 *(978-1-60818-338-8(6))* Creative Co., The.

—Seedlings: Bulldozers. 2014. (Seedlings Ser.). (ENG.). 24p. (J). (gr. -1-k). pap. 7.99 *(978-0-89812-883-3(8),* Creative Paperbacks) Creative Co., The.

Gilbert, Sara. Bulldozers. 2009. (Machines That Build Ser.). (J). (gr. 1-5). 24.25 *(978-1-58341-725-6(7),* Creative Education) Creative Co., The.

Gilbert, Sara & Clark, Tracey. Bulldozers. 2011. (Machines That Build Ser.). (ENG.). 24p. (J). (gr. 1-17). pap. 7.99 *(978-1-897563-70-0(1),* Creative Paperbacks) Creative Co., The.

Hayes, Amy. Big Bulldozers. 2015. (Machines That Work Ser.). (ENG., Illus.). 24p. (J). (gr. 1-1). pap. 8.22 *(978-1-5026-0388-3(8))* Cavendish Square Publishing.

Kawa, Katie. Bulldozers. 2011. (Big Machines Ser.). (Illus.). 24p. (gr. k-2). 69.20 *(978-1-4339-6886-0(X));* (J). pap. 8.15 *(978-1-4339-5552-5(0));* (J). lib. bdg. 22.60 *(978-1-4339-5550-1(4));* (SPA & ENG., (J). lib. bdg. 22.60 *(978-1-4339-5574-7(1))* Stevens, Gareth Publishing LLLP.

Lennie, Charles. Bulldozers, 1 vol. 2014. (Construction Machines Ser.). (ENG.). 24p. (J). (gr. 4-8). lib. bdg. 28.50 *(978-1-62970-015-1(0))* ABDO Publishing Co.

Martin, M. T. Bulldozers. 2006. (Mighty Machines Ser.). (ENG., Illus.). 24p. (J). (gr. k-3). lib. bdg. 25.95 *(978-1-60014-043-3(2))* Bellwether Media.

Mezzanotte, Jim. Giant Bulldozers. 2005. (Giant Vehicles Ser.). (Illus.). 24p. (gr. 1-4). pap. 8.15 *(978-0-8368-4917-2(5));* lib. bdg. 23.00 *(978-0-8368-4910-3(8))* Stevens, Gareth Publishing LLLP. (Gareth Stevens Learning Library).

—Niveladoras. Acosta, Tatiana & Gutierrez, Guillermo, trs. 2005. (Vehiculos Gigantes (Giant Vehicles) Ser.). (SPA., Illus.). 24p. (gr. 1-4). lib. bdg. 23.00 *(978-0-8368-5989-8(8),* Gareth Stevens Learning Library) Stevens, Gareth Publishing LLLP.

Osier, Dan. Bulldozers, 1 vol., 1. 2014. (Construction Site Ser.). (ENG.). 24p. (J). (gr. k-2). 23.60 *(978-1-4777-2859-8(7),* PowerKids Pr.) Rosen Publishing Group, Inc., The.

Randolph, Joanne. Bulldozers. 2009. (Earth Movers Ser.). 24p. (gr. k-1). 37.50 *(978-1-61512-233-2(8),* PowerKids Pr.) Rosen Publishing Group, Inc., The.

—Earth Movers, 6 bks. Incl. Bulldozers. lib. bdg. 18.75 *(978-0-8239-6025-5(0));* Wheel Loaders. lib. bdg. 18.75 *(978-0-8239-6026-2(9));* 24p. (J). (gr. 1). 2002. (Illus.). Set lib. bdg. 88.50 *(978-0-8239-7113-8(9),* PowerKids Pr.) Rosen Publishing Group, Inc., The.

Reinke, Beth Bence. Bulldozers Push! 2017. (Bumba Books (tm) — Construction Zone Ser.). (ENG.). 24p. (J). (gr. -1-1). 25.32 ***(978-1-5124-3358-6(6))*** Lerner Publishing Group.

Schuh, Mari C. Bulldozers. 2017. (Spot Mighty Machines Ser.). (ENG.). 16p. (gr. k-3). 17.95 ***(978-1-68151-099-6(5))*** Amicus Publishing.

Tourville, Amanda Doering. Bulldozers, 1 vol. Trover, Zachary, illus. 2009. (Mighty Machines Ser.). (ENG.). 32p. (J). (gr. -1-3). 28.50 *(978-1-60270-621-7(2))* Magic Wagon.

Wiseman, Blaine. Bulldozers. 2010. (J). pap. 9.95 *(978-1-61690-143-1(8))* Weigl Pubs., Inc.

—Mighty Bulldozers. 2010. (World of Wonder Ser.). 24p. (J). (gr. 2-4). lib. bdg. 25.70 *(978-1-61690-142-4(X))* Weigl Pubs., Inc.

BULLDOZERS—FICTION

Baxter, Nicola. The Trouble with Tippers. Ball, Geoff, illus. 2012. (ENG.). 24p. (J). (gr. -1-k). pap. 6.99 *(978-1-84322-783-0(5),* Armadillo) Anness Publishing GBR. Dist: National Bk. Network.

Biro, Val. Gumdrop & the Bulldozer. (Illus.). 32p. (J). *(978-0-340-71444-7(1));* pap. *(978-0-340-71445-4(X))* Hodder & Stoughton.

Dronsfield, Paul, illus. The Bulldozer. 2009. (My Shiny Little Truck Bks.). (ENG.). 10p. (J). bds. 3.95 *(978-1-58117-858-6(1),* Intervisual/Piggy Toes) Bendon, Inc.

Fleming, Candace. Bulldozer's Big Day. Rohmann, Eric, illus. 2015. (Bulldozer Bks.). (ENG.). 40p. (J). (gr. -1-2). 17.99 *(978-1-4814-0097-8(5),* Atheneum Bks. for Young Readers) Simon & Schuster Children's Publishing.

Gabel, Stacey. The Bulldozers Dig a Pond. 2008. (Illus.). 24p. pap. 13.95 *(978-1-59858-779-1(X))* Dog Ear Publishing, LLC.

Melling, David & Whybrow, Ian. The Flying Diggers. 2010. (ENG., Illus.). 32p. (J). (gr. -1-k). pap. 9.99 *(978-0-340-90313-1(9))* Hodder & Stoughton GBR. Dist: Hachette Bk. Group.

Sharp, Euan. Diggedy Dozer in Ned at Night. 2009. 32p. pap. 13.90 *(978-0-557-04447-4(2))* Lulu Pr., Inc.

Stoddard, Jeffery, Pete & Pillar: A Story of Friendship Based on John 15:13: the Big Rain. Stoddard, Jeffery, illus. 2007. (Pete & Pillar Ser.). (ENG., Illus.). 32p. (J). (gr. -1-2). 12.99 *(978-1-59317-203-9(6))* Warner Pr., Inc.

BULLFIGHTS—FICTION

Aryal, Aimee. Hello, Ralphie! Perez, Gerry, illus. 2007. 24p. (J). lib. bdg. 14.95 *(978-1-932888-34-8(9))* Mascot Bks., Inc.

Deutsch, Stacia. The Book of Life Movie Novelization. 2014. (Book of Life Ser.). (ENG., Illus.). 144p. (J). (gr. 3-7). pap. 6.99 *(978-1-4814-2351-9(7),* Simon Spotlight) Simon Spotlight.

Leaf, Munro. The Story of Ferdinand. 2011. (gr. k-3). lib. bdg. 14.75 *(978-0-613-30144-2(7),* Turtleback) Turtleback Bks.

Reel FX Inc. Staff, et al, illus. A Tale of Two Friends. 2014. (Book of Life Ser.). (ENG.). 32p. (J). (gr. k-2). pap. 3.99 *(978-1-4814-2573-5(0),* Simon Spotlight) Simon Spotlight.

Wojciechowska, Maia. Shadow of a Bull. 2011. 8.32 *(978-0-7848-3457-2(1),* Everbind) Marco Bk. Co.

—Shadow of a Bull. 2007. (ENG.). 160p. (J). (gr. 3-7). pap. 6.99 *(978-1-4169-3395-3(6),* Simon & Schuster/Paula Wiseman Bks.) Simon & Schuster/Paula Wiseman Bks.

BULLIES

Berry, Joy. Help Me Be Good about Being Bullied. 2009. (Help Me Be Good Ser.). 32p. pap. 7.95 *(978-1-60577-125-0(2))* Berry, Joy Enterprises.

—Help Me Be Good Bullying. Bartholomew, illus. 2010. (Help Me Be Good Ser.). (ENG.). 32p. (J). (gr. -1-2). pap. 4.99 *(978-1-60577-140-3(6))* Berry, Joy Enterprises.

Doering, Amanda F. & Higgins, Melissa. No More Bullies. Shin, Simone, illus. 2015. (No More Bullies Ser.). (ENG.). 24p. (gr. k-3). 103.96 *(978-1-4795-8007-1(4))* Picture Window Bks.

Eniwaye, Olu O. Country Bully & the City Bully: A Children's Book. 2004. (J). per. 7.95 *(978-1-59427-028-4(7))* Aglob Publishing.

Johnston, Marianne. Dealing with Bullying / Qué hacer con los Bravucones. 2009. (Conflict Resolution Library / Biblioteca solución de conflictos Ser.). (ENG & SPA.). 24p. (gr. 2-3). 42.50 *(978-1-60853-413-5(8),* Editorial Buenas Letras) Rosen Publishing Group, Inc., The.

McGraw, Jay & Björkman, Manns. Life Strategies for Dealing with Bullies. Björkman, Steve, illus. 2008. (ENG.). 192p. (J). (gr. 4-8). 17.99 *(978-1-4169-7473-4(3),* Aladdin) Simon & Schuster Children's Publishing.

Morris, Daphne. Trevor Romain's Tips, Strategies & Activities for Dealing with Bullies Resource Guide. 2006. (J). spiral bd. 24.99 *(978-0-9787783-6-1(7))* Romain, Trevor Co., The.

—Trevor Romain's Tips, Strategies & Activities for Dealing with Cliques Resource Guide. 2006. (J). (gr. 2-6). spiral bd. 24.99 *(978-0-9787783-7-8(5))* Romain, Trevor Co., The.

Soske, Becky. Just the Way He Wanted Me to Be. Haisch, Joshua, illus. 2007. 32p. (J). (gr. -1-3). per. 11.99 *(978-1-59879-339-0(X))* Lifevest Publishing, Inc.

Toews, Rita Y. The Bully: A Discussion & Activity Story. Ljungberg, Jon, illus. I.t. ed. 2004. (ENG.). 40p. (J). *(978-0-9736224-0-9(7))* Birds Hill Publishing.

Williams, Sam. Are You a Bully? 2012. (ENG., Illus.). 24p. (gr. k-2). pap. 8.95 *(978-1-61810-267-6(2))* Rourke Educational Media.

BULLIES—FICTION

Abreu, Raquel, illus. Little Ruth Reddingford (and the Wolf) An Old Tale retold by Hank Wesselman, PH. D. 2004. 32p. (J). per. 15.95 *(978-0-9740190-0-0(3))* Illumination Arts Publishing Co., Inc.

Achor, Shawn & Blankson, Amy. Ripple's Effect. O'Malley, Judy, ed. Rebora, Cecilia, illus. 2012. (ENG.). 32p. (J). (gr. -1-k). 18.95 *(978-0-9829938-7-3(0))* March 4th, Inc.

Adams, W. Royce. The Computer's Nerd. 2011. 154p. (gr. 4-7). 22.99 *(978-0-9712206-9-0(7))* Rairarubia Bks.

Aguirre, Ann. Mortal Danger. 2014. (Immortal Game Ser.: 1). (ENG.). 384p. (YA). (gr. 7). 17.99 *(978-1-250-02464-0(1),* 9781250024640) Feiwel & Friends.

Albee, Sarah. Clever Trevor. Billin-Frye, Paige, illus. 2003. (Science Solves It! Ser.). 32p. (J). pap. 5.95 *(978-1-57565-123-1(8))* Kane Press, Inc.

—Trevor el Ingenioso. Billin-Frye, Paige, illus. 2008. (Science Solves It! en Espanol Ser.).Tr. of Clever Trevor. (SPA.). 32p. (J). (gr. -1-3). pap. 5.95 *(978-1-57565-263-4(3))* Kane Press, Inc.

—Trevor el Ingenioso; Clever Trevor. 2008. pap. 34.95 *(978-0-7613-3868-0(3))* Kane Press, Inc.

Alexander, Claire. Lucy & the Bully, 1 vol. Alexander, Claire, illus. 2008. (ENG., Illus.). 32p. (J). (gr. -1-3). 16.99 *(978-0-8075-4786-1(7))* Whitman, Albert & Co.

Alexander, Jill S. The Sweetheart of Prosper County. 2010. (ENG.). 240p. (YA). (gr. 7-12). pap. 18.99 *(978-0-312-54857-5(5),* 9780312548575) Square Fish.

Alexander, Michael. Until Wishes Are Fulfilled II: Alec's Story. 2007. 204p. per. 15.50 *(978-1-84426-468-1(8))* Upfront Publishing Ltd. GBR. Dist: Printondemand-worldwide.com.

Alger, Horatio. Frank & Fearless or the Fortunes of Jasper Kent. 2007. 228p. 20.99 *(978-1-4280-7465-1(1));* per. 14.99 *(978-1-4280-7470-5(8))* IndyPublish.com.

Alpert, Sandra F. Horrible Howard: The Bully & Coward. Date not set. (Bully Busting Ser.: Bk. 1). (Illus.). (Orig.). (J). (gr. k-5). pap. *(978-1-884931-02-4(2))* Global Commitment Publishing.

Anderson, Jeff. Zack Delacruz: Me & My Big Mouth. (Zack Delacruz Ser.). (ENG., Illus.). 176p. (J). (gr. 5-8). 2016. pap. 6.95 *(978-1-4549-2127-1(7))* 2015. 12.95 *(978-1-4549-1499-0(8))* Sterling Publishing Co., Inc.

Anderson, John David. Posted. 2017. 384p. (J). (gr. 3-7). 16.99 *(978-0-06-233820-4(X),* Walden Pond Pr.) HarperCollins Pubs.

Anglin, M. R. Lucas: Guardian of Truth. 2012. 192p. pap. 8.00 *(978-1-60039-195-8(8))* Lamp Post Inc.

Applegate, Katherine. Never Swipe a Bully's Bear. Biggs, Brian, illus. 2008. (Roscoe Riley Rules Ser.: 2). (ENG.). 96p. (J). (gr. 1-5). 15.99 *(978-0-06-114884-2(9));* pap. 4.99 *(978-0-06-114883-5(0))* HarperCollins Pubs.

Arena, Felice & Kettle, Phil. Hit the Beach. Vane, Mitch, illus. 2004. (J). pap. *(978-1-59336-361-1(3))* Mondo Publishing.

Arnold, Louise. Golden & Grey: An Unremarkable Boy & a Rather Remarkable Ghost. 2006. (ENG., Illus.). 272p. (J). (gr. 3-7). reprint ed. pap. 6.99 *(978-0-689-87585-4(1),* McElderry, Margaret K. Bks.) McElderry, Margaret K. Bks.

—Golden & Grey: The Nightmares That Ghosts Have. 2007. (ENG.). 304p. (J). (gr. 3-7). pap. 5.99 *(978-0-689-87587-8(8),* McElderry, Margaret K. Bks.) McElderry, Margaret K. Bks.

Babcock, Nona Burroughs. Little Wolf's Adventure: A Medicine Dream & Warrior Ghosts. 2008. 212p. 24.95 *(978-0-595-49087-5(5));* pap. 14.95 *(978-0-595-46072-4(0))* iUniverse, Inc.

Bailey, Kevin. Anthony Meets the Playground Bully. 2009. 20p. pap. 13.50 *(978-1-60860-072-4(6),* Eloquent Bks.) Strategic Book Publishing & Rights Agency (SBPRA).

Barkow, Henriette. Tom & Sofia Start School. Lamont, Priscilla, illus. 2004. 32p. (J). (ENG & HIN.). pap. *(978-1-84444-570-7(4));* (ENG & GRE.). pap. *(978-1-84444-568-4(2));* (ENG & GER.). pap. *(978-1-84444-567-7(4));* (FRE & ENG.). pap. *(978-1-84444-566-0(6));* (ENG & ALB.). pap. *(978-1-84444-560-8(7));* (ENG & GUJ.). pap. *(978-1-84444-569-1(0));* (ENG & ARA.). pap. *(978-1-84444-561-5(5));* (ENG & BEN.). pap. *(978-1-84444-562-2(3));* (CHI & ENG.). pap. *(978-1-84444-563-9(1));* (ENG & CHI.). pap. *(978-1-84444-564-6(X));* (ENG & PER.). pap. *(978-1-84444-565-3(8))* Mantra Lingua.

Baskin, Nora Raleigh. Runt. 2013. (ENG., Illus.). 208p. (J). (gr. 3-7). 15.99 *(978-1-4424-5807-9(0),* Simon & Schuster Bks. For Young Readers) Simon & Schuster Bks. For Young Readers.

Bateman, Teresa. The Bully Blockers Club. Urbanovic, Jackie, illus. 2004. (ENG.). 32p. (J). (gr. 1-3). 6.99 *(978-0-8075-0919-7(1))* Whitman, Albert & Co.

Bauer, Michael Gerard. Don't Call Me Ishmael. 2007. 255p. (YA). (gr. 9-12). lib. bdg. 17.89 *(978-0-06-134835-8(X),* HarperTeen) HarperCollins Pubs.

Becker, Helaine. Let Sleeping Dogs Lie, 1 vol. 2016. (Dirk Daring, Secret Agent Ser.: 2). (ENG., Illus.). 240p. (J). (gr. 3-6). pap. 9.95 *(978-1-4598-1038-9(4))* Orca Bk. Pubs. USA.

Belavilas, Charlotte. Walter, the Carpenter Bee. 2007. pap. 9.00 *(978-0-8059-8504-7(2))* Dorrance Publishing Co., Inc.

Bellingham, Brenda. Lilly Traps the Bullies. MacDonald, Clarke, illus. 2011. (Formac First Novels Ser.). (ENG.). 64p. (J). (gr. 2-3). 14.95 *(978-0-88780-961-3(8),* 9780887809613); pap. 5.95 *(978-0-88780-959-0(6),* 9780887809590) Formac Publishing Co., Ltd. CAN. Dist: Casemate Pubs. & Bk. Distributors, LLC.

Berenstain, Jan & Berenstain, Mike. Berenstain Bears & the Gift of Courage, 1 vol. Berenstain, Stan, illus. 2010. (Berenstain Bears/Living Lights Ser.). (ENG.). 32p. (J). (gr. -1-2). pap. 3.99 *(978-0-310-71256-5(4))* Zonderkidz.

Berman, Ali. Misdirected: A Novel. 2014. (ENG., Illus.). 290p. (YA). (gr. 7). 18.95 *(978-1-60980-573-9(9),* Triangle Square) Seven Stories Pr.

Big Bad Bully. 2006. (ENG.). 32p. (J). pap. 12.99 *(978-0-9758709-1-4(2))* Send The Light Distribution LLC.

Blagden, Scott. Dear Life, You Suck: A Novel. 2015. (ENG.). 320p. (YA). (gr. 9). pap. 9.99 *(978-0-544-33621-6(6),* HMH Books For Young Readers) Houghton Mifflin Harcourt Publishing Co.

Blahitka, Vira. Joad the Toad. 2013. 32p. pap. *(978-1-4602-1881-5(7))* FriesenPress.

Blake-Brekke, Carri. Billy Bully Bug: Learns a Lesson in Hawaii. Melton, Jodi, illus. 2003. (Mrs. B's Story Time... With a Twist! Ser.). 20p. (J). pap. 11.95 incl. audio compact disk *(978-0-9720549-2-8(8))* Mom's Pride Enterprises.

Boelts, Maribeth. The PS Brothers. 2011. (ENG.). 144p. (J). (gr. 2-5). pap. 6.99 *(978-0-547-57717-3(6))* Houghton Mifflin Harcourt Publishing Co.

Bolger, Kevin. Zombiekins. 2010. (ENG.). 208p. (J). (gr. 4-7). 10.99 *(978-1-59514-177-4(4),* Razorbill) Penguin Young Readers Group.

Boston, Ruth. Super Hero for A Day. 2007. 152p. per. 13.95 *(978-1-4327-1427-7(9))* Outskirts Pr., Inc.

Bottner, Barbara. Miss Brooks' Story Nook (where Tales Are Told & Ogres Are Welcome) Emberley, Michael, illus. 2014. (ENG.). 40p. (J). (gr. k-4). 16.99 *(978-0-449-81328-7(2),* Knopf Bks. for Young Readers) Random Hse. Children's Bks.

Bowles, Paula. Scary Mary. 2012. (ENG., Illus.). 24p. (J). *(978-1-58925-110-6(5))* Tiger Tales.

Bracken, Beth. The Little Bully, 1 vol. Bell, Jennifer A., illus. 2012. (Little Boost Ser.). (ENG.). 32p. (gr. k-3). lib. bdg. 23.99 *(978-1-4048-6795-6(3),* Little Boost) Picture Window Bks.

Brennan, Eileen. Bad Astrid. Dunnick, Regan, illus. 2013. (ENG.). 40p. (J). (gr. -1-2). 15.99 *(978-0-375-85580-1(7),* Random Hse. Bks. for Young Readers) Random Hse. Children's Bks.

—Bad Astrid. Dunnick, Regan, illus. 2013. (J). *(978-0-449-81427-7(0))* Random Hse., Inc.

Briggs, Andy. Council of Evil. 2009. 1.00 *(978-1-4074-4313-3(5))* Recorded Bks., Inc.

Brill, Calista. Tugboat Bill & the River Rescue. Carpenter, Tad, illus. 2017. 40p. (J). (gr. -1-3). 17.99 *(978-0-06-236618-4(1))* HarperCollins Pubs.

Brouwer, Sigmund. Justine McKeen vs. the Queen of Mean, 1 vol. Whamond, Dave, illus. 2014. (Orca Echoes Ser.). (ENG.). 64p. (J). (gr. 2-3). pap. 6.95 *(978-1-4598-0397-8(3))* Orca Bk. Pubs. USA.

Buckley, Michael. Attack of the Bullies. 2013. (Nerds Ser.). (ENG.). 336p. (YA). (gr. 3-7). 16.95 *(978-1-4197-0857-2(0),* Amulet Bks.) Abrams, Inc.

Buckner, Chuck. The Death of Arkie Baker. 2008. 84p. pap. 8.86 *(978-1-4357-4105-8(6))* Lulu Pr., Inc.

Butler, Dori Hillestad. Trading Places with Tank Talbott. 2003. (ENG.). 144p. (J). (gr. 3-7). 15.99 *(978-0-8075-1708-6(9))* Whitman, Albert & Co.

—The Truth about Truman School, 1 vol. (ENG.). (J). (gr. 3-7). 2009. 192p. pap. 7.99 *(978-0-8075-8096-7(1))* 2008. (Illus.). 176p. lib. bdg. 15.99 *(978-0-8075-8095-0(3))* Whitman, Albert & Co.

Cabot, Meg. The New Girl. 2008. (Allie Finkle's Rules for Girls Ser.: 2). (ENG.). 240p. (J). (gr. 3-7). 15.99 *(978-0-545-04049-5(3),* Scholastic Pr.) Scholastic, Inc.

Cannon, Sherrill S. Manner-Man. 2013. 28p. pap. 12.50 *(978-1-62212-478-7(2),* Strategic Bk. Publishing) Strategic Book Publishing & Rights Agency (SBPRA).

Carlson, Melody. Girl Power, 1 vol. 2016. (Faithgirlz / Girls of Harbor View Ser.). (ENG.). 272p. (J). pap. 9.99 *(978-0-310-75361-2(9))* Zonderkidz.

Carlson, Nancy. Henry & the Bully. 2012. (ENG.). 32p. (J). (gr. -1-1). pap. 6.99 *(978-0-14-242120-8(0),* Puffin Books) Penguin Young Readers Group.

—Loudmouth George & the Sixth Grade Bully. 20th anniv. ed. 2005. (Nancy Carlson's Neighborhood Ser.). (Illus.). 32p. (gr. k-2). 15.95 *(978-1-57505-218-2(0))* Lerner Publishing Group.

—Loudmouth George & the Sixth-Grade Bully. 20th anniv. rev. ed. 2003. (Nancy Carlson's Neighborhood Ser.). (ENG., Illus.). 32p. (J). (gr. k-2). pap. 6.95 *(978-1-57505-549-7(X))* Lerner Publishing Group.

Castle, M. E. Cloneward Bound. 2013. (Clone Chronicles Ser.: No. 2). (ENG.). 272p. (J). (gr. 3-7). pap. 6.99 *(978-1-60684-473-1(3),* Darby Creek) Lerner Publishing Group.

—Game of Clones. (Clone Chronicles Ser.: No. 3). (ENG.). 256p. (J). (gr. 3-7). 2014. 15.99 *(978-1-60684-234-8(X))*No. 3. 2015. pap. 6.99 *(978-1-60684-538-7(1))* Lerner Publishing Group. (Darby Creek).

—Popular Clone. 2012. (Clone Chronicles: No. 1). (ENG.). 320p. (J). (gr. 3-7). pap. 6.99 *(978-1-60684-414-4(8));* 15.99 *(978-1-60684-232-4(3))* Lerner Publishing Group. (Darby Creek).

Chmakova, Svetlana. Brave. 2017. (J). lib. bdg. 22.10 ***(978-0-606-40456-3(2))*** Turtleback Bks.

Christopher, Matt. Lacrosse Face-Off. 2010. (Matt Christopher Sports Library). 128p. (J). (gr. 4-6). lib. bdg. 26.60 *(978-1-59953-355-1(3))* Norwood Hse. Pr.

—Lacrosse Face-Off. 2006. (ENG.). 128p. (J). (gr. 3-7). per. 15.99 *(978-0-316-79641-5(7))* Little, Brown Bks. for Young Readers.

Clarke, David. Snake Bite: A Novel. 2009. 188p. 23.95 *(978-0-595-71833-7(7));* pap. 13.95 *(978-0-595-48406-5(9))* iUniverse, Inc.

Clements, Andrew. Bully Buster. 2014. (Jake Drake Ser. Bk. 1 Ser.). (ENG.). 80p. (J). (gr. 2-5). 9.24 *(978-1-63245-290-0(1))* Lectorum Pubns., Inc.

—Bully Buster. Frazee, Marla & Pedersen, Janet, illus. 2008. (Jake Drake Ser.: Bk. 1). 67p. (gr. 2-5). 15.00 *(978-0-7569-9001-5(7))* Perfection Learning Corp.

—Bully Buster. Pedersen, Janet & Frazee, Marla, illus. 2007. (Jake Drake Ser.: Bk. 1). (ENG.). 80p. (J). (gr. 2-5). pap. 5.99 *(978-1-4169-3933-7(4),* Atheneum Bks. for Young Readers) Simon & Schuster Children's Publishing.

Clevenger, Lee. IncrediBoy: Be Careful What You Wish. 2004. 267p. (J). pap. 12.95 *(978-0-9764052-0-7(2))* Thomas Max Publishing.

Codell, Esmé Raji. Vive la Paris. 2006. (ENG.). 224p. (gr. 4-7). 15.99 *(978-0-7868-5124-9(4))* Hyperion Pr.

Cody, Matthew. Powerless. 2011. (Supers of Noble's Green Ser.). (ENG.). 288p. (J). (gr. 3-7). 7.99 *(978-0-375-84489-8(9),* Yearling) Random Hse. Children's Bks.

Cohen, Miriam. Tough Jim, 1 vol. Himler, Ronald, illus. (ENG.). 32p. (J). (gr. -1-3). 2008. 15.95 *(978-1-59572-071-9(5))* 2007. pap. 5.95 *(978-1-59572-072-6(3))* Star Bright Bks., Inc.

Cole, Frank. The Adventures of Hashbrown Winters. 2009. (J). pap. 7.99 *(978-1-59955-303-0(1))* Cedar Fort, Inc./CFI Distribution.

Coleman, Evelyn. Freedom Train. 2012. (ENG.). 160p. (J). (gr. 3-7). pap. 7.99 *(978-1-4424-3652-7(2),* McElderry, Margaret K. Bks.) McElderry, Margaret K. Bks.

—Freedom Train. Riley, David, illus. 2008. (ENG.). 160p. (J). (gr. 3-7). 17.99 *(978-0-689-84716-5(5),* McElderry, Margaret K. Bks.) McElderry, Margaret K. Bks.

Collard, Sneed B., III. Dog Sense, 1 vol. (ENG.). 192p. (J). (gr. 3-7). 2008. pap. 7.95 *(978-1-56145-460-0(5))* 2005. 14.95 *(978-1-56145-351-1(X))* Peachtree Pubs.

Collins, Ross. Medusa Jones. 2008. (J). *(978-0-439-90101-7(4),* Levine, Arthur A. Bks.) Scholastic, Inc.

Cooper, Jay. Mutant Rat Attack! 2017. (Spy Next Door Ser.: 1). (ENG.). 144p. (J). (gr. 2-5). 9.99 *(978-0-545-93297-4(1),* Scholastic Pr.) Scholastic, Inc.

Coville, Bruce. The Monster's Ring. Coville, Katherine, illus. 2008. (Magic Shop Book Ser.: 1). (ENG.). 128p. (J). (gr. 5-7). pap. 6.99 *(978-0-15-206442-6(7))* Houghton Mifflin Harcourt Publishing Co.

Crutcher, Chris. Period 8. 2013. 288p. (YA). (gr. 9). (ENG.). 17.99 *(978-0-06-191480-5(0));* lib. bdg. 18.89 *(978-0-06-191481-2(9))* HarperCollins Pubs. (Greenwillow Bks.).

Cuyler, Margery. Bullies Never Win. Howard, Arthur, illus. 2009. (ENG.). 32p. (J). (gr. k-3). 17.99 *(978-0-689-86187-1(7),* Simon & Schuster Bks. For Young Readers) Simon & Schuster Bks. For Young Readers.

Dahl, Michael. Eye of the Monster, 1 vol. Piatti, Federico, illus. 2010. (Dragonblood Ser.). (ENG.). 40p. (gr. 1-3). lib. bdg. 23.99 *(978-1-4342-1928-2(3),* Zone Bks.) Stone Arch Bks.

Dail, Maggie. Getting to First Base - Chris Struggles to Read. 2006. 157p. pap. 13.95 *(978-1-4116-8125-5(8))* Lulu Pr., Inc.

Daly, Joseph M. Strange Town Volume One: The Woods Behind Trevor Malone's House. 2007. 265p. (YA). pap. 9.99 net. *(978-0-9779921-0-2(1))* Wolfs Corner Publishing.

Daly, Niki. Nicholas & the Wild Ones: How to Beat the Bullies. 2016. (ENG.). 32p. (J). (gr. -1-3). 18.99 *(978-1-84780-853-0(0),* Frances Lincoln Children's Bks.) Quarto Publishing Group UK GBR. Dist: Hachette Bk. Group.

Davies, Matt. Ben Rides On. 2013. (ENG., Illus.). 32p. (J). (gr. -1-2). 17.99 (978-1-59643-794-4(4), 9781596437944) Roaring Brook Pr.

Davis, Mandy. Superstar. 2017. 336p. (J). (gr. 3-7). 16.99 (978-0-06-237777-7(9)) HarperCollins Pubs.

dePaola, Tomie. Trouble in the Barkers' Class. dePaola, Tomie, illus. 2006. (Barker Twins Ser.). (ENG., Illus.). 32p. (J). (gr. -1-3). reprint ed. pap. 6.99 (978-0-14-240585-7(X), Puffin Books) Penguin Young Readers Group.

DePino, Catherine S. Blue Cheese Breath & Stinky Feet: How to Deal with Bullies. Matthews, Bonnie, illus. 2004. 48p. (J). 14.95 (978-1-59147-111-0(7)); pap. 9.95 (978-1-59147-112-7(5)) American Psychological Assn. (Magination Pr.).

Dewdney, Anna. Llama Llama & the Bully Goat. 2013. (Llama Llama Ser.). (ENG., Illus.). 40p. (J). (gr. -1-k). 17.99 (978-0-670-01395-1(1), Viking Books for Young Readers) Penguin Young Readers Group.

Dinbergs, Holly Smith. Bowling Buddies. Foye, Lloyd, illus. 2005. (Girlz Rock! Ser.). (J). pap. (978-1-59336-699-5(X)) Mondo Publishing.

Disney Book Group Staff. Sheriff Callie's Wild West Toby Braves the Bully. Disney Storybook Art Team, illus. 2015. (ENG.). 16p. (J). (gr. -1-k). pap. 6.99 (978-1-4847-1562-8(4)) Disney Pr.

Disney Press Staff. Sheriff Callie's Wild West: Toby Braves the Bully. 2015. (J). lib. bdg. 17.20 (978-0-606-35914-6(1)) Turtleback Bks.

Dolan, Penny. Little Troll. Smith, Lisa, illus. 2008. (Tadpoles Ser.). (ENG.). 24p. (J). (gr. -1-3). lib. bdg. (978-0-7787-3856-5(6)) Crabtree Publishing Co.

Don't Bully Me. 2004. (J). (ENG & GUJ.). (978-1-84444-556-1(9)); (ENG & FRE.). (978-1-84444-555-4(0)); (PER & ENG.). (978-1-84444-554-7(2)); (CRO & ENG.). (978-1-84444-553-0(4)); (ENG & HIN.). (978-1-84444-557-8(7)) Mantra Lingua.

Douglas, Marjory Stoneman & Milkweed Editions Staff. Alligator Crossing. Nicholson, Trudy, illus. 2003. (ENG.). 192p. (J). (gr. 3-8). pap. 7.95 (978-1-57131-644-8(2)) Milkweed Editions.

Downer, Denise. Tombstone Twins Package: Soul Mates. Frampton, Otis, illus. 2013. (ENG.). 41p. (J). (gr. 2-4). pap. 35.70 (978-1-4342-3955-6(1)) Stone Arch Bks.

Durant, Alan. Humpty Dumpty's Great Fall. Heming, Leah-Ellen, illus. 2012. (ENG.). 32p. (J). (978-0-7787-8028-1(7)); pap. (978-0-7787-8039-7(2)) Crabtree Publishing Co.

Earhart, Kristin. Puppy Powers #2: Wag, You're It! 2014. (Puppy Powers Ser.: 2). (ENG., Illus.). 96p. (J). (gr. 2-5). pap. 4.99 (978-0-545-61760-4(X), Scholastic Paperbacks) Scholastic, Inc.

Edgerton, Martha. Civility Matters: Anna Moves to the Big City. 2011. 38p. pap. 16.95 (978-1-4626-4211-3(X)) America Star Bks.

Edwards, Michelle. Stinky Stern Forever. 2007. (Jackson Friends Bks.). (Illus.). 49p. (gr. 1-4). 15.95 (978-0-7569-8198-3(0)) Perfection Learning Corp.

—Stinky Stern Forever: A Jackson Friends Book. 2007. (Jackson Friends Ser.). (ENG., Illus.). 56p. (J). (gr. 1-4). pap. 6.95 (978-0-15-206101-2(0)) Houghton Mifflin Harcourt Publishing Co.

Elder, Joshua. Mail Order Ninja, 1 vol., Vol. 1. Owen, Erich, illus. 2009. (Tokyopop Ser.). (ENG.). 96p. (gr. 2-6). 25.65 (978-1-59961-568-4(1)) Spotlight.

—Mail Order Ninja Vol. 2: Timmy Strikes Back, 1 vol. Owen, Erich, illus. 2009. (Tokyopop Ser.). (ENG.). 104p. (gr. 2-6). 25.65 (978-1-59961-569-1(X)) Spotlight.

Emberley, Ed. Bye-Bye, Big Bad Bullybug! Emberley, Ed, illus. 2007. (ENG., Illus.). 32p. (J). (gr. -1-3). 14.99 (978-0-316-01762-6(0)) Little, Brown Bks. for Young Readers.

Emily Breaks Free - Evaluation Guide. 2006. (J). (978-1-55942-404-2(4)) Witcher Productions.

English, Karen. Dog Days. Freeman, Laura, illus. 2014. (Carver Chronicles Ser.). (ENG.). 128p. (J). (gr. 1-4). pap. 5.99 (978-0-544-33912-5(6), HMH Books For Young Readers) Houghton Mifflin Harcourt Publishing Co.

Erickson, John R. The Case of the Car-Barkaholic Dog. Holmes, Gerald L., illus. 2011. (Hank the Cowdog Ser.). (ENG.). 115p. (J). (gr. 3-6). pap. 5.99 (978-1-59188-117-9(X)) Maverick Bks., Inc.

Fabian, Cynthia. Can't & Able: An Inspirational Story. Stevens, Daniel, illus. 2012. 28p. pap. 12.50 (978-1-61204-327-2(5), Strategic Bk. Publishing) Strategic Book Publishing & Rights Agency (SBPRA).

Fairchild Hawks, Lyn. How Wendy Redbird Dancing Survived the Dark Ages of Nought. 2013. (ENG.). 286p. (C). pap. 16.99 (978-0-9888837-2-7(4)) Hawks, Lyn.

Farmer, Tom. Once upon a Daydream: The Story of Patrick & the Clumsy Camel. 2013. 44p. pap. 17.44 (978-1-4669-6912-4(1)) Trafford Publishing.

The Fearsome Four: Individual Title Six-Packs. (Bookweb Ser.). 32p. (gr. 3-18). 34.00 (978-0-7635-3932-0(5)) Rigby Education.

Fields, T. S. Missing in the Mountains. 2008. (ENG.). 108p. (J). (gr. 4-7). pap. 6.95 (978-0-87358-950-5(5)) Cooper Square Publishing Llc.

Fitzgerald, Mary. Jodie Has Jagged Edges. 2012. (ENG.). 21p. (J). pap. 22.95 (978-1-4327-8839-1(6)) Outskirts Pr., Inc.

Fitzpatrick, Melody. Operation Josh Taylor. 2015. (Hannah Smart Ser.: 1). (ENG., Illus.). 112p. (J). (gr. 4-7). pap. 12.99 (978-1-4597-3134-9(4)) Dundurn CAN. Dist: Ingram Publisher Services.

Fleming, David. Saturday Boy. 2013. (ENG.). 272p. (J). (gr. 5). 16.99 (978-0-670-78551-3(2), Viking Books for Young Readers) Penguin Young Readers Group.

Flores-Galbis, Enrique. 90 Miles to Havana. 2012. (ENG.). 304p. (J). (gr. 4-7). pap. 7.99 (978-1-250-00559-5(0), 9781250005595) Square Fish.

Fogg, K. L. Widow's Revenge: A Novel. 2007. 355p. (J). (978-1-59811-319-8(4)) Covenant Communications.

Fontes, Justine. Henry's Turn. Hefferan, Rob, illus. 2004. (J). (978-1-59336-004-7(5)); pap. (978-1-59336-005-4(3)) Mondo Publishing.

Fowler, Josephine A. Lilly's Faith. 2012. 32p. (-18). pap. 19.99 (978-1-4772-8688-3(8)) AuthorHouse.

Frost, Lesley. Mr Bothers. Cassetta, Andrea, illus. 2007. 52p. per. 12.95 (978-1-934246-59-7(X)) Peppertree Pr., The.

Fry, Michael. Zero Tolerance. Fry, Michael, illus. 2013. (Odd Squad Book Ser.). (ENG., Illus.). 240p. (J). (gr. 3-7). 12.99 (978-1-4231-7099-0(7)) Hyperion Pr.

Galan, Alvaro. Billy Bully. Simpson, Steve, illus. 2009. (ENG.). 32p. (J). (gr. -1-3). pap. 3.99 (978-0-545-11012-9(2)) Scholastic, Inc.

Gallagher, Diana G. Beware! The Complicated Life of Claudia Cristina Cortez, 1 vol. Garvey, Brann, illus. 2009. (Claudia Cristina Cortez Ser.). (ENG.). 88p. (gr. 2-3). 26.65 (978-1-4342-1575-8(X), Claudia Cristina Cortez) Stone Arch Bks.

Gardner, Graham. Inventing Elliot. 2005. (ENG.). 192p. (YA). (gr. 7-7). 5.99 (978-0-14-240344-0(X), Speak) Penguin Young Readers Group.

—Inventing Elliot. 2005. 181p. (YA). 13.65 (978-0-7569-5704-9(4)) Perfection Learning Corp.

Garlick, Nicholas. Storm Horse. 2017. (J). pap. **(978-0-545-90415-5(3))** Scholastic, Inc.

Garza, Xavier. Rooster Joe & the Bully / el Gallo Joe y el Abusón. 2016. (ENG & SPA.). 128p. (J). (gr. 5-8). pap. 9.95 (978-1-55885-835-0(0), Piñata Books) Arte Publico Pr.

Gervay, Susanne. Being Jack. Wilcox, Cathy, illus. 2015. 167p. (J). (978-1-61067-455-3(3)) Kane Miller.

—I Am Jack. Cathy, Wilcox, illus. 2013. (ENG.). 144p. (J). pap. 5.99 (978-1-61067-128-6(7)) Kane Miller.

Gibbs, Stuart. Poached. 2014. (FunJungle Ser.). (ENG., Illus.). 352p. (J). (gr. 3-7). 17.99 (978-1-4424-6777-4(0), Simon & Schuster Bks. For Young Readers) Simon & Schuster Bks. For Young Readers.

Gilman, Grace. Dixie & the Good Deeds. McConnell, Sarah, illus. 2013. (I Can Read Level 1 Ser.). (ENG.). 32p. (J). (gr. -1-3). 16.99 (978-0-06-208657-0(X)); pap. 3.99 (978-0-06-208643-3(X)) HarperCollins Pubs.

Glassman, Miriam. Call Me Oklahoma! 2013. (ENG.). 128p. (J). (gr. 2-7). 16.95 (978-0-8234-2742-0(0)) Holiday Hse., Inc.

Goff, John. The Take Over. Evans, Patricia, ed. 2012. 196p. (J). pap. 18.99 (978-0-9841934-8-6(0)) Bryson Taylor Publishing.

Gorman, Carol. A Midsummer Night's Dork. 2004. (ENG.). 224p. (J). 15.99 (978-0-06-050718-3(7)) HarperCollins Pubs.

Gownley, Jim. Amelia vs. the Sneeze Barf: #1, 1 vol. Gownley, Jim, illus. 2011. (Amelia Rules! Ser.). (ENG., Illus.). 36p. 24.21 (978-1-59961-787-9(0)) Spotlight.

Grabenstein, Chris. I Funny: A Middle School Story. Patterson, James, ed. Park, Laura, illus. 2012. 303p. (J). 11.99 (978-0-316-22638-7(6), 1351607) Little Brown & Co.

—Riley Mack & the Other Known Troublemakers. 2012. (Riley Mack Ser.: 1). (ENG.). 272p. (J). (gr. 3-7). 16.99 (978-0-06-202620-0(8)) HarperCollins Pubs.

Green, D. L. Zeke Meeks vs the Stinkin' Science Fair, 1 vol. Alves, Josh, illus. 2012. (Zeke Meeks Ser.). (ENG.). 128p. (gr. 2-2). pap. 5.95 (978-1-4048-7222-6(1)); lib. bdg. 22.65 (978-1-4048-6802-1(X)) Picture Window Bks. (Zeke Meeks).

Greene, Jacqueline. Secrets at Camp Nokomis: A Rebecca Mystery. Hirsch, Jennifer, ed. Tibbles, JeanPaul, illus. 2010. (ENG.). 192p. (J). (gr. 4-8). pap. 6.95 (978-1-59369-657-3(4)) American Girl Publishing, Inc.

Griffin, Adele. The Julian Game. 2011. (ENG.). 208p. (YA). (gr. 7-18). 7.99 (978-0-14-241973-1(7), Speak) Penguin Young Readers Group.

Grindley, Sally. Feather Wars. 2003. (ENG.). 1p. (J). pap. 12.99 (978-0-7475-6338-9(1)) Bloomsbury Publishing Plc GBR. Dist: Independent Pubs. Group.

Hahn, Mary Downing. Stepping on the Cracks. 2009. (ENG.). 224p. (J). (gr. 5-7). pap. 7.99 (978-0-547-07660-7(6)) Houghton Mifflin Harcourt Publishing Co.

—Where I Belong. 2014. (ENG.). 240p. (J). (gr. 5-7). 16.99 (978-0-544-23020-0(5)) Houghton Mifflin Harcourt Publishing Co.

Hannan, Peter. My Big Mouth: 10 Songs I Wrote That Almost Got Me Killed. Hannan, Peter, illus. 2011. (ENG., Illus.). 240p. (J). (gr. 3-7). 16.99 (978-0-545-16210-4(6), Scholastic Pr.) Scholastic, Inc.

Harmon, Michael. Brutal. 2011. (ENG.). 240p. (YA). (gr. 9). pap. 8.99 (978-0-440-23995-6(8), Knopf Bks. for Young Readers) Random Hse. Children's Bks.

Harpster, Steve, illus. Betty Stops the Bully: An Emotional Literacy Book. 2004. (Emotional Literacy Ser.). 44p. (J). (gr. 2-18). 14.95 (978-0-9747789-1-4(5), 67313) CTC Publishing.

Harrington, Janice N. Catching a Story Fish. 2016. (ENG.). 224p. (J). (gr. 2-7). 17.95 (978-1-62979-429-7(5), Wordsong) Boyds Mills Pr.

Harris, Patricia. The Cat & the Dog. 2017. (Farmyard Tales Ser.). 24p. (gr. 4-6). pap. 8.25 **(978-1-5383-2178-2(5),** PowerKids Pr.) Rosen Publishing Group, Inc., The.

Harrison, Emma. Toe the Line: A Rival High Novel. 2008. (YA). (978-1-4114-0526-4(9), Spark Publishing Group) Sterling Publishing Co., Inc.

Hautman, Pete. Blank Confession. (ENG.). 176p. (YA). (gr. 7). 2011. pap. 10.99 (978-1-4169-1328-3(9)) 2010. 16.99 (978-1-4169-1327-6(0)) Simon & Schuster Bks. For Young Readers. (Simon & Schuster Bks. For Young Readers).

Hawley, Bobby. By Golly, Molly, You're Right. 2006. 48p. pap. 16.95 (978-1-4241-2085-7(3)) PublishAmerica, Inc.

Hayes, Geoffrey. Benny & Penny in the Toy Breaker. Mouly, Francoise, ed. Hayes, Geoffrey, illus. 2010. (Benny & Penny Ser.). (ENG., Illus.). 32p. (J). (gr. -1-3). 12.95 (978-1-935179-07-8(1)) TOON Books / RAW Junior, LLC.

Hellman, Charles. Adventures in Sportsand - the Baseball Bully (with accompanying CD) The Baseball Bully. Tiritilli, Robert, illus. 2008. (Adventures in SportsLand: the Bully Ser.). 32p. pap. 19.95 (978-0-935938-27-2(3)) Stogo, Malcolm Assocs.

—Adventures in SportsLand - the Basketball Bully (with accompanying CD) Tiritilli, Robert, illus. 2008. (Adventures in SportsLand: the Bully Ser.). 32p. (J). (gr. -1-3). 19.95 (978-0-935938-28-9(1)) Stogo, Malcolm Assocs.

—Adventures in SportsLand - the Football Bully (with accompanying CD) Tiritilli, Robert, illus. 2008. (Adventures in SportsLand: the Bully Ser.). 32p. (J). (gr. -1-3). 19.95 (978-0-935938-30-2(3)) Williams, Michael.

—Adventures in SportsLand - the Soccer Bully (with accompanying CD) Tiritilli, Robert, illus. 2008. (Adventures in SportsLand: the Bully Ser.). 32p. (gr. -1-3). pap. 19.95 (978-0-935938-26-5(5)) Stogo, Malcolm Assocs.

Hellman, Charles S. The Baseball Bully. Tiritilli, Robert A., illus. 2013. 34p. pap. 9.25 (978-0-935938-19-7(2)) LuckySports.

—The Football Bully. Tiritilli, Robert A., illus. 2013. 34p. pap. 9.25 (978-0-935938-22-7(2)) LuckySports.

—The Hockey Bully. Tiritilli, Robert A., illus. 2013. 34p. pap. 9.25 (978-0-935938-23-4(0)) LuckySports.

—The Volleyball Bully. Tiritilli, Robert A., illus. 2013. 34p. pap. 9.25 (978-0-935938-53-1(2)) LuckySports.

Hellman, Charles S. & Tiritilli, Robert A. The Tennis Bully. 2013. 34p. pap. 9.25 (978-0-935938-24-1(9)) LuckySports.

Helmetag Murdock, Kita. Future Flash. 2014. (ENG.). 208p. (J). (gr. 2-7). 12.95 (978-1-62873-822-3(7), Sky Pony Pr.) Skyhorse Publishing Co., Inc.

Heneghan, James. Hit Squad, 1 vol. 2003. (Orca Soundings Ser.). (ENG.). 128p. (YA). (gr. 8-12). pap. 9.95 (978-1-55143-269-4(2)) Orca Bk. Pubs. USA.

—Hit Squad. 2004. (Orca Soundings Ser.). 106p. 19.95 (978-0-7569-4300-4(0)) Perfection Learning Corp.

—Payback, 1 vol. 2008. (ENG.). 184p. (J). (gr. 4-9). pap. 8.95 (978-0-88899-704-3(3)) Groundwood Bks. CAN. Dist: Publishers Group West (PGW).

Hepler, Linda McGhee. How to Survive Seventh Grade (If You're Lucky) 2008. 146p. pap. 24.95 (978-1-60563-610-8(X)) America Star Bks.

Herold, Mariette. Luvable Lucind: Jacob & the Bullies. 2011. 40p. pap. 17.99 (978-1-4520-2356-4(5)) AuthorHouse.

Hickey, Laura L. What's in the Woods. 2012. 84p. pap. 19.95 (978-1-4626-9025-1(4)) America Star Bks.

Higbee, Heidi. It Could Happen... on the Bus. Hezlep, Amber, illus. 2012. 32p. (J). pap. 16.95 (978-0-9882940-0-4(1)) Bryson Taylor Publishing.

Hoena, Blake & Hoena, Blake A. The Ghost Trap. Bardin, Dave, illus. 2016. (Monster Heroes Ser.). (ENG.). 32p. (gr. 1-2). lib. bdg. 21.32 (978-1-4965-3757-7(2)) Stone Arch Bks.

Hoena, Blake A. & Gonzalez, Jorge. Kickoff Blitz. Ruiz, Alfonso, illus. 2010. (Sports Illustrated Kids Graphic Novels Ser.). 56p. pap. 0.50 (978-1-4342-3205-2(0)); (ENG.). (gr. 2-3). pap. 7.19 (978-1-4342-2292-3(6)); (ENG.). (gr. 2-3). 26.65 (978-1-4342-1909-1(7)) Stone Arch Bks.

Hoffman, Mary. Bravo, Grace! 2011. (ENG.). 112p. (J). (gr. 3-7). 5.99 (978-0-14-241850-5(1), Puffin Books) Penguin Young Readers Group.

Hoffmire, A. B., illus. & as told by. The Ogre Bully. Hoffmire, A. B., as told by. 2007. (Story Cove Ser.). (ENG.). 32p. (J). (gr. -1-3). 3.95 (978-0-87483-803-9(7)) August Hse. Pubs., Inc.

Hole, Stian & Bartlett, Don. Garmann's Street. 2010. (ENG.). 44p. (J). (gr. 1-5). 17.00 (978-0-8028-5357-8(9), Eerdmans Bks For Young Readers) Eerdmans, William B. Publishing Co.

Holland, Cheron. The Bully: Carmen & Artela. 2013. (ENG.). 40p. (J). pap. 12.95 (978-1-4787-1030-1(6)) Outskirts Pr., Inc.

Holm, Jennifer L. & Holm, Matthew. Super Amoeba. Holm, Jennifer L. & Holm, Matthew, illus. 2011. (Squish Ser.: No. 1). (ENG., Illus.). 96p. (J). (gr. 3-7). pap. 6.99 (978-0-375-84389-1(2)); lib. bdg. 12.99 (978-0-375-93783-5(8)) Random Hse. Children's Bks. (Random Hse. Bks. for Young Readers).

Homan, Michael. Grendel Gander the Sinister Goose. Duggins, Peat, illus. 2012. 48p. pap. 14.95 (978-1-60808-049-6(8), WriteLife Publishing) Boutique of Quality Books Publishing Co., Inc.

Hoole, Elissa Janine. Sometimes Never, Sometimes Always. 2013. (ENG.). 360p. (YA). pap. 9.99 (978-0-7387-3722-5(4), Flux) North Star Editions.

Hopkins, Ellen. Rumble. 2016. lib. bdg. 24.50 (978-0-606-38277-9(1)) Turtleback Bks.

Howard, Ryan & Howard, Krystle. My New Team. Madrid, Erwin, illus. 2015. (Little Rhino Ser.: 1). (ENG.). 112p. (J). (gr. 2-5). pap. 4.99 (978-0-545-67490-4(5), Scholastic Paperbacks) Scholastic, Inc.

Hudson, Marilyn A. Elephant Hips Are Expensive! A Tale of the Sooner State. Fulco, Haley, illus. 2007. 50p. (J). per. (978-0-9778850-2-2(X), WhorlBooks Thumbprints) Whorl Bks.

Hueller, Andy. Skipping Stones at the Center of the Earth: A Middle Grade Novel. 2011. (J). pap. 8.99 (978-1-59955-488-4(7), Bonneville Bks.) Cedar Fort, Inc./CFI Distribution.

Jackson, Al, Jr. Adventures of Middle School: The Handbook. 2013. (ENG.). 60p. (YA). pap. 12.95 (978-1-4787-0892-6(1)) Outskirts Pr., Inc.

Jackson, Vicky, illus. Poepal's Purpose. l.t. ed. 2005. 20p. (J). 7.95 (978-0-9718741-0-7(7)) Tawa Productions.

Jacobs, John Hornor. The Shibboleth. 2014. (Twelve-Fingered Boy Trilogy: Bk. 2). 408p. (YA). (gr. 9-12). 17.95 (978-0-7613-9008-4(1), Carolrhoda Lab™) Lerner Publishing Group.

—The Twelve-Fingered Boy. (Twelve-Fingered Boy Trilogy Ser.: Bk. 1). (ENG.). 280p. (YA). (gr. 9-12). 2014. pap. 9.95 (978-1-4677-3706-7(2)) 2013. 17.95 (978-0-7613-9007-7(3)) Lerner Publishing Group.

Jacobs, Z. D. Ari & the Dybbuk. 2012. 144p. (gr. 4-6). pap. 14.95 (978-1-4685-3671-3(0)) AuthorHouse.

James, Howe. Pinky & Rex & the Bully. 2014. (Pinky & Rex Ser.). (ENG.). 48p. (J). (gr. 1-3). 8.24 (978-1-63245-347-1(9)) Lectorum Pubns., Inc.

Jenkins, Emily. Invisible Inkling. Bliss, Harry, illus. (Invisible Inkling Ser.: 1). (ENG.). (J). (gr. 1-5). 2012. 176p. pap. 5.99 (978-0-06-180222-5(0)) 2011. 160p. 16.99 (978-0-06-180220-1(4)) HarperCollins Pubs.

Jennings, Patrick. The Lightning Bugs. Alter, Anna, illus. 2003. (ENG.). 56p. (J). (gr. k-3). tchr. ed. 15.95 (978-0-8234-1673-8(9)) Holiday Hse., Inc.

—Odd, Weird & Little. 2014. (ENG.). 160p. (J). (gr. 3-7). 15.99 (978-1-60684-374-1(5), Carolrhoda Bks.) Lerner Publishing Group.

Jeremiah, Omari. Paperboy 3: The School of Doom. Rollins, Bernie, illus. 2006. 75p. pap. 12.99 (978-1-929188-13-0(7)) Morton Bks.

Johnson, Charles & Johnson, Elisheba. The Adventures of Emery Jones, Boy Science Wonder: Bending Time. Johnson, Charles, illus. 2013. (Illus.). 110p. pap. 9.99 (978-1-62015-181-5(2), Booktrope Editions) Booktrope.

Johnson, Jeremy. Rallo's Goal. 2016. (What's Your Dream? Ser.). (ENG.). 96p. (gr. 3-4). lib. bdg. 25.32 (978-1-4965-3444-6(1)) Capstone Press of Coughlan Cos.

Johnston, Tamra L. Libby the Little Leprechaun: And the Majestic Roller Coaster. 2012. 50p. pap. 21.99 (978-1-4772-0752-9(X)) AuthorHouse.

—Libby the Little Leprechaun: Exploring the Opposite Side of South Africa. 2012. 50p. pap. 21.99 (978-1-4772-0782-6(1)) AuthorHouse.

Jones, H. Lena. Trapped on Planet Liska. 2006. 180p. pap. 19.95 (978-1-4241-0989-0(2)) America Star Bks.

Jones-Sorge, Jennifer Elaine. Monsters, Monsters, Monsters! The Power in Me Is Bigger Then Any Monster I've Ever Met! 2012. 48p. pap. 24.95 (978-1-4626-7555-5(7)) America Star Bks.

Jules, Jacqueline. Freddie Ramos Makes a Splash. Benítez, Miguel, illus. 2013. (Zapato Power Ser.: Book 4). (ENG.). 96p. (J). (gr. 1-5). pap. 4.99 (978-0-8075-9486-5(5)) Whitman, Albert & Co.

—Freddie Ramos Makes a Splash Bk. 4. Benítez, Miguel, illus. 2012. (Zapato Power Ser.: Book 4). (ENG.). 96p. (J). (gr. 1-5). 14.99 (978-0-8075-9485-8(7)) Whitman, Albert & Co.

—Freddie Ramos Zooms to the Rescue. Benítez, Miguel, illus. 2012. (Zapato Power Ser.: Book 3). (ENG.). 96p. (J). (gr. 1-5). pap. 4.99 (978-0-8075-9484-1(9)) Whitman, Albert & Co.

Karpes, H. R. Morris... the Downside-Up Bat. 2013. (ENG., Illus.). 32p. (J). (gr. -1-k). 11.95 (978-1-62087-987-0(5), 620987, Sky Pony Pr.) Skyhorse Publishing Co., Inc.

Katschke, Judy & Nickle, John. The Ant Bully: Movie Novel. 2006. (Illus.). 88p. (J). (978-1-4156-8331-6(X)) Scholastic, Inc.

Kelly, Erin Entrada. Blackbird Fly. Peterschmidt, Betsy, illus. 2016. 320p. (J). (gr. 3-7). pap. 6.99 (978-0-06-223862-7(0), Greenwillow Bks.) HarperCollins Pubs.

Kessler, Jackie Morse. Loss. 2012. (Riders of the Apocalypse Ser.: 3). (ENG.). 272p. (YA). (gr. 7). pap. 8.99 (978-0-547-71215-4(4)) Houghton Mifflin Harcourt Publishing Co.

—Loss. 2012. (Riders of the Apocalypse Ser.: 3). lib. bdg. 19.65 (978-0-606-24742-9(4), Turtleback) Turtleback Bks.

Kessler, Liz. Emily Windsnap & the Monster from the Deep. Gibb, Sarah, illus. 2012. (Emily Windsnap Ser.: 2). (ENG.). 240p. (J). (gr. 3-7). pap. 5.99 (978-0-7636-6018-5(3)) Candlewick Pr.

—Emily Windsnap & the Monster from the Deep. 2012. (Emily Windsnap Ser.: 2). lib. bdg. 16.00 (978-0-606-25573-8(7), Turtleback) Turtleback Bks.

Key, Watt. Alabama Moon. (Alabama Moon Ser.: 1). (ENG.). (J). (gr. 5-9). 2008. 304p. pap. 8.99 (978-0-312-38428-9(9), 9780312384289) 2010. 320p. pap. 8.99 (978-0-312-64480-2(9), 9780312644802) Square Fish.

Kimmelman, Leslie. The Three Bully Goats. Terry, Will, illus. 2012. (J). (978-1-61913-136-1(6)) Weigl Pubs., Inc.

—The Three Bully Goats. Terry, Will, illus. 2011. (ENG.). 32p. (J). (gr. -1-3). 16.99 (978-0-8075-7900-8(9)) Whitman, Albert & Co.

King, A. S. Everybody Sees the Ants. 2011. (ENG.). 288p. (YA). (gr. 10-17). 18.00 (978-0-316-12928-2(3)) Little Brown & Co.

—Everybody Sees the Ants. 2012. (ENG.). 320p. (YA). (gr. 10-17). pap. 10.00 (978-0-316-12927-5(5)) Little, Brown Bks. for Young Readers.

King, Daren. Frightfully Friendly Ghosties: School of Meanies. Roberts, David, illus. 2014. (ENG.). 128p. (J). (gr. k-3). 12.99 (978-1-62365-349-1(5), Quercus) Quercus NA.

Klein, Abby. Don't Sit on My Lunch! Mckinley, John & McKinley, John, illus. 2005. (Ready, Freddy! Ser.: 4). (ENG.). 96p. (J). (gr. -1-3). 5.99 (978-0-439-55602-6(3), Blue Sky Pr., The) Scholastic, Inc.

—Thanksgiving Turkey Trouble. McKinley, John, illus. 2008. (Ready, Freddy! Ser.: Bk. 15). 95p. (gr. -1-3). 16.00 (978-0-7569-8838-8(1)) Perfection Learning Corp.

Kocek, Sara. Promise Me Something. 2013. (ENG.). 320p. (YA). (gr. 8-12). 16.99 (978-0-8075-6641-1(1)) Whitman, Albert & Co.

Korman, Gordon. Jackpot. 2014. (Swindle Ser.: 6). (ENG.). 208p. (J). (gr. 3-7). 16.99 (978-0-545-56146-4(9), Scholastic Pr.) Scholastic, Inc.

—Jackpot. 2014. (Swindle Ser.: 6). lib. bdg. 17.20 (978-0-606-36032-6(8)) Turtleback Bks.

Korman, Gordon. Restart. 2017. (ENG.). 256p. (J). (gr. 3-7). 16.99 **(978-1-338-05377-7(9),** Scholastic Pr.) Scholastic, Inc.

Krackow, Eric T. The Lollipop Monster, 1 vol. 2011. (ENG., Illus.). 64p. (J). 16.99 (978-0-7643-3773-4(4), 9780764337734, Schiffer Publishing Ltd) Schiffer Publishing, Ltd.

Kroll, Steven. Jungle Bullies, 0 vols. Nguyen, Vincent, illus. 2006. (ENG.). 34p. (J). (gr. -1-2). pap. 7.99 (978-0-7614-5620-9(1), 9780761456209, Amazon Children's Publishing) Amazon Publishing.

Krosoczka, Jarrett J. Peanut Butter & Jellyfish. 2014. (ENG.). 40p. (J). (gr. -1-2). 16.99 (978-0-375-87036-1(9), Knopf Bks. for Young Readers) Random Hse. Children's Bks.

Kruse, Donald W. Fleas, Please. Crank, Donny, illus. 2012. 48p. pap. 12.95 (978-1-59663-858-7(3), Castle Keep Pr.) Rock, James A. & Co. Pubs.

Lachtman, Ofelia Dumas. Pepita & the Bully: Pepita y la Peleonera. Baeza Ventura, Gabriela, tr. Pardo DeLange, Alex, illus. 2011. (SPA & ENG.). 32p. (J). (gr. -1-3). 16.95 (978-1-55885-689-9(7), Piñata Books) Arte Publico Pr.

Laks, Shan. The Tale of Brave Ritchie: Be Aware of Strangers; Beat the Bullies & Exercise Changes Health. 2012. 76p. pap. 42.05 (978-1-4797-2882-4(9)) Xlibris Corp.

Lange, Erin Jade. Dead Ends. 2013. (ENG.). 336p. (YA). (gr. 9). 17.99 (978-1-61963-080-2(X), 9781619630802, Bloomsbury USA Childrens); 288p. pap. 17.99 (978-1-61963-081-9(8)) Bloomsbury Publishing USA.

Latimer, Alex. Lion vs Rabbit, 1 vol. Latimer, Alex, illus. 2013. (ENG., Illus.). 32p. (J). (gr. -1-3). 15.95 (978-1-56145-709-0(4)) Peachtree Pubs.

Latimer, Alex. Lion vs. Rabbit, 1 vol. Latimer, Alex, illus. 2017. (ENG., Illus.). 32p. (J). (gr. -1-3). pap. 7.95 **(978-1-56145-898-1(8))** Peachtree Pubs.

Lears, Laurie. Stay Away from Rat Boy! Hansen, Red, illus. 2009. (ENG.). 32p. (J). (gr. 2-3). 16.99 (978-0-8075-6789-0(2)) Whitman, Albert & Co.

Lee, Jenny. Elvis & the Underdogs. Light, Kelly, illus. 2013. (Elvis & the Underdogs Ser.: 1). (ENG.). 304p. (J). (gr. 3-7). 16.99 (978-0-06-223554-1(0)) HarperCollins Pubs.

Lemke, Donald. Revealed!, 1 vol. Holgate, Douglas, illus. 2008. (Zinc Alloy Ser.). (ENG.). 40p. (gr. 1-3). 23.99 (978-1-4342-0763-0(3), Graphic Sparks) Stone Arch Bks.

—Revealed! Zinc Alloy, 1 vol. Holgate, Douglas, illus. 2008. (Graphic Sparks Ser.). (ENG.). 40p. (gr. 1-3). pap. 5.95 (978-1-4342-0859-0(1), Graphic Sparks) Stone Arch Bks.

—Super Zero, 1 vol. Holgate, Douglas, illus. 2008. (Zinc Alloy Ser.). (ENG.). 40p. (gr. 1-3). 23.99 (978-1-4342-0762-3(5)); pap. 5.95 (978-1-4342-0858-3(3)) Stone Arch Bks. (Graphic Sparks).

Lennon, Maria T. Confessions of a So-Called Middle Child. 2014. (ENG.). 304p. (J). (gr. 3-7). pap. 6.99 (978-0-06-212691-7(1)) HarperCollins Pubs.

Lester, Helen. Hooway for Wodney Wat, 1 vol. Munsinger, Lynn, illus. 2011. (ENG.). 32p. (J). (gr. -1-3). audio compact disk 10.99 (978-0-547-55217-0(3)) Houghton Mifflin Harcourt Publishing Co.

Levy, Janice. Flip-Flop & the Bully Frogs Gruff, 1 vol. Madden, Colleen M., illus. 2011. (Flip-Flop Adventure Ser.). (ENG.). 32p. (J). (gr. k-3). 28.50 (978-1-61641-653-9(X)) Magic Wagon.

Linden, Dianne. Peacekeepers. (J). 82p. stu. ed. 9.95 (978-1-55050-297-8(2)); 2003. (ENG., Illus.). 208p. (gr. 3-6). pap. 7.95 (978-1-55050-271-8(9)) Coteau Bks. CAN. Dist: Fitzhenry & Whiteside, Ltd., Orca Bk. Pubs. USA.

Little China's Not So Mean after All. 2012. 28p. 24.95 (978-1-4137-7549-5(7)) America Star Bks.

Ludwig, Trudy. Confessions of a Former Bully. Adams, Beth, illus. (ENG.). 48p. (J). 2012. (gr. 3-7). pap. 7.99 (978-0-307-93113-9(7), Dragonfly Bks.) 2010. (gr. 1-4). 15.99 (978-1-58246-309-4(3), Tricycle Pr.) Random Hse. Children's Bks.

—Confessions of a Former Bully. 2012. lib. bdg. 18.40 (978-0-606-26382-5(9), Turtleback) Turtleback Bks.

—Just Kidding. Gustavson, Adam, illus. 2006. (ENG.). 32p. (J). (gr. 1-4). 15.99 (978-1-58246-163-2(5), Tricycle Pr.) Random Hse. Children's Bks.

—My Secret Bully. Marble, Abigail, illus. (ENG.). 32p. (J). (gr. 1-4). 2015. 7.99 (978-0-553-50940-3(3), Dragonfly Bks.) 2005. 15.99 (978-1-58246-159-5(7), Tricycle Pr.) Random Hse. Children's Bks.

Lukachko, Mary Louise. Peter the Blue Penguin. 2012. 28p. pap. 24.95 (978-1-4626-8186-0(7)) America Star Bks.

Lundstrom, Norma Niemi. The Chubby Girl. 2013. 12p. pap. 7.99 (978-1-4624-0556-5(8), Inspiring Voices) Author Solutions, Inc.

Lupica, Mike. Hot Hand, 1 vol. 2012. (Comeback Kids Ser.). (ENG.). 176p. (J). (gr. 4-8). lib. bdg. 27.07 (978-1-59961-175-4(9)) Spotlight.

—The Only Game. 2015. (Home Team Ser.). (ENG., Illus.). 320p. (J). (gr. 3-7). 16.99 (978-1-4814-0995-7(6), Simon & Schuster Bks. For Young Readers) Simon & Schuster Bks. For Young Readers.

—The Only Game. 2016. (Home Team Ser.). lib. bdg. 18.40 (978-0-606-38252-6(6)) Turtleback Bks.

Lyons, C. J. Broken. 2014. (ENG.). 320p. (YA). (gr. 7-12). pap. 9.99 (978-1-4022-9230-9(9)) Sourcebooks, Inc.

Mackall, Dandi Daley. Larger-Than-Life Lara. 2016. (ENG.). 176p. 14.99 (978-1-4964-1429-8(2)) Tyndale Hse. Pubs.

MacKenzie, Catherine. The Dark Blue Bike at No 17: Tammy & Jake Learn about Friendship & Bullying. 2003. (Tales from Canterbury Place Ser.). (ENG., Illus.). 160p. (J). mass mkt. 6.99 (978-1-85792-732-0(X)) Christian Focus Pubns. GBR. Dist: Send The Light Distribution LLC.

MacPhail, Catherine. Hide & Seek. 2012. (Stoke Books Titles Ser.). 72p. (J). (gr. 5-8). pap. 7.95 (978-1-78112-024-8(2)); lib. bdg. 22.60 (978-1-78112-023-1(4)) Stoke Bks.

Maddox, Jake. Beach Bully. 2013. (Jake Maddox Sports Stories Ser.). (ENG.). 72p. (gr. 2-3). pap. 35.70 (978-1-4342-6234-9(0)) Stone Arch Bks.

—Board Battle, 1 vol. Aburtov, Jesus Aburto, illus. 2013. (Jake Maddox Sports Stories Ser.). (ENG.). 72p. (gr. 2-3). pap. 5.95 (978-1-4342-6208-0(1)) Stone Arch Bks.

—Board Battle. 2013. (Jake Maddox Sports Stories Ser.). (ENG.). 72p. (gr. 2-3). pap. 35.70 (978-1-4342-6235-6(9)) Stone Arch Bks.

—Board Battle, 1 vol. Aburtov, Jesus Aburto, illus. 2013. (Jake Maddox Sports Stories Ser.). (ENG.). 72p. (gr. 2-3). lib. bdg. 25.32 (978-1-4342-5975-2(7)) Stone Arch Bks.

—On the Line, 1 vol. Tiffany, Sean, illus. 2006. (Jake Maddox Sports Stories Ser.). (ENG.). 72p. (gr. 2-3). 25.32 (978-1-59889-062-4(X)); pap. 5.95 (978-1-59889-240-6(1)) Stone Arch Bks.

—Paintball Problems. 2013. (Jake Maddox Sports Stories Ser.). (ENG.). 72p. (gr. 2-3). pap. 35.70 (978-1-4342-6237-0(5)) Stone Arch Bks.

Mammay, Judith. Knowing Joseph. (ENG., Illus.). 256p. (J). (gr. 2-7). 2009. pap. 8.95 (978-1-933831-06-0(5)) 2008. 13.95 (978-1-933831-05-3(7)) Blooming Tree Pr.

Manning, Matthew K. Superman Battles the Billionaire Bully. Beavers, Ethen, illus. 2017. (DC Super Hero Stories Ser.). (ENG.). 56p. (gr. 1-3). lib. bdg. 25.32 (978-1-4965-4634-0(2), DC Super Heroes) Stone Arch Bks.

Mantra Lingua Staff. Don't Bully Me. 2004. (ENG & WEL., Illus.). 64p. (J). (978-1-84444-548-6(8)); (978-1-84444-549-3(6)); (978-1-84444-550-9(X)); (978-1-84444-551-6(8)); (978-1-84444-552-3(6)) Mantra Lingua.

Manushkin, Fran. No More Teasing, 1 vol. Lyon, Tammie, illus. 2009. (Katie Woo Ser.). (ENG.). 32p. (gr. k-2). 21.32 (978-1-4048-5492-5(4)) Picture Window Bks.

Manushkin, Fran & Lyon, Tammie. Basta de Burlas, 1 vol. Lyon, Tammie, illus. 2012. (Katie Woo en Español Ser.). (SPA., Illus.). 32p. (gr. k-2). pap. 6.95 (978-1-4048-7677-4(4)); lib. bdg. 21.32 (978-1-4048-7525-8(5)) Picture Window Bks.

Mara, Cate. The Great Kieranski & the Bardbuy. 2012. 114p. pap. (978-0-9873204-2-1(4)) Breedles Publishing.

Marcionette, Jake. Just Jake. Villa, Victor Rivas, illus. 2014. (Just Jake Ser.: No. 1). (ENG.). 160p. (J). (gr. 3-7). 11.99 (978-0-448-46692-7(9), Grosset & Dunlap) Penguin Young Readers Group.

Marino, Peter. Dough Boy. 2005. (ENG.). 176p. (YA). (gr. 7-12). 17.95 (978-0-8234-1873-2(1)) Holiday Hse., Inc.

Martin, Timothy. Wimps Like Me, 1 vol. 2010. 112p. pap. 19.95 (978-1-4489-7004-9(0)) America Star Bks.

Marzullo, Re. Sped. 2013. 214p. pap. 9.99 (978-0-9889618-0-7(6)) Sauvignon Pr.

McGowan, Anthony. The Knife That Killed Me. 2011. (ENG.). 224p. (YA). (gr. 9). pap. 8.99 (978-0-375-85516-0(5), Ember) Random Hse. Children's Bks.

McKay, Hilary. Indigo's Star. 2006. (ENG.). 272p. (J). (gr. 3-7). reprint ed. per. 7.99 (978-1-4169-1403-7(X), McElderry, Margaret K. Bks.) McElderry, Margaret K. Bks.

McKee, David. Elmer & the Big Bird. McKee, David, illus. 2012. (Andersen Press Picture Bks). (ENG., Illus.). 32p. (J). (gr. -1-3). 16.95 (978-1-4677-0319-2(2)) Lerner Publishing Group.

McKnight, Marty. Jim Nasium Is a Hockey Hazard. Jones, Chris B., illus. 2015. (Jim Nasium Ser.). (ENG.). 88p. (gr. 2-3). pap. 5.95 (978-1-4965-0524-8(7)) Stone Arch Bks.

McLelland, Michael J. Beating the Bully. Kirk, Andrea Cope, illus. 2007. 16p. (J). 15.99 (978-1-59955-006-0(7)) Cedar Fort, Inc./CFI Distribution.

McMullan, Kate. Four Eyes. Alley, R. W., illus. 2013. (Pearl & Wagner Ser.: 4). (ENG.). 48p. (J). (gr. 1-3). pap. 3.99 (978-0-448-47781-7(5), Penguin Young Readers) Penguin Young Readers Group.

McNish, Cliff. Angel. 2008. (Exceptional Reading & Language Arts Titles for Intermediate Grades Ser.). 311p. (YA). (gr. 8-12). 16.95 (978-0-8225-8900-6(1)) Lerner Publishing Group.

McPhee, Peter. New Blood, 1 vol. 2007. (Lorimer SideStreets Ser.). (ENG.). 168p. (YA). (gr. 9-12). 9.95 (978-1-55028-996-1(9), 9781550289961) Lorimer, James & Co., Ltd., Pubs. CAN. Dist: Casemate Pubs. & Bk. Distributors, LLC.

Medina, Meg. Yaqui Delgado Quiere Darte una Paliza. 2016. (ENG & SPA.). 304p. (YA). (gr. 9). pap. 7.99 (978-0-7636-7940-8(2)) Candlewick Pr.

—Yaqui Delgado Wants to Kick Your Ass. (ENG., 272p. (YA). (gr. 9). 2014. Illus.). pap. 7.99 (978-0-7636-7164-8(9)) 2013. 16.99 (978-0-7636-5859-5(6)) Candlewick Pr.

Meister, Cari. Bus Ride Bully, 1 vol. Simard, Remy, illus. (My First Graphic Novel Ser.). (ENG.). 32p. (gr. k-2). 2011. pap. 6.25 (978-1-4342-3101-7(1)) 2010. 24.65 (978-1-4342-2059-2(1)) Stone Arch Bks. (My First Graphic Novel).

Menard, Michele R. The Moon Means Business. 2013. 48p. pap. 14.50 (978-0-9887969-2-8(9)) Four Menards, The.

Michener, Tara. No Longer Besties: And Other Assorted Teenage Drama. 2011. 192p. (gr. 10-12). pap. 14.99 (978-1-4634-0118-4(3)) AuthorHouse.

Miller, Ashley Edward & Stentz, Zack. Colin Fischer. 2012. (Colin Fischer Ser.: 1). (ENG.). 256p. (YA). (gr. 7). 17.99 (978-1-59514-578-9(8), Razorbill) Penguin Young Readers Group.

Mills, Arthur. The Crawl Space. Mills, Arthur & Tichelaar, Tyler, eds. 2012. (ENG., Illus.). 254p. (J). pap. 9.99 (978-0-9860166-0-8(8)) Branching Plot Bks.

mitchell, Ed. You never can tell what's least expected Most. 2008. 228p. pap. 16.95 (978-1-4092-2539-3(9)) Lulu Pr., Inc.

Mitchell, Ed. You Never Can Tell What's Least Expected Most. 2009. 232p. pap. 18.95 (978-1-4092-5434-8(8)) Lulu Pr., Inc.

Montes, Marisa. A Crazy Mixed-Up Spanglish Day. Cepeda, Joe, illus. 2004. (Get Ready for Gabi Ser.). 120p. (gr. 2-5). 14.00 (978-0-7569-3403-3(6)) Perfection Learning Corp.

—A Crazy Mixed-Up Spanglish Day. Cepeda, Joe, illus. 2003. (Get Ready for Gabi Ser.). 128p. (J). 12.95 (978-0-439-51710-2(9), Scholastic Paperbacks) Scholastic, Inc.

Morpurgo, Michael. Snakes & Ladders. Wilson, Anne, illus. 2006. (Yellow Bananas Ser.). (ENG.). 48p. (J). (gr. -1-3). lib. bdg. (978-0-7787-0952-7(3)) Crabtree Publishing Co.

Morrison, Kevin. I Can Speak Bully. Kemble, Mai S., illus. 2009. 32p. (J). 14.95 (978-0-8091-6744-9(1), Ambassador Bks.) Paulist Pr.

Moss, Marissa. Amelia's Bully Survival Guide. Moss, Marissa, illus. 2006. (Amelia Ser.). (ENG., Illus.). 40p. (J). (gr. 2-5). 9.95 (978-1-4169-0907-1(9), Simon & Schuster/Paula Wiseman Bks.) Simon & Schuster/Paula Wiseman Bks.

Moss, Peggy. Say Something, 1 vol. Lyon, Lea, illus. 2004. (ENG.). 32p. (gr. 2-7). 16.95 (978-0-88448-261-1(8), 884261) Tilbury Hse. Pubs.

Mull, Brandon. Pingo & the Playground Bully. Dorman, Brandon, illus. 2012. (Pingo Ser.: 2). (ENG.). 32p. (J). (gr. k-3). 17.99 (978-1-60907-178-3(6), Shadow Mountain) Shadow Mountain Publishing.

Mullarkey, Lisa. TJ Zaps a Nightmare: Stopping Blackmail Bullying #5, 1 vol. LaCoste, Gary, illus. 2012. (TJ Trapper, Bully Zapper Ser.). (ENG.). 80p. (J). (gr. 2-5). lib. bdg. 27.07 (978-1-61641-909-7(1), Calico Chapter Bks) Magic Wagon.

—TJ Zaps the Freeze Out: Stopping the Silent Treatment #3, 1 vol. LaCoste, Gary, illus. 2012. (TJ Trapper, Bully Zapper Ser.). (ENG.). 80p. (J). (gr. 2-5). lib. bdg. 27.07 (978-1-61641-907-3(5), Calico Chapter Bks) Magic Wagon.

—TJ Zaps the New Kid: Stopping a Social Bully #1, 1 vol. LaCoste, Gary, illus. 2012. (TJ Trapper, Bully Zapper Ser.). (ENG.). 80p. (J). (gr. 2-5). lib. bdg. 27.07 (978-1-61641-905-9(9), Calico Chapter Bks) Magic Wagon.

—TJ Zaps the One-Upper: Stopping One-Upping & Cell Phone Bullying #2, 1 vol. LaCoste, Gary, illus. 2012. (TJ Trapper, Bully Zapper Ser.). (ENG.). 80p. (J). (gr. 2-5). lib. bdg. 27.07 (978-1-61641-906-6(7), Calico Chapter Bks) Magic Wagon.

—TJ Zaps the Rumor Mill: Stopping Gossip #4, 1 vol. LaCoste, Gary, illus. 2012. (TJ Trapper, Bully Zapper Ser.). (ENG.). 80p. (J). (gr. 2-5). lib. bdg. 27.07 (978-1-61641-908-0(3), Calico Chapter Bks) Magic Wagon.

—TJ Zaps the Smackdown: Stopping a Physical Bully #6, 1 vol. LaCoste, Gary, illus. 2012. (TJ Trapper, Bully Zapper Ser.). (ENG.). 80p. (J). (gr. 2-5). lib. bdg. 27.07 (978-1-61641-910-3(5), Calico Chapter Bks) Magic Wagon.

Murphy, Stuart J. Freda Stops a Bully. Jones, Tim, illus. 2012. (I See I Learn Ser.). (ENG.). 32p. (J). (-k). 14.95 (978-1-58089-466-1(6)); pap. 6.95 (978-1-58089-467-8(4)) Charlesbridge Publishing, Inc.

Murray, Stuart A. P. Todd Goes for the Goal. 2012. (Champion Sports Story Ser.). 104p. (J). (gr. 3-18). pap. 10.95 (978-1-4644-0000-1(8)); lib. bdg. 27.94 (978-0-7660-3887-5(4)) Enslow Pubs., Inc.

Myers, Walter Dean. Shooter. (ENG.). 2004. 224p. (J). 15.99 (978-0-06-029519-6(8), HarperTeen) 2005. 256p. (YA). (gr. 9-17). reprint ed. pap. 9.99 (978-0-06-447290-6(6), Amistad) HarperCollins Pubs.

Nagda, Ann Whitehead. Tarantula Power! 2007. (ENG., Illus.). 96p. (J). (gr. 2-5). 15.95 (978-0-8234-1991-3(6)) Holiday Hse., Inc.

Nathoo, Aalaynah. The World above Us!!! 2012. 16p. pap. 15.99 (978-1-4772-3222-4(2)) AuthorHouse.

Naylor, Phyllis Reynolds. Roxie & the Hooligans. Boiger, Alexandra, illus. 2007. 115p. (gr. 2-5). 16.00 (978-0-7569-8284-3(7)) Perfection Learning Corp.

—Roxie & the Hooligans. Boiger, Alexandra, illus. (ENG.). 128p. (J). 2007. (gr. 3-5). pap. 6.99 (978-1-4169-0244-7(9), Simon & Schuster/Paula Wiseman Bks.) 2006. (gr. 2-5). 17.99 (978-1-4169-0243-0(0), Atheneum Bks. for Young Readers) Simon & Schuster Children's Publishing.

Nesbø, Jo. Doctor Proctor's Fart Powder. Chace, Tara F., tr. Lowery, Mike, illus. 2010. (Doctor Proctor's Fart Powder Ser.). (ENG.). 288p. (J). (gr. 3-7). pap. 7.99 (978-1-4169-7973-9(5), Aladdin) Simon & Schuster Children's Publishing.

—Doctor Proctor's Fart Powder. Chace, Tara, tr. from GER. Lowery, Mike, illus. 2009. (Doctor Proctor's Fart Powder Ser.). (ENG.). 272p. (J). (gr. 3-7). 17.99 (978-1-4169-7972-2(7), Aladdin) Simon & Schuster Children's Publishing.

—Doctor Proctor's Fart Powder. 2010. (Dr. Proctor's Fart Powder Ser.: 1). lib. bdg. 18.40 (978-0-606-15419-2(1), Turtleback) Turtleback Bks.

Nettles Jr, J. H. Hit Em' with Words, 1 vol. Jones, Joff, illus. 2010. 22p. 24.95 (978-1-4489-4102-5(4)) PublishAmerica, Inc.

Nikolet, C. T. From Bullies to Friends. Howe, Cindy T., illus. 2008. 25p. pap. 24.95 (978-1-60610-121-6(8)) America Star Bks.

Nnabuchi, Afam. Emeka Transforms in the Pit. 2013. 78p. (J). pap. 12.95 (978-1-4772-9679-0(4)) AuthorHouse.

Nolen, Jerdine. Plantzilla Goes to Camp. Catrow, David, illus. 2006. (ENG.). 32p. (J). (gr. k-3). 17.99 (978-0-689-86803-0(0), Simon & Schuster/Paula Wiseman Bks.) Simon & Schuster/Paula Wiseman Bks.

O'Connor, George. Ker-Splash! O'Connor, George, illus. 2010. (ENG., Illus.). 40p. (J). (gr. -1-3). 19.99 (978-1-4424-2196-7(7), Simon & Schuster Bks. For Young Readers) Simon & Schuster Bks. For Young Readers.

O'Dell, Kathleen. Agnes Parker... Girl in Progress. 2004. (ENG.). 176p. (J). (gr. 2-5). reprint ed. 6.99 (978-0-14-240228-3(1), Puffin Books) Penguin Young Readers Group.

O'Ryan, Ray. Journey to Juno. Jack, Colin, illus. 2013. (Galaxy Zack Ser.: 2). (ENG.). 128p. (J). (gr. k-4). 17.99 (978-1-4424-5391-3(5)); pap. 5.99 (978-1-4424-5390-6(7)) Little Simon. (Little Simon).

—Journey to Juno. 2013. (Galaxy Zack Ser.: 2). lib. bdg. 16.00 (978-0-606-32443-4(7), Turtleback) Turtleback Bks.

Park, Louise. New Girl. May, Kyla & Matthews, Melanie, illus. 2015. (Star Girl Ser.). (ENG.). 80p. (gr. 1-4). lib. bdg. 22.65 (978-1-4795-8275-4(1)) Picture Window Bks.

Parker, Robert B. Chasing the Bear. 2010. (ENG.). 176p. (YA). (gr. 7-18). 8.99 (978-0-14-241573-3(1), Speak) Penguin Young Readers Group.

Parnell, Robyn. The Mighty Quinn. DeYoe, Katie & DeYoe, Aaron, illus. 2013. (ENG.). 272p. (gr. 2-7). pap. 10.95 (978-1-938063-10-7(4), Mighty Media Junior Readers) Mighty Media Pr.

Pascal, Francine. The Ruling Class. 2010. (ENG.). 208p. (YA). (gr. 9). pap. 10.99 (978-1-4424-1423-5(5), Simon Pulse) Simon Pulse.

Patterson, James & Grabenstein, Chris. I Funny: A Middle School Story. Park, Laura, illus. (I Funny Ser.: 1). (ENG.). 320p. (J). (gr. 3-7). 2015. pap. 8.00 (978-0-316-20692-1(X)) 2013. 13.99 (978-0-316-32200-3(8)) Little Brown & Co. (Jimmy Patterson).

Payne, C. C. Lula Bell on Geekdom, Freakdom, & the Challenges of Bad Hair, 0 vols. 2012. (ENG.). 276p. (J). (gr. 3-7). 16.99 (978-0-7614-6225-5(2), 9780761462255, Amazon Children's Publishing) Amazon Publishing.

Penn, Audrey & Gibson, Barbara L. Chester Raccoon & the Big Bad Bully. 2008. (Kissing Hand Ser.). (ENG., Illus.). 32p. (J). (gr. -1-3). 16.95 (978-1-933718-15-6(3)) Tanglewood Pr.

Peretti, Frank E. Hangman's Curse. 2008. 352p. (YA). mass mkt. 7.99 (978-1-4003-1016-6(4)) Nelson, Thomas Inc.

Perry, Fred. Grossery Games. 2012. (ENG., Illus.). 128p. (J). (gr. 4-7). pap. 10.99 (978-0-9850925-5-9(6), 9780985092559) Antarctic Pr., Inc.

Pinkwater, Daniel M. Yo-Yo Man. Davis, Jack E., illus. 2007. (ENG.). 32p. (J). (gr. -1-3). 16.99 (978-0-06-055502-3(5)) HarperCollins Pubs.

Pitts, Constance. Chulita the Blind Cat. 2007. (Illus.). 48p. (J). (978-0-9652902-2-7(0)) Beevinwood, Inc.

Pixley, Marcella. Freak. 2013. (ENG.). 160p. (YA). (gr. 7-10). pap. 10.99 (978-1-250-02742-9(X), 9781250027429) Square Fish.

Pointon, Janet. A Matter of Choice. 2008. 82p. pap. 11.51 (978-1-4092-3108-0(9)) Lulu Pr., Inc.

Polacco, Patricia. Bully. Polacco, Patricia, illus. 2012. (ENG., Illus.). 48p. (J). (gr. 2-5). 17.99 (978-0-399-25704-9(7), G.P. Putnam's Sons Books for Young Readers) Penguin Young Readers Group.

Potter, Noel Gyro. A Very Sticky Situation, 1 vol. Cannon, Joseph, illus. 2008. (Adventures of Marshall & Art Ser.). (ENG.). 32p. (gr. -1-4). 28.50 (978-1-60270-201-1(2), Looking Glass Library) ABDO Publishing Co.

Preller, James. Bystander. 2011. (ENG.). 256p. (YA). (gr. 5-9). pap. 8.99 (978-0-312-54796-7(X), 9780312547967) Square Fish.

Prochaska, Dan J. Courage, 1 vol. 2009. 48p. pap. 16.95 (978-1-61582-995-8(4)) PublishAmerica, Inc.

Prose, Francine. Bullyville. 2007. 260p. (YA). (gr. 7-12). 16.99 (978-0-06-057497-0(6)); lib. bdg. 17.89 (978-0-06-057498-7(4)) HarperCollins Pubs. (HarperTeen).

—Bullyville. 2011. 10.36 (978-0-7848-3625-5(6), Everbind) Marco Bk. Co.

R. N., Lavanya. The Bookworm. Suleman, Shilo Shiv, illus. 2013. (ENG.). 32p. (J). (gr. k). pap. 9.95 (978-81-8190-180-4(0)) Karadi Tales Co. Pvt, Ltd. IND. Dist: Consortium Bk. Sales & Distribution.

Recorvits, Helen & Recorvits, H. Yoon & the Jade Bracelet. Swiatkowska, Gabi, illus. 2008. (ENG.). 32p. (J). (gr. -1-3). 18.99 (978-0-374-38689-4(7), 9780374386894, Farrar, Straus & Giroux (BYR)) Farrar, Straus & Giroux.

Reeves, Pamela. United We Stand, a Story about Two Bullies. LaGrange, Tiffany, illus. 2009. 24p. pap. 12.95 (978-1-936051-36-6(2)) Peppertree Pr., The.

Ripken, Cal, Jr. & Cowherd, Kevin. Super Slugger. 2013. (ENG.). 200p. (YA). (gr. 3-7). pap. 6.99 (978-1-4231-4004-7(4)) Hyperion Pr.

Robert, Na'ima bint. Don't Bully Me. Mistry, Nilesh, illus. 2004. (POL, ENG & KUR.). 24p. (J). pap. (978-1-84444-558-5(5)) Mantra Lingua.

Roberts, Daniel. Douglas Diggly Super Spy. 2012. 180p. pap. 12.50 (978-1-105-49212-9(5)) Lulu Pr., Inc.

Rose, Sandra. My Mom Has Wheels. Talbott, Sherri, illus. 2009. 28p. pap. 24.95 (978-1-60836-889-1(0)) America Star Bks.

Roy, James. Max Quigley: Technically Not a Bully. 2009. (ENG., Illus.). 208p. (J). (gr. 2-5). 14.99 (978-0-547-15263-9(9)) Houghton Mifflin Harcourt Publishing Co.

Rue, Nancy N. Sophie's Friendship Fiasco. 2009. (Faithgirlz! Ser.: No. 7). (ENG.). 128p. (J). pap. 6.99 (978-0-310-71842-0(2)) Zonderkidz.

Russell, Rachel Renée. Locker Hero. Russell, Rachel Renée, illus. 2016. (Misadventures of Max Crumbly Ser.: 1). (ENG., Illus.). 320p. (J). (gr. 4-8). 13.99 (978-1-4814-6001-9(3), Aladdin) Simon & Schuster Children's Publishing.

Rylander, Chris. The Fourth Stall. (Fourth Stall Ser.: 1). (ENG.). (J). (gr. 3-7). 2011. 320p. 16.99 (978-0-06-199496-8(0))Pt. III. 2013. 304p. 16.99 (978-0-06-212005-2(0)) HarperCollins Pubs. (Waldon Pond Pr.).

Salisbury, Graham. Calvin Coconut: Rocket Ride. Rogers, Jacqueline, illus. 2013. (Calvin Coconut Ser.). (ENG.). 160p. (J). (gr. 2-5). pap. 6.99 (978-0-375-86508-4(X), Yearling) Random Hse. Children's Bks.

—Trouble Magnet. Rogers, Jacqueline, illus. 2010. (Calvin Coconut Ser.). (ENG.). 160p. (J). (gr. 3-7). pap. 6.99 (978-0-375-84600-7(X), Yearling) Random Hse. Children's Bks.

Salom, Susie. Kyle Finds Her Way. 2016. (ENG.). 256p. (J). (gr. 4-7). 16.99 (978-0-545-85266-1(8), Levine, Arthur A. Bks.) Scholastic, Inc.

Salusso, S. T. Billy the Roly Poly Bug. 2012. 24p. pap. 13.00 (978-1-4269-6134-2(0)) Trafford Publishing.

Samuels, Arthur. Old Flames: Teen Bullies & Prep School Cruelty. 2013. 238p. pap. 14.00 (978-0-9882394-4-9(2)) Dr. Joyce STARR Publishing.

Satera, Diane. The Angel of Wild Springs: Jaiden & the Sacred Stones. 2010. 168p. 23.99 (978-1-4520-3460-7(5)); pap. 11.99 (978-1-4520-3461-4(3)) AuthorHouse.

Sathre, Vivian. J. B. Wigglebottom & the Parade of Pets: True Ringside Tales, BBQ, & down-Home Recipies. O'Neill, Catharine, illus. 2013. (ENG.). 96p. (J). (gr. 2-5). pap. 13.99 (978-1-4814-2159-1(X), Atheneum Bks. for Young Readers) Simon & Schuster Children's Publishing.

Sazaklis, John. The Dangers of Dog Walking. Robinson, Lee, illus. 2016. (Billy Burger, Model Citizen Ser.). (ENG.). 96p. (gr. 2-3). lib. bdg. 22.65 (978-1-4965-2587-1(6)) Stone Arch Bks.

Schizas, Lea. Bubba & Giganto: Odds Against Us. 2008. 68p. (J). pap. (978-0-9797513-6-3(5)) 4RV Publishing, LLC.

Schneider, Richard H. The Christmas Pea Coat. Bond, Higgins, illus. 2004. 32p. (J). 14.95 (978-0-8249-5474-1(2), Ideal Pubns.) Worthy Publishing.

Scieszka, Jon. Zoom! Boom! Bully. Shannon, David et al, illus. 2008. (Jon Scieszka's Trucktown Ser.). (ENG.). 24p. (J). (gr. -1-1). pap. 3.99 (978-1-4169-4139-2(8), Simon Spotlight) Simon Spotlight.

Scott, Kevin. Stevie Wonderboy. 2009. 72p. pap. 11.49 (978-1-4490-5839-5(6)) AuthorHouse.

Seeger, Laura Vaccaro. Bully. Seeger, Laura Vaccaro, illus. 2013. (ENG., Illus.). 40p. (J). (gr. -1-3). 17.99 (978-1-59643-630-5(1), 9781596436305) Roaring Brook Pr.

Seyforth, Edward L. A Horribly Frightening Deception, 1 vol. 2009. 75p. pap. 19.95 (978-1-61546-260-5(0)) America Star Bks.

Shepard, Aaron. Timothy Tolliver & the Bully Basher. 2005. 48p. (J). pap. 2.99 (978-0-938497-24-0(3)); lib. bdg. 15.00 (978-0-938497-23-3(5)) Shepard Pubns. (Skyhook Pr.).

Shepard, Sara. The Good Girls. 2015. 341p. (J). (978-0-06-239115-5(1)) HarperCollins Pubs.

Simon, Coco. Alexis Gets Frosted. 2013. (Cupcake Diaries: 12). (ENG., Illus.). 160p. (J). (gr. 3-7). pap. 6.99 (978-1-4424-6867-2(X), Simon Spotlight) Simon Spotlight.

—Alexis Gets Frosted. 2013. (Cupcake Diaries: 12). lib. bdg. 17.20 (978-0-606-27026-7(4), Turtleback) Turtleback Bks.

Sims, Harold "Catman". Kevin Tames the Bullies. 2011. (Illus.). 32p. (J). pap. 12.95 (978-0-9827611-7-5(1), Catch the Spirit of Appalachia) Ammons Communications, Ltd.

Singhose, Rose. Granny's giggles book Four. 2010. 38p. pap. 16.95 (978-0-557-59965-3(2)) Lulu Pr., Inc.

Slater, David Michael. Comin' Through, 1 vol. Rooney, Ronnie, illus. 2007. (Missy Swiss & More Ser.). (ENG.). 32p. (gr. -1-4). 28.50 (978-1-60270-008-6(7), Looking Glass Library) ABDO Publishing Co.

Smith, Lane. Return to Augie Hobble. 2015. (ENG., Illus.). 288p. (J). (gr. 3-7). 16.99 (978-1-62672-054-1(1), 9781626720541) Roaring Brook Pr.

—Return to Augie Hobble. 2017. (J). lib. bdg. 18.40 (978-0-606-38550-3(9)) Turtleback Bks.

Sommer, Carl. King of the Pond. Budwine, Greg, illus. 2014. (J). pap. (978-1-57537-956-2(2)) Advance Publishing, Inc.

—King of the Pond(El Rey Del Estanque) Budwine, Greg, illus. 2009. (Another Sommer-Time Story Bilingual Ser.). (SPA & ENG.). 48p. (J). lib. bdg. 16.95 (978-1-57537-156-6(1)) Advance Publishing, Inc.

—The Rebel. Vignolo, Enrique, illus. 2009. (Quest for Success Ser.). (ENG.). 56p. (YA). pap. 4.95 (978-1-57537-282-2(7)); lib. bdg. 12.95 (978-1-57537-257-0(6)) Advance Publishing, Inc.

—The Rebel(El Rebelde) Vignolo, Enrique, illus. 2009. (Quest for Success Bilingual Ser.). (ENG & SPA.). 104p. (YA). lib. bdg. 14.95 (978-1-57537-231-0(2)) Advance Publishing, Inc.

—Spike the Rebel! Vignolo, Enrique, illus. (J). 2014. pap. (978-1-57537-967-8(8)) 2007. (ENG.). 48p. (gr. -1-3). lib. bdg. 16.95 (978-1-57537-072-9(7)) 2007. (ENG.). 48p. 16.95 incl. audio compact disk (978-1-57537-522-9(2)) 2007. (ENG.). 48p. 23.95 incl. audio compact disk (978-1-57537-722-3(5)) 2007. (ENG.). 48p. (gr. -1-3). lib. bdg. 9.95 (978-1-57537-023-1(9)) Advance Publishing, Inc.

—Spike the Rebel!(pua, el Rebelde!) Vignolo, Enrique, illus. 2009. (Another Sommer-Time Story Bilingual Ser.). (SPA & ENG.). 48p. (J). lib. bdg. 16.95 (978-1-57537-167-2(7)) Advance Publishing, Inc.

Spinelli, Jerry. Jake & Lily. 2012. 352p. (J). (gr. 3-7). (ENG.). 16.99 (978-0-06-028135-9(9)); lib. bdg. 16.89 (978-0-06-028136-6(7)) HarperCollins Pubs.

Springstubb, Tricia. Phoebe & Digger. Newman, Jeff, illus. 2013. (ENG.). 32p. (J). (gr. -1-2). 16.99 (978-0-7636-5281-4(4)) Candlewick Pr.

Starkey, Scott. The Call of the Bully. 2013. (How to Beat the Bully Ser.). (ENG.). 272p. (J). (gr. 3-7). 15.99 (978-1-4424-5674-7(4), Simon & Schuster/Paula Wiseman Bks.) Simon & Schuster/Paula Wiseman Bks.

—The Call of the Bully: A Rodney Rathbone Novel. 2014. (How to Beat the Bully Ser.). (ENG., Illus.). 272p. (J). (gr. 3-7). pap. 6.99 (978-1-4424-5675-4(2), Simon & Schuster/Paula Wiseman Bks.) Simon & Schuster/Paula Wiseman Bks.

—How to Beat the Bully Without Really Trying. (How to Beat the Bully Ser.). (ENG.). 272p. (J). (gr. 3-7). 2013. pap. 7.99 (978-1-4424-8473-3(X)) 2012. 15.99 (978-1-4424-1685-7(8)) Simon & Schuster/Paula Wiseman Bks. (Simon & Schuster/Paula Wiseman Bks.).

Stavans, Ilan. Golemito. Villegas, Teresa, illus. 2013. (ENG.). 32p. (J). 16.95 (978-1-58838-292-4(3), NewSouth Bks.) NewSouth, Inc.

Stevens, Eric. Finn Reeder, Flu Fighter: How I Survived a Worldwide Pandemic, the School Bully, & the Craziest Game of Dodge Ball Ever. Fraser, Kay, illus. 2009. (Finn Reeder Ser.). (ENG.). 80p. (gr. 2-3). lib. bdg. 26.65 (978-1-4342-2450-7(3)) Capstone Digital.

—Flu Fighter: How I Survived a Worldwide Pandemic, the School Bully, & the Craziest Game of Dodge Ball Ever. Fraser, Kay, illus. 2010. (Finn Reeder Ser.). (ENG.). 80p. (gr. 3-4). 9.99 (978-1-4342-2562-7(3)) Capstone Digital.

Stewart, Trenton Lee. The Extraordinary Education of Nicholas Benedict. Sudyka, Diana, illus. (Mysterious Benedict Society Ser.). (ENG.). (J). (gr. 3-7). 2013. 496p. pap. 9.99 (978-0-316-17620-0(6)) 2012. 480p. 18.99 (978-0-316-17619-4(2)) Little, Brown Bks. for Young Readers.

—The Extraordinary Education of Nicholas Benedict. 2013. (Mysterious Benedict Society Ser.: 0). (J). lib. bdg. 19.65 (978-0-606-31743-6(0), Turtleback) Turtleback Bks.

Stine, R. L. Don't Scream! 2012. (J). 137p. (978-0-545-48408-4(1)); (Goosebumps Hall of Horrors Ser.: 5). (ENG.). 160p. (gr. 3-7). pap. 6.99 (978-0-545-28937-5(8), Scholastic Paperbacks) Scholastic, Inc.

—Don't Scream! 2012. (Goosebumps HorrorLand: Hall of Horrors Ser.: 5). lib. bdg. 17.20 (978-0-606-23727-7(5), Turtleback) Turtleback Bks.

—Dudes, the School Is Haunted!, 1 vol. Park, Trip, illus. 2011. (Rotten School Ser.: No. 7). (ENG.). 128p. (gr. 2-5). 24.21 (978-1-59961-831-9(1)) Spotlight.

—Weirdo Halloween. 2010. (Goosebumps Horrorland Ser.: 16). (ENG.). 240p. (J). (gr. 3-7). 7.99 (978-0-545-16197-8(5), Scholastic Paperbacks) Scholastic, Inc.

Suen, Anastasia. Game Over: Dealing with Bullies, 1 vol. Ebbeler, Jeff, illus. 2008. (Main Street School - Kids with Character Ser.). (ENG.). 32p. (gr. -1-4). 28.50 (978-1-60270-270-7(5), Looking Glass Library) ABDO Publishing Co.

—New Girl: An Up2U Character Education Adventure, 1 vol. Dippold, Jane, illus. 2013. (Up2U Adventures Ser.). (ENG.). 80p. (J). (gr. 2-5). lib. bdg. 27.07 (978-1-61641-968-4(7), Calico Chapter Bks) Magic Wagon.

Sulkowski, Jennifer Suzanne. A Pony Named Napoleon. 2013. 74p. 30.95 (978-1-59299-979-8(4)); pap. 22.95 (978-1-59299-978-1(6)) Inkwater Pr.

Summers, Courtney. Some Girls Are. 2010. (ENG.). 256p. (YA). (gr. 9-18). pap. 11.99 (978-0-312-57380-5(4), 9780312573805, St. Martin's Griffin) St. Martin's Pr.

Susanne, Gervay & Gervay, Susanne. Being Jack. Wilcox, Cathy, illus. 2016. (ENG.). 192p. (J). pap. 5.99 (978-1-61067-379-2(4)) Kane Miller.

Tacang, Brian. Bully-Be-Gone: The Misadventures of Millicent Madding #1. 2006. (Illus.). 216p. (J). (gr. 3-7). 17.89 (978-0-06-073912-6(6)) HarperCollins Pubs.

Tanner-Moore, Margie. What Noah Knows. 2010. 49p. pap. 10.00 (978-0-557-45753-3(X)) Lulu Pr., Inc.

Taylor, Chloe. Stitches & Stones. Zhang, Nancy, illus. 2013. (Sew Zoey Ser.: 4). (ENG.). 176p. (J). (gr. 3-7). 16.99 (978-1-4424-9803-7(X));Bk. 4. pap. 5.99 (978-1-4424-9802-0(1)) Simon Spotlight. (Simon Spotlight).

Tennapel, Doug. Tommysaurus Rex. 2013. (ENG., Illus.). 144p. (J). (gr. 4-7). pap. 10.99 (978-0-545-48383-4(2), Graphix) Scholastic, Inc.

TenNapel, Doug. Tommysaurus Rex. 2013. (ENG., Illus.). 144p. (J). (gr. 3-7). 19.99 (978-0-545-48382-7(4), Graphix) Scholastic, Inc.

Thomas, Isabel. Emma Peror's New Clothes. Waters, Erica-Jane, illus. 2016. (Fairy Tales Today Ser.). (ENG.). 24p. (gr. 1-2). 9.95 (978-1-4795-8751-3(6)) Picture Window Bks.

Thompson, Colin. The Floods #2: School Plot. Scrambly, Crab, illus. 2008. (Floods Ser.). (J). (ENG.). 224p. 15.99 (978-0-06-113861-4(4)); 256p. lib. bdg. 16.89 (978-0-06-113855-3(X)) HarperCollins Pubs.

Tingle, Tim. Danny Blackgoat, Navajo Prisoner. 2013. (PathFinders Ser.). (ENG.). 151p. (YA). pap. 9.95 (978-1-939053-03-9(X), 7th Generation) Book Publishing Co.

Tokarz, Brenda. Curious Jane's: A Balloon Adventure. 2012. (ENG.). (J). pap. 9.95 (978-1-4507-7092-7(4)) Independent Pub.

Trevino, David. A Colorful Carnival of Kids in the Kingdom of Marbles: Mission #2. 2012. 156p. pap. 24.95 (978-1-4626-5377-5(4)) America Star Bks.

—A Colorful Carnival of Kids in the Kingdom of Marbles: Mission #3. 2012. 176p. pap. 19.95 (978-1-4626-9247-7(8)) America Star Bks.

Trish Lynch Marquis. Pesty Neighbor. 2009. 28p. pap. 14.99 (978-1-4389-9011-8(1)) AuthorHouse.

Trouble in the Barkers' Class. 2005. (J). 29.95 incl. audio compact disk (978-0-8045-4134-3(5)); 27.95 incl. audio (978-0-8045-6935-4(5)) Spoken Arts, Inc.

Vail, Rachel. Rules, Tools, & Maybe a Bully. 2015. (Justin Case Ser.: 3). (J). lib. bdg. 17.20 (978-0-606-37279-4(2)) Turtleback Bks.

Van Draanen, Wendelin. Secret Identity. Biggs, Brian, illus. 2006. (Shredderman Ser.: Bk. 1).Tr. of Al Haqiqa Wara ¿Al Fatak¿. (ENG.). 144p. (J). (gr. 1-4). reprint ed. 6.99 (978-0-440-41912-9(3), Yearling) Random Hse. Children's Bks.

—Shredderman: Secret Identity. Biggs, Brian, illus. unabr. ed. 2006. (Shredderman Ser.: Bk. 1).Tr. of Shredderman - Al Haqiqa Wara ¿Al Fatak¿. (J). (gr. 2-4). audio 24.95 (978-1-59519-762-7(1)) Live Oak Media.

—Shredderman: Secret Identity. unabr. ed. 2006. (Shredderman Ser.: Bk. 1).Tr. of Shredderman - Al Haqiqa Wara ¿Al Fatak¿. (Illus.). (J). (gr. 2-4). pap. 28.95 incl. audio compact disk (978-1-59519-763-4(X)) Live Oak Media.

Vernon, Ursula. Dragonbreath. Vernon, Ursula, illus. (Dragonbreath Ser.: 1). (ENG., Illus.). 160p. (J). (gr. 3-7). 2012. pap. 6.99 (978-0-14-242095-9(6), Puffin Books) 2009. 12.99 (978-0-8037-3363-3(1), Dial Bks) Penguin Young Readers Group.

—No Such Thing as Ghosts. 5th ed. 2011. (Dragonbreath Ser.: 5). (ENG.). 208p. (J). (gr. 3-7). 12.99 (978-0-8037-3527-9(8), Dial Bks) Penguin Young Readers Group.

Villareal, Ray. Alamo Wars. 2008. 187p. (J). (gr. 6-18). pap. 10.95 (978-1-55885-513-7(0), Piñata Books) Arte Publico Pr.

Volponi, Paul. Crossing Lines. 2011. (ENG.). 256p. (YA). (gr. 7). E-Book (978-1-101-52904-1(0)); 16.99 (978-0-670-01214-5(9)) Penguin Young Readers Group. (Viking Books for Young Readers).

Wallace, Jason. Out of Shadows. (ENG., Illus.). 272p. (J). (gr. 10). 2012. pap. 8.95 (978-0-8234-2436-8(7)) 2011. 17.95 (978-0-8234-2342-2(5)) Holiday Hse., Inc.

Walton, K. M. Cracked. 2012. (ENG.). 336p. (YA). (gr. 9). pap. 11.99 (978-1-4424-2917-8(8), Simon Pulse) Simon Pulse.

Wardlaw, Lee. 101 Ways to Bug Your Friends & Enemies. 2011. (ENG.). 288p. (J). (gr. 5-18). 6.99 (978-0-14-241949-6(4), Puffin Books) Penguin Young Readers Group.

Warner, Sally. The Dragon Slayer! Biggs, Brian, illus. 2013. (EllRay Jakes Ser.: 4). (ENG.). 144p. (J). (gr. 1-3). 14.99 (978-0-670-78497-4(4), Viking Books for Young Readers) Penguin Young Readers Group.

—Ellray Jakes Is a Rock Star! 2012. (EllRay Jakes Ser.: 2). lib. bdg. 16.00 (978-0-606-23633-1(3), Turtleback) Turtleback Bks.

—EllRay Jakes Is Not a Chicken! 2012. (EllRay Jakes Ser.: 1). lib. bdg. 16.00 (978-0-606-23632-4(5), Turtleback) Turtleback Bks.

—EllRay Jakes the Dragon Slayer. 2013. (EllRay Jakes Ser.: 4). lib. bdg. 16.00 (978-0-606-32136-5(5), Turtleback) Turtleback Bks.

—Ellray Jakes the Dragon Slayer, No. 4. Biggs, Brian, illus. 2013. (EllRay Jakes Ser.: 4). (ENG.). 144p. (J). (gr. 1-3). pap. 5.99 (978-0-14-242358-5(0), Puffin Books) Penguin Young Readers Group.

—Super Emma. Harper, Jamie, illus. 2008. (Emma Ser.). (ENG.). 112p. (J). (gr. 3-7). 5.99 (978-0-14-241088-2(8), Puffin Books) Penguin Young Readers Group.

Washakie, John. Yuse: The Bully & the Bear. Cox, Jon, illus. 2nd ed. 2004. 47p. (J). 14.95 (978-0-9759806-0-6(2)) Painted Pony, Inc.

Watkins, Greg. A Big Beaked, Big Bellied Bird Named Bill, 1 vol. Watkins, Greg, illus. 2006. (Big Bill & Buddies Ser.). (ENG., Illus.). 32p. (J). (gr. k-3). 16.99 (978-1-58980-441-8(4)) Pelican Publishing Co., Inc.

Watkins, Steve. Down Sand Mountain. (ENG., Illus.). 336p. (YA). (gr. 7). 2011. pap. 7.99 (978-0-7636-4835-0(3)) 2008. 16.99 (978-0-7636-3839-9(0)) Candlewick Pr.

Watts, Kevin. The Snowman Capers of Finneus Bleek. 2013. 76p. pap. 9.95 (978-1-4908-1176-5(1), WestBow Pr.) Author Solutions, Inc.

Weston Woods Staff, creator. Goggles! 2011. 29.95 (978-0-439-85317-0(6)) 2004. (J). 18.95 (978-1-55592-417-1(4)) 2004. (J). 38.75 (978-1-55592-418-8(2)) Weston Woods Studios, Inc.

—Ready, Freddy! #4: Don't Sit on My Lunch! 2011. 20.95 (978-0-545-05006-7(5)) Weston Woods Studios, Inc.

Wiggins, Thalia. Greg & the Cheat Sheets, 1 vol. Tate, Don, illus. 2012. (Making Choices: the Mcnair Cousins Ser.). (ENG.). 64p. 27.07 (978-1-61641-630-0(0), Calico Chapter Bks) Magic Wagon.

Wilhelm, Doug. The Revealers. 2011. (ENG.). 240p. (YA). (gr. 5-9). pap. 7.99 (978-0-312-56374-5(4), 9780312563745) Square Fish.

Willey, Margaret. Four Secrets. Hauser, Bill, illus. (ENG.). 288p. (YA). (gr. 7-12). 2014. pap. 9.95 (978-1-4677-1626-0(X), Carolrhoda Lab™) 2012. 17.95 (978-0-7613-8535-6(5)) Lerner Publishing Group.

Winerip, Michael. Adam Canfield Watch Your Back! 2009. (Adam Canfield of the Slash Ser.: 2). (ENG., Illus.). 352p. (J). (gr. 3-7). 7.99 (978-0-7636-4412-3(9)) Candlewick Pr.

Winkler, Henry & Oliver, Lin. Zero to Hero. 2012. (Ghost Buddy Ser.: 1). (ENG.). 176p. (J). (gr. 3-7). pap. 5.99 (978-0-545-29882-7(2), Scholastic Paperbacks) Scholastic, Inc.

Wisdom, Gail Ann. Trouble with Bullies. 2013. 48p. pap. 20.45 (978-1-4908-0026-4(3), WestBow Pr.) Author Solutions, Inc.

Wise, Rachel. Everyone's a Critic. 2013. (Dear Know-It-All Ser.: 5). (ENG.). 160p. (J). (gr. 3-7). 15.99 (978-1-4424-6821-4(1)); pap. 5.99 (978-1-4424-6820-7(3)) Simon Spotlight. (Simon Spotlight).

Wolf, Elaine. Camp. 2012. (ENG.). 256p. (YA). (gr. 6-17). 16.95 (978-1-61608-657-2(2), 608657, Sky Pony Pr.) Skyhorse Publishing Co., Inc.

Wyn, Dafydd. Hunting the Man in the Moon. 2015. (ENG.). 192p. (J). pap. 13.00 (978-1-84771-833-4(7)) Y Lolfa GBR. Dist: Dufour Editions, Inc.

Yagmin, Daniel, Jr., illus. Norton B. Nice. 2009. (J). (978-1-60108-018-9(2)) Red Cygnet Pr.

Yee, Lisa. Warp Speed. (ENG.). 320p. (J). 2013. (gr. 3-7). pap. 6.99 (978-0-545-15400-0(6)) 2011. (gr. 4-7). 16.99 (978-0-545-12276-4(7)) Scholastic, Inc. (Levine, Arthur A. Bks.).

Young, Steve. Winchell Mink: The Misadventure Begins. 2004. 144p. (J). 16.89 (978-0-06-053500-1(8)) HarperCollins Pubs.

BULLYING

Adams, Brenda Thompson. All about Abby: Abby Learns a Lesson about Bullying. 2012. 24p. 24.95 (978-1-4626-4935-8(1)) America Star Bks.

Adams, Herschelle. Color Bind. 2011. 49p. (J). pap. 21.95 (978-1-4327-6977-2(4)); pap. 19.95 (978-1-4327-6336-7(9)) Outskirts Pr., Inc.

Adams, Lisa K. Dealing with Teasing/Que Hacer con Las Burlas. Velazquez De Leon, Mauricio, tr. from SPA. 2008. (Conflict Resolution Library / Biblioteca Solución de Conflictos Ser.). (SPA., Illus.). 24p. (J). (gr. k-3). lib. bdg. 22.60 (978-1-4042-7663-5(7)) Rosen Publishing Group, Inc., The.

Adams, Sabrina. Everything You Need to Know about Trolls & Cybermobs. 2017. (Need to Know Library). 64p. (J). (gr. 12-11). 34.45 **(978-1-5081-7420-2(2))**; pap. 12.95 **(978-1-5081-7418-9(0))** Rosen Publishing Group, Inc., The. (Rosen Young Adult).

Alexander, Jenny. Bullies, Bigmouths & So-Called Friends. 2nd ed. 2006. (ENG., Illus.). 128p. (J). (gr. 4-6). per. 9.99 (978-0-340-91184-6(0), Hodder Children's Books) Hachette Children's Group GBR. Dist: Hachette Bk. Group.

Banas, Sharon L. Dealing with Bullying. 2009. (Character Education Ser.). (Illus.). 112p. (gr. 6-12). 35.00 (978-1-60413-121-5(7), Chelsea Hse.) Facts On File, Inc.

Berry, Joy. Help Me Be Good Bullying. Bartholomew, illus. 2010. (Help Me Be Good Ser.). (ENG.). 32p. (J). (gr. -1-2). pap. 4.99 (978-1-60577-140-3(6)) Berry, Joy Enterprises.

Berry, Joy Wilt. A Book about Being Bullied. 2005. (Illus.). (J). (978-0-7172-8578-5(2)) Scholastic, Inc.

—A Book about Teasing. 2005. (Illus.). (J). (978-0-7172-8580-8(4)) Scholastic, Inc.

Bingham, Jane. Taking Action Against Bullying. 2009. (Taking Action Ser.). (Illus.). 48p. (YA). (gr. 5-9). lib. bdg. 29.25 (978-1-4358-5343-0(1)) Rosen Publishing Group, Inc., The.

Birky, Joy. Bully Bill. Thompson, Chad, illus. 2007. 40p. (J). (gr. 3-7). per. 12.99 (978-0-8361-9382-4(2)) Herald Pr.

Blanco, Jodee. Bullied Kids Speak Out: We Survived-How You Can Too. 2015. (ENG.). 206p. pap. 15.99 (978-1-4405-7953-0(9)) Adams Media Corp.

Blunt, Lucy. Beating the Bullies: How Did Ben Help Himself? (Large Print 16pt) 2012. 84p. pap. (978-1-4596-4751-0(3)) ReadHowYouWant.com, Ltd.

Bowen, Shane. Out of the Darkness. 2010. 220p. pap. 21.95 (978-0-557-26249-6(6)) Lulu Pr., Inc.

Brezina, Corona. Helping a Friend Who Is Being Bullied. 2016. (How Can I Help? Friends Helping Friends Ser.). 00064p. (J). (gr. 6-6). pap. 12.95 (978-1-4994-6452-8(5)) Rosen Publishing Group, Inc., The.

Brezina, Corona. Standing up to Bullying at School. 2017. (LGBTQ+ Guide to Beating Bullying Ser.). 64p. (J). (gr. 12-11). pap. 12.95 **(978-1-5081-7429-5(6)**, Rosen Young Adult) Rosen Publishing Group, Inc., The.

Brown, Pamela. Annie's Attitude on Bullying. 2011. 40p. pap. (978-1-4269-6978-2(3)) Trafford Publishing (UK) Ltd.

Brown, Tracy. Cyberbullying: Online Safety. 2013. (Illus.). 80p. (YA). (gr. 7-12). 33.25 (978-1-4488-9450-5(6)) Rosen Publishing Group, Inc., The.

Burstein, John. Why Are You Picking on Me? Dealing with Bullies. 2009. (Slim Goodbody's Life Skills 101 Ser.). (ENG., Illus.). 32p. (J). (gr. 3-6). pap. (978-0-7787-4808-3(1)); lib. bdg. (978-0-7787-4792-5(1)) Crabtree Publishing Co.

Carls, Beth & Looper, Amy, eds. I Wish I Knew What to Do: On What to Say to Get Bullies to Leave You Alone. 2005. (Illus.). (YA). per. 14.95 (978-0-9773689-0-7(4)) MindOH! Foundation, The.

Cassidy, Mike. The Skinny on Bullying: Legend of Gretchen. 2010. (Skinny On Ser.). (Illus.). 128p. (J). (gr. 5-18). pap. 12.95 (978-0-9824390-1-2(6), Skinny On (tm), The) Rand Media Co.

Cerullo, Claudio V. Stop Bullying Me. 2012. 40p. pap. 24.95 (978-1-4626-5645-5(5)) America Star Bks.

Crabtree Publishing Company Staff & Pegis, Jessica. Bullying. 2012. (ENG.). 48p. (J). (978-0-7787-2181-9(7)); (Illus.). pap. (978-0-7787-2188-8(4)) Crabtree Publishing Co.

Crabtree Publishing Company Staff & Rivkin, Jennifer. Physical Bullying. 2012. (ENG., Illus.). 48p. (J). (978-0-7787-7914-8(9)) Crabtree Publishing Co.

—Verbal Bullying. 2012. (ENG.). 48p. (J). (978-0-7787-7916-2(5)) Crabtree Publishing Co.

Crabtree Publishing Company Staff & Stuckey, Rachel. Cyber Bullying. 2012. (ENG.). 48p. (J). (978-0-7787-7913-1(0)) Crabtree Publishing Co.

Crabtree Staff & Rivkin, Jennifer. Physical Bullying. 2012. (ENG., Illus.). 48p. (J). pap. (978-0-7787-7919-3(X)) Crabtree Publishing Co.

—Verbal Bullying. 2012. (ENG., Illus.). 48p. (J). pap. (978-0-7787-7921-6(1)) Crabtree Publishing Co.

Crabtree Staff & Stuckey, Rachel. Cyber Bullying. 2012. (ENG., Illus.). 48p. (J). pap. (978-0-7787-7918-6(1)) Crabtree Publishing Co.

Crabtree Staff & Webb, Margaret. Social Bullying. 2012. (ENG., Illus.). 48p. (J). pap. (978-0-7787-7920-9(3)) Crabtree Publishing Co.

Craver, Marcella Marino. Shield Up! Pinelli, Amerigo, illus. 2014. 64p. (J). pap. (978-1-4338-1651-2(2), Magination Pr.) American Psychological Assn.

Crist, James J. What to Do When You're Cranky & Blue. 2013. (ENG., Illus.). 128p. (J). (gr. 4-8). pap. 10.99 (978-1-57542-430-9(4)) Free Spirit Publishing, Inc.

Cunningham, Anne C., ed. Public Shaming. 2017. (Opposing Viewpoints Ser.). 224p. (YA). (gr. 10-12). pap. 33.80 **(978-1-5345-0033-4(2))**; lib. bdg. 48.80 **(978-1-5345-0023-5(5))** Greenhaven Publishing LLC. (Greenhaven Publishing).

Curatola Knowles, Carmela N. Piano & Laylee & the Cyberbully. 2011. (J). (978-1-56484-294-7(0)) International Society for Technology in Education.

—Piano & Laylee & the Cyberbully. Lewellen, Emily, illus. 2011. (J). pap. (978-1-56484-279-4(7)) International Society for Technology in Education.

Dailey, D. C. Billy the Bully. l.t. ed. 2005. (Illus.). 32p. (J). 10.95 (978-1-929662-04-3(1)) Brighter Horizons Publishing.

—Billy the Bully Educators Edition. l.t. ed. 2005. (Illus.). 36p. (J). 15.95 (978-1-929662-05-0(X)) Brighter Horizons Publishing.

—Mindy the Meanie. l.t. ed. 2005. (Illus.). 34p. (J). 10.95 (978-1-929662-06-7(8)) Brighter Horizons Publishing.

—Mindy the Meanie Educators Edition. l.t. ed. 2005. (Illus.). 36p. (J). 15.95 (978-1-929662-07-4(6)) Brighter Horizons Publishing.

Doering, Amanda. Insults Aren't Funny: What to Do about Verbal Bullying. Shin, Simone, illus. 2015. (No More Bullies Ser.). (ENG.). 24p. (gr. k-3). lib. bdg. 25.99 (978-1-4795-6942-7(9)) Picture Window Bks.

—Sometimes Jokes Aren't Funny: What to Do about Hidden Bullying. Shin, Simone, illus. 2015. (No More Bullies Ser.). (ENG.). 24p. (gr. k-3). lib. bdg. 25.99 (978-1-4795-6943-4(7)) Picture Window Bks.

Donovan, Sandy. How Can I Deal with Bullying? A Book about Respect. 2014. (Show Your Character Ser.). (ENG., Illus.). 32p. (gr. 1-3). lib. bdg. 26.60 (978-1-4677-1362-7(7), Lerner Pubns.) Lerner Publishing Group.

Ellis, Deborah. We Want You to Know: Kids Talk about Bullying, 1 vol. 2010. (ENG.). 136p. (YA). (gr. 6-12). 21.95 (978-1-55050-417-0(7)) Coteau Bks. CAN. Dist: Orca Bk. Pubs. USA.

Ellis, Deborah & Reed, Fred. We Want You to Know: Kids Talk about Bullying, 1 vol. 2011. (ENG.). 120p. (J). (gr. 6-12). pap. 14.95 (978-1-55050-463-7(0)) Coteau Bks. CAN. Dist: Orca Bk. Pubs. USA.

Etingoff, Kim. Bully on Campus & Online. Stephens, Ronald, ed. 2014. (Safety First Ser.: 11). 48p. (J). (gr. 5-18). 20.95 (978-1-4222-3045-9(7)) Mason Crest.

Everly, Nita. Early Social Behavior Books Can You Stand up for Yourself. 2007. (J). spiral bd. 11.95 (978-0-7606-0740-4(0)) LinguiSystems, Inc.

Falligant, Erin & American Girl Editors, eds. Stand up for Yourself Journal: Quizzes & Questions to Help You Stand Strong Against Bullying. Martini, Angela, illus. 2011. (ENG.). 64p. (J). spiral bd. 9.95 (978-1-59369-910-9(7)) American Girl Publishing, Inc.

Ferguson, Addy. Antibullying Clubs. 2014. (Stand up: Bullying Prevention Ser.). (Illus.). 24p. (J). (gr. k-3). pap. 49.50 (978-1-4777-6623-1(5), PowerKids Pr.) Rosen Publishing Group, Inc., The.

—Are You a Bully? 2013. (Stand up: Bullying Prevention Ser.). (ENG., Illus.). 24p. (J). (gr. 3-6). pap. 8.25 (978-1-4488-9790-2(4)); lib. bdg. 22.60 (978-1-4488-9666-0(5)) Rosen Publishing Group, Inc., The. (PowerKids Pr.).

—Bullying with Words: Teasing, Name-Calling, & Rumors. 2013. (Stand up: Bullying Prevention Ser.). (ENG., Illus.). 24p. (J). (gr. 3-6). pap. 8.25 (978-1-4488-9798-8(X)); lib. bdg. 22.60 (978-1-4488-9670-7(3)) Rosen Publishing Group, Inc., The. (PowerKids Pr.).

—Group Bullying: Exclusion & Ganging Up. 2013. (Stand up: Bullying Prevention Ser.). (ENG., Illus.). 24p. (J). (gr. 3-6). pap. 8.25 (978-1-4488-9796-4(3)); lib. bdg. 22.60 (978-1-4488-9669-1(X)) Rosen Publishing Group, Inc., The. (PowerKids Pr.).

—How to Deal with an Adult Bully. 2014. (Stand up: Bullying Prevention Ser.). 24p. (J). (gr. k-3). pap. 49.50 (978-1-4777-6622-4(7), PowerKids Pr.) Rosen Publishing Group, Inc., The.

—Online Bullying. 2013. (Stand up: Bullying Prevention Ser.). (ENG., Illus.). 24p. (J). (gr. 3-6). pap. 8.25 (978-1-4488-9794-0(7)); lib. bdg. 22.60 (978-1-4488-9668-4(1)) Rosen Publishing Group, Inc., The. (PowerKids Pr.).

—What to Do When You Are Bullied for Being Different. 2014. (Stand up: Bullying Prevention Ser.). 24p. (J). (gr. k-3). lib. bdg. 23.60 (978-1-4777-6892-1(0), PowerKids Pr.) Rosen Publishing Group, Inc., The.

—What to Do When Your Brother or Sister Is a Bully. 2014. (Stand up: Bullying Prevention Ser.). 24p. (J). (gr. k-3). pap. 49.50 (978-1-4777-6621-7(9), PowerKids Pr.) Rosen Publishing Group, Inc., The.

—What to Do When Your Friends Are Bullies. 2014. (Stand up: Bullying Prevention Ser.). 24p. (J). (gr. k-3). lib. bdg. 23.60 (978-1-4777-6877-8(7), PowerKids Pr.) Rosen Publishing Group, Inc., The.

—What You Can Do to Stop Bullying. 2013. (Stand up: Bullying Prevention Ser.). (ENG., Illus.). 24p. (J). (gr. 3-6). pap. 8.25 (978-1-4488-9792-6(0)); lib. bdg. 22.60 (978-1-4488-9667-7(3)) Rosen Publishing Group, Inc., The. (PowerKids Pr.).

Fieldler, Julie. How to Deal with Teasing. 2007. (Let's Work It Out Ser.). (ENG., Illus.). 24p. (J). (gr. 3-7). lib. bdg. 22.60 (978-1-4042-3675-2(9), PowerKids Pr.) Rosen Publishing Group, Inc., The.

Finn, Carrie. Kids Talk about Bullying, 1 vol. Muehlenhardt, Amy Bailey, illus. 2006. (Kids Talk Jr Ser.). (ENG.). 32p. (gr. -1-2). lib. bdg. 26.65 (978-1-4048-2315-0(8)) Picture Window Bks.

Frankel, Erin. Dare!, Bk. 2. Heaphy, Paula, illus. 2012. (Weird! Ser.). (ENG.). 48p. (J). (gr. k-4). 15.99 (978-1-57542-399-9(5)) Free Spirit Publishing, Inc.

—Nobody! a Story about Overcoming Bullying in Schools. 2015. lib. bdg. 20.85 (978-0-606-36921-3(X)) Turtleback Bks.

—Tough!, Bk. 3. Heaphy, Paula, illus. 2013. (Weird! Ser.). (ENG.). 48p. (J). (gr. k-4). pap. 9.99 (978-1-57542-438-5(X)) Free Spirit Publishing, Inc.

—Weird! Heaphy, Paula, illus. 2013. (Weird! Ser.). (ENG.). 48p. (J). (gr. k-4). pap. 9.99 (978-1-57542-437-8(1)) Free Spirit Publishing, Inc.

Freedman, Jeri. Online Safety. 2011. (J). 167.70 (978-1-4488-4858-4(X), Rosen Reference); (Illus.). 48p. (YA). (gr. 5-9). lib. bdg. 29.25 (978-1-4488-4577-4(7)) Rosen Publishing Group, Inc., The.

Friedman, Lauri S. Cyberbullying. 2010. (Introducing Issues with Opposing Viewpoints Ser.). (ENG., Illus.). 144p. 36.95 (978-0-7377-5117-8(7), Greenhaven Pr., Inc.) Cengage Gale.

Friedman, Lauri S., ed. Bullying. 2010. (Writing the Critical Essay: an Opposing Viewpoints Guide Ser.). (ENG.). 128p. 33.75 *(978-0-7377-5024-9(3)*, Greenhaven Pr., Inc.) Cengage Gale.

Gallo, Diane. William Wolf & the Three Little Kids: A Tale of a Playground Bully. 2011. 20p. pap. 24.95 *(978-1-4626-3291-6(2))* America Star Bks.

Gerdes, Louise. Cyberbullying. Greenhaven Press Editors, ed. 2011. (At Issue Ser.). (ENG.). 128p. (gr. 10-12). pap. 27.80 *(978-0-7377-5563-3(6)*, Greenhaven Pr., Inc.) Cengage Gale.

Golus, Carrie. Take a Stand! What You Can Do about Bullying. Desrocher, Jack, illus. 2008. (Health Zone Ser.). 64p. (YA). (gr. 4-7). lib. bdg. 30.60 *(978-0-8225-7554-2(X))* Lerner Publishing Group.

—Take A Stand! What You Can Do about Bullying. 2009. pap. 52.95 *(978-0-7613-4689-0(9))* Lerner Publishing Group.

Greenhaven Press Editors, ed. Cyberbullying. 2011. (At Issue Ser.). 128p. (YA). (gr. 9-12). 34.45 *(978-0-7377-5562-6(8))* Cengage Gale.

Guillain, Charlotte. Coping with Bullying, 1 vol. 2011. (Real Life Issues Ser.). (ENG.). 48p. (gr. 6-8). 32.65 *(978-1-4329-4761-3(3))* Heinemann-Raintree.

Hall, Megan Kelley & Jones, Carrie. Dear Bully: 70 Authors Tell Their Stories. 2011. (ENG.). 384p. (YA). (gr. 8). 17.99 *(978-0-06-206098-3(8))*; pap. 9.99 *(978-0-06-206097-6(X))* HarperCollins Pubs. (HarperTeen).

Hall, Pamela. A Bully-Free Bus, 1 vol. Ostrom, Bob, illus. 2012. (Bully-Free World Ser.). (ENG.). 24p. (J). (gr. -1-4). 27.07 *(978-1-61641-844-1(3))* Magic Wagon.

—A Bully-Free Party, 1 vol. Ostrom, Bob, illus. 2012. (Bully-Free World Ser.). (ENG.). 24p. (J). (gr. -1-4). 27.07 *(978-1-61641-845-8(1))* Magic Wagon.

—A Bully-Free Playground, 1 vol. Ostrom, Bob, illus. 2012. (Bully-Free World Ser.). (ENG.). 24p. (J). (gr. -1-4). 27.07 *(978-1-61641-846-5(X))* Magic Wagon.

—A Bully-Free School, 1 vol. Ostrom, Bob, illus. 2012. (Bully-Free World Ser.). (ENG.). 24p. (J). (gr. -1-4). 27.07 *(978-1-61641-847-2(8))* Magic Wagon.

—Making a Bully-Free World, 1 vol. Ostrom, Bob, illus. 2012. (Bully-Free World Ser.). (ENG.). 24p. (J). (gr. -1-4). 27.07 *(978-1-61641-848-9(6))* Magic Wagon.

—Staying Bully-Free Online, 1 vol. Ostrom, Bob, illus. 2012. (Bully-Free World Ser.). (ENG.). 24p. (J). (gr. -1-4). 27.07 *(978-1-61641-849-6(4))* Magic Wagon.

Hamilton, Jill. Bullying & Hazing. 2008. (Issues That Concern You Ser.). (ENG., Illus.). 144p. (gr. 10-12). lib. bdg. 42.00 *(978-0-7377-4183-4(X)*, LML02109-243087, Greenhaven Pr., Inc.) Cengage Gale.

Hanson, Anders. No Bullies Allowed! The Kids' Book of Dealing with Bullies, 1 vol. 2014. (What We Stand For Ser.). (ENG.). 24p. (gr. 5-10). lib. bdg. 25.65 *(978-1-62403-296-7(6)*, Super SandCastle) ABDO Publishing Co.

Hanson-Harding, Alexandra. How to Beat Physical Bullying. 2012. (Beating Bullying Ser.). (ENG., Illus.). 48p. (YA). (gr. 5-8). pap. 11.75 *(978-1-4488-6813-1(0))*; lib. bdg. 27.95 *(978-1-4488-6808-7(4))* Rosen Publishing Group, Inc., The. (Rosen Reference).

Harold, Elsie Louise. Stop Bullying: An ABC Guide for Children & the Adults Who Interact with Them. Harold, Elsie Louise, illus. 2004. (Illus.). (J). spiral bd. 14.99 *(978-0-9764644-0-2(3))* Harold, Elsie L.

Haugen, David M. Bullying. Greenhaven Press Editors, ed. 2014. (Teen Rights & Freedoms Ser.). (ENG., Illus.). 176p. (gr. 10-12). lib. bdg. 42.00 *(978-0-7377-6399-7(X)*, Greenhaven Pr., Inc.) Cengage Gale.

Head, Honor. How to Handle Cyberbullying. 2014. (Under Pressure Ser.). (Illus.). 48p. (gr. 4-7). 37.10 *(978-1-59920-826-8(1))* Black Rabbit Bks.

Heller Korin, Ellen S. Asperger Syndrome an Owner's Manual: What You, Your Parents & Your Teachers Need to Know. 2006. (YA). wbk. ed. 17.95 *(978-1-931282-91-8(9))* Autism Asperger Publishing Co.

Herweck, Diana. Safe & Sound: Stop Bullying. 2017. (Time for Kids Nonfiction Readers Ser.). lib. bdg. 20.85 ***(978-0-606-40261-3(6))*** Turtleback Bks.

Higgins, Melissa. I Am Caring, 1 vol. 2014. (I Don't Bully Ser.). (ENG.). 24p. (gr. k-1). lib. bdg. 21.99 *(978-1-4765-4070-2(5)*, Pebble Bks.) Capstone Press of Coughlan Cos.

—I Don't Bully, 1 vol. 2014. (I Don't Bully Ser.). (ENG.). 24p. (gr. k-1). lib. bdg. 131.94 *(978-1-4765-7009-9(4)*, Pebble Bks.) Capstone Press of Coughlan Cos.

—Pushing Isn't Funny: What to Do about Physical Bullying. Shin, Simone, illus. 2015. (No More Bullies Ser.). (ENG.). 24p. (gr. k-3). lib. bdg. 25.99 *(978-1-4795-6941-0(0))* Picture Window Bks.

—Teasing Isn't Funny: What to Do about Emotional Bullying. Shin, Simone, illus. 2015. (No More Bullies Ser.). (ENG.). 24p. (gr. k-3). lib. bdg. 25.99 *(978-1-4795-6940-3(2))* Picture Window Bks.

Hile, Lori. Bullying, 1 vol. 2012. (Teen Issues Ser.). (ENG.). 56p. (gr. 6-10). lib. bdg. 34.65 *(978-1-4329-6534-1(4))* Heinemann-Raintree.

Hix, Zack. Bully Bad. 2013. 50p. pap. 11.95 *(978-1-935256-37-3(8))* L'Edge Pr.

Hoeffner, Betty. Stop Bullying Handbook: A Guide for Students & Their Friends. 2013. 66p. pap. 15.00 *(978-0-9759004-1-3(2))* Hey U.G.L.Y., Inc.

Hudec-Ignatescu, Donna. Time Out. 2011. 24p. pap. 15.99 *(978-1-4653-3541-8(2))* Xlibris Corp.

Hunter, Nick. Cyber Bullying, 1 vol. 2011. (Hot Topics Ser.). (ENG.). 56p. (gr. 7-8). pap. 10.95 *(978-1-4329-5544-1(6))*; 34.65 *(978-1-4329-4869-6(5))* Heinemann-Raintree. (NA-h).

Hurt, Avery Elizabeth. Working with Your School to Create a Safe Environment. 2017. (LGBTQ+ Guide to Beating Bullying Ser.). 64p. (J). (gr. 12-11). 34.45 ***(978-1-5081-7435-6(0)***, Rosen Young Adult) Rosen Publishing Group, Inc., The.

Jacobs, Thomas A. Teen Cyberbullying Investigated: Where Do Your Rights End & Consequences Begin? 2010. (ENG.). 208p. (YA). (gr. 6-18). pap. 15.99 *(978-1-57542-339-5(1))* Free Spirit Publishing, Inc.

Jakubiak, David. A Smart Kid's Guide to Online Bullying. 2009. 24p. (YA). pap. 8.25 *(978-1-4358-3348-7(1))* Rosen Publishing Group, Inc., The.

Jakubiak, David J. A Smart Kid's Guide to Online Bullying. (J). 2010. 49.50 *(978-1-4358-3349-4(X))* 2009. (Illus.). 24p. (gr. 2-6). 22.60 *(978-1-4042-8114-1(2))* Rosen Publishing Group, Inc., The. (PowerKids Pr.).

Johnston, Marianne. Dealing with Bullying / Qué hacer con los Bravucones. 2009. (Conflict Resolution Library / Biblioteca solución de conflictos Ser.). (ENG & SPA.). 24p. (gr. 2-3). 42.50 *(978-1-60853-413-5(8)*, Editorial Buenas Letras) Rosen Publishing Group, Inc., The.

—Dealing with Bullying/Que Hacer con Los Bravucones. Velazquez De Leon, Mauricio, tr. from ENG. 2008. (Conflict Resolution Library / Biblioteca Solución de Conflictos Ser.). (SPA., Illus.). 24p. (J). (gr. k-3). lib. bdg. 22.60 *(978-1-4042-7658-1(0))* Rosen Publishing Group, Inc., The.

—Dealing with Fighting / Qué hacer con las Peleas. 2009. (Conflict Resolution Library / Biblioteca solución de conflictos Ser.). (ENG & SPA.). 24p. (gr. 2-3). 42.50 *(978-1-60853-414-2(6)*, Editorial Buenas Letras) Rosen Publishing Group, Inc., The.

Jones, Jen. How Much Do You Know about Bullying?, 1 vol. 2011. (Friendship Quizzes Ser.). (ENG.). 32p. (gr. 3-4). lib. bdg. 27.99 *(978-1-4296-6540-7(8)*, Snap Bks.) Capstone Press of Coughlan Cos.

Jones, Kip. The Power of Bystanders: Willie Bohanon & Friends Learn to Handle Bullying Like a Boss. Isely, Chad, illus. 2015. (ENG.). 32p. (J). pap. 10.95 *(978-1-934490-79-2(2))* Boys Town Pr.

Kamberg, Mary-Lane. I Have Been Bullied — Now What?, 1 vol. 2015. (ENG.). 112p. (YA). 35.60 *(978-1-4777-7978-1(7)*, Rosen Young Adult) Rosen Publishing Group, Inc., The.

Kaufman Goodstein, Phyllis & Verdick, Elizabeth. Stand up to Bullying! (Upstanders to the Rescue!) 2014. (Laugh & Learn Ser.). (ENG., Illus.). 128p. (J). (gr. 3-8). pap. 8.95 *(978-1-57542-483-5(5))* Free Spirit Publishing, Inc.

Kravetz, Jonathan. How to Deal with Bullies. (Let's Work It Out Ser.). 24p. (gr. 2-3). 2009. 42.50 *(978-1-61514-257-6(6)*, PowerKids Pr.) 2007. (Illus.). (J). lib. bdg. 22.60 *(978-1-4042-3670-7(8))* Rosen Publishing Group, Inc., The.

Ladin, Marc J. The Playground Bully Blues. Margolis, Al, illus. 2010. 26p. pap. 14.95 *(978-1-60844-377-2(9))* Dog Ear Publishing, LLC.

Landau, Jennifer. Dealing with Bullies, Cliques, & Social Stress. 2012. (Middle School Survival Handbook Ser.). (ENG., Illus.). 64p. (YA). (gr. 5-8). pap. 12.95 *(978-1-4488-8321-9(0))*; lib. bdg. 31.95 *(978-1-4488-8313-4(X))* Rosen Publishing Group, Inc., The. (Rosen Reference).

—How to Beat Psychological Bullying. 2012. (Beating Bullying Ser.). (ENG., Illus.). 48p. (J). (gr. 5-8). pap. 11.75 *(978-1-4488-6815-5(7))*; lib. bdg. 27.95 *(978-1-4488-6809-4(2))* Rosen Publishing Group, Inc., The. (Rosen Reference).

Leigh, Susan K. God, I Need to Talk to You about Bullying. Clark, Bill, illus. 2005. 16p. (J). pap. 1.19 *(978-0-7586-0796-6(2))* Concordia Publishing Hse.

Le'Taxione. A Bully's Behavior. 2011. 30p. (J). pap. 18.95 *(978-1-4327-4950-7(1))* Outskirts Pr., Inc.

L'Heureux, Christine. Caillou & the Big Bully. Brignaud, Pierre, illus. 2015. (Hand in Hand Ser.). (ENG.). 24p. (J). (gr. -1-k). 5.95 *(978-2-89718-199-4(0))* Caillouet, Gerry.

Lindeen, Mary. Digital Safety Smarts: Preventing Cyberbullying. 2016. (Searchlight Books (tm) — What Is Digital Citizenship? Ser.). (ENG.). 40p. (J). (gr. 3-5). 30.65 *(978-1-4677-9488-6(0)*, Lerner Pubns.) Lerner Publishing Group.

Lindsay, Jabari. Gangs: Deal with It Before Wrong Seems Right, 1 vol. 2012. (Lorimer Deal with It Ser.). (ENG., Illus.). 32p. (YA). (gr. 4-6). pap. 12.95 *(978-1-55277-917-0(3)*, 9781552779170) Lorimer, James & Co., Ltd., Pubs. CAN. Dist: Casemate Pubs. & Bk. Distributors, LLC.

Lite, Lori. Children's Wellness Curriculum: Lessons, Stories & Techniques Designed to Decrease Bullying, Anxiety, Anger & Obesity While Promoting Self-Esteem & Healthy Food Choices. 2007. (J). (gr. k-5). 89.95 incl. audio compact disk *(978-0-9787781-2-5(X)*, 5) Stress Free Pubs.

Living with Peer Pressure & Bullying. 2010. (Teen's Guides). (Illus.). 176p. (gr. 6-12). pap. 14.95 *(978-0-8160-7915-5(3)*, Checkmark Bks.) Facts On File, Inc.

Lohmann, Raychelle Cassada & Taylor, Julia V. The Bullying Workbook for Teens: Activities to Help You Deal with Social Aggression & Cyberbullying. 2013. (ENG.). 152p. (YA). (gr. 6-12). pap. 17.95 *(978-1-60882-450-2(0)*, Instant Help Books) New Harbinger Pubns.

Lovegrove, Emily. Help! I'm Being Bullied. 2007. (Illus.). 167p. per. *(978-1-905170-34-0(3))* Accent Pr. Ltd.

MacCarald, Clara. Beating Bullying at Home & in Your Community. 2017. (LGBTQ+ Guide to Beating Bullying Ser.). 64p. (J). (gr. 12-11). 34.45 ***(978-1-5081-7424-0(5))***; pap. 12.95 ***(978-1-5081-7422-6(9))*** Rosen Publishing Group, Inc., The. (Rosen Young Adult).

MacEachern, Robyn. Cyberbullying: And Ctrl Alt Delete It, 1 vol. Charette, Geraldine, illus. (Lorimer Deal with It Ser.). (ENG.). 32p. (J). 2010. (gr. 4-6). 24.95 *(978-1-55277-496-0(1)*, 9781552774960) 2009. (gr. 5-12). pap. 12.95 *(978-1-55277-037-5(0)*, 9781552770375) Lorimer, James & Co., Ltd., Pubs. CAN. Dist: Casemate Pubs. & Bk. Distributors, LLC, Orca Bk. Pubs. USA.

MacKay, Jennifer, ed. Bullying. 2012. (Hot Topics Ser.). (ENG., Illus.). 128p. (gr. 7-10). lib. bdg. 33.95 *(978-1-4205-0814-7(8)*, Lucent Bks.) Cengage Gale.

MacRae, Sloan. Respecting the Contributions of Disabled Americans. 2012. (Stop Bullying Now! Ser.). (ENG., Illus.). 24p. (J). (gr. 3-6). pap. 8.25 *(978-1-4488-7518-4(8))*; lib. bdg. 22.60 *(978-1-4488-7445-3(9))* Rosen Publishing Group, Inc., The. (PowerKids Pr.).

Marsico, Katie. Bullying. 2013. 80p. (YA). (gr. 7-12). 34.21 *(978-1-60870-849-9(7))*; pap. 17.64 *(978-1-62712-126-2(9))* Cavendish Square Publishing.

Martineau, Susan. Dealing with Bullying. 2011. (Positive Steps Ser.). 32p. (gr. 2-5). lib. bdg. 31.35 *(978-1-59920-491-8(6))* Black Rabbit Bks.

Mayrock, Aija. The Survival Guide to Bullying: Written by a Teen. rev. ed. 2015. (ENG., Illus.). 160p. (J). (gr. 7). pap. 9.99 *(978-0-545-86053-6(9))* Scholastic, Inc.

McAneney, Caitlin. Bullies, 1 vol. 2015. (ENG., Illus.). 24p. (J). pap. 8.25 *(978-1-4777-5785-7(6))*; lib. bdg. 23.60 *(978-1-4777-5784-0(8))* Rosen Publishing Group, Inc., The. (PowerKids Pr.).

—I Have Been Cyberbullied. Now What? 2015. (Teen Life 411 Ser.). (ENG., Illus.). 112p. (J). (gr. 6-7). 35.60 *(978-1-4994-6138-1(0)*, Rosen Young Adult) Rosen Publishing Group, Inc., The.

Meyer, Susan. Combatting Slut Shaming. 2016. (Combatting Shaming & Toxic Communities Ser.). 64p. (J). (gr. 7-7). 34.45 *(978-1-5081-7115-7(7))* Rosen Publishing Group, Inc., The.

Miles, Lisa & Chown, Xanna Eve. How to Survive Mean Girls. 2013. (Girl Talk Ser.). 48p. (J). (gr. 5-8). pap. 70.50 *(978-1-4777-0722-7(0)*, Rosen Reference); (ENG., Illus.). pap. 11.75 *(978-1-4777-0721-0(2)*, Rosen Classroom); (ENG., Illus.). lib. bdg. 29.25 *(978-1-4777-0707-4(7)*, Rosen Reference) Rosen Publishing Group, Inc., The.

Minton, Eric. Cyberbullies, 1 vol., 1. 2014. (Stay Safe Online Ser.). (ENG.). 32p. (J). (gr. 4-6). 26.25 *(978-1-4777-2936-6(4)*, PowerKids Pr.) Rosen Publishing Group, Inc., The.

Mooney, Carla. Bullying. 2016. (Matters of Opinion Ser.). (ENG., Illus.). 64p. (J). (gr. 4-6). lib. bdg. 27.93 *(978-1-59953-754-2(0))* Norwood Hse. Pr.

Morris, Daphne. Trevor Romain's Tips, Strategies & Activities for Dealing with Bullies Resource Guide. 2006. (J). spiral bd. 24.99 *(978-0-9787783-6-1(7))* Romain, Trevor Co., The.

—Trevor Romain's Tips, Strategies & Activities for Dealing with Cliques Resource Guide. 2006. (J). (gr. 2-6). spiral bd. 24.99 *(978-0-9787783-7-8(5))* Romain, Trevor Co., The.

Murray, Molly. Everyone Just Yell No at the Bullies! That Should Help to Stop Them! 2011. 48p. pap. 19.33 *(978-1-4567-6327-5(X))* AuthorHouse.

Navarre, Sam. Masculinity, Bullying, & Aggression: A Guy's Guide. 2011. (Young Man's Guide to Contemporary Issues Ser.). (ENG.). 104p. (J). (gr. 9-12). lib. bdg. 34.60 *(978-1-4488-5525-4(X))* Rosen Publishing Group, Inc., The.

Nelson, Drew. Dealing with Cyberbullies. 2012. (Cyberspace Survival Guide Ser.). (Illus.). 32p. (J). (gr. 3-6). 26.60 *(978-1-4339-7220-1(4))*; pap. 10.50 *(978-1-4339-7221-8(2))* Stevens, Gareth Publishing LLLP. (Gareth Stevens Learning Library).

Noll, Kathy. Encounters with Every-Day Angels (Workbook) Can You See the Angels (A Workbook on Bullying & Character Development) 2004. (Illus.). 65p. (J). ring bd., wbk. ed. 12.95 *(978-0-937004-03-6(0))* Unicorn Pr.

Owings, Lisa. Punishing Bullies: Zero Tolerance vs. Working Together. 2015. (Perspectives Flip Books: Issues Ser.). (ENG.). 64p. (gr. 5-6). 33.99 *(978-0-7565-4995-4(7))* Compass Point Bks.

Patchin, Justin W. & Hinduja, Sameer. Words Wound: Delete Cyberbullying & Make Kindness Go Viral. 2013. (ENG., Illus.). 208p. (YA). (gr. 7-12). pap. 15.99 *(978-1-57542-451-4(7))* Free Spirit Publishing, Inc.

Perdew, Laura. Bullying, 1 vol. 2014. (Essential Issues Set 4 Ser.). (ENG.). 112p. (J). (gr. 6-12). lib. bdg. 35.64 *(978-1-62403-418-3(7)*, Essential Library) ABDO Publishing Co.

Perron, Brigitte. I'm a Champ. 2010. 32p. 14.95 *(978-1-4269-1176-7(9))* Trafford Publishing.

Pitt, Steve. Teasing: Deal with It Before the Joke's on You, 1 vol. Geoffroi, Remie, illus. 2007. (Lorimer Deal with It Ser.). (ENG.). 32p. (J). (gr. 4-8). pap., instr.'s gde. ed. 12.95 *(978-1-55028-946-6(2)*, 9781550289466) Lorimer, James & Co., Ltd., Pubs. CAN. Dist: Orca Bk. Pubs. USA.

Raatma, Lucia. Bullying. 2013. (21st Century Junior Library: Character Education Ser.). (ENG., Illus.). 24p. (J). (gr. 1-4). 25.64 *(978-1-62431-152-9(0)*, 202928); pap. 12.79 *(978-1-62431-284-7(5)*, 202930) Cherry Lake Publishing.

—Stop Bullying. 2013. (True Book™—Guides to Life Ser.). (ENG., Illus.). 48p. (J). pap. 6.95 *(978-0-531-23921-6(7))*; lib. bdg. 29.00 *(978-0-531-25521-6(2))* Scholastic Library Publishing.

Rawl, Paige, et al. Positive. 2014. (ENG.). 288p. (YA). (gr. 8). 18.99 *(978-0-06-234251-5(7))* HarperCollins Pubs.

Riad, Hala. There Is a Bully in My Tummy. 2012. 20p. pap. 24.95 *(978-1-4626-2914-5(8))* America Star Bks.

Richards, Melissa. I Didn't Know I Was a Bully: A Meaningful & Memorable Reproducible Story Plus Six Literatur-Based Lessons on Bullying Behaviors. 2005. pap. 19.95 *(978-1-57543-138-3(6))* MAR*CO Products, Inc.

Rische, Stephanie. My Princesses Learn to Be Brave. Heyworth, Heather, illus. 2014. (ENG.). 24p. (J). 6.99 *(978-1-4143-9661-3(9))* Tyndale Hse. Pubs.

Robertson, Warden Howard. The 411 on Bullying, Gangs, Drugs & Jail: The Formula for Staying in School & Out of Jail. 2013. 82p. pap. 10.95 *(978-1-4787-0571-0(X))* Outskirts Pr., Inc.

Roleff, Tamara, ed. Cyberbullying. 2012. (Issues That Concern You Ser.). (ENG., Illus.). 144p. (gr. 7-10). lib. bdg. 36.95 *(978-0-7377-5692-0(6))* Cengage Gale.

Romain, Trevor. Bullying Is a Pain in the Brain, Revised & Updated Edition. 2016. lib. bdg. 19.60 *(978-0-606-37930-4(4))* Turtleback Bks.

Ryan, Peter. Online Bullying. 2011. (Teen Mental Health Ser.). (Illus.). 48p. (YA). (gr. 7-12). lib. bdg. 29.25 *(978-1-4488-4588-0(2))* Rosen Publishing Group, Inc., The.

Scherer, Lauri S. Cyber Bullying. Greenhaven Press Staff, ed. 2015. (Introducing Issues with Opposing Viewpoints Ser.). (ENG., Illus.). 144p. (J). (gr. 7-10). lib. bdg. 42.00 *(978-0-7377-7234-0(4)*, Greenhaven Pr., Inc.) Cengage Gale.

Schwartz, Heather E. Cyberbullying, 6 vols. 2013. (Tech Safety Smarts Ser.). (ENG.). 32p. (gr. 3-4). 47.70 *(978-1-62065-799-7(6)*, Fact Finders); lib. bdg. 27.32 *(978-1-4296-9944-0(2))*; (Illus.). pap. 8.10 *(978-1-62065-798-0(8))* Capstone Press of Coughlan Cos.

Shapiro, Ouisie. Bullying & Me: Schoolyard Stories, 1 vol. Vote, Steven, photos by. 2010. (ENG., Illus.). 32p. (J). (gr. 3-7). 16.99 *(978-0-8075-0921-0(3))* Whitman, Albert & Co.

Slavens, Elaine. Bullying: Deal with It Before Push Comes to Shove. Kerrigan, Brooke, illus. 3rd ed. 2014. (Lorimer Deal with It Ser.). (ENG.). 32p. (J). (gr. 4-6). pap. 12.95 *(978-1-4594-0653-7(2)*, 9781459406537) Lorimer, James & Co., Ltd., Pubs. CAN. Dist: Casemate Pubs. & Bk. Distributors, LLC.

Slavens, Elaine & Pitt, Steve. Teasing: Before the Joke's on You, 1 vol. Geoffroi, Remie, illus. 2010. (Lorimer Deal with It Ser.). (ENG.). 32p. (J). (gr. 4-6). 24.95 *(978-1-55277-497-7(X)*, 9781552774977) Lorimer, James & Co., Ltd., Pubs. CAN. Dist: Casemate Pubs. & Bk. Distributors, LLC.

Smartphone Bullying. 2014. (Stand up: Bullying Prevention Ser.). (Illus.). 24p. (J). (gr. k-3). pap. 49.50 *(978-1-4777-6624-8(3)*, PowerKids Pr.) Rosen Publishing Group, Inc., The.

Soliz, Adela. Bullying. 2009. (Social Issues Firsthand Ser.). (ENG., Illus.). 128p. (YA). (gr. 10-12). lib. bdg. 33.75 *(978-0-7377-3833-9(2)*, LML02109-234572, Greenhaven Pr., Inc.) Cengage Gale.

Sonneborn, Liz. How to Beat Verbal Bullying. 2012. (Beating Bullying Ser.). (ENG., Illus.). 48p. (YA). (gr. 5-8). pap. 11.75 *(978-1-4488-6819-3(X)*, Rosen Reference) Rosen Publishing Group, Inc., The.

Spilsbury, Louise. Say No to Bullying. 2014. (ENG., Illus.). 64p. (J). (gr. 4-6). pap. 9.99 *(978-1-4380-0401-3(X))* Barron's Educational Series, Inc.

Spivet, Bonnie. Stopping Cyberbullying. 2011. (CyberSmarts: Staying Safe Online Ser.). (ENG.). 24p. (J). (gr. 4-6). pap. 10.00 *(978-1-4488-6420-1(8))*; lib. bdg. 21.25 *(978-1-4488-6413-3(5))* Rosen Publishing Group, Inc., The. (PowerKids Pr.).

Sprague, Susan & Schwartz, S. Coping with Cliques: A Workbook to Help Girls Deal with Gossip, Put-Downs, Bullying & Other Mean Behavior. 2008. (Instant Help Ser.). (ENG.). 168p. (YA). (gr. 6-12). pap. 16.95 *(978-1-57224-613-3(8)*, Instant Help Books) New Harbinger Pubns.

Stand kup against bullies K-2. 2005. pap. 18.95 *(978-1-57543-132-1(7))* MAR*CO Products, Inc.

Stand Up: Bullying Prevention: Set 2. 2014. (Stand up: Bullying Prevention Ser.). 24p. (J). (gr. k-3). 141.60 *(978-1-4777-6632-3(4)*, PowerKids Pr.) Rosen Publishing Group, Inc., The.

Stand Up: Bullying Prevention: Sets 1-2. 2014. (Stand up: Bullying Prevention Ser.). 24p. (J). (gr. k-3). 283.20 *(978-1-4777-6900-3(5))*; pap. 99.00 *(978-1-4777-7266-9(9))* Rosen Publishing Group, Inc., The. (PowerKids Pr.).

Steen, Joel. Home Room 7b. 2005. 64p. pap. 16.95 *(978-1-4137-9822-7(5))* PublishAmerica, Inc.

Stewart, Gail B. Teens & Bullying. 2015. (ENG., Illus.). 80p. (J). lib. bdg. *(978-1-60152-908-4(2))* ReferencePoint Pr., Inc.

Subramanian, Mathangi. Bullying: The Ultimate Teen Guide. 2014. (It Happened to Me Ser.: 38). (ENG., Illus.). 232p. 50.00 *(978-0-8108-9054-1(2))* Rowman & Littlefield Publishers, Inc.

Tarshis, Thomas Paul. Living with Peer Pressure & Bullying. 2010. (Teen's Guides). (Illus.). 176p. (gr. 6-12). 34.95 *(978-0-8160-7914-8(5))* Facts On File, Inc.

Tate, Brucetta McClue. Jolly Meets Cyber Air Bully. 2012. 44p. pap. 21.99 *(978-1-4685-8719-7(6))* AuthorHouse.

Terry-Bryant, Wincey. Bullying Is Wrong. 2012. (ENG.). (J). pap. 9.95 *(978-1-4675-0857-5(8))* Independent Pub.

Thompson, Stephen, ed. Teens at Risk. 2013. (Opposing Viewpoints Ser.). (ENG., Illus.). 224p. (gr. 10-12). pap. 33.80 *(978-0-7377-6431-4(7))*; lib. bdg. 48.80 *(978-0-7377-6430-7(9))* Cengage Gale. (Greenhaven Pr., Inc.).

Truesdell, Ann. How to Handle Cyberbullies. Petelinsek, Kathleen, illus. 2013. (Explorer Library: Information Explorer Ser.). (ENG.). 32p. (J). (gr. 4-8). 28.50 *(978-1-62431-127-7(X)*, 202828); pap. 14.21 *(978-1-62431-259-5(4)*, 202830) Cherry Lake Publishing.

Utterly Global Youth Empowerment. Anti-Bullying Club/Project Manual. 2013. 84p. 99.00 *(978-0-9891338-2-1(6))* Utterly Global.

Vandawalker, Marianne. Conquering Bullies: 27 Game-Oriented Guidance Lessons for Grades 2-5 & 12 Story-Based Guidance Lessons for Grades K-12. 2005. pap. 29.95 *(978-1-57543-136-9(X))* MAR*CO Products, Inc.

Williams, Julie-Anne. Bully Me Not. 2013. 52p. pap. *(978-0-646-90927-1(4))* Williams, Julie.

Williams, Sam. Are You a Bully? 2012. (ENG., Illus.). 24p. (gr. k-2). pap. 8.95 *(978-1-61810-267-6(2))* Rourke Educational Media.

Winkler, Kathleen. Are You Being Bullied? How to Deal with Taunting, Teasing, & Tormenting. 2014. (Got Issues? Ser.). (Illus.). 112p. (gr. 6-12). (J). 33.27 *(978-0-7660-5953-5(7))*; (YA). pap. 10.95 *(978-0-7660-5954-2(5))* Enslow Pubs., Inc.

—Bullying: How to Deal with Taunting, Teasing, & Tormenting. 2005. (Issues in Focus Today Ser.). (Illus.). 104p. (J). (gr. 6-13). lib. bdg. 33.27 *(978-0-7660-2355-0(9))* Enslow Pubs., Inc.

World Book, Inc Staff, contrib. by. Bullied by Boys. 2013. (J). *(978-0-7166-2071-6(5))* World Bk., Inc.

—Bullied by Friends. 2013. (J). *(978-0-7166-2072-3(3))* World Bk., Inc.

—Bullied by Girls. 2013. (J). *(978-0-7166-2073-0(1))* World Bk., Inc.

—Bullied by Groups. 2013. (J). *(978-0-7166-2074-7(X))* World Bk., Inc.

—Bullied in Cyberspace. 2013. (J). *(978-0-7166-2075-4(8))* World Bk., Inc.

—Bullied to Belong. 2013. 48p. (J). *(978-0-7166-2076-1(6))* World Bk., Inc.

Yearling, Tricia. How Do I Stay Safe from Cyberbullies? 2015. (Online Smarts Ser.). (ENG.). 32p. (J). (gr. 3-4). pap. 10.52 *(978-0-7660-6849-0(8))*; (Illus.). 25.27 *(978-0-7660-6851-3(X))* Enslow Pubs., Inc.

BULLYING—FICTION

Achor, Shawn & Blankson, Amy. Ripple's Effect. O'Malley, Judy, ed. Rebora, Cecilia, illus. 2012. (ENG.). 32p. (J). (gr. -1-k). 18.95 *(978-0-9829938-7-3(0))* March 4th, Inc.

Adams, W. Royce. The Computer's Nerd. 2011. 154p. (gr. 4-7). 22.99 *(978-0-9712206-9-0(7))* Rairarubia Bks.

Ahlstrom, Susan. Project: Owen Ritter. 2011. 108p. pap. 15.99 *(978-1-4568-8559-5(6))* Xlibris Corp.

Alexiou, Michelle. A Bully for Bert: Playground Escapades. 2012. (ENG.). 45p. (J). pap. 26.95 *(978-1-4327-8370-9(X))*; pap. 22.95 *(978-1-4327-8364-8(5))* Outskirts Pr., Inc.

Aliaga, Roberto. Dorothy: A Different Kind of Friend. 2013. (ENG., Illus.). 28p. (J). (gr. -1-k). 16.95 *(978-84-15619-81-9(2))* Eastern National.

Allen, Bryony. Otoli. 2011. 144p. (YA). pap. *(978-1-907728-12-9(0))* Pneuma Springs Publishing.

Almond, David. The Tightrope Walkers. 2016. (ENG.). 336p. (YA). (gr. 9). pap. 9.99 *(978-0-7636-9104-2(6))* Candlewick Pr.

Aloha Potter! Evaluation Guide: Evaluation Guide. 2006. (J). *(978-1-55942-397-7(8))* Witcher Productions.

Amos, Angela. 'Twas the Fight Before Christmas. 2013. 34p. pap. 12.95 *(978-1-4327-8204-7(5))* Outskirts Pr., Inc.

Anderson, Georgia Lee. Bullying Is Wrong. Fox, Tom Paul, illus. 2012. (ENG.). 26p. pap. 14.95 *(978-1-57258-882-0(9),* Aspect Bk.) TEACH Services, Inc.

Anderson, Jeff. Zack Delacruz: Me & My Big Mouth. (Zack Delacruz Ser.). (ENG., Illus.). 176p. (J). (gr. 5-8). 2016. pap. 6.95 *(978-1-4549-2127-1(7))* 2015. 12.95 *(978-1-4549-1499-0(8))* Sterling Publishing Co., Inc.

Anderson, Jennifer. King of the Lake. 2013. 144p. (YA). pap. 10.99 *(978-0-62237-217-1(4))* Turquoise Morning Pr.

Anderson, John David. Insert Coin to Continue. 2016. (ENG., Illus.). 336p. (J). (gr. 3-7). 16.99 *(978-1-4814-4704-1(1),* Aladdin) Simon & Schuster Children's Publishing.

Anderson, Phil. The Thomas Family Values. 2012. 84p. pap. 13.95 *(978-1-4772-2529-5(3))* AuthorHouse.

Arcos, Carrie. Crazy Messy Beautiful. 2017. (ENG.). 320p. (YA). (gr. 7). 17.99 *(978-0-399-17553-4(9),* Philomel Bks.) Penguin Young Readers Group.

Armstrong, Gregory D. The Day Buddy Flew. 2013. 42p. (J). 21.99 *(978-0-578-12191-8(3))* Armstrong, Greg.

—Don't Laugh at Me. 2013. 32p. 21.99 *(978-0-578-12368-4(1))* Armstrong, Greg.

Arnold, Beth. Elijah Makes New Friends. Arnold, Beth, illus. 2012. (Illus.). 30p. pap. 9.99 *(978-0-9860272-3-9(5))* Get Happy Tips, LLC.

Asher, Diana Harmon. Sidetracked. 2017. (ENG.). 240p. (J). (gr. 3-7). 16.99 ***(978-1-4197-2601-9(3),*** Amulet Bks.) Abrams, Inc.

Assunto, Cecelia. God Did Make Little Green Apples. DeMatte, Darcey, illus. 2012. 30p. (J). pap. 12.95 *(978-1-61314-028-4(2))* Innovo Publishing, LLC.

Atwood, Megan. The Bridge of Death. 2012. (Paranormalists Ser.: 4). (ENG.). 104p. (YA). (gr. 6-12). pap. 7.95 *(978-0-8225-9090-3(5),* Darby Creek); lib. bdg. 27.93 *(978-0-7613-8335-2(2))* Lerner Publishing Group.

Aunt Fezzie. Happy-Feliz & Fatso's Heroic School Adventures: Heroes vs. Bullies. 2013. 32p. pap. 13.99 *(978-1-4808-0134-9(8))* Archway Publishing.

Bachelor, G. M. No Home Should Be Without. 2012. 24p. 24.95 *(978-1-62709-052-0(5))* America Star Bks.

Bailey, Charles. Slick Glickman, Unlikely Hero. 2008. 164p. 22.95 *(978-0-595-49014-1(X))*; pap. 12.95 *(978-0-595-48014-2(4))* iUniverse, Inc.

Baker, Patrick. Fuzzy the Bear. 2013. 24p. pap. 14.95 *(978-1-4669-8942-9(4))* Trafford Publishing.

Banting, Celia. I Only Said Yes So That They'd Like Me. 2006. (Illus.). 224p. (YA). per. 14.99 *(978-0-9786648-1-7(7))* Wighita Pr.

Baratz-Logsted, Lauren. Crazy Beautiful. 2011. (ENG.). 204p. (YA). (gr. 7). pap. 12.95 *(978-0-547-40310-6(0))* Houghton Mifflin Harcourt Publishing Co.

Barclay, Jane. JoJo the Giant. Melo, Esperanca, illus. 2012. (ENG.). 32p. (J). (gr. -1-1). 17.95 *(978-0-88776-976-4(4),* Tundra Bks.) Tundra Bks. CAN. Dist: Penguin Random Hse. LLC.

Barnes, Brenda J. Silas Watts: The Highly Electric Lightning Bug. Williams, Nancy E., ed. Forrest, Grace Metzger, illus. 2013. 28p. (J). pap. 17.98 *(978-1-938526-36-7(8))* Roxby Media Ltd. GBR. Dist: Laurus Co., The.

Barraza, Cindy Lou. Mexiroo Says, So What!! 2012. 32p. pap. 12.99 *(978-1-890900-78-6(8))* Insight Publishing Group.

Barreintez, Elsa. I'm Only Eight, by Reynaldo: I Survived Being Eight. 2010. 46p. pap. 14.95 *(978-1-4327-5489-1(0))* Outskirts Pr., Inc.

Bashline, Trent. How Jake & Daisy Stopped Bullying at Dogwood Elementary. 2011. 32p. pap. 12.79 *(978-1-4634-2895-2(2))* AuthorHouse.

Baskin, Nora Raleigh. Runt. (ENG., Illus.). 208p. (J). (gr. 3-7). 2014. pap. 6.99 *(978-1-4424-5808-6(9))* 2013. 15.99 *(978-1-4424-5807-9(0))* Simon & Schuster Bks. For Young Readers. (Simon & Schuster Bks. For Young Readers).

Bass, Patrik Henry. The Zero Degree Zombie Zone. Craft, Jerry, illus. 2014. (ENG.). 144p. (J). (gr. 3-7). 16.99 *(978-0-545-13210-7(X),* Scholastic Pr.) Scholastic, Inc.

Bates, Penny. A Murder of Crows. 2004. (Shades Ser.). 60p. (J). pap. *(978-0-237-52648-1(4))* Evans Brothers, Ltd.

Bauer, Michael Gerard. Don't Call Me Ishmael. 2007. 255p. (YA). (gr. 9-12). lib. bdg. 17.89 *(978-0-06-134835-8(X),* HarperTeen) HarperCollins Pubs.

Bauer, Michael Gerard & Bauer, Michael G. Don't Call Me Ishmael. 2007. (ENG.). 272p. (YA). (gr. 9-12). 17.99 *(978-0-06-134834-1(1),* Greenwillow Bks.) HarperCollins Pubs.

Bear, F. T. Connor Finn: The Secret of Snow. 2013. 258p. pap. *(978-0-646-91485-5(5))* F. T. Bear.

Bedford, David A. Angela. 2009. 190p. 25.50 *(978-1-60860-755-6(0),* Eloquent Bks.) Strategic Book Publishing & Rights Agency (SBPRA).

Beeson, Paul & Beeson, Lady Jan. Zeela the Zebra of a Different Color. Beeson, Jan, illus. 2013. 38p. pap. 12.99 *(978-0-9890482-5-5(X))* Beeson, Jan.

Bell, Aaron. Jak's Story. 2010. (ENG., Illus.). 96p. (YA). (gr. 4). pap. 10.99 *(978-1-55488-710-1(0))* Dundurn CAN. Dist: Ingram Publisher Services.

Benedis-Grab, Daphne. Army Brats. 2017. (ENG.). 240p. (J). (gr. 3-7). 17.99 *(978-0-545-93205-9(X),* Scholastic Pr.) Scholastic, Inc.

Benoit, Charles. Cold Calls. (ENG.). (gr. 7). 2016. 304p. (YA). pap. 8.99 *(978-0-544-54121-4(9),* HMH Books For Young Readers) 2014. 288p. (J). 17.99 *(978-0-544-23950-0(4))* Houghton Mifflin Harcourt Publishing Co.

Bentley, Sue. Firelight Friends #10. Swan, Angela, illus. 2014. (Magic Kitten Ser.: 10). (ENG.). 128p. (J). (gr. 1-3). 5.99 *(978-0-448-46788-7(7),* Grosset & Dunlap) Penguin Young Readers Group.

Berk, Josh. The Dark Days of Hamburger Halpin. 2011. (ENG.). 258p. (YA). (gr. 7). pap. 8.99 *(978-0-375-84625-0(5),* Ember) Random Hse. Children's Bks.

Bernal, Estela. Can You See Me Now? 2014. (ENG.). (YA). pap. 10.95 *(978-1-55885-783-4(4),* Piñata Books) Arte Publico Pr.

Bietz, Kara. Until I Break. 2016. (ENG.). 256p. (YA). (gr. 8-12). 16.99 *(978-0-8075-7438-6(4))* Whitman, Albert & Co.

Bingham, Mark Jay. Woolie & the Bully. 2013. 52p. 30.95 *(978-1-4582-0843-9(5))*; pap. 23.95 *(978-1-4582-0844-6(3))* Author Solutions, Inc. (Abbott Pr.).

Biro, Sharon. Snaggleloopus. 2008. (Illus.). 36p. pap. 24.95 *(978-1-60474-118-6(X))* America Star Bks.

Bledsoe Jr, Reuben Booo. Bullybuster. 2013. (ENG.). 98p. (J). pap. 14.95 *(978-1-4787-1215-2(5))* Outskirts Pr., Inc.

Blevins, Wiley. Bear's Bad Day: Bullies Can Change. Clegg, Dave, illus. 2015. (ENG.). 24p. (J). (gr. k-2). lib. bdg. 19.99 *(978-1-63440-012-1(7))* Red Chair Pr.

—Go, Billy, Go! Being Yourself. Gordon, John, illus. 2015. (ENG.). 24p. (J). (gr. k-2). lib. bdg. 19.99 *(978-1-63440-003-9(8))* Red Chair Pr.

—How to Deal with Bullies Superhero-Style: Response to Bullying. Palen, Debbie, illus. 2015. (ENG.). 24p. (gr. k-2). lib. bdg. 19.99 *(978-1-63440-009-1(7))* Red Chair Pr.

—The on-Again, off-Again Friend: Standing up for Friends. Alley, R. W., illus. 2015. (ENG.). 24p. (J). (gr. k-2). lib. bdg. 19.99 *(978-1-63440-015-2(1))* Red Chair Pr.

—Stella... Almost: Self-Confidence. Nez, John Abbott, illus. 2015. (ENG.). 24p. (J). (gr. k-2). lib. bdg. 19.99 *(978-1-63440-006-0(2),* 1392169) Red Chair Pr.

Blount, Patty. Send. 2012. (ENG.). 304p. (YA). (gr. 7-12). pap. 8.99 *(978-1-4022-7337-7(1))* Sourcebooks, Inc.

Blume-D'Ausilio, Carole Ed. D. The Bronx Bully. 2011. 28p. pap. 15.99 *(978-1-4628-5235-2(1))* Xlibris Corp.

Bologna, Barbara. Bullied over Sandman's Falls. 2012. 52p. pap. 11.95 *(978-0-9851184-7-1(4))* Barringer Publishing.

Bost, Richard. Taekwon Tales. 2012. 120p. pap. 9.99 *(978-0-9848626-1-0(7))* ImBost Inc.

Bouncy & the Bully: Book One of Bouncy's Adventures. 2013. 28p. pap. 13.95 *(978-1-4624-0788-0(9),* Inspiring Voices) Author Solutions, Inc.

Bowles, B. R. Pauley the Pancake Boy. 2012. 24p. 24.95 *(978-1-4626-6026-1(6))* America Star Bks.

Boyce, Frank Cottrell. The Astounding Broccoli Boy. 2015. 384p. (J). (gr. 3-7). 16.99 *(978-0-06-240017-8(7),* Walden Pond Pr.) HarperCollins Pubs.

Bracken, Beth. The Little Bully, 1 vol. Bell, Jennifer A., illus. 2012. (Little Boost Ser.). (ENG.). 32p. (gr. k-3). lib. bdg. 23.99 *(978-1-4048-6795-6(3),* Little Boost) Picture Window Bks.

Bradford, Wilson D. The Bear & the Price. Abby, Mitchell, illus. 2012. 48p. (-18). pap. 12.00 *(978-0-9848651-2-3(8))* True Path Pubs.

Brenda, Jones. No, I Don't Want to Play Today: An African Tale about Bullying. 2010. 40p. pap. 14.95 *(978-1-60911-387-2(X),* Eloquent Bks.) Strategic Book Publishing & Rights Agency (SBPRA).

Brenner, Vida. The Magic Music Shop. Sharp, Mary, ed. Sharpnack, Joe, illus. 2013. 102p. pap. 12.95 *(978-1-57216-094-1(2))* Penfield Bks.

Brezenoff, Steve. New in Town, 1 vol. Percival, Tom, illus. 2012. (Ravens Pass Ser.). (ENG.). 96p. (gr. 2-3). pap. 6.15 *(978-1-4342-4210-5(2))*; lib. bdg. 25.32 *(978-1-4342-3793-4(1))* Stone Arch Bks.

Brown, Gavin. Josh Baxter Levels Up. 2016. (ENG., Illus.). 192p. (J). (gr. 3-7). 12.99 *(978-0-545-77294-5(X),* Scholastic Pr.) Scholastic, Inc.

Brown, Herman. A Cut Too Far. 2015. (ENG.). 96p. (YA). (gr. 6-12). 27.99 *(978-1-4677-5709-6(8))* Lerner Publishing Group.

Brown, Jeffrey. Jedi Academy. 2015. (Star Wars: Jedi Academy Ser.). (ENG.). 112p. (J). (gr. 3-7). 9.99 *(978-0-545-85278-4(1))* Scholastic, Inc.

Brown, Liz. The Bully. (Illus.). 90p. *(978-1-897039-08-3(5))* High Interest Publishing (HIP).

Bryant, Annie. Just Kidding. 2009. (Beacon Street Girls Ser.: 10). (ENG.). 256p. (J). (gr. 4-8). pap. 7.99 *(978-1-4169-6440-7(1),* Aladdin) Simon & Schuster Children's Publishing.

Buckner, Chuck. The Death of Arkie Baker. 2008. 84p. pap. 8.86 *(978-1-4357-4105-8(6))* Lulu Pr., Inc.

Bully Busters in the Adventures of Wooly Bully. 2003. (Illus.). 100p. (J). per. 8.95 *(978-0-9770294-0-2(9))* Better Me Bks., Inc.

Burgess, Starr. Counselor Dynamite Befuddles the Bullyville Crew. Guiza, Victor, illus. 2013. 52p. (J). 19.95 *(978-1-60131-156-6(7),* Castlebridge Bks.) Big Tent Bks.

Burton-Hupp, Lynne. Venus the Very Proper Fly Trap. 2009. 28p. pap. 24.95 *(978-1-60563-993-2(1))* America Star Bks.

Bush, Martha Faircloth. Helping Hurting Children: a Journey of Healing: Children's Workbook. 2013. 174p. pap. 19.95 *(978-1-4497-8527-7(1),* WestBow Pr.) Author Solutions, Inc.

Bustard, Anne. Anywhere but Paradise. 2015. (ENG.). 288p. (gr. 5). 16.99 *(978-1-60684-585-1(3))*; (J). 16.99 *(978-1-5124-0110-3(2))* Lerner Publishing Group. (Carolrhoda Bks.).

Butcher, Kristin. Cabin Girl, 1 vol. 2014. (Orca Currents Ser.). (ENG.). 128p. (J). (gr. 5-9). pap. 9.95 *(978-1-4598-0649-8(2))* Orca Bk. Pubs. USA.

Butler, Heather. Adam & the Tattooed Angel. Buckley, Joel, illus. 2004. 64p. pap. *(978-1-84427-043-9(2))* Scripture Union.

Butterfield, MaryAnn Milton. You Are Too a Bully! 2013. 126p. (gr. 4-6). 28.99 *(978-1-4582-0968-9(7))*; pap. 11.99 *(978-1-4582-0969-6(5))* Author Solutions, Inc. (Abbott Pr.).

Button, Lana. Willow Finds a Way. Howells, Tania, illus. 2013. (Willow Ser.). (ENG.). 32p. (J). (gr. -1-2). 16.95 *(978-1-55453-842-3(4))* Kids Can Pr., Ltd. CAN. Dist: Hachette Bk. Group.

Cafaro, Phyllis. The Legend of Captain McFinn & Friends. 2012. (ENG., Illus.). 24p. pap. 19.99 *(978-0-9799283-1-4(1),* 9780979928314) Cold River Pubns.

Cafaro, Phyllis C. Captain Mcfinn & Friends Encounter the Bully Bunker. 2012. (ENG., Illus.). 24p. (J). 17.99 *(978-0-9859482-2-1(1),* 9780985948221); pap. 9.99 *(978-0-9859482-3-8(X),* 9780985948238) Cold River Pubns.

Cafege, Adam. Of Petals & Hope: Sunny Sunflower Triumphs over Bullying. Calindas, Marconi, illus. 2013. 36p. pap. 24.95 *(978-0-9840204-4-7(6))* Pacific Raven Pr.

Cannella, Nicole DeRosa. The Ribbit Exhibit: One frog's tale of a leap of Faith. 2011. 28p. pap. 13.59 *(978-1-4634-2435-0(3))* AuthorHouse.

Canning, Charlie. The 89th Temple. 2012. (ENG.). 211p. pap. 14.95 *(978-1-4787-1763-8(7))* Outskirts Pr., Inc.

Cannon, Sherrill S. Gimme-Jimmy. 2012. 32p. pap. 13.00 *(978-1-61897-267-5(7),* Strategic Bk. Publishing) Strategic Book Publishing & Rights Agency (SBPRA).

Cardarelli, Mario. Kid Jack Adventures: Prevent Bullying. 2011. 48p. pap. 15.49 *(978-1-4567-2296-8(4))* AuthorHouse.

Cardoza, Kristina. Pinky Bunny's First Day of Kindergarten. 2011. 16p. pap. 8.75 *(978-1-4634-8753-9(3))* AuthorHouse.

Caroll, Robin. Samantha Sanderson on the Scene, 1 vol. 2014. (FaithGirlz / Samantha Sanderson Ser.). (ENG.). 256p. (J). pap. 8.99 *(978-0-310-74247-0(1))* Zonderkidz.

Carradice, Phil & Thomas, Frances. Hannah Goes to War. 2005. (ENG.). 144p. pap. 12.95 *(978-1-84323-461-6(0))* Beekman Bks., Inc.

Carson, Jana. We Both Read-The New Tribe. Treatner, Meryl, illus. 2013. 44p. (J). pap. 4.99 *(978-1-60115-264-0(7))*; 9.95 *(978-1-60115-263-3(9))* Treasure Bay, Inc.

Casanova, Mary. Chrissa Stands Strong, Bks. 2. England, Tamara, ed. Jones, Richard, illus. 2009. (ENG.). 130p. (YA). (gr. 3-18). pap. 6.95 *(978-1-59369-567-5(5),* American Girl) American Girl Publishing, Inc.

Cazet, Denys. Snail & Slug. Cazet, Denys, illus. 2016. (ENG., Illus.). 32p. (J). (gr. -1-3). 17.99 *(978-1-4814-4506-1(5),* Atheneum/Richard Jackson Bks.) Simon & Schuster Children's Publishing.

Chand, Emlyn. Farsighted. 2012. 260p. pap. 12.95 *(978-0-9839308-3-9(X))* Blue Crown Pr.

CHaracter Ed & the Magical Lesson of the Bully. 2004. (J). pap. 15.95 *(978-1-59526-181-6(8))* Aeon Publishing Inc.

Charles, Rie. No More Dragons. 2010. (ENG., Illus.). 112p. (J). (gr. 5-7). pap. 9.95 *(978-1-926607-12-2(0),* Napoleon & Co.) Dundurn CAN. Dist: Ingram Publisher Services.

Choyce, Lesley. Rat, 1 vol. 2012. (Orca Soundings Ser.). (ENG.). 128p. (YA). (gr. 8-12). pap. 9.95 *(978-1-4598-0300-8(0))*; lib. bdg. 16.95 *(978-1-4598-0301-5(9))* Orca Bk. Pubs. USA.

Christopher, Matt. Lacrosse Firestorm. 2008. (ENG.). 144p. (J). (gr. 3-7). pap. 5.99 *(978-0-316-01631-5(4))* Little, Brown Bks. for Young Readers.

Clampitt, Ed & Fortier, Robert. Team Dawg Trevor's Bully Problem. 2007. (J). per. 14.99 *(978-0-9749378-2-3(7))* Team Dawg Productions, Inc.

Clarke, Kevin & Dutton, Demi. Jenny Can't Read: A Story about Dyslexia & Its Effect on Self-Esteem. 2012. 90p. pap. 13.66 *(978-1-4772-1909-6(9))* AuthorHouse.

Clay, Dorian. Freddie Loses His Game. 2012. 64p. pap. 5.95 *(978-1-938056-04-8(3))* ARIVA Publishing.

—Freddie Loses His Game. Clay, Dorian, illus. 2012. (Illus.). 64p. pap. 12.99 *(978-1-938056-03-1(5))* ARIVA Publishing.

Clements, Andrew. Bully Buster. Frazee, Marla & Pedersen, Janet, illus. 2008. (Jake Drake Ser.: Bk. 1). 67p. (gr. 2-5). 15.00 *(978-0-7569-9001-5(7))* Perfection Learning Corp.

—Bully Buster. Pedersen, Janet & Frazee, Marla, illus. 2007. (Jake Drake Ser.: Bk. 1). (ENG.). 80p. (J). (gr. 2-5). pap. 5.99 *(978-1-4169-3933-7(4),* Atheneum Bks. for Young Readers) Simon & Schuster Children's Publishing.

Clements, Andrew. The Losers Club. 2017. (ENG.). 240p. (J). (gr. 3-7). 16.99 ***(978-0-399-55755-2(5),*** Random Hse. Bks. for Young Readers) Random Hse. Children's Bks.

Cogswell, Jackie Chirco. Super Luke Faces His Bully: GiggleHeart Adventures #2. Johannes, Shelley, illus. 2011. 224p. (J). 14.99 *(978-0-9820490-2-0(1))*; pap. 9.99 *(978-0-9820490-1-3(3))* Divine Inspiration Publishing, LLC.

Cohen, Joshua C. Leverage. 2012. (ENG.). 432p. (YA). (gr. 9). pap. 8.99 *(978-0-14-242086-7(7),* Speak) Penguin Young Readers Group.

Cole, Henry. Eddie the Bully. 2016. (ENG.). 40p. (J). (gr. -1-3). 17.99 *(978-1-4998-0181-1(5))* Little Bee Books Inc.

Cole, Kathryn. A Tattle-Tell Tale: A Story about Getting Help, 1 vol. Leng, Qin, illus. 2016. (I'm a Great Little Kid Ser.). (ENG.). 24p. (J). (gr. 1-3). 15.95 *(978-1-927583-92-0(6))* Second Story Pr. CAN. Dist: Orca Bk. Pubs. USA.

Collins, Paul. Lucy & the Red Street Boyz. Bocquée, Christian, illus. 2015. (Legends in Their Own Lunchbox Ser.). (ENG.). 56p. (gr. 2-3). pap. 7.99 *(978-1-4966-0260-2(9),* Legends in Their Own Lunchbox) Capstone Classroom.

Compagnucci, Veronica M. Emily Finds Her Voice. 2013. 40p. pap. 24.95 *(978-1-63004-288-2(9))* America Star Bks.

Conlin, Judy. Crissy,the Cross-Eyed Cat. 2012. 28p. pap. 19.99 *(978-1-4685-0789-8(3))* AuthorHouse.

Conner, Deborah N. The Bully Magnet. 2012. 28p. pap. 15.99 *(978-1-4653-7731-9(X))* Xlibris Corp.

Connolly, Patrick. The Adventures of Funny, the Amazing Fish-Bunny. 2013. (ENG.). 70p. (YA). pap. 13.95 *(978-1-4787-0440-9(3))* Outskirts Pr., Inc.

Cook, Jeremy. Illusion of Time, 1 vol. 2010. 118p. pap. 19.95 *(978-1-4489-6235-8(8))* America Star Bks.

Cook, Julia. Tease Monster: (a Book about Teasing vs. Bullying) DuFalla, Anita, illus. 2013. (Building Relationships Ser.). (ENG.). 32p. (J). pap. 10.95 *(978-1-934490-47-1(4))* Boys Town Pr.

Cook, Julia. Technology Tail: A Digital Footprint Story. DuFalla, Anita, illus. 2017. (ENG.). 32p. (J). (gr. 1-6). pap. 10.95 ***(978-1-944882-13-6(8))*** Boys Town Pr.

Cook, Katie. Little Big Benny: The Wicked Itch. 2012. 138p. pap. 9.99 *(978-0-9883554-2-2(6))* Katie Cook.

Cooper, Nelle. Princess Lil. 2013. 82p. (J). pap. 9.00 *(978-1-936442-16-4(7))* Fresh Ink Group.

Coppard, Yvonne. Bully. 2008. 92p. (gr. -1-7). pap. *(978-1-904529-36-1(4),* Back to Front) Solidus.

Cosgrove, Stephen. Pickles & the P-Flock Bullies. James, Robin, illus. 2014. (ENG.). 32p. (J). (gr. k-3). 16.99 *(978-1-57061-887-1(9),* Little Bigfoot) Sasquatch Bks.

Coughlin, Denise. Dragon in My Pocket. Kastan, Bill, illus. 2005. (J). *(978-0-9765905-0-7(6))* Rose Valley Publishing.

Cox, Phil Roxbee. Don't Be Greedy, Graham. Tyler, Jenny, ed. McCafferty, Jan, illus. 2006. (Cautionary Tales Ser.). 24p. (J). (gr. -1). lib. bdg. 15.99 *(978-1-58086-972-0(6),* Usborne) EDC Publishing.

Crichlow, Giselle. Just Call Me Shaun. 2010. 24p. 11.99 *(978-1-4490-5222-5(3))* AuthorHouse.

Crocker, Mike. It's Not Your Fault. 2012. (ENG.). pap. *(978-1-4675-2292-2(9))* Independent Pub.

Curtin, Ann. Dreamcatcher. 2015. 201p. (YA). *(978-1-61271-246-8(0))* Zumaya Pubns. LLC.

Curtiss, A. B. & Curtiss, A. B. Hanner & the Bullies. Brown, Jason, illus. 2012. 140p. pap. 9.99 *(978-0-932529-63-3(1))* Oldcastle Publishing.

Dalton, Annie. Lilac Peabody. Griff, illus. 2009. (ENG.). (J). No. 1. 80p. pap. 5.99 *(978-0-00-713771-8(0))*No. 2. 96p. pap. 5.99 *(978-0-00-713772-5(9))* HarperCollins Pubs. Ltd. GBR. (HarperCollins Children's Bks.). Dist: HarperCollins Pubs.

—Lilac Peabody & Honeysuckle Hope, No. 4. Griff, illus. 2009. (ENG.). 96p. (J). (gr. 2-4). pap. 5.99 *(978-0-00-713774-9(5))* HarperCollins Pubs. Ltd. GBR. Dist: HarperCollins Pubs.

Daly, Niki. Nicholas & the Wild Ones: How to Beat the Bullies. 2016. (ENG.). 32p. (J). (gr. -1-3). 18.99 *(978-1-84780-853-0(0),* Frances Lincoln Children's Bks.) Quarto Publishing Group UK GBR. Dist: Hachette Bk. Group.

Daniel, Martha Ann. Mimi Mouse Meets Roger Rat: A Tail of Bullying. 2012. 32p. (-18). pap. 19.99 *(978-1-4772-8295-3(5))* AuthorHouse.

Daniels, Miriam Rs. Bully-Free School. 2011. 32p. pap. 21.99 *(978-1-4568-6613-6(3))* Xlibris Corp.

Davidson, Danica. Escape from the Overworld. 2015. (Unofficial Overworld Adventure Ser.). (ENG.). 112p. (J). (gr. 1-7). pap. 7.99 *(978-1-63450-103-3(9),* Sky Pony Pr.) Skyhorse Publishing Co., Inc.

Davis, Deon M. Beanie & the Bully. 2012. 28p. pap. 19.99 *(978-1-4685-7483-8(3))* AuthorHouse.

Davis, Lane. I Swear. (ENG., Illus.). 288p. (YA). (gr. 9). 2013. pap. 10.99 *(978-1-4424-3507-0(0))* 2012. 16.99 *(978-1-4424-3506-3(2))* Simon & Schuster Bks. For Young Readers. (Simon & Schuster Bks. For Young Readers).

Davis, Lois. Happy to Be Me. 2013. 20p. pap. 24.95 *(978-1-63000-789-8(7))* America Star Bks.

Davis, Samira And Edwina. Nikko & Sierra's Adventures: I Hate Knuckle Sandwiches. 2011. 24p. pap. 11.32 *(978-1-4634-0408-6(5))* AuthorHouse.

Dawe, Ted. Into the River. 2016. (ENG.). 304p. (J). (gr. 7). 17.99 *(978-1-943818-19-8(3))* Polis Bks.

Day-Bivins, Pat. Bullies Beware! Larkins, Mona & Anderson, Jan, illus. 2006. (ENG.). 32p. (J). (gr. -1). 16.95 *(978-0-9742806-5-3(8))* Heart to Heart Publishing, Inc.

de Kinder, Jan. Red. 2015. (ENG., Illus.). 32p. (J). 16.00 *(978-0-8028-5446-9(X),* Eerdmans Bks For Young Readers) Eerdmans, William B. Publishing Co.

Dee, Carole. The Bully Returns to Margaret. 2012. 36p. pap. 10.95 *(978-1-4626-7766-5(5))* America Star Bks.

Deekster, Deek. Ozzie Rozzie. 2005. 41p. (YA). pap. 7.85 *(978-1-4116-6420-3(5))* Lulu Pr., Inc.

DeFelice, Cynthia. Fort. 2015. (ENG.). 208p. (J). (gr. 3-7). 16.99 *(978-0-374-32427-8(1),* 9780374324278, Farrar, Straus & Giroux (BYR)) Farrar, Straus & Giroux.

—Fort. 2016. (ENG.). 224p. (J). pap. 6.99 *(978-1-250-07973-2(X),* 9781250079732) Square Fish.

—Fort. 2016. (J). lib. bdg. 17.20 *(978-0-606-38552-7(5))* Turtleback Bks.

Delos, Louis & Sharma, Vicky. Tomorrow Will Be a New Day. 2011. 20p. pap. *(978-1-4269-7318-5(7))* Trafford Publishing (UK) Ltd.

Deuker, Carl. Gutless. (ENG.). 336p. (YA). (gr. 7). 2017. pap. 9.99 ***(978-1-328-74206-3(7))*** 2016. 17.99 *(978-0-544-64961-3(3))* Houghton Mifflin Harcourt Publishing Co. (HMH Books For Young Readers).

Deutsch, Stacia. Rotten Apple #1: Mean Ghouls. 2012. (Rotten Apple Ser.). (ENG.). 192p. (J). (gr. 3-7). pap. 5.99 *(978-0-545-39823-7(1),* Scholastic Paperbacks) Scholastic, Inc.

Devine, Eric. Press Play. 2014. (ENG.). 368p. (YA). (gr. 3-17). pap. 9.95 *(978-0-7624-5512-6(8),* Running Pr. Kids) Running Pr. Bk. Pubs.

Dickey, R. A. Knuckleball Ned. Bowers, Tim, illus. 2014. (ENG.). 32p. (J). (gr. -1-k). 17.99 *(978-0-8037-4038-9(7),* Dial Bks) Penguin Young Readers Group.

Diesen, Deborah. The Pout-Pout Fish & the Bully-Bully Shark. Hanna, Dan, illus. 2017. (Pout-Pout Fish Adventure Ser.). (ENG.). 32p. (J). 16.99 ***(978-0-374-30402-7(5),*** 9780374304027, Farrar, Straus & Giroux (BYR)) Farrar, Straus & Giroux.

Diggle, David Mark. Ewan: From Bullied to Superhero in One Afternoon. Diggle, Daniel James, illus. 2011. 24p. (J). pap. *(978-0-9871657-0-1(4))* Diggle de Doo Productions Pty, Ltd.

Dinardo, Jeff. The Fable of the Bully Dragon: Facing Your Fears. Coloji, Livia, illus. 2015. (ENG.). 24p. (J). (gr. k-2). lib. bdg. 19.99 *(978-1-63440-000-8(3))* Red Chair Pr.

Dipucchio, Kelly. Super Manny Stands Up! Graegin, Stephanie, illus. 2017. (Super Manny Ser.). (ENG.). 40p. (J). (gr. -1-3). 17.99 *(978-1-4814-5960-0(0))* Simon & Schuster Children's Publishing.

Domogala, Sophia Z. Buzzin' with Kindness. 2012. 24p. pap. 15.99 *(978-1-4797-5023-8(9))* Xlibris Corp.

Donzelli, Janine. I Am Like You, & You Are Like Me. 2012. 24p. pap. 17.99 *(978-1-4685-4128-1(5))* AuthorHouse.

Doodler, Todd H. Super Fly: The World's Smallest Superhero! 2015. (Super Fly Ser.). (ENG., Illus.). 208p. (J). (gr. k-2). 15.99 *(978-1-61963-379-7(5),* 9781619633797, Bloomsbury USA Childrens) Bloomsbury Publishing USA.

Dowell, Frances O'Roark. Phineas L. MacGuire ... Gets Cooking! McDaniels, Preston, illus. 2015. (From the Highly Scientific Notebooks of Phineas L. MacGuire Ser.). (ENG.). 224p. (J). (gr. 3-7). pap. 6.99 *(978-1-4814-0100-5(9))* Simon & Schuster Children's Publishing.

Downer, Denise. Soul Mates. Frampton, Otis, illus. 2013. (Tombstone Twins Ser.). (ENG.). 48p. (gr. 1-3). lib. bdg. 23.99 *(978-1-4342-2248-0(9))* Stone Arch Bks.

—Tombstone Twins: Soul Mates, 1 vol. Frampton, Otis, illus. 2013. (Tombstone Twins Ser.). (ENG.). 48p. (gr. 1-3). pap. 5.95 *(978-1-4342-3873-3(3))* Stone Arch Bks.

Dudley, Blanche R. Siggy & the Bullies. 2013. 42p. 22.50 *(978-1-4575-1994-9(1))*; pap. 11.95 *(978-1-4575-1993-2(3))* Dog Ear Publishing, LLC.

Dungy, Tony & Dungy, Lauren. Justin & the Bully. Newton, Vanessa Brantley, illus. 2012. (Tony & Lauren Dungy Ready-To-Reads Ser.). (ENG.). 32p. (J). (gr. k-2). pap. 3.99 *(978-1-4424-5718-8(X),* Simon Spotlight) Simon Spotlight.

Duracell and the National Center for Missing & Exploited Children (NCMEC), creator. The Great Tomato Adventure: A Story about Smart Safety Choices. 2007. 0.00 *(978-0-9795307-0-8(9))* Duracell & the National Ctr. for Missing & Exploited Children (NCMEC).

Dwyer, Cynthia. Four-Eyed Philip. Schuepbach, Lynnette, illus. 2007. (J). 14.95 *(978-0-9793296-0-9(4))* Grannie Annie Family Story Celebration, The.

Dyan, Penelope. Smile! Dyan, Penelope, illus. 2012. (Illus.). 34p. pap. 11.95 *(978-1-61477-028-2(X))* Bellissima Publishing, LLC.

—Woolly Bully! Dyan, Penelope, illus. 2013. (Illus.). 34p. pap. 11.95 *(978-1-61477-069-5(7))* Bellissima Publishing, LLC.

Earhart, Kristin. Puppy Powers #2: Wag, You're It! 2014. (Puppy Powers Ser.: 2). (ENG., Illus.). 96p. (J). (gr. 2-5). pap. 4.99 *(978-0-545-61760-4(X),* Scholastic Paperbacks) Scholastic, Inc.

Eash, Sara. Adeline. 2011. 28p. pap. 15.99 *(978-1-4568-7099-7(8))* Xlibris Corp.

Edmonds, Lin. Jaden & the Terrible Terrible Toad. 2011. 36p. pap. 15.14 *(978-1-4634-1112-1(X))* AuthorHouse.

Edwards, Michelle. Stinky Stern Forever. 2007. (Jackson Friends Bks.). (Illus.). 49p. (gr. 1-4). 15.95 *(978-0-7569-8198-3(0))* Perfection Learning Corp.

Elliott, Sherria L. My Shaking Eyes. Moore, Sasha & Tilak, Brian, illus. 2013. 30p. pap. 12.99 *(978-0-9846963-2-1(6))* 4Elliott Publishing, Inc.

Ellis, Ann Dee. This Is What I Did. 2011. 9.68 *(978-0-7848-3387-2(7),* Everbind) Marco Bk. Co.

Ely, Lesley & Dunbar, Polly. Measuring Angels. Dunbar, Polly, illus. 2008. (ENG., Illus.). 32p. (J). (gr. -1-3). 16.95 *(978-1-84507-639-9(7),* Frances Lincoln) Quarto Publishing Group UK GBR. Dist: Hachette Bk. Group.

Endacott, C. R. Afflatus. 2008. 232p. pap. 15.95 *(978-0-595-52418-1(4))* iUniverse, Inc.

Erlings, Fridrik. Boy on the Edge. 2014. (ENG.). 240p. (YA). (gr. 9). 16.99 *(978-0-7636-6680-4(7))* Candlewick Pr.

Erno, Jeff. Bullied. 2nd ed. 2016. (ENG., Illus.). (J). 24.99 ***(978-1-63477-944-9(4),*** Harmony Ink Pr.) Dreamspinner Pr.

—You Belong with Me. 2016. (ENG., Illus.). (J). 24.99 ***(978-1-63477-998-2(3))*** 2013. 164p. pap. 14.99 *(978-1-62380-533-3(3))* Dreamspinner Pr. (Harmony Ink Pr.).

Erno, Jeff. You Belong with Me [Library Edition]. 2013. 164p. pap. 14.99 *(978-1-62380-922-5(3),* Harmony Ink Pr.) Dreamspinner Pr.

Evans, Courtney. Percy the Penguin, 1 vol. 2010. 26p. pap. 24.95 *(978-1-4489-4881-9(9))* PublishAmerica, Inc.

Eyre, Lindsay. The Mean Girl Meltdown. 2015. (Sylvie Scruggs Ser.: 2). (ENG., Illus.). 160p. (J). (gr. 2-5). pap. 5.99 *(978-0-545-62030-7(9),* Levine, Arthur A. Bks.) Scholastic, Inc.

Farber, E. S. Fish Finelli (Book 2) Operation Fireball. Beene, Jason, illus. 2015. (Fish Finelli Ser.). (ENG.). 184p. (J). (gr. 3-7). pap. 6.99 *(978-1-4521-2875-7(8))* Chronicle Bks. LLC.

—Fish Finelli (Book 3) Warrick, Jessica, illus. 2016. (Fish Finelli Ser.). (ENG.). 176p. (J). (gr. 3-7). 15.99 *(978-1-4521-3815-2(X))* Chronicle Bks. LLC.

—Operation Fireball. Beene, Jason, illus. 2014. (Fish Finelli Ser.). (ENG.). 172p. (J). (gr. 3-7). 15.99 *(978-1-4521-1083-7(2))* Chronicle Bks. LLC.

Field, C. D. The Medicine Tree. 2015. (ENG.). 108p. (YA). (gr. 3-4). mass mkt. 11.95 *(978-1-78554-535-1(3),* 5ff504aa-2872-45d0-b48e-8fde50a9662c) Austin, Stan AUS. Dist: Bookmasters Distribution.

Fields, Jan. Tattletale Traitor, 1 vol. 2014. (Meri's Mirror Ser.). (ENG., Illus.). 80p. (J). (gr. 2-5). lib. bdg. 27.07 *(978-1-62402-010-0(0),* Calico Chapter Bks) Magic Wagon.

—Terrible Twin Mania, 1 vol. 2014. (Meri's Mirror Ser.). (ENG.). 80p. (J). (gr. 2-5). lib. bdg. 27.07 *(978-1-62402-011-7(9),* Calico Chapter Bks) Magic Wagon.

Finley, Danielle. Confronting a Bully, 1 vol. Davenport, Chris, illus. 2009. 12p. pap. 24.95 *(978-1-61546-146-2(9))* America Star Bks.

Fleming, Bryn. Jasper & Willie: Wildfire. 2015. (Range Riders Ser.). (ENG.). 130p. (J). 28.99 *(978-1-941821-92-3(8));* pap. 9.99 *(978-1-941821-71-8(5))* Graphic Arts Ctr. Publishing Co. (West Winds Pr.).

Flores-Galbis, Enrique. 90 Miles to Havana. 2012. (ENG.). 304p. (J). (gr. 4-7). pap. 7.99 *(978-1-250-00559-5(0),* 9781250005595) Square Fish.

Ford, Adam B. Jam-Bo, Litta-Girl, & the Bullies. Huddleston, Courtney, illus. 2013. 44p. pap. 12.95 *(978-0-9794104-9-9(5))* H Bar Pr.

Fowler, Josephine A. Lilly's Faith. 2012. 32p. (-18). pap. 19.99 *(978-1-4772-8688-3(8))* AuthorHouse.

Frankel, Erin. Dare!, Bk. 2. Heaphy, Paula, illus. 2013. (Weird! Ser.). (ENG.). 48p. (J). (gr. k-4). pap. 9.99 *(978-1-57542-439-2(8))* Free Spirit Publishing, Inc.

—Nobody! A Story about Overcoming Bullying in Schools. Heaphy, Paula, illus. 2015. (ENG.). 48p. (J). (gr. k-4). 15.99 *(978-1-57542-495-8(9))* Free Spirit Publishing, Inc.

French, Simon. My Cousin's Keeper. 2014. (ENG.). 240p. (J). (gr. 3-7). 16.99 *(978-0-7636-6279-0(8))* Candlewick Pr.

Frizzell, Colin. Chill, 1 vol. 2006. (Orca Soundings Ser.). (ENG.). 128p. (YA). (gr. 8-12). per. 9.95 *(978-1-55143-507-7(1))* Orca Bk. Pubs. USA.

Fuller, Kimberly. H a Carter. 2012. 138p. 28.99 *(978-1-105-83103-4(5))* Lulu Pr., Inc.

Funny, Ania. The Power of Ania to Change the World of Bullying. 2012. 28p. pap. 15.99 *(978-1-4797-4599-9(5))* Xlibris Corp.

Fusek Peters, Andrew. The Ant & the Big Bad Bully Goat. Wadham, Anna, illus. 2010. (Traditional Tales with a Twist Ser.). (ENG.). 32p. (J). (gr. -1-2). audio compact disk *(978-1-84643-348-1(7))* Child's Play International Ltd.

Gaffney, Linda. My Daddy Does GOOD Things, Too! Dabney, Undra & Goetting, Nickalas, illus. 2006. 55p. per. 10.99 *(978-0-9787501-0-7(1))* Gaffney, Linda.

Gagnon, Jilly. #famous. 2017. 384p. (YA). (gr. 8). 17.99 *(978-0-06-243003-8(3),* Tegen, Katherine Bks) HarperCollins Pubs.

Gale, Emily. My Explosive Diary. Dreidemy, Joëlle, illus. 2014. (Eliza Boom Ser.: 1). (ENG.). 128p. (J). (gr. 1-4). 15.99 *(978-1-4814-0650-5(7),* Simon & Schuster/Paula Wiseman Bks.) Simon & Schuster/Paula Wiseman Bks.

Gale, Eric Kahn. The Bully Book. (ENG.). (J). (gr. 3-7). 2013. 256p. pap. 6.99 *(978-0-06-212513-2(3))* 2012. 240p. 16.99 *(978-0-06-212511-8(7))* HarperCollins Pubs.

Galveston, Louise. By the Grace of Todd. 2015. (ENG., Illus.). 272p. (J). (gr. 3-7). pap. 8.99 *(978-1-59514-678-6(4),* Razorbill) Penguin Young Readers Group.

Garden, Nancy. Endgame. 2012. (ENG., Illus.). 304p. (YA). (gr. 7-12). pap. 6.99 *(978-0-15-206377-1(3))* Houghton Mifflin Harcourt Publishing Co.

Gardener, Amanda & Sealey, Nanlie. Freddy the White Flamingo. 2013. 28p. pap. 12.99 *(978-1-60820-900-2(8))* MLR Pr., LLC.

Garland, Betsy. The Golden Rule. 2012. 28p. pap. 16.99 *(978-1-4624-0172-7(4),* Inspiring Voices) Author Solutions, Inc.

Garlick, Nicholas. Storm Horse. 2017. (J). pap. ***(978-0-545-90415-5(3))*** Scholastic, Inc.

Garton, Carol. Isabella Barella. 2013. (ENG.). 300p. (YA). 32.95 *(978-1-4787-1339-5(9));* pap. 17.95 *(978-1-4787-1490-3(5))* Outskirts Pr., Inc.

Garvin, Jeff. Symptoms of Being Human. 2016. 352p. (YA). (gr. 9). 17.99 *(978-0-06-238286-3(1))* HarperCollins Pubs.

Gaydos, Nora. Now I'm Growing! Hands Are Not for Hurting. Gutierrez, Akemi, illus. 2012. (ENG.). 30p. (J). (gr. -1-17). 8.99 *(978-1-60169-222-1(6))* Innovative Kids.

Gemeinhart, Dan. Scar Island. 2017. (ENG.). 256p. (J). (gr. 3-7). 16.99 *(978-1-338-05384-5(1),* Scholastic Pr.) Scholastic, Inc.

Georgiana, Vanessa. Lulu: And the Garden of Life. 2013. 104p. (gr. 4-6). pap. 8.99 *(978-1-4582-0936-8(9),* Abbott Pr.) Author Solutions, Inc.

Gervay, Susanne. I Am Jack. Cathy, Wilcox, illus. 2013. (ENG.). 144p. (J). pap. 5.99 *(978-1-61067-128-6(7))* Kane Miller.

Gibsen, Cole. Life Unaware. 2015. 284p. (YA). ***(978-1-62844-152-9(6))*** Entangled Publishing, LLC.

Gidney, Craig Laurance. Bereft. 2013. (ENG.). 170p. (J). (gr. 7). pap. 9.95 *(978-0-9849146-4-7(1))* Tiny Stachel Pr.

Gill, Jean. On the Other Hand. 2005. (ENG.). 126p. (J). pap. 11.95 *(978-0-86243-771-8(7))* Y Lolfa GBR. Dist: Dufour Editions, Inc.

Gino, Alex. George. 2015. (ENG.). 208p. (J). (gr. 3-7). 16.99 *(978-0-545-81254-2(2),* Scholastic Pr.) Scholastic, Inc.

Glynn, Eoin. Mischief at Se. 2009. 232p. pap. 14.49 *(978-1-4389-4919-2(7))* AuthorHouse.

Goldblatt, Mark. Twerp. 2014. (ENG.). 288p. (J). (gr. 4-7). 7.99 *(978-0-375-97145-7(9),* Yearling) Random Hse. Children's Bks.

Good, Dinah. Stay Away from Mean Jean! 2012. 48p. pap. 19.56 *(978-1-4685-2862-6(9))* AuthorHouse.

Goodman, Gabriel. Lightning's Run. 2014. (Bareknuckle Ser.). (ENG.). 104p. (YA). (gr. 6-12). pap. 7.95 *(978-1-4677-2162-2(X),* Darby Creek) Lerner Publishing Group.

Gordon, David. Extremely Cute Animals Operating Heavy Machinery. Gordon, David, illus. 2016. (ENG., Illus.). 48p. (J). (gr. -1-3). 17.99 *(978-1-4169-2441-8(8),* Simon & Schuster Bks. For Young Readers) Simon & Schuster Bks. For Young Readers.

Gosselin, Jake & Gosselin, Laura. The Pinkaboos: Bitterly & the Giant Problem. 2016. (Pinkaboos Ser.: 1). (ENG.). 96p. (J). pap. 7.99 *(978-1-4494-7831-5(X))* Andrews McMeel Publishing.

Gottesfeld, Jeff. The Code. 2014. (Red Rhino Ser.). (J). lib. bdg. 18.40 *(978-0-606-36199-6(5))* Turtleback Bks.

Gough, Erin. Get It Together, Delilah! 2017. (ENG., Illus.). 336p. (YA). 16.99 *(978-1-4521-5187-8(3))* Chronicle Bks. LLC.

Grabenstein, Chris. I Funny: A Middle School Story. Patterson, James, ed. Park, Laura, illus. 2012. 303p. (J). 11.99 *(978-0-316-22638-7(6),* 1351607) Little Brown & Co.

Grant, Myrna. Ivan & the Hidden Bible. 2006. (Flamingo Fiction 9-13s Ser.). (ENG., Illus.). 144p. (J). (gr. 4-7). per. 6.99 *(978-1-84550-133-4(0),* 9394aef3-942b-4824-b0b8-0ae3449d32e0) Christian Focus Pubns. GBR. Dist: Bookmasters Distribution.

Gray, Kes. Leave Me Alone: A Tale of What Happens When You Stand up to a Bully. Wildish, Lee, illus. 2011. 32p. (J). (gr. -1-2). pap. 8.99 *(978-0-7641-4736-4(6))* Barron's Educational Series, Inc.

Green, D. L. Zeke Meeks vs the Stinkin' Science Fair, 1 vol. Alves, Josh, illus. 2012. (Zeke Meeks Ser.). (ENG.). 128p. (gr. 2-2). pap. 5.95 *(978-1-4048-7222-6(1));* lib. bdg. 22.65 *(978-1-4048-6802-1(X))* Picture Window Bks. (Zeke Meeks).

—Zeke Meeks vs the Stinky Soccer Team. Alves, Josh, illus. 2015. (Zeke Meeks Ser.). (ENG.). 128p. (gr. 2-2). 22.65 *(978-1-4795-5768-4(4),* Zeke Meeks) Picture Window Bks.

Greene, Stephanie. Princess Posey & the First-Grade Boys. Sisson, Stéphanie Roth, illus. 2014. (Princess Posey, First Grader Ser.: 8). (ENG.). 96p. (J). (gr. k-3). pap. 5.99 *(978-0-14-242735-4(7),* Puffin Books) Penguin Young Readers Group.

Groenendyk, Doretta. Bully 101, 1 vol. 2013. (ENG., Illus.). 24p. (J). (gr. -1-3). 18.95 *(978-1-894838-84-9(X))* Acorn Pr., The CAN. Dist: Orca Bk. Pubs. USA.

Guillain, Adam & Guillain, Charlotte. Emma Peror's New Clothes. Waters, Erica-Jane, illus. 2015. (Fairy Tales Today Ser.). (ENG.). 24p. (gr. 1-2). 23.99 *(978-1-4795-8617-2(X))* Picture Window Bks.

Gulley Sr, Wayne A. Michelangelo Tangelo - a Bully No More. Gulley, Robin, ed. Gulley SR, Wayne A., illus. 2012. 40p. pap. 13.99 *(978-0-9843505-5-1(1))* Gulley, Wayne.

Hallam, Gwion. Creadyn. 2005. (WEL.). 176p. pap. 5.99 *(978-1-84323-247-6(2))* Gomer Pr. GBR. Dist: Gomer Pr.

Hamlin, Robyn Maria. Polly Dactyl's Magic Castle Missions. 2011. 64p. pap. 31.99 *(978-1-4628-5146-1(0))* Xlibris Corp.

Hancock, Carl. Marlborough Blues. 2015. (ENG.). 347p. pap. 13.95 *(978-1-78455-401-9(4),* 6f7befcb-7511-4f07-a6b2-54737e692b98) Austin, Stan AUS. Dist: Bookmasters Distribution.

Hardin, Lori. Squiggly & the Bully. 2006. (ENG., Illus.). spiral bd. 9.95 *(978-1-57166-407-5(6))* Quixote Pr.

Harkrader, Lisa. Cool Beans: The Further Adventures of Beanboy. 2014. (ENG., Illus.). 272p. (J). (gr. 5-7). 16.99 *(978-0-544-03094-3(X)),* HMH Books For Young Readers) Houghton Mifflin Harcourt Publishing Co.

Harnest, Faye. Girl Fight, 1 vol. 2011. (Lorimer SideStreets Ser.). (ENG.). 112p. (YA). (gr. 9-12). 16.95 *(978-1-55277-866-1(5),* 9781552778661); pap. 9.95 *(978-1-55277-865-4(7),* 9781552778654) Lorimer, James & Co., Ltd., Pubs. CAN. Dist: Casemate Pubs. & Bk. Distributors, LLC.

Harrison, Cora. Wolf in the Midnight Forest. (ENG., Illus.). 240p. pap. 5.95 *(978-0-86327-882-2(5))* Wolfhound Pr. IRL. Dist: Interlink Publishing Group, Inc.

Harrold, A. F. The Song from Somewhere Else. Pinfold, Levi, illus. 2017. (ENG.). 240p. (J). 16.99 *(978-1-68119-401-1(5),* 9781681194011, Bloomsbury USA Childrens) Bloomsbury Publishing USA.

Hartt-Sussman, Heather. Noni Speaks Up. Côté, Geneviève, illus. 2016. (ENG.). 24p. (J). (gr. -1-2). 16.99 *(978-1-77049-839-6(7),* Tundra Bks.) Tundra Bks. CAN. Dist: Penguin Random Hse. LLC.

Hayes, Geoffrey. Benny & Penny in the Toy Breaker, 1 vol. 2013. (Toon Bks). (ENG.). 36p. (J). (gr. 1-2). lib. bdg. 27.07 *(978-1-61479-149-2(X))* Spotlight.

—Benny & Penny in the Toy Breaker. 2013. (Toon Books Level 2 Ser.). lib. bdg. 14.75 *(978-0-606-31598-2(5),* Turtleback) Turtleback Bks.

Haynes, Marilee. Pictures of Me. 2016. 149p. (J). pap. *(978-0-8198-6019-4(0))* Pauline Bks. & Media.

Hayward, Linda. Monster Bug. Palmisciano, Diane, illus. 2004. 32p. (J). lib. bdg. 20.00 *(978-1-4242-1097-8(6))* Fitzgerald Bks.

Hemingway, Edward. Bad Apple: A Tale of Friendship. Hemingway, Edward, illus. 2015. (ENG., Illus.). 32p. (J). (gr. -1-k). 8.99 *(978-0-14-751748-7(6),* Puffin Books) Penguin Young Readers Group.

Hen, Horseradish. You Have Permission. 2010. 50p. pap. 21.00 *(978-0-557-50939-3(4))* Lulu Pr., Inc.

Henderson, Lauren. Kiss Me Kill Me. 2009. (ENG.). 272p. (YA). (gr. 9). pap. 8.99 *(978-0-385-73488-2(3),* Delacorte Pr.) Random Hse. Children's Bks.

Hendry, Frances. Wee Malkie. Lt. ed. 2007. 240p. per. *(978-1-905665-19-8(9))* Pollinger In Print.

Heneghan, James. Payback, 1 vol. 2008. (ENG.). 184p. (J). (gr. 4-9). pap. 8.95 *(978-0-88899-704-3(3))* Groundwood Bks. CAN. Dist: Publishers Group West (PGW).

Hensley, Joy N. Rites of Passage. 2014. (ENG.). 416p. (YA). (gr. 8). 17.99 *(978-0-06-229519-4(5),* HarperTeen) HarperCollins Pubs.

Herold, Mariette. Luvable Lucind: Jacob & the Bullies. 2011. 40p. pap. 17.99 *(978-1-4520-2356-4(5))* AuthorHouse.

Higbee, Heidi. It Could Happen... on the Bus. Hezlep, Amber, illus. 2012. 32p. (J). pap. 16.95 *(978-0-9882940-0-4(1))* Bryson Taylor Publishing.

Higgins, M. G. I'm Just Me. 2014. (Gravel Road Ser.). (YA). lib. bdg. 20.80 *(978-0-606-35220-8(1))* Turtleback Bks.

Hileman, Linda L. Dawn's Secret. 2006. (J). per. 9.95 *(978-1-59571-117-5(1))* Word Association Pubs.

Hill, Ryan. J P Trouble. 2012. 32p. pap. 12.95 *(978-1-886057-15-9(X))* Warren Publishing, Inc.

Hoena, Blake. Daring, 1 vol. Cano, Fernando, illus. 2014. (Tony Hawk: Live2Skate Ser.). (ENG.). 72p. (gr. 4-5). lib. bdg. 25.32 *(978-1-4342-9139-4(1))* Stone Arch Bks.

—School Bus Bully. Regan, Dana, illus. 2014. (Jess & Jaylen Ser.). (ENG.). 48p. (J). (gr. 1-4). 27.07 *(978-1-63143-440-2(3),* 208264) Child's World, Inc., The.

Hoena, Blake & Hoena, Blake A. The Ghost Trap. Bardin, Dave, illus. 2016. (Monster Heroes Ser.). (ENG.). 32p. (gr. 1-2). lib. bdg. 21.32 *(978-1-4965-3757-7(2))* Stone Arch Bks.

Holland, Cheron. The Bully: Carmen & Artela. 2013. (ENG.). 40p. (J). pap. 12.95 *(978-1-4787-1030-1(6))* Outskirts Pr., Inc.

Holmes, Kathryn. The Distance Between Lost & Found. 2016. 320p. (YA). (gr. 8). pap. 9.99 *(978-0-06-231727-8(X),* HarperTeen) HarperCollins Pubs.

Holt, K. A. Rhyme Schemer. 2014. (ENG., Illus.). 176p. (J). (gr. 5-9). 15.99 *(978-1-4521-2700-2(X))* Chronicle Bks. LLC.

Hopkins, Cathy. Teen Queens & Has-Beens. 2010. (Truth or Dare Ser.). (ENG.). 192p. (YA). (gr. 7). pap. 9.99 *(978-1-4424-1416-7(2),* Simon Pulse) Simon Pulse.

Hopkins, Mildred Elaine. Friends to the Rescue. 2013. 94p. pap. 8.00 *(978-0-9840237-1-4(2))* Gran Gran Series.

Hoston, William T. No Bullies in the Huddle - Redskins - Casebound. rev. ed. 2015. (ENG.). 23.99 *(978-1-4652-6892-1(8))* Kendall Hunt Publishing Co.

—No Bullies in the Huddle - Redskins - Perfect Bound. rev. ed. 2014. (ENG.). 17.99 *(978-1-4652-6893-8(6))* Kendall Hunt Publishing Co.

House, B. J. What's Wrong with Pauly? Cash, Paul, illus. 2013. 36p. 11.99 *(978-0-9835843-6-0(2),* Lonely Swan Bks.) Cosmic Gargoyle Creative Solutions.

Housenick, Nicole. It's All about Sam-Or Is It? Sam's Terrible Day-Or Billy's? 2013. 36p. pap. 16.99 *(978-1-4525-7396-0(4),* Balboa Pr.) Author Solutions, Inc.

Hughes, Mair Wynn & West, Alex. Ragsi Ragsan. 2005. (WEL., Illus.). 13p. pap. *(978-0-86243-455-7(6))* Y Lolfa.

Imes, Jarold, adapted by. U Can't Break Me. 2007. 148p. (YA). pap. 10.99 *(978-1-934195-03-1(0))* Tinsley Phelps, LLC.

Inagaki, Riichiro. Eyeshield 21, Vol. 8. Murata, Yusuke, illus. 2006. (Eyeshield 21 Ser.: 8). (ENG.). 208p. pap. 9.99 *(978-1-4215-0637-1(8))* Viz Media.

Jackson, A. Isaiah J. Jiffy: You, You, You. Bully! 2005. 50p. pap. 16.95 *(978-1-4137-8524-1(7))* PublishAmerica, Inc.

Jacobs, John Hornor. The Shibboleth. 2014. (Twelve-Fingered Boy Trilogy: Bk. 2). 408p. (YA). (gr. 9-12). 17.95 *(978-0-7613-9008-4(1),* Carolrhoda Lab™) Lerner Publishing Group.

Jacobs, Sherry. "Bobby the Bully" 2012. 32p. pap. 21.99 *(978-1-4797-1069-0(5))* Xlibris Corp.

James-Carde, Genice. Go Away Bully! 2012. 20p. pap. 13.77 *(978-1-4669-2188-7(9))* Trafford Publishing.

Javaherbin, Mina. Goal! Ford, A. G., illus. 2012. (ENG.). 40p. (J). (gr. 1-4). pap. 6.99 *(978-0-7636-5822-9(7))* Candlewick Pr.

Jazwierska, Jennifer & Popiel, Candice Bataille. Discovery of Glow. 2008. (Glowmundo Ser.). (J). (gr. 2-6). pap. 12.95 *(978-0-9814930-0-8(9))* Elora Media, LLC.

Jefferson, Courtney. Shoo Bobby Don't Bother Me. 2010. 28p. pap. 19.95 *(978-1-4490-6570-6(8))* AuthorHouse.

Jeffs, Dixie. Pokey's Chance. 2013. 24p. pap. 24.95 *(978-1-62709-292-0(7))* America Star Bks.

Jenkins, Emily. Invisible Inkling. Bliss, Harry, illus. (Invisible Inkling Ser.: 1). (ENG.). (J). (gr. 1-5). 2012. 176p. pap. 5.99 *(978-0-06-180222-5(0))* 2011. 160p. 16.99 *(978-0-06-180220-1(4))* HarperCollins Pubs.

Jensen, Olivia. Thomas & the Bully. 2009. 16p. pap. 8.49 *(978-1-4389-1848-8(8))* AuthorHouse.

Johnson, Christopher L. I Don't Have Crooked Legs. 2013. 130p. 28.99 *(978-1-4497-8355-6(4));* pap. 11.99 *(978-1-4497-8356-3(2))* Author Solutions, Inc. (WestBow Pr.).

Johnson, Jeremy. Rallo's Goal. 2016. (What's Your Dream? Ser.). (ENG.). 96p. (gr. 3-4). lib. bdg. 25.32 *(978-1-4965-3444-6(1))* Capstone Press of Coughlan Cos.

Johnson, Ken & Myers, Bill. The Big Lie: A Star in the Breaking / The Not-so-Great Escape. 2015. (McGee & Me! Ser.). (ENG.). 256p. (J). pap. 9.99 *(978-1-4964-0329-2(0))* Tyndale Hse. Pubs.

Johnson Mockler, Nicole. Alex Has Had Enough! Mockler, Sean, illus. 2011. 64p. pap. *(978-1-77067-334-2(2))* FriesenPress.

Johnson, Tina Marie. Heaven Dolly: Little Miss Attitude. 2012. pap. 8.95 *(978-0-7414-7470-4(0))* Infinity Publishing.

Johnston, Tony. The Spoon in the Bathroom Wall. 2006. (ENG., Illus.). 144p. (J). (gr. 2-5). pap. 10.95 *(978-0-15-205625-4(4))* Houghton Mifflin Harcourt Publishing Co.

Jones, Jen. Delaney vs. the Bully. Franco, Paula, illus. 2015. (Sleepover Girls Ser.). (ENG.). 128p. (gr. 3-5). lib. bdg. 22.65 *(978-1-4965-0541-5(7))* Stone Arch Bks.

Jones, Nicky. Toby Fletcher's Fly-Away Tree. 2013. 182p. pap. *(978-1-78299-798-6(9))* FeedARead.com.

Jovanovic, Katerina. The Blue Vase, 1 vol. Bisaillon, Josée, illus. 2015. (ENG.). 120p. (J). (gr. 2-5). pap. 10.95 *(978-1-896580-91-3(2))* Tradewind Bks. CAN. Dist: Orca Bk. Pubs. USA.

Katschke, Judy & Nickle, John. The Ant Bully: Movie Novel. 2006. (Illus.). 88p. (J). *(978-1-4156-8331-6(X))* Scholastic, Inc.

Keene, Carolyn. Identity Theft. 34th ed. 2009. (Nancy Drew (All New) Girl Detective Ser.: 34). (ENG.). 176p. (J). (gr. 3-7). pap. 5.99 *(978-1-4169-6831-3(8),* Aladdin) Simon & Schuster Children's Publishing.

—Secret Sabotage, Bk. 1. 2010. (Nancy Drew (All New) Girl Detective Ser.: 42). (ENG.). 144p. (J). (gr. 3-7). pap. 5.99 *(978-1-4169-9069-7(0),* Aladdin) Simon & Schuster Children's Publishing.

Kelly, Erin Entrada. Blackbird Fly. Peterschmidt, Betsy, illus. 2015. (ENG.). 304p. (J). (gr. 3-7). 16.99 *(978-0-06-223861-0(2),* Greenwillow Bks.) HarperCollins Pubs.

—Hello, Universe. Roxas, Isabel, illus. 2017. 320p. (J). (gr. 3-7). 16.99 *(978-0-06-241415-1(1),* Greenwillow Bks.) HarperCollins Pubs.

Kelly, Lynda. Blister Parkin & the Bullies. 2013. 188p. pap. *(978-1-903053-39-3(0))* Kelly Pubns.

Kemnitz, Dianna. Meet Jack & His New Friend. 2011. 36p. pap. 24.95 *(978-1-4560-8776-0(2))* America Star Bks.

Kerbel, Deborah. Girl on the Other Side. 2009. (ENG., Illus.). 152p. (YA). (gr. 6-18). pap. 10.99 *(978-1-55488-443-8(8),* Dundurn Pr.) Dundurn CAN. Dist: Ingram Publisher Services.

Kerick, Mia. The Red Sheet. 2016. (ENG., Illus.). (J). 24.99 ***(978-1-63477-974-6(6))*** 2014. 190p. pap. 14.99 *(978-1-62798-715-8(0))* Dreamspinner Pr. (Harmony Ink Pr.).

Kevin, Henkes. Chrysanthemum. 2014. (ENG.). 32p. (J). (gr. k-3). 11.24 *(978-1-63245-281-8(2))* Lectorum Pubns., Inc.

King, Sharon. Oops Was Bullied? Hey, Why Did You Hurt Me That Way? LaRoe, Misty Bailey, illus. 2013. (ENG.). 32p. (J). pap. 16.95 *(978-1-4787-1364-7(X))* Outskirts Pr., Inc.

Kingfisher, Rupert. Madame Pamplemousse & the Enchanted Sweet Shop. 2011. (ENG., Illus.). 176p. (YA). (gr. 3-6). 16.99 *(978-1-4088-0505-3(7),* 9781408805053, Bloomsbury USA Childrens) Bloomsbury Publishing USA.

Kinney, Jeff. Hard Luck. 2013. (Diary of a Wimpy Kid Ser.: Bk. 8). (ENG., Illus.). 224p. (J). (gr. 3-7). 13.95 *(978-1-4197-1132-9(6),* Amulet Bks.) Abrams, Inc.

—Hard Luck. 2013. (Diary of a Wimpy Kid Ser.: 8). (J). lib. bdg. 25.70 *(978-0-606-32062-7(8),* Turtleback) Turtleback Bks.

Kinsella, Sophie, pseud. Finding Audrey. (ENG.). 304p. (YA). (gr. 7). 2016. pap. 9.99 *(978-0-553-53653-9(2),* Ember) 2015. 18.99 *(978-0-553-53651-5(6),* Delacorte Pr.) Random Hse. Children's Bks.

—Finding Audrey. 2016. lib. bdg. 20.85 *(978-0-606-38874-0(5))* Turtleback Bks.

Klein, Abby. Thanks for Giving. McKinley, John, illus. 2009. (Ready, Freddy! Reader List: No. 4). 32p. (J). pap. *(978-0-545-14176-5(1))* Scholastic, Inc.

Kline, Suzy. Horrible Harry & the Hallway Bully. Wummer, Amy, illus. (Horrible Harry Ser.: 31). (ENG.). 80p. (J). 2015. (gr. 1-3). 4.99 *(978-0-14-750967-3(X),* Puffin Books) 2014. (gr. 2-4). 14.99 *(978-0-670-01551-1(2),* Viking Books for Young Readers) Penguin Young Readers Group.

—Horrible Harry & the Hallway Bully. 2015. (Horrible Harry Ser.: 31). lib. bdg. 14.75 *(978-0-606-36776-9(4))* Turtleback Bks.

Knapp, J. Richard. Bobby's Story: An Amazing Story of Teen Courage. 2006. (ENG.). 224p. (YA). per. 14.95 *(978-0-9774761-7-6(0),* Books To Believe In) Thornton Publishing, Inc.

Kogler, Jennifer. The Otherworldlies. 2008. 400p. (J). lib. bdg. 17.89 *(978-0-06-073960-7(6));* (ENG.). (gr. 5-18). 16.99 *(978-0-06-073959-1(2))* HarperCollins Pubs. (Eos).

Korman, Gordon. Jackpot. 2014. (Swindle Ser.: 6). (ENG.). 208p. (J). (gr. 3-7). pap. 6.99 *(978-0-545-56147-1(7));* 16.99 *(978-0-545-56146-4(9))* Scholastic, Inc. (Scholastic Pr.).

—Jackpot. 2014. (Swindle Ser.: 6). lib. bdg. 17.20 *(978-0-606-36032-6(8))* Turtleback Bks.

—Unleashed. 2015. (Swindle Ser.: 7). (ENG.). 208p. (J). (gr. 3-7). 16.99 *(978-0-545-70935-4(0),* Scholastic Pr.) Scholastic, Inc.

Koss, Amy Goldman. Poison Ivy. 2008. (ENG.). 192p. (J). (gr. 5-9). pap. 8.99 *(978-0-312-38453-1(X),* 9780312384531) Square Fish.

Krackow, Eric T. The Lollipop Monster, 1 vol. 2011. (ENG., Illus.). 64p. (J). 16.99 *(978-0-7643-3773-4(4),* 9780764337734, Schiffer Publishing Ltd) Schiffer Publishing, Ltd.

—The Lollipop Monster's Christmas, 1 vol. 2014. (ENG., Illus.). 64p. (J). (gr. 5-8). 16.99 *(978-0-7643-4743-6(8),* 9780764347436) Schiffer Publishing, Ltd.

Kraus, Daniel. Rotters. 2012. (ENG.). 464p. (YA). (gr. 9). pap. 10.99 *(978-0-385-73858-3(7),* Ember) Random Hse. Children's Bks.

Kravitz, Danny. Tommy Mcknight & the Great Election. 2016. (Presidential Politics Ser.). (ENG.). 96p. (gr. 3-4). lib. bdg. 26.65 *(978-1-4965-2585-7(X)*, Connect) Stone Arch Bks.
—Tommy McKnight & the Great Election. 2016. (J). pap. *(978-1-4965-2752-3(6))* Stone Arch Bks.
Krokos, Dan. The Black Stars. 2015. (ENG., Illus.). 304p. (J). (gr. 3-8). pap. 21.99 *(978-0-7653-7668-8(7)*, 9780765376688, Starscape) Doherty, Tom Assocs., LLC.
Kropp, Paul. Scarface. 88p. *(978-0-9731237-3-9(7))* High Interest Publishing (HIP).
Kshir, Donna M. & Potter, Sandra Dawn. I Was A Teen Abuser: One Boy's Struggle to Gain Self-Control. 2010. 38p. pap. 7.50 *(978-0-557-67211-0(2))* Lulu Pr., Inc.
Kucharski, Linda. Sneak the Sneaker. 2010. 44p. pap. 15.50 *(978-1-60911-487-9(6)*, Eloquent Bks.) Strategic Book Publishing & Rights Agency (SBPRA).
Kumiega, Michelle. The Bunnies Who Learn Not to Bully. 2011. 24p. pap. 24.95 *(978-1-4560-6742-7(7))* America Star Bks.
Lamb, Jowana. Makhi & the Run Away Elephant. 2012. 28p. pap. 15.99 *(978-1-4771-3820-5(X))* Xlibris Corp.
Lampley, Titra. Jazzy Dolls & Swaggro's Get's Revenge on Bullies. 2012. 42p. 16.95 *(978-1-4626-6137-4(8))* America Star Bks.
Lang, Diane & Buchanan, Michael. The Fat Boy Chronicles. 2010. (Fat Boy Chronicles Ser.). (ENG.). 224p. (J). (gr. 7-11). pap. 9.95 *(978-1-58536-543-2(2)*, 202220) Sleeping Bear Pr.
Lasky, Ricki & Siqueiros, Paula. The Brave Adventures of Captain Courage: The Bully. 2012. (Illus.). (J). 14.95 *(978-1-62086-095-3(3))* Mascot Bks., Inc.
Leamon, Kevin. Oh No. Not Again! 2010. 27p. 14.95 *(978-0-557-63078-3(9))* Lulu Pr., Inc.
Leblanc, Louise. Maddie Stands Tall. Cummins, Sarah, tr. from FRE. Gay, Marie-Louise, illus. 2005. (Formac First Novels Ser.: 54). (ENG.). 64p. (J). (gr. 2-5). 14.95 *(978-0-88780-683-4(X)*, 9780887806834) Formac Publishing Co., Ltd. CAN. Dist: Casemate Pubs. & Bk. Distributors, LLC.
—Maddie Stands Tall, 1 vol. Cummins, Sarah, tr. from FRE. Gay, Marie-Louise, illus. 2005. (Formac First Novels Ser.: 54). (ENG.). 64p. (J). (gr. 2-5). 4.95 *(978-0-88780-682-7(1)*, 9780887806827) Formac Publishing Co., Ltd. CAN. Dist: Casemate Pubs. & Bk. Distributors, LLC.
Lee, Kathy. River Rapids. 2011. 144p. pap. *(978-1-84427-508-3(6))* Scripture Union.
Lennon, Maria T. Confessions of a So-Called Middle Child. 2013. (ENG.). 288p. (J). (gr. 3-7). 16.99 *(978-0-06-212690-0(3))* HarperCollins Pubs.
Leveen, Tom. Random. 2014. (ENG., Illus.). 224p. (YA). (gr. 9). 17.99 *(978-1-4424-9956-0(7)*, Simon Pulse) Simon Pulse.
Lewis, Fiona. Dreaming in Color. 2011. (ENG.). 304p. (J). (gr. 7). pap. 16.95 *(978-0-9845318-5-1(8))* Tiny Stachel Pr.
Linke, Glenn Colin. The Gargantuan Boy. 2011. 102p. pap. 30.50 *(978-1-60976-079-3(4)*, Eloquent Bks.) Strategic Book Publishing & Rights Agency (SBPRA).
Littman, Sarah Darer. Backlash. 2015. (ENG.). 336p. (J). (gr. 7). 17.99 *(978-0-545-65126-4(3)*, Scholastic Pr.) Scholastic, Inc.
Lo, Catherine. How It Ends. 2016. (ENG.). 304p. (YA). (gr. 9). 17.99 *(978-0-544-54006-4(9)*, HMH Books For Young Readers) Houghton Mifflin Harcourt Publishing Co.
Logan, Kenneth. True Letters from a Fictional Life. 2016. 336p. (J). (gr. 8). 17.99 *(978-0-06-238025-8(7)*, HarperTeen) HarperCollins Pubs.
Lopez, Patricia A. Carly & Boey. 2009. 56p. pap. 16.95 *(978-1-61546-836-2(6))* America Star Bks.
Love, D. Anne. Defying the Diva. 2008. (ENG., Illus.). 272p. (YA). (gr. 7-12). 17.99 *(978-1-4169-3481-3(2)*, McElderry, Margaret K. Bks.) McElderry, Margaret K. Bks.
Luck, Gail. Bumduggle Davis Bites off More Than He Can Chew: Or You Can't Make an Omelette Without Breaking Eggs. 2012. 170p. pap. 13.50 *(978-1-62212-380-3(8)*, Strategic Bk. Publishing) Strategic Book Publishing & Rights Agency (SBPRA).
Ludwig, Trudy. Confessions of a Former Bully. 2012. lib. bdg. 18.40 *(978-0-606-26382-5(9)*, Turtleback) Turtleback Bks.
—My Secret Bully. Marble, Abigail, illus. 2015. (ENG.). 32p. (J). (gr. 1-4). 7.99 *(978-0-553-50940-3(3)*, Dragonfly Bks.) Random Hse. Children's Bks.
Lupica, Mike. Hot Hand, 1 vol. 2012. (Comeback Kids Ser.). (ENG.). 176p. (J). (gr. 4-8). lib. bdg. 27.07 *(978-1-59961-175-4(9))* Spotlight.
Lynch, Jane, et al. Marlene, Marlene, Queen of Mean. Tusa, Tricia, illus. 2014. (ENG.). 32p. (J). (gr. -1-2). lib. bdg. 19.99 *(978-0-375-97329-1(X)*, Random Hse. Bks. for Young Readers) Random Hse. Children's Bks.
Maciel, Amanda. Tease. (ENG.). 336p. (YA). (gr. 9). 2015. pap. 9.99 *(978-0-06-230531-2(X))* 2014. 17.99 *(978-0-06-230530-5(1))* HarperCollins Pubs.
Mack, Kelvin. Bullies Need Friends Too. 2011. 20p. 13.99 *(978-1-4269-6182-3(0))* Trafford Publishing.
MacPhail, Cathy. Run, Zan, Run. 2012. (ENG.). 192p. (YA). pap. 12.99 *(978-1-4088-1733-9(0)*, 9781408817339, Bloomsbury USA Childrens) Bloomsbury Publishing USA.
Maddox, Jake. Beach Bully, 1 vol. Aburtov, illus. 2013. (Jake Maddox Sports Stories Ser.). (ENG.). 72p. (gr. 2-3). pap. 5.95 *(978-1-4342-6206-6(5))* Stone Arch Bks.
—Beach Bully. 2013. (Jake Maddox Sports Stories Ser.). (ENG.). 72p. (gr. 2-3). pap. 35.70 *(978-1-4342-6234-9(0))* Stone Arch Bks.
—Beach Bully, 1 vol. Aburtov, Jesus, illus. 2013. (Jake Maddox Sports Stories Ser.). (ENG.). 72p. (gr. 2-3). lib. bdg. 25.32 *(978-1-4342-5973-8(0))* Stone Arch Bks.
—Board Battle, 1 vol. Aburtov, Jesus Aburto, illus. 2013. (Jake Maddox Sports Stories Ser.). (ENG.). 72p. (gr. 2-3). pap. 5.95 *(978-1-4342-6208-0(1))* Stone Arch Bks.
—Board Battle. 2013. (Jake Maddox Sports Stories Ser.). (ENG.). 72p. (gr. 2-3). pap. 35.70 *(978-1-4342-6235-6(9))* Stone Arch Bks.
—Board Battle, 1 vol. Aburtov, Jesus Aburto, illus. 2013. (Jake Maddox Sports Stories Ser.). (ENG.). 72p. (gr. 2-3). lib. bdg. 25.32 *(978-1-4342-5975-2(7))* Stone Arch Bks.
—En la línea de Ataque. Heck, Claudia M., tr. from ENG. Tiffany, Sean, illus. 2012. (Jake Maddox en Español Ser.). (SPA.). 72p. (gr. 2-3). 25.32 *(978-1-4342-3813-9(X))* Stone Arch Bks.
—Paintball Problems, 1 vol. Aburtov, Jesus Aburto, illus. 2013. (Jake Maddox Sports Stories Ser.). (ENG.). 72p. (gr. 2-3). pap. 5.95 *(978-1-4342-6207-3(3))* Stone Arch Bks.
—Paintball Problems. 2013. (Jake Maddox Sports Stories Ser.). (ENG.). 72p. (gr. 2-3). pap. 35.70 *(978-1-4342-6237-0(5))* Stone Arch Bks.
—Paintball Problems, 1 vol. Aburtov, Jesus Aburto, illus. 2013. (Jake Maddox Sports Stories Ser.). (ENG.). 72p. (gr. 2-3). lib. bdg. 25.32 *(978-1-4342-5974-5(9))* Stone Arch Bks.
—Second-Chance Soccer, 1 vol. Ray, Mike, illus. 2014. (Jake Maddox JV Ser.). (ENG.). 96p. (gr. 3-4). 25.99 *(978-1-4342-9154-7(5))* Stone Arch Bks.
Maddox, Jake. Squad Struggles. Wood, Katie, illus. 2017. (Jake Maddox Girl Sports Stories Ser.). (ENG.). 72p. (gr. 2-3). lib. bdg. 25.32 ***(978-1-4965-4971-6(6))*** Stone Arch Bks.
Mader, Ph. D. Lothar & Mader, Lothar. Fartface: Stop Teasing Me, Bulliback... 2010. 30p. 14.95 *(978-0-615-24577-5(3))* Mader, Lothar.
Madge, Amy. The Adventures of Kwun-Gee & Uba Dooba Boy. 2012. 24p. 29.95 *(978-1-4626-9270-5(2))* America Star Bks.
Madrzak, Carole. The Arronna Crystal. 2012. 234p. pap. 24.95 *(978-1-4137-9968-2(X))* America Star Bks.
Manci, Arlene. The Grumpy Troll, 1 vol. Rawcliffe, Lee, illus. 2009. 25p. pap. 19.95 *(978-1-4489-2456-1(1))* PublishAmerica, Inc.
Mandel, Lee. Barf for Lunch. 2012. 184p. pap. 8.99 *(978-0-9831996-4-9(7))* Creative Dragon Pr.
Maness, Rowan. Bombshell. 2017. (ENG., Illus.). 320p. (YA). (gr. 9). 18.99 ***(978-1-4814-4164-3(7)***, Simon Pulse) Simon Pulse.
Manushkin, Fran & Lyon, Tammie. Basta de Burlas, 1 vol. Lyon, Tammie, illus. 2012. (Katie Woo en Español Ser.). (SPA., Illus.). 32p. (gr. k-2). pap. 6.95 *(978-1-4048-7677-4(4))*; lib. bdg. 21.32 *(978-1-4048-7525-8(5))* Picture Window Bks.
Marie, K. Beulah the Lunchroom Bully. Cook, Monique, illus. 2011. 20p. pap. 24.95 *(978-1-4560-5224-9(1))* America Star Bks.
Martin, Bridgitt. Bunny & the Amazing Gift: God Cares for All His Creation. 2013. 28p. pap. 13.99 *(978-1-4908-0952-6(X)*, WestBow Pr.) Author Solutions, Inc.
Masessa, Ed. Wandmaker. 2016. (ENG.). 336p. (J). (gr. 3-7). 12.99 *(978-0-545-86174-8(8)*, Scholastic Pr.) Scholastic, Inc.
Mathews, Temple. The New Kid. 2010. (New Kid Ser.). (ENG.). 288p. (J). (gr. 6-11). pap. 9.99 *(978-1-935618-27-0(X))* BenBella Bks.
Mathieu, Jennifer. The Truth about Alice. 2014. (ENG.). 208p. (YA). (gr. 7). 16.99 *(978-1-59643-909-2(2)*, 9781596439092) Roaring Brook Pr.
McAuslan, Fiona & Nicholson, Peter. The Resolving Bullying Book. 2010. (Resolving Bks). (ENG., Illus.). 76p. (J). pap. 9.95 *(978-1-84730-223-6(8))* Veritas Pubns. IRL. Dist: Dufour Editions, Inc.
McCaffrey, Kate. Destroying Avalon. 2006. (ENG.). 240p. (J). pap. 13.00 *(978-1-921064-57-9(9))* Fremantle Pr. AUS. Dist: Independent Pubs. Group.
McCarney, Rosemary. Tilt Your Head Rosie the Red, 1 vol. Cathcart, Yvonne, illus. 2015. (Rosie the Red Ser.). (ENG.). 24p. (J). (gr. 1-3). 15.95 *(978-1-927583-59-3(4))* Second Story Pr. CAN. Dist: Orca Bk. Pubs. USA.
McCombs, A. Lisa. Abby. 2011. 184p. *(978-1-77067-327-4(X))* FriesenPress.
McCombs, Lisa A. Abby. 2011. 184p. pap. *(978-1-77067-328-1(8))* FriesenPress.
McDaniels, Preston, illus. Phineas L. MacGuire ... Gets Cooking! 2014. (From the Highly Scientific Notebooks of Phineas L. MacGuire Ser.). (ENG.). 208p. (J). (gr. 3-7). 16.99 *(978-1-4814-0099-2(1)*, Atheneum Bks. for Young Readers) Simon & Schuster Children's Publishing.
McEwan, Jamie. Rufus the Scrub Does Not Wear a Tutu. Margeson, John, illus. 2006. 64p. (J). (gr. 2-3). 14.95 *(978-1-58196-060-0(3)*, Darby Creek) Lerner Publishing Group.
McGann, Erika. The Demon Notebook. 2014. (Demon Notebook Ser.: 1). (ENG.). 288p. (J). (gr. 3-6). pap. 6.99 *(978-1-4022-9538-6(3)*, 9781402295386, Sourcebooks Jabberwocky) Sourcebooks, Inc.
Mcgill, Leslie. The Game. 2015. (Cap Central Ser.: 5). (YA). lib. bdg. 20.80 *(978-0-606-37192-6(3))* Turtleback Bks.
McGinn, William. The Blacktop Brothers. 2012. 154p. (gr. 10-12). pap. 13.42 *(978-1-4669-6530-0(4))* Trafford Publishing.
McGlotham, L. R. E. I Didn't Do Nuthin' Bailin, Jill, ed. Brennan, Lisa, illus. 2013. 42p. 18.99 *(978-0-9892711-5-8(3))* Mindstir Media.
McGrath, Maureen Julie. The Tale of the Cat with the Crooked Tail. 2013. 24p. pap. 13.50 *(978-1-62516-859-7(4)*, Strategic Bk. Publishing) Strategic Book Publishing & Rights Agency (SBPRA).
McKinley, Mary. Beau, Lee, the Bomb & Me. 2014. (Rusty Winters Ser.: 1). (ENG.). 256p. (YA). (gr. 13). pap. 9.95 *(978-1-61773-255-3(9)*, K-Teen) Kensington Publishing Corp.
McLaughlin, Richard. The Skunk with the Stinky Attitude. Wilson, Mark, illus. 2013. 44p. (YA). pap. 13.75 *(978-1-939625-49-6(1))* Inkwell Books LLC.
McNutt, Dave. Safety Dave & Daisy Take on the Bullies. 2012. 16p. pap. 8.95 *(978-1-4772-7503-0(7))* AuthorHouse.
Medina, Meg. Yaqui Delgado Wants to Kick Your Ass. (ENG., 272p. (YA). (gr. 9). 2014. Illus.). pap. 7.99 *(978-0-7636-7164-8(9))* 2013. 16.99 *(978-0-7636-5859-5(6))* Candlewick Pr.
Meistle, Jarrod. Victor the Vampire & the Bully. 2012. 28p. pap. 14.99 *(978-1-4691-3879-4(4))* Xlibris Corp.
Mello, Mary. Johnny Makes a Friend. 2012. 30p. 24.95 *(978-1-4512-1248-8(8))* America Star Bks.
Mesker, Erma Medrano. Bullies on the Prowl on a Hallow's Eve. 2011. 56p. (gr. 4-6). pap. 27.98 *(978-1-4567-5622-2(2))* AuthorHouse.
Messner, Kate. Sea Monster & the Bossy Fish. Rash, Andy, illus. 2013. (ENG.). 40p. (J). (gr. -1-k). 16.99 *(978-1-4521-1253-4(3))* Chronicle Bks. LLC.
Middleton, Dana. The Infinity Year of Avalon James. 2016. (ENG.). 224p. (J). 16.99 *(978-1-250-08569-6(1)*, 9781250085696) Feiwel & Friends.
Miller, Janet. Little House on the Highway - a Story of a Homeless Family & School Bullying. 2011. 200p. pap. 19.95 *(978-1-257-83540-9(8))* Lulu Pr., Inc.
Miller, Sam J. The Art of Starving. 2017. 384p. (YA). (gr. 8). 17.99 ***(978-0-06-245671-7(7)***, HarperTeen) HarperCollins Pubs.
Milot, Carryanne. Austin & the Bully. Proulx, Denis, illus. 2012. 40p. pap. *(978-1-77097-970-3(0))* FriesenPress.
Milway, Katie Smith. The Banana-Leaf Ball: How Play Can Change the World. Evans, Shane W., illus. 2017. (CitizenKid Ser.). (ENG.). 32p. (J). (gr. 3-7). 18.95 *(978-1-77138-331-8(3))* Kids Can Pr., Ltd. CAN. Dist: Hachette Bk. Group.
Mitchell, Julie & Konye, Paul. The Bully. 2008. (Rigby Focus Forward: Level K Ser.). (Illus.). 24p. (J). (gr. 4-7). pap. *(978-1-4190-3784-9(6)*, Rigby) Pearson Education Australia.
Mitchell, Marvin T. Bully Me No More: How Everyone Can Be Bullied! 2013. 16p. pap. 10.00 *(978-1-62212-669-9(6)*, Strategic Bk. Publishing) Strategic Book Publishing & Rights Agency (SBPRA).
Mitchell, P. S. I Don't Wanna Be Me. 2013. 48p. 15.95 *(978-0-615-80354-8(7))* Mitchell, P. S.
M.J.Higgy. The Bombay Bear. 2012. (Illus.). 16p. pap. 18.30 *(978-1-4685-8193-5(7))* AuthorHouse.
Montes de Oca, Sharron. Animal Town. 2017. (ENG.). 44p. (J). pap. 15.95 ***(978-1-78693-365-2(9)***, 9781786933652) Austin, Stan AUS. Dist: Bookmasters Distribution.
Montreuil, Gaetane. Leelo. Goodway, Simon, illus. 2013. 50p. pap. *(978-1-926633-67-1(9))* Titles on Demand.
Moore, Monica A. Everyday Heroes. 2006. (ENG.). 52p. per. 12.95 *(978-1-59800-563-9(4))* Outskirts Pr., Inc.
Moreira, Carol. Membrane, 1 vol. 2013. (ENG.). 269p. pap. *(978-1-927746-05-9(1))*; 282p. pap. *(978-1-927746-04-2(3))* Fierce ink Pr. Co-Op, Ltd.
Morgan, Anna & Turkienicz, Rachael. My (Worst) Best Sleepover Party, 1 vol. 2007. (ENG., Illus.). 128p. (J). (gr. 2-5). pap. 7.95 *(978-1-897187-20-3(3))* Second Story Pr. CAN. Dist: Orca Bk. Pubs. USA.
Moskowitz, Hannah. Not Otherwise Specified: A Novel. 2015. (ENG., Illus.). 304p. (YA). (gr. 9). pap. 11.99 *(978-1-4814-0595-9(0)*, Simon Pulse) Simon Pulse.
Moss, Peggy & Lyon, Lea. Say Something, 1 vol. 2008. (ENG., Illus.). 32p. (J). (gr. 1-7). pap. 7.95 *(978-0-88448-310-6(X))* Tilbury Hse. Pubs.
—Say Something: 10TH Anniversary Edition. 2013. (ENG., Illus.). 32p. (gr. 2-7). pap. 7.95 *(978-0-88448-360-1(6)*, 884360) Tilbury Hse. Pubs.
Mostoller, Marcia. Emma's Dilemm. 2011. 42p. pap. 16.95 *(978-1-4560-9859-9(4))* America Star Bks.
Mullarkey, Lisa. TJ Zaps a Nightmare: Stopping Blackmail Bullying #5, 1 vol. LaCoste, Gary, illus. 2012. (TJ Trapper, Bully Zapper Ser.). (ENG.). 80p. (J). (gr. 2-5). lib. bdg. 27.07 *(978-1-61641-909-7(1)*, Calico Chapter Bks) Magic Wagon.
—TJ Zaps the Freeze Out: Stopping the Silent Treatment #3, 1 vol. LaCoste, Gary, illus. 2012. (TJ Trapper, Bully Zapper Ser.). (ENG.). 80p. (J). (gr. 2-5). lib. bdg. 27.07 *(978-1-61641-907-3(5)*, Calico Chapter Bks) Magic Wagon.
—TJ Zaps the New Kid: Stopping a Social Bully #1, 1 vol. LaCoste, Gary, illus. 2012. (TJ Trapper, Bully Zapper Ser.). (ENG.). 80p. (J). (gr. 2-5). lib. bdg. 27.07 *(978-1-61641-905-9(9)*, Calico Chapter Bks) Magic Wagon.
—TJ Zaps the One-Upper: Stopping One-Upping & Cell Phone Bullying #2, 1 vol. LaCoste, Gary, illus. 2012. (TJ Trapper, Bully Zapper Ser.). (ENG.). 80p. (J). (gr. 2-5). lib. bdg. 27.07 *(978-1-61641-906-6(7)*, Calico Chapter Bks) Magic Wagon.
—TJ Zaps the Rumor Mill: Stopping Gossip #4, 1 vol. LaCoste, Gary, illus. 2012. (TJ Trapper, Bully Zapper Ser.). (ENG.). 80p. (J). (gr. 2-5). lib. bdg. 27.07 *(978-1-61641-908-0(3)*, Calico Chapter Bks) Magic Wagon.
—TJ Zaps the Smackdown: Stopping a Physical Bully #6, 1 vol. LaCoste, Gary, illus. 2012. (TJ Trapper, Bully Zapper Ser.). (ENG.). 80p. (J). (gr. 2-5). lib. bdg. 27.07 *(978-1-61641-910-3(5)*, Calico Chapter Bks) Magic Wagon.
Murcray, Rod. Tuttle Stories. McDaniel, Rick, illus. 2012. 40p. pap. 14.95 *(978-1-61897-654-3(0)*, Strategic Bk. Publishing) Strategic Book Publishing & Rights Agency (SBPRA).
Murdoch, Patricia. Exposure, 1 vol. 2006. (Orca Soundings Ser.). (ENG.). 128p. (YA). (gr. 8-12). per. 9.95 *(978-1-55143-493-3(8))* Orca Bk. Pubs. USA.
Nass, Marcia. How to be a Bully... NOT! Moon, Poppy, illus. 2011. 56p. (J). pap. 16.95 *(978-1-59850-101-8(1))* Youthlight, Inc.
Nelson, Sheila K. The Backpack Bears' Adventure: No Bullies Allowed. Kerber, Kathy, illus. 2010. 24p. pap. 14.99 *(978-1-4490-9726-4(X))* AuthorHouse.
Nettles, Sarah A. Benjamin, the Bully & the Butterfly. 2012. 24p. pap. 17.99 *(978-1-4772-7195-7(3))* AuthorHouse.
Nighthawk, Tori. Don't Judge a Bird by Its Feathers. Nighthawk, Tori, illus. 2013. (ENG., Illus.). 60p. (J). (gr. -1-3). 17.99 *(978-0-9858811-9-1(4))* Stone, Anne Publishing.
Nobleman, Marc Tyler. Brave Like My Brother. 2016. (ENG.). 112p. (J). (gr. 2-5). 15.99 *(978-0-545-88035-0(1)*, Scholastic Pr.) Scholastic, Inc.
Nolan, Alan. Conor's Caveman: The Amazing Adventures of Ogg. 2016. (ENG., Illus.). 144p. (J). pap. 11.00 *(978-1-84717-732-2(8))* O'Brien Pr., Ltd., The IRL. Dist: Dufour Editions, Inc.
Nolan, Nancy. Mr. Munson's Itvice on Bullying. Scadden, Kathryn, illus. 2015. (J). 16.95 *(978-1-59298-907-2(1))* Beaver's Pond Pr., Inc.
Nosy Crow Staff. Bizzy Bear: Let's Get to Work! Davies, Benji, illus. 2012. (Bizzy Bear Ser.). (ENG.). 8p. (J). (gr. k — 1). bds. 6.99 *(978-0-7636-5899-1(5)*, Nosy Crow) Candlewick Pr.
Nydam, Anne. The Bad Advice of Grandma Hasenfuss. 2010. 112p. pap. 14.00 *(978-0-557-26037-9(X))* Lulu Pr., Inc.
Oakes, Cory Putman. Dinosaur Boy. 2015. (Dinosaur Boy Ser.: 1). (ENG.). 224p. (J). (gr. 3-7). 12.99 *(978-1-4926-0537-9(9)*, 9781492605379, Sourcebooks Jabberwocky) Sourcebooks, Inc.
O'Connor, George. Ker-Splash! O'Connor, George, illus. 2010. (ENG., Illus.). 40p. (J). (gr. -1-3). 19.99 *(978-1-4424-2196-7(7)*, Simon & Schuster Bks. For Young Readers) Simon & Schuster Bks. For Young Readers.
Ode to Bobby B Billy. 2013. (Illus.). 140p. pap. 24.95 *(978-0-9894379-1-2(4))* Jots & Tittles Publishing.
Olsen, Sylvia. White Girl, 1 vol. 2004. (ENG., Illus.). 200p. (YA). (gr. 7-12). pap. 9.95 *(978-1-55039-147-3(X))* Sono Nis Pr. CAN. Dist: Orca Bk. Pubs. USA.
Onwusilikam, Ify Chinedum. The Drama Queen. 2009. 56p. pap. 10.00 *(978-1-60860-126-4(9)*, Strategic Bk. Publishing) Strategic Book Publishing & Rights Agency (SBPRA).
Opio, Leoncio. The Adventures of Mr. Nimbus & the School House Bullies. 2012. 98p. pap. 19.95 *(978-1-4626-9442-6(X))* America Star Bks.
Orme, Helen. Leave Her Alone. 2008. (Siti's Sisters Ser.). (ENG., Illus.). 36p. pap. *(978-1-84167-742-2(6))* Ransom Publishing Ltd.
Osborn, Kelly. The Green Knight. 2006. 64p. pap. 19.95 *(978-1-4241-1741-3(0))* America Star Bks.
Otoshi, Kathryn. One. pap. *(978-0-9723946-5-9(6))*; 2008. (ENG., Illus.). 32p. (J). (gr. -1). 17.95 *(978-0-9723946-4-2(8))* KO Kids Bks.
P. Cotton & Clyde & the Chameleons. 2011. 28p. (gr. -1 — 1). pap. 13.99 *(978-1-4520-9675-9(9))* AuthorHouse.
Palmer, Tom. Boys United. 2009. (Football Academy Ser.). (ENG., Illus.). 176p. (J). (gr. 2-4). pap. 10.99 *(978-0-14-132467-8(8))* Penguin Bks., Ltd. GBR. Dist: Independent Pubs. Group.
—The Real Thing, Bk. 3. 3rd ed. 2009. (Football Academy Ser.). (ENG., Illus.). 176p. (J). (gr. 2-4). pap. 10.99 *(978-0-14-132469-2(4))* Penguin Bks., Ltd. GBR. Dist: Independent Pubs. Group.
Pam, Miss. Never Never Be a Bully. Stutz, Chris, illus. 2011. 24p. pap. 24.95 *(978-1-4626-4325-7(6))* America Star Bks.
Pasnak, William. The Ginger Princess, 1 vol. 2006. (Lorimer Streetlights Ser.). (ENG.). 96p. (J). (gr. 2-5). 7.95 *(978-1-55028-952-7(7)*, 9781550289527) Lorimer, James & Co., Ltd., Pubs. CAN. Dist: Casemate Pubs. & Bk. Distributors, LLC.
Patterson, James & Grabenstein, Chris. I Even Funnier: A Middle School Story. Park, Laura, illus. 2013. (I Funny Ser.: 2). (ENG.). 368p. (J). (gr. 3-7). 13.99 *(978-0-316-20697-6(0)*, Jimmy Patterson) Little Brown & Co.
—I Funny: A Middle School Story. Park, Laura, illus. (I Funny Ser.: 1). (ENG.). 320p. (J). (gr. 3-7). 2015. pap. 8.00 *(978-0-316-20692-1(X))* 2013. 13.99 *(978-0-316-32200-3(8))* Little Brown & Co. (Jimmy Patterson).
Patterson, James & Tebbetts, Chris. Just My Rotten Luck. Park, Laura, illus. 2015. (Middle School Ser.: 7). (ENG.). 320p. (J). (gr. 3-7). 13.99 *(978-0-316-28477-6(7)*, Jimmy Patterson) Little Brown & Co.
Patterson, Trina Dawkins. A Tale of Two Cookies: A Message of Kindness & Acceptance. Wilson, Bonnita, illus. 2011. (ENG.). 32p. (J). (gr. -1-3). pap. 10.99 *(978-0-9819860-9-8(9))* Amber Skye Publishing LLC.
Pavón, Mar. Clucky & the Magic Kettle. 2013. (ENG., Illus.). 30p. (J). (gr. -1-k). 15.95 *(978-84-15619-44-4(8))* Eastern National.
Pearl, David R. & Pearl, Tamara R. Stop the Bully. Ahrin, Jacob, illus. 2013. 26p. pap. *(978-0-646-90104-6(4))* Be Positive Solutions.
Pendziwol, Jean E. The Tale of Sir Dragon: Dealing with Bullies for Kids (and Dragons) Gourbault, Martine, illus. 2007. (ENG.). 32p. (J). (gr. -1-2). 15.95 *(978-1-55453-135-6(7))* Kids Can Pr., Ltd. CAN. Dist: Hachette Bk. Group.
Pendziwol, Jean E. & Gourbault, Martine. The Tale of Sir Dragon: Dealing with Bullies for Kids (and Dragons) Gourbault, Martine, illus. 2007. (ENG., Illus.). 32p. (J). (gr. -1-2). pap. 7.95 *(978-1-55453-136-3(5))* Kids Can Pr., Ltd. CAN. Dist: Hachette Bk. Group.
Pernikoff, Doug. So What If Im a Bully. 2009. 40p. 11.99 *(978-0-9816923-3-3(8))* Cochran, Russ Co., The.
Perry, Fred. Grossery Games. 2012. (ENG., Illus.). 128p. (J). (gr. 4-7). pap. 10.99 *(978-0-9850925-5-9(6)*, 9780985092559) Antarctic Pr., Inc.
Perry, Laurie. Kaycee's New School, 1 vol. 2009. 48p. pap. 16.95 *(978-1-61582-638-4(6))* America Star Bks.
Peters, Andrew. Rabbit Cooks up a Cunning Plan! Roberts, Bruno, illus. 2010. (Traditional Tales with a Twist Ser.). (ENG.). 32p. (J). (gr. -1-2). audio compact disk *(978-1-84643-349-8(5))* Child's Play International Ltd.
Peters, Andrew Fusek. The Ant & the Big Bad Bully Goat. Wadham, Anna, illus. 2007. (Traditional Tales with a Twist Ser.). (ENG.). 32p. (J). (gr. 2-2). pap. *(978-1-84643-079-4(8))* Child's Play International Ltd.
—Rabbit Cooks up a Cunning Plan! Robert, Bruno, illus. 2007. (Traditional Tales with a Twist Ser.). (ENG.). 32p. (J). (gr. 2-2). pap. *(978-1-84643-097-8(6))* Child's Play International Ltd.
Peters, Julie Anne. By the Time You Read This, I'll Be Dead. 2011. (ENG.). 240p. (J). (gr. 5-9). pap. 9.99 *(978-1-4231-3021-5(9))* Hyperion Pr.
Peterson, Tina L. Oscar & the Amazing Gravity Repellent. Bonet, Xavier, illus. 2015. (Middle-Grade Novels Ser.). (ENG.). 224p. (gr. 4-7). lib. bdg. 26.65 *(978-1-4965-0000-7(8))* Stone Arch Bks.
Philippou, Stefanie. Sammy Learns to Say I Am Sorry. 2011. 28p. pap. 21.99 *(978-1-4653-6352-7(1))* Xlibris Corp.
Phillips, Dee. Friends?, 1 vol. 2014. (Right Now! Ser.). (ENG.). 48p. (YA). (gr. 9-12). pap. 8.95 *(978-1-62250-882-2(3))* Saddleback Educational Publishing, Inc.
Phillips, Ruby Ann. Fortune Cookie Fiasco. Isik, Semur, illus. 2015. (Krystal Ball Ser.). (ENG.). 112p. (gr. 2-3). lib. bdg. 25.32 *(978-1-4795-5874-2(5))* Picture Window Bks.
—The Great & Powerful, 1 vol. Isik, Semur, illus. 2014. (Krystal Ball Ser.). (ENG.). 112p. (gr. 2-3). 25.32 *(978-1-4795-2179-1(5))* Picture Window Bks.
Pilkey, Dav. Ricky Ricotta's Mighty Robot. Santat, Dan, illus. 2014. (Ricky Ricotta Ser.: 1). (ENG.). 112p. (J). (gr. -1-3). pap. 5.99 *(978-0-545-63009-2(6))*; lib. bdg. 15.99 *(978-0-545-63106-8(8))* Scholastic, Inc.
—Ricky Ricotta's Mighty Robot. 2014. (Ricky Ricotta's Mighty Robot Ser.: 1). lib. bdg. 16.00 *(978-0-606-35799-9(8))* Turtleback Bks.
Pixley, Marcella. Freak. 2013. (ENG.). 160p. (YA). (gr. 7-10). pap. 10.99 *(978-1-250-02742-9(X)*, 9781250027429) Square Fish.
Polacco, Patricia. Bully. Polacco, Patricia, illus. 2012. (ENG., Illus.). 48p. (J). (gr. 2-5). 17.99 *(978-0-399-25704-9(7)*, G.P. Putnam's Sons Books for Young Readers) Penguin Young Readers Group.

Polacco, Patricia. Mr. Lincoln's Way. 2017. lib. bdg. 19.65 **(978-0-606-39783-4(3))** Turtleback Bks.
Pollock, A. K. I Am Joshua: Heart Matters Series. 2013. 214p. (gr. 4-6). pap. 17.95 *(978-1-4497-9726-3(1)*, WestBow Pr.) Author Solutions, Inc.
Porcelli-Munisteri, Nadia. Who Are You Calling a Bully? 2013. (ENG.). 34p. (J). pap. 14.95 *(978-1-4787-1703-4(3))* Outskirts Pr., Inc.
Preller, James. The Fall. 2015. (ENG.). 208p. (J). (gr. 4-9). 16.99 *(978-0-312-64301-0(2)*, 9780312643010) Feiwel & Friends.
Pride, Dana L. So How Is That a Bully? 2012. 200p. pap. 9.95 *(978-0-9852739-0-3(9))* Everlasting Publishing.
Prignano, Barbara. The Tiny Tomato & His Terrific Manners. Kalpart, illus. 2013. 32p. pap. 12.95 *(978-1-62857-080-9(6)*, Strategic Bk. Publishing) Strategic Book Publishing & Rights Agency (SBPRA).
Principe, Tami. The Green Rabbit: Rabbits Aren't Supposed to Be Green! 2012. 32p. pap. 10.95 *(978-1-4626-7509-8(3))* America Star Bks.
Prostko, Andrea. Strike One! 2010. 220p. pap. 13.95 *(978-1-60911-546-3(5)*, Eloquent Bks.) Strategic Book Publishing & Rights Agency (SBPRA).
Rad, Charles J. A Bus & Below. 2008. 96p. pap. 16.50 *(978-1-84753-871-0(1))* Lulu Pr., Inc.
Ramsey, Jo. Nail Polish & Feathers. 2016. (ENG., Illus.). (YA). (gr. 9-12). 24.99 **(978-1-63533-050-2(5))** 2013. 210p. pap. 14.99 *(978-1-62798-088-3(1))* Dreamspinner Pr. (Harmony Ink Pr.).
Rankin, Heather & Rankin, Heather. All It Takes Is One Friend. 2012. 46p. pap. *(978-0-9878945-0-2(1))* Our Farm Bks.
Ransom, Jeanie Franz. Big Red & the Little Bitty Wolf: A Tale about Bullies. Zivoin, Jennifer, illus. 2016. 32p. (J). *(978-1-4338-2048-9(X)*, Magination Pr.) American Psychological Assn.
Rateau, Loy. David's Prayers: A Boy's Perseverance of Conquering the Enemy. 2005. 17.00 *(978-0-8059-9834-4(9))* Dorrance Publishing Co., Inc.
Read, Sara. The Teenagers Guide to Self-Destruction. 2008. 92p. pap. 12.99 *(978-1-4343-6962-8(5))* AuthorHouse.
Reavis, Vicky 'A' Blevins. The Night Before Christmas. 2013. 72p. pap. 17.95 *(978-1-4241-2838-9(2))* America Star Bks.
Reed, Emma & Reed, Jennifer. Romeo's Rescue. Movshina, Marina, illus. 2012. 24p. pap. 10.95 *(978-1-61633-247-1(6))* Guardian Angel Publishing, Inc.
Reeves, Pamela. United We Stand, a Story about Two Bullies. LaGrange, Tiffany, illus. 2009. 24p. pap. 12.95 *(978-1-936051-36-6(2))* Peppertree Pr., The.
Renert, Gerry. Nathan & the Really Big Bully. Bradshaw, Carrie, illus. 2012. (ENG.). 32p. 16.95 *(978-1-62167-072-8(4)*, Raven Tree Pr.,Csi) Continental Sales, Inc.
Revell, Mike. Stonebird. 2016. (ENG.). 288p. (J). (gr. 5-9). pap. 9.99 *(978-1-68144-514-4(X))* Quercus NA.
Revenge of the Bully. 2014. (How to Beat the Bully Ser.). (ENG., Illus.). 288p. (J). (gr. 3-7). 17.99 *(978-1-4424-5677-8(9)*, Simon & Schuster/Paula Wiseman Bks.) Simon & Schuster/Paula Wiseman Bks.
Reynolds, Eleanor Davenport. Why Aren't You My Friend? the Story of Bullying, Diversity, & Friendship. 2nd ed. 2013. 140p. pap. 11.95 *(978-0-9882209-5-9(4))* Wyatt Hse. Publishing.
Reynolds, Wendy. Moby for Justice. 2006. 17.00 *(978-0-8059-8861-1(0))* Dorrance Publishing Co., Inc.
Richard, Ramonda. Robert the Bully. 2012. 28p. pap. 24.95 *(978-1-4626-7170-0(5))* America Star Bks.
Riggi, Samantha K. Wesley Reece: Fourth Grade Hero. 2011. 52p. (gr. 4-6). pap. 9.99 *(978-1-4634-1640-9(7))* AuthorHouse.
Rivers, Karen. The Girl in the Well Is Me. (ENG.). 224p. (J). (gr. 5-8). 2017. pap. 6.95 *(978-1-61620-696-3(9))* 2016. 16.95 *(978-1-61620-569-0(5))* Algonquin Bks. of Chapel Hill.
Roberts, Jeyn. When They Fade. 2016. (ENG.). 352p. (YA). (gr. 9). 17.99 *(978-0-385-75413-2(2)*, Knopf Bks. for Young Readers) Random Hse. Children's Bks.
Roberts, Willo Davis. The Kidnappers. 2016. (ENG., Illus.). 208p. (J). (gr. 3-7). pap. 6.99 *(978-1-4814-4904-5(4)*, Aladdin) Simon & Schuster Children's Publishing.
Rowe, W. W. Jerry's Madness. 2015. (ENG., Illus.). 98p. (J). (gr. 3-7). pap. 8.95 *(978-1-936012-68-8(5))* Larson Pubns.
Roytman, Arkady. How to Beat a Bully Sticker Activity Book. 2011. (Dover Little Activity Books Stickers Ser.). (ENG.). 4p. (J). (gr. -1-2). pap. 1.50 *(978-0-486-48187-6(5))* Dover Pubns., Inc.
Ruben, Pamela J. Don't Pick on Pepper! Take a Journey with Pepper as She Takes on a Schoolyard Bully with Brainpower, Humor, & a Dash of Spice! Ruben, Anthony R., ed. 2004. 31p. (J). 12.95 *(978-0-9764813-1-7(6))* Peppery Pr.
Ruby, Laura. Bad Apple. 2009. (ENG.). 256p. (YA). (gr. 8-18). 16.99 *(978-0-06-124330-1(2)*, HarperTeen) HarperCollins Pubs.
—Bone Gap. 368p. (YA). (gr. 9). 2016. pap. 9.99 *(978-0-06-231762-9(8))* 2015. (ENG.). 17.99 *(978-0-06-231760-5(1))* HarperCollins Pubs.
—Bone Gap. 2016. (YA). lib. bdg. 20.85 *(978-0-606-38739-2(0))* Turtleback Bks.
Rud, Jeff. Crossover, 1 vol. 2008. (Orca Sports Ser.). (ENG.). 176p. (YA). (gr. 6-10). pap. 9.95 *(978-1-55143-981-5(6))* Orca Bk. Pubs. USA.
Rue, Nancy. So Not Okay, 1 vol. 2014. (Mean Girl Makeover Ser.). (ENG.). 304p. (J). pap. 9.99 *(978-1-4003-2370-8(3))* Nelson, Thomas Inc.
—Sorry I'm Not Sorry: An Honest Look at Bullying from the Bully, 1 vol. 2015. (Mean Girl Makeover Ser.). (ENG.). 288p. (J). pap. 9.99 *(978-1-4003-2372-2(X))* Nelson, Thomas Inc.
—You Can't Sit with Us - Mean Girl Makeover, 1 vol. 2014. (Mean Girl Makeover Ser.). (ENG.). 224p. (J). pap. 9.99 *(978-1-4003-2371-5(1))* Nelson, Thomas Inc.
Ryan, Darlene. Responsible, 1 vol. 2007. (Orca Soundings Ser.). (ENG.). (YA). (gr. 8-12). 128p. pap. 9.95 *(978-1-55143-685-2(X))*; 112p. lib. bdg. 14.95 *(978-1-55143-687-6(6))* Orca Bk. Pubs. USA.
Rylander, Chris. The Fourth Stall. 2012. (Fourth Stall Ser.: 1). (ENG.). 336p. (J). (gr. 3-7). pap. 6.99 *(978-0-06-199497-5(9)*, Waldon Pond Pr.) HarperCollins Pubs.
Saigeon, Lori. Fight for Justice, 1 vol. 2009. (ENG.). 128p. (J). (gr. 3-6). pap. 7.95 *(978-1-55050-405-7(3))* Coteau Bks. CAN. Dist: Orca Bk. Pubs. USA.
Sanchez, Lorrie Christel & Blank, Carol. Virgil: The Bully from Cyberspace. Margolis, Al, illus. 2013. 54p. (J). 20.99 *(978-0-9891338-0-7(X))* Utterly Global.
—Virgil: The Bully from Cyberspace Teacher Edition. Margolis, Al, illus. 2013. 88p. 99.00 *(978-0-9891338-1-4(8))* Utterly Global.
Sauceda, Vickie. Doobie Kind & Mean Gene. 2013. 22p. pap. 9.99 *(978-1-62697-509-5(4))* Salem Author Services.
Sauer, Tammi. Ginny Louise & the School Field Day. Munsinger, Lynn, illus. 2016. (ENG.). 32p. (J). (gr. -1-k). 16.99 *(978-1-4847-3044-7(5))* Disney Pr.
—Ginny Louise & the School Showdown. Munsinger, Lynn, illus. 2015. (ENG.). 32p. (J). (gr. -1-k). 16.99 *(978-1-4231-6853-9(4))* Disney Pr.
Sazaklis, John. The Dangers of Dog Walking. Robinson, Lee, illus. 2016. (Billy Burger, Model Citizen Ser.). (ENG.). 96p. (gr. 2-3). lib. bdg. 22.65 *(978-1-4965-2587-1(6))* Stone Arch Bks.
Scelsa, Kate. Fans of the Impossible Life. 2015. (ENG.). 368p. (YA). (gr. 9). 17.99 *(978-0-06-233175-5(2))* HarperCollins Pubs.
Schizas, Lea. Bubba & Giganto: Odds Against Us. 2008. 68p. (J). pap. *(978-0-9797513-6-3(5))* 4RV Publishing, LLC.
Schmatz, Pat. Mousetraps. Hauser, Bill, illus. 2008. (ENG.). 192p. (YA). (gr. 7-12). 17.95 *(978-0-8225-8657-9(6)*, Carolrhoda Bks.) Lerner Publishing Group.
Schmitt, Sarah. It's a Wonderful Death. 2015. (ENG.). 320p. (J). (gr. 6). 17.99 *(978-1-63450-173-6(X)*, Sky Pony Pr.) Skyhorse Publishing Co., Inc.
Schneider, Rosemary. Bully Paws. 2011. 40p. pap. 18.46 *(978-1-4567-6294-0(X))* AuthorHouse.
Schraff, Anne. I Am Underdog. 2014. (Red Rhino Ser.). (J). lib. bdg. 18.40 *(978-0-606-36198-9(7))* Turtleback Bks.
—Vengeance, 1 vol. unabr. ed. 2012. (Urban Underground Ser.). (ENG.). 204p. (YA). (gr. 9-12). pap. 9.95 *(978-1-61651-961-2(4))* Saddleback Educational Publishing, Inc.
Schraff, Anne E. Vengeance. 2012. (Urban Underground — Cesar Chavez High School Ser.: 29). (YA). lib. bdg. 20.80 *(978-0-606-26599-7(6)*, Turtleback) Turtleback Bks.
Schulz, Charles M., creator. Peanuts: Be Brave: Peanuts Wisdom to Carry You Through. 2013. (ENG., Illus.). 72p. (J). (gr. -1-17). 7.95 *(978-0-7624-4861-6(X)*, Running Pr. Kids) Running Pr. Bk. Pubs.
Schwab, Victoria. Second Chances. 2014. (Everyday Angel Ser.: 2). (ENG.). 208p. (J). (gr. 3-7). pap. 6.99 *(978-0-545-52847-4(X)*, Scholastic Paperbacks) Scholastic, Inc.
Scott-Coleman, Brenda. The Girl with Many Faces. 2012. 40p. pap. 20.99 *(978-1-4772-8409-4(5))* AuthorHouse.
Scott, Ladena Mae. Bossy Rossy. 2013. 36p. pap. 18.41 *(978-1-4669-8965-8(3))* Trafford Publishing.
Scruggs, Sheldon. Tyler: The Strongest Boy on the Block. 2012. 140p. pap. 12.95 *(978-1-4575-1355-8(2))* Dog Ear Publishing, LLC.
Seyforth, Edward L. A Horribly Frightening Deception, 1 vol. 2009. 75p. pap. 19.95 *(978-1-61546-260-5(0))* America Star Bks.
Sheehan, Nikki. Swan Boy. 2016. (ENG.). 240p. (gr. 3-8). pap. 10.99 *(978-1-78074-924-2(4))* Oneworld Pubns. GBR. Dist: Publishers Group West (PGW).
ShelFish. Dots Dots Polka Dots, 1 vol. 2010. 46p. 24.95 *(978-1-4512-1427-7(8))* PublishAmerica, Inc.
Sher, Emil. Young Man with Camera. Wyman, David, photos by. 2015. (ENG., Illus.). 240p. (J). (gr. 7). 17.99 *(978-0-545-54131-2(X)*, Levine, Arthur A. Bks.) Scholastic, Inc.
Simon, Coco. Alexis Gets Frosted. (Cupcake Diaries: 12). (ENG., Illus.). 160p. (J). (gr. 3-7). 2014. 17.99 *(978-1-4424-9612-5(6))* 2013. pap. 6.99 *(978-1-4424-6867-2(X))* Simon Spotlight. (Simon Spotlight).
—Alexis Gets Frosted. 2013. (Cupcake Diaries: 12). lib. bdg. 17.20 *(978-0-606-27026-7(4)*, Turtleback) Turtleback Bks.
Simone, Kriss. Fairy Forest. 2007. 86p. pap. 7.78 *(978-1-84799-156-0(4))* Lulu Pr., Inc.
Simukka, Salla. As Red As Blood. Witesman, Owen Frederick, tr. from FIN. 2017. (As Red As Blood Ser.: 1). (ENG.). 256p. (J). (gr. 9). 17.99 *(978-1-5247-1341-6(4)*, Crown Books For Young Readers) Random Hse. Children's Bks.
Slater, Teddy. Patty & the Pink Princesses. Springer, Sally, illus. 2007. (J). pap. *(978-0-439-89707-5(6))* Scholastic, Inc.
Slater, Teddy & Harraid-Pilz, Marilee. Here Comes Smelly Nellie. 2007. (No Bullies Allowed Ser.). (Illus.). (J). *(978-0-439-89705-1(X))* Scholastic, Inc.
—Jake's Secret. 2007. (Illus.). (J). *(978-0-439-89708-2(4))* Scholastic, Inc.
Slater, Teddy & Springer, Sally. Trouble for Trudy. 2007. (No Bullies Allowed Ser.). (Illus.). (J). *(978-0-439-89709-9(2))* Scholastic, Inc.
Sledge-Yancy, Barbara. The Red Haired Hare. 2011. 40p. pap. 17.49 *(978-1-4568-6647-1(8))* Xlibris Corp.
Smith, Clyde. The Bashful Bull of Buchanan County. 2012. 24p. pap. 24.95 *(978-1-4626-8111-2(5))* America Star Bks.
Smith, Clyde R. The Bully of Glendale Pond. Perin, Pauline, illus. 2012. 24p. (-18). pap. 24.95 *(978-1-4626-7795-5(9))* America Star Bks.
Smith, Dawn K. The Hulk of Cranberry Lake: Don't Be a Bully. 2012. 24p. pap. 12.45 *(978-1-4497-6614-6(5)*, WestBow Pr.) Author Solutions, Inc.
Smith, James. The Wonderer of Time. 2006. 52p. pap. 16.95 *(978-1-4241-3316-1(5))* PublishAmerica, Inc.
Snyder, Karen Lee. Loony Lori. 2012. (ENG.). 28p. (J). pap. 14.95 *(978-1-4787-1799-7(8))* Outskirts Pr., Inc.
Sonnenblick, Jordan. The Secret Sheriff of Sixth Grade. 2017. (ENG.). 208p. (J). (gr. 4-7). 16.99 **(978-0-545-86320-9(1)**, Scholastic Pr.) Scholastic, Inc.
Somson, Bob. The Juice Box Bully: Empowering Kids to Stand up for Others. 2010. (ENG., Illus.). 32p. (J). (gr. k-5). pap. 10.95 *(978-1-933916-72-9(9))* Early Learning Foundation, LLC.
Sosa, Cynthia. Sebastian, the Small Trunk Elephant. 2013. 32p. pap. 13.00 *(978-1-62516-622-7(2)*, Strategic Bk. Publishing) Strategic Book Publishing & Rights Agency (SBPRA).
Spears, Kat. The Boy Who Killed Grant Parker. 2016. (ENG.). 320p. (YA). 18.99 *(978-1-250-08886-4(0)*, 9781250088864, St. Martin's Griffin) St. Martin's Pr.
Staake, Bob. Bluebird. Staake, Bob, illus. 2013. (ENG., Illus.). 40p. (J). (gr. -1-3). 17.99 *(978-0-375-87037-8(7)*, Schwartz & Wade Bks.) Random Hse. Children's Bks.
Standiford, Natalie. The Only Girl in School. 2016. (ENG.). 224p. (J). (gr. 3-7). 16.99 *(978-0-545-82996-0(8)*, Scholastic Pr.) Scholastic, Inc.
Stanley, Betty J. The Dupree Family Says No to Bullying. 2012. 56p. pap. 24.99 *(978-1-4772-9663-9(8))* AuthorHouse.
Starkey, Scott. The Call of the Bully. 2013. (How to Beat the Bully Ser.). (ENG.). 272p. (J). (gr. 3-7). 15.99 *(978-1-4424-5674-7(4)*, Simon & Schuster/Paula Wiseman Bks.) Simon & Schuster/Paula Wiseman Bks.
Staunton, Ted. Ace's Basement, 1 vol. 2013. (Orca Currents Ser.). (ENG.). 112p. (J). (gr. 5-9). pap. 9.95 *(978-1-4598-0437-1(6))*; lib. bdg. 16.95 *(978-1-4598-0438-8(4))* Orca Bk. Pubs. USA.
Ster, Caroline Rose. Face 2 Face. Jones, Emily, illus. 2011. 110p. (J). pap. 16.95 *(978-1-61660-002-0(0))* Reflections Publishing, Inc.
Stevens, Gary J. If I Called You a Hippopotamus! Stead, April-Nicole, illus. 2010. 24p. pap. 11.50 *(978-1-60911-280-6(6)*, Eloquent Bks.) Strategic Book Publishing & Rights Agency (SBPRA).
Stevenson, Robin. Attitude, 1 vol. 2013. (Orca Limelights Ser.). (ENG.). 144p. (J). (gr. 6-9). pap. 9.95 *(978-1-4598-0382-4(5))* Orca Bk. Pubs. USA.
Stewart, H. E. Walrus's Gift, 1 vol. 2011. (ENG.). 32p. (J). (gr. -1-3). 18.00 *(978-0-9693852-7-1(7))* Tudor Hse. GBR. Dist: Orca Bk. Pubs. USA.
Stick & Stone. 2016. *(978-0-545-93814-3(7))* Weston Woods Studios, Inc.
Sticks Stones & Stumped. 2006. (Illus.). 26p. (J). 19.95 *(978-0-9773738-0-2(0))* Bryson Taylor Publishing.
Stine, R. L. Rotten School - Dudes, the School Is Haunted! Park, Trip, illus. 2009. (Rotten School Ser.: No. 7). 128p. (J). pap. 4.99 *(978-0-06-078820-9(6)*, Harper Trophy) HarperCollins Pubs.
Stokes, Paula. This Is How It Happened. 2017. 384p. (YA). (gr. 8). 17.99 *(978-0-06-237993-1(3)*, HarperTeen) HarperCollins Pubs.
Stoudemire, Amar'e. Home Court. 2012. (STAT: Standing Tall & Talented Ser.: 1). lib. bdg. 16.00 *(978-0-606-26169-2(9)*, Turtleback) Turtleback Bks.
Struyk-Bonn, Chris. Nice Girls Endure. 2016. (ENG.). 256p. (gr. 9-12). 16.95 *(978-1-63079-047-9(8))* Switch Pr.
StVil, Lola. Girls Like Me. 2016. (ENG.). 320p. (YA). (gr. 7). 17.99 *(978-0-544-70674-3(9)*, HMH Books For Young Readers) Houghton Mifflin Harcourt Publishing Co.
Suen, Anastasia. New Girl: An Up2U Character Education Adventure, 1 vol. Dippold, Jane, illus. 2013. (Up2U Adventures Ser.). (ENG.). 80p. (J). (gr. 2-5). lib. bdg. 27.07 *(978-1-61641-968-4(7)*, Calico Chapter Bks) Magic Wagon.
Suen, Anastasia & Maddox, Jake. BMX Bully, 1 vol. Tiffany, Sean, illus. 2006. (Jake Maddox Sports Stories Ser.). (ENG.). 72p. (gr. 2-3). pap. 5.95 *(978-1-59889-236-9(3))* Stone Arch Bks.
Sulkowski, Jennifer Suzanne. A Pony Named Napoleon. 2013. 74p. 30.95 *(978-1-59299-979-8(4))*; pap. 22.95 *(978-1-59299-978-1(6))* Inkwater Pr.
Sullivan, Ayn Cates. Sparkle & the Light. duCray, Belle Crow, illus. 2013. (ENG.). (J). (gr. 1-4). 19.99 *(978-0-9884537-0-8(3))* Infinite Light Publishing.
Sullivan, Kevin & Goldman, Leslie. Anne & the Bully. 2010. (Anne of Green Gables for Young Readers Ser.). (ENG.). 64p. (J). (gr. 2-4). pap. 4.95 *(978-0-9736803-8-6(5))* Davenport Pr. CAN. Dist: Independent Pubs. Group.
Summers, Courtney. All the Rage. (ENG.). 336p. (YA). 2016. pap. 10.99 *(978-1-250-06915-3(7)*, 9781250069153) 2015. (gr. 9-13). 18.99 *(978-1-250-02191-5(X)*, 9781250021915) St. Martin's Pr. (St. Martin's Griffin).
Sunderland, Margot & Hancock, Nicky. A Wibble Called Bipley (And a Few Honks), 2 vols. Armstrong, Nicky, tr. Armstrong, Nicky, illus. 2010. (Helping Children with Feelings Ser.). (ENG.). 40p. (C). pap. 15.95 *(978-0-86388-494-8(6)*, Y329775, Routledge) Taylor & Francis Group GBR. Dist: Taylor & Francis Group.
Taylor, Chet. Last, but Not Least. 2007. (Illus.). 20p. (J). per. 11.99 *(978-0-9797574-8-8(7))* Dragonfly Publishing, Inc.
Teague, Monica. Diary of a Teenager in Junior High. 2011. 32p. pap. 16.95 *(978-1-4560-8552-0(2))* America Star Bks.
Temple, Mary V. How Jedaiah Changed Junk-Food-Nation-Land. 2011. 40p. pap. 20.76 *(978-1-4634-4102-9(9))* AuthorHouse.
Terrian, Michael W. Chalie's Brand New Coat. 2011. 24p. pap. 12.50 *(978-1-4670-3858-4(X))* AuthorHouse.
Terry, Judith A. Why Bully Me? 2012. 16p. pap. 17.99 *(978-1-4685-7392-3(6))* AuthorHouse.
Thaler, Mike. The Bully from the Black Lagoon. Lee, Jared, illus. (J). 2008. (ENG.). 32p. (gr. -1-3). pap. 3.99 *(978-0-545-06521-4(6)*, Cartwheel Bks.) 2004. *(978-0-439-68072-1(7))* Scholastic, Inc.
—The Bully from the Black Lagoon, 1 vol. Lee, Jared, illus. 2012. (Black Lagoon Set 2 Ser.: No. 2). (ENG.). 32p. (J). (gr. 1-4). lib. bdg. 24.21 *(978-1-59961-953-8(9))* Spotlight.
The Equality Of Genders Project. Billy Conquers the Bully. 2009. 16p. pap. 8.49 *(978-1-4389-5376-2(3))* AuthorHouse.
Thomas, Leah. Because You'll Never Meet Me. (ENG.). (YA). 2017. 368p. pap. 9.99 *(978-1-68119-021-1(4)*, 9781681190211) 2015. 352p. (gr. 9-12). 17.99 *(978-1-61963-590-6(9)*, 9781619635906) Bloomsbury Publishing USA. (Bloomsbury USA Childrens).
—Because You'll Never Meet Me. 2017. (YA). lib. bdg. 20.85 **(978-0-606-40347-4(7))** Turtleback Bks.
Thompson, Holly. Falling into the Dragon's Mouth. Huynh, Matt, illus. 2016. (ENG.). 352p. (J). 17.99 *(978-1-62779-134-2(5)*, 9781627791342, Holt, Henry & Co. Bks. For Young Readers) Holt, Henry & Co.
—Orchards. 2012. (ENG.). 336p. (YA). (gr. 7). pap. 9.99 *(978-0-385-73978-8(8)*, Ember) Random Hse. Children's Bks.
The Tiger's Stripes & the Water Buffalo's Teeth. 2010. 40p. 19.57 *(978-1-4269-3110-9(7))* Trafford Publishing.
Tilley. Damaged. 2011. (ENG.). 260p. (gr. 9-13). pap. 11.95 *(978-988-18967-0-4(3))* Haven Bks.
Tobias, Anne B. Harry Meets a Bully. Tobias, Tom, illus. 2008. 16p. pap. 9.95 *(978-0-9822540-3-5(2))* Peppertree Pr., The.
Todesco, Angelique. The Way of the Pendant. 2007. 196p. pap. 19.95 *(978-1-84753-846-8(0))* Lulu Pr., Inc.
Toews, Rita. The Bully: A Discussion & Activity Story. Ljungberg, Jon, illus. 2011. 40p. (J). pap. 11.95 *(978-1-59850-102-5(X))* Youthlight, Inc.
Tokarz, Brenda. Curious Jane's: A Balloon Adventure. 2012. (ENG.). (J). pap. 9.95 *(978-1-4507-7092-7(4))* Independent Pub.
Tougas, Shelley. A Patron Saint for Junior Bridesmaids. 2016. (ENG.). 272p. (J). 16.99 *(978-1-62672-403-7(2)*, 9781626724037) Roaring Brook Pr.
Toz, Karen Pokras. Millicent Marie Is Not My Name. 2012. (ENG.). (J). 162p. pap. 7.99 *(978-0-9848608-5-2(1))*; 2nd ed. mass mkt. 8.99 **(978-0-9962843-4-9(6))** Grand Daisy Pr.
Tracey, Andrée. Buddies NOT Bullies Rule! 2016. (Dover Coloring Bks.). (ENG.). 32p. (J). (gr. k-3). pap. 3.99 *(978-0-486-80148-3(9))* Dover Pubns., Inc.
Tutu, Desmond. Desmond & the Very Mean Word. Ford, A. G., illus. 2012. (ENG.). 32p. (J). (gr. 1-4). 15.99 *(978-0-7636-5229-6(6))* Candlewick Pr.
Usher, Carolyn. Chip Takes Off. 2013. (ENG.). 167p. (YA). pap. 8.95 *(978-1-4787-1637-2(1))* Outskirts Pr., Inc.
Vagner, Bohdanka. Bullying, Change, Friendship & Trust. Montgomerie, Genevieve, illus. 2013. 106p. pap. *(978-1-921883-51-4(0)*, MBS Pr.) Pick-a-Woo Woo Pubs.
Valdez-Moore, Pura J. Tippy the Special Star. 2008. 24p. pap. 24.95 *(978-1-4241-9943-3(3))* America Star Bks.
Van Dusen, Ross, illus. Crocka Dog in the Evil Forest. 2015. (J). *(978-1-936744-54-1(6)*, Rio Grande Bks.) LPD Pr.
—How Crocka Dog Came to Be. 2015. (J). *(978-1-936744-39-8(2))* LPD Pr.
VanDenberg, Saidat. Tadias & the Pitbully Tree. 2012. 36p. pap. 21.99 *(978-1-4797-0172-8(6))* Xlibris Corp.
Vandygrift, Wendy. Lilly Lamoo & the Stray Gray Hair: A Book about Bad Hair, Bullies & Being Your Best. 2011. 24p. (J). 16.95 *(978-1-4327-7109-6(4))* Outskirts Pr., Inc.
Vergo, Franny. Jonathan Ray & His Superhero Pack: Be Bully-Free. 2012. 44p. pap. 18.50 *(978-1-4772-4558-3(8))* AuthorHouse.
Vernon, Ursula. Dragonbreath. 2012. (Dragonbreath Ser.: 1). lib. bdg. 17.20 *(978-0-606-26665-9(8)*, Turtleback) Turtleback Bks.
Vicente, Alidis. The Shameless Shenanigans of Mister Malo / Las Terribles Travesuras de Mister Malo: The Mister Malo Series / Serie Mister Malo. 2017. (ENG & SPA.). 115p. (J). (gr. 4-8). pap. 9.95 **(978-1-55885-853-4(9)**, Piñata Books) Arte Publico Pr.
Vogel, Peter C. Mike Duffy & His Adventure Witht the World's Smallest Person. 2008. 112p. pap. 9.95 *(978-1-59526-796-2(4)*, Llumina Pr.) Aeon Publishing Inc.
Vrabel, Beth. Pack of Dorks. (Pack of Dorks Ser.). (ENG.). 240p. (J). (gr. 2-7). 2015. pap. 7.99 *(978-1-5107-0179-3(6))* 2014. 15.95 *(978-1-62914-623-2(4))* Skyhorse Publishing Co., Inc. (Sky Pony Pr.).
Walker, Rachael. Angel Starlight & the Wish Book. 2006. 204p. per. *(978-1-905529-52-0(X))* Grosvenor Hse. Publishing Ltd.
Wallace, Jason. Out of Shadows. 2012. (ENG., Illus.). 272p. (J). (gr. 10). pap. 8.95 *(978-0-8234-2436-8(7))* Holiday Hse., Inc.
Wallace, Nancy K. Presumed Missing, 1 vol. Chronister, Amanda, illus. 2013. (Abby & the Book Bunch Ser.). (ENG.). 80p. (J). (gr. 2-5). 27.07 *(978-1-61641-917-2(2))* Magic Wagon.
Walters, Eric & Williams, Jerome. Triple Threat, 1 vol. 2004. (Orca Young Readers Ser.). (ENG., Illus.). 144p. (J). (gr. 3-6). pap. 6.95 *(978-1-55143-359-2(1))* Orca Bk. Pubs. USA.
Walton, Evangeline. The Misadventures of Rufus & Misha: Two Dogs Who Are Smart Enough to Go to School. 2013. 24p. pap. 14.93 *(978-1-4669-9970-1(5))* Trafford Publishing.
Wark, L. A. Tuffy Tufferson Is a Bully. 2012. 36p. pap. 14.50 *(978-1-4669-1066-9(6))* Trafford Publishing.
Warner, Sally. EllRay Jakes Is a Rock Star, 2 vols. Harper, Jamie, illus. 2012. (EllRay Jakes Ser.: 2). (ENG.). 128p. (J). (gr. 1-3). 5.99 *(978-0-14-241989-2(3)*, Puffin Books) Penguin Young Readers Group.
—EllRay Jakes Is Not a Chicken, 1 vol. Harper, Jamie, illus. 2012. (EllRay Jakes Ser.: 1). (ENG.). 128p. (J). (gr. 1-3). 5.99 *(978-0-14-241988-5(5)*, Puffin Books) Penguin Young Readers Group.
—Super Emma. Harper, Jamie, illus. 2008. (Emma Ser.). (ENG.). 112p. (J). (gr. 3-7). 5.99 *(978-0-14-241088-2(8)*, Puffin Books) Penguin Young Readers Group.
Washington, Angel D. Always Remember You Are Loved: When a Child Seeks Guidance on Cyber & Peer Bullying. Perry, Curtis, illus. 2012. 40p. pap. 9.95 *(978-0-9860041-1-7(1))* Angel's Diary.
Washington, Kathleen. The School Bully. 2006. 9.00 *(978-0-8059-8201-5(9))* Dorrance Publishing Co., Inc.
Watkins, Greg. A Big Beaked, Big Bellied Bird Named Bill. Watkins, Greg, illus. 2005. (Illus.). 30p. 13.95 *(978-0-9761318-1-6(1)*, 1239651) Cute & Cuddly Productions, Inc.
Watts, Jan. Zipline. 2010. 94p. pap. 25.50 *(978-1-4452-6040-2(9))* Lulu Pr., Inc.
Webb, Dave. Barkley Rules. 2011. 148p. pap. 9.99 *(978-1-4575-0607-9(6))* Dog Ear Publishing, LLC.
Webb Quest, Sara. Aydil Vice & Her Disgustin' Hair Knots. 2008. 72p. pap. 7.00 *(978-1-4357-5150-7(7))* Lulu Pr., Inc.
Weber, Lori. Picture Me, 1 vol. 2013. (ENG.). 168p. (YA). (gr. 8-12). pap. 12.95 *(978-1-4594-0510-3(2)*, 9781459405103) Lorimer, James & Co., Ltd., Pubs. CAN. Dist: Casemate Pubs. & Bk. Distributors, LLC.
Weeks, Sarah & Varadarajan, Gita. Save Me a Seat. 2016. (ENG.). 240p. (J). (gr. 3-7). 16.99 *(978-0-545-84660-8(9)*, Scholastic Pr.) Scholastic, Inc.
Weinberger, Justin. Reformed. 2017. (ENG.). 208p. (J). (gr. 3-7). 16.99 *(978-0-545-90252-6(5)*, Scholastic Pr.) Scholastic, Inc.
Wells, Rosemary. Felix Stands Tall. Wells, Rosemary, illus. 2015. (ENG., Illus.). 32p. (J). (gr. k-3). 14.99 *(978-0-7636-6111-3(2))* Candlewick Pr.

—Stella's Starliner. Wells, Rosemary, illus. 2014. (ENG., Illus.). 32p. (J). (gr. -1-3). 15.99 *(978-0-7636-1495-9(5))* Candlewick Pr.

Welvaert, Scott R. The 13th Floor. 2015. (ENG., Illus.). 96p. (J). *(978-1-63235-056-5(4))* Pr. Room Editions LLC.

Wheiler, Robert. Wink's , Boo, & Who! 2012. 64p. pap. 13.49 *(978-1-105-49858-9(1))* Lulu Pr., Inc.

White, Tara. I Like Who I Am, 1 vol. 2010. (ENG., Illus.). 44p. pap. 12.95 *(978-1-894778-63-3(4))* Theytus Bks., Ltd. CAN. Dist: Univ. of Toronto Pr.

Wiggins, Thalia. Greg & the Cheat Sheets, 1 vol. Tate, Don, illus. 2012. (Making Choices: the Mcnair Cousins Ser.). (ENG.). 64p. 27.07 *(978-1-61641-630-0(0),* Calico Chapter Bks) Magic Wagon.

Wilde, Jeanne Wilkins. Two Dogs Long & Half a Dog High. 2013. 20p. pap. 15.99 *(978-1-4817-0594-3(6))* AuthorHouse.

Wilhelm, Hans. Noodles & the Bully. 2012. (Illus.). (J). *(978-0-545-34499-9(9))* Scholastic, Inc.

Wilkenstanley, Ellen. Berryville Bully. 2011. 24p. pap. 11.50 *(978-1-61204-527-6(8),* Strategic Bk. Publishing) Strategic Book Publishing & Rights Agency (SBPRA).

Williams, Felisha. I'm No Bully, Am I? 2012. 24p. (-18). pap. 15.99 *(978-1-4797-0973-1(5))* Xlibris Corp.

—The Milk Chocolate Kid. 2012. 24p. (-18). pap. 15.99 *(978-1-4797-0971-7(9))* Xlibris Corp.

Williams, Rachel. Alex & the Bully. 2006. (Illus.). 88p. pap. *(978-1-84401-651-8(X))* Athena Pr.

Williamson, Pam. Sweet & Sour Milk. 2011. 24p. pap. 12.79 *(978-1-4634-0725-4(4))* AuthorHouse.

Willink, Jocko. Way of the Warrior Kid: From Wimpy to Warrior the Navy SEAL Way. Bozak, Jon, illus. 2017. (Way of the Warrior Kid Ser.: 1). (ENG.). 192p. (J). 13.99 ***(978-1-250-15107-0(4),*** 9781250151070) Feiwel & Friends.

Willis, Jeanne. Troll Stinks. Ross, Tony, illus. 2017. (Andersen Press Picture Bks.). (ENG.). 32p. (gr. -1-3). 35.99 ***(978-1-5124-3964-9(9))*** Lerner Publishing Group.

Wilson, Jacqueline. Monster Eyeballs. Lewis, Stephen, illus. 2nd ed. 2016. (Reading Ladder Ser.). (ENG.). 48p. (J). (gr. k-2). pap. 7.99 *(978-1-4052-8199-7(5))* Egmont Bks., Ltd. GBR. Dist: Independent Pubs. Group.

Winerip, Michael. Adam Canfield Watch Your Back! 2009. (Adam Canfield of the Slash Ser.: 2). (ENG., Illus.). 352p. (J). (gr. 3-7). 7.99 *(978-0-7636-4412-3(9))* Candlewick Pr.

Winkler, Henry & Oliver, Lin. The Life of Me (Enter at Your Own Risk) 2008. (Hank Zipzer Ser.: No. 14). (Illus.). 186p. (gr. 3-7). 16.00 *(978-0-7569-8819-7(5))* Perfection Learning Corp.

—Zero to Hero. 2012. (Ghost Buddy Ser.: 1). (ENG.). 176p. (J). (gr. 3-7). pap. 5.99 *(978-0-545-29882-7(2),* Scholastic Paperbacks) Scholastic, Inc.

Wisdom, Gail Ann. Trouble with Bullies. 2013. 48p. pap. 20.45 *(978-1-4908-0026-4(3),* WestBow Pr.) Author Solutions, Inc.

Wishinsky, Frieda. Camp Disaster. 2016. (Orca Currents Ser.). lib. bdg. 20.80 *(978-0-606-38697-5(1))* Turtleback Bks.

—Dimples Delight. Laliberete, Louise-Andree, illus. 2005. (SPA.). 61p. (J). lib. bdg. 20.00 *(978-1-4242-1252-1(9))* Fitzgerald Bks.

—Dimples Delight, 1 vol. Laliberté, Louise-Andrée, illus. 2005. (Orca Echoes Ser.). (ENG.). 64p. (J). (gr. 2-3). per. 6.95 *(978-1-55143-362-2(1))* Orca Bk. Pubs. USA.

Wolf, Elaine. Camp: A Novel. 2015. (ENG.). 272p. (J). (gr. 6). pap. 9.99 *(978-1-63220-422-6(3),* Sky Pony Pr.) Skyhorse Publishing Co., Inc.

Wolk, Lauren. Wolf Hollow. 2016. (ENG.). 304p. (J). (gr. 5-7). 16.99 *(978-1-101-99482-5(7),* Dutton Books for Young Readers) Penguin Young Readers Group.

Wong, Janet S. & Wong, Janet G. Minn & Jake. Cote, Genevieve, illus. 2008. (ENG.). 160p. (J). (gr. 2-5). pap. 9.99 *(978-0-374-40021-7(0),* 9780374400217, Farrar, Straus & Giroux (BYR)) Farrar, Straus & Giroux.

Woods, Jeanne & Lugo, Patricia. Bonita Bones & the Halloween Surprise. 2012. 24p. pap. 17.99 *(978-1-4772-4103-5(5))* AuthorHouse.

Woodson, Jacqueline. Feathers. 2010. lib. bdg. 19.65 *(978-0-606-14654-8(7),* Turtleback) Turtleback Bks.

Woodson, Vera. Lady Bug, Beetle Boy, & Friends: Bullies Be Gone! 2013. (ENG., Illus.). (J). 14.95 *(978-1-62086-049-6(X))* Mascot Bks., Inc.

Yang, Gene Luen. Animal Crackers: A Gene Luen Yang Collection. 2012. (ENG., Illus.). 216p. (YA). pap. 14.95 *(978-1-59362-183-4(3),* 9781593621834) Slave Labor Bks.

Yatscoff, Edward R. Archie's Gold. 2013. 200p. pap. *(978-0-9869678-7-0(4))* Yatscoff, Edward R.

Young, Suzanne. All in Pieces. 2016. (ENG., Illus.). 272p. (YA). (gr. 9). 17.99 *(978-1-4814-1883-6(1),* Simon Pulse) Simon Pulse.

Zorn, Claire. Protected. 2017. (ENG.). 288p. (YA). (gr. 6-12). 17.99 ***(978-1-4926-5213-7(X))*** Sourcebooks, Inc.

50 Cent Staff. Playground. Akana, Lizzi, illus. 2012. (ENG.). 320p. (YA). (gr. 7). pap. 9.99 *(978-1-59514-478-2(1),* Razorbill) Penguin Young Readers Group.

BULLION

see Gold; Money; Silver

BUMPPO, NATTY (FICTITIOUS CHARACTER)—FICTION

Cooper, James Fenimore. The Last of the Mohicans. Wyeth, N. C., illus. 2013. (Scribner Classics Ser.). (ENG.). 368p. (J). (gr. 5). 24.99 *(978-1-4424-8130-5(7),* Atheneum Bks. for Young Readers) Simon & Schuster Children's Publishing.

BUNNICULA (FICTITIOUS CHARACTER)—FICTION

Howe, James. Harold & Chester Stories. Date not set. (Bunnicula & Friends Ser.). (J). (gr. k-3). *(978-0-688-10298-2(0));* lib. bdg. *(978-0-688-10299-9(9))* HarperCollins Pubs.

—Howliday Inn. unabr. ed. 2004. (Bunnicula Ser.). 195p. (J). (gr. 3-7). pap. 29.00 incl. audio *(978-0-8072-8382-0(7),* YA179SP, Listening Library) Random Hse. Audio Publishing Group.

—Nighty-Nightmare. unabr. ed. 2004. (Bunnicula Ser.). 128p. (J). (gr. 3-7). pap. 29.00 incl. audio *(978-0-8072-8397-4(5),* YA201SP, Listening Library) Random Hse. Audio Publishing Group.

BUNYAN, JOHN, 1628-1688

Barr, Gladys H. The Tinker's Armor: The Story of John Bunyan. Hutchinson, William, illus. 2011. 176p. 42.95 *(978-1-258-05498-4(1))* Literary Licensing, LLC.

Edwards, Andrew & Thornton, Fleur. John Bunyan: The Story of How a Hooligan & Soldier Became a Preacher, Prisoner & Famous Writer. 2005. (Footsteps of the Past Ser.). (Illus.). 32p. (J). (gr. -1-7). pap. 5.00 *(978-1-903087-81-7(3))* DayOne Pubns. GBR. Dist: Send The Light Distribution LLC.

BUNYAN, PAUL (LEGENDARY CHARACTER)

Blair, Eric. Paul Bunyan, 1 vol. Robledo, Sol, tr. from ENG. Chambers-Goldberg, Micah, illus. 2006. (Read-It! Readers en Español: Cuentos Exagerados Ser.).Tr. of Paul Bunyan. (SPA.). 32p. (gr. k-3). 21.32 *(978-1-4048-1657-2(7),* Easy Readers) Picture Window Bks.

Furgang, Kathy. Paul Bunyan & Paul Bunyan (Spanish) 6 English, 6 Spanish Adaptations. 2011. (ENG & SPA.). (J). 75.00 net. *(978-1-4108-5640-1(2))* Benchmark Education Co.

—Paul Bunyan (Spanish) Set Of 6. 2011. (SPA.). (J). 38.00 net. *(978-1-4108-4823-9(X))* Benchmark Education Co.

Gleeson, Brian. Paul Bunyan, 1 vol. Meyerowitz, Rick, illus. 2004. (Rabbit Ears-A Classic Tale Ser.). (ENG.). 40p. (gr. k-5). 25.65 *(978-1-59197-767-4(3))* Spotlight.

Kellogg, Steven. Paul Bunyan. Kellogg, Steven, illus. 20th anniv. ed. 2004. (ENG., Illus.). 48p. (J). (gr. -1-3). pap. 6.99 *(978-0-688-05800-5(0))* HarperCollins Pubs.

—Paul Bunyan. 2004. (J). (gr. k-3). 17.20 *(978-0-8085-6790-5(X),* Turtleback) Turtleback Bks.

Krensky, Stephen. Paul Bunyan. 2008. pap. 40.95 *(978-0-8225-9295-2(9))* Lerner Publishing Group.

McCaslin, Nellie. Paul Bunyan: Lumberjack. 2003. (Players Press Nellie McCaslin Ser.). 55p. (Orig.). (J). (gr. 1-6). pap. 5.00 *(978-0-88734-477-0(1))* Players Pr., Inc.

McDonnell, Julia. The Legend of Paul Bunyan. 2017. (Famous Legends Ser.). 32p. (J). (gr. 2-3). pap. 10.50 ***(978-1-5382-0376-7(6))*** Stevens, Gareth Publishing LLLP.

BURGLARS

see Robbers and Outlaws

BURIAL

see Cemeteries; Funeral Rites and Ceremonies; Mounds and Mound Builders

BURIED CITIES

see Extinct Cities

BURIED TREASURE

Addario, Yvonne. Treasure Diving with Captain Dom - Special Archival Section: Special Archival Section. 2007. (ENG., Illus.). 56p. (YA). per. 15.99 *(978-0-9743414-1-5(X))* Adventure in Discovery.

Barber, Nicola. Tomb Explorers, 1 vol. 2013. (Treasure Hunters Ser.). (ENG.). 48p. (gr. 5-8). pap. 9.25 *(978-1-4109-4962-2(1));* lib. bdg. 29.99 *(978-1-4109-4955-4(9))* Heinemann-Raintree.

Bearce, Stephanie. Top Secret Files: Pirates & Buried Treasure: Secrets, Strange Tales, & Hidden Facts about Pirates. rev. ed. 2015. (Top Secret Files of History Ser.: 0). (ENG., Illus.). 125p. (J). (gr. 4-7). pap. 8.95 *(978-1-61821-421-8(7))* Prufrock Pr.

Brezina, Corona. Treasure Hunters. 2009. (Extreme Careers Ser.). 64p. (gr. 5-5). 58.50 *(978-1-61512-415-2(2),* Rosen Reference) Rosen Publishing Group, Inc., The.

Butts, Ed. X Doesn't Mark the Spot: Tales of Pirate Gold, Buried Treasure, & Lost Riches. 2008. (ENG., Illus.). 88p. (J). (gr. 5-18). pap. 12.95 *(978-0-88776-808-8(3),* Tundra Bks.) Tundra Bks. CAN. Dist: Penguin Random Hse. LLC.

Callery, Sean. Treasure Hunt. 2011. (ENG.). 24p. (J). pap. *(978-0-7787-7874-5(6));* (gr. 3-6). *(978-0-7787-7852-3(5))* Crabtree Publishing Co.

Claybourne, A. & Young, Charles A. Treasure Hunting. 2004. (Illus.). 96p. (YA). (gr. 5-18). lib. bdg. 22.95 *(978-1-58086-163-2(6))* EDC Publishing.

Eggleton, Jill. Treasures. 2007. (Connectors Ser.). (gr. 2-5). pap. *(978-1-877453-17-5(X))* Global Education Systems Ltd.

Fuhr, Ute & Sautai, Raoul. Let's Look for Lost Treasure. 2012. (ENG., Illus.). 38p. (J). (gr. k-3). pap. 11.99 *(978-1-85103-291-4(6))* Moonlight Publishing, Ltd. GBR. Dist: Independent Pubs. Group.

Hunter, Nick. Ancient Treasures, 1 vol. 2013. (Treasure Hunters Ser.). (ENG., Illus.). 48p. (gr. 5-8). pap. 9.25 *(978-1-4109-4957-8(5));* lib. bdg. 29.99 *(978-1-4109-4950-9(8))* Heinemann-Raintree.

—Pirate Treasure, 1 vol. 2013. (Treasure Hunters Ser.). (ENG., Illus.). 48p. (gr. 5-8). pap. 9.25 *(978-1-4109-4960-8(5));* lib. bdg. 29.99 *(978-1-4109-4953-0(2))* Heinemann-Raintree.

—Shipwrecks, 1 vol. 2013. (Treasure Hunters Ser.). (ENG.). 48p. (gr. 5-8). pap. 9.25 *(978-1-4109-4961-5(3));* lib. bdg. 29.99 *(978-1-4109-4954-7(0))* Heinemann-Raintree.

Hunter, Nick, et al. Treasure Hunters. 2013. (Treasure Hunters Ser.). (ENG.). 48p. (gr. 5-8). pap. 53.94 *(978-1-4109-4963-9(X));* lib. bdg. 179.94 *(978-1-4109-4956-1(7))* Heinemann-Raintree.

Jameson, W. C. Atlantic Coast: Legends of Sunken Pirate Treasures, Mysterious Caches, & Jinxed Ships, from Maine to Florida. 2006. (Buried Treasure Ser.). (ENG.). 192p. (J). (gr. 4-17). pap. 14.95 *(978-0-87483-484-0(8))* August Hse. Pubs., Inc.

—Buried Treasures of New England. 2005. (Buried Treasure Ser.). (ENG.). 192p. (J). (gr. 4-17). pap. 11.95 *(978-0-87483-485-7(6))* August Hse. Pubs., Inc.

—Buried Treasures of the Mid-Atlantic States: Legends of Island Treasure, Jewelry Caches & Secret Tunnels. 2006. (Buried Treasure Ser.). (ENG., Illus.). 192p. (J). (gr. 4-17). pap. 14.95 *(978-0-87483-531-1(3))* August Hse. Pubs., Inc.

Kerrigan, Juliet. Underwater Treasure. 2016. (ENG.). 32p. (J). (gr. 2-3). pap. 8.95 *(978-0-00-816384-6(7))* HarperCollins Pubs. Ltd. GBR. Dist: Independent Pubs. Group.

Lamb, Lee. Oak Island Family: The Restall Hunt for Buried Treasure. 2012. (ENG., Illus.). 136p. (YA). pap. 19.99 *(978-1-4597-0342-1(1))* Dundurn CAN. Dist: Ingram Publisher Services.

—Oak Island Family: The Restall Hunt for Buried Treasure (Large Print 16pt) 2013. 204p. pap. *(978-1-4596-6324-4(1))* ReadHowYouWant.com, Ltd.

Leonard, Barry, ed. Treasure Trove of an Ancient Egyptian Child. 2005. (Illus.). 24p. (J). (gr. 4-8). 27.00 *(978-0-7567-8939-8(7))* DIANE Publishing Co.

Liu-Perkins, Christine. At Home in Her Tomb: Lady Dai & the Ancient Chinese Treasures of Mawangdui. Brannen, Sarah S., illus. 2014. (ENG.). 80p. (J). (gr. 4-7). lib. bdg. 19.95 *(978-1-58089-370-1(8))* Charlesbridge Publishing, Inc.

—At Home in Her Tomb: Lady Dai & the Ancient Chinese Treasures of Mawangdui. 2014. 80p. pap. 19.95 *(978-1-60734-615-9(X))* Charlesbridge Publishing, Inc.

Malam, John. Buried Treasure. 2009. (Amazing History Ser.). (Illus.). 32p. (J). (gr. 2-6). pap. 7.95 *(978-1-59920-208-2(5))* Black Rabbit Bks.

Matsen, Bradford. The Incredible Search for the Treasure Ship Atocha. 2003. (Incredible Deep-Sea Adventures Ser.). (Illus.). 48p. (J). lib. bdg. 25.27 *(978-0-7660-2193-8(9))* Enslow Pubs., Inc.

Mazurkiewicz, Jessica. Treasure Hunt. 2009. (Dover Little Activity Bks.). (ENG.). 64p. (J). (gr. k-3). pap., act. bk. ed. 1.99 *(978-0-486-47042-9(3))* Dover Pubns., Inc.

McCune, Susan. The Treasure Map, 01 vols., 1. 2016. (Rosen REAL Readers: Social Studies Nonfiction / Fiction: Family, Community, & the World Ser.). (ENG.). 8p. (J). pap. 5.46 *(978-1-5081-1881-7(7),* Rosen Classroom) Rosen Publishing Group, Inc., The.

Meissner, David & Richardson, Kim. Call of the Klondike: A True Gold Rush Adventure. 2013. (ENG., Illus.). 168p. (J). (gr. 4). 16.95 *(978-1-59078-823-3(0),* Calkins Creek) Boyds Mills Pr.

Nilsen, Anna. Pirates Galore: The Biggest Treasure Hunt Ever! 2008. (ENG., Illus.). 32p. (J). (gr. 2-7). pap. 8.99 *(978-1-921049-97-2(9))* Little Hare Bks. AUS. Dist: Independent Pubs. Group.

O'Brien, Cynthia. Lost Treasures. 2015. (ENG.). 32p. (J). *(978-0-7787-8071-7(6))* Crabtree Publishing Co.

Owen, James A. & Owen, Jeremy. Lost Treasures of the Pirates of the Caribbean. Owen, James A., illus. 2011. (ENG., Illus.). 32p. (J). (gr. 3-7). pap. 16.99 *(978-1-4424-3093-8(1),* Simon & Schuster Bks. For Young Readers) Simon & Schuster Bks. For Young Readers.

Peters, Gregory N. Looking for Lost Treasure, 1 vol. 2014. (Real World Adventures Ser.). (ENG.). 48p. (gr. 4-12). 31.99 *(978-1-4765-8471-3(0))* Capstone Press of Coughlan Cos.

Red Bird Press Staff. Secret Spex Treasure Hunt. 2004. (Secret Picture Search Ser.). 18p. (J). pap. 5.95 *(978-1-902626-66-6(4))* Red Bird Publishing GBR. Dist: Weatherhill, Inc.

Redmond, Shirley Raye. The Oak Island Treasure Pit. 2011. (Mysterious Encounters Ser.). 48p. lib. bdg. 29.00 *(978-0-7377-5140-6(1),* Kidhaven) Cengage Gale.

Roytman, Arkady. Treasures of King Tut's Tomb Stained Glass Coloring Book. 2009. (Dover Stained Glass Coloring Book Ser.). (ENG., Illus.). 32p. (J). (gr. -1-5). pap. 6.99 *(978-0-486-46996-6(4))* Dover Pubns., Inc.

Schwartz, Alvin. Gold & Silver, Silver & Gold: Tales of Hidden Treasure. Christiana, David, illus. 2009. (ENG.). 144p. (J). (gr. 4-8). pap. 15.99 *(978-0-374-42582-1(5),* 9780374425821, Farrar, Straus & Giroux (BYR)) Farrar, Straus & Giroux.

Scott, Caitlin. Treasure Hunting: Looking for Lost Riches. 2016. (High Five Reading - Red Ser.). (ENG.). 48p. (gr. 3-4). pap. 9.39 *(978-1-5157-3687-5(3),* High Five Reading (RBL)) Capstone Press of Coughlan Cos.

Silverberg, Robert A. Treasures Beneath the Sea. 2003. 90p. pap. 29.00 *(978-0-7581-0537-0(1))* Textbook Pubs.

Spilsbury, Louise. Coastal Treasure Hunter. 2010. (ENG.). 32p. (J). *(978-0-7787-9907-8(7));* pap. *(978-0-7787-9928-3(X))* Crabtree Publishing Co.

Stadther, Michael. 101 New Puzzles Clues, Maps, Tantalizing Tales: And Stories of Real Treasure. Stadther, Michael, illus. 2006. (Treasure's Trove Ser.). (ENG., Illus.). 112p. (J). pap. 12.99 *(978-1-4169-2655-9(0))* Treasure Trove, Inc.

Stephens, David R. Treasure Hunters. 2013. (Discovery Education: Sensational True Stories Ser.). (ENG., Illus.). 32p. (J). (gr. 3-6). pap. 10.00 *(978-1-4777-0101-0(X));* lib. bdg. 25.25 *(978-1-4777-0058-7(7))* Rosen Publishing Group, Inc., The. (PowerKids Pr.).

Stilton, Geronimo. The Search for Sunken Treasure. 2006. (Geronimo Stilton Ser.: No. 25). (ENG., Illus.). 128p. (J). (gr. 2-5). pap. 7.99 *(978-0-439-84116-0(X),* Scholastic Paperbacks) Scholastic, Inc.

Tucker, Rosalyn. Pirate Treasure. 2015. (Pirates Ahoy! Ser.). (ENG.). 24p. (gr. k-1). lib. bdg. 26.65 *(978-1-4914-2114-7(2),* Pebble Plus) Capstone Press of Coughlan Cos.

Walsh, Liza Gardner. Treasure Hunters Handbook. 2014. (ENG., Illus.). 112p. (J). (gr. k-7). 16.95 *(978-1-60893-278-8(8))* Down East Bks.

Whelon, Chuck. Treasure Hunter Activity Book. 2011. (Dover Children's Activity Bks.). (ENG., Illus.). 48p. (J). (gr. 2-5). pap. 4.99 *(978-0-486-47878-4(5))* Dover Pubns., Inc.

White, Graham. A Maze Adventure: Search for Pirate Treasure. 2009. (ENG., Illus.). 32p. (J). (gr. 4-7). pap. 8.95 *(978-1-4263-0459-0(5),* National Geographic Children's Bks.) National Geographic Society.

BURIED TREASURE—FICTION

Abdo, Kenny. Triple Take, 1 vol. Doucet, Bob, illus. 2013. (Haven't Got a Clue! Ser.). (ENG.). 80p. (J). (gr. 3-6). lib. bdg. 27.07 *(978-1-61641-955-4(5),* Calico Chapter Bks) Magic Wagon.

Aguilar, Jose. Jovenes piratas/Youngs Pirates. 2008. 36p. *(978-84-934160-7-2(X))* Atalante.

Allende, Isabel. Kingdom of the Golden Dragon. 2009. (City of the Beasts Ser.: Bk. 2).Tr. of Reino del Dragón de Oro. (ENG.). 480p. pap. 14.99 *(978-0-06-182512-5(3),* Harper Perennial) HarperCollins Pubs.

Amato, Carol J. The Lost Treasure of the Golden Sun. 2005. 172p. (J). *(978-0-9713756-3-5(1))* Stargazer Publishing Co.

Anderson, Janet. The Last Treasure. 2004. (ENG.). 272p. (J). (gr. 3-7). 8.99 *(978-0-14-240217-7(6),* Puffin Books) Penguin Young Readers Group.

Anderson, John David. The Dungeoneers. 2015. (ENG.). 448p. (J). (gr. 3-7). 16.99 *(978-0-06-233814-3(5),* Walden Pond Pr.) HarperCollins Pubs.

Anderson, Scoular. Pirate Treasure. Anderson, Scoular, illus. 2009. (Get Set Readers Ser.). (Illus.). 32p. (J). (gr. -1-2). lib. bdg. 22.60 *(978-1-60754-266-7(8))* Windmill Bks.

Angstrom, Gwen R. The Eemlets & Grandma Eema Stories, Book 1: From Rainbow to Sunshine. 2006. 67p. pap. 16.95 *(978-1-4241-1257-9(5))* PublishAmerica, Inc.

Armstrong, Ashley Sage-Taylor. The Adventures of Starlight & Sunny: I Am Me! Who Are You?, How to Find Good Quality Friends & Stand up for One Another, with Positive Morals, Pi. 2013. 52p. pap. *(978-1-927863-00-8(7))* Armstrong, Ashley.

Awdry, W. Legend of the Lost Treasure. 2015. (Little Golden Book Ser.). (ENG., Illus.). 24p. (J). (-k). 4.99 *(978-0-553-52074-3(1),* Golden Bks.) Random Hse. Children's Bks.

—Sodor's Legend of the Lost Treasure. 2015. (Big Golden Book Ser.). (ENG., Illus.). 32p. (J). (gr. -1-2). 9.99 *(978-0-553-52076-7(8),* Golden Bks.) Random Hse. Children's Bks.

Barbie. Barbie Fall Movie Sliding Tab. 2015. (Barbie Movie Tie-In Ser.: 1). (ENG.). 12p. (J). (gr. -1-1). bds. 10.99 *(978-0-7944-3529-5(7))* Studio Fun International.

Barbo, Maria S. Treasure Hunt, 1 vol. 2013. (Scooby-Doo! Picture Clue Bks.). (ENG.). 24p. (J). (gr. -1-1). lib. bdg. 24.21 *(978-1-61479-040-2(X),* Essential Library) ABDO Publishing Co.

Bateson, Maggie. My Pirate Adventure: A Pop-up & Play Book. Eaves, Ed, illus. 2008. (ENG.). 20p. (J). (gr. 4-7). 23.50 *(978-0-230-53036-2(2),* Macmillan) Pan Macmillan GBR. Dist: Trans-Atlantic Pubns., Inc.

Batson, Wayne Thomas. Isle of Fire, 1 vol. 2009. (ENG.). 352p. pap. 9.99 *(978-1-4003-1512-3(3))* Nelson, Thomas Inc.

—Isle of Swords, 1 vol. 2008. (ENG.). 352p. pap. 9.99 *(978-1-4003-1363-1(5))* Nelson, Thomas Inc.

Beeson, Jan. Mysterious World of the Puffins the Treasure Hunt Book 1. 2013. 74p. pap. 19.99 *(978-0-9890482-0-0(9))* Beeson, Jan.

Beil, Michael D. The Red Blazer Girls: the Secret Cellar. 2012. (Red Blazer Girls Ser.). (ENG., Illus.). 288p. (J). (gr. 5). 17.99 *(978-0-375-86741-5(4),* Knopf Bks. for Young Readers) Random Hse. Children's Bks.

—The Secret Cellar. 2013. (Red Blazer Girls Ser.). (ENG., Illus.). 288p. (J). (gr. 5). pap. 8.99 *(978-0-375-86495-7(4),* Yearling) Random Hse. Children's Bks.

Bell, Lindzi. Sherlock Times Three, 1 vol. 2009. 62p. pap. 19.95 *(978-1-61582-028-3(0))* America Star Bks.

Benton, Lynne. Pirate Pete. Chapman, Neil, illus. 2008. (Tadpoles Ser.). (ENG.). 24p. (J). (gr. -1-3). pap. *(978-0-7787-3892-3(2))* Crabtree Publishing Co.

Berenstain, Stan & Berenstain, Jan. The Berenstain Bears' Seashore Treasure. Berenstain, Jan, illus. 2005. (I Can Read Level 1 Ser.). (ENG., Illus.). 32p. (J). (gr. k-3). pap. 3.99 *(978-0-06-058341-5(X))* HarperCollins Pubs.

Bessen, Luc. Arthur & the Minimoys. Sowchek, Ellen, tr. from FRE. 2005. (ENG.). 240p. (J). 15.99 *(978-0-06-059623-1(6))* HarperCollins Pubs.

Besson, Luc. Arthur & the Forbidden City. Sowchek, Ellen, tr. 2006. (ENG., Illus.). 192p. (J). (gr. 3-7). pap., pap. 5.99 *(978-0-06-059628-6(7),* Harper Trophy) HarperCollins Pubs.

—Arthur & the Forbidden City. 2005. (ENG., Illus.). 192p. (J). 15.99 *(978-0-06-059626-2(0))* HarperCollins Pubs.

—Arthur & the Minimoys. 2005. (Illus.). 240p. (J). lib. bdg. 16.89 *(978-0-06-059624-8(4))* HarperCollins Pubs.

Bleu, Kennedy. Cotter Otter in Treasure Water. Goembel, Ponder, illus. 2014. (ENG.). 24p. (J). pap. 24.95 *(978-1-63004-814-3(3))* America Star Bks.

Bloom, Suzanne. Treasure. 2012. (Goose & Bear Stories Ser.). (ENG.). 32p. (J). (gr. -1-1). pap. 7.95 *(978-1-59078-920-9(2))* Boyds Mills Pr.

Blum, Alex A., et al. Treasure Island. 2015. (Classics Illustrated Ser.: 21). (ENG., Illus.). 48p. pap. 9.95 *(978-1-906814-47-2(3))* Classic Comic Store, Ltd. GBR. Dist: Casemate Pubs. & Bk. Distributors, LLC.

Blyton, Enid. The Ship of Adventure. Cobb, Rebecca, illus. unabr. ed. 2014. (Adventure Ser.: 6). (ENG.). 288p. (J). (gr. 4-7). pap. 9.99 *(978-1-4472-6280-0(8))* Pan Macmillan GBR. Dist: Independent Pubs. Group.

Bodeen, S. A. Found. 2017. (Shipwreck Island Ser.: 4). (ENG.). 160p. (J). 16.99 *(978-1-250-02783-2(7),* 9781250027832) Feiwel & Friends.

Bondanella Filutze, Ann M. On Gramma's Rocker: Animal Tales & Other Short Stories. 2013. 84p. pap. 27.95 *(978-1-4624-0498-8(7),* Inspiring Voices) Author Solutions, Inc.

Bostick, B. k. Huber Hill & the Brotherhood of Coronado. 2012. 14.99 *(978-1-59955-981-0(1))* Cedar Fort, Inc./CFI Distribution.

—Huber Hill & the Dead Man's Treasure. 2011. (J). *(978-1-59955-911-7(0),* Bonneville Bks.) Cedar Fort, Inc./CFI Distribution.

Broadhurst, Sherree. Bella Finds the Hidden Treasure. 2009. 28p. pap. 12.25 *(978-1-60693-815-7(0),* Eloquent Bks.) Strategic Book Publishing & Rights Agency (SBPRA).

Brown, Jeff. Flat Stanley & the Lost Treasure. Pamintuan, Macky, illus. 2016. (I Can Read Level 2 Ser.). 32p. (J). (gr. -1-3). pap. 3.99 *(978-0-06-236595-8(9))* HarperCollins Pubs.

—Flat Stanley & the Lost Treasure. 2016. (Flat Stanley: I Can Read Ser.). (J). lib. bdg. 13.55 *(978-0-606-38757-6(9))* Turtleback Bks.

Bryant, Jen. Kaleidoscope Eyes. 2010. (ENG.). 272p. (J). (gr. 3-7). 7.99 *(978-0-440-42190-0(X),* Yearling) Random Hse. Children's Bks.

Bucky Badger A Children's Story: Treasure. 2005. (J). 9.99 *(978-0-9765510-2-7(0))* Badgerland Bks. LLC.

Butterworth, Nick. The Treasure Hunt. Butterworth, Nick, illus. 2011. (Tales from Percy's Park Ser.). (ENG., Illus.). 32p. (J). (gr. k-2). pap. 11.00 *(978-0-00-715517-0(4),* HarperCollins Children's Bks.) HarperCollins Pubs. Ltd. GBR. Dist: HarperCollins Pubs.

Campbell, Julie. The Secret of the Mansion. Stevens, Mary, illus. 2003. (Trixie Belden Ser.: No. 1). (ENG.). 272p. (J). (gr. 3-7). 6.99 *(978-0-375-82412-8(X),* Random Hse. Bks. for Young Readers) Random Hse. Children's Bks.

Campos, Llanos & Campos Martinez, Llanos. The Treasure of Barracuda. Sardà, Júlia, illus. 2016. (ENG.). 156p. (J). (gr. 3-7). 15.95 *(978-1-939775-14-6(0))* March 4th, Inc.

Candlewick Press, Candlewick. Peppa Pig & the Treasure Hunt. 2015. (Peppa Pig Ser.). (ENG.). 32p. (J). (-k). 12.99 *(978-0-7636-7703-9(5),* Candlewick Entertainment) Candlewick Pr.

Candlewick Press Editors. Peppa Pig & the Treasure Hunt. 2016. (Peppa Pig Ser.). lib. bdg. 16.00 *(978-0-606-37936-6(3))* Turtleback Bks.

Carris, Joan D. A Ghost of a Chance. 2003. (Legends of the Carolinas Ser.). 155p. (J). 8.95 *(978-1-928556-40-4(X))* Coastal Carolina Pr.

Chalfoun, Michelle. The Treasure of Maria Mamoun. 2016. (ENG.). 352p. (J). 16.99 *(978-0-374-30340-2(1)*, 9780374303402, Farrar, Straus & Giroux (BYR)) Farrar, Straus & Giroux.

Chase, L. P. Elliott Stone & the Mystery of the Backyard Treasure. 2008. 122p. (J). pap. 11.95 *(978-0-7414-4804-0(1))* Infinity Publishing.

Chedru, Delphine. What Happens When... 2013. (ENG., Illus.). 32p. (J). (gr. k-2). 15.95 *(978-1-84976-103-1(5))* Tate Publishing, Ltd. GBR. Dist: Abrams, Inc.

Cheshire, Simon. The Treasure of Dead Man's Lane & Other Case Files: Saxby Smart, Private Detective: Book 2. Alley, R. W., illus. 2011. (Saxby Smart, Private Detective Ser.: 2). (ENG.). 224p. (J). (gr. 3-7). pap. 8.99 *(978-0-312-67434-2(1)*, 9780312674342) Square Fish.

Chin, Oliver. Baltazar & the Flying Pirates. Roth, Justin, illus. 2009. (ENG.). 36p. (J). (gr. -1-3). 15.95 *(978-1-59702-018-3(4))* Immedium.

Coerr, Eleanor. Mieko & the Fifth Treasure. 2003. (ENG., Illus.). 80p. (J). (gr. 4-7). 5.99 *(978-0-698-11990-1(8)*, Puffin Books) Penguin Young Readers Group.

Collard, Sneed B., III. Double Eagle, 1 vol. 2011. (ENG.). 256p. pap. 7.95 *(978-1-56145-599-7(7)*, Peachtree Junior) Peachtree Pubs.

Collingwood, Harry. The Castaways. 2008. 172p. 25.95 *(978-1-60664-710-3(5))*; pap. 13.95 *(978-1-60664-209-2(X))* Rodgers, Alan Bks.

—The Cruise of The 'Esmeralda' 2009. 220p. pap. 15.95 *(978-1-60664-391-4(6))* Rodgers, Alan Bks.

—The Strange Adventures of Eric Blackburn. 2008. 164p. 25.95 *(978-1-60664-711-0(3))* Rodgers, Alan Bks.

Condon, Bill. Riley & the Treasure. Hopgood, Andrew, illus. 2015. (Legends in Their Own Lunchbox Ser.). (ENG.). 56p. (gr. 2-3). pap. 7.99 *(978-1-4966-0258-9(7)*, Legends in Their Own Lunchbox) Capstone Classroom.

Cosson, M. J. The Pirate, Big Fist, & Me, 1 vol. Garvey, Brann, illus. 2006. (Vortex Bks.). (ENG.). 112p. (gr. 2-3). 26.65 *(978-1-59889-068-6(9)*, Vortex Bks.) Stone Arch Bks.

Coulton, Mia. Pirate Fish. Coulton, Mia, photos by. 2007. (ENG., Illus.). pap. 5.35 *(978-1-933624-15-0(9))* Maryruth Bks., Inc.

Cowell, Cressida. How to Be a Pirate. 2010. (ENG., Illus.). 240p. (J). pap. *(978-0-340-99908-0(X)*, Hodder Children's Books) Hachette Children's Group GBR. Dist: Hachette Bk. Group.

—How to Be a Pirate. (How to Train Your Dragon Ser.: 2). (ENG.). (J). (gr. 3-7). 2010. 240p. pap. 8.99 *(978-0-316-08528-1(6))* 2005. (Illus.). 224p. 13.99 *(978-0-316-15598-4(5))* Little, Brown Bks. for Young Readers.

—How to Seize a Dragon's Jewel. 2014. (How to Train Your Dragon Ser.: 10). (ENG., Illus.). 416p. (J). (gr. 3-7). pap. 8.00 *(978-0-316-24408-4(2))* Little, Brown Bks. for Young Readers.

Dadey, Debbie. Treasure in Trident City. Avakyan, Tatevik, illus. 2014. (Mermaid Tales Ser.: 8). (ENG.). 128p. (J). (gr. 1-4). pap. 5.99 *(978-1-4424-8266-1(4)*, Aladdin) Simon & Schuster Children's Publishing.

Dadey, Debby & Dadey, Debbie. Treasure in Trident City, 1 vol., Bk. 8. 2015. (Mermaid Tales Ser.). (ENG.). 120p. (J). (gr. 2-4). 24.21 *(978-1-61479-329-8(8)*, Spotlight) ABDO Publishing Co.

Dale, Penny. Dinosaur Pirates! Dale, Penny, illus. 2017. (ENG., Illus.). 32p. (J). (-k). 15.99 *(978-0-7636-9330-5(8)*, Nosy Crow) Candlewick Pr.

Davies, Linda. Longbow Girl. 2016. (ENG.). 336p. (J). (gr. 7). 17.99 *(978-0-545-85345-3(1)*, Chicken Hse., The) Scholastic, Inc.

Day, Jan. Pirate Pink & Treasures of the Reef, 1 vol. Mason, Janeen, illus. 2003. (ENG.). 32p. (J). (gr. k-3). 16.99 *(978-1-58980-086-1(9))* Pelican Publishing Co., Inc.

Dean, James. Pete the Cat & the Treasure Map. Dean, James, illus. 2017. (Pete the Cat Ser.). (Illus.). 24p. (J). (gr. -1-3). pap. 4.99 *(978-0-06-240441-1(5)*, HarperFestival) HarperCollins Pubs.

DeMuth, Robert R. Grandpa's Treasures. 2006. (ENG., Illus.). 22p. (J). (gr. 2-4). pap. *(978-1-933255-20-0(X))* DNA Pr.

Deshpande, Shashi. 3 Novels. 2006. 379p. *(978-0-14-333511-5(1)*, Puffin) Penguin Publishing Group.

Desrosiers, Sylvie. Mais Qui Va Trouver le Tresor? 2003. (Roman Jeunesse Ser.). (FRE.). 96p. (YA). (gr. 4-7). pap. *(978-2-89021-175-9(4))* Diffusion du livre Mirabel (DLM).

Dorman, Brandon. Pirates of the Sea! Dorman, Brandon, illus. 2011. (ENG., Illus.). 32p. (J). (gr. -1-3). 16.99 *(978-0-06-204068-8(5)*, Greenwillow Bks.) HarperCollins Pubs.

Dower, Laura. Sunny & the Secret Passage. 2013. (Palace Puppies Ser.: 4). (J). lib. bdg. 14.75 *(978-0-606-35108-9(6)*, Turtleback) Turtleback Bks.

Dubisch, Mike, illus. The Haunted Cabin Mystery. 2009. (Boxcar Children Graphic Novels Ser.: 9). (ENG.). 32p. (J). (gr. 1-5). pap. 6.99 *(978-0-8075-3180-8(4))* Whitman, Albert & Co.

Duddle, Jonny. The Jolley-Rogers & the Monster's Gold. Duddle, Jonny, illus. 2017. (ENG., Illus.). 160p. (J). (gr. 1-4). pap. 6.99 *(978-0-7636-9292-6(1)*, Templar) Candlewick Pr.

—The Pirate Cruncher. Duddle, Jonny, illus. 2010. (ENG., Illus.). 38p. (J). (gr. -1-2). 15.99 *(978-0-7636-4876-3(0)*, Templar) Candlewick Pr.

Dunagan, Ted M. Secret of the Satilfa. 2010. (ENG.). 208p. (J). (gr. 3-18). 21.95 *(978-1-58838-249-8(4)*, NewSouth Bks.) NewSouth, Inc.

Durbin, Amanda. Tree Houses & Treasures. 2013. 24p. pap. 24.95 *(978-1-63004-353-7(2))* America Star Bks.

Edwards, Amelia. The Treasure Hunt, 1 vol. 2013. (Fiction Readers Ser.). (ENG., Illus.). 24p. (J). (gr. 2-2). pap. 6.99 *(978-1-4333-5522-6(1))* Shell Educational Publishing.

Emmett, Jonathan. The Treasure of Captain Claw. Cox, Steve, illus. 2012. (ENG.). 32p. (J). (gr. -1-k). pap. 9.99 *(978-1-84616-741-6(8))* Hodder & Stoughton GBR. Dist: Hachette Bk. Group.

Enderle, Dotti. Book 13: Yo Ho No!, 1 vol. 2014. (Ghost Detectors Set 3 Ser.). (ENG., Illus.). 80p. (J). (gr. 2-5). lib. bdg. 27.07 *(978-1-62402-001-8(1)*, Calico Chapter Bks) Magic Wagon.

—Hidden, 1 vol. Gentry, T. Kyle, illus. 2007. (ENG.). 104p. (J). (gr. 3-7). per. 8.95 *(978-1-58980-481-4(3))* Pelican Publishing Co., Inc.

Fairlie, Emily. The Lost Treasure of Tuckernuck. Caparo, Antonio Javier, illus. 2013. (Tuckernuck Mysteries Ser.: 1). (ENG.). 320p. (J). (gr. 3-7). pap. 6.99 *(978-0-06-211891-2(9)*, Tegen, Katherine Bks) HarperCollins Pubs.

Farber, E. S. Fish Finelli (Book 1) Seagulls Don't Eat Pickles. Beene, Jason, illus. 2014. (Fish Finelli Ser.). (ENG.). 168p. (J). (gr. 3-7). pap. 6.99 *(978-1-4521-2853-5(7))* Chronicle Bks. LLC.

Farber, Erica. Fish Finelli: Seagulls Don't Eat Pickles. Beene, Jason, illus. 2013. (Fish Finelli Ser.). (ENG.). 155p. (J). (gr. 2-5). 15.99 *(978-1-4521-0820-9(X))* Chronicle Bks. LLC.

Ferrone, John M. Gus & the Pirate Treasure. Ferrone, John M., illus. Date not set. (Illus.). 36p. (J). (gr. -1-5). pap. 16.95 *(978-1-928811-01-5(9))* Story Stuff, Inc.

Ficklin, Jonene H. Orinoco Intrigue. 2005. (YA). 14.95 *(978-0-9761188-1-7(5))* Victor's Crown Publishing.

Finotti, M. C. The Treasure of Amelia Island. 2008. (Florida Historical Fiction for Youth Ser.). (ENG., Illus.). 97p. (J). (gr. 3-7). 14.95 *(978-1-56164-416-2(1))* Pineapple Pr., Inc.

Finotti, M. C. & National Geographic Learning Staff. The Treasure of Amelia Island. 2012. (ENG.). 108p. (C). pap. 14.95 *(978-1-56164-536-7(2))* National Geographic School Publishing, Inc.

Fleischman, Sid. The Ghost in the Noonday Sun. Sís, Peter, illus. 2007. (ENG.). 256p. (J). (gr. 3-7). per. 5.99 *(978-0-06-134502-9(4)*, Greenwillow Bks.) HarperCollins Pubs.

Francis, Pauline, retold by. Treasure Island. 2010. (Essential Classics - Adventure Ser.). (Illus.). 48p. pap. *(978-0-237-54085-2(1))* Evans Brothers, Ltd.

Freedman, Claire. Pirates Love Underpants. Cort, Ben, illus. 2013. (Underpants Bks.). (ENG.). 32p. (J). (gr. -1-2). 17.99 *(978-1-4424-8512-9(4)*, Simon & Schuster/Paula Wiseman Bks.) Simon & Schuster/Paula Wiseman Bks.

Fuerst, Jeffrey B. & Benchmark Education Co., LLC. Robert Louis Stevenson's Treasure Island: My Sea Adventure Israel Hands. Hondru, Ovi, illus. 2014. (Text Connections Ser.). (J). (gr. 3). *(978-1-4509-9652-5(3))* Benchmark Education Co.

Gelsey, James. Scooby-Doo! & the Gruesome Goblin, 1 vol. 2013. (Scooby-Doo Mysteries Set 2 Ser.). (ENG.). 64p. (J). (gr. 3-6). lib. bdg. 24.21 *(978-1-61479-045-7(0))* ABDO Publishing Co.

—Scooby-Doo! & the Howling Wolfman, 1 vol. 2013. (Scooby-Doo Mysteries Set 2 Ser.). (ENG.). 64p. (J). (gr. 3-6). lib. bdg. 24.21 *(978-1-61479-046-4(9))* ABDO Publishing Co.

Gelsey, James & Duendes Del Sur Staff. Scooby-Doo & the Sunken Ship, 1 vol. 2011. (Scooby-Doo Mysteries Ser.). (ENG., Illus.). 64p. (J). (gr. 3-6). 24.21 *(978-1-59961-893-7(1))* Spotlight.

Gerwitz, Felice. Literature No. 3: Keys to the Past: Unlocked. 2003. (Truth Seeker's Mystery Ser.: 3). (YA). stu. ed., per. 6.50 *(978-1-931941-06-8(8))* Media Angels, Inc.

Gerwitz, Felice & Gerwitz, Christina. Keys to the Past: Unlocked, Vol. 3. 2003. (Truth Seeker's Mystery Ser.). (YA). per. 8.99 *(978-0-9700385-8-6(5))* Media Angels, Inc.

Ghani, Samna. The Shoe, the Necklace, & the Giant. Williams, Nancy E., ed. Cappoen, Jennifer Tipton, illus. 2012. 48p. (J). pap. 9.95 *(978-1-938526-18-3(X))* Roxby Media Ltd. GBR. Dist: Laurus Co., The.

Giff, Patricia Reilly. Hunter Moran Digs Deep. Sheban, Chris, illus. 2014. (ENG.). 160p. (J). (gr. 3-7). 16.95 *(978-0-8234-3165-6(7))* Holiday Hse., Inc.

Girard, Thomas. The Nameless Treasure. Girard, Thomas, illus. 2013. (Illus.). 58p. pap. *(978-0-9918736-0-9(2))* Bric-a-brac Bks.

Golden Books Staff. Pirate Pups! (Paw Patrol) Petrossi, Fabrizio, illus. 2016. (Little Golden Book Ser.). (ENG.). 24p. (J). (gr. -1-k). 4.99 *(978-0-553-53888-5(8)*, Golden Bks.) Random Hse. Children's Bks.

Gould, Susan Lynn. A Gift from Grandma. Verkruysse, Toni, illus. 2013. 56p. pap. 20.50 *(978-1-61897-230-9(8)*, Strategic Bk. Publishing) Strategic Book Publishing & Rights Agency (SBPRA).

Graphman, Wm. Matthew. Chel & Riley Adventures: The K9 Kidnapping Adventure. 2011. 80p. (gr. 4-6). pap. 9.99 *(978-1-4567-9574-0(0))* AuthorHouse.

Greene, Rhonda Gowler. No Pirates Allowed! Said Library Lou. Ajhar, Brian, illus. 2013. (ENG.). 40p. (J). (gr. 1-3). 15.95 *(978-1-58536-796-2(6)*, 202364) Sleeping Bear Pr.

Griffiths, Andy. Treasure Fever! 2008. (Schooling Around Ser.: No. 1). 198p. (J). pap. *(978-0-545-09222-7(1))* Scholastic, Inc.

Gutman, Dan. Mr. Burke Is Berserk! Paillot, Jim, illus. 2012. (My Weirder School Ser.: 4). 112p. (J). (gr. 1-5). (ENG.). pap. 4.99 *(978-0-06-196922-5(2))*; lib. bdg. 15.89 *(978-0-06-196923-2(0))* HarperCollins Pubs.

—Mr. Burke Is Berserk! 2012. (My Weirder School Ser.: 4). (J). lib. bdg. 14.75 *(978-0-606-23571-6(X)*, Turtleback) Turtleback Bks.

Haggard, H. Rider. King Solomon's Mines. Marcos, Pablo, illus. 2005. (Great Illustrated Classics Ser.). 239p. (J). (gr. 3-8). 21.35 *(978-1-59679-244-9(2)*, Abdo & Daughters) ABDO Publishing Co.

Hall, Kirsten. Buried Treasure: All about Using a Map. Luedecke, Bev, illus. 2003. (Beastieville Ser.). 32p. (J). 19.50 *(978-0-516-22894-5(3)*, Children's Pr.) Scholastic Library Publishing.

Harrison, Paula. The Lost Gold. 2013. (Rescue Princesses Ser.: 7). lib. bdg. 14.75 *(978-0-606-32374-1(0)*, Turtleback) Turtleback Bks.

Hergé. Red Rackham's Treasure. 2012. Orig. Title: Tresor de Rackham le Rouge. (ENG., Illus.). 64p. (J). (gr. 3-17). 60.00 *(978-0-316-23054-4(5))* Little, Brown Bks. for Young Readers.

—The Secret of the Unicorn. 2012. Orig. Title: Secret de la Licorne. (ENG., Illus.). 64p. (J). (gr. 3-17). 60.00 *(978-0-316-23055-1(3))* Little, Brown Bks. for Young Readers.

Hergé, et al. The Secret of the Unicorn. 2003. Orig. Title: Secret de la Licorne. (ENG.). 64p. *(978-1-4052-0810-9(4))* Egmont Bks., Ltd.

Hicks, Clifford B. Alvin Fernald's Incredible Buried Treasure. Bradfield, Roger, illus. 2009. (J). 17.95 *(978-1-930900-43-1(0))* Purple Hse. Pr.

—Alvin's Secret Code. Sokol, Bill, illus. 2015. (J). pap. 9.99 *(978-1-930900-85-1(6))* Purple Hse. Pr.

Higginson, Sheila Sweeny. Cubby's Mixed-Up Map. 2014. (Jake & the Never Land Pirates Ser.). (J). lib. bdg. 14.75 *(978-0-606-35262-8(7))* Turtleback Bks.

Hillan, Pamela & Dyan, Penelope. The Hidden Treasure at Dragon Lake. 2013. 112p. pap. 8.95 *(978-1-61477-101-2(4))* Bellissima Publishing, LLC.

Hobbs, Will. Leaving Protection. 2005. (ENG.). 192p. (J). (gr. 5-18). pap. 8.99 *(978-0-380-73312-5(9))* HarperCollins Pubs.

—Leaving Protection. 2005. 178p. (gr. 5-9). 19.00 *(978-0-7569-5121-4(6))* Perfection Learning Corp.

Hoena, Blake. Robert Louis Stevenson's Treasure Island, 1 vol. 2013. (Can You Survive? Ser.). (ENG.). 160p. (J). (gr. 4-6). pap. 8.95 *(978-0-9883662-6-8(6))* Lake 7 Creative, LLC.

Horsfall, S. J. Jodie & Lilly... & the Fake Mansion. 2009. 58p. pap. 7.50 *(978-0-557-12474-9(3))* Lulu Pr., Inc.

Hubbard, L. Ron, contrib. by. Tomb of the Ten Thousand Dead: Literature Guide for Teachers & Librarians Based on Common Core ELA Standards for Classrooms 6-9. 2013. (Stories from the Golden Age Ser.). (ENG.). 35p. (gr. 6-9). pap., tchr. ed. 14.95 *(978-1-61986-219-7(0))* Galaxy Pr., LLC.

Jacques, Brian. Doomwyte. 2010. (Redwall Ser.: 20). (ENG.). 368p. (J). (gr. 5). pap. 8.99 *(978-0-441-01778-2(9)*, Ace Bks.) Penguin Publishing Group.

—Doomwyte. Elliot, David, illus. 2011. (Redwall Ser.). (ENG.). 384p. (J). (gr. 5-18). 8.99 *(978-0-14-241853-6(6)*, Firebird) Penguin Young Readers Group.

Jakubowski, Michele. Mick's Buried Treasure. Pinelli, Amerigo, illus. 2016. (Sleuths of Somerville Ser.). (ENG.). 144p. (gr. 4-6). lib. bdg. 25.99 *(978-1-4965-3178-0(7))* Stone Arch Bks.

Jepson, Gill. Out of Time: The Secret of the Swan. 2011. (ENG.). 144p. pap. *(978-1-84876-612-9(2))* Troubador Publishing Ltd.

Johnson, Janet. The Last Great Adventure of the PB & J Society. 2016. (ENG.). 256p. (gr. 4-8). 12.95 *(978-1-62370-636-4(X))* Capstone Young Readers of Coughlan Cos.

The Jupiter Pirates - Curse of the Iris. 2014. (Jupiter Pirates Ser.: 2). (ENG.). 352p. (J). (gr. 3-7). 16.99 *(978-0-06-223023-2(9))* HarperCollins Pubs.

Keats, Israel. The Zephyr Conspiracy. 2017. (Level Up Ser.). (ENG.). (YA). (gr. 6-12). 120p. pap. 7.99 ***(978-1-5124-5361-4(7))***; lib. bdg. 26.65 ***(978-1-5124-3985-4(1))*** Lerner Publishing Group. (Darby Creek).

Keene, Carolyn. Secret of Shadow Ranch. 2015. (Nancy Drew Ser.: 5). (ENG.). 192p. (J). (gr. 3-7). 8.99 *(978-0-448-48905-6(8)*, Grosset & Dunlap) Penguin Young Readers Group.

Kelly, David A. The Wrigley Riddle. Meyers, Mark, illus. 2013. (Ballpark Mysteries Ser.: Bk. 6). (ENG.). 112p. (J). (gr. 1-4). pap. 4.99 *(978-0-307-97776-2(5)*, Random Hse. Bks. for Young Readers) Random Hse. Children's Bks.

—The Wrigley Riddle. 2013. (Ballpark Mysteries Ser.: Bk. 6). lib. bdg. 14.75 *(978-0-606-26998-8(3)*, Turtleback) Turtleback Bks.

Kelman, Marcy & Disney Book Group Staff. Trick or Treasure? Disney Storybook Artists Staff, illus. 2013. (ENG.). 24p. (J). (gr. -1-k). pap. 5.99 *(978-1-4231-7140-9(3))* Disney Pr.

Kendrick, Robert. Treasure Quest: Journey to the Jungle. 2004. (ENG.). 46p. 24.95 *(978-1-4137-1467-8(6))* PublishAmerica, Inc.

Kennedy Center Staff. Teddy Roosevelt & the Treasure of Ursa Major. Hoyt, Ard, illus. 2011. (ENG.). 128p. (J). (gr. 2-5). pap. 5.99 *(978-1-4169-4860-5(0)*, Simon & Schuster Bks. For Young Readers) Simon & Schuster Bks. For Young Readers.

Kidd, Rob. Jack Sparrow: The Siren Song. Orpinas, Jean-Paul, illus. 2006. 122p. (J). lib. bdg. 16.00 *(978-1-4242-1571-3(4))* Fitzgerald Bks.

Kimpton, Diana. Princess Ellie's Treasure Hunt No. 10. Finlay, Lizzie, illus. 10th ed. 2008. (ENG.). 96p. (gr. -1-3). pap. 3.99 *(978-1-4231-1414-7(0))* Hyperion Pr.

King, Trey. Deep Sea Treasure Dive. 2016. (LEGO City 8X8 Ser.). lib. bdg. 13.55 *(978-0-606-38106-2(6))* Turtleback Bks.

Kirby, Stan. Captain Awesome & the Mummy's Treasure. O'Connor, George, illus. 2015. (Captain Awesome Ser.: 15). (ENG.). 128p. (J). (gr. k-4). pap. 5.99 *(978-1-4814-4438-5(7)*, Little Simon) Little Simon.

Kositsky, Lynne. Minerva's Voyage. 2009. (ENG., Illus.). 240p. (YA). (gr. 6-18). pap. 10.99 *(978-1-55488-439-1(X)*, Dundurn Pr.) Dundurn CAN. Dist: Ingram Publisher Services.

Kruse, Donald W. Where's the Gold. Shipman, Josie, illus. 2012. 50p. pap. 12.95 *(978-1-59663-857-0(5)*, Castle Keep Pr.) Rock, James A. & Co. Pubs.

La Rose, Melinda & Ward, Kelly. Treasure of the Tides. 2014. (Illus.). (J). *(978-1-4844-3449-9(8))* Disney Publishing Worldwide.

Lacey, Josh. Island of Thieves. 2013. (ENG.). 240p. (J). (gr. 5-7). pap. 7.99 *(978-0-544-10485-3(4))* Houghton Mifflin Harcourt Publishing Co.

Lacey, Josh & Pakenham, Sarah. Island of Thieves. 2012. (ENG.). 240p. (J). (gr. 5-7). 15.99 *(978-0-547-76327-9(1))* Houghton Mifflin Harcourt Publishing Co.

Langridge, Roger. The Muppet Show Comic Book: The Treasure of Peg-Leg Wilson. Langridge, Roger, illus. 2010. (Muppet Show Ser.). (ENG., Illus.). 112p. (J). 24.99 *(978-1-60886-530-7(4))*; (gr. 4-7). pap. 9.99 *(978-1-60886-504-8(5))* Boom! Studios.

Lanthier, Jennifer. The Legend of the Lost Jewels. 2008. (ENG.). 240p. (J). (gr. 5-9). pap. 9.99 *(978-0-00-639161-6(3))* HarperCollins Pubs.

Lapidot, Gila. Shakel Shakelovitz Finds a Treasure. 2013. 40p. pap. *(978-965-550-200-8(7))* Contento De Semrik.

Larose, Melinda. Treasure of the Tides. 2014. (Jake & the Never Land Pirates Ser.). (J). lib. bdg. 13.55 *(978-0-606-35269-7(4))* Turtleback Bks.

LaRose, Melinda & Disney Book Group Staff. Jake Hatches a Plan, Pre-Level 1. Disney Storybook Art Team, illus. 2012. (World of Reading Ser.). (ENG.). 32p. (J). (gr. -1-k). pap. 3.99 *(978-1-4231-5542-3(4))* Disney Pr.

Larson, Hope. Compass South. Mock, Rebecca, illus. 2016. (Four Points Ser.: 1). (ENG.). 224p. (J). 17.99 *(978-0-374-30043-2(7)*, 9780374300432, Farrar, Straus & Giroux (BYR)) Farrar, Straus & Giroux.

Latsch, Oliver, tr. from GER. The Pirate Pig. 2015. (ENG., Illus.). 80p. (J). (gr. 2-5). 9.99 *(978-0-385-37544-3(1)*, Random Hse. Bks. for Young Readers) Random Hse. Children's Bks.

Lawrence, Caroline. The Dolphins of Laurentum. 2005. (Roman Mysteries Ser.). (Illus.). 161p. (J). (gr. 6-9). 13.65 *(978-0-7569-6538-9(1))* Perfection Learning Corp.

Leavey, Peggy Dymond. Treasure at Turtle Lake. 2007. (ENG.). 152p. (J). (gr. 4-18). per. 9.95 *(978-1-894917-49-0(9)*, Napoleon & Co.) Dundurn CAN. Dist: Ingram Publisher Services.

Lerangis, Peter. Journals: The Key. 2015. (Seven Wonders Journals: 3). (ENG.). 96p. (J). (gr. 3-7). pap. 2.99 *(978-0-06-223892-4(2))* HarperCollins Pubs.

—The Key. 2015. (Seven Wonders Journals: 3). (J). lib. bdg. 12.35 *(978-0-606-36487-4(0))* Turtleback Bks.

Lerangis, Peter. Max Tilt: Fire the Depths. 2017. (Max Tilt Ser.: 1). 368p. (J). (gr. 3-7). 17.99 ***(978-0-06-244100-3(0))*** HarperCollins Pubs.

Litwin, Mike. The Big Cowhuna. Litwin, Mike, illus. 2015. (Welcome to Bermooda! Ser.: 3). (ENG., Illus.). 160p. (J). (gr. 1-5). 14.99 *(978-0-8075-8720-1(6))* Whitman, Albert & Co.

—Crown of the Cowibbean. Litwin, Mike, illus. 2014. (Welcome to Bermooda! Ser.: 2). (ENG., Illus.). 144p. (J). (gr. 1-5). 14.99 *(978-0-8075-8719-5(2))* Whitman, Albert & Co.

Lloyd, Natalie. The Key to Extraordinary. 2016. (ENG.). 240p. (J). (gr. 3-7). 16.99 *(978-0-545-55274-5(5)*, Scholastic Pr.) Scholastic, Inc.

Long, Ethan. Clara & Clem under the Sea. Long, Ethan, illus. 2014. (Penguin Young Readers, Level 1 Ser.). (ENG., Illus.). 32p. (J). (gr. k-1). pap. 3.99 *(978-0-448-47812-8(9)*, Penguin Young Readers) Penguin Young Readers Group.

Looper, Grace W. Great-Grandpa's Hidden Treasure. 2006. (YA). pap. *(978-1-933523-18-7(2))* Bella Rosa Bks.

The Lost Treasure of Skull Island. 2012. (Illus.). (J). *(978-1-4351-4328-9(0))* Barnes & Noble, Inc.

Lowitz, Leza & Oketani, Shogo. Jet Black & the Ninja Wind. 2013. (ENG., Illus.). 320p. (J). (gr. 7-12). 17.99 *(978-4-8053-1284-1(X))* Tuttle Publishing.

Lynch, Brendan Denis. The Document. 2012. 218p. pap. 8.99 *(978-0-9825243-2-9(3))* 1776 Pr.

Mack, Harry. The Treasure Mystery Clues. 2011. 70p. pap. 19.95 *(978-1-4626-2487-4(1))* America Star Bks.

MacPhail, C. & Cosson, M. J. The Pirate, Big Fist, & Me, 1 vol. Garvey, Brann, illus. 2006. (Vortex Bks.). (ENG.). 112p. (gr. 2-3). 7.19 *(978-1-59889-279-6(7)*, Vortex Bks.) Stone Arch Bks.

Mahle, Melissa & Dennis, Kathryn. Lost in Petra. 2012. (Anatolia Steppe Mysteries: 1). (ENG., Illus.). 246p. (J). pap. 10.99 *(978-0-9852273-0-2(3))* SpyGirls Pr.

Makura, Sho. Panda Man & the Treasure Hunt. Kato, Haruhi, illus. 2011. (ENG.). 96p. (J). (gr. 1-4). pap. 7.99 *(978-1-4215-3521-0(1))* Viz Media.

Markell, Denis. Click Here to Start. 2016. (ENG.). 320p. (J). (gr. 5-7). 16.99 *(978-1-101-93187-5(6)*, Delacorte Bks. for Young Readers) Random Hse. Children's Bks.

Marsh, Carole. The Mystery of Blackbeard the Pirate. Marsh, Carole, photos by. 2009. (Real Kids, Real Places Ser.). (Illus.). 150p. (J). 18.99 *(978-0-635-06992-4(X)*, Marsh, Carole Mysteries) Gallopade International.

Masefield, John. The Midnight Folk. Hilder, Rowland, illus. 2008. (ENG.). 256p. (J). (gr. 4-7). 17.95 *(978-1-59017-290-2(6)*, NYR Children's Collection) New York Review of Bks., Inc., The.

Mazurick, Shannon K. Gemm: The Treasure Hunt with Griffin. 2012. 32p. pap. 19.99 *(978-1-4772-7740-9(4))* AuthorHouse.

McCaughren, Tom. Legend of the Golden Key. 2nd rev. ed. 2012. (McCaughren's Legends Trilogy Ser.). (ENG., Illus.). 190p. (J). pap. 14.95 *(978-1-85635-803-3(8))* Mercier Pr., Ltd., The IRL. Dist: Dufour Editions, Inc.

—Legend of the Golden Key. (Illus.). 96p. 3.95 *(978-0-900068-73-7(6))* Penguin Publishing Group.

McGinty, Sean. The End of FUN. 2016. (ENG.). 416p. (YA). (gr. 9-17). 17.99 *(978-1-4847-2211-4(6))* Hyperion Bks. for Children.

—The End of Fun. 2017. (ENG.). 416p. (YA). (gr. 9-17). pap. 9.99 *(978-1-4847-2214-5(0))* Hyperion Bks. for Children.

McKay, Lise Y. The Mysterious Well. 2012. 130p. pap. 14.95 *(978-1-59663-865-5(6)*, Mount Helicon Pr.) Rock, James A. & Co. Pubs.

McMullan, Kate. Class Trip to the Cave of Doom, 3 vols. Basso, Bill, illus. 2003. (Dragon Slayers' Academy Ser.: 3). (ENG.). 112p. (J). (gr. 2-5). pap. 5.99 *(978-0-448-43110-9(6)*, Grosset & Dunlap) Penguin Young Readers Group.

—Class Trip to the Cave of Doom, 1 vol. Basso, Bill, illus. 2006. (Dragon Slayers' Academy Ser.: No. 3). (ENG.). 112p. (gr. 1-7). 24.21 *(978-1-59961-123-5(6))* Spotlight.

McNee, Ian, illus. Treasure Island. 2006. 158p. (J). (gr. 5-9). per. 4.99 *(978-0-7945-1230-9(5)*, Usborne) EDC Publishing.

McOmber, Rachel B., ed. McOmber Phonics Storybooks: The Confection Connection. rev. ed. (Illus.). (J). *(978-0-944991-73-2(4))* Swift Learning Resources.

Meadows, Daisy. The Fairy Treasure Hunt. 2012. (Rainbow Magic — Scholastic Reader Ser.). lib. bdg. 13.55 *(978-0-606-23912-7(X)*, Turtleback) Turtleback Bks.

Mertz, Alyssa. The Lucky Farm Boy, 1 vol. Crum, A. M., illus. 2009. 28p. pap. 24.95 *(978-1-60813-892-0(5))* PublishAmerica, Inc.

Messer, Celeste M. The Ghost of Piper's Landing. Hoeffner, Deb, illus. 2004. 82-92p. 4.95 *(978-0-9702171-7-2(X))* AshleyAlan Enterprises.

Meyer, L. A. Rapture of the Deep: Being an Account of the Further Adventures of Jacky Faber, Soldier, Sailor, Mermaid, Spy. 2011. (Bloody Jack Adventures Ser.: 7). (ENG.). 464p. (YA). (gr. 9). pap. 9.99 *(978-0-547-55120-3(7))* Houghton Mifflin Harcourt Publishing Co.

Michaels, Craig. Blackbeard's Treasure. 2008. (J). *(978-0-936389-99-8(0))* Tudor Pubs., Inc.

Miller, Bobbi. Big River's Daughter. 2013. (ENG.). 224p. (J). (gr. 2-7). 16.95 *(978-0-8234-2752-9(8))* Holiday Hse., Inc.

Miller, Judith J. Hidden Treasure. Beers, Robert Lee, illus. 2013. 24p. pap. 10.95 *(978-1-61633-419-2(3))* Guardian Angel Publishing, Inc.

Milliner, Donna L. The Kingdom of Wish & Why. Snyder, Ronda, illus. 2013. 30p. pap. 11.95 *(978-1-938743-06-1(7))* Reimann Bks.

Mills, Judith Christine & Mills, Judith C. The Painted Chest. rev. ed. 2008. (ENG., Illus.). 32p. (J). (gr. k). *(978-1-55263-809-5(X))* Me to We.

Milway, Alex. Pigsticks & Harold & the Pirate Treasure. Milway, Alex, illus. 2016. (ENG., Illus.). 64p. (J). (gr. k-4). 12.99 *(978-0-7636-8157-9(1))* Candlewick Pr.

Miraucourt, Christophe. Pirate Treasure. 2015. (Race Further with Reading Ser.). (ENG., Illus.). 48p. (J). *(978-0-7787-2031-7(4))* Crabtree Publishing Co.

Mone, Gregory. Fish. 2010. (J). *(978-0-545-11631-2(7),* Scholastic Pr.) Scholastic, Inc.

Mongredien, Sue & Taylor, Dan. The Best Pirate: With Pirate Hat, Eyepatch, & Treasure! 2016. (ENG.). 32p. (J). (gr. -1-2). pap. 7.99 *(978-1-4380-0948-3(8))* Barron's Educational Series, Inc.

Moore, Ashley L. The Story of Princess K. 2012. 20p. pap. 24.95 *(978-1-4626-6800-7(3))* America Star Bks.

Morgan, Winter. Terror on a Treasure Hunt: An Unofficial Minetrapped Adventure, #3. 2016. (Unofficial Minetrapped Adventure Ser.: 3). (ENG.). 112p. (J). (gr. 1-7). pap. 7.99 *(978-1-5107-0599-9(6),* Sky Pony Pr.) Skyhorse Publishing Co., Inc.

Muller, Carrie & Halsey, Jacqueline. The Terrible, Horrible, Smelly Pirate, 1 vol. Orchard, Eric, illus. 2008. (ENG.). 32p. (J). (gr. k-3). pap. 11.95 *(978-1-55109-655-1(2))* Nimbus Publishing, Ltd. CAN. Dist: Orca Bk. Pubs. USA.

Mussi, Sarah. The Door of No Return. (ENG.). 400p. (YA). (gr. 7). 2009. pap. 10.99 *(978-1-4169-6825-2(3))* 2008. 17.99 *(978-1-4169-1550-8(8))* McElderry, Margaret K. Bks. (McElderry, Margaret K. Bks.).

Myers, Walter Dean. The Mouse Rap. 3rd ed. (J). pap. 3.95 *(978-0-13-800087-5(5))* Prentice Hall (Schl. Div.).

—The Righteous Revenge of Artemis Bonner. 2003. (J). (gr. 5-18). 23.00 *(978-0-8446-7250-2(5))* Smith, Peter Pub., Inc.

Naranjo, K. L. The Adventures of Ariel & Eden & the Lost Treasures of Zion. 2013. 50p. pap. 10.95 *(978-1-62516-835-1(7),* Strategic Bk. Publishing) Strategic Book Publishing & Rights Agency (SBPRA).

National Geographic Learning Staff. The Secret under the Tree. Life, Kay, illus. 2010. (Rise & Shine Ser.: 7). (ENG.). 32p. (C). (gr. 1-3). pap. 13.95 *(978-0-8075-0643-1(5))* National Geographic School Publishing, Inc.

Nesbit, E. The House of Arden. 2006. 184p. (gr. 3-7). per. 14.95 *(978-1-59818-967-4(0));* 26.95 *(978-1-59818-181-4(5))* Aegypan.

—The House of Arden. 2006. (New York Review Children's Collection). (ENG.). 260p. (J). (gr. 4-7). 17.95 *(978-1-59017-202-5(7),* NYR Children's Collection) New York Review of Bks., Inc., The.

—New Treasure Seekers. 2009. 172p. (gr. 4-7). pap. 13.95 *(978-1-60664-293-1(6))* Rodgers, Alan Bks.

—The Story of the Treasure Seekers: Being the Adventures of the Bastable Children in Search of A Fortune. 2006. 132p. (gr. 4-7). per. 10.95 *(978-1-59818-963-6(8));* 24.95 *(978-1-59818-172-2(6))* Aegypan.

Nesbit, Troy. Diamond Cave Mystery. 2013. (Wilderness Mystery Ser.). (ENG., Illus.). 280p. (J). (gr. 3-7). pap. 12.95 *(978-1-58979-809-0(0))* Taylor Trade Publishing.

Oboh, Rolic. Treasure Hunt. 2006. 108p. pap. 7.99 *(978-1-84426-318-9(5))* Upfront Publishing Ltd. GBR. Dist: Printondemand-worldwide.com.

Oechsle, Michael. The Lost Cipher. (ENG.). 272p. (J). (gr. 3-7). 2017. pap. 9.99 ***(978-0-8075-8065-3(1))*** 2016. 14.99 *(978-0-8075-8063-9(5))* Whitman, Albert & Co.

Ogden, Charles. Nod's Limbs. Carton, Rick, illus. 2007. (Edgar & Ellen Ser.: 6). (ENG.). 224p. (J). (gr. 3-7). 24.99 *(978-1-4169-1501-0(X),* Simon & Schuster/Paula Wiseman Bks.) Simon & Schuster/Paula Wiseman Bks.

O'Hearn, Michael. The el Dorado Map. 2015. (Middle-Grade Novels Ser.). (ENG.). 320p. (gr. 4-7). lib. bdg. 26.65 *(978-1-4965-0158-5(6))* Stone Arch Bks.

Olson, D. A. The Treasure Map. 2011. 36p. pap. 24.95 *(978-1-4626-3655-6(1))* America Star Bks.

Orsi, Tea & Panaro, Carlo. Tinker Bell & the Lost Treasure. Razzi, Manuela et al, illus. 2013. (Disney Fairies Ser.: 12). (ENG.). 64p. (J). (gr. 1-6). pap. 7.99 *(978-1-59707-428-5(4),* 9781597074285) Papercutz.

Osborne, Mary Pope. Piratas Despues del Mediodia. 2003. (Magic Tree House Ser.: 4). (SPA.). (gr. 3-6). lib. bdg. 16.00 *(978-0-613-64578-2(2),* Turtleback) Turtleback Bks.

Osteen, Victoria. Unexpected Treasures. Palmisciano, Diane, illus. 2009. (ENG.). 32p. (J). (gr. -1-3). 17.99 *(978-1-4169-5550-4(X),* Little Simon Inspirations) Little Simon Inspirations.

O'Toole, Detra. Ty-Ty Quackers & the Hidden Treasure: Biblical Lessons with Barnyard Fun. 2009. 32p. pap. 13.99 *(978-1-4343-6799-0(1))* AuthorHouse.

Owens, Greg. Rupert the Wrong-Word Pirate. Beaky, Suzanne, illus. 2006. (J). *(978-1-58987-143-4(X))* Kindermusik International.

Padma, T. V., et al. Growing Gold. 2007. (Story Cove Ser.). (ENG., Illus.). 32p. (J). (gr. -1-3). pap. 4.95 *(978-0-87483-860-2(6))* August Hse. Pubs., Inc.

Papp, Robert, illus. The Creature in Ogopogo Lake. 2006. (Boxcar Children Mysteries Ser.: 108). (ENG.). 128p. (J). (gr. 1-5). per. 6.99 *(978-0-8075-1337-8(7))* Whitman, Albert & Co.

Parish, Peggy. Key to the Treasure. 154p. (J). pap. 4.50 *(978-0-8072-1398-8(5),* Listening Library) Random Hse. Audio Publishing Group.

Parker, Danny. Lola's Toybox: the Treasure Trove. 2017. (Lola's Toy Box Ser.: 3). (ENG.). 96p. (J). (gr. k-2). pap. 6.99 ***(978-1-76012-438-0(9))*** Hardie Grant Egmont Pty, Ltd. AUS. Dist: Independent Pubs. Group.

Patterson, James & Grabenstein, Chris. Danger down the Nile. Neufeld, Juliana, illus. 2014. (Treasure Hunters Ser.). (ENG.). 480p. (J). (gr. 3-7). 14.99 *(978-0-316-37086-8(X),* Jimmy Patterson) Little Brown & Co.

—Secret of the Forbidden City. Neufeld, Juliana, illus. 2015. (Treasure Hunters Ser.: 3). (ENG.). 448p. (J). (gr. 3-7). 14.99 *(978-0-316-28480-6(7),* Jimmy Patterson) Little Brown & Co.

—Treasure Hunters. Neufeld, Juliana, illus. (Treasure Hunters Ser.: 1). (ENG.). 480p. (J). (gr. 3-7). 2015. pap. 8.00 *(978-0-316-20757-7(8))* 2013. 14.99 *(978-0-316-20756-0(X))* Little Brown & Co. (Jimmy Patterson).

—Treasure Hunters. 2015. (Treasure Hunters Ser.: 1). (J). lib. bdg. 18.45 *(978-0-606-37305-0(5))* Turtleback Bks.

Patterson, James, et al. Treasure Hunters. Neufeld, Juliana, illus. 2013. 451p. (J). *(978-0-316-24262-2(4))* Little Brown & Co.

Pavanello, Roberto. The Pirate with the Golden Tooth, 1 vol. Zeni, Marco, tr. from ITA. Pisapia, Blasco & Brughera, Pamela, illus. (Echo & the Bat Pack Ser.). (ENG.). 128p. (gr. 2-3). 2013. 9.95 *(978-1-4342-4888-6(7))* 2012. 25.32 *(978-1-4342-3836-8(9),* Echo & the Bat Pack) Stone Arch Bks.

—Treasure in the Graveyard, 1 vol. Zeni, Marco, tr. from ITA. Pisapia, Blasco & Brughera, Pamela, illus. 2012. (Echo & the Bat Pack Ser.). (ENG.). 128p. (gr. 2-3). 9.95 *(978-1-4342-4248-8(X))* Stone Arch Bks.

Payson, Howard. Boy Scouts' Mountain Camp. 2005. (Illus.). pap. 28.95 *(978-1-885529-54-1(6))* Stevens Publishing.

Penn, Audrey & Miller, Joshua. Blackbeard & the Gift of Silence. 2009. (ENG.). 350p. (J). (gr. 2-7). pap. 8.95 *(978-1-933718-32-3(3))* Tanglewood Pr.

—Blackbeard & the Sandstone Pillar: When Lightning Strikes. 2009. (ENG.). 350p. (J). (gr. 2-7). pap. 8.95 *(978-1-933718-31-6(5))* Tanglewood Pr.

Peschke, Marci. Dead Man's Map, 1 vol. Smith, Tod G., illus. 2008. (Vortex Bks.). (ENG.). 112p. (gr. 2-3). pap. 7.19 *(978-1-59889-921-4(X),* 1271328, Vortex Bks.) Stone Arch Bks.

—Pirate Queen. Mourning, Tuesday, illus. (Kylie Jean Ser.). (ENG.). 112p. (gr. 2-3). 2015. pap. 5.95 *(978-1-4795-8020-0(1))* 2013. 8.95 *(978-1-4048-8103-7(4))* 2013. lib. bdg. 22.65 *(978-1-4048-7581-4(6))* Picture Window Bks. (Kylie Jean).

Pigott, Louise. Squirrel Me Timbers. 2016. (Fiction Picture Bks.). (ENG., Illus.). 24p. (gr. k-1). lib. bdg. 24.65 *(978-1-4795-9177-0(7),* Fiction Picture Bks.) Picture Window Bks.

Prager, Ellen. The Shark Whisperer. Caparo, Antonio Javier, illus. 2014. (Tristan Hunt & the Sea Guardians Ser.). (ENG.). 288p. (J). (gr. 3-7). pap. 9.95 *(978-1-938063-44-2(9),* Mighty Media Junior Readers) Mighty Media Pr.

Preus, Margi. Enchantment Lake: A Northwoods Mystery. 2015. (ENG.). 200p. (YA). 16.95 *(978-0-8166-8302-4(6))* Univ. of Minnesota Pr.

Prior, Natalie Jane & Prior, Natalie. Lily Quench & the Treasure of Mote Ely, Vol. 3. 2004. (ENG., Illus.). 160p. (J). (gr. 3-7). 6.99 *(978-0-14-240022-7(X),* Puffin Books) Penguin Young Readers Group.

Proysen, Alf. Mrs Pepperpot & the Treasure: A Classic Story with a Touch of Magic. Offen, Hilda, illus. 2013. (ENG.). 32p. (J). (gr. k-2). pap. 10.99 *(978-1-84941-866-9(7),* Red Fox) Random House Children's Books GBR. Dist: Independent Pubs. Group.

Pryor, Bonnie. Captain Hannah Pritchard: The Hunt for Pirate Gold. 2011. (Historical Fiction Adventures (HFA) Ser.). (Illus.). 160p. (J). (gr. 3-18). pap. 10.95 *(978-1-59845-283-9(5));* (gr. 4-7). lib. bdg. 29.27 *(978-0-7660-3817-2(3))* Enslow Pubs., Inc.

Publications International Ltd. Staff, ed. Lights & Music Treasury. 2010. 160p. (J). bds. 16.98 *(978-1-4127-7911-1(1))* Phoenix International Publications, Inc.

Ragan, Lyn. Berc's Inner Voice. 2013. 24p. 21.95 *(978-0-9860205-4-4(0))* HourGlass Publishing.

—Berc's Inner Voice. Meyer, Alison, illus. 2013. 24p. pap. 14.95 *(978-0-9860205-3-7(2))* HourGlass Publishing.

Ralphson, G. Harvey. Boy Scouts in a Motor Boat or Adventures. 2005. pap. 26.95 *(978-1-885529-50-3(3))* Stevens Publishing.

Reasoner, Charles. Inside Jolly Roger's Pirate Ship. Reasoner, Charles, illus. 2007. (Story Book Ser.). (Illus.). 12p. (J). (gr. k). bds. *(978-1-84666-149-5(8),* Tide Mill Pr.) Top That! Publishing PLC.

Reichs, Kathy & Reichs, Brendan. Seizure. 2013. (Virals Ser.: 2). (ENG.). 512p. (J). (gr. 5). pap. 9.99 *(978-1-59514-486-7(2),* Puffin Books) Penguin Young Readers Group.

—Seizure. 2013. (Virals Ser.: 2). lib. bdg. 20.85 *(978-0-606-30050-6(3),* Turtleback) Turtleback Bks.

Rey, H. A. Curious George Travel Activity Kit. 2010. (Curious George Ser.). (ENG., Illus.). 64p. (J). (gr. -1-3). 12.99 *(978-0-547-25875-1(5))* Houghton Mifflin Harcourt Publishing Co.

Rhodes, O. K. & Spencer, Octavia. The Case of the Time-Capsule Bandit. To, Vivienne, illus. 2013. (Randi Rhodes, Ninja Detective Ser.: 1). (ENG.). 224p. (J). (gr. 3-7). 16.99 *(978-1-4424-7681-3(8),* Simon & Schuster Bks. For Young Readers) Simon & Schuster Bks. For Young Readers.

Rhyne, Nancy. The Crab Boys. 2007. (J). pap. 6.95 *(978-0-87844-183-9(2))* Sandlapper Publishing Co., Inc.

Riddell, Andrew G. The Curse of Blackbeard's Ghost. 2010. 122p. (gr. 4-6). pap. 10.95 *(978-1-4502-6952-0(4))* iUniverse, Inc.

Rodkey, Geoff. Blue Sea Burning. 2015. (Chronicles of Egg Ser.: 3). (ENG.). 400p. (J). (gr. 5). 7.99 *(978-0-14-751443-1(6),* Puffin Books) Penguin Young Readers Group.

—Deadweather & Sunrise. 2013. (Chronicles of Egg Ser.: 1). (ENG.). 320p. (J). (gr. 5). pap. 7.99 *(978-0-14-242662-3(8),* Puffin Books) Penguin Young Readers Group.

Rokker, H. M. The Adventures of Ralph in the Search for Blackbeard's Gold, 1 vol. 2009. 41p. pap. 24.95 *(978-1-60474-259-6(3))* America Star Bks.

Rothwell, David. The Voyage of the Pilchard. 2009. 162p. pap. 13.95 *(978-1-4092-1071-9(5))* Lulu Pr., Inc.

Roy, Ron. Mayflower Treasure Hunt. Gurney, John Steven, illus. 2nd ed. 2007. (to Z Mysteries Ser.: 2). (ENG.). 128p. (J). (gr. 1-4). per. 5.99 *(978-0-375-83937-5(2),* Random Hse. Bks. for Young Readers) Random Hse. Children's Bks.

—Mayflower Treasure Hunt. Gurney, John Steven, illus. 2007. (to Z Mysteries Ser.: 28). 114p. (gr. 4-7). lib. bdg. 16.00 *(978-1-4177-9141-5(1),* Turtleback) Turtleback Bks.

Ryan, Jessica. The Mystery of Arroyo Seco. Stone, David, illus. 2011. 186p. 42.95 *(978-1-258-08470-7(8))* Literary Licensing, LLC.

Sachar, Louis. Buracos. pap. 29.95 *(978-85-336-1280-8(X))* Livraria Martins Editora BRA. Dist: Distribooks, Inc.

—Holes. 2008. (KOR., Illus.). 334p. (J). pap. *(978-89-364-5602-3(4))* Chang-jag and Bipyeong Co.

—Holes. 10th ed. 2008. (ENG., Illus.). 272p. (J). (gr. 4-8). 18.99 *(978-0-374-33266-2(5),* 9780374332662, Farrar, Straus & Giroux (BYR)) Farrar, Straus & Giroux.

—Holes. 2008. (ENG.). (J). 39.99 *(978-0-7393-7103-9(7))* Findaway World, LLC.

—Holes. 2014. (CHI & ENG.). 246p. (J). (gr. 4-8). pap. *(978-7-5442-7158-5(7))* Fukuinkan Shoten.

—Holes. 2009. 9.14 *(978-0-7848-1394-2(9),* Everbind) Marco Bk. Co.

—Holes. 240p. (J). (gr. 4-6). pap. 5.99 *(978-0-8072-8073-7(9),* Listening Library) Random Hse. Audio Publishing Group.

—Holes, 4 vols. (J). 2006. 46.75 *(978-1-4193-6136-4(8))* 2004. 1.25 *(978-1-4025-6758-2(8))* Recorded Bks., Inc.

—Holes. l.t. ed. 2003. 288p. pap. 10.95 *(978-0-7862-6190-1(0))* Thorndike Pr.

Salerni, Dianne K. The Caged Graves. 2014. (ENG.). 336p. (YA). (gr. 7). pap. 8.99 *(978-0-544-33622-3(4),* HMH Books For Young Readers) Houghton Mifflin Harcourt Publishing Co.

Santillo, LuAnn. Stubs. Santillo, LuAnn, ed. 2003. (Half-Pint Kids Readers Ser.). (Illus.). 7p. (J). (gr. -1-1). pap. 1.00 *(978-1-59256-097-4(0))* Half-Pint Kids, Inc.

Schade, Susan. Riff Raff the Mouse Pirate. Kennedy, Anne, illus. 2014. (I Can Read Level 2 Ser.). (ENG.). 24p. (J). (gr. -1-3). pap. 3.99 *(978-0-06-230507-7(7))* HarperCollins Pubs.

Schaub, Michelle. The Lost Pirate. 2006. (Early Explorers Ser.). (J). pap. *(978-1-4108-6109-2(0))* Benchmark Education Co.

Schiro, Michael. Treasure Hunt: Level R, 6 vols. (Raging Rivers Ser.). 128p. (gr. 3-6). 36.95 *(978-0-322-05897-2(X))* Wright Group/McGraw-Hill.

Scholastic, Inc. Staff & Duendes Del Sur Staff, contrib. by. Scooby-Doo! & the Mummy's Curse. 2005. (Illus.). 24p. (J). *(978-1-4156-3913-9(2))* Scholastic, Inc.

Scholastic, Inc. Staff & King, Trey. Deep Sea Treasure Dive. Hyland, Greg, illus. 2016. (Lego City Ser.). (ENG.). 24p. (J). (gr. 2-5). pap. 3.99 *(978-0-545-90591-6(5))* Scholastic, Inc.

Schulz, Heidi. Hook's Revenge. Hendrix, John, illus. 2015. (Hook's Revenge Ser.: Bk. 2). (ENG.). 344p. (J). (gr. 3-7). 16.99 *(978-1-4847-1717-2(1))* Hyperion Bks. for Children.

Schwarz, Viviane. How to Find Gold. Schwarz, Viviane, illus. 2016. (ENG., Illus.). 32p. (J). (-k). 16.99 *(978-0-7636-8104-3(0))* Candlewick Pr.

Scollon, William & Disney Book Group Staff. The Great Treasure Hunt. Disney Storybook Art Team, illus. 2013. (ENG.). 10p. (J). (gr. -1-k). bds. 8.99 *(978-1-4231-6396-1(6))* Disney Pr.

—The Key to Skull Rock, Level 1. Disney Storybook Art Team, illus. 2013. (World of Reading Ser.). (ENG.). 32p. (J). (gr. -1-k). pap. 3.99 *(978-1-4231-6397-8(4))* Disney Pr.

Scotton, Rob. Russell & the Lost Treasure. Scotton, Rob, illus. 2006. (ENG., Illus.). 32p. (J). (gr. -1-2). 15.99 *(978-0-06-059851-8(4))* HarperCollins Pubs.

Selfors, Suzanne. Smells Like Treasure. 2012. (Smells Like Dog Ser.: 2). (ENG.). 432p. (J). (gr. 3-7). pap. 8.99 *(978-0-316-04402-8(4))* Little, Brown Bks. for Young Readers.

Shannon, Terry Miller. Leela's Treasure. Smillie, Natalie, illus. 2016. (Spring Forward Ser.). (J). (gr. 1). *(978-1-4900-9380-2(X))* Benchmark Education Co.

Shealy, Dennis. Treasure Island. 2017. (Little Golden Book Ser.). (ENG., Illus.). 24p. (J). (-k). 4.99 *(978-1-101-93836-2(6),* Golden Bks.) Random Hse. Children's Bks.

Shulman, Polly & Airgood, Ellen. The Poe Annex. 2015. (ENG.). 272p. (J). (gr. 5). 16.99 *(978-0-399-16614-3(9),* Nancy Paulsen Books) Penguin Young Readers Group.

Simner, Janni Lee. Secret of the Three Treasures. 2006. (ENG.). 160p. (YA). (gr. 8-12). 16.95 *(978-0-8234-1914-2(2))* Holiday Hse., Inc.

Simon, Nadine. The Treasured Dream. 2009. 52p. pap. 9.95 *(978-1-60693-274-2(8),* Eloquent Bks.) Strategic Book Publishing & Rights Agency (SBPRA).

Skye, Lucy. The Adventure of Maisie Voyager. 2012. (ENG.). 240p. (J). pap. 15.95 *(978-1-84905-287-0(5),* 4927) Kingsley, Jessica Pubs. GBR. Dist: Macmillan Distribution Ltd.

Smith, Steven K. Summer of the Woods. 2013. 158p. pap. 7.99 *(978-0-9893414-1-7(0))* MyBoys3 Pr.

Snowden, Gary. The Lost Treasure of Hawkins Cave. Pierce Clark, Donna, illus. 2013. 112p. pap. 7.99 *(978-1-938768-10-1(8))* Gypsy Pubns.

Snyder, Zilpha Keatley. The Treasures of Weatherby. 2008. (ENG.). 240p. (J). (gr. 3-7). pap. 7.99 *(978-1-4169-1399-3(8),* Atheneum Bks. for Young Readers) Simon & Schuster Children's Publishing.

Specter, Baron. Drama at Dungeon Rock: #6, 1 vol. Evans, Dustin, illus. 2010. (Ghostly Graphic Adventures Ser.). (ENG.). 32p. (J). (gr. 3-6). 28.50 *(978-1-60270-775-7(8))* ABDO Publishing Co.

—The Star Island Spirits: #5, 1 vol. Evans, Dustin, illus. 2010. (Ghostly Graphic Adventures Ser.). (ENG.). 32p. (J). (gr. 3-6). 28.50 *(978-1-60270-774-0(X))* ABDO Publishing Co.

Stadther, Michael. Secrets of the Alchemist Dar. Stadther, Michael, illus. 2006. (Treasure's Trove Ser.). (ENG., Illus.). 144p. (J). 21.99 *(978-1-4169-2653-5(4));* 39.99 *(978-1-4169-2661-0(5))* Treasure Trove, Inc.

Standish, Joyce, ed. The Adventures of Ryan Lincoln. Cooper, Nicole, illus. 2012. 46p. (J). pap. 10.00 *(978-0-9716244-5-0(3))* TLS Publishing.

Stevens, Linda M. Unlocking the Hidden Treasures. 2009. 28p. pap. 24.95 *(978-1-61546-454-8(9))* America Star Bks.

Stevenson, Robert Louis. Treasure Island. Corvino, Lucy, illus. 2005. (Classic Starts(tm) Ser.). (ENG.). 160p. (J). (gr. 2-4). 6.95 *(978-1-4027-1318-7(5))* Sterling Publishing Co., Inc.

—Treasure Island. 2009. (Foundation Classics Ser.). (Illus.). 56p. (J). (gr. 5-9). lib. bdg. 27.95 *(978-1-60754-543-9(8))* Windmill Bks.

—Treasure Island. Lawrence, John, illus. 2009. (Candlewick Illustrated Classics Ser.). (ENG.). 272p. (J). (gr. 4-7). 24.99 *(978-0-7636-4445-1(5))* Candlewick Pr.

—Treasure Island. 2016. (ENG., Illus.). (J). pap. ***(978-3-7433-2049-9(5))*** Creation Pubs.

—Treasure Island. 2016. (ENG., Illus.). (J). 26.95 ***(978-1-358-35578-3(9))*** Creative Media Partners, LLC.

—Treasure Island. 2005. 116p. per. 5.95 *(978-1-4209-2258-5(0))* Digireads.com Publishing.

—Treasure Island. 2004. reprint ed. pap. 1.99 *(978-1-4192-9097-8(5))* Kessinger Publishing, LLC.

—Treasure Island. (Young Collector's Illustrated Classics Ser.). (Illus.). 192p. (J). (gr. 3-7). 9.95 *(978-1-56156-456-9(7))* Kidsbooks, LLC.

—Treasure Island. Rhead, Louis, illus. 2015. (J). pap. *(978-1-4677-7821-3(4),* First Avenue Editions) Lerner Publishing Group.

—Treasure Island. 2014. (Word Cloud Classics Ser.). (ENG., Illus.). 208p. pap. 14.99 *(978-1-62686-256-2(7),* Thunder Bay Pr.) Readerlink Distribution Services, LLC.

—Treasure Island, 1 vol. Gully, Mario & Davidson, Pat, illus. 2009. (Treasure Island Ser.). (ENG.). 24p. (gr. 5-8). 24.21 *(978-1-59961-601-8(7));*Pt. 2. 24.21 *(978-1-59961-602-5(5))* Spotlight.

—Treasure Island. Corvino, Lucy, illus. abr. ed. 2010. (Classic Starts(tm) Ser.). (ENG.). 160p. (J). (gr. 2-4). cd-rom 9.95 *(978-1-4027-7358-7(7))* Sterling Publishing Co., Inc.

—Treasure Island: The Treasure Map. Comport, Sally Wern, illus. 2008. (Easy Reader Classics Ser.). (ENG.). 32p. (gr. -1-3). lib. bdg. 24.21 *(978-1-59961-342-0(5))* Spotlight.

—Treasure Island: With a Discussion of Courage. 2003. (Values in Action Illustrated Classics Ser.). (J). *(978-1-59203-054-5(8))* Learning Challenge, Inc.

—Treasure Island: With Story of the Treasure of Normon Island. Date not set. (J). (gr. 5-6). reprint ed. lib. bdg. 22.95 *(978-0-89190-236-2(8),* American Reprint Co.) Amereon Ltd.

Stevenson, Robert Louis & Ballaz, Jesus. Treasure Island. 2007. (Illustrated Classics Ser.). (Illus.). 40p. (gr. 3-6). lib. bdg. 26.00 *(978-0-8368-7665-9(2),* Gareth Stevens Learning Library) Stevens, Gareth Publishing LLLP.

Stevenson, Robert Louis & Gaston, Charles Robert. Treasure Island. 2016. (ENG., Illus.). (J). 25.95 ***(978-1-358-93415-5(0))*** Creative Media Partners, LLC.

Stevenson, Robert Louis & Vance, Hiram Albert. Treasure Island. 2016. (ENG., Illus.). (J). 25.95 ***(978-1-358-73513-4(1));*** 25.95 ***(978-1-359-06744-9(2))*** Creative Media Partners, LLC.

Stevenson, Robert Louis, et al. Treasure Island. 2016. (ENG., Illus.). (J). 26.95 ***(978-1-357-83050-2(5))*** Creative Media Partners, LLC.

Stevenson, Steve. The Treasure of the Bermuda Triangle. 2014. (Agatha Girl of Mystery Ser.: 6). lib. bdg. 17.20 *(978-0-606-35700-5(9))* Turtleback Bks.

Stilton, Geronimo. Cavemice: Surfing for Secrets. 2015. (Geronimo Stilton Cavemice Ser.: 8). (ENG., Illus.). 128p. (J). (gr. 2-5). pap. 7.99 *(978-0-545-74617-5(5),* Scholastic Paperbacks) Scholastic, Inc.

—Ghost Pirate Treasure. 2012. (Creepella Von Cacklefur Ser.: 3). (ENG.). 128p. (J). (gr. 2-5). pap. 7.99 *(978-0-545-30744-4(9),* Scholastic Paperbacks) Scholastic, Inc.

—Ghost Pirate Treasure. 2012. (Geronimo Stilton — Creepella Von Cacklefur Ser.: 3). lib. bdg. 18.40 *(978-0-606-23931-8(6),* Turtleback) Turtleback Bks.

—Lost Treasure of the Emerald Eye. Wolf, Matt, illus. 2004. (Geronimo Stilton Ser.: No. 1). 116p. (J). lib. bdg. 10.00 *(978-1-4242-0695-7(2))* Fitzgerald Bks.

—Lost Treasure of the Emerald Eye. Wolf, Matt & Keys, Larry, illus. 2004. (Geronimo Stilton Ser.: 1). (ENG.). 128p. (J). (gr. 2-5). pap. 7.99 *(978-0-439-55963-8(4),* Scholastic Paperbacks) Scholastic, Inc.

—The Temple of the Ruby of Fire. 2004. (Geronimo Stilton Ser.: 14). (ENG., Illus.). 128p. (J). (gr. 2-5). pap. 7.99 *(978-0-439-66163-8(3),* Scholastic Paperbacks) Scholastic, Inc.

—The Treasure of Easter Island. 2015. (Geronimo Stilton Ser.: 6). (ENG., Illus.). 128p. (J). (gr. 2-5). pap. 7.99 *(978-0-545-74614-4(0),* Scholastic Paperbacks) Scholastic, Inc.

—Valley of the Giant Skeletons. 2008. (Illus.). 111p. (J). lib. bdg. 15.38 *(978-1-4242-4303-7(3))* Fitzgerald Bks.

—Valley of the Giant Skeletons. 2008. (Geronimo Stilton Ser.). (Illus.). 110p. (gr. 2-5). 17.00 *(978-0-7569-8805-0(5))* Perfection Learning Corp.

—Valley of the Giant Skeletons. 2008. (Geronimo Stilton Ser.: 32). (ENG., Illus.). 128p. (J). (gr. 2-5). pap. 7.99 *(978-0-545-02132-6(4),* Scholastic Paperbacks) Scholastic, Inc.

Stilton, Thea. Thea Stilton & the Tropical Treasure. 2015. (Thea Stilton Ser.: 22). (ENG.). 176p. (J). (gr. 2-5). pap. 8.99 *(978-0-545-83552-7(6),* Scholastic Paperbacks) Scholastic, Inc.

Stowell, Louie. Wind-Up Pirate Ship. Fox, Christyan, illus. 2010. (Wind-up Bks). 13p. (J). bds. 29.99 *(978-0-7945-2835-5(X),* Usborne) EDC Publishing.

Suen, Anastasia. The Pirate Map: A Robot & Rico Story. Laughead, Mike, illus. 2010. (Robot & Rico Ser.). (ENG.). 32p. (gr. 1-2). pap. 6.25 *(978-1-4342-2301-2(9))* Stone Arch Bks.

Suits, Barbara Bradford. The Hidden Treasure. 2013. 48p. pap. 7.95 *(978-1-61286-199-9(7))* Avid Readers Publishing Group.

Sumner Johnson, Janet. The Last Great Adventure of the PB & J Society. 2016. (Middle-Grade Novels Ser.). (ENG.). 256p. (gr. 4-7). lib. bdg. 26.65 *(978-1-4965-2695-3(3))* Stone Arch Bks.

Swender, Jennifer & Jacobs, Paul DuBois. Treasure Hunt. Laberis, Stephanie, illus. 2016. (Animal Inn Ser.: 2). (ENG.). 112p. (J). (gr. 2-5). pap. 5.99 *(978-1-4814-6226-6(1),* Aladdin) Simon & Schuster Children's Publishing.

Swindells, Robert. Blackout. 2011. (ENG.). 224p. (J). (gr. 3-6). pap. 9.99 *(978-0-552-56154-9(1))* Transworld Publishers Ltd. GBR. Dist: Independent Pubs. Group.

Sylvester, Kevin. Neil Flambé & the Duel in the Desert. Sylvester, Kevin, illus. 2017. (Neil Flambe Capers Ser.: 6). (ENG., Illus.). 304p. (J). (gr. 3-7). pap. 7.99 *(978-1-4814-1042-7(3),* Simon & Schuster Bks. For Young Readers) Simon & Schuster Bks. For Young Readers.

Taylor, Dereen. The Lost Treasure of the Jungle Temple: Peek Inside the 3D Windows! Hutchinson, Tim, illus. 2013. (ENG.). 12p. (J). (gr. 1-8). 16.99 *(978-1-84322-822-6(X),* Armadillo) Anness Publishing GBR. Dist: National Bk. Network.

Taylor, Martin. The Lost Treasure of the Sunken City. Catling, Andy, illus. 2012. (J). *(978-1-4351-4330-2(2))* Barnes & Noble, Inc.

Taylor, S. S. The Expeditioners & the Treasure of Drowned Man's Canyon. Roy, Katherine, illus. 2013. (ENG.). 384p. pap. 12.95 *(978-1-938073-71-7(1))* McSweeney's Publishing.

Taylor, Theodore. Teetoncey & Ben O'Neal. 2004. (ENG., Illus.). 240p. (J). (gr. 2-5). pap. 15.95 *(978-0-15-205297-3(6))* Houghton Mifflin Harcourt Publishing Co.

Thompson, Lisa. Digging for Buried Treasure. Cantell, Brenda, illus. 2006. (Treasure Trackers Ser.). 80p. (J). (gr. 3-4). lib. bdg. 19.00 *(978-0-7910-8872-2(3),* Chelsea Hse.) Facts On File, Inc.

Tipton, R. Kent. Kid Posse & the Phantom Robber. 2003. (ENG., Illus.). (J). pap. 14.95 *(978-1-878044-89-1(3))* Mayhaven Publishing, Inc.

Tougas, Shelley. Finders Keepers. 2015. (ENG.). 288p. (J). (gr. 3-7). 16.99 *(978-1-59643-990-0(4),* 9781596439900) Roaring Brook Pr.

Treasure Hunt: Individual Title Six-Packs. (Chiquilibros Ser.). (gr. k-1). 23.00 *(978-0-7635-0415-1(7))* Rigby Education.

Treasury of Classic Stories. 2008. (Treasuries Ser.). 192p. *(978-1-4075-1209-9(9))* Parragon, Inc.

Trees, Annie Mae. The Last Days of Summer: A Mystery of Two Children & Their Grandma Set Out on an Adventure. 2012. 40p. pap. 24.95 *(978-1-4626-6103-9(3))* America Star Bks.

Trout, Richard E. Cayman Gold: Lost Treasure of Devils Grotto, 1 vol. 2005. (MacGregor Family Adventure Ser.: 1). (ENG., Illus.). 224p. (YA). (gr. 5-12). 15.95 *(978-1-58980-323-7(X))* Pelican Publishing Co., Inc.

Tyre, Lisa Lewis & Airgood, Ellen. Last in a Long Line of Rebels. 2015. (ENG.). 288p. (J). (gr. 5). 16.99 *(978-0-399-16838-3(9),* Nancy Paulsen Books) Penguin Young Readers Group.

Vail, Emily Blake. The Search for Ole Ben's Treasure. 2011. 82p. 24.99 *(978-1-4568-9874-8(4));* pap. 15.99 *(978-1-4568-9873-1(6))* Xlibris Corp.

Vaughan, Marcia. The Treasure of Ghostwood Gully: A Southwest Mystery. Terry, Will, illus. 2004. (ENG.). 32p. (J). (gr. 1-3). 15.95 *(978-0-87358-858-4(4))* Cooper Square Publishing Llc.

Vogel, Sean. Celtic Run. 2012. 159p. *(978-0-9850814-0-9(6))* MB Publishing, LLC.

Voorhees, Coert. In Too Deep. 2014. (ENG.). 336p. (YA). (gr. 7-12). pap. 8.99 *(978-1-4231-4473-1(2))* Hyperion Bks. for Children.

Walker, Lane. The Hunt for Scarface. 2014. (ENG.). 161p. (YA). (gr. 7-13). pap. 9.99 *(978-1-58169-518-2(7),* Evergreen Pr.) Genesis Communications, Inc.

Walker, Richard. The Barefoot Book of Pirates. Whelan, Olwyn, illus. 2008. (Barefoot Bks.). (ENG.). 64p. (J). 19.99 *(978-1-84686-237-3(X))* Barefoot Bks., Inc.

Walley, Nathan R. The Treasure of Frank & Jesse James. 2008. 188p. 26.92 *(978-1-4251-6920-6(1))* Trafford Publishing.

Warner, Gertrude Chandler. The Haunted Cabin Mystery, 1 vol. Bloodworth, Mark, illus. 2010. (Boxcar Children Graphic Novels Ser.). (ENG.). 32p. (J). (gr. 2-5). 28.50 *(978-1-60270-717-7(0))* ABDO Publishing Co.

Warner, Gertrude Chandler, creator. The Creature in Ogopogo Lake. 2006. (Boxcar Children Mysteries Ser.: 108). (ENG., Illus.). 128p. (J). (gr. 1-5). lib. bdg. 14.99 *(978-0-8075-1336-1(9))* Whitman, Albert & Co.

Warner, Penny. The Code Busters Club, Case #2: the Haunted Lighthouse. 2013. (Code Busters Club Ser.). (ENG.). 208p. (J). (gr. 4-7). pap. 6.99 *(978-1-60684-455-7(5),* Darby Creek) Lerner Publishing Group.

—Mystery of the Pirate's Treasure. 2013. (Code Busters Club Ser.). (ENG.). 192p. (J). (gr. 4-7). 16.99 *(978-1-60684-457-1(1),* Darby Creek) Lerner Publishing Group.

Wasserman, Robin & Soderberg, Erin. X Marks the Spot. 2015. (Puppy Pirates Ser.: No. 2). (ENG., Illus.). 96p. (J). (gr. 1-4). 4.99 *(978-0-553-51170-3(X),* Random Hse. Bks. for Young Readers) Random Hse. Children's Bks.

Watson, Philip & Ofiesh, Nicole. The Treasure Chest. 2011. 52p. 20.50 *(978-1-4269-5350-7(X));* pap. 10.50 *(978-1-4269-5269-2(4))* Trafford Publishing.

Wealth, Viktoria. Aadom Kingdom of the Dragons' Light: Book-I. 2003. 214p. (YA). pap. 14.95 *(978-0-595-28175-6(3))* iUniverse, Inc.

White, Ruth. The Treasure of Way down Deep. 2013. (ENG.). 176p. (J). (gr. 5-9). 16.99 *(978-0-374-38067-0(8),* 9780374380670, Farrar, Straus & Giroux (BYR)) Farrar, Straus & Giroux.

Wild, Margaret. The Treasure Box. Blackwood, Freya, illus. 2017. (ENG.). 40p. (J). (gr. k-3). 16.99 *(978-0-7636-9084-7(8))* Candlewick Pr.

Wilhelm, Doug. Curse of the Pirate Mist. 2011. (Illus.). 144p. (J). pap. 6.99 *(978-1-937133-02-3(8))* Chooseco LLC.

Wilson, John. Stolen, 1 vol. 2013. (Orca Currents Ser.). (ENG.). 128p. (J). (gr. 5-9). 16.95 *(978-1-4598-0376-3(0));* pap. 9.95 *(978-1-4598-0375-6(2))* Orca Bk. Pubs. USA.

Wilson, N. D. Leepike Ridge. 2008. (ENG., Illus.). 256p. (J). (gr. 3-7). 6.99 *(978-0-375-83874-3(0),* Yearling) Random Hse. Children's Bks.

Winfield, Arthur M. Rover Boys on Treasure Isle or the Stran. 2006. pap. 30.95 *(978-1-4286-4112-9(2))* Kessinger Publishing, LLC.

Wolk, Lauren. Beyond the Bright Sea. 2017. (ENG.). 304p. (J). (gr. 5). 16.99 ***(978-1-101-99485-6(1),*** Dutton Books for Young Readers) Penguin Young Readers Group.

Wolverton, Barry. The Vanishing Island. Stevenson, Dave, illus. (Chronicles of the Black Tulip Ser.: 1). (J). (gr. 3-7). 2016. 368p. pap. 6.99 *(978-0-06-222191-9(4))* 2015. (ENG.). 352p. 16.99 *(978-0-06-222190-2(6))* HarperCollins Pubs. (Waldon Pond Pr.).

—The Vanishing Island. Stevenson, Dave, illus. 2016. (Chronicles of the Black Tulip Ser.: Vol. 1). (ENG.). 368p. (J). (gr. 3-7). 17.20 *(978-0-606-39260-0(2))* Turtleback Bks.

Wooster, Devin Ann. Barbie & Her Sisters in the Great Puppy Adventure. 2015. (Barbie Chapters Ser.). (ENG.). 64p. (J). (gr. 1-4). pap. 5.99 *(978-0-553-53764-2(4),* Random Hse. Bks. for Young Readers) Random Hse. Children's Bks.

Wygand, Melissa. Where the Pirates Arrgh! (SpongeBob SquarePants) Martinez, Heather, illus. 2013. (Little Golden Book Ser.). (ENG.). 24p. (J). (-k). 3.99 *(978-0-307-98174-5(6),* Golden Bks.) Random Hse. Children's Bks.

Zhang, Kat. The Emperor's Riddle. 2017. (ENG., Illus.). 256p. (J). (gr. 3-7). 16.99 ***(978-1-4814-7862-5(1),*** Aladdin) Simon & Schuster Children's Publishing.

Ziegler-Sullivan, Ursula. Pirate Pups! Petrossi, Fabrizio, illus. 2016. (J). *(978-1-4806-9717-1(6),* Golden Bks.) Random Hse. Children's Bks.

BURMA

Aung San Suu Kyi. 2014. (Making a Difference: Leaders Who Are Changing the World Ser.). 48p. (J). (gr. 5-8). 25.85 *(978-1-62275-430-4(1))* Rosen Publishing Group, Inc., The.

Bjorklund, Ruth. Aung San Suu Kyi. 2013. 112p. (gr. 7-12). (J). 39.93 *(978-0-7614-4957-7(4));* (YA). pap. 19.99 *(978-1-62712-115-6(3))* Cavendish Square Publishing.

Burling, Alexis. Aung San Suu Kyi: Burmese Politician & Activist for Democracy. 2017. (J). ***(978-1-5383-8070-3(6));*** pap. ***(978-1-5383-8069-7(2))*** Rosen Publishing Group, Inc., The.

Hare, Eric B. Jungle Heroes & Other Stories. 2005. (Illus.). 106p. (J). 9.99 *(978-0-8163-2063-9(2))* Pacific Pr. Publishing Assn.

Harris, Nathaniel. Burma (Myanmar) 2009. (Global Hotspots Ser.). 32p. (gr. 5-18). lib. bdg. 18.56 *(978-0-7614-4758-0(X))* Marshall Cavendish Corp.

K/H (Pathways). Pathways: Grade 6 Dr. Rabbit Trade Book. rev. ed. 2011. (ENG.). 30p. pap. 11.00 *(978-0-7575-4840-6(7))* Kendall Hunt Publishing Co.

Mara, Wil. Burma. 2016. (Enchantment of the World Ser.). (ENG., Illus.). 144p. (J). lib. bdg. 40.00 *(978-0-531-23294-1(8),* Children's Pr.) Scholastic Library Publishing.

O'Keefe, Sherry. Aung San Suu Kyi. 2012. (Champion of Freedom Ser.). (J). (gr. 7-12). 28.95 *(978-1-59935-168-1(4))* Reynolds, Morgan Inc.

Rodger, Ellen. A Refugee's Journey from Myanmar. 2017. 32p. (J). ***(978-0-7787-3674-5(1))*** Crabtree Publishing Co.

Rose, Simon. Aung San Suu Kyi. 2011. (J). (gr. 4-6). pap. 12.95 *(978-1-61690-834-8(3),* AV2 by Weigl); (Illus.). 24p. (YA). (gr. 3-6). 27.13 *(978-1-61690-833-1(5))* Weigl Pubs., Inc.

Rush, Elizabeth. M Is for Myanmar. 2011. (Alphabetical World Ser.). (ENG.). 40p. (J). (gr. k-4). 12.95 *(978-1-934159-28-6(X))* ThingsAsian Pr.

Streissguth, Thomas. Myanmar in Pictures. 2007. (Visual Geography (Lerner) Ser.). (Illus.). 80p. (YA). (gr. 7-12). lib. bdg. 31.93 *(978-0-8225-7146-9(3))* Twenty First Century Bks.

Yin, Saw Myat & Elias, Josie. Myanmar. 3rd rev. ed. 2011. (Cultures of the World: 3rd Edition 1 Ser.). (Illus.). 144p. (J). (gr. 6). 47.07 *(978-1-60870-786-7(5))* Marshall Cavendish Corp.

Zahler, Diane. Than Shwe's Burma. 2009. (Dictatorships Ser.). (ENG.). 160p. (gr. 9-12). 38.60 *(978-0-8225-9097-2(2))* Lerner Publishing Group.

BURMA—FICTION

Fenn, G. Manville. The Rajah of Dah. 2011. 194p. 26.95 *(978-1-4638-9697-3(2))* Rodgers, Alan Bks.

Hare, Eric B. Curse Proof. 2007. (Illus.). 95p. (J). 10.99 *(978-0-8163-2208-4(2))* Pacific Pr. Publishing Assn.

Howat, Irene. Adoniram Judson: Danger on the Streets of Gold. 2007. (Trailblazers Ser.). (ENG.). 160p. (J). mass mkt. 8.99 *(978-1-85792-660-6(9),* aa09dd00-c28c-4172-8dee-7bb4c77f28dc) Christian Focus Pubns. GBR. Dist: Bookmasters Distribution.

Perkins, Mitali. Bamboo People. 2010. (ENG.). 288p. (J). (gr. 5-9). 17.95 *(978-1-58089-328-2(7))* Charlesbridge Publishing, Inc.

Smith, Roland. Elephant Run. 2009. (ENG.). 336p. (J). (gr. 5-6). pap. 6.99 *(978-1-4231-0401-8(3))* Hyperion Pr.

BURNETT, FRANCES HODGSON, 1849-1924

Collins, Carolyn Strom & Eriksson, Christina Wyss. Inside the Secret Garden: A Treasury of Crafts, Recipes, & Activities. Tudor, Tasha, illus. 2004. 130p. (J). (gr. 2-8). reprint ed. 25.00 *(978-0-7567-7630-5(9))* DIANE Publishing Co.

BURR, AARON, 1756-1836

Brown, Don. Aaron & Alexander: The Most Famous Duel in American History. 2015. (ENG., Illus.). 32p. (J). (gr. k-4). 17.99 *(978-1-59643-998-6(X),* 9781596439986) Roaring Brook Pr.

Greeley, August. Pistols & Politics: Alexander Hamilton Duels Aaron Burr. 2004. (Primary Sources of Famous People in American History Ser.). (ENG.). 32p. (gr. 4-8). pap. 10.00 *(978-0-8239-4327-2(5),* Rosen Classroom) Rosen Publishing Group, Inc., The.

—Pistols & Politics: Alexander Hamilton's Great Duel. 2009. (Great Moments in American History Ser.). 32p. (gr. 3-3). 47.90 *(978-1-61513-149-5(3))* Rosen Publishing Group, Inc., The.

Lucas, Eileen. The Aaron Burr Treason Trial. 2003. (Headline Court Cases Ser.). (Illus.). 112p. (J). (gr. 6-12). lib. bdg. 27.94 *(978-0-7660-1765-8(6))* Enslow Pubs., Inc.

Melton, Buckner F. Aaron Burr: The Rise & Fall of an American Politician. 2009. (Library of American Lives & Times Ser.). 112p. (gr. 5-5). 69.20 *(978-1-60853-468-5(5))* Rosen Publishing Group, Inc., The.

Perrin, Pat. The Mystery of the Deadly Duel. 2004. (Illus.). 64p. pap. 9.00 *(978-0-7891-5996-0(1))* Perfection Learning Corp.

Seeley, M. H. 20 Fun Facts about Aaron Burr. 2017. (Fun Fact File: Founding Fathers Ser.). 32p. (gr. 2-3). 25.25 ***(978-1-5382-0281-4(6))*** Stevens, Gareth Publishing LLLP.

St. George, Judith. The Duel: The Parallel Lives of Alexander Hamilton & Aaron Burr. 2016. lib. bdg. 20.85 *(978-0-606-38853-5(2))* Turtleback Bks.

BURROUGHS, JOHN, 1837-1921

Bloodgood, Dorothy U. A Post Card Portrait with Memorabilia of John Burroughs Literary Naturalist. 2nd ed. 2004. (Illus.). 48p. per. 11.95 *(978-0-910746-33-5(8))* Hope Farm Pr. & Bookshop.

BURTON, RICHARD FRANCIS, SIR, 1821-1890

Young, Serinity. Richard Francis Burton: Explorer, Scholar, Spy. 2006. (Great Explorations Ser.). (Illus.). 80p. (gr. 6-7). lib. bdg. 22.95 *(978-0-7614-2222-8(6),* Benchmark Bks.) Marshall Cavendish Corp.

BURYING GROUNDS

see Cemeteries

BUS DRIVERS

Gorman, Jacqueline Laks. Bus Drivers. Andersen, Gregg, photos by. 2010. (People in My Community Ser.). (Illus.). 24p. (gr. k-3). pap. 8.15 *(978-1-4339-3336-3(5))* Stevens, Gareth Publishing LLLP.

Gorman, Jacqueline Laks & Laks Gorman, Jacqueline. Bus Drivers. Andersen, Gregg, photos by. 2010. (People in My Community Ser.). (Illus.). 24p. (gr. k-3). 22.60 *(978-1-4339-3335-6(7))* Stevens, Gareth Publishing LLLP.

Jeffries, Joyce. Meet the Bus Driver. 2012. (People Around Town Ser.). (Illus.). 24p. (gr. k-2). 69.20 *(978-1-4339-8059-6(2));* (J). 22.60 *(978-1-4339-7324-6(3));* (J). pap. 8.15 *(978-1-4339-7325-3(1))* Stevens, Gareth Publishing LLLP.

—Meet the Bus Driver /Te Presento A Los Conductores de AutobúS. 2012. (People Around Town / Gente de mi ciudad Ser.). (SPA & ENG., Illus.). 24p. (J). (gr. k-2). 22.60 *(978-1-4339-7384-0(7))* Stevens, Gareth Publishing LLLP.

Laks Gorman, Jacqueline. Bus Drivers / Conductores de Autobuses. Andersen, Gregg, photos by. 2010. (People in My Community / Mi comunidad Ser.). (SPA., Illus.). 24p. (gr. k-3). pap. 8.15 *(978-1-4339-3754-5(9))* Stevens, Gareth Publishing LLLP.

Mitchell, Melanie. School Bus Drivers. 2005. (Pull Ahead Books: Community Helpers Ser.). 32p. (gr. k-3). (ENG.). pap. 7.95 *(978-0-8225-5472-1(0));* (Illus.). (J). 22.60 *(978-0-8225-1695-8(0))* Lerner Publishing Group.

Murray, Julie. Bus Drivers, 1 vol. 2010. (Buddy Bks.). (ENG.). 32p. (J). (gr. 2-5). 27.07 *(978-1-61613-504-1(2))* ABDO Publishing Co.

Owen, Ann. Taking You Places: A Book about Bus Drivers, 1 vol. Thomas, Eric, illus. 2003. (Community Workers Ser.). (ENG.). 24p. (J). (gr. -1-3). per. 8.95 *(978-1-4048-0484-5(6))* Picture Window Bks.

Rivera, Sheila. Bus Driver. 2004. (First Step Nonfiction Ser.). (J). pap. 3.95 *(978-0-8225-5362-5(7),* Lerner Pubns.) Lerner Publishing Group.

Watts, Franklin & Phillips, Hannah. Bus Driver. 2017. (Here to Help Ser.). (ENG., Illus.). 24p. (J). (gr. k-2). 16.99 *(978-1-4451-3993-7(6),* Franklin Watts) Hachette Children's Group GBR. Dist: Hachette Bk. Group.

BUS DRIVERS—FICTION

Anstee, Ashlyn. Are We There, Yeti? Anstee, Ashlyn, illus. 2015. (ENG., Illus.). 40p. (J). (gr. -1-3). 17.99 *(978-1-4814-3089-0(0),* Simon & Schuster Bks. For Young Readers) Simon & Schuster Bks. For Young Readers.

Bass, Barbara. Gus the Bus Driver. 2010. 32p. 17.95 *(978-1-4269-3460-5(2))* Trafford Publishing.

Grant, Vicki. Cochonnet: (Pigboy), 1 vol. 2011. (FRE.). 112p. (J). (gr. 5-9). pap. 9.95 *(978-1-4598-0006-9(0))* Orca Bk. Pubs. USA.

Jasper, Rick & Reece, Richard. The Late Bus. 2011. (Night Fall Ser.). (ENG.). 112p. (YA). (gr. 6-12). pap. 7.95 *(978-0-7613-7812-9(X))* Lerner Publishing Group.

Marin, Cheech. Captain Cheech. Ramirez, Orlando L., illus. 2008. 32p. (J). (gr. -1-3). lib. bdg. 17.89 *(978-0-06-113208-7(X))* HarperCollins Pubs.

—Cheech y el Autobus Fantasma. Fabiancic, Miriam, tr. Ramirez, Orlando L., illus. 2009. (SPA.). 32p. (J). (gr. -1-3). 17.99 *(978-0-06-113214-8(4),* Rayo) HarperCollins Pubs.

Russell, Joyce. My First Bus Ride to School. 2011. 28p. 12.03 *(978-1-4567-1111-5(3))* AuthorHouse.

Scala, Vincent. Beep Beep Goes the Bus Driver, 1 vol. 2013. (ENG., Illus.). 32p. (J). 16.99 *(978-0-7643-4493-0(5),* 9780764344930) Schiffer Publishing, Ltd.

Seltzer, Eric & Hall, Kirsten. Dog on His Bus. Braun, Sebastien, illus. 2012. (Penguin Young Readers, Level 2 Ser.). (ENG.). 32p. (J). (gr. 1-2). pap. 3.99 *(978-0-448-45904-2(3),* Penguin Young Readers) Penguin Young Readers Group.

—Dog on His Bus. Braun, Sebastien, illus. 2012. (Penguin Young Readers Level 2 Ser.). lib. bdg. 13.55 *(978-0-606-25815-9(9),* Turtleback) Turtleback Bks.

Thaler, Mike. The School Bus Driver from the Black Lagoon, 1 vol. Lee, Jared, illus. 2012. (Black Lagoon Set 2 Ser.: No. 2). (ENG.). 32p. (J). (gr. 1-4). lib. bdg. 24.21 *(978-1-59961-957-6(1))* Spotlight.

Toombs, Robert. Dottie the Bus Driver in Bicycle Safety. Barnett, Linda, illus. 2013. 24p. pap. 9.99 *(978-0-9885180-6-3(6))* Mindstir Media.

Whisler, Barbara. Shag Finds a Home. Jackson, Kay, illus. 2008. 24p. pap. 24.95 *(978-1-60703-730-9(0))* America Star Bks.

Wick, Kimberly. Katie's First Day of School: The Adventures of Mrs. Swirlie. 2009. 36p. pap. 15.49 *(978-1-4389-2257-7(4))* AuthorHouse.

Willems, Mo. Don't Let the Pigeon Drive the Bus! Willems, Mo, illus. 2012. (Pigeon Ser.). (ENG., Illus.). 40p. (J). (gr. -1-k). pap. 19.99 *(978-1-4231-4514-1(3))* Hyperion Pr.

—Don't Let the Pigeon Stay Up Late! Willems, Mo, illus. 2006. (Pigeon Ser.). (ENG., Illus.). 40p. (J). (gr. -1-k). 16.99 *(978-0-7868-3746-5(2))* Hyperion Pr.

—¡No Dejes Que la Paloma Conduzca el Autobús! Willems, Mo, illus. 2011.Tr. of Don't Let the Pigeon Drive the Bus. (SPA & ENG., Illus.). 40p. (J). (gr. -1-k). pap. 7.99 *(978-1-4231-4052-8(4))* Hyperion Pr.

Willems, Mo & Scieszka, Jon, narrated by. Don't Let the Pigeon Drive the Bus! 2011. (J). (gr. -1-1). 29.95 *(978-0-545-13453-8(6))* Weston Woods Studios, Inc.

BUSES

Ashley, Susan. En Autobús. 2003. (Weekly Reader Early Learning Library). (SPA., Illus.). 24p. (gr. 1-4). pap. 8.15 *(978-0-8368-3639-8(4),* Weekly Reader Leveled Readers) Stevens, Gareth Publishing LLLP.

—Going by Bus. 2003. (Weekly Reader Early Learning Library). (Illus.). 24p. (gr. 1-4). pap. 8.15 *(978-0-8368-3834-3(3),* Weekly Reader Leveled Readers) Stevens, Gareth Publishing LLLP.

Baby's Very First Bus Book. 2017. (Baby's Very First Bus Book Ser.). (ENG.). (J). bds. 8.99 ***(978-0-7945-3997-9(1),*** Usborne) EDC Publishing.

Beck, Isabel L., et al. Trophies Kindergarten: My Bus. 2003. (Trophies Ser.). (gr. k-6). 13.80 *(978-0-15-329522-5(8))* Harcourt Schl. Pubs.

Bloom, Paul. Rules on the Bus. 2015. (School Rules Ser.). (ENG., Illus.). 24p. (J). (gr. k-k). pap. 8.15 *(978-1-4824-2653-3(6))* Stevens, Gareth Publishing LLLP.

Burch, Lynda S. Wicky Wacky Things that Go! Busses. Burch, Lynda S., photos by. 2004. (Illus.). 28p. (J). E-Book 9.95 incl. cd-rom *(978-1-933090-06-1(5))* Guardian Angel Publishing, Inc.

Faircloth, Harry W. My First Bus Ride. Anderson, Billie Ann, illus. Date not set. 26p. (J). (gr. -1-4). pap. 9.95 *(978-0-9668650-1-1(4))* Maximilian Pr. Pubs.

Garrett, Winston. Let's Ride the School Bus! 2014. (Public Transportation Ser.). 24p. (J). (gr. k-2). pap. 49.50 *(978-1-4777-6517-3(4),* PowerKids Pr.) Rosen Publishing Group, Inc., The.

—¡Vamos a Tomar el Autobús Escolar! / Let's Ride the School Bus! de la Vega, Eida, ed. 2014. (Transporte Público / Public Transportation Ser.). (SPA & ENG.). 24p. (J). (gr. k-2). 23.60 *(978-1-4777-6787-0(8),* PowerKids Pr.) Rosen Publishing Group, Inc., The.

Gorman, Jacqueline Laks. Bus Drivers. Andersen, Gregg, photos by. 2010. (People in My Community Ser.). (Illus.). 24p. (gr. k-3). pap. 8.15 *(978-1-4339-3336-3(5))* Stevens, Gareth Publishing LLLP.

Gorman, Jacqueline Laks & Laks Gorman, Jacqueline. Bus Drivers. Andersen, Gregg, photos by. 2010. (People in My Community Ser.). (Illus.). 24p. (gr. k-3). 22.60 *(978-1-4339-3335-6(7))* Stevens, Gareth Publishing LLLP.

Hamilton, Robert M. On a Bus. 2012. (Going Places Ser.). (ENG.). 24p. (J). (gr. k-2). pap. 8.15 *(978-1-4339-6275-2(6));* lib. bdg. 22.60 *(978-1-4339-6273-8(X))* Stevens, Gareth Publishing LLLP.

Hanson, Anders. Let's Go by Bus, 1 vol. 2008. (Let's Go Ser.). (ENG., Illus.). 24p. (J). (gr. k-3). lib. bdg. 24.21 *(978-1-59928-895-6(8),* SandCastle) ABDO Publishing Co.

Hort, Lenny. Seals on the Bus. Karas, G. Brian & Karas, G., illus. 2008. (ENG.). 32p. (J). (gr. -1-k). pap. 26.99 *(978-0-8050-8678-2(1),* 9780805086782, Holt, Henry & Co. Bks. For Young Readers) Holt, Henry & Co.

Jeffries, Joyce. Meet the Bus Driver. 2012. (People Around Town Ser.). (Illus.). 24p. (gr. k-2). 69.20 *(978-1-4339-8059-6(2))* Stevens, Gareth Publishing LLLP.

—Meet the Bus Driver /Te Presento A Los Conductores de AutobúS. 2012. (People Around Town / Gente de mi ciudad Ser.). (SPA & ENG., Illus.). 24p. (J). (gr. k-2). 22.60 *(978-1-4339-7384-0(7))* Stevens, Gareth Publishing LLLP.

Jennings, Rosemary. Safe on the School Bus. 2016. (Safety Smarts Ser.). 00024p. (J). (gr. k-1). pap. 8.25 *(978-1-4994-2786-8(7),* PowerKids Pr.) Rosen Publishing Group, Inc., The.

Katz, Karen. The Babies on the Bus. Katz, Karen, illus. 2013. (ENG., Illus.). 28p. (J). (gr. -1-k). bds. 7.99 *(978-0-8050-9779-5(1),* 9780805097795, Holt, Henry & Co. Bks. For Young Readers) Holt, Henry & Co.

Laks Gorman, Jacqueline. Bus Drivers / Conductores de Autobuses. Andersen, Gregg, photos by. 2010. (People in My Community / Mi comunidad Ser.). (SPA., Illus.). 24p. (gr. k-3). pap. 8.15 *(978-1-4339-3754-5(9))* Stevens, Gareth Publishing LLLP.

Lassieur, Allison. Buses in Action. 2012. (Transportation Zone Ser.). (ENG.). 24p. (J). (gr. 1-2). pap. 41.70 *(978-1-4296-8394-4(5));* lib. bdg. 25.32 *(978-1-4296-7689-2(2))* Capstone Press of Coughlan Cos. (First Facts).

Manolis, Kay. School Buses. 2008. (Mighty Machines Ser.). (ENG., Illus.). 24p. (J). (gr. k-3). lib. bdg. 25.95 *(978-1-60014-180-5(3))* Bellwether Media.

Mattern, Joanne. Staying Safe on the School Bus. 2007. (Safety First Ser.). (Illus.). 24p. (gr. k-3). pap. 8.15 *(978-0-8368-7802-8(7));* lib. bdg. 22.00 *(978-0-8368-7795-3(0))* Stevens, Gareth Publishing LLLP. (Weekly Reader Leveled Readers).

—Staying Safe on the School Bus/La Seguridad en el Autobús Escol Ar. 2007. (Safety First / la Seguridad Es lo Primero Ser.). (SPA., Illus.). 24p. (gr. k-3). lib. bdg. 22.00 *(978-0-8368-8060-1(9),* Weekly Reader Leveled Readers) Stevens, Gareth Publishing LLLP.

Mitchell, Melanie. School Bus Drivers. 2005. (Pull Ahead Books: Community Helpers Ser.). 32p. (gr. k-3). (ENG.). pap. 7.95 *(978-0-8225-5472-1(0));* (Illus.). (J). 22.60 *(978-0-8225-1695-8(0))* Lerner Publishing Group.

Morey, Allan. School Buses. 2014. (Illus.). 24p. (J). lib. bdg. 25.65 *(978-1-62031-108-0(9),* Bullfrog Bks.) Jump! Inc.

Murray, Julie. Bus Drivers, 1 vol. 2010. (Buddy Bks.). (ENG.). 32p. (J). (gr. 2-5). 27.07 *(978-1-61613-504-1(2))* ABDO Publishing Co.

Orr, Tamra B. Pondering Pollution. 2014. (Explorer Library: Follow the Clues Ser.). (ENG., Illus.). 32p. (J). (gr. 4-8). 28.50 *(978-1-62431-779-8(0),* 203312) Cherry Lake Publishing.

Peppas, Lynn. Big Buses. 2011. (ENG.). 32p. (J). lib. bdg. *(978-0-7787-2726-2(2));* (Vehicles on the Move Ser.: No. 12). pap. *(978-0-7787-2733-0(5))* Crabtree Publishing Co.

Peters, Elisa. Let's Ride the City Bus! 2014. (Public Transportation Ser.). 24p. (J). (gr. k-2). 23.60 *(978-1-4777-6482-4(8),* PowerKids Pr.) Rosen Publishing Group, Inc., The.

—¡Vamos a Tomar el Autobús! / Let's Ride the City Bus! de la Vega, Eida, ed. 2014. (Transporte Público / Public Transportation Ser.). (SPA & ENG.). 24p. (J). (gr. k-2). 23.60 *(978-1-4777-6777-1(0),* PowerKids Pr.) Rosen Publishing Group, Inc., The.

Raatma, Lucia. Staying Safe on the School Bus, 1 vol. 2011. (Staying Safe Ser.). (ENG.). 24p. (gr. 1-2). pap. 7.29 *(978-1-4296-7199-6(8));* pap. 41.70 *(978-1-4296-7200-9(5));* lib. bdg. 25.32 *(978-1-4296-6823-1(7))* Capstone Press of Coughlan Cos. (First Facts).

Randolph, Joanne. Let's Draw a School Bus with Shapes. Muschinske, Emily, illus. 2005. (Let's Draw with Shapes Ser.). 24p. (J). (gr. k-1). lib. bdg. 22.60 *(978-1-4042-2791-0(1),* PowerKids Pr.) Rosen Publishing Group, Inc., The.

—Let's Draw a School Bus with Shapes: Vamos a Dibujar un Autobus Escolar Usando Figuras. Muschinske, Emily, illus. 2005. (Let's Draw with Shapes / Vamos a Dibujar con Figuras Ser.). (ENG & SPA.). (J). 22.60 *(978-1-4042-7557-7(6),* PowerKids Pr.) Rosen Publishing Group, Inc., The.

Rau, Dana Meachen. Buses. 2009. (Bookworms Ser.). 24p. (gr. k-1). 15.95 *(978-0-7614-4077-2(1))* Marshall Cavendish Corp.

—Buses/En Autobuses. 2009. (Bookworms Ser.). (SPA & ENG.). 24p. (gr. k-1). lib. bdg. 15.95 *(978-0-7614-4766-5(0))* Marshall Cavendish Corp.

Rustad, Martha. Tanya Takes the School Bus. Becker, Paula, illus. 2017. (Cloverleaf Books (tm) — off to School Ser.). (ENG.). (J). (gr. k-2). pap. 7.99 ***(978-1-5124-5580-9(6)***, Millbrook Pr.) Lerner Publishing Group.

Rustad, Martha E. H. Tanya Takes the School Bus. Becker, Paula J., illus. 2017. (Cloverleaf Books (tm) — off to School Ser.). (ENG.). 24p. (J). (gr. k-2). 25.32 ***(978-1-5124-3939-7(8)***, Millbrook Pr.) Lerner Publishing Group.

Sévigny, Eric, illus. The School Bus. 2003. (Clubhouse Ser.). (ENG.). 24p. (J). (gr. -1-1). pap. 3.99 *(978-2-89450-421-5(7))* Caillouet, Gerry.

Smith, K. Be Safe on the Bus: Learning the B Sound. 2009. (PowerPhonics Ser.). 24p. (gr. 1-1). 39.90 *(978-1-60851-434-2(X)*, PowerKids Pr.) Rosen Publishing Group, Inc., The.

Tourville, Amanda Doering. Manners on the School Bus (Comportamiento y Modales en el Autobús Escolar) Lensch, Chris, illus. 2011. (¡Así Debemos Ser!: Buenos Modales, Buen Comportamiento/Way to Be!: Manners Ser.). (ENG, SPA & MUL.). 24p. (gr. -1-2). lib. bdg. 26.65 *(978-1-4048-6696-6(5))* Picture Window Bks.

Zuehlke, Jeffrey. Buses. 2004. (Pull Ahead Books-Mighty Movers Ser.). (ENG., Illus.). 32p. (gr. k-3). pap. 7.95 *(978-0-8225-2380-2(9))*; lib. bdg. 22.60 *(978-0-8225-1538-8(5))* Lerner Publishing Group.

BUSES—FICTION

Adler, David A. Bones & the Big Yellow Mystery, No. 1. Newman, Barbara Johansen, illus. 2008. (Bones Ser.: 1). (ENG.). 32p. (J). (gr. 1-3). mass mkt. 3.99 *(978-0-14-241042-4(X)*, Penguin Young Readers) Penguin Young Readers Group.

Allen, Richard L. Kindergarteners on Their First School Bus. 2012. 34p. pap. 9.95 *(978-1-60414-636-3(2))* Fideli Publishing, Inc.

Allyson, Libby. Scottie Rides the Bus. 2004. 27p. pap. 24.95 *(978-1-4137-3298-6(4))* PublishAmerica, Inc.

The Anywhere Everywhere Bus, 6 vols., Pack. (gr. k-1). 23.00 *(978-0-7635-9065-9(7))* Rigby Education.

Barlow, Andrew. Jellytoes Misses the Bus. Barlow, Andrew, illus. 2005. (Jellytoes Ser.). (ENG., Illus.). 32p. (J). per. 8.95 *(978-0-9764336-0-6(5))* MJS Publishing Group LLC.

Barton, Byron. My Bus Board Book. Barton, Byron, illus. 2015. (ENG., Illus.). 38p. (J). (gr. -1 — 1). bds. 7.99 *(978-0-06-228738-0(9)*, Greenwillow Bks.) HarperCollins Pubs.

Bass, Barbara. Gus the Bus Driver. 2010. 32p. 17.95 *(978-1-4269-3460-5(2))* Trafford Publishing.

Blance, Ellen & Cook, Tony. Monster on the Bus. Date not set. (Illus.). 24p. pap. 129.15 *(978-0-582-18595-1(5))* Addison-Wesley Longman, Ltd. GBR. Dist: Trans-Atlantic Pubns., Inc.

Britan, Denise G. Harry Meets Sam. 2011. 24p. pap. 12.99 *(978-1-4628-6756-1(1))* Xlibris Corp.

Brooks, Felicity & Durber, Matt. Busy Bus. Crisp, Dan, illus. 2007. (Play Bks). 10p. (J). bds. 10.99 *(978-0-7945-1701-4(3)*, Usborne) EDC Publishing.

Brown, Marc. Arthur Lost & Found. 2004. (Arthur Adventure Ser.). (J). (gr. k-3). spiral bd. *(978-0-616-11102-4(9))* Canadian National Institute for the Blind/Institut National Canadien pour les Aveugles.

Cabral, Jeane. All Aboard the Yellow School Bus: Follow the Bus Through the Pages on a Counting Adventure! Top That Publishing Staff, ed. Petrlik, Andrea, illus. 2008. (Story Book Ser.). 20p. (J). (gr. -1). *(978-1-84666-543-1(4)*, Tide Mill Pr.) Top That! Publishing PLC.

Carter, Denzel T. Our Bus Trip. 2015. (Rosen REAL Readers: STEM & STEAM Collection). (ENG.). 8p. pap. 5.46 *(978-1-4994-9718-2(0)*, Rosen Classroom) Rosen Publishing Group, Inc., The.

Carter, Shawn. Sheldon's First School Bus Ride. 2012. 16p. pap. 15.99 *(978-1-4685-4932-4(4))* AuthorHouse.

Christian, Reinar Carl, Sr. Nate: The New Bus on the Block! l.t. ed. 2005. (Illus.). 41p. (J). 16.99 *(978-0-9769866-0-7(4))* Meritage Publishing.

Cole, Joanna. The Magic School Bus & the Climate Challenge. Degen, Bruce, illus. 2010. (Magic School Bus Ser.). (ENG.). 48p. (J). (gr. 2-5). 16.99 *(978-0-590-10826-3(3)*, Scholastic Pr.) Scholastic, Inc.

—The Science Fair Expedition. Degen, Bruce, illus. 2006. (Magic School Bus Ser.). (ENG.). 56p. (J). (gr. 2-5). 17.99 *(978-0-590-10824-9(7)*, Scholastic) Scholastic, Inc.

Crandell, Bethany. Summer on the Short Bus. 2014. (ENG.). 256p. (YA). (gr. 2-17). pap. 9.95 *(978-0-7624-4951-4(9)*, Running Pr. Kids) Running Pr. Bk. Pubs.

Crow, Melinda Melton. Brave Fire Truck, 1 vol. Thompson, Chad, illus. 2011. (Wonder Wheels Ser.). (ENG.). 32p. (gr. -1-1). pap. 6.25 *(978-1-4342-3384-4(7))*; lib. bdg. 22.65 *(978-1-4342-3029-4(5))* Stone Arch Bks.

—Field Trip for School Bus, 1 vol. Thompson, Chad, illus. 2012. (Wonder Wheels Ser.). (ENG.). 32p. (gr. -1-1). pap. 6.25 *(978-1-4342-4237-2(4))*; lib. bdg. 22.65 *(978-1-4342-4019-4(3))* Stone Arch Bks.

—Helpful Tractor, 1 vol. Thompson, Chad, illus. 2011. (Wonder Wheels Ser.). (ENG.). 32p. (gr. -1-1). pap. 6.25 *(978-1-4342-3382-0(0))*; lib. bdg. 22.65 *(978-1-4342-3027-0(9))* Stone Arch Bks.

—Lucky School Bus, 1 vol. Thompson, Chad, illus. 2011. (Wonder Wheels Ser.). (ENG.). 32p. (gr. -1-1). pap. 6.25 *(978-1-4342-3381-3(2))*; lib. bdg. 22.65 *(978-1-4342-3026-3(0))* Stone Arch Bks.

Cuyler, Margery. The Little School Bus. Kolar, Bob, illus. 2014. (Little Vehicles Ser.). (ENG.). 32p. (J). (gr. -1-1). 12.99 *(978-0-8050-9435-0(0)*, 9780805094350, Holt, Henry & Co. Bks. For Young Readers) Holt, Henry & Co.

Dave, Safety. Safety Dave & Daisy Ride the Bus. 2011. 16p. 8.95 *(978-1-4520-7218-0(3))* AuthorHouse.

De la Peña, Matt. Last Stop on Market Street. Robinson, Christian, illus. 2015. (ENG.). 32p. (J). 16.99 *(978-0-399-25774-2(8)*, G.P. Putnam's Sons Books for Young Readers) Penguin Publishing Group.

Demarest, Chris L. Bus. 2017. (ENG., Illus.). 16p. (J). (— 1). bds. 6.99 *(978-0-544-87087-1(5)*, HMH Books For Young Readers) Houghton Mifflin Harcourt Publishing Co.

DeMico, Judy. The Bus Trip, 1 vol. Johnson, Catherine LeAnn, illus. 2010. 26p. pap. 24.95 *(978-1-4489-2767-8(6))* PublishAmerica, Inc.

Derrick, Patricia. Mr. Walrus & the Old School Bus. Martinez, J-P Loppo, illus. 2007. 32p. 18.95 incl. audio compact disk *(978-1-933818-13-9(1))* Animalations.

Dubuc, Marianne & Ghione, Yvette. The Bus Ride. Dubuc, Marianne, illus. 2015. (ENG., Illus.). 40p. (J). (gr. -1-2). 15.95 *(978-1-77138-209-0(0))* Kids Can Pr., Ltd. CAN. Dist: Hachette Bk. Group.

Edmondson, Frank. Mr. Frank's Magic School Bus: Rainbow's End Adventure. Edmondson, Brad, illus. 2007. 20p. per. 24.95 *(978-1-4241-8617-4(X))* America Star Bks.

—Mr. Frank's Magic School Bus: Rainbow's End Adventure, 1 vol. Edmondson, Brad, illus. 2010. 20p. 24.95 *(978-1-4512-1042-2(6))* PublishAmerica, Inc.

Ella, Peter Leo. Class Party on the Big Yellow School Bus. Ella, Peter Leo, illus. 2013. (Illus.). 28p. pap. *(978-9980-86-513-7(X))* University of Papua New Guinea Press.

Gomi, Taro. Bus Stops. 2013. (ENG., Illus.). 34p. (J). (gr. -1-7). bds. 6.99 *(978-1-4521-0755-4(6))* Chronicle Bks. LLC.

Graham, Bob. A Bus Called Heaven. Graham, Bob, illus. 2012. (ENG., Illus.). 40p. (J). (gr. -1-2). 16.99 *(978-0-7636-5893-9(6))* Candlewick Pr.

Gulbis, Stephen, illus. The Wheels on the Bus. 2003. 22p. (YA). *(978-1-85602-454-9(7)*, Pavilion Children's Books) Pavilion Bks.

Hay un esqueleto en el Autobus: Individual Title Six-Packs. (Literatura 2000 Ser.). (SPA.). (gr. 2-3). 33.00 *(978-0-7635-1094-7(7))* Rigby Education.

Hofmeister, Alan, et al. The Bus. (Reading for All Learners Ser.). (Illus.). (J). pap. *(978-1-56861-122-8(6))* Swift Learning Resources.

Huneke, Amanda. A Monster on the Bus, 1 vol. Wolek, Guy, illus. 2013. (Monster on the Loose Ser.). (ENG.). 32p. (J). (gr. -1-4). 28.50 *(978-1-61641-933-2(4))* Magic Wagon.

Jessi Swanson And Jessica Swanson & Swanson, Jessica. An Adventurous Day for Lucy. 2011. 28p. pap. 24.95 *(978-1-4626-2426-3(X))* America Star Bks.

Liu, Julia. Gus, the Dinosaur Bus. Lynn, Bei, illus. 2013. (ENG.). 32p. (J). (gr. -1-3). 12.99 *(978-0-547-90573-0(4))* Houghton Mifflin Harcourt Publishing Co.

Maria Muirhead. Smoking = Problems: Flora-Lee's Journal. 2010. 56p. pap. 8.95 *(978-1-4502-0645-7(X))* iUniverse, Inc.

Marie, Lynne. Hedgehog Goes to Kindergarten. Kennedy, Anne, illus. 2011. (J). pap. *(978-0-545-29874-2(1))* Scholastic, Inc.

Marin, Cheech. Captain Cheech. Ramirez, Orlando L., illus. 2008. 32p. (J). (gr. -1-3). lib. bdg. 17.89 *(978-0-06-113208-7(X))* HarperCollins Pubs.

—Cheech the School Bus Driver. Ramirez, Orlando L., illus. 2007. 32p. (J). (gr. -1-3). lib. bdg. 17.89 *(978-0-06-113202-5(0))* HarperCollins Pubs.

McDaid, Mark. Billy the Bus. 2006. (Illus.). 48p. pap. *(978-1-84401-714-0(1))* Athena Pr.

McMullan, Kate. I'm Smart! McMullan, Jim, illus. 2017. 40p. (J). (gr. -1-3). 17.99 *(978-0-06-244923-8(0))* HarperCollins Pubs.

Meister, Cari. Bus Ride Bully, 1 vol. Simard, Remy, illus. (My First Graphic Novel Ser.). (ENG.). 32p. (gr. k-2). 2011. pap. 6.25 *(978-1-4342-3101-7(1))* 2010. 24.65 *(978-1-4342-2059-2(1))* Stone Arch Bks. (My First Graphic Novel).

Montes, Juan Mari. Diario del Autobus a de la Linea 3. 2006. (SPA., Illus.). 96p. (J). *(978-84-667-5192-6(0))* Grupo Anaya, S.A.

MOONEY, Tara. The Big Blue Bus. 2010. 23p. 16.95 *(978-1-4461-5055-9(0))* Lulu Pr., Inc.

Morgan, Vicky S. Jim & Me & Theo T. 2011. 28p. pap. 21.99 *(978-1-4568-8124-5(8))* Xlibris Corp.

Nosy Crow Staff. The Wheels on the Bus: Sing along with Me! Huang, Yu-Hsuan, illus. 2016. (Sing along with Me! Ser.). (ENG.). (J). (-k). bds. 8.99 *(978-0-7636-8648-2(4)*, Nosy Crow) Candlewick Pr.

Nothing Ever Happens 6 Packs. Individual Title. (gr. -1-2). 27.00 *(978-0-7635-9467-1(9))* Rigby Education.

O'Connor, Jane. Fancy Nancy at the Museum. Enik, Ted & Glasser, Robin Preiss, illus. 2008. (I Can Read Level 1 Ser.). (ENG.). 32p. (J). (gr. -1-3). 16.99 *(978-0-06-123608-2(X))*; pap. 3.99 *(978-0-06-123607-5(1))* HarperCollins Pubs.

O'Connor, Jane & Harper Collins / LeapFrog. Fancy Nancy at the Museum. Glasser, Robin Preiss, illus. 2008. (Fancy Nancy Ser.). (J). 13.99 *(978-1-59319-940-1(6))* LeapFrog Enterprises, Inc.

Paquette, Ammi-Joan. Bunny Bus. Withrow, Lesley Breen, illus. 2017. (ENG.). 32p. (J). 16.99 *(978-0-374-30225-2(1)*, 9780374302252, Farrar, Straus & Giroux (BYR)) Farrar, Straus & Giroux.

Phillips, Linda. My Bus Adventure: My Bus Ride. 2009. 24p. pap. 11.49 *(978-1-4490-1675-3(8))* AuthorHouse.

Polak, Monique. 121 Express, 1 vol. 2008. (Orca Currents Ser.). (ENG.). (J). (gr. 5-9). 144p. pap. 9.95 *(978-1-55143-976-1(X))*; 112p. lib. bdg. 16.95 *(978-1-55143-978-5(6))* Orca Bk. Pubs. USA.

Quivers, Anthony S. Lil' Johnny's First Day of School. 2010. 24p. 13.99 *(978-1-4520-4149-0(0))* AuthorHouse.

Robinson, Hilary. Ted's Party Bus. 2009. (ENG., Illus.). 24p. (J). pap. *(978-0-7787-3901-2(5))*; lib. bdg. *(978-0-7787-3870-1(1))* Crabtree Publishing Co.

Roth, Carol. The Little School Bus. Paparone, Pamela, illus. 2004. (ENG.). 32p. (J). (gr. k-1). pap. 7.95 *(978-0-7358-1905-4(X))* North-South Bks., Inc.

Russell, Joyce. My First Bus Ride to School. 2011. 28p. 12.03 *(978-1-4567-1111-5(3))* AuthorHouse.

Scala, Vincent. Beep Beep Goes the Bus Driver, 1 vol. 2013. (ENG., Illus.). 32p. (J). 16.99 *(978-0-7643-4493-0(5)*, 9780764344930) Schiffer Publishing, Ltd.

Seltzer, Eric & Hall, Kirsten. Dog on His Bus. Braun, Sebastien, illus. 2012. (Penguin Young Readers, Level 2 Ser.). (ENG.). 32p. (J). (gr. 1-2). pap. 3.99 *(978-0-448-45904-2(3)*, Penguin Young Readers) Penguin Young Readers Group.

—Dog on His Bus. Braun, Sebastien, illus. 2012. (Penguin Young Readers Level 2 Ser.). lib. bdg. 13.55 *(978-0-606-25815-9(9)*, Turtleback) Turtleback Bks.

Shea, Therese. Un alboroto en el autobús (A Fuss on the Bus) 2007. (Lecturas del barrio (Neighborhood Readers) Ser.). (SPA.). 12p. 33.50 *(978-1-4042-7081-7(7)*, Rosen Classroom) Rosen Publishing Group, Inc., The.

—A Fuss on the Bus. (Neighborhood Readers Ser.). 12p. 2007. (SPA.). 33.50 *(978-1-4042-7080-0(9))* 2006. (ENG.). (gr. -1-3). pap. 5.90 *(978-1-4042-5744-3(6))* Rosen Publishing Group, Inc., The. (Rosen Classroom).

—The School Bus Mystery. 2006. (Neighborhood Readers Ser.). (ENG.). 16p. (gr. 1-3). pap. 6.50 *(978-1-4042-6982-8(7)*, Rosen Classroom) Rosen Publishing Group, Inc., The.

Silvano, Wendi. Just One More. Gamboa, Ricardo, illus. 2007. (ENG.). 36p. (J). reprint ed. pap. 11.95 *(978-0-9744446-5-9(0))* All About Kids Publishing.

The Skeleton on the Bus: Individual Title Six-Packs. (Literatura 2000 Ser.). (gr. 2-3). 33.00 *(978-0-7635-0183-9(2))* Rigby Education.

Slater, Teddy. Safety in the Bus. Smith, Jamie, illus. 2010. 16p. (J). *(978-0-545-24602-6(4))* Scholastic, Inc.

Tattum, Stephan. The Bus. 2005. (J). 4.95 *(978-1-59792-004-9(5))* F.A.S.T. Learning LLC.

Thaler, Mike. The School Bus Driver from the Black Lagoon, 1 vol. Lee, Jared, illus. 2012. (Black Lagoon Set 2 Ser.: No. 2). (ENG.). 32p. (J). (gr. 1-4). lib. bdg. 24.21 *(978-1-59961-957-6(1))* Spotlight.

Towson, Robert. The Wrong Bus, 1 vol. 2010. 34p. 24.95 *(978-1-4489-4345-6(0))* PublishAmerica, Inc.

Wheels on the Bus. 2005. (J). bds. 6.99 *(978-0-9753127-7-3(4))* Family Bks. at Home.

Williams, Sam. School Bus Bunny Bus. Trotter, Stuart, illus. 2006. (ENG.). 10p. (J). (gr. -1-1). 12.95 *(978-1-905417-17-9(9))* Boxer Bks., Ltd. GBR. Dist: Sterling Publishing Co., Inc.

BUSH, GEORGE, 1924-

Childress, Diana. George H. W. Bush. 2007. (Presidential Leaders Ser.). (Illus.). 112p. (J). (gr. 3-7). lib. bdg. 29.27 *(978-0-8225-1510-4(5)*, Lerner Pubns.) Lerner Publishing Group.

Elston, Heidi. George H. W. Bush, 1 vol. 2009. (United States Presidents Ser.). (ENG., Illus.). 40p. (YA). (gr. 3-6). 27.07 *(978-1-60453-443-6(5))* ABDO Publishing Co.

Margaret, Amy. George Bush Presidential Library. (Presidential Libraries Ser.). 24p. 2009. (gr. 3-3). 42.50 *(978-1-60851-484-7(6))* 2004. (Illus.). (J). lib. bdg. 22.60 *(978-0-8239-6273-0(3))* Rosen Publishing Group, Inc., The. (PowerKids Pr.).

Miller, Mirella S. George H. W. Bush. 2017. (Premier Presidents Ser.). (ENG.). 24p. (J). (gr. 1-4). lib. bdg. 27.07 *(978-1-5038-1645-9(1)*, 211488) Child's World, Inc., The.

O'Shei, Tim & Marren, Joe. George H. W. Bush: A MyReportLinks. Com Book. 2003. (Presidents Ser.). (Illus.). 48p. (J). lib. bdg. 25.26 *(978-0-7660-5132-4(3)*, MyReportLinks.com Bks.) Enslow Pubs., Inc.

Parker, Lewis. How to Draw the Life & Times of George H. W. Bush. 2009. (Kid's Guide to Drawing the Presidents of the United States of America Ser.). 32p. (gr. 4-4). 50.50 *(978-1-61511-138-1(7)*, PowerKids Pr.) Rosen Publishing Group, Inc., The.

Parker, Lewis K. How to Draw the Life & Times of George H. W. Bush. 2007. (Kid's Guide to Drawing the Presidents of the United States of America Ser.). (Illus.). 32p. (YA). (gr. 2-5). 26.50 *(978-1-4042-3017-0(3))* Rosen Publishing Group, Inc., The.

Venezia, Mike. George Bush. Venezia, Mike, illus. 2008. (Getting to Know the U. S. Presidents Ser.). (ENG., Illus.). 32p. (J). (gr. 3-4). pap. 7.95 *(978-0-516-25536-1(3)*, Children's Pr.) Scholastic Library Publishing.

Welch, Catherine A. George H. W. Bush. 2009. pap. 52.95 *(978-0-7613-4952-5(9))* 2008. (ENG.). 48p. (gr. 3-6). 27.93 *(978-0-8225-8895-5(1)*, Lerner Pubns.) Lerner Publishing Group.

BUSH, GEORGE W. (GEORGE WALKER), 1946-

Burgan, Michael. George W. Bush. 2011. (Presidents & Their Times 5 Ser.). (Illus.). 96p. (J). (gr. 6). 34.21 *(978-1-60870-184-1(0))* Marshall Cavendish GBR. Dist: Marshall Cavendish Corp.

Donnelly, Matt. George W. Bush. 2005. (Encyc of Presidents, 2ND Ser.). (ENG., Illus.). 112p. (YA). (gr. 5-9). 34.00 *(978-0-516-22972-0(9))* Scholastic Library Publishing.

Fry, Sonali. Let's Read About — George W. Bush. Heyer, Carol, illus. 2003. (Scholastic First Biographies Ser.). (J). pap. *(978-0-439-45953-2(2))* Scholastic, Inc.

Gormley, Beatrice. George W. Bush: Our 43rd President. 2015. (Real-Life Story Ser.). (ENG., Illus.). 256p. (J). (gr. 3-7). 17.99 *(978-1-4814-4645-7(2)*, Aladdin) Simon & Schuster Children's Publishing.

Haskell, L. S. George W. Bush. 2016. (Premier Presidents Ser.). (ENG.). 24p. (J). (gr. 1-4). 27.07 *(978-1-5038-0908-6(0)*, 210744) Child's World, Inc., The.

Heppermann, Christine & Friedman, Richard D. Bush v. Gore: The Florida Recounts of the 2000 Presidential Election, 1 vol. 2012. (Landmark Supreme Court Cases Ser.). (ENG., Illus.). 160p. (J). (gr. 6-12). 37.07 *(978-1-61783-471-4(8))* ABDO Publishing Co.

Hughes, Libby. George W. Bush: From Texas to the White House. 2003. (Great Life Stories Ser.). (ENG., Illus.). 128p. (J). 30.50 *(978-0-531-12310-2(3)*, Watts, Franklin) Scholastic Library Publishing.

Kachurek, Sandra J. George W. Bush. 2004. (United States Presidents Ser.). (Illus.). 128p. (J). lib. bdg. 26.60 *(978-0-7660-2040-5(1))* Enslow Pubs., Inc.

Langley, Andrew. Bush, Blair, & Iraq: Days of Decision, 1 vol. Della-Rovere, Cynthia, illus. 2013. (Days of Decision Ser.). (ENG.). 64p. (gr. 7-8). pap. 10.95 *(978-1-4329-7640-8(0))* Heinemann-Raintree.

Lansford, Tom & Watson, Robert P. George W. Bush. 2004. (gr. 10-12). 22.45 *(978-0-7377-2598-8(2)*, Greenhaven Pr., Inc.) Cengage Gale.

Lee, Sally. George W. Bush, 1 vol. (Presidential Biographies Ser.). (ENG.). 24p. (gr. k-1). 2014. pap. 6.29 *(978-1-4765-9628-0(X)*, Pebble Bks.) 2012. (Illus.). lib. bdg. 26.65 *(978-1-4296-8586-3(7)*, Pebble Plus) Capstone Press of Coughlan Cos.

Mara, Wil. George W. Bush. 2003. (Rookie Biographies Ser.). (ENG.). 32p. (J). (gr. 1-2). pap. 4.95 *(978-0-516-27838-4(X)*, Children's Pr.) Scholastic Library Publishing.

Marquez, Heron. George W. Bush. (Presidential Leaders Ser.). (Illus.). 112p. (gr. 6-12). 2005. (J). lib. bdg. 29.27 *(978-0-8225-1507-4(5)*, Lerner Pubns.) 2005. lib. bdg. 27.93 *(978-0-8225-4995-6(6))* 2003. (YA). 7.95 *(978-0-8225-5001-3(6)*, Carolrhoda Bks.) Lerner Publishing Group.

Mattern, Joanne. Laura Bush, 1 vol. 2008. (First Ladies Set 1 Ser.). (ENG., Illus.). 32p. (YA). (gr. 1-4). 27.07 *(978-1-59928-791-1(9))* ABDO Publishing Co.

McNeese, Tim. George W. Bush: First President of the New Century. 2004. (Notable Americans Ser.). (Illus.). 112p. (YA). (gr. 6-12). 21.95 *(978-1-883846-85-5(4)*, First Biographies) Reynolds, Morgan Inc.

O'Shei, Tim & Marren, Joe. George W. Bush: A MyReportLinks. Com Book. 2003. (Presidents Ser.). (Illus.). 48p. (J). lib. bdg. 25.26 *(978-0-7660-5133-1(1)*, MyReportLinks.com Bks.) Enslow Pubs., Inc.

Rauf, Don. How George W. Bush Fought the Wars in Iraq & Afghanistan. 2017. (Presidents at War Ser.). 128p. (J). (gr. 8-8). lib. bdg. 37.27 ***(978-0-7660-8533-6(3))*** Enslow Pubs., Inc.

Rumsch, BreAnn. George W. Bush, 1 vol. 2009. (United States Presidents Ser.). (ENG., Illus.). 40p. (YA). (gr. 3-6). 27.07 *(978-1-60453-444-3(3))* ABDO Publishing Co.

Schmidt, Roderic. How to Draw the Life & Times of George W. Bush. (Kid's Guide to Drawing the Presidents of the United States of America Ser.). 32p. 2009. (gr. 4-4). 50.50 *(978-1-61511-139-8(5)*, PowerKids Pr.) 2007. (Illus.). (YA). (gr. 2-5). 26.50 *(978-1-4042-3019-4(X))* Rosen Publishing Group, Inc., The.

Sergis, Diana K. Bush vs. Gore: Controversial Presidential Election Case. 2003. (Landmark Supreme Court Cases Ser.). (Illus.). 128p. (J). lib. bdg. 26.60 *(978-0-7660-2095-5(9))* Enslow Pubs., Inc.

Sherman, Patrice. George W. Bush: Gobernado de Texas y Presidente de los Estados Unidos / George W. Bush - Texan Governor & U. S. President. 2013. (Primary Source Readers Ser.). (SPA.). lib. bdg. 19.65 *(978-0-606-31875-4(5)*, Turtleback) Turtleback Bks.

—George W. Bush: Texan Governor & U. S. President, 1 vol. 2012. (Primary Source Readers Ser.). (ENG.). 32p. (J). (gr. 3-3). pap. 8.99 *(978-1-4333-5054-2(8))* Teacher Created Materials, Inc.

Thompson, William & Thompson, Dorcas. George W. Bush. 2004. (Childhoods of the Presidents Ser.). (Illus.). 48p. (J). (gr. 4-18). lib. bdg. 17.95 *(978-1-59084-281-2(2))* Mason Crest.

Wukovits, John F. George W Bush: People in the News. 2004. (Illus.). 111p. (J). (gr. 4-8). reprint ed. 22.00 *(978-0-7567-7902-3(2))* DIANE Publishing Co.

Zahensky, Kenneth. George W. Bush. 2016. (J). lib. bdg. *(978-1-68048-526-4(1))* Rosen Publishing Group, Inc., The.

Zahensky, Kenneth, ed. George W. Bush. 2017. (Pivotal Presidents: Profiles in Leadership Ser.). 80p. (J). (gr. 12-13). 33.90 ***(978-1-68048-629-2(2)***, Britannica Educational Publishing) Rosen Publishing Group, Inc., The.

Zollman, Pam. George W. Bush: President in a Turbulent World. 2006. (People to Know Today Ser.). (Illus.). 128p. (J). (gr. 6-9). lib. bdg. 33.27 *(978-0-7660-2628-5(0))* Enslow Pubs., Inc.

BUSHMEN

see San (African People)

BUSINESS

see also Advertising; Banks and Banking; Credit; Department Stores; Economic History; Industrial Management; Manufactures; Marketing; Markets; Merchants; Occupations; Real Estate Business; Sales Personnel; Small Business

Advanced Principles of Entrepreneurship. 2003. pap., stu. ed. 15.00 *(978-1-890859-11-4(7))* National Foundation for Teaching Entrepreneurship, The.

Advanced Principles of Entrepreneurship, Student Text. 2003. (YA). pap. 35.00 *(978-1-890859-10-7(9))* National Foundation for Teaching Entrepreneurship, The.

Andrews, Carolyn & Thompson, Gare. What Is Importing & Exporting? 2009. (ENG., Illus.). 32p. (J). (gr. 2-5). lib. bdg. *(978-0-7787-4443-6(4))* Crabtree Publishing Co.

Bell, Lonnie. The Story of Coca-Cola. 2003. (Built for Success Ser.). (Illus.). 48p. (J). 28.50 *(978-1-58340-292-4(6))* Black Rabbit Bks.

—The Story of the Ford Motor Company. 2003. (Built for Success Ser.). (Illus.). 48p. (J). 28.50 *(978-1-58340-293-1(4))* Black Rabbit Bks.

Berman, Ron. Fashion. 2012. (Urban Entrepreneurs Ser.). (ENG., Illus.). 40p. (gr. 3-8). pap. 9.95 *(978-1-61570-516-0(3))* Scobre Pr. Corp.

—Food. 2012. (Urban Entrepreneurs Ser.). (ENG., Illus.). 40p. (gr. 3-8). pap. 9.95 *(978-1-61570-517-7(1))* Scobre Pr. Corp.

—Innovators. 2012. (Urban Entrepreneurs Ser.). (ENG., Illus.). 40p. (gr. 3-8). pap. 9.95 *(978-1-61570-518-4(X))* Scobre Pr. Corp.

Black, Cassandra. When I'm Big & Grown: When I'm Big & Grown: I Want to Be an Entrepreneur When I Grow Up. Tucker, Tracey, illus. 2012. (ENG.). 32p. (J). pap. *(978-0-9822503-7-2(1))* Stone Cottage Bks.

Bryant, Jill. Phenomenal Female Entrepreneurs, 1 vol. 2013. (Women's Hall of Fame Ser.). (ENG.). 128p. (J). (gr. 6-8). pap. 10.95 *(978-1-927583-12-8(8))* Second Story Pr. CAN. Dist: Orca Bk. Pubs. USA.

Carlson Berne, Emma. Run Your Own Yard-Work Business. 2014. (Young Entrepreneurs Ser.). 32p. (J). (gr. 4-6). pap. 10.00 *(978-1-4777-3010-2(9)*, PowerKids Pr.) Rosen Publishing Group, Inc., The.

Celebrity Entrepreneurs. 2015. (Celebrity Entrepreneurs Ser.). (ENG.). 48p. (J). (gr. 5-5). 188.16 *(978-1-5026-0282-4(2))*; 77.58 *(978-1-5026-0326-5(8))* Cavendish Square Publishing.

Chappell, Mike & Nuttall, Chris. Business & the European Union. 2003. (ENG., Illus.). 80p. pap. *(978-0-7487-7112-7(3))* Nelson Thornes Ltd.

Connolly, Sean & Pipe, Jim. The Stock Market. 2011. (On the Edge Ser.). 32p. (YA). (gr. 3-6). 28.50 *(978-1-59920-518-2(1))* Black Rabbit Bks.

DaSilva-Gordon, Maria. Top 10 Secrets for Making Money & Even More Money. 2013. 64p. (YA). (gr. 7-12). 31.95 *(978-1-4488-9359-1(3))*; pap. 12.95 *(978-1-4488-9373-7(9))*;

pap. 77.70 *(978-1-4488-9374-4(7))* Rosen Publishing Group, Inc., The.

Dryden, Emma D. & DiOrio, Rana. What Does It Mean to Be an Entrepreneur? Min, Ken, illus. 2016. (ENG.). 32p. (J). (gr. -1-3). 17.95 *(978-1-939775-12-2(4))* March 4th, Inc.

Erickson, Christian. Biz4Kids Business Start-up Kit NEIGHBORHOOD BUSINESSES. 2005. (YA). 29.95 *(978-0-9745218-2-4(5))* Round Cow Media Group.

Erickson, Christian, creator. Biz4KidsBusiness Start-up Guide - Lawn Care. 2004. (Illus.). (J). *(978-0-9745218-0-0(9))* Round Cow Media Group.

Farese, Lois Schneider, et al. Sports & Entertainment Marketing. 2004. (Advanced Marketing Modules Ser.). (ENG., Illus.). 416p. (gr. 9-12). stu. ed., per. 59.48 *(978-0-07-861401-9(5)*, 0078614015) McGraw-Hill Higher Education.

Frisch, Aaron. The Story of Nike. 2003. (Built for Success Ser.). (Illus.). 48p. (J). lib. bdg. 19.95 *(978-1-58340-295-5(0))* Black Rabbit Bks.

Gagne, Tammy. Start Your Petsitting Service. 2017. (Build Your Business Ser.). (ENG.). 32p. (gr. 3-4). lib. bdg. 27.99 ***(978-1-5157-6689-6(6))*** Capstone Press of Coughlan Cos.

Gay, Kathlyn. Women Entrepreneurs. 2016. (Defying Convention: Women Who Changed the Rules Ser.). (Illus.). 128p. (J). 37.27 *(978-0-7660-8143-7(5))* Enslow Pubs., Inc.

Gilbert, Sara. The Story of Pixar. 2015. (Built for Success Ser.). (J). lib. bdg. 23.30 *(978-0-606-37010-3(2))* Turtleback Bks.

Gillespie, Andrew. As Business Studies. 2010. 204p. pap. 13.95 *(978-1-4441-1542-0(1))* Hodder Education Group GBR. Dist: Trans-Atlantic Pubns., Inc.

—Business Studies. 2010. 204p. pap. 13.95 *(978-1-4441-1543-7(X))* Hodder Education Group GBR. Dist: Trans-Atlantic Pubns., Inc.

The Global Marketplace, 1 vol., Set. Incl. Booms, Bubbles, & Busts: The Economic Cycle. Hollander, Barbara. (Illus.). 34.65 *(978-1-4329-3932-8(7))*; Business Without Borders: Globalization. Leppman, Elizabeth & Andrews, David. 34.65 *(978-1-4329-3933-5(5))*; Money Matters: An Introduction to Economics. Hollander, Barbara. 34.65 *(978-1-4329-3929-8(7))*; (gr. 6-9). (Global Marketplace Ser.). (ENG.). 56p. 2010. Set lib. bdg. 103.95 *(978-1-4329-3930-4(0)*, NA-h) Heinemann-Raintree.

Gregory, Joy. Disney. 2017. (J). ***(978-1-5105-2364-7(2))*** SmartBook Media, Inc.

Hoovegen, Margaret. What Is Social Entrepreneurship? 2016. (Your Start-Up Starts Now! a Guide to Entrepreneurship Ser.). (ENG., Illus.). 48p. (J). (gr. 5-8). *(978-0-7787-2757-6(2))* Crabtree Publishing Co.

Hyde, Natalie. What Is Entrepreneurship? 2016. (Your Start-Up Starts Now! a Guide to Entrepreneurship Ser.). (ENG., Illus.). 48p. (J). (gr. 5-8). *(978-0-7787-2758-3(0))* Crabtree Publishing Co.

Industrie und Dienstleistungen. (Duden Abiturhilfen Ser.). (GER.). 112p. (YA). (gr. 12-13). *(978-3-411-06111-2(1))* Bibliographisches Institut & F. A. Brockhaus AG DEU. Dist: International Bk. Import Service, Inc.

Islam, Sabirul. The World at Your Feet: Three Strikes to a Successful Entrepreneurial Life. 2010. (Illus.). 120p. pap. *(978-0-462-09952-1(0))* Marshall Cavendish.

Jacobson, Ryan. Get a Job Helping Others. Cannell, Jon, illus. 2014. (You're in Business! Ser.). 40p. (J). (gr. 5-9). lib. bdg. 27.93 *(978-1-4677-3836-1(0)*, Lerner Pubns.) Lerner Publishing Group.

Kenney, Karen Latchana. David Karp: The Mastermind Behind Tumblr. 2015. (Gateway Biographies Ser.). (ENG., Illus.). 48p. (gr. 4-8). 34.65 *(978-1-4677-5975-5(9)*, Lerner Digital) Lerner Publishing Group.

Kiefer, Jeanne. Jobs for Kids: A Smart Kid's Q & A Guide. Green, Anne Canevari, illus. 2003. (Single Titles Ser.). 112p. (gr. 5-8). lib. bdg. 25.90 *(978-0-7613-2611-3(1)*, Millbrook Pr.) Lerner Publishing Group.

Koh, Frederick. The 10 Most Outstanding Entrepreneurs. 2008. (J). 14.99 *(978-1-55448-498-0(7))* Scholastic Library Publishing.

Koya, Lena & Niver, Heather Moore. Networking: Building Social & Professional Connections. 2017. (J). ***(978-1-5081-7724-1(4))*** Rosen Publishing Group, Inc., The.

Leavitt, Amie Jane. Start Your Yard Work Business. 2017. (Build Your Business Ser.). (ENG.). 32p. (gr. 3-4). lib. bdg. 27.99 ***(978-1-5157-6692-6(6))*** Capstone Press of Coughlan Cos.

Linderman, Dianne. My Cookie Business. Johnson, Dolores, illus. 2005. 32p. (J). 8.95 *(978-0-9704876-0-5(6))* First Mom's Club, The.

—My Fishing Business. Johnson, Dolores, illus. 2005. 32p. (J). 8.95 *(978-0-9704876-2-9(2))* First Mom's Club, The.

—My Pony Ride Business. Johnson, Dolores, illus. 2005. 32p. (J). 8.95 *(978-0-9704876-1-2(4))* First Mom's Club, The.

Loewen, Nancy. Lemons & Lemonade: A Book about Supply & Demand. Fitzpatrick, Brad & Jensen, Brian, illus. 2005. (Money Matters Ser.). (ENG.). 24p. (gr. 1-3). 26.65 *(978-1-4048-0956-7(2))* Picture Window Bks.

Lopez, Eduardo. 20 Great Career-Building Activities Using Instagram & Snapchat. 2016. (Social Media Career Building Ser.). 00064p. (J). (gr. 7-7). 34.45 *(978-1-5081-7272-7(2))* Rosen Publishing Group, Inc., The.

Lüsted, Marcia Amidon. What Are Producers & Consumers? 2016. (Let's Find Out! Ser.). 32p. (J). (gr. 3-2). lib. bdg. 24.45 *(978-1-68048-403-8(6)*, Britannica Educational Publishing) Rosen Publishing Group, Inc., The.

MacGregor, Lucy. Choosing a Career as an Entrepreneur. 2005. (World of Work Ser.). (Illus.). 64p. (YA). (gr. 7-12). lib. bdg. 31.95 *(978-0-8239-3329-7(6))* Rosen Publishing Group, Inc., The.

Mara, Wil. American Entrepreneurship. 2013. (True Book(tm), a — Great American Business Ser.). (ENG.). 48p. (J). 31.00 *(978-0-531-24775-4(9))*; pap. 6.95 *(978-0-531-28461-2(1))* Scholastic Library Publishing.

Maurer, Tracy Nelson. John Deere, That's Who! Zeltner, Tim, illus. 2017. (ENG.). 40p. (J). 17.99 *(978-1-62779-129-8(9)*, 9781627791298, Holt, Henry & Co. Bks. For Young Readers) Holt, Henry & Co.

Meyer, Terry Teague. Social Entrepreneurship: Doing Well While Doing Good. 2014. (Digital & Information Literacy Ser.). (Illus.). 48p. (J). (gr. 5-8). 30.25 *(978-1-4777-7651-3(6)*, Rosen Reference) Rosen Publishing Group, Inc., The.

Moriarty, J. T. The Rise of American Capitalism: The Growth of American Banks. 2009. (America's Industrial Society in the 19th Century Ser.). 32p. (gr. 4-4). 47.90 *(978-1-61511-346-0(0))* Rosen Publishing Group, Inc., The.

Mozer, Mindy. Big Data & You. 2014. (Digital & Information Literacy Ser.). 48p. (YA). (gr. 5-8). 30.25 *(978-1-4777-7643-8(5))* Rosen Publishing Group, Inc., The.

Murley, Leon & Wilson, Antoine. The Distribution of Goods & Services. 2011. 77.70 *(978-1-4488-4750-1(6)*, Rosen Reference); (ENG.). 64p. (YA). (gr. 5-8). pap. 12.95 *(978-1-4488-4718-1(4)*, Rosen Reference); (YA). (gr. 5-9). lib. bdg. 31.95 *(978-1-4488-4710-5(9))* Rosen Publishing Group, Inc., The.

Musolf, Nell. The Story of Microsoft. 2011. (ENG., Illus.). 48p. (J). (gr. 5-17). pap. *(978-1-897563-05-2(1))* Saunders Bk. Co.

Nelson, Sandi. A Fly on the Wall Street. Beckstrand, Jared, illus. 2013. 23p. (J). 19.99 *(978-1-938690-29-7(X))* Salem Author Services.

Norwood, R. Edward. Kids under$Tanding Money. 2009. 48p. pap. 19.95 *(978-1-4389-4053-3(X))* AuthorHouse.

Nugent, Samantha. Yard Worker. 2017. (J). ***(978-1-4896-5902-6(1)**, AV2 by Weigl)* Weigl Pubs., Inc.

Ostrovsky, Alexandr. Birthday: Companies-Products-Services. Ostrovsky, Alexsandr, illus. (Childrens Ser.). (Illus.). (Orig.). (J). pap. 14.95 *(978-0-934393-17-1(6))* Rector Pr., Ltd.

—Clouds: Companies-Products-Services. Ostrovsky, Alexsandr, illus. (Childrens Ser.). (Illus.). (Orig.). (J). pap. 14.95 *(978-0-934393-20-1(6))* Rector Pr., Ltd.

Porterfield, Jason. How a Depression Works. 2009. (Real World Economics Ser.). (Illus.). 80p. (YA). (gr. 7-12). lib. bdg. 33.25 *(978-1-4358-5322-5(9))* Rosen Publishing Group, Inc., The.

Rajczak, Kristen. Mujeres en Los Negocios (Women in Business) 2015. (Ellas Abrieron Camino (Women Groundbreakers) Ser.). (ENG & SPA.). 32p. (J). (gr. 4-5). 26.25 *(978-1-4994-0513-2(8)*, PowerKids Pr.) Rosen Publishing Group, Inc., The.

Roberts, Sherry J. Fundamentals of Business Communication. 2011. (ENG.). 476p. (gr. 9-14). 99.96 *(978-1-60525-472-2(X))* Goodheart-Willcox Pub.

Roza, Greg. Great Networking Skills. (Work Readiness Ser.). 64p. 2009. (gr. 6-6). 58.50 *(978-1-60854-826-2(0))* 2008. (Illus.). (YA). (gr. 8-12). lib. bdg. 31.95 *(978-1-4042-1420-0(8))* Rosen Publishing Group, Inc., The.

Simons, Rae. Entrepreneurship. 2010. (Junior Library of Money). 64p. (YA). (gr. 7-18). pap. 9.95 *(978-1-4222-1883-9(X))*; lib. bdg. 22.95 *(978-1-4222-1764-1(7))* Mason Crest.

Small, Cathleen. How to Start an Online Business. 2015. (J). lib. bdg. *(978-1-62713-541-2(3))* Cavendish Square Publishing.

—20 Great Career-Building Activities Using Facebook. 2016. (Social Media Career Building Ser.). 00064p. (J). (gr. 7-7). 34.45 *(978-1-5081-7262-8(5))* Rosen Publishing Group, Inc., The.

Suen, Anastasia. How to Start a Lemonade Stand. 2015. (ENG.). 24p. (gr. k-3). 28.50 *(978-1-63430-356-9(3))* Rourke Educational Media.

Sutherland, Adam. Be a Young Entrepreneur! Be Inspired to Be a Business Whiz. 2016. (ENG.). 64p. (J). (gr. 3-7). pap. 9.99 *(978-1-4380-0872-1(4))* Barron's Educational Series, Inc.

Swanson, Jennifer A. Smart Strategies for Turning an Idea into a Product or Service. 2014. (Financial Security & Life Success for Teens Ser.). 80p. (YA). (gr. 7-12). 34.25 *(978-1-4777-7634-6(6))* Rosen Publishing Group, Inc., The.

Tangerine Press Staff & Scholastic, Inc. Staff, contrib. by. Kid Biz. 2004. (Illus.). 62p. (J). *(978-0-439-69986-0(X))* Scholastic, Inc.

Thompson, Helen. Understanding Business Math & Budgets. Madrian, Brigitte, ed. 2013. (Young Adult Library of Small Business & Finance Ser.; 10). 64p. (J). (gr. 7-18). 22.95 *(978-1-4222-2921-7(1))* Mason Crest.

Wolfe, Mike & Sprengelmeyer, Lily. Kid Pickers: How to Turn Junk into Treasure. Right, Mike, illus. 2013. (ENG.). 128p. (J). (gr. 2-7). 19.99 *(978-1-250-00848-0(4)*, 9781250008480); pap. 14.99 *(978-1-250-01930-1(3)*, 9781250019301) Feiwel & Friends.

BUSINESS—BIOGRAPHY

Aaseng, Nathan. Business Builders in Broadcasting. 2005. (Business Builders Ser.: Vol. 8). (Illus.). 160p. (J). (gr. 5-18). lib. bdg. 24.95 *(978-1-881508-83-0(8))* Oliver Pr., Inc.

—Business Builders in Sweets & Treats. 2005. (Business Builders Ser.: Vol. 9). (Illus.). 160p. (J). (gr. 5-18). lib. bdg. 24.95 *(978-1-881508-84-7(6))* Oliver Pr., Inc.

Arrathoon, Leigh A. Men Who Changed the World Vol. I: The Henry Ford Story. Davio, John, ed. Hajdyla, Ken, illus. 56p. (J). (gr. 5-6). pap. 5.95 *(978-0-9648564-5-5(X))* Archus Pr., LLC.

Bailey, Tom. A.G. Gaston: Visionary Businessman. 2003. (Alabama Roots Biography Ser.). (Illus.). 111p. (J). pap. *(978-1-878561-99-2(5))* Seacoast Publishing, Inc.

Boyd, Aaron. Smart Money: The Story of Bill Gates. rev. exp. ed. 2004. (American Business Leaders Ser.). (Illus.). 128p. (YA). (gr. 6-12). 23.95 *(978-1-931798-32-7(X))* Reynolds, Morgan Inc.

Brackett, Virginia. Steve Jobs: Computer Genius of Apple. 2003. (Internet Biographies Ser.). (Illus.). 48p. (J). (gr. 4-10). lib. bdg. 23.93 *(978-0-7660-1970-6(5))* Enslow Pubs., Inc.

Brennan, Patricia. Who Is Bill Gates? 2013. (Who Is...? Ser.). lib. bdg. 16.00 *(978-0-606-30038-4(4)*, Turtleback) Turtleback Bks.

Brown, Jonatha A. Bill Gates. 2004. (People We Should Know Ser.). (Illus.). 24p. (gr. 1-4). pap. 8.15 *(978-0-8368-4317-0(7))*; lib. bdg. 22.00 *(978-0-8368-4310-1(X))* Stevens, Gareth Publishing LLLP. (Weekly Reader Leveled Readers).

Burgan, Michael. Who Is Richard Branson? Hammond, Ted, illus. 2015. 105p. (J). *(978-1-4844-6180-8(0)*, Grosset & Dunlap) Penguin Young Readers Group.

—Who Was Henry Ford? Hammond, Ted & Harrison, Nancy, illus. 2014. (Who Was? Ser.). (ENG.). 112p. (J). (gr. 3-7). 5.99 *(978-0-448-47957-6(5)*, Grosset & Dunlap) Penguin Young Readers Group.

Business Leaders Set, vols. 13, vol. 13. Incl. Faces Behind Beauty. Langley, Wanda. (Illus.). 160p. lib. bdg. 28.95 *(978-1-59935-097-4(1))*; Michael Dell. Friedman, Lauri S. 128p. lib. bdg. 28.95 *(978-1-59935-083-7(1))*; Oprah Winfrey. Hasday, Judy L. (Illus.). 128p. lib. bdg. 28.95 *(978-1-59935-096-7(3))*; Ralph Lauren. Weatherly, Myra. 112p. lib. bdg. 28.95 *(978-1-59935-084-4(X))*; Russell Simmons. Baughan, Brain. 112p. lib. bdg. 28.95 *(978-1-59935-075-2(0))*; Steve Jobs. Corrigan, Jim. 128p. lib. bdg. 27.95 *(978-1-59935-076-9(9))*; Warren Buffett. Johnson, Anne Janette. 128p. lib. bdg. 28.95 *(978-1-59935-080-6(7))*; (YA). (gr. 7-12). 2008. 2008. Set lib. bdg. 376.35 *(978-1-59935-094-3(7))* Reynolds, Morgan Inc.

Byman, Jeremy. J. P. Morgan: Banker to a Growing Nation. 2004. (American Business Leaders Ser.). (Illus.). 112p. (YA). (gr. 6-12). 23.95 *(978-1-883846-60-2(9)*, First Biographies) Reynolds, Morgan Inc.

Carlson Berne, Emma. Run Your Own Yard Sale. 2014. (Young Entrepreneurs Ser.). 32p. (J). (gr. 4-6). pap. 10.00 *(978-1-4777-3008-9(7)*, PowerKids Pr.) Rosen Publishing Group, Inc., The.

Cooper, Sharon Katz. Milton Hershey's Sweet Idea: A Chocolate Kingdom. Lokus, Rex & Sánchez, Alvaro Iglesias, illus. 2015. (Story Behind the Name Ser.). (ENG.). 32p. (gr. 2-3). lib. bdg. 28.65 *(978-1-4795-7137-6(7))* Picture Window Bks.

Cornell, Kari. Facebook Founder & Internet Entrepreneur Mark Zuckerberg. 2016. (STEM Trailblazer Bios Ser.). (ENG.). 32p. (J). (gr. 2-5). 26.65 *(978-1-4677-9527-2(5)*, Lerner Pubns.) Lerner Publishing Group.

Corrigan, Jim. Business Leaders: Steve Jobs. 2009. (KOR., Illus.). 304p. (J). pap. *(978-89-7677-617-4(8))* Myeongjinculpan Co., Ltd.

—Steve Jobs. 2008. (Business Leaders Ser.). 128p. (YA). (gr. 7-12). lib. bdg. 27.95 *(978-1-59935-076-9(9))* Reynolds, Morgan Inc.

Demuth, Patricia Brennan. Who Is Bill Gates? Hammond, Ted & Harrison, Nancy, illus. 2013. (Who Was? Ser.). (ENG.). 112p. (J). (gr. 3-7). pap. 5.99 *(978-0-448-46332-2(6)*, Grosset & Dunlap) Penguin Young Readers Group.

Di Piazza, Domenica. Google Cybersecurity Expert Parisa Tabriz. 2017. (J). ***(978-1-5415-0007-5(5))*** Lerner Publishing Group.

Doak, Robin S. Mark Zuckerberg. 2015. (ENG., Illus.). 48p. (J). lib. bdg. *(978-0-531-21594-4(6)*, Orchard Bks.) Scholastic, Inc.

Doeden, Matt. Steve Jobs: Technology Innovator & Apple Genius. 2012. (Gateway Biographies Ser.). (ENG.). 48p. (gr. 4-8). lib. bdg. 26.60 *(978-1-4677-0215-7(3)*, Lerner Pubns.) Lerner Publishing Group.

Donohue, Moira Rose. Maggie L. Walker. 2012. (Illus.). 32p. (J). *(978-1-935884-62-0(X))*; pap. *(978-1-935884-68-2(9))* State Standards Publishing, LLC.

Duffield, Katy. Chad Hurley, Steve Chen, Jawed Karim: You Tube Creators. 2008. (Innovators Ser.). (ENG., Illus.). 48p. (J). (gr. 4-8). pap. 29.95 *(978-0-7377-4270-1(4)*, LML02109-243873, Kidhaven) Cengage Gale.

Eboch, M. M. Milton Hershey: Young Chocolatier. Henderson, Meryl, illus. 2008. (Childhood of Famous Americans Ser.). (ENG.). 224p. (J). (gr. 3-7). pap. 6.99 *(978-1-4169-5569-6(0)*, Simon & Schuster/Paula Wiseman Bks.) Simon & Schuster/Paula Wiseman Bks.

Fandel, Jennifer & Milgrom, Al. George Eastman & the Kodak Camera, 1 vol. Purcell, Gordon & Milgrom, Al, illus. 2007. (Inventions & Discovery Ser.). (ENG.). 32p. (gr. 3-4). 30.65 *(978-0-7368-6848-8(8)*, Graphic Library) Capstone Press of Coughlan Cos.

Ganchinello, Sheena. Tim Westergren & Pandora. 2013. (Internet Biographies Ser.). (ENG., Illus.). 128p. (YA). (gr. 7-12). lib. bdg. 34.60 *(978-1-4488-9526-7(X)*, Rosen Classroom) Rosen Publishing Group, Inc., The.

Garty, Judy. Jeff Bezos: Business Genius of Amazon.com. 2003. (Internet Biographies Ser.). (Illus.). 48p. (J). (gr. 4-10). lib. bdg. 25.27 *(978-0-7660-1972-0(1))* Enslow Pubs., Inc.

Gillam, Scott. Steve Jobs: Apple ICon, 1 vol. 2012. (Essential Lives Set 2 Ser.). (ENG.). 112p. (J). (gr. 6-12). lib. bdg. 35.64 *(978-1-60453-997-4(6)*, Essential Library) ABDO Publishing Co.

Goldsmith, Bonnie. William Randolph Hearst: Newspaper Magnate, 1 vol. 2009. (Publishing Pioneers Ser.). (ENG., Illus.). 112p. (J). (gr. 6-12). lib. bdg. 35.64 *(978-1-60453-763-5(9)*, Essential Library) ABDO Publishing Co.

Goldsworthy, Steve. Steve Jobs. 2011. (J). (gr. 4-6). pap. 12.95 *(978-1-61690-675-7(8)*, AV2 by Weigl); (Illus.). 24p. (YA). (gr. 3-6). 27.13 *(978-1-61690-670-2(7))* Weigl Pubs., Inc.

Great Entrepreneurs in U. S. History. 2016. (Great Entrepreneurs in U. S. History Ser.). 32p. (gr. 5-5). pap. 70.50 *(978-1-4994-2446-1(9)*, PowerKids Pr.) Rosen Publishing Group, Inc., The.

Green, Sara. Bill Gates. 2014. (Tech Icons Ser.). (ENG., Illus.). 24p. (J). (gr. 3-8). lib. bdg. 25.95 *(978-1-60014-987-0(1)*, Pilot Bks.) Bellwether Media.

—Elon Musk. 2014. (Tech Icons Ser.). (ENG., Illus.). 24p. (J). (gr. 3-8). lib. bdg. 25.95 *(978-1-60014-988-7(X)*, Pilot Bks.) Bellwether Media.

—Jeff Bezos. 2014. (Tech Icons Ser.). (ENG., Illus.). 24p. (J). (gr. 3-8). lib. bdg. 25.95 *(978-1-60014-989-4(8)*, Pilot Bks.) Bellwether Media.

—Marissa Mayer. 2014. (Tech Icons Ser.). (ENG., Illus.). 24p. (J). (gr. 3-8). lib. bdg. 25.95 *(978-1-60014-991-7(X)*, Pilot Bks.) Bellwether Media.

—Mark Zuckerberg. 2014. (Tech Icons Ser.). (ENG., Illus.). 24p. (J). (gr. 3-8). lib. bdg. 25.95 *(978-1-60014-992-4(8)*, Pilot Bks.) Bellwether Media.

—Steve Jobs. 2014. (Tech Icons Ser.). (ENG., Illus.). 24p. (J). (gr. 3-8). lib. bdg. 25.95 *(978-1-60014-994-8(4)*, Pilot Bks.) Bellwether Media.

Hunter, Nick. Steve Jobs, 1 vol. 2012. (Titans of Business Ser.). (ENG.). 48p. (gr. 4-6). pap. 8.99 *(978-1-4329-6435-1(6))*; lib. bdg. 32.00 *(978-1-4329-6428-3(3))* Heinemann-Raintree. (NA-h).

Isabella, Jude. Steve Jobs: Visionary Entrepreneur of the Digital Age. 2013. (ENG.). 112p. (J). E-Book ***(978-1-4271-8936-3(6))***; (Illus.). *(978-0-7787-1189-6(7))*; (Illus.). pap. *(978-0-7787-1191-9(9))* Crabtree Publishing Co.

Jackson, Aurelia. Amazon(r): How Jeff Bezos Built the World's Largest Online Store. 2014. (Wizards of Technology Ser.: 10). 64p. (J). (gr. 7-18). 23.95 *(978-1-4222-3179-1(8))* Mason Crest.

—Google(Tm) How Larry Page & Sergey Brin Changed the Way We Search the Web. 2014. (Illus.). 64p. (J). *(978-1-4222-3178-4(X))* Mason Crest.

Kallen, Stuart A. Elon Musk & Tesla. 2015. (ENG., Illus.). 80p. (J). lib. bdg. *(978-1-60152-870-4(1))* ReferencePoint Pr., Inc.

—Jeff Bezos & Amazon. 2015. (ENG., Illus.). 80p. (J). lib. bdg. *(978-1-60152-872-8(8))* ReferencePoint Pr., Inc.

Kamberg, Mary-Lane. Evan Williams, Biz Stone, Jack Dorsey, & Twitter. 2012. (Internet Biographies Ser.). (ENG., Illus.). 128p. (J). (gr. 7-12). lib. bdg. 34.60 *(978-1-4488-6913-8(7))* Rosen Publishing Group, Inc., The.

Kampff, Joseph. Jay Z: Rapper & Businessman. 2016. (Exceptional African Americans Ser.). (ENG.). 24p. (J). (gr. 3-3). pap. 9.35 *(978-0-7660-7252-7(5))* Enslow Pubs., Inc.

Kawa, Katie. Milton Hershey & the Chocolate Industry. 2016. (Great Entrepreneurs in U. S. History Ser.). (Illus.). 32p. (J). (gr. 5-5). pap. 11.75 *(978-1-4994-2135-4(4)*, PowerKids Pr.) Rosen Publishing Group, Inc., The.

Kenney, Karen Latchana. David Karp: The Mastermind Behind Tumblr. 2013. (Gateway Biographies Ser.). (ENG., Illus.). 48p. (gr. 4-8). lib. bdg. 26.60 *(978-1-4677-1285-9(X)*, Lerner Pubns.) Lerner Publishing Group.

Kent, Jacqueline C. Business Builders in Cosmetics. 2003. (Business Builders Ser.: Vol. 7). (Illus.). 160p. (gr. 5-18). lib. bdg. 22.95 *(978-1-881508-82-3(X))* Oliver Pr., Inc.

Kerns, Ann. Martha Stewart. 2006. (Biography Ser.). (Illus.). 111p. (J). (gr. 3-7). lib. bdg. 29.27 *(978-0-8225-6613-7(3)*, Twenty-First Century Bks.) Lerner Publishing Group.

Kjelle, Marylou Morano. Bill Gates: Microsoft Founder & Philanthropist, 1 vol. 2014. (Newsmakers Ser.). (ENG.). 48p. (gr. 3-6). lib. bdg. 32.79 *(978-1-62403-641-5(4))* ABDO Publishing Co.

Klein, Adria F. Steve Jobs. 2009. pap. 13.25 *(978-1-60559-071-4(1))* Hameray Publishing Group, Inc.

Krieg, Katherine. Sam Walton: Founder of the Walmart Empire, 1 vol. 2013. (Essential Lives Set 8 Ser.). (ENG., Illus.). 112p. (J). (gr. 6-12). lib. bdg. 35.64 *(978-1-61783-898-9(5)*, Essential Library) ABDO Publishing Co.

Kupperberg, Paul. Jerry Yang. 2009. (Asian Americans of Achievement Ser.). (Illus.). 128p. (YA). (gr. 7-12). 35.00 *(978-1-60413-569-5(7))* Facts On File, Inc.

Kurlansky, Mark. Frozen in Time: Clarence Birdseye's Outrageous Idea about Frozen Food. 2014. (ENG.). 176p. (J). (gr. 5). lib. bdg. 18.99 *(978-0-375-99135-6(2)*, Delacorte Bks. for Young Readers) Random Hse. Children's Bks.

La Bella, Laura. Hulu & Jason Kilar, 1 vol. 2015. (ENG.). 128p. (YA). 35.60 *(978-1-4777-7921-7(3)*, Rosen Young Adult) Rosen Publishing Group, Inc., The.

Lesinski, Jeanne. Bill Gates. pap. 9.95 *(978-0-8225-5745-6(2))* Lerner Publishing Group.

Lesinski, Jeanne M. Bill Gates. 2007. (Illus.). 112p. (J). (gr. 6-9). per. 7.95 *(978-0-8225-7027-1(0)*, Lerner Pubns.); lib. bdg. 29.27 *(978-0-8225-7363-0(6)*, Twenty-First Century Bks.) Lerner Publishing Group.

—Bill Gates: Entrepreneur & Philanthropist. 2008. (Lifeline Biographies Ser.). 112p. (YA). (gr. 7-12). lib. bdg. 33.26 *(978-1-58013-570-2(6))* Lerner Publishing Group.

Llanas, Sheila Griffin. Caleb Davis Bradham: Pepsi-Cola Inventor, 1 vol. 2014. (Food Dudes Set 2 Ser.). (ENG.). 32p. (J). (gr. 8-12). lib. bdg. 27.07 *(978-1-62403-315-5(6)*, Checkerboard Library) ABDO Publishing Co.

—Colonel Harland Sanders: KFC Creator, 1 vol. 2014. (Food Dudes Set 2 Ser.). (ENG.). 32p. (gr. 8-12). 27.07 *(978-1-62403-318-6(0))* ABDO Publishing Co.

—Dave Thomas: Wendy's Founder, 1 vol. 2014. (Food Dudes Set 2 Ser.). (ENG.). 32p. (J). (gr. 8-12). 27.07 *(978-1-62403-319-3(9))* ABDO Publishing Co.

—John Pemberton: Coca-Cola Developer, 1 vol. 2014. (Food Dudes Set 2 Ser.). (ENG.). 32p. (J). (gr. 8-12). lib. bdg. 27.07 *(978-1-62403-317-9(2)*, Checkerboard Library) ABDO Publishing Co.

—Tom Monaghan: Domino's Pizza Innovator, 1 vol. 2014. (Food Dudes Set 2 Ser.). (ENG.). 32p. (gr. 8-12). 27.07 *(978-1-62403-316-2(4))* ABDO Publishing Co.

Mara, Wil. Sam Walton: Rethinking Retail. 2013. (ENG.). 48p. (J). pap. 6.95 *(978-0-531-28464-3(6))* Scholastic Library Publishing.

—Sam Walton: The man Who Invented Walmart. 2013. (True Book(tm), a — Great American Business Ser.). (ENG.). 48p. (J). 31.00 *(978-0-531-24778-5(3))* Scholastic Library Publishing.

Mattern, Joanne. Ben & Jerry: Ice Cream Manufacturers, 1 vol. 2014. (Food Dudes Set 1 Ser.). (ENG.). 32p. (gr. 3-6). lib. bdg. 27.07 *(978-1-62403-491-6(8)*, Checkerboard Library) ABDO Publishing Co.

—Clarence Birdseye: Frozen Food Innovator, 1 vol. 2014. (Food Dudes Set 1 Ser.). (ENG.). 32p. (gr. 3-6). lib. bdg. 27.07 *(978-1-62403-492-3(6)*, Checkerboard Library) ABDO Publishing Co.

—Food Dudes Set 1, 1 vol. 2014. (Food Dudes Set 1 Ser.: 8). (ENG.). 32p. (gr. 3-6). lib. bdg. 216.56 *(978-1-62403-490-9(X)*, Checkerboard Library) ABDO Publishing Co.

—Kellogg Family: Breakfast Cereal Pioneers, 1 vol. 2014. (Food Dudes Set 1 Ser.). (ENG., Illus.). 32p. (J). (gr. 3-6). lib. bdg. 27.07 *(978-1-62403-495-4(0)*, Checkerboard Library) ABDO Publishing Co.

—Milton Hershey: Hershey's Chocolate Creator, 1 vol. 2014. (Food Dudes Set 1 Ser.). (ENG.). 32p. (gr. 3-6). lib. bdg. 27.07 *(978-1-62403-494-7(2)*, Checkerboard Library) ABDO Publishing Co.

—Ray Kroc: McDonald's Restaurants Builder, 1 vol. (Food Dudes Set 1 Ser.). (ENG., Illus.). 32p. (J). (gr. 3-6). 2014. lib. bdg. 27.07 *(978-1-62403-496-1(9)*, Checkerboard Library) 2011. 27.07 *(978-1-61613-559-1(X))* ABDO Publishing Co.

—Robert Cade: Gatorade Inventor, 1 vol. 2014. (Food Dudes Set 1 Ser.). (ENG.). 32p. (gr. 3-6). lib. bdg. 27.07 *(978-1-62403-493-0(4)*, Checkerboard Library) ABDO Publishing Co.

—William Wrigley Jr. Wrigley's Chewing Gum Founder, 1 vol. 2014. (Food Dudes Set 1 Ser.). (ENG.). 32p. (gr. 3-6). lib. bdg. 27.07 *(978-1-62403-498-5(5)*, Checkerboard Library) ABDO Publishing Co.

McAneney, Caitie. Madam C. J. Walker & Her Beauty Empire. 2016. (Great Entrepreneurs in U. S. History Ser.). (Illus.). 32p. (J). (gr. 5-5). pap. 11.75 (978-1-4994-2131-6(1), PowerKids Pr.) Rosen Publishing Group, Inc., The.

McPherson, Stephanie Sammartino. Levi Strauss. 2007. (History Maker Bios Ser.). (Illus.). 48p. (J). (gr. 3-7). lib. bdg. 26.60 (978-0-8225-6581-9(1), Lerner Pubns.) Lerner Publishing Group.

Miklowitz, Gloria D. Bill Gates. 2004. (ENG., Illus.). 37p. (J). (gr. 2-5). pap. 7.33 (978-0-7685-1214-4(X), Dominie Elementary) Pearson Schl.

Morales, Leslie. Esther Dyson: Internet Visionary. 2003. (Internet Biographies Ser.). (Illus.). 48p. (J). (gr. 4-10). lib. bdg. 23.93 (978-0-7660-1973-7(X)) Enslow Pubs., Inc.

Mueller, Marilyn J. Thank You God for Everything! Gracias a Dios por Todo. 2007. pap. 11.00 (978-0-8059-8648-8(0)) Dorrance Publishing Co., Inc.

Nagelhout, Ryan. Elon Musk: Space Entrepreneur. 2017. (People in the News Ser.). 104p. (YA). (gr. 7-7). lib. bdg. 39.40 **(978-1-5345-6035-2(1)**, Lucent Pr.) Greenhaven Publishing LLC.

Nakaya, Andrea C. Reed Hastings & Nexflix. 2015. (ENG., Illus.). 80p. (J). lib. bdg. (978-1-60152-878-0(7)) ReferencePoint Pr., Inc.

Parker, Lewis K. Cornelius Vanderbilt & the Railroad Industry. (American Tycoons Ser.). 24p. 2009. (gr. 3-3). 42.50 (978-1-61511-389-7(4)) 2003. (Illus.). (J). lib. bdg. 22.60 (978-0-8239-6450-5(7)) Rosen Publishing Group, Inc., The. (PowerKids Pr.).

—Henry Ford & the Automobile Industry. 2009. (American Tycoons Ser.). 24p. (gr. 3-3). 42.50 (978-1-61511-390-3(8), PowerKids Pr.) Rosen Publishing Group, Inc., The.

—John Jacob Astor & the Fur Trade. 2003. (American Tycoons Ser.). (Illus.). 24p. (J). lib. bdg. 22.60 (978-0-8239-6447-5(7), PowerKids Pr.) Rosen Publishing Group, Inc., The.

Paxson, Jillip Naysinthe, told to. The First Thirty. anniv. ed. 2015. (ENG.). 96p. (YA). (gr. 5-16). pap. 10.00 (978-0-9758794-1-2(3)) IdeaList Enterprises, Inc.

Paxson, Jillip Naysinthe & Siegman, Greg Forbes. The First Thirty. 2005. 96p. (YA). per. 10.00 (978-0-9758794-0-5(5)) IdeaList Enterprises, Inc.

Peters, Craig. Bill Gates: Software Genius of Microsoft. 2003. (Internet Biographies Ser.). (Illus.). 48p. (J). (gr. 4-10). lib. bdg. 23.93 (978-0-7660-1969-0(1)) Enslow Pubs., Inc.

—Larry Ellison: Database Genius of Oracle. 2003. (Internet Biographies Ser.). (Illus.). 48p. (J). (gr. 4-10). lib. bdg. 23.93 (978-0-7660-1974-4(8)) Enslow Pubs., Inc.

—Steve Case: Internet Genius of America Online. 2003. (Internet Biographies Ser.). (Illus.). 48p. (J). (gr. 4-10). lib. bdg. 25.27 (978-0-7660-1971-3(3)) Enslow Pubs., Inc.

Porterfield, Jason. Niklas Zennstrom & Skype. 2013. (Internet Biographies Ser.). (ENG., Illus.). 128p. (YA). (gr. 7-12). lib. bdg. 34.60 (978-1-4488-9527-4(8), Rosen Classroom) Rosen Publishing Group, Inc., The.

Rajczak, Kristen. Instagram & Kevin Systrom & Mike Krieger, 1 vol. 2015. (ENG., Illus.). 128p. (J). lib. bdg. 35.60 (978-1-4777-7917-0(5), Rosen Young Adult) Rosen Publishing Group, Inc., The.

Richardson, Adele D. The Story of Microsoft. 2003. (Built for Success Ser.). (Illus.). 48p. (J). 28.50 (978-1-58340-294-8(2)) Black Rabbit Bks.

Robinson, Tom. Jeff Bezos: Amazon.com Architect, 1 vol. 2009. (Publishing Pioneers Ser.). (ENG., Illus.). 112p. (J). (gr. 6-12). lib. bdg. 35.64 (978-1-60453-759-8(0), Essential Library) ABDO Publishing Co.

Roza, Greg. Bill & Melinda Gates. 2014. (Making a Difference: Leaders Who Are Changing the World Ser.). 48p. (J). (gr. 5-8). pap. 14.05 (978-1-62275-452-6(2)) Rosen Publishing Group, Inc., The.

Santos, Rita. Donald Trump: Businessman & President. 2017. (Junior Biographies Ser.). 24p. (gr. 3-4). lib. bdg. 22.60 **(978-0-7660-8666-1(6))** Enslow Pubs., Inc.

Schuette, Sarah L. Wallace Famous Amos, 1 vol. 2014. (Business Leaders Ser.). (ENG.). 24p. (gr. k-1). lib. bdg. 21.99 (978-1-4765-9639-6(5), Pebble Bks.) Capstone Press of Coughlan Cos.

Schulte, Mary. Helen Griener: Cofounder of iRobot Corporation. 2009. (Innovators Ser.). (ENG., Illus.). 48p. (gr. 4-8). lib. bdg. 34.60 (978-0-7377-4404-0(9), LML02109-245405, Kidhaven) Cengage Gale.

Schuman, Michael A. Bill Gates: Computer Mogul & Philanthropist. 2007. (People to Know Today Ser.). (Illus.). 128p. (J). (gr. 3-7). lib. bdg. 33.27 (978-0-7660-2693-3(0)) Enslow Pubs., Inc.

Scott, Celicia. Twitter: How Jack Dorsey Changed the Way We Communicate. 2014. (Wizards of Technology Ser.: 10). 64p. (J). (gr. 7-18). 23.95 (978-1-4222-3187-6(9)) Mason Crest.

Shea, Therese. Steve Jobs & Apple. 2012. (Internet Biographies Ser.). (ENG., Illus.). 128p. (YA). (gr. 7-12). lib. bdg. 34.60 (978-1-4488-6910-7(2)) Rosen Publishing Group, Inc., The.

Shores, Erika L. Sam Walton, 1 vol. 2014. (Business Leaders Ser.). (ENG.). 24p. (gr. k-1). lib. bdg. 21.99 (978-1-4765-9642-6(5), Pebble Bks.) Capstone Press of Coughlan Cos.

Slater, Lee. Crayola Creators: Edwin Binney & C. Harold Smith, 1 vol. 2016. (Toy Trailblazers Ser.). (ENG., Illus.). 32p. (J). (gr. 3-6). 27.07 (978-1-62403-976-8(6)) ABDO Publishing Co.

—Play-Doh Pioneer: Joseph Mcvicker, 1 vol. 2016. (Toy Trailblazers Ser.). (ENG., Illus.). 32p. (J). (gr. 3-6). lib. bdg. 27.07 (978-1-62403-978-2(2), Checkerboard Library) ABDO Publishing Co.

Staley, Erin. Nick Swinmurn, Tony Hsieh, & Zappos. 2013. (Internet Biographies Ser.). (ENG., Illus.). 128p. (YA). (gr. 7-12). lib. bdg. 34.60 (978-1-4488-9529-8(4), Rosen Classroom) Rosen Publishing Group, Inc., The.

Steve Jobs & Apple. 2011. (Graphic Nonfiction Biographies Ser.). (ENG.). 48p. (YA). (gr. 5-8). (978-1-4488-5546-9(2)); pap. (978-1-4488-5645-9(0)) Rosen Publishing Group, Inc., The. (Rosen Reference).

Sutherland, Adam. Virgin. 2017. (Big Business Ser.). (ENG., Illus.). 32p. (J). (gr. 4-6). pap. 11.99 (978-0-7502-8922-1(8), Wayland) Hachette Children's Group GBR. Dist: Hachette Bk. Group.

Vance, Ashlee. Elon Musk & the Quest for a Fantastic Future Young Readers' Edition. 2017. 288p. (J). (gr. 3). pap. 6.99 (978-0-06-246327-2(6)); (Illus.). 16.99 (978-0-06-246328-9(4)) HarperCollins Pubs.

Viegas, Jennifer. Pierre Omidyar: The Founder of Ebay. 2006. (Internet Career Biographies Ser.). (Illus.). 112p. (YA). (gr. 7-12). lib. bdg. 34.60 (978-1-4042-0715-8(5)) Rosen Publishing Group, Inc., The.

Washburne, Sophie & Sheen, Barbara. Steve Jobs: Computer Visionary. 2017. (People in the News Ser.). 104p. (J). (gr. 7-7). lib. bdg. 39.40 **(978-1-5345-6031-4(9)**, Lucent Pr.) Greenhaven Publishing LLC.

Weil, Jamie. Jeff Bezos: Founder of Amazon. com, 1 vol. 2014. (Newsmakers Ser.). (ENG.). 48p. (gr. 3-6). lib. bdg. 32.79 (978-1-62403-640-8(6)) ABDO Publishing Co.

—Mark Zuckerberg: Creator of Facebook, 1 vol. 2014. (Newsmakers Ser.). (ENG.). 48p. (gr. 3-6). lib. bdg. 32.79 (978-1-62403-647-7(3)) ABDO Publishing Co.

Weston, Michael R. Jerry Yang & David Filo: The Founders of Yahoo! (Internet Career Biographies Ser.). 112p. 2009. (gr. 8-8). 63.90 (978-1-61513-590-5(1)) 2006. (Illus.). (YA). (gr. 7-12). lib. bdg. 34.60 (978-1-4042-0718-9(X)) Rosen Publishing Group, Inc., The.

White, Casey. Sergey Brin & Larry Page: The Founders of Google. 2009. (Internet Career Biographies Ser.). 112p. (gr. 8-8). 63.90 (978-1-61513-597-4(9)) Rosen Publishing Group, Inc., The.

Woog, Adam. Zuckerberg. 2009. (Innovators Ser.). (ENG., Illus.). 64p. (J). 29.95 (978-0-7377-4566-5(5)) Cengage Gale.

Wooten, Sara McIntosh. Donald Trump: From Real Estate to Reality TV. 2008. (People to Know Today Ser.). (Illus.). 128p. (J). (gr. k-6). lib. bdg. 33.27 (978-0-7660-2890-6(9)) Enslow Pubs., Inc.

Wooten, Sara McIntosh. Donald Trump: Real Estate Mogul & President. 2017. (Influential Lives Ser.). 128p. (J). (gr. 7-8). lib. bdg. 37.27 **(978-0-7660-8499-5(X))** Enslow Pubs., Inc.

Wukovits, John F. Booker T. Washington & Entrepreneurship. 2008. (Lucent Library of Black History Ser.). (ENG., Illus.). 128p. (gr. 7-10). 39.40 (978-1-4205-0052-3(X), Lucent Bks.) Cengage Gale.

Wybomy, Shelia. Frederick W. Smith: Founder of FedEx. 2007. (Innovators Ser.). (ENG., Illus.). 64p. (J). (gr. 4-8). lib. bdg. 28.75 (978-0-7377-3861-2(8), LML02109-234922, Kidhaven) Cengage Gale.

BUSINESS, CHOICE OF

see Vocational Guidance

BUSINESS—FICTION

Bacigalupi, Paolo. The Doubt Factory. 2014. (ENG.). 496p. (YA). (gr. 10-17). 18.00 (978-0-316-22075-0(2)) Little Brown & Co.

Bair, Sheila. Isabel's Car Wash. Stead, Judy, illus. 2012. (J). 34.28 (978-1-61913-118-7(8)) Weigl Pubs., Inc.

Bouani, Jennifer. Tyler & His Solve-A-Matic Machine: (1st Edition) 2006. (Future Business Leaders' Ser.). (Illus.). 118p. (J). (gr. 4-7). per. 6.99 (978-0-9779265-0-3(8)) Bouje Publishing, LLC.

Boyce, Frank Cottrell. Framed. (J). (gr. 3). 2008. (Illus.). 320p. per. 8.99 (978-0-06-073404-6(3)) 2006. 306p. lib. bdg. 17.89 (978-0-06-073403-9(5)) HarperCollins Pubs.

Butcher, Kristin. Zach & Zoe: Bully & the Beagle, 1 vol. 2009. (Lorimer Streetlights Ser.). (ENG.). 120p. (J). (gr. 2-4). 8.95 (978-1-55277-427-4(9), 9781552774274) Lorimer, James & Co., Ltd., Pubs. CAN. Dist: Casemate Pubs. & Bk. Distributors, LLC.

Chapman, Allen. Bart Sterlings Road to Success. rev. ed. 2006. (ENG.). 204p. 27.95 (978-1-4218-2015-6(3), 1st World Library - Literary Society) 1st World Publishing, Inc.

Doyle, Brian. Pure Spring, 1 vol. 2008. (ENG.). 160p. (J). (gr. 5-9). pap. 8.95 (978-0-88899-775-3(2)) Groundwood Bks. CAN. Dist: Publishers Group West (PGW).

Driscoll, Laura. Project Popcorn: Mean/Median/Mode. Ng-Benitez, Shirley, illus. 2017. (Math Matters (r) Ser.). (ENG.). 32p. (J). (gr. k-3). 5.95 (978-1-57565-865-0(8)) Kane Press, Inc.

Eburne, Tim. Zebra Stripes: A Tail of Personal Branding. 2012. (Illus.). 48p. pap. 31.99 (978-1-4691-4536-5(7)) Xlibris Corp.

Fisher, Anne. Look What Brains Can Do! 2005. reprint ed. pap. 20.95 (978-1-4179-9453-3(3)) Kessinger Publishing, LLC.

Fowler, Leona. Sasha's Silly Sock Business: Working at the Same Time. 2017. (Computer Science for the Real World Ser.). 16p. (gr. 7-8). pap. 7.95 **(978-1-5383-5222-9(2)**, Rosen Classroom) Rosen Publishing Group, Inc., The.

Froese, Dorothy Cheever. Captain Rhino's Progress: An Allegory of the Workplace. 2003. (Illus.). 32p. pap. 9.00 (978-1-890437-86-2(7)) Western Reflections Publishing Co.

Gadson, Denise. Penelope's World Famous Cookies. 2011. 32p. pap. 12.95 (978-1-4327-6850-8(6)) Outskirts Pr., Inc.

Gallagher, Diana G. Advice about Work & Play: Claudia Cristina Cortez Uncomplicates Your Life. Garvey, Brann, illus. 2010. (Claudia Cristina Cortez Ser.). (ENG.). 80p. (gr. 2-3). pap. 6.10 (978-1-4342-2253-4(5)); 26.65 (978-1-4342-1908-4(9)) Stone Arch Bks. (Claudia Cristina Cortez).

Goss, Anthony & Blair, Janet. The Golden Dog Bone. 2012. 50p. 24.95 (978-1-4626-5929-6(2)) America Star Bks.

Harper, Michael J. & Arrington, Jay. The Little Entrepreneur: Takes Flight. 2005. 66p. (J). per. 9.95 (978-0-9764161-3-5(1)) Harper-Arrington Publishing.

Harris, Andy. Tick-Tock Grandad's Sweetshop Skills for Life. 2009. 20p. pap. 9.99 (978-1-60693-933-8(5), Eloquent Bks.) Strategic Book Publishing & Rights Agency (SBPRA).

Hibbitts, Mark. Alfie Potts: Alfie & the Mind Virus. Purchase, Brendan, illus. 2011. (ENG.). 40p. (J). (978-1-907498-60-2(5), Book Shaker) Lean Marketing Pr.

—Alfie Potts: Alfie & the Seminar. Purchase, Brendan, illus. 2011. (ENG.). 40p. pap. (978-1-907498-75-6(3), Book Shaker) Lean Marketing Pr.

Hipscher, Jerome. White Slavery. 2004. 78p. (YA). pap. 8.95 (978-0-595-31441-6(4)) iUniverse, Inc.

Holding, James Malcolm, 3rd, et al. The Mullet Masters. 2007. pap. 8.00 (978-0-8059-7147-7(5)) Dorrance Publishing Co., Inc.

Holt, Kimberly Willis. Piper Reed Gets a Job. Davenier, Christine, illus. 2009. (Piper Reed Ser.: 3). (ENG.). 160p. (J). (gr. 3-6). 14.99 (978-0-8050-8199-2(2), 9780805081992, Holt, Henry & Co. Bks. For Young Readers) Holt, Henry & Co.

Hood, Sue. Monkey Business. Chapman, Susan, illus. 2005. (J). bds. (978-1-890647-17-9(9)) TOMY International, Inc.

Hutchins, Hazel. Mattland. Petricic, Dusan, illus. 3rd ed. 2008. (ENG.). 32p. (J). (gr. -1-2). pap. 8.95 (978-1-55451-120-4(8), 9781554511204) Annick Pr., Ltd. CAN. Dist: Publishers Group West (PGW).

Irwin, Inez. Maida's Little Shop. 2006. 41.99 (978-1-4219-7069-1(4)) IndyPublish.com.

Jamieson, Mark. Ico Island. 2007. (J). pap. 11.95 (978-0-9792518-0-1(X)) Gequalsa.

Kelly, Katy. Melonhead & the We-Fix-It Company. Johnson, Gillian, illus. 2014. (Melonhead Ser.). (ENG.). 240p. (J). (gr. 3-7). 6.99 (978-0-307-92970-9(1), Yearling) Random Hse. Children's Bks.

Kim, Byung-Gyu & Hao, K. T. The 100th Customer. Ferri, Giuliano, illus. 2005. (ENG.). 32p. (J). (gr. -1-17). 15.95 (978-1-933327-03-7(0)) Purple Bear Bks., Inc.

LeFlore, Lyah B. Can't Hold Me Down. Warfield, D. L., illus. 2010. (Come Up Ser.). (ENG.). 272p. (J). (gr. 9-18). pap. 8.99 (978-1-4169-7964-7(6), Simon Pulse) Simon Pulse.

Lesczynski, Jim. The Walton Street Tycoons. 2007. 269p. (YA). pap. 9.95 (978-0-9791283-0-1(7)) East River Pr.

Ludwig, Elisa. Pretty Crooked. 2012. (Pretty Crooked Trilogy Ser.: 1). (ENG.). 368p. (YA). (gr. 8). 17.99 (978-0-06-206606-0(4), Tegen, Katherine Bks) HarperCollins Pubs.

Martin, Ann M. Needle & Thread. Andreasen, Dan, illus. 2007. 205p. (J). pap. (978-0-545-03660-3(7)) Scholastic, Inc.

Mayer, Mercer. The Best Yard Sale. Mayer, Mercer, illus. 2010. (Little Critter Ser.). (ENG., Illus.). 24p. (J). (gr. -1-2). pap. 3.99 (978-0-06-147799-7(0), HarperFestival) HarperCollins Pubs.

McCormick, Michelle. Priscilla Willa, Party Planner. 2013. (ENG.). 94p. (YA). pap. 9.95 (978-1-4787-1444-6(1)) Outskirts Pr., Inc.

Moonjar, ed. Conversations to Go - Money. 2005. 36p. 9.95 (978-0-9724282-5-5(9)) Moonjar, LLC.

—Noom & Raj Start Business. 2005. 36p. 19.95 (978-0-9724282-2-4(4)) Moonjar, LLC.

Myers, Madeleine M. Pocketful of Feathers. 2012. 160p. 41.95 (978-1-258-25346-2(1)); pap. 26.95 (978-1-258-25472-8(7)) Literary Licensing, LLC.

Nowell, Daphne A. Juana Meets Gabriel, the Small Business Angel: What if you Don't Want to Wait Around for a Prince Charming? 2008. (Illus.). 24p. (J). 17.95 (978-0-9798909-1-8(8)) Business Angel Pr.

Pants Builds a Business. 2004. (J). per. 7.99 (978-0-9755959-4-7(6)) Girl Named Pants, Inc., A.

Parker, David. Our Class Works Together. Lucas, Margeaux, illus. 2007. (J). (978-0-545-00384-1(9)) Scholastic, Inc.

Paulsen, Gary. Lawn Boy Returns. 2011. (ENG.). 112p. (J). (gr. 3-7). pap. 5.99 (978-0-553-49430-3(9), Yearling) Random Hse. Children's Bks.

Pinkowski, Vern V. A Twisted Pig's Tale. 2008. 144p. pap. 11.95 (978-0-595-46595-8(1), iUniverse, Inc.) iUniverse, Inc.

Pinkowski, Vernon V. A Twisted Pig's Tale. 2008. 148p. 21.95 (978-0-595-49022-6(0), iUniverse, Inc.) iUniverse, Inc.

Poyner, James R. Toy-Maker's Apprentice. 2006. 67p. per. 12.00 (978-1-60002-282-1(0), 4145) Mountain Valley Publishing, LLC.

Romer, Ruth. The Great Lemonade Standoff. 2005. (J). pap. (978-1-4108-4200-8(2)) Benchmark Education Co.

Rozen, Anna. The Merchant of Noises. Scarbrough, Carl W., tr. from FRE. Avril, Francois, illus. 2006. (ENG.). 28p. (J). (gr. 3-7). 18.95 (978-1-56792-321-6(6)) Godine, David R. Pub.

Rylander, Chris. The Fourth Stall, Pt. II. 2012. (Fourth Stall Ser.: 2). (ENG.). 288p. (J). (gr. 3-7). 16.99 (978-0-06-199630-6(0), Waldon Pond Pr.) HarperCollins Pubs.

Schaefer, Laura. The Teashop Girls. Rim, Sujean, illus. 2009. (ENG.). 272p. (J). (gr. 4-9). pap. 6.99 (978-1-4169-6794-1(X), Simon & Schuster/Paula Wiseman Bks.) Simon & Schuster/Paula Wiseman Bks.

Shoup, Andrew J. Andy & Elmer's Apple Dumpling Adventure. 2nd ed. 2007. (J). 16.95 (978-0-9720436-3-2(2)) TokoBooks, LLC.

—Andy & Elmer's Apple Dumpling Adventure Coloring & Activity Book. Shoup, Andrew J., illus. 2007. (Illus.). 36p. (J). 3.95 (978-0-9720436-2-5(4)) TokoBooks, LLC.

Stockton, Frank Richard. What Might Have Been Expected. 2009. 128p. 23.95 (978-1-60664-676-2(1)) Rodgers, Alan Bks.

Stratemeyer, Edward. The Rover Boys in Business or the Search. 2004. reprint ed. pap. 22.95 (978-1-4191-8116-0(5)) Kessinger Publishing, LLC.

—The Rover Boys in Business or the Search for the Missing Bonds. 2004. reprint ed. pap. 1.99 (978-1-4192-8116-7(X)) Kessinger Publishing, LLC.

Weissman, Elissa Brent. The Short Seller. (ENG.). (J). (gr. 3-7). 2014. 272p. pap. 8.99 (978-1-4424-5256-5(0)) 2013. (Illus.). 256p. 15.99 (978-1-4424-5255-8(2)) Simon & Schuster Children's Publishing.

White-Hill, Carol. Dreams Do Come True. 2009. 16p. pap. 12.99 (978-1-4490-0641-9(8)) AuthorHouse.

Wiebe, Trina. Lizards Don't Wear Lip Gloss. Sarrazin, Marisol, illus. 2004. (Abby & Tess Pet-Sitters Ser.). 91p. 15.95 (978-0-7569-3425-5(7)) Perfection Learning Corp.

Yeamans Simrell, Elizabeth. Only Mr. Bromley Will Do. 2008. 26p. 14.25 (978-0-615-22279-0(X)) Dash & Doodles Productions.

BUSINESS—HISTORY

Moriarty, J. T. The Birth of American Capitalism: The Growth of American Banks. 2004. (America's Industrial Society in the 19th Century Ser.). (Illus.). 32p. (gr. 5-8). pap. 10.00 (978-0-8239-4280-0(5)) Rosen Publishing Group, Inc., The.

BUSINESS, SMALL

see Small Business

BUSINESS—VOCATIONAL GUIDANCE

Business & Construction. 2010. (Green Careers Ser.). (Illus.). 160p. (C). (gr. 9-18). 32.95 (978-0-8160-8149-3(2), Ferguson Publishing Co.) Facts On File, Inc.

Careers in Focus: Business. 3rd rev. ed. 2010. (Careers in Focus Ser.). (Illus.). 192p. (gr. 6-12). 32.95 (978-0-8160-8016-8(X), Ferguson Publishing Co.) Facts On File, Inc.

Stinson, Paul. Sales, Marketing, Business & Finance. 2008. (Great Careers with a High School Diploma Ser.). 110p. (C). (gr. 9). 32.95 (978-0-8160-7051-0(2), Ferguson Publishing Co.) Facts On File, Inc.

What Can I Do Now: Business & Finance. 2010. (What Can I Do Now? Ser.). 240p. (gr. 6-12). 32.95 (978-0-8160-8081-6(X)) Facts On File, Inc.

Yomtov, Nel. Starting Your Own Business. 2013. (True Book(tm), a — Great American Business Ser.). (ENG.). 48p. (J). 31.00 (978-0-531-24779-2(1)); pap. 6.95 (978-0-531-28465-0(4)) Scholastic Library Publishing.

BUSINESS COLLEGES

see Business Education

BUSINESS CORRESPONDENCE

see Commercial Correspondence

BUSINESS DEPRESSIONS

see Depressions; Economic History

BUSINESS EDUCATION

see also Secretaries

James, Jack. How to Let Your Parents Raise a Millionaire: A Kid-to-Kid View on How to Make Money Make a Difference & Have Fun Doing Both. 2012. (ENG.). 115p. pap. 14.95 (978-1-61448-248-2(9)) Morgan James Publishing.

Orr, Tamra. What Degree Do I Need to Pursue a Career in Business?, 1 vol. 2015. (ENG.). 80p. (YA). 34.60 (978-1-4777-7853-1(5), Rosen Young Adult) Rosen Publishing Group, Inc., The.

Rosen Publishing Staff. The Right Degree for Me, 1 vol. 2015. (Right Degree for Me Ser.). (ENG.). 80p. (YA). 207.60 (978-1-4777-7877-7(2), Rosen Young Adult) Rosen Publishing Group, Inc., The.

The Vo-Tech Track to Success in Business. 2014. (Learning a Trade, Preparing for a Career Ser.). (Illus.). 80p. (J). (gr. 7-12). 34.25 (978-1-4777-7722-0(9)) Rosen Publishing Group, Inc., The.

BUSINESS ENGLISH

see English Language—Business English

BUSINESS ETHICS

see also Success

Checkmark Books, creator. Professional Ethics & Etiquette. 2nd rev. ed. 2007. (Mastering Career Skills Ser.). (Illus.). 144p. per. 12.95 (978-0-8160-7117-3(9), Checkmark Bks.) Facts On File, Inc.

Fischer, James. Business & Ethics. Madrian, Brigitte, ed. 2013. (Young Adult Library of Small Business & Finance Ser.: 10). 64p. (J). (gr. 7-18). 22.95 (978-1-4222-2914-9(9)); (Illus.). pap. 12.95 (978-1-4222-2981-1(5)) Mason Crest.

BUSINESS FAILURES

see Bankruptcy

BUSINESS LETTERS

see Commercial Correspondence

BUSINESS SCHOOLS

see Business Education

BUTTERFLIES

see also Caterpillars; Moths

Adams, Alison. Butterflies & Moths. 2011. (Early Connections Ser.). (J). (978-1-61672-629-4(6)) Benchmark Education Co.

Alinsky, Shelby. National Geographic Readers: Flutter, Butterfly! 2015. (Readers Ser.). (ENG., Illus.). 24p. (J). (-k). pap. 3.99 (978-1-4263-2117-7(1), National Geographic Children's Bks.) National Geographic Society.

Allen, Judy. Are You a Butterfly? Humphries, Tudor, illus. 2003. (Backyard Bks.). (ENG.). 28p. (J). (gr. k-3). pap. 6.99 (978-0-7534-5608-8(7), 9780753456088, Kingfisher) Roaring Brook Pr.

Amstutz, Lisa J. Butterflies. 2016. (Little Critters Ser.). (ENG., Illus.). 24p. (gr. k-1). lib. bdg. 21.99 (978-1-5157-1935-9(9), Pebble Bks.) Capstone Press of Coughlan Cos.

Appleby, Alex. I See a Butterfly. 2013. (In My Backyard Ser.). (Illus.). 24p. (J). (gr. k-2). pap. 8.15 (978-1-4339-8544-7(6)); lib. bdg. 22.60 (978-1-4339-8543-0(8)) Stevens, Gareth Publishing LLLP.

—I See a Butterfly: Puedo Ver una Mariposa. 2013. (In My Backyard / en Mi Jardín Ser.). (SPA & ENG., Illus.). 24p. (J). (gr. k-2). lib. bdg. 22.60 (978-1-4339-8792-2(9)) Stevens, Gareth Publishing LLLP.

Appleton-Smith, Laura & Blackaby, Susan. Butterfly Life Cycle. 2014. (Book to Remember Ser.). (ENG., Illus.). 26p. (J). pap. 8.95 (978-1-60541-153-8(1), Books To Remember) Flyleaf Publishing.

Ashley, Susan. Butterflies. (Incredible World of Insects Ser.). (Illus.). 24p. 2011. (J). (gr. 1-3). pap. 8.15 (978-1-4339-4580-9(0)) 2011. (J). (gr. 1-3). lib. bdg. 22.60 (978-1-4339-4579-3(7)) 2004. (gr. k-3). pap. 8.15 (978-0-8368-4059-9(3), Weekly Reader Leveled Readers) 2004. (gr. k-3). lib. bdg. 22.00 (978-0-8368-4052-0(6), Weekly Reader Leveled Readers) Stevens, Gareth Publishing LLLP.

Aston, Dianna Hutts. A Butterfly Is Patient. Long, Sylvia, illus. 2011. (ENG.). 40p. (J). (gr. k-5). 16.99 (978-0-8118-6479-4(0)) Chronicle Bks. LLC.

—A Butterfly Is Patient. Long, Sylvia, illus. 2015. (ENG.). 40p. (J). (gr. k-3). 7.99 (978-1-4521-4124-4(X)) Chronicle Bks. LLC.

—A Butterfly Is Patient. 2015. (J). lib. bdg. 18.40 (978-0-606-36918-3(X)) Turtleback Bks.

Axt, Katie. Can You See the Butterfly? 2015. (1G Bugs Ser.). (ENG., Illus.). 20p. (J). pap. 5.99 (978-1-63437-092-9(9)) American Reading Co.

Bach, Rachel. Butterflies. 2017. (Spot Creepy Crawlies Ser.). (ENG.). 16p. (J). (gr. k-3). 17.95 **(978-1-68151-107-8(X))** Amicus Publishing.

Bader, Bonnie. Fly, Butterfly. 2014. (Penguin Core Concepts Ser.). (ENG.). 32p. (J). (gr. -1-k). 3.99 (978-0-448-47919-4(2), Grosset & Dunlap) Penguin Young Readers Group.

Bailer, Darice. How Do Caterpillars Become Butterflies? 2009. (Tell Me Why, Tell Me How Ser.). 32p. (gr. 3-5). 29.93 (978-0-7614-3987-5(0)) Marshall Cavendish Corp.

Bair, Heather. Flying High with Butterflies: A Pre-K/ K Complete Supplemental Unit. Bruner, Garth, illus. 2004. per. 9.95 (978-1-891541-03-2(X)) Insect Lore.

—I Spy a Butterfly: A Second Grade Complete Supplemental Unit. Bruner, Garth, illus. 2005. per. 9.95 (978-1-891541-05-6(6)) Insect Lore.

—O'H Me O'H My A Butterfly: A First Grade Complete Supplemental Unit. Bruner, Garth, illus. 2005. per. 9.95 (978-1-891541-04-9(8)) Insect Lore.

Barnard, Edward S. Butterflies. (Amazing Animals Ser.). 48p. 2009. (gr. 2-6). pap. 10.50 (978-1-4339-2011-0(5), Gareth Stevens Learning Library) 2008. (YA). (gr. 3-6). lib. bdg. 28.00 (978-0-8368-9094-5(9)) Stevens, Gareth Publishing LLLP.

—Butterflies. 2006. (Illus.). 45p. (J). (978-1-59939-111-3(2), Reader's Digest Young Families, Inc.) Studio Fun International.

Barry, Frances. Caterpillar to Butterfly. 2010. (J). (978-0-7636-4261-7(4)) Candlewick Pr.

Bentley, Dawn. Good Night, Sweet Butterflies. Cahoon, Heather, illus. 2007. (ENG.). 14p. (J). 5.99 (978-1-4169-1296-5(7), Little Simon) Little Simon.

Berger, Melvin & Berger, Gilda. Butterflies. 2011. (Illus.). 16p. (J). pap. (978-0-545-24447-3(1)) Scholastic, Inc.

—A Caterpillar Grows Up. 2008. (Illus.). 32p. (J). (978-0-439-02527-0(3)) Scholastic, Inc.

Best, B. J. Butterflies. 2016. (Migrating Animals Ser.). 24p. (J). pap. 8.22 (978-1-5026-2090-3(1)) Cavendish Square Publishing.

Beylon, Cathy & Barbaresi, Nina. I Love Butterflies. 2007. (Dover Nature Coloring Book Ser.). (ENG., Illus.). 32p. (J). (gr. -1-2). pap. 4.99 (978-0-486-45659-1(5)) Dover Pubns., Inc.

Bishop, Nic. Butterflies & Moths. Bishop, Nic, photos by. 2009. (Nic Bishop Ser.). (ENG., Illus.). 48p. (J). (gr. -1-3). 17.99 (978-0-439-87757-2(1)) Scholastic, Inc.

Bredeson, Carmen. Monarch Butterflies up Close. 2006. (Zoom in on Animals! Ser.). (Illus.). 24p. (J). (gr. -1-3). lib. bdg. 22.60 (978-0-7660-2494-6(6), Enslow Elementary) Enslow Pubs., Inc.

Bredeson, Carmen & Cousins, Lindsey. Can You Find These Butterflies? 2012. (All about Nature Ser.). 24p. (J). (gr. -1-1). (Illus.). pap. 7.95 (978-1-4644-0069-8(5), Enslow Elementary); 22.60 (978-0-7660-3980-3(3)) Enslow Pubs., Inc.

Bronson, Cary. I am Not a Flying Elephant Fish! A Children's Science Book on the Butterfly. Gorner, William, illus. l.t. ed. 2004. 32p. (J). lib. bdg. 14.95 (978-0-9746094-0-9(4)) Connect With Your Kid Bks.

Burns, Loree Griffin. Handle with Care: An Unusual Butterfly Journey. Harasimowicz, Ellen, illus. 2014. (ENG.). 32p. (gr. 1-4). lib. bdg. 26.60 (978-0-7613-9342-9(0), Millbrook Pr.) Lerner Publishing Group.

Butterflies. (Color & Learn Ser.). 36p. (J). (gr. 1-5). pap. (978-1-882210-10-7(7)) Action Publishing, Inc.

Butterflies, Vol. 3. 2005. (Bugs, Bugs, Bugs Ser.). (YA). (gr. k-3). 118.80 (978-0-7368-4205-1(5), Pebble Bks.) Capstone Press of Coughlan Cos.

Butterfly & Caterpillar. 2003. 38.95 (978-0-8136-4171-3(3)) Modern Curriculum Pr.

Bygrave, Linda. Butterfly. (Illus.). 24p. (YA). (gr. 1-18). lib. bdg. 22.80 (978-1-931983-52-5(6)) Chrysalis Education.

Calder, Joan Z. Airplanes in the Garden: Monarch Butterflies Take Flight. l.t. alt. ed. 2014. (ENG., Illus.). 32p. (J). 16.95 (978-0-9832962-1-8(9)) Willow Creek Pr., Inc.

Caldwell, Charlotte. Kirby's Journal: Backyard Butterfly Magic. 2015. (Young Palmetto Bks.). (ENG., Illus.). 56p. (J). (gr. 4-6). pap. 17.95 (978-1-61117-553-0(4)) Univ. of South Carolina Pr.

Cardenas, Ernesto A. Butterflies. 2009. pap. 4.95 (978-1-60698-064-4(5)) Milo Educational Bks. & Resources.

Catt, Thessaly. Migrating with the Monarch Butterfly. 2011. (Animal Journeys Ser.). (Illus.). 24p. (YA). (gr. 1-4). lib. bdg. 22.60 (978-1-4488-2546-2(6)) Rosen Publishing Group, Inc., The.

Chavez, R. J. Bob. Bye Bye Butterfly: A True-Life Children's Butterfly Adventure. 2006. (ENG.). (J). 3.99 (978-0-9778110-0-7(X)) R.J. Bob Chavez Images.

Conlon, Mara. Butterflies & Friends: An Art Activity Book for Adventurous Artists of All Ages. Zschock, Martha, illus. 2009. (Scratch & Sketch Ser.). 64p. (J). (gr. 1). spiral bd., act. bk. ed. 12.99 (978-1-59359-841-9(6)) Peter Pauper Pr. Inc.

Cooper, Jason. Butterflies. 2005. (ENG., Illus.). 24p. (gr. k-2). per. 8.95 (978-1-59515-739-3(5)) Rourke Educational Media.

Cooper, Sharon Katz. When Butterflies Cross the Sky: The Monarch Butterfly Migration. Brunet, Joshua S., illus. 2015. (Extraordinary Migrations Ser.). (ENG.). 24p. (gr. 2-3). pap. 8.95 (978-1-4795-6100-1(2)); lib. bdg. 26.65 (978-1-4795-6076-9(6)) Picture Window Bks.

Corley, Nikolett. Zendoodle Coloring: Birds & Butterflies: Delicate Beauties to Color & Display. 2017. (ENG., Illus.). 128p. pap. 13.99 (978-1-250-12823-2(4), 9781250128232, St. Martin's Griffin) St. Martin's Pr.

Cullis, Megan. Butterflies Coloring Book. Cooper, Jenny, illus. 2012. (Coloring Bks). 32p. (J). pap. 5.99 (978-0-7945-3113-3(X), Usborne) EDC Publishing.

Cussen, Sarah. Those Beautiful Butterflies. Weaver, Steve, illus. 2008. (Those Amazing Animals Ser.). (ENG.). 55p. (J). (gr. k-4). lib. bdg. 14.95 (978-1-56164-414-8(5)); (gr. 1-5). pap. 9.95 (978-1-56164-415-5(3)) Pineapple Pr., Inc.

De la Bédoyère, Camilla. Lifecycles Caterpillar to Butterfly SchoIBC SS. 2009. 24p. (J). (978-1-59566-709-0(1)) QEB Publishing Inc.

Delano, Marfe Ferguson. Explore My World Butterflies. 2014. (Explore My World Ser.). (ENG.). 32p. (J). (gr. -1-2). pap. 4.99 (978-1-4263-1699-9(2), National Geographic Children's Bks.) National Geographic Society.

Dickmann, Nancy. A Butterfly's Life, 1 vol. 2010. (Watch It Grow Ser.). (ENG., Illus.). 24p. (gr. -1-1). 22.65 (978-1-4329-4138-3(0)); pap. 6.29 (978-1-4329-4147-5(X)) Heinemann-Raintree. (Acorn).

—La Vida de la Mariposa, 1 vol. 2011. (¡Mira Cómo Crece! Ser.). (Illus.). 24p. (gr. -1-1). (SPA & ENG.). 22.65 (978-1-4329-5271-6(4)); (ENG & SPA., pap. 6.29 (978-1-4329-5283-9(8)) Heinemann-Raintree. (Bellota).

Dominquez, Amalia. Busy, Busy Butterfly. 2004. (Illus.). 24p. bds. 8.95 (978-1-932915-01-3(X)) Sandvik Publishing.

Dorling Kindersley Publishing Staff. Butterfly & Moth. 2012. (DK Eyewitness Bks.). (ENG., Illus.). 72p. (J). (gr. 3-7). 16.99 (978-0-7566-9298-8(9), DK Children) Dorling Kindersley Publishing, Inc.

Dorling Kindersley Publishing Staff, creator. Butterflies. 2006. (Ultimate Sticker Bks.). (ENG., Illus.). 16p. (J). (gr. k-3). pap. 6.99 (978-0-7566-2096-7(1), DK Children) Dorling Kindersley Publishing, Inc.

Earhart, Kristin, et al. The Magic School Bus & the Butterfly Bunch. Bracken, Carolyn, illus. 2010. 32p. (J). (978-0-545-16727-7(2)) Scholastic, Inc.

Eckart, Edana. Monarch Butterfly. 2005. (Welcome Bks.). (ENG., Illus.). 24p. (J). (gr. -1-2). pap. 4.95 (978-0-516-25166-0(X), Children's Pr.) Scholastic Library Publishing.

Edwards, Roberta. Flight of the Butterflies. Kayganich, Bob, illus. 2010. (Penguin Young Readers, Level 3 Ser.). (ENG.). 48p. (J). (gr. 1-3). mass mkt. 3.99 (978-0-448-45396-5(7), Penguin Young Readers) Penguin Young Readers Group.

Engle, Margarita. Summer Birds: The Butterflies of Maria Merian. Paschkis, Julie, illus. 2010. (ENG.). 32p. (J). (gr. k-3). 17.99 (978-0-8050-8937-0(3), 9780805089370, Holt, Henry & Co. Bks. For Young Readers) Holt, Henry & Co.

Enslow, Brian. Counting Butterflies 1-2-3. 2011. (All about Counting Bugs 1-2-3 Ser.). (Illus.). 24p. (J). (gr. -1-18). pap. 7.95 (978-1-59845-246-4(0), Enslow Elementary); (gr. k-3). lib. bdg. 22.60 (978-0-7660-3921-6(8)) Enslow Pubs., Inc.

Farndon, John. Butterflies & Moths: A Comprehensive Guide to the Brief But BrilliantLives of These Fascinating Creatures, With over 200 Pictures. 2015. (ENG., Illus.). 64p. (J). (gr. -1-k). 12.99 (978-1-86147-407-0(5), Armadillo) Anness Publishing GBR. Dist: National Bk. Network.

Fiedler, Heidi. Butterflies: A Close-Up Photographic Look Inside Your World. 2017. (Up Close Ser.). (ENG., Illus.). (J). (gr. k-6). lib. bdg. 27.99 **(978-1-942875-37-6(1)**, Walter Foster Jr) Quarto Publishing Group USA.

French, Vivian. Caterpillar Caterpillar: Read & Wonder. Voake, Charlotte, illus. 2009. (Read & Wonder Ser.). (ENG.). 32p. (J). (gr. -1-3). pap. 6.99 (978-0-7636-4263-1(0)) Candlewick Pr.

Frisch, Aaron. Butterflies. 2014. 24p. (978-1-60818-457-6(9)) Creative Co., The.

—Seedlings: Butterflies. 2015. (Seedlings Ser.). (ENG.). 24p. (J). (gr. -1-1). pap. 7.99 (978-1-62832-039-8(7), Creative Paperbacks) Creative Co., The.

Frost, Helen. Monarch & Milkweed. Gore, Leonid, illus. 2008. (ENG.). 40p. (J). (gr. -1-3). 17.99 (978-1-4169-0085-6(3), Atheneum Bks. for Young Readers) Simon & Schuster Children's Publishing.

Gallagher, Debbie. Butterflies. 2011. (Mighty Minibeasts Ser.). 32p. (gr. 2). 28.50 (978-1-60870-544-3(7)) Marshall Cavendish Corp.

Ganeri, Anita. Butterflies & Caterpillars. Axworthy, Ann, illus. 2012. (Animal Families Ser.). 24p. (J). (gr. -1-k). 12.79 (978-1-60753-097-8(X)) Amicus Publishing.

—Butterflies & Caterpillars. Axworthy, Ani, illus. 2010. (Animal Families Ser.). (ENG.). 14p. (J). bds. 10.99 (978-1-84089-641-1(8)) Evans Brothers, Ltd. GBR. Dist: Independent Pubs. Group.

Goddard, Jolyon. Monarch Butterfly. 2008. (Nature's Children Ser.). (Illus.). 52p. (J). (978-0-7172-6240-3(5)) Grolier, Ltd.

Goldish, Meish. Beautiful Butterflies. 2008. (No Backbone! Ser.). (Illus.). 24p. (J). (gr. k-3). lib. bdg. 21.28 (978-1-59716-587-7(5)) Bearport Publishing Co., Inc.

Gordon, Sharon. Guess Who Changes. 2007. (J). pap. 6.99 (978-0-7614-3318-7(X)) Marshall Cavendish Corp.

Goryl, Madeline, illus. The Butterfly Coloring Book. 2015. (ENG.). 80p. (J). (gr. -1). pap. 5.99 (978-1-63220-523-0(8), Sky Pony Pr.) Skyhorse Publishing Co., Inc.

Gregory, Josh. From Butterfly Wings to Display Technology. 2014. (21st Century Skills Innovation Library: Innovations from Nature Ser.). (ENG., Illus.). 32p. (J). (gr. 4-8). pap. 14.21 (978-1-62431-760-6(X), 203285); lib. bdg. 28.50 (978-1-62431-754-5(5), 203284) Cherry Lake Publishing.

—Monarch Butterflies. 2016. (Nature's Children Ser.). (ENG., Illus.). 48p. (J). pap. 6.95 (978-0-531-22520-2(8), Children's Pr.) Scholastic Library Publishing.

Guillain, Charlotte. Life Story of a Butterfly, 1 vol. 2014. (Animal Life Stories Ser.). (ENG., Illus.). 32p. (gr. 1-3). 27.32 (978-1-4846-0487-8(3), Heinemann First Library) Heinemann-Raintree.

Hansen, Grace. Butterflies, 1 vol. 2014. (Insects Ser.). (ENG.). 24p. (J). (gr. 4-8). lib. bdg. 28.50 (978-1-62970-039-7(8)) ABDO Publishing Co.

—Mariposas. 2015. (Insectos Ser.). (SPA., Illus.). 24p. (gr. k-1). pap. 7.95 (978-1-4966-0479-8(2)) Capstone Classroom.

Hayes, Amy. A Caterpillar Becomes a Butterfly. 2016. (Transformations in Nature Ser.). (ENG., Illus.). 24p. (J). (gr. 1-1). pap. 8.22 (978-1-5026-0822-2(7)) Cavendish Square Publishing.

Heiligman, Deborah. From Caterpillar to Butterfly. Weissman, Bari, illus. 2015. (Let's-Read-And-Find-Out Science 1 Ser.). (ENG.). 32p. (J). (gr. -1-3). pap. 6.99 (978-0-06-238183-5(0)) HarperCollins Pubs.

—From Caterpillar to Butterfly Big Book. Weissman, Bari, illus. 2008. (Let's-Read-And-Find-Out Science 1 Ser.). (ENG.). 32p. (J). (gr. -1-3). pap. 24.99 (978-0-06-111975-0(X), Collins) HarperCollins Pubs.

Heliadore. The Butterfly. Heliadore, illus. 2012. (ENG., Illus.). 36p. (J). (gr. -1-k). spiral bd. 12.99 (978-1-85103-404-8(8)) Moonlight Publishing, Ltd. GBR. Dist: Independent Pubs. Group.

Héliadore, et al. The Butterfly. 2006. (ENG., Illus.). 36p. (J). (gr. k-3). pap. 11.99 (978-1-85103-240-2(1)) Moonlight Publishing, Ltd. GBR. Dist: Independent Pubs. Group.

Hengel, Katherine. Cool Birds & Bugs: Great Things to Do in the Great Outdoors, 1 vol. 2016. (ENG., Illus.). 32p. (J). (978-1-62403-694-1(5)) ABDO Publishing Co.

Herrington, Lisa M. Butterflies & Moths. 2015. (Rookie Read-About(tm) Science: What's the Difference? Ser.). (ENG., Illus.). 32p. (J). lib. bdg. 25.00 (978-0-531-21485-5(0), Children's Pr.) Scholastic Library Publishing.

—Caterpillar to Butterfly. 2014. (Rookie Read-About(r) Science - Life Cycles Ser.). (ENG.). 32p. (J). lib. bdg. 23.00 (978-0-531-21055-0(3)) Scholastic Library Publishing.

—It's a Good Thing There Are Butterflies. 2014. (Rookie Read-About(r) Science — It's a Good Thing... Ser.). (ENG.). 32p. (J). pap. 5.95 (978-0-531-22835-7(5)); lib. bdg. 25.00 (978-0-531-22363-5(9)) Scholastic Library Publishing.

Hewitt, Sally. Life Cycles: From Caterpillar to Butterfly. 2004. (QEB Start Talking Ser.). (Illus.). 24p. (J). lib. bdg. 15.95 (978-1-59566-002-2(X)) QEB Publishing Inc.

Ho, Cammie. Butterfly Butterfly. 2016. (Life Cycle Bks.). (ENG., Illus.). 27p. (J). (gr. k-2). pap. 7.99 (978-1-943241-03-3(1)) Phonic Monic.

Hoffman, Don. Wanderer: The Monarch Butterfly. 2004. 7.95 (978-1-930401-21-1(3)) Central Coast Bks./Pr.

Holden, Pam. Caterpillar to Butterfly. 2015. (ENG., Illus.). 16p. (-1). pap. (978-1-77654-078-5(6), Red Rocket Readers) Flying Start Bks.

Howard, Fran. Butterflies [Scholastic]. 2010. (Bugs, Bugs, Bugs! Ser.). 24p. pap. 0.52 (978-1-4296-5054-0(0), Pebble Plus) Capstone Press of Coughlan Cos.

Hudak, Heather C. Butterflies. 2008. (World of Wonder Ser.). (Illus.). 24p. (J). (gr. k-3). pap. 8.95 (978-1-59036-867-1(3)); lib. bdg. 24.45 (978-1-59036-866-4(5)) Weigl Pubs., Inc.

Hunt, Joni Phelps. A Shimmer of Butterflies: The Brief, Brilliant Life of a Magical Insect. León, Vicki, ed. 2nd ed. 2005. (Jean-Michel Cousteau Presents Ser.). Orig. Title: Butterflies. (ENG., Illus.). 48p. (J). pap. 9.95 (978-0-9666490-6-2(0)) London Town Pr.

Hurtig, Jennifer. Butterflies. (J). 2012. (978-1-61913-261-0(3)) 2012. (978-1-61913-064-7(5)) 2007. (Illus.). 24p. (gr. -1-3). lib. bdg. 24.45 (978-1-59036-683-7(2)) Weigl Pubs., Inc.

—Butterflies. Hudak, Heather C., ed. 2007. (Backyard Animals Ser.). (Illus.). 24p. (J). (gr. -1-3). pap. 8.95 (978-1-59036-684-4(0)) Weigl Pubs., Inc.

Huseby, Victoria. Butterfly. 2008. (Illus.). 24p. (J). 25.65 (978-1-59920-174-0(7)) Black Rabbit Bks.

Jackman, Vernon. Bunnies & Butterflies in the Backyard & the Pirates Who Know Where They Live: Stories That Help Children Learn & Remember Their Address & Telephone Number. Theagene, Jeannisse, illus. l.t. ed. 2010. (ENG.). 32p. (J). pap. 6.99 (978-0-9829371-1-2(3)) New Kid Safety.

Jeunesse, Gallimard & Delafosse, Claude. Butterflies. Heliadore, illus. 2007. (First Discovery Book Ser.). (ENG.). 24p. (J). (gr. -1-k). 5.99 (978-0-439-91087-3(0)) Scholastic, Inc.

Johnson, Jinny. Butterfly. Woods, Michael, illus. 2010. (J). 28.50 (978-1-59920-352-2(9)) Black Rabbit Bks.

—What's It Like to Be... Butterfly? Sanzi, Desiderio, illus. 2011. (What's It Like to Be... ? Ser.). 24p. (J). (gr. -1-k). 25.65 (978-1-60753-185-2(2)) Amicus Publishing.

Kalman, Bobbie. Caterpillars to Butterflies. 2008. (It's Fun to Learn about Baby Animals Ser.). (ENG., Illus.). 24p. (J). (gr. k-3). pap. (978-0-7787-3974-6(0), 1294250) Crabtree Publishing Co.

—I Can Write a Book about Butterflies. 2012. (ENG.). 32p. (J). (978-0-7787-7987-2(4)); pap. (978-0-7787-7996-4(3)) Crabtree Publishing Co.

—The Life Cycle of a Butterfly. 2007. (ENG.). 32p. (J). (978-0-7787-7700-7(6)) Crabtree Publishing Co.

Kalman, Bobbie & Johnson, Robin. Endangered Butterflies. 2006. (Earth's Endangered Animals Ser.). (ENG., Illus.). 32p. (J). (gr. 4-7). pap. (978-0-7787-1916-8(2)) Crabtree Publishing Co.

Kant, Tanya. How a Caterpillar Grows into a Butterfly. Franklin, Carolyn, illus. 2008. (Amaze Ser.). (ENG.). 32p. (J). 27.00 (978-0-531-24046-5(0)); (gr. -1-3). pap. 8.95 (978-0-531-23800-4(8)) Scholastic Library Publishing. (Children's Pr.).

—The Migration of a Butterfly. Franklin, Carolyn, illus. 2008. (Amaze Ser.). (ENG.). 32p. (J). 27.00 (978-0-531-24048-9(7)); (gr. -1-3). pap. 8.95 (978-0-531-23802-8(4)) Scholastic Library Publishing. (Children's Pr.).

Kay, Jill. Caterpillars & Butterflies. 2013. (InfoMax Readers Ser.). (ENG.). 24p. (J). (gr. 2-3). pap. 49.50 (978-1-4777-2264-0(5)); pap. 8.25 (978-1-4777-2263-3(7)) Rosen Publishing Group, Inc., The. (Rosen Classroom).

Kelly, Irene. It's a Butterfly's Life. 2007. (ENG., Illus.). 32p. (J). (gr. -1-3). 16.95 (978-0-8234-1860-2(X)) Holiday Hse., Inc.

Kij, Krysia. Becoming a Butterfly. 2008. (Real Readers - Upper Emergent Ser.). (ENG., Illus.). 12p. (gr. 1-2). pap. 5.90 (978-0-8239-8203-5(3)) Rosen Publishing Group, Inc., The.

King, Anthea. Where Do Butterflies Go ... ?? 2013. 32p. pap. (978-1-4602-1743-6(8)) FriesenPress.

Kissock, Heather. Butterflies. 2016. (J). **(978-1-4896-5393-2(7))** Weigl Pubs., Inc.

Knudsen, Shannon. Eggs, Legs, Wings: A Butterfly Life Cycle, 1 vol. Smith, Simon, illus. (First Graphics: Nature Cycles Ser.). (ENG.). 24p. (gr. 1-2). 2011. pap. 6.29 (978-1-4296-6228-4(X)) 2011. pap. 35.70 (978-1-4296-6397-7(9)) 2010. lib. bdg. 23.99 (978-1-4296-5367-1(1)) Capstone Press of Coughlan Cos.

—From Egg to Butterfly. 2012. (Start to Finish, Second Series: Nature's Cycles Ser.). (ENG.). 24p. (gr. k-3). lib. bdg. 23.93 (978-0-7613-6562-4(1)) Lerner Publishing Group.

Kralovansky, Susan. Moth or Butterfly?, 1 vol. 2014. (This or That? Ser.). (ENG.). 24p. (gr. 5-10). lib. bdg. 25.65 (978-1-62403-288-2(5), Super SandCastle) ABDO Publishing Co.

Lawrence, Ellen. A Butterfly's Life. (Animal Diaries: Life Cycles Ser.). 24p. (J). 2016. (ENG.). (gr. k-3). pap. 7.95 (978-1-944998-41-7(1)) 2012. (gr. -1-3). lib. bdg. 23.93 (978-1-61772-413-8(0)) Bearport Publishing Co., Inc.

Leaf, Christina. Butterflies. 2017. (Insects up Close Ser.). (ENG., Illus.). 24p. (J). (gr. k-3). lib. bdg. 25.95 **(978-1-62617-659-1(0)**, Blastoff! Readers) Bellwether Media.

Leigh, Autumn. From Caterpillar to Butterfly: A Life Cycle. 2009. (Real Life Readers Ser.). 16p. (gr. 2-3). pap. 7.05 (978-1-4358-0223-0(3), Rosen Classroom) Rosen Publishing Group, Inc., The.

Life Cycles: From Caterpillar to Butterfly. 2005. (J). per. 8.95 (978-1-59566-129-6(8)) QEB Publishing Inc.

Ljung, Kiki. Build A... Butterfly. 2017. (Build A... Ser.). (ENG.). 12p. (J). (gr. k-3). bds. 12.99 **(978-1-84780-922-3(7)**, Frances Lincoln Children's Bks.) Quarto Publishing Group UK GBR. Dist: Hachette Bk. Group.

Llewellyn, Claire. Asi Nace una Mariposa. Giraldo, Maria Cristina, tr. Mendez, Simon, illus. 2003. (Colección Así Nace... / Starting Life Collection Ser.). (SPA.). 24p. (gr. k-6). pap. 14.95 (978-1-59437-788-4(X)) Santillana USA Publishing Co., Inc.

Lockwood, Sophie. Butterflies. 2007. (World of Insects Ser.). (ENG., Illus.). 40p. (J). (gr. 3-6). 31.36 (978-1-59296-820-6(1), 200973) Child's World, Inc., The.

Lundgren, Julie K. Butterflies & Moths. 2010. (ENG., Illus.). 24p. (gr. 1-4). pap. 8.95 (978-1-61590-547-8(2)) Rourke Educational Media.

Macheske, Felicia. Bright & Beautiful: Butterfly. 2016. (Guess What Ser.). (ENG., Illus.). 24p. (J). (gr. k-2). 28.50 (978-1-63470-721-3(4), 207595) Cherry Lake Publishing.

Malam, John. Grow Your Own Butterfly Farm, 1 vol. 2011. (Grow It Yourself! Ser.). (ENG.). 32p. (gr. k-2). 27.32 (978-1-4329-5109-2(2), Heinemann First Library) Heinemann-Raintree.

Marabout & Abrams Noterie Staff. Butterflies. 2015. (ENG., Illus.). 144p. pap. 9.95 (978-1-4197-1980-6(7), Abrams Noterie) Abrams, Inc.

Markovics, Joyce L. Las Mariposas Monarca. 2014. (¿a dónde Van en Invierno? Ser.). (SPA.). 24p. (J). (gr. -1-3). lib. bdg. 23.93 (978-1-62724-458-9(1)) Bearport Publishing Co., Inc.

—Monarch Butterflies. 2015. (Illus.). 24p. (J). lib. bdg. (978-1-62724-316-2(X)) Bearport Publishing Co., Inc.

Marsh, Laura. Caterpillar to Butterfly. 2012. (Readers Ser.). (ENG., Illus.). 32p. (J). (gr. -1-1). pap. 3.99 (978-1-4263-0920-5(1), National Geographic Children's Bks.) National Geographic Society.

—Great Migrations Butterflies. 2010. (Readers Ser.). (ENG., Illus.). 48p. (J). (gr. 2-4). 13.90 (978-1-4263-0740-9(3)); pap. 3.99 (978-1-4263-0739-3(X)) National Geographic Society. (National Geographic Children's Bks.).

—National Geographic Readers: Caterpillar to Butterfly. 2012. (Readers Ser.). (ENG., Illus.). 32p. (J). (gr. -1-1). lib. bdg. 13.90 (978-1-4263-0921-2(X), National Geographic Children's Bks.) National Geographic Society.

Mazurkiewicz, Jessica. Butterfly Fun Activity Book. 2009. (Dover Little Activity Bks.). (ENG., Illus.). 64p. (J). (gr. k-3). pap. 1.99 (978-0-486-47198-3(5)) Dover Pubns., Inc.

—Creative Haven Beautiful Butterfly Designs Coloring Book. 2013. (Adult Coloring Ser.). (ENG.). 64p. (gr. 3). pap. 5.99 (978-0-486-49456-2(X)) Dover Pubns., Inc.

—3-D Coloring Book — Butterflies. 2011. (Dover 3-D Coloring Book Ser.). (ENG., Illus.). 32p. (J). (gr. 3-5). pap. 5.99 (978-0-486-48161-6(1)) Dover Pubns., Inc.

McAneney, Caitlin. Life Cycle of a Butterfly. 2013. (Rosen Readers Ser.). (ENG.). 24p. (J). (gr. 2-3). pap. 8.25 (978-1-4777-2237-4(8)); pap. 49.50 (978-1-4777-2238-1(6)) Rosen Publishing Group, Inc., The. (Rosen Classroom).

Meachen Rau, Dana. The Butterfly in the Sky. 2006. (Nature Ser.). (SPA., Illus.). 24p. (gr. k-1). lib. bdg. 15.95 (978-0-7614-2311-9(7), Benchmark Bks.) Marshall Cavendish Corp.

—Fly, Butterfly, Fly! 2007. (Go, Critter, Go! Ser.). (SPA & ENG., Illus.). 24p. (gr. k-1). lib. bdg. 15.95 (978-0-7614-2649-3(3), Benchmark Bks.) Marshall Cavendish Corp.

—Fly, Butterfly, Fly!/Vuela Mariposa, Vuela! 2007. (Go, Critter, Go!/¡Vamos Criaturita, Vamos! Ser.). (SPA & ENG., Illus.). 24p. (gr. k-1). lib. bdg. 15.95 (978-0-7614-2814-5(3), Benchmark Bks.) Marshall Cavendish Corp.

—La Mariposa en el Aire. 2006. (Naturaleza Ser.). (SPA., Illus.). 24p. (gr. k-1). lib. bdg. 15.95 (978-0-7614-2416-1(4), Benchmark Bks.) Marshall Cavendish Corp.

—Vuela Mariposa, Vuela! 2007. (¡Vamos Criaturita, Vamos! Ser.). (SPA & ENG., Illus.). 24p. (gr. k-1). lib. bdg. 15.95 (978-0-7614-2790-2(2), Benchmark Bks.) Marshall Cavendish Corp.

Merritt, Robin. The Life Cycle of a Butterfly. 2011. (Life Cycles Ser.). (ENG., Illus.). 32p. (J). (gr. k-3). lib. bdg. 29.93 (978-1-60973-143-4(3), 201168) Child's World, Inc., The.

Migrating with the Monarch Butterfly. 2011. (Animal Journeys Ser.). (Illus.). 24p. (J). pap. 8.25 (978-1-4488-2676-6(4), PowerKids Pr.) Rosen Publishing Group, Inc., The.

Milbourne, Anna. Butterfly. 2005. 24p. (J). 9.99 (978-0-7945-1052-7(3), Usborne) EDC Publishing.

Miles, Lisa. Origami Birds & Butterflies. 2013. (Amazing Origami Ser.). 32p. (J). (gr. 2-5). pap. 63.00 (978-1-4339-9646-7(4)); pap. 10.50 (978-1-4339-9645-0(6)); (ENG., Illus.). lib. bdg. 26.60 (978-1-4339-9644-3(8)) Stevens, Gareth Publishing LLLP.

Mitchell, Melanie S. Butterflies. 2003. (First Step Nonfiction - Animal Life Cycles Ser.). (ENG., Illus.). 24p. (gr. k-2). pap. 6.95 (978-0-8225-4599-6(3), Lerner Pubns.); lib. bdg. 23.93 (978-0-8225-4598-9(5)) Lerner Publishing Group.

Monroe, Mary Alice. A Butterfly Called Hope, 1 vol. Bergwerf, Barbara J., illus. 2013. (ENG.). 32p. (J). (gr. -1-4). 17.95 (978-1-60718-854-4(6)); pap. 9.95 (978-1-60718-856-8(2)) Arbordale Publishing.

Morris, Neil & Morris, Ting. Butterfly. 2003. (Illus.). 32p. (J). lib. bdg. 27.10 (978-1-58340-379-2(5)) Black Rabbit Bks.

Murawski, Darlyne. Face to Face with Butterflies. 2010. (Face to Face with Animals Ser.). (ENG., Illus.). 32p. (J). (gr. 1-4). 16.95 (978-1-4263-0618-1(0)); 25.90 (978-1-4263-0619-8(9)) National Geographic Society. (National Geographic Children's Bks.).

Murcia, Rebecca Thatcher. Threat to the Monarch Butterfly. 2007. (On the Verge of Extinction Ser.). (Illus.). 32p. (YA). (gr. 2-5). lib. bdg. 25.70 (978-1-58415-587-4(6)) Mitchell Lane Pubs., Inc.

Murray, Julie. Butterflies, 1 vol. (Big Buddy Bks.). (ENG.). (J). 2010. 32p. (gr. 2-5). 28.50 (978-1-61613-483-9(6)) 2003. 24p. (gr. 1-4). 25.65 (978-1-57765-718-7(7)) ABDO Publishing Co.

—Monarch Butterflies, 1 vol. 2007. (Life Cycles Ser.). (ENG.). 24p. (gr. 4-7). 25.65 (978-1-59928-708-9(0), Buddy Bks.) ABDO Publishing Co.

National Geographic Kids Staff. Caterpillar to Butterfly. 2016. (Look & Learn Ser.). (ENG., Illus.). 24p. (J). (-k). bds. 6.99 (978-1-4263-2306-5(9), National Geographic Children's Bks.) National Geographic Society.

Natural History Museum Staff. Sensational Butterflies Sticker Book. 2013. (ENG.). 14p. (J). (gr. -1-1). pap. 6.99 (978-0-565-09328-0(2)) Natural History Museum Pubns. GBR. Dist: Independent Pubs. Group.

Nelson, Sara. Butterflies. 2007. (Nature Watch Ser.). (ENG., Illus.). 48p. (J). (gr. 4-8). lib. bdg. 27.93 (978-0-8225-6766-0(0), Lerner Pubns.) Lerner Publishing Group.

Opler, Paul. Butterflies of North America: An Activity & Coloring Book. 2004. (ENG.). 84p. (J). (gr. 3-17). pap. 9.95 *(978-1-57098-435-8(2))* Rinehart, Roberts Pubs.

Orenstein, Ronald. Weird Butterflies & Moths. Marent, Thomas, photos by. 2016. (ENG., Illus.). 64p. (J). (gr. 5-8). pap. 9.95 *(978-1-77085-814-5(8)*, 9781770858145) Firefly Bks., Ltd.

Pallotta, Jerry. Butterfly Colors & Counting. Bersani, Shennen, illus. 2013. (ENG.). 10p. (J). (— 1). bds. 5.95 *(978-1-57091-899-5(6))* Charlesbridge Publishing, Inc.

—Butterfly Counting. Bersani, Shennen, illus. 2015. (ENG.). 32p. (J). (gr. -1-2). 17.95 *(978-1-57091-414-0(1))* Charlesbridge Publishing, Inc.

Parsonage, Betty. Butterfly Wings. 2003. (Illus.). 50p. 12.95 *(978-1-59094-013-6(X)*, 159094013X) Jawbone Publishing Corp.

Pasternak, Carol. How to Raise Monarch Butterflies: A Step-by-Step Guide for Kids. 2012. (ENG., Illus.). 48p. (J). (gr. 1-7). 19.95 *(978-1-77085-001-9(5)*, 9781770850019); pap. 9.95 *(978-1-77085-002-6(3)*, 9781770850026) Firefly Bks., Ltd.

Pavone, Bree. If I Were a Butterfly. 2017. (I'm a Bug! Ser.). 24p. (gr. 4-6). 23.60 ***(978-1-5081-5720-5(0)**, PowerKids Pr.)* Rosen Publishing Group, Inc., The.

Pendergast, George. A Butterfly's Life Cycle. 2015. (Cycles in Nature Ser.). (ENG., Illus.). 24p. (J). (gr. 1-2). lib. bdg. 22.60 *(978-1-4824-1650-3(6))* Stevens, Gareth Publishing LLLP.

Pyle, Robert Michael & Peterson, Roger Tory. Butterflies. Peterson, Roger Tory, ed. Hughes, Sarah Anne, illus. 2nd ed. 2013. (Peterson Field Guide Color-In Bks.). (ENG.). 64p. (J). 8.95 *(978-0-544-03339-9(6))* Houghton Mifflin Harcourt Publishing Co.

QEB Start Reading & Talking National Book Stores Edition: Life Cycles: from Caterpillar to Butterfly. 2006. (J). per. *(978-1-59566-252-1(9))* QEB Publishing Inc.

Rabe, Tish. My, Oh My — A Butterfly! All about Butterflies. Ruiz, Aristides & Mathieu, Joe, illus. 2007. (Cat in the Hat's Learning Library). (ENG.). 48p. (J). (gr. -1-3). 9.99 *(978-0-375-82882-9(6)*, Random Hse. Bks. for Young Readers) Random Hse. Children's Bks.

Reagan, Naomi. Butterflies & Moths: Represent & Interpret Data. 2014. (Rosen Common Core Math Readers Ser.). (ENG., Illus.). 24p. (J). (gr. 3-4). pap. 8.25 *(978-1-4777-4901-2(2)*, Rosen Classroom) Rosen Publishing Group, Inc., The.

The Really Big Butterfly Coloring Book ' A Teaching & Learning Tool. 2004. Orig. Title: Same. (J). per. 7.95 *(978-0-9729753-2-2(2))* Really Big Coloring Bks., Inc.

Reher, Matt. All about Butterflies. 2015. (2G Bugs Ser.). (ENG., Illus.). 36p. (J). pap. 5.99 *(978-1-63437-097-4(X))* American Reading Co.

Rice, Dona Herweck. A Butterfly's Life, 1 vol. 2nd rev. ed. 2013. (Nonfiction Readers Ser.). (ENG., Illus.). 20p. (J). (gr. 1-1). pap. 19.96 *(978-1-4807-1020-7(2))* Shell Educational Publishing.

—A Butterfly's Life, 1 vol. 2nd rev. ed. 2011. (TIME for KIDS(r) Nonfiction Readers Ser.). (ENG.). 20p. (J). (gr. 1-1). 4.99 *(978-1-4333-3587-7(5))* Teacher Created Materials, Inc.

—La Vida de una Mariposa, 1 vol. 2nd rev. ed. 2012. (Nonfiction Readers Ser.). (SPA.). 20p. (J). (gr. 1-1). pap. 4.99 *(978-1-4333-4420-6(3))* Teacher Created Materials, Inc.

Riggs, Kate. Butterfly. 2012. (Grow with Me Ser.). (Illus.). 32p. (J). (gr. 3-8). 19.95 *(978-1-60818-215-2(0)*, Creative Education) Creative Co., The.

—Grow with Me: Butterfly. 2013. (Grow with Me Ser.). (ENG.). 32p. (J). (gr. 1-3). pap. 9.99 *(978-0-89812-768-3(8)*, Creative Paperbacks) Creative Co., The.

Ring, Elizabeth. Monarch Butterfly of Aster Way. Lee, Katie, illus. (ENG.). 32p. (J). (gr. -1-2). 2005. pap. 7.65 *(978-1-931465-40-3(1)*, S5017)Incl. toy. 2003. 9.95 *(978-1-56899-573-1(3)*, PB5067) Soundprints.

Romeu, Emma. A Forest for the Monarch Butterfly. Vigil, Luis Gerardo Sanchez & Broeck, Fabricio Vanden, illus. 2005. (Colección Animales de América / Animals of the Americas Ser.). (SPA.). 48p. (gr. 3-5). pap. 11.95 *(978-1-59437-844-7(4))* Santillana USA Publishing Co., Inc.

Roop, Connie & Roop, Peter. Millions of Monarchs. Maydak, Michael S., illus. 2003. 30p. (J). *(978-0-439-43965-7(5))* Scholastic, Inc.

Rudolph, Jessica. Butterfly. 2017. (See Them Grow Ser.). (ENG., Illus.). 24p. (J). (gr. -1-3). 17.95 ***(978-1-68402-038-6(7))*** Bearport Publishing Co., Inc.

Rupp, Kristina. The Life of a Butterfly. 2015. (1B Bugs Ser.). (ENG., Illus.). 28p. (J). pap. 5.99 *(978-1-63437-093-6(7))* American Reading Co.

Rustad, Martha E. H. Butterflies. 2007. (World of Insects Ser.). (ENG., Illus.). 24p. (J). (gr. k-3). lib. bdg. 25.95 *(978-1-60014-075-4(0))* Bellwether Media.

Ryder, Joanne. Where Butterflies Grow. Cherry, Lynne, illus. 2014. 32p. pap. 7.00 *(978-1-61003-313-8(2))* Center for the Collaborative Classroom.

Salzmann, Mary Elizabeth. Fluttering Butterflies, 1 vol. 2012. (Bug Bks.). (ENG.). 24p. (J). (gr. k-3). 24.21 *(978-1-61783-191-1(3)*, SandCastle) ABDO Publishing Co.

Samuel, Anna. Glitter Butterflies Stickers. 2004. (Dover Stickers Ser.). (ENG., Illus.). 2p. (gr. -1). 1.50 *(978-0-486-43537-4(7))* Dover Pubns., Inc.

Schlaepfer, Gloria G. Butterflies. 2005. (Animalways Ser.). (Illus.). 104p. (J). (gr. 4-7). lib. bdg. 24.95 *(978-0-7614-1745-3(1))* Marshall Cavendish Corp.

Scholastic, Inc. Staff, contrib. by. What Happens Next? Caterpillar to Butterfly. 2013. (ENG.). 12p. (J). bds. 6.95 *(978-0-531-27256-5(7))* Scholastic Library Publishing.

Schuh, Mari. Butterflies. 2013. (ENG., Illus.). 24p. (J). lib. bdg. 25.65 *(978-1-62031-053-3(8))* Jump! Inc.

Scott, Rose Marie. Gentle Ones. Scott, Rose Marie, illus. 2003. (Illus.). 60p. (J). lib. bdg. 22.95 *(978-1-59098-395-9(5))* Wooster Bk. Co., The.

Sexton, Colleen. The Life Cycle of a Butterfly. 2010. (Life Cycles Ser.). (ENG., Illus.). 24p. (J). (gr. k-3). lib. bdg. 25.95 *(978-1-60014-306-9(7)*, Blastoff! Readers) Bellwether Media.

Shingu, Susumu. Traveling Butterflies. 2015. (ENG., Illus.). 48p. (J). (gr. k-3). 19.95 *(978-1-77147-148-0(4)*, Owlkids) Owlkids Bks. Inc. CAN. Dist: Publishers Group West (PGW).

Shulman, Lisa. How Penguins & Butterflies Grow, 6 vols., Set. 2004. (Phonics Readers Books 37-72 Ser.). (ENG.). 8p. (gr. k-1). pap. 35.70 *(978-0-7368-4053-8(2)*, Phonics Readers) Capstone Press of Coughlan Cos.

Sibbett, Jr., Ed, Ed. Butterfly GemGlow Stained Glass Coloring Book. 2009. (Dover Nature Stained Glass Coloring Book Ser.). (ENG., Illus.). 32p. (J). (gr. 1-5). pap. 7.99 *(978-0-486-47147-1(0))* Dover Pubns., Inc.

Silverman, Buffy. Can You Tell a Butterfly from a Moth? 2011. (Lightning Bolt Books (tm) — Animal Look-Alikes Ser.). (ENG.). 32p. (gr. k-2). pap. 7.95 *(978-0-7613-7844-0(8))*; (Illus.). lib. bdg. 26.60 *(978-0-7613-6731-4(4))* Lerner Publishing Group.

—Can You Tell A Butterfly from A Moth? 2011. (Animal Look-Alikes Ser.). pap. 45.32 *(978-0-7613-8383-3(2))* Lerner Publishing Group.

Simon, Seymour. Butterflies. 2011. (ENG.). 32p. (J). (gr. k-4). 17.99 *(978-0-06-191493-5(2)*, Collins) HarperCollins Pubs.

Slade, Suzanne. Butterflies. 2009. (Under the Microscope: Backyard Bugs Ser.). 24p. (gr. 2-3). 42.50 *(978-1-60854-613-8(6)*, PowerKids Pr.) Rosen Publishing Group, Inc., The.

—A Monarch Butterfly's Journey, 1 vol. Swan, Susan, illus. 2011. (Follow It! Ser.). (ENG.). 24p. (gr. 1-3). pap. 7.49 *(978-1-4048-7029-1(6))*; lib. bdg. 26.65 *(978-1-4048-6655-3(8))* Picture Window Bks.

Smith, A. G. Beautiful Butterflies Stained Glass Coloring Book. 2003. (Dover Nature Stained Glass Coloring Book Ser.). (ENG., Illus.). 32p. (J). (gr. 3-5). pap. 7.99 *(978-0-486-43061-4(8))* Dover Pubns., Inc.

Soffer, Ruth. Butterflies & Flowers to Paint or Color. 2005. (Dover Art Coloring Book Ser.). (ENG., Illus.). 48p. (gr. 3-8). per. 5.99 *(978-0-486-44496-3(1))* Dover Pubns., Inc.

Spilsbury, Louise. Caterpillar Capers. 2011. (ENG., Illus.). 24p. (J). pap. *(978-0-7787-7876-9(2))*; (gr. 3-6). *(978-0-7787-7854-7(1))* Crabtree Publishing Co.

Stein, Lori. Butterfly Treats & Hummingbird Sweets. 2011. (PACKtivities Ser.: 1). (ENG.). 48p. (J). (gr. k-3). 9.99 *(978-1-935703-36-5(6))* Downtown Bookworks.

Stewart, Melissa. Butterflies. Recher, Andrew, illus. 2007. (Our Wild World Ser.). (ENG.). 48p. (J). (gr. 2-5). 10.95 *(978-1-55971-966-7(4))*; pap. 7.95 *(978-1-55971-967-4(2))* Cooper Square Publishing Llc.

—Butterfly or Moth? How Do You Know? 2011. (Which Animal Is Which? Ser.). (Illus.). 24p. (J). (gr. k-18). pap. 7.95 *(978-1-59845-235-8(5)*, Enslow Elementary); lib. bdg. 22.60 *(978-0-7660-3678-9(2))* Enslow Pubs., Inc.

—A Place for Butterflies, 1 vol. Bond, Higgins, illus. 2006. (ENG.). 32p. (J). (gr. 1-5). 16.95 *(978-1-56145-357-3(9))* Peachtree Pubs.

—A Place for Butterflies, Revised Edition, 1 vol. Bond, Higgins, illus. 2nd ed. 2014. (Place for... Ser.). (ENG.). 32p. (J). (gr. 1-5). pap. 7.95 *(978-1-56145-784-7(1))* Peachtree Pubs.

—Zoom in on Butterflies. 2014. (Zoom in on Insects! Ser.). 24p. (J). 22.60 *(978-0-7660-4211-7(1))*; pap. 7.95 *(978-1-4644-0365-1(1)*, Enslow Elementary) Enslow Pubs., Inc.

Stewart, Melissa & American Museum of Natural History. Caterpillar to Butterfly. 2016. (Science for Toddlers Ser.). (ENG., Illus.). 24p. (J). (gr. -1 — 1). bds. 7.95 *(978-1-4549-1406-8(8))* Sterling Publishing Co., Inc.

Stidworthy, John. Queen Alexandra's Birdwing: The World's Largest Butterfly. 2007. (SuperSized! Ser.). (Illus.). 24p. (J). (gr. k-3). lib. bdg. 21.28 *(978-1-59716-395-8(3)*, 1265940) Bearport Publishing Co., Inc.

Sundance/Newbridge LLC Staff. A Butterfly Is Born. 2007. (Early Science Ser.). (gr. k-3). 18.95 *(978-1-4007-6224-8(3))*; pap. 6.10 *(978-1-4007-6220-0(0))* Sundance/Newbridge Educational Publishing.

Swinburne, Stephen R. A Butterfly Grows. 2009. (Green Light Readers Level 2 Ser.). (ENG., Illus.). 24p. (J). (gr. -1-3). pap. 3.99 *(978-0-15-206416-7(8))* Houghton Mifflin Harcourt Publishing Co.

Tan, Richard. Bugs, Bugs, Bugs. 2015. (Rosen REAL Readers: STEM & STEAM Collection). (ENG.). 8p. pap. 5.46 *(978-1-4994-9703-8(2)*, Rosen Classroom) Rosen Publishing Group, Inc., The.

Time for Kids Editors. Butterflies! 2006. (Time for Kids Science Scoops Ser.). (ENG., Illus.). 32p. (J). (gr. 1-3). pap. 3.99 *(978-0-06-078213-9(7))* HarperCollins Pubs.

Time for Kids Magazine Staff, ed. Butterflies! 2006. (Time for Kids Science Scoops Ser.). (Illus.). 32p. (gr. 1-3). 14.00 *(978-0-7569-6676-8(0))* Perfection Learning Corp.

Tomio, Stacy. Ranger Rick's Amazing Animals: Caterpillars & Butterflies. 2016. (Ranger Rick: Amazing Animals Ser.). (ENG., Illus.). 40p. (J). (gr. 2-7). pap. 7.95 *(978-1-63076-204-9(0))* Muddy Boots Pr.

Trueit, Trudi Strain. Caterpillars & Butterflies. 2011. (Backyard Safari Ser.). 32p. (gr. 3). 28.50 *(978-1-60870-243-5(X))* Marshall Cavendish GBR. Dist: Marshall Cavendish Corp.

Trumbauer, Lisa. The Life Cycle of a Butterfly. 2016. (Life Cycles Ser.). (ENG.). 24p. (gr. k-1). pap. 6.29 *(978-1-5157-4228-9(8)*, Pebble Bks.) Capstone Press of Coughlan Cos.

Tuchman, Gail. Scholastic Discover More Reader Level 1: Busy Butterflies. 2014. (Scholastic Discover More Readers Ser.). (ENG.). 32p. (J). (gr. 1-2). pap. 3.99 *(978-0-545-67951-0(6)*, Scholastic Reference) Scholastic, Inc.

Turnbull, S. Caterpillars & Butterflies. 2004. (Beginners Ser.). 32p. (J). (gr. 1-18). (ENG.). pap. 4.95 *(978-0-7945-0378-9(0))*; lib. bdg. 12.95 *(978-1-58086-506-7(2))* EDC Publishing.

Turnbull, Stephanie. Caterpillars & Butterflies. Guille, Rosanne & Mayer, Uwe, illus. 2007. (Usborne Beginners Ser.). 32p. (J). (gr. -1-3). 4.99 *(978-0-7945-1337-5(9)*, Usborne) EDC Publishing.

Twinn, M. Metamorphoses: Butterfly. 2006. (Metamorphoses Ser.). (ENG., Illus.). 16p. (J). (gr. 1-5). bds. *(978-1-84643-013-8(5))* Child's Play International Ltd.

UG, Philippe. In the Butterfly Garden. 2015. (ENG., Illus.). 16p. (J). (gr. -1-3). 19.95 *(978-3-7913-7207-5(6))* Prestel Verlag GmbH & Co KG. DEU. Dist: Penguin Random Hse. LLC.

Upgrade kit dsm-3 Butterflies&moths. (J). 2004. *(978-1-59242-526-6(7))* 2003. *(978-1-59242-409-2(0))* Delta Education, LLC.

Wallace, Karen. Born to Be a Butterfly. 2010. (DK Readers Ser.). (ENG., Illus.). 32p. (J). (gr. k-2). 3.99 *(978-0-7566-6281-3(8)*, DK Children) Dorling Kindersley Publishing, Inc.

Wallace, Nancy Elizabeth. Fly, Monarch! Fly!, 0 vols. 2012. (ENG.). 42p. (J). (gr. k-3). pap. 7.99 *(978-0-7614-6246-0(5)*, 9780761462460, Amazon Children's Publishing) Amazon Publishing.

Waters, Kate. Monarch Butterflies. 2009. (Growing Reader Level 3 Ser.). (Illus.). 32p. (J). pap. *(978-0-545-07234-2(4))* Scholastic, Inc.

Watts, Barrie. Butterfly. 2003. 32p. (J). lib. bdg. 24.25 *(978-1-58340-234-4(9))* Black Rabbit Bks.

Waxman, Laura Hamilton. Let's Look at Monarch Butterflies. 2010. (Lightning Bolt Bks.). (gr. k-2). (Illus.). 32p. (J). lib. bdg. 25.26 *(978-0-7613-3886-4(1)*, 1312738, Lerner Pubns.); pap. 45.32 *(978-0-7613-6980-6(5))*; (ENG., Illus.). 32p. (J). pap. 7.95 *(978-0-7613-6039-1(5)*, 1312738) Lerner Publishing Group.

Wells, E. A. The Butterfly Weed Patch. 2012. 32p. pap. *(978-1-105-50787-8(4))* Lulu.com.

Wenger, Shaunda. Watch a Butterfly Grow. 2006. (Early Explorers Ser.). (J). pap. *(978-1-4108-6100-9(7))* Benchmark Education Co.

Weston Woods Staff, creator. Waiting for Wings. 2004. 29.95 *(978-1-55592-152-1(3))* Weston Woods Studios, Inc.

Wildlife Education, Ltd Staff, contrib. by. Butterflies. 2007. (Illus.). (J). *(978-1-932396-36-2(5))* Wildlife Education, Ltd.

Wimmer, Teresa. Butterflies. 2015. (J). pap. *(978-1-62832-212-5(8)*, Creative Paperbacks) Creative Co., The.

Winnick, Nick. Butterflies. 2010. pap. 9.95 *(978-1-60596-929-9(X))*; 24p. (J). (gr. 2-4). lib. bdg. 25.70 *(978-1-60596-928-2(1))* Weigl Pubs., Inc.

Woodward, John. Butterfly. 2010. (Garden Minibeasts up Close Ser.). 32p. (gr. 2-4). 30.00 *(978-1-60413-899-3(8)*, Chelsea Clubhouse) Facts On File, Inc.

World Book, Inc. Staff, contrib. by. Butterflies of the United States & Canada. 2004. (World Book's Science & Nature Guides Ser.). (Illus.). 80p. (J). *(978-0-7166-4211-4(5))* World Bk., Inc.

—Monarchs & Other Butterflies. 2005. (World Book's Animals of the World Ser.). (Illus.). 64p. (J). *(978-0-7166-1271-1(2))* World Bk., Inc.

Zemlicka, Shannon. Del Huevo a la Mariposa. 2006. (De Principio a Fin (Start to Finish) Ser.). (Illus.). 24p. (J). (gr. -1-3). per. 5.95 *(978-0-8225-6631-1(1)*, Ediciones Lerner) Lerner Publishing Group.

—Del Huevo a la Mariposa. Translations.com Staff, tr. from ENG. 2006. (De Principio a Fin (Start to Finish) Ser.). (SPA., Illus.). 24p. (gr. 3-5). lib. bdg. 19.93 *(978-0-8225-6494-2(7)*, Ediciones Lerner) Lerner Publishing Group.

—From Egg to Butterfly. 2012. (Start to Finish, Second Series: Nature's Cycles Ser.). (ENG.). 24p. (gr. k-3). pap. 39.62 *(978-0-7613-9291-0(2))*; pap. 6.95 *(978-0-7613-8573-8(8))* Lerner Publishing Group.

BUTTERFLIES—FICTION

Akey, Maureen. The Adventures of Molly the Monarch Butterfly & Friends¬Series: Molly. 2009. 28p. pap. 14.99 *(978-1-4389-4229-2(X))* AuthorHouse.

Albanell, Pep. El Grito de la Botella. Tobella, Montse, illus. 2004.Tr. of Scream from the Bottle. (SPA.). (J). pap. 7.99 *(978-84-236-6701-7(4))* Edebé ESP. Dist: Lectorum Pubns., Inc.

Alsop - Jinks, A. G. Kylie & the Butterfly. 2011. 16p. pap. 8.32 *(978-1-4634-0859-6(5))* AuthorHouse.

Ana, Moh. Kookaburra Tales: Shy Not, My Friend. 2013. 16p. pap. 17.03 *(978-1-4669-3193-0(0))* Trafford Publishing.

Andersen, Hans Christian. IceMaiden & Other Tales. 2006. pap. *(978-1-4068-0421-8(5))* Echo Library.

Anderson, T. N. Chiko & the Butterfly. 2009. 70p. pap. 7.00 *(978-0-557-10395-9(9))* Lulu Pr., Inc.

Andrews, Andy. The Boy Who Changed the World. 2010. 16.99 *(978-1-4003-1718-9(5))* Nelson, Thomas Inc.

Argiento, Cindy. Doris in Dreamland. 2007. pap. 8.00 *(978-0-8059-7461-4(X))* Dorrance Publishing Co., Inc.

Ariel, A. D. The Ant & the Butterfly. 2016. (Spring Forward Ser.). (J). (gr. 1). *(978-1-4900-2239-0(2))* Benchmark Education Co.

Atkins, Carla. Kiara & the Butterfly. 2012. 52p. pap. 24.99 *(978-1-4685-2323-2(6))* AuthorHouse.

Baer, Julie. Love Me Later. 2005. (Illus.). 28p. (J). (gr. -1-3). 16.99 *(978-1-932188-03-5(7))* Bollix Bks.

Baker, Bill. The Butterfly. RUZICKA, Carol, illus. 2012. 46p. pap. 15.00 *(978-0-9859132-0-5(7))* Asbury Heritage Publishing.

Barsy, Kalman. El Cocodrilo Lloron. Gastaldo, Walter, illus. 2004. (Yellow Ser.). (SPA.). 31p. (J). (gr. k-3). pap. 5.95 *(978-1-57581-433-9(1))* Santillana USA Publishing Co., Inc.

Batten, Scott A. Johnny the Phoenix. 2008. 64p. pap. 23.95 *(978-1-4343-7297-0(9))* AuthorHouse.

Baumann, Jessica. Bella-Blue Butterfly's Purple Surprise. Kordich, Melinda, illus. 2013. 30p. pap. 9.99 *(978-1-937165-38-3(8))* Orange Hat Publishing.

Bekis, Joanne. Bubble & Butterfly. 2009. 20p. pap. 10.50 *(978-1-60693-696-2(4)*, Strategic Bk. Publishing) Strategic Book Publishing & Rights Agency (SBPRA).

Benitez, Diana. The Butterfly Keeper. 2011. 102p. pap. 19.95 *(978-1-4626-2616-8(5))* America Star Bks.

Berkove, Lawrence I. How Butterflies Got Colored Wings. Barshishat, Malka Michaela, illus. 2017. (J). pap. ***(978-1-5011-4872-9(9))*** Meadowbrook Pr.

Beus, Bryan. Westly: A Spider's Tale. Beus, Bryan, illus. 2015. (Illus.). 171p. (J). 15.99 *(978-1-62972-068-5(2)*, Shadow Mountain) Deseret Bk. Co.

Bezdek, Mirasol. Your & You're: Betty the Butterfly. 2013. 44p. pap. 16.90 *(978-1-300-62695-4(X))* Lulu Pr., Inc.

Bickford, Janette. Vern & His Butterfly Migration. 2013. 16p. pap. 12.68 *(978-1-4669-5032-0(3))* Trafford Publishing.

Blaine, Dalton. Bella's Butterfly: Over & over Again. 2017. (Computer Science for the Real World Ser.). 16p. (gr. 7-8). pap. 7.95 ***(978-1-5383-5218-2(4)**, Rosen Classroom)* Rosen Publishing Group, Inc., The.

Blaylock, Kathy. Adventures of Buddy Fairy & Friends. 2007. 48p. 16.95 *(978-1-4137-9195-2(6))* America Star Bks.

Blocker, Adam P. Joshua & the Spider. Taylor, Josh, illus. 2013. (ENG.). 72p. 17.99 *(978-1-939418-08-1(9))* Writer of the Round Table Pr.

Bohn, Kendall. Fantasy Adventure. 2008. (Kaleidoscopia Coloring Book Ser.). (Illus.). 56p. (J). (gr. -1-7). 8.95 *(978-0-929636-83-2(X))* Syren Bk. Co.

Boies, Jennifer. Bonnie Butterfly. 2010. 20p. pap. 11.99 *(978-1-4490-4913-3(3))* AuthorHouse.

Boone, Sheila. Free As a Butterfly. Knox, Susi Grell, illus. 2003. 32p. (J). (gr. -1-3). pap. 7.95 *(978-1-891577-80-2(8))* Image Pr., Inc.

—Free As a Butterfly. 2003. (J). pap. 6.95 *(978-1-891577-81-9(6))* Images Pr.

Boynton, Cara. Sam's Secret World. 2006. (ENG.). 48p. per. 16.95 *(978-1-4241-4529-4(5))* PublishAmerica, Inc.

Brantley, Meg. Love Family Adventures. 2009. 116p. pap. 11.99 *(978-1-60791-786-1(6))* Salem Author Services.

Brewster, Frank. Little Yellow Butterfly Book. 2012. (ENG.). (J). pap. 2012.00 *(978-1-4675-1844-4(1))* Independent Pub.

Brown, Monica. Butterflies on Carmen Street/Mariposas en la Calle Carmen. Ward, April, illus. 2007. (SPA & ENG.). 32p. (J). (gr. -1-2). 16.95 *(978-1-55885-484-0(3)*, Piñata Books) Arte Publico Pr.

Brown, Rhonda Sue. Misty the Butterfly, 1 vol. 2010. 16p. pap. 24.95 *(978-1-4489-2005-1(1))* PublishAmerica, Inc.

Bunton, M. Catherine. Butterfly Peddler. 2008. 88p. pap. 9.95 *(978-1-59526-990-4(8)*, Llumina Pr.) Aeon Publishing Inc.

—The Fairy Tale Keeper. 2012. 134p. pap. 8.95 *(978-1-60594-783-9(0))* Aeon Publishing Inc.

Butler, Alberta J. The Little White Butterflies. 2012. 36p. pap. 18.41 *(978-1-4669-5658-2(5))* Trafford Publishing.

The Butterfly Farm Burglar, 6 vols., Vol. 3. (Woodland Mysteriestm Ser.). 133p. (gr. 3-7). 42.50 *(978-0-322-02374-1(2))* Wright Group/McGraw-Hill.

A Butterfly's Tale. 2005. (J). per. 12.95 *(978-1-59700-082-6(5))* Island Heritage Publishing.

Cain, Sheridan. The Crunching Munching Caterpillar. Tickle, Jack, illus. (J). 2013. (ENG.). 20p. (gr. -1). 9.99 *(978-1-58925-616-3(6))* 2005. 18p. bds. 6.95 *(978-1-58925-757-3(X))* Tiger Tales.

—Crunching Munching Caterpillar. Tickle, Jack, illus. 2003. 32p. (J). tchr. ed. 15.95 *(978-1-58925-025-3(7))* Tiger Tales.

Calabrese, Paul. The Good Bug Book ... (and Other Cool Creatures) 2012. 24p. pap. 15.99 *(978-1-4797-4131-1(0))* Xlibris Corp.

Cameron, Kristy. The Other Side of the Window. Ian, Shickle, illus. 2013. 28p. pap. *(978-0-9859790-2-7(X))* LP Publishing.

Carle, Eric. The Very Hungry Caterpilar. Carle, Eric, illus. 2011. (ENG & SPA., Illus.). 32p. (J). (gr. -1-k). 21.99 *(978-0-399-25604-2(0)*, Philomel Bks.) Penguin Young Readers Group.

Carter, Todd. A Monarch Universe Package Set: Children's Picture Book. 2007. (Illus.). 34p. (J). pap. 32.95 incl. cd-rom *(978-0-9800222-3-0(1))* UPfirst.com Bks.

Charles, Faustin. The Selfish Crocodile Book of Words. Terry, Michael, illus. 2012. (Selfish Crocodile Ser.). (ENG.). 12p. (J). (gr. -1-k). bds. 10.99 *(978-1-4088-1452-9(8)*, 9781408814529, Bloomsbury USA Childrens) Bloomsbury Publishing USA.

Churchill, Vicky & Fuge, Charles. Butterfly Kiss. (Illus.). 28p. (J). pap. *(978-0-340-68614-0(6))* Hodder & Stoughton.

Clarke, Ella. I Am So Beautiful, 1 vol. rev. ed. 2013. (Fiction Readers Ser.). (ENG., Illus.). 20p. (J). (gr. 1-1). 4.99 *(978-1-4333-5485-4(3))*; pap. 15.96 *(978-1-4807-1141-9(1))* Shell Educational Publishing.

Clarke, Wanda Marie. The Butterfly Ball. 2012. 32p. pap. 13.95 *(978-1-4497-2211-1(3)*, WestBow Pr.) Author Solutions, Inc.

Collett, Debra. The Reluctant Butterfly. 2013. (Illus.). 32p. pap. 13.95 *(978-1-4908-1245-8(8)*, WestBow Pr.) Author Solutions, Inc.

Collier, Wayne Evans. Grumpy the Grasshopper. Goodman, Larry, illus. 2012. 20p. pap. 24.95 *(978-1-4626-6844-1(5))* America Star Bks.

Corlett, Mary Lee. Belle: The Amazing, Astonishingly Magical Journey of an Artfully Painted Lady. Saroff, Phyllis, illus. 12th ed. 2011. (ENG.). 52p. (J). (gr. 3-4). pap. 25.00 *(978-1-59373-084-0(5))* Bunker Hill Publishing, Inc.

—Belle's Wild Ride: The Artful Adventure of a Butterfly & a Cabbie. Cayless, Sophie, illus. 2015. (ENG.). 32p. (J). (gr. 3-7). 17.95 *(978-1-907804-51-9(X))* Giles, D. Ltd. GBR. Dist: Consortium Bk. Sales & Distribution.

Cueva, Susana & Shibaja, Calixto. Lita the Hardworking Worm/Lita la Trabajadora. 2012. (ENG & SPA.). 26p. pap. 9.99 *(978-0-9883927-1-7(2))* Carsume.

Danley, Jerry J. Billy Black Ant's Exciting Adventures. Hilley, Thomas, illus. 2012. 56p. pap. 12.99 *(978-0-9885180-5-6(8))* Mindstir Media.

De Sena, Joseph. The Butterfly & the Bunny's Tail. Anfuso, Dennis, illus. 2007. 60p. per. 19.95 *(978-1-4327-0404-9(4))* Outskirts Pr., Inc.

Dehghanpisheh, Corine. Buddy's Dream. Dehghanpisheh, Corine, illus. 2013. (Illus.). 34p. pap. 12.95 *(978-0-9851930-4-1(2))* Dehghanpisheh, Corine.

Delgato, Carolyn A. Jiggy & his Hiccups, 1 vol. 2010. 30p. 24.95 *(978-1-4512-0927-3(4))* PublishAmerica, Inc.

Deshmukh, Manisha. Chinu's Day Out. 2008. 24p. pap. 11.49 *(978-1-4389-0601-0(3))* AuthorHouse.

Dickens, Sara Jo. Kamer's Quest for Blue Lupine. Nancy, Scheibe, illus. 2014. (J). 18.95 *(978-1-59298-923-2(3))* Beaver's Pond Pr., Inc.

Donaldson, Julia. Where's My Mom? Scheffler, Axel, illus. 2008. (ENG.). 32p. (J). (gr. -1-2). 18.99 *(978-0-8037-3228-5(7)*, Dial Bks) Penguin Young Readers Group.

Downs, Jay & Downs, Jeanie. The Flutterfly. 2010. 68p. pap. 25.49 *(978-1-4520-1860-7(X))* AuthorHouse.

Ebel, Sherry. Cassie's Magic Doors the Butterfly Garden. 2012. 36p. pap. 21.99 *(978-1-4797-0108-7(4))* Xlibris Corp.

Edwards, Pamela Duncan. Clara Caterpillar. 2014. 17.00 *(978-1-63419-653-6(8))* Perfection Learning Corp.

Eldridge, VonDa. Wiggles the Worm, 1 vol. 2010. 26p. pap. 24.95 *(978-1-4489-2547-6(9))* PublishAmerica, Inc.

Farahay, Michael L. The Butterfly, The Bee & The Spider. Farahay, Naomi E., ed. 2007. 80p. pap. 36.95 *(978-1-4303-2623-6(9))* Lulu Pr., Inc.

Farnsworth-Simpson, Patricia Ann. The Wonderful Butterbee Angel's. 2010. 125p. pap. 14.50 *(978-1-4092-8762-9(9))* Lulu Pr., Inc.

Feldman, Karen. Glorious Wings. 2011. 36p. pap. 24.95 *(978-1-4560-8352-6(X))* America Star Bks.

A
B

Flint-Warren, Cathrine. To Dance with the Yellow Butterfly. 2007. 28p. per. 18.95 *(978-1-4327-0491-9(5))* Outskirts Pr., Inc.

Flowers, Elizabeth. Butterfly George. 2012. 24p. pap. 24.95 *(978-1-4626-8308-6(8))* America Star Bks.

Flowers, J. J. Juan Pablo & the Butterflies. 2017. (ENG., Illus.). 224p. (YA). (gr. 9-12). 17.99 *(978-1-5072-0214-2(8)*, Simon Pulse) Simon Pulse.

Föger, Regina. Butterfly Letter: A Tale about Life after Life. 2012. (GER & ENG., Illus.). 44p. pap. 21.99 *(978-1-4771-0882-6(3))* Xlibris Corp.

Fontenot, Mary Alice. Clovis Crawfish & Bertile's Bon Voyage, 1 vol. Blazek, Scott R., illus. 2008. (Clovis Crawfish Ser.). (ENG.). 32p. (J). (gr. k-3). 16.99 *(978-1-58980-541-5(0))* Pelican Publishing Co., Inc.

—Clovis Crawfish & Petit Papillon, 1 vol. Graves, Keith, illus. 2009. (Clovis Crawfish Ser.). (ENG.). 32p. (J). (gr. k-3). 16.99 *(978-1-58980-772-3(3))* Pelican Publishing Co., Inc.

—Clovis Crawfish & Silvie Sulphur, 1 vol. Buckner, Julie Dupre, illus. 2004. (Clovis Crawfish Ser.). (ENG & FRE.). 32p. (J). (gr. k-3). 16.99 *(978-1-56554-864-0(7))* Pelican Publishing Co., Inc.

Fox, Erin. A Butterfly's Dream. 2012. 16p. pap. 12.68 *(978-1-4669-2066-8(1))* Trafford Publishing.

Freeman, Gayle. Football Friends. 2008. 16p. pap. 8.49 *(978-1-4343-5611-6(6))* AuthorHouse.

Gambino, Dolores. Flutter the Butterfly Who Found a Home with Jesus. 2011. 24p. pap. 11.32 *(978-1-4634-4882-0(1))* AuthorHouse.

Gardener, Amanda & Sealey, Nanlie. Butterfly Pavilion. 2013. 24p. pap. 10.99 *(978-1-60820-898-2(2))* MLR Pr., LLC.

Gigliotti, Sallie B. I'm Sorry, Said Denny. 2009. 20p. pap. 10.99 *(978-1-4343-9999-1(0))* AuthorHouse.

Gilbert, Diana. Guided by the Light. 2007. 48p. per. 16.95 *(978-1-4241-7016-6(8))* America Star Bks.

Gill, Mehmaz S. The Yellow Butterfly. Ward, Lindsay, illus. 2010. (ENG.). 24p. (J). (gr. k-2). 17.95 *(978-1-933979-71-7(2)*, 45f00f36-ed1a-4633-929a-2bb04d2073f4) Bright Sky Pr.

Gillingham, Sara & Chronicle Books Staff. In My Flower. Siminovich, Lorena, illus. 2009. (ENG.). 12p. (J). (gr. -1 — 1). bds. 8.99 *(978-0-8118-7339-0(0))* Chronicle Bks. LLC.

Gist, Richard. Ayshus on the Inside. 2013. 104p. *(978-1-4602-1899-0(X))*; pap. *(978-1-4602-1900-3(7))* FriesenPress.

Goebig, Ed. Jake & Julia Save the Butterfly. 2012. 24p. pap. 15.99 *(978-1-4771-4289-9(4))* Xlibris Corp.

Gold, Willa. Stella & Tulip: A Home for Us. 2010. (ENG.). 36p. (J). (gr. k-2). 17.99 *(978-0-930773-95-3(0))* Black Heron Pr.

Golden Books. The Little Grumpy Cat That Wouldn't (Grumpy Cat) Golden Books, illus. 2016. (Little Golden Book Ser.). (ENG., Illus.). 24p. (J). (gr. -1-1). 4.99 *(978-0-399-55354-7(1)*, Golden Bks.) Random Hse. Children's Bks.

Goldman, Judy. Uncle Monarch & the Day of the Dead. Moreno, Rene King, illus. 2008. (ENG.). 32p. (J). (gr. 2-4). 16.95 *(978-1-59078-425-9(1))* Boyds Mills Pr.

Gonzalez, Blanca Maciel. Cathy Meets Sofi. 2011. 40p. pap. 21.99 *(978-1-4568-9575-4(3))* Xlibris Corp.

Good Night Sweet Butterflies. 2003. (J). *(978-0-9740149-0-6(7))* White Heat Ltd.

Graham, Othello Leneer. The Animal Sisters. 2012. 20p. pap. 17.99 *(978-1-4772-6550-5(3))* AuthorHouse.

Grateful Steps Publishing & Tipton, Angela. Butterflies Don't Crawl. Irvine, Wil, illus. 2009. 32p. (J). 16.95 *(978-1-935130-14-7(5))* Grateful Steps.

Grosso, Salvatore. The Butterfly & the Dinosaur: A true story of fiction Inspired by a Beautiful Butterfly. 2010. 32p. pap. 16.99 *(978-1-4490-6603-1(8))* AuthorHouse.

Gudino Kieffer, E. Giraluna (Moonflower) (J). 22.50 *(978-950-04-1280-3(2))* Emecé Editores S.A. ARG. Dist: AIMS International Bks., Inc.

Guerrera, Debra. The Adventures of Baby Caterpillar & His Traveling Butterfly Family. 2011. 28p. pap. 15.99 *(978-1-4628-9982-1(X))* Xlibris Corp.

Hansen, Roland. The Story of a Butterfly Called Bee. 2010. 32p. pap. 9.96 *(978-0-9843426-2-4(1))* G Publishing LLC.

Haque, Mary Baca. Madalynn the Monarch Butterfly & Her Quest to Michoacan. Jones, Francisco Lancaster, tr. from ENG. du Houx, Emily, illus. 2003. (ENG & SPA.). 64p. pap. 14.00 *(978-1-882190-52-2(1))* Polar Bear & Co.

Harris, Nikki. Adventures in Friendship for Benji Butterfly & Tom Turkey. 2013. 24p. pap. 24.95 *(978-1-63004-741-2(4))* America Star Bks.

Harrold, Yvette. With Butterfly Eyes. Henriksen, Rebecca, illus. 2009. 36p. pap. 15.49 *(978-1-4490-0946-5(8))* AuthorHouse.

Hart, Kim. Beatrice & Raymond: A Universal MessagesTM Book. 2012. 32p. pap. 16.99 *(978-1-4772-4951-2(6))* AuthorHouse.

Haskins, Lori. Butterfly Fever. Smath, Jerry, illus. 2004. 31p. (J). lib. bdg. 20.00 *(978-1-4242-1087-9(9))* Fitzgerald Bks.

—Locura Por Las Marisposas (Butterfly Fever) Smath, Jerry, illus. 2009. (Science Solves It! (r) en Espanol Ser.). (SPA.). (gr. 1-3). pap. 33.92 *(978-0-7613-4799-6(2))* Lerner Publishing Group.

Haskins, Lori & Ramirez, Alma. Locura por las Mariposas. Smath, Jerry, illus. 2009. (Science Solves It! en Espanol Ser.). (SPA.). 32p. (J). (gr. 1-3). pap. 5.95 *(978-1-57565-284-9(6))* Kane Press, Inc.

Heyden, Linda Vander. Mr. Mcginty's Monarchs. Ewen, Eileen R., illus. 2016. (ENG.). 32p. (J). (gr. 1-4). pap. 16.99 *(978-1-58536-612-5(9)*, 204034) Sleeping Bear Pr.

Hildreth, Joann R. Nicholas James & Missy. Aughe, Roger, illus. 2011. 28p. pap. 24.95 *(978-1-4626-0041-0(7))* America Star Bks.

Himes, John. Beauty. 2012. 24p. pap. 17.99 *(978-1-4772-9440-6(6))* AuthorHouse.

Holland, Diane. Sally Butterfield Goes Fishing! 2005. 49p. pap. 16.95 *(978-1-4137-9767-1(9))* America Star Bks.

Hood, Susan. Caterpillar Spring, Butterfly Summer. Gévry, Claudine, illus. 2003. (ENG.). 10p. (J). (gr. k-3). bds. 12.99 *(978-0-7944-0149-8(X))* Reader's Digest Assn., Inc., The.

Hooser, Betty J. Kids with Large Insects & Flowers & Unusual Things. 2012. 32p. 24.95 *(978-1-4626-4784-2(7))* America Star Bks.

Horácek, Petr. Butterfly Butterfly: A Book of Colors. Horácek, Petr, illus. 2007. (ENG., Illus.). 16p. (J). (gr. -1-2). 15.99 *(978-0-7636-3343-1(7))* Candlewick Pr.

Horan, Pamela. Newman the Gnome. 2012. 66p. pap. 17.95 *(978-1-4626-9461-7(6))* America Star Bks.

Houston, Rebecca. My Butterfly. 2013. 20p. pap. 24.95 *(978-1-62709-079-7(7))* America Star Bks.

Hoyland, Christa. The Beautiful Butterfly. 2004. (J). *(978-0-9759530-4-4(4))* Jostens Bks.

Hurth, Barbi. The Butterfly & the Bee. Meyer, Chloe, illus. 2008. 32p. pap. 24.95 *(978-1-60610-226-8(5))* America Star Bks.

Huxley, Sheila M. One Lovely Summer: The Stories of One Little Butterfly & His Friends. 2009. (Illus.). 48p. pap. 19.49 *(978-1-4389-2987-3(0))* AuthorHouse.

I Wish I Could Fly: Lonely Caterpillar/the Lonely Butterfly. l.t. ed. 2006. (Illus.). 60p. (J). (gr. -1-3). per. 17.99 *(978-1-59879-196-9(6))* Lifevest Publishing, Inc.

Image Books Staff & Chronicle Books Staff. Little Butterfly. van der Put, Klaartje, illus. 2006. (Little Finger Puppet Board Bks.: FING). (ENG.). 12p. (J). (gr. -1 — 1). bds. 6.99 *(978-0-8118-5645-4(3))* Chronicle Bks. LLC.

ImageBooks Staff & Chronicle Books Staff. Little Fox: Finger Puppet Book. Put, Klaartje van der, illus. 2015. (ENG.). 12p. (J). (gr. -1 — 1). bds. 6.99 *(978-1-4521-4230-2(0))* Chronicle Bks. LLC.

Jackson, Ovetta. Beanie & Skooda & the Buddifly Gang. 2012. 32p. pap. 19.99 *(978-1-4685-3131-2(X))* AuthorHouse.

James, J. Alison. Eucalyptus Wings. Demi, illus. 2012. (ENG.). 36p. (J). (gr. k-3). 17.99 *(978-1-4424-7484-0(X)*, Atheneum Bks. for Young Readers) Simon & Schuster Children's Publishing.

Jefferson, E. Louis. The Little Caterpillar-A Story of Kindness. 2012. 38p. pap. 17.00 *(978-1-105-76076-1(6))* Lulu Pr., Inc.

—The Little Caterpillar-A Story of Kindness-Companion Coloring Book. 2012. 52p. pap. 8.00 *(978-1-105-92194-0(8))* Lulu Pr., Inc.

Jewell, M. B. Tales of Amanda O' 2008. 80p. pap. 15.99 *(978-1-4363-2215-7(4))* Xlibris Corp.

Johnson, Gerald J. J. Betty, the Chubby Butterfly. Miltenberger, Jeri and Dave, illus. 2011. 24p. pap. 24.95 *(978-1-4489-3990-9(9))* America Star Bks.

Johnston, Jan. Amélie the Most Amazing Butterfly: I Do So Love Being a Butterfly ... 2013. (Illus.). 24p. pap. 17.99 *(978-1-4817-8018-6(2))* AuthorHouse.

Johnston, Kayla & Johnston, David. Butterflies in My Belly. 2010. 16p. pap. 10.99 *(978-1-4490-5339-0(4))* AuthorHouse.

Johnston, Tony. Isabel's House of Butterflies. Guevara, Susan, illus. 2005. 32p. pap. 6.95 *(978-1-58685-844-5(0))*; (ENG.). (J). (gr. 3-4). per. 7.99 *(978-1-57805-128-1(2))* Gibbs Smith, Publisher.

Jonas, Gennevive. Mary Loves Butterflies. Barrett, Karlish, illus. 2012. 40p. pap. 24.95 *(978-1-62709-061-2(4))* America Star Bks.

Kann, Victoria. Pinkalicious & the Little Butterfly. Kann, Victoria, illus. 2016. (Pinkalicious Ser.). (Illus.). 24p. (J). (gr. -1-3). pap. 4.99 *(978-0-06-241071-9(7)*, HarperFestival) HarperCollins Pubs.

Katz, Susan B. All Year Round. Ojala, Eiko, illus. 2016. (ENG.). 32p. (J). (gr. -1-1). 17.99 *(978-0-545-74100-2(9)*, Orchard Bks.) Scholastic, Inc.

Keene, Carolyn. Butterfly Blues. Francis, Peter, illus. 2015. (Nancy Drew & the Clue Crew Ser.: 40). (ENG.). 96p. (J). (gr. 1-4). pap. 5.99 *(978-1-4814-1470-8(4)*, Aladdin) Simon & Schuster Children's Publishing.

Kemp, Michelle. Flutter by Butterfly. 2012. 28p. pap. 24.95 *(978-1-4626-6181-7(5))* America Star Bks.

Kennedy, Kirk. Mr. Blue Butterfly. Nazario, Rafael, illus. 2013. (ENG.). (J). (gr. -1-3). 14.95 *(978-1-62086-256-8(5))* Mascot Bks., Inc.

Kessler, Liz. Philippa Fisher & the Dream-Maker's Daughter. 2009. (Philippa Fisher Ser.: 2). (ENG., Illus.). 288p. (J). (gr. 3-7). 15.99 *(978-0-7636-4202-0(9))* Candlewick Pr.

Kiesling Garrett, Doris. The Butterfly Book das Schmetterling Buch. 2013. 76p. pap. 25.24 *(978-1-4669-7803-4(1))* Trafford Publishing.

Kleven, Elisa. Glasswings: A Butterfly's Story. 2013. (ENG., Illus.). 32p. (J). (gr. -1-k). 16.99 *(978-0-8037-3742-6(4)*, Dial Bks) Penguin Young Readers Group.

Kline, Lpc. Flutter Flies Away: A Book about Rules. 2009. 32p. pap. 14.99 *(978-1-4389-9747-6(7))* AuthorHouse.

Knight, P. B. The Little Orange & Red Butterfly, 1 vol. 2009. 16p. pap. 19.95 *(978-1-60749-693-9(3))* PublishAmerica, Inc.

Kompelien, Tracy. Monarch Butterfly, 1 vol. Chawla, Neena, illus. 2007. (Critter Chronicles Ser.). (ENG.). 24p. (J). (gr. k-3). lib. bdg. 24.21 *(978-1-59928-454-5(5)*, SandCastle) ABDO Publishing Co.

Koontz, Robin Michal & Elliott, Rebecca. Butterfly Spring. 2009. (Rhyme Time Readers Ser.). (Illus.). (J). *(978-0-545-08359-1(1))* Scholastic, Inc.

Krakower, Harold. Sugarland. 2008. 28p. pap. 12.50 *(978-1-934925-12-6(8)*, Eloquent Bks.) Strategic Book Publishing & Rights Agency (SBPRA).

—Sugarland: Volume 2 Trouble in Sugarland. 2009. 28p. pap. 12.50 *(978-1-4490-1880-1(7))* AuthorHouse.

Kuhn, Douglas Wolcik. The Summer of the Monarch Butterflies. 2012. 28p. pap. 24.95 *(978-1-4626-9302-3(4))* America Star Bks.

Kurtz, Jane. Lanie's Real Adventures. Papp, Robert, illus. 2010. (American Girl Today Ser.). (ENG.). 112p. (YA). (gr. 3-18). 12.95 *(978-1-59369-685-6(X))* American Girl Publishing, Inc.

Laughter in the Wind. 2004. (Illus.). (J). 17.95 *(978-0-9753417-0-4(7))* Cheerful Cherub.

Lewis, Terence. Bani a Butterfly Adventure. 2012. 30p. pap. 8.99 *(978-1-62230-329-8(6))* Salem Author Services.

Liautaud, Judy. Lulu Turns on the Night Light. Liautaud, Judy, illus. 2013. (Illus.). 24p. pap. 12.95 *(978-1-883841-19-5(4))* City Creek Pr., Inc.

Lighthipe, Mindy. Mother Monarch, 1 vol. 2010. (ENG., Illus.). 32p. (J). 19.99 *(978-0-7643-3400-9(X)*, 9780764334009) Schiffer Publishing, Ltd.

Logan, Laura. Little Butterfly. Logan, Laura, illus. 2016. (Illus.). 32p. (J). (gr. -1-3). 14.99 *(978-0-06-228126-5(7))* HarperCollins Pubs.

Lorraine, Nancy. The Butterfly Adventure. Herron, Dorothy, illus. 2nd ed. 2013. 50p. 22.50 *(978-0-9886194-9-4(0))* ProsePress.

—Tatty, the Lonely Monarch. Herron, Dorothy, illus. 2013. 48p. pap. 17.50 *(978-0-9893063-8-6(0))* ProsePress.

Luis y la Mariposa: Individual Title Six-Packs. (Literatura 2000 Ser.). (SPA.). (gr. 2-3). 33.00 *(978-0-7635-1263-7(X))* Rigby Education.

Lurie, Craig. Butterflies, Ladybugs, & Bumble Bees & the wonderful world this could Be ... . 2011. 36p. (gr. -1). pap. 14.95 *(978-1-4567-6300-8(8))* AuthorHouse.

Lynch, Lauren Boehm. The Yellow Butterfly. DeBroeck, Sarah, illus. 2011. 28p. pap. 24.95 *(978-1-4560-0982-3(6))* America Star Bks.

MacKay, Elly. Butterfly Park. 2015. (ENG., Illus.). 40p. (J). (gr. -1-17). 16.95 *(978-0-7624-5339-9(7)*, Running Pr. Kids) Running Pr. Bk. Pubs.

Macri, Rebecca. Pip: A Very Special Little Caterpillar. 2010. 32p. (J). 16.95 *(978-1-886057-61-6(3))* Warren Publishing, Inc.

Madden, Michelle. The Butterfly Garden. 2008. 24p. pap. 24.95 *(978-1-60813-375-8(3))* America Star Bks.

Madison, Alan. Velma Gratch & the Way Cool Butterfly. Hawkes, Kevin, illus. 2007. (ENG.). 40p. (J). (gr. -1-3). 17.99 *(978-0-375-83597-1(0)*, Schwartz & Wade Bks.) Random Hse. Children's Bks.

—Velma Gratch & the Way Cool Butterfly. Hawkes, Kevin, illus. 2012. (ENG.). 40p. (J). (gr. -1-3). pap. 7.99 *(978-0-307-97804-2(4)*, Dragonfly Bks.) Random Hse. Children's Bks.

Maier, Inger M. Ben's Flying Flowers. Bogade, Maria, illus. 2012. (J). 14.95 *(978-1-4338-1133-3(2))*; pap. 9.95 *(978-1-4338-1132-6(4))* American Psychological Assn. (Magination Pr.).

Margolis, Amy. Butterflies & Magical Wings, 1. 2006. (Illus.). 44p. (J). pap. 16.99 *(978-0-9776692-0-2(3))* Margolis, Amy Publishing.

Markle, Sandra. Butterfly Tree, 1 vol. Wu, Leslie, illus. 2011. (ENG.). 32p. (J). (gr. -1-3). 16.95 *(978-1-56145-539-3(3))* Peachtree Pubs.

Marks, Kathi. Butterflies are Special: The Most Beautiful Butterfly. 2006. (ENG.). 48p. per. 9.95 *(978-1-59800-572-1(3))* Outskirts Pr., Inc.

Marrero-Bond, Stephanie. Flor la Maripos. 2009. 24p. pap. 14.49 *(978-1-4343-9609-9(6))* AuthorHouse.

Martin-Larranaga, Ana, illus. Butterfly at Home. 2007. (Butterfly Bks.). (J). bds. 5.95 *(978-1-58925-804-4(5))* Tiger Tales.

—Butterfly in the Garden. 2007. (Butterfly Bks.). (J). bds. 5.95 *(978-1-58925-803-7(7))* Tiger Tales.

—Butterfly in the Town. 2007. (Butterfly Bks.). (J). bds. 5.95 *(978-1-58925-805-1(3))* Tiger Tales.

—Butterfly on the Farm. 2007. (Butterfly Bks.). (J). bds. 5.95 *(978-1-58925-802-0(9))* Tiger Tales.

McCreadie, Sandi. Thistle Fables. 2013. 64p. pap. 23.99 *(978-1-4808-0313-8(8))* Archway Publishing.

McGee, Warner, illus. Diego Saves a Butterfly. 2007. (Go, Diego, Go! Ser.: 3). (ENG.). 24p. (J). (gr. -1-1). pap. 3.99 *(978-1-4169-3364-9(6)*, Simon Spotlight/Nickelodeon) Simon Spotlight/Nickelodeon.

McGrath, Maureen. Spunky's Special Friend. 2009. (Illus.). 24p. pap. 13.50 *(978-1-60693-735-8(9)*, Eloquent Bks.) Strategic Book Publishing & Rights Agency (SBPRA).

McJarrow, Shandy. The Adventures of Papilio the Butterfly. 2009. 112p. 20.95 *(978-1-4401-3850-8(8))*; pap. 10.95 *(978-1-4401-3840-9(0))* iUniverse, Inc.

McKee, David. Elmer & Butterfly. McKee, David, illus. 2015. (ENG., Illus.). 32p. (J). (gr. -1-3). 16.99 *(978-1-4677-6326-4(8))* Lerner Publishing Group.

McKee, David, illus. Elmer & Butterfly. 2015. (J). 17.32 *(978-1-4677-6327-1(6))* Lerner Publishing Group.

McMahon, Michele. The Butterfly Promise. 2010. 24p. 12.99 *(978-1-4520-1510-1(4))* AuthorHouse.

McNamara, Margaret. Butterfly Garden. Gordon, Mike, illus. 2012. (Robin Hill School Ser.). (ENG.). 32p. (J). (gr. -1-1). 15.99 *(978-1-4424-3643-5(3))*; pap. 3.99 *(978-1-4424-3642-8(5))* Simon Spotlight. (Simon Spotlight).

—Butterfly Garden. 2012. (Robin Hill School Ready-To-Read Ser.). lib. bdg. 13.55 *(978-0-606-23694-2(5)*, Turtleback) Turtleback Bks.

Mead, Purnima. Bibia Meets Gripper. 2013. 24p. pap. 12.45 *(978-1-4497-9751-5(2)*, WestBow Pr.) Author Solutions, Inc.

—Bibia Tells Her Story! 2010. 24p. 14.50 *(978-1-4490-4753-5(X))* AuthorHouse.

Mead, Purnima & Kerber, Kathy. Bibia, the Butterfly. 2009. 24p. pap. 18.50 *(978-1-4389-6644-1(X))* AuthorHouse.

Mescall, Ron. The Adventures of Goo Goo Malou: A Parent's Guide for Teaching Values. 2009. 24p. pap. 10.96 *(978-1-4269-0836-1(9))* Trafford Publishing.

Meserve, Adria. Cleopatra Silverwing. 2004. (ENG., Illus.). 32p. (J). (gr. k-2). pap. 9.99 *(978-0-09-943228-9(5)*, Red Fox) Random House Children's Books GBR. Dist: Independent Pubs. Group.

Mitchell, Sandra. Butterfly Buddies. 2012. 20p. pap. 15.99 *(978-1-4772-0273-9(0))* AuthorHouse.

Mitchell, Tammy. Rachel & the Magical Butterfly. 2011. 36p. 15.14 *(978-1-4520-8390-2(8))* AuthorHouse.

Mohr, Janet. Flight of Change. 2007. 48p. pap. 16.95 *(978-1-4241-0793-3(8))* America Star Bks.

A Monarch Universe CD: Children's Picture Book. 2007. (J). cd-rom 22.95 *(978-0-9800222-2-3(3))* UPfirst.com Bks.

Moncure, Jane Belk. Butterfly Express: A Book about Life Cycles. Billin-Frye, Paige, illus. 2013. (Magic Castle Readers Ser.). (ENG.). 32p. (J). (gr. -1-2). 25.64 *(978-1-62323-588-8(X)*, 206323) Child's World, Inc., The.

Moody, Gloria. Two Beautiful Butterflies. Doering, Kimber, illus. l.t. ed. 2005. 25p. (YA). per. 8.99 *(978-1-59879-002-3(1))* Lifevest Publishing, Inc.

Morris, Lynn. Belinda the Butterfly's Beautiful Colors. 2011. 48p. (gr. -1). pap. 19.26 *(978-1-4567-3521-0(7))* AuthorHouse.

Moss, Yvonne. The Butterfly Princess. 2011. 16p. (gr. -1). pap. 9.49 *(978-1-4567-4044-3(X))* AuthorHouse.

Musgrave, Sugin. Butterfly in the Sky: Daddy's Little Girl. 2008. 32p. 14.00 *(978-1-4389-2218-8(3))* AuthorHouse.

Nana, Old. The Girl Who Converses with Butterflies. 2012. 24p. pap. 11.50 *(978-1-61204-972-4(9)*, Strategic Bk. Publishing) Strategic Book Publishing & Rights Agency (SBPRA).

Neale, Karen. The Boy Who Burped Butterflies. 2012. 32p. pap. 32.70 *(978-1-4771-3999-8(0))* Xlibris Corp.

Nesbit, E. Butterfly Alphabet Counter. 2003. 185p. (J). 95.70 *(978-0-590-70231-7(9))* Scholastic, Inc.

Nettles, Sarah A. Benjamin, the Bully & the Butterfly. 2012. 24p. pap. 17.99 *(978-1-4772-7195-7(3))* AuthorHouse.

Newman, Yvette. Missy's Day with Butterflies. 2007. 84p. pap. 11.96 *(978-1-4357-0172-4(0))* Lulu Pr., Inc.

O Flatharta, Antoine. Hurry & the Monarch. So, Meilo, illus. 2009. (ENG.). 40p. (J). (gr. k-3). pap. 7.99 *(978-0-385-73719-7(X)*, Dragonfly Bks.) Random Hse. Children's Bks.

O'Connor, Crystal Ball. Gift/ Book Combo. Hollinger, Valerie Bunch, illus. 2005. (J). 25.00 *(978-0-9774038-0-6(7))* Monarch Pubs.

—Jake & the Migration of the Monarch. Hollinger, Valerie Bunch, illus. 2005. 32p. (J). 17.95 *(978-0-615-12659-3(6))* Monarch Pubs.

—Jake & the Migration of the Monarch with CD. Hollinger, Valerie Bunch, illus. 2005. (J). audio compact disk 18.95 *(978-0-9774038-3-7(1))* Monarch Pubs.

—Jake y la Migraci'on de la Monarca. Brenes-Sotela, Guillermo J. & Quave, Gloria Martinez, trs. from ENG. Hollinger, Valerie Bunch, illus. 2005. (SPA.). (J). 17.95 *(978-0-9774038-2-0(3))* Monarch Pubs.

O'Connor, Jane. Bonjour, Butterfly. Glasser, Robin Preiss, illus. (Fancy Nancy Ser.). (ENG.). 32p. (J). (gr. -1-2). 2012. 9.99 *(978-0-06-221053-1(X))* 2008. 17.99 *(978-0-06-123588-7(1))* HarperCollins Pubs.

—Fancy Nancy: Bonjour, Butterfly. Glasser, Robin Preiss, illus. 2008. (Fancy Nancy Ser.). (J). 203.88 *(978-0-06-158245-5(X))* HarperCollins Pubs.

Oelschlager, Vanita. Farfalla: A Story of Loss & Hope. Blackwood, Kristin, illus. 2012. (ENG.). 40p. (J). (gr. -1-3). 15.95 *(978-0-9832904-0-7(7))* VanitaBooks.

Oelschlager, Vanita & Blackwood, Kristin. Farfalla: A Story of Loss & Hope. 2012. (ENG., Illus.). 40p. (J). (gr. -1-3). pap. 8.95 *(978-0-9832904-3-8(1))* VanitaBooks.

O'Neal, Kerry. I Wish I Could Fly/I Can Fly! The Lonely Caterpillar BOOK I & the Lonely Butterfly BOOK II. O'Neal, Kerry, illus. l.t. ed. 2006. (Illus.). 60p. (J). 29.99 *(978-1-59879-197-6(4))* Lifevest Publishing, Inc.

OSullivan, Michaeleen, tr. A Monarch Universe: Children's Picture Book. 2007. (Illus.). 34p. (J). pap. 22.95 *(978-0-9800222-0-9(7))* UPfirst.com Bks.

Owens, Lucy. My Lime Green Butterfly. 2011. 40p. pap. 22.65 *(978-1-4568-7103-1(X))* Xlibris Corp.

Parker, Emma. The Butterfly on the Subway. 2010. (Illus.). pap. *(978-1-877547-81-2(6))* First Edition Ltd.

Pascual, Dennis Mark. The Adventures of Dj the Butterfly & Friends Series Presents Dj's Birthday Party. 2012. 20p. pap. 10.15 *(978-1-105-35838-8(0))* Lulu Pr., Inc.

Patterson, Christine. On the Wings of a Butterfly. 2004. 21p. (J). per. 10.68 *(978-1-4116-0669-2(8))* Lulu Pr., Inc.

Peet, Joy. Sophia's Flutterfly. 2008. 19p. pap. 24.95 *(978-1-60610-806-2(9))* America Star Bks.

Perry, Valerie J. Trilby Learns a Lesson. 2011. 26p. pap. 14.00 *(978-1-60976-659-7(8)*, Eloquent Bks.) Strategic Book Publishing & Rights Agency (SBPRA).

Perugini, Donna. The Adventures of Amelia Airheart Butterfly. 2010. 36p. pap. 9.99 *(978-0-88144-537-4(1))* Yorkshire Publishing Group.

—Do Angels Go Camping? 2010. 32p. (Orig.). pap. 9.99 *(978-0-88144-536-7(3))* Yorkshire Publishing Group.

Peterson, Kay. Tillie the Turtle. 2012. 24p. pap. 15.99 *(978-1-4691-8414-2(1))* Xlibris Corp.

Pinkham, Mark Amaru. Love Me Later. 2005. 202p. 14.95 *(978-1-932188-02-8(9))* Adventures Unlimited Pr.

Pledger, Maurice. Billy Bunny & the Butterflies. 2013. (ENG., Illus.). 16p. (J). bds. 10.95 *(978-1-60710-808-5(9)*, Silver Dolphin Bks.) Readerlink Distribution Services, LLC.

Porter, Gene Stratton-. A Girl of the Limberlost. 2011. 266p. pap. 17.99 *(978-1-61279-071-8(2))* Publishing in Motion.

Portes, Andrea. The Fall of Butterflies. 2016. 400p. (YA). (gr. 9). 17.99 *(978-0-06-231367-6(3)*, HarperTeen) HarperCollins Pubs.

—The Fall of Butterflies. 2017. (ENG.). (YA). (gr. 9). lib. bdg. 20.85 ***(978-0-606-40045-9(1))*** Turtleback Bks.

Pova, Rosie. Ladybug & Caterpillar: The Way to Friendship. 2008. 16p. pap. 24.95 *(978-1-60474-950-2(4))* America Star Bks.

Prida, Isabel Suarez de la. El Caracol de las Mariposas. (Barril Sin Fondo Ser.).Tr. of Shell of the Butterflies. (SPA., Illus.). (J). (gr. 3-5). pap. 8.76 *(978-968-6465-76-1(6))* Casa de Estudios de Literatura y Talleres Artisticos Amaquemecan A.C. MEX. Dist: Lectorum Pubns., Inc.

Prior, R. W. The Great Monarch Butterfly Chase. Loven, Beth Glick, illus. 2013. (ENG.). 32p. (J). (gr. -1-3). 16.99 *(978-1-4814-2157-7(3)*, Simon & Schuster Bks. For Young Readers) Simon & Schuster Bks. For Young Readers.

Quinn, Susan. Little Bear & the Butterflies. Pedler, Caroline, illus. 2014. 24p. (J). ***(978-1-4351-5922-8(5))*** Barnes & Noble, Inc.

Randolph, Joanne. Bella: A Butterfly's Story. 2009. (Nature Stories Ser.). (Illus.). 24p. (J). (gr. -1-2). pap. 8.15 *(978-1-60754-099-1(1))*; lib. bdg. 22.60 *(978-1-60754-098-4(3))* Windmill Bks.

Rea, Ba. Monarch! Come Play with Me. Rea, Ba, illus. 2006. (Illus.). 32p. (J). per. 10.95 *(978-0-9657472-5-7(5))* Bas Relief, LLC.

Reason, Diane. Travis the Traveling Turtle & the Beautiful Butterfly. 2011. 32p. pap. 14.98 *(978-1-4634-0206-8(6))* AuthorHouse.

Reid, Alastair. A Balloon for a Blunderbuss. Gill, Bob, illus. 2008. (ENG.). 36p. (gr. -1-3). 14.95 *(978-0-7148-4873-0(5))* Phaidon Pr., Inc.

Richman, Karyn. The Land Where All Things Become Beautiful. 2011. 204p. pap. 15.99 *(978-1-61215-926-3(5))* Salem Author Services.

Rift. The Wise Little Butterfly, 1 vol. Rift, illus. 2009. (Illus.). 39p. pap. 19.95 *(978-1-61546-493-7(X))* PublishAmerica, Inc.

Ring, Elizabeth & Smithsonian Institution Staff. onarch Butterfly of Aster Way (Mariposa Monarcha de la Calle Aster) 2008. (MUL.). 16p. 14.95 *(978-1-59249-846-8(9))* Soundprints.

Rivers-Moore, Debbie. Little Bunny's Butterflies. Fox, Lisa, illus. 2012. (Springtime Shakers Ser.). (ENG.). 8p. (J). bds. 5.99 *(978-0-7641-6488-0(0))* Barron's Educational Series, Inc.
Robinson, Zan D. Ferdie the Fay Meets Flutterey the Butterfly: A Forest Fable. Maxwell, Jeremy, illus. (Ferdie the Fay Adventure Ser.: No. 1). 52p. (Orig.). (J). (gr. -1-4). *(978-0-9635587-4-9(9))* Connors, E. W. Publishing Co.
Rockhill, Dennis. Meadow Dance. 2007. (Wonderlands Ser.).Tr. of Danza de la Pradera. (ENG., Illus.). 32p. (J). (gr. -1-3). per. 7.95 *(978-1-932748-70-3(9),* Raven Tree Pr.,Csi) Continental Sales, Inc.
Rogers, Suzanne J. Cody Meets A Butterfly. 2008. 72p. pap. 19.95 *(978-1-4327-2069-8(4))* Outskirts Pr., Inc.
Rose, Jasmine. The Last Caterpillar Princess. 2011. 16p. pap. 8.64 *(978-1-4634-1953-0(8))* AuthorHouse.
Rosenthal, S. L. Mama, Where Do Our Butterflies Go in the Winter? 2011. 40p. pap. 24.95 *(978-1-4560-7498-2(9))* America Star Bks.
Roy, Alene Adele. The Legend of Dragonfly Pond: Coloring Book. 2008. 56p. pap. 11.99 *(978-1-4343-4628-5(5))* AuthorHouse.
Runton, Andy. Owly & Wormy, Friends All Aflutter! Runton, Andy, illus. 2011. (ENG., Illus.). 40p. (J). (gr. -1-2). 16.99 *(978-1-4169-5774-4(X),* Atheneum Bks. for Young Readers) Simon & Schuster Children's Publishing.
Ruth, Nick. The Dark Dreamweaver. Concannon, Sue, illus. 2007. (Remin Chronicles: 1). (ENG.). 256p. (J). (gr. 4-7). per. 11.95 *(978-0-9745603-5-9(9))* Imaginator Pr.
Sandoval, Anna. Tickle a Daisy. 2007. 28p. per. 24.95 *(978-1-4241-8470-5(3))* America Star Bks.
Sasso, Sandy Eisenberg. Butterflies under Our Hats. Rothenberg, Joani Keller, illus. 2006. (ENG.). 32p. (J). (gr. -1-3). 16.95 *(978-1-55725-474-0(5))* Paraclete Pr., Inc.
Satterfield, April. Leah Bug & Her Flying Friends. Guthrie, Lewis, illus. 2011. 20p. pap. 24.95 *(978-1-4560-8422-6(4))* America Star Bks.
Schaeffer-Stumpf, Dawn. Fluttah Fluttah Butterfly. 2003. (Illus.). 24p. (J). per. 14.95 *(978-0-9747147-0-7(4))* MK Publishing.
Schmauss, Judy Kentor. The Caterpillar. Collier, Mary, illus. 2006. (Reader's Clubhouse Level 1 Reader Ser.). (ENG.). 24p. (J). (gr. 1-4). pap. 4.99 *(978-0-7641-3286-5(5))* Barron's Educational Series, Inc.
Sims, Stacy. Rainbow Butterflies. 2007. 39p. 25.95 *(978-0-615-15922-5(2))* Blue Peach Publishing.
Singh, Jay. Once upon a Time in a Forest Far Away. 2009. 394p. pap. 33.12 *(978-1-4251-9122-1(3))* Trafford Publishing.
Sirotzky, Sara. Red Rose & Blue Butterfly. Weber, Andra, illus. 2012. (ENG.). 32p. (J). (gr. -1-3). 17.95 *(978-1-4507-9594-4(3))* Ampersand, Inc.
Smith, Gloria. Annie Elf & Flippy Butterfly. 2012. 24p. 24.95 *(978-1-4626-9835-6(2));* 20p. pap. 24.95 *(978-1-4626-6636-2(1))* America Star Bks.
Smith, Sarah. The Butterfly House. 2014. (ENG., Illus.). 32p. (gr. -1-3). 19.95 *(978-1-84976-205-2(8))* Tate Publishing, Ltd. GBR. Dist: Abrams, Inc.
Sommers, Audrey. Mickey the Monarch. Mattie, Dugan, ed. Bhuiyan, Julia, illus. 2013. 42p. pap. 14.95 *(978-0-9851996-2-3(8))* HMSI, Inc.
Soundar, Chitra. Chasing the Pot of Gold. Amrein, Paul, illus. 2006. 32p. (J). E-Book 5.00 incl. cd-rom *(978-1-933090-36-8(7))* Guardian Angel Publishing, Inc.
Stone, Kazuko G. & Keido, Ippo. The Butterfly's Dream: Children's Stories from China. 2003. (ENG., Illus.). 1p. 15.95 *(978-0-8048-3480-3(6))* Tuttle Publishing.
The Story of the Mexican Jumping Bean, 6 vols. (Multicultural Programs Ser.). 16p. (gr. 1-6). 25.95 *(978-0-7802-8312-1(0))* Wright Group/McGraw-Hill.
Sullivan, Melody. Lillibit's Dream. Grof, Stanislav, illus. 2011. (ENG.). 32p. (J). 19.95 *(978-1-59275-000-9(1))* Hanford Mead Pubs., Inc.
Sundgaard, Arnold. The Lamb & the Butterfly. Carle, Eric, illus. 2013. (ENG.). 32p. (J). (gr. -1-k). 17.99 *(978-0-545-44326-5(1),* Orchard Bks.) Scholastic, Inc.
Surman-Hobbs, Debbi. The Little Brown Moth, 1 vol. 2010. 34p. pap. 24.95 *(978-1-4489-8620-0(6))* PublishAmerica, Inc.
Swope, Sam. Gotta Go! Gotta Go! Riddle, Sue, illus. 2004. (ENG.). 32p. (J). (gr. -1-1). reprint ed. pap. 8.99 *(978-0-374-42786-3(0),* 9780374427863) Square Fish.
Taylor, Chad. We Catch Butterflies. 2016. (Rosen REAL Readers: STEM & STEAM Collection). 8p. (gr. 1-k). pap. 5.46 *(978-1-5081-2607-2(0),* Rosen Classroom) Rosen Publishing Group, Inc., The.
Taylor-Gaines, Lonnetta. Fia & the Butterfly: 7 Stories for Character Education. 2005. 13.00 *(978-0-8059-9848-1(9))* Dorrance Publishing Co., Inc.
Thomas Nelson. Butterfly Art. 2015. (ENG.). 80p. (J). (gr. 3-9). pap. *(978-1-78393-715-8(7))* Make Believe Ideas.
Thompson, Holly Sue. Molly, the Good Furry Friend. Thompson, Kristi June, illus. 2011. 36p. pap. 14.75 *(978-1-60911-431-2(0),* Eloquent Bks.) Strategic Book Publishing & Rights Agency (SBPRA).
Tillis, Dionne. Willameana Whitney White & the Magical Butterfly. 2012. 24p. pap. 17.99 *(978-1-4685-7286-5(5))* AuthorHouse.
Tony & the Butterfly: Individual Title Six-Packs. (Literatura 2000 Ser.). (gr. 2-3). 33.00 *(978-0-7635-0243-0(X))* Rigby Education.
Turnbull, Kathie. Because Everyone Needs a Friend. 2009. 20p. pap. 12.50 *(978-1-60693-372-5(8),* Eloquent Bks.) Strategic Book Publishing & Rights Agency (SBPRA).
Uihlein, Mary. Hello Little Owl, I Am Hermit Crab! Uihlein, Mary, illus. 2013. (Illus.). 28p. 24.95 *(978-1-61493-159-1(3));* pap. 12.95 *(978-1-61493-158-4(5))* Peppertree Pr., The.
Valko, Danna. Dee & Maya Are Best Friends. 2013. (Illus.). *(978-1-62510-726-8(9)); (978-1-62563-112-1(X))* Tate Publishing, Ltd.
Wagner, Fiona. The Little Cat. 2005. 15p. (J). 9.99 *(978-1-4116-5568-3(0))* Lulu Pr., Inc.
Wagner, Linda. Lady Flatterley. 2008. 44p. pap. 22.95 *(978-1-4327-3233-2(1))* Outskirts Pr., Inc.
Watson, Jean. Onyx the Butterfly. 2007. 160p. pap. 58.25 *(978-1-4303-2408-9(2))* Lulu Pr., Inc.
Watson, Kenneth C. The Big Yellow Butterfly. 2010. 36p. 15.69 *(978-1-4490-5974-3(0))* AuthorHouse.
Weimer, Heidi R. How Do I Kiss You? Sharp, Chris, illus. 2008. (ENG.). 18p. (J). (gr. -1-k). bds. 12.99 *(978-0-8249-1814-9(2),* Ideal Pubns.) Worthy Publishing.
Wenger, Shaunda. Caterpillar Can't Wait! 2006. (Early Explorers Ser.). (J). pap. *(978-1-4108-6101-6(5))* Benchmark Education Co.
Weston, Laura. The Butterfly Garden. Weston, Laura, illus. 2017. (ENG., Illus.). 12p. (J). (-k). bds. 14.99 *(978-0-7636-9317-6(0),* Big Picture Press) Candlewick Pr.
Wethington, Constance. The Butterfly's Ball. 2013. 20p. pap. 24.95 *(978-1-4626-8640-7(0))* America Star Bks.
White, Kittie. The Magic Butterfly: And Other Tales. 2008. (ENG.). 52p. pap. 11.99 *(978-1-4196-9096-9(5))* CreateSpace Independent Publishing Platform.
Williams, Rufus. The Frog & the Butterfly. 2012. 88p. pap. 10.00 *(978-1-61897-380-1(0),* Strategic Bk. Publishing) Strategic Book Publishing & Rights Agency (SBPRA).
Williams, Zachary. What Will It Be? 2006. (Neighborhood Readers Ser.). (ENG.). 16p. (gr. 1-3). pap. 6.50 *(978-1-4042-7252-1(6),* Rosen Classroom) Rosen Publishing Group, Inc., The.
Wilson, Hannah & Parrish, Emma. Flutterby Butterfly: A Hide-and-Seek Book. 2015. (Slide-And-Seek Ser.). (ENG., Illus.). 10p. (J). (gr. -1-k). bds. 8.99 *(978-1-4998-0029-6(0))* Little Bee Books Inc.
Woodbridge, Nancy Garfield. A Bouquet of Fairy Tales. 2012. 108p. 24.99 *(978-1-4771-4493-0(5));* pap. 15.99 *(978-1-4771-4492-3(7))* Xlibris Corp.
Wyttenbach, Bigna A. Francis-von. Coronets, Butterflies & Roses. 2004. 49p. pap. 10.00 *(978-1-4134-7785-6(2))* Xlibris Corp.
Yusuf. Butterfly & Bumble Bee: Adventure in Yellow Stone National Park. 2010. 16p. 8.49 *(978-1-4520-4022-6(2))* AuthorHouse.
Zimmerman, Kathleen. Oscar's First Flight. Feldmeier Sims, Julie & Hartman, John, illus. 2005. 44p. (J). per. 16.95 *(978-0-9744330-0-4(4))* Kat Tales Publishing.

BUTTONS

Formaro, Amanda. Button Mania: Buttons, Bottlecaps, & Beyond! 2015. (ENG., Illus.). 72p. (J). (gr. k-6). pap. 8.99 *(978-0-7944-3339-0(1),* Reader's Digest Children's Bks.) Studio Fun International.
Rylance, Ulrike. Emma in Buttonland. Morby, Connie Stradling, tr. from GER. Leffler, Silke, illus. 2013. (ENG.). 120p. (J). (gr. 1-5). 12.95 *(978-1-62087-992-4(1),* 620992, Sky Pony Pr.) Skyhorse Publishing Co., Inc.

BUYERS GUIDES

see Consumer Education; Shopping

BY-PRODUCTS

see Waste Products

BYRD, RICHARD EVELYN, 1888-1957

Burleigh, Robert. Black Whiteness: Admiral Byrd Alone in the Antarctic. Krudop, Walter Lyon, illus. 2011. (ENG.). 40p. (J). (gr. 2-5). pap. 19.99 *(978-1-4424-5334-0(6),* Atheneum Bks. for Young Readers) Simon & Schuster Children's Publishing.
Seiple, Samantha. Byrd & Igloo: A Polar Adventure. 2013. (J). (ENG.). 192p. (gr. 3-7). 18.99 *(978-0-545-56276-8(7));* (Illus.). 186p. *(978-0-545-61642-3(5))* Scholastic, Inc. (Scholastic Pr.).
Steinberg, Alfred. Admiral Richard E Byrd. Beck, Charles, illus. 2011. 128p. 40.95 *(978-1-258-01853-5(5))* Literary Licensing, LLC.

BYZANTINE EMPIRE

Boone, Mary. Byzantine Empire. 2012. (Explore Ancient Worlds Ser.). (J). (gr. 3-6). lib. bdg. 29.95 *(978-1-61228-281-7(4))* Mitchell Lane Pubs., Inc.
The Byzantine Empire in the Age of Justinian (NCHS) (YA). (gr. 6-9). spiral bd., tchr.'s planning gde. ed. 11.00 *(978-0-382-40980-6(9))* Cobblestone Publishing Co.
The Byzantine Empire in the Age of Justinian (NCHS) Grades 6-9. (J). tchr. ed. 15.50 *(978-0-382-40981-3(7))* Cobblestone Publishing Co.
DeCarlo, Carolyn. The Byzantine Empire. 2017. (J). ***(978-1-68048-859-3(7));*** lib. bdg. ***(978-1-68048-780-0(9))*** Rosen Publishing Group, Inc., The. (Britannica Educational Publishing).
Feldman, Ruth Tenzer. The Fall of Constantinople. 2008. (Pivotal Moments in History Ser.). (ENG., Illus.). 160p. (gr. 9-12). lib. bdg. 38.60 *(978-0-8225-5918-4(8))* Lerner Publishing Group.
Phillips, Robin. Who in the World Was the Acrobatic Empress? The Story of Theodora. unabr. ed. 2010. (ENG.). 1p. audio compact disk 12.95 *(978-1-933339-39-9(X),* 333939) Well-Trained Mind Pr.
Rodgers, Kelly. The Byzantine Empire: A Society That Shaped the World, 1 vol. 2012. (Primary Source Readers Ser.). (ENG.). 32p. (J). (gr. 5-5). pap. 8.99 *(978-1-4333-5001-6(7))* Teacher Created Materials, Inc.
Stefoff, Rebecca. The Medieval World. 2004. (World Historical Atlases Ser.). (Illus.). 48p. (gr. 5). 26.95 *(978-0-7614-1642-5(0),* Benchmark Bks.) Marshall Cavendish Corp.
VanVoorst, Jennifer Fretland. The Byzantine Empire, 1 vol. 2012. (Exploring the Ancient World Ser.). (ENG., Illus.). 48p. (gr. 5-6). pap. 9.10 *(978-0-7565-4586-4(2))* Compass Point Bks.
—The Byzantine Empire, 1 vol. 2012. (Exploring the Ancient World Ser.). (ENG., Illus.). 48p. (gr. 5-6). 29.32 *(978-0-7565-4565-9(X))* Compass Point Bks.

C

CABEZA DE VACA, ALVAR NUNEZ, 1490?-1557

Johnston, Lissa J. & Núñez Cabeza de Vaca, Alvar. Crossing a Continent: The Incredible Journey of Cabeza de Vaca. 2005. 82p. (J). pap. 9.95 *(978-1-57168-183-6(3),* Eakin Pr.) Eakin Pr.

CABINET OFFICERS

Alexander, Heather & dePaola, Tomie. Who Is Hillary Clinton? Harrison, Nancy & Putra, Dede, illus. 2016. (Who Was? Ser.). (ENG.). 112p. (J). (gr. 3-7). lib. bdg. 15.99 *(978-0-399-54234-3(5),* Grosset & Dunlap) Penguin Young Readers Group.
Banting, Erinn. Condoleeza Rice. 2007. (Remarkable People Ser.). (Illus.). 24p. (J). (gr. 3-7). lib. bdg. 24.45 *(978-1-59036-639-4(5))* Weigl Pubs., Inc.
—Condoleezza Rice. 2007. (Remarkable People Ser.). (Illus.). 24p. (J). (gr. 3-7). pap. 8.95 *(978-1-59036-640-0(9))* Weigl Pubs., Inc.
Blashfield, Jean F. Hillary Clinton. 2010. (Leading Women Ser.). 96p. (YA). (gr. 7-12). 39.93 *(978-0-7614-4954-6(X))* Marshall Cavendish Corp.
Blumenthal, Karen. Hillary Rodham Clinton: A Woman Living History. 2016. (ENG., Illus.). 448p. (J). 18.99 *(978-1-250-06014-3(1),* 9781250060143) Feiwel & Friends.
Burgan, Michael. Hillary Clinton, 1 vol. 2014. (Extraordinary Women Ser.). (ENG.). 48p. (gr. 6-6). lib. bdg. 32.65 *(978-1-4109-5941-6(4))* Heinemann-Raintree.
Byman, Jeremy. Madam Secretary: The Story of Madeleine Albright. rev. exp. ed. 2004. (Notable Americans Ser.). (Illus.). 128p. (YA). (gr. 6-12). 23.95 *(978-1-931798-34-1(6))* Reynolds, Morgan Inc.
Corey, Shana. Hillary Clinton: the Life of a Leader. Gustavson, Adam, illus. 2016. (Step into Reading Ser.). (ENG.). 48p. (J). (gr. k-3). 3.99 *(978-1-101-93235-3(X),* Random Hse. Bks. for Young Readers) Random Hse. Children's Bks.
Cunningham, Anne C. Women Political Leaders. 2016. (Defying Convention: Women Who Changed the Rules Ser.). 128p. (J). 37.27 *(978-0-7660-8141-3(9))* Enslow Pubs., Inc.
Cunningham, Kevin. Condoleezza Rice. 2009. (Journey to Freedom Ser.). (ENG., Illus.). 32p. (J). (gr. 4-7). 29.93 *(978-1-60253-120-8(X),* 200386) Child's World, Inc., The.
Ditchfield, Christin. Condoleezza Rice: America's Leading Stateswoman. 2006. (Great Life Stories Ser.). (ENG., Illus.). 112p. (J). (gr. 6-8). lib. bdg. 30.50 *(978-0-531-13874-8(7),* Watts, Franklin) Scholastic Library Publishing.
Doak, Robin S. Hillary Clinton. 2013. (True Book™—Biographies Ser.). (ENG., Illus.). 48p. (J). pap. 6.95 *(978-0-531-23877-6(6));* lib. bdg. 29.00 *(978-0-531-21906-5(2))* Scholastic Library Publishing.
Emert, Phyllis Raybin. Attorneys General: Enforcing the Law. 2005. (In the Cabinet Ser.). (Illus.). 176p. (J). (gr. 7-18). lib. bdg. 24.95 *(978-1-881508-66-3(8))* Oliver Pr., Inc.
Epstein, Dwayne. Hillary Clinton. 2010. (People in the News Ser.). (Illus.). 128p. (J). 33.95 *(978-1-4205-0268-8(9),* Lucent Bks.) Cengage Gale.
Feinstein, Stephen. Colin Powell. 2007. (African-American Heroes Ser.). (Illus.). 24p. (J). (gr. 1-3). lib. bdg. 22.60 *(978-0-7660-2761-9(9),* Enslow Elementary) Enslow Pubs., Inc.
Fitzgerald, Stephanie. Hillary Clinton. rev. ed. 2017. (Rookie Biographies(tm) Ser.). (ENG., Illus.). 32p. (J). lib. bdg. 25.00 ***(978-0-531-22931-6(9))*** Scholastic Library Publishing.
—Rookie Biographies: Hillary Clinton (Revised Edition) 2017. (Rookie Biographies Ser.). (ENG., Illus.). 32p. (J). pap. 5.95 ***(978-0-531-23406-8(1))*** Scholastic Library Publishing.
Harness, Cheryl. Hillary Clinton: American Woman of the World. 2016. (Real-Life Story Ser.). (ENG., Illus.). 192p. (J). (gr. 3-7). 17.99 *(978-1-4814-6057-6(9),* Aladdin) Simon & Schuster Children's Publishing.
Lee, Sally. Hillary Clinton, 1 vol. 2010. (First Ladies Ser.). (ENG.). 24p. (gr. k-1). lib. bdg. 26.65 *(978-1-4296-5327-5(2),* Pebble Plus) Capstone Press of Coughlan Cos.
Levinson, Cynthia. Hillary Rodham Clinton: Do All the Good You Can. 2016. (Illus.). 352p. (J). (gr. 3-7). pap. 6.99 *(978-0-06-238729-5(4))* HarperCollins Pubs.
Markel, Michelle. Hillary Rodham Clinton: Some Girls Are Born to Lead. Pham, LeUyen, illus. 2016. 40p. (J). (gr. -1-3). 17.99 *(978-0-06-238122-4(9))* HarperCollins Pubs.
Mattern, Joanne. Attorney General. 2003. (America's Leaders Ser.). (Illus.). 32p. (J). 24.94 *(978-1-56711-278-8(1),* Blackbirch Pr., Inc.) Cengage Gale.
McAuliffe, Bill. The Presidential Cabinet. 2016. (Illus.). 48p. (J). 39.95 *(978-1-60818-673-0(3),* Creative Education) Creative Co., The.
Porterfield, Jason. What Is the Executive Branch? 2015. (Let's Find Out! Government Ser.). (ENG., Illus.). 32p. (J). (gr. 2-3). 23.45 *(978-1-62275-922-4(2),* Britannica Educational Publishing) Rosen Publishing Group, Inc., The.
Rajczak, Michael. Meet the President's Cabinet. 2012. (Guide to Your Government Ser.). (Illus.). 32p. (J). (gr. 4-6). 26.60 *(978-1-4339-7260-7(3));* pap. 10.50 *(978-1-4339-7261-4(1))* Stevens, Gareth Publishing LLLP. (Gareth Stevens Learning Library).
Strum, Richard. Henry Knox: Washington's Artilleryman. 2006. (Forgotten Heroes of the American Revolution Ser.). (Illus.). 88p. (J). (gr. 5-11). lib. bdg. 23.95 *(978-1-59556-013-1(0))* OTTN Publishing.
Strum, Richard M. Henry Knox: Washington's Artilleryman. 2006. (J). pap. *(978-1-59556-018-6(1))* OTTN Publishing.
Summers, Portia. Hillary Clinton: Politician & Activist. 2017. (Junior Biographies Ser.). 24p. (J). (gr. 3-4). lib. bdg. 22.60 ***(978-0-7660-8670-8(4))*** Enslow Pubs., Inc.
Tieck, Sarah. Hillary Rodham Clinton, 1 vol. 2010. (First Biographies Set 6 Ser.). (ENG.). 32p. (J). (gr. 1-4). 27.07 *(978-1-60453-983-7(6))* ABDO Publishing Co.
Winter, Jonah & Colón, Raúl. Hillary. 2016. (ENG., Illus.). 40p. (J). (gr. -1-3). 17.99 *(978-0-553-53388-0(6),* Schwartz & Wade Bks.) Random Hse. Children's Bks.

CABINETWORK

see also Woodwork

Merrill, Amy French. A Day in the Life of a Colonial Cabinetmaker. 2009. (Library of Living & Working in Colonial Times Ser.). 24p. (gr. 3-3). 42.50 *(978-1-60853-729-7(3),* PowerKids Pr.) Rosen Publishing Group, Inc., The.

CABINS

see Log Cabins

CABOT, JOHN, -1498?

Anderson, Zachary. John Cabot: Searching for a Westward Passage to Asia. 2015. (Incredible Explorers Ser.). (ENG., Illus.). 64p. (J). (gr. 7-7). 34.21 *(978-1-5026-0173-5(7))* Cavendish Square Publishing.
Dalrymple, Lisa & O'Brien, Cynthia. Explore with John Cabot. 2015. (Travel with the Great Explorers Ser.). (ENG., Illus.). 32p. (J). (gr. 3-6). *(978-0-7787-1702-7(X))* Crabtree Publishing Co.
Donohue, Moira Rose. John Cabot. 2014. (Illus.). 24p. (J). *(978-1-938813-15-3(4))* State Standards Publishing, LLC.
Mass, Wendy. John Cabot: Early Explorer. 2004. (Explorers! Ser.). (Illus.). 48p. (J). lib. bdg. 25.27 *(978-0-7660-2144-0(0))* Enslow Pubs., Inc.
Morey, Allan. John Cabot. 2003. (Explorers of the Unknown Ser.). (J). pap. *(978-1-58417-098-3(0))* Lake Street Pubs.
Petrie, Kristin. John Cabot, 1 vol. 2004. (Explorers Set 1 Ser.). (ENG.). 32p. (gr. k-6). 27.07 *(978-1-59197-593-9(X),* Checkerboard Library) ABDO Publishing Co.
Rengel, Marian. John Cabot: The Ongoing Search for a Westward Passage to Asia. (Library of Explorers & Exploration Ser.). 112p. (gr. 5-8). 2009. 66.50 *(978-1-60853-609-2(2))* 2003. (Illus.). (J). lib. bdg. 34.60 *(978-0-8239-3626-7(0))* Rosen Publishing Group, Inc., The. (Rosen Reference).
Rice, Earle, Jr. John Cabot. 2006. (Profiles in American History Ser.). (Illus.). 48p. (J). (gr. 3-7). lib. bdg. 29.95 *(978-1-58415-451-8(9))* Mitchell Lane Pubs., Inc.
Roberts, Steven. John Cabot. 2013. (Jr. Graphic Famous Explorers Ser.). (ENG., Illus.). 24p. (J). (gr. 3-6). pap. 10.60 *(978-1-4777-0129-4(X));* lib. bdg. 25.25 *(978-1-4777-0072-3(2))* Rosen Publishing Group, Inc., The. (PowerKids Pr.).

CABOT, JOHN, -1498?—FICTION

Garfield, Henry. The Lost Voyage of John Cabot. 2007. (ENG., Illus.). 320p. (YA). (gr. 7). pap. 16.95 *(978-1-4169-5460-6(0),* Simon Pulse) Simon Pulse.

CACTUS

Benchmark Education Company, LLC Staff, compiled by. Cactus & Canyons & Ecosystems. 2005. spiral bd. 225.00 *(978-1-4108-5806-1(5))* Benchmark Education Co.
—Cactus & Canyons & Regions. 2005. spiral bd. 225.00 *(978-1-4108-5805-4(7))* Benchmark Education Co.
Cole, Tayler. Cacti Barely Need Water! 2016. (World's Weirdest Plants Ser.). 00024p. (J). pap. 8.15 ***(978-1-4824-5603-5(6))*** Stevens, Gareth Publishing LLLP.
Morrison, Yvonne. Stuck on Cactus: American Desert Life. 2007. (Shockwave: Life Science & Medicine Ser.). (ENG., Illus.). 36p. (J). (gr. 3-5). 25.00 *(978-0-531-17768-6(8),* Children's Pr.) Scholastic Library Publishing.
Owings, Lisa. From Seed to Cactus. 2017. (Start to Finish, Second Ser.). (ENG.). (J). (gr. k-3). 24p. 23.99 *(978-1-5124-3445-3(0));* pap. 6.99 ***(978-1-5124-5624-0(1))*** Lerner Publishing Group.
Rae, Rowena. Cacti. 2016. (Illus.). 24p. (J). *(978-1-5105-1405-8(8))* SmartBook Media, Inc.
Troller, Leah. The Cactus Book. 2017. (1-3Y Our Natural World Ser.). (ENG.). 16p. pap. 5.99 ***(978-1-63437-841-3(5))*** American Reading Co.

CAESAR, CAIUS JULIUS

see Caesar, Julius

CAESAR, JULIUS

Abbott, Jacob. Julius Caesar. 2009. (J). pap. 12.00 *(978-1-59128-060-6(5))* Canon Pr.
—Julius Caesar. 2009. 206p. pap. 10.95 *(978-1-59915-141-0(3))* Yesterday's Classics.
Albee, Sarah. Julius Caesar, Cleopatra. 2011. (Readers' & Writers' Genre Workshop Ser.). (YA). pap. *(978-1-4509-3023-9(9))* Benchmark Education Co.
Bailey, Gerry & Foster, Karen. Julius Caesar's Sandals. Noyes, Leighton, illus. 2008. (Stories of Great People Ser.). (ENG.). 40p. (J). (gr. 3-6). pap. *(978-0-7787-3717-9(9));* lib. bdg. *(978-0-7787-3695-0(4))* Crabtree Publishing Co.
Baum, Margaux & Thorne, James. Julius Caesar. 2016. (Leaders of the Ancient World Ser.). 00112p. (J). (gr. 6-6). 37.10 *(978-1-5081-7248-2(X))* Rosen Publishing Group, Inc., The.
Crompton, Samuel Willard. Julius Caesar. 2003. (Ancient World Leaders Ser.). (Illus.). 112p. (J). (gr. 6-12). 30.00 *(978-0-7910-7220-2(7),* Chelsea Hse.) Facts On File, Inc.
Dugan, Christine. Julius Caesar: Roman Leader, 1 vol. 2007. (Primary Source Readers Ser.). (ENG.). 32p. (J). (gr. 4-4). pap. 8.99 *(978-0-7439-0433-9(8))* Shell Educational Publishing.
Firth, Rachel. Julius Caesar. 2007. (Famous Lives Gift Bks). (Illus.). 64p. (J). 8.99 *(978-0-7945-1595-9(9),* Usborne) EDC Publishing.
Galford, Ellen. Julius Caesar: The Boy Who Conquered an Empire. 2007. (National Geographic World History Biographies Ser.). (ENG., Illus.). 64p. (J). (gr. 3-7). 17.95 *(978-1-4263-0064-6(6));* lib. bdg. 27.90 *(978-1-4263-0065-3(4))* National Geographic Society. (National Geographic Children's Bks.).
Goldberg, Jan. Julius Caesar. 2004. (ZB Reads Trio Books). (Illus.). 106p. (gr. 5-7). pap. 5.50 *(978-0-7367-1800-4(1))* Zaner-Bloser, Inc.
Gormley, Beatrice. Julius Caesar: Young Statesman. 2006. (Childhood of World Figures Ser.). (ENG.). 256p. (J). (gr. 3-7). pap. 12.99 *(978-1-4169-1281-1(9),* Simon & Schuster/Paula Wiseman Bks.) Simon & Schuster/Paula Wiseman Bks.
Greenblatt, Miriam. Julius Caesar & the Roman Republic. 2005. (Rulers & Their Times Ser.). (Illus.). 96p. (J). (gr. 3-7). lib. bdg. 29.93 *(978-0-7614-1836-8(9),* Benchmark Bks.) Marshall Cavendish Corp.
Hess, Debra. On Trial in Rome: Cicero Versus Caesr. 2007. (Read on! Special Edition: Level AA Ser.). (Illus.). 23p. pap. 18.51 *(978-1-4190-3517-3(7))* Steck-Vaughn.
Hunter, Nick. Julius Caesar, 1 vol. Edwards, Mat, illus. 2013. (Hero Journals). (ENG.). 48p. (gr. 4-6). pap. 9.95 *(978-1-4109-5363-6(7),* NA-r) Heinemann-Raintree.
—Julius Caesar, 1 vol. 2013. (Hero Journals). (ENG., Illus.). 48p. (gr. 4-6). 33.32 *(978-1-4109-5356-8(4),* NA-r) Heinemann-Raintree.
Jeffrey, Gary. Julius Caesar: The Life of a Roman General. 2009. (Graphic Nonfiction Biographies Ser.). (ENG.). 48p. (YA). (gr. 4-5). 58.50 *(978-1-61513-020-7(9),* Rosen Reference) Rosen Publishing Group, Inc., The.
Jeffrey, Gary & Petty, Kate. Julius Caesar: The Life of a Roman General. 2005. (Graphic Nonfiction Biographies Ser.). (ENG., Illus.). 48p. (J). (gr. 4-7). lib. bdg. 31.95 *(978-1-4042-0239-9(0),* 1241097) Rosen Publishing Group, Inc., The.

C
D

Kent, Zachary. Julius Caesar: Ruler of the Roman World. 2006. (Rulers of the Ancient World Ser.). (Illus.). 160p. (YA). (gr. 6-9). lib. bdg. 29.27 (978-0-7660-2563-9(2)) Enslow Pubs., Inc.

Leoni, Cristiana. In Caesar's Rome with Cicero. Cappon, Manuela, illus. 2008. (Come See My City Ser.). 48p. (gr. 4-8). lib. bdg. 28.50 (978-0-7614-4328-5(2), Benchmark Bks.) Marshall Cavendish Corp.

Mattern, Joanne. Julius Caesar. 2017. (Junior Biography From Ancient Civilization Ser.). (gr. 4-6). 29.95 (978-1-68020-024-9(0)) Mitchell Lane Pubs., Inc.

Medina, Nico. Who Was Julius Caesar? Foley, Tim, illus. 2014. (Who Was? Ser.). (ENG.). 112p. (J). (gr. 3-7). pap. 5.99 (978-0-448-48083-1(2), Grosset & Dunlap) Penguin Young Readers Group.

—Who Was Julius Caesar? 2014. (Who Was... ? Ser.). lib. bdg. 16.00 (978-0-606-36173-6(1)) Turtleback Bks.

Rinaldo, Denise. Julius Caesar: Dictator for Life. (Wicked History Ser.). (ENG.). 128p. (J). 2010. (gr. 6-12). pap. 5.95 (978-0-531-22822-7(3), Watts, Franklin) 2009. (gr. 5-9). 31.00 (978-0-531-21276-9(9)) Scholastic Library Publishing.

Whiting, Jim. The Life & Times of Julius Caesar. 2005. (Biography from Ancient Civilizations Ser.). (Illus.). 48p. (J). (gr. -1-7). lib. bdg. 29.95 (978-1-58415-337-5(7)) Mitchell Lane Pubs., Inc.

CAESAR, JULIUS—DRAMA

Shakespeare, William. Henry V. 2008. (Easy Reading Shakespeare Ser.). (ENG., Illus.). 72p. pap., act. bk. ed. 10.95 (978-1-55576-336-7(7), EDSC502B) EDCON Publishing Group.

CAFETERIAS

see Restaurants

CAILLOU (FICTITIOUS CHARACTER)—FICTION

Brignaud, Pierre, illus. Baby Caillou Looks Around: Animals (A Toddler's Search & Find Book) 2014. (Baby Caillou Ser.). (ENG.). 10p. (J). bds. 6.99 (978-2-89718-150-5(8)) Caillouet, Gerry.

—Caillou - My First Dictionary. rev. ed. 2007. (My First Dictionary Ser.). (ENG.). 16p. (J). (gr. -1-k). bds. 12.95 (978-2-89450-627-1(9)) Caillouet, Gerry.

—Caillou - My Little Library. 2017. (ENG.). 72p. (J). (gr. -1-k). 9.99 (978-2-89718-359-2(4)) Caillouet, Gerry.

—Caillou: Jobs People Do. 2011. (My First Dictionary Ser.). (ENG.). 16p. (J). (gr. -1-k). bds. 12.95 (978-2-89450-831-2(X)) Caillouet, Gerry.

Brignaud, Pierre & Sévigny, Eric, illus. Caillou - Learning for Fun - Ages 3-4. 2013. (Coloring & Activity Book Ser.). (ENG.). 64p. (J). (gr. -1-k). 6.99 (978-2-89718-049-2(8)) Caillouet, Gerry.

—Caillou - Learning for Fun!, Ages 4-5. 2013. (Coloring & Activity Book Ser.). (ENG.). 64p. (J). (gr. -1-k). 6.99 (978-2-89718-050-8(1)) Caillouet, Gerry.

Caillou. 2003. 32p. pap., wbk. ed. 14.95 incl. cd-rom (978-1-57791-028-2(1)); 32p. pap., wbk. ed. 14.95 incl. cd-rom (978-1-57791-015-2(X)); 32p. pap., wbk. ed. 14.95 incl. cd-rom (978-1-57791-014-5(1)); 32p. pap., wbk. ed. 14.95 incl. cd-rom (978-1-57791-013-8(3)); 32p. pap., wbk. ed. 14.95 incl. cd-rom (978-1-57791-012-1(5)); cd-rom 19.95 (978-1-57791-019-0(2)) Brighter Minds Children's Publishing.

Chouette Publishing Staff. Caillou: Storybook Treasury. Sévigny, Eric, illus. 2014. (ENG.). 240p. (J). (gr. -1-k). 15.99 (978-2-89718-149-9(4)) Caillouet, Gerry.

Paradis, Anne. Baby Caillou Looks Around - The Seasons. 2014. (Baby Caillou Ser.). (ENG., Illus.). 10p. (J). bds. 6.99 (978-2-89718-154-3(0)) Caillouet, Gerry.

—Caillou - The Best Day Ever! Sévigny, Eric, illus. 2013. (Caillou (Board Books) Ser.). (ENG.). 24p. (J). (gr. -1-1). bds. 9.99 (978-2-89718-097-3(8)) Caillouet, Gerry.

—Caillou, Fun All Day! Brignaud, Pierre & Sevigny, Eric, illus. 2015. (ENG.). 10p. (J). (gr. -1 — 1). bds. 16.99 (978-2-89718-197-0(4)) Caillouet, Gerry.

—Caillou, My House: Includes 4 Chunky Board Books. Brignaud, Pierre, illus. 2015. (ENG.). 40p. (J). (gr. -1-k). 16.99 (978-2-89718-224-3(5)) Caillouet, Gerry.

—Caillou: the Little Christmas Artist. Sévigny, Eric, illus. 2013. (Coloring & Activity Book Ser.). (ENG.). 64p. (J). (gr. -1-1). 8.99 (978-2-89718-065-2(X)) Caillouet, Gerry.

Pierre Brignaud, Pierre, illus. Baby Caillou: My Farm Friends: A Finger Fun Book. 2015. (Baby Caillou Ser.). (ENG.). 16p. (J). (— 1). bds. 6.99 (978-2-89718-177-2(X)) Caillouet, Gerry.

Rudel-Tessier, Melanie. Caillou: Happy Easter! Brignaud, Pierre, illus. 2012. (Confetti Ser.). (ENG.). 24p. (J). (gr. -1-1). pap. 4.99 (978-2-89450-947-0(2)) Caillouet, Gerry.

Sanschagrin, Joceline. Caillou at the Doctor. Brignaud, Pierre, illus. 3rd ed. 2013. (Step by Step Ser.). (ENG.). 24p. (J). (gr. -1-k). bds. 5.99 (978-2-89718-058-4(7)) Caillouet, Gerry.

—Caillou: It's Mine! Brignaud, Pierre, illus. 3rd ed. 2013. (Step by Step Ser.). (ENG.). 24p. (J). (gr. -1-k). bds. 5.99 (978-2-89718-059-1(5)) Caillouet, Gerry.

Sévigny, Eric, illus. Caillou: Watches Rosie. rev. ed. 2008. (Playtime Ser.). (ENG.). 24p. (J). (gr. -1-1). pap. 4.95 (978-2-89450-635-6(X)) Caillouet, Gerry.

—Caillou Around Town. 2nd ed. 2013. (Coloring & Activity Book Ser.). (ENG.). 16p. (J). (gr. -1-1). bds. 9.99 (978-2-89718-045-4(5)) Caillouet, Gerry.

—Caillou, Search & Count: Fun Adventures! 2013. (Coloring & Activity Book Ser.). (ENG.). 16p. (J). (gr. -1-1). bds. 9.99 (978-2-89718-034-8(X)) Caillouet, Gerry.

CAKE

Besel, Jen. Custom Confections, 1 vol. 2014. (Custom Confections Ser.). (ENG.). 48p. (gr. 4-5). 95.97 (978-1-4914-0862-9(6)) Capstone Press of Coughlan Cos.

Besel, Jennifer M. Baking Bliss! Baked Desserts to Make & Devour, 1 vol. 2014. (Custom Confections Ser.). (ENG., Illus.). 48p. (gr. 4-5). lib. bdg. 31.99 (978-1-4914-0859-9(6)) Capstone Press of Coughlan Cos.

Blake, Susannah. Cookies & Cakes. 2009. (Make & Eat Ser.). (ENG.). 24p. (J). (gr. 3-5). pap. 9.40 (978-1-4358-2933-6(6), PowerKids Pr.) Rosen Publishing Group, Inc., The.

—Cookies & Cakes. Crawford, Andy, photos by. 2009. (Make & Eat Ser.). (Illus.). 24p. (J). (gr. 3-5). 25.25 (978-1-4358-2859-9(3), PowerKids Pr.) Rosen Publishing Group, Inc., The.

Boon, Fiona, ed. The Great Fairy Baking Competition. Ede, Lara, illus. Snaith, Andy, photos by. 2013. (ENG.). 64p. (J). 12.99 (978-1-78235-591-5(X)) Make Believe Ideas GBR. Dist: Nelson, Thomas Inc.

Brown, Sonja. David Lawrence & his Game Day Chocolate Chip Pancakes. 2011. 32p. (gr. -1). pap. 14.39 (978-1-4567-5641-3(9)) AuthorHouse.

Cookbook Resources, ed. Super Simple Cupcake Recipes. 2010. 256p. (J). pap. (978-1-59769-046-1(5)) Cookbook Resources, LLC.

Cutler, Paris. Planet Cake Clever Creations for Kids. 2014. (ENG., Illus.). 192p. pap. 19.95 (978-1-62686-096-4(3), Thunder Bay Pr.) Readerlink Distribution Services, LLC.

Favorite Brand Name Recipes Editors, ed. Party Cakes. 2010. 144p. spiral bd. 10.98 (978-1-60553-255-4(X), PIL Kids) Publications International, Ltd.

Forrest-Pruzan Creative Staff. Make Me a Cake! A Delicious Game of Creative Cake-Making. 2010. (ENG.). 72p. (J). (gr. -1-17). bds. 16.99 (978-0-8118-6936-2(9)) Chronicle Bks. LLC.

Giulieri, Anne. Cooking Pancakes, 1 vol. Meldrum, Ned, photos by. 2012. (Engage Literacy Red Ser.). (ENG., Illus.). 32p. (gr. k-2). pap. 5.99 (978-1-4296-8950-2(1), Engage Literacy) Capstone Press of Coughlan Cos.

Hamlyn. Princess Cupcakes, Kit. 2012. (ENG., Illus.). 64p. (gr. -1-17). pap. 19.99 (978-0-600-62194-2(4), Hamlyn) Octopus Publishing Group GBR. Dist: Hachette Bk. Group.

Kuskowski, Alex. Cool Cake Mix Cupcakes: Fun & Easy Baking Recipes for Kids!, 1 vol. 2014. (Cool Cupcakes & Muffins Ser.). (ENG.). 32p. (gr. 8-12). 28.50 (978-1-62403-299-8(0)) ABDO Publishing Co.

—Cool Filled Cupcakes: Fun & Easy Baking Recipes for Kids!, 1 vol. 2014. (Cool Cupcakes & Muffins Ser.). (ENG.). 32p. (gr. 8-12). 28.50 (978-1-62403-300-1(8)) ABDO Publishing Co.

—Cool Fun Cupcakes: Fun & Easy Baking Recipes for Kids!, 1 vol. 2014. (Cool Cupcakes & Muffins Ser.). (ENG.). 32p. (gr. 8-12). 28.50 (978-1-62403-301-8(6)) ABDO Publishing Co.

Larrew, Brekka Hervey. Cheesecake Cupcakes & Other Cake Recipes. 2008. (Fun Foods for Cool Cooks Ser.). (ENG.). 32p. (gr. 3-4). 27.99 (978-1-4296-2016-1(1), Snap Bks.) Capstone Press of Coughlan Cos.

Maurer, Tracy Nelson. Cupcakes, Cookies, & Cakes. 2009. (Illus.). 32p. (J). lib. bdg. 29.95 (978-1-60694-346-5(4)) Rourke Educational Media.

Meachen Rau, Dana. Cake. 2008. (What's Cooking? Ser.). 24p. (gr. k-1). lib. bdg. 15.95 (978-0-7614-2896-1(8), Benchmark Bks.) Marshall Cavendish Corp.

—Pasteles. 2008. (Qué Preparamos Hoy? Ser.). (SPA.). 24p. (gr. k-1). lib. bdg. 15.95 (978-0-7614-3441-2(0), Benchmark Bks.) Marshall Cavendish Corp.

Miller, Pat. The Hole Story of the Doughnut. Kirsch, Vincent X., illus. 2016. (ENG.). 40p. (J). (gr. 1-4). 17.99 (978-0-544-31961-5(3), HMH Books For Young Readers) Houghton Mifflin Harcourt Publishing Co.

Patchett, Fiona, et al. Children's Book of Baking. Allman, Howard, photos by. 2007. (Children's Cooking Ser.). (ENG., Illus.). 96p. (J). 17.99 (978-0-7945-1438-9(3), Usborne) EDC Publishing.

Price, Pamela S. Cool Cookies & Bars: Easy Recipes for Kids to Bake, 1 vol. 2010. (Cool Baking Ser.). (ENG.). 32p. (gr. 3-6). 28.50 (978-1-60453-775-8(2), Checkerboard Library) ABDO Publishing Co.

Rau, Dana Meachen. Dessert Designer: Creations You Can Make & Eat! 2013. pap. 12.95 (978-1-62065-688-4(4)) Capstone Pr., Inc.

—Dessert Designer: Creations You Can Make & Eat!, 1 vol. 2013. (Craft It Yourself Ser.). (ENG.). 112p. (gr. 3-4). pap. 12.95 (978-1-62370-006-5(X)) Capstone Young Readers of Coughlan Cos.

—Piece of Cake! Decorating Awesome Cakes, 1 vol. 2012. (Dessert Designer Ser.). (ENG., Illus.). 32p. (gr. 3-4). lib. bdg. 27.99 (978-1-4296-8618-1(9), Snap Bks.) Capstone Press of Coughlan Cos.

—Smart Cookie: Designing Creative Cookies, 1 vol. 2012. (Dessert Designer Ser.). (ENG., Illus.). 32p. (gr. 3-4). lib. bdg. 27.99 (978-1-4296-8619-8(7), Snap Bks.) Capstone Press of Coughlan Cos.

—What's up, Cupcake? Creating Amazing Cupcakes, 1 vol. 2012. (Dessert Designer Ser.). (ENG., Illus.). 32p. (gr. 3-4). lib. bdg. 27.99 (978-1-4296-8617-4(0), Snap Bks.) Capstone Press of Coughlan Cos.

Schuette, Sarah L. Birthday Cakes, 1 vol. 2010. (Happy Birthday! Ser.). (ENG.). 24p. (gr. k-1). lib. bdg. 26.65 (978-1-4296-3998-9(9), Pebble Plus) Capstone Press of Coughlan Cos.

Shaw-Russell, Susan & Activity Books Staff. Build Your Own Cupcake Sticker Activity Book. 2011. (Dover Little Activity Books Stickers Ser.). (ENG.). 4p. (J). (gr. k-3). 1.99 (978-0-486-48243-9(X)) Dover Pubns., Inc.

Suen, Anastasia. How to Bake a Cake. 2015. (ENG.). 24p. (gr. k-3). 28.50 (978-1-63430-357-6(1)) Rourke Educational Media.

Tuminelly, Nancy. Cool Cake & Cupcake Food Art: Easy Recipes That Make Food Fun to Eat!, 1 vol. 2011. (Cool Food Art Ser.). (ENG.). 32p. (gr. 3-6). 28.50 (978-1-61613-362-7(7), Checkerboard Library) ABDO Publishing Co.

Turnbull, Stephaniel & Turnbull, Stephanie. Cool Stuff to Bake. 2014. (Cool Stuff Ser.). 32p. (gr. 2-5). 31.35 (978-1-62588-186-1(X)) Black Rabbit Bks.

Walton, Ruth. Let's Bake a Cake. 2013. (Let's Find Out Ser.). (Illus.). 32p. (gr. k-5). 28.50 (978-1-59771-386-3(4)) Sea-To-Sea Pubns.

Wheatley, Abigail. Children's Cupcake Kit. 2015. (Children's Cupcake Kit Ser.). (ENG.). 64p. (J). (gr. k-5). 19.99 (978-0-7945-3463-9(5), Usborne) EDC Publishing.

826 Valencia Writing Project Student Staff. A Time to Eat Cake. 2012. (ENG., Illus.). 73p. (J). (gr. k). pap. 12.00 (978-1-934750-27-8(1)) 826 Valencia.

CALAMITIES

see Disasters

CALCULATING MACHINES

see Calculators

CALCULATORS

Here are entered works on present-day calculators as well as on calculators and mechanical computers of pre-1945 vintage. Works on modern electronic computers first developed after 1945 are entered under Computers.

see also Arithmetic; Computers

Arvoy, Marsha & Nardi, Dorianne. Using a Calculator. 2010. (ENG., Illus.). 24p. (J). (978-0-7787-5252-3(6)); pap. (978-0-7787-5299-8(2)) Crabtree Publishing Co.

Bitter. Math Calc Explorer 10-Pk. 2004. (gr. 4-6). suppl. ed. 230.04 (978-0-201-23163-2(8)) Addison-Wesley Educational Pubs., Inc.

Hagler, Gina. ADA Lovelace, 01 vols., 1. 2016. (Tech Pioneers Ser.). (ENG.). 112p. (J). 35.60 (978-1-4994-6282-1(4), Rosen Young Adult) Rosen Publishing Group, Inc., The.

Johnson, Rebecca L. Crunching Numbers. 2007. (Reading Expeditions Ser.). (ENG., Illus.). 24p. (J). pap. 14.95 (978-0-7922-4592-6(X)) CENGAGE Learning.

CALCULUS

Analysis III: Integralrechnung. (Duden Abiturhilfen Ser.). (GER.). 112p. (YA). (gr. 12-13). (978-3-411-70182-7(X)) Bibliographisches Institut & F. A. Brockhaus AG DEU. Dist: International Bk. Import Service, Inc.

Calculus Without Tears Vol. 2: Easy Lessons for Learning Calculus for Students from the 4th Grade up - Newton's Apple. 2005. spiral bd. 19.95 net. (978-0-9764138-1-3(7)) Berkeley Science Bks.

Cohen, Don. Calculus for Young People, 2 vols. 2006. (YA). cd-rom 64.95 (978-0-9779493-1-1(1)) VirTru Powers.

Cohen, Donald. Calculus by & for Young People - Ages 7, Yes 7 & Up (CD-ROM) 2006. cd-rom 17.95 (978-0-9779493-0-4(3)) Don Cohen-The Mathman.

Fannon, Paul, et al. Mathematics Higher Level Calculus for the IB Diploma 2013. (IB Diploma Ser.). (ENG., Illus.). 186p. pap. 18.44 (978-1-107-63289-9(7)) Cambridge Univ. Pr.

Flannery, William Davis. Calculus Without Tears Vol. 1: Easy Lessons for Learning Calculus for Students from the 4th Grade up - Constant Velocity Motion, vols. 4. 2004. (ENG.). 154p. spiral bd. 19.95 net. (978-0-9764138-0-6(9)) Berkeley Science Bks.

McRae, W. David. Calculus Student Activity Book. 2003. (Illus.). stu. ed., per., wbk. ed. 22.00 (978-1-931680-26-4(4), Expert Systems for Teachers) Teaching Point, Inc.

Stewart, Scott. Calculus. 5th ed. 2003. (ENG.). 480p. (C). pap. 37.95 (978-0-534-39331-1(4)) Brooks/Cole.

Waner, Stefan & Costenoble, Steven R. Student Solutions Manual for Applied Calculus. 3rd ed. 2003. (C). pap. 26.95 (978-0-534-41960-8(7)) Brooks/Cole.

CALDECOTT MEDAL

Bankston, John. Randolph J. Caldecott & the Story of the Caldecott Medal. 2003. (Great Achiever Awards Ser.). (Illus.). 48p. (J). (gr. 4-8). lib. bdg. 29.95 (978-1-58415-200-2(1)) Mitchell Lane Pubs., Inc.

CALENDARS

see also Almanacs

Adamson, Tom & Adamson, Heather. How Do You Measure Time?, 1 vol. 2010. (Measure It! Ser.). (ENG.). 32p. (gr. 1-2). lib. bdg. 27.32 (978-1-4296-4459-4(1), Aplus Bks.) Capstone Press of Coughlan Cos.

Bailer, Darice. Measuring Time with a Calendar. Petelinsek, Kathleen, illus. 2014. (Explorer Junior Library: Math Explorer Junior Ser.). (ENG.). 24p. (J). (gr. 1-4). 28.50 (978-1-62431-649-4(2), 203108) Cherry Lake Publishing.

Boswell, Kelly. Timelines, Timelines, Timelines!, 1 vol. 2013. (Displaying Information Ser.). (ENG.). 32p. (gr. 1-2). 27.32 (978-1-4765-0261-8(7)); pap. 8.95 (978-1-4765-3338-4(5)) Capstone Press of Coughlan Cos. (Aplus Bks.).

Brimner, Larry Dane. The Official M&M's(r) Brand History of the Calendar. Pellaton, Karen E., illus. 2004. 32p. (YA). 16.95 (978-1-57091-431-7(1)); pap. 6.95 (978-1-57091-432-4(X)) Charlesbridge Publishing, Inc.

Brode, Robyn & Nations, Susan. April. 2nd rev. ed. 2009. (Months of the Year Ser.). (ENG.). 24p. (J). (gr. -1-3). lib. bdg. 22.00 (978-1-4339-1920-6(6), Weekly Reader Leveled Readers) Stevens, Gareth Publishing LLLP.

—January. 2nd rev. ed. 2009. (Months of the Year Ser.). (ENG.). 24p. (J). (gr. -1-3). pap. 8.15 (978-1-4339-2094-3(8), Weekly Reader Leveled Readers) Stevens, Gareth Publishing LLLP.

Bryce, Frank & MacCall, Terry. How the Days of the Week Got Their Names, 1 vol. 2009. 109p. pap. 19.95 (978-1-61546-639-9(8)) America Star Bks.

Clark, Claire. How Long Is a Year?, 1 vol. 2012. (Calendar Ser.). (ENG., Illus.). 24p. (gr. k-1). lib. bdg. 26.65 (978-1-4296-7594-9(2), Pebble Plus) Capstone Press of Coughlan Cos.

Clark, Claire & Shaskan, Trisha Speed. How Long Is a Month?, 1 vol. 2012. (Calendar Ser.). (ENG.). 24p. (gr. k-1). lib. bdg. 26.65 (978-1-4296-7593-2(4), Pebble Plus) Capstone Press of Coughlan Cos.

Cleary, Brian P. A Second, a Minute, a Week with Days in It: A Book about Time. Gable, Brian, illus. (ENG.). 32p. (gr. k-3). 2015. pap. 6.95 (978-1-4677-2050-2(X)) 2013. lib. bdg. 16.95 (978-0-8225-7883-3(2)) Lerner Publishing Group. (Millbrook Pr.).

Doward, Jan S. Sweeeet! God's Awesome Plan for You. 2010. (J). pap. 15.99 (978-0-8280-2510-2(X)) Review & Herald Publishing Assn.

Esparza, Thomas, Jr., prod. Esther's Playhouse, Disk E. 2004. (Illus.). (J). cd-rom (978-1-879817-46-3(2), Children) Star Light Pr.

Flood, Nancy Bo. The Navajo Year, Walk Through Many Seasons: Activities for Learning & Exploring. Ruffenach, Jessie E., ed. Whitethorne, Billy & Whitethorne, Bahe, Jr., illus. 2006. (ENG.). 48p. (J). (gr. 4-7). pap. 7.95 (978-1-893354-98-2(9)) Salina Bookshelf Inc.

Formichelli, Linda & Martin, W. Eric. Timekeeping: Explore the History & Science of Telling Time with 15 Projects. Carbaugh, Sam, illus. 2012. (Build It Yourself Ser.). (ENG.). 128p. (J). (gr. 3-7). 21.95 (978-1-61930-136-8(9)) Open City Bks.

Formichelli, Linda, et al. Timekeeping: Explore the History & Science of Telling Time with 15 Projects. Carbaugh, Samuel, illus. 2012. (Build It Yourself Ser.). (ENG.). 128p. (J). (gr. 3-7). pap. 15.95 (978-1-61930-033-0(8)) Open City Bks.

Gregoire, Maryellen. Fun Days! 2011. (Wonder Readers Emergent Level Ser.). (ENG.). 8p. (gr. -1-1). pap. 35.94 (978-1-4296-8214-5(0), Wonder Readers) Capstone Press of Coughlan Cos.

Grosshauser, Peter, illus. My Week. 2010. (My World Ser.). (ENG.). 24p. (J). (gr. -1-1). lib. bdg. 22.60 (978-1-60754-951-2(4)) Windmill Bks.

Hibbert, Clare. My Busy Week. 2011. (Busy Times Ser.). (ENG., Illus.). 24p. (J). 19.99 (978-0-237-54264-1(1)) Evans Brothers, Ltd. GBR. Dist: Independent Pubs. Group.

Hill, Nancy S. The One Year Did You Know Devotions 2. 2009. (ENG., Illus.). 416p. (J). pap. 13.99 (978-1-4143-2014-4(0), Tyndale Kids) Tyndale Hse. Pubs.

Kesselring, Mari. April, 1 vol. Dumm, Brian Caleb, illus. 2009. (Months of the Year Ser.). (ENG.). 24p. (gr. -1-2). 27.07 (978-1-60270-631-6(X), Looking Glass Library- Nonfiction) Magic Wagon.

—August, 1 vol. Collier-Morales, Roberta, illus. 2009. (Months of the Year Ser.). (ENG.). 24p. (gr. -1-2). 27.07 (978-1-60270-635-4(2), Looking Glass Library- Nonfiction) Magic Wagon.

—December, 1 vol. Billin-Frye, Paige, illus. 2009. (Months of the Year Ser.). (ENG.). 24p. (gr. -1-2). 27.07 (978-1-60270-639-2(5), Looking Glass Library- Nonfiction) Magic Wagon.

—February, 1 vol. Billin-Frye, Paige, illus. 2009. (Months of the Year Ser.). (ENG.). 24p. (gr. -1-2). 27.07 (978-1-60270-629-3(8), Looking Glass Library- Nonfiction) Magic Wagon.

—January, 1 vol. Billin-Frye, Paige, illus. 2009. (Months of the Year Ser.). (ENG.). 24p. (gr. -1-2). 27.07 (978-1-60270-628-6(X), Looking Glass Library- Nonfiction) Magic Wagon.

—July, 1 vol. Collier-Morales, Roberta, illus. 2009. (Months of the Year Ser.). (ENG.). 24p. (gr. -1-2). 27.07 (978-1-60270-634-7(4), Looking Glass Library- Nonfiction) Magic Wagon.

—June, 1 vol. Collier-Morales, Roberta, illus. 2009. (Months of the Year Ser.). (ENG.). 24p. (gr. -1-2). 27.07 (978-1-60270-633-0(6), Looking Glass Library- Nonfiction) Magic Wagon.

—March, 1 vol. Dumm, Brian Caleb, illus. 2009. (Months of the Year Ser.). (ENG.). 24p. (gr. -1-2). 27.07 (978-1-60270-630-9(1), Looking Glass Library- Nonfiction) Magic Wagon.

—May, 1 vol. Dumm, Brian Caleb, illus. 2009. (Months of the Year Ser.). (ENG.). 24p. (gr. -1-2). 27.07 (978-1-60270-632-3(8), Looking Glass Library- Nonfiction) Magic Wagon.

—November, 1 vol. Rooney, Ronnie, illus. 2009. (Months of the Year Ser.). (ENG.). 24p. (gr. -1-2). 27.07 (978-1-60270-638-5(7), Looking Glass Library- Nonfiction) Magic Wagon.

—October, 1 vol. Rooney, Ronnie, illus. 2009. (Months of the Year Ser.). (ENG.). 24p. (gr. -1-2). 27.07 (978-1-60270-637-8(9), Looking Glass Library- Nonfiction) Magic Wagon.

—September, 1 vol. Rooney, Ronnie, illus. 2009. (Months of the Year Ser.). (ENG.). 24p. (gr. -1-2). 27.07 (978-1-60270-636-1(0), Looking Glass Library- Nonfiction) Magic Wagon.

Kompelien, Tracy. I Know the Days in Many Ways!, 1 vol. 2007. (Math Made Fun Ser.). (ENG., Illus.). 24p. (J). (gr. k-3). lib. bdg. 24.21 (978-1-59928-531-3(2), SandCastle) ABDO Publishing Co.

Kummer, Patricia K. The Calendar. 2005. (Inventions That Shaped the World Ser.). (Illus.). 80p. (J). (gr. 5-8). 17.60 (978-0-7569-6854-0(2)) Perfection Learning Corp.

Macdonald, Fiona. You Wouldn't Want to Live Without Clocks & Calendars! Antram, David, illus. 2015. (You Wouldn't Want to Live Without... Ser.). (ENG.). 32p. (J). lib. bdg. 29.00 (978-0-531-21928-7(3), Watts, Franklin) Scholastic Library Publishing.

Maestro, Betsy. The Story of Clocks & Calendars. Maestro, Giulio, illus. 2004. (ENG.). 48p. (J). (gr. 2-7). pap. 9.99 (978-0-06-058945-5(0)) HarperCollins Pubs.

Marrero, Alba. Diego's Busy Week: Learn the days of the week as you tag along with a boy named Diego. 2009. 20p. pap. 10.99 (978-1-4389-5201-7(5)) AuthorHouse.

Mitten, Luana K. Mi Calendario: Los Meses Del Año/My Calendar: Months of the Year. 2008. (SPA & ENG., Illus.). 24p. (J). 22.79 (978-1-60472-492-9(7)) Rourke Educational Media.

—My Calendar: Days of the Week. 2008. (My Calendar Ser.). (Illus.). 24p. (J). (gr. -1-k). lib. bdg. 22.79 (978-1-60472-409-7(9)) Rourke Educational Media.

Morris, Sheila L. Sweet Baby's Fun Months of the Year. 2013. 16p. pap. 9.99 (978-1-61897-424-2(6), Strategic Bk. Publishing) Strategic Book Publishing & Rights Agency (SBPRA).

Nelson, Robin. A Day. 2005. (First Step Nonfiction Ser.). (Illus.). 24p. (gr. k-2). 17.27 (978-0-8225-0177-0(5)) Lerner Publishing Group.

—A Week. 2005. (First Step Nonfiction Ser.). (Illus.). 24p. (gr. k-2). 17.27 (978-0-8225-0178-7(3)) Lerner Publishing Group.

Randolph, Joanne. All about the Months. (It's about Time Ser.). 24p. 2009. (gr. 1-1). 42.50 (978-1-61513-632-2(0), PowerKids Pr.) 2007. (Illus.). (J). (gr. k-2). lib. bdg. 22.60 (978-1-4042-3769-8(0)) Rosen Publishing Group, Inc., The.

—All about the Months/Los Meses. 2009. (It's about Time/Los libros del tiempo Ser.). (SPA.). 24p. (gr. 1-1). 42.50 (978-1-61513-628-5(2), Editorial Buenas Letras) Rosen Publishing Group, Inc., The.

Scheunemann, Pam. Time to Learn about Weeks & Months, 1 vol. 2008. (Time Ser.). (ENG., Illus.). 24p. (J). (gr. k-3). lib. bdg. 24.21 (978-1-60453-020-9(0)) ABDO Publishing Co.

Shepherd, Jodie. Days of the Week. 2015. (Rookie Toddler(r) Ser.). (ENG.). 12p. (J). bds. 6.95 (978-0-531-20568-6(1)) Scholastic Library Publishing.

Snyder, Jane. Days of the Week: Learning Ordinal Numbers. 2009. (Math for the REAL World Ser.). 12p. (gr. 1-2). pap. 5.90 (978-0-8239-8913-3(5), Rosen Classroom) Rosen Publishing Group, Inc., The.

Sper, Emily. The Kids' Fun Book of Jewish Time. Sper, Emily, illus. 2006. (HEB & ENG., Illus.). 24p. (J). (gr. -1-1). 16.99 (978-1-58023-311-8(2), 1260461, Jewish Lights Publishing) LongHill Partners, Inc.

Steffora, Tracey. Relojes y Calendarios. 2011. (Medir el Tiempo Ser.). (SPA.). 24p. (gr. -1-1). pap. 6.29 *(978-1-4329-5635-6(3),* Bellota) Heinemann-Raintree.

Studio Mouse Staff. Time to Learn!, 4 vols. rev. ed. 2007. (ENG., Illus.). 4x20p. (J). (gr. -1-k). 14.99 *(978-1-59069-564-7(X))* Studio Mouse LLC.

Vogel, Julia. Measuring Time: The Calendar. Marten, Luanne, illus. 2012. (Simple Measurement Ser.). (ENG.). 24p. (J). (gr. -1-2). 27.07 *(978-1-61473-281-5(7),* 204986) Child's World, Inc., The.

Wesley, Milliana, ed. My Week. Grosshauser, Peter, illus. 2010. (My World Ser.). (ENG.). 24p. (J). (gr. -1-1). pap. 8.15 *(978-1-61533-035-5(6))* Windmill Bks.

CALHOUN, JOHN C. (JOHN CALDWELL), 1782-1850

Silate, Jennifer. The Calhoun-Randolph Debate on the Eve of the War of 1812: A Primary Source Investigation. 2004. (Great Historic Debates & Speeches Ser.). (Illus.). 64p. (YA). (gr. 5-9). lib. bdg. 31.95 *(978-1-4042-0150-7(5))* Rosen Publishing Group, Inc., The.

—The Calhoun-Randolph Debate on the Eve of the War Of 1812: A Primary Source Investigation. 2009. (Great Historic Debates & Speeches Ser.). 64p. (gr. 5-8). 58.50 *(978-1-61513-124-2(8))* Rosen Publishing Group, Inc., The.

CALIFORNIA

Bodden, Valerie. California. 2010. (Let's Explore America Ser.). (J). (gr. k-2). 19.95 *(978-1-58341-832-1(6))* Creative Co., The.

Bogue, Gary. Raccoon Next Door: And Other Creatures of the Urban Wilderness. Todd, Chuck, illus. 2003. 196p. pap. 16.95 *(978-1-890771-71-3(6))* Heyday.

Brant, Cherie. Legends of Ventura County. 2003. per. 9.99 *(978-0-9722936-4-8(7),* Legends1) Del Sol Pubns.

Brown, Vinson. The Californian Wildlife Region. 3rd rev. ed. 2003. (Illus.). 302p. (J). pap. 14.95 *(978-0-87961-201-6(0))* Naturegraph Pubs., Inc.

Burgan, Michael & McGeveran, William. California. 2014. (It's My State! (r) Ser.). 80p. (J). (gr. 4-8). lib. bdg. 34.21 *(978-1-62712-629-8(5))* Cavendish Square Publishing.

California: Grades 4-9. (Teaching with Primary Sources Ser.). (J). tchr. ed., ring bd. 32.95 *(978-0-382-40871-7(3))* Cobblestone Publishing Co.

The California Mission Activity Book. 2003. (Missions of California Ser.). (Illus.). 144p. (gr. 4-6). pap. 19.95 *(978-0-404-28506-7(6),* Rosen Classroom) Rosen Publishing Group, Inc., The.

Dennis, Brian, et al. Nubs: The True Story of a Mutt, a Marine & a Miracle. 2009. (ENG., Illus.). 40p. (J). (gr. -1-3). 18.99 *(978-0-316-05318-1(X))* Little, Brown Bks. for Young Readers.

Doeden, Matt. The Winchester Mystery House: A Chilling Interactive Adventure. 2016. (You Choose: Haunted Places Ser.). (ENG., Illus.). 112p. (gr. 3-4). lib. bdg. 31.99 *(978-1-5157-2577-0(4),* You Choose Bks.) Capstone Press of Coughlan Cos.

Domeniconi, David. Golden Numbers: A California Number Book. Carroll, Pam, illus. 2008. (Count Your Way Across the U. S. A. Ser.). (ENG.). 40p. (J). 17.95 *(978-1-58536-173-1(9))* Sleeping Bear Pr.

Downey, Tika. California: The Golden State. (Illus.). 24p. (J). 2010. pap. 8.25 *(978-1-4358-3340-1(6),* 1300524) 2009. lib. bdg. 22.60 *(978-1-4042-8110-3(X),* 1300524) Rosen Publishing Group, Inc., The. (PowerKids Pr.).

Fandel, Jennifer. Golden Gate Bridge. 2006. (Modern Wonders of the World Ser.). (Illus.). 32p. (J). (gr. 4-7). 18.95 *(978-1-58341-437-8(1),* 1262897, Creative Education) Creative Co., The.

Furstinger, Nancy. Los Angeles, 1 vol. 2005. (Cities Set 1 Ser.). (ENG., Illus.). 32p. (gr. k-6). 27.07 *(978-1-59197-861-9(0),* Checkerboard Library) ABDO Publishing Co.

Gamble, Adam. Good Night San Diego. Kelly, Cooper, illus. 2006. (Good Night Our World Ser.). (ENG.). 20p. (J). (gr. k — 1). bds. 9.95 *(978-0-9777979-6-7(1))* Good Night Bks.

Guia del Maestro: Gente y Lugares. 2003. (MacMillan/McGraw-Hill. Estudios Sociales Ser.). (ENG & SPA.). (gr. 1-18). *(978-0-02-149965-6(9))* Macmillan/McGraw-Hill Schl. Div.

Imagineers Staff & Wright, Alex. The Imagineering Field Guide to Disneyland. 2008. (ENG.). 128p. (gr. -1-17). pap., instr.'s gde. ed. 9.99 *(978-1-4231-0975-4(9),* Disney Editions) Disney Pr.

Johnson, Michael & Yenne, Bill. Native Tribes of California & the Southwest. 2004. (Native Tribes of North America Ser.). (Illus.). 64p. (gr. 5-12). lib. bdg. 34.00 *(978-0-8368-5609-5(0),* Gareth Stevens Secondary Library) Stevens, Gareth Publishing LLLP.

Kirchner, Jason. California. 2016. (States Ser.). (ENG., Illus.). 32p. (gr. 3-4). lib. bdg. 27.32 *(978-1-5157-0391-4(6))* Next Page Pr., The.

Koontx, Jayne. California Central Coast Coloring Book. 2005. (J). 8.95 *(978-1-930401-35-8(3))* Central Coast Bks./Pr.

La Bella, Laura. California: Past & Present. 2009. (J). 70.50 *(978-1-4358-5579-3(5));* (J). pap. 11.75 *(978-1-4358-5578-6(7));* (ENG., Illus.). 48p. (YA). lib. bdg. 29.25 *(978-1-4358-5290-7(7))* Rosen Publishing Group, Inc., The. (Rosen Reference).

Labastida, Roberta. My Ancestor's Village. 2003. (Illus.). 32p. (J). 9.95 *(978-0-932653-61-1(8))* Sunbelt Pubns., Inc.

Lindeen, Mary. Griz Finds Gold: A Story about California, 1 vol. 2008. (Fact & Fable: State Stories Ser.). (ENG., Illus.). 24p. (J). (gr. -1-2). 25.65 *(978-1-60453-183-1(5))* ABDO Publishing Co.

Marsh, Carole. The Big California Reproducible Activity Book. 2004. (Carole Marsh California Bks.). (Illus.). 96p. (J). (gr. 2-6). pap. 9.95 *(978-0-7933-9457-9(0))* Gallopade International.

—California Current Events Projects: 30 Cool, Activities, Crafts, Experiments & More for Kids to Do to Learn about Your State! 2003. (California Experience Ser.). 32p. (gr. k-8). pap. 5.95 *(978-0-635-02024-6(6),* Marsh, Carole Bks.) Gallopade International.

—California Geography Projects: 30 Cool, Activities, Crafts, Experiments & More for Kids to Do to Learn about Your State! 2003. (California Experience Ser.). 32p. (gr. k-5). pap. 5.95 *(978-0-635-01824-3(1),* Marsh, Carole Bks.) Gallopade International.

—California Government Projects: 30 Cool, Activities, Crafts, Experiments & More for Kids to Do to Learn about Your State! 2003. (California Experience Ser.). 32p. (gr. k-5). pap. 5.95 *(978-0-635-01924-0(8),* Marsh, Carole Bks.) Gallopade International.

—California People Projects: 30 Cool, Activities, Crafts, Experiments & More for Kids to Do to Learn about Your State! 2003. (California Experience Ser.). 32p. (gr. k-5). pap. 5.95 *(978-0-635-01974-5(4),* Marsh, Carole Bks.) Gallopade International.

—California Symbols & Facts Projects: 30 Cool, Activities, Crafts, Experiments & More for Kids to Do to Learn about Your State! 2003. (California Experience Ser.). 32p. (gr. k-5). pap. 5.95 *(978-0-635-01873-1(X),* Marsh, Carole Bks.) Gallopade International.

Martin, Michael & Ingram, Scott. California. 2003. (World Almanac Biblioteca de los Estados). (SPA., Illus.). 48p. (gr. 4-9). pap. 14.05 *(978-0-8368-5549-4(3),* Gareth Stevens Learning Library) Stevens, Gareth Publishing LLLP.

McNeil, Niki, et al. HOCPP 1084 California. 2006. spiral bd. 24.00 *(978-1-60308-084-2(8))* In the Hands of a Child.

—HOCPP 1090 Native Americans of California. 2006. spiral bd. 19.50 *(978-1-60308-090-3(2))* In the Hands of a Child.

—HOCPP 1098 Disneyland. 2006. spiral bd. 16.00 *(978-1-60308-098-9(8))* In the Hands of a Child.

Obregon, Jose Maria. California. 2005. (Bilingual Library of the United States of America Ser.: Set 1). (ENG & SPA., Illus.). 32p. (J). (gr. 3-6). lib. bdg. 25.25 *(978-1-4042-3069-9(6))* Rosen Publishing Group, Inc., The.

Obregón, José María. California. 2009. (Bilingual Library of the United States of America Ser.). 32p. (gr. 2-2). 47.90 *(978-1-60853-345-9(X),* Editorial Buenas Letras) Rosen Publishing Group, Inc., The.

O'Dell, Scott & Berg, Rea. The Cruise of the Arctic Star: A Voyage from San Diego to the Columbia River. 2008. (Illus.). xiv, 206p. *(978-1-893103-25-2(0))* Beautiful Feet Bks.

O'Donnell, Kerri. The California Gold Rush: Multiplying & Dividing Using Three- & Four-Digit Numbers. 2009. (PowerMath: Proficiency Plus Ser.). 32p. (gr. 4-5). 47.90 *(978-1-60851-419-9(6),* PowerKids Pr.) Rosen Publishing Group, Inc., The.

Orr, Tamra & Orr, Tamra B. California. 2005. (Portraits of the States Ser.). (Illus.). 32p. (gr. 2-6). pap. 10.50 *(978-0-8368-4640-9(0),* Gareth Stevens Learning Library) Stevens, Gareth Publishing LLLP.

Orr, Tamra B. California. 144p. (J). 2014. (America the Beautiful Ser.: 3). (ENG.). lib. bdg. 40.00 *(978-0-531-24877-5(1))* 2011. (America the Beautiful, Third Ser.). pap. 12.95 *(978-0-531-22924-8(6),* Children's Pr.) Scholastic Library Publishing.

—California. 2005. (Portraits of the States Ser.). (Illus.). 32p. (gr. 2-6). lib. bdg. 26.00 *(978-0-8368-4621-8(4),* Gareth Stevens Learning Library) Stevens, Gareth Publishing LLLP.

Pearce, Claudia & Worley, Karen E. San Diego Zoo. Bohn, Ken & Garrison, Ron, illus. Bohn, Ken & Garrison, Ron, photos by. 2003. (Great Zoos of the United States Ser.). 24p. (J). lib. bdg. 22.60 *(978-0-8239-6321-8(7),* PowerKids Pr.) Rosen Publishing Group, Inc., The.

Pelta, Kathy. California. 2012. (J). lib. bdg. 25.26 *(978-0-7613-4523-7(X),* Lerner Pubns.) Lerner Publishing Group.

Peterson, Sheryl. California. 2008. (This Land Called America Ser.). 32p. (YA). (gr. 3-6). lib. bdg. 22.95 *(978-1-58341-630-3(7))* Creative Co., The.

Puck. 123 California. Somers, Kevin, illus. 2008. (Cool Counting Bks.). (ENG.). 22p. (J). (gr. k — 1). bds. 7.95 *(978-0-9796213-3-8(X))* Duo Pr. LLC.

Pulte, Therese Marie. Laguna Beach: A Visual Souvenir. 2004. (Illus.). 80p. (YA). lib. bdg. *(978-0-9746557-0-3(8),* Destination Pubs.) Pulte, Therese Marie.

Quasha, Jennifer. How to Draw California's Sights & Symbols. 2009. (Kid's Guide to Drawing America Ser.). 32p. (gr. k-k). 50.50 *(978-1-61511-047-6(X),* PowerKids Pr.) Rosen Publishing Group, Inc., The.

Riggs, Kate. Golden Gate Bridge. 2009. (Now That's Big Ser.). (J). (gr. 1-5). 24.25 *(978-1-58341-704-1(4),* Creative Education) Creative Co., The.

Robison, Greg. Coachella. 2009. (Monster Music Festivals Ser.). 48p. (gr. 5-8). pap. 11.75 *(978-1-4358-5120-7(X),* Rosen Classroom) Rosen Publishing Group, Inc., The.

Savage, Jeff. California: A MyReportLinks. Com Book. 2003. (States Ser.). (Illus.). 48p. (J). (gr. 4-10). lib. bdg. 25.26 *(978-0-7660-5113-3(7),* MyReportLinks.com Bks.) Enslow Pubs., Inc.

Smith, Rich. California, 1 vol. 2009. (United States Ser.). (ENG., Illus.). 48p. (YA). (gr. 2-5). 27.07 *(978-1-60453-640-9(3))* ABDO Publishing Co.

Steele, Christy. California & the Southwest Join the United States. 2005. (America's Westward Expansion Ser.). (Illus.). 48p. (gr. 5-12). lib. bdg. 31.00 *(978-0-8368-5786-3(0),* Gareth Stevens Secondary Library) Stevens, Gareth Publishing LLLP.

Turner, Rich, photos by. Delta Skies Fine Art Folio 2003. (Illus.). *(978-0-9762410-4-1(8))* Turner, Rich Photographs.

Weintraub, Aileen. Point Pinos Light: The West Coast's Oldest Continuously Active Lighthouse. 2003. (Great Lighthouses of North America Ser.). (Illus.). 24p. (J). 22.60 *(978-0-8239-6173-3(7),* PowerKids Pr.) Rosen Publishing Group, Inc., The.

Williams, Jack S. The Chumash of California. 2009. (Library of Native Americans Ser.). 64p. (gr. 4-4). 58.50 *(978-1-60853-744-0(7),* PowerKids Pr.) Rosen Publishing Group, Inc., The.

—The Luiseno of California. 2009. (Library of Native Americans Ser.). 64p. (gr. 4-4). 58.50 *(978-1-60853-752-5(8),* PowerKids Pr.) Rosen Publishing Group, Inc., The.

Yasuda, Anita. What's Great about California? 2014. (Our Great States Ser.). (Illus.). 32p. (J). (gr. 2-5). lib. bdg. 26.60 *(978-1-4677-3349-6(0),* Lerner Pubns.) Lerner Publishing Group.

Zelver, Patricia. Wonderful Towers of Watts. Lessac, Frané, illus. 2005. (ENG.). 32p. (J). (gr. k-5). pap. 10.95 *(978-1-59078-255-2(0))* Boyds Mills Pr.

CALIFORNIA—BIOGRAPHY

Benge, Janet & Benge, Geoff. Louis Zamperini: Redemption. 2014. (ENG.). 218p. (YA). pap. 9.99 *(978-1-62486-049-2(4))* Emerald Bks.

Cortez, Linda. When I Was Little. Shrum, Edgar, illus. 2009. 44p. pap. 19.99 *(978-1-4389-5934-4(6))* AuthorHouse.

Gasnick, Roy M. & Grycan, Julien. Serra: American Founding Father. 2010. (ENG., Illus.). 35p. pap. 2.95 *(978-0-86716-942-3(7))* Franciscan Media.

Goranson, Christopher D. Danny Harf: Wakeboarding Superstar. 2009. (Extreme Sports Biographies Ser.). 64p. (gr. 3-4). 58.50 *(978-1-61512-461-9(6),* Rosen Reference) Rosen Publishing Group, Inc., The.

Grabowski, John F. Alton Brown. 2012. (J). *(978-1-61900-007-0(5));* pap. *(978-1-61900-008-7(3))* Eldorado Ink.

Grinapol, Corinne. Harvey Milk: Pioneering Gay Politician, 1 vol. 2015. (ENG., Illus.). 112p. (J). 35.60 *(978-1-4777-7899-9(3),* Rosen Young Adult) Rosen Publishing Group, Inc., The.

Kostecki-Shaw, Jenny Sue. Luna & Me: The True Story of a Girl Who Lived in a Tree to Save a Forest. Kostecki-Shaw, Jenny Sue, illus. 2015. (ENG., Illus.). 40p. (J). (gr. k-4). 18.99 *(978-0-8050-9976-8(X),* 9780805099768, Holt, Henry & Co. Bks. For Young Readers) Holt, Henry & Co.

Krinard, Susan. Dark of the Moon. l.t. ed. 2008. 475p. (J). 23.95 *(978-1-4104-0956-0(2))* Thorndike Pr.

Lynetter, Rachel. Julia Butterfly Hill: Saving the Ancient Redwoods. 2007. (Young Heros Ser.). (ENG., Illus.). 48p. (J). (gr. 4-7). lib. bdg. 30.50 *(978-0-7377-3628-1(3),* Kidhaven) Cengage Gale.

Mahaney, Ian F. Danny Harf: Wakeboarding Champion. (Extreme Sports Biographies Ser.). 24p. 2009. (gr. 3-4). 42.50 *(978-1-61512-462-6(4),* PowerKids Pr.) 2005. (Illus.). (YA). (gr. 2-5). 22.60 *(978-1-4042-2743-9(1))* Rosen Publishing Group, Inc., The.

Mattern, Joanne. America's Gold Rush: John Sutter & the Discovery of Gold in California. 2009. (Great Moments in American History Ser.). 32p. (gr. 3-3). 47.90 *(978-1-61513-139-6(6))* Rosen Publishing Group, Inc., The.

McNeese, Tim. The Donner Party: A Doomed Journey. 2009. (Milestones in American History Ser.). (Illus.). 160p. (gr. 6-12). 35.00 *(978-1-60413-025-6(3),* Chelsea Hse.) Facts On File, Inc.

Milkweed Editions Staff. The California Coast: A Literary Field Guide. St. Antoine, Sara, ed. 2005. (Stories from Where We Live Ser.). (ENG., Illus.). 248p. (J). pap. 10.95 *(978-1-57131-653-0(1))* Milkweed Editions.

Nussbaum, Ben. Junipero Serra: A Spanish Missionary. 2017. (Primary Source Readers Ser.). (Illus.). 32p. (gr. 4-4). 9.99 ***(978-1-4258-3235-3(0))*** Teacher Created Materials, Inc.

Olson, Nathan. Levi Strauss & Blue Jeans. Barnett, Charles, III et al, illus. 2006. (Inventions & Discovery Ser.). (ENG.). 32p. (gr. 3-4). pap. 8.10 *(978-0-7368-9646-7(5),* Graphic Library) Capstone Press of Coughlan Cos.

Osial, Heather L. Californians Who Made a Difference. 2017. (Primary Source Readers Ser.). 32p. (gr. 4-4). 9.99 ***(978-1-4258-3247-6(4))*** Teacher Created Materials, Inc.

Perissinotto, Giorgio Sabino Antonio, ed. & tr. from SPA. The California Recollections of Angustias de la Guerra Ord: (Occurrences in Hispanic California) Perissinotto, Giorgio Sabino Antonio, tr. 2004. (ENG & SPA.). xxi, 172p. *(978-0-88382-157-2(5))* Academy of American Franciscan History.

Run of the Mill: A True Life, Napa Valley Adventure. 2004. (YA). lib. bdg. *(978-0-9760276-0-7(7))* Pastime Pubns.

Schraff, Anne E. Jaime Escalante: Inspirational Math Teacher. 2008. (Latino Biography Library). (Illus.). 128p. (J). (gr. k-6). lib. bdg. 33.27 *(978-0-7660-2967-5(0))* Enslow Pubs., Inc.

Sheff, Nic. Tweak: Growing up on Methamphetamines. 2009. (ENG.). (YA). (gr. 9). lib. bdg. 23.60 ***(978-1-61383-809-9(3))*** Perfection Learning Corp.

—Tweak: Growing up on Methamphetamines. (ENG., Illus.). (YA). (gr. 9-18). 2009. 352p. pap. 13.99 *(978-1-4169-7219-8(6))* 2008. 336p. 16.99 *(978-1-4169-1362-7(9))* Simon & Schuster Children's Publishing. (Atheneum Bks. for Young Readers).

—We All Fall Down: Living with Addiction. (ENG.). (YA). (gr. 10-17). 2012. 384p. pap. 10.99 *(978-0-316-08081-1(0))* 2011. 368p. 17.99 *(978-0-316-08082-8(9))* Little, Brown Bks. for Young Readers.

Weber, Terri. Oscar de la Hoya. 2004. (J). pap. *(978-1-932724-31-8(1));* lib. bdg. *(978-1-932724-30-1(3))* Panda Publishing, L.L.C. (Bios for Kids).

Wong, Li Keng. Good Fortune: My Journey to Gold Mountain, 1 vol. 2008. (ENG., Illus.). 144p. (J). (gr. 3-7). pap. 8.95 *(978-1-56145-464-8(8))* Peachtree Pubs.

Zimmerman, Robert. Switchfoot. 2009. (Contemporary Musicians & Their Music Ser.). 48p. (gr. 6-6). 53.00 *(978-1-61511-946-2(9))* Rosen Publishing Group, Inc., The.

CALIFORNIA—FICTION

Abbott, Hailey. The Other Boy. 2008. (ENG.). 272p. (YA). (gr. 9-18). pap. 8.99 *(978-0-06-125383-6(9),* HarperTeen) HarperCollins Pubs.

Acton, Vanessa. Aftershock. 2017. (Day of Disaster Ser.). (ENG.). 112p. (gr. 6-12). (J). 26.65 *(978-1-5124-2777-6(2));* (YA). 12.99 ***(978-1-5124-3502-3(3),*** Darby Creek); (YA). 39.99 ***(978-1-5124-2785-1(3),*** Darby Creek); (YA). 39.99 ***(978-1-5124-3500-9(7),*** Darby Creek) Lerner Publishing Group.

—Skeleton Tower. 2016. (Atlas of Cursed Places Ser.). (ENG.). 104p. (YA). (gr. 6-12). lib. bdg. 26.65 *(978-1-5124-1322-9(4),* Darby Creek) Lerner Publishing Group.

Adkins, Kurt. The Summer of Mucus Mcbain. 2013. 188p. (gr. 4-6). pap. 13.99 *(978-1-4582-1138-5(X),* Abbott Pr.) Author Solutions, Inc.

Aguayo, Sal. The Tiny Detective. 2008. 48p. pap. 16.95 *(978-1-60703-859-7(5))* America Star Bks.

Alderson, Sarah. Losing Lila. 2013. (ENG.). 352p. (J). pap. 10.00 *(978-0-85707-197-2(1),* Simon & Schuster Children's) Simon & Schuster, Ltd. GBR. Dist: Simon & Schuster, Inc.

Alegre, Mari. Destiny. 2011. 174p. 29.99 *(978-1-4568-2040-4(0));* pap. 19.99 *(978-1-4568-2039-8(7))* Xlibris Corp.

Alegria, Malin. Sofi Mendoza's Guide to Getting Lost in Mexico. 2008. (ENG.). 304p. (YA). (gr. 7). pap. 10.99 *(978-0-689-87812-1(5),* Simon & Schuster Bks. For Young Readers) Simon & Schuster Bks. For Young Readers.

Alger, Horatio. Joe's Luck. 2005. 28.95 *(978-1-4218-1455-1(2));* 264p. pap. 13.95 *(978-1-4218-1555-8(9))* 1st World Publishing, Inc. (1st World Library - Literary Society).

—Joe's Luck: Or, Always Wide Awake. 2006. (ENG.). 172p. pap. 19.99 *(978-1-4264-6426-3(6))* 2006. (ENG.). 176p. pap. 19.99 *(978-1-4264-0883-0(8))* 2007. 186p. pap. 21.99 *(978-1-4264-6500-0(9))* 2006. (ENG.). 170p. pap. 21.99 *(978-1-4264-0864-9(1))* Creative Media Partners, LLC.

—Joe's Luck: Or, Always Wide Awake. 2006. pap. *(978-1-4065-0713-3(X))* Dodo Pr.

—Tom Temple's Career. reprint ed. pap. 79.00 *(978-1-4047-3611-5(5))* Classic Textbooks.

Alphin, Elaine Marie. Picture Perfect. 2003. (ENG., Illus.). 256p. (YA). (gr. 5-12). 15.95 *(978-0-8225-0535-8(5))* Lerner Publishing Group.

An, Na. A Step from Heaven. 2016. (ENG., Illus.). 160p. (YA). (gr. 7). 17.99 *(978-1-4814-4235-0(X));* pap. 10.99 *(978-1-4814-4236-7(8))* Simon & Schuster Children's Publishing. (Atheneum/Caitlyn Dlouhy Books).

Appleton, Victor. The Moving Picture Boys on the Coast or Showing up the Perils of the Deep. 2004. reprint ed. pap. 24.95 *(978-1-4179-1612-2(5))* Kessinger Publishing, LLC.

Archer, Natalie J. Willy, 1 vol. 2009. 50p. pap. 16.95 *(978-1-4489-2935-1(0))* America Star Bks.

Arcos, Carrie. Out of Reach. (ENG.). (YA). (gr. 9). 2013. Illus.). 272p. pap. 9.99 *(978-1-4424-4054-8(6))* 2012. 256p. 16.99 *(978-1-4424-4053-1(8))* Simon Pulse. (Simon Pulse).

Ardis, C. The Hill: Oh What A Day Series. 2012. 116p. 23.99 *(978-1-4685-3700-0(8));* pap. 14.95 *(978-1-4685-3701-7(6))* AuthorHouse.

Asher, Jay. What Light. 2016. (ENG.). 272p. (YA). (gr. 7). 18.99 *(978-1-59514-551-2(6),* Razorbill) Penguin Young Readers Group.

—What Light. 2017. lib. bdg. 22.10 ***(978-0-606-40488-4(0))*** Turtleback Bks.

Babcock, Nona Burroughs. Little Wolf's Adventure: A Medicine Dream & Warrior Ghosts. 2008. 212p. 24.95 *(978-0-595-49087-5(5));* pap. 14.95 *(978-0-595-46072-4(0))* iUniverse, Inc.

Baker, Ken. How I Got Skinny, Famous, & Fell Madly in Love. 2014. (ENG.). 272p. (YA). (gr. 2-17). pap. 9.95 *(978-0-7624-5014-5(2),* Running Pr. Kids) Running Pr. Bk. Pubs.

Ball, Jeff. Son Who Returns. 2014. (ENG.). (YA). pap. 9.95 *(978-1-939053-04-6(8),* 7th Generation) Book Publishing Co.

Barnes, Jennifer Lynn. All in ((the Naturals #3)) 2016. (Naturals Ser.). (ENG.). 400p. (YA). (gr. 7-12). pap. 9.99 *(978-1-4847-2367-8(8))* Hyperion Bks. for Children.

Barnett, Mac. It Happened on a Train. Rex, Adam, illus. (Brixton Brothers Ser.: 3). (ENG.). (J). (gr. 3-7). 2012. 304p. pap. 7.99 *(978-1-4169-7820-6(8))* 2011. 288p. 17.99 *(978-1-4169-7819-0(4))* Simon & Schuster Bks. For Young Readers. (Simon & Schuster Bks. For Young Readers).

Barwin, Steven. Desert Slam. 2017. (Orca Soundings Ser.). lib. bdg. 20.80 ***(978-0-606-40453-2(8))*** Turtleback Bks.

Beaty, Janice C. Jarod & the Mystery of the Joshua Trees: A National Park Adventure Series Book. 2015. (Illus.). 108p. (J). pap. *(978-1-63293-037-8(4))* Sunstone Pr.

Beckler, Bruce. The Secrets of the Green Mansion. l.t. ed. 2004. (Illus.). 240p. (J). per. 13.99 *(978-0-9745210-1-5(9))* Myers Publishing Co.

Beckler, Marion. Carrie: A Story of Early San Diego. 2011. 140p. 40.95 *(978-1-258-06804-2(4))* Literary Licensing, LLC.

Benavidez, Max. Historia de Carlito/ Carlito's Story. 2006. 121p. pap. 8.95 *(978-1-60448-004-7(1))* Lectura Bks.

Bennett, Jenn. Alex, Approximately. 2017. (ENG., Illus.). 400p. (YA). (gr. 9). 17.99 *(978-1-4814-7877-9(X),* Simon Pulse) Simon Pulse.

Bennett, Marilyn J. The Poinsettia Adventure. 2010. 60p. pap. 21.99 *(978-1-4490-7108-0(2))* AuthorHouse.

Benson, Linda. Finding Chance. Lane, Nancy, illus. 2006. 112p. (J). *(978-1-59336-696-4(5))* Mondo Publishing.

Birdsall, Bridget. Double Exposure. 2014. (ENG.). 304p. (J). (gr. 6). 16.95 *(978-1-62914-606-5(4),* Sky Pony Pr.) Skyhorse Publishing Co., Inc.

Birney, Betty G. The Princess & the Peabodys. 2007. (ENG.). 256p. (J). (gr. 5-9). 15.99 *(978-0-06-084720-3(4))* HarperCollins Pubs.

Block, F. L. My Miserable Life. Hemingway, Edward, illus. 2016. (ENG.). 192p. (J). 13.99 *(978-0-8050-9628-6(0),* 9780805096286, Holt, Henry & Co. Bks. For Young Readers) Holt, Henry & Co.

Block, Francesca Lia. Teen Spirit. 2014. (ENG.). 240p. (YA). (gr. 9). 17.99 *(978-0-06-200809-1(9),* HarperTeen) HarperCollins Pubs.

Bocks, Eric Stephen. Wing over Wendover. 2012. 86p. pap. 12.95 *(978-1-4685-6179-1(0))* AuthorHouse.

Boone, Sheila. Free As a Butterfly. Knox, Susi Grell, illus. 2003. 32p. (J). (gr. -1-3). pap. 7.95 *(978-1-891577-80-2(8))* Image Pr., Inc.

Bragaw, Jennie M. The Marble Harvest. 2012. 60p. pap. 31.99 *(978-1-4691-8569-9(5))* Xlibris Corp.

Breslin, Theresa. Prisoner in Alcatraz. 2012. (Stoke Books Titles Ser.). (ENG.). 80p. (YA). (gr. 8-12). pap. 6.95 *(978-1-78112-124-5(9));* lib. bdg. 22.60 *(978-1-78112-125-2(7))* Lerner Publishing Group.

Brothers Washburn Staff, contrib. by. Mojave Green: Dimensions in Death. 2014. (Dimensions in Death Ser.: 2). (ENG.). 328p. (YA). (gr. 7). pap. 14.99 *(978-1-939967-85-5(6),* Jolly Fish Pr.) North Star Editions.

Brown, Jeff. Flat Stanley's Worldwide Adventures #12: Escape to California. Pamintuan, Macky, illus. 2014. (Flat Stanley's Worldwide Adventures Ser.: 12). (ENG.). 128p. (J). (gr. 1-5). pap. 4.99 *(978-0-06-218990-5(5))* HarperCollins Pubs.

Brown, Maureen E. Tanker's Adventures in Monterey. Brown, Michael D., illus. 2007. 24p. (J). 13.95 *(978-0-615-16200-3(2))* TankerToys.

Buchanan, Paul & Buchanan, P. The Last Place I Want to Be, 1 vol. 2009. 176p. (J). pap. 7.99 *(978-0-8254-2408-3(9))* Kregel Pubns.

Bulla, Clyde Robert. The Secret Valley. 19.00 *(978-0-8446-6997-7(0))* Smith, Peter Pub., Inc.

Bunting, Eve. The Lambkins. Keegan, Jonathan, illus. 2005. (ENG.). 192p. (J). (gr. 5-18). 15.99 *(978-0-06-059906-5(5),* Cotler, Joanna Books) HarperCollins Pubs.

C
D

—A Sudden Silence. 2007. (ENG., Illus.). 144p. (YA). (gr. 7-12). pap. 7.99 *(978-0-15-205868-5(0))* Houghton Mifflin Harcourt Publishing Co.

Burggraaf, Deborah. Crow No More. Lumsden, Matt, illus. 2011. 28p. (J). pap. 10.95 *(978-0-9845161-8-6(2))* Protective Hands Communications.

Burnett, Frances Hodgson. The Head of the House of Coombe. 2008. 252p. 29.95 *(978-1-60664-769-1(5))*; pap. 15.95 *(978-1-60664-142-2(5))* Aegypan.

Buzbee, Lewis. Steinbeck's Ghost. 2010. (ENG.). 368p. (J). (gr. 5-9). pap. 18.99 *(978-0-312-60211-6(1)*, 9780312602116) Square Fish.

Cable, Ken. Track of the Hunter. 2013. 192p. pap. 10.95 *(978-0-9837873-3-4(6))* Reader Publishing Group.

Cabot, Meg. Shadowland & Ninth Key. 2010. (Mediator Ser.). (ENG.). 544p. (YA). (gr. 8). pap. 9.99 *(978-0-06-204020-6(0)*, HarperTeen) HarperCollins Pubs.

Cantor, Jillian. Searching for Sky. 2014. (ENG.). 288p. (YA). (gr. 7-12). 17.99 *(978-1-61963-351-3(5)*, 9781619633513, Bloomsbury USA Childrens) Bloomsbury Publishing USA.

Carson, Rae. Like a River Glorious. Hendrix, John, illus. (Gold Seer Trilogy Ser.: 2). (YA). (gr. 8). 2017. (ENG.). 432p. pap. 9.99 ***(978-0-06-224295-2(4))*** 2016. 416p. 17.99 *(978-0-06-224294-5(6))* HarperCollins Pubs. (Greenwillow Bks.).

Carson, Rae. Walk on Earth a Stranger. 2015. (Gold Seer Trilogy Ser.: 1). (ENG.). 448p. (YA). (gr. 8). 17.99 *(978-0-06-224291-4(1)*, Greenwillow Bks.) HarperCollins Pubs.

Casey, Grandpa. The Trilogy: Three adventures of the Müsh-Mice. Brennan, Lisa, illus. 2011. 48p. pap. 24.95 *(978-1-4626-2095-1(7))* America Star Bks.

Castan, Mike. Fighting for Dontae. 2012. (ENG.). 144p. (YA). 16.95 *(978-0-8234-2348-4(4))* Holiday Hse., Inc.

Castro-Bran, Rose. The Adventures of Port Herman Lighthouse. 2008. 32p. pap. 14.95 *(978-1-4343-6547-7(6))* AuthorHouse.

Castro, Shirley. The Pelican Family Series — Stelly & the Sticky, Gooey Taffy. Castro, Christopher, illus. 2011. 36p. (J). 15.00 *(978-0-9790307-3-4(0))* Castro, Shirley.

Chaban, Liz. Jules of the World: The California Caper. 2012. 42p. pap. 18.99 *(978-1-105-92248-0(0))* Lulu Pr., Inc.

Chambers, Vickie. In the Silence of the Hills. Taylor, LaVonne, ed. (Illus.). (YA). (gr. 9-12). *(978-0-9627735-1-8(4))* Excellence Enterprises.

Cheaney, J. B. I Don't Know How the Story Ends. 2016. (ENG.). 320p. (J). (gr. 4-7). 18.40 *(978-0-606-39304-1(8))* Turtleback Bks.

Chin, Jason. Redwoods. Chin, Jason, illus. 2009. (ENG., Illus.). 40p. (J). (gr. -1-3). 18.99 *(978-1-59643-430-1(9)*, 9781596434301) Roaring Brook Pr.

Choldenko, Gennifer. Al Capone Does My Homework. 2013. Bk. 3. (ENG.). 224p. (J). (gr. 5). 17.99 *(978-0-8037-3472-2(7)*, Dial Bks) Penguin Publishing Group.

—Al Capone Does My Homework. 2014. (ENG.). 240p. (J). (gr. 5). pap. 7.99 *(978-0-14-242522-0(2)*, Puffin Books) Penguin Young Readers Group.

—Al Capone Does My Homework. 2014. (Tale from Alcatraz (Al Capone) Ser.: 3). lib. bdg. 18.40 *(978-0-606-35714-2(9))* Turtleback Bks.

—Al Capone Does My Shirts. (Tales from Alcatraz Ser.). (ENG., Illus.). (J). (gr. 5-18). 2004. 240p. 17.99 *(978-0-399-23861-1(1)*, G.P. Putnam's Sons Books for Young Readers) 2006. 288p. reprint ed. pap. 7.99 *(978-0-14-240370-9(9)*, Puffin Books) Penguin Young Readers Group.

—Al Capone Does My Shirts. 2006. (Illus.). 317p. (J). (gr. 4-7). per. 10.95 *(978-0-7862-8927-1(9))* Thorndike Pr.

—Al Capone Shines My Shoes. (ENG.). (J). (gr. 5-18). 2011. 304p. 7.99 *(978-0-14-241718-8(1)*, Puffin Books) 2009. 288p. 17.99 *(978-0-8037-3460-9(3)*, Dial Bks) Penguin Young Readers Group.

—Al Capone Shines My Shoes. 2011. (Tale from Alcatraz (Al Capone) Ser.: 2). lib. bdg. 18.40 *(978-0-606-23072-8(6)*, Turtleback) Turtleback Bks.

Christopher, Matt. Catching Waves. 2006. (ENG.). 128p. (J). (gr. 3-7). per. 15.99 *(978-0-316-05848-3(3))* Little, Brown Bks. for Young Readers.

Clark, Brenda. Spiro Goes West: More Adventures of Spiro the Shooting Star. 2008. 57p. pap. 16.95 *(978-1-60474-770-6(6))* America Star Bks.

Colbert, Brandy. Little & Lion. 2017. (ENG.). 336p. (YA). (gr. 9-17). 17.99 ***(978-0-316-34900-0(3))*** Little, Brown Bks. for Young Readers.

Coley, Liz. Pretty Girl-13. 2013. (ENG.). 352p. (YA). (gr. 9). 17.99 *(978-0-06-212737-2(3)*, Tegen, Katherine Bks) HarperCollins Pubs.

Conkling, Winifred. Sylvia & Aki. (ENG.). 160p. (J). 2013. (gr. 4-7). 6.99 *(978-1-58246-345-2(X)*, Yearling) 2011. (Illus.). (gr. 3-7). 16.99 *(978-1-58246-337-7(9)*, Tricycle Pr.) Random Hse. Children's Bks.

Corman, Dick. Noah Knows. 2006. 183p. (YA). pap. 12.95 *(978-0-9655749-3-8(8))* Corman Productions.

Cornfield, Lynda Ellis. Rocks for Clean Oceans. 2009. 28p. pap. 13.99 *(978-1-4389-8417-9(0))* AuthorHouse.

Corwin, Susan Simon. The Cryptic Cat. Corwin, Stuart, illus. 2006. 99p. (YA). *(978-0-9790632-0-6(5))* Lucky Duck Designs.

Crabtree, Julie. Discovering Pig Magic. 2008. (ENG.). 144p. (J). (gr. 2-8). 16.95 *(978-1-57131-683-7(3))*; pap. 6.95 *(978-1-57131-684-4(1))* Milkweed Editions.

Crum, Sally. Race to the River: The Ancient Journey Continues. 2009. (YA). pap. 12.95 *(978-1-932738-72-8(X))* Western Reflections Publishing Co.

Culbertson, Kim. Catch a Falling Star. 2014. (ENG.). 304p. (J). (gr. 7). 17.99 *(978-0-545-62704-7(4)*, Scholastic Pr.) Scholastic, Inc.

—The Possibility of Now. 2016. (Point Ser.). (ENG.). 304p. (J). (gr. 7). 17.99 *(978-0-545-73146-1(1))* Scholastic, Inc.

Currier, Katrina Saltonstall. Kai's Journey to Gold Mountain: An Angel Island Story. 2004. 40p. 16.95 *(978-0-9667352-7-7(7))*; (Illus.). 44p. (J). pap. 10.95 *(978-0-9667352-4-6(2))* Angel Island Assoc.

Darke, J. A. Attack of the Mud Creatures. Evergreen, Nelson, illus. 2015. (Spine Shivers Ser.). (ENG.). 128p. (gr. 3-4). lib. bdg. 26.65 *(978-1-4965-0220-9(5))* Stone Arch Bks.

Daswani, Kavita. Lovetorn. 2012. (ENG.). 256p. (YA). (gr. 8). 17.99 *(978-0-06-167311-5(0)*, HarperTeen) HarperCollins Pubs.

De la Peña, Matt. I Will Save You. 2011. (ENG.). 320p. (YA). (gr. 9). pap. 9.99 *(978-0-385-73828-6(5)*, Ember) Random Hse. Children's Bks.

—Mexican WhiteBoy. 2010. (ENG.). 256p. (YA). (gr. 9). pap. 9.99 *(978-0-440-23938-3(9)*, Ember) Random Hse. Children's Bks.

—Mexican WhiteBoy. 2010. lib. bdg. 20.85 *(978-0-606-12316-7(4)*, Turtleback) Turtleback Bks.

—We Were Here. 2010. (ENG.). 368p. (YA). (gr. 9). pap. 9.99 *(978-0-385-73670-1(3)*, Ember) Random Hse. Children's Bks.

Deal, Paul. Lighting Candles. 2003. 122p. (YA). 20.95 *(978-0-595-65804-6(0))*; pap. 10.95 *(978-0-595-28457-3(4))* iUniverse, Inc.

Dean, Zoey. Blonde Ambition. 2004. (A-List Ser.: 3). (ENG.). 240p. (YA). (gr. 10-17). pap. 9.99 *(978-0-316-73474-5(8)*, Poppy) Little, Brown Bks. for Young Readers.

del Toro, Guillermo & Kraus, Daniel. Trollhunters. Murray, Sean, illus. (Trollhunters Ser.). (ENG.). 320p. (YA). (gr. 7-12). 2016. pap. 9.99 ***(978-1-368-01218-8(3)***, 1380291) 2015. 18.99 *(978-1-4231-2598-3(3)*, 1380291) Hyperion Bks. for Children.

Dell'orco, Antonio. The Wolf Lion & Whistle: Two Children's Stories. 2013. 68p. 22.95 *(978-0-9755471-8-2(6))* Divine Mercy Pr.

Deol, Gunleen. Sleepover Disaster. 2010. 60p. pap. 10.49 *(978-1-4520-6559-5(4))* AuthorHouse.

Dickman, Jacqueline Rosett. Rebecca & Mom: Friends Forever, 1 vol. 2010. 116p. pap. 19.95 *(978-1-4489-4088-2(5))* America Star Bks.

Diego, Marene. Hyper Spin, 1 vol. 2010. 190p. pap. 24.95 *(978-1-4489-2490-5(1))* America Star Bks.

Dixon, Franklin W. Running on Fumes. 2005. 150p. (J). lib. bdg. 16.92 *(978-1-4242-0384-0(8))* Fitzgerald Bks.

Doherty, Dave, illus. There Once Was a Place Called P.O.P. 2008. 93p. (J). 61.99 *(978-1-4363-6190-3(7))* Xlibris Corp.

Dolenz, Ami. Harold & Agatha: The Mysterious Jewel. 2013. 176p. *(978-1-4602-0520-4(0))*; pap. *(978-1-4602-0420-7(4))* FriesenPress.

Dubyn, Bj. The Thrilling & Dynamic Adventures of Barbara Ann, Her Kid Brother, Billy, Jr., & Manfred the Magnificent, Their Parrot. 2008. 104p. pap. 15.99 *(978-1-4363-2652-0(4))* Xlibris Corp.

Dugan, David J. The Missing Prince of Distria. 2008. 36p. pap. 24.95 *(978-1-60563-587-3(1))* America Star Bks.

Dumas, Firoozeh. It Ain't So Awful, Falafel. 2017. (ENG.). 384p. (J). (gr. 5-7). pap. 7.99 ***(978-1-328-74096-0(X)***, HMH Books For Young Readers) Houghton Mifflin Harcourt Publishing Co.

Duval, Alex. Bloodlust - Initiation. 2010. (Vampire Beach Ser.: 1). (ENG.). 416p. (YA). (gr. 9). pap. 9.99 *(978-1-4424-0693-3(3)*, Simon Pulse) Simon Pulse.

—Vampire Beach 2 - Ritual - Legacy. 2011. (Vampire Beach Ser.: 2). (ENG.). 448p. (YA). (gr. 9). pap. 9.99 *(978-1-4424-0694-0(1)*, Simon Pulse) Simon Pulse.

Elliott, Eric. Dear Miss Karana. 2016. 117p. (J). pap. *(978-1-59714-323-3(5))* Heyday.

Enos, Deanna. The Wooden Garden of Romano Gabriel, 1 vol. 2008. (ENG.). 36p. 24.95 *(978-1-60563-234-6(1))* America Star Bks.

Everett McNeil. The Cave of Gold: A Tale of California In '49. 2007. (ENG.). 256p. pap. 21.99 *(978-1-4346-3814-4(6))*; 284p. pap. 23.99 *(978-1-4346-3815-1(4))* Creative Media Partners, LLC.

Feldman, Ruth Tenzer. The Ninth Day. 2013. (Blue Thread Saga Ser.). (ENG., Illus.). 288p. (YA). pap. 13.95 *(978-1-932010-65-7(3)*, 9781932010657) Ooligan Pr.

Ferguson, J. M. Bubbles the Little Pig, 1 vol. 2008. (ENG.). 44p. 24.95 *(978-1-60474-229-9(1))* America Star Bks.

Ferguson, Tina. The Day I Disappeared. 2005. 83p. pap. 16.95 *(978-1-4137-9243-0(X))* PublishAmerica, Inc.

Fields, Jan. Tame Tahoe Tessie, 1 vol. Brundage, Scott, illus. 2014. (Monster Hunters Ser.). (ENG.). 80p. (J). (gr. 8-12). 27.07 *(978-1-62402-047-6(X))* Magic Wagon.

Fleischman, Sid. Bandit's Moon. Smith, Jos. A., illus. 2008. (ENG.). 192p. (J). (gr. 3-7). pap. 6.99 *(978-0-06-145096-9(0)*, Greenwillow Bks.) HarperCollins Pubs.

—The Giant Rat of Sumatra. Hendrix, John, illus. 208p. (J). (gr. 5-18). 2005. 15.99 *(978-0-06-074238-6(0))* 2006. (ENG.). reprint ed. pap. 6.99 *(978-0-06-074240-9(2)*, Greenwillow Bks.) HarperCollins Pubs.

Flemmer, Chip. Out of Texas, 1 vol. 2010. 183p. pap. 24.95 *(978-1-4489-2918-4(0))* America Star Bks.

Flor Ada, Alma. El Vuelo de los Colibries. Jacobson, Judith, illus. 32p. (J). (gr. 3-6). pap. 9.95 *(978-1-56492-211-3(1))* Laredo Publishing Co., Inc.

Flor Ada, Alma & Zubizarreta, Gabriel M. Dancing Home. (ENG., (J). (gr. 3-7). 2013. Illus.). 176p. pap. 7.99 *(978-1-4424-8175-6(7))* 2011. 160p. 15.99 *(978-1-4169-0088-7(8))* Simon & Schuster Children's Publishing. (Atheneum Bks. for Young Readers).

—Nacer Bailando (Dancing Home) 2011. (SPA.). 160p. (J). (gr. 3-7). lib. bdg. 16.99 *(978-1-4424-2061-8(8)*, Atheneum Bks. for Young Readers) Simon & Schuster Children's Publishing.

Frazier, Sundee T. Cleo Edison Oliver in Persuasion Power. 2017. (ENG.). 256p. (J). (gr. 3-7). 16.99 *(978-0-545-82239-8(4)*, Levine, Arthur A. Bks.) Scholastic, Inc.

Frederick, Heather Vogel. Home for the Holidays. 2011. (Mother-Daughter Book Club Ser.). (ENG.). 352p. (J). (gr. 4-7). 18.99 *(978-1-4424-0685-8(2)*, Simon & Schuster Bks. For Young Readers) Simon & Schuster Bks. For Young Readers.

Freeman, Martha. The Spy Wore Shades. Date not set. 160p. (YA). (gr. 3-18). pap. 4.99 *(978-0-06-440957-5(0))* HarperCollins Pubs.

French, S. Terrell. Operation Redwood. 2011. (ENG.). 368p. (J). (gr. 3-7). pap. 9.95 *(978-0-8109-9720-2(7)*, Amulet Bks.) Abrams, Inc.

Freymann-Weyr, Garret. French Ducks in Venice. McGuire, Erin, illus. 2011. (ENG.). 56p. (J). (gr. k-4). 16.99 *(978-0-7636-4173-3(1))* Candlewick Pr.

Friesen, Jonathan. Rush. 2010. (ENG.). 320p. (YA). (gr. 7-18). 9.99 *(978-0-14-241258-9(9)*, Speak) Penguin Young Readers Group.

Gamble, Adam. Buenas Noches, California. Kelly, Cooper, illus. 2012. (Buenas Noches Ser.). (SPA & ENG.). 24p. (J). (gr. k — 1). bds. 9.95 *(978-1-60219-070-2(4))* Good Night Bks.

—Good Night California. Kelly, Cooper, illus. 2008. (Good Night Our World Ser.). (ENG.). 26p. (J). (gr. k — 1). bds. 9.95 *(978-1-60219-021-4(6))* Good Night Bks.

Garcia, Cristina. I Wanna Be Your Shoebox. 2009. (ENG.). 208p. (J). (gr. 3-7). pap. 6.99 *(978-1-4169-7904-3(2)*, Simon & Schuster Bks. For Young Readers) Simon & Schuster Bks. For Young Readers.

Gennifer, Choldenko. Al Capone Does My Shirts. 2014. (ENG.). 240p. (J). (gr. 6-12). 12.24 *(978-1-63245-251-1(0))* Lectorum Pubns., Inc.

Gibson, Marley. The Counseling. 2010. (ENG.). 264p. (YA). (gr. 7). pap. 8.99 *(978-0-547-39307-0(5))* Houghton Mifflin Harcourt Publishing Co.

Giles, Katharine. The Princess of Skye, an Archer Adventure. 2013. (ENG.). 280p. (YA). pap. 12.99 *(978-1-939927-79-8(X))* Telemachus Pr., LLC.

Glazer, Maryann. The Adventures of Teddy Bark-Lee: Teddy Comes Home. 2009. 28p. pap. 13.99 *(978-1-4389-4569-9(8))* AuthorHouse.

Gonzalez, Genaro. A So-Called Vacation. 2009. 192p. (YA). (gr. 9-18). pap. 10.95 *(978-1-55885-545-8(9)*, Piñata Books) Arte Publico Pr.

Goo, Maurene. Since You Asked... 2013. (YA). pap. *(978-0-545-44822-2(0))*; (ENG.). 272p. (J). (gr. 7). 17.99 *(978-0-545-44821-5(2))* Scholastic, Inc. (Scholastic Pr.).

Graham, Rosemary. Thou Shalt Not Dump the Skater Dude: And Other Commandments I Have Broken. 2008. (ENG.). 288p. (YA). (gr. 7-18). 8.99 *(978-0-14-240851-3(4)*, Speak) Penguin Young Readers Group.

Gregory, Kristiana. Bronte's Book Club. 2008. (ENG., Illus.). 160p. (J). (gr. 3-7). pap. 7.95 *(978-0-8234-2209-8(7))*; 16.95 *(978-0-8234-2136-7(8))* Holiday Hse., Inc.

Gunn, Robin Jones. Christy Miller Collection, Vol 1, Vol. 1. 2005. (Christy Miller Collection: Bks. 1-3). (ENG., Illus.). 496p. (J). (gr. 7-12). 16.99 *(978-1-59052-584-5(1)*, Multnomah) Doubleday Religious Publishing Group, The.

Gurevich, Margaret. All or Nothing. Hagel, Brooke, illus. 2016. (Chloe by Design Ser.). (ENG.). 96p. (gr. 5-8). lib. bdg. 25.32 *(978-1-4965-3263-3(5))* Stone Arch Bks.

—Back to Basics. Hagel, Brooke, illus. 2016. (Chloe by Design Ser.). (ENG.). 96p. (gr. 5-8). lib. bdg. 25.32 *(978-1-4965-3261-9(9))* Stone Arch Bks.

—Chloe by Design: Measuring Up. Hagel, Brooke, illus. 2016. (Chloe by Design Ser.). (ENG.). 384p. (gr. 4-8). 14.95 *(978-1-62370-727-9(7))* Capstone Young Readers of Coughlan Cos.

—Design Diva, 1 vol. Hagel, Brooke, illus. 2014. (Chloe by Design Ser.). (ENG.). 96p. (gr. 5-8). 25.32 *(978-1-4342-9177-6(4))* Stone Arch Bks.

—The Final Cut. Hagel, Brooke, illus. 2016. (Chloe by Design Ser.). (ENG.). 96p. (gr. 5-8). lib. bdg. 25.32 *(978-1-4965-3264-0(3))* Stone Arch Bks.

—The First Cut, 1 vol. Hagel, Brooke, illus. 2014. (Chloe by Design Ser.). (ENG.). 96p. (gr. 5-8). 25.32 *(978-1-4342-9178-3(2))* Stone Arch Bks.

—Made to Measure. Hagel, Brooke, illus. 2016. (Chloe by Design Ser.). (ENG.). 96p. (gr. 5-8). lib. bdg. 25.32 *(978-1-4965-3262-6(7))* Stone Arch Bks.

Haden, Robbie. Run Girl Run. 2013. 116p. 28.95 *(978-1-4525-6779-2(4))*; pap. 11.99 *(978-1-4525-6777-8(8))* Author Solutions, Inc. (Balboa Pr.).

Hansen, Doug, illus. California, the Magic Island. 2016. 45p. (J). *(978-1-59714-332-5(4))* Heyday.

Hansen, Doug & Aesop. Aesop in California. 2013. (J). 16.95 *(978-1-59714-235-9(2))* Heyday.

Harmon, Michael. Brutal. 2011. (ENG.). 240p. (YA). (gr. 9). pap. 8.99 *(978-0-440-23995-6(8)*, Knopf Bks. for Young Readers) Random Hse. Children's Bks.

Harris, Loretta. The Rise of Death Valley. 2007. 41p. (YA). 1.99 *(978-0-9786681-0-5(3))* Triumphant Living Enterprises, Inc.

Harris, Michael. TEENAGERS II: High School Blowout!!! 2010. 153p. pap. 16.50 *(978-0-557-61163-8(6))* Lulu Pr., Inc.

Harris, Rachel. A Tale of Two Centuries. 2013. (Entangled Teen Ser.). (ENG.). 320p. (YA). (gr. 7-12). pap. 9.99 *(978-1-62266-012-4(9)*, 9781622660124) Entangled Publishing, LLC.

Haskins, Lori. Butterfly Fever. Smath, Jerry, illus. 2004. 31p. (J). lib. bdg. 20.00 *(978-1-4242-1087-9(9))* Fitzgerald Bks.

—Locura Por Las Mariposas (Butterfly Fever) Smath, Jerry, illus. 2009. (Science Solves It! (r) en Espanol Ser.). (SPA.). (gr. 1-3). pap. 33.92 *(978-0-7613-4799-6(2))* Lerner Publishing Group.

Hayes, Sadie. The Social Code. 2013. (Start-Up Ser.: 1). (ENG., Illus.). 320p. (YA). (gr. 7-12). pap. 9.99 *(978-1-250-03565-3(1)*, 9781250035653, St. Martin's Griffin) St. Martin's Pr.

Hazelton, Tanya & Bonanni, Constance. Ian's Golden Passage. 2009. 168p. pap. 9.99 *(978-1-935105-33-6(7))* Avid Readers Publishing Group.

Heimbuch, Carol Jo. Condor Caper. Martin, Fred, illus. 2008. 128p. pap. 11.50 *(978-1-59330-560-4(5))* Aventine Pr.

Henty, George Alfred. Captain Bayley's Heir: A Tale of the California Gold Fields. 2011. 314p. pap. 19.95 *(978-1-61179-115-0(4))* Fireship Pr.

Hernandez, David. No More Us for You. 2009. (YA). 281p. lib. bdg. 17.89 *(978-0-06-117334-9(7))*; (ENG.). 288p. (gr. 9-18). 16.99 *(978-0-06-117333-2(9))* HarperCollins Pubs. (HarperTeen).

—Suckerpunch. 2007. (ENG.). 224p. (YA). (gr. 9-18). 17.99 *(978-0-06-117330-1(4)*, HarperTeen) HarperCollins Pubs.

Hernandez, Natalie. Stowaway to California: Adventures with Father Junipero Serra, 3. 2003. (Illus.). 138p. (J). per. 10.95 *(978-1-885852-29-8(0))* James Stevenson Pub.

Hernandez, Natalie Nelson. Aventuras Con Padre Serra. 2003. (SPA., Illus.). 112p. (J). per. 10.95 *(978-1-885852-30-4(4))* James Stevenson Pub.

—Captain Sutter's Fort: Adventures with John A. Sutter. 2003. (Illus.). 108p. (J). per. 9.95 *(978-1-885852-28-1(2))* James Stevenson Pub.

Herrera, Juan Felipe & Cuevas, Ernesto, illus. Featherless. 2013.Tr. of Desplumado. (SPA & ENG.). 32p. (J). pap. 8.95 *(978-0-89239-303-9(3))* Lee & Low Bks., Inc.

Hill, Susanna Leonard. Airplane Flight! Larrañaga, Ana Martin, illus. 2009. (ENG.). 12p. (J). (gr. -1-k). bds. 7.99 *(978-1-4169-7832-9(1)*, Little Simon) Little Simon.

Hillan, Pamela & Dyan, Penelope. The Discovery in the Old Mine. Weigand, John, photos by. 2013. (Illus.). 116p. pap. 8.95 *(978-1-61477-095-4(6))* Bellissima Publishing, LLC.

Hiti, Samuel, creator. End Times - Tiempos Finales Vol. 1: English / Spanish. 2004. Orig. Title: Bloody Demon Guts. (Illus.). 128p. (YA). per. 9.95 net. *(978-0-9755193-0-1(1))* La Luz Comics.

Hoeffner, Karol Ann. Surf Ed. 2010. (ENG.). 288p. (YA). (gr. 9). pap. 13.99 *(978-1-4424-1418-1(9)*, Simon Pulse) Simon Pulse.

Hogan, Mary. Pretty Face. (ENG.). 224p. (J). 2009. pap. 8.99 *(978-0-06-084113-3(3))* 2008. (gr. 9-18). 16.99 *(978-0-06-084111-9(7))* HarperCollins Pubs. (HarperTeen).

—The Serious Kiss. 2005. (ENG.). 256p. (YA). (gr. 8). pap. 7.99 *(978-0-06-072208-1(8)*, HarperTeen); (gr. 7-18). 16.99 *(978-0-06-072206-7(1))* HarperCollins Pubs.

Holt, Stephen & Lewis, Oscar. We Were There with the California Forty-Niners. Lufkin, Raymond, illus. 2011. 186p. 42.95 *(978-1-258-05988-0(6))* Literary Licensing, LLC.

Hope, Laura Lee. The Bobbsey Twins on Blueberry Island. 2007. (ENG.). 136p. pap. 18.99 *(978-1-4346-3610-2(0))* Creative Media Partners, LLC.

Hopkins, Ellen. Identical. (ENG.). (YA). (gr. 9-18). 2010. 592p. pap. 12.99 *(978-1-4169-5006-6(0))* 2008. 576p. 17.99 *(978-1-4169-5005-9(2))* McElderry, Margaret K. Bks. (McElderry, Margaret K. Bks.).

Humphries, Jessie. Killing Ruby Rose, 0 vols. 2014. (Ruby Rose Ser.: 1). (ENG.). 304p. (YA). (gr. 9-12). pap. 9.99 *(978-1-4778-2006-3(X)*, 9781477820063, Amazon Children's Publishing) Amazon Publishing.

Hunt, Wayne. Zack & the Validators: Good As Gold. 2011. 138p. pap. 19.99 *(978-1-4653-5816-5(1))* Xlibris Corp.

Hurwitz, Laura. Disappear Home. 2015. (ENG.). 256p. (J). (gr. 8-12). 16.99 *(978-0-8075-2468-8(9))* Whitman, Albert & Co.

I DOUBLE Dare You. 2008. (Illus.). 36p. (J). *(978-0-9792686-5-6(6))* Lehman Publishing.

Irwin, Bindi, et al. Surfing with Turtles: Bindi Wildlife Adventures. 2013. (Bindi's Wildlife Adventures Ser.: 8). (ENG.). 112p. (J). (gr. 3-6). pap. 4.99 *(978-1-4022-8094-8(7)*, Sourcebooks Jabberwocky) Sourcebooks, Inc.

Isaacs, Anne. The Ghosts of Luckless Gulch. Santat, Dan, illus. 2008. (ENG.). 48p. (J). (gr. k-3). 18.99 *(978-1-4169-0201-0(5)*, Atheneum Bks. for Young Readers) Simon & Schuster Children's Publishing.

Jacobs, Lily. The Littlest Bunny in California: An Easter Adventure. Dunn, Robert, illus. 2015. (ENG.). 32p. (J). (-3). 9.99 *(978-1-4926-1042-7(9)*, Sourcebooks Jabberwocky) Sourcebooks, Inc.

—The Littlest Bunny in San Diego. Dunn, Robert, illus. 2016. (ENG.). 32p. (J). (-7). 9.99 *(978-1-4926-3348-8(8)*, 9781492633488, Sourcebooks Jabberwocky) Sourcebooks, Inc.

Jacquemain, Patti. Journey of the Great Bear: Through California's Golden Past. Jacquemain, Patti, illus. 2006. (Illus.). (J). *(978-0-929702-10-0(7))* Mission Creek Studios.

James, Eric. A Halloween Scare in California. Le Ray, Marina, illus. 2014. (ENG.). 32p. (J). (-5). 9.99 *(978-1-4926-0570-6(0)*, 9781492605706, Sourcebooks Jabberwocky) Sourcebooks, Inc.

—Santa's Sleigh Is on Its Way to California. Dunn, Robert, illus. 2015. (ENG.). 32p. (J). (-2). 12.99 *(978-1-4926-2747-0(X)*, Sourcebooks Jabberwocky) Sourcebooks, Inc.

James, Helen Foster & Loh, Virginia Shin-Mui. Paper Son: Lee's Journey to America. Ong, Wilson, illus. 2013. (Tales of Young Americans Ser.). (ENG.). 32p. (J). (gr. 1-4). 16.99 *(978-1-58536-833-4(4)*, 202366) Sleeping Bear Pr.

James, Larry W. Captain Petey: An Adventure at Sea. Ramos, Violet M., ed. James, Larry W. & Freshman, Floris R., illus. 2003. 28p. pap. 6.99 *(978-0-9742154-0-2(6))* Cross Pointe Printing.

Jay, Stacey. Juliet Immortal. 2012. (ENG.). 324p. (YA). (gr. 9). pap. 9.99 *(978-0-385-74017-3(4)*, Ember) Random Hse. Children's Bks.

—Romeo Redeemed. 2013. (ENG.). 384p. (YA). (gr. 9). pap. 9.99 *(978-0-385-74019-7(0)*, Ember) Random Hse. Children's Bks.

Jiménez, Francisco. Taking Hold: From Migrant Childhood to Columbia University. 2017. (ENG.). 208p. (YA). (gr. 9). pap. 8.99 ***(978-1-328-74209-4(1)***, HMH Books For Young Readers) Houghton Mifflin Harcourt Publishing Co.

Johnson, Annabel. A Rock Candy Dream. 2009. 140p. 22.49 *(978-1-4389-4233-9(8))*; pap. 11.99 *(978-1-4389-4234-6(6))* AuthorHouse.

Johnston, Tony. Levi Strauss Gets a Bright Idea: A Fairly Fabricated Story of a Pair of Pants. Innerst, Stacy, illus. 2011. (ENG.). 32p. (J). (gr. -1-3). 16.99 *(978-0-15-206145-6(2))* Houghton Mifflin Harcourt Publishing Co.

Jones, Kelly. Unusual Chickens for the Exceptional Poultry Farmer. Kath, Katie, illus. 2015. (ENG.). 224p. (J). (gr. 3-7). 16.99 *(978-0-385-75552-8(X)*, Knopf Bks. for Young Readers) Random Hse. Children's Bks.

Jones, Patrick. Always Faithful. 2015. (ENG.). 112p. (YA). (gr. 6-12). lib. bdg. 27.99 *(978-1-4677-8052-0(9)*, Darby Creek) Lerner Publishing Group.

—Guarding Secrets. 2015. (J). 9.99 *(978-1-4677-7694-3(7))*; (ENG.). 96p. (gr. 6-12). lib. bdg. 27.99 *(978-1-4677-5801-7(9))* Lerner Publishing Group.

Juan, Felipe Herrera. Coralito's Bay: Bahia de Coralito. 2004. (SPA & ENG.). 41p. 14.95 *(978-0-9742810-0-1(X))* Monterey Bay Sanctuary Foundation.

Kadence, Sam. On the Right Track. 2016. (ENG., Illus.). (YA). (gr. 9-12). 24.99 ***(978-1-63533-057-1(2))*** 2013. 184p. pap. 14.99 *(978-1-62798-069-2(5))* Dreamspinner Pr. (Harmony Ink Pr.).

Karr, Kathleen. Exiled: Memoirs of a Camel, 0 vols. 2006. (ENG.). 242p. (gr. 5-8). pap. 9.99 *(978-0-7614-5291-1(5)*, 9780761452911, Amazon Children's Publishing) Amazon Publishing.

Kashyap, Keshni. Tina's Mouth: An Existential Comic Diary. Araki, Mari, illus. 10th ed. 2012. (ENG.). 256p. 18.95

(978-0-618-94519-1(9)) Houghton Mifflin Harcourt Publishing Co.

Keene, Carolyn. California Schemin' 2011. (Nancy Drew (All New) Girl Detective Ser.: 45). (ENG.). 160p. (J). (gr. 3-7). pap. 5.99 (978-1-4424-2295-7(5), Aladdin) Simon & Schuster Children's Publishing.

—Mystery at Malachite Mansion. 2011. (Nancy Drew (All New) Girl Detective Ser.: 46). (ENG.). 144p. (J). (gr. 3-7). pap. 5.99 (978-1-4424-2297-1(1), Aladdin) Simon & Schuster Children's Publishing.

—Stalk, Don't Run. 2012. (Nancy Drew (All New) Girl Detective Ser.: 47). (ENG.). 160p. (J). (gr. 3-7). pap. 5.99 (978-1-4424-2299-5(8), Aladdin) Simon & Schuster Children's Publishing.

Kellerman, Faye & Kellerman, Aliza. Prism. 2009. 272p. (YA). (gr. 7-18). lib. bdg. 17.89 (978-0-06-168722-8(7), HarperTeen) HarperCollins Pubs.

Kennedy, Marlane. Disaster Strikes #1: Earthquake Shock. 2014. (Disaster Strikes Ser.: 1). (ENG.). 128p. (J). (gr. 2-5). pap. 4.99 (978-0-545-53044-6(X), Scholastic Paperbacks) Scholastic, Inc.

Keonna-E'nea. Momzilla, 1 vol. Joane', E'nea, illus. 2009. 18p. pap. 24.95 (978-1-60749-607-6(0)) America Star Bks.

Key, Janet Rhyme. Rosa in Bloom. 2013. 86p. (J). pap. 13.95 (978-1-4817-1956-8(4)) AuthorHouse.

The Kicks Collection: Saving the Team; Sabotage Season; Win or Lose. 2014. (Kicks Ser.). (ENG., Illus.). 544p. (J). (gr. 3-7). pap. 20.99 (978-1-4814-2478-3(5), Simon & Schuster Bks. For Young Readers) Simon & Schuster Bks. For Young Readers.

Kidd, Ronald. The Year of the Bomb. 2009. (ENG.). 208p. (YA). (gr. 7). pap. 5.99 (978-1-4169-9625-5(7)); 16.99 (978-1-4169-5892-5(4)) Simon & Schuster Bks. For Young Readers. (Simon & Schuster Bks. For Young Readers).

—Year of the Bomb. 2009. 208p. 5.99 (978-1-4169-9504-3(8)) Studio Fun International.

Kirby, Jessi. Moonglass. (ENG.). (YA). (gr. 7). 2012. 256p. pap. 9.99 (978-1-4424-1695-6(5)) 2011. 240p. 16.99 (978-1-4424-1694-9(7)) Simon & Schuster Bks. For Young Readers. (Simon & Schuster Bks. For Young Readers).

Kirkpatrick, Teresa. The Adventures of Four Friends on Vacation, 1 vol. 2009. 119p. pap. 19.95 (978-1-60836-927-0(7)) America Star Bks.

Knight, Karsten. Wildefire. 2011. (ENG.). 400p. (YA). (gr. 9-18). 16.99 (978-1-4424-2117-2(7), Simon & Schuster Bks. For Young Readers) Simon & Schuster Bks. For Young Readers.

Konnikova, Svetlana. Grapette, the Runaway Who Rolled Away: A Timeless Tale of Love & Family: A Child Discovering the World. Smishliaev, Anatoli, illus. 2007. (Grapette's Adventures Ser.). (ENG.). 32p. (J). (gr. k-2). 15.95 (978-0-9791758-0-0(1)) Aurora Pubs., Inc.

Korman, Gordon. Son of the Mob (repackage) 2017. (ENG.). 240p. (J). (gr. 5-9). pap. 8.99 **(978-1-4847-9845-4(7))** Hyperion Bks. for Children.

Koss, Amy Goldman. Kailey. Howe, Philip, illus. 2003. (American Girl of Today Ser.). (ENG.). 160p. (J). pap. 6.95 (978-1-58485-591-0(6)) American Girl Publishing, Inc.

Lachtman, Ofelia Dumas. The Trouble with Tessa. 2005. 122p. (J). (gr. 3-7). per. 9.95 (978-1-55885-448-2(7), Piñata Books) Arte Publico Pr.

Lazo, Dorina. Children of the San Joaquin Valley. Hires, Josh, photos by. 2005. (Illus.). 35p. (YA). (gr. 7-12). pap. 15.00 (978-0-938911-28-9(7)) Individualized Education Systems/Poppy Lane Publishing.

Leavitt, Lindsey. Going Vintage. 2013. (ENG.). 320p. (YA). (gr. 7-12). 16.99 (978-1-59990-787-1(9), 9781599907871, Bloomsbury USA Childrens) Bloomsbury Publishing USA.

Lee, Melicent Humason & Lee, Leslie W., illus. Indians of the Oaks. 2nd ed. 2007. xiv, 244p. (J). pap. (978-0-937808-50-4(4)) San Diego Museum of Man.

Lee, Milly. Landed. Choi, Yangsook, illus. 2006. (ENG.). 40p. (J). (gr. 2-6). 17.99 (978-0-374-34314-9(4), 9780374343149, Farrar, Straus & Giroux (BYR)) Farrar, Straus & Giroux.

Lee, Stacey. Outrun the Moon. 2017. lib. bdg. 22.10 **(978-0-606-40097-8(4))** Turtleback Bks.

Lemke, Donald B. Drop In, 1 vol., Vol. 1. Majado, Caio et al, illus. 2011. (Tony Hawk's 900 Revolution Ser.). (ENG.). 128p. (gr. 3-4). pap. 7.19 (978-1-4342-3451-3(7)); lib. bdg. 26.65 (978-1-4342-3214-4(X)) Stone Arch Bks. (Tony Hawk's 900 Revolution).

L'Engle, Madeleine. The Moon by Night, Bk. 2. 2008. (Austin Family Ser.: 2). (ENG.). 288p. (J). (gr. 6-12). pap. 9.99 (978-0-312-37932-2(3), 9780312379322) Square Fish.

Lenhard, Elizabeth. Power of Five. 2004. 158p. (J). lib. bdg. 16.92 (978-1-4242-0795-4(9)) Fitzgerald Bks.

Levitin, Sonia. Boom Town. Smith, Cat Bowman, illus. 2004. 30p. (J). (gr. -1-3). 14.65 (978-0-7569-3185-8(1)) Perfection Learning Corp.

Lin, Grace. The Year of the Rat. 2009. (Pacy Lin Novel Ser.). (ENG.). 208p. (J). (gr. 3-7). pap. 7.00 (978-0-316-03361-9(8)) Little, Brown Bks. for Young Readers.

Liparulo, Robert. House of Dark Shadows, 1 vol. 2009. (Dreamhouse Kings Ser.: 1). (ENG.). 304p. pap. 9.99 (978-1-59554-727-9(4)) Nelson, Thomas Inc.

—Watcher in the Woods, 1 vol. 2009. (Dreamhouse Kings Ser.: 2). (ENG.). 304p. pap. 9.99 (978-1-59554-726-6(2)) Nelson, Thomas Inc.

Longo, Jennifer. Six Feet over It. 2014. (ENG.). 352p. (YA). (gr. 7). 17.99 (978-0-449-81871-8(3), Random Hse. Bks. for Young Readers) Random Hse. Children's Bks.

Look, Lenore. Ruby Lu, Brave & True. Wilsdorf, Anne, illus. 2006. (Ruby Lu Ser.). 105p. (J). (gr. 1-5). 11.65 (978-0-7569-6553-2(5)) Perfection Learning Corp.

Lord, Emery. When We Collided. 2017. (ENG.). 368p. (YA). pap. 9.99 (978-1-68119-203-1(9), 9781681192031, Bloomsbury USA Childrens) Bloomsbury Publishing USA.

Lorsch-Saltzman, Laurie. Josh & George. 2011. 32p. pap. 24.95 (978-1-4560-6552-2(1)) America Star Bks.

Lowell, Susan. I Am Lavina Cumming: A Novel of the American West. 2005. (Historical Fiction for Young Readers Ser.). (ENG., Illus.). 200p. (J). pap. 8.00 (978-1-57131-655-4(8)) Milkweed Editions.

Ludwig, Elisa. Pretty Sly. 2014. (Pretty Crooked Trilogy Ser.: 2). (ENG.). 336p. (YA). (gr. 8). 17.99 (978-0-06-206609-1(9), Tegen, Katherine Bks) HarperCollins Pubs.

Lupita Manana. 3rd ed. (J). pap., stu. ed. (978-0-13-772500-7(0)) Prentice Hall (Schl. Div.).

Lynch, Janet Nichols. Messed Up. 2009. (ENG.). 320p. (YA). (gr. 7-18). 17.95 (978-0-8234-2185-5(6)) Holiday Hse., Inc.

MacAndrew, Richard. A Little Trouble in California Level Starter/Beginner, 1 vol. 2011. (ENG.). 48p. pap. 11.00 (978-84-8323-982-7(5)) Cambridge Univ. Pr.

MacPherson, M. j. The Magic Thread: Overcoming challenges during World War II, a young girl discovers secrets that change adversity into Adventure. 2009. 208p. pap. 17.95 (978-0-595-52812-7(0)) iUniverse, Inc.

Madigan, L. K. The Mermaid's Mirror. 2011. (ENG.). 320p. (YA). (gr. 7). pap. 8.99 (978-0-547-57735-7(4)) Houghton Mifflin Harcourt Publishing Co.

Madison, Mike. No Time to Nap. Peterson, Mary, illus. 2007. (J). (gr. -1-3). (978-1-59714-046-1(5)) Heyday.

Magsamen, Sandra. I Love California (an ABC Adventure) 2015. (ENG.). 40p. (J). (-5). 12.99 (978-1-4926-2837-8(9), Sourcebooks Jabberwocky) Sourcebooks, Inc.

Marciniak, Christine. Lights, Camera, All! 2013. 232p. pap. 13.99 (978-1-61271-214-7(2)) Zumaya Pubns. LLC.

Margolis, Leslie. Everybody Bugs Out. (Annabelle Unleashed Ser.). (ENG.). (YA). (gr. 3-12). 2012. 224p. pap. 6.99 (978-1-59990-828-1(X), 9781599908281) 2011. 208p. 15.99 (978-1-59990-526-6(4), 9781599905266) Bloomsbury Publishing USA. (Bloomsbury USA Childrens).

—Girls Acting Catty. (Annabelle Unleashed Ser.). (ENG.). (YA). (gr. 3-6). 2010. 208p. pap. 6.99 (978-1-59990-520-4(5), 9781599905204) 2009. 192p. 15.99 (978-1-59990-237-1(0), 9781599902371) Bloomsbury Publishing USA. (Bloomsbury USA Childrens).

—One Tough Chick. 2013. (Annabelle Unleashed Ser.). (ENG.). 176p. (YA). (gr. 3-6). 15.99 (978-1-59990-961-5(8), 9781599909615, Bloomsbury USA Childrens) Bloomsbury Publishing USA.

Marlow, Susan K. Andrea Carter & the Dangerous Decision, 1 vol. 2007. (Circle C Adventures Ser.). 144p. (J). pap. 7.99 (978-0-8254-3357-3(6)) Kregel Pubns.

—Andrea Carter & the Family Secret, 1 vol. 2008. (Circle C Adventures Ser.). 144p. (J). pap. 7.99 (978-0-8254-3365-8(7)) Kregel Pubns.

—Andrea Carter & the Price of Truth, 1 vol. 2017. (Circle C Adventures Ser.: 6). 144p. (J). pap. 8.99 **(978-0-8254-4505-7(1))** Kregel Pubns.

—Andrea Carter & the San Francisco Smugglers: A Novel, 1 vol. 2008. (Circle C Adventures Ser.). 144p. (J). pap. 7.99 (978-0-8254-3446-4(7)) Kregel Pubns.

—Andrea Carter's Tales from the Circle C Ranch, 1 vol. 2015. (Illus.). 160p. (J). pap. 7.99 (978-0-8254-4379-4(2)) Kregel Pubns.

—Heartbreak Trail: An Andrea Carter Book, 1 vol. 2015. (Circle C Milestones Ser.: 2). 168p. (YA). pap. 9.99 (978-0-8254-4368-8(7)) Kregel Pubns.

—River of Peril, 1 vol. 2014. (Goldtown Adventures Ser.: 4). 144p. (J). pap. 7.99 (978-0-8254-4297-1(4)) Kregel Pubns.

—Thick As Thieves: An Andrea Carter Book, 1 vol. 2015. (Circle C Milestones Ser.: 1). 176p. (YA). pap. 9.99 (978-0-8254-4367-1(9)) Kregel Pubns.

Marsh, Carole. Mystery on California Mission Trail. 2003. 160p. (J). (gr. 2-8). pap. 7.99 (978-0-635-01656-0(7)) Gallopade International.

—The Mystery on the California Mission Trail. 2009. (Real Kids, Real Places Ser.). (Illus.). 147p. (J). lib. bdg. 18.99 (978-0-635-06994-8(6), Marsh, Carole Mysteries) Gallopade International.

—The Mystery on the California Mission Trail (Hardcover) 2003. 160p. (gr. 2-8). 14.95 (978-0-635-01658-4(3)) Gallopade International.

Martin, Ann M. Dawn on the Coast. (Baby-Sitters Club Ser.: No. 23). 10p. (J). (gr. 3-7). pap. 3.95 (978-0-590-42007-5(0)) Scholastic, Inc.

Martin, Anne E. Flip Flops for Paige. 2007. (Illus.). 36p. (J). per. 14.99 (978-1-59879-243-0(1)) Lifevest Publishing, Inc.

Martinusen-Coloma, Cindy. Ruby Unscripted, 1 vol. 2009. (ENG.). 272p. (YA). (gr. 7-18). pap. 12.99 (978-1-59554-356-1(2)) Nelson, Thomas Inc.

Matas, Carol & Nodelman, Perry. The Curse of the Evening Eye. 2009. (Ghosthunters Ser.). (ENG.). 216p. (J). (gr. 3-7). pap. (978-1-55470-145-2(7)) Me to We.

Mazer, Harry. A Boy No More. 2007. 136p. (gr. 5-9). 16.00 (978-0-7569-8112-9(3)) Perfection Learning Corp.

McBride, Shaylah. All the Stars in the Sky. 2011. 106p. pap. 19.95 (978-1-4489-9678-0(3)) America Star Bks.

McDonald, Abby. Sophomore Switch. 2010. (ENG., Illus.). 304p. (YA). (gr. 9). pap. 8.99 (978-0-7636-4774-2(8)) Candlewick Pr.

McIntosh, Kenneth. Close-Up: Forensic Photography. 2009. (J). pap. 24.95 (978-1-4222-1455-8(9)) Mason Crest.

—Close-Up: Forensic Photography, 5 vols. Sanborn, Casey, illus. 2007. (Crime Scene Club Ser.: Bk. 5). 144p. (YA). (gr. 9-12). lib. bdg. 24.95 (978-1-4222-0251-7(8)) Mason Crest.

McNeal, Laura. Dark Water. 2011. (ENG.). 324p. (YA). (gr. 7). pap. 9.99 (978-0-375-84330-3(2), Ember) Random Hse. Children's Bks.

McVoy, Terra Elan. Drive Me Crazy. 2015. (ENG.). 288p. (J). (gr. 3-7). 16.99 (978-0-06-232243-2(5), Tegen, Katherine Bks) HarperCollins Pubs.

Mead, Richelle. Bloodlines. 2012. (Bloodlines Ser.: 1). (ENG.). 448p. (YA). (gr. 7-18). pap. 10.99 (978-1-59514-473-7(0), Razorbill) Penguin Young Readers Group.

—The Golden Lily. (Bloodlines Ser.: 2). (ENG.). (YA). (gr. 7). 2013. 448p. pap. 10.99 (978-1-59514-602-1(4)) 2012. 432p. 18.99 (978-1-59514-318-1(1)) Penguin Young Readers Group. (Razorbill).

Mellor, Colleen Kelly. Grandpa & the Truck Book One. Irwin, Dana, illus. 2012. 34p. pap. 9.99 (978-0-9856770-0-8(7)) truckerkidzPr.

Menard, Michele R. The Moon Means Business. 2013. 48p. pap. 14.50 (978-0-9887969-2-8(9)) Four Menards, The.

Michael Ray Knauff. Roubidoux: A Story for 12-Year Olds & Those Who Wish They Still Were. 2009. 128p. pap. 10.99 (978-1-4389-5391-5(7)) AuthorHouse.

Michaels, Robbie. A Star Is Born. 2016. (ENG., Illus.). (J). 24.99 **(978-1-63477-930-2(4))** 2012. 200p. pap. 14.99 (978-1-61372-730-0(5)) Dreamspinner Pr. (Harmony Ink Pr.).

Milani, Joan. The Secret Society of the Palos Verdes Lizards. Schartup, Adam, illus. 2013. (ENG.). (J). 14.95 (978-1-62086-346-6(4)) Mascot Bks., Inc.

Mincin, Sabrina. Catching a Shooting Star. 2012. 28p. pap. 12.95 (978-1-4575-0862-2(1)) Dog Ear Publishing, LLC.

Montes, Marisa. A Crazy Mixed-Up Spanglish Day. Cepeda, Joe, illus. 2004. (Get Ready for Gabi Ser.). 120p. (gr. 2-5). 14.00 (978-0-7569-3403-3(6)) Perfection Learning Corp.

—A Crazy Mixed-Up Spanglish Day. Cepeda, Joe, illus. 2003. (Get Ready for Gabi Ser.: 1). 128p. (J). 12.95 (978-0-439-51710-2(9), Scholastic Paperbacks) Scholastic, Inc.

Moodley, Ermila. Path to My African Eyes. 2007. 173p. (J). (gr. 6-13). per. 15.95 (978-1-933491-09-7(4)) Just Us Bks., Inc.

Morgan, Alex. Sabotage Season. (Kicks Ser.). (ENG., Illus.). (J). (gr. 3-7). 2014. 192p. pap. 6.99 (978-1-4424-8576-1(0)) 2013. 176p. 15.99 (978-1-4424-8574-7(4)) Simon & Schuster Bks. For Young Readers. (Simon & Schuster Bks. For Young Readers).

—Shaken Up. 2015. (Kicks Ser.). (ENG., Illus.). 128p. (J). (gr. 3-7). 16.99 (978-1-4814-5100-0(6), Simon & Schuster Bks. For Young Readers) Simon & Schuster Bks. For Young Readers.

—Win or Lose. 2014. (Kicks Ser.). (ENG., Illus.). 160p. (J). (gr. 3-7). 15.99 (978-1-4424-8580-8(9), Simon & Schuster Bks. For Young Readers) Simon & Schuster Bks. For Young Readers.

Murphy, Pat. The Wild Girls. 2008. (ENG.). 304p. (YA). (gr. 7-18). 8.99 (978-0-14-241245-9(7), Speak) Penguin Young Readers Group.

Myers, Bill. The Enemy Closes In, 1 vol. 2009. (Elijah Project Ser.). (ENG.). 128p. (J). (gr. 4-7). pap. 6.99 (978-0-310-71194-0(0)) Zonderkidz.

Myers, Bill & Riordan, James. On the Run, 1 vol. 2009. (Elijah Project Ser.). (ENG.). 128p. (J). (gr. 4-7). pap. 4.99 (978-0-310-71193-3(2)) Zonderkidz.

Myracle, Lauren. Awesome Blossom. 2013. (Flower Power Ser.). (ENG.). 272p. (J). (gr. 4-8). 17.95 (978-1-4197-0405-5(2), Amulet Bks.) Abrams, Inc.

—Awesome Blossom: A Flower Power Book. 2013. (Flower Power Ser.). (ENG.). 272p. (J). (gr. 3-7). pap. 7.95 (978-1-4197-0791-9(4), Amulet Bks.) Abrams, Inc.

—Oopsy Daisy. 2012. (Flower Power Ser.). (ENG.). 368p. (J). (gr. 3-7). pap. 8.95 (978-1-4197-0418-5(4), Amulet Bks.) Abrams, Inc.

Mystery of the Desert Giant: Hardy Boys Mystery Stories. 2011. 190p. (gr. 5-9). 42.95 (978-1-258-10226-5(9)) Literary Licensing, LLC.

Neely, M. W. Saving the Kilda Street Zoo. 2012. 218p. 29.99 (978-1-4771-0179-7(9)); pap. 19.99 (978-1-4771-0178-0(0)) Xlibris Corp.

Neighbors, Jolene. Nobody's Dog. 2010. 107p. pap. 14.95 (978-1-4327-5957-5(4)) Outskirts Pr., Inc.

Nelson, Jandy. I'll Give You the Sun. 2015. (CHI.). 384p. (YA). (gr. 9). pap. (978-986-359-180-1(7)) Ecus Publishing Hse.

—I'll Give You the Sun. 2014. (ENG.). 384p. (YA). (gr. 9). 17.99 (978-0-8037-3496-8(4), Dial Bks) Penguin Publishing Group.

—I'll Give You the Sun. 2015. (ENG.). 400p. (YA). (gr. 9-12). pap. 10.99 (978-0-14-242576-3(1), Speak) Penguin Young Readers Group.

—I'll Give You the Sun. 2015. (ENG.). 400p. (YA). (gr. 9). 21.30 (978-1-68065-512-4(4)) Perfection Learning Corp.

—I'll Give You the Sun. 2015. lib. bdg. 22.10 (978-0-606-37572-6(4)) Turtleback Bks.

Nelson, Theresa. Ruby Electric. 2004. 264p. (J). (gr. 5-7). 13.65 (978-0-7569-3530-6(X)) Perfection Learning Corp.

—Ruby Electric. 2004. (ENG.). 272p. (J). (gr. 5-7). reprint ed. pap. 12.99 (978-0-689-87146-7(5), Atheneum Bks. for Young Readers) Simon & Schuster Children's Publishing.

Noël, Alyson. Art Geeks & Prom Queens. 2011. (ENG.). 240p. (YA). (gr. 7-12). pap. 9.99 (978-0-312-61922-0(7), 9780312619220, St. Martin's Griffin) St. Martin's Pr.

—Forever Summer. 2011. (ENG.). 464p. (YA). (gr. 8-12). pap. 9.99 (978-0-312-60439-4(4), 9780312604394, St. Martin's Griffin) St. Martin's Pr.

—Laguna Cove. 2006. (ENG.). 224p. (YA). (gr. 8-13). pap. 9.99 (978-0-312-34869-4(X), 9780312348694, St. Martin's Griffin) St. Martin's Pr.

Norris, Elizabeth. Unraveling. (Unraveling Ser.: 1). (ENG.). (YA). (gr. 8). 2013. 480p. pap. 9.99 (978-0-06-210374-1(1)) 2012. 464p. 17.99 (978-0-06-210373-4(3)) HarperCollins Pubs.

Nuchols, Galand A. Dragon Hatchling. 2007. 144p. per. 11.95 (978-0-595-46346-6(0)) iUniverse, Inc.

Ockler, Sarah. Twenty Boy Summer. 2010. (ENG.). 320p. (YA). (gr. 7-17). pap. 10.99 (978-0-316-05158-3(6)) Little, Brown Bks. for Young Readers.

O'Dell, Scott. La Isla de los Delfines Azules. (SPA., Illus.). (YA). (gr. 5-8). 7.96 net. (978-1-56137-541-7(1), NU5722) Novel Units, Inc.

—Island of the Blue Dolphins. Lewin, Ted, illus. gif. ed. 2010. (ENG.). 192p. (J). (gr. 2-5). 22.00 (978-0-547-42483-5(3)) Houghton Mifflin Harcourt Publishing Co.

Okei-san: The Girl from Wakamatsu. 2006. (J). pap. 11.95 (978-0-9642112-8-5(9)) Barsotti Bks.

Oliver, Lin. Almost Identical. 2012. (Almost Identical Ser.: 1). (ENG.). 224p. (J). (gr. 3-7). pap. 7.99 (978-0-448-45191-6(3), Grosset & Dunlap) Penguin Young Readers Group.

—Double-Crossed #3. 2013. (Almost Identical Ser.: 3). (ENG.). 224p. (J). (gr. 3-7). pap. 7.99 (978-0-448-45193-0(X), Grosset & Dunlap) Penguin Young Readers Group.

—Revenge of the Itty-Bitty Brothers. Gilpin, Stephen, illus. (Who Shrunk Daniel Funk? Ser.: 3). (ENG.). 176p. (J). (gr. 3-7). 2010. pap. 6.99 (978-1-4169-0962-0(1)) 2009. 14.99 (978-1-4169-0961-3(3)) Simon & Schuster Bks. For Young Readers. (Simon & Schuster Bks. For Young Readers).

—Two-Faced, No. 2. 2012. (Almost Identical Ser.: 2). (ENG.). 224p. (J). (gr. 3-7). pap. 7.99 (978-0-448-45192-3(1), Grosset & Dunlap) Penguin Young Readers Group.

Olney, Ross R. Time Dial, 1 vol. 2010. 134p. pap. 24.95 (978-1-4489-4371-5(X)) America Star Bks.

O'Neill, Elizabeth. Alfred Visits California. 2006. (Illus.). 24p. (J). (gr. -1-3). pap. 12.00 (978-0-9771836-9-2(6)) Global Business Information Strategies, Inc.

Ostow, Micol. Family. (ENG.). 384p. (J). (gr. 9). 2013. pap. 9.99 (978-1-60684-393-2(1)) 2011. 17.99 (978-1-60684-155-6(6)) Lerner Publishing Group. (Carolrhoda Lab™).

PaleoJoe & Caszatt-Allen, Wendy. Secret Sabertooth. 2007. (PaleoJoe's Dinosaur Detective Club Ser.: 3). (ENG., Illus.). 168p. (J). (gr. 2-5). pap. 8.95 (978-1-934133-10-1(8), Mackinac Island Press, Inc.) Charlesbridge Publishing, Inc.

Pandora. Ankh: Conquering the Seven Deadly Sins. 2013. 100p. pap. 10.95 (978-1-62212-908-9(3), Strategic Bk. Publishing) Strategic Book Publishing & Rights Agency (SBPRA).

Parks, Kathy. The Lifeboat Clique. 2016. 336p. (YA). (gr. 8). 17.99 (978-0-06-239396-8(0), Tegen, Katherine Bks) HarperCollins Pubs.

Partridge, Elizabeth. Dogtag Summer. (ENG.). 240p. (YA). (gr. 3-12). 2012. pap. 7.99 (978-1-59990-829-8(8), 9781599908298) 2011. 16.99 (978-1-59990-183-1(8), 9781599901831) Bloomsbury Publishing USA. (Bloomsbury USA Childrens).

Patron, Susan. Behind the Masks: The Diary of Angeline Reddy - Bodie, California 1880. 2012. (Dear America Ser.). (ENG.). 304p. (J). (gr. 3-7). 12.99 (978-0-545-30437-5(7)) Scholastic, Inc.

—Lucky Breaks. Phelan, Matt, illus. (ENG.). (J). (gr. 3-7). 2010. 208p. pap. 7.99 (978-1-4169-9772-6(5)) 2009. 192p. 16.99 (978-1-4169-3998-6(9)) Simon & Schuster Children's Publishing. (Atheneum Bks. for Young Readers).

—Lucky for Good. McGuire, Erin, illus. 2012. (ENG.). 224p. (J). (gr. 3-7). pap. 6.99 (978-1-4169-9059-8(3), Atheneum Bks. for Young Readers) Simon & Schuster Children's Publishing.

—Lucky for Good. McGuire, Erin K., illus. 2011. (ENG.). 224p. (J). (gr. 3-7). 16.99 (978-1-4169-9058-1(5), Atheneum Bks. for Young Readers) Simon & Schuster Children's Publishing.

Pearce, Jonathan. The Far Side of the Moon: A California Story. 2nd ed. 2004. 150p. (J). pap. 15.95 (978-1-59411-011-5(5)) Writers' Collective, The.

Pearson, Ridley. Disney Lands. 2015. (Kingdom Keepers: Bk. 1). (ENG., Illus.). 352p. (J). (gr. 4-7). 17.99 (978-1-4231-8431-7(9)) Hyperion Bks. for Children.

—The Return: Legacy of Secrets. 2016. (Kingdom Keepers Ser.: Bk. 2). (ENG., Illus.). 394p. (J). (gr. 5-9). 17.99 (978-1-4231-8432-4(7)) Hyperion Bks. for Children.

Peralta, Joaquin. Emma Snow: At the Edge of the World. 2009. 206p. (J). pap. 17.00 (978-1-934376-19-5(1)) Balona Bks.

Perrin, Randy, et al. Time Like a River. 2004. 144p. (gr. 5-18). 14.95 (978-1-57143-061-8(X)) RDR Bks.

Peterson, J. D. R. & Reimer, Diana. Priscilla Bailey: A Story of the Great Depression. 2009. 196p. 24.95 (978-1-4401-3929-1(6)); pap. 14.95 (978-1-4401-3927-7(X)) iUniverse, Inc.

Peterson, Kathryn. Reilly's Leap of Faith, 1 vol. 2010. 48p. pap. 16.95 (978-1-4512-0154-3(0)) America Star Bks.

Pfitsch, Patricia Curtis. Riding the Flume. 2004. (Aladdin Historical Fiction Ser.). 232p. (gr. 5-9). 15.00 (978-0-7569-2938-1(5)) Perfection Learning Corp.

—Riding the Flume. 2004. (ENG., Illus.). 240p. (J). (gr. 5-9). pap. 11.99 (978-0-689-86692-0(5), Simon & Schuster/Paula Wiseman Bks.) Simon & Schuster/Paula Wiseman Bks.

Pike, Aprilynne. Life after Theft. 2013. (Life after Theft Ser.). (ENG.). 352p. (YA). (gr. 8). 17.99 (978-0-06-199900-0(8), HarperTeen) HarperCollins Pubs.

Politi, Leo. Song of the Swallows. 2009. (ENG., Illus.). 32p. 16.95 (978-0-89236-989-8(2)) Oxford Univ. Pr., Inc.

Porter, Sarah. The Twice Lost. 2014. (Lost Voices Trilogy Ser.: 3). (ENG.). 480p. (YA). (gr. 7). pap. 8.99 (978-0-547-48255-2(8), HMH Books For Young Readers) Houghton Mifflin Harcourt Publishing Co.

Portman, Frank. Andromeda Klein. 2010. (ENG.). 432p. (YA). (gr. 9). pap. 9.99 (978-0-385-73526-1(X), Delacorte Bks. for Young Readers) Random Hse. Children's Bks.

Preble, Laura. The Queen Geek Social Club. 2006. (ENG.). 336p. (YA). (gr. 7-18). 15.00 (978-0-425-21164-9(9), Berkley) Penguin Publishing Group.

Prentice-Hall Staff. The Red Pony. 2nd ed. (J). stu. ed. (978-0-13-717133-0(1)) Prentice Hall (Schl. Div.).

Prinz, Yvonne. If You're Lucky. 2016. (ENG.). 288p. (YA). (gr. 9-12). pap. 9.95 (978-1-61620-639-0(X)) Algonquin Bks. of Chapel Hill.

—The Vinyl Princess. 2011. 336p. (J). pap. 8.99 (978-0-06-171585-3(9), HarperTeen) 2009. (ENG.). 320p. (YA). (gr. 8-18). 16.99 (978-0-06-171583-9(2)) HarperCollins Pubs.

Purves, William C. Fairmont Forever. 2011. 180p. pap. 13.95 (978-1-4502-3878-6(5)) iUniverse, Inc.

Quince, Lia. Abby & Jules. 2009. (978-1-933791-14-2(4)) Finial Publishing.

Rader, Laura. The Twelve Days of Christmas in California. Rader, Laura, illus. 2009. (Twelve Days of Christmas in America Ser.). (ENG., Illus.). 40p. (J). (gr. k-3). 12.95 (978-1-4027-6247-5(X)) Sterling Publishing Co., Inc.

Ralphson, G. Harvey. Boy Scouts in Death Valley. 2005. pap. 27.95 (978-1-885529-51-0(1)) Stevens Publishing.

RealBuzz Studios Staff. Let There Be Lighten Up! 2007. (Goofyfoot Gurl Ser.: No. 1). 96p. (YA). pap. 4.97 (978-1-59789-573-6(3), Barbour Bks.) Barbour Publishing, Inc.

Redbank, Tennant. The Haunted Boardwalk. 2016. (Barbie Chapters Ser.). (ENG., Illus.). 64p. (J). (gr. 1-4). lib. bdg. 12.99 (978-0-375-97412-0(1), Random Hse. Bks. for Young Readers) Random Hse. Children's Bks.

Reichardt, Marisa. Underwater. 2016. (ENG.). 288p. (YA). 17.99 (978-0-374-36886-9(4), 9780374368869, Farrar, Straus & Giroux (BYR)) Farrar, Straus & Giroux.

Reinhardt, Dana. The Summer I Learned to Fly. 2012. (ENG.). 224p. (YA). (gr. 7). pap. 8.99 (978-0-385-73955-9(9), Ember) Random Hse. Children's Bks.

Renae, Cameo. Hidden Wings. 2013. 270p. pap. 13.99 (978-1-939769-21-3(3)) Crushing Hearts and Black Butterfly Publishing.

Richardson, Nikki. A Beautiful Lie, 1 vol. 2009. 168p. pap. 24.95 (978-1-61582-927-9(X)) America Star Bks.

Rio, Adam del & Arroyo, David. Vines of the Earth. Rio, Adam del & Arroyo, David, illus. 2006. (SPA & ENG., Illus.). 27p. (978-0-9772852-7-3(8)); pap. (978-0-9772852-6-6(X)) Lectura Bks.

C
D

Ritter, John H. The Boy Who Saved Baseball. 2005. (ENG.). 224p. (J). (gr. 3-7). pap. 7.99 *(978-0-14-240286-3(9)*, Puffin Books) Penguin Young Readers Group.

—Desperado Who Stole Baseball. 2010. (ENG.). 288p. (J). (gr. 5-18). 7.99 *(978-0-14-241507-8(3)*, Puffin Books) Penguin Young Readers Group.

—Under the Baseball Moon. 2008. (ENG., Illus.). 320p. (J). (gr. 5-18). 9.99 *(978-0-14-241090-5(X)*, Puffin Books) Penguin Young Readers Group.

—Under the Baseball Moon. 2008. (Illus.). 283p. (gr. 8-12). 17.00 *(978-0-7569-8934-7(5))* Perfection Learning Corp.

Roberts, Tina. Dream Watchman: Quest for the Missing Tailsman Book I. 2011. 244p. pap. 15.95 *(978-1-60976-636-8(9)*, Eloquent Bks.) Strategic Book Publishing & Rights Agency (SBPRA).

Rocklin, Joanne. One Day & One Amazing Morning on Orange Street. 2012. (ENG., Illus.). 240p. (J). (gr. 3-7). pap. 8.95 *(978-1-4197-0181-8(9)*, Amulet Bks.) Abrams, Inc.

Roderman, Anna Marie. Two Tales of Courage. 2004. 116p. (YA). pap. 7.95 *(978-0-87714-318-5(8))* i-5 Publishing LLC.

Rodrigue, Nancy Temple. Hidden Mickey Adventures 2: Peter & the Missing Mansion, vol. 2. (Hidden Mickey Adventures Ser.: 2). (ENG.). 2015. 182p. (YA). (gr. 4-17). lib. bdg. 29.99 *(978-1-938319-19-8(2)*, DOUBLE-R BKS.) 2nd ed. 2017. 198p. (gr. 5-17). pap. 14.99 ***(978-1-938319-31-0(1)***, DOUBLE R Bks.) Rodrigue & Sons Co./Double R Books Publishing.

Roe, D. J. The Impossible Dream. 2008. 59p. pap. 16.95 *(978-1-60610-173-5(0))* America Star Bks.

Romano, Juliana. First There Was Forever. 2016. (ENG.). 416p. (YA). (gr. 9). pap. 10.99 *(978-0-14-751391-5(X)*, Speak) Penguin Young Readers Group.

Romeyn, Debra. Passage to Monterey. May, Dan, tr. May, Dan, illus. 2003. (Adventures of Juan & Mariano Ser.: No. 1). 39p. (J). pap. 9.95 *(978-0-9729016-0-4(4))* Gossamer Bks.

Rosner, Hannah. The Ambulance Club. 2005. 87p. pap. 19.95 *(978-1-4137-7492-4(X))* America Star Bks.

Ross, Emily. Half in Love with Death. 2015. (ENG.). 224p. (YA). 17.99 *(978-1-4405-8903-4(8)*, Simon Pulse) Simon Pulse.

Ross, Sylvia. Lion Singer. Ross, Sylvia, illus. 2005. (Illus.). 33p. (J). (gr. 3-7). 12.95 *(978-1-59714-009-6(0)*, Great Valley Bks.) Heyday.

Rowe, Vicki J. Yellow Roses. 2012. 64p. pap. 15.99 *(978-1-4771-2636-3(8))* Xlibris Corp.

Rubcic, Michael. Native Soul. 2004. 216p. (Orig.). (J). pap. 14.95 *(978-0-9746848-0-2(5))* Native Sun Pr.

Rubino, M. Gayle. The Truth about Scuttlebutt. 2012. 32p. pap. 19.95 *(978-1-4772-0348-4(6))* AuthorHouse.

Ruiz, Joseph J. Angel on Daniel's Shoulder. 2004. (SPA & ENG., Illus.). 108p. (J). pap. 12.95 *(978-0-86534-402-0(7))* Sunstone Pr.

Rusch, Brian. The Bear Who Barked Like a Dog. 2011. 122p. pap. 12.50 *(978-1-60976-005-2(0)*, Eloquent Bks.) Strategic Book Publishing & Rights Agency (SBPRA).

Ryan, Pam Muñoz. Echo. 2015. (ENG., Illus.). 512p. (J). (gr. 5-9). 19.99 *(978-0-439-87402-1(5)*, Scholastic Pr.) Scholastic, Inc.

—Esperanza Rising. 2005. (Reader's Workshop Ser.). (ENG.). 264p. (C). pap. 19.95 *(978-0-7362-2817-6(9))* CENGAGE Learning.

—Esperanza Rising. unabr. ed. 2004. (Middle Grade Cassette Librariestm Ser.). 272p. (J). (gr. 4-7). pap. 36.00 incl. audio *(978-0-8072-1726-9(3)*, S YA 281 SP, Listening Library) Random Hse. Audio Publishing Group.

—Esperanza Rising. 2016. (gr. 5-8). lib. bdg. 17.20 *(978-0-613-53807-7(2)*, Turtleback) Turtleback Bks.

—Yo, Naomi León. 2005. (SPA.). 272p. (J). (gr. 3-7). pap. 6.99 *(978-0-439-75572-6(7)*, Scholastic en Espanol) Scholastic, Inc.

Salvatierra, Dante. The Latchkey Kids & the Escape from California. 2008. 260p. pap. 14.50 *(978-1-4357-0876-1(8))* Lulu Pr., Inc.

Sanchez, Alex. So Hard to Say. Weiss, Jennifer, ed. 2006. (ENG., Illus.). 232p. (YA). (gr. 7-12). reprint ed. pap. 11.99 *(978-1-4169-1189-0(8)*, Simon & Schuster Bks. For Young Readers) Simon & Schuster Bks. For Young Readers.

Sanderson, Nancy. Horse of the Four Winds. 2011. 152p. (gr. 10-12). pap. 14.50 *(978-1-4634-4802-8(3))* AuthorHouse.

—Summer of the Dancing Horse. 2010. 200p. pap. 14.49 *(978-1-4520-6891-6(7))* AuthorHouse.

Sandoval, Victor. Roll over, Big Toben. 2003. 128p. (J). pap. 9.95 *(978-1-55885-401-7(0)*, Piñata Books) Arte Publico Pr.

Sands, Kathryn Ann. How Chili Willie Got His Name. 2013. 24p. pap. 17.99 *(978-1-4817-0641-4(1))* AuthorHouse.

Sayles, Carol L. Turn the Turtle Rightside. 2007. (ENG.). 156p. (J). (gr. 4-7). per. *(978-1-933255-25-5(0))* DNA Pr.

Scaglione, Rebecca L. Jack: The trilogy ... the Truth. 2007. 204p. per. 14.95 *(978-0-595-47331-1(8))* iUniverse, Inc.

Schaefer, Jack. Old Ramon. West, Harold E., illus. 2016. (ENG.). 112p. (J). pap. 19.95 *(978-0-8263-5764-9(4))* Univ. of New Mexico Pr.

Schneider, Robyn. The Beginning of Everything. (ENG.). 352p. (YA). (gr. 8). 2014. pap. 9.99 *(978-0-06-221714-1(3)*, Tegen, Katherine Bks) 2013. 17.99 *(978-0-06-221713-4(5))* HarperCollins Pubs.

Schorner-Wendel, Gretchen & Schorner, Adam Anthony. Becka Goes to San Diego. 2009. (Becka & the Big Bubble Ser.). (Illus.). 32p. (J). (gr. -1-2). 22.60 *(978-1-60754-113-4(0))*; pap. 10.55 *(978-1-60754-114-1(9))* Windmill Bks.

Schraff, Anne. Memories Are Forever. 2008. (Passages Ser.). 135p. lib. bdg. 13.95 *(978-0-7569-8405-2(X))* Perfection Learning Corp.

Schwartz, Joel. The Extraordinary Pupfish of Calaveras County. 2008. 216p. 25.95 *(978-1-4401-0892-1(7))* iUniverse, Inc.

Scott, Michael. The Sorceress. (Secrets of the Immortal Nicholas Flamel Ser.: 3). (ENG.). 512p. (YA). (gr. 7-18). 2010. pap. 10.99 *(978-0-385-73530-8(8)*, Ember) 2009. 17.99 *(978-0-385-73529-2(4)*, Delacorte Bks. for Young Readers) Random Hse. Children's Bks.

—The Sorceress. 2010. (Secrets of the Immortal Nicholas Flamel Ser.: 3). lib. bdg. 22.10 *(978-0-606-14133-8(2)*, Turtleback) Turtleback Bks.

—The Sorceress the Secrets of the Immortal Nicholas Flamel. l.t. ed. 2009. (Secrets of the Immortal Nicholas Flamel Ser.). (ENG.). 614p. (YA). 23.95 *(978-1-4104-2092-3(2))* Thorndike Pr.

—The Warlock. 2012. (Secrets of the Immortal Nicholas Flamel Ser.: 5). (ENG.). 400p. (YA). (gr. 7). pap. 10.99 *(978-0-385-73534-6(0)*, Ember) Random Hse. Children's Bks.

—The Warlock. 2012. (Secrets of the Immortal Nicholas Flamel Ser.: 5). lib. bdg. 22.10 *(978-0-606-26411-2(6)*, Turtleback) Turtleback Bks.

Serros, Michele. ¡Scandalosa! A Honey Blonde Chica Novel. 2008. (ENG.). 320p. (YA). (gr. 9). pap. 14.99 *(978-1-4169-1594-2(X)*, Simon Pulse) Simon Pulse.

Service, Pamela F. Alien Contact. Gorman, Mike, illus. (Alien Agent Ser.: 5). (ENG.). 144p. (J). (gr. 4-6). 2010. lib. bdg. 16.95 *(978-0-7613-5363-8(1)*, Carolrhoda Bks.)No. 5. 2011. pap. 5.95 *(978-0-7613-7297-4(0)*, Darby Creek) Lerner Publishing Group.

—#5 Alien Contact. Gorman, Mike, illus. 2011. (Alien Agent Ser.). pap. 33.92 *(978-0-7613-8347-5(6)*, Darby Creek) Lerner Publishing Group.

Sheinmel, Courtney. Sincerely: Sincerely, Sophie; Sincerely, Katie. 2010. (ENG.). 400p. (J). (gr. 3-7). 15.99 *(978-1-4169-4010-4(3)*, Simon & Schuster Bks. For Young Readers) Simon & Schuster Bks. For Young Readers.

—Sincerely: Sincerely, Sophie, Sincerely, Katie. 2011. (ENG.). 416p. (J). (gr. 3-7). pap. 7.99 *(978-1-4169-4022-7(7)*, Simon & Schuster Bks. For Young Readers) Simon & Schuster Bks. For Young Readers.

—Stella Batts Something Blue. Bell, Jennifer A., illus. 2014. (Stella Batts Ser.). (ENG.). 162p. (J). (gr. 1-3). 9.99 *(978-1-58536-851-8(2)*, 203016) Sleeping Bear Pr.

—Superstar. Bell, Jennifer A., illus. 2015. (Stella Batts Ser.). (ENG.). 184p. (J). (gr. 1-3). pap. 5.99 *(978-1-58536-856-3(3)*, 203956) Sleeping Bear Pr.

Sheinmel, Courtney & Bell, Jennifer A. Stella Batts: Hair Today, Gone Tomorrow. 2012. (Stella Batts Ser.). (ENG., Illus.). (J). (gr. 1-3). 152p. pap. 5.99 *(978-1-58536-191-5(7)*, 202269); 160p. lib. bdg. 9.99 *(978-1-58536-189-2(5)*, 202268) Sleeping Bear Pr.

Sibley, Linda. David Joins the California Gold Rush. 2004. 96p. pap. 6.65 *(978-0-7891-6002-7(1))* Perfection Learning Corp.

Silvano, Wendi. Love Is All Around California. Czernichowska, Joanna, illus. 2016. (ENG.). 32p. (J). (-10). 12.99 *(978-1-4926-2909-2(X)*, Sourcebooks Jabberwocky) Sourcebooks, Inc.

Simmons, Andra. What Anna Loves. Capaldi, Gina, illus. 2006. 24p. (J). (gr. -1-3). 15.95 *(978-1-59714-044-7(9))* Heyday.

Simmons, Michael. Pool Boy. 2005. 164p. (gr. 7). 17.95 *(978-0-7569-5064-4(3))* Perfection Learning Corp.

—Pool Boy. 2005. (ENG.). 192p. (YA). (gr. 7). reprint ed. pap. 7.99 *(978-0-385-73196-6(5)*, Delacorte Bks. for Young Readers) Random Hse. Children's Bks.

Singleton, Linda Joy. Last Dance. 2005. (Seer Ser.: 2). (ENG.). 264p. (YA). pap. 9.95 *(978-0-7387-0638-2(8)*, Flux) Llewellyn Pubns.

Skilton, Sarah. High & Dry. 2014. (ENG.). 272p. (YA). (gr. 9-17). 16.95 *(978-1-4197-0929-6(1)*, Amulet Bks.) Abrams, Inc.

Skurzynski, Gloria & Ferguson, Alane. Valley of Death: A Mystery in Death Valley National Park. 2008. (Mysteries in Our National Park Ser.). (ENG., Illus.). 160p. (J). (gr. 3-7). per. 4.99 *(978-1-4263-0178-0(2)*, National Geographic Children's Bks.) National Geographic Society.

Smallman, Steve. Santa Is Coming to California. Dunn, Robert, illus. 2012. (ENG.). 32p. (J). (-3). 9.99 *(978-1-4022-7515-9(3)*, Sourcebooks Jabberwocky) Sourcebooks, Inc.

—Santa Is Coming to San Diego. Dunn, Robert, illus. 2014. (ENG.). 32p. (J). (-3). 9.99 *(978-1-4926-0688-8(X)*, Sourcebooks Jabberwocky) Sourcebooks, Inc.

—Santa Is Coming to San Jose. Dunn, Robert, illus. 2015. (ENG.). 32p. (J). (-3). 9.99 *(978-1-4926-2641-1(4)*, Sourcebooks Jabberwocky) Sourcebooks, Inc.

—Santa Is Coming to Santa Cruz. Dunn, Robert, illus. 2013. (ENG.). 32p. (J). (-3). 9.99 *(978-1-4022-9057-2(8)*, Sourcebooks Jabberwocky) Sourcebooks, Inc.

Smiley, Jane. Gee Whiz. Clayton, Elaine, illus. 2013. (Horses of Oak Valley Ranch Ser.: Bk. 5). (ENG.). 272p. (J). (gr. 5). 16.99 *(978-0-375-86969-3(7)*, Knopf Bks. for Young Readers) Random Hse. Children's Bks.

—Gee Whiz, Bk. 5. 2014. (Horses of Oak Valley Ranch Ser.: Bk. 5). (ENG.). 272p. (J). (gr. 5). 7.99 *(978-0-375-87132-0(2)*, Yearling) Random Hse. Children's Bks.

—The Georges & the Jewels. 2010. (Horses of Oak Valley Ranch Ser.: Bk. 1). (ENG.). 240p. (J). (gr. 5). 6.99 *(978-0-375-86228-1(5)*, Yearling) Random Hse. Children's Bks.

—A Good Horse. 2011. (Horses of Oak Valley Ranch Ser.: Bk. 2). (ENG.). 256p. (J). (gr. 5). 6.99 *(978-0-375-86230-4(7)*, Yearling) Random Hse. Children's Bks.

—Pie in the Sky. 2013. (Horses of Oak Valley Ranch Ser.). (ENG.). 272p. (J). (gr. 5). 6.99 *(978-0-375-87131-3(4)*, Yearling) Random Hse. Children's Bks.

—True Blue. 2012. (Horses of Oak Valley Ranch Ser.: Bk. 3). (ENG.). 304p. (J). (gr. 5). 6.99 *(978-0-375-86232-8(3)*, Yearling) Random Hse. Children's Bks.

Smith, Andrew. 100 Sideways Miles. 2014. (ENG., Illus.). 288p. (YA). (gr. 9). 17.99 *(978-1-4424-4495-9(9)*, Simon & Schuster Bks. For Young Readers) Simon & Schuster Bks. For Young Readers.

Smith, D. James. The Boys of San Joaquin. 2006. (ENG.). 240p. (J). (gr. 3-7). pap. 11.99 *(978-1-4169-1619-2(9)*, Atheneum Bks. for Young Readers) Simon & Schuster Children's Publishing.

—It Was September When We Ran Away the First Time. 2012. (ENG.). 240p. (J). (gr. 3-7). pap. 11.99 *(978-1-4169-3810-1(9)*, Atheneum Bks. for Young Readers) Simon & Schuster Children's Publishing.

—Probably the World's Best Story about a Dog & the Girl Who Loved Me. 2011. (ENG.). 256p. (J). pap. 5.99 *(978-1-4169-9652-1(4)*, Atheneum Bks. for Young Readers) Simon & Schuster Children's Publishing.

—Probably the World's Best Story about a Dog & The Girl Who Loved Me. 2010. (ENG.). 240p. (J). (gr. 4-7). pap. 11.99 *(978-1-4424-2194-3(0)*, Atheneum Bks. for Young Readers) Simon & Schuster Children's Publishing.

Smith, Sherri L. Pasadena. 2016. (ENG.). 240p. (YA). (gr. 9). 17.99 *(978-1-101-99625-6(0)*, G.P. Putnam's Sons Books for Young Readers) Penguin Young Readers Group.

Snedden, Genevra Sis. Docas the Indian Boy of Santa Clara. 2005. pap. 21.95 *(978-1-4179-2695-4(3))* Kessinger Publishing, LLC.

Spradlin, Michael P. & Smith, Roland. Alcatraz. 2014. (I, Q Ser.). (ENG.). 272p. (J). (gr. 5-7). pap. 9.99 *(978-1-58536-825-9(3)*, 203727) Sleeping Bear Pr.

Spreng, Robert C. The Tahoe Tiger & the Lahontan Lion. 2008. 38p. pap. 14.50 *(978-0-557-02370-7(X))* Lulu Pr., Inc.

Stalcup. La Loncheria. Arroyo, illus. 2008. (SPA & ENG.). 28p. (J). pap. 8.95 *(978-1-60448-006-1(8))* Lectura Bks.

—La Loncheria. Arroyo, illus. 2008. (SPA & ENG.). 28p. (J). 15.95 *(978-1-60448-005-4(X))* Lectura Bks.

Standiford, Natalie. Breaking up Is Really, Really Hard to Do. 2005. (ENG.). 224p. (YA). (gr. 7-17). pap. 18.99 *(978-0-316-11041-9(8))* Little, Brown Bks. for Young Readers.

—The Dating Game, No. 1. 2005. (ENG.). 224p. (YA). (gr. 7-17). pap. 18.99 *(978-0-316-11040-2(X))* Little, Brown Bks. for Young Readers.

—Ex-Rating. 4th rev. ed. 2006. (ENG.). 224p. (YA). (gr. 7-17). per. 17.99 *(978-0-316-15876-3(3))* Little, Brown Bks. for Young Readers.

—Speed Dating. 5th ed. 2006. (ENG.). 224p. (J). (gr. 8-12). per. 18.99 *(978-0-316-11530-8(4))* Little, Brown Bks. for Young Readers.

Steinkellner, Teddy. Trash Can Days: A Middle School Saga. 2013. (Trash Can Days Ser.). (ENG.). 352p. (J). (gr. 5-9). 16.99 *(978-1-4231-6632-0(9))* Disney Pr.

Stevenson, Sarah Jamila. The Latte Rebellion. 2011. (ENG., Illus.). 336p. (YA). (gr. 9-18). pap. 9.95 *(978-0-7387-2278-8(2)*, Flux) North Star Editions.

Stiefvater, Maggie. Sinner. 2015. (Shiver Ser.). (ENG.). 368p. (J). (gr. 9). pap. 10.99 *(978-0-545-65459-3(9))* Scholastic, Inc.

Stites, Clara. Lixia of Gold Mountain: A Story of Early California. 2015. (ENG., Illus.). 100p. (J). pap. 8.95 *(978-1-56474-421-0(3)*, Fithian Pr) Daniel & Daniel, Pubs., Inc.

—Rosalba of Santa Juanita: A California Story. 2015. (ENG., Illus.). 100p. (J). pap. 8.95 *(978-1-56474-394-7(2)*, Fithian Pr) Daniel & Daniel, Pubs., Inc.

Stokes, Phil. Phillip & Dickie. 2004. 384p. (YA). 28.95 *(978-0-9744360-0-5(3))* Da Wong Bks.

Stone, Jeff. Five Ancestors Out of the Ashes #2: Lion. 2014. (Five Ancestors Out of the Ashes Ser.). (ENG.). 256p. (J). (gr. 4-7). 6.99 *(978-0-375-87099-6(7)*, Yearling) Random Hse. Children's Bks.

—Lion. 2013. (Five Ancestors Out of the Ashes Ser.). (ENG.). 240p. (J). (gr. 4-7). 16.99 *(978-0-375-87019-4(9)*, Random Hse. Bks. for Young Readers) Random Hse. Children's Bks.

Strasnick, Lauren. Nothing Like You. 2010. (ENG.). 240p. (YA). (gr. 9). pap. 8.99 *(978-1-4169-8265-4(5)*, Simon Pulse) Simon Pulse.

—Then You Were Gone. (ENG., 272p. (YA). (gr. 9). 2014. Illus.). pap. 9.99 *(978-1-4424-2716-7(7))* 2013. 16.99 *(978-1-4424-2715-0(9))* Simon Pulse. (Simon Pulse).

Strasser, Todd. The Wave. 2013. (ENG.). 144p. (YA). (gr. 7). pap. 9.99 *(978-0-307-97912-4(1)*, Ember) Random Hse. Children's Bks.

Sugiura, Misa. It's Not Like It's a Secret. 2017. 400p. (YA). (gr. 8). 17.99 *(978-0-06-247341-7(7)*, HarperTeen) HarperCollins Pubs.

Sully, Katherine. Night-Night California. Kolanovic, Dubravka & Poole, Helen, illus. 2016. (ENG.). 20p. (J). (-1). bds. 9.99 *(978-1-4926-3939-8(7)*, 9781492639398, Sourcebooks Jabberwocky) Sourcebooks, Inc.

Summers, Gillian. Shadows of the Redwood Bk. 1, Bk. 1. 2010. (Faire Folk Saga Ser.: 4). (ENG.). 336p. (YA). (gr. 7-18). pap. 9.95 *(978-0-7387-1552-0(2)*, Flux) North Star Editions.

Summy, Barrie. I So Don't Do Mysteries. 2009. (ENG.). 288p. (J). (gr. 3-7). 6.99 *(978-0-385-73603-9(7)*, Yearling) Random Hse. Children's Bks.

Tamaki, Mariko. Saving Montgomery Sole. 2016. (ENG.). 240p. (YA). 17.99 *(978-1-62672-271-2(4)*, 9781626722712) Roaring Brook Pr.

—Saving Montgomery Sole. 2017. (ENG.). 240p. (YA). pap. 9.99 *(978-1-250-10440-3(8)*, 9781250104403) Square Fish.

Tara, Stephanie Lisa. Eliza's Forever Trees. Walton, Alex, illus. 2012. 290p. (J). pap. 9.99 net. *(978-1-61254-067-2(8))* Brown Books Publishing Group.

Tashjian, Janet. My Life as a Stuntboy. Tashjian, Jake, illus. 2011. (My Life Ser.: 2). (ENG.). 272p. (J). (gr. 4-7). 15.99 *(978-0-8050-8904-2(7)*, 9780805089042, Holt, Henry & Co. Bks. For Young Readers) Holt, Henry & Co.

Telgemeier, Raina. Ghosts. Telgemeier, Raina, illus. 2016. (ENG., Illus.). 256p. (J). (gr. 3-7). 24.99 *(978-0-545-54061-2(5)*, Graphix) Scholastic, Inc.

To Be Perfectly Honest: A Novel Based on an Untrue Story. 2014. (ENG., Illus.). 496p. (YA). (gr. 7). pap. 11.99 *(978-0-689-87605-9(X)*, Simon & Schuster Bks. For Young Readers) Simon & Schuster Bks. For Young Readers.

Trevor, Simeon. I'm Going to Fly SomeDay. 2004. 36p. spiral bd. 13.93 *(978-1-4116-2072-8(0))* Lulu Pr., Inc.

Turner, Ginger. Gold Mine! The California Gold Rush Story. 2004. (Illus.). 46p. (J). per. 15.95 *(978-0-9742502-2-9(8))* Gossamer Bks., LLC.

Turner, Ginger & Shimpi, Shekhar. Gold Mine! The California Gold Rush Story. 2004. (Illus.). 44p. (J). pap. 15.95 *(978-0-9742502-3-6(6))* Gossamer Bks., LLC.

Uncle Markie. Piglettè & Bobo Christmas in Palm Springs. 2003. (YA). ring bd. 9.95 *(978-1-933129-10-5(7))* Studio 403.

—Piglettè & Bobo in Berkeley. 2003. (YA). ring bd. 9.95 *(978-1-933129-07-5(7))* Studio 403.

—Piglettè & BoBoTrash Orange County. 2003. (YA). ring bd. 9.95 *(978-1-933129-09-9(3))* Studio 403.

Van Dolzer, Krista. The Sound of Life & Everything. 2015. (ENG.). 272p. (J). (gr. 5). 16.99 *(978-0-399-16775-1(7)*, G.P. Putnam's Sons Books for Young Readers) Penguin Young Readers Group.

Van Dyne, Edith. Aunt Jane's Nieces Out West. 2007. (ENG.). 180p. pap. 21.99 *(978-1-4264-4188-2(6))*; 164p. pap. 19.99 *(978-1-4264-4145-5(2))* Creative Media Partners, LLC.

Van Syckle, A. & Schwartz, Josh. The OC: 'twas the Night Before Chrismukkah. 2005. 206p. (YA). *(978-1-4156-3915-3(9))* Scholastic, Inc.

VanDycke, Lilian Claudine. The Mystery Fire. 2012. 56p. pap. *(978-1-77097-382-4(6))* FriesenPress.

Vega, Diego. The Iron Brand. 2007. (Young Zorro Ser.). 240p. (YA). (gr. 3-7). pap. 6.99 *(978-0-06-083947-5(3)*, Rayo) HarperCollins Pubs.

Velásquez, Gloria. Rudy's Memory Walk. 2009. (Roosevelt High School Ser.). 140p. (YA). (gr. 6-18). pap. 9.95 *(978-1-55885-593-9(9))* Arte Publico Pr.

Ventura, Marne. Edgy Estella Aces the Sleepover Party. Trinidad, Leo, illus. 2016. (Worry Warriors Ser.). (ENG.). 96p. (gr. 2-4). lib. bdg. 25.99 *(978-1-4965-3610-5(X))* Stone Arch Bks.

—Nervous Nellie Fights First-Day Frenzy. Trinidad, Leo, illus. 2016. (Worry Warriors Ser.). (ENG.). 96p. (gr. 2-4). lib. bdg. 25.99 *(978-1-4965-3613-6(4))* Stone Arch Bks.

Viguié, Debbie. The Spring of Candy Apples, 1 vol. 2009. (Sweet Seasons Novel Ser.). (ENG.). 208p. (YA). (gr. 8-11). pap. 9.99 *(978-0-310-71753-9(1))* Zondervan.

Villasenor, Victor. The Stranger & the Red Rooster: El Forastero y el Gallo Rojo. Ventura, Gabriela Baeza, tr. Jara, Jose, illus. 2005. (ENG & SPA.). 26p. (J). (gr. -1-2). 16.95 *(978-1-55885-420-8(7)*, Piñata Books) Arte Publico Pr.

Wait for Me. 2007. 169p. (gr. 4-7). 18.00 *(978-0-7569-7959-1(5))* Perfection Learning Corp.

Walls, P. Abby: El oro de California. 2003. (Abby Ser.).Tr. of Abby: California Gold. pap. 6.99 *(978-0-7899-0969-5(3))* Editorial Unilit.

Walser, Jo. Chasing the Rising Moon. 2012. 452p. pap. 14.95 *(978-1-935807-04-9(8))* Stansbury Publishing.

Warner, Penny. Mystery of the Pirate's Treasure. 2013. (Code Busters Club Ser.). (ENG.). 192p. (J). (gr. 4-7). 16.99 *(978-1-60684-457-1(1)*, Darby Creek) Lerner Publishing Group.

—The Secret of the Puzzle Box. 2016. (Code Busters Club Ser.: 6). (ENG.). 192p. (gr. 3-6). 16.99 *(978-1-5124-0307-7(5))*; 33.32 *(978-1-5124-0900-0(6))* Lerner Publishing Group. (Darby Creek).

Warner, Sally. EllRay Jakes Is a Rock Star, 2 vols. Harper, Jamie, illus. 2012. (EllRay Jakes Ser.: 2). (ENG.). 128p. (J). (gr. 1-3). 5.99 *(978-0-14-241989-2(3)*, Puffin Books) Penguin Young Readers Group.

—Ellray Jakes Is a Rock Star! 2012. (EllRay Jakes Ser.: 2). lib. bdg. 16.00 *(978-0-606-23633-1(3)*, Turtleback) Turtleback Bks.

—EllRay Jakes Is Not a Chicken, 1 vol. Harper, Jamie, illus. 2012. (EllRay Jakes Ser.: 1). (ENG.). 128p. (J). (gr. 1-3). 5.99 *(978-0-14-241988-5(5)*, Puffin Books) Penguin Young Readers Group.

—EllRay Jakes Is Not a Chicken! 2012. (EllRay Jakes Ser.: 1). lib. bdg. 16.00 *(978-0-606-23632-4(5)*, Turtleback) Turtleback Bks.

—Ellray Jakes Rocks the Holidays! 2014. (EllRay Jakes Ser.: 7). lib. bdg. 16.00 *(978-0-606-36188-0(X))* Turtleback Bks.

—EllRay Jakes the Recess King! Biggs, Brian, illus. 2015. (EllRay Jakes Ser.: 8). (ENG.). 176p. (J). (gr. 1-3). 5.99 *(978-0-14-751252-9(2)*, Puffin Books); 14.99 *(978-0-451-46911-3(9)*, Viking Books for Young Readers) Penguin Young Readers Group.

—Rocks the Holidays! Biggs, Brian, illus. 2014. (EllRay Jakes Ser.: 7). (ENG.). 160p. (J). (gr. 1-3). 14.99 *(978-0-451-46909-0(7)*, Viking Books for Young Readers) Penguin Young Readers Group.

Wells, Rosemary. On the Blue Comet. Ibatoulline, Bagram, illus. 2012. (ENG.). 336p. (J). (gr. 5). pap. 8.99 *(978-0-7636-5815-1(4))* Candlewick Pr.

Wells, Shannon Nicole. Gold! A Tall Tale. 2009. (J). pap. 7.00 *(978-1-61623-111-8(4))* Independent Pub.

Wendel, Gretchen Schorner & Schorner, Adam Anthony. Becka Goes to San Diego. Renthrope, Damon, illus. 2008. (ENG.). 32p. (J). (gr. -1-3). 11.99 *(978-1-933754-51-2(6))* Waterside Publishing.

West, Kasie. On the Fence. 2014. (ENG.). 304p. (YA). (gr. 8). pap. 9.99 *(978-0-06-223567-1(2)*, HarperTeen) HarperCollins Pubs.

White, Kiersten. The Chaos of Stars. (ENG.). (YA). 2014. 304p. (gr. 8). pap. 9.99 *(978-0-06-213587-2(2))* 2013. 288p. (gr. 8). 17.99 *(978-0-06-213592-6(9))* 2013. 288p. pap. *(978-0-06-229412-8(1))* HarperCollins Pubs. (HarperTeen).

Whitmore, Hugh. The Three Madelines. Wilson, Raylene Jenee & Gibbons, Deanna, illus. 2012. 124p. pap. 15.95 *(978-0-9848314-4-9(4))* Sincerity Publishing.

Wiggin, Kate Douglas. A Summer in a Canyon. 2007. 140p. 24.95 *(978-1-60312-626-7(0))* Aegypan.

Willard, Eliza, et al. Love Is in the Air. 2004. (ENG.). 128p. *(978-0-00-718094-3(2))* HarperCollins Pubs. Australia.

Williams-Garcia, Rita. One Crazy Summer. 2009. (KOR.). 272p. (J). pap. *(978-89-7199-494-8(0))* Dolbegae Publishing Co.

—One Crazy Summer. (J). (gr. 4-7). 2011. (ENG.). 240p. pap. 7.99 *(978-0-06-076090-8(7))* 2010. (ENG.). 224p. 16.99 *(978-0-06-076088-5(5))* 2010. 224p. lib. bdg. 16.89 *(978-0-06-076089-2(3))* HarperCollins Pubs. (Amistad).

—One Crazy Summer. (J). 2011. 1.25 *(978-1-4498-2201-9(0))* 2010. 69.75 *(978-1-4498-2197-5(9))* 2010. 67.75 *(978-1-4498-2199-9(5))* Recorded Bks., Inc.

—One Crazy Summer. 2011. (J). lib. bdg. 17.20 *(978-0-606-23555-6(8)*, Turtleback) Turtleback Bks.

—P. S. Be Eleven. 2013. 288p. (J). (gr. 3-7). lib. bdg. 17.89 *(978-0-06-193863-4(7)*, Amistad) HarperCollins Pubs.

Williams, Patricia de Belloy. Pioneers-1937. 2003. (Illus.). 409p. (J). per. 14.99 *(978-1-932176-00-1(4))* Beluga-Duga Pr.

Willner-Pardo, Gina. The Hard Kind of Promise. 2011. (ENG.). 204p. (J). (gr. 5-7). pap. 12.99 *(978-0-547-55017-6(0))* Houghton Mifflin Harcourt Publishing Co.

Wilsdon, Christina. Lights! Action! California! Hockerman, Dennis, illus. 2006. 26p. (J). 7.99 *(978-1-59939-009-3(4))* Cornerstone Pr.

Wilson, Diane Lee. Tracks. (ENG., (J). (gr. 5-9). 2013. Illus.). 304p. pap. 6.99 *(978-1-4424-2014-4(6))* 2012. 288p. 16.99 *(978-1-4424-2013-7(8))* McElderry, Margaret K. Bks. (McElderry, Margaret K. Bks.).

Winters, Cat. In the Shadow of Blackbirds. 2013. (ENG., Illus.). 400p. (YA). (gr. 7-17). 17.95 *(978-1-4197-0530-4(X)*, Amulet Bks.) Abrams, Inc.

Wong, Janet S. Minn & Jake's Almost Terrible Summer. Côté, Geneviève, illus. 2008. (ENG.). 112p. (J). (gr. 2-5). 15.99 *(978-0-374-34977-6(0)*, 9780374349776, Farrar, Straus & Giroux (BYR)) Farrar, Straus & Giroux.

Yamada, Debbie Leung. Striking It Rich: Treasures from Gold Mountain. Tang, You-shan, illus. l.t. ed. 2004. 128p. (J). (gr. 4-8). pap. 13.95 *(978-1-879965-21-8(6))* Polychrome Publishing Corp.

Yee, Lisa. The Kidney Hypothetical: or How to Ruin Your Life in Seven Days:Or How to Ruin Your Life in Seven Days. 2015. (ENG.). 272p. (J). (gr. 7). 17.99 *(978-0-545-23094-0(2))* Scholastic, Inc.

—The Kidney Hypothetical, or, How to Ruin Your Life in Seven Days. 2016. (ENG.). 272p. (J). (gr. 7). pap. 9.99 *(978-0-545-23095-7(0))* Scholastic, Inc.

—Warp Speed. (ENG.). 320p. (J). 2013. (gr. 3-7). pap. 6.99 *(978-0-545-15400-0(6))* 2011. (gr. 4-7). 16.99 *(978-0-545-12276-4(7))* Scholastic, Inc. (Levine, Arthur A. Bks.).

Yep, Laurence & Yep, Kathleen S. The Dragon's Child: A Story of Angel Island. 2011. (ENG.). 160p. (J). (gr. 3-7). pap. 5.99 *(978-0-06-201815-1(9))* HarperCollins Pubs.

Yin. Coolies. Soentpiet, Chris K., illus. 2003. (ENG.). 40p. (J). (gr. 2-5). 7.99 *(978-0-14-250055-2(0)*, Puffin Books) Penguin Young Readers Group.

Young, Andrea. Finny & the Boy from Horse Mountain. (ENG.). 320p. (J). (gr. 6). 2016. pap. 9.99 *(978-1-63450-166-8(7))* 2013. 16.95 *(978-1-62087-682-4(5)*, 620682) Skyhorse Publishing Co., Inc. (Sky Pony Pr.).

Young, Karen Romano. Doodlebug: A Novel in Doodles. 2012. (ENG., Illus.). 128p. (J). (gr. 3-7). pap. 7.99 *(978-1-250-01020-9(9)*, 9781250010209) Square Fish.

—Stuck in the Middle (of Middle School) A Novel in Doodles. 2013. (ENG., Illus.). 112p. (J). (gr. 3-7). 12.99 *(978-0-312-55596-2(2)*, 9780312555962) Feiwel & Friends.

—Stuck in the Middle (of Middle School) A Novel in Doodles. 2014. (ENG., Illus.). 128p. (J). (gr. 3-7). pap. 6.99 *(978-1-250-03997-2(5)*, 9781250039972) Square Fish.

Zarr, Sara. Story of a Girl. 2008. (ENG.). 224p. (YA). (gr. 7-17). per. 10.99 *(978-0-316-01454-0(0))* Little, Brown Bks. for Young Readers.

Zaugg, Sandra L. Secret of the Desert Lights: A Story about Following God's Laws. 2009. (J). pap. 9.99 *(978-0-8163-2294-7(5))* Pacific Pr. Publishing Assn.

—Secret of the Yellow Van: A Book about Dealing with Loss. 2008. (J). pap. 8.99 *(978-0-8163-2246-6(5))* Pacific Pr. Publishing Assn.

Zehring Fischer, Nancy. Children of the Mission. 2013. 52p. pap. 7.95 *(978-1-61170-129-6(5))* Robertson Publishing.

Zink, Michelle. Lies I Told. 2015. (Lies I Told Ser.: 1). (ENG.). 352p. (YA). (gr. 8). 17.99 *(978-0-06-232712-3(7))* HarperCollins Pubs.

Zolty, H. Calli the Bear: the Story of a Little Bear Who Explores California & Helps Children Learn about the Golden State. 2006. 56p. pap. 19.98 *(978-1-4116-4889-0(7))* Lulu Pr., Inc.

CALIFORNIA—GOLD DISCOVERIES

Altman, Linda Jacobs. The California Gold Rush. 2012. (Stories in American History Ser.). (Illus.). 128p. (J). (gr. 5-18). 33.27 *(978-0-7660-3953-7(6))*; pap. *(978-1-4644-0023-8(4))* Enslow Pubs., Inc.

—The California Gold Rush: Stories in American History. 2012. (Stories in American History Ser.). (Illus.). 128p. (J). (gr. 5-18). pap. 10.95 *(978-1-4644-0023-0(7))* Enslow Pubs., Inc.

Aretha, David. The Gold Rush to California's Riches. 2006. (Wild History of the American West Ser.). (Illus.). 128p. (J). (gr. 5-9). lib. bdg. 34.60 *(978-1-59845-012-5(3)*, MyReportLinks.com Bks.) Enslow Pubs., Inc.

Benoit, Peter. The California Gold Rush. 2012. (Cornerstones of Freedom, Third Ser.). (ENG., Illus.). 64p. (J). pap. 8.95 *(978-0-531-28153-6(1))*; lib. bdg. 30.00 *(978-0-531-23053-4(8))* Scholastic Library Publishing.

Blashfield, Jean F. The California Gold Rush & The '49ers. 2017. (Landmarks in U. S. History Ser.). (ENG.). 32p. (gr. 3-4). lib. bdg. 27.32 ***(978-1-5157-7116-6(4)***, Fact Finders) Capstone Press of Coughlan Cos.

Brown, Don. Gold! Gold from the American River! January 24 1848 - The Day the Gold Rush Began. Brown, Don, illus. 2011. (Actual Times Ser.: 3). (ENG., Illus.). 64p. (J). (gr. 1-5). 17.99 *(978-1-59643-223-9(3)*, 9781596432239) Roaring Brook Pr.

—Gold! Gold from the American River! January 24, 1848: the Day the Gold Rush Began. Brown, Don, illus. 2014. (Actual Times Ser.: 3). (ENG., Illus.). 64p. (J). (gr. 1-5). 8.99 *(978-1-250-04060-2(4)*, 9781250040602) Square Fish.

Brown, Rachel K. Sacramento: Daily Life in Western Mining Town. 2003. (J). pap. *(978-1-58417-078-5(6))*; lib. bdg. *(978-1-58417-015-0(8))* Lake Street Pubs.

Caswell, Max. My Life During the Gold Rush. 2017. (My Place in History Ser.). 24p. (J). (gr. 2-3). pap. 8.15 ***(978-1-5382-0297-5(2))*** Stevens, Gareth Publishing LLLP.

Collins, Terry. Stake a Claim! Nickolas Flux & the California Gold Rush, 1 vol. Ginevra, Dante, illus. 2014. (Nickolas Flux History Chronicles Ser.). (ENG.). 32p. (gr. 3-4). lib. bdg. 30.65 *(978-1-4765-3944-7(8)*, Graphic Library) Capstone Press of Coughlan Cos.

Craats, Rennay. Gold Rush. 2003. (Real Life Stories Ser.). (Illus.). 24p. (J). lib. bdg. 24.45 *(978-1-59036-078-1(8))* Weigl Pubs., Inc.

Crewe, Sabrina & Uschan, Michael V. La Fiebre del Oro en California. 2006. (Hitos de la historia de Estados Unidos (Landmark Events in American History) Ser.). (SPA., Illus.). 48p. (gr. 5-12). lib. bdg. 27.00 *(978-0-8368-7466-2(8)*, Gareth Stevens Secondary Library) Stevens, Gareth Publishing LLLP.

—La Fiebre del oro en California. 2006. (Hitos de la historia de Estados Unidos (Landmark Events in American History) Ser.). (SPA.). 48p. (gr. 5-12). pap. 11.70 *(978-0-8368-7473-0(0)*, Gareth Stevens Learning Library) Stevens, Gareth Publishing LLLP.

Crewe, Sabrina, et al. The California Gold Rush. 2010. (ENG., Illus.). 32p. (C). (gr. 3-6). lib. bdg. 41.95 *(978-0-8368-3393-5(7))* National Geographic School Publishing, Inc.

Davies, Monika. The Gold Rush. 2017. (Primary Source Readers Ser.). 32p. (gr. 4-4). 9.99 ***(978-1-4258-3238-4(5))*** Teacher Created Materials, Inc.

Doeden, Matt. John Sutter & the California Gold Rush, 1 vol. Barnett, Charles, III et al, illus. 2005. (Graphic History Ser.). (ENG.). 32p. (gr. 3-4). 30.65 *(978-0-7368-4370-6(1)*, Graphic Library) Capstone Press of Coughlan Cos.

Flores, Mina. The Gold Rush: Gold Seekers, Miners, & Merchants. 2016. (Spotlight on American History Ser.). (Illus.). 24p. (J). (gr. 6-4). 26.25 *(978-1-5081-4942-2(9)*, PowerKids Pr.) Rosen Publishing Group, Inc., The.

Fradin, Dennis Brindell. The California Gold Rush. 2008. (Turning Points in U. S. History Ser.). 48p. (gr. 3-18). lib. bdg. 31.36 *(978-0-7614-3012-4(1)*, Benchmark Bks.) Marshall Cavendish Corp.

Friedman, Mel. The California Gold Rush. 2010. (True Book Ser.). (ENG., Illus.). 48p. (J). (gr. 2-5). 29.00 *(978-0-531-20581-5(9))* Scholastic Library Publishing.

George, Lynn. What Do You Know about the Gold Rush? (20 Questions: History Ser.). 24p. (gr. 2-3). 2009. 42.50 *(978-1-60854-959-7(3)*, PowerKids Pr.) 2008. (J). lib. bdg. 22.60 *(978-1-4042-4188-6(4))* Rosen Publishing Group, Inc., The.

Gildenstein, Melanie & O'Donnell, Kerri. A Primary Source Investigation of the Gold Rush. 2015. (Uncovering American History Ser.). (ENG., Illus.). 64p. (J). (gr. 5-6). 32.95 *(978-1-4994-3511-5(8)*, Rosen Central) Rosen Publishing Group, Inc., The.

Goff, Elizabeth Hudson & Uschan, Michael V. The California Gold Rush. 2006. (Graphic Histories Ser.). (Illus.). 32p. (gr. 5-8). pap. 10.50 *(978-0-8368-6254-6(6))* Stevens, Gareth Publishing LLLP.

Goff, Elizabeth Hudson, et al. The California Gold Rush. Floor, Guus, illus. 2006. (Graphic Histories Ser.). 32p. (gr. 5-8). lib. bdg. 27.00 *(978-0-8368-6202-7(3))* Stevens, Gareth Publishing LLLP.

Hall, Brianna. Strike It Rich! The Story of the California Gold Rush, 1 vol. 2014. (Adventures on the American Frontier Ser.). (ENG.). 32p. (gr. 3-4). 27.32 *(978-1-4914-0184-2(2)*, Fact Finders) Capstone Press of Coughlan Cos.

Hayhurst, Chris. John Sutter: California Pioneer / Pionero de California. 2009. (Famous People in American History/Grandes personajes en la historia de los Estados Unidos Ser.). (ENG & SPA.). 32p. (gr. 2-3). 47.90 *(978-1-61512-549-4(3)*, Editorial Buenas Letras) Rosen Publishing Group, Inc., The.

—John Sutter: Pionero de California (John Sutter: California Pioneer) 2009. (Grandes personajes en la historia de los Estados Unidos (Famous People in American History) Ser.). (SPA.). 32p. (gr. 2-3). 47.90 *(978-1-61512-803-7(4)*, Editorial Buenas Letras) Rosen Publishing Group, Inc., The.

Holub, Joan. What Was the Gold Rush? Tomkinson, Tim, illus. 2013. (What Was? Ser.). (ENG.). 112p. (J). (gr. 3-7). pap. 5.99 *(978-0-448-46289-9(3)*, Penguin Workshop) Penguin Young Readers Group.

—What Was the Gold Rush? 2013. (What Was... ? Ser.). lib. bdg. 16.00 *(978-0-606-29972-5(6)*, Turtleback) Turtleback Bks.

Howell, Brian. U. S. Growth & Change in the 19th Century, 1801 to 1861. 2011. (Explorer Library: Language Arts Explorer Ser.). (ENG.). 32p. (gr. 4-8). lib. bdg. 28.50 *(978-1-61080-202-4(0)*, 201180) Cherry Lake Publishing.

—U.S. Growth & Change in the 19th Century. 2011. (Explorer Library: Language Arts Explorer Ser.). (ENG.). 32p. (gr. 4-8). pap. 14.21 *(978-1-61080-290-1(X)*, 201213) Cherry Lake Publishing.

Jeffrey, Gary. The Gold Rush. Boccanfuso, Emanuele, illus. 2012. (Graphic History of the American West Ser.). (ENG.). 24p. (J). (gr. 3-8). pap. 8.15 *(978-1-4339-6741-2(3)*, Gareth Stevens Learning Library) Stevens, Gareth Publishing LLLP.

Johnson, Robin. California Gold Rush! 2013. (ENG., Illus.). 48p. (J). *(978-0-7787-1170-4(6))*; pap. *(978-0-7787-1178-0(1))* Crabtree Publishing Co.

Jordan, Shirley. California Gold Rush: Moments in History. 2003. (Cover-To-Cover Books). (Illus.). 64p. pap. 9.00 *(978-0-7891-5554-2(0))*; (J). (gr. 4-7). lib. bdg. 17.95 *(978-0-7569-0633-7(4))* Perfection Learning Corp.

Kraft, Eric. Gold Rush! & ¡la fiebre del Oro! 6 English, 6 Spanish Adaptations. 2011. (ENG & SPA.). (J). 97.00 net. *(978-1-4108-5699-9(2))* Benchmark Education Co.

Landau, Elaine. The California Gold Rush: Would You Go for the Gold? (What Would You Do? Ser.). (Illus.). 48p. (J). 2010. pap. 8.95 *(978-1-59845-193-1(6))* 2008. (gr. 3-4). lib. bdg. 25.27 *(978-0-7660-2901-9(8))* Enslow Pubs., Inc. (Enslow Elementary).

—The Gold Rush in California: Would You Catch Gold Fever? 2015. (What Would You Do? Ser.). 48p. (J). (gr. 3-4). 25.27 *(978-0-7660-6300-6(3))*; pap. 8.95 *(978-0-7660-6301-3(1)*, Enslow Elementary) Enslow Pubs., Inc.

Levy, Janey. Life During the Gold Rush. 2013. (What You Didn't Know about History Ser.). (Illus.). 24p. (J). (gr. 2-5). pap. 8.15 *(978-1-4339-8430-3(X))*; lib. bdg. 22.60 *(978-1-4339-8429-7(6))* Stevens, Gareth Publishing LLLP.

Lüsted, Marcia Amidon. The California Gold Rush: A History Perspectives Book. 2014. (Perspectives Library). (ENG., Illus.). 32p. (J). (gr. 4-8). 28.50 *(978-1-63137-615-3(2)*, 205243) Cherry Lake Publishing.

Lynette, Rachel. The Gold Rush. 2013. (Pioneer Spirit: the Westward Expansion Ser.). 24p. (J). (gr. 3-6). 22.60 *(978-1-4777-0784-5(0))*; pap. 49.50 *(978-1-4777-0902-3(9))*; (ENG., Illus.). pap. 8.25 *(978-1-4777-0901-6(0))* Rosen Publishing Group, Inc., The. (PowerKids Pr.).

Madison, Amelia & Shoup, Kate. Life As a Prospector in the California Gold Rush. 2016. (Life As... Ser.). (ENG., Illus.). 32p. (J). (gr. 3-3). 28.50 *(978-1-5026-1780-4(3))* Cavendish Square Publishing.

Mattern, Joanne. America's Gold Rush: John Sutter & the Discovery of Gold in California. 2009. (Great Moments in American History Ser.). 32p. (gr. 3-3). 47.90 *(978-1-61513-139-6(6))* Rosen Publishing Group, Inc., The.

Micklos, John, Jr. The Gold Rush. 2016. (Primary Source History Ser.). (ENG., Illus.). 32p. (gr. 3-4). lib. bdg. 27.32 *(978-1-4914-8486-9(1)*, Fact Finders) Capstone Press of Coughlan Cos.

Morlock, Theresa. The Gold Rush. 2017. (J). pap. ***(978-1-68048-788-6(4)***, Britannica Educational Publishing) Rosen Publishing Group, Inc., The.

O'Donnell, Kerri. The California Gold Rush: Multiplying & Dividing Using Three- & Four-Digit Numbers. (PowerMath Ser.). 32p. 2009. (ENG., Illus.). (gr. 5-6). pap. 10.00 *(978-1-4042-5131-1(6)*, PowerKids Pr.) 2005. (Illus.). (YA). (gr. 5-9). lib. bdg. 25.25 *(978-1-4042-2934-1(5))* 2005. 47.50 *(978-1-4042-5221-9(5)*, Rosen Classroom) Rosen Publishing Group, Inc., The.

—A Timeline of the California Gold Rush. 2009. (Real Life Readers Ser.). 32p. (gr. 4-5). pap. 10.00 *(978-1-4358-0161-5(X)*, Rosen Classroom); (gr. 4-4). 47.90 *(978-1-61511-366-8(5)*, PowerKids Pr.); (J). (gr. 3-4). lib. bdg. 25.25 *(978-1-4358-2989-3(1)*, PowerKids Pr.) Rosen Publishing Group, Inc., The.

Olson, Tod. How to Get Rich in the California Gold Rush: An Adventurer's Guide to the Fabulous Riches Discovered in 1848. Allred, Scott, illus. 2008. (ENG.). 48p. (J). (gr. 5-9). lib. bdg. 25.90 *(978-1-4263-0316-6(5)*, National Geographic Children's Bks.) National Geographic Society.

Onsgard, Bethany. Life During the California Gold Rush, 1 vol. 2014. (Daily Life in US History Ser.). (ENG., Illus.). 48p. (J). (gr. 3-6). lib. bdg. 32.79 *(978-1-62403-624-8(4))* ABDO Publishing Co.

Quasha, Jennifer. Gold Rush: Hands-on Projects about Mining the Riches of California. 2009. (Great Social Studies Projects Ser.). 24p. (gr. 3-3). 42.50 *(978-1-61513-209-6(0)*, PowerKids Pr.) Rosen Publishing Group, Inc., The.

Raabe, Emily. The Gold Rush: California or Bust! (Westward Ho! Ser.). 24p. 2009. (gr. 2-3). 42.50 *(978-1-60854-762-3(0))* 2003. (Illus.). (J). lib. bdg. 22.60 *(978-0-8239-6494-9(9))* Rosen Publishing Group, Inc., The. (PowerKids Pr.).

Rau, Margaret. The Wells Fargo Book of the Gold Rush. 2003. (Illus.). 143p. (J). (gr. 3-7). reprint ed. 18.00 *(978-0-7567-6878-2(0))* DIANE Publishing Co.

Raum, Elizabeth. The California Gold Rush: An Interactive History Adventure. 2016. (You Choose: History Ser.). (ENG.). 112p. (gr. 3-4). pap. 6.95 *(978-1-5157-4254-8(7)*, You Choose Bks.) Capstone Press of Coughlan Cos.

Rivera, Sheila. California Gold Rush, 1 vol. 2004. (American Moments Ser.). (ENG., Illus.). 48p. (gr. 4-8). 27.07 *(978-1-59197-281-5(7)*, Abdo & Daughters) ABDO Publishing Co.

Schanzer, Rosalyn. Gold Fever! Tales from the California Gold Rush. 2007. (ENG., Illus.). 48p. (J). (gr. 4-7). per. 6.95 *(978-1-4263-0040-0(9)*, National Geographic Children's Bks.) National Geographic Society.

Schuetz, Kari. Bodie: The Gold-Mining Ghost Town. 2017. (Abandoned Places Ser.). (ENG., Illus.). 24p. (J). (gr. 3-7). lib. bdg. 25.95 ***(978-1-62617-694-2(9)***, Torque Bks.) Bellwether Media.

Shoup, Kate. The California Gold Rush. 2016. (Expanding America Ser.). (ENG., Illus.). 96p. (J). (gr. 8-8). lib. bdg. 42.79 *(978-1-5026-0968-7(1))* Cavendish Square Publishing.

Shoup, Kate. The Gold Rush. 2017. (J). ***(978-1-5026-2640-0(3))*** Cavendish Square Publishing.

Sonneborn, Liz. The California Gold Rush. 2008. (Milestones in American History Ser.). (Illus.). 128p. (YA). (gr. 7-12). 35.00 *(978-1-60413-051-5(2))* Facts On File, Inc.

Thompson, Linda. The California Gold Rush. 2005. (Expansion of America Ser.). (Illus.). 48p. (gr. 4-8). 20.95 *(978-1-59515-222-0(9))* Rourke Educational Media.

Thornton, Jeremy. The Gold Rush: Chinese Immigrants Come to America (1848-1882) (Primary Sources of Immigration & Migration in America Ser.). 24p. 2009. (gr. 3-4). 42.50 *(978-1-60851-784-8(5))* 2004. (Illus.). (J). lib. bdg. 22.60 *(978-0-8239-6833-6(2))* Rosen Publishing Group, Inc., The. (PowerKids Pr.).

—The Gold Rush: Chinese Immigrants Come to America, 1848-1882. 2004. (Primary Sources of Immigration & Migration in America Ser.). (ENG., Illus.). 24p. (gr. 4-8). pap. 9.40 *(978-0-8239-8959-1(3)*, PowerKids Pr.) Rosen Publishing Group, Inc., The.

Uschan, Michael V. The California Gold Rush. 2003. (Landmark Events in American History Ser.). (Illus.). 48p. (gr. 5-12). pap. 14.05 *(978-0-8368-5402-2(0))*; lib. bdg. 31.00 *(978-0-8368-5374-2(1))* Stevens, Gareth Publishing LLLP. (Gareth Stevens Secondary Library).

Watson, Stephanie. A Timeline History of the California Gold Rush. 2015. (ENG., Illus.). 48p. (J). (gr. 5-8). 30.65 *(978-1-4677-8580-8(6))* Lerner Publishing Group.

CALIFORNIA—HISTORY

Abbink, Emily. Monterey Bay Area Missions. 2007. (Exploring California Missions Ser.). (ENG., Illus.). 64p. (gr. 4-7). lib. bdg. 27.93 *(978-0-8225-0887-8(7)*, Lerner Pubns.) Lerner Publishing Group.

Altman, Linda Jacobs. California. 2nd rev. ed. 2005. (Celebrate the States Ser.). (Illus.). 144p. (gr. 6-7). lib. bdg. 42.79 *(978-0-7614-1737-8(0)*, Benchmark Bks.) Marshall Cavendish Corp.

—The California Gold Rush: Stories in American History. 2012. (Stories in American History Ser.). (Illus.). 128p. (J). (gr. 5-18). pap. 10.95 *(978-1-4644-0023-0(7))* Enslow Pubs., Inc.

Anderson, Zachary. Discovering Mission La Purísima Concepción. 2014. (California Missions Ser.). (Illus.). 48p. (J). (gr. 4-6). lib. bdg. 31.36 *(978-1-62713-094-3(2))* Cavendish Square Publishing.

—Discovering Mission Nuestra Señora de la Soledad. 2014. (California Missions Ser.). 48p. (J). (gr. 4-6). 31.36 *(978-1-62713-079-0(9))* Cavendish Square Publishing.

—Discovering Mission San Antonio de Padua. 2014. (California Missions Ser.). (Illus.). 48p. (J). (gr. 4-6). lib. bdg. 31.36 *(978-1-62713-082-0(9))* Cavendish Square Publishing.

Baker, Gayle. Cambria: A HarborTown History. 2003. (Illus.). 96p. per. 8.95 *(978-0-9710984-2-8(5))* HarborTown Histories.

—Newport Beach: A HarborTown History. 2004. (Illus.). 112p. per. 9.95 *(978-0-9710984-3-5(3))* HarborTown Histories.

—Santa Barbara: A HarborTown History. 2003. (Illus.). 96p. per. 8.95 *(978-0-9710984-1-1(7))* HarborTown Histories.

Bakker, T. C. Alcatraz Believe It or Not. House, Charles, illus. 2016. 110p. ***(978-1-932519-36-5(X))*** Golden Gate National Parks Conservancy.

Bauer, Marion Dane & Rucker, Justin. Celebrating California: 50 States to Celebrate. Canga, C. B., illus. 2013. (Green Light Readers Level 3 Ser.). (ENG.). 40p. (J). (gr. 1-4). 12.99 *(978-0-547-98385-1(9))*; pap. 3.99 *(978-0-547-89697-7(2))* Houghton Mifflin Harcourt Publishing Co.

Behrens, June. Central Coast Missions in California. 2007. (Exploring California Missions Ser.). (Illus.). 64p. (J). lib. bdg. 27.93 *(978-0-8225-0897-7(4))*, Lerner Pubns.) Lerner Publishing Group.

Benoit, Peter. The California Gold Rush. 2012. (Cornerstones of Freedom, Third Ser.). (ENG., Illus.). 64p. (J). pap. 8.95 *(978-0-531-28153-6(1))*; lib. bdg. 30.00 *(978-0-531-23053-4(8))* Scholastic Library Publishing.

Blake, Kevin. Salton Sea Resort: Death in the Desert. 2015. (Abandoned: Towns Without People Ser.). (ENG.). 32p. (J). (gr. 2-7). lib. bdg. 26.60 *(978-1-62724-523-4(5))* Bearport Publishing Co., Inc.

Blake, Kevin & Sturdivant, Brad. Bodie: The Town That Belongs to Ghosts. 2015. (Abandoned: Towns Without People Ser.). (ENG.). 32p. (J). (gr. 2-7). lib. bdg. 26.60 *(978-1-62724-524-1(3))* Bearport Publishing Co., Inc.

Blashfield, Jean F. The California Gold Rush & The '49ers. 2017. (Landmarks in U. S. History Ser.). (ENG.). 32p. (gr. 3-4). lib. bdg. 27.32 ***(978-1-5157-7116-6(4)***, Fact Finders) Capstone Press of Coughlan Cos.

Boule, Mary Null. California Native American Tribes: Mohave Tribe, 28 booklets. Liddell, Daniel & Basta, Mary, illus. (California Native American Tribes). 52p. (J). (gr. 3-6). pap. 7.95 *(978-1-877599-73-6(5))* Merryant Pubs.

Brower, Pauline. Inland Valleys Missions in California. 2007. (Exploring California Missions Ser.). (ENG., Illus.). 64p. (gr. 4-7). lib. bdg. 27.93 *(978-0-8225-0899-1(0)*, Lerner Pubns.) Lerner Publishing Group.

Brown, Don. Gold! Gold from the American River! January 24 1848 - The Day the Gold Rush Began. Brown, Don, illus. 2011. (Actual Times Ser.: 3). (ENG., Illus.). 64p. (J). (gr. 1-5). 17.99 *(978-1-59643-223-9(3)*, 9781596432239) Roaring Brook Pr.

Brown, Rachel K. Sacramento: Daily Life in Western Mining Town. 2003. (J). pap. *(978-1-58417-078-5(6))* Lake Street Pubs.

Buckley, Jeannette. Discovering Mission San Juan Capistrano. 2016. (California Missions Ser.). (ENG.). 48p. (J). (gr. 4-4). pap. 12.95 *(978-1-5026-1217-5(8))* Cavendish Square Publishing.

—Discovering Mission San Luis Obispo de Tolosa. 2014. (California Missions Ser.). (Illus.). 48p. (J). (gr. 4-6). lib. bdg. 31.36 *(978-1-62713-091-2(8))* Cavendish Square Publishing.

—Discovering Mission San Luis Rey de Francia. (California Missions Ser.). 48p. (J). (gr. 4-4). 2016. (ENG.). pap. 12.95 *(978-1-5026-1226-7(7))* 2014. 31.36 *(978-1-62713-112-4(4))* Cavendish Square Publishing.

Burgan, Michael & McGeveran, William. California. 2nd rev. ed. 2010. (It's My State! Ser.). 80p. (gr. 3-18). lib. bdg. 31.36 *(978-1-60870-045-5(3))* Marshall Cavendish Corp.

California Missions. 2014. (California Missions Ser.). 48p. (J). (gr. 4-6). 658.56 *(978-1-62713-148-3(5))* Cavendish Square Publishing.

Campbell, Wallis. Angel Island. 2006. (Illus.). 48p. (J). pap. *(978-1-59034-808-6(7))* Mondo Publishing.

Cantillo, Oscar. Discovering Mission San Fernando Rey de España. (California Missions Ser.). 48p. (J). (gr. 4-4). 2016. (ENG.). pap. 12.95 *(978-1-5026-1224-3(0))* 2014. lib. bdg. 31.36 *(978-1-62713-106-3(X))* Cavendish Square Publishing.

—Discovering Mission San Francisco de Asís. 2014. (J). lib. bdg. *(978-1-62713-061-5(6))* Musa Publishing.

—Discovering Mission San Francisco de Solano. 2014. (California Missions Ser.). 48p. (J). (gr. 4-6). lib. bdg. 31.36 *(978-1-62713-055-4(1))* Cavendish Square Publishing.

Caron, Mona, illus. Many Worlds: Native Life along the Anza Trail. 2012. (ENG.). 24p. (J). pap. 7.95 *(978-1-59714-167-3(4))* Heyday.

Caswell, Max. My Life During the Gold Rush. 2017. (My Place in History Ser.). 24p. (J). (gr. 2-3). pap. 8.15 ***(978-1-5382-0297-5(2))*** Stevens, Gareth Publishing LLLP.

Ching, Jacqueline. Mission San Fernando Rey de Espana. 2009. (Missions of California Ser.). 64p. (gr. 4-4). 58.50 *(978-1-60854-028-0(6)*, PowerKids Pr.) Rosen Publishing Group, Inc., The.

—Mission San Rafael Arcangel. (Missions of California Ser.). 64p. 2009. (gr. 4-4). 58.50 *(978-1-60854-036-5(7))* 2003. (J). 26.50 *(978-0-8239-5886-3(8))* Rosen Publishing Group, Inc., The. (PowerKids Pr.).

—Mission Santa Ines. 2009. (Missions of California Ser.). 64p. (gr. 4-4). 58.50 *(978-1-60854-042-6(1)*, PowerKids Pr.) Rosen Publishing Group, Inc., The.

Ching, Jacqueline & Connelly, Jack. Discovering Mission San Rafael Arcángel. 2014. (California Missions Ser.). (Illus.). 48p. (J). (gr. 4-6). lib. bdg. 31.36 *(978-1-62713-058-5(6))* Cavendish Square Publishing.

Coleman, Wim & Perrin, Pat. The Rebellious Californians & the Brave Struggle to Join the Nation. 2006. (Wild History of the American West Ser.). (Illus.). 128p. (J). (gr. 5-9). lib. bdg. 34.60 *(978-1-59845-015-6(8)*, MyReportLinks.com Bks.) Enslow Pubs., Inc.

Collins, Terry. Stake a Claim! Nickolas Flux & the California Gold Rush, 1 vol. Ginevra, Dante, illus. 2014. (Nickolas Flux History Chronicles Ser.). (ENG.). 32p. (gr. 3-4). lib. bdg. 30.65 *(978-1-4765-3944-7(8)*, Graphic Library) Capstone Press of Coughlan Cos.

Connelly, Jack. Discovering Mission Santa Bárbara. 2014. (California Missions Ser.). 48p. (J). (gr. 4-6). lib. bdg. 31.36 *(978-1-62713-100-1(0))* Cavendish Square Publishing.

Crewe, Sabrina & Uschan, Michael V. La Fiebre del Oro en California. 2006. (Hitos de la historia de Estados Unidos (Landmark Events in American History) Ser.). (SPA., Illus.). 48p. (gr. 5-12). lib. bdg. 27.00 *(978-0-8368-7466-2(8)*, Gareth Stevens Secondary Library) Stevens, Gareth Publishing LLLP.

—La Fiebre del oro en California. 2006. (Hitos de la historia de Estados Unidos (Landmark Events in American History) Ser.). (SPA.). 48p. (gr. 5-12). pap. 11.70 *(978-0-8368-7473-0(0)*, Gareth Stevens Learning Library) Stevens, Gareth Publishing LLLP.

Crewe, Sabrina, et al. The California Gold Rush. 2010. (ENG., Illus.). 32p. (C). (gr. 3-6). lib. bdg. 41.95 *(978-0-8368-3393-5(7))* National Geographic School Publishing, Inc.

C
D

Davies, Monika. The Gold Rush. 2017. (Primary Source Readers Ser.). 32p. (gr. 4-4). 9.99 ***(978-1-4258-3238-4(5))*** Teacher Created Materials, Inc.

De Capua, Sarah. California. 2003. (Rookie Read-about Science Ser.). (Illus.). 31p. (J). (gr. -1-3). 13.60 *(978-0-7569-7136-6(5))* Perfection Learning Corp.

—California. 2005. (Rookie Espanol: Geografia Ser.). (SPA., Illus.). 32p. (J). (gr. k-2). pap. 5.95 *(978-0-516-25513-2(4)*, Children's Pr.) Scholastic Library Publishing.

Dickmann, Nancy. Earth's Landforms. 2016. (Earth Figured Out Ser.). (ENG., Illus.). 32p. (J). (gr. 4-4). pap. 10.58 *(978-1-5026-0866-6(9)*, 1399805) Cavendish Square Publishing.

Ditchfield, Christin. Spanish Missions. 2006. (True Bks.). (Illus.). 48p. (J). (gr. 3-7). pap. 6.95 *(978-0-516-21746-8(1)*, Children's Pr.) Scholastic Library Publishing.

Doak, Robin Santos. California, 1542-1850. 2006. (National Geographic Voices from ColonialAmerica Ser.). (ENG., Illus.). 112p. (J). (gr. 5-9). 21.95 *(978-0-7922-6391-3(X))*; lib. bdg. 32.90 *(978-0-7922-6861-1(X))* National Geographic Society. (National Geographic Children's Bks.).

Draper, Allison Stark. Mission San Fransisco de Solano. (Missions of California Ser.). 64p. (gr. 4-4). 2009. 58.50 *(978-1-60854-029-7(4)*, PowerKids Pr.) 2003. (Illus.). (J). 26.50 *(978-0-8239-5884-9(1))* Rosen Publishing Group, Inc., The.

—Mission San Juan Bautista. 2009. (Missions of California Ser.). 64p. (gr. 4-4). 58.50 *(978-1-60854-032-7(4)*, PowerKids Pr.) Rosen Publishing Group, Inc., The.

Duffield, Katy S. California History for Kids: Missions, Miners, & Moviemakers in the Golden State, Includes 21 Activities. 2012. (For Kids Ser.). (ENG., Illus.). 144p. (J). (gr. 4). pap. 16.95 *(978-1-56976-532-6(4))* Chicago Review Pr., Inc.

Durrie, Karen. California: The Golden State. 2012. (J). *(978-1-61913-329-7(6))*; pap. *(978-1-61913-330-3(X))* Weigl Pubs., Inc.

Dyan, Penelope. Beaching It! a Kid's Guide to la Jolla, California. Weigand, John, photos by. 2013. (Illus.). 34p. pap. 11.95 *(978-1-61477-092-3(1))* Bellissima Publishing, LLC.

—Beyond the Trees! a Kid's Guide to Lake Tahoe, Us. Weigand, John D., photos by. 2012. (Illus.). 34p. pap. 11.95 *(978-1-61477-027-5(1))* Bellissima Publishing, LLC.

—By the Bay! a Kid's Guide to San Diego, California. Weigand, John D., photos by. 2013. (Illus.). 34p. pap. 11.95 *(978-1-61477-087-9(5))* Bellissima Publishing, LLC.

—Cruisin' 4 Fun! a Kid's Guide to Santa Cruz, Californi. Weigand, John, photos by. 2013. (Illus.). 34p. pap. 11.95 *(978-1-61477-082-4(4))* Bellissima Publishing, LLC.

—Fun in the Sun! a Kids' Guide to Santa Barbara, Californi. Weigand, John D., photos by. 2012. (Illus.). 34p. pap. 11.95 *(978-1-61477-051-0(4))* Bellissima Publishing, LLC.

—Island Style! a Kid's Guide to Coronado, California. Weigand, John D., photos by. 2013. (Illus.). 34p. pap. 11.95 *(978-1-61477-090-9(5))* Bellissima Publishing, LLC.

—It's Magic! a Kid's Guide to Monterey, California. Weigand, John D., photos by. 2013. (Illus.). 34p. pap. 11.95 *(978-1-61477-119-7(7))* Bellissima Publishing, LLC.

—Yummy Solvang! a Kid's Guide to Solvang, Californi. Weigand, John D., photos by. 2012. (Illus.). 34p. pap. 11.95 *(978-1-61477-052-7(2))* Bellissima Publishing, LLC.

Eastman, Gail. Anna's Home by the River: A Children's History of Anaheim. Bates, Bob, illus. 2007. 199p. (J). pap. *(978-0-9797419-0-6(4))* Tesoro Publishing.

Edgar, Kathleen J. Mission San Diego de Alcala. 2009. (Missions of California Ser.). 64p. (gr. 4-4). 58.50 *(978-1-60854-027-3(8)*, PowerKids Pr.) Rosen Publishing Group, Inc., The.

—Mission San Francisco de Asis. 2009. (Missions of California Ser.). 64p. (gr. 4-4). 58.50 *(978-1-60854-024-2(3)*, PowerKids Pr.) Rosen Publishing Group, Inc., The.

—Mission San Miguel Arcangel. 2009. (Missions of California Ser.). 64p. (gr. 4-4). 58.50 *(978-1-60854-035-8(9)*, PowerKids Pr.) Rosen Publishing Group, Inc., The.

Edgar, Kathleen J. & Edgar, Susan E. Mission San Carlos Borromeo Del Rio Carmelo. 2003. (Missions of Californiatm Ser.). (Illus.). 64p. (YA). (gr. 4-7). 26.50 *(978-0-8239-5890-0(6))* Rosen Publishing Group, Inc., The.

—Mission San Francisco de Asis. 2003. (Missions of Californiatm Ser.). (Illus.). 64p. (J). (gr. 4-18). 26.50 *(978-0-8239-5887-0(6))* Rosen Publishing Group, Inc., The.

Edgar, Kathleen J., et al. Discovering Mission San Carlos Borromeo Del Carmelo. 2014. (California Missions Ser.). 48p. (J). (gr. 4-6). lib. bdg. 31.36 *(978-1-62713-076-9(4))* Cavendish Square Publishing.

—Discovering Mission San Juan Capistrano. 2014. (California Missions Ser.). (Illus.). 48p. (J). (gr. 4-6). lib. bdg. 31.36 *(978-1-62713-085-1(3))* Cavendish Square Publishing.

—Discovering Mission San Miguel Arcángel. 2014. (California Missions Ser.). 48p. (J). (gr. 4-6). lib. bdg. 31.36 *(978-1-62713-088-2(8))* Cavendish Square Publishing.

Ferut, Michael. Winchester Mystery House. 2014. (Scariest Places on Earth Ser.). (ENG., Illus.). 24p. (J). (gr. 3-7). lib. bdg. 25.95 *(978-1-60014-998-6(7)*, Torque Bks.) Bellwether Media.

Freedman, Russell. Angel Island: Gateway to Gold Mountain. 2014. (ENG., Illus.). 96p. (J). (gr. 5-7). 17.99 *(978-0-547-90378-1(2))* Houghton Mifflin Harcourt Publishing Co.

—Angel Island: Gateway to Gold Mountain. 2016. lib. bdg. 22.10 ***(978-0-606-39677-6(2))*** Turtleback Bks.

Friedman, Mel. The California Gold Rush. 2010. (True Book Ser.). (ENG., Illus.). 48p. (J). pap. 6.95 *(978-0-531-21244-8(0))*; (gr. 2-5). 29.00 *(978-0-531-20581-5(9))* Scholastic Library Publishing.

Fun & Educational Places to go with Kids & Adults in Southern California - 8th Edition: Fun Places to go with Kids. 2009. 878p. pap. 24.95 *(978-0-9646737-9-3(7))* Fun Places Publishing.

Gendell, Megan. Spanish Missions of California. 2010. (True Book(tm), a — Spanish Missions Ser.). (Illus.). 48p. (J). (gr. 2-5). 31.00 *(978-0-531-20577-8(0))* Scholastic Library Publishing.

—The Spanish Missions of California. 2010. (True Book Ser.). (ENG.). 48p. (J). (gr. 3-5). pap. 6.95 *(978-0-531-21240-0(8)*, Children's Pr.) Scholastic Library Publishing.

George, Lynn. What Do You Know about the Gold Rush? (20 Questions: History Ser.). 24p. (gr. 2-3). 2009. 42.50 *(978-1-60854-959-7(3)*, PowerKids Pr.) 2008. (J). lib. bdg. 22.60 *(978-1-4042-4188-6(4))* Rosen Publishing Group, Inc., The.

Goff, Elizabeth Hudson & Uschan, Michael V. The California Gold Rush. 2006. (Graphic Histories Ser.). (Illus.). 32p. (gr. 5-8). pap. 10.50 *(978-0-8368-6254-6(6))* Stevens, Gareth Publishing LLLP.

Goff, Elizabeth Hudson, et al. The California Gold Rush. Floor, Guus, illus. 2006. (Graphic Histories Ser.). 32p. (gr. 5-8). lib. bdg. 27.00 *(978-0-8368-6202-7(3))* Stevens, Gareth Publishing LLLP.

Goldstein, Margaret J. You Are Now on Indian Land: The American Indian Occupation of Alcatraz Island, California, 1969. 2011. (Civil Rights Struggles around the World Ser.). (ENG.). 160p. (gr. 9-12). lib. bdg. 38.60 *(978-0-7613-5769-8(6))* Lerner Publishing Group.

Gordon, Nick. Alcatraz. 2013. (Scariest Places on Earth Ser.). (ENG., Illus.). 24p. (J). (gr. 3-7). lib. bdg. 25.95 *(978-1-60014-945-0(6)*, Torque Bks.) Bellwether Media.

Greathouse, Lisa E. California's Spanish Missions. 2017. (Primary Source Readers Ser.). (Illus.). 32p. (gr. 4-4). 9.99 ***(978-1-4258-3234-6(2))*** Teacher Created Materials, Inc.

Greve, Tom. Angel Island. 2015. (ENG.). 32p. (gr. 3-6). 32.79 *(978-1-63430-044-5(0))* Rourke Educational Media.

Haines, Serena. Exploration of California. 2017. (Primary Source Readers Ser.). 32p. (gr. 4-4). 9.99 ***(978-1-4258-3233-9(4))*** Teacher Created Materials, Inc.

Hall, Brianna. Strike It Rich! The Story of the California Gold Rush, 1 vol. 2014. (Adventures on the American Frontier Ser.). (ENG.). 32p. (gr. 3-4). 27.32 *(978-1-4914-0184-2(2)*, Fact Finders) Capstone Press of Coughlan Cos.

Hamilton, Sam. Discovering Mission San Buenaventura. 2014. (California Missions Ser.). 48p. (J). (gr. 4-6). lib. bdg. 31.36 *(978-1-62713-103-2(5))* Cavendish Square Publishing.

—Discovering Mission San Diego de Alcalá. 2014. (California Missions Ser.). 48p. (J). (gr. 4-6). lib. bdg. 31.36 *(978-1-62713-109-4(4))* Cavendish Square Publishing.

Hamilton, Sam C. Discovering Mission San Buenaventura. 2016. (California Missions Ser.). (ENG.). 48p. (J). (gr. 4-4). pap. 12.95 *(978-1-5026-1223-6(2))* Cavendish Square Publishing.

—Discovering Mission San Carlos Borromeo Del Rio Carmelo. 2016. (California Missions Ser.). (ENG.). 48p. (J). (gr. 4-4). pap. 12.95 *(978-1-5026-1214-4(3))* Cavendish Square Publishing.

Hardwick, Michael R. La Purisima Concepcion: The Enduring History of a California Mission. 2015. (Brief History Ser.). (ENG., Illus.). 144p. pap. 19.99 *(978-1-62619-984-2(1)*, History Pr., The) Arcadia Publishing.

Haunted! Alcatraz. 2013. (History's Most Haunted Ser.). 32p. (J). (gr. 3-6). pap. 63.00 *(978-1-4339-9245-2(0))* Stevens, Gareth Publishing LLLP.

Hawley, Linda Gallo. Nature Adventures: A Guidebook of Nature Facts, Songs, & Hikes in San Diego County. 2017. (ENG., Illus.). (J). (gr. 3-7). pap. 12.95 ***(978-1-941384-28-2(5))*** Sunbelt Pubns., Inc.

Hayhurst, Chris. John Sutter: California Pioneer. 2009. (Primary Sources of Famous People in American History Ser.). 32p. (gr. 2-3). 47.90 *(978-1-60851-696-4(2))* Rosen Publishing Group, Inc., The.

—John Sutter: California Pioneer / Pionero de California. 2009. (Famous People in American History/Grandes personajes en la historia de los Estados Unidos Ser.). (ENG & SPA.). 32p. (gr. 2-3). 47.90 *(978-1-61512-549-4(3)*, Editorial Buenas Letras) Rosen Publishing Group, Inc., The.

—John Sutter: Pionero de California (John Sutter: California Pioneer) 2009. (Grandes personajes en la historia de los Estados Unidos (Famous People in American History) Ser.). (SPA.). 32p. (gr. 2-3). 47.90 *(978-1-61512-803-7(4)*, Editorial Buenas Letras) Rosen Publishing Group, Inc., The.

Herrera, Matthew D. History Guide to Old Mission San Luis Obispo de Tolosa. 2003. (Illus.). 77p. 9.95 *(978-0-9723720-1-5(6))* Tixlini Scriptorium, Inc.

Hill, William E. The California Trail: Yesterday & Today. 2017. ***(978-0-87004-604-9(7))*** Caxton Pr.

Holub, Joan. What Was the Gold Rush? Tomkinson, Tim, illus. 2013. (What Was? Ser.). (ENG.). 112p. (J). (gr. 3-7). pap. 5.99 *(978-0-448-46289-9(3)*, Penguin Workshop) Penguin Young Readers Group.

—What Was the Gold Rush? 2013. (What Was... ? Ser.). lib. bdg. 16.00 *(978-0-606-29972-5(6)*, Turtleback) Turtleback Bks.

Hyde, Natalie. Alcatraz. 2013. (ENG.). 48p. (J). *(978-0-7787-1098-1(X))*; pap. *(978-0-7787-1104-9(8))* Crabtree Publishing Co.

James, Helen Foster & Wilbur, Helen L. Little California. Urban, Helle, illus. 2011. (My Little State Ser.). (ENG.). 22p. (J). 9.95 *(978-1-58536-538-8(6))* Sleeping Bear Pr.

Jaskol, Julie & Lewis, Brian. City of Angels: In & Around Los Angeles. Kleven, Elisa, illus. 2008. (J). *(978-1-883318-85-7(8))* Angel City Pr.

Jerome, Kate B. Lucky to Live in NorCal. 2017. (Arcadia Kids Ser.). (ENG., Illus.). 32p. (J). 16.99 ***(978-0-7385-2770-3(X))*** Arcadia Publishing.

—Lucky to Live in Socal. 2017. (Arcadia Kids Ser.). (ENG., Illus.). 32p. (J). 16.99 ***(978-0-7385-2768-0(8))*** Arcadia Publishing.

—The Wise Animal Handbook NorCal. 2017. (Arcadia Kids Ser.). (ENG., Illus.). 32p. (J). 16.99 ***(978-0-7385-2836-6(6))*** Arcadia Publishing.

—The Wise Animal Handbook Socal. 2017. (Arcadia Kids Ser.). (ENG., Illus.). 32p. (J). 16.99 ***(978-0-7385-2843-4(9))*** Arcadia Publishing.

Johnson, Robin. California Gold Rush! 2013. (ENG., Illus.). 48p. (J). *(978-0-7787-1170-4(6))*; pap. *(978-0-7787-1178-0(1))* Crabtree Publishing Co.

Jordan, Shirley. California Gold Rush: Moments in History. 2003. (Cover-To-Cover Books). (Illus.). 64p. pap. 9.00 *(978-0-7891-5554-2(0))*; (J). (gr. 4-7). lib. bdg. 17.95 *(978-0-7569-0633-7(4))* Perfection Learning Corp.

Kallio, Jamie. Angel Island Immigration: A History Perspectives Book. 2014. (Perspectives Library). (ENG.). 32p. (J). (gr. 4-8). 28.50 *(978-1-63137-614-6(4)*, 205239) Cherry Lake Publishing.

Korte, Nicole M. California in the 20th Century. 2017. (Primary Source Readers Ser.). 32p. (gr. 4-4). 9.99 ***(978-1-4258-3244-5(X))*** Teacher Created Materials, Inc.

Landau, Elaine. The Gold Rush in California: Would You Catch Gold Fever? 2015. (What Would You Do? Ser.). 48p. (J). (gr. 3-4). 25.27 *(978-0-7660-6300-6(3))*; pap. 8.95 *(978-0-7660-6301-3(1)*, Enslow Elementary) Enslow Pubs., Inc.

Larson, Kirsten W. The West: Arizona, California, Nevada. 2015. (Let's Explore the States Ser.). (Illus.). 64p. (J). (gr. 5). 23.95 *(978-1-4222-3337-5(5))* Mason Crest.

Lemke, Nancy. Southern Coast Missions in California. 2007. (Exploring California Missions Ser.). (ENG., Illus.). 64p. (gr. 4-7). lib. bdg. 27.93 *(978-0-8225-1935-5(6)*, Lerner Pubns.) Lerner Publishing Group.

Lopez, Elizabeth Anderson. California: Becoming a State. 2017. (Primary Source Readers Ser.). 32p. (gr. 4-4). 9.99 ***(978-1-4258-3240-7(7))*** Teacher Created Materials, Inc.

Lynette, Rachel. The Gold Rush. 2013. (Pioneer Spirit: the Westward Expansion Ser.). 24p. (J). (gr. 3-6). 22.60 *(978-1-4777-0784-5(0))*; pap. 49.50 *(978-1-4777-0902-3(9))*; (ENG., Illus.). pap. 8.25 *(978-1-4777-0901-6(0))* Rosen Publishing Group, Inc., The. (PowerKids Pr.).

Madison, Amelia & Shoup, Kate. Life As a Prospector in the California Gold Rush. 2016. (Life As... Ser.). (ENG., Illus.). 32p. (J). (gr. 3-3). 28.50 *(978-1-5026-1780-4(3))* Cavendish Square Publishing.

Margaret, Amy. Mission San Buenaventura. (Missions of California Ser.). 64p. (gr. 4-4). 2009. 58.50 *(978-1-60854-026-6(X)*, PowerKids Pr.) 2003. (Illus.). (J). 26.50 *(978-0-8239-5888-7(4))* Rosen Publishing Group, Inc., The.

—Mission San Jose de Guadalupe. 2009. (Missions of California Ser.). 64p. (gr. 4-4). 58.50 *(978-1-60854-031-0(6)*, PowerKids Pr.) Rosen Publishing Group, Inc., The.

—Mission Santa Barbara. (Missions of California Ser.). 64p. (gr. 4-4). 2009. 58.50 *(978-1-60854-037-2(5)*, PowerKids Pr.) 2003. (Illus.). (J). 26.50 *(978-0-8239-5880-1(9))* Rosen Publishing Group, Inc., The.

—Mission Santa Clara de Asis. (Missions of California Ser.). 64p. (gr. 4-4). 2009. 58.50 *(978-1-60854-038-9(3)*, PowerKids Pr.) 2003. (Illus.). (J). 26.50 *(978-0-8239-5883-2(3))* Rosen Publishing Group, Inc., The.

Marschner, Janice. California's Arab Americans. 2003. (Illus.). 160p. lib. bdg. 18.95 *(978-0-9677069-7-9(1))* Coleman Ranch Pr.

Marsh, Carole. California History Projects: 30 Cool, Activities, Crafts, Experiments & More for Kids to Do to Learn about Your State! 2003. (California Experience Ser.). 32p. (gr. k-5). pap. 5.95 *(978-0-635-01774-1(1)*, Marsh, Carole Bks.) Gallopade International.

—Exploring California Through Project-Based Learning. 2016. (ENG.). (J). pap. 9.99 *(978-0-635-12329-9(0))* Gallopade International.

Mattern, Joanne. America's Gold Rush: John Sutter & the Discovery of Gold in California. 2009. (Great Moments in American History Ser.). 32p. (gr. 3-3). 47.90 *(978-1-61513-139-6(6))* Rosen Publishing Group, Inc., The.

McGinty, Alice B. Mission San Gabriel Arcangel. (Missions of California Ser.). 64p. (gr. 4-4). 2009. 58.50 *(978-1-60854-030-3(8)*, PowerKids Pr.) 2003. (Illus.). (J). 26.50 *(978-0-8239-5892-4(2))* Rosen Publishing Group, Inc., The.

McGinty, Alice B. & Stevens, Madeline. Discovering Mission San Gabriel Arcángel. 2014. (California Missions Ser.). 48p. (J). (gr. 4-6). lib. bdg. 31.36 *(978-1-62713-115-5(9))* Cavendish Square Publishing.

Medina, Nico. Where Is Alcatraz? Groff, David, illus. 2016. (Where Is? Ser.). (ENG.). 112p. (J). (gr. 3-7). lib. bdg. 15.99 *(978-0-399-54232-9(9)*, Grosset & Dunlap) Penguin Young Readers Group.

Meyers, Haily & Meyers, Kevin. All Aboard California, 1 vol. Meyers, Haily, illus. 2015. (ENG., Illus.). 22p. (J). bds. 9.99 *(978-1-4236-4080-6(2))* Gibbs Smith, Publisher.

Minch, John, et al. Caminos de Baja California: Geologia y Biologica Para Su Viaje. Minch, Jason, ed. Ledesma Vazquez, Jorge, tr. Minch, Edwin, illus. Minch, John, photos by. 2003. (SPA.). 192p. per. 23.95 *(978-0-9631090-2-6(2))* Minch, John Publishing.

The Missions of California, 21 bks. Incl. Mission la Purisima Concepcion. Ostrow, Kim. 2000. lib. bdg. 25.50 *(978-0-8239-5498-8(6))*; Mission Nuestra Senora de la Soledad. Ostrow, Kim. 2000. lib. bdg. 25.50 *(978-0-8239-5500-8(1))*; Mission San Antonio de Padua. Serafin, Kim. 2000. lib. bdg. 25.50 *(978-0-8239-5489-6(7))*; Mission San Buenaventura. Margaret, Amy. 2000. lib. bdg. 25.50 *(978-0-8239-5496-4(X))*; Mission San Carlos Borromeo del Rio Carmela. Edgar, Kathleen J. & Edgar, Susan E. 2000. lib. bdg. 25.50 *(978-0-8239-5488-9(9))*; Mission San Diego de Alcala. Edgar, Kathleen J. & Edgar, Susan E. 2000. lib. bdg. 25.50 *(978-0-8239-5487-2(0))*; Mission San Fernando Rey de Espana. Ching, Jacqueline. 2000. lib. bdg. 25.50 *(978-0-8239-5503-9(6))*; Mission San Francisco de Asis. Edgar, Kathleen J. & Edgar, Susan E. 2000. lib. bdg. 25.50 *(978-0-8239-5492-6(7))*; Mission San Francisco de Solano. Draper, Allison Stark. 2000. lib. bdg. 25.50 *(978-0-8239-5507-7(9))*; Mission San Gabriel Arcangel. McGinty, Alice B. 2000. lib. bdg. 25.50 *(978-0-8239-5490-2(0))*; Mission San Jose de Guadalupe. Margaret, Amy. 2000. lib. bdg. 25.50 *(978-0-8239-5495-7(1))*; Mission San Juan Bautista. Draper, Allison Stark. 2000. lib. bdg. 25.50 *(978-0-8239-5501-5(X))*; Mission San Luis Obispo de Tolosa. Edgar, Kathleen J. & Edgar, Susan E. 2000. lib. bdg. 25.50 *(978-0-8239-5491-9(9))*; Mission San Luis Rey de Francia. Quasha, Jennifer. 1999. lib. bdg. 25.50 *(978-0-8239-5504-6(4))*; Mission San Miguel Arcangel. Edgar, Kathleen J. & Edgar, Nancy A. 2000. lib. bdg. 25.50 *(978-0-8239-5502-2(8))*; Mission San Rafael Arcangel. Ching, Jacqueline. 2000. lib. bdg. 25.50 *(978-0-8239-5506-0(0))*; Mission Santa Barbara. Margaret, Amy. 2000. lib. bdg. 25.50 *(978-0-8239-5497-1(8))*; Mission Santa Clara de Asis. Margaret, Amy. 2000. lib. bdg. 25.50 *(978-0-8239-5494-0(3))*; Mission Santa Cruz. Ostrow, Kim. 2000. lib. bdg. 25.50 *(978-0-8239-5499-5(4))*; Mission Santa Ines. Ching, Jacqueline. 2000. lib. bdg. 25.50 *(978-0-8239-5505-3(2))*; 64p. (J). (gr. 4). (Illus.). Set lib. bdg. 535.50 *(978-0-8239-5706-4(3)*, MISET, PowerKids Pr.) Rosen Publishing Group, Inc., The.

Monteverde, Matthew. Notre Dame vs. USC. 2013. (J). *(978-1-4777-1164-4(3))*; pap. *(978-1-4777-1163-7(5))*; lib. bdg. *(978-1-4777-1158-3(9))* Rosen Publishing Group, Inc., The. (PowerKids Pr.).

Morlock, Theresa. The Gold Rush. 2017. (J). ***(978-1-5383-0050-3(8))***; pap. ***(978-1-68048-788-6(4))*** Rosen Publishing Group, Inc., The. (Britannica Educational Publishing).

Murray, Julie. California, 1 vol. 2006. (Buddy Book Ser.). (ENG., Illus.). 32p. (gr. k-4). 27.07 *(978-1-59197-664-6(2)*, Buddy Bks.) ABDO Publishing Co.

Nagelhout, Ryan. Haunted! Alcatraz. 2013. 32p. (J). (gr. 3-6). 26.60 *(978-1-4339-9243-8(4))*; pap. 10.50 *(978-1-4339-9244-5(2))* Stevens, Gareth Publishing LLLP.

Newman, Lauren. California. 2017. (True Book — My United States Ser.). (ENG.). 48p. (J). pap. 7.95 ***(978-0-531-23282-8(4)***, Children's Pr.) Scholastic Library Publishing.

Newman, Patricia. Sea Otter Heroes: The Predators That Saved an Ecosystem. 2017. (Nonfiction — Grades 4-8 Ser.). (ENG.). 56p. (J). (gr. 4-8). 16.99 ***(978-1-5124-3884-0(7))***; 47.99 ***(978-1-5124-2844-5(2))***; 47.99 ***(978-1-5124-3885-7(5))***; (Illus.). 31.99 *(978-1-5124-2631-1(8))* Lerner Publishing Group. (Millbrook Pr.).

Nuñes, Sofia. Discovering Mission Santa Clara de Asís. 2016. (California Missions Ser.). (ENG.). 48p. (J). (gr. 4-4). pap. 12.95 *(978-1-5026-1211-3(9))* Cavendish Square Publishing.

—Discovering Mission Santa Cruz. 2016. (California Missions Ser.). (ENG.). 48p. (J). (gr. 4-4). pap. 12.95 *(978-1-5026-1212-0(7))* Cavendish Square Publishing.

—Discovering Mission Santa Inés. 2014. (California Missions Ser.). (Illus.). 48p. (J). (gr. 4-6). lib. bdg. 31.36 *(978-1-62713-097-4(7))* Cavendish Square Publishing.

—Discovering Mission Santa Inés. 2016. (California Missions Ser.). (ENG.). 48p. (J). (gr. 4-4). pap. 12.95 *(978-1-5026-1221-2(6))* Cavendish Square Publishing.

O'Donnell, Kerri. A Timeline of the California Gold Rush. 2009. (Real Life Readers Ser.). 32p. (gr. 4-5). pap. 10.00 *(978-1-4358-0161-5(X)*, Rosen Classroom); (gr. 4-4). 47.90 *(978-1-61511-366-8(5)*, PowerKids Pr.); (J). (gr. 3-4). lib. bdg. 25.25 *(978-1-4358-2989-3(1)*, PowerKids Pr.) Rosen Publishing Group, Inc., The.

Ogintz, Eileen. The Kid's Guide to San Diego. 2014. (Kid's Guides Ser.). (ENG., Illus.). 160p. pap. 12.95 *(978-1-4930-0152-1(3))* Globe Pequot Pr., The.

Oliver, Marilyn Tower. The Infamous Alcatraz Prison in United States History. 2015. (In United States History Ser.). 96p. (J). (gr. 5-12). 27.94 *(978-0-7660-6320-4(8))*; pap. 10.95 *(978-0-7660-6321-1(6))* Enslow Pubs., Inc.

Oney, Yannick. First American Colonies. 2004. (World Discovery History Readers Ser.). (Illus.). 32p. (J). pap. *(978-0-439-66555-1(8))* Scholastic, Inc.

Ostrow, Kim. Mission Nuestra Senora de la Soledad. (Missions of California Ser.). 64p. (gr. 4-4). 2009. 58.50 *(978-1-60854-021-1(9)*, PowerKids Pr.) 2003. (Illus.). (J). 26.50 *(978-0-8239-5882-5(5))* Rosen Publishing Group, Inc., The.

—Mission Santa Cruz. 2009. (Missions of California Ser.). 64p. (gr. 4-4). 58.50 *(978-1-60854-041-9(3)*, PowerKids Pr.) Rosen Publishing Group, Inc., The.

Ostrow, Kim & Nuñes, Sofia. Discovering Mission Santa Cruz. 2014. (California Missions Ser.). (Illus.). 48p. (J). (gr. 4-6). lib. bdg. 31.36 *(978-1-62713-070-7(5))* Cavendish Square Publishing.

Parker, Janice. California. 2011. (Guide to American States Ser.). (Illus.). 48p. (J). (gr. 3-6). 29.99 *(978-1-61690-777-8(0))*; *(978-1-61690-452-4(6))* Weigl Pubs., Inc.

—California: The Golden State. 2016. (J). ***(978-1-5105-2083-7(X))***; *(978-1-5105-0659-6(4))* SmartBook Media, Inc.

—California: The Golden State. 2016. (J). *(978-1-4896-4827-3(5))* Weigl Pubs., Inc.

People of the California Missions. (Illus.). (J). (gr. k-5). 151.50 *(978-0-8239-7263-0(1))* Rosen Publishing Group, Inc., The.

Perissinotto, Giorgio Sabino Antonio, ed. & tr. from SPA. The California Recollections of Angustias de la Guerra Ord: (Occurrences in Hispanic California) Perissinotto, Giorgio Sabino Antonio, tr. 2004. (ENG & SPA.). xxi, 172p. *(978-0-88382-157-2(5))* Academy of American Franciscan History.

Person, Stephen. Ghostly Alcatraz Island. 2010. (HorrorScapes Ser.). 32p. (YA). (gr. 4-7). lib. bdg. 25.27 *(978-1-936087-97-6(9))* Bearport Publishing Co., Inc.

Philipp, Cathy. On the Trail Again: Malibu to Santa Barbara, 1. Philipp, Cathy et al, photos by. 2004. (Illus.). 252p. per. *(978-0-9655848-1-4(X))* Philipp, Cathy Publishing.

Price-Wright, Heather. Mexican Rule of California. 2017. (Primary Source Readers Ser.). 32p. (gr. 4-4). 9.99 ***(978-1-4258-3236-0(9))*** Teacher Created Materials, Inc.

Quasha, Jennifer. Mission San Luis Rey de Francia. 2009. (Missions of California Ser.). 64p. (gr. 4-4). 58.50 *(978-1-60854-034-1(0)*, PowerKids Pr.) Rosen Publishing Group, Inc., The.

Raabe, Emily. The Gold Rush: California or Bust! 2009. (Westward Ho! Ser.). 24p. (gr. 2-3). 42.50 *(978-1-60854-762-3(0)*, PowerKids Pr.) Rosen Publishing Group, Inc., The.

Raum, Elizabeth. Birth & Death of a City. 2007. (Illus.). 32p. (J). *(978-1-4062-0505-3(2))*; *(978-1-4062-0480-3(3))* Steck-Vaughn.

Roberts, Helen M. Miguel & the Pirates: A Tale of Mission Santa Cruz. Lawrence, Muriel, illus. 2011. 28p. 35.95 *(978-1-258-02882-4(4))* Literary Licensing, LLC.

Ryan, Pam Muñoz. Nuestra California. López, Rafael, illus. 2008.Tr. of Our California. (SPA & ENG.). 48p. (J). (gr. 1-4). 17.95 *(978-1-58089-226-1(4))* Charlesbridge Publishing, Inc.

—Our California. López, Rafael, illus. 2008. (ENG.). 48p. (J). (gr. 1-4). 18.95 *(978-1-58089-116-5(0))*; per. 9.95 *(978-1-58089-117-2(9))* Charlesbridge Publishing, Inc.

Serafin, Kim. Mission San Antonio de Padua. (Missions of California Ser.). 64p. (gr. 4-4). 2009. 58.50 *(978-1-60854-025-9(1)*, PowerKids Pr.) 2003. (Illus.). (J). 26.50 *(978-0-8239-5891-7(4))* Rosen Publishing Group, Inc., The.

Shea, Therese. The Bigfoot Trail. 2014. (Scariest Places on Earth Ser.). 24p. (J). (gr. 2-5). pap. 8.15 *(978-1-4824-0928-4(3))* Stevens, Gareth Publishing LLLP.

Shoup, Kate. The California Gold Rush. 2016. (Expanding America Ser.). (ENG., Illus.). 96p. (J). (gr. 8-8). lib. bdg. 42.79 *(978-1-5026-0968-7(1))* Cavendish Square Publishing.

Silverman, Steve. The Story of the Sacramento Kings. 2010. (NBA — A History of Hoops Ser.). 48p. (YA). (gr. 5-18). 23.95 *(978-1-58341-960-1(8),* Creative Education) Creative Co., The.

Stevens, Madeline. Discovering Mission San José. 2014. (California Missions Ser.). (Illus.). 48p. (J). (gr. 4-6). lib. bdg. 31.36 *(978-1-62713-064-6(0))* Cavendish Square Publishing.

—Discovering Mission San Juan Bautista. 2014. (California Missions Ser.). (Illus.). 48p. (J). (gr. 4-6). lib. bdg. 31.36 *(978-1-62713-073-8(X))* Cavendish Square Publishing.

Tatlock, Ann. My Home Is My Castle Hearst Castle: Hearst Castle. 2015. (ENG., Illus.). 48p. (J). 29.95 *(978-1-62469-138-6(2))* Purple Toad Publishing, Inc.

Thompson, Gare. When the Mission Padre Came to the Rancho: The Early California Adventures of Rosalinda & Simon Delgado. 2004. (I Am American Ser.). (ENG., Illus.). 40p. (J). (gr. 3-7). pap. 6.99 *(978-0-7922-6945-8(4),* National Geographic Children's Bks.) National Geographic Society.

Thompson, Gare & National Geographic Learning Staff. Missions & Ranchos. 2007. (Reading Expeditions Ser.). (ENG., Illus.). 40p. (J). pap. 19.95 *(978-0-7922-4548-3(2))* CENGAGE Learning.

Thornton, Jeremy. The Gold Rush: Chinese Immigrants Come to America (1848-1882) (Primary Sources of Immigration & Migration in America Ser.). 24p. 2009. (gr. 3-4). 42.50 *(978-1-60851-784-8(5))* 2004. (Illus.). (J). lib. bdg. 22.60 *(978-0-8239-6833-6(2))* Rosen Publishing Group, Inc., The. (PowerKids Pr.).

—The Gold Rush: Chinese Immigrants Come to America, 1848-1882. 2004. (Primary Sources of Immigration & Migration in America Ser.). (ENG., Illus.). 24p. (gr. 4-8). pap. 9.40 *(978-0-8239-8959-1(3),* PowerKids Pr.) Rosen Publishing Group, Inc., The.

Tieck, Sarah. California, 1 vol. 2012. (Explore the United States Ser.). (ENG.). 32p. (J). (gr. 2-5). lib. bdg. 28.50 *(978-1-61783-343-4(6),* Big Buddy Bks.) ABDO Publishing Co.

Tracy, Kathleen. San Diego. 2009. (Class Trip Ser.). (Illus.). 48p. (J). (gr. 2-5). lib. bdg. 29.95 *(978-1-58415-810-3(7))* Mitchell Lane Pubs., Inc.

Uschan, Michael V. The California Gold Rush. 2003. (Landmark Events in American History Ser.). (Illus.). 48p. (gr. 5-12). pap. 14.05 *(978-0-8368-5402-2(0));* lib. bdg. 31.00 *(978-0-8368-5374-2(1))* Stevens, Gareth Publishing LLLP. (Gareth Stevens Secondary Library).

Watson, Stephanie. The Escape from Alcatraz, 1 vol. 2012. (Unsolved Mysteries (el) Ser.). (ENG.). 112p. (J). (gr. 6-12). lib. bdg. 35.64 *(978-1-61783-303-8(7),* Essential Library) ABDO Publishing Co.

—A Timeline History of the California Gold Rush. 2015. (ENG., Illus.). 48p. (J). (gr. 5-8). 30.65 *(978-1-4677-8580-8(6))* Lerner Publishing Group.

Weintraub, Aileen. Point Pinos Light: The West Coast's Oldest Continuously Active Lighthouse. 2009. (Great Lighthouses of North America Ser.). 24p. (gr. 3-3). 42.50 *(978-1-61513-132-7(9),* PowerKids Pr.) Rosen Publishing Group, Inc., The.

Wertz, Michael. ABC Oakland. 2017. (J). *(978-1-59714-371-4(5))* Heyday.

Williams, Dinah. Haunted Hollywood. 2015. (Scary Places Ser.). (ENG.). 32p. (J). (gr. 4-8). lib. bdg. 26.60 *(978-1-62724-519-7(7))* Bearport Publishing Co., Inc.

—Secrets of Disneyland: Weird & Wonderful Facts about the Happiest Place on Earth. 2013. (ENG., Illus.). 160p. (J). (gr. 2-4). 8.95 *(978-1-4549-0813-5(0))* Sterling Publishing Co., Inc.

Williams, Jack. The Miwok of California. 2009. (Library of Native Americans Ser.). 64p. (gr. 4-4). 58.50 *(978-1-60853-753-2(6),* PowerKids Pr.) Rosen Publishing Group, Inc., The.

—The Modoc of California. 2009. (Library of Native Americans Ser.). 64p. (gr. 4-4). 58.50 *(978-1-60853-754-9(4),* PowerKids Pr.) Rosen Publishing Group, Inc., The.

—The Mojave of California. 2009. (Library of Native Americans Ser.). 64p. (gr. 4-4). 58.50 *(978-1-60853-755-6(2),* PowerKids Pr.) Rosen Publishing Group, Inc., The.

—The Mono of California. 2009. (Library of Native Americans Ser.). 64p. (gr. 4-4). 58.50 *(978-1-60853-756-3(0),* PowerKids Pr.) Rosen Publishing Group, Inc., The.

Williams, Jack S. Craftsmen & Craftswomen. 2004. (People of the California Missions Ser.). (Illus.). 64p. (YA). (gr. 3-6). lib. bdg. 26.50 *(978-0-8239-6280-8(6))* Rosen Publishing Group, Inc., The.

—Craftsmen & Craftswomen of the California Mission Frontier. 2009. (People of the California Missions Ser.). 64p. (gr. 4-4). 58.50 *(978-1-60851-156-3(1),* PowerKids Pr.) Rosen Publishing Group, Inc., The.

—Indians of the California Mission Frontier. 2009. (People of the California Missions Ser.). 64p. (gr. 4-4). 58.50 *(978-1-60851-157-0(X),* PowerKids Pr.) Rosen Publishing Group, Inc., The.

—The Ohlone of California. 2009. (Library of Native Americans Ser.). 64p. (gr. 4-4). 58.50 *(978-1-60853-757-0(9),* PowerKids Pr.) Rosen Publishing Group, Inc., The.

—Padres of the California Mission Frontier. 2009. (People of the California Missions Ser.). 64p. (gr. 4-4). 58.50 *(978-1-60851-158-7(8),* PowerKids Pr.) Rosen Publishing Group, Inc., The.

—Sailors, Merchants, & Muleteers of the California Mission Frontier. 2009. (People of the California Missions Ser.). 64p. (gr. 4-4). 58.50 *(978-1-60851-159-4(6),* PowerKids Pr.) Rosen Publishing Group, Inc., The.

—Soldiers & Their Families of the California Mission Frontier. 2009. (People of the California Missions Ser.). 64p. (gr. 4-4). 58.50 *(978-1-60851-160-0(X),* PowerKids Pr.) Rosen Publishing Group, Inc., The.

—Townspeople & Ranchers of the California Mission Frontier. 2009. (People of the California Missions Ser.). 64p. (gr. 4-4). 58.50 *(978-1-60851-161-7(8),* PowerKids Pr.) Rosen Publishing Group, Inc., The.

Williams, Jack S. & Davis, Thomas L. Padres of the California Mission Frontier. 2004. (People of the California Missions Ser.). (Illus.). 64p. (J). lib. bdg. 26.50 *(978-0-8239-6283-9(0),* PowerKids Pr.) Rosen Publishing Group, Inc., The.

—Sailors, Merchants, & Muleteers. 2004. (People of the California Missions Ser.). (Illus.). 64p. (J). lib. bdg. 26.50 *(978-0-8239-6282-2(2))* Rosen Publishing Group, Inc., The.

—Soldiers & Their Families of the California Mission Frontier. 2004. (People of the California Missions Ser.). (Illus.). 64p. (J). lib. bdg. 26.50 *(978-0-8239-6285-3(7))* Rosen Publishing Group, Inc., The.

—Townspeople & Ranchers of the California Mission Frontier. 2004. (People of the California Missions Ser.). (Illus.). 64p. (J). lib. bdg. 26.50 *(978-0-8239-6284-6(9),* PowerKids Pr.) Rosen Publishing Group, Inc., The.

Yasuda, Anita. What's Great about California? 2014. (Our Great States Ser.). (ENG., Illus.). 32p. (gr. 2-5). pap. 7.95 *(978-1-4677-4535-2(9))* Lerner Publishing Group.

Zuchora-Walske, Christine. The Dust Bowl: A History Perspectives Book. 2013. (Perspectives Library). (ENG., Illus.). 32p. (J). (gr. 4-8). 28.50 *(978-1-62431-417-9(1),* 202788); pap. 14.21 *(978-1-62431-493-3(7),* 202790) Cherry Lake Publishing.

CALIFORNIA ANGELS (BASEBALL TEAM)

see Los Angeles Angels of Anaheim (Baseball Team)

CALISTHENICS

see Exercise

CALLIGRAPHY

Hanson, Anders. Cool Calligraphy: The Art of Creativity for Kids, 1 vol. 2009. (Cool Art Ser.). (ENG.). 32p. (gr. 3-6). 28.50 *(978-1-60453-145-9(2),* Checkerboard Library) ABDO Publishing Co.

Marlborough, Max. Hand Drawn Lettering. 2016. (ENG., Illus.). 128p. pap. ***(978-1-910706-42-8(6))*** Barron's Educational Series, Inc.

Olive, Guillaume & He, Zihong. My First Book of Chinese Calligraphy. 2010. (ENG., Illus.). 96p. (J). (gr. 2-6). spiral bd. 19.95 *(978-0-8048-4104-7(7))* Tuttle Publishing.

Phillips, Karen. Lettering in Crazy, Cool, Quirky Style. 2006. (ENG., Illus.). 56p. (J). (gr. 3-7). 18.95 *(978-1-57054-428-6(X))* Klutz.

Pratt, L. Chinese Calligraphy Kit (Bag) 2009. 32p. pap. 11.99 *(978-1-60130-121-5(9),* Usborne) EDC Publishing.

Tanahashi, Kazuaki. Heart of the Brush: The Splendor of East Asian Calligraphy. 2016. (ENG., Illus.). 400p. pap. 27.95 *(978-1-61180-134-7(6))* Shambhala Pubns., Inc.

Top That Publishing Staff, ed. Calligraphy Skills. (Illus.). 48p. 2005. *(978-1-84510-302-6(5))* 2004. *(978-1-84510-319-4(X))* Top That! Publishing PLC.

Wamaar, Dawn. DIY Lettering. 2017. (DIY Ser.). (ENG., Illus.). (J). (gr. 3-8). lib. bdg. 34.65 ***(978-1-942875-26-0(6),*** Walter Foster Jr) Quarto Publishing Group USA.

Wamaar, Dawn. Words to Live By: Creative Lettering, Coloring, & Inspirations. 2016. (ENG.). 128p. (J). (gr. 3-7). pap. 12.95 *(978-1-63322-100-0(8),* Walter Foster Jr) Quarto Publishing Group USA.

Winters, Eleanor. Calligraphy for Kids. 2007. (ENG., Illus.). 128p. (J). (gr. 3-7). pap. 9.95 *(978-1-4027-3912-5(5))* Sterling Publishing Co., Inc.

Young, Caroline. Calligraphy: From Beginner to Expert. Lyon, Chris, illus. 2006. (Usborne Guide Ser.). 48p. (J). (gr. 6). lib. bdg. 16.99 *(978-1-58086-934-8(3),* Usborne) EDC Publishing.

CALVERT FAMILY

Marsh, Carole. Lords of Baltimore, Founders of Maryland. 2004. 12p. (gr. k-4). 2.95 *(978-0-635-02368-1(7))* Gallopade International.

Mills, Clifford W. Lord Baltimore. 2010. (Leaders of the Colonial Era Ser.). 128p. (gr. 5-8). 35.00 *(978-1-60413-738-5(X),* Chelsea Hse.) Facts On File, Inc.

Whiting, Jim. The Maryland Colony: Lord Baltimore. 2007. (Building America Ser.). (Illus.). 48p. (J). (gr. 4-8). lib. bdg. 29.95 *(978-1-58415-547-8(7))* Mitchell Lane Pubs., Inc.

CALVIN, JEAN, 1509-1564

Carr, Simonetta. John Calvin. Taglietti, Emanuele, illus. 2008. (ENG.). 63p. (J). 18.00 *(978-1-60178-055-3(9))* Reformation Heritage Bks.

Davis, Thomas J. John Calvin. 2004. (Spiritual Leaders & Thinkers Ser.). (Illus.). 120p. (C). (gr. 9-13). 30.00 *(978-0-7910-8100-6(1),* Chelsea Hse.) Facts On File, Inc.

CAMBODIA

Behnke, Alison. Angkor Wat. 2008. (Unearthing Ancient Worlds Ser.). (ENG.). 80p. (gr. 5-8). lib. bdg. 30.60 *(978-0-8225-7585-6(X))* Lerner Publishing Group.

Diep, Bridgette. Trip Through Cambodia. Vaing, Jocelang, illus. 32p. (J). (gr. -1-3). 14.95 *(978-0-87592-054-2(3))* Scroll Pr., Inc.

Dorling Kindersley Publishing Staff, et al. Jungle Adventure. 2015. (DK Adventures Ser.). (ENG., Illus.). 128p. (J). (gr. 3-7). pap. 5.99 *(978-1-4654-2931-5(X),* DK Children) Dorling Kindersley Publishing, Inc.

—Jungle Adventures. 2015. (DK Adventures Ser.). (ENG., Illus.). 128p. (J). (gr. 3-7). 16.99 *(978-1-4654-2930-8(1),* DK Children) Dorling Kindersley Publishing, Inc.

Elizabeth Anne Biddle. A Girl Called Nothing: A Tale of Cambodia. 2010. 124p. pap. 13.95 *(978-1-4502-2017-0(7))* iUniverse, Inc.

Kras, Sara Louise. Cambodia. 2005. (Enchantment of the World Ser.). (ENG., Illus.). 144p. (YA). (gr. 5-9). 39.00 *(978-0-516-23679-7(2))* Scholastic Library Publishing.

Lord, Michelle. A Song for Cambodia, 1 vol. Arihara, Shino, illus. 2008. (ENG.). 32p. (J). (gr. 1-6). 16.95 *(978-1-60060-139-2(1))* Lee & Low Bks., Inc.

Mara, Wil. Cambodia. 2017. (Enchantment of the World Ser.). (ENG.). 144p. (J). lib. bdg. 40.00 ***(978-0-531-23573-7(4),*** Children's Pr.) Scholastic Library Publishing.

Marshall Cavendish. The Khmer Rouge. 2011. (Great Escapes Ser.). (Illus.). 80p. (J). (gr. 6). 34.21 *(978-1-60870-474-3(2))* Marshall Cavendish Corp.

Max, Jill. Strangers in Black: A Young Boy's Struggle to Survive in Khmer Rouge Cambodia. 2006. (J). pap. *(978-0-88092-617-1(1));* lib. bdg. *(978-0-88092-616-4(3))* Royal Fireworks Publishing Co.

Miller, Caitlyn & Cooke, Barbara. Cambodia. 3rd enl. ed. 2016. (Cultures of the World (Third Edition) (r) Ser.). 144p. (J). lib. bdg. 47.07 *(978-1-5026-2229-7(7))* Cavendish Square Publishing.

O'Neal, Claire. We Visit Cambodia. 2014. (ENG., Illus.). 63p. (J). (gr. 4-8). lib. bdg. 33.95 *(978-1-61228-475-0(2))* Mitchell Lane Pubs., Inc.

Sheehan, Sean & Cooke, Barbara. Cambodia. 2nd rev. ed. 2006. (Cultures of the World Ser.). (Illus.). 144p. (gr. 6-7). lib. bdg. 42.79 *(978-0-7614-2071-2(1),* Benchmark Bks.) Marshall Cavendish Corp.

Sherman, Benjamin. Gregory's Paper Airplane. 2010. 32p. 11.95 *(978-1-4497-0719-4(X),* WestBow Pr.) Author Solutions, Inc.

Simmons, Walter. Cambodia. 2012. (Exploring Countries Ser.). (ENG., Illus.). 32p. (J). (gr. 3-7). lib. bdg. 26.95 *(978-1-60014-726-5(7),* Blastoff! Readers) Bellwether Media.

Taus-Bolstad, Stacy & Goldstein, Margaret J. Cambodia in Pictures. 2nd rev. expurg. ed. 2004. (Visual Geography Series, Second Ser.). (ENG., Illus.). 80p. (gr. 5-12). 31.93 *(978-0-8225-1994-2(1))* Lerner Publishing Group.

CAMBODIA—FICTION

Base, Graeme. The Last King of Angkor Wat. 2014. (ENG., Illus.). 36p. (J). (gr. k-2). 17.95 *(978-1-4197-1354-5(X),* Abrams Bks. for Young Readers) Abrams, Inc.

Flanagan, Liz, et al. Dara's Clever Trap: A Story from Cambodia. Peluso, Martina, illus. 2014. (Princess Stories Ser.). 48p. (J). (gr. 1-5). pap. 8.99 *(978-1-78285-103-5(8))* Barefoot Bks., Inc.

Ho & Ho, Minfong. The Stone Goddess. 2006. (Reader's Workshop Ser.). (ENG., Illus.). 200p. (C). pap. 19.95 *(978-0-7362-3160-2(9))* CENGAGE Learning.

Hunt, Elizabeth Singer. The Secret of the Sacred Temple. Williamson, Brian, illus. 2008. (Secret Agent Jack Stalwart Ser.: 5). (ENG.). 128p. (J). (gr. 1-4). per. 5.99 *(978-1-60286-003-2(3),* Weinstein Bks.) Perseus Bks. Group.

Lipp, Frederick. Running Shoes. Gaillard, Jason, illus. 2008. 32p. (J). (gr. 2-5). 16.95 *(978-1-58089-175-2(6));* pap. 7.95 *(978-1-58089-176-9(4))* Charlesbridge Publishing, Inc.

Lord, Michelle & Hoshino, Felicia. Little Sap & Monsieur Rodin, 1 vol. (ENG., Illus.). 32p. (J). 2015. pap. 9.95 *(978-1-62014-226-4(0))* 2006. (gr. 1-5). 16.95 *(978-1-58430-248-3(8))* Lee & Low Bks., Inc.

McCormick, Patricia. Never Fall Down. 224p. (YA). (gr. 9). 2013. (ENG.). pap. 9.99 *(978-0-06-173095-5(5))* 2012. (ENG.). 17.99 *(978-0-06-173093-1(9))* 2012. lib. bdg. 18.89 *(978-0-06-173094-8(7))* HarperCollins Pubs.

O'Brien, Anne Sibley. A Path of Stars. O'Brien, Anne Sibley, illus. 2012. (ENG., Illus.). 40p. (J). (gr. k-3). 15.95 *(978-1-57091-735-6(3))* Charlesbridge Publishing, Inc.

pierSath, Chath. Sinat & the Instrument of the Heart: A Story of Cambodia. Nath, Vann & Pouriseth, Phal, illus. 2010. (Make Friends Around the World Ser.). (ENG.). 32p. (J). (gr. k-3). 9.95 *(978-1-60727-116-1(8));* 9.95 *(978-1-60727-098-0(6));* 9.95 *(978-1-60727-117-8(6));* 19.95 *(978-1-60727-097-3(8));* 16.95 *(978-1-60727-087-4(0));* pap. 6.95 *(978-1-60727-088-1(9))* Soundprints.

Smith, Icy. Half Spoon of Rice: A Survival Story of the Cambodian Holocaust. Nhem, Sopaul, illus. 2009. (J). (gr. 2-7). 19.95 *(978-0-9821675-8-8(X))* East West Discovery Pr.

CAMELS

Barnes, Julia. Camels & Llamas at Work. 2006. (Animals at Work Ser.). (Illus.). 32p. (gr. 3-6). lib. bdg. 26.00 *(978-0-8368-6222-5(8),* Gareth Stevens Learning Library) Stevens, Gareth Publishing LLLP.

Borgert-Spaniol, Megan. Baby Camels. 2016. (Super Cute! Ser.). (ENG., Illus.). 24p. (J). (gr. k-3). 25.95 *(978-1-62617-387-3(7),* Blastoff! Readers) Bellwether Media.

—Camels. 2012. (Animal Safari Ser.). (ENG., Illus.). 24p. (J). (gr. k-3). lib. bdg. 25.95 *(978-1-60014-715-9(1),* Blastoff! Readers) Bellwether Media.

Camels. (Butterfly Collection). 8.95 *(978-0-86685-491-7(6),* LDL54E) Librairie du Liban Pubns. FRA. Dist: International Bk. Ctr., Inc.

Camels & Their Cousins: Level J, 6 vols. 128p. (gr. 2-3). 40.50 *(978-0-7699-0995-0(7))* Shortland Pubns. (U. S. A.) Inc.

Clark, Willow. Camels. 2012. (Animals of Asia Ser.). (ENG., Illus.). 24p. (J). (gr. 1-5). pap. 8.25 *(978-1-4488-7489-7(0));* lib. bdg. 22.60 *(978-1-4488-7416-3(5))* Rosen Publishing Group, Inc., The. (PowerKids Pr.).

Davin, Rose. Camels. 2017. (Meet Desert Animals Ser.). (ENG., Illus.). 24p. (gr. k-1). lib. bdg. 26.65 *(978-1-5157-4600-3(3),* Pebble Plus) Capstone Press of Coughlan Cos.

Dawson, Susie. Camels. 2009. (Illus.). 52p. (J). ***(978-0-7172-8060-5(8))*** Grolier, Ltd.

Durrie, Karen. I Am a Camel. (J). 2013. (Illus.). 24p. pap. *(978-1-61913-232-0(X))* 2012. 27.13 *(978-1-61913-231-3(1))* Weigl Pubs., Inc.

—Yo Soy un Camello. 2014. (SPA., Illus.). 24p. (J). *(978-1-62127-565-7(5))* Weigl Pubs., Inc.

Fisher, Doris. Army Camels: Texas Ships of the Desert, 1 vol. Buckner, Julie, illus. 2013. (ENG.). 32p. (J). (gr. k-3). 16.99 *(978-1-4556-1823-1(3))* Pelican Publishing Co., Inc.

Ganeri, Anita & Anita, Ganeri. Los Camellos Tienen Jorobas. 2003. (Enciclopedia Me Pregunto Por Que). (SPA., Illus.). 32p. (J). (gr. 3-5). 12.99 *(978-84-241-2167-9(8),* EV2029) Everest Editora ESP. Dist: Lectorum Pubns., Inc.

Gareth Stevens Publishing Staff, contrib. by. Camels. 2004. (All about Wild Animals Ser.). (Illus.). 32p. (gr. k-4). lib. bdg. 26.00 *(978-0-8368-4181-7(6),* Gareth Stevens Learning Library) Stevens, Gareth Publishing LLLP.

Gish, Melissa. Camels. 2012. (Living Wild Ser.). (Illus.). 48p. (J). (gr. 5-12). 23.95 *(978-1-60818-166-7(9),* Creative Education) Creative Co., The.

—Living Wild: Camels. 2013. (Living Wild Ser.). (ENG., Illus.). 48p. (J). (gr. 4-7). pap. 12.00 *(978-0-89812-773-7(4),* Creative Paperbacks) Creative Co., The.

Goldish, Meish. Camel. 2015. (Desert Animals Searchin' for Shade Ser.). (ENG.). 24p. (J). (gr. -1-3). lib. bdg. 23.93 *(978-1-62724-536-4(7))* Bearport Publishing Co., Inc.

Gray, Susan H. Camels Have Humps. 2014. (Tell Me Why Library). (ENG.). 24p. (J). (gr. 2-5). 25.64 *(978-1-63188-001-8(2),* 205411) Cherry Lake Publishing.

Hasselius, Michelle M. Alpacas. 2016. (Farm Animals Ser.). (ENG.). 24p. (gr. k-1). lib. bdg. 26.65 *(978-1-5157-0924-4(8))* Capstone Press of Coughlan Cos.

Heos, Bridget. Do You Really Want to Meet a Camel? Fabbri, Daniele, illus. 2017. (Do You Really Want to Meet... Wild Animals? Ser.). (ENG.). 24p. (J). (gr. 1-3). pap. 8.99 *(978-1-68152-116-9(4))* Amicus.

—Do You Really Want to Meet a Camel? Fabbri, Daniele, illus. 2016. (Do You Really Want to Meet... Wild Animals? Ser.). (ENG.). 24p. (J). (gr. k-3). 20.95 *(978-1-60753-945-2(4))* Amicus Publishing.

How the Camel Got his Hump: Level J, 6 vols. 128p. (gr. 2-3). 41.95 *(978-0-7699-0991-2(4))* Shortland Pubns. (U. S. A.) Inc.

Jango-Cohen, Judith. Camels. 2004. (Animals Animals Ser.). (Illus.). 48p. (YA). (gr. 3-6). 29.93 *(978-0-7614-1750-7(8))* Marshall Cavendish Corp.

Morey, Allan. Camels Are Awesome! 2015. (Awesome Asian Animals Ser.). (ENG., Illus.). 32p. (gr. 1-2). lib. bdg. 27.32 *(978-1-4914-3904-3(1))* Capstone Press of Coughlan Cos.

Riggs, Kate. Amazing Animals: Camels. 2014. (Amazing Animals Ser.). (ENG.). 24p. (J). (gr. 1-3). pap. 8.99 *(978-0-89812-925-0(7),* Creative Paperbacks) Creative Co., The.

—Camels. (J). 2015. *(978-1-60818-513-9(3))* 2014. 25.65 *(978-1-60818-346-3(7))* Creative Co., The. (Creative Education).

—Seedlings: Camels. 2015. (Seedlings Ser.). (ENG.). 24p. (J). (gr. -1-1). pap. 7.99 *(978-1-62832-113-5(X),* Creative Paperbacks) Creative Co., The.

Schuh, Mari. Camels. 2015. (Illus.). 24p. (J). lib. bdg. 25.65 *(978-1-62031-174-5(7),* Bullfrog Bks.) Jump! Inc.

Sirota, Lyn A. Camels, 1 vol. 2010. (Asian Animals Ser.). (ENG.). 24p. (gr. k-1). pap. 7.29 *(978-1-4296-4844-8(9));* pap. 41.70 *(978-1-4296-5094-6(X))* Capstone Press of Coughlan Cos. (Pebble Plus).

Taylor, Trace. Camels of Asia. 2008. (1-3Y Wild Animals Ser.). (ENG.). 24p. (J). (gr. k-2). pap. 5.99 *(978-1-59301-750-7(2))* American Reading Co.

Turnbull, Stephanie. Camel. 2013. (Big Beasts Ser.). (Illus.). 24p. (gr. k-3). 28.50 *(978-1-62588-164-9(9))* Black Rabbit Bks.

—Camel. 2015. (ENG., Illus.). 24p. (J). pap. 8.95 *(978-1-77092-211-2(3))* RiverStream Publishing.

Williams, Zella. Llamas & Other Latin American Camels: Llamas y Otros Camélidos de Latinoamérica. 2009. (Animals of Latin America / Animales de Latinoamérica Ser.). (SPA & ENG.). 24p. pap. 8.25 *(978-1-4358-3388-3(0));* (Illus.). (J). (gr. 1-3). lib. bdg. 22.60 *(978-1-4042-8128-8(2))* Rosen Publishing Group, Inc., The. (PowerKids Pr.).

Winner, Cherie. Camels. 2007. (Nature Watch Ser.). (ENG., Illus.). 48p. (gr. 4-8). lib. bdg. 27.93 *(978-1-57505-870-2(7),* Lerner Pubns.) Lerner Publishing Group.

Zeiger, Jennifer. Camels. 2015. (ENG.). 48p. (J). pap. 6.95 *(978-0-531-21189-2(4),* Orchard Bks.) Scholastic Library Publishing.

CAMELS—FICTION

Abbott, Donna. Cjam, the Unique Camel. 2008. 24p. pap. 24.95 *(978-1-60610-228-2(1))* America Star Bks.

Aguiar, Judy Lee. The Littlest Camel: And the Journey of the Three Kings. Rodriguez, Tom, illus. 2008. 176p. (J). per. *(978-0-9725231-2-7(X))* Turnapaige & Reed Moore.

Antieau, Kim. Broken Moon. 2007. (ENG.). 192p. (YA). (gr. 9-12). 16.99 *(978-1-4169-1767-0(5),* McElderry, Margaret K. Bks.) McElderry, Margaret K. Bks.

Banks, Celia. Issy's Gift: A Story about Giving. 2006. (Illus.). 41p. 14.99 *(978-0-9764460-7-1(3))* HonorNet.

Bradfield, Jolly Roger. Benjamin Dilley's Thirsty Camel. Bradfield, Jolly Roger, illus. 2012. (ENG., Illus.). 64p. (J). (gr. 4-7). 18.95 *(978-1-930900-60-8(0))* Purple Hse. Pr.

Brasch, Nicolas & Parton, Daron. The Riddle of the Camel Race. 2008. (Rigby Focus Forward: Level L Ser.). (Illus.). 24p. (gr. -1-3). pap. *(978-1-4190-3820-4(6),* Rigby) Pearson Education Australia.

Burton, Thomas. Bluey & Dingo's Outback Adventure. 2011. 40p. 15.66 *(978-1-4567-7006-8(3))* AuthorHouse.

Carr, Fran. Wilbur Runs Away. 2004. (Illus.). 80p. pap. *(978-1-84401-304-3(9))* Athena Pr.

Casello-Atassi, Rosemarie. Camel's Tales: The Journey to Bethlehem. 2013. 86p. pap. 15.99 *(978-1-4797-7565-1(7))* Xlibris Corp.

Christie, Gerschutz. Samuel the Camel & the Lone Star. 2006. (Eyes of the Stable Ser.). (ENG.). 128p. pap. 7.50 *(978-1-933341-19-4(X))* CRM.

Darnell, Cynthia. Cameron Asks, What If... 2009. 18p. pap. 24.95 *(978-1-60836-836-5(X))* America Star Bks.

Davies, Stephen. Sophie & the Albino Camel. 2009. 1.00 *(978-1-4074-4344-7(5))* Recorded Bks., Inc.

Davis, Gene. Dromedarius & Camela. 2006. lib. bdg. 18.95 *(978-1-59094-115-7(2))* Jawbone Publishing Corp.

DeStefano, Anthony. Roxy the Ritzy Camel. Cowdrey, Richard, illus. 2016. (ENG.). 36p. (J). (gr. -1-3). 14.99 *(978-0-7369-6634-4(X))* Harvest Hse. Pubs.

Diamond, Lorraine. I Want a Camel for a Pet, 1 vol. 2009. 13p. pap. 24.95 *(978-1-61546-425-8(5))* America Star Bks.

Diedrich, Ann Goshia. Randal the Flannel Camel. 2012. 24p. pap. 17.99 *(978-1-4685-8822-4(2))* AuthorHouse.

Docherty, Thomas. To the Beach. Docherty, Thomas, illus. 2009. (ENG., Illus.). 40p. (J). (gr. -1-2). 15.99 *(978-0-7636-4429-1(3),* Templar) Candlewick Pr.

Dowell, F. M. C. The Little Palace. 2004. (YA). per. 14.95 *(978-1-932205-48-0(9))* Word Association Pubs.

Fischer, Jean & Thomas Nelson Publishing Staff. A Star for Me, 1 vol. Steele-Morgan, Alexandra, illus. 2014. (ENG.). 20p. (J). bds. 14.99 *(978-0-529-11212-5(4))* Nelson, Thomas Inc.

French, Jackie. The Camel Who Crossed Australia. 2008. 256p. *(978-0-7322-8543-2(7))* HarperCollins Pubs. Australia.

Friedman, J. S. Casablanca. Beatrice, Chris, illus. 2013. (Maurice's Valises: Moral Tails in an Immoral World Ser.: Vol. 3). (ENG.). 45p. (J). (gr. k-4). pap. *(978-94-91613-09-8(X))* Mouse Prints Pr.

Hall, Stephen M. The Shepherd's Son. 2013. 36p. 25.99 *(978-1-4808-0112-7(7));* pap. 16.99 *(978-1-4808-0078-6(3))* Archway Publishing.

Hanna, Margaret Leis. Canneh, the Reluctant Christmas Camel. Weltner, Dave, illus. l.t. ed. 2003. 26p. (J). 7.95 *(978-0-9706654-7-8(4))* Sprite Pr.

CD

Hanson, Sandy. A Camel's Story: A Search for the Messiah. Hanson, Sandy & Delage, Kristi, illus. 2005. 53p. (J). lib. bdg. 21.95 *(978-0-9763271-0-3(4))* MK Publishing.

—A Camel's Story, I Met the Lamb. 2012. 62p. 24.99 *(978-1-61996-615-4(8))*; pap. 14.99 *(978-1-61996-614-7(X))* Salem Author Services.

Harber, Chris. Simon the Policeman on Safari - Claude the Camel. Harber, Hulya, illus. 2013. 24p. pap. *(978-0-7552-1552-2(4)*, Bright Pen) Authors OnLine, Ltd.

Hash, Stella. The Christmas Caravan. 2011. 32p. pap. 24.95 *(978-1-4626-0533-0(8))* America Star Bks.

Heyer, Carol. Humphrey's First Christmas. Heyer, Carol, illus. 2008. (ENG., Illus.). 32p. (J). (gr. -1-3). 14.99 *(978-0-8249-5559-5(5)*, Ideal Pubns.) Worthy Publishing.

—Humphrey's First Palm Sunday. Heyer, Carol, illus. 2012. (Illus.). 32p. (J). 14.99 *(978-0-8249-5636-3(2)*, Ideal Pubns.) Worthy Publishing.

James, Robert. How the Camel Got His Hump. 2012. (ENG., Illus.). 24p. (J). pap. *(978-0-7787-7900-1(9))* Crabtree Publishing Co.

Johnston, Annie Fellows. In the Desert of Waiting the Legend of Camel Back Mountain. 2005. reprint ed. pap. 15.95 *(978-1-4179-3370-9(4))* Kessinger Publishing, LLC.

Jones, Christianne C. How the Camel Got Its Hump, 1 vol. Rooney, Ronnie, illus. 2011. (My First Classic Story Ser.). (ENG.). 32p. (gr. k-3). pap. 7.10 *(978-1-4048-7358-2(9)*, My First Classic Story) Picture Window Bks.

Jones, Christianne C. & Kipling, Rudyard. How the Camel Got Its Hump, 1 vol. Rooney, Ronnie, illus. 2010. (My First Classic Story Ser.). (ENG.). 32p. (gr. k-3). lib. bdg. 22.65 *(978-1-4048-6075-9(4)*, My First Classic Story) Picture Window Bks.

Karr, Kathleen. Exiled: Memoirs of a Camel, 0 vols. 2006. (ENG.). 242p. (gr. 5-8). pap. 9.99 *(978-0-7614-5291-1(5)*, 9780761452911, Amazon Children's Publishing) Amazon Publishing.

Katrana, Carol. Charlie, the Christmas Camel: A Christmas Story to Remember. 2012. 120p. (gr. 4-6). pap. 16.95 *(978-1-4772-7710-2(2))* AuthorHouse.

Kipling, Rudyard. How the Camel Got His Hump, 1 vol. Raglin, Tim, illus. 2005. (Rabbit Ears: A Classic Tale Ser.). (ENG.). 28p. (gr. 2-7). 25.65 *(978-1-59197-749-0(5))* Spotlight.

—How the Camel Got His Hump: The Graphic Novel, 1 vol. Rodriguez, Pedro, illus. 2012. (Graphic Spin Ser.). (ENG.). 40p. (gr. 1-3). pap. 5.95 *(978-1-4342-3879-5(2))*; lib. bdg. 23.99 *(978-1-4342-3202-1(6))* Stone Arch Bks. (Graphic Revolve).

Laird, Elizabeth. Lost Riders, 1. unabr. ed. 2010. (ENG., Illus.). 304p. (J). (gr. 4-7). pap. 8.99 *(978-0-330-45209-0(6))* Macmillan Pubs., Ltd. GBR. Dist: Independent Pubs. Group.

Law, Felicia. Cairo the Camel: A Tale of Responsibility. Danson, Lesley, illus. 2010. (Animal Fair Values Ser.). (ENG.). 32p. (J). (gr. -1-3). pap. 10.55 *(978-1-60754-911-6(5))*; lib. bdg. 22.60 *(978-1-60754-903-1(4))* Windmill Bks.

Mills, Joyce C. & Crowley, Richard J. Sammy the Elephant & Mr. Camel: A Story to Help Children Overcome Bedwetting. Pillo, Cary, illus. 2nd ed. 2005. 32p. (J). 14.95 *(978-1-59147-247-6(4))*; pap. 9.95 *(978-1-59147-248-3(2))* American Psychological Assn. (Magination Pr.).

Nimmo, Jenny. The Stones of Ravenglass. 2012. (Chronicles of the Red King Ser.). (ENG.). 272p. (J). (gr. 3-7). 16.99 *(978-0-439-84674-5(9)*, Scholastic Pr.) Scholastic, Inc.

Ondaatje, Griffin. The Camel in the Sun, 1 vol. Wolfsgruber, Linda, illus. 2013. (ENG.). 32p. (J). (gr. k). 17.95 *(978-1-55498-381-0(9))* Groundwood Bks. CAN. Dist: Publishers Group West (PGW).

Peet, Mal & Graham, Elspeth. Mysterious Traveler. Lynch, P. J., illus. 2013. (ENG.). 48p. (J). (gr. k-3). 15.99 *(978-0-7636-6232-5(1))* Candlewick Pr.

Phillips, Dixie & Sharon, et al. Camiles Journey Master Playbook with Musical Scores. 2012. 44p. pap. 29.95 *(978-1-61633-196-2(8))* Guardian Angel Publishing, Inc.

Plante, Raymond. Un Dromadaire Chez Marilou Polaire. Favreau, Marie-Claude, illus. 2003. (Premier Roman Ser.). (FRE.). 64p. (J). (gr. 1-4). pap. *(978-2-89021-608-2(X))* Diffusion du livre Mirabel (DLM).

—Marilou Keeps a Camel. Favreau, Marie-Claude, illus. 2004. 61p. (J). lib. bdg. 12.00 *(978-1-4242-1232-3(4))* Fitzgerald Bks.

—Marilou Keeps a Camel, 1 vol. Cummins, Sarah, tr. from FRE. Favreau, Marie-Claude, illus. 2004. (Formac First Novels Ser.: 50). (ENG.). 64p. (J). (gr. 1-5). 4.95 *(978-0-88780-634-6(1)*, 9780887806346); 14.95 *(978-0-88780-635-3(X)*, 9780887806353) Formac Publishing Co., Ltd. CAN. Dist: Casemate Pubs. & Bk. Distributors, LLC.

Rennison, Louise. Away Laughing on a Fast Camel: Even More Confessions of Georgia Nicolson. (Confessions of Georgia Nicolson Ser.: No. 5). 2004. (Illus.). 288p. (J). lib. bdg. 16.89 *(978-0-06-058935-6(3))* 2006. (ENG.). 304p. (YA). (gr. 8). reprint ed. pap. 9.99 *(978-0-06-058936-3(1))* HarperCollins Pubs. (HarperTeen).

Sayle, Stephen. Cam & Zara the Travel Bugs: Egypt. 2011. 36p. pap. 15.25 *(978-1-4567-6978-9(2))* AuthorHouse.

Tewkesbury, Alexa. The Camel Who Found Christmas. 2007. (ENG., Illus.). 32p. (J). *(978-1-85345-427-1(3))* Crusade for World Revival.

Viknesh, R. My Fantasy Your Treat. 2012. 32p. pap. 28.55 *(978-1-4669-2733-9(X))* Trafford Publishing.

Waines, Frances Drummond. Humpi, the Orphan Camel, 1 vol. 2010. 104p. pap. 19.95 *(978-1-4489-3963-3(1))* America Star Bks.

Wardell, Joe. Doodey the Combat Camel. Bane, T. Glenn, illus. 2012. 20p. pap. 12.95 *(978-0-615-58866-7(2))* Little Clive Pr.

Weed, Thurlow R. Camel Fables from the Sailors of the Sudan. 2004. 84p. pap. 15.95 *(978-0-7414-2229-3(8))* Infinity Publishing.

CAMERAS

Anderson, Lynne. Taking Photographs. 2011. (Early Connections Ser.). (J). *(978-1-61672-621-8(0))* Benchmark Education Co.

Berry, Ron. My First Family Photo Album. Sharp, Chris, illus. 2008. (ENG.). 12p. (J). bds. 8.99 *(978-0-8249-6722-2(4)*, Ideal Pubns.) Worthy Publishing.

Bodden, Valerie. Photography. 2008. (Media Sources Ser.). (J). pap. 9.95 *(978-0-89812-531-3(6))*; (Illus.). 24p. lib. bdg. 24.25 *(978-1-58341-558-0(0))* Creative Co., The. (Creative Education).

Davis, Lynn. George Eastman, 1 vol. 2016. (ENG., Illus.). 24p. (J). *(978-1-62403-722-1(4))* ABDO Publishing Co.

Fandel, Jennifer & Milgrom, Al. George Eastman & the Kodak Camera, 1 vol. Purcell, Gordon, illus. 2007. (Inventions & Discovery Ser.). (ENG.). 32p. (gr. 3-4). pap. 8.10 *(978-0-7368-7900-2(5)*, Graphic Library) Capstone Press of Coughlan Cos.

Greathead, Helen. My Smartphone & Other Digital Accessories. 2016. (Illus.). 32p. (J). *(978-0-7787-2715-6(7))* Crabtree Publishing Co.

Hotchkins, Dewayne. My Camera. 2016. (Rosen REAL Readers: STEM & STEAM Collection). 8p. (gr. 1-k). pap. 5.46 *(978-1-5081-2622-5(4)*, Rosen Classroom) Rosen Publishing Group, Inc., The.

Kallen, Stuart A. Digital Cameras & Camcorders. 2014. (Technology 360 Ser.). (ENG., Illus.). 128p. (gr. 10-10). lib. bdg. 39.90 *(978-1-4205-0165-0(8)*, LML02109-246077, Lucent Bks.) Cengage Gale.

Kulling, Monica. It's a Snap! George Eastman's First Photograph. Slavin, Bill, illus. (Great Idea Ser.). (ENG.). 32p. (J). (gr. k-3). 2013. pap. 7.95 *(978-1-77049-513-5(4))* 2009. 17.95 *(978-0-88776-881-1(4))* Tundra Bks. CAN. (Tundra Bks.). Dist: Penguin Random Hse. LLC.

Kuskowski, Alex & Craig, Diane. Super Simple Camera Projects: Inspiring & Educational Science Activities, 1 vol. 2016. (ENG., Illus.). 32p. (J). *(978-1-62403-730-6(5))* ABDO Publishing Co.

Nagelhout, Ryan. The Problem with Early Cameras. 2015. (Bloopers of Invention Ser.). (ENG., Illus.). 24p. (J). (gr. 2-3). pap. 8.15 *(978-1-4824-2756-1(7))* Stevens, Gareth Publishing LLLP.

Oxlade, Chris. Cameras: With 9 Easy-to-Do Experiments & 230 Exciting Pictures. 2016. (ENG., Illus.). 64p. 12.99 *(978-1-86147-663-0(9)*, Armadillo) Anness Publishing GBR. Dist: National Bk. Network.

Oxlade, Chris & Ganeri, Anita. The Camera, 1 vol. 2010. (Tales of Invention Ser.). (ENG.). 32p. (gr. 3-5). 30.65 *(978-1-4329-3828-4(2)*, NA-h) Heinemann-Raintree.

Petrie, Kristin. Cameras, 1 vol. 2009. (Everyday Inventions Ser.). (ENG., Illus.). 32p. (gr. 3-6). 27.07 *(978-1-60453-085-8(5)*, Checkerboard Library) ABDO Publishing Co.

Pobst, Sandy. The Camera. 2005. (Great Inventions Ser.). (Illus.). 48p. (gr. 5-12). lib. bdg. 31.00 *(978-0-8368-5801-3(8)*, Gareth Stevens Secondary Library) Stevens, Gareth Publishing LLLP.

Richter, Joanne. Inventing the Camera. 2006. (Breakthrough Inventions Ser.). (ENG., Illus.). 32p. (J). (gr. 4-7). pap. *(978-0-7787-2836-8(6))*; lib. bdg. *(978-0-7787-2814-6(5))* Crabtree Publishing Co.

Salzmann, Mary Elizabeth. Camera, 1 vol. 2016. (ENG., Illus.). 24p. (J). *(978-1-62403-709-2(7))* ABDO Publishing Co.

Skog, Jason. Taking the Shot. 2012. (Photography for Teens Ser.). (ENG.). 48p. (gr. 5-7). lib. bdg. 29.32 *(978-0-7565-4490-4(4)*, CPB Grades 4-8) Compass Point Bks.

Skog, Jason & Kalz, Jill. Displaying the Shot. 2012. (Photography for Teens Ser.). (ENG.). 48p. (gr. 5-7). 29.32 *(978-0-7565-4491-1(2)*, CPB Grades 4-8) Compass Point Bks.

Spence, Kelly. Maker Projects for Kids Who Love Photography. 2016. (Be a Maker! Ser.). (ENG.). 32p. (J). (gr. 5-8). *(978-0-7787-2578-7(2))* Crabtree Publishing Co.

Stefoff, Rebecca. The Camera. 2007. (Great Inventions Ser.). (Illus.). 128p. (gr. 8-18). lib. bdg. 29.95 *(978-0-7614-2596-0(9)*, Benchmark Bks.) Marshall Cavendish Corp.

Trueit, Trudi Strain. The Camera. 2006. (Inventions That Shaped the World Ser.). (ENG., Illus.). 80p. (J). (gr. 5-8). pap. 9.95 *(978-0-531-13900-4(X)*, Watts, Franklin) Scholastic Library Publishing.

Turnbull, Stephaniel. Cool Stuff to Photograph. 2014. (Cool Stuff Ser.). 32p. (gr. 2-5). 31.35 *(978-1-62588-190-8(8))* Black Rabbit Bks.

CAMP COOKING

see Outdoor Cooking

CAMPAIGNS, POLITICAL

see Politics, Practical

CAMPAIGNS, PRESIDENTIAL

see Presidents—United States—Election

CAMPING

see also Backpacking; Outdoor Cooking; Outdoor Life; Tents; Wilderness Survival

Aiken, Zora & Aiken, David. Camp ABC: A Place for Outdoor Fun, 1 vol. Aiken, David, illus. 2013. (ENG., Illus.). 32p. (J). 16.99 *(978-0-7643-4423-7(4)*, 9780764344237) Schiffer Publishing, Ltd.

Armour, Christopher. 40 Daily Devotions. 2010. (Wisdom Series Ser.: 0). (ENG., Illus.). 144p. pap. 6.95 *(978-1-882959-55-6(8))* Foxglove Pr.

Bailer, Darice. Austin & Alex Learn about Adjectives. Girouard, Patrick, illus. 2014. (Language Builders Ser.). (ENG.). 32p. (J). (gr. 2-4). pap. 11.94 *(978-1-60357-703-8(3))*; lib. bdg 25.27 *(978-1-59953-668-2(4))* Norwood Hse. Pr.

Beylon, Cathy. At Day Camp. 2005. (Dover Coloring Bks.). (ENG., Illus.). 32p. (J). (gr. -1-5). 2.95 *(978-0-486-44431-4(7))* Dover Pubns., Inc.

Bliss, Dominic. My First Camping Book: 35 Easy & Fun Camping Activities for Children Aged 7 Years+ 2015. (ENG., Illus.). 112p. (J). (gr. 7-11). pap. 14.95 *(978-1-78249-198-9(8)*, CICO Books) Ryland Peters & Small GBR. Dist: WIPRO.

Camping. 2013. (Adventures in the Great Outdoors Ser.). 32p. (J). (gr. 3-6). pap. 70.50 *(978-1-61533-812-2(8)*, PowerKids Pr.) Rosen Publishing Group, Inc., The.

Camps & Retreats to Go: Above & Beyond. 2004. spiral bd. 132.00 *(978-0-9743687-2-6(5))* Connection.

Cardenas, Ernesto A. With My Senses. 2009. 19.95 *(978-1-60698-029-3(7))*; pap. 3.95 *(978-1-60698-027-9(0))* Milo Educational Bks. & Resources.

Champion, Neil. Camping & Hiking. 2011. (Get Outdoors Ser.). (Illus.). 32p. (J). (gr. 4-6). lib. bdg. 25.25 *(978-1-4488-3295-8(0)*, PowerKids Pr.) Rosen Publishing Group, Inc., The.

—Fire & Cooking. 2010. (Survive Alive Ser.). 32p. (J). (gr. 3-6). 28.50 *(978-1-60753-039-8(2))* Amicus Publishing.

—Fire & Cooking. 2012. (Illus.). 32p. (gr. 3-7). pap. 8.95 *(978-1-926722-57-3(4))* Saunders Bk. Co. CAN. Dist: RiverStream Publishing.

—Wild Trail: Hiking & Camping. 2013. (Illus.). 32p. (J). lib. bdg. 28.50 *(978-1-59920-809-1(1))* Black Rabbit Bks.

Champion, Neil & Ganeri, Anita. Fire & Cooking. 2011. (How the World Makes Music Ser.). 32p. (gr. 4-7). lib. bdg. 31.35 *(978-1-59920-480-2(0))* Black Rabbit Bks.

Conners, Christine & Conners, Tim. Scout's Deck of Outdoor Recipe Cards. 2015. (ENG., Illus.). 64p. 14.95 *(978-1-4930-0811-7(0)*, Falcon Guides) Globe Pequot Pr., The.

Davis, James (Jim) W. Out-takes of 55 Years of Camping 2004. (Illus.). 168p. (YA). per. 5.95 *(978-0-9760960-0-9(5))* Davis, James (Jim).

Donahue, Jill Urban. Cómo Contener el Fuego. Masheris, Bob, illus. 2011. (Cómo Mantenernos Seguros/How to Be Safe Ser.).Tr. of Contain the Flame. (SPA, ENG & MUL.). 24p. (gr. k-2). 26.65 *(978-1-4048-6887-8(9))* Picture Window Bks.

Early Bird Books Staff. Going Camping. Date not set. 1.95 *(978-0-394-86704-5(1)*, Random Hse. Bks. for Young Readers) Random Hse. Children's Bks.

Eckart, Edana. I Can Go Camping. 2003. (Wel-Sports Ser.). (ENG., Illus.). 24p. (J). 19.00 *(978-0-516-24280-4(6)*, Children's Pr.) Scholastic Library Publishing.

Encarnacion, Elizabeth. The Girls' Guide to Campfire Activities. 2008. (ENG., Illus.). 124p. (J). (gr. 5-18). pap. 12.95 *(978-1-60433-003-8(1)*, Applesauce Pr.) Cider Mill Pr. Bk. Pubs., LLC.

Erwin, Wesley. Boundary Waters ABC, 1 vol. Kemp, Kathie, illus. 2014. (ENG.). 64p. (J). (gr. -1-k). 12.95 *(978-1-59193-498-1(2))* Adventure Pubns.

Evans, Lynette. Camp Extreme. 2008. (Illus.). 36p. pap. *(978-0-531-15492-2(0))* Children's Pr., Ltd.

—Camp Extreme. 2007. (Shockwave: the Human Experience Ser.). (ENG., Illus.). 36p. (J). (gr. 3-5). 25.00 *(978-0-531-17758-7(0)*, Children's Pr.) Scholastic Library Publishing.

Frisch, Nate. Camping. 2017. (J). *(978-1-60818-685-3(7)*, Creative Education) Creative Co., The.

Gingold, Janet. My Adventure as a Camper: Advanced My Adventure. 2007. 44p. (J). pap. 8.99 *(978-1-59092-407-5(X))* Blue Forge Pr.

Green, Sara. Camping. 2012. (Outdoor Adventures Ser.). (ENG., Illus.). 24p. (J). (gr. 3-8). lib. bdg. 25.95 *(978-1-60014-794-4(1)*, Pilot Bks.) Bellwether Media.

Gulick, Luther & Luther Gulick. Camp Fire Girls. 2009. (ENG., Illus.). 100p. (J). (gr. 4-7). pap. 9.95 *(978-1-4290-9103-9(7))* Applewood Bks.

Hardyman, Robyn. Camping. 2013. (Adventures in the Great Outdoors Ser.). (ENG., Illus.). 32p. (J). (gr. 3-6). pap. 11.75 *(978-1-61533-811-5(X)*, PowerKids Pr.) Rosen Publishing Group, Inc., The.

—Camping. 2013. (Adventures in the Great Outdoors Ser.). (ENG., Illus.). 32p. (J). (gr. 3-6). lib. bdg. 26.50 *(978-1-61533-747-7(4))* Windmill Bks.

Harris, Carolyn. RV in NZ: How to Spend Your Winters Freedom Camping South — Way South — in New Zealand. 2004. (Illus.). 140p. pap. 17.00 *(978-0-9748552-0-2(0))* Marble Mountain Pr.

Harvey, Roger. Caillou Goes Camping. Sévigny, Eric, illus. 2012. (Clubhouse Ser.). (ENG.). 24p. (J). (gr. -1-1). pap. 3.99 *(978-2-89450-856-5(5))* Caillouet, Gerry.

The Hiking & Camping Coloring Book. 2004. (J). mass mkt. *(978-0-9745863-8-0(2))* Cypress Knees Publishing.

Howard, Melanie A. Camping for Kids, 1 vol. 2012. (Into the Great Outdoors Ser.). (ENG.). 32p. (gr. 3-4). pap. 7.95 *(978-1-4296-9266-3(9))*; lib. bdg. 27.99 *(978-1-4296-8423-1(2))* Capstone Press of Coughlan Cos.

James, Helen Foster. S Is for S'Mores: A Camping Alphabet. Judge, Lita, illus. rev. ed. 2007. (ENG.). 40p. (J). (gr. k-6). 17.95 *(978-1-58536-302-5(2))* Sleeping Bear Pr.

Johnson, Nerissa & Parra, Angelo. Teen Reflections, Then & Now. 2011. (Readers' & Writers' Genre Workshop Ser.). (YA). pap. *(978-1-4509-3025-3(5))* Benchmark Education Co.

Klein, Adam G. Camping, 1 vol. 2008. (Outdoor Adventure! Ser.). (ENG.). 32p. (gr. k-6). 27.07 *(978-1-59928-957-1(1)*, Checkerboard Library) ABDO Publishing Co.

Lecreux, Michele & Gallais, Celia. The Boy's Book of Adventure: The Little Guidebook for Smart & Resourceful Boys. Millet, Esao & Millet, Jocelyn, illus. 2013. (ENG.). 128p. (J). (gr. 3-7). 14.99 *(978-0-7641-6611-2(5))* Barron's Educational Series, Inc.

Lundgren, Julie K. Camping. 2009. (Illus.). 24p. (J). (gr. 4-8). lib. bdg. 27.07 *(978-1-60694-367-0(7))* Rourke Educational Media.

Mableton, Barry & Ching, Jacqueline. Camping, 01 vols., 1. 2016. (Outdoor Life Ser.). (ENG.). 64p. (J). 32.95 *(978-1-4994-6227-2(1)*, Rosen Young Adult) Rosen Publishing Group, Inc., The.

Mason, Paul. Hiking & Camping: The World's Top Hikes & Camping Spots, 1 vol. 2011. (Passport to World Sports Ser.). (ENG.). 32p. (gr. 3-4). lib. bdg. 27.99 *(978-1-4296-6863-7(6)*, Edge Bks.) Capstone Press of Coughlan Cos.

More Eternal Camping-Grounds. 2004. (YA). *(978-0-9753721-3-5(0))* Fame's Eternal Bks., LLC.

Morey, Allan. Camping. 2016. (Great Outdoors Ser.). (ENG.). 32p. (J). (gr. 1-4). 20.95 *(978-1-60753-796-0(6))* Amicus Publishing.

Nani. Special Time with Grandm: Grandma & the Camping Trip. 2011. 24p. pap. 11.32 *(978-1-4670-2614-7(X))* AuthorHouse.

Nickens, T. Eward. Field & Stream's Guide to Camping. 2015. (Field & Stream's Guide to the Outdoors Ser.). (ENG., Illus.). 96p. (J). (gr. 6-8). 35.95 *(978-1-4824-2298-6(0))* Stevens, Gareth Publishing LLLP.

Pimental, Annette Bay & Lo, Rich. Mountain Chef: How One Man Lost His Groceries, Changed His Plans, & Helped Cook up the National Park Service. 2016. (ENG., Illus.). 40p. (J). (gr. 1-4). 16.95 *(978-1-58089-711-2(8))* Charlesbridge Publishing, Inc.

Rober, Harold. Going Camping. 2017. (Bumba Books (tm) — Fun Firsts Ser.). (ENG.). 24p. (J). (gr. -1-1). 12.99 ***(978-1-5124-3678-5(X))***; 38.65 ***(978-1-5124-3677-8(1))***; 38.65 ***(978-1-5124-2746-2(2))*** Lerner Publishing Group. (Lerner Pubns.).

Rober, Harold T. Going Camping. 2017. (Bumba Books (tm) — Fun Firsts Ser.). (ENG., Illus.). 24p. (J). (gr. -1-1). 25.32 *(978-1-5124-2550-5(8))* Lerner Publishing Group.

Ruth, Angie. My Adventure Camping. 2006. 44p. (J). 8.99 *(978-1-59092-414-3(2))* Blue Forge Pr.

Ruurs, Margriet. When We Go Camping. Kiss, Andrew, illus. 2004. (ENG.). 32p. (J). (gr. 1-4). pap. 8.95 *(978-0-88776-685-5(4)*, Tundra Bks.) Tundra Bks. CAN. Dist: Penguin Random Hse. LLC.

Scholastic, Inc. Staff & Campbell, Guy. The Boys' Book of Survival: How to Survive Anything, Anywhere. 2009. (Best at Everything Ser.). (ENG., Illus.). 128p. (J). (gr. 3-7). 10.99 *(978-0-545-08536-6(5))* Scholastic, Inc.

Sesame Street Staff, creator. Sesame Street: Elmo & Me! Boxed Set. 2011. 40p. (J). bds. 12.99 *(978-1-60745-166-2(2))* Flying Frog Pubs.

Shah, Nupur. Let's Go Camping. rev. ed. 2011. (1-3Y in My World Ser.). (ENG., Illus.). 16p. (J). (gr. k-1). pap. 5.99 *(978-1-61541-415-4(0))* American Reading Co.

Shava, Ryder. Camping with My Cousins, 01 vols., 1. 2016. (Rosen REAL Readers: Social Studies Nonfiction / Fiction: Family, Community, & the World Ser.). (ENG.). 8p. (J). pap. 5.46 *(978-1-5081-1641-7(5)*, Rosen Classroom) Rosen Publishing Group, Inc., The.

Slade, Suzanne. Let's Go Camping. (Adventures Outdoors Ser.). 32p. 2009. (gr. 4-5). 47.90 *(978-1-61511-267-8(7))* 2007. (Illus.). (J). (gr. 3-7). lib. bdg. 25.25 *(978-1-4042-3650-9(3))* Rosen Publishing Group, Inc., The. (PowerKids Pr.).

Taylor, Trace & Sanchez, Lucia M. Vamos de acampada (Let's Go Camping) 2011. (Lugares adonde voy Ser.). (SPA.). 16p. pap. 39.62 *(978-1-61541-418-5(5))* American Reading Co.

Taylor, Trace, et al. Vamos de Acampada: Let's Go Camping. 2011. (2Y Lugares Adonde Voy Ser.). (SPA.). 16p. (J). (gr. k-2). pap. 6.99 *(978-1-61541-417-8(7))* American Reading Co.

Tomljanovic, Tatiana. Camping. (J). 2013. 27.13 *(978-1-62127-354-7(7))* 2013. pap. 12.95 *(978-1-62127-360-8(1))* 2007. (Illus.). 24p. (gr. 4-7). lib. bdg. 24.45 *(978-1-59036-657-8(3))* 2007. (Illus.). 24p. (gr. 4-7). per. 8.95 *(978-1-59036-658-5(1))* Weigl Pubs., Inc.

Turnbull, Stephanie. Fun & Games. 2016. (Sleepover Secrets Ser.). 24p. (gr. 2-6). 28.50 *(978-1-62588-380-3(3)*, Smart Apple Media) Black Rabbit Bks.

Ventura, Marne. A Camper's Guide to an Awesome Camping Trip. 2017. (Go-To Guides). (ENG., Illus.). 32p. (gr. 3-4). lib. bdg. 27.99 *(978-1-5157-3662-2(8)*, Snap Bks.) Capstone Press of Coughlan Cos.

Walter Foster Creative Team & Winner, Cherie. Kids' Guide to Camping: All You Need to Know about Having Fun in the Outdoors. 2017. (Ranger Rick Kids' Guides). (ENG., Illus.). 96p. (J). (gr. 3-7). 14.95 ***(978-1-63322-381-3(7)***, Walter Foster Jr) Quarto Publishing Group USA.

Willow Creek Press, creator. What Camping Can Teach Us: Life's Lessons Learned from the Great Outdoors. 2006. (ENG., Illus.). 32p. 12.95 *(978-1-59543-290-2(6))* Willow Creek Pr., Inc.

York, M. J. Camping. 2014. (Great Outdoors Ser.). (ENG.). 24p. (J). (gr. 2-5). 28.50 *(978-1-62687-327-8(5)*, 207167) Child's World, Inc., The.

CAMPING—FICTION

Aldridge, Janet. Meadow Brook Girls Afloat. l.t. ed. 2006. (ENG.). 156p. pap. 21.99 *(978-1-4264-0859-5(5))* Creative Media Partners, LLC.

—Meadow Brook Girls Afloat: Or the Stormy Cruise of the Red Rover. 2006. 160p. pap. 19.99 *(978-1-4264-0878-6(1))* Creative Media Partners, LLC.

—The Meadow-Brook Girls under Canvas (Ill. 2006. pap. *(978-1-4065-0695-2(8))* Dodo Pr.

Allen, Quinc. The Outdoor Chums: The First Tour of the. 2004. reprint ed. pap. 20.95 *(978-1-4191-7642-5(0))* Kessinger Publishing, LLC.

Allen, Quincy. The Outdoor Chums at Cabin Point: Or the Golden Cup Mystery. 2007. (ENG.). 154p. pap. 19.99 *(978-1-4346-3238-8(5))*; 166p. pap. 21.99 *(978-1-4346-3239-5(3))* Creative Media Partners, LLC.

—The Outdoor Chums at Cabin Point or the Golden Cup Mystery. 2007. 160p. 95.99 *(978-1-4280-7590-0(9))*; per. 89.99 *(978-1-4280-7608-2(5))* IndyPublish.com.

Amery, Heather. Camping Out. Cartwright, Stephen, illus. 2005. (Usborne Farmyard Tales Ser.). 16p. (J). (gr. -1-17). pap., pap. 5.95 *(978-0-7945-0750-3(6)*, Usborne) EDC Publishing.

Anglen, Becca. Nightmare in the Woods. McKeown, Christian, illus. 2007. 36p. (J). pap. 9.00 *(978-0-8059-7655-7(8))* Dorrance Publishing Co., Inc.

Auerbach, Annie. Grosse Adventures - Trouble at Twilight Cave. 2007. (Grosse Adventures Ser.). (Illus.). 96p. per. 4.99 *(978-1-59816-051-2(6))* TOKYOPOP, Inc.

Baldwin, Faith. Judy: A Story of Divine Corners. Beebe, Robb, illus. 2011. 264p. 47.95 *(978-1-258-08877-4(0))* Literary Licensing, LLC.

Ball, Nate. Alien in My Pocket #6: Forces of Nature. Pamintuan, Macky, illus. 2015. (Alien in My Pocket Ser.: 6). (ENG.). 144p. (J). (gr. 1-5). pap. 4.99 *(978-0-06-221633-5(3))* HarperCollins Pubs.

Ballantyne, R. M. Red Rooney: Or, the Last of the Crew. 2007. (R. M. Ballantyne Collection). (Illus.). 408p. 22.00 *(978-1-934554-08-1(1))* Vision Forum, Inc., The.

Ballantyne, Robert Michael. Red Rooney: The Last of the Crew. 2007. (ENG.). 270p. pap. 21.99 *(978-1-4346-3693-5(3))*; 302p. pap. 24.99 *(978-1-4346-3741-3(7))* Creative Media Partners, LLC.

Banks, Steven. Pick a Dad, Any Dad! Moore, Harry, illus. 2005. (Fairly Odd Parents Ser.: 7). 24p. (J). lib. bdg. 15.00 *(978-1-59054-804-2(3))* Fitzgerald Bks.

Barbour, Ralph Henry. The Lilac Girl. 2006. (Illus.). pap. *(978-1-4065-0778-2(4))* Dodo Pr.

Barnholdt, Lauren. Hailey Twitch & the Campground Itch. Beaky, Suzanne, illus. 2011. (Hailey Twitch Ser.: 3). (ENG.). 144p. (J). (gr. 2-4). pap. 8.99 *(978-1-4022-2446-1(X)*, Sourcebooks Jabberwocky) Sourcebooks, Inc.

Barshaw, Ruth McNally. Ellie McDoodle: Have Pen, Will Travel. Barshaw, Ruth McNally, illus. 2nd ed. 2011. (Ellie Mcdoodle Ser.). (ENG., Illus.). 192p. (YA). (gr. 3-6). pap. 7.99

(978-1-59990-715-4(1), 9781599907154, Bloomsbury USA Childrens) Bloomsbury Publishing USA.
—Have Pen, Will Travel. Barshaw, Ruth McNally, illus. 2013. (Ellie Mcdoodle Diaries). (ENG., Illus.). 192p. (YA). (gr. 3-6). 12.99 (978-1-61963-173-1(3), 9781619631731, Bloomsbury USA Childrens) Bloomsbury Publishing USA.
Baum, Robert. Portal Masters: A New Beginning. 2004. 282p. (YA). 27.95 (978-0-595-66942-4(5)) iUniverse, Inc.
Beasley, David R. Canoe Trip. Milner, Elizabeth B., illus. 2006. 129p. (YA). per. 15.00 (978-0-915317-21-9(4)) Davus Publishing.
Beaty, Janice J. & Beaty, Lillian C., illus. Jarod & the Mystery of the Utah Arches: A National Park Adventure Series Book. 2016. 118p. (J). pap. (978-1-63293-122-1(2)) Sunstone Pr.
Beauregard, Lynda. The Yucky Duck Rescue: A Mystery about Pollution. Torres, German, illus. 2013. (Summer Camp Science Mysteries Ser.: 8). (ENG.). 48p. (gr. 3-6). lib. bdg. 29.27 (978-1-4677-0170-9(X), Graphic Universe™) Lerner Publishing Group.
Benson, Irene Elliott. Ethel Hollister's Second Summer As a Campfire Girl. 2007. 84p. per. (978-1-4065-4834-1(0)) Dodo Pr.
—How Ethel Hollister Became a Campfire Girl. 2007. 108p. per. (978-1-4065-4835-8(9)) Dodo Pr.
Beresford, Elisabeth. Wombles Camping & Cloudberries. (Illus.). 15p. (J). (gr. k-6). pap. (978-0-340-73584-8(8)) Hodder & Stoughton.
Birney, Betty G. Humphrey's Creepy-Crawly Camping Adventure. Burris, Priscilla, illus. 2015. (Humphrey's Tiny Tales Ser.: 3). (ENG.). 96p. (J). (gr. k-3). 4.99 (978-0-14-751459-2(2), Puffin Books); 14.99 (978-0-399-17227-4(0), G.P. Putnam's Sons Books for Young Readers) Penguin Young Readers Group.
—Humphrey's Creepy-Crawly Camping Adventure. 2015. (Humphrey's Tiny Tales Ser.: 3). lib. bdg. 14.75 (978-0-606-36772-1(1)) Turtleback Bks.
Blakeney, Crystal Denise. Paradise & Cove Go Camping. 2012. 20p. pap. 17.99 (978-1-4772-7587-0(8)) AuthorHouse.
Bonehill, Ralph. Guns & Snowshoes. 2006. 27.95 (978-1-4218-3002-5(7)); pap. 12.95 (978-1-4218-3102-2(3)) 1st World Publishing, Inc.
—Guns & Snowshoes: Or, the Winter Outing of the Young Hunters. 2006. 160p. pap. 19.99 (978-1-4264-3173-9(2)) 2007. (ENG.). 174p. pap. 21.99 (978-1-4264-3208-8(9)) Creative Media Partners, LLC.
Bowman, Chaliece. Sarah's Camping Trip. 2012. 20p. pap. 17.99 (978-1-4772-5531-5(1)) AuthorHouse.
Bradman, Tony. The Three Little Pigs Go Camping, 1 vol. Warburton, Sarah, illus. 2014. (After Happily Ever After Ser.). (ENG.). 56p. (gr. 2-3). lib. bdg. 25.32 (978-1-4342-7952-1(9), After Happily Ever After) Stone Arch Bks.
Brandes, Wendy L. Claire's Cursed Camping Trip. Lorenzet, Eleonora, illus. 2016. (Summer Camp Ser.). (ENG.). 96p. (gr. 4-6). lib. bdg. 24.65 (978-1-4965-2600-7(7)) Stone Arch Bks.
Brasch, Nicolas & Nickel, Adam. Dad & Dan Go Camping. 2008. (Rigby Focus Forward: Level G Ser.). (Illus.). 24p. (J). (gr. 4-7). pap. (978-1-4190-3705-4(6), Rigby) Pearson Education Australia.
Broekstra, Lorette. Baby Bear Goes Camping. 2004. (Baby Bear Ser.). (Illus.). 32p. (J). 5.99 (978-1-85854-408-3(4)) Brimax Books Ltd. GBR. Dist: Byeway Bks.
Brooks, Walter R. Freddy Goes Camping. Wiese, Kurt, illus. 2014. (ENG.). 272p. (gr. 4-13). pap. 10.99 (978-1-4683-0831-0(9), 460831) Overlook Pr., The.
Brown, Jeff. Flat Stanley Goes Camping. Pamintuan, Macky, illus. 2013. (I Can Read Level 2 Ser.). (ENG.). 32p. (J). (gr. -1-3). 16.99 (978-0-06-143013-8(7)); pap. 3.99 (978-0-06-143015-2(3)) HarperCollins Pubs.
—Flat Stanley Goes Camping. 2013. (J). lib. bdg. 13.55 (978-0-606-31815-0(1), Turtleback) Turtleback Bks.
Budbill, David. Bones on Black Spruce Mountain. 2004. 117p. (J). (978-0-9657144-6-4(2)); pap. (978-0-9657144-7-1(0)) Onion River Pr.
—Snowshoe Trek to Otter River. 2005. (J). pap. (978-0-9657144-9-5(7)) Onion River Pr.
Burries-Hall, Tracy. Honey the Firefly: Honey the Firefly & the Cub Scout. 2010. 28p. 13.99 (978-1-4520-2550-6(9)) AuthorHouse.
Butler, T. Lee. The Ghost on Tanner's Mountain. 2008. 96p. pap. 11.94 (978-1-4357-5963-3(X)) Lulu Pr., Inc.
Calame, Don. Dan vs. Nature. 2016. (ENG.). 384p. (YA). (gr. 9). 17.99 (978-0-7636-7071-9(5)) Candlewick Pr.
Cammuso, Frank. Cookie Catastrophe. 2014. (Misadventures of Salem Hyde Ser.: 3). (J). lib. bdg. 17.15 (978-0-606-36149-1(9)) Turtleback Bks.
—The Misadventures of Salem Hyde: Cookie Catastrophe. 2014. (Misadventures of Salem Hyde Ser.). (ENG., Illus.). 96p. (J). (gr. 1-4). 14.95 (978-1-4197-1198-5(9), Amulet Bks.) Abrams, Inc.
Camping Caper: Coloring/Activity Book (English) incl. Stickers. 2007. (Illus.). (J). 2.99 (978-1-933934-65-5(4)) Mighty Kids Media.
Camping Caper: Picture Book (English) 8x8. 2007. (Illus.). (J). 5.99 (978-1-933934-64-8(6)) Mighty Kids Media.
Candlewick Press, Candlewick. Peppa Pig & the Camping Trip. 2016. (Peppa Pig Ser.). (ENG., Illus.). 32p. (J). (-k). 12.99 (978-0-7636-8741-0(3), Candlewick Entertainment) Candlewick Pr.
Capucilli, Alyssa Satin. Biscuit Goes Camping. Schories, Pat, illus. 2015. (My First I Can Read Ser.). (ENG.). 32p. (J). (gr. -1-3). pap. 3.99 (978-0-06-223693-7(8)) HarperCollins Pubs.
Carson, Janet. Camping with Colleen. 2006. (Neighborhood Readers Ser.). (ENG.). 8p. (gr. 1-3). pap. 5.15 (978-1-4042-6803-6(0), Rosen Classroom) Rosen Publishing Group, Inc., The.
Carson, Penny & Hess, Amy. Simon Goes Camping. 2008. 19p. 10.95 (978-1-4357-1560-8(8)) Lulu Pr., Inc.
Carter, Herbert. The Boy Scouts' First Camp Fire. 2007. 124p. per. (978-1-4068-4409-2(8)) Echo Library.
Catt, Louis & Cummings, Fiona. Mega Sleepover Club 5. 2011. (Sleepover Club Ser.). (ENG.). 320p. (J). pap., pap., pap. 11.99 (978-0-00-712843-3(6), HarperCollins Children's Bks.) HarperCollins Pubs. Ltd. GBR. Dist: HarperCollins Pubs.
Chancellor, Deborah. Camping Trip. Fairclough, Chris, illus. 2005. (Reading Corner Ser.). 24p. (J). (gr. k-3). lib. bdg. 22.80 (978-1-59771-010-7(5)) Sea-To-Sea Pubns.
Chapman, Allen. Frank Roscoes Secret or the Darewell Chu. 2007. pap. (978-1-4065-1431-5(4)) Dodo Pr.
Clements, Andrew. Because Your Mommy Loves You. Alley, R. W., illus. 2012. (ENG.). 32p. (J). (gr. -1-3). 16.99 (978-0-547-25522-4(5)) Houghton Mifflin Harcourt Publishing Co.
—A Week in the Woods. 2004. (ENG.). 208p. (J). (gr. 4-8). reprint ed. pap. 7.99 (978-0-689-85802-4(7), Atheneum Bks. for Young Readers) Simon & Schuster Children's Publishing.
Conforto, Lisa. The Very Compromising Adventures of Thumby Blackstone, 1 vol. 2010. 34p. 24.95 (978-1-4512-0270-0(9)) PublishAmerica, Inc.
Cousins, Lucy. Maisy Goes Camping. Cousins, Lucy, illus. 2009. (Maisy Ser.). (ENG., Illus.). 32p. (J). (gr. k-k). pap. 6.99 (978-0-7636-4368-3(8)) Candlewick Pr.
—Maisy Goes Camping. 2009. (Maisy First Experiences Ser.). lib. bdg. 17.20 (978-0-606-06667-9(5), Turtleback) Turtleback Bks.
Cowan, Charlotte. Moose with Loose Poops. Neal, Penelope, illus. 2008. (Dr. Hippo Ser.). (ENG.). 32p. (J). (gr. -1-2). 17.95 (978-0-9753516-5-9(6)) Hippocratic Pr., The.
Cox, Steve, illus. Is That You, Monster? Check Inside the Secret Pockets If You Dare! 2013. (ENG.). 22p. (J). (gr. -1-1). 12.99 (978-0-7641-6608-2(5)) Barron's Educational Series, Inc.
Coyle, Carmela Lavigna. Do Princesses Make Happy Campers? Gordon, Mike, illus. 2015. (ENG.). 32p. (J). (gr. -1-2). 15.95 (978-1-63076-054-0(4)) Taylor Trade Publishing.
Crisis Maximus! Individual Title Six-Packs. (Bookweb Ser.). 32p. (gr. 6-18). 34.00 (978-0-7578-0902-6(2)) Rigby Education.
Crow, Melinda Melton. Rocky & Daisy Go Camping, 1 vol. Brownlow, Mike, illus. 2013. (My Two Dogs Ser.). (ENG.). 32p. (gr. 2-3). pap. 5.95 (978-1-4342-6117-5(4)) Stone Arch Bks.
Cummings, Priscilla. The Journey Back. 2013. (ENG.). 272p. (J). (gr. 5). pap. 7.99 (978-0-14-242290-8(8), Puffin Books) Penguin Young Readers Group.
Daniels, Darla. Carrie Goes Camping. 2011. 24p. pap. 16.95 (978-1-4626-0642-9(3)) America Star Bks.
Davis, Jacky. I Love You, Bingo. 2015. (Penguin Young Readers Level 2 Ser.). lib. bdg. 13.55 (978-0-606-37578-8(3)) Turtleback Bks.
Davis, Jacky & Soman, David. Ladybug Girl & Bingo. Soman, David, illus. 2012. (Ladybug Girl Ser.). (ENG., Illus.). 40p. (J). (gr. -1-k). 16.99 (978-0-8037-3582-8(0), Dial Bks) Penguin Young Readers Group.
Davis, Jim & Michiels, Cedric. Unfair Weather. Dargaud Media Staff & Ellipsanime Staff, illus. 2013. (Garfield Show Ser.). (ENG.). 64p. (J). (gr. 1-5). 11.99 (978-1-59707-433-9(0), 9781597074339) Papercutz.
Davis, Terry. Camping with Dad: The Mystery of Valley Gulch. 2006. (ENG.). 148p. per. 24.95 (978-1-4241-5659-7(9)) America Star Bks.
deRubertis, Barbara. Maxwell Moose's Mountain Monster. Alley, R. W., illus. 2011. (Animal Antics A to Z Ser.). 32p. (J). pap. 45.32 (978-0-7613-7659-0(3)); (ENG.). lib. bdg. 22.60 (978-1-57565-334-1(6)); (ENG.). (gr. -1-3). pap. 7.95 (978-1-57565-325-9(7)) Kane Press, Inc.
deRubertis, Barbara & DeRubertis, Barbara. Maxwell Moose's Mountain Monster. Alley, R. W., illus. 2012. (Animal Antics A to Z Ser.). 32p. (J). (gr. 2 — 1). cd-rom 7.95 (978-1-57565-406-5(7)) Kane Press, Inc.
Deshone, Jerry Michael. Bear in Mind. 2011. 24p. pap. 24.95 (978-1-4626-2973-2(3)) America Star Bks.
Disney Press Editors. Training Army Al. 2014. (Doc Mcstuffins 8X8 Ser.). (J). lib. bdg. 13.55 (978-0-606-35910-8(9)) Turtleback Bks.
Dixon, Franklin W. Camping Chaos. 2014. (Hardy Boys: Secret Files Ser.: 16). lib. bdg. 16.00 (978-0-606-36100-2(6)) Turtleback Bks.
—The Madman of Black Bear Mountain. 2016. (Hardy Boys Adventures Ser.: 12). (ENG., Illus.). 144p. (J). (gr. 3-7). pap. 6.99 (978-1-4814-3880-3(8), Aladdin) Simon & Schuster Children's Publishing.
Doerrfeld, Cori. A Perfect View. Doerrfeld, Cori & Page, Tyler, illus. 2017. (Cici: a Fairy's Tale Ser.: 3). (ENG.). 48p. (J). (gr. 2-5). 26.65 (978-1-4677-6154-3(0)); pap. 7.99 (978-1-5124-3068-4(4)); E-Book 19.99 **(978-1-5124-2700-4(4)**, 9781512427004) Lerner Publishing Group. (Graphic Universe™).
Doller, Trish. The Devil You Know. 2015. (ENG.). 256p. (YA). (gr. 9). 17.99 (978-1-61963-416-9(3), 9781619634169, Bloomsbury USA Childrens) Bloomsbury Publishing USA.
Eastman, Peter. Fred & Ted Go Camping. 2005. (Beginner Books(R) Ser.). (ENG., Illus.). 48p. (J). (gr. -1-2). 9.99 (978-0-375-82965-9(2), Random Hse. Bks. for Young Readers) Random Hse. Children's Bks.
Elkins, Stephen. Know God, No Fear. Reisch, Jessie, illus. 2003. 32p. (J). (gr. k-5). 14.99 (978-0-8054-2658-8(2)) B&H Publishing Group.
Emerson, Carl. Monster Boy & the Scary Scouts, 1 vol. Levin, Lon, illus. 2010. (Monster Boy Set 2 Ser.). (ENG.). 32p. (J). (gr. k-3). 28.50 (978-1-60270-778-8(2)) ABDO Publishing Co.
Emert, Sarah. Chanler & Friends: Backyard Camping. 2013. (ENG.). 30p. (J). pap. 7.99 (978-1-936815-81-4(8)) Yawn's Bks. & More, Inc.
Farber, Erica. Kooky Campout. Scarry, Huck, illus. 2015. (Richard Scarry's Great Big Schoolhouse Ser.). (ENG.). 24p. (J). (gr. 1-2). 12.95 (978-1-4027-9914-3(4)) Sterling Publishing Co., Inc.
Fitzhugh, Percy Keese. Pee-Wee Harris & Roy Blakeley's Adventures in Camp. l.t. ed. 2007. (ENG.). 282p. pap. 23.99 (978-1-4346-1532-9(4)) Creative Media Partners, LLC.
Flo & Wendell Explore. 2014. (ENG.). 32p. (J). (gr. -1-k). 17.99 (978-0-8037-3930-7(3), Dial Bks) Penguin Young Readers Group.
Foggo, Cheryl. I Have Been in Danger, 1 vol. Hotchkiss, Conrad & Graham, Heather, illus. 2005. (In the Same Boat Ser.: No. 3). (ENG.). 184p. (J). (gr. 4-6). pap. 7.95 (978-1-55050-185-8(2)) Coteau Bks. CAN. Dist: Fitzhenry & Whiteside, Ltd.
Forever Lost. 2011. (Hardy Boys (All New) Undercover Brothers Ser.: 36). (ENG.). 160p. (J). (gr. 3-7). pap. 6.99 (978-1-4424-0264-5(4), Aladdin) Simon & Schuster Children's Publishing.
Frenette, Liza. Dead End. Gillis, Jane, illus. 2005. x, 65p. (J). (978-1-59531-001-9(0)) North Country Bks., Inc.
Frisch, Aaron. A Night on the Range. Sheban, Chris, illus. 2013. (ENG.). 32p. (J). (gr. -1-17). pap. 7.99 (978-0-89812-829-1(3), Creative Paperbacks) Creative Co., The.
Frueh, Pamela. Me & My Best Cousin Joy. 2007. 80p. pap. 8.95 (978-1-4303-2193-4(8)) Lulu Pr., Inc.
Gangsei, Jan. The Wild Bunch. 2017. (Max Ser.). (ENG., Illus.). 192p. (J). (gr. 4-8). pap. 7.99 **(978-1-4814-6828-2(6)**, Aladdin) Simon & Schuster Children's Publishing.
Garis, Howard R. The Curlytops on Star Island. 2009. 120p. 22.95 (978-1-60664-611-3(7)); pap. 10.95 (978-1-60664-343-3(6)) Rodgers, Alan Bks.
Garland, Sarah. Eddie's Tent: And How to Go Camping. 2015. (ENG., Illus.). 40p. (J). (gr. -1-2). 17.99 (978-1-84780-408-2(X), Frances Lincoln) Quarto Publishing Group UK GBR. Dist: Hachette Bk. Group.
Gelsey, James & Duendes Del Sur Staff. Scooby-Doo & the Zombie's Treasure, 1 vol. 2011. (Scooby-Doo Mysteries Ser.). (ENG., Illus.). 64p. (J). (gr. 3-6). 24.21 (978-1-59961-896-8(6)) Spotlight.
Giff, Patricia Reilly. Bears Beware. Bright, Alasdair, illus. 2012. (Zigzag Kids Ser.). (ENG.). 80p. (J). (gr. 1-4). pap. 4.99 (978-0-375-85913-7(6), Yearling) Random Hse. Children's Bks.
Goodman, Nancy. The Camping Kids Adventures. 2010. 74p. pap. 10.99 (978-1-60957-474-1(5)) Salem Author Services.
Goscinny, René. Nicholas on Vacation. Bell, Anthea, tr. Sempé, Jean-Jacques, illus. 2013. (ENG.). 136p. (J). (gr. 1-4). pap. 9.95 (978-0-7148-6224-8(X)) Phaidon Pr., Inc.
Gownley, Jim. Amelia in Speak Softee to Me: #5, 1 vol. Gownley, Jim, illus. 2011. (Amelia Rules! Ser.). (ENG., Illus.). 36p. 24.21 (978-1-59961-791-6(9)) Spotlight.
Graham, Oakley. 3 Go Camping. 2017. (Learning Journeys Ser.). (ENG.). 24p. (J). (gr. -1-2). 12.99 **(978-1-78445-313-8(7))** Top That! Publishing PLC GBR. Dist: Independent Pubs. Group.
Grant, Katy. Friends Fornever. 2008. (Summer Camp Secrets Ser.). (ENG.). 240p. (J). (gr. 3-7). pap. 7.99 (978-1-4169-3578-0(9), Aladdin) Simon & Schuster Children's Publishing.
Grant, Robert. Jack in the Bush or A Summer on a Salmon River. 2005. pap. 33.95 (978-1-4179-5573-2(2)) Kessinger Publishing, LLC.
Hancock, H. Irving. The High School Boys in Summer Camp. 2007. 180p. per. (978-1-4065-1985-3(5)) Dodo Pr.
Hapka, Catherine, pseud. The Camping Trip. 2014. (Pony Scouts: I Can Read! Ser.). (J). lib. bdg. 13.55 (978-0-606-35069-3(1), Turtleback) Turtleback Bks.
Hapka, Cathy, pseud. Mystery in the Whispering Woods. 2013. (LEGO Friends Chapter Bks.: 3). lib. bdg. 14.75 (978-0-606-32394-9(5), Turtleback) Turtleback Bks.
Harper, Charise Mericle. Just Grace & the Super Sleepover. 2014. (Just Grace Ser.: 11). (ENG., Illus.). 208p. (J). (gr. 1-4). 15.99 (978-0-544-04584-2(X)) Houghton Mifflin Harcourt Publishing Co.
Harris, Evelyn. Two Harrises & One Day Go Camping. 2010. 28p. pap. 12.99 (978-1-4500-9252-4(7)) Xlibris Corp.
Harvey, Jacqueline. Alice-Miranda at Camp. 2015. 10. 352p. (J). (gr. 3-7). 9.99 (978-1-74275-761-2(8)) Random Hse. Australia AUS. Dist: Independent Pubs. Group.
Hayes, Joe. The Lovesick Skunk. Castro L., Antonio, illus. (ENG.). 32p. (J). 2016. 7.95 (978-1-941026-04-5(4)) 2010. 16.95 (978-1-933693-81-1(9)) Cinco Puntos Pr.
Herbert Carter. The Boy Scouts' First Camp Fire. 2007. 224p. per. 12.95 (978-1-4218-4548-7(2)); 27.95 (978-1-4218-4464-0(8)) 1st World Publishing, Inc. (1st World Library - Literary Society).
Hermes, Patricia. Emma Dilemma & the Camping Nanny, 0 vols. Carter, Abby, illus. 2009. (Emma Dilemma Ser.: 4). (ENG.). 144p. (J). (gr. 3-6). 15.99 (978-0-7614-5534-9(5), 9780761455349, Amazon Children's Publishing) Amazon Publishing.
Heyliger, William. Jerry Hicks, Explorer. Salg, Bert, illus. 2011. 210p. 44.95 (978-1-258-08964-1(5)) Literary Licensing, LLC.
Hill, Kirkpatrick. Winter Camp. 2007. (ENG.). 192p. (J). (gr. 3-7). pap. 10.99 (978-1-4169-6455-1(X), Simon & Schuster/Paula Wiseman Bks.) Simon & Schuster/Paula Wiseman Bks.
Hillan, Pamela & Dyan, Penelope. The Discovery in the Old Mine. Weigand, John, photos by. 2013. (Illus.). 116p. pap. 8.95 (978-1-61477-095-4(6)) Bellissima Publishing, LLC.
Hillert, Margaret. Dear Dragon Goes to the Carnival. Schimmell, David, illus. 2010. (BeginningtoRead Ser.). 32p. (J). (gr. k-2). lib. bdg. 22.60 (978-1-59953-346-9(4)) Norwood Hse. Pr.
Hines, Anna Grossnickle, illus. Whistling. 2003. 40p. (J). 16.89 (978-0-06-050236-2(3)) HarperCollins Pubs.
Hiris, Monica. Just Like Mom. Sierra, Holly, illus. 2005. (ENG.). 8p. (gr. k-1). pap. 7.95 (978-1-57874-088-8(6), Kaeden Bks.) Kaeden Corp.
Hofmeister, Alan, et al. In the Tent. (Reading for All Learners Ser.). (Illus.). (J). pap. (978-1-56861-132-7(3)) Swift Learning Resources.
Holden, Pam. Message from Camp, 6 pack. Webb, Philip, illus. 2009. (Red Rocket Readers Ser.). (ENG.). 16p. (gr. 2-2). pap. (978-1-877363-64-1(2), Red Rocket Readers) Flying Start Bks.
Holt, Kimberly Willis. Piper Reed, Campfire Girl. Davenier, Christine, illus. 2010. (Piper Reed Ser.: 4). (ENG.). 160p. (J). (gr. 3-6). 15.99 (978-0-8050-9006-2(1), 9780805090062, Holt, Henry & Co. Bks. For Young Readers) Holt, Henry & Co.
—Piper Reed, Campfire Girl. Davenier, Christine, illus. 2011. (Piper Reed Ser.: 4). (ENG.). 176p. (J). (gr. 3-6). pap. 6.99 (978-0-312-67482-3(1), 9780312674823) Square Fish.
Hooker, Karen. Camping. Biddle, Bruce, illus. l.t. ed. 2003. (ENG.). 16p. (gr. k-1). pap. 7.95 (978-1-879835-32-0(0), Kaeden Bks.) Kaeden Corp.
Hooks, Gwendolyn. The Noisy Night: A Pet Club Story, 1 vol. Byrne, Mike, illus. 2010. (Pet Club Ser.). (ENG.). 32p. (gr. 1-2). 22.65 (978-1-4342-2049-3(4)); pap. 6.25 (978-1-4342-2793-5(6)) Stone Arch Bks.
Hope, Laura Lee. Bunny Brown & His Sister Sue at Camp R. 2006. 26.95 (978-1-4218-2972-2(X)); pap. 11.95 (978-1-4218-3072-8(8)) 1st World Publishing, Inc.
—The Outdoor Girls of Deepdale: Or Camping & Tramping for Fun & Health. 2007. (ENG.). 136p. pap. 18.99 (978-1-4346-2152-8(9)); 150p. pap. 19.99 (978-1-4346-2212-9(6)) Creative Media Partners, LLC.
Hope, Lee Laura. The Outdoor Girls in a Winter Camp or Glorious Days on Skates & Ice Boats. 2007. 156p. 41.99 (978-1-4280-7498-9(8)); per. 35.99 (978-1-4280-7509-2(7)) IndyPublish.com.
Howard, Becky L. Harrison Goes Camping. Pine, Margherita N., ed. Howard, Becky L., illus. 2nd ed. 2012. (Illus.). 26p. (-18). pap. 11.98 (978-0-9848782-1-5(1)) Palmetto Street Publishing.
Howe, James. Nighty-Nightmare. Morrill, Leslie, illus. 2007. (Bunnicula & Friends Ser.). (ENG.). 144p. (J). (gr. 3-7). pap. 6.99 (978-1-4169-3966-5(0), Atheneum Bks. for Young Readers) Simon & Schuster Children's Publishing.
Idle, Molly. Camp Rex. Idle, Molly, illus. 2014. (ENG., Illus.). 40p. (J). (gr. -1-k). 16.99 (978-0-670-78573-5(3), Viking Books for Young Readers) Penguin Young Readers Group.
Inkpen, Mick. Kipper's Monster. 2008. (ENG., Illus.). 32p. (J). (gr. -1-12). pap. 10.99 (978-0-340-93208-7(2)) Hodder & Stoughton GBR. Dist: Hachette Bk. Group.
Jaimet, Kate. Edge of Flight, 1 vol. 2012. (Orca Sports Ser.). (ENG.). 160p. (YA). (gr. 6-10). pap. 9.95 (978-1-4598-0160-8(1)) Orca Bk. Pubs. USA.
Janni, Rebecca. Nellie Sue, Happy Camper. Avril, Lynne, illus. 2013. (Every Cowgirl Ser.). (ENG.). 32p. (J). (gr. 1-2). 14.99 (978-0-448-46507-4(8)); mass mkt. 3.99 (978-0-448-46387-2(3)) Penguin Young Readers Group. (Penguin Young Readers).
Joyner, Andrew. Boris Sees the Light. 2013. (Boris Ser.: 4). (ENG.). 80p. (J). (gr. k-2). pap. 4.99 (978-0-545-48454-1(5)) Scholastic, Inc.
—Boris Sees the Light. 2013. (Boris Ser.: 4). lib. bdg. 14.75 (978-0-606-32363-5(5), Turtleback) Turtleback Bks.
Juhasz, Mike. Posey & Mosey Go Camping. Juhasz, Brenda, illus. 2008. 16p. pap. 24.95 (978-1-60610-258-9(3)) America Star Bks.
Kalar, Bonnie. Neal Camps Out. Spreen, Kathe, illus. Date not set. 12p. (J). (gr. -1-2). pap. (978-1-891619-39-7(X)) Corona Pr.
Keene, Carolyn. Secret at Mystic Lake. 2014. (Nancy Drew Diaries: 6). (ENG., Illus.). 160p. (J). (gr. 3-7). pap. 6.99 (978-1-4814-0012-1(6), Aladdin) Simon & Schuster Children's Publishing.
Keyser, Amber J. The Way Back from Broken. 2015. (ENG.). 216p. (YA). (gr. 6-12). 18.99 (978-1-4677-8817-5(1), Carolrhoda Lab™); 18.99 (978-1-4677-7590-8(8)) Lerner Publishing Group.
Kimpton, Diana. Princess Ellie's Moonlight Mystery. 2015. (Pony-Crazed Princess Ser.). (ENG.). 96p. (J). (gr. k-5). pap. 4.99 (978-0-7945-3431-8(7), Usborne) EDC Publishing.
Kittredge, James M. The Three Little Explorers, 1 vol. Reyes, Glendalys, illus. 2010. 16p. pap. 24.95 (978-1-4489-8973-7(6)) PublishAmerica, Inc.
Klein, Abby. Camping Catastrophe! McKinley, John, illus. 2008. (Ready, Freddy! Ser.: Bk. 14). 95p. (J). (gr. -1-3). 11.65 (978-0-7569-8837-1(3)) Perfection Learning Corp.
—Camping Catastrophe! McKinley, John, illus. 2008. (Ready, Freddy! Ser.: 14). (ENG.). 96p. (J). (gr. -1-3). 5.99 (978-0-439-89594-1(4), Blue Sky Pr., The) Scholastic, Inc.
Klein, Adria F. Sammy Saw & the Campout, 1 vol. Rowland, Andrew, illus. 2012. (Tool School Ser.). (ENG.). 32p. (gr. 1-3). pap. 6.25 (978-1-4342-4234-1(X)); lib. bdg. 22.65 (978-1-4342-4022-4(3)) Stone Arch Bks.
Knesek, Marian. Zane & the Armadillo. Leipsic, Regina, illus. 2012. 26p. 24.95 (978-1-4626-6685-0(X)) America Star Bks.
Kropp, Joseph P. Hickok's Gold. 2006. (J). 11.95 (978-1-890905-25-5(9)) Day to Day Enterprises.
Krulik, Nancy. Hey! Who Stole the Toilet?, 8 vols. Blecha, Aaron, illus. 2012. (George Brown, Class Clown Ser.: 8). (ENG.). 128p. (J). (gr. 2-4). pap. 5.99 (978-0-448-45576-1(5), Grosset & Dunlap) Penguin Young Readers Group.
—Hey! Who Stole the Toilet? 2012. (George Brown, Class Clown Ser.: 8). lib. bdg. 14.75 (978-0-606-26075-6(7), Turtleback) Turtleback Bks.
Kvasnosky, Laura McGee. The Big Picture. Kvasnosky, Laura McGee, illus. 2010. (Zelda & Ivy Ser.). (ENG., Illus.). 48p. (J). (gr. k-4). 14.99 (978-0-7636-4180-1(4)) Candlewick Pr.
—Zelda & Ivy - The Big Picture. Kvasnosky, Laura McGee, illus. 2013. (Candlewick Sparks Ser.). (ENG., Illus.). 48p. (J). (gr. k-4). pap. 3.99 (978-0-7636-6637-8(8)) Candlewick Pr.
Lawrence, Antoinette & Lewis, Terry. My Dad, My Granddad, & Me. 2013. (ENG.). 32p. (J). pap. 12.95 (978-1-4787-0013-5(0)) Outskirts Pr., Inc.
Leblanc, Margaret Ann. Ms Maddy & the Lake Adventure. 2008. 89p. pap. 19.95 (978-1-60474-003-5(5)) America Star Bks.
Leonard, Marcia. Mi Dia de Campamento. Translations.com Staff, tr. from ENG. Handelman, Dorothy, photos by. 2007. (Lecturas para niños de Verdad - Nivel 1 (Real Kids Readers - Level 1) Ser.).Tr. of My Camp-Out. (SPA., Illus.). 32p. (gr. k-2). per. 5.95 (978-0-8225-7798-0(4), Ediciones Lerner) Lerner Publishing Group.
—Mi Dia de Campamento; My Camp Out. 2008. pap. 34.95 (978-0-8225-9496-3(X)) Lerner Publishing Group.
Look, Lenore. Alvin Ho: Allergic to Camping, Hiking, & Other Natural Disasters. Pham, LeUyen, illus. 2010. (Alvin Ho Ser.). (ENG.). 192p. (J). (gr. 1-4). 6.99 (978-0-375-85750-8(8), Yearling) Random Hse. Children's Bks.
Lundy, Charlotte. Thank You, Peter. Waldrep, Evelyn L., ed. Blackley, Mary Beth, illus. 2003. 32p. (gr. k-3). 15.95 (978-0-9670280-8-8(6)) Bay Light Publishing.
Mackay, Gregory. Anders & the Volcano. 2017. (Anders Ser.: 2). (ENG.). 176p. (J). (gr. 1-6). pap. 9.99 **(978-1-76029-003-0(3))** Allen & Unwin AUS. Dist: Independent Pubs. Group.
Maddox, Jake. Volcano! A Survive! Story. Tiffany, Sean, illus. 2009. (Jake Maddox Sports Stories Ser.). (ENG.). 72p. (gr. 2-3). 25.32 (978-1-4342-1208-5(4)) Stone Arch Bks.

—Wild Hike. Tiffany, Sean, illus. 2008. (Jake Maddox Sports Stories Ser.). (ENG.). 72p. (gr. 2-3). 25.32 *(978-1-4342-0785-2(4))*; pap. 5.95 *(978-1-4342-0881-1(8))* Stone Arch Bks.

Manning, Jane. Millie Fierce Sleeps Out. Manning, Jane, illus. 2014. (Millie Fierce Ser.). (ENG., Illus.). 32p. (J). (gr. -1-2). 16.99 *(978-0-399-16093-6(0)*, Philomel Bks.) Penguin Young Readers Group.

Manushkin, Fran. Katie Goes Camping, 1 vol. Lyon, Tammie, illus. 2010. (Katie Woo Ser.). (ENG.). 32p. (gr. k-2). lib. bdg. 21.32 *(978-1-4048-5731-5(1))* Picture Window Bks.

Marguerita, Ann. Fannie Annie & Her Little White Shoes. 2008. (Illus.). 68p. per. *(978-1-84748-259-4(7))* Athena Pr.

Matheis, Mickie. Camp Berry. Thomas, Laura, illus. 2014. (Strawberry Shortcake Ser.). (ENG.). 32p. (J). (gr. 1-3). pap. 3.99 *(978-0-448-48153-1(7)*, Penguin Young Readers) Penguin Young Readers Group.

Matt & Dave. Yuck's Robotic Butt Blast. Baines, Nigel, illus. 2013. (Yuck Ser.). (ENG.). 112p. (J). (gr. 2-5). pap. 4.99 *(978-1-4424-8309-5(1)*, Simon & Schuster/Paula Wiseman Bks.) Simon & Schuster/Paula Wiseman Bks.

Matthews, Morgan & Sinden, David. Yuck's Robotic Butt Blast. Baines, Nigel, illus. 2013. (Yuck Ser.). (ENG.). 112p. (J). (gr. 2-5). 15.99 *(978-1-4424-8308-8(3)*, Simon & Schuster/Paula Wiseman Bks.) Simon & Schuster/Paula Wiseman Bks.

May, Eleanor. Where's Albert? Counting & Skip Counting. Melmon, Deborah, illus. 2017. (Mouse Math (r) Ser.). (ENG.). 32p. (gr. -1-1). lib. bdg. 22.65 *(978-1-57565-855-1(0))* Kane Press, Inc.

—Where's Albert? Counting & Skip Counting. Melmon, Deborah, illus. 2017. (Mouse Math (r) Ser.). (ENG.). 32p. (gr. -1-1). 7.95 *(978-1-57565-858-2(5))* Kane Press, Inc.

—Who Needs It? Sims, Blanche, illus. 2009. (Social Studies Connects Ser.). 32p. (J). (gr. 1-3). pap. 5.95 *(978-1-57565-281-8(1))* Kane Press, Inc.

—Who Needs It? Sims, Blanche, illus. 2009. (Social Studies Connects (r) Ser.). (ENG.). (gr. 1-3). pap. 33.92 *(978-0-7613-4804-7(2))* Lerner Publishing Group.

Mccormick, Scott. Camping Catastrophe! Lazzell, R. H., illus. 2016. (Mr. Pants Ser.: 4). (ENG.). 128p. (J). (gr. k-3). 12.99 *(978-0-525-42812-1(7)*, Dial Bks) Penguin Young Readers Group.

McDonald, Kirsten. The Green Surprise, 1 vol. Meza, Erika, illus. 2016. (Carlos & Carmen Ser.). (ENG.). 32p. (J). (gr. k-3). 27.07 *(978-1-62402-138-1(7))* Magic Wagon.

Meadows, Daisy. Caitlin the Ice Bear Fairy. 2012. (Illus.). 65p. (J). *(978-0-545-42602-2(2))* Scholastic, Inc.

—Sophia the Snow Swan Fairy. 2012. (Illus.). 65p. (J). *(978-0-545-42600-8(6))* Scholastic, Inc.

Mealue, Monique. Johnny Goes Camping. 2011. 28p. pap. 15.99 *(978-1-4634-2488-6(4))* AuthorHouse.

Meddaugh, Susan. Martha Camps Out. 2011. (Martha Speaks Ser.). (ENG., Illus.). 24p. (J). (gr. -1-3). 12.99 *(978-0-547-55618-5(7))*; pap. 3.99 *(978-0-547-55619-2(5))* Houghton Mifflin Harcourt Publishing Co.

Meunier, Sylvain. Raffi's Island Adventure, 1 vol. Cummins, Sarah, tr. from FRE. Eudes-Pascal, Elisabeth, illus. 2008. (Formac First Novels Ser.). (ENG.). 64p. (J). (gr. 2-5). 5.95 *(978-0-88780-755-8(0)*, 9780887807558) Formac Publishing Co., Ltd. CAN. Dist: Casemate Pubs. & Bk. Distributors, LLC.

Meyer, Susan. Matthew & Tall Rabbit Go Camping. Huntington, Amy, illus. 2008. (ENG.). 32p. (J). (gr. -1-3). 15.95 *(978-0-89272-769-8(1))* Down East Bks.

Meyers, Haily & Meyers, Kevin. My First: Camping, 1 vol. 2016. (ENG., Illus.). 22p. (J). bds. 9.99 *(978-1-4236-4236-7(8))* Gibbs Smith, Publisher.

Miles, Ellen. Lucky. 2010. (Puppy Place Ser.: 15). (ENG.). 96p. (J). (gr. 2-5). 4.99 *(978-0-545-08347-8(8)*, Scholastic Paperbacks) Scholastic, Inc.

Moroni, Lisa. Watch Out for the Crocodile. 2014. (Illus.). 32p. (J). (gr. -1-3). 17.95 *(978-1-877579-89-9(0))* Gecko Pr. NZL. Dist: Lerner Publishing Group.

Muncaster, Harriet. Isadora Moon Goes Camping. 2017. (Isadora Moon Ser.: 2). (ENG.). 128p. (J). (gr. 1-4). 5.99 ***(978-0-399-55827-6(6))***; 14.99 ***(978-0-399-55825-2(X))***; lib. bdg. 17.99 ***(978-0-399-55826-9(8))*** Random Hse. Children's Bks. (Random Hse. Bks. for Young Readers).

Nees, Susan. Field Trip. 2014. (Missy's Super Duper Royal Deluxe Ser.: 4). (ENG.). 80p. (J). (gr. k-2). pap. 4.99 *(978-0-545-43854-4(3))* Scholastic, Inc.

No Extras: Individual Title, 6 packs. (Literatura 2000 Ser.). (gr. 1-2). 28.00 *(978-0-7635-0103-7(4))* Rigby Education.

Nolen, Jerdine, et al. Bradford Street Buddies: Backyard Camp-Out. Henninger, Michelle, illus. 2015. (Green Light Readers Level 3 Ser.). (ENG.). 48p. (J). (gr. 1-4). pap. 3.99 *(978-0-544-36844-6(4)*, HMH Books For Young Readers) Houghton Mifflin Harcourt Publishing Co.

—Bradford Street Buddies: Backyard Camp-Out. Henninger, Michelle, illus. 2015. (Green Light Readers Level 3 Ser.). (ENG.). 48p. (J). (gr. 1-4). 12.99 *(978-0-544-36843-9(6)*, HMH Books For Young Readers) Houghton Mifflin Harcourt Publishing Co.

Nordqvist, Sven. The Camping Trip: The Adventures of Pettson & Findus. Nordqvist, Sven, illus. 2017. (ENG., Illus.). 32p. (J). (gr. -1-3). 17.95 *(978-0-7358-4277-9(9))* North-South Bks., Inc.

O'Connor, Jane. Stellar Stargazer! Glasser, Robin Preiss, illus. 2011. (Fancy Nancy Ser.). (ENG.). 32p. (J). (gr. -1-2). 12.99 *(978-0-06-191523-9(8))* HarperCollins Pubs.

O'Connor, Miles. The Tree That Moved. 2012. (ENG.). pap. 3.99 *(978-1-4675-1647-1(3))* Independent Pub.

O'Hara, Mo. Fins of Fury. Jagucki, Marek, illus. 2015. (My Big Fat Zombie Goldfish Ser.: Bk. 3). (ENG.). 224p. (J). (gr. 2-5). 12.99 *(978-1-250-02921-8(X)*, 9781250029218) Feiwel & Friends.

Orme, Helen. Wet! 2008. (Siti's Sisters Ser.). (ENG., Illus.). 36p. pap. *(978-1-84167-688-3(8))* Ransom Publishing Ltd.

Orr, Wendy. The Princess & Her Panther. Stringer, Lauren, illus. 2010. (ENG.). 40p. (J). (gr. -1-3). 16.99 *(978-1-4169-9780-1(6)*, Beach Lane Bks.) Beach Lane Bks.

Orton, W. George. Bob Hunt in Canada. 2007. 168p. 95.99 *(978-1-4280-7682-2(4))*; per. 89.99 *(978-1-4280-7702-7(2))* IndyPublish.com.

Osterhold, Jared, illus. OLIVIA Goes Camping. 2011. (Olivia TV Tie-In Ser.). (ENG.). 24p. (J). (gr. -1-1). 15.99 *(978-1-4424-2253-7(X))*; pap. 3.99 *(978-1-4424-2135-6(5))* Simon Spotlight. (Simon Spotlight).

Parish, Peggy. Amelia Bedelia Goes Camping. Sweat, Lynn, illus. 2003. (I Can Read Level 2 Ser.). (ENG.). 64p. (J). (gr. k-3). pap. 3.99 *(978-0-06-051106-7(0)*, Greenwillow Bks.) HarperCollins Pubs.

—Amelia Bedelia Goes Camping. 2003. (Amelia Bedelia: I Can Read! Ser.: 10). (J). (gr. k-3). lib. bdg. 13.55 *(978-0-613-62664-4(8)*, Turtleback) Turtleback Bks.

Parker, Emma. Summer Camp. 2010. (Illus.). pap. *(978-1-877561-27-6(4))* First Edition Ltd.

Parvensky Barwell, Catherine A. Tommi Goes Camping, 4 vols. Barwell, Matthew W. et al, eds. Parvensky Barwell, Catherine A., illus. 2006. (Illus.). 40p. (J). 14.95 *(978-0-9774409-3-1(1)*, TL004) ILT Publishing.

Paterson, Brian. Zigby Camps Out. 2003. (Zigby Ser.). (ENG., Illus.). 32p. (J). (gr. -1-2). pap. 8.99 *(978-0-00-713180-8(1)*, HarperCollins Children's Bks.) HarperCollins Pubs. Ltd. GBR. Dist: Independent Pubs. Group.

Patterson, James & Tebbetts, Chris. Save Rafe! Park, Laura, illus. 2014. (Middle School Ser.: 6). (ENG.). 288p. (J). (gr. 3-7). 13.99 *(978-0-316-32212-6(1)*, Jimmy Patterson) Little Brown & Co.

Patterson, James & Tebbetts, Christopher. Save Rafe! Park, Laura, illus. 2014. 269p. (J). *(978-0-316-28629-9(X))* Little Brown & Co.

Pearson, Yvonne. Sadie Braves the Wilderness. Ritz, Karen, illus. 2017. (ENG.). 32p. (J). (gr. -1-2). 16.95 ***(978-1-68134-038-8(0))*** Minnesota Historical Society Pr.

Penn, Tony. The Misadventures of Michael Mcmichaels: The Creepy Campers, vol. 3. Martin, Brian, illus. 2017. (Michael Mcmichaels Ser.: 3). (ENG.). 84p. (J). pap. 7.95 ***(978-1-944882-10-5(3))*** Boys Town Pr.

Penrose, Margaret. Dorothy Dale s Camping Days. 2007. (ENG.). 148p. pap. 18.99 *(978-1-4264-9201-3(4))* Creative Media Partners, LLC.

—Dorothy Dale's Camping Days. l.t. ed. 2007. (ENG.). 166p. pap. 21.99 *(978-1-4264-9258-7(8))* Creative Media Partners, LLC.

Percival, Tom. Herman's Vacation. 2016. (ENG., Illus.). 32p. (J). 17.99 *(978-1-61963-990-4(4)*, 9781619639904, Bloomsbury USA Childrens) Bloomsbury Publishing USA.

Percy Keese, Fitzhugh. Pee-Wee Harris & Roy Blakeley's Adventures in Camp. 2007. (ENG.). 262p. pap. 21.99 *(978-1-4346-1438-4(7))* Creative Media Partners, LLC.

Perry, Chrissie. Private List for Camp Success. 2017. (Penelope Perfect Ser.: 2). lib. bdg. 16.00 ***(978-0-606-40211-8(X))*** Turtleback Bks.

Perugini, Donna. Do Angels Go Camping? 2010. 32p. (Orig.). pap. 9.99 *(978-0-88144-536-7(3))* Yorkshire Publishing Group.

Pierce, Seth J. Camporee of Doom. 2009. (J). pap. 12.99 *(978-0-8163-2364-7(X))* Pacific Pr. Publishing Assn.

Pittar, Gill. Milly & Molly Go Camping. 2004. (Illus.). 28p. *(978-1-86972-003-2(2))* Milly Molly Bks.

Powell-Tuck, Maudie. Pirates Aren't Afraid of the Dark! Edgson, Alison, illus. 2014. (ENG.). 32p. (J). (gr. -1-3). 16.99 *(978-1-58925-165-6(2))* Tiger Tales.

Quarles, Pamela. Jake & Josh Go Camping. Denison, Susan, illus. 2007. 40p. per. 14.00 *(978-1-59858-407-3(3))* Dog Ear Publishing, LLC.

Quay, Emma. Good Night, Sleep Tight: A Book about Bedtime. Walker, Anna, illus. 2011. (ENG.). 24p. (J). (gr. -1 — 1). bds. 5.99 *(978-0-8037-3581-1(2)*, Dial Bks) Penguin Young Readers Group.

Ransome, Arthur. Swallowdale. Ransome, Arthur, illus. 2010. (Swallows & Amazons Ser.). (Illus.). 431p. (YA). pap. 14.95 *(978-1-56792-421-3(2))* Godine, David R. Pub.

—Swallowdale. 2014. (ENG., Illus.). 464p. (gr. 4-13). 24.95 *(978-1-4683-0956-0(0)*, 460956) Overlook Pr., The.

Redenbaugh, Vicki. Skar's Picnic ... A Bear's Tale. Redenbaugh, Vicki, illus. 2005. (Illus.). (J). 14.95 *(978-1-59091-034-4(6))* Eastern National.

Reid, Roger. Longleaf. 2007. 133p. (J). (gr. 3-7). 19.95 *(978-1-58838-194-1(3)*, Junebug Bks.) NewSouth, Inc.

Reimiller, Diane. Brayden & Ryan's Summer Vacation. Jastrzebski, Brandy, illus. 2012. 24p. pap. 24.95 *(978-1-4626-7792-4(4))* America Star Bks.

Remkiewicz, Frank. Gus Gets Scared. 2011. (Scholastic Reader Pre-Level 1 Ser.). (ENG., Illus.). 24p. (J). (gr. k-1). pap. 3.99 *(978-0-545-24471-8(4)*, Cartwheel Bks.) Scholastic, Inc.

Remsburg, Rebecca. The Camping Trip, 1 vol. 2010. 22p. pap. 24.95 *(978-1-4489-2508-7(8))* PublishAmerica, Inc.

Rey, Margret. Margret & H. A. Rey's Curious George Goes Camping. Vipah Interactive, illus. 2015. 24p. pap. 4.00 *(978-1-61003-550-7(X))* Center for the Collaborative Classroom.

Rey, Margret & Rey, H. A. Curious George Goes Camping, 1 vol. 2007. (Read along Book & CD Ser.). (ENG., Illus.). 24p. (J). (gr. -1-3). audio compact disk 10.99 *(978-0-618-73764-2(2))* Houghton Mifflin Harcourt Publishing Co.

Richards, Natalie D. One Was Lost. (ENG., (YA). (gr. 7-12). 2017. Illus.). 23.99 ***(978-1-4926-6232-7(1))*** 2016. 320p. pap. 10.99 *(978-1-4926-1574-3(9)*, 9781492615743) Sourcebooks, Inc.

Richardson, Timarlay A. Billy Bean & the Chocolate Dragon. 2013. 44p. pap. 11.95 *(978-0-9840456-7-9(8))* Universal Publishing LLC.

Rippin, Sally. The Big Adventure. Spartels, Stephanie, illus. 2015. 41p. (J). *(978-1-61067-453-9(7))* Kane Miller.

—The Big Adventure: Hey Jack! Spartels, Stephanie, illus. 2016. (ENG.). 48p. (J). pap. 4.99 *(978-1-61067-393-8(X))* Kane Miller.

—The Midnight Feast. Fukuoka, Aki, illus. (J). 2013. (ENG.). 48p. pap. 4.99 *(978-1-61067-097-5(3))* 2012. 44p. *(978-1-61067-134-7(1))* Kane Miller.

River Runners: Individual Title Six-Packs. (Action Packs Ser.). 120p. (gr. 3-5). 44.00 *(978-0-7635-8398-9(7))* Rigby Education.

Robert, Lytle. Mr. Blair's Labyrinth. Gayle, Vandercook, illus. 2011. (J). 10.95 *(978-0-9798088-4-5(7))* EDCO Publishing, Inc.

Ross, Tony. I Want to Do It Myself! Ross, Tony, illus. 2011. (Andersen Press Picture Bks). (ENG., Illus.). 32p. (J). (gr. -1-3). 16.95 *(978-0-7613-7412-1(4))* Lerner Publishing Group.

Roy, Lillian Elizabeth. The Woodcraft Girls at Camp. Barbour, H. S., illus. 2011. 348p. 51.95 *(978-1-258-10242-5(0))* Literary Licensing, LLC.

Royther, Chris. Abi's First Camping Days, 1 vol. 2010. 32p. pap. 24.95 *(978-1-4489-5002-7(3))* PublishAmerica, Inc.

Ruelle, Karen Gray. The Monster in Harry's Backyard. Ruelle, Karen Gray, illus. 2003. (Holiday House Readers Ser.). (ENG., Illus.). 32p. (J). (gr. k-3). 4.95 *(978-0-8234-1783-4(2))* Holiday Hse., Inc.

Runton, Andy. Owly & Wormy, Bright Lights & Starry Nights. Runton, Andy, illus. 2012. (ENG., Illus.). 40p. (J). (gr. -1-3). 17.99 *(978-1-4169-5775-1(8)*, Atheneum Bks. for Young Readers) Simon & Schuster Children's Publishing.

Rylant, Cynthia. Poppleton in Spring. Teague, Mark, illus. 2009. (Scholastic Reader Level 3 Ser.). (ENG.). 48p. (J). (gr. -1-3). pap. 3.99 *(978-0-545-07867-2(9)*, Cartwheel Bks.) Scholastic, Inc.

Saddleback Educational Publishing Staff, ed. Camp, 1 vol. unabr. ed. 2011. (Heights Ser.). (ENG.). 50p. (gr. 5-8). pap. 7.95 *(978-1-61651-284-2(9))* Saddleback Educational Publishing, Inc.

Salisbury, Graham. Night of the Howling Dogs. 2009. (ENG.). 208p. (YA). (gr. 7-7). mass mkt. 6.99 *(978-0-440-23839-3(0)*, Laurel Leaf) Random Hse. Children's Bks.

Sander, Sonia. Scooby-Doo in Keepaway Camp, 1 vol. 2016. (Scooby-Doo! Set 3 Ser.). (ENG., Illus.). 32p. (J). (gr. k-3). lib. bdg. 24.21 *(978-1-61479-407-3(3)*, 1401183) Spotlight.

Saunders, Karen. Suzy P. & the Trouble with Three. 2014. (Suzy P. Ser.). (ENG.). 352p. (J). (gr. 4-7). pap. 10.99 *(978-1-84877-369-1(2))* Bonnier Publishing GBR. Dist: Independent Pubs. Group.

Savage, J. Scott. Evil Twins. Holgate, Doug, illus. (Case File 13 Ser.: 3). (ENG.). (J). (gr. 3-7). 2015. 288p. pap. 6.99 *(978-0-06-213338-0(1))* 2014. 272p. 14.99 *(978-0-06-213337-3(3))* HarperCollins Pubs.

Schulz, Charles. Where Is Woodstock?, 1 vol. 2013. (Peanuts Picture Bks.). (ENG.). 24p. (J). (gr. -1-4). lib. bdg. 24.21 *(978-1-61479-033-4(7))* ABDO Publishing Co.

Scotton, Rob. Good Night, Sleep Tight. Scotton, Rob & Eberz, Robert, illus. 2011. (I Can Read Level 1 Ser.). (ENG.). 32p. (J). (gr. -1-3). pap. 3.99 *(978-0-06-197855-5(8))* HarperCollins Pubs.

—Splat the Cat: Good Night, Sleep Tight. Scotton, Rob & Eberz, Robert, illus. 2011. (I Can Read Level 1 Ser.). (ENG.). 32p. (J). (gr. -1-3). 16.99 *(978-0-06-197856-2(6))* HarperCollins Pubs.

Scripture Teachers: Solomon & Friends Learn about Trusting God. 2003. pap. *(978-0-9712894-2-0(5))* Lighthouse Christian Products Co.

Selig, Josh. The Small Potatoes Go Camping. Gibbons, Cassandra, illus. 2013. (J). lib. bdg. *(978-1-4844-0111-8(5)*, Grosset & Dunlap) Penguin Publishing Group.

Seton, Ernest Thompson. Two Little Savages. 2011. (Dover Children's Classics Ser.). (ENG., Illus.). 320p. (J). (gr. 3-8). pap. 14.95 *(978-0-486-20985-2(7))* Dover Pubns., Inc.

—Two Little Savages: The Adventures of Two Boys Who Lived As American Indians. Seton, Ernest Thompson, illus. 2010. (ENG., Illus.). 313p. (J). (gr. 4-7). pap. 18.00 *(978-1-60419-033-5(7))* Axios Pr.

Shubin, Masha. The Camp Caper: A Shubin Cousins Adventure. Hayes, Kathy & Hayes, David, illus. 2013. 88p. pap. 6.95 *(978-0-9792145-1-6(3))* Anno Domini.

Shultz, Charles M. & Bailer, Darice. Snoopy: Flying Ace to the Rescue, 1 vol. Lo Bianco, Peter, illus. 2011. (Peanuts Ready-To-Reads Ser.). (ENG.). 32p. (gr. -1-2). lib. bdg. 24.21 *(978-1-59961-807-4(9))* Spotlight.

Simon, Francesca. Horrid Henry. 2009. (Horrid Henry Ser.). lib. bdg. 17.20 *(978-0-606-06765-2(5)*, Turtleback) Turtleback Bks.

Singer, Marilyn. I'm Gonna Climb a Mountain in My Patent Leather Shoes. Avril, Lynne, illus. 2014. (ENG.). 40p. (J). (gr. k-2). 16.95 *(978-1-4197-0336-2(6)*, Abrams Bks. for Young Readers) Abrams, Inc.

Sloyer, Elliot. The Safety Pin: Summer Camp Stories. Guiza, Victor, illus. 2014. (ENG.). 32p. (J). 16.95 *(978-1-60131-182-5(6)*, Castlebridge Bks.) Big Tent Bks.

Snyder, Karen. Camp Charlie, the Adventures of Grandma Lipstick. LaGrange, Tiffany, illus. 2013. 20p. pap. 12.95 *(978-1-61493-218-5(2))* Peppertree Pr., The.

Spalding, Andrea. An Island of My Own. 2008. (ENG., Illus.). 112p. (YA). (gr. 8-12). pap. 11.99 *(978-1-55002-635-1(6)*, Sandcastle Bks.) Dundurn CAN. Dist: Ingram Publisher Services.

Sprague, Howard Lee. Snowflake's Vacation. Borrajero, Judy, illus. 2011. 40p. pap. 9.95 *(978-1-881276-16-6(3))* Serey/Jones Pubs.

Spurr, Elizabeth. In the Woods, 1 vol. Oliphant, Manelle, illus. 2012. (ENG.). 22p. (J). bds. 6.95 *(978-1-56145-582-9(2))* Peachtree Pubs.

St. Pierre, Connie. Camping with Mommy. 2013. 48p. pap. *(978-1-4602-3850-9(8))* FriesenPress.

Stanek, Robert, pseud. Bugville Critters Go to Camp. 2011. 34p. pap. 5.99 *(978-1-57545-261-6(8)*, Reagent Pr. Bks. for Young Readers) RP Media.

Staunton, Ted. Campfire Morgan. Slavin, Bill, illus. 2007. (Formac First Novels Ser.: 36). (ENG.). 64p. (J). (gr. 2-5). 14.95 *(978-0-88780-725-1(9)*, 9780887807251); 5.95 *(978-0-88780-721-3(6)*, 9780887807213) Formac Publishing Co., Ltd. CAN. Dist: Casemate Pubs. & Bk. Distributors, LLC.

Steinberg, Laya. Thesaurus Rex Finds a Friend. Harter, Debbie, illus. 2006. (J). *(978-1-905236-48-0(4))* Barefoot Bks., Inc.

Steinkraus, Kyla. Camping Out. Reese, Bob, illus. 2011. (ENG.). 24p. (J). (gr. 2-3). pap. 8.95 *(978-1-61236-031-7(9))* Rourke Educational Media.

—Vamos a Acampar. 2012. (SPA & ENG.). 24p. (gr. 2-3). pap. 8.95 *(978-1-61810-549-3(3))* Rourke Educational Media.

Stern, Jacqueline. Mystery of the Whispering Walls. 2004. (J). 148p. pap. *(978-1-57168-844-6(7))*; (Hollow Tree Mystery Ser.: Bk. 6). (Illus.). v, 142p. *(978-1-57168-850-7(1)*, Eakin Pr.) Eakin Pr.

Strange, Jason. The Mothman's Shadow, 1 vol. Parks, Phil, illus. 2011. (Jason Strange Ser.). (ENG.). 72p. (gr. 2-3). pap. 6.25 *(978-1-4342-3093-5(7))* Stone Arch Bks.

—The Mothman's Shadow, 1 vol. Soleiman, Serg & Parks, Phil, illus. 2011. (Jason Strange Ser.). (ENG.). 72p. (gr. 2-3). lib. bdg. 25.32 *(978-1-4342-2965-6(3))* Stone Arch Bks.

Stratemeyer, Edward. The Mystery at Putnam Hall: Or the School Chums' Strange Discovery. 2007. (ENG.). 186p. pap. 19.99 *(978-1-4346-1186-4(8))*; 204p. pap. 22.99 *(978-1-4346-1257-1(0))* Creative Media Partners, LLC.

Suen, Anastasia. La Noche de Terror. Heck, Claudia M., tr. from ENG. Laughead, Mike, illus. 2012. (Robot y Rico/Robot & Rico Ser.).Tr. of Scary Night. (MUL, SPA & ENG.). 32p. (gr. 1-2). pap. 5.05 *(978-1-4342-3918-1(7))*; lib. bdg. 22.65 *(978-1-4342-3779-8(6))* Stone Arch Bks. (Bilingual Stone Arch Readers).

—The Scary Night: A Robot & Rico Story, 1 vol. Laughead, Mike, illus. 2009. (Robot & Rico Ser.). (ENG.). 32p. (gr. 1-2). 22.65 *(978-1-4342-1628-1(4))* Stone Arch Bks.

Swinger-Ellbogen, Sue. Campfire Kids, 1 vol. 2010. 54p. pap. 16.95 *(978-1-4489-5493-3(2))* America Star Bks.

Toombs, Tom. The Big Camping Adventure: Little Tommy Learns Lessons from the Great Outdoors. Wells-Smith, Abby, illus. 2013. 32p. pap. 12.95 *(978-1-61314-035-2(5))* Innovo Publishing, LLC.

Toretto, Jordana. The Runaway Children. 2013. 30p. pap. 16.95 *(978-1-63004-706-1(6))* America Star Bks.

Trenowden, Mark. The Miracle of Bean's Bullion. 2012. 192p. pap. *(978-1-84667-041-1(1))* Derwent Pr., The.

Turner, Darlene. Tommy Gets Lost! Rottinger, Amy, illus. 2012. 24p. pap. 12.95 *(978-1-61244-064-4(9))* Halo Publishing International.

Van Draanen, Wendelin. Sammy Keyes & the Wild Things. Biggs, Brian, illus. 2008. (Sammy Keyes Ser.: 11). (ENG.). 320p. (J). (gr. 5-7). 7.99 *(978-0-440-42112-2(8)*, Yearling) Random Hse. Children's Bks.

Van Dusen, Chris. A Camping Spree with Mr. Magee. 2003. (Mr. Mcgee Ser.: MCGE). (ENG., Illus.). 36p. (J). (gr. -1-7). 15.99 *(978-0-8118-3603-6(7))* Chronicle Bks. LLC.

van Genechten, Guido. Ricky Is Brave. van Genechten, Guido, illus. 2011. (Ricky Ser.). (ENG., Illus.). 32p. (J). (gr. -1-k). 16.95 *(978-1-60537-097-2(5))* Cobblestone Publishing Co.

Vandercook, Margaret. The Camp Fire Girls at Sunrise Hill. 2007. 96p. per. *(978-1-4068-3817-6(9))* Echo Library.

Wargin, Kathy-jo. Frank & Beans & the Scary Campout, 1 vol. Lewis, Anthony, illus. 2010. (I Can Read! / Frank & Beans Ser.). (ENG.). 32p. (J). pap. 3.99 *(978-0-310-71850-5(3))* Zonderkidz.

Wargin, Kathy-jo & Bendall-Brunello, John, illus. Scare a Bear. 2010. (ENG.). 32p. (J). (gr. -1-3). 15.95 *(978-1-58536-430-5(4))* Sleeping Bear Pr.

Warner, Penny. The Mystery of the Missing Mustangs. 2012. 107p. (J). *(978-0-88166-411-9(1))* Meadowbrook Pr.

Wasserman, Robin. Search for Scooby Snacks, 1 vol. 2013. (Scooby-Doo! Picture Clue Bks.). (ENG.). 24p. (J). (gr. -1-1). lib. bdg. 24.21 *(978-1-61479-039-6(6)*, Essential Library) ABDO Publishing Co.

Watts, Jan. Zipline. 2010. 94p. pap. 25.50 *(978-1-4452-6040-2(9))* Lulu Pr., Inc.

Wissinger, Tamera Will. Gone Camping: A Novel in Verse. Cordell, Matthew, illus. 2017. (ENG.). 112p. (J). (gr. 1-4). 15.99 *(978-0-544-63873-0(5)*, HMH Books For Young Readers) Houghton Mifflin Harcourt Publishing Co.

Wooderson, Philip. Arf & the Happy Campers. 2004. *(978-0-7136-7639-6(6)*, A&C Black) Bloomsbury Publishing Plc.

Yep, Laurence. Skunk Scout. 2009. (Journeys Ser.). (ENG.). 192p. (gr. 5-5). pap. 7.45 *(978-0-547-07397-2(6))* Houghton Mifflin Harcourt Publishing Co.

Yerushalmi, Miriam. Let's Go Camping & Discover Our Nature. Perez, Esther Ido, illus. 2007. 28p. (J). (gr. 2-4). 16.50 *(978-0-911643-38-1(9))* Aura Printing, Inc.

Young, Jessica. Nature Calls. Secheret, Jessica, illus. 2015. (Finley Flowers Ser.). (ENG.). 128p. (gr. 2-3). 8.95 *(978-1-4795-5879-7(6)*, Finley Flowers) Picture Window Bks.

CAMPS

Brooks, Marigold. It's Time for Summer Camp. 2017. (Let's Tell Time Ser.). 24p. (gr. 4-6). 23.60 ***(978-1-5081-5726-7(X)***, PowerKids Pr.) Rosen Publishing Group, Inc., The.

Bussell, Linda. Using Division at Sports Camp. 2008. (Math in Our World Ser.). (Illus.). 24p. (J). (gr. 2-5). pap. 8.15 *(978-0-8368-9387-8(5))*; lib. bdg. 22.00 *(978-0-8368-9288-8(7))* Stevens, Gareth Publishing LLLP. (Weekly Reader Leveled Readers).

—Vamos a Usar la División en el Campamento de Deportes. 2008. (Matemáticas en Nuestro Mundo - Nivel 3 (Math in Our World - Level 3) Ser.). (SPA.). 24p. (J). (gr. 2-5). lib. bdg. 22.00 *(978-0-8368-9296-3(8)*, Weekly Reader Leveled Readers) Stevens, Gareth Publishing LLLP.

Deem, James M. Auschwitz: Voices from the Death Camp. 2011. (Holocaust Through Primary Sources Ser.). (Illus.). 128p. (J). (gr. 6-18). pap. 10.95 *(978-1-59845-346-1(7))* Enslow Pubs., Inc.

Evans, Lynette. Camp Extreme. 2008. (Illus.). 36p. pap. *(978-0-531-15492-2(0))* Children's Pr., Ltd.

Gish, Sarah. The Summer Book 2006: A Guide to Houston Day Camps & Classes for Kids & Teens. 2006. spiral bd. 12.95 *(978-0-9728507-3-5(2))* Gish Creative.

Marx, Trish. Sharing Our Homeland: Palestinian & Jewish Children at Summer Peace Camp, 1 vol. Karp, Cindy, illus. 2010. (ENG.). 48p. (J). (gr. 1-6). 19.95 *(978-1-58430-260-5(7))* Lee & Low Bks., Inc.

Thrash, Maggie. Honor Girl: A Graphic Memoir. Thrash, Maggie, illus. 2015. (ENG., Illus.). 272p. (YA). (gr. 9). 19.99 *(978-0-7636-7382-6(X))* Candlewick Pr.

Ventura, Marne & Peschke, Marci. Kylie Jean Summer Camp Craft Queen, 1 vol. Mourning, Tuesday, illus. 2014. (Kylie Jean Craft Queen Ser.). (ENG.). 32p. (gr. 2-3). lib. bdg. 26.65 *(978-1-4795-2193-7(0))* Picture Window Bks.

Walker, Nan. Day Camp. 2011. (Early Connections Ser.). (J). *(978-1-61672-347-7(5))* Benchmark Education Co.

CAMPS—FICTION

Adler, David A. The Summer Camp Mysteries. Allen, Joy, illus. 2007. (Cam Jansen Ser.). (ENG.). 128p. (J). (gr. 2-5). 5.99 *(978-0-14-240742-4(9)*, Puffin Books) Penguin Young Readers Group.

Alexander, Louise. The Legend of Everfree. 2016. (My Little Pony 8X8 Picture Bks.). (J). lib. bdg. 14.75 *(978-0-606-39193-1(2))* Turtleback Bks.

Altiero, Carl. Alvora & Vulture Mountain. 2011. 86p. pap. 19.95 *(978-1-4512-8263-4(X))* America Star Bks.

Amore, Dani, et al. Samurai Summer, 0 vols. Carlsson, Per, tr. 2013. (ENG.). 256p. (YA). (gr. 7-12). 17.99 *(978-1-4778-1654-7(2),* 9781477816547, Amazon Children's Publishing) Amazon Publishing.

Aronskind, Ofer. That Same Summer. 2008. 156p. pap. 12.95 *(978-0-595-50605-7(4))* iUniverse, Inc.

Bacon, Lee. The Nameless Hero. 2014. (Joshua Dread Ser.: 2). (ENG., Illus.). 304p. (J). (gr. 4-7). 7.99 *(978-0-307-92997-6(3),* Yearling) Random Hse. Children's Bks.

Bader, Bonnie. Benny the Big Shot Goes to Camp. Warren, Shari, illus. 2003. (Penguin Young Readers, Level 3 Ser.: No. 2). (ENG.). 48p. (J). (gr. 1-3). mass mkt. 3.99 *(978-0-448-42894-9(6),* Penguin Young Readers) Penguin Young Readers Group.

Barrows, Annie. Ivy + Bean - Make the Rules. Blackall, Sophie, illus. 2012. (Ivy & Bean Ser.). (ENG.). 127p. (J). (gr. 1-5). 14.99 *(978-1-4521-0295-5(3))* Chronicle Bks. LLC.

—Ivy + Bean Make the Rules, Bk. 9. Blackall, Sophie, illus. 2013. (Ivy & Bean Ser.: 9). (ENG.). 144p. (J). (gr. 1-5). pap. 5.99 *(978-1-4521-1148-3(0))* Chronicle Bks. LLC.

—Ivy + Bean Make the Rules. 2013. (Ivy & Bean Ser.: 9). (J). lib. bdg. 16.00 *(978-0-606-32296-6(5),* Turtleback) Turtleback Bks.

Bassoff, Leah & DeLuca, Laura. Lost Girl Found, 1 vol. 2014. (ENG., Illus.). 192p. (J). (gr. 7). 16.95 *(978-1-55498-416-9(5))* Groundwood Bks. CAN. Dist: Publishers Group West (PGW).

Basye, Dale E. Snivel: the Fifth Circle of Heck. Dob, Bob, illus. 2013. (Heck Ser.). (ENG.). 448p. (J). (gr. 4-7). 8.99 *(978-0-375-86806-1(2),* Yearling) Random Hse. Children's Bks.

Beaty, Andrea. Attack of the Fluffy Bunnies. 2012. (Fluffy Bunnies Ser.). (ENG.). 192p. (YA). (gr. 2-8). pap. 7.95 *(978-1-4197-0519-9(9),* Amulet Bks.) Abrams, Inc.

Beauregard, Lynda. The Hunt for Hidden Treasure: A Mystery about Rocks. Mogorrón, Guillermo, illus. 2012. (Summer Camp Science Mysteries Ser.: 3). (ENG.). 48p. (gr. 3-6). pap. 39.62 *(978-0-7613-9270-5(X));* pap. 6.95 *(978-0-7613-8545-5(2));* lib. bdg. 29.27 *(978-0-7613-5690-5(8))* Lerner Publishing Group. (Graphic Universe™).

—In Search of the Fog Zombie: A Mystery about Matter. Helmer, Der-Shing, illus. 2012. (Summer Camp Science Mysteries Ser.: 1). (ENG.). 48p. (gr. 3-6). pap. 39.62 *(978-0-7613-9268-2(8),* Graphic Universe™); pap. 6.95 *(978-0-7613-8544-8(4),* Graphic Universe™); lib. bdg. 29.27 *(978-0-7613-5689-9(4))* Lerner Publishing Group.

—The Missing Cuckoo Clock: A Mystery about Gravity. Helmer, Der-Shing, illus. 2013. (Summer Camp Science Mysteries Ser.: 5). (ENG.). 48p. (gr. 3-6). pap. 6.95 *(978-1-4677-0733-6(3));* lib. bdg. 29.27 *(978-1-4677-0167-9(X))* Lerner Publishing Group. (Graphic Universe™).

—The Nighttime Cabin Thief: A Mystery about Light. Helmer, Der-Shing, illus. 2012. (Summer Camp Science Mysteries Ser.: 2). (ENG.). 48p. (gr. 3-6). pap. 39.62 *(978-0-7613-9269-9(6),* Graphic Universe™); pap. 6.95 *(978-0-7613-8543-1(6),* Graphic Universe™); lib. bdg. 29.27 *(978-0-7613-5692-9(4))* Lerner Publishing Group.

—Summer Camp Science Mysteries. Helmer, Der-Shing, illus. 2012. (Summer Camp Science Mysteries Ser.). (ENG.). 48p. (gr. 3-6). pap. 52.82 *(978-0-7613-9272-9(6));*Pack, Set. pap. 316.92 *(978-0-7613-9273-6(4))* Lerner Publishing Group. (Graphic Universe™).

—Summer Camp Science Mysteries: Spring 2012 New Releases. Helmer, Der-Shing, illus. 2012. (Summer Camp Science Mysteries Ser.). 48p. (J). (gr. 3-6). lib. bdg. 117.08 *(978-0-7613-5688-2(6),* Graphic Universe™) Lerner Publishing Group.

—The Werewolf Chase: A Mystery about Adaptations. Torres, German, illus. 2012. (Summer Camp Science Mysteries Ser.: 4). (ENG.). 48p. (gr. 3-6). pap. 39.62 *(978-0-7613-9271-2(8),* Graphic Universe™); pap. 6.95 *(978-0-7613-8542-4(8),* Graphic Universe™); lib. bdg. 29.27 *(978-0-7613-5691-2(6))* Lerner Publishing Group.

—The Whispering Lake Ghosts: A Mystery about Sound. Torres, German, illus. 2013. (Summer Camp Science Mysteries Ser.: 6). (ENG.). 48p. (gr. 3-6). pap. 6.95 *(978-1-4677-0734-3(1));* lib. bdg. 29.27 *(978-1-4677-0168-6(8))* Lerner Publishing Group. (Graphic Universe™).

—The Yucky Duck Rescue: A Mystery about Pollution. Torres, German, illus. 2013. (Summer Camp Science Mysteries Ser.: 8). (ENG.). 48p. (gr. 3-6). pap. 6.95 *(978-1-4677-0736-7(8),* Graphic Universe™) Lerner Publishing Group.

Bee, Clair. Ten Seconds to Play: A Chip Hilton Sports Story. 2011. 222p. (gr. 8-12). 44.95 *(978-1-258-09715-8(X))* Literary Licensing, LLC.

Bell, Cathleen Davitt. Little Blog on the Prairie. 2011. (ENG.). 288p. (YA). (gr. 7). pap. 9.99 *(978-1-59990-677-5(5),* 9781599906775, Bloomsbury USA Childrens) Bloomsbury Publishing USA.

Bentley, Sue. Firelight Friends #10. Swan, Angela, illus. 2014. (Magic Kitten Ser.: 10). (ENG.). 128p. (J). (gr. 1-3). 5.99 *(978-0-448-46788-7(7),* Grosset & Dunlap) Penguin Young Readers Group.

Birney, Betty G. Summer According to Humphrey. (Humphrey Ser.: 6). (ENG.). (J). (gr. 3-7). 2011. 192p. 5.99 *(978-0-14-241818-5(8),* Puffin Books) 2010. 176p. 14.99 *(978-0-399-24732-3(7),* G.P. Putnam's Sons Books for Young Readers) Penguin Young Readers Group.

Bosch, Pseudonymous. Bad Luck. (Bad Bks.: 2). (ENG., Illus.). (J). (gr. 3-7). 2017. 304p. pap. 7.99 *(978-0-316-32044-3(7))* 2016. 288p. 17.00 *(978-0-316-32042-9(0))* Little, Brown Bks. for Young Readers.

—Bad Luck. 2017. (Bad Bks.: 2). (J). lib. bdg. 18.40 *(978-0-606-39475-8(3))* Turtleback Bks.

—Bad Magic. 2014. (ENG.). (J). 384p. 153.00 *(978-0-316-37696-9(5));* (Bad Bks.: 1). 400p. (gr. 3-7). 17.00 *(978-0-316-32038-2(2))* Little, Brown Bks. for Young Readers.

—Bad Magic. 2015. (Bad Bks.: 1). (J). lib. bdg. 18.45 *(978-0-606-37522-1(8))* Turtleback Bks.

Bossley, Michele Martin. Bio-Pirate, 1 vol. 2008. (Orca Currents Ser.). (ENG.). (J). (gr. 5-9). 112p. 16.95 *(978-1-55143-895-5(X));* 128p. pap. 9.95 *(978-1-55143-893-1(3))* Orca Bk. Pubs. USA.

Bowe, Julie. My Extra Best Friend. 2013. (Friends for Keeps Ser.: 5). (ENG.). 240p. (J). (gr. 3-7). pap. 6.99 *(978-0-14-242603-6(2),* Puffin Books) Penguin Young Readers Group.

Bradford, Karleen. Ghost Wolf, 1 vol. Cormack, Allan & Drew-Brook, Deborah, illus. 2005. (Orca Echoes Ser.). (ENG.). 64p. (J). (gr. 2-3). per. 6.95 *(978-1-55143-341-7(9))* Orca Bk. Pubs. USA.

Brammer, Deb. Moose. 2007. 132p. (YA). (gr. 8-12). per. 8.99 *(978-1-59166-722-3(4))* BJU Pr.

Brandes, Wendy L. Claire's Cursed Camping Trip. Lorenzet, Eleonora, illus. 2016. (Summer Camp Ser.). (ENG.). 96p. (gr. 4-6). lib. bdg. 24.65 *(978-1-4965-2600-7(7))* Stone Arch Bks.

—Emily's Pranking Problem. Lorenzet, Eleonora, illus. 2016. (Summer Camp Ser.). (ENG.). 96p. (gr. 4-6). lib. bdg. 24.65 *(978-1-4965-2599-4(X))* Stone Arch Bks.

—MJ's Camp Crisis. Lorenzet, Eleonora, illus. 2016. (Summer Camp Ser.). (ENG.). 96p. (gr. 4-6). lib. bdg. 24.65 *(978-1-4965-2598-7(1))* Stone Arch Bks.

—Nina's Not Boy Crazy! (She Just Likes Boys) Lorenzet, Eleonora, illus. 2016. (Summer Camp Ser.). (ENG.). 96p. (gr. 4-6). lib. bdg. 24.65 *(978-1-4965-2601-4(5))* Stone Arch Bks.

—Summer Camp, 4 vols. Lorenzet, Eleonora, illus. 2016. (Summer Camp Ser.). (ENG.). 96p. (gr. 4-6). 98.60 *(978-1-4965-2749-3(6))* Stone Arch Bks.

Bruchac, Joseph. Bearwalker. Comport, Sally Wern, illus. 2010. (ENG.). 240p. (J). (gr. 5). pap. 6.99 *(978-0-06-112315-3(3))* HarperCollins Pubs.

Bunting, Eve. I Don't Want to Go to Camp. Cocca-Leffler, Maryann, illus. 2003. (ENG.). 32p. (J). (gr. -1-1). pap. 8.95 *(978-1-59078-074-9(4))* Boyds Mills Pr.

Burford, Dinah. If I Could Talk, I Would Say the Adventures of Miss Pink. 2011. 28p. pap. 13.99 *(978-1-4634-4181-4(9))* AuthorHouse.

Burgess, Pauline. Pony Palace Camp. 2014. (Pony Friends Forever Ser.). (ENG., Illus.). 128p. (J). pap. 12.00 *(978-0-85640-923-3(5))* Blackstaff Pr., Ltd. GBR. Dist: Dufour Editions, Inc.

Burleigh, Cyril. The Hilltop Boys on the River. 2005. 26.95 *(978-1-4218-0327-2(5),* 1st World Library - Literary Society) 1st World Publishing, Inc.

—The Hilltop Boys on the River. 2006. (ENG.). 118p. pap. 18.99 *(978-1-4264-6538-3(6))* Creative Media Partners, LLC.

Butcher, Kristin. Cabin Girl, 1 vol. 2014. (Orca Currents Ser.). (ENG.). 128p. (J). (gr. 5-9). pap. 9.95 *(978-1-4598-0649-8(2))* Orca Bk. Pubs. USA.

Calonita, Jen. Sleepaway Girls. 2010. (ENG.). 320p. (J). (gr. 7-17). pap. 18.99 *(978-0-316-01718-3(3),* Poppy) Little, Brown Bks. for Young Readers.

—Summer State of Mind. 2014. (ENG.). 256p. (YA). (gr. 7-17). pap. 10.00 *(978-0-316-09115-2(4),* Poppy) Little, Brown Bks. for Young Readers.

Camp Day's. 2003. (J). per. *(978-1-57657-955-8(7))* Paradise Pr., Inc.

Campbell, L. A. Cartboy Goes to Camp. 2014. (Cartboy Ser.: 2). (ENG., Illus.). 224p. (J). (gr. 3-7). 12.99 *(978-0-7653-3327-8(9),* 9780765333278, Starscape) Doherty, Tom Assocs., LLC.

Carey, Benedict. Island of the Unknowns. 2011. (ENG., Illus.). 288p. (YA). (gr. 3-7). pap. 6.95 *(978-0-8109-9663-2(4),* Amulet Bks.) Abrams, Inc.

—The Unknowns: A Mystery. 2009. (ENG., Illus.). 272p. (YA). (gr. 3-7). 17.95 *(978-0-8109-7991-8(8),* Amulet Bks.) Abrams, Inc.

Carlson, Nancy. Arnie Goes to Camp. Carlson, Nancy, illus. 2012. (Nancy Carlson Picture Bks). (Illus.). 32p. (J). (gr. k-2). 56.72 *(978-0-7613-9302-3(1));* (ENG., 9.95 *(978-0-7613-8947-7(4))* Lerner Publishing Group. (Carolrhoda Bks.).

Cavanaugh, Nancy. Just Like Me. 2016. (ENG.). 256p. (J). (gr. 3-7). 16.99 *(978-1-4926-0427-3(5),* 9781492604273, Sourcebooks Jabberwocky) Sourcebooks, Inc.

Chapman, Brenda. Where Trouble Leads. 2007. (Jennifer Bannon Mystery Ser.: 3). (ENG., Illus.). 136p. (YA). (gr. 5-18). per. 9.95 *(978-1-894917-44-5(8),* Napoleon & Co.) Dundurn CAN. Dist: Ingram Publisher Services.

Chapman, Clay McLeod. Camp Cannibal. 2014. (Tribe Novel Ser.). (ENG.). 320p. (J). (gr. 3-7). 16.99 *(978-1-4231-5222-4(0))* Hyperion Bks. for Children.

Cheasebro, Margaret. The Healing Tree. 2015. (ENG.). 304p. (YA). 15.95 *(978-1-937240-60-8(6))* Casa de Snapdragon LLC.

Cherry, Alison. Willows vs. Wolverines. 2017. (Mix Ser.). (ENG., Illus.). 352p. (J). (gr. 4-8). 17.99 *(978-1-4814-6354-6(3),* Simon & Schuster/Paula Wiseman Bks.) Simon & Schuster/Paula Wiseman Bks.

Childs, Tera Lynn. Goddess Boot Camp. 2010. (ENG.). 272p. (YA). (gr. 7-18). pap. 7.99 *(978-0-14-241665-5(7),* Speak) Penguin Young Readers Group.

Christopher, Matt. Hook Shot Hero: A Nothin' but Net Sequel. 2011. (ENG.). 144p. (J). (gr. 3-7). pap., pap. 5.99 *(978-0-316-10296-4(2))* Little, Brown Bks. for Young Readers.

Cobb, Amy. Band Camp Rules. 2016. (Band Geeks Set 2 Ser.). (ENG., Illus.). (J). (gr. 3-6). lib. bdg. 27.07 ***(978-1-62402-172-5(7))*** ABDO Publishing Co.

Cole, Brock. The Goats. 2003. 20.75 *(978-0-8446-7238-0(6))* Smith, Peter Pub., Inc.

—The Goats. Cole, Brock, illus. 2010. (ENG., Illus.). 192p. (YA). (gr. 7-10). pap. 9.99 *(978-0-312-61191-0(9),* 9780312611910) Square Fish.

Combs, Sarah. Breakfast Served Anytime. 2016. (ENG.). 272p. (YA). (gr. 7). pap. 7.99 *(978-0-7636-8752-6(9))* Candlewick Pr.

Conford, Ellen. Annabel the Actress Starring in Camping It Up. Andriani, Renee W., illus. 2005. (Annabel the Actress Ser.). 60p. (J). (gr. 2-5). 11.65 *(978-0-7569-5555-7(6))* Perfection Learning Corp.

—Annabel the Actress Starring in Camping It Up. Andriani, Renee W., illus. 2013. (ENG.). 64p. (J). (gr. 2-5). pap. 13.99 *(978-1-4814-0147-0(5),* Simon & Schuster Bks. For Young Readers) Simon & Schuster Bks. For Young Readers.

Connelly, Neil. The Miracle Stealer. 2010. (ENG.). 240p. (J). (gr. 9-18). 17.99 *(978-0-545-13195-7(2),* Levine, Arthur A. Bks.) Scholastic, Inc.

Connelly, Neil O. The Miracle Stealer. 2012. (ENG.). 240p. (J). (gr. 9-9). pap. 9.99 *(978-0-545-13312-8(2),* Levine, Arthur A. Bks.) Scholastic, Inc.

Cotler, Steve. Cheesie Mack Is Cool in a Duel. McCauley, Adam, illus. (Cheesie Mack Ser.). (ENG.). 240p. (J). (gr. 3-7). 2013. 6.99 *(978-0-375-86395-0(8),* Yearling) 2012. 15.99 *(978-0-375-86438-4(5),* Random Hse. Bks. for Young Readers) Random Hse. Children's Bks.

Coven, Wanda. Heidi Heckelbeck Goes to Camp! Burris, Priscilla, illus. 2013. (Heidi Heckelbeck Ser.: 8). (ENG.). 128p. (J). (gr. k-2). 15.99 *(978-1-4424-6481-0(X));* pap. 5.99 *(978-1-4424-6480-3(1))* Little Simon. (Little Simon).

—Heidi Heckelbeck Goes to Camp! 2013. (Heidi Heckelbeck Ser.: 8). lib. bdg. 16.00 *(978-0-606-32031-3(8),* Turtleback) Turtleback Bks.

Coyle, Carmela Lavigna. Thank You, Aunt Tallulah! MacPherson, Bruce, illus. 2006. (ENG.). 32p. (J). (gr. -1-3). 15.95 *(978-0-87358-891-1(6))* Cooper Square Publishing Llc.

Crandell, Bethany. Summer on the Short Bus. 2014. (ENG.). 256p. (YA). (gr. 2-17). pap. 9.95 *(978-0-7624-4951-4(9),* Running Pr. Kids) Running Pr. Bk. Pubs.

Cummings, Troy. Flurry of the Snombies. 2015. (Notebook of Doom Ser.: 7). (ENG., Illus.). 96p. (J). (gr. 1-3). 15.99 *(978-0-545-79551-7(6));* pap. 4.99 *(978-0-545-79550-0(8))* Scholastic, Inc.

Daher, Anita. On the Trail of the Bushman, 1 vol. 2009. (Orca Young Readers Ser.). (ENG.). 128p. (J). (gr. 3-6). pap. 7.95 *(978-1-55469-013-8(7))* Orca Bk. Pubs. USA.

Dairman, Tara. The Stars of Summer. 2015. (All Four Stars Ser.: Bk. 2). (ENG.). 336p. (J). (gr. 3-7). 16.99 *(978-0-399-17069-0(3),* G.P. Putnam's Sons Books for Young Readers) Penguin Young Readers Group.

Danziger, Paula. There's a Bat in Bunk Five. 2006. (ENG.). 208p. (J). (gr. 5-18). 8.99 *(978-0-14-240681-6(3),* Puffin Books) Penguin Young Readers Group.

Danziger, Paula, et al. Amber Brown Horses Around. Lewis, Anthony, illus. (Amber Brown Ser.: 12). (ENG.). (J). 2015. 224p. (gr. 3-7). 5.99 *(978-0-14-751552-0(1),* Puffin Books) 2014. 208p. (gr. 2-5). 14.99 *(978-0-399-16170-4(8),* G.P. Putnam's Sons Books for Young Readers) Penguin Young Readers Group.

Darling, Angela. Maddie's Camp Crush. 2013. (Crush Ser.: 2). (ENG.). 160p. (J). (gr. 3-7). pap. 5.99 *(978-1-4424-8334-7(2));* (Illus.). 15.99 *(978-1-4424-8335-4(0))* Simon Spotlight. (Simon Spotlight).

Davidowitz, Stacy. Camp Rolling Hills. (Camp Rolling Hills Ser.: 3). (ENG., Illus.). (J). (gr. 3-7). 2017. 240p. pap. 8.95 *(978-1-4197-2291-2(3))*Bk. 1. 2016. 256p. pap. 8.95 *(978-1-4197-1885-4(1))* Abrams, Inc. (Amulet Bks.).

—Crossing Over, Bk. 2. 2016. (Camp Rolling Hills Ser.: 2). (ENG., Illus.). 240p. (J). (gr. 3-7). pap. 8.95 *(978-1-4197-1880-9(0),* Amulet Bks.) Abrams, Inc.

Davis, Heather. Never Cry Werewolf. 2010. (ENG.). 224p. (YA). (gr. 8). pap. 9.99 *(978-0-06-134925-6(9),* HarperTeen) HarperCollins Pubs.

de Gramont, Nina. Every Little Thing in the World. (ENG., Illus.). 288p. (YA). (gr. 9). 2011. pap. 8.99 *(978-1-4169-8015-5(6))* 2010. 16.99 *(978-1-4169-8013-1(X))* Simon & Schuster Children's Publishing. (Atheneum Bks. for Young Readers).

de los Santos, Marisa & Teague, David. Connect the Stars. 2015. (ENG.). 352p. (J). (gr. 3-7). 16.99 *(978-0-06-227465-6(1))* HarperCollins Pubs.

deGroat, Diane. Good Night, Sleep Tight, Don't Let the Bedbugs Bite! deGroat, Diane, illus. 2008. (ENG., Illus.). 32p. (J). (gr. -1-3). pap. 6.99 *(978-0-06-134061-1(8))* HarperCollins Pubs.

Destiny, A. & Kahler, A. R. Love Is in the Air. 2015. 221p. (YA). *(978-1-4814-2377-9(0),* Simon Pulse) Simon Pulse.

Destiny, A. & Lenhard, Elizabeth. Our Song. 2015. 225p. (YA). *(978-1-4424-8407-8(1),* Simon Pulse) Simon Pulse.

Digby, Anne. Summer Camp at Trebizon. 2016. (Trebizon Ser.). (ENG., Illus.). 192p. (J). (gr. 3-6). pap. 10.99 ***(978-1-4052-8069-3(7))*** Egmont Bks., Ltd. GBR. Dist: Independent Pubs. Group.

Dokey, Cameron. Boys Camp: Zack's Story. Orback, Craig, illus. 2015. (ENG.). 128p. (J). (gr. 1-5). pap. 9.95 *(978-1-62914-805-2(9),* Sky Pony Pr.) Skyhorse Publishing Co., Inc.

—Zack's Story, Bk. 1. Orback, Craig, illus. 2013. (ENG.). 128p. (J). (gr. 2-5). 14.95 *(978-1-62087-528-5(4),* 620528, Sky Pony Pr.) Skyhorse Publishing Co., Inc.

Downing, Erin. Drive Me Crazy. 2009. (Romantic Comedies Ser.). (ENG.). 240p. (YA). (gr. 7-18). mass mkt. 6.99 *(978-1-4169-7484-0(9),* Simon Pulse) Simon Pulse.

Draper, Sharon M. Shadows of Caesar's Creek. Watson, Jesse Joshua, illus. 2011. (Clubhouse Mysteries Ser.: 3). (ENG.). 128p. (J). (gr. 3-7). 15.99 *(978-1-4424-2712-9(4));* pap. 5.99 *(978-1-4424-2711-2(6))* Simon & Schuster Children's Publishing. (Aladdin).

—The Space Mission Adventure. Watson, Jesse Joshua, illus. 2012. (Clubhouse Mysteries Ser.: 4). (ENG.). 112p. (J). (gr. 3-7). 15.99 *(978-1-4424-4225-2(5));* pap. 5.99 *(978-1-4424-4226-9(3))* Simon & Schuster Children's Publishing. (Aladdin).

Draus, Naudia Burtwell. My Grandma Wears A Number: How One Girl Survived World War Ii. 2011. 40p. (gr. 4-6). pap. 19.57 *(978-1-4269-3351-6(7))* Trafford Publishing.

Durbin, William. Blackwater Ben. 2014. (Fesler-Lampert Minnesota Heritage Ser.). (ENG., Illus.). 216p. pap. 11.95 *(978-0-8166-9192-0(4))* Univ. of Minnesota Pr.

Durbin, William & Durbin, Barbara. Dead Man's Rapids. 2017. (J). pap. ***(978-1-5179-0224-7(X))*** Univ. of Minnesota Pr.

Dussling, Jennifer. Gotcha! Nez, John, illus. 2003. (Science Solves It! Ser.). 32p. (J). pap. 5.95 *(978-1-57565-124-8(6))* Kane Press, Inc.

Dussling, Jennifer A. The Longest Yawn. Sims, Blanche, illus. 2005. (Science Solves It! Ser.). 32p. (J). (gr. -1-3). pap. 5.95 *(978-1-57565-160-6(2))* Kane Press, Inc.

Edmonds, Lin. Jaden & the Terrible Terrible Toad. 2011. 36p. pap. 15.14 *(978-1-4634-1112-1(X))* AuthorHouse.

Edwards, Marnie. Magical Mix-Ups: Spells & Surprises. Hodgkinson, Leigh, illus. 2014. (Magical Mix-Ups Ser.). (ENG.). (J). (gr. 2-5). pap. 6.99 *(978-0-7636-6610-1(6),* Nosy Crow) Candlewick Pr.

Ellis, Ann Dee. You May Already Be a Winner. 2017. (ENG.). 352p. (J). (gr. 5-9). 16.99 ***(978-1-101-99385-9(5),*** Dial Bks) Penguin Young Readers Group.

Ellis, Deborah. Mud City. 2013. 156p. pap. *(978-1-4596-6445-6(0))* ReadHowYouWant.com, Ltd.

Emerson, Kevin. The Lost Code. 2012. (Atlanteans Ser.: 1). (ENG.). 448p. (YA). (gr. 8). 17.99 *(978-0-06-206279-6(4),* Tegen, Katherine Bks) HarperCollins Pubs.

FableVision. Spf 40. Reynolds, Peter H., illus. 2013. (Zebrafish Ser.). (ENG.). 128p. (J). (gr. 5-9). 19.99 *(978-1-4169-9708-5(3),* Atheneum Bks. for Young Readers) Simon & Schuster Children's Publishing.

FableVision Staff. Spf 40. Reynolds, Peter H., illus. 2013. (Zebrafish Ser.). (ENG.). 128p. (J). (gr. 5-9). pap. 9.99 *(978-1-4169-9709-2(1),* Atheneum Bks. for Young Readers) Simon & Schuster Children's Publishing.

Fitzhugh, Keese Percy. Tom Slade at Temple Camp. 2007. (ENG.). 124p. pap. 18.99 *(978-1-4346-3188-6(5));* 138p. pap. 19.99 *(978-1-4346-3189-3(3))* Creative Media Partners, LLC.

—Tom Slade's Double Dare. 2007. 148p. 41.99 *(978-1-4280-7506-1(2));* per. 35.99 *(978-1-4280-7492-7(9))* IndyPublish.com.

Fitzhugh, Percy. Tom Slade on Mystery Trail. 2006. pap. 12.95 *(978-1-55742-910-0(3))* Wildside Pr., LLC.

Fitzhugh, Percy K. Tom Slade on Mystery Trail. 2005. (Illus.). pap. 24.95 *(978-1-885529-88-6(0))* Stevens Publishing.

—Tom Slade's Double Dare. 2005. (Illus.). pap. 26.95 *(978-1-885529-86-2(4))* Stevens Publishing.

Fleming, Denise. Buster Goes to Cowboy Camp. Fleming, Denise, illus. 2008. (ENG., Illus.). 40p. (J). (gr. -1-2). 16.95 *(978-0-8050-7892-3(4),* 9780805078923, Holt, Henry & Co. Bks. For Young Readers) Holt, Henry & Co.

Flower, Amanda. Andi under Pressure, 1 vol. 2014. (Andi Boggs Novel Ser.). (ENG.). 176p. (J). 10.99 *(978-0-310-73702-5(8))* Zonderkidz.

—Andi under Pressure: An Andi Boggs Novel. 2014. 176p. (J). pap. *(978-0-310-74022-3(3))* Zondervan.

Fox, Tamar. No Baths at Camp. Vasquez, Natalia, illus. 2013. (ENG.). 32p. (J). (gr. -1-3). pap. 7.95 *(978-0-7613-8121-1(X));* lib. bdg. 17.95 *(978-0-7613-8120-4(1))* Lerner Publishing Group. (Kar-Ben Publishing).

Frederick, Heather Vogel. Mother-Daughter Book Camp. 2016. (Mother-Daughter Book Club Ser.). (ENG., Illus.). 336p. (J). (gr. 5-9). 16.99 *(978-1-4424-7183-2(2),* Simon & Schuster Bks. For Young Readers) Simon & Schuster Bks. For Young Readers.

Freedman, Sharon. Hey Guys: A Story about Going to Day Camp. Nelson, Megan, illus. 2004. (ENG.). 39p. 24.95 *(978-1-4137-2422-6(1))* PublishAmerica, Inc.

Freeman, Martha. Campfire Cookies. 2016. (Secret Cookie Club Ser.). (ENG., Illus.). 288p. (J). (gr. 3-7). 16.99 *(978-1-4814-4821-5(8),* Simon & Schuster/Paula Wiseman Bks.) Simon & Schuster/Paula Wiseman Bks.

Frey, Hildegard G. The Camp Fire Girls at School or the Wolelo Weavers. 2004. reprint ed. pap. 1.99 *(978-1-4192-5575-5(4));* pap. 21.95 *(978-1-4191-5575-8(X))* Kessinger Publishing, LLC.

—The Camp Fire Girls Go Motoring: Or along the Road That Leads the Way. 2007. (ENG.). 148p. pap. 18.99 *(978-1-4264-5040-2(0));* 166p. pap. 21.99 *(978-1-4264-5341-0(8))* Creative Media Partners, LLC.

—The Camp Fire Girls in the Maine Woods: Or the Winnebagos Go Camping. 2007. (ENG.). 152p. pap. 19.99 *(978-1-4264-9375-1(4));* 168p. pap. 21.99 *(978-1-4264-9756-8(3))* Creative Media Partners, LLC.

Frey, Hildegard Gertrude. The Camp Fire Girls Do Their Bit: Or over the Top with the Winnebagos. 2007. 158p. pap. 19.99 *(978-1-4346-2281-5(9));* (ENG.). 176p. pap. 21.99 *(978-1-4346-2339-3(4))* Creative Media Partners, LLC.

Friedman, Laurie. Campfire Mallory. 2009. pap. 34.95 *(978-0-7613-4787-3(9))* Lerner Publishing Group.

—Campfire Mallory. Kalis, Jennifer, illus. (Mallory Ser.: 9). (ENG.). 176p. (J). (gr. 2-5). 2009. pap. 5.95 *(978-1-58013-841-3(1),* First Avenue Editions) 2008. lib. bdg. 15.95 *(978-0-8225-7657-0(0),* Carolrhoda Bks.) Lerner Publishing Group.

Friedman, Laurie B. Love or Something Like It. 2015. (J). 5.99 *(978-1-4677-7790-2(0));* (Mostly Miserable Life of April Sinclair Ser.: 4). (ENG.). 184p. (gr. 5-9). 17.95 *(978-1-4677-0928-6(X))* Lerner Publishing Group.

Gaard, Betty. Jericho Ride. 2003. (Illus.). 165p. (J). pap. 8.99 *(978-1-57924-968-7(X))* BJU Pr.

Gallagher, Diana G. Camp Can't: The Complicated Life of Claudia Cristina Cortez, 1 vol. Garvey, Brann, illus. 2007. (Claudia Cristina Cortez Ser.). (ENG.). 88p. (gr. 2-3). per. 6.10 *(978-1-59889-878-1(7),* Claudia Cristina Cortez) Stone Arch Bks.

Gemmell, N. J. Coco Banjo Has Been Unfriended. 2016. (Coco Banjo Ser.: 2). (ENG.). 192p. (J). (gr. 1-3). pap. 9.99 *(978-0-85798-735-8(6))* Random Hse. Australia AUS. Dist: Independent Pubs. Group.

Gendreau, Paula. The Adventures of Lilly Lou: The First Day at Camp Who Who. 2009. 16p. pap. 8.49 *(978-1-4389-5950-4(8))* AuthorHouse.

George, J. A. Camp Aconyte. 2008. 65p. pap. 19.95 *(978-1-60610-631-0(7))* America Star Bks.

Gibbs, Stuart. Spy Camp. (Spy School Ser.). (ENG., Illus.). (J). (gr. 3-7). 2014. 352p. pap. 7.99 *(978-1-4424-5754-6(6))* 2013. 336p. 17.99 *(978-1-4424-5753-9(8))* Simon & Schuster Bks. For Young Readers. (Simon & Schuster Bks. For Young Readers).

Gibson, Marley. The Counseling. 2010. (ENG.). 264p. (YA). (gr. 7). pap. 8.99 *(978-0-547-39307-0(5))* Houghton Mifflin Harcourt Publishing Co.

Goelman, Ari. The Path of Names. 2013. (Illus.). 339p. (J). pap. *(978-0-545-47431-3(0),* Levine, Arthur A. Bks.) Scholastic, Inc.

Gottesfeld, Jeff. Little Miss Miss, 1 vol. 2015. (Red Rhino Ser.). (ENG.). 68p. (J). (gr. 4-6). pap. 7.95 *(978-1-62250-952-2(8))* Saddleback Educational Publishing, Inc.

Graff, Lisa. A Clatter of Jars. 2016. (ENG.). 224p. (J). (gr. 3-7). 16.99 *(978-0-399-17499-5(0),* Philomel Bks.) Penguin Young Readers Group.

C
D

Grant, Katy. Acting Out. 2008. (Summer Camp Secrets Ser.). (ENG.). 240p. (J). (gr. 3-7). pap. 7.99 *(978-1-4169-3577-3(0),* Aladdin) Simon & Schuster Children's Publishing.
—Fearless. 2010. (Summer Camp Secrets Ser.). (ENG.). 240p. (J). (gr. 3-7). pap. 7.99 *(978-1-4169-9162-5(X),* Aladdin) Simon & Schuster Children's Publishing.
—Rumors. 2010. (Summer Camp Secrets Ser.). (ENG.). 256p. (J). (gr. 3-7). pap. 6.99 *(978-1-4169-9163-2(8),* Aladdin) Simon & Schuster Children's Publishing.
—Tug-of-War. 2010. (Summer Camp Secrets Ser.). (ENG.). 256p. (J). (gr. 3-7). pap. 7.99 *(978-1-4169-9161-8(1),* Aladdin) Simon & Schuster Children's Publishing.
Graydon, William Murray. Canoe Boys & Campfires: Adventures on Winding Waters. 2007. (ENG.). 204p. per. 20.99 *(978-1-4346-4409-1(X));* 214p. per. 22.99 *(978-1-4346-4410-7(3))* Creative Media Partners, LLC.
Greene, Jacqueline. Secrets at Camp Nokomis: A Rebecca Mystery. Hirsch, Jennifer, ed. Tibbles, JeanPaul, illus. 2010. (ENG.). 192p. (J). (gr. 4-8). pap. 6.95 *(978-1-59369-657-3(4))* American Girl Publishing, Inc.
Greenwald, Tommy. Charlie Joe Jackson's Guide to Summer Vacation. Coovert, J. P., illus. (Charlie Joe Jackson Ser.: 3). (ENG.). 240p. (J). (gr. 5-7). 2014. 13.99 *(978-1-62672-031-2(2),* 9781626720312) 2013. 14.99 *(978-1-59643-757-9(X),* 9781596437579) Roaring Brook Pr.
Guiza, Vic, illus. Bat in the Bunk: Summer Camp Stories Seires. 2015. (ENG.). 32p. (J). (gr. 1-18). 19.99 *(978-0-9863743-0-2(X))* Summer Camp Stories LLC.
Gundel, Jean. The Mystery Key at Camp Green Meadow. Robertson, R. H., illus. 2011. (J). pap. 14.95 *(978-1-59571-730-6(7))* Word Association Pubs.
Gunderson, Jessica. I Broke into Gymnastics Camp, 1 vol. Santillan, Jorge H., illus. 2012. (Sports Illustrated Kids Victory School Superstars Ser.). (ENG.). 56p. (gr. 1-3). pap. 5.95 *(978-1-4342-3869-6(5));* lib. bdg. 26.65 *(978-1-4342-2245-9(4))* Stone Arch Bks.
Gutman, Dan. Back to School, Weird Kids Rule! 2014. (My Weird School Ser.). (J). lib. bdg. 16.00 *(978-0-606-35502-5(2))* Turtleback Bks.
Hancock, H. Irving. The High School Boys in Summer Camp. rev. ed. 2006. 216p. 27.95 *(978-1-4218-1750-7(0));* pap. 12.95 *(978-1-4218-1850-4(7))* 1st World Publishing, Inc. (1st World Library - Literary Society).
—The High School Boys in Summer Camp. 2007. 180p. per. *(978-1-4065-1985-3(5))* Dodo Pr.
Hanson, Bonnie Compton. Escape from Camp Porcupine. 2004. (Ponytail Girls Ser.). (Illus.). 192p. (J). pap. 7.99 *(978-1-58411-033-0(3),* Legacy Pr.) Rainbow Pubs. & Legacy Pr.
Hapka, Catherine, pseud. Blue Ribbon Summer. 2014. (Marguerite Henry's Ponies of Chincoteague Ser.: 2). (ENG., Illus.). 208p. (J). (gr. 3-7). pap. 6.99 *(978-1-4814-0339-9(7),* Aladdin) Simon & Schuster Children's Publishing.
—True Riders. 2015. (Marguerite Henry's Ponies of Chincoteague Ser.: 6). (ENG., Illus.). 192p. (J). (gr. 3-7). 17.99 *(978-1-4814-3972-5(3),* Aladdin) Simon & Schuster Children's Publishing.
Harkrader, Lisa. Daisy Diaz Shakes up Camp. Nez, John A., illus. 2009. (Social Studies Connects Complete Set Ser.). 32p. (J). (gr. k-7). pap. 5.95 *(978-1-57565-292-4(7))* Kane Press, Inc.
Hasty, Vicki Sterling. Eliza & the Analogies of Burnshire. 2009. 150p. pap. 24.95 *(978-1-60813-216-4(1))* America Star Bks.
Hay, Sam. Night of the Howling Hound, No. 3. Cooper, Simon, illus. 2014. (Undead Pets Ser.: 3). (ENG.). 112p. (J). (gr. 1-3). 5.99 *(978-0-448-47797-8(1),* Grosset & Dunlap) Penguin Young Readers Group.
—Night of the Howling Hound. 2014. (Undead Pets Ser.: 3). lib. bdg. 16.00 *(978-0-606-36219-1(3))* Turtleback Bks.
Heath, Kathy. Camp Crazy Kids. 2006. 157p. pap. 24.95 *(978-1-4241-0260-0(X))* PublishAmerica, Inc.
Henry, April. Shock Point. 2008. (ENG.). 192p. (YA). (gr. 7-18). 7.99 *(978-0-14-241240-4(6),* Speak) Penguin Young Readers Group.
Herrera, Robin. Hope Is a Ferris Wheel. 2014. (ENG., Illus.). 272p. (YA). (gr. 3-7). 16.95 *(978-1-4197-1039-1(7),* Amulet Bks.) Abrams, Inc.
Higgins, Nadia. Zombie Camp: Zombie Zappers Book 1. (Zombie Zappers Ser.). 64p. (J). 2014. (gr. 5-9). pap. 9.95 *(978-1-62285-000-6(9))* 2013. 15.95 *(978-1-62285-003-7(3))* Enslow Pubs., Inc.
Higginson, Hadley. Keeker & the Pony Camp Catastrophe, Bk. 5. Perrett, Lisa, illus. 2007. (Keeker & the Sneaky Pony Ser.: KEEK). (ENG.). 56p. (J). (gr. k-3). per. 4.99 *(978-0-8118-5597-6(X))* Chronicle Bks. LLC.
Hill, C. J. Slayers. 2013. (Slayers Ser.: 1). (ENG.). 400p. (YA). (gr. 7). pap. 9.99 *(978-0-312-67514-1(3))* Square Fish.
—Slayers: Friends & Traitors. 2014. (Slayers Ser.: 2). (ENG.). 416p. (YA). (gr. 7). pap. 10.99 *(978-1-250-05079-3(0),* 9781250050793) Square Fish.
Hill, Kirkpatrick. Bo at Ballard Creek. Pham, LeUyen, illus. 2014. (ENG.). 304p. (J). (gr. 3-7). pap. 7.99 *(978-1-250-04425-9(1),* 9781250044259) Square Fish.
Hillan, Pamela & Dyan, Penelope. The Discovery in the Old Mine. Weigand, John, photos by. 2013. (Illus.). 116p. pap. 8.95 *(978-1-61477-095-4(6))* Bellissima Publishing, LLC.
Hillyer, Lexa. Proof of Forever. 352p. (YA). (gr. 8). 2016. pap. 9.99 *(978-0-06-233038-3(1))* 2015. (ENG.). 17.99 *(978-0-06-233037-6(3))* HarperCollins Pubs. (HarperTeen).
Hinbest, Wendy. Frizzy Tizzy Camps In. 2011. 20p. pap. 11.95 *(978-1-4583-5826-4(7))* Lulu Pr., Inc.
Holm, Jennifer L. & Holm, Matthew. Camp Babymouse. 2007. (Babymouse Ser.: 6). lib. bdg. 17.20 *(978-1-4177-8070-9(3),* Turtleback) Turtleback Bks.
—The Power of the Parasite. Holm, Jennifer L. & Holm, Matthew, illus. 2012. (Squish Ser.: No. 3). (ENG., Illus.). 96p. (J). (gr. 2-5). pap. 6.99 *(978-0-375-84391-4(4));* lib. bdg. 12.99 *(978-0-375-93785-9(4))* Random Hse. Children's Bks. (Random Hse. Bks. for Young Readers).
—The Power of the Parasite. 2012. (Squish Ser.: 3). lib. bdg. 17.20 *(978-0-606-26405-1(1),* Turtleback) Turtleback Bks.
Hooper, Mary. The Revolting Holiday. Vayssiere, Frederique, illus. 2008. (Katie Ser.). (ENG.). 96p. (J). (gr. 2-4). pap. 8.95 *(978-0-7475-8614-2(4))* Bloomsbury Publishing Plc GBR. Dist: Independent Pubs. Group.
Hope, Lee Laura. The Outdoor Girls in a Winter Camp: Glorious Days on Skates & Ice Boats. 2007. (ENG.). 138p. pap. 18.99 *(978-1-4346-3216-6(4));* 152p. pap. 21.99 *(978-1-4346-3217-3(2))* Creative Media Partners, LLC.
Hubler, Marsha. Summer Camp Adventure, 1 vol. 2009. (Keystone Stables Ser.). (ENG.). 128p. (J). pap. 7.99 *(978-0-310-71795-9(7))* Zonderkidz.
Hunter, C. C. Awake at Dawn. 2011. (Shadow Falls Novel Ser.: 2). (ENG.). 400p. (YA). (gr. 7-12). pap. 10.99 *(978-0-312-62468-2(9),* 9780312624682, St. Martin's Griffin) St. Martin's Pr.
—Born at Midnight. (Shadow Falls Novel Ser.: 1). (ENG.). 416p. (YA). (gr. 7-12). 2013. mass mkt. 9.99 *(978-1-250-04680-2(7),* 9781250046802, St. Martin's Paperbacks) 2011. pap. 10.99 *(978-0-312-62467-5(0),* 9780312624675, St. Martin's Griffin) St. Martin's Pr.
—Chosen at Nightfall. 2013. (Shadow Falls Novel Ser.: 5). (ENG.). (YA). (gr. 7). 432p. mass mkt. 9.99 *(978-1-250-04765-6(X),* 9781250047656, St. Martin's Paperbacks); 416p. pap. 10.99 *(978-1-250-01289-0(9),* 9781250012890, St. Martin's Griffin) St. Martin's Pr.
—Eternal. 2014. (Shadow Falls: after Dark Ser.: 2). (ENG.). 400p. (YA). mass mkt. 9.99 *(978-1-250-07016-6(3),* 9781250070166, St. Martin's Paperbacks); (gr. 7-12). 19.99 *(978-1-250-05630-6(6),* St. Martin's Griffin) St. Martin's Pr.
—Eternal: Shadow Falls: After Dark. 2014. (Shadow Falls: after Dark Ser.: 2). (ENG.). 400p. (YA). (gr. 7-12). pap. 9.99 *(978-1-250-04461-7(8),* 9781250044617, St. Martin's Griffin) St. Martin's Pr.
—Next Chapter: Taken at Dusk - Whispers at Moonrise, 2 bks. in 1. 2014. (Shadow Falls Novel Ser.). (ENG.). 784p. (YA). (gr. 8-12). pap. 13.99 *(978-1-250-06695-4(6),* 9781250066954, St. Martin's Griffin) St. Martin's Pr.
—Reborn. 2014. (Shadow Falls: after Dark Ser.: 1). (ENG.). 400p. (YA). (gr. 7). pap. 10.99 *(978-1-250-03591-2(0),* 9781250035912, St. Martin's Griffin) St. Martin's Pr.
—Taken at Dusk. 2012. (Shadow Falls Novel Ser.: 3). (ENG.). 400p. (YA). (gr. 7-12). pap. 10.99 *(978-0-312-62469-9(7),* 9780312624699, St. Martin's Griffin) St. Martin's Pr.
—Taken at Dusk: A Shadow Falls Novel. 2013. (Shadow Falls Novel Ser.: 3). (ENG.). 400p. (YA). (gr. 7-12). mass mkt. 9.99 *(978-1-250-04681-9(5),* 9781250046819, St. Martin's Paperbacks) St. Martin's Pr.
—Whispers at Moonrise. (Shadow Falls Novel Ser.: 4). (ENG.). 400p. (YA). (gr. 7-12). 2013. mass mkt. 9.99 *(978-1-250-04682-6(3),* 9781250046826, St. Martin's Paperbacks) 2012. pap. 10.99 *(978-1-250-01191-6(4),* 9781250011916, St. Martin's Griffin) St. Martin's Pr.
Jackson, Melanie. Queen of Disguises, 1 vol. 2009. (Dinah Galloway Ser.). (ENG.). 176p. (J). (gr. 4-8). pap. 9.95 *(978-1-55469-037-4(4))* Orca Bk. Pubs. USA.
Jazynka, Kitson. Nate's Story, Bk. 2. Orback, Craig, illus. 2013. (ENG.). 144p. (J). (gr. 2-5). 14.95 *(978-1-62087-981-8(6),* 620981, Sky Pony Pr.) Skyhorse Publishing Co., Inc.
Jazynka, Kitson & Tripp, Valerie. Boys Camp: Zee's Story. Orback, Craig, illus. 2015. (ENG.). 144p. (J). (gr. 1-5). 14.99 *(978-1-62914-754-3(0),* Sky Pony Pr.) Skyhorse Publishing Co., Inc.
Jobling, Curtis. The Beast of Bone Creek. 2016. (Max Helsing: Monster Hunter Ser.: 2). (ENG., Illus.). 304p. (J). (gr. 5). 16.99 *(978-0-451-47480-3(5),* Viking Books for Young Readers) Penguin Young Readers Group.
Johnson, Harriet McBryde. Accidents of Nature. rev. ed. 2006. (ENG.). 240p. (YA). (gr. 7-12). 19.99 *(978-0-8050-7634-9(4),* Holt, Henry & Co. Bks. For Young Readers) Holt, Henry & Co.
—Accidents of Nature. rev. l.t. ed. 2007. (Thorndike Literacy Bridge Ser.). 273p. (YA). (gr. 7-12). 22.95 *(978-0-7862-9182-3(6))* Thorndike Pr.
Johnson, Rebecca. Rainforest Camp: Juliet, Nearly a Vet (Book 12) May, Kyla, illus. 2017. (Juliet, Nearly a Vet Ser.: 12). (ENG.). 96p. (J). (gr. 3-5). 8.99 ***(978-0-14-350704-8(4))*** Random Hse. Australia AUS. Dist: Independent Pubs. Group.
Johnson, Regan. Hold on to Your Tail: Letters from Camp Lizard. Johnson, Regan, illus. 2008. (Letters From Camp Lizard Ser.). (ENG., Illus.). 112p. (J). (gr. 1-5). pap. 7.95 *(978-1-933831-04-6(9))* Blooming Tree Pr.
Jones, Christianne. Fuchsia Fierce. Canby, Kelly, illus. 2016. (Fiction Picture Bks.). (ENG.). 32p. (gr. 1-2). lib. bdg. 22.65 *(978-1-5158-0553-3(0),* Fiction Picture Bks.) Picture Window Bks.
Jones, Christianne C. Eric No Juega, 1 vol. Ruiz, Carlos, tr. Demski, James, Jr., illus. 2006. (Read-It! Readers en Español: Story Collection).Tr. of Eric Won't Do It. (SPA.). 24p. (gr. -1-3). 21.32 *(978-1-4048-1683-1(6),* Easy Readers) Picture Window Bks.
—Fuchsia Fierce. Canby, Kelly, illus. 2016. (ENG.). 32p. (gr. 1-2). 15.95 *(978-1-62370-786-6(2))* Capstone Young Readers of Coughlan Cos.
Jones, Jen. Faith & the Camp Snob, No. 1. 2011. (Team Cheer Ser.). (ENG.). 112p. (gr. 4-4). lib. bdg. 25.32 *(978-1-4342-2994-6(7),* Team Cheer) Stone Arch Bks.
—Faith & the Camp Snob: # 1, 1 vol. 2012. (Team Cheer Ser.). (ENG.). 112p. (gr. 4-4). pap. 7.19 *(978-1-4342-4249-5(8),* Team Cheer) Stone Arch Bks.
Jules, Jacqueline. Freddie Ramos Makes a Splash. Benitez, Miguel, illus. 2013. (Zapato Power Ser.: Book 4). (ENG.). 96p. (J). (gr. 1-5). pap. 4.99 *(978-0-8075-9486-5(5))* Whitman, Albert & Co.
—Freddie Ramos Makes a Splash Bk. 4. Benitez, Miguel, illus. 2012. (Zapato Power Ser.: Book 4). (ENG.). 96p. (J). (gr. 1-5). 14.99 *(978-0-8075-9485-8(7))* Whitman, Albert & Co.
—Freddie Ramos Zooms to the Rescue. Benitez, Miguel, illus. 2012. (Zapato Power Ser.: Book 3). (ENG.). 96p. (J). (gr. 1-5). pap. 4.99 *(978-0-8075-9484-1(9))* Whitman, Albert & Co.
—Picnic at Camp Shalom. Melmon, Deborah, illus. 2011. (ENG.). 32p. (J). (gr. k-3). pap. 7.95 *(978-0-7613-6662-1(8),* Kar-Ben Publishing) Lerner Publishing Group.
Jules, Jacqueline & Hechtkopf, Jacqueline. Picnic at Camp Shalom. Melmon, Deborah, illus. 2011. (Kar-Ben Favorites Ser.). (ENG.). 32p. (J). (gr. k-3). 17.95 *(978-0-7613-6661-4(X),* Kar-Ben Publishing) Lerner Publishing Group.
Kasischke, Laura. Boy Heaven. 2006. 275p. (YA). (gr. 9-12). 16.99 *(978-0-06-081314-7(8));* lib. bdg. 17.89 *(978-0-06-081315-4(6))* HarperCollins Pubs. (HarperTeen).
Keene, Carolyn. Cooking Camp Disaster. Pamintuan, Macky, illus. 2013. (Nancy Drew & the Clue Crew Ser.: 35). (ENG.). 96p. (J). (gr. 1-4). pap. 4.99 *(978-1-4169-9466-4(1),* Aladdin) Simon & Schuster Children's Publishing.
—The Sign in the Smoke. 2016. (Nancy Drew Diaries: 12). (ENG., Illus.). 272p. (J). (gr. 3-7). pap. 6.99 *(978-1-4814-3816-2(6),* Aladdin) Simon & Schuster Children's Publishing.
Kenneally, Miranda. Things I Can't Forget. 2013. (Hundred Oaks Ser.: Bk. 3). (ENG.). 320p. (YA). (gr. 7-12). pap. 9.99 *(978-1-4022-7190-8(5),* 9781402271908) Sourcebooks, Inc.
Kidd, Virginia Bates. The Children's Escape. 2011. 90p. pap. 19.95 *(978-1-4560-5406-9(6))* America Star Bks.
Kimmelman, Leslie. Sam & Charlie (and Sam Too) at Camp! Owl, William, illus. 2015. (ENG.). 48p. (J). (gr. k-3). 13.99 *(978-0-8075-7217-7(9))* Whitman, Albert & Co.
Kirby, Stan. Captain Awesome Goes to Superhero Camp. O'Connor, George, illus. 2015. (Captain Awesome Ser.: 14). (ENG.). 128p. (J). (gr. k-4). pap. 5.99 *(978-1-4814-3153-8(6),* Little Simon) Little Simon.
Klausner, Julie. Art Girls Are Easy. 2013. (ENG.). 240p. (YA). (gr. 10-17). pap. 18.99 *(978-0-316-24362-9(0),* Poppy) Little, Brown Bks. for Young Readers.
Kloepfer, John. Galaxy's Most Wanted. Edwards, Nick, illus. 2014. (Galaxy's Most Wanted Ser.: 1). (ENG.). 224p. (J). (gr. 3-7). 12.99 *(978-0-06-223101-7(4))* HarperCollins Pubs.
—Galaxy's Most Wanted #2: into the Dorkness. Edwards, Nick, illus. 2016. (Galaxy's Most Wanted Ser.: 2). 272p. (J). (gr. 3-7). pap. 6.99 *(978-0-06-223109-3(X))* HarperCollins Pubs.
—Galaxy's Most Wanted #3: Starship Bloopers. Edwards, Nick, illus. 2016. (Galaxy's Most Wanted Ser.: 3). 240p. (J). (gr. 3-7). 12.99 *(978-0-06-223106-2(5))* HarperCollins Pubs.
—Into the Dorkness. Edwards, Nick, illus. 2015. (Galaxy's Most Wanted Ser.: 2). (ENG.). 256p. (J). (gr. 3-7). 12.99 *(978-0-06-223104-8(9))* HarperCollins Pubs.
Knudsen, Michelle. Revenge of the Evil Librarian. 2017. (ENG.). (YA). (gr. 9). 16.99 *(978-0-7636-8828-8(2))* Candlewick Pr.
Knudson, Mike. Cool Campers. 2011. (Raymond & Graham Ser.). (ENG.). 160p. (J). (gr. 3-7). 6.99 *(978-0-14-241875-8(7),* Puffin Books) Penguin Young Readers Group.
Koffsky, Ann D. Noah's Swim-A-Thon. 2010. (J). *(978-0-8074-1168-1(X))* URJ Pr.
Konigsburg, E. L. The Outcasts of 19 Schuyler Place. 2005. 296p. (J). (gr. 5). 13.65 *(978-0-7569-6307-1(9))* Perfection Learning Corp.
—The Outcasts of 19 Schuyler Place. (ENG.). 304p. (J). (gr. 5-9). 2004. 16.95 *(978-0-689-86636-4(4))* 2006. reprint ed. pap. 7.99 *(978-0-689-86637-1(2))* Simon & Schuster Children's Publishing. (Atheneum Bks. for Young Readers).
Korngold, Jamie. Sadie, Ori, & Nuggles Go to Camp. Fortenberry, Julie, illus. 2014. (ENG.). 24p. (J). (gr. -1-1). 17.95 *(978-1-4677-0424-3(5),* Kar-Ben Publishing) Lerner Publishing Group.
Krosoczka, Jarrett J. Lunch Lady & the Summer Camp Shakedown. 2010. (Lunch Lady Ser.). (ENG.). 96p. (J). (gr. 3-7). pap. 6.99 *(978-0-375-86095-9(9));* lib. bdg. 12.99 *(978-0-375-96095-6(3))* Random Hse. Children's Bks. (Knopf Bks. for Young Readers).
Krulik, Nancy. Camp Rules! John and Wendy Staff, illus. 2007. (Katie Kazoo, Switcheroo Ser.: No. 5). (ENG.). 160p. (J). (gr. 2-4). pap. 5.99 *(978-0-448-44542-7(5),* Grosset & Dunlap) Penguin Young Readers Group.
—Get Lost!, 6 vols. John and Wendy Staff, illus. 2006. (Katie Kazoo, Switcheroo Ser.: 6). (ENG.). 80p. (J). (gr. 2-4). pap. 4.99 *(978-0-448-43101-7(7),* Grosset & Dunlap) Penguin Young Readers Group.
Larry Sweitzer. The Ghost, the Eggheads, & Babe Ruth's Piano: A Novel. 2009. 180p. 23.95 *(978-1-4401-7103-1(3));* pap. 13.95 *(978-1-4401-7104-8(1))* iUniverse, Inc.
Larson, Hope. Chiggers. Larson, Hope, illus. 2008. (ENG., Illus.). 176p. (J). (gr. 5-9). pap. 11.99 *(978-1-4169-3587-2(8),* Simon & Schuster/Paula Wiseman Bks.) Simon & Schuster Children's Publishing.
Laughton, Geoff. At the Lake. 2016. (ENG., Illus.). (J). 24.99 ***(978-1-63477-937-1(1),*** Harmony Ink Pr.) Dreamspinner Pr.
Leblanc, Margaret. Ms. Maddy Comes to Town. 2006. 76p. pap. 19.95 *(978-1-4241-4103-6(6))* America Star Bks.
Lenhard, Elizabeth. The Ball of Clay That Rolled Away, 0 vols. Wolff, Jason, illus. 2012. (Shofar Ser.: 0). (ENG.). 24p. (J). (gr. k-3). 16.99 *(978-0-7614-6142-5(6),* 9780761461425, Amazon Children's Publishing) Amazon Publishing.
Leoni, Nancy. Toby Goes to Camp, 1 vol. Leoni, Nancy, illus. 2009. (Illus.). 21p. pap. 24.95 *(978-1-61546-417-3(4))* America Star Bks.
Lester, Helen. Tacky Goes to Camp. Munsinger, Lynn, illus. 2009. (Tacky the Penguin Ser.). (ENG.). 32p. (J). (gr. -1-3). 16.00 *(978-0-618-98812-9(2))* Houghton Mifflin Harcourt Publishing Co.
—Tacky Goes to Camp. 2012. (Tacky the Penguin Ser.). lib. bdg. 17.20 *(978-0-606-23992-9(8),* Turtleback) Turtleback Bks.
Lieberman, Leanne. Off Pointe, 1 vol. 2014. (Orca Limelights Ser.). (ENG.). 128p. (J). (gr. 6-9). pap. 9.95 *(978-1-4598-0280-3(2))* Orca Bk. Pubs. USA.
London, Jonathan. Froggy Goes to Camp. Remkiewicz, Frank, illus. 2010. (Froggy Ser.). (ENG.). 32p. (J). (gr. -1-k). pap. 6.99 *(978-0-14-241604-4(5),* Puffin Books) Penguin Young Readers Group.
Longley, Joshua. Barnaby's Buccaneers. 2011. 240p. (gr. 4-6). 25.95 *(978-1-4620-6112-9(5));* pap. 15.95 *(978-1-4620-6110-5(9))* iUniverse, Inc.
Lord, Emery. The Names They Gave Us. 2017. (ENG.). 400p. (YA). 17.99 *(978-1-61963-958-4(0),* 9781619639584, Bloomsbury USA Childrens) Bloomsbury Publishing USA.
Lupica, Mike. Summer Ball. 2008. (ENG.). 272p. (J). (gr. 3-7). 7.99 *(978-0-14-241153-7(1),* Puffin Books) Penguin Young Readers Group.
—Summer Ball. 2008. (Illus.). 244p. (gr. 5-9). 18.00 *(978-0-7569-8825-8(X))* Perfection Learning Corp.
Lynch, Chris. Slot Machine. 2003. 23.00 *(978-0-8446-7249-6(1))* Smith, Peter Pub., Inc.
Maddox, Jake. On the Speedway, 1 vol. Tiffany, Sean, illus. 2011. (Jake Maddox Sports Stories Ser.). (ENG.). 208p. (gr. 2-3). pap. 7.95 *(978-1-4342-3030-0(9))* Stone Arch Bks.
—Speed Camp, 1 vol. Tiffany, Sean, illus. 2009. (Jake Maddox Sports Stories Ser.). (ENG.). 72p. (gr. 2-3). 25.32 *(978-1-4342-1602-1(0))* Stone Arch Bks.
Mahle, Melissa & Dennis, Kathryn. Camp Secret. Wong, Liz, illus. 2013. (Junior Spies Ser.: 1). (ENG.). 268p. (J). pap. 10.99 *(978-0-9852273-4-0(6))* SpyGirls Pr.
Mann, Jennifer Ann. Sunny Sweet Can So Get Lost. 2015. (Sunny Sweet Ser.). (ENG., Illus.). 208p. (YA). (gr. 3-6). 15.99 *(978-1-61963-505-0(4),* 9781619635050, Bloomsbury USA Childrens) Bloomsbury Publishing USA.
Mantell, Paul, text. Nothin' but Net. 2003. (Matt Christopher Sports Ser.). 136p. (J). (gr. 3-7). 12.65 *(978-0-7569-3021-9(9))* Perfection Learning Corp.
Martin, Ann M. Ten Good & Bad Things about My Life (So Far) 2013. (ENG.). 288p. (J). (gr. 4-7). pap. 7.99 *(978-1-250-03413-7(2),* 9781250034137) Square Fish.
Matheis, Mickie. Camp Berry. Thomas, Laura, illus. 2014. (Strawberry Shortcake Ser.). (ENG.). 32p. (J). (gr. -1-3). pap. 3.99 *(978-0-448-48153-1(7),* Penguin Young Readers) Penguin Young Readers Group.
Matlin, Marlee. Deaf Child Crossing. 2004. (ENG., Illus.). 208p. (J). (gr. 3-7). pap. 7.99 *(978-0-689-86696-8(8),* Simon & Schuster Bks. For Young Readers) Simon & Schuster Bks. For Young Readers.
Mattern, Joanne. Batter Up! 2005. (J). pap. *(978-1-4108-4193-3(6))* Benchmark Education Co.
Maurer, Jayne. Grandpa Goes to Horse Camp. 2012. 40p. 16.95 *(978-1-62709-874-8(7));* pap. 16.95 *(978-1-62709-141-1(6))* America Star Bks.
Mays, Stan. Wicked Little Camp Story. 2005. 248p. pap. 14.95 *(978-1-59113-674-3(1))* Booklocker.com, Inc.
McCoy, Mary. Camp So-And-So. 2017. (ENG.). 424p. (YA). (gr. 8-12). 18.99 *(978-1-5124-1597-1(9));* 9.99 ***(978-1-5124-3428-6(0),*** Carolrhoda Lab™); 38.65 ***(978-1-5124-3429-3(9),*** Carolrhoda Lab™); 38.65 ***(978-1-5124-2693-9(8),*** Carolrhoda Lab™) Lerner Publishing Group.
McFarlane, Susannah. On the Ball: EJ12 Girl Hero. 2017. (Illus.). 128p. (J). pap. 5.99 *(978-1-61067-507-9(X))* Kane Miller.
McKy, Katie. Wolf Camp. Leick, Bonnie, illus. 2009. (ENG.). 32p. (J). (gr. -1-3). pap. 8.95 *(978-1-933718-25-5(0))* Tanglewood Pr.
McVoy, Terra Elan. The Summer of Firsts & Lasts. (ENG.). (YA). (gr. 9). 2012. 448p. pap. 9.99 *(978-1-4424-0214-0(8))* 2011. 432p. 16.99 *(978-1-4424-0213-3(X))* Simon Pulse. (Simon Pulse).
Meadows, Daisy. Ashley the Dragon Fairy. 2012. (Illus.). (J). (Magical Animal Fairies Ser.: 1). (ENG.). 80p. (gr. 2-5). pap. 4.99 *(978-0-545-38417-9(6),* Scholastic Paperbacks); 65p. *(978-0-545-42595-7(6))* Scholastic, Inc.
—Ava the Sunset Fairy. 2011. (Illus.). 63p. (J). *(978-0-545-38040-9(5))* Scholastic, Inc.
—Cara the Camp Fairy. 2011. (Rainbow Magic Ser.). (Illus.). (J). (ENG.). 176p. (gr. 2-5). pap. 6.99 *(978-0-545-30877-9(1),* Scholastic Paperbacks); 165p. *(978-0-545-31656-9(1))* Scholastic, Inc.
—Erin the Phoenix Fairy. 2012. (Illus.). 64p. (J). *(978-0-545-42597-1(2))* Scholastic, Inc.
—Lara the Black Cat Fairy. 2012. (Illus.). 65p. (J). *(978-0-545-42596-4(4))* Scholastic, Inc.
—Rihanna the Seahorse Fairy. 2012. (Illus.). 65p. (J). *(978-0-545-42599-5(9))* Scholastic, Inc.
Melkonian, Sheyda Mia. Nika Goes to Camp. OConner, Kim, illus. 2011. 28p. pap. 14.95 *(978-1-4575-0524-9(X))* Dog Ear Publishing, LLC.
Michaels, Craig. Blackbeard's Treasure. 2008. (J). *(978-0-936389-99-8(0))* Tudor Pubs., Inc.
Michener, Tara. Summer Camp Survival. 2010. 76p. pap. 10.99 *(978-1-4520-6297-6(8))* AuthorHouse.
Mike, Marion. Abagail Goes to Camp. 2009. 32p. pap. 12.99 *(978-1-4389-3090-9(9))* AuthorHouse.
Miller, Sibley. Horsey Trails. Chang, Tara Larsen & Gershman, Jo, illus. 2011. (Wind Dancers Ser.: 11). (ENG.). 80p. (J). (gr. 1-4). pap. 16.99 *(978-0-312-60544-5(7),* 9780312605445) Feiwel & Friends.
Millner, Denene. Miss You, Mina. 2010. 163p. (J). pap. *(978-0-545-25106-8(0))* Scholastic, Inc.
Mlynowski, Sarah. Spells & Sleeping Bags. 2008. (Magic in Manhattan Ser.: No. 3). (ENG.). 320p. (YA). (gr. 7-12). pap. 8.99 *(978-0-385-73388-5(7),* Delacorte Pr.) Random Hse. Children's Bks.
Moldavsky, Goldy. No Good Deed. 2017. (ENG.). 352p. (J). (gr. 9). 17.99 ***(978-0-545-86751-1(7))*** Scholastic, Inc.
Monninger, Joseph. Breakdown. 2014. (Stay Alive Ser.: 3). lib. bdg. 16.00 *(978-0-606-35854-5(4))* Turtleback Bks.
Montgomery, Lewis B. The Case of the Missing Moose. Wummer, Amy, illus. 2011. (Milo & Jazz Mysteries Ser.). 96p. (J). 22.60 *(978-1-57565-331-0(1));* pap. 39.62 *(978-0-7613-7607-1(0));* (ENG.). (gr. 2-6). pap. 6.95 *(978-1-57565-322-8(2))* Kane Press, Inc.
Morgan, Melissa J. Alex's Challenge. 2005. (Camp Confidential Ser.: 4). (ENG.). 160p. (J). (gr. 3-7). mass mkt. 4.99 *(978-0-448-43876-4(3),* Grosset & Dunlap) Penguin Young Readers Group.
—Best (Boy) Friend Forever. 2006. (Camp Confidential Ser.: 9). (ENG.). 160p. (J). (gr. 3-7). pap. 4.99 *(978-0-448-44325-6(2),* Grosset & Dunlap) Penguin Young Readers Group.
—Golden Girls. 2007. (Camp Confidential Ser.: 16). (ENG.). 160p. (J). (gr. 3-7). pap. 4.99 *(978-0-448-44541-0(7),* Grosset & Dunlap) Penguin Young Readers Group.
—In It to Win It. 2010. (Camp Confidential Ser.: 25). (ENG.). 160p. (J). (gr. 4-7). pap. 4.99 *(978-0-448-45402-3(5),* Grosset & Dunlap) Penguin Young Readers Group.
—Jenna's Dilemma. 2005. (Camp Confidential Ser.: 2). (ENG.). 160p. (J). (gr. 3-7). 4.99 *(978-0-448-43738-5(4),* Grosset & Dunlap) Penguin Young Readers Group.
—Natalie's Secret. 2005. (Camp Confidential Ser.: 1). (ENG.). 160p. (J). (gr. 3-7). 4.99 *(978-0-448-43737-8(6),* Grosset & Dunlap) Penguin Young Readers Group.
—Over & Out. 2006. (Camp Confidential Ser.: 10). (ENG.). 160p. (J). (gr. 3-7). pap. 4.99 *(978-0-448-44326-3(0),* Grosset & Dunlap) Penguin Young Readers Group.

—Politically Incorrect. 2010. (Camp Confidential Ser.: 23). (ENG.). 176p. (J). (gr. 3-7). pap. 4.99 *(978-0-448-45267-8(7),* Grosset & Dunlap) Penguin Young Readers Group.

—Reality Bites, 15 vols. 2007. (Camp Confidential Ser.: 15). (ENG.). 160p. (J). (gr. 3-7). pap. 4.99 *(978-0-448-44539-7(5),* Grosset & Dunlap) Penguin Young Readers Group.

—Suddenly Last Summer. 2008. (Camp Confidential Ser.: 20). (ENG.). 160p. (J). (gr. 3-7). pap. 4.99 *(978-0-448-44881-7(5),* Grosset & Dunlap) Penguin Young Readers Group.

—Sunrise. 2009. (Summer Confidential Ser.: 1). (ENG.). 240p. (J). (gr. 5-6). pap. 7.99 *(978-0-448-44988-3(9),* Grosset & Dunlap) Penguin Young Readers Group.

—Topsy-Turvy. 2010. (Camp Confidential Ser.: 24). (ENG.). 160p. (J). (gr. 3-7). pap. 4.99 *(978-0-448-45372-9(X),* Grosset & Dunlap) Penguin Young Readers Group.

—Twilight. 2009. (Summer Confidential Ser.: 3). (ENG.). 240p. (J). (gr. 5-18). pap. 7.99 *(978-0-448-44990-6(0),* Grosset & Dunlap) Penguin Young Readers Group.

Morrill, Lauren. Being Sloane Jacobs. 2015. (ENG.). 352p. (YA). (gr. 7). pap. 9.99 *(978-0-385-74180-4(4),* Ember) Random Hse. Children's Bks.

Moss, Marissa. Amelia's Itchy-Twitchy, Lovey-Dovey Summer at Camp Mosquito. Moss, Marissa, illus. 2008. (Amelia Ser.). (ENG., Illus.). 80p. (J). (gr. 5-8). 12.99 *(978-1-4169-4722-6(1),* Simon & Schuster/Paula Wiseman Bks.) Simon & Schuster/Paula Wiseman Bks.

—Amelia's Summer Survival Guide: Amelia's Longest, Biggest, Most-Fights-Ever Family Reunion; Amelia's Itchy-Twitchy, Lovey-Dovey Summer at Camp Mosquito. Moss, Marissa, illus. 2011. (Amelia Ser.). (ENG., Illus.). 160p. (J). (gr. 5-8). 12.99 *(978-1-4424-2331-2(5),* Simon & Schuster/Paula Wiseman Bks.) Simon & Schuster/Paula Wiseman Bks.

Mostoller, Marcia. Emma's Summer Camp Dilemm. 2011. 64p. pap. 19.95 *(978-1-4626-2814-8(1))* America Star Bks.

Mullarkey, Lisa. Carly, 1 vol. Franco, Paula, illus. 2016. (Pony Girls Ser.). (ENG.). 112p. (J). (gr. 1-4). 27.07 *(978-1-62402-127-5(1))* Magic Wagon.

—Daniela, 1 vol. Franco, Paula, illus. 2016. (Pony Girls Ser.). (ENG.). 112p. (J). (gr. 1-4). 27.07 *(978-1-62402-128-2(X))* Magic Wagon.

—A Feast of Fun, 1 vol. Franco, Paula, illus. 2016. (ENG.). 112p. (J). lib. bdg. *(978-1-62402-163-3(8))* Magic Wagon.

—Gabriela, 1 vol. Franco, Paula, illus. 2016. (Pony Girls Ser.). (ENG.). 112p. (J). (gr. 1-4). 27.07 *(978-1-62402-129-9(8))* Magic Wagon.

—Kianna, 1 vol. Franco, Paula, illus. 2016. (Pony Girls Ser.). (ENG.). 112p. (J). (gr. 1-4). 27.07 *(978-1-62402-130-5(1))* Magic Wagon.

—Trail Ride Troubles, 1 vol. 2014. (Storm Cliff Stables Ser.). (ENG.). 112p. (J). (gr. 7-11). lib. bdg. 27.07 *(978-1-62402-052-0(6),* Calico Chapter Bks) Magic Wagon.

Myracle, Lauren. Thirteen Plus One. 2011. (Winnie Years Ser.). (ENG.). 304p. (J). (gr. 5-18). 7.99 *(978-0-14-241901-4(X),* Puffin Books) Penguin Young Readers Group.

Naylor, Phyllis Reynolds. I Like Him, He Likes Her: Alice Alone; Simply Alice; Patiently Alice. 2010. (Alice Ser.). (ENG.). 640p. (YA). (gr. 7). pap. 12.99 *(978-1-4424-0978-1(9),* Atheneum Bks. for Young Readers) Simon & Schuster Children's Publishing.

Night, P. J. Together Forever. 2012. (Creepover Ser.: 8). lib. bdg. 16.00 *(978-0-606-26339-9(X),* Turtleback) Turtleback Bks.

Nixon, Joan Lowery. Nightmare. 2005. 166p. (gr. 5-7). 17.00 *(978-0-7569-5239-6(5))* Perfection Learning Corp.

—Nightmare. 2005. (ENG.). 176p. (J). (gr. 3-7). 6.99 *(978-0-440-23773-0(4),* Yearling) Random Hse. Children's Bks.

Nolan, Han. Pregnant Pause. 2012. (ENG.). 352p. (YA). (gr. 9). pap. 8.99 *(978-0-547-85414-4(5))* Houghton Mifflin Harcourt Publishing Co.

Nolen, Jerdine. Plantzilla Goes to Camp. Catrow, David, illus. 2006. (ENG.). 32p. (J). (gr. k-3). 17.99 *(978-0-689-86803-0(0),* Simon & Schuster/Paula Wiseman Bks.) Simon & Schuster/Paula Wiseman Bks.

Numeroff, Laura Joffe, et al. The Jellybeans & the Big Camp Kickoff. 2011. (ENG., Illus.). 32p. (J). (gr. k-2). 17.95 *(978-0-8109-9765-3(7),* Abrams Bks. for Young Readers) Abrams, Inc.

O'Connor, Jane. Yours till Niagara Falls, Abby. Apple, Margot, illus. 2008. (ENG.). 128p. (J). (gr. 3-7). 7.99 *(978-0-14-241151-3(5),* Puffin Books) Penguin Young Readers Group.

Oechsle, Michael. The Lost Cipher. 2017. (ENG.). 272p. (J). (gr. 3-7). pap. 9.99 ***(978-0-8075-8065-3(1))*** Whitman, Albert & Co.

Olsen, Mary-Kate & Olsen, Ashley. Camp Rock 'N' Roll. 2005. (ENG.). 112p. *(978-0-00-718091-2(8))* HarperCollins Pubs. Australia.

—Love, Set, Match. 2005. (ENG., Illus.). 112p. *(978-0-00-715885-0(8))* HarperCollins Pubs. Australia.

O'Ryan, Ray. Space Camp. Kraft, Jason, illus. 2016. (Galaxy Zack Ser.: 14). (ENG.). 128p. (J). (gr. k-4). pap. 5.99 *(978-1-4814-6300-3(4),* Little Simon) Little Simon.

Padian, Maria. Jersey Tomatoes Are the Best. 2012. (ENG.). 352p. (YA). (gr. 7). pap. 9.99 *(978-0-375-86563-3(2),* Ember) Random Hse. Children's Bks.

Paley, Sasha. Huge. 2008. (ENG.). 272p. (YA). (gr. 7-12). pap. 8.99 *(978-1-4169-5795-9(2),* Simon & Schuster Bks. For Young Readers) Simon & Schuster Bks. For Young Readers.

Parker, Emma. Summer Camp. 2010. (Illus.). pap. *(978-1-877561-27-6(4))* First Edition Ltd.

Patterson, James & Tebbetts, Chris. How I Survived Bullies, Broccoli, & Snake Hill. Park, Laura, illus. 2013. (Middle School Ser.: 4). (ENG.). 336p. (J). (gr. 3-7). 14.00 *(978-0-316-23175-6(4),* Jimmy Patterson) Little Brown & Co.

Pearce, Jacqueline. Siege, 1 vol. 2014. (Orca Currents Ser.). (ENG.). 136p. (J). (gr. 5-9). pap. 9.95 *(978-1-4598-0751-8(0))* Orca Bk. Pubs. USA.

Penner, Lucille Recht. A Limpiar el Campamento; Clean Sweep Campers. 2008. pap. 34.95 *(978-1-58013-758-4(X))* Kane Press, Inc.

Peschke, Marci. Summer Camp Queen, 1 vol. Mourning, Tuesday, illus. 2013. (Kylie Jean Ser.). (ENG.). 112p. (gr. 2-3). lib. bdg. 22.65 *(978-1-4048-7583-8(2),* Kylie Jean) Picture Window Bks.

Peterson, Donna. Pip Goes to Camp. 2012. 9.99 *(978-1-4621-1077-3(0))* Cedar Fort, Inc./CFI Distribution.

Polak, Monique. Forensics Squad Unleashed, 1 vol. 2016. (ENG.). 208p. (J). (gr. 3-6). pap. 9.95 *(978-1-4598-0979-6(3))* Orca Bk. Pubs. USA.

Post, Cynthia W. Carrie Flower: Goes to Camp. 2011. pap. 15.95 *(978-0-7414-6462-0(4))* Infinity Publishing.

Prager, Ellen. The Shark Rider. Caparo, Antonio Javier, illus. 2015. (Tristan Hunt & the Sea Guardians Ser.: 2). (ENG.). 326p. (J). (gr. 3-7). pap. 9.95 *(978-1-938063-51-0(1),* Mighty Media Junior Readers) Mighty Media Pr.

—The Shark Whisperer. Caparo, Antonio Javier, illus. 2014. (Tristan Hunt & the Sea Guardians Ser.). (ENG.). 288p. (J). (gr. 3-7). pap. 9.95 *(978-1-938063-44-2(9),* Mighty Media Junior Readers) Mighty Media Pr.

—Stingray City. Caparo, Antonio Javier, illus. 2016. (Tristan Hunt & the Sea Guardians Ser.: 3). (ENG.). 292p. (J). (gr. 2-7). pap. 9.95 *(978-1-938063-70-1(8),* Mighty Media Junior Readers) Mighty Media Pr.

Quintero, Sofia. Show & Prove. 2015. (ENG.). 352p. (YA). (gr. 7). 17.99 *(978-0-375-84707-3(3),* Knopf Bks. for Young Readers) Random Hse. Children's Bks.

Ransom, Candice. Rebel Mckenzie. 2013. (ENG.). 288p. (J). (gr. 3-7). pap. 7.99 *(978-1-4231-6388-6(5))* Hyperion Pr.

Rasheed, Leila. Doughnuts, Dreams & Drama Queens. 2013. (Fantastic Diary of Bathsheba Claric de Trop Ser.). 299p. (J). pap. 5.99 *(978-0-7945-3030-3(3),* Usborne) EDC Publishing.

Reisner, Molly & Ostrow, Kim. Camp Spongebob. Martinez, Heather, illus. 2005. (Spongebob Squarepants Ser.). 32p. (gr. k-2). 14.00 *(978-0-7569-5424-6(X))* Perfection Learning Corp.

Renna, G. M. Meticulous Nicholas Goes to Camp. 2009. 64p. pap. 10.49 *(978-1-4490-2784-1(9))* AuthorHouse.

Rennison, Louise. Withering Tights. (Misadventures of Tallulah Casey Ser.: 1). (ENG.). (YA). (gr. 8). 2012. 304p. pap. 8.99 *(978-0-06-179933-4(5))* 2011. 288p. 16.99 *(978-0-06-179931-0(9))* HarperCollins Pubs. (HarperTeen).

Rich, Juliann. Caught in the Crossfire. 2014. (ENG.). 264p. (J). (gr. 7). pap. 11.95 *(978-1-62639-070-6(3))* Bold Strokes Bks.

Riordan, Rick. The Battle of the Labyrinth, Bk. 4. (Percy Jackson & the Olympians Ser.). (ENG.). (J). (gr. 5-9). 2009. 400p. pap. 7.99 *(978-1-4231-0149-9(9))* 2008. 384p. 17.99 *(978-1-4231-0146-8(4))* Hyperion Pr.

—The Battle of the Labyrinth. 2011. 9.68 *(978-0-7848-3442-8(3),* Everbind) Marco Bk. Co.

—The Battle of the Labyrinth. l.t. ed. 2008. (Percy Jackson & the Olympians Ser.: Bk. 4). (ENG.). 462p. (J). (gr. 4-7). 23.95 *(978-1-4104-1018-4(8))* Thorndike Pr.

—The Battle of the Labyrinth. 2009. (Percy Jackson & the Olympians Ser.: 4). (J). lib. bdg. 18.40 *(978-0-606-02158-6(2),* Turtleback) Turtleback Bks.

—The Demigod Files. James, Steve, illus. 2009. (ENG.). 160p. (J). (gr. 5-6). 12.99 *(978-1-4231-2166-4(X))* Hyperion Pr.

—From Percy Jackson: Camp Half-Blood Confidential: Your Real Guide to the Demigod Training Camp. 2017. (Trials of Apollo Ser.). (ENG.). 192p. (J). (gr. 3-7). 9.99 *(978-1-4847-8555-3(X))* Hyperion Bks. for Children.

—The House of Hades, Bk. 4. 2015. (Heroes of Olympus Ser.). (ENG.). 720p. (J). (gr. 5-9). pap. 9.99 *(978-1-4231-4677-3(8))* Hyperion Bks. for Children.

—The Lightning Thief. (Percy Jackson & the Olympians Ser.: Bk. 1). (ENG.). (J). (gr. 5-9). 2005. 384p. 17.99 *(978-0-7868-5629-9(7))*Bk. 1. 2006. 416p. reprint ed. per. 7.99 *(978-0-7868-3865-3(5))* Disney Publishing Worldwide.

—The Lightning Thief. 2008. (J). 54.99 *(978-0-7393-7113-8(4))* Findaway World, LLC.

—The Lightning Thief. 2006. (Percy Jackson & the Olympians Ser.: Bk. 1). 377p. (J). (gr. 5-12). 15.65 *(978-0-7569-6603-4(5))* Perfection Learning Corp.

—The Lightning Thief. rev. l.t. ed. 2006. (Percy Jackson & the Olympians Ser.: 1). (ENG.). 483p. (gr. 5-18). 22.95 *(978-0-7862-8225-8(8))* Thorndike Pr.

—The Lightning Thief. 2006. (Percy Jackson & the Olympians Ser.: 1). (J). lib. bdg. 18.40 *(978-1-4177-3247-0(4),* Turtleback) Turtleback Bks.

—The Lost Hero. 2011. (Heroes of Olympus Ser.: Bk. 1). (ENG.). 576p. pap. 9.99 *(978-1-4231-5537-9(8))* Disney Pr.

—The Lost Hero. 2010. (Heroes of Olympus Ser.). (ENG.). 576p. (YA). (gr. 5-9). pap. 12.00 *(978-1-4231-4265-2(9))* Hyperion Bks. for Children.

—The Lost Hero. (Heroes of Olympus Ser.). (ENG.). (J). (gr. 5-9). 2012. 592p. pap. 9.99 *(978-1-4231-1346-1(2))* 2010. 576p. 19.99 *(978-1-4231-1339-3(X))* Hyperion Pr.

—The Lost Hero. l.t. ed. 2010. (Heroes of Olympus Ser.: Bk. 1). (ENG.). 708p. 23.99 *(978-1-4104-3359-6(5))* Thorndike Pr.

—The Lost Hero. 2012. (Heroes of Olympus Ser.: 1). (J). lib. bdg. 20.85 *(978-0-606-23615-7(5),* Turtleback) Turtleback Bks.

—The Mark of Athena. 2012. (Heroes of Olympus Ser.). (ENG.). 608p. (J). (gr. 5-17). 19.99 *(978-1-4231-4060-3(5))* Hyperion Pr.

—The Mark of Athena. l.t. ed. 2012. (Heroes of Olympus Ser.: Bk. 3). (ENG.). 698p. 23.99 *(978-1-4104-5205-4(0))* Thorndike Pr.

—The Mark of Athena. 2014. (Heroes of Olympus Ser.: 3). (J). lib. bdg. 20.85 *(978-0-606-35255-0(4))* Turtleback Bks.

—The Sea of Monsters, Bk. 2. Tk, illus. 2nd rev. ed. 2007. (Percy Jackson & the Olympians Ser.: Bk. 2). (ENG.). 320p. (J). (gr. 5-9). pap. 7.99 *(978-1-4231-0334-9(3))* Disney Publishing Worldwide.

—The Sea of Monsters. l.t. ed. 2006. (Percy Jackson & the Olympians Ser.: Bk. 2). 361p. (J). (gr. 5-9). 22.95 *(978-0-7862-9074-1(9))* Thorndike Pr.

—The Sea of Monsters. 2007. (Percy Jackson & the Olympians Ser.: 2). 279p. (J). (gr. 4-7). lib. bdg. 18.40 *(978-1-4177-7612-2(9),* Turtleback) Turtleback Bks.

—The Son of Neptune. (Heroes of Olympus Ser.: Bk. 2). (ENG.). (J). (gr. 5-9). 2013. 560p. pap. 9.99 *(978-1-4231-4199-0(7))* 2011. (Illus.). 544p. 19.99 *(978-1-4231-4059-7(1))* Hyperion Pr.

—The Son of Neptune. l.t. ed. 2011. (Heroes of Olympus Ser.: Bk. 2). (ENG.). 616p. 23.99 *(978-1-4104-4122-5(9))* Thorndike Pr.

—The Son of Neptune. 2013. (Heroes of Olympus Ser.: 2). (J). lib. bdg. 20.85 *(978-0-606-31759-7(7),* Turtleback) Turtleback Bks.

—The Son of Neptune: The Graphic Novel. 2017. (Heroes of Olympus Ser.). (ENG.). 192p. (J). (gr. 5-9). 21.99 *(978-1-4847-1621-2(3))* Disney Pr.

Riordan, Rick & Venditti, Robert. The Lightning Thief. Futaki, Attila & Villarrubia, Jose, illus. 2010. (Percy Jackson & the Olympians Ser.). (ENG.). 128p. (J). (gr. 5-9). 21.99 *(978-1-4231-1696-7(8));* pap. 12.99 *(978-1-4231-1710-0(7))* Hyperion Pr.

Ritchie, Polly. A Pocket Full of Frogs. 2007. 124p. pap. 10.00 *(978-0-9795103-2-8(5))* Ascended Ideas.

Rock, J. K. Camp Forget-Me-Not. 2014. (Camp Boyfriend Ser.: 3). (ENG.). 272p. (YA). (gr. 4-6). pap. 9.95 *(978-1-939392-30-5(6),* Spencer Hill Contemporary) Spencer Hill Pr.

Rodman, Mary Ann. Camp K-9, 1 vol. Hayashi, Nancy, illus. 2011. (ENG.). 32p. (J). (gr. -1-3). 15.95 *(978-1-56145-561-4(X))* Peachtree Pubs.

Roesti, Delores. Mareena Maree Mulligan & the Flying Wheelchair: Book 2: The Busybodies. 2008. 102p. pap. 10.95 *(978-0-7414-4477-6(1))* Infinity Publishing.

Roter, Jordan. Camp Rules. 2007. 260p. (J). *(978-1-4287-4603-9(X),* Dutton Adult) Penguin Publishing Group.

Roth, Judith L. & Rothshank, Brooke, illus. Julia's Words. 2008. (J). (gr. -1-3). pap. 12.99 *(978-0-8361-9417-3(9))* Herald Pr.

Roy, Lillian Elizabeth. The Woodcraft Girls at Camp. Barbour, H. S., illus. 2011. 348p. 51.95 *(978-1-258-10242-5(0))* Literary Licensing, LLC.

Roy, Ron. Detective Camp. Gurney, John Steven, illus. 2006. (to Z Mysteries Ser.: No. 1). (ENG.). 144p. (J). (gr. 1-4). per. 5.99 *(978-0-375-83534-6(2),* Random Hse. Bks. for Young Readers) Random Hse. Children's Bks.

Rubino, M. Gayle. The Truth about Scuttlebutt. 2012. 32p. pap. 19.95 *(978-1-4772-0348-4(6))* AuthorHouse.

Sachar, Louis. Hoyos. 2003. (SPA.). (gr. 5-8). lib. bdg. 25.75 *(978-0-613-64523-2(5),* Turtleback) Turtleback Bks.

Saddleback Educational Publishing, ed. Mudslide, 1 vol. 2013. (Heights Ser.). (ENG.). 51p. (gr. 5-8). 7.95 *(978-1-62250-049-9(0))* Saddleback Educational Publishing, Inc.

Sanrio. Hello Kitty Goes to Camp. 2015. (Hello Kitty Ser.). (J). lib. bdg. 17.15 *(978-0-606-37240-4(7))* Turtleback Bks.

Sauer, Tammi. Cowboy Camp. Reed, Mike, illus. (ENG.). (J). (gr. -1-k). 2015. 24p. bds. 6.95 *(978-1-4549-1389-4(4))* 2014. 32p. pap. 6.95 *(978-1-4549-1360-3(6))* 2005. 32p. 14.95 *(978-1-4027-2224-0(9))* Sterling Publishing Co., Inc.

—Princess in Training. Berger, Joe, illus. (ENG.). 40p. (J). (gr. -1-3). 2015. 6.99 *(978-0-544-45609-9(2),* HMH Books For Young Readers) 2012. 16.99 *(978-0-15-206599-7(7))* Houghton Mifflin Harcourt Publishing Co.

Schanback, Mindy. Princess from Another Planet. 2005. (ENG.). 254p. (J). (gr. 5-9). 16.95 *(978-0-8234-1847-3(2))* Holiday Hse., Inc.

Schroeder, Lisa. Caitlin's Lucky Charm. 2014. (Charmed Life Ser.: 1). lib. bdg. 16.00 *(978-0-606-35849-1(8))* Turtleback Bks.

—Charmed Life #1: Caitlin's Lucky Charm. 2014. (Charmed Life Ser.: 1). (ENG.). 192p. (J). (gr. 3-7). pap. 5.99 *(978-0-545-60372-0(2))* Scholastic, Inc.

Scott, Rosanna. Peter & Friends at Camp. Fargo, Todd, illus. l.t. ed. 2006. (Turtle Books). 32p. (J). (gr. k-4). pap. 9.95 *(978-0-944727-51-5(4));* lib. bdg. 15.95 *(978-0-944727-52-2(2))* Jason & Nordic Pubs. (Turtle Bks.).

Service, Pamela F. Camp Alien. 2010. pap. 33.92 *(978-0-7613-6955-4(4))* Lerner Publishing Group.

—Camp Alien. Gorman, Mike, illus. (Alien Agent Ser.: 2). (ENG.). 160p. (J). (gr. 4-6). 2010. pap. 5.95 *(978-0-7613-5247-1(3))* 2009. 16.95 *(978-0-8225-8656-2(8),* Carolrhoda Bks.) Lerner Publishing Group.

Seuling, Barbara. Robert Goes to Camp. Brewer, Paul, illus. 2007. (Robert Bks.). (ENG.). 160p. (J). (gr. k-4). 16.95 *(978-0-8126-2753-4(9))* Cricket Bks.

Sheinmel, Courtney. Positively. 2010. (ENG.). 240p. (J). (gr. 4-9). pap. 6.99 *(978-1-4424-0622-3(4),* Simon & Schuster Bks. For Young Readers) Simon & Schuster Bks. For Young Readers.

Simon, Coco. Emma All Stirred Up! (Cupcake Diaries: 7). (ENG., 160p. (J). (gr. 3-7). 2013. Illus.). 17.99 *(978-1-4424-8567-9(1))* 2012. pap. 6.99 *(978-1-4424-5078-3(9))* Simon Spotlight. (Simon Spotlight).

—Emma All Stirred Up! 2012. (Cupcake Diaries: 7). lib. bdg. 17.20 *(978-0-606-26309-2(8),* Turtleback) Turtleback Bks.

Singer, Marilyn. Tallulah's Tap Shoes. Boiger, Alexandra, illus. 2015. (ENG.). 48p. (J). (gr. -1-3). 16.99 *(978-0-544-23687-5(4))* Houghton Mifflin Harcourt Publishing Co.

Sisco, Joann Ellen. Midnight at Faraway Farm. 2008. 79p. pap. 19.95 *(978-1-60474-777-5(3))* America Star Bks.

Small, Lily. Kylie the Kitten. 2017. (Fairy Animals of Misty Wood Ser.). (ENG., Illus.). 144p. (J). pap. 5.99 ***(978-1-250-12698-6(3),*** 9781250126986, Holt, Henry & Co. Bks. For Young Readers) Holt, Henry & Co.

Smallcomb, Pam. Camp Buccaneer. Lichtenheld, Tom, illus. 2005. 58p. (J). lib. bdg. 15.00 *(978-1-59054-897-4(3))* Fitzgerald Bks.

Snider, Cindy Gay. Finding Anna Bee. Chambers, Mary, illus. 2007. 163p. (J). (gr. 3-7). per. 9.99 *(978-0-8361-9392-3(X))* Herald Pr.

Snyder, Laurel. Camp Wonderful Wild, 0 vols. Whitt, Carlynn, illus. 2013. (ENG.). 32p. (J). (gr. -1-3). 17.99 *(978-1-4778-1652-3(6),* 9781477816523, Amazon Children's Publishing) Amazon Publishing.

Sookraj, Esther. Good with Words Bueno con las Palabras. 2010. 24p. pap. 15.99 *(978-1-4500-4169-0(8))* Xlibris Corp.

Souders, Taryn. How to (Almost) Ruin Your Summer. 2016. (ENG.). 240p. (J). (gr. 3-7). pap. 7.99 *(978-1-4926-3774-5(2),* 9781492637745, Sourcebooks Jabberwocky) Sourcebooks, Inc.

Sparkes, Ali. Frog Freakout. Collins, Ross, illus. 2014. (S. W. I. T. C. H. Ser.: 7). (ENG.). 88p. (J). (gr. 2-5). lib. bdg. 27.93 *(978-1-4677-2111-0(5),* Darby Creek) Lerner Publishing Group.

—Newt Nemesis. Collins, Ross, illus. 2014. (S. W. I. T. C. H. Ser.: 8). (ENG.). 88p. (J). (gr. 2-5). lib. bdg. 27.93 *(978-1-4677-3233-8(6),* Darby Creek) Lerner Publishing Group.

Squires, Megan. The Rules of Regret, 0 vols. 2014. (ENG.). 290p. (YA). (gr. 9-12). pap. 9.99 *(978-1-4778-2488-7(X),* 9781477824887, Skyscape) Amazon Publishing.

Standish, Burt L. Frank Merriwell's Happy Camp. Rudman, Jack, ed. 2003. (Frank Merriwell Ser.). pap. 9.95 *(978-0-8373-9140-3(7))* Merriwell, Frank Inc.

Stanek, Robert, pseud. Go to Camp. 2010. 34p. pap. 8.99 *(978-1-57545-178-7(6),* Reagent Pr. Bks. for Young Readers) RP Media.

Stanton, Angie. Snapshot. 2013. (Jamieson Brothers Ser.: 2). (ENG.). 416p. (YA). (gr. 9). pap. 9.99 *(978-0-06-227256-0(X),* HarperTeen) HarperCollins Pubs.

Starkey, Scott. The Call of the Bully. 2013. (How to Beat the Bully Ser.). (ENG.). 272p. (J). (gr. 3-7). 15.99 *(978-1-4424-5674-7(4),* Simon & Schuster/Paula Wiseman Bks.) Simon & Schuster/Paula Wiseman Bks.

—The Call of the Bully: A Rodney Rathbone Novel. 2014. (How to Beat the Bully Ser.). (ENG., Illus.). 272p. (J). (gr. 3-7). pap. 6.99 *(978-1-4424-5675-4(2),* Simon & Schuster/Paula Wiseman Bks.) Simon & Schuster/Paula Wiseman Bks.

Sternberg, Julie. Like Bug Juice on a Burger. Cordell, Matthew, illus. (Eleanor Ser.). (ENG.). (J). (gr. 1-4). 2016. 192p. pap. 6.95 *(978-1-4197-2049-9(X))* 2013. 176p. 15.95 *(978-1-4197-0190-0(8))* Abrams, Inc. (Amulet Bks.).

Stewart, Elizabeth. Blue Gold: A Novel. 2014. (ENG., Illus.). 304p. (YA). (gr. 7-12). 21.95 *(978-1-55451-635-3(8),* 9781554516353) Annick Pr., Ltd. CAN. Dist: Publishers Group West (PGW).

Stewart, Jane L. The Camp Fire Girls at Long Lake. rev. ed. 2006. (ENG.). 140p. 25.95 *(978-1-4218-2057-6(9),* 1st World Library - Literary Society) 1st World Publishing, Inc.

—The Camp Fire Girls at Long Lake: Bessie King in Summer Camp. 2007. 112p. pap. 18.99 *(978-1-4346-2295-2(9));* (ENG.). 126p. pap. 19.99 *(978-1-4346-2353-9(X))* Creative Media Partners, LLC.

—The Camp Fire Girls at Long Lake or Bessie King in Summer Camp. 2004. reprint ed. pap. 1.99 *(978-1-4192-5574-8(6));* pap. 15.95 *(978-1-4191-5574-1(1))* Kessinger Publishing, LLC.

Stine, R. L. Welcome to Camp Nightmare. 2010. (Classic Goosebumps Ser.: 14). (ENG.). 160p. (J). (gr. 3-7). 6.99 *(978-0-545-15889-3(3),* Scholastic Paperbacks) Scholastic, Inc.

Stratemeyer, Edward. The Rover Boys in Camp. 2007. 252p. 27.95 *(978-1-4218-4147-2(9));* per. 12.95 *(978-1-4218-4245-5(9))* 1st World Publishing, Inc. (1st World Library - Literary Society).

Taback, Simms. Postcards from Camp. Taback, Simms, illus. 2011. (ENG., Illus.). 40p. (J). (gr. -1-3). 17.99 *(978-0-399-23973-1(1),* Nancy Paulsen Books) Penguin Young Readers Group.

Taylor, Chloe. Knot Too Shabby! Zhang, Nancy, illus. 2014. (Sew Zoey Ser.: 7). (ENG.). 176p. (J). (gr. 3-7). pap. 5.99 *(978-1-4814-1398-5(8),* Simon Spotlight) Simon Spotlight.

Temple, Bob. The Ghost of J. Stokely. Nitzsche, Shane, illus. 2008. (Shade Bks.). (ENG.). 80p. (gr. 2-3). 25.32 *(978-1-4342-0796-8(X),* Shade Bks.) Stone Arch Bks.

Thaler, Mike. Church Summer Cramp, 1 vol. Lee, Jared, illus. 2009. (Tales from the Back Pew Ser.). (ENG.). 32p. (J). (gr. 1-4). pap. 3.99 *(978-0-310-71592-4(X))* Zonderkidz.

Thomas Nelson Publishing Staff. Camping the Bug-A-Boo Way: Go for the Gold Against Camp Hot Foot! 2008. cd-rom 19.95 *(978-0-9754280-7-8(1))* Nelson, Thomas Inc.

Thompson, Dan. Li'l Rip Haywire Adventures: Escape from Camp Cooties. 2016. (ENG., Illus.). 208p. (J). 13.99 *(978-1-4494-7051-7(3))* Andrews McMeel Publishing.

Tolan, Stephanie S. Applewhites at Wit's End. (Applewhites Ser.: 2). (J). (gr. 5). 2013. (ENG.). 288p. pap. 6.99 *(978-0-06-057940-1(4))* 2012. (ENG.). 272p. 16.99 *(978-0-06-057938-8(2))* 2012. 272p. lib. bdg. 17.89 *(978-0-06-057939-5(0))* HarperCollins Pubs.

Twitty, Mary F. Ashley Visits Urchin Village. 2008. 92p. pap. 51.99 *(978-1-4363-5578-0(8))* Xlibris Corp.

Vail, Rachel. Shells, Smells, & the Horrible Flip-Flops of Doom. Cordell, Matthew, illus. 2012. (Justin Case Ser.: 2). (ENG.). 192p. (J). (gr. 2-4). 16.99 *(978-1-250-00081-1(5),* 9781250000811) Feiwel & Friends.

—Shells, Smells, & the Horrible Flip-Flops of Doom. Cordell, Matthew, illus. 2013. (Justin Case Ser.: 2). (ENG.). 208p. (J). (gr. 2-4). pap. 6.99 *(978-1-250-02723-8(3),* 9781250027238) Square Fish.

Vandercook, Margaret. The Camp Fire Girls at Sunrise Hill. 2004. reprint ed. pap. 19.95 *(978-1-4191-5576-5(8));* pap. 1.99 *(978-1-4192-5576-2(2))* Kessinger Publishing, LLC.

VanRiper, Gary & VanRiper, Justin. The Secret of the Skeleton Key. 2006. (Adirondack Kids Ser.: Vol. 6). 71p. (J). (gr. 2-7). pap. 9.95 *(978-0-9707044-6-7(1))* Adirondack Kids Pr.

Verdi, Jessica. The Summer I Wasn't Me. 2014. (ENG.). 352p. (YA). (gr. 7-12). pap. 9.99 *(978-1-4022-7788-7(1),* 9781402277887) Sourcebooks, Inc.

Vernon, Ursula. Revenge of the Horned Bunnies, No. 6. 6th ed. 2012. (Dragonbreath Ser.: 6). (ENG.). 208p. (J). (gr. 3-7). 12.99 *(978-0-8037-3677-1(0),* Dial Bks) Penguin Young Readers Group.

Vrabel, Beth. Pack of Dorks. 2016. (Pack of Dorks Ser.). (ENG.). 240p. (J). (gr. 2-7). 16.99 *(978-1-63450-181-1(0),* Sky Pony Pr.) Skyhorse Publishing Co., Inc.

Watters, Shannon & Stevenson, Noelle. Band Together. 2016. (Lumberjanes Ser.: 5). lib. bdg. 26.95 *(978-0-606-39484-0(2))* Turtleback Bks.

Wedekind, Annie. A Horse of Her Own. 2009. (ENG.). 288p. (YA). (gr. 5-9). pap. 8.99 *(978-0-312-58146-6(7),* 9780312581466) Square Fish.

Weissman, Elissa Brent. Nerd Camp. (ENG., 272p. (J). (gr. 3-7). 2012. Illus.). pap. 6.99 *(978-1-4424-1704-5(8))* 2011. 17.99 *(978-1-4424-1703-8(X))* Simon & Schuster Children's Publishing. (Atheneum Bks. for Young Readers).

—Nerd Camp 2.0. Willis, Drew, illus. (ENG.). (J). (gr. 3-7). 2015. 304p. pap. 7.99 *(978-1-4424-5295-4(1))* 2014. 288p.

C D

17.99 *(978-1-4424-5294-7(3)*, Atheneum Bks. for Young Readers) Simon & Schuster Children's Publishing.
Wells, Helen. Cherry Ames, Camp Nurse. 2007. (Cherry Ames Nurse Stories Ser.). 224p. (YA). (gr. 7-12). 14.95 *(978-0-8261-0417-5(7))* Springer Publishing Co., Inc.
Wells, Tina. Friends Forever? 2013. (Mackenzie Blue Ser.: 3). (ENG.). 208p. (J). (gr. 3-7). pap. 6.99 *(978-0-06-158316-2(2))* HarperCollins Pubs.
Wing, Natasha. The Night Before Summer Camp. Pierce, Mindy & M, Pierce, illus. 2007. (Night Before Ser.). (ENG.). 32p. (J). (gr. -1-3). pap. 4.99 *(978-0-448-44639-4(1)*, Grosset & Dunlap) Penguin Young Readers Group.
Wishinsky, Frieda. Camp Disaster, 1 vol. 2016. (Orca Currents Ser.). (ENG.). 144p. (J). (gr. 5-9). pap. 9.95 *(978-1-4598-1114-0(3))* Orca Bk. Pubs. USA.
—Camp Disaster. 2016. (Orca Currents Ser.). lib. bdg. 20.80 *(978-0-606-38697-5(1))* Turtleback Bks.
Withers, Pam. Camp Wild, 1 vol. (Orca Currents Ser.). (ENG.). 112p. (J). (gr. 5-9). 2006. 14.95 *(978-1-55143-557-2(8))* 2005. (Illus.). per. 9.95 *(978-1-55143-361-5(3))* Orca Bk. Pubs. USA.
—Camp Wild. 2006. (Orca Currents Ser.). 104p. (gr. 5-9). lib. bdg. 19.95 *(978-0-7569-6878-6(X))* Perfection Learning Corp.
Wojciechowski, Susan. Beany Goes to Camp. Natti, Susanna, illus. 2005. (Beany Adventures Ser.). 104p. (J). (gr. 4-7). 13.65 *(978-0-7569-6499-3(7))* Perfection Learning Corp.
Wojtowycz, David, illus. Elephant Joe, Brave Firefighter! 2015. (Step into Reading Ser.). (ENG.). 32p. (J). (gr. -1-1). 12.99 *(978-0-375-97203-4(X)*, Random Hse. Bks. for Young Readers) Random Hse. Children's Bks.
Wolf, Elaine. Camp. 2012. (ENG.). 256p. (YA). (gr. 6-17). 16.95 *(978-1-61608-657-2(2)*, 608657, Sky Pony Pr.) Skyhorse Publishing Co., Inc.
Wooster, Devin Ann. Sing It Out. 2015. (Step into Reading Ser.). (ENG., Illus.). 24p. (J). (gr. -1-1). 4.99 *(978-0-553-52438-3(0)*, Random Hse. Bks. for Young Readers) Random Hse. Children's Bks.
Young, Jessica. Nature Calls. Secheret, Jessica, illus. 2015. (Finley Flowers Ser.). (ENG.). 128p. (gr. 2-3). 8.95 *(978-1-4795-5879-7(6)*, Finley Flowers) Picture Window Bks.
Younge-Ullman, Danielle. Everything Beautiful Is Not Ruined. 2017. (ENG.). 368p. (YA). (gr. 9). 17.99 *(978-0-425-28759-0(9)*, Viking Books for Young Readers) Penguin Young Readers Group.
Zuill, Andrea. Wolf Camp. 2016. (ENG., Illus.). 40p. (J). (gr. -1-3). 16.99 *(978-0-553-50912-0(8)*, Schwartz & Wade Bks.) Random Hse. Children's Bks.

CANADA

Anness Publishing Ltd. Let's Look & See: Canadian Animals. 2014. (ENG., Illus.). 24p. (J). (gr. -1-k). bds. 6.99 *(978-1-86147-377-6(X)*, Armadillo) Anness Publishing GBR. Dist: National Bk. Network.
Bannatyne-Cugnet, Jo. A Prairie Alphabet. Moore, Yvette, illus. 2009. (ABC Our Country Ser.). (ENG.). 32p. (J). (gr. 1-4). pap. 7.95 *(978-0-88776-937-5(3)*, Tundra Bks.) Tundra Bks. CAN. Dist: Penguin Random Hse. LLC.
Beckett, Harry. Manitoba. 2003. (Eye on Canada Ser.). (Illus.). 32p. (J). pap. 9.95 *(978-1-894705-01-1(7))* Weigl Pubs., Inc.
Bellefontaine, Kim. ABC of Canada. Gürth, Per-Henrik, illus. 2006. (ENG.). 30p. (J). (gr. -1 — 1). bds. 8.95 *(978-1-55337-979-9(9))* Kids Can Pr., Ltd. CAN. Dist: Hachette Bk. Group.
—Canada 123. Gürth, Per-Henrik, illus. 2008. (ENG.). 24p. (J). (gr. -1 — 1). bds. 8.95 *(978-1-55453-235-3(3))* Kids Can Pr., Ltd. CAN. Dist: Hachette Bk. Group.
—Canada 123. Gürth, Per-Henrik, illus. 2006. (ENG.). 24p. (J). (gr. -1-1). 15.95 *(978-1-55337-897-6(0))* Kids Can Pr., Ltd. CAN. Dist: Hachette Bk. Group.
Blades, Heather. Focus on Canada. 2006. (World in Focus Ser.). (Illus.). 64p. (gr. 5-12). lib. bdg. 34.00 *(978-0-8368-6215-7(5)*, Gareth Stevens Secondary Library) Stevens, Gareth Publishing LLLP.
Blevins, Wiley. Canada. 2017. (Follow Me Around Ser.). (J). lib. bdg. 27.00 ***(978-0-531-23708-3(7)***, Children's Pr.) Scholastic Library Publishing.
Braun, Eric. Canada in Pictures. 2nd ed. 2003. (Visual Geography Series, Second Ser.). (ENG., Illus.). 80p. (gr. 5-12). 31.93 *(978-0-8225-4679-5(5))* Lerner Publishing Group.
Canadian Books Staff. Canadian Scented Book. 2005. (Illus.). 12p. 6.95 *(978-0-9762524-5-0(7))* Gimme Gimme Toys & Games, Inc.
Corrigan, Kathleen. Canada Today. 2016. (Canada Through Time Ser.). (ENG.). 32p. (gr. 1-4). lib. bdg. 29.99 *(978-1-4109-8122-6(3)*, Read Me!) Heinemann-Raintree.
Crosby, Sidney, et al. Sidney Crosby. 2015. (Quotes from the Greatest Athletes Ser.). (ENG., Illus.). 24p. (J). lib. bdg. 12.95 *(978-1-4896-3377-4(4)*, AV2 by Weigl) Weigl Pubs., Inc.
Downie, Mary Alice. A Pioneer Alphabet. Gerber, Mary Jane, illus. 2009. (ABC Our Country Ser.). (ENG.). 32p. (J). (gr. k-3). pap. 7.95 *(978-0-88776-961-0(6)*, Tundra Bks.) Tundra Bks. CAN. Dist: Penguin Random Hse. LLC.
Faryon, Cynthia J. Real Justice: Guilty of Being Weird: The Story of Guy Paul Morin, 1 vol. 2012. (Lorimer Real Justice Ser.). (ENG., Illus.). 144p. (YA). (gr. 8-12). 18.95 *(978-1-4594-0093-1(3)*, 9781459400931); pap. 12.95 *(978-1-4594-0092-4(5)*, 9781459400924) Lorimer, James & Co., Ltd., Pubs. CAN. Dist: Casemate Pubs. & Bk. Distributors, LLC.
—Sentenced to Life at Seventeen: The Story of David Milgaard, 1 vol. 2012. (Lorimer Real Justice Ser.). (ENG., Illus.). 120p. (J). (gr. 8-12). 18.95 *(978-1-4594-0169-3(7)*, 9781459401693) Lorimer, James & Co., Ltd., Pubs. CAN. Dist: Casemate Pubs. & Bk. Distributors, LLC.
Foran, Jill. La Vie de Famille: Le Début de la Colonie. Karvonen, Tanjah, tr. from ENG. 2011. (FRE., Illus.). 24p. (gr. 3-6). *(978-1-77071-419-9(7))* Weigl Educational Pubs. Ltd.
Geiger, Beth. Geography of Canada: Set Of 6. 2011. (Navigators Ser.). (J). pap. 50.00 net. *(978-1-4108-6262-4(3))* Benchmark Education Co.
Ghione, Yvette & Gürth, Per-Henrik. Oh, Canada! Gürth, Per-Henrik, illus. 2009. (ENG., Illus.). 32p. (J). (gr. -1-2). 15.99 *(978-1-55453-374-9(0))* Kids Can Pr., Ltd. CAN. Dist: Hachette Bk. Group.
Golden, Nancy. Exploring Canada with the Five Themes of Geography. 2005. (Library of the Western Hemisphere). (Illus.). 24p. (gr. 3-8). pap. 8.25 *(978-0-8239-4629-7(0))* Rosen Publishing Group, Inc., The.
Greenwood, Barbara. The Kids Book of Canada. MacRae, Jock, illus. 2007. (Kids Book Of Ser.). (ENG.). 60p. (J). (gr. 3-7). 14.95 *(978-1-55453-226-1(4))* Kids Can Pr., Ltd. CAN. Dist: Hachette Bk. Group.
Gürth, Per-Henrik. Canada All Year. Gürth, Per-Henrik, illus. 2011. (ENG., Illus.). 32p. (J). (gr. -1-1). 14.95 *(978-1-55453-709-9(6))* Kids Can Pr., Ltd. CAN. Dist: Hachette Bk. Group.
—Canada in Words. Gürth, Per-Henrik, illus. 2012. (ENG., Illus.). 32p. (J). (gr. -1-1). 14.95 *(978-1-55453-710-5(X))* Kids Can Pr., Ltd. CAN. Dist: Hachette Bk. Group.
Gurtler, Janet. Beaver. 2011. 24p. (YA). (gr. 2-4). *(978-1-77071-662-9(9))*; pap. *(978-1-77071-668-1(8))* Weigl Educational Pubs. Ltd.
Hamilton, Janice. Canada. 2007. (Country Explorers Ser.). (ENG., Illus.). 48p. (gr. 2-4). lib. bdg. 29.27 *(978-0-8225-7128-5(5)*, Lerner Pubns.) Lerner Publishing Group.
Harrison, Ted. A Northern Alphabet. 2009. (ABC Our Country Ser.). (ENG., Illus.). 32p. (J). (gr. 1-4). pap. 7.99 *(978-0-88776-960-3(8)*, Tundra Bks.) Tundra Bks. CAN. Dist: Penguin Random Hse. LLC.
—O Canada. 2004. (J). (gr. k-3). spiral bd. *(978-0-616-03038-7(X))* Canadian National Institute for the Blind/Institut National Canadien pour les Aveugles.
James, Soloman & Salt, Allan. Little Book of Animals. 2010. (OJI & ENG., Illus.). 43p. *(978-0-9745168-6-8(4))* Cotsen Occasional Pr.
Junior Worldmark Encyclopedia of the Canadian Provinces. 5th rev. ed. 2007. (ENG., Illus.). 312p. (J). 106.00 *(978-1-4144-1060-9(3)*, UXL) Cengage Gale.
Kaplan, Leslie C. A Primary Source Guide to Canada. 2005. (Countries of the World). (Illus.). 24p. (J). (gr. -1-3). lib. bdg. 22.60 *(978-1-4042-2750-7(4)*, PowerKids Pr.) Rosen Publishing Group, Inc., The.
Kissock, Heather, ed. Disasters. 2011. 48p. (gr. 5-8). *(978-1-77071-674-2(2))*; pap. *(978-1-77071-677-3(7))* Weigl Educational Pubs. Ltd.
Laidlaw, Rob. Elephant Journey: The True Story of Three Zoo Elephants & Their Rescue from Captivity. Deines, Brian, illus. 2016. (ENG.). 40p. (J). (gr. 1-4). 19.95 *(978-1-927485-77-4(0))* Pajama Pr. CAN. Dist: Ingram Publisher Services.
Laws, Gordon D. & Laws, Lauren M. The Northwest Territories. 2003. (Exploring Canada Ser.). (ENG., Illus.). 112p. (J). 30.85 *(978-1-59018-049-5(6)*, Lucent Bks.) Cengage Gale.
Lindeen, Mary. Welcome to North America, 1 vol. 2011. (Wonder Readers Fluent Level Ser.). (ENG.). 32p. (gr. -1-2). pap. 5.99 *(978-1-4296-7974-9(3)*, Wonder Readers) Capstone Press of Coughlan Cos.
MacDonald, Barry. Everything Real Justin Bieber Fans Should Know & Do. 2012. (ENG.). 192p. (J). (gr. 7). pap. 12.95 *(978-1-60078-770-6(3))* Triumph Bks.
Mara, Wil. Canada. 2017. (Enchantment of the World Ser.). (ENG.). 144p. (J). lib. bdg. 40.00 ***(978-0-531-23572-0(6)***, Children's Pr.) Scholastic Library Publishing.
Marsh, Carole. Canada: The Maple Leaf Melting Pot Country! 2009. (It's Your World Ser.). 48p. (J). (gr. 2-9). pap. 7.99 *(978-0-635-06816-3(8))* Gallopade International.
Match Game Staff. Canada Scented Memory Game. 2005. pap. 19.95 *(978-0-9762524-1-2(4))* Gimme Gimme Toys & Games, Inc.
Mattern, Joanne. Let's Visit Canada: The Metric System. 2009. (PowerMath Ser.). (Illus.). 24p. (gr. 3-4). pap. 8.25 *(978-0-8239-8872-3(4)*, PowerKids Pr.) Rosen Publishing Group, Inc., The.
McCarthy, Pat. Canada: A MyReportLinks. com Book. 2004. (Top Ten Countries of Recent Immigrants Ser.). (Illus.). 48p. (J). lib. bdg. 26.60 *(978-0-7660-5176-8(5)*, MyReportLinks.com Bks.) Enslow Pubs., Inc.
McDonnell, Ginger. Next Stop - Canada, 1 vol. 2nd rev. ed. 2011. (Nonfiction Readers Ser.). (ENG.). 24p. (J). (gr. 2-2). pap. 6.99 *(978-1-4333-3611-9(1))* Teacher Created Materials, Inc.
McNamara, Margaret. Canada. 2006. (J). pap. *(978-1-4108-6458-1(8))* Benchmark Education Co.
Nations of the World: Canada. (Time Traveler Ser.). 32p. (gr. 3-6). 6.99 *(978-0-513-02377-2(1)*, TSD23771) Denison, T. S. & Co., Inc.
Owens, Ann-Maureen & Yealland, Jane. Our Flag: The Story of Canada's Maple Leaf. Slavin, Bill & Melo, Esperança, illus. 2014. (ENG.). 32p. (J). (gr. 2-5). 17.95 *(978-1-77138-111-6(6))*; pap. 9.95 *(978-1-77138-112-3(4))* Kids Can Pr., Ltd. CAN. Dist: Hachette Bk. Group.
Pang, Guek Cheng. Canada. 2nd rev. ed. 2004. (Cultures of the World Ser.). 144p. (gr. 6). 42.79 *(978-0-7614-1788-0(5)*, Benchmark Bks.) Marshall Cavendish Corp.
Pohl, Kathleen. Descubramos Canadá. 2007. (Descubramos países del mundo (Spanish- Looking at Countries) Ser.). (SPA.). 32p. (gr. 1-5). pap. 10.50 *(978-0-8368-8189-9(3)*, Gareth Stevens Learning Library) Stevens, Gareth Publishing LLLP.
—Looking at Canada. 2007. (Looking at Countries Ser.). (Illus.). 32p. (gr. 1-5). pap. 10.50 *(978-0-8368-8175-2(3))*; lib. bdg. 26.00 *(978-0-8368-8168-4(0))* Stevens, Gareth Publishing LLLP. (Gareth Stevens Learning Library).
Richardson, Adele. Canada. 2006. (My First Look at: Countries Ser.). (Illus.). 24p. (J). lib. bdg. 15.95 *(978-1-58341-444-6(4)*, Creative Education) Creative Co., The.
Ruth, Angie. My Adventure in Canada. 2007. 44p. (J). 8.99 *(978-1-59092-424-2(X))* Blue Forge Pr.
Sonneborn, Liz. Canada. 2011. (Enchantment of the World Ser.). (ENG., Illus.). 144p. (J). (gr. 5-9). lib. bdg. 40.00 *(978-0-531-25351-9(1))* Scholastic Library Publishing.
Staunton, Ted. Gold Rush. Geoffroi, Remie, illus. 2008. (Dreadful Truth Ser.). (ENG.). 104p. (YA). (gr. 3-8). *(978-0-88780-747-3(X))* Formac Publishing Co., Ltd.
Sutoski, Jennifer. Terry Fox. 2015. (Canadian Biographies Ser.). (ENG., Illus.). 24p. (gr. k-1). lib. bdg. 26.65 *(978-1-4914-7836-3(5)*, Pebble Plus) Capstone Press of Coughlan Cos.
Triumph Books Staff. Believe. 2012. (ENG.). 112p. (YA). (gr. 7). pap. 12.95 *(978-1-60078-792-8(4))* Triumph Bks.
Trottier, Maxine. One Is Canada. 2004. (Illus.). (J). (gr. 1-5). spiral bd. *(978-0-616-01797-5(9))* Canadian National Institute for the Blind/Institut National Canadien pour les Aveugles.
Ulmer, Mike. M Is for Maple: A Canadian Alphabet. Rose-Popp, Melanie, illus. rev. ed. 2004. (Discover the World Ser.). (ENG.). 48p. (J). (gr. -1-1). pap. 8.95 *(978-1-58536-235-6(2)*, 202276) Sleeping Bear Pr.
Ulmer, Mike & Ulmer, Michael. M Is for Maple: A Canadian Alphabet. Rose, Melanie, illus. rev. abr. ed. 2007. (Discover the World Ser.). (ENG.). 32p. (J). (gr. -1-1). 8.99 *(978-1-58536-345-2(6)*, 202380) Sleeping Bear Pr.
Verstraete, Larry. G Is for Golden Boy: A Manitoba Alphabet. Lund, Brian, illus. 2009. (Discover Canada Province by Province Ser.). (ENG.). 40p. (J). (gr. k-8). 17.95 *(978-1-58536-364-3(2))* Sleeping Bear Pr.
Williams, Brian. Canada. 2007. (Countries of the World Ser.). (ENG., Illus.). 64p. (J). (gr. 5-5). lib. bdg. 27.90 *(978-1-4263-0025-7(5)*, National Geographic Children's Bks.) National Geographic Society.
—Canada - National Geographic. 2009. (Countries of the World Ser.). (ENG., Illus.). 64p. (J). (gr. 5). pap. 12.95 *(978-1-4263-0573-3(7)*, National Geographic Children's Bks.) National Geographic Society.
Zocchi, Judy. In Canada. Brodie, Neale, illus. 2005. (Global Adventures II Ser.). 32p. (J). per. 10.95 *(978-1-59646-169-7(1))* Dingles & Co.
—In Canada/en Canada. Brodie, Neale, illus. 2005. (Global Adventures II Ser.).Tr. of En Canada. (ENG & SPA.). 32p. (J). per. 10.95 *(978-1-59646-171-0(3))* Dingles & Co.
—In Cuba. Brodie, Neale, illus. 2005. (Global Adventures II Ser.). 32p. (J). per. 10.95 *(978-1-59646-161-1(6))* Dingles & Co.

CANADA—BIOGRAPHY

Argyle, Ray. The Boy in the Picture: The Craigellachie Kid & the Driving of the Last Spike. 2010. (ENG., Illus.). 152p. (YA). pap. 19.99 *(978-1-55488-787-3(9))* Dundurn CAN. Dist: Ingram Publisher Services.
Azzarelli, Ally. Justin Bieber: Teen Music Superstar. 2011. (Hot Celebrity Biographies Ser.). (Illus.). 48p. (J). (gr. 5-18). pap. 8.95 *(978-1-59845-287-7(8))*; lib. bdg. 25.27 *(978-0-7660-3873-8(4))* Enslow Pubs., Inc.
Bailey, Katharine. Radisson & des Groseilliers: Fur Traders of the North. 2006. (In the Footsteps of Explorers Ser.). (ENG., Illus.). 32p. (J). (gr. 3-7). lib. bdg. *(978-0-7787-2422-3(0)*, 1253444) Crabtree Publishing Co.
Baldwin, Garrett. The Justin Bieber Album. 2010. (ENG., Illus.). 64p. (gr. 3-11). pap. 12.95 *(978-0-85965-464-7(8))* Plexus Publishing, Ltd. GBR. Dist: Publishers Group West (PGW).
Barghoorn, Linda. Craig Kielburger: Champion for Children's Rights & Youth Activism. 2017. (Illus.). 32p. (J). ***(978-0-7787-3420-8(X))*** Crabtree Publishing Co.
Batten, Jack. Oscar Peterson: The Man & His Jazz. 2012. (ENG., Illus.). 192p. (YA). (gr. 5). 19.95 *(978-1-77049-269-1(0)*, Tundra Bks.) Tundra Bks. CAN. Dist: Penguin Random Hse. LLC.
Benge, Janet & Benge, Geoff. Christian Heroes - Then & Now - Rowland Bingham: Into Africa's Interior. 2003. (Christian Heroes Ser.). (Illus.). 181p. per. 8.99 *(978-1-57658-282-4(5))* YWAM Publishing.
Bieber, Justin. Justin Bieber: Just Getting Started. 2012. (ENG.). 240p. (J). (gr. 3-7). 21.99 *(978-0-06-220208-6(1))* HarperCollins Pubs.
—Justin Bieber - First Step 2 Forever: My Story. 2012. (ENG.). 240p. (J). (gr. 3-7). pap. 12.99 *(978-0-06-209158-1(1))* HarperCollins Pubs.
Blohm, Craig E. Great Cartoonists. 2016. (ENG.). 80p. (J). (gr. 5-12). *(978-1-60152-996-1(1))* ReferencePoint Pr., Inc.
Bloom, Ronny. Justin Bieber. 2011. (SPA.). 192p. (YA). 14.95 *(978-84-666-4680-2(9))* Ediciones B ESP. Dist: Spanish Pubs., LLC.
Bodden, Valerie. Justin Bieber: Musical Phenom, 1 vol. 2012. (Contemporary Lives Set 1 Ser.). (ENG.). 112p. (J). (gr. 6-12). lib. bdg. 35.64 *(978-1-61783-321-2(5))* ABDO Publishing Co.
Bogart, Jo Ellen. Capturing Joy: The Story of Maud Lewis. Lang, Mark, illus. 2011. (ENG.). 32p. (J). (gr. 3-7). pap. 8.95 *(978-1-77049-262-2(3)*, Tundra Bks.) Tundra Bks. CAN. Dist: Penguin Random Hse. LLC.
Bolte, Mari. Justin Bieber. 2012. (Star Biographies Ser.). (ENG.). 32p. (gr. 3-4). pap. 47.70 *(978-1-4296-9457-5(2))*; (Illus.). lib. bdg. 27.99 *(978-1-4296-8665-5(0))* Capstone Press of Coughlan Cos. (Snap Bks.).
Boone, Mary & Sprinkel, Katy. Bieber Fever. 2011. (ENG., Illus.). 112p. (J). (gr. 7). pap. 12.95 *(978-1-60078-634-1(0))* Triumph Bks.
Bradley, Michael. Pro Hockey's Underdogs: Players & Teams Who Shocked the Hockey World. 2017. (Sports Shockers! Ser.). (ENG.). 32p. (gr. 3-4). lib. bdg. 27.99 ***(978-1-5157-8045-8(7))*** Capstone Press of Coughlan Cos.
Brickweg, Jason. Chris Jericho. 2013. (Pro Wrestling Champions Ser.). (ENG., Illus.). 24p. (J). (gr. 3-7). lib. bdg. 25.95 *(978-1-60014-902-3(2)*, Torque Bks.) Bellwether Media.
—Santino Marella. 2013. (Illus.). 24p. (J). *(978-0-531-26807-0(1))*; (ENG., (gr. 3-7). lib. bdg. 25.95 *(978-1-60014-904-7(9)*, Torque Bks.) Bellwether Media.
Brignall, Richard. Big League Dreams: Baseball Hall of Fame's First African-Canadian, Fergie Jenkins, 1 vol. 2010. (Lorimer Recordbooks Ser.). (ENG., Illus.). 152p. (gr. 8-12). 9.95 *(978-1-55277-486-1(4)*, 9781552774861) Lorimer, James & Co., Ltd., Pubs. CAN. Dist: Casemate Pubs. & Bk. Distributors, LLC.
—Big Train: The Legendary Ironman of Sport, Lionel Conacher, 1 vol. 2009. (Lorimer Recordbooks Ser.). (ENG., Illus.). 168p. (YA). (gr. 6-12). 16.95 *(978-1-55277-451-9(1)*, 9781552774519); 9.95 *(978-1-55277-450-2(3)*, 9781552774502) Lorimer, James & Co., Ltd., Pubs. CAN. Dist: Casemate Pubs. & Bk. Distributors, LLC.
—China Clipper: Pro Football's First Chinese-Canadian Player, Normie Kwong, 1 vol. 2010. (Lorimer Recordbooks Ser.). (ENG., Illus.). 152p. (YA). (gr. 7-12). mass mkt. 9.95 *(978-1-55277-527-1(5)*, 9781552775271) Lorimer, James & Co., Ltd., Pubs. CAN. Dist: Casemate Pubs. & Bk. Distributors, LLC.
—Fearless: The Story of George Chuvalo, Canada's Greatest Boxer, 1 vol. 2009. (Lorimer Recordbooks Ser.). (ENG., Illus.). 160p. (YA). (gr. 7-12). 16.95 *(978-1-55277-436-6(8)*, 9781552774366); 9.95 *(978-1-55277-435-9(X)*, 9781552774359) Lorimer, James & Co., Ltd., Pubs. CAN. Dist: Casemate Pubs. & Bk. Distributors, LLC.
Brooker, Marion Fargey. Hold the Oxo! A Teenage Soldier Writes Home. 2011. (Canadians at War Ser.: 6). (ENG., Illus.). 144p. (YA). pap. 14.99 *(978-1-55488-870-2(0))* Dundurn CAN. Dist: Ingram Publisher Services.
Brown, Don. Mack Made Movies. Brown, Don, illus. 2008. (Illus.). (J). (gr. 2-5). 25.95 incl. audio compact disk *(978-1-4301-0432-2(5))*; pap. 16.95 incl. audio *(978-1-4301-0431-5(7))*; pap. 39.95 incl. audio compact disk *(978-1-4301-0436-0(8))*;Set. pap. 37.95 incl. audio *(978-1-4301-0433-9(3))* Live Oak Media.
Burgan, Michael. Sidney Crosby. 2015. (Hockey Superstars Ser.). (ENG.). 32p. (gr. 3-4). lib. bdg. 27.99 *(978-1-4914-2138-3(X))* Capstone Press of Coughlan Cos.
Burlingame, Jeff. Avril Lavigne: Celebrity with Heart. 2010. (Celebrities with Heart Ser.). 112p. (J). (gr. 7-12). 33.27 *(978-0-7660-3407-5(0))*; (Illus.). pap. 10.95 *(978-1-59845-204-4(5))* Enslow Pubs., Inc.
Burns, Kylie. Sidney Crosby. 2013. (ENG., Illus.). 32p. (J). *(978-0-7787-0038-8(0))*; pap. *(978-0-7787-0068-5(2))* Crabtree Publishing Co.
Butts, Ed. She Dared: True Stories of Heroines, Scoundrels, & Renegades. Collins, Heather, illus. 2005. (ENG.). 128p. (J). (gr. 5-9). pap. 8.95 *(978-0-88776-718-0(4)*, Tundra Bks.) Tundra Bks. CAN. Dist: Penguin Random Hse. LLC.
Carr, Annaleise. Annaleise Carr: How I Conquered Lake Ontario to Help Kids Battling Cancer, 1 vol. 2014. (Lorimer Recordbooks Ser.). (ENG., Illus.). 144p. (YA). (gr. 7-12). 16.95 *(978-1-4594-0632-2(X)*, 9781459406322); pap. 9.95 *(978-1-4594-0631-5(1)*, 9781459406315) Lorimer, James & Co., Ltd., Pubs. CAN. Dist: Casemate Pubs. & Bk. Distributors, LLC.
Charleyboy, Lisa & Leatherdale, Mary Beth. Dreaming in Indian: Contemporary Native American Voices. 2016. (ENG., Illus.). 128p. (J). (gr. 6). pap. 12.95 *(978-1-55451-686-5(2))* Annick Pr., Ltd. CAN. Dist: Publishers Group West (PGW).
Conover, David & Conover, David, Sr. Once upon an Island. 2nd ed. 2003. (Illus.). 207p. per. 17.95 *(978-0-9707399-1-9(5)*, 425-485-2813) San Juan Publishing.
Corporate Contributor. Steve Nash. 2012. (ENG.). 32p. (J). *(978-0-7787-7618-5(2))*; pap. *(978-0-7787-7631-4(X))* Crabtree Publishing Co.
Crabtree, Marc. Meet My Neighbor, the Chef. 2009. (Meet my Neighbor Ser.). (ENG., Illus.). 24p. (J). (gr. k-2). lib. bdg. *(978-0-7787-4571-6(6))* Crabtree Publishing Co.
—Meet My Neighbor, the Doctor. 2013. (ENG., Illus.). 24p. (J). *(978-0-7787-0871-1(3))*; pap. *(978-0-7787-0875-9(6))* Crabtree Publishing Co.
—Meet My Neighbor, the Librarian. 2012. (ENG., Illus.). 24p. (J). *(978-0-7787-4559-4(7))*; pap. *(978-0-7787-4564-8(3))* Crabtree Publishing Co.
—Meet My Neighbor, the News Camera Operator. 2012. (ENG., Illus.). 24p. (J). *(978-0-7787-4560-0(0))*; pap. *(978-0-7787-4565-5(1))* Crabtree Publishing Co.
Crompton, Samuel Willard. Robert de la Salle. 2009. (Great Explorers Ser.). (Illus.). 112p. (J). (gr. 6-12). 30.00 *(978-1-60413-419-3(4)*, Chelsea Hse.) Facts On File, Inc.
Crump, Jennifer. Canada on Fire: The War of 1812. 2011. (Canadians at War Ser.: 4). (ENG., Illus.). 208p. (YA). (gr. 6). pap. 19.99 *(978-1-55488-753-8(4))* Dundurn CAN. Dist: Ingram Publisher Services.
Dakers, Diane. Chris Hadfield: Inspiring New Generations to Explore Space. 2015. (Crabtree Groundbreaker Biographies Ser.). (ENG., Illus.). 112p. (J). (gr. 5-8). *(978-0-7787-2558-9(8))* Crabtree Publishing Co.
Danakas, John. Choice of Colours: The Pioneering African-American Quarterbacks Who Changed the Face of Football. 2007. (Lorimer Recordbooks Ser.). (ENG., Illus.). (YA). 120p. (gr. 4-9). 16.95 *(978-1-55028-993-0(4)*, 9781550289930); 128p. (gr. 7-12). 9.95 *(978-1-55028-991-6(8)*, 9781550289916) Lorimer, James & Co., Ltd., Pubs. CAN. Dist: Casemate Pubs. & Bk. Distributors, LLC.
De Medeiros, Michael. Steve Nash. 2008. (Remarkable People Ser.). (Illus.). 24p. (J). (gr. 4-6). pap. 8.95 *(978-1-59036-991-3(2))*; lib. bdg. 24.45 *(978-1-59036-990-6(4))* Weigl Pubs., Inc.
Debon, Nicolas. Four Pictures by Emily Carr, 1 vol. (ENG., Illus.). 40p. (J). 2007. (gr. 2-7). pap. 6.95 *(978-0-88899-814-9(7))* 2003. (gr. k-4). 15.95 *(978-0-88899-532-2(6))* Groundwood Bks. CAN. Dist: Publishers Group West (PGW).
Doeden, Matt. Carey Price. 2015. (Hockey Superstars Ser.). (ENG.). 32p. (gr. 3-4). lib. bdg. 27.99 *(978-1-4914-2140-6(1))* Capstone Press of Coughlan Cos.
—Phil Kessel. 2015. (Hockey Superstars Ser.). (ENG., Illus.). 32p. (gr. 3-9). pap. 7.95 *(978-1-4914-9022-8(5))*; lib. bdg. 27.99 *(978-1-4296-8278-7(7))* Capstone Press of Coughlan Cos.
—Steven Stamkos. 2015. (Hockey Superstars Ser.). (ENG.). 32p. (gr. 3-4). lib. bdg. 27.99 *(978-1-4914-2139-0(8))* Capstone Press of Coughlan Cos.
—Wayne Gretzky. 2007. (Sports Heroes & Legends Ser.). (ENG., Illus.). 120p. (gr. 5-12). lib. bdg. 30.60 *(978-0-8225-7165-0(X))* Lerner Publishing Group.
Donaldson, Chelsea. Canadian Biographies. 2014. (Canadian Biographies Ser.). (ENG.). 24p. (gr. k-1). 106.60 *(978-1-4914-1961-8(X))*; pap. 27.80 *(978-1-4914-1980-9(6))* Capstone Press of Coughlan Cos. (Pebble Plus).
—Chris Hadfield, 1 vol. 2014. (Canadian Biographies Ser.). (ENG.). 24p. (gr. k-1). 26.65 *(978-1-4914-1957-1(1)*, Pebble Plus) Capstone Press of Coughlan Cos.
—Hayley Wickenheiser, 1 vol. 2014. (Canadian Biographies Ser.). (ENG.). 24p. (gr. k-1). 26.65 *(978-1-4914-1958-8(X)*, Pebble Plus) Capstone Press of Coughlan Cos.
Down, Heather, text. Postcards from Space: The Chris Hadfield Story. 2014. (Illus.). 48p. *(978-1-894813-68-6(5))* Winterickle Pr.
Dubé, Jean-Claude. The Chevalier de Montmagny: First Governor of New France. Rapley, Elizabeth, tr. from FRE. 2005. (French America Ser.). (ENG., Illus.). 430p. 65.00 *(978-0-7766-3028-1(8))* Univ. of Ottawa Pr./Presses de l'Universite d'Ottawa CAN. Dist: Two Rivers Distribution.
Dublin, Anne. June Callwood: A Life of Action, 1 vol. 2007. (ENG., Illus.). 156p. (J). (gr. 3-12). pap. 14.95

(978-1-897187-14-2(9)) Second Story Pr. CAN. Dist: Orca Bk. Pubs. USA.

Edwards, Ethan. Meet Steve Nash: Basketball's Ultimate Team Player. 2009. (All-Star Players Ser.). 32p. (gr. 4-5). 47.90 (978-1-61511-295-1(2)); (Illus.). (J). lib. bdg. 23.95 (978-1-4042-4489-4(1)) Rosen Publishing Group, Inc., The. (PowerKids Pr.).

Edwards, Frank B. Robert Munsch: Portrait of an Extraordinary Canadian, 1 vol. 2009. (Larger Than Life Ser.). (ENG.). 71p. (J). (gr. 2-4). (978-1-55455-138-5(2)) Fitzhenry & Whiteside, Ltd.

Emery, Joanna. Caring for a Colony: The Story of Jeanne Mance. Thompson, Allister, ed. Wysotski, Chrissie, illus. 2005. (Stories of Canada Ser.: 8). (ENG.). 72p. (J). (gr. 4-7). 18.95 (978-1-894917-07-0(3), Napoleon & Co.) Dundurn CAN. Dist: Ingram Publisher Services.

Frederick, Shane. John Tavares. 2015. (Hockey Superstars Ser.). (ENG., Illus.). 32p. (gr. 3-9). pap. 7.95 (978-1-4914-9025-9(X)); lib. bdg. 27.99 (978-1-62065-158-2(0)) Capstone Press of Coughlan Cos.

Frisch, Aaron. Justin Bieber. 2013. (Illus.). 24p. (J). 25.65 (978-1-60818-330-2(0), Creative Education) Creative Co., The.

Fryer, Mary Beacock. Bold, Brave, & Born to Lead: Major General Isaac Brock & the Canadas. 2004. (ENG., Illus.). 264p. (YA). pap. 9.99 (978-1-55002-501-9(5)) Dundurn CAN. Dist: Ingram Publisher Services.

—Champlain: Peacemaker & Explorer. 2011. (ENG., Illus.). 152p. (YA). (gr. 6). pap. 19.99 (978-1-55488-940-2(5)) Dundurn CAN. Dist: Ingram Publisher Services.

Gaetz, Dayle. Catriona le May Doan: La Plus Rapide des Patineuses. 2004. (FRE., Illus.). (J). (978-2-7650-0745-6(4)) Les Editions de la Cheneliere, Inc.

Gagne, Tammy. Day by Day with Justin Bieber. 2011. (Day by Day with... Ser.). (Illus.). 32p. (J). (gr. -1-2). lib. bdg. 25.70 (978-1-58415-984-1(7)) Mitchell Lane Pubs., Inc.

Gagne, Tammy. The Weeknd. 2017. lib. bdg. 25.70 **(978-1-68020-124-6(7))** Mitchell Lane Pubs., Inc.

Gerstner, Joanne C. Toronto Raptors, 1 vol. 2011. (Inside the NBA Ser.). (ENG., Illus.). 48p. (J). (gr. 3-6). lib. bdg. 32.79 (978-1-61783-176-8(X)) ABDO Publishing Co.

Goodall, Lian. Photographing Greatness: The Story of Karsh. Thompson, Samantha, illus. 2007. (Stories of Canada Ser.: 11). (ENG.). 96p. (J). 21.99 (978-1-894917-34-6(0), Napoleon & Co.) Dundurn CAN. Dist: Ingram Publisher Services.

—Singing Towards the Future: The Story of Portia White. 2nd ed. 2008. (Stories of Canada Ser.: 6). (ENG.). 72p. (J). pap. 18.99 (978-1-894917-55-1(3), Napoleon & Co.) Dundurn CAN. Dist: Ingram Publisher Services.

Gosman, Gillian. Justin Bieber. 2012. (Kid Stars! Ser.). (ENG., Illus.). 24p. (J). (gr. 1-6). pap. 8.25 (978-1-4488-6339-6(2)); lib. bdg. 22.60 (978-1-4488-6190-3(X)) Rosen Publishing Group, Inc., The. (PowerKids Pr.).

Goyette, Linda. Rocky Mountain Kids, 1 vol. 2008. (ENG., Illus.). 128p. (J). (gr. 3-7). pap. (978-1-897142-32-5(3)) Brindle & Glass Publishing.

Gravel, Élise. The Great Antonio, Level 3. 2016. (ENG., Illus.). 64p. (J). (gr. -1-4). 12.95 (978-1-943145-08-9(3), 9781943145089) TOON Books / RAW Junior, LLC.

Graves, Will. Best Hockey Players of All Time, 1 vol. 2014. (Sports' Best Ever Ser.). (ENG.). 64p. (gr. 3-6). lib. bdg. 32.79 (978-1-62403-620-0(1), SportsZone) ABDO Publishing Co.

Hamilton, John. Georges St-Pierre. 2010. (Xtreme UFC Ser.). 32p. (gr. 3-9). 27.07 (978-1-61613-479-2(8), A&D Xtreme) ABDO Publishing Co.

Harte, Harlee. I Justin Bieber. 2010. 144p. pap. 4.95 (978-1-60747-777-8(7), Pickwick Pr.) Phoenix Bks., Inc.

Haugen, Brenda. Johnathan Toews. 2015. (Hockey Superstars Ser.). (ENG., Illus.). 32p. (gr. 3-9). lib. bdg. 27.99 (978-1-62065-157-5(2)) Capstone Press of Coughlan Cos.

—Jonathan Toews. 2015. (Hockey Superstars Ser.). (ENG.). 32p. (gr. 3-9). pap. 7.95 (978-1-4914-9024-2(1)) Capstone Press of Coughlan Cos.

Hawley, Samuel. I Just Ran: Percy Williams, World's Fastest Human. 2011. (ENG., Illus.). 332p. pap. 23.95 (978-1-55380-126-9(1)) Ronsdale Pr. CAN. Dist: SPD-Small Pr. Distribution.

Hearn, Emily & Milne, Marywinn, eds. Our New Home: Immigrant Children Speak, 1 vol. 2008. (ENG., Illus.). 128p. (J). (gr. 4-8). pap. 13.95 (978-1-897187-32-6(7)) Orca Bk. Pubs. USA.

Herman, Gail & Harrison, Nancy. Who Is Wayne Gretzky? 2015. (Who Is...? Ser.). lib. bdg. 16.00 (978-0-606-36595-6(8)) Turtleback Bks.

Higgins, Nadia. Carly Rae Jepsen: Call Her Amazing. 2013. (Pop Culture Bios Ser.). (ENG.). 32p. (gr. 3-6). lib. bdg. 26.60 (978-1-4677-1306-1(6), Lerner Pubns.); (Illus.). pap. 7.95 (978-1-4677-1547-8(6)) Lerner Publishing Group.

—Justin Bieber: Pop & R & B Idol. 2012. (Pop Culture Bios Ser.). (ENG., Illus.). 32p. (gr. 3-6). pap. 7.95 (978-1-4677-0295-9(1)); lib. bdg. 26.60 (978-1-4677-0294-2(3), Lerner Pubns.) Lerner Publishing Group.

Jablonski, Patricia Edward. Saint Andre Bessette: Miracles in Montreal. Kiwak, Barbara, illus. 2010. (J). (gr. 4-7). pap. 7.95 (978-0-8198-7140-4(0)) Pauline Bks. & Media.

Janveau, Teri-Lynn & Thompson, Allister. Sailing for Glory: The Story of Captain Angus Walters & the Bluenose. Thompson, Samantha, illus. 2006. (Stories of Canada Ser.: 10). (ENG.). 72p. (J). 18.95 (978-1-894917-09-4(X), Napoleon & Co.) Dundurn CAN. Dist: Ingram Publisher Services.

Jordan-Fenton, Christy & Pokiak-Fenton, Margaret. Fatty Legs: A True Story. Amini-Holmes, Liz, illus. 9th ed. 2010. (ENG.). 112p. (J). (gr. 4-7). pap. 12.95 (978-1-55451-246-1(8), 9781554512461) Annick Pr., Ltd. CAN. Dist: Publishers Group West (PGW).

—When I Was Eight. Grimard, Gabrielle, illus. 2nd ed. 2013. (ENG.). 32p. (J). (gr. 1-4). 21.95 (978-1-55451-491-5(6), 9781554514915); pap. 9.95 (978-1-55451-490-8(8), 9781554514908) Annick Pr., Ltd. CAN. Dist: Publishers Group West (PGW).

Jordan-Fenton, Christy, et al. Fatty Legs: A True Story. Amini-Holmes, Liz, illus. 8th ed. 2010. (ENG.). 112p. (J). (gr. 4-7). 21.95 (978-1-55451-247-8(6), 9781554512478) Annick Pr., Ltd. CAN. Dist: Publishers Group West (PGW).

Kaufmann, Anne. Glenn Gould: Sketches of Solitude. Koci, Rudin, illus. 2013. (978-0-9868657-9-4(6)) Brownridge Publishing.

Kimmich, Ian. Steve Nash. (Role Model Athletes Ser.). (Illus.). 64p. (YA). 2010. (gr. 7-12). 22.95 (978-1-4222-0485-6(5)) 2007. pap. 9.95 (978-1-4222-0773-4(0)) Mason Crest.

Kirkpatrick, Rob. Wayne Gretzky: Hockey All-Star. 2009. (Great Record Breakers in Sports Ser.). 24p. (gr. 3-3). 42.50 (978-1-61513-192-1(2), PowerKids Pr.) Rosen Publishing Group, Inc., The.

Kissock, Heather. Robert Munsch. 2008. (My Favorite Writer Ser.). (Illus.). 32p. (YA). (gr. 5-18). pap. 8.95 (978-1-59036-925-8(4)); lib. bdg. 26.00 (978-1-59036-924-1(6)) Weigl Pubs., Inc.

Knelman, Martin. Mike's World: The Life of Mike Myers. 2003. (ENG., Illus.). 268p. (gr. 5-12). pap. 16.95 (978-1-55297-661-6(0), 9781552976616) Firefly Bks., Ltd.

Konieczny, Vladimir. Struggling for Perfection: The Story of Glenn Gould. Wysotski, Chrissie, illus. 2009. (Stories of Canada Ser.: 5). (ENG.). 104p. (J). (gr. 4-7). per. 18.99 (978-1-894917-48-3(0), Napoleon & Co.) Dundurn CAN. Dist: Ingram Publisher Services.

Kortemeier, Todd. Jonathan Toews. 2016. (Illus.). 32p. (J). (978-1-62143-289-0(0)) Pr. Room Editions LLC.

Langley, Andrew. Chris Hadfield & Living on the International Space Station. 2015. (Adventures in Space Ser.). (ENG., Illus.). 48p. (J). (gr. 4-6). 33.32 (978-1-4846-2517-0(X)) Heinemann-Raintree.

LeClair, Danielle. Sidney Crosby: Ma Vie. Karvonen, Tanjah, tr. from ENG. 2011. (FRE., Illus.). 24p. (YA). (gr. 2-4). (978-1-77071-430-4(8)) Weigl Educational Pubs. Ltd.

Leclaire, Danielle. Sidney Crosby. 2010. (Illus.). 24p. (978-1-77071-596-7(7)); pap. (978-1-77071-602-5(5)) Weigl Educational Pubs. Ltd.

Lewis, Wendy A. Fire on the Water: The Red-Hot Career of Superstar Rower Ned Hanlan, 1 vol. 2007. (Lorimer Recordbooks Ser.). (ENG & GER., Illus.). 112p. (J). (gr. 4-6). 9.95 (978-1-55028-972-5(1), 9781550289725) Lorimer, James & Co., Ltd., Pubs. CAN. Dist: Casemate Pubs. & Bk. Distributors, LLC.

Lewis, Wendy A. & Lewis, Wendy. Fire on the Water: The Red-Hot Career of Superstar Rower Ned Hanlan. 2007. (Lorimer Recordbooks Ser.). (ENG., Illus.). 112p. (J). (gr. 4-6). 16.95 (978-1-55028-973-2(X), 9781550289732) Lorimer, James & Co., Ltd., Pubs. CAN. Dist: Casemate Pubs. & Bk. Distributors, LLC.

MacKay, Jennifer. James Cameron. Greenhaven Press Editors, ed. 2013. (People in the News Ser.). (ENG., Illus.). 128p. (gr. 7-10). lib. bdg. 39.40 (978-1-4205-0885-7(7), Lucent Bks.) Cengage Gale.

MacLeod, Elizabeth. The Kids Book of Great Canadian Women. Mantha, John, illus. 2006. (Kids Book Of Ser.). (ENG.). 64p. (J). (gr. 3-7). 19.95 (978-1-55337-820-4(2)) Kids Can Pr., Ltd. CAN. Dist: Hachette Bk. Group.

—The Kids Book of Great Canadians. Mantha, John, illus. 2008. (Kids Book Of Ser.). (ENG.). 64p. (J). (gr. 3-7). pap. 14.95 (978-1-55453-255-1(8)) Kids Can Pr., Ltd. CAN. Dist: Hachette Bk. Group.

Manson, Ainslie. Boy in Motion: Rick Hansen's Story. Benoit, Renné, illus. 2009. (ENG.). 48p. (J). (gr. k-3). pap. 12.00 (978-1-55365-427-8(7)) Greystone Books Ltd. CAN. Dist: Publishers Group West (PGW).

—Roll On: Rick Hansen Wheels Around the World, 1 vol. Lightburn, Ron, illus. 2013. (ENG.). 40p. (J). (gr. k-5). pap. 10.95 (978-1-77100-268-4(9)) Greystone Books Ltd. CAN. Dist: Publishers Group West (PGW).

Mara, Wil. James Cameron. 2014. (Great Filmmakers Ser.). 80p. (YA). (gr. 8-11). lib. bdg. 35.64 (978-1-62712-951-0(0)) Cavendish Square Publishing.

McClellan, Ray. Chris Jericho. 2014. (Wrestling Superstars Ser.). (ENG., Illus.). 24p. (J). (gr. 3-7). 25.95 (978-1-62617-140-4(8), Epic Bks.) Bellwether Media.

McConnell, Craig, ed. Theo Tams: Inside the Music. 2009. (ENG., Illus.). 48p. pap. 14.95 (978-1-894917-84-1(7), Napoleon & Co.) Dundurn CAN. Dist: Ingram Publisher Services.

McMahon, Dave. Sidney Crosby: Hockey's Golden Boy, 1 vol. 2011. (Playmakers Ser.). (ENG., Illus.). 32p. (J). (gr. 3-6). 27.07 (978-1-61714-745-6(1)) ABDO Publishing Co.

McNiven, Kelly. Carly Rae Jepsen. 2013. (ENG., Illus.). 32p. (J). (978-0-7787-0021-0(6)); pap. (978-0-7787-0042-5(9)) Crabtree Publishing Co.

Millar, Ruth. Saskatchewan Heroes & Rogues. 2004. (ENG., Illus.). 240p. (gr. 7-18). pap. 17.95 (978-1-55050-289-3(1)) Coteau Bks. CAN. Dist: Fitzhenry & Whiteside, Ltd.

Morganelli, Adrianna. Rick Hansen: Improving Life for People with Disabilities. 2016. (Illus.). 32p. (J). (978-0-7787-2692-0(4)) Crabtree Publishing Co.

Morrison, Jessica. Wayne Gretzky: Greatness on Ice. 2010. (Crabtree Groundbreaker Biographies Ser.). (ENG., Illus.). 112p. (J). pap. (978-0-7787-2548-0(0)); (gr. 5-8). lib. bdg. (978-0-7787-2539-8(1)) Crabtree Publishing Co.

Mortillaro, Nicole. Connor Mcdavid. 2015. (Hockey Superstars Ser.). (ENG., Illus.). 32p. (gr. 3-9). lib. bdg. 27.99 (978-1-4914-9021-1(7)) Capstone Press of Coughlan Cos.

—Something to Prove: The Story of Hockey Tough Guy Bobby Clarke, 1 vol. 2010. (Lorimer Recordbooks Ser.). (ENG., Illus.). 96p. (gr. 8-12). 16.95 (978-1-55277-481-6(3), 9781552774816); pap. 9.95 (978-1-55277-480-9(5), 9781552774809) Lorimer, James & Co., Ltd., Pubs. CAN. Dist: Casemate Pubs. & Bk. Distributors, LLC.

—Willie O'Ree: The Story of the First Black Player in the NHL, 1 vol. 2012. (Lorimer Recordbooks Ser.). (ENG., Illus.). (YA). (gr. 7-12). 118p. 16.95 (978-1-4594-0196-9(4), 9781459401969); 120p. pap. 9.95 (978-1-4594-0195-2(6), 9781459401952) Lorimer, James & Co., Ltd., Pubs. CAN. Dist: Casemate Pubs. & Bk. Distributors, LLC.

Nagelhout, Ryan. Sidney Crosby. 2016. (Sports MVPs Ser.). 24p. (J). (gr. 2-1). 22.60 (978-1-4824-4643-2(X)) Stevens, Gareth Publishing LLLP.

Nagle, Jeanne. Sidney Crosby: One of the NHL's Top Scorers. 2015. (Living Legends of Sports Ser.). (ENG.). 48p. (J). (gr. 5-6). pap. 14.05 (978-1-68048-125-9(8), Britannica Educational Publishing) Rosen Publishing Group, Inc., The.

Nicholson, Lorna Schultz. Winning Gold: Canada's Incredible 2002 Olympic Victory in Women's Hockey, 1 vol. 2009. (Lorimer Recordbooks Ser.). (ENG., Illus.). 112p. (J). (gr. 8-12). pap. 9.95 (978-1-55277-472-4(4), 9781552774724) Lorimer, James & Co., Ltd., Pubs. CAN. Dist: Casemate Pubs. & Bk. Distributors, LLC.

Older, Jules. Snowmobile: Bombardier's Dream Machine. Lauritano, Michael, illus. 2012. (ENG.). 64p. (J). (gr. 3-7). pap. 6.95 (978-1-58089-335-0(X)) Charlesbridge Publishing, Inc.

Osier, Dan. Steve Nash. 2011. (Basketball's MVPs Ser.). 24p. (J). (ENG.). pap. 8.85 (978-1-4488-2634-6(9)); (Illus.). (gr. 3-6). lib. bdg. 22.60 (978-1-4488-2525-7(3)) Rosen Publishing Group, Inc., The. (PowerKids Pr.).

Otfinoski, Steve. Drake: Actor & Hip-Hop Artist, 1 vol. 2013. (Contemporary Lives Set 2 Ser.). (ENG.). 112p. (J). (gr. 6-12). lib. bdg. 35.64 (978-1-61783-618-3(4), Essential Library) ABDO Publishing Co.

Owens, Ann-Maureen & Yealland, Jane. Canadian Exploration. Mantha, John, illus. 2008. (Kids Book Of Ser.). (ENG.). 56p. (J). (gr. 3-7). pap. 14.95 (978-1-55453-257-5(4)) Kids Can Pr., Ltd. CAN. Dist: Hachette Bk. Group.

Peppas, Lynn. Justin Bieber. 2011. (ENG.). 32p. (J). pap. (978-0-7787-7612-3(3)); (gr. 3-6). lib. bdg. (978-0-7787-7607-9(7)) Crabtree Publishing Co.

Pezzi, Bryan. Craig Kielburger. 2010. (Illus.). 24p. (978-1-77071-597-4(5)); pap. (978-1-77071-603-2(3)) Weigl Educational Pubs. Ltd.

—Craig Kielburger: Ma Vie. Karvonen, Tanjah, tr. from ENG. 2011. (FRE., Illus.). 24p. (YA). (gr. 2-4). (978-1-77071-428-1(6)) Weigl Educational Pubs. Ltd.

—David Suzuki. 2010. (Illus.). 24p. (978-1-77071-595-0(9)); pap. (978-1-77071-601-8(7)) Weigl Educational Pubs. Ltd.

—David Suzuki: Ma Vie. Karvonen, Tanjah, tr. from ENG. 2011. (FRE., Illus.). 24p. (YA). (gr. 2-4). (978-1-77071-429-8(4)) Weigl Educational Pubs. Ltd.

—Emily Carr. 2010. (Illus.). 24p. (978-1-77071-599-8(1)); pap. (978-1-77071-605-6(X)) Weigl Educational Pubs. Ltd.

—Terry Fox. 2010. (Illus.). 24p. (978-1-77071-598-1(3)); pap. (978-1-77071-604-9(1)) Weigl Educational Pubs. Ltd.

—Terry Fox: Ma Vie. Karvonen, Tanjah, tr. from ENG. 2011. (FRE., Illus.). 24p. (YA). (gr. 2-4). (978-1-77071-431-1(6)) Weigl Educational Pubs. Ltd.

Powell, Marie. Explore with Jacques Cartier. 2014. (ENG., Illus.). 32p. (J). pap. (978-0-7787-1432-3(2)) Crabtree Publishing Co.

Rabjohn, R. H. & Wilson, John. A Soldier's Sketchbook: The Illustrated First World War Diary of R.H. Rabjohn. 2017. (ENG., Illus.). 112p. (J). (gr. 5). 16.99 (978-1-77049-854-9(0), Tundra Bks.) Tundra Bks. CAN. Dist: Penguin Random Hse. LLC.

Rajczak, Kristen. Justin Bieber. 2011. (Rising Stars Ser.). (Illus.). 32p. (J). (gr. 3-6). pap. 10.50 (978-1-4339-5896-0(1)); lib. bdg. 25.25 (978-1-4339-5894-6(5)) Stevens, Gareth Publishing LLLP.

Robertson, David. The Ballad of Nancy April: Shawnadithit. Henderson, Scott B., illus. 2014. (Tales from Big Spirit Ser.: 6). (ENG.). 32p. (J). (gr. 4-6). pap. (978-1-55379-477-6(X), 7a5bbbca-e620-446e-8c13-29bf73a0b984, HighWater Pr.) Portage & Main Pr.

—The Scout: Tommy Prince. Henderson, Scott B., illus. 2014. (Tales from Big Spirit Ser.: 6). (ENG.). 32p. (J). (gr. 4-6). pap. (978-1-55379-478-3(8), 78912685-2d85-4153-9f88-b7d8feb31ffe, HighWater Pr.) Portage & Main Pr.

—The Slave Woman: Thanadelthur. Tien, Wai, illus. 2014. (Tales from Big Spirit Ser.: 6). (ENG.). 32p. (J). (gr. 4-6). pap. (978-1-55379-479-0(6), 51f7764c-c947-4547-8ce4-63887e0f4e03, HighWater Pr.) Portage & Main Pr.

Robertson, Sebastian. Rock & Roll Highway: The Robbie Robertson Story. Gustavson, Adam, illus. 2014. (ENG.). 40p. (J). (gr. 1-4). 17.99 (978-0-8050-9473-2(3), 9780805094732, Holt, Henry & Co. Bks. For Young Readers) Holt, Henry & Co.

Roza, Greg. Sidney Crosby. 2011. (Today's Sports Greats Ser.). (Illus.). 32p. (gr. 4-6). (J). pap. 10.50 (978-1-4339-5876-2(7), Gareth Stevens Learning Library); (YA). lib. bdg. 26.60 (978-1-4339-5874-8(0)) Stevens, Gareth Publishing LLLP.

Rudnicki, Richard. Cyrus Eaton, 1 vol. 2016. (ENG., Illus.). 40p. (J). (gr. 2-7). 19.95 (978-1-77108-396-6(4)) Nimbus Publishing, Ltd. CAN. Dist: Orca Bk. Pubs. USA.

Saddleback Educational Publishing Staff. Drake, 1 vol. 2013. (Hip-Hop Biographies Ser.). (ENG.). 48p. (YA). (gr. 9-12). 11.95 (978-1-62250-013-0(X)) Saddleback Educational Publishing, Inc.

Saunders, Gary L. My Life with Trees: A Sylvan Journey. 2015. (ENG.). 256p. pap. (978-1-55447-151-5(6)) Gaspereau Pr.

Savage, Jeff. Sidney Crosby. 2009. (Amazing Athletes Ser.). (gr. 2-5). (J). 23.93 (978-0-7613-4054-6(8)); (ENG.). 32p. pap. 7.95 (978-0-7613-4139-0(0), First Avenue Editions) Lerner Publishing Group.

Sawyer, Sarah. Avril Lavigne. 48p. 2009. (Illus.). (gr. 7-12). pap. 11.75 (978-1-4358-5128-3(5), Rosen Classroom) 2009. (gr. 6-6). 53.00 (978-1-61511-923-3(X)) 2008. (Illus.). (J). lib. bdg. 29.25 (978-1-4042-1820-8(3)) Rosen Publishing Group, Inc., The.

Schwartzenberger, Tina. Don Cherry. 2010. (Illus.). 24p. (978-1-77071-625-4(4)) Weigl Educational Pubs. Ltd.

Shardlow, Tom & Wysotski, Chrissie. Mapping the Wilderness: The Story of David Thompson. 2006. (Stories of Canada Ser.: 9). (ENG., Illus.). 72p. (J). 18.95 (978-0-929141-85-5(7), Napoleon & Co.) Dundurn CAN. Dist: Ingram Publisher Services.

Singh, Rina. Pitseolak Ashoona: Une Artiste Inuite. 2004. (FRE., Illus.). (J). (978-2-7650-0741-8(1)) Les Editions de la Cheneliere, Inc.

Sjonger, Rebecca. Knockout! How "Little Giant" Tommy Burns Became the World Heavyweight Champion, 1 vol. 2008. (Lorimer Recordbooks Ser.). (ENG., Illus.). 136p. (J). (gr. 2-12). 16.95 (978-1-55277-004-7(4), 9781552770047); (gr. 7-12). 9.95 (978-1-55277-003-0(6), 9781552770030) Lorimer, James & Co., Ltd., Pubs. CAN. Dist: Casemate Pubs. & Bk. Distributors, LLC.

Skrypuch, Marsha Forchuk. Last Airlift: A Vietnamese Orphan's Rescue from War. 2013. (ENG., Illus.). 120p. (J). (gr. 3-7). pap. 9.95 (978-0-9869495-1-7(5)) Pajama Pr. CAN. Dist: Ingram Publisher Services.

—One Step at a Time: A Vietnamese Child Finds Her Way. (ENG., Illus.). 128p. (J). (gr. 3-7). 2014. pap. 12.95 (978-1-927485-02-6(9)) 2013. 13.95 (978-1-927485-01-9(0)) Pajama Pr. CAN. Dist: Ingram Publisher Services.

Spray, John. Next Round: A Young Athlete's Journey to Gold. 2016. (ENG., Illus.). 112p. (J). (gr. 5-9). pap. 9.95 (978-1-77278-001-7(4)) Pajama Pr. CAN. Dist: Ingram Publisher Services.

St. Stephen's Community House Staff. It's Not All Black & White: Multiracial Youth Speak Out. 2012. (ENG., Illus.). 120p. (YA). (gr. 7-12). pap. 12.95 (978-1-55451-380-2(4), 9781554513802) Annick Pr., Ltd. CAN. Dist: Publishers Group West (PGW).

Staunton, Ted. The Dreadful Truth: Canadian Crime. Geoffroi, Remie, illus. 2006. (Dreadful Truth Ser.). (ENG.). 104p. (J). (gr. 3-8). (978-0-88780-705-3(4)) Formac Publishing Co., Ltd.

Sutoski, Jennifer. Barbara Reid. 2015. (Canadian Biographies Ser.). (ENG., Illus.). 24p. (gr. k-1). lib. bdg. 26.65 (978-1-4914-7838-7(1), Pebble Plus) Capstone Press of Coughlan Cos.

—Canadian Biographies Set 2. 2015. (Canadian Biographies Ser.). (ENG.). 24p. (gr. k-1). lib. bdg. 159.90 (978-1-4914-7839-4(X), Pebble Plus) Capstone Press of Coughlan Cos.

—Carey Price. 2015. (Canadian Biographies Ser.). (ENG., Illus.). 24p. (gr. k-1). lib. bdg. 26.65 (978-1-4914-7835-6(7), Pebble Plus) Capstone Press of Coughlan Cos.

—Hedley. 2015. (Canadian Biographies Ser.). (ENG., Illus.). 24p. (gr. k-1). lib. bdg. 26.65 (978-1-4914-7837-0(3), Pebble Plus) Capstone Press of Coughlan Cos.

—Patrick Chan. 2015. (Canadian Biographies Ser.). (ENG., Illus.). 24p. (gr. k-1). lib. bdg. 26.65 (978-1-4914-7834-9(9), Pebble Plus) Capstone Press of Coughlan Cos.

—Stephen Harper. 2015. (Canadian Biographies Ser.). (ENG.). 24p. (gr. k-1). lib. bdg. 26.65 (978-1-4914-7833-2(0), Pebble Plus) Capstone Press of Coughlan Cos.

Sutoski, Jennifer & Donaldson, Chelsea. Canadian Biographies: Set 1-2. 2015. (Canadian Biographies Ser.). (ENG.). 24p. (gr. k-1). pap. 69.50 (978-1-4914-7848-6(9), Pebble Plus) Capstone Press of Coughlan Cos.

—Canadian Biographies Set 1-2. 2015. (Canadian Biographies Ser.). (ENG.). 24p. (gr. k-1). lib. bdg. 266.50 (978-1-4914-7840-0(3), Pebble Plus) Capstone Press of Coughlan Cos.

Ternier Gordon, Irene. Grey Owl (Junior Edition) 2007. (Amazing Stories Junior Ser.). (Illus.). 96p. pap. (978-1-55439-723-5(5)) Altitude Publishing Canada Ltd.

Tieck, Sarah. Carly Rae Jepsen: Pop Star, 1 vol. 2013. (Big Buddy Biographies Set 10 Ser.). (ENG.). 32p. (J). (gr. 2-5). lib. bdg. 28.50 (978-1-61783-858-3(6), Big Buddy Bks.) ABDO Publishing Co.

—Justin Bieber: Pop Music Superstar, 1 vol. 2012. (Big Buddy Biographies Ser.). (ENG.). 32p. (J). (gr. 2-5). 28.50 (978-1-61783-224-6(3)) ABDO Publishing Co.

—Justin Bieber: Singing Sensation, 1 vol. 2010. (Big Buddy Bks.). (ENG.). 32p. (J). (gr. 2-5). 28.50 (978-1-61613-974-2(9)) ABDO Publishing Co.

Toyne, Jessica. Justin Bieber. 2015. (Pop Icons Ser.). (Illus.). 64p. (J). (gr. 7). lib. bdg. 23.95 (978-1-4222-3247-7(6)) Mason Crest.

Tracy, Kathleen. Justin Bieber. 2010. (Robbie Reader Ser.). (Illus.). 32p. (YA). (gr. 2-5). lib. bdg. 25.70 (978-1-58415-895-0(6)) Mitchell Lane Pubs., Inc.

Upjohn, Rebecca, et al. Patrick's Wish, 1 vol. 2010. (ENG., Illus.). 24p. (J). (gr. 1-3). 7.95 (978-1-897187-70-8(X)) Second Story Pr. CAN. Dist: Orca Bk. Pubs. USA.

Wallace, Ian. The Slippers' Keeper, 1 vol. 2015. (ENG., Illus.). 36p. (J). (gr. k-3). 18.95 (978-1-55498-414-5(9)) Groundwood Bks. CAN. Dist: Publishers Group West (PGW).

Warner, Jody Nyasha. Viola Desmond Won't Be Budged, 1 vol. Rudnicki, Richard & Junaid, Bushra, illus. 2010. (ENG.). 32p. (J). (gr. k-4). 18.95 (978-0-88899-779-1(5)) Groundwood Bks. CAN. Dist: Publishers Group West (PGW).

Watson, Cindy. Out of Darkness: The Jeff Healey Story. 2010. (ENG., Illus.). 144p. (YA). (gr. k-6). pap. 19.99 (978-1-55488-706-4(2), 9781554887064) Dundurn CAN. Dist: Ingram Publisher Services.

Wearing, Judy. Roberta Bondar: Canada's First Woman in Space. 2010. (Crabtree Groundbreaker Biographies Ser.). (ENG., Illus.). 112p. (J). (gr. 5-8). lib. bdg. (978-0-7787-2540-4(5)) Crabtree Publishing Co.

Weaver, Janice. Hudson. Craig, David, illus. 2010. (ENG.). 48p. (J). (gr. 3-7). 22.95 (978-0-88776-814-9(8), Tundra Bks.) Tundra Bks. CAN. Dist: Penguin Random Hse. LLC.

Whitfield, Simon & Dheensaw, Cleve. Simon Says Gold: Simon Whitfield's Pursuit of Athletic Excellence, 1 vol. 2009. (ENG., Illus.). 128p. (J). (gr. 5-12). pap. 14.00 (978-1-55469-141-8(9)) Orca Bk. Pubs. USA.

Wilson, Janet. Severn & the Day She Silenced the World, 1 vol. 2014. (Kids' Power Book Ser.: 5). (ENG., Illus.). 184p. (J). (gr. 6-8). pap. 14.95 (978-1-927583-23-4(3)) Second Story Pr. CAN. Dist: Orca Bk. Pubs. USA.

—Shannen & the Dream for a School, 1 vol. 2011. (Kids' Power Ser.). (ENG & CRE., Illus.). 132p. (J). (gr. 6-8). pap. 14.95 (978-1-926920-30-6(9)) Second Story Pr. CAN. Dist: Orca Bk. Pubs. USA.

Yasuda, Anita. Hannah Taylor. 2011. 24p. (YA). (gr. 2-4). (978-1-77071-646-9(7)); pap. (978-1-77071-650-6(5)) Weigl Educational Pubs. Ltd.

—Hannah Taylor: Ma Vie. Karvonen, Tanjah, tr. from ENG. 2011. (FRE., Illus.). 24p. (YA). (gr. 2-4). (978-1-77071-434-2(0)) Weigl Educational Pubs. Ltd.

—Justin Bieber. 2011. 24p. (YA). (gr. 2-4). (978-1-77071-647-6(5)); pap. (978-1-77071-651-3(3)) Weigl Educational Pubs. Ltd.

—Justin Bieber. 2011. (J). (gr. 4-6). pap. 12.95 (978-1-61690-672-6(3), AV2 by Weigl); (Illus.). 24p. (YA). (gr. 3-6). 27.13 (978-1-61690-667-2(7)) Weigl Pubs., Inc.

—Justin Bieber: Ma Vie. Karvonen, Tanjah, tr. from ENG. 2011. (FRE., Illus.). 24p. (YA). (gr. 2-4). (978-1-77071-432-8(4)) Weigl Educational Pubs. Ltd.

—Mike Meyers. 2012. (J). (978-1-61913-587-1(6)); pap. (978-1-61913-593-2(0)) Weigl Pubs., Inc.

C D

—Nikki Yanofsky. 2011. 24p. (YA). (gr. 2-4). pap. *(978-1-77071-652-0(1))* Weigl Educational Pubs. Ltd.

—Nikki Yanofsky: Ma Vie. Karvonen, Tanjah, tr. from ENG. 2011. (FRE., Illus.). 24p. (YA). (gr. 2-4). *(978-1-77071-433-5(2))* Weigl Educational Pubs. Ltd.

Zweig, Eric. Star Power: The Legend & Lore of Cyclone Taylor, 1 vol. 2007. (Lorimer Recordbooks Ser.). (ENG., Illus.). 104p. (YA). (gr. 4-8). 8.95 *(978-1-55028-995-4(0),* 9781550289954); *(978-1-55028-997-8(7))* Lorimer, James & Co., Ltd., Pubs. CAN. Dist: Casemate Pubs. & Bk. Distributors, LLC.

CANADA—DISCOVERY AND EXPLORATION

see America—Discovery and Exploration

CANADA—FICTION

Aksomitis, Linda. Adeline's Dream, 1 vol. 2005. (From Many Peoples Ser.). (ENG.). 216p. (J). (gr. 4-7). per. 7.95 *(978-1-55050-323-4(5))* Coteau Bks. CAN. Dist: Orca Bk. Pubs. USA.

Alma, Ann. Skateway to Freedom. 2nd ed. 2008. (ENG.). 136p. (YA). (gr. 5-8). pap. 11.99 *(978-1-55002-719-8(0))* Dundurn CAN. Dist: Ingram Publisher Services.

Ames, Allison. Susie & Sasha's Tea Party, 1 vol. 2010. 48p. 24.95 *(978-1-4489-4895-6(9))* PublishAmerica, Inc.

Anderson, Laurie Halse. Acting Out, 14 vols. 2012. (Vet Volunteers Ser.: 14). (ENG.). 144p. (J). (gr. 3-7). pap. 6.99 *(978-0-14-241676-1(2),* Puffin Books) Penguin Young Readers Group.

Anderson, Susannah. Susie. 2010. 60p. pap. 8.50 *(978-1-4116-2175-6(1))* Lulu Pr., Inc.

Andrews, Jan. When Apples Grew Noses & White Horses Flew: Tales of Ti-Jean, 1 vol. Petricic, Dusan, illus. 2011. (ENG.). 72p. (J). (gr. 1-5). 16.95 *(978-0-88899-952-8(6))* Groundwood Bks. CAN. Dist: Publishers Group West (PGW).

Arkin, Alan. Cassie Loves Beethoven. l.t. ed. 2003. (Children's Large Print Ser.). 28.95 *(978-1-58118-108-1(6))* LRS.

Armstrong, Kelley. The Gathering. (Darkness Rising Ser.: 1). (YA). (gr. 8). 2012. 384p. pap. 9.99 *(978-0-06-179703-3(0))* 2011. 368p. 17.99 *(978-0-06-179702-6(2))* HarperCollins Pubs.

—The Gathering. (Darkness Rising Ser.: Bk. 1). (YA). 1.25 *(978-1-4498-6189-6(X));* 100.75 *(978-1-4498-6186-5(5));* 2013. 102.75 *(978-1-4498-6184-1(9))* Recorded Bks., Inc.

—The Rising. 2013. (Darkness Rising Ser.: 3). 416p. (YA). (gr. 8). 17.99 *(978-0-06-179708-8(1))* HarperCollins Pubs.

Austen, Catherine. Walking Backward, 1 vol. 2009. (ENG., Illus.). 176p. (J). (gr. 4-7). pap. 9.95 *(978-1-55469-147-0(8))* Orca Bk. Pubs. USA.

Badoe, Adwoa. Nana's Cold Days, 1 vol. Junaid, Bushra, illus. 2009. (ENG.). 24p. (J). (gr. k-k). pap. 6.95 *(978-0-88899-937-5(2))* Groundwood Bks. CAN. Dist: Publishers Group West (PGW).

Banks, Lynne Reid. Uprooted - A Canadian War Story. 2015. (ENG.). 336p. (J). pap. 8.99 *(978-0-00-813235-4(6),* HarperCollins Children's Bks.) HarperCollins Pubs. Ltd. GBR. Dist: HarperCollins Pubs.

Bannatyne-Cugnet, Jo. The Day I Became a Canadian: A Citizenship Scrapbook. Zhang, Song Nan, illus. 2008. (ENG.). 24p. (J). (gr. 2-4). pap. 10.95 *(978-0-88776-892-7(X),* Tundra Bks.) Tundra Bks. CAN. Dist: Penguin Random Hse. LLC.

Bauer, A. C. E. Gil Marsh. 2013. (ENG.). 192p. (YA). (gr. 7). pap. 7.99 *(978-0-375-87374-4(0),* Ember) Random Hse. Children's Bks.

Bayle, B. J. Red River Rising: A Novel (Large Print 16pt) 2013. 332p. (gr. 5-8). pap. *(978-1-4596-6330-5(6))* ReadHowYouWant.com, Ltd.

—Shadow Riders. 2010. (ENG.). 256p. (YA). (gr. 7). pap. 10.99 *(978-1-55488-724-8(0))* Dundurn CAN. Dist: Ingram Publisher Services.

Beaty, Mary, et al. George Johnson's War, 1 vol. 2003. (ENG., Illus.). 224p. (J). (gr. 7-18). pap. 8.95 *(978-0-88899-468-4(0))* Groundwood Bks. CAN. Dist: Publishers Group West (PGW).

Beemink, Joe. Nowhere Wild. 2015. (ENG.). 304p. (J). 17.99 *(978-1-4434-2243-7(6))* HarperCollins Pubs.

Beha, Eileen. Tango: The Tale of an Island Dog. 2010. (ENG.). 256p. (YA). (gr. 3-6). pap. 7.99 *(978-1-59990-485-6(3),* 9781599904856, Bloomsbury USA Childrens) Bloomsbury Publishing USA.

Belaney, Archibald Stansfeld. On the Trail: Pages from the Writings of Grey Owl. Reynolds, E. E., ed. 2011. (ENG.). 130p. pap. 21.99 *(978-1-107-60015-7(4))* Cambridge Univ. Pr.

Belasen, Amy & Osborn, Jacob. Jenny Green's Killer Junior Year. 2008. (ENG.). 304p. (YA). (gr. 9-18). pap. 14.99 *(978-1-4169-6792-7(3),* Simon Pulse) Simon Pulse.

Bell, Loman. Old Glory Faces the Hurricane. Bell, Loman, illus. 2013. (Illus.). 46p. pap. *(978-0-9918033-2-3(9))* Wood Islands Prints.

Benton, Doug. The Hummingbird Goose, 1 vol. 2009. 64p. pap. 19.95 *(978-1-61546-746-4(7))* America Star Bks.

Bioletti, Lucy. Nanabozho & the Maple Trees: A Tale from Canada. Molinari, Carlo, illus. 2016. 24p. (J). pap. *(978-1-927244-64-7(1))* Flying Start Bks.

—Nanabozho & the Maple Trees (Big Book Edition) A Tale from Canada. 2016. (ENG., Illus.). 24p. (J). pap. *(978-1-927244-74-6(9))* Flying Start Bks.

Blum, Vicki. Spitt to the Rescue. unabr. ed. 2004. 115p. (J). (gr. 3-6). pap. 7.95 *(978-1-932280-59-3(6),* 80596) Granite Publishing & Distribution.

Boeve, Eunice. The Summer of the Crow. 2013. 306p. pap. 14.95 *(978-1-939054-06-7(0))* Rowe Publishing and Design.

Boissery, Beverley. Sophie's Rebellion. 2005. (ENG.). 224p. (J). pap. 12.99 *(978-1-55002-566-8(X))* Dundurn CAN. Dist: Ingram Publisher Services.

Bourgeois, Paulette. Postal Workers. LaFave, Kim, illus. 2005. 32p. (J). lib. bdg. 15.38 *(978-1-4242-1192-0(1))* Fitzgerald Bks.

Brandeis, Madeline. Little Anne of Canad. 2011. 176p. 42.95 *(978-1-258-09048-7(1))* Literary Licensing, LLC.

Breen, Krista Michelle. Hardware - the Trouble with Phillip. 2013. 160p. pap. *(978-0-9735241-1-6(1))* Groundskeeper's Cottage.

Brennan, Ann. The Hawthorn Bush. 2005. (Illus.). 163p. pap. *(978-0-88887-316-3(6))* Borealis Pr.

Brooks, Bertha. The Big Fishing Trip. 2004. (Illus.). 32p. (J). 12.00 *(978-1-58374-086-6(4))* Chicago Spectrum Pr.

Brooks, Martha. Bone Dance, 1 vol. 2005. (ENG.). 184p. (J). (gr. 6-16). pap. 8.95 *(978-0-88899-336-6(6))* Groundwood Bks. CAN. Dist: Publishers Group West (PGW).

Brouwer, Sigmund. Devil's Pass, 1 vol. 2012. (Seven (the Series) Ser.). (ENG., Illus.). 256p. (J). (gr. 5-10). pap. 9.95 *(978-1-55469-938-4(X))* Orca Bk. Pubs. USA.

—Tiger Threat, 1 vol. 2006. (Orca Sports Ser.). (ENG.). 176p. (YA). (gr. 6-10). per. 9.95 *(978-1-55143-639-5(6))* Orca Bk. Pubs. USA.

Brown, Jeff. The Intrepid Canadian Expedition. Pamintuan, Macky, illus. 2009. (Flat Stanley's Worldwide Adventures Ser.: 4). (ENG.). 112p. (J). (gr. 2-5). 15.99 *(978-0-06-142997-2(X))* HarperCollins Pubs.

—The Intrepid Canadian Expedition. 2009. (Flat Stanley's Worldwide Adventures Ser.: 4). (J). lib. bdg. 14.75 *(978-0-606-10068-7(7),* Turtleback) Turtleback Bks.

—The Intrepid Canadian Expedition Vol. 4. Pamintuan, Macky, illus. 2009. (Flat Stanley's Worldwide Adventures Ser.: 4). (ENG.). 112p. (J). (gr. 2-5). pap. 4.99 *(978-0-06-142996-5(1))* HarperCollins Pubs.

Bruchac, Joseph. Crazy Horse's Vision. Nelson, S. D., illus. 2006. (gr. 1-4). 20.45 *(978-0-7569-6691-1(4))* Perfection Learning Corp.

Buffie, Margaret. Who Is Frances Rain? 20th ed. 2007. (ENG.). 184p. (J). (gr. 7-9). 7.95 *(978-1-55453-209-4(4))* Kids Can Pr., Ltd. CAN. Dist: Hachette Bk. Group.

Campbell, Nicola I. Shin-Chi's Canoe. LaFave, Kim, illus. 2008. (ENG.). 40p. (J). (gr. -1-2). 18.95 *(978-0-88899-857-6(0))* Groundwood Bks. CAN. Dist: Publishers Group West (PGW).

Carter, Anne Laurel. Under a Prairie Sky, 1 vol. Daniel, Alan & Daniel, Lea, illus. 2004. (ENG.). 32p. (J). (gr. -1-3). pap. 7.95 *(978-1-55143-282-3(X))* Orca Bk. Pubs. USA.

Chan, Marty. The Mystery of the Graffiti Ghoul. 2006. (ENG.). 192p. (J). per. 10.95 *(978-1-897235-00-3(3))* Thistledown Pr., Ltd. CAN. Dist: Univ. of Toronto Pr.

Charles, Veronika Martenova. It's Not about the Apple! Parkins, David, illus. 2010. (Easy-To-Read Wonder Tales Ser.). (ENG.). 64p. (J). (gr. k-3). pap. 5.95 *(978-0-88776-955-9(1),* Tundra Bks.) Tundra Bks. CAN. Dist: Penguin Random Hse. LLC.

—It's Not about the Crumbs! Parkins, David, illus. 2010. (Easy-To-Read Wonder Tales Ser.). (ENG.). 64p. (J). (gr. k-3). pap. 5.95 *(978-0-88776-953-5(5),* Tundra Bks.) Tundra Bks. CAN. Dist: Penguin Random Hse. LLC.

—It's Not about the Hunter! Parkins, David, illus. 2010. (Easy-To-Read Wonder Tales Ser.). (ENG.). 56p. (J). (gr. k-3). pap. 5.95 *(978-0-88776-948-1(9),* Tundra Bks.) Tundra Bks. CAN. Dist: Penguin Random Hse. LLC.

—It's Not about the Pumpkin! Parkins, David, illus. 2010. (Easy-To-Read Wonder Tales Ser.). (ENG.). 64p. (J). (gr. k-3). pap. 5.95 *(978-0-88776-949-8(7),* Tundra Bks.) Tundra Bks. CAN. Dist: Penguin Random Hse. LLC.

—It's Not about the Rose! Parkins, David, illus. 2010. (Easy-To-Read Wonder Tales Ser.). (ENG.). 64p. (J). (gr. k-3). pap. 5.95 *(978-0-88776-954-2(3),* Tundra Bks.) Tundra Bks. CAN. Dist: Penguin Random Hse. LLC.

Childress, Mildred Tickfer. Esmerelda the Silly Goose. Zipperer, Susan Johnson, illus. 2004. 52p. (J). (gr. -1-3). 11.95 *(978-1-887774-17-8(3),* Wynden) Canmore Pr.

Citra, Becky. Strawberry Moon, 1 vol., Vol. 5. 2005. (Orca Young Readers Ser.: Book #5). (ENG., Illus.). 96p. (J). (gr. 3-6). per. 5.95 *(978-1-55143-367-7(2))* Orca Bk. Pubs. USA.

Cook, Jacqueline. The Little Bear Who Worried Too Much: Suzie Bear Goes to London. 2011. 34p. (gr. 1-4). pap. 13.50 *(978-1-60976-875-1(2),* Eloquent Bks.) Strategic Book Publishing & Rights Agency (SBPRA).

Cooper, Susan. The Boggart. 2004. 196p. (gr. 3-7). 17.00 *(978-0-7569-3932-8(1))* Perfection Learning Corp.

Cumyn, Alan. The Secret Life of Owen Skye. 2nd ed. 2008. (ENG.). 176p. (J). (gr. 3-7). pap. 9.95 *(978-0-88899-867-5(8))* Groundwood Bks. CAN. Dist: Publishers Group West (PGW).

Curtis, Christopher Paul. The Madman of Piney Woods. (Illus.). (J). 2016. (ENG.). 384p. (gr. 3-7). pap. 7.99 *(978-0-545-15665-3(3))* 2014. 363p. *(978-0-545-63376-5(1))* 2014. (ENG., 384p. (gr. 3-7). 16.99 *(978-0-545-15664-6(5))* Scholastic, Inc. (Scholastic Pr.).

Cutting, Michael. Goosebumps Mixed Floor. 2003. (Illus.). 19p. (J). 266.50 *(978-0-590-55093-2(4))* Scholastic, Inc.

Dance, Jennifer. Red Wolf. 2014. (ENG., Illus.). 256p. (YA). pap. 12.99 *(978-1-4597-0810-5(5),* 9781459708105) Dundurn CAN. Dist: Ingram Publisher Services.

Davidge, James. Driftwood Ellesmere. Palmer, Judd, illus. 2010. (Driftwood Saga Ser.). (ENG.). 216p. (J). (gr. 8-12). 7.95 *(978-1-896209-61-4(5))* Bayeux Arts, Inc. CAN. Dist: Chicago Distribution Ctr.

Dekker, James. Scum, 1 vol. 2008. (Orca Soundings Ser.). (ENG.). 112p. (YA). (gr. 8-12). pap. 9.95 *(978-1-55143-924-2(7))* Orca Bk. Pubs. USA.

Dekker, James C. Scum, 1 vol. 2008. (Orca Soundings Ser.). (ENG.). 112p. (YA). (gr. 8-12). 16.95 *(978-1-55143-926-6(3))* Orca Bk. Pubs. USA.

Dell, Pamela. Half-Breed: A Story of Two Boys During the Klondike Gold Rush. 2003. (Scrapbooks of America Ser.). (ENG., Illus.). 48p. (J). (gr. 3-6). 32.79 *(978-1-59187-044-9(5),* 200809) Child's World, Inc., The.

Denman, K. L. Mirror Image, 1 vol. 2007. (Orca Currents Ser.). (ENG.). 128p. (J). (gr. 5-9). per. 9.95 *(978-1-55143-665-4(5))* Orca Bk. Pubs. USA.

Diamond, Corinna. The Mystical Manifestations of Morgan. 2012. 16p. pap. 7.99 *(978-1-4525-6321-3(7))* Balboa Pr.

Doupe, Pauline Wood. My Arctic Circle of Friends. Fawcett, Vicki, illus. Belair, Brenda Brousseau, photos by. 2009. 24p. pap. 16.98 *(978-1-4251-8097-3(3))* Trafford Publishing.

Dowding, Philippa. The Gargoyle at the Gates. 2012. (Lost Gargoyle Ser.: 3). (ENG.). 192p. (J). pap. 10.99 *(978-1-4597-0394-0(4),* 9781459703940) Dundurn CAN. Dist: Ingram Publisher Services.

Doyle, Brian. Boy O'Boy, 1 vol. 2005. (ENG.). 162p. (YA). pap. 6.95 *(978-0-88899-654-1(3))* Groundwood Bks. CAN. Dist: Publishers Group West (PGW).

—Easy Avenue, 1 vol. 2nd ed. 2004. (ENG.). 122p. (YA). pap. 6.95 *(978-0-88899-605-3(5))* Groundwood Bks. CAN. Dist: Publishers Group West (PGW).

—Hey, Dad!, 1 vol. 3rd ed. 2006. (ENG.). 112p. (J). (gr. 4-8). pap. 6.95 *(978-0-88899-708-1(6))* Groundwood Bks. CAN. Dist: Publishers Group West (PGW).

—Mary Ann Alice. braille ed. 2003. (J). (gr. 2). spiral bd. *(978-0-616-15266-9(3))* Canadian National Institute for the Blind/Institut National Canadien pour les Aveugles.

—Mary Ann Alice, 1 vol. 2nd ed. 2003. (ENG.). 168p. (J). (gr. 9-13). pap. 9.95 *(978-0-88899-551-3(2))* Groundwood Bks. CAN. Dist: Publishers Group West (PGW).

—Spud in Winter, 1 vol. 2nd ed. 2006. (ENG.). 140p. (J). (gr. 2-7). pap. 5.95 *(978-0-88899-755-5(8))* Groundwood Bks. CAN. Dist: Publishers Group West (PGW).

—Uncle Ronald, 1 vol. 2nd ed. 2004. (ENG.). 138p. (J). (gr. 4). pap. 9.95 *(978-0-88899-621-3(7))* Groundwood Bks. CAN. Dist: Publishers Group West (PGW).

Durkin, Shawn & Doherty, Catherine. Shola's Game: A Novel. (Illus.). 93p. *(978-1-897039-17-5(4))* High Interest Publishing (HIP).

Dyer, K. C. A Walk Through a Window. 2009. (ENG.). 240p. (J). (gr. 5-7). pap. 12.50 *(978-0-385-66637-4(3),* Doubleday Canada) Penguin Random House Canada Young Readers CAN. Dist: Penguin Random Hse. LLC.

Erdrich, Louise. Chickadee. Erdrich, Louise, illus. 2012. (Birchbark House Ser.: 4). (Illus.). 208p. (J). (gr. 3-7). (ENG.). 16.99 *(978-0-06-057790-2(8));* lib. bdg. 17.89 *(978-0-06-057791-9(6))* HarperCollins Pubs.

Feagan, Robert. Arctic Thunder. 2010. (ENG.). 288p. (YA). (gr. 7). pap. 12.99 *(978-1-55488-700-2(3))* Dundurn CAN. Dist: Ingram Publisher Services.

—Napachee. 2005. 128p. (YA). (gr. 3-8). pap., tchr. ed. *(978-0-88878-403-2(1),* Sandcastle Bks.) Dundurn.

Flitcroft, Jean. The Pacific Giants. 2014. (Cryptid Files Ser.: No. 3). 240p. (gr. 4-8). (J). lib. bdg. 27.93 *(978-1-4677-3266-6(4));* (ENG.). (YA). pap. 7.95 *(978-1-4677-3485-1(3))* Lerner Publishing Group. (Darby Creek).

Francis, Pauline, retold by. White Fang. 2010. (Essential Classics - Adventure Ser.). (Illus.). 48p. pap. *(978-0-237-54101-9(7))* Evans Brothers, Ltd.

Friend, Larry. Icy the Iceberg. Makis, Sidney, illus. 2008. 28p. pap. 13.95 *(978-1-4327-3777-1(5))* Outskirts Pr., Inc.

Gaetz, Dayle Campbell. Something Suspicious in Saskatchewan, 1 vol. 2006. (ENG.). 208p. (J). (gr. 4-7). per. 7.95 *(978-1-55143-565-7(9))* Orca Bk. Pubs. USA.

Gamble, Adam & Adams, David J. Good Night Canada. Kelly, Cooper, illus. 2010. (Good Night Our World Ser.). (ENG.). 28p. (J). (gr. k — 1). bds. 9.95 *(978-1-60219-038-2(0))* Good Night Bks.

Garvie, Maureen. Amy by Any Other Name. 2009. (ENG.). 256p. (YA). (gr. 7-18). pap. *(978-1-55470-142-1(2))* Me to We.

Gary, Paulsen. Hatchet. 2014. (ENG.). 192p. (J). (gr. 3-3). 12.24 *(978-1-63245-105-7(0))* Lectorum Pubns., Inc.

Gilmore, Rachna. Roses for Gita. Priestley, Alice, illus. 2004. 24p. (J). *(978-1-85269-369-5(X)); (978-1-85269-367-1(3))* Mantra Lingua.

Glaze, Dave. The Light-Fingered Gang, 1 vol. 2005. (1912: the Mackenzie Davis Files Ser.). (ENG.). 168p. (J). (gr. 3-7). per. 7.95 *(978-1-55050-326-5(X))* Coteau Bks. CAN. Dist: Orca Bk. Pubs. USA.

Goodwin, Vincent. Wendigo, 1 vol. 2014. (Graphic Horror Set 3 Ser.). (ENG.). 32p. (J). (gr. 5-8). lib. bdg. 28.50 *(978-1-62402-018-6(6),* Graphic Planet) Magic Wagon.

Grovet, Heather. Blondie's Big Ride. 2008. (Illus.). 95p. (J). pap. 5.97 *(978-0-8163-2225-1(2))* Pacific Pr. Publishing Assn.

Gummer, Chiele. A Family of Geese. 2013. 34p. pap. 16.95 *(978-1-4808-0026-7(0))* Archway Publishing.

Gushue, Brenda. Through the Storm, 1 vol. 2009. 48p. pap. 12.95 *(978-1-4489-8898-3(5))* PublishAmerica, Inc.

Halsey, Jacqueline. Bluenose Adventure. Orchard, Eric, illus. 2013. (ENG.). 32p. (J). (gr. -1-3). 16.95 *(978-1-4595-0280-2(9),* 9781459502802) Formac Publishing Co., Ltd. CAN. Dist: Casemate Pubs. & Bk. Distributors, LLC.

Harelkin, Mary. Tunnels of Treachery, 1 vol. 2003. (Moose Jaw Adventure Ser.: Vol. 3). (ENG., Illus.). 304p. (J). (gr. 4-7). pap. 7.95 *(978-1-55050-270-1(0))* Coteau Bks. CAN. Dist: Orca Bk. Pubs. USA.

Harlow, Joan Hiatt. Secret of the Night Ponies. 2009. (ENG.). 336p. (J). (gr. 3-7). 16.99 *(978-1-4169-0783-1(1),* McElderry, Margaret K. Bks.) McElderry, Margaret K. Bks.

Hasiuk, Brenda. Your Constant Star, 1 vol. 2014. (ENG.). 248p. (YA). (gr. 8-12). pap. 12.95 *(978-1-4598-0368-8(X))* Orca Bk. Pubs. USA.

Hébert-Collins, Sheila. Jean-Paul Hébert Was There/Jean-Paul Hébert Etait Là, 1 vol. Bergeron, John W., illus. 2004. (ENG & FRE.). 32p. (J). (gr. k-3). 16.99 *(978-1-56554-928-9(7))* Pelican Publishing Co., Inc.

Heim, Barbara. The Hudson Beavers & the New Neighbourhood. 2012. (ENG.). 42p. (J). pap. 11.95 *(978-1-938586-36-1(0))* Writer's Cramp, Inc.

—The Hudson Beavers Build a Lodge. 2013. (ENG.). 44p. (J). 13.95 *(978-1-938586-45-3(X))* Writer's Cramp, Inc.

Heneghan, James B. Torn Away, 1 vol. 2003. (ENG.). 256p. (YA). (gr. 8-12). pap. 9.95 *(978-1-55143-263-2(3))* Orca Bk. Pubs. USA.

Heywood, La Abuelita Geny. Proto: ¿Qué hacer cuando un dinosaurio nace en tu Jardin? 2010. 52p. pap. 22.49 *(978-1-4490-5628-5(8))* AuthorHouse.

Hobbs, Will. Never Say Die. 224p. (J). (gr. 3-7). 2014. (ENG.). pap. 6.99 *(978-0-06-170880-0(1))* 2013. (ENG.). 16.99 *(978-0-06-170878-7(X))* 2013. lib. bdg. 17.89 *(978-0-06-170879-4(8))* HarperCollins Pubs.

Hodgkins, Dorothy. Darlington's Margaret. 2009. 82p. pap. 12.20 *(978-1-4251-8668-5(8))* Trafford Publishing.

Hoffpauir, J. R. Wibeau Flies! 2013. 26p. pap. 14.95 *(978-1-62838-118-4(3))* Page Publishing Inc.

Hope, Kathleen. Jack Eagle the Pirate & Other Mysterious Tales. 2012. (Illus.). 48p. pap. 24.40 *(978-1-4678-9611-5(X))* AuthorHouse.

Hopkinson, Nalo. The Chaos. (ENG., 256p. (YA). (gr. 9). 2013. Illus.). pap. 9.99 *(978-1-4424-5926-7(3))* 2012. 16.99 *(978-1-4169-5488-0(0))* McElderry, Margaret K. Bks. (McElderry, Margaret K. Bks.).

Horvath, Polly. The Night Garden. 2017. (ENG.). 304p. (J). 16.99 ***(978-0-374-30452-2(1),*** 9780374304522, Farrar, Straus & Giroux (BYR)) Farrar, Straus & Giroux.

Horvath, Polly. Northward to the Moon. 2012. (ENG.). 256p. (J). (gr. 5-8). 7.99 *(978-0-307-92980-8(9),* Yearling) Random Hse. Children's Bks.

Howse, Jennifer. Le Lendemain de Noël: Les Célébrations Canadiennes. Karvonen, Tanjah, tr. from ENG. 2011. (FRE.). 24p. (gr. k-3). *(978-1-77071-395-6(6))* Weigl Educational Pubs. Ltd.

Hrdlitschka, Shelley. Sister Wife, 1 vol. 2008. (ENG.). 280p. (YA). (gr. 7-12). pap. 12.95 *(978-1-55143-927-3(1))* Orca Bk. Pubs. USA.

Humphrey, Anna. Mission (un)Popular. 2013. (ENG.). 416p. (J). (gr. 5-9). pap. 6.99 *(978-1-4231-2321-7(2))* Hyperion Pr.

Innis-Weissneder, Emma May. Silky: The Dog That Saved the Day. Sherrard, Laura, illus. 2008. (ENG.). 65p. pap. 9.00 *(978-1-894372-43-5(3))* DreamCatcher Publishing CAN. Dist: Univ. of Toronto Pr.

Jacobs, Lily. The Littlest Bunny in Canada: An Easter Adventure. Dunn, Robert, illus. 2015. (ENG.). 32p. (J). (-3). 11.99 *(978-1-4926-1045-8(3),* Sourcebooks Jabberwocky) Sourcebooks, Inc.

—The Littlest Bunny in Vancouver: An Easter Adventure. Dunn, Robert, illus. 2015. (ENG.). 32p. (J). (-3). 11.99 *(978-1-4926-1222-3(7),* Sourcebooks Jabberwocky) Sourcebooks, Inc.

James, Eric. A Halloween Scare in Canada. Le Ray, Marina, illus. 2014. (ENG.). 32p. (J). (-5). 9.99 *(978-1-4926-0573-7(5),* 9781492605737, Sourcebooks Jabberwocky) Sourcebooks, Inc.

—A Halloween Scare in Vancouver. Le Ray, Marina, illus. 2015. (ENG.). 32p. (J). (-5). 11.99 *(978-1-4926-2406-6(3),* 9781492624066, Sourcebooks Jabberwocky) Sourcebooks, Inc.

—Santa's Sleigh Is on Its Way to Canada: A Christmas Adventure. Dunn, Robert, illus. 2016. (ENG.). 32p. (J). (-2). 12.99 *(978-1-4926-4321-0(1),* 9781492643210, Sourcebooks Jabberwocky) Sourcebooks, Inc.

—Santa's Sleigh Is on It's Way to Nova Scotia: A Christmas Adventure. Dunn, Robert, illus. 2016. (ENG.). 32p. (J). (-2). 12.99 *(978-1-4926-4508-5(7),* 9781492645085, Sourcebooks Jabberwocky) Sourcebooks, Inc.

Jenkins Bathe, Bettina. Violet the Pilot in Canada. 2004. (Illus.). 20p. (J). 14.35 *(978-1-4120-3215-5(6))* Trafford Publishing.

Johnston, E. K. Prairie Fire. 2015. (J). 18.99 *(978-1-4677-6181-9(8));* (ENG.). 304p. (gr. 6-12). 18.99 *(978-1-4677-3909-2(X))* Lerner Publishing Group.

—The Story of Owen: Dragon Slayer of Trondheim. 2014. 312p. (J). (gr. 6-12). 17.95 *(978-1-4677-1066-4(0),* Carolrhoda Lab™) Lerner Publishing Group.

Johnston, Julie. Hero of Lesser Causes. pap. 6.95 *(978-0-7737-5850-6(X))* Stoddart Kids CAN. Dist: Fitzhenry & Whiteside, Ltd.

—Hero of Lesser Causes. 2003. (ENG.). 232p. (J). (gr. 5). pap. 10.95 *(978-0-88776-649-7(8),* Tundra Bks.) Tundra Bks. CAN. Dist: Penguin Random Hse. LLC.

Johnston, Wayne M. North Fork. 2016. (ENG.). 210p. (YA). (gr. 7-12). pap. 14.95 *(978-1-936364-20-6(4))* Black Heron Pr.

Jones, Wendy Lou. Bastian - Defender of Golden Downs. 2013. 234p. pap. 10.95 *(978-0-9777110-3-1(X))* Royal Knight Inc.

Keeley, Catherine. The Secrets of Phantom Valley. 2003. 101p. (YA). pap. 10.95 *(978-0-7414-1831-9(2))* Infinity Publishing.

Kelly, David A. The Rookie Blue Jay. Meyers, Mark, illus. 2015. (Ballpark Mysteries Ser.: 10). (ENG.). 112p. (J). (gr. 1-4). 4.99 *(978-0-385-37875-8(0),* Random Hse. Bks. for Young Readers) Random Hse. Children's Bks.

Kent, Jennifer McGrath. Chocolate River Rescue, 1 vol. 2007. (ENG.). 112p. (J). (gr. 2-5). pap. 8.95 *(978-1-55109-600-1(5))* Nimbus Publishing, Ltd. CAN. Dist: Orca Bk. Pubs. USA.

Keyser, Amber J. The Way Back from Broken. 2015. (ENG.). 216p. (YA). (gr. 6-12). 18.99 *(978-1-4677-8817-5(1),* Carolrhoda Lab™); 18.99 *(978-1-4677-7590-8(8))* Lerner Publishing Group.

Kimmel, Elizabeth Cody. Suddenly Supernatural 4: Crossing Over. 2011. (Suddenly Supernatural Ser.: 4). (ENG.). 256p. (J). (gr. 3-7). pap. 5.99 *(978-0-316-13345-6(0))* Little, Brown Bks. for Young Readers.

Koops, Sheena. Voice of the Valley, 1 vol. 2006. (ENG.). 224p. (YA). (gr. 8-12). per. 8.95 *(978-1-55143-514-5(4))* Orca Bk. Pubs. USA.

Kositsky, Lynne. Claire by Moonlight. 2005. (ENG.). 280p. (J). (gr. 7). pap. 9.95 *(978-0-88776-659-6(5),* Tundra Bks.) Tundra Bks. CAN. Dist: Penguin Random Hse. LLC.

Kovacs, Deborah. Catie Copley's Great Escape. Williams, Jared T., illus. 2009. (J). 17.95 *(978-1-56792-382-7(8));* (ENG.). 32p. (gr. -1-3). 17.95 *(978-1-56792-379-7(8))* Godine, David R. Pub.

Kropp, Paul. Scarface. 88p. *(978-0-9731237-3-9(7))* High Interest Publishing (HIP).

Kuepfer, Sharon (Durksen) Schnupp. Little Prairie Girl: Are We Rich ... or Poor? 2009. (ENG., Illus.). 115p. pap. 7.95 *(978-1-60126-187-8(X))* Masthof Pr.

Kusugak, Michael. The Littlest Sled Dog, 1 vol. Krykorka, Vladyana, illus. 2010. (ENG.). 32p. (J). (gr. -1-3). pap. 10.95 *(978-1-55469-174-6(5))* Orca Bk. Pubs. USA.

Kyi, Tanya Lloyd. Anywhere but Here. 2013. (ENG., Illus.). 320p. (YA). (gr. 9). 17.99 *(978-1-4424-8070-4(X));* pap. 9.99 *(978-1-4424-8069-8(6))* Simon Pulse. (Simon Pulse).

Leavitt, Martine. Blue Mountain. 2014. (ENG.). 176p. (J). (gr. 3-7). 15.99 *(978-0-374-37864-6(9),* 9780374378646, Farrar, Straus & Giroux (BYR)) Farrar, Straus & Giroux.

—Heck Superhero!, 1 vol. 2005. (ENG.). 144p. pap. 12.95 *(978-0-88995-333-8(3))* Red Deer Pr. CAN. Dist: Ingram Publisher Services.

—Heck, Superhero. 2003. (ENG.). 172p. (J). (gr. 4-7). 16.95 *(978-1-886910-94-2(4),* Lemniscaat) Boyds Mills Pr.

Leblanc, Margaret Ann. Ms Maddy & the Lake Adventure. 2008. 89p. pap. 19.95 *(978-1-60474-003-5(5))* America Star Bks.

Lewis, Cindy (Didas). Time to Head South with Cindy the Canadian Goose, 1 vol. 2010. 56p. pap. 16.95 *(978-1-4489-3879-7(1))* America Star Bks.

Loccisano, Rina. Baby Dario Is Born. Baker, David, illus. 2012. 36p. pap. 24.95 *(978-1-4560-6099-2(6))* America Star Bks.

London, Jack. The Call of the Wild. Corvino, Lucy, illus. 2005. (Classic Starts(tm) Ser.). (ENG.). 160p. (J). (gr. 2-4). 6.95 *(978-1-4027-1274-6(X))* Sterling Publishing Co., Inc.

—Colmillo Blanco. 2003. (Advanced Reading Ser.: Vol. 56).Tr. of White Fang. (SPA., Illus.). 268p. (J). (gr. 4-7). 11.95 *(978-84-239-9030-6(3))* Espasa Calpe, S.A. ESP. Dist: Planeta Publishing Corp.

—Colmillo Blanco.Tr. of White Fang. (SPA.). (J). 8.00 *(978-958-04-7143-1(6))* Norma S.A. COL. Dist: Distribuidora Norma, Inc.

—Colmillo Blanco. 2006. (Clasicos Juveniles Ser.).Tr. of White Fang. (SPA., Illus.). 279p. pap. 13.95 *(978-84-263-5246-0(4))* Vives, Luis Editorial (Edelvives) ESP. Dist: Lectorum Pubns., Inc.

—White Fang. Andreasen, Dan, illus. 2006. (Classic Starts(tm) Ser.). (ENG.). 160p. (J). (gr. 2-4). 6.95 *(978-1-4027-2500-5(0))* Sterling Publishing Co., Inc.

—White Fang: With a Discussion of Resilience. Walker, Karen, illus. 2003. (Values in Action Illustrated Classics Ser.). 191p. (J). *(978-1-59203-038-5(6))* Learning Challenge, Inc.

—White Fang Study Guide. 2003. (Saddleback Classics Ser.). (Illus.). 48p. (J). (gr. 4-7). per. 17.95 *(978-1-56254-536-9(1)*, SP5361) Saddleback Educational Publishing, Inc.

Lottridge, Celia Barker. Wings to Fly, 1 vol. 3rd ed. 2007. (ENG.). 144p. (J). (gr. 2-7). pap. 8.95 *(978-0-88899-844-6(9))* Groundwood Bks. CAN. Dist: Publishers Group West (PGW).

Louis HéMon Staff. Maria Chapdelaine. 2005. pap. *(978-1-4065-0017-2(8))* Dodo Pr.

Lovell, Brandy. Crazy Colours. Mitchell, Tina, illus. 2011. 42p. pap. *(978-0-9867761-0-6(6))* Bing Long Bks.

MacGregor, Roy. Face-Off at the Alamo. 2013. (Screech Owls Ser.). (ENG.). 176p. (J). (gr. 4-7). pap. 8.95 *(978-1-77049-418-3(9)*, Tundra Bks.) Tundra Bks. CAN. Dist: Penguin Random Hse. LLC.

—Sudden Death in New York City. 2013. (Screech Owls Ser.). (ENG.). 176p. (J). (gr. 4-7). pap. 8.95 *(978-1-77049-415-2(4)*, Tundra Bks.) Tundra Bks. CAN. Dist: Penguin Random Hse. LLC.

MacLachlan, Patricia. More Perfect Than the Moon. 2005. 16.00 *(978-0-7569-5437-6(1))* Perfection Learning Corp.

Manzer, Jenny. Save Me, Kurt Cobain. 2016. (ENG.). 272p. (YA). (gr. 7). 17.99 *(978-0-553-52126-9(8)*, Delacorte Pr.) Random Hse. Children's Bks.

Martin, Ruth. The Little Moose. Boey, Stephanie, illus. 2008. (ENG.). 35p. (J). *(978-1-55168-332-4(6))* Fenn, H. B. & Co., Ltd.

Martinez, Jessica. The Space Between Us. (ENG., (YA). (gr. 9). 2013. Illus.). 416p. pap. 9.99 *(978-1-4424-2056-4(1))* 2012. 400p. 16.99 *(978-1-4424-2055-7(3))* Simon Pulse. (Simon Pulse).

Maruno, Jennifer. Totem, 0 vols. 2014. (ENG.). 168p. (YA). pap. 10.99 *(978-1-4597-1934-7(4)*, 9781459719347) Dundurn CAN. Dist: Ingram Publisher Services.

—Warbird. 2010. (ENG., Illus.). 120p. (J). (gr. 4-7). pap. 9.95 *(978-1-926607-11-5(2)*, Napoleon & Co.) Dundurn CAN. Dist: Ingram Publisher Services.

Matheson, Shirlee Smith. Gambler's Daughter. 2009. (ENG.). 144p. (YA). pap. 11.99 *(978-1-55002-718-1(2)*, Sandcastle Bks.) Dundurn CAN. Dist: Ingram Publisher Services.

—Jailbird Kid. 2010. (ENG.). 168p. (YA). (gr. 6). pap. 10.99 *(978-1-55488-704-0(6))* Dundurn CAN. Dist: Ingram Publisher Services.

Matson, Stacey. A Year in the Life of a Complete & Total Genius. 2015. (Arthur Bean Stories Ser.: 0). (ENG.). 272p. (J). (gr. 3-7). 15.99 *(978-1-4926-2074-7(2)*, 9781492620747, Sourcebooks Jabberwocky) Sourcebooks, Inc.

McClintock, Norah. Bang, 1 vol. 2007. (Orca Soundings Ser.). (ENG.). 112p. (YA). (gr. 8-12). per. 9.95 *(978-1-55143-654-8(X))* Orca Bk. Pubs. USA.

McDonald, Abby. Boys, Bears, & a Serious Pair of Hiking Boots. (ENG., Illus.). 304p. (YA). (gr. 9). 2011. pap. 7.99 *(978-0-7636-4994-4(5))* 2010. 16.99 *(978-0-7636-4382-9(3))* Candlewick Pr.

McIntyre, Sandra. Les Canots: Les Emblèmes Canadiens. McMann, Julie, tr. from ENG. 2011. (FRE.). 24p. (YA). (gr. 2-4). *(978-1-77071-407-6(3))* Weigl Educational Pubs. Ltd.

—Les Carcajous: Les Animaux du Canada. Karvonen, Tanjah, tr. from ENG. 2011. (FRE.). 24p. (gr. 3-6). *(978-1-77071-417-5(0))* Weigl Educational Pubs. Ltd.

McKay, Sharon E. Esther. 2004. (ENG.). 336p. (J). pap. *(978-0-14-331204-8(9))* Penguin Canada.

McMiller, Theresa R. Bessie Goes All over the World. 2012. 28p. pap. 24.95 *(978-1-4626-9464-8(0))* America Star Bks.

McNamee, Graham. Acceleration. 2012. (ENG.). 240p. (YA). (gr. 7). pap. 9.99 *(978-0-307-97595-9(9)*, Ember) Random Hse. Children's Bks.

—Bonechiller. 2012. (ENG.). 304p. (YA). (gr. 7). pap. 9.99 *(978-0-307-97593-5(2)*, Ember) Random Hse. Children's Bks.

McPhee, Peter. New Blood, 1 vol. 2007. (Lorimer SideStreets Ser.). (ENG.). 168p. (YA). (gr. 9-12). 9.95 *(978-1-55028-996-1(9)*, 9781550289961) Lorimer, James & Co., Ltd., Pubs. CAN. Dist: Casemate Pubs. & Bk. Distributors, LLC.

McRae, David. Blood of the Donnellys. 2007. (ENG.). 144p. (J). (gr. 8). pap. 11.99 *(978-1-55002-754-9(9))* Dundurn CAN. Dist: Ingram Publisher Services.

Mok, Carmen. Ride the Big Machines Across Canada. 2015. (My Big Machines Ser.). (ENG.). 14p. (J). bds. 10.50 *(978-1-4434-3810-0(3))* HarperCollins Pubs.

Montgomery, L. M. Anne of Avonlea. l.t. ed. 2006. (ENG.). pap. *(978-1-4068-3173-3(5))* Echo Library.

—Anne of Avonlea. 2011. (Oxford Children's Classics Ser.). (ENG.). 336p. (YA). (gr. 3-18). 9.95 *(978-0-19-276359-4(8))* Oxford Univ. Pr., Inc.

—Emily Climbs: Emily of New Moon Series. 2014. (Emily Ser.: 2). (ENG.). 368p. (YA). (gr. 5-12). pap. 8.99 *(978-1-4022-8915-6(4))* Sourcebooks, Inc.

—Emily's Quest. 2014. (Emily Ser.: 3). (ENG.). 256p. (YA). (gr. 5-12). pap. 8.99 *(978-1-4022-8918-7(9))* Sourcebooks, Inc.

Morrill, Lauren. Being Sloane Jacobs. 2015. (ENG.). 352p. (YA). (gr. 7). pap. 9.99 *(978-0-385-74180-4(4)*, Ember) Random Hse. Children's Bks.

Morrison, Jessica. La Fête du Travail: Les Célébrations Canadiennes. Karvonen, Tanjah, tr. from ENG. 2011. (FRE.). 24p. (gr. k-3). *(978-1-77071-397-0(2))* Weigl Educational Pubs. Ltd.

—Le Jour de la SaintJeanBaptiste: Les Célébrations Canadiennes. Karvonen, Tanjah, tr. from ENG. 2011. (FRE.). 24p. (gr. k-3). *(978-1-77071-399-4(9))* Weigl Educational Pubs. Ltd.

—Le Jour de L'Action de Grâce: Les Célébrations Canadiennes. Karvonen, Tanjah, tr. from ENG. 2011. (FRE.). 24p. (gr. k-3). *(978-1-77071-400-7(6))* Weigl Educational Pubs. Ltd.

Munsch, Robert. Munsch Mini-Treasury One. Martchenko, Michael, illus. 5th ed. 2010. (Munsch for Kids Ser.). (ENG.). 144p. (J). (gr. -1-2). 18.95 *(978-1-55451-273-7(5)*, 9781554512737) Annick Pr., Ltd. CAN. Dist: Publishers Group West (PGW).

—Munsch Mini-Treasury Two. 4th ed. 2010. (Munsch for Kids Ser.). (ENG., Illus.). 136p. (J). (gr. -1-2). 18.95 *(978-1-55451-274-4(3)*, 9781554512744) Annick Pr., Ltd. CAN. Dist: Publishers Group West (PGW).

Nicolas, Ron. Northern Lights: A Wilderness Adventure. 2005. 228p. (YA). per. 15.85 *(978-0-9770043-2-4(5))* New Global Publishing.

Oborowsky, S. L. S. Ivy: The Stem of a Rose. 2011. (ENG.). 112p. (YA). pap. 10.95 *(978-1-59299-654-4(X))* Inkwater Pr.

O'Brien, Jack. Silver Chief's Revenge. Wiese, Kurt, illus. 2011. 222p. 44.95 *(978-1-258-09709-7(5))* Literary Licensing, LLC.

Ooten, Tara Broeckel. Justin Bieber - Fame. 2011. (ENG., Illus.). 40p. (YA). pap. 7.99 *(978-1-4507-3538-4(X))* Bluewater Productions, Inc.

Orton, W. George. Bob Hunt in Canada. 2007. 168p. 95.99 *(978-1-4280-7682-2(4))*; per. 89.99 *(978-1-4280-7702-7(2))* IndyPublish.com.

Oxley, J. Mcdonald. The Young Woodsman: Life in the Forests of Canada. 2007. 90p. pap. 16.99 *(978-1-4346-4267-7(4))*; 100p. pap. 18.99 *(978-1-4346-4268-4(2))* Creative Media Partners, LLC.

Paperny, Myra. The Greenies. 2007. (ENG.). 304p. (J). mass mkt. 6.99 *(978-0-00-639356-6(X)*, Harper Trophy) HarperCollins Pubs.

Parkinson, Curtis. Man Overboard! 2012. (ENG., Illus.). 152p. (J). (gr. 4-7). pap. 9.95 *(978-1-77049-298-1(4)*, Tundra Bks.) Tundra Bks. CAN. Dist: Penguin Random Hse. LLC.

Patton, Anne. Through Flood & Fire: A Second Barr Colony Adventure, 1 vol. 2015. (ENG., Illus.). 192p. (J). (gr. 4-6). pap. 9.95 *(978-1-55050-640-2(4))* Coteau Bks. CAN. Dist: Orca Bk. Pubs. USA.

Paulsen, Gary. Hatchet. 2003. (ENG.). 160p. (J). mass mkt. 9.99 *(978-0-330-31045-1(3)*, Pan) Pan Macmillan GBR. Dist: Trafalgar Square Publishing.

—Hatchet. Willis, Drew, illus. 20th anniv. ed. 2007. (ENG.). 192p. (J). (gr. 5-9). 19.99 *(978-1-4169-2508-8(2)*, Simon & Schuster Bks. For Young Readers) Simon & Schuster Bks. For Young Readers.

—Hatchet. 2006. 18.40 *(978-1-4177-6883-7(5)*, Turtleback) Turtleback Bks.

—Hatchet: With Related Readings. 2004. (EMC Masterpiece Series Access Editions). (J). 11.99 *(978-0-8219-2960-5(7))* EMC/Paradigm Publishing.

Pavlick, Leon E. & PAVLICK, A. N. N. M. Foxes on the Ridge. Calvert, Lissa, illus. 2012. 48p. pap. *(978-1-77097-852-2(6))* FriesenPress.

Payson, Howard. The Boy Scouts at the Canadian Border. 2005. pap. 30.95 *(978-1-885529-49-7(X))* Stevens Publishing.

Pearce, Jacqueline. The Reunion, 1 vol. 2003. (Orca Young Readers Ser.). (ENG., Illus.). 96p. (J). (gr. 3-6). pap. 4.99 *(978-1-55143-230-4(7))* Orca Bk. Pubs. USA.

Pellerin, Mona. Peetie & the Marsh Aliens, 1 vol. 2010. 58p. pap. 16.95 *(978-1-4489-7017-9(2))* America Star Bks.

Perkins, Lynne Rae. Pictures from Our Vacation. Perkins, Lynne Rae, illus. 2007. (Illus.). 32p. (J). (gr. k-3). 17.89 *(978-0-06-085098-2(1)*, Greenwillow Bks.) HarperCollins Pubs.

Perkins, Lynne Rae & Perkins, Lynne R. Pictures from Our Vacation. Perkins, Lynne Rae, illus. 2007. (ENG., Illus.). 32p. (J). (gr. k-3). 17.99 *(978-0-06-085097-5(3)*, Greenwillow Bks.) HarperCollins Pubs.

Pinkerton, Robert E. The Fourth Norwood. 2011. 350p. 51.95 *(978-1-258-09433-1(9))* Literary Licensing, LLC.

Pinter, Karin. Niki Owl: Leap of Faith. 2012. 172p. (gr. 4-6). 27.99 *(978-1-4772-8023-2(5))* AuthorHouse.

Pogue, Carolyn. Gwen, 1 vol. 2009. (ENG.). 160p. (YA). (gr. 9-12). pap. *(978-1-894549-80-6(5)*, Sumach Pr.) Canadian Scholars.

Pratt, Laura. La Fête des Mères: Les Célébrations Canadiennes. Karvonen, Tanjah, tr. from ENG. 2011. (FRE.). 24p. (gr. k-3). *(978-1-77071-398-7(0))* Weigl Educational Pubs. Ltd.

Prendergast, G. S. Zero Repeat Forever. 2017. (Nahx Invasions Ser.: 1). (ENG., Illus.). 496p. (YA). (gr. 9). 17.99 ***(978-1-4814-8184-7(3)**, Simon & Schuster Bks. For Young Readers)* Simon & Schuster Bks. For Young Readers.

Prendergast, Gabrielle. Zero Repeat Forever. 2017. (YA). pap. ***(978-1-4814-8185-4(1)**, Simon & Schuster Bks. For Young Readers)* Simon & Schuster Bks. For Young Readers.

Pugliano-Martin, Carol. Glooscap Makes the Seasons: A Canadian Legend. 2006. (J). pap. *(978-1-4108-7159-6(2))* Benchmark Education Co.

Radford, Megan. Canada Doodles, 1 vol. Cook, Peter, illus. 2014. (ENG.). 240p. pap. 9.99 *(978-1-4236-3621-2(X))* Gibbs Smith, Publisher.

Ralphson, G. Harvey. Boy Scouts in a Motor Boat or Adventures. 2005. pap. 26.95 *(978-1-885529-50-3(3))* Stevens Publishing.

Ravel, Edeet. The Saver, 1 vol. (ENG.). (J). (gr. 8). 2010. 216p. pap. 8.95 *(978-0-88899-883-5(X))* 2008. 192p. 17.95 *(978-0-88899-882-8(1))* Groundwood Bks. CAN. Dist: Publishers Group West (PGW).

Reid, Charles. Ghost of Heroes Past. 2010. (ENG., Illus.). 170p. pap. 10.95 *(978-1-55380-102-3(4))* Ronsdale Pr. CAN. Dist: SPD-Small Pr. Distribution.

Renshaw, Douglas. Around Our Feeder with George the Groundhog & Friends. Lamb, Janie, illus. 2008. 48p. pap. 24.95 *(978-1-60610-657-0(0))* America Star Bks.

Rice, Luanne. The Beautiful Lost. 2017. (ENG.). 304p. (J). (gr. 7). 18.99 ***(978-1-338-11107-1(8))*** Scholastic, Inc.

Richardson, Faith. Tree Root & River Rat. 2003. (Illus.). 248p. (J). 21.95 *(978-0-9744989-4-2(7))*; pap. 12.95 *(978-0-9744989-5-9(5))* Fox Song Bks.

Richler, Mordecai. Jacob Two-Two's First Spy Case. Petricic, Dusan, illus. 2009. (Jacob Two-Two Ser.). (ENG.). 168p. (J). (gr. 4-7). 10.95 *(978-0-88776-927-6(6))* Tundra Bks. CAN. Dist: Random Hse., Inc.

Rivera, Raquel. Arctic Adventures: Tales from the Lives of Inuit Artists, 1 vol. Marton, Jirina, illus. 2007. (ENG.). 36p. (J). (gr. 2-18). 18.95 *(978-0-88899-714-2(0))* Groundwood Bks. CAN. Dist: Publishers Group West (PGW).

Roberge, Tracy. Jacob & Alec Move to Hong Kong. 2011. 32p. pap. 17.99 *(978-1-257-01739-3(X))* Lulu Pr., Inc.

Roberts, Ken. Thumb & the Bad Guys. 2013. 104p. pap. *(978-1-4596-6491-3(4))* ReadHowYouWant.com, Ltd.

Robinson, C. Black Souls. 2008. 193p. 34.99 *(978-1-4357-0724-5(9))* Lulu Pr., Inc.

Rose, Simon. Les Loonies: Les Emblèmes Canadiens. McMann, Julie, tr. from ENG. 2011. (FRE.). 24p. (YA). (gr. 2-4). *(978-1-77071-409-0(X))* Weigl Educational Pubs. Ltd.

Ross, Jeff. The Drop, 1 vol. 2011. (Orca Sports Ser.). (ENG.). 168p. (YA). (gr. 6-10). pap. 9.95 *(978-1-55469-392-4(6))* Orca Bk. Pubs. USA.

Sherrard, Valerie. Three Million Acres of Flame. 2007. (ENG.). 200p. (YA). pap. 10.99 *(978-1-55002-727-3(1)*, Boardwalk Bks.) Dundurn CAN. Dist: Ingram Publisher Services.

Signore, Marco. The Hunting Pack: Allosaurus. Bacchin, Matteo, illus. 2009. (Dinosaurs: Ser.). (ENG.). 64p. (J). (gr. 4-9). 15.95 *(978-0-7892-1011-1(8)*, Abbeville Kids) Abbeville Pr., Inc.

Silvano, Wendi. Love Is All Around Canada. Czernichowska, Joanna, illus. 2016. (ENG.). 32p. (J). (-10). 12.99 *(978-1-4926-2910-8(3)*, Sourcebooks Jabberwocky) Sourcebooks, Inc.

Silverthorne, Judith. The Secret of Sentinel Rock, 1 vol. 2006. (From Many Peoples Ser.). (ENG.). 168p. (J). (gr. 3-6). pap. 7.95 *(978-1-55050-103-2(8))* Coteau Bks. CAN. Dist: Orca Bk. Pubs. USA.

—The Secret of the Stone House, 1 vol. 2005. (From Many Peoples Ser.). (ENG., Illus.). 224p. (J). (gr. 4-7). pap. 7.95 *(978-1-55050-325-8(1))* Coteau Bks. CAN. Dist: Orca Bk. Pubs. USA.

Silverthorne, Judith & Coteau Books Staff. Dinosaur Hideout, 1 vol. 2006. (Dinosaur Adventure Ser.). (ENG.). 220p. (J). (gr. 4-7). pap. 6.95 *(978-1-55050-226-8(3))* Coteau Bks. CAN. Dist: Orca Bk. Pubs. USA.

Sinclair, Mehded Maryam. When Wings Expand. 2013. (ENG., Illus.). 150p. (J). (gr. 5-9). pap. 9.95 *(978-0-86037-499-2(8))* Kube Publishing Ltd. GBR. Dist: Consortium Bk. Sales & Distribution.

Skrypuch, Marsha Forchuk. Dance of the Banished, 1 vol. 2015. (ENG., Illus.). 288p. (YA). (gr. 7-11). pap. 12.95 *(978-1-927485-65-1(7))* Pajama Pr. CAN. Dist: Ingram Publisher Services.

Smallman, Steve. Santa Is Coming to Canada. Dunn, Robert, illus. 2013. (ENG.). 32p. (J). (-3). 11.99 *(978-1-4022-8839-5(5)*, Sourcebooks Jabberwocky) Sourcebooks, Inc.

—Santa Is Coming to Ottawa. Dunn, Robert, illus. 2013. (ENG.). 32p. (J). (-3). 11.99 *(978-1-4022-8994-1(4)*, Sourcebooks Jabberwocky) Sourcebooks, Inc.

Soggie, Neil. The Young-Dogs of Elbow. 2007. (ENG.). 112p. per. 32.99 *(978-0-7618-3813-5(9))* Hamilton Bks.

Spalding, Andrea. Sarah May & the New Red Dress. 2004. (Illus.). (J). (gr. k-3). spiral bd. *(978-0-616-01782-1(0))* Canadian National Institute for the Blind/Institut National Canadien pour les Aveugles.

Stafford, Liliana. Snow Bear. Davis, Lambert, illus. 32p. (J). pap. *(978-0-88899-441-7(9))* Groundwood Bks.

Stanek, Mary Beth. The Fire Keepers: Mystery at Manitou Beach. Stanek, Mary Beth, illus. Stanek, Linda, photos by. 2003. (Illus.). (J). pap. 20.00 *(978-0-9747556-0-1(5))* Stanek, Mary Beth.

Steiner, Barbara. Mystery at Chilkoot Pass. 2009. (Mysteries Through Time Ser.). 144 - 176p. (YA). (gr. 4-8). 31.95 *(978-1-60754-435-7(0))*; pap. 15.25 *(978-1-60754-434-0(2))* Windmill Bks.

Stellings, Caroline. The Contest, 1 vol. 2009. (ENG.). 160p. (J). (gr. 4-7). pap. 9.95 *(978-0-9779183-5-5(1)*, 7th Generation) Book Publishing Co.

Stevenson, Robin. Impossible Things, 1 vol. 2008. (ENG.). 192p. (J). (gr. 4-8). pap. 8.95 *(978-1-55143-736-1(8))* Orca Bk. Pubs. USA.

—Out of Order, 1 vol. 2007. (ENG.). 232p. (YA). (gr. 7-12). per. 9.95 *(978-1-55143-693-7(0))* Orca Bk. Pubs. USA.

Stroud, Bettye. The Patchwork Path: A Quilt Map to Freedom. Bennett, Erin Susanne, illus. 2007. (ENG.). 32p. (J). (gr. k-3). pap. 7.99 *(978-0-7636-3519-0(7))* Candlewick Pr.

Stuchner, Joan Betty. The Kugel Valley Klezmer Band. Row, Richard, illus. 2005. 30p. (J). (gr. 2-6). reprint ed. 16.00 *(978-0-7567-8605-2(3))* DIANE Publishing Co.

—The Kugel Valley Klezmer Band. Row, Richard, illus. 2009. (PJ Library). (ENG.). 32p. (J). (gr. -1-3). pap. 7.95 *(978-1-56656-782-4(3)*, Crocodile Bks.) Interlink Publishing Group, Inc.

Stute, Lela Labree & Stute, Lela LaBree. Three Pugs & a Canadian Spy. 2011. 74p. pap. 26.90 *(978-1-257-82229-4(2))* Lulu Pr., Inc.

Sully, Katherine. Night-Night Canada. Poole, Helen, illus. 2017. (ENG.). 20p. (J). (-1). bds. 9.99 *(978-1-4926-4769-0(1)*, 9781492647690, Sourcebooks Jabberwocky) Sourcebooks, Inc.

Summers, Gillian. The Quicksilver Faire: The Scions of Shadow Trilogy, Book 2. 2011. (Faire Folk Saga Ser.: 5). (ENG.). 336p. (YA). pap. 9.95 *(978-0-7387-1571-1(9)*, Flux) North Star Editions.

Taylor, Betty Ann. Mari's Miracle. 2013. 32p. pap. 16.99 *(978-1-4808-0230-8(1))* Archway Publishing.

Taylor, Cora. Champlain & Cartier, 1 vol. 2004. (Ghost Voyages Ser.: No. 4). (ENG., Illus.). 128p. (J). (gr. 3-6). pap. 7.95 *(978-1-55050-374-6(X))* Coteau Bks. CAN. Dist: Orca Bk. Pubs. USA.

Torres, J. The Collected Alison Dare Little Miss Adventures. Bone, J., illus. 2005. (J). *(978-1-4156-1359-7(1))* Oni Pr., Inc.

Trottier, Maxine. Migrant, 1 vol. Arsenault, Isabelle, illus. 2011. (ENG.). 40p. (J). (gr. -1-2). 18.95 *(978-0-88899-975-7(5))* Groundwood Bks. CAN. Dist: Publishers Group West (PGW).

Troughton, Ruth. The Invisible Ones. 2003. 88p. pap. 9.95 *(978-0-595-29592-0(4))* iUniverse, Inc.

Udvari, Joseph G. Courage. 2012. 132p. pap. *(978-1-84961-169-5(6))* RealTime Publishing.

Ulmer, Mike. The Gift of the Inuksuk. Rose, Melanie, illus. rev. ed. 2004. (ENG.). 32p. (J). (gr. k-6). 17.95 *(978-1-58536-214-1(X))* Sleeping Bear Pr.

Unrau, Adela. A Big Change, 1 vol. Friesen, Anni, illus. 2010. 16p. pap. 24.95 *(978-1-4489-7672-0(3))* PublishAmerica, Inc.

Wallace, Ian. The True Story of Trapper Jack's Left Big Toe. (Illus.). 32p. (J). 18.95 *(978-0-88899-415-8(X))* Groundwood Bks. CAN. Dist: Publishers Group West (PGW).

Walsh, Ann, ed. Beginnings: Stories of Canada's Past. 2005. (ENG., Illus.). 228p. (J). pap. 12.95 *(978-0-921870-87-6(6))* Ronsdale Pr. CAN. Dist: Literary Pr. Group of Canada.

Warner, Gertrude Chandler, creator. The Mystery at the Calgary Stampede. 2015. (Boxcar Children Mysteries Ser.: 140). (ENG.). 128p. (J). (gr. 1-5). 15.99 *(978-0-8075-2840-2(4))* Whitman, Albert & Co.

Warren, Bertie. Sammie's Journey to Freedom. 2006. (ENG.). 52p. per. 16.95 *(978-1-4241-5142-4(2))* America Star Bks.

Warring, Molly-Ann. Paradise Acres. 2005. 518p. *(978-0-88887-312-5(3))* Borealis Pr.

Warwick, Ellen. The Twelve Days of Christmas in Canada. Smith, Kim, illus. 2016. (Twelve Days of Christmas in America Ser.). (ENG.). 22p. (J). (— 1). bds. 9.50 *(978-1-4549-2056-4(4))* Sterling Publishing Co., Inc.

—The Twelve Days of Christmas in Canada. Smith, Kimberly, illus. 2015. (Twelve Days of Christmas in America Ser.). (ENG.). 40p. (J). (gr. k). 12.95 *(978-1-4549-1431-0(9))* Sterling Publishing Co., Inc.

Welvaert, Scott R. The Mosquito King: An Agate & Buck Adventure, 1 vol. Garvey, Brann, illus. 2007. (Agate & Buck Adventure Ser.). (ENG.). 112p. (gr. 2-3). 26.65 *(978-1-59889-857-6(4)*, Vortex Bks.) Stone Arch Bks.

West, Karen L. Tommy the Squirrel Wants to Be Human. 2009. 24p. pap. 12.99 *(978-1-4389-8096-6(5))* AuthorHouse.

White, Howard. The Airplane Ride. Guzek, Greta, illus. unabr. ed. 2006. (ENG.). 32p. (J). bds. 16.95 *(978-0-88971-224-9(7))* Harbour Publishing Co., Ltd. CAN. Dist: Midpoint Trade Bks., Inc.

Wiseman, Blaine. La Fête des Pères: Les Célébrations Canadiennes. Karvonen, Tanjah, tr. from ENG. 2011. (FRE.). 24p. (gr. k-3). *(978-1-77071-396-3(4))* Weigl Educational Pubs. Ltd.

Wiseman, Eva. Kanada. 2006. (ENG., Illus.). 264p. (YA). (gr. 5). pap. 9.95 *(978-0-88776-729-6(X)*, Tundra Bks.) Tundra Bks. CAN. Dist: Penguin Random Hse. LLC.

Wishinsky, Frieda. Make It Fair!, No. 15. Lewis-MacDougall, Patricia Ann & Owlkids Books Inc. Staff, illus. 2010. (Canadian Flyer Adventures Ser.: 15). (ENG.). 96p. (J). (gr. 1-4). pap. 7.95 *(978-1-897349-99-1(8)*, Maple Tree Pr.) Owlkids Bks. Inc. CAN. Dist: Publishers Group West (PGW).

—On the Case. Franson, Leanne et al, illus. 2009. (Canadian Flyer Adventures Ser.: 12). (ENG.). 96p. (J). (gr. 1-4). pap. 7.95 *(978-1-897349-55-7(6)*, Owlkids) Owlkids Bks. Inc. CAN. Dist: Publishers Group West (PGW).

Wishinsky, Frieda & Griffiths, Dean. Far from Home. Franson, Leanne & Owlkids Books Inc. Staff, illus. 2008. (Canadian Flyer Adventures Ser.: 11). (ENG.). 96p. (J). (gr. 1-4). pap. 7.95 *(978-1-897349-43-4(2)*, Maple Tree Pr.) Owlkids Bks. Inc. CAN. Dist: Publishers Group West (PGW).

Woodbury, Mary. Flight of the Tiger Moth, 1 vol. 2007. (ENG.). 240p. (YA). (gr. 7-11). per. 8.95 *(978-1-55050-364-7(2))* Coteau Bks. CAN. Dist: Orca Bk. Pubs. USA.

Wyeth, Sharon Dennis. Message in the Sky Bk. 3: Corey's Underground Railroad Diary. 2003. (My America Ser.). (ENG.). 112p. (J). 10.95 *(978-0-439-37057-8(4)*, Scholastic Pr.) Scholastic, Inc.

Wynne-Jones, Tim. Blink & Caution. (ENG., Illus.). 352p. (YA). (gr. 9). 2012. pap. 8.99 *(978-0-7636-5697-3(6))* 2011. 16.99 *(978-0-7636-3983-9(4))* Candlewick Pr.

—The Boy in the Burning House. braille ed. 2003. (J). (gr. 2). spiral bd. *(978-0-616-15275-1(2))* Canadian National Institute for the Blind/Institut National Canadien pour les Aveugles.

—The Boy in the Burning House. 2003. (ENG.). 224p. (J). (gr. 5-9). pap. 12.99 *(978-0-374-40887-9(4)*, 9780374408879, Farrar, Straus & Giroux (BYR)) Farrar, Straus & Giroux.

—The Boy in the Burning House, 1 vol. (ENG.). 232p. pap. 8.95 *(978-0-88899-500-1(8))* Groundwood Bks. CAN. Dist: Publishers Group West (PGW).

—Lord of the Fries & Other Stories: Other Stories. pap. 9.95 *(978-0-88899-274-1(2))* Groundwood Bks. CAN. Dist: Publishers Group West (PGW).

—Rex Zero, King of Nothing. 2013. (ENG.). 240p. (J). (gr. 3-7). pap. 6.99 *(978-0-312-67478-6(3)*, 9780312674786) Square Fish.

—The Uninvited. 2010. (ENG., Illus.). 368p. (YA). (gr. 9). pap. 8.99 *(978-0-7636-4826-8(4))* Candlewick Pr.

Yee, Paul. Learning to Fly, 1 vol. 2008. (Orca Soundings Ser.). (ENG.). (YA). (gr. 8-12). 112p. 16.95 *(978-1-55143-955-6(7))*; 136p. pap. 9.95 *(978-1-55143-953-2(0))* Orca Bk. Pubs. USA.

—Money Boy. 2013. 192p. pap. *(978-1-4596-6450-0(7))* ReadHowYouWant.com, Ltd.

—Shu-Li & Tamara, 1 vol. Wang, Shaoli, illus. 2008. (ENG.). 72p. (J). (gr. 1-4). per. 7.95 *(978-1-896580-93-7(9))* Tradewind Bks. CAN. Dist: Orca Bk. Pubs. USA.

—Tales from Gold Mountain, 1 vol. Ng, Simon, illus. 2011. (ENG.). 64p. (J). (gr. 1-5). pap. 14.95 *(978-1-55498-125-0(5))* Groundwood Bks. CAN. Dist: Publishers Group West (PGW).

—What Happened This Summer, 1 vol. 2006. (ENG., Illus.). 178p. (YA). (gr. 8-12). per. 10.95 *(978-1-896580-88-3(2))* Tradewind Bks. CAN. Dist: Orca Bk. Pubs. USA.

Young, Elizabeth L. Dozens & Dozens of Cousins & Cousins. Perkins, Ruth, illus. 2012. 30p. 20.95 *(978-1-61633-353-9(7))*; pap. 12.95 *(978-1-61633-352-2(9))* Guardian Angel Publishing, Inc.

Zhang, Crystal. Lil' P & His Big Problem, 1 vol. 2010. 32p. pap. 24.95 *(978-1-4489-8319-3(3))* PublishAmerica, Inc.

C
D

CANADA—HISTORY

Aloian, Molly. Cultural Traditions in Canada. 2014. (ENG., Illus.). 32p. (J). *(978-0-7787-0297-9(9))* Crabtree Publishing Co.

—Remembrance Day. 2010. (ENG., Illus.). 32p. (J). *(978-0-7787-4765-9(4))*; pap. *(978-0-7787-4783-3(2))* Crabtree Publishing Co.

Andra-Warner, Elle. Hudson's Bay Company Adventures: Tales of Canada's Early Fur Traders. 2006. (Amazing Stories Ser.). (ENG.). 96p. (J). pap. 9.95 *(978-1-55439-700-6(6)*, 9781554397006) Lorimer, James & Co., Ltd., Pubs. CAN. Dist: Casemate Pubs. & Bk. Distributors, LLC.

Andrekson, Judy. Brigadier: Gentle Hero. Parkins, David, illus. 2009. (True Horse Stories Ser.). (ENG.). 96p. (J). (gr. 4-7). pap. 7.95 *(978-0-88776-904-7(7)*, Tundra Bks.) Tundra Bks. CAN. Dist: Penguin Random Hse. LLC.

Argyle, Ray. The Boy in the Picture: The Craigellachie Kid & the Driving of the Last Spike. 2010. (ENG., Illus.). 152p. (YA). pap. 19.99 *(978-1-55488-787-3(9))* Dundurn CAN. Dist: Ingram Publisher Services.

Bailey, Katharine. Radisson & des Groseilliers: Fur Traders of the North. 2006. (In the Footsteps of Explorers Ser.). (ENG., Illus.). 32p. (J). (gr. 3-7). lib. bdg. *(978-0-7787-2422-3(0)*, 1253444); (gr. 4-7). pap. *(978-0-7787-2458-2(1)*, 1253444) Crabtree Publishing Co.

Baldwin, Douglas. War of 1812. 2011. 48p. (J). (gr. 8-10). *(978-1-77071-628-5(9))*; pap. *(978-1-77071-629-2(7))* Weigl Educational Pubs. Ltd.

—1920: Canadian Decades. 2011. 48p. (C). (gr. 4-6). *(978-1-77071-712-1(9))* Weigl Educational Pubs. Ltd.

—1930: Canadian Decades. 2011. 48p. (C). (gr. 4-6). *(978-1-77071-713-8(7))*; pap. *(978-1-77071-724-4(2))* Weigl Educational Pubs. Ltd.

Baldwin, Douglas & Baldwin, Patricia. 1920: Canadian Decades. 2011. 48p. (C). (gr. 4-6). pap. *(978-1-77071-723-7(4))* Weigl Educational Pubs. Ltd.

Barlas, Robert & Tompsett, Norm. Canada. 2010. (Festivals of the World Ser.). 32p. (gr. 3). 28.50 *(978-1-60870-095-0(X))* Marshall Cavendish Corp.

Beckett, Harry. Nunavut. 2003. (Eye on Canada Ser.). 32p. (J). pap. 9.95 *(978-1-894705-02-8(5))* Weigl Pubs., Inc.

Bellefontaine, Kim. Canada 123. Gürth, Per-Henrik, illus. 2011. (ENG.). 24p. (J). (gr. -1-1). 7.95 *(978-1-55453-659-7(6))* Kids Can Pr., Ltd. CAN. Dist: Hachette Bk. Group.

Bercuson, David. How Canada Became Canada, 10 vols., Set. 2005. (Illus.). 88p. (J). (gr. 5-18). lib. bdg. 219.50 *(978-1-4222-0000-1(0)*, 1247970) Mason Crest.

Bowers, Vivien. Hey Canada! Pavlovic, Milan, illus. 2012. (ENG.). 74p. (J). (gr. 2-5). 19.95 *(978-1-77049-255-4(0)*, Tundra Bks.) Tundra Bks. CAN. Dist: Penguin Random Hse. LLC.

—Wow Canada! Exploring This Land from Coast to Coast to Coast. Eastman, Dianne et al, illus. 2nd ed. 2010. (Wow Canada! Ser.). (ENG.). 160p. (J). (gr. 3-6). 24.95 *(978-1-897349-82-3(3)*, Maple Tree Pr.); pap. 19.95 *(978-1-897349-83-0(1)*, Owlkids) Owlkids Bks. Inc. CAN. Dist: Publishers Group West (PGW).

Brezina, Corona. Jacques Cartier. 2016. (Spotlight on Explorers & Colonization Ser.). 00048p. (J). (gr. 6-6). pap. 11.75 *(978-1-5081-7206-2(4))* Rosen Publishing Group, Inc., The.

Brouwer, Sigmund. Innocent Heroes. 2017. (ENG., Illus.). 208p. (J). (gr. 4-7). 16.99 *(978-1-101-91846-3(2)*, Tundra Bks.) Tundra Bks. CAN. Dist: Penguin Random Hse. LLC.

Bruchac, Marge. Malian's Song. Maughan, William L., illus. 2006. (Vermont Folklife Center Children's Book Ser.). (ENG.). 32p. (J). (gr. -1-3). 16.95 *(978-0-916718-26-8(3))* Vermont Folklife Ctr.

Burrell, Bill. The Path to Glory. 2011. 24p. pap. *(978-1-4269-9427-2(3))* Trafford Publishing (UK) Ltd.

Corrigan, Jim. Filipino Immigration. 2005. (Changing Face of North America Ser.). (Illus.). 112p. (YA). lib. bdg. 24.95 *(978-1-59084-684-1(2))* Mason Crest.

Corrigan, Kathleen. Building a Nation. 2016. (Canada Through Time Ser.). (ENG., Illus.). 32p. (gr. 1-4). lib. bdg. 29.99 *(978-1-4109-8120-2(7)*, Read Me!) Heinemann-Raintree.

—Canada Through Time. 2016. (Canada Through Time Ser.). (ENG.). 32p. (gr. 1-4). 149.95 *(978-1-4109-8133-2(9)*, Read Me!) Heinemann-Raintree.

—First Nations & Early Explorers. 2016. (Canada Through Time Ser.). (ENG., Illus.). 32p. (gr. 1-4). lib. bdg. 29.99 *(978-1-4109-8119-6(3)*, Read Me!) Heinemann-Raintree.

—Immigration & the Founding of New Communities. 2016. (Canada Through Time Ser.). (ENG., Illus.). 32p. (gr. 1-4). lib. bdg. 29.99 *(978-1-4109-8121-9(5)*, Read Me!) Heinemann-Raintree.

Covello, Paul. Canada ABC. 2016. 30p. (J). bds. 10.50 *(978-1-4434-4884-0(2))* HarperCollins Pubs.

Craats, Rennay. 1910: Canadian Decades. 2011. 48p. (C). (gr. 4-6). *(978-1-77071-711-4(0))* Weigl Educational Pubs. Ltd.

—1970: Canadian Decades. 2011. 48p. (C). (gr. 4-6). *(978-1-77071-717-6(X))*; pap. *(978-1-77071-728-2(5))* Weigl Educational Pubs. Ltd.

Creasey, Eleanor. On Remembrance Day. 2014. (ENG., Illus.). 40p. (J). 19.99 *(978-1-4597-2166-1(7))* Dundurn CAN. Dist: Ingram Publisher Services.

Crewe, Sabrina. Canadian Coins. 2015. (Canadian Symbols Ser.). (ENG.). 24p. (gr. k-1). lib. bdg. 26.65 *(978-1-4914-7093-0(3)*, Pebble Plus) Capstone Press of Coughlan Cos.

—Canadian Symbols. 2015. (Canadian Symbols Ser.). (ENG.). 24p. (gr. k-1). lib. bdg. 133.25 *(978-1-4914-7095-4(X)*, Pebble Plus) Capstone Press of Coughlan Cos.

Crooks, Claire V. Engagement et Responsabilisation des Jeunes Autochtones: Trousse D'Outils DestinéE Aux Fournisseurs des Services. 2010. (FRE.). 168p. pap. 45.99 *(978-1-4269-1299-3(4))* Trafford Publishing.

Crump, Jennifer. The War of 1812: Heroes of a Great Canadian Victory. 2007. (Amazing Stories Ser.). (ENG.). 96p. (J). pap. 9.95 *(978-1-55439-711-2(1)*, 9781554397112) Lorimer, James & Co., Ltd., Pubs. CAN. Dist: Casemate Pubs. & Bk. Distributors, LLC.

Dendy, Christina. Underground Railroad: Defining Moments in Canadian History. 2011. (Illus.). 32p. (gr. 5-8). *(978-1-77071-691-9(2))* Weigl Educational Pubs. Ltd.

Doeden, Matt. Sidney Crosby: Hockey Superstar. 2012. (Superstar Athletes Ser.). (ENG.). 24p. (gr. 1-2). pap. 41.70 *(978-1-4296-8495-8(X))* Capstone Press of Coughlan Cos.

Dooling, Sandra. Japanese Internment: Defining Moments in Canadian History. 2011. (Illus.). 32p. (gr. 5-8). *(978-1-77071-688-9(2))* Weigl Educational Pubs. Ltd.

—Last Spike in CPR: Defining Moments in Canadian History. 2011. (Illus.). 32p. (gr. 5-8). *(978-1-77071-689-6(0))* Weigl Educational Pubs. Ltd.

Dowdy, Penny. British North America Act: Defining Moments in Canadian History/Graphic Novels. 2010. (Illus.). 32p. *(978-1-77071-614-8(9))* Weigl Educational Pubs. Ltd.

—The Famous Five: Defining Moments in Canadian History/Graphic Novels. 2010. (Illus.). 32p. *(978-1-77071-616-2(5))* Weigl Educational Pubs. Ltd.

—The October Crisis: Defining Moments in Canadian History/Graphic Novels. 2010. (Illus.). 32p. *(978-1-77071-613-1(0))* Weigl Educational Pubs. Ltd.

Dueck, Adele. Nettie's Journey, 1 vol. 2005. (From Many Peoples Ser.). (ENG., Illus.). 216p. (J). (gr. 4-7). per. 7.95 *(978-1-55050-322-7(7))* Coteau Bks. CAN. Dist: Orca Bk. Pubs. USA.

Dyan, Penelope. Oh Victoria! a Kid's Guide to Victoria, Bc. Canada. Weigand, John D., photos by. 2013. (Illus.). 34p. pap. 11.95 *(978-1-61477-108-1(1))* Bellissima Publishing, LLC.

Freedman, Jeri. Careers in Child Care, 1 vol. 2015. (ENG.). 80p. (J). 34.25 *(978-1-4777-7884-5(5)*, Rosen Young Adult) Rosen Publishing Group, Inc., The.

Friesen, Helen Lepp. Maple Syrup. 2011. 24p. (YA). (gr. 2-4). *(978-1-77071-660-5(2))*; pap. *(978-1-77071-666-7(1))* Weigl Educational Pubs. Ltd.

Funk, Jack. Outside, the Women Cried: The Story of the Surrender by Chief Thunderchild's Band of Their Reserve near Delmas, Saskatchewan 1908. 2007. 108p. per. 12.95 *(978-0-595-43557-9(2))* iUniverse, Inc.

Gaines, Jena. Haitian Immigration. 2003. (Changing Face of North America Ser.). (Illus.). 112p. (J). lib. bdg. *(978-1-59084-691-9(5))* Mason Crest.

Ganeri, Anita. Canada. Isik, Semur, illus. 2015. (Country Guides, with Benjamin Blog & His Inquisitive Dog Ser.). (ENG.). 32p. (gr. 1-3). 29.99 *(978-1-4109-6847-0(2)*, Read Me!) Heinemann-Raintree.

Geiger, Beth. Geography of Canada: Text Pairs. 2008. (Bridges/Navigators Ser.). (J). (gr. 6). 81.00 *(978-1-4108-8438-1(4))* Benchmark Education Co.

Goldsmith, Rose. How Did the Vikings Come to Canada? 2014. (Little Books of Answers: Level F Ser.). (Illus.). 16p. (gr. k-2). pap. 7.95 *(978-1-927136-51-5(2))* Three Crows Media NZL. Dist: RiverStream Publishing.

Goldsworthy, Kaite. Canada. 2013. (J). *(978-1-62127-251-9(6))*; pap. *(978-1-62127-257-1(5))* Weigl Pubs., Inc.

Gordon, Sharon. Canada. 2015. (Exploring World Cultures Ser.). (ENG., Illus.). 32p. (J). (gr. 3-4). pap. 10.58 *(978-1-5026-0585-6(6))* Cavendish Square Publishing.

Goyette, Linda. Rocky Mountain Kids, 1 vol. 2008. (ENG., Illus.). 128p. (J). (gr. 3-7). pap. *(978-1-897142-32-5(3))* Brindle & Glass Publishing.

Grambo, Rebecca L. Digging Canadian History, 1 vol. 2006. (ENG., Illus.). 64p. (J). (gr. 2-6). pap. *(978-1-55285-757-1(3))* Whitecap Bks., Ltd.

Grant, Vicki. The Halifax Citadel. Pilsworth, Graham, illus. 2003. (Dreadful Truth Ser.). (ENG.). 80p. (J). (gr. 3-8). *(978-0-88780-599-8(X))* Formac Publishing Co., Ltd.

Hacker, Carlotta. The Kids Book of Canadian History. Mantha, John, illus. 2009. (Kids Book Of Ser.). (ENG.). 72p. (J). (gr. 3-7). 14.95 *(978-1-55453-328-2(7))* Kids Can Pr., Ltd. CAN. Dist: Hachette Bk. Group.

—1950: Canadian Decades. 2011. 48p. (C). (gr. 4-6). *(978-1-77071-715-2(3))*; pap. *(978-1-77071-726-8(9))* Weigl Educational Pubs. Ltd.

Hazleton, Amie. Sieur de la Salle: An Explorer of the Great West. 2017. (World Explorers Ser.). (ENG., Illus.). 32p. (gr. 3-4). lib. bdg. 27.32 *(978-1-5157-4206-7(7))* Capstone Press of Coughlan Cos.

Henry, Natasha L. Talking about Freedom: Celebrating Emancipation Day in Canada. 2012. (ENG., Illus.). 174p. (YA). (gr. 6). pap. 19.99 *(978-1-4597-0048-2(1))* Dundurn CAN. Dist: Ingram Publisher Services.

Hernandez, Romel. Immigration from Central America. 2005. (Changing Face of North America Ser.). (Illus.). 112p. (YA). lib. bdg. 24.95 *(978-1-59084-688-9(5))* Mason Crest.

Hickman, Pamela & Taraschi-Carr, Gola. Righting Canada's Wrongs: the Komagata Maru & Canada's Anti-Indian Immigration Policies in the Twentieth Century. 2014. (Righting Canada's Wrongs Ser.). (ENG., Illus.). 104p. (YA). (gr. 8-12). 34.95 *(978-1-4594-0437-3(8)*, 9781459404373) Lorimer, James & Co., Ltd., Pubs. CAN. Dist: Casemate Pubs. & Bk. Distributors, LLC.

Hodge, Deborah. The Kids Book of Canada's Railway: And How the CPR Was Built. Mantha, John, illus. 2008. (Kids Book Of Ser.). (ENG.). 48p. (J). (gr. 3-7). pap. 14.95 *(978-1-55453-256-8(6))* Kids Can Pr., Ltd. CAN. Dist: Hachette Bk. Group.

—The Kids Book of Canadian Immigration. Mantha, John, illus. 2006. (Kids Book Of Ser.). (ENG.). 64p. (J). (gr. 3-7). 19.95 *(978-1-55337-484-8(3))* Kids Can Pr., Ltd. CAN. Dist: Hachette Bk. Group.

Honovich, Nancy. Immigration from the Former Yugoslavia. 2005. (Changing Face of North America Ser.). (Illus.). 112p. (YA). lib. bdg. 24.95 *(978-1-59084-690-2(7))* Mason Crest.

Horn, Bernd. Battle Cries in the Wilderness: The Struggle for North America in the Seven Years' War. 2011. (Canadians at War Ser.: 5). (ENG., Illus.). 152p. (YA). pap. 19.99 *(978-1-55488-919-8(7))* Dundurn CAN. Dist: Ingram Publisher Services.

—Men of Steel: Canadian Paratroopers in Normandy 1944. 2010. (Canadians at War Ser.: 2). (ENG., Illus.). 120p. (YA). (gr. 6). pap. 19.99 *(978-1-55488-708-8(9))* Dundurn CAN. Dist: Ingram Publisher Services.

Hudak, Heather C. A Refugee's Journey from Yemen. 2017. 32p. (J). ***(978-0-7787-3677-6(6))*** Crabtree Publishing Co.

Hurley, Michael. Canada, 1 vol. 2012. (Countries Around the World Ser.). (ENG.). 48p. (gr. 3-6). lib. bdg. 33.32 *(978-1-4329-6095-7(4)*, NA-h) Heinemann-Raintree.

Hyde, Natalie. Cryptic Canada: Unsolved Mysteries from Coast to Coast. Hammill, Matt & Owlkids Books Inc. Staff, illus. 2012. (ENG.). 48p. (J). (gr. 3-7). pap. 12.95 *(978-1-926973-43-2(7)*, Owlkids) Owlkids Bks. Inc. CAN. Dist: Publishers Group West (PGW).

—Internment Camps. 2016. (Uncovering the Past: Analyzing Primary Sources Ser.). (ENG., Illus.). 48p. (J). (gr. 5-8). *(978-0-7787-2860-3(9))* Crabtree Publishing Co.

Innes, Stephanie & Endrulat, Harry. Bear on the Homefront, 1 vol. Deines, Brian, illus. 2014. (ENG.). 32p. (J). (gr. k-3). 17.95 *(978-1-927485-13-2(4))* Pajama Pr. CAN. Dist: Ingram Publisher Services.

Johnson, Michael. Iroquois: People of the Longhouse. 2013. (ENG., Illus.). 160p. 35.00 *(978-1-77085-218-1(2)*, 9781770852181) Firefly Bks., Ltd.

Jordan-Fenton, Christy & Pokiak-Fenton, Margaret. Not My Girl. Grimard, Gabrielle, illus. 2014. (ENG.). 36p. (J). (gr. 1-4). 21.95 *(978-1-55451-625-4(0)*, 9781554516254); pap. 9.95 *(978-1-55451-624-7(2)*, 9781554516247) Annick Pr., Ltd. CAN. Dist: Publishers Group West (PGW).

Juarez, Christine. Canada, 1 vol. 2013. (Countries Ser.). (ENG.). 24p. (gr. k-1). 26.65 *(978-1-4765-3075-8(0)*, Pebble Plus); pap. 6.95 *(978-1-4765-3515-9(9)*, Pebble Bks.) Capstone Press of Coughlan Cos.

Kalman, Bobbie. Canada: The Culture. 3rd rev. ed. 2009. (Lands, Peoples, & Cultures Ser.). (ENG., Illus.). 32p. (J). (gr. 4-5). pap. *(978-0-7787-9654-1(X))* Crabtree Publishing Co.

—Canada: The Land. 3rd rev. ed. 2009. (Lands, Peoples, & Cultures Ser.). (ENG., Illus.). 32p. (J). (gr. 4-5). pap. *(978-0-7787-9652-7(3))* Crabtree Publishing Co.

—Canada - The People. 3rd rev. ed. 2009. (Lands, Peoples, & Cultures Ser.). (ENG., Illus.). 32p. (J). (gr. 4-5). pap. *(978-0-7787-9653-4(1))*; *(978-0-7787-9283-3(8))* Crabtree Publishing Co.

—Conoce Canadá. 2009. (SPA.). 32p. (J). *(978-0-7787-8197-4(6))*; (gr. 2-5). pap. *(978-0-7787-8217-9(4))* Crabtree Publishing Co.

—Spotlight on Canada. 2007. (Spotlight on My Country Ser.). (ENG., Illus.). 32p. (J). (gr. 4-7). pap. *(978-0-7787-3476-5(5))* Crabtree Publishing Co.

Kaplan, Leslie C. A Primary Source Guide to Canada. 2009. (Countries of the World). 24p. (gr. 2-3). 42.50 *(978-1-61512-026-0(2)*, PowerKids Pr.) Rosen Publishing Group, Inc., The.

Kauffman, Dorothy. Letters from Canada & Mexico. 2005. (Oxford Picture Dictionary for the Content Areas Ser.). (ENG., Illus.). 22p. pap. 7.56 *(978-0-19-430951-6(7))* Oxford Univ. Pr., Inc.

Kenney, Karen Latchana. Canada, 1 vol. 2013. (Countries of the World Set 2 Ser.). (ENG.). 144p. (J). (gr. 6-12). lib. bdg. 37.07 *(978-1-61783-627-5(3)*, Essential Library) ABDO Publishing Co.

Kissock, Heather, ed. Entertainment. 2011. 48p. (gr. 5-8). *(978-1-77071-673-5(4))*; pap. *(978-1-77071-676-6(9))* Weigl Educational Pubs. Ltd.

—Trends. 2011. 48p. (gr. 5-8). *(978-1-77071-672-8(6))*; pap. *(978-1-77071-675-9(0))* Weigl Educational Pubs. Ltd.

Knudsen, Anders. Antoine de la Mothe Cadillac: French Settlements at Detroit & Louisiana. 2006. (In the Footsteps of Explorers Ser.). (ENG., Illus.). 32p. (J). (gr. 3-9). lib. bdg. *(978-0-7787-2429-2(8))*; (gr. 4-7). pap. *(978-0-7787-2465-0(4))* Crabtree Publishing Co.

Kusugak, Michael. T Is for Territories: A Yukon, Northwest Territories, & Nunavut Alphabet. 2013. (Discover Canada Province by Province Ser.). (ENG., Illus.). 40p. (J). (gr. 1-4). 17.95 *(978-1-58536-207-3(7)*, 202273) Sleeping Bear Pr.

Kylie, Aaron. Canadian Geographic Canada for Kids: 1000 Awesome Facts. 2015. (ENG., Illus.). 248p. (J). (gr. 4-8). pap. 17.95 *(978-1-77085-581-6(5)*, 9781770855816) Firefly Bks., Ltd.

Laxer, James. Tecumseh, 1 vol. Rudnicki, Richard, illus. 2012. (ENG.). 56p. (J). (gr. 3). 19.95 *(978-1-55498-123-6(9))* Groundwood Bks. CAN. Dist: Publishers Group West (PGW).

Le Sueur, William Dawson. W. I. MacKenzie. reprint ed. 150.00 *(978-0-7222-6950-3(1))* Library Reprints, Inc.

Leighton, Douglas. The Canadian Rockies, 1 vol. 2005. (ENG., Illus.). 112p. pap. *(978-1-55153-233-2(6))* RMB Rocky Mountain Bks.

Libal, Joyce. Migrant Youth: Falling Between the Cracks. 2009. (Youth in Rural North America Ser.). (Illus.). 96p. (YA). (gr. 3-7). lib. bdg. 22.95 *(978-1-4222-0020-9(5))* Mason Crest.

Lindeen, Mary. Welcome to North America, 1 vol. (Wonder Readers: Social Studies). (ENG.). (gr. -1-2). 2012. 20p. lib. bdg. 22.65 *(978-1-4296-9617-3(6))* 2011. 16p. pap. 35.94 *(978-1-4296-8204-6(3))* Capstone Press of Coughlan Cos. (Wonder Readers).

Lingen, Marissa. Chinese Immigration. 2005. (Changing Face of North America Ser.). (Illus.). 112p. (YA). lib. bdg. 24.95 *(978-1-59084-694-0(X))* Mason Crest.

Lynch, Wayne. Wayne Lynch's Canadian Rockies Wildlife for Kids. 2011. 22.95 *(978-1-926983-05-9(X))* Summerthought Publishing Ltd. CAN. Dist: Alpen Bks.

MacKinnon, Christopher. Canadian Sports Sites for Kids: Places Named for Speedsters, Scorers, & Other Sportsworld Citizens. 2012. (ENG., Illus.). 144p. (J). pap. 14.99 *(978-1-4597-0705-4(2))* Dundurn CAN. Dist: Ingram Publisher Services.

—Canadian Sports Sites for Kids: Places Named for Speedsters, Scorers, & Other Sportsworld Citizens (Large Print 16pt) 2013. 208p. pap. *(978-1-4596-6305-3(5))* ReadHowYouWant.com, Ltd.

MacLeod, Elizabeth. Canada Year by Year. Smith, Sydney, illus. 2016. (ENG.). 96p. (J). (gr. 3-7). 21.95 *(978-1-77138-397-4(6))* Kids Can Pr., Ltd. CAN. Dist: Hachette Bk. Group.

—The Kids Book of Canada at War. Mantha, John, illus. 2007. (Kids Book Of Ser.). (ENG.). 72p. (J). (gr. 3-7). 19.95 *(978-1-55453-003-8(2))* Kids Can Pr., Ltd. CAN. Dist: Hachette Bk. Group.

Macleod, Steve. 2000-10: Canadian Decades. 2011. 48p. (C). (gr. 4-6). lib. bdg. *(978-1-77071-720-6(X))* Weigl Educational Pubs. Ltd.

—200010: Canadian Decades. 2011. 48p. (C). (gr. 4-6). pap. *(978-1-77071-731-2(5))* Weigl Educational Pubs. Ltd.

Mallory, Enid. Captain Fitz: FitzGibbon, Green Tiger of the War of 1812. 2011. (Canadians at War Ser.: 7). (ENG., Illus.). 208p. (YA). (gr. 6). pap. 19.99 *(978-1-4597-0118-2(6))* Dundurn CAN. Dist: Ingram Publisher Services.

Markovics, Adam. Canada. 2016. (Countries We Come From Ser.). (ENG.). 32p. (J). (gr. -1-3). lib. bdg. 19.95 *(978-1-944998-27-1(6))* Bearport Publishing Co., Inc.

Matthews, Carolyn. True Stories of Rescue & Survival: Canada's Unknown Heroes. 2008. (ENG., Illus.). 176p. (YA). (gr. 6-18). pap. 19.99 *(978-1-55002-851-5(0))* Dundurn CAN. Dist: Ingram Publisher Services.

Maury, Rob. Immigration from the Middle East. 2005. (Changing Face of North America Ser.). (Illus.). 112p. (YA). lib. bdg. 24.95 *(978-1-59084-695-7(8))* Mason Crest.

McDonnell, Ginger. Next Stop - Canada, 1 vol. 2nd rev. ed. 2013. (Nonfiction Readers Ser.). (ENG., Illus.). 24p. (J). (gr. 2-2). pap. 23.96 *(978-1-4807-1038-2(5))* Shell Educational Publishing.

McKinley, Herald. Myths of the Native Americans. 2016. (World Mythologies Ser.). (ENG., Illus.). 96p. (J). (gr. 6-6). 42.79 *(978-1-5026-0990-8(8))* Cavendish Square Publishing.

McNamara, Margaret. Discover Canada. 2006. (J). pap. *(978-1-4108-6461-1(8))* Benchmark Education Co.

Meyer, Edith Patterson. The Friendly Frontier: The Story of the Canadian-American Border. Mars, W. T., illus. 2011. 304p. 48.95 *(978-1-258-09384-6(7))* Literary Licensing, LLC.

Miller, Susan Hoskins. Canada. 2015. (One World, Many Countries Ser.). (ENG.). 32p. (J). (gr. 1-4). 28.50 *(978-1-63407-039-3(9)*, 208880) Child's World, Inc., The.

Moore, Christopher. The Big Book of Canada. Slavin, Bill, illus. 2017. (ENG.). 256p. (J). (gr. 4-7). 34.99 *(978-1-101-91894-4(2)*, Tundra Bks.) Tundra Bks. CAN. Dist: Penguin Random Hse. LLC.

—Champlain. Back, Francis, illus. 2004. (ENG.). 56p. (J). (gr. 3-7). 18.95 *(978-0-88776-657-2(9)*, Tundra Bks.) Tundra Bks. CAN. Dist: Penguin Random Hse. LLC.

Morrison, J. A. & Goldsworthy, Steve. English-French Relations. 2010. (Illus.). 48p. *(978-1-55388-690-7(9))*; pap. *(978-1-55388-695-2(X))* Weigl Educational Pubs. Ltd.

Murray, Julie. Canada, 1 vol. 2013. (Explore the Countries Ser.). (ENG.). 40p. (J). (gr. 2-5). lib. bdg. 29.93 *(978-1-61783-806-4(3)*, Big Buddy Bks.) ABDO Publishing Co.

Murray, Laura K. Lululemon Athletica. 2015. (Illus.). 48p. (J). *(978-1-60818-558-0(3)*, Creative Education) Creative Co., The.

Napier, Matt. Little Canada. 2012. (Little Country Ser.). (ENG., Illus.). 22p. (J). (gr. k-3). 9.95 *(978-1-58536-178-6(X))* Sleeping Bear Pr.

Nelson, Sheila. Britain's Canada, 1613-1770. 2007. (How Canada Became Canada Ser.). (Illus.). 87p. (YA). (gr. 3-7). lib. bdg. 21.95 *(978-1-4222-0003-2(5))* Mason Crest.

—Canada's Changing Society, 1984-the Present. 2007. (How Canada Became Canada Ser.). (Illus.). 87p. (YA). (gr. 3-7). lib. bdg. 21.95 *(978-1-4222-0009-4(4)*, 1247977) Mason Crest.

—From the Atlantic to the Pacific: Canadian Expansion, 1867-1909. 2007. (How Canada Became Canada Ser.). (Illus.). 87p. (YA). (gr. 3-7). lib. bdg. 21.95 *(978-1-4222-0005-6(1)*, 1247971) Mason Crest.

—Redefining Canada: A Developing Identity, 1960-1984. 2007. (How Canada Became Canada Ser.). (Illus.). 87p. (YA). (gr. 3-7). lib. bdg. 21.95 *(978-1-4222-0008-7(6)*, 1247976) Mason Crest.

Nicholson, Lorna Schultz. Winning Gold: Canada's Incredible 2002 Olympic Victory in Women's Hockey, 1 vol. 2010. (Lorimer Recordbooks Ser.). (ENG., Illus.). 112p. (J). (gr. 8-12). 16.95 *(978-1-55277-473-1(2)*, 9781552774731) Lorimer, James & Co., Ltd., Pubs. CAN. Dist: Casemate Pubs. & Bk. Distributors, LLC.

Noonan, Sheila Smith. Korean Immigration. 2005. (Changing Face of North America Ser.). (Illus.). 112p. (YA). lib. bdg. 24.95 *(978-1-59084-693-3(1))* Mason Crest.

Oachs, Emily Rose. Canada. 2017. (Country Profiles Ser.). (ENG., Illus.). 32p. (J). (gr. 3-8). lib. bdg. 26.95 ***(978-1-62617-677-5(9)***, Blastoff! Discovery) Bellwether Media.

Owens, L. L. A Journey with Sieur de la Salle. 2017. (Primary Source Explorers Ser.). (ENG.). 40p. (J). (gr. 3-5). 30.65 *(978-1-5124-0775-4(5))* Lerner Publishing Group.

Parker, Janice. 1980: Canadian Decades. 2011. 48p. (C). (gr. 4-6). *(978-1-77071-718-3(8))*; pap. *(978-1-77071-729-9(3))* Weigl Educational Pubs. Ltd.

Parkes, Elle. Let's Explore Canada. 2017. (Bumba Books (tm) — Let's Explore Countries Ser.). (ENG.). 24p. (J). (gr. -1-1). 25.32 ***(978-1-5124-3361-6(6))*** Lerner Publishing Group.

Pelletier, Mia. A Children's Guide to Arctic Birds, 1 vol. Christopher, Danny, illus. 2014. (ENG.). 32p. (J). (gr. k-2). 16.95 *(978-1-927095-67-6(0))* Inhabit Media Inc. CAN. Dist: Independent Pubs. Group.

Pitt, Steve. To Stand & Fight Together: Richard Pierpoint & the Coloured Corps of Upper Canada. 2008. (Canadians at War Ser.: 1). (ENG., Illus.). 144p. (YA). (gr. 4-8). pap. 19.99 *(978-1-55002-731-0(X))* Dundurn CAN. Dist: Ingram Publisher Services.

Pohl, Kathleen. Descubramos Canada. 2007. (Descubramos Países del Mundo (Looking at Countries) Ser.). (SPA., Illus.). 32p. (gr. 1-5). lib. bdg. 26.00 *(978-0-8368-8182-0(6)*, Gareth Stevens Learning Library) Stevens, Gareth Publishing LLLP.

Powell, Marie. Explore with Jacques Cartier. 2014. (ENG., Illus.). 32p. (J). pap. *(978-0-7787-1432-3(2))* Crabtree Publishing Co.

Qitsualik-Tinsley, Rachel & Qitsualik-Tinsley, Sean. Tuniit: Mysterious Folk of the Arctic, 1 vol. Bigham, Sean, illus. 2014. (ENG.). 60p. (J). (gr. 2-4). 16.95 *(978-1-927095-76-8(X))* Inhabit Media Inc. CAN. Dist: Independent Pubs. Group.

Rinker, Kimberly. Immigration from the Dominican Republic. 2005. (Changing Face of North America Ser.). (Illus.). 112p. (YA). lib. bdg. 24.95 *(978-1-59084-689-6(3))* Mason Crest.

Robertson, David Alexander. Sugar Falls: A Residential School Story. Henderson, Scott B., illus. 2012. (ENG.). 40p. (YA). (gr. 9-12). pap. *(978-1-55379-334-2(X)*, 9781553793342, HighWater Pr.) Portage & Main Pr.

Rodger, Ellen. A Refugee's Journey from South Sudan. 2017. 32p. (J). ***(978-0-7787-3676-9(8))*** Crabtree Publishing Co.

—A Refugee's Journey from the Democratic Republic of the Congo. 2017. (Leaving My Homeland Ser.). (ENG., Illus.).

32p. (J). pap. ***(978-0-7787-3156-6(1))*** Crabtree Publishing Co.

Rogers, Stan. Northwest Passage, 1 vol. James, Matt, illus. 2013. (ENG.). 56p. (J). (gr. k). 24.95 *(978-1-55498-153-3(0))* Groundwood Bks. CAN. Dist: Publishers Group West (PGW).

Rose, Simon. Le Flambeau Olympique: Les Emblèmes Canadiens. McMann, Julie, tr. from ENG. 2011. (FRE.). 24p. (YA). (gr. 2-4). *(978-1-77071-411-3(1))* Weigl Educational Pubs. Ltd.

Sakany, Lois. Canada: A Primary Source Cultural Guide. 2009. (Primary Sources of World Cultures Ser.). 128p. (gr. 4-5). 79.90 *(978-1-60851-917-0(1))* Rosen Publishing Group, Inc., The.

Salomons, Elizabeth. 1900: Canadian Decades. 2011. 48p. (C). (gr. 4-6). *(978-1-77071-710-7(2))*; pap. *(978-1-77071-721-3(8))* Weigl Educational Pubs. Ltd.

Samuels, Barbara. Canada's Immigrant Cultures: Multiculturalism in Canada. 2011. 32p. (gr. 5-8). *(978-1-77071-705-3(6))*; pap. *(978-1-77071-708-4(0))* Weigl Educational Pubs. Ltd.

—Canada's Multicultural Society Today: Multiculturalism in Canada. 2011. 32p. (gr. 5-8). *(978-1-77071-706-0(4))*; pap. *(978-1-77071-709-1(9))* Weigl Educational Pubs. Ltd.

—Multiculturalism in Early Canada: Multiculturalism in Canada. 2011. 32p. (gr. 5-8). *(978-1-77071-704-6(8))* Weigl Educational Pubs. Ltd.

Saracuse, Tara. Island Kids, 1 vol. 2010. (Courageous Kids Ser.). (ENG.). 240p. (J). (gr. 4-7). pap. *(978-1-897142-43-1(9))* Brindle & Glass Publishing.

Seidlitz, Lauri. 1990: Canadian Decades. 2011. 48p. (C). (gr. 4-6). *(978-1-77071-719-0(6))*; pap. *(978-1-77071-730-5(7))* Weigl Educational Pubs. Ltd.

Sexton, Colleen. Canada. 2010. (Exploring Countries Ser.). (ENG., Illus.). 32p. (J). (gr. 3-7). lib. bdg. 26.95 *(978-1-60014-475-2(6)*, Blastoff! Readers) Bellwether Media.

Shipton, Rosemary. 1960: Canadian Decades. 2011. 48p. (C). (gr. 4-6). *(978-1-77071-716-9(1))*; pap. *(978-1-77071-727-5(7))* Weigl Educational Pubs. Ltd.

Skrypuch, Marsha Forchuk. Adrift at Sea: A Vietnamese Boy's Story of Survival. Deines, Brian, illus. 2016. (ENG.). 40p. (J). (gr. 1-4). 18.95 *(978-1-77278-005-5(7))* Pajama Pr. CAN. Dist: Ingram Publisher Services.

Sleeping Bear Press. Diary of a Canadian Kid. Moore, Cyd, illus. 2012. (Country Journal Ser.). (ENG.). 128p. (J). (gr. 4-8). pap. 11.95 *(978-1-58536-812-9(1)*, 202346) Sleeping Bear Pr.

Staunton, Ted. Confederation. Pilsworth, Graham, illus. 2004. (Dreadful Truth Ser.). (ENG.). 80p. (J). (gr. 3-8). *(978-0-88780-630-8(9))* Formac Publishing Co., Ltd.

Stewart, Mark. The United States & Canada. 2016. (Regions of the World Ser.). (ENG.). 64p. (gr. 6-9). pap. 9.99 *(978-1-4846-3814-9(X)*, NA-h) Heinemann-Raintree.

Walker, Sally M. Winnie: The True Story of the Bear Who Inspired Winnie-the-Pooh. Voss, Jonathan D., illus. 2015. (ENG.). 40p. (J). (gr. -1-3). 17.99 *(978-0-8050-9715-3(5)*, 9780805097153, Holt, Henry & Co. Bks. For Young Readers) Holt, Henry & Co.

Warner, Jody Nyasha. Viola Desmond Won't Be Budged, 1 vol. Rudnicki, Richard & Junaid, Bushra, illus. 2010. (ENG.). 32p. (J). (gr. k-4). 18.95 *(978-0-88899-779-1(5))* Groundwood Bks. CAN. Dist: Publishers Group West (PGW).

Weil, Ann. Meet Our New Student from Quebec. 2009. (Meet Our New Student Ser.). 48p. (J). (gr. 2-5). 29.95 *(978-1-58415-778-6(X))* Mitchell Lane Pubs., Inc.

Welldon, Christine. Pier 21 - Listen to My Story, 1 vol. 2012. (ENG.). 96p. (J). (gr. 2-5). pap. 15.95 *(978-1-55109-909-5(8))* Nimbus Publishing, Ltd. CAN. Dist: Orca Bk. Pubs. USA.

Yasuda, Anita. Political Leaders. 2010. (Illus.). 48p. *(978-1-55388-691-4(7))*; pap. *(978-1-55388-696-9(8))* Weigl Educational Pubs. Ltd.

Zelenyi, Alexander & Zelenyj, Alexander. Marquette & Jolliet: Quest for the Mississippi. 2006. (In the Footsteps of Explorers Ser.). (ENG., Illus.). 32p. (J). (gr. 4-7). pap. *(978-0-7787-2467-4(0))*; lib. bdg. *(978-0-7787-2431-5(X))* Crabtree Publishing Co.

Zocchi, Judy. In Canada. Brodie, Neale, illus. 2005. (Global Adventures II Ser.). 32p. (J). pap. 10.95 *(978-1-59646-168-0(3))*; lib. bdg. 21.65 *(978-1-59646-083-6(0))* Dingles & Co.

—In Canada/en Canada. Brodie, Neale, illus. 2005. (Global Adventures II Ser.).Tr. of En Canada. (ENG & SPA.). 32p. (J). pap. 10.95 *(978-1-59646-170-3(5))*; lib. bdg. 21.65 *(978-1-59646-084-3(9))* Dingles & Co.

CANADA—HISTORY—FICTION

Baxter, Jean Rae. Freedom Bound. 2012. (ENG., Illus.). 246p. pap. 11.95 *(978-1-55380-143-6(1))* Ronsdale Pr. CAN. Dist: SPD-Small Pr. Distribution.

Beveridge, Cathy. Stormstruck. 2006. (ENG., Illus.). 214p. (J). pap. *(978-1-55380-041-5(9))* Ronsdale Pr.

Boissery, Beverley. Sophie's Treason. 2006. (ENG.). 224p. (J). pap. 12.99 *(978-1-55002-642-9(9))* Dundurn CAN. Dist: Ingram Publisher Services.

Brooks, Martha. Queen of Hearts. 2011. (ENG.). 224p. (YA). (gr. 7-12). 17.99 *(978-0-374-34229-6(6)*, 9780374342296, Farrar, Straus & Giroux (BYR)) Farrar, Straus & Giroux.

Chan, Gillian. An Ocean Apart: The Gold Mountain Diary of Chin Mei-Ling. 2004. (Dear Canada Ser.). (ENG., Illus.). 224p. (J). *(978-0-7791-1353-8(5))* Scholastic Canada, Ltd.

Crook, Connie Brummel. Acts of Courage: Laura Secord & the War of 1812. 2012. (ENG., Illus.). 272p. (J). (gr. 5-9). pap. 11.95 *(978-0-9869495-7-9(4))* Pajama Pr. CAN. Dist: Ingram Publisher Services.

—Meyers' Creek, 1 vol. 2nd ed. 2014. (ENG.). 212p. pap. *(978-1-55455-351-8(2))* Fitzhenry & Whiteside, Ltd.

Dinsdale, Christopher. The Emerald Key. 2013. 356p. pap. *(978-1-4596-6395-4(0))* ReadHowYouWant.com, Ltd.

Dyer, K. C. Facing Fire. 2010. (ENG.). 224p. pap. 12.95 *(978-0-385-66638-1(1)*, Doubleday Can) Doubleday Canada, Ltd. CAN. Dist: Random Hse., Inc.

Frazier, Angie. The Midnight Tunnel: A Suzanna Snow Mystery. 2011. (ENG.). 288p. (J). (gr. 3-7). 17.99 *(978-0-545-20862-8(9)*, Scholastic Pr.) Scholastic, Inc.

Golden, Christopher & Lebbon, Tim. The Wild. Ruth, Greg, illus. 2011. (Secret Journeys of Jack London Ser.: 1). (ENG.). 368p. (YA). (gr. 5-18). 15.99 *(978-0-06-186317-2(3)*, HarperTeen) HarperCollins Pubs.

Gunderson, Jessica. Passage to Fortune: Searching for Saguenay. Kurtz, Rory, illus. 2016. (Discovering the New World Ser.). (ENG.). 96p. (gr. 3-4). pap. 7.95 *(978-1-4965-3482-8(4)*, Connect) Stone Arch Bks.

Guyatt, Ben. Billy Green Saves the Day. 2009. (ENG.). 160p. (J). (gr. 7-18). pap. 10.99 *(978-1-55488-041-6(6)*, Dundurn Pr.) Dundurn CAN. Dist: Ingram Publisher Services.

Harlow, Joan Hiatt. Secret of the Night Ponies. 2010. (ENG.). 352p. (J). (gr. 3-7). pap. 7.99 *(978-1-4169-0784-8(X)*, McElderry, Margaret K. Bks.) McElderry, Margaret K. Bks.

Henty, George Alfred. With Wolfe in Canad: The Winning of a Continent. 2011. 378p. pap. 19.95 *(978-1-61179-149-5(9))* Fireship Pr.

Jocelyn, Marthe. Mable Riley: A Reliable Record of Humdrum, Peril, & Romance. 2007. 279p. (gr. 4-7). 17.00 *(978-0-7569-8183-9(2))* Perfection Learning Corp.

Kerz, Anna. The Gnome's Eye, 1 vol. 2010. (ENG.). 224p. (J). (gr. 4-7). pap. 9.95 *(978-1-55469-195-1(8))* Orca Bk. Pubs. USA.

Kessler, Deirdre. Born: A Foal, Five Kittens & Confederation, 1 vol. Jones, Brenda, illus. 2015. (ENG.). 48p. (J). (gr. k-2). pap. 12.95 *(978-1-927502-33-4(0))* Acorn Pr., The CAN. Dist: Orca Bk. Pubs. USA.

London, Jack. The Call of the Wild. 2014. iv, 96p. (J). pap. *(978-1-4677-4602-1(9)*, First Avenue Editions) Lerner Publishing Group.

—The Call of the Wild & White Fang. McKowen, Scott, illus. 2004. (Sterling Unabridged Classics Ser.). (ENG.). 312p. (J). (gr. 5). 9.95 *(978-1-4027-1455-9(6))* Sterling Publishing Co., Inc.

—White Fang, 1 vol. VanArsdale, Anthony, illus. 2011. (Calico Illustrated Classics Ser.: No. 3). (ENG.). 112p. (J). (gr. 3-6). 27.07 *(978-1-61641-112-1(0))* Magic Wagon.

Lunn, Janet. Laura Secord: A Story of Courage. Newhouse, Maxwell, illus. 2012. (ENG.). 32p. (J). (gr. 2-4). pap. 9.95 *(978-1-77049-384-1(0)*, Tundra Bks.) Tundra Bks. CAN. Dist: Penguin Random Hse. LLC.

MacPhee, Bill. Stella, Nothing Has Changed. 2008. 312p. 28.50 *(978-1-60693-230-8(6)*, Strategic Bk. Publishing) Strategic Book Publishing & Rights Agency (SBPRA).

Marlowe, Paul. Sporeville. 2007. (Wellborn Conspiracy Ser.: Bk. 1). 250p. (YA). (gr. 8-12). pap. 10.95 *(978-0-9739505-4-0(4))* Sybertooth, Inc. CAN. Dist: Lightning Source, Inc.

Matas, Carol. Turned Away: The World War II Diary of Devorah Bernstein. 2005. (Dear Canada Ser.). (ENG., Illus.). 208p. (J). *(978-0-439-96946-8(8))* Scholastic Canada, Ltd.

McDivitt, Barry. The Youngest Spy. 2007. (ENG.). 176p. (YA). (gr. 3-9). per. 12.95 *(978-1-897235-17-1(8))* Thistledown Pr., Ltd. CAN. Dist: Univ. of Toronto Pr.

Messner, Kate. Champlain & the Silent One. Gulley, Martha, illus. 2008. (J). *(978-1-59531-050-7(9))* North Country Bks., Inc.

Montgomery, L. M. Anne of Avonlea. 2005. pap. *(978-1-905432-15-8(1))* Dodo Pr.

—Anne of Avonlea. Andreasen, Dan, illus. 2009. (Classic Starts(tm) Ser.). (ENG.). 160p. (J). (gr. 2-4). 6.95 *(978-1-4027-5424-1(8))* Sterling Publishing Co., Inc.

—Anne of Avonlea. McKowen, Scott, illus. 2008. (Sterling Unabridged Classics Ser.). (ENG.). 256p. (J). 9.95 *(978-1-4027-5428-9(0))* Sterling Publishing Co., Inc.

—Anne of Green Gables. 400p. 2005. 33.95 *(978-1-4218-0660-0(6)*, 1st World Library - Literary Society) 2004. per. 16.95 *(978-1-59540-110-6(5))* 1st World Publishing, Inc.

—Anne of Green Gables. 2009. 292p. 27.99 *(978-1-60512-375-2(7))*; pap. 14.99 *(978-1-60512-475-9(3))* Akasha Publishing, LLC. (Akasha Classics).

—Anne of Green Gables. 2008. 316p. 29.99 *(978-0-554-23545-5(5))* 2008. 316p. 28.99 *(978-0-554-32848-5(8))* 2007. (ENG.). 312p. pap. 24.99 *(978-1-4264-4662-7(4))* Creative Media Partners, LLC.

—Anne of Green Gables. 2008. (Anne of Green Gables Ser.). (ENG.). 366p. (J). (gr. 4-7). pap. 9.95 *(978-0-9782552-6-8(7))* Davenport Pr. CAN. Dist: Independent Pubs. Group.

—Anne of Green Gables. 2007. per. 6.99 *(978-1-4209-2922-5(4))* Digireads.com Publishing.

—Anne of Green Gables. 2007. 284p. per. *(978-1-4065-6399-3(4))* Dodo Pr.

—Anne of Green Gables. 2007. 572p. *(978-1-84702-773-3(3))* 2006. pap. *(978-1-4068-2170-3(5))* Echo Library.

—Anne of Green Gables. 2008. 316p. pap. 16.95 *(978-1-60096-565-4(2))*; pap. 16.95 *(978-1-60096-101-4(0))* Editorium, The.

—Anne of Green Gables. 2009. 242p. pap. 8.58 *(978-0-217-43952-7(7))* General Bks. LLC.

—Anne of Green Gables. 2005. (My First Classics Ser.). 112p. (J). (gr. k-3). pap. 4.99 *(978-0-06-079147-6(0)*, HarperFestival) HarperCollins Pubs.

—Anne of Green Gables. 2005. 21.99 *(978-1-4142-5125-7(4))* IndyPublish.com.

—Anne of Green Gables. 2008. (ENG.). 376p. (gr. k-12). pap. 14.95 *(978-0-7710-9368-5(3)*, New Can Library) McClelland & Stewart CAN. Dist: Penguin Random Hse. LLC.

—Anne of Green Gables. Rubio, Mary Henley & Waterston, Elizabeth, eds. 2007. (Norton Critical Editions Ser.: 0). (ENG., Illus.). 464p. (C). (gr. 9-12). per. 15.02 *(978-0-393-92695-8(8)*, 92695) Norton, W. W. & Co., Inc.

—Anne of Green Gables. 2003. (ENG.). 320p. (gr. 5-7). 5.95 *(978-0-451-52882-7(4)*, Signet) Penguin Publishing Group.

—Anne of Green Gables. 2003. 320p. (J). (gr. 4-7). 12.60 *(978-0-7569-1848-4(0))* Perfection Learning Corp.

—Anne of Green Gables. 2009. 224p. pap. 15.45 *(978-1-4385-1847-3(1)*, Book Jungle) Standard Pubns., Inc.

—Anne of Green Gables. 2008. (Modern Library Classics Ser.). (ENG.). 320p. pap. 9.00 *(978-0-8129-7903-9(6)*, Modern Library) Random House Publishing Group.

—Anne of Green Gables. rev. ed. 2007. 280p. pap. 21.99 *(978-1-4264-4611-5(X))* Creative Media Partners, LLC.

—Anne of Green Gables. l.t. ed. 2006. pap. *(978-1-4068-3174-0(3))* Echo Library.

—Anne of Green Gables. 2004. reprint ed. pap. 27.95 *(978-1-4191-0717-7(8))*; pap. 1.99 *(978-1-4192-0717-4(2))* Kessinger Publishing, LLC.

—Anne of Green Gables. l.t. ed. 2009. (World Classics Ser.). 288p. pap. 21.95 *(978-1-59688-123-5(2))* Large Print Bk. Co., The.

—Anne of the Island. 2006. (ENG.). pap. *(978-1-4068-2171-0(3))*; pap. *(978-1-4068-3175-7(1))* Echo Library.

—Anne of the Island. 2004. reprint ed. pap. 1.99 *(978-1-4192-0718-1(0))*; pap. 30.95 *(978-1-4179-0885-1(8))* Kessinger Publishing, LLC.

—Anne of the Island. l.t. ed. 2004. 396p. 26.00 *(978-1-58287-640-5(1))* North Bks.

—Anne of the Island. 2010. (Puffin Classics Ser.). (ENG.). 368p. (J). (gr. 5-7). pap. 5.99 *(978-0-14-132736-5(7)*, Puffin Books) Penguin Young Readers Group.

—Magic for Marigold. 2014. (ENG.). 336p. (YA). (gr. 5-12). pap. 8.99 *(978-1-4022-8921-7(9))* Sourcebooks, Inc.

Montgomery, L. M & Castelao, Patricia. Anne of Green Gables, 1 vol. 2012. (Calico Illustrated Classics Ser.: No. 4). (ENG., Illus.). 112p. (J). (gr. 3-6). 27.07 *(978-1-61641-612-6(2))* Magic Wagon.

Munday, Evan. Loyalist to a Fault: The Dead Kid Detective Agency #3. 2015. (Dead Kid Detective Agency Ser.: 3). (ENG., Illus.). 320p. (J). (gr. 2-7). pap. 11.95 *(978-1-77041-074-9(0))* Purple Bear Bks., Inc.

Nervelle, Rosemarie. The Witch of Beaver Creek Mine. 2nd ed. 2007. (ENG.). 160p. (J). (gr. 3-7). pap. 9.95 *(978-0-89272-763-6(2))* Down East Bks.

Oppel, Kenneth. The Boundless. Tierney, Jim, illus. 2014. (ENG.). 336p. (J). (gr. 3-7). 17.99 *(978-1-4424-7288-4(X)*, Simon & Schuster Bks. For Young Readers) Simon & Schuster Bks. For Young Readers.

Skelton, John. Band of Acadians. 2009. (ENG.). 168p. (J). (gr. 5-18). pap. 10.99 *(978-1-55488-040-9(8))* Dundurn CAN. Dist: Ingram Publisher Services.

Sutherland, Robert. The Schooner's Revenge. 2008. (ENG.). 176p. (J). pap. 11.99 *(978-0-00-200853-2(X)*, Harper Trophy) HarperCollins Pubs.

Terrell, Brandon. Pluck & Perfection. Max, Iman, illus. 2016. (Time Machine Magazine Ser.). (ENG.). 128p. (gr. 3-4). lib. bdg. 22.65 *(978-1-4965-2595-6(7))* Capstone Press of Coughlan Cos.

Trottier, Maxine. The Death of My Country: The Plains of Abraham Diary of Geneviève Aubuchon. 2005. (Dear Canada Ser.). (ENG., Illus.). 216p. *(978-0-439-96762-4(7))* Scholastic Canada, Ltd.

Watson, Krista M. Pépère's Fiddle. 2008. (J). *(978-0-9717214-5-6(9))* Sunnyside Pr.

Wells, Helen. Cherry Ames, Island Nurse. 2007. (Cherry Ames Nurse Stories Ser.). 224p. (J). (gr. 3-7). 14.95 *(978-0-8261-0423-6(1))* Springer Publishing Co., Inc.

Welvaert, Scott R. The Mosquito King: An Agate & Buck Adventure, 1 vol. Garvey, Brann, illus. 2008. (Vortex Bks.). (ENG.). 112p. (gr. 2-3). pap. 6.95 *(978-1-59889-923-8(6)*, Vortex Bks.) Stone Arch Bks.

Wilson, John. The Flags of War: Fields of Conflict-The American Civil War, Part One. 2015. (ENG.). 192p. pap. 12.95 *(978-1-77203-070-9(8))* Heritage Hse. CAN. Dist: Orca Bk. Pubs. USA.

Wishinsky, Frieda. Hurry, Freedom. Griffiths, Dean & Owlkids Books Inc. Staff, illus. 2008. (Canadian Flyer Adventures Ser.: 7). (ENG.). 96p. (J). (gr. 1-4). per. 9.95 *(978-1-897349-15-1(7)*, Maple Tree Pr.) Owlkids Bks. Inc. CAN. Dist: Publishers Group West (PGW).

Wishinsky, Frieda & Griffiths, Dean. Lost in the Snow. Franson, Leanne & Owlkids Books Inc. Staff, illus. 2008. (Canadian Flyer Adventures Ser.: 10). (ENG.). 96p. (J). (gr. 1-4). pap. 7.95 *(978-1-897349-41-0(6)*, Owlkids) Owlkids Bks. Inc. CAN. Dist: Publishers Group West (PGW).

Wynne-Jones, Tim. Rex Zero & the End of the World. 2013. (ENG.). 208p. (J). (gr. 3-7). pap. 8.99 *(978-0-312-64460-4(4)*, 9780312644604) Square Fish.

CANADA—HISTORY—TO 1763 (NEW FRANCE)

Aretha, David. La Salle: French Explorer of the Mississippi. 2009. (Great Explorers of the World Ser.). (Illus.). 112p. (J). (gr. 7-12). lib. bdg. 33.27 *(978-1-59845-098-9(0))* Enslow Pubs., Inc.

Donaldson-Forbes, Jeff. Jacques Cartier. 2009. (Primary Source Library of Famous Explorers Ser.). 24p. (gr. 4-4). 42.50 *(978-1-60854-126-3(6)*, PowerKids Pr.) Rosen Publishing Group, Inc., The.

—Jacques Marquette & Louis Jolliet. 2009. (Primary Source Library of Famous Explorers Ser.). 24p. (gr. 4-4). 42.50 *(978-1-60854-127-0(4)*, PowerKids Pr.) Rosen Publishing Group, Inc., The.

—La Salle. 2009. (Primary Source Library of Famous Explorers Ser.). 24p. (gr. 4-4). 42.50 *(978-1-60854-129-4(0)*, PowerKids Pr.) Rosen Publishing Group, Inc., The.

Donohue, Moira Rose. Jacques Cartier. 2013. (Illus.). 24p. (J). *(978-1-938813-03-0(0))* State Standards Publishing, LLC.

Dubé, Jean-Claude. The Chevalier de Montmagny: First Governor of New France. Rapley, Elizabeth, tr. from FRE. 2005. (French America Ser.). (ENG., Illus.). 430p. 65.00 *(978-0-7766-3028-1(8))* Univ. of Ottawa Pr./Presses de l'Universite d'Ottawa CAN. Dist: Two Rivers Distribution.

Harkins, Susan Sales & Harkins, William H. The Life & Times of Father Jacques Marquette. 2008. (Profiles in American History Ser.). (Illus.). 48p. (J). (gr. 4-8). lib. bdg. 29.95 *(978-1-58415-528-7(0))* Mitchell Lane Pubs., Inc.

MacLeod, Elizabeth. Samuel de Champlain. Mantha, John, illus. 2008. (Kids Can Read Ser.). (ENG.). 32p. (J). (gr. 1-3). 14.95 *(978-1-55453-049-6(0))* Kids Can Pr., Ltd. CAN. Dist: Hachette Bk. Group.

Morganelli, Adrianna. Samuel de Champlain: From New France to Cape Cod. 2005. (In the Footsteps of Explorers Ser.). (ENG., Illus.). 32p. (J). (gr. 4-5). pap. *(978-0-7787-2450-6(6))* Crabtree Publishing Co.

O'Brien, Cynthia. Explore with Samuel de Champlain. 2014. (ENG., Illus.). 32p. (J). *(978-0-7787-1256-5(7))*; pap. *(978-0-7787-1260-2(5))* Crabtree Publishing Co.

—Explore with Sieur de la Salle. 2014. (ENG., Illus.). 32p. (J). *(978-0-7787-1430-9(6))* Crabtree Publishing Co.

Parker, Lewis K. French Colonies in the Americas. (European Colonies in the Americas Ser.). 24p. 2009. (gr. 2-2). 42.50 *(978-1-61512-318-6(0))* 2003. (Illus.). (J). lib. bdg. 22.60 *(978-0-8239-6473-4(6))* Rosen Publishing Group, Inc., The. (PowerKids Pr.).

Payment, Simone. La Salle: Claiming the Mississippi River for France. (Library of Explorers & Exploration Ser.). 112p. (gr. 5-8). 2009. 66.50 *(978-1-60853-610-8(6))* 2004. (Illus.). lib. bdg. 34.60 *(978-0-8239-3628-1(7))* Rosen Publishing Group, Inc., The. (Rosen Reference).

Petrie, Kristin. Jacques Cartier, 1 vol. 2004. (Explorers Set 1 Ser.). (ENG., Illus.). 32p. (gr. k-6). 27.07 *(978-1-59197-594-6(8)*, Checkerboard Library) ABDO Publishing Co.

—Marquette & Jolliet, 1 vol. 2007. (Explorers Set 2 Ser.). (ENG., Illus.). 32p. (gr. 4-7). 27.07 *(978-1-59679-745-1(2)*, Checkerboard Library) ABDO Publishing Co.

—La Salle, 1 vol. 2007. (Explorers Set 2 Ser.). (ENG., Illus.). 32p. (gr. 4-7). 27.07 *(978-1-59679-750-5(9)*, Checkerboard Library) ABDO Publishing Co.

Sherman, Josepha. Samuel de Champlain: Explorer of the Great Lakes Region & Founder of Quebec. 2009. (Library of Explorers & Exploration Ser.). 112p. (gr. 5-8). 66.50 *(978-1-60853-611-5(4)*, Rosen Reference) Rosen Publishing Group, Inc., The.

Vietze, Andrew. Samuel de Champlain. 2016. (Spotlight on Explorers & Colonization Ser.). 00048p. (J). (gr. 6-6). 31.75 *(978-1-5081-7230-7(7))*; pap. 11.75 *(978-1-5081-7227-7(7))* Rosen Publishing Group, Inc., The.

Woog, Adam. Jacques Cartier. 2009. (Great Explorers Ser.). (Illus.). 112p. (gr. 6-12). 30.00 *(978-1-60413-430-8(5)*, Chelsea Hse.) Facts On File, Inc.

Worth, Richard. New France, 1534-1763. 2007. (National Geographic Voices from ColonialAmerica Ser.). (ENG., Illus.). 112p. (J). (gr. 5-9). 21.95 *(978-1-4263-0147-6(2))*; lib. bdg. 32.90 *(978-1-4263-0148-3(0))* National Geographic Society. (National Geographic Children's Bks.).

CANADA—HISTORY—1914-1945

Baldwin, Douglas & Baldwin, Patricia. World War II. 2010. (Illus.). 48p. *(978-1-55388-720-1(4))* Weigl Educational Pubs. Ltd.

Baldwin, Douglas & Baldwin, Patricia L. World War II. 2010. (Illus.). 48p. pap. *(978-1-55388-724-9(7))* Weigl Educational Pubs. Ltd.

Baldwin, Douglas & Kissock, Heather. World War I. 2010. (Illus.). 48p. *(978-1-55388-719-5(0))*; pap. *(978-1-55388-723-2(9))* Weigl Educational Pubs. Ltd.

Craats, Rennay. 1910: Canadian Decades. 2011. 48p. (C). (gr. 4-6). pap. *(978-1-77071-722-0(6))* Weigl Educational Pubs. Ltd.

—1940: Canadian Decades. 2011. 48p. (C). (gr. 4-6). *(978-1-77071-714-5(5))*; pap. *(978-1-77071-725-1(0))* Weigl Educational Pubs. Ltd.

Nelson, Sheila. A Nation Is Born: World War I & Independence, 1910-1929. 2007. (How Canada Became Canada Ser.). (Illus.). 87p. (YA). (gr. 3-7). lib. bdg. 21.95 *(978-1-4222-0006-3(X)*, 1247972) Mason Crest.

Smith, Robert W. The Great Depression. 2006. (Spotlight on America Ser.). (ENG., Illus.). 48p. (gr. 5-9). per. 9.99 *(978-1-4206-3218-7(3))* Teacher Created Resources, Inc.

Wilson, John. Bitter Ashes: The Story of WW II. 2010. (ENG., Illus.). 96p. (J). (gr. 6-9). 20.95 *(978-1-894917-90-2(1)*, Napoleon & Co.) Dundurn CAN. Dist: Ingram Publisher Services.

World Book, Inc Staff, contrib. by. Canadian Independence. 2010. (J). *(978-0-7166-1502-6(9))* World Bk., Inc.

CANADA—POLITICS AND GOVERNMENT

Dendy, Christina. Bringing Home the Constitution: Defining Moments in Canadian History. 2011. (Illus.). 32p. (gr. 5-8). *(978-1-77071-686-5(6))* Weigl Educational Pubs. Ltd.

Hudak, Heather C. Roles & Responsibilities of Canadian Citizens: Government of Canada. 2010. (Illus.). 32p. pap. *(978-1-55388-684-6(4))* Weigl Educational Pubs. Ltd.

Hudak, Heather C., ed. Federal Government. 2010. (Illus.). 32p. *(978-1-55388-677-8(1))* Weigl Educational Pubs. Ltd.

—Roles & Responsibilities of Canadian Citizens: Government of Canada. 2010. (Illus.). 32p. *(978-1-55388-680-8(1))* Weigl Educational Pubs. Ltd.

Libal, Autumn. The True Costs of Prisons. 2017. (J). ***(978-1-4222-3781-6(8))*** Mason Crest.

Rodger, Ellen. How Does the Canadian Government Work? 2013. (ENG.). 32p. (J). *(978-0-7787-0903-9(5))*; pap. *(978-0-7787-0908-4(6))* Crabtree Publishing Co.

Smith, Roger & McIntosh, Martha. Juveniles Growing up in Prison. 2017. (J). ***(978-1-4222-3783-0(4))*** Mason Crest.

World Book, Inc Staff, contrib. by. Canadian Independence. 2010. (J). *(978-0-7166-1502-6(9))* World Bk., Inc.

Yasuda, Anita. Political Leaders. 2010. (Illus.). 48p. *(978-1-55388-691-4(7))*; pap. *(978-1-55388-696-9(8))* Weigl Educational Pubs. Ltd.

—Provincial & Territorial Governments. 2010. (Illus.). 32p. *(978-1-55388-678-5(X))*; pap. *(978-1-55388-682-2(8))* Weigl Educational Pubs. Ltd.

CANADA—ROYAL CANADIAN MOUNTED POLICE

see Royal Canadian Mounted Police

CANADA—SOCIAL LIFE AND CUSTOMS

Aloian, Molly. Canada Day. 2009. (Celebrations in My World Ser.). (ENG., Illus.). 32p. (J). (gr. k-2). pap. *(978-0-7787-4770-3(0))*; (gr. 1-3). *(978-0-7787-4752-9(2))* Crabtree Publishing Co.

Challen, Paul. The Culture & Crafts of Canada. 2015. (Cultural Crafts Ser.). (ENG.). 32p. (J). (gr. 4-6). pap. 11.75 *(978-1-4994-1118-8(9)*, PowerKids Pr.) Rosen Publishing Group, Inc., The.

Cooper, John, Jr. Season of Rage: Hugh Burnett & the Struggle for Civil Rights. 2005. (ENG., Illus.). 80p. (J). (gr. 5-12). pap. 9.95 *(978-0-88776-700-5(1)*, Tundra Bks.) Tundra Bks. CAN. Dist: Penguin Random Hse. LLC.

Craats, Rennay. The Blacksmith: Pioneers of Canada. 2011. 24p. (YA). (gr. 2-4). *(978-1-77071-681-0(5))*; pap. *(978-1-77071-685-8(8))* Weigl Educational Pubs. Ltd.

—Le Forgeron: Le Début de la Colonie. Karvonen, Tanjah, tr. from ENG. 2011. (FRE., Illus.). 24p. (gr. 3-6). *(978-1-77071-418-2(9))* Weigl Educational Pubs. Ltd.

—Le Magasin Général: Le Début de la Colonie. Karvonen, Tanjah, tr. from ENG. 2011. (FRE., Illus.). 24p. (gr. 3-6). *(978-1-77071-420-5(0))* Weigl Educational Pubs. Ltd.

Foran, Jill. La Petite école: Le Début de la Colonie. Karvonen, Tanjah, tr. from ENG. 2011. (FRE., Illus.). 24p. (gr. 3-6). *(978-1-77071-421-2(9))* Weigl Educational Pubs. Ltd.

C
D

—The School House: Pioneers of Canada. 2011. 24p. (YA). (gr. 2-4). (978-1-77071-680-3(7)); pap. (978-1-77071-684-1(X)) Weigl Educational Pubs. Ltd.
Granfield, Linda. Cowboy: An Album. (J). 9.99 (978-1-55054-230-1(3)) Da Capo Pr., Inc.
Gray Smith, Monique. Speaking Our Truth: A Journey of Reconciliation, 1 vol. 2017. (ENG.). 160p. (J). (gr. 3-7). 29.95 (978-1-4598-1583-4(1)) Orca Bk. Pubs. USA.
Hamilton, Janice. Canada. 2008. pap. 40.95 (978-0-8225-9299-0(1)) Lerner Publishing Group.
Hickman, Pamela & Cavalluzzo, Jean Smith. Righting Canada's Wrongs: Italian Canadian Internment in the Second World War. 2012. (Righting Canada's Wrongs Ser.). (ENG., Illus.). 112p. (gr. 8-12). 34.95 (978-1-4594-0095-5(X), 9781459400955) Lorimer, James & Co., Ltd., Pubs. CAN. Dist: Casemate Pubs. & Bk. Distributors, LLC.
Kalman, Bobbie. A Visual Dictionary of Victorian Life. 2010. (Crabtree Visual Dictionaries Ser.). (ENG.). 32p. (J). (gr. 1-7). lib. bdg. (978-0-7787-3507-6(9)) Crabtree Publishing Co.
Kissock, Heather, ed. Trends. 2011. 48p. (gr. 5-8). (978-1-77071-672-8(6)); pap. (978-1-77071-675-9(0)) Weigl Educational Pubs. Ltd.
Lappi, Megan. The Church: Pioneers of Canada. 2011. 24p. (YA). (gr. 2-4). (978-1-77071-678-0(5)); pap. (978-1-77071-682-7(3)) Weigl Educational Pubs. Ltd.
Mac, Janie. The Moon over Canada. 2013. 20p. pap. 13.77 (978-1-4669-9005-0(8)) Trafford Publishing.
McGill, Jordan. Farm Life: Pioneers of Canada. 2011. 24p. (YA). (gr. 2-4). (978-1-77071-679-7(3)); pap. (978-1-77071-683-4(1)) Weigl Educational Pubs. Ltd.
Middleton, Kathy. Canada's 150th Birthday. 2017. (Illus.). 32p. (J). (978-0-7787-4108-4(7)) Crabtree Publishing Co.
Morrison, Jessica. Christmas. 2010. (Illus.). 24p. (978-1-55388-607-5(0)); pap. (978-1-55388-608-2(9)) Weigl Educational Pubs. Ltd.
—Easter. 2010. (Illus.). 24p. (978-1-55388-610-5(0)); pap. (978-1-55388-611-2(9)) Weigl Educational Pubs. Ltd.
Peppas, Lynn. Victoria Day. 2012. (ENG.). 32p. (J). (978-0-7787-4088-9(9)); pap. (978-0-7787-4093-3(5)) Crabtree Publishing Co.
Sheen, Barbara, ed. Foods of Canada. 2012. (Taste of Culture Ser.). (ENG., Illus.). 64p. (J). (gr. 3-6). lib. bdg. 30.45 (978-0-7377-5947-1(X), Kidhaven) Cengage Gale.
Silvey, Diane. The Kids Book of Aboriginal Peoples in Canada. Mantha, John, illus. 2012. (Kids Book Of Ser.). (ENG.). 64p. (J). (gr. 3-7). 14.95 (978-1-55453-930-7(1)) Kids Can Pr., Ltd. CAN. Dist: Hachette Bk. Group.
Snyder, Gail. Growing up in Canada. 2017. (Growing up Around the World Ser.). (ENG.). 80p. (YA). (gr. 5-12). (978-1-68282-207-4(9)) ReferencePoint Pr., Inc.
World Book, Inc Staff, contrib. by. A Christmas Train Across Canada. 2014. (J). (978-0-7166-0828-8(6)) World Bk., Inc.
Zocchi, Judy. In Canada. Brodie, Neale, illus. 2005. (Global Adventures II Ser.). 32p. (J). pap. 10.95 (978-1-59646-168-0(3)); lib. bdg. 21.65 (978-1-59646-083-6(0)) Dingles & Co.
—In Canada/en Canada. Brodie, Neale, illus. 2005. (Global Adventures II Ser.).Tr. of En Canada. (ENG & SPA.). 32p. (J). pap. 10.95 (978-1-59646-170-3(5)); lib. bdg. 21.65 (978-1-59646-084-3(9)) Dingles & Co.

CANADIAN INDIANS

see Indians of North America—Canada

CANADIAN POETRY—COLLECTIONS

Booth, David. Doctor Knickerbocker & Other Rhymes. 2004. (Illus.). (J). (gr. k-3). spiral bd. (978-0-616-01563-6(1)); spiral bd. (978-0-616-01564-3(X)) Canadian National Institute for the Blind/Institut National Canadien pour les Aveugles.
Clarke, George Elliott. Lasso the Wind: Aurelia's Verses & Other Poems, 1 vol. Tooke, Susan, illus. 2014. (ENG.). 64p. (J). (gr. 3-6). 24.95 (978-1-77108-050-7(7)) Nimbus Publishing, Ltd. CAN. Dist: Orca Bk. Pubs. USA.
Fitch, Sheree. If I Had a Million Onions, 1 vol. Yayo, illus. 2005. (ENG.). 64p. (J). (gr. 2-5). 15.95 (978-1-896580-78-4(5)) Tradewind Bks. CAN. Dist: Orca Bk. Pubs. USA.
Hamilton, Jen, ed. Canadian Poems for Canadian Kids. Fearon, Merrill, illus. 2005. (ENG.). 64p. pap. 14.95 (978-0-9736675-0-9(8)) Subway Bks. CAN. Dist: Univ. of Toronto Pr.
Stone, Tiffany. Floyd the Flamingo: And His Flock of Friends, 1 vol. Shoemaker, Kathryn, illus. 2004. (ENG.). 64p. (J). (gr. 2-5). per. 7.95 (978-1-896580-58-6(0)) Tradewind Bks. CAN. Dist: Orca Bk. Pubs. USA.

CANAL, ANTONIO, CALLED CANALETTO, 1697-1768

see Canaletto, 1697-1768

CANALETTO, 1697-1768

Rice, Earle, Jr. Canaletto. 2007. (Art Profiles for Kids Ser.). (Illus.). 48p. (YA). (gr. 4-7). lib. bdg. 29.95 (978-1-58415-561-4(2)) Mitchell Lane Pubs., Inc.

CANALS

Anderson, Dale. Building the Panama Canal. 2004. (Landmark Events in American History Ser.). (Illus.). 48p. (J). (gr. 5-12). pap. 14.05 (978-0-8368-5422-0(5), Gareth Stevens Secondary Library) Stevens, Gareth Publishing LLLP.
Benoit, Peter. The Panama Canal. 2013. (ENG.). 64p. (J). 30.00 (978-0-531-28205-2(8)); pap. 8.95 (978-0-531-27670-9(8)) Scholastic Library Publishing.
Crewe, Sabrina & Anderson, Dale. Building the Panama Canal. 2005. (Events That Shaped America Ser.). (Illus.). 32p. (gr. 3-6). lib. bdg. 26.00 (978-0-8368-3413-0(5), Gareth Stevens Learning Library) Stevens, Gareth Publishing LLLP.
Honders, Christine. How Do Canals Work? 2016. (STEM Waterworks Ser.). 32p. (J). (gr. 5-5). pap. 11.75 (978-1-4994-1995-5(3), PowerKids Pr.) Rosen Publishing Group, Inc., The.
Latham, Donna. Canals & Dams: Investigate Feats of Engineering with 25 Projects. Christensen, Andrew, illus. 2013. (Build It Yourself Ser.). (ENG.). 128p. (J). (gr. 3-7). 21.95 (978-1-61930-169-6(5)); pap. 16.95 (978-1-61930-165-8(2)) Open City Bks.
Leake, Diyan. Canals, 1 vol. 2014. (Water, Water Everywhere! Ser.). (ENG., Illus.). 24p. (gr. -1-1). 22.65 (978-1-4846-0451-9(2), Acorn) Heinemann-Raintree.
Pascal, Janet. What Is the Panama Canal? 2014. (What Is... ? Ser.). lib. bdg. 16.00 (978-0-606-35688-6(6)) Turtleback Bks.
Pascal, Janet B. What Is the Panama Canal? Foley, Tim & Harper, Fred, illus. 2014. (What Was? Ser.). (ENG.). 112p. (J). (gr. 3-7). 5.99 (978-0-448-47899-9(4), Penguin Workshop) Penguin Young Readers Group.
Ryckman, Tatiana. The Panama Canal. 2017. (J). (978-1-5026-2692-9(6)) Cavendish Square Publishing.
Stefoff, Rebecca. Panama Canal. 2016. (Engineering Wonders Ser.). (ENG., Illus.). 32p. (gr. 3-4). lib. bdg. 27.32 (978-1-4914-8198-1(6), Fact Finders) Capstone Press of Coughlan Cos.
Vander Hook, Sue. Building the Panama Canal, 1 vol. 2010. (Essential Events Set 4 Ser.). (ENG.). 112p. (J). (gr. 6-12). lib. bdg. 35.64 (978-1-60453-942-4(9)) ABDO Publishing Co.

CANALS—FICTION

Burton, Lynne. The Adventures on Ken's Canal: Volume 1. 2011. 32p. pap. 13.75 (978-1-61204-511-5(1), Eloquent Bks.) Strategic Book Publishing & Rights Agency (SBPRA).
—The Adventures on Ken's Canal: Volume 2. 2011. 32p. pap. 13.75 (978-1-61204-510-8(3), Eloquent Bks.) Strategic Book Publishing & Rights Agency (SBPRA).
—The Adventures on Ken's Canal: Volume 3. 2011. 30p. pap. 13.75 (978-1-61204-509-2(X), Eloquent Bks.) Strategic Book Publishing & Rights Agency (SBPRA).
Freymann-Weyr, Garret. French Ducks in Venice. McGuire, Erin, illus. 2011. (ENG.). 56p. (J). (gr. k-4). 16.99 (978-0-7636-4173-3(1)) Candlewick Pr.
Howard, Ellen. The Gate in the Wall. 2007. (ENG.). 160p. (J). (gr. 3-7). pap. 9.95 (978-1-4169-6796-5(6), Simon & Schuster/Paula Wiseman Bks.) Simon & Schuster/Paula Wiseman Bks.
Stacy, Dorothy. Erie Canal Cousins. Stacy, Dorothy, illus. 2007. (Illus.). 110p. (J). per. 9.95 (978-0-9792947-0-9(3)) Blackberry Hill Pr.

CANARIES—FICTION

Folgueira, Rodrigo. Bob the Dog. Bernatene, Poly, illus. 2014. (J). (978-1-4351-5774-3(5)) Barnes & Noble, Inc.
Foreman, Michael. Cat & Canary. 2004. (ENG., Illus.). 32p. (J). pap. 8.99 (978-1-84270-287-1(4)) Andersen Pr. GBR. Dist: Trafalgar Square Publishing.
Rosenberg, Madelyn. Canary in the Coal Mine. 2013. (ENG., Illus.). 192p. (J). (gr. 2-7). 16.95 (978-0-8234-2600-3(9)) Holiday Hse., Inc.
Scherer, Catherine W. Simon & Barklee in China, Book 1 - the Southeast. 2007. (Another Country Calling Ser.). (J). per. 15.00 (978-0-9714502-6-4(9), Explorer Media) Simon & Barklee, Inc./ExplorerMedia.
Stanton, Andy. Sterling & the Canary. 2012. (Stoke Books Titles Ser.). 64p. (J). (gr. 5-8). pap. 7.95 (978-1-78112-030-9(7)); lib. bdg. 22.60 (978-1-78112-029-3(3)) Stoke Bks.
Yolen, Jane. Elsie's Bird. Small, David, illus. 2010. (ENG.). 40p. (J). (gr. k-3). 17.99 (978-0-399-25292-1(4), Philomel Bks.) Penguin Young Readers Group.

CANARY ISLANDS—FICTION

Grahame, Howard. The Wishing Book 2 - Return to Mars. 2009. 102p. (J). pap. (978-1-905809-80-6(8)) Pneuma Springs Publishing.
Howard, Grahame. The Wishing Book 3 - Extermination. 2010. 170p. (J). pap. (978-1-905809-90-5(5)) Pneuma Springs Publishing.

CANCER

see also Leukemia

Alagna, Magdalena. Everything You Need to Know about Chemotherapy. 2009. (Need to Know Library). 64p. (gr. 5-5). 58.50 (978-1-60854-056-3(1)) Rosen Publishing Group, Inc., The.
Ammary, Neyal J. In Mommy's Garden: A Book to Help Explain Cancer to Young Children. Risch, Christopher, illus. 2004. 34p. (J). per. 10.95 (978-0-9754221-0-6(3)) Canyon Beach Visual Communications.
Anniss, Matt. Fighting Cancer. 2014. (Tiny Battlefields Ser.). 48p. (YA). (gr. 6-8). pap. 84.30 (978-1-4824-1308-3(6)) Stevens, Gareth Publishing LLLP.
Aronson, Virginia. Everything You Need to Know about Breast Health & Examinations. 2005. (Need to Know Library). (Illus.). 64p. (YA). (gr. 7-12). lib. bdg. 31.95 (978-0-8239-3224-5(9), NTBRHE) Rosen Publishing Group, Inc., The.
Bankston, John. Lance Armstrong. 2004. (Blue Banner Biography Ser.). (Illus.). 32p. (J). lib. bdg. 25.70 (978-1-58415-334-4(2)) Mitchell Lane Pubs., Inc.
Barraclough, Sue. I Know Someone with Cancer, 1 vol. 2011. (Understanding Health Issues Ser.). (ENG.). 32p. (gr. 1-3). 27.32 (978-1-4329-4564-0(5), Heinemann First Library) Heinemann-Raintree.
Barton, Jenna. C Is for Cure. 2012. 72p. pap. 24.45 (978-1-4525-6069-4(2)) Balboa Pr.
Benson, Michael. Lance Armstrong, Cyclist. 2003. (Ferguson Career Biographies Ser.). (Illus.). 144p. (gr. 6-12). 25.00 (978-0-8160-5479-4(7), Ferguson Publishing Co.) Facts On File, Inc.
Bickerstaff, Linda. Kidney Cancer. 2011. (Cancer & Modern Science Ser.). (J). lib. bdg. 31.95 (978-1-4488-1309-4(3)) Rosen Publishing Group, Inc., The.
Bozzone, Donna M. Cancer Genetics. 2007. (Biology of Cancer Ser.). (Illus.). 126p. (C). lib. bdg. 35.00 (978-0-7910-8818-0(9), Chelsea Hse.) Facts On File, Inc.
—Causes of Cancer. 2007. (Biology of Cancer Ser.). 136p. (C). (gr. 9). 35.00 (978-0-7910-8819-7(7), Chelsea Hse.) Facts On File, Inc.
Bryfonski, Dedria. Breast Cancer. 2016. (Opposing Viewpoints Ser.). (ENG.). 224p. (gr. 7-12). 48.80 (978-0-7377-7550-1(5), Greenhaven Pr., Inc.) Cengage Gale.
Calloway, Jill Trotta. There's an Elephant in My Room: A child's unforgettable journey through cancer proved hope was stronger than Fear. 2010. 44p. pap. 16.99 (978-1-4490-8244-4(0)) AuthorHouse.
Cancer & Modern Science. (Illus.). (YA). (gr. 7-12). 175.50 (978-1-4042-0627-4(2)) Rosen Publishing Group, Inc., The.
Cancer Journal for the Survivor in You. 2004. (YA). spiral bd. 9.95 (978-0-9749216-0-0(2)) Rivers, Swannee.
Capaccio, George. Cancer Treatments. 2013. (Illus.). 64p. (J). (gr. 6-9). 34.21 (978-1-60870-466-8(1)) Cavendish Square Publishing.
Cappacio, George. Cancer Treatments. 2013. (Advances in Medicine Ser.). 64p. (J). (gr. 6-9). pap. 15.28 (978-1-62712-009-8(2)) Cavendish Square Publishing.
Clifford, Mikaela Rae. Live & Love it Up! When Life Gets You Down. 2010. 32p. pap. 14.99 (978-1-4520-5868-9(7)) AuthorHouse.
Cooper, Heather, et al. Jacob Has Cancer: His Friends Want to Help. McMillion, Lindsey, illus. 2012. (ENG.). 16p. (J). (gr. k-2). pap. 3.50 (978-1-60443-012-7(5)) American Cancer Society, Inc.
Donovan, Sandy. Lance Armstrong. (Amazing Athletes Ser.). (Illus.). 32p. (J). 2005. (gr. 3-4). lib. bdg. 23.93 (978-0-8225-3691-8(9)) 2004. (gr. 2-5). per. 5.95 (978-0-8225-2039-9(7)) Lerner Publishing Group.
Dorfman, Elsa, photos by. No Hair Day. 2004. (Wgbh Specials Ser.). (Illus.). (gr. 7-18). 19.95 (978-1-57807-730-4(3), WG1205) WGBH Boston Video.
Dreyer, ZoAnn. Living with Cancer. (Teen's Guides). (gr. 6-12). 2008. 208p. per. 14.95 (978-0-8160-7561-4(1), Checkmark Bks.) 2007. (Illus.). 192p. 34.95 (978-0-8160-6484-7(9)) Facts On File, Inc.
Earl, Esther, et al. This Star Won't Go Out: The Life & Words of Esther Grace Earl. 2014. (ENG., Illus.). 384p. (J). (gr. 7). 19.99 (978-0-525-42636-3(1), Dutton Books for Young Readers) Penguin Young Readers Group.
Egan, Tracie. Skin Cancer: Current & Emerging Trends in Detection & Treatment. 2005. (Cancer & Modern Science Ser.). (Illus.). 64p. (J). (gr. -1-7). lib. bdg. 31.95 (978-1-4042-0390-7(7)) Rosen Publishing Group, Inc., The.
Ellwood, Nancy. Lance Armstrong: With a Discussion of Determination. 2004. (Values in Action Ser.). (J). (978-1-59203-073-6(4)) Learning Challenge, Inc.
Fead, Beverlye Hyman, et al. Nana, What's Cancer? Bersani, Shennen, illus. 2009. (ENG.). 64p. (J). (gr. -1-7). pap. 14.95 (978-1-60443-010-3(9), 1604430109) American Cancer Society, Inc.
Filigenzi, Courtney. My Cancer Days. Tadgell, Nicole, illus. 2015. (ENG.). 24p. (J). (gr. 2-4). 12.95 (978-1-60443-091-2(5)) American Cancer Society, Inc.
Fitzmaurice, John. Miracles from Maddie. Cedar, Emily, illus. 2010. 52p. pap. 21.25 (978-1-4490-5332-1(7)) AuthorHouse.
Forest, Chris. What You Need to Know about Cancer. 2015. (Focus on Health Ser.). (ENG., Illus.). 32p. (gr. 3-4). pap. 7.95 (978-1-4914-4899-1(7)) Capstone Press of Coughlan Cos.
Fredericks, Carrie. Breast Cancer. 2008. (Perspectives on Diseases & Disorders Ser.). (ENG., Illus.). 159p. (YA). (gr. 10-12). lib. bdg. 38.95 (978-0-7377-4244-2(5), LML02109-243156, Greenhaven Pr., Inc.) Cengage Gale.
Freedman, Jeri. Lymphoma: Current & Emerging Trends in Detection & Treatment. (Cancer & Modern Science Ser.). 64p. 2009. (gr. 5-5). 58.50 (978-1-61511-782-6(2)) 2005. (Illus.). (J). (gr. -1-7). lib. bdg. 31.95 (978-1-4042-0389-1(3)) Rosen Publishing Group, Inc., The.
—Ovarian Cancer: Current & Emerging Trends in Detection & Treatment. 2009. (Cancer & Modern Science Ser.). 64p. (gr. 5-5). 58.50 (978-1-61511-783-3(0)) Rosen Publishing Group, Inc., The.
Giddens, Sandra. Coping with Chemotherapy. 2009. (Coping Ser.). 192p. (gr. 7-12). 63.90 (978-1-61511-995-0(7)) Rosen Publishing Group, Inc., The.
Giddens, Sandra & Giddens, Owen. Coping with Chemotherapy. 2005. (Coping Ser.). (Illus.). 192p. (YA). (gr. 7-12). lib. bdg. 34.60 (978-0-8239-3361-7(X)) Rosen Publishing Group, Inc., The.
Greenfield, Nancy Reuben. When Mommy Had a Mastectomy. Butler, Ralph M., illus. 2016. 40p. (gr. -1-3). 14.95 (978-0-910155-60-1(7)) Bartleby Pr.
Greenhaven Press Editors & Fisanick, Christina, eds. Ovarian Cancer. 2012. (Perspectives on Diseases & Disorders Ser.). (ENG., Illus.). 144p. (gr. 10-12). 38.95 (978-0-7377-5781-1(7), Greenhaven Pr., Inc.) Cengage Gale.
Gutman, Bill. Lance Armstrong: A Biography. 2009. (ENG.). 192p. (YA). (gr. 7). pap. 9.99 (978-1-4169-9845-7(4), Simon Pulse) Simon Pulse.
Hasan, Heather. Bone Cancer. 2009. (Cancer & Modern Science Ser.). lib. bdg. 31.95 (978-1-4358-5010-1(6)) Rosen Publishing Group, Inc., The.
—Cervical Cancer: Current & Emerging Trends in Detection & Treatment. 2009. (Cancer & Modern Science Ser.). 64p. (gr. 5-5). 58.50 (978-1-61511-774-1(1)) Rosen Publishing Group, Inc., The.
Hecht, Alan. Cancer Treatment Drugs. 2010. (Understanding Drugs Ser.). 136p. (YA). (gr. 9-12). 34.95 (978-1-60413-535-0(2)) Facts On File, Inc.
Horton, Nancy Jane & Horton, Carter. The Big, Fat, Bald Head! 2011. (978-1-77069-252-7(5)) Word Alive Pr.
Johanson, Paula. Breast Cancer Prevention. (Girls' Health Ser.). 48p. 2009. (gr. 5-6). 53.00 (978-1-61512-728-3(3), Rosen Reference) 2007. (Illus.). (YA). (gr. 7-12). lib. bdg. 29.25 (978-1-4042-1947-2(1)) Rosen Publishing Group, Inc., The.
Jones, Brenn. Learning about Resilience from the Life of Lance Armstrong. 2009. (Character Building Book Ser.). 24p. (gr. 2-3). 42.50 (978-1-60854-967-2(4), PowerKids Pr.) Rosen Publishing Group, Inc., The.
Kenny, Paraic & Bozzone, Donna M. Stages of Cancer Development. 2007. (Biology of Cancer Ser.). 136p. (C). (gr. 9). 35.00 (978-0-7910-8825-8(1), Chelsea Hse.) Facts On File, Inc.
Kramer, Barbara. Lance Armstrong: Determined to Beat the Odds. 2005. (Awesome Values in Famous Lives Ser.). (Illus.). 48p. (J). (gr. 4-7). lib. bdg. 25.27 (978-0-7660-2377-2(X), Enslow Elementary) Enslow Pubs., Inc.
Lance Armstrong. 2004. (J). 31.36 (978-0-7614-1761-3(3)) Marshall Cavendish Corp.
Langwith, Jacqueline. Lung Cancer. Gale Editors, ed. 2010. (Perspectives on Diseases & Disorders Ser.). (ENG., Illus.). 144p. (gr. 12-12). 44.30 (978-0-7377-5002-7(2), Greenhaven Pr., Inc.) Cengage Gale.
Levy, Janey. Esophageal Cancer. 2011. (Cancer & Modern Science Ser.). (J). lib. bdg. 31.95 (978-1-4488-1310-0(7)) Rosen Publishing Group, Inc., The.
Lew, Kristi. The Truth about Cancer: Understanding & Fighting a Deadly Disease. 2009. (Issues in Focus Today Ser.). (Illus.). 104p. (J). (gr. 6). lib. bdg. 33.27 (978-0-7660-3068-8(7)) Enslow Pubs., Inc.
Lewis, Alaric. When Someone You Love Has Cancer: A Guide to Help Kids Cope. Alley, R. W., illus. 2005. (Elf-Help Books for Kids Ser.). 32p. per. 7.95 (978-0-87029-395-5(8)) Abbey Pr.
Magee, Elaine. Tell Me What to Eat to Help Prevent Breast Cancer. (Tell Me What to Eat Ser.). 168p. 2009. (gr. 9-9). 63.90 (978-1-60853-306-0(9)) 2008. (Illus.). (J). lib. bdg. 35.95 (978-1-4042-1839-0(4)) Rosen Publishing Group, Inc., The.
Marquardt, Meg. Curing Cancer. (J). 2017. (978-1-62143-516-7(4)) 2016. (ENG., Illus.). 32p. pap. 9.95 (978-1-63235-392-4(X)) Pr. Room Editions LLC.
Martin, Chia & Martin, Carrie. The Rainbow Feelings of Cancer: A Book for Children Who Have a Loved One with Cancer. 2nd rev. ed. 2016. (ENG., Illus.). 32p. pap. 19.95 (978-1-942493-13-6(4)) Hohm Pr.
Massari, Francesca. Everything You Need to Know about Cancer. 2005. (Need to Know Library). (Illus.). 64p. (YA). (gr. 7-12). lib. bdg. 31.95 (978-0-8239-3164-4(1), NTCANC) Rosen Publishing Group, Inc., The.
McAuliffe, Bill. Cancer. 2011. (Living with Disease Ser.). (Illus.). 48p. (J). (gr. 5-8). lib. bdg. 34.25 (978-1-60818-073-8(5), 1331495, Creative Education) Creative Co., The.
McKinnell, Robert G. Prevention of Cancer. 2008. (Biology of Cancer Ser.). (Illus.). 144p. (C). (gr. 9). lib. bdg. 35.00 (978-0-7910-8827-2(8), Chelsea Hse.) Facts On File, Inc.
Meyers, Barbara & Mays, Lydia. The Long & the Short of It: A Tale about Hair. Bersani, Shennen, illus. 2011. (ENG.). 32p. (J). (gr. 2-4). 14.95 (978-1-60443-017-2(6)) American Cancer Society, Inc.
Miss Riedel. Superheroes Breathe Cancer Away: (a Little Book for Children Living with Cancer in Their Lives.) 2012. 28p. pap. 17.99 (978-1-4685-7981-9(9)) AuthorHouse.
Moehn, Heather. Everything You Need to Know When Someone You Know Has Leukemia. 2005. (Need to Know Library). (Illus.). 64p. (YA). (gr. 7-12). lib. bdg. 31.95 (978-0-8239-3121-7(8), NTLEUK) Rosen Publishing Group, Inc., The.
Moore-Mallinos, Jennifer & Roca, Nuria. Mom Has Cancer! Fabrega, Marta, illus. 2008. (Let's Talk about It Ser.). (ENG.). 32p. (J). (gr. -1-2). pap. 7.99 (978-0-7641-4074-7(4)) Barron's Educational Series, Inc.
My Book about Cancer: A Workbook to Help Children Deal with the Diagnosis & Treatment of a Father with Cancer. 2003. (ACE.). (J). 6.00 (978-1-890504-33-5(5), INPU0546D) Oncology Nursing Society.
Nelson, Sheila & Walker, Ida. Youth with Cancer: Facing the Shadows. 2007. (Helping Youth with Mental, Physical, & Social Challenges Ser.). (Illus.). 128p. (YA). (gr. 8-12). pap. 14.95 (978-1-4222-0439-9(1)) Mason Crest.
Orr, Tamra. Frequently Asked Questions about Bone Cancer. 2009. (FAQ: Teen Life Ser.). 64p. (gr. 5-6). 58.50 (978-1-61512-568-5(X)) Rosen Publishing Group, Inc., The.
—Liver Cancer. 2009. (Cancer & Modern Science Ser.). lib. bdg. 31.95 (978-1-4358-5009-5(2)) Rosen Publishing Group, Inc., The.
—Liver Cancer: Current & Emerging Trends in Detection & Treatment. 2009. (Cancer & Modern Science Ser.). 64p. (gr. 5-5). 58.50 (978-1-61511-778-9(4)) Rosen Publishing Group, Inc., The.
—Ovarian Tumors & Cysts. 2009. (Library of Sexual Health Ser.). 64p. (gr. 6-6). 58.50 (978-1-60853-847-8(8)) Rosen Publishing Group, Inc., The.
Owens, Jim. The Survivorship Net: A Parable for the Family, Friends, & Caregivers of People with Cancer. Cass, Bill, illus. 2010. (ENG.). 48p. (gr. 2). 14.95 (978-1-60443-018-9(4)) American Cancer Society, Inc.
Perna, Maria. Meatballs, Oddballs, & Curveballs. 2012. 28p. pap. 24.95 (978-1-4626-6950-9(6)) PublishAmerica, Inc.
Pezzi, Bryan. Terry Fox. 2010. (Illus.). 24p. (978-1-77071-598-1(3)); pap. (978-1-77071-604-9(1)) Weigl Educational Pubs. Ltd.
Rauf, Don, et al. What You Can Do about Breast Cancer. 2015. (Contemporary Diseases & Disorders Ser.). (ENG., Illus.). 128p. (J). (gr. 7-7). 37.27 (978-0-7660-7032-5(8)) Enslow Pubs., Inc.
Rawlins, Trey. When Mommy Had Cancer. 2013. 26p. pap. 13.95 (978-1-4497-9600-6(1), WestBow Pr.) Author Solutions, Inc.
Riddering, Marggie & Riddering, David. Atravesando el Valle. 2005. (SPA.). (YA). 9.95 (978-0-9765977-0-4(5)) Riddering, Marggie.
Riddering, Margie & Riddering, David. Walking through the Valley. 2nd ed. 2005. (YA). 9.95 (978-0-9765977-1-1(3)) Riddering, Marggie.
Rocha, Toni L. Coping When Someone in Your Family Has Cancer. (Coping Ser.). 192p. (gr. 7-12). 2009. 63.90 (978-1-61511-988-2(4)) 2005. (Illus.). (YA). lib. bdg. 34.60 (978-0-8239-3195-8(1)) Rosen Publishing Group, Inc., The.
Sachedina, Shenin. Metu & Lee Learn about Breast Cancer. 2007. (Illus.). 32p. (J). (gr. k-5). 14.99 (978-0-9778648-0-5(4)) Sachedina, Dr. Shenin Medical Education Products.
Schmidt, Rebecca C., contrib. by. My Book about Cancer: A Workbook to Help Children Deal with the Diagnosis & Treatment of a Father with Cancer. 2003. (Illus.). 54p. (J). (gr. 3-7). pap. 6.00 (978-1-890504-36-6(X), INPU0546M) Oncology Nursing Society.
Scientific American Staff. Tackling Cancer. 2009. (Scientific American Cutting-Edge Science Ser.). 120p. (gr. 9-9). 63.90 (978-1-60853-080-9(9)) Rosen Publishing Group, Inc., The.
Shapiro, Dean & Sheen, Barbara. Prostate Cancer. 2008. (Diseases & Disorders Ser.). (ENG., Illus.). 104p. (YA). (gr. 7-12). lib. bdg. 34.95 (978-1-59018-593-3(5), LML02109-198421) Cengage Gale.
Sheen, Barbara. Lung Cancer. 2007. (Diseases & Disorders Ser.). (ENG., Illus.). 104p. (YA). (gr. 8-12). lib. bdg. 34.95 (978-1-4205-0043-1(0), Lucent Bks.) Cengage Gale.
Silver, Alex, et al. Our Mom Is Getting Better. 2007. (ENG., Illus.). 32p. (J). (gr. -1-3). 14.95 (978-0-944235-85-0(9), 9780944235850) American Cancer Society, Inc.

Silver, Emily, et al. Our Dad Is Getting Better. 2007. (ENG., Illus.). 32p. (J). (gr. -1-3). 14.95 *(978-0-944235-86-7(7),* 9780944235867) American Cancer Society, Inc.

Silver, Maya & Silver, Marc. My Parent Has Cancer & It Really Sucks. 2013. (ENG.). 272p. (YA). (gr. 7-12). pap. 17.99 *(978-1-4022-7307-0(X),* 9781402273070) Sourcebooks, Inc.

Silverstein, Alvin, et al. The Breast Cancer Update. 2007. (Disease Update Ser.). (Illus.). 128p. (J). (gr. 3-7). lib. bdg. 33.27 *(978-0-7660-2747-3(3))* Enslow Pubs., Inc.

—Cancer. 2005. (Twenty-First Century Medical Library). (Illus.). 121p. (YA). (gr. 7-12). lib. bdg. 27.93 *(978-0-7613-2833-9(5))* Lerner Publishing Group.

Skin Cancer. 2007. (Biology of Cancer Ser.). (Illus.). 168p. (C). (gr. 9-12). lib. bdg. 35.00 *(978-0-7910-8938-5(X),* Chelsea Hse.) Facts On File, Inc.

Slomski, Genevieve T. Living with Cancer, 1 vol. 2012. (Living with Health Challenges Set 1 Ser.). (ENG.). 112p. (J). (gr. 6-12). lib. bdg. 35.64 *(978-1-61783-124-9(7),* Essential Library) ABDO Publishing Co.

Smith, Cynthia & Wishbone. Dogs Get Cancer Too: A True Story. 2010. 48p. 19.49 *(978-1-4490-4129-8(9))* AuthorHouse.

Snyder, R. Bradley & Engelsgjerd, Marc. What Every Child Needs to Know about Cancer. Kempe, Barbara, ed. 2014. (ENG.). 22p. (-k). 8.95 *(978-1-940705-01-9(0))* Need To Know Publishing.

Squire, Ann O. Cancer. 2015. (ENG., Illus.). 48p. (J). lib. bdg. *(978-0-531-21472-5(9),* Orchard Bks.) Scholastic, Inc.

Sterling Casil, Amy. Pancreatic Cancer: Current & Emerging Trends in Detection & Treatment. 2009. (Cancer & Modern Science Ser.). 64p. (gr. 5-5). 58.50 *(978-1-61511-784-0(9))* Rosen Publishing Group, Inc., The.

Stewart, Gail B. Alexandra Scott: Champion for Cancer Research. 2006. (Young Heroes Ser.). (ENG., Illus.). 64p. (J). (gr. 4-7). lib. bdg. 28.75 *(978-0-7377-3613-7(5),* Kidhaven) Cengage Gale.

Stokes, Mark. Prostate Cancer: Current & Emerging Trends in Detection & Treatment. (Cancer & Modern Science Ser.). 64p. 2009. (gr. 5-5). 58.50 *(978-1-61511-785-7(7))* 2005. (Illus.). (YA). (gr. 7-12). lib. bdg. 31.95 *(978-1-4042-0391-4(5))* Rosen Publishing Group, Inc., The.

Students & Teachers at Christian Academy. Cutting Class: The St. Baldrick's Story of Christian Academy of Louisville Rock Creek. 2008. (Illus.). 32p. 16.95 *(978-0-929915-77-7(1))* Headline Bks., Inc.

Sundquist, Josh. We Should Hang Out Sometime: Embarrassingly, a True Story. 2014. (ENG., Illus.). 336p. (YA). (gr. 7-17). 18.00 *(978-0-316-25102-0(X))* Little Brown & Co.

Tanner, Jerome E. Myeloma. 2008. (Biology of Cancer Ser.). (Illus.). 119p. (C). (gr. 9). lib. bdg. 35.00 *(978-0-7910-8824-1(3),* Chelsea Hse.) Facts On File, Inc.

Tate, M. My Little Life: A Cancer Survivor's Story As Told by Nature. Tate, M., photos by. 2004. (Illus.). (YA). pap. 10.00 *(978-0-9761969-0-7(5))* Heads First (1st).

Therrien, Patricia. An Enemy Within: Overcoming Cancer & Other Life-Threatening Diseases. (Survivors Ser.). 2010. 128p. (YA). (gr. 7-12). 24.95 *(978-1-4222-0450-4(2))* 2009. (J). pap. 24.95 *(978-1-4222-1463-3(X))* Mason Crest.

Thomas, Cristine. Can I Catch Cancer? Explaing cancer to Children. Thomas, Cristine, illus. 2007. (Illus.). 44p. (J). 10.95 *(978-0-9778796-9-4(0))* Brittany's Bks.

Thompson, Gabrielle. The ABCs of Childhood Cancer. 2008. (Illus.). (J). *(978-1-59298-247-9(6))* Beaver's Pond Pr., Inc.

Thornton, Catherine. Why Mum? A Small Child Dealing with a Big Problem. 2005. (ENG.). 20p. (J). pap. 9.95 *(978-1-85390-891-0(6))* Veritas Pubns. IRL. Dist: Dufour Editions, Inc.

Thornton, Denise. Living with Cancer: The Ultimate Teen Guide. 2011. (It Happened to Me Ser.: 30). (ENG.). 190p. 45.00 *(978-0-8108-7277-6(3))* Scarecrow Pr., Inc.

USA Today Health Reports Set: Diseases & Disorders, 11 vols. Incl. ADHD. Farrar, Amy. 112p. 2010. lib. bdg. 34.60 *(978-0-7613-5455-0(7));* AIDS. Sonenklar, Carol. 128p. 2011. lib. bdg. 34.60 *(978-0-8225-8581-7(2));* Anorexia & Bulimia. Sonenklar, Carol. 128p. 2010. lib. bdg. 34.60 *(978-0-8225-6786-8(5));* Asthma. Murphy, Wendy. 128p. 2011. 34.60 *(978-0-7613-5457-4(3));* Autism Spectrum Disorders. Rodriguez, Ana Maria. 128p. 2011. lib. bdg. 34.60 *(978-0-7613-5883-1(8));* Depression. Moragne, Wendy. 128p. 2011. 34.60 *(978-0-7613-5882-4(X));* Food Poisoning & Foodborne Diseases. Landau, Elaine. (Illus.). 128p. 2010. lib. bdg. 34.60 *(978-0-8225-7290-9(7));* Hepatitis. Goldsmith, Connie. (Illus.). 128p. 2010. lib. bdg. 34.60 *(978-0-8225-6787-5(3));* Influenza. Goldsmith, Connie. 128p. 2010. lib. bdg. 34.60 *(978-0-7613-5881-7(1));* Obsessive-Compulsive Disorder. Pedrick, Cherry. 112p. 2011. lib. bdg. 34.60 *(978-0-7613-5884-8(6));* Skin Cancer. Goldsmith, Connie. 128p. 2010. 34.60 *(978-0-7613-5469-7(7));* (gr. 6-12). (USA TODAY Health Reports: Diseases & Disorders Ser.). (ENG., Illus.). 2011. Set lib. bdg. 692.00 *(978-0-7613-5880-0(3))* Lerner Publishing Group.

Van Dernoot, Peter R. & van Dernoot, Peter R. Talking with My Treehouse Friends about Cancer: An Activity Book for Children of Parents with Cancer. Opsahl, Gail Kohler, illus. 2007. (ENG.). 24p. (J). (gr. 1-7). pap. 12.95 *(978-1-55591-630-5(9))* Fulcrum Publishing.

Victory in the Valleys: A Journey Through the Valleys of Life Including Cancer & Death. 2004. (YA). pap. 12.99 *(978-0-9753818-0-9(6))* Victory Pr.

Watters, Debbie, et al. Where's Mom's Hair? A Family's Journey Through Cancer, 1 vol. Hogan, Sophie, photos by. 2005. (ENG., Illus.). 32p. (J). (gr. -1-5). per. 14.95 *(978-1-896764-94-8(0))* Second Story Pr. CAN. Dist: Orca Bk. Pubs. USA.

What If. . . . Someone I Love Has Cancer. 2003. (J). per. 19.95 incl. cd-rom *(978-0-9676189-1-3(6))* Star Pr., The.

Wyborny, Sheila. Hodgkin's Disease. 2008. (Diseases & Disorders Ser.). (ENG., Illus.). 128p. (gr. 7-10). lib. bdg. 39.90 *(978-1-59018-674-9(5),* LML02109-221239, Lucent Bks.) Cengage Gale.

Zweber, Rhonda. Mommy's Hats. 2009. 36p. pap. 18.50 *(978-1-60860-204-9(4),* Eloquent Bks.) Strategic Book Publishing & Rights Agency (SBPRA).

CANCER—FICTION

Adams, Karen S. Introducing Marlon! Your Cancer-Fighting Friend! A Story to Help a Child Learn How to Use Visual Imagery to Fight Cancer. 2008. 20p. pap. 11.49 *(978-1-4343-7840-8(3))* AuthorHouse.

Albert, Louise. Less Than Perfect. 2003. (ENG.). 224p. (J). (gr. 7-18). tchr. ed. 17.95 *(978-0-8234-1688-2(7))* Holiday Hse., Inc.

Amarone, Morgan. Madison's Journey. Ruocco, Paul, illus. 2011. 30p. (J). pap. 16.99 *(978-0-9841934-5-5(6))* Bryson Taylor Publishing.

Anderson, Laurie Halse. Say Good-Bye, No. 5. 2008. (Vet Volunteers Ser.: 5). (ENG.). 160p. (J). (gr. 3-7). 7.99 *(978-0-14-241100-1(0),* Puffin Books) Penguin Young Readers Group.

Aparici Martin, Irene. Mom Goes to War. 2013. (ENG., Illus.). 24p. (J). (gr. 2-4). 15.95 *(978-84-15503-20-0(2))* Eastern National.

Bell, Juliet. Kepler's Dream. 2013. (ENG.). 256p. (J). (gr. 5). pap. 6.99 *(978-0-14-242648-7(2),* Puffin Books) Penguin Young Readers Group.

Bennett, Sophia. The Look. 2013. (J). (ENG.). 336p. (gr. 7). 17.99 *(978-0-545-46438-3(2)); (978-0-545-46439-0(0))* Scholastic, Inc. (Chicken Hse., The).

Bobrow, Laura J. He Listens. 2004. (YA). 9.95 *(978-0-9716489-4-4(8))* Pastorpreneur Ministries.

Bostic, Megan. Never Eighteen. 2012. (ENG.). 208p. (YA). (gr. 7). pap. 8.99 *(978-0-547-55076-3(6))* Houghton Mifflin Harcourt Publishing Co.

Brittany's Books, illus. & creator. I Can Too! African American Girls. Brittany's Books, creator. 2006. 44p. (J). lib. bdg. 9.95 *(978-0-9778796-8-7(2))* Brittany's Bks.

Bryce, Celia. Anthem for Jackson Dawes. 2013. (ENG.). 240p. (YA). (gr. 7-12). 16.99 *(978-1-59990-975-2(8),* 9781599909752, Bloomsbury USA Childrens) Bloomsbury Publishing USA.

Buckingham, Dorothea N. Staring down the Dragon. 2006. (ENG.). 226p. (YA). (gr. 7-12). pap. 10.95 *(978-0-9724577-3-6(9))* Sydney Pr., LLC.

Buckley, Colleen. Grandma Kathy Has Cancer. Sponaugle, Kim, illus. 2007. 24p. per. 11.50 *(978-1-59858-422-6(7))* Dog Ear Publishing, LLC.

Byrne, Jean Livingstone. Legends of Newgrange. 2014. 54p. pap. 12.99 *(978-1-84386-818-7(0))* Vanguard Pr.

Caldwell, V. M. Runt: Story of a Boy. 2006. (ENG.). 208p. (J). (gr. 2-8). 16.95 *(978-1-57131-662-2(0));* (gr. 3-7). per. 6.95 *(978-1-57131-661-5(2))* Milkweed Editions.

Castrovilla, Selene. The Girl Next Door. 2010. 240p. (YA). (gr. 9-12). 16.95 *(978-1-934813-15-7(X))* Westside Bks.

Chambers, Cindy & Miller, Gabriella. Beamer Learns about Cancer: The Beamer Book Series. 2013. 32p. pap. 14.95 *(978-1-4575-2246-8(2))* Dog Ear Publishing, LLC.

Cheng, Andrea. Brushing Mom's Hair. Wong, Nicole, illus. 2009. (ENG.). 64p. (J). (gr. 5-8). 17.95 *(978-1-59078-599-7(1),* Front Street) Boyds Mills Pr.

Chilman-Blair, Kim & Taddeo, John. Medikidz Explain Brain Tumours: What's up with Rachel? 2010. (Illus.). 32p. (J). pap. *(978-1-906935-09-2(2))* Medikidz Ltd.

Conklin, Melanie. Counting Thyme. 2016. (ENG.). 320p. (J). (gr. 5). 16.99 *(978-0-399-17330-1(7),* G.P. Putnam's Sons Books for Young Readers) Penguin Young Readers Group.

Crow, Matthew. The Brilliant Light of Amber Sunrise. 2015. (ENG., Illus.). 304p. (YA). (gr. 9). 17.99 *(978-1-4814-1873-7(4),* Simon Pulse) Simon Pulse.

Cummins, Chris. Bigsbie - A Bunny's Tale of Surviving Cancer. 2007. 107p. pap. 15.00 *(978-1-4116-5785-4(3))* Lulu Pr., Inc.

Curtis, Marci Lyn. The One Thing. 2015. (ENG., Illus.). 336p. (YA). (gr. 7-12). 17.99 *(978-1-4847-0902-3(0))* Hyperion Bks. for Children.

Daley-Prado, M. J. Grandma,What Is Cancer? 2007. 20p. 13.95 *(978-1-4357-0204-2(2))* Lulu Pr., Inc.

De Kockere, Geert & Dom, An. Dragon Fire. Van Hemeldonck, Tineke, illus. 2015. (ENG.). 32p. (J). (gr. -1-k). 16.99 *(978-1-63220-599-5(8),* Sky Pony Pr.) Skyhorse Publishing Co., Inc.

DeLand, M. Maitland. The Great Katie Kate Tackles Questions about Cancer. 2010. (Illus.). 30p. (J). (gr. -1-1). 14.95 *(978-1-60832-027-1(8),* Greenleaf Book Group Pr.) Greenleaf Book Group.

Delmonte, Ellis. Miracle Girl. 2007. (ENG.). 208p. (YA). per. *(978-0-9555096-4-3(5))* Hawkwood Bks.

Ditmars, Maribeth R. The Bald-Headed Princess: Cancer, Chemo, & Courage. 2010. 80p. (J). (gr. 3-8). 14.95 *(978-1-4338-0737-4(8));* pap. 9.95 *(978-1-4338-0738-1(6))* American Psychological Assn. (Magination Pr.).

Fallon, Kevin A. Rest in Peas: What Does that Mean? 2005. per. 12.95 *(978-1-59196-943-3(3))* Instant Pub.

Fehler, Gene. Never Blame the Umpire, 1 vol. 2010. (ENG.). 192p. (J). (gr. 4-7). 12.99 *(978-0-310-71941-0(0))* Zonderkidz.

Filigenzi, Courtney & Bersani, Shennen. Let My Colors Out. Bersani, Shennen, illus. 2009. (ENG., Illus.). 16p. (J). (gr. -1-k). pap. 11.95 *(978-1-60443-011-0(7),* 1604430117) American Cancer Society, Inc.

Forest, G. Daddy's Different: A Look at Brain Injury Through a Child's Eyes. 2013. 34p. 21.95 *(978-1-4575-1742-6(6))* Dog Ear Publishing, LLC.

Gemeinhart, Dan. The Honest Truth. 2015. (ENG.). 240p. (J). (gr. 3-7). 16.99 *(978-0-545-66573-5(6),* Scholastic Pr.) Scholastic, Inc.

Gervay, Susanne. Always Jack. Wilcox, Cathy, illus. 2013. 148p. (J). *(978-1-61067-226-9(7))* Kane Miller.

Gervay, Susanne & Wilcox, Cathy. Always Jack. 2014. (ENG.). 160p. (J). pap. 5.99 *(978-1-61067-130-9(9))* Kane Miller.

Gibson, Marley. Radiate. 2012. (ENG.). 416p. (YA). (gr. 7). pap. 21.99 *(978-0-547-61728-2(3))* Houghton Mifflin Harcourt Publishing Co.

Green, John. The Fault in Our Stars. 2013. (ENG & JPN.). 337p. (YA). (gr. 9-12). pap. *(978-4-00-116405-3(1))* Iwanami Shoten.

—The Fault in Our Stars. 2013. (CHI & ENG.). 304p. (YA). (gr. 9-12). pap. *(978-7-5448-3122-2(1))* Jieli Publishing Hse.

—The Fault in Our Stars. 2013. (ENG.). 336p. pap. *(978-0-14-134565-9(9))* Penguin Bks., Ltd.

—The Fault in Our Stars. 2014. (ENG.). 336p. (YA). (gr. 9). pap. 12.99 *(978-0-14-242417-9(X),* Penguin Books) Penguin Publishing Group.

—The Fault in Our Stars. 2012. *(978-0-525-42641-7(8));* (ENG., Illus.). 336p. (YA). (gr. 9-18). 19.99 *(978-0-525-47881-2(7),* Dutton Books for Young Readers) Penguin Young Readers Group.

—The Fault in Our Stars. 2014. (ENG.). (YA). (gr. 9). lib. bdg. 23.60 ***(978-1-62765-362-6(7))*** Perfection Learning Corp.

—The Fault in Our Stars. l.t. ed. 2012. (ENG.). 364p. (J). (gr. 8-12). 23.99 *(978-1-4104-5001-2(5))* Thorndike Pr.

—The Fault in Our Stars. 2014. lib. bdg. 24.50 *(978-0-606-35633-6(9))* Turtleback Bks.

Greves, Julie, et al. Upside down & Backwards: A Sibling's Journey Through Childhood Cancer. 2014. (Illus.). 112p. (J). *(978-1-4338-1637-6(7),* Magination Pr.) American Psychological Assn.

Griffin, Paul. When Friendship Followed Me Home. 2016. (ENG.). 256p. (J). (gr. 5-9). 16.99 *(978-0-8037-3816-4(1),* Dial Bks) Penguin Young Readers Group.

Grovet, Heather. Blondie's Big Ride. 2008. (Illus.). 95p. (J). pap. 5.97 *(978-0-8163-2225-1(2))* Pacific Pr. Publishing Assn.

Gurtler, Janet. I'M Not Her. 2011. (ENG.). 304p. (YA). (gr. 7-12). pap. 12.99 *(978-1-4022-5636-3(1),* 9781402256363) Sourcebooks, Inc.

Haley, Olivia. Jellybeans. 2008. 52p. pap. 20.50 *(978-1-4259-7781-8(2))* AuthorHouse.

Hall, Noelle Chason & Joanne Beeker Clurman. Sweetpea County's Secret Quilt. Caprara, Collette, illus. 2011. 28p. pap. 24.95 *(978-1-4626-2248-1(8))* America Star Bks.

Hannigan, Katherine. Ida B: ... And Her Plans to Maximize Fun, Avoid Disaster, & (Possibly) Save the World. 2004. 256p. (gr. 4-18). lib. bdg. 16.89 *(978-0-06-073025-3(0));* (ENG.). (J). 17.99 *(978-0-06-073024-6(2),* Greenwillow Bks.) HarperCollins Pubs.

—Ida B: And Her Plans to Maximize Fun Avoid Disaster, & (Possibly) Save the World. 2011. (ENG.). 272p. (J). (gr. 5-9). reprint ed. pap. 6.99 *(978-0-06-073026-0(9),* Greenwillow Bks.) HarperCollins Pubs.

Hermes, Patricia. You Shouldn't Have to Say GoodBye: It's Hard Losing the Person You Love The Most. 2008. (ENG.). 128p. (J). (gr. 4-7). pap. 8.99 *(978-1-4022-1325-0(5),* Sourcebooks Jabberwocky) Sourcebooks, Inc.

Hobbs, Valerie. Defiance. 2009. (ENG.). 144p. (J). (gr. 5-8). pap. 8.99 *(978-0-312-53581-0(3),* 9780312535810) Square Fish.

I Can Too! Cancer Kids Can Too Caucasian Series. l.t. ed. 2006. (Illus.). 44p. (J). *(978-0-9778796-3-2(1))* Brittany's Bks.

Jablonski, Carla. Thicker Than Water. 2007. (ENG.). 272p. (YA). (gr. 9-12). 8.99 *(978-1-59514-123-1(5),* Razorbill) Penguin Young Readers Group.

Jacobson, Jennifer Richard. The Complete History of Why I Hate Her. 2010. (ENG.). 192p. (YA). (gr. 7-18). 16.99 *(978-0-689-87800-8(1),* Atheneum/Richard Jackson Bks.) Simon & Schuster Children's Publishing.

Jacoby, Sue. The Sneakies in Las Vegas: A Coby Jay Adventure. 2012. 128p. (gr. 4-6). 22.60 *(978-1-4669-6672-7(6));* pap. 12.60 *(978-1-4669-6670-3(X))* Trafford Publishing.

Jamison, Lori. Running for Dave. (Illus.). 86p. *(978-1-897039-11-3(5))* High Interest Publishing (HIP).

Jones, F. Thomas. Backstep Forward. 2011. 184p. 24.59 *(978-1-4520-8441-1(6));* pap. 14.03 *(978-1-4520-8440-4(8))* AuthorHouse.

Kats, Jewel. Jenny & Her Dog Both Fight Cancer: A Tale of Chemotherapy & Caring. 2015. (J). pap. *(978-1-61599-279-9(0))* Loving Healing Pr., Inc.

Kennedy, J. Aday. Itcha Itcha Goo Goo Blues. Foster, Jack, illus. 2012. 20p. pap. 10.95 *(978-1-61633-294-5(8))* Guardian Angel Publishing, Inc.

Kephart, Beth. House of Dance. 2010. (ENG.). 272p. (J). (gr. 8). pap. 10.99 *(978-0-06-142930-9(9))* 2008. 263p. (YA). (gr. 7-18). lib. bdg. 17.89 *(978-0-06-142929-3(5))* HarperCollins Pubs. (HarperTeen).

Koss, Amy Goldman. Side Effects. 2006. 143p. (J). *(978-1-4287-0203-5(2))* Roaring Brook Pr.

—Side Effects. 2010. (ENG.). 160p. (YA). (gr. 4-7). pap. 8.99 *(978-0-312-60276-5(6),* 9780312602765) Square Fish.

Kuhn, Tom B. Little Chick: Learns to Trust in the Lord, 1 vol. Kuhn, Douglas W., illus. 2009. 23p. pap. 24.95 *(978-1-60836-929-4(3))* America Star Bks.

LaCaille, Link. Smoken Careers: Roots, Rock, Rap & Reggae Book 2, 1 vol. 2010. 44p. pap. 24.95 *(978-1-4489-2136-2(8))* PublishAmerica, Inc.

Langill, Jill. Sweet Tea for Frankenstein. 2010. 212p. pap. 14.95 *(978-1-4490-6480-8(9))* AuthorHouse.

Lee, Kathy. The Runaway Train. 2011. 144p. pap. *(978-1-84427-505-2(1))* Scripture Union.

Link, Amy. My Mommy Wears a Wig. 2009. 16p. pap. 17.95 *(978-1-4490-0218-3(8))* AuthorHouse.

Loftin, Nikki. Wish Girl. 2015. (ENG.). 256p. (J). (gr. 3-7). 16.99 *(978-1-59514-686-1(5),* Razorbill) Penguin Young Readers Group.

López, Diana. Ask My Mood Ring How I Feel. 2013. (ENG.). 336p. (J). (gr. 3-7). 17.00 *(978-0-316-20996-0(1))* Little Brown & Co.

Lopez, Khrystle M. & Lopez, Yolanda C. Princess Khrystle & the Monster Cancer: An informative fairytale version about brain cancer in Children. 2005. (ENG., Illus.). 63p. (gr. -1-3). 24.95 *(978-0-9772565-0-1(2))* Princess Khrystle & Prince Michael, Inc.

Mangskau, Monica. My Grandpa the Super Hero. 2010. 16p. 9.49 *(978-1-4343-8088-3(2))* AuthorHouse.

Matthies, Jana. The Goodbye Cancer Garden, 1 vol. Valiant, Kristi, illus. 2011. (ENG.). 32p. (J). (gr. 1-3). 16.99 *(978-0-8075-2994-2(X))* Whitman, Albert & Co.

McBride, Linda Ray. Mema Has Cancer, 1 vol. DeNault, Shirl, illus. 2008. (ENG.). 29p. 24.95 *(978-1-60610-833-8(6))* America Star Bks.

McCall, Guadalupe Garcia. Under the Mesquite. 2013. (ENG., Illus.). 224p. (J). (gr. 7-18). 17.95 *(978-1-60060-429-4(3))* Lee & Low Bks., Inc.

McCowan, Linda. Cancer Rhymes with Dancer. 2007. (Illus.). 24p. (J). (gr. -1-3). pap. 12.95 *(978-0-9814596-0-8(9))* McCowan, Linda.

McDaniel, Lurlene. Breathless. 2010. (ENG.). 180p. (YA). (gr. 7). mass mkt. 7.99 *(978-0-440-24016-7(6),* Delacorte Bks. for Young Readers) Random Hse. Children's Bks.

—Garden of Angels. 2005. 272p. (gr. 7). 16.50 *(978-0-7569-5756-8(7))* Perfection Learning Corp.

—Letting Go of Lisa. 2007. (ENG.). 192p. (YA). (gr. 7-12). mass mkt. 6.99 *(978-0-440-23868-3(4),* Laurel Leaf) Random Hse. Children's Bks.

McGraw, Jason. Beating the Odds. 2007. 30p. 47.88 *(978-0-615-13681-3(8))* McGraw, Jason A.

Mendenhall, Gaylee. My Teacher Is Bald! 2011. 28p. pap. 14.99 *(978-1-4634-5032-8(X))* AuthorHouse.

Mills, Wendy. Positively Beautiful. (ENG.). 368p. (YA). 2016. pap. 9.99 *(978-1-68119-025-9(7),* 9781681190259) 2015. (gr. 9). 17.99 *(978-1-61963-341-4(8),* 9781619633414) Bloomsbury Publishing USA. (Bloomsbury USA Childrens).

Murphy, Sally. Toppling. James, Rhian Nest, illus. 2012. (ENG.). 128p. (J). (gr. 3-7). 15.99 *(978-0-7636-5921-9(5))* Candlewick Pr.

Myers, Caron. Captain Steven: The Little Pirate who fought the Big C to Rule the Big Sea. 2011. 32p. 12.99 *(978-1-4567-5936-0(1))* AuthorHouse.

Ness, Patrick. A Monster Calls: Inspired by an Idea from Siobhan Dowd. (ENG.). 240p. (YA). (gr. 7). 2016. pap. 9.99 *(978-0-7636-9215-5(8))* 2015. pap. 12.00 *(978-0-7636-8081-7(8))* Candlewick Pr.

—A Monster Calls: Inspired by an Idea from Siobhan Dowd. Kay, Jim, illus. (ENG.). 224p. (YA). (gr. 7). 2013. pap. 12.00 *(978-0-7636-6065-9(5))* 2011. 16.99 *(978-0-7636-5559-4(7))* Candlewick Pr.

—A Monster Calls: Inspired by an Idea from Siobhan Dowd. 2011. (Playaway Children Ser.). (YA). (gr. 7-12). 54.99 *(978-1-4558-4499-9(3))* Findaway World, LLC.

—A Monster Calls: Inspired by an Idea from Siobhan Dowd. 2013. lib. bdg. 23.30 *(978-0-606-31603-3(5),* Turtleback) Turtleback Bks.

Nicklas, Rita. The B-Liminator & I Fight Cancer. 2009. 40p. pap. 18.50 *(978-0-557-04764-2(1))* Lulu Pr., Inc.

Owens, Connie S. Aunt Lucy Has Cancer. 2003. (J). pap. 5.99 *(978-1-59317-008-0(4))* Warner Pr., Inc.

Padian, Maria. Brett McCarthy: Work in Progress. 2009. (ENG.). 288p. (YA). (gr. 7). pap. 8.99 *(978-0-440-24055-6(7),* Knopf Bks. for Young Readers) Random Hse. Children's Bks.

Patterson, James & Raymond, Emily. First Love. 2017. (ENG., Illus.). 384p. mass mkt. 7.99 ***(978-1-4555-8500-7(9),*** Jimmy Patterson) Little Brown & Co.

—First Love. Illingworth, Sasha, photos by. 2015. (ENG., Illus.). 336p. (YA). (gr. 10-17). pap. 9.99 *(978-0-316-20703-4(9),* Jimmy Patterson) Little Brown & Co.

—First Love. 2014. (ENG.). 560p. (YA). pap. 16.00 *(978-1-4555-8501-4(7),* Jimmy Patterson) Little Brown & Co.

—First Love. 2014. (YA). lib. bdg. 28.20 *(978-0-606-35894-1(3))* Turtleback Bks.

Patterson, Michael. Blam! O'Reilly, Sean Patrick, ed. 2011. (Illus.). 80p. (YA). pap. 14.95 *(978-1-926914-04-6(X))* Arcana Studio, Inc.

Paulsen, Gary. Notes from the Dog. 2011. (ENG.). 144p. (YA). (gr. 7). pap. 6.99 *(978-0-375-85542-9(4),* Ember) Random Hse. Children's Bks.

Perry, Jolene. The Next Door Boys. 2011. (YA). *(978-1-59955-910-0(2),* Bonneville Bks.) Cedar Fort, Inc./CFI Distribution.

Polacco, Patricia. The Lemonade Club. Polacco, Patricia, illus. 2007. (ENG., Illus.). 48p. (J). (gr. 1-4). 17.99 *(978-0-399-24540-4(5),* Philomel Bks.) Penguin Young Readers Group.

Preller, James. Six Innings. 2010. (ENG.). 176p. (YA). (gr. 4-9). pap. 7.99 *(978-0-312-60240-6(5),* 9780312602406) Square Fish.

Price, David. Sly the Fox & Advice from la Princessa Roja. 2008. (Illus.). 34p. (J). 14.95 *(978-0-9779701-2-4(4))* Wishingstone Publishing.

Prusha, Crystal. The Day I Beat Mr. C. 2010. 12p. 8.32 *(978-1-4520-9366-6(0))* AuthorHouse.

Quillen, Donna Mc. I Can't Wait. 2011. 50p. 24.99 *(978-1-4628-8475-9(X));* pap. 15.99 *(978-1-4628-8474-2(1))* Xlibris Corp.

Reed, Amy. Invincible. 2015. (ENG.). 336p. (YA). (gr. 9). 17.99 *(978-0-06-229957-4(3),* Tegen, Katherine Bks) HarperCollins Pubs.

Richter, Jutta. The Summer of the Pike. Brailovsky, Anna, tr. from GER. Buchholz, Quint, illus. 2006. (ENG.). 132p. (J). (gr. 2-8). 16.95 *(978-1-57131-671-4(X));* (gr. 8-12). per. 6.95 *(978-1-57131-672-1(8))* Milkweed Editions.

Rivers, Karen. Love, Ish. 2017. (ENG.). 288p. (J). (gr. 4-8). 16.95 *(978-1-61620-570-6(9))* Algonquin Bks. of Chapel Hill.

Rovere, Amy. And Still They Bloom: A Family's Journey of Loss & Healing. Spector, Joel, illus. 2012. (ENG.). 48p. (J). (gr. 4-7). 14.95 *(978-1-60443-036-3(2))* American Cancer Society, Inc.

Sauer, Tammi. Dear Jack. 2004. 164p. (YA). mass mkt. 6.99 *(978-0-9753367-0-0(3))* Onstage Publishing, LLC.

Sawyer, Jacqueline. Little Racer Big Heart. 2012. 28p. pap. 16.95 *(978-1-62709-783-3(X))* America Star Bks.

Schwab, Victoria. New Beginnings. 2014. (Everyday Angel Ser.: 1). (J). (ENG.). 208p. (gr. 3-7). pap. 6.99 *(978-0-545-52846-7(1),* Scholastic Paperbacks); 195p. pap. *(978-0-545-68443-9(9))* Scholastic, Inc.

Scott, Liz, et al. Alex & the Amazing Lemonade Stand. Howard, Pam, illus. 2005. 32p. (gr. -1-5). 15.95 *(978-0-9753200-0-6(9))* PAJE Publishing Co.

Shannon Simmons. The Community Club: #1 Aubrey & the Fight for Life. 2009. 112p. pap. 10.95 *(978-1-4401-7616-6(7))* iUniverse, Inc.

Sherrard, Valerie. Kate. 2003. (ENG.). 200p. (YA). pap. 8.99 *(978-1-55002-476-0(0))* Dundurn CAN. Dist: Ingram Publisher Services.

Shofner, Corabel. Almost Paradise. 2017. (ENG.). 304p. (J). 16.99 *(978-0-374-30378-5(9),* 9780374303785, Farrar, Straus & Giroux (BYR)) Farrar, Straus & Giroux.

Sinclair, Mehded Maryam. When Wings Expand. 2013. (ENG., Illus.). 150p. (J). (gr. 5-9). pap. 9.95 *(978-0-86037-499-2(8))* Kube Publishing Ltd. GBR. Dist: Consortium Bk. Sales & Distribution.

Sinykin, Sheri. Giving up the Ghost, 1 vol. (ENG.). (YA). 2011. 240p. pap. 7.95 *(978-1-56145-572-0(5))* 2007. 224p. (gr. 4-7). pap. 14.95 *(978-1-56145-423-5(0))* Peachtree Pubs.

Skuy, David. Striker, 1 vol. 2013. (ENG.). 216p. (J). (gr. 4-7). 19.95 *(978-1-4594-0512-7(9),* 9781459405127); pap. 12.95

C
D

(978-1-4594-0513-4(7), 9781459405134) Lorimer, James & Co., Ltd., Pubs. CAN. Dist: Casemate Pubs. & Bk. Distributors, LLC.

Sliwerski, Jessica Reid. Cancer Hates Kisses. Song, Mika, illus. 2017. (ENG.). 40p. (J). (-k). 17.99 **(978-0-7352-2781-1(0)**, Dial Bks) Penguin Young Readers Group.

Slote, Alfred. Hang Tough, Paul Mather. 2013. 146p. pap. 11.99 (978-0-9886988-3-3(8)) Arborville Bks.

Smith, Jennifer Dawn Deconinck. If I Could Float on A Cloud, Where Would I Go? 2010. 64p. pap. 12.99 (978-1-4520-3628-1(4)) AuthorHouse.

Sonnenblick, Jordan. After Ever After. (ENG.). 272p. (J). 2014. pap. 9.99 (978-0-545-72287-2(X)) 2010. (gr. 7-12). 17.99 (978-0-439-83706-4(5), Scholastic Pr.) Scholastic, Inc.

Stiverson, Charlotte L. Nellie's Walk. Aitken, Kati, illus. 2016. (J). (978-1-935864-62-2(9)) Oncology Nursing Society.

Stone, Heather Duffy. Over the Tracks. 2015. (ENG.). 96p. (YA). (gr. 6-12). 27.99 (978-1-4677-5711-9(X)) Lerner Publishing Group.

Stork, Francisco X. The Last Summer of the Death Warriors. 2010. (ENG.). 352p. (J). (gr. 9-7). 18.99 (978-0-545-15133-7(3), Levine, Arthur A. Bks.) Scholastic, Inc.

Stuart, Duncan. The Whole of the Moon. 200p. (YA). (gr. 8-18). pap. (978-1-877135-05-7(4), Longacre Pr.) Random Hse. New Zealand.

Sutherland, Eileen. Mom & the Polka-Dot Boo-Boo: A Gentle Story Explaining Breast Cancer to a Young Child. Sutherland, Eileen & Sutherland, Maggie, illus. 2007. (ENG.). 24p. (J). (gr. -1-k). 14.95 (978-0-944235-87-4(5), 9780944235874) American Cancer Society, Inc.

Swanson, Julie A. Going for the Record. 2004. 223p. (YA). pap. 8.00 (978-0-8028-5273-1(4)) Eerdmans, William B. Publishing Co.

Theis, Patricia & Theis, Matthew. Clarabelle the Cat Loses Her Hair. Norhelm, Karen, illus. 2008. 24p. pap. 12.95 (978-1-59858-865-1(6)) Dog Ear Publishing, LLC.

Thomas, Cristine Leeann. I Can Too! Cancer Kids Can Too African American Series. Thomas, Cristine Leeann, illus. 2006. (Illus.). (J). (978-0-9778796-4-9(X)) Brittany's Bks.

Townsend, Lois Ritter. Our Journey Through Breast Cancer: -a story based on a teacher's journey through breast cancer with her kindergarten Class. 2005. (Illus.). 20p. (J). pap. 6.99 (978-1-933570-93-8(8)) Aardvark Global Publishing.

Victoria, Lisa, illus. Clara's Gift from the Heart. 2006. (J). 17.95 (978-0-9674602-9-1(8)) Blue Marlin Pubns.

Vigna, Judith. When Eric's Mom Fought Cancer. 2004. (J). (gr. 1-5). spiral bd. (978-0-616-03063-9(0)) Canadian National Institute for the Blind/Institut National Canadien pour les Aveugles.

Vlahos, Len. Life in a Fishbowl. 2017. (ENG.). 336p. (YA). 17.99 (978-1-68119-035-8(4), 9781681190358, Bloomsbury USA Childrens) Bloomsbury Publishing USA.

Walsh, Ann. Whatever. 2013. (ENG.). 200p. pap. 11.95 (978-1-55380-259-4(4)) Ronsdale Pr. CAN. Dist: SPD-Small Pr. Distribution.

Wang, An. Anywhere but Here. 2006. 107p. (J). (gr. 6-8). per. 9.95 (978-0-88100-140-2(6)) National Writers Pr., The.

Waters-Porter, Amber Rae. Rachael's Auntie Is Bald-Headed. 2010. (ENG.). 16p. pap. 9.49 (978-1-4490-7755-6(2)) AuthorHouse.

Willner, Judy. How My Sun Got Its Smile: The Story of Deana Vega. 2010. 48p. pap. 20.99 (978-1-4520-7720-8(7)) AuthorHouse.

Wood, Debra. William Warrior Bear. Blake, Joshua Aaron, illus. l.t. ed. 2005. 30p. (J). per. 12.95 (978-1-59879-001-6(3)) Lifevest Publishing, Inc.

Wright, Gina. My Mommy Has Breast Cancer. 2009. 32p. pap. 13.49 (978-1-4490-2150-4(6)) AuthorHouse.

Wunder, Wendy. The Probability of Miracles. 2012. (ENG., Illus.). 336p. (YA). (gr. 9). pap. 9.99 (978-1-59514-480-5(3), Razorbill) Penguin Young Readers Group.

Wylie, Sarah. All These Lives, 1 vol. 2012. (ENG.). 256p. (YA). (gr. 7-12). 24.99 (978-0-374-30208-5(1), 9780374302085, Farrar, Straus & Giroux (BYR)) Farrar, Straus & Giroux.

CANDLES

Best, B. J. Wax to Candle. 2016. (How It Is Made Ser.). 24p. (J). pap. 8.22 (978-1-5026-2118-4(5)) Cavendish Square Publishing.

Check, Laura. Create Your Own Candles: 30 Easy-To-Make Designs. 2004. (Quick Starts for Kids! Ser.). (J). pap. (978-1-885593-52-8(X), Ideal Pubns.) Worthy Publishing.

Mooney, Carla. Light Your Way: Make a Candle. 2010. (Creative Adventure Guides). 48p. (J). (gr. 3-6). lib. bdg. 26.60 (978-1-59953-387-2(1)) Norwood Hse. Pr.

Tolhurst, Marilyn. Lights & Candles. Date not set. (Sense of History Ser.). (Illus.). 24p. pap. 27.69 (978-0-582-04026-7(4)) Addison-Wesley Longman, Ltd. GBR. Dist: Trans-Atlantic Pubns., Inc.

Yonck, Barbara. Candle Crafts. Date not set. (Illus.). (J). (gr. 4-8). lib. bdg. 8.95 (978-0-87460-376-7(5)) Lion Bks.

CANDY

see Confectionery

CANNED FOODS

see Canning and Preserving

CANNING AND PRESERVING

Cefrey, Holly. The Inventions of Amanda Jones: The Vacuum Method of Canning & Food Preservation. 2009. (19th Century American Inventors Ser.). 24p. (gr. 2-3). 42.50 (978-1-60854-950-4(X), PowerKids Pr.) Rosen Publishing Group, Inc., The.

Mecozzi, Maureen. The Uncanny Can. 2007. (Shockwave: Science in Practice Ser.). (ENG., Illus.). 36p. (J). (gr. 3-5). 25.00 (978-0-531-17584-2(7), Children's Pr.) Scholastic Library Publishing.

Owings, Lisa. From Strawberry to Jam. 2015. (Start to Finish, Second Ser.). (ENG.). 24p. (J). (gr. k-3). pap. 6.95 (978-1-4677-6110-9(9)); lib. bdg. 23.93 (978-1-4677-6022-5(6)) Lerner Publishing Group. (Lerner Pubns.).

Parker, Lewis K. The Inventions of Amanda Jones: The Vacuum Method of Canning & Food Preservation. 2003. (19th Century American Inventors Ser.). (Illus.). 24p. (J). lib. bdg. 22.60 (978-0-8239-6445-1(0), PowerKids Pr.) Rosen Publishing Group, Inc., The.

CANNON

see Ordnance

CANOES AND CANOEING

Bevis, Mary. Old Woman Winter. Powell, Consie, illus. 2010. 32p. (J). (gr. 1-2). pap. 9.95 (978-0-9819307-6-3(X)) Raven Productions, Inc.

Champion, Neil. Wild Water: Canoeing & Kayaking. 2013. (Illus.). 32p. (J). lib. bdg. 28.50 (978-1-59920-812-1(1)) Black Rabbit Bks.

De Medeiros, James. Kayaking. 2007. (Outdoor Adventures (Weigl Hardcover) Ser.). (Illus.). 24p. (J). lib. bdg. 24.45 (978-1-59036-663-9(8)); (gr. 4-7). per. 8.95 (978-1-59036-664-6(6)) Weigl Pubs., Inc.

Doeden, Matt. Canoeing. 2017. (Great Outdoors Ser.). (ENG., Illus.). 32p. (J). (gr. 1-3). pap. 9.99 (978-1-68152-076-6(1)) Amicus.

—Let's Go Canoeing. 2016. (Great Outdoors Ser.). (ENG., Illus.). 32p. (J). (gr. 1-4). 20.95 (978-1-60753-801-1(6)) Amicus Publishing.

—Rock Climbing. 2016. (Great Outdoors Ser.). (ENG., Illus.). 32p. (J). (gr. 1-4). 20.95 (978-1-60753-797-7(4)) Amicus Publishing.

Frisch-Schmoll, Joy. Canoeing. 2017. (J). (978-1-60818-686-0(5), Creative Education) Creative Co., The.

Green, Sara. Canoeing. 2012. (Outdoor Adventures Ser.). (ENG., Illus.). 24p. (J). (gr. 3-8). lib. bdg. 25.95 (978-1-60014-795-1(X), Pilot Bks.) Bellwether Media.

—Kayaking. 2013. (Outdoor Adventures Ser.). (ENG., Illus.). 24p. (J). (gr. 3-8). lib. bdg. 25.95 (978-1-60014-891-0(3), Pilot Bks.) Bellwether Media.

Hamilton, S. L. White Water. 2010. (Xtreme Sports Ser.). 32p. (gr. 3-9). 27.07 (978-1-61613-006-0(7), A&D Xtreme) ABDO Publishing Co.

Hardyman, Robyn. Kayaking & Canoeing. 2013. (Adventures in the Great Outdoors Ser.). (ENG., Illus.). 32p. (J). (gr. 3-6). lib. bdg. 26.50 (978-1-61533-750-7(4)) Windmill Bks.

Labrecque, Ellen. Whitewater Kayaking. 2011. (Extreme Sports Ser.). (ENG., Illus.). 32p. (J). (gr. 2-5). lib. bdg. 28.50 (978-1-60973-187-8(5), 201138) Child's World, Inc., The.

Maloney, Brenna. National Geographic Kids Chapters: White Water! 2017. (NGK Chapters Ser.). (ENG.). 112p. (J). (gr. 2-5). lib. bdg. 15.90 **(978-1-4263-2823-7(0)**, National Geographic Children's Bks.) National Geographic Society.

—White Water! 2017. (NGK Chapters Ser.). (ENG., Illus.). 112p. (J). (gr. 2-5). pap. 5.99 **(978-1-4263-2822-0(2)**, National Geographic Children's Bks.) National Geographic Society.

McIntyre, Sandra. Canoes: Canadian Icons. 2010. (Illus.). 24p. (978-1-77071-575-2(4)); pap. (978-1-77071-582-0(7)) Weigl Educational Pubs. Ltd.

Norris, Ashley P. Watson. How to Canoe & Kayak Like a Pro. 2014. (Outdoor Sports Skills Ser.). (Illus.). 48p. (J). (gr. 4-10). 14.95 (978-1-62285-244-4(3)) Enslow Pubs., Inc.

Rock, Lois. Canoeing & Kayaking. 2009. (Get Outdoors Ser.). (Illus.). 32p. (J). (ENG.). pap. 10.00 (978-1-4358-3049-3(0)); (gr. 4-6). lib. bdg. 25.25 (978-1-4358-3041-7(5)) Rosen Publishing Group, Inc., The. (PowerKids Pr.).

Slade, Suzanne. Let's Go Canoeing & Kayaking. (Adventures Outdoors Ser.). 32p. 2009. (gr. 4-5). 47.90 (978-1-61511-268-5(5)) 2007. (Illus.). (J). (gr. 3-7). lib. bdg. 25.25 (978-1-4042-3649-3(X)) Rosen Publishing Group, Inc., The. (PowerKids Pr.).

Tobin, Jennifer & Tobin, Adriana. ABCs of the BWCAW: A Fun Guide to the Boundary Waters Canoe Area Wilderness. Tobin, Jennifer, photos by. 2003. (Illus.). 60p. (YA). bds. 17.95 (978-0-9742555-0-7(5)) MyHandiwork.

Turnbull, Stephanie. Canoeing & Kayaking. 2016. (Adventure Sports Ser.). 24p. (gr. 2-6). 28.50 (978-1-62588-382-7(X), Smart Apple Media) Black Rabbit Bks.

York, M. J. Canoeing. 2014. (Great Outdoors Ser.). (ENG.). 24p. (J). (gr. 2-5). 28.50 (978-1-62687-328-5(3), 207168) Child's World, Inc., The.

Young, Jeff C. Running the Rapids: White-Water Rafting, Canoeing, & Kayaking, 1 vol. 2011. (Adrenaline Adventure Ser.). (ENG., Illus.). 32p. (J). (gr. 3-6). 27.07 (978-1-61613-551-5(4)) ABDO Publishing Co.

CANOES AND CANOEING—FICTION

Ballantyne, R. M. Blown to Bits; or, the Lonely Man of Rak. 2006. pap. (978-1-4065-0515-3(3)) Dodo Pr.

Bryson, Jamie S. The War Canoe. 2nd ed. 2009. (ENG., Illus.). 180p. (YA). (gr. 8-12). pap. 9.95 (978-0-88240-758-6(9), Alaska Northwest Bks.) Graphic Arts Ctr. Publishing Co.

Campbell, Nicola I. Shin-Chi's Canoe. LaFave, Kim, illus. 2008. (ENG.). 40p. (J). (gr. -1-2). 18.95 (978-0-88899-857-6(0)) Groundwood Bks. CAN. Dist: Publishers Group West (PGW).

Casanova, Mary. One-Dog Canoe. Hoyt, Ard, illus. 2003. (ENG.). 32p. (J). (gr. -1-1). 18.99 (978-0-374-35638-5(6), 9780374356385, Farrar, Straus & Giroux (BYR)) Farrar, Straus & Giroux.

—One-Dog Canoe. Hoyt, Ard, illus. 2009. (ENG.). 32p. (J). (gr. -1-1). pap. 7.99 (978-0-312-56118-5(0), 9780312561185) Square Fish.

Disney Storybook Art Team, illus. Moana Read-Along Storybook & CD. 2016. (Read-Along Storybook & CD Ser.). (ENG.). 32p. (J). (gr. 1-3). pap. 6.99 (978-1-4847-4361-4(X)) Disney Pr.

Hobbs, Will. Downriver. 2012. (ENG., Illus.). 208p. (J). (gr. 5-9). pap. 7.99 (978-1-4424-4547-5(5), Atheneum Bks. for Young Readers) Simon & Schuster Children's Publishing.

—Take Me to the River. (ENG.). (J). (gr. 5). 2012. 208p. pap. 6.99 (978-0-06-074146-4(5)) 2011. 192p. 15.99 (978-0-06-074144-0(9)) HarperCollins Pubs.

Hobbs, Will & Hobbs, William. Wild Man Island. 2003. (ENG.). 192p. (J). (gr. 5-18). pap. 5.99 (978-0-380-73310-1(2)) HarperCollins Pubs.

Hobbs, William. Ghost Canoe. 2004. 195p. (J). (gr. 5-9). pap. 38.00 incl. audio (978-0-8072-0450-4(1), Listening Library) Random Hse. Audio Publishing Group.

Howe, James. Houndsley & Catina Plink & Plunk. Gay, Marie-Louise, illus. 2013. (Candlewick Sparks Ser.). (ENG.). 48p. (J). (gr. k-4). pap. 3.99 (978-0-7636-6640-8(8)) Candlewick Pr.

—Plink & Plunk. Gay, Marie-Louise, illus. 2009. (Houndsley & Catina Ser.). (ENG.). 48p. (J). (gr. k-4). 15.99 (978-0-7636-3385-1(2)) Candlewick Pr.

Jazynka, Kitson & Tripp, Valerie. Boys Camp: Zee's Story. Orback, Craig, illus. 2015. (ENG.). 144p. (J). (gr. 1-5). 14.99 (978-1-62914-754-3(0), Sky Pony Pr.) Skyhorse Publishing Co., Inc.

Jimmy. My Kayak Lives in a Tree at the Beach, 1 vol. 2009. 18p. pap. 24.95 (978-1-60749-210-8(5)) America Star Bks.

Martone, Ginny. Trouble at Big Bear Falls. 2011. 90p. pap. 19.95 (978-1-4626-2558-1(4)) America Star Bks.

Matthews, T. J. The Canoeing Safari. Rheburg, Judy, illus. 2004. (J). (978-0-938978-35-0(7)) Wycliffe Bible Translators.

McIntyre, Sandra. Les Canots: Les Emblèmes Canadiens. McMann, Julie, tr. from ENG. 2011. (FRE.). 24p. (YA). (gr. 2-4). (978-1-77071-407-6(3)) Weigl Educational Pubs. Ltd.

Medley, Shari. The Adventure of a Lifetime! LaGrange, Tiffany, illus. 2009. 24p. pap. 10.95 (978-1-936051-20-5(6)) Peppertree Pr., The.

Mikaelsen, Ben. Red Midnight. 2003. 212p. (gr. 5-9). 17.00 (978-0-7569-1550-6(3)) Perfection Learning Corp.

Nixon-Roulet, Mary F. Kalitan Our Little Alaskan Cousin. 2004. reprint ed. pap. 1.99 (978-1-4192-2838-4(2)); pap. 15.95 (978-1-4191-2838-7(8)) Kessinger Publishing, LLC.

Panagopoulos, Janie Lynn. Mark of the Bear Claw. 2004. (J). 15.95 (978-0-938682-78-3(4)) River Road Pubns., Inc.

Peratrovich, Roy A., Jr. Little Whale: A Story of the Last Tlingit War Canoe. 2016. (ENG., Illus.). 64p. (J). pap. 16.95 (978-1-60223-295-2(4)) Univ. of Alaska Pr.

Petersen, P. J. Wild River. 2013. (ENG.). 128p. (J). (gr. 4-7). 6.99 (978-0-375-84624-3(7), Yearling) Random Hse. Children's Bks.

RH Disney. Quest for the Heart. RH Disney, illus. 2016. (Step into Reading Ser.). (ENG., Illus.). 32p. (J). (gr. -1-1). lib. bdg. 12.99 (978-0-7364-8226-4(1), RH/Disney) Random Hse. Children's Bks.

Robinson, Gary. Tribal Journey. 2013. (YA). 111p. (978-1-939053-87-9(0)); (ENG.). 120p. pap. 9.95 (978-1-939053-01-5(3), 7th Generation) Book Publishing Co.

Roddy, Lee. The Dangerous Canoe Race. 2006. (Ladd Family Adventure Ser.: Vol. 4). (Illus.). 137p. (Orig.). (J). (gr. 4-7). per. 7.99 (978-0-88062-253-0(9)) Mott Media.

Salvati, Elizabeth A. Counting Your Way down the Toccoa River Canoe Trail. 2011. 24p. pap. 12.95 (978-1-4567-5773-1(3)) AuthorHouse.

Saunders, Harry M. Teenagers on an Adventure: Journey of Two Boys & a Girl. 2013. 168p. pap. 19.95 (978-1-62709-466-5(0)) America Star Bks.

Thomas Nelson Publishing Staff. Camping the Bug-A-Boo Way: Go for the Gold Against Camp Hot Foot! 2008. cd-rom 19.95 (978-0-9754280-7-8(1)) Nelson, Thomas Inc.

Trout, Richard. Sign of the Dragon, 1 vol. 2007. (MacGregor Family Adventure Ser.: 5). (ENG.). 272p. (YA). (gr. 5-12). 16.99 (978-1-58980-476-0(7)) Pelican Publishing Co., Inc.

Tuzee, John & Tuzee, Diane. Charlie Canoe & Other Boats, Too. Kasun, Mike, illus. 2006. (J). (978-0-9755348-2-3(3)) Kids Life Pr.

Weaver, Jenny. Following the Raven. 2003. (ENG.). 113p. (YA). (gr. 5-8). pap. 14.95 (978-1-878044-91-4(5)) Mayhaven Publishing, Inc.

Withers, Pam. Camp Wild, 1 vol. 2006. (Orca Currents Ser.). (ENG.). 112p. (J). (gr. 5-9). 14.95 (978-1-55143-557-2(8)) Orca Bk. Pubs. USA.

—Camp Wild. 2006. (Orca Currents Ser.). 104p. (gr. 5-9). lib. bdg. 19.95 (978-0-7569-6878-6(X)) Perfection Learning Corp.

CAPE COD (MASS.)

Briggett, Marlissa. The Compleat Day Tripper-Cape Cod: The Cape's Best Classic & Eclectic Destinations for Kids & Grown-Ups! Pierce, Charlotte, ed. 2008. (Illus.). 80p. per. (978-0-9776396-2-5(2)) Pierce Pr.

Clark, Admont G. The Boy Who Saved a Cape Cod Town: And Other Cape Cod Stories. Fraser, Richard M., illus. 2006. 56p. (J). (gr. 6-12). per. 12.95 (978-0-9785766-0-8(8)) On Cape Pubns.

Penta, Mark, creator. Cape Cod Invasion! 2007. (Illus.). 32p. 17.95 (978-1-933212-49-4(7), Commonwealth Editions) Applewood Bks.

CAPE COD (MASS.)—FICTION

Adler, Cs. The Magic of the Glits: A Tale of Loss, Love, & Lasting Friendship. 2007. 112p. per. 7.95 (978-1-58348-838-6(3), iUniverse Star) iUniverse, Inc.

Barbo, Theresa Mitchell & Webster, W. Russell. The Daring Coast Guard Rescue of the Pendleton Crew. Marshall, Julia, illus. 2013. Orig. Title: The Daring Coast Guard Rescue of the Pendleton Crew. (ENG.). 128p. (J). (gr. 4-7). 14.99 (978-1-62619-095-5(X), History Pr., The) Arcadia Publishing.

Chandler, Elizabeth. Evercrossed. (Kissed by an Angel Ser.). (ENG.). (YA). (gr. 7). 2012. 304p. pap. 9.99 (978-1-4424-0915-6(0)) 2011. 288p. 16.99 (978-1-4424-0914-9(2)) Simon Pulse. (Simon Pulse).

—Everlasting. (Kissed by an Angel Ser.). (ENG.). (YA). (gr. 7). 2013. 336p. pap. 9.99 (978-1-4424-0917-0(7)) 2012. 320p. 16.99 (978-1-4424-0921-7(5)) Simon Pulse. (Simon Pulse).

Clark, Mary Higgins. Ghost Ship. Minor, Wendell, illus. 2007. (ENG.). 40p. (J). (gr. 1-5). 17.99 (978-1-4169-3514-8(2), Simon & Schuster/Paula Wiseman Bks.) Simon & Schuster/Paula Wiseman Bks.

Conway, K. R. Stormfront, vol. 2. 2014. (The Undertow Ser.). 428p. (YA). (gr. 7-17). pap. 15.95 (978-0-9897763-4-9(4)) Conway, Kathleen R.

Demas, Corinne. Returning to Shore. 2014. 208p. (YA). (gr. 6-12). 17.95 (978-1-4677-1328-3(7), Carolrhoda Lab™) Lerner Publishing Group.

Ehrlich, Esther. Nest. 2014. (ENG.). 336p. (J). (gr. 5-7). 16.99 (978-0-385-38607-4(9), Lamb, Wendy Bks.) Random Hse. Children's Bks.

Feil, Hila. Blue Moon. 2007. (ENG., Illus.). 272p. (YA). (gr. 7). pap. 17.99 (978-0-15-205933-0(4)) Houghton Mifflin Harcourt Publishing Co.

Gamble, Adam. Good Night Cape Cod. Andert, John, illus. 2007. (Good Night Our World Ser.). (ENG.). 20p. (J). (gr. k — 1). bds. 9.95 (978-1-60219-004-7(6)) Good Night Bks.

—Good Night Cape Cod. Andert, John, illus. 2005. (J). bds. 9.95 (978-0-9758502-5-1(3)) On Cape Pubns.

Harrington, Kim. Clarity. (ENG.). 256p. (J). (gr. 9-9). 2012. pap. 8.99 (978-0-545-23051-3(9)) 2011. 16.99 (978-0-545-23050-6(0)) Scholastic, Inc.

—Perception. 2012. (ENG.). 288p. (J). (gr. 9). 16.99 (978-0-545-23053-7(5)) Scholastic, Inc.

Holland, Robert. The Black Queen. 2003. (Books Boys Want to Read). 220p. (J). pap. 12.00 (978-0-9720922-1-0(8)) Frost Hollow Pubs., LLC.

Howland, Leila. The Brightest Stars of Summer. 2017. (Silver Sisters Ser.: 2). 384p. (J). (gr. 3-7). pap. 6.99 (978-0-06-231873-2(X)) HarperCollins Pubs.

—The Brightest Stars of Summer: A Silver Sisters Story. 2016. (Silver Sisters Ser.: 2). (Illus.). 368p. (J). (gr. 3-7). 16.99 (978-0-06-231872-5(1)) HarperCollins Pubs.

—The Forget-Me-Not Summer. Kim, Ji-Hyuk, illus. 2015. (Silver Sisters Ser.: 1). (ENG.). 352p. (J). (gr. 3-7). 16.99 (978-0-06-231869-5(1)) HarperCollins Pubs.

Hunter, Sara Hoagland. Every Turtle Counts. Spellman, Susan, illus. 2014. (ENG.). 36p. (J). 16.95 (978-1-931807-25-8(6)) Randall, Peter E. Pub.

Johnson, Angela. Looking for Red. 2003. (ENG., Illus.). 128p. (YA). (gr. 7). pap. 6.99 (978-0-689-86388-2(8), Simon Pulse) Simon Pulse.

Maizel, Rebecca. Between Us & the Moon. 2015. (ENG.). 384p. (YA). (gr. 9). 17.99 (978-0-06-232761-1(5)) HarperCollins Pubs.

Marsh, Carole. The Mystery at Cape Cod. 2010. (Real Kids, Real Places Ser.). (Illus.). 158p. (J). pap. 18.99 (978-0-635-07594-9(6), Marsh, Carole Mysteries) Gallopade International.

—The Mystery at Cape Cod. Friedlander, Randolyn, illus. 2010. (Real Kids, Real Places Teacher Guides). 32p. (J). pap. 7.99 (978-0-635-07600-7(4)) Gallopade International.

—The Mystery at Death Valley. 2010. (Real Kids, Real Places Ser.). (Illus.). 158p. (J). pap. 7.99 (978-0-635-07596-3(2), Marsh, Carole Mysteries) Gallopade International.

Millet, Lydia. The Fires Beneath the Sea. 2012. (Dissenters Ser.). (ENG.). 256p. (J). (gr. 3-7). pap. 12.00 (978-1-931520-47-8(X), Big Mouth Hse.) Small Beer Pr.

Paratore, Coleen Murtagh. Catching the Sun. 2010. (J). (978-0-618-45780-9(1)) Houghton Mifflin Harcourt Publishing Co.

—The Cupid Chronicles. 2008. (Wedding Planner's Daughter Ser.). (ENG.). 224p. (J). (gr. 4-8). pap. 6.99 (978-1-4169-5484-2(8), Aladdin) Simon & Schuster Children's Publishing.

—The Wedding Planner's Daughter. 2005. (Wedding Planner's Daughter Ser.). (ENG.). 208p. (J). (gr. 3-7). 15.95 (978-0-689-87340-9(9), Simon & Schuster Bks. For Young Readers) Simon & Schuster Bks. For Young Readers.

—Willa by Heart. 2008. (Wedding Planner's Daughter Ser.). (ENG.). 240p. (J). (gr. 3-7). 15.99 (978-1-4169-4076-0(6), Simon & Schuster Bks. For Young Readers) Simon & Schuster Bks. For Young Readers.

—Willa by Heart. 2009. (Wedding Planner's Daughter Ser.). (ENG.). 240p. (J). (gr. 4-8). pap. 6.99 (978-1-4169-7470-3(9), Aladdin) Simon & Schuster Children's Publishing.

—Wish I Might. 2011. (ENG.). 176p. (J). (gr. 5-9). pap. 6.99 (978-0-545-09402-3(X), Scholastic Paperbacks) Scholastic, Inc.

—Wish I Might: From the Life of Willa Havisham. 2010. (ENG.). 176p. (J). (gr. 5-9). 16.99 (978-0-545-09406-1(2), Scholastic Pr.) Scholastic, Inc.

Pennypacker, Sara. Summer of the Gypsy Moths. (ENG.). 288p. (J). (gr. 3-7). 2013. pap. 6.99 (978-0-06-196422-0(0)) 2012. 15.99 (978-0-06-196420-6(4)) HarperCollins Pubs.

Reisfeld, Randi. No Strings Attached: CC (Cape Cod); Partiers Preferred. 2013. (ENG., Illus.). 624p. (YA). (gr. 9). pap. 9.99 (978-1-4424-5978-6(6), Simon Pulse) Simon Pulse.

Rossiter, Nan Parson. The Fo'c'sle: Henry Beston's Outermost House. 2012. (Illus.). 32p. (J). (gr. 5-18). 17.95 (978-1-56792-433-6(6)) Godine, David R. Pub.

Shankman, Ed. The Cods of Cape Cod. O'Neill, Dave, illus. 2009. (Shankman & O'Neill Ser.). (ENG.). 32p. (gr. -1-3). 14.95 (978-1-933212-78-4(0), Commonwealth Editions) Applewood Bks.

Smallman, Steve. Santa Is Coming to Cape Cod. Dunn, Robert, illus. 2013. (ENG.). 32p. (J). (-3). 9.99 (978-1-4022-9078-7(0), Sourcebooks Jabberwocky) Sourcebooks, Inc.

Zschock, Martha Day & Zschock, Martha. Hello, Cape Cod! 2009. (Hello! Ser.). (ENG., Illus.). 16p. (gr. -1-k). bds. 9.95 (978-0-9819430-1-5(2), Commonwealth Editions) Applewood Bks.

CAPITAL PUNISHMENT

Berlatsky, Noah. Capital Punishment. 2010. (Global Viewpoints Ser.). (Illus.). 224p. (J). 40.45 (978-0-7377-4663-1(7)); pap. 27.95 (978-0-7377-4664-8(5)) Cengage Gale. (Greenhaven Pr., Inc.).

Devaney, Sherri. Ripped from the Headlines: The Death Penalty. 2007. (Ripped from the Headlines Ser.). (YA). (gr. 7-12). 23.95 (978-1-60217-012-4(6)) Erickson Pr.

Friedman, Lauri S. The Death Penalty. 2010. (Introducing Issues with Opposing Viewpoints Ser.). (ENG., Illus.). 144p. 36.95 (978-0-7377-4938-0(5), Greenhaven Pr., Inc.) Cengage Gale.

Golston, Sydele E. Death Penalty. 2009. (Hot Topics Ser.). (Illus.). 128p. (YA). (gr. 7-10). lib. bdg. 33.95 (978-1-4205-0048-6(1), LML02109-240036, Lucent Bks.) Cengage Gale.

Herda, D. J. The Death Penalty: Furman V. Georgia. 2016. (US Supreme Court Landmark Cases Ser.). 128p. (J). 37.27 (978-0-7660-8430-8(2)) Enslow Pubs., Inc.

—Furman V. Georgia: The Death Penalty Case. rev. ed. 2010. (Landmark Supreme Court Cases, Gold Edition Ser.). (Illus.). 112p. (J). (gr. 6-18). 33.27 (978-0-7660-3428-0(3)) Enslow Pubs., Inc.

Kerrigan, Michael. Capital Punishment, Vol. 20. Gomez, Manny, ed. 2016. (Crime & Detection Ser.). (Illus.). 96p. (J). (gr. 7). 24.95 (978-1-4222-3473-0(8)) Mason Crest.

Kuklin, Susan. No Choirboy: Murder, Violence, & Teenagers on Death Row. 2014. (ENG., Illus.). 240p. (YA). (gr. 9-13). pap. 12.99 (978-1-250-04445-7(6), 9781250044457) Square Fish.

Manzano, Megan. The Death Penalty. 2017. (J). **(978-1-5345-0208-6(4))** Greenhaven Publishing LLC.

Marzilli, Alan. Capital Punishment. 2nd rev. ed. 2008. (Point/Counterpoint Ser.). (Illus.). 120p. (C). (gr. 9). 35.00 (978-0-7910-9796-0(X), Chelsea Hse.) Facts On File, Inc.

Meister, Deborah. What Catholic Teens Should Know about Capital Punishment. Larkin, Jean, ed. 2003. (What Catholic Teens Should Know Ser.). (Illus.). 8p. (YA). 7.95 *(978-0-89837-193-2(7),* 440610) Pflaum Publishing Group.

Murray, Hallie. Preventing Cruel & Unusual Punishment: The Eighth Amendment. 2017. (Bill of Rights Ser.). 48p. (gr. 5-6). 27.93 ***(978-0-7660-8563-3(5))*** Enslow Pubs., Inc.

Park, Peggy J. Is the Death Penalty Just? 2014. (In Controversy Ser.). (ENG., Illus.). 80p. (J). lib. bdg. *(978-1-60152-714-1(4))* ReferencePoint Pr., Inc.

parks, peggy. The Death Penalty. 2011. (Compact Research Ser.). 96p. (YA). (gr. 7-12). lib. bdg. 27.95 *(978-1-60152-158-3(8))* ReferencePoint Pr., Inc.

Roensch, Greg. Furman V. Georgia: Cruel & Unusual Punishment. 2007. (Great Supreme Court Decisions Ser.). (Illus.). 112p. (YA). (gr. 5-9). lib. bdg. 32.95 *(978-0-7910-9382-5(4))* Facts On File, Inc.

Smith, Rich. Eighth Amendment: The Right to Mercy, 1 vol. 2007. (Bill of Rights Ser.). (ENG.). 32p. (gr. 3-7). 27.07 *(978-1-59928-920-5(2),* Abdo & Daughters) ABDO Publishing Co.

Stearman, Kaye. The Debate about the Death Penalty. 2007. (Ethical Debates Ser.). (Illus.). 48p. (YA). (gr. 5-9). lib. bdg. 29.25 *(978-1-4042-3752-0(6))* Rosen Publishing Group, Inc., The.

Stefoff, Rebecca. Furman V. Georgia: Debating the Death Penalty. 2007. (Supreme Court Milestones Ser.). (Illus.). 128p. (gr. 7-18). lib. bdg. 42.79 *(978-0-7614-2583-0(7),* Benchmark Bks.) Marshall Cavendish Corp.

Ward, Adam. Critical World Issues: Capital Punishment, Vol. 16. 2016. (Critical World Issues Ser.: Vol. 16). (ENG., Illus.). 112p. (J). (gr. 7-12). 25.95 *(978-1-4222-3649-9(8))* Mason Crest.

Watkins, Christine. The Ethics of Capital Punishment. 2011. (At Issue Ser.). 128p. (ENG.). (gr. 12-12). lib. bdg. 39.40 *(978-0-7377-5171-0(1));* (J). pap. 24.45 *(978-0-7377-5172-7(X))* Cengage Gale. (Greenhaven Pr., Inc.).

CAPITALISM

see also Socialism

Bailey, Diane. How Markets Work. 2011. (Real World Economics Ser.). (ENG.). 80p. (YA). (gr. 7-12). lib. bdg. 33.25 *(978-1-4488-5564-3(0))* Rosen Publishing Group, Inc., The.

Burgan, Michael. American Capitalism. 2012. (ENG.). 64p. (J). lib. bdg. 30.00 *(978-0-531-23054-1(6));* (gr. 4-6). pap. 8.95 *(978-0-531-28154-3(X))* Scholastic Library Publishing.

Clark, Brenda & Commers, Judy. Entrepreneurship. 2012. (ENG.). 560p. (gr. 9-12). 93.28 *(978-1-60525-782-2(6))* Goodheart-Willcox Pub.

Davidson, Tish. African Americans in Business. 2012. (J). pap. *(978-1-4222-2390-1(6))* Mason Crest.

—African Americans in Business. Hill, Marc Lamont, ed. 2012. (Major Black Contributions from Emancipation to Civil Rights Ser.). 64p. (J). (gr. 5). 22.95 *(978-1-4222-2377-2(9))* Mason Crest.

Earl, C. F. What Does It Mean to Be an Entrepreneur? Madrian, Brigitte, ed. 2013. (Young Adult Library of Small Business & Finance Ser.: 10). 64p. (J). (gr. 7-18). 22.95 *(978-1-4222-2922-4(X))* Mason Crest.

Hess, Karl. Capitalism for Kids: Growing up to Be Your Own Boss. Williams, Jane A. & Daniels, Kathryn, eds. rev. ed. 2006. (ENG.). 196p. (YA). pap. 14.95 *(978-0-942617-35-1(5))* Bluestocking Pr.

Hobbs, Mike. Communications. 2013. (Young Entrepreneurs' Club Ser.). 48p. (gr. 5-11). 37.10 *(978-1-59920-920-3(9))* Black Rabbit Bks.

—Fashion. 2013. (Young Entrepreneurs' Club Ser.). 48p. (gr. 5-11). lib. bdg. 37.10 *(978-1-59920-922-7(5))* Black Rabbit Bks.

—Food & Drink. 2013. (Young Entrepreneurs' Club Ser.). (Illus.). 48p. (gr. 5-11). lib. bdg. 37.10 *(978-1-59920-923-4(3))* Black Rabbit Bks.

MacGregor, Lucy. Choosing a Career as an Entrepreneur. 2009. (World of Work Ser.). 64p. (gr. 5-5). 58.50 *(978-1-60854-326-7(9))* Rosen Publishing Group, Inc., The.

Merino, Noël. Capitalism. 2010. (Current Controversies Ser.). (Illus.). 240p. 40.95 *(978-0-7377-4699-0(8));* pap. 28.45 *(978-0-7377-4700-3(5))* Cengage Gale. (Greenhaven Pr., Inc.).

Merino, Noël, ed. Capitalism. 2012. (Global Viewpoints Ser.). (ENG., Illus.). 224p. (gr. 10-12). pap. 31.70 *(978-0-7377-5647-0(0),* Greenhaven Pr., Inc.); (YA). (gr. 9-12). 40.45 *(978-0-7377-5646-3(2))* Cengage Gale.

Orr, Tamra. Understanding Economic Systems. 2011. (Real World Economics Ser.). (ENG.). 80p. (YA). (gr. 7-12). lib. bdg. 33.25 *(978-1-4488-5568-1(3))* Rosen Publishing Group, Inc., The.

Smalbach, Richard, ed. Capitalism. 2014. (Political & Economic Systems Ser.). 312p. (YA). (gr. 9-12). 45.00 *(978-1-62275-359-8(3))* Rosen Publishing Group, Inc., The.

Small, Cathleen. How to Start an Online Business. 2015. (J). lib. bdg. *(978-1-62713-541-2(3))* Cavendish Square Publishing.

CAPITALISTS AND FINANCIERS

American Tycoons. (Illus.). (J). (gr. 3-6). 103.50 *(978-0-8239-7290-6(9),* Reading Power) Rosen Publishing Group, Inc., The.

Gale Research Staff. Industrial Revolution: Biographies. 2003. (Industrial Revolution Reference Library). (ENG., Illus.). 240p. (J). (gr. 6-10). 106.00 *(978-0-7876-6514-2(2),* GML00502-182382, UXL) Cengage Gale.

Kishel, Ann-Marie. Cashier. 2007. (First Step Nonfiction Ser.). (J). pap. 3.95 *(978-0-8225-6843-8(8))* Lerner Publishing Group.

Lupo, Tamar. Warren Buffett. 2007. (Remarkable People Ser.). (Illus.). 24p. (J). (gr. 4-7). pap. 8.95 *(978-1-59036-652-3(2));* lib. bdg. 24.45 *(978-1-59036-651-6(4))* Weigl Pubs., Inc.

Machajewski, David. John Pierpont Morgan & the Banking Industry. 2016. (Great Entrepreneurs in U. S. History Ser.). (Illus.). 32p. (J). (gr. 5-5). pap. 11.75 *(978-1-4994-2127-9(3),* PowerKids Pr.) Rosen Publishing Group, Inc., The.

Mullenbach, Cheryl. The Industrial Revolution for Kids: The People & Technology That Changed the World, with 21 Activities. 2014. (For Kids Ser.). (ENG., Illus.). 144p. (J). (gr. 4). pap. 16.95 *(978-1-61374-690-5(3))* Chicago Review Pr., Inc.

Parker, Lewis K. J. Pierpont Morgan & Wall Street. (American Tycoons Ser.). 24p. 2009. (gr. 3-3). 42.50 *(978-1-61511-391-0(6))* 2003. (Illus.). (J). lib. bdg. 22.60 *(978-0-8239-6449-9(3))* Rosen Publishing Group, Inc., The. (PowerKids Pr.).

Phan, Sandy. Cecil Rhodes: The Man Who Expanded an Empire, 1 vol. 2012. (Primary Source Readers Ser.). (ENG.). 32p. (J). (gr. 4-4). pap. 8.99 *(978-1-4333-5016-0(5))* Teacher Created Materials, Inc.

Ryan, Bernard Jr. Warren Buffett: Financier. 2005. (Ferguson Career Biographies Ser.). (Illus.). 144p. (gr. 6-12). 25.00 *(978-0-8160-5894-5(6),* Ferguson Publishing Co.) Facts On File, Inc.

Sammons, Sandra Wallus. Henry Flagler, Builder of Florida. 2010. (Pineapple Press Biography Ser.). (ENG.). 64p. (J). (gr. 4-7). pap. 8.95 *(978-1-56164-467-4(6))* Pineapple Pr., Inc.

CAPTAIN UNDERPANTS (FICTITIOUS CHARACTER)—FICTION

Captain Underpants & the Tyrannical Retaliation of the Turbo Toilet 2000. 2014. (Captain Underpants Ser.: Bk. 11). (ENG., Illus.). 224p. (J). (gr. 2-5). 9.99 *(978-0-545-50490-4(2))* Scholastic, Inc.

Howard, Kate. Official Handbook (Captain Underpants Movie) 2017. (Captain Underpants Movie Ser.). (ENG., Illus.). 64p. (J). (gr. 2-5). pap. 5.99 ***(978-1-338-19656-6(1))*** Scholastic, Inc.

Pilger, Seamus. Underpantsed! Gilpin, Stephen, illus. 2016. (Fart Squad Ser.: 5). 112p. (J). (gr. 1-5). pap. 4.99 *(978-0-06-229053-3(3))* HarperCollins Pubs.

Pilkey, Dav. The Adventures of Captain Underpants. 2004. (Captain Underpants Ser.: No. 1). (J). lib. bdg. 19.95 *(978-0-439-68434-7(X),* Scholastic, Inc.) Scholastic, Inc.

—El Capitan Calzoncillos y la Furia de la Supermujer Macroelastica. 2003. (Captain Underpants Ser.: 5). (SPA & ENG., Illus.). 176p. (J). (gr. 2-5). pap. 5.99 *(978-0-439-53820-6(3),* Scholastic en Espanol) Scholastic, Inc.

—Captain Underpants & the Attack of the Talking Toilets. Pilkey, Dav, illus. 2014. (Captain Underpants Ser.: Bk. 2). (ENG., Illus.). 160p. (J). (gr. 2-5). 9.99 *(978-0-545-59932-0(6))* Scholastic, Inc.

—Captain Underpants & the Attack of the Talking Toilets. 2004. (Captain Underpants Ser.: No. 2). (J). lib. bdg. 19.95 *(978-0-439-68436-1(6),* Scholastic, Inc.) Scholastic, Inc.

—Captain Underpants & the Big, Bad Battle of the Bionic Booger Boy Part 1: The Night of the Nasty Nostril Nuggets. 2003. (Captain Underpants Ser.: 6). (ENG., Illus.). 176p. (J). (gr. 2-5). 18.99 *(978-0-439-37609-9(2))* Scholastic, Inc.

—Captain Underpants & the Big, Bad Battle of the Bionic Booger Boy Part 1: The Night of the Nasty Nostril Nuggets. Pilkey, Dav, illus. 2003. (Captain Underpants Ser.: 6). (ENG., Illus.). 176p. (J). (gr. 2-5). pap. 5.99 *(978-0-439-37610-5(6))* Scholastic, Inc.

—Captain Underpants & the Big, Bad Battle of the Bionic Booger Boy Part 2: The Revenge of the Ridiculous Robo-Boogers. Pilkey, Dav, illus. 2003. (Captain Underpants Ser.: 7). (ENG., Illus.). 176p. (J). (gr. 2-5). 18.99 *(978-0-439-37611-2(4));* pap. 5.99 *(978-0-439-37612-9(2))* Scholastic, Inc.

—Captain Underpants & the Invasion of the Incredibly Naughty Cafeteria Ladies from Outer Space: Color Edition. 2014. (Captain Underpants Ser.: 3). (ENG., Illus.). 160p. (J). (gr. 2-5). 9.99 *(978-0-545-69470-4(1))* Scholastic, Inc.

—Captain Underpants & the Perilous Plot of Professor Poopypants. (Captain Underpants Ser.: 4). (J). 2015. (ENG.). 160p. (gr. 3). 9.99 *(978-0-545-87187-7(5))* 2004. lib. bdg. 19.95 *(978-0-439-68440-8(4),* Scholastic, Inc.) Scholastic, Inc.

—Captain Underpants & the Perilous Plot of Professor Poopypants. 2015. (Captain Underpants Color Edition Ser.: 4). lib. bdg. 20.85 *(978-0-606-38063-8(9))* Turtleback Bks.

—Captain Underpants & the Revolting Revenge of the Radioactive Robo-Boxers. Pilkey, Dav, illus. 2013. (Captain Underpants Ser.: 10). (ENG., Illus.). 192p. (J). (gr. 2-5). 9.99 *(978-0-545-17536-4(4))* Scholastic, Inc.

—Captain Underpants & the Revolting Revenge of the Radioactive Robo-Boxers. 2013. (Captain Underpants Ser.: 10). lib. bdg. 20.85 *(978-0-606-31563-0(2),* Turtleback) Turtleback Bks.

—Captain Underpants & the Sensational Saga of Sir Stinks-a-Lot. Pilkey, Dav, illus. 2015. (Captain Underpants Ser.: 12). (ENG., Illus.). 208p. (J). (gr. 2). 9.99 *(978-0-545-50492-8(9))* Scholastic, Inc.

—Captain Underpants & the Sensational Saga of Sir Stinks-a-Lot. Pilkey, Dav, illus. 2015. (Captain Underpants Ser.: 12). (ENG., Illus.). 208p. (J). (gr. 2). lib. bdg. 20.85 *(978-0-606-37924-3(X))* Turtleback Bks.

—Captain Underpants & the Terrifying Return of Tippy Tinkletrousers. Pilkey, Dav, illus. 2012. (Captain Underpants Ser.: 9). (ENG., Illus.). 304p. (J). (gr. 2-5). 9.99 *(978-0-545-17534-0(8))* Scholastic, Inc.

—Captain Underpants & the Terrifying Return of Tippy Tinkletrousers. 2012. (Captain Underpants Ser.: 9). lib. bdg. 20.85 *(978-0-606-26523-2(6),* Turtleback) Turtleback Bks.

—Captain Underpants & the Tyrannical Retaliation of the Turbo Toilet 2000. 2014. (Captain Underpants Ser.: 11). lib. bdg. 20.85 *(978-0-606-36264-1(9))* Turtleback Bks.

—Captain Underpants & the Wrath of the Wicked Wedgie Woman. 2004. (Captain Underpants Ser.: No. 5). (J). lib. bdg. 19.95 *(978-0-439-68441-5(2),* Scholastic, Inc.) Scholastic, Inc.

—Captain Underpants Color Collection. Pilkey, Dav, illus. 2015. (Captain Underpants Ser.). (ENG., Illus.). 160p. (J). (gr. 2-5). 29.97 *(978-0-545-87011-5(9))* Scholastic, Inc.

CAR WHEELS

see Wheels

CARBINES

see Rifles

CARBON

see also Diamonds

Gardner, Jane P. Carbon. 2017. (Chemistry of Everyday Elements Ser.). (ENG.). (YA). (gr. 7-12). 23.95 ***(978-1-4222-3839-4(3))*** Mason Crest.

Loria, Laura. The Carbon Cycle. 2017. (J). ***(978-1-5383-0025-1(7))*** Rosen Publishing Group, Inc., The.

Saucerman, Linda. Carbon. 2009. (Understanding the Elements of the Periodic Table Ser.). 48p. (gr. 6-6). 53.00 *(978-1-60854-642-8(X),* Rosen Reference) Rosen Publishing Group, Inc., The.

Slade, Suzanne. The Carbon Cycle. 2007. 28p. (gr. 3-7). pap. 21.25 *(978-1-4358-3828-4(9),* PowerKids Pr.) Rosen Publishing Group, Inc., The.

Summers, Marilee. C Is for Carbon. Wojtko, Kimberlee, illus. 2004. 61p. (J). per. 24.95 *(978-0-9753078-0-9(0))* MackStorm Productions, Inc.

Wu, Ronald W. Carbon. 2005. (Understanding the Elements of the Periodic Table Ser.). (Illus.). 48p. (YA). (gr. 5-9). lib. bdg. 29.25 *(978-1-4042-0155-2(6))* Rosen Publishing Group, Inc., The.

CARCINOMA

see Cancer

CARD GAMES

see Cards

CARD TRICKS

see also Fortune-Telling

Barnhart, Norm. Dazzling Card Tricks, 1 vol. 2013. (Magic Manuals Ser.). (ENG., Illus.). 32p. (gr. 3-4). lib. bdg. 27.99 *(978-1-4765-0133-8(5))* Capstone Press of Coughlan Cos.

Card Tricks. Date not set. 48p. (J). 7.98 *(978-0-7525-9817-8(1))* Parragon, Inc.

Card Tricks Kid Kit. 2004. (Illus.). 32p. (J). 8.99 *(978-1-58086-455-8(4));* (gr. 2-18). 8.99 *(978-1-58086-439-8(2))* EDC Publishing.

Charney, Steve. Cool Card Tricks, 1 vol. 2010. (Easy Magic Tricks Ser.). (ENG.). 24p. (gr. 1-2). lib. bdg. 25.32 *(978-1-4296-4515-7(6),* First Facts) Capstone Press of Coughlan Cos.

Fulves, Karl. More Self-Working Card Tricks: 88 Fool-Proof Card Miracles for the Amateur Magician. 2011. (Dover Magic Bks.). (ENG., Illus.). 160p. (Orig.). (gr. 6-18). pap. 10.95 *(978-0-486-24580-5(2))* Dover Pubns., Inc.

Gross, Peter & Walter Foster Jr. Creative Team. 101 Ways to Amaze & Entertain: Amazing Magic & Hilarious Jokes to Try on Your Friends & Family. 2015. (101 Things Ser.). (ENG., Illus.). 144p. (J). (gr. 3-7). pap. 12.95 *(978-1-63322-042-3(7))* Quarto Publishing Group USA.

Magic Card Tricks. 2004. (Whizz Kits Ser.). (Illus.). 48p. (J). *(978-1-84229-943-2(3))* Top That! Publishing PLC.

Megram, Paul. My First Magic Book: 35 Fun Tricks & Illusions for Children Aged 7 Years + 2014. (ENG., Illus.). 112p. (J). (gr. 7-11). pap. 14.95 *(978-1-78249-158-3(9),* CICO Books) Ryland Peters & Small GBR. Dist: WIPRO.

Turnbull, Stephanie. Card Tricks. 2011. (ENG., Illus.). 32p. (J). pap. 10.95 *(978-1-77092-041-5(2))* Saunders Bk. Co. CAN. Dist: RiverStream Publishing.

—Easy Card Tricks. 2014. (Beginner Magic Ser.). (Illus.). 24p. (J). (gr. 2-5). pap. 8.95 *(978-1-77092-154-2(0))* Saunders Bk. Co. CAN. Dist: RiverStream Publishing.

—Easy Coin Tricks. 2014. (Beginner Magic Ser.). (ENG., Illus.). 24p. (J). (gr. 2-5). pap. 8.95 *(978-1-77092-155-9(9))* Saunders Bk. Co. CAN. Dist: RiverStream Publishing.

Zenon, Paul. Cool Card Tricks: Techniques for the Advanced Magician. 2007. (Amazing Magic Ser.). (Illus.). 64p. (YA). (gr. 5-8). lib. bdg. 31.95 *(978-1-4042-1085-1(7))* Rosen Publishing Group, Inc., The.

—Gimmicks & Card Tricks: Illusions for the Intermediate Magician. 2008. (Amazing Magic Ser.). (ENG., Illus.). 64p. (gr. 5-8). pap. 14.05 *(978-1-4042-1758-4(4),* Rosen Reference) Rosen Publishing Group, Inc., The.

—Simple Sleight-of-Hand: Card & Coin Tricks for the Beginning Magician. (Amazing Magic Ser.). (Illus.). 64p. (gr. 5-8). 2008. (ENG.). per. 14.05 *(978-1-4042-1757-7(6),* Rosen Reference) 2007. (YA). lib. bdg. 31.95 *(978-1-4042-1070-7(9))* Rosen Publishing Group, Inc., The.

CARDIAC DISEASES

see Heart—Diseases

CARDINALS (BIRDS)

Dealia, Yancey. The Cardinal Nest: Where the Life Cycle Begins. Ted, Hood, Jr., photos by. 2013. (Illus.). 30p. (J). pap. 9.95 *(978-0-578-05005-8(6))* Four Seasons Publishing.

Murray, Julie. Cardinals, 1 vol. 2003. (Buddy Book Ser.). (ENG.). 24p. (J). (gr. 1-4). 25.65 *(978-1-57765-704-0(7))* ABDO Publishing Co.

Shea, Therese. A Bird Watcher's Guide to Cardinals. 2016. (Backyard Bird Watchers Ser.). (ENG., Illus.). 32p. (J). (gr. 2-3). pap. 10.50 *(978-1-4824-3840-6(2))* Stevens, Gareth Publishing LLLP.

CARDS

see also Card Tricks; Fortune-Telling

Age of Dinosaurs Playing Cards. (Additional Educational Games & Activities for Children Ser.). pap. 6.00 *(978-0-88079-709-2(6),* DIN54) U.S. Games Systems, Inc.

Allyson, Jackie. Antonio the Magician Esfandiari. 2007. (Superstars of Poker Ser.). (Illus.). 64p. (YA). pap. 7.95 *(978-1-4222-0370-5(0))* Mason Crest.

—Chris Jesus Ferguson. (Superstars of Poker Ser.). (Illus.). 64p. (YA). 2009. (gr. 4-7). lib. bdg. 22.95 *(978-1-4222-0218-0(6))* 2007. pap. 7.95 *(978-1-4222-0371-2(9))* Mason Crest.

—Doyle Texas Dolly Brunson. (Superstars of Poker Ser.). (Illus.). 64p. (YA). 2009. (gr. 4-7). lib. bdg. 22.95 *(978-1-4222-0216-6(X))* 2007. pap. 7.95 *(978-1-4222-0368-2(9))* Mason Crest.

—Gus the Great Dane Hansen. (Superstars of Poker Ser.). (Illus.). 64p. (YA). 2009. (gr. 4-7). lib. bdg. 22.95 *(978-1-4222-0219-7(4))* 2007. pap. 7.95 *(978-1-4222-0372-9(7))* Mason Crest.

—Phil Unabomber Laak. 2007. (Superstars of Poker Ser.). (Illus.). 64p. (YA). pap. 7.95 *(978-1-4222-0376-7(X))* Mason Crest.

Alyson, Jackie. Howard the Professor Lederer. 2007. (Superstars of Poker: Texas Hold'em Ser.). (Illus.). 64p. (YA). (gr. 3-7). pap. 7.95 *(978-1-4222-0377-4(8))* Mason Crest.

Amery, Heather. Donkey Cards. Cartwright, Stephen, illus. 2004. (Farmyard Tales Card Games Ser.). 52p. (J). 8.95 *(978-0-7945-0326-0(8),* Usborne) EDC Publishing.

Animals Bingo: Player Cards & Master Cards & Caller Markers & Blank Markers. 2006. (Journeys Ser.). 46.60 *(978-1-4042-5488-6(9),* Rosen Classroom) Rosen Publishing Group, Inc., The.

Bagley, Val. Who Said Book of Mormon Match Game. 2004. 8.95 *(978-1-57734-527-5(4))* Covenant Communications, Inc.

Barry, Sheila Anne, et al. Giant Book of Card Games/Giant Book of Card Tricks: Flip Book. Sterling Publishing Company Staff, ed. (Illus.). 512p. pap. 9.98 *(978-1-4027-0467-3(4))* Sterling Publishing Co., Inc.

Blister Pack Staff. Phase 10 Card Game. 8.00 *(978-1-57281-141-6(2),* PH8220) U.S. Games Systems, Inc.

Bustamante, Frank & Gray, Dan, eds. The Testimony of Jacob Hollow. Bustamante, Frank et al, illus. alt. ed. 2003. (YA). bds. 19.95 *(978-0-9728526-0-9(3))* Third World Games, Inc.

Card Games. Date not set. 48p. (J). 7.98 *(978-0-7525-9816-1(3))* Parragon, Inc.

Carson-Dellosa Publishing Staff. Go Fish. 2006. (ENG., Illus.). 54p. (gr. -1-2). 2.99 *(978-0-7696-4839-2(8),* Brighter Child) Carson-Dellosa Publishing, LLC.

Cartwright, Stephen, illus. Fairytale Snap. 2005. (Snap Card Games Ser.). 52p. (J). 8.95 *(978-0-7945-0905-7(3),* Usborne) EDC Publishing.

Cassidy, Maura A. Go Ask Anyone! 2003. 56p. (YA). mass mkt. *(978-0-9742866-4-8(8))* Go Ask Anyone, Inc.

—Go Ask Your Girlfriends! 2003. 56p. (YA). mass mkt. *(978-0-9742866-5-5(6))* Go Ask Anyone, Inc.

—Go Ask Your Grandparent! 2003. 56p. (YA). mass mkt. *(978-0-9742866-2-4(1))* Go Ask Anyone, Inc.

—Go Ask Your Mother! 2003. 56p. (YA). mass mkt. *(978-0-9742866-1-7(3))* Go Ask Anyone, Inc.

—Go Ask Your Teenager! 2003. 56p. (YA). mass mkt. *(978-0-9742866-3-1(X))* Go Ask Anyone, Inc.

Changing Earth Word-picture match cards, Memory game cards, Labeled picture Cards. 2008. (Journeys Ser.). 46.60 *(978-1-4042-9519-3(4),* Rosen Classroom) Rosen Publishing Group, Inc., The.

Cordill, Lloyd. Card Wars Official Guide. 2016. (Adventure Time Ser.). (ENG., Illus.). 176p. (J). (gr. 3-7). pap. 12.99 *(978-0-399-54163-6(2),* Cartoon Network Books) Penguin Young Readers Group.

Daniel, Andy, et al. Bid-It! Card Game. 2003. 9.95 *(978-1-929645-17-6(1))* Enginuity, LLC.

—LINX Card Game. 2003. 9.95 *(978-1-929645-19-0(8))* Enginuity, LLC.

Deck, Upper. Dinosaur King Blister. 2008. audio 3.99 *(978-1-59945-540-2(4))* Upper Deck Co., LLC,The.

—Dinosaur King Starter. 2008. audio 9.99 *(978-1-59945-666-9(4))* Upper Deck Co., LLC,The.

Donaldson, Terry, et al, creators. The Lord of the Rings Tarot Gravity Feed Counter Display. 2004. (Illus.). 108.00 *(978-1-57281-162-1(5),* DLR6) U.S. Games Systems, Inc.

Empyrean, Inc. 2004. (YA). 12.99 *(978-0-9749460-1-6(X))* Versal Technologies, Inc.

Ewing, Susan. Cats! Train Your Owner! Cider Mill Press Staff, ed. Mullen, Lana, illus. 2008. (My-T-Smart(tm) Flash Cards Ser.). (ENG.). 32p. 14.95 *(978-1-933662-77-0(8))* Cider Mill Pr. Bk. Pubs., LLC.

Faidutti, Bruno. Terra: Game. 2004. 25.00 *(978-92-3-010870-0(7))* UNESCO Publishing FRA. Dist: Renouf Publishing Co., Ltd.

Falconer, Ian. Olivia Matching Game. 2013. (ENG., Illus.). 72p. (J). (gr. -1 — 1). bds. 14.99 *(978-1-4521-1180-3(4))* Chronicle Bks. LLC.

FitzGerald, Jerry. Dragon Hunt Card Game. 8.00 *(978-1-57281-098-3(X),* WDH66) U.S. Games Systems, Inc.

Flaherty, Patrick. Why Scouting? A Collection of Thoughts & Stories about Our Family's Experiences with the Boy Scout Program. McLaughlin, Pat, ed. 2004. 96p. per. 9.95 *(978-0-9724178-6-0(9))* Teckni-Corp, Ltd.

Flaherty, Patrick J. Camping Challenge: Card Game for Campers. 2003. (Illus.). 54p. (YA). mass mkt. 6.95 *(978-0-9724178-4-6(2))* Teckni-Corp, Ltd.

Foley, Mariena. Family Game Night: Poker for Kids! 2013. 24p. pap. 4.99 *(978-1-61933-517-2(4))* FastPrncil, Inc.

Frank, Paul. Matching Game. 2008. (ENG., Illus.). 72p. (J). (gr. -1-17). bds. 14.95 *(978-0-8118-6352-0(2))* Chronicle Bks. LLC.

Get the Goods Card Game. 8.00 *(978-1-57281-081-5(5),* GTG100) U.S. Games Systems, Inc.

Gill, Bill Pojo. Duel Masters. 2004. (Pojo's... Ser.). (ENG., Illus.). 80p. (J). (gr. 4-6). pap. 9.95 *(978-1-57243-700-5(6))* Triumph Bks.

Girard, Alexander. Alexander Girard Memory Game. 2012. (ENG.). 15.95 *(978-1-934429-76-1(7))* AMMO Bks., LLC.

Gulliver, A. & Cartwright, S. Snap. 2004. (Treasury of Farmyard Tales Ser.). (J). 8.95 *(978-0-7945-0325-3(X))* EDC Publishing.

Harrison, Erica. Monster Snap. Harrison, Erica, illus. 2007. (Card Games Ser.). (Illus.). 52p. (J). 8.99 *(978-0-7945-1449-5(9),* Usborne) EDC Publishing.

Hiron. Rhombo Continuo. 12.00 *(978-1-57281-110-2(2),* RCT48) U.S. Games Systems, Inc.

Ho, Oliver. The Ultimate Book of Family Card Games. 2013. (ENG., Illus.). 128p. (gr. 3). pap. 9.95 *(978-1-4027-5041-0(2))* Sterling Publishing Co., Inc.

Holt, Deloris L. Black History Playing Card Deck: With 52 Portraits of Distinguished Black Americans. Newman, Langley, illus. (History Channel Ser.). 120p. pap. 12.00 *(978-1-57281-422-6(5),* HCBH55) U.S. Games Systems, Inc.

Janner, Hans. Hans Janner, Sr. Playing Cards: Boxed, Custom Designed, Deluxe Poker-Size Playing Cards. 2006. 11.95 *(978-0-9748721-2-4(1))* Fish Decoy.com, Ltd.

Kern Alphabet Card Games. (Illus.). 60.00 *(978-1-57281-133-1(1),* DAZ12) U.S. Games Systems, Inc.

Kern, Donna. Animal Alphabet. Kern, Donna, illus. (Illus.). 60.00 *(978-1-57281-296-3(6),* DAA12) U.S. Games Systems, Inc.

—Kern Alphabet Card Games. Kern, Donna, illus. (Illus.). 5.00 *(978-1-57281-092-1(0),* AZ54) U.S. Games Systems, Inc.

Lewis, Barbara A. & Free Spirit Publishing Staff. What Do You Stand For? Character Building. 2006. (ENG., Illus.). 60p. (gr. 1-6). 13.99 *(978-1-57542-217-6(4))* Free Spirit Publishing, Inc.

Lu, Nick, illus. Bumper-To-Bumper Cars & Trucks Flash Cards. 2017. (ENG.). 20p. (J). 14.99 *(978-1-4521-5503-6(8))* Chronicle Bks. LLC.

—Bumper-To-Bumper Stroller Cars. 2017. (ENG.). 10p. (J). 9.99 *(978-1-4521-5504-3(6))* Chronicle Bks. LLC.

C
D

MacColl, Gail. The Book of Cards for Kids. 2007. (ENG., Illus.). 128p. (J). (gr. -1-4). pap. 14.95 (978-0-7611-4800-5(0), 14800) Workman Publishing Co., Inc.

Mother Goose Nursery Rhymes I. (Mother Goose Nursery Rhymes Ser.). (Illus.). 6.00 (978-0-88079-647-7(2), NR541) U.S. Games Systems, Inc.

My Big Art Show: A Card Game + Book for Art Experts. 2014. (ENG., Illus.). 60p. (J). (gr. 2-5). 24.95 (978-0-500-65039-4(X), 565039) Thames & Hudson.

Numbers League: Adventures in Addiplication. 2006. (SPA, FRE, GER & ENG.). (J). 19.95 (978-0-9768848-1-1(X)) Bent Castle Workshops.

Numbers League Infinity Level Expansion. 2007. (J). 9.95 (978-0-9768848-3-5(6)) Bent Castle Workshops.

O'Reilly, Wenda. Go Fish for Art. 2004. 238.80 (978-1-889613-53-6(3)) Birdcage Pr.

Ouija Oracle Card Game. 2004. 72.00 (978-1-57281-135-5(8), DOUJ6); 12.00 (978-1-57281-047-1(5), OUJ52) U.S. Games Systems, Inc.

Panian, Angie & Panian, Tyler. Creature Clash! Card Game. 2014. (ENG., Illus.). 100p. (J). (gr. 1-4). 14.99 (978-1-4521-1266-4(5)) Chronicle Bks. LLC.

Parr, Todd. Todd Parr Feelings Flash Cards. 2010. (ENG.). 20p. (J). (gr. -1 — 1). 14.99 (978-0-8118-7145-7(2)) Chronicle Bks. LLC.

Peleg Pete's Deck of Royal Rogues: Pirate Playing Cards. 2007. (YA). (978-0-9768848-2-8(8)) Bent Castle Workshops.

Peterson, Oscar. Oscar Peterson Playing Cards: Boxed, Custom-designed, Poker-size Playing Cards. 2006. 11.95 (978-0-9748721-3-1(X)) Fish Decoy.com, Ltd.

Phase 10 Card Game. 7.00 (978-1-57281-140-9(4), PH9225) U.S. Games Systems, Inc.

Prap, Lila. Whyld Animals Kid Kit. 2010. (Kid Kits Ser.). 32p. (J). pap. 9.99 (978-1-60130-219-9(3), Usborne) EDC Publishing.

Rain Forest Card Games. (Additional Educational Games & Activities for Children Ser.). 10.00 (978-1-57281-307-6(5), RF48); 60.00 (978-1-57281-338-0(5), DRF6) U.S. Games Systems, Inc.

Reynolds, Charles. Card Magic. 6.95 (978-1-59093-001-4(0), Eager Minds Pr.) Warehousing & Fulfillment Specialists, LLC (WFS, LLC).

Rogge, Robie. Peekaboo! Stroller Cards: on the Farm. Huang, Yu-Hsuan, illus. 2017. (ENG.). 10p. (J). 9.99 (978-1-4521-5385-8(X)) Chronicle Bks. LLC.

Roycroft, Mitch. Chris Moneymaker. 2007. (Superstars of Poker Ser.). (Illus.). 64p. (YA). pap. 7.95 (978-1-4222-0378-1(6)) Mason Crest.

—Daniel Kid Poker Negreanu. 2007. (Superstars of Poker Ser.). (Illus.). 64p. (YA). pap. 7.95 (978-1-4222-0379-8(4)) Mason Crest.

—Greg Fossilman Raymer. (Superstars of Poker Ser.). (Illus.). 64p. (YA). 2009. (gr. 3-7). lib. bdg. 22.95 (978-1-4222-0228-9(3)) 2007. pap. 7.95 (978-1-4222-0380-4(8)) Mason Crest.

—Jennifer Harman. 2007. (Superstars of Poker Ser.). (Illus.). 64p. (YA). pap. 7.95 (978-1-4222-0373-6(5)) Mason Crest.

—Johnny Orient Express Chan. 2007. (Superstars of Poker Ser.). (Illus.). 64p. (YA). pap. 7.95 (978-1-4222-0369-9(7)) Mason Crest.

—Phil the Poker Brat Hellmuth. 2007. (Superstars of Poker Ser.). 64p. (YA). pap. 7.95 (978-1-4222-0374-3(3)) Mason Crest.

—Phil Tiger Woods of Poker Ivey. 2007. (Superstars of Poker Ser.). (Illus.). 64p. (YA). pap. 7.95 (978-1-4222-0375-0(1)) Mason Crest.

Scarry, Richard. Best Busytown. 2013. (ENG., Illus.). 118p. (J). (gr. -1-2). pap., act. bk. ed. 14.95 (978-1-4027-7315-0(3)) Sterling Publishing Co., Inc.

Simons, Rae. Texas Hold'em: The Learning Curve of Life. 2009. (Superstars of Poker Ser.). (Illus.). 64p. (YA). (gr. 4-7). lib. bdg. 22.95 (978-1-4222-0229-6(1)) Mason Crest.

—Texas Hold'em: the Learning Curve of Life. 2007. (Superstars of Poker: Texas Hold'em Ser.). (Illus.). 64p. (YA). (gr. 4-7). pap. 7.95 (978-1-4222-0381-1(6)) Mason Crest.

Smith, Dan & Nickoloff, Michael, eds. Portable Adventures: 8th Grade. Smith, Dan, illus. 2003. (Illus.). (YA). bds. 12.95 (978-0-9728526-2-3(X)) Third World Games, Inc.

—Portable Adventures: Lair of the Rat King. Smith, Dan, illus. 2003. (Illus.). (YA). bds. 12.95 (978-0-9728526-1-6(1)) Third World Games, Inc.

Stone. Lucky 13 Card Game. 10.00 (978-1-57281-200-0(1), LK55) U.S. Games Systems, Inc.

Superstars of Poker: Texas Hold-em, 14 vols., Set. Incl. Antonio the Magician Esfandiari. Allyson, Jackie. (gr. 3-7). lib. bdg. 22.95 (978-1-4222-0217-3(8)); Chris Jesus Ferguson. Allyson, Jackie. (gr. 4-7). lib. bdg. 22.95 (978-1-4222-0218-0(6)); Chris Moneymaker. Roycroft, Mitch. (gr. 4-7). lib. bdg. 22.95 (978-1-4222-0225-8(9)); Doyle Texas Dolly Brunson. Allyson, Jackie. (gr. 4-7). lib. bdg. 22.95 (978-1-4222-0216-6(X)); Greg Fossilman Raymer. Roycroft, Mitch. (gr. 3-7). lib. bdg. 22.95 (978-1-4222-0228-9(3)); Gus the Great Dane Hansen. Allyson, Jackie. (gr. 4-7). lib. bdg. 22.95 (978-1-4222-0219-7(4)); Howard the Professor Lederer. Allyson, Jackie. (gr. 3-7). lib. bdg. 22.95 (978-1-4222-0223-4(2)); Jennifer Harman. Roycroft, Mitch. (gr. 3-7). lib. bdg. 22.95 (978-1-4222-0227-2(5)); Johnny Orient Express Chan. Roycroft, Mitch. (gr. 4-7). lib. bdg. 22.95 (978-1-4222-0224-1(0)); Phil the Poker Brat Hellmuth. Roycroft, Mitch. (gr. 4-7). lib. bdg. 22.95 (978-1-4222-0220-3(8)); Phil Tiger Woods of Poker Ivey. Roycroft, Mitch. (gr. 4-7). lib. bdg. 22.95 (978-1-4222-0221-0(6)); Phil Unabomber Laak. Allyson, Jackie. (gr. 3-7). lib. bdg. 22.95 (978-1-4222-0222-7(4)); Texas Hold'em: The Learning Curve of Life. Simons, Rae. (gr. 4-7). lib. bdg. 22.95 (978-1-4222-0229-6(1)); (Illus.). 64p. (YA). 2009. 2007. Set lib. bdg. 321.30 (978-1-4222-0215-9(1)) Mason Crest.

Teddy Bear Playig Cards/Games. (Mother Goose Nursery Rhymes Ser.). 72.00 (978-1-57281-134-8(X), DTB12) U.S. Games Systems, Inc.

Tullet, Hervé. Hervé Tullet's Zazazoom! A Game of Imagination. 2016. (ENG., Illus.). 25p. (J). (gr. -1-4). bds. 14.99 (978-1-4521-5874-7(6)) Chronicle Bks. LLC.

U S Games Systems, Inc., creator. Guardian Angel Cards. 2004. (Kids' Classics Ser.). 19.95 (978-1-57281-444-8(6), CCBP168) U.S. Games Systems, Inc.

Wizkids, creator. Star War Pocketmodel TCG Trading Card Game: Imperial Power-up Pack. 2007. 14.99 (978-1-59041-416-3(0)) WizKids, LLC.

Yu-gi-oh. Yu-gi-oh Duelist Genesis Blister. 2008. 3.99 (978-1-59945-576-1(5)) Upper Deck Co., LLC,The.

—Yu-gi-oh Premium Pack 2. 2008. 4.99 (978-1-59945-658-4(3)) Upper Deck Co., LLC,The.

CARDS, GREETING

see Greeting Cards

CARE BEARS (FICTITIOUS CHARACTERS)—FICTION

Care Bears Coloring Books. 2004. (J). act. bk. ed. 1.29 (978-0-7666-0921-1(9), 99390) Modern Publishing.

Flasterstein, Ran. Care Bears Lullaby: A Night Light Book. Moore, Saxton, illus. 2007. 8p. (J). bds. 12.95 incl. audio compact disk (978-1-57791-303-0(5), Little Melody Pr.) Brighter Minds Children's Publishing.

Lee, Quinlan B. Phonics: 12 Book Reading Program, 12 vols. 2006. (Illus.). (978-0-439-78949-3(4)); (978-0-439-78947-9(8)); (978-0-439-78948-6(6)); (978-0-439-78938-7(9)); (978-0-439-78939-4(7)); (978-0-439-78940-0(0)); (978-0-439-78941-7(9)); (978-0-439-78942-4(7)); (978-0-439-78943-1(5)); (978-0-439-78944-8(3)); (978-0-439-78945-5(1)); (978-0-439-78946-2(X)) Scholastic, Inc.

Sander, Sonia. Plant a Garden. Moore, Saxton & McGee, Warner, illus. 2008. (Care Bears Ser.). (ENG.). 24p. (J). (gr. -1-3). pap. 3.99 (978-0-545-00908-9(1), Scholastic) Scholastic, Inc.

Welcome to Care-a-Lot! 2007. (Care Bears Bonus Fun Bks.). (Illus.). 40p. (J). (gr. -1-3). 3.99 (978-0-7666-0948-8(0), 55310) Modern Publishing.

CAREERS

see Occupations; Professions; Vocational Guidance

see subject headings with the subdivision Vocational Guidance

CAREY, WILLIAM, 1761-1834

Edwards, Andrew & Thornton, Fleur. William Carey: The Story of a Country Boy & Shoe Mender Whose Big Dreams Took Him to India. 2005. (Footsteps of the Past Ser.). (Illus.). 32p. pap. 5.00 (978-1-84625-012-5(9)) DayOne Pubns. GBR. Dist: Send The Light Distribution LLC.

CARIBBEAN AREA

Bentley, Joyce. St. Lucia. 2005. (Illus.). 32p. 18.95 (978-1-59389-227-2(6)) Chrysalis Education.

Boyd, Judy. Central America & the Caribbean, Vol. 10. 2016. (Social Progress & Sustainability Ser.). (Illus.). 80p. (J). (gr. 7). 24.95 (978-1-4222-3493-8(2)) Mason Crest.

Brooks, Susie. St. Lucia. 2006. (Our Lives, Our World Ser.). (J). (978-1-59389-290-6(X)) Chrysalis Education.

Furgang, Kathy. Mount Pelee: The Biggest Volcano Eruption of the 20th Century. 2009. (Volcanoes of the World Ser.). 24p. (gr. 3-3). 42.50 (978-1-60854-731-9(0), PowerKids Pr.) Rosen Publishing Group, Inc., The.

Grateful Steps Publishing House, prod. Jammin' Geography: Caribbean Cruise. 2010. (ENG., Illus.). 48p. (J). 19.95 (978-1-935130-21-5(8)) Grateful Steps.

Green, Jen. Caribbean Sea & Gulf of Mexico. 2006. (Oceans & Seas Ser.). (Illus.). 48p. (gr. 5-12). pap. 14.05 (978-0-8368-6280-5(5)); lib. bdg. 31.00 (978-0-8368-6272-0(4)) Stevens, Gareth Publishing LLLP. (Gareth Stevens Secondary Library).

Guek Cheng, P. & Pang, Guek Cheng. Grenada. 2nd rev. ed. 2010. (Cultures of the World 21 Ser.). 144p. (gr. 6). lib. bdg. 42.79 (978-1-60870-216-9(2)) Marshall Cavendish GBR. Dist: Marshall Cavendish Corp.

Henderson, James D., ed. Discovering the Caribbean, 11 vols., Set. (Illus.). 64p. (YA). (gr. 5-18). lib. bdg. (978-1-59084-503-5(X)) Mason Crest.

Hernandez, Romel. Caribbean Islands: Facts & Figures, Vol. 11. Henderson, James D., ed. 2015. (Discovering the Caribbean: History, Politics, & Culture Ser.). (Illus.). 64p. (J). (gr. 7). lib. bdg. 22.95 (978-1-4222-3309-2(X)) Mason Crest.

Katchur, Matthew & Sterngass, Jon. Spanish Settlement in North America: 1822-1898. Overmyer-Velazquez, Mark, ed. 2006. (Latino-American History Ser.). (Illus.). 106p. (YA). (gr. 5-9). lib. bdg. 35.00 (978-0-8160-6442-7(3)) Facts On File, Inc.

Malam, John. You Wouldn't Want to... Be a Pirate's Prisoner! Antram, David, illus. rev. ed. 2012. (ENG.). 32p. (J). lib. bdg. 29.00 (978-0-531-27502-3(7)) Scholastic Library Publishing.

—You Wouldn't Want to Be a Pirate's Prisoner! Horrible Things You'd Rather Not Know. Antram, David, illus. rev. ed. 2012. (You Wouldn't Want to...: History of the World Ser.). (ENG.). 40p. (J). pap. 9.95 (978-0-531-28027-0(6)) Scholastic Library Publishing.

McDonnell, Ginger. Next Stop: The Caribbean, 1 vol. 2nd rev. ed. 2013. (Nonfiction Readers Ser.). (ENG., Illus.). 24p. (J). (gr. 2-2). pap. 23.96 (978-1-4807-1039-9(3)) Shell Educational Publishing.

—Next Stop: The Caribbean, 1 vol. 2nd rev. ed. 2011. (Nonfiction Readers Ser.). (ENG.). 24p. (J). (gr. 2-2). pap 6.99 (978-1-4333-3612-6(X)) Teacher Created Materials, Inc.

Newland, Sonya. Sailing the Caribbean Islands. 2016. (Travelling Wild Ser.). (ENG., Illus.). 32p. (J). (gr. 4-6). 17.99 (978-0-7502-9865-0(0), Wayland) Hachette Children's Group GBR. Dist: Hachette Bk. Group.

Orr, Tamra. St. Lucia. 2nd ed. 2007. (Cultures of the World Ser.). (Illus.). 144p. (gr. 6). lib. bdg. 42.79 (978-0-7614-2569-4(1), Benchmark Bks.) Marshall Cavendish Corp.

Picayo, Mario. A Caribbean Journey from A to Y: (Read & Discover What Happened to the Z) Griswold, Earleen, illus. 2007. (ENG & FRE.). 64p. (J). 19.95 (978-0-9725611-8-1(8), Campanita Bks.) Editorial Campana.

Popper, Garry. Winston in the Caribbean. Johnson, Andi, illus. 2004. 36p. (gr. -1-7). 4.00 (978-1-84161-061-0(5)) Ravette Publishing, Ltd. GBR. Dist: Parkwest Pubns., Inc.

Powell, Jillian. Caribbean Carnival. 2016. (ENG., Illus.). 32p. (J). (gr. 2-3). pap. 8.95 (978-0-00-816383-9(9)) HarperCollins Pubs. Ltd. GBR. Dist: Independent Pubs. Group.

—Caribe. 2007. (Descubramos paises del mundo (Looking at Countries) Ser.). (SPA., Illus.). 32p. (gr. 1-5). lib. bdg. 26.00 (978-0-8368-7957-5(0), Gareth Stevens Learning Library) Stevens, Gareth Publishing LLLP.

—Descubramos paises del Caribe. 2007. (Descubramos paises del mundo (Looking at Countries) Ser.). (SPA.). 32p. (gr. 1-5). pap. 10.50 (978-0-8368-7964-3(3), Gareth Stevens Learning Library) Stevens, Gareth Publishing LLLP.

—Looking at Caribbean Countries. 2007. (Looking at Countries Ser.). (Illus.). 32p. (gr. 1-5). pap. 10.50 (978-0-8368-7674-1(1)); lib. bdg. 26.00 (978-0-8368-7667-3(9)) Stevens, Gareth Publishing LLLP. (Gareth Stevens Learning Library).

Sebastian, Emily. The Colonial & Postcolonial Experience in Latin America & the Caribbean. 2016. (Colonial & Postcolonial Experience Ser.). 00128p. (J). (gr. 10-10). 54.00 (978-1-5081-0439-1(5)) Rosen Publishing Group, Inc., The.

Silva Lee, Alfonso. My Island & I: The Nature of the Caribbean. Hayskar, Bonnie J., ed. Lago, Alexis, illus. 2010. 32p. (J). pap. 9.95 (978-1-929165-14-8(5)) PANGAEA.

Sullivan, Laura L. Sir Henry Morgan. 2015. (J). lib. bdg. (978-1-62713-308-1(9)) Cavendish Square Publishing.

Temko, Florence. Traditional Crafts from the Caribbean. 2005. (Culture Crafts Ser.). (Illus.). 64p. (gr. 3-8). 23.93 (978-0-8225-2937-8(8)) Lerner Publishing Group.

Waters, Rosa. Bob Marley & the Wailers. 2008. (Pop Rock Ser.). (Illus.). 64p. (YA). (gr. 7-18). lib. bdg. 22.95 (978-1-4222-0192-3(9)) Mason Crest.

Weintraub, Aileen. Henry Morgan: 17th-Century Buccaneer. 2009. (Library of Pirates Ser.). 24p. (gr. 3-3). 42.50 (978-1-60853-812-6(5), PowerKids Pr.) Rosen Publishing Group, Inc., The.

Wojahn, Rebecca Hogue & Wojahn, Donald. A Coral Reef Food Chain: A Who-Eats-What Adventure in the Caribbean Sea. 2009. (Follow That Food Chain Ser.). (ENG.). 64p. (gr. 3-5). 30.60 (978-0-8225-7611-2(2)) Lerner Publishing Group.

CARIBBEAN AREA—FICTION

Agard, John & Nichols, Grace. Full Moon Night in Silk Cotton Tree Village: A Collection of Caribbean Folk Tales. Woods, Rosie, illus. 2016. (ENG.). 48p. (J). pap. 9.95 (978-0-00-814724-2(8)) HarperCollins Pubs. Ltd. GBR. Dist: Independent Pubs. Group.

Anderson, Al. Adventures with Bingo Borden. Agora Publications Staff, tr. Kurzyca, Krystyna Emilia, illus. 2010. 77p. (J). pap. 9.50 (978-1-887250-46-7(8)) Agora Pubns., Inc.

Applin, Barbara & Simon, Veronica, eds. Treasure House 1: A Caribbean Anthology. 2006. (ENG., Illus.). 220p. (J). (gr. 3-5). per. 11.95 (978-1-4050-3094-6(1)) Macmillan Caribbean GBR. Dist: Interlink Publishing Group, Inc.

Baptiste, Tracey. The Jumbies. (ENG.). 240p. (J). (gr. 3-7). 2016. pap. 6.95 (978-1-61620-592-8(X)) 2015. 15.95 (978-1-61620-414-3(1)) Algonquin Bks. of Chapel Hill.

Baptiste, Tracey. The Rise of the Jumbies. 2017. (Jumbies Ser.). (ENG.). 256p. (J). (gr. 3-7). 16.95 **(978-1-61620-665-9(9))** Algonquin Bks. of Chapel Hill.

Bell, Ted. The Time Pirate. 2011. (Nick Mciver Adventures Through Time Ser.: 2). (ENG., Illus.). 480p. (J). (gr. 5-9). pap. 10.99 (978-0-312-66549-4(0), 9780312665494) Square Fish.

Bousquet, Anthea. Counting St. Lucian Style: A delightfully illustrated counting rhyme set in the Caribbean island of St. Lucia. Sandiford, Ted, illus. 2011. 16p. (J). pap. (978-976-8238-01-6(1)) Maryli Pubs.

Bruton, Georgia. Escape. 2012. 210p. pap. 11.95 (978-1-938083-10-5(5)) Silver Knight Publishing, LLC.

Burchett, Jan & Vogler, Sara. Ocean S. O. S. Le Feyer, Diane, illus. 2013. (Wild Rescue Ser.). (ENG.). 152p. (gr. 3-6). 9.95 (978-1-4342-4891-6(7)) Stone Arch Bks.

—Ocean S. O. S. Le Feyer, Diane & Kennedy, Sam, illus. 2012. (Wild Rescue Ser.). (ENG.). 152p. (gr. 3-6). lib. bdg. 25.32 (978-1-4342-3771-2(0)) Stone Arch Bks.

Campbell, Hazel. Juice Box & Scandal. 2nd ed. 2005. (ENG., Illus.). 100p. pap. 4.49 (978-976-8184-65-8(5)) Penguin Publishing Group.

Cohen, Miriam. Down in the Subway, 1 vol. Greenberg, Melanie Hope, illus. 2003. (ENG.). 32p. (J). (gr. k-3). pap. 6.95 (978-1-932065-24-4(5)); 15.95 (978-1-932065-08-4(3)) Star Bright Bks., Inc.

Crowley-Ranelli, D. Holiday Island: Santa in a Bathing Suit? 2009. 56p. pap. 9.95 (978-1-60860-268-1(0), Eloquent Bks.) Strategic Book Publishing & Rights Agency (SBPRA).

Dalton, Annie. Making Waves: Mission - Foil the Pirates. 2010. (Mel Beeby, Agent Angel Ser.: 7). (ENG.). 208p. (J). (gr. 4-7). pap. 9.99 (978-0-00-720477-9(9)) HarperCollins Pubs. Ltd. GBR. Dist: HarperCollins Pubs.

Daniels, J. M. The Secret of the Little Dutch Doll. 2009. 68p. pap. 25.49 (978-1-4343-9356-2(9)) AuthorHouse.

Derenge, Garett. The Adventures of Iggy the Iguana. 2013. (ENG.). 30p. (J). pap. 13.95 (978-1-4787-1290-9(2)) Outskirts Pr., Inc.

Disney Book Group & Rudnick, Elizabeth. Pirates of the Caribbean: Dead Men Tell No Tales Novelization. Disney Storybook Art Team, illus. 2017. (ENG.). 272p. (J). (gr. 5-9). 16.99 (978-1-4847-8719-9(6)) Disney Pr.

Disney Book Group & Rusu, Meredith. Pirates of the Caribbean: Dead Men Tell No Tales: the Brightest Star in the North. Disney Storybook Art Team, illus. 2017. (ENG.). 240p. (J). (gr. 3-7). 12.99 (978-1-4847-8720-5(X)) Disney Pr.

Disney Book Group, et al. Pirates of the Caribbean. Disney Storybook Art Team & Wall, Mike, illus. 2017. (Disney Parks Presents Ser.). (ENG.). 32p. (J). (gr. -1-k). 17.99 (978-1-4847-2786-7(X)) Disney Pr.

Dixon, Franklin W. Ship of Secrets. 2014. (Hardy Boys: Secret Files Ser.: 15). lib. bdg. 14.75 (978-0-606-35781-4(5)) Turtleback Bks.

Doan, Lisa. Jack the Castaway. Stevanovic, Ivica, illus. 2014. (Berenson Schemes Ser.: 1). (ENG.). 152p. (J). (gr. 4-6). 17.95 (978-1-4677-1076-3(8), Darby Creek) Lerner Publishing Group.

Ferris, Aimee. Girl Overboard. 2007. (S. A. S. S. Ser.). (ENG., Illus.). 224p. (YA). (gr. 7-18). 7.99 (978-0-14-240799-8(2), Speak) Penguin Young Readers Group.

Fitzgerald, D. M. The True Story of the Big Red Onion. Cudd, Savannah, illus. 2013. 36p. 18.99 (978-0-9890288-7-5(9)); pap. 10.99 (978-0-9890288-5-1(2)) Mindstir Media.

Fontanez, Edwin. On This Beautiful Island. Fontanez, Edwin, illus. l.t. ed. 2004. (Illus.). 32p. (J). 16.95 (978-0-9640868-6-9(7), 1241077) Exit Studio.

Fuerst, Jeffrey B. & Benchmark Education Co., LLC. Robert Louis Stevenson's Treasure Island: My Sea Adventure Israel Hands. Hondru, Ovi, illus. 2014. (Text Connections Ser.). (J). (gr. 3). (978-1-4509-9652-5(3)) Benchmark Education Co.

Gazarik, Rebecca Renee. The Caribbean Caribou's Ancient Discovery. Patterson, Aaron James, ed. Gazarik, Rebecca Renee, illus. 2012. (Illus.). 36p. (J). (978-0-9802258-2-2(5)) Gazarik, Rebecca.

Geneviève Douyon Flambert. Grace: The Mystical Caribbean Mission. 2009. 152p. 22.95 (978-0-595-50709-2(3)); pap. 12.95 (978-0-595-51639-1(4)) iUniverse, Inc.

Gershator, Phillis. Sambalena Show-Off. 2011. (ENG.). 32p. (J). (gr. -1-3). pap. 16.99 (978-1-4424-3410-3(4), Simon & Schuster Bks. For Young Readers) Simon & Schuster Bks. For Young Readers.

Gill, Patricia. Pabi, Beega & the Mongoose Monster. 2009. 28p. pap. 14.99 (978-1-4490-2566-3(8)) AuthorHouse.

Gilligan, Shannon. Ghost Island. Newton, Keith, illus. 2008. (Dragonlarks Ser.). 80p. (J). (gr. k-3). pap. 7.99 (978-1-933390-57-4(3)) Chooseco LLC.

Grandoit, Jean. In the Quest for Inshalla: Simbies of the Caribbean at the World Under. 2010. 68p. pap. 25.49 (978-1-4520-3900-8(3)) AuthorHouse.

Haas, Abigail. Dangerous Girls. (ENG., Illus.). 400p. (YA). (gr. 9). 2014. pap. 10.99 (978-1-4424-8660-7(0)) 2013. 16.99 (978-1-4424-8659-1(7)) Simon Pulse. (Simon Pulse).

Halfmann, Janet. Hermit Crab's Home: Safe in a Shell. Dacey, Bob, illus. 2007. (ENG.). 32p. (J). pap. 6.95 (978-1-59249-733-1(0)) Soundprints.

—Hermit Crab's Home: Safe in a Shell. Dacey, Bob & Bandelin, Debra, illus. 2007. (Smithsonian Oceanic Collection). (ENG.). 32p. (J). (gr. -1-3). 16.95 (978-1-59249-732-4(2)) Soundprints.

Hall, Desis. Christmas in Jamaica & Other Stories. 2012. 64p. pap. (978-1-908690-06-7(2)) Abba Pr.

Hallworth, Grace. Sing Me a Story: Song-And-Dance Tales from the Caribbean. Clementson, John, illus. 2013. (ENG.). 48p. (J). (gr. 1-4). 9.99 (978-1-84780-426-6(8), Frances Lincoln) Quarto Publishing Group UK GBR. Dist: Hachette Bk. Group.

Hamilton, Tisha. Piratas del Caribe. el viaje al fin del Mundo: Pirates of the Caribbean: at the World's End. 2007. (Illus.). 38p. (J). (978-970-718-532-6(5), Silver Dolphin en Español) Advanced Marketing, S. de R. L. de C. V.

Hearn, Julie. Hazel. 2009. (ENG.). 400p. (YA). (gr. 7-18). 17.99 (978-1-4169-2504-0(X), Atheneum Bks. for Young Readers) Simon & Schuster Children's Publishing.

Hillhouse, Joanne C. With Grace: By Joanne C. Hillhouse. Ward, Cherise, illus. 2017. (J). pap. (978-1-934370-62-9(2)) Editorial Campana.

Hitchcock, Jan Hoag. Rosie's Flight. 2011. 36p. pap. 24.95 (978-1-4560-8889-7(0)) America Star Bks.

Hodge, Merle. For the Life of Laetitia. 2003. 21.25 (978-0-8446-7246-5(7)) Smith, Peter Pub., Inc.

Hohn, Nadia L. & Luxbacher, Irene. Malaika's Costume, 1 vol. 2016. (ENG., Illus.). 32p. (J). (gr. -1-2). 18.95 (978-1-55498-754-2(7)) Groundwood Bks. CAN. Dist: Publishers Group West (PGW).

Johnson, David. Toby the Blow Fish: A Fish on A Quest & Learns A Life Lesson. 2011. (ENG.). 16p. pap. 9.95 (978-1-4327-6680-1(5)) Outskirts Pr., Inc.

Kidd, Rob. City of Gold, 1 vol. Orpinas, Jean-Paul, illus. 2009. (Pirates of the Caribbean, Jack Sparrow Ser.: Bk. 7). (ENG.). 128p. (gr. 3-6). 24.21 (978-1-59961-529-5(0)) Spotlight.

Kloepfer, John. The Zombie Chasers - Zombies of the Caribbean. DeGrand, David, illus. 2014. (Zombie Chasers Ser.: 6). (ENG.). 224p. (J). (gr. 3-7). 16.99 (978-0-06-229024-3(X)) HarperCollins Pubs.

Laurie, Peter. Mauby & the Hurricane. 2007. (Illus.). 56p. pap. 16.00 (978-1-4050-7718-7(2)) Macmillan Caribbean GBR. Dist: Interlink Publishing Group, Inc.

Lawrence, Iain. The Buccaneers. 2003. (High Seas Trilogy). (Illus.). 244p. (gr. 5-9). 16.50 (978-0-7569-1454-7(X)) Perfection Learning Corp.

—The Buccaneers. 2003. (ENG., Illus.). 256p. (J). (gr. 3-7). 7.99 (978-0-440-41671-5(X), Yearling) Random Hse. Children's Bks.

Lessac, Frané. Island Counting 1 2 3. Lessac, Frané, illus. 2007. (ENG., Illus.). 24p. (J). (— 1). bds. 6.99 (978-0-7636-3518-3(9)) Candlewick Pr.

Lindsay, Fitzroy A. Two Aliens Looking in My Window. 2012. 36p. pap. 20.99 (978-1-4772-5333-5(5)) AuthorHouse.

Mann, Elizabeth. Little Man: A Novel. 2014. (ENG., Illus.). 208p. (J). (gr. 5-7). 18.95 (978-1-931414-49-4(1), 9781931414494) Mikaya Pr.

Martínez, Rueben. Once upon a Time: Traditional Latin American Tales. Unger, David, tr. from SPA. Colón, Raúl, illus. 2010. (ENG & SPA.). 96p. (J). (gr. k-5). 19.99 (978-0-06-146895-7(9), Rayo) HarperCollins Pubs.

Meyer, Kim Shapiro. The Journey of the Coconut. Shapiro, Pepper, illus. 2012. 34p. 24.95 (978-1-4626-5576-2(9)); 36p. pap. 24.95 (978-1-4626-8641-4(9)) America Star Bks.

Meyer, L. A. Rapture of the Deep: Being an Account of the Further Adventures of Jacky Faber, Soldier, Sailor, Mermaid, Spy. 2011. (Bloody Jack Adventures Ser.: 7). (ENG.). 464p. (YA). (gr. 9). pap. 9.99 (978-0-547-55120-3(7)) Houghton Mifflin Harcourt Publishing Co.

Mitchell, Carol. Another Day. Ward, Cherise, illus. 2013. 206p. pap. 8.99 (978-0-9899305-0-5(5)) CaribbeanReads.

Mumford, Carole. Caribbean Cruise Summer Vacation: A Magnificent Six Adventure, 1 vol. 2009. 96p. pap. 16.95 (978-1-61546-760-0(2)) PublishAmerica, Inc.

Noël, Alyson. Shimmer. 2011. pap. (978-0-545-39923-4(8)) Scholastic, Inc.

—Shimmer. 2011. (Riley Bloom Book Ser.: 2). (ENG.). 208p. (J). (gr. 4-7). pap. 9.99 (978-0-312-64825-1(1), 9780312648251) Square Fish.

—Shimmer. 2011. (Riley Bloom Ser.: 2). (J). lib. bdg. 20.85 (978-0-606-21683-8(9), Turtleback) Turtleback Bks.

Norris, Zack. The Secret of Skull Island. 2012. (Double Detectives Ser.). (ENG.). 144p. (J). (gr. 3-7). pap. 4.95 (978-1-4027-7912-1(7)) Sterling Publishing Co., Inc.

Patrick, Wendy. When Passion Wins. 2012. 186p. (gr. 4-6). pap. 14.50 (978-1-4669-7131-8(2)) Trafford Publishing.

Pearson Education Staff. Pirates of the Caribbean the Curse of the Black Pearl. 2nd ed. 2008. (ENG.). 48p. pap. 11.99 (978-1-4058-8170-8(4)) Pearson Education.

Perisic, Zoran. An Alien Called Freddy. 2012. 152p. pap. 9.95 *(978-1-60594-907-9(8),* Lumina Pr.) Aeon Publishing Inc.

Picayo, Mario. Fun, Fun, One Crab on the Run. Byer, Stacey, illus. 2012. (J). *(978-1-934370-27-8(4))* Editorial Campana.

Pirates of the Caribbean Dead Mans Chest. 2006. incl. audio compact disk *(978-1-4054-7260-9(X))* Parragon Bk. Service Ltd.

Prager, Ellen. Stingray City. Caparo, Antonio Javier, illus. 2016. (Tristan Hunt & the Sea Guardians Ser.: 3). (ENG.). 292p. (J). (gr. 2-7). pap. 9.95 *(978-1-938063-70-1(8),* Mighty Media Junior Readers) Mighty Media Pr.

Publications International Ltd. Staff. Interactive Sound Pirates of the Caribbean 3. 2007. 24p. (J). 16.98 *(978-1-4127-8111-4(6))* Publications International, Ltd.

Publications International Ltd. Staff, ed. Look & Find Pirates of the Caribbean 3. 2007. 24p. (J). 7.10 *(978-1-4127-8019-3(5))* Publications International, Ltd.

Quetel, Julie. The Adventures of Shayne & His Flying Grandma. 2011. 60p. (gr. -1). pap. 10.49 *(978-1-4490-5553-0(2))* AuthorHouse.

Reid-Tulloch, Joseth. Manu's Special Day. 2012. 16p. pap. 14.99 *(978-1-4520-9150-1(1))* AuthorHouse.

Roach, Tregenza A. The Lesson Box. Samuel, Karen L., illus. 2012. (J). *(978-1-934370-25-4(8))* Editorial Campana.

Robertson, Barry & Smith, Jeff. Pirates of the "I Don't Care" -Ibbean: A Kids' Musical about Storing up Treasures in Heaven. 2007. (ENG.). 104p. pap. 7.99 *(978-0-8341-7595-2(9),* 0834175959) Lillenas Publishing Co.

Roy, Lillian Elizabeth. Polly's Southern Cruise: The Polly Brewster Series. Barbour, H. S., illus. 2011. 294p. 48.95 *(978-1-258-10514-3(4))* Literary Licensing, LLC.

Sabatini, Rafael. The King's Messenger. 2004. reprint ed. pap. 1.99 *(978-1-4192-6824-3(4))* Kessinger Publishing, LLC.

Santomenna, Joan E. & Santomenna, Marco D. Caribbean Capers. 2003. (Illus.). 144p. (YA). (gr. 3-9). pap. 9.95 *(978-0-9643407-2-5(0))* WindSpirit Publishing.

Sheley, Kristen. Partners in Time #5: A Change of Course. 2010. 236p. 25.95 *(978-1-4502-6658-1(4));* pap. 15.95 *(978-1-4502-6657-4(6))* iUniverse, Inc.

Shusterman, Neal. Ship Out of Luck. 2014. (ENG.). 320p. (YA). (gr. 7). pap. 7.99 *(978-0-14-242624-1(5),* Puffin Books) Penguin Young Readers Group.

Simon, Veronica & Applin, Barbara, eds. Treasure House 2: A Caribbean Anthology. 2nd ed. 2007. (ENG., Illus.). 248p. (J). *(978-1-4050-2734-2(7))* Macmillan Caribbean.

Snowballs & Coconuts. 2006. 56p. pap. 7.75 *(978-0-8341-2295-6(2),* 083-412-2952) Beacon Hill Pr. of Kansas City.

St. Aubyn, Douglas. Caribbean Fables. 2007. 72p. pap. *(978-976-8054-72-2(7))* Paria Publishing Co., Ltd.

Stevenson, Robert Louis. Treasure Island. Lawrence, John, illus. 2009. (Candlewick Illustrated Classics Ser.). (ENG.). 272p. (J). (gr. 4-7). 24.99 *(978-0-7636-4445-1(5))* Candlewick Pr.

Stevenson, Robert Louis. Treasure Island. 2016. (ENG., Illus.). (J). pap. **(978-3-7433-2049-9(5))** Creation Pubs.

—Treasure Island. 2016. (ENG., Illus.). (J). 26.95 **(978-1-358-35578-3(9))** Creative Media Partners, LLC.

—Treasure Island. Rhead, Louis, illus. 2015. (J). pap. *(978-1-4677-7821-3(4),* First Avenue Editions) Lerner Publishing Group.

—Treasure Island. 2014. (Word Cloud Classics Ser.). (ENG., Illus.). 208p. pap. 14.99 *(978-1-62686-256-2(7),* Thunder Bay Pr.) Readerlink Distribution Services, LLC.

—Treasure Island. Corvino, Lucy, illus. abr. ed. 2010. (Classic Starts(tm) Ser.). (ENG.). 160p. (J). (gr. 2-4). cd-rom 9.95 *(978-1-4027-7358-7(7))* Sterling Publishing Co., Inc.

Stevenson, Robert Louis & Ballaz, Jesus. Treasure Island. 2007. (Illustrated Classics Ser.). (Illus.). 40p. (gr. 3-6). lib. bdg. 26.00 *(978-0-8368-7665-9(2),* Gareth Stevens Learning Library) Stevens, Gareth Publishing LLLP.

Stevenson, Robert Louis & Gaston, Charles Robert. Treasure Island. 2016. (ENG., Illus.). (J). 25.95 **(978-1-358-93415-5(0))** Creative Media Partners, LLC.

Stevenson, Robert Louis & Vance, Hiram Albert. Treasure Island. 2016. (ENG., Illus.). (J). 25.95 **(978-1-358-73513-4(1));** 25.95 **(978-1-359-06744-9(2))** Creative Media Partners, LLC.

Stevenson, Robert Louis, et al. Treasure Island. 2016. (ENG., Illus.). (J). 26.95 **(978-1-357-83050-2(5))** Creative Media Partners, LLC.

Taylor, Jessica. A Map for Wrecked Girls. 2017. (ENG.). 368p. (YA). (gr. 9). 17.99 **(978-0-7352-2811-5(6),** Dial Bks) Penguin Young Readers Group.

Taylor, Theodore. Timothy of the Cay. 2007. (ENG., Illus.). 176p. (J). (gr. 5-7). pap. 6.99 *(978-0-15-206320-7(X))* Houghton Mifflin Harcourt Publishing Co.

Toybox Innovations & Toybox Innovations, creators. At Worlds End. 2007. (Pirates of the Caribbean Ser.). (ENG., Illus.). (J). (gr. -1-3). pap. *(978-0-7634-2186-1(3))* Walt Disney Records.

Triana, Gaby. The Temptress Four. 2008. 247p. (YA). (gr. 7). lib. bdg. 17.89 *(978-0-06-088568-7(8),* HarperTeen) HarperCollins Pubs.

Vaid, Raj. A Case of Cold Feet: The Super Sleuth - Mystery #2. 2011. 68p. pap. 9.99 *(978-1-4520-6981-4(6))* AuthorHouse.

Wright, Kiyah. Vacation Fun. 2011. 24p. pap. 14.95 *(978-1-4634-4055-8(3))* AuthorHouse.

CARIBOU

Borgert-Spaniol, Megan. Caribou. 2017. (North American Animals Ser.). (ENG., Illus.). 24p. (J). (gr. k-3). lib. bdg. 25.95 **(978-1-62617-636-2(1),** Blastoff! Readers) Bellwether Media.

Catt, Thessaly. Migrating with the Caribou. 2011. (Animal Journeys Ser.). (Illus.). 24p. (YA). (gr. 1-4). 22.60 *(978-1-4488-2541-7(5))* Rosen Publishing Group, Inc., The.

French, Vivian. Caribou Journey. Flather, Lisa, illus. 2003. (Fantastic Journeys Ser.). 32p. (J). *(978-1-84089-216-1(1))* Zero to Ten, Ltd.

Gagne, Tammy. Caribou. 2017. (Animals of North America (paperback) Ser.). (ENG., Illus.). 32p. (J). (gr. 3-5). pap. 9.95 **(978-1-63517-089-4(3),** Focus Readers) North Star Editions.

Hirsch, Rebecca. Caribou Migration. 2012. (Animal Migrations Ser.). (ENG., Illus.). 32p. (J). (gr. 2-5). lib. bdg. 29.93 *(978-1-60973-618-7(4),* 201195) Child's World, Inc., The.

Hirsch, Rebecca E. Caribou: A Tundra Journey. 2016. (Illus.). 32p. (J). *(978-1-4896-4513-5(6))* Weigl Pubs., Inc.

Hiscock, Bruce. The Big Caribou Herd: Life in the Arctic National Wildlife Refuge. Hiscock, Bruce, illus. 2003. (ENG., Illus.). 32p. (J). (gr. 2-4). 16.95 *(978-1-59078-010-7(8))* Boyds Mills Pr.

Jackson, Tom. Caribou. 2008. (Nature's Children Ser.). (Illus.). 52p. (J). *(978-0-7172-6219-9(7))* Grolier, Ltd.

Jeffries, Joyce. Caribou, 01 vols., 1. 2016. (North America's Biggest Beasts Ser.). (ENG., Illus.). 24p. (J). pap. 8.25 *(978-1-5081-4285-0(8),* PowerKids Pr.) Rosen Publishing Group, Inc., The.

Johnson, Jinny. Caribou. 2014. (North American Mammals Ser.). 24p. (gr. 2-5). 28.50 *(978-1-62588-033-8(2))* Black Rabbit Bks.

—Caribou. 2014. (North American Mammals Ser.). (ENG., Illus.). 24p. (J). (gr. -1-4). pap. 8.95 *(978-1-77092-168-9(0))* Saunders Bk. Co. CAN. Dist: RiverStream Publishing.

Markovics, Joyce L. Caribou: And Reindeer, Too. 2011. (Built for Cold Ser.). 32p. (YA). (gr. 1-4). lib. bdg. 25.27 *(978-1-61772-130-4(1));* (J). (gr. 4-5). lib. bdg., E-Book 49.22 *(978-1-61772-220-2(0))* Bearport Publishing Co., Inc.

Migrating with the Caribou. 2011. (Animal Journeys Ser.). (Illus.). 24p. (J). pap. 8.25 *(978-1-4488-2666-7(7),* PowerKids Pr.) Rosen Publishing Group, Inc., The.

Miller, Debbie S. A Caribou Journey. 2010. (ENG., Illus.). 32p. (J). 15.95 *(978-1-60223-097-2(8));* pap. 9.95 *(978-1-60223-096-5(X))* Univ. of Alaska Pr.

Miller, Sara Swan. Caribou of the Arctic. 2009. (Brrr! Polar Animals Ser.). (ENG., Illus.). 24p. (J). (gr. k-5). pap. 8.25 *(978-1-4358-3148-3(9),* 1291792, PowerKids Pr.); 24p. (gr. 2-3). 42.50 *(978-1-61511-745-1(8),* PowerKids Pr.); (J). (gr. k-3). lib. bdg. 22.60 *(978-1-4358-2744-8(9))* Rosen Publishing Group, Inc., The.

Owens, Mary Beth. The Caribou Alphabet: A Tilbury House Nature Book. Owens, Mary Beth, illus. exp. ed. 2015. (Tilbury House Nature Book Ser.: 0). (ENG., Illus.). 36p. (gr. -1-3). pap. 8.95 *(978-0-88448-446-2(7),* 884446) Tilbury Hse. Pubs.

Patrick, Roman. Caribou. 2010. (Animals That Live in the Tundra Ser.). (ENG.). 24p. (J). (gr. -1-3). pap. 8.15 *(978-1-4339-3897-9(9));* lib. bdg. 22.60 *(978-1-4339-3896-2(0))* Stevens, Gareth Publishing LLLP.

Quinlan, Susan E. Caribou. 2004. (Nature Watch Ser.). (ENG., Illus.). 48p. (gr. 4-8). lib. bdg. 27.93 *(978-1-57505-579-4(1))* Lerner Publishing Group.

CARIBOU—FICTION

Coles, Michael Joseph, et al. The Land of Caring Bou. Banks, Timothy, illus. 2006. (J). *(978-0-87483-814-5(2))* August Hse. Pubs., Inc.

Hobbs, Will. Never Say Die. 224p. (J). (gr. 3-7). 2014. (ENG.). pap. 6.99 *(978-0-06-170880-0(1))* 2013. (ENG.). 16.99 *(978-0-06-170878-7(X))* 2013. lib. bdg. 17.89 *(978-0-06-170879-4(8))* HarperCollins Pubs.

Manceau, Édouard. The Race, 0 vols. Owlkids Books Inc. Staff & Quinn, Sarah, trs. from FRE. 2014. (ENG & FRE., Illus.). 64p. (J). (gr. -1-4). 17.95 *(978-1-77147-055-1(0),* Owlkids) Owlkids Bks. Inc. CAN. Dist: Publishers Group West (PGW).

CARICATURES AND CARTOONS

see Cartoons and Comics

CARILLONS

see Bells

CARLSBAD CAVERNS (N.M.)

Burnham, Brad. Carlsbad Caverns: America's Largest Underground Chamber. (Famous Caves of the World Ser.). 24p. 2009. (gr. 3-4). 42.50 *(978-1-61512-494-7(2),* PowerKids Pr.) 2003. (Illus.). (J). lib. bdg. 22.60 *(978-0-8239-6256-3(3))* Rosen Publishing Group, Inc., The.

Herweck Rice, Dona. Travel Adventures: Carlsbad Caverns: Identifying Arithmetic Patterns (Grade 3) 2017. (Mathematics Readers Ser.). (Illus.). 32p. (gr. 3-3). 8.99 **(978-1-4807-5798-1(5))** Teacher Created Materials, Inc.

CARNEGIE, ANDREW, 1835-1919

De Capua, Sarah. Andrew Carnegie. 2007. (21st Century Skills Library: Life Skills Biographies Ser.). (ENG., Illus.). 48p. (gr. 4-8). lib. bdg. 31.36 *(978-1-60279-067-4(1),* 200038) Cherry Lake Publishing.

Edge, Laura Bufano. Andrew Carnegie. 2004. (Lerner Biographies Ser.). (Illus.). 128p. (J). (gr. 6-12). lib. bdg. 27.93 *(978-0-8225-4965-9(4))* Lerner Publishing Group.

Gillam, Scott. Andrew Carnegie: Industrial Giant & Philanthropist, 1 vol. 2009. (Essential Lives Set 3 Ser.). (ENG., Illus.). 112p. (J). (gr. 6-12). lib. bdg. 35.64 *(978-1-60453-521-1(0))* ABDO Publishing Co.

Kent, Zachary. Andrew Carnegie: Industrialist & Philanthropist. 2015. (Legendary American Biographies Ser.). 96p. (J). (gr. 6-12). pap. 10.95 *(978-0-7660-6436-2(0))* Enslow Pubs., Inc.

Larsen, Andrew. Andrew Carnegie: The Man Who Loved Libraries. Maurey, Katty, illus. 2017. (ENG.). 32p. (J). (gr. 1-5). 16.95 **(978-1-77147-267-8(7))** Owlkids Bks. Inc. CAN. Dist: Publishers Group West (PGW).

Parker, Lewis K. Andrew Carnegie & the Steel Industry. (American Tycoons Ser.). 24p. 2009. (gr. 3-3). 42.50 *(978-1-61511-388-0(6))* 2003. (Illus.). (J). lib. bdg. 22.60 *(978-0-8239-6448-2(5))* Rosen Publishing Group, Inc., The. (PowerKids Pr.).

Rajczak Nelson, Kristen. Andrew Carnegie & the Steel Industry. 2016. (Great Entrepreneurs in U. S. History Ser.). (Illus.). 32p. (J). (gr. 5-5). pap. 11.75 *(978-1-4994-2115-6(X),* PowerKids Pr.) Rosen Publishing Group, Inc., The.

CARNIVALS

see Festivals

CARNIVOROUS PLANTS

Aaseng, Nathan. Weird Meat-Eating Plants. 2011. (Bizarre Science Ser.). (Illus.). 48p. (J). (gr. 5-18). pap. 8.95 *(978-1-59845-223-5(1));* lib. bdg. 25.27 *(978-0-7660-3672-7(3))* Enslow Pubs., Inc.

Batten, Mary. Hungry Plants. Mirocha, Paul, illus. 2004. (Step into Reading Ser.). (ENG.). 48p. (J). (gr. 2-4). pap. 3.99 *(978-0-375-82533-0(9),* Random Hse. Bks. for Young Readers) Random Hse. Children's Bks.

Collard, Sneed B., III. Tough Terminators. 2004. (It's Nature! Ser.). (Illus.). 32p. (J). (gr. 3-6). pap. 7.95 *(978-1-55971-633-8(9),* Creative Publishing International) Quarto Publishing Group USA.

Gould, Margee. Meat-Eating Plants. 2012. (Strangest Plants on Earth Ser.). (Illus.). 24p. (J). (gr. 2-5). lib. bdg. 22.60 *(978-1-4488-4988-8(8))* Rosen Publishing Group, Inc., The.

Johnson, Rebecca L. Carnivorous Plants. 2007. (Nature Watch Ser.). (Illus.). 48p. (J). (gr. 3-7). lib. bdg. 25.26 *(978-0-8225-6563-5(3),* Lerner Pubns.) Lerner Publishing Group.

Jones, Keisha. Plants That Eat. 2016. (Plant Defenses Ser.). (Illus.). 24p. (J). (gr. 3-3). pap. 8.25 *(978-1-4994-2139-2(7),* PowerKids Pr.) Rosen Publishing Group, Inc., The.

Lawler, Janet. Scary Plants! 2017. (Smithsonian Ser.). (ENG., Illus.). 48p. (J). (gr. 1-3). pap. 3.99 *(978-0-451-53371-5(2),* Penguin Young Readers) Penguin Young Readers Group.

Lawrence, Ellen. Meat-Eating Plants: Toothless Wonders. 2012. (Science Slam: Plant-Ology Ser.). 24p. (J). (gr. -1-3). lib. bdg. 23.93 *(978-1-61772-589-0(7))* Bearport Publishing Co., Inc.

MacDonald, Margaret. Meat-Eating Plants. 2011. (Learn-Abouts Ser.). (Illus.). 16p. (J). pap. 7.95 *(978-1-59920-619-6(6))* Black Rabbit Bks.

Owen, Ruth. How Do Meat-Eating Plants Catch Their Food? 2014. (World of Plants Ser.). 32p. (J). (gr. 2-5). lib. bdg. 26.25 *(978-1-4777-7153-2(0),* PowerKids Pr.) Rosen Publishing Group, Inc., The.

Willebrant, Avery. Meat-Eating Plants. 2009. (Real Life Readers Ser.). 16p. (gr. 2-3). pap. 7.05 *(978-1-4358-0077-9(X),* Rosen Classroom) Rosen Publishing Group, Inc., The.

Willis, John. Carnivorous Plants. 2016. (Illus.). 24p. (J). *(978-1-5105-1407-2(4))* SmartBook Media, Inc.

CAROLS

Amery, H. The Usborne Book of Christmas Carols. 2004. 32p. (J). pap. 6.95 incl. audio *(978-0-7945-0600-1(3))* EDC Publishing.

Austin, Glenda. More Christmas Classics. 2005. (ENG.). 16p. pap. 4.99 *(978-0-87718-101-9(2),* 0877181012) Willis Music Co.

Baker-Smith, Grahame. The Twelve Days of Christmas: Panorama Pops. Baker-Smith, Grahame, illus. 2017. (Panorama Pops Ser.). (ENG., Illus.). 30p. (J). (gr. k-4). 8.99 **(978-0-7636-9485-2(1))** Candlewick Pr.

Betts, Jan & Roberts, Timothy. Sing Nowell: 34 Favourite Carols to Sing & Play, 1 vol. 2008. (Songbooks Ser.). (ENG., Illus.). 64p. (J). pap. 32.95 incl. audio compact disk **(978-1-4081-0424-8(5))** HarperCollins Pubs. Ltd. GBR. Dist: Independent Pubs. Group.

Bonnet, Rosalinde. Very First Christmas Carols. 2011. (Very First Words Board Book Ser.). 12p. (J). ring bd. 6.99 *(978-0-7945-3117-1(2),* Usborne) EDC Publishing.

Boys Choir of Harlem Staff. O Holy Night: Christmas with the Boys Choir of Harlem. Ringgold, Faith, illus. 2004. 40p. (J). 19.89 *(978-0-06-051819-6(7))* HarperCollins Pubs.

Christmas Coloring Fun Christmas Carols. 2004. (J). per. 6.95 *(978-1-885920-47-8(4))* Pyramid Publishing, Inc.

Davidson, Susanna. Christmas Carol (Picture Book) 2007. (Picture Book Classics Ser.). 24p. (J). 9.99 *(978-0-7945-1894-3(X),* Usborne) EDC Publishing.

Dickens, Charles. A Christmas Carol. 2008. (Orig.). (gr. 5-8). lib. bdg. 16.00 *(978-0-613-63928-6(6),* Turtleback) Turtleback Bks.

Ebina, Hiro. Joy to the World! Warabe, Kimika, illus. 2006. (JPN.). 12p. (J). (gr. -1-k). bds. 9.95 *(978-0-8198-3985-5(X))* Pauline Bks. & Media.

Griffin, Rachel & Barefoot Books. Twelve Days of Christmas. 2015. (Illus.). 32p. (J). (gr. k-5). 14.99 *(978-1-78285-221-6(2))* Barefoot Bks., Inc.

Jackson, Mary Helene. Weaver of Song: The Birth of Silent Night. Winstead, Leo, illus. l.t. ed. 2009. 40p. (J). 16.95 *(978-0-9825713-0-9(5))* Clifton Carriage House Pr.

Jaroszko, Mike, illus. Away in a Manger Devotional. 2008. pap. 2.29 *(978-0-7586-1449-0(7))* Concordia Publishing Hse.

Julian, Alison, illus. The 12 Days of Christmas. 2005. (J). *(978-1-74157-281-0(9))* Hinkler Bks. Pty, Ltd.

Litchfield, Jo, illus. First Book of Christmas Carols. 2004. (First Book of Christmas Carols Ser.). 24p. (J). 9.95 *(978-0-7945-0596-7(1),* Usborne) EDC Publishing.

Long, Laurel. The Twelve Days of Christmas. Long, Laurel, illus. 2014. (ENG., Illus.). 32p. (J). (gr. -1-2). pap. 8.99 *(978-0-14-751286-4(7),* Puffin Books) Penguin Young Readers Group.

Manson, Christopher, illus. Good King Wenceslas. 2004. 25p. (J). (gr. k-4). reprint ed. 15.00 *(978-0-7567-8226-9(0))* DIANE Publishing Co.

Moore, Clement C. A Christmas Carol. (Illus.). 12p. (J). 4.95 *(978-1-58989-103-6(1))* Thurman Hse., LLC.

National Gallery of Art Staff. Hark! The Herald Angels Sing: The National Gallery, London. (Illus.). 48p. (J). (gr. k-18). *(978-0-7112-0814-8(X))* ReiseArt Buchhandlung GmbH.

Neale, John M. Good King Wenceslas. Ladwig, Tim, illus. 2005. (ENG.). 32p. (J). (gr. k-17). 17.00 *(978-0-8028-5209-0(2),* Eerdmans Bks For Young Readers) Eerdmans, William B. Publishing Co.

Newsom, Tom, illus. The First Noel. 2006. 14p. (J). (gr. k-4). reprint ed. 8.00 *(978-1-4223-5413-1(X))* DIANE Publishing Co.

Okun, Milton, ed. Christmas Carols for Piano Duet. 63p. (YA). pap. 14.95 *(978-0-89524-948-7(0),* 02505651) Cherry Lane Music Co.

Rauenhorst, Linda. Fröhliche Weihnachten: Learning Songs & Traditions in German. Collier, Roberta, illus. 2007. (Teach Me Ser.). (GER & ENG.). 32p. (J). (gr. -1-3). 19.95 *(978-1-59972-063-0(9))* Teach Me Tapes, Inc.

Rindt, Lindsay. Summer Time Carols. 2010. 36p. pap. 15.49 *(978-1-4490-5774-9(8))* AuthorHouse.

Ringgold, Faith, illus. O Holy Night: Christmas with the Boys Choir of Harlem. 2006. 30p. (J). (gr. 4-8). 19.00 *(978-1-4223-5512-1(8))* DIANE Publishing Co.

Scarry, Richard. Richard Scarry's Favorite Christmas Carols. 2009. (ENG., Illus.). 24p. (J). (gr. -1-3). 14.95 *(978-1-4027-5824-9(3))* Sterling Publishing Co., Inc.

Sneesby, Frederick. A Believer's Christmas. 2008. 92p. pap. 15.25 *(978-1-4389-0031-5(7))* AuthorHouse.

Spirin, Gennady. We Three Kings. 2007. (ENG., Illus.). 32p. (J). (gr. -1-5). 17.99 *(978-0-689-82114-1(X),* Atheneum Bks. for Young Readers) Simon & Schuster Children's Publishing.

St. James, Rebecca. Friendly Beasts: An Old English Christmas Carol, 1 vol. Vojtech, Anna, illus. 2012. (ENG.). 32p. (J). 16.99 *(978-0-310-72012-6(5))* Zonderkidz.

Stern, Leonard & Price, Roger. Christmas Carol Mad Libs: Very Merry Songs & Stories. 2007. (Mad Libs Ser.). (ENG., Illus.). 48p. (J). (gr. 3-7). 4.99 *(978-0-8431-2676-1(0),* Mad Libs) Penguin Young Readers Group.

Tada, Joni Eareckson & Wolgemuth, Bobbie. Christmas Carols for a Kid's Heart, Vol. 3. Martinez, Sergio, illus. 2004. (Hymns for a Kid's Heart Ser.: 3). 96p. (J). 21.99 incl. audio compact disk *(978-1-58134-626-8(3))* Crossway.

Traditional. O Little Town of Bethlehem. Beauvois, Nathalie, illus. 2014. 16p. (J). bds. 12.99 *(978-0-8249-1933-7(5),* Ideal Pubns.) Worthy Publishing.

Twin Sisters(r), et al. The Best Thing about Christmas Sing-Along Storybook. 2016. (ENG.). 12p. (J). (-5). 9.99 *(978-1-63409-805-2(6))* Barbour Publishing, Inc.

Tyrrell, Frances, illus. The Huron Carol. 2004. 32p. 16.00 *(978-0-8028-5263-2(7))* Eerdmans, William B. Publishing Co.

We Wish You a Merry Christmas. Date not set. 6p. (J). (gr. 1-18). bds. 6.99 *(978-0-694-01558-0(X))* HarperCollins Pubs.

Weston Woods Staff, creator. The Little Drummer Boy. 2011. 18.95 *(978-0-439-93213-4(0));* 38.75 *(978-0-439-93227-1(0))* Weston Woods Studios, Inc.

Wheeler, Jody. The First Noel. 2010. (Illus.). 24p. (J). (gr. -1-3). 14.99 *(978-0-8249-5621-9(4),* Ideal Pubns.) Worthy Publishing.

CARPENTRY

Here are entered works dealing with the construction of a wooden building or the wooden portion of any building. Works that treat the making and finishing of fine woodwork, such as furniture or interior details, are entered under Cabinet Work.

see also Building; Cabinetwork; Woodwork

Baker, Maryann. My Mom Is a Carpenter: Relate Addition & Subtraction to Length. 2014. (Rosen Common Core Math Readers Ser.). (ENG.). 24p. (J). (gr. 2-3). pap. 8.25 *(978-1-4777-4813-8(X),* Rosen Classroom) Rosen Publishing Group, Inc., The.

Burgan, Michael. The Carpenter. 2013. (Colonial People 3 Ser.). 48p. (J). (gr. 4-8). pap. 12.93 *(978-1-62712-045-6(9))* Cavendish Square Publishing.

Clement, Mark. Kid's Carpenter's Workbook. 2005. (Illus.). (J). 12.95 *(978-0-9754212-6-0(3))* CenterLine Media.

Cohn, Jessica. On the Job in Construction. Scheuer, Lauren, illus. 2016. (Core Content Social Studies — on the Job Ser.). (ENG.). 32p. (J). (gr. 2-5). lib. bdg. 26.65 *(978-1-63440-109-8(3))* Red Chair Pr.

Freese, Joan. Carpenters. 2005. (Pull Ahead Bks.). (Illus.). 32p. (J). (gr. 3-7). lib. bdg. 22.60 *(978-0-8225-2800-5(2),* Lerner Pubns.) Lerner Publishing Group.

Harrison, Scott. Choosing a Career in Carpentry. 2009. (World of Work Ser.). 64p. (gr. 5-5). 58.50 *(978-1-60854-330-4(7))* Rosen Publishing Group, Inc., The.

Hindman, Susan. Carpenter. 2010. (21st Century Skills Library: Cool Careers Ser.). (ENG.). 32p. (gr. 4-8). lib. bdg. 28.50 *(978-1-60279-935-6(0),* 200615) Cherry Lake Publishing.

Kishel, Ann-Marie. Carpenter. 2007. (First Step Nonfiction Ser.). (J). pap. 3.95 *(978-0-8225-6842-1(X))* Lerner Publishing Group.

Labrecque, Ellen. Carpenter. 2016. (21st Century Skills Library: Cool Vocational Careers Ser.). (ENG., Illus.). 32p. (J). (gr. 4-7). 29.93 *(978-1-63471-059-6(2),* 208316) Cherry Lake Publishing.

Marsico, Katie. Levels. 2013. (21st Century Junior Library: Basic Tools Ser.). (ENG.). 24p. (J). (gr. 2-5). 25.64 *(978-1-62431-172-7(5),* 203008); pap. 12.79 *(978-1-62431-304-2(3),* 203010) Cherry Lake Publishing.

Ross, Allison J. & Harrison, Scott. Choosing a Career in Carpentry. 2005. (World of Work Ser.). (Illus.). 64p. (YA). (gr. 7-12). lib. bdg. 31.95 *(978-0-8239-3294-8(X))* Rosen Publishing Group, Inc., The.

Roza, Greg. A Career as a Carpenter. 2010. (Essential Careers Ser.). (ENG.). 80p. (YA). lib. bdg. 33.25 *(978-1-4358-9472-3(3))* Rosen Publishing Group, Inc., The.

Small, Cathleen. Carpenter. 2016. (Careers in Construction Ser.). (ENG., Illus.). 112p. (J). (gr. 7-7). lib. bdg. 42.79 *(978-1-5026-0984-7(3))* Cavendish Square Publishing.

CARPENTRY—FICTION

Down, Reg. The Magic Knot: And other Tangles. 2007. (Illus.). 100p. (J). per. 14.95 *(978-0-9794452-0-0(5))* Lightly Pr.

Enos, Deanna. The Wooden Garden of Romano Gabriel, 1 vol. 2008. (ENG.). 36p. 24.95 *(978-1-60563-234-6(1))* America Star Bks.

Hale, Marian. Dark Water Rising. 2010. (ENG.). 256p. (J). (gr. 5-9). pap. 7.99 *(978-0-312-62908-3(7),* 9780312629083) Square Fish.

Hesse, Karen. Sable. Sewall, Marcia, illus. 2010. (ENG.). 96p. (J). (gr. 2-5). pap. 7.99 *(978-0-312-37610-9(3),* 9780312376109) Square Fish.

Jacob's Gift. 2004. (Max Lucado Ser.). 32p. 19.99 incl. DVD *(978-1-4003-0182-9(3))* Nelson, Thomas Inc.

Joslin, Steve. The Working Class Meets the Carpenter. 2004. 25p. (J). pap. 12.99 *(978-1-4116-1223-5(X))* Lulu Pr., Inc.

McCaughrean, Geraldine. The Jesse Tree. Willey, Bee, illus. 2005. 93p. (J). (gr. k). 20.00 *(978-0-8028-5288-5(2),* Eerdmans Bks For Young Readers) Eerdmans, William B. Publishing Co.

Ruiz-Flores, Lupe. The Woodcutter's Gift/el Regalo del Lenador. Ventura, Gabriela Baeza, tr. from ENG. Jerome, Elaine, illus. 2007. (SPA & ENG.). 32p. (J). (gr. -1-2). 16.95 *(978-1-55885-489-5(4),* Piñata Books) Arte Publico Pr.

Shelby, Anne. The Man Who Lived in a Hollow Tree. Hazelaar, Cor, illus. 2009. (ENG.). 40p. (J). (gr. -1-2). 17.99 *(978-0-689-86169-7(9),* Atheneum/Richard Jackson Bks.) Simon & Schuster Children's Publishing.

Widmer, Kirsten & Buxton, Sarah. Workshops That Work! 30 Days of Mini-Lessons That Help Launch & Establish All-Important Routines for an Effective Reading & Writing Workshop. 2004. (ENG.). 160p. pap. 20.99 *(978-0-439-44406-4(3),* Teaching Resources) Scholastic, Inc.

C
D

CARRIAGES AND CARTS

Petersen, Christine. The Wheelwright. 2013. 48p. (J). (gr. 4-8). 29.93 *(978-1-60870-419-4(X))*; pap. 12.93 *(978-1-62712-049-4(1))* Cavendish Square Publishing.

CARRIERS, AIRCRAFT

see Aircraft Carriers

CARROLL, CHARLES, 1737-1832

Lomask, Milton. Charles Carroll & the American Revolution. Polseno, Jo, illus. 2011. 188p. 42.95 *(978-1-258-07263-6(7))* Literary Licensing, LLC.

CARROLL, JOHN, 1735-1815

Betz, Eva K. Priest, Patriot & Leader: The Story of Archbishop Carroll. Dougherty, Charles L., illus. 2011. 188p. 42.95 *(978-1-258-03693-5(2))* Literary Licensing, LLC.

CARROLL, LEWIS, 1832-1898

Cadavid, Jorge. Lewis Carroll -Los Juegos del Lenguaje. 2005. (SPA.). 128p. (YA). *(978-958-30-1833-6(3))* Panamericana Editorial.

CARS (AUTOMOBILES)

see Automobiles

CARS, ARMORED (TANKS)

see Tanks (Military Science)

CARSON, KIT, 1809-1868

Beals, Frank Lee. Kit Carson. Merryweather, Jack, illus. 2011. 194p. 42.95 *(978-1-258-08971-9(8))* Literary Licensing, LLC.

Calvert, Patricia. Kit Carson: He Led the Way. 2006. (Great Explorations Ser.). (Illus.). 80p. (gr. 6-7). lib. bdg. 22.95 *(978-0-7614-2223-5(4))*, Benchmark Bks.) Marshall Cavendish Corp.

Ellis, Edward S. The Life of Kit Carson: Hunter, Trapper, Guide, Indian Agent & Colonel U. S. A. 2007. 176p. per. *(978-1-4065-2477-2(8))* Dodo Pr.

Ellis, Edward Sylvester. The Life of Kit Carson: The Life of Kit Carson. 2007. (ENG.). 180p. pap. 19.99 *(978-1-4264-5784-5(7))* Creative Media Partners, LLC.

Ericson, Emma. Who Was Kit Carson? 2013. (InfoMax Readers Ser.). (ENG.). 24p. (J). (gr. 2-3). pap. 8.25 *(978-1-4777-2292-3(0))*; pap. 49.50 *(978-1-4777-2293-0(9))* Rosen Publishing Group, Inc., The. (Rosen Classroom).

Rich, Karissa. Kit Carson: Legendary Mountain Man. 2013. (Rosen Readers Ser.). (ENG.). 24p. (J). (gr. 2-3). pap. 49.50 *(978-1-4777-2314-2(5))*; pap. 8.25 *(978-1-4777-2313-5(7))* Rosen Publishing Group, Inc., The. (Rosen Classroom).

Sanford, William R. & Green, Carl R. Kit Carson: Courageous Mountain Man. 2012. (Courageous Heroes of the American West Ser.). 48p. (J). pap. 8.95 *(978-1-4644-0094-0(6))*; (Illus.). (gr. 5-18). 22.60 *(978-0-7660-4011-3(9))* Enslow Pubs., Inc.

CARSON, KIT, 1809-1868—FICTION

Osborne, Mary Pope. Adaline Falling Star. unabr. ed. 2004. (Middle Grade Cassette Librariestm Ser.). 176p. (J). (gr. 3-7). pap. 29.00 incl. audio *(978-0-8072-1195-3(8))*, S YA 319 SP, Listening Library) Random Hse. Audio Publishing Group.

CARSON, RACHEL, 1907-1964

Archer, Jules. To Save the Earth: The American Environmental Movement. 2016. (Jules Archer History for Young Readers Ser.). (ENG., Illus.). 200p. (J). (gr. 6). 16.99 *(978-1-63450-196-5(9))*, Sky Pony Pr.) Skyhorse Publishing Co., Inc.

Bruchac, Joseph & Locker, Thomas. Rachel Carson: Preserving a Sense of Wonder. 2009. (ENG., Illus.). 32p. (gr. 3-5). pap. 12.95 *(978-1-55591-695-4(3))* Fulcrum Publishing.

Dal Fuoco, Gina. Rachel Carson: Nature's Guardian, 1 vol. 2007. (Science Readers Ser.). (SPA & ENG.). 32p. (J). (gr. 3-3). pap. 8.99 *(978-0-7439-0566-4(0))* Shell Educational Publishing.

Domblewski, Carol. Citizens Who Made a Difference: Set Of 6. 2011. (Navigators Ser.). (J). pap. 44.00 net. *(978-1-4108-5097-3(8))* Benchmark Education Co.

Ehrlich, Amy. Rachel: The Story of Rachel Carson. Minor, Wendell, illus. 2008. (ENG.). 32p. (J). (gr. -1-3). pap. 7.99 *(978-0-15-206324-5(2))* Houghton Mifflin Harcourt Publishing Co.

Fabiny, Sarah. Who Was Rachel Carson? Putra, Dede & Harrison, Nancy, illus. 2014. (Who Was? Ser.). (ENG.). 112p. (J). (gr. 3-7). 5.99 *(978-0-448-47959-0(1))*, Grosset & Dunlap) Penguin Young Readers Group.

—Who Was Rachel Carson? 2014. (Who Was... ? Ser.). lib. bdg. 16.00 *(978-0-606-36171-2(5))* Turtleback Bks.

Fontes, Ron. Rachel Carson. 2005. (Rookie Biographies Ser.). (ENG., Illus.). 32p. (J). (gr. 1-2). 4.95 *(978-0-516-26819-4(8))*, Children's Pr.) Scholastic Library Publishing.

Gillam, Scott. Rachel Carson: Pioneer of Environmentalism, 1 vol. 2010. (Essential Lives Set 5 Ser.). (ENG.). 112p. (J). (gr. 6-12). lib. bdg. 35.64 *(978-1-61613-511-9(5))* ABDO Publishing Co.

Gow, Mary. Rachel Carson: Ecologist & Activist. 2005. (Great Minds of Science Ser.). (Illus.). 128p. (J). (gr. 4-10). lib. bdg. 27.94 *(978-0-7660-2503-5(9))* Enslow Pubs., Inc.

Heitkamp, Kristina Lyn. Rachel Carson: Pioneering Environmental Activist. 2017. (J). ***(978-1-5383-8075-8(7))***; pap. ***(978-1-5383-8074-1(9))*** Rosen Publishing Group, Inc., The.

Hile, Lori. Rachel Carson: Environmental Pioneer, 1 vol. 2014. (Women in Conservation Ser.). (ENG., Illus.). 48p. (gr. 3-6). 33.32 *(978-1-4846-0471-7(7))*; pap. 8.99 *(978-1-4846-0476-2(8))* Heinemann-Raintree. (Heinemann InfoSearch).

Hustad, Douglas. Environmentalist Rachel Carson. 2016. (STEM Trailblazer Bios Ser.). (ENG., Illus.). 32p. (J). (gr. 2-5). lib. bdg. 26.65 *(978-1-5124-0787-7(9))* Lerner Publishing Group.

James, Emily. Rachel Carson. 2017. (Great Scientists & Inventors Ser.). (ENG., Illus.). 24p. (gr. k-1). lib. bdg. 26.65 *(978-1-5157-3881-7(7))* Capstone Press of Coughlan Cos.

Lantier, Patricia. Rachel Carson: Fighting Pesticides & Other Chemical Pollutants. 2009. (Voices for Green Choices Ser.). (ENG., Illus.). 48p. (J). (gr. 5-9). pap. *(978-0-7787-4676-8(3))*; lib. bdg. *(978-0-7787-4663-8(1))* Crabtree Publishing Co.

Lawlor, Laurie. Rachel Carson & Her Book That Changed the World. Beingessner, Laura, illus. 2014. (ENG.). 32p. (J). (gr. k-5). 7.99 *(978-0-8234-3193-9(2))* Holiday Hse., Inc.

Levine, Ellen. Rachel Carson. 2008. (Up Close Ser.). (ENG., Illus.). 224p. (YA). (gr. 7-18). 7.99 *(978-0-14-241046-2(2))*, Puffin Books) Penguin Young Readers Group.

Marsh, Carole. Rachel Carson: Excellent Ecologist. 2004. (1000 Readers Ser.). (Illus.). 14p. (J). (gr. k-4). pap. 2.95 *(978-0-635-02524-1(8))* Gallopade International.

Miller, Marie-Therese. Rachel Carson. 2011. (Conservation Heroes Ser.). (Illus.). 136p. (YA). (gr. 6-12). 35.00 *(978-1-60413-950-1(1))*, Chelsea Hse.) Facts On File, Inc.

Piddock, Charles. Rachel Carson: A Voice for the Natural World. 2009. (Life Portraits Ser.). (Illus.). 112p. (YA). (gr. 7-12). lib. bdg. 36.00 *(978-1-4339-0058-7(0))* Stevens, Gareth Publishing LLLP.

Quaratiello, Arlene R. Rachel Carson: A Biography, 1 vol. 2004. (Greenwood Biographies Ser.). (Illus.). 168p. (C). 43.00 *(978-0-313-32388-1(7))*, GR2388, Greenwood) ABC-CLIO, LLC.

Rachel Carson, Escritora Y Cientifica. 2003. (Notas Biograficas Ser.). pap. 48.95 *(978-0-8136-5886-5(1))* Modern Curriculum Pr.

Rivera, Sheila. Rachel Carson: A Life of Responsibility. 2007. (Pull Ahead Bks.). (Illus.). 32p. (J). (gr. 3-7). lib. bdg. 22.60 *(978-0-8225-6462-1(9))*, Lerner Pubns.) Lerner Publishing Group.

Rock, Meghan. Rachel Carson: Marine Biologist & Winner of the National Book Award. 2016. (Women in Science Ser.). 128p. (J). 45.64 *(978-1-5026-2319-5(6))* Cavendish Square Publishing.

Scherer, Glenn & Fletcher, Marty. Who on Earth Is Rachel Carson? Mother of the Environmental Movement. 2009. (Scientists Saving the Earth Ser.). (Illus.). 112p. (J). (gr. 5-9). lib. bdg. 33.27 *(978-1-59845-116-0(2))* Enslow Pubs., Inc.

Simon, Charnan. Rachel Carson: Author & Environmentalist. 2003. (Our People Ser.). (ENG., Illus.). 32p. (J). (gr. 3-6). 29.93 *(978-1-59296-011-8(1))*, 200650) Child's World, Inc., The.

Tremblay, E. A. Rachel Carson. 2003. (Women in Science Ser.). (Illus.). 112p. (gr. 6-12). 30.00 *(978-0-7910-7244-8(4))*, Chelsea Hse.) Facts On File, Inc.

Venezia, Mike. Rachel Carson: Clearing the Way for Environmental Protection. Venezia, Mike, illus. (Getting to Know the World's Greatest Inventors & Scientists Ser.). (ENG., Illus.). 32p. (J). 2010. (gr. 3-4). pap. 6.95 *(978-0-531-20778-9(1))*, Children's Pr.) 2009. (gr. 2-5). 28.00 *(978-0-531-23704-5(4))* Scholastic Library Publishing.

Wade, Mary Dodson. Amazing Champion of the Earth Rachel Carson. (Amazing Americans Ser.). (Illus.). 24p. (J). 2013. (gr. k-3). pap. 7.95 *(978-0-7660-5975-7(8))*, Enslow Elementary) 2009. (gr. 1-3). lib. bdg. 22.60 *(978-0-7660-3283-5(3))* Enslow Pubs., Inc.

Wheeler, Jill C. Rachel Carson: Extraordinary Environmentalist, 1 vol. 2012. (Women in Science Ser.). (ENG., Illus.). 32p. (J). (gr. 3-6). lib. bdg. 27.07 *(978-1-61783-446-2(7))*, Checkerboard Library) ABDO Publishing Co.

CARTER, HOWARD, 1874-1939

Bennett, Doraine. Jimmy Carter: Georgia, My State Biographies. l.t. ed. 2008. (ENG., Illus.). 24p. (J). (gr. k-2). pap. 22.60 *(978-1-935077-07-7(4))* State Standards Publishing, LLC.

Harvey, Gill. Tutankhamun. McNee, Ian, illus. 2006. (Usborne Young Reading Ser.). 64p. (J). (gr. 3-7). 8.99 *(978-0-7945-1271-2(2))*, Usborne) EDC Publishing.

Woods, Michael & Woods, Mary B. The Tomb of King Tutankhamen. 2008. (Unearthing Ancient Worlds Ser.). (ENG., Illus.). 80p. (gr. 5-8). lib. bdg. 30.60 *(978-0-8225-7506-1(X))* Lerner Publishing Group.

Zoehfeld, Kathleen Weidner. The Curse of King Tut's Mummy. Nelson, Jim, illus. 2007. (Totally True Adventures Ser.). (ENG.). 112p. (J). (gr. 2-5). per. 4.99 *(978-0-375-83862-0(7))*, Random Hse. Bks. for Young Readers) Random Hse. Children's Bks.

CARTER, JIMMY, 1924-

Anderson, Sheila. Jimmy Carter. 2008. pap. 40.95 *(978-0-8225-9472-7(2))* Lerner Publishing Group.

—Jimmy Carter: A Life of Friendship. 2008. (Pull Ahead Books-Biographies Ser.). (ENG.). 32p. (gr. k-3). pap. 7.95 *(978-0-8225-8618-0(5))*; (Illus.). lib. bdg. 22.60 *(978-0-8225-8585-5(5))*, Lerner Pubns.) Lerner Publishing Group.

Bennett, Doraine. Jimmy Carter: Georgia, My State Biographies. l.t. ed. 2008. (ENG., Illus.). 24p. (J). (gr. k-2). 22.60 *(978-1-935077-00-8(7))* State Standards Publishing, LLC.

Elston, Heidi M. D. Jimmy Carter, 1 vol. 2009. (United States Presidents Ser.). (ENG., Illus.). 40p. (YA). (gr. 3-6). 27.07 *(978-1-60453-445-0(1))* ABDO Publishing Co.

Gherman, Beverly. Jimmy Carter. 2003. (Presidential Leaders Ser.). (ENG., Illus.). 112p. (gr. 6-12). 29.27 *(978-0-8225-0816-8(8))*, Lerner Pubns.) Lerner Publishing Group.

Haldy, Emma E. Jimmy Carter. Bane, Jeff, illus. 2016. (My Early Library: My Itty-Bitty Bio Ser.). (ENG.). 24p. (J). (gr. k-1). 28.50 *(978-1-63471-014-5(2))*, 208006) Cherry Lake Publishing.

January, Brendan & Seidman, David. Jimmy Carter: Peacemaker & President. 2004. (Great Life Stories Ser.). (ENG., Illus.). 127p. (J). 30.50 *(978-0-531-12374-4(X))*, Watts, Franklin) Scholastic Library Publishing.

Kent, Deborah. Jimmy Carter. 2005. (Encyc of Presidents, 2ND Ser.). (ENG., Illus.). 112p. (YA). (gr. 5-9). 34.00 *(978-0-516-22975-1(3))* Scholastic Library Publishing.

Kramer, Barbara. Jimmy Carter: A Life of Service. 2005. (Awesome Values in Famous Lives Ser.). (Illus.). 48p. (J). (gr. 3-7). lib. bdg. 25.27 *(978-0-7660-2379-6(6))*, Enslow Elementary) Enslow Pubs., Inc.

Margaret, Amy. Jimmy Carter Library & Museum. (Presidential Libraries Ser.). 24p. 2009. (gr. 3-3). 42.50 *(978-1-60851-486-1(2))* 2004. (Illus.). (J). lib. bdg. 22.60 *(978-0-8239-6271-6(7))* Rosen Publishing Group, Inc., The. (PowerKids Pr.).

Marsh, Carole. Jimmy Carter. 2003. 12p. (gr. k-4). 2.95 *(978-0-635-02126-7(9))* Gallopade International.

Rice, Dona. Jimmy Carter: For the People. 2016. (Primary Source Readers Ser.). (Illus.). 32p. (gr. 2-2). 8.99 *(978-1-4938-2561-5(5))* Teacher Created Materials, Inc.

Rissman, Rebecca. James Carter. 2017. (Premier Presidents Ser.). (ENG.). 24p. (J). (gr. 1-4). lib. bdg. 27.07 *(978-1-5038-1648-0(6))*, 211491) Child's World, Inc., The.

Ryan, Bernard. Jimmy Carter: U. S. President & Humanitarian. 2006. (Ferguson Career Biographies Ser.). (Illus.). 138p. (gr. 6-12). 25.00 *(978-0-8160-5903-4(9))*, Ferguson Publishing Co.) Facts On File, Inc.

Venezia, Mike. Jimmy Carter: Thirty-Ninth President 1977-1981. Venezia, Mike, illus. 2007. (Getting to Know the U. S. Presidents Ser.). (ENG., Illus.). 32p. (J). (gr. 3-4). 28.00 *(978-0-516-22643-9(6))*, Children's Pr.) Scholastic Library Publishing.

Waxman, Laura Hamilton. Jimmy Carter. 2006. (History Maker Biographies Ser.). (ENG., Illus.). 48p. (gr. 3-6). lib. bdg. 27.93 *(978-0-8225-5939-9(0))*, Lerner Pubns.) Lerner Publishing Group.

Whitelaw, Nancy. Jimmy Carter: President & Peacemaker. 2004. (Twentieth Century Leaders Ser.). (Illus.). 128p. (YA). (gr. 6-12). 23.95 *(978-1-931798-18-1(4))* Reynolds, Morgan Inc.

Wilson, Natashya & Natashya, Wilson. How to Draw the Life & Times of James Earl Carter Jr. 2007. (Kid's Guide to Drawing the Presidents of the United States of America Ser.). (Illus.). 32p. (YA). (gr. 2-5). 26.50 *(978-1-4042-3015-6(7))* Rosen Publishing Group, Inc., The.

CARTIER, JACQUES, 1491-1557

Donaldson-Forbes, Jeff. Jacques Cartier. 2009. (Primary Source Library of Famous Explorers Ser.). 24p. (gr. 4-4). 42.50 *(978-1-60854-126-3(6))*, PowerKids Pr.) Rosen Publishing Group, Inc., The.

Donohue, Moira Rose. Jacques Cartier. 2013. (Illus.). 24p. (J). *(978-1-938813-03-0(0))* State Standards Publishing, LLC.

Kjelle, Marylou Morano. Jacques Cartier. 2006. (What's So Great About... ? Ser.). (Illus.). 32p. (YA). (gr. 2-4). lib. bdg. 25.70 *(978-1-58415-481-5(0))* Mitchell Lane Pubs., Inc.

Lackey, Jennifer. Jacques Cartier: Exploring the St. Lawrence River. 2006. (In the Footsteps of Explorers Ser.). (ENG., Illus.). 32p. (J). (gr. 4-7). pap. *(978-0-7787-2466-7(2))* Crabtree Publishing Co.

Morey, Allan. Jacques Cartier. 2003. (Explorers of the Unknown Ser.). (J). *(978-1-58417-038-9(7))*; pap. *(978-1-58417-101-0(4))* Lake Street Pubs.

Petrie, Kristin. Jacques Cartier, 1 vol. 2004. (Explorers Set 1 Ser.). (ENG., Illus.). 32p. (gr. k-6). 27.07 *(978-1-59197-594-6(8))*, Checkerboard Library) ABDO Publishing Co.

Powell, Marie. Explore with Jacques Cartier. 2014. (ENG., Illus.). 32p. (J). pap. *(978-0-7787-1432-3(2))* Crabtree Publishing Co.

Woog, Adam. Jacques Cartier. 2009. (Great Explorers Ser.). (Illus.). 112p. (gr. 6-12). 30.00 *(978-1-60413-430-8(5))*, Chelsea Hse.) Facts On File, Inc.

CARTOGRAPHY

Here are entered works on the general science of map-making, including map projection and the mapping of large areas. Works on the mapping of small areas and the drawing of maps in elementary schools are entered under Map Drawing. Works on cartography applied to a particular subject are entered under that subject subdivided by the subdivision Maps, e.g. Geology—Maps.

see also Map Drawing; Maps

Aberg, Rebecca. Latitud y Longitud. 2005. (Rookie Espanol Geografia Ser.). (ENG & SPA., Illus.). 32p. (J). (gr. k-2). lib. bdg. 19.50 *(978-0-516-25240-7(2))*, Children's Pr.) Scholastic Library Publishing.

Ashley, Susan. I Can Read a Map. 2004. (I Can Do It! Ser.). (Illus.). 24p. (gr. k-3). pap. 8.15 *(978-0-8368-4331-6(2))*; lib. bdg. 21.00 *(978-0-8368-4324-8(X))* Stevens, Gareth Publishing LLLP. (Weekly Reader Leveled Readers).

Ball, Jacqueline A. & Ball, Jacqueline A. Mapping Earth. 2004. (Discovery Channel School Science Ser.). (Illus.). 32p. (gr. 4-8). lib. bdg. 26.00 *(978-0-8368-3382-9(1))*, Gareth Stevens Learning Library) Stevens, Gareth Publishing LLLP.

Besel, Jennifer M. Map Scales, 1 vol. 2013. (Maps Ser.). (ENG.). 24p. (gr. k-1). 26.65 *(978-1-4765-3083-3(1))*, Pebble Plus); pap. 6.95 *(978-1-4765-3523-4(X))*, Pebble Bks.) Capstone Press of Coughlan Cos.

Boothroyd, Jennifer. Map My Country. 2013. (First Step Nonfiction - Map It Out Ser.). (ENG., Illus.). 24p. (gr. k-2). lib. bdg. 23.93 *(978-1-4677-1113-5(6))*, Lerner Pubns.) Lerner Publishing Group.

—Map My Home. 2013. (First Step Nonfiction - Map It Out Ser.). (ENG., Illus.). 24p. (gr. k-2). pap. 6.95 *(978-1-4677-1530-0(1))*; lib. bdg. 23.93 *(978-1-4677-1110-4(1))*, Lerner Pubns.) Lerner Publishing Group.

—Map My Room. 2013. (First Step Nonfiction - Map It Out Ser.). (ENG., Illus.). 24p. (gr. k-2). pap. 6.95 *(978-1-4677-1532-4(8))*; lib. bdg. 23.93 *(978-1-4677-1109-8(8))*, Lerner Pubns.) Lerner Publishing Group.

Boston, Paul, illus. In Space. 2017. (Find Your Way Ser.). (ENG.). 32p. (J). (gr. k-3). 14.95 *(978-1-68297-047-8(7))*, QED Publishing) Quarto Publishing Group UK GBR. Dist: Hachette Bk. Group.

Bow, James. Mapping the Future. 2017. (Mapping in the Modern World Ser.). (ENG., Illus.). 32p. (J). ***(978-0-7787-3238-9(X))***; pap. ***(978-0-7787-3244-0(4))*** Crabtree Publishing Co.

Brown, Cynthia Light & McGinty, Patrick. Mapping & Navigation: Explore the History & Science of Finding Your Way with 20 Projects. Hetland, Beth, illus. 2013. (Build It Yourself Ser.). (ENG.). 128p. (J). (gr. 3-7). 21.95 *(978-1-61930-194-8(6))*; pap. 16.95 *(978-1-61930-198-6(9))* Open City Bks.

Burrows, Terry. Codes, Ciphers, & Cartography: Math Goes to War. 2017. (STEM on the Battlefield Ser.). (ENG., Illus.). 48p. (J). (gr. 4-6). 31.99 ***(978-1-5124-3927-4(4))***, Lerner Pubns.) Lerner Publishing Group.

Burstein, John. Making Maps: Where's the Party? 2003. (Weekly Reader Early Learning Library). (Illus.). 24p. (J). (gr. k-4). pap. 8.15 *(978-0-8368-3826-8(2))*, Weekly Reader Leveled Readers) Stevens, Gareth Publishing LLLP.

Campbell, Mel. Caminando con Mapas/Walk on Maps. Mallick, David, tr. from ENG. 2006. (My First Math Discovery Ser.). (SPA., Illus.). 24p. (J). (gr. -1-3). lib. bdg. 22.79 *(978-1-60044-287-2(0))* Rourke Educational Media.

Chancellor, Deborah. Maps & Mapping. 2011. (Discover Science Ser.). (ENG., Illus.). 56p. (J). (gr. k-3). pap. 7.99 *(978-0-7534-6718-3(6))*, 9780753467183, Kingfisher) Roaring Brook Pr.

Cooke, Tim. The Changing Face of Maps. 2017. 32p. (J). ***(978-0-7787-3221-1(5))*** Crabtree Publishing Co.

—Mapping Human Activity. 2017. (Illus.). 32p. (J). ***(978-0-7787-3222-8(3))*** Crabtree Publishing Co.

—Maps & Exploration. 2010. (Understanding Maps of Our World Ser.). 48p. (YA). (gr. 4-7). lib. bdg. 31.00 *(978-1-4339-3512-1(0))*; (Illus.). (gr. 6-8). pap. 14.05 *(978-1-4339-3513-8(9))*, Gareth Stevens Secondary Library) Stevens, Gareth Publishing LLLP.

—Maps Today. 2010. (Understanding Maps of Our World Ser.). 48p. (YA). (gr. 4-7). lib. bdg. 31.00 *(978-1-4339-3521-3(X))*; (Illus.). (J). (gr. 6-8). pap. 14.05 *(978-1-4339-3522-0(8))*, Gareth Stevens Secondary Library) Stevens, Gareth Publishing LLLP.

George, Enzo. Mapping in a Digital World. 2017. (Mapping in the Modern World Ser.). (ENG., Illus.). 32p. (J). ***(978-0-7787-3223-5(1))***; pap. ***(978-0-7787-3241-9(X))*** Crabtree Publishing Co.

—Mental Maps & Mapping the Mind. 2017. (Mapping in the Modern World Ser.). (ENG., Illus.). 32p. (J). ***(978-0-7787-3237-2(1))***; pap. ***(978-0-7787-3243-3(6))*** Crabtree Publishing Co.

Gray, Leon. Global Positioning System: Who's Tracking You? 2013. (Ask the Experts Ser.). (Illus.). 48p. (J). (gr. 6-8). 31.95 *(978-1-4339-8639-0(6))*; pap. 14.05 *(978-1-4339-8640-6(X))* Stevens, Gareth Publishing LLLP. (Gareth Stevens Secondary Library).

Hammond World Atlas Corporation Staff, ed. Globes in a Box. 2008. (Hammond Ser.). 64p. (J). (gr. 5-18). 19.95 *(978-0-8437-1825-6(0))* Hammond World Atlas Corp.

Harasymiw, Mark. Mapping South America. 2013. (Mapping the World Ser.). 24p. (J). (gr. 2-5). pap. 48.90 *(978-1-4339-9121-9(7))*; (ENG., Illus.). pap. 8.15 *(978-1-4339-9120-2(9))* Stevens, Gareth Publishing LLLP.

Harasymiw, Mark & Harasymiw, Mark J. Mapping South America. 2013. 24p. (J). (gr. 2-5). 22.60 *(978-1-4339-9119-6(5))* Stevens, Gareth Publishing LLLP.

Henzel, Cynthia Kennedy. Creating Modern Maps, 1 vol. 2008. (On the Map Ser.). (ENG.). 32p. (gr. k-6). 27.07 *(978-1-59928-949-6(0))*, Checkerboard Library) ABDO Publishing Co.

—Mapmaking, 1 vol. 2008. (On the Map Ser.). (ENG.). 32p. (gr. k-6). 27.07 *(978-1-59928-950-2(4))*, Checkerboard Library) ABDO Publishing Co.

—Mapping History, 1 vol. 2008. (On the Map Ser.). (ENG.). 32p. (gr. k-6). 27.07 *(978-1-59928-951-9(2))*, Checkerboard Library) ABDO Publishing Co.

—Measuring the World, 1 vol. 2008. (On the Map Ser.). (ENG.). 32p. (gr. k-6). 27.07 *(978-1-59928-952-6(0))*, Checkerboard Library) ABDO Publishing Co.

Hibbert, Clare. Around the World in 80 Maps. 2017. (ENG., Illus.). 96p. (J). (gr. 3-7). 19.95 ***(978-0-2281-0010-2(0))***, 9780228100102) Firefly Bks., Ltd.

Hoe, Susan C. Environments. 2008. (Maps & Mapping Ser.). 32p. (gr. 1-5). pap. 10.50 *(978-0-8368-9331-1(X))*, Gareth Stevens Learning Library) Stevens, Gareth Publishing LLLP.

—Habitats. 2008. (Maps & Mapping Ser.). 32p. (gr. 1-5). (J). lib. bdg. 26.00 *(978-0-8368-9205-5(4))*; pap. 10.50 *(978-0-8368-9332-8(8))* Stevens, Gareth Publishing LLLP. (Gareth Stevens Learning Library).

—Resources. 2008. (Maps & Mapping Ser.). 32p. (gr. 1-5). (J). lib. bdg. 26.00 *(978-0-8368-9206-2(2))*; pap. 10.50 *(978-0-8368-9333-5(6))* Stevens, Gareth Publishing LLLP. (Gareth Stevens Learning Library).

—Where We Live. 2008. (Maps & Mapping Ser.). 32p. (gr. 1-5). pap. 10.50 *(978-0-8368-9334-2(4))*, Gareth Stevens Learning Library) Stevens, Gareth Publishing LLLP.

Hoe, Susan C. & Hoe, Susan C. Environments. 2008. (Maps & Mapping Ser.). 32p. (J). (gr. 1-5). lib. bdg. 26.00 *(978-0-8368-9204-8(6))*, Gareth Stevens Learning Library) Stevens, Gareth Publishing LLLP.

—Where We Live. 2008. (Maps & Mapping Ser.). 32p. (J). (gr. 1-5). lib. bdg. 26.00 *(978-0-8368-9207-9(0))*, Gareth Stevens Learning Library) Stevens, Gareth Publishing LLLP.

Hollingum, Ben. Travel Maps. 2010. (Understanding Maps of Our World Ser.). (Illus.). 48p. (YA). (gr. 4-7). lib. bdg. 31.00 *(978-1-4339-3506-0(6))*; (J). (gr. 6-8). pap. 14.05 *(978-1-4339-3507-7(4))*, Gareth Stevens Secondary Library) Stevens, Gareth Publishing LLLP.

Hudak, Heather C. Mapping. 2007. (Social Studies Essential Skills Ser.). (Illus.). 24p. (J). (gr. 4-7). lib. bdg. 24.45 *(978-1-59036-761-2(8))*; per. 8.95 *(978-1-59036-762-9(6))* Weigl Pubs., Inc.

Jankowski, Emily. Mapping North America. 2013. 24p. (J). (gr. 2-5). 22.60 *(978-1-4339-9114-1(4))*; pap. 48.90 *(978-1-4339-9116-5(0))*; (ENG., Illus.). pap. 8.15 *(978-1-4339-9115-8(2))* Stevens, Gareth Publishing LLLP.

Jordan, Ashley. Maddie's Map Adventure. 2013. (InfoMax Readers Ser.). (ENG.). 24p. (J). (gr. 2-3). pap. 49.50 *(978-1-4777-2299-2(8))*; (Illus.). pap. 8.25 *(978-1-4777-2298-5(X))* Rosen Publishing Group, Inc., The. (Rosen Classroom).

Kachur, Matthew. Making Maps & Cómo hacer un Mapa: 6 English, 6 Spanish Adaptations. 2011. (ENG & SPA.). (J). 97.00 net. *(978-1-4108-5693-7(3))* Benchmark Education Co.

Leithauser, Jessica. Maps Show Us the Way. 2006. (Rosen Real Readers Big Bookstm Ser.). (ENG., Illus.). 12p. (gr. 1-2). 33.50 *(978-1-4042-6218-8(0))* Rosen Publishing Group, Inc., The.

Leithauser, Jessica & National Geographic Learning Staff. Maps Show Us the Way. 2012. (ENG., Illus.). 12p. (C). (gr. 1-2). pap. 9.95 *(978-0-8239-6357-7(8))* National Geographic School Publishing, Inc.

Levy, Janey. Mapping America's Westward Expansion: Applying Geographic Tools & Interpreting Maps. (Critical Thinking in American History Ser.). 48p. 2009. (gr. 5-8). 53.00 *(978-1-61512-095-6(5))*, Rosen Reference) 2005. (Illus.). (J). (gr. k-3). lib. bdg. 29.25 *(978-1-4042-0416-4(4))* Rosen Publishing Group, Inc., The.

—Mapping Australia. 2013. 24p. (J). (gr. 2-5). 22.60 *(978-1-4339-9104-2(7))* Stevens, Gareth Publishing LLLP.

—The Silk Road: Using a Map Scale to Measure Distances. 2009. (PowerMath: Proficiency Plus Ser.). 32p. (gr. 4-5). 47.90 *(978-1-60851-423-6(4)*, PowerKids Pr.) Rosen Publishing Group, Inc., The.

Linde, Barbara. Mapping Europe. 2013. (Mapping the World Ser.). 24p. (J). (gr. 2-5). pap. 48.90 *(978-1-4339-9111-0(X))*; (ENG., Illus.). pap. 8.15 *(978-1-4339-9110-3(1))* Stevens, Gareth Publishing LLLP.

Linde, Barbara & Linde, Barbara M. Mapping Europe. 2013. 24p. (J). (gr. 2-5). 22.60 *(978-1-4339-9109-7(8))* Stevens, Gareth Publishing LLLP.

Linde, Barbara M. Mapping Asia. 2013. 24p. (J). (gr. 2-5). 22.60 *(978-1-4339-9099-1(7))*; pap. 8.15 *(978-1-4339-9100-4(4))*; pap. 48.90 *(978-1-4339-9101-1(2))* Stevens, Gareth Publishing LLLP.

Mapping Antarctica. 2013. (Mapping the World Ser.). 24p. (J). (gr. 2-5). pap. 48.90 *(978-1-4339-9096-0(2))* Stevens, Gareth Publishing LLLP.

Mapping Australia. 2013. (Mapping the World Ser.). 24p. (J). (gr. 2-5). pap. 48.90 *(978-1-4339-9106-6(3))* Stevens, Gareth Publishing LLLP.

Mapping the World. 2013. (Mapping the World Ser.). 24p. (J). (gr. 2-5). 158.20 *(978-1-4339-9674-0(X))*; pap. 342.30 *(978-1-4339-9760-0(6))*; pap. 57.05 *(978-1-4339-9759-4(2))* Stevens, Gareth Publishing LLLP.

Matteson, Adrienne. Using Digital Maps. Petelinsek, Kathleen, illus. 2013. (Explorer Library: Information Explorer Ser.). (ENG.). 32p. (J). (gr. 4-8). 28.50 *(978-1-62431-129-1(6)*, 202836); pap. 14.21 *(978-1-62431-261-8(6)*, 202838) Cherry Lake Publishing.

Meachen Rau, Dana. Los Mapas. 2008. (Planeta Es Importante Ser.). (SPA.). 32p. (gr. 1-2). lib. bdg. 15.95 *(978-0-7614-3468-9(2)*, Benchmark Bks.) Marshall Cavendish Corp.

—Maps. 2008. (Earth Matters Ser.). 32p. (gr. 1-2). lib. bdg. 15.95 *(978-0-7614-3046-9(6)*, Benchmark Bks.) Marshall Cavendish Corp.

—Maps/Los Mapas. 2008. (Earth Matters/El Planeta Es Importante Ser.). (SPA & ENG.). 32p. (gr. k-1). lib. bdg. 15.95 *(978-0-7614-3493-1(3)*, Benchmark Bks.) Marshall Cavendish Corp.

Oleksy, Walter. Maps in History. 2003. (Watts Library). (ENG., Illus.). 64p. (J). (gr. 5-7). pap. 8.95 *(978-0-531-16633-8(3)*, Watts, Franklin) Scholastic Library Publishing.

Owen, James A. & Owen, Jeremy. Lost Treasures of the Pirates of the Caribbean. Owen, James A., illus. 2011. (ENG., Illus.). 32p. (J). (gr. 3-7). pap. 16.99 *(978-1-4424-3093-8(1)*, Simon & Schuster Bks. For Young Readers) Simon & Schuster Bks. For Young Readers.

Panchyk, Richard. Charting the World: Geography & Maps from Cave Paintings to GPS with 21 Activities. 2011. (For Kids Ser.). (ENG.). 144p. (J). (gr. 4). pap. 18.95 *(978-1-56976-344-5(5))* Chicago Review Pr., Inc.

Rockett, Paul. Mapping Africa. 2016. (Illus.). 32p. (J). *(978-0-7787-2612-8(6))* Crabtree Publishing Co.

—Mapping Asia. 2016. (Illus.). 32p. (J). *(978-0-7787-2613-5(4))* Crabtree Publishing Co.

—Mapping Australia & Oceania, & Antarctica. 2016. (Illus.). 32p. (J). *(978-0-7787-2614-2(2))* Crabtree Publishing Co.

—Mapping Europe. 2016. (Mapping the Continents Ser.). (ENG., Illus.). 32p. (J). (gr. 3-6). *(978-0-7787-2615-9(0))* Crabtree Publishing Co.

—Mapping North America. 2016. (Illus.). 32p. (J). *(978-0-7787-2616-6(9))* Crabtree Publishing Co.

—Mapping South America. 2016. (Illus.). 32p. (J). *(978-0-7787-2617-3(7))* Crabtree Publishing Co.

Ross, Val. The Road to There: Mapmakers & Their Stories. (ENG., Illus.). 152p. (J). (gr. 5). 2009. pap. 15.95 *(978-0-88776-933-7(0))* 2003. 22.95 *(978-0-88776-621-3(8))* Tundra Bks. CAN. (Tundra Bks.). Dist: Penguin Random Hse. LLC.

Roza, Greg. Mapping Antarctica. 2013. 24p. (J). (gr. 2-5). 22.60 *(978-1-4339-9094-6(6))*; pap. 8.15 *(978-1-4339-9095-3(4))* Stevens, Gareth Publishing LLLP.

Samuels, Charlie. Mapping the Physical World. 2017. (Mapping in the Modern World Ser.). (ENG.). 32p. (J). ***(978-0-7787-3236-5(3))***; pap. ***(978-0-7787-3242-6(8))*** Crabtree Publishing Co.

Somervill, Barbara A. The Story Behind Maps, 1 vol. 2011. (True Stories Ser.). (ENG.). 32p. (gr. 3-3). 30.65 *(978-1-4329-5443-7(1)*, NA-h) Heinemann-Raintree.

Waldron, Melanie. Mapping Communities, 1 vol. 2013. (Let's Get Mapping! Ser.). (ENG., Illus.). 32p. (gr. 2-4). 30.65 *(978-1-4109-4900-4(1))*; pap. 8.29 *(978-1-4109-4907-3(9))* Heinemann-Raintree. (Raintree Perspectives).

—Mapping the Land & Weather, 1 vol. 2013. (Let's Get Mapping! Ser.). (ENG., Illus.). 32p. (gr. 2-4). 30.65 *(978-1-4109-4902-8(8))*; pap. 8.29 *(978-1-4109-4909-7(5))* Heinemann-Raintree. (Raintree Perspectives).

—Mapping the World, 1 vol. 2013. (Let's Get Mapping! Ser.). (ENG., Illus.). 32p. (gr. 2-4). 30.65 *(978-1-4109-4903-5(6))*; pap. 8.29 *(978-1-4109-4910-3(9))* Heinemann-Raintree. (Raintree Perspectives).

Walker, Rob. Mapping Towns & Cities. 2010. (Mapping Our World Ser.). 32p. (gr. 4). 28.50 *(978-1-60870-120-9(4))* Marshall Cavendish Corp.

Wood, Alix. Hunting on the Map. 2014. (Fun with Map Skills Ser.). (Illus.). 32p. (J). (gr. 3-6). lib. bdg. 26.25 *(978-1-4777-6980-5(3)*, PowerKids Pr.) Rosen Publishing Group, Inc., The.

Zelon, Helen. The Endeavor SRTM: Mapping the Earth. 2009. (Space Missions Ser.). 24p. (gr. 3-4). 42.50 *(978-1-60853-118-9(X)*, PowerKids Pr.) Rosen Publishing Group, Inc., The.

CARTOONING

ABDO Publishing Company Staff. Comic Book Creators. 2006. (Comic Book Creators Ser.). 32p. 162.42 *(978-1-59928-296-1(8)*, Abdo & Daughters) ABDO Publishing Co.

Allen, Chris, et al. How to Draw Adventure Friends & Other Cartoon Heroes. 2013. (ENG., Illus.). 128p. (YA). pap. 19.95 *(978-0-9850925-8-0(0)*, 9780985092580) Antarctic Pr., Inc.

Ames, Lee J. Draw 50 Famous Cartoons. 2012. (Draw 50 Ser.). lib. bdg. 20.85 *(978-0-606-26439-6(6)*, Turtleback) Turtleback Bks.

Antram, David. Draw Caricatures. David Antram, illus. 2017. (Step-By-Step Ser.). 32p. (gr. 3-8). 31.35 ***(978-1-911242-20-8(2))*** Book Hse. GBR. Dist: Black Rabbit Bks.

—Drawing Manga Pets. 2015. (Art Class: the Art of Drawing Manga Ser.). (ENG., Illus.). 32p. (gr. 2-6). 31.35 *(978-1-62588-353-7(6))* Black Rabbit Bks.

—Drawing Manga Villians. 2015. (Art Class: the Art of Drawing Manga Ser.). (ENG., Illus.). 32p. (gr. 2-6). 31.35 *(978-1-62588-354-4(4))* Black Rabbit Bks.

—How to Draw Manga Warriors. 2010. (How to Draw Ser.). (Illus.). 32p. (YA). (gr. 6-18). pap. 11.75 *(978-1-4488-1609-5(2))*; lib. bdg. 26.50 *(978-1-4488-1581-4(9))* Rosen Publishing Group, Inc., The. (PowerKids Pr.).

—Manga Action Figures. 2012. (How to Draw Ser.). (ENG.). 32p. (J). (gr. 4-6). pap. 11.75 *(978-1-4488-6469-0(0))*; lib. bdg. 26.50 *(978-1-4488-6460-7(7))* Rosen Publishing Group, Inc., The. (PowerKids Pr.).

Artell, Mike. Funny Cartooning for Kids. 2014. (ENG., Illus.). 128p. (J). (gr. 3). pap. 9.95 *(978-1-4027-8475-0(9))* Sterling Publishing Co., Inc.

Asquith, Ros. How to Draw Cartoons. Asquith, Ros, illus. 2006. (Collins Big Cat Ser.). (ENG., Illus.). 56p. (J). (gr. 2-2). pap. 7.99 *(978-0-00-718697-6(5))* HarperCollins Pubs. Ltd. GBR. Dist: Independent Pubs. Group.

Barnhart, Duane & Barnhart, Angie. Cartooning Basics: Creating the Characters & More. 4th ed. 2004. (Illus.). 88p. (J). per. 12.99 *(978-0-9657136-4-1(4)*, 1235827) Cartoon Connections Pr.

Barr, Steve. 1-2-3 Draw Cartoon People. 2014. 64p. pap. 9.00 *(978-1-61003-322-0(1))* Center for the Collaborative Classroom.

—1-2-3 Draw Cartoon People: A Step-By-Step Guide. 2016. (ENG., Illus.). 66p. (J). (gr. k-5). pap. 6.99 *(978-0-939217-98-4(8))* Peel Productions, Inc.

Beauvais, Den. Dragonfly Flipz Sampler. 2003. (Illus.). 96p. per. 3.99 *(978-0-9745213-0-5(2)*, Dragonfly Flipz) Dragonfly Entertainment.

Beginner's Guide to Drawing Cartoons. Date not set. (I Can Draw Ser.). (Illus.). 128p. (J). 7.98 *(978-1-4054-0543-0(0))* Parragon, Inc.

Bellen-Berthézène, Cyndie. Cartoon How-To. Workman, Terry & Workman, Lisa, illus. 2005. 48p. (J). *(978-0-439-81332-7(8))* Scholastic, Inc.

Belmonte, David. Creating Horror Comics. 2015. (Illus.). 32p. (J). *(978-1-4777-5924-0(7)*, PowerKids Pr.) Rosen Publishing Group, Inc., The.

Bergin, Mark & Antram, David. How to Draw Cartoons. 2010. (How to Draw Ser.). (Illus.). 32p. (YA). (gr. 6-18). pap. 11.75 *(978-1-4488-1597-5(5))*; lib. bdg. 26.50 *(978-1-4488-1576-0(2))* Rosen Publishing Group, Inc., The. (PowerKids Pr.).

Bishop-Stephens, Will. How to Create Animation in 10 Easy Lessons: Create 2-D, 3-d, & Digital Animation Without a Hollywood Budget. 2016. (Super Skills Ser.). (ENG.). 64p. (J). (gr. 3-7). 12.95 *(978-1-63322-182-6(2)*, Walter Foster Jr) Quarto Publishing Group USA.

Booth, Scott, illus. How to Draw Superheroes & Super Villains. 2003. 64p. (J). *(978-0-439-55133-5(1))* Scholastic, Inc.

Bray, Adam, et al. Marvel Absolutely Everything You Need to Know. 2016. (ENG., Illus.). 240p. (J). (gr. 3-7). 19.99 *(978-1-4654-5262-7(1)*, DK Children) Dorling Kindersley Publishing, Inc.

Broadbent, Paul. Being A Cartoonist. 2007. (Trackers-Math Ser.). (gr. 2-5). pap. 5.00 *(978-1-59055-937-6(1))* Pacific Learning, Inc.

Burgess, Mary. The Most Wonderful Place. 2012. 44p. pap. 21.99 *(978-1-4772-6796-7(4))* AuthorHouse.

Camagajevac, Seb. Creating Fantasy Comics. 2015. (J). *(978-1-4777-5904-2(2))* Rosen Publishing Group, Inc., The.

Cameron, Neill. How to Make Awesome Comics. 2017. (ENG.). 64p. (J). (gr. 2-5). pap. 8.99 ***(978-1-338-13273-1(3))*** Scholastic, Inc.

Campos, Leo. Creating Manga Comics, 1 vol. 2015. (ENG., Illus.). 32p. (J). lib. bdg. 27.50 *(978-1-4777-5926-4(3)*, PowerKids Pr.) Rosen Publishing Group, Inc., The.

Chambers, Ailin. Manga. 2014. (Ready, Set, Draw! Ser.). 32p. (J). (gr. 2-5). 26.60 *(978-1-4824-0918-5(6))* Stevens, Gareth Publishing LLLP.

Chiacchiera, Moreno. Creating Funny Comics. 2015. (Illus.). 32p. *(978-1-4777-5912-7(3))* Rosen Publishing Group, Inc., The.

Clay, Adam. How to Draw Cartoons: An Easy Step-By-Step Guide. 2012. (ENG., Illus.). 128p. (J). pap. 10.95 *(978-1-84837-495-9(X))* Arcturus Publishing GBR. Dist: Bookmasters Distribution.

Cohen, Sherman. Cartooning: Character Design - Learn the Art of Cartooning Step by Step. 2006. (How to Draw & Paint Ser.). (ENG., Illus.). 32p. pap. 8.95 *(978-1-56010-967-9(X)*, 156010967X) Quarto Publishing Group USA.

Comics: Investigate the History & Technology of American Cartooning. 2014. (Build It Yourself Ser.). (ENG., Illus.). 128p. (J). (gr. 3-7). pap. 17.95 *(978-1-61930-254-9(3))* Open City Bks.

Comikers. Pen & Ink. 2006. (ENG., Illus.). 114p. (YA). pap. 19.95 *(978-1-56970-917-7(3)*, 9781569709177) Digital Manga Publishing.

Cook, Trevor & Miles, Lisa. Drawing Manga. 2011. (Drawing Is Fun Ser.). (Illus.). 32p. (J). (gr. 1-3). pap. 10.50 *(978-1-4339-5067-4(7)*, Gareth Stevens Learning Library); lib. bdg. 26.60 *(978-1-4339-5024-7(3))* Stevens, Gareth Publishing LLLP.

Coope, Katy. How to Draw Manga Characters. Coope, Katy, illus. 2008. (Collins Big Cat Ser.). (ENG., Illus.). 56p. (J). (gr. 5-6). pap. 8.99 *(978-0-00-723102-7(4))* HarperCollins Pubs. Ltd. GBR. Dist: Independent Pubs. Group.

Creative Team at Walter Foster Publishing Staff. How to Draw Teenage Mutant Ninja Turtles: Learn to Draw Leonardo, Raphael, Donatello, & Michelangelo Step by Step! 2013. (Licensed Learn to Draw Ser.). (ENG., Illus.). 64p. (J). (gr. 3-7). pap. 9.95 *(978-1-60058-296-7(6)*, 1600582966) Quarto Publishing Group USA.

—Spongebob Squarepants - The Bikini Bottom Collection. 2012. (Licensed Learn to Draw Ser.). (ENG., Illus.). 64p. (J). (gr. 1-3). pap. 9.95 *(978-1-60058-297-4(4)*, 1600582974) Quarto Publishing Group USA.

Curto, Rosa M. Super Simple Cartooning for Kids. 2016. (Super Simple... Bks.). (ENG., Illus.). 96p. (J). (gr. 2-6). pap. 11.99 *(978-1-4380-0826-4(0))* Barron's Educational Series, Inc.

Disney Storybook Artists Staff. Enchanted Princesses: Learn to Draw Ariel, Cinderella, Belle, Rapunzel, & All of Your Favorite Disney Princesses! 2012. (Licensed Learn to Draw Ser.). (ENG., Illus.). 64p. (J). (gr. 1-17). pap. 9.95 *(978-1-60058-305-6(9)*, 1600583059) Quarto Publishing Group USA.

—Favorite Fairies: Learn to Draw the Magical World of Tinker Bell, Silver Mist, Rosetta, & All of Your Favorite Disney Fairies! 2012. (Licensed Learn to Draw Ser.). (ENG., Illus.). 64p. (J). (gr. 1-3). pap. 9.95 *(978-1-60058-298-1(2)*, 1600582982) Quarto Publishing Group USA.

—Learn to Draw Disney Villains: Featuring Favorite Villains, Including Captain Hook, Cruella de Vil, Jafar, & Others! 2012. (Licensed Learn to Draw Ser.). (ENG., Illus.). 144p. (J). (gr. 1-3). pap. 19.95 *(978-1-60058-261-5(3)*, 1600582613, Walter Foster Jr) Quarto Publishing Group USA.

—Learn to Draw Disney's Phineas & Ferb Drawing Book & Kit: Includes Everything You Need to Draw Candace, Agent P, & Your Other Favorite Characters from the Hit Show! 2012. (Licensed Learn to Draw Ser.). (ENG., Illus.). 32p. (J). (gr. 1-3). pap. 19.99 *(978-1-60058-331-5(8)*, 1600583318) Quarto Publishing Group USA.

—Learn to Draw Disney's Planes; Featuring Dusty Crophopper, Skipper Riley, Ripslinger, el Chupacabra, & All Your Favorite Characters! 2013. (Licensed Learn to Draw Ser.). (ENG., Illus.). 64p. (J). (gr. 1-3). pap. 9.95 *(978-1-60058-383-4(0)*, 1600583830, Walter Foster Jr) Quarto Publishing Group USA.

—Your Favorite Disney/Pixar Characters: Featuring Woody, Buzz Lightyear, Lightning McQueen, Mater, & Other Favorite Characters. 2013. (Licensed Learn to Draw Ser.). (ENG., Illus.). 64p. (J). (gr. 1-3). pap. 9.95 *(978-1-60058-371-1(7)*, 1600583717) Quarto Publishing Group USA.

Dobbyn, Nigel. Creating Science Fiction Comics. 2015. (Illus.). 32p. (J). *(978-1-4777-5932-5(8)*, PowerKids Pr.) Rosen Publishing Group, Inc., The.

Dorling Kindersley Publishing Staff. Marvel Comics 75 Years of Cover Art. 2014. (ENG., Illus.). 320p. *(978-1-4093-4751-4(6))* Dorling Kindersley Publishing, Inc.

Drawing Cartoons. 2004. (I-Quest Ser.). (J). *(978-1-84229-756-8(2))* Top That! Publishing PLC.

DreamWorks Animation Creative Team. Learn to Draw DreamWorks Animation's Kung Fu Panda: Featuring Po, Tigress, Master Shifu, & All Your Favorite New Characters from Kung Fu Panda 3! 2016. (Licensed Learn to Draw Ser.). (ENG.). 64p. (J). (gr. 1-3). pap. 9.95 *(978-1-63322-060-7(5)*, Walter Foster Jr) Quarto Publishing Group USA.

Dunn, Ben. How to Draw Manga. 2004. (Illus.). 344p. (YA). pap. 3.25 *(978-1-59412-063-3(3))* Mud Puddle, Inc.

Edgers, Geoff. Who Is Stan Lee? Laznicka, Mike et al, illus. 2014. (Who Was? Ser.). (ENG.). 112p. (J). (gr. 3-7). pap. 5.99 *(978-0-448-48236-1(3)*, Grosset & Dunlap) Penguin Young Readers Group.

Elder, Jeremy. Manga Mazes. 2009. (Dover Children's Activity Bks.). (ENG., Illus.). 48p. (J). (gr. -1-5). pap. 4.99 *(978-0-486-47329-1(5))* Dover Pubns., Inc.

Farris, D. & Brookes, Kate. Activators Cartooning. (Illus.). iv, 122p. (J). pap. *(978-0-340-71518-5(9))* Hodder & Stoughton.

Ferrer, María, tr. from JPN. Cómo Dibujar Manga Vol. 1: Personajes. 2004. (SPA., Illus.). 82p. (YA). pap. 19.95 *(978-1-59497-038-2(6))* Public Square Bks.

Garbot, Dave. Crazy, Zany Cartoon Characters: Learn to Draw 20 Weird, Wacky Characters! 2014. (Cartooning for Kids Ser.). (ENG., Illus.). 64p. (J). (gr. 1-3). pap. 8.95 *(978-1-60058-385-8(7)*, 1600583857) Quarto Publishing Group USA.

—Fairy Tale Fun: Learn to Draw More Than 20 Cartoon Princesses, Fairies, & Adventure Characters. 2014. (Cartooning for Kids Ser.). (ENG., Illus.). 64p. (J). (gr. 1-3). pap. 8.95 *(978-1-60058-451-0(9))* Quarto Publishing Group USA.

—Furry & Feathered Friends. 2015. (Cartooning for Kids Ser.). (ENG., Illus.). 64p. (J). (gr. k-5). 33.32 *(978-1-939581-49-5(4))* Quarto Publishing Group USA.

—Furry & Feathered Friends: Learn to Draw More Than 20 Cute Cartoon Critters. 2014. (Cartooning for Kids Ser.). (ENG., Illus.). 64p. (J). (gr. 1-3). pap. 8.95 *(978-1-60058-450-3(0))* Quarto Publishing Group USA.

—Mashup Mania: Learn to Draw 20 Laughable, Loony Characters! 2015. (Cartooning for Kids Ser.). (ENG., Illus.). 64p. (J). (gr. 1-3). pap. 8.95 *(978-1-60058-491-6(8))* Quarto Publishing Group USA.

—Mean 'n' Messy Monsters: Learn to Draw 25 Spooky, Kooky Monsters! 2014. (Cartooning for Kids Ser.). (ENG., Illus.). 64p. (J). (gr. 1-3). pap. 8.95 *(978-1-60058-392-6(X)*, 160058392X) Quarto Publishing Group USA.

—Silly Sports: Learn to Draw 20 Awesomely Athletic Characters! 2015. (Cartooning for Kids Ser.). (ENG., Illus.). 64p. (J). (gr. 1-3). pap. 8.95 *(978-1-60058-492-3(6))* Quarto Publishing Group USA.

Gilbert, James. Big Jims Ten Years & Still Cartooning. 2005. (J). 9.95 *(978-1-59971-024-2(2))* Aardvark Global Publishing.

Glossop, Jennifer. Tattoo You! Color & Make Your Own Temporary Tattoo Designs. Klund, Barbara, illus. 2004. 30p. (J). (gr. k-4). reprint ed. pap. 8.00 *(978-0-7567-8260-3(0))* DIANE Publishing Co.

Gray, Peter. Animals. (Drawing Manga Ser.). 32p. 2009. (gr. 4-4). 50.50 *(978-1-61512-196-0(X))* 2006. (Illus.). (YA). (gr. 3-6). lib. bdg. 26.50 *(978-1-4042-3329-4(6))* Rosen Publishing Group, Inc., The.

—Female Action Figures. 2009. (Drawing Manga Ser.). 32p. (gr. 4-4). 50.50 *(978-1-61512-197-7(8))* Rosen Publishing Group, Inc., The.

—Heroes & Villains. (Drawing Manga Ser.). 32p. 2009. (gr. 4-4). 50.50 *(978-1-61512-198-4(6))* 2006. (Illus.). (YA). (gr. 3-6). lib. bdg. 26.50 *(978-1-4042-3330-0(X))* Rosen Publishing Group, Inc., The.

—Male Action Figures. 2009. (Drawing Manga Ser.). 32p. (gr. 4-4). 50.50 *(978-1-61512-199-1(4))* Rosen Publishing Group, Inc., The.

—Monsters. 2006. (Drawing Manga Ser.). (Illus.). 32p. (YA). (gr. 3-6). lib. bdg. 26.50 *(978-1-4042-3331-7(8))* Rosen Publishing Group, Inc., The.

—Robots. 2009. (Drawing Manga Ser.). 32p. (gr. 4-4). 50.50 *(978-1-61512-201-1(X))* Rosen Publishing Group, Inc., The.

Gray, Peter C. Female Action Figures. 2006. (Drawing Manga Ser.). (Illus.). 32p. (J). (gr. 3-6). lib. bdg. 26.50 *(978-1-4042-3327-0(X))* Rosen Publishing Group, Inc., The.

—Male Action Figures. 2006. (Drawing Manga Ser.). (Illus.). 32p. (YA). (gr. 3-6). lib. bdg. 26.50 *(978-1-4042-3328-7(8))* Rosen Publishing Group, Inc., The.

—Robots. 2006. (Drawing Manga Ser.). (Illus.). 32p. (YA). (gr. 3-6). lib. bdg. 26.50 *(978-1-4042-3332-4(6))* Rosen Publishing Group, Inc., The.

Green, Barry. 101 Fairies. Green, Dan, illus. 2009. (How to Draw 101... Ser.). (ENG.). 48p. (J). (gr. k). pap. 4.99 *(978-1-84666-852-4(2))* Top That! Publishing PLC GBR. Dist: Independent Pubs. Group.

Hamilton, Sue. Jack Kirby, 1 vol. 2006. (Comic Book Creators Ser.). (ENG.). 32p. (YA). (gr. 3-6). 27.07 *(978-1-59928-298-5(4))* ABDO Publishing Co.

—Joe Simon, 1 vol. 2006. (Comic Book Creators Ser.). (ENG.). 32p. (YA). (gr. 3-6). 27.07 *(978-1-59928-300-5(X))* ABDO Publishing Co.

—Joe Sinnott, 1 vol. 2006. (Comic Book Creators - 6 Titles Ser.). (ENG.). 32p. (YA). (gr. 3-6). 27.07 *(978-1-59928-299-2(2))* ABDO Publishing Co.

—John Buscema, 1 vol. 2006. (Comic Book Creators - 6 Titles Ser.). (ENG., Illus.). 32p. (YA). (gr. 3-6). 27.07 *(978-1-59928-297-8(6))* ABDO Publishing Co.

—John Romita, Sr, 1 vol. 2006. (Comic Book Creators - 6 Titles Ser.). (ENG.). 32p. (YA). (gr. 3-6). 27.07 *(978-1-59928-302-9(6))* ABDO Publishing Co.

Harat, Christopher. Draw Manga. 2006. 25p. (gr. 5). pap. 16.99 *(978-0-9776925-0-7(7))* Loew-Cornell, Inc.

Hart, Chris. Manga Mania Romance: Drawing Shojo Girls & Bishie Boys. 2008. (Manga Mania(tm) Ser.). (ENG., Illus.). 144p. (gr. 5-18). pap. 19.95 *(978-1-933027-43-2(6)*, Hart, Chris Bks.) Sixth&Spring Bks.

Hart, Christopher. Cartoon Faces: How to Draw Faces, Features & Expressions. 2014. (Cartoon Academy Ser.). (ENG., Illus.). 144p. pap. 19.95 *(978-1-936096-74-9(9))* Sixth&Spring Bks.

—Draw Manga! 2003. (XTreme Art Ser.). (ENG., Illus.). 64p. (J). (gr. 2-4). 7.99 *(978-0-8230-0369-3(8)*, Watson-Guptill) Potter/TenSpeed/Harmony.

—Draw Manga Super Cute Characters Drawing Kit. 2006. (Illus.). 24p. (J). (gr. k-4). 16.99 *(978-0-9776925-3-8(1))* Loew-Cornell, Inc.

—Drawing Animals Shape by Shape: Create Cartoon Animals with Circles, Squares, Rectangles & Triangles. 2015. (Drawing Shape by Shape Ser.). (ENG., Illus.). 176p. (J). (gr. -1). pap. 14.95 *(978-1-936096-95-4(1)*, Hart, Chris Bks.) Sixth&Spring Bks.

—How to Draw Amazing Comic Book Characters Drawing Kit. 2006. (How to Draw Ser.). (Illus.). 24p. (J). (gr. 3-9). 16.99 *(978-0-9776925-4-5(X))* Loew-Cornell, Inc.

—How to Draw Cartoon Animals Drawing Kit. 2006. (How to Draw Ser.). (Illus.). 24p. (J). (gr. 1-7). 16.99 *(978-0-9776925-6-9(6))* Loew-Cornell, Inc.

—Kids Draw Manga Shoujo. 2005. (Kids Draw Ser.). (ENG., Illus.). 64p. (J). (gr. 2-4). pap. 11.95 *(978-0-8230-2622-7(1)*, Watson-Guptill) Potter/TenSpeed/Harmony.

—Magna Martial Arts Masters Drawing Kit. 2006. (Illus.). 24p. (J). (gr. 3-9). 16.99 *(978-0-9776925-1-4(5))* Loew-Cornell, Inc.

—Magna Teen Characters Drawing Kit. 2006. (Illus.). 24p. (J). (gr. 3-9). 16.99 *(978-0-9776925-2-1(3))* Loew-Cornell, Inc.

—Xtreme Art: Ultimate Book of Trace-and-Draw Manga. 2009. (ENG., Illus.). 192p. (J). pap. 21.95 *(978-0-8230-9806-4(0)*, Watson-Guptill) Potter/TenSpeed/Harmony.

—You Can Draw Cartoon Animals: A Simple Step-by-Step Drawing Guide! 2009. (ENG., Illus.). 120p. (J). (gr. 1-3). pap., instr.'s gde. ed. 12.95 *(978-1-60058-611-8(2)*, 1600586112) Quarto Publishing Group USA.

—Young Artists Draw Manga. 2011. (ENG.). 144p. (J). (gr. 3-7). pap. 14.99 *(978-0-8230-2657-9(4)*, Watson-Guptill) Potter/TenSpeed/Harmony.

Hyung, Min-Woo, illus. Justice N Mercy, Vol. 1. 2005. 120p. pap. 39.99 *(978-1-59532-980-6(3))* TOKYOPOP, Inc.

Jones, Richard & Santillan, Jorge. Manga Animals. 2012. (Learn to Draw Manga Ser.). (ENG., Illus.). 32p. (J). (gr. 4-6). pap. 11.75 *(978-1-4488-7943-4(4))*; lib. bdg. 26.50 *(978-1-4488-7872-7(1))* Rosen Publishing Group, Inc., The. (PowerKids Pr.).

—Manga Dragons. 2012. (Learn to Draw Manga Ser.). (ENG., Illus.). 32p. (J). (gr. 4-6). pap. 11.75 *(978-1-4488-7945-8(0))*; lib. bdg. 26.50 *(978-1-4488-7874-1(8))* Rosen Publishing Group, Inc., The. (PowerKids Pr.).

—Manga Martial Arts Figures. 2012. (Learn to Draw Manga Ser.). (ENG., Illus.). 32p. (J). (gr. 4-6). pap. 11.75 *(978-1-4488-7946-5(9))*; lib. bdg. 26.50 *(978-1-4488-7875-8(6))* Rosen Publishing Group, Inc., The. (PowerKids Pr.).

—Manga Superheroes. 2012. (Learn to Draw Manga Ser.). (ENG., Illus.). 32p. (J). (gr. 4-6). pap. 11.75 *(978-1-4488-7948-9(5))*; lib. bdg. 26.50 *(978-1-4488-7877-2(2))* Rosen Publishing Group, Inc., The. (PowerKids Pr.).

Joyce, John. Black John the Bogus Pirate - Cartoon Workbook of Marine Beasts. Joyce, John, illus. 2012. (ENG., Illus.). 20p. (J). *(978-0-9557637-8-6(9))* Sprindrift Pr.

Keely, Jack & Van Osten, Carson. Cartooning 1: Learn the Basics of Cartooning. 2004. (How to Draw & Paint Ser.). (ENG., Illus.). 32p. (gr. k-6). pap. 8.95 *(978-1-56010-487-2(2)*, 1560104872) Quarto Publishing Group USA.

Kovacs, Vic. Get into Cartooning. 2016. (Get-Into-It Guides). (ENG.). 32p. (J). (gr. 3-6). *(978-0-7787-2638-8(X))* Crabtree Publishing Co.

LaBaff, Stephanie. Draw Cartoon People in 4 Easy Steps: Then Write a Story. LaBaff, Tom, illus. 2012. (Drawing in 4 Easy Steps Ser.). 48p. (J). (gr. 3-18). 25.27 *(978-0-7660-3843-1(2))* Enslow Pubs., Inc.

Labaff, Stephanie. Draw Cartoon People in 4 Easy Steps: Then Write a Story. LaBaff, Tom, illus. 2012. (Drawing in 4 Easy Steps Ser.). 48p. (J). (gr. 3-18). pap. 8.95

C D

(978-1-4644-0016-2(4), Enslow Elementary) Enslow Pubs., Inc.

Lee, Frank. Telling the Story in Your Graphic Novel. 2012. (How to Draw Your Own Graphic Novel Ser.). (ENG., Illus.). 32p. (J). (gr. 4-6). pap. 12.30 *(978-1-4488-6453-9(4));* lib. bdg. 26.50 *(978-1-4488-6434-8(8))* Rosen Publishing Group, Inc., The. (PowerKids Pr.).

Lee, Stan. Stan Lee's How to Draw Superheroes. 2013. lib. bdg. 39.15 *(978-0-606-31949-2(2),* Turtleback) Turtleback Bks.

Levy, Barbara Soloff & Drawing Staff. ART START Funny Characters: How to Draw with Simple Shapes. 2010. (Dover How to Draw Ser.). (ENG., Illus.). 64p. (J). (gr. k-3). pap. 4.99 *(978-0-486-47679-7(0))* Dover Pubns., Inc.

Lewis, Siân, et al. Cartwnio gydag Elwyn Ioan. 2005. (WEL.). 48p. pap. *(978-0-903131-18-6(8))* Urdd Gobaith Cymru.

Manga University Staff. Manga Without Borders: Japanese Comic Art from All Four Corners of the World. 2006. (ENG & JPN., Illus.). 64p. pap. 14.99 *(978-4-921205-05-8(1),* 9784921205058) Japanime Co., Ltd. JPN. Dist: Diamond Comic Distributors, Inc.

Marvis, Barbara J. Charles Schulz. 2004. (Robbie Reader Ser.). (Illus.). 32p. (J). (gr. 1-4). lib. bdg. 25.70 *(978-1-58415-289-7(3))* Mitchell Lane Pubs., Inc.

Milbourne, A. Drawing Cartoons. 2004. (Art School Ser.). (ENG., Illus.). 64p. (J). pap. 8.99 *(978-0-7945-0372-7(1))* EDC Publishing.

Milbourne, Anna. Drawing Cartoons: Internet-Linked. McCafferty, Jan, illus. 2006. (Art School Ser.). 64p. (J). (gr. 5). lib. bdg. 16.95 *(978-1-58086-507-4(0))* EDC Publishing.

Miller, Raymond H. Matt Groening. 2005. (Inventors & Creators Ser.). (ENG., Illus.). 48p. (gr. 4-8). 27.00 *(978-0-7377-3158-3(3),* Greenhaven Pr., Inc.) Cengage Gale.

Navarra, Nino, illus. How to Draw Nickelodeon Teenage Mutant Ninja Turtles: /step-By-Step Illustrations by Niño Navarra. 2014. 64p. (J). *(978-1-939581-17-4(6))* Quarto Publishing Group USA.

Nishida, Masaki. Drawing Manga Animals. (How to Draw Manga Ser.). 24p. 2009. (gr. 3-3). 47.90 *(978-1-61513-437-3(9),* PowerKids Pr.) 2007. (Illus.). (J). (gr. 4-7). lib. bdg. 25.25 *(978-1-4042-3846-6(8))* Rosen Publishing Group, Inc., The.

—Drawing Manga Dinosaurs. (How to Draw Manga Ser.). 24p. 2009. (gr. 3-3). 47.90 *(978-1-61513-438-0(7),* PowerKids Pr.) 2007. (Illus.). (J). (gr. -1-3). lib. bdg. 25.25 *(978-1-4042-3845-9(X))* Rosen Publishing Group, Inc., The.

—Drawing Manga Insects. (How to Draw Manga Ser.). 24p. (gr. 3-3). 2009. 47.90 *(978-1-61513-439-7(5),* PowerKids Pr.) 2007. (Illus.). (J). lib. bdg. 25.25 *(978-1-4042-3847-3(6))* Rosen Publishing Group, Inc., The.

—Drawing Manga Martial Arts Figures. (How to Draw Manga Ser.). 24p. (gr. 3-3). 2009. 47.90 *(978-1-61513-440-3(9),* PowerKids Pr.) 2007. (Illus.). (J). lib. bdg. 25.25 *(978-1-4042-3850-3(6))* Rosen Publishing Group, Inc., The.

—Drawing Manga Medieval Castles & Knights. 2007. (How to Draw Manga Ser.: Vol. 4). (Illus.). 24p. (J). (gr. 4-7). lib. bdg. 25.25 *(978-1-4042-3849-7(2))* Rosen Publishing Group, Inc., The.

—Drawing Manga Vehicles. (How to Draw Manga Ser.). 24p. 2009. (gr. 3-3). 47.90 *(978-1-61513-442-7(5),* PowerKids Pr.) 2007. (Illus.). (J). (gr. 5-8). lib. bdg. 25.25 *(978-1-4042-3848-0(4))* Rosen Publishing Group, Inc., The.

Nobleman, Marc Tyler. Bill the Boy Wonder: The Secret Co-Creator of Batman. Templeton, Ty, illus. 2012. (J). pap. 17.95 *(978-1-58089-290-2(6));* (ENG.). 48p. (gr. 3-7). 17.95 *(978-1-58089-289-6(2))* Charlesbridge Publishing, Inc.

Orr, Tamra. Manga Artists. 2008. (Extreme Careers Ser.). (Illus.). 64p. (YA). (gr. 5-9). lib. bdg. 31.95 *(978-1-4042-1854-3(8))* Rosen Publishing Group, Inc., The.

Orr, Tamra B. Manga Artists. 2009. (Extreme Careers Ser.). 64p. (gr. 5-5). 58.50 *(978-1-61512-400-8(4),* Rosen Reference) Rosen Publishing Group, Inc., The.

Pinder, Andrew. Icky, Sticky, Slimy Doodles: Gross, Full-Color Pictures to Complete & Create. 2013. (ENG., Illus.). 160p. (J). (gr. -1-17). pap. 12.95 *(978-0-7624-4972-9(1),* Running Pr. Kids) Running Pr. Bk. Pubs.

Platten, Carl. Once upon a Dragon: A Colouring Book. 2012. 48p. 24.99 *(978-1-4691-9369-4(8));* pap. 15.99 *(978-1-4691-9368-7(X))* Xlibris Corp.

Powell, Marc & Neal, David. How to Draw Action Manga. 2015. (Ultimate Manga Ser.). (ENG., Illus.). 32p. (J). (gr. 3-4). pap. 11.75 *(978-1-4994-1138-6(3),* 1391131, PowerKids Pr.) Rosen Publishing Group, Inc., The.

—How to Draw Cute Manga. 2015. (Ultimate Manga Ser.). (ENG., Illus.). 32p. (J). (gr. 3-4). pap. 11.75 *(978-1-4994-1139-3(1),* 1391132, PowerKids Pr.) Rosen Publishing Group, Inc., The.

—How to Draw Dramatic Manga. 2015. (Ultimate Manga Ser.). (ENG., Illus.). 32p. (J). (gr. 3-4). pap. 11.75 *(978-1-4994-1141-6(3),* 1391133, PowerKids Pr.) Rosen Publishing Group, Inc., The.

Publications International Ltd. Staff, ed. Disney Pixar: School Memory Keeper. 2011. 48p. (J). spiral bd. 16.98 *(978-1-4508-1137-8(X))* Phoenix International Publications, Inc.

QEB Learn Art National Book Stores Edition: Cartooning. 2006. (J). per. *(978-1-59566-279-8(0))* QEB Publishing Inc.

Rechlin, Ted. What to Doodle? Manga! 2011. (Dover Doodle Bks.). (ENG., Illus.). 64p. (J). (gr. 2-5). pap. 5.99 *(978-0-486-48290-3(1))* Dover Pubns., Inc.

Robins, Deri. Cartooning. 2004. (QEB Learn Art Ser.). (Illus.). 32p. (J). lib. bdg. 18.95 *(978-1-59566-044-2(5))* QEB Publishing Inc.

Roche, Art. Art for Kids: Comic Strips - Create Your Own Comic Strips from Start to Finish. 2011. (Art for Kids Ser.). (ENG., Illus.). 112p. (J). (gr. 3-18). pap. 9.95 *(978-1-4027-8474-3(0))* Sterling Publishing Co., Inc.

—Art for Kids: Cartooning: The Only Cartooning Book You'll Ever Need to Be the Artist You've Always Wanted to Be. 2010. (Art for Kids Ser.). (ENG., Illus.). 112p. (J). (gr. 3-12). pap. 9.95 *(978-1-4027-7515-4(6))* Sterling Publishing Co., Inc.

Running Press Staff. The Peanuts Gang Loves to Doodle: Create & Complete Full-Color Pictures with Charlie Brown, Snoopy, & Friends. 2013. (ENG., Illus.). 128p. (J). (gr. -1-17). pap. 12.95 *(978-0-7624-5093-0(2),* Running Pr. Kids) Running Pr. Bk. Pubs.

Ryan, Nellie, et al. Gorgeous Doodles: Pretty, Full-Color Pictures to Create & Complete. 2013. (ENG., Illus.). 128p. (J). (gr. -1-17). pap. 12.95 *(978-0-7624-4971-2(3),* Running Pr. Kids) Running Pr. Bk. Pubs.

Saddleback Educational Publishing Staff, ed. Walt Disney, 1 vol. unabr. ed. 2008. (Graphic Biographies Ser.). (ENG., Illus.). 25p. (YA). (gr. 9-12). pap. 7.95 *(978-1-59905-230-4(X))* Saddleback Educational Publishing, Inc.

Sage, Alison. What Is CGI? Band 06/Orange. Stuart, Jon, illus. 2007. (Collins Big Cat Ser.). (ENG.). 24p. (J). (gr. 1-2). pap. 6.99 *(978-0-00-718667-9(3))* HarperCollins Pubs. Ltd. GBR. Dist: Independent Pubs. Group.

Sautter, Aaron. How to Draw Comic Heroes, 1 vol. Martin, Cynthia, illus. 2007. (Drawing Cool Stuff Ser.). (ENG.). 32p. (gr. 3-4). 27.99 *(978-1-4296-0074-3(8),* Edge Bks.) Capstone Press of Coughlan Cos.

Singh, Asavari. How to Draw the Craziest, Creepiest Characters, 1 vol. James, Martin et al, illus. 2011. (Drawing Ser.). (ENG.). 48p. (gr. 3-4). lib. bdg. 31.99 *(978-1-4296-6595-7(5))* Capstone Press of Coughlan Cos.

—How to Draw the Most Exciting, Awesome Manga, 1 vol. James, Martin et al, illus. 2011. (Drawing Ser.). (ENG.). 48p. (gr. 3-4). lib. bdg. 31.99 *(978-1-4296-6593-3(9))* Capstone Press of Coughlan Cos.

Southgate, Anna & Li, Yishan. Drawing Manga Mecha, Weapons, & Wheels. 2012. (Manga Mania Ser.). (ENG., Illus.). 80p. (YA). (gr. 5-8). 33.25 *(978-1-4488-9242-6(2));* pap. 14.05 *(978-1-4488-9265-5(1))* Rosen Publishing Group, Inc., The. (Rosen Reference).

—Drawing Manga Men. 2012. (Manga Mania Ser.). (ENG., Illus.). 80p. (YA). (gr. 5-8). 33.25 *(978-1-4488-9240-2(6));* pap. 14.05 *(978-1-4488-9261-7(9))* Rosen Publishing Group, Inc., The. (Rosen Reference).

—Drawing Manga Women. 2012. (Manga Mania Ser.). (ENG., Illus.). 80p. (YA). (gr. 5-8). 33.25 *(978-1-4488-9239-6(2));* pap. 14.05 *(978-1-4488-9259-4(7))* Rosen Publishing Group, Inc., The. (Rosen Reference).

Southgate, Anna & Sparrow, Keith. Drawing Manga Expressions & Poses. 2011. (J). 84.30 *(978-1-4488-4808-9(3));* pap. 14.05 *(978-1-4488-4804-1(0));* lib. bdg. 33.25 *(978-1-4488-4800-3(8))* Rosen Publishing Group, Inc., The. (Rosen Reference).

—Drawing Manga Weapons, Vehicles, & Accessories. 2011. (Illus.). 80p. (J). 84.30 *(978-1-4488-4809-6(1));* pap. 14.05 *(978-1-4488-4805-8(9));* lib. bdg. 33.25 *(978-1-4488-4801-0(6))* Rosen Publishing Group, Inc., The. (Rosen Reference).

Stowell, Louie. Write & Draw Your Own Comics IR. 2015. (Write Your Own Bks.). (ENG.). (J). (gr. 5-12). 15.99 *(978-0-7945-2121-9(5),* Usborne) EDC Publishing.

Sturm, James & Arnold, Andrew. Adventures in Cartooning: Characters in Action. 2013. (Adventures in Cartooning Ser.). (J). lib. bdg. 22.10 *(978-0-606-32306-2(6),* Turtleback) Turtleback Bks.

—Adventures in Cartooning Christmas Special. 2012. (Adventures in Cartooning Ser.). (J). lib. bdg. 20.85 *(978-0-606-26709-0(3),* Turtleback) Turtleback Bks.

Sturm, James, et al. Christmas Special! Sturm, James, illus. 2012. (Adventures in Cartooning Ser.). (ENG., Illus.). 64p. (J). (gr. 1-5). pap. 9.99 *(978-1-59643-730-2(8),* 9781596437302, First Second Bks.) Roaring Brook Pr.

—Sleepless Knight. 2015. (Adventures in Cartooning Ser.). (ENG., Illus.). 40p. (J). (gr. -1-k). 14.99 *(978-1-59643-651-0(4),* 9781596436510, First Second Bks.) Roaring Brook Pr.

Takarai, Saori. Manga Moods: 40 Faces + 80 Phrases. 2010. (ENG., Illus.). 96p. (YA). 9.99 *(978-4-921205-13-3(2),* 9784921205133) Japanime Co., Ltd. JPN. Dist: Diamond Comic Distributors, Inc.

Tallarico, Tony, Sr. & Drawing Staff. Drawing & Cartooning Monsters: A Step-by-Step Guide for the Aspiring Monster-Maker. 2010. (Dover How to Draw Ser.). (ENG., Illus.). 96p. (J). (gr. 3-6). pap. 6.99 *(978-0-486-47278-2(7))* Dover Pubns., Inc.

Tatchell, Judy. How to Draw Cartoons & Caricatures. Bave, Terry et al, illus. rev. ed. 2006. (How to Draw Ser.). 40p. (J). (gr. 4-7). pap. 5.99 *(978-0-7945-1374-0(3),* Usborne) EDC Publishing.

Taylor, Des. Cartoons & Manga. 2012. (Master This! Ser.). (Illus.). 32p. (J). lib. bdg. 25.25 *(978-1-4488-5283-3(8),* PowerKids Pr.) Rosen Publishing Group, Inc., The.

Top That Publishing Staff, ed. Shadow on Wall. 2004. (Wicked Tattoos Ser.). (Illus.). 16p. (J). pap. *(978-1-84510-112-1(X))* Top That! Publishing PLC.

Toy Story - Learn to Draw. 2013. (Learn to Draw Ser.: 4). 32p. (gr. -1-2). 12.99 *(978-1-62588-923-2(2))* Black Rabbit Bks.

Ursell, Martin. You Can Draw Cartoons: A Step-By-Step Guide to Drawing Great Cartoons. 2014. (You Can Draw Ser.). (ENG., Illus.). 32p. (J). (gr. 1-4). pap. 7.99 *(978-1-902915-14-2(3))* B Small Publishing GBR. Dist: Independent Pubs. Group.

Uschan, Michael V. Comic Art. 2012. (Eye on Art Ser.). (ENG., Illus.). 128p. (J). (gr. 7-10). lib. bdg. 39.40 *(978-1-4205-0862-8(8),* Lucent Bks.) Cengage Gale.

Visca, Curt. How to Draw Cartoon Careers. 2009. (Kid's Guide to Drawing Ser.). 24p. (gr. 3-3). 47.90 *(978-1-61511-012-4(7),* PowerKids Pr.) Rosen Publishing Group, Inc., The.

—How to Draw Cartoon Fish. 2003. (Kid's Guide to Drawing Ser.). (Illus.). 24p. (J). lib. bdg. 25.25 *(978-0-8239-6159-7(1),* PowerKids Pr.) Rosen Publishing Group, Inc., The.

—How to Draw Cartoon Holiday Symbols. 2009. (Kid's Guide to Drawing Ser.). 24p. (gr. 3-3). 47.90 *(978-1-61511-015-5(1),* PowerKids Pr.) Rosen Publishing Group, Inc., The.

—How to Draw Cartoon Spacecraft & Astronauts in Action. 2009. (Kid's Guide to Drawing Ser.). 24p. (gr. 3-3). 47.90 *(978-1-61511-019-3(4),* PowerKids Pr.) Rosen Publishing Group, Inc., The.

—How to Draw Cartoon Symbols of the United States. 2009. (Kid's Guide to Drawing Ser.). 24p. (gr. 3-3). 47.90 *(978-1-61511-020-9(8),* PowerKids Pr.) Rosen Publishing Group, Inc., The.

—How to Draw Cartoon Symbols of the Wild West. 2009. (Kid's Guide to Drawing Ser.). 24p. (gr. 3-3). 47.90 *(978-1-61511-021-6(6),* PowerKids Pr.) Rosen Publishing Group, Inc., The.

Visca, Curt & Visca, Kelley. How to Draw Cartoon Careers. 2004. (Kid's Guide to Drawing Ser.). (Illus.). 24p. (YA). (gr. 2-5). lib. bdg. 25.25 *(978-0-8239-6725-4(5))* Rosen Publishing Group, Inc., The.

—How to Draw Cartoon Crustaceans. 2003. (Kid's Guide to Drawing Ser.). (Illus.). 24p. (J). lib. bdg. 25.25 *(978-0-8239-6158-0(3),* PowerKids Pr.) Rosen Publishing Group, Inc., The.

—How to Draw Cartoon Holiday Symbols. 2004. (Kid's Guide to Drawing Ser.). (Illus.). 24p. (YA). (gr. 2-5). lib. bdg. 25.25 *(978-0-8239-6726-1(3))* Rosen Publishing Group, Inc., The.

—How to Draw Cartoon Rodents. 2003. (Kid's Guide to Drawing Ser.). (Illus.). 24p. (J). lib. bdg. 25.25 *(978-0-8239-6161-0(3),* PowerKids Pr.) Rosen Publishing Group, Inc., The.

—How to Draw Cartoon Spacecraft & Astronauts in Action. 2004. (Kid's Guide to Drawing Ser.). (Illus.). 24p. (J). lib. bdg. 25.25 *(978-0-8239-6729-2(8),* PowerKids Pr.) Rosen Publishing Group, Inc., The.

—How to Draw Cartoon Symbols of the United States. 2004. (Kid's Guide to Drawing Ser.). (Illus.). 24p. (J). lib. bdg. 25.25 *(978-0-8239-6727-8(1),* PowerKids Pr.) Rosen Publishing Group, Inc., The.

—How to Draw Cartoon Symbols of the Wild West. 2004. (Kid's Guide to Drawing Ser.). (Illus.). 24p. (J). lib. bdg. 25.25 *(978-0-8239-6728-5(X),* PowerKids Pr.) Rosen Publishing Group, Inc., The.

Visca, Kelley & Visca, Curt. How to Draw Cartoon Birds. 2003. (Kid's Guide to Drawing Ser.). (Illus.). 24p. (J). lib. bdg. 25.25 *(978-0-8239-6156-6(7),* PowerKids Pr.) Rosen Publishing Group, Inc., The.

Visca, Kelly. How to Draw Cartoon Birds. 2009. (Kid's Guide to Drawing Ser.). 24p. (gr. 3-3). 47.90 *(978-1-61511-011-7(9),* PowerKids Pr.) Rosen Publishing Group, Inc., The.

—How to Draw Cartoon Crustaceans. 2009. (Kid's Guide to Drawing Ser.). 24p. (gr. 3-3). 47.90 *(978-1-61511-013-1(5),* PowerKids Pr.) Rosen Publishing Group, Inc., The.

—How to Draw Cartoon Fish. 2009. (Kid's Guide to Drawing Ser.). 24p. (gr. 3-3). 47.90 *(978-1-61511-014-8(3),* PowerKids Pr.) Rosen Publishing Group, Inc., The.

—How to Draw Cartoon Rodents. 2009. (Kid's Guide to Drawing Ser.). 24p. (gr. 3-3). 47.90 *(978-1-61511-018-6(6),* PowerKids Pr.) Rosen Publishing Group, Inc., The.

Walter Foster Creative Team. Learn to Draw the Best of Nickelodeon: Featuring Characters from Your Favorite TV Shows, Including SpongeBob SquarePants, the Teenage Mutant Ninja Turtles, the Fairly OddParents, & More! 2013. (Licensed Learn to Draw Ser.). (ENG., Illus.). 64p. (J). (gr. 1-3). pap. 9.95 *(978-1-60058-343-8(1),* 1600583431) Quarto Publishing Group USA.

Walter Foster Creative Team, ed. How to Draw Transformers. 2008. 32p. pap. 5.95 *(978-1-60058-119-9(6))* Quarto Publishing Group USA.

Walter Foster Jr. Creative Team. Learn to Draw Angry Birds: Bad Piggies: Featuring All Your Favorite Crafty, Crazy Pigs, Including King Pig, Foreman Pig, Corporal Pig, & More! 2014. (Licensed Learn to Draw Ser.). (ENG., Illus.). 64p. (J). (gr. 1-17). pap. 9.95 *(978-1-60058-448-0(9))* Quarto Publishing Group USA.

Whitten, Samantha & Lee, Jeannie, illus. How to Draw Manga Chibis & Cute Critters. 2013. (Walter Foster Studio Ser.). 128p. (J). (gr. 3-8). 35.65 *(978-1-936309-93-1(9))* Quarto Publishing Group USA.

Zalme, Ron, illus. How to Draw Sinnoh Superstars. 2010. 32p. (J). pap. *(978-0-545-22625-7(2))* Scholastic, Inc.

CARTOONS, ANIMATED

see Animated Films

CARTOONS AND COMICS

see also Pictures; Wit And Humor, Pictorial

Aaron, Jason. Wolverine & the X-Men by Jason Aaron - Volume 3. 2013. (ENG., Illus.). 112p. (J). (gr. 4-17). pap. 16.99 *(978-0-7851-6000-7(0),* Marvel Pr.) Disney Publishing Worldwide.

Abadzis, Nick. Laika. 2014. (YA). lib. bdg. 22.10 *(978-0-606-36130-9(8))* Turtleback Bks.

—Pigs Might Fly. Dye, Jerel, illus. 2017. (Pigs Might Fly Ser.). (ENG.). 208p. (J). pap. 15.99 *(978-1-62672-086-2(X),* 9781626720862, First Second Bks.) Roaring Brook Pr.

Abdo, Kenny. Comic Relief, 1 vol. Doucet, Bob, illus. 2013. (Haven't Got a Clue! Ser.). (ENG.). 80p. (J). (gr. 3-6). lib. bdg. 27.07 *(978-1-61641-951-6(2),* Calico Chapter Bks) Magic Wagon.

Abdo Publishing. Amelia Rules! Set 2, 1 vol. 2013. (Amelia Rules! Set 2 Ser.: 6). (ENG.). 36p. (J). (gr. 3-6). lib. bdg. 145.26 *(978-1-61479-067-9(1),* Essential Library) ABDO Publishing Co.

—Nascar Heroes, 1 vol. 2013. (NASCAR Heroes Ser.: 8). (ENG.). 32p. (J). (gr. 3-9). lib. bdg. 216.56 *(978-1-61783-659-6(1),* SportsZone) ABDO Publishing Co.

ABDO Publishing. Scooby-Doo Comic Readers. 2016. (Scooby-Doo Comic Readers Ser.: 6). (ENG.). 32p. (J). (gr. k-3). lib. bdg. 145.26 *(978-1-61479-450-9(2),* Graphic Planet) Magic Wagon.

Abdo Publishing. Scooby-Doo Graphic Novels Set 3, 1 vol. 2013. (Scooby-Doo Graphic Novels Set 3 Ser.: 6). (ENG.). 24p. (J). (gr. 2-6). lib. bdg. 145.26 *(978-1-61479-048-8(5),* Essential Library) ABDO Publishing Co.

—Scooby-Doo Mysteries Set 2, 1 vol. 2013. (Scooby-Doo Mysteries Set 2 Ser.: 6). (ENG.). 64p. (J). (gr. 3-6). lib. bdg. 145.26 *(978-1-61479-041-9(8),* Essential Library) ABDO Publishing Co.

—Skylanders: The Kaos Trap. 2015. (Skylanders: the Kaos Trap Ser.: Vol. 4). (ENG.). 24p. (J). (gr. 2-5). lib. bdg. 96.84 *(978-1-61479-384-7(0))* ABDO Publishing Co.

—Star Wars Digests Set 2, 1 vol. 2013. (Star Wars Digests Set 2 Ser.: 4). (ENG.). 80p. (J). (gr. 4-8). lib. bdg. 108.28 *(978-1-61479-055-6(8),* Essential Library) ABDO Publishing Co.

ABDO Publishing Company Staff. Archie Set of 6, 6 vols., Set. 2007. (Archie Ser.). (ENG., Illus.). 80p. 96.84 *(978-1-59961-257-7(7))* Spotlight.

—Betty & Veronica, 6 vols., Set. 2007. (Betty & Veronica Ser.). (Illus.). 80p. 145.26 *(978-1-59961-264-5(X))* Spotlight.

—Hardy Boys - 3 Titles. 2005. (Hardy Boys Ser.). (ENG., Illus.). 88p. (gr. 3-8). 72.63 *(978-1-59961-060-3(4))* Spotlight.

—Jughead with Archie - 6 Titles, 6 vols., Set. 2007. (Jughead with Archie Ser.). (ENG., Illus.). 80p. 145.26 *(978-1-59961-271-3(2))* Spotlight.

—Kid Squad Saves the World, 1 vol. 2014. (Kid Squad Saves the World Ser.: 6). (ENG.). 112p. (J). (gr. 8-12). lib. bdg. 162.42 *(978-1-62402-036-0(4),* Calico Chapter Bks) Magic Wagon.

—Mr. & Mrs. Green - 4 Titles. 2007. (Mr. & Mrs. Green Ser.). (ENG., Illus.). 70p. 108.28 *(978-1-59961-299-7(2))* Spotlight.

—Storm Cliff Stables, 1 vol. 2014. (Storm Cliff Stables Ser.: 4). (ENG.). 112p. (J). (gr. 7-11). lib. bdg. 108.28 *(978-1-62402-048-3(8),* Calico Chapter Bks) Magic Wagon.

ABDO Publishing Company Staff & Howard, Lee. Scooby-Doo Comic Storybook. Alcadia SNC Staff, illus. 2014. (Scooby-Doo Comic Storybook Ser.: 4). (ENG.). 32p. (J). (gr. 5-9). lib. bdg. 96.84 *(978-1-61479-280-2(1),* Graphic Planet) Magic Wagon.

ABDO Publishing Company Staff & Wood, Brian. Star Wars: In the Shadow of Yavin. D'Anda, Carlos, illus. 2014. (Star Wars: in the Shadow of Yavin Ser.: 6). (ENG.). 24p. (J). (gr. 9-14). lib. bdg. 145.26 *(978-1-61479-285-7(2),* Graphic Planet) Magic Wagon.

Abirached, Zeina. I Remember Beirut. 2014. (ENG.). 96p. pap. 9.95 *(978-1-4677-4458-4(1),* Graphic Universe™) Lerner Publishing Group.

Abnett, Dan. This Ghost Is Toast! Williams, Anthony, illus. 2007. (Real Ghostbusters Ser.). (ENG.). 96p. per. 8.95 *(978-1-84576-143-1(X),* Titan Bks. Ltd. GBR. Dist: Penguin Random Hse. LLC.

Abnett, Dan & Lanning, Andy. Marvel's Guardians of the Galaxy Prelude. Alves, Wellington et al, illus. 2014. (ENG.). 168p. (J). (gr. 4-17). pap. 14.99 *(978-0-7851-5410-5(8))* Marvel Worldwide, Inc.

—Penguins of Madagascar: The Great Drain Robbery. 2015. (ENG., Illus.). 112p. (J). (gr. 1-4). pap. 14.99 *(978-1-78276-695-7(2))* Titan Bks. Ltd. GBR. Dist: Penguin Random Hse. LLC.

—Shrek & Kung Fu Panda, Vol. 2. 2016. (ENG., Illus.). 64p. (J). (gr. 1-4). pap. 6.99 *(978-1-78276-247-8(7))* Titan Bks. Ltd. GBR. Dist: Penguin Random Hse. LLC.

Abnett, Dan, et al. Dreamworks Classics, Shrek & Madagascar, Game On, Vol. 3. Gallant, S., illus. 2016. (ENG.). 64p. (J). (gr. 3-7). pap. 6.99 *(978-1-78276-248-5(5))* Titan Bks. Ltd. GBR. Dist: Penguin Random Hse. LLC.

—Shrek & Madagascar, Vol. 1. 2015. (ENG., Illus.). 64p. (J). (gr. 1-4). pap. 6.99 *(978-1-78276-246-1(9))* Titan Bks. Ltd. GBR. Dist: Penguin Random Hse. LLC.

Aboff, Marcie & Gray-Wilburn, Renée. First Graphics: Wild Earth. Sotirovski, Aleksandar, illus. 2012. (First Graphics: Wild Earth Ser.). (ENG.). 24p. (gr. 1-2). pap. 25.16 *(978-1-4296-8374-6(0));* pap. 142.80 *(978-1-4296-8375-3(9));* lib. bdg. 71.97 *(978-1-4296-8146-9(2))* Capstone Press of Coughlan Cos.

Acampora, Michael V. Battle of the Blue Lanterns, 1 vol. Schoening, Dan, illus. 2011. (Green Lantern Ser.). (ENG.). 56p. (gr. 2-3). pap. 4.95 *(978-1-4342-3085-0(6));* lib. bdg. 26.65 *(978-1-4342-2608-2(5))* Stone Arch Bks. (DC Super Heroes).

Achi, Taro. Mamoru the Shadow Protector Volume 1. 2008. (ENG., Illus.). 176p. (YA). pap. 9.95 *(978-1-59796-183-7(3))* DrMaster Pubns. Inc.

Aclin, Justin. Akaneiro. Marshall, Dave, ed. Lolos, Vasilis & Atiyeh, Michael, illus. 2013. (ENG.). 72p. 14.99 *(978-1-61655-194-0(1))* Dark Horse Comics.

Adams, Matthew R. Kord & Harley. O'Reilly, Sean Patrick, ed. 2011. (Illus.). 50p. (YA). pap. 19.95 *(978-0-9809204-7-5(7))* Arcana Studio, Inc.

Adamson, Thomas K. The First Moon Landing, 1 vol. Purcell, Gordon & Beatty, Terry, illus. 2006. (Graphic History Ser.). (ENG.). 32p. (gr. 3-4). per. 8.10 *(978-0-7368-9654-2(6),* Graphic Library) Capstone Press of Coughlan Cos.

Adaptor. Graphic Horror Set 3. 2014. (Graphic Horror Set 3 Ser.: 6). 32p. (J). (gr. 5-8). lib. bdg. 171.00 *(978-1-62402-012-4(7),* Graphic Planet) Magic Wagon.

The Adirondack. 2006. (YA). per. *(978-1-59872-344-1(8))* Instant Pub.

Adrien, Gilles & Broders, Alain. The Planet of the Giant. Élyum Studio, illus. 2013. (Little Prince Ser.: 9). (ENG.). 56p. (J). (gr. 4-8). pap. 7.95 *(978-1-4677-1518-8(2));* lib. bdg. 26.60 *(978-0-7613-8759-6(5))* Lerner Publishing Group. (Graphic Universe™).

Aguirre, Jorge. Dragons Beware! 2015. (Chronicles of Claudette Ser.). (ENG., Illus.). 160p. (J). (gr. 2-5). pap. 14.99 *(978-1-59643-878-1(9),* 9781596438781, First Second Bks.) Roaring Brook Pr.

—Giants Beware! Rosado, Rafael, illus. 2012. (Chronicles of Claudette Ser.). (ENG.). 208p. (J). (gr. 2-5). pap. 15.99 *(978-1-59643-582-7(8),* 9781596435827, First Second Bks.) Roaring Brook Pr.

Aguirre-Sacasa, Roberto. Archie Meets Glee. Parent, Dan, illus. 2013. (Archie & Friends All-Stars Ser.: 20). (ENG.). 112p. (gr. 5). pap. 12.99 *(978-1-936975-45-7(9),* Archie Comics) Archie Comic Pubns., Inc.

—Chilling Adventures of Sabrina. Hack, Robert, illus. 2016. (Chilling Adventures of Sabrina Ser.). (ENG.). 176p. pap. 17.99 *(978-1-62738-987-7(3))* Archie Comic Pubns., Inc.

Aikawa, Yu. Dark Edge. 2005. (Dark Edge Ser.). (Illus.). (YA). Vol. 3. (ENG.). 200p. pap. 9.95 *(978-1-59796-030-4(6))* Vol. 4. 208p. pap. 9.95 *(978-1-59796-024-3(1))* DrMaster Pubns. Inc.

—Dark Edge, Vol. 6. Aikawa, Yu, illus. 2006. (Dark Edge Ser.). (ENG., Illus.). 200p. (YA). pap. 9.95 *(978-1-59796-026-7(8))* DrMaster Pubns. Inc.

Akira, Shouko. Times Two. Akira, Shouko, illus. 2005. (Times Two Ser.). (ENG., Illus.). 200p. (YA). pap. 9.99 *(978-1-59116-736-5(1))* Viz Media.

Albright, Kendra S. & Gavigan, Karen W., eds. AIDS in the Endzone. Petrulis, Sarah, illus. 2014. (Young Palmetto Bks.). (ENG.). 40p. pap. 12.95 *(978-1-61117-424-3(4))* Univ. of South Carolina Pr.

Alex, Ben. Great Bible Stories. 2010. (ENG., Illus.). 37p. (gr. k-5). pap. 5.95 *(978-87-7247-026-9(7))* Scandinavia Publishing Hse. DNK. Dist: Destiny Image Pubs.

Alexander. Phonic Comics: Princess School - Level 1. 2011. (ENG., Illus.). 24p. (J). (gr. 1-17). pap. 3.99 (978-1-60169-110-1(6)) Innovative Kids.

Alixe, Pascal & Klein, Nic, illus. The Iron Nail - Captain America, Vol. 4. 2014. (ENG.). 144p. (J). (gr. 4-17). 24.99 (978-0-7851-8953-4(X)) Marvel Worldwide, Inc.

Allison, John. Bad Machinery Volume 1 - Pocket Edition: The Case of the Team Spirit. 2017. (ENG., Illus.). 136p. (J). pap. 9.99 (978-1-62010-387-6(7), 9781620103876) Oni Pr., Inc.

Allison, John. Bad Machinery Volume 2: The Case of the Good Boy. 2014. (ENG., Illus.). 136p. (YA). pap. 19.99 (978-1-62010-114-8(9), 9781620101148) Oni Pr., Inc.

Almand, M. Nicholas. Orphan Blade. 2014. (ENG., Illus.). 160p. (YA). pap. 19.99 (978-1-62010-120-9(3), 9781620101209) Oni Pr., Inc.

Amano, Shiro. Chain of Memories, Vol. 2. 2nd rev. ed. 2007. (Kingdom Hearts Ser.). (Illus.). 232p. (gr. 4-7). pap. 9.99 (978-1-59816-638-5(7), Tokyopop Kids) TOKYOPOP, Inc.

Amara, Philip. So, You Want to Be a Comic Book Artist? The Ultimate Guide on How to Break into Comics! 2012. (Be What You Want Ser.). (ENG., Illus.). 176p. (J). (gr. 3-7). 17.99 (978-1-58270-358-9(2)); pap. 9.99 (978-1-58270-357-2(4)) Aladdin/Beyond Words.

Ambrose, Adrianne. What I Learned from Being a Cheerleader. 2010. 202p. pap. 12.95 (978-1-935661-94-8(9), Bell Bridge Bks.) BelleBks., Inc.

Ambrosio, Stefano. Mouse Magic. Pastrovicchio, Lorenzo, illus. 2010. (ENG.). 112p. (J). 24.99 (978-1-60886-550-5(9)); Vol. 1. pap. 9.99 (978-1-60886-541-3(X)) Boom! Studios.

—Wizards of Mickey - Grand Tournament, Vol. 2. Pastrovicchio, Lorenzo & Magic Eye Studios, illus. 2010. (Wizards of Mickey Ser.). (ENG.). 128p. (J). (gr. 3-6). pap. 9.99 (978-1-60886-564-2(9)) Boom! Studios.

Ameet Studio, Ameet. The Hands of Time. 2017. (LEGO Ninjago Ser.). (ENG.). 32p. (J). (gr. 2-5). pap. 8.99 (978-1-338-11368-6(2)) Scholastic, Inc.

—The Otherworldly League! 2016. (LEGO DC Super Heroes Ser.: Bk. 1). (ENG.). 32p. (J). (gr. 2-5). pap., act. bk. ed. 8.99 (978-1-338-04744-8(2)) Scholastic, Inc.

American Graphic. 2011. (American Graphic Ser.). (ENG.). 32p. (gr. 3-4). pap. 381.60 (978-1-4296-7344-0(3), Graphic Library) Capstone Press of Coughlan Cos.

American Graphic, 8 vols., Set. Incl. Bambino: The Story of Babe Ruth's Legendary 1927 Season. Yomtov, Nelson. Foley, Tim, illus. 2010. lib. bdg. 30.65 (978-1-4296-5473-9(2)); Biography of Malcolm X. Gunderson, Jessica. Hayden, Seitu, illus. 2010. lib. bdg. 30.65 (978-1-4296-5471-5(6)); Elvis: A Graphic Novel. Collins, Terry. Melcher, Michele, illus. 2010. lib. bdg. 30.65 (978-1-4296-5476-0(7)); Obama: The Historic Election of America's 44th President. Biskup, Agnieszka. Hayden, Seitu, illus. 2011. lib. bdg. 30.65 (978-1-4296-6016-7(3)); Robert E. Lee: The Story of the Great Confederate General. Collins, Terry. Mallea, Cristian, illus. 2010. lib. bdg. 30.65 (978-1-4296-5475-3(9)); Sarah Palin: Political Rebel. Yomtov, Nelson. D'Ottavi, Francesca, illus. 2011. lib. bdg. 30.65 (978-1-4296-6018-1(X)); Thunder Rolling down the Mountain: The Story of Chief Joseph & the Nez Perce. Biskup, Agnieszka. Zimmerman, Rusty, illus. 2010. lib. bdg. 30.65 (978-1-4296-5472-2(4)); (gr. 3-4). (American Graphic Ser.). (ENG.). 32p. 2011. Set lib. bdg. 214.55 (978-1-4296-6585-8(8), Graphic Library) Capstone Press of Coughlan Cos.

Amstel, Marsha. The Horse-Riding Adventure of Sybil Ludington, Revolutionary War Messenger. Hammond, Ted & Carbajal, Richard Pimentel, illus. 2011. (History's Kid Heroes Set III Ser.). pap. 51.02 (978-0-7613-7636-1(4), Graphic Universe™) Lerner Publishing Group.

—The Horse-Riding Adventure of Sybil Ludington, Revolutionary War Messenger. Hammond, Ted & Carbajal, Richard, illus. 2011. (History's Kid Heroes Ser.). (ENG.). 32p. (gr. 3-5). 26.60 (978-0-7613-6181-7(2)); pap. 8.95 (978-0-7613-7073-4(0), Graphic Universe™) Lerner Publishing Group.

Andersen, Hans Christian. Los Cisnes Salvajes.Tr. of Wild Swans. (SPA., Illus.). 48p. (J). (gr. 3-5). 9.56 (978-84-241-5524-7(6)) Everest Editora ESP. Dist: Lectorum Pubns., Inc.

Andersen, Hans Christian, illus. Thumbelina. 2004.Tr. of Tommelise. 32p. 3.99 (978-1-894998-17-8(0)) Lake, Jack Productions, Inc. CAN. Dist: Hushion Hse. Publishing, Ltd.

Andersen, Hans Christian & Capstone Press Editors. La Bella y la Bestia: La Novela Grafica. Feldman, Luke, illus. 2010. (Graphic Spin en Español Ser.). (SPA.). 40p. (gr. 1-3). lib. bdg. 25.32 (978-1-4342-1899-5(6), Graphic Spin en Español) Stone Arch Bks.

Andersen, Hans Christian & Capstone Press Staff. Caperucita Roja. Rivas, Victor, illus. 2010. (Graphic Spin en Español Ser.). (SPA.). 40p. (gr. 1-3). lib. bdg. 25.32 (978-1-4342-1903-9(8), Graphic Spin en Español) Stone Arch Bks.

—Cenicienta. Feely, Maria Luisa, tr. Timmins, Jeffrey Stewart, illus. 2010. (Graphic Spin en Español Ser.). (SPA.). 40p. (gr. 1-3). lib. bdg. 25.32 (978-1-4342-1900-8(3), Graphic Spin en Español) Stone Arch Bks.

—Hansel y Gretel: La Novela Grafica. Dietrich, Sean, illus. 2010. (Graphic Spin en Español Ser.). (SPA.). 40p. (gr. 1-3). lib. bdg. 25.32 (978-1-4342-1901-5(1), Graphic Spin en Español) Stone Arch Bks.

—Jack y los Frijoles Magicos. Tercio, Ricardo, illus. 2010. (Graphic Spin en Español Ser.). (SPA.). 40p. (gr. 1-3). lib. bdg. 25.32 (978-1-4342-1902-2(X), Graphic Spin en Español) Stone Arch Bks.

—Rumpelstiltskin: La Novela Grafica. Valdez Y Alanis, Erik, illus. 2010. (Graphic Spin en Español Ser.). (SPA.). 40p. (gr. 1-3). lib. bdg. 25.32 (978-1-4342-1904-6(6), Graphic Spin en Español) Stone Arch Bks.

Andersen, Hans Christian & Maguire, Thomas Aquinas. The Wild Swans. 2012. (ENG., Illus.). 104p. (J). (gr. k). 24.95 (978-1-897476-36-9(1)) Simply Read Bks. CAN. Dist: Ingram Publisher Services.

Andersen, Hans Christian & Stone Arch Books Staff. La Bella y la Bestia: La Novela Grafica, 1 vol. Feldman, Luke, illus. 2010. (Graphic Spin en Español Ser.). (SPA & ENG.). 40p. (gr. 1-3). pap. 5.95 (978-1-4342-2269-5(1), Graphic Spin en Español) Stone Arch Bks.

—Caperucita Roja. Rivas, Victor, illus. 2010. (Graphic Spin en Español Ser.). (SPA & ENG.). 40p. (gr. 1-3). pap. 5.95 (978-1-4342-2315-9(9), Graphic Spin en Español) Stone Arch Bks.

—Cenicienta: La Novela Grafica. Timmins, Jeffrey Stewart, illus. 2010. (Graphic Spin en Español Ser.). (SPA & ENG.). 40p. (gr. 1-3). pap. 5.95 (978-1-4342-2270-1(5), Graphic Spin en Español) Stone Arch Bks.

—Hansel y Gretel: La Novela Grafica. Dietrich, Sean, illus. 2010. (Graphic Spin en Español Ser.). (SPA & ENG.). 40p. (gr. 1-3). pap. 5.95 (978-1-4342-2271-8(3), Graphic Spin en Español) Stone Arch Bks.

—Jack y los Frijoles Magicos. Tercio, Ricardo, illus. 2010. (Graphic Spin en Español Ser.). (SPA & ENG.). 40p. (gr. 1-3). pap. 5.95 (978-1-4342-2272-5(1), Graphic Spin en Español) Stone Arch Bks.

—Rumpelstiltskin: La Novela Grafica, 1 vol. Alanis, Erik Valdez Y., illus. 2010. (Graphic Spin en Español Ser.). (ENG & SPA.). 40p. (gr. 1-3). pap. 5.95 (978-1-4342-2273-2(X), Graphic Spin en Español) Stone Arch Bks.

Anderson, Andrea Patrice. Heaven's Diary: Our Gift from God. 2006. 37.00 (978-0-8059-8845-1(9)) Dorrance Publishing Co., Inc.

Anderson, Brian. The Adventures of Commander Zack Proton & the Warlords of Nibblecheese. Holgate, Douglas, illus. 2006. (Adventures of Commander Zack Proton Ser.: 2). (ENG.). 112p. (J). (gr. 2-5). pap. 5.99 (978-1-4169-1365-8(3), Aladdin) Simon & Schuster Children's Publishing.

Anderson, Matt & Durning, Tim. Cut the Rope: Strange Delivery. 2012. (ENG., Illus.). 104p. pap. 9.99 (978-1-937676-04-9(8), 9781937676049) Ape Entertainment.

Anderson, Matt & Hutchins, Eric. White Picket Fences: Double Feature One-shot. 2008. (Illus.). 52p. (YA). pap. 6.95 (978-0-9801314-9-9(9)) Ape Entertainment.

Anderson, Matt & Lambert, Chad. Kung Fu Panda Vol. 2: It's Elemental & Other Stories. 2012. (ENG., Illus.). 24p. pap., pap. 6.95 (978-1-936340-56-9(9), 9781936340569) Ape Entertainment.

Anderson, Rob. Twilight Sparkle & Shining Armor, 1 vol. Mebberson, Amy, illus. 2016. (ENG.). 24p. (J). (978-1-61479-512-4(6)) Spotlight.

Anderson, Ted. Pinkie Pie, 1 vol. Bates, Ben, illus. 2015. (ENG.). 24p. (J). (978-1-61479-333-5(6)) Spotlight.

Anderson, Ted, et al. My Little Pony: Pony Tales Volume 2: Pony Tales Volume 2. Mebberson, Amy, illus. 2014. (My Little Pony Ser.). (ENG.). 104p. pap. 17.99 (978-1-61377-873-9(2), 9781613778739) Idea & Design Works, LLC.

Ando, Natsumi. Arisa 1. 2012. (Arisa Ser.). (ENG., Illus.). 208p. pap. 10.99 (978-1-61262-335-1(2)) Kodansha America, Inc.

Ando, Yuma. Sherlock Bones. 2014. (Sherlock Bones Ser.). (ENG., Illus.). 200p. pap. 10.99 (978-1-61262-545-4(2)) Kodansha America, Inc.

—Sherlock Bones, Vol. 3. Sato, Yuki, illus. 2014. (Sherlock Bones Ser.). (ENG.). 200p. pap. 10.99 (978-1-61262-446-4(4)) Kodansha America, Inc.

—Sherlock Bones, Vol. 4. 2014. (Sherlock Bones Ser.). (ENG., Illus.). 200p. pap. 10.99 (978-1-61262-447-1(2)) Kodansha America, Inc.

Andrews, Kaare. Spider-Man Legend of the Spider-Clan, 3 vols. Young, Skott, illus. 2003. (Mangaverse Ser.: Vol. 3). 128p. (YA). pap. 11.99 (978-0-7851-1114-6(X)) Marvel Worldwide, Inc.

Angleberger, Tom. Rocket & Groot: Stranded on Planet Stripmall! Angleberger, Tom, illus. 2016. (Marvel Middle Grade Novel Ser.). (ENG., Illus.). 224p. (J). (gr. 3-7). 13.99 (978-1-4847-1452-2(0), Marvel Pr.) Disney Publishing Worldwide.

—Rocket & Groot: Keep on Truckin'! Angleberger, Tom, illus. 2017. (Marvel Middle Grade Novel Ser.). (ENG., Illus.). 272p. (J). (gr. 3-7). 13.99 (978-1-4847-8141-8(4), Marvel Pr.) Disney Publishing Worldwide.

Angleberger, Tom. Rocket & Groot: Stranded on Planet Strip Mall! Angleberger, Tom, illus. 2017. (Marvel Middle Grade Novel Ser.). (ENG., Illus.). 224p. (J). (gr. 3-7). pap. 7.99 (978-1-368-01392-5(9), Marvel Pr.) Disney Publishing Worldwide.

Ankylosaurus: The Armored Dinosaur. 2009. (Graphic Dinosaurs Ser.). (ENG., Illus.). 32p. (J). 50.50 (978-1-61531-880-3(1), PowerKids Pr.) Rosen Publishing Group, Inc., The.

Annable, Graham. Further Grickle. 2003. (ENG., Illus.). 128p. pap. 14.95 (978-1-891867-55-2(5)) Alternative Comics.

Antram, David. Draw Caricatures. David Antram, illus. 2017. (Step-By-Step Ser.). 32p. (gr. 3-8). 31.35 (978-1-911242-20-8(2)) Book Hse. GBR. Dist: Black Rabbit Bks.

Anzai, Nobuyuki. Flame of Recca. 2007. (Flame of Recca Ser.: 22). (ENG., Illus.). 192p. pap. 9.99 (978-1-4215-0893-1(1)) Viz Media.

Anzai, Nobuyuki & Caselman, Lance. Flame of Recca. Anzai, Nobuyuki, illus. (Flame of Recca Ser.: 19). (ENG., Illus.). 2006. 208p. pap. 9.99 (978-1-4215-0455-1(3)) 2006. 208p. pap. 9.99 (978-1-4215-0454-4(5)) 2005. 200p. pap. 9.99 (978-1-4215-0131-4(7)) Vol. 14. 2005. 184p. pap. 9.99 (978-1-4215-0014-0(0)) Viz Media.

Aoki, Takao. Beyblade. Aoki, Takao, illus. 2004. (ENG., Illus.). 200p. (YA). pap. 7.99 (978-1-59116-621-4(7)) Viz Media.

—Beyblade: Beyblade Extreme Rotation Shoot, Vol. 2. Aoki, Takao, illus. 2004. (Beyblade Ser.). (ENG., Illus.). 192p. (YA). pap. 7.99 (978-1-59116-697-9(7)) Viz Media.

Aptekar, Devan. Darkseid's Revenge. Gordon, Eric A. & Gordon, Steven E., illus. 2012. (ENG.). 24p. (J). (gr. -1-3). pap. 3.99 (978-0-06-188533-4(9), HarperFestival) HarperCollins Pubs.

Arai, Kiyoko. Beauty Pop, Vol. 1. 2006. (ENG., Illus.). 208p. pap. 8.99 (978-1-4215-0575-6(4)) Viz Media.

Arakawa, Hiromu. Fullmetal Alchemist (3-in-1 Edition), Vol. 7, 3 in 1. 7th ed. 2014. (ENG., Illus.). 568p. pap. 14.99 (978-1-4215-5494-5(1)) Viz Media.

Araujo, André, illus. Avengers A. I. , 12,000 A. D. 2014. (ENG.). 136p. (YA). (gr. 8-17). pap. 16.99 (978-0-7851-8492-8(9)) Marvel Worldwide, Inc.

Archie Superstars, Archie. Archie 1000 Page Comics Gala. 2015. (Archie 1000 Page Digests Ser.). (ENG., Illus.). 1000p. (J). (gr. 4-7). pap. 14.99 (978-1-62738-999-0(7)) Archie Comic Pubns., Inc.

—Archie Comics Spectacular: Block Party. 2015. (Archie Comics Spectaculars Ser.). (ENG., Illus.). 128p. (J). (gr. 4-7). pap. 5.99 (978-1-62738-800-9(1)) Archie Comic Pubns., Inc.

Archie Superstars Staff. Archie 1000 Page Comics Bonanza. 2014. (Archie 1000 Page Digests Ser.: 5). (ENG., Illus.). 1000p. (J). (gr. 4-7). 14.99 (978-1-61988-903-3(X)) Archie Comic Pubns., Inc.

—Archie Giant Comics Jackpot! 2016. (Archie Giant Comics Digests Ser.). (ENG., Illus.). 480p. (J). (gr. 4-7). pap. 7.99 (978-1-62738-802-3(8)) Archie Comic Pubns., Inc.

—The Best of Archie Comics. (ENG., Illus.). 416p. (J). (gr. 4-7). 2014. (Best of Betty & Veronica Ser.: 1). 9.99 (978-1-936975-88-4(2))Bk. 3. 2013. (Best of Archie Comics Ser.: 3). 9.99 (978-1-936975-61-7(0)) Archie Comic Pubns., Inc.

—The Best of Archie Comics: 75 Years, 75 Stories. 2015. (Best of Archie Comics Ser.). (ENG., Illus.). 640p. (J). (gr. 4-7). pap. 14.99 (978-1-62738-992-1(X)) Archie Comic Pubns., Inc.

Ariga, Hitoshi. Mega Man Gigamix, 2 vols., Vol. 3. 2011. (ENG., Illus.). 224p. (J). pap. 13.95 (978-1-926778-31-0(6), 9781926778310) URON Entertainment Corp. CAN. Dist: Diamond Comic Distributors, Inc.

Aristophane. Zabime Sisters. Madden, Matt, tr. from FRE. Aristophane, illus. 2010. (ENG., Illus.). 96p. (YA). (gr. 7-18). pap. 16.99 (978-1-59643-638-1(7), First Second Bks.) Roaring Brook Pr.

Arlon, Penelope. Big Book of Animals. 2017. (LEGO Nonfiction Ser.). (ENG.). 128p. (J). (gr. -1-3). 14.99 (978-1-338-13007-2(2)) Scholastic, Inc.

Armstrong, Robert. The Great Comic Caper. 2015. (ENG.). 86p. (J). (gr. 7-9). mass mkt. 10.95 (978-1-78554-096-7(3), abf15feb-c238-4382-aa9a-3de445005139) Austin, Stan AUS. Dist: Bookmasters Distribution.

Arnold, Robyn. Branli Says Bye-Bye to Binky. 2007. 32p. 16.50 (978-0-615-15292-9(9)) Robyn Z Moon Publishing.

Art Baltazar Comic Book Staff. Tiny Titans - Aw Yeah Titans! 2013. (ENG., Illus.). 128p. (J). (gr. 2-5). pap. 12.99 (978-1-4012-3812-4(2)) DC Comics.

Artibani, Francesco, et al. Donald Duck Adventures, Vol. 19. Clark, John, ed. 2006. (ENG., Illus.). 128p. (YA). pap. 7.95 (978-1-888472-31-8(6), 9781888472318) Gemstone Publishing, Inc.

Aryal, Aimee. Go, Pack, Go! De Angel, Miguel, illus. 2007. 24p. (J). (gr. -1-3). 14.95 (978-1-932888-94-2(2)) Mascot Bks., Inc.

—Hello, Ralphie! Perez, Gerry, illus. 2007. 24p. (J). lib. bdg. 14.95 (978-1-932888-34-8(9)) Mascot Bks., Inc.

Asada, Miho. Stitch! 2017. (ENG., Illus.). 176p. (J). pap. 10.99 (978-1-4278-5694-4(X), 9781427856944) TOKYOPOP, Inc.

Ashbe, Jeanne. Cu Cu! 2003. (SPA.). 36p. (978-84-8470-053-1(4)) Corimbo, Editorial S.L.

—Eso No Se Hace! 2003. (SPA.). 32p. (J). 6.80 (978-84-95150-25-7(5)) Corimbo, Editorial S.L. ESP. Dist: Lectorum Pubns., Inc.

Asrar, Mahmud & Bennett, Joe, illus. Indestructible Hulk - Humanity Bomb, Vol. 4. 2014. (ENG.). 144p. (J). (gr. 4-17). 24.99 (978-0-7851-5480-8(9)) Marvel Worldwide, Inc.

Asso, B. & Bergese, F. Cinebook Recounts: Battle of Britain. movie tie-in ed. 2010. (Cinebook Recounts Ser.). (ENG., Illus.). 48p. pap. 11.95 (978-1-84918-025-2(3)) CineBook GBR. Dist: National Bk. Network.

Asso, Bernard & Bergèse, Francis. Battle of Britain. 2008. (ENG., Illus.). 48p. pap. 11.95 (978-1-905460-39-7(2)) CineBook GBR. Dist: National Bk. Network.

Asso, Bernard & Rideau, Joel. Biggles Recounts the Falklands War: Volume 1. Chauvin, Daniel & Uderzo, Marcel, illus. 2007. (ENG.). 48p. per. 9.99 (978-1-905460-22-9(8)) CineBook GBR. Dist: National Bk. Network.

Auerbach, Annie. Grosse Adventures - Trouble at Twilight Cave. 2007. (Grosse Adventures Ser.). (Illus.). 96p. per. 4.99 (978-1-59816-051-2(6)) TOKYOPOP, Inc.

Avengers Staff, et al. Meet Captain America No. 2. 2011. (Avengers: Earth's Mightiest Heroes! Ser.). (ENG.). 24p. (J). (gr. 1-2). pap. 3.99 (978-1-4231-4296-6(9)) Marvel Worldwide, Inc.

Avery, Ben. Tunnel Twist-Up, 1 vol., Vol. 4. Gaudiamo, Adi Darda, illus. 2008. (Z Graphic Novels / TimeFlyz Ser.). (ENG.). 160p. (J). (gr. 4-7). pap. 6.99 (978-0-310-71364-7(1)) Zondervan.

Avery, Ben & Zondervan Staff. Time Trap, 1 vol. Wong, Scott, illus. 2009. (Z Graphic Novels / TimeFlyz Ser.). (ENG.). 160p. (J). pap. 6.99 (978-0-310-71366-1(8)) Zondervan.

Avi. City of Light, City of Dark. Floca, Brian, illus. 2013. (ENG.). 192p. (J). (gr. 3-7). 19.99 (978-0-545-54256-2(1)); pap. 12.99 (978-0-545-39880-0(0)) Scholastic, Inc. (Graphix).

Bagley, Mark, illus. Ultimate Spider-Man Vol. 11: Carnage. 2007. (ENG.). 144p. (J). (gr. -1-17). pap. 12.99 (978-0-7851-1403-1(3)) Marvel Worldwide, Inc.

Bailey, Michael. Cartoon Nation, 6 bks., Set. Incl. Citizenship. Skog, Jason. Brown, Kelly, illus. 30.65 (978-1-4296-1331-6(9)); Political Elections. Miller, Davis Worth & Brevard, Katherine M. Barnett, Charles, III, illus. 30.65 (978-1-4296-1333-0(5)); Political Parties. Burgan, Michael & Hoena, Blake A. Barnett, Charles et al, illus. lib. bdg. 30.65 (978-1-4296-1334-7(3)); 32p. (gr. 3-4). (Cartoon Nation Ser.). (ENG.). 2008. 91.95 (978-1-4296-1675-1(X), Graphic Library) Capstone Press of Coughlan Cos.

Baker-King, Lisa. The Zealous Zebecs from the Midnight Ocean's Zenith. 2015. (ENG., Illus.). 58p. (J). pap. 10.95 (978-1-63047-437-9(1)) Morgan James Publishing.

Baldwin, Christopher. Little Dee & the Penguin. 2016. (ENG., Illus.). 128p. (J). (gr. 3-7). pap. 10.99 (978-0-8037-4108-9(1)); lib. bdg. 17.99 (978-1-101-99429-0(0)) Penguin Young Readers Group. (Dial Bks).

Baldwin, Stephen. Spirit, No. 1. Simko, Joe, illus. 2006. (ENG.). 208p. (gr. 8-12). per. 9.99 (978-0-8054-4357-8(6)) B&H Publishing Group.

—Spirit Warriors: Number Three. 2007. (Spirit Warriors Ser.). (Illus.). 208p. (YA). per. 9.99 (978-0-8054-4356-1(8)) B&H Publishing Group.

Baldwin, Stephen & Rosato, Bruno. Spirit Warriors: Number Two. Simko, Joe & Tidwell, Jeral, illus. 2007. (Spirit Warriors Ser.). 208p. (YA). per. 9.99 (978-0-8054-4355-4(X)) B&H Publishing Group.

Ball, Georgia & Disney Editors. Disney Frozen Comics Collection. 2016. (ENG.). 96p. (J). (gr. 4-7). 20.85 (978-0-606-39075-0(8)) Turtleback Bks.

Baltazar, Art. Aw Yeah Comics! Vol. 2: Time for... . Adventure! Baltazar, Franco, illus. 2015. (ENG.). 168p. (J). (gr. 3-7). pap. 12.99 (978-1-61655-689-1(7)) Dark Horse Comics.

—The Green Team - Teen Trillionaires, Vol. 1. 2014. (ENG., Illus.). 192p. (YA). pap. 16.99 (978-1-4012-4641-9(9)) DC Comics.

Baltazar, Art, illus. DC Super-Pets, 12 vols., Set. Incl. Attack of the Invisible Cats. Sonneborn, Scott. lib. bdg. 23.99 (978-1-4048-6481-8(4)); Backward Bowwow. Stephens, Sarah Hines. lib. bdg. 23.99 (978-1-4048-6480-1(6)); Battle Bugs of Outer Space. Mason, Jane B. lib. bdg. 23.99 (978-1-4048-6482-5(2)); Fastest Pet on Earth. Bright, J. E. lib. bdg. 23.99 (978-1-4048-6264-7(1)); Heroes of the High Seas. Bright, J. E. 23.99 (978-1-4048-6263-0(3)); Hopping Hero. Sazaklis, John. lib. bdg. 23.99 (978-1-4048-6477-1(6)); Midway Monkey Madness. Stephens, Sarah. lib. bdg. 23.99 (978-1-4048-6305-7(2)); Pooches of Power! Stephens, Sarah. lib. bdg. 23.99 (978-1-4048-6306-4(0)); Royal Rodent Rescue. Sazaklis, John. lib. bdg. 23.99 (978-1-4048-6307-1(9)); Salamander Smackdown! Sazaklis, John. lib. bdg. 23.99 (978-1-4048-6478-8(4)); Super Hero Splash Down. Mason, Jane B. lib. bdg. 23.99 (978-1-4048-6357-6(5)); Superpowered Pony. Stephens, Sarah Hines. lib. bdg. 23.99 (978-1-4048-6479-5(2)); (gr. 2-2). (DC Super-Pets Ser.). (ENG., Illus.). 56p. 2011. Set lib. bdg. 287.88 (978-1-4048-6774-1(0), DC Super-Pets) Picture Window Bks.

Baltazar, Art & Aureliani, Franco. Adventures Begin! Baltazar, Art, illus. 2013. (Superman Family Adventures Ser.). (ENG., Illus.). 32p. (gr. 1-2). 22.60 (978-1-4342-4786-5(4)) Stone Arch Bks.

—And Now... Braniac!, 1 vol. 2014. (Superman Family Adventures Ser.). (ENG., Illus.). 32p. (gr. 1-2). 22.60 (978-1-4342-6478-7(5)) Stone Arch Bks.

—And Now... Ma Kent!, 1 vol. 2014. (Superman Family Adventures Ser.). (ENG., Illus.). 32p. (gr. 1-2). 22.60 (978-1-4342-9006-9(9)) Stone Arch Bks.

—Attack of the Toyman!, 1 vol. 2014. (Superman Family Adventures Ser.). (ENG., Illus.). 32p. (gr. 1-2). 22.60 (978-1-4342-6476-3(9)) Stone Arch Bks.

—Aw Yeah Comics! and. . Action!, Vol. 1: Baltazar, Art, illus. 2014. (ENG., Illus.). 152p. (J). (gr. 3-7). pap. 12.99 (978-1-61655-558-0(0)) Dark Horse Comics.

—Because You Demanded It... Darkseid!, 1 vol. 2014. (Superman Family Adventures Ser.). (ENG., Illus.). 32p. (gr. 1-2). 22.60 (978-1-4342-9005-2(0)) Stone Arch Bks.

—Bounty Hunter, 1 vol. Brizuela, Dario, illus. 2012. (Green Lantern: the Animated Ser.). (ENG.). 32p. (gr. 2-3). 22.60 (978-1-4342-4835-0(6)) Stone Arch Bks.

—By Hook or by Web, 1 vol. Norton, Mike, illus. 2012. (Young Justice Ser.). (ENG.). 32p. (gr. 2-3). 22.60 (978-1-4342-4556-4(X)) Stone Arch Bks.

—Counterfeits, 1 vol. Brizuela, Dario, illus. 2013. (Green Lantern: the Animated Ser.). (ENG.). 32p. (gr. 2-3). 22.60 (978-1-4342-5566-2(2)) Stone Arch Bks.

—Enter - Nightwing! Baltazar, Art & Aureliani, Franco, illus. 2012. (Tiny Titans Ser.). (ENG., Illus.). 32p. (gr. 1-2). lib. bdg. 22.60 (978-1-4342-4540-3(3)) Stone Arch Bks.

—Enter Bizarro!, 1 vol. 2013. (Superman Family Adventures Ser.). (ENG., Illus.). 32p. (gr. 1-2). 22.60 (978-1-4342-4790-2(2)) Stone Arch Bks.

—General Zod Dogs!, 1 vol. 2014. (Superman Family Adventures Ser.). (ENG., Illus.). 32p. (gr. 1-2). 22.60 (978-1-4342-6479-4(3)) Stone Arch Bks.

—Goldface Attacks!, 1 vol. Brizuela, Dario, illus. 2014. (Green Lantern: the Animated Ser.). (ENG.). 32p. (gr. 2-3). 22.60 (978-1-4342-6482-4(3)) Stone Arch Bks.

—Green Lantern: the Animated Series. Brizuela, Dario, illus. 2013. (Green Lantern: the Animated Ser.). (ENG.). 32p. (gr. 2-3). 90.40 (978-1-4342-8828-8(5)) Stone Arch Bks.

—Hack & You Shall Find, 1 vol. Norton, Mike, illus. 2012. (Young Justice Ser.). (ENG.). 32p. (gr. 2-3). 22.60 (978-1-4342-4555-7(1)) Stone Arch Bks.

—Haunted, 1 vol. Norton, Mike, illus. 2012. (Young Justice Ser.). (ENG.). 32p. (gr. 2-3). lib. bdg. 22.60 (978-1-4342-4553-3(5)) Stone Arch Bks.

—Invisible Destroyer. Brizuela, Dario, illus. 2013. (Green Lantern: the Animated Ser.). (ENG.). 32p. (gr. 2-3). 22.60 (978-1-4342-4796-4(1)) Stone Arch Bks.

—Meet Tiny Titans East!, 1 vol. Baltazar, Art & Aureliani, Franco, illus. 2013. (Tiny Titans Ser.). (ENG., Illus.). 32p. (gr. 1-2). lib. bdg. 22.60 (978-1-4342-4696-7(5)) Stone Arch Bks.

—Menace of Metallo! Baltazar, Art, illus. 2013. (Superman Family Adventures Ser.). (ENG., Illus.). 32p. (gr. 1-2). 22.60 (978-1-4342-4794-0(5)) Stone Arch Bks.

—Monkey Business, 1 vol. Norton, Mike, illus. 2012. (Young Justice Ser.). (ENG.). 32p. (gr. 2-3). 22.60 (978-1-4342-4554-0(3)) Stone Arch Bks.

—Monkey Metropolis!, 1 vol. Baltazar, Art, illus. 2013. (Superman Family Adventures Ser.). (ENG., Illus.). 32p. (gr. 1-2). 22.60 (978-1-4342-4791-9(0)) Stone Arch Bks.

—The Mysterious Alien Menace!, 1 vol. 2014. (Superman Family Adventures Ser.). (ENG., Illus.). 32p. (gr. 1-2). 22.60 (978-1-4342-6477-0(7)) Stone Arch Bks.

—Patrick Vol. 4: Wolf Boy. 2008. (Patrick the Wolf Boy Ser.). (Illus.). 144p. pap. 12.99 (978-1-932796-83-4(5)) Devil's Due Publishing, Inc.

—Penguins in the Batcave!, 1 vol. Baltazar, Art & Aureliani, Franco, illus. 2012. (Tiny Titans Ser.). (ENG., Illus.). 32p. (gr. 1-2). 22.60 (978-1-4342-4539-7(X)) Stone Arch Bks.

—Report Card Pickup!, 1 vol. Baltazar, Art & Aureliani, Franco, illus. 2013. (Tiny Titans Ser.). (ENG., Illus.). 32p. (gr. 1-2). lib. bdg. 22.60 (978-1-4342-4699-8(X)) Stone Arch Bks.

—Sidekick City Elementary, 1 vol. Baltazar, Art & Aureliani, Franco, illus. 2012. (Tiny Titans Ser.). (ENG., Illus.). 32p. (gr. 1-2). lib. bdg. 22.60 (978-1-4342-4528-1(4)) Stone Arch Bks.

—Super-Pets!, 1 vol. Baltazar, Art, illus. 2013. (Superman Family Adventures Ser.). (ENG., Illus.). 32p. (gr. 1-2). 22.60 (978-1-4342-4792-6(9)) Stone Arch Bks.

—Superman Family Adventures, 1 vol. (Superman Family Adventures Ser.). (ENG.). 32p. (gr. 1-2). 2014. 271.20

(978-1-4342-8766-3(1)) 2013. 135.60
(978-1-4342-8829-5(3)) Stone Arch Bks.
—Tiny Titans. Baltazar, Art & Aureliani, Franco, illus. 2013. (Tiny Titans Ser.). (ENG., Illus.). 32p. (gr. 1-2). 90.40 (978-1-4342-4853-4(4)); 113.00 (978-1-4342-4854-1(2)) Stone Arch Bks.
—Tiny Titans vs. the Fearsome Five, 1 vol. Baltazar, Art & Aureliani, Franco, illus. 2012. (Tiny Titans Ser.). (ENG., Illus.). 32p. (gr. 1-2). lib. bdg. 22.60 (978-1-4342-4538-0(1)) Stone Arch Bks.
—Titans in Space, 1 vol. Baltazar, Art & Aureliani, Franco, illus. 2013. (Tiny Titans Ser.). (ENG., Illus.). 32p. (gr. 1-2). lib. bdg. 22.60 (978-1-4342-4698-1(1)) Stone Arch Bks.
—Welcome to the Treehouse, 1 vol. Baltazar, Art & Aureliani, Franco, illus. 2013. (Tiny Titans Ser.). (ENG., Illus.). 32p. (gr. 1-2). lib. bdg. 22.60 (978-1-4342-4697-4(3)) Stone Arch Bks.
—Who Is the Purple Superman?, 1 vol. Baltazar, Art, illus. 2013. (Superman Family Adventures Ser.). (ENG., Illus.). 32p. (gr. 1-2). 22.60 (978-1-4342-4793-3(7)) Stone Arch Bks.
—Young Justice. 2013. (Young Justice Ser.). (ENG.). 32p. (gr. 2-3). 180.80 (978-1-4342-8835-6(8)); 90.40 (978-1-4342-8834-9(X)) Stone Arch Bks.
Baltazar, Art & Baltazar, Franco. Aw Yeah Titans! 2013. (Tiny Titans Ser.: 8). lib. bdg. 24.50 (978-0-606-32095-5(4), Turtleback) Turtleback Bks.
Baltazar, Art & Franco. Itty Bitty Hellboy. Allie, Scott, ed. Baltazar, Art, illus. 2014. (ENG., Illus.). 128p. (J). (gr. 3-7). pap. 9.99 (978-1-61655-414-9(2)) Dark Horse Comics.
—Return to the Treehouse. 2015. (ENG., Illus.). 128p. (J). (gr. 2-5). pap. 12.99 (978-1-4012-5492-6(6)) DC Comics.
Baltazar, Art, et al. Campfire Secrets, 1 vol. 2013. (Young Justice Ser.). (ENG.). 32p. (gr. 2-3). 22.60 (978-1-4342-6037-6(2)) Stone Arch Bks.
—Fears, 1 vol. Jones, Christopher, illus. 2013. (Young Justice Ser.). (ENG.). 32p. (gr. 2-3). 22.60 (978-1-4342-6038-3(0)) Stone Arch Bks.
—Hal Versus Atrocitus, 1 vol. Brizuela, Dario, illus. 2014. (Green Lantern: the Animated Ser.). (ENG.). 32p. (gr. 2-3). 22.60 (978-1-4342-6481-7(5)) Stone Arch Bks.
—Trouble in the Arena!, 1 vol. Brizuela, Dario, illus. 2014. (Green Lantern: the Animated Ser.). (ENG.). 32p. (gr. 2-3). 22.60 (978-1-4342-4787-2(2)) Stone Arch Bks.
—True Colors, 1 vol. Brizuela, Dario, illus. 2013. (Green Lantern: the Animated Ser.). (ENG.). 32p. (gr. 2-3). 22.60 (978-1-4342-4795-7(3)) Stone Arch Bks.
Baltazar, Arthur & Franco. Aw Yeah Comics! Make Way... for Awesome!, Vol. 3. Baltazar, Arthur et al, illus. 2016. (ENG.). 144p. (J). (gr. 3-7). pap. 12.99 (978-1-5067-0045-8(4)) Dark Horse Comics.
Banda, Lo Hartog Van. Fingers. Morris Publishing Company Staff, illus. 2013. (Lucky Luke Ser.: 37). (ENG.). 48p. (J). (gr. 3-12). pap. 11.95 (978-1-84918-138-9(1)) CineBook GBR. Dist: National Bk. Network.
Bannister, illus. The Calling. 2010. (Elsewhere Chronicles Ser.: Bk. 4). 48p. (J). (gr. 2-5). lib. bdg. 27.93 (978-0-7613-6068-1(9), Graphic Universe™) Lerner Publishing Group.
Bar-el, Dan. That One Spooky Night. Huyck, David, illus. 2012. (ENG.). 80p. (J). (gr. 2-5). 8.95 (978-1-55453-752-5(5)); 16.95 (978-1-55453-751-8(7)) Kids Can Pr., Ltd. CAN. Dist: Hachette Bk. Group.
Baraitser, Marion. Home Number One. 2006. (Illus.). 63p. (YA). pap. (978-0-9529426-7-2(4)) Loki Books Ltd.
Baraou, Anne & Sardon, Vincent. The Skeleton Family: The Neighbors from Elsewhere. 2005. (Illus.). 64p. (978-1-59687-825-9(8), ipicturebooks) ibooks, Inc.
Barber, John. Transformers: Official Movie Adaptation: Vol 1, 1 vol. Moreno, Jorge Jimenez, illus. 2012. (Transformers: Dark of the Moon Official Movie Adaptation Ser.). (ENG.). 24p. (J). 24.21 (978-1-59961-966-8(0), Graphic Novels) Spotlight.
—Transformers: Official Movie Adaptation: Vol 2, 1 vol. Moreno, Jorge Jimenez, illus. 2012. (Transformers: Dark of the Moon Official Movie Adaptation Ser.). (ENG.). 24p. (J). 24.21 (978-1-59961-967-5(9), Graphic Novels) Spotlight.
—Transformers: Official Movie Adaptation: Vol 4, 1 vol. Moreno, Jorge Jimenez, illus. 2012. (Transformers: Dark of the Moon Official Movie Adaptation Ser.). (ENG.). 24p. (J). 24.21 (978-1-59961-969-9(5), Graphic Novels) Spotlight.
—Transformers: Official Movie Adaption: Vol 3, 1 vol. Moreno, Jorge Jimenez, illus. 2012. (Transformers: Dark of the Moon Official Movie Adaptation Ser.). (ENG.). 24p. (J). 24.21 (978-1-59961-968-2(7), Graphic Novels) Spotlight.
Bargellini, Demetrio & Stilton, Geronimo. The Coliseum Con. Cooper-McGuinness, Nanette, tr. 2009. (Geronimo Stilton Graphic Novels Ser.). (ENG., Illus.). 56p. (J). (gr. 2-6). 9.99 (978-1-59707-172-7(2), 9781597071727) Papercutz.
Bargellini, Demetrio, et al. The Secret of the Sphinx. Cooper-McGuinness, Nanette, tr. 2009. (Geronimo Stilton Graphic Novels Ser.). (ENG., Illus.). 56p. (J). (gr. 2-6). 9.99 (978-1-59707-159-8(5), 9781597071598) Papercutz.
Barichella, Thomas. The Star Snatcher's Planet. 2013. (Little Prince Ser.: 5). (ENG., Illus.). 56p. (J). (gr. 4-8). pap. 7.95 (978-1-4677-0737-4(6)); lib. bdg. 26.60 (978-0-7613-8755-8(2)) Lerner Publishing Group. (Graphic Universe™).
Barks, Carl. The Golden Helmet Starring Walt Disney's Donald Duck. 2015. (ENG., Illus.). 128p. pap. 12.99 (978-1-60699-852-6(8), 699852) Fantagraphics Bks.
—Sheriff of Bullet Valley: Starring Walt Disney's Donald Duck. 2015. (ENG., Illus.). 96p. pap. 9.99 (978-1-60699-820-5(X), 699820) Fantagraphics Bks.
—Walt Disney's Donald Duck: Trick or Treat. 2015. (Carl Barks Library: 0). (ENG., Illus.). 232p. 29.99 (978-1-60699-874-8(9), 699874) Fantagraphics Bks.
Barks, Carl, et al. Uncle Scrooge #387. 2009. 64p. pap. 7.99 (978-1-60360-087-3(6)) Gemstone Publishing, Inc.
—Uncle Scrooge #389. 2009. 64p. pap. 7.99 (978-1-60360-089-7(2)) Gemstone Publishing, Inc.
—Walt Disney's Christmas Parade #5. 2008. (Illus.). 80p. pap. 9.50 (978-1-60360-005-7(1)) Gemstone Publishing, Inc.
—Walt Disney's Comics & Stories #702. 2009. 64p. pap. 7.99 (978-1-60360-092-7(2)) Gemstone Publishing, Inc.
—Walt Disney's Comics & Stories #704. 2009. 64p. pap. 7.99 (978-1-60360-094-1(9)) Gemstone Publishing, Inc.
—Walt Disney's Vacation Parade Volume 5. Clark, John, ed. 2008. (ENG., Illus.). 80p. pap. 9.95 (978-1-60360-031-6(0), 9781603600316) Gemstone Publishing, Inc.
—Walt Disney's Vacation Parade Volume 6. 2009. 80p. pap. 9.99 (978-1-60360-096-5(5)) Gemstone Publishing, Inc.
Barlow, Jeremy. Star Wars Adventures: Boba Fett & the Ship of Fear, 1 vol. 2013. (Star Wars Digests Set 2 Ser.). (ENG.). 80p. (J). (gr. 4-7). lib. bdg. 27.07 (978-1-61479-056-3(6), Essential Library) ABDO Publishing Co.
Barlow, Jeremy & Soriano, Carlo. Star Wars Adventures: Princess Leia & the Royal Ransom, 1 vol. 2012. (Star Wars Digests Ser.). (ENG., Illus.). 80p. (J). (gr. 4-7). 27.07 (978-1-59961-902-6(4)) Spotlight.
Baron, Mike. Nexus Omnibus Volume 3. Warner, Chris, ed. 2013. (ENG., Illus.). 424p. pap. 24.99 (978-1-61655-036-3(8)) Dark Horse Comics.
Baron, Mike & Horse, Dark. Nexus Omnibus Volume 4. Wright, Brendan, ed. 2013. (ENG., Illus.). 416p. 24.99 (978-1-61655-037-0(6)) Dark Horse Comics.
Barosso, Abramo, et al. Uncle Scrooge #386. 2009. 64p. pap. 7.99 (978-1-60360-086-6(8)) Gemstone Publishing, Inc.
Barrie, J. M. J. M. Barrie's Peter Pan. White, Stephen, illus. 2016. (ENG.). 96p. (J). (gr. 2-4). pap. (978-1-78027-290-0(1)) Birlinn, Ltd.
—Peter Pan, 1 vol. Dunn, Ben, illus. 2007. (Graphic Classics). (ENG.). 32p. (gr. 3-7). 28.50 (978-1-60270-052-9(4), Graphic Planet- Fiction) ABDO Publishing Co.
Barriman, Lydia. The Runaway Puppy: A Mystery with Probability. Grutzik, Becky, illus. 2010. (Manga Math Mysteries Ser.: 8). (ENG.). 48p. (gr. 3-5). 29.27 (978-0-7613-4910-5(3)) Lerner Publishing Group.
—Thr Runaway Puppy: A Mystery with Probability. Grutzik, Becky, illus. 2011. (Manga Math Mysteries Ser.: 8). (ENG.). 46p. (gr. 3-5). pap. 6.95 (978-0-7613-8137-2(6), Graphic Universe™) Lerner Publishing Group.
—#8 the Runaway Puppy: A Mystery with Probability. Grutzik, Becky, illus. 2011. (Manga Math Mysteries Set II Ser.). pap. 39.62 (978-0-7613-8365-9(4), Graphic Universe™) Lerner Publishing Group.
Barroux. Line of Fire: Diary of an Unknown Soldier. Ardizzone, Sarah, tr. from FRE. 2014. (ENG., Illus.). 96p. (J). (gr. 5-8). pap. 16.99 (978-1-907912-39-9(8)) Phoenix Yard Bks. GBR. Dist: Independent Pubs. Group.
Bateman, Jordan. Dunamis Heroes: Issue #1: the Lost Kingdom. Save, Ken, illus. 2007. 120p. (J). per. (978-0-9781953-0-4(2)) Dunamis Media.
Batman: Comic Chapter Books, 1 vol. 2014. (Batman: Comic Chapter Bks.). (ENG.). 32p. (gr. k-2). pap. 11.90 (978-1-4342-9534-7(6), DC Super Heroes) Stone Arch Bks.
Batman vs. Superman: Their Greatest Battles. 2015. lib. bdg. 20.85 (978-0-606-37886-4(3)) Turtleback Bks.
Battle, Craig. Max Finder Mystery Collected Casebook, Vol. 6. Pérez, Ramón, illus. 2012. (Max Finder Mystery Collected Casebook Ser.: 6). (ENG.). 96p. (J). (gr. 3-6). pap. 9.95 (978-1-926973-21-0(6), Owlkids) Owlkids Bks. Inc. CAN. Dist: Publishers Group West (PGW).
Baum, L. Frank. The Wizard of Oz. Michael, Cavallaro et al, illus. 2005. (ENG.). 176p. (J). (gr. 3-7). 10.99 (978-0-14-240471-3(3), Puffin Books) Penguin Young Readers Group.
Beatty, Scott. Murder in Mind, Vol. 4. Guice, Butch et al, illus. 2004. (Ruse Ser.: Vol. 4). 160p. (YA). pap. 15.95 (978-1-59314-047-2(9)) CrossGeneration Comics, Inc.
—Scarecrow's Panic Plot. Vecchio, Luciano, illus. 2015. (Batman: Comic Chapter Bks.). (ENG.). 88p. (gr. 3-7). lib. bdg. 21.32 (978-1-4965-0512-5(3)) Stone Arch Bks.
Beatty, Scott, et al. In the Mouth of the Whale. Vecchio, Luciano, illus. 2015. (Beware the Batman Ser.). (ENG.). 32p. (gr. 2-3). lib. bdg. 22.60 (978-1-4342-9740-2(3)) Stone Arch Bks.
Beauregard, Lynda. The Great Space Case: A Mystery about Astronomy. Helmer, Der-Shing, illus. 2013. (Summer Camp Science Mysteries Ser.: 7). (ENG.). 48p. (gr. 3-6). pap. 6.95 (978-1-4677-0735-0(X)); lib. bdg. 29.27 (978-1-4677-0169-3(6)) Lerner Publishing Group. (Graphic Universe™).
—The Hunt for Hidden Treasure: A Mystery about Rocks. Mogorrón, Guillermo, illus. 2012. (Summer Camp Science Mysteries Ser.: 3). (ENG.). 48p. (gr. 3-6). pap. 39.62 (978-0-7613-9270-5(X)); pap. 6.95 (978-0-7613-8545-5(2)); lib. bdg. 29.27 (978-0-7613-5690-5(8)) Lerner Publishing Group. (Graphic Universe™).
—In Search of the Fog Zombie: A Mystery about Matter. Helmer, Der-Shing, illus. 2012. (Summer Camp Science Mysteries Ser.: 1). (ENG.). 48p. (gr. 3-6). pap. 39.62 (978-0-7613-9268-2(8), Graphic Universe™); pap. 6.95 (978-0-7613-8544-8(4), Graphic Universe™); lib. bdg. 29.27 (978-0-7613-5689-9(4)) Lerner Publishing Group.
—The Missing Cuckoo Clock: A Mystery about Gravity. Helmer, Der-Shing, illus. 2013. (Summer Camp Science Mysteries Ser.: 5). (ENG.). 48p. (gr. 3-6). pap. 6.95 (978-1-4677-0733-6(3)); lib. bdg. 29.27 (978-1-4677-0167-9(X)) Lerner Publishing Group. (Graphic Universe™).
—The Nighttime Cabin Thief: A Mystery about Light. Helmer, Der-Shing, illus. 2012. (Summer Camp Science Mysteries Ser.: 2). (ENG.). 48p. (gr. 3-6). pap. 39.62 (978-0-7613-9269-9(6), Graphic Universe™); pap. 6.95 (978-0-7613-8543-1(6), Graphic Universe™); lib. bdg. 29.27 (978-0-7613-5692-9(4)) Lerner Publishing Group.
—The Werewolf Chase: A Mystery about Adaptations. Torres, German, illus. 2012. (Summer Camp Science Mysteries Ser.: 4). (ENG.). 48p. (gr. 3-6). pap. 39.62 (978-0-7613-9271-2(8), Graphic Universe™); pap. 6.95 (978-0-7613-8542-4(8), Graphic Universe™); lib. bdg. 29.27 (978-0-7613-5691-2(6)) Lerner Publishing Group.
—The Whispering Lake Ghosts: A Mystery about Sound. Torres, German, illus. 2013. (Summer Camp Science Mysteries Ser.: 6). (ENG.). 48p. (gr. 3-6). pap. 6.95 (978-1-4677-0734-3(1)); lib. bdg. 29.27 (978-1-4677-0168-6(8)) Lerner Publishing Group. (Graphic Universe™).
—The Yucky Duck Rescue: A Mystery about Pollution. Torres, German, illus. 2013. (Summer Camp Science Mysteries Ser.: 8). (ENG.). 48p. (gr. 3-6). pap. 6.95 (978-1-4677-0736-7(8)); lib. bdg. 29.27 (978-1-4677-0170-9(X)) Lerner Publishing Group. (Graphic Universe™).
Bedard, Tony. Most Haunted, Vol. 2. Moline, Karl et al, illus. 2004. (Route 666 Traveler Ser.: Vol. 2). 160p. (YA). pap. 9.95 (978-1-59314-055-7(X)) CrossGeneration Comics, Inc.
—Mystic: The Mathemagician, Vol. 6. Lopresti, Aaron et al, illus. 2004. (Mystic Ser.). 160p. (YA). pap. 15.95 (978-1-59314-039-7(8)) CrossGeneration Comics, Inc.
—Route 666 Traveler: Highway of Horror. Moline, Karl et al, illus. 2004. (Route 666 Traveler Ser.). 160p. (YA). pap. 9.95 (978-1-59314-041-0(X)) CrossGeneration Comics, Inc.
Beddor, Frank & Cavalier, Liz. Hatter M: The Looking Glass Wars - Love of Wonder. Wrobel, C. J., ed. 2010. (ENG., Illus.). 176p. (gr. 7). pap. 14.99 (978-0-9892221-4-3(4)) Automatic Pictures Publishing.
—Mad with Wonder. Wrobel, C. J., ed. 2009. (ENG., Illus.). 208p. (gr. 7). 24.99 (978-0-9818737-1-8(5)); Vol. 2. pap. 14.95 (978-0-9818737-2-5(3)) Automatic Pictures Publishing.
—The Nature of Wonder, Vol. 3. Wrobel, C. J., ed. 2010. (ENG., Illus.). 192p. (gr. 7). 24.99 (978-0-9818737-4-9(X)) Automatic Pictures Publishing.
—The Nature of Wonder, Vol. 3. Wrobel, C. J., ed. 2010. (ENG., Illus.). 192p. (gr. 7). pap. 14.95 (978-0-9818737-5-6(8)) Automatic Pictures Publishing.
—Zen of Wonder, Vol. 4. 2013. (ENG., Illus.). 140p. (gr. 7). pap. 14.95 (978-0-9818737-8-7(2)) Automatic Pictures Publishing.
—Zen of Wonder, Vol. 4. 2013. (ENG., Illus.). 142p. (gr. 7). 24.99 (978-0-9818737-7-0(4)) Automatic Pictures Publishing.
Beechen, Adam. Darkseid's Inferno!, 1 vol. Beavers, Ethen, illus. 2013. (Justice League Unlimited Ser.). (ENG.). 32p. (gr. 2-3). 22.60 (978-1-4342-6043-7(7)) Stone Arch Bks.
—Divide & Conquer, 1 vol. Barberi, Carlo & Wong, Walden, illus. 2013. (Justice League Unlimited Ser.). (ENG.). 32p. (gr. 2-3). lib. bdg. 22.60 (978-1-4342-4713-1(9)) Stone Arch Bks.
—Justice League Unlimited. 2013. (Justice League Unlimited Ser.). (ENG.). 32p. (gr. 2-3). 180.80 (978-1-4342-8832-5(3)); 90.40 (978-1-4342-8833-2(1)); 90.40 (978-1-4342-3936-5(5)) Stone Arch Bks.
—Small Time, 1 vol. Barberi, Carlo & Wong, Walden, illus. 2013. (Justice League Unlimited Ser.). (ENG.). 32p. (gr. 2-3). 22.60 (978-1-4342-4715-5(5)) Stone Arch Bks.
—UFO! (SpongeBob SquarePants) Saunders, Zina, illus. 2005. (SpongeBob SquarePants Ser.). (ENG.). 32p. (J). pap. 3.99 (978-0-689-87202-0(X), Simon Spotlight/Nickelodeon) Simon Spotlight/Nickelodeon.
Beechen, Adam & Age, Heroic. Mad Mod Is in Vogue!, 1 vol. Vedder, Erik, illus. 2014. (Teen Titans GO! Ser.). (ENG.). 32p. (gr. 2-3). 22.60 (978-1-4342-9216-2(9)) Stone Arch Bks.
Beechen, Adam & Wong, Walden. In the Dimming Light, 1 vol. Barberi, Carlo, illus. 2013. (Justice League Unlimited Ser.). (ENG.). 32p. (gr. 2-3). 22.60 (978-1-4342-6042-0(9)) Stone Arch Bks.
—Monitor Duty, 1 vol. Barberi, Carlo, illus. 2013. (Justice League Unlimited Ser.). (ENG.). 32p. (gr. 2-3). 22.60 (978-1-4342-6041-3(0)) Stone Arch Bks.
—Who Is the Question?, 1 vol. Barberi, Carlo, illus. 2013. (Justice League Unlimited Ser.). (ENG.). 32p. (gr. 2-3). 22.60 (978-1-4342-6044-4(5)) Stone Arch Bks.
Beecroft, Simon. Jedi Adventures. 2009. (Star Wars: the Clone Wars DK Readers Ser.). lib. bdg. 13.55 (978-0-606-06254-1(8), Turtleback) Turtleback Bks.
Beeuwsaert, Matt. I Got Game. Beeuwsaert, Matt, illus. 2003. (Illus.). 176p. per. 14.95 (978-0-9724358-0-2(8)) Beex Art Bks.
Behling, Steve. Daring Dino Rescue! (Rusty Rivets) Lovett, Nate, illus. 2017. (Big Golden Book Ser.). (ENG.). 48p. (J). (gr. -1-2). 9.99 **(978-1-5247-1678-3(2)**, Golden Bks.) Random Hse. Children's Bks.
Behling, Steve. Iron Man: Invasion of the Space Phantoms. 2016. (Mighty Marvel Chapter Bks.). (J). lib. bdg. 16.00 (978-0-606-38305-9(0)) Turtleback Bks.
Behling, Steve & Sotomayor, Chris. Iron Man: Invasion of the Space Phantoms. Pham, Khoi, illus. 2016. (Mighty Marvel Chapter Book Ser.). (ENG.). 128p. (J). (gr. 3-7). pap. 5.99 (978-1-4847-3269-4(3), Marvel Pr.) Disney Publishing Worldwide.
Beka. African Folk Fever. 2012. (Dance Class Graphic Novels Ser.). (ENG., Illus.). 48p. (J). 10.99 (978-1-59707-363-9(6), 9781597073639) Papercutz.
—A Funny Thing Happened on the Way to Paris..., No. 4. 2013. (Dance Class Graphic Novels Ser.). (ENG., Illus.). 48p. (J). (gr. 1-7). 10.99 (978-1-59707-384-4(9), 9781597073844) Papercutz.
—Romeo & Juliets. 2012. (Dance Class Graphic Novels Ser.). (ENG., Illus.). 48p. (J). 10.99 (978-1-59707-317-2(2), 9781597073172) Papercutz.
—We'll Win with Big Class & Huge Style. 2008. (Rugger Boys Ser.: 2). (ENG., Illus.). 48p. pap. 11.95 (978-1-905460-44-1(9)) CineBook GBR. Dist: National Bk. Network.
—Why Are We Here Again? Poupard et al, illus. 2007. (Rugger Boys Ser.: 1). (ENG.). 48p. (J). (gr. 4-7). per. 9.99 (978-1-905460-33-5(3)) CineBook GBR. Dist: National Bk. Network.
Bell, Christine. Oh No! the Television Won't Work! 2005. (Illus.). 52p. pap. (978-1-84401-340-1(5)) Athena Pr.
Belle, Magnolia. Teen Titans Go! - Read at Your Own Risk. 2015. (ENG., Illus.). 24p. (J). (gr. -1-3). pap. 3.99 (978-0-316-37725-6(2)) Little, Brown Bks. for Young Readers.
Belshe, Judy. The Fry Family Goes to Hollywood. 2007. (Illus.). 50p. (J). spiral bd. 10.00 (978-0-9655530-4-9(3)) Snuggle Up Bks.
Bendis, Brian Michael. Takio. Oeming, Michael Avon, illus. 2011. (ENG.). 96p. (J). (gr. -1-17). 9.95 (978-0-7851-5326-9(8)) Marvel Worldwide, Inc.
Bendis, Brian Michael, et al. What If... ? Why Not?, Vol. 1. 2005. (Marvel Heroes Ser.). (Illus.). 152p. pap. 16.99 (978-0-7851-1593-9(5)) Marvel Worldwide, Inc.
Benedetti, Hervé & Robin, Nicolas. The Planet of the Tortoise Driver. Élyum Studio Staff, illus. 2013. (Little Prince Ser.: 8). (ENG.). 56p. (J). (gr. 4-8). pap. 7.95 (978-1-4677-0740-4(6), Graphic Universe™) Lerner Publishing Group.
Benedetti, Hervé, et al. The Planet of the Tortoise Driver. Élyum Studio Staff, illus. 2013. (Little Prince Ser.: 8). (ENG.). 56p. (J). (gr. 4-8). lib. bdg. 26.60 (978-0-7613-8758-9(7), Graphic Universe™) Lerner Publishing Group.
Benintendi, Stephen F. PowerMark 3-pk Issues 1-3. 2004. (J). 7.95 (978-0-9729135-7-7(2)) PowerMark Productions.
—PowerMark 3-pk Issues 4-6. 2004. (YA). 7.95 (978-0-9729135-8-4(0)) PowerMark Productions.
—PowerMark 3-pk Issues 7-9. 2004. (YA). 7.95 (978-0-9729135-9-1(9)) PowerMark Productions.
—PowerMark Issue 22: Unlikely Heroes. 2004. (YA). 2.95 (978-0-9717876-1-2(1)) PowerMark Productions.
—PowerMark Issue 23: Prodigal. 2004. (YA). 2.95 (978-0-9717876-2-9(X)) PowerMark Productions.
—PowerMark Issue 24: Apocalypse. 2004. (YA). 2.95 (978-0-9717876-3-6(8)) PowerMark Productions.
—PowerMark LightQuest Issue 1: The Hunted. 2004. (YA). 2.95 (978-0-9725121-4-5(4)) PowerMark Productions.
—PowerMark Seeker Series Issue 4: Redemption. 2003. (ENG & SPA.). (J). 1.75 (978-0-9729135-4-6(8)) PowerMark Productions.
—PowerMark Seeker Series Issue 5: Transformation. 2003. (ENG & SPA.). (J). 1.75 (978-0-9729135-5-3(6)) PowerMark Productions.
—PowerMark Seeker Series Issue 6: The Pathway. 2003. (ENG & SPA.). (J). 1.75 (978-0-9729135-6-0(4)) PowerMark Productions.
—PowerMark Series One Autographed Box Set: Issues 1-12. aut. ed. 2003. 50.00 (978-0-9717876-4-3(6)) PowerMark Productions.
Benintendi, Steve. The Mission, 3 vols. 2003. (Powermark Comics Ser.). (Illus.). 40p. (J). pap. 2.95 (978-0-9705669-0-4(5)) PowerMark Productions.
—PM Seeker Series # 7 Masquerade: Halloween Edition. 2005. (Illus.). 20p. (J). pap. 7.25 (978-0-9749339-1-7(0)) PowerMark Productions.
—PowerMark Issue 10 5-Pack. 2004. (Powermark Comics Ser.). (Illus.). 32p. pap. 14.75 (978-0-9747026-2-9(5)) PowerMark Productions.
—Underfire. 2003. (Powermark Comics Ser.). (Illus.). 32p. (J). pap. 2.95 (978-0-9705669-2-8(1)) PowerMark Productions.
Benjamin, Paul. Monsters, Inc: Laugh Factory. Mebberson, Amy, illus. 2010. (ENG.). 112p. (J). pap. 9.99 (978-1-60886-508-6(8)) Boom! Studios.
Benjamin, Paul & Rosa, Don. Monsters, Inc: Laugh Factory. Mebberson, Amy & Rosa, Don, illus. 2010. (ENG.). 112p. (J). 24.99 (978-1-60886-533-8(9)) Boom! Studios.
Bennett, Chris. Robots & Dinosaurs. 2012. (ENG.). 127p. (J). pap. 16.99 (978-1-926780-26-9(4)) Key Publishing Hse., Inc., The CAN. Dist: Bookmasters Distribution.
Bergen, Lara Rice. Phonics Comics: the Fearless Four - Level 2. Semple, Dave, illus. 2007. (ENG.). 24p. (J). (gr. 1-17). per. 3.99 (978-1-58476-564-6(X)) Innovative Kids.
Bergèse, Francis. Ghost Squadron. 2013. (Buck Danny Ser.: 3). (ENG., Illus.). 56p. (J). (gr. 5-12). pap. 13.95 (978-1-84918-137-2(3)) CineBook GBR. Dist: National Bk. Network.
Bergese, Francis. Spitfire Parade, Vol. 1. 2009. (ENG., Illus.). 54p. pap. 11.95 (978-1-905460-54-0(6)) CineBook GBR. Dist: National Bk. Network.
Bermejo, Lee. The Vigilante Business. 2016. (We Are Robin Ser.: 1). lib. bdg. 26.95 (978-0-606-38580-0(0)) Turtleback Bks.
Berrill, Jack. Under the Friday Night Lights! A Gil Thorp Football Collection. 2004. (Illus.). 328p. per. 32.95 (978-0-930099-14-5(1)) Take Five Pubs.
Berrios, Frank. The Big Book of the DC Super Friends. Golden Books, illus. 2015. (Big Golden Book Ser.). (ENG.). 48p. (J). (gr. k-4). 9.99 (978-0-553-50773-7(7), Golden Bks.) Random Hse. Children's Bks.
—A Day in the Sun. 2014. lib. bdg. 13.55 (978-0-606-35546-9(4)) Turtleback Bks.
Bersson, Robert & Shoup, Dolores. Stripes & Stars. Bersson, Robert & Trobaugh, Scott, illus. l.t. ed. 2003. 40p. (J). (gr. 1-4). per. 16.95 (978-0-9740585-0-4(5)) Legacy Group Productions, LLC.
Berts, Peter, et al. Fish to Fry. Ellipsanime Staff & Dargaud Media Staff, illus. 2011. (Garfield Graphic Novels Ser.). (ENG.). 32p. (J). (gr. 1-6). 7.99 (978-1-59707-266-3(4), 9781597072663) Papercutz.
Bethel, Ellie. Michael Recycle. Colombo, Alexandra, illus. 2008. (Michael Recycle Ser.). (ENG.). 28p. (J). (gr. 2-5). 15.99 (978-1-60010-224-0(7), 9781600102240) Idea & Design Works, LLC.
Bidaud, Agnès. The Planet of Libris. Élyum Studio, illus. 2013. (Little Prince Ser.: 11). (ENG.). 48p. (J). (gr. 4-8). pap. 7.95 (978-1-4677-1520-1(4)); lib. bdg. 26.60 (978-0-7613-8761-9(7)) Lerner Publishing Group. (Graphic Universe™).
Big Idea Entertainment, LLC. Dave & the Giant Pickle. Jones, Cory, illus. 2016. (VeggieTales Ser.: 1). (ENG.). 32p. (J). (gr. -1-3). pap. 3.99 (978-1-4336-8538-5(8), B&H Kids) B&H Publishing Group.
—VeggieTales SuperComics: Vol 1. Jones, Cory, illus. 2015. (VeggieTales Super Comics Ser.: 1). (ENG.). 104p. (J). (gr. -1-3). pap. 12.99 (978-1-4336-8534-7(5), B&H Kids) B&H Publishing Group.
—VeggieTales SuperComics: Vol 2. Jones, Cory, illus. 2015. (VeggieTales Super Comics Ser.). (ENG.). 104p. (J). (gr. -1-3). pap. 12.99 (978-1-4336-8535-4(3), B&H Kids) B&H Publishing Group.
—VeggieTales SuperComics: Vol 3. Jones, Cory, illus. 2015. (VeggieTales Super Comics Ser.: 1). (ENG.). 104p. (J). (gr. -1-3). pap. 12.99 (978-1-4336-8536-1(1), B&H Kids) B&H Publishing Group.
—VeggieTales SuperComics: Vol 4. Jones, Cory, illus. 2015. (VeggieTales Super Comics Ser.: 1). (ENG.). 104p. (J). (gr. -1-3). pap. 12.99 (978-1-4336-8537-8(X), B&H Kids) B&H Publishing Group.
—VeggieTales SuperComics: Vol 6. Jones, Cory, illus. 2016. (VeggieTales Ser.: 1). (ENG.). 32p. (J). (gr. -1-3). pap. 3.99 (978-1-4336-8539-2(6), B&H Kids) B&H Publishing Group.
Biskup, Agnieszka. Aliens & Energy. Aón, Carlos, illus. 2011. (Monster Science Ser.). (ENG.). 32p. (gr. 3-4). pap. 47.70 (978-1-4296-7326-6(5), Graphic Library) Capstone Press of Coughlan Cos.
—The Amazing Work of Scientists with Max Axiom, Super Scientist, 1 vol. Baez, Marcelo, illus. 2013. (Graphic Science & Engineering in Action Ser.). (ENG.). 32p. (gr. 3-4). pap.

8.10 *(978-1-62065-701-0(5))*; lib. bdg. 30.65 *(978-1-4296-9936-5(1))* Capstone Press of Coughlan Cos. (Graphic Library).

—D-Day: June 6 1944, 1 vol. 2014. (24-Hour History Ser.). (ENG., Illus.). 48p. (gr. 3-5). lib. bdg. 33.32 *(978-1-4329-9295-8(3)*, NA-h) Heinemann-Raintree.

—Egypt's Mysterious Pyramids: An Isabel Soto Archaeology Adventure. Stewart, Roger, illus. 2012. (Graphic Expeditions Ser.). (ENG.). 32p. (gr. 3-4). pap. 47.70 *(978-1-4296-8472-9(0)*, Graphic Library) Capstone Press of Coughlan Cos.

—George Washington: The Rise of America's First President, 1 vol. Mallea, Cristian, illus. 2012. (American Graphic Ser.). (ENG.). 32p. (gr. 3-4). lib. bdg. 30.65 *(978-1-4296-8621-1(9)*, Graphic Library) Capstone Press of Coughlan Cos.

—Graphic Expeditions. Stewart, Roger, illus. 2012. (Graphic Expeditions Ser.). (ENG.). 32p. (gr. 3-4). pap. 667.80 *(978-1-4296-8474-3(7))*; lib. bdg. 61.30 *(978-1-4296-8174-2(8))* Capstone Press of Coughlan Cos. (Graphic Library).

—The Incredible Work of Engineers with Max Axiom, Super Scientist, 1 vol. Baez, Marcelo, illus. 2013. (Graphic Science & Engineering in Action Ser.). (ENG.). 32p. (gr. 3-4). pap. 8.10 *(978-1-62065-705-8(8))*; lib. bdg. 30.65 *(978-1-4296-9937-2(X))* Capstone Press of Coughlan Cos. (Graphic Library).

—The Remarkable World of Robots: Max Axiom STEM Adventures. 2017. (STEM Adventures Ser.). (ENG.). 32p. (gr. 3-4). lib. bdg. 30.65 ***(978-1-5157-7391-7(4)***, Graphic Library) Capstone Press of Coughlan Cos.

—Super Cool Chemical Reaction Activities with Max Axiom. Baez, Marcelo, illus. 2015. (Max Axiom Science & Engineering Activities Ser.). (ENG.). 32p. (gr. 3-4). lib. bdg. 30.65 *(978-1-4914-2077-5(4)*, Graphic Library) Capstone Press of Coughlan Cos.

—Thunder Rolling down the Mountain: The Story of Chief Joseph & the Nez Perce, 1 vol. Zimmerman, Rusty, illus. (American Graphic Ser.). (ENG.). 32p. (gr. 3-4). 2011. pap. 8.10 *(978-1-4296-6270-3(0))* 2011. pap. 47.70 *(978-1-4296-6437-0(1))* 2010. lib. bdg. 30.65 *(978-1-4296-5472-2(4))* Capstone Press of Coughlan Cos. (Graphic Library).

Biskup, Agnieszka & Enz, Tammy. Super Cool Science & Engineering Activities. 2015. (ENG., Illus.). 128p. (gr. 3-4). pap. 14.95 *(978-1-62370-232-8(1))* Capstone Young Readers of Coughlan Cos.

Biskup, Agnieszka & Sohn, Emily. Ciencia Gráfica. Martin, Cynthia & Dominguez, Richard, illus. 2013. (Ciencia Gráfica Ser.). (SPA.). 32p. (gr. 3-4). lib. bdg. 245.20 *(978-1-62065-186-5(6))* Capstone Press of Coughlan Cos.

—Ciencia Gráfica. Martin, Cynthia & Dominguez, Richard, illus. 2013. (Ciencia Gráfica Ser.). (SPA.). 32p. (gr. 3-4). lib. bdg. 122.60 *(978-1-62065-185-8(8))* Capstone Press of Coughlan Cos.

Biskup, Agnieszka, et al. Comprender el Calentamiento Global con Max Axiom, Supercientífico. Strictly Spanish Translation Services Staff, tr. from ENG. Martin, Cynthia & Anderson, Bill, illus. 2012. (Ciencia Gráfica Ser.). (SPA.). 32p. (gr. 3-4). lib. bdg. 30.65 *(978-1-4296-9235-9(9))* Capstone Press of Coughlan Cos.

—The Dynamic World of Chemical Reactions with Max Axiom. 2010. (Graphic Science Ser.). (ENG., Illus.). 32p. (gr. 3-4). pap. 8.10 *(978-1-4296-5635-1(2)*, Graphic Library) Capstone Press of Coughlan Cos.

—The Surprising World of Bacteria with Max Axiom, Super Scientist, 1 vol. 2010. (Graphic Science Ser.). (ENG.). 32p. (gr. 3-4). pap. 8.10 *(978-1-4296-4863-9(5))*; lib. bdg. 30.65 *(978-1-4296-3975-0(X))* Capstone Press of Coughlan Cos. (Graphic Library).

—Uncovering Mummies: An Isabel Soto Archaeology Adventure. 2016. (Graphic Expeditions Ser.). (ENG., Illus.). 32p. pap. 8.10 *(978-1-5157-6190-7(8)*, Graphic Library) Capstone Press of Coughlan Cos.

Blabey, Aaron. The Bad Guys. 2017. (Bad Guys Ser.: bk.4). (ENG.). 144p. (J). (gr. 2-5). pap. 5.99 ***(978-1-338-08753-6(3)***, Scholastic Paperbacks) Scholastic, Inc.

Black, Holly. Kin. Naifeh, Ted, illus. (Good Neighbors Ser.: 1). (ENG.). 144p. (J). (gr. 7). 2009. pap. 12.99 *(978-0-439-85565-5(9))* 2008. 16.99 *(978-0-439-85562-4(4))* Scholastic, Inc. (Graphix).

—Kind. Naifeh, Ted, illus. 2010. (Good Neighbors Ser.: 3). (ENG.). 128p. (J). (gr. 3-7). 16.99 *(978-0-439-85564-8(0)*, Graphix) Scholastic, Inc.

—Kith. Naifeh, Ted, illus. 2010. (Good Neighbors Ser.: 2). (ENG.). 128p. (J). (gr. 3-7). pap. 12.99 *(978-0-439-85566-2(7)*, Graphix) Scholastic, Inc.

Black, Jake. Attack of the Man-Bat! Vecchio, Luciano, illus. 2015. (Batman: Comic Chapter Bks.). (ENG.). 88p. (gr. 3-7). lib. bdg. 21.32 *(978-1-4965-0513-2(1))* Stone Arch Bks.

Black, Jake & Beatty, Scott. Batman: Comic Chapter Books, 2 vols. 2015. (Batman: Comic Chapter Bks.). (ENG., Illus.). 88p. (gr. 3-7). 42.64 *(978-1-4965-1997-9(3))* Stone Arch Bks.

Black, Jake & Meredith Books Staff. Race Against Crime. Wallace, Loston, illus. 2008. 24p. (J). pap. 3.99 *(978-0-696-23958-8(2))* Meredith Bks.

—Robo Monster. Stewart, Scott, illus. 2008. 22p. (J). pap. 3.99 *(978-0-696-23957-1(4))* Meredith Bks.

Blackbird. Mr. Hookworm. Blackbird, illus. 2006. (Illus.). (J). per. 18.00 *(978-0-9789798-6-7(9)*, 978-0-9789798-6-7) Blackbird's World Publishing Co.

Blackman, Haden & Caldwell, Ben. Star Wars: Clone Wars Adventures, 1 vol. 2012. (Star Wars Digests Ser.). (ENG., Illus.). 96p. (J). (gr. 4-7). 27.07 *(978-1-59961-904-0(0))* Spotlight.

Blackman, Haden & The Fillbach Brothers. Star Wars: Clone Wars Adventures, 1 vol. 2012. (Star Wars Digests Ser.). (ENG., Illus.). 96p. (J). (gr. 4-7). 27.07 *(978-1-59961-906-4(7))*; 27.07 *(978-1-59961-905-7(9))* Spotlight.

Bladek, John. Lost in Ghostville. 2016. (Middle-Grade Novels Ser.). (ENG.). 208p. (gr. 4-7). lib. bdg. 25.99 *(978-1-4965-3360-9(7))* Stone Arch Bks.

Blanquet, Stephane. Toys in the Basement. 2010. (ENG., Illus.). 32p. 14.99 *(978-1-60699-402-3(6)*, 699402) Fantagraphics Bks.

Blaylock, Josh. Misplaced. O'Reilly, Sean Patrick, ed. 2011. (Illus.). 126p. (YA). pap. 14.95 *(978-1-926914-17-6(1))* Arcana Studio, Inc.

Bliss, Harry. Luke on the Loose. Bliss, Harry, illus. 2009. (ENG., Illus.). 32p. (J). (gr. -1-3). 12.95 *(978-1-935179-00-9(4))* TOON Books / RAW Junior, LLC.

—Luke on the Loose. 2014. (Toon Books Level 2 Ser.). lib. bdg. 14.75 *(978-0-606-32101-3(2)*, Turtleback) Turtleback Bks.

Block, Shelly, et al. Uncle Scrooge, No. 351. Clark, John, ed. 2006. (ENG., Illus.). 64p. pap. 6.95 *(978-1-888472-15-8(4)*, 9781888472158) Gemstone Publishing, Inc.

Bloodworth, Mark, illus. The Castle Mystery. 2010. (Boxcar Children Graphic Novels Ser.: 12). (ENG.). 32p. (J). (gr. 1-5). pap. 6.99 *(978-0-8075-1080-3(7))* Whitman, Albert & Co.

Bloom, Carol A. The Wishing Closet. (Magic Mansion Mystery Ser.: Bk. 2). 124p. (J). (gr. 3-6). 9.99 *(978-0-88092-476-4(4))* Royal Fireworks Publishing Co.

Bloomsbury. Lift-The-Flap Friends: Dinosaurs. 2016. (ENG.). 14p. (J). bds. 9.99 *(978-1-68119-099-0(0)*, 9781681190990, Bloomsbury Activity Bks.) Bloomsbury Publishing USA.

Blum, Geoffrey & Barks, Carl. Uncle Scrooge #377. Clark, John, ed. 2008. (ENG., Illus.). 64p. pap. 7.99 *(978-1-60360-033-0(7)*, 9781603600330) Gemstone Publishing, Inc.

Bobillo, Juan & Dragotta, Nick, illus. FF, Vol. 3. 2013. (ENG.). 128p. (J). (gr. 4-17). pap. 16.99 *(978-0-7851-6313-8(1))* Marvel Worldwide, Inc.

Bolte, Mari. Triceratops: Three-Horned Giant. Dove, Jason, illus. 2012. (First Graphics: Dinosaurs Ser.). (ENG.). 24p. (gr. 1-2). pap. 35.70 *(978-1-4296-8365-4(1))* Capstone Press of Coughlan Cos.

Bolte, Marissa. Arrested for Witchcraft! Nickolas Flux & the Salem Witch Trials, 1 vol. Ginevra, Dante, illus. 2014. (Nickolas Flux History Chronicles Ser.). (ENG.). (gr. 3-4). 40p. pap. 7.95 *(978-1-4765-5151-7(0))*; 32p. lib. bdg. 30.65 *(978-1-4765-3947-8(2))* Capstone Press of Coughlan Cos. (Graphic Library).

Bolton, Chris A. Smash: Trial by Fire. Bolton, Kyle, illus. 2013. (ENG.). 160p. (J). (gr. 4-7). 18.99 *(978-0-7636-5596-9(1))* Candlewick Pr.

Bones. Wolf's Rain, Vol. 2. Lida, Toshitsugu, illus. 2005. (ENG.). 184p. pap. 9.99 *(978-1-59116-718-1(3))* Viz Media.

Bonner, Hannah. When Dinos Dawned, Mammals Got Munched, & Pterosaurs Took Flight: A Cartoon Prehistory of Life in the Triassic. 2012. (ENG., Illus.). 48p. (J). (gr. 3-7). lib. bdg. 25.90 *(978-1-4263-0863-5(9)*, National Geographic Children's Bks.) National Geographic Society.

—When Fish Got Feet, When Bugs Were Big, & When Dinos Dawned: A Cartoon Prehistory of Life on Earth. 2015. (ENG., Illus.). 128p. (J). (gr. 3-7). pap. 12.99 *(978-1-4263-2104-7(X)*, National Geographic Children's Bks.) National Geographic Society.

Bonner, Hannah & National Geographic Kids Staff. When Dinos Dawned, Mammals Got Munched, & Pterosaurs Took Flight: A Cartoon PreHistory of Life in the Triassic. 2012. (ENG., Illus.). 48p. (J). (gr. 3-7). 17.95 *(978-1-4263-0862-8(0)*, National Geographic Children's Bks.) National Geographic Society.

Bonneval, Gwen de & Smith, Owen. William & the Lost Spirit. Smith, Anne Collins, tr. from FRE. Bonhomme, Matthieu, illus. 2013. (ENG.). 160p. (J). (gr. 8-12). lib. bdg. 30.60 *(978-0-7613-8567-7(3)*, Graphic Universe™) Lerner Publishing Group.

Borando, Silvia. The Cat Book: A Minibombo Book. Borando, Silvia, illus. 2017. (Minibombo Ser.). (ENG., Illus.). 32p. (J). (-k). 9.99 *(978-0-7636-9472-2(X))* Candlewick Pr.

Bostic, Charles. Da' art of Ravenous Redd. 2010. 32p. pap. 23.96 *(978-0-557-46640-5(7))* Lulu Pr., Inc.

Bouchard, Hervé. Harvey: How I Became Invisible, 1 vol. Mixter, Helen, tr. from FRE. Nadeau, Janice, illus. 2017. (ENG.). 168p. (J). (gr. 4). pap. 14.95 *(978-1-77306-005-7(8))* Groundwood Bks. CAN. Dist: Publishers Group West (PGW).

Bowen, Carl. Jak & the Magic Nano-Beans: a Graphic Novel. Lozano, Omar, illus. 2016. (Far Out Fairy Tales Ser.). (ENG.). 40p. (gr. 3-4). lib. bdg. 25.32 *(978-1-4965-2510-9(8)*, Far Out Fairy Tales) Stone Arch Bks.

—Loki & Thor. Smith, Tod & Lokus, Rex, illus. 2016. (Norse Myths: a Viking Graphic Novel Ser.). (ENG.). 56p. (gr. 3-4). pap. 5.95 *(978-1-4965-3494-1(8))*; lib. bdg. 27.99 *(978-1-4965-3490-3(5))* Stone Arch Bks.

—Quarterback Rush, 1 vol. Garcia, Eduardo, illus. 2014. (Sports Illustrated Kids Graphic Novels Ser.). (ENG.). 72p. (gr. 2-5). 26.65 *(978-1-4342-6489-3(0))* Stone Arch Bks.

—Thor vs. the Giants: A Viking Graphic Novel. Garcia, Eduardo, illus. 2016. (Norse Myths: a Viking Graphic Novel Ser.). (ENG.). 56p. (gr. 3-4). pap. 5.95 *(978-1-4965-3491-0(3))*; lib. bdg. 27.99 *(978-1-4965-3487-3(5))* Stone Arch Bks.

Bowen, Carl & Fuentes, Benny. BMX Breakthrough, 1 vol. Sandoval, Gerardo, illus. 2011. (Sports Illustrated Kids Graphic Novels Ser.). (ENG.). 56p. (gr. 2-3). pap. 7.19 *(978-1-4342-3401-8(0))*; lib. bdg. 26.65 *(978-1-4342-2240-4(3))* Stone Arch Bks.

Bowen, Carl & Poe, Edgar Allen. The Murders in the Rue Morgue, 1 vol. Dimaya, Emerson & Calero, Dennis, illus. 2013. (Edgar Allan Poe Graphic Novels Ser.). (ENG.). 72p. (gr. 2-3). 27.99 *(978-1-4342-3033-1(3))*; pap. 6.10 *(978-1-4342-4259-4(5))* Stone Arch Bks.

Bowen, Carl, et al. Norse Myths, 4 vols. Smith, Tod & Garcia, Eduardo, illus. 2016. (Norse Myths: a Viking Graphic Novel Ser.). (ENG.). 56p. (gr. 3-4). 111.96 *(978-1-4965-3519-1(7))* Stone Arch Bks.

Bowser, Milton, illus. Cartoon Stories from the Teachings of Buddha. l.t. ed. 2003. (Cartoon Ser.). (JPN & SPA.). 72p. (YA). 10.00 *(978-0-940178-34-2(6)*, Buddha 1) Sitare, Ltd.

Boyd, Bentley. George Washington Leads the Way. 2011. (Mount Vernon Comix Ser.). (Illus.). 24p. (J). (gr. 3-9). pap. 6.95 *(978-1-933122-44-1(7))* Chester Comix, LLC.

—Government. 2nd ed. 2010. (Chester the Crab's Comix with Content Ser.). (Illus.). 24p. pap. 6.95 *(978-1-933122-38-0(2))* Chester Comix, LLC.

—Moving & Grooving. 2009. (Chester Comix Ser.). (Illus.). 24p. pap. 6.95 *(978-1-933122-36-6(6))* Chester Comix, LLC.

—Reconstruction Junction. 2010. (Chester Comix Ser.). (Illus.). 24p. pap. *(978-1-933122-43-4(9))* Chester Comix, LLC.

Braddock, Paige. Jane's World, Vol. 4. 2006. (ENG., Illus.). 160p. pap. 15.00 *(978-0-9766707-3-5(9)*, 9780976670735) Girl Twirl Comics.

—Stinky Cecil in Operation Pond Rescue. 2015. (Stinky Cecil Ser.: 1). (ENG.). 128p. (J). pap. 9.99 *(978-1-4494-5711-2(8))* Andrews McMeel Publishing.

—Stinky Cecil in Terrarium Terror. 2016. (Stinky Cecil Ser.: 2). (ENG.). 128p. (J). pap. 9.99 *(978-1-4494-7186-6(2))* Andrews McMeel Publishing.

Bradley, Jessica, illus. Comics Land. 2013. (Comics Land Ser.). (ENG.). 32p. (gr. k-2). lib. bdg. 202.56 *(978-1-4342-6063-5(1))*; lib. bdg. 101.28 *(978-1-4342-6062-8(3))*; lib. bdg. 63.60 *(978-1-4342-8516-4(2))*; lib. bdg. 101.28 *(978-1-4342-4104-7(1))* Stone Arch Bks.

Bradshaw, Nick & Bachalo, Chris, illus. Wolverine & the X-Men by Jason Aaron - Volume 2. 2013. (ENG.). 104p. (J). (gr. 4-17). pap. 16.99 *(978-0-7851-5682-6(8)*, Marvel Pr.) Disney Publishing Worldwide.

Brallier, Max. Quest for Gem Magic. 2015. (Steven Universe Ser.). (ENG.). 80p. (J). (gr. 3-7). 7.99 *(978-0-8431-8317-7(9)*, Cartoon Network Books) Penguin Young Readers Group.

Brancatelli, Joe, et al. Creepy Archives Volume 18. Simon, Philip, ed. 2014. (ENG., Illus.). 288p. 49.99 *(978-1-61655-269-5(7))* Dark Horse Comics.

Branch, Ken & Tanguay, Dave. Mr. Who? Mr. Atom! 2015. (Billy Batson & the Magic of Shazam! Ser.). (ENG., Illus.). 32p. (gr. 2-3). lib. bdg. 22.60 *(978-1-4342-9656-6(3))* Stone Arch Bks.

Bravest Warriors Presents: Catbug's Treasure Book. 2014. (ENG.). 108p. (J). 12.99 *(978-1-4215-6392-3(4))* Viz Media.

Bravo, Emile. The Hunger of the Seven Squat Bears. 2011. (Squat Bears Ser.). (ENG., Illus.). 32p. (J). (gr. k-17). 14.99 *(978-0-316-08361-4(5)*, Yen Pr.) Orbit.

Brewer, Heather. Eighth Grade Bites. Laud, Julia, illus. 2013. (Chronicles of Vladimir Tod Ser.: 1). (ENG.). 144p. (YA). (gr. 7). pap. 12.99 *(978-0-8037-3811-9(0)*, Dial Bks) Penguin Young Readers Group.

Brewster, Chad, et al. Bob's Burgers. 2015. (ENG., Illus.). 120p. (YA). pap. 17.99 *(978-1-60690-660-6(7)*, 9781606906606, Dynamite Entertainment) Dynamic Forces, Inc.

Briggs, Raymond. The Snowman. 2013. (ENG.). 34p. (J). (—1). bds. 6.99 *(978-0-385-37869-7(6)*, Random Hse. Bks. for Young Readers) Random Hse. Children's Bks.

Bright, J. E. Batman Versus Man-Bat. Gordon, Steven E. & Gordon, Eric A., illus. 2012. (I Can Read Level 2 Ser.). (ENG.). 32p. (J). (gr. -1-3). pap. 3.99 *(978-0-06-188523-5(1))* HarperCollins Pubs.

—Cosmic Clash. Kiernan, Kenny, illus. 2016. (LEGO DC Super Heroes Ser.). (ENG.). 64p. (J). (gr. -1-3). pap. 4.99 *(978-0-545-86801-3(7))* Scholastic, Inc.

—Heroes of the High Seas, 1 vol. Baltazar, Art, illus. 2011. (DC Super-Pets Ser.). (ENG.). 56p. (gr. 2-2). 23.99 *(978-1-4048-6263-0(3)*, DC Super-Pets) Picture Window Bks.

—Reader. Lee, Paul, illus. 2016. (Lego City Ser.). (ENG.). 32p. (J). (gr. -1-3). pap. 3.99 *(978-0-545-91386-7(1))* Scholastic, Inc.

Bright, J. E., adapted by. Raven Rocks! 2015. (J). *(978-0-316-37734-8(1))* Little Brown & Co.

Brighter Child Publishing Staff, creator. Marvel Super Hero Fact Book. 2006. (Marvel Ser.). (Illus.). 12p. (J). bds. 9.95 *(978-1-57791-298-9(5))* Brighter Minds Children's Publishing.

Brightwood, Laura, illus. I Am A Frog. Brightwood, Laura, . 2007. (J). DVD *(978-1-934409-02-2(2))* 3-C Institute for Social Development.

—King's New Suit. Brightwood, Laura, . 2007. (J). DVD *(978-1-934409-05-3(7))* 3-C Institute for Social Development.

—Lion & Mousie. Brightwood, Laura, . 2007. (J). DVD *(978-1-934409-00-8(6))* 3-C Institute for Social Development.

—Little Freddie & His Whistle. Brightwood, Laura, . 2007. (J). DVD *(978-1-934409-01-5(4))* 3-C Institute for Social Development.

—Look What You've Done. Brightwood, Laura, . 2007. (J). DVD *(978-1-934409-03-9(0))* 3-C Institute for Social Development.

—Wolf under the Bed. Brightwood, Laura, . 2007. (J). DVD *(978-1-934409-04-6(9))* 3-C Institute for Social Development.

—The Woodsman & His Ax. Brightwood, Laura, . 2007. (J). DVD *(978-1-934409-07-7(3))* 3-C Institute for Social Development.

Brill, Marlene Targ. The Rough-Riding Adventure of Bronco Charlie, Pony Express Rider. Trover, Zachary, illus. 2010. (History's Kid Heroes Ser.). (ENG.). 32p. (gr. 3-5). pap. 8.95 *(978-0-7613-6195-4(2)*, Graphic Universe™); lib. bdg. 26.60 *(978-0-7613-6176-3(6))* Lerner Publishing Group.

—The Underground Railroad Adventure of Allen Jay, Antislavery Activist. Hammond, Ted & Carbajal, Richard Pimentel, illus. 2011. (History's Kid Heroes Set III Ser.). pap. 51.02 *(978-0-7613-8622-3(X))*; (ENG.). 32p. (gr. 3-5). pap. 8.95 *(978-0-7613-7806-8(5))* Lerner Publishing Group. (Graphic Universe™).

—The Underground Railroad Adventure of Allen Jay, Antislavery Activist. Hammond, Ted & Carbajal, Richard, illus. 2011. (History's Kid Heroes Ser.). (ENG.). 32p. (gr. 3-5). lib. bdg. 26.60 *(978-0-7613-7804-4(9))* Lerner Publishing Group.

Britt, Fanny. Louis Undercover, 1 vol. Arsenault, Isabelle, illus. 2017. (ENG.). 160p. (J). (gr. 5-9). 19.95 ***(978-1-55498-859-4(4))*** Groundwood Bks. CAN. Dist: Publishers Group West (PGW).

Brockington, Drew. CatStronauts: Mission Moon. 2017. (CatStronauts Ser.: 1). (ENG., Illus.). 160p. (J). (gr. 1-5). 16.99 *(978-0-316-30747-5(5))*; pap. 7.99 *(978-0-316-30745-1(9))* Little Brown & Co.

—CatStronauts: Race to Mars. 2017. (CatStronauts Ser.: 2). (ENG.). 184p. (J). (gr. 1-5). 16.99 *(978-0-316-30748-2(3))* Little, Brown Bks. for Young Readers.

Brontë, Emily. Wuthering Heights by Emily Bront' The Graphic Novel. 2012. (Classic Graphic Novel Collection). (ENG.). 160p. (gr. 7-10). lib. bdg. 39.40 *(978-1-4205-0841-3(5)*, Lucent Bks.) Cengage Gale.

Brooks, Brian. Oopsy Daisy's Bad Day. Brooks, Brian, illus. 2007. (Illus.). 62p. (J). reprint ed. 13.00 *(978-1-4223-9004-7(7))* DIANE Publishing Co.

Brosgol, Vera. Anya's Ghost. Brosgol, Vera, illus. 2011. (ENG., Illus.). 224p. (YA). (gr. 7-12). 22.99 *(978-1-59643-713-5(8)*, 9781596437135); pap. 17.99 *(978-1-59643-552-0(6)*, 9781596435520) Roaring Brook Pr. (First Second Bks.).

—Anya's Ghost. Brosgol, Vera, illus. 2014. (ENG., Illus.). 240p. (YA). (gr. 7). pap. 10.99 *(978-1-250-04001-5(9)*, 9781250040015) Square Fish.

Brown, Bruce. Jack & the Zombie Box. O'Reilly, Sean Patrick, ed. 2011. (Illus.). 46p. (J). pap. 5.95 *(978-1-926914-01-5(5))* Arcana Studio, Inc.

—Mwumba. O'Reilly, Sean Patrick, ed. 2011. (Illus.). 48p. (J). pap. 7.95 *(978-1-897548-03-5(6))* Arcana Studio, Inc.

Brown, Bruce, et al. Brit - Awol, 3 vols., Vol. 2. Kirkman, Robert, ed. 2008. (ENG., Illus.). 160p. (YA). pap. 14.99 *(978-1-58240-864-4(5)*, 9781582408644) Image Comics.

Brown, Jeffrey. Jedi Academy. 2015. (Star Wars: Jedi Academy Ser.). (ENG.). 112p. (J). (gr. 3-7). 9.99 *(978-0-545-85278-4(1))* Scholastic, Inc.

—Lucy & Andy Neanderthal. 2016. (Lucy & Andy Neanderthal Ser.: 1). (ENG., Illus.). 224p. (J). (gr. 3-7). 12.99 *(978-0-385-38835-1(7)*, Crown Books For Young Readers) Random Hse. Children's Bks.

—Lucy & Andy Neanderthal: the Stone Cold Age. 2017. (Lucy & Andy Neanderthal Ser.: 2). (ENG., Illus.). 224p. (J). (gr. 3-7). 12.99 ***(978-0-385-38838-2(1)***, Crown Books For Young Readers) Random Hse. Children's Bks.

Brown, Jeffrey. Sulk. 2009. (Sulk Ser.: 3). (ENG., Illus.). 64p. pap. 6.00 *(978-1-60309-055-1(X)*, 9781603090551) Top Shelf Productions.

Bruneau, Clotilde, et al. The Planet of Ashkabaar. 2015. (Little Prince Ser.: 22). (ENG., Illus.). 48p. (J). (gr. 4-8). 26.60 *(978-0-7613-8773-2(0)*, Graphic Universe™) Lerner Publishing Group.

—The Planet of Bamalias. 2015. (ENG., Illus.). 48p. (J). (gr. 4-8). pap. 7.95 *(978-1-4677-6026-3(9)*, Graphic Universe™) Lerner Publishing Group.

—The Planet of Coppelius. 2014. (Little Prince Ser.: 20). (ENG., Illus.). 48p. (J). (gr. 4-8). lib. bdg. 26.60 *(978-0-7613-8770-1(6)*, Graphic Universe™) Lerner Publishing Group.

—The Planet of Okidians. 2015. (Little Prince Ser.: 21). (ENG., Illus.). 48p. (J). (gr. 4-8). lib. bdg. 26.60 *(978-0-7613-8771-8(4)*, Graphic Universe™) Lerner Publishing Group.

—The Planet of the Cublix. 2014. (Little Prince Ser.: 19). (ENG., Illus.). 48p. (J). (gr. 4-8). lib. bdg. 26.60 *(978-0-7613-8769-5(2)*, Graphic Universe™) Lerner Publishing Group.

—The Planet of the Snake. Nautilus Studio Staff, illus. 2015. (ENG.). 48p. (J). (gr. 4-8). pap. 7.95 *(978-1-4677-6027-0(7)*, Graphic Universe™) Lerner Publishing Group.

—The Planet of Time. Smith, Owen, tr. from FRE. 2014. (Illus.). 48p. (J). (gr. 4-8). lib. bdg. 26.60 *(978-0-7613-8768-8(4)*, Graphic Universe™) Lerner Publishing Group.

Brunswick, Glen. Non-Humans Volume 1: Runaway American Dream TP: Runaway American Dream TP. 2013. (Illus.). 120p. (YA). pap. 14.99 *(978-1-60706-666-8(1))* Image Comics.

Brusha, Joe. Dinosaurs & Prehistoric Predators. Dehart, Andy, ed. 2011. (ENG., Illus.). 120p. (gr. 4-9). pap. 9.99 *(978-0-9827507-4-2(9)*, 9780982750742) Zenescope Entertainment.

—Top 10 Deadliest Sharks. 2011. (ENG., Illus.). 200p. (J). pap. 9.99 *(978-1-937068-90-5(0)*, 9781937068905) Zenescope Entertainment.

Brusha, Joe, et al. Worlds Most Dangerous Animals. 2012. (ENG., Illus.). 120p. pap. 9.99 *(978-0-9827507-3-5(0)*, 9780982750735) Zenescope Entertainment.

Bruzzone, Catherine. Lucy the Cat at the Farm: Lucie le Chat a la Ferme. Beaton, Clare, illus. 2005. (Lucy Cat Ser.). (ENG & FRE.). 24p. (J). (gr. -1-1). pap. 7.99 *(978-1-902915-11-1(9))* B Small Publishing GBR. Dist: Independent Pubs. Group.

—Lucy the Cat in Town: Lucie le Chat en Ville. Beaton, Clare, illus. 2005. (Lucy Cat Ser.). (ENG & FRE.). 24p. (J). (gr. -1-1). pap. 7.99 *(978-1-902915-15-9(1))* B Small Publishing GBR. Dist: Independent Pubs. Group.

Bryant, Clive, ed. Sweeney Todd: The Demon Barber of Fleet Street. Shalvey, Declan et al, illus. 2012. (ENG.). 176p. pap. 16.95 *(978-1-907127-09-0(7)*, Classical Comics, Ltd.); pap. 16.95 *(978-1-907127-10-6(0)*, Classical Comics, Ltd.); (gr. 9). lib. bdg. 24.95 *(978-1-907127-82-3(8))* Classical Comics GBR. Dist: Publishers Group West (PGW).

Bryson, Karen Mueller. The Incredibly Awesome Adventures of Puggie Liddel, the Graphic Novel. Tisdel, L. L, illus. 2013. 108p. pap. *(978-1-927384-09-1(5))* Zeta Comics.

Bucki, Jo Dee & O'Malley, John. Maya Visits a Hospital: Love Is the Best Medicine, 110 vols. Hicks, Mindy, ed. Matthews, Ashley, illus. l.t. ed. 2007. 32p. (J). per. 4.95 *(978-0-9769069-0-2(2))* TAOH Inspired Education, LLC.

Buffagni, Matteo, illus. Avengers Assemble. 2014. (ENG.). 112p. (YA). (gr. 8-17). pap. 16.99 *(978-0-7851-6798-3(6))* Marvel Worldwide, Inc.

Bugtime Adventures - Blessing in Disguise. 2005. (J). 3.95 *(978-1-933262-26-0(5))* Lightning Bug Flix.

Bui-Quang, Phuong-Mai. Tea Club. 2006. (YA). per. 10.95 *(978-1-59971-581-0(3))* Aardvark Global Publishing.

Bunn, Cullen. Doom Maidens. 2013. (ENG., Illus.). 144p. (YA). (gr. 8-17). pap. 15.99 *(978-0-7851-6848-5(6))* Marvel Worldwide, Inc.

—Terrible Lizard. 2015. (ENG., Illus.). 136p. (J). pap. 19.99 *(978-1-62010-236-7(6)*, 9781620102367) Oni Pr., Inc.

Bunyan, Noah F. Lightning Man #1. 2011. 28p. pap. 21.99 *(978-1-4653-3628-6(1))* Xlibris Corp.

Burgan, Michael. Hot Iron: The Adventures of a Civil War Powder Boy. Rodriquez, Pedro, illus. 2007. (Historical Fiction Ser.). (ENG.). 56p. (gr. 2-3). pap. 6.25 *(978-1-59889-406-6(4)*, Graphic Flash) Stone Arch Bks.

Burks, James. Bird & Squirrel on the Edge! 2015. (Bird & Squirrel Ser.). (ENG., Illus.). 144p. (J). (gr. 2-5). 18.99 *(978-0-545-80425-7(6)*, Graphix) Scholastic, Inc.

—Bird & Squirrel on the Run! 2012. (Bird Squirrel Ser.). (Illus.). 125p. (J). lib. bdg. 19.65 *(978-0-606-26211-8(3)*, Turtleback) Turtleback Bks.

C
D

—Gabby & Gator. 2015. (ENG., Illus.). 192p. (J). (gr. 1-17). pap. 10.00 (978-0-316-25935-4(7), Yen Pr.) Orbit.

Burnham, Erik. Ghostbusters, Vol. 2. Schoening, Dan, illus. 2012. (Ghostbusters Ser.). (ENG.). 104p. pap. 17.99 (978-1-61377-279-9(3), 9781613772799) Idea & Design Works, LLC.

—The New Ghostbusters. 2016. lib. bdg. 30.60 (978-0-606-38722-4(6)) Turtleback Bks.

—Teenage Mutant Ninja Turtles: New Animated Adventures: Volume 4, 1 vol. 2016. (Teenage Mutant Ninja Turtles: New Animated Adventures Ser.). (ENG.). 24p. (J). lib. bdg. 24.21 (978-1-61479-462-2(6), Graphic Planet) Magic Wagon.

Burns, Jason M. Megamind: Bad, Blue, Brilliant. 2011. (ENG., Illus.). 52p. pap. 6.95 (978-1-936340-49-1(6), 9781936340491) Ape Entertainment.

—Sesame Street: I Is for Imagination: I Is for Imagination. 2016. 32p. (J). 7.99 (978-1-937676-91-9(9)) Ape Entertainment.

Burrell, Carol klio. Secret Diary. Neel, Julien, illus. 2012. (Lou! Ser.: 1). (ENG.). 48p. (J). (gr. 6-9). lib. bdg. 27.93 (978-0-7613-8776-3(5), Graphic Universe™) Lerner Publishing Group.

—Summertime Blues. Neel, Julien, illus. 2012. (Lou! Ser.: 2). (ENG.). 48p. (J). (gr. 6-9). lib. bdg. 27.93 (978-0-7613-8777-0(3), Graphic Universe™) Lerner Publishing Group.

Burton, Tim. Frankenweenie: A Graphic Novel. 2014. (J). lib. bdg. 26.95 (978-0-606-35261-1(9)) Turtleback Bks.

Buscema, John & Byrne, John, illus. Avengers: The Legacy of Thanos. 2014. (ENG.). 256p. (J). (gr. 4-17). pap. 34.99 (978-0-7851-8891-9(6)) Marvel Worldwide, Inc.

Busch, Robbie. Scooby-Doo in Barnstormin' Banshee, 1 vol. Williams, Anthony, illus. 2010. (Scooby-Doo Graphic Novels Ser.: No. 1). (ENG.). 24p. (J). (gr. 2-5). 24.21 (978-1-59961-691-9(2)) Spotlight.

—Scooby-Doo in Don't Play Dummy with Me, 1 vol. Deporter, Vincent, illus. 2010. (Scooby-Doo Graphic Novels Ser.: No. 1). (ENG.). 24p. (J). (gr. 2-5). 24.21 (978-1-59961-693-3(9)) Spotlight.

—Scooby-Doo in Ready-to-Werewolf, 1 vol. Matchette, Karen, illus. 2010. (Scooby-Doo Graphic Novels Ser.: No. 1). (ENG.). 24p. (J). (gr. 2-5). 24.21 (978-1-59961-696-4(3)) Spotlight.

—Scooby-Doo in the Agony of de Feet!, 1 vol. Pope, Robert, illus. 2010. (Scooby-Doo Graphic Novels Ser.: No. 1). (ENG.). 24p. (J). (gr. 2-5). 24.21 (978-1-59961-690-2(4)) Spotlight.

Busiek, Kurt. Marvels: The Platinum Edition Slipcase. 2014. (ENG., Illus.). 512p. (J). (gr. 4-17). 200.00 (978-0-7851-5471-6(X)) Marvel Worldwide, Inc.

—Wizard's Tale. 2013. (ENG., Illus.). 144p. pap. 19.99 (978-1-61377-593-6(8), 9781613775936) Idea & Design Works, LLC.

Butch, Hartman. The Fairly Oddparents Vol. 6: Gone Too Far. 2005. (Illus.). 96p. (J). pap. 7.99 (978-1-59532-898-4(X)) TOKYOPOP, Inc.

Byerly, Kenny. Teenage Mutant Ninja Turtles: New Animated Adventures: Volume 1, 1 vol. 2016. (Teenage Mutant Ninja Turtles: New Animated Adventures Ser.). (ENG.). 24p. (J). lib. bdg. 24.21 (978-1-61479-459-2(6), Graphic Planet) Magic Wagon.

—Teenage Mutant Ninja Turtles: New Animated Adventures: Volume 2, 1 vol. 2016. (Teenage Mutant Ninja Turtles: New Animated Adventures Ser.). (ENG.). 24p. (J). lib. bdg. 24.21 (978-1-61479-460-8(X), Graphic Planet) Magic Wagon.

Byerly, Kenny Sternin & Eisinger, Justin. Teenage Mutant Ninja Turtles Animated: Never Say Xever/The Gauntlet, Vol. 2. 2013. (Illus.). 112p. (J). pap. 7.99 (978-1-61377-753-4(1), 9781613777534) Idea & Design Works, LLC.

Cabot, Meg. Homecoming. Coronado, Jinky, illus. 2008. (Avalon High Coronation Ser.: Bk. 2). (ENG.). 192p. (YA). (gr. 8-18). pap. 9.99 (978-0-06-117709-5(1)) HarperCollins Pubs.

Cadic, Oliver, et al. Queen Margot - The Bloody Wedding. 2007. (Queen Margot Ser.: 2). (ENG., Illus.). 48p. (J). (gr. -1-12). pap. 13.95 (978-1-905460-19-9(8)) CineBook GBR. Dist: National Bk. Network.

Cadic, Olivier & Gheysens, Francois. Queen Margot - The Age of Innocence. Derenne, Juliette & Barroux, Sophie, illus. 2007. (Queen Margot Ser.: 1). (ENG.). 48p. (J). (gr. 4-7). per. 13.95 (978-1-905460-10-6(4)) CineBook GBR. Dist: National Bk. Network.

Cammuso, Frank. Big Birthday Bash. 2014. (Misadventures of Salem Hyde Ser.). (ENG., Illus.). 96p. (J). (gr. 1-4). 14.95 (978-1-4197-1025-4(7), Amulet Bks.) Abrams, Inc.

—Cookie Catastrophe, Bk. 3. 2014. (Misadventures of Salem Hyde Ser.). (ENG., Illus.). 96p. (J). (gr. 1-4). pap. 6.95 (978-1-4197-1199-2(7), Amulet Bks.) Abrams, Inc.

—Cookie Catastrophe. 2014. (Misadventures of Salem Hyde Ser.: 3). (J). lib. bdg. 17.15 (978-0-606-36149-1(9)) Turtleback Bks.

—The Dodgeball Chronicles. 2008. (Knights of the Lunch Table Ser.: 1). (ENG., Illus.). 144p. (J). (gr. 2-5). pap. 10.99 (978-0-439-90322-6(X), Graphix) Scholastic, Inc.

—The Dragon Players. 2009. (Knights of the Lunch Table Ser.: 2). (ENG.). 128p. (J). (gr. 4-7). pap. 10.99 (978-0-439-90323-3(8), Graphix) Scholastic, Inc.

—The Misadventures of Salem Hyde: Cookie Catastrophe. 2014. (Misadventures of Salem Hyde Ser.). (ENG., Illus.). 96p. (J). (gr. 1-4). 14.95 (978-1-4197-1198-5(9), Amulet Bks.) Abrams, Inc.

—The Misadventures of Salem Hyde: Dinosaur Dilemma. 2015. (Misadventures of Salem Hyde Ser.: 4). (ENG., Illus.). 96p. (J). (gr. 2-4). 14.95 (978-1-4197-1534-1(8), Amulet Bks.) Abrams, Inc.

—The Misadventures of Salem Hyde: Spelling Trouble. 2013. (Misadventures of Salem Hyde Ser.: 1). (J). lib. bdg. 17.15 (978-0-606-33440-2(8), Turtleback) Turtleback Bks.

Campbell, Jan-Ives. League of Super Groovy Crimefighters Trade Paperback. Massey, Mitch & Kelleher, Michael, illus. 2003. (YA). per. 12.95 (978-0-9744216-0-5(X)) Ancient Studios.

Camper, Cathy. Lowriders to the Center of the Earth. 2016. (ENG., Illus.). 128p. (J). (gr. 3-7). 22.99 (978-1-4521-2343-1(8)) Chronicle Bks. LLC.

—Lowriders to the Center of the Earth, Bk. 2. Raul, Gonzalez, illus. 2016. (ENG.). 128p. (J). (gr. 3-7). pap. 9.99 (978-1-4521-3836-7(2)) Chronicle Bks. LLC.

Campi, Alex de. Kat & Mouse, Vol. 1. 2017. (ENG., Illus.). 96p. (YA). pap. 5.99 (978-1-59816-548-7(8), 9781598165487) TOKYOPOP, Inc.

—Valentine Volume 1: Ice of Death TP: Ice of Death TP. 2012. (ENG., Illus.). 352p. (YA). pap. 24.99 (978-1-60706-624-8(6), 9781607066248) Image Comics.

Caniff, Milton. The Complete Terry & the Pirates, 1934-1936, 6 vols., Vol. 1. 2007. (Terry & the Pirates Ser.: 1). (ENG., Illus.). 368p. 49.99 (978-1-60010-100-7(3), 9781600101007) Idea & Design Works, LLC.

Cappoccia, Héloïse. The Planet of the Overhearers. 2013. (Little Prince Ser.: 7). (ENG., Illus.). 56p. (J). (gr. 4-8). pap. 7.95 (978-1-4677-0739-8(2)); lib. bdg. 26.60 (978-0-7613-8757-2(9)) Lerner Publishing Group. (Graphic Universe™).

Capstone Press. First Graphics: My Community, 1 vol. 2010. (First Graphics: My Community Ser.). (ENG.). 32p. lib. bdg. 106.60 (978-1-4296-5935-2(1)) Capstone Press of Coughlan Cos.

—First Graphics: Seasons, 1 vol. 2010. (First Graphics: Seasons Ser.). (ENG.). 32p. lib. bdg. 106.60 (978-1-4296-5936-9(X)) Capstone Press of Coughlan Cos.

Capstone Press Staff. John Henry - Hammerin' Hero. Evergreen, Nelson, illus. 2010. (Graphic Spin Ser.). (ENG.). 40p. (gr. 1-3). lib. bdg. 25.32 (978-1-4342-1898-6(8), Graphic Revolve) Stone Arch Bks.

—The Legend of Johnny Appleseed. Lamoreaux, Michelle, illus. 2010. (Graphic Spin Ser.). (ENG.). 40p. (gr. 1-3). lib. bdg. 25.32 (978-1-4342-1895-7(3), Graphic Revolve) Stone Arch Bks.

—Pecos Bill, Colossal Cowboy. Weber, Lisa K., illus. 2010. (Graphic Spin Ser.). (ENG.). 40p. (gr. 1-3). lib. bdg. 25.32 (978-1-4342-1896-4(1), Graphic Revolve) Stone Arch Bks.

—Rapunzel. Timmins, Jeffrey Stewart, illus. 2009. (Graphic Spin Ser.). (ENG.). 40p. (gr. 1-3). pap. 5.95 (978-1-4342-1392-1(7), Graphic Revolve) Stone Arch Bks.

—Sleeping Beauty. Dietrich, Sean, illus. 2009. (Graphic Spin Ser.). (ENG.). 40p. (gr. 1-3). pap. 5.95 (978-1-4342-1393-8(5), Graphic Revolve) Stone Arch Bks.

—Snow White. Valdez Y Alanis, Erik, illus. 2009. (Graphic Spin Ser.). (ENG.). 40p. (gr. 1-3). pap. 5.95 (978-1-4342-1394-5(3), Graphic Revolve) Stone Arch Bks.

—The Three Little Pigs. Blecha, Aaron, illus. 2010. (Graphic Spin Ser.). (ENG.). 40p. (gr. 1-3). pap. 5.95 (978-1-4342-1395-2(1), Graphic Revolve) Stone Arch Bks.

Caramagna, Joe. Iron Man & the Armor Wars. 2013. (Iron Man & the Armor Wars Ser.: 4). 24p. (J). (gr. 2-6). lib. bdg. 96.84 (978-1-61479-163-8(5)) Spotlight.

—Iron Man & the Armor Wars Part 1: Down & Out in Beverly Hills Hosted. 2013. (Iron Man & the Armor Wars Ser.). (Illus.). 24p. (J). (gr. 2-6). lib. bdg. 24.21 (978-1-61479-164-5(3)) Spotlight.

—Iron Man & the Armor Wars Part 2: The Big Red Machine. 2013. (Iron Man & the Armor Wars Ser.). (Illus.). 24p. (J). (gr. 2-6). lib. bdg. 24.21 (978-1-61479-165-2(1)) Spotlight.

—Iron Man & the Armor Wars Part 3: How I Learned to Love the Bomb. 2013. (Iron Man & the Armor Wars Ser.). (Illus.). 24p. (J). (gr. 2-6). lib. bdg. 24.21 (978-1-61479-166-9(X)) Spotlight.

—Iron Man & the Armor Wars Part 4: The Golden Avenger Strikes Back. 2013. (Iron Man & the Armor Wars Ser.). (Illus.). 24p. (J). (gr. 2-6). lib. bdg. 24.21 (978-1-61479-167-6(8)) Spotlight.

—Marvel Universe Avengers Assemble Volume 2. 2014. (ENG., Illus.). 88p. (J). (gr. -1-17). pap. 9.99 (978-0-7851-8880-3(0)) Marvel Worldwide, Inc.

—Marvel Universe Guardians of the Galaxy: Cosmic Team-Up. Buscema, Sal, illus. 2014. (ENG.). 96p. (J). (gr. -1-17). pap. 9.99 (978-0-7851-9031-8(7)) Marvel Worldwide, Inc.

Caramagna, Joe, text. Amazing Spider-Man, Vol. 4. 2012. (ENG., Illus.). 96p. (J). (gr. -1-17). pap. 6.99 (978-0-7851-6613-9(0)) Marvel Worldwide, Inc.

Carbone, Courtney. Wonder Woman to the Rescue! (DC Super Friends) Doescher, Erik & Random House, illus. 2016. (Step into Reading Ser.). (ENG.). 24p. (J). (gr. -1-1). 4.99 (978-1-101-93308-4(9), Random Hse. Bks. for Young Readers) Random Hse. Children's Bks.

Carew, Kieran. 1 Block Down. Yan, Stan, illus. 2004. 24p. (YA). 2.95 (978-0-9755041-2-3(6)) Squid Works.

Carlin, Mike. The Flintstones & the Jetsons. 2017. (ENG., Illus.). 144p. (gr. 3-7). pap. 12.99 (978-1-4012-7240-1(1)) DC Comics.

Carlson, Bryce. Wall- E: Out There. Luthi, Morgan, illus. 2010. (ENG.). 112p. (J). (gr. 3-6). pap. 9.99 (978-1-60886-568-0(1)) Boom! Studios.

Cartoon Nation, Set. 2009. (Cartoon Nation Ser.). (ENG., Illus.). 32p. (gr. 3-4). lib. bdg. 61.30 (978-1-4296-3687-2(4), Graphic Library) Capstone Press of Coughlan Cos.

Cartoon Stickers. 2004. (Art Rom Create Your Own... Ser.). (Illus.). 24p. (J). pap. incl. audio compact disk (978-1-84229-737-7(6)) Top That! Publishing PLC.

Caselli, Stefano, illus. Avengers World Vol. 1: A. I. M. Empire. 2014. (ENG.). 120p. (J). (gr. 4-17). pap. 16.99 (978-0-7851-8981-7(5)) Marvel Worldwide, Inc.

Casey, Joe. Godland Finale. 2013. (Illus.). 72p. (YA). pap. 6.99 (978-1-60706-819-8(2)) Image Comics.

—Haunt, Vol. 4. 2012. (ENG., Illus.). 140p. (YA). pap. 14.99 (978-1-60706-588-3(6), 9781607065883) Image Comics.

—Rock Bottom. 2012. (ENG., Illus.). 120p. (YA). 19.99 (978-1-60706-619-4(X), 9781607066194) Image Comics.

Casey, Joe & Reed, Brian. The Amazing Spider-Man: The One & Only. Weeks, Lee et al, illus. 2014. (ENG.). 168p. (J). (gr. 4-17). pap. 16.99 (978-0-7851-9010-3(4)) Marvel Worldwide, Inc.

Cassaday, John, illus. Astonishing X-Men - Gifted, Vol. 1. gif. ed. 2006. (ENG.). 152p. (YA). (gr. 8-17). pap. 14.99 (978-0-7851-1531-1(5)) Marvel Worldwide, Inc.

Castellan, Andrea. Mickey Mouse & the Orbiting Nightmare. 2011. (ENG., Illus.). 128p. (J). pap. 9.99 (978-1-60886-630-4(0)) Boom! Studios.

Castellan, Andrea "Casty". Mickey Mouse & the World to Come. Castellan, Andrea "Casty" & Mazzon, Michelle, illus. 2010. (ENG.). 112p. (J). (gr. 3-6). pap. 9.99 (978-1-60886-562-8(2)) Boom! Studios.

Castellucci, Cecil. Shade the Changing Girl Vol. 1: Earth Girl Made Easy. Zarcone, Marley, illus. 2017. (Young Animal Ser.). (ENG.). 144p. pap. 16.99 (978-1-4012-7099-5(9)) DC Comics.

Castro, Nachie. The Man in the Ant Hill, 1 vol. Marvel Illustrators, illus. 2012. (Avengers: Earth's Mightiest Heroes! Ser.). (ENG.). 24p. (J). (gr. -1-4). lib. bdg. 24.21 (978-1-61479-004-4(3)) Spotlight.

Catholic Answers, creator. The Truth Is Out There: Brendan & Erc in Exile, Volume 1. 2013. (ENG., Illus.). 119p. (J). (gr. 4-7). pap. 12.95 (978-1-938983-39-9(4)) Catholic Answers, Inc.

Cauvin, Raoul. Bluecoats - Greenhorn, Vol. 4. Lambil, Willy, illus. 4th ed. 2011. (Bluecoats Ser.: 4). (ENG.). 48p. (gr. 3-17). pap. 11.95 (978-1-84918-066-5(0)) CineBook GBR. Dist: National Bk. Network.

—The Blues in the Mud. Lambil, Willy, illus. 2014. (Bluecoats Ser.: 7). (ENG.). 48p. pap. 11.95 (978-1-84918-183-9(7)) CineBook GBR. Dist: National Bk. Network.

—Bronco Benny. Lambil, Willy, illus. 2013. (Bluecoats Ser.: 6). (ENG.). 48p. pap. 11.95 (978-1-84918-146-4(2)) CineBook GBR. Dist: National Bk. Network.

—Cedric 1 - High-Risk Class. Laudec, Calvinaoul, illus. 2008. (Cedric Ser.: 1). (ENG.). 48p. pap. 11.95 (978-1-905460-68-7(6)) CineBook GBR. Dist: National Bk. Network.

—Cedric Vol. 4: Hot & Cold. Laudec, illus. 2013. (Cedric Ser.: 4). (ENG.). 48p. pap. 11.95 (978-1-84918-158-7(6)) CineBook GBR. Dist: National Bk. Network.

—The Navy Blues. Lambil, Willy, illus. 2009. (Bluecoats Ser.: 2). (ENG.). 46p. (J). (gr. 4-7). pap. 11.95 (978-1-905460-82-3(1)) CineBook GBR. Dist: National Bk. Network.

—Robertsonville Prison, Volume 1. Lambil, Willy, illus. 2009. (Bluecoats Ser.: 1). (ENG.). 46p. (J). (gr. -1-17). pap. 11.95 (978-1-905460-71-7(6)) CineBook GBR. Dist: National Bk. Network.

—Rumberley. Lambil, Willy, illus. 2012. (Bluecoats Ser.: 5). (ENG.). 48p. (J). (gr. 3-8). pap. 11.95 (978-1-84918-108-2(X)) CineBook GBR. Dist: National Bk. Network.

Cerami, Matteo, et al. The Planet of the Grand Buffoon. Smith, Anne & Smith, Owen, trs. from FRE. Elyum Studio, illus. 2014. (Little Prince Ser.: 14). (ENG.). 48p. (J). (gr. 4-8). lib. bdg. 26.60 (978-0-7613-8764-0(1), Graphic Universe™) Lerner Publishing Group.

Cerasi, Chris. Star Wars Adventures: Chewbacca & the Slavers of the Shadowlands, 1 vol. 2013. (Star Wars Digests Set 2 Ser.). (ENG.). 80p. (J). (gr. 4-8). lib. bdg. 27.07 (978-1-61479-057-0(4), Essential Library) ABDO Publishing Co.

Chabert, Jack. Mystery of the Map. Merritt, Kory, illus. 2016. (Poptropica Ser.: bk.1). (ENG.). 112p. (J). (gr. 1-4). 9.95 (978-1-4197-2067-3(8), Amulet Bks.) Abrams, Inc.

Chabot, Jacob. Hello Kitty: Work of Art. 2014. lib. bdg. 18.40 (978-0-606-36123-1(5)) Turtleback Bks.

—Hello Kitty - It's about Time. McGinty, Ian et al, illus. 2015. (ENG.). 64p. (J). pap. 7.99 (978-1-4215-7769-2(0)) Viz Media.

Chabot, Jacob & Mcginty, Ian. Delicious! 2014. (Hello Kitty Graphic Novel Ser.). lib. bdg. 18.40 (978-0-606-35470-7(0)) Turtleback Bks.

Chad, Jon. Leo Geo & His Miraculous Journey Through the Center of the Earth. Chad, Jon, illus. 2012. (ENG., Illus.). 36p. (J). (gr. 2-5). 15.99 (978-1-59643-661-9(1), 9781596436619) Roaring Brook Pr.

—Leo Geo & the Cosmic Crisis. Chad, Jon, illus. 2013. (ENG., Illus.). 40p. (J). (gr. 2-6). 16.99 (978-1-59643-822-4(3), 9781596438224) Roaring Brook Pr.

Chan, Queenie. The Dreaming Collection. 2010. (ENG., Illus.). 576p. pap. 19.99 (978-1-4278-1871-3(1)) TOKYOPOP, Inc.

Chankhamma, Shari. The Sisters' Luck. 2010. (ENG., Illus.). 144p. (YA). pap. 12.95 (978-1-59362-190-2(6), 9781593621902) Slave Labor Bks.

Chantler, Scott. The Captive Prince. Chantler, Scott, illus. 2012. (Three Thieves Ser.: 3). (ENG., Illus.). 116p. (J). (gr. 4-7). 17.95 (978-1-55453-776-1(2)); pap. 7.95 (978-1-55453-777-8(0)) Kids Can Pr., Ltd. CAN. Dist: Hachette Bk. Group.

—Pirates of the Silver Coast. Chantler, Scott, illus. 2014. (Three Thieves Ser.). (ENG., Illus.). 96p. (J). (gr. 4-7). 17.95 (978-1-894786-53-9(X)); pap. 7.95 (978-1-894786-54-6(8)) Kids Can Pr., Ltd. CAN. Dist: Hachette Bk. Group.

—Tower of Treasure. Chantler, Scott, illus. 2010. (Three Thieves Ser.). (ENG., Illus.). 112p. (J). (gr. 4-7). pap. 7.95 (978-1-55453-415-9(1)) Kids Can Pr., Ltd. CAN. Dist: Hachette Bk. Group.

Charlton, Dan & Weiss, Stacy. Silver Surfer, Vol. 2. 2005. (Silver Surfer Ser.: Vol. 2). (Illus.). 192p. (YA). pap. 19.99 (978-0-7851-1575-5(7)) Marvel Worldwide, Inc.

Charlesworth, Kate & Gribbin, John. The Cartoon History of Time. 2013. (ENG., Illus.). 64p. pap. 19.95 (978-0-486-49097-7(1)) Dover Pubns., Inc.

Cheatham, Mark. Aliens! 2012. (Jr. Graphic Monster Stories Ser.). (ENG.). 24p. (J). (gr. 3-6). pap. 10.60 (978-1-4488-6403-4(8)); lib. bdg. 25.25 (978-1-4488-6222-1(1)) Rosen Publishing Group, Inc., The. (PowerKids Pr.).

—Witches! 2012. (Jr. Graphic Monster Stories Ser.). (ENG.). 24p. (J). (gr. 3-6). pap. 10.60 (978-1-4488-6407-2(0)); lib. bdg. 25.25 (978-1-4488-6224-5(8)) Rosen Publishing Group, Inc., The. (PowerKids Pr.).

Check, S. A., et al. Pink Panther, Vol. 1. 2016. (ENG., Illus.). 128p. (J). pap. 19.99 (978-1-945205-04-0(0), 9781945205040) American Mythology Productions.

Chen, Wei Dong. Blood & Renewal. Liang, Xiao Long, illus. 2015. (Outlaws of the Marsh Ser.). (ENG.). 176p. (YA). (gr. 6-12). pap. 9.99 (978-89-98341-90-9(5)) Lerner Publishing Group.

—Etched in Blood. Long Liang, Xiao, illus. 2013. (Three Kingdoms Ser.: 5). 176p. (YA). (gr. 5-12). lib. bdg. 29.27 (978-89-94208-98-5(4)) Lerner Publishing Group.

—The Expulsion of Sun Wu Kong. Peng, Chao, illus. 2013. (Monkey King Ser.: 7). 176p. (YA). (gr. 6-12). lib. bdg. 29.27 (978-89-94208-75-6(5)) Lerner Publishing Group.

—The Family Plot. Long Liang, Xiao, illus. 2013. (Three Kingdoms Ser.: 2). 176p. (YA). (gr. 5-12). lib. bdg. 29.27 (978-89-94208-92-3(5)) Lerner Publishing Group.

—Fight to the Death. Peng, Chao, illus. 2013. (Monkey King Ser.: 11). 176p. (YA). (gr. 6-12). lib. bdg. 29.27 (978-89-94208-79-4(8)) Lerner Publishing Group.

—Heroes & Chaos. Long Liang, Xiao, illus. 2013. (Three Kingdoms Ser.: 1). 176p. (YA). (gr. 5-12). lib. bdg. 29.27 (978-89-94208-90-9(9)) Lerner Publishing Group.

—The Lost Children. Peng, Chao, illus. 2013. (Monkey King Ser.: 12). 176p. (YA). (gr. 6-12). lib. bdg. 29.27 (978-89-94208-80-0(1)) Lerner Publishing Group.

—Monkey King: Birth of the Stone Monkey. Peng, Chao, illus. 2012. (Monkey King Ser.: 1). (ENG.). 176p. (gr. 5-8). lib. bdg. 29.27 (978-89-94208-69-5(0)) JR Comics KOR. Dist: Lerner Publishing Group.

—Monkey King: Enemies & a New Friend. Peng, Chao, illus. 2012. (Monkey King Ser.: 4). (ENG.). 176p. (gr. 5-8). lib. bdg. 29.27 (978-89-94208-72-5(0)) JR Comics KOR. Dist: Lerner Publishing Group.

—Monkey King: Journey to the West. Peng, Chao, illus. 2012. (Monkey King Ser.: 3). (ENG.). 176p. (gr. 5-8). lib. bdg. 29.27 (978-89-94208-71-8(2)) JR Comics KOR. Dist: Lerner Publishing Group.

—Monkey King: The Bane of Heaven. Peng, Chao, illus. 2012. (Monkey King Ser.: 2). (ENG.). 176p. (gr. 5-8). lib. bdg. 29.27 (978-89-94208-70-1(4)) JR Comics KOR. Dist: Lerner Publishing Group.

—Monkey King: The Sacred Tree. Peng, Chao, illus. 2012. (Monkey King Ser.: 6). (ENG.). 176p. (gr. 5-8). lib. bdg. 29.27 (978-89-94208-74-9(7)) JR Comics KOR. Dist: Lerner Publishing Group.

—Monkey King: Three Trials. Peng, Chao, illus. 2012. (Monkey King Ser.: 5). (ENG.). 176p. (gr. 5-8). lib. bdg. 29.27 (978-89-94208-73-2(9)) JR Comics KOR. Dist: Lerner Publishing Group.

—The Realm of the Infant King. Peng, Chao, illus. 2013. (Monkey King Ser.: 10). 176p. (YA). (gr. 6-12). lib. bdg. 29.27 (978-89-94208-78-7(X)) Lerner Publishing Group.

—Revenge & Betrayal. Long Liang, Xiao, illus. 2013. (Three Kingdoms Ser.: 4). 176p. (YA). (gr. 5-12). lib. bdg. 29.27 (978-89-94208-96-1(8)) Lerner Publishing Group.

—The Stolen Kingdom. Peng, Chao, illus. 2013. (Monkey King Ser.: 9). 176p. (YA). (gr. 6-12). lib. bdg. 29.27 (978-89-94208-77-0(1)) Lerner Publishing Group.

—The Timely Rain. Liang, Xiao Long, illus. 2015. (Outlaws of the Marsh Ser.). (ENG.). 176p. (YA). (gr. 6-12). pap. 9.99 (978-89-98341-91-6(3)) Lerner Publishing Group.

—To Pledge Allegiance. Long Liang, Xiao, illus. 2013. (Three Kingdoms Ser.: 3). 176p. (YA). (gr. 5-12). lib. bdg. 29.27 (978-89-94208-94-7(1)) Lerner Publishing Group.

—Treasures of the Mountain Kings. Peng, Chao, illus. 2013. (Monkey King Ser.: 8). 176p. (YA). (gr. 6-12). lib. bdg. 29.27 (978-89-94208-76-3(3)) Lerner Publishing Group.

Chen, Wei Dong & Liang, Xiao Long. Blood & Honor, Vol. 6. 2013. (Three Kingdoms Ser.: 6). (ENG., Illus.). 176p. (gr. 5-12). pap. 8.95 (978-89-94208-99-2(2)) JR Comics KOR. Dist: Lerner Publishing Group.

—The Brotherhood Restored, Vol. 7. Liang, Xiao Long, illus. 2013. (Three Kingdoms Ser.: 7). (ENG., Illus.). 176p. (gr. 5-12). pap. 9.99 (978-89-94208-67-1(4)) JR Comics KOR. Dist: Lerner Publishing Group.

—Etched in Blood, Vol. 5. 2013. (Three Kingdoms Ser.: 5). (ENG., Illus.). 176p. (YA). (gr. 5-12). pap. 9.99 (978-89-94208-97-8(6)) Lerner Publishing Group.

—The Family Plot, Vol. 2. 2013. (Three Kingdoms Ser.: 2). (ENG., Illus.). 176p. (YA). (gr. 5-12). pap. 9.99 (978-89-94208-91-6(7)) Lerner Publishing Group.

—Revenge & Betrayal, Vol. 4. 2013. (Three Kingdoms Ser.: 4). (ENG., Illus.). 176p. (YA). (gr. 5-12). pap. 9.99 (978-89-94208-95-4(X)) Lerner Publishing Group.

—Three Kingdoms, Vol. 9. Liang, Xiao Long, illus. 2013. (Three Kingdoms Ser.: 9). (ENG., Illus.). 176p. (gr. 5-12). pap. 9.99 (978-89-98341-22-0(0)) JR Comics KOR. Dist: Lerner Publishing Group.

—To Pledge Allegiance, Vol. 3. 2013. (Three Kingdoms Ser.: 3). (ENG., Illus.). 176p. (YA). (gr. 5-12). pap. 9.99 (978-89-94208-93-0(3)) Lerner Publishing Group.

Cheshire, Simon. The Treasure of Dead Man's Lane & Other Case Files: Saxby Smart, Private Detective: Book 2. Alley, R. W., illus. 2011. (Saxby Smart, Private Detective Ser.: 2). (ENG.). 224p. (J). (gr. 3-7). pap. 8.99 (978-0-312-67434-2(1), 9780312674342) Square Fish.

Cheung, Jim, et al, illus. Young Avengers. 2010. (ENG.). 352p. (YA). (gr. 8-17). pap. 34.99 (978-0-7851-4907-1(4)) Marvel Worldwide, Inc.

Chickasaw Adventures: More than Warriors. 2005. (J). (978-1-4265-0002-2(5)) Layne Morgan Media, Inc.

Chickasaw Adventures: Tears at Fort Coffee. 2004. (J). (978-0-9762904-2-1(1)) Layne Morgan Media, Inc.

Chickasaw Adventures: The Battle of Akia. 2004. (J). (978-0-9762904-1-4(3)) Layne Morgan Media, Inc.

Chickasaw Adventures: The Civil War. 2005. (J). (978-1-4265-0000-8(9)) Layne Morgan Media, Inc.

Chickasaw Adventures: The Making of a Storyteller. 2004. (J). (978-0-9762904-3-8(X)) Layne Morgan Media, Inc.

Chickasaw Adventures: War with the Creeks. 2005. (J). (978-1-4265-0001-5(7)) Layne Morgan Media, Inc.

Chickasaw Adventures No. 1: The Journey Begins. 2004. (J). (978-0-9762904-0-7(5)) Layne Morgan Media, Inc.

Chilman-Blair, Kim. Medikidz Explain Swine Flu. 2010. (Superheroes on a Medical Mission Ser.). (Illus.). 40p. (YA). pap. 11.75 (978-1-4488-1843-3(5)); (gr. 5-8). lib. bdg. 29.25 (978-1-4358-9457-0(X)) Rosen Publishing Group, Inc., The. (Rosen Reference).

—Superheroes on a Medical Mission, 6 vols., Set 2. Incl. Medikidz Explain ADHD. Taddeo, John. lib. bdg. 29.25 (978-1-4358-9456-3(1)); Medikidz Explain Autism. Taddeo, John. lib. bdg. 29.25 (978-1-4358-9460-0(X)); Medikidz Explain Depression. Deloache, Shawn. lib. bdg. 29.25 (978-1-4358-9455-6(3)); Medikidz Explain HIV. Taddeo, John. lib. bdg. 29.25 (978-1-4358-9458-7(8)); Medikidz Explain Sleep Apnea. Deloache, Shawn. lib. bdg. 29.25 (978-1-4358-9459-4(6)); Medikidz Explain Swine Flu. lib. bdg. 29.25 (978-1-4358-9457-0(X)); (YA). (gr. 5-8). (Illus.). 40p. 2010. Set lib. bdg. 175.50 (978-1-4358-9570-6(3), Rosen Reference) Rosen Publishing Group, Inc., The.

Chilman-Blair, Kim & DeLoache, Shawn. Medikidz Explain Burns: What's up with Harry? 2013. (Illus.). 32p. (J). pap. (978-1-906935-18-4(1)) Medikidz Ltd.

—Medikidz Explain Childhood Glaucoma: What's up with Scott? 2012. (Illus.). 32p. (J). pap. *(978-1-906935-67-2(X))* Medikidz Ltd.
—Medikidz Explain Clinical Trials: What's up with Sara? 2012. (Illus.). 32p. (J). pap. *(978-1-906935-81-8(5))* Medikidz Ltd.
Chilman-Blair, Kim & Deloache, Shawn. Medikidz Explain Depression. 2010. (Superheroes on a Medical Mission Ser.). (Illus.). 40p. (YA). pap. 11.75 *(978-1-4488-1837-2(0))*; (gr. 5-8). lib. bdg. 29.25 *(978-1-4358-9455-6(3))* Rosen Publishing Group, Inc., The. (Rosen Reference).
—Medikidz Explain Depression: What's up with James? 2010. (Illus.). 32p. (J). pap. *(978-1-906935-10-8(6))* Medikidz Ltd.
Chilman-Blair, Kim & DeLoache, Shawn. Medikidz Explain Having an Operation. 2012. (Illus.). 16p. (J). pap. *(978-1-906935-82-5(3))* Medikidz Ltd.
—Medikidz Explain Malaria: What's up with Ken? 2011. (Illus.). 32p. (J). pap. *(978-1-906935-19-1(X))* Medikidz Ltd.
—Medikidz Explain Parkinson's Disease: What's up with Alys' Grandad? 2013. (Illus.). 32p. (J). pap. *(978-1-906935-80-1(7))* Medikidz Ltd.
—MediKidz Explain Severe Asthma: What's up with Tim? 2012. (Illus.). 32p. (J). pap. *(978-1-906935-76-4(9))* Medikidz Ltd.
Chilman-Blair, Kim & Deloache, Shawn. Medikidz Explain Sleep Apnea. 2010. (Superheroes on a Medical Mission Ser.). 40p. (YA). (ENG.). pap. 11.75 *(978-1-4488-1841-9(9))*; (Illus.). (gr. 5-8). lib. bdg. 29.25 *(978-1-4358-9459-4(6))* Rosen Publishing Group, Inc., The. (Rosen Reference).
Chilman-Blair, Kim & DeLoache, Shawn. Medikidz Explain Slipped Hip: What's up with Jacob? 2nd ed. 2012. (Illus.). 32p. (J). pap. *(978-1-906935-14-6(9))* Medikidz Ltd.
—MediKidz Explain Type 1 Diabetes: What's up with Ashleigh? 2nd ed. 2012. (Illus.). 32p. (J). pap. *(978-1-906935-87-0(4))* Medikidz Ltd.
—Medikidz Explain Ulcerative Colitis: What's up with Sarah? 2013. (Illus.). 32p. (J). pap. *(978-1-906935-85-6(8))* Medikidz Ltd.
Chilman-Blair, Kim & Hersov, Kate. Medikidz Explain Haemophilia: What's up with Louis? Deloache, Shawn, illus. 2011. 32p. (J). pap. *(978-1-906935-29-0(7))* Medikidz Ltd.
—Medikidz Explain Inflammatory Bowel Disease: What's up with Adam? Deloache, Shawn, illus. 2011. 32p. (J). pap. *(978-1-906935-65-8(3))* Medikidz Ltd.
Chilman-Blair, Kim & Kipiniak, Chris. Medikidz Explain Hepatitis A: What's up with George? 2011. (Illus.). 32p. (J). pap. *(978-1-906935-72-6(6))* Medikidz Ltd.
—Medikidz Explain Kidney Transplants: What's up with Jonah? 2012. (Illus.). 32p. (J). pap. *(978-1-906935-69-6(6))* Medikidz Ltd.
—Medikidz Explain Seasonal Flu: What's up with Tom? 2011. (Illus.). 32p. (J). pap. *(978-1-906935-44-3(0))* Medikidz Ltd.
Chilman-Blair, Kim & Lee, Tony. MediKidz Explain HIV: What's up with Jason? 2012. (Illus.). 32p. (J). pap. *(978-1-906935-88-7(2))* Medikidz Ltd.
Chilman-Blair, Kim & Rimmer, Ian. Medikidz Explain Eczema: What's up with Kenzie? 2013. (Illus.). 24p. (J). pap. *(978-1-906935-12-2(2))* Medikidz Ltd.
—Medikidz Explain Multiple Sclerosis: What's up with Ryan's Mum? 2012. (Illus.). 32p. (J). pap. *(978-1-906935-78-8(5))* Medikidz Ltd.
Chilman-Blair, Kim & Taddeo, John. Medikidz Explain ADHD. 2010. (Superheroes on a Medical Mission Ser.). 40p. (YA). (ENG.). pap. 11.75 *(978-1-4488-1833-4(8))*; (Illus.). (gr. 5-8). lib. bdg. 29.25 *(978-1-4358-9456-3(1))* Rosen Publishing Group, Inc., The. (Rosen Reference).
—Medikidz Explain Autism. 2010. (Superheroes on a Medical Mission Ser.). (Illus.). 40p. (YA). pap. 11.75 *(978-1-4488-1835-8(4))*; (gr. 5-8). lib. bdg. 29.25 *(978-1-4358-9460-0(X))* Rosen Publishing Group, Inc., The. (Rosen Reference).
—Medikidz Explain Brain Tumours: What's up with Rachel? 2010. (Illus.). 32p. (J). pap. *(978-1-906935-09-2(2))* Medikidz Ltd.
—Medikidz Explain HIV. 2010. (Superheroes on a Medical Mission Ser.). (Illus.). 40p. (YA). pap. 11.75 *(978-1-4488-1839-6(7))*; (gr. 5-8). lib. bdg. 29.25 *(978-1-4358-9458-7(8))* Rosen Publishing Group, Inc., The. (Rosen Reference).
Chilman-Blair, Kim, et al. Medikidz Explain Dystonia Management. 2013. (Illus.). 16p. (J). pap. *(978-1-906935-90-0(4))* Medikidz Ltd.
—Medikidz Explain Living with ADHD. Copter, Steve, illus. 2014. 16p. (J). pap. *(978-1-906935-84-9(X))* Medikidz Ltd.
Chimeno del Campo, Ana Belén. El Preste Juan: Mito y Leyenda en la Literatura Infantil y Juvenil Contemporánea. 2009. (Europäische Hochschulschriften. Reihe 24: Ibero-Romanische Sprachen und Literaturen Ser.). (SPA & POR., Illus.). 128p. pap. 33.95 *(978-3-631-58935-9(2))* Lang, Peter GmbH, Internationaler Verlag der Wissenschaften DEU. Dist: Lang, Peter.
Ching, Jerry Yu & Onghai, Mike. The Greatest King. Ching, Jerry Yu, illus. 2nd I.t. ed. 2003. (Illus.). 52p. *(978-0-9743215-0-9(8))* WebCartoons, LLC.
Chmakova, Svetlana. Awkward. 2015. (ENG., Illus.). 224p. (J). (gr. 5-17). pap. 11.00 *(978-0-316-38130-7(6)*, Yen Pr.) Orbit.
—Awkward. 2015. (J). lib. bdg. 22.10 *(978-0-606-38218-2(6))* Turtleback Bks.
Christie, Robert. Into the Outlands. Lang, Deborah, illus. 2016. (Quirk's Quest Ser.). (ENG.). 128p. (J). 16.99 *(978-1-62672-233-0(1)*, 9781626722330, First Second Bks.) Roaring Brook Pr.
Christopher, Danny. Putuguq & Kublu, 1 vol. Arijanto, Astrid, illus. 2017. (ENG.). 40p. (J). (gr. k-2). pap. 5.95 ***(978-1-77227-143-0(8))*** Inhabit Media Inc. CAN. Dist: Independent Pubs. Group.
Christopher, Neil. The Country of Wolves, 1 vol. Pérez, Ramón, illus. 2015. (ENG.). 108p. (YA). (gr. 7). pap. 19.95 *(978-1-927095-35-5(2))* Inhabit Media Inc. CAN. Dist: Independent Pubs. Group.
Chronicle Books Staff. Nickelodeon Nighttime Book. (J). 16.95 *(978-0-8118-4628-8(8))* Chronicle Bks. LLC.
Chwast, Seymour & Lofting, Hugh. Dr. Dolittle. Chwast, Seymour, illus. 2015. (ENG., Illus.). 40p. (J). (gr. 4-7). 18.99 *(978-1-56846-258-5(1)*, Creative Editions) Creative Co., The.
Cibos, Lindsay. Peach Fuzz, 1 vol., Vol. 1. Hodges, Jared, illus. 2009. (Tokyopop Ser.). (ENG.). 160p. (gr. 2-6). 25.65 *(978-1-59961-571-4(1))* Spotlight.
—Peach Fuzz Vol. 2: Show & Tell, 1 vol. Hodges, Jared, illus. 2009. (Tokyopop Ser.). (ENG.). 176p. (gr. 2-6). 25.65 *(978-1-59961-572-1(X))* Spotlight.
—Peach Fuzz Vol. 3: Prince Edwin, 1 vol. Hodges, Jared, illus. 2009. (Tokyopop Ser.). (ENG.). 176p. (gr. 2-6). 25.65 *(978-1-59961-573-8(8))* Spotlight.
Ciencia Gráfica. 2013. (Ciencia Grfica Ser.). (SPA.). 32p. (gr. 3-4). pap. 95.40 *(978-1-62065-987-8(5))* Capstone Press of Coughlan Cos.
Ciencin, Scott. Attack of the Cling-Ons, 1 vol. Crowther, Jeff, illus. 2011. (Graphic Sparks Ser.). (ENG.). 40p. (gr. 1-3). pap. 5.95 *(978-1-4342-3067-6(8)*, Graphic Sparks) Stone Arch Bks.
—Point-Blank Paintball, 1 vol. Aburtov, illus. 2010. (Sports Illustrated Kids Graphic Novels Ser.). (ENG.). 32p. pap. 1.00 *(978-1-4342-2137-7(7))* Stone Arch Bks.
Ciencin, Scott & Cano, Fernando. Power at the Plate, 1 vol. Esparza, Andres et al, illus. 2011. (Sports Illustrated Kids Graphic Novels Ser.). (ENG.). 56p. (gr. 2-3). pap. 7.19 *(978-1-4342-3400-1(2))*; lib. bdg. 26.65 *(978-1-4342-2239-8(X))* Stone Arch Bks.
Ciencin, Scott & Fuentes, Benny. End Zone Thunder, 1 vol. Sandoval, Gerardo, illus. 2010. (Sports Illustrated Kids Graphic Novels Ser.). (ENG.). 56p. (gr. 2-3). 26.65 *(978-1-4342-2010-3(9))*; pap. 7.19 *(978-1-4342-2784-3(7))* Stone Arch Bks.
—Full Court Flash, 1 vol. Sandoval, Gerardo, illus. 2011. (Sports Illustrated Kids Graphic Novels Ser.). (ENG.). 56p. (gr. 2-3). pap. 7.19 *(978-1-4342-3074-4(0))*; lib. bdg. 26.65 *(978-1-4342-2225-1(X))* Stone Arch Bks.
Ciencin, Scott & Maese, Fares. Avalanche Freestyle, 1 vol. Aburto, Jesus & Esparza, Andres, illus. 2010. (Sports Illustrated Kids Graphic Novels Ser.). (ENG.). 56p. (gr. 2-3). 26.65 *(978-1-4342-2009-7(5))*; pap. 7.19 *(978-1-4342-2783-6(9))* Stone Arch Bks.
—BMX Blitz, 1 vol. Aburto, Jesus & Esparza, Andres, illus. 2011. (Sports Illustrated Kids Graphic Novels Ser.). (ENG.). 56p. (gr. 2-3). pap. 7.19 *(978-1-4342-3071-3(6))* Stone Arch Bks.
—BMX Blitz, 1 vol. Esparza, Andres & Aburto, Jesus, illus. 2011. (Sports Illustrated Kids Graphic Novels Ser.). (ENG.). 56p. (gr. 2-3). lib. bdg. 26.65 *(978-1-4342-2222-0(5))* Stone Arch Bks.
Ciencin, Scott, et al. Hoop Rat, 1 vol. Aburto, Jesus & Cano, Fernando M., illus. 2011. (Sports Illustrated Kids Graphic Novels Ser.). (ENG.). 56p. (gr. 2-3). pap. 7.19 *(978-1-4342-3069-0(4))* Stone Arch Bks.
—Point-Blank Paintball, 1 vol. Aburto, Jesus, illus. 2010. (Sports Illustrated Kids Graphic Novels Ser.). (ENG.). 56p. (gr. 2-3). pap. 7.19 *(978-1-4342-2293-0(4))*; 26.65 *(978-1-4342-1914-5(3))* Stone Arch Bks.
—Snowboard Standoff, 1 vol. Esparza, Andres et al, illus. 2011. (Sports Illustrated Kids Graphic Novels Ser.). (ENG.). 56p. (gr. 2-3). pap. 7.19 *(978-1-4342-3403-2(7))* Stone Arch Bks.
—Snowboard Standoff, 1 vol. Aburto, Jesus et al, illus. 2011. (Sports Illustrated Kids Graphic Novels Ser.). (ENG.). 56p. (gr. 2-3). lib. bdg. 26.65 *(978-1-4342-2242-8(X))* Stone Arch Bks.
Cinebook. Halloween. Jeffrey, Erica, tr. from FRE. 2007. (Melusine Ser.: 2). (ENG., Illus.). 48p. (J). (gr. 4-7). pap. 11.95 *(978-1-905460-34-2(1))* CineBook GBR. Dist: National Bk. Network.
Cipriano, Sal. Adventures of Bio Boy: The Best of Season One. 2006. (Illus.). 128p. (YA). pap. 12.99 *(978-0-9738388-4-8(1))* Speakeasy Comics CAN. Dist: Diamond Bk. Distributors.
CLAMP. X, Vol. 6. 6th ed. 2013. (ENG., Illus.). 192p. pap. 19.99 *(978-1-4215-4046-7(0))* Viz Media.
Clamp Staff. Blood-C Volume 3. Simon, Philip, ed. Kotone, Ranmaru, illus. 2014. (ENG.). 192p. pap. 12.99 *(978-1-61655-314-2(6))* Dark Horse Comics.
—Cardcaptor Sakura, 4 vols., Bk. 4. Horn, Carl Gustav, ed. 2012. (ENG., Illus.). 592p. pap. 19.99 *(978-1-59582-889-7(3))* Dark Horse Comics.
—Cardcaptor Sakura, 4 vols., Vol. 1. 2010. (ENG., Illus.). 600p. pap. 19.99 *(978-1-59582-522-3(3))* Dark Horse Comics.
—Cardcaptor Sakura. 2005. (Illus.). 192p. Vol. 5. 5th rev. ed. pap. 9.99 *(978-1-59182-882-2(1))* Vol. 6. rev. ed. pap. 9.99 *(978-1-59182-883-9(X))* TOKYOPOP, Inc. (Tokyopop Kids).
Clanton, Ben. Super Narwhal & Jelly Jolt. 2017. (Narwhal & Jelly Book Ser.). (ENG., Illus.). 64p. (J). (gr. 1-4). 12.99 *(978-1-101-91829-6(2)*, Tundra Bks.) Tundra Bks. CAN. Dist: Penguin Random Hse. LLC.
Clare, Cassandra. The Mortal Instruments: City of Bones; City of Ashes; City of Glass; City of Fallen Angels; City of Lost Souls; City of Heavenly Fire. 2014. (Mortal Instruments Ser.). (ENG., Illus.). 3248p. (YA). (gr. 9). 137.99 *(978-1-4814-4296-1(1)*, McElderry, Margaret K. Bks.) McElderry, Margaret K. Bks.
Claremont, Chris. X-Men Forever. 2011. (ENG., Illus.). 120p. (J). (gr. 4-17). pap. 16.99 *(978-0-7851-4665-0(2))* Marvel Worldwide, Inc.
Clark, John, ed. Mickey Mouse Adventures, Vol. 5. 2005. (ENG., Illus.). 128p. (YA). pap. 7.95 *(978-0-911903-70-6(4)*, 9780911903706) Gemstone Publishing, Inc.
—Mystery of the Old Mansion, Vol. 6. 2005. (ENG., Illus.). 128p. (YA). pap. 7.95 *(978-0-911903-71-3(2)*, 9780911903713) Gemstone Publishing, Inc.
Clark, Pat. Katz & Dogz Rule. 2013. 48p. pap. 12.99 *(978-1-935711-32-2(6))* Peak City Publishing, LLC.
Clark, Todd. The Ice Cream Kid: Brain Freeze! 2014. (ENG.). 176p. (J). 13.99 *(978-1-4494-4424-2(5))* Andrews McMeel Publishing.
Clark, Wook Jin. Megagogo, Vol. 1. 2014. (ENG., Illus.). 176p. (YA). pap. 19.99 *(978-1-62010-117-9(3)*, 9781620101179) Oni Pr., Inc.
Clarke, Carol Page. The Cuddly Mogs. 2006. (Illus.). 72p. pap. *(978-1-84401-620-4(X))* Athena Pr.
Clarrain, Dean. Teenage Mutant Ninja Turtles Adventures Volume 9. Allan, Chris & Kazaleh, Mike, illus. 2015. (Teenage Mutant Ninja Turtles Ser.). (ENG.). 140p. pap. 19.99 *(978-1-63140-208-1(0)*, 9781631402081) Idea & Design Works, LLC.
Clay, Kathryn, et al. First Graphics: Dinosaurs. Dove, Jason, illus. 2012. (First Graphics: Dinosaurs Ser.). (ENG.). 24p. (gr. 1-2). lib. bdg. 71.97 *(978-1-4296-8143-8(8))* Capstone Press of Coughlan Cos.
Clements, Richmond. Turning Tiger Special Edition. Finbow, Alexander, ed. 2012. (Illus.). 56p. pap. 7.99 *(978-1-926914-87-9(2))* Arcana Studio, Inc.
Cliff, Tony. Delilah Dirk & the King's Shilling. 2016. (ENG., Illus.). 272p. (YA). pap. 17.99 *(978-1-62672-155-5(6)*, 9781626721555, First Second Bks.) Roaring Brook Pr.
Cohen, Ivan & Eltaeb, Gabe. Tattooed Man Trouble!, 1 vol. Vecchio, Luciano, illus. 2014. (Green Lantern: the Animated Ser.). (ENG.). 32p. (gr. 2-3). 22.60 *(978-1-4342-6480-0(7))* Stone Arch Bks.
Cohen, Ivan, et al. Beware the Batman, Vol. 1. 2015. (ENG., Illus.). 144p. (J). (gr. 2-5). pap. 12.99 *(978-1-4012-4936-6(1))* DC Comics.
—Beware the Batman. Vecchio, Luciano & Brizuela, Dario, illus. 2015. (Beware the Batman Ser.). (ENG.). 32p. (gr. 2-3). 90.40 *(978-1-4965-0302-2(3))* Stone Arch Bks.
—Law & Disorder. Vecchio, Luciano, illus. 2015. (Beware the Batman Ser.). (ENG.). 32p. (gr. 2-3). lib. bdg. 22.60 *(978-1-4342-9738-9(1))* Stone Arch Bks.
—The Son of the Man-Bat. Vecchio, Luciano, illus. 2015. (Beware the Batman Ser.). (ENG.). 32p. (gr. 2-3). lib. bdg. 22.60 *(978-1-4342-9741-9(1))* Stone Arch Bks.
Cohn, Ariel. The Zoo Box. Steinke, Aron Nels, illus. 2014. (ENG.). 48p. (J). (gr. k-2). 17.99 *(978-1-62672-052-7(5)*, 9781626720527, First Second Bks.) Roaring Brook Pr.
Colan, Gene & Heck, Don, illus. The Invincible Iron Man. 2014. (ENG.). 264p. (J). (gr. -1-17). pap. 24.99 *(978-0-7851-8843-8(6))* Marvel Worldwide, Inc.
Cole, Bob. Power Reading: Comic Book/Dr. Little. Sirrell, Terri, illus. 2005. 36p. (J). (gr. 2-4). vinyl bd. *(978-1-883186-77-7(3)*, PPSFC1) National Reading Styles Institute, Inc.
—Power Reading: Comic Book/Jungle Book. Connor, Robin, illus. 2005. 62p. (J). (gr. 3-18). vinyl bd. 39.95 *(978-1-883186-74-6(9)*, PPCLC2) National Reading Styles Institute, Inc.
—Power Reading: Comic Book/Superhero. Ford, David, illus. 2005. 34p. (J). (gr. 2-4). vinyl bd. 29.95 *(978-1-883186-79-1(X)*, PPSFC2) National Reading Styles Institute, Inc.
—Power Reading: Comic Book/Time Warp. Ford, David, illus. 2005. 36p. (J). (gr. 3-4). vinyl bd. 29.95 *(978-1-883186-69-2(2)*, PPSFC3) National Reading Styles Institute, Inc.
—Power Reading: Comic Book/Treasure Island. Lee, Ioe, illus. 2005. 70p. (J). (gr. 4-6). vinyl bd. *(978-1-883186-78-4(1)*, PPCLC3) National Reading Styles Institute, Inc.
—Power Reading: Comic Book/Wizard of OZ. Sirrell, Terri, illus. 2005. 60p. (J). (gr. 3-4). vinyl bd. 39.95 *(978-1-883186-80-7(3)*, PPCLC1) National Reading Styles Institute, Inc.
Colfer, Eoin. The Supernaturalist. 2012. (Supernaturalist Ser.). (ENG.). 272p. (J). (gr. 5-9). pap. 7.99 *(978-1-4231-4679-7(4))* Hyperion Pr.
Colfer, Eoin & Donkin, Andrew. Artemis Fowl the Opal Deception Graphic Novel. Rigano, Giovanni & Lamanna, Paolo, illus. 2014. (Artemis Fowl Ser.: 4). (ENG.). 112p. (J). (gr. 5-9). pap. 12.99 *(978-1-4231-4549-3(6))* Hyperion Bks. for Children.
—The Eternity Code. Rigano, Giovanni & Lamanna, Paolo, illus. 2013. (Artemis Fowl Ser.: 3). (ENG.). 112p. (J). (gr. 5-9). 19.99 *(978-1-4231-4527-1(5))* Hyperion Pr.
—Eternity Code. Rigano, Giovanni & Lamanna, Paolo, illus. 2013. (Artemis Fowl Ser.: 3). (ENG.). 112p. (J). (gr. 5-9). pap. 12.99 *(978-1-4231-4577-6(1))* Hyperion Pr.
Collar, Orpheus & Riordan, Rick. The Throne of Fire. Collar, Orpheus, illus. 2015. (Kane Chronicles Ser.). (ENG., Illus.). 160p. (J). (gr. 5-9). 21.99 *(978-1-4847-1490-4(3))* Hyperion Bks. for Children.
Collicutt, Paul. Murder on the Robot City Express. Collicutt, Paul, illus. 2010. (Robot City Ser.: 4). (ENG., Illus.). 48p. (J). (gr. 3-7). pap. 8.99 *(978-0-7636-5015-5(3)*, Templar) Candlewick Pr.
—Rust Attack! Collicutt, Paul, illus. 2009. (Robot City Ser.: 2). (ENG., Illus.). 48p. (J). (gr. 3-7). pap. 8.99 *(978-0-7636-4594-6(X)*, Templar) Candlewick Pr.
Collin, Renaud. Minions - Evil Panic, Vol. 2. Lapuss, Stephane, illus. 2016. (ENG.). 48p. (J). (gr. 3-7). 14.99 *(978-1-78276-556-1(5))* Titan Bks. Ltd. GBR. Dist: Penguin Random Hse. LLC.
Collins, Terry. The Assassination of John F. Kennedy: November 22 1963, 1 vol. 2014. (24-Hour History Ser.). (ENG., Illus.). 48p. (gr. 3-5). lib. bdg. 33.32 *(978-1-4329-9294-1(5)*, NA-h) Heinemann-Raintree.
—The Assassination of Martin Luther King, Jr: April 4 1968, 1 vol. 2014. (24-Hour History Ser.). (ENG., Illus.). 48p. (gr. 3-5). lib. bdg. 33.32 *(978-1-4329-9296-5(1)*, NA-h) Heinemann-Raintree.
—King of Pop: The Story of Michael Jackson, 1 vol. Byers, Michael, illus. 2012. (American Graphic Ser.). (ENG.). 32p. (gr. 3-4). pap. 8.10 *(978-1-4296-7994-7(8))*; 30.65 *(978-1-4296-6015-0(5))*; pap. 47.70 *(978-1-4296-8476-7(3))* Capstone Press of Coughlan Cos. (Graphic Library).
—Robert E. Lee: The Story of the Great Confederate General. Mallea, Cristian, illus. (American Graphic Ser.). (ENG.). 32p. (gr. 3-4). 2011. pap. 47.70 *(978-1-4296-6436-3(3))* 2010. lib. bdg. 30.65 *(978-1-4296-5475-3(9))* Capstone Press of Coughlan Cos. (Graphic Library).
—True Stories of World War II. Kinsella, Pat, illus. 2012. (Stories of War Ser.). (ENG.). 32p. (gr. 3-4). pap. 47.70 *(978-1-4296-9347-9(9)*, Graphic Library) Capstone Press of Coughlan Cos.
Collins, Terry & Schulz, Barbara. Escape from Pompeii: An Isabel Soto Archaeology Adventure, 1 vol. 2010. (Graphic Expeditions Ser.). (ENG., Illus.). 32p. (gr. 3-4). pap. 8.10 *(978-1-4296-5634-4(4)*, Graphic Library) Capstone Press of Coughlan Cos.
Collins, Terry & Weakland, Mark. Unmasking Monsters with Scooby-Doo! Comia, Christian et al, illus. 2015. (Unmasking Monsters with Scooby-Doo! Ser.). (ENG.). 24p. (gr. 1-2). lib. bdg. 155.94 *(978-1-4914-1797-3(8))* Capstone Press of Coughlan Cos.
Collins, Terry, et al. Escape from Pompeii: An Isabel Soto Archaeology Adventure, 1 vol. 2010. (Graphic Expeditions Ser.). (ENG., Illus.). 32p. (gr. 3-4). lib. bdg. 30.65 *(978-1-4296-4771-7(X)*, Graphic Library) Capstone Press of Coughlan Cos.
—Getting to the Bottom of Global Warming: An Isabel Soto Investigation. 2010. (Graphic Expeditions Ser.). (ENG.). 32p. (gr. 3-4). pap. 47.70 *(978-1-4296-5143-1(1)*, Graphic Library) Capstone Press of Coughlan Cos.
—Getting to the Bottom of Global Warming: An Isabel Soto Investigation. Schulz, Barbara, illus. 2010. (Graphic Expeditions Ser.). (ENG.). 32p. (gr. 3-4). lib. bdg. 30.65 *(978-1-4296-3972-9(5)*, Graphic Library) Capstone Press of Coughlan Cos.
—Nickolas Flux History Chronicles, 1 vol. Simmons, Mark, illus. 2014. (Nickolas Flux History Chronicles Ser.). (ENG.). 32p. (gr. 3-4). 122.60 *(978-1-4914-0255-9(5)*, Graphic Library) Capstone Press of Coughlan Cos.
Colossal, Eric. Feasts of Fury. 2016. (Rutabaga the Adventure Chef Ser.: 2). (J). lib. bdg. 20.80 *(978-0-606-38205-2(4))* Turtleback Bks.
—Rutabaga: The Adventure Chef. 2015. (Rutabaga the Adventure Chef Ser.). (ENG., Illus.). 128p. (J). (gr. 3-7). 16.95 *(978-1-4197-1380-4(9)*, Amulet Bks.) Abrams, Inc.
—Rutabaga the Adventure Chef: Book 2: Feasts of Fury. 2016. (Rutabaga the Adventure Chef Ser.). (ENG., Illus.). 128p. (J). (gr. 3-7). 16.95 *(978-1-4197-1658-4(1)*, Amulet Bks.) Abrams, Inc.
Comeau, Joey. Ninja-Rella. Lozano, Omar, illus. 2015. (Far Out Fairy Tales Ser.). (ENG.). 40p. (gr. 3-4). lib. bdg. 25.32 *(978-1-4342-9647-4(4))* Stone Arch Bks.
Comeau, Joey & Holmes, Mike. Bravest Warriors, Vol. 2. Holmes, Mike, illus. 2014. (Bravest Warriors Ser.: 2). (ENG., Illus.). 128p. (J). (gr. 4). pap. 14.99 *(978-1-60886-352-5(2))* Boom! Studios.
The Complete Graphica Collection (2013) 2013. (Graphica Ser.). (ENG., Illus.). 24–48p. (gr. 3-8). 16041.10 *(978-1-4777-0643-5(7)*, Rosen Classroom) Rosen Publishing Group, Inc., The.
Conner, Daniel. The Tempest, 1 vol. Martin, Cynthia, illus. 2008. (Graphic Shakespeare Ser.). (ENG.). 48p. (gr. 5-10). 29.93 *(978-1-60270-194-6(6)*, Graphic Planet- Fiction) ABDO Publishing Co.
Constantine, Clélia. The Planet of Ludokaa. Élyum Studio, illus. 2013. (Little Prince Ser.: 12). (ENG.). 48p. (J). (gr. 4-8). pap. 7.95 *(978-1-4677-1521-8(2))*; lib. bdg. 26.60 *(978-0-7613-8762-6(5))* Lerner Publishing Group. (Graphic Universe™).
Conway, Gerry. Break-Up! 2011. (Hardy Boys the New Case Files Ser.). (ENG., Illus.). 64p. (J). (gr. 3-7). pap. 6.99 *(978-1-59707-242-7(7)*, 9781597072427) Papercutz.
—Break-Up! Henrique, Paulo, illus. 2011. (Hardy Boys the New Case Files Ser.: 2). (ENG.). 64p. (J). (gr. 3-7). 10.99 *(978-1-59707-243-4(5)*, 9781597072434) Papercutz.
—Nancy Drew: Together with the Hardy Boys. 2011. (Nancy Drew the New Case Files Ser.). (ENG., Illus.). 64p. (J). (gr. 3-7). pap. 7.99 *(978-1-59707-262-5(1)*, 9781597072625) Papercutz.
Cook, Greg. Friends Is Friends. 2016. (ENG., Illus.). 208p. (gr. 9). 19.99 *(978-1-59643-105-8(9)*, 9781596431058, First Second Bks.) Roaring Brook Pr.
Cook, Katie. Friendship Is Magic, Vol. 1. Price, Andy, illus. 2014. (My Little Pony Ser.). (ENG.). 104p. pap. 17.99 *(978-1-61377-605-6(5)*, 9781613776056) Idea & Design Works, LLC.
—My Little Pony: Friendship Is Magic Part 1: Friendship Is Magic Part 1. Price, Andy, illus. 2013. (My Little Pony Ser.). (ENG.). 52p. (J). (gr. 2-5). pap. 6.99 *(978-1-61377-628-5(4)*, 9781613776285) Idea & Design Works, LLC.
—My Little Pony: Friendship Is Magic Part 2: Friendship Is Magic Part 2. Price, Andy, illus. 2014. (My Little Pony Ser.). (ENG.). 52p. (J). (gr. 2-5). pap. 6.99 *(978-1-61377-860-9(0)*, 9781613778609) Idea & Design Works, LLC.
—My Little Pony: Friendship Is Magic Volume 3: Friendship Is Magic Volume 3. Price, Andy, illus. 2014. (My Little Pony Ser.). (ENG.). 104p. pap. 17.99 *(978-1-61377-854-8(6)*, 9781613778548) Idea & Design Works, LLC.
—Rarity, 1 vol. Price, Andy, illus. 2015. (ENG.). 24p. (J). *(978-1-61479-335-9(2))* Spotlight.
Cooke, C. W. Fame: The Cast of Glee. 2011. (ENG., Illus.). 40p. (YA). pap. 7.99 *(978-1-4507-4429-4(X))* Bluewater Productions, Inc.
—Lady Gaga - Fame. 2012. (ENG., Illus.). 40p. (YA). pap. 7.99 *(978-1-4507-4920-6(8))* Bluewater Productions, Inc.
—Wrath of the Titans: Cyclops. 2012. (ENG.). 40p. pap. 7.99 *(978-1-4507-8964-6(1))* Bluewater Productions, Inc.
Coover, Colleen & Tobin, Paul. Adventure Time: The Flip Side. 2014. lib. bdg. 33.05 *(978-0-606-36120-0(0))* Turtleback Bks.
Corderoy, Tracey. The Grunt & the Grouch. 2013. (Grunt & the Grouch Ser.). (ENG.). 112p. (gr. 1-3). 101.28 *(978-1-4342-4852-7(6))* Stone Arch Bks.
Cornell, Paul & Venditti, Robert. Demon Knights - The Gathering Storm, Vol. 3. 2014. (ENG., Illus.). 256p. pap. 19.99 *(978-1-4012-4269-5(3))* DC Comics.
Corsetto, Danielle. Adventure Time Volume 1: Playing with Fire (Color Edition) 2016. lib. bdg. 26.95 *(978-0-606-38733-0(1))* Turtleback Bks.
Cosentino, Ralph. Batman: The Story of the Dark Knight. Cosentino, Ralph, illus. 2008. (ENG., Illus.). 40p. (J). (gr. -1-2). 16.99 *(978-0-670-06255-3(3)*, Viking Books for Young Readers) Penguin Young Readers Group.
—Wonder Woman: The Story of the Amazon Princess. Cosentino, Ralph, illus. 2011. (ENG., Illus.). 40p. (J). (gr. -1-2). 16.99 *(978-0-670-06256-0(1)*, Viking Books for Young Readers) Penguin Young Readers Group.
Cosson, M. J. Sherlock Holmes & A Scandal in Bohemia. rev. ed. 2010. pap. 39.62 *(978-0-7613-6954-7(6))* Lerner Publishing Group.
—Sherlock Holmes & the Adventure at the Abbey Grange. 2nd rev. ed. 2010. pap. 39.62 *(978-0-7613-6957-8(0))* Lerner Publishing Group.
—Sherlock Holmes & the Adventure of the Blue Gem. 3rd rev. ed. 2010. pap. 39.62 *(978-0-7613-6959-2(7))* Lerner Publishing Group.
Costi, Vincent. The Planet of the Gargand. Smith, Anne & Smith, Owen, trs. from FRE. Élyum Studio, illus. 2014. (Little Prince Ser.: 15). (ENG.). 48p. (J). (gr. 4-8). lib. bdg. 26.60 *(978-0-7613-8765-7(X)*, Graphic Universe™) Lerner Publishing Group.

C
D

Coudray, Jean-Luc. A Goofy Guide to Penguins: TOON Level 1. Coudray, Philippe, illus. 2016. (ENG.). 40p. (J). (gr. k). 12.95 *(978-1-935179-96-2(9))* TOON Books / RAW Junior, LLC.

Coudray, Philippe. Benjamin Bear in Brain Storms! 2015. (Benjamin Bear Ser.). (ENG., Illus.). 40p. (J). (gr. -1-3). 12.95 *(978-1-935179-82-5(9))* TOON Books / RAW Junior, LLC.

—Benjamin Bear in Bright Ideas! 2013. (Benjamin Bear Ser.). (ENG., Illus.). 32p. (J). (gr. -1-3). 12.95 *(978-1-935179-22-1(5))* TOON Books / RAW Junior, LLC.

—Benjamin Bear in Fuzzy Thinking. 2013. (Benjamin Bear Ser.). (ENG., Illus.). 32p. (J). (gr. -1-3). pap. 6.99 *(978-1-935179-25-2(X))* TOON Books / RAW Junior, LLC.

Coverly, Dave. Dogs Are People, Too: A Collection of Cartoons to Make Your Tail Wag. 2015. (ENG., Illus.). 224p. (J). (gr. 2-7). pap. 12.99 *(978-1-62779-042-0(X)*, 9781627790420, Holt, Henry & Co. Bks. For Young Readers) Holt, Henry & Co.

Cowsill, Alan. World War One, 1914-1918. Sharma, Lalit Kumar, illus. 2014. (Campfire Graphic Novels Ser.). (ENG.). 114p. (YA). (gr. 8-12). pap. 12.99 *(978-93-80741-85-7(5)*, Campfire) Steerforth Pr.

Coy, John & Reonegro, Antonio. Around the World, 1 vol. 2015. (ENG.). 32p. (J). pap. 10.95 *(978-1-62014-224-0(4))* Lee & Low Bks., Inc.

—Around the World. Lynch, Tom, illus. 2005. (ENG.). 32p. (J). (gr. 1-7). 17.95 *(978-1-58430-244-5(5))* Lee & Low Bks., Inc.

Craddock, Erik. BC Mambo. Craddock, Erik, illus. 2009. (Stone Rabbit Ser.: Bk. 1). (ENG., Illus.). 96p. (J). (gr. 3-7). pap. 6.99 *(978-0-375-84360-0(4)*, Random Hse. Bks. for Young Readers) Random Hse. Children's Bks.

—Dragon Boogie. Craddock, Erik, illus. 2012. (Stone Rabbit Ser.: Vol. 7). (ENG., Illus.). 96p. (J). (gr. 2-5). pap. 6.99 *(978-0-375-86912-9(3)*, Random Hse. Bks. for Young Readers) Random Hse. Children's Bks.

—Dragon Boogie. 2012. (Stone Rabbit Ser.: 7). lib. bdg. 17.20 *(978-0-606-23868-7(9)*, Turtleback) Turtleback Bks.

—Pirate Palooza. Craddock, Erik, illus. 2009. (Stone Rabbit Ser.: Bk. 2). (ENG., Illus.). 96p. (J). (gr. 3-7). pap. 6.99 *(978-0-375-85660-0(9)*, Random Hse. Bks. for Young Readers) Random Hse. Children's Bks.

—Robot Frenzy. 2013. (Stone Rabbit Ser.: 8). lib. bdg. 17.20 *(978-0-606-27004-5(3)*, Turtleback) Turtleback Bks.

—Stone Rabbit #6: Night of the Living Dust Bunnies. Craddock, Erik, illus. 2011. (Stone Rabbit Ser.: 6). (ENG., Illus.). 96p. (J). (gr. 3-7). pap. 6.99 *(978-0-375-86724-8(4)*, Random Hse. Bks. for Young Readers) Random Hse. Children's Bks.

—Stone Rabbit #8: Robot Frenzy. Craddock, Erik, illus. 2013. (Stone Rabbit Ser.). (ENG., Illus.). 96p. (J). (gr. 2-5). pap. 6.99 *(978-0-375-86913-6(1))*; lib. bdg. 12.99 *(978-0-375-96913-3(6))* Random Hse. Children's Bks. (Random Hse. Bks. for Young Readers).

Craft, Jerry. Mama's Boyz: Because Learning Shouldn't Stop at 3 o'Clock!: Home Schoolin', 2 vols. 2007. (Illus.). 112p. (YA). per. 9.95 *(978-0-9796132-0-3(5))* Mama's Boyz, Inc.

Creanga, Ion. The Old Man's Daughter & the Old Woman's Daughter / Fata Babei Si Fata Mosneagului. Todd Kaplan, Delia Angelescu, tr. Gimlin, Mihaela, illus. 2013. 42p. pap. 17.95 *(978-1-936629-30-5(5))* Reflection Publishing.

Crilley, Mark. Akiko Flights of Fancy. exp. ed. 2007. (Illus.). 264p. pap. 24.95 *(978-1-57989-088-9(1))* Sirius Entertainment, Inc.

—Brody's Ghost Volume 6. Crilley, Mark, illus. 2015. (ENG., Illus.). 112p. pap. 7.99 *(978-1-61655-461-3(4))* Dark Horse Comics.

—Spring. Crilley, Mark, illus. 2007. (Miki Falls Ser.: 1). (ENG., Illus.). 176p. (YA). (gr. 8-12). pap. 8.99 *(978-0-06-084616-9(X))* HarperCollins Pubs.

—Summer. Crilley, Mark, illus. 2007. (Miki Falls Ser.: 2). (ENG., Illus.). 176p. (YA). (gr. 8-12). pap. 8.99 *(978-0-06-084617-6(8))* HarperCollins Pubs.

—Winter. Crilley, Mark, illus. 2008. (Miki Falls Ser.: 4). (ENG., Illus.). 176p. (YA). (gr. 8-12). pap. 8.99 *(978-0-06-084619-0(4))* HarperCollins Pubs.

Crippa, Luca, et al. The Discovery of America. Cooper-McGuinness, Nanette, tr. de Pretto, Lorenzo, illus. 2009. (Geronimo Stilton Graphic Novels Ser.). (ENG.). 56p. (J). (gr. 2-6). 9.99 *(978-1-59707-158-1(7)*, 9781597071581) Papercutz.

Criswell, Ginger. Recycle Michael. 2012. (Illus.). 24p. 12.99 *(978-1-60010-906-5(3))* Idea & Design Works, LLC.

Croall, Marie. Ali Baba: Fooling the Forty Thieves [an Arabian Tale]. Hilinski, Clint, illus. 2009. (Graphic Myths & Legends Ser.). (ENG.). 48p. (gr. 4-8). pap. 8.95 *(978-1-58013-887-1(X))* Lerner Publishing Group.

—Sinbad: Sailing into Peril. Hilinski, Clint, illus. 2007. (Graphic Myths & Legends Ser.). (ENG.). 48p. (gr. 4-8). lib. bdg. 27.93 *(978-0-8225-6375-4(4))* Lerner Publishing Group.

Croall, Marie P. Marwe: Into the Land of the Dead - An East African Folktale. Lago, Ray & Hamilton, Craig, illus. 2008. (Graphic Myths & Legends Ser.). (ENG.). 48p. (gr. 4-8). 27.93 *(978-0-8225-7134-6(X)*, Graphic Universe™) Lerner Publishing Group.

—My Boyfriend Is a Monster - Under His Spell. Park, Hyeondo, illus. 2011. (My Boyfriend Is a Monster Ser.: 4). (ENG.). 128p. (YA). (gr. 7-12). pap. 9.95 *(978-0-7613-7076-5(5)*, Graphic Universe™) Lerner Publishing Group.

—School of Evil. Carruthers, Sandy, illus. 2010. (Twisted Journeys (r) Ser.: 13). (ENG.). 112p. (J). (gr. 4-7). pap. 7.95 *(978-0-8225-9271-6(1)*, Graphic Universe™); lib. bdg. 27.93 *(978-0-8225-9263-1(0))* Lerner Publishing Group.

—Under His Spell, 4 vols., No. 4. Park, Hyeondo, illus. 2011. (My Boyfriend Is a Monster Ser.: 4). (ENG.). 128p. (YA). (gr. 7-12). 29.27 *(978-0-7613-5602-8(9))* Lerner Publishing Group.

Croall, Marie P. & Jolley, Dan. Agent Mongoose & the Attack of the Giant Insects. Wendt, Matt, illus. 2010. (Twisted Journeys (r) Ser.: 15). (ENG.). 112p. (J). (gr. 4-7). lib. bdg. 27.93 *(978-0-8225-9251-8(7))* Lerner Publishing Group.

Crompton, Laurie Boyle. Blaze (Or, Love in the Time of Supervillains) 2013. (ENG.). 320p. (YA). (gr. 7-12). pap. 8.99 *(978-1-4022-7343-8(6))* Sourcebooks, Inc.

Cronin, Doreen. Wiggle, 1 vol. Menchin, Scott, illus. 2006. (Doreen Cronin: Click-Clack & More Ser.). (ENG.). 36p. (gr. -1-3). lib. bdg. 24.21 *(978-1-59961-093-1(0))* Spotlight.

Cronn-Mills, Kirstin. Original Fake. Johnson, E. Eero, illus. 2016. (ENG.). 352p. (YA). (gr. 7). 17.99 *(978-0-399-17326-4(9)*, G.P. Putnam's Sons Books for Young Readers) Penguin Young Readers Group.

Crow, Melinda Melton. Little Lizard's New Baby, 1 vol. Rowland, Andrew, illus. 2011. (Little Lizards Ser.). (ENG.). 32p. (gr. -1-1). pap. 6.25 *(978-1-4342-3047-8(3))* Stone Arch Bks.

—Little Lizard's New Friend, 1 vol. Rowland, Andrew, illus. 2011. (Little Lizards Ser.). (ENG.). 32p. (gr. -1-1). pap. 6.25 *(978-1-4342-3048-5(1))* Stone Arch Bks.

—Little Lizard's New Pet, 1 vol. Rowland, Andrew, illus. 2011. (Little Lizards Ser.). (ENG.). 32p. (gr. -1-1). pap. 6.25 *(978-1-4342-3049-2(X))*; lib. bdg. 22.65 *(978-1-4342-2508-5(9))* Stone Arch Bks.

—Little Lizard's New Shoes, 1 vol. Rowland, Andrew, illus. 2011. (Little Lizards Ser.). (ENG.). 32p. (gr. -1-1). pap. 6.25 *(978-1-4342-3050-8(3))*; lib. bdg. 22.65 *(978-1-4342-2509-2(7))* Stone Arch Bks.

Cunningham, Scott. Scooby-Doo in Terror Is Afoot!, 1 vol. Neely, Scott, illus. 2010. (Scooby-Doo Graphic Novels Ser.: No. 1). (ENG.). 24p. (J). (gr. 2-5). 24.21 *(978-1-59961-698-8(X))* Spotlight.

Curnow, Bobby. Applejack, 1 vol. Hickey, Brenda, illus. 2015. (ENG.). 24p. (J). *(978-1-61479-331-1(X))* Spotlight.

Custard, P. T. Kid Canine - Superhero! Custard, P. T. & Pearson, David, illus. 2008. 32p. (J). 13.95 *(978-0-9785317-1-3(X))* Black Plum Bks.

Cuthbert, Jennifer. The Adventures of Lollipop. 2004. 28p. 4.95 *(978-0-9732053-0-5(X))* Peppermint Publishing CAN. Dist: Hushion Hse. Publishing, Ltd.

Dahl, Michael. Alien Snow, 1 vol. Glass House Graphics Staff, illus. 2011. (Good vs Evil Ser.). (ENG.). 48p. (gr. 1-2). pap. 6.29 *(978-1-4342-3444-5(4)*, Good vs Evil) Stone Arch Bks.

—Dragon in the Desert, 1 vol. Vue, Tou, illus. 2010. (Dragonblood Ser.). (ENG.). 40p. (gr. 1-3). pap. 6.25 *(978-1-4342-2309-8(4)*, Zone Bks.) Stone Arch Bks.

—Dragon Theft Auto, 1 vol. Rong, Yap Kun, illus. 2010. (Dragonblood Ser.). (ENG.). 40p. (gr. 1-3). pap. 6.25 *(978-1-4342-2310-4(8)*, Zone Bks.) Stone Arch Bks.

—Dungeon of Seven Dooms, 1 vol. 2011. (Good vs Evil Ser.). (ENG.). 48p. (gr. 1-2). lib. bdg. 23.99 *(978-1-4342-2091-2(5)*, Good vs Evil) Stone Arch Bks.

—Good Morning, Superman! Lozano, Omar, illus. 2017. (DC Super Heroes Ser.). (ENG.). 32p. (gr. -1-2). lib. bdg. 22.65 *(978-1-5158-0970-8(6)*, DC Super Heroes) Stone Arch Bks.

—Guardian of Earth, 1 vol. Schoening, Dan, illus. 2011. (Green Lantern Ser.). (ENG.). 56p. (gr. 2-3). pap. 4.95 *(978-1-4342-3081-2(3))*; lib. bdg. 26.65 *(978-1-4342-2611-2(5))* Stone Arch Bks. (DC Super Heroes).

—The Last Super Hero, 1 vol. Schoening, Dan, illus. 2011. (Green Lantern Ser.). (ENG.). 56p. (gr. 2-3). pap. 4.95 *(978-1-4342-3082-9(1))*; lib. bdg. 26.65 *(978-1-4342-2612-9(3))* Stone Arch Bks. (DC Super Heroes).

—The Marshmallow Mermaid. Crowther, Jeff, illus. 2010. (Graphic Sparks Ser.). (ENG.). 40p. (gr. 1-3). pap. 5.95 *(978-1-4342-2802-4(9)*, Graphic Sparks) Stone Arch Bks.

—The Museum Monsters. Schoening, Dan, illus. (Superman Ser.). (ENG.). 56p. (gr. 2-3). 2013. pap. 4.95 *(978-1-4342-1372-3(2))* 2009. lib. bdg. 26.65 *(978-1-4342-1157-6(6))* Stone Arch Bks. (DC Super Heroes).

—Stowaway Monster, 1 vol. Pellegrino, Richard, illus. 2010. (Dragonblood Ser.). (ENG.). 40p. (gr. 1-3). pap. 6.25 *(978-1-4342-2312-8(4)*, Zone Bks.) Stone Arch Bks.

—Sugar Hero. Crowther, Jeff, illus. (Graphic Sparks Ser.). (ENG.). 40p. (gr. 1-3). 2010. pap. 5.95 *(978-1-4342-2801-7(0))* 2009. lib. bdg. 23.99 *(978-1-4342-1587-1(3))* Stone Arch Bks. (Graphic Sparks).

—Terror Beach, 1 vol. Pellegrino, Richard, illus. 2010. (Dragonblood Ser.). (ENG.). 40p. (gr. 1-3). pap. 6.25 *(978-1-4342-2313-5(2)*, Zone Bks.) Stone Arch Bks.

—Trial of the Amazons, 1 vol. Schoening, Dan, illus. 2010. (Wonder Woman Ser.). (ENG.). 56p. (gr. 2-3). lib. bdg. 26.65 *(978-1-4342-1883-4(X)*, DC Super Heroes) Stone Arch Bks.

—Twilight of the Gods: A Viking Graphic Novel. Garcia, Eduardo, illus. 2016. (Norse Myths: a Viking Graphic Novel Ser.). (ENG.). 56p. (gr. 3-4). lib. bdg. 27.99 *(978-1-4965-3489-7(1))* Stone Arch Bks.

Dahl, Michael & Nickel, Scott. The Dozer Strikes! Jennings, C. S., illus. 2010. (Incredible Rockhead Ser.). (ENG.). 40p. (gr. 1-3). lib. bdg. 23.99 *(978-1-4342-1894-0(5)*, Graphic Sparks) Stone Arch Bks.

—The Green Queen of Mean. Crowther, Jeff, illus. 2010. (Graphic Sparks Ser.). (ENG.). 40p. (gr. 1-3). pap. 5.95 *(978-1-4342-2803-1(7)*, Graphic Sparks) Stone Arch Bks.

Dahl, Michael, et al. Five Riddles for Robin, 1 vol. Schigiel, Gregg, illus. 2013. (Batman Ser.). (ENG.). 56p. (gr. 2-3). pap. 4.95 *(978-1-4342-1366-2(8)*, DC Super Heroes) Stone Arch Bks.

—The Last Son of Krypton. 2009. (Superman Ser.). (ENG., Illus.). 56p. (gr. 2-3). lib. bdg. 26.65 *(978-1-4342-1155-2(X)*, DC Super Heroes) Stone Arch Bks.

—Last Son of Krypton. 2013. (Superman Ser.). (ENG., Illus.). 56p. (gr. 2-3). pap. 4.95 *(978-1-4342-1370-9(6)*, DC Super Heroes) Stone Arch Bks.

Dale, Jeremy. Battle at Three Rivers, Vol. 3. 2014. (ENG., Illus.). 96p. (YA). pap. 8.99 *(978-1-939352-55-2(X)*, 9781939352552) Action Lab Entertainment.

—Into the Woods. 2014. (ENG., Illus.). 96p. (J). pap. 8.99 *(978-1-939352-50-7(9)*, 9781939352507) Action Lab Entertainment.

—Strange Creatures, Vol. 2. 2014. (ENG., Illus.). 96p. (J). pap. 8.99 *(978-1-939352-52-1(5)*, 9781939352521) Action Lab Entertainment.

David, B. The Littlest Pirate King. 2010. (ENG., Illus.). 48p. 16.99 *(978-1-60699-403-0(4)*, 699403) Fantagraphics Bks.

David, Peter. Hand in Hand: Part 1. 2013. (Wolverine First Class Set 2 Ser.). (Illus.). 24p. (J). (gr. 2-6). lib. bdg. 24.21 *(978-1-61479-176-8(7))* Spotlight.

—Hand in Hand: Part 2. 2013. (Wolverine First Class Set 2 Ser.). (Illus.). 24p. (J). (gr. 2-6). lib. bdg. 24.21 *(978-1-61479-177-5(5))* Spotlight.

—Nothing to Lose. Cross, Chris, illus. 2003. (Captain Marvel Ser.). 144p. (YA). pap. 12.99 *(978-0-7851-1104-7(2))* Marvel Worldwide, Inc.

—Rock Gods. 2013. (Wolverine First Class Set 2 Ser.). (Illus.). 24p. (J). (gr. 2-6). lib. bdg. 24.21 *(978-1-61479-180-5(5))* Spotlight.

—X-Factor - Hell on Earth War, Vol. 20. 2013. (ENG., Illus.). 160p. (YA). (gr. 8-17). pap. 15.99 *(978-0-7851-6700-6(5))* Marvel Worldwide, Inc.

David, Peter & Van Lente, Fred. Wolverine First Class Set 2. 2013. (Wolverine First Class Set 2 Ser.: 6). 24p. (J). (gr. 2-6). lib. bdg. 145.26 *(978-1-61479-175-1(9))* Spotlight.

David, Peter, et al. Amazing Spider-Man Epic Collection: Ghosts of the Past. Buscema, Sal & Frenz, Ron, illus. 2014. (ENG.). 472p. (J). (gr. 4-17). pap. 34.99 *(978-0-7851-8916-9(5))* Marvel Worldwide, Inc.

—The Return of the Worthy. 2007. (Star Trek (Titan Books) Ser.). (ENG., Illus.). 160p. per. 14.95 *(978-1-84576-319-0(X)*, Titan Bks.) Titan Bks. Ltd. GBR. Dist: Penguin Random Hse. LLC.

Davidge, James. The Duchess Ranch of Old John Ware. Prodor, Bob, illus. 2010. (ENG.). 104p. pap. 10.95 *(978-1-897411-18-6(9))* Bayeux Arts, Inc. CAN. Dist: Chicago Distribution Ctr.

—Mathemagick: The Point & the Invisible Hand. Davidge, Jesse, illus. 2014. (ENG.). 64p. (YA). pap. 9.95 *(978-1-897411-80-3(4))* Bayeux Arts, Inc. CAN. Dist: Chicago Distribution Ctr.

Davidge, James & Davidge, Jesse. Mathemagick: Apples & Origins - Featuring Hypatia of the Wandering Stars. 2013. (ENG.). 32p. (YA). pap. 6.95 *(978-1-897411-76-6(6))* Bayeux Arts, Inc. CAN. Dist: Chicago Distribution Ctr.

—Mathemagick: The War of Flat & Wonder. 2014. (ENG., Illus.). 48p. (YA). pap. 9.95 *(978-1-897411-81-0(2))* Bayeux Arts, Inc. CAN. Dist: Chicago Distribution Ctr.

Davis, Alan. Killraven. Davis, Alan, illus. 2003. (Spider-Man Ser.). (Illus.). 144p. (YA). pap. 16.99 *(978-0-7851-1083-5(6))* Marvel Worldwide, Inc.

Davis, Alan, et al. The Road to Onslaught. Cruz, Roger et al, illus. 2014. (ENG.). 440p. (J). (gr. 4-17). pap. 39.99 *(978-0-7851-8830-8(4))* Marvel Worldwide, Inc.

Davis, Daniel M. & Davis, Dawna Jo. Klawberry: Good Girl. Bad World. McClellan, Sara, ed. ltd. ed. 2007. (Illus.). per. 20.00 *(978-0-9774173-3-9(6))* Steam Crow Pr.

Davis, Darren G. & Larner, Bob. Atlas: Greetings from Earth. 2011. (ENG., Illus.). 96p. (J). pap. 7.99 *(978-1-4507-3535-3(5))* Bluewater Productions, Inc.

Davis, Eleanor. Flop to the Top! TOON Level 3. Weing, Drew, illus. 2015. (ENG.). 40p. (J). (gr. k). 12.95 *(978-1-935179-89-4(6))* TOON Books / RAW Junior, LLC.

—The Secret Science Alliance. Davis, Eleanor, illus. 2009. (ENG., Illus.). 160p. (YA). (gr. 3-6). pap. 16.99 *(978-1-59990-396-5(2)*, 9781599903965, Bloomsbury USA Childrens) Bloomsbury Publishing USA.

—The Secret Science Alliance & the Copycat Crook. Davis, Eleanor, illus. 2009. (ENG., Illus.). 160p. (J). (gr. 3-6). 18.99 *(978-1-59990-142-8(0)*, 9781599901428, Bloomsbury USA Childrens) Bloomsbury Publishing USA.

Davis, Jim. Fat Cat, No.1. 2003. (Garfield Ser.). (gr. 5-8). lib. bdg. 29.40 *(978-0-613-68581-8(4)*, Turtleback) Turtleback Bks.

—Garfield: Sticht Zu. Goetting, Waltraud & Bartoszko, Alexandra, trs. from ENG. (Garfield Ser.: Vol. 10). (GER., Illus.). 128p. (J). pap. 10.95 *(978-3-8105-0754-9(7))* Kruger, Wolfgang Verlag, GmbH DEU. Dist: Distribooks, Inc.

—Garfield & Co. Boxed Set Vol. #1-4. 2012. (Garfield Graphic Novels Ser.). (ENG., Illus.). 128p. (J). (gr. 1-6). 29.99 *(978-1-59707-342-4(3)*, 9781597073424) Papercutz.

—Garfield Benimmt sich Daneben. Goetting, Waltraud & Bartoszko, Alexandra, trs. from ENG. (GER., Illus.). 128p. (J). pap. *(978-3-8105-0890-4(X))* Kruger, Wolfgang Verlag, GmbH DEU. Dist: International Bk. Import Service, Inc.

—Garfield Blast sich Auf. Goetting, Waltraud & Bartoszko, Alexandra, trs. from ENG. (Garfield Ser.: Vol. 20). (GER., Illus.). 128p. (J). pap. *(978-3-8105-0884-3(5))* Kruger, Wolfgang Verlag, GmbH DEU. Dist: International Bk. Import Service, Inc.

—Garfield Bleibt sich Treu. Goetting, Waltraud & Bartoszko, Alexandra, trs. from ENG. (Garfield Ser.: Vol.19). (GER., Illus.). 128p. (J). pap. *(978-3-8105-0880-5(2))* Kruger, Wolfgang Verlag, GmbH DEU. Dist: International Bk. Import Service, Inc.

—Garfield Caution - Wide Load. 2013. (Garfield Ser.: 56). (ENG., Illus.). 96p. pap. 14.00 *(978-0-345-52596-3(5)*, Ballantine Bks.) Random House Publishing Group.

—Garfield Dreht Durch. Goetting, Waltraud & Bartoszko, Alexandra, trs. from ENG. (Garfield Ser.: Vol. 22). (GER., Illus.). 128p. (J). pap. *(978-3-8105-0886-7(1))* Kruger, Wolfgang Verlag, GmbH DEU. Dist: International Bk. Import Service, Inc.

—Garfield Gets in a Pickle. 2012. (Garfield Ser.: 54). lib. bdg. 25.75 *(978-0-606-26835-6(9)*, Turtleback) Turtleback Bks.

—Garfield Halt die Ohren Steif. Goetting, Waltraud & Bartoszko, Alexandra, trs. from ENG. (Garfield Ser.: Vol. 23). (GER., Illus.). 128p. (J). pap. *(978-3-8105-0889-8(6))* Kruger, Wolfgang Verlag, GmbH DEU. Dist: International Bk. Import Service, Inc.

—Garfield Hangt Ab. Bartoszko, Alexandra, tr. from ENG. (Garfield Ser.: Vol. 32). (GER., Illus.). 128p. (J). pap. *(978-3-8105-0918-5(3))* Kruger, Wolfgang Verlag, GmbH DEU. Dist: International Bk. Import Service, Inc.

—Garfield Hat Genug. Goetting, Waltraud & Bartoszko, Alexandra, trs. from ENG. (Garfield Ser.: Vol. 18). (GER., Illus.). 128p. (J). pap. *(978-3-8105-0833-1(0))* Kruger, Wolfgang Verlag, GmbH DEU. Dist: International Bk. Import Service, Inc.

—Garfield Hat Schwein. Bartoszko, Alexandra, tr. from ENG. (Garfield Ser.: Vol. 31). (GER., Illus.). 128p. (J). pap. *(978-3-8105-0897-3(7))* Kruger, Wolfgang Verlag, GmbH DEU. Dist: International Bk. Import Service, Inc.

—Garfield Haut Rein. Goetting, Waltraud & Bartoszko, Alexandra, trs. from ENG. (Garfield Ser.: Vol. 17). (GER., Illus.). 128p. (J). pap. *(978-3-8105-0779-2(2))* Kruger, Wolfgang Verlag, GmbH DEU. Dist: International Bk. Import Service, Inc.

—Garfield Hebt Ab. Goetting, Waltraud & Bartoszko, Alexandra, trs. from ENG. (Garfield Ser.: Vol. 16). (GER., Illus.). 128p. (J). pap. *(978-3-8105-0776-1(8))* Kruger, Wolfgang Verlag, GmbH DEU. Dist: International Bk. Import Service, Inc.

—Garfield ist Spitze. Goetting, Waltraud & Bartoszko, Alexandra, trs. from ENG. (Garfield Ser.: Vol. 11). (GER., Illus.). 128p. (J). pap. *(978-3-8105-0757-0(1))* Kruger, Wolfgang Verlag, GmbH DEU. Dist: International Bk. Import Service, Inc.

—Garfield Kratzt die Kurve. Goetting, Waltraud & Bartoszko, Alexandra, trs. from ENG. (Garfield Ser.: Vol. 28). (GER., Illus.). 128p. (J). pap. *(978-3-8105-0894-2(2))* Kruger, Wolfgang Verlag, GmbH DEU. Dist: International Bk. Import Service, Inc.

—Garfield Lasst nicht Locker. Goetting, Waltraud & Bartoszko, Alexandra, trs. from ENG. (Garfield Ser.: Vol. 14). (GER., Illus.). 128p. (J). pap. *(978-3-8105-0771-6(7))* Kruger, Wolfgang Verlag, GmbH DEU. Dist: International Bk. Import Service, Inc.

—Garfield Legts Drauf An. Goetting, Waltraud & Bartoszko, Alexandra, trs. from ENG. (Garfield Ser.: Vol. 25). (GER.). 128p. (J). pap. *(978-3-8105-0891-1(8))* Kruger, Wolfgang Verlag, GmbH DEU. Dist: International Bk. Import Service, Inc.

—Garfield Nimmt den Mund Voll. Goetting, Waltraud & Bartoszko, Alexandra, trs. from ENG. (Garfield Ser.: Vol. 21). (GER., Illus.). 128p. (J). pap. *(978-3-8105-0885-0(3))* Kruger, Wolfgang Verlag, GmbH DEU. Dist: International Bk. Import Service, Inc.

—Garfield Nimmt's Leicht. Bartoszko, Alexandra, tr. from ENG. (Garfield Ser.: Vol. 29). (GER., Illus.). 128p. (J). pap. *(978-3-8105-0895-9(0))* Kruger, Wolfgang Verlag, GmbH DEU. Dist: International Bk. Import Service, Inc.

—Garfield Platzt aus allen Naehten. Bartoszko, Alexandra, tr. from ENG. (Garfield Ser.: Vol. 33). (GER., Illus.). 128p. (J). pap. *(978-3-8105-0919-2(1))* Kruger, Wolfgang Verlag, GmbH DEU. Dist: International Bk. Import Service, Inc.

—Garfield Riecht den Braten. Bartoszko, Alexandra, tr. from ENG. (Garfield Ser.: Vol. 34). (GER., Illus.). 128p. (J). pap. *(978-3-8105-0920-8(5))* Kruger, Wolfgang Verlag, GmbH DEU. Dist: International Bk. Import Service, Inc.

—Garfield Spielt auf Zeit. Goetting, Waltraud & Bartoszko, Alexandra, trs. from ENG. (Garfield Ser.: Vol. 13). (GER., Illus.). 128p. (J). pap. *(978-3-8105-0759-4(8))* Kruger, Wolfgang Verlag, GmbH DEU. Dist: International Bk. Import Service, Inc.

—Garfield Streicht Ein. Goetting, Waltraud & Bartoszko, Alexandra, trs. from ENG. (Garfield Ser.: Vol. 12). (GER., Illus.). 128p. (J). pap. *(978-3-8105-0758-7(X))* Kruger, Wolfgang Verlag, GmbH DEU. Dist: International Bk. Import Service, Inc.

—Garfield Waechst & Gegeiht. Bartoszko, Alexandra, tr. from ENG. (Garfield Ser.: Vol. 30). (GER., Illus.). 128p. (J). pap. *(978-3-8105-0896-6(9))* Kruger, Wolfgang Verlag, GmbH DEU. Dist: International Bk. Import Service, Inc.

—Garfield Will es Wissen. Goetting, Waltraud & Bartoszko, Alexandra, trs. from ENG. (Garfield Ser.: Vol. 26). (GER., Illus.). 128p. (J). pap. *(978-3-8105-0892-8(6))* Kruger, Wolfgang Verlag, GmbH DEU. Dist: International Bk. Import Service, Inc.

—Garfield Zeigt die Krallen. Goetting, Waltraud & Bartoszko, Alexandra, trs. from ENG. (Garfield Ser.: Vol. 27). (GER., Illus.). 128p. (J). pap. *(978-3-8105-0893-5(4))* Kruger, Wolfgang Verlag, GmbH DEU. Dist: International Bk. Import Service, Inc.

Davis, Jim & Evanier, Mark. Catzilla. Ellipsanime Staff & Dargaud Media, illus. 2011. (Garfield Graphic Novels Ser.). (ENG.). 32p. (J). (gr. 1-6). 7.99 *(978-1-59707-278-6(8)*, 9781597072786) Papercutz.

—Garfield & Co. #7: Home for the Holidays. Ellipsanime Staff & Dargaud Media, illus. 2012. (Garfield Graphic Novels Ser.). (ENG.). 32p. (J). (gr. 1-6). 7.99 *(978-1-59707-370-7(9)*, 9781597073707) Papercutz.

Davis, Jim & Michiels, Cedric. Jon's Night Out. Ellipsanime Staff & Dargaud Media, illus. 2013. (Garfield Show Ser.). (ENG.). 64p. (J). (gr. 1-5). 11.99 *(978-1-59707-444-5(6)*, 9781597074445); pap. 7.99 *(978-1-59707-443-8(8)*, 9781597074438) Papercutz.

—Unfair Weather. Dargaud Media Staff & Ellipsanime Staff, illus. 2013. (Garfield Show Ser.). (ENG.). 64p. (J). (gr. 1-5). 11.99 *(978-1-59707-433-9(0)*, 9781597074339); pap. 7.99 *(978-1-59707-422-3(5)*, 9781597074223) Papercutz.

Davis, Jim, et al. A Game of Cat & Mouse. Dargaud Media Staff & Ellipsanime Staff, illus. 2012. (Garfield Graphic Novels Ser.). (ENG.). 32p. (J). (gr. 1-6). 7.99 *(978-1-59707-300-4(8)*, 9781597073004) Papercutz.

—Garfield & Co. #6: Mother Garfield. Ellipsanime Staff, illus. 2012. (Garfield Graphic Novels Ser.). (ENG.). 32p. (J). (gr. 1-6). 7.99 *(978-1-59707-318-9(0)*, 9781597073189) Papercutz.

—Secret Agent X, Bk. 8. Ellipsanime Staff & Dargaud Media Staff, illus. 2013. (Garfield Graphic Novels Ser.). (ENG.). 32p. (J). (gr. 1-6). 7.99 *(978-1-59707-360-8(1)*, 9781597073608) Papercutz.

Davis, Katie. The Curse of Addy Mcmahon. 2008. (ENG., Illus.). 288p. (J). (gr. 5-9). 16.99 *(978-0-06-128711-4(3)*, Greenwillow Bks.) HarperCollins Pubs.

—The Curse of Addy McMahon. 2008. (Illus.). 288p. (J). (gr. 5-9). lib. bdg. 17.89 *(978-0-06-128712-1(1)*, Greenwillow Bks.) HarperCollins Pubs.

Davison, Max. Home Collection, Vol. 1. Hebb, Matt & Dalton, Alex, illus. 2016. (ENG.). 112p. (J). (gr. 3-7). pap. 12.99 *(978-1-78276-698-8(7))* Titan Bks. Ltd. GBR. Dist: Penguin Random Hse. LLC.

Davison, Max & Cooper, Chris. Cat about Town. Bartolini, Egle & Alvarez, Dave, illus. 2016. (ENG.). 64p. (J). (gr. 1-4). pap. 6.99 *(978-1-78585-332-6(5))* Titan Bks. Ltd. GBR. Dist: Penguin Random Hse. LLC.

—Puss in Boots Collection - Amazing Tales!, Vol. 1. Bartolini, Egle & Alvarez, Dave, illus. 2016. (ENG.). 112p. (J). (gr. 1-4). pap. 12.99 *(978-1-78585-318-0(X))* Titan Bks. Ltd. GBR. Dist: Penguin Random Hse. LLC.

Dc Comics Editors. Batman Arkham Poison Ivy. 2016. lib. bdg. 33.05 *(978-0-606-39204-4(1))* Turtleback Bks.

DC Comics Staff. Batman Jumbo Color & Activity Book. Meredith Books Staff et al, eds. 2005. 400p. (J). pap. 5.99 *(978-0-696-22722-6(3))* Meredith Bks.

—DC Super Friends: Girl Power! 2017. (ENG., Illus.). 16p. (J). bds. 10.99 *(978-0-374-30397-6(5)*, 9780374303976, Farrar, Straus & Giroux (BYR)) Farrar, Straus & Giroux.

—DC Super Friends: the Missing Batmobile. 2016. (ENG., Illus.). 16p. (J). bds. 10.99 *(978-0-374-30395-2(9)*, 9780374303952, Farrar, Straus & Giroux (BYR)) Farrar, Straus & Giroux.

—DC Super Friends Wipe Clean Activity Book. 2017. (ENG.). 56p. (J). spiral bd. 12.99 *(978-0-374-30398-3(3)*, 9780374303983, Farrar, Straus & Giroux (BYR)) Farrar, Straus & Giroux.

—DC Super Heroes Storybook Collection. 2012. (ENG., Illus.). 192p. (J). (gr. -1-3). 11.99 *(978-0-06-212398-5(X))* HarperCollins Pubs.

DC Super Friends, 1 vol. (DC Super Friends Ser.). (ENG.). 32p. (gr. 1-2). 2014. 271.20 *(978-1-4342-9525-5(7))* 2013. 180.80 *(978-1-4342-4856-5(9))* Stone Arch Bks.

DC Super Hero Books for Libraries. 2013. (DC Super Heroes Ser.). (ENG.). 3823.26 *(978-1-4342-6566-1(8))* Stone Arch Bks.

DC Super Heroes. 2013. (DC Super Heroes Ser.). (ENG.). 56p. (gr. 2-3). 133.25 *(978-1-4342-6064-2(X))*; 106.60 *(978-1-4342-6065-9(8))* Stone Arch Bks. (DC Super Heroes).

De Bonneval, Gwen. William & the Lost Spirit. Smith, Anne, tr. Bonhomme, Matthieu, illus. 2013. (ENG.). 160p. (YA). (gr. 8-12). pap. 9.95 *(978-1-4677-0807-4(0)*, Graphic Universe™) Lerner Publishing Group.

de Campi, Alex. Agent Boo, Vol. 1. 2017. (ENG., Illus.). 96p. pap. 4.99 *(978-1-59816-802-0(9)*, 9781598168020) TOKYOPOP, Inc.

—Kat & Mouse. 2017. (ENG., Illus.). 96p. pap. 5.99 *(978-1-59816-549-4(6)*, 9781598165494) TOKYOPOP, Inc.

De Campi, Alex. Kat & Mouse, Vol. 3. 2017. (ENG., Illus.). 96p. pap. 5.99 *(978-1-59816-550-0(X)*, 9781598165500) TOKYOPOP, Inc.

—Kat & Mouse Vol. 1: Teacher Torture, 1 vol. Manfredi, Federica, illus. 2009. (Tokyopop Ser.). (ENG.). 96p. (gr. 2-6). 25.65 *(978-1-59961-564-6(9))* Spotlight.

—Kat & Mouse Vol. 2: Tripped, 1 vol. Manfredi, Federica, illus. 2009. (Tokyopop Ser.). (ENG.). 96p. (gr. 2-6). 25.65 *(978-1-59961-565-3(7))* Spotlight.

—Kat & Mouse Vol. 3: The Ice Storm, 1 vol. Manfredi, Federica, illus. 2009. (Tokyopop Ser.). (ENG.). 96p. (gr. 2-6). 25.65 *(978-1-59961-566-0(5))* Spotlight.

—Pinkie Pie & Applejack, 1 vol. McNeil, Carla Speed, illus. 2016. (ENG.). 24p. (J). *(978-1-61479-508-7(8))* Spotlight.

De Gieter, Lucien. The Evil Mummies. Spear, Luke, tr. from FRE. 2010. (Papyrus Ser.: 4). (ENG., Illus.). 46p. (J). (gr. 4-7). pap. 11.95 *(978-1-84918-027-6(X))* CineBook GBR. Dist: National Bk. Network.

—Imhotep's Transformation. Spear, Luke, tr. from FRE. 2008. (Papyrus Ser.: 2). (ENG., Illus.). 48p. pap. 11.95 *(978-1-905460-50-2(3))* CineBook GBR. Dist: National Bk. Network.

—The Rameses' Revenge. Spear, Luke, tr. from FRE. 2007. (Papyrus Ser.: 1). (ENG., Illus.). 48p. (J). (gr. 4-7). pap. 11.95 *(978-1-905460-35-9(X))* CineBook GBR. Dist: National Bk. Network.

de Groot, Bob & Morris Publishing Company Staff. The One-Armed Bandits, Vol. 33. 2012. (Lucky Luke Ser.: 33). (ENG., Illus.). 48p. (J). (gr. 3-12). pap. 11.95 *(978-1-84918-111-2(X))* CineBook GBR. Dist: National Bk. Network.

De Saint-Exupéry, Antoine. The Little Prince Graphic Novel. Sfar, Joann, illus. 2013. (Little Prince Ser.). (ENG.). 112p. (J). (gr. 5-7). 12.99 *(978-0-547-33800-2(7))* Houghton Mifflin Harcourt Publishing Co.

—Le Petit Prince Graphic Novel. Sfar, Joann, illus. 2010. (FRE & ENG.). 112p. (J). (gr. 5-7). 22.00 *(978-0-547-44330-0(7))* Houghton Mifflin Harcourt Publishing Co.

Deacon, Kristen, et al. Boo the World's Cutest Dog Volume 1. 2017. (ENG., Illus.). 104p. (J). 12.99 *(978-1-5241-0233-3(4)*, 9781524102333, Dynamite Entertainment) Dynamic Forces, Inc.

Dean, Myers Walter. Monster. 2014. (ENG.). 304p. (J). (gr. 12-12). 14.24 *(978-1-63245-060-9(7))* Lectorum Pubns., Inc.

DeBlois, Dean, et al. The Serpent's Heir. Wheatley, Doug, illus. 2017. (ENG.). 80p. (gr. 4-7). pap. 10.99 *(978-1-61655-931-1(4))* Dark Horse Comics.

DeCarlo, Mike, et al. Shell Shocker, 1 vol. Doescher, Erik, illus. 2011. (Flash Ser.). (ENG.). 56p. (J). (gr. 2-3). lib. bdg. 26.65 *(978-1-4342-2615-0(8)*, DC Super Heroes) Stone Arch Bks.

Defalco, Tom. Spider-Man: The Ultimate Guide. 2004. (Illus.). 168p. (J). (gr. 4-10). reprint ed. 25.00 *(978-0-7567-7419-6(5))* DIANE Publishing Co.

—Spider-Man Bk. 1: The Complete Alien Costume Saga. Leonardi, Rick et al, illus. 2014. (ENG.). 488p. (J). (gr. 4-17). pap. 44.99 *(978-0-7851-8867-4(3))* Marvel Worldwide, Inc.

Defalco, Tom, et al. Thor Epic Collection: War of the Pantheons. Frenz, Ron et al, illus. 2013. (ENG.). 472p. (J). (gr. 4-17). pap. 34.99 *(978-0-7851-8788-2(X))* Marvel Worldwide, Inc.

Defilippis, Nunzio & Weir, Christina. The Avalon Chronicles, Vol. 2. 2013. (ENG., Illus.). 152p. (YA). 19.99 *(978-1-934964-90-3(5)*, 9781934964903) Oni Pr., Inc.

—Avalon Chronicles Volume 1: Once in a Blue Moon. 2012. (ENG., Illus.). 152p. 19.99 *(978-1-934964-75-0(1)*, 9781934964750) Oni Pr., Inc.

Defoe, Daniel. Robinson Crusoe. Cabrera, Eva, illus. 2015. (Graphic Revolve: Common Core Editions Ser.). (ENG.). 72p. (gr. 2-3). lib. bdg. 27.99 *(978-1-4965-0371-8(6))* Stone Arch Bks.

Dehoratius. Follow Your Fates Exile of Aeneas. 2010. (Illus.). x, 113p. (J). pap. 12.00 *(978-0-86516-709-4(5))* Bolchazy-Carducci Pubs.

del Rio, Tania. Sabrina the Teenage Witch: the Magic Within 1. 2013. (Sabrina Manga Ser.). (ENG., Illus.). 256p. (J). (gr. 4-7). 10.99 *(978-1-936975-39-6(4)*, Archie Comics) Archie Comic Pubns., Inc.

—Sabrina the Teenage Witch: the Magic Within 3. 2013. (Sabrina Manga Ser.: 3). (ENG., Illus.). 256p. (J). (gr. 4-7). pap. 10.99 *(978-1-936975-60-0(2)*, Archie Comics) Archie Comic Pubns., Inc.

—Sabrina the Teenage Witch: the Magic Within 4. 2014. (Sabrina Manga Ser.: 4). (ENG., Illus.). 272p. (J). (gr. 4-7). pap. 10.99 *(978-1-936975-76-1(9)*, Archie Comics) Archie Comic Pubns., Inc.

Delashmutt, Amy. Hello, Cy! Torgeson, Sarah, illus. 2007. 24p. (J). lib. bdg. 14.95 *(978-1-932888-53-9(5))* Mascot Bks., Inc.

Delisi, Don. Junk Pyle. 2012. 36p. pap. 20.99 *(978-1-4772-5699-2(7))* AuthorHouse.

Delporte, Peyo, et al. The Smurfs & the Howlibird. 2011. (Smurfs Graphic Novels Ser.). (ENG., Illus.). 56p. (J). (gr. 2-5). 10.99 *(978-1-59707-261-8(3)*, 9781597072618) Papercutz.

Delporte, Yvan. The Purple Smurfs. Peyo, illus. 2010. (Smurfs Graphic Novels Ser.). (ENG.). 56p. (J). (gr. 2-5). pap. 6.99 *(978-1-59707-206-9(0)*, 9781597072069) Papercutz.

—The Smurfs & the Magic Flute. Peyo, illus. 2010. (Smurfs Graphic Novels Ser.). (ENG.). 64p. (J). (gr. 2-5). pap. 5.99 *(978-1-59707-208-3(7)*, 9781597072083) Papercutz.

Delporte, Yvan & Peyo. The Purple Smurf, No. 1. 2010. (Smurfs Graphic Novels Ser.). (ENG., Illus.). 56p. (J). (gr. 2-5). 12.99 *(978-1-59707-207-6(9)*, 9781597072076) Papercutz.

—The Smurf King. 2010. (Smurfs Graphic Novels Ser.). (ENG., Illus.). 64p. (J). (gr. 2-5). 10.99 *(978-1-59707-225-0(7)*, 9781597072250) Papercutz.

—The Smurfs & the Magic Flute. 2010. (Smurfs Graphic Novels Ser.). (ENG., Illus.). 64p. (J). (gr. 2-5). 10.99 *(978-1-59707-209-0(5)*, 9781597072090) Papercutz.

Delsante, Vito. Babe Ruth. Martinez, Andrés Vera, illus. 2009. (Before They Were Famous Ser.). (ENG.). 128p. (J). (gr. 3-7). pap. 8.99 *(978-1-4169-5071-4(0)*, Simon & Schuster/Paula Wiseman Bks.) Simon & Schuster/Paula Wiseman Bks.

DeMatteis, J. M. & Kleid, Neil, texts. Spider-Man: Kraven's Last Hunt. 2014. (ENG., Illus.). 288p. (YA). (gr. 8-17). 24.99 *(978-0-7851-8970-1(X))* Marvel Worldwide, Inc.

DeMatteis, J. M., et al. Son of the Goblin. 2004. (Spider-Man Ser.). (Illus.). 144p. (YA). pap. 15.99 *(978-0-7851-1563-2(3))* Marvel Worldwide, Inc.

Dembicki, Matt. Xoc: The Journey of a Great White. 2012. (ENG., Illus.). 120p. 19.99 *(978-1-934964-85-9(9)*, 9781934964859) Oni Pr., Inc.

Demers, Tristan. Comic Collection (Shopkins) 2017. (Shopkins Ser.). (ENG.). 80p. (J). (gr. -1-3). pap. 7.99 ***(978-1-338-14857-2(5))*** Scholastic, Inc.

Depken, Kristen L. Dream Closet. 2013. (Barbie Step into Reading Level 3 Ser.). lib. bdg. 13.55 *(978-0-606-32194-5(2)*, Turtleback) Turtleback Bks.

Derib & Jeffrey, Erica. Yakari & Great Eagle. 2007. (Yakari Ser.: 1). (ENG., Illus.). 48p. (J). (gr. 4-7). per. 11.95 *(978-1-905460-04-5(X))* CineBook GBR. Dist: National Bk. Network.

Derib, et al. Yakari & the White Buffalo. 2007. (Yakari Ser.: 2). (ENG., Illus.). 48p. (J). (gr. 4-7). per. 11.95 *(978-1-905460-05-2(8))* CineBook GBR. Dist: National Bk. Network.

d'Errico, Camilla & Sanders, Scott. Camilla d'Errico's Burn. d'Errico, Camilla, illus. 2009. (ENG., Illus.). 160p. (YA). (gr. 7-18). pap. 9.99 *(978-1-4169-7873-2(9)*, Simon Pulse) Simon Pulse.

Desbordes, Astrid & Martin, Pauline. Daydreams of a Solitary Hamster. 2010. (ENG., Illus.). 56p. (J). (gr. 1-2). 17.95 *(978-1-59270-093-6(4))* Enchanted Lion Bks., LLC.

Desfile de Walt Disney. (Coleccion Estrella). (SPA., Illus.). 64p. (YA). 14.95 *(978-950-11-0008-2(1)*, SGM008) Sigmar ARG. Dist: Continental Bk. Co., Inc.

Despeyroux, Denise & Poe, Edgar Allen. Dark Graphic Tales by Edgar Allan Poe. Serratosa, Miquel, illus. 2012. (Dark Graphic Novels Ser.). 96p. (J). (gr. 5-9). 31.94 *(978-0-7660-4086-1(0))* Enslow Pubs., Inc.

Deutsch, Barry. Hereville: How Mirka Caught a Fish. 2015. (Hereville Ser.: 3). (ENG., Illus.). 144p. (J). (gr. 3-7). 17.95 *(978-1-4197-0800-8(7)*, Amulet Bks.) Abrams, Inc.

Deutsch, Barry & Hansen Literary Agency Staff. Hereville: How Mirka Got Her Sword. 2010. (Hereville Ser.). (ENG., Illus.). 144p. (J). (gr. 3-7). 17.99 *(978-0-8109-8422-6(9)*, Amulet Bks.) Abrams, Inc.

Dexter & His Mystery Friend. 2004. (J). per. 15.99 *(978-0-9753533-5-6(7))* Golden Eagle Publishing Hse., Inc.

Dexter & Milly the Caterpiller. 2004. (J). per. 15.99 *(978-0-9753533-4-9(9))* Golden Eagle Publishing Hse., Inc.

Dexter Rescues Matt the Duckling. 2004. (J). per. 15.99 *(978-0-9753533-3-2(0))* Golden Eagle Publishing Hse., Inc.

Dexter the Hamster Gets Lost. 2004. (J). per. 15.99 *(978-0-9753533-2-5(2))* Golden Eagle Publishing Hse., Inc.

Dezago, Todd. Casper & the Spectrals TP. 2011. (Illus.). 96p. pap. 7.99 *(978-0-9561259-6-5(4))* Ardden Entertainment GBR. Dist: Diamond Bk. Distributors.

Diamond Comic Distributors, Inc., contrib. by. Eternal Challenge: The Art of Street Fighter. 2005. (ENG.). 270p. pap. 34.99 *(978-1-932796-24-7(X)*, 9781932796247) Devil's Due Publishing, Inc.

Dickens, Charles. A Christmas Carol. Sanchez Almara, Dono & Almara, Dono Sanchez, illus. 2015. (Graphic Revolve: Common Core Editions Ser.). (ENG.). 72p. (gr. 2-3). lib. bdg. 27.99 *(978-1-4965-0370-1(8))* Stone Arch Bks.

—A Christmas Carol & the Remembrance of Mugby. 2012. (Classics Illustrated Deluxe Graphic Nove Ser.). (ENG., Illus.). 96p. (J). (gr. 2-8). pap. 11.99 *(978-1-59707-345-5(8)*, 9781597073455) Papercutz.

—Great Expectations: The Graphic Novel. 2010. (Classic Graphic Novel Collection). (ENG.). 160p. (YA). (gr. 7-12). 34.80 *(978-1-4205-0372-2(3))* Cengage Gale.

Dickens, Charles & Dauvillier, Loïc. Oliver Twist. 70th anniv. ed. 2012. (Classics Illustrated Deluxe Graphic Nove Ser.). (ENG., Illus.). 240p. (J). (gr. 3-9). pap. 19.99 *(978-1-59707-307-3(5)*, 9781597073073) Papercutz.

Dietrich, Sean, illus. Hansel & Gretel: The Graphic Novel, 1 vol. 2008. (Graphic Spin Ser.). (ENG.). 40p. (gr. 1-3). 25.32 *(978-1-4342-0767-8(6)*, Graphic Revolve) Stone Arch Bks.

DiMartino, Michael Dante & Konietzko, Bryan, creators. Avatar, Vol. 5. 2007. (Avatar Ser.). (Illus.). 104p. pap. 7.99 *(978-1-59816-929-4(7)*, Tokyopop Kids) TOKYOPOP, Inc.

Ding, Yuhui Andrew. Warrior Soul. 2009. 28p. pap. 15.99 *(978-1-4415-6734-5(8))* Xlibris Corp.

Dini, Paul. Men of Steel, 1 vol. Burchett, Rick & Austin, Terry, illus. 2012. (Superman Adventures Ser.). (ENG.). 32p. (gr. 2-3). lib. bdg. 22.60 *(978-1-4342-4549-6(7))* Stone Arch Bks.

Disney. Yo Ho! Let's Go! 2013. (Dress-Up Ser.: 1). (ENG.). 24p. (J). (gr. -1-1). 11.99 *(978-0-7944-2843-3(6))* Reader's Digest Assn., Inc., The.

Disney Book Club Staff. Disney Junior Music Player Storybook. 2013. (Music Player Storybook Ser.: 1). (ENG.). 32p. (J). (gr. -1-2). 19.99 *(978-0-7944-3011-5(2))* Reader's Digest Assn., Inc., The.

—Pirates of the Caribbean - On Stranger Tides: Six Sea Chanties - An Original Graphic Novel Anthology. 2011. (ENG.). 128p. (YA). (gr. 8-18). pap. 10.99 *(978-1-4231-3320-9(X))* Disney Pr.

Disney Book Group. 5-Minute Spider-Man Stories. Disney Book Group, illus. 2013. (5-Minute Stories Ser.). (ENG., Illus.). 192p. (J). (gr. 1-3). 12.99 *(978-1-4231-7786-9(X))* Marvel Worldwide, Inc.

Disney Book Group Staff. Iron Man vs. Titanium Man. Disney Storybook Artists Staff, illus. 2013. (Marvel Super Hero vs. Book Ser.). (ENG.). 24p. (J). (gr. -1-k). pap. 3.99 *(978-1-4231-5469-3(X))* Marvel Worldwide, Inc.

—Star Wars: Return of the Jedi Read-Along Storybook & CD. 2015. (Read-Along Storybook & CD Ser.). (ENG.). 32p. (J). (gr. 1-3). pap. 6.99 *(978-1-4847-0685-5(4)*, Disney Lucasfilm Press) Disney Publishing Worldwide.

—These Are the Avengers Level 1 Reader. 2012. (World of Reading Ser.). (ENG.). 32p. (J). (gr. -1-k). pap. 3.99 *(978-1-4231-5398-6(7)*, Marvel Pr.) Disney Publishing Worldwide.

—World of Reading Avengers Boxed Set: Level 1 - Purchase Includes Marvel EBook! Disney Book Group Staff, illus. 2015. (World of Reading Ser.: 2). (ENG., Illus.). 192p. (J). (gr. 1-3). pap. 12.99 *(978-1-4847-0438-7(X)*, Marvel Pr.) Disney Publishing Worldwide.

—5-Minute Marvel Stories. 2012. (5-Minute Stories Ser.). (ENG., Illus.). 192p. (J). (gr. -1 — 1). 12.99 *(978-1-4231-6722-8(8))* Marvel Worldwide, Inc.

Disney Book Group Staff & Macri, Thomas. These Are the X-Men Level 1. Disney Storybook Artists Staff & Bachs, Ramon, illus. 2013. (World of Reading Ser.). (ENG.). 32p. (J). (gr. -1-k). pap. 3.99 *(978-1-4231-7083-9(0))* Marvel Worldwide, Inc.

Disney Book Group Staff & Peterson, Scott. Meet the Marvel Super Heroes: Includes a Poster of Your Favorite Super Heroes! 2013. (ENG., Illus.). 144p. (J). (gr. 1-3). 12.99 *(978-1-4231-6142-4(4))* Marvel Worldwide, Inc.

Disney Book Group Staff, et al. Shake to Assemble. Disney Book Group Staff et al, illus. 2015. (ENG.). 48p. (J). (gr. -1-k). 12.99 *(978-1-4231-7826-2(2)*, Marvel Pr.) Disney Publishing Worldwide.

Disney Editors. Disney Descendants: Wicked World Cinestory Comic, Volume 2. 2016. (J). lib. bdg. 20.85 *(978-0-606-39425-3(7))* Turtleback Bks.

—Disney Descendants Cinestory Comic, Volume 1, 1. 2016. (J). lib. bdg. 20.85 *(978-0-606-38727-9(7))* Turtleback Bks.

—Disney Descendants Wicked World Cinestory Comic, Volume 3, 3. 2017. (J). lib. bdg. 20.85 ***(978-0-606-39833-6(3))*** Turtleback Bks.

—Disney-Pixar Finding Nemo Cinestory Comic. 2016. (J). lib. bdg. 26.95 *(978-0-606-38732-3(3))* Turtleback Bks.

—Disney Tangled Movie Comic. 2017. (ENG.). 64p. (J). (gr. 4-7). 18.40 *(978-0-606-39085-9(5))* Turtleback Bks.

Disney Frozen Staff. Disney Frozen Movie Theater: Storybook & Movie Projector. 2013. (Movie Theater Ser.: 1). (ENG.). 32p. (J). (gr. -1-1). 19.99 *(978-0-7944-2895-2(9))* Reader's Digest Assn., Inc., The.

Disney Minnie Mouse Staff. Disney Minnie. 2013. (Carry along Play Book Ser.: 1). (ENG.). 14p. (J). (gr. -1-2). 14.99 *(978-0-7944-2897-6(5)*, Reader's Digest Children's Bks.) Studio Fun International.

Disney Pixar Editors. Disney Pixar Finding Dory Comics Collection. 2016. (J). lib. bdg. 20.85 *(978-0-606-39074-3(X))* Turtleback Bks.

—Disney Pixar Finding Dory Movie Comic. 2017. lib. bdg. 18.40 *(978-0-606-39083-5(9))* Turtleback Bks.

—Disney Pixar Finding Nemo Movie Comic. 2017. lib. bdg. 18.40 *(978-0-606-39082-8(0))* Turtleback Bks.

Disney Staff. The Story of Clarabelle Cow. 2004. (Illus.). 96p. (J). 35.00 incl. audio compact disk *(978-1-55709-357-8(1))* Applewood Bks.

—The Story of Pluto the Pup. 2004. (Illus.). 96p. (J). 35.00 incl. audio compact disk *(978-1-55709-356-1(3))* Applewood Bks.

Disney Storybook Art Team, illus. Frozen Fever Read-Along Storybook & CD. 2015. (Read-Along Storybook & CD Ser.). (ENG.). 32p. (J). (gr. 1-3). pap. 6.99 *(978-1-4847-4197-9(8))* Disney Pr.

Disney Storybook Artists Staff. Your Favorite Disney Pixar Characters. 2011. (Learn to Draw Favorite Characters Ser.). (Illus.). 32p. (J). (gr. k-3). 28.50 *(978-1-936309-22-1(X))* Quarto Publishing Group USA.

Dixon, Chuck. Airboy, Vol. 1. Truman, Timothy et al, illus. 2014. (Airboy Ser.: 1). (ENG.). 308p. pap. 29.99 *(978-1-61377-900-2(3)*, 9781613779002) Idea & Design Works, LLC.

—Perdition's Gate, Vol. 6. Eaglesham, Dale et al, illus. 2004. (Sigil Ser.: Vol. 6). 160p. (YA). pap. 15.95 *(978-1-59314-048-9(7))* CrossGeneration Comics, Inc.

—Resurrection, Vol. 5. Cariello, Sergio et al, illus. 2004. (Crux Ser.: Vol. 5). 160p. (YA). pap. 15.95 *(978-1-59314-053-3(3))* CrossGeneration Comics, Inc.

—Way of the Rat Traveler, Vol. 1. 2003. (Way of the Rat Traveler Ser.). (Illus.). 160p. (YA). pap. 9.95 *(978-1-59314-032-8(0))* CrossGeneration Comics, Inc.

Dixon, Chuck & Kwapisz, Gary. Civil War Adventure: Book One. 2015. (Dover Graphic Novels Ser.). (ENG., Illus.). 144p. pap. 9.95 *(978-0-486-79509-6(8))* Dover Pubns., Inc.

Dixon, Franklin W. Comic con Artist. 21st ed. 2008. (Hardy Boys (All New) Undercover Brothers Ser.: 21). (ADY & ENG., Illus.). 192p. (J). (gr. 3-7). pap. 5.99 *(978-1-4169-5498-9(8))*, Aladdin) Simon & Schuster Children's Publishing.

—Pushed. 18th ed. 2007. (Hardy Boys (All New) Undercover Brothers Ser.: 18). (ENG., Illus.). 160p. (J). (gr. 3-7). pap. 5.99 *(978-1-4169-4802-5(3)*, Aladdin) Simon & Schuster Children's Publishing.

d'Lacey, Chris. Alexander's Army. 2015. (UFiles Ser.: 2). (ENG.). 304p. (J). (gr. 3-7). 16.99 *(978-0-545-60880-0(5)*, Scholastic Pr.) Scholastic, Inc.

Dobel, Jean-Marc, et al. The Planet of the Bubble Gob. Smith, Anne Collins & Smith, Owen, trs. from FRE. 2014. (Little Prince Ser.: 17). (ENG., Illus.). 48p. (J). (gr. 4-8). lib. bdg. 26.60 *(978-0-7613-8767-1(6)*, Graphic Universe™) Lerner Publishing Group.

Doering Tourville, Amanda. Transportation in the City, 1 vol. Thompson, Jeffrey, illus. 2011. (First Graphics: My Community Ser.). (ENG.). 24p. (gr. 1-2). pap. 6.29 *(978-1-4296-6233-8(6))*; pap. 35.70 *(978-1-4296-6403-5(7))* Capstone Press of Coughlan Cos.

Doerrfeld, Cori. A Perfect View. Doerrfeld, Cori & Page, Tyler, illus. 2017. (Cici: a Fairy's Tale Ser.: 3). (ENG.). 48p. (J). (gr. 2-5). 26.65 *(978-1-4677-6154-3(0))*; pap. 7.99 *(978-1-5124-3068-4(4))*; E-Book 19.99 ***(978-1-5124-2700-4(4)***, 9781512427004) Lerner Publishing Group. (Graphic Universe™).

—Truth in Sight. Doerrfeld, Cori & Page, Tyler, illus. 2016. (Cici: a Fairy's Tale Ser.: 2). (ENG.). 48p. (J). (gr. 2-5). lib. bdg. 26.65 *(978-1-4677-6153-6(2)*, Graphic Universe™) Lerner Publishing Group.

Donaldson, Julia. Charlie Cook's Favorite Book. Scheffler, Axel, illus. 2008. (ENG.). 32p. (J). (gr. -1-k). pap. 7.99 *(978-0-14-241138-4(8)*, Puffin Books) Penguin Young Readers Group.

Dong Chen, Wei. Band of Brothers. Peng, Chao, illus. 2013. (Monkey King Ser.: 18). (ENG.). 176p. (gr. 6-12). pap. 9.99 *(978-89-94208-63-3(1))* JR Comics KOR. Dist: Lerner Publishing Group.

—Battle of Red Cliffs. Liang, Xiao Long, illus. 2013. (Three Kingdoms Ser.: 11). (ENG.). 176p. (gr. 5-12). pap. 9.99 *(978-89-98341-24-4(7))* JR Comics KOR. Dist: Lerner Publishing Group.

—The Dual. Peng, Chao, illus. 2013. (Monkey King Ser.: 14). (ENG.). 176p. (gr. 6-12). pap. 9.99 *(978-89-94208-59-6(3))* JR Comics KOR. Dist: Lerner Publishing Group.

—Expulsion of Sun Wu. Peng, Chao, illus. 2013. (Monkey King Ser.: 7). (ENG.). 176p. (YA). (gr. 6-12). pap. 9.99 *(978-89-94208-51-0(8))* Lerner Publishing Group.

—Fanning the Flames. Peng, Chao, illus. 2013. (Monkey King Ser.: 15). (ENG.). 176p. (gr. 6-12). pap. 9.99 *(978-89-94208-60-2(7))* JR Comics KOR. Dist: Lerner Publishing Group.

—Fight to the Death. Peng, Chao, illus. 2013. (Monkey King Ser.: 11). (ENG.). 176p. (YA). (gr. 6-12). pap. 9.99 *(978-89-94208-56-5(9))* Lerner Publishing Group.

—The Fortunate Sons. Long Liang, Xiao, illus. 2013. (Three Kingdoms Ser.: 8). (ENG.). 176p. (gr. 5-12). pap. 9.99 *(978-89-98341-21-3(2))* JR Comics KOR. Dist: Lerner Publishing Group.

—Golden Temple. Peng, Chao, illus. 2013. (Monkey King Ser.: 16). (ENG.). 176p. (gr. 6-12). pap. 9.99 *(978-89-94208-61-9(5))* JR Comics KOR. Dist: Lerner Publishing Group.

—The Journey Ends. Peng, Chao, illus. 2013. (Monkey King Ser.: 20). (ENG.). 176p. (gr. 6-12). pap. 9.99 *(978-89-94208-65-7(8))* JR Comics KOR. Dist: Lerner Publishing Group.

—Lost Children. Peng, Chao, illus. 2013. (Monkey King Ser.: 12). (ENG.). 176p. (YA). (gr. 6-12). pap. 9.99 *(978-89-94208-57-2(7))* Lerner Publishing Group.

—Masters & Disciples. Peng, Chao, illus. 2013. (Monkey King Ser.: 19). (ENG.). 176p. (gr. 6-12). pap. 9.99 *(978-89-94208-64-0(X))* JR Comics KOR. Dist: Lerner Publishing Group.

—Realm of Infant King. Peng, Chao, illus. 2013. (Monkey King Ser.: 10). (ENG.). 176p. (YA). (gr. 6-12). pap. 9.99 *(978-89-94208-54-1(2))* Lerner Publishing Group.

—The Seven Sisters. Peng, Chao, illus. 2013. (Monkey King Ser.: 17). (ENG.). 176p. (gr. 6-12). pap. 9.99 *(978-89-94208-62-6(3))* JR Comics KOR. Dist: Lerner Publishing Group.

—Stolen Kingdom. Peng, Chao, illus. 2013. (Monkey King Ser.: 9). (ENG.). 176p. (YA). (gr. 6-12). pap. 9.99 *(978-89-94208-53-4(4))* Lerner Publishing Group.

—Treasures of the Mountain Kings. Peng, Chao, illus. 2013. (Monkey King Ser.: 8). (ENG.). 176p. (YA). (gr. 6-12). pap. 9.99 *(978-89-94208-52-7(6))* Lerner Publishing Group.

—Trust & Temptation. Peng, Chao, illus. 2013. (Monkey King Ser.: 13). (ENG.). 176p. (gr. 6-12). pap. 9.99 *(978-89-94208-58-9(5))* JR Comics KOR. Dist: Lerner Publishing Group.

—Wagers & Vows. Liang, Xiao Long, illus. 2013. (Three Kingdoms Ser.: 12). (ENG.). 176p. (gr. 5-12). pap. 9.99 *(978-89-98341-25-1(5))* JR Comics KOR. Dist: Lerner Publishing Group.

—War of Words. Long Liang, Xiao, illus. 2013. (Three Kingdoms Ser.: 10). (ENG.). 176p. (gr. 5-12). pap. 9.99 *(978-89-98341-23-7(9))* JR Comics KOR. Dist: Lerner Publishing Group.

Dong Chen, Wei & Peng, Chao. Bane of Heaven. 2012. (Monkey King Ser.: 2). (ENG., Illus.). 176p. (gr. 5-8). pap. 9.99 *(978-89-94208-46-6(1))* JR Comics KOR. Dist: Lerner Publishing Group.

—Birth of Stone Monkey. 2012. (Monkey King Ser.: 1). (ENG., Illus.). 176p. (gr. 5-8). pap. 9.99 *(978-89-94208-45-9(3))* JR Comics KOR. Dist: Lerner Publishing Group.

—Enemies & New Friend. 2012. (Monkey King Ser.: 4). (ENG., Illus.). 176p. (gr. 5-8). pap. 9.99 *(978-89-94208-48-0(8))* JR Comics KOR. Dist: Lerner Publishing Group.

—Journey to the West. 2012. (Monkey King Ser.: 3). (ENG., Illus.). 176p. (gr. 5-8). pap. 9.99 *(978-89-94208-47-3(X))* JR Comics KOR. Dist: Lerner Publishing Group.

—Sacred Tree. 2012. (Monkey King Ser.: 6). (ENG., Illus.). 176p. (gr. 5-8). pap. 9.99 *(978-89-94208-50-3(X))* JR Comics KOR. Dist: Lerner Publishing Group.

—Three Trials. 2012. (Monkey King Ser.: 5). (ENG., Illus.). 176p. (gr. 5-8). pap. 9.99 *(978-89-94208-49-7(6))* JR Comics KOR. Dist: Lerner Publishing Group.

Doodler, Todd H. Rise of the Evil Army. 2017. (Super Fly Ser.: 4). (J). lib. bdg. 17.20 ***(978-0-606-39594-6(9))*** Turtleback Bks.

—Super Fly 4: Rise of the Evil Army. 2017. (Super Fly Ser.). (ENG., Illus.). 128p. (J). pap. 6.99 *(978-1-61963-387-2(6)*, 9781619633872, Bloomsbury USA Childrens) Bloomsbury Publishing USA.

—Super Fly vs. Furious Flea! 2016. (Super Fly Ser.). (ENG., Illus.). 128p. (J). pap. 6.99 *(978-1-61963-384-1(1)*,

9781619633841, Bloomsbury USA Childrens) Bloomsbury Publishing USA.

Doran, Colleen. Coda, Vol. 4. ltd. ed. 2007. (Distant Soil Ser.). (Illus.). 164p. (YA). lib. bdg. 29.95 (978-1-58240-525-4(5)) Image Comics.

—A Distant Soil: the Gathering TP: The Gathering TP. 2013. (Illus.). 240p. (YA). pap. 16.99 (978-1-60706-689-7(0)) Image Comics.

Dorison, Guillaume, et al. The Planet of the Firebird. Fayolle, Diane & Benoit, Jérôme, illus. 2012. (Little Prince Ser.: 2). (ENG.). 56p. (J). (gr. 4-8). lib. bdg. 26.60 (978-0-7613-8752-7(8), Graphic Universe™) Lerner Publishing Group.

—The Planet of Wind. Fayolle, Diane & Benoit, Jérôme, illus. 2012. (Little Prince Ser.: 1). (ENG.). 56p. (J). (gr. 4-8). lib. bdg. 26.60 (978-0-7613-8751-0(X), Graphic Universe™) Lerner Publishing Group.

Dorison, Xavier. The Emerald Maze, Vol. 3. Lauffray, Mathieu, illus. 2012. (Long John Silver Ser.: 3). (ENG.). 56p. pap. 13.95 (978-1-84918-105-1(5)) CineBook GBR. Dist: National Bk. Network.

—Lady Vivian Hastings. Saincantin, Jerome, tr. from FRE. Lauffray, Mathieu, illus. 2011. (Long John Silver Ser.: 1). (ENG.). 56p. pap. 13.95 (978-1-84918-062-7(8)) CineBook GBR. Dist: National Bk. Network.

—Long John Silver Vol. 4: Guiana-Capac. Lauffray, Mathieu, illus. 2014. (Long John Silver Ser.: 4). (ENG.). 64p. pap. 15.95 (978-1-84918-175-4(6)) CineBook GBR. Dist: National Bk. Network.

—Neptune Vol. 2: Long John Silver. Lauffray, Mathieu, illus. 2011. (Long John Silver Ser.: 2). (ENG.). 56p. pap. 13.95 (978-1-84918-072-6(5)) CineBook GBR. Dist: National Bk. Network.

Dorison, Xavier & Nury, Fabian. Century Club. Ross, C., illus. 2012. (Spooks Ser.: 2). (ENG.). 56p. (J). (gr. 10-12). pap. 13.95 (978-1-84918-129-7(2)) CineBook GBR. Dist: National Bk. Network.

Dorison, Xavier & Nury, Fabien. El Santero Vol. 3: Spooks. Rossi, Christian, illus. 2014. (Spooks Ser.: 3). (ENG.). 56p. pap. 13.95 (978-1-84918-170-9(5)) CineBook GBR. Dist: National Bk. Network.

—Spooks - The 46th State, Vol. 4. Rossi, Christian, illus. 2014. (Spooks Ser.: 4). (ENG.). 64p. pap. 15.95 (978-1-84918-185-3(3)) CineBook GBR. Dist: National Bk. Network.

Dorkin, Evan & Dyer, Sarah. Calla Cthulhu. Humiston, Erin & Mudron, Bill, illus. 2017. (ENG.). 136p. (gr. 5-9). pap. 12.99 **(978-1-5067-0293-3(7))** Dark Horse Comics.

Dorling Kindersley Publishing Staff. The Amazing Book of Marvel Spider-Man. 2017. (ENG.). 48p. (J). (gr. k-4). 14.99 **(978-1-4654-5561-1(2)**, DK Children) Dorling Kindersley Publishing, Inc.

—DK Readers L3: LEGO DC Comics Super Heroes: Batman's Missions: LEGO DC Comics Super Heroes: Batman's Missions. 2015. (DK Readers Ser.). (ENG.). 64p. (J). (gr. 2-4). 14.99 (978-1-4654-3013-7(X), DK Children) Dorling Kindersley Publishing, Inc.

—LEGO DC Comics Super Heroes Character Encyclopedia. 2016. (ENG., Illus.). 208p. (J). (gr. 1-3). 18.99 (978-1-4654-4454-7(8), DK Children) Dorling Kindersley Publishing, Inc.

—Marvel Good vs Evil. 2016. (Ultimate Sticker Collections). (ENG.). 96p. (J). (gr. 1-4). pap. 12.99 (978-1-4654-5159-0(5), DK Children) Dorling Kindersley Publishing, Inc.

—Star Wars: Jedi Battles. 2013. (DK Adventures Ser.). lib. bdg. 16.00 (978-0-606-35319-9(4)) Turtleback Bks.

—Star Wars: Sith Wars. 2013. (DK Adventures Ser.). lib. bdg. 16.00 (978-0-606-35320-5(8)) Turtleback Bks.

—Super Heroes - Ready for Action! 2013. (LEGO DC Universe DK Readers Ser.). lib. bdg. 13.55 (978-0-606-31474-9(1), Turtleback) Turtleback Bks.

—Ultimate Sticker Collection: DC Comics Wonder Woman. 2017. (Ultimate Sticker Collections). (ENG.). 96p. (J). (gr. 1-4). pap. 12.99 (978-1-4654-6076-9(4), DK Children) Dorling Kindersley Publishing, Inc.

—Ultimate Sticker Collection: Marvel's Guardians of the Galaxy. 2017. (Ultimate Sticker Collections). (ENG.). 96p. (J). (gr. 2-5). pap. 12.99 (978-1-4654-5555-0(8), DK Children) Dorling Kindersley Publishing, Inc.

Dorling Kindersley Publishing Staff & Manning, Matthew. Iron Man: The Ultimate Guide to the Armored Super Hero. 2010. (ENG., Illus.). 200p. (J). (gr. 3-7). 24.99 (978-0-7566-5749-9(0), DK Children) Dorling Kindersley Publishing, Inc.

Dorling Kindersley Publishing Staff & Manning, Matthew K. Wolverine. 2009. (ENG., Illus.). 200p. (J). (gr. 8-12). 24.99 (978-0-7566-4547-2(6), DK Children) Dorling Kindersley Publishing, Inc.

Dougall, Alastair & Dorling Kindersley Publishing Staff. Spider-Man - Glow in the Dark. 2006. (Ultimate Sticker Bks.). (ENG., Illus.). 16p. (J). (gr. k-3). pap. 6.99 (978-0-7566-1999-2(8), DK Children) Dorling Kindersley Publishing, Inc.

Doupe, Pauline Wood. My Arctic Circle of Friends. Fawcett, Vicki, illus. Belair, Brenda Brousseau, photos by. 2009. 24p. pap. 16.98 (978-1-4251-8097-3(3)) Trafford Publishing.

Downer, Denise. Soul Mates. Frampton, Otis, illus. 2013. (Tombstone Twins Ser.). (ENG.). 48p. (gr. 1-3). lib. bdg. 23.99 (978-1-4342-2248-0(9)) Stone Arch Bks.

—Tombstone Twins: Soul Mates, 1 vol. Frampton, Otis, illus. 2013. (Tombstone Twins Ser.). (ENG.). 48p. (gr. 1-3). pap. 5.95 (978-1-4342-3873-3(3)) Stone Arch Bks.

—Tombstone Twins Package: Soul Mates. Frampton, Otis, illus. 2013. (ENG.). 41p. (J). (gr. 2-4). pap. 35.70 (978-1-4342-3955-6(1)) Stone Arch Bks.

Doyle, Arthur Conan. El Sabueso de Los Baskerville, 1 vol. Ferran, Adriana & Ferran, Daniel, illus. 2010. (Classic Fiction Ser.). (SPA.). 72p. (gr. 2-3). 27.99 (978-1-4342-2325-8(6), Graphic Revolve en Español) Stone Arch Bks.

—Sherlock Holmes & the Adventure of Black Peter. Rohrbach, Sophie & Morrow, J. T., illus. 2012. (On the Case with Holmes & Watson Ser.: 11). (ENG.). 48p. (J). (gr. 4-6). lib. bdg. 27.93 (978-0-7613-7092-5(7)) Lerner Publishing Group.

—Sherlock Holmes & the Adventure of the Cardboard Box. Rohrbach, Sophie & Morrow, J. T., illus. 2012. (On the Case with Holmes & Watson Ser.: 12). (ENG.). 48p. (J). (gr. 4-6). lib. bdg. 27.93 (978-0-7613-7090-1(0)) Lerner Publishing Group.

—Sherlock Holmes & the Three Garridebs. Rohrbach, Sophie & Morrow, J. T., illus. 2012. (On the Case with Holmes & Watson Ser.: 13). (ENG.). 48p. (J). (gr. 4-6). lib. bdg. 27.93 (978-0-7613-7091-8(9)) Lerner Publishing Group.

—#07 Sherlock Holmes & the Redheaded League. Rohrbach, Sophie & Morrow, Jt, illus. 2011. (On the Case with Holmes & Watson Set II Ser.). pap. 39.62 (978-0-7613-7609-5(7), Graphic Universe™) Lerner Publishing Group.

—#08 Sherlock Holmes & the Adventure at the Copper Beeches. Rohrbach, Sophie & Morrow, Jt, illus. 2011. (On the Case with Holmes & Watson Set II Ser.). (J). pap. 39.62 (978-0-7613-7610-1(0), Graphic Universe™) Lerner Publishing Group.

—#09 Sherlock Holmes & the Adventure of the Six Napoleons. Rohrbach, Sophie & Morrow, Jt, illus. 2011. (On the Case with Holmes & Watson Set II Ser.). pap. 39.62 (978-0-7613-7611-8(9), Graphic Universe™) Lerner Publishing Group.

—#10 Sherlock Holmes & the Boscombe Valley Mystery. Rohrbach, Sophie & Morrow, Jt, illus. 2011. (On the Case with Holmes & Watson Set II Ser.). pap. 39.62 (978-0-7613-7612-5(7), Graphic Universe™) Lerner Publishing Group.

Dragoon, Leigh. The Class of Classics. Sheron, Jessica, illus. 2017. (ENG.). 112p. (J). (gr. 3-7). pap. 9.99 (978-0-316-33741-0(2)) Little Brown & Co.

The Dreamer Who Unlocked the Secrets of the Universe... 2004. (Illus.). 126p. (YA). pap. 11.11 (978-0-9749196-1-4(6)) Don Quixote Publishing Co. Inc.

Dreamworks Editors. Dreamworks Trolls Cinestory Comic. 2016. (J). lib. bdg. 26.95 **(978-0-606-39834-3(1))** Turtleback Bks.

Duarte, Gustavo. Monsters! & Other Stories. Hahn, Sierra, ed. Duarte, Gustavo, illus. 2014. (ENG., Illus.). 152p. pap. 12.99 (978-1-61655-309-8(X)) Dark Horse Comics.

Dubisch, Mike, illus. Mike's Mystery, No. 5. 2009. (Boxcar Children Graphic Novels Ser.). (ENG.). 32p. (J). (gr. 2-5). 6.99 (978-0-8075-2871-6(4)) Whitman, Albert & Co.

—Mystery Ranch. 2009. (Boxcar Children Graphic Novels Ser.: 4). (ENG.). 32p. (J). (gr. 1-5). 6.99 (978-0-8075-2870-9(6)) Whitman, Albert & Co.

—The Pizza Mystery. 2010. (Boxcar Children Graphic Novels Ser.: 11). (ENG.). 32p. (J). (gr. 1-5). pap. 6.99 (978-0-8075-6537-7(7)) Whitman, Albert & Co.

Dubisch, Mike & Bloodworth, Mark, illus. The Amusement Park Mystery. 2010. (Boxcar Children Graphic Novels Ser.: 10). (ENG.). 32p. (J). (gr. 1-5). pap. 6.99 (978-0-8075-0321-8(5)) Whitman, Albert & Co.

Dubos, Delphine. The Planet of Tear-Eaters. Smith, Anne & Smith, Owen, trs. from FRE. Élyum Studio, illus. 2014. (Little Prince Ser.: 13). (ENG.). 48p. (J). (gr. 4-8). lib. bdg. 26.60 (978-0-7613-8763-3(3), Graphic Universe™) Lerner Publishing Group.

—The Planet of Wind. Burrell, Carol klio, tr. Élyum Studio Staff, illus. 2012. (Little Prince Ser.: 1). (ENG.). 56p. (J). (gr. 4-8). pap. 7.95 (978-0-8225-9422-2(6), Graphic Universe™) Lerner Publishing Group.

Dufaux, Jean. Blackmore Vol. 2: Lament of the Lost Moors, Volume 2. Rosinski, Grzegorz, illus. 2014. (Lament of the Lost Moors Ser.: 2). (ENG.). 64p. pap. 15.95 (978-1-84918-187-7(X)) CineBook GBR. Dist: National Bk. Network.

—Siobhan. Rosinski, Grzegorz, illus. 2014. (Lament of the Lost Moors Ser.: 1). (ENG.). 64p. pap. 15.95 (978-1-84918-169-3(1)) CineBook GBR. Dist: National Bk. Network.

Duggan, Gerry. Nova, Vol. 3. Baldeon, David, illus. 2014. (ENG.). 152p. (J). (gr. 4-17). pap. 19.99 (978-0-7851-8957-2(2)) Marvel Worldwide, Inc.

Dumas, Alexandre. The Man in the Iron Mask, 1 vol. 2010. (Illustrated Classics Ser.). (ENG., Illus.). 64p. (YA). (gr. 9-12). per. 9.95 (978-1-56254-920-6(0)) Saddleback Educational Publishing, Inc.

Dunn, Joe. The Bombing of Pearl Harbor, 1 vol. Wight, Joseph & Espinosa, Rod, illus. 2007. (Graphic History Ser.). (ENG.). 32p. (gr. 3-6). 28.50 (978-1-60270-074-1(5), Graphic Planet-Nonfiction) ABDO Publishing Co.

Dunn, Joeming. Cask of Amontillado, 1 vol. 2014. (Graphic Horror Set 3 Ser.). (ENG.). 32p. (J). (gr. 5-8). lib. bdg. 28.50 (978-1-62402-015-5(1), Graphic Planet) Magic Wagon.

—The Eyes: A Graphic Novel Tour, 1 vol. Espinosa, Rod, illus. 2009. (Graphic Body Ser.). (ENG.). 32p. (J). (gr. 3-6). 28.50 (978-1-60270-684-2(0)) ABDO Publishing Co.

—Fallujah. Dunn, Ben, illus. 2016. (Graphic Warfare Ser.). (ENG.). 32p. (J). (gr. 3-8). 28.50 (978-1-61641-980-6(6)) Magic Wagon.

—Graphic Adventures: The Human Body, 6 vols., Set. Espinosa, Rod, illus. Incl. Brain: A Graphic Novel Tour. Espinosa, Rod. 28.50 (978-1-60270-683-5(2)); Eyes: A Graphic Novel Tour. 28.50 (978-1-60270-684-2(0)); Heart: A Graphic Novel Tour. Espinosa, Rod. 28.50 (978-1-60270-685-9(9)); Kidneys: A Graphic Novel Tour. 28.50 (978-1-60270-686-6(7)); Liver: A Graphic Novel Tour. 28.50 (978-1-60270-687-3(5)); Lungs: A Graphic Novel Tour. 28.50 (978-1-60270-688-0(3)); (J). (gr. 3-6). (Graphic Body Ser.). (Illus.). 32p. 2009. 171.00 (978-1-60270-682-8(4), Graphic Planet- Nonfiction) ABDO Publishing Co.

—Graphic Warfare. 2016. (Graphic Warfare Ser.: 6). (ENG.). 32p. (J). (gr. 3-8). lib. bdg. 171.00 (978-1-61641-977-6(6), Graphic Planet) Magic Wagon.

—The Kidneys: A Graphic Novel Tour, 1 vol. Espinosa, Rod, illus. 2009. (Graphic Body Ser.). (ENG.). 32p. (J). (gr. 3-6). 28.50 (978-1-60270-686-6(7)) ABDO Publishing Co.

—The Lighthouse Mystery. Dunn, Ben, illus. 2010. (Boxcar Children Graphic Novels Ser.: 14). (ENG.). 32p. (J). (gr. 2-5). pap. 6.99 (978-0-8075-4547-8(3)) Whitman, Albert & Co.

—The Liver: A Graphic Novel Tour, 1 vol. Espinosa, Rod, illus. 2009. (Graphic Body Ser.). (ENG.). 32p. (J). (gr. 3-6). 28.50 (978-1-60270-687-3(5)) ABDO Publishing Co.

—The Lungs: A Graphic Novel Tour, 1 vol. Espinosa, Rod, illus. 2009. (Graphic Body Ser.). (ENG.). 32p. (J). (gr. 3-6). 28.50 (978-1-60270-688-0(3)) ABDO Publishing Co.

—Macbeth, 1 vol. Hutchinson, David, illus. 2008. (Graphic Shakespeare Ser.). (ENG.). 48p. (gr. 5-10). 29.93 (978-1-60270-190-8(3), Graphic Planet- Fiction) ABDO Publishing Co.

—Mountain Top Mystery, No. 15. Dunn, Ben, illus. 2010. (Boxcar Children Graphic Novels Ser.: 15). (ENG.). 32p. (J). (gr. 1-5). pap. 6.99 (978-0-8075-5294-0(1)) Whitman, Albert & Co.

—Raven, 1 vol. 2014. (Graphic Horror Set 3 Ser.). (ENG.). 32p. (J). (gr. 5-8). lib. bdg. 28.50 (978-1-62402-017-9(8), Graphic Planet) Magic Wagon.

—Romeo & Juliet, 1 vol. Espinosa, Rod, illus. 2008. (Graphic Shakespeare Ser.). (ENG.). 48p. (gr. 5-10). 29.93 (978-1-60270-193-9(8), Graphic Planet- Fiction) ABDO Publishing Co.

—Tet Offensive. Dunn, Ben, illus. 2016. (Graphic Warfare Ser.). (ENG.). 32p. (J). (gr. 3-8). 28.50 (978-1-61641-983-7(0)) Magic Wagon.

—The Woodshed Mystery. Dunn, Ben, illus. 2010. (Boxcar Children Graphic Novels Ser.: 13). (ENG.). 32p. (J). (gr. 1-5). pap. 6.99 (978-0-8075-9208-3(0)) Whitman, Albert & Co.

Dunn, Joeming & Dunn, Ben. Richard Nixon: 37th U. S. President, 1 vol. 2011. (Presidents of the United States Bio-Graphics Ser.). (ENG., Illus.). 32p. (YA). (gr. 3-6). 28.50 (978-1-61641-647-8(5)) Magic Wagon.

Dunn, Joeming & Espinosa De Santayana, Rodrigo De. Ulysses S. Grant: 18th U. S. President, 1 vol. 2011. (Presidents of the United States Bio-Graphics Ser.). (ENG., Illus.). 32p. (YA). (gr. 3-6). 28.50 (978-1-61641-646-1(7)) Magic Wagon.

Dunn, Joeming & Espinosa, Rod. The Brain: A Graphic Novel Tour, 1 vol. Espinosa, Rod, illus. 2009. (Graphic Body Ser.). (ENG., Illus.). 32p. (J). (gr. 3-6). 28.50 (978-1-60270-683-5(2)) ABDO Publishing Co.

—The Heart: A Graphic Novel Tour, 1 vol. Espinosa, Rod, illus. 2009. (Graphic Body Ser.). (ENG., Illus.). 32p. (J). (gr. 3-6). 28.50 (978-1-60270-685-9(9)) ABDO Publishing Co.

Dunn, Joeming & Warner, Gertrude Chandler. The Lighthouse Mystery, 1 vol., Bk. 14. Dunn, Ben, illus. 2011. (Boxcar Children Graphic Novels Ser.). (ENG.). 32p. (J). (gr. 2-5). 28.50 (978-1-61641-122-0(8)) ABDO Publishing Co.

—The Woodshed Mystery, 1 vol., Bk. 13. Dunn, Ben, illus. 2011. (Boxcar Children Graphic Novels Ser.). (ENG.). 32p. (J). (gr. 2-5). 28.50 (978-1-61641-121-3(X)) ABDO Publishing Co.

Dunn, Joeming W. Gettysburg. Dunn, Ben, illus. 2016. (Graphic Warfare Ser.). (ENG.). 32p. (J). (gr. 3-8). 28.50 (978-1-61641-981-3(4)) Magic Wagon.

Dunn, Rebecca. Hamlet, 1 vol. Dunn, Ben, illus. 2008. (Graphic Shakespeare Ser.). (ENG.). 48p. (gr. 5-10). 29.93 (978-1-60270-188-5(1), Graphic Planet- Fiction) ABDO Publishing Co.

Duopress Labs Staff. Messi, Superstar: His Records, His Life, His Epic Awesomeness. 2016. (ENG., Illus.). 140p. (J). (gr. 3-7). pap. 14.99 (978-1-938093-57-9(7)) Duo Pr. LLC.

Dye, Troy & Kelesides, Tom. Goblin Chronicles 01A. 2008. (YA). 3.50 (978-0-9801314-0-6(5)) Ape Entertainment.

—Goblin Chronicles #1B. 2008. (YA). 3.50 (978-0-9801314-1-3(3)) Ape Entertainment.

—Goblin Chronicles #2A. 2008. (Illus.). 32p. (J). 3.50 (978-0-9801314-2-0(1)) Ape Entertainment.

—Goblin Chronicles #2B. 2008. (Illus.). 32p. (J). 3.50 (978-0-9801314-3-7(X)) Ape Entertainment.

Eastman, Kevin B. & Waltz, Tom. Sins of the Fathers. Kuhn, Andy, illus. 2013. (Teenage Mutant Ninja Turtles Ser.). (ENG.). 104p. pap. 17.99 (978-1-61377-568-4(7), 9781613775684) Idea & Design Works, LLC.

—Teenage Mutant Ninja Turtles Volume 2: Enemies Old, Enemies New: Enemies Old, Enemies New. Duncan, Dan & Santolouco, Mateus, illus. 2016. (Teenage Mutant Ninja Turtles Ser.). (ENG.). 104p. pap. 17.99 (978-1-61377-288-1(2), 9781613772881) Idea & Design Works, LLC.

Eastman, Kevin B., et al. Teenage Mutant Ninja Turtles Volume 1: Change Is Constant: Change Is Constant. Duncan, Dan, illus. 2012. (Teenage Mutant Ninja Turtles Ser.). (ENG.). 104p. pap. 17.99 (978-1-61377-139-6(8), 9781613771396) Idea & Design Works, LLC.

Eaton, Maxwell, III. Birds vs. Bunnies. 2013. (Flying Beaver Brothers Ser.). (ENG., Illus.). 96p. (J). (gr. 1-4). pap. 7.99 (978-0-449-81022-4(4), Knopf Bks. for Young Readers) Random Hse. Children's Bks.

—Birds vs. Bunnies. 2013. (Flying Beaver Brothers Ser.: 4). lib. bdg. 18.40 (978-0-606-32234-8(5), Turtleback) Turtleback Bks.

—The Flying Beaver Brothers & the Crazy Critter Race. 2015. (Flying Beaver Brothers Ser.). (ENG., Illus.). 96p. (J). (gr. 1-4). pap. 7.99 (978-0-385-75469-9(8), Knopf Bks. for Young Readers) Random Hse. Children's Bks.

—The Flying Beaver Brothers & the Fishy Business. 2012. (Flying Beaver Brothers Ser.). (ENG.). 96p. (J). (gr. 1-4). pap. 7.99 (978-0-375-86448-3(2), Knopf Bks. for Young Readers) Random Hse. Children's Bks.

—The Flying Beaver Brothers & the Fishy Business. 2012. (Flying Beaver Brothers Ser.: 2). lib. bdg. 18.40 (978-0-606-23870-0(0), Turtleback) Turtleback Bks.

—The Flying Beaver Brothers & the Hot Air Baboons. 2014. (Flying Beaver Brothers Ser.). (ENG., Illus.). 96p. (J). (gr. 1-4). pap. 6.99 (978-0-385-75466-8(3), Knopf Bks. for Young Readers) Random Hse. Children's Bks.

—The Flying Beaver Brothers & the Mud-Slinging Moles. 2013. (Flying Beaver Brothers Ser.). (ENG., Illus.). 96p. (J). (gr. 1-4). pap. 7.99 (978-0-449-81019-4(4), Knopf Bks. for Young Readers) Random Hse. Children's Bks.

—The Flying Beaver Brothers & the Mud-Slinging Moles. 2013. (Flying Beaver Brothers Ser.: 3). lib. bdg. 17.20 (978-0-606-32233-1(7), Turtleback) Turtleback Bks.

Edgar Allan Poe. 2013. (Edgar Allan Poe Graphic Novels Ser.). (ENG.). 72p. (gr. 2-3). 111.96 (978-1-4342-4129-0(7)) Stone Arch Bks.

Edgar Allan Poe Graphic Novels. 2013. (Edgar Allan Poe Graphic Novels Ser.). (ENG.). 72p. (gr. 2-3). pap. 23.80 (978-1-4342-4351-5(5)) Stone Arch Bks.

Edginton, Ian. Assassin's Creed Last Descendants - Locus. Wijngaard, Caspar & Farrell, Triona, illus. 2017. (ENG.). 112p. (gr. 7). pap. 16.99 (978-1-78276-313-0(9)) Titan Bks. Ltd. GBR. Dist: Penguin Random Hse. LLC.

Edison, Richard E. Trouble on the Blue Planet. Santillan, Mariano, illus. 2012. 47p. (J). 4.99 (978-0-8280-2655-0(6)) Review & Herald Publishing Assn.

Edmondson, Nathan. The Activity Volume 3. 2015. (ENG., Illus.). 160p. (YA). pap. 16.99 (978-1-60706-759-7(5), 9781607067597) Image Comics.

—Black Widow - The Finely Woven Thread, Vol. 1. 2014. (ENG., Illus.). 144p. (YA). (gr. 8-17). pap. 17.99 (978-0-7851-8819-3(3)) Marvel Worldwide, Inc.

—Where Is Jake Ellis? 2016. (ENG., Illus.). 124p. (YA). pap. 14.99 (978-1-60706-744-3(7), 9781607067443) Image Comics.

—Who Is Jake Ellis?, Vol. 1. 2011. (ENG., Illus.). 136p. (YA). pap. 16.99 (978-1-60706-459-6(6), 9781607064596) Image Comics.

Edwards, Neil & Pierfederici, Mirco, illus. Dark Avengers: Masters of Evil. 2013. (ENG.). 160p. (YA). (gr. 8-17). pap. 14.99 (978-0-7851-6847-8(8)) Marvel Worldwide, Inc.

Ehrenhaft, Daniel. Drawing a Blank: Or How I Tried to Solve a Mystery, End a Feud, & Land the Girl of My Dreams. Ristow, Trevor, illus. 2009. (ENG.). 352p. (J). pap. 8.99 (978-0-06-075254-5(8), HarperTeen) HarperCollins Pubs.

Ehrmann, Johanna. The Life of a Colonial Wigmaker. 2013. (Jr. Graphic Colonial America Ser.). (ENG., Illus.). 24p. (J). (gr. 3-6). pap. 10.60 (978-1-4777-1431-7(6)); lib. bdg. 25.25 (978-1-4777-1307-5(7)) Rosen Publishing Group, Inc., The. (PowerKids Pr.).

—Theseus & the Minotaur, 1 vol., 1. 2014. (Jr. Graphic Myths: Greek Heroes Ser.). (ENG.). 24p. (J). (gr. 3-6). 26.25 (978-1-4777-6236-3(1), PowerKids Pr.) Rosen Publishing Group, Inc., The.

Eickhoff, Kim, et al. Bamboo Zoo: Meet Lester Panda & his Friends! 2005. (Bamboo Zoo Ser.: Bk. 1). (Illus.). (J). per. 9.95 (978-0-9774493-0-9(0)) Bamboo Zoo, LLC.

Eisner, Will. Sundiata: A Legend of Africa. 2003. (ENG., Illus.). 32p. pap. 7.95 (978-1-56163-340-1(2)) NBM Publishing Co.

Eisner, Will, illus. & retold by. Sundiata: A Legend of Africa. Eisner, Will, retold by. 2003. (ENG.). 32p. (gr. k-3). 15.95 (978-1-56163-332-6(1)) NBM Publishing Co.

Eisner, Will & Melville, Herman. Moby Dick. 2003. (ENG., Illus.). 32p. (J). pap. 7.95 (978-1-56163-294-7(5)) NBM Publishing Co.

Ejsing, Jesper. Jarvis: the Sorcerer's Apprentice: The Sorcerer's Apprentice. 2010. (Illus.). 608p. (YA). 19.95 (978-1-58994-321-6(X)) Fantasy Flight Games.

Elder, Jeremy. ComicQuest ZOMBIES UNLEASHED. 2013. (Dover Children's Activity Bks.). (ENG.). 48p. (J). (gr. 3-8). pap. 4.99 (978-0-486-49943-7(X)) Dover Pubns., Inc.

Elder, Joshua. Mail Order Ninja, 1 vol., Vol. 1. Owen, Erich, illus. 2009. (Tokyopop Ser.). (ENG.). 96p. (gr. 2-6). 25.65 (978-1-59961-568-4(1)) Spotlight.

—Mail Order Ninja Vol. 2: Timmy Strikes Back, 1 vol. Owen, Erich, illus. 2009. (Tokyopop Ser.). (ENG.). 104p. (gr. 2-6). 25.65 (978-1-59961-569-1(X)) Spotlight.

Eliopoulis, Chris, text. Franklin Richards: Son of a Genius Ultimate Collection - Book 1. 2010. (ENG., Illus.). 208p. (J). (gr. -1-17). pap., pap. 19.99 (978-0-7851-4924-8(4)) Marvel Worldwide, Inc.

Eliopoulos, Chris. Does a Great Job, 1 vol. Eliopoulos, Chris, illus. 2013. (Mr. Puzzle Ser.). (ENG., Illus.). 40p. (gr. 1-3). lib. bdg. 23.99 (978-1-4342-6025-3(9)) Stone Arch Bks.

—Mr. Puzzle. Eliopoulos, Chris, illus. 2013. (Mr. Puzzle Ser.). (ENG., Illus.). 40p. (gr. 1-3). 95.96 (978-1-4342-6347-6(9)) Stone Arch Bks.

—Mr. Puzzle Super Collection!, 1 vol. Eliopoulos, Chris, illus. 2013. (Mr. Puzzle Ser.). (ENG., Illus.). 128p. (gr. 3-6). pap. 7.95 (978-1-62370-035-5(3)) Capstone Young Readers of Coughlan Cos.

—No Instructions Needed, 1 vol. Eliopoulos, Chris, illus. 2013. (Mr. Puzzle Ser.). (ENG., Illus.). 40p. (gr. 1-3). lib. bdg. 23.99 (978-1-4342-6026-0(7)) Stone Arch Bks.

—Okie Dokie Donuts: Open for Business! Open for Business! 2011. (ENG., Illus.). 48p. (J). (gr. 2-5). 9.95 (978-1-60309-068-1(1), 9781603090681) Top Shelf Productions.

—A Perfect Fit, 1 vol. Eliopoulos, Chris, illus. 2013. (Mr. Puzzle Ser.). (ENG., Illus.). 40p. (gr. 1-3). lib. bdg. 23.99 (978-1-4342-6024-6(0)) Stone Arch Bks.

—Piece by Piece, 1 vol. Eliopoulos, Chris, illus. 2013. (Mr. Puzzle Ser.). (ENG., Illus.). 40p. (gr. 1-3). lib. bdg. 23.99 (978-1-4342-6027-7(5)) Stone Arch Bks.

Eliopoulos, Christopher. Cosmic Commandos. Eliopoulos, Christopher, illus. 2017. (ENG., Illus.). 192p. (J). (gr. 3-7). 13.99 **(978-1-101-99448-1(7)**, Dial Bks) Penguin Young Readers Group.

Eliopulos, Nick & Random House Staff. DC Super Friends: Flying High. Wallace, Loston et al, illus. 2008. (Step into Reading Ser.). (ENG.). 32p. (J). (gr. -1-1). pap. 3.99 (978-0-375-85208-4(5), Random Hse. Bks. for Young Readers) Random Hse. Children's Bks.

Eliot, Jan. The First Collection of the Syndicated Cartoon Strip, No. 1. 2004. 128p. pap. 10.95 (978-0-9674102-2-7(3)) Four Panel Pr.

Ellis, Warren. Doom 2099: The Complete Collection by Warren Ellis. Klein, David et al, illus. 2013. (ENG.). 424p. (J). (gr. 4-17). pap. 39.99 (978-0-7851-6754-9(4), Marvel Pr.) Disney Publishing Worldwide.

—Iron Man: Armor Wars. Kurth, Steve, illus. 2010. (ENG.). 112p. (YA). (gr. 8-17). pap. 14.99 (978-0-7851-4430-4(7)) Marvel Worldwide, Inc.

Emerson, Marcus. Recess Warriors: Hero Is a Four Letter Word. Emerson, Marcus, illus. 2017. (Recess Warriors Ser.). (ENG., Illus.). 144p. (J). pap. 12.99 (978-1-62672-708-3(2), 9781626727083) Roaring Brook Pr.

Ende, Michael & Michael, Ende. El Largo Camino Hacia Santa Cruz. Kehn, Regina, illus. (SPA.). 64p. (J). (gr. 3-5). 6.95 (978-84-241-3354-2(4), EV3073) Everest Editora ESP. Dist: Lectorum Pubns., Inc.

Englar, Xavier & Niz, Xavier W. The Mystery of the Roanoke Colony, 1 vol. Denton, Shannon E., illus. 2006. (Graphic History Ser.). (ENG.). 32p. (gr. 3-4). per. 8.10 (978-0-7368-9657-3(0), Graphic Library) Capstone Press of Coughlan Cos.

Englehart, Steve. Jurassic Park: Aftershocks!: Vol. 5, 1 vol. 2013. (Jurassic Park Ser.). (ENG.). 32p. (J). (gr. 4-8). lib. bdg. 24.21 (978-1-61479-187-4(2)) Spotlight.

—Jurassic Park: Animals vs. Gods!: Vol. 9, 1 vol. 2013. (Jurassic Park Ser.). (ENG.). 32p. (J). (gr. 4-8). lib. bdg. 24.21 *(978-1-61479-191-1(0))* Spotlight.

—Jurassic Park: Animals vs. Man!: Vol. 8, 1 vol. 2013. (Jurassic Park Ser.). (ENG.). 32p. (J). (gr. 4-8). lib. bdg. 24.21 *(978-1-61479-190-4(2))* Spotlight.

—Jurassic Park: Dark Cargo!: Vol. 6, 1 vol. 2013. (Jurassic Park Ser.). (ENG.). 32p. (J). (gr. 4-8). lib. bdg. 24.21 *(978-1-61479-188-1(0))* Spotlight.

—Jurassic Park: Gods vs. Men!: Vol. 10, 1 vol. 2013. (Jurassic Park Ser.). (ENG.). 32p. (J). (gr. 4-8). lib. bdg. 24.21 *(978-1-61479-192-8(9))* Spotlight.

—Jurassic Park: Raptors Attack!: Vol. 7, 1 vol. 2013. (Jurassic Park Ser.). (ENG.). 32p. (J). (gr. 4-8). lib. bdg. 24.21 *(978-1-61479-189-8(9))* Spotlight.

Enna, Bruno. Double Duck. Soffritti, Donald, illus. 2010. (ENG.). 112p. (J). pap. 9.99 *(978-1-60886-545-1(2))* Boom! Studios.

Enos, Joel, ed. Bravest Warriors: The Search for Catbug. Brown, Alan et al, illus. 2014. (ENG.). 64p. (J). 14.99 *(978-1-4215-7177-5(3))* Viz Media.

Enz, Tammy. Amazing Story of Cell Phone Technology. Pop Art Properties Staff, illus. 2013. (STEM Adventures Ser.). (ENG.). 32p. (gr. 3-4). pap. 8.95 *(978-1-4765-3457-2(8))* Capstone Press of Coughlan Cos.

—Super Cool Construction Activities with Max Axiom. Baez, Marcelo, illus. 2015. (Max Axiom Science & Engineering Activities Ser.). (ENG.). 32p. (gr. 3-4). lib. bdg. 30.65 *(978-1-4914-2078-2(2)*, Graphic Library) Capstone Press of Coughlan Cos.

—Super Cool Mechanical Activities with Max Axiom. Baez, Marcelo, illus. 2015. (Max Axiom Science & Engineering Activities Ser.). (ENG.). 32p. (gr. 3-4). lib. bdg. 30.65 *(978-1-4914-2080-5(4)*, Graphic Library) Capstone Press of Coughlan Cos.

Erickson, Timothy Ronald. Death's Whisper Recoil, 2. Erickson, Timothy Ronald, illus. 2003. (Illus.). (YA). pap. 14.95 *(978-1-59492-001-1(X))* Erickson, Tim.

Espinosa, Frank. Journey to the Hidden Sea, Vol. 1. 2006. (ENG., Illus.). 304p. (YA). pap. 19.99 *(978-1-58240-585-8(9)*, 9781582405858) Image Comics.

—Rocketo: The Journey to the Hidden Sea. 2006. (Illus.). 200p. (YA). pap. 19.99 *(978-0-9738966-4-0(7))* Speakeasy Comics CAN. Dist: Diamond Bk. Distributors.

Espinosa, Rod. Benjamin Franklin, 1 vol. Espinosa, Rod, illus. 2007. (Bio-Graphics Ser.). (ENG., Illus.). 32p. (gr. 3-6). 28.50 *(978-1-60270-066-6(4)*, Graphic Planet- Nonfiction) ABDO Publishing Co.

—Courageous Princess Vol. 1: Beyond the Hundred Kingdoms. Espinosa, Rod, illus. 3rd ed. 2015. (ENG., Illus.). 250p. (J). (gr. 3-7). 19.99 *(978-1-61655-722-5(2))* Dark Horse Comics.

—The Courageous Princess Pocket Manga. 2012. (Illus.). 232p. pap. 14.99 *(978-0-9841107-9-7(8))* Antarctic Pr., Inc.

—The Dragon Queen. Espinosa, Rod, illus. 2015. (Courageous Princess Ser.). (ENG., Illus.). 180p. (J). (gr. 3-7). 19.99 *(978-1-61655-724-9(9))* Dark Horse Comics.

—George Washington, 1 vol. Espinosa, Rod, illus. 2007. (Bio-Graphics Ser.). (ENG., Illus.). 32p. (gr. 3-7). 28.50 *(978-1-60270-067-3(2)*, Graphic Planet- Nonfiction) ABDO Publishing Co.

—The Unremembered Lands. Espinosa, Rod, illus. 2015. (ENG., Illus.). 166p. (J). (gr. 3-7). 19.99 *(978-1-61655-723-2(0))* Dark Horse Comics.

Evanier, Mark. Garfield. Barker, Gary, illus. (Garfield Ser.: 3). (ENG.). 112p. (J). (gr. 2). 2014. pap. 13.99 *(978-1-60886-348-8(4))* Vol. 1. 2012. pap. 13.99 *(978-1-60886-287-0(9))* Boom! Studios.

Evanier, Mark & Barker, Gary. Garfield Vol. 2: I'll Give You All the Ten Seconds to Get off the Comic Racks! Barker, Gary, illus. 2013. (Garfield Ser.). (ENG., Illus.). 112p. (J). (gr. 2). pap. 13.99 *(978-1-60886-303-7(4))* Boom! Studios.

Evanovich, Alex & Evanovich, Janet. Troublemaker. Jackson, Dan, illus. 2011. (Alex Barnaby Ser.: Bk. 3). (ENG.). 112p. pap. 16.99 *(978-1-59582-722-7(6))* Dark Horse Comics.

Evans, Dustin, illus. Costume Craziness, 1 vol. 2013. (Mystical Pencil Ser.). (ENG.). 32p. (J). (gr. 3-6). 28.50 *(978-1-61641-926-4(1))* Magic Wagon.

—Dinosaur Drama, 1 vol. 2013. (Mystical Pencil Ser.). (ENG.). 32p. (J). (gr. 3-6). 28.50 *(978-1-61641-927-1(X))* Magic Wagon.

—A Medieval Mess, 1 vol. 2013. (Mystical Pencil Ser.). (ENG.). 32p. (J). (gr. 3-6). 28.50 *(978-1-61641-928-8(8))* Magic Wagon.

—Raging Robots, 1 vol. 2013. (Mystical Pencil Ser.). (ENG.). 32p. (J). (gr. 3-6). 28.50 *(978-1-61641-929-5(6))* Magic Wagon.

Everheart, Chris. Demolition Day, 1 vol. Arcana Studio Staff, illus. 2010. (Recon Academy Ser.). (ENG.). 64p. (gr. 3-3). 26.65 *(978-1-4342-1917-6(8)*, Recon Academy) Stone Arch Bks.

—The Hidden Face of Fren-Z, 1 vol. 2009. (Recon Academy Ser.). (ENG.). 64p. (gr. 3-3). lib. bdg. 26.65 *(978-1-4342-1165-1(7)*, Recon Academy) Stone Arch Bks.

—Mixed Signals, 1 vol. Arcana Studio Staff, illus. 2010. (Recon Academy Ser.). (ENG.). 64p. (gr. 3-3). 26.65 *(978-1-4342-1915-2(1)*, Recon Academy) Stone Arch Bks.

—Nuclear Distraction, 1 vol. 2009. (Recon Academy Ser.). (ENG.). 64p. (gr. 3-3). lib. bdg. 26.65 *(978-1-4342-1167-5(3)*, Recon Academy) Stone Arch Bks.

—Prep Squadron, 1 vol. 2009. (Recon Academy Ser.). (ENG.). 64p. (gr. 3-3). lib. bdg. 26.65 *(978-1-4342-1168-2(1)*, Recon Academy) Stone Arch Bks.

—Shadow Cell Scam, 1 vol. 2009. (Recon Academy Ser.). (ENG.). 64p. (gr. 3-3). lib. bdg. 26.65 *(978-1-4342-1166-8(5)*, Recon Academy) Stone Arch Bks.

—Storm Surge, 1 vol. Arcana Studio Staff, illus. 2010. (Recon Academy Ser.). (ENG.). 64p. (gr. 3-3). 26.65 *(978-1-4342-1918-3(6)*, Recon Academy) Stone Arch Bks.

—Teen Agent, 1 vol. Arcana Studio Staff, illus. 2010. (Recon Academy Ser.). (ENG.). 64p. (gr. 3-3). 26.65 *(978-1-4342-1916-9(X)*, Recon Academy) Stone Arch Bks.

Ewing, Garen. The Rainbow Orchid, Vol. 1. Ewing, Garen, illus. 2012. (Rainbow Orchid Ser.: 1). (ENG., Illus.). 48p. (J). (gr. 4-7). pap. 10.99 *(978-1-4052-4853-2(X))* Egmont Bks., Ltd. GBR. Dist: Independent Pubs. Group.

FableVision. Spf 40. Reynolds, Peter H., illus. 2013. (Zebrafish Ser.). (ENG.). 128p. (J). (gr. 5-9). 19.99 *(978-1-4169-9708-5(3)*, Atheneum Bks. for Young Readers) Simon & Schuster Children's Publishing.

FableVision Staff. Spf 40. Reynolds, Peter H., illus. 2013. (Zebrafish Ser.). (ENG.). 128p. (J). (gr. 5-9). pap. 9.99 *(978-1-4169-9709-2(1)*, Atheneum Bks. for Young Readers) Simon & Schuster Children's Publishing.

Fackrell, David. Princess, the Collection, Vol. 1. 2005. 78p. pap. 19.99 *(978-1-4116-5820-2(5))* Lulu Pr., Inc.

Faerber, Jay. Near Death Volume 2 TP. 2012. (ENG., Illus.). 136p. (YA). pap. 14.99 *(978-1-60706-590-6(8)*, 9781607065906) Image Comics.

Faerber, Jay, et al. Universal Heroes. 2006. (Illus.). 136p. (YA). pap. 13.99 *(978-0-7851-1857-2(8))* Marvel Worldwide, Inc.

Fajardo, Alexis E. Kid Beowulf: The Song of Roland. 2017. lib. bdg. 24.50 ***(978-0-606-40301-6(9))*** Turtleback Bks.

Fake, Vol. 8. 2004. (YA). pap. 9.99 *(978-1-59182-454-1(0))* TOKYOPOP, Inc.

Fandel, Jennifer, et al. Louis Pasteur & Pasteurization, 1 vol. Wilson, Keith et al, illus. 2007. (Inventions & Discovery Ser.). (ENG.). 32p. (gr. 3-4). 30.65 *(978-0-7368-6844-0(5)*, Graphic Library) Capstone Press of Coughlan Cos.

Farago, Andrew. Teenage Mutant Ninja Turtles: The Ultimate Visual History. 2014. (ENG., Illus.). 192p. 50.00 *(978-1-60887-185-8(1))* Insight Editions.

Farshtey, Greg & Scholastic, Inc. Staff. Zane - Ninja of Ice. 2011. (Lego Ninjago Ser.). (ENG.). 80p. (J). (gr. 2-5). pap. 4.99 *(978-0-545-34828-7(5))* Scholastic, Inc.

Farshtey, Greg, et al. Night of the Nindroids. 2014. (Illus.). 63p. (J). *(978-1-4844-1967-0(7))* Papercutz.

Faulkner, Matt. Gaijin: American Prisoner of War. 2014. (ENG., Illus.). 144p. (J). (gr. 3-7). 19.99 *(978-1-4231-3735-1(3))* Hyperion Bks. for Children.

Faust, Daniel R. After Earth: Living on a Different Planet. 2008. (Jr. Graphic Environmental Dangers Ser.). (ENG.). 24p. (J). 47.90 *(978-1-61532-099-8(7)*, PowerKids Pr.) Rosen Publishing Group, Inc., The.

Fawkes, Ray. The Better House Trap, Vol. 3. 2012. (ENG., Illus.). 72p. (J). pap. 7.99 *(978-1-934964-76-7(X)*, 9781934964767) Oni Pr., Inc.

Fein, Eric. The Fisherman & the Genie, 1 vol. Garcia, Eduardo, illus. 2010. (Classic Fiction Ser.). (ENG.). 72p. (gr. 2-3). 27.99 *(978-1-4342-2134-6(2))*; pap. 7.15 *(978-1-4342-2777-5(4))* Stone Arch Bks. (Graphic Revolve).

—Mystery at Manzanar: A WWII Internment Camp Story, 1 vol. Hartman, Kurt, illus. 2008. (Historical Fiction Ser.). (ENG.). 56p. (gr. 2-3). pap. 6.25 *(978-1-4342-0847-7(8)*, Graphic Flash) Stone Arch Bks.

Fein, Eric & Fuentes, Benny. Skateboard Breakdown, 1 vol. Sandoval, Gerardo, illus. 2010. (Sports Illustrated Kids Graphic Novels Ser.). (ENG.). 56p. (gr. 2-3). 26.65 *(978-1-4342-2011-0(7))*; pap. 7.19 *(978-1-4342-2785-0(5))* Stone Arch Bks.

—Wild Pitch, 1 vol. Sandoval, Gerardo, illus. 2011. (Sports Illustrated Kids Graphic Novels Ser.). (ENG.). 56p. (gr. 2-3). pap. 7.19 *(978-1-4342-3073-7(2))*; lib. bdg. 26.65 *(978-1-4342-2221-3(7))* Stone Arch Bks.

Fein, Eric, et al. Parasite's Power Drain, 1 vol. McManus, Shawn, illus. (Superman Ser.). (ENG.). 56p. (gr. 2-3). 2013. pap. 4.95 *(978-1-4342-2261-9(6))* 2010. lib. bdg. 26.65 *(978-1-4342-1882-7(1))* Stone Arch Bks. (DC Super Heroes).

Feldstein, Al. Weird Science, Vol. 2. 2007. (ENG., Illus.). 212p. (YA). 49.95 *(978-1-888472-69-1(3)*, 9781888472691, William M. Gaines Agent, INC.) Diamond Bk. Distributors.

Fendler, Donn & Plourde, Lynn. Lost Trail: Nine Days Alone in the Wilderness, 1 vol. Bishop, Ben, illus. 2011. (ENG.). 72p. (J). (gr. 4-7). pap. 14.95 *(978-0-89272-945-6(7))* Down East Bks.

Fenton, Sue Fenton, creator. Professor Mel T. Lingual's Coloring Book of Signs: Promoting Language Study & Cultural Awareness. 2005. (Illus.). 58p. (YA). 18.95 *(978-0-9762900-2-5(2)*, #MFP 114) Madame Fifi Pubns.

Ferber, Brenda. The Yuckiest, Stinkiest, Best Valentine Ever. Arnold, Tedd, illus. 2015. (ENG.). 32p. (J). (gr. -1-2). 8.99 *(978-0-14-751709-8(5)*, Puffin Books) Penguin Young Readers Group.

Ferdowsi. Rostam: Tales from the Shahnameh. 2007. (ENG., Illus.). 32p. (YA). 5.95 *(978-0-9770213-2-1(7))* Hyperwerks Entertainment.

Fernández, Leandro, illus. The Punisher. 2006. (ENG.). 144p. (gr. 13-17). pap. 15.99 *(978-0-7851-1899-2(3))* Marvel Worldwide, Inc.

Fernandez, Nacho. La nueva era del sueno vol. 2: Los desiertos del Norte: The New Age of Dreams vol. 2: the Deserts of the North. 2007. (SPA.). 48p. 22.95 *(978-1-59497-398-7(9))* Public Square Bks.

Ferri, Jean-Yves. Asterix & the Picts. Conrad, Didier, illus. 2013. (ENG.). 48p. (J). (gr. 4-7). 17.99 *(978-1-4440-1167-8(7)*, Orion) Orion Publishing Group, Ltd. GBR. Dist: Hachette Bk. Group.

Ferri, Jean-Yves, et al. Asterix & the Missing Scroll. Conrad, Didier, illus. 2016. (Asterix Ser.). (ENG.). 48p. (J). (gr. 2-4). pap. 12.99 *(978-1-5101-0046-6(6)*, Orion Children's Bks.) Hachette Children's Group GBR. Dist: Hachette Bk. Group.

—Asterix & the Picts. Conrad, Didier, illus. 2014. (ENG.). 48p. (J). (gr. 4-6). pap. 12.99 *(978-1-4440-1169-2(3)*, Orion) Orion Publishing Group, Ltd. GBR. Dist: Hachette Bk. Group.

Ferrier, Florian, et al. The Ghosts in the Clouds. Ferrier, Katherine, illus. 2017. (Hotel Strange Ser.: 4). (ENG.). 40p. (gr. 2-5). 26.65 *(978-1-4677-8587-7(3)*, Graphic Universe™) Lerner Publishing Group.

—Wake up, Spring. Ferrier, Katherine, illus. 2015. (ENG.). 40p. (J). (gr. 2-5). 26.65 *(978-1-4677-8584-6(9)*, Graphic Universe™) Lerner Publishing Group.

Ferrier, Katherine & Ferrier, Florian. His Royal Majesty of the Mushrooms. Ferrier, Katherine, illus. 2016. (Hotel Strange Ser.: 3). (ENG., Illus.). 40p. (J). (gr. 2-5). lib. bdg. 26.65 *(978-1-4677-8586-0(5)*, Graphic Universe™) Lerner Publishing Group.

Ferry, Pasqual, illus. Ultimate X-Men Fantastic Four. 2006. (ENG.). 152p. (J). (gr. 4-17). pap. 12.99 *(978-0-7851-2292-0(3))* Marvel Worldwide, Inc.

Festival de Walt Disney. (Coleccion Estrella). (SPA., Illus.). 64p. (J). 14.95 *(978-950-11-0003-7(0)*, SGM003) Sigmar ARG. Dist: Continental Bk. Co., Inc.

Feuti, Norm. The King of Kazoo. 2016. (ENG.). 208p. (J). (gr. 2-5). 22.99 *(978-0-545-77088-0(2)*, Graphix) Scholastic, Inc.

Fialkov, Joshua Hale. X-Men: To Serve & Protect. Coipel, Olivier & Donovan, Deric, illus. 2011. (ENG.). 136p. (J). (gr. 4-17). pap. 14.99 *(978-0-7851-5228-6(8))* Marvel Worldwide, Inc.

Figley, Marthy Rhodes & Figley, Marty Rhodes. The Prison-Ship Adventure of James Forten, Revolutionary War Captive. Hammond, Ted & Carbajal, Richard, illus. 2011. (History's Kid Heroes Ser.). (ENG.). 32p. (gr. 3-5). 26.60 *(978-0-7613-6183-1(9))*; pap. 8.95 *(978-0-7613-7075-8(7)*, Graphic Universe™) Lerner Publishing Group.

Figley, Marty Rhodes. The Prairie Adventure of Sarah & Annie, Blizzard Survivors. Hammond, Ted & Carbajal, Richard Pimentel, illus. 2011. (History's Kid Heroes Set III Ser.). pap. 51.02 *(978-0-7613-8621-6(1))*; (ENG.). 32p. (gr. 3-5). pap. 8.95 *(978-0-7613-7808-2(1))* Lerner Publishing Group. (Graphic Universe™).

—The Prairie Adventure of Sarah & Annie, Blizzard Survivors. Hammond, Ted & Carbajal, Richard, illus. 2011. (History's Kid Heroes Ser.). (ENG.). 32p. (gr. 3-5). lib. bdg. 26.60 *(978-0-7613-7805-1(7))* Lerner Publishing Group.

—The Prison-Ship Adventure of James Forten, Revolutionary War Captive. Hammond, Ted & Carbajal, Richard, illus. 2011. (History's Kid Heroes Ser.). 32p. pap. 51.02 *(978-0-7613-7637-8(2)*, Graphic Universe™) Lerner Publishing Group.

Fillbach Brothers. Star Wars: Clone Wars Adventures, 1 vol. 2013. (Star Wars Digests Set 2 Ser.). (ENG.). 80p. (J). (gr. 4-8). lib. bdg. 27.07 *(978-1-61479-058-7(2))*; lib. bdg. 27.07 *(978-1-61479-059-4(0))* ABDO Publishing Co. (Essential Library).

Fillbach, Brothers & The Fillbach Brothers. Star Wars: Clone Wars Adventures, 1 vol. 2012. (Star Wars Digests Ser.). (ENG., Illus.). (J). (gr. 4-7). 88p. 27.07 *(978-1-59961-909-5(1))*; 96p. 27.07 *(978-1-59961-907-1(5))* Spotlight.

Finals Crisis. 2016. (DC Super Hero Girls Ser.: 1). lib. bdg. 20.85 *(978-0-606-38779-8(X))* Turtleback Bks.

Finch, David, illus. Disassembled. 2006. (ENG.). 176p. (YA). (gr. 8-17). pap. 15.99 *(978-0-7851-1482-6(3))* Marvel Worldwide, Inc.

Finger, Bill & Cameron, Don. Batman Arkham: Scarecrow. 2016. lib. bdg. 33.05 *(978-0-606-38632-6(7))* Turtleback Bks.

Fingeroth, David. Age of the Avengers. 2015. (ENG.). 12p. (J). (gr. k-2). 10.99 *(978-0-7944-3270-6(0)*, Reader's Digest Children's Bks.) Studio Fun International.

Finnegan, Delphine. Justice League Classic: Mind Games. Roberts, Jeremy et al, illus. 2016. 24p. (J). (gr. -1-3). pap. 3.99 *(978-0-06-236075-5(2)*, HarperFestival) HarperCollins Pubs.

First Graphics - My Community, 7 vols. 2010. (First Graphics: My Community Ser.). (ENG.). 24p. (gr. 1-2). lib. bdg. 71.97 *(978-1-4296-5373-2(6))* Capstone Press of Coughlan Cos.

First Graphics - Seasons. 2010. (First Graphics: Seasons Ser.). (ENG.). 24p. (gr. 1-2). pap. 142.80 *(978-1-4296-5698-6(0))*; pap. 18.87 *(978-1-4296-5696-2(4))* Capstone Press of Coughlan Cos.

First Graphics: Manners Matter. 2011. (First Graphics: Manners Matter Ser.). (ENG.). 24p. (gr. 1-2). pap. 142.80 *(978-1-4296-6396-0(0))* Capstone Press of Coughlan Cos.

First Graphics: My Community. (First Graphics: My Community Ser.). (ENG.). 24p. (gr. 1-2). 2011. pap. 249.90 *(978-1-4296-6405-9(3))* 2010. pap. 142.80 *(978-1-4296-5618-4(2))* Capstone Press of Coughlan Cos.

First Graphics: Nature Cycles. 2011. (First Graphics: Nature Cycles Ser.). (ENG.). 24p. (gr. 1-2). pap. 142.80 *(978-1-4296-6401-1(0))* Capstone Press of Coughlan Cos.

First Graphics: Manners Matter. 2010. (First Graphics: Manners Matter Ser.). (ENG.). 24p. (gr. 1-2). lib. bdg. 95.96 *(978-1-4296-5334-3(5))* Capstone Press of Coughlan Cos.

First Graphics: Nature Cycles. 2010. (First Graphics: Nature Cycles Ser.). (ENG.). 24p. (gr. 1-2). pap. 25.16 *(978-1-4296-6232-1(8))* Capstone Press of Coughlan Cos.

First Graphics: Seasons Collection. 2010. (First Graphics: Seasons Ser.). (ENG.). 24p. (gr. 1-2). pap. 18.87 *(978-1-4296-5697-9(2))* Capstone Press of Coughlan Cos.

Fisch, Sholly. April Fools, 1 vol. Brizuela, Dario, illus. 2012. (DC Super Friends Ser.). (ENG.). 32p. (gr. 1-2). lib. bdg. 22.60 *(978-1-4342-4544-1(6))* Stone Arch Bks.

—Challenge of the Super Friends, 1 vol. Brizuela, Dario, illus. 2013. (DC Super Friends Ser.). (ENG.). 32p. (gr. 1-2). lib. bdg. 22.60 *(978-1-4342-4701-8(5))* Stone Arch Bks.

—DC Super Friends. 2013. (DC Super Friends Ser.). (ENG.). 32p. (gr. 1-2). 90.40 *(978-1-4342-4855-8(0))* Stone Arch Bks.

—Hungry for Power, 1 vol. Brizuela, Dario, illus. 2012. (DC Super Friends Ser.). (ENG.). 32p. (gr. 1-2). lib. bdg. 22.60 *(978-1-4342-4541-0(1))* Stone Arch Bks.

—Monkey Business, 1 vol. McKenny, Stewart & Moy, Phil, illus. 2013. (DC Super Friends Ser.). (ENG.). 32p. (gr. 1-2). 22.60 *(978-1-4342-4700-1(7))* Stone Arch Bks.

—Nothing to Fear, 1 vol. McKenny, Stewart & Moy, Phil, illus. 2013. (DC Super Friends Ser.). (ENG.). 32p. (gr. 1-2). lib. bdg. 22.60 *(978-1-4342-4703-2(1))* Stone Arch Bks.

—Scooby-Doo in Fangs, but No Fangs!, 1 vol. 2013. (Scooby-Doo Graphic Novels Set 3 Ser.). (ENG.). 24p. (J). (gr. 2-6). lib. bdg. 24.21 *(978-1-61479-051-8(5)*, Essential Library) ABDO Publishing Co.

—Scooby-Doo in Trick or Treat!, 1 vol. Staton, Joe, illus. 2010. (Scooby-Doo Graphic Novels Ser.: No. 1). (ENG.). 24p. (J). (gr. 2-5). 24.21 *(978-1-59961-699-5(8))* Spotlight.

—Scooby-Doo! Team-Up. 2015. (ENG., Illus.). 128p. (J). (gr. 2-5). pap. 12.99 *(978-1-4012-4946-5(9))* DC Comics.

—Wanted - The Super Friends. McKenny, Stewart & Moy, Philip, illus. 2012. (DC Super Friends Ser.). (ENG.). 32p. (gr. 1-2). lib. bdg. 22.60 *(978-1-4342-4543-4(8))* Stone Arch Bks.

Fisch, Sholly & Age, Heroic. Happy Birthday, Superman!, 1 vol. Bone, J., illus. 2014. (DC Super Friends Ser.). (ENG.). 32p. (gr. 1-2). 22.60 *(978-1-4342-9222-3(3))* Stone Arch Bks.

—Season of Light, 1 vol. Brizuela, Dario, illus. 2014. (DC Super Friends Ser.). (ENG.). 32p. (gr. 1-2). 22.60 *(978-1-4342-9223-0(1))* Stone Arch Bks.

—Who Is the Mystery Bat-Squad?, 1 vol. Clugston, Chynna, illus. 2014. (DC Super Friends Ser.). (ENG.). 32p. (gr. 1-2). 22.60 *(978-1-4342-9224-7(X))* Stone Arch Bks.

Fisch, Sholly & Ottolini, Horacio. Dinosaur Round-Up, 1 vol. Brizuela, Dario & Staton, Joe, illus. 2012. (DC Super Friends Ser.). (ENG.). 32p. (gr. 1-2). lib. bdg. 22.60 *(978-1-4342-4542-7(X))* Stone Arch Bks.

Fisch, Sholly, et al. The All-New Batman: the Brave & the Bold. 2015. (All-New Batman: the Brave & the Bold Ser.). (ENG., Illus.). 32p. (gr. 2-3). lib. bdg. 90.40 *(978-1-4965-0544-6(1))* Stone Arch Bks.

—Bottle of the Planets. 2015. (All-New Batman: the Brave & the Bold Ser.). (ENG., Illus.). 32p. (gr. 2-3). lib. bdg. 22.60 *(978-1-4342-9658-0(X))* Stone Arch Bks.

—The Bride & the Bold. 2015. (All-New Batman: the Brave & the Bold Ser.). (ENG., Illus.). 32p. (gr. 2-3). lib. bdg. 22.60 *(978-1-4342-9661-0(X))* Stone Arch Bks.

—Clobbered by Clayface! 2015. (All-New Batman: the Brave & the Bold Ser.). (ENG., Illus.). 32p. (gr. 2-3). lib. bdg. 22.60 *(978-1-4342-9663-4(6))* Stone Arch Bks.

—Go! - Party, Party!, Vol. 1. 2015. (ENG., Illus.). 128p. (J). (gr. 2-5). pap. 12.99 *(978-1-4012-5242-7(7))* DC Comics.

—Manhandled by Manhunters! 2015. (All-New Batman: the Brave & the Bold Ser.). (ENG., Illus.). 32p. (gr. 2-3). lib. bdg. 22.60 *(978-1-4342-9662-7(8))* Stone Arch Bks.

—Starro & the Pirates, 1 vol. 2014. (DC Super Friends Ser.). (ENG., Illus.). 32p. (gr. 1-2). 22.60 *(978-1-4342-9225-4(8))* Stone Arch Bks.

—That Holiday Feeling. 2015. (All-New Batman: the Brave & the Bold Ser.). (ENG., Illus.). 32p. (gr. 2-3). lib. bdg. 22.60 *(978-1-4342-9659-7(8))* Stone Arch Bks.

—Through the Looking Glass! 2015. (All-New Batman: the Brave & the Bold Ser.). (ENG., Illus.). 32p. (gr. 2-3). lib. bdg. 22.60 *(978-1-4342-9660-3(1))* Stone Arch Bks.

Fisher, Martin & Davison, Max. Home. 2015. (ENG., Illus.). 64p. (J). (gr. 1-4). Vol. 1. pap. 6.99 *(978-1-78276-228-7(0))* Vol. 2. pap. 6.99 *(978-1-78276-229-4(9))* Titan Bks. Ltd. GBR. Dist: Penguin Random Hse. LLC.

Fleur, Leo La. The Errand. Oehlers, Adam, illus. 2017. (ENG.). 44p. (J). (gr. 1-5). 16.95 ***(978-1-77229-024-0(6))*** Simply Read Bks. CAN. Dist: Ingram Publisher Services.

Flor Ada, Alma & Campoy, F. Isabel. Ratoncito Prez, Cartero. Escriva, Sandra Lopez, illus. 2015. (Santillana USA Ser.).Tr. of New Job for Pérez, the Mouse. (SPA.). 32p. (J). (gr. 6-6). pap. 15.95 *(978-1-63113-547-7(3)*, Santillana) Santillana USA Publishing Co., Inc.

Fly Chronicles. 2005. (Illus.). per. 12.95 *(978-0-9740567-9-1(0))* Active Images.

Flynn, Ian. Mega Man 3: Return of Dr. Wily. Bates, Ben, illus. 2012. (Mega Man Ser.: 3). (ENG.). 112p. (gr. 4-7). pap. 11.99 *(978-1-936975-11-2(4)*, Archie Comics) Archie Comic Pubns., Inc.

—Mega Man 4: Spiritus Ex Machina. 2012. (Mega Man Ser.: 4). (ENG.). 112p. (gr. 4-7). pap. 11.99 *(978-1-936975-27-3(0)*, Archie Comics) Archie Comic Pubns., Inc.

Flynn, Ian & Spaziante, Patrick. Let the Games Begin. 2011. (Mega Man Ser.: 1). (ENG., Illus.). 112p. (gr. 4-7). pap. 11.95 *(978-1-879794-85-6(3)*, Archie Comics) Archie Comic Pubns., Inc.

Foglio, Kaja & Foglio, Phil. Agatha Heterodyne & the Clockwork Princess: A Gaslamp Fantasy with Adventure, Romance & Mad Science. Foglio, Kaja & Foglio, Phil, eds. 2013. (ENG., Illus.). 112p. (YA). pap. 25.00 *(978-1-890856-39-7(8)*, 9781890856397) Studio Foglio, LLC.

Foley, Ryan. The Treasured Thief. Nagar, Sachin, illus. 2012. (Campfire Graphic Novels Ser.). (ENG.). 64p. (YA). (gr. 3-7). pap. 9.99 *(978-93-80741-11-6(1)*, Campfire) Steerforth Pr.

Follet, René. The Fascinating Madame Tussaud. Duchateau, illus. 2008. (Expresso Collection). (ENG.). 104p. pap. 19.95 *(978-1-905460-36-6(8))* CineBook GBR. Dist: National Bk. Network.

Fontana, Shea. Summer Olympus. 2017. (DC Super Hero Girls Ser.: 3). lib. bdg. 20.85 ***(978-0-606-40123-4(7))*** Turtleback Bks.

Fontes, Justine & Fontes, Ron. Atalanta: The Race Against Destiny. Yeates, Thomas, illus. 2008. (Graphic Myths & Legends Ser.). (ENG.). 48p. (gr. 4-8). per. 8.95 *(978-0-8225-6569-7(2))* Lerner Publishing Group.

—Casebook: Bigfoot. 2009. (Top Secret Graphica Mysteries Ser.). (Illus.). 48p. (YA). (gr. 2-6). 29.25 *(978-1-60754-594-1(2))*; pap. 11.75 *(978-1-60754-595-8(0))* Windmill Bks.

—Casebook: Ghosts & Poltergeists. 2009. (Top Secret Graphica Mysteries Ser.). (Illus.). 48p. (YA). (gr. 2-6). 29.25 *(978-1-60754-597-2(7))*; pap. 11.75 *(978-1-60754-598-9(5))* Windmill Bks.

—The Fifth Musketeer. Meconis, Dylan, illus. 2012. (Twisted Journeys Ser.: 19). (ENG.). 112p. (J). (gr. 4-7). pap. 7.95 *(978-0-7613-8550-9(9))*; pap. 45.32 *(978-0-7613-9289-7(0))*; lib. bdg. 27.93 *(978-0-7613-4594-7(9))* Lerner Publishing Group. (Graphic Universe™).

—Sunjata: Warrior King of Mali [A West African Legend]. Carruthers, Sandy, illus. 2009. (Graphic Myths & Legends Ser.). (ENG.). 48p. (gr. 4-8). pap. 8.95 *(978-1-58013-891-8(8))* Lerner Publishing Group.

—The Trojan Horse: The Fall of Troy [a Greek Myth]. Purcell, Gordon, illus. 2015. (Graphic Myths & Legends Ser.). (ENG.). 48p. (gr. 4-8). 21.32 *(978-1-4677-5985-4(6))*, Lerner Digital) Lerner Publishing Group.

Fontes, Ron. El Caballo de Troya: La Caida de Troya: un Mito Griego. Purcell, Gordon & Schulz, Barbara, illus. 2007. (Mitos y leyendas en viñetas (Graphic Myths & Legends) Ser.).Tr. of Trojan Horse. (SPA.). 48p. (J). (gr. 4-7). per. 8.95 *(978-0-8225-7970-0(7)*, Ediciones Lerner) Lerner Publishing Group.

—Sunjata: Warrior King of Mali: A West African Legend. Carruthers, Sandy, illus. 2008. (Graphic Myths & Legends Ser.). 48p. (J). (gr. 3-7). lib. bdg. 26.60 *(978-0-8225-6758-5(X)*, Graphic Universe™) Lerner Publishing Group.

Fontes, Ron & Fontes, Justine. Captured by Pirates. Witt, David, illus. 2007. (Twisted Journeys (r) Ser.: 1). (ENG.). 112p. (J). (gr. 4-7). lib. bdg. 27.93 *(978-0-8225-6201-6(4)*, Graphic Universe™); per. 7.95 *(978-0-8225-6202-3(2))* Lerner Publishing Group.

—The Trojan Horse: The Fall of Troy - A Greek Legend. Purcell, Gordon & Schulz, Barbara, illus. 2007. (Graphic Myths & Legends Ser.). (ENG.). 48p. (gr. 4-8). per. 8.95 *(978-0-8225-6484-3(X))* Lerner Publishing Group.

Fontes, Ron, et al. The Trojan Horse: The Fall of Troy. Purcell, Gordon, illus. 2006. (Graphic Myths & Legends Ser.). (ENG.). 48p. (gr. 4-8). 27.93 *(978-0-8225-3085-5(6))* Lerner Publishing Group.
Forbes, Jake T., ed. Tokyopop Manga Sampler: 2002. (Illus.). 190p. (YA). mass mkt. *(978-0-681-88644-5(7)*, TOKYOPOP Manga) TOKYOPOP, Inc.
Forlini, Victoria, ed. Batman Begins Stencil Activity Book. 2005. (Illus.). 22p. (J). bds., act. bk. ed. 9.95 *(978-0-696-22590-1(5))* Meredith Bks.
Forney, Ellen. Monkey Food: The Complete I was Seven in '75 Collection. Forney, Ellen, illus. 2005. (Illus.). 142p. (YA). reprint ed. pap. 13.00 *(978-0-7567-8610-6(X))* DIANE Publishing Co.
Fosgitt, Jay P. Little Green Men. 2010. (ENG., Illus.). 100p. (YA). pap. 9.95 *(978-1-936340-01-9(1)*, 9781936340019) Ape Entertainment.
—Little Green Men: Small Package, Big Fun! GN: Small Package, Big Fun! GN. 2012. (ENG., Illus.). 48p. pap. 6.95 *(978-1-936340-63-7(1)*, 9781936340637) Ape Entertainment.
Fountain, Bill. Raven: The Sleeping Glass Heart. 2005. (Illus.). 24p. (YA). 5.00 *(978-0-9773461-0-3(2))* Level Ground Pr.
Fox, Gardner. The Atom, Vol. 2. rev. ed. 2003. (ENG., Illus.). 216p. (YA). 49.95 *(978-1-4012-0014-5(1))* DC Comics.
Foxe, Steve. Hot Pursuit! (DC Super Friends) Random House, illus. 2017. (Pictureback(R) Ser.). (ENG.). 24p. (J). (gr. -1-2). pap. 5.99 ***(978-1-5247-1715-5(0)**, Random Hse. Bks. for Young Readers) Random Hse. Children's Bks.
Frampton, Otis. Oddly Normal, Bk. 2. 2015. (Oddly Normal Ser.: 2). lib. bdg. 20.85 *(978-0-606-37601-3(1))* Turtleback Bks.
—Oddly Normal, Book 3. 2016. (Oddly Normal Ser.: 3). lib. bdg. 20.85 *(978-0-606-38577-0(0))* Turtleback Bks.
—Red Riding Hood, Superhero. Frampton, Otis, illus. 2015. (Far Out Fairy Tales Ser.). (ENG., Illus.). 40p. (gr. 3-4). lib. bdg. 25.32 *(978-1-4342-9650-4(4))* Stone Arch Bks.
Francesc Bargada Studios Staff & Staff, Di I. Around the World in 80 Bucks. 2010. (Uncle Scrooge Ser.). (ENG., Illus.). 128p. (J). (gr. 3-6). pap. 9.99 *(978-1-60886-566-6(5))* Boom! Studios.
Francis, Suzanne & Marsham, Liz. Ariel Is Fearless/Jasmine Is Helpful (Disney Princess) Disney Storybook Art Team Staff & Thomas, Jeffrey, illus. 2017. (Step into Reading Ser.). (ENG.). 48p. (J). (gr. -1-1). lib. bdg. 12.99 ***(978-0-7364-9018-4(3)**, RH/Disney) Random Hse. Children's Bks.
Franco. Itty Bitty Comics: Grimmiss Island. Baltazar, Art, illus. 2015. (Itty Bitty Comics Ser.). (ENG.). 104p. (J). (gr. 3-7). pap. 12.99 *(978-1-61655-768-3(0))* Dark Horse Comics.
Frank, Vincent. The Six Pack. 2010. 48p. (J). pap. 18.99 *(978-1-4490-9471-3(6))* AuthorHouse.
Franquin, André. The Marsupilami Thieves. 2013. (Spirou & Fantasio Ser.: 5). (ENG., Illus.). 64p. (J). (gr. 3-12). pap. 15.95 *(978-1-84918-167-9(5))* CineBook GBR. Dist: National Bk. Network.
Fred. Cast Away on the Letter A. Fred, illus. 2013. (Philemon Adventures Ser.). (ENG., Illus.). 48p. (J). (gr. 2-7). 16.95 *(978-1-935179-63-4(2))* TOON Books / RAW Junior, LLC.
French, Renee. Barry's Best Buddy. French, Renee, illus. 2013. (ENG., Illus.). 32p. (J). (gr. -1-3). 12.95 *(978-1-935179-21-4(7))* TOON Books / RAW Junior, LLC.
—The Soap Lady. French, Renee, illus. 2005. (Illus.). 111p. (J). (gr. 4-8). reprint ed. 20.00 *(978-0-7567-9419-4(6))* DIANE Publishing Co.
Fridolfs, Derek. Fort Solitude (DC Comics: Secret Hero Society #2) Nguyen, Dustin, illus. 2016. (DC Comics: Secret Hero Society Ser.: 2). (ENG.). 176p. (J). (gr. 3-7). 12.99 *(978-0-545-87684-1(2))* Scholastic, Inc.
Friedman, Michael Jan, et al. Convergence. Erwin, Steve et al, illus. 2008. (ENG.). 176p. pap. 14.95 *(978-1-84576-320-6(3)*, Titan Bks.) Titan Bks. Ltd. GBR. Dist: Penguin Random Hse. LLC.
Friesen, Christi. Under the Sea. 2006. (CF Sculpture Ser.). (ENG., Illus.). 48p. per. 9.95 *(978-0-9728177-0-7(0))* Don't Eat Any Bugs Productions.
Friesen, Ray. A Cheese Related Mishap & Other Stories. 2005. (Lookit! Ser.). (ENG., Illus.). 100p. per. 8.95 *(978-0-9728177-6-9(X))* Don't Eat Any Bugs Productions.
—Lookit!, Vol. 2. 2004. (YA). per. 4.95 *(978-0-9728177-3-8(5))* Don't Eat Any Bugs Prodns.
—Pirate Penguin vs Ninja Chicken Volume 1: Troublems with Frenemies: Troublems with Frenemies. 2011. (Pirate Penguin vs Ninja Chicken Ser.). (ENG., Illus.). 96p. (J). (gr. 2-5). 9.95 *(978-1-60309-071-1(1)*, 9781603090711) Top Shelf Productions.
—RQW, Vol. 3. 2003. (YA). 2.95 *(978-0-9728177-2-1(7))* Don't Eat Any Bugs Prodns.
—RQW Comics #1-4 Collection. 2004. (YA). 10.00 *(978-0-9728177-5-2(1))* Don't Eat Any Bugs Prodns.
—Yarg! & Other Stories. 2006. (Lookit! Ser.). (ENG., Illus.). 104p. (gr. 3-6). per. 11.95 *(978-0-9728177-9-0(4))* Don't Eat Any Bugs Productions.
From the Dust #1: The Last King of Judah. 2012. (ENG.). pap. 14.99 *(978-0-9859884-1-8(X))* Spider Comics.
Fuentes, Benny & Hoena, Blake A. Sack Attack!, 1 vol. Sandoval, Gerardo, illus. 2011. (Sports Illustrated Kids Graphic Novels Ser.). (ENG.). 56p. (gr. 2-3). pap. 7.19 *(978-1-4342-3404-9(5))*; lib. bdg. 26.65 *(978-1-4342-2243-5(8))* Stone Arch Bks.
Fujieda, Toru, creator. Dragon Girl. (Dragon Girl Ser.: 1). (ENG., Illus.). (J). (gr. 8-17). 2010. 496p. pap. 20.99 *(978-0-7595-3166-6(8))* Vol. 2. 2011. 464p. pap. 20.99 *(978-0-7595-3167-3(6))* Orbit. (Yen Pr.).
Fujii, Hideaki. LBX Vol. 1: New Dawn Raisers. 2014. (ENG., Illus.). 192p. (J). pap. 9.99 *(978-1-4215-7695-4(3))* Viz Media.
—LBX Vol. 2: Artemis Begins. 2014. (ENG., Illus.). 184p. (J). pap. 9.99 *(978-1-4215-7696-1(1))* Viz Media.
—LBX: World Battle, Vol. 6. 2015. (ENG., Illus.). 152p. (J). pap. 9.99 *(978-1-4215-7700-5(3))* Viz Media.
—LBX: World Changer, Vol. 3. 2015. (ENG., Illus.). 192p. (J). pap. 9.99 *(978-1-4215-7697-8(X))* Viz Media.
Fujinari, Yuuki. Ugly Duckling's Love Revolution, Vol. 3. 2011. (Ugly Duckling's Love Revolution Ser.: 3). (ENG., Illus.). 192p. (gr. 8-17). pap. 11.99 *(978-0-7595-3177-2(3)*, Yen Pr.) Orbit.
Fujishima, Kosuke. Oh My Goddess! Fujishima, Kosuke, illus. (Oh My Goddess! Ser.). (ENG., Illus.). Vol. 25. 2007. 176p. pap. 10.95 *(978-1-59307-644-3(4))* Vol. 34. 2010. 144p. pap. 10.99 *(978-1-59582-448-6(0))* Dark Horse Comics.
—Oh My Goddess! Volume 36. 2010. (ENG., Illus.). 152p. pap. 10.99 *(978-1-59582-581-0(9))* Dark Horse Comics.
—Oh My Goddess! Volume 43. Horn, Carl Gustav, ed. Fujishima, Kosuke, illus. 2013. (ENG., Illus.). 176p. pap. 12.99 *(978-1-61655-082-0(1))* Dark Horse Comics.
Furman, Simon. Dangerous Dangers of the Deep. 2014. lib. bdg. 17.20 *(978-0-606-35606-0(1))* Turtleback Bks.
—Dragon Down. 2014. lib. bdg. 17.20 *(978-0-606-35605-3(3))* Turtleback Bks.
—Dragons Vol.4: The Stowaway. 2015. (Riders of Berk Ser.). (ENG., Illus.). 64p. (J). (gr. 3-7). pap. 6.99 *(978-1-78276-079-5(2))* Titan Bks. Ltd. GBR. Dist: Penguin Random Hse. LLC.
—Dragons - Defenders of Berk Vol. 1: The Endless Night. Florean, Arianna, illus. 2016. (ENG.). 64p. (J). (gr. 3-7). pap. 6.99 *(978-1-78276-214-0(0))* Titan Bks. Ltd. GBR. Dist: Penguin Random Hse. LLC.
—Dragons: Defenders of Berk Volume 1. Nazif, Iwan & Lawrence, Jack, illus. 2016. (ENG.). 112p. (J). (gr. 1-4). pap. 12.99 *(978-1-78585-678-5(2))* Titan Bks. Ltd. GBR. Dist: Penguin Random Hse. LLC.
—Dragons: Riders of Berk Collection Volume 3. Nasif, Iwan, illus. 2016. (ENG.). 112p. (J). (gr. 1-4). pap. 12.99 *(978-1-78585-177-3(2))* Titan Bks. Ltd. GBR. Dist: Penguin Random Hse. LLC.
—Riders of Berk - Tales from Berk, Vol. 1. 2016. (ENG., Illus.). 64p. (J). (gr. 3-7). pap. 12.99 *(978-1-78276-696-4(0))* Titan Bks. Ltd. GBR. Dist: Penguin Random Hse. LLC.
Furman, Simon & Ferreyra, Lucas. Kung Fu Panda, Vol. 1. Robinson, Lee & Simmonds-Hurn, Zak, illus. 2016. (ENG.). 64p. (J). (gr. 3-7). pap. 6.99 *(978-1-78276-268-3(X))* Titan Bks. Ltd. GBR. Dist: Penguin Random Hse. LLC.
Furman, Simon & Nazif, Iwan. Dragons - Riders of Berk. 2015. (ENG., Illus.). 112p. (J). 22.99 *(978-1-78276-766-4(5))* Titan Bks. Ltd. GBR. Dist: Penguin Random Hse. LLC.
—Dragons - Riders of Berk, Vol. 2. Lawrence, Jack, illus. 2016. (ENG.). 112p. (J). (gr. 3-7). pap. 12.99 *(978-1-78585-176-6(4))* Titan Bks. Ltd. GBR. Dist: Penguin Random Hse. LLC.
Furman, Simon & Titan Comics Staff. The Legend of Ragnarok, Vol. 5. 2015. (Riders of Berk Ser.). (ENG., Illus.). 64p. (J). (gr. 3-7). pap. 6.99 *(978-1-78276-080-1(6))* Titan Bks. Ltd. GBR. Dist: Penguin Random Hse. LLC.
Furman, Simon, et al. Kung Fu Panda - Sleep-Fighting, Vol. 2. 2016. (ENG., Illus.). 64p. (J). (gr. 3-7). pap. 6.99 *(978-1-78276-269-0(8))* Titan Bks. Ltd. GBR. Dist: Penguin Random Hse. LLC.
Fushimi, Tsukasa. Oreimo Volume 4. Jefferson, Jemiah, ed. 2013. (ENG., Illus.). 168p. pap. 10.99 *(978-1-61655-221-3(2))* Dark Horse Comics.
Gage, Christos. What You Want, Not What You Need. Allie, Scott & Hahn, Sierra, eds. 2014. (ENG., Illus.). 136p. pap. 17.99 *(978-1-61655-253-4(0))* Dark Horse Comics.
Gagné, Michel. The Saga of Rex. 2010. (ENG., Illus.). 200p. (J). (gr. 4-7). pap. 17.99 *(978-1-60706-322-3(0)*, 9781607063223) Image Comics.
Gaiman, NEil. El Dia Que Cambié a Mi Padre por dos Peces de Colores. Ferrer, Maria, tr. from ENG. 2005. (Single Volume Ser.). (SPA., Illus.). 56p. 28.95 *(978-1-59497-076-4(9))* Public Square Bks.
—The Graveyard Book Graphic Novel. 2015. (J). Vol. 1. lib. bdg. 20.85 *(978-0-606-37613-6(5))* Vol. 2. lib. bdg. 20.85 *(978-0-606-37614-3(3))* Turtleback Bks.
—The Graveyard Book Graphic Novel Single Volume. Russell, P. Craig, illus. 368p. (J). (gr. 3-7). 2017. pap. 20.00 ***(978-0-06-242189-0(1))** 2016. 35.00 *(978-0-06-242188-3(3))* HarperCollins Pubs.
—The Graveyard Book Graphic Novel Single Volume Special Limited Edition. Russell, P. Craig, illus. 2016. 384p. (J). (gr. 3-7). 175.00 *(978-0-06-239449-1(5))* HarperCollins Pubs.
—Los Lobos de la Pared. McKean, Dave, illus. 2006.Tr. of Wolves in the Wall. (SPA.). 64p. 22.95 *(978-1-59497-222-5(2))* Public Square Bks.
—The Wolves in the Walls. McKean, Dave, illus. 2005. (ENG.). 56p. (J). (gr. k). reprint ed. pap. 6.99 *(978-0-380-81095-6(6))* HarperCollins Pubs.
Gaines, Bill, et al. The Vault of Horror, Vol. 3. Chabon, Daniel, ed. Craig, Johnny, illus. 2014. (ENG.). 200p. 49.99 *(978-1-61655-292-3(1))* Dark Horse Comics.
Gale Editor, ed. A Christmas Carol: The Graphic Novel. 2011. (Classic Graphic Novel Collection Ser.). 160p. (YA). (gr. 7-12). lib. bdg. 34.80 *(978-1-4205-0630-3(7))* Cengage Gale.
Gallagher, Mike. Sabrina Animated. Manak, Dave, illus. 2011. (Archie & Friends All-Stars Ser.: 13). (ENG.). 128p. (J). (gr. 4-7). pap. 9.95 *(978-1-879794-80-1(2)*, Archie Comics) Archie Comic Pubns., Inc.
Gamache, Line. Hello, Me Pretty. Cochrane, KerryAnn, tr. from FRE. 2007. (ENG., Illus.). 64p. per. *(978-1-894994-23-1(X))* Conundrum Pr.
Gardner, Matt. Alabaster Shadows. 2015. (ENG., Illus.). 184p. (J). pap. 12.99 *(978-1-62010-264-0(1)*, 9781620102640) Oni Pr., Inc.
Garing, Ken. Planetoid Volume 1 TP. 2013. (ENG., Illus.). 164p. (YA). pap. 15.99 *(978-1-60706-813-6(3)*, 9781607068136) Image Comics.
Gasnick, Roy M. & Grycan, Julien. Serra: American Founding Father. 2010. (ENG., Illus.). 35p. pap. 2.95 *(978-0-86716-942-3(7))* Franciscan Media.
Gaston County Museum of Art & History, ed. The Secret Adventures of Hamster Sam: Attack of the Evil Boll Weevils! 2008. (Illus.). 32p. (J). 15.95 *(978-0-9798445-0-8(9))* DM Creative.
Gatou, Shouji. Full Metal Panic - Overload!, Vol. 5. Nagai, Tomohiro, illus. 2006. (Full Metal Panic: Overload! Ser.). 200p. (YA). pap. 9.99 *(978-1-4139-0342-3(8))* ADV Manga.
Gauvin, Edward, tr. I Remember Beirut. 2014. (ENG., Illus.). 96p. (gr. 8-12). lib. bdg. 29.27 *(978-1-4677-3822-4(0)*, Graphic Universe™) Lerner Publishing Group.
Gavila, Robert. Nisha: Montana. 2004. (YA). 2.25 *(978-0-9748466-0-6(0))* Gavila Publishing.
Gay, Francis. The Friendship Book. 2005. (Illus.). 180p. 9.95 *(978-1-84535-050-5(2))* Thomson, D.C. & Co., Ltd. GBR. Dist: APG Sales & Distribution Services.
Gaydos, Nora. Phonics Comics: Pony Tales - Level 1. Hamilton, Pamela, illus. 2007. (ENG.). 24p. (J). (gr. 1-17). per. 3.99 *(978-1-58476-553-0(4))* Innovative Kids.
Gecko, Gabriel, et al, illus. Iron Man/War Machine: Hands of the Mandarin. 2013. (ENG.). 280p. (J). (gr. 4-17). pap. 24.99 *(978-0-7851-8428-7(7))* Marvel Worldwide, Inc.
Gerani, Gary. Dinosaurs Attack. Trimpe, Herb et al, illus. 2014. (ENG.). 136p. pap. 19.99 *(978-1-61377-862-3(7)*, 9781613778623) Idea & Design Works, LLC.
Gerra, Laurent. The Man from Washington. 2013. (Lucky Luke Ser.: 39). (ENG., Illus.). 48p. pap. 11.95 *(978-1-84918-149-5(7))* CineBook GBR. Dist: National Bk. Network.
—Tying the Knot, Vol. 45. 2014. (Lucky Luke Ser.: 45). (ENG., Illus.). 48p. pap. 11.95 *(978-1-84918-188-4(8))* CineBook GBR. Dist: National Bk. Network.
Gerrold, David, et al. Diary of a Stinky Dead Kid, No. 8. Hack, Robert et al, illus. 2009. (Tales from the Crypt Graphic Novels Ser.). (ENG.). 96p. (J). (gr. 5-12). pap. 7.95 *(978-1-59707-163-5(3)*, 9781597071635); 12.95 *(978-1-59707-164-2(1)*, 9781597071642) Papercutz.
—Wickeder. Parker, Rick et al, illus. 2010. (Tales from the Crypt Graphic Novels Ser.). (ENG.). 64p. (J). (gr. 5-12). pap. 6.99 *(978-1-59707-215-1(X)*, 9781597072151); 10.99 *(978-1-59707-216-8(8)*, 9781597072168) Papercutz.
Ghiglione, Marco. Ultraheroes Vol. 1: Save the World. Secchi, Riccardo, illus. 2010. (Disney's Hero Squad Ser.). (ENG.). 112p. (J). pap. 9.99 *(978-1-60886-543-7(6))* Boom! Studios.
Ghiglione, Marco & Randolph, Grace. Ultraheroes: Save the World. Secchi, Riccardo & Randolph, Grace, illus. 2010. (Disney's Hero Squad Ser.: 1). (ENG.). 112p. (J). pap. 24.99 *(978-1-60886-552-9(5))* Boom! Studios.
Gianatti, Silvia, et al. Tinker Bell & Her Magical Arrival. Melaranci, Elisabetta & Urbano, Emilio, illus. 2012. (Disney Fairies Ser.: 9). (ENG.). 64p. (J). (gr. 1-6). 11.99 *(978-1-59707-324-0(5)*, 9781597073240); pap. 7.99 *(978-1-59707-323-3(7)*, 9781597073233) Papercutz.
Giarrusso, Chris. G-Man Coming Home. 2013. (ENG., Illus.). 128p. (J). pap. 9.99 *(978-1-60706-571-5(1)*, 9781607065715) Image Comics.
—G-Man Learning to Fly, Vol. 1. 2010. (ENG., Illus.). 96p. (J). pap. 9.99 *(978-1-60706-270-7(4)*, 9781607062707) Image Comics.
—The G-Man Super Journal: Awesome Origins. 2015. (ENG.). 240p. (J). 13.99 *(978-1-4494-5844-7(0))* Andrews McMeel Publishing.
—G-Man Volume 2: Cape Crisis: Cape Crisis. 2010. (ENG., Illus.). 128p. (J). pap. 9.99 *(978-1-60706-271-4(2)*, 9781607062714) Image Comics.
Gifford, Clive. Dead or Alive? Horne, Sarah, illus. 2015. (ENG.). 48p. (J). (gr. 2-4). 14.99 *(978-1-4052-6858-5(1))* Egmont Bks., Ltd. GBR. Dist: Independent Pubs. Group.
Gilbert, Janet, et al. Uncle Scrooge, Vol. 354. Clark, John, ed. 2006. (ENG., Illus.). 64p. pap. 6.95 *(978-1-888472-23-3(5)*, 9781888472233) Gemstone Publishing, Inc.
Gilbert, Michael T., et al. Mickey Mouse Adventures, Vol. 8. Clark, John, ed. 2006. (ENG., Illus.). 128p. (YA). pap. 7.95 *(978-1-888472-09-7(X)*, 9781888472097) Gemstone Publishing, Inc.
—Walt Disney's Comics & Stories #693. Clark, John, ed. 2008. (ENG., Illus.). 64p. pap. 7.99 *(978-1-60360-038-5(8)*, 9781603600385) Gemstone Publishing, Inc.
Gilliam, David. Gingertown. Gilliam, David, illus. 2012. 216p. (J). 29.99 *(978-1-60131-122-1(2))* Big Tent Bks.
Gilroy, Henry. The Clone Wars: Hero of the Confederacy Vol. 1: Breaking Bread with the Enemy!, 1 vol. Koschak, Brian, illus. 2011. (Star Wars: the Clone Wars Ser.: No. 2). (ENG.). 24p. (J). (gr. 7-12). 24.21 *(978-1-59961-841-8(9))* Spotlight.
—The Clone Wars: Hero of the Confederacy Vol. 2: A Hero Rises, 1 vol. Koschak, Brian, illus. 2011. (Star Wars: the Clone Wars Ser.: No. 2). (ENG.). 24p. (J). (gr. 7-12). 24.21 *(978-1-59961-842-5(7))* Spotlight.
—The Clone Wars: Hero of the Confederacy Vol. 3: the Destiny of Heroes, 1 vol. Koschak, Brian, illus. 2011. (Star Wars: the Clone Wars Ser.: No. 2). (ENG.). 24p. (J). (gr. 7-12). 24.21 *(978-1-59961-843-2(5))* Spotlight.
—The Clone Wars: In Service of the Republic Vol. 1: the Battle of Khorm, 1 vol. Hepburn, Scott, illus. 2011. (Star Wars: the Clone Wars Ser.: No. 2). (ENG.). 24p. (J). (gr. 7-12). 24.21 *(978-1-59961-838-8(9))* Spotlight.
—The Clone Wars: In Service of the Republic Vol. 2: A Frozen Doom!, 1 vol. Hepburn, Scott, illus. 2011. (Star Wars: the Clone Wars Ser.: No. 2). (ENG.). 24p. (J). (gr. 7-12). 24.21 *(978-1-59961-839-5(7))* Spotlight.
—The Clone Wars: In Service of the Republic Vol. 3: Blood & Snow, 1 vol. Hepburn, Scott, illus. 2011. (Star Wars: the Clone Wars Ser.: No. 2). (ENG.). 24p. (J). (gr. 7-12). 24.21 *(978-1-59961-840-1(0))* Spotlight.
Gilson. Melusine Vol. 3: The Vampires' Ball. 2008. (Melusine Ser.: 3). (ENG., Illus.). 48p. (J). (gr. 4-7). pap. 11.95 *(978-1-905460-69-4(4))* CineBook GBR. Dist: National Bk. Network.
Ginevra, Dante, contrib. by. Peril in Pompeii! Nickolas Flux & the Eruption of Mount Vesuvius, 1 vol. 2014. (Nickolas Flux History Chronicles Ser.). (ENG., Illus.). 32p. (gr. 3-4). lib. bdg. 30.65 *(978-1-4914-0251-1(2)*, Graphic Library) Capstone Press of Coughlan Cos.
Given, Cate. The Great Pogo Stick. Hill-Peterson, Jodi, illus. 2006. (J). *(978-0-9790057-0-1(1))* Paws In the Sand Publishing.
Glass, Bryan J. L. Mice Templar, Vol. 3. 2012. (ENG., Illus.). 250p. (YA). 29.99 *(978-1-60706-457-2(X)*, 9781607064572) Image Comics.
Glass, Calliope. Disney Tails We Love Marie. Disney Storybook Art Team, illus. 2015. (Disney Tails Ser.). (ENG.). 10p. (J). (gr. -1 — 1). bds. 6.99 *(978-1-4847-1373-0(7))* Disney Pr.
Glymph, Rikimah. Are You My Friend? 2006. (Illus.). 32p. (J). lib. bdg. 17.95 *(978-1-934190-00-5(4))* Ocean Front Bk. Publishing, Inc.
Goddard, Drew, et al. No Future for You, 8 vols., Vol. 2. Jeanty, Georges et al, illus. 2008. (Buffy the Vampire Slayer Ser.). (ENG.). 320p. pap. 15.99 *(978-1-59307-963-5(X))* Dark Horse Comics.
Goh, Colin & Woo, Yen Yen. Enter the Dumpling, Vol. 1. Lee, Soo, illus. 2013. (ENG.). 144p. (J). pap. 12.99 *(978-0-9881899-0-4(9)*, 9780988189904) Yumcha Studios LLC.
The Golden Bird. rev. ed. 2006. 152p. 26.95 *(978-1-4218-2343-0(8))*; pap. 11.95 *(978-1-4218-2443-7(4))* 1st World Publishing, Inc. (1st World Library - Literary Society).
Golden Books. Marvel Heroes Little Golden Book Favorites #1 (Marvel) Golden Books, illus. 2016. (Little Golden Book Favorites Ser.). (ENG., Illus.). 80p. (J). (gr. k-k). 7.99 *(978-0-307-97653-6(X)*, Golden Bks.) Random Hse. Children's Bks.
Golden Books, illus. DC Super Friends Little Golden Book Favorites #2 (DC Super Friends) 2016. (Little Golden Book Favorites Ser.). (ENG.). 80p. (J). (-k). 7.99 *(978-1-101-94023-5(9)*, Golden Bks.) Random Hse. Children's Bks.
—DC Super Friends Little Golden Book Favorites (DC Super Friends) 2013. (Little Golden Book Favorites Ser.). (ENG.). 80p. (J). (-k). 6.99 *(978-0-449-81621-9(4)*, Golden Bks.) Random Hse. Children's Bks.
—Disney Junior Little Golden Book Library (Disney Junior), 5 vols. 2013. (ENG.). 120p. (J). (-k). 24.95 *(978-0-7364-3076-0(8)*, Golden/Disney) Random Hse. Children's Bks.
Golden, Christopher, illus. Omnibus, 7 vols., Vol. 4. 2008. (ENG.). 408p. pap. 24.95 *(978-1-59307-968-0(0))* Dark Horse Comics.
Goldfield, Rebecca & Short, Mike. Captive of Friendly Cove: Based on the Secret Journals of John Jewitt. 2015. (ENG., Illus.). 168p. (J). (gr. 7-7). pap. 25.95 *(978-1-936218-11-0(9))* Fulcrum Publishing.
Goldman, Steven & Goldman, Dan. Everyman: Be the People. Bucco, Joe, illus. 2004. 96p. per. 6.00 *(978-0-9759152-0-2(7))* KINJIN Global.
Goldsmann, Henri. Secret Agent Spanky Sheep in the mystery of: the Pooperous Pizza Plunderer. 2006. 140p. pap. 11.99 *(978-1-4116-8094-4(4))* Lulu Pr., Inc.
Golightly, Holly. School Bites: Blood Drinking 101, 2. 2005. (Illus.). 64p. (YA). per. *(978-0-9745367-3-6(3))* BroadSword Comics/ Jim Balent Studios.
Golightly, Holly, creator. School Bites. 2004. 64p. (YA). per. *(978-0-9745367-2-9(5)*, SB1A) BroadSword Comics/ Jim Balent Studios.
Golliher, Bill. Best of Sabrina the Teenage Witch. G!, Holly, illus. 2011. (Archie & Friends All-Stars Ser.: 15). (ENG.). 128p. (J). (gr. 4-7). pap. 9.95 *(978-1-879794-75-7(6)*, Archie Comics) Archie Comic Pubns., Inc.
Gonnard, Christel. The Planet of the Night Globes. 2013. (Little Prince Ser.: 6). (ENG., Illus.). 56p. (J). (gr. 4-8). pap. 7.95 *(978-1-4677-0738-1(4))*; lib. bdg. 26.60 *(978-0-7613-8756-5(0))* Lerner Publishing Group. (Graphic Universe™).
Gonnard, Christel & Pilot, Cédric. The Planet of Bamalias. Smith, Anne & Smith, Owen, trs. Nautilus Studio, illus. 2015. (Little Prince Ser.: 23). (ENG.). 48p. (J). (gr. 4-8). 26.65 *(978-1-4677-6198-7(2)*, Graphic Universe™) Lerner Publishing Group.
Gonnard, Christel, et al. The Planet of Okidians. 2015. (Little Prince Ser.: 21). (ENG., Illus.). 48p. (J). (gr. 4-8). pap. 7.95 *(978-1-4677-6024-9(2)*, Graphic Universe™) Lerner Publishing Group.
Gonzalez, Jorge & Collodi, Carlo. Pinocchio, 1 vol. Ruiz, Alfonso, illus. 2009. (Classic Fiction Ser.).Tr. of Avventure di Pinocchio. (ENG.). 72p. (gr. 2-3). lib. bdg. 27.99 *(978-1-4342-1583-3(0)*, Graphic Revolve) Stone Arch Bks.
Gonzalez, Jorge & Shakespeare, William. Romeo & Juliet, 1 vol. Cabrera, Eva, illus. 2011. (Shakespeare Graphics Ser.). (ENG.). 88p. (gr. 2-3). pap. 7.15 *(978-1-4342-3448-3(7))*; lib. bdg. 27.99 *(978-1-4342-2563-4(1))* Stone Arch Bks. (Shakespeare Graphics).
Goodin, Robert. The Kurdles. 2015. (ENG., Illus.). 64p. 24.99 *(978-1-60699-832-8(3)*, 699832) Fantagraphics Bks.
Goodwin, Archie. Secret Agent Corrigan, 1977-1980, 5 vols., Vol. 5. Williamson, Al, illus. 2013. (X-9 Ser.). (ENG.). 288p. 49.99 *(978-1-61377-542-4(3)*, 9781613775424) Idea & Design Works, LLC.
Goodwin, Vincent. The Adventure of the Cardboard Box, 1 vol. Dunn, Ben, illus. 2013. (Graphic Novel Adventures of Sherlock Holmes Set 3 Ser.). (ENG.). 48p. (J). (gr. 3-8). lib. bdg. 29.93 *(978-1-61641-971-4(7)*, Graphic Planet) Magic Wagon.
—The Adventure of the Dying Detective, 1 vol. Dunn, Ben, illus. 2013. (Graphic Novel Adventures of Sherlock Holmes Set 3 Ser.). (ENG.). 48p. (J). (gr. 3-8). lib. bdg. 29.93 *(978-1-61641-972-1(5)*, Graphic Planet) Magic Wagon.
—The Adventure of the Priory School, 1 vol. Dunn, Ben, illus. 2013. (Graphic Novel Adventures of Sherlock Holmes Set 3 Ser.). (ENG.). 48p. (J). (gr. 3-8). lib. bdg. 29.93 *(978-1-61641-973-8(3)*, Graphic Planet) Magic Wagon.
—The Adventure of the Red Circle, 1 vol. Dunn, Ben, illus. 2013. (Graphic Novel Adventures of Sherlock Holmes Set 3 Ser.). (ENG.). 48p. (J). (gr. 3-8). lib. bdg. 29.93 *(978-1-61641-974-5(1)*, Graphic Planet) Magic Wagon.
—The Adventure of the Second Stain, 1 vol. Dunn, Ben, illus. 2013. (Graphic Novel Adventures of Sherlock Holmes Set 3 Ser.). (ENG.). 48p. (J). (gr. 3-8). lib. bdg. 29.93 *(978-1-61641-975-2(X)*, Graphic Planet) Magic Wagon.
—The Adventure of the Six Napoleons, 1 vol. Dunn, Ben, illus. 2013. (Graphic Novel Adventures of Sherlock Holmes Set 3 Ser.). (ENG.). 48p. (J). (gr. 3-8). lib. bdg. 29.93 *(978-1-61641-976-9(8)*, Graphic Planet) Magic Wagon.
—Body-Snatcher, 1 vol. 2014. (Graphic Horror Set 3 Ser.). (ENG.). 32p. (J). (gr. 5-8). lib. bdg. 28.50 *(978-1-62402-013-1(5)*, Graphic Planet) Magic Wagon.
—Call of Cthulhu, 1 vol. 2014. (Graphic Horror Set 3 Ser.). (ENG., Illus.). 32p. (J). (gr. 5-8). lib. bdg. 28.50 *(978-1-62402-014-8(3)*, Graphic Planet) Magic Wagon.
—Moonlit Road, 1 vol. 2014. (Graphic Horror Set 3 Ser.). (ENG.). 32p. (J). (gr. 5-8). lib. bdg. 28.50 *(978-1-62402-016-2(X)*, Graphic Planet) Magic Wagon.
—Othello, 1 vol. Allen, Chris, illus. 2008. (Graphic Shakespeare Ser.). (ENG.). 48p. (gr. 5-10). 29.93 *(978-1-60270-192-2(X)*, Graphic Planet- Fiction) ABDO Publishing Co.
—Wendigo, 1 vol. 2014. (Graphic Horror Set 3 Ser.). (ENG.). 32p. (J). (gr. 5-8). lib. bdg. 28.50 *(978-1-62402-018-6(6)*, Graphic Planet) Magic Wagon.

Goodwin, Vincent & Shakespeare, William. Twelfth Night, 1 vol. Martin, Cynthia, illus. 2008. (Graphic Shakespeare Ser.). (ENG.). 48p. (gr. 5-10). 29.93 *(978-1-60270-195-3(4),* Graphic Planet- Fiction) ABDO Publishing Co.

Gorgas, Paula Blais. Little Lost Leprechaun. Taylor, Chet, illus. l.t. ed. 2005. 20p. (J). 17.99 *(978-0-9755888-4-0(2))* Dragonfly Publishing, Inc.

Gormon: The Sentinel Awakes. 2004. per. 2.75 *(978-0-9762294-0-7(4))* Corbett Features.

Gos & Peyo. The Astrosmurf. 2011. (Smurfs Graphic Novels Ser.). (ENG., Illus.). 56p. (J). (gr. 2-5). 10.99 *(978-1-59707-251-9(6),* 9781597072519) Papercutz.

Gos, Charles & Peyo. The Astrosmurf. 2011. (Smurfs Graphic Novels Ser.). (ENG., Illus.). 56p. (J). (gr. 2-5). pap. 5.99 *(978-1-59707-250-2(8),* 9781597072502) Papercutz.

Goscinny, René. Asterix & Caesar's Gift. Uderzo, Albert, illus. 2004. (ENG.). 48p. pap. 12.99 *(978-0-7528-6646-8(X),* Orion) Orion Publishing Group, Ltd. GBR. Dist: Hachette Bk. Group.

—Asterix & Obelix's Birthday. Uderzo, Albert, illus. 2010. (ENG.). 56p. (J). (gr. 4-6). pap. 12.99 *(978-1-4440-0095-5(0),* Orion) Orion Publishing Group, Ltd. GBR. Dist: Hachette Bk. Group.

—Asterix & the Golden Sickle. Uderzo, Albert, illus. 2004. (ENG.). 48p. pap. 12.99 *(978-0-7528-6613-0(3),* Orion) Orion Publishing Group, Ltd. GBR. Dist: Hachette Bk. Group.

—Asterix & the Goths. Uderzo, Albert, illus. 2004. (ENG.). 48p. 17.99 *(978-0-7528-6614-7(1),* Orion) Orion Publishing Group, Ltd. GBR. Dist: Hachette Bk. Group.

—Asterix & the Roman Agent. Uderzo, Albert, illus. 2004. (ENG.). 48p. 17.99 *(978-0-7528-6632-1(X),* Orion) Orion Publishing Group, Ltd. GBR. Dist: Hachette Bk. Group.

—Asterix et les Goths. (FRE.). (J). pap. 21.95 *(978-2-01-210003-9(1))* Hachette Groupe Livre FRA. Dist: Distribooks, Inc.

—Asterix in Belgium. Uderzo, Albert, illus. 2005. (ENG.). 48p. 17.99 *(978-0-7528-6649-9(4));* pap. 12.99 *(978-0-7528-6650-5(8))* Orion Publishing Group, Ltd. GBR. (Orion). Dist: Hachette Bk. Group.

—Asterix in Corsica. Uderzo, Albert, illus. 2004. (ENG.). 48p. pap. 12.99 *(978-0-7528-6644-4(3),* Orion) Orion Publishing Group, Ltd. GBR. Dist: Hachette Bk. Group.

—Asterix le Gaulois. 2005. audio compact disk 45.00 *(978-0-320-06624-5(X))* French & European Pubns., Inc.

—Asterix le Gaulois. (FRE.). (J). pap. 21.95 *(978-2-01-210133-3(X))* Hachette Groupe Livre FRA. Dist: Distribooks, Inc.

—Asterix Omnibus 2: Asterix the Gladiator; Asterix & the Banquet; Asterix & Cleopatra. Uderzo, Albert, illus. 2011. (ENG.). 156p. (J). (gr. 4-6). pap. 22.99 *(978-1-4440-0424-3(7),* Orion) Orion Publishing Group, Ltd. GBR. Dist: Hachette Bk. Group.

—Asterix Omnibus 3: Asterix & the Big Fight; Asterix in Britain; Asterix & the Normans. Uderzo, Albert, illus. 2012. (ENG.). 156p. (J). (gr. 4-7). pap. 22.99 *(978-1-4440-0475-5(1),* Orion) Orion Publishing Group, Ltd. GBR. Dist: Hachette Bk. Group.

—Asterix Omnibus 4: Asterix the Legionary; Asterix & the Chieftain's Shield; Asterix at the Olympic Games. Uderzo, Albert, illus. 2012. (ENG.). 152p. (J). (gr. 4-6). pap. 22.99 *(978-1-4440-0487-8(5),* Orion) Orion Publishing Group, Ltd. GBR. Dist: Hachette Bk. Group.

—Asterix Omnibus 6: Asterix in Switzerland; the Mansion of the Gods; Asterix & the Laurel Wreath. Uderzo, Albert, illus. (ENG.). (J). (gr. 4-7). 2013. 156p. pap. 22.99 *(978-1-4440-0491-5(3))* 2012. 152p. 29.99 *(978-1-4440-0489-2(1))* Orion Publishing Group, Ltd. GBR. (Orion). Dist: Hachette Bk. Group.

—Asterix Omnibus 7: Asterix & the Soothsayer - Asterix in Corsica - And Asterix & Caesar's Gift. Uderzo, Albert, illus. 2013. (ENG.). 156p. (J). (gr. 4-7). 29.99 *(978-1-4440-0835-7(8),* Orion) Orion Publishing Group, Ltd. GBR. Dist: Hachette Bk. Group.

—Asterix Omnibus 7: Asterix & the Soothsayer, Asterix in Corsica, & Asterix & Caesar's Gift. Uderzo, Albert, illus. 2014. (ENG.). 156p. (J). (gr. 4-6). pap. 22.99 *(978-1-4440-0836-4(6),* Orion) Orion Publishing Group, Ltd. GBR. Dist: Hachette Bk. Group.

—Asterix Omnibus 8: Asterix & the Great Crossing; Obelix & Co; Asterix in Belgium. Uderzo, Albert, illus. 2014. (ENG.). 156p. (J). (gr. 4-6). pap. 22.99 *(978-1-4440-0838-8(2),* Orion) Orion Publishing Group, Ltd. GBR. Dist: Hachette Bk. Group.

—Asterix Omnibus 9. Uderzo, Albert, illus. 2014. (ENG.). 152p. (J). (gr. 4-6). 29.99 *(978-1-4440-0967-5(2),* Orion) Orion Publishing Group, Ltd. GBR. Dist: Hachette Bk. Group.

—Asterix on the Warpath: Pop-Up. 2015. (ENG., Illus.). 14p. (J). (gr. 4-6). 35.00 *(978-1-5101-0042-8(3),* Asterix) Hachette Children's Group GBR. Dist: Hachette Bk. Group.

—The Bounty Hunter, Vol. 26. Morris Publishing Company Staff, illus. 2011. (Lucky Luke Ser.: 26). (ENG.). 48p. pap. 11.95 *(978-1-84918-059-7(8))* CineBook GBR. Dist: National Bk. Network.

—The Caliph's Vacation. 2009. (Iznogoud Ser.: 2). (ENG., Illus.). 48p. (J). (gr. 4-7). pap. 11.95 *(978-1-905460-61-8(9))* CineBook GBR. Dist: National Bk. Network.

—A Cure for the Daltons, Vol. 23. Morris, Alfred, illus. 2010. (Lucky Luke Ser.: 23). (ENG.). 48p. (J). (gr. 3-17). pap. 11.95 *(978-1-84918-034-4(2))* CineBook GBR. Dist: National Bk. Network.

—Daltons in the Blizzard. 2009. (Lucky Luke Ser.: 15). (ENG., Illus.). 48p. (gr. 3-17). pap. 11.95 *(978-1-905460-76-2(7))* CineBook GBR. Dist: National Bk. Network.

—The Dashing White Cowboy. Morris, illus. 2009. (Lucky Luke Ser.: 14). (ENG.). 46p. (J). (gr. -1-17). pap. 11.95 *(978-1-905460-66-3(X))* CineBook GBR. Dist: National Bk. Network.

—The Grand Vizier Iznogoud, Vol. 9. Tabary, illus. 2012. (Iznogoud Ser.: 9). (ENG.). 52p. (J). (gr. 3-12). pap. 13.95 *(978-1-84918-131-0(4))* CineBook GBR. Dist: National Bk. Network.

—Grande Traversee. (FRE., Illus.). 48p. (J). pap. 21.95 *(978-2-01-210154-8(2))* Hachette Groupe Livre FRA. Dist: Distribooks, Inc.

—How Obelix Fell into the Magic Potion: When He Was a Little Boy. Uderzo, Albert, illus. 2010. (ENG.). 32p. (YA). (gr. 7-17). pap. 12.99 *(978-1-4440-0094-8(2),* Orion) Orion Publishing Group, Ltd. GBR. Dist: Hachette Bk. Group.

—In the Shadow of the Derricks. 2007. (Lucky Luke Ser.: 5). (ENG., Illus.). 48p. (gr. -1). per. 11.95 *(978-1-905460-17-5(1))* CineBook GBR. Dist: National Bk. Network.

—Iznogoud - The Infamous, Vol. 7. Tabary, illus. 2011. (Iznogoud Ser.: 7). (ENG.). 48p. (gr. 3-17). pap. 11.95 *(978-1-84918-074-0(1))* CineBook GBR. Dist: National Bk. Network.

—Iznogoud & the Magic Carpet. Tabary, illus. 2010. (Iznogoud Ser.: 6). (ENG.). 46p. (J). (gr. 3-17). pap. 11.95 *(978-1-84918-044-3(X))* CineBook GBR. Dist: National Bk. Network.

—Iznogoud Vol. 10: Iznogoud the Relentless. Tabary, Jean, illus. 2013. (Iznogoud Ser.: 10). (ENG.). 48p. (J). (gr. 3-12). pap. 11.95 *(978-1-84918-181-5(0))* CineBook GBR. Dist: National Bk. Network.

—Jesse James. Morris, Alfred, illus. 2007. (Lucky Luke Ser.: 4). (ENG.). 48p. (J). (gr. 4-7). per. 11.95 *(978-1-905460-14-4(7))* CineBook GBR. Dist: National Bk. Network.

—Lucky Luke Versus Joss Jamon. Morris, illus. 27th ed. 2011. (Lucky Luke Ser.: 27). (ENG.). 48p. (gr. 3-17). pap. 11.95 *(978-1-84918-071-9(7))* CineBook GBR. Dist: National Bk. Network.

—Ma Dalton. 2007. (Lucky Luke Ser.: 6). (ENG., Illus.). 48p. (J). (gr. 4-7). pap. 11.95 *(978-1-905460-18-2(X))* CineBook GBR. Dist: National Bk. Network.

—Omnibus 1: Asterix the Gaul; Asterix & the Golden Sickle; Asterix & the Goths. Uderzo, Albert, illus. 2011. (ENG.). 152p. (J). (gr. 4-6). pap. 22.99 *(978-1-4440-0423-6(9),* Orion) Orion Publishing Group, Ltd. GBR. Dist: Hachette Bk. Group.

—Omnibus 5: Asterix & the Cauldron; Asterix in Spain; Asterix & the Roman Agent. Uderzo, Albert, illus. 2013. (ENG.). 156p. (J). (gr. 4-6). pap. 22.99 *(978-1-4440-0490-8(5),* Orion) Orion Publishing Group, Ltd. GBR. Dist: Hachette Bk. Group.

—Omnibus 8: Asterix & the Great Crossing; Obelix & Co.; & Asterix in Belgium. Uderzo, Albert, illus. 2013. (ENG.). 152p. (J). (gr. 4-6). 29.99 *(978-1-4440-0837-1(4),* Orion) Orion Publishing Group, Ltd. GBR. Dist: Hachette Bk. Group.

—The Rivals of Painful Gulch. Morris Publishing Company Staff, illus. 2009. (Lucky Luke Ser.: 12). (ENG.). 48p. pap. 11.95 *(978-1-905460-60-1(0))* CineBook GBR. Dist: National Bk. Network.

—The Stagecoach. Morris Publishing Company Staff, illus. 2011. (Lucky Luke Ser.: 25). (ENG.). 48p. (J). (gr. 3-17). pap. 11.95 *(978-1-84918-052-8(0))* CineBook GBR. Dist: National Bk. Network.

—The Tenderfoot. Morris, Alfred, illus. 2008. (Lucky Luke Ser.: 13). (ENG.). 48p. (J). (gr. -1-17). pap. 11.95 *(978-1-905460-65-6(1))* CineBook GBR. Dist: National Bk. Network.

—Tortillas for the Daltons. Spear, Luke, tr. from FRE. Morris, Ting, illus. 2008. (Lucky Luke Ser.: 10). (ENG.). 48p. pap. 11.95 *(978-1-905460-49-6(X))* CineBook GBR. Dist: National Bk. Network.

—The Wagon Train. Morris, Jean, illus. 2008. (Lucky Luke Ser.: 9). (ENG.). 48p. pap. 11.95 *(978-1-905460-40-3(6))* CineBook GBR. Dist: National Bk. Network.

—Western Circus. Morris, Alfred, illus. 2008. (Lucky Luke Ser.: 11). (ENG.). 48p. pap. 11.95 *(978-1-905460-55-7(4))* CineBook GBR. Dist: National Bk. Network.

—The Wicked Wiles of Iznogoud, Vol. 1. Tabary, Armelle, illus. 2008. (Iznogoud Ser.: 1). (ENG.). 48p. (J). (gr. -1-12). pap. 13.95 *(978-1-905460-46-5(5))* CineBook GBR. Dist: National Bk. Network.

Goscinny, René, text. Asterix le Gaulois. (FRE.). pap. 21.95 *(978-2-01-210001-5(5))* Hachette Groupe Livre FRA. Dist: Distribooks, Inc.

Goscinny, René & Morris Publishing Company Staff. Billy the Kid. 2009. (Lucky Luke Ser.: 1). (ENG., Illus.). 46p. (J). (gr. 4-7). pap. 11.95 *(978-1-905460-11-3(2))* CineBook GBR. Dist: National Bk. Network.

—The Dalton Cousins. 2011. (Lucky Luke Ser.: 28). (ENG., Illus.). 48p. (gr. 3-17). pap. 11.95 *(978-1-84918-076-4(8))* CineBook GBR. Dist: National Bk. Network.

—The Daltons Redeem Themselves. 2012. (Lucky Luke Ser.: 36). (ENG., Illus.). 48p. (J). (gr. 3-12). pap. 11.95 *(978-1-84918-132-7(2))* CineBook GBR. Dist: National Bk. Network.

—Emperor Smith. 2010. (Lucky Luke Ser.: 22). (ENG., Illus.). 47p. (J). (gr. 4-7). pap. 11.95 *(978-1-84918-026-9(1))* CineBook GBR. Dist: National Bk. Network.

—Rails on the Prairie. 2012. (Lucky Luke Ser.: 32). (ENG., Illus.). 48p. (J). (gr. 3-12). pap. 11.95 *(978-1-84918-104-4(7))* CineBook GBR. Dist: National Bk. Network.

Goscinny, René & Spear, Luke. Barbed Wire on the Prairie. Spear, Luke, tr. from FRE. Morris, Ting, illus. 2007. (Lucky Luke Ser.: 7). (ENG.). 48p. (J). (gr. 4-7). pap. 11.95 *(978-1-905460-24-3(4))* CineBook GBR. Dist: National Bk. Network.

Goscinny, René & Tabary, Jean. A Carrot for Iznogoud, Vol. 5. 2010. (Iznogoud Ser.: 5). (ENG., Illus.). 48p. (J). (gr. 4-7). pap. 11.95 *(978-1-84918-021-4(0))* CineBook GBR. Dist: National Bk. Network.

Goscinny, René & Uderzo, Albert. Asterix & Obelix's Birthday: The Golden Book. 2009. (ENG., Illus.). 56p. 17.99 *(978-1-4440-0027-6(6),* Orion) Orion Publishing Group, Ltd. GBR. Dist: Hachette Bk. Group.

—Asterix & the Banquet. Uderzo, Albert, illus. 2004. (ENG., Illus.). 48p. pap. 12.99 *(978-0-7528-6609-3(5),* Orion) Orion Publishing Group, Ltd. GBR. Dist: Hachette Bk. Group.

—Asterix & the Cauldron. Uderzo, Albert, illus. 2004. (ENG., Illus.). 48p. pap. 12.99 *(978-0-7528-6629-1(X),* Orion) Orion Publishing Group, Ltd. GBR. Dist: Hachette Bk. Group.

—Asterix & the Chieftain's Shield. Uderzo, Albert, illus. 2004. (ENG., Illus.). 48p. pap. 12.99 *(978-0-7528-6625-3(7),* Orion) Orion Publishing Group, Ltd. GBR. Dist: Hachette Bk. Group.

—Asterix & the Chieftan's Shield. 2004. (ENG., Illus.). 48p. 17.99 *(978-0-7528-6624-6(9),* Orion) Orion Publishing Group, Ltd. GBR. Dist: Hachette Bk. Group.

—Asterix & the Goths. Uderzo, Albert, illus. 2004. (ENG., Illus.). 48p. pap. 12.99 *(978-0-7528-6615-4(X),* Orion) Orion Publishing Group, Ltd. GBR. Dist: Hachette Bk. Group.

—Asterix & the Great Crossing. 2004. (ENG., Illus.). 48p. pap. 12.99 *(978-0-7528-6648-2(6),* Orion) Orion Publishing Group, Ltd. GBR. Dist: Hachette Bk. Group.

—Asterix & the Laurel Wreath. Uderzo, Albert, illus. 2004. (ENG., Illus.). 48p. pap. 12.99 *(978-0-7528-6637-6(0),* Orion) Orion Publishing Group, Ltd. GBR. Dist: Hachette Bk. Group.

—Asterix & the Normans. Uderzo, Albert, illus. 2004. (ENG., Illus.). 48p. pap. 12.99 *(978-0-7528-6623-9(0),* Orion) Orion Publishing Group, Ltd. GBR. Dist: Hachette Bk. Group.

—Asterix & the Roman Agent. Uderzo, Albert, illus. 2004. (ENG., Illus.). 48p. pap. 12.99 *(978-0-7528-6633-8(8),* Orion) Orion Publishing Group, Ltd. GBR. Dist: Hachette Bk. Group.

—Asterix & the Soothsayer. Uderzo, Albert, illus. 2004. (ENG., Illus.). 48p. pap. 12.99 *(978-0-7528-6642-0(7),* Orion) Orion Publishing Group, Ltd. GBR. Dist: Hachette Bk. Group.

—Asterix el Galo. Uderzo, Albert, illus. 2009. (SPA., Illus.). 54p. 19.95 *(978-84-345-6719-1(9))* Grupo Anaya, S.A. ESP. Dist: Baker & Taylor Bks.

—Asterix in Corsica. Uderzo, Albert, illus. 2004. (ENG., Illus.). 48p. 17.99 *(978-0-7528-6643-7(5),* Orion) Orion Publishing Group, Ltd. GBR. Dist: Hachette Bk. Group.

—Asterix Omnibus 10: Asterix & the Magic Carpet; Asterix & the Secret Weapon; Asterix & Obelix All at Sea. 2011. (ENG., Illus.). 156p. (J). (gr. 4-6). pap. 22.99 *(978-1-4440-0425-0(5),* Orion) Orion Publishing Group, Ltd. GBR. Dist: Hachette Bk. Group.

—Asterix Omnibus 5: Includes Asterix & the Cauldron, Asterix in Spain, & Asterix & the Roman Agent. 2012. (ENG., Illus.). 152p. (J). (gr. 4-6). 29.99 *(978-1-4440-0488-5(3),* Orion) Orion Publishing Group, Ltd. GBR. Dist: Hachette Bk. Group.

—Asterix the Gladiator. Uderzo, Albert, illus. 2004. (ENG., Illus.). 48p. pap. 12.99 *(978-0-7528-6611-6(7),* Orion) Orion Publishing Group, Ltd. GBR. Dist: Hachette Bk. Group.

—The Gaul. Uderzo, Albert, illus. 2004. (ENG., Illus.). 48p. pap. 12.99 *(978-0-7528-6605-5(2),* Orion) Orion Publishing Group, Ltd. GBR. Dist: Hachette Bk. Group.

—The Mansions of the Gods. Uderzo, Albert, illus. 2004. (ENG., Illus.). 48p. 17.99 *(978-0-7528-6638-3(9),* Orion) Orion Publishing Group, Ltd. GBR. Dist: Hachette Bk. Group.

—Obelix & Co. 2005. (ENG., Illus.). 48p. 17.99 *(978-0-7528-6651-2(6),* Orion) Orion Publishing Group, Ltd. GBR. Dist: Hachette Bk. Group.

—Omnibus 9: Asterix & the Great Divide; Asterix & the Black Gold; Asterix & Son. 2015. (Asterix Ser.). (ENG., Illus.). 152p. (J). (gr. 4-6). pap. 22.99 *(978-1-4440-0966-8(4),* Asterix) Hachette Children's Group GBR. Dist: Hachette Bk. Group.

—Le Tour de Gaule d'Asterix. (Asterix Adventure Ser.). (FRE., Illus.). 48p. pap. 19.95 *(978-2-205-00146-4(9))* Dargaud Publishing Co. FRA. Dist: Distribooks, Inc.

—La Vuelta a la Galia. (SPA.). 48p. 9.95 *(978-84-7510-132-3(1))* Grijalbo-Dargaud, S.A. Editores ESP. Dist: Distribooks, Inc.

Goscinny, René & Uderzo, M. El Adivino. (SPA., Illus.). (J). 24.95 *(978-0-8288-6082-6(3),* S26630) French & European Pubns., Inc.

—Der Arvernerschild. (GER., Illus.). (J). 24.95 *(978-0-8288-4914-2(5))* French & European Pubns., Inc.

—La Cizana. (SPA., Illus.). (J). 24.95 *(978-0-8288-4961-6(7))* French & European Pubns., Inc.

—El Combate de los Jefes. (SPA., Illus.). (J). 24.95 *(978-0-8288-4962-3(5))* French & European Pubns., Inc.

—El Escudo Arverno. (SPA., Illus.). (J). 24.95 *(978-0-8288-4965-4(X))* French & European Pubns., Inc.

—Falx Aurea. (LAT., Illus.). (J). 24.95 *(978-0-8288-4966-1(8))* French & European Pubns., Inc.

—Das Geschenk Casars. (GER., Illus.). (J). 24.95 *(978-0-8288-4967-8(6))* French & European Pubns., Inc.

—Die Goldene Sichel. (GER., Illus.). (J). 24.95 *(978-0-8288-4969-2(2))* French & European Pubns., Inc.

—La Gran Travesia. (SPA., Illus.). (J). 24.95 *(978-0-8288-5124-4(7))* French & European Pubns., Inc.

—Die Grosse Uberfahrt. (GER., Illus.). (J). 24.95 *(978-0-8288-4972-2(2))* French & European Pubns., Inc.

—La Hoz de Oro. (SPA., Illus.). (J). 24.95 *(978-0-8288-4973-9(0))* French & European Pubns., Inc.

—Der Kampf der Hauptlinge. (GER., Illus.). (J). 24.95 *(978-0-8288-4974-6(9))* French & European Pubns., Inc.

—Der Kupferkessel. (GER., Illus.). (J). 24.95 *(978-0-8288-4975-3(7))* French & European Pubns., Inc.

—Los Laureles del Cesar. (SPA., Illus.). (J). 24.95 *(978-0-8288-4976-0(5))* French & European Pubns., Inc.

—Die Lorbeeren des Casar. (GER., Illus.). (J). 24.95 *(978-0-8288-4978-4(1))* French & European Pubns., Inc.

—Die Normannen. (GER., Illus.). (J). 24.95 *(978-0-8288-4980-7(3))* French & European Pubns., Inc.

—El Regalo del Cesar. (SPA., Illus.). (J). 24.95 *(978-0-8288-4900-5(5))* French & European Pubns., Inc.

—La Residencia de los Dioses. (SPA., Illus.). (J). 24.95 *(978-0-8288-4901-2(3))* French & European Pubns., Inc.

—Der Seher. (GER., Illus.). (J). 24.95 *(978-0-8288-5125-1(5))* French & European Pubns., Inc.

—Le Tour de Gaulle. (FRE., Illus.). (J). 24.95 *(978-0-8288-4908-1(0))* French & European Pubns., Inc.

—Die Trabantenstadt. (GER., Illus.). (J). 24.95 *(978-0-8288-4910-4(2))* French & European Pubns., Inc.

—La Vuelta a la Galia. (SPA., Illus.). (J). 24.95 *(978-0-8288-4911-1(0))* French & European Pubns., Inc.

Goscinny, René, et al. Lucky Luke: The Dashing White Cowboy. 2008. (ENG.). 48p. (J). (gr. 2-4). pap. *(978-81-8386-014-7(1))* India Research Pr. IND. Dist: Independent Pubs. Group.

—Lucky Luke - Jesse James. 2008. (ENG.). 48p. (J). (gr. 2-4). pap. *(978-81-8386-016-1(8))* India Research Pr. IND. Dist: Independent Pubs. Group.

—Lucky Luke - Ma Dalton. 2008. (ENG.). 48p. (J). (gr. 2-4). pap. *(978-81-8386-015-4(X))* India Research Pr. IND. Dist: Independent Pubs. Group.

—Lucky Luke - the Tender Foot. 2008. (ENG.). 48p. (J). (gr. 2-4). pap. *(978-81-8386-017-8(6))* India Research Pr. IND. Dist: Independent Pubs. Group.

Gottfredson, Floyd, et al. Walt Disney's Comics & Stories #700. 2008. 80p. pap. 9.99 *(978-1-60360-057-6(4))* Gemstone Publishing, Inc.

Gould, Jane H. George Washington Carver. 2013. (Jr. Graphic American Inventors Ser.). (ENG., Illus.). 24p. (J). (gr. 3-6). pap. 10.60 *(978-1-4777-0141-6(9));* lib. bdg. 25.25 *(978-1-4777-0078-5(1))* Rosen Publishing Group, Inc., The. (PowerKids Pr.).

—John Adams. 2012. (Jr. Graphic Founding Fathers Ser.). (ENG., Illus.). 24p. (J). (gr. 3-6). pap. 10.60 *(978-1-4488-7993-9(0));* lib. bdg. 25.25 *(978-1-4488-7899-4(3))* Rosen Publishing Group, Inc., The. (PowerKids Pr.).

Gownley, Jim. Amelia & the Gym Class System: #2, 1 vol. Gownley, Jim, illus. 2011. (Amelia Rules! Ser.). (ENG., Illus.). 36p. 24.21 *(978-1-59961-788-6(9))* Spotlight.

—Amelia & the Other Side of Yuletide: #4, 1 vol. Gownley, Jim, illus. 2011. (Amelia Rules! Ser.). (ENG., Illus.). 36p. 24.21 *(978-1-59961-790-9(0))* Spotlight.

—Amelia in Loosely in Disguise & Frightened: #3, 1 vol. Gownley, Jim, illus. 2011. (Amelia Rules! Ser.). (ENG., Illus.). 36p. 24.21 *(978-1-59961-789-3(7))* Spotlight.

—Amelia in Speak Softee to Me: #5, 1 vol. Gownley, Jim, illus. 2011. (Amelia Rules! Ser.). (ENG., Illus.). 36p. 24.21 *(978-1-59961-791-6(9))* Spotlight.

—Amelia in What Makes You Happy: #6, 1 vol. Gownley, Jim, illus. 2011. (Amelia Rules! Ser.). (ENG., Illus.). 36p. 24.21 *(978-1-59961-792-3(7))* Spotlight.

—Amelia vs. the Sneeze Barf: #1, 1 vol. Gownley, Jim, illus. 2011. (Amelia Rules! Ser.). (ENG., Illus.). 36p. 24.21 *(978-1-59961-787-9(0))* Spotlight.

Gownley, Jimmy. The Amelia Rules! Collection: The Whole World's Crazy; What Makes You Happy; Superheroes; When the Past Is a Present; the Tweenage Guide to Not Being Unpopular; True Things (Adults Don't Want Kids to Know); the Meaning of Life ... & Other Stuff; Her Permanent Record. Gownley, Jimmy, illus. 2016. (Amelia Rules! Ser.). (ENG., Illus.). 1392p. (J). (gr. 2-7). pap. 96.99 *(978-1-4814-9755-8(3),* Atheneum Bks. for Young Readers) Simon & Schuster Children's Publishing.

—The Dumbest Idea Ever! 2014. (ENG., Illus.). 240p. (J). (gr. 4-7). 24.99 *(978-0-545-45346-2(1),* Graphix) Scholastic, Inc.

—Her Permanent Record. 2012. (Amelia Rules! Ser.: 8). lib. bdg. 23.30 *(978-0-606-26885-1(5),* Turtleback) Turtleback Bks.

—The Meaning of Life ... & Other Stuff. Gownley, Jimmy, illus. 2011. (Amelia Rules! Ser.). (ENG., Illus.). 160p. (J). (gr. 2-7). 19.99 *(978-1-4169-8613-3(8));* pap. 11.99 *(978-1-4169-8612-6(X))* Simon & Schuster Children's Publishing. (Atheneum Bks. for Young Readers).

—Superheroes. Gownley, Jimmy, illus. 2011. (Amelia Rules! Ser.). (ENG., Illus.). 176p. (J). (gr. 2-7). 19.99 *(978-1-4424-4540-6(8),* Atheneum Bks. for Young Readers) Simon & Schuster Children's Publishing.

—True Things: Adults Don't Want Kids to Know. Gownley, Jimmy, illus. 2010. (Amelia Rules! Ser.). (ENG., Illus.). 176p. (J). (gr. 2-7). 19.99 *(978-1-4169-8611-9(1));* pap. 11.99 *(978-1-4169-8609-6(X))* Simon & Schuster Children's Publishing. (Atheneum Bks. for Young Readers).

—The Tweenage Guide to Not Being Unpopular. Gownley, Jimmy, illus. 2010. (Amelia Rules! Ser.). (ENG., Illus.). 192p. (J). (gr. 2-7). pap. 12.99 *(978-1-4169-8608-9(1),* Atheneum Bks. for Young Readers) Simon & Schuster Children's Publishing.

—A Very Ninja Christmas. Gownley, Jimmy, illus. 2009. (Amelia Rules! Ser.). (ENG., Illus.). 80p. (J). (gr. 2-7). pap. 7.99 *(978-1-4169-8959-2(5),* Atheneum Bks. for Young Readers) Simon & Schuster Children's Publishing.

—What Makes You Happy. Gownley, Jimmy, illus. 2011. (Amelia Rules! Ser.). (ENG., Illus.). 176p. (J). (gr. 2-7). 19.99 *(978-1-4424-4539-0(4),* Atheneum Bks. for Young Readers) Simon & Schuster Children's Publishing.

—When the Past Is a Present. Gownley, Jimmy, illus. 2011. (Amelia Rules! Ser.). (ENG., Illus.). 176p. (J). (gr. 2-7). 19.99 *(978-1-4424-4541-3(6),* Atheneum Bks. for Young Readers) Simon & Schuster Children's Publishing.

—The Whole World's Crazy. Gownley, Jimmy, illus. 2011. (Amelia Rules! Ser.). (ENG., Illus.). 176p. (J). (gr. 2-7). 21.99 *(978-1-4424-4538-3(6),* Atheneum Bks. for Young Readers) Simon & Schuster Children's Publishing.

Graham, Brandon & Roy, Simon. Prophet Volume 2: Brothers TP: Brothers TP. 2013. (ENG., Illus.). 172p. (YA). pap. 14.99 *(978-1-60706-749-8(8),* 9781607067498) Image Comics.

Graham, Brandon, et al. Prophet Volume 3: Empire TP: Empire TP. 2014. (ENG., Illus.). 128p. (YA). pap. 14.99 *(978-1-60706-858-7(3),* 9781607068587) Image Comics.

Graham-Larkin, Debbie. Magic in the Air. 2005. (Graham Cracker Kids Adventure Ser.). (Illus.). (J). pap. 12.95 *(978-0-9716475-1-0(8))* Graham Cracker Kids.

Gran, Meredith & Udzenija, Mario. Doodle Jump. 2015. (ENG., Illus.). 152p. (J). 12.99 *(978-1-60690-704-7(2),* 9781606907047, Dynamite Entertainment) Dynamic Forces, Inc.

Granados, Lucia, illus. Bemba's Secret Garden. 2006. (ENG.). 57p. (J). per. 16.95 *(978-0-9790110-0-9(0))* Tpprince Esquire International.

Graphic Expeditions. 2010. (Graphic Expeditions Ser.). 32p. lib. bdg. 293.20 *(978-1-4296-5860-7(6),* Graphic Library) Capstone Press of Coughlan Cos.

Graphic History. 2016. (Graphic History Ser.). (ENG.). 32p. (gr. 3-4). lib. bdg. 582.35 *(978-1-5157-4019-3(6),* Graphic Library) Capstone Press of Coughlan Cos.

Graphic Myths & Legends, 22 bks., Set. 2008. (J). (gr. 4-8). lib. bdg. 585.20 *(978-0-8225-8402-5(6),* Carolrhoda Bks.) Lerner Publishing Group.

Graphic Revolve: Common Core Editions, 1 vol. 2014. (Graphic Revolve: Common Core Editions Ser.). (ENG.). 72p. (gr. 2-3). 559.80 *(978-1-4965-0115-8(2),* Graphic Revolve) Stone Arch Bks.

Graphic Science. (Graphic Science Ser.). (ENG.). 32p. (gr. 3-4). 2016. lib. bdg. 459.75 *(978-1-5157-4022-3(6))* 2010. pap. 15.90 *(978-1-4296-4996-4(8))* 2010. lib. bdg. 61.30 *(978-1-4296-4450-1(8))* Capstone Press of Coughlan Cos. (Graphic Library).

Graphic Science Collection. 2010. (Graphic Science Ser.). (ENG.). 32p. (gr. 3-4). pap. 174.90 *(978-1-4296-5148-6(2),* Graphic Library) Capstone Press of Coughlan Cos.

Graphic Sparks. 2014. (Graphic Sparks Ser.). (ENG.). (gr. 1-3). pap. 273.94 *(978-1-4965-0319-0(8)*, Graphic Sparks) Stone Arch Bks.

Gravel, Élise. If Found, Please Return to Elise Gravel. Adriance, Shira, tr. from FRE. 2017. (ENG., Illus.). 100p. (J). 17.95 ***(978-1-77046-278-6(3)***, 9781770462786) Drawn & Quarterly Pubns. CAN. Dist: Macmillan.

Gray-Wilburn, Renée. Earthquakes! Sotirovski, Aleksandar, illus. 2012. (First Graphics: Wild Earth Ser.). (ENG.). 24p. (gr. 1-2). pap. 35.70 *(978-1-4296-8370-8(8))* Capstone Press of Coughlan Cos.

Grecian, Alexander. Rocketbots: Trouble in Time: Trouble in Time. 2010. 48p. (YA). 12.99 *(978-1-60706-183-0(X))* Image Comics.

Green, K. C. Regular Show Vol. 1. 2014. lib. bdg. 26.95 *(978-0-606-35467-7(0))* Turtleback Bks.

Greenberger, Robert, et al. Robin's First Flight. Schigiel, Gregg, illus. 2013. (Batman Ser.). (ENG.). 56p. (gr. 2-3). pap. 4.95 *(978-1-4342-2262-6(4)*, DC Super Heroes) Stone Arch Bks.

Greg, Neri. Yummy: The Last Days of a Southside Shorty. 2014. (ENG.). 94p. (YA). (gr. k-3). 21.20 *(978-1-63245-250-4(2))* Lectorum Pubns., Inc.

Gregori, Anthony, illus. Meet the Itslts. l.t. ed. 2007. 40p. (J). lib. bdg. 9.99 *(978-0-9769360-1-5(1))* Adam Hill Pubns.

Greig, Allison. Stacey's Adventures. 2006. (Illus.). 64p. pap. *(978-1-84401-035-6(X))* Athena Pr.

Grell, Mike. Green Arrow Vol. 5: Black Arrow. 2016. lib. bdg. 33.05 *(978-0-606-38630-2(0))* Turtleback Bks.

Griep, Heinrich & Laguna, Fabio. Scooby-Doo in Sumo A-Go-Go, 1 vol. 2012. (Scooby-Doo Graphic Novels Ser.: No. 2). (ENG., Illus.). 24p. (J). (gr. 2-5). 24.21 *(978-1-59961-923-1(7))* Spotlight.

Griep, Terrence, Jr. Scooby-Doo in Screechy Keen, 1 vol. Matchette, Karen, illus. 2010. (Scooby-Doo Graphic Novels Ser.: No. 1). (ENG.). 24p. (J). (gr. 2-5). 24.21 *(978-1-59961-697-1(1))* Spotlight.

Griffith, Andrew, illus. Transformers: Movie Prequel: Foundation: Vol 1: Dark of the Moon, 1 vol. 2012. (Transformers: Dark of the Moon Movie Prequel Ser.). (ENG.). 24p. (J). 24.21 *(978-1-59961-971-2(7)*, Graphic Novels) Spotlight.

—Transformers: Movie Prequel: Foundation: Vol 2, 1 vol. 2012. (Transformers: Dark of the Moon Movie Prequel Ser.). (ENG.). 24p. (J). 24.21 *(978-1-59961-972-9(5)*, Graphic Novels) Spotlight.

—Transformers: Movie Prequel: Foundation: Vol 3, 1 vol. 2012. (Transformers: Dark of the Moon Movie Prequel Ser.). (ENG.). 24p. (J). 24.21 *(978-1-59961-973-6(3)*, Graphic Novels) Spotlight.

—Transformers: Movie Prequel: Foundation: Vol 4, 1 vol. 2012. (Transformers: Dark of the Moon Movie Prequel Ser.). (ENG.). 24p. (J). 24.21 *(978-1-59961-974-3(1)*, Graphic Novels) Spotlight.

Grimaldi. My Amazing Dinosaur. Burrell, Carol klio, tr. from FRE. Bannister, illus. 2014. (Tib & Tumtum Ser.: 2). (ENG.). 48p. (J). (gr. 2-5). lib. bdg. 26.60 *(978-1-4677-1298-9(1)*, Graphic Universe™) Lerner Publishing Group.

—Welcome to the Tribe! Bannister, illus. 2013. (Tib & Tumtum Ser.: 1). (ENG.). 48p. (J). (gr. 2-5). pap. 6.95 *(978-1-4677-1522-5(0))*; lib. bdg. 26.60 *(978-1-4677-1297-2(3))* Lerner Publishing Group. (Graphic Universe™).

Grimaldi, Flora. My Amazing Dinosaur. Burrell, Carol klio, tr. Bannister, illus. 2014. (Tib & Tumtum Ser.: 2). (ENG.). 48p. (J). (gr. 2-5). pap. 7.95 *(978-1-4677-2181-3(6)*, Graphic Universe™) Lerner Publishing Group.

Grimm, Jacob, et al. The Elves & the Shoemaker: A Grimm Graphic Novel, 1 vol. Rodriquez, Pedro, illus. 2011. (Graphic Spin Ser.). (ENG.). 40p. (gr. 1-3). lib. bdg. 25.32 *(978-1-4342-2553-5(4)*, Graphic Revolve) Stone Arch Bks.

Grimm, Wilhelm K. & Grimm, Jacob. Grimm's Fairy Tales Volume 2. 2011. (Illus.). 200p. (YA). 16.99 *(978-1-61377-048-1(0))* Idea & Design Works, LLC.

Gritton, Steve. The Super Dupers. Gritton, Steve, illus. 2013. (Illus.). 30p. pap. 9.29 *(978-0-9795361-8-2(9))* Bad Frog Art/SMG Bks.

Groening, Matt. Bart Simpson - Out to Lunch. 2012. (ENG., Illus.). 128p. pap. 15.99 *(978-0-06-211533-1(2)*, Collins Design) HarperCollins Pubs.

—Simpsons Comics Colossal Compendium Volume 2. 2014. (ENG., Illus.). 176p. pap. 17.99 *(978-0-06-233609-5(6)*, Collins Design) HarperCollins Pubs.

—Simpsons Comics Colossal Compendium Volume 3. 2015. (ENG., Illus.). 176p. pap. 17.99 *(978-0-06-236059-5(0)*, Collins Design) HarperCollins Pubs.

—Simpsons Comics Colossal Compendium: Volume 5. 2017. 176p. pap. 17.99 ***(978-0-06-256754-3(3)***, Collins Design) HarperCollins Pubs.

Groening, Matt. Simpsons Comics Knockout. 2017. 128p. pap. 15.99 *(978-0-06-256891-5(4)*, Collins Design) HarperCollins Pubs.

Groot, Bob de. Jade Vol. 5. Rodrigue, illus. 2008. (Clifton Ser.: 5). (ENG.). 48p. pap. 11.95 *(978-1-905460-52-6(X))* CineBook GBR. Dist: National Bk. Network.

Groot, De. Black Moon. Spear, Luke, tr. from FRE. Rodrigue, illus. 2007. (Clifton Ser.: 4). (ENG.). 48p. (J). (gr. 4-7). pap. 9.99 *(978-1-905460-30-4(9))* CineBook GBR. Dist: National Bk. Network.

Gross, Scott. Scooby-Doo & the Aliens of Area 49, 1 vol. 2013. (Scooby-Doo Graphic Novels Set 3 Ser.). (ENG.). 24p. (J). (gr. 2-6). lib. bdg. 24.21 *(978-1-61479-049-5(3)*, Essential Library) ABDO Publishing Co.

Grotholt, Yannick. Playing with Fire. 2016. (LEGO Legends of Chima Graphic Novels Ser.: 6). (J). lib. bdg. 18.40 *(978-0-606-38370-7(0))* Turtleback Bks.

—Wings for a Lion. 2015. (LEGO Legends of Chima Graphic Novels Ser.: 5). (J). lib. bdg. 18.40 *(978-0-606-37293-0(8))* Turtleback Bks.

Gruber, Ben. The Next Generation, Vol. 4. 2009. (Illus.). 112p. pap. 7.99 *(978-1-60010-388-9(X))* Diamond Bk. Distributors.

Grunberg, Greg. Nightmare Escape. Tumbloom, Lucas, illus. 2016. (Dream Jumper Ser.: 1). (ENG.). 208p. (J). (gr. 3-7). 24.99 *(978-0-545-82603-7(9)*, Graphix) Scholastic, Inc.

Guard, Candy. Turning to Jelly, 1. Guard, Candy, illus. unabr. ed. 2014. (ENG., Illus.). 224p. (J). (gr. 4-6). pap. 9.99 *(978-1-4472-5610-6(7))* Pan Macmillan GBR. Dist: Independent Pubs. Group.

Guarente, Gabe. Satan's Prep: A Graphic Novel. 2014. (ENG., Illus.). 112p. (J). (gr. 6). 17.95 *(978-1-62873-592-5(9)*, Sky Pony Pr.) Skyhorse Publishing Co., Inc.

Guibert, Emmanuel. A Beautiful Cow. 2014. (Ariol Ser.: 4). (J). lib. bdg. 24.50 *(978-0-606-35103-4(5)*, Turtleback) Turtleback Bks.

—Happy as a Pig... 2013. (Ariol Ser.: 3). (J). lib. bdg. 24.50 *(978-0-606-32310-9(4)*, Turtleback) Turtleback Bks.

—Just a Donkey Like You & Me. 2013. (Ariol Graphic Novels Ser.). (ENG., Illus.). 124p. (J). (gr. 1-5). pap. 12.99 *(978-1-59707-399-8(7)*, 9781597073998) Papercutz.

—Just a Donkey Like You & Me. 2013. (Ariol Ser.: 1). (J). lib. bdg. 24.50 *(978-0-606-28692-3(6)*, Turtleback) Turtleback Bks.

—The Little Rats of the Opera. 2017. (Ariol Ser.: 10). (J). lib. bdg. 24.50 ***(978-0-606-39879-4(1))*** Turtleback Bks.

—Sardine in Outer Space 5. Pezzali, Walter & Sfar, Joann, illus. 5th ed. 2008. (Sardine in Outer Space Ser.: 5). (ENG.). 112p. (J). (gr. 1-5). pap. 17.99 *(978-1-59643-380-9(9)*, 9781596433809, First Second Bks.) Roaring Brook Pr.

—The Thunder Horse. 2013. (Ariol Ser.: 2). (J). lib. bdg. 24.50 *(978-0-606-31910-2(7)*, Turtleback) Turtleback Bks.

—Top Dog. 2016. (Ariol Ser.: 7). (J). lib. bdg. 24.50 *(978-0-606-37581-8(3))* Turtleback Bks.

—Where's Petula? 2015. (Ariol Ser.: 7). (J). lib. bdg. 20.85 *(978-0-606-37284-8(9))* Turtleback Bks.

Guibert, Emmanuel & Sfar, Joann. Sardine in Outer Space. Watson, Sasha, tr. from FRE. Sfar, Joann & Pezzali, Walter, illus. deluxe ed. 2006. (Sardine in Outer Space Ser.: 1). (ENG.). 128p. (J). (gr. 1-5). pap. 16.99 *(978-1-59643-126-3(1)*, 9781596431263, First Second Bks.) Roaring Brook Pr.

—Sardine in Outer Space, Vol. 3. Brizzi, Elisabeth & Siegel, Alexis, trs. from FRE. Sfar, Joann & Pezzali, Walter, illus. 3rd rev. ed. 2007. (Sardine in Outer Space Ser.: 3). (ENG.). 112p. (J). (gr. 1-5). pap. 17.99 *(978-1-59643-128-7(8)*, 9781596431287, First Second Bks.) Roaring Brook Pr.

Guillain, Charlotte. Animal Fairy Tales, 1 vol. Beacon, Dawn, illus. 2014. (Animal Fairy Tales Ser.). (ENG.). 24p. (gr. 1-2). lib. bdg. 119.95 *(978-1-4109-6116-7(8)*, NA-r) Heinemann-Raintree.

Gulledge, Laura Lee. Page by Paige. 2011. (ENG., Illus.). 192p. (YA). (gr. 7-17). 18.95 *(978-0-8109-9721-9(5))*; pap. 9.95 *(978-0-8109-9722-6(3))* Abrams, Inc. (Amulet Bks.).

Gunderson, J. Fire & Snow: A Tale of the Alaskan Gold Rush. Townsend, Shannon, illus. 2007. (Historical Fiction Ser.). (ENG.). 56p. (gr. 2-3). pap. 6.25 *(978-1-59889-405-9(6)*, Graphic Flash) Stone Arch Bks.

—The Last Rider: The Final Days of the Pony Express. Ruiz, Jose Alfonso Ocampo & Woodman, Ned, illus. 2007. (Historical Fiction Ser.). (ENG.). 56p. (gr. 2-3). pap. 6.25 *(978-1-59889-407-3(2)*, Graphic Flash) Stone Arch Bks.

Gunderson, Jessica. Jay-Z: Hip-Hop Icon. Kinsella, Pat, illus. 2012. (American Graphic Ser.). (ENG.). 32p. (gr. 3-4). pap. 47.70 *(978-1-4296-8475-0(5)*, Graphic Library) Capstone Press of Coughlan Cos.

—Secret Weapons: A Tale of the Revolutionary War, 1 vol. Aburto, Jesus, illus. 2008. (Historical Fiction Ser.). (ENG.). 56p. (gr. 2-3). pap. 6.25 *(978-1-4342-0848-4(6)*, Graphic Flash) Stone Arch Bks.

Gunderson, Jessica & Collins, Terry. American Graphic. Kinsella, Pat & Byers, Michael, illus. 2012. (American Graphic Ser.). (ENG.). 32p. (gr. 3-4). pap. 15.90 *(978-1-4296-9505-3(6))*; pap. 72.90 *(978-1-4296-8477-4(1))*; pap. 477.00 *(978-1-4296-8478-1(X))*; lib. bdg. 61.30 *(978-1-4296-8178-0(0))*; lib. bdg. 275.85 *(978-1-4296-8179-7(9))* Capstone Press of Coughlan Cos. (Graphic Library).

Gunderson, Jessica & Gonzalez, Jorge. Full Court Pressure, 1 vol. Ruiz, Alfonso, illus. 2010. (Sports Illustrated Kids Graphic Novels Ser.). (ENG.). 56p. (gr. 2-3). pap. 7.19 *(978-1-4342-2291-6(8))*; 26.65 *(978-1-4342-1911-4(9))* Stone Arch Bks.

Gunderson, Jessica Sarah. Sacagawea: Journey into the West, 1 vol. Martin, Cynthia & Schulz, Barbara, illus. 2006. (Graphic Biographies Ser.). (ENG.). 32p. (gr. 3-4). per. 8.10 *(978-0-7368-9663-4(5)*, Graphic Library) Capstone Press of Coughlan Cos.

Gunpowder Girl & the Outlaw Squaw. 2005. (Illus.). per. 12.95 *(978-0-9766761-0-2(9))* Active Images.

Guy, Joseph. One Childs Cry for Hope. 2010. 32p. 18.60 *(978-0-557-28780-2(4))* Lulu Pr., Inc.

H., Yves & Hermann. Manhattan Beach 1957. 2003. (Illus.). 56p. (YA). (gr. 11-18). 12.95 *(978-1-931724-23-4(7))* Diamond Select Toys & Collectibles.

Haibara, Yak & Haibara, Yak. Sengoku Basara: Samurai Legends Volume 2: Samurai Legends Volume 2, 2 vols. 2013. (ENG., Illus.). 424p. (YA). pap. 19.99 *(978-1-926778-59-4(6)*, 9781926778594) URON Entertainment Corp. CAN. Dist: Diamond Comic Distributors, Inc.

Hale, Nathan. Alamo All-Stars. 2016. (Nathan Hale's Hazardous Tales Ser.: 6). (ENG., Illus.). 128p. (J). (gr. 3-7). 12.95 *(978-1-4197-1902-8(5)*, Amulet Bks.) Abrams, Inc.

—Alamo All-Stars. 2017. (Nathan Hale's Hazardous Tales Ser.). (J). lib. bdg. 24.45 ***(978-0-606-40709-0(X))*** Turtleback Bks.

Hale, Shannon. Real Friends. Pham, LeUyen, illus. 2017. (ENG.). 224p. (J). pap. 12.99 *(978-1-62672-785-4(6)*, 9781626727854, First Second Bks.) Roaring Brook Pr.

Hama, Larry, text. Captain America: The Death of Captain America Prose Novel. 2014. (ENG., Illus.). 344p. (J). (gr. 4-17). 24.99 *(978-0-7851-8996-1(3))* Marvel Worldwide, Inc.

Hama, Larry & Dixon, Chuck. G. I. JOE: the IDW Collection Volume 1: The IDW Collection Volume 1. Mutti, Andrea et al, illus. 2013. (G. I. Joe Ser.). (ENG.). 352p. 49.99 *(978-1-61377-549-3(0)*, 9781613775493) Idea & Design Works, LLC.

Hama, Larry, et al. G. I. Joe Vol. 6: A Real American Hero. Frenz, Ron & Buscema, Sal, illus. 2013. (G. I. Joe Ser.). (ENG.). 128p. pap. 19.99 *(978-1-61377-582-0(2)*, 9781613775820) Idea & Design Works, LLC.

Hamazaki, Tatsuya. . hack //Legend of the Twilight, Volume 1: Kaplan SAT/ACT Vocabulary-Building Manga. Izumi, Rei, illus. 2007. (Kaplan SAT/ACT Score-Raising Manga Ser.). 192p. pap. 9.99 *(978-1-4277-5497-4(7))* Kaplan Publishing.

Hamme, Van. Giants. Rosinski, illus. 2013. (Thorgal Ser.: 14). (ENG.). 48p. pap. 11.95 *(978-1-84918-156-3(X))* CineBook GBR. Dist: National Bk. Network.

Han, Xuemei. The Radish & the Girl with Long Hair. Han, Xuemei, illus. 2008. (Illus.). (J). per. *(978-0-9763168-6-2(2))* DigitalKu.

Hankins, Jim. Teddy Scares Volume 3. 2008. (Illus.). 52p. (YA). pap. 6.95 *(978-0-9791050-2-9(1))* Ape Entertainment.

Hanley, Victoria. Seize the Story: A Handbook for Teens Who Like to Write. 2008. (ENG.). 208p. (J). (gr. 6). pap. 15.95 *(978-1-877673-81-8(1))* Cottonwood Pr., Inc.

Hansen, Amy S. How Do We Stay on Earth? A Gravity Mystery, 1 vol. Scott, Korey, illus. 2011. (First Graphics: Science Mysteries Ser.). (ENG.). 24p. (gr. 1-2). pap. 6.29 *(978-1-4296-7174-3(2))*; pap. 35.70 *(978-1-4296-7178-1(5))* Capstone Press of Coughlan Cos.

—Where Does the Sun Go at Night? An Earth Science Mystery, 1 vol. Scott, Korey, illus. 2011. (First Graphics: Science Mysteries Ser.). (ENG.). 24p. (gr. 1-2). pap. 6.29 *(978-1-4296-7176-7(9))*; pap. 35.70 *(978-1-4296-7180-4(7))* Capstone Press of Coughlan Cos.

Hansen, Justin LaRocca. Brothers Unite. 2016. (Secondhand Heroes Ser.). (ENG., Illus.). 160p. (J). (gr. 3-7). pap. 10.99 *(978-0-8037-4094-5(8)*, Dial Bks) Penguin Young Readers Group.

—In the Trenches. 2017. (Secondhand Heroes Ser.). (ENG., Illus.). 160p. (J). (gr. 3-7). pap. 10.99 *(978-0-8037-4095-2(6)*, Dial Bks) Penguin Young Readers Group.

Hansen, Marc. Ralph Snart Adventures: Comic Collection #2. 2007. (Illus.). 128p. (YA). pap. 14.95 *(978-0-9794643-1-7(5))* Hansen, Marc Stuff!

Hansen, Marc. Ralph Snart Adventures: Comic Collection #1. Hansen, Marc, . 2007. (Illus.). (YA). per. 14.95 *(978-0-9794643-0-0(7))* Hansen, Marc Stuff!

Harbo, Christopher L., et al. The Secrets of Martial Arts: An Isabel Soto History Adventure. 2010. (Graphic Expeditions Ser.). (ENG.). 32p. (gr. 3-4). pap. 47.70 *(978-1-4296-5146-2(6))*; lib. bdg. 30.65 *(978-1-4296-3973-6(3))* Capstone Press of Coughlan Cos. (Graphic Library).

Hardcastle, Michael. Hit It!, 1 vol. Moulder, Bob, illus. 2006. (Graphic Quest Ser.). (ENG.). 88p. (gr. 3-3). per. 6.95 *(978-1-59889-164-5(2)*, Graphic Quest) Stone Arch Bks.

Hardman, John. Mr. Bump in: Lights, Camera, Bump!, Vol. 1. Britton, Matthew, illus. 2012. (ENG.). 80p. (J). pap. 6.99 *(978-1-4215-4074-0(6))* Viz Media.

Harkrader, Lisa. The Adventures of Beanboy. 2012. (ENG., Illus.). 240p. (J). (gr. 5-7). 12.99 *(978-0-547-55078-7(2))* Houghton Mifflin Harcourt Publishing Co.

—Cool Beans: The Further Adventures of Beanboy. 2014. (ENG., Illus.). 272p. (J). (gr. 5-7). 16.99 *(978-0-544-03904-9(1)*, HMH Books For Young Readers) Houghton Mifflin Harcourt Publishing Co.

Harper, Benjamin. Far Out Fairy Tales. Cano, Fern, illus. 2016. (Far Out Fairy Tales Ser.). (ENG.). 40p. (gr. 3-4). pap. 11.90 *(978-1-4965-3135-3(3)*, Far Out Fairy Tales) Stone Arch Bks.

—Hansel & Gretel & Zombies: a Graphic Novel. Cano, Fern, illus. 2016. (Far Out Fairy Tales Ser.). (ENG.). 40p. (gr. 3-4). lib. bdg. 25.32 *(978-1-4965-2509-3(4)*, Far Out Fairy Tales) Stone Arch Bks.

Harper, Benjamin & Poe, Edgar Allen. The Tell-Tale Heart, 1 vol. Calero, Dennis, illus. 2013. (Edgar Allan Poe Graphic Novels Ser.). (ENG.). 72p. (gr. 2-3). lib. bdg. 27.99 *(978-1-4342-3023-2(6))* Stone Arch Bks.

Harper, Charise Mericle. The Ball. 2013. (Bean Dog & Nugget Ser.). lib. bdg. 14.75 *(978-0-606-31944-7(1)*, Turtleback) Turtleback Bks.

—The Cookie. 2013. (Bean Dog & Nugget Ser.). lib. bdg. 14.75 *(978-0-606-31945-4(X)*, Turtleback) Turtleback Bks.

Harrington, Sean. Jack-in-the-Box Madness. 2006. (Illus.). 32p. (YA). 4.99 *(978-0-9778042-0-7(8))* Harrington Artwerkes Booksellers.

Harris, Joe. Wars in Toyland. 2013. (ENG., Illus.). 104p. 19.99 *(978-1-934964-93-4(X)*, 9781934964934) Oni Pr., Inc.

Hart, Christopher. Draw Manga! 2003. (XTreme Art Ser.). (ENG., Illus.). 64p. (J). (gr. 2-4). 7.99 *(978-0-8230-0369-3(8)*, Watson-Guptill) Potter/TenSpeed/Harmony.

Hartzell, Andy. Fox Bunny Funny. 2007. (ENG., Illus.). 104p. pap. 10.00 *(978-1-891830-97-6(X)*, 9781891830976) Top Shelf Productions.

Hasbro. G. I. Joe Valor vs. Venom, Vol. 1. (Illus.). 96p. (YA). pap. 7.99 *(978-1-59182-816-7(3))* TOKYOPOP, Inc.

Haspiel, Dean. Mo & Jo: Fighting Together Forever. Lynch, Jay, illus. 2013. (ENG.). 40p. (J). (gr. -1-3). pap. 4.99 *(978-1-935179-37-5(3))* TOON Books / RAW Junior, LLC.

Hatke, Ben. Little Robot. 2015. (ENG., Illus.). 144p. (J). (gr. 1-4). 16.99 *(978-1-62672-080-0(0)*, 9781626720800, First Second Bks.) Roaring Brook Pr.

Hawkins, Matt. Think Tank, Vol. 1. 2012. (ENG., Illus.). 120p. (YA). pap. 14.99 *(978-1-60706-660-6(2)*, 9781607066606) Image Comics.

—Think Tank, Vol. 2. 2013. (ENG., Illus.). 160p. (YA). pap. 14.99 *(978-1-60706-745-0(5)*, 9781607067450) Image Comics.

Hawthorne, Mike, illus. Machine Teen: History 101001. 2012. (ENG.). 120p. (J). (gr. 4-17). pap. 14.99 *(978-0-7851-6486-9(3))* Marvel Worldwide, Inc.

Hayes, Geoffrey. Benny & Penny in Just Pretend, 1 vol. 2013. (Toon Bks). (ENG.). 36p. (J). (gr. 1-2). lib. bdg. 27.07 *(978-1-61479-148-5(1))* Spotlight.

—Benny & Penny in Just Pretend. 2013. (Benny & Penny Ser.). (ENG., Illus.). 32p. (J). pap. 4.99 *(978-1-935179-26-9(8)*, 9781935179269) TOON Books / RAW Junior, LLC.

—Benny & Penny in Just Pretend. Hayes, Geoffrey, illus. 2008. (Benny & Penny Ser.). (ENG., Illus.). 32p. (J). (gr. -1-3). 12.95 *(978-0-9799238-0-7(8))* TOON Books / RAW Junior, LLC.

—Benny & Penny in Just Pretend. 2013. (Toon Books Level 2 Ser.). lib. bdg. 14.75 *(978-0-606-31597-5(7)*, Turtleback) Turtleback Bks.

—Benny & Penny in Lights Out! Hayes, Geoffrey, illus. 2012. (Benny & Penny Ser.). (ENG., Illus.). 32p. (J). (gr. -1-3). 12.95 *(978-1-935179-20-7(9))* TOON Books / RAW Junior, LLC.

—Benny & Penny in Lost & Found. Hayes, Geoffrey, illus. 2013. (Benny & Penny Ser.). (ENG., Illus.). 40p. (J). (gr. -1-3). 12.95 *(978-1-935179-64-1(0))* TOON Books / RAW Junior, LLC.

—Benny & Penny in the Big No-No! Mouly, Francoise, ed. Hayes, Geoffrey, illus. 2009. (Benny & Penny Ser.). (ENG., Illus.). 32p. (J). (gr. -1-3). 12.95 *(978-0-9799238-9-0(1))* TOON Books / RAW Junior, LLC.

—Benny & Penny in the Big No-No! 2014. (Toon Books Level 1 Ser.). lib. bdg. 14.75 *(978-0-606-32102-0(0)*, Turtleback) Turtleback Bks.

—Benny & Penny in the Toy Breaker, 1 vol. 2013. (Toon Bks). (ENG.). 36p. (J). (gr. 1-2). lib. bdg. 27.07 *(978-1-61479-149-2(X))* Spotlight.

—Benny & Penny in the Toy Breaker. Hayes, Geoffrey, illus. 2013. (Benny & Penny Ser.). (ENG., Illus.). 32p. (J). (gr. -1-3). pap. 6.99 *(978-1-935179-28-3(4))* TOON Books / RAW Junior, LLC.

—Benny & Penny in the Toy Breaker. 2013. (Toon Books Level 2 Ser.). lib. bdg. 14.75 *(978-0-606-31598-2(5)*, Turtleback) Turtleback Bks.

—Patrick Eats His Peas & Other Stories. Hayes, Geoffrey, illus. 2013. (ENG., Illus.). 32p. (J). (gr. -1-3). 12.95 *(978-1-935179-34-4(9))* TOON Books / RAW Junior, LLC.

Hayes, Geoffrey & Rosenstiehl, Agnes. Toon Books. 2013. (Toon Bks: 10). 36p. (J). (gr. k-3). lib. bdg. 270.70 *(978-1-61479-147-8(3))* Spotlight.

Heck, Don, et al, illus. Invaders Classic Vol. 1: The Complete Collection. 2014. (ENG.). 512p. (J). (gr. 4-17). pap. 39.99 *(978-0-7851-9057-8(0))* Marvel Worldwide, Inc.

Heer, Margreet de. Science: A Discovery in Comics. 2013. (Discovery in Comics Ser.). (ENG., Illus.). 194p. 19.99 *(978-1-56163-750-8(5))* NBM Publishing Co.

Helfand, Lewis. Mother Teresa: Saint of the Slums. Banerjee, Sankha & Nagar, Sachin, illus. 2013. (Campfire Graphic Novels Ser.). (ENG.). 88p. (YA). (gr. 5). pap. 11.99 *(978-93-80028-70-5(9)*, Campfire) Steerforth Pr.

—They Changed the World: Bell, Edison & Tesla. Kumar, Naresh, illus. 2014. (Campfire Graphic Novels Ser.). (ENG.). 102p. (YA). (gr. 8-12). pap. 12.99 *(978-93-80741-87-1(1)*, Campfire) Steerforth Pr.

Heller, Sarah & Reader's Digest Staff. Disney Fairies Music Player. 2008. (RD Innovative Book & Player Format Ser.). (ENG.). 36p. (J). 24.99 *(978-0-7944-1300-2(5))* Reader's Digest Assn., Inc., The.

Hellman, Charles. Fun Is... 2005. 124p. (gr. 4-7). per. 9.95 *(978-0-935938-16-6(8))* LuckySports.

Hello Kitty: Fashion Music Wonderland. 2015. (ENG.). 48p. (J). pap. 6.99 *(978-1-4215-5903-2(X))* Viz Media.

Hello, Phillie Phanatic! 2007. (J). 17.95 *(978-1-932888-85-0(3))* Mascot Bks., Inc.

Hergé. Aventures de Tintin au Pays des Soviets. (FRE.). 21.95 *(978-2-203-00100-8(3))* Casterman, Editions FRA. Dist: Distribooks, Inc.

—The Black Island. 2012. (Adventures of Tintin: Young Readers Edition Ser.). (ENG., Illus.). 96p. (J). (gr. 3-17). pap. 11.00 *(978-0-316-13387-6(6))* Little, Brown Bks. for Young Readers.

—El Cetro de Ottokar. 2007. (Aventuras de Tintin Ser.). (SPA., Illus.). 62p. reprint ed. 22.95 *(978-1-59497-345-1(8))* Public Square Bks.

—Cigars of the Pharaoh. 2011. (Adventures of Tintin: Young Readers Edition Ser.). Tr. of Cigares du Pharoan. (ENG., Illus.). 96p. (J). (gr. 3-17). pap. 11.00 *(978-0-316-13388-3(4))* Little, Brown Bks. for Young Readers.

—The Crab with the Golden Claws. 2012. (Adventures of Tintin: Young Readers Edition Ser.). (ENG., Illus.). 96p. (J). (gr. 3-17). pap. 8.99 *(978-0-316-19876-9(5))* Little, Brown Bks. for Young Readers.

—La Isla Negra. 2007. (Aventuras de Tintin Ser.). (SPA., Illus.). 62p. reprint ed. 22.95 *(978-1-59497-344-4(X))* Public Square Bks.

—King Ottokar's Sceptre. 2012. (Adventures of Tintin: Young Readers Edition Ser.). (ENG., Illus.). 96p. (J). (gr. 3-17). pap. 8.99 *(978-0-316-13383-8(3))* Little, Brown Bks. for Young Readers.

—Prisoners of the Sun. 2014. (Adventures of Tintin: Young Readers Edition Ser.). (ENG., Illus.). 96p. (J). (gr. 3-17). pap. 9.00 *(978-0-316-40917-9(0))* Little, Brown Bks. for Young Readers.

—Red Rackham's Treasure. Orig. Title: Tresor de Rackham le Rouge. (ENG., Illus.). (J). (gr. 3-17). 2012. 64p. 60.00 *(978-0-316-23054-4(5))* 2011. 96p. pap. 9.99 *(978-0-316-13384-5(1))* Little, Brown Bks. for Young Readers.

—The Secret of the Unicorn. Orig. Title: Secret de la Licorne. (ENG., Illus.). (J). (gr. 3-17). 2012. 64p. 60.00 *(978-0-316-23055-1(3))* 2011. 96p. pap. 9.99 *(978-0-316-13386-9(8))* Little, Brown Bks. for Young Readers.

—The Seven Crystal Balls. 2014. (Adventures of Tintin: Young Readers Edition Ser.). (ENG., Illus.). 96p. (J). (gr. 3-17). pap. 9.00 *(978-0-316-40918-6(9))* Little, Brown Bks. for Young Readers.

—The Shooting Star. 2012. (Adventures of Tintin: Young Readers Edition Ser.). (ENG., Illus.). 96p. (J). (gr. 3-7). pap. 8.99 *(978-0-316-19875-2(7))* Little, Brown Bks. for Young Readers.

—Tintin: El cangrejo de las pinzas de Oro. 2007. (SPA., Illus.). 64p. reprint ed. 22.95 *(978-1-59497-346-8(6))* Public Square Bks.

—Tintin & Alph-Art. 2007. (Adventures of Tintin: Original Classic Ser.). (ENG., Illus.). 64p. (gr. 3-17). pap. 11.99 *(978-0-316-00375-9(1))* Little, Brown Bks. for Young Readers.

—Tintin et le Lac aux Requins. (FRE.). 21.95 *(978-2-203-00122-0(4))* Casterman, Editions FRA. Dist: Distribooks, Inc.

—Tintin in the Land of the Soviets. 2007. (Adventures of Tintin: Original Classic Ser.). (ENG., Illus.). 144p. (J). (gr. 3-17). pap. 13.99 *(978-0-316-00374-2(3))* Little, Brown Bks. for Young Readers.

—Le Tresor de Rackham le Rouge. (Tintin Ser.). (FRE., Illus.). 62p. (J). pap. 21.95 *(978-2-203-00111-4(9))* Casterman, Editions FRA. Dist: Distribooks, Inc.

Hergé, et al. The Secret of the Unicorn. 2003. Orig. Title: Secret de la Licorne. (ENG.). 64p. *(978-1-4052-0810-9(4))* Egmont Bks., Ltd.

Hernandez, Gilbert. The Adventures of Venus. 2012. (ENG., Illus.). 104p. (gr. 4-9). 9.99 *(978-1-60699-540-2(5)*, 699540) Fantagraphics Bks.

Hester, Phil. T. H. U. N. D. E. R. Agents Volume 1. 2014. (T. H. U. N. D. E. R. Agents Ser.). (ENG., Illus.). 104p. pap. 17.99 *(978-1-61377-861-6(9)*, 9781613778616) Idea & Design Works, LLC.

Hickman, Jonathan. Avengers - Rogue Planet, Vol. 5. 2014. (ENG., Illus.). 136p. (YA). (gr. 8-17). 24.99 *(978-0-7851-5477-8(9))* Marvel Worldwide, Inc.

Hicks, Faith Erin. The Adventures of Superhero Girl (Expanded Edition) 2017. (ENG., Illus.). 128p. (gr. 5-9). 16.99 ***(978-1-5067-0336-7(4))*** Dark Horse Comics.

—Friends with Boys. Hicks, Faith Erin, illus. 2012. (ENG., Illus.). 224p. (YA). (gr. 7-11). pap. 16.99 *(978-1-59643-556-8(9)*, 9781596435568, First Second Bks.) Roaring Brook Pr.

—The Nameless City. 2016. (Nameless City Ser.: 1). (ENG., Illus.). 240p. (J). pap. 14.99 *(978-1-62672-156-2(4)*, 9781626721562, First Second Bks.) Roaring Brook Pr.

Hicks, Faith Erin & Druckmann, Neil. The Last of Us: American Dreams. Wright, Brendan, ed. 2013. (ENG., Illus.). 96p. pap. 16.99 *(978-1-61655-212-1(3))* Dark Horse Comics.

Hicks, Rebecca. Little Vampires. Hicks, Rebecca, illus. 2007. (Illus.). 56p. per. 8.95 *(978-0-9799290-0-7(8))* Lunasea Studios.

Hidaka, Banri. V. B. Rose Volume 10. 2010. (Illus.). 208p. pap. 10.99 *(978-1-4278-1160-8(1))* TOKYOPOP, Inc.

—V. B. Rose Volume 9. 2010. (Illus.). 192p. pap. 10.99 *(978-1-4278-0927-8(5))* TOKYOPOP, Inc.

Hidalgo, Pablo. The Phantom Menace. 2012. (Star Wars Ser.). (ENG.). 64p. (J). (gr. -1-3). 9.99 *(978-0-545-38986-0(0))* Scholastic, Inc.

Hiiragi, Aoi. Baron: The Cat Returns. Hiiragi, Aoi, illus. 2005. (Baron Ser.). (ENG., Illus.). 224p. pap. 9.99 *(978-1-59116-956-7(9))* Viz Media.

Hikawa, Kyoko. From Far Away, Vol. 2. Hikawa, Kyoko, illus. 2005. (ENG., Illus.). 184p. pap. 9.99 *(978-1-59116-601-6(2))* Viz Media.

Hilgenberg, Bob & Muir, Roberto. Tinker Bell & the Great Fairy Rescue. Storino, Sara & Zanotta, Roberta, illus. movie tie-in ed. 2010. (Disney Fairies Ser.). (ENG.). 56p. (J). (gr. 1-6). 9.99 *(978-1-59707-232-8(X)*, 9781597072328) Papercutz.

Hillenburg, Stephen. SpongeBob Comics: Book 1: Silly Sea Stories. 2017. (SpongeBob Comics Ser.). (ENG., Illus.). 112p. (J). (gr. 3-7). pap. 10.95 ***(978-1-4197-2319-3(7)***, Amulet Bks.) Abrams, Inc.

—SpongeBob Comics: Book 2: Aquatic Adventurers, Unite! 2017. (SpongeBob Comics Ser.). (ENG., Illus.). 112p. (J). (gr. 3-7). pap. 10.95 ***(978-1-4197-2320-9(0)***, Amulet Bks.) Abrams, Inc.

Hillenburg, Stephen. Spongebob Squarepants Bikini Bottom's Most Wanted. 2006. (Nickelodeon Ser.). (Illus.). 91p. (J). (gr. 4-7). per. 14.99 *(978-1-59532-471-9(2)*, Tokyopop Kids) TOKYOPOP, Inc.

Hillenburg, Steven. SpongeBob SquarePants: Another Day Another Dollar, Vol. 5. 2004. (Nickelodeon Ser.). (Illus.). 96p. pap. 14.99 *(978-1-59532-209-8(4)*, Tokyopop Kids) TOKYOPOP, Inc.

Hillenburg, Steven, creator. Crime & Funishment Vol. 4, 7 vols. 2004. (Illus.). 96p. (gr. 2-5). pap. 14.99 *(978-1-59182-576-0(8)*, Tokyopop Kids) TOKYOPOP, Inc.

—Saves the Day, Vol. 8. 2005. (Nickelodeon Ser.). (Illus.). 88p. pap. 14.99 *(978-1-59532-679-9(0)*, Tokyopop Kids) TOKYOPOP, Inc.

Hiller, Sandra J. The Life of a Colonial Printer. 2013. (Jr. Graphic Colonial America Ser.). 24p. (J). (gr. 3-6). pap. 63.60 *(978-1-4777-1430-0(8))*; (ENG., Illus.). pap. 10.60 *(978-1-4777-1429-4(4))*; (ENG., Illus.). lib. bdg. 25.25 *(978-1-4777-1306-8(9))* Rosen Publishing Group, Inc., The. (PowerKids Pr.).

Himekawa, Akira. The Legend of Zelda Box Set, 10 vols. 2011. (ENG., Illus.). 2000p. (J). pap. 79.99 *(978-1-4215-4242-3(0))* Viz Media.

—The Legend of Zelda, Vol. 10. Himekawa, Akira, illus. 2010. (ENG., Illus.). 200p. (J). (gr. 2-5). pap. 9.99 *(978-1-4215-3724-5(9))* Viz Media.

—The Legend of Zelda, Vol. 5. Himekawa, Akira, illus. 2009. (ENG., Illus.). 200p. (J). pap. 9.99 *(978-1-4215-2331-6(0))* Viz Media.

—The Legend of Zelda, Vol. 9. Himekawa, Akira, illus. 2010. (ENG., Illus.). 192p. (YA). pap. 9.99 *(978-1-4215-2335-4(3))* Viz Media.

Hinds, Gareth. Macbeth. Hinds, Gareth, illus. 2015. (ENG., Illus.). 152p. (YA). (gr. 7). 21.99 *(978-0-7636-6943-0(1))* Candlewick Pr.

Hinds, Gareth, illus. & adapted by. Beowulf. Hinds, Gareth, adapted by. 2007. (ENG.). 128p. (J). (gr. 5-12). pap. 12.99 *(978-0-7636-3023-2(3))* Candlewick Pr.

Hino, Hideshi. The Bug Boy No. 2: Hino Horror: A Graphic Novel. Hino, Hideshi, illus. 2005. (Illus.). 204p. (YA). (gr. 4-9). reprint ed. pap. 10.00 *(978-0-7567-9709-6(8))* DIANE Publishing Co.

Hirsch, Andy. Varmints. 2016. (ENG., Illus.). 224p. (J). pap. 16.99 *(978-1-62672-279-8(X)*, 9781626722798, First Second Bks.) Roaring Brook Pr.

Hiwatari, Saki. Please Save My Earth, Vol. 18. Hiwatari, Saki, illus. 2006. (Please Save My Earth Ser.: 18). (ENG., Illus.). 208p. pap. 9.99 *(978-1-4215-0551-0(7))* Viz Media.

—Please Save My Earth, Vol. 17. Hiwatari, Saki, illus. 2006. (ENG., Illus.). 208p. pap. 9.99 *(978-1-4215-0550-3(9))* Viz Media.

Hoban, Russell. Jim's Lion. Deacon, Alexis, illus. 2014. (ENG.). 64p. (J). (gr. 1-4). 15.99 *(978-0-7636-6517-3(7))* Candlewick Pr.

Hoena, B. A. Jason & the Argonauts: A Graphic Retelling. 2015. (Ancient Myths Ser.). (ENG., Illus.). 32p. (gr. 3-4). lib. bdg. 30.65 *(978-1-4914-2072-0(3)*, Graphic Library) Capstone Press of Coughlan Cos.

Hoena, B. A. & Barrie, J. M. Peter Pan. Cano, Fernando, illus. 2015. (Graphic Revolve: Common Core Editions Ser.). (ENG.). 72p. (gr. 2-3). lib. bdg. 27.99 *(978-1-4965-0372-5(4))* Stone Arch Bks.

Hoena, Blake, retold by. The 12 Labors of Hercules: A Graphic Retelling. 2015. (Ancient Myths Ser.). (ENG.). 32p. (gr. 3-4). lib. bdg. 30.65 *(978-1-4914-2071-3(5)*, Graphic Library) Capstone Press of Coughlan Cos.

Hoena, Blake A. Beyond the Black Hole. Harpster, Steve, illus. 2008. (Graphic Sparks Ser.). (ENG.). 40p. (gr. 1-3). pap. 5.95 *(978-1-4342-0855-2(9)*, Graphic Sparks) Stone Arch Bks.

—Eek & Ack Early Chapter Books, 1 vol. 2014. (Eek & Ack Early Chapter Bks.). (ENG.). 32p. (gr. k-2). 90.60 *(978-1-4342-8457-0(3))* Stone Arch Bks.

—Eek & Ack vs the Wolfman, 1 vol. Harpster, Steve, illus. 2009. (Eek & Ack Ser.). (ENG.). 40p. (gr. 1-3). lib. bdg. 23.99 *(978-1-4342-1189-7(4)*, Graphic Sparks) Stone Arch Bks.

—Ooze Slingers from Outer Space. Harpster, Steve, illus. 2007. (Graphic Sparks Ser.). (ENG.). 40p. (gr. 1-3). per. 5.95 *(978-1-59889-410-3(2)*, Graphic Sparks) Stone Arch Bks.

—The Puzzling Pluto Plot: Eek & Ack, 1 vol. Harpster, Steve, illus. 2008. (Graphic Sparks Ser.). (ENG.). 40p. (gr. 1-3). pap. 5.95 *(978-1-4342-0502-5(9)*, Graphic Sparks) Stone Arch Bks.

—Swamp Sting!, 1 vol. Facio, Sebastian, illus. 2011. (Graphic Sparks Ser.). (ENG.). 40p. (gr. 1-3). pap. 5.95 *(978-1-4342-3065-2(1))*; lib. bdg. 23.99 *(978-1-4342-2960-1(2))* Stone Arch Bks. (Graphic Sparks).

—Under the Red Sun, 1 vol. Schoening, Dan, illus. (Superman Ser.). (ENG.). 56p. (gr. 2-3). 2013. pap. 4.95 *(978-1-4342-1375-4(7))* 2009. lib. bdg. 26.65 *(978-1-4342-1159-0(2))* Stone Arch Bks. (DC Super Heroes).

Hoena, Blake A. & Fuentes, Benny. Spotlight Striker, 1 vol. Sandoval, Gerardo, illus. 2010. (Sports Illustrated Kids Graphic Novels Ser.). (ENG.). 56p. (gr. 2-3). 26.65 *(978-1-4342-2128-5(8))*; pap. 7.19 *(978-1-4342-2787-4(1))* Stone Arch Bks.

Hoena, Blake A. & Gonzalez, Jorge. Kickoff Blitz. Ruiz, Alfonso, illus. 2010. (Sports Illustrated Kids Graphic Novels Ser.). 56p. pap. 0.50 *(978-1-4342-3205-2(0))*; (ENG.). (gr. 2-3). pap. 7.19 *(978-1-4342-2292-3(6))*; (ENG.). (gr. 2-3). 26.65 *(978-1-4342-1909-1(7))* Stone Arch Bks.

Hoena, Blake A., et al. Poison Ivy's Deadly Garden, 1 vol. (Batman Ser.). (ENG., Illus.). 56p. (gr. 2-3). 2013. pap. 4.95 *(978-1-4342-1368-6(4))* 2009. lib. bdg. 26.65 *(978-1-4342-1152-1(5))* Stone Arch Bks. (DC Super Heroes).

Hoffman, Mary. The Sword in the Stone. Ginevra, Dante, illus. 2014. (Collins Big Cat Progress Ser.). (ENG.). 32p. (J). (gr. 4-5). pap. 7.99 *(978-0-00-751935-4(4))* HarperCollins Pubs. Ltd. GBR. Dist: Independent Pubs. Group.

Hoffmann, Heinrich. Slovenly Kate & Other Stories: From the Struwwelpeter Library. Hosemann, Theodor, illus. 2012. (Dover Children's Classics Ser.). (ENG.). 96p. (J). (gr. 3-5). pap. 12.99 *(978-0-486-49032-8(7))* Dover Pubns., Inc.

Holm, Jennifer L. Detention! 2017. (Comics Squad Ser.: 3). lib. bdg. 18.40 ***(978-0-606-40230-9(6))*** Turtleback Bks.

—Eighth Grade Is Making Me Sick: Ginny Davis's Year in Stuff. Castaldi, Elicia, illus. 2015. (Ginny Davis's Year in Stuff Ser.). (ENG.). 128p. (J). (gr. 3-7). pap. 7.99 *(978-0-375-87219-8(1)*, Yearling) Random Hse. Children's Bks.

—I'm Grumpy (My First Comics) Holm, Matthew, illus. 2016. (ENG.). 24p. (J). (— 1). 7.99 *(978-0-553-53344-6(4)*, Random Hse. Bks. for Young Readers) Random Hse. Children's Bks.

—I'm Silly! (My First Comics) Holm, Matthew, illus. 2017. (ENG.). 22p. (J). (— 1). bds. 7.99 ***(978-0-553-53348-4(7)***, Random Hse. Bks. for Young Readers) Random Hse. Children's Bks.

—I'm Sunny! (My First Comics) Holm, Matthew, illus. 2016. (ENG.). 24p. (J). (— 1). 7.99 *(978-0-553-53346-0(0)*, Random Hse. Bks. for Young Readers) Random Hse. Children's Bks.

—Sunny Side Up. 2015. lib. bdg. 24.50 *(978-0-606-37759-1(X))* Turtleback Bks.

Holm, Jennifer L. Swing It, Sunny. Holm, Matthew, illus. 2017. (Sunny Ser.: 2). (ENG.). 224p. (J). (gr. 3-7). 24.99 ***(978-0-545-74170-5(X))***; pap. 12.99 ***(978-0-545-74172-9(6))*** Scholastic, Inc. (Graphix).

Holm, Jennifer L. & Holm, Matthew. Babymouse for President. Holm, Jennifer L. & Holm, Matthew, illus. 2012. (Babymouse Ser.: 16). (ENG., Illus.). 96p. (J). (gr. 2-5). 12.99 *(978-0-375-96780-1(X))*; pap. 6.99 *(978-0-375-86780-4(5))* Random Hse. Children's Bks. (Random Hse. Bks. for Young Readers).

—Babymouse Goes for the Gold. Holm, Jennifer L. & Holm, Matthew, illus. 2016. (Babymouse Ser.: 20). (ENG., Illus.). 96p. (J). (gr. 2-5). pap. 6.99 *(978-0-307-93163-4(3)*, Random Hse. Bks. for Young Readers) Random Hse. Children's Bks.

—Babymouse Tales from the Locker Presents Lights, Camera, Messy Whiskers. 2017. (Babymouse Tales from the Locker Ser.: 1). (ENG., Illus.). 208p. (J). (gr. 3-7). 13.99 *(978-0-399-55438-4(6)*, Random Hse. Bks. for Young Readers) Random Hse. Children's Bks.

—Bad Babysitter. Holm, Jennifer L. & Holm, Matthew, illus. 2015. (Babymouse Ser.: 19). (ENG., Illus.). 96p. (J). (gr. 2-5). pap. 6.99 *(978-0-307-93162-7(5)*, Random Hse. Bks. for Young Readers) Random Hse. Children's Bks.

—Beach Babe. 2008. (Babymouse Ser.: No. 3). (Illus.). 91p. (gr. 2-5). 17.00 *(978-0-7569-8345-1(2))* Perfection Learning Corp.

—Beach Babe. 2006. (Babymouse Ser.: 3). (ENG., Illus.). 96p. (J). (gr. 2-5). pap. 6.99 *(978-0-375-83231-4(9))*;No. 3. lib. bdg. 12.99 *(978-0-375-93231-1(3))* Random Hse. Children's Bks. (Random Hse. Bks. for Young Readers).

—Brave New Pond. Holm, Jennifer L. & Holm, Matthew, illus. 2011. (Squish Ser.: No. 2). (ENG., Illus.). 96p. (J). (gr. 3-7). 12.99 *(978-0-375-93784-2(6))*; pap. 6.99 *(978-0-375-84390-7(6))* Random Hse. Children's Bks. (Random Hse. Bks. for Young Readers).

—Burns Rubber. 2010. (Babymouse Ser.: 12). lib. bdg. 17.20 *(978-0-606-07025-6(7)*, Turtleback) Turtleback Bks.

—Camp Babymouse. 2007. (Babymouse Ser.: 6). (ENG., Illus.). 96p. (J). (gr. 2-5). pap. 6.99 *(978-0-375-83988-7(7))*; lib. bdg. 12.99 *(978-0-375-93988-4(1))* Random Hse. Children's Bks. (Random Hse. Bks. for Young Readers).

—Captain Disaster. Holm, Jennifer L. & Holm, Matthew, illus. 2012. (Squish Ser.: No. 4). (ENG., Illus.). 96p. (J). (gr. 2-5). pap. 6.99 *(978-0-375-84392-1(2))*; lib. bdg. 12.99 *(978-0-375-93786-6(2))* Random Hse. Children's Bks. (Random Hse. Bks. for Young Readers).

—Captain Disaster. 2012. (Squish Ser.: 4). lib. bdg. 17.20 *(978-0-606-26812-7(X)*, Turtleback) Turtleback Bks.

—Deadly Disease of Doom. Holm, Jennifer L. & Holm, Matthew, illus. 2015. (Squish Ser.). (ENG., Illus.). 96p. (J). (gr. 2-5). lib. bdg. 12.99 *(978-0-307-98306-0(4)*, Random Hse. Bks. for Young Readers) Random Hse. Children's Bks.

—Dragonslayer. Holm, Jennifer L. & Holm, Matthew, illus. 2009. (Babymouse Ser.: 11). (ENG., Illus.). 96p. (J). (gr. 2-5). pap. 6.99 *(978-0-375-85712-6(5)*, Random Hse. Bks. for Young Readers) Random Hse. Children's Bks.

—Extreme Babymouse. Holm, Jennifer L. & Holm, Matthew, illus. 2013. (Babymouse Ser.: 17). (ENG., Illus.). 96p. (J). (gr. 2-5). pap. 6.99 *(978-0-307-93160-3(9))*; lib. bdg. 12.99 *(978-0-375-97096-2(7))* Random Hse. Children's Bks. (Random Hse. Bks. for Young Readers).

—Extreme Babymouse. 2013. (Babymouse Ser.: 17). lib. bdg. 17.20 *(978-0-606-26999-5(1)*, Turtleback) Turtleback Bks.

—Fear the Amoeba. Holm, Jennifer L. & Holm, Matthew, illus. 2014. (Squish Ser.: No. 6). (ENG., Illus.). 96p. (J). (gr. 2-5). 12.99 *(978-0-307-98303-9(X))*;No. 6. pap. 6.99 *(978-0-307-98302-2(1))* Random Hse. Children's Bks. (Random Hse. Bks. for Young Readers).

—Fear the Amoeba. 2014. (Squish Ser.: 6). lib. bdg. 17.20 *(978-0-606-36025-8(5))* Turtleback Bks.

—Game On! Holm, Jennifer L. & Holm, Matthew, illus. 2013. (Squish Ser.: No. 5). (ENG., Illus.). 96p. (J). (gr. 2-5). lib. bdg. 12.99 *(978-0-307-98300-8(5))*;No. 5. pap. 6.99 *(978-0-307-98299-5(8))* Random Hse. Children's Bks. (Random Hse. Bks. for Young Readers).

—Game On! 2013. (Squish Ser.: 5). lib. bdg. 17.20 *(978-0-606-31946-1(8)*, Turtleback) Turtleback Bks.

—Happy Birthday, Babymouse! Holm, Jennifer L. & Holm, Matthew, illus. 2014. (Babymouse Ser.: 18). (ENG., Illus.). 96p. (J). (gr. 2-5). 12.99 *(978-0-375-97097-9(5)*, Random Hse. Bks. for Young Readers) Random Hse. Children's Bks.

—Happy Birthday, Babymouse. Holm, Jennifer L. & Holm, Matthew, illus. 2014. (Babymouse Ser.: 18). (ENG., Illus.). 96p. (J). (gr. 2-5). pap. 6.99 *(978-0-307-93161-0(7)*, Random Hse. Bks. for Young Readers) Random Hse. Children's Bks.

—Happy Birthday, Babymouse. 2014. (Babymouse Ser.: 18). lib. bdg. 17.20 *(978-0-606-35567-4(7))* Turtleback Bks.

—Heartbreaker. 2006. (Babymouse Ser.: 5). (ENG., Illus.). 96p. (J). (gr. 2-5). lib. bdg. 12.99 *(978-0-375-93798-9(6)*, Random Hse. Bks. for Young Readers) Random Hse. Children's Bks.

—Mad Scientist. Holm, Jennifer L. & Holm, Matthew, illus. 2011. (Babymouse Ser.: No. 14). (ENG., Illus.). 96p. (J). (gr. 2-5). pap. 6.99 *(978-0-375-86574-9(8))*; lib. bdg. 12.99 *(978-0-375-96574-6(2))* Random Hse. Children's Bks. (Random Hse. Bks. for Young Readers).

—The Musical. Holm, Jennifer L. & Holm, Matthew, illus. 2009. (Babymouse Ser.: 10). (ENG., Illus.). 96p. (J). (gr. 2-5). pap. 6.99 *(978-0-375-84388-4(4))*; lib. bdg. 12.99 *(978-0-375-93791-0(9))* Random Hse. Children's Bks. (Random Hse. Bks. for Young Readers).

—Our Hero. 2005. (Babymouse Ser.: 2). (ENG., Illus.). 96p. (J). (gr. 2-5). pap. 6.99 *(978-0-375-83230-7(0))*; lib. bdg. 12.99 *(978-0-375-93230-4(5))* Random Hse. Children's Bks. (Random Hse. Bks. for Young Readers).

—The Power of the Parasite. Holm, Jennifer L. & Holm, Matthew, illus. 2012. (Squish Ser.: No. 3). (ENG., Illus.). 96p. (J). (gr. 2-5). pap. 6.99 *(978-0-375-84391-4(4))*; lib. bdg. 12.99 *(978-0-375-93785-9(4))* Random Hse. Children's Bks. (Random Hse. Bks. for Young Readers).

—The Power of the Parasite. 2012. (Squish Ser.: 3). lib. bdg. 17.20 *(978-0-606-26405-1(1)*, Turtleback) Turtleback Bks.

—Queen of the World! 2005. (Babymouse Ser.: 1). (ENG., Illus.). 96p. (J). (gr. 2-5). pap. 6.99 *(978-0-375-83229-1(7))*; lib. bdg. 12.99 *(978-0-375-93229-8(1))* Random Hse. Children's Bks. (Random Hse. Bks. for Young Readers).

—Rock Star. 2006. (Babymouse Ser.: 4). (ENG., Illus.). 96p. (J). (gr. 2-5). pap. 6.99 *(978-0-375-83232-1(7))*; lib. bdg. 12.99 *(978-0-375-93232-8(1))* Random Hse. Children's Bks. (Random Hse. Bks. for Young Readers).

—Squish #8: Pod vs. Pod. Holm, Jennifer L. & Holm, Matthew, illus. 2016. (Squish Ser.). (ENG., Illus.). 96p. (J). (gr. 2-5). pap. 6.99 *(978-0-307-98308-4(0))*; lib. bdg. 12.99 *(978-0-307-98309-1(9))* Random Hse. Children's Bks. (Random Hse. Bks. for Young Readers).

—Super Amoeba. Holm, Jennifer L. & Holm, Matthew, illus. 2011. (Squish Ser.: No. 1). (ENG., Illus.). 96p. (J). (gr. 3-7). pap. 6.99 *(978-0-375-84389-1(2))*; lib. bdg. 12.99 *(978-0-375-93783-5(8))* Random Hse. Children's Bks. (Random Hse. Bks. for Young Readers).

—A Very Babymouse Christmas. Holm, Jennifer L. & Holm, Matthew, illus. 2011. (Babymouse Ser.: 15). (ENG., Illus.). 96p. (J). (gr. 2-5). 12.99 *(978-0-375-96779-5(6))*; pap. 6.99 *(978-0-375-86779-8(1))* Random Hse. Children's Bks. (Random Hse. Bks. for Young Readers).

Holm, Jennifer L., et al. Comics Squad: Recess! 2014. (Comics Squad Ser.). (ENG., Illus.). 144p. (J). (gr. 2-5). pap. 7.99 *(978-0-385-37003-5(2)*, Random Hse. Bks. for Young Readers) Random Hse. Children's Bks.

—Comics Squad #3: Detention! 2017. (Comics Squad Ser.: 3). (ENG., Illus.). 160p. (J). (gr. 2-5). pap. 7.99 ***(978-0-553-51267-0(6))***; lib. bdg. 12.99 ***(978-0-553-51268-7(4))*** Random Hse. Children's Bks. (Random Hse. Bks. for Young Readers).

—Sunny Side Up. 2015. (Illus.). 216p. (J). ***(978-0-545-89934-5(6)***, Graphix) Scholastic, Inc.

Holm, Kirsten C. Everyday Life in Ancient China. 2012. (Jr. Graphic Ancient Civilizations Ser.). (ENG.). 24p. (J). (gr. 3-6). pap. 10.60 *(978-1-4488-6395-2(3))*; lib. bdg. 25.25 *(978-1-4488-6218-4(3))* Rosen Publishing Group, Inc., The. (PowerKids Pr.).

—Everyday Life in Ancient Rome. 2012. (Jr. Graphic Ancient Civilizations Ser.). (ENG.). 24p. (J). (gr. 3-6). pap. 10.60 *(978-1-4488-6389-1(9))*; lib. bdg. 25.25 *(978-1-4488-6215-3(9))* Rosen Publishing Group, Inc., The. (PowerKids Pr.).

Holm, Matthew & Holm, Jennifer L. Lunch! 2016. (Comics Squad Ser.: 2). lib. bdg. 18.40 *(978-0-606-38446-9(4))* Turtleback Bks.

Holm, Matthew, et al. Comics Squad #2: Lunch! 2016. (Comics Squad Ser.). (ENG., Illus.). 144p. (J). (gr. 2-5). pap. 7.99 *(978-0-553-51264-9(1)*, Random Hse. Bks. for Young Readers) Random Hse. Children's Bks.

Homan, Michael. Grendel Gander the Sinister Goose. Duggins, Peat, illus. 2012. 48p. pap. 14.95 *(978-1-60808-049-6(8)*, WriteLife Publishing) Boutique of Quality Books Publishing Co., Inc.

Hongo, Akiyoshi. Digimon, 5 vols., Vol. 4. 4th rev. ed. 2003. (Illus.). 164p. (gr. 2-18). pap. 9.99 *(978-1-59182-159-5(2))* TOKYOPOP, Inc.

Hooks, Gwendolyn. The Cat Food Mystery: A Pet Club Story, 1 vol. Byrne, Mike, illus. 2011. (Pet Club Ser.). (ENG.). 32p. (gr. 1-2). pap. 6.25 *(978-1-4342-3051-5(1))*; lib. bdg. 22.65 *(978-1-4342-2511-5(9))* Stone Arch Bks.

—The Lucky Charm: A Pet Club Story, 1 vol. Byrne, Mike, illus. 2011. (Pet Club Ser.). (ENG.). 32p. (gr. 1-2). pap. 6.25 *(978-1-4342-3052-2(X))* Stone Arch Bks.

—Pet Costume Party: A Pet Club Story, 1 vol. Byrne, Mike, illus. 2011. (Pet Club Ser.). (ENG.). 32p. (gr. 1-2). pap. 6.25 *(978-1-4342-3053-9(8))*; lib. bdg. 22.65 *(978-1-4342-2513-9(5))* Stone Arch Bks.

—The Pet Wash: A Pet Club Story, 1 vol. Byrne, Mike, illus. 2011. (Pet Club Ser.). (ENG.). 32p. (gr. 1-2). pap. 6.25 *(978-1-4342-3054-6(6))*; lib. bdg. 22.65 *(978-1-4342-2514-6(3))* Stone Arch Bks.

Hoopmann, Kathy. Blue Bottle Mystery - the Graphic Novel: An Asperger Adventure. 2015. (Asperger Adventures Ser.). (ENG., Illus.). 64p. (J). 18.95 *(978-1-84905-650-2(1)*, 7952) Kingsley, Jessica Pubs. GBR. Dist: Macmillan Distribution Ltd.

Horowitz, Anthony. Skeleton Key. Kanako & Yuzuru, illus. 2009. (Alex Rider Ser.: Bk. 3). (ENG.). 176p. (J). (gr. 5-18). pap. 14.99 *(978-0-399-25418-5(8)*, Philomel Bks.) Penguin Young Readers Group.

Horowitz, Anthony & Johnston, Antony. Point Blank. Yuzuru & Kanako, illus. 2007. (Alex Rider Ser.). (ENG.). 176p. (J). (gr. 5-18). 14.99 *(978-0-399-25026-2(3)*, Philomel Bks.) Penguin Young Readers Group.

Horowitz, Jeanine. My First Playing Lesson. l.t. ed. 2006. (Illus.). 32p. (J). lib. bdg. *(978-1-934190-04-3(7))* Ocean Front Bk. Publishing, Inc.

Horton, Steve. Amala's Blade - Spirits of Naamaron, Vol. 1. Warner, Chris, ed. 2014. (ENG., Illus.). 144p. pap. 18.99 *(978-1-61655-332-6(4))* Dark Horse Comics.

Hotton, Rick. Holy Mole: Life Is What You Make It: Subtle Wisdom from an Unconventional Comic Strip. 2013. (ENG.). 96p. pap. *(978-1-62343-164-8(6))* Willow Creek Pr., Inc.

Houghton, Shane. Reed Gunther Volume 2 TP. 2012. (ENG., Illus.). 172p. pap. 14.99 *(978-1-60706-556-2(8)*, 9781607065562) Image Comics.

Houser, Jody. Faith. 2016. (Faith Ser.: 1). lib. bdg. 20.85 *(978-0-606-38942-6(3))* Turtleback Bks.

Houts, Amy. Down on the Farm, 1 vol. Harpster, Steve, illus. 2011. (My First Graphic Novel Ser.). (ENG.). 32p. (gr. k-2). pap. 6.25 *(978-1-4342-3063-8(5))*; lib. bdg. 24.65 *(978-1-4342-2516-0(X))* Stone Arch Bks. (My First Graphic Novel).

Howard, Josh. Dead@17: Blood of Saints. Howard, Josh, illus. 2004. (Illus.). 112p. (YA). per. 14.95 *(978-0-9754193-1-1(5))* Viper Comics.

Howard, Kate. The Misadventures of Jibanyan, Bk. 1. 2016. (Yo-Kai Watch Ser.: 1). (ENG.). 64p. (J). (gr. 2-5). pap. 4.99 *(978-1-338-05462-0(7))* Scholastic, Inc.

—Ninja vs. Ninja. 2015. (Ninjago Readers Ser.: 12). (Illus.). 32p. (J). lib. bdg. 13.55 *(978-0-606-37079-0(X))* Turtleback Bks.

Howard, Lee. Scooby-Doo & the High Tech House of the Future, 1 vol. 2016. (Scooby-Doo Comic Readers Ser.). (ENG.). 32p. (J). (gr. k-3). lib. bdg. 24.21 *(978-1-61479-452-3(9)*, Graphic Planet) Magic Wagon.

—Scooby-Doo & the Unnatural, 1 vol. 2016. (Scooby-Doo Comic Readers Ser.). (ENG.). 32p. (J). (gr. k-3). lib. bdg. 24.21 *(978-1-61479-453-0(7)*, Graphic Planet) Magic Wagon.

—Scooby-Doo in Mummy Scares Best, 1 vol. 2016. (Scooby-Doo Comic Readers Ser.). (ENG.). 32p. (J). (gr. k-3). lib. bdg. 24.21 *(978-1-61479-455-4(3)*, Graphic Planet) Magic Wagon.

—Scooby-Doo in There's No Creature Like Snow Creature, 1 vol. 2016. (Scooby-Doo Comic Readers Ser.). (ENG.). 32p. (J). (gr. k-3). lib. bdg. 24.21 *(978-1-61479-456-1(1)*, Graphic Planet) Magic Wagon.

Howard, Lee & Khan, Nahnatchka. A Haunted Halloween, 1 vol. 2014. (Scooby-Doo Comic Storybook Ser.). (ENG.). 32p. (J). (gr. 5-9). 24.21 *(978-1-61479-281-9(X))* Spotlight.

—A Merry Scary Holiday, 1 vol. 2014. (Scooby-Doo Comic Storybook Ser.). (ENG.). 32p. (J). (gr. 5-9). 24.21 *(978-1-61479-282-6(8))* Spotlight.

Hubert. Adrian & the Tree of Secrets. 2014. (ENG., Illus.). 128p. (gr. 6). pap. 18.95 *(978-1-55152-556-3(9))* Arsenal Pulp Pr. CAN. Dist: Consortium Bk. Sales & Distribution.

Huddleston, Courtney & Zirkel, Scott. A Bit Haywire. Huddleston, Courtney, illus. 2006. (Illus.). 112p. per. 11.95 *(978-0-9777883-5-4(0))* Viper Comics.

Hudson Goff, Elizabeth & Uschan, Michael V. El Ataque a Pearl Harbor. 2007. (Historias Graficas (Graphic Histories) Ser.). (SPA.). 32p. (gr. 5-8). lib. bdg. 27.00 *(978-0-8368-7892-9(2))* Stevens, Gareth Publishing LLLP.

—El ataque a Pearl Harbor (the Bombing of Pearl Harbor) 2007. (Historias Graficas (Graphic Histories) Ser.). (SPA.). 32p. (gr. 5-8). pap. 10.50 *(978-0-8368-7899-8(X))* Stevens, Gareth Publishing LLLP.

Huelin, Jodi. Batman Versus Bane. Tong, Andie, illus. 2012. (I Can Read Book 2 Ser.). (ENG.). 32p. (J). (gr. -1-3). pap. 3.99 *(978-0-06-213224-6(5))* HarperCollins Pubs.

—Tools of the Trade. Gordon, Steven E., illus. 2012. (I Can Read Book 2 Ser.). (ENG.). 32p. (J). (gr. k-3). pap. 3.99 *(978-0-06-213223-9(7))* HarperCollins Pubs.

Hughes, Emily C. Marvel's Avengers - The Doodle Book. 2015. (ENG., Illus.). 128p. (J). (gr. 1-17). pap. 12.99 *(978-0-316-34085-4(5))* Little, Brown Bks. for Young Readers.

Hulk. 2003. (J). per. *(978-1-57657-856-8(9))* Paradise Pr., Inc.

Hunter, Derek. Brainwash Escape Victims, Vol. 2. 2006. (ENG., Illus.). 144p. (YA). pap. 12.95 *(978-1-59362-051-6(9)*, 9781593620516) Slave Labor Bks.

Hunter, Erin. Into the Woods. Hudson, Don, illus. 2008. (Warriors Manga Ser.: 1). (ENG.). 112p. (J). (gr. 3-7). pap. 7.99 *(978-0-06-154792-8(1))* HarperCollins Pubs.

—Kallik's Adventure. Kurkoski, Bettina M., illus. 2011. (Seekers Manga Ser.). (ENG.). 112p. (J). (gr. 3-7). pap. 7.99 *(978-0-06-172383-4(5))* HarperCollins Pubs.

—The Lost Warrior, 3 vols. 2007. (Warriors Manga Ser.: No. 1). (ENG., Illus.). 112p. (J). (gr. 3-7). pap. 6.99 *(978-0-06-124020-1(6))* HarperCollins Pubs.

—The Rise of Scourge. Kurkoski, Bettina M., illus. 2008. (Warriors Manga Ser.: No. 3). (ENG.). 112p. (J). (gr. 3-7). pap. 6.99 *(978-0-06-147867-3(9))* HarperCollins Pubs.

Hunter, Erin. Warriors: Graystripe's Adventure: The Lost Warrior, Warrior's Refuge, Warrior's Return. Barry, James L., illus. 2017. (Warriors Manga Ser.). 272p. (J). (gr. 3-7). pap. 12.99 ***(978-0-06-257300-1(4))*** HarperCollins Pubs.

Hunter, Erin & Jolley, Dan. Escape from the Forest. Hudson, Don, illus. 2008. (Warriors Manga Ser.: 2). (ENG.). 112p. (J). (gr. 3-7). pap. 7.99 *(978-0-06-154793-5(X))* HarperCollins Pubs.

—Warrior's Return, 3 vols. Barry, James L., illus. 2008. (Warriors Manga Ser.: No. 3). (ENG.). 112p. (J). (gr. 3-7). pap. 6.99 *(978-0-06-125233-4(6))* HarperCollins Pubs.

Husted, Ursula. Making Rain. 2004. 56p. (J). per. 9.95 *(978-0-9753225-0-5(8))* Atomic Fruit Pr.

Hutton, Laurie S. & Marsham, Liz. Wonder Woman Classic - A Hero for All. Hood, Josh et al, illus. 2017. 24p. (J). (gr. -1-3). pap. 3.99 *(978-0-06-236081-6(7),* HarperFestival) HarperCollins Pubs.

Hyperion. Meridian Magic. 2nd ed. 2005. (W. I. T. C. H. Graphic Novels Ser.: Bk. 2). (ENG.). 125p. (J). pap. 4.99 *(978-0-7868-5576-6(2),* Volo) Hyperion Bks. for Children.

I-Haun. Real - Fake Princess. 2006. (Real/Fake Princess Ser.). (ENG., Illus.). 200p. (YA). pap. 9.95 *(978-1-59796-080-9(2))* DrMaster Pubns. Inc.

—Real/Fake Princess, Vol. 4. Zhao, Yun, tr. 2007. (Real/Fake Princess Ser.). (ENG., Illus.). 200p. pap. 9.95 *(978-1-59796-082-3(9))* DrMaster Pubns. Inc.

I-Huan. Real - Fake Princess, Set, Vols. 1-5. 2007. (ENG., Illus.). 200p. (YA). pap. 34.95 *(978-1-59796-074-8(8))* DrMaster Pubns. Inc.

I-Huan & I-Haun. Real Fake Princess, Vol. 3. 2006. (Real/Fake Princess Ser.). (ENG., Illus.). 200p. (YA). pap. 9.95 *(978-1-59796-081-6(0))* DrMaster Pubns. Inc.

Ihara, Shigekatsu. Pokémon Vol. 8: Diamond & Pearl Adventure! Ihara, Shigekatsu, illus. 2010. (ENG., Illus.). 192p. (J). pap. 9.99 *(978-1-4215-3671-2(4))* Viz Media.

—Pokémon: Diamond & Pearl Adventure!, Vol. 3. Ihara, Shigekatsu, illus. 2009. (ENG., Illus.). 200p. (J). pap. 9.99 *(978-1-4215-2574-7(7))* Viz Media.

—Pokémon: Diamond & Pearl Adventure!, Vol. 6. Ihara, Shigekatsu, illus. 2010. (ENG., Illus.). 192p. (J). pap. 9.99 *(978-1-4215-3170-0(4))* Viz Media.

—Pokémon: Diamond & Pearl Adventure!, Vol. 7. Ihara, Shigekatsu, illus. 2010. (ENG., Illus.). 192p. (J). pap. 9.99 *(978-1-4215-3491-6(6))* Viz Media.

Iinuma, Yuuki. Itsuwaribito, Vol. 14. 2015. (ENG.). 192p. pap. 9.99 *(978-1-4215-6525-5(0))* Viz Media.

Ilka, Benjamin Alexander. A Boy & His Shadow. Ilka, Benjamin Alexander, illus. (Illus.). (YA). Pt. 1. 2005. per. 4.95 net. *(978-0-9779504-0-9(9))*Pt. 2. 2006. 3.95 net. *(978-0-9779504-1-6(7))* Hogan Publishing LLC.

Immonen, Stuart, illus. Magnetic North. 2006. (ENG.). 128p. (YA). (gr. 8-17). pap. 12.99 *(978-0-7851-1906-7(X))* Marvel Worldwide, Inc.

Inagaki, Riichird & Inagaki, Riichiro. Eyeshield 21, Vol. 1. Murata, Yusuke, illus. 2005. (ENG.). 208p. (gr. 11-17). pap. 9.99 *(978-1-59116-752-5(3))* Viz Media.

Inagaki, Riichiro. Eyeshield 21. Murata, Yusuke, illus. (Eyeshield 21 Ser.: 5). (ENG.). Vol. 5. 2005. 200p. pap. 9.99 *(978-1-4215-0113-0(9))* Vol. 8. 2006. 208p. pap. 9.99 *(978-1-4215-0637-1(8))* Viz Media.

—Eyeshield 21, Vol. 12. Murata, Yusuke, illus. 2007. (ENG.). 208p. pap. 9.99 *(978-1-4215-1061-3(8))* Viz Media.

—Eyeshield 21, Vol. 13. Murata, Yusuke, illus. 2007. (ENG.). 216p. pap. 7.99 *(978-1-4215-1062-0(6))* Viz Media.

—Eyeshield 21, Vol. 9. Murata, Yusuke, illus. 2006. (ENG.). 208p. (gr. 11). pap. 9.99 *(978-1-4215-0638-8(6))* Viz Media.

Inagaki, Riichiro & Toriyama, Akira. Dragon Ball Z, Vol. 19. Inagaki, Riichiro & Toriyama, Akira, illus. 2005. (ENG., Illus.). 184p. (gr. -1-13). pap. 9.99 *(978-1-59116-751-8(5))* Viz Media.

Inoue, Kazurou. Midori Days. Inoue, Kazurou, illus. 2006. (Midori Days Ser.). (ENG., Illus.). 208p. Vol. 6. pap. 9.99 *(978-1-4215-0495-7(2))* Vol. 7. pap. 9.99 *(978-1-4215-0496-4(0))* Viz Media.

Inoue, Momota. Pokémon the Movie: Kyurem vs. The Sword of Justice. 2013. (ENG.). 192p. (J). pap. 9.99 *(978-1-4215-5690-1(1))* Viz Media.

—Pokémon the Movie: White, Vol. 1. movie tie-in ed. 2012. (ENG.). 192p. (J). pap. 9.99 *(978-1-4215-4954-5(9))* Viz Media.

Inzana, Ryan. Ichiro. (ENG., Illus.). 288p. (YA). (gr. 7). 2014. pap. 12.99 *(978-0-547-61789-3(5),* HMH Books For Young Readers) 2012. 24.99 *(978-0-547-25269-8(2))* Houghton Mifflin Harcourt Publishing Co.

Irvine, Alex. Captain America: The First Avenger. 2014. (Marvel Cinematic Universe Ser.). (ENG.). 160p. (J). (gr. 3-7). 12.99 *(978-0-316-25632-2(3))* Little, Brown Bks. for Young Readers.

—Phase One: Iron Man. 2014. (Marvel Cinematic Universe Ser.). (ENG.). 256p. (J). (gr. 3-7). 10.99 *(978-0-316-25634-6(X))* Little, Brown Bks. for Young Readers.

—Phase One: Marvel's the Avengers. 2015. (Marvel Cinematic Universe Ser.). (ENG., Illus.). 240p. (J). (gr. 3-7). 12.99 *(978-0-316-25637-7(4))* Little, Brown Bks. for Young Readers.

—Phase One: the Incredible Hulk. 2015. (Marvel Cinematic Universe Ser.). (ENG.). 192p. (J). (gr. 3-7). 10.99 *(978-0-316-25633-9(1))* Little, Brown Bks. for Young Readers.

—Phase One: Thor. 2015. (Marvel Cinematic Universe Ser.). (ENG.). 224p. (J). (gr. 3-7). 10.99 *(978-0-316-25635-3(8))* Little, Brown Bks. for Young Readers.

—Phase Two: Marvel's Captain America: the Winter Soldier. 2016. (Marvel Cinematic Universe Ser.). (ENG., Illus.). 208p. (J). (gr. 3-7). 10.99 *(978-0-316-25678-0(1))* Little, Brown Bks. for Young Readers.

Irving, Washington, et al. Halloween Classics, Vol. 23. Pomplun, Tom, ed. 2012. (ENG., Illus.). 144p. (YA). pap. 17.95 *(978-0-9825630-5-2(1),* 9780982563052) Eureka Productions.

Isaac, Lowell. Mr. Cat & the End of the World. 2013. 36p. pap. 20.99 *(978-1-4817-0297-3(1))* AuthorHouse.

Izubuchi, Yutaka. Rahxephon. Momose, Takeaki, illus. 2004. (Rahxephon Ser.). (ENG.). (YA). 192p. pap. 9.95 *(978-1-59116-407-4(9))*; Vol. 2. 200p. pap. 9.95 *(978-1-59116-427-2(3))*; Vol. 3. 200p. pap. 9.95 *(978-1-59116-428-9(1))* Viz Media.

Izubuchi, Yutaka & Ohnogi, Hiroshi. Rahxephon, Vol. 3. 2006. (RahXephon (Dr Masterbook) Ser.). (ENG., Illus.). 200p. (YA). pap. 7.95 *(978-1-59796-002-1(0))* DrMaster Pubns. Inc.

Izumi, Kaneyoshi. Doubt!!, Vol. 1. Izumi, Kaneyoshi, illus. 2005. (ENG., Illus.). 192p. pap. 9.99 *(978-1-59116-908-6(9))* Viz Media.

—Seiho Boys' High School!, Vol. 3. Izumi, Kaneyoshi, illus. 2010. (ENG., Illus.). 200p. pap. 9.99 *(978-1-4215-3733-7(8))* Viz Media.

Jablonski, Carla. Defiance, Bk. 2. Purvis, Leland, illus. 2011. (Resistance Ser.: 2). (ENG.). 128p. (YA). (gr. 7-12). pap. 18.99 *(978-1-59643-292-5(6),* 9781596432925, First Second Bks.) Roaring Brook Pr.

—Resistance, Bk. 1. Purvis, Leland, illus. 2010. (Resistance Ser.: 1). (ENG.). 128p. (YA). (gr. 7-12). pap. 17.99 *(978-1-59643-291-8(8),* 9781596432918, First Second Bks.) Roaring Brook Pr.

—Victory: Resistance Book 3. Purvis, Leland, illus. 2012. (Resistance Ser.: 3). (ENG.). 128p. (YA). (gr. 7-3). pap. 17.99 *(978-1-59643-293-2(4),* 9781596432932, First Second Bks.) Roaring Brook Pr.

Jackson, Robert, Jr. The Amazing Liberteens. 2004. (YA). per. 9.95 *(978-0-9761420-0-3(7))* Jackson, Robert.

Jacobs, Edgar P. Atlantis Mystery. 2012. (Blake & Mortimer Ser.: 12). (ENG., Illus.). 72p. (J). (gr. 5-12). pap. 15.95 *(978-1-84918-107-5(1))* CineBook GBR. Dist: National Bk. Network.

—Blake & Mortimer Vol. 15: The Secret of the Swordfish Part 1. 2013. (Blake & Mortimer Ser.: 15). (ENG., Illus.). 64p. pap. 15.95 *(978-1-84918-148-8(9))* CineBook GBR. Dist: National Bk. Network.

—Blake & Mortimer Vol. 17: the Secret of the Swordfish Part 3. 2014. (Blake & Mortimer Ser.: 17). (ENG., Illus.). 64p. pap. 15.95 *(978-1-84918-174-7(8))* CineBook GBR. Dist: National Bk. Network.

—The Mystery of the Great Pyramid. (Blake & Mortimer Ser.: 2). (ENG., Illus.). Pt. 1. 2007. 72p. pap. 15.95 *(978-1-905460-37-3(6))*Pt. 2. 2008. 56p. pap. 15.95 *(978-1-905460-38-0(4))* CineBook GBR. Dist: National Bk. Network.

—S. O. S. Meteors. 2009. (Blake & Mortimer Ser.: 6). (ENG., Illus.). 64p. pap. 15.95 *(978-1-905460-97-7(X))* CineBook GBR. Dist: National Bk. Network.

—The Secret of the Swordfish. 2013. (Blake & Mortimer Ser.: 16). (ENG., Illus.). 64p. pap. 15.95 *(978-1-84918-161-7(6))* CineBook GBR. Dist: National Bk. Network.

—The Yellow "M" 2007. (Blake & Mortimer Ser.: 1). (ENG., Illus.). 72p. per. 15.95 *(978-1-905460-21-2(X))* CineBook GBR. Dist: National Bk. Network.

Jacobson, Ryan. Caught in a Pickle, 1 vol. Garcia, Eduardo & Ferrara, Eduardo, illus. 2011. (B-Team Ser.). (ENG.). 40p. (gr. 1-3). lib. bdg. 23.99 *(978-1-4342-2606-8(9),* Graphic Sparks) Stone Arch Bks.

Jakobsen, Lars. The Mysterious Manuscript. Jakobsen, Lars, illus. 2012. (Mortensen's Escapades Ser.: 1). (ENG., Illus.). 48p. (gr. 6-12). pap. 6.95 *(978-0-8225-9409-3(9))*; lib. bdg. 27.93 *(978-0-7613-7883-9(9))* Lerner Publishing Group. (Graphic Universe™).

—The Red Ruby. Jakobsen, Lars, illus. 2013. (Mortensen's Escapades Ser.: 3). (ENG., Illus.). 48p. (gr. 6-12). pap. 6.95 *(978-1-4677-0729-9(5),* Graphic Universe™) Lerner Publishing Group.

—The Santa Fe Jail. Jakobsen, Lars, illus. 2012. (Mortensen's Escapades Ser.: 2). (ENG., Illus.). 48p. (gr. 6-12). pap. 6.95 *(978-0-8225-9421-5(8))*; lib. bdg. 27.93 *(978-0-7613-7886-0(3))* Lerner Publishing Group. (Graphic Universe™).

—The Secret Mummy. Jakobsen, Lars, illus. 2013. (Mortensen's Escapades Ser.: 4). (ENG., Illus.). 48p. (gr. 6-12). pap. 6.95 *(978-1-4677-0730-5(9))*; lib. bdg. 27.93 *(978-0-7613-7915-7(0))* Lerner Publishing Group. (Graphic Universe™).

Jakobsen, Lars & Chapman, Robyn. The Red Ruby. Jakobsen, Lars, illus. 2013. (Mortensen's Escapades Ser.: 3). (ENG., Illus.). 48p. (gr. 6-12). lib. bdg. 27.93 *(978-0-7613-7914-0(2),* Graphic Universe™) Lerner Publishing Group.

Jamieson, Victoria. The Great Pet Escape. Jamieson, Victoria, illus. 2016. (Pets on the Loose! Ser.). (ENG.). 64p. (J). 15.99 *(978-1-62779-105-2(1),* 9781627791052, Holt, Henry & Co. Bks. For Young Readers) Holt, Henry & Co.

Jamiol, Paul. Bikers Are Animals: A Children's Book on Motorcycling. Habib, Linda, ed. 2009. 38p. pap. 14.95 *(978-1-60844-232-4(2))* Dog Ear Publishing, LLC.

Janry, illus. Spirou & Fantasio - Valley of the Exiles. 2013. (Spirou & Fantasio Ser.: 4). Orig. Title: Vol. 4. (ENG.). 48p. pap. 11.95 *(978-1-84918-157-0(8))* CineBook GBR. Dist: National Bk. Network.

Janry, Tome, illus. Spirou & Fantasio in Moscow, Vol. 6. 2014. (Spirou & Fantasio Ser.: 6). (ENG.). 48p. pap. 11.95 *(978-1-84918-193-8(4))* CineBook GBR. Dist: National Bk. Network.

Jansson, Tove. Club Life in Moominvalley. 2016. (Moomin Ser.). (ENG., Illus.). 40p. pap. 9.95 *(978-1-77046-243-4(0),* 9781770462434) Drawn & Quarterly Pubns. CAN. Dist: Macmillan.

—Moomin & the Golden Tail. 2014. (Moomin Ser.). (ENG., Illus.). 56p. (J). (gr. 4-7). pap. 9.95 *(978-1-77046-133-8(7),* 9781770461338) Drawn & Quarterly Pubns. CAN. Dist: Macmillan.

—Moomin & the Martians. 2015. (Moomin Ser.). (ENG., Illus.). 56p. (J). (gr. -1-5). pap. 9.95 *(978-1-77046-203-8(1),* 9781770462038) Drawn & Quarterly Pubns. CAN. Dist: Macmillan.

—Moomin & the Sea. 2013. (Moomin Ser.). (ENG., Illus.). 56p. (J). (gr. 4-7). pap. 9.95 *(978-1-77046-123-9(X),* 9781770461239) Drawn & Quarterly Pubns. CAN. Dist: Macmillan.

—Moomin Begins a New Life. 2017. (Moomin Ser.). (ENG., Illus.). 40p. pap. 9.95 *(978-1-77046-271-7(6),* 9781770462717) Drawn & Quarterly Pubns. CAN. Dist: Macmillan.

—Moomin Builds a House. 2013. (Moomin Ser.). (ENG., Illus.). 48p. (J). (gr. 4-7). pap. 9.95 *(978-1-77046-108-6(6),* 9781770461086) Drawn & Quarterly Pubns. CAN. Dist: Macmillan.

—Moomin Falls in Love. 2013. (Moomin Ser.). (ENG., Illus.). 48p. (J). (gr. 4-7). pap. 9.95 *(978-1-77046-107-9(8),* 9781770461079) Drawn & Quarterly Pubns. CAN. Dist: Macmillan.

—Moomin on the Riviera. 2014. (ENG., Illus.). 48p. (J). pap. 9.95 *(978-1-77046-169-7(8),* 9781770461697) Drawn & Quarterly Pubns. CAN. Dist: Macmillan.

—Moominmamma's Maid. 2015. (Moomin Ser.). (ENG., Illus.). 48p. (J). pap. 9.95 *(978-1-77046-216-8(3),* 9781770462168) Drawn & Quarterly Pubns. CAN. Dist: Macmillan.

—Moomin's Desert Island. 2014. (Moomin Ser.). (ENG., Illus.). 48p. (J). (gr. 4-7). pap. 9.95 *(978-1-77046-134-5(5),* 9781770461345) Drawn & Quarterly Pubns. CAN. Dist: Macmillan.

—Moomin's Winter Follies. 2012. (Moomin Ser.). (ENG., Illus.). 48p. (J). (gr. 4-7). pap. 9.95 *(978-1-77046-098-0(5),* 9781770460980) Drawn & Quarterly Pubns. CAN. Dist: Macmillan.

—Moominvalley Turns Jungle. 2012. (Moomin Ser.). (ENG., Illus.). 48p. (J). (gr. 4-7). pap. 9.95 *(978-1-77046-097-3(7),* 9781770460973) Drawn & Quarterly Pubns. CAN. Dist: Macmillan.

Jarvis, James & Waterman, Russell. Vortigern's Machine: And the Great Sage of Wisdom. Jarvis, James, illus. 2006. (Illus.). 48p. per. 24.00 *(978-3-89955-098-6(6))* Die Gestalten Verlag DEU. Dist: Prestel Publishing.

Jeanne, DuPrau. The City of Ember. 2014. (Books of Ember Ser. Bk. 1 Ser.). (ENG.). 288p. (J). (gr. 12-12). 11.24 *(978-1-63245-182-8(4))* Lectorum Pubns., Inc.

Jeanty, Georges, et al. The Core, Vol. 5. Allie, Scott & Hahn, Sierra, eds. 2014. (ENG., Illus.). 168p. pap. 17.99 *(978-1-61655-254-1(9))* Dark Horse Comics.

Jeeva Raghunath & Nayar, Deeya. Malli. Nancy Raj, illus. 2005. (HIN & ENG.). 16p. (J). *(978-81-8146-089-9(8))* Tulika Pubs.

Jeffrey, Gary. African Myths. 2009. (Graphic Mythology Ser.). (ENG.). 48p. (YA). (gr. 4-5). 58.50 *(978-1-61512-976-8(6),* Rosen Reference) Rosen Publishing Group, Inc., The.

—Autopsies: Pathologists at Work. Riley, Terry, illus. 2008. (Graphic Forensic Science Ser.). (ENG.). 48p. (gr. 5-8). per. 14.05 *(978-1-4042-1447-7(X))*; (YA). lib. bdg. 31.95 *(978-1-4042-1446-0(1))* Rosen Publishing Group, Inc., The.

—Battle for the Atlantic. 2012. (ENG., Illus.). 48p. (J). *(978-0-7787-4192-3(3))*; pap. *(978-0-7787-4199-2(0))* Crabtree Publishing Co.

—The Black Death. 2014. (ENG., Illus.). 48p. (J). *(978-0-7787-0400-3(9))*; pap. *(978-0-7787-0406-5(8))* Crabtree Publishing Co.

—Castles. 2014. (ENG., Illus.). 48p. (J). *(978-0-7787-0396-9(7))* Crabtree Publishing Co.

—The Dark Ages & the Vikings. 2014. (ENG., Illus.). 48p. (J). *(978-0-7787-0401-0(7))* Crabtree Publishing Co.

—The Eastern Front. 2012. (ENG., Illus.). 48p. (J). *(978-0-7787-4194-7(X))*; pap. *(978-0-7787-4201-2(6))* Crabtree Publishing Co.

—Gallipoli & the Southern Theaters. 2013. (ENG., Illus.). 48p. (J). pap. *(978-0-7787-0917-6(5))* Crabtree Publishing Co.

—Julius Caesar: The Life of a Roman General. 2009. (Graphic Nonfiction Biographies Ser.). (ENG.). 48p. (YA). (gr. 4-5). 58.50 *(978-1-61513-020-7(9),* Rosen Reference) Rosen Publishing Group, Inc., The.

—Knights. 2014. (ENG., Illus.). 48p. (J). *(978-0-7787-0398-3(3))*; pap. *(978-0-7787-0404-1(1))* Crabtree Publishing Co.

—Lawrence of Arabia & the Middle East & Africa. 2013. (ENG., Illus.). 48p. (J). *(978-0-7787-0912-1(4))*; pap. *(978-0-7787-0918-3(3))* Crabtree Publishing Co.

—Malcolm X & the Fight for African American Unity. 2012. (Graphic History of the Civil Rights Movement Ser.). (Illus.). 24p. (J). (gr. 3-8). pap. 8.15 *(978-1-4339-7488-5(6))*; lib. bdg. 23.95 *(978-1-4339-7487-8(8))* Stevens, Gareth Publishing LLLP.

—North Africa & the Mediterranean. 2012. (ENG., Illus.). 48p. (J). *(978-0-7787-4193-0(1))*; pap. *(978-0-7787-4200-5(8))* Crabtree Publishing Co.

—On the Eastern Front. 2013. (ENG., Illus.). 48p. (J). *(978-0-7787-0910-7(8))*; pap. *(978-0-7787-0916-9(7))* Crabtree Publishing Co.

—On the Western Front. 2013. (ENG., Illus.). 48p. (J). *(978-0-7787-0909-1(4))*; pap. *(978-0-7787-0915-2(9))* Crabtree Publishing Co.

—The Oregon Trail. Poluzzi, Allesandro, illus. 2012. (Graphic History of the American West Ser.). (ENG.). 24p. (J). (gr. 3-8). pap. 8.15 *(978-1-4339-6745-0(6),* Gareth Stevens Learning Library); (gr. 4-7). lib. bdg. 23.95 *(978-1-4339-6743-6(X))* Stevens, Gareth Publishing LLLP.

—The Pony Express. Riley, Terry, illus. 2012. (Graphic History of the American West Ser.). (ENG.). 24p. (J). (gr. 3-8). pap. 8.15 *(978-1-4339-6749-8(9),* Gareth Stevens Learning Library); (gr. 4-7). lib. bdg. 23.95 *(978-1-4339-6747-4(2))* Stevens, Gareth Publishing LLLP.

—Rebellion & Revolt. 2014. (ENG., Illus.). 48p. (J). *(978-0-7787-0399-0(1))* Crabtree Publishing Co.

—The Secret War. 2012. (ENG., Illus.). 48p. (J). *(978-0-7787-4195-4(8))*; pap. *(978-0-7787-4202-9(4))* Crabtree Publishing Co.

—Solving Crimes with Trace Evidence. Richardson, Peter, illus. 2008. (Graphic Forensic Science Ser.). (ENG.). 48p. (gr. 5-8). per. 14.05 *(978-1-4042-1432-3(1))*; (YA). lib. bdg. 31.95 *(978-1-4042-1431-6(3))* Rosen Publishing Group, Inc., The.

—The Soviet War in Afghanistan. Spender, Nik, illus. 2013. (ENG.). 48p. (J). *(978-0-7787-1235-0(4))*; pap. *(978-0-7787-1239-8(7))* Crabtree Publishing Co.

—War at Sea. 2013. (ENG., Illus.). 48p. (J). *(978-0-7787-0913-8(2))*; pap. *(978-0-7787-0923-7(X))* Crabtree Publishing Co.

—War in the Air. 2013. (ENG., Illus.). 48p. (J). *(978-0-7787-0914-5(0))*; pap. *(978-0-7787-0924-4(8))* Crabtree Publishing Co.

—War in the Pacific. 2012. (ENG., Illus.). 48p. (J). *(978-0-7787-4197-8(4))*; pap. *(978-0-7787-4204-3(0))* Crabtree Publishing Co.

—Werewolves: Stories of Deadly Shapeshifters. 2011. (Graphic Tales of the Supernatural Ser.). (Illus.). 48p. (YA). pap. 14.05 *(978-1-4488-1911-9(3))*; lib. bdg. 31.95 *(978-1-4488-1901-0(6))* Rosen Publishing Group, Inc., The. (Rosen Reference).

—The Western Front. 2012. (ENG., Illus.). 48p. (J). *(978-0-7787-4196-1(6))*; pap. *(978-0-7787-4203-6(2))* Crabtree Publishing Co.

Jeffrey, Gary & Riley, Terry, illus. The Cuban Missile Crisis. 2013. (ENG.). 48p. (J). *(978-0-7787-1233-6(8))*; pap. *(978-0-7787-1237-4(0))* Crabtree Publishing Co.

—The Korean War. 2013. (ENG.). 48p. (J). *(978-0-7787-1234-3(6))*; pap. *(978-0-7787-1238-1(9))* Crabtree Publishing Co.

Jeffrey, Gary & Spender, Nik, illus. The Vietnam War. 2013. (ENG.). 48p. (J). *(978-0-7787-1236-7(2))*; pap. *(978-0-7787-1240-4(0))* Crabtree Publishing Co.

Jenkins, Paul. Here There Be the Monsters, Vol. 3. Scott, Damion, illus. 2004. (Spider-Man Ser.). 144p. (YA). 9.99 *(978-0-7851-1333-1(9))* Marvel Worldwide, Inc.

Jensen, Jeff. X-Factor. Ranson, Arthur, illus. 2003. (X-Men Ser.: Vol. 1). 96p. (YA). pap. 9.99 *(978-0-7851-1016-3(X))* Marvel Worldwide, Inc.

Jensen, Lars, et al. Donald Duck Adventures, Vol. 18. Clark, John, ed. 2006. (ENG., Illus.). 128p. (YA). pap. 7.95 *(978-1-888472-30-1(8),* 9781888472301) Gemstone Publishing, Inc.

Jensen Shaffer, Jody. Vampires & Light, 6 vols. Gervasio, illus. 2013. (Monster Science Ser.). (ENG.). 32p. (gr. 3-4). 47.70 *(978-1-62065-821-5(6),* Graphic Library) Capstone Press of Coughlan Cos.

Jippes, Daan, et al. Donald Duck Family, Vol. 2. 2009. 64p. pap. 8.99 *(978-1-60360-099-6(X))* Gemstone Publishing, Inc.

—Walt Disney's Comics & Stories #703. 2009. 64p. pap. 7.99 *(978-1-60360-093-4(0))* Gemstone Publishing, Inc.

Job. The River of Forgetfulness. Dérib, illus. 2013. (Yakari Ser.: 10). (ENG.). 48p. pap. 11.95 *(978-1-84918-140-2(3))* CineBook GBR. Dist: National Bk. Network.

—Yakari & Nanabozo. Derib, illus. 2014. (Yakari Ser.: 11). (ENG.). 48p. pap. 11.95 *(978-1-84918-177-8(2))* CineBook GBR. Dist: National Bk. Network.

—Yakari & the Coyote. Dérib, illus. 2012. (Yakari Ser.: 9). (ENG.). 48p. (J). (gr. 1-6). pap. 11.95 *(978-1-84918-101-3(2))* CineBook GBR. Dist: National Bk. Network.

—Yakari & the Grizzly. Dérib, illus. 2007. (Yakari Ser.: 4). (ENG.). 46p. (J). (gr. 4-7). per. 9.99 *(978-1-905460-16-8(3))* CineBook GBR. Dist: National Bk. Network.

—Yakari in the Land of Wolves. 2009. (Yakari Ser.: 6). (ENG., Illus.). 46p. pap. 11.95 *(978-1-905460-29-8(5))* CineBook GBR. Dist: National Bk. Network.

Job & Dérib. Yakari & the White Fleece. 2011. (Yakari Ser.: 8). (ENG., Illus.). 48p. pap. 11.95 *(978-1-84918-055-9(5))* CineBook GBR. Dist: National Bk. Network.

Job, et al. Yakari & the Beavers. 2007. (Yakari Ser.: 3). (ENG., Illus.). 48p. (J). (gr. 4-7). per. 11.95 *(978-1-905460-09-0(0))* CineBook GBR. Dist: National Bk. Network.

Jocelyn, Marthe & Scrimger, Richard. Viminy Crowe's Comic Book. Dávila, Claudia, illus. (ENG.). 336p. (J). (gr. 4-7). 2017. pap. 9.99 *(978-1-101-91893-7(4))* 2014. 17.99 *(978-1-77049-479-4(0))* Tundra Bks. CAN. (Tundra Bks.). Dist: Penguin Random Hse. LLC.

Joffo, Joseph. A Bag of Marbles: The Graphic Novel. 2013. 128p. pap. 29.27 *(978-1-4677-1651-2(0))* Lerner Publishing Group.

—A Bag of Marbles: The Graphic Novel. Gauvin, Edward, tr. Bailly, Vincent, illus. 2013. (ENG.). 128p. (gr. 7-12). pap. 9.95 *(978-1-4677-1516-4(6))*; lib. bdg. 29.27 *(978-1-4677-0700-8(7))* Lerner Publishing Group. (Graphic Universe™).

Johnson, Alaya. The Goblin King. Gandy, Meg, illus. 2009. (Twisted Journeys (r) Ser.: 10). (ENG.). 112p. (J). (gr. 4-7). pap. 7.95 *(978-0-8225-9259-4(2))* Lerner Publishing Group.

Johnson, Alaya Dawn. Detective Frankenstein. Ota, Yuko, illus. 2011. (Twisted Journeys (r) Ser.: 17). (ENG.). 112p. (J). (gr. 4-7). pap. 7.95 *(978-0-8225-8943-3(5))*; pap. 45.32 *(978-0-7613-7613-2(5))*; lib. bdg. 27.93 *(978-0-8225-8942-6(7))* Lerner Publishing Group. (Graphic Universe™).

—The Goblin King, No. 10. Gandy, Meg & Olson, Meagan, illus. 2009. (Twisted Journeys (r) Ser.: 10). (ENG.). 112p. (J). (gr. 4-7). 27.93 *(978-0-8225-9253-2(3),* Graphic Universe™) Lerner Publishing Group.

Johnson, Gee. All I Can Be. 2015. (2G Graphic Novels Ser.). (ENG., Illus.). 36p. (J). pap. 5.99 *(978-1-63437-083-7(X))* American Reading Co.

Johnson, Lauren. Beastly Basketball, 1 vol. Garcia, Eduardo, illus. 2014. (Sports Illustrated Kids Graphic Novels Ser.). (ENG.). 72p. (gr. 2-5). lib. bdg. 26.65 *(978-1-4342-6490-9(4))* Stone Arch Bks.

Johnson, Mike. Galileo Seven Part 1, 1 vol. 2013. (Star Trek Ser.). (ENG.). 24p. (J). (gr. 6-12). lib. bdg. 24.21 *(978-1-61479-159-1(7))* Spotlight.

—Galileo Seven Part 2, 1 vol. 2013. (Star Trek Ser.). (ENG.). 24p. (J). (gr. 6-12). lib. bdg. 24.21 *(978-1-61479-160-7(0))* Spotlight.

—Star Trek. 2013. (Star Trek Ser.: 4). 24p. (J). (gr. 6-12). lib. bdg. 96.84 *(978-1-61479-158-4(9))* Spotlight.

—Where No Man Has Gone Before Part 1, 1 vol. 2013. (Star Trek Ser.). (ENG.). 24p. (J). (gr. 6-12). lib. bdg. 24.21 *(978-1-61479-161-4(9))* Spotlight.

—Where No Man Has Gone Before Part 2, 1 vol. 2013. (Star Trek Ser.). (ENG.). 24p. (J). (gr. 6-12). lib. bdg. 24.21 *(978-1-61479-162-1(7))* Spotlight.

Johnson, Mike & Parrott, Ryan. Star Trek: Starfleet Academy. Charm, Derek, illus. 2016. (Star Trek Ser.). (ENG.). 120p. (J). pap. 19.99 *(978-1-63140-663-8(9))*, 9781631406638) Idea & Design Works, LLC.

Johnson, Mike & Scott, Mairghread. Transformers Prime: Rage of the Dinobots: Rage of the Dinobots. Padilla, Agustin, illus. 2013. (Transformers Ser.). (ENG.). 104p. pap. 17.99 *(978-1-61377-606-3(3))*, 9781613776063) Idea & Design Works, LLC.

Johnson, R. Kikuo. The Shark King. Loeffler, Trade & Johnson, R. Kikuo, illus. 2012. (ENG.). 40p. (J). (gr. -1-3). 12.95 *(978-1-935179-16-0(0))* TOON Books / RAW Junior, LLC.

—The Shark King. Johnson, R. Kikuo, illus. 2013. (ENG., Illus.). 40p. (J). (gr. -1-3). pap. 4.99 *(978-1-935179-60-3(8))* TOON Books / RAW Junior, LLC.

Johnson, Regan. Hold on to Your Tail: Letters from Camp Lizard. Johnson, Regan, illus. 2008. (Letters From Camp Lizard Ser.). (ENG., Illus.). 112p. (J). (gr. 1-5). pap. 7.95 *(978-1-933831-04-6(9))* Blooming Tree Pr.

Jolley, Dan. Agent Mongoose & the Hypno-Beam Scheme. Wendt, Matt, illus. 2009. (Twisted Journeys (r) Ser.: 9). (ENG.). 112p. (J). (gr. 4-7). 27.93 *(978-0-8225-6203-0(0))*; pap. 7.95 *(978-0-8225-6204-7(9))* Lerner Publishing Group.

—Alien Adventure on Planet J. Wendt, Matt, illus. 2008. (Twisted Journeys (r) Ser.: 8). (ENG.). 112p. (J). (gr. 4-7). 27.93 *(978-0-8225-6998-5(1))*, Graphic Universe™) Lerner Publishing Group.

—Alien Incident on Planet J. Wendt, Matt, illus. 2008. (Twisted Journeys (r) Ser.: 8). (ENG.). 112p. (J). (gr. 4-7). pap. 7.95 *(978-0-8225-8876-4(5))* Lerner Publishing Group.

—Attack of the Mutant Meteors. Witt, David, illus. 2010. (Twisted Journeys (r) Ser.: 14). (ENG.). 112p. (J). (gr. 4-7). pap. 7.95 *(978-0-8225-9255-6(X))*, Graphic Universe™); lib. bdg. 27.93 *(978-0-8225-9249-5(5))* Lerner Publishing Group.

—Escape from Pyramid X. Wendt, Matt, illus. 2007. (Twisted Journeys (r) Ser.: 2). (ENG.). (J). (gr. 4-7). pap. 45.32 *(978-0-8225-9466-6(8))*; 112p. lib. bdg. 27.93 *(978-0-8225-6777-6(6))*, Graphic Universe™); 112p. per. 7.95 *(978-0-8225-6779-0(2))* Lerner Publishing Group.

—Guan Yu: Blood Brothers to the End [A Chinese Legend]. Randall, Ron, illus. 2009. (Graphic Myths & Legends Ser.). (ENG.). 48p. (gr. 4-8). pap. 8.95 *(978-1-58013-890-1(X))* Lerner Publishing Group.

—The Hero Twins: Against the Lords of Death [A Mayan Myth]. Witt, David, illus. 2009. (Graphic Myths & Legends Ser.). (ENG.). 48p. (gr. 4-8). pap. 8.95 *(978-1-58013-892-5(6))* Lerner Publishing Group.

—My Boyfriend Bites, 3 vols., No. 3. Martinez, Alitha E., illus. 2011. (My Boyfriend Is a Monster Ser.: 3). (ENG.). 128p. (YA). (gr. 7-12). 29.27 *(978-0-7613-5599-1(5))* Lerner Publishing Group.

—My Boyfriend Is a Monster - My Boyfriend Bites. Martinez, Alitha E., illus. 2011. (My Boyfriend Is a Monster Ser.: 3). (ENG.). 128p. (YA). (gr. 7-12). pap. 9.95 *(978-0-7613-7078-9(1))*, Graphic Universe™) Lerner Publishing Group.

—Odysseus: Escaping Poseidon's Curse. Yeates, Thomas, illus. 2008. (Graphic Myths & Legends Ser.). (ENG.). 48p. (gr. 4-8). pap. 8.95 *(978-0-8225-8515-2(4))* Lerner Publishing Group.

—Odysseus: Escaping Poseidon's Curse [a Greek Legend]. Yeates, Thomas, illus. 2015. (Graphic Myths & Legends Ser.). (ENG.). 48p. (gr. 4-8). 21.32 *(978-1-4677-5983-0(X))*, Lerner Digital) Lerner Publishing Group.

—Pigling: A Cinderella Story [A Korean Tale]. Timmons, Anne, illus. 2009. (Graphic Myths & Legends Ser.). (ENG.). 48p. (gr. 4-8). pap. 8.95 *(978-1-58013-825-3(X))* Lerner Publishing Group.

—Shipwrecked on Mad Island, No. 11. Huddleston, Courtney, illus. 2009. (Twisted Journeys (r) Ser.: 11). (ENG.). 112p. (J). (gr. 4-7). 27.93 *(978-0-8225-7911-3(1))*, Graphic Universe™) Lerner Publishing Group.

—The Time Travel Trap. Wendt, Matt, illus. 2008. (Twisted Journeys (r) Ser.: 6). (ENG.). 112p. (J). (gr. 4-7). per. 7.95 *(978-0-8225-8874-0(9))* Lerner Publishing Group.

—Vampire Hunt. Titus, Gregory, illus. 2008. (Twisted Journeys (r) Ser.: 7). (ENG.). 112p. (J). (gr. 4-7). 27.93 *(978-0-8225-8877-1(3))*, Graphic Universe™); pap. 7.95 *(978-0-8225-8879-5(X))* Lerner Publishing Group.

—Wrapped up in You. Nourigat, Natalie, illus. 2012. (My Boyfriend Is a Monster Ser.: 6). (ENG.). 128p. (YA). (gr. 7-12). pap. 9.95 *(978-0-8225-9425-3(0))*; lib. bdg. 29.27 *(978-0-7613-6856-4(6))* Lerner Publishing Group. (Graphic Universe™).

Jolley, Dan & Croall, Marie P. Agent Mongoose & the Attack of the Giant Insects. Wendt, Matt, illus. 2010. (Twisted Journeys (r) Ser.: 15). (ENG.). 112p. (J). (gr. 4-7). pap. 7.95 *(978-0-8225-9257-0(6))*, Graphic Universe™) Lerner Publishing Group.

Jolley, Dan & Nelson, O. T. The Girl Who Owned a City: The Graphic Novel. Jones, Joëlle, illus. 2012. (Single Titles Ser.). (ENG.). 128p. (YA). (gr. 5-12). pap. *(978-0-7613-5634-9(7))*, Graphic Universe™) Lerner Publishing Group.

Jones, Blake. Kevin the ninja kid Collection 1. 2010. 56p. pap. 12.70 *(978-0-557-49076-9(6))* Lulu Pr., Inc.

Jones, Bruce & Austen, Chuck. The Call of Duty Vol. 2: The Precinct, 2 vols. Mandrake, Tom & Zezelj, Danijel, illus. 2003. (Call Ser.). 128p. (YA). pap. 9.99 *(978-0-7851-0974-7(9))* Marvel Worldwide, Inc.

Jones, Carl L. Aaron Burrd, the Paranoid Bird with Acute Acrophobi. Vicki, Jones, ed. 2008. 88p. pap. 16.00 *(978-0-9748266-2-2(6))* Grampa Jones's Publishing Co.

Jones, Christianne C. Bella's Boat Surprise, 1 vol. Sullivan, Mary, illus. 2010. (My First Graphic Novel Ser.). (ENG.). 32p. (gr. k-2). pap. 6.25 *(978-1-4342-2287-9(X))*, My First Graphic Novel) Stone Arch Bks.

—Morning Mystery, 1 vol. Simard, Remy, illus. 2010. (My First Graphic Novel Ser.). (ENG.). 32p. (gr. k-2). lib. bdg. 24.65 *(978-1-4342-1890-2(2))*, My First Graphic Novel) Stone Arch Bks.

—Rah-Rah Ruby!, 1 vol. Doerrfeld, Cori, illus. 2009. (My First Graphic Novel Ser.). (ENG.). 32p. (gr. k-2). pap. 6.25 *(978-1-4342-1412-6(5))*, My First Graphic Novel) Stone Arch Bks.

Jones, James Lucas & Torres, J., eds. Yo Gabba Gabba: Comic Book Time. 2011. (Illus.). 128p. (J). 24.99 *(978-1-934964-49-1(2))* Oni Pr., Inc.

Jones, Kip. The Power of a Positive No: Willie Bohanon & Friends Learn the Power of Resisting Peer Pressure. Isely, Chad, illus. 2016. (Urban Character Education Ser.: Vol. 4). (ENG.). 32p. (J). pap. 10.95 *(978-1-944882-06-8(5))* Boys Town Pr.

—The Power of an Attitude of Gratitude: Willie Bohanon & Friends Learn the Power of Showing Appreciation. Isely, Chad, illus. 2016. (Urban Character Education Ser.: Vol. 3). (ENG.). 40p. (J). pap. 10.95 *(978-1-934490-92-1(X))* Boys Town Pr.

—The Power of Self-D: Willie Bohanon & Friends Learn the Power of Self-Determination. Isely, Chad, illus. 2014. (ENG.). 32p. (J). pap. 10.95 *(978-1-934490-66-2(0))* Boys Town Pr.

Joyce, Sandie May. Aunt Sandie Goes to School - the Comics. 2008. 55p. pap. 22.50 *(978-0-557-02295-3(9))* Lulu Pr., Inc.

Jozev. Claws of Darkness. 2006. (Journal of the Vampire Hunter; Claws of Darkness Ser.). (ENG., Illus.). 64p. (YA). pap. 5.95 *(978-1-59796-090-8(X))* DrMaster Pubns. Inc.

—Journal of the Vampire Hunter Vol. 3: Claws of Darkness. Zhao, Yun, tr. 2006. (Journal of the Vampire Hunter; Claws of Darkness Ser.). (ENG., Illus.). 64p. (YA). pap. 5.95 *(978-1-59796-088-5(8))* DrMaster Pubns. Inc.

—Journal of the Vampire Hunter Vol. 4: Claws of Darkness. 2006. (Journal of the Vampire Hunter; Claws of Darkness Ser.). (ENG., Illus.). 64p. (YA). pap. 5.95 *(978-1-59796-089-2(6))* DrMaster Pubns. Inc.

Jr. Graphic Ghost Stories. 2014. (Jr. Graphic Ghost Stories Ser.). 24p. (J). (gr. 3-6). pap. 381.60 *(978-1-4777-7209-6(X))*, PowerKids Pr.) Rosen Publishing Group, Inc., The.

Jurgens, Dan. Brave New Worlds. 2016. (Batman Beyond Ser.: 1). lib. bdg. 26.95 *(978-0-606-38627-2(0))* Turtleback Bks.

Jurgens, Dan, et al. Thor Vol. 3: Gods on Earth, 3 vols. Raney, Tom & Bennett, Davis, illus. 2003. (Thor Ser.). 248p. (YA). pap. 21.99 *(978-0-7851-1126-9(3))* Marvel Worldwide, Inc.

Kaczmarczyk, Kyle J. The Misadventures of Silent Boy - Volume II: the Stupid Strikes Back. 2005. 52p. (YA). pap. 17.99 *(978-1-4116-5231-6(2))* Lulu Pr., Inc.

Kaishaku. Eternal Alice Rondo, Vol. 4. 2007. (ENG., Illus.). 192p. pap. 9.95 *(978-1-59796-123-3(X))* DrMaster Pubns. Inc.

Kakinouchi, Narumi. My Codename Is Charmer, Vol. 3. 208p. pap. 12.95 *(978-1-932575-08-8(1))* International Comics & Entertainment L.L.C.

Kalman, Bobbie & Jeffrey, Gary. Gallipoli & the Southern Theaters. 2013. (ENG.). 48p. (J). *(978-0-7787-0911-4(6))* Crabtree Publishing Co.

Kamata, Suzanne. Gadget Girl: The Art of Being Invisible. 2013. (ENG., Illus.). 256p. (YA). pap. 14.95 *(978-1-936846-38-2(1))* GemmaMedia.

Kamimura, Gin, illus. Pokemon the Movie: Hoopa & the Clash of Ages, Vol. 1. 2016. (ENG.). 192p. (J). pap. 9.99 *(978-1-4215-8782-0(3))* Viz Media.

Kaminsky, Stuart M. Fever Pitch. 2003. (ENG., Illus.). 48p. (gr. 11-18). pap. 6.95 *(978-0-9710129-9-8(7))*, 9780971012998) Moonstone.

Kamio, Yoko. Boys over Flowers, Vol. 15. 2005. (Boys over Flowers Ser.). (ENG., Illus.). 192p. pap. 9.99 *(978-1-4215-0136-9(8))* Viz Media.

—Boys over Flowers, Vol. 18. Kamio, Yoko, illus. 2006. (Boys over Flowers Ser.). (ENG., Illus.). 208p. pap. 9.99 *(978-1-4215-0532-9(0))* Viz Media.

—Boys over Flowers, Vol. 11. Kamio, Yoko, illus. 2005. (ENG., Illus.). 184p. (YA). pap. 9.99 *(978-1-59116-747-1(7))* Viz Media.

Kanata, Konami. Chi's Sweet Home, Vol. 11. 2014. (Chi's Sweet Home Ser.). (ENG., Illus.). 152p. (gr. k-12). pap. 13.95 *(978-1-939130-51-8(4))*, Vertical) Vertical, Inc.

—Chi's Sweet Home, Volume 12. 2015. (Chi's Sweet Home Ser.). (ENG., Illus.). 176p. (J). (gr. 2-5). pap. 13.95 *(978-1-941220-25-2(8))*, Vertical) Kodansha America, Inc.

Kane, Bob. Comic con & Labor Day. Nguyen, Dustin, illus. 2015. (Batman: Li'l Gotham Ser.). (ENG.). 32p. (gr. 2-3). lib. bdg. 22.60 *(978-1-4342-9736-5(5))* Stone Arch Bks.

—Month of Waters & Independence Day. Nguyen, Dustin, illus. 2015. (Batman: Li'l Gotham Ser.). (ENG.). 32p. (gr. 2-3). lib. bdg. 22.60 *(978-1-4342-9666-5(0))* Stone Arch Bks.

—Sandwich Day & Our Family Album. Nguyen, Dustin, illus. 2015. (Batman: Li'l Gotham Ser.). (ENG.). 32p. (gr. 2-3). lib. bdg. 22.60 *(978-1-4342-9737-2(3))* Stone Arch Bks.

—Tropical Getaway & Bird Watching. Nguyen, Dustin, illus. 2015. (Batman: Li'l Gotham Ser.). (ENG.). 32p. (gr. 2-3). lib. bdg. 22.60 *(978-1-4342-9735-8(7))* Stone Arch Bks.

Kane, Gil, et al, illus. Thor Epic Collection: A Kingdom Lost. 2014. (ENG.). 480p. (J). (gr. 4-17). pap. 34.99 *(978-0-7851-8862-9(2))* Marvel Worldwide, Inc.

Kaneyoshi, Izumi. Doubt!!, Vol. 4. Kaneyoshi, Izumi, illus. 2005. (Doubt Ser.: 4). (ENG., Illus.). 192p. pap. 9.99 *(978-1-59116-984-0(4))* Viz Media.

Kanietzko, Bryan & DiMartino, Michael Dante. Avatar. 2007. (Illus.). 96p. pap. 7.99 *(978-1-59816-928-7(9))*, Tokyopop Kids) TOKYOPOP, Inc.

Kaplan, Arie. The New Kid from Planet Glorf, 1 vol. Bradley, Jessica, illus. 2013. (Comics Land Ser.). (ENG.). 32p. (gr. k-2). 7.95 *(978-1-4342-4272-3(2))*; lib. bdg. 25.32 *(978-1-4342-4032-3(0))* Stone Arch Bks.

Kardy, Glenn. Kanji de Manga Vol. 1: The Comic Book That Teaches You How to Read & Write Japanese!, 33 vols. 2005. (JPN & ENG., Illus.). 144p. (YA). pap. 9.99 *(978-4-921205-02-7(7))*, 9784921205027) Japanime Co., Ltd. JPN. Dist: Diamond Comic Distributors, Inc.

—Kanji de Manga Volume 2: the Comic Book That Teaches You How to Read & Write Japanese! Vol. 2: The Comic Book That Teaches You How to Read & Write Japanese!, 33 vols. 2005. (JPN & ENG., Illus.). 112p. (YA). pap. 9.99 *(978-4-921205-03-4(5))*, 9784921205034) Japanime Co., Ltd. JPN. Dist: Diamond Comic Distributors, Inc.

—Kanji de Manga Volume 3: the Comic Book That Teaches You How to Read & Write Japanese! The Comic Book That Teaches You How to Read & Write Japanese!, Vol. 3. 2005. (JPN & ENG., Illus.). 112p. (YA). pap. 9.99 *(978-4-921205-04-1(3))*, 9784921205041) Japanime Co., Ltd. JPN. Dist: Diamond Comic Distributors, Inc.

Kariya, Tetsu. Oishinbo: Izakaya — Pub Food, Vol. 7. Hanasaki, Akira, illus. 2010. (ENG.). 276p. pap. 12.99 *(978-1-4215-2145-9(8))* Viz Media.

Katayama, Kyoichi. Yami No Matsuei. Kazui, Kazumi, illus. 2005. (Socrates in Love Ser.: Vol. 1). (ENG.). 192p. pap. 8.99 *(978-1-4215-0199-4(6))* Viz Media.

Katschke, Judy. Phonics Comics. Baumann, Marty, illus. 2006. (ENG.). 24p. (J). (gr. 1-17). per. 3.99 *(978-1-58476-411-3(2))*, IKIDS) Innovative Kids.

—Teeny Genie. Jennings, C. S., illus. 2009. (ENG.). 24p. (J). (gr. 1-17). pap. 3.99 *(978-1-58476-813-5(4))* Innovative Kids.

Kawahara, Kazune. High School Debut (3-in-1 Edition), Vol. 1. 3rd ed. 2014. (ENG., Illus.). 544p. pap. 14.99 *(978-1-4215-6588-0(9))* Viz Media.

Kawahara, Yumiko. Dolls, 1. Kawahara, Yumiko, illus. 2004. (Dolls Ser.: 1). (ENG., Illus.). 200p. pap. 9.99 *(978-1-59116-508-8(3))* Viz Media.

Kawamoto, Kemon, illus. Pokémon the Movie: Volcanion & the Mechanical Marvel. 2017. (Pokemon Ser.). (ENG.). 200p. (J). pap. 9.99 ***(978-1-4215-9419-4(6))*** Viz Media.

Kawashita, Mizuki. Ichigo 100% (JPN., Illus.). (YA). Vol. 1. 191p. pap. *(978-4-08-873304-3(5))* Vol. 2. 188p. pap. *(978-4-08-873326-5(6))* Vol. 3. 182p. pap. *(978-4-08-873369-2(X))* Vol. 4. 190p. pap. *(978-4-08-873412-5(2))* Vol. 5. 187p. pap. *(978-4-08-873438-5(6))* Vol. 6. 186p. pap. *(978-4-08-873496-5(3))* Vol. 8. 185p. pap. *(978-4-08-873537-5(4))* Vol. 9. 180p. pap. *(978-4-08-873577-1(3))* Vol. 10. 189p. pap. *(978-4-08-873597-9(8))* Vol. 11. 186p. pap. *(978-4-08-873629-7(X))* Vol. 12. 190p. pap. *(978-4-08-873650-1(8))* Vol. 13. 190p. pap. *(978-4-08-873669-3(9))* Shuei-Sha.

Kayser, Eric. Champion: Graphic Novel Series. 3rd ed. 2007. (YA). 2.95 *(978-0-9785605-2-2(3))* Oasis Studios Inc.

Kayser, Eric, creator. Champion: Graphic Novel Series, 1st vol., 10bks. (Illus.). (YA). 2006. 32p. 2.95 *(978-0-9785605-0-8(7))* abr. ed. 2007. 28p. 2.95 *(978-0-9785605-3-9(1))* 2nd abr. ed. 2007. 28p. 2.95 *(978-0-9785605-1-5(5))* Vol. 1. 5th ed. 2007. (ENG.). 28p. 2.95 *(978-0-9785605-4-6(X))* Oasis Studios Inc.

Kearby, Mike. The Trail Drives, No. 2. White, Mack, illus. 2015. (Texas Tales Illustrated Ser.). (ENG.). 24p. pap. 5.95 *(978-0-87565-608-3(0))* Texas Christian Univ. Pr.

Keatinge, Joe. Hell Yeah! Volume 1: Last Days on Earth TP: Last Days on Earth TP. 2012. (ENG., Illus.). 128p. (YA). pap. 9.99 *(978-1-60706-607-1(6))*, 9781607066071) Image Comics.

Keeling, Evan. CrumbSnatchers. 2008. 60p. (J). per. 5.95 *(978-0-9796902-4-2(2))* Silent Devil Productions.

Keenan, Sheila. Dogs of War. Fox, Nathan, illus. 2013. (ENG.). 176p. (J). (gr. 3-7). pap. 12.99 *(978-0-545-12888-9(9))*, Graphix) Scholastic, Inc.

Keenan, Sheila & Stine, R. L. Scary Summer. Haspiel, Dean et al, illus. 2007. (Goosebumps Graphix Ser.: 3). (ENG.). 144p. (J). (gr. 3-7). pap. 9.99 *(978-0-439-85782-6(1))* Scholastic, Inc.

Keil, Melissa. The Incredible Adventures of Cinnamon Girl, 1 vol. Lawrence, Mike, illus. 2016. (ENG.). 300p. (YA). (gr. 7-10). 17.95 *(978-1-56145-905-6(4))* Peachtree Pubs.

Kelly, Joe, et al. Justice League Elite, Vol. 1. rev. ed. 2005. (ENG., Illus.). 208p. (YA). pap. 19.99 *(978-1-4012-0481-5(3))* DC Comics.

—Megamind Movie Prequel. 2010. (ENG., Illus.). 52p. (J). pap. 6.95 *(978-1-934944-94-3(7))*, 9781934944943) Ape Entertainment.

Kelly, Mij. A Bed of Your Own. McQuillan, Mary, illus. 2011. 32p. (J). (gr. -1-1). pap. 8.99 *(978-0-7641-4768-5(4))* Barron's Educational Series, Inc.

Kelly, Neil & Dorling Kindersley Publishing Staff. Glow in the Dark - Marvel Heroes. 2006. (Ultimate Sticker Bks.). (ENG., Illus.). 16p. (J). (gr. 1-3). pap. 6.99 *(978-0-7566-2002-8(3))*, DK Children) Dorling Kindersley Publishing, Inc.

Kelman, Ari & Fetter-Vorm, Jonathan. Battle Lines: A Graphic History of the Civil War. Fetter-Vorm, Jonathan, illus. 2015. (ENG., Illus.). 224p. 26.00 *(978-0-8090-9474-5(6))*, 9780809094745, Hill & Wang) Farrar, Straus & Giroux.

Kennedy, Mike. Thrill of the Hunt. 2004. (ENG., Illus.). 96p. pap. 6.95 *(978-1-59307-257-5(0))* Dark Horse Comics.

Kenny, Michael Daedalus. Little Miss Sunshine in: Here Comes the Sun!, Vol. 2. 2012. (ENG.). 80p. (J). pap. 6.99 *(978-1-4215-4071-9(1))* Viz Media.

—Mr. Strong: Good Thing I Came Along, Vol. 1. Corbera, Gabriel, illus. 2013. (ENG.). 80p. (J). pap. 6.99 *(978-1-4215-4073-3(8))* Viz Media.

Kerns, Ann. I Date Dead People. Gorman, Mike & Görrissen, Janina, illus. 2012. (My Boyfriend Is a Monster Ser.: 5). (ENG.). 128p. (YA). (gr. 7-12). pap. 9.95 *(978-0-7613-8549-3(5))*, Graphic Universe™) Lerner Publishing Group.

—I Date Dead People. Görrissen, Janina, illus. 2012. (My Boyfriend Is a Monster Ser.: 5). (ENG.). 128p. (YA). (gr. 7-12). lib. bdg. 29.27 *(978-0-7613-6007-0(7))* Lerner Publishing Group.

Kesel, Barbara. Fluttershy, 1 vol. Fleecs, Tony, illus. 2015. (ENG.). 24p. (J). *(978-1-61479-332-8(8))* Spotlight.

—Radiant, Vol. 2. Perez, George et al, illus. 2004. (Solus Ser.: Vol. 2). 160p. (YA). pap. 15.95 *(978-1-59314-057-1(6))* CrossGeneration Comics, Inc.

Keyser, Amber J., et al. Decoding Genes with Max Axiom, Super Scientist, 1 vol. 2010. (Graphic Science Ser.). (ENG.). 32p. (gr. 3-4). pap. 8.10 *(978-1-4296-4862-2(7))*; lib. bdg. 30.65 *(978-1-4296-3976-7(8))* Capstone Press of Coughlan Cos. (Graphic Library).

Khalili, Davood. Developing Olympian Character, 1 vol. 2010. 32p. pap. 24.95 *(978-1-4489-5281-6(6))* PublishAmerica, Inc.

Kibuishi, Kazu. Amulet, Bks. 1-7, Set. Kibuishi, Kazu, illus. 2016. (Amulet Ser.). (ENG., Illus.). 1344p. (J). (gr. 3-7). pap., pap., pap. 90.93 *(978-1-338-04564-2(4))* Scholastic, Inc.

—The Cloud Searchers. (Amulet Ser.: 3). (ENG.). 208p. (J). (gr. 3-7). 2015. 24.99 *(978-0-545-20884-0(X))* 2010. pap. 12.99 *(978-0-545-20885-7(8))* Scholastic, Inc. (Graphix).

—Copper. 2010. lib. bdg. 24.50 *(978-0-606-14274-8(6))*, Turtleback) Turtleback Bks.

—Escape from Lucien. 2015. (Amulet Ser.: 6). (ENG., Illus.). 224p. (J). (gr. 3-7). 24.99 *(978-0-545-84899-2(7))*, Graphix) Scholastic, Inc.

—The Hidden Doors. 2014. (Explorer Ser.: 3). (ENG., Illus.). 128p. (J). (gr. 4-17). 19.95 *(978-1-4197-0882-4(1))*, Amulet Bks.) Abrams, Inc.

—The Last Council. 2015. (Amulet Ser.: 4). (ENG.). 224p. (J). (gr. 3-7). 24.99 *(978-0-545-20886-4(6))*, Graphix) Scholastic, Inc.

—The Lost Islands. 2013. (Explorer Ser.). (ENG., Illus.). 128p. (J). (gr. 3-7). 19.95 *(978-1-4197-0881-7(3))*; pap. 10.95 *(978-1-4197-0883-1(X))* Abrams, Inc. (Amulet Bks.).

—The Lost Islands. 2013. (Explorer Ser.: 1). (J). lib. bdg. 22.05 *(978-0-606-33456-3(4))*, Turtleback) Turtleback Bks.

—The Mystery Boxes. 2012. (Explorer Ser.: 2). (YA). lib. bdg. 22.05 *(978-0-606-23820-5(4))*, Turtleback) Turtleback Bks.

—Prince of the Elves. 2015. (Amulet Ser.: 5). (ENG.). 208p. (J). (gr. 3-7). 24.99 *(978-0-545-20888-8(2))*, Graphix) Scholastic, Inc.

—The Stonekeeper. 2008. (Amulet Ser.: 1). (ENG., Illus.). 192p. (J). (gr. 3-7). 24.99 *(978-0-439-84680-6(3))*; pap. 12.99 *(978-0-439-84681-3(1))* Scholastic, Inc. (Graphix).

—The Stonekeeper's Curse. 2009. (Amulet Ser.: 2). (ENG., Illus.). 224p. (J). (gr. 3-7). pap. 12.99 *(978-0-439-84683-7(8))*; (gr. 4-7). 24.99 *(978-0-439-84682-0(X))* Scholastic, Inc. (Graphix).

Kibuishi, Kazu, ed. The Mystery Boxes. 2012. (Explorer Ser.). (ENG., Illus.). 128p. (gr. 4-17). pap. 10.95 *(978-1-4197-0009-5(X))*; (YA). 19.95 *(978-1-4197-0010-1(3))* Abrams, Inc. (Amulet Bks.).

Kibuishi, Kazu, illus. Firelight. 2016. 197p. (J). *(978-1-4806-9909-0(8))* Baker & Taylor, CATS.

Kidd, Ronald. Undercover Kid: The Comic Book King. Sklar, Andy, illus. 2007. (All Aboard Mystery Reader Ser.). (ENG.). 48p. (J). pap. 3.99 *(978-0-448-44438-3(0))*, Grosset & Dunlap) Penguin Publishing Group.

The Kids Guide to Pet Jokes, Rhymes & Riddles: For Kids Who Love Pets. 2006. (J). 7.95 *(978-0-9744749-3-9(2))* Crazy Pet Pr., The.

Kientz, Chris & Hockensmith, Steve. Claws & Effect. Nielsen, Lee, illus. 2016. (Secret Smithsonian Adventures Ser.: 2). (ENG.). 64p. (gr. 4-7). pap. 10.95 *(978-1-58834-567-7(X))*, Smithsonian Bks.) Smithsonian Institution Scholarly Pr.

—The Wrong Wrights. Keane, John & Nielsen, Lee, illus. 2016. (Secret Smithsonian Adventures Ser.: 1). (ENG.). 64p. (J). (gr. 4-7). pap. 10.95 *(978-1-58834-541-7(6))*, Smithsonian Bks.) Smithsonian Institution Scholarly Pr.

Kiernan, Kenny, illus. Save the Day! 2013. (J). *(978-1-4844-0146-0(8))* Scholastic, Inc.

Kim, Derek Kirk. Vanishing Point. Kim, Derek Kirk, illus. 2012. (Tune Ser.: 1). (ENG., Illus.). 160p. pap. 17.99 *(978-1-59643-516-2(X))*, 9781596435162, First Second Bks.) Roaring Brook Pr.

Kindt, Matt. Super Spy. 2007. (Super Spy Ser.). (ENG., Illus.). 304p. pap. 19.95 *(978-1-891830-96-9(1))*, 9781891830969) Top Shelf Productions.

King, Frank. Nina & Skeezix: The Problem of the Lost Ring. 2005. pap. 26.95 *(978-1-4179-9654-4(4))* Kessinger Publishing, LLC.

King, Trey. The Last Laugh! Kiernan, Kenny, illus. 2013. (LEGO DC Superheroes Ser.). (ENG.). 32p. (J). (gr. -1-3). pap. 3.99 *(978-0-545-48029-1(9))* Scholastic, Inc.

—The Legend Begins. 2013. (LEGO Legends of Chima: Comic Reader Ser.: 1). lib. bdg. 13.55 *(978-0-606-32012-2(1))*, Turtleback) Turtleback Bks.

—Save the Day! Kiernan, Kenny, illus. 2013. (LEGO DC Superheroes Ser.). (ENG.). 32p. (J). (gr. -1-3). pap. 3.99 *(978-0-545-48028-4(0))* Scholastic, Inc.

—Sidekick Showdown! Wang, Sean, illus. 2016. (LEGO DC Super Heroes Ser.). (ENG.). 24p. (J). (gr. -1-3). pap. 3.99 *(978-1-338-04742-4(6))* Scholastic, Inc.

—Sidekick Showdown! Wang, Sean, illus. 2016. (LEGO DC Super Heroes 8X8 Ser.). (ENG.). 24p. (J). (gr. -1-3). 13.55 *(978-0-606-39149-8(5))* Turtleback Bks.

—Star Wars: a Very Vader Valentine's Day. Cook, Katie, illus. 2013. (ENG.). 16p. (J). (gr. 3-7). pap. 6.99 *(978-0-545-51560-3(2))* Scholastic, Inc.

—La Vuelta Al Mundo! Wang, Sean, illus. 2016. (LEGO DC Super Heroes 8X8 Ser.). (ENG & SPA.). 24p. (J). (gr. -1-3). 13.55 *(978-0-606-39150-3(6))* Turtleback Bks.

Kinney, Jeff. Do-It-Yourself. rev. ed. 2011. (Diary of a Wimpy Kid Ser.). (ENG., Illus.). 224p. (J). (gr. 3-7). 13.95 *(978-0-8109-8995-5(6))*, Amulet Bks.) Abrams, Inc.

Kinney, Sarah & Petrucha, Stefan. Secret Sand Sleuths. 2013. (Nancy Drew & the Clue Crew Ser.). (ENG., Illus.). 64p. (J). (gr. k-3). pap. 7.99 *(978-1-59707-376-9(8))*, 9781597073769);Bk. 2. 11.99 *(978-1-59707-377-6(6))*, 9781597073776) Papercutz.

Kinney, Sarah, et al. Walt Disney's Vacation Parade, No. 3. Clark, John, ed. 2006. (ENG., Illus.). 80p. pap. 8.95 *(978-1-888472-34-9(0))*, 9781888472349) Gemstone Publishing, Inc.

Kinney, Scott. Kozmik. O'Reilly, Sean Patrick, ed. 2013. (Illus.). 78p. (J). pap. 14.95 *(978-1-927424-51-3(8))* Arcana Studio, Inc.

Kipling, Rudyard. How the Camel Got His Hump: The Graphic Novel, 1 vol. Rodriguez, Pedro, illus. 2012. (Graphic Spin Ser.). (ENG.). 40p. (gr. 1-3). pap. 5.95 *(978-1-4342-3879-5(2))*; lib. bdg. 23.99 *(978-1-4342-3202-1(6))* Stone Arch Bks. (Graphic Revolve).

—How the Elephant Got His Trunk: The Graphic Novel, 1 vol. Rodriguez, Pedro, illus. 2012. (Graphic Spin Ser.). (ENG.). 40p. (gr. 1-3). pap. 5.95 *(978-1-4342-3880-1(6))*; lib. bdg. 23.99 *(978-1-4342-3222-9(0))* Stone Arch Bks. (Graphic Revolve).

—How the Leopard Got His Spots. Rodriguez, Pedro, illus. 2012. (Graphic Spin Ser.). (ENG.). 40p. (gr. 1-3). lib. bdg. 23.99 *(978-1-4342-3223-6(9))*, Graphic Revolve) Stone Arch Bks.

—How the Rhinoceros Got His Skin: The Graphic Novel, 1 vol. Rodriguez, Pedro, illus. 2012. (Graphic Spin Ser.). (ENG.). 40p. (gr. 1-3). pap. 5.95 *(978-1-4342-3882-5(2))*, Graphic Revolve) Stone Arch Bks.

—How the Rhinoceros Got His Skin: The Graphic Novel, 1 vol. Rodriguez, Pedro, illus. 2012. (Graphic Spin Ser.). (ENG.). 40p. (gr. 1-3). lib. bdg. 23.99 *(978-1-4342-3025-6(2))*, Graphic Revolve) Stone Arch Bks.

C
D

—Just So Comics: Tales of the World's Wildest Beasts. Rodriguez, Pedro, illus. 2013. (Graphic Spin Ser.). (ENG.). 144p. (gr. 3-6). pap. 12.95 *(978-1-4342-4880-0(1))* Stone Arch Bks.

Kirby, Stan. Captain Awesome & the Missing Elephants. 2014. (Captain Awesome Ser.: 10). lib. bdg. 16.00 *(978-0-606-35440-0(9))* Turtleback Bks.

—Captain Awesome vs. Nacho Cheese Man. O'Connor, George, illus. 2012. (Captain Awesome Ser.: 2). (ENG.). 128p. (J). (gr. -1-2). 16.99 *(978-1-4424-4091-3(0))*; (gr. k-4). pap. 5.99 *(978-1-4424-3563-6(1))* Little Simon. (Little Simon).

—Captain Awesome vs. Nacho Cheese Man. 2012. (Captain Awesome Ser.: 2). lib. bdg. 16.00 *(978-0-606-26323-8(3),* Turtleback) Turtleback Bks.

Kirkham, Tyler & Kirkham, Rian. My Best Friend's a Booger. O'Reilly, Sean Patrick, ed. 2012. (Illus.). 32p. pap. 6.95 *(978-1-926914-36-7(8))* Arcana Studio, Inc.

Kirkman, Rick & Scott, Jerry. Gross! A Baby Blues Collection. 2016. (Baby Blues Ser.: 40). (ENG., Illus.). 208p. pap. 18.99 *(978-1-4494-7781-3(X))* Andrews McMeel Publishing.

Kirkman, Robert. Genesis, Vol. 1. 2009. (ENG., Illus.). 120p. pap. 14.99 *(978-1-58240-572-8(7),* 9781582405728) Image Comics.

—Masters of the Universe: He-Man's Icons of Evil. Neves, Diogenes & Walker, Cory, illus. 2004. (Masters of the Universe Ser.). 160p. (YA). pap. 9.95 *(978-1-59314-040-3(1))* CrossGeneration Comics, Inc.

—No Turning Back, Vol. 25. 2016. (Walking Dead Ser.: 25). lib. bdg. 26.95 *(978-0-606-38027-0(2))* Turtleback Bks.

—Super Dinosaur. (ENG., Illus.). Vol. 1. 2011. 128p. (J). pap. 9.99 *(978-1-60706-420-6(0),* 9781607064206) Vol. 2. 2012. 112p. pap. 12.99 *(978-1-60706-568-5(1),* 9781607065685) Vol. 3. 2013. 112p. pap. 12.99 *(978-1-60706-667-5(X),* 9781607066675) Image Comics.

—Super Dinosaur, Vol. 4. 2015. (ENG., Illus.). 128p. (YA). pap. 12.99 *(978-1-60706-843-3(5),* 9781607068433) Image Comics.

Kirshenblatt, Shane. Dorothy Gale - Journey to Oz. 2005. 64p. Vol. 2. 7.99 *(978-1-894998-89-5(8))* Vol. 3. 7.99 *(978-1-894998-90-1(1))* Lake, Jack Productions, Inc. CAN. Dist: Hushion Hse. Publishing, Ltd.

Kishimoto, Masashi. Naruto: Chapter Book, Vol. 2. Kishimoto, Masashi, illus. 2008. (ENG., Illus.). 80p. (J). (gr. 1-5). pap. 4.99 *(978-1-4215-2213-5(6))* Viz Media.

—Zatch Bell. 2004. 192p. pap. 9.95 *(978-1-59116-679-5(9))* Viz Media.

Kishimoto, Seishi. O-Parts Hunter, Vol. 3. Kishimoto, Seishi, illus. 2007. (O-Parts Hunter Ser.: 3). (ENG., Illus.). 200p. pap. 9.99 *(978-1-4215-0857-3(5))* Viz Media.

—O-Parts Hunter, Vol. 2. Kishimoto, Seishi, illus. 2007. (ENG., Illus.). 200p. pap. 9.99 *(978-1-4215-0856-6(7))* Viz Media.

Kitamura, Satoshi. Comic Adventures of Boots. Kitamura, Satoshi, illus. 2012. (ENG., Illus.). 32p. (J). (gr. k-4). pap. 10.99 *(978-1-84270-908-5(9))* Andersen Pr. GBR. Dist: Independent Pubs. Group.

Kiyuduki, Satoko. Ga - Geijutsuka Art Design Class. 2014. (GA: Geijutsuka Art Design Class Ser.: 6). (ENG., Illus.). 128p. (J). (gr. 8-17). pap. 17.00 *(978-0-316-33589-8(4),* Yen Pr.) Orbit.

—Shoulder-a-Coffin Kuro, Vol. 4. 2014. (Shoulder-A-Coffin, Kuro Ser.: 4). (ENG., Illus.). 128p. (gr. 8-17). pap. 17.00 *(978-0-316-33588-1(6),* Yen Pr.) Orbit.

Klio Burrell, Carol. Welcome to the Tribe!, 1. 2013. 48p. pap. 26.60 *(978-1-4677-1656-7(1))* Lerner Publishing Group.

Klitzner, Irene. Sean Michael K. Whistles the Wrong Way! Who, Carrie Lou, illus. 2011. 48p. (J). 18.95 *(978-0-692-01275-8(3))* Attitude Pie Publishing.

Knife, Ivan M. Uses the. Black Thursday. 2010. 108p. pap. 15.99 *(978-1-4500-6311-1(X))* Xlibris Corp.

Knisley, Lucy. Heart: Seed Snow Circuit. 2007. 20p. pap. 10.00 *(978-0-9789427-7-9(9),* Epigraph Bks.) Monkfish Bk. Publishing Co.

Knudsen, Shannon. Seed, Sprout, Fruit: An Apple Tree Life Cycle, 1 vol. Smith, Simon, illus. 2011. (First Graphics: Nature Cycles Ser.). (ENG.). 24p. (gr. 1-2). pap. 6.29 *(978-1-4296-6230-7(1))* Capstone Press of Coughlan Cos.

Koch, Falynn. Science Comics: Bats: Learning to Fly. Koch, Falynn, illus. 2017. (Science Comics Ser.). (ENG., Illus.). 128p. (J). pap. 12.99 *(978-1-62672-408-2(3),* 9781626724082, First Second Bks.) Roaring Brook Pr.

Kochalka, James. Dragon Puncher Book 1. 2010. (Dragon Puncher Ser.: 1). (ENG., Illus.). 40p. (J). (gr. 2-5). 9.95 *(978-1-60309-057-5(6),* 9781603090575) Top Shelf Productions.

—Dragon Puncher Book 2: Dragon Puncher Island: Dragon Puncher Island. 2011. (Dragon Puncher Ser.: 2). (ENG., Illus.). 40p. (J). (gr. 2-5). 9.95 *(978-1-60309-085-8(1),* 9781603090858) Top Shelf Productions.

—The Glorkian Warrior & the Mustache of Destiny. 2016. (Glorkian Warrior Ser.: 3). (ENG., Illus.). 128p. (J). pap. 14.99 *(978-1-62672-022-0(3),* 9781626720220, First Second Bks.) Roaring Brook Pr.

—The Glorkian Warrior Delivers a Pizza. Kochalka, James, illus. 2014. (Glorkian Warrior Ser.: 1). (ENG., Illus.). 112p. (J). (gr. k-4). pap. 12.99 *(978-1-59643-917-7(3),* 9781596439177, First Second Bks.) Roaring Brook Pr.

—The Happy Apples, Bk. 3. 2009. (Johnny Boo Ser.: 3). (ENG., Illus.). 40p. (J). (gr. 2-5). 9.95 *(978-1-60309-041-4(X),* 9781603090414) Top Shelf Productions.

—Johnny Boo Book 5: Johnny Boo Does Something! Johnny Boo Does Something! 2013. (Johnny Boo Ser.: 5). (ENG., Illus.). 40p. (J). (gr. 2-5). 9.95 *(978-1-60309-084-1(3),* 9781603090841) Top Shelf Productions.

—Johnny Boo Meets Dragon Puncher. 2015. (Johnny Boo Ser.). (ENG., Illus.). 40p. (J). (gr. 2-5). 9.99 *(978-1-60309-368-2(0),* 9781603093682) Top Shelf Productions.

—The Mean Little Boy. 2010. (Johnny Boo Ser.: 4). (ENG., Illus.). 40p. (J). (gr. 2-5). 9.95 *(978-1-60309-059-9(2),* 9781603090599) Top Shelf Productions.

Kokoro, Natsume & Natsume, Kokoro. Lovephobia Volume 2. 2012. (ENG., Illus.). 200p. (YA). pap. 12.95 *(978-1-56970-283-3(7),* 9781569702833) Digital Manga Publishing.

Komikwerks. 2003. (Illus.). (YA). Vol. 1. 116p. per. 9.95 *(978-0-9742803-0-1(5))* Vol. 2. per. 9.95 *(978-0-9742803-1-8(3))* Komikwerks, LLC.

Komorn, Julie & Lenhard, Elizabeth, adapted by. The Light of Meridian. 2004. (W. I. T. C. H. Ser.: Bk. 7). (Illus.). 144p. (J). lib. bdg. 16.92 *(978-1-4242-0794-7(0))* Fitzgerald Bks.

Komura, Ayumi. Mixed Vegetables, Vol. 8. Komura, Ayumi, illus. 2010. (Mixed Vegetables Ser.: 8). (ENG., Illus.). 208p. pap. 9.99 *(978-1-4215-3235-6(2))* Viz Media.

Konishi, Noriyuki. Yo-kai Watch, Vol. 1. 2015. (ENG., Illus.). 192p. (J). pap. 9.99 *(978-1-4215-8251-1(1))* Viz Media.

—Yo-kai Watch, Vol. 2. 2015. (ENG., Illus.). 192p. (J). pap. 9.99 *(978-1-4215-8252-8(X))* Viz Media.

Koontz, Robin. Hide & Seek Moon: The Moon Phases. Davidson, Chris, illus. 2011. (First Graphics: Nature Cycles Ser.). (ENG.). 24p. (gr. 1-2). pap. 35.70 *(978-1-4296-6398-4(7))* Capstone Press of Coughlan Cos.

—Water Goes Round: The Water Cycle, 1 vol. Davidson, Chris, illus. 2011. (First Graphics: Nature Cycles Ser.). (ENG.). 24p. (gr. 1-2). pap. 6.29 *(978-1-4296-6231-4(X))* Capstone Press of Coughlan Cos.

Koontz, Robin Michal. Hide & Seek Moon: The Moon Phases, 1 vol. Davidson, Chris, illus. 2010. (First Graphics: Nature Cycles Ser.). (ENG.). 24p. (gr. 1-2). 23.99 *(978-1-4296-5365-7(5))* Capstone Press of Coughlan Cos.

—Water Goes Round: The Water Cycle, 1 vol. Davidson, Chris, illus. 2010. (First Graphics: Nature Cycles Ser.). (ENG.). 24p. (gr. 1-2). lib. bdg. 23.99 *(978-1-4296-5364-0(7))* Capstone Press of Coughlan Cos.

Korhonen, Kari, et al. Uncle Scrooge #355. Clark, John, ed. Hernandez, Tino Santanach, illus. 2006. (ENG.). 64p. pap. 6.95 *(978-1-888472-24-0(3),* 9781888472240) Gemstone Publishing, Inc.

—Walt Disney's Comics & Stories #705. 2009. 64p. pap. 7.99 *(978-1-60360-095-8(7))* Gemstone Publishing, Inc.

Korte, Steve. Curse of the Stage Fright. Neely, Scott, illus. 2016. (Scooby-Doo Comic Chapter Bks.). (ENG.). 88p. (gr. 3-7). pap. 5.95 *(978-1-4965-3587-0(1))* Capstone Press of Coughlan Cos.

—DC Super-Pets Character Encyclopedia, 1 vol. Baltazar, Art, illus. 2013. (DC Super-Pets Ser.). (ENG.). 128p. (gr. 1-3). 26.60 *(978-1-4795-2030-5(6),* DC Super-Pets) Picture Window Bks.

—Wonder Woman - I Am an Amazon Warrior. Ferguson, Lee, illus. 2017. (I Can Read Level 2 Ser.). 32p. (J). (gr. -1-3). pap. 3.99 ***(978-0-06-268184-3(2))*** HarperCollins Pubs.

—Wonder Woman Movie Deluxe Junior Novel. 2017. 144p. (J). (gr. 1-5). 9.99 ***(978-0-06-268190-4(7),*** HarperFestival) HarperCollins Pubs.

—Wonder Woman Movie ICR #2. Ferguson, Lee & Roberts, Jeremy, illus. 2017. (I Can Read Level 2 Ser.). 32p. (J). (gr. -1-3). pap. 3.99 ***(978-0-06-268186-7(9))*** HarperCollins Pubs.

—Wonder Woman Movie Junior Novel. 2017. 144p. (J). (gr. 1-5). pap. 6.99 ***(978-0-06-268188-1(5),*** HarperFestival) HarperCollins Pubs.

Korte, Steve, et al. Scooby-Doo Comic Chapter Books. Neely, Scott, illus. 2016. (Scooby-Doo Comic Chapter Bks.). (ENG.). 88p. (gr. 3-7). 109.28 *(978-1-4965-3603-7(7))* Capstone Press of Coughlan Cos.

Kotecki, Jason. Stupid Swimming Lessons: Kim & Jason Annual #3. 2004. 134p. per. 13.95 *(978-0-9715253-2-0(3))* JBiRD iNK, Ltd.

Kouga, Yun. Crown of Love, Vol. 1. 2010. (ENG., Illus.). 192p. pap. 9.99 *(978-1-4215-3193-9(3))* Viz Media.

—Crown of Love, Vol. 2. 2010. (ENG., Illus.). 200p. pap. 9.99 *(978-1-4215-3194-6(1))* Viz Media.

Kovac, Tommy. Wonderland #1. 2006. (Illus.). 24p. (YA). pap. 3.50 *(978-1-59362-039-4(X),* Slave Labor Graphics) Slave Labor Bks.

—Wonderland #2: The Tulgey Wood & the Treacle Well. 2006. (Illus.). 3.50 *(978-1-59362-050-9(0))* Slave Labor Bks.

Kreie, Chris & Maese, Fares. Shot Clock Slam. Aburto, Jesus & Esparza, Andres, illus. 2010. (Sports Illustrated Kids Graphic Novels Ser.). (ENG.). 56p. (gr. 2-3). pap. 7.19 *(978-1-4342-2786-7(3))* Stone Arch Bks.

Kreie, Chris, et al. Battle for Home Plate, 1 vol. Aburtov, Jesus Aburto, illus. 2010. (Sports Illustrated Kids Graphic Novels Ser.). (ENG.). 56p. (gr. 2-3). pap. 7.19 *(978-1-4342-2290-9(X))* Stone Arch Bks.

—Battle for Home Plate, 1 vol. Aburto, Jesus, illus. 2010. (Sports Illustrated Kids Graphic Novels Ser.). (ENG.). 56p. (gr. 2-3). 26.65 *(978-1-4342-1913-8(5))* Stone Arch Bks.

Kress, Earl. Scooby-Doo in Hear No Evil, 1 vol. Delaney, John, illus. 2010. (Scooby-Doo Graphic Novels Ser.: No. 1). (ENG.). 24p. (J). (gr. 2-5). 24.21 *(978-1-59961-694-0(7))* Spotlight.

Krohn, Katherine. Encountering Bigfoot: Eyewitness Accounts, 1 vol. Byers, Michael, illus. 2014. (Eyewitness to the Unexplained Ser.). (ENG.). 32p. (gr. 3-4). 30.65 *(978-1-4914-0243-6(1),* Graphic Library) Capstone Press of Coughlan Cos.

Krohn, Katherine & Milgrom, Al. The Whirlwind World of Hurricanes with Max Axiom, Super Scientist. 2010. (Graphic Science Ser.). (ENG., Illus.). 32p. (gr. 3-4). pap. 8.10 *(978-1-4296-5636-8(0),* Graphic Library) Capstone Press of Coughlan Cos.

Kroll, Steve. Nina in That Makes Me Mad!, 1 vol. 2013. (Toon Bks). (ENG.). 36p. (J). (gr. 1-2). lib. bdg. 27.07 *(978-1-61479-153-9(8))* Spotlight.

Krosoczka, Jarrett J. Lunch Lady & the Author Visit Vendetta. 2009. (Lunch Lady Ser.). (ENG.). 96p. (J). (gr. 3-7). pap. 6.99 *(978-0-375-86094-2(0),* Knopf Bks. for Young Readers) Random Hse. Children's Bks.

—Lunch Lady & the Cyborg Substitute. 2009. (Lunch Lady Ser.). (ENG.). 96p. (J). (gr. 3-7). pap. 6.99 *(978-0-375-84683-0(2),* Knopf Bks. for Young Readers) Random Hse. Children's Bks.

—Lunch Lady & the Field Trip Fiasco. 2011. (Lunch Lady Ser.). (ENG.). 96p. (J). (gr. 3-7). pap. 6.99 *(978-0-375-86730-9(9),* Knopf Bks. for Young Readers) Random Hse. Children's Bks.

—Lunch Lady & the Mutant Mathletes. 2012. (Lunch Lady Ser.). (ENG., Illus.). 96p. (J). (gr. 2-5). pap. 6.99 *(978-0-375-87028-6(8))*; lib. bdg. 12.99 *(978-0-375-97028-3(2))* Random Hse. Children's Bks. (Knopf Bks. for Young Readers).

—Lunch Lady & the Mutant Mathletes. 2012. (Lunch Lady Ser.: 7). lib. bdg. 17.20 *(978-0-606-23871-7(9),* Turtleback) Turtleback Bks.

—Lunch Lady & the Picture Day Peril. 2012. (Lunch Lady Ser.). (ENG., Illus.). 96p. (J). (gr. 2-5). pap. 6.99 *(978-0-375-87035-4(0))*; lib. bdg. 12.99 *(978-0-375-97035-1(5))* Random Hse. Children's Bks. (Knopf Bks. for Young Readers).

—Lunch Lady & the Picture Day Peril. 2012. (Lunch Lady Ser.: 8). lib. bdg. 17.20 *(978-0-606-26811-0(1),* Turtleback) Turtleback Bks.

—Lunch Lady & the Schoolwide Scuffle. 2014. (Lunch Lady Ser.). (ENG., Illus.). 96p. (J). (gr. 2-5). pap. 6.99 *(978-0-385-75279-4(2))*; lib. bdg. 12.99 *(978-0-385-75280-0(6))* Random Hse. Children's Bks. (Knopf Bks. for Young Readers).

—Lunch Lady & the Schoolwide Scuffle. 2014. (Lunch Lady Ser.: 10). lib. bdg. 17.20 *(978-0-606-32235-5(3),* Turtleback) Turtleback Bks.

—Lunch Lady & the Video Game Villain. 2013. (Lunch Lady Ser.). (ENG.). 96p. (J). (gr. 2-5). pap. 6.99 *(978-0-307-98079-3(0))*; lib. bdg. 12.99 *(978-0-307-98080-9(4))* Random Hse. Children's Bks. (Knopf Bks. for Young Readers).

—Lunch Lady & the Video Game Villain. 2013. (Lunch Lady Ser.: 9). lib. bdg. 17.20 *(978-0-606-27003-8(5),* Turtleback) Turtleback Bks.

—A New Class. 2016. (Star Wars: Jedi Academy Ser.: 4). (ENG.). 176p. (J). (gr. 3-7). 12.99 *(978-0-545-87573-8(0))* Scholastic, Inc.

Krueger, Jim & Rogers, Bud. Child of Destiny, 1 vol. Padilla, Ariel, illus. 2008. (Z Graphic Novels / Tomo Ser.). (ENG.). 160p. (J). (gr. 4-7). pap. 6.99 *(978-0-310-71302-9(1))* Zondervan.

Krueger, Jim & Zondervan Staff. Betrayal of Trust, 1 vol. Rogers, Bud, ed. Padilla, Ariel, illus. 2009. (Z Graphic Novels / Tomo Ser.). (ENG.). 160p. (J). pap. 6.99 *(978-0-310-71306-7(4))* Zondervan.

Krukar, Jeff, et al. Melting Down: A Comic for Kids with Asperger's Disorder & Challenging Behavior (the Orp Library) 2013. 74p. pap. 12.99 *(978-1-939418-20-3(8))* Writer of the Round Table Pr.

Krulik, Nancy E. It's a Bird, It's a Plane, It's Toiletman! 2016. (George Brown, Class Clown Ser.: 17). lib. bdg. 14.75 *(978-0-606-38417-9(0))* Turtleback Bks.

Kruse, Jan, et al. Walt Disney's Spring Fever Volume 3. 2009. 80p. pap. 9.99 *(978-1-60360-097-2(3))* Gemstone Publishing, Inc.

Kubert, Andy. Cry Wolf, Vol. 10. 2007. (ENG., Illus.). 96p. (YA). (gr. 8-17). pap. 8.99 *(978-0-7851-1405-5(X))* Marvel Worldwide, Inc.

Kunkel, Mike. Billy Batson & the Magic. Kunkel, Mike, illus. 2015. (Billy Batson & the Magic of Shazam! Ser.). (ENG., Illus.). 32p. (gr. 2-3). 226.00 *(978-1-4965-0290-2(6))* Stone Arch Bks.

—Billy Batson & the Magic of Shazam!, 1 vol. Kunkel, Mike, illus. 2014. (Billy Batson & the Magic of Shazam! Ser.). (ENG., Illus.). 32p. (gr. 2-3). 90.40 *(978-1-4342-9524-8(9))* Stone Arch Bks.

—Brother vs. Brother!, 1 vol. Kunkel, Mike, illus. 2014. (Billy Batson & the Magic of Shazam! Ser.). (ENG., Illus.). 32p. (gr. 2-3). 22.60 *(978-1-4342-9228-5(2))* Stone Arch Bks.

—Herobear & the Kid Vol. 1 the Inheritance. Kunkel, Mike, illus. 2014. (Herobear & the Kid Ser.: 1). (ENG., Illus.). 128p. (J). (gr. 3). pap. 19.99 *(978-1-60886-366-2(2))* Boom! Studios.

—Magic Words!, 1 vol. Kunkel, Mike, illus. 2014. (Billy Batson & the Magic of Shazam! Ser.). (ENG., Illus.). 32p. (gr. 2-3). 22.60 *(978-1-4342-9209-4(6))* Stone Arch Bks.

—Perilous Peril!, 1 vol. Kunkel, Mike, illus. 2014. (Billy Batson & the Magic of Shazam! Ser.). (ENG., Illus.). 32p. (gr. 2-3). 22.60 *(978-1-4342-9227-8(4))* Stone Arch Bks.

—The World's Mightiest Mortal!, 1 vol. Kunkel, Mike, illus. 2014. (Billy Batson & the Magic of Shazam! Ser.). (ENG., Illus.). 32p. (gr. 2-3). 22.60 *(978-1-4342-9226-1(6))* Stone Arch Bks.

Kupperberg, Paul. Scooby-Doo & the Night of the Undead!, 1 vol. 2013. (Scooby-Doo Graphic Novels Set 3 Ser.). (ENG.). 24p. (J). (gr. 2-6). lib. bdg. 24.21 *(978-1-61479-050-1(7),* Essential Library) ABDO Publishing Co.

—Scooby-Doo in over the Boardwalk, 1 vol. 2013. (Scooby-Doo Graphic Novels Set 3 Ser.). (ENG., Illus.). 24p. (J). (gr. 2-6). lib. bdg. 24.21 *(978-1-61479-052-5(3),* Essential Library) ABDO Publishing Co.

—Scooby-Doo in Read All about It!, 1 vol. 2013. (Scooby-Doo Graphic Novels Set 3 Ser.). (ENG.). 24p. (J). (gr. 2-6). lib. bdg. 24.21 *(978-1-61479-053-2(1),* Essential Library) ABDO Publishing Co.

Kupperberg, Paul & Loughridge, Lee. The Kid Who Saved Superman, 1 vol. Ku, Min Sung, illus. (Superman Ser.). (ENG.). 56p. (gr. 2-3). 2013. pap. 4.95 *(978-1-4342-1937-4(2))* 2009. lib. bdg. 26.65 *(978-1-4342-1936-7(4))* Stone Arch Bks. (DC Super Heroes).

Kupperberg, Paul, et al. Super-Villain Showdown, 1 vol. Doescher, Erik, illus. 2013. (Superman Ser.). (ENG.). 56p. (gr. 2-3). pap. 4.95 *(978-1-4342-1736-3(1),* DC Super Heroes) Stone Arch Bks.

Kurtz, Rob. Meet the Robots. 2011. 20p. pap. 5.99 *(978-1-60010-512-8(2))* Idea & Design Works, LLC.

—Robots to the Rescue! 2011. 32p. pap. 3.99 *(978-1-60010-513-5(0))* Idea & Design Works, LLC.

Kurtz, Scott. Rides Again, Vol. 3. 2005. (ENG., Illus.). 144p. pap. 11.99 *(978-1-58240-553-7(0),* 9781582405537) Toonhound Studios, LLC.

Kusaka, Hidenori. Pokémon Adventures Vol. 3: Black & White. Yamamoto, Satoshi, illus. 2014. (ENG.). 208p. (J). pap. 9.99 *(978-1-4215-6178-3(6))* Viz Media.

—Pokémon Adventures: Black & White, Vol. 4. Yamamoto, Satoshi, illus. 2014. (ENG.). 200p. (J). pap. 9.99 *(978-1-4215-6180-6(8))* Viz Media.

—Pokémon Adventures: Diamond & Pearl/Platinum, Vol. 10. Yamamoto, Satoshi, illus. 2014. (ENG.). 208p. (J). pap. 9.99 *(978-1-4215-5406-8(2))* Viz Media.

—Pokémon Adventures, Vol. 21. Yamamoto, Satoshi, illus. 2014. (ENG.). 208p. (J). pap. 9.99 *(978-1-4215-3555-5(6))* Viz Media.

—Pokémon Black & White Box Set 2, Vols. 9-14, Set. Yamamoto, Satoshi, illus. 2014. (ENG.). 504p. (J). pap. 25.99 *(978-1-4215-7774-6(7))* Viz Media.

—Pokémon Black & White, Vol. 12. Yamamoto, Satoshi, illus. 2013. (ENG.). 96p. (J). pap. 4.99 *(978-1-4215-5896-7(3))* Viz Media.

—Pokémon Black & White, Vol. 13. Yamamoto, Satoshi, illus. 2013. (ENG.). 96p. (J). pap. 4.99 *(978-1-4215-5897-4(1))* Viz Media.

—Pokémon Black & White, Vol. 14. Yamamoto, Satoshi, illus. 2014. (ENG.). 88p. (J). pap. 4.99 *(978-1-4215-6766-2(0))* Viz Media.

—Pokémon Black & White, Vol. 15. Yamamoto, Satoshi, illus. 2014. (ENG.). 80p. (J). pap. 4.99 *(978-1-4215-6767-9(9))* Viz Media.

—Pokémon Black & White, Vol. 16. Yamamoto, Satoshi, illus. 2014. (ENG.). 80p. (J). pap. 4.99 *(978-1-4215-6768-6(7))* Viz Media.

—Pokémon Black & White, Vol. 17. Yamamoto, Satoshi, illus. 2014. (ENG.). 88p. (J). pap. 4.99 *(978-1-4215-6769-3(5))* Viz Media.

—Pokémon Black & White, Vol. 18. Yamamoto, Satoshi, illus. 2014. (ENG.). 96p. (J). pap. 4.99 *(978-1-4215-7602-2(3))* Viz Media.

—Pokémon Black & White, Vol. 19. Yamamoto, Satoshi, illus. 2014. (ENG.). 80p. (J). pap. 4.99 *(978-1-4215-7603-9(1))* Viz Media.

—Pokémon Black & White, Vol. 20. Yamamoto, Satoshi, illus. 2015. (ENG.). 80p. (J). pap. 4.99 *(978-1-4215-7604-6(X))* Viz Media.

—Pokémon X Y. Yamamoto, Satoshi, illus. (ENG.). (J). Vol. 1. 2014. 96p. pap. 4.99 *(978-1-4215-7980-1(4))* Vol. 2. 2015. 112p. pap. 4.99 *(978-1-4215-7834-7(4))* Vol. 5. 2015. 96p. pap. 4.99 *(978-1-4215-8250-4(3))* Viz Media.

—Pokémon X Y, Vol. 6. Yamamoto, Satoshi, illus. 2016. (ENG.). 96p. (J). pap. 4.99 *(978-1-4215-8335-8(6))* Viz Media.

—Pokémon X Y, Vol. 7. 2016. (ENG., Illus.). 96p. (J). pap. 4.99 *(978-1-4215-8777-6(7))* Viz Media.

Kusaka, Hidenori & Harukaze, Santa. Pokémon Pocket Comics Vol. 1: Black & White. 2013. (ENG., Illus.). 320p. (J). pap. 9.99 *(978-1-4215-5910-0(2))* Viz Media.

Kutner, Richard, tr. from FRE. Oedipus: Trapped by Destiny: A TOON Graphic. Pommaux, Yvan, illus. 2016. (TOON Graphic Mythology Ser.). (ENG.). 48p. (J). (gr. 2-7). 16.95 *(978-1-935179-95-5(0))* TOON Books / RAW Junior, LLC.

—The Suspended Castle: a Philemon Adventure: A TOON Graphic. Fred, illus. 2015. (Philemon Adventures Ser.). (ENG.). 56p. (J). (gr. 2). 16.95 *(978-1-935179-86-3(1))* TOON Books / RAW Junior, LLC.

—The Wild Piano. Fred, illus. 2015. (Philemon Adventures Ser.). (ENG.). 48p. (J). (gr. 2-7). 16.95 *(978-1-935179-83-2(7))* TOON Books / RAW Junior, LLC.

Kwon, Min, illus. Snow Biz, Vol. 5. 2006. (Serenity Ser.: Vol. 5). 96p. (YA). (gr. 7-12). per. 7.97 *(978-1-59310-874-8(5),* Barbour Bks.) Barbour Publishing, Inc.

Laban, Terry. Donald Duck Adventures, Vol. 17. Clark, John, ed. Andersen, Flemming & Gonzalez, Jose Antonio, illus. 2006. (ENG.). 128p. (YA). (gr. 3-7). pap. 7.95 *(978-1-888472-12-7(X),* 9781888472127) Gemstone Publishing, Inc.

Labatt, Mary. Mummy Mayhem. Rioux, Jo-Anne, illus. 2010. (Sam & Friends Mystery Ser.). (ENG.). 96p. (J). (gr. 2-5). 16.95 *(978-1-55453-470-8(4))*; pap. 7.95 *(978-1-55453-471-5(2))* Kids Can Pr., Ltd. CAN. Dist: Hachette Bk. Group.

—Witches' Brew. Rioux, Jo-Anne, illus. 2011. (Sam & Friends Mystery Ser.). (ENG.). 96p. (J). (gr. 2-5). 16.95 *(978-1-55453-472-2(0))*; pap. 7.95 *(978-1-55453-473-9(9))* Kids Can Pr., Ltd. CAN. Dist: Hachette Bk. Group.

Labrune, Jean-Baptiste & Fischer, Jérémie. The Night Watchman. 2015. (ENG., Illus.). 192p. (J). (gr. 3-7). 15.00 *(978-3-89955-749-7(2))* Die Gestalten Verlag DEU. Dist: Penguin Random Hse. LLC.

Lancett, Peter. Fear in the Dark (Blue Series), 1 vol. 2015. (Dark Man Ser.). (ENG.). 36p. (YA). (gr. 9-12). pap. 7.95 *(978-1-68021-128-3(5))* Saddleback Educational Publishing, Inc.

Land, Greg, illus. Crossover. 2006. (ENG.). 144p. (YA). (gr. 8-17). pap. 12.99 *(978-0-7851-1802-2(0))* Marvel Worldwide, Inc.

Landers, Ace. The Padawan Menace. 2012. (Lego Star Wars Ser.). (ENG.). 32p. (J). (gr. 2-5). pap. 3.99 *(978-0-545-40450-1(9),* Scholastic Paperbacks) Scholastic, Inc.

—R2-D2 & C-3P0's Guide to the Galaxy. 2016. (Lego Star Wars Ser.). (ENG.). 128p. (J). (gr. 2-5). 12.99 *(978-0-545-94894-4(0))* Scholastic, Inc.

—The Yoda Chronicles Trilogy. 2014. (Lego Star Wars Ser.). (ENG.). 96p. (J). (gr. -1-3). 7.99 *(978-0-545-62901-0(2))* Scholastic, Inc.

Landmann, Bimba. The Incredible Voyage of Ulysses. 2010. (ENG., Illus.). 60p. (J). (gr. 4-7). 19.95 *(978-1-60606-012-4(0))* Getty Pubns.

Langridge, Roger. Family Reunion. Langridge, Roger & Mebberson, Amy, illus. 2010. (Muppet Show Ser.). (ENG.). 112p. (J). pap. 9.99 *(978-1-60886-587-1(8))* Boom! Studios.

—The Muppet Show Comic Book: The Treasure of Peg-Leg Wilson. Langridge, Roger, illus. 2010. (Muppet Show Ser.). (ENG., Illus.). 112p. (J). 24.99 *(978-1-60886-530-7(4))*; (gr. 4-7). pap. 9.99 *(978-1-60886-504-8(5))* Boom! Studios.

—On the Road. Langridge, Roger, illus. 2010. (Muppet Show Ser.). (ENG., Illus.). 112p. (J). pap. 9.99 *(978-1-60886-516-1(9))* Boom! Studios.

—Snarked, Vol. 3. 2013. (Snarked Ser.). (ENG., Illus.). 112p. (J). (gr. 4). pap. 14.99 *(978-1-60886-295-5(X))* Boom! Studios.

Langridge, Roger, text. The Muppets Omnibus. 2014. (ENG., Illus.). 600p. (J). (gr. -1-17). 59.99 *(978-0-7851-8792-9(8))* Marvel Worldwide, Inc.

Langridge, Roger & Cox, Alex. Adventure Time Vol. 2: Sugary Shorts Mathematical Edition. 2016. lib. bdg. 33.05 *(978-0-606-38730-9(7))* Turtleback Bks.

Lansdale, John L., et al. Something Wicca This Way Comes, No. 7. Romberger, James et al, illus. 7th ed. 2009. (Tales from the Crypt Graphic Novels Ser.: 7). (ENG.). 96p. (J). (gr.

5-12). 12.95 *(978-1-59707-151-2(X)*, 9781597071512) Papercutz.

Lapointe, Stéphanie. Grandfather & the Moon, 1 vol. Tanaka, Shelley, tr. from FRE. Rogé, illus. 2017. (ENG.). 100p. (J). (gr. 4-8). 18.95 *(978-1-55498-961-4(2))* Groundwood Bks. CAN. Dist: Publishers Group West (PGW).

Lark, Michael, et al, illus. Daredevil the Man Without Fear! 2017. (ENG.). 472p. (YA). (gr. 8-17). 75.00 ***(978-1-302-90859-1(6))*** Marvel Worldwide, Inc.

LaRocque, Greg. Crybaby: Extinction. Castillo, Cesar & Burruss, Melissa, illus. 2005. (YA). per. 9.99 *(978-1-933570-86-0(5))* Aardvark Global Publishing.

Larosa, Lewis, illus. In the Beginning. 2006. (ENG.). 144p. (gr. 13-17). pap. 14.99 *(978-0-7851-1391-1(6))* Marvel Worldwide, Inc.

Larsen, Erik. Savage Dragon on Trial TP. 2013. (ENG., Illus.). 128p. (YA). pap. 16.99 *(978-1-60706-755-9(2)*, 9781607067559) Image Comics.

Larsen, Erik, et al. Image Comics. ltd. ed. 2005. (ENG., Illus.). 128p. (YA). 75.00 *(978-1-58240-257-4(4)*, 9781582402574) Image Comics.

Larson, Hope. Knife's Edge: A Graphic Novel. Mock, Rebecca, illus. 2017. (Four Points Ser.: 2). (ENG.). 224p. (J). 19.99 *(978-0-374-30044-9(5)*, 9780374300449, Farrar, Straus & Giroux (BYR)) Farrar, Straus & Giroux.

—Mercury. Larson, Hope, illus. 2010. (ENG., Illus.). 240p. (YA). (gr. 7-18). 19.99 *(978-1-4169-3585-8(1))*; pap. 15.99 *(978-1-4169-3588-9(6))* Simon & Schuster Children's Publishing. (Atheneum Bks. for Young Readers).

Larson, Mitch & McCarthy, Meghan. When Cutie Calls. 2014. (My Little Pony Ser.). (ENG., Illus.). 128p. (J). (gr. 2-5). pap. 7.99 *(978-1-61377-830-2(9)*, 9781613778302) Idea & Design Works, LLC.

Lash, Batton, et al. The Scrapyard Detectives: Collected Cases. 2007. (Illus.). 102p. (J). (gr. 3-5). per. *(978-0-9797193-0-1(5))* Diversity Foundation, The.

Lasseter, John, et al. Disney Graphic Novels Planes 1. 2015. (J). lib. bdg. 18.40 *(978-0-606-37580-1(5))* Turtleback Bks.

Last, Shari. Rebel Heroes. 2017. (Star Wars DK Readers Level 3 Ser.). lib. bdg. 13.55 ***(978-0-606-39898-5(8))*** Turtleback Bks.

Laurel Associates. Kidnapped Study Guide: The Complete Adventures of David Balfour. 2006. (Classics Ser.). (Illus.). 48p. (YA). per. 17.95 *(978-1-56254-874-2(3))* Saddleback Educational Publishing, Inc.

Lawrence, James. Buck Rogers in the 25th Century - The Gray Morrow Years, 1979-1981, Vol. 1. Herman, Daniel, ed. 2013. (ENG., Illus.). 240p. (YA). 49.99 *(978-1-61345-034-5(6)*, 9781613450345) Hermes Pr.

Lawrence, Mike. Star Scouts. 2017. (Star Scouts Ser.: 1). (ENG., Illus.). 192p. (J). pap. 14.99 *(978-1-62672-280-4(3)*, 9781626722804, First Second Bks.) Roaring Brook Pr.

Lawson, Jim & Dooney, Michael. Paleo: Tales of the Late Cretaceous. 2003. (Illus.). 172p. (YA). reprint ed. pap. 12.95 *(978-0-9661985-3-9(0)*, Empty Sky) Zeromayo Studios, LLP.

Layman, John S. Armageddon & Son. 2005. (ENG., Illus.). 96p. (YA). pap. 9.95 *(978-1-932664-33-1(5)*, 9781932664331) Oni Pr., Inc.

Le Gall, Frank. Freedom! Balthazar, Flore, illus. 2012. (Miss Annie Ser.). 48p. (J). (gr. 2-4). pap. 39.62 *(978-0-7613-9281-1(5))*; (ENG.). lib. bdg. 29.27 *(978-0-7613-7884-6(7))* Lerner Publishing Group. (Graphic Universe™).

—Miss Annie. Balthazar, Flore, illus. 2012. (Miss Annie Ser.). 48p. (J). (gr. 2-4). lib. bdg. 58.54 *(978-0-7613-8902-6(4)*, Graphic Universe™) Lerner Publishing Group.

—Miss Annie: 6Pack Set. Balthazar, Flore, illus. 2012. (Miss Annie Ser.). 48p. (J). (gr. 2-4). pap. 79.23 *(978-0-7613-9284-2(X)*, Graphic Universe™) Lerner Publishing Group.

—Miss Annie: Single Copy Set. Balthazar, Flore, illus. 2012. (Miss Annie Ser.). 48p. (J). (gr. 2-4). pap. 13.21 *(978-0-7613-9283-5(1)*, Graphic Universe™) Lerner Publishing Group.

—Rooftop Cat. Balthazar, Flore, illus. 2012. (Miss Annie Ser.). 48p. (J). (gr. 2-4). pap. 39.62 *(978-0-7613-9282-8(3))*; (ENG.). pap. 6.95 *(978-0-7613-8547-9(9))*; (ENG.). lib. bdg. 29.27 *(978-0-7613-7885-3(5))* Lerner Publishing Group. (Graphic Universe™).

Le Gall, Frank & Doo, Robin. Freedom! Balthazar, Flore, illus. 2012. (Miss Annie Ser.: 1). (ENG.). 48p. (J). (gr. 2-4). pap. 6.95 *(978-0-7613-8546-2(0)*, Graphic Universe™) Lerner Publishing Group.

Lee, Frank. Drawing the Heroes in Your Graphic Novel. 2012. (How to Draw Your Own Graphic Novel Ser.). (ENG.). 32p. (J). (gr. 4-6). pap. 12.30 *(978-1-4488-6447-8(X))*; lib. bdg. 26.50 *(978-1-4488-6432-4(1))* Rosen Publishing Group, Inc., The. (PowerKids Pr.).

—Drawing the Villains in Your Graphic. 2012. (How to Draw Your Own Graphic Novel Ser.). (ENG.). 32p. (J). (gr. 4-6). pap. 12.30 *(978-1-4488-6449-2(6))*; lib. bdg. 26.50 *(978-1-4488-6433-1(X))* Rosen Publishing Group, Inc., The. (PowerKids Pr.).

Lee, Kanani K. M. & Wallenta, Adam. The Incredible Plate Tectonics Comic: The Adventures of Geo, Vol. 1. 2014. (ENG., Illus.). 40p. (J). (gr. 2-8). pap. 7.95 *(978-1-59327-549-5(8))* No Starch Pr., Inc.

Lee, SangEun. 13th Boy, 12 vols., Vol. 5. 2010. (13th Boy Ser.: 5). (ENG., Illus.). 192p. (YA). (gr. 8-17). pap. 10.99 *(978-0-7595-2998-4(1)*, Yen Pr.) Orbit.

Lee, Stan. Balder the Brave. 2013. (Thor: Tales of Asgard Ser.). (Illus.). 24p. (J). (gr. 4-8). lib. bdg. 24.21 *(978-1-61479-169-0(4))* Spotlight.

—Boyhood of Thor! 2013. (Thor: Tales of Asgard Ser.). (Illus.). 24p. (J). (gr. 4-8). lib. bdg. 24.21 *(978-1-61479-170-6(8))* Spotlight.

—Challenge! 2013. (Thor: Tales of Asgard Ser.). (Illus.). 24p. (J). (gr. 4-8). lib. bdg. 24.21 *(978-1-61479-171-3(6))* Spotlight.

—The Fantastic Four. 2013. (ENG., Illus.). 832p. (J). (gr. -1-17). 99.99 *(978-0-7851-8567-3(4))* Marvel Worldwide, Inc.

—The Fantastic Four Omnibus, Vol. 1. 2013. (ENG., Illus.). 848p. (J). (gr. -1-17). 99.99 *(978-0-7851-8566-6(6))* Marvel Worldwide, Inc.

—Quest for the Mystic Mountain! 2013. (Thor: Tales of Asgard Ser.). (Illus.). 24p. (J). (gr. 4-8). lib. bdg. 24.21 *(978-1-61479-172-0(4))* Spotlight.

—Thor: Tales of Asgard. 2013. (Thor: Tales of Asgard Ser.: 6). 24p. (J). (gr. 4-8). lib. bdg. 145.26 *(978-1-61479-168-3(6))* Spotlight.

—To the Death! 2013. (Thor: Tales of Asgard Ser.). (Illus.). 24p. (J). (gr. 4-8). lib. bdg. 24.21 *(978-1-61479-173-7(2))* Spotlight.

—When Speaks the Dragon! 2013. (Thor: Tales of Asgard Ser.). (Illus.). 24p. (J). (gr. 4-8). lib. bdg. 24.21 *(978-1-61479-174-4(0))* Spotlight.

Lee, Stan & Moore, Stuart. Power Lines. Cullins, Paris, illus. 2016. (Zodiac Ser.). (ENG.). 64p. (J). 12.99 *(978-1-62991-445-9(2)*, 9781629914459) Papercutz.

Lee, T. S. The Oprah Winfrey Story: The First Oprah Winfrey Comic Biography. 2010. 190p. (J). pap. 14.95 *(978-0-9819542-6-4(X))* DASANBOOKS.

—The Stephen Hawking Story: The First Stephen Hawking Comic Biography. 2010. 179p. (J). pap. 14.95 *(978-0-9819542-9-5(4))* DASANBOOKS.

—The Stephen Spielberg Story: The First Stephen Spielberg Comic Biogrhaphy. 2010. 177p. (J). pap. 14.95 *(978-0-9819542-7-1(8))* DASANBOOKS.

—The Thomas Edison Story: The First Thomas Edison Comic Biography. 2010. 179p. (J). pap. 14.95 *(978-0-9819542-5-7(1))* DASANBOOKS.

Lefevre-Garros. The Wright Brothers. 2009. (ENG., Illus.). 48p. pap. 11.95 *(978-1-905460-73-1(2))* CineBook GBR. Dist: National Bk. Network.

Lehman, John, et al. Canine Classics, Vol. 25. Pomplun, Tom & Lehman, John, eds. 2014. (ENG., Illus.). 144p. (YA). pap. 19.95 *(978-0-9825630-8-3(6)*, 9780982563083) Eureka Productions.

Leigh, Savanah-Rose. Trunks & Amelia. 2012. 48p. pap. 9.89 *(978-1-4669-3803-8(X))* Trafford Publishing.

Leigh, Susan K. Luther: Echoes of the Hammer. 2011. 144p. pap. 12.99 *(978-0-7586-2382-9(8))* Concordia Publishing Hse.

Leijten, Aileen. Lint Boy. 2017. (ENG., Illus.). 128p. (J). (gr. 2-5). 16.99 *(978-0-544-52860-4(3))* Houghton Mifflin Harcourt Publishing Co.

Leitha, Dan. Welcome to Life after Eden. 2003. (YA). per. 12.00 *(978-1-893345-15-7(7))* Answers in Genesis Ministries.

Leloup, Roger. The Curious Trio. 2012. (Yoko Tsuno Ser.: 7). (ENG., Illus.). 48p. (J). (gr. 3-12). pap. 11.95 *(978-1-84918-127-3(6))* CineBook GBR. Dist: National Bk. Network.

—The Devil's Organ. 2013. (Yoko Tsuno Ser.: 8). (ENG., Illus.). 48p. (J). (gr. 3-12). pap. 11.95 *(978-1-84918-164-8(0))* CineBook GBR. Dist: National Bk. Network.

—The Dragon of Hong Kong - Yoko Tsuno, Vol. 5. 2010. (Yoko Tsuno Ser.: 5). (ENG., Illus.). 46p. (J). (gr. 3-17). pap. 11.95 *(978-1-84918-041-2(5))* CineBook GBR. Dist: National Bk. Network.

—On the Edge of Life. 2007. (Yoko Tsuno Ser.: 1). (ENG., Illus.). 48p. (J). (gr. 4-7). pap. 11.95 *(978-1-905460-32-8(5))* CineBook GBR. Dist: National Bk. Network.

—The Prey & the Ghost. 2009. (Yoko Tsuno Ser.: 3). (ENG., Illus.). 48p. pap. 11.95 *(978-1-905460-56-4(2))* CineBook GBR. Dist: National Bk. Network.

—The Time Spiral. 2008. (Yoko Tsuno Ser.: 2). (ENG., Illus.). 48p. pap. 11.95 *(978-1-905460-43-4(0))* CineBook GBR. Dist: National Bk. Network.

Lemaître, Pascal, illus. Pinocchio. 2014. (Cartoon Classics Ser.). (ENG.). 144p. (J). (gr. 2-5). 12.99 *(978-0-8050-9699-6(X)*, 9780805096996, Holt, Henry & Co. Bks. For Young Readers) Holt, Henry & Co.

Lemke, Amy J. Dinosaurs for Breakfast, 1 vol. Bradley, Jessica, illus. 2013. (Comics Land Ser.). (ENG.). 32p. (gr. k-2). 7.95 *(978-1-4342-4270-9(6))* Stone Arch Bks.

—Snorkeling with Sea-Bots, 1 vol. Bradley, Jessica, illus. 2013. (Comics Land Ser.). (ENG.). 32p. (gr. k-2). 7.95 *(978-1-4342-4271-6(4))*; lib. bdg. 25.32 *(978-1-4342-4030-9(4))* Stone Arch Bks.

—Too Short for the Court, 1 vol. Harpster, Steve, illus. 2012. (My First Graphic Novel Ser.). (ENG.). 32p. (gr. k-2). pap. 6.25 *(978-1-4342-3862-7(8))*; lib. bdg. 24.65 *(978-1-4342-3282-3(4))* Stone Arch Bks. (My First Graphic Novel).

Lemke, Amy J. & Lemke, Donald B. Frank 'n' Beans, 1 vol. Bradley, Jessica, illus. 2013. (Comics Land Ser.). (ENG.). 32p. (gr. k-2). 7.95 *(978-1-4342-6284-4(7))*; lib. bdg. 25.32 *(978-1-4342-4988-3(3))* Stone Arch Bks.

—My Little Bro-Bot, 1 vol. Bradley, Jessica, illus. 2013. (Comics Land Ser.). (ENG.). 32p. (gr. k-2). 7.95 *(978-1-4342-6285-1(5))*; lib. bdg. 25.32 *(978-1-4342-4989-0(1))* Stone Arch Bks.

Lemke, Donald. Batman - Winter Wasteland. Gordon, Steven E. & Gordon, Eric A., illus. 2014. (I Can Read Level 2 Ser.). (ENG.). 32p. (J). (gr. -1-3). pap. 3.99 *(978-0-06-221004-3(1))* HarperCollins Pubs.

—Batman Classic: Batman Versus the Riddler. Gordon, Steven E. & Gordon, Eric A., illus. 2014. (I Can Read Level 2 Ser.). (ENG.). 32p. (J). (gr. -1-3). pap. 3.99 *(978-0-06-221008-1(4))* HarperCollins Pubs.

—Batman Classic: Poison Ivy's Scare Fair. Tong, Andie, illus. 2017. 24p. (J). (gr. -1-3). pap. 3.99 *(978-0-06-236077-9(9)*, HarperFestival) HarperCollins Pubs.

—Batman Versus the Riddler. 2014. (Batman Classic I Can Read Level 2 Ser.). (J). lib. bdg. 13.55 *(978-0-606-35474-5(3))* Turtleback Bks.

—Coldfinger: Zinc Alloy. Holgate, Douglas, illus. 2010. (Graphic Sparks Ser.). (ENG.). 40p. (gr. 1-3). pap. 5.95 *(978-1-4342-2314-2(0)*, Graphic Sparks) Stone Arch Bks.

—Diver Down, 1 vol. Glass House Graphics Staff, illus. 2011. (Good vs Evil Ser.). (ENG.). 48p. (gr. 1-2). pap. 6.29 *(978-1-4342-3446-9(0)*, Good vs Evil) Stone Arch Bks.

—The Joker's Ice Scream. 2015. (Batman Classic I Can Read Level 2 Ser.). (J). lib. bdg. 13.55 *(978-0-606-37607-5(0))* Turtleback Bks.

—Justice League Classic: Storm Surge. Spaziante, Patrick, illus. 2017. 24p. (J). (gr. -1-3). pap. 3.99 *(978-0-06-236079-3(5)*, HarperFestival) HarperCollins Pubs.

—Revealed!, 1 vol. Holgate, Douglas, illus. 2008. (Zinc Alloy Ser.). (ENG.). 40p. (gr. 1-3). 23.99 *(978-1-4342-0763-0(3)*, Graphic Sparks) Stone Arch Bks.

—Revealed! Zinc Alloy, 1 vol. Holgate, Douglas, illus. 2008. (Graphic Sparks Ser.). (ENG.). 40p. (gr. 1-3). pap. 5.95 *(978-1-4342-0859-0(1)*, Graphic Sparks) Stone Arch Bks.

—Super Zero, 1 vol. Holgate, Douglas, illus. 2008. (Zinc Alloy Ser.). (ENG.). 40p. (gr. 1-3). 23.99 *(978-1-4342-0762-3(5))*; pap. 5.95 *(978-1-4342-0858-3(3))* Stone Arch Bks. (Graphic Sparks).

—Superman Classic: Bizarro's Last Laugh. Spaziante, Patrick, illus. 2017. (I Can Read Level 2 Ser.). 32p. (J). (gr. -1-3). pap. 3.99 *(978-0-06-236089-2(2))* HarperCollins Pubs.

—Winter Wasteland. 2014. (Batman Classic I Can Read Level 2 Ser.). (J). lib. bdg. 13.55 *(978-0-606-36458-4(7))* Turtleback Bks.

Lemke, Donald B. The Awakening, 1 vol. 2011. (Good vs Evil Ser.). (ENG.). 48p. (gr. 1-2). lib. bdg. 23.99 *(978-1-4342-2089-9(3)*, Good vs Evil) Stone Arch Bks.

—Coldfinger, 1 vol. Holgate, Douglas, illus. 2009. (Zinc Alloy Ser.). (ENG.). 40p. (gr. 1-3). lib. bdg. 23.99 *(978-1-4342-1586-4(5)*, Graphic Sparks) Stone Arch Bks.

—Diver Down, 1 vol. 2011. (Good vs Evil Ser.). (ENG.). 48p. (gr. 1-2). lib. bdg. 23.99 *(978-1-4342-2092-9(3)*, Good vs Evil) Stone Arch Bks.

—The Invincible Boy-Bot. 2012. (Zinc Alloy Ser.). (ENG.). 128p. (gr. 1-3). pap. 8.95 *(978-1-4342-4597-7(7))* Stone Arch Bks.

—Spokes on the Water, 1 vol. Holgate, Douglas, illus. 2011. (Bike Rider Ser.). (ENG.). 40p. (gr. 1-3). lib. bdg. 23.99 *(978-1-4342-2537-5(2)*, Graphic Sparks) Stone Arch Bks.

—Wheelies of Justice, 1 vol. Holgate, Douglas, illus. 2010. (Bike Rider Ser.). (ENG.). 40p. (gr. 1-3). lib. bdg. 23.99 *(978-1-4342-1892-6(9)*, Graphic Sparks) Stone Arch Bks.

—Zinc Alloy vs Frankenstein, 1 vol. Holgate, Douglas, illus. (Graphic Sparks Ser.). (ENG.). 40p. (gr. 1-3). 2010. pap. 5.95 *(978-1-4342-1391-4(9))* 2009. lib. bdg. 23.99 *(978-1-4342-1188-0(6))* Stone Arch Bks. (Graphic Sparks).

Lemke, Donald B. & Pattison, Ronda. Captured off Guard: The Attack on Pearl Harbor, 1 vol. St. Aubin, Claude, illus. 2008. (Historical Fiction Ser.). (ENG.). 56p. (gr. 2-3). pap. 6.25 *(978-1-4342-0493-6(6)*, Graphic Flash) Stone Arch Bks.

Lemke, Donald B., et al. Fun House of Evil, 1 vol. 2013. (Batman Ser.). (ENG., Illus.). 56p. (gr. 2-3). pap. 4.95 *(978-1-4342-1367-9(6)*, DC Super Heroes) Stone Arch Bks.

—Wrath of the Weather Wizard, 1 vol. Doescher, Erik, illus. 2011. (Flash Ser.). (ENG.). 56p. (gr. 2-3). pap. 4.95 *(978-1-4342-3090-4(2))*; lib. bdg. 26.65 *(978-1-4342-2613-6(1))* Stone Arch Bks. (DC Super Heroes).

Lendler, Ian. The Stratford Zoo Midnight Revue Presents Macbeth. Giallongo, Zack, illus. 2014. (Stratford Zoo Ser.). (ENG.). 80p. (J). (gr. 2-5). pap. 12.99 *(978-1-59643-915-3(7)*, 9781596439153, First Second Bks.) Roaring Brook Pr.

—The Stratford Zoo Midnight Revue Presents Romeo & Juliet. Lendler, Ian, illus. 2015. (Stratford Zoo Ser.). (ENG., Illus.). 96p. (J). (gr. 2-5). pap. 13.99 *(978-1-59643-916-0(5)*, 9781596439160, First Second Bks.) Roaring Brook Pr.

Lenhard, Elizabeth. Different Path. 2004. (W. I. T. C. H. Ser.: Bk. 13). 158p. (J). lib. bdg. 16.92 *(978-1-4242-0791-6(6))* Fitzgerald Bks.

Leo & LEO, Inc Staff. Aldebaran Vol. 1, 3 vols., Vol. 1. LEO, Inc Staff, illus. 2008. (Aldebaran Ser.: 1). (ENG., Illus.). 104p. pap. 19.95 *(978-1-905460-57-1(0))* CineBook GBR. Dist: National Bk. Network.

Lepp, Royden. Visitor in the Field, Vol. 1. Lepp, Royden, illus. 2016. (Rust Ser.: 1). (ENG., Illus.). 176p. (J). (gr. 5). pap. 14.99 *(978-1-60886-894-0(X)*, Archaia Entertainment) Boom! Studios.

LernerClassroom Editors. Mallory Teaching Guide. 2009. pap. 7.95 *(978-0-8225-7448-4(9))* Lerner Publishing Group.

Leroux, Gaston. Graphic Horror, 6 vols., Set 2. Espinosa, Rod, illus. Incl. Phantom of the Opera. (Illus.). 32p. (gr. 5-8). 2009. 28.50 *(978-1-60270-679-8(4)*, Graphic Planet- Fiction); (Graphic Horror Set 2 Ser.). (Illus.). 32p. 2009. 171.00 *(978-1-60270-675-0(1)*, Graphic Planet- Fiction) ABDO Publishing Co.

Leth, Kate. Adventure Time Vol. 4. 2014. lib. bdg. 24.50 *(978-0-606-36119-4(7))* Turtleback Bks.

Léturgie, Jean & Fauche, Xavier. The Daily Star. Morris, illus. 2013. (Lucky Luke Ser.: 41). (ENG.). 48p. pap. 11.95 *(978-1-84918-160-0(8))* CineBook GBR. Dist: National Bk. Network.

Liang, Kuan & Yung, Kao. Magic Lover's Tower, Vol. 1. 2008. (ENG., Illus.). 176p. (YA). pap. 9.95 *(978-1-59796-153-0(1))* DrMaster Pubns. Inc.

Lichtenheld, Tom. What Are You So Grumpy About? Lichtenheld, Tom, illus. 2007. (ENG., Illus.). 40p. (J). (gr. -1-3). 7.99 *(978-0-316-06589-4(7))* Little, Brown Bks. for Young Readers.

Lickens, Alice. How to Be a Cowboy. Lickens, Alice, illus. 2016. (ENG., Illus.). 32p. (J). (gr. -1-2). 16.99 *(978-1-84365-241-0(2)*, Pavilion) Pavilion Bks. GBR. Dist: Independent Pubs. Group.

The Life of a Colonial Wigmaker. 2013. (Jr. Graphic Colonial America Ser.). 24p. (J). (gr. 3-6). pap. 63.60 *(978-1-4777-1432-4(4)*, PowerKids Pr.) Rosen Publishing Group, Inc., The.

Lijewski, Christy. Next Exit, Vol. 1. 2006. (ENG., Illus.). 168p. (YA). pap. 12.95 *(978-1-59362-037-0(3)*, 9781593620370) Slave Labor Bks.

Limke, Jeff. Arthur & Lancelot: The Fight for Camelot. Yeates, Thomas, illus. 2008. (Graphic Myths & Legends Ser.). (ENG.). 48p. (gr. 4-8). pap. 8.95 *(978-0-8225-8513-8(8))* Lerner Publishing Group.

—Arthur & Lancelot: The Fight for Camelot - An English Legend. Yeates, Thomas, illus. 2007. (Graphic Myths & Legends Ser.). (ENG.). 48p. (J). (gr. 4-8). lib. bdg. 27.93 *(978-0-8225-6296-2(0)*, Graphic Universe™) Lerner Publishing Group.

—Arthur & Lancelot: The Fight for Camelot [an English Legend]. Yeates, Thomas, illus. 2015. (Graphic Myths & Legends Ser.). (ENG.). 48p. (gr. 4-8). 21.32 *(978-1-4677-5979-3(1)*, Lerner Digital) Lerner Publishing Group.

—Isis & Osiris: To the Ends of the Earth. Witt, David, illus. 2007. (Graphic Myths & Legends Ser.). (ENG.). 48p. (gr. 4-8). per. 8.95 *(978-0-8225-6482-9(3))* Lerner Publishing Group.

—Isis y Osiris: Hasta el Fin del Mundo: Un Mito Egipcio. Witt, David, illus. 2007. (Mitos y leyendas en viñetas (Graphic Myths & Legends) Ser.). (SPA & ENG.). 48p. (J). (gr. 4-7). per. 8.95 *(978-0-8225-7971-7(5)*, Ediciones Lerner) Lerner Publishing Group.

—King Arthur: Excalibur Unsheathed. Yeates, Thomas, illus. 2007. (Graphic Myths & Legends Ser.). (ENG.). 48p. (gr. 4-8). per. 8.95 *(978-0-8225-6483-6(1))* Lerner Publishing Group.

—El Rey Arturo: La Espada Excalibur Desenvainada: Una Leyenda Inglesa. Translations.com Staff, tr. from ENG. Yeates, Thomas, illus. 2007. (Mitos y leyendas en viñetas (Graphic Myths & Legends) Ser.).Tr. of King Arthur - Excalibur Unsheathed [An English Legend. (SPA.). 48p. (gr. 4-8). per. 8.95 *(978-0-8225-7968-7(5))* Lerner Publishing Group.

—Theseus: Battling the Minotaur. McCrea, John, illus. 2008. (Graphic Myths & Legends Ser.). (ENG.). 48p. (gr. 4-8). pap. 8.95 *(978-0-8225-8517-6(0))* Lerner Publishing Group.

—The Treasure of Mount Fate. Hilinski, Clint, illus. 2007. (Twisted Journeys (r) Ser.: 4). (ENG.). 112p. (J). (gr. 4-7). lib. bdg. 27.93 *(978-0-8225-6205-4(7)*, Graphic Universe™); per. 7.95 *(978-0-8225-6206-1(5))* Lerner Publishing Group.

—Tristan & Isolde: The Warrior & the Princess - A British Legend. Randall, Ron, illus. 2008. (Graphic Myths & Legends Ser.). (ENG.). 48p. (J). (gr. 4-8). lib. bdg. 27.93 *(978-0-8225-7526-9(4)*, Graphic Universe™) Lerner Publishing Group.

Lindgren, Astrid & Nyman, Ingrid. Pippi Won't Grow Up. Nunnally, Tiina, tr. from SWE. 2014. (ENG., Illus.). 56p. (J). 14.95 *(978-1-77046-168-0(X)*, 9781770461680) Drawn & Quarterly Pubns. CAN. Dist: Macmillan.

Lindgren, Astrid & Vang Nyman, Ingrid. Pippi Fixes Everything. Nunnally, Tiina, tr. from SWE. 2013. (ENG., Illus.). 56p. (J). 14.95 *(978-1-77046-131-4(0)*, 9781770461314) Drawn & Quarterly Pubns. CAN. Dist: Macmillan.

Lindsay, Ryan K. Rainbow Dash, 1 vol. Fleecs, Tony, illus. 2015. (ENG.). 24p. (J). *(978-1-61479-334-2(4))* Spotlight.

Liniers. Written & Drawn by Henrietta. 2015. (ENG., Illus.). 64p. (J). (gr. k). 12.95 *(978-1-935179-90-0(X))* TOON Books / RAW Junior, LLC.

Linsner, Joseph Michael. Three Tiers, Vol. 3. 2006. (ENG., Illus.). 176p. (YA). 39.99 *(978-1-58240-573-5(5)*, 9781582405735) Image Comics.

Lipkowitz, Daniel & Dorling Kindersley Publishing Staff. Batman, Visual Dictionary. 2012. (ENG.). 96p. (J). (gr. 2-5). 21.99 *(978-0-7566-9787-7(5)*, DK Children) Dorling Kindersley Publishing, Inc.

Litchmore, Michael. The MB Force: Heroes at the Best! 2007. 56p. pap. 9.00 *(978-0-8059-7399-0(0))* Dorrance Publishing Co., Inc.

Little, Troy. Second Chances. 2014. (Powerpuff Girls Ser.). (ENG., Illus.). 152p. pap. 19.99 *(978-1-61377-906-4(2)*, 9781613779064) Idea & Design Works, LLC.

Littlefield, Holly. The Rooftop Adventure of Minnie & Tessa, Factory Fire Survivors. Hammond, Ted & Carbajal, Richard, illus. 2011. (History's Kid Heroes Ser.). 32p. pap. 51.02 *(978-0-7613-7639-2(9))*; (ENG.). (gr. 3-5). pap. 8.95 *(978-0-7613-7071-0(4))* Lerner Publishing Group. (Graphic Universe™).

—The Rooftop Adventure of Minnie & Tessa, Factory Fire Survivors. Trover, Zachary et al, illus. 2011. (History's Kid Heroes Ser.). (ENG.). 32p. (gr. 3-5). 26.60 *(978-0-7613-6179-4(0))* Lerner Publishing Group.

Litwin, Mike. The Amazing IncrediBull. Litwin, Mike, illus. 2015. (Welcome to Bermooda! Ser.: 4). (ENG., Illus.). 160p. (J). (gr. 1-5). 14.99 *(978-0-8075-8713-3(3))* Whitman, Albert & Co.

Lobdell, Scott. Haley Danelle's Top Eight! 2008. (Hardy Boys Graphic Novels Ser.: 14). (ENG., Illus.). 96p. (J). (gr. 3-7). pap. 7.95 *(978-1-59707-113-0(7)*, 9781597071130) Papercutz.

—Live Free, Die Hardy!, No. 15. 2008. (Hardy Boys Graphic Novels Ser.: 15). (ENG., Illus.). 96p. (J). (gr. 3-7). pap. 7.95 *(978-1-59707-123-9(4)*, 9781597071239) Papercutz.

—The Opposite Numbers. Rendon, Daniel et al, illus. 2006. 111p. (J). *(978-1-4156-9815-0(5))* Papercutz.

Lobdell, Scott, et al. X-Force: Phalanx Covenant. Cruz, Roger et al, illus. 2013. (ENG.). 256p. (J). (gr. 4-17). 39.99 *(978-0-7851-6271-1(2))* Marvel Worldwide, Inc.

Loeb, Jeph. Blue. Sale, Tim, illus. 2003. (Spider-Man Ser.). 160p. (YA). 21.99 *(978-0-7851-1062-0(3))* Marvel Worldwide, Inc.

Lofficier, Randy & Lofficier, Jean-Marc. Robonocchio. Martiniere, Stephan, illus. 2004. (FRE.). 128p. (YA). per. 14.95 *(978-1-932983-04-3(X)*, Black Coat Pr.) HollywoodComics.com, LLC.

Loggia, Wendy & Roberts, Christa. Employee Handbook. 2014. (Regular Show Ser.). (ENG.). 80p. (J). (gr. 3-7). 6.99 *(978-0-8431-7743-5(8)*, Price Stern Sloan) Penguin Young Readers Group.

Loisillier, Maud & Morel, Diane. The Planet of Jade. Smith, Owen & Collins Smith, Anne, trs. ELyum Studio, illus. 2012. (Little Prince Ser.: 4). (ENG.). 56p. (J). (gr. 4-8). pap. 7.95 *(978-1-4677-0263-8(3)*, Graphic Universe™) Lerner Publishing Group.

Loisillier, Maud, et al. The Planet of Jade. 2012. (Little Prince Ser.: 4). (ENG., Illus.). 56p. (J). (gr. 4-8). lib. bdg. 26.60 *(978-0-7613-8754-1(4)*, Graphic Universe™) Lerner Publishing Group.

London, Jack. White Fang, 1 vol. Martin, Cynthia, illus. 2007. (Graphic Classics). (ENG.). 32p. (gr. 4-7). 28.50 *(978-1-60270-055-0(9)*, Graphic Planet- Fiction) ABDO Publishing Co.

London, Jack, et al. Jack London, Vol. 5. Pomplun, Tom, ed. 2nd ed. 2016. (ENG., Illus.). 144p. (YA). pap. 11.95 *(978-0-9746648-8-0(X)*, 9780974664880) Eureka Productions.

Lord, Michelle. Tide Pool Trouble, 1 vol. Harpster, Steve, illus. 2011. (My First Graphic Novel Ser.). (ENG.). 32p. (gr. k-2). pap. 6.25 *(978-1-4342-3059-1(7))*; lib. bdg. 24.65 *(978-1-4342-2517-7(8))* Stone Arch Bks. (My First Graphic Novel).

Loux, Matthew. Salt Water Taffy: Caldera's Revenge! 2011. (ENG., Illus.). 72p. pap. 5.99 *(978-1-934964-62-0(X)*, 9781934964620) Oni Pr., Inc.

—Salt Water Taffy Pt. 2: Caldera's Revenge! 2011. (ENG., Illus.). 80p. pap. 5.99 (978-1-934964-63-7(8), 9781934964637) Oni Pr., Inc.

Lu, Marie. Champion: The Graphic Novel. 2017. (Legend Graphic Novels Ser.: 3). lib. bdg. 26.95 **(978-0-606-39796-4(5))** Turtleback Bks.

—Legend. Kaaris, illus. 2015. (Legend Ser.). (ENG.). 160p. (YA). (gr. 7). pap. 14.99 (978-0-399-17189-5(4), G.P. Putnam's Sons Books for Young Readers) Penguin Young Readers Group.

—Prodigy: The Graphic Novel. 2016. (Legend Graphic Novels Ser.: 2). lib. bdg. 26.95 (978-0-606-38425-4(1)) Turtleback Bks.

Lucas Film Book Group & Ferrari, Alessandro. Star Wars: Prequel Trilogy Graphic Novel. 2017. (ENG., Illus.). 208p. (J). (gr. 3-7). 19.99 (978-1-368-00274-5(9), Disney Lucasfilm Press) Disney Publishing Worldwide.

Lucas Film Book Group & Simonson, Louise. A New Hope: The Rise of a Hero. Simonson, Walter, illus. 2017. (ENG.). 48p. (J). (gr. 1-3). 10.99 (978-1-4847-9933-8(X), Disney Lucasfilm Press) Disney Publishing Worldwide.

LucasFilm Book Group. Star Wars: Oversize Graphic Novel. Kawaii Studio Staff & Pastrovicchio, Alessandro, illus. 2016. (ENG.). 208p. (J). (gr. 3-7). 19.99 (978-1-4847-3784-2(9), Disney Lucasfilm Press) Disney Publishing Worldwide.

LucasFilm Press Staff. Star Wars: Before the Awakening. Noto, Phil, illus. 2015. E-Book (978-1-4847-3550-3(1)) Disney Publishing Worldwide.

Luciani, Brigitte. The Carnival. Tharlet, Eve, illus. 2014. (ENG.). 32p. (J). pap. 6.95 (978-1-4677-4204-7(X)); lib. bdg. 25.26 (978-1-4677-4203-0(1), Graphic Universe™) Lerner Publishing Group.

—A Hubbub. Gauvin, Edward, tr. from FRE. Tharlet, Eve, illus. 2010. (Mr. Badger & Mrs. Fox Ser.: 2). (ENG.). 32p. (J). (gr. k-3). pap. 6.95 (978-0-7613-5632-5(0), Graphic Universe™);Bk. 2. 25.26 (978-0-7613-5626-4(6)) Lerner Publishing Group.

—Peace & Quiet. Burrell, Carol, tr. Tharlet, Eve, illus. 2012. (Mr. Badger & Mrs. Fox Ser.: 4). (ENG.). 32p. (J). (gr. k-3). pap. 6.95 (978-0-8225-9163-4(4)); lib. bdg. 25.26 (978-0-7613-8520-2(7)) Lerner Publishing Group. (Graphic Universe™).

—What a Team! Gauvin, Edward, tr. from FRE. Tharlet, Eve, illus. 2011. (Mr. Badger & Mrs. Fox Ser.: 3). (ENG.). 32p. (J). (gr. k-3). 25.26 (978-0-7613-5627-1(4)); pap. 6.95 (978-0-7613-5633-2(9), Graphic Universe™) Lerner Publishing Group.

Lucke, Deb. The Lunch Witch. No. 1. 2015. (Lunch Witch Ser.). (ENG., Illus.). 180p. (J). (gr. 1-5). pap. 14.99 (978-1-62991-162-5(3), 9781629911625) Papercutz.

Lyga, Barry. The Astonishing Adventures of Fanboy & Goth Girl. 2007. (ENG.). 320p. (YA). (gr. 7-12). pap. 9.99 (978-0-618-91652-8(0)) Houghton Mifflin Harcourt Publishing Co.

—Mangaman. Doran, Colleen, illus. 2011. (ENG.). 144p. (YA). (gr. 7). 19.99 (978-0-547-42315-9(2)) Houghton Mifflin Harcourt Publishing Co.

Lynch, Brian. Leonardo. 1 vol. Campbell, Ross, illus. 2015. (ENG.). 24p. (J). (978-1-61479-339-7(5)) Spotlight.

—Michelangelo. 1 vol. Kuhn, Andy, illus. 2015. (ENG.). 24p. (J). (978-1-61479-340-3(9)) Spotlight.

—Raphael. 1 vol. Urru, Franco, illus. 2015. (ENG.). 24p. (J). (978-1-61479-341-0(7)) Spotlight.

Lynch, Brian & Waltz, Tom. Donatello. 1 vol. Schiti, Valerio, illus. 2015. (ENG.). 24p. (J). (978-1-61479-338-0(7)) Spotlight.

Lynch, Jay. Mo & Jo: Fighting Together Forever. Haspiel, Dean, illus. 2008. (ENG.). 40p. (J). (gr. -1-3). 12.95 (978-0-9799238-5-2(9)) TOON Books / RAW Junior, LLC.

—Otto's Backwards Day. Cammuso, Frank, illus. 2013. (ENG.). 32p. (J). (gr. -1-3). 12.95 (978-1-935179-33-7(0)) TOON Books / RAW Junior, LLC.

—Otto's Orange Day. Cammuso, Frank, illus. 2013. (ENG.). 40p. (J). (gr. -1-3). pap. 4.99 (978-1-935179-27-6(6)) TOON Books / RAW Junior, LLC.

—Otto's Orange Day. Mouly, Francoise, ed. Cammuso, Frank, illus. 2008. (ENG.). 40p. (J). (gr. -1-3). 12.95 (978-0-9799238-2-1(4)) TOON Books / RAW Junior, LLC.

Lynch, Jay & Cammuso, Frank. Otto's Orange Day. 1 vol. 2013. (Toon Bks). (ENG.). 36p. (J). (gr. 2-3). lib. bdg. 27.07 (978-1-61479-154-6(6)) Spotlight.

—Otto's Orange Day. 2013. (Toon Books Level 3 Ser.). lib. bdg. 14.75 (978-0-606-32103-7(9), Turtleback) Turtleback Bks.

Lynch, Jay & Haspiel, Dean. Mo & Jo: Fighting Together Forever. 1 vol. 2013. (Toon Bks). (ENG.). 40p. (J). (gr. 2-3). lib. bdg. 27.07 (978-1-61479-152-2(X)) Spotlight.

Ma, Wing Shing & Lau, Ding Kin. Chinese Hero Vol. 3: Tales of the Blood Sword. Yang, Sue & Stone, Benjamin, eds. Zhao, Yun, tr. from CHI. 2007. (ENG., Illus.). 280p. (YA). pap. 19.95 (978-1-59796-117-2(5)) DrMaster Pubns. Inc.

Macan, Darko. Soldier X. Kordey, Igor, illus. 2003. 144p. (YA). pap. 12.99 (978-0-7851-1013-2(5)) Marvel Worldwide, Inc.

Macauley, Jo. Secrets & Spies. 1 vol. 2014. (Secrets & Spies Ser.). (ENG.). 224p. (gr. 4-7). 106.60 (978-1-4342-9618-4(0)) Stone Arch Bks.

MacDonald, Kimber. The Misfits, Level 3. Swain, Wilson, illus. 2006. (ENG.). 24p. (J). (gr. 1-17). per. 3.99 (978-1-58476-421-2(X), IKIDS) Innovative Kids.

Machetto, Augusto, et al. A Present for Tinker Bell. Urbano, Emilio et al, illus. 2011. (Disney Fairies Ser.: 6). (ENG.). 64p. (J). (gr. 1-6). pap. 7.99 (978-1-59707-256-4(7), 9781597072564) Papercutz.

—Tinker Bell & the Lucky Rainbow. Dalena, Antonello et al, illus. 2012. (Disney Fairies Ser.: 10). (ENG.). 64p. (J). (gr. 1-6). 11.99 (978-1-59707-368-4(7), 9781597073684) Papercutz.

Mack, Stan & Champlin, Susan. Fight for Freedom. 2012. (Cartoon Chronicles of America Ser.). (ENG., Illus.). 128p. (J). (gr. 5-7). pap. 10.99 (978-1-59990-835-9(2), 9781599908359, Bloomsbury USA Childrens) Bloomsbury Publishing USA.

Mackay, Gregory. Anders & the Volcano. 2017. (Anders Ser.: 2). (ENG.). 176p. (J). (gr. 1-6). pap. 9.99 **(978-1-76029-003-0(3))** Allen & Unwin AUS. Dist: Independent Pubs. Group.

Mackie, Howard & Kavanagh, Terry. Gambit Classic - Volume 2. Janson, Klaus, illus. 2013. (ENG.). 208p. (J). (gr. 4-17). pap. 29.99 (978-0-7851-6790-7(0)) Marvel Worldwide, Inc.

Mackie, Howard, et al. X-Men - Age of Apocalypse Omnibus Companion. Dodson, Terry et al, illus. 2014. (ENG.). 992p. (J). (gr. 4-17). 99.99 (978-0-7851-8514-7(3)) Marvel Worldwide, Inc.

Macri, Thomas. The Story of the X-Men Level 2 Reader. Olliffe, Pat, illus. 2013. (World of Reading Ser.). (ENG.). 32p. (J). (gr. 1-3). pap. 3.99 (978-1-4231-7224-6(8)) Marvel Worldwide, Inc.

Maddox, Jake. Comeback Catcher. Muniz, Berenice, illus. 2017. (Jake Maddox Graphic Novels Ser.). (ENG.). 72p. (gr. 2-5). lib. bdg. 26.65 (978-1-4965-3700-3(9)) Stone Arch Bks.

—Impact Books, 10 bks., Set. Tiffany, Sean, illus. 2007. (Jake Maddox Sports Stories Ser.). (ENG.). 72p. (gr. 2-3). 253.20 (978-1-59889-462-2(5)) Stone Arch Bks.

—Jake Maddox Graphic Novels. 2017. (Jake Maddox Graphic Novels Ser.). (ENG.). 72p. (gr. 2-5). 106.60 (978-1-4965-3747-8(5)) Stone Arch Bks.

—Jake Maddox JV. 1 vol. Ray, Mike, illus. 2014. (Jake Maddox JV Ser.). (ENG.). 96p. (gr. 3-4). 103.96 (978-1-4342-9380-0(7)) Stone Arch Bks.

—Soccer Switch. Aburtov, Jesus Aburto, illus. 2017. (Jake Maddox Graphic Novels Ser.). (ENG.). 72p. (gr. 2-5). lib. bdg. 26.65 (978-1-4965-3699-0(1)) Stone Arch Bks.

Maese, Fares & Shakespeare, William. A Midsummer Night's Dream. 1 vol. Esparza, Andres et al, illus. 2011. (Shakespeare Graphics Ser.). (ENG.). 88p. (gr. 2-3). pap. 7.15 (978-1-4342-3449-0(5), Shakespeare Graphics) Stone Arch Bks.

Magnat, Julien. The Planet of the Snake. Smith, Anne & Smith, Owen, trs. Nautilus Studio, illus. 2015. (Little Prince Ser.: 24). (ENG.). 48p. (J). (gr. 4-8). 26.65 (978-1-4677-6199-4(0), Graphic Universe™) Lerner Publishing Group.

Magnat, Julien, et al. The Curse of the Cat People. Ellipsanime Staff & Dargaud Media Staff, illus. 2011. (Garfield Graphic Novels Ser.). (ENG.). 32p. (J). (gr. 1-6). 7.99 (978-1-59707-267-0(2), 9781597072670) Papercutz.

Magnet, Julien. The Planet of the Firebird. Klio Burrell, Carol, tr. ÉLyum Studio, illus. 2012. (Little Prince Ser.: 2). (ENG.). 56p. (J). (gr. 4-8). pap. 7.95 (978-0-8225-9423-9(4), Graphic Universe™) Lerner Publishing Group.

Magno, Carlos, illus. Transformers: Movie Prequel: Rising Storm: Vol 1. 1 vol. 2012. (Transformers: Dark of the Moon Movie Prequel Ser.). (ENG.). 24p. (J). 24.21 (978-1-59961-975-0(X), Graphic Novels) Spotlight.

—Transformers: Movie Prequel: Rising Storm: Vol 2. 1 vol. 2012. (Transformers: Dark of the Moon Movie Prequel Ser.). (ENG.). 24p. (J). 24.21 (978-1-59961-976-7(8), Graphic Novels) Spotlight.

—Transformers: Movie Prequel: Rising Storm: Vol 3. 1 vol. 2012. (Transformers: Dark of the Moon Movie Prequel Ser.). (ENG.). 24p. (J). 24.21 (978-1-59961-977-4(6), Graphic Novels) Spotlight.

—Transformers: Movie Prequel: Rising Storm: Vol 4. 1 vol. 2012. (Transformers: Dark of the Moon Movie Prequel Ser.). (ENG.). 24p. (J). 24.21 (978-1-59961-978-1(4), Graphic Novels) Spotlight.

Maihack, Mike. The Golden Lion. 2017. (Cleopatra in Space Ser.: 4). (ENG.). 208p. (J). (gr. 3-7). pap. 12.99 **(978-0-545-83872-8(X)**, Graphix) Scholastic, Inc.

—The Golden Lion. Maihack, Mike, illus. 2017. (Cleopatra in Space Ser.: 4). (ENG., Illus.). 208p. (J). (gr. 3-7). 22.99 **(978-0-545-83871-9(1)**, Graphix) Scholastic, Inc.

—Secret of the Time Tablets (Cleopatra in Space #3) 2016. (Cleopatra in Space Ser.: 3). (ENG.). 192p. (J). (gr. 3-7). pap. 12.99 (978-0-545-83867-2(3), Graphix) Scholastic, Inc.

—Target Practice. 2014. (Cleopatra in Space Ser.: 1). (ENG.). 176p. (J). (gr. 3-7). 22.99 (978-0-545-52842-9(9), Graphix) Scholastic, Inc.

—The Thief & the Sword. 2015. (Cleopatra in Space Ser.: 2). (ENG., Illus.). 192p. (J). (gr. 3-7). 22.99 (978-0-545-52844-3(5), Graphix) Scholastic, Inc.

MAKOTO, Mizobuchi. Pokémon: Arceus & the Jewel of Life. MAKOTO, Mizobuchi, illus. 2011. (ENG., Illus.). 200p. (J). pap. 9.99 (978-1-4215-3802-0(4)) Viz Media.

Makura, Sho. Panda Man & the Treasure Hunt. Kato, Haruhi, illus. 2011. (ENG.). 96p. (J). (gr. 1-4). pap. 7.99 (978-1-4215-3521-0(1)) Viz Media.

—Panda Man to the Rescue! Kato, Haruhi, illus. 2010. (ENG.). 96p. (J). pap. 7.99 (978-1-4215-3520-3(3)) Viz Media.

—Panda Man vs. Chiwanda. Kato, Haruhi, illus. 2011. (ENG.). 96p. (J). (gr. 1-4). pap. 7.99 (978-1-4215-3522-7(X)) Viz Media.

Malam, John, retold by. Oliver Twist. 2014. (Graphic Classics Ser.). 48p. (gr. 3-6). 37.10 (978-1-908973-89-4(7)) Book Hse. GBR. Dist: Black Rabbit Bks.

Malbrough, Page. Fire Proves Iron: Grounded Stars. Malbrough, Michael & Fisher, G. W., illus. 2004. 80p. (YA). per. 9.95 (978-0-9758883-0-8(7)) Malbrough, Michael.

Maleev, Alex, et al, illus. The Road to Civil War. 2007. (ENG.). 160p. (YA). (gr. 8-17). pap. 14.99 (978-0-7851-1974-6(4)) Marvel Worldwide, Inc.

Maloza, Herve. The Secret of Creation. 2011. 36p. 16.86 (978-1-4520-9878-4(6)) AuthorHouse.

The Man of Steel. 2013. (Man of Steel Ser.). (ENG.). 88p. (gr. 2-3). 106.60 (978-1-4342-4812-1(7)); 213.20 (978-1-4342-4811-4(9)); pap. 23.80 (978-1-4342-4864-0(X)); pap. 47.60 (978-1-4342-4863-3(1)) Stone Arch Bks. (DC Super Heroes).

Mandracchia, Charles, 8th, illus. & creator. Showtoonz Mandracchia, Charles, 8th, creator. 2nd l.t. ed. 2005. 38p. (J). per. 995.00 net. (978-0-9721957-2-0(6), Mandracchia Bks.) Mandracchia, Charles.

Mangual, Cynthia Ines. 3 Super Hero Tales (DC Super Friends) Random House & Doescher, Erik, illus. 2017. (Padded Board Book Ser.). (ENG.). 30p. (J). (— 1). bds. 11.99 **(978-1-5247-1714-8(2)**, Random Hse. Bks. for Young Readers) Random Hse. Children's Bks.

Manning, Matthew. Batgirl: New Hero of the Night (Backstories) Spaziante, Patrick, illus. 2017. (Backstories Ser.). (ENG.). 128p. (J). (gr. 3-7). pap. 5.99 (978-1-338-11741-7(6)) Scholastic, Inc.

Manning, Matthew K. Batman Character Encyclopedia. 2016. (ENG., Illus.). 208p. (J). (gr. k-4). 16.99 (978-1-4654-4498-1(X), DK Children) Dorling Kindersley Publishing, Inc.

—Batman Tangles with Terror. Beavers, Ethen, illus. 2017. (DC Super Hero Stories Ser.). (ENG.). 56p. (gr. 1-3). lib. bdg. 25.32 (978-1-4965-4632-6(6), DC Super Heroes) Stone Arch Bks.

—Catwoman's Nine Lives. 1 vol. Vecchio, Luciano, illus. 2014. (Batman: Comic Chapter Bks.). (ENG.). 88p. (gr. 3-7). 21.32 (978-1-4342-9132-5(4)) Stone Arch Bks.

—DC Super Hero Stories. Beavers, Ethen, illus. 2017. (DC Super Hero Stories Ser.). (ENG.). 56p. (gr. 1-3). 101.28 (978-1-4965-4636-4(9), DC Super Heroes) Stone Arch Bks.

—Go Slow. Lima, Dijjo & Furuzono, Carlos, illus. 2016. (EOD Soldiers Ser.). (ENG.). 40p. (gr. 4-8). lib. bdg. 26.65 (978-1-4965-3109-4(4)) Stone Arch Bks.

—The List. Lima, Rico et al, illus. 2016. (EOD Soldiers Ser.). (ENG.). 40p. (gr. 4-8). lib. bdg. 26.65 (978-1-4965-3110-0(8)) Stone Arch Bks.

—The Mist. Lima, Rico & Bello, Thiago Dal, illus. 2016. (EOD Soldiers Ser.). (ENG.). 40p. (gr. 4-8). lib. bdg. 26.65 (978-1-4965-3108-7(6)) Stone Arch Bks.

—Mystery of the Mist Monster. Neely, Scott, illus. 2016. (Scooby-Doo Comic Chapter Bks.). (ENG.). 88p. (gr. 3-7). lib. bdg. 27.32 (978-1-4965-3586-3(3)) Capstone Press of Coughlan Cos.

—Secret of the Haunted Cave. Neely, Scott, illus. 2016. (Scooby-Doo Comic Chapter Bks.). (ENG.). 88p. (gr. 3-7). lib. bdg. 27.32 (978-1-4965-3585-6(5)) Capstone Press of Coughlan Cos.

—Two Sides. Lima, Dijjo & Furuzono, Carlos, illus. 2016. (EOD Soldiers Ser.). (ENG.). 40p. (gr. 4-8). lib. bdg. 26.65 (978-1-4965-3107-0(8)) Stone Arch Bks.

Manning, Matthew K. & Poe, Edgar Allen. The Fall of the House of Usher. 1 vol. Jimenz, Jim & Calero, Dennis, illus. 2013. (Edgar Allan Poe Graphic Novels Ser.). (ENG.). 72p. (gr. 2-3). 27.99 (978-1-4342-3024-9(4)); pap. 6.10 (978-1-4342-4258-7(7)) Stone Arch Bks.

Manning, Matthew K., et al. The Attack of Professor Zoom!. 1 vol. 2011. (Flash Ser.). (ENG., Illus.). 56p. (gr. 2-3). pap. 4.95 (978-1-4342-3091-1(0)); lib. bdg. 26.65 (978-1-4342-2614-3(X)) Stone Arch Bks. (DC Super Heroes).

—Little Green Men. (Superman Ser.). (ENG., Illus.). 56p. (gr. 2-3). 2013. pap. 4.95 (978-1-4342-2259-6(4)) 2010. lib. bdg. 26.65 (978-1-4342-1881-0(3)) Stone Arch Bks. (DC Super Heroes).

—Two-Face's Double Take. McManus, Shawn, illus. (Batman Ser.). (ENG.). 56p. (gr. 2-3). 2013. pap. 4.95 (978-1-4342-2264-0(0)) 2010. lib. bdg. 26.65 (978-1-4342-1878-0(3)) Stone Arch Bks. (DC Super Heroes).

Manning, Mick. William Shakespeare: Scenes from the Life of the World's Greatest Writer. Granström, Brita, illus. 2017. (ENG.). 48p. (J). (gr. 3-7). pap. 11.99 (978-1-84780-759-5(3), Frances Lincoln Children's Bks.) Quarto Publishing Group UK GBR. Dist: Hachette Bk. Group.

Marathon, creator. Trouble in the Tropics. 2005. (Totally Spies! Ser.: Vol. 3). (Illus.). pap. 14.99 (978-1-59532-817-5(3), Tokyopop Kids) TOKYOPOP, Inc.

Marazano, Richard. Civilisation. 2 vols. Ponzio, Jean-Michel, illus. 2010. (Chimpanzee Complex Ser.: 3). (ENG.). 55p. pap. 13.95 (978-1-84918-043-6(1)) CineBook GBR. Dist: National Bk. Network.

March, Julia. Ultimate Sticker Collection: Spider-Man. 2017. (Ultimate Sticker Collections). (ENG.). 96p. (J). (gr. 1-4). pap. 12.99 **(978-1-4654-6192-6(2)**, DK Children) Dorling Kindersley Publishing, Inc.

Marcoux, Tom. Crystal Pegasus. 2012. 92p. pap. 18.24 (978-0-9800511-9-3(3)) Marcoux, Tom Media, LLC.

Marder, Larry. Beanworld: Tales of the Beanworld. Schutz, Diana, ed. Marder, Larry, illus. 2012. (ENG., Illus.). 64p. 14.99 (978-1-59582-897-2(4)) Dark Horse Comics.

Marini, Enrico & Dufaux, Jean. Rapaces, Vol. 4. 2005. (SPA., Illus.). 56p. pap. 17.95 (978-1-59497-107-5(2)) Public Square Bks.

Mariolle, Mathieu. Changing Moon. MiniKim et al, illus. 2010. (Nola's Worlds Ser.: 1). (ENG.). 136p. (J). (gr. 6-9). 30.60 (978-0-7613-6502-0(8)) Lerner Publishing Group.

—Changing Moon. Jeffrey, Erica Olson, tr. from FRE. MiniKim et al, illus. 2010. (Nola's Worlds Ser.: 1). (ENG.). 136p. (J). (gr. 6-9). pap. 9.95 (978-0-7613-6538-9(9), Graphic Universe™) Lerner Publishing Group.

—Even for a Dreamer Like Me. MiniKim et al, illus. 2010. (Nola's Worlds Ser.: 3). (ENG.). 128p. (J). (gr. 6-9). 30.60 (978-0-7613-6505-1(2)) Lerner Publishing Group.

—Even for a Dreamer Like Me. Jeffrey, Erica Olson, tr. from FRE. MiniKim et al, illus. 2010. (Nola's Worlds Ser.: 3). (ENG.). 136p. (J). (gr. 6-9). pap. 9.95 (978-0-7613-6541-9(9), Graphic Universe™) Lerner Publishing Group.

—Ferrets & Ferreting Out. Buffiere, Mélanie & Lajic, Maïté, illus. 2010. (Nola's Worlds Ser.: 2). (ENG.). 136p. (J). (gr. 6-9). pap. 9.95 (978-0-7613-6542-6(7), Graphic Universe™) Lerner Publishing Group.

—Ferrets & Ferreting Out. MiniKim et al, illus. 2010. (Nola's Worlds Ser.: 2). (ENG.). 136p. (J). (gr. 6-9). 30.60 (978-0-7613-6504-4(4)) Lerner Publishing Group.

Marko, Cyndi. This Little Piggy: An Owner's Manual. Marko, Cyndi, illus. 2017. (Pix Ser.). (ENG., Illus.). 64p. (J). (gr. 1-4). 14.99 **(978-1-4814-6826-8(X)**, Aladdin) Simon & Schuster Children's Publishing.

Marks, Melanie. Phonics Comics: Spooky Sara - Level 3, Level 3. Ball, Victoria, illus. 2006. (ENG.). 24p. (J). (gr. 1-17). per. 3.99 (978-1-58476-473-1(2), IKIDS) Innovative Kids.

—Phonics Comics: Super Sam - Level 3: Issue 1. Collins, Daryl, illus. 2006. (ENG.). 24p. (J). (gr. 1-17). per. 3.99 (978-1-58476-420-5(1), IKIDS) Innovative Kids.

Marr, Melissa. Desert Tales. 2013. (Wicked Lovely Ser.). (ENG.). 272p. (YA). (gr. 8). pap. 9.99 (978-0-06-228756-4(7)) HarperCollins Pubs.

—Resolve. Xian Nu Studio, illus. 2011. (Wicked Lovely: Desert Tales Ser.: 3). (ENG.). 176p. (YA). (gr. 8-18). pap. 9.99 (978-0-06-149350-8(3)) HarperCollins Pubs.

Marsh, Robert. Monster & Me. 1 vol. Percival, Tom, illus. 2009. (Monster & Me Ser.). (ENG.). 40p. (gr. 1-3). lib. bdg. 23.99 (978-1-4342-1589-5(X), Graphic Sparks) Stone Arch Bks.

—Monster in the Outfield. 1 vol. Percival, Tom, illus. 2009. (Monster & Me Ser.). (ENG.). 40p. (gr. 1-3). lib. bdg. 23.99 (978-1-4342-1590-1(3), Graphic Sparks) Stone Arch Bks.

—Monster Moneymaker. 1 vol. Percival, Tom, illus. 2010. (Monster & Me Ser.). (ENG.). 40p. (gr. 1-3). lib. bdg. 23.99 (978-1-4342-1891-9(0), Graphic Sparks) Stone Arch Bks.

Marsham, Liz. DK Readers L3: DC Comics Wonder Woman: Warrior for Justice! 2017. (DK Readers Ser.). (ENG.). 64p. (J). (gr. 2-4). 14.99 (978-1-4654-6065-3(9), DK Children) Dorling Kindersley Publishing, Inc.

Marsham, Liz. Wonder Woman Classic: Maze of Magic. Ferguson, Lee, illus. 2017. (I Can Read Level 2 Ser.). 32p. (J). (gr. -1-3). pap. 3.99 **(978-0-06-236093-9(0))** HarperCollins Pubs.

Martin, Ann M. Kristy's Great Idea. Telgemeier, Raina, illus. rev. ed. 2015. (Baby-Sitters Club Graphix Ser.: 1). (ENG.). 192p. (J). (gr. 3-7). 24.99 (978-0-545-81386-0(7), Graphix) Scholastic, Inc.

Martin, Gary & Zondervan Bibles Staff. The Sword of Revenge. 1 vol. Rogers, Bud, ed. Cariello, Sergio, illus. 2009. (Z Graphic Novels / Son of Samson Ser.). (ENG.). 160p. (J). pap. 6.99 (978-0-310-71285-5(8)) Zondervan.

Martin, Gary & Zondervan Staff. The Heroes of God. 1 vol. Cariello, Sergio, illus. 2009. (Z Graphic Novels / Son of Samson Ser.). (ENG.). 160p. (J). pap. 6.99 (978-0-310-71284-8(X)) Zondervan.

Martin, Gary, et al. The Maiden of Thunder. 1 vol. Cariello, Sergio & Lanphear, Dave, illus. 2008. (Z Graphic Novels / Son of Samson Ser.). (ENG.). 160p. (J). (gr. 4-7). pap. 6.99 (978-0-310-71281-7(5)) Zondervan.

Martin, George R. R. & Avery, Ben. The Sworn Sword. 0 vols. 2014. (Game of Thrones Ser.). (ENG., Illus.). 184p. (YA). pap. 14.95 (978-1-4778-4929-3(7), 9781477849293, Jet City Comics) Amazon Publishing.

Martz, John. A Cat Named Tim & Other Stories. 2014. (ENG., Illus.). 52p. (gr. -1-k). 19.95 (978-1-927668-10-8(7)) Koyama Pr. CAN. Dist: Consortium Bk. Sales & Distribution.

Maruto, Fumiaki. How to Raise a Boring Girlfriend, Vol. 4. 2016. (How to Raise a Boring Girlfriend Ser.: 4). (ENG., Illus.). 176p. (gr. 11-17). pap. 13.00 (978-0-316-31085-7(9), Yen Pr.) Orbit.

—How to Raise a Boring Girlfriend, Vol. 5. 2017. (How to Raise a Boring Girlfriend Ser.: 5). (ENG., Illus.). 176p. (gr. 11-17). pap. 13.00 (978-0-316-31647-7(4), Yen Pr.) Orbit.

Marvel. Marvel Super Heroes Assemble! Tattoos, Fantastic Facts, & Amazing Activites. 2014. (ENG.). 24p. (J). (gr. -1-1). pap. 7.99 (978-0-7944-3008-5(2), Reader's Digest Children's Bks.) Studio Fun International.

—Marvel's Guardians of the Galaxy, Vol. 2. 2017. (ENG., Illus.). 12p. (J). (gr. -1-1). pap. 6.99 (978-0-316-27170-7(5)) Little, Brown Bks. for Young Readers.

—Marvel's the Avengers Storybook Collection. 2015. (ENG., Illus.). 192p. (J). (gr. -1-3). 11.99 (978-0-316-25631-5(5)) Little, Brown Bks. for Young Readers.

Marvel. Meet Spidey. 2017. (ENG., Illus.). 32p. (J). (gr. -1-3). pap. 4.99 **(978-0-316-43834-6(0))** Little, Brown Bks. for Young Readers.

Marvel & Busse, R. R. Meet the Team! 2017. (Passport to Reading Level 2 Ser.). (ENG., Illus.). 32p. (J). (gr. -1-3). pap. 4.99 (978-0-316-27167-7(5)) Little, Brown Bks. for Young Readers.

—Revenge of the Ravagers. 2017. (ENG., Illus.). 24p. (J). (gr. -1-3). pap. 4.99 (978-0-316-27161-5(6)) Little, Brown Bks. for Young Readers.

Marvel & Busse, R. R. The Tangled Web of Super Tech. 2017. (ENG., Illus.). 32p. (J). (gr. -1-3). pap. 5.99 **(978-0-316-43822-3(7))** Little, Brown Bks. for Young Readers.

Marvel & Cho, Charles. The Return of Rocket & Groot. 2017. (ENG., Illus.). 24p. (J). (gr. -1-3). pap. 4.99 (978-0-316-27162-2(4)) Little, Brown Bks. for Young Readers.

Marvel & May, Tallulah. Mayhem at the Monument. 2017. (ENG., Illus.). 32p. (J). (gr. -1-3). pap. 4.99 **(978-0-316-43831-5(6))** Little, Brown Bks. for Young Readers.

Marvel & McCann, Jim. Guardians of the Galaxy, Vol. 2. 2017. (ENG.). 176p. (J). (gr. 3-7). 9.99 (978-0-316-27163-9(2)) Little, Brown Bks. for Young Readers.

Marvel & McCann, Jim. The Stick-Like-Spidey. 2017. (ENG.). 160p. (J). (gr. 3-7). 9.99 **(978-0-316-43818-6(9))**; pap. 6.99 **(978-0-316-43817-9(0))** Little, Brown Bks. for Young Readers.

Marvel & Wyatt, Chris. Marvel's Avengers: Age of Ultron: the Deluxe Junior Novel. 2015. (ENG., Illus.). 144p. (J). (gr. 3-7). 9.99 (978-0-316-30105-3(1)) Little, Brown Bks. for Young Readers.

Marvel, et al. Best of Wolverine, Vol. 1. 2004. (Wolverine Ser.). (Illus.). 320p. 29.99 (978-0-7851-1370-6(3)) Marvel Worldwide, Inc.

Marvel Book Group. Captain America: the First Avenger Read-Along Storybook & CD. 2016. (Read-Along Storybook & CD Ser.). (ENG.). 32p. (J). (gr. -1-k). pap. 6.99 (978-1-4847-5131-2(0), Marvel Pr.) Disney Publishing Worldwide.

—Iron-Man 2. 2016. (Read-Along Storybook & CD Ser.). (ENG.). 32p. (J). (gr. -1-k). pap. 6.99 (978-1-4847-8630-7(0), Marvel Pr.) Disney Publishing Worldwide.

—Iron Man Read-Along Storybook & CD. 2016. (Read-Along Storybook & CD Ser.). (ENG.). 32p. (J). (gr. -1-k). pap. 6.99 (978-1-4847-5182-4(5), Marvel Pr.) Disney Publishing Worldwide.

—World of Reading: Avengers the New Team: Level 1. 2015. (World of Reading Ser.). (ENG.). 32p. (J). (gr. -1-1). pap. 3.99 (978-1-4847-1454-6(7), Marvel Pr.) Disney Publishing Worldwide.

—World of Reading: Hawkeye This Is Hawkeye. 2015. (World of Reading Ser.). (ENG.). 32p. (J). (gr. 1-3). pap. 3.99 (978-1-4847-2591-7(3), Marvel Pr.) Disney Publishing Worldwide.

Marvel Book Group & Wong, Clarissa S. World of Reading Falcon: This Is Falcon: Level 1. Lim, Ron & Rosenberg, Rachelle, illus. 2015. (World of Reading Ser.). (ENG.). 32p. (J). (gr. 1-3). pap. 3.99 (978-1-4847-2259-6(0), Marvel Pr.) Disney Publishing Worldwide.

Marvel Comics, text. Annihilation Omnibus. 2014. (ENG., Illus.). 880p. (YA). (gr. 8-17). 125.00 *(978-0-7851-8889-6(4))* Marvel Worldwide, Inc.

—Marvel's Agents of S. H. I. E. L. D. 2014. (ENG., Illus.). 240p. (J). (gr. -1-17). 49.99 *(978-0-7851-8998-5(X))* Marvel Worldwide, Inc.

—Max Ride: Final Flight. 2017. (ENG., Illus.). 136p. (J). (gr. 4-17). 24.99 *(978-1-302-90333-6(0))* Marvel Worldwide, Inc.

—Toy Story: Tales from the Toy Chest. 2012. (ENG., Illus.). 96p. (J). (gr. -1-17). pap. 9.99 *(978-0-7851-6506-4(1))* Marvel Worldwide, Inc.

—Women of Power Standee Punch-Out Book. 2017. (ENG., Illus.). 18p. (YA). (gr. 8-17). 24.99 *(978-1-302-90456-2(6))* Marvel Worldwide, Inc.

Marvel Comics Staff, creator. Ultimate X-Men, Bk. 1. 2006. (ENG., Illus.). 336p. (J). (gr. -1-17). pap. 24.99 *(978-0-7851-2187-9(0))* Marvel Worldwide, Inc.

Marvel Comics Staff & Kirby, Jack, texts. Devil Dinosaur. 2014. (ENG., Illus.). 184p. (J). (gr. 4-17). pap. 24.99 *(978-0-7851-9037-0(6))* Marvel Worldwide, Inc.

Marvel Heroes. 2015. *(978-1-4508-9771-6(1)*, PIL Kids) Publications International, Ltd.

Marvel Press Book Group. Astonishing Adventures!, 3 Bks In 1. 2016. (Mighty Marvel Chapter Book Ser.: 1). (ENG.). 400p. (J). (gr. 3-7). pap. 11.99 *(978-1-4847-6731-3(4)*, Marvel Pr.) Disney Publishing Worldwide.

—Mighty Numbers. 2016. (ENG.). 20p. (J). (gr. -1 — 1). bds. 7.99 *(978-1-4847-3271-7(5)*, Marvel Pr.) Disney Publishing Worldwide.

—5-Minute Avengers Stories. 2015. (5-Minute Stories Ser.). (ENG.). 192p. (J). (gr. 1-3). 12.99 *(978-1-4847-4331-7(8)*, Marvel Pr.) Disney Publishing Worldwide.

Marvel Press Group & Disney Book Group Staff. Marvel Super Heroes. Disney Book Group Staff, illus. 2013. (Storybook Collection). (ENG., Illus.). 304p. (J). (gr. -1-k). 15.99 *(978-1-4231-7223-9(X))* Marvel Worldwide, Inc.

Marvel Press Group Staff, et al. The X-Men. Oliffe, Pat et al, illus. 2nd ed. 2014. (Origin Story Ser.). (ENG.). 48p. (J). (gr. 1-3). 8.99 *(978-1-4231-7226-0(4))* Marvel Worldwide, Inc.

Marvel Press Staff & Palacios, Tomas. Suits of Armor. Disney Book Group Staff, illus. 2013. (ENG.). 24p. (J). (gr. -1-k). pap. 3.99 *(978-1-4231-7246-8(9))* Marvel Worldwide, Inc.

Marz, Ron. Artifacts, Vol. 5. 2013. (ENG., Illus.). 160p. (YA). pap. 16.99 *(978-1-60706-664-4(5)*, 9781607066644) Image Comics.

—Mystic Traveler: The Demon Queen, Vol. 2. Peterson, Brandon et al, illus. 2004. (Mystic Traveler Ser.). 160p. (YA). pap. 9.95 *(978-1-59314-037-3(1))* CrossGeneration Comics, Inc.

—Scion Vol. 6: The Royal Wedding. Cheung, Jim et al, illus. 2004. (Scion Ser.). 160p. (YA). pap. 15.95 *(978-1-59314-034-2(7))* CrossGeneration Comics, Inc.

—Witchblade Redemption, Vol. 4. 2012. (ENG., Illus.). 160p. pap. 19.99 *(978-1-60706-424-4(3)*, 9781607064244) Image Comics.

Marz, Ron, et al. Progeny Volume 1 TP. 2013. (ENG., Illus.). 144p. (YA). pap. 16.99 *(978-1-60706-748-1(X)*, 9781607067481) Image Comics.

Mashima, Hiro. Rave. 2006. (Rave Ser.). (SPA., Illus.). reprint ed. Vol. 1. 185p. pap. 10.95 *(978-1-59497-175-4(7))* Vol. 3. 184p. pap. 10.95 *(978-1-59497-177-8(3))* Vol. 4. 188p. per. 10.95 *(978-1-59497-178-5(1))* Vol. 5. 192p. pap. 10.95 *(978-1-59497-179-2(X))* Vol. 6. 200p. pap. 10.95 *(978-1-59497-180-8(3))* Public Square Bks.

—Rave: Volume 2, Vol. 2. 2006. (Rave Ser.). (SPA., Illus.). 180p. reprint ed. pap. 10.95 *(978-1-59497-176-1(5))* Public Square Bks.

—Rave: Volume 7, Vol. 7. 2006. (Rave Ser.). (SPA., Illus.). 189p. reprint ed. pap. 10.95 *(978-1-59497-199-0(4))* Public Square Bks.

—Rave: Volume 9, Vol. 9. 2006. (Rave Ser.). (SPA., Illus.). 189p. reprint ed. pap. 10.95 *(978-1-59497-201-0(X))* Public Square Bks.

—Rave Master. Vol. 4. pap. 7.99 *(978-1-59532-792-5(4))* Vol. 5. (Illus.). 200p. pap. 7.99 *(978-1-59532-793-2(2))* TOKYOPOP, Inc.

—Rave, Volume 8, Vol. 8. 2006. (Rave Ser.). (SPA., Illus.). 171p. reprint ed. pap. 10.95 *(978-1-59497-200-3(1))* Public Square Bks.

Mason, Jane B., et al. Captain Cold's Arctic Eruption, 1 vol. Doescher, Erik, illus. 2011. (Flash Ser.). (ENG.). 56p. (gr. 2-3). pap. 4.95 *(978-1-4342-3089-8(9))*; lib. bdg. 26.65 *(978-1-4342-2617-4(4))* Stone Arch Bks. (DC Super Heroes).

Matas, Toni. St. Ignatius of Loyola, Leading the Way. Picanyol, illus. 2013. (J). 8.95 *(978-0-8198-7298-2(9))* Pauline Bks. & Media.

Matheny, Bill, et al. Alfred to the Rescue?! 2015. (Batman Strikes! Ser.). (ENG., Illus.). 32p. (gr. 2-3). lib. bdg. 22.60 *(978-1-4342-9664-1(4))* Stone Arch Bks.

—Bane on the Rampage!, 1 vol. 2014. (Batman Strikes! Ser.). (ENG., Illus.). 32p. (gr. 2-3). 22.60 *(978-1-4342-4788-9(0))* Stone Arch Bks.

—Bane's Breaking In! 2015. (Batman Strikes! Ser.). (ENG., Illus.). 32p. (gr. 2-3). lib. bdg. 22.60 *(978-1-4342-9665-8(2))* Stone Arch Bks.

—The Batman Is on Fire!, 1 vol. 2014. (Batman Strikes! Ser.). (ENG., Illus.). 32p. (gr. 2-3). 22.60 *(978-1-4342-9229-2(0))* Stone Arch Bks.

—Batman Strikes!, 1 vol. 2014. (Batman Strikes! Ser.). (ENG., Illus.). 32p. (gr. 2-3). 90.40 *(978-1-4342-9518-7(4))*; 90.40 *(978-1-4342-8928-5(1))* Stone Arch Bks.

—Batman Strikes, 1 vol. 2014. (Batman Strikes! Ser.). (ENG., Illus.). 32p. (gr. 2-3). 180.80 *(978-1-4342-9600-9(8))* Stone Arch Bks.

—Catwoman Gets Busted by the Batman, 1 vol. 2014. (Batman Strikes! Ser.). (ENG., Illus.). 32p. (gr. 2-3). 22.60 *(978-1-4342-9211-7(8))* Stone Arch Bks.

—Frozen Solid by Mr. Freeze!, 1 vol. 2014. (Batman Strikes! Ser.). (ENG., Illus.). 32p. (gr. 2-3). 22.60 *(978-1-4342-9212-4(6))* Stone Arch Bks.

—Going... Batty!, 1 vol. 2014. (Batman Strikes! Ser.). (ENG., Illus.). 32p. (gr. 2-3). 22.60 *(978-1-4342-6484-8(X))* Stone Arch Bks.

—In the Clutches of the Penguin!, 1 vol. 2014. (Batman Strikes! Ser.). (ENG., Illus.). 32p. (gr. 2-3). 22.60 *(978-1-4342-6483-1(1))* Stone Arch Bks.

—Joker's Wild!, 1 vol. 2014. (Batman Strikes! Ser.). (ENG., Illus.). 32p. (gr. 2-3). 22.60 *(978-1-4342-6485-5(8))* Stone Arch Bks.

—Man-Bat's Sneak Attack! 2015. (Batman Strikes! Ser.). (ENG., Illus.). 32p. (gr. 2-3). lib. bdg. 22.60 *(978-1-4342-9655-9(5))* Stone Arch Bks.

—Sanity Plea! 2015. (Batman Strikes! Ser.). (ENG., Illus.). 32p. (gr. 2-3). lib. bdg. 22.60 *(978-1-4342-9743-3(8))* Stone Arch Bks.

—Scarface Is Gonna Go Boom!, 1 vol. 2014. (Batman Strikes! Ser.). (ENG., Illus.). 32p. (gr. 2-3). 22.60 *(978-1-4342-9210-0(X))* Stone Arch Bks.

Matheson, Dan. Before: The Smith & Miya Collection. 2016. (ENG., Illus.). (J). (gr. 3-6). pap. ***(978-1-925590-11-1(9))*** Vivid Publishing.

Matsumoto, Tomo. Beauty is the Beast, Vol. 4. Matsumoto, Tomo, illus. 2006. (ENG., Illus.). 208p. pap. 8.99 *(978-1-4215-0354-7(9))* Viz Media.

Matsuura, Tokihiko. Tuxedo Gin, Vol. 10. Matsuura, Tokihiko, illus. 2005. (Tuxedo Gin Ser.: 10). (ENG., Illus.). 200p. pap. 9.95 *(978-1-59116-695-5(0))* Viz Media.

Matte, Johane, et al. Flight Explorer, Vol. 1. Kibuishi, Kazu, ed. Armstrong, Matthew S., illus. 2008. (ENG.). 112p. (YA). pap. 16.00 *(978-0-345-50313-8(9)*, Villard Bks.) Random House Publishing Group.

Matthews, Alex. Penguins of Madagascar, Vol. 1. Fereyra, Lucas, illus. 2015. (ENG.). 64p. (J). (gr. 1-4). pap. 6.99 *(978-1-78276-251-5(5))* Titan Bks. Ltd. GBR. Dist: Penguin Random Hse. LLC.

Matthews, Andrew. Gulliver's Travels. Horrocks, Steve, illus. 2014. (Collins Big Cat Progress Ser.). (ENG.). 32p. (J). (gr. 5-6). pap. 7.99 *(978-0-00-751937-8(0))* HarperCollins Pubs. Ltd. GBR. Dist: Independent Pubs. Group.

Mayer, Kirsten. I Am Aquaman. Smith, Andy & Vancata, Brad, illus. 2013. (I Can Read Level 2 Ser.). (ENG.). 32p. (J). (gr. -1-3). pap. 3.99 *(978-0-06-221003-6(3))* HarperCollins Pubs.

Mayhall, Robin. He Loves Me, He Loves Me Not. Cella, Kristen & Tiede, Dirk, illus. 2013. (My Boyfriend Is a Monster Ser.: 7). (ENG.). 128p. (YA). (gr. 7-12). lib. bdg. 29.27 *(978-0-7613-6005-6(0)*, Graphic Universe™) Lerner Publishing Group.

—He Loves Me, He Loves Me Not. Cella, Kristen et al, illus. 2013. (My Boyfriend Is a Monster Ser.: 7). (ENG.). 128p. (YA). (gr. 7-12). pap. 9.95 *(978-0-7613-8548-6(7)*, Graphic Universe™) Lerner Publishing Group.

—The Quest for Dragon Mountain. Martinez, Alitha E., illus. 2010. (Twisted Journeys (r) Ser.: 16). (ENG.). 112p. (J). (gr. 4-7). pap. 7.95 *(978-0-8225-9267-9(3)*, Graphic Universe™) Lerner Publishing Group.

McAdams Moore, Carol. Phonics Comics: Cave Dave - Level 1. Dammer, Mike, illus. 2007. (ENG.). 24p. (J). (gr. 1-17). per. 3.99 *(978-1-58476-552-3(6))* Innovative Kids.

McAnulty, Stacy. Goldie Blox & the Three Dares. 2017. (Goldie Blox Ser.). lib. bdg. 17.20 ***(978-0-606-40255-2(1))*** Turtleback Bks.

—Goldie Blox Rules the School! 2017. (Goldie Blox Ser.). lib. bdg. 17.20 ***(978-0-606-40256-9(X))*** Turtleback Bks.

McCann, Jesse L., et al. Bad Moon Rising, 1 vol. 2014. (Krypto the Superdog Ser.). (ENG., Illus.). 32p. (gr. 1-2). 22.60 *(978-1-4342-6475-6(0))* Stone Arch Bks.

—Crisis of Infinite Kryptos, 1 vol. 2014. (Krypto the Superdog Ser.). (ENG., Illus.). 32p. (gr. 1-2). 22.60 *(978-1-4342-6471-8(8))* Stone Arch Bks.

—Here Comes Krypto, 1 vol. 2014. (Krypto the Superdog Ser.). (ENG., Illus.). 32p. (gr. 1-2). 22.60 *(978-1-4342-4785-8(6))* Stone Arch Bks.

—Houndin' the Mail Carrier!, 1 vol. 2014. (Krypto the Superdog Ser.). (ENG., Illus.). 32p. (gr. 1-2). 22.60 *(978-1-4342-6472-5(6))* Stone Arch Bks.

—The Purr-Fect Crime, 1 vol. 2014. (Krypto the Superdog Ser.). (ENG., Illus.). 32p. (gr. 1-2). 22.60 *(978-1-4342-6474-9(2))* Stone Arch Bks.

—Three Naughty Doggies!, 1 vol. 2014. (Krypto the Superdog Ser.). (ENG., Illus.). 32p. (gr. 1-2). 22.60 *(978-1-4342-6473-2(4))* Stone Arch Bks.

McClintock, Norah. I, Witness, 1 vol. Deas, Mike, illus. 2012. (ENG.). 144p. (YA). (gr. 8-12). pap. 16.95 *(978-1-55469-789-2(1))* Orca Bk. Pubs. USA.

—Tru Detective, 1 vol. Hughes, Steven, illus. 2015. (ENG.). 128p. (YA). (gr. 10-12). pap. 19.95 *(978-1-4598-0379-4(5))* Orca Bk. Pubs. USA.

McCLOUD, Scott. Be Careful What You Wish For... Burchett, Rick & Austin, Terry, illus. 2012. (Superman Adventures Ser.). (ENG.). 32p. (gr. 2-3). lib. bdg. 22.60 *(978-1-4342-4550-2(0))* Stone Arch Bks.

—Distant Thunder, 1 vol. Burchett, Rick & Austin, Terry, illus. 2012. (Superman Adventures Ser.). (ENG.). 32p. (gr. 2-3). 22.60 *(978-1-4342-4551-9(9))* Stone Arch Bks.

—Eye to Eye, 1 vol. Burchett, Rick & Austin, Terry, illus. 2012. (Superman Adventures Ser.). (ENG.). 32p. (gr. 2-3). lib. bdg. 22.60 *(978-1-4342-4552-6(7))* Stone Arch Bks.

—Seonimod, 1 vol. Austin, Terry & Burchett, Rick, illus. 2013. (Superman Adventures Ser.). (ENG.). 32p. (gr. 2-3). lib. bdg. 22.60 *(978-1-4342-4711-7(2))* Stone Arch Bks.

—Superman Adventures. 2013. (Superman Adventures Ser.). (ENG.). 32p. (gr. 1-2). 90.40 *(978-1-4342-4859-6(3))* Stone Arch Bks.

—Tiny Problems!, 1 vol. Austin, Terry & Burchett, Rick, illus. 2013. (Superman Adventures Ser.). (ENG.). 32p. (gr. 2-3). lib. bdg. 22.60 *(978-1-4342-4712-4(0))* Stone Arch Bks.

McCollum, Rick, et al. Teenage Mutant Ninja Turtles Classics Volume 5. 2013. (Teenage Mutant Ninja Turtles Ser.). (ENG., Illus.). 132p. pap. 19.99 *(978-1-61377-639-1(X)*, 9781613776391) Idea & Design Works, LLC.

McCool, Ben. Souljacker: #2. Rousseau, Craig, illus. 2012. (Captain America: the Korvac Saga Ser.). 24p. (J). (gr. 3-5). lib. bdg. 24.21 *(978-1-61479-020-4(5))* Spotlight.

—The Star Lord: #4. Rousseau, Craig, illus. 2012. (Captain America: the Korvac Saga Ser.). 24p. (J). (gr. 3-5). lib. bdg. 24.21 *(978-1-61479-022-8(1))* Spotlight.

—Strange Days: #1. Rousseau, Craig, illus. 2012. (Captain America: the Korvac Saga Ser.). 24p. (J). (gr. 3-5). lib. bdg. 24.21 *(978-1-61479-019-8(1))* Spotlight.

—The Traveler: #3. Rousseau, Craig, illus. 2012. (Captain America: the Korvac Saga Ser.). 24p. (J). (gr. 3-5). lib. bdg. 24.21 *(978-1-61479-021-1(3))* Spotlight.

McCool, Ben, et al. Grumpy Cat & Pokey, Vol. 3. 2017. (ENG., Illus.). 104p. (J). 12.99 *(978-1-5241-0246-3(6)*, 9781524102463, Dynamite Entertainment) Dynamic Forces, Inc.

McCoola, Marika. Baba Yaga's Assistant. 2015. (ENG., Illus.). 136p. (J). (gr. 5). 16.99 *(978-0-7636-6961-4(X))* Candlewick Pr.

Mccormick, Scott. It's Go Time! 2015. (Mr. Pants Ser.). lib. bdg. 18.40 *(978-0-606-38216-8(X))* Turtleback Bks.

—Slacks, Camera, Action! 2015. (Mr. Pants Ser.). lib. bdg. 18.40 *(978-0-606-38217-5(8))* Turtleback Bks.

Mccraken, Craig, et al. Power Party, Vol. 1. Carolan, Sean & Denson, Abby, illus. 2013. (Powerpuff Girls Ser.). (ENG.). 148p. pap. 19.99 *(978-1-61377-733-6(7)*, 9781613777336) Idea & Design Works, LLC.

McCranie, Stephen. Food Fight!, 2 vols. McCranie, Stephen, illus. 2nd ed. 2012. (Mal & Chad Ser.: 2). (ENG., Illus.). 224p. (J). (gr. 3-7). 9.99 *(978-0-399-25657-8(1)*, Philomel Bks.) Penguin Young Readers Group.

McCurniskey, Gavin. Shackleton: A Graphic Account: the Voyage of the James Caird. Butler, David, illus. 2016. (ENG.). 96p. (J). pap. 16.00 *(978-1-84889-281-1(0))* Collins Pr., The IRL. Dist: Dufour Editions, Inc.

McDaniel, Scott, et al, illus. Daredevil & Elektra: Fall from Grace. 2014. (ENG.). 464p. (J). (gr. 4-17). pap. 44.99 *(978-0-7851-8516-1(X))* Marvel Worldwide, Inc.

McDermott, Michael, et al. Smosh. 2017. (ENG., Illus.). 184p. pap. 19.99 ***(978-1-5241-0280-7(6)***, 9781524102807, Dynamite Entertainment) Dynamic Forces, Inc.

McDonald, Fiona. Ghost Doll & Jasper. 2012. (ENG., Illus.). 112p. (J). (gr. 2-7). 12.95 *(978-1-62087-174-4(2)*, 620174, Sky Pony Pr.) Skyhorse Publishing Co., Inc.

McDonald, John. The Tempest: The Graphic Novel. Gale Editor, ed. 2011. (Classic Graphic Novel Collection). (ENG.). 160p. (gr. 7-10). lib. bdg. 39.40 *(978-1-4205-0632-7(3))* Cengage Gale.

McDonnell, Patrick. Mutts: Tiere sind auch nur Menschen. Dickerhof-Kranz, Susanne, tr. from ENG. (GER., Illus.). 64p. (J). Vol. 1. pap. *(978-3-8105-1250-5(8))* Vol. 2. pap. *(978-3-8105-1251-2(6))* Vol. 3. pap. *(978-3-8105-1252-9(4))* Vol. 4. pap. *(978-3-8105-1253-6(2))* Vol. 5. pap. *(978-3-8105-1254-3(0))* Vol. 6. pap. *(978-3-8105-1255-0(9))* Kruger, Wolfgang Verlag, GmbH DEU. Dist: International Bk. Import Service, Inc.

—The Mutts Diaries. 2016. (ENG., Illus.). 226p. (J). (gr. 3-7). 29.99 *(978-1-4494-7380-8(6))* Andrews McMeel Publishing.

Mcginty, Ian. Surprise! 2014. (Hello Kitty Graphic Novel Ser.). lib. bdg. 18.40 *(978-0-606-35471-4(9))* Turtleback Bks.

McGinty, Ian. Welcome to Showside. 2016. (ENG., Illus.). 176p. (J). pap. 19.99 *(978-1-940878-07-2(1)*, 9781940878072) Z2 Comics.

McGraw, Royal, et al. Grumpy Cat, Vol. 1. 2016. (ENG., Illus.). 104p. (J). 12.99 *(978-1-60690-796-2(4)*, 9781606907962, Dynamite Entertainment) Dynamic Forces, Inc.

McGreal, Pat & McGreal, Carol. Uncle Scrooge #385. 2008. 64p. pap. 7.99 *(978-1-60360-062-0(0))* Gemstone Publishing, Inc.

McGreal, Pat, et al. Uncle Scrooge #390. 2009. 64p. pap. 7.99 *(978-1-60360-090-3(6))* Gemstone Publishing, Inc.

—Walt Disney's Comics & Stories #701. 2009. 64p. pap. 7.99 *(978-1-60360-091-0(4))* Gemstone Publishing, Inc.

McGregor, Don. Flights. Lima, Sidney, illus. 4th rev. ed. 2006. (Zorro Ser.). (ENG.). 96p. (J). pap. 7.95 *(978-1-59707-026-3(2))* Papercutz.

McGregor, Don & Lima, Sidney. Flights. 4th rev. ed. 2006. (Zorro Ser.). (ENG., Illus.). 96p. (J). 12.95 *(978-1-59707-027-0(0))* Papercutz.

McGuinness, Ed & Stewart, Cameron, illus. Amazing X-Men, Voi. 1. 2014. (ENG.). 136p. (YA). (gr. 8-17). pap. 17.99 *(978-0-7851-8821-6(5))* Marvel Worldwide, Inc.

Mchale, Pat. Over the Garden Wall. 2016. lib. bdg. 33.05 *(978-0-606-39002-6(2))* Turtleback Bks.

McIntosh, Kenneth. Things Fall Apart: Forensic Engineering. 2007. (Crime Scene Club: Fact & Fiction Ser.). (Illus.). 144p. (YA). (gr. 8-12). pap. 9.95 *(978-1-4222-0880-9(X))* Mason Crest.

McKay, Sharon E. & Lafrance, Daniel. War Brothers: The Graphic Novel. Lafrance, Daniel, illus. 2013. (ENG., Illus.). 176p. (YA). (gr. 9-12). 2nd ed. 27.95 *(978-1-55451-489-2(4)*, 9781554514892) 3rd ed. pap. 18.95 *(978-1-55451-488-5(6)*, 9781554514885) Annick Pr., Ltd. CAN. Dist: Publishers Group West (PGW).

McLeese, Don. Spartans. 2009. (ENG., Illus.). 32p. (gr. 4-8). pap. 9.95 *(978-1-60694-545-2(9))* Rourke Educational Media.

McLeod, Bob, illus. The New Mutants, Vol. 1. 2006. (ENG.). 240p. (J). (gr. 4-17). pap. 24.99 *(978-0-7851-2194-7(3))* Marvel Worldwide, Inc.

McMullan, Kate. Dragon Slayers' Academy Set 2. Basso, Bill, illus. 2007. (Dragon Slayers' Academy Ser.). (ENG.). 112p. 145.26 *(978-1-59961-375-8(1))* Spotlight.

—I'm Smart! McMullan, Jim, illus. 2017. 40p. (J). (gr. -1-3). 17.99 *(978-0-06-244923-8(0))* HarperCollins Pubs.

McNiven, Steve, illus. The Sentry, Vol. 2. 2006. (ENG.). 152p. (J). (gr. 4-17). pap. 14.99 *(978-0-7851-1672-1(9))* Marvel Worldwide, Inc.

Mead, Richelle. Shadow Kiss. Vieceli, Emma, illus. 2013. (Vampire Academy Ser.: 3). (ENG.). 160p. (YA). (gr. 7). pap. 12.99 *(978-1-59514-431-7(5)*, Razorbill) Penguin Young Readers Group.

—Shadow Kiss. 2013. (Vampire Academy (Graphic Novels) Ser.: 3). lib. bdg. 24.50 *(978-0-606-34129-5(3)*, Turtleback) Turtleback Bks.

—Vampire Academy. Vieceli, Emma, illus. 2011. (Vampire Academy Ser.: 1). (ENG.). 144p. (J). (gr. 7-18). pap. 12.99 *(978-1-59514-429-4(3)*, Razorbill) Penguin Young Readers Group.

Mebberson, Amy, et al. Disney Princess Comics Collection. 2016. (ENG.). 96p. (J). (gr. 4-7). 20.85 *(978-0-606-39073-6(1))* Turtleback Bks.

Meddaugh, Susan. Canine Comics: Six Daring Doggie Adventures. (Martha Speaks Ser.). (ENG., Illus.). 112p. (J). (gr. 1-4). 2014. pap. 5.99 *(978-0-544-22056-0(0)*, HMH Books For Young Readers) 2013. 9.99 *(978-0-547-86784-7(0))* Houghton Mifflin Harcourt Publishing Co.

Meister, Cari. Airplane Adventure, 1 vol. Janovitz, Marilyn, illus. 2010. (My First Graphic Novel Ser.). 32p. (gr. k-2). (ENG.). pap. 6.25 *(978-1-4342-2286-2(1))*; pap. 4.95 *(978-1-4342-3602-9(1))* Stone Arch Bks. (My First Graphic Novel).

—Bus Ride Bully, 1 vol. Simard, Remy, illus. (My First Graphic Novel Ser.). (ENG.). 32p. (gr. k-2). 2011. pap. 6.25 *(978-1-4342-3101-7(1))* 2010. 24.65 *(978-1-4342-2059-2(1))* Stone Arch Bks. (My First Graphic Novel).

—Clues in the Attic, 1 vol. Simard, Remy, illus. 2010. (My First Graphic Novel Ser.). (ENG.). 32p. (gr. k-2). pap. 6.25 *(978-1-4342-2283-1(7)*, My First Graphic Novel) Stone Arch Bks.

—Dump Truck Day, 1 vol. Emmerson, Michael, illus. 2010. (My First Graphic Novel Ser.). (ENG.). 32p. (gr. k-2). pap. 6.25 *(978-1-4342-2288-6(8)*, My First Graphic Novel) Stone Arch Bks.

—Fall Is Fun, 1 vol. Lingenfelter, Jim, illus. 2010. (First Graphics: Seasons Ser.). (ENG.). 24p. (gr. 1-2). pap. 6.29 *(978-1-4296-5623-8(9))*; pap. 35.70 *(978-1-4296-5692-4(1))* Capstone Press of Coughlan Cos.

—First Graphics - Seasons, Set. Lingenfelter, Jim, illus. Incl. Fall Is Fun. lib. bdg. 23.99 *(978-1-4296-4731-1(0))*; Spring Is Special. lib. bdg. 23.99 *(978-1-4296-4729-8(9))*; Summer Is Super. lib. bdg. 23.99 *(978-1-4296-4730-4(2))*; Winter Is Wonderful. lib. bdg. 23.99 *(978-1-4296-4732-8(9))*; (Illus.). (gr. 1-2). (First Graphics: Seasons Ser.). (ENG.). 24p. 2010. Set lib. bdg. 95.96 *(978-1-4296-4733-5(7))* Capstone Press of Coughlan Cos.

—Goalkeeper Goof, 1 vol. Doerrfeld, Cori, illus. 2009. (My First Graphic Novel Ser.). (ENG.). 32p. (gr. k-2). pap. 6.25 *(978-1-4342-1409-6(5))*; lib. bdg. 24.65 *(978-1-4342-1292-4(0))* Stone Arch Bks. (My First Graphic Novel).

—The Kickball Kids, 1 vol. Olson, Julie, illus. 2009. (My First Graphic Novel Ser.). (ENG.). 32p. (gr. k-2). pap. 6.25 *(978-1-4342-1410-2(9))*; lib. bdg. 24.65 *(978-1-4342-1294-8(7))* Stone Arch Bks. (My First Graphic Novel).

—Lily's Lucky Leotard, 1 vol. Ho, Jannie, illus. 2009. (My First Graphic Novel Ser.). (ENG.). 32p. (gr. k-2). pap. 6.25 *(978-1-4342-1411-9(7))*; lib. bdg. 24.65 *(978-1-4342-1296-2(3))* Stone Arch Bks. (My First Graphic Novel).

—Moopy on the Beach, 1 vol. Messner, Dennis, illus. 2010. (Monster Friends Ser.). (ENG.). 32p. (gr. 2-3). pap. 6.25 *(978-1-4342-2304-3(3))*; lib. bdg. 22.65 *(978-1-4342-1874-2(0))* Stone Arch Bks.

—Shark in the Library!, 1 vol. Simard, Remy, illus. (My First Graphic Novel Ser.). (ENG.). 32p. (gr. k-2). 2011. pap. 6.25 *(978-1-4342-3104-8(6))* 2010. 24.65 *(978-1-4342-2058-5(3))* Stone Arch Bks. (My First Graphic Novel).

—Snorp on the Slopes, 1 vol. Messner, Dennis, illus. 2010. (Monster Friends Ser.). (ENG.). 32p. (gr. 2-3). pap. 6.25 *(978-1-4342-2306-7(X))*; lib. bdg. 22.65 *(978-1-4342-1873-5(2))* Stone Arch Bks.

—Spring Is Special, 1 vol. Lingenfelter, Jim, illus. 2010. (First Graphics: Seasons Ser.). (ENG.). 24p. (gr. 1-2). pap. 6.29 *(978-1-4296-5621-4(2))*; pap. 35.70 *(978-1-4296-5693-1(X))* Capstone Press of Coughlan Cos.

—T-Ball Trouble, 1 vol. Ho, Jannie, illus. 2009. (My First Graphic Novel Ser.). (ENG.). 32p. (gr. k-2). pap. 6.25 *(978-1-4342-1413-3(3))*; lib. bdg. 24.65 *(978-1-4342-1300-6(5))* Stone Arch Bks. (My First Graphic Novel).

Meister, Cari & Stone Arch Books Staff. Train Trip, 1 vol. Janovitz, Marilyn, illus. 2010. (My First Graphic Novel Ser.). (ENG.). 32p. (gr. k-2). pap. 6.25 *(978-1-4342-2289-3(6)*, My First Graphic Novel) Stone Arch Bks.

Melo, Filipe. The Incredible Adventures of Dog Mendonca & Pizzaboy Vol. 2: Apocalypse. Simon, Philip, ed. 2014. (ENG., Illus.). 152p. pap. 14.99 *(978-1-61655-267-1(0))* Dark Horse Comics.

Melville, Herman. Cities of the Fantastic: Brusel. Eisner, Will, illus. 2003. (Cities of the Fantastic Ser.). (ENG.). 120p. 19.95 *(978-1-56163-291-6(0))* NBM Publishing Co.

—Moby Dick. Eisner, Will, illus. 2003. (ENG.). 32p. (J). (gr. 4-7). 15.95 *(978-1-56163-293-0(7))* NBM Publishing Co.

—Moby Dick, 1 vol. Espinosa, Rod, illus. 2007. (Graphic Classics). (ENG.). 32p. (gr. 3-6). 28.50 *(978-1-60270-051-2(6)*, Graphic Planet- Fiction) ABDO Publishing Co.

Melville, Herman, et al. Moby Dick. (Classics Illustrated Ser.). (Illus.). 52p. (YA). pap. 4.95 *(978-1-57209-003-3(0))* Classics International Entertainment, Inc.

Meomi (Firm) Staff. Meomi Journal. 2008. 128p. spiral bd. 9.99 *(978-1-59617-699-7(7))* Dark Horse Comics.

Meredith Books Staff. Batman Activity Kit. 2008. (Illus.). 32p. (J). 14.99 *(978-0-696-23961-8(2))* Meredith Bks.

—Batman Sticker Story Adventure. 2008. (Illus.). 16p. (J). pap. 5.99 *(978-0-696-23960-1(4))* Meredith Bks.

Meredith Books Staff, ed. Madagascar Activity Book & Floor Puzzle. 10p. (J). bds. 12.95 *(978-0-696-22701-1(0))* Meredith Bks.

—Madagascar Stencil Activity Book with Stickers. 22p. (J). bds. 12.95 *(978-0-696-22702-8(9))* Meredith Bks.

Meredith, Randy. Marvel Heros: Mix & Match Storybook. Barberi, Carlo, illus. 2006. 8p. (J). 8.95 *(978-1-57791-299-6(3)*, Penny Candy Pr.) Brighter Minds Children's Publishing.

Merritt, Kory. The Dreadful Fate of Jonathan York. 2015. (ENG.). 128p. (J). pap. 9.99 *(978-1-4494-7100-2(5))* Andrews McMeel Publishing.

Meunier, Henri. A Beary Merry Christmas. Choux, Nathalie, illus. 2017. (Super-Duper Duo Ser.). (ENG.). 32p. (J). (gr. -1-3). 8.99 ***(978-1-328-76678-6(0)***, HMH Books For Young Readers) Houghton Mifflin Harcourt Publishing Co.

Meyer, Marissa. Wires & Nerve. Holgate, Douglas, illus. 2017. (Wires & Nerve Ser.). (ENG.). 240p. (YA). 21.99 *(978-1-250-07826-1(1)*, 9781250078261) Feiwel & Friends.

Midorikawa, Yuki. Natsume's Book of Friends. Midorikawa, Yuki, illus. (ENG., Illus.). Vol. 1. 2010. 208p. pap. 9.99 *(978-1-4215-3243-1(3))* Vol. 3. 2010. 200p. pap. 9.99 *(978-1-4215-3245-5(X))* Vol. 4. 2010. 200p. pap. 9.99 *(978-1-4215-3246-2(8))* Vol. 15. 2014. 192p. pap. 9.99 *(978-1-4215-5967-4(6))* Viz Media.

—Natsume's Book of Friends, Vol. 2. Midorikawa, Yuki, illus. 2010. (ENG., Illus.). 208p. pap. 9.99 (978-1-4215-3244-8(1)) Viz Media.

A Midsummer Nightsquo;s Dream by William Shakespeare: The Graphic Novel. 2012. (Classic Graphic Novel Collection). (ENG.). (gr. 7-10). lib. bdg. 34.80 (978-1-4205-0840-6(7), Lucent Bks.) Cengage Gale.

Midthun, Joseph. Addition. Hiti, Samuel, illus. 2013. (Building Blocks of Mathematics Ser.). 32p. (J). pap. 169.00 (978-0-7166-1432-6(4)) World Bk., Inc.

—Division. Hiti, Samuel, illus. 2013. (Building Blocks of Mathematics Ser.). 32p. pap. 169.00 (978-0-7166-1433-3(2)) World Bk., Inc.

—Fractions. Hiti, Samuel, illus. 2013. (Building Blocks of Mathematics Ser.). 32p. (J). pap. 169.00 (978-0-7166-1435-7(9)) World Bk., Inc.

—Multiplication. Hiti, Samuel, illus. 2013. (Building Blocks of Mathematics Ser.). 32p. (J). pap. 169.00 (978-0-7166-1437-1(5)) World Bk., Inc.

Mignola, Mike. The Chained Coffin & Others, Vol. 3. 2nd ed. 2004. (Hellboy Ser.). (ENG., Illus.). 176p. pap. 19.99 (978-1-59307-091-5(8)) Dark Horse Comics.

—Wake the Devil. Brosseau, Pat & Sinclair, James, illus. 2nd ed. 2004. (Hellboy Ser.). (ENG.). 144p. pap. 17.99 (978-1-59307-095-3(0)) Dark Horse Comics.

Miller, Bryan Q. The Guardian, Vol. 1. 2013. (ENG., Illus.). 144p. pap. 14.99 (978-1-4012-3824-7(6)) DC Comics.

Miller, John Jackson, et al. Star Wars - Knights of the Old Republic, 9 vols., Vol. 1. 2007. (Illus.). 152p. (978-1-84576-371-8(8)) Titan Bks. Ltd.

Miller, Megan. Quest for the Golden Apple: A Graphic Novel for Minecrafters. 2015. (ENG., Illus.). 192p. (J). (gr. 2-7). pap. 11.99 (978-1-5107-0410-7(8), Sky Pony Pr.) Skyhorse Publishing Co., Inc.

Miller, Megan & Stevens, Cara J. Revenge of the Zombie Monks: An Unofficial Graphic Novel for Minecrafters, #2. 2016. (ENG., Illus.). 192p. (J). (gr. 2-7). pap. 11.99 (978-1-5107-0727-6(1), Sky Pony Pr.) Skyhorse Publishing Co., Inc.

Miller, Mike S. Confession, 1 vol. Ninaltowski, Eric, illus. 2008. (Z Graphic Novels / Hand of the Morning Star Ser.). (ENG.). 160p. (YA). (gr. 8-11). pap. 6.99 (978-0-310-71371-5(4)) Zondervan.

Miller, Mona. Hero of the Month! Random House, illus. 2017. (Pictureback(R) Ser.). (ENG.). 16p. (J). (gr. -1-2). pap. 5.99 **(978-1-5247-6604-7(6)**, Random Hse. Bks. for Young Readers) Random Hse. Children's Bks.

Milligan, Peter. Good Omens, Vol. 1. Allred, Mike, illus. 2003. (X-Statix Ser.). 128p. (YA). pap. 11.99 (978-0-7851-1059-0(3)) Marvel Worldwide, Inc.

—X-Force: Famous, Mutant & Mortal. Allred, Mike, illus. 2003. (X-Statix Ser.). 352p. (YA). 29.99 (978-0-7851-1023-1(2)) Marvel Worldwide, Inc.

Milway, Alex. Pigsticks & Harold & the Incredible Journey. Milway, Alex, illus. 2014. (ENG., Illus.). 84p. (J). (gr. k-4). 12.99 (978-0-7636-6615-6(7)) Candlewick Pr.

—Pigsticks & Harold & the Tuptown Thief. Milway, Alex, illus. 2017. (Candlewick Sparks Ser.). (ENG., Illus.). 80p. (J). (gr. k-4). pap. 3.99 (978-0-7636-9400-5(2)) Candlewick Pr.

—Pigsticks & Harold & the Tuptown Thief. Milway, Alex, illus. 2017. (Candlewick Sparks Ser.). (ENG., Illus.). (J). (gr. k-4). lib. bdg. 13.55 **(978-0-606-39840-4(6))** Turtleback Bks.

Mishkin, Dan. The Warren Commission Report: A Graphic Investigation into the Kennedy Assassination. Colón, Ernie & Drozd, Jerzy, illus. 2014. (ENG.). 160p. 29.95 (978-1-4197-1230-2(6), Abrams ComicArts) Abrams, Inc.

Mitsui-Kids. A Duel on the Dark Side, 3 vols. Shogakukan, ed. 2004. (Teen Ser.). (Illus.). 96p. pap. 14.99 (978-1-59532-064-3(4), Tokyopop Kids) TOKYOPOP, Inc.

Miyaki, Tetsuichiro. Pokémon. Yamamoto, Satoshi, illus. 2013. (J). **(978-1-4844-1630-3(9))** Viz Media.

Miyasaka, Kaho. Kare First Love, 10 vols. Miyasaka, Kaho, illus. (Kare First Love Ser.). (ENG., Illus.). 2006. 208p. pap. 9.99 (978-1-4215-0547-3(9)) 2006. 208p. pap. 9.99 (978-1-4215-0546-6(0)) 2005. 192p. pap. 9.99 (978-1-4215-0139-0(2)) Viz Media.

Miyazaki, Hayao. The Art of Howl's Moving Castle. Miyazaki, Hayao, illus. 2005. (ENG., Illus.). 256p. 34.99 (978-1-4215-0049-2(3)) Viz Media.

—The Art of Porco Rosso, Vol. 1. Searleman, Eric, ed. Miyazaki, Hayao, illus. 2005. (ENG., Illus.). 208p. 34.99 (978-1-59116-704-4(3)) Viz Media.

—Howls Moving Castle Picture Book. Miyazaki, Hayao, illus. 2005. (ENG., Illus.). 184p. 19.99 (978-1-4215-0090-4(6)) Viz Media.

—Kiki's Delivery Service, Vol. 3. 2006. (Kiki's Delivery Service Film Comics Ser.: 3). (ENG., Illus.). 208p. pap. 9.99 (978-1-59116-784-6(1)) Viz Media.

—Kiki's Delivery Service Film Comic, Vol. 4. 2006. Orig. Title: Majo No Takkyubin. (ENG., Illus.). 208p. pap. 9.99 (978-1-4215-0595-4(9)) Viz Media.

—Kiki's Delivery Service Picture Book, Vol. 1. 2006. (ENG., Illus.). 208p. pap. 19.99 (978-1-4215-0596-1(7)) Viz Media.

—My Neighbor Totoro Picture Book (New Edition) 2013. (ENG., Illus.). 112p. (J). 19.99 (978-1-4215-6122-6(0)) Viz Media.

Mizobuchi, Makoto. The Complete Pokémon Pocket Guide, Vol. 1. 2017. (Pokemon Ser.: 1). (ENG.). 256p. (J). pap. 10.99 **(978-1-4215-9543-6(5))** Viz Media.

—The Complete Pokémon Pocket Guide, Vol. 2. 2017. (Pokemon Ser.: 2). (ENG.). 256p. (J). pap. 10.99 **(978-1-4215-9544-3(3))** Viz Media.

Modan, Rutu. Maya Makes a Mess. Modan, Rutu, illus. 2012. (ENG., Illus.). 32p. (J). (gr. -1-3). 12.95 (978-1-935179-17-7(9)) TOON Books / RAW Junior, LLC.

Modern Publishing Staff. ABCs! 2007. (Disney Bath Time Bubble Bks.). (Illus.). (J). (gr. -1-k). 4.99 (978-0-7666-2551-8(6)) Modern Publishing.

Monda, Joseph, creator. The Unnaturals. 2007. (Illus.). 32p. (YA). 3.50 (978-0-615-15138-0(8)) Wild Mind Creations.

Mongillo, Michael. The Philistine: Anthology/Chronology, 1 book. Zittel, Michael, illus. 2003. 216p. (YA). pap. 24.95 (978-0-9743086-0-9(9)) United Comics.

Monlongo, Jorge & Chabot, Jacob. Hello Kitty: Just Imagine. Monlongo, Jorge, illus. 2014. (ENG., Illus.). 64p. (J). pap. 7.99 (978-1-4215-7362-5(8)) Viz Media.

Montes, Graciela. Federico Dice No. (SPA.). 16p. pap. 9.95 (978-950-07-1158-6(3)) Editorial Sudamericana S.A. ARG. Dist: Distribooks, Inc.

—Federico Se Hizo Pis. (SPA.). pap. 9.95 (978-950-07-0851-7(5)) Editorial Sudamericana S.A. ARG. Dist: Distribooks, Inc.

Mooney, Carla. The Forest Surprise, 1 vol. Harpster, Steve, illus. 2011. (My First Graphic Novel Ser.). (ENG.). 32p. (gr. k-2). pap. 6.25 (978-1-4342-3064-5(3)); lib. bdg. 24.65 (978-1-4342-2520-7(8)) Stone Arch Bks. (My First Graphic Novel).

Mooney, Stephen. Half Past Danger. 2014. (ENG., Illus.). 200p. 29.99 (978-1-61377-849-4(X), 9781613778494) Idea & Design Works, LLC.

Moore, Alan, intro. Brickman Begins! 2005. (Illus.). 148p. per. 9.99 (978-0-9740567-8-4(2)) Active Images.

Moore, B. Clay, et al. Put the Book Back on the Shelf: A Belle & Sebastian Anthology. 2006. (ENG., Illus.). 144p. (YA). pap. 19.99 (978-1-58240-600-8(6), 9781582406008) Image Comics.

Moore, Stuart. The Age of Bronze. Cullins, Paris & Henrique, Paulo, illus. 2017. (Zodiac Ser.: 3). (ENG.). 64p. (J). 12.99 (978-1-62991-485-5(1), 9781629914855) Papercutz.

Moreci, Michael & Seeley, Steve. Murder, Death, & the Devil, Vol. 1. 2012. (ENG., Illus.). 160p. (YA). pap. 14.99 (978-1-60706-657-6(2), 9781607066576) Image Comics.

Morgan, Lori. Healing the Bruises, 1 vol. Kaulbach, Kathy R., illus. 2013. (ENG.). 32p. (J). (gr. 1-4). 16.95 (978-1-4595-0283-3(3), 9781459502833) Formac Publishing Co., Ltd. CAN. Dist: Casemate Pubs. & Bk. Distributors, LLC.

Mori, Kotaro. Stray Little Devil. (Stray Little Devil Ser.). (ENG., Illus.). (YA). Vol. 1. 2006. 200p. pap. 9.95 (978-1-59796-043-4(8)) Vol. 2. 2006. 200p. pap. 9.95 (978-1-59796-044-1(6)) Vol. 3. 2006. 200p. pap. 9.95 (978-1-59796-045-8(4)) Vol. 4. 2007. 208p. pap. 9.95 (978-1-59796-046-5(2)) DrMaster Pubns. Inc.

Morimoto, Sango. Taro & the Magic Pencil. Morimoto, Sango, illus. 2010. (ENG., Illus.). 104p. (J). pap. 7.99 (978-1-4215-3524-1(6)) Viz Media.

—Taro & the Terror of Eats Street. Morimoto, Sango, illus. 2011. (Adventures of Taro Ser.). (ENG., Illus.). 96p. (J). (gr. 1-4). pap. 7.99 (978-1-4215-3525-8(4)) Viz Media.

Morita, Hiroyuki. The Cat Returns Picture Book. Searleman, Eric, ed. Hiiragi, Aoi, illus. 2007. (Cat Returns Ser.: 1). (ENG.). 112p. (J). (gr. -1). 14.99 (978-1-4215-1498-7(2)) Viz Media.

Moriyama, Daisuke. Chrono Crusade. 2004. (Illus.). (YA). Vol. 2. 200p. pap. 9.99 (978-1-4139-0104-7(2)) Vol. 3. 198p. pap. 9.99 (978-1-4139-0045-3(3)) ADV Manga.

Morris, illus. The Bluefeet Are Coming! 2014. (Lucky Luke Ser.: 43). (ENG.). 48p. pap. 11.95 (978-1-84918-173-0(X)) CineBook GBR. Dist: National Bk. Network.

—Doc Doxey's Elixir. 2013. (Lucky Luke Ser.: 38). (ENG.). 48p. pap. 11.95 (978-1-84918-141-9(1)) CineBook GBR. Dist: National Bk. Network.

—Lucky Luke Versus Pat Poker. 2014. (Lucky Luke Ser.: 44). (ENG.). 48p. pap. 11.95 (978-1-84918-179-2(9)) CineBook GBR. Dist: National Bk. Network.

—Phil Wire. 2013. (Lucky Luke Ser.: 40). (ENG.). 48p. pap. 11.95 (978-1-84918-155-6(1)) CineBook GBR. Dist: National Bk. Network.

Morris & Goscinny, René. Dalton City. 2007. (Lucky Luke Ser.: 3). (ENG., Illus.). 48p. (J). (gr. 4-7). pap. 11.95 (978-1-905460-13-7(9)) CineBook GBR. Dist: National Bk. Network.

Morris, Alfred, illus. The Judge. 2010. (Lucky Luke Ser.: 24). (ENG.). 46p. (J). (gr. 3-17). pap. 11.95 (978-1-84918-045-0(8)) CineBook GBR. Dist: National Bk. Network.

Morris, Elizabeth. The Quest for the Tellings. Troy, Michael, illus. 2012. 52p. (-18). pap. (978-1-78222-055-8(0)) Paragon Publishing, Rothersthorpe.

Morris Publishing Company Staff & Goscinny, René. The Daltons' Escape, Vol. 30. 2011. (Lucky Luke Ser.: 30). (ENG., Illus.). 48p. pap. 11.95 (978-1-84918-091-7(1)) CineBook GBR. Dist: National Bk. Network.

Mortensen, Lori. The Cat That Disappeared, 1 vol. Simard, Remy, illus. 2010. (My First Graphic Novel Ser.). (ENG.). 32p. (gr. k-2). pap. 6.25 (978-1-4342-2282-4(9)); lib. bdg. 24.65 (978-1-4342-1887-2(2)) Stone Arch Bks. (My First Graphic Novel).

—A Day at the Fire Station. Thompson, Jeffrey, illus. 2010. (First Graphics: My Community Ser.). (ENG.). 24p. (gr. 1-2). pap. 35.70 (978-1-4296-5613-9(1)) Capstone Press of Coughlan Cos.

—The End Zone, 1 vol. Sullivan, Mary, illus. 2009. (My First Graphic Novel Ser.). (ENG.). 32p. (gr. k-2). pap. 6.25 (978-1-4342-1408-9(7), My First Graphic Novel) Stone Arch Bks.

—Going to the Dentist, 1 vol. Thompson, Jeffrey, illus. 2010. (First Graphics: My Community Ser.). (ENG.). 24p. (gr. 1-2). 23.99 (978-1-4296-4507-2(5)); pap. 35.70 (978-1-4296-5611-5(5)) Capstone Press of Coughlan Cos.

—The Lost Lunch, 1 vol. Simard, Remy, illus. (My First Graphic Novel Ser.). (ENG.). 32p. (gr. k-2). 2011. pap. 6.25 (978-1-4342-3103-1(8)) 2010. 24.65 (978-1-4342-2014-1(1)) Stone Arch Bks. (My First Graphic Novel).

—Manners Matter in the Classroom. Hunt, Lisa, illus. (First Graphics: Manners Matter Ser.). (ENG.). 24p. (gr. 1-2). 2011. pap. 35.70 (978-1-4296-6392-2(8)) 2010. lib. bdg. 23.99 (978-1-4296-5333-6(7)) Capstone Press of Coughlan Cos.

—Manners Matter in the Library, 1 vol. Hunt, Lisa, illus. 2010. (First Graphics: Manners Matter Ser.). (ENG.). 24p. (gr. 1-2). lib. bdg. 23.99 (978-1-4296-5330-5(2)) Capstone Press of Coughlan Cos.

—Manners Matter on a Field Trip. Hunt, Lisa, illus. (First Graphics: Manners Matter Ser.). (ENG.). 24p. (gr. 1-2). 2011. pap. 35.70 (978-1-4296-6394-6(4)) 2010. lib. bdg. 23.99 (978-1-4296-5331-2(0)) Capstone Press of Coughlan Cos.

—Manners Matter on the Playground. Hunt, Lisa, illus. (First Graphics: Manners Matter Ser.). (ENG.). 24p. (gr. 1-2). 2011. pap. 35.70 (978-1-4296-6395-3(2)) 2010. lib. bdg. 23.99 (978-1-4296-5332-9(9)) Capstone Press of Coughlan Cos.

—The Missing Monster Card, 1 vol. Simard, Remy, illus. 2010. (My First Graphic Novel Ser.). (ENG.). 32p. (gr. k-2). pap. 6.25 (978-1-4342-2284-8(5)); lib. bdg. 24.65 (978-1-4342-1888-9(0)) Stone Arch Bks. (My First Graphic Novel).

—A Visit to the Police Station Set. Thompson, Jeffrey, illus. Incl. Going to the Dentist. (ENG., Illus.). 24p. (gr. 1-2). 2010. 23.99 (978-1-4296-4507-2(5)); (First Graphics: My Community Ser.). (ENG.). 24p. 2010. Set lib. bdg. 47.98 o.p. (978-1-4296-4513-3(X)) Capstone Press of Coughlan Cos.

—Working on the Farm, 1 vol. Thompson, Jeffrey, illus. 2010. (First Graphics: My Community Ser.). (ENG.). 24p. (gr. 1-2). pap. 6.29 (978-1-4296-5616-0(6)); pap. 35.70 (978-1-4296-5617-7(4)) Capstone Press of Coughlan Cos.

Moscowitz, Moshe & Resnick, Yael. The Queen of Persia. Sokoloff, David, illus. 2004. 107p. (978-1-930925-09-0(3), Shazak Productions) Torah Excel.

Mosier, Scott & Son, Eugene, illus. Marvel Universe Ultimate Spider-Man Volume 6. 2014. (ENG.). 88p. (J). (gr. -1-17). pap. 9.99 (978-0-7851-8815-5(0)) Marvel Worldwide, Inc.

Moss, Marissa. The Fake Friend! Moss, Marissa, illus. 2012. (Daphne's Diary of Daily Disasters Ser.). (ENG., Illus.). 96p. (J). (gr. 2-5). 9.99 (978-1-4424-4014-2(7)); pap. 5.99 (978-1-4424-4015-9(5)) Simon & Schuster/Paula Wiseman Bks. (Simon & Schuster/Paula Wiseman Bks.).

—The Vampire Dare! Moss, Marissa, illus. 2011. (Daphne's Diary of Daily Disasters Ser.). (ENG., Illus.). 80p. (J). (gr. 2-5). pap. 5.99 (978-1-4424-1737-3(4), Simon & Schuster/Paula Wiseman Bks.) Simon & Schuster/Paula Wiseman Bks.

Motomi, Kyousuke. Dengeki Daisy , Vol. 16. 2015. (ENG.). 192p. pap. 9.99 (978-1-4215-7771-5(2)) Viz Media.

Mowry, Chris. Revenge of the Fallen: Defiance, 1 vol., Vol. 1. Khanna, Dan, illus. 2010. (Transformers: Revenge of the Fallen Movie Prequel Ser.). (ENG.). 24p. (J). (gr. 3-6). 24.21 (978-1-59961-721-3(8)) Spotlight.

—Revenge of the Fallen: Defiance, 1 vol. Khanna, Dan & Griffith, Andrew, illus. 2010. (Transformers: Revenge of the Fallen Movie Prequel Ser.). (ENG.). 24p. (J). (gr. 3-6). Vol. 2. 24.21 (978-1-59961-722-0(6)) Vol. 3. 24.21 (978-1-59961-723-7(4)) Spotlight.

—Revenge of the Fallen: Defiance, 1 vol., Vol. 4. Duendes del Sur, illus. 2010. (Transformers: Revenge of the Fallen Movie Prequel Ser.). (ENG.). 24p. (J). (gr. 3-6). 24.21 (978-1-59961-724-4(2)) Spotlight.

Muell, Jason. Descendants. 2017. (ENG.). 80p. (J). pap. 10.99 **(978-1-4278-5687-6(7)**, 9781427856876) TOKYOPOP, Inc.

Mulazzi, Paola, et al. Disney Fairies Graphic Novel #4: Tinker Bell to the Rescue. Urbano, Emilio et al, illus. 2010. (Disney Fairies Ser.: 4). (ENG.). 80p. (J). (gr. 1-6). 12.99 (978-1-59707-230-4(3)); pap. 7.99 (978-1-59707-200-7(1), 9781597072007) Papercutz.

—Tinker Bell & the Pirate Adventure, Vol. 5. Urbano, Emilio et al, illus. 2011. (Disney Fairies Ser.: 5). (ENG.). 64p. (J). (gr. 1-6). pap. 7.99 (978-1-59707-240-3(0), 9781597072403) Papercutz.

—Tinker Bell the Perfect Fairy. Urbano, Emilio et al, illus. 2012. (Disney Fairies Ser.: 7). (ENG.). 64p. (J). (gr. 1-6). 11.99 (978-1-59707-282-3(6), 9781597072823) Papercutz.

Murayama, Kei. A Centaur's Life, Vol. 2. 2014. (Centaur's Life Ser.). (ENG., Illus.). 175p. pap. 12.99 (978-1-62692-000-2(1), 9781626920002) Seven Seas Entertainment, LLC.

Murozumi, Hikaru & Inokuma, Shinobu. The School of Water Business. (Illus.). (YA). 206p. pap. (978-4-09-153102-5(4)); Vol. 4. 2005. (JPN., 205p. mass mkt. (978-4-09-153104-9(0)); Vol. 5. (JPN., 205p. mass mkt. (978-4-09-153105-6(9)) Shogakukan.

Murphy, Hugh. T-Rex Trying. 2013. (ENG., Illus.). 128p. (gr. 12). 13.00 (978-0-452-29902-3(0), Plume) Penguin Publishing Group.

Murphy, Stephen & Zulli, Michael. The Puma Blues. 2015. (Dover Graphic Novels Ser.). (ENG., Illus.). 480p. 34.95 (978-0-486-79813-4(5)) Dover Pubns., Inc.

Muth, Jon J. & Buscema, John, illus. Galactus the Devourer. 2014. (ENG.). 184p. (J). (gr. 4-17). pap. 24.99 (978-0-7851-8562-8(3)) Marvel Worldwide, Inc.

Nagpal, Saraswati. Draupadi: The Fire-Born Princess. Chandu & Manu, illus. 2013. (Campfire Graphic Novels Ser.). (ENG.). 116p. (YA). (gr. 5-12). pap. 12.99 (978-93-80741-09-3(X), Campfire) Steerforth Pr.

Naifeh, Ted. Courtney Crumrin: The Coven of Mystics. 2012. (ENG., Illus.). 144p. 24.99 (978-1-934964-80-4(8), 9781934964804) Oni Pr., Inc.

—Courtney Crumrin Volume 4: Monstrous Holiday Special Edition: Monstrous Holiday Special Edition. 2013. (ENG., Illus.). 128p. (YA). 24.99 (978-1-934964-92-7(1), 9781934964927) Oni Pr., Inc.

Naifeh, Ted & Wucinich, Warren. Courtney Crumrin Volume 5: the Witch Next Door: The Witch Next Door. 2014. (ENG., Illus.). 144p. (J). 24.99 (978-1-934964-96-5(4), 9781934964965) Oni Pr., Inc.

Nalbandian, Paisely Lineyeia. Treasure Seekers. 2011. 28p. pap. 15.99 (978-1-4415-1375-5(2)) Xlibris Corp.

Nanatsuki, Kyoichi. Project Arms, Vol. 13. Nanatsuki, Kyoichi, illus. 2006. (Project Arms Ser.). (ENG., Illus.). 208p. pap. 9.99 (978-1-4215-0502-2(9)) Viz Media.

Napton, Robert Place. Son of Merlin Volume 1 TP. 2013. (ENG., Illus.). 160p. (YA). pap. 19.99 (978-1-60706-795-5(1), 9781607067955) Image Comics.

Nasu, Yukie. Here Is Greenwood. Nasu, Yukie, illus. 2005. (Here Is Greenwood Ser.). (ENG., Illus.). (YA). Vol. 2. 216p. pap. 9.99 (978-1-59116-605-4(5)) Vol. 3. 200p. pap. 9.99 (978-1-59116-606-1(3)) Viz Media.

Nasu, Yukie & Smith, Joe. Here is Greenwood, 1. Nasu, Yukie, illus. 2004. (ENG., Illus.). 208p. (YA). pap. 9.99 (978-1-59116-604-7(7)) Viz Media.

Natsume, Kokoro. Lovephobia, Vol. 3. 2016. (Illus.). 200p. (YA). pap. 12.95 (978-1-56970-300-7(0)) Digital Manga Publishing.

Neary, Paul, illus. S. H. I. E. L. D. Nick Fury vs. S. H. I. E. L. D. 2013. (ENG.). 304p. (J). (gr. 4-17). pap. 29.99 (978-0-7851-8500-0(3)) Marvel Worldwide, Inc.

Neel, Julien. Down in the Dumps. Neel, Julien, illus. 2012. (Lou! Ser.: 3). (ENG., Illus.). 48p. (J). (gr. 6-9). pap. 8.95 (978-0-8225-9165-8(0), Graphic Universe™) Lerner Publishing Group.

—Lou! Neel, Julien, illus. 2012. (Lou! Ser.). (Illus.). 48p. (J). (gr. 4-8). lib. bdg. 55.86 (978-0-7613-8903-3(2), Graphic Universe™) Lerner Publishing Group.

—Lou! 6Pack Set. Neel, Julien, illus. 2012. (Lou! Ser.). (Illus.). 48p. (J). (gr. 4-8). pap. 102.03 (978-0-7613-9288-0(2), Graphic Universe™) Lerner Publishing Group.

—Lou! Single Copy Set. Neel, Julien, illus. 2012. (Lou! Ser.). (Illus.). 48p. (J). (gr. 4-8). pap. 17.01 (978-0-7613-9287-3(4), Graphic Universe™) Lerner Publishing Group.

—The Perfect Summer. Neel, Julien, illus. 2012. (Lou! Ser.: 4). (ENG., Illus.). 48p. (J). (gr. 6-9). pap. 8.95 (978-0-8225-9169-6(3), Graphic Universe™) Lerner Publishing Group.

—Secret Diary. Neel, Julien, illus. 2012. (Lou! Ser.). (Illus.). 48p. (J). (gr. 4-8). pap. 51.02 (978-0-7613-9285-9(8)); (ENG., (gr. 6-9). pap. 8.95 (978-0-7613-8868-5(0)) Lerner Publishing Group. (Graphic Universe™).

—Summertime Blues. Neel, Julien, illus. 2012. (Lou! Ser.). (Illus.). 48p. (J). (gr. 4-8). pap. 51.02 (978-0-7613-9286-6(6)); (ENG., (gr. 6-9). pap. 8.95 (978-0-7613-8869-2(9)) Lerner Publishing Group. (Graphic Universe™).

Neel, Julien & Burrell, Carol klio. Down in the Dumps. Neel, Julien, illus. 2012. (Lou! Ser.: 3). (ENG., Illus.). 48p. (J). (gr. 6-9). lib. bdg. 27.93 (978-0-7613-8779-4(X), Graphic Universe™) Lerner Publishing Group.

—The Perfect Summer. Neel, Julien, illus. 2012. (Lou! Ser.: 4). (ENG., Illus.). 48p. (J). (gr. 6-9). lib. bdg. 27.93 (978-0-7613-8780-0(3), Graphic Universe™) Lerner Publishing Group.

Nelly. Nelly Music Manga. (Illus.). 96p. (J). pap. 7.99 (978-1-59182-834-1(1)) TOKYOPOP, Inc.

Nelson, John. Collision Course: Asteroids & Earth. 2008. (Jr. Graphic Environmental Dangers Ser.). (ENG.). 24p. (J). 47.90 (978-1-61532-098-1(9), PowerKids Pr.) Rosen Publishing Group, Inc., The.

—Polar Ice Caps in Danger: Expedition to Antarctica. 2008. (Jr. Graphic Environmental Dangers Ser.). (ENG.). 24p. (J). 47.90 (978-1-61532-097-4(0), PowerKids Pr.) Rosen Publishing Group, Inc., The.

Nelson, O. T. The Girl Who Owned a City. 2012. (Exceptional Reading & Language Arts Titles for Intermediate Grades Ser.). (ENG.). 208p. (YA). (gr. 5-12). pap. 9.95 (978-0-7613-5086-6(1)) Lerner Publishing Group.

Neri, Greg. Grand Theft Horse: A Graphic Novel. Wilkin, Corban, illus. 2016. (YA). (978-1-4677-9463-3(5), Graphic Universe™) Lerner Publishing Group.

Nguyen, Hoang & Gardner, Paul. Daughters of Stone, Vol. 2. 2013. (ENG., Illus.). 128p. (YA). pap. 14.99 (978-1-60706-789-4(7), 9781607067894) Image Comics.

Nguyen, Taohuu. Mighty Mite 2: Zoo Gone Wild. Nguyen, Taohuu, illus. 2007. (Illus.). (J). 14.95 (978-0-9788469-2-3(3)) Amazing Factory, The.

—Mighty Mite 3: Good Mites, Bad Mites. Nguyen, Taohuu, illus. 2007. (Illus.). (J). 14.95 (978-0-9790302-3-9(4)) Amazing Factory, The.

Nichols, Kaitlyn. Draw the DC Universe: Learn to Draw the Heroes & the Villains. 2011. (ENG.). 104p. (J). spiral bd. 19.99 (978-0-545-34619-1(3)) Klutz.

Nickel, Scott. Attack of the Mutant Lunch Lady. Smith, Andy J., illus. 2008. (Graphic Sparks Ser.). (ENG.). 40p. (gr. 1-3). per. 5.95 (978-1-4342-0501-8(0), Graphic Sparks) Stone Arch Bks.

—Attack of the Mutant Lunch Lady: A Buzz Beaker Brainstorm, 1 vol. Smith, Andy J., illus. 2008. (Buzz Beaker Brainstorm Ser.). (ENG.). 40p. (gr. 1-3). lib. bdg. 23.99 (978-1-4342-0451-6(0), Graphic Sparks) Stone Arch Bks.

—Back to the Ice Age. Corts, Enrique, illus. 2008. (Graphic Sparks Ser.). (ENG.). 40p. (gr. 1-3). pap. 5.95 (978-1-4342-0500-1(2), Graphic Sparks) Stone Arch Bks.

—Backyard Bug Battle: A Buzz Beaker Brainstorm, 1 vol. Smith, Andy J., illus. 2006. (Buzz Beaker Brainstorm Ser.). (ENG.). 40p. (gr. 1-3). lib. bdg. 23.99 (978-1-59889-054-9(9)); per. 5.95 (978-1-59889-224-6(X)) Stone Arch Bks. (Graphic Sparks).

—Billions of Bats. Smith, Andy J., illus. 2007. (Graphic Sparks Ser.). (ENG.). 40p. (gr. 1-3). per. 5.95 (978-1-59889-408-0(0), Graphic Sparks) Stone Arch Bks.

—Blast to the Past. Harpster, Steve, illus. 2006. (Graphic Sparks Ser.). (ENG.). 40p. (gr. 1-3). 5.95 (978-1-59889-167-6(7), Graphic Sparks) Stone Arch Bks.

—The Boy Who Burped Too Much, 1 vol. Harpster, Steve, illus. 2006. (Graphic Sparks Ser.). (ENG.). 40p. (gr. 1-3). 23.99 (978-1-59889-037-2(9), Graphic Sparks) Stone Arch Bks.

—Buzz Beaker vs Dracula: A Buzz Beaker Brainstorm, 1 vol. Smith, Andy J., illus. 2009. (Buzz Beaker Brainstorm Ser.). (ENG.). 40p. (gr. 1-3). lib. bdg. 23.99 (978-1-4342-1191-0(6), Graphic Sparks) Stone Arch Bks.

—Curse of the Red Scorpion, 1 vol. Harpster, Steve, illus. 2006. (Graphic Sparks Ser.). (ENG.). 40p. (gr. 1-3). per. 5.95 (978-1-59889-169-0(3)); 23.99 (978-1-59889-034-1(4)) Stone Arch Bks. (Graphic Sparks).

—Dognapped! Jimmy Sniffles. Harpster, Steve, illus. 2006. (Graphic Sparks Ser.). (ENG.). 40p. (gr. 1-3). per. 5.95 (978-1-59889-226-0(6), Graphic Sparks) Stone Arch Bks.

—Double Trouble, 1 vol. Harpster, Steve, illus. 2007. (Jimmy Sniffles Ser.). (ENG.). 40p. (gr. 1-3). lib. bdg. 23.99 (978-1-59889-314-4(9)); per. 5.95 (978-1-59889-411-0(0)) Stone Arch Bks. (Graphic Sparks).

—The Incredible Rockhead, 1 vol. Jennings, C. S., illus. 2009. (Incredible Rockhead Ser.). (ENG.). 40p. (gr. 1-3). lib. bdg. 23.99 (978-1-4342-1591-8(1), Graphic Sparks) Stone Arch Bks.

—The Incredible Rockhead vs Papercut!, 1 vol. Jennings, C. S., illus. 2010. (Incredible Rockhead Ser.). (ENG.). 40p. (gr. 1-3). 23.99 (978-1-4342-1976-3(3), Graphic Sparks) Stone Arch Bks.

—Invasion of the Gym Class Zombies. Luxich, Matt, illus. 2008. (Graphic Sparks Ser.). (ENG.). 40p. (gr. 1-3). pap. 5.95 (978-1-4342-0503-2(7)); lib. bdg. 23.99 (978-1-4342-0453-0(7)) Stone Arch Bks. (Graphic Sparks).

—Jimmy Sniffles Dognapped! 2007. (J). (gr. 3-5). 31.92 incl. cd-rom (978-1-4342-0372-4(7)); 21.52 incl. audio compact disk (978-1-4342-0379-3(4)) Stone Arch Bks.

—Race on the River, 1 vol. Harpster, Steve, illus. 2011. (My First Graphic Novel Ser.). (ENG.). 32p. (gr. k-2). pap. 6.25 (978-1-4342-3061-4(9)); lib. bdg. 24.65 (978-1-4342-2521-4(6)) Stone Arch Bks. (My First Graphic Novel).

—Robot Rampage: A Buzz Beaker Brainstorm. Smith, Andy J., illus. 2006. (Graphic Sparks Ser.). (ENG.). 40p. (gr. 1-3).

per. 5.95 *(978-1-59889-227-7(4),* Graphic Sparks) Stone Arch Bks.
—Rock, Paper, Scissorlegz. Jennings, C. S., illus. 2012. (Incredible Rockhead Ser.). (ENG.). 128p. (gr. 1-3). pap. 8.95 *(978-1-4342-4596-0(9))* Stone Arch Bks.
—Secret of the Summer School Zombies, 1 vol. Luxich, Matt, illus. 2008. (School Zombies Ser.). (ENG.). 40p. (gr. 1-3). 23.99 *(978-1-4342-0760-9(9));* pap. 5.95 *(978-1-4342-0856-9(7))* Stone Arch Bks. (Graphic Sparks).
—The Super-Powered Sneeze. Harpster, Steve, illus. 2007. (Graphic Sparks Ser.). (ENG.). 40p. (gr. 1-3). per. 5.95 *(978-1-59889-409-7(9),* Graphic Sparks) Stone Arch Bks.
—T. Rex vs Robo-Dog 3000. Corts, Enrique, illus. 2008. (Graphic Sparks Ser.). (ENG.). 40p. (gr. 1-3). pap. 5.95 *(978-1-4342-0857-6(5),* Graphic Sparks) Stone Arch Bks.
—Wind Power Whiz Kid: A Buzz Beaker Brainstorm. Smith, Andy J., illus. 2008. (Graphic Sparks Ser.). (ENG.). 40p. (gr. 1-3). pap. 5.95 *(978-1-4342-0854-5(0),* Graphic Sparks) Stone Arch Bks.
Nickel, Scott & Dahl, Michael. The Evil Echo, 1 vol. Crowther, Jeff, illus. 2010. (Princess Candy Ser.). (ENG.). 40p. (gr. 1-3). 23.99 *(978-1-4342-1977-0(1));* pap. 5.95 *(978-1-4342-2804-8(5))* Stone Arch Bks. (Graphic Sparks).
Nickel, Scott, et al. The Incredible Rockhead & the Spectacular Scissorlegz, 1 vol. Jennings, C. S., illus. 2010. (Incredible Rockhead Ser.). (ENG.). 40p. (gr. 1-3). 23.99 *(978-1-4342-2127-8(X),* Graphic Sparks) Stone Arch Bks.
Nickelodeon Staff. All Grown up: Coup Deville, Vol. 2. Rau, Zachary, ed. 2005. (Nick All Grown Up Ser.). (Illus.). 96p. (J). (gr. 3-17). per. 14.99 *(978-1-59532-723-9(1),* Tokyopop Kids) TOKYOPOP, Inc.
Nickelodeon Staff, creator. All Grown Up. 2005. (Illus.). 96p. pap. 14.99 *(978-1-59532-722-2(3),* Tokyopop Kids) TOKYOPOP, Inc.
—The Amanda Show. 2005. (Illus.). 96p. pap. 7.99 *(978-1-59532-721-5(5),* Tokyopop Kids) TOKYOPOP, Inc.
Nicolle, Ethan. Kill the Devil. 2008. (ENG., Illus.). 120p. (YA). pap. 10.95 *(978-1-59362-099-8(3),* 9781593620998) Slave Labor Bks.
Nicolle, Malachai. Axe Cop, Vol. 1. 2011. (ENG., Illus.). 144p. (J). (gr. 5-12). pap. 14.99 *(978-1-59582-681-7(5))* Dark Horse Comics.
—Axe Cop, Vol. 3. 2012. (ENG., Illus.). 120p. (J). (gr. 5-12). pap. 14.99 *(978-1-59582-911-5(3))* Dark Horse Comics.
—Bad Guy Earth, Vol. 1. 2011. (ENG., Illus.). 120p. (J). (gr. 5-12). pap. 14.99 *(978-1-59582-825-5(7))* Dark Horse Comics.
Niles, Steve & Santoro, Matt. Breath of Bones: a Tale of the Golem: A Tale of the Golem. Allie, Scott, ed. Wachter, Dave, illus. 2014. (ENG.). 80p. 14.99 *(978-1-61655-344-9(8))* Dark Horse Comics.
Nishi, Yoshiyuki. Muhyo & Roji's Bureau of Supernatural Investigation, Vol. 18. Nishi, Yoshiyuki, illus. 2010. (ENG., Illus.). 192p. pap. 9.99 *(978-1-4215-2840-3(1))* Viz Media.
Nishimori, Hiroyuki. Cheeky Angel. Nishimori, Hiroyuki, illus. (Cheeky Angel Ser.). (ENG., Illus.). Vol. 8. 2005. 192p. pap. 9.99 *(978-1-59116-976-6(8))* Vol. 13. 2006. 208p. pap. 9.99 *(978-1-4215-0447-6(2))* Viz Media.
N'Leh, Anne-Claire. The Planet of Trainiacs. Élyum Studio, illus. 2013. (Little Prince Ser.: 10). (ENG.). 56p. (J). (gr. 4-8). pap. 7.95 *(978-1-4677-1519-5(0));* lib. bdg. 26.60 *(978-0-7613-8760-2(9))* Lerner Publishing Group. (Graphic Universe™).
Nobleman, Marc Tyler. Vocabulary Cartoon of the Day: 180 Reproducible Cartoons That Expand Students' Vocabularies to Help Them Become Better Readers & Writers. 2010. (Vocabulary Cartoon of the Day Ser.). (ENG.). 96p. (gr. 2-3). pap. 14.99 *(978-0-545-14713-2(1),* Teaching Resources) Scholastic, Inc.
Nobleman, Marc Tyler, et al. Rescue in the Bermuda Triangle: An Isabel Soto Investigation. 2010. (Graphic Expeditions Ser.). (ENG., Illus.). 32p. (gr. 3-4). pap. 47.70 *(978-1-4296-5713-6(8),* Graphic Library) Capstone Press of Coughlan Cos.
Nocenti, Ann. Typhoid Mary, 4 vols. Romita, John, Jr., illus. 2003. (Daredevil Legends Ser.: Vol. 4). 224p. (YA). pap. 19.99 *(978-0-7851-1041-5(0))* Marvel Worldwide, Inc.
Nolan, Alan. Destination: Homicide! 2012. (ENG., Illus.). 80p. (J). pap. 12.95 *(978-1-84717-256-3(3))* O'Brien Pr., Ltd., The IRL. Dist: Dufour Editions, Inc.
Nordling, Lee. Andrew the Seeker. Roberts, Scott, illus. 2017. (Game for Adventure Ser.). (ENG.). 32p. (J). (gr. k-3). 25.32 *(978-1-5124-1330-4(5),* Graphic Universe™) Lerner Publishing Group.
—Belinda the Unbeatable. Roberts, Scott, illus. 2017. (Game for Adventure Ser.). (ENG.). 32p. (J). (gr. k-3). pap. 6.99 ***(978-1-5124-5413-0(3));*** lib. bdg. 25.32 ***(978-1-5124-1331-1(3))*** Lerner Publishing Group. (Graphic Universe™).
—BirdCatDog. Bosch, Meritxell, illus. 2014. (J). lib. bdg. 25.32 *(978-1-4677-4522-2(7),* Graphic Universe™) Lerner Publishing Group.
—BirdCatDog. 2014. (ENG.). 32p. pap. 6.95 *(978-1-4677-4523-9(5))* Lerner Publishing Group.
—Fishfishfish. Bosch, Meritxell, illus. 2015. (Three-Story Bks.). (ENG.). 32p. (J). (gr. k-3). lib. bdg. 25.26 *(978-1-4677-4575-8(8),* Graphic Universe™) Lerner Publishing Group.
—FishFishFish. Bosch, Meritxell, illus. 2015. (Three-Story Bks.). (ENG.). 32p. (J). (gr. k-3). pap. 6.95 *(978-1-4677-4576-5(6),* Graphic Universe™) Lerner Publishing Group.
—SheHeWe. Bosch, Meritxell, illus. 2015. (ENG.). 32p. (J). (gr. k-3). pap. 6.95 *(978-1-4677-4578-9(2));* lib. bdg. 25.26 *(978-1-4677-4574-1(X))* Lerner Publishing Group. (Graphic Universe™).
North, Ryan. Adventure Time, Vol. 3. 2013. (Adventure Time Graphic Novels Ser.: 3). lib. bdg. 26.95 *(978-0-606-35462-2(X))* Turtleback Bks.
—Adventure Time Volume 2. 2013. (Adventure Time Graphic Novels Ser.: 2). lib. bdg. 26.95 *(978-0-606-35461-5(1))* Turtleback Bks.
—Dinosaur Comics. North, Ryan, illus. 2005. (Illus.). 112p. 14.99 *(978-0-7560-0518-4(3))* Teacher's Discovery.
North, Ryan & Paroline, Shelli. Adventure Time Vol.4 - Mathematical Edition. 2014. (Illus.). 144p. *(978-1-78276-171-6(3),* Titan Bks.) Titan Bks. Ltd.
Norton, Mike & Hopeless, Dennis. The Answer!, Vol.1. Thorpe, Patrick, ed. 2013. (ENG., Illus.). 120p. pap. 12.99 *(978-1-61655-197-1(6))* Dark Horse Comics.
Novik, Naomi. Will Supervillains Be on the Final? Liberty Vocational. Li, Yishan, illus. 2011. (ENG.). 192p. pap. 10.99 *(978-0-345-51656-5(7),* Del Rey) Random House Publishing Group.
Nuhfer, Heather. Hopes & Screams. 2014. (Monster High Ser.). (ENG., Illus.). 112p. (J). (gr. 3-7). pap. 10.00 *(978-0-316-25433-5(9))* Little, Brown Bks. for Young Readers.
Nutrition Adventures with the Nutri Gang, Race Day, Issue #1: The Nutri Gang. 2007. (J). 2.99 *(978-0-9792383-0-7(7))* KJ Pubns.
Nykko. Book Six: The Tower of Shadows. Bannister, illus. 2013. (Elsewhere Chronicles Ser.: 6). (ENG.). 48p. (J). (gr. 4-8). pap. 6.95 *(978-1-4677-1517-1(4));* lib. bdg. 27.93 *(978-1-4677-1233-0(7))* Lerner Publishing Group.
—The Elsewhere Chronicles. 2009. (Elsewhere Chronicles Ser.). (ENG.). (J). (gr. 4-8). pap. 39.62 *(978-0-7613-5088-0(8));*Pack, Set. pap. 237.69 *(978-0-7613-5090-3(X))* Lerner Publishing Group.
—The Parting. Bannister, illus. 2011. (Elsewhere Chronicles Ser.: 5). (ENG.). 48p. (J). (gr. 4-8). pap. 6.95 *(978-0-7613-7524-1(4))* Lerner Publishing Group.
—The Parting, Bk. 5. Bannister, illus. 2011. (Elsewhere Chronicles Ser.: 5). (ENG.). 48p. (J). (gr. 4-8). lib. bdg. 27.93 *(978-0-7613-6632-4(6))* Lerner Publishing Group.
—The Shadow Door. Bannister, illus. 2009. (Elsewhere Chronicles Ser.: Bk. 1). (ENG.). 48p. (J). (gr. 4-8). pap. 8.99 *(978-0-7613-3963-2(9));* lib. bdg. 27.93 *(978-0-7613-4459-9(4))* Lerner Publishing Group.
—The Shadow Spies. Bannister, illus. 2009. (Elsewhere Chronicles Ser.: Bk. 2). (ENG.). 48p. (J). (gr. 4-8). pap. 6.95 *(978-0-7613-3964-9(7))* Lerner Publishing Group.
Nytra, David. The Secret of the Stone Frog. Nytra, David, illus. 2012. (Leah & Alan Adventures Ser.). (ENG., Illus.). 80p. (J). (gr. 2-7). 14.95 *(978-1-935179-18-4(7))* TOON Books / RAW Junior, LLC.
—Windmill Dragons: A Leah & Alan Adventure - A Toon Graphic. 2015. (Leah & Alan Adventures Ser.). (ENG., Illus.). 120p. (J). (gr. 2). 18.95 *(978-1-935179-88-7(8))* TOON Books / RAW Junior, LLC.
O'brien, John. Look ... Look Again! 2012. (ENG.). 64p. (J). (gr. 3). 18.95 *(978-1-59078-894-3(X))* Boyds Mills Pr.
Oceanak, Karla. Bogus: An Aldo Zelnick Comic Novel. Spanjer, Kendra, illus. 2016. (Aldo Zelnick Comic Novel Ser.: 2). (ENG.). 160p. (J). (gr. 3-7). pap. 8.95 *(978-1-934649-66-4(X))* Bailiwick Pr.
—Cahoots. Spanjer, Kendra, illus. 2011. (Aldo Zelnick Comic Novel Ser.: 3). (ENG.). 151p. (J). (gr. 3-7). 12.95 *(978-1-934649-08-4(2))* Bailiwick Pr.
—Cahoots: An Aldo Zelnick Comic Novel. Spanjer, Kendra, illus. 2016. (Aldo Zelnick Comic Novel Ser.: 3). (ENG.). 160p. (J). (gr. 1-8). pap. 8.95 *(978-1-934649-67-1(8))* Bailiwick Pr.
—Dumbstruck. Spanjer, Kendra, illus. 2011. (Aldo Zelnick Comic Novel Ser.: 4). (ENG.). 160p. (J). (gr. 3-7). 12.95 *(978-1-934649-16-9(3))* Bailiwick Pr.
—Dumbstruck: An Aldo Zelnick Comic Novel. Spanjer, Kendra, illus. 2016. (Aldo Zelnick Comic Novel Ser.: 4). (ENG.). 160p. (J). (gr. 1-8). pap. 8.95 *(978-1-934649-68-8(6))* Bailiwick Pr.
—Egghead: An Aldo Zelnick Comic Novel. Spanjer, Kendra, illus. 2016. (Aldo Zelnick Comic Novel Ser.: 5). (ENG.). 160p. (J). (gr. 1-8). pap. 8.95 *(978-1-934649-69-5(4))* Bailiwick Pr.
—Finicky: An Aldo Zelnick Comic Novel. Spanjer, Kendra, illus. 2016. (Aldo Zelnick Comic Novel Ser.: 6). (ENG.). 160p. (J). (gr. 1-8). pap. 8.95 *(978-1-934649-70-1(8))* Bailiwick Pr.
—Glitch. Spanjer, Kendra, illus. 2012. (Aldo Zelnick Comic Novel Ser.: 7). (ENG.). 160p. (J). (gr. 3-7). 12.95 *(978-1-934649-25-1(2))* Bailiwick Pr.
—Glitch: An Aldo Zelnick Comic Novel. Spanjer, Kendra, illus. 2016. (Aldo Zelnick Comic Novel Ser.: 7). (ENG.). 160p. (J). (gr. 1-8). pap. 8.95 *(978-1-934649-71-8(6))* Bailiwick Pr.
—Hotdogger: An Aldo Zelnick Comic Novel. Spanjer, Kendra, illus. 2016. (Aldo Zelnick Comic Novel Ser.: 8). (ENG.). 160p. (J). (gr. 1-8). pap. 8.95 *(978-1-934649-72-5(4))* Bailiwick Pr.
—Ignoramus. Spanjer, Kendra, illus. 2013. (Aldo Zelnick Comic Novel Ser.: 9). (ENG.). 160p. (J). (gr. 3-7). 12.95 *(978-1-934649-41-1(4))* Bailiwick Pr.
—Ignoramus: An Aldo Zelnick Comic Novel. Spanjer, Kendra, illus. 2016. (Aldo Zelnick Comic Novel Ser.: 9). (ENG.). 160p. (J). (gr. 1-8). pap. 8.95 *(978-1-934649-73-2(2))* Bailiwick Pr.
—Jackpot: An Aldo Zelnick Comic Novel. Spanjer, Kendra, illus. 2016. (Aldo Zelnick Comic Novel Ser.: 10). (ENG.). 160p. (J). (gr. 1-8). pap. 8.95 *(978-1-934649-74-9(0))* Bailiwick Pr.
O'Connor, Eddie, et al. Donald Duck Adventures, Vol. 16. Clark, John, ed. 2006. (ENG., Illus.). 128p. (YA). pap. 7.95 *(978-1-888472-11-0(1),* 9781888472110) Gemstone Publishing, Inc.
O'Connor, George. Athena Bk. 2: Grey-Eyed Goddess. O'Connor, George, illus. 2010. (Olympians Ser.: 2). (ENG., Illus.). 80p. (J). (gr. 4-9). 17.99 *(978-1-59643-649-7(2),* 9781596436497); pap. 10.99 *(978-1-59643-432-5(5),* 9781596434325) Roaring Brook Pr. (First Second Bks.).
—Hera: The Goddess & Her Glory. O'Connor, George, illus. 2011. (Olympians Ser.: 3). (ENG., Illus.). 80p. (J). (gr. 4-9). 17.99 *(978-1-59643-724-1(3),* 9781596437241); pap. 10.99 *(978-1-59643-433-2(3),* 9781596434332) Roaring Brook Pr. (First Second Bks.).
Odin, Jey. Chicken Fighter. 2011. (ENG.). 128p. (YA). pap., pap. 14.95 *(978-0-9831823-5-1(3),* 9780983182351) Antarctic Pr., Inc.
Odjick, Jay & Tenascon, Patrick. Kagagi: the Raven: The Raven. O'Reilly, Sean Patrick, ed. 2011. (Illus.). 78p. (YA). pap. 14.95 *(978-1-926914-29-9(5))* Arcana Studio, Inc.
O'Doherty, David. Danger Is Everywhere: A Handbook for Avoiding Danger. Judge, Chris, illus. 2017. (Danger Is Everywhere Ser.: 1). (ENG.). 272p. (J). (gr. 3-7). pap. 6.99 *(978-0-316-50183-5(2))* Little, Brown Bks. for Young Readers.
O'Donnell, Liam. Blackbeard's Sword: The Pirate King of the Carolinas. Spoor, Mike, illus. 2007. (Historical Fiction Ser.). (ENG.). 56p. (gr. 2-3). pap. 6.25 *(978-1-59889-404-2(8),* Graphic Flash) Stone Arch Bks.
—Food Fight, 1 vol. Deas, Mike, illus. 2010. (Graphic Guides). (ENG.). 64p. (J). (gr. 3-7). pap. 9.95 *(978-1-55469-067-1(6))* Orca Bk. Pubs. USA.
—Power Play, 1 vol. Deas, Mike, illus. 2011. (Graphic Guides). (ENG.). 64p. (J). (gr. 3-7). pap. 9.95 *(978-1-55469-069-5(2))* Orca Bk. Pubs. USA.
—Tank & Fizz: the Case of the Slime Stampede, 1 vol. Deas, Mike, illus. 2015. (Tank & Fizz Ser.: 1). (ENG.). 152p. (J). (gr. 3-6). pap. 9.95 *(978-1-4598-0810-2(X))* Orca Bk. Pubs. USA.
—Understanding Photosynthesis with Max Axiom, Super Scientist, 1 vol. Dominguez, Richard & Barnett, Charles, III, illus. 2007. (Graphic Science Ser.). (ENG.). 32p. (gr. 3-4). per. 8.10 *(978-0-7368-7893-7(9),* 1264938, Graphic Library) Capstone Press of Coughlan Cos.
O'Donnell, Liam & Anderson, Bill. The World of Food Chains with Max Axiom, Super Scientist. Martin, Cynthia, illus. 2016. (Graphic Science Ser.). (ENG.). 32p. (gr. 3-4). pap. 8.10 *(978-1-5157-4642-3(9),* Graphic Library) Capstone Press of Coughlan Cos.
O'Donnell, Liam & Barnett, Charles, III. Cómo Comprender la Fotosíntesis con Max Axiom, Supercientífico. Dominguez, Richard, illus. 2013. (Ciencia Gráfica Ser.). (SPA.). 32p. (gr. 3-4). pap. 8.10 *(978-1-62065-984-7(0));* lib. bdg. 30.65 *(978-1-62065-180-3(7))* Capstone Press of Coughlan Cos.
O'Donnell, Liam & Battle, Craig. Max Finder Mystery Collected Casebook, Vol. 4. Pérez, Ramón & Owlkids Books Inc. Staff, illus. 2010. (Max Finder Mystery Collected Casebook Ser.: 4). (ENG.). 96p. (J). (gr. 3-6). pap. 9.95 *(978-1-897349-80-9(7))* Owlkids Bks. Inc. CAN. Dist: Publishers Group West (PGW).
Oeming, Michael Avon & Glass, Bryan J. L. Mice Templar Volume 4. 1 HC. 2013. (ENG., Illus.). 248p. (YA). 29.99 *(978-1-60706-822-8(2),* 9781607068228) Image Comics.
—Mice Templar Volume 4. 1: Legend Part 1 TP: Legend Part 1 TP. 2014. (ENG., Illus.). 304p. (YA). pap. 17.99 *(978-1-60706-857-0(5),* 9781607068570) Image Comics.
Ogden, Charles, ed. Edgar & Ellen Graphic Novelty: A Comics Collection. 2009. (Edgar & Ellen Ser.). (ENG.). 112p. (J). (gr. 3-7). pap. 7.99 *(978-1-4169-5004-2(4),* Simon & Schuster/Paula Wiseman Bks.) Simon & Schuster/Paula Wiseman Bks.
Ohnogi, Hiroshi. Rahxephon, Vol. 4. 2006. (RahXephon (Dr Masterbook) Ser.). (ENG., Illus.). 200p. (YA). pap. 7.95 *(978-1-59796-003-8(9))* DrMaster Pubns. Inc.
—Rahxephon, Vol. 5. 2006. (RahXephon (Dr Masterbook) Ser.). (ENG., Illus.). 200p. (YA). pap. 7.95 *(978-1-59796-004-5(7))* DrMaster Pubns. Inc.
Ohtaka, Shinobu. Magi: The Labyrinth of Magic, Vol. 1. 2013. (ENG., Illus.). 200p. pap. 9.99 *(978-1-4215-5951-3(X))* Viz Media.
—The Strongest Bride on Earth, 12 vols. 2012. (Sumomomo, Momomo Ser.: 12). (ENG., Illus.). 240p. (gr. 11-17). pap. 13.00 *(978-0-316-20470-5(6),* Yen Pr.) Orbit.
Okonkwo, Chidi, creator. Destiny, Neo Genesis, Vol. 6. 2004. 32p. (YA). 2.95 *(978-0-9758863-5-9(5))* Vizione Productions Inc.
Olien, Rebecca. How Do We Know about Dinosaurs? A Fossil Mystery, 1 vol. McDee, Katie, illus. 2011. (First Graphics: Science Mysteries Ser.). (ENG.). 24p. (gr. 1-2). pap. 6.29 *(978-1-4296-7173-6(4));* pap. 35.70 *(978-1-4296-7177-4(7))* Capstone Press of Coughlan Cos.
Olsen, Lauri. Pacific Bound: The Adventures of Lewis & Clark. Toonz Animation, ed. 2005. (Illus.). 44p. (J). 18.95 *(978-0-9742502-5-0(2))* Gossamer Bks., LLC.
—Pacific Bound: The Adventures of Lewis & Clark. 2004. (Illus.). 46p. (J). per. 15.95 *(978-0-9742502-4-3(4))* Gossamer Bks., LLC.
Olson, Nathan. John F. Kennedy: American Visionary, 1 vol. Bascle, Brian, illus. 2007. (Graphic Biographies Ser.). (ENG.). 32p. (gr. 3-4). per. 8.10 *(978-0-7368-7904-0(8),* 1264943, Graphic Library) Capstone Press of Coughlan Cos.
Olson, Nathan, et al. Theodore Roosevelt: Bear of a President, 1 vol. Martin, Cynthia et al, illus. 2007. (Graphic Biographies Ser.). (ENG.). 32p. (gr. 3-4). per. 8.10 *(978-0-7368-7901-9(3),* 1264944, Graphic Library) Capstone Press of Coughlan Cos.
O'Neill, Josh, et al, eds. Little Nemo's Big Dreams: A Toon Graphic. 2015. (ENG., Illus.). 72p. (J). (gr. 6). 16.95 *(978-1-935179-87-0(X))* TOON Books / RAW Junior, LLC.
O'Neill, Sean. Rocket Robinson & the Secret of the Saint. 2016. (Rocket Robinson Ser.). (ENG.). 240p. (J). (gr. 4-7). pap. 19.95 *(978-0-9893655-2-9(2))* Independent Pubs. Group.
Onion Head Monster Attacks. 2007. (YA). per. 12.95 *(978-0-9793676-0-1(3))* Friedrich, Paul.
Onion Head Monster Attacks (XL) 2006. per. 19.99 *(978-0-9793676-3-2(8))* Friedrich, Paul.
Onion Head Monster Bombastic. 2007. (YA). per. 12.95 *(978-0-9793676-1-8(1))* Friedrich, Paul.
Onion Head Monster Catastrophic. 2007. per. 11.99 *(978-0-9793676-2-5(X))* Friedrich, Paul.
Ooten, Tara Broeckel. Justin Bieber - Fame. 2011. (ENG., Illus.). 40p. (YA). pap. 7.99 *(978-1-4507-3538-4(X))* Bluewater Productions, Inc.
Orchard, Eric. Bera the One-Headed Troll. 2016. (ENG., Illus.). 128p. (J). 17.99 *(978-1-62672-106-7(8),* 9781626721067, First Second Bks.) Roaring Brook Pr.
—Maddy Kettle Book 1: the Adventure of the Thimblewitch: The Adventure of the Thimblewitch. 2014. (ENG., Illus.). 96p. (J). (gr. 2-5). pap. 14.95 *(978-1-60309-072-8(X),* 9781603090728) Top Shelf Productions.
Orci, Roberto, et al. Transformers Official Movie Adaptation Issue #2, 1 vol. Milne, Alex, illus. 2008. (Transformers: Official Movie Adaptation Ser.). (ENG.). 24p. (J). (gr. 2-7). 24.21 *(978-1-59961-482-3(0))* Spotlight.
—Transformers Official Movie Adaptation Issue #3, 1 vol. Milne, Alex, illus. 2008. (Transformers: Official Movie Adaptation Ser.). (ENG.). 24p. (J). (gr. 2-7). 24.21 *(978-1-59961-483-0(9))* Spotlight.
—Transformers Official Movie Adaptation Issue #4, 1 vol. Milne, Alex, illus. 2008. (Transformers: Official Movie Adaptation Ser.). (ENG.). 24p. (J). (gr. 2-7). 24.21 *(978-1-59961-484-7(7))* Spotlight.
O'Reilly, Sean. The Abominable Snow Kid, 1 vol. 2012. (Mighty Mighty Monsters Ser.). (ENG.). 48p. (gr. 2-3). lib. bdg. 23.99 *(978-1-4342-3892-4(X))* Stone Arch Bks.
—Abominable Snow Kid. 2013. (Mighty Mighty Monsters Ser.). (ENG., Illus.). 48p. (gr. 2-3). pap. 6.10 *(978-1-4342-4227-3(7))* Stone Arch Bks.
—The Gremlin's Curse, 1 vol. 2012. (Mighty Mighty Monsters Ser.). (ENG.). 48p. (gr. 2-3). lib. bdg. 23.99 *(978-1-4342-3894-8(6))* Stone Arch Bks.
—Gremlin's Curse. 2013. (Mighty Mighty Monsters Ser.). (ENG., Illus.). 48p. (gr. 2-3). pap. 6.10 *(978-1-4342-4228-0(5))* Stone Arch Bks.
—Hide & Shriek!, 1 vol. Arcana Studio Staff, illus. 2011. (Mighty Mighty Monsters Ser.). (ENG.). 48p. (gr. 2-3). pap. 6.10 *(978-1-4342-3417-9(7))* Stone Arch Bks.
—Hide & Shriek!, 1 vol. 2010. (Mighty Mighty Monsters Ser.). (ENG., Illus.). 48p. (gr. 2-3). lib. bdg. 23.99 *(978-1-4342-2148-3(2))* Stone Arch Bks.
—Homesick Witch, 1 vol. (Mighty Mighty Monsters Ser.). (ENG., 48p. (gr. 2-3). 2013. Illus.). pap. 6.10 *(978-1-4342-4225-9(0))* 2012. lib. bdg. 23.99 *(978-1-4342-3893-1(8))* Stone Arch Bks.
—The King of Halloween Castle, 1 vol. 2010. (Mighty Mighty Monsters Ser.). (ENG., Illus.). 48p. (gr. 2-3). lib. bdg. 23.99 *(978-1-4342-2150-6(4))* Stone Arch Bks.
—Lost in Spooky Forest, 1 vol. Arcana Studio Staff, illus. 2011. (Mighty Mighty Monsters Ser.). (ENG.). 48p. (gr. 2-3). pap. 6.10 *(978-1-4342-3418-6(5))* Stone Arch Bks.
—Lost in Spooky Forest, 1 vol. 2010. (Mighty Mighty Monsters Ser.). (ENG.). 48p. (gr. 2-3). lib. bdg. 23.99 *(978-1-4342-2149-0(0))* Stone Arch Bks.
—The Missing Mummy, 1 vol. Arcana Studio Staff, illus. 2012. (Mighty Mighty Monsters Ser.). (ENG.). 48p. (gr. 2-3). pap. 6.10 *(978-1-4342-4609-7(4))* Stone Arch Bks.
—The Missing Mummy, 1 vol. 2011. (Mighty Mighty Monsters Ser.). (ENG.). 48p. (gr. 2-3). lib. bdg. 23.99 *(978-1-4342-3218-2(2))* Stone Arch Bks.
—Monster Beach, 1 vol. 2011. (Mighty Mighty Monsters Ser.). (ENG.). 48p. (gr. 2-3). lib. bdg. 23.99 *(978-1-4342-3217-5(4))* Stone Arch Bks.
—Monster Beach, 1 vol. Arcana Studio Staff, illus. 2012. (Mighty Mighty Monsters Ser.). (ENG.). 48p. (gr. 2-3). pap. 6.10 *(978-1-4342-4608-0(6))* Stone Arch Bks.
—The Monster Crooks, 1 vol. 2011. (Mighty Mighty Monsters Ser.). (ENG.). 48p. (gr. 2-3). lib. bdg. 23.99 *(978-1-4342-3216-8(6))* Stone Arch Bks.
—The Monster Crooks, 1 vol. Arcana Studio Staff, illus. 2012. (Mighty Mighty Monsters Ser.). (ENG.). 48p. (gr. 2-3). pap. 6.10 *(978-1-4342-4610-3(8))* Stone Arch Bks.
—Monster Mansion, 1 vol. 2010. (Mighty Mighty Monsters Ser.). (ENG.). 48p. (gr. 2-3). lib. bdg. 23.99 *(978-1-4342-2152-0(0))* Stone Arch Bks.
—My Missing Monster, 1 vol. 2010. (Mighty Mighty Monsters Ser.). (ENG.). 48p. (gr. 2-3). lib. bdg. 23.99 *(978-1-4342-2153-7(9))* Stone Arch Bks.
—New Monster in School, 1 vol. Arcana Studio, Arcana, illus. 2010. (Mighty Mighty Monsters Ser.). (ENG.). 48p. (gr. 2-3). lib. bdg. 23.99 *(978-1-4342-2151-3(2))* Stone Arch Bks.
—The Scare Fair, 1 vol. 2011. (Mighty Mighty Monsters Ser.). (ENG.). 48p. (gr. 2-3). lib. bdg. 23.99 *(978-1-4342-3220-5(4))* Stone Arch Bks.
—The Scare Fair, 1 vol. Arcana Studio Staff, illus. 2012. (Mighty Mighty Monsters Ser.). (ENG.). 48p. (gr. 2-3). pap. 6.10 *(978-1-4342-4611-0(6))* Stone Arch Bks.
—Science Fair Nightmare, 1 vol. (Mighty Mighty Monsters Ser.). (ENG., 48p. (gr. 2-3). 2013. Illus.). pap. 6.10 *(978-1-4342-4226-6(9))* 2012. lib. bdg. 23.99 *(978-1-4342-3891-7(1))* Stone Arch Bks.
—The Toy Snatcher, 1 vol. Arcana Studio Staff, illus. 2012. (Mighty Mighty Monsters Ser.). (ENG.). 48p. (gr. 2-3). pap. 6.10 *(978-1-4342-4612-7(4))* Stone Arch Bks.
—The Wolfboy's Wish, 1 vol. Arcana Studio Staff, illus. 2012. (Mighty Mighty Monsters Ser.). (ENG.). 48p. (gr. 2-3). pap. 6.10 *(978-1-4342-4613-4(2))* Stone Arch Bks.
Orme, David. Bugs & Spiders. Mongiovi, Jorge, illus. 2010. (Fact to Fiction Ser.). 36p. pap. 7.45 *(978-0-7891-7990-6(3))* Perfection Learning Corp.
—Strange Creatures. Lindblad, Stefan, illus. 2010. (Fact to Fiction Grafx Ser.). 36p. pap. 7.45 *(978-0-7891-7994-4(6))* Perfection Learning Corp.
Orsi, Tea. Tinker Bell & Her Magical Friends. 2016. (Disney Fairies Graphic Novels Ser.: 18). (J). lib. bdg. 18.40 *(978-0-606-38371-4(9))* Turtleback Bks.
—Tinker Bell & the Legend of the NeverBeast. 2015. (Disney Fairies Graphic Novels Ser.: 17). (J). lib. bdg. 18.40 *(978-0-606-37295-4(4))* Turtleback Bks.
—Tinker Bell & the Secret of the Wings. 2014. (Disney Fairies Graphic Novels Ser.: 15). (J). lib. bdg. 18.40 *(978-0-606-35533-9(2))* Turtleback Bks.
Orsi, Tea & Panaro, Carlo. Disney Fairies Graphic Novel #13: Tinker Bell & the Pixie Hollow Games. Razzi, Manuela et al, illus. 2013. (Disney Fairies Ser.: 13). (ENG.). 64p. (J). (gr. 1-6). 11.99 *(978-1-59707-447-6(0),* 9781597074476); pap. 7.99 *(978-1-59707-446-9(2),* 9781597074469) Papercutz.
—Tinker Bell & the Lost Treasure. Razzi, Manuela et al, illus. 2013. (Disney Fairies Ser.: 12). (ENG.). 64p. (J). (gr. 1-6). 11.99 *(978-1-59707-429-2(2),* 9781597074292); pap. 7.99 *(978-1-59707-428-5(4),* 9781597074285) Papercutz.
O'Ryan, Ray. Hello, Nebulon! 2013. (Galaxy Zack Ser.: 1). lib. bdg. 16.00 *(978-0-606-32442-7(9),* Turtleback) Turtleback Bks.
O'Ryan, Ray. Ready, Set, Blast Off! 2017. (Galaxy Zack Ser.: 15). lib. bdg. 16.00 ***(978-0-606-39737-7(X))*** Turtleback Bks.
Oshima, Towa. High School Girls, Vol. 5. 2005. (High School Girls Ser.). (ENG., Illus.). 200p. (YA). pap. 9.95 *(978-1-59796-058-8(6))* DrMaster Pubns. Inc.
—High School Girls Volume 1-6 Set. 2007. (ENG., Illus.). 200p. pap. 44.95 *(978-1-59796-072-4(1))* DrMaster Pubns. Inc.
Ota, Yuko & Panagariya, Ananth. Adventure Time: Candy Capers. 2014. lib. bdg. 33.05 *(978-0-606-35468-4(9))* Turtleback Bks.
Ottaviani, Jim. T-Minus: The Race to the Moon. Cannon, Zander & Cannon, Kevin, illus. 2009. (ENG.). 128p. (J). (gr. 3-7). pap. 15.99 *(978-1-4169-4960-2(7),* Aladdin) Simon & Schuster Children's Publishing.

Pacheco, Carlos & Klein, Nic, illus. Captain America, Vol. 3. 2014. (ENG.). 136p. (J). (gr. 4-17). 24.99 *(978-0-7851-8951-0(3))* Marvel Worldwide, Inc.

Page, Frank. Sometimes a Squirrel Is Just a Squirrel. 2005. 106p. pap. 9.99 *(978-1-4116-6062-5(5))* Lulu Pr., Inc.

Page, Philip, et al. Great Expectations. 2003. (Illus.). 64p. pap. 19.95 *(978-0-340-87161-4(X))* Hodder Education Group GBR. Dist: Trans-Atlantic Pubns., Inc.

Pagotto, Toni. Pope John Paul II. Toppi, Sergio, illus. 2006. (Comic Book Ser.). 64p. (J). pap. 7.95 *(978-0-8198-5957-0(5))* Pauline Bks. & Media.

Pak, Greg. The Totally Awesome Hulk, Volume 1. 2016. (J). lib. bdg. 30.60 *(978-0-606-38351-6(4))* Turtleback Bks.

Pak, Greg, et al. X-Men - X-Termination. Buffagni, Matteo et al, illus. 2013. (ENG.). 184p. (YA). (gr. 8-17). pap. 24.99 *(978-0-7851-8443-0(0))* Marvel Worldwide, Inc.

Palmer, Barbara E. Recoverbee Says Learn with Me. 2011. 28p. pap. 24.95 *(978-1-4560-4983-6(6))* America Star Bks.

Panagariya, Ananth & Hirsh, Ananth. Buzz! 2013. (ENG., Illus.). 144p. (J). pap. 19.99 *(978-1-62010-088-2(6),* 9781620100882) Oni Pr., Inc.

Parent, Dan. Betty & Veronica: Best Friends Forever. 2012. (Archie & Friends All-Stars Ser.: 16). (ENG.). 128p. (J). (gr. 4-7). pap. 9.99 *(978-1-879794-76-4(4),* Archie Comics) Archie Comic Pubns., Inc.

—Kevin Keller: Drive Me Crazy. 2013. (ENG., Illus.). 112p. (YA). (gr. 7). pap. 11.99 *(978-1-936975-58-7(0))* Archie Comic Pubns., Inc.

Parham, Keelan. Let's Toon Caricatures. 2003. (Illus.). 128p. per. 18.95 *(978-0-9725638-0-2(6))* Lunar Donut Pr.

Park, Min-Seo. Blazin' Barrels, Vol. 2. Park, Min-Seo, illus. 2nd rev. ed. 2005. (Illus.). 192p. pap. 9.99 *(978-1-59532-559-4(X))* TOKYOPOP, Inc.

Park, So Hee, creator. The Royal Palace. (Goong Ser.: 15). (ENG., Illus.). (gr. 8-17). 2014. 352p. pap. 25.00 *(978-0-7595-3159-8(5))* 2014. 368p. pap. 25.00 *(978-0-7595-3158-1(7))* Vol. 13. 2013. 384p. pap. 25.00 *(978-0-7595-3157-4(9))* Orbit. (Yen Pr.).

—The Royal Palace, Vol. 16. 2014. (Goong Ser.: 16). (ENG., Illus.). 384p. (gr. 8-17). 25.00 *(978-0-7595-3160-4(9),* Yen Pr.) Orbit.

Parker, Jake. Rescue on Tankium, No. 3. 2011. (Missile Mouse Ser.: 2). (ENG.). 160p. (J). (gr. 3-7). pap. 10.99 *(978-0-545-11717-3(8),* Graphix) Scholastic, Inc.

—Rescue on Tankium3. 2011. (Missile Mouse Ser.: 2). (ENG.). 160p. (J). (gr. 3-7). 21.99 *(978-0-545-11716-6(X),* Graphix) Scholastic, Inc.

Parker, Jeff. Attack of 50 Foot Girl! Kirk, Leonard, illus. 2014. (Avengers Set 4 Ser.). (ENG.). 24p. (J). (gr. 9-14). lib. bdg. 24.21 *(978-1-61479-293-2(3))* Spotlight.

—Avenging Seven. Kirk, Leonard, illus. 2014. (Avengers Set 4 Ser.). (ENG.). 24p. (J). (gr. 9-14). lib. bdg. 24.21 *(978-1-61479-294-9(1))* Spotlight.

—Bringers of Storm. Cafu, illus. 2014. (Avengers Set 4 Ser.). (ENG.). 24p. (J). (gr. 9-14). lib. bdg. 24.21 *(978-1-61479-295-6(X))* Spotlight.

—Ego: The Loving Planet. Santacruz, Juan, illus. 2012. (Avengers Set 3 Ser.). 24p. (J). (gr. 2-6). lib. bdg. 24.21 *(978-1-61479-014-3(0))* Spotlight.

—Even a Hawkeye Can Cry. Scott, Steve, illus. 2014. (Avengers Set 4 Ser.). (ENG.). 24p. (J). (gr. 9-14). lib. bdg. 24.21 *(978-1-61479-296-3(8))* Spotlight.

—High Serpent Society. Santacruz, Juan, illus. 2012. (Avengers Set 3 Ser.). 24p. (J). (gr. 2-6). lib. bdg. 24.21 *(978-1-61479-015-0(9))* Spotlight.

—Medieval Women. Santacruz, Juan, illus. 2012. (Avengers Set 3 Ser.). 24p. (J). (gr. 2-6). lib. bdg. 24.21 *(978-1-61479-016-7(7))* Spotlight.

—A Not-So-Beautiful Mind. Santacruz, Juan, illus. 2012. (Avengers Set 3 Ser.). 24p. (J). (gr. 2-6). lib. bdg. 24.21 *(978-1-61479-017-4(5))* Spotlight.

Parker, Jeff, ed. Perfect World, Vol. 3. Molina, Jorge et al, illus. 2011. (ENG.). 144p. (J). (gr. 4-17). pap. 16.99 *(978-0-7851-4666-7(0))* Marvel Worldwide, Inc.

Parker, Jeff, et al. Wonderland, Vol. 1. Allie, Scott & Hahn, Sierra, eds. 2013. (ENG., Illus.). 144p. pap. 17.99 *(978-1-61655-145-2(3))* Dark Horse Comics.

Parks, James & Costa, Ben. The Road to Epoli. 2017. (Rickety Stitch & the Gelatinous Goo Ser.: Bk. 1). (ENG.). 208p. (YA). (gr. 7). 18.99 ***(978-0-399-55613-5(3))***; pap. 14.99 ***(978-0-399-55614-2(1))*** Random Hse. Children's Bks. (Knopf Bks. for Young Readers).

Pastis, Stephan. Beginning Pearls. 2013. lib. bdg. 20.85 *(978-0-606-31764-1(3),* Turtleback) Turtleback Bks.

—Skip School, Fly to Space: A Pearls Before Swine Collection. 2015. (Pearls Before Swine Kids Ser.: 3). (ENG., Illus.). 224p. (J). pap. 9.99 *(978-1-4494-3637-7(4))* Andrews McMeel Publishing.

—Stephan's Web: A Pearls Before Swine Collection. 2016. (Pearls Before Swine Ser.: 26). (ENG.). 128p. pap. 14.99 *(978-1-4494-8202-2(3))* Andrews McMeel Publishing.

Patrick, Jean L. S. The Baseball Adventure of Jackie Mitchell, Girl Pitcher vs. Babe Ruth. Hammond, Ted & Carbajal, Richard, illus. 2011. (History's Kid Heroes Ser.). 32p. pap. 51.02 *(978-0-7613-7635-4(6),* Graphic Universe™) Lerner Publishing Group.

—The Baseball Adventure of Jackie Mitchell, Girl Pitcher vs. Babe Ruth. Trover, Zachary et al, illus. 2011. (History's Kid Heroes Ser.). (ENG.). 32p. (gr. 3-5). 26.60 *(978-0-7613-6180-0(4))* Lerner Publishing Group.

Patterson, James. The Manga. 2012. (Daniel X: the Manga Ser.: 3). lib. bdg. 24.55 *(978-0-606-26463-1(9),* Turtleback) Turtleback Bks.

Patterson, James & Rust, Ned. Daniel X. Kye, SeungHui, illus. 2011. (Daniel X: the Manga Ser.: 2). (ENG.). 208p. (gr. 7-17). pap. 12.99 *(978-0-316-07765-1(8),* Yen Pr.) Orbit.

Patterson, Michael. Blam! O'Reilly, Sean Patrick, ed. 2011. (Illus.). 80p. (YA). pap. 14.95 *(978-1-926914-04-6(X))* Arcana Studio, Inc.

Pattison, Darcy. The Scary Slopes, 1 vol. Harpster, Steve, illus. 2011. (My First Graphic Novel Ser.). (ENG.). 32p. (gr. k-2). lib. bdg. 24.65 *(978-1-4342-2534-4(8),* My First Graphic Novel) Stone Arch Bks.

Pauline Comics Series, 10 bks., Set. Incl. James Alberione Vol. 10: Hero for the Gospel. Richards, Virginia Helen, ed. Wickenhiser, Mary D., tr. 80p. (gr. 5-9). 1996. pap. 2.95 *(978-0-8198-3964-0(7))*; Vol. 1. St. Maximilian Kolbe. Laferte, Jean-Marie & Jeanson, Brigitte. Trouve', Marianne L., tr. 32p. (gr. 3-8). 1995. pap. 1.95 *(978-0-8198-6978-4(3))*; Vol. 3. St. Elizabeth. Lang, Justin & Wehrung, Juliette. Trouve', Marianne L., tr. Retailleau, Jean, illus. 32p. (gr. 3-8). 1995. pap. 1.95 *(978-0-8198-6981-4(3),* 332-325); Vol. 4. St. Joan of Arc. Berthier, Rene & Segault, Marie. Trouve', Marianne L., tr. Le Sourd, Bruno, illus. 32p. (gr. 3-8). 1995. pap. 1.95 *(978-0-8198-6975-3(9))*; Vol. 5. St. Clare of Assisi. Dhombre, Pierre. Trouve', Marianne L., tr. De La Fuente, Victor, illus. 32p. (gr. 3-8). 1995. pap. 1.95 *(978-0-8198-6976-0(7))*; Vol. 6. St. Martin. Trouve', Marianne L. & Maric, Raymond, trs. Frisano, Pierre & Alluard, Marie, illus. 32p. (gr. 3-8). 1995. pap. 1.95 *(978-0-8198-6980-7(5),* 332-324); Vol. 7. St. Bernadette. Berthier, Rene & Sigault, Marie. Trouve', Marianne L., tr. Garel, Roland, illus. 32p. (gr. 3-8). 1995. pap. 1.95 *(978-0-8198-6977-7(5))*; Vol. 8. St. Vincent de Paul. Garel, Roland. Trouve', Marianne L., tr. 32p. (gr. 3-8). 1995. pap. 1.95 *(978-0-8198-6982-1(1))*; Vol. 9. St. Bernard of Clairvaux. Monk of Citeaux Staff. Trouve', Marianne L., tr. De La Fuente, Victor, illus. 32p. (gr. 3-8). 1995. pap. 1.95 *(978-0-8198-6979-1(1),* 332-323); (J). Set pap. 18.45 *(978-0-8198-5903-7(6))* Pauline Bks. & Media.

Pearce, Jacqueline. Manga Touch, 1 vol. 2007. (Orca Currents Ser.). (ENG.). (J). (gr. 5-9). 136p. pap. 9.95 *(978-1-55143-746-0(5))*; 112p. lib. bdg. 14.95 *(978-1-55143-748-4(1))* Orca Bk. Pubs. USA.

Pearl, Michael & Bulanadi, Danny. Good & Evil Pt. 2: Abraham, Pt. 2. 2007. (ENG., Illus.). 12p. (J). pap. 2.99 *(978-0-9786372-5-5(9))* No Greater Joy Ministries, Inc.

Pearson, Luke, illus. Hilda & the Bird Parade. 2013. (Hildafolk Ser.). (ENG.). 44p. (J). (gr. k). 24.00 *(978-1-909263-06-2(0))* Flying Eye Bks. GBR. Dist: Consortium Bk. Sales & Distribution.

—Hilda & the Troll. 2013. (Hildafolk Ser.). (ENG.). 40p. (J). (gr. k). 18.95 *(978-1-909263-14-7(1))* Flying Eye Bks. GBR. Dist: Consortium Bk. Sales & Distribution.

Pearson, Ridley. Shell Game. 2013. (Kingdom Keepers Ser.: 5). (J). lib. bdg. 19.65 *(978-0-606-27067-0(1),* Turtleback) Turtleback Bks.

Peirce, Lincoln. Big Nate: From the Top. 2010. (Big Nate Ser.: 1). (ENG., Illus.). 224p. (J). (gr. 2-7). pap. 9.99 *(978-1-4494-0232-7(1))* Andrews McMeel Publishing.

—Big Nate: I Can't Take It! 2013. (ENG., Illus.). 224p. pap. 9.99 *(978-1-4494-2937-9(8))* Andrews McMeel Publishing.

—Big Nate: Mr. Popularity. Peirce, Lincoln, illus. 2014. (Big Nate Ser.). (ENG., Illus.). 224p. (J). (gr. 3-7). pap. 9.99 *(978-0-06-208700-3(2))* HarperCollins Pubs.

—Big Nate: Revenge of the Cream Puffs. 2016. (Big Nate Ser.: 15). (ENG.). 184p. (J). (gr. 3-7). pap. 9.99 *(978-1-4494-6228-4(6))* Andrews McMeel Publishing.

—Big Nate: The Crowd Goes Wild! Peirce, Lincoln, illus. 2014. (Big Nate Ser.). (ENG., Illus.). 224p. (J). 9.99 *(978-1-4494-3634-6(X))* Andrews McMeel Publishing.

—Big Nate: Thunka, Thunka, Thunka. 2016. (Big Nate Ser.: Vol. 14). (ENG., Illus.). (J). (gr. 3-6). 29.99 ***(978-1-4494-7581-9(7))*** Andrews McMeel Publishing.

—Big Nate — Genius Mode. Peirce, Lincoln, illus. 2013. (Big Nate Ser.). (ENG., Illus.). 224p. (J). (gr. 3-7). pap. 9.99 *(978-0-06-208698-3(7))* HarperCollins Pubs.

—Big Nate — Genius Mode. 2013. (Big Nate Graphic Novels Ser.). (J). lib. bdg. 20.85 *(978-0-606-31802-0(X),* Turtleback) Turtleback Bks.

—Big Nate — Great Minds Think Alike. 2014. (Big Nate Graphic Novels Ser.). lib. bdg. 20.85 *(978-0-606-35229-1(5))* Turtleback Bks.

—Big Nate — Here Goes Nothing. 2012. (Big Nate Graphic Novels Ser.: 6). (J). lib. bdg. 20.85 *(978-0-606-26526-3(0),* Turtleback) Turtleback Bks.

—Big Nate — Welcome to My World. 2015. (Big Nate Ser.: 13). (ENG., Illus.). 176p. (J). pap. 9.99 *(978-1-4494-6226-0(X))* Andrews McMeel Publishing.

—Big Nate - Say Good-Bye to Dork City. 2015. (Big Nate Ser.). (ENG., Illus.). 224p. (J). 9.99 *(978-1-4494-6225-3(1))* Andrews McMeel Publishing.

—Big Nate - The Crowd Goes Wild! 2014. (Big Nate Graphic Novels Ser.). lib. bdg. 20.85 *(978-0-606-36143-9(X))* Turtleback Bks.

—Big Nate & Friends. 2011. (Illus.). 224p. (J). *(978-1-60744-837-2(8))*; *(978-0-545-46801-5(9))* Andrews McMeel Publishing.

—Big Nate Makes the Grade. 2012. (Big Nate Graphic Novels Ser.). (Illus.). 224p. lib. bdg. 20.85 *(978-0-606-26308-5(X),* Turtleback) Turtleback Bks.

—Big Nate Out Loud. 2011. (Big Nate Ser.: 2). (ENG., Illus.). 224p. (J). pap. 9.99 *(978-1-4494-0718-6(8))* Andrews McMeel Publishing.

—Big Nate: Thunka, Thunka, Thunka. 2016. (ENG., Illus.). 176p. (J). (gr. 3-6). pap. 9.99 *(978-1-4494-6227-7(8))* Andrews McMeel Publishing.

—Big Nate's Greatest Hits. 2015. (ENG., Illus.). 376p. (J). pap. 12.99 *(978-1-4494-6489-9(0))* Andrews McMeel Publishing.

—Epic Big Nate. 2016. (ENG.). 472p. 50.00 *(978-1-4494-7195-8(1))* Andrews McMeel Publishing.

—Great Minds Think Alike. 2014. (Big Nate Ser.: 8). (ENG.). 224p. (J). 9.99 *(978-1-4494-3635-3(8))* Andrews McMeel Publishing.

—Here Goes Nothing. Peirce, Lincoln, illus. 2012. (Big Nate Comix Ser.: 2). (ENG., Illus.). 224p. (J). (gr. 3-7). pap. 9.99 *(978-0-06-208696-9(0))* HarperCollins Pubs.

—I Can't Take It! 2013. (Big Nate Graphic Novels Ser.). lib. bdg. 20.85 *(978-0-606-32313-0(9),* Turtleback) Turtleback Bks.

—Thunka, Thunka, Thunka. 2016. (Big Nate Graphic Novels Ser.). lib. bdg. 20.85 *(978-0-606-38234-2(8))* Turtleback Bks.

—What Could Possibly Go Wrong? Peirce, Lincoln, illus. 2012. (Big Nate Comix Ser.: 1). (ENG., Illus.). 224p. (J). (gr. 3-7). pap. 9.99 *(978-0-06-208694-5(4))* HarperCollins Pubs.

—What's a Little Noogie Between Friends? 2017. (Big Nate Ser.: 16). (ENG.). 176p. (J). pap. 9.99 *(978-1-4494-6229-1(4))* Andrews McMeel Publishing.

Pell, Jason. Woody & the Noble. O'Reilly, Sean Patrick, ed. 2011. (Illus.). 80p. (YA). pap. 14.95 *(978-1-926914-33-6(3))* Arcana Studio, Inc.

Pelleschi, Andrea. Juan Ponce de Leon. 2013. (Jr. Graphic Famous Explorers Ser.). (ENG., Illus.). 24p. (J). (gr. 3-6). pap. 10.60 *(978-1-4777-0131-7(1))*; lib. bdg. 25.25 *(978-1-4777-0073-0(0))* Rosen Publishing Group, Inc., The. (PowerKids Pr.).

Pennac, D. & Benacquista, E. Lone Riders. 2013. (Lucky Luke Ser.: 42). (ENG., Illus.). 48p. (J). (gr. 3-12). pap. 11.95 *(978-1-84918-168-6(3))* CineBook GBR. Dist: National Bk. Network.

Pennac, Daniel & Benacquista, Tonino. Lucky Luke Versus the Pinkertons. Achdé, illus. 2012. (Lucky Luke Ser.: 31). (ENG.). 48p. pap. 11.95 *(978-1-84918-098-6(9))* CineBook GBR. Dist: National Bk. Network.

Penny, Anne. Scraper. 2006. (Illus.). 56p. pap. *(978-1-84401-921-2(7))* Athena Pr.

Perritano, John. Radical Republicans: The Struggle for Equality. 2008. (Graphic America Ser.). (ENG., Illus.). 32p. (J). (gr. 3-6). lib. bdg. *(978-0-7787-4187-9(7))* Crabtree Publishing Co.

Perry, Fred. Gold Digger, Vol. 8. 2006. (ENG., Illus.). 200p. (YA). pap. 9.99 *(978-0-9768043-0-7(1),* 9780976804307) Antarctic Pr., Inc.

—Gold Digger Platinum, Vol. 4. 2012. (ENG., Illus.). 132p. (YA). pap. 14.95 *(978-0-9850925-0-4(5),* 9780985092504) Antarctic Pr., Inc.

Peters, Stephanie True. Sleeping Beauty, Magic Master: A Graphic Novel. Lopez, Alex, illus. 2016. (Far Out Fairy Tales Ser.). (ENG.). 40p. (gr. 3-4). lib. bdg. 25.32 *(978-1-4965-3784-3(X),* Far Out Fairy Tales) Stone Arch Bks.

Peters, Stephanie True & Cano, Fernando M. Track Team Titans, 1 vol. Aburto, Jesus et al, illus. 2011. (Sports Illustrated Kids Graphic Novels Ser.). (ENG.). 56p. (gr. 2-3). pap. 7.19 *(978-1-4342-3072-0(4))*; lib. bdg. 26.65 *(978-1-4342-2224-4(1))* Stone Arch Bks.

Peterson, Brandon, illus. Ultimate X-Men - The Tempest, Vol. 9. 2006. (ENG.). 112p. (J). (gr. -1-17). pap. 10.99 *(978-0-7851-1404-8(1))* Marvel Worldwide, Inc.

Peterson, Brandon & Brereton, Dan. Giant Killer. 2006. (ENG., Illus.). 128p. (YA). pap. 14.99 *(978-1-58240-539-1(5),* 9781582405391) Image Comics.

Peterson, Megan Cooley & Rustad, Martha E. H. Encountering Chupacabra & Other Cryptids: Eyewitness Accounts, 1 vol. Stevens, Matt, illus. 2014. (Eyewitness to the Unexplained Ser.). (ENG.). 32p. (gr. 3-4). 30.65 *(978-1-4914-0242-9(3),* Graphic Library) Capstone Press of Coughlan Cos.

Petranek, Michael. The Joker's Big Break. 2016. (LEGO Batman Movie Ser.). (ENG.). 24p. (J). (gr. -1-3). pap. 4.99 *(978-1-338-11217-7(1))* Scholastic, Inc.

Petrucha, Stefan. Breaking Down, No. 2. Parker, Rick, illus. 2011. (Papercutz Slices Ser.: 2). (ENG.). 64p. (J). (gr. 5-12). 10.99 *(978-1-59707-245-8(1),* 9781597072458) Papercutz.

—Harry Potty & the Deathly Boring. 2010. (Papercutz Slices Ser.). (ENG., Illus.). 64p. (J). (gr. 5-12). pap. 7.99 *(978-1-59707-217-5(6),* 9781597072175) Papercutz.

—Mr. Cheeters Is Missing. 6th rev. ed. 2006. (Nancy Drew Graphic Novels: Girl Detective Ser.: 6). (ENG., Illus.). 96p. (J). (gr. 3-7). pap. 7.95 *(978-1-59707-030-0(0),* 9781597070300) Papercutz.

—Papercutz Slices #5: the Farting Dead. 2013. (Papercutz Slices Ser.). (ENG., Illus.). 64p. (J). (gr. 5-12). 11.99 *(978-1-59707-454-4(3),* 9781597074544) Papercutz.

—Prilla's Talent. Magic Eye Studios Staff et al, illus. 2010. (Disney Fairies Ser.: 1). (ENG.). 80p. (J). (gr. 1-6). pap. 7.99 *(978-1-59707-186-4(2),* 9781597071864);No. 1. 12.99 *(978-1-59707-187-1(0))* Papercutz.

Petrucha, Stefan & Kinney-Petrucha, Margo. Percy Jackson & the Ovolactovegetarians, No. 3. 2011. (Papercutz Slices Ser.). (ENG., Illus.). 64p. (J). (gr. 5-12). pap. 6.99 *(978-1-59707-264-9(8),* 9781597072649) Papercutz.

Petrucha, Stefan & Kinney, Sarah. City under the Basement. Murase, Sho, illus. 2009. (Nancy Drew Graphic Novels: Girl Detective Ser.: 18). (ENG.). 96p. (J). (gr. 3-7). pap. 7.95 *(978-1-59707-154-3(4),* 9781597071543); 18th ed. 12.95 *(978-1-59707-155-0(2),* 9781597071550) Papercutz.

—Cliffhanger. Murase, Sho, illus. 2009. (Nancy Drew Graphic Novels: Girl Detective Ser.: 19). (ENG.). 96p. (J). (gr. 3-7). 12.95 *(978-1-59707-166-6(8),* 9781597071666) Papercutz.

—High School Musical Mystery. 2010. (Nancy Drew Graphic Novels: Girl Detective Ser.). (ENG., Illus.). 96p. (J). (gr. 3-7). pap. 8.99 *(978-1-59707-178-9(1),* 9781597071789) Papercutz.

—Nancy Drew: High School Musical Mystery II - "The Lost Verse" 2010. (Nancy Drew Graphic Novels: Girl Detective Ser.). (ENG., Illus.). 96p. (J). (gr. 3-7). pap. 8.99 *(978-1-59707-195-6(1),* 9781597071956) Papercutz.

—Night of the Living Chatchke. 2009. (Nancy Drew Graphic Novels: Girl Detective Ser.). (ENG., Illus.). 96p. (J). (gr. 3-7). pap. 7.95 *(978-1-59707-143-7(9),* 9781597071437) Papercutz.

—Night of the Living Chatchke. Murase, Sho, illus. 17th ed. 2009. (Nancy Drew Graphic Novels: Girl Detective Ser.: 17). (ENG.). 96p. (J). (gr. 3-7). 12.95 *(978-1-59707-144-4(7),* 9781597071444) Papercutz.

—Sleight of Dan. 14th ed. 2008. (Nancy Drew Graphic Novels: Girl Detective Ser.: 14). (ENG., Illus.). 112p. (J). (gr. 3-7). pap. 7.95 *(978-1-59707-107-9(2),* 9781597071079) Papercutz.

—Small Volcanoes. 2012. (ENG., Illus.). 64p. (J). (gr. 3-7). 10.99 *(978-1-59707-355-4(5),* 9781597073554);No. 1. pap. 6.99 *(978-1-59707-354-7(7),* 9781597073547) Papercutz.

—Tiger Counter. 2008. (Nancy Drew Graphic Novels: Girl Detective Ser.: 15). (ENG., Illus.). 96p. (J). (gr. 3-7). 12.95 *(978-1-59707-119-2(6),* 9781597071192) Papercutz.

—Vampire Slayer, No. 2. 2010. (Nancy Drew the New Case Files Ser.). (ENG., Illus.). 64p. (J). (gr. 3-7). pap. 6.99 *(978-1-59707-233-5(8),* 9781597072335) Papercutz.

—What Goes Up... 2009. (Nancy Drew Graphic Novels: Girl Detective Ser.: 16). (ENG., Illus.). 96p. (J). (gr. 3-7). 12.95 *(978-1-59707-135-2(8),* 9781597071352) Papercutz.

Petrucha, Stefan, et al. The Fake Heir. Ross, Daniel Vaughn, illus. 2006. (J). *(978-1-59707-060-7(2))* Papercutz.

—Papercutz Slices Boxed Set: Vol #1-3. 2012. (ENG., Illus.). 192p. (J). (gr. 5-12). 19.99 *(978-1-59707-274-8(5),* 9781597072748) Papercutz.

Pettinato, Laura. Thirteen Americas: American Revolution & Constitution. Tiwari, Saral, illus. 2004. (J). 18.95 *(978-0-9742502-7-4(9))* Gossamer Bks., LLC.

—Thirteen Americas: The Declaration of Independence. Tiwari, Saral, illus. 2nd ed. 2004. (J). lib. bdg. *(978-0-9742502-6-7(0))* Gossamer Bks., LLC.

Petty, J. T. & Pope, Paul. The Fall of the House of West. Rubin, David, illus. 2015. 157p. (J). ***(978-1-5182-0095-3(8),*** First Second Bks.) Roaring Brook Pr.

Peyo. The Aerosmurf. 2013. (Smurfs Graphic Novels Ser.). (ENG., Illus.). 56p. (J). (gr. 2-5). 10.99 *(978-1-59707-427-8(6),* 9781597074278); pap. 5.99 *(978-1-59707-426-1(8),* 9781597074261) Papercutz.

—The Baby Smurf. 2013. (Smurfs Graphic Novels Ser.). (ENG., Illus.). 56p. (J). (gr. 1-5). pap. 5.99 *(978-1-59707-381-3(4),* 9781597073813) Papercutz.

—Benny Breakiron #2: Madame Adolphine. 2013. (Benny Breakiron Ser.). (ENG., Illus.). 64p. (J). (gr. 2-12). 11.99 *(978-1-59707-436-0(5),* 9781597074360) Papercutz.

—Meet Smurfette. Peyo, illus. 2011. (Smurfs Classic Ser.). (ENG., Illus.). 24p. (J). (gr. -1-2). pap. 3.99 *(978-1-4424-2290-2(4),* Simon Spotlight) Simon Spotlight.

—The Return of the Smurfette. 2012. (Smurfs Graphic Novels Ser.). (ENG., Illus.). 56p. (J). (gr. 2-5). pap. 5.99 *(978-1-59707-292-2(3),* 9781597072922) Papercutz.

—The Smurflings. 2013. (Smurfs Graphic Novels Ser.). (ENG., Illus.). 56p. (J). (gr. 2-5). 10.99 *(978-1-59707-408-7(X),* 9781597074087); pap. 5.99 *(978-1-59707-407-0(1),* 9781597074070) Papercutz.

—The Smurfs #14: the Baby Smurf. 2013. (Smurfs Graphic Novels Ser.). (ENG., Illus.). 56p. (J). (gr. 1-5). 10.99 *(978-1-59707-382-0(2),* 9781597073820) Papercutz.

—The Smurfs Anthology #2. 2013. (Smurfs Anthology Ser.). (ENG., Illus.). 192p. (J). (gr. 6-5). 19.99 *(978-1-59707-445-2(4),* 9781597074452) Papercutz.

—The Smurfs Christmas. 2013. (Smurfs Graphic Novels Ser.). (ENG., Illus.). 56p. (J). (gr. 2-5). 10.99 *(978-1-59707-452-0(7),* 9781597074520); pap. 5.99 *(978-1-59707-451-3(9),* 9781597074513) Papercutz.

—The Smurfs Graphic Novels Boxed Set: Vol. #10-12. 2013. (Smurfs Graphic Novels Ser.). (ENG., Illus.). 168p. (J). (gr. 2-5). 17.99 *(978-1-59707-386-8(5),* 9781597073868) Papercutz.

Peyo & Delporte, Yvan. The Smurf Olympics. 2012. (Smurfs Graphic Novels Ser.). (ENG., Illus.). 56p. (J). (gr. 2-5). 10.99 *(978-1-59707-302-8(4),* 9781597073028); pap. 7.99 *(978-1-59707-301-1(6),* 9781597073011) Papercutz.

—Smurf Soup. 2012. (Smurfs Graphic Novels Ser.). (ENG., Illus.). 56p. (J). (gr. 1-6). pap. 5.99 *(978-1-59707-358-5(X),* 9781597073585) Papercutz.

—Smurf vs. Smurf. 2012. (Smurfs Graphic Novels Ser.). (ENG., Illus.). 56p. (J). (gr. 2-5). 10.99 *(978-1-59707-321-9(0),* 9781597073219); pap. 5.99 *(978-1-59707-320-2(2),* 9781597073202) Papercutz.

—The Smurfette. 2011. (Smurfs Graphic Novels Ser.). (ENG., Illus.). 64p. (J). (gr. 2-5). pap. 5.99 *(978-1-59707-236-6(2),* 9781597072366);No. 4. 10.99 *(978-1-59707-237-3(0),* 9781597072373) Papercutz.

—The Smurfs, 3 Vols., Set. 2011. (Smurfs Graphic Novels Ser.). (ENG., Illus.). 184p. (J). (gr. 2-5). 17.99 *(978-1-59707-273-1(7),* 9781597072731) Papercutz.

—The Smurfs #10: the Return of the Smurfette. 2012. (Smurfs Graphic Novels Ser.). (ENG., Illus.). 56p. (J). (gr. 2-5). 10.99 *(978-1-59707-293-9(1),* 9781597072939) Papercutz.

—The Smurfs #13: Smurf Soup. 2012. (Smurfs Graphic Novels Ser.). (ENG., Illus.). 56p. (J). (gr. 1-6). 10.99 *(978-1-59707-359-2(8),* 9781597073592) Papercutz.

—The Smurfs #9: Gargamel & the Smurfs. 2011. (Smurfs Graphic Novels Ser.). (ENG., Illus.). 56p. (J). (gr. 2-5). 10.99 *(978-1-59707-290-8(7),* 9781597072908); pap. 5.99 *(978-1-59707-289-2(3),* 9781597072892) Papercutz.

—The Smurfs & the Egg. 2011. (Smurfs Graphic Novels Ser.). (ENG., Illus.). 64p. (J). (gr. 2-5). 10.99 *(978-1-59707-247-2(8),* 9781597072472); pap. 5.99 *(978-1-59707-246-5(X),* 9781597072465) Papercutz.

—The Smurfs Anthology. 2013. (Smurfs Anthology Ser.). (ENG., Illus.). 192p. (J). (gr. 6-5). 19.99 *(978-1-59707-417-9(9),* 9781597074179) Papercutz.

—The Smurfs Graphic Novels Boxed Set: Vol. #7-9. Gos, illus. 2012. (Smurfs Graphic Novels Ser.). (ENG.). 168p. (J). (gr. 2-5). 17.99 *(978-1-59707-340-0(7),* 9781597073400) Papercutz.

Peyo, et al. The Smurfs, Set, Vols. 4-6. 2012. (Smurfs Graphic Novels Ser.). (ENG., Illus.). 184p. (J). (gr. 2-5). 17.99 *(978-1-59707-306-6(7),* 9781597073066) Papercutz.

—The Smurfs #8: the Smurf Apprentice. 2011. (Smurfs Graphic Novels Ser.). (ENG., Illus.). 56p. (J). (gr. 2-5). 10.99 *(978-1-59707-280-9(X),* 9781597072809); pap. 5.99 *(978-1-59707-279-3(6),* 9781597072793) Papercutz.

—The Smurfs & the Howlibird. 2011. (Smurfs Graphic Novels Ser.). (ENG., Illus.). 56p. (J). (gr. 2-5). pap. 5.99 *(978-1-59707-260-1(5),* 9781597072601) Papercutz.

Pham, Thien. Sumo. Pham, Thien, illus. 2012. (ENG., Illus.). 112p. (YA). (gr. 9-12). pap. 14.99 *(978-1-59643-581-0(X),* First Second Bks.) Roaring Brook Pr.

Phelan, Matt. Around the World. Phelan, Matt, illus. 2014. (ENG., Illus.). 240p. (J). (gr. 4-7). pap. 12.99 *(978-0-7636-6925-6(3))* Candlewick Pr.

—Bluffton. Phelan, Matt, illus. 2013. (ENG., Illus.). 240p. (J). (gr. 4-7). 22.99 *(978-0-7636-5079-7(X))* Candlewick Pr.

—Bluffton: My Summers with Buster. Phelan, Matt, illus. 2017. (ENG., Illus.). 232p. (J). (gr. 4-7). pap. 12.99 *(978-0-7636-8706-9(5))* Candlewick Pr.

—Bluffton: My Summers with Buster. Phelan, Matt, illus. 2017. (ENG., Illus.). (J). (gr. 4-7). lib. bdg. 24.50 ***(978-0-606-39837-4(6))*** Turtleback Bks.

Phelan, Matt. The Storm in the Barn. 2011. (ENG., Illus.). 208p. (J). (gr. 5). pap. 14.99 *(978-0-7636-5290-6(3))* Candlewick Pr.

Phillips, Samantha. Crow: Part 1, Vol. 1. 2006. (ENG., Illus.). 24p. (YA). 3.50 *(978-0-9785891-0-3(6),* 0001) MANGACANDY, LLC.

Pike, Jay Scott, et al, illus. Marvel Masterworks: Atlas Era Jungle Adventures - Volume 3. 2013. (ENG.). 280p. (J). (gr. -1-17). 74.99 *(978-0-7851-5927-8(4),* Marvel Pr.) Disney Publishing Worldwide.

Pilkey, Dav. The Adventures of Captain Underpants. Pilkey, Dav, illus. 2013. (Captain Underpants Ser.: 1). (ENG., Illus.). 144p. (J). (gr. 2-5). 9.99 *(978-0-545-49908-8(9))* Scholastic, Inc.

—The Adventures of Captain Underpants. 2013. (Captain Underpants Color Edition Ser.: 1). lib. bdg. 20.85 *(978-0-606-32441-0(0),* Turtleback) Turtleback Bks.

—The Adventures of Super Diaper Baby. Pilkey, Dav, illus. 2014. (ENG., Illus.). 144p. (J). (gr. 3-7). 9.99 *(978-0-545-66544-5(2))* Scholastic, Inc.

—The Adventures of Super Diaper Baby. 2014. (Super Diaper Baby Ser.: 1). lib. bdg. 20.85 *(978-0-606-36273-3(8))* Turtleback Bks.

—El Capitan Calzoncillos y la Ridicula Historia de los Seres del Inodoro Morado. 2008. (Captain Underpants Ser.). (SPA., Illus.). 176p. (J). (gr. 2-5). pap. 5.99 *(978-0-545-02583-6(4),* Scholastic en Espanol) Scholastic, Inc.

—Captain Underpants & the Invasion of the Incredibly Naughty Cafeteria Ladies from Outer Space: Color Edition. 2014. (Captain Underpants Ser.: 3). (ENG., Illus.). 160p. (J). (gr. 2-5). 9.99 *(978-0-545-69470-4(1))* Scholastic, Inc.

Pinto, Ferando. Little Heroes. 2012. (ENG.). (J). pap. 14.99 *(978-1-4507-8573-0(5))* Independent Pub.

Pires, Curt. The Fiction. 2016. lib. bdg. 26.95 *(978-0-606-38936-5(9))* Turtleback Bks.

Pittman, Eddie. Red's Planet. 2016. (Red's Planet Ser.). (ENG., Illus.). 192p. (J). (gr. 3-7). 19.95 *(978-1-4197-1907-3(6),* Amulet Bks.) Abrams, Inc.

—Red's Planet. 2016. (Red's Planet Ser.: 1). (J). lib. bdg. 20.80 *(978-0-606-38203-8(8))* Turtleback Bks.

Piven, Hanoch. What Athletes Are Made Of. Piven, Hanoch, illus. 2015. (ENG., Illus.). 40p. (J). (gr. 1-5). 19.99 *(978-1-4814-7508-2(8),* Atheneum Bks. for Young Readers) Simon & Schuster Children's Publishing.

Pizer, Carol. Michael Jackson, 1 vol. Saddleback Educational Publishing Staff, ed. unabr. ed. 2011. (Graphic Biographies Ser.). (ENG.). 25p. (YA). (gr. 9-12). pap. 7.95 *(978-1-61651-265-1(2))* Saddleback Educational Publishing, Inc.

Plumeri, Arnaud. Dinosaurs: In the Beginning... 2014. (Dinosaurs Graphic Novels Ser.). (ENG., Illus.). 64p. (J). (gr. 3-9). 10.99 *(978-1-59707-490-2(X),* 9781597074902) Papercutz.

PM Seeker Series #8 Jesus, Someone Who Cares. 2005. (J). pap. 2.95 *(978-0-9749339-6-2(1))* PowerMark Productions.

Poe, Edgar Allen. The Tell-Tale Heart Package. Calero, Dennis, illus. 2013. (ENG.). 62p. (J). (gr. 5-8). pap. 35.70 *(978-1-4342-4285-3(4))* Stone Arch Bks.

Poe, Edgar Allen & Harper, Benjamin. The Tell-Tale Heart, 1 vol. Calero, Dennis, illus. 2013. (Edgar Allan Poe Graphic Novels Ser.). (ENG.). 72p. (gr. 2-3). pap. 6.10 *(978-1-4342-4261-7(7))* Stone Arch Bks.

Poe, Mark Andrew. Inkadink. 2017. (ENG., Illus.). 180p. (YA). 24.95 *(978-1-943785-10-0(4),* 9781943785100) Rabbit Pubs.

Poe, Marshall. A House Divided. Lindner, Ellen & Purvis, Leland, illus. 2009. (Turning Points Ser.). (ENG.). 128p. (J). (gr. 3-7). pap. 8.99 *(978-1-4169-5057-8(5),* Simon & Schuster/Paula Wiseman Bks.) Simon & Schuster/Paula Wiseman Bks.

Pokemon 1: Advanced Box Set [2 Discs / Subtitles / Box Set]. 2005. 39.98 incl. DVD *(978-1-4215-0214-4(3))* Viz Media.

Polette, Nancy. Gifted or Goof Off? Fact & Fiction of the Famous. 2004. (J). pap. 11.95 *(978-1-931334-23-5(4))* Pieces of Learning.

Pommaux, Yvan. Orpheus in the Underworld. Kutner, Richard, tr. from FRE. 2015. (TOON Graphic Mythology Ser.). (ENG., Illus.). 56p. (J). (gr. 2-7). 16.95 *(978-1-935179-84-9(5))* TOON Books / RAW Junior, LLC.

Ponti, Claude. Adele in Sand Land: TOON Level 1. 2017. (ENG., Illus.). 48p. (J). (gr. -1). 12.95 *(978-1-943145-16-4(4),* 9781943145164) TOON Books / RAW Junior, LLC.

—Chick & Chickie in Play All Day! 2013. (Toon Books Level 1 Ser.). lib. bdg. 14.75 *(978-0-606-31595-1(0),* Turtleback) Turtleback Bks.

—Chick & Chickie Play All Day!, 1 vol. 2013. (Toon Bks). (ENG.). 36p. (J). (gr. k-1). lib. bdg. 27.07 *(978-1-61479-150-8(3))* Spotlight.

—Chick & Chickie Play All Day! Ponti, Claude, illus. (ENG., Illus.). (J). (gr. -1-3). 2013. 32p. pap. 4.99 *(978-1-935179-29-0(2))* 2012. 36p. 12.95 *(978-1-935179-14-6(4))* TOON Books / RAW Junior, LLC.

Poon, Janice. Claire & the Bakery Thief. Poon, Janice, illus. 2008. (ENG., Illus.). 104p. (J). (gr. 2-5). 15.95 *(978-1-55453-286-5(8));* pap. 7.95 *(978-1-55453-245-2(0))* Kids Can Pr., Ltd. CAN. Dist: Hachette Bk. Group.

—Claire & the Water Wish. Poon, Janice, illus. 2009. (ENG., Illus.). 120p. (J). (gr. 2-5). 7.95 *(978-1-55453-382-4(1));* 15.95 *(978-1-55453-381-7(3))* Kids Can Pr., Ltd. CAN. Dist: Hachette Bk. Group.

Pope, Paul. Sugary Shorts. 2013. (Adventure Time Ser.: 1). (ENG.). 144p. (J). (gr. 4). 34.99 *(978-1-60886-333-4(6))* Boom! Studios.

Pope, Paul & Petty, J. T. The Fall of the House of West. Rubín, David, illus. 2015. (Battling Boy Ser.: 2). (ENG.). 160p. (J). (gr. 5). pap. 9.99 *(978-1-62672-010-7(X),* 9781626720107, First Second Bks.) Roaring Brook Pr.

Pope, Paul, et al. The Fall of the House of West. 2015. (J). lib. bdg. 20.85 *(978-0-606-37806-2(5))* Turtleback Bks.

Porter, Alan J. Cars: Radiator Springs. Carreres, Albert, illus. 2010. (World of Cars Ser.). (ENG.). 112p. (J). pap. 9.99 *(978-1-60886-502-4(9))* Boom! Studios.

—Cars: Route 66 Dash! Gladfelter, Allen, illus. 2010. (Cars Ser.). (ENG.). 112p. (J). (gr. 3-6). pap. 9.99 *(978-1-60886-585-7(1))* Boom! Studios.

—Cars Vol. 2: Radiator Springs. Carreres, Albert, illus. 2010. (World of Cars Ser.). (ENG.). 112p. (J). 24.99 *(978-1-60886-528-4(2))* Boom! Studios.

—Rally Race. Magic Eye Studios, illus. 2010. (Cars Ser.). (ENG.). 112p. (J). (gr. 3-6). pap. 9.99 *(978-1-60886-517-8(7))* Boom! Studios.

Pose File. 2nd ed. 2004. pap. 29.95 *(978-1-932453-48-5(2))* Antarctic Pr., Inc.

Posner-Sanchez, Andrea & Hitchcock, Laura. Moana Little Golden Book (Disney Moana) RH Disney & Sastrawinata-Lemay, Griselda, illus. 2016. (Little Golden Book Ser.). (ENG.). 24p. (J). (-k). 4.99 *(978-0-7364-3603-8(0),* Golden/Disney) Random Hse. Children's Bks.

Pow! 2014. (Peanuts Kids Ser.: 3). (ENG., Illus.). 224p. (J). 9.99 *(978-1-4494-5826-3(2))* Andrews McMeel Publishing.

Powell, Martin. The Seven Voyages of Sinbad, 1 vol. Pérez, Daniel et al, illus. 2010. (Classic Fiction Ser.). (ENG.). 72p. (gr. 2-3). 27.99 *(978-1-4342-1987-9(9),* Graphic Revolve) Stone Arch Bks.

—The Seven Voyages of Sinbad. Pérez, Daniel et al, illus. 2010. (Classic Fiction Ser.). (ENG.). 72p. (gr. 2-3). pap. 7.15 *(978-1-4342-2775-1(8),* Graphic Revolve) Stone Arch Bks.

Powell, Martin, et al. Graphic Revolve: Common Core Editions, 4 vols. 2015. (Graphic Revolve: Common Core Editions Ser.). (ENG.). 72p. (gr. 2-3). 111.96 *(978-1-4965-2004-3(1))* Stone Arch Bks.

PowerMark 3-pk Issues 10-12. 2004. (YA). 7.95 *(978-0-9725121-6-9(0))* PowerMark Productions.

Press, Pikachu. Catch Pikachu! DELUXE Look & Listen Set. 2012. (ENG.). 48p. (J). 16.99 *(978-1-60438-171-9(X))* Pokemon, USA, Inc.

—Guide to Pokemon Legends. 2012. (ENG.). 32p. (J). 17.99 *(978-1-60438-175-7(2))* Pokemon, USA, Inc.

—Super Pokemon Pop-Up! Black Kyurem. 2013. (ENG.). 5p. (J). (gr. 3-6). 9.99 *(978-1-60438-179-5(5))* Pokemon, USA, Inc.

Price, Roger & Mad Libs Staff. Give Me Liberty or Give Me Mad Libs. 2015. (Mad Libs Ser.). (ENG., Illus.). 48p. (J). (gr. 3-7). pap. 4.99 *(978-0-8431-8298-9(9),* Mad Libs) Penguin Young Readers Group.

Priest, Christopher. Brothers & Keepers. 2005. (Captain America & the Falcon Ser.: Vol. 2). (Illus.). 168p. (YA). pap. 17.99 *(978-0-7851-1568-7(4))* Marvel Worldwide, Inc.

Proimos, James, Jr. Apocalypse Meow Meow. Proimos, James, Jr., illus. 2015. (ENG., Illus.). 224p. (J). (gr. 3-6). 13.99 *(978-1-61963-472-5(4),* 9781619634725, Bloomsbury USA Childrens) Bloomsbury Publishing USA.

Proimos, James. The Complete Adventures of Johnny Mutton. 2014. (ENG., Illus.). 160p. (J). (gr. 1-4). 12.99 *(978-0-544-32404-6(8),* HMH Books For Young Readers) Houghton Mifflin Harcourt Publishing Co.

Proimos, James, III & Proimos, James, Jr. Apocalypse Bow Wow. Proimos, James, III & Proimos, James, Jr., illus. (ENG., Illus.). 224p. (J). 2016. pap. 7.99 *(978-1-68119-088-4(5),* 9781681190884) 2015. (gr. 3-6). 13.99 *(978-1-61963-442-8(2),* 9781619634428) Bloomsbury Publishing USA. (Bloomsbury USA Childrens).

Protobunker Studio Staff & Wells, H. G. La Guerra de los Mundos. Ruiz, Alfonso, illus. 2010. (Classic Fiction Ser.). (SPA.). 72p. (gr. 2-3). 27.99 *(978-1-4342-2322-7(1),* Graphic Revolve en Español) Stone Arch Bks.

Publications International Ltd. Staff, ed. Batman: The Brave & the Bold (My First Library) 2010. 10p. (J). bds. 12.98 *(978-1-60553-856-3(6))* Phoenix International Publications, Inc.

—Captain America Large Play a Sound. 2011. 24p. (J). 14.98 *(978-1-4508-1608-3(8))* Publications International, Ltd.

—Green Lantern Large Play a Sound. 2011. 24p. (J). 12.98 *(978-1-4508-1606-9(1))* Publications International, Ltd.

—Look & Find - Captain America: The First Avenger. 2011. 24p. (J). 3.75 net. *(978-1-4508-1877-3(3))* Phoenix International Publications, Inc.

—Look & Find Green Lantern. 2011. 24p. (J). 7.98 *(978-1-4508-1179-8(5))* Publications International, Ltd.

—Marvel Heroes. 2007. (J). 9.98 *(978-1-4127-8449-8(2))* Phoenix International Publications, Inc.

—Marvel Heroes. 2007. (J). 7.10 *(978-1-4127-6665-4(6))* Publications International, Ltd.

—Record A Story: My Grandma Is Special. 2011. 20p. (J). bds. 19.99 *(978-1-4508-1352-5(6))* Phoenix International Publications, Inc.

—Record a Story: My Grandpa Is Special. 2011. 20p. (J). bds. 25.98 *(978-1-4508-1381-5(X))* Phoenix International Publications, Inc.

—Thomas & Friends: Let's Go, Thomas! 2010. 14p. (J). 17.98 *(978-1-4508-0212-3(5))* Phoenix International Publications, Inc.

Pujol, Miquel, et al. Uncle Scrooge #388. 2009. 64p. pap. 7.99 *(978-1-60360-088-0(4))* Gemstone Publishing, Inc.

—Uncle Scrooge: Timeless Tales Volume 1: Timeless Tales Volume 1. 2016. (Uncle Scrooge Ser.). (ENG., Illus.). 240p. 29.99 *(978-1-63140-566-2(7),* 9781631405662) Idea & Design Works, LLC.

Pullman, Philip. The Golden Compass Graphic Novel, Volume 2. 2016. (His Dark Materials Ser.). (ENG.). 80p. (J). (gr. 5). 18.99 *(978-0-553-53512-9(9),* Knopf Bks. for Young Readers) Random Hse. Children's Bks.

Purves, Jeff, et al, illus. Hulk Visionaries, Vol. 3. 2006. (ENG.). 192p. (J). (gr. 4-17). pap. 19.99 *(978-0-7851-2095-7(5))* Marvel Worldwide, Inc.

Pyle, Howard. The Merry Adventures of Robin Hood, 1 vol. Dunn, Ben, illus. 2007. (Graphic Classics). (ENG.). 32p. (gr. 3-6). 28.50 *(978-1-60270-053-6(2),* Graphic Planet- Fiction) ABDO Publishing Co.

Pyle, Kevin C. Take What You Can Carry. Pyle, Kevin C., illus. 2012. (ENG., Illus.). 176p. (YA). (gr. 7-12). pap. 14.99 *(978-0-8050-8286-9(7),* 9780805082869) Square Fish.

Pyle, Kevin C. & Cunningham, Scott. Bad for You: Exposing the War on Fun! Pyle, Kevin C., illus. 2014. (ENG., Illus.). 192p. (YA). (gr. 7). pap. 12.99 *(978-0-8050-9289-9(7),* Holt, Henry & Co. Bks. For Young Readers) Holt, Henry & Co.

Qitsualik-Tinsley, Rachel, et al. Stories of Survival & Revenge: From Inuit Folklore, 1 vol. 2015. (ENG., Illus.). 80p. (YA). (gr. 7). pap. 12.95 *(978-1-77227-001-3(6))* Inhabit Media Inc. CAN. Dist: Independent Pubs. Group.

Quackenbush, Robert. Detective Mole. 2010. 68p. (J). (gr. k-4). pap. 8.95 *(978-1-4502-1529-9(7))* iUniverse, Inc.

Quesada, Joe & Tieri, Frank. Iron Man by Joe Quesada. Martinez, Alitha et al, illus. 2013. (ENG.). 232p. (J). (gr. 4-17). pap. 24.99 *(978-0-7851-6736-5(6))* Marvel Worldwide, Inc.

The Quest. 2nd ed. 2003. 170p. (YA). per. 10.95 *(978-0-9713292-7-0(3))* Aim Higher Bks.

*quino. MAFALDA 3. (SPA., Illus.). 94p. 12.95 *(978-84-264-4503-2(9))* Editorial Lumen ESP. Dist: Distribooks, Inc.

Quino. Mafalda 9. 2003. (SPA., Illus.). 85p. per. 11.90 *(978-950-515-609-2(X))* De La Flor ARG. Dist: LD Bks., Inc.

R, Disney. The Incredibles. Stein, Erin, ed. 2005. (Illus.). 93p. pap. 14.99 *(978-1-59532-720-8(7),* Tokyopop Kids) TOKYOPOP, Inc.

Radice, Teresa, et al. Tinker Bell & the Wings of Rani. Vetro, Daniela et al, illus. 2010. (Disney Fairies Ser.: 2). (ENG.). 80p. (J). (gr. 1-6). pap. 7.99 *(978-1-59707-226-7(5),* 9781597072267) Papercutz.

Rafter, Dan. Atlas. 2010. (ENG., Illus.). 96p. pap. 9.99 *(978-1-61623-931-2(X))* Bluewater Productions, Inc.

—Gearz. 2010. (ENG., Illus.). 96p. (YA). pap. 17.99 *(978-1-61623-929-9(8))* Bluewater Productions, Inc.

Ragawa, Marimo. Baby & Me, Vol. 2. Ragawa, Marimo, illus. 2006. (Baby & Me Ser.). (ENG., Illus.). 208p. pap. 8.99 *(978-1-4215-0573-2(8))* Viz Media.

Ragawa, Marimo & Marimo, Ragawa. Baby & Me, Vol. 5. Robertson, Ian, ed. Ragawa, Marimo & Marimo, Ragawa, illus. 2007. (Baby & Me Ser.: 5). (ENG., Illus.). 192p. pap. 8.99 *(978-1-4215-1008-8(1))* Viz Media.

Raiku, Makoto. Animal Land 7. 2013. (Animal Land Ser.). (ENG., Illus.). 200p. (gr. 8-12). pap. 10.99 *(978-1-61262-249-1(6))* Kodansha America, Inc.

—Animal Land 8. 2013. (Animal Land Ser.). (ENG., Illus.). 208p. (gr. 8-12). pap. 10.99 *(978-1-61262-250-7(X))* Kodansha America, Inc.

—Animal Land 9. 2014. (Animal Land Ser.). (ENG., Illus.). 208p. pap. 10.99 *(978-1-61262-546-1(0))* Kodansha America, Inc.

Raiku, Makoto, contrib. by. Zatchbell!, Vol. 3. 2005. 200p. 9.99 *(978-1-4215-0208-3(9))* Viz Media.

Ralph, Brian. Cave In. 2013. (ENG., Illus.). 96p. (J). (gr. 7-12). pap. 14.95 *(978-1-77046-094-2(2),* 9781770460942) Drawn & Quarterly Pubns. CAN. Dist: Macmillan.

—Reggie-12. 2013. (ENG., Illus.). 96p. (YA). 21.95 *(978-1-77046-132-1(9),* 9781770461321) Drawn & Quarterly Pubns. CAN. Dist: Macmillan.

Ramirez, David. Minimonsters (En Español) 2004. (SPA., Illus.). 48p. 19.95 *(978-1-59497-073-3(4))* Public Square Bks.

Ramos, Humberto, et al, illus. Spider-Man - Trouble on the Horizon. 2013. (ENG.). 112p. (J). (gr. 4-17). pap. 16.99 *(978-0-7851-6004-5(3))* Marvel Worldwide, Inc.

Rand, Jason. Helios. 2007. (Illus.). 152p. (YA). pap. 15.99 *(978-0-9738966-3-3(9))* Speakeasy Comics CAN. Dist: Diamond Bk. Distributors.

Randolph, Grace. Muppet Peter Pan. Mebberson, Amy, illus. 2010. (Muppet Show Ser.). (ENG.). 112p. (J). pap. 9.99 *(978-1-60886-507-9(X))* Boom! Studios.

Randolph, Grace & Barks, Carl. Muppet Peter Pan. Mebberson, Amy, illus. 2010. (Muppet Show Ser.). (ENG.). 112p. (J). 24.99 *(978-1-60886-531-4(2))* Boom! Studios.

Randolph, Grace, et al. Fraggle Rock: Tails & Tales. Beedle, Tim, ed. Cook, Katie & Ashworth, Nichol, illus. 2011. (Fraggle Rock Ser.: 2). (ENG.). 136p. (J). (gr. 4). 19.95 *(978-1-936393-13-8(1))* Boom Entertainment, Inc.

Random House. The Mutant Files (Teenage Mutant Ninja Turtles) Random House, illus. 2014. (Pictureback(R) Ser.). (ENG., Illus.). 24p. (J). (gr. -1-2). 5.99 *(978-0-385-38746-0(6),* Random Hse. Bks. for Young Readers) Random Hse. Children's Bks.

Raney, Tom, et al, illus. The Infinity War. 2006. (ENG.). 400p. (J). (gr. 4-17). pap. 29.99 *(978-0-7851-2105-3(6))* Marvel Worldwide, Inc.

Ransom, Candice. The Life-Saving Adventure of Sam Deal, Shipwreck Rescuer. Trover, Zachary, illus. 2010. (History's Kid Heroes Ser.). (ENG.). 32p. (gr. 3-5). pap. 8.95 *(978-0-7613-6196-1(0),* Graphic Universe™); lib. bdg. 26.60 *(978-0-7613-6177-0(4))* Lerner Publishing Group.

—The Rescue Adventure of Stenny Green, Hindenburg Crash Eyewitness. Hammond, Ted & Carbajal, Richard, illus. 2011. (History's Kid Heroes Ser.). 32p. pap. 51.02 *(978-0-7613-7638-5(0),* Graphic Universe™); (ENG.). (gr. 3-5). 26.60 *(978-0-7613-6178-7(2));* (ENG.). (gr. 3-5). pap. 8.95 *(978-0-7613-7070-3(6),* Graphic Universe™) Lerner Publishing Group.

—The Underground Adventure of Arly Dunbar, Cave Explorer. Hammond, Ted & Carbajal, Richard Pimentel, illus. 2011. (History's Kid Heroes Set III Ser.). pap. 51.02 *(978-0-7613-7640-8(2),* Graphic Universe™) Lerner Publishing Group.

—The Underground Adventure of Arly Dunbar, Cave Explorer. Hammond, Ted & Carbajal, Richard, illus. 2011. (History's Kid Heroes Ser.). (ENG.). 32p. (gr. 3-5). (J). 26.60 *(978-0-7613-6182-4(0));* pap. 8.95 *(978-0-7613-7074-1(9),* Graphic Universe™) Lerner Publishing Group.

Rao, Lisa. Iron Man: I Am Iron Man! Guidi, Guido, illus. 2008. (I Can Read Bks.). 32p. (J). (gr. -1-2). pap. 3.99 *(978-0-06-082193-7(0),* Harper Trophy) HarperCollins Pubs.

Rao, Sirish. The Old Animals' Forest Band. Bai, Durga, illus. 2008. 40p. (J). (gr. -1-2). (ENG.). *(978-81-86211-45-8(4));* *(978-81-86211-41-0(1))* Tara Publishing.

Rasheed, M. Monsters 101, Book One. 2007. 152p. pap. 15.00 *(978-1-4303-2946-6(7))* Lulu Pr., Inc.

Rau, Dana Meachen. Go Bot, Robot! Jung, Wook Jin, illus. 2013. (Step into Reading Ser.). (ENG.). 32p. (J). (gr. -1-1). 3.99 *(978-0-375-87083-5(0),* Random Hse. Bks. for Young Readers) Random Hse. Children's Bks.

—Go Bot, Robot! Jung, Wook Jin, illus. 2013. 32p. (J). *(978-0-449-81429-1(7))* Random Hse., Inc.

—Robot, Go Bot! 2013. (Step into Reading Level 1 Ser.). lib. bdg. 13.55 *(978-0-606-31935-5(2),* Turtleback) Turtleback Bks.

Rauch, Earl Mac. Buckaroo Banzai TP Vol 02 No Matter Where You Go. 2014. (ENG., Illus.). 158p. (YA). pap. 16.95 *(978-1-936814-72-5(2),* 9781936814725) Moonstone.

Rauch, Mac & Richter, W. D. BUCKAROO BANZAI: TPB Vol. 1: Return of the Screw: TPB Vol. 1: Return of the Screw. 2014. (ENG., Illus.). 120p. (YA). pap. 15.95 *(978-1-936814-71-8(4),* 9781936814718) Moonstone.

Raum, Elizabeth. True Stories of the Revolutionary War, 1 vol. Kinsella, Pat, illus. 2012. (Stories of War Ser.). (ENG.). 32p. (gr. 3-4). 30.65 *(978-1-4296-8674-7(X));* pap. 47.70 *(978-1-4296-9343-1(6));* pap. 8.10 *(978-1-4296-9342-4(8))* Capstone Press of Coughlan Cos. (Graphic Library).

Raum, Elizabeth, et al. Stories of War. 2012. (Stories of War Ser.). (ENG.). 32p. (gr. 3-4). lib. bdg. 122.60 *(978-1-4296-9164-2(6),* Graphic Library) Capstone Press of Coughlan Cos.

Raymond, Roger & Savoy, Darryl. Ralph Filmore: Paranormal Investigator. O'Reilly, Sean Patrick, ed. 2012. (Illus.). 78p. (J). pap. 14.95 *(978-1-926914-31-2(7))* Arcana Studio, Inc.

Real Bout High School, Vol. 6. 2005. (YA). pap. 9.99 *(978-1-59182-523-4(7))* TOKYOPOP, Inc.

RealBuzz Studios Staff. Hits & Misses. 2007. 128p. (YA). No. 1. pap. 4.97 *(978-1-59789-569-9(5))*No. 2. pap. 4.97 *(978-1-59789-570-5(9))*No. 3. pap. 4.97 *(978-1-59789-571-2(7))*No. 4. pap. 4.97 *(978-1-59789-572-9(5))* Barbour Publishing, Inc. (Barbour Bks.).

—Let There Be Lighten Up! 2007. (Goofyfoot Gurl Ser.: No. 1). 96p. (YA). pap. 4.97 *(978-1-59789-573-6(3),* Barbour Bks.) Barbour Publishing, Inc.

—Space Cadet vs Drama Queen Terror from the Tarantula Nebula: Life Camera Action Book 1. 2007. 128p. (YA). pap. 4.97 *(978-1-59789-577-4(6),* Barbour Bks.) Barbour Publishing, Inc.

Rechlin, Ted. ComicQuest TIME TRAVEL TROUBLE. 2013. (Dover Children's Activity Bks.). (ENG.). 48p. (J). (gr. 3-8). pap. 4.99 *(978-0-486-49949-9(9))* Dover Pubns., Inc.

Rechlin, Ted & Stickers. Mecha Robot Stickers. 2011. (Dover Little Activity Books Stickers Ser.). (ENG.). 4p. (J). (gr. k-3). pap. 1.50 *(978-0-486-48275-0(8))* Dover Pubns., Inc.

Reed, M. K. Science Comics: Dinosaurs. Flood, Joe, illus. 2016. (Science Comics Ser.). (ENG.). 128p. (J). pap. 12.99 *(978-1-62672-143-2(2),* 9781626721432, First Second Bks.) Roaring Brook Pr.

Reger, Rob. Emily the Strange Vol. 3: The 13th Hour. 2011. (ENG., Illus.). 104p. (J). (gr. 5-12). pap. 14.99 *(978-1-59582-700-5(5))* Dark Horse Comics.

Reger, Rob & Huehner, Mariah. The Battle of the Bands. Gibbons, Jim, ed. Ivie, Emily & Parker, Buzz, illus. 2014. (Emily & the Strangers Ser.: Vol. 1). (ENG.). 80p. (J). (gr. 5-12). 12.99 *(978-1-61655-323-4(5))* Dark Horse Comics.

—Breaking the Record, Vol. 2. Farris, Cat, illus. 2015. (ENG.). 1p. (J). (gr. 5-12). 12.99 *(978-1-61655-598-6(X))* Dark Horse Comics.

Reid, Alastair. Supposing. Gill, Bob, illus. 2010. (ENG.). 48p. (J). (gr. -1-3). 15.95 *(978-1-59017-369-5(4),* NYR Children's Collection) New York Review of Bks., Inc., The.

Remender, Rick. Castaway in Dimension Z, Bk. 2. 2014. (ENG., Illus.). 136p. (J). (gr. 4-17). pap. 19.99 *(978-0-7851-6656-6(4))* Marvel Worldwide, Inc.

—Uncanny Avengers - Avenge the Earth, Vol. 4. 2014. (ENG., Illus.). 136p. (J). (gr. 4-17). 24.99 *(978-0-7851-5423-5(X))* Marvel Worldwide, Inc.

Remender, Rick & Comtois, Joelle. Girl Afraid, 4 vols., Vol. 1. 2006. (ENG., Illus.). 104p. (YA). per. 12.99 *(978-1-58240-543-8(3),* 9781582405438) Image Comics.

Renner, Benjamin. The Big Bad Fox. 2017. (ENG., Illus.). 192p. (J). pap. 15.99 *(978-1-62672-331-3(1),* 9781626723313, First Second Bks.) Roaring Brook Pr.

Renner, C. J., et al. Soccer Longshot, 1 vol. Maese, Fares & Aburto, Jesus, illus. 2011. (Sports Illustrated Kids Graphic Novels Ser.). (ENG.). 56p. (gr. 2-3). pap. 7.19 *(978-1-4342-3402-5(9))* Stone Arch Bks.

—Soccer Longshot, 1 vol. Maese, Fares, illus. 2011. (Sports Illustrated Kids Graphic Novels Ser.). (ENG.). 56p. (gr. 2-3). lib. bdg. 26.65 *(978-1-4342-2241-1(1))* Stone Arch Bks.

Rex, Michael. The Egg of Misery. 2012. (Fangbone Ser.: 2). lib. bdg. 16.00 *(978-0-606-23635-5(X),* Turtleback) Turtleback Bks.

—Fangbone! Third-Grade Barbarian. 2012. (Illus.). 120p. (J). *(978-0-545-44042-4(4),* Putnam Juvenile) Penguin Publishing Group.

—Third-Grade Barbarian. 2012. (Fangbone Ser.: 1). lib. bdg. 18.40 *(978-0-606-23634-8(1),* Turtleback) Turtleback Bks.

Reynolds, Aaron. The Dung Beetle Bandits, 1 vol. Lervold, Erik, illus. 2007. (Tiger Moth Ser.). (ENG.). 40p. (gr. 1-3). lib. bdg. 23.99 *(978-1-59889-317-5(3),* Graphic Sparks) Stone Arch Bks.

—The Dung Beetle Bandits: Tiger Moth. Lervold, Erik, illus. 2007. (Graphic Sparks Ser.). (ENG.). 40p. (gr. 1-3). pap. 5.95 *(978-1-59889-412-7(9),* Graphic Sparks) Stone Arch Bks.

—The Fortune Cookies of Weevil: Tiger Moth. Lervold, Erik, illus. 2007. (Graphic Sparks Ser.). (ENG.). 40p. (gr. 1-3). pap. 5.95 *(978-1-59889-413-4(7),* Graphic Sparks) Stone Arch Bks.

—Insect Ninja: Tiger Moth. Lervold, Erik, illus. 2006. (Graphic Sparks Ser.). (ENG.). 40p. (gr. 1-3). per. 5.95 *(978-1-59889-228-4(2),* Graphic Sparks) Stone Arch Bks.

—Kung Pow Chicken: Tiger Moth. Lervold, Erik, illus. 2008. (Graphic Sparks Ser.). (ENG.). 40p. (gr. 1-3). pap. 5.95 *(978-1-4342-0505-6(3),* Graphic Sparks) Stone Arch Bks.

—The Pest Show on Earth, 1 vol. Lervold, Erik, illus. 2008. (Tiger Moth Ser.). (ENG.). 40p. (gr. 1-3). lib. bdg. 23.99 *(978-1-4342-0454-7(5),* Graphic Sparks) Stone Arch Bks.

—The Pest Show on Earth: Tiger Moth, 1 vol. Lervold, Erik, illus. 2008. (Graphic Sparks Ser.). (ENG.). 40p. (gr. 1-3). per. 5.95 *(978-1-4342-0504-9(5),* Graphic Sparks) Stone Arch Bks.

—Tiger Moth: Adventures of an Insect Ninja, 1 vol. Lervold, Erik, illus. 2011. (Tiger Moth Ser.). (ENG.). 128p. (gr. 2-5). pap. 7.95 *(978-1-4342-3032-4(5),* Graphic Sparks) Stone Arch Bks.

—Tiger Moth & the Dragon Kite Contest. Lervold, Erik, illus. 2006. (Tiger Moth Ser.). (ENG.). 40p. (gr. 1-3). per. 5.95 *(978-1-59889-229-1(0),* Graphic Sparks) Stone Arch Bks.

Reynolds, Aaron & Wells, Rosemary. Caveboy Dave: More Scrawny Than Brawny. McAndrew, Phil, illus. 2016. (Caveboy Dave Ser.: 1). (ENG.). 256p. (J). (gr. 3-7). bds. 12.99 *(978-0-14-751658-9(7),* Viking Books for Young Readers) Penguin Young Readers Group.

RH Disney. Moana Deluxe Step into Reading #1 (Disney Moana) RH Disney, illus. 2016. (Step into Reading Ser.). (ENG., Illus.). 24p. (J). (gr. -1-1). pap. 4.99 *(978-0-7364-3644-1(8),* RH/Disney) Random Hse. Children's Bks.

—Quest for the Heart. RH Disney, illus. 2016. (Step into Reading Ser.). (ENG., Illus.). 32p. (J). (gr. -1-1). pap. 4.99 *(978-0-7364-3646-5(4),* RH/Disney) Random Hse. Children's Bks.

—Where Monsters Live. RH Disney, illus. 2016. (Pictureback(R) Ser.). (ENG., Illus.). 24p. (J). (gr. -1-2). 4.99 *(978-0-7364-3649-6(9),* RH/Disney) Random Hse. Children's Bks.

Ribeiro, Nelson. Jughead with Archie in Power Play. Gorelick, Victor, illus. 2007. (Jughead with Archie Ser.). (ENG.). 80p. (J). (gr. 3-6). 24.21 *(978-1-59961-275-1(5))* Spotlight.

C
D

Ribeiro, Nelson, et al. Betty & Veronica in Trendsetter. 2007. (Betty & Veronica Ser.). (ENG., Illus.). 80p. (J). (gr. 3-6). 24.21 (978-1-59961-268-3(2)) Spotlight.

Ribiero, Nelson & Spotlight Editors. Laugh with Mammoth Madness. Gorelick, Victor, illus. 2007. (Archie Digest Library). (ENG.). 80p. (J). (gr. 3-6). 24.21 (978-1-59961-281-2(X)) Spotlight.

—Laugh with Snack Swap. Gorelick, Victor, illus. 2007. (Archie Digest Library). (ENG.). 80p. (J). (gr. 3-6). 24.21 (978-1-59961-282-9(8)) Spotlight.

—Laugh with Stampede. Gorelick, Victor, illus. 2007. (Archie Digest Library). (ENG.). 80p. (J). (gr. 3-6). 24.21 (978-1-59961-283-6(6)) Spotlight.

Ricard, Anouk. Anna & Froga: Completely Bubu. Dascher, Helge, tr. from FRE. 2017. (Anna & Froga Ser.). (ENG., Illus.). 208p. (J). pap. 19.95 **(978-1-77046-292-2(9)**, 9781770462922) Drawn & Quarterly Pubns. CAN. Dist: Macmillan.

—Anna & Froga: Thrills, Spills, & Gooseberries. Dascher, Helge, tr. from FRE. 2014. (Anna & Froga Ser.). (ENG., Illus.). 40p. (J). (gr. k-4). 14.95 (978-1-77046-156-7(6), 9781770461567) Drawn & Quarterly Pubns. CAN. Dist: Macmillan.

—Anna & Froga: Wanna Gumball? Dascher, Helge, tr. from FRE. 2012. (Anna & Froga Ser.). (ENG., Illus.). 40p. (J). (gr. k-4). 14.95 (978-1-77046-070-6(5), 9781770460706) Drawn & Quarterly Pubns. CAN. Dist: Macmillan.

—Fore! Dascher, Helge, tr. from FRE. 2015. (Anna & Froga Ser.). (ENG., Illus.). 40p. (J). (gr. k-4). 14.95 (978-1-77046-204-5(X), 9781770462045) Drawn & Quarterly Pubns. CAN. Dist: Macmillan.

—I Dunno, What Do You Want to Do? Dascher, Helge, tr. from FRE. 2013. (Anna & Froga Ser.). (ENG., Illus.). 40p. (J). (gr. k-4). 14.95 (978-1-77046-120-8(5), 9781770461208) Drawn & Quarterly Pubns. CAN. Dist: Macmillan.

Rich, Jamie S. A Boy & a Girl. 2013. (ENG., Illus.). 168p. (YA). pap. 19.99 (978-1-62010-089-9(4), 9781620100899) Oni Pr., Inc.

—Love the Way You Love. Ellerby, Marc, illus. 2006. (J). (978-1-932664-52-2(1)) Oni Pr., Inc.

—Spell Checkers Volume 3: Careless Whisper: Careless Whisper. 2013. (ENG., Illus.). 144p. (YA). pap. 11.99 (978-1-62010-094-3(0), 9781620100943) Oni Pr., Inc.

—The World Is Flat. 2013. (ENG., Illus.). 168p. (YA). pap. 14.99 (978-1-60706-791-7(9), 9781607067917) Image Comics.

Richard, Laurent. The Championship! Gauvin, Edward, tr. Ryser, Nicolas, illus. 2014. (ENG.). 64p. (J). (gr. 2-5). pap. 6.95 (978-1-4677-4459-1(X)); (Tao, the Little Samurai Ser.: 4). lib. bdg. 29.27 (978-1-4677-2097-7(6)) Lerner Publishing Group. (Graphic Universe™).

—Clowns & Dragons! Gauvin, Edward, tr. from FRE. Ryser, Nicolas, illus. 2014. (Tao, the Little Samurai Ser.: 3). (ENG.). 56p. (J). (gr. 2-5). lib. bdg. 29.27 (978-1-4677-2096-0(8), Graphic Universe™) Lerner Publishing Group.

—Ninjas & Knock Outs! Gauvin, Edward, tr. from FRE. Ryser, Nicolas, illus. 2014. (Tao, the Little Samurai Ser.: 2). (ENG.). 64p. (J). (gr. 2-5). lib. bdg. 29.27 (978-1-4677-3272-7(9), Graphic Universe™) Lerner Publishing Group.

—Pranks & Attacks! Gauvin, Edward, tr. from FRE. Ryser, Nicolas, illus. 2014. (Tao, the Little Samurai Ser.: 1). (ENG.). 64p. (J). (gr. 2-5). lib. bdg. 29.27 (978-1-4677-2095-3(X), Graphic Universe™) Lerner Publishing Group.

—Wild Animals! Gauvin, Edward, tr. from FRE. Ryser, Nicolas, illus. 2014. (Tao, the Little Samurai Ser.: 5). (ENG.). 64p. (J). (gr. 2-5). lib. bdg. 29.27 (978-1-4677-2098-4(4), Graphic Universe™) Lerner Publishing Group.

Richards, Barnaby. Blip! Toon Level 1. 2016. (ENG., Illus.). 40p. (J). (gr. -1-k). 12.95 (978-1-935179-98-6(5)) TOON Books / RAW Junior, LLC.

Richards, C. E., illus. King Arthur. 2010. (Classic Fiction Ser.). 72p. 4.75 (978-1-4342-2603-7(4), Graphic Revolve) Stone Arch Bks.

Richards, Kitty. Meet the Sparkplugs, Level 3. Simard, Remy, illus. 2006. (ENG.). 24p. (J). (gr. 1-17). per. 3.99 (978-1-58476-419-9(8), IKIDS) Innovative Kids.

—Phonics Comics: Twisted Tales - Level 3, Level 3. Juarez, Fernando, illus. 2006. (ENG.). 24p. (J). (gr. 1-17). per. 3.99 (978-1-58476-514-1(3), IKIDS) Innovative Kids.

Richards, Kitty & Disney Book Group Staff. Goodnight, Thumper! Tyminski, Lori & Gordon, Dean, illus. 2007. (ENG.). 16p. (J). (gr. -1-k). bds. 5.99 (978-1-4231-0077-5(8)) Disney Pr.

Richards, Lynne. The Fearless Four: Braced for Battle. Semple, Dave, illus. 2009. (ENG.). 24p. (J). (gr. 1-17). pap. 3.99 (978-1-58476-814-2(2)) Innovative Kids.

Richardson, Mike. The Return of the Gremlins. 2009. (Illus.). 88p. pap. 12.95 (978-1-59582-170-6(8)) Dark Horse Comics.

Rideau, J. & Asso, B. The Falklands War. Chauvin, D. & Uderzo, M., illus. 2011. (Cinebook Recounts Ser.). (ENG.). 48p. pap. 11.95 (978-1-84918-056-6(3)) CineBook GBR. Dist: National Bk. Network.

Rieber, John Ney. Reloaded Vol. I: In the Name of Patriotism. Lim, Ron & Millet, Jason, illus. 2005. 144p. pap. 12.95 (978-1-932796-23-0(1)) Devil's Due Publishing, Inc.

Rimmer, Ian. The Bootiful Game. Hansen, Jimmy & Williamson, Brian, illus. 2005. (Wallace & Gromit Ser.). (ENG.). 48p. pap. 8.95 (978-1-84023-948-5(4), Titan Bks.) Titan Bks. Ltd. GBR. Dist: Penguin Random Hse. LLC.

Rinaldi, Francis. Brock Lee & the Salad Kids. 2005. 20p. 7.53 (978-1-4116-5552-2(4)) Lulu Pr., Inc.

Rinaldo, Jessica. Key to the Gate Book 1. 2005. 324p. (YA). pap. 14.98 (978-1-4116-5262-0(2)) Lulu Pr., Inc.

Riordan, Rick. The Sea of Monsters. 2011. 9.68 (978-0-7848-3440-4(7), Everbind) Marco Bk. Co.

—The Son of Neptune: The Graphic Novel. 2017. (Heroes of Olympus Ser.). (ENG.). 192p. (J). (gr. 5-9). 21.99 (978-1-4847-1621-2(3)) Disney Pr.

Rioux, Jo. The Golden Twine. Rioux, Jo, illus. 2012. (Cat's Cradle Ser.: 1). (ENG., Illus.). 112p. (J). (gr. 4-7). 9.95 (978-1-55453-637-5(5)) Kids Can Pr., Ltd. CAN. Dist: Hachette Bk. Group.

Risso, Eduardo. Mysteries of the Red Moon, Vol. 3. 2006. (SPA.). 48p. pap. 16.95 (978-1-59497-163-1(3)) Public Square Bks.

Risso, Eduardo & Trillo, Carlos. Los Misterios de la Luna Roja Vol. 2: El Ataque del Circo. 2006. (SPA., Illus.). 72p. (J). (gr. 1). per. 16.95 (978-1-59497-162-4(5)) Public Square Bks.

Rix, Jamie. Panda Panic: Running Wild. 2013. (Awesome Animals Ser.). (ENG., Illus.). 192p. (J). (gr. 2-6). pap. 6.99 (978-1-4380-0308-5(0)) Barron's Educational Series, Inc.

Rizy, Brock, illus. Emily Edison: Volume 1. 2006. 139p. (gr. 8-18). pap. 12.95 (978-0-9777883-2-3(6)) Viper Comics.

Roba, Jean. It's a Dog's Life. 2013. (Billy & Buddy Ser.: 4). (ENG., Illus.). 48p. (J). (gr. 3-12). pap. 11.95 (978-1-84918-171-6(3)) CineBook GBR. Dist: National Bk. Network.

Robbins, Trina. The Bark in Space. Page, Tyler, illus. 2013. (Chicagoland Detective Agency Ser.: 5). (ENG.). 64p. (gr. 4-8). (J). lib. bdg. 29.27 (978-0-7613-8166-2(X)); pap. 6.95 (978-1-4677-0725-1(2)) Lerner Publishing Group. (Graphic Universe™).

—The Big Flush. Page, Tyler, illus. 2012. (Chicagoland Detective Agency Ser.: 4). (ENG.). 64p. (gr. 4-8). pap. 6.95 (978-0-8225-9161-0(8)); lib. bdg. 29.27 (978-0-7613-8165-5(1)) Lerner Publishing Group. (Graphic Universe™).

—The Drained Brains Caper. Page, Tyler, illus. 2010. (Chicagoland Detective Agency Ser.: 1). (ENG.). 64p. (gr. 4-8). pap. 6.95 (978-0-7613-5635-6(5), Graphic Universe™) Lerner Publishing Group.

—Freedom Songs: A Tale of the Underground Railroad, 1 vol. Millet, Jason, illus. 2008. (Historical Fiction Ser.). (ENG.). 56p. (gr. 2-3). pap. 6.25 (978-1-4342-0495-0(2), Graphic Flash) Stone Arch Bks.

—The Maltese Mummy. Page, Tyler, illus. 2011. (Chicagoland Detective Agency Ser.: 2). (ENG.). 64p. (gr. 4-8). 29.27 (978-0-7613-4615-9(5)); pap. 6.95 (978-0-7613-5636-3(3), Graphic Universe™) Lerner Publishing Group.

—A Match Made in Heaven. Ota, Yuko & Studio, Xian Nu, illus. 2013. (My Boyfriend Is a Monster Ser.: 8). (ENG.). 128p. (YA). (gr. 7-12). pap. 9.95 (978-1-4677-0732-9(5), Graphic Universe™) Lerner Publishing Group.

—A Match Made in Heaven. Xian Nu Studio Staff, illus. 2013. (My Boyfriend Is a Monster Ser.: 8). (ENG.). 128p. (YA). (gr. 7-12). lib. bdg. 29.27 (978-0-7613-6857-1(4), Graphic Universe™) Lerner Publishing Group.

—A Midterm Night's Scheme. Page, Tyler, illus. 2014. (Chicagoland Detective Agency Ser.: 6). (ENG.). 64p. (gr. 4-8). lib. bdg. 29.27 (978-0-7613-8167-9(8), Graphic Universe™) Lerner Publishing Group.

—Night of the Living Dogs. Page, Tyler, illus. 2012. (Chicagoland Detective Agency Ser.). 64p. (J). (gr. 4-8). pap. 39.62 (978-0-7613-9313-9(7), Graphic Universe™) Lerner Publishing Group.

—The Night of the Living Dogs. Page, Tyler, illus. 2012. (Chicagoland Detective Agency Ser.: 3). (ENG.). 64p. (gr. 4-8). pap. 6.95 (978-0-7613-5637-0(1), Graphic Universe™) Lerner Publishing Group.

Roberts, Daniel. The Dragon, the Princess & the Peanut Butter Sandwiches. 2009. 36p. pap. 16.99 (978-1-4389-8277-9(1)) AuthorHouse.

—Three Funky Monkeys. 2011. 36p. pap. 16.99 (978-1-4634-4732-8(9)) AuthorHouse.

Roberts, Ken. The Thumb in the Box. 2013. 56p. pap. (978-1-4596-6500-2(7)) ReadHowYouWant.com, Ltd.

Roberts, Rachel. Omnibus Collection No. 1, Bk. 1-3. 2012. (Avalon: Web of Magic Ser.: 1). (ENG., Illus.). 640p. (YA). (gr. 3-6). pap. 14.95 (978-1-935934-29-5(5), 9781935934295) Seven Seas Entertainment, LLC.

Roberts, Scott. Patty Cake & Friends. 2006. (ENG., Illus.). 96p. pap. 12.95 (978-1-59362-030-1(6), 9781593620301) Slave Labor Bks.

Roberts, Steven. Francisco Vasquez de Coronado. 2013. (Jr. Graphic Famous Explorers Ser.). (ENG., Illus.). 24p. (J). (gr. 3-6). pap. 10.60 (978-1-4777-0125-6(7)); lib. bdg. 25.25 (978-1-4777-0070-9(6)) Rosen Publishing Group, Inc., The. (PowerKids Pr.).

—John Cabot. 2013. (Jr. Graphic Famous Explorers Ser.). (ENG., Illus.). 24p. (J). (gr. 3-6). pap. 10.60 (978-1-4777-0129-4(X)); lib. bdg. 25.25 (978-1-4777-0072-3(2)) Rosen Publishing Group, Inc., The. (PowerKids Pr.).

Robertson, David. Betty: The Helen Betty Osborne Story, 1 vol. Henderson, Scott B., illus. 2016. (ENG.). 32p. (YA). (gr. 9-12). pap. 16.00 (978-1-55379-544-5(X), 155379544X, HighWater Pr.) Portage & Main Pr. CAN. Dist: Orca Bk. Pubs. USA.

—The Scout: Tommy Prince. Henderson, Scott B., illus. 2014. (Tales from Big Spirit Ser.: 6). (ENG.). 32p. (J). (gr. 4-6). pap. (978-1-55379-478-3(8), 78912685-2d85-4153-9f88-b7d8feb31ffe, HighWater Pr.) Portage & Main Pr.

—The Slave Woman: Thanadelthur. Tien, Wai, illus. 2014. (Tales from Big Spirit Ser.: 6). (ENG.). 32p. (J). (gr. 4-6). pap. (978-1-55379-479-0(6), 51f7764c-c947-4547-8ce4-63887e0f4e03, HighWater Pr.) Portage & Main Pr.

—Will I See, 1 vol. Chomichuk, G. M. B., illus. 2017. (ENG.). 56p. (YA). (gr. 10-12). pap. 18.95 (978-1-55379-674-9(8), HighWater Pr.) Portage & Main Pr. CAN. Dist: Orca Bk. Pubs. USA.

—7 Generations: A Plains Cree Saga, 1 vol. Henderson, Scott B., illus. 2016. (7 Generations Ser.). (ENG.). 136p. (YA). (gr. 9-12). pap. 34.00 (978-1-55379-355-7(2), 9781553793557, HighWater Pr.) Portage & Main Pr. CAN. Dist: Orca Bk. Pubs. USA.

Robertson, David Alexander. Ends/Begins. Henderson, Scott B., illus. 2010. (7 Generations Ser.: 3). (ENG.). 32p. (YA). (gr. 9-12). pap. (978-1-55379-262-8(9), 72bc3568-4f12-4574-9f82-146597fa1b3a, HighWater Pr.) Portage & Main Pr.

—The Pact. Henderson, Scott B., illus. 2011. (7 Generations Ser.: 4). (ENG.). 32p. (YA). pap. (978-1-55379-230-7(0), 9781553792307, HighWater Pr.) Portage & Main Pr.

—Scars. Henderson, Scott B., illus. 2010. (7 Generations Ser.: 2). (ENG.). 32p. (YA). pap. (978-1-55379-228-4(9), 4ae83eb9-baca-4c13-a381-ea5771ba95b7, HighWater Pr.) Portage & Main Pr.

—Stone. Henderson, Scott B., illus. 2010. (7 Generations Ser.: 1). (ENG.). 32p. (YA). pap. (978-1-55379-227-7(0), 4ae83eb9-baca-4c13-a381-ea5771ba95b7, HighWater Pr.) Portage & Main Pr.

—Sugar Falls: A Residential School Story. Henderson, Scott B., illus. 2012. (ENG.). 40p. (YA). (gr. 9-12). pap. (978-1-55379-334-2(X), 9781553793342, HighWater Pr.) Portage & Main Pr.

Robico. My Little Monster 1. 2014. (My Little Monster Ser.). (ENG., Illus.). 176p. (YA). (gr. 9). pap. 10.99 (978-1-61262-597-3(5)) Kodansha America, Inc.

—My Little Monster 2. 2014. (My Little Monster Ser.). (ENG., Illus.). 176p. (YA). (gr. 9). pap. 10.99 (978-1-61262-598-0(3)) Kodansha America, Inc.

—My Little Monster 3. 2014. (My Little Monster Ser.). (ENG., Illus.). 176p. (YA). (gr. 9). pap. 10.99 (978-1-61262-599-7(1)) Kodansha America, Inc.

—My Little Monster 4. 2014. (My Little Monster Ser.). (ENG., Illus.). 176p. (YA). pap. 10.99 (978-1-61262-600-0(9)) Kodansha America, Inc.

Robinson, Fiona. The 3-2-3 Detective Agency: The Disappearance of Dave Warthog. 2009. (ENG., Illus.). 80p. (J). (gr. 1-4). 18.95 (978-0-8109-8489-9(X), Amulet Bks.) Abrams, Inc.

Robinson, Jimmie. Evil & Malice - Save the World! 2009. (ENG., Illus.). 128p. (J). pap. 14.99 (978-1-60706-091-8(4), 9781607060918) Image Comics.

—Five Weapons: Make the Grade. 2013. (ENG., Illus.). 144p. (YA). pap. 15.99 (978-1-60706-779-5(X), 9781607067795) Image Comics.

Roche, Art. The Knights of Boo'Gar. 2017. (ENG.). 176p. (J). pap. 9.99 (978-1-4494-7987-9(1)) Andrews McMeel Publishing.

Rodda, Emily. Deltora Quest 1. Niwano, Makoto, illus. 2011. (Deltora Quest Ser.). (ENG.). 202p. (gr. 8-12). pap. 10.99 (978-1-935429-28-9(0)) Kodansha America, Inc.

—Deltora Quest 2. Niwano, Makoto, illus. 2011. (Deltora Quest Ser.). (ENG.). 206p. (gr. 8-12). pap. 10.99 (978-1-935429-29-6(9)) Kodansha America, Inc.

—Deltora Quest 3. Niwano, Makoto, illus. 2011. (Deltora Quest Ser.). (ENG.). 208p. (gr. 8-12). pap. 10.99 (978-1-935429-30-2(2)) Kodansha America, Inc.

—Deltora Quest 4. Niwano, Makoto, illus. 2012. (Deltora Quest Ser.). (ENG.). 208p. (gr. 8-12). pap. 10.99 (978-1-935429-31-9(0)) Kodansha America, Inc.

—Deltora Quest 5. 2012. (Deltora Quest Ser.). (ENG., Illus.). 208p. (gr. 8-12). pap. 10.99 (978-1-61262-011-4(6)) Kodansha America, Inc.

—Deltora Quest 6. 2012. (Deltora Quest Ser.). (ENG., Illus.). 200p. (gr. 8-12). pap. 10.99 (978-1-61262-012-1(4)) Kodansha America, Inc.

—Deltora Quest 7. 2012. (Deltora Quest Ser.). (ENG., Illus.). 200p. (gr. 8-12). pap. 10.99 (978-1-61262-013-8(2)) Kodansha America, Inc.

—Deltora Quest 8. 2012. (Deltora Quest Ser.). (ENG., Illus.). 200p. (gr. 8-12). pap. 10.99 (978-1-61262-014-5(0)) Kodansha America, Inc.

—Deltora Quest 9. 2012. (Deltora Quest Ser.). (ENG., Illus.). 200p. (gr. 8-12). pap. 10.99 (978-1-61262-015-2(9)) Kodansha America, Inc.

Rodi, Robert & Richards, Cliff. Rogue: Going Rogue. 2005. (X-Men Ser.). (Illus.). 144p. pap. 14.99 (978-0-7851-1336-2(3)) Marvel Worldwide, Inc.

Rodriguez, Alfredo. Redfoot. O'Reilly, Sean Patrick, ed. 2011. (Illus.). 43p. pap. 8.95 (978-1-926914-59-6(7)) Arcana Studio, Inc.

Rodriguez, David. Finding Gossamyr, Vol. 1. Nelson, Angela, ed. 2013. (ENG., Illus.). 132p. 24.95 (978-0-9832161-6-2(9), 9780983216162) Th3rd World Studios.

—Shadowgirls - Season One. Nelson, Angela, ed. 2013. (ENG., Illus.). 240p. (YA). 29.95 (978-0-9832161-1-7(8), 9780983216117) Th3rd World Studios.

Rodriguez, Jason, ed. Colonial Comics: New England, 1620 ¿ 1750. 2014. (Colonial Comics Ser.). (ENG., Illus.). 208p. (gr. 4). pap. 29.95 (978-1-938486-30-2(7)) Fulcrum Publishing.

Rodríguez, Pedro. Chilling Tales of Horror: Dark Graphic Short Stories. 2012. (Dark Graphic Novels Ser.). (Illus.). 96p. (J). (gr. 5-9). 31.94 (978-0-7660-4085-4(2)) Enslow Pubs., Inc.

Rodriguez, Robert & Roberson, Chris. Shark Boy & Lava Girl Adventures: Return to Planet Drool. Toader, Alex, illus. 2005. (Shark Boy & Lava Girl Adventures Ser.: Book 2). 150p. (J). (978-1-933104-05-8(8)) Troublemaker Publishing, LP.

Rogers, Bud & Krueger, Jim. Secret Alliance, 1 vol. Padilla, Ariel, illus. 2008. (Z Graphic Novels / Tomo Ser.). (ENG.). 160p. (J). pap. 6.99 (978-0-310-71304-3(8)) Zondervan.

Rogers, Bud & Martin, Gary. The Witch of Endor, 1 vol. Cariello, Sergio, illus. 2008. (Z Graphic Novels / Son of Samson Ser.). (ENG.). 160p. (J). pap. 6.99 (978-0-310-71283-1(1)) Zonderkidz.

Rogers, Bud, et al. Truth Revealed, 1 vol. Padilla, Ariel, illus. 2009. (Z Graphic Novels / Tomo Ser.). (ENG.). 160p. (J). pap. 6.99 (978-0-310-71305-0(6)) Zondervan.

Rogers, Buddy & Avery, Ben. Power Play, 1 vol. Wong, Scott, illus. 2008. (Z Graphic Novels / TimeFlyz Ser.). (ENG.). 160p. (J). pap. 6.99 (978-0-310-71365-4(X)) Zondervan.

Rogers, John. Dungeons & Dragons Volume 3: Down: Down. Ponce, Andres & Arranz, Nacho, illus. 2012. (Dungeons & Dragons Ser.). (ENG.). 132p. 21.99 (978-1-61377-178-5(9), 9781613771785) Idea & Design Works, LLC.

Rogers, John & Di Vito, Andrea. First Encounters, Vol. 2. Alcazar, Vicente et al, illus. 2012. (Dungeons & Dragons Ser.). (ENG.). 156p. pap. 19.99 (978-1-61377-534-9(2), 9781613775349) Idea & Design Works, LLC.

Rogers, Simon. Information Graphics: Human Body. Grundy, Peter, illus. 2014. (ENG.). 80p. (J). (gr. 1-4). 17.99 (978-0-7636-7123-5(1), Big Picture Press) Candlewick Pr.

Rohmer, Sax, pseud, et al. Adventure Classics, Vol. 12. Pomplun, Tom, ed. 2005. (ENG., Illus.). 144p. pap. 11.95 (978-0-9746648-4-2(7), 9780974664842) Eureka Productions.

Roland, Timothy. Our Crazy Class Election. 2007. (Illus.). 90p. (J). (978-0-545-00401-5(2)) Scholastic, Inc.

Rolt, Molly. The Chocci-Croc & Other Stories. 2006. 64p. pap. (978-1-84401-890-1(3)) Athena Pr.

Roman, Annette. Passage 2: HIV/AIDS — First Love. Ng, Leandro, illus. 2005. (1 World Manga Ser.: Vol. 2). (ENG.). 40p. (J). pap. 3.99 (978-0-8213-6406-2(5)) World Bank Pubns.

—1 World Manga. Ng, Leandro, illus. (1 World Manga Ser.: Vol. 3). (ENG.). 2006. 40p. pap. 3.99 (978-1-4215-0366-0(2)) Vol. 1. 2005. 40p. pap. 3.99 (978-1-4215-0364-6(6)) Vol. 2. 2005. 40p. pap. 3.99 (978-1-4215-0365-3(4)) Vol. 5. 2007. 240p. pap. 3.99 (978-1-4215-1169-6(X)) Viz Media.

Roman, Dave. Astronaut Academy: Re-Entry. Roman, Dave, illus. 2013. (Astronaut Academy Ser.: 2). (ENG., Illus.). 192p. (J). (gr. 5-9). pap. 9.99 (978-1-59643-621-3(2), 9781596436213, First Second Bks.) Roaring Brook Pr.

—Teen Boat! The Race for Boatlantis. Green, John, illus. 2015. (ENG.). 160p. (YA). (gr. 7). 14.99 (978-0-547-86563-8(5)) Houghton Mifflin Harcourt Publishing Co.

—Zero Gravity. Roman, Dave, illus. 2011. (Astronaut Academy Ser.: 1). (ENG., Illus.). 192p. (J). (gr. 5-9). 17.99 (978-1-59643-756-2(1), 9781596437562, First Second Bks.) Roaring Brook Pr.

Romita, John & Ditko, Steve, illus. X-Men - The Hidden Year, Vol. 2. 2012. (ENG.). 304p. (J). (gr. 4-17). pap. 34.99 (978-0-7851-6055-7(8)) Marvel Worldwide, Inc.

Roop, Peter & Roop, Connie. The Stormy Adventure of Abbie Burgess, Lighthouse Keeper. Trover, Zachary, illus. 2010. (History's Kid Heroes Ser.). (ENG.). 32p. (gr. 3-5). pap. 8.95 (978-0-7613-6191-6(X), Graphic Universe™) Lerner Publishing Group.

—The Top-Secret Adventure of John Darragh, Revolutionary War Spy. Trover, Zachary, illus. 2010. (History's Kid Heroes Ser.). (ENG.). 32p. (gr. 3-5). pap. 8.95 (978-0-7613-6193-0(6), Graphic Universe™) Lerner Publishing Group.

Rosa, Don. Walt Disney Uncle Scrooge & Donald Duck: Treasure under Glass: The Don Rosa Library Vol. 3. 2015. (Don Rosa Library: 0). (ENG., Illus.). 192p. 29.99 (978-1-60699-836-6(6), 699836) Fantagraphics Bks.

Rosa, Don, et al. Uncle Scrooge #347. Clark, John, ed. 2005. (ENG., Illus.). 64p. (YA). pap. 6.95 (978-1-888472-00-4(6), 9781888472004) Gemstone Publishing, Inc.

Rose, Simon. The Emerald Curse, 1 vol. Nugent, Cynthia, illus. 384th ed. 2006. (ENG.). 96p. (J). (gr. 3-6). per. 7.95 (978-1-896580-90-6(4)) Tradewind Bks. CAN. Dist: Orca Bk. Pubs. USA.

Rosen, Lucy. Friends & Foes. Gordon, Steven E. & Gordon, Eric A., illus. 2013. (I Can Read Level 2 Ser.). (ENG.). 32p. (J). (gr. -1-3). pap. 3.99 (978-0-06-223595-4(8)) HarperCollins Pubs.

—I Am Bane. Cohn, Scott, illus. 2012. (Dark Knight Rises Ser.). (ENG.). 24p. (J). (gr. -1-2). pap. 3.99 (978-0-06-213222-2(9), HarperFestival) HarperCollins Pubs.

—Superman Phonics Fun. 2012. (My First I Can Read Ser.). (ENG., Illus.). 12p. (J). (gr. -1-3). pap. 12.99 (978-0-06-188541-9(X)) HarperCollins Pubs.

Rosen, Michael. Send for a Superhero! McEwen, Katharine, illus. 2014. (ENG.). 40p. (J). (gr. -1-2). 16.99 (978-0-7636-6438-1(3)) Candlewick Pr.

Rosenstiehl, Agnes. Silly Lilly & the Four Seasons, 1 vol. 2013. (Toon Bks). (ENG.). 36p. (J). (gr. k-1). lib. bdg. 27.07 (978-1-61479-155-3(4)) Spotlight.

—Silly Lilly & the Four Seasons. 2013. (ENG., Illus.). 32p. (J). (gr. -1-3). pap. 4.99 (978-1-935179-23-8(3)) TOON Books / RAW Junior, LLC.

—Silly Lilly in What Will I Be Today?, 1 vol. 2013. (Toon Bks). (ENG.). 36p. (J). (gr. k-1). lib. bdg. 27.07 (978-1-61479-156-0(2)) Spotlight.

Rosinski & Van Hamme, Jean. Chlid of the Stars. Rosinski, Adolf, illus. 2007. (Thorgal Ser.: 1). (ENG.). 96p. per. 19.95 (978-1-905460-23-6(6)) CineBook GBR. Dist: National Bk. Network.

Ross, Donald. The Scribble Squad in the Weird Weird West. 2016. (ENG., Illus.). 256p. (J). 13.99 (978-1-4494-6921-4(3)) Andrews McMeel Publishing.

Roussin, Simon. Forever Young: the Boy Who Couldn't Die: A TOON Graphic. 2016. (ENG., Illus.). 48p. (J). (978-1-943145-10-2(5)) TOON Books / RAW Junior, LLC.

Rowles, Chuck, et al. Drunk & Disorderly Vol. 2: The Drunk Duck Collection. Rowles, Chuck et al, illus. 2004. (YA). per. 14.95 (978-0-9748960-1-4(2)) Drunk Duck Comics.

Rozum, John. Scooby-Doo in Yankee Doodle Danger, 1 vol. 2013. (Scooby-Doo Graphic Novels Set 3 Ser.). (ENG.). 24p. (J). (gr. 2-6). lib. bdg. 24.21 (978-1-61479-054-9(X), Essential Library) ABDO Publishing Co.

Rucka, Greg. Journey to Star Wars: The Force Awakens — Shattered Empire. 2015. (Star Wars Graphic Novels Ser.). (YA). lib. bdg. 29.40 (978-0-606-37933-5(9)) Turtleback Bks.

Rudnick, Elizabeth. Hulk Versus the World, 1 vol. Marvel Illustrators, illus. 2012. (Avengers: Earth's Mightiest Heroes! Ser.). (ENG.). 24p. (J). (gr. -1-4). lib. bdg. 24.21 (978-1-61479-002-0(7)) Spotlight.

—Iron Man Is Born, 1 vol. Marvel Illustrators, illus. 2012. (Avengers: Earth's Mightiest Heroes! Ser.). (ENG.). 24p. (J). (gr. -1-4). lib. bdg. 24.21 (978-1-61479-003-7(5)) Spotlight.

Ruiz, Emilio. Waluk. 2013. 56p. pap. 23.95 (978-1-4677-2057-1(7)) Lerner Publishing Group.

—Waluk. Oliverio, Daniel, tr. Miralles, Ana, illus. 2013. (ENG.). 56p. (J). (gr. 2-5). pap. 7.95 (978-1-4677-1606-2(5)); lib. bdg. 26.60 (978-1-4677-1598-0(0)) Lerner Publishing Group. (Graphic Universe™).

Ruiz, Jackson. It's Cool in the Furnace: The first graphic novel by Jackson Ruiz. 2010. 32p. pap. 16.99 (978-1-4520-2634-3(3)) AuthorHouse.

Rumble, Chris. My Dad Is Coming to Career Day but Hopefully the Earth Will Be Destroyed. 2013. 218p. pap. 8.95 (978-0-9832491-2-2(1)) Thunder Enlightening.

Runberg, Sylvain. Orbital Vol. 5: Justice. Pelle, Serge, illus. 2014. (Orbital Ser.: 5). (ENG.). 56p. pap. 13.95 (978-1-84918-172-3(1)) CineBook GBR. Dist: National Bk. Network.

Russell, Rachel Renée. Tales from a Not-So-Friendly Frenemy. 2016. (Dork Diaries: 11). lib. bdg. 25.75 **(978-0-606-39887-9(2))** Turtleback Bks.

Rusu, Meredith. Python's Revenge. 2017. (LEGO Ninjago Chapter Bks.: 11). lib. bdg. 14.75 **(978-0-606-39733-9(7))** Turtleback Bks.

—Pythor's Revenge. 2017. (LEGO Ninjago Ser.). (ENG.). 80p. (J). (gr. 2-5). pap. 4.99 (978-1-338-11796-7(3)) Scholastic, Inc.

—Yo-Kai Watch. Scholastic, illus. 2016. (Yo-Kai Watch Ser.). (ENG.). 32p. (J). (gr. -1-3). pap. 3.99 *(978-1-338-05444-6(9))* Scholastic, Inc.

Ryan, Paul, et al, illus. Iron Man Epic Collection: War Games. 2014. (ENG.). 504p. (J). (gr. 4-17). pap. 39.99 *(978-0-7851-8550-5(X))* Marvel Worldwide, Inc.

—Squadron Supreme. 2013. (ENG.). 368p. (J). (gr. 4-17). pap. 34.99 *(978-0-7851-8469-0(4))* Marvel Worldwide, Inc.

Ryan, Sara. Bad Houses. Hahn, Sierra, ed. 2013. (ENG., Illus.). 152p. pap. 19.99 *(978-1-59582-993-1(8))* Dark Horse Comics.

Sacks, Nathan & Paty, Miss. May's Wild Walk. MissPaty, illus. 2017. (Whiskers Sisters Ser.: 1). (ENG.). 40p. (J). (gr. k-3). 26.65 ***(978-1-5124-2527-7(3)***, Graphic Universe™) Lerner Publishing Group.

Saddleback Educational Publishing Staff, ed. Abraham Lincoln, 1 vol. unabr. ed. 2008. (Graphic Biographies Ser.). (ENG., Illus.). 25p. (YA). (gr. 9-12). per. 7.95 *(978-1-59905-211-3(3))* Saddleback Educational Publishing, Inc.

—Alexander Graham Bell, 1 vol. unabr. ed. 2008. (Graphic Biographies Ser.). (ENG., Illus.). 25p. (YA). (gr. 9-12). pap. 7.95 *(978-1-59905-213-7(X))* Saddleback Educational Publishing, Inc.

—Amelia Earhart, 1 vol. unabr. ed. 2008. (Graphic Biographies Ser.). (ENG., Illus.). 25p. (YA). (gr. 9-12). pap. 7.95 *(978-1-59905-214-4(8))* Saddleback Educational Publishing, Inc.

—Babe Ruth, 1 vol. unabr. ed. 2008. (Graphic Biographies Ser.). (ENG., Illus.). 25p. (YA). (gr. 9-12). pap. 7.95 *(978-1-59905-215-1(6))* Saddleback Educational Publishing, Inc.

—The Beatles, 1 vol. unabr. ed. 2008. (Graphic Biographies Ser.). (ENG., Illus.). 25p. (YA). (gr. 9-12). pap. 7.95 *(978-1-59905-216-8(4))* Saddleback Educational Publishing, Inc.

—Benjamin Franklin, 1 vol. unabr. ed. 2008. (Graphic Biographies Ser.). (ENG., Illus.). 25p. (YA). (gr. 9-12). pap. 7.95 *(978-1-59905-217-5(2))* Saddleback Educational Publishing, Inc.

—Charles Lindbergh, 1 vol. unabr. ed. 2008. (Graphic Biographies Ser.). (ENG., Illus.). 25p. (YA). (gr. 9-12). pap. 7.95 *(978-1-59905-218-2(0))* Saddleback Educational Publishing, Inc.

—Daniel Boone, 1 vol. unabr. ed. 2008. (Graphic Biographies Ser.). (ENG., Illus.). 25p. (YA). (gr. 9-12). pap. 7.95 *(978-1-59905-219-9(9))* Saddleback Educational Publishing, Inc.

—Davy Crockett, 1 vol. unabr. ed. 2008. (Graphic Biographies Ser.). (ENG., Illus.). 25p. (YA). (gr. 9-12). pap. 7.95 *(978-1-59905-220-5(2))* Saddleback Educational Publishing, Inc.

—Elvis Presley, 1 vol. unabr. ed. 2008. (Graphic Biographies Ser.). (ENG., Illus.). 25p. (YA). (gr. 9-12). pap. 7.95 *(978-1-59905-221-2(0))* Saddleback Educational Publishing, Inc.

—Franklin Roosevelt, 1 vol. unabr. ed. 2008. (Graphic Biographies Ser.). (ENG., Illus.). 25p. (YA). (gr. 9-12). pap. 7.95 *(978-1-59905-222-9(9))* Saddleback Educational Publishing, Inc.

—George Washington, 1 vol. unabr. ed. 2008. (Graphic Biographies Ser.). (ENG., Illus.). 25p. (YA). (gr. 9-12). pap. 7.95 *(978-1-59905-223-6(7))* Saddleback Educational Publishing, Inc.

—Houdini, 1 vol. unabr. ed. 2008. (Graphic Biographies Ser.). (ENG., Illus.). 25p. (YA). (gr. 9-12). pap. 7.95 *(978-1-59905-224-3(5))* Saddleback Educational Publishing, Inc.

—Jackie Robinson, 1 vol. unabr. ed. 2008. (Graphic Biographies Ser.). (ENG., Illus.). 25p. (YA). (gr. 9-12). pap. 7.95 *(978-1-59905-225-0(3))* Saddleback Educational Publishing, Inc.

—Marie Curie, 1 vol. unabr. ed. 2008. (Graphic Biographies Ser.). (ENG., Illus.). 25p. (YA). (gr. 9-12). pap. 7.95 *(978-1-59905-226-7(1))* Saddleback Educational Publishing, Inc.

—Martin Luther King Jr., 1 vol. unabr. ed. 2008. (Graphic Biographies Ser.). (ENG., Illus.). 25p. (YA). (gr. 9-12). pap. 7.95 *(978-1-59905-227-4(X))* Saddleback Educational Publishing, Inc.

—Thomas Jefferson, 1 vol. unabr. ed. 2008. (Graphic Biographies Ser.). (ENG., Illus.). 25p. (YA). (gr. 9-12). pap. 7.95 *(978-1-59905-229-8(6))* Saddleback Educational Publishing, Inc.

—Walt Disney, 1 vol. unabr. ed. 2008. (Graphic Biographies Ser.). (ENG., Illus.). 25p. (YA). (gr. 9-12). pap. 7.95 *(978-1-59905-230-4(X))* Saddleback Educational Publishing, Inc.

Sagara, Sou & Okomeken. The Hentai Prince & the Stony Cat. 2012. (ENG., Illus.). 200p. (YA). pap. 12.95 *(978-1-56970-285-7(3)*, 9781569702857) Digital Manga Publishing.

Saguchi, Kensaku. Biographical Comics: Christopher Columbus: The Merchant Adventurer. Miyazoe, Ikuo, illus. 2012. (Biographical Comic Ser.). (ENG.). 152p. (J). (gr. 3-6). 18.99 *(978-1-4215-4973-6(5))*; pap. 9.99 *(978-1-4215-4974-3(3))* Shogakukan JPN. Dist: Simon & Schuster, Inc.

Saijyo, Shinji. Iron Wok Jan!, Vol. 13. 2005. (Iron Wok Jan! Ser.). (ENG., Illus.). 200p. (YA). pap. 9.95 *(978-1-59796-031-1(4))* DrMaster Pubns. Inc.

Saito, Chiho. Revolutionary Girl Utena. Be-Papas, illus. 2003. (Revolutionary Girl Utena Ser.: 3). (ENG.). 200p. pap. 9.95 *(978-1-56931-812-6(3))* Viz Media.

Sakai, Stan. The Adventures of Nilson Groundthumper & Hermy. Wright, Brendan, ed. Sakai, Stan, illus. 2013. (ENG., Illus.). 112p. 14.99 *(978-1-61655-341-8(3))* Dark Horse Comics.

—Usagi Yojimbo Vol. 3: Al Filo de la Vida y la Muerte. 2007. (SPA., Illus.). 200p. reprint ed. pap. 15.95 *(978-1-59497-319-2(9))* Public Square Bks.

—Usagi Yojimbo Vol. 4: Estaciones. 2007. (SPA., Illus.). 200p. reprint ed. pap. 15.95 *(978-1-59497-320-8(2))* Public Square Bks.

—Usagi Yojimbo Vol. 5: Segadora. 2007. (SPA., Illus.). 256p. reprint ed. pap. 17.95 *(978-1-59497-321-5(0))* Public Square Bks.

—Usagi Yojimbo Vol. 7: Samurai (en Español) 2007. (SPA., Illus.). 144p. reprint ed. pap. 14.95 *(978-1-59497-323-9(7))* Public Square Bks.

—The Usagi Yojimbo Saga, Vol. 2, Bk. 2. 2015. (ENG., Illus.). 672p. pap. 24.99 *(978-1-61655-610-5(2))* Dark Horse Comics.

—Usagi Yojimbo Saga Volume 3. Sakai, Stan, illus. 2015. (ENG., Illus.). 616p. pap. 24.99 *(978-1-61655-611-2(0))* Dark Horse Comics.

—Usagi Yojimbo Saga Volume 3 Ltd. Ed. Sakai, Stan, illus. 2015. (ENG., Illus.). 618p. 79.99 *(978-1-61655-673-0(0))* Dark Horse Comics.

Sala, Richard. Cat Burglar Black. Sala, Richard, illus. 2009. (ENG., Illus.). 128p. (J). (gr. 6-9). pap. 17.99 *(978-1-59643-144-7(X)*, 9781596431447, First Second Bks.) Roaring Brook Pr.

Salamoff, Paul. The Cast of Doctor Who. 2012. (ENG., Illus.). 40p. pap. 7.99 *(978-1-4507-8451-1(8))* Bluewater Productions, Inc.

Salamoff, Paul J. Bo Obama: The White House Tails. 2010. (ENG.). 40p. pap. 6.99 *(978-1-61623-925-1(5))* Bluewater Productions, Inc.

Salane, Jeffrey. The Lego Movie. Kiernan, Kenny, illus. 2013. (ENG.). 64p. (J). (gr. 2-5). pap. 5.99 *(978-0-545-62462-6(2))* Scholastic, Inc.

Salazar, Souther. Destined for Dizzyness. Salazar, Souther, illus. 2005. (Illus.). 48p. pap. 5.95 *(978-0-9766848-1-7(0))* Buenaventura Pr.

Sanchez, Ricardo. Spotlight Soccer, 1 vol. Waryanto, Ian, illus. 2014. (Sports Illustrated Kids Graphic Novels Ser.). (ENG.). 72p. (gr. 2-5). 26.65 *(978-1-4342-4165-8(3))* Stone Arch Bks.

Sander, Sonia. Scooby-Doo & the Chocolate Phantom, 1 vol. 2016. (Scooby-Doo Comic Readers Ser.). (ENG.). 32p. (J). (gr. k-3). lib. bdg. 24.21 *(978-1-61479-451-6(0)*, Graphic Planet) Magic Wagon.

Sane, Justin. Heart of a Corpse; an Undead Engagement Part One. Sane, Justin, illus. 2012. (Illus.). 34p. pap. 5.95 *(978-1-59362-243-5(0)*, Slave Labor Graphics) Slave Labor Bks.

Sanjo, Riku. Beet the Vandel Buster, Vol. 1. Inada, Koji, illus. 2004. (ENG.). 200p. pap. 7.99 *(978-1-59116-690-0(X))* Viz Media.

—Beet the Vandel Buster, Vol. 4. Inada, Koji, illus. 2005. (ENG.). 208p. pap. 7.99 *(978-1-59116-750-1(7))* Viz Media.

Sanna, Alessandro, creator. The River. 2014. (ENG., Illus.). 110p. (J). (gr. k). 22.95 *(978-1-59270-149-0(3))* Enchanted Lion Bks., LLC.

Sarda, Bruno. Mickey & Donald: the Search for the Zodiac Stone. Vita, Massimo de & Valussi, Franco, illus. 2016. (Mickey Mouse Ser.). (ENG.). 368p. 39.99 *(978-1-63140-706-2(6)*, 9781631407062) Idea & Design Works, LLC.

Satterlee, Chuck. Smoke & Mirror Vol. 1: Time & Again. 2006. (Illus.). 152p. (YA). pap. 15.99 *(978-0-9738966-2-6(0))* Speakeasy Comics CAN. Dist: Diamond Bk. Distributors.

Satterwhite, William. Stealth, Vol. 1. 2005. 44p. (YA). pap. 5.75 *(978-1-4116-2395-8(9))* Lulu Pr., Inc.

Sautter, Aaron, et al. Searching for UFOs: An Isabel Soto Investigation, 1 vol. 2010. (Graphic Expeditions Ser.). (ENG.). 32p. (gr. 3-4). lib. bdg. 30.65 *(978-1-4296-3974-3(1)*, Graphic Library) Capstone Press of Coughlan Cos.

Sava, Scott Christian. Animal Crackers. 2011. (Illus.). 152p. pap. 11.99 *(978-1-60010-619-4(6))* Idea & Design Works, LLC.

—Gary the Pirate. 2008. (Illus.). 112p. 12.95 *(978-0-9789168-5-5(9))* Blue Dream Studios.

—Hyperactive. 2008. (Illus.). 112p. 12.95 *(978-0-9789168-4-8(0))* Blue Dream Studios.

—Magic Carpet. 2010. (Illus.). 110p. (J). pap. 11.99 *(978-1-60010-563-0(7))* Idea & Design Works, LLC.

—My Grandparents Are Secret Agents. 2008. (Illus.). 112p. (J). 12.95 *(978-0-9789168-6-2(7))* Blue Dream Studios.

Savage, Doug. Laser Moose & Rabbit Boy. 2016. (ENG.). 144p. (J). pap. 9.99 *(978-1-4494-7094-4(7))* Andrews McMeel Publishing.

Sazaklis, John. Batman Classic - Eternal Enemies. Tong, Andie, illus. 2013. (ENG.). 24p. (J). (gr. -1-3). pap. 3.99 *(978-0-06-220997-9(3)*, HarperFestival) HarperCollins Pubs.

—The Fate of Krypton. Roberts, Jeremy, illus. 2013. (Man of Steel Ser.). (ENG.). 24p. (J). (gr. -1-3). pap. 3.99 *(978-0-06-223593-0(1)*, HarperFestival) HarperCollins Pubs.

—Fowl Play. Gordon, Steven E. & Gordon, Eric A., illus. 2012. (ENG.). 24p. (J). (gr. -1-3). pap. 3.99 *(978-0-06-188536-5(3)*, HarperFestival) HarperCollins Pubs.

—Goat on a Boat, 1 vol. Bradley, Jessica, illus. 2013. (Comics Land Ser.). (ENG.). 32p. (gr. k-2). 7.95 *(978-1-4342-6282-0(0))*; lib. bdg. 25.32 *(978-1-4342-4944-9(1))* Stone Arch Bks.

—I Am the Flash. 2014. (Justice League Classic: I Can Read! Ser.). (J). lib. bdg. 13.55 *(978-0-606-35073-0(X)*, Turtleback) Turtleback Bks.

—Justice League Classic - I Am the Flash. Gordon, Steven E. & Gordon, Eric A., illus. 2014. (I Can Read Level 2 Ser.). (ENG.). 32p. (J). (gr. -1-3). pap. 3.99 *(978-0-06-221005-0(X))* HarperCollins Pubs.

—Marvel Avengers Assemble: Rise of the Avengers: Freeze Frame 1. 2015. (ENG.). 80p. (J). (gr. k-5). pap. 6.99 *(978-0-7944-3271-3(9))* Studio Fun International.

—Superman Saves Smallville. Roberts, Jeremy, illus. 2013. (Man of Steel Ser.). (ENG.). 24p. (J). (gr. -1-3). pap. 3.99 *(978-0-06-223603-6(2)*, HarperFestival) HarperCollins Pubs.

Sazaklis, John, retold by. Marvel Ultimate Spider-Man: Spider-Man & His Amazing Friends. 2016. (ENG.). 80p. (J). (gr. 1-4). pap. 6.99 *(978-0-7944-3391-8(X))* Studio Fun International.

Sazaklis, John & Farley, John. Attack of the Toyman. Smith, Andy, illus. 2012. (ENG.). 24p. (J). (gr. -1-3). pap. 3.99 *(978-0-06-188535-8(5)*, HarperFestival) HarperCollins Pubs.

Sazaklis, John & Merkel, Joe F. Day of the Undead. Tong, Andie, illus. 2013. (ENG.). 24p. (J). (gr. -1-3). pap. 3.99 *(978-0-06-220999-3(X)*, HarperFestival) HarperCollins Pubs.

Sazaklis, John & Roberts, Jeremy. Fright Club. Farley, Rick & Smith, Andy, illus. 2012. (ENG.). 24p. (J). (gr. -1-2). pap. 3.99 *(978-0-06-188534-1(7)*, HarperFestival) HarperCollins Pubs.

Scarpa, Romano, et al. Uncle Scrooge: the Eternal Knot: The Eternal Knot. 2016. (Uncle Scrooge Ser.). (ENG., Illus.). 120p. (J). (gr. 2-5). pap. 12.99 *(978-1-63140-639-3(6)*, 9781631406393) Idea & Design Works, LLC.

Schauer, M. RIP, M. D. Vosburg, M., illus. 2010. (ENG.). 88p. pap. 12.99 *(978-1-60699-369-9(0)*, 699369) Fantagraphics Bks.

Schmitt, Michel-Yves. Snowball Truce! Caut, Vincent, illus. 2013. (Where's Leopold? Ser.: 2). (ENG.). 32p. (J). (gr. 2-4). pap. 6.95 *(978-1-4677-1523-2(9)*, Graphic Universe™) Lerner Publishing Group.

—Your Pajamas Are Showing! Caut, Vincent, illus. 2013. (Where's Leopold? Ser.: 1). (ENG.). 40p. (J). (gr. 2-4). pap. 6.95 *(978-1-4677-0871-5(2))*; lib. bdg. 25.26 *(978-1-4677-0769-5(4))* Lerner Publishing Group. (Graphic Universe™).

Scholastic. Day of the Departed (LEGO Ninjago: Reader) 2016. (Lego Ninjago Ser.). (ENG.). 32p. (J). (gr. -1-3). pap. 3.99 *(978-1-338-11369-3(0))* Scholastic, Inc.

Scholastic & Arlon, Penelope. Bug off! (LEGO Nonfiction) 2017. (LEGO Nonfiction Ser.). (ENG.). 32p. (J). (gr. -1-3). pap. 4.99 *(978-1-338-13015-7(3))* Scholastic, Inc.

Scholastic Editors. Princess Leia. 2016. (Backstories Ser.: Vol. 7). (ENG., Illus.). 128p. (J). (gr. 3-7). 16.00 *(978-0-606-39146-7(0))* Turtleback Bks.

—The Quest for the Crystal. 2015. (Ninjago Readers Ser.: 14). lib. bdg. 13.55 *(978-0-606-38109-3(0))* Turtleback Bks.

Scholastic, Inc. Staff & Kogge, Michael. Cross Fire. 2016. (Batman vs. Superman: Dawn of Justice Ser.). (ENG.). 144p. (J). (gr. 2-5). lib. bdg. 16.00 *(978-0-606-38097-3(3))* Turtleback Bks.

Schroeder, Niels Olaf. Berlin Brain Odyssee - a trip into the Brain. 2010. 32p. pap. 18.50 *(978-1-4452-3979-8(5))* Lulu Pr., Inc.

Schulz, Charles. Alle Achtung. Herbst, Gabriele & Rolle, Ekkehard, trs. from ENG. (Snoopy & die Peanuts Ser.: Vol. 5). (GER., Illus.). 128p. (J). pap. *(978-3-8105-1818-7(2))* Kruger, Wolfgang Verlag, GmbH DEU. Dist: International Bk. Import Service, Inc.

—Alles Peanuts. Herbst, Gabriele & Rolle, Ekkehard, trs. from ENG. (Snoopy & die Peanuts Ser.: Vol. 26). (GER., Illus.). 96p. (J). pap. *(978-3-8105-1871-2(9))* Kruger, Wolfgang Verlag, GmbH DEU. Dist: International Bk. Import Service, Inc.

—Allzeit Bereit. Herbst, Gabriele & Rolle, Ekkehard, trs. from ENG. (Snoopy & die Peanuts Ser.: Vol. 35). (GER., Illus.). 96p. (J). pap. *(978-3-8105-1891-0(3))* Kruger, Wolfgang Verlag, GmbH DEU. Dist: International Bk. Import Service, Inc.

— An der Langen Leine. Herbst, Gabriele & Rolle, Ekkehard, trs. from ENG. (Snoopy & die Peanuts Ser.: Vol. 30). (GER., Illus.). 96p. (J). pap. *(978-3-8105-1880-4(8))* Kruger, Wolfgang Verlag, GmbH DEU. Dist: International Bk. Import Service, Inc.

—Auf den Hund Gekommen. Herbst, Gabriele & Rolle, Ekkehard, trs. from ENG. (Snoopy & die Peanuts Ser.: Vol. 34). (GER., Illus.). 96p. (J). pap. *(978-3-8105-1888-0(3))* Kruger, Wolfgang Verlag, GmbH DEU. Dist: International Bk. Import Service, Inc.

—Christmas Is Together-Time. Schulz, Charles, illus. 2006. (Peanuts(r) Ser.). (ENG., Illus.). 72p. 6.95 *(978-1-933662-37-4(9))* Cider Mill Pr. Bk. Pubs., LLC.

—Cowabunga! 2013. (Peanuts Kids Ser.: 1). (ENG., Illus.). 224p. (J). 9.99 *(978-1-4494-5079-3(2))* Andrews McMeel Publishing.

—Den Wind im Ruecken. Herbst, Gabriele & Rolle, Ekkehard, trs. from ENG. (Snoopy & die Peanuts Ser.: Vol. 6). (GER., Illus.). 96p. (J). pap. *(978-3-8105-1819-4(0))* Kruger, Wolfgang Verlag, GmbH DEU. Dist: International Bk. Import Service, Inc.

—Einfach Genial. Herbst, Gabriele & Rolle, Ekkehard, trs. from ENG. (Snoopy & die Peanuts Ser.: Vol. 31). (GER., Illus.). 96p. (J). pap. *(978-3-8105-1881-1(6))* Kruger, Wolfgang Verlag, GmbH DEU. Dist: International Bk. Import Service, Inc.

—Einfach Unschlagbar. Herbst, Gabriele & Rolle, Ekkehard, trs. from ENG. (Snoopy & die Peanuts Ser.: Vol. 1). (GER., Illus.). 96p. (J). pap. *(978-3-8105-1811-8(5))* Kruger, Wolfgang Verlag, GmbH DEU. Dist: International Bk. Import Service, Inc.

—Grundlos Gluecklich. Herbst, Gabriele & Rolle, Ekkehard, trs. from ENG. (Snoopy & die Peanuts Ser.: Vol. 37). (GER., Illus.). 96p. (J). pap. *(978-3-8105-1893-4(X))* Kruger, Wolfgang Verlag, GmbH DEU. Dist: International Bk. Import Service, Inc.

—Gut Aufgelegt. Herbst, Gabriele & Rolle, Ekkehard, trs. from ENG. (Snoopy & die Peanuts Ser.: Vol. 12). (GER., Illus.). 96p. (J). pap. *(978-3-8105-1828-6(X))* Kruger, Wolfgang Verlag, GmbH DEU. Dist: International Bk. Import Service, Inc.

—Herzlich Unverschaemt. Herbst, Gabriele & Rolle, Ekkehard, trs. from ENG. (Snoopy & die Peanuts Ser.: Vol. 9). (GER., Illus.). 128p. (J). pap. *(978-3-8105-1823-1(9))* Kruger, Wolfgang Verlag, GmbH DEU. Dist: International Bk. Import Service, Inc.

—Himmel & Hoelle. Herbst, Gabriele & Rolle, Ekkehard, trs. from ENG. (Snoopy & die Peanuts Ser.: Vol. 23). (GER., Illus.). 96p. (J). pap. *(978-3-8105-1867-5(0))* Kruger, Wolfgang Verlag, GmbH DEU. Dist: International Bk. Import Service, Inc.

—Hoch die Tassen. Herbst, Gabriele & Rolle, Ekkehard, trs. from ENG. (Snoopy & die Peanuts Ser.: Vol. 36). (GER., Illus.). 96p. (J). pap. *(978-3-8105-1892-7(1))* Kruger, Wolfgang Verlag, GmbH DEU. Dist: International Bk. Import Service, Inc.

—I Need All the Friends I Can Get. 2006. (Peanuts(r) Ser.). (ENG., Illus.). 72p. 5.95 *(978-1-933662-39-8(5))* Cider Mill Pr. Bk. Pubs., LLC.

—Immer Dabei. Herbst, Gabriele & Rolle, Ekkehard, trs. from ENG. (Snoopy & die Peanuts Ser.: Vol. 27). (GER., Illus.). 96p. (J). pap. *(978-3-8105-1872-9(7))* Kruger, Wolfgang Verlag, GmbH DEU. Dist: International Bk. Import Service, Inc.

—Kaum zu Bremsen. Rolle, Ekkehard, tr. from ENG. (Snoopy & die Peanuts Ser.: Vol. 11). (GER., Illus.). 128p. (J). pap. *(978-3-8105-1827-9(1))* Kruger, Wolfgang Verlag, GmbH DEU. Dist: International Bk. Import Service, Inc.

—The Many Faces of Snoopy. 2006. (ENG., Illus.). 352p. per. 22.00 *(978-0-345-47983-9(1)*, Ballantine Bks.) Random House Publishing Group.

—Pfoten Hoch! Herbst, Gabriele & Rolle, Ekkehard, trs. from ENG. (Snoopy & die Peanuts Ser.: Vol. 33). (GER., Illus.). 96p. (J). pap. *(978-3-8105-1887-3(5))* Kruger, Wolfgang Verlag, GmbH DEU. Dist: International Bk. Import Service, Inc.

—Schwer in Fahrt. Herbst, Gabriele & Rolle, Ekkehard, trs. from ENG. (Snoopy & die Peanuts Ser.: Vol. 7). (GER., Illus.). 128p. (J). pap. *(978-3-8105-1820-0(4))* Kruger, Wolfgang Verlag, GmbH DEU. Dist: International Bk. Import Service, Inc.

—Snoopy's Thanksgiving. 2014. (Peanuts Seasonal Ser.: 0). (ENG., Illus.). 64p. 9.99 *(978-1-60699-778-9(5)*, 699778) Fantagraphics Bks.

—Suppertime! 2006. (Peanuts(r) Ser.). (ENG., Illus.). 72p. 5.95 *(978-1-933662-38-1(7))* Cider Mill Pr. Bk. Pubs., LLC.

—Voll auf die Schnauze. Herbst, Gabriele & Rolle, Ekkehard, trs. from ENG. (Snoopy & die Peanuts Ser.: Vol. 32). (GER., Illus.). 96p. (J). pap. *(978-3-8105-1886-6(7))* Kruger, Wolfgang Verlag, GmbH DEU. Dist: International Bk. Import Service, Inc.

—Voll im Griff. Herbst, Gabriele & Rolle, Ekkehard, trs. from ENG. (Snoopy & die Peanuts Ser.: Vol. 13). (GER., Illus.). 128p. (J). pap. *(978-3-8105-1829-3(8))* Kruger, Wolfgang Verlag, GmbH DEU. Dist: International Bk. Import Service, Inc.

—You Can Be Anything! 2009. (ENG.). 48p. (J). (gr. -1-3). 12.95 *(978-0-7624-3583-8(6)*, Running Pr. Kids) Running Pr. Bk. Pubs.

Schulz, Charles & Houghton, Shane. Peanuts, Vol. 2. Braddock, Paige, illus. 2013. (Peanuts Ser.). (ENG.). 112p. (J). (gr. 1). pap. 13.99 *(978-1-60886-299-3(2))* Boom! Studios.

Schulz, Charles & Pastis, Stephan. Happiness Is a Warm Blanket, Charlie Brown! Scott, Bob, illus. 2011. (Peanuts Ser.). (ENG.). 96p. (gr. 3). pap. 9.99 *(978-1-60886-681-6(5))* Boom! Studios.

Schulz, Charles & Scott, Vicki. It's Tokyo, Charlie Brown! Braddock, Paige, illus. 2012. (Peanuts Ser.). (ENG.). 96p. (J). (gr. 2). pap. 9.99 *(978-1-60886-270-2(4))* Boom! Studios.

Schulz, Charles M. Batter up, Charlie Brown! 2014. (ENG., Illus.). 64p. 9.99 *(978-1-60699-725-3(4)*, 699725) Fantagraphics Bks.

—Be Joyful: Peanuts Wisdom to Carry You Through. 2014. (ENG., Illus.). 72p. (J). (gr. k-17). 7.95 *(978-0-7624-4719-0(2)*, Running Pr. Kids) Running Pr. Bk. Pubs.

—Waiting for the Great Pumpkin. 2014. (Peanuts Seasonal Ser.: 0). (ENG., Illus.). 64p. 9.99 *(978-1-60699-772-7(6)*, 699772) Fantagraphics Bks.

Schwartz, Simon. First Man: The Voyages of Matthew Henson. Watkinson, Laura, tr. from GER. 2015. (ENG., Illus.). 160p. (J). (gr. 8-12). 31.99 *(978-1-4677-5842-0(6)*, Graphic Universe™) Lerner Publishing Group.

—The Other Side of the Wall. Watkinson, Laura, tr. from GER. 2015. (ENG., Illus.). 112p. (J). (gr. 7-12). lib. bdg. 29.32 *(978-1-4677-5840-6(X)*, Graphic Universe™) Lerner Publishing Group.

Schwarz, Viviane. Shark & Lobster's Amazing Undersea Adventure. Stewart, Joel, illus. 2006. 34p. (J). *(978-1-4156-8140-4(6))* Candlewick Pr.

Schweizer, Chris. The Creeps: Book 1: Night of the Frankenfrogs. 2015. (ENG., Illus.). 128p. (J). (gr. 3-7). 17.95 *(978-1-4197-1379-8(5)*, Amulet Bks.) Abrams, Inc.

—The Creeps: Curse of the Attack-O-Lanterns. 2016. (Creeps Ser.: 3). (ENG., Illus.). 128p. (J). (gr. 3-7). 17.95 *(978-1-4197-2190-8(9)*, Amulet Bks.) Abrams, Inc.

—The Crogan Adventures. 2015. (ENG., Illus.). 224p. (J). pap. 17.99 *(978-1-62010-243-5(9)*, 9781620102435) Oni Pr., Inc.

—Tricky Coyote Tales. Thomas, Chad, illus. 2011. (Tricky Journeys Ser.: 1). (ENG.). (J). (gr. 2-4). pap. 39.62 *(978-0-7613-8625-4(4))*;No. 1. 64p. pap. 6.95 *(978-0-7613-7859-4(6))*;No. 1. 64p. lib. bdg. 27.93 *(978-0-7613-6601-0(6))* Lerner Publishing Group.

—Tricky Fox Tales. Paroline, Shelli & Paroline, Michelle, illus. 2011. (Tricky Journeys Ser.: 3). (ENG.). (J). (gr. 2-4). pap. 39.62 *(978-0-7613-8627-8(0))* Lerner Publishing Group.

—Tricky Fox Tales. Paroline, Shelli, illus. 2011. (Tricky Journeys Ser.: 3). (ENG.). 64p. (J). (gr. 2-4). pap. 6.95 *(978-0-7613-7861-7(8))* Lerner Publishing Group.

—Tricky Fox Tales, No. 3. Paroline, Shelli & Paroline, Michelle, illus. 2011. (Tricky Journeys Ser.: 3). (ENG.). 64p. (J). (gr. 2-4). lib. bdg. 27.93 *(978-0-7613-6605-8(9))* Lerner Publishing Group.

—Tricky Monkey Tales. Thomas, Chad, illus. 2011. (Tricky Journeys Ser.: 6). (ENG.). (J). (gr. 2-4). pap. 39.62 *(978-0-7613-8630-8(0))*; 64p. pap. 6.95 *(978-0-7613-7860-0(X))*;No. 6. 64p. lib. bdg. 27.93 *(978-0-7613-6611-9(3))* Lerner Publishing Group.

—Tricky Rabbit Tales. Giallongo, Zack, illus. 2011. (Tricky Journeys Ser.: 2). (ENG.). (J). (gr. 2-4). pap. 39.62 *(978-0-7613-8626-1(2))*; 64p. pap. 6.95 *(978-0-7613-7862-4(6))*;No. 2. 64p. lib. bdg. 27.93 *(978-0-7613-6607-2(5))* Lerner Publishing Group.

—Tricky Raven Tales. Witt, David, illus. 2011. (Tricky Journeys Ser.: 4). (ENG.). (J). (gr. 2-4). pap. 39.62 *(978-0-7613-8628-5(9))*;No. 4. 64p. pap. 6.95 *(978-0-7613-7863-1(4))*;No. 4. 64p. lib. bdg. 27.93 *(978-0-7613-6603-4(2))* Lerner Publishing Group.

—Tricky Spider Tales. Huddleston, Courtney, illus. 2011. (Tricky Journeys Ser.: 5). (ENG.). (J). (gr. 2-4). pap. 39.62 *(978-0-7613-8629-2(7))*; 64p. pap. 6.95 *(978-0-7613-7864-8(2))*;No. 5. 64p. lib. bdg. 27.93 *(978-0-7613-6609-6(1))* Lerner Publishing Group.

—The Trolls Will Feast! 2016. (Creeps Ser.). (ENG., Illus.). 128p. (J). (gr. 3-7). 17.95 *(978-1-4197-1882-3(7)*, Amulet Bks.) Abrams, Inc.

Scotford, Groenewald & Scotford, Tina. A Bush Buffet in the Land of Kachoo. 2014. (Land of Kachoo Ser.). (ENG.). 32p. (J). (gr. k-2). pap. 10.95 *(978-1-4314-0761-3(5))* Jacana Media ZAF. Dist: Independent Pubs. Group.

—The Mighty Elephant in the Land of Kachoo: The Land of Kachoo Series. Groenewald, Frans, illus. 2014. (Land of Kachoo Ser.). (ENG.). 32p. (J). (gr. k-2). pap. 10.95

C
D

(978-1-4314-0759-0(3)) Jacana Media ZAF. Dist: Independent Pubs. Group.

Scott, Cavan. Penguins of Madagascar Volume 4. Ferreyra, Lucas, illus. 2016. (ENG.). 64p. (J). (gr. 1-4). 6.99 (978-1-78276-254-6(X)) Titan Bks. Ltd. GBR. Dist: Penguin Random Hse. LLC.

Scott, Cavan & Matthews, Alex. Penguins Collection 2. Ferrerya, Lucas, illus. 2016. (ENG.). 112p. (gr. 1-4). pap. 12.99 (978-1-78585-316-6(3)) Titan Bks. Ltd. GBR. Dist: Penguin Random Hse. LLC.

Scott, Cavan, et al. Penguins of Madagascar Vol. 2: Operation Heist. Bartolini, Egle, illus. 2015. (ENG.). 64p. (J). (gr. 1-4). pap. 6.99 (978-1-78276-252-2(3)) Titan Bks. Ltd. GBR. Dist: Penguin Random Hse. LLC.

Scott, Jerry. Chillax. Borgman, Jim, illus. 2013. (Zits Ser.: 1). (ENG.). 256p. (YA). (gr. 8). pap. 9.99 (978-0-06-222851-2(X), HarperTeen) HarperCollins Pubs.

Seagle, Steven T. Frankie Stein. 2010. (ENG., Illus.). 48p. 14.99 (978-1-60706-191-5(0), 9781607061915) Image Comics.

—Solstice. Norman, Justin & Starkings, Richard, illus. 2005. per. 12.95 (978-0-9766761-1-9(7)) Active Images.

Secchi, Richard & Salati, Giorgio. Race for the Ultrapods, Vol. 2. Turconi, Stefano et al, illus. 2010. (Disney's Hero Squad Ser.). (ENG.). 128p. (J). (gr. 4-7). pap. 9.99 (978-1-60886-560-4(6)) Boom! Studios.

Sechrist, Darren. Taming the West. 2008. (ENG.). 32p. (J). pap. (978-0-7787-4215-9(6)) Crabtree Publishing Co.

—Westward, Ho! 2008. (ENG.). 32p. (J). pap. (978-0-7787-4217-3(2)) Crabtree Publishing Co.

Seeley, Tim. Bloodstrike Vol. 1: Reborn under a Bad Sign. 2012. (ENG., Illus.). 160p. (YA). pap. 14.99 (978-1-60706-625-5(4), 9781607066255) Image Comics.

—Rebirth, Vol. 2. 2012. (ENG., Illus.). 160p. (YA). pap. 16.99 (978-1-60706-637-8(8), 9781607066378) Image Comics.

Seeley, Tim, et al. Rebirth, Vol. 4. 2013. (ENG., Illus.). 160p. (YA). pap. 16.99 (978-1-60706-800-6(1), 9781607068006) Image Comics.

Seidman, David, et al. Deadly Double. 2013. (Superman Ser.). (ENG., Illus.). 56p. (gr. 2-3). pap. 4.95 (978-1-4342-1726-4(4), DC Super Heroes) Stone Arch Bks.

Seifert, Brandon. Disney Kingdoms: Seekers of the Weird. 2014. (ENG., Illus.). 120p. (J). (gr. -1-17). 24.99 (978-0-7851-5452-5(3)) Marvel Worldwide, Inc.

—Witch Doctor Volume 2: Mal Practice TP: Mal Practice TP. 2013. (ENG., Illus.). 176p. (YA). pap. 14.99 (978-1-60706-693-4(9), 9781607066934) Image Comics.

Sellner, Joelle. Punky Brewster: Punky Power. Vamos, Lesley, illus. 2016. (ENG.). 256p. pap. 12.99 (978-1-941302-19-4(X)) Lion Forge, LLC, The.

Sente, Yves. The Sarcophagi of the Sixth Coninent, Pt. 1, Vol. 9. Juillard, André, illus. 2011. (Blake & Mortimer Ser.: 9). (ENG.). 64p. (gr. 5-17). pap. 15.95 (978-1-84918-067-2(9)) CineBook GBR. Dist: National Bk. Network.

Sente, Yves & Juillard, Andre. The Gondwana Shrine. 2012. (Blake & Mortimer Ser.: 11). (ENG., Illus.). 64p. pap. 15.95 (978-1-84918-094-8(6)) CineBook GBR. Dist: National Bk. Network.

—The Oath of the Five Swords, Vol. 18. 2014. (Blake & Mortimer Ser.: 18). (ENG., Illus.). 72p. pap. 15.95 (978-1-84918-191-4(8)) CineBook GBR. Dist: National Bk. Network.

—The Sarcophagi of the Sixth Continent, Pt. 2. 2011. (Blake & Mortimer Ser.: 10). (ENG., Illus.). 64p. pap. 15.95 (978-1-84918-077-1(6)) CineBook GBR. Dist: National Bk. Network.

Server, David & Lanzing, Jackson. Penguins of Madagascar, Vol. 2. 2011. (ENG.). 52p. (J). pap. 6.95 (978-1-936340-30-9(5), 9781936340309) Ape Entertainment.

Sesen, Cihan. Stop the Rain, Issue #1. 2010. 45p. pap. 12.99 (978-0-557-48426-3(X)) Lulu Pr., Inc.

Sewell, Anna. Black Beauty. l.t. ed. 2010. (ENG.). 260p. pap. 22.95 (978-1-4104-2390-0(5), Kennebec Large Print) Cengage Gale.

Sfar, Joann & Trondheim, Lewis. La Mazmorra: Corazón de Pato. Abuli, Enrique Sánchez, tr. from FRE. 2004. Orig. Title: Le Donjon: Coeur de Canard. (SPA., Illus.). 48p. pap. 16.95 (978-1-59497-057-3(2)) Public Square Bks.

—La Mazmorra: El Cementerio de los Dragones. Abuli, Enrique Sánchez, tr. from FRE. 2004. Orig. Title: Donjon Crepuscule 101: le Cimetiere des Dragons. (SPA., Illus.). 48p. pap. 16.95 (978-1-59497-060-3(2)) Public Square Bks.

—La Mazmorra: La Princesa de los Barbaros. Abuli, Enrique Sánchez, tr. from FRE. 2004. Orig. Title: Donjon Zenith 3: la Princesse des Barbares. (SPA., Illus.). 48p. pap. 16.95 (978-1-59497-059-7(9)) Public Square Bks.

—La Mazmorra: Sortilegios e Infortunios. Abuli, Enrique Sánchez, tr. from FRE. 2005. Orig. Title: Donjon Zenith 4: Sortilege et Avatar. (SPA., Illus.). 48p. pap. 16.95 (978-1-59497-063-4(7)) Public Square Bks.

—La Mazmorra: Un Justiciero en Apuros. Abuli, Enrique Sánchez, tr. from FRE. 2004. Orig. Title: Donjon Potron-minet -98: un Justicier dans L'Ennui. (SPA., Illus.). 48p. (J). pap. 16.95 (978-1-59497-062-7(9)) Public Square Bks.

Shaffer, Jody Jensen. Vampires & Light, 1 vol. Gervasio, illus. 2013. (Monster Science Ser.). (ENG.). 32p. (gr. 3-4). lib. bdg. 30.65 (978-1-4296-9928-0(0), Graphic Library) Capstone Press of Coughlan Cos.

Shakespeare, William. Henry V: The Graphic Novel. 2010. (Classic Graphic Novel Collection). (ENG.). 160p. (gr. 7-12). 39.40 (978-1-4205-0371-5(5)) Cengage Gale.

—Julius Caesar. Mahbab, Mustashrik, illus. 2008. (ENG.). 208p. (YA). (gr. 7-11). pap. 12.95 (978-0-8109-7072-4(4), Amulet Bks.) Abrams, Inc.

—Julius Caesar, 1 vol. Garcia, Eduardo, illus. 2011. (Shakespeare Graphics Ser.). (ENG.). 88p. (gr. 2-3). pap. 7.15 (978-1-4342-3450-6(9)); lib. bdg. 27.99 (978-1-4342-2631-0(X)) Stone Arch Bks. (Shakespeare Graphics).

—Macbeth. Deas, Robert, illus. 2008. (ENG.). 208p. (YA). (gr. 7-11). pap. 12.95 (978-0-8109-7073-1(2), Amulet Bks.) Abrams, Inc.

—Macbeth, 1 vol. Pérez, Daniel & Ferran, Daniel, illus. 2011. (Shakespeare Graphics Ser.). (ENG.). 88p. (gr. 2-3). pap. 7.15 (978-1-4342-3447-6(9), Shakespeare Graphics) Stone Arch Bks.

—Macbeth, 1 vol. Ferran, Daniel, illus. 2011. (Shakespeare Graphics Ser.). (ENG.). 88p. (gr. 2-3). lib. bdg. 27.99 (978-1-4342-2506-1(2), Shakespeare Graphics) Stone Arch Bks.

Shakespeare, William & Appignanesi, Richard. Hamlet. Vieceli, Emma, illus. 2007. (ENG.). 204p. (J). (gr. 2-8). pap. 12.95 (978-0-8109-9324-2(4), Abrams Bks. for Young Readers) Abrams, Inc.

—Romeo & Juliet. Leong, Sonia, illus. 2007. (ENG.). 208p. (J). (gr. 2-8). pap. 14.95 (978-0-8109-9325-9(2), Abrams Bks. for Young Readers) Abrams, Inc.

Shan, Darren, pseud. Vampire Mountain, Vol. 4. 2010. (Cirque du Freak, the Manga Ser.: 4). lib. bdg. 24.55 (978-0-606-14433-9(1), Turtleback) Turtleback Bks.

Shanower, Eric. Adventures in Oz Volume 1. 2014. (Adventures in Oz Ser.). (ENG., Illus.). 160p. (J). (gr. 2-5). 34.99 (978-1-63140-150-3(5), 9781631401503) Idea & Design Works, LLC.

—Oz: Road to Oz. 2013. (ENG., Illus.). 136p. (J). (gr. -1-17). pap. 16.99 (978-0-7851-6405-0(7)) Marvel Worldwide, Inc.

—Wonderful Wizard of Oz: Vol. 3, 1 vol. 2014. (ENG.). 24p. 24.21 (978-1-61479-228-4(3)) ABDO Publishing Co.

Shapiro, David R. Terra Tempo: The Four Corners of Time. Herndon, Christopher, illus. 2013. (Terra Tempo Ser.). (ENG.). 264p. (J). pap. 17.99 (978-0-9844422-6-3(X)) Craigmore Creations.

—Terra Tempo Vol. 3: The Academy of Planetary Evolution. Herndon, Christopher, illus. 2014. (Terra Tempo Ser.). (ENG.). 182p. (J). (gr. 2-4). pap. 17.99 (978-1-940052-09-0(2)) Craigmore Creations.

Shaskan, Trisha Speed. Art Panels, BAM! Speech Bubbles, POW! Writing Your Own Graphic Novel, 1 vol. Shaskan, Stephen, illus. 2010. (Writer's Toolbox Ser.). (ENG.). 32p. (gr. 2-4). pap. 8.95 (978-1-4048-6393-4(1)) Picture Window Bks.

—The Case of the Missing Mola Lisa! Shaskan, Stephen, illus. 2017. (Q & Ray Ser.: 1). (ENG.). 48p. (gr. 2-5). 26.65 (978-1-5124-1147-8(7), Graphic Universe™) Lerner Publishing Group.

Shaw, Murray & Cosson, M. J. Sherlock Holmes & a Scandal in Bohemia. Rohrbach, Sophie, illus. 2010. (On the Case with Holmes & Watson Ser.: 1). (ENG.). 48p. (J). (gr. 4-6). pap. 6.95 (978-0-7613-6197-8(9), Graphic Universe™) Lerner Publishing Group.

—Sherlock Holmes & the Adventure at the Abbey Grange. Rohrbach, Sophie, illus. 2010. (On the Case with Holmes & Watson Ser.: 2). (ENG.). 48p. (J). (gr. 4-6). pap. 6.95 (978-0-7613-6200-5(2), Graphic Universe™) Lerner Publishing Group.

—Sherlock Holmes & the Adventure of the Blue Gem. Rohrbach, Sophie, illus. 2010. (On the Case with Holmes & Watson Ser.: 3). (ENG.). 48p. (J). (gr. 4-6). pap. 6.95 (978-0-7613-6202-9(9), Graphic Universe™) Lerner Publishing Group.

—Sherlock Holmes & the Adventure of the Dancing Men. Rohrbach, Sophie, illus. 2010. (On the Case with Holmes & Watson Ser.: 4). (ENG.). 48p. (J). (gr. 4-6). pap. 6.95 (978-0-7613-6199-2(5), Graphic Universe™) Lerner Publishing Group.

—Sherlock Holmes & the Adventure of the Speckled Band. Rohrbach, Sophie, illus. 2010. (On the Case with Holmes & Watson Ser.: 5). (ENG.). 48p. (J). (gr. 4-6). 27.93 (978-0-7613-6186-2(3)); pap. 6.95 (978-0-7613-6198-5(7), Graphic Universe™) Lerner Publishing Group.

—Sherlock Holmes & the Adventure of the Sussex Vampire. Rohrbach, Sophie, illus. 2010. (On the Case with Holmes & Watson Ser.: 6). (ENG.). 48p. (J). (gr. 4-6). pap. 6.95 (978-0-7613-6201-2(0), Graphic Universe™) Lerner Publishing Group.

Shaw, Scott. Shrek - Living Green, Vol. 2. 2012. (ENG.). 52p. pap. 6.95 (978-1-936340-19-4(4), 9781936340194) Ape Entertainment.

Shelley, Mary. Frankenstein, 1 vol. Ho, Jason, illus. 2007. (Graphic Horror Ser.). (ENG.). 32p. (gr. 4-7). 28.50 (978-1-60270-059-8(1), Graphic Planet- Fiction) ABDO Publishing Co.

—Frankenstein. Williams, Anthony, illus. 2014. (ENG.). 32p. pap. 8.95 (978-1-78404-356-8(7)) Arcturus Publishing GBR. Dist: Bookmasters Distribution.

—Gris Grimly's Frankenstein. Grimly, Gris, illus. 2015. (ENG.). 208p. (YA). (gr. 8). pap. 16.99 (978-0-06-186298-4(3)) HarperCollins Pubs.

Shelley, Mary, et al. Frankenstein. 2004. (ENG.). 112p. pap. 20.00 (978-0-582-82301-3(3)) Pearson Education, Ltd. GBR. Dist: Trans-Atlantic Pubns., Inc.

Shen, Prudence. Nothing Can Possibly Go Wrong. Hicks, Faith Erin, illus. 2013. (ENG.). 288p. (YA). (gr. 7). pap. 17.99 (978-1-59643-659-6(X), 9781596436596, First Second Bks.) Roaring Brook Pr.

Shepard, Aaron. The Monkey King: A Superhero Tale of China, Retold from the Journey to the West. 2008. (Ancient Fantasy Ser.: 4). (J). 44p. lib. bdg. 6.00 (978-0-938497-41-7(3)); 50p. lib. bdg. 15.00 (978-0-938497-40-0(5)) Shepard Pubns. (Skyhook Pr.).

Sherry, Kevin. Remy Sneakers vs. the Robo-Rats. Sherry, Kevin, illus. 2017. (Remy Sneakers Ser.: 1). (ENG., Illus.). 128p. (J). (gr. 2-5). 9.99 **(978-1-338-03460-8(X)**, Scholastic Pr.) Scholastic, Inc.

Shiina, Karuho. Kimi ni Todoke: From Me to You, Vol. 18. Shiina, Karuho, illus. 2014. (ENG., Illus.). 176p. pap. 9.99 (978-1-4215-5917-9(X)) Viz Media.

Shipton, Paul. Get the Fruit! Dunton, Trevor, illus. 2004. (Collins Big Cat Ser.). (ENG.). 24p. (J). (gr. -1-k). pap. 5.99 (978-0-00-718529-0(4)) HarperCollins Pubs. Ltd. GBR. Dist: Independent Pubs. Group.

Shirodaira, Kyo & Mizuno, Eita. The Bonds of Reasoning Vol. 6. (JPN., Illus.). (YA). 182p. pap. (978-4-7575-0790-6(9)); 185p. pap. (978-4-7575-0678-7(3)); Vol. 1. 189p. pap. (978-4-7575-0175-1(7)); Vol. 2. 190p. pap. (978-4-7575-0271-0(0)); Vol. 8. 190p. pap. (978-4-7575-0854-5(9)); Vol. 10. 187p. pap. (978-4-7575-1099-9(3)); Vol. 11. 205p. pap. (978-4-7575-1186-6(8)); Vol. 12. 183p. pap. (978-4-7575-1252-8(X)) Enix Corp.

Shogakukan & Mitsui-Kids, illus. Duel Masters Vol. 3: The Champion of Tomorrow. 2004. (Teen Ser.). 96p. pap. 14.99 (978-1-59532-065-0(2), Tokyopop Kids) TOKYOPOP, Inc.

Shone, Rob. Spartacus: The Life of a Roman Gladiator. 2009. (Graphic Nonfiction Biographies Ser.). (ENG.). 48p. (YA). (gr. 4-5). 58.50 (978-1-61513-028-3(4), Rosen Reference) Rosen Publishing Group, Inc., The.

—Tyrannosaurus: The Tyrant Lizard. 2008. (Graphic Dinosaurs Ser.). (ENG., Illus.). 32p. (gr. 2-5). pap. 12.30 (978-1-4042-9627-5(1), 1270754, PowerKids Pr.) Rosen Publishing Group, Inc., The.

Shouoto, Aya. He's My Only Vampire, Vol. 10. 2017. (He's My Only Vampire Ser.: 10). (ENG., Illus.). 176p. (gr. 11-17). pap. 13.00 (978-0-316-39912-8(4), Yen Pr.) Orbit.

—He's My Only Vampire, Vol. 4. 2015. (He's My Only Vampire Ser.: 4). (ENG., Illus.). 160p. (gr. 11-17). pap. 13.00 (978-0-316-26168-5(8), Yen Pr.) Orbit.

—He's My Only Vampire, Vol. 9. 2016. (He's My Only Vampire Ser.: 9). (ENG., Illus.). 160p. (gr. 11-17). pap. 13.00 (978-0-316-34584-2(9), Yen Pr.) Orbit.

Shreve, Steve. The Adventures of Benny, 0 vols. 2013. (ENG.). 160p. (J). (gr. 3-6). pap. 9.99 (978-1-4778-1607-3(0), 9781477816073, Amazon Children's Publishing) Amazon Publishing.

Siegel, Siena Cherson. To Dance: A Ballerina's Graphic Novel. Siegel, Mark, illus. 2006. (ENG.). 64p. (J). (gr. 3-9). 19.99 (978-0-689-86747-7(6), Atheneum/Richard Jackson Bks.); pap. 10.99 (978-1-4169-2687-0(9), Atheneum Bks. for Young Readers) Simon & Schuster Children's Publishing.

Sierra, Sergio A. & Shelley, Mary. Frankenstein by Mary Shelley. Ribas, Meritxell, illus. 2012. (Dark Graphic Novels Ser.). 96p. (J). (gr. 5-9). 31.94 (978-0-7660-4084-7(4)) Enslow Pubs., Inc.

Siglain, Michael. Breakout!, 1 vol. Marvel Illustrators, illus. 2012. (Avengers: Earth's Mightiest Heroes! Ser.). (ENG.). 24p. (J). (gr. -1-4). lib. bdg. 24.21 (978-1-61479-001-3(9)) Spotlight.

Silbaugh, Michael John. Crosseyed Puzzle. 2009. 28p. pap. 15.99 (978-1-4415-8779-4(9)) Xlibris Corp.

Silberberg, Alan. The Awesome, Almost 100% True Adventures of Matt & Craz. Silberberg, Alan, illus. (ENG., Illus.). 336p. (J). (gr. 4-8). 2014. pap. 7.99 (978-1-4169-9433-6(5)) 2013. 16.99 (978-1-4169-9432-9(7)) Simon & Schuster Children's Publishing. (Aladdin).

Silver Dolphin en Español Editors. Disney Serie Aprendizaje: Disney Learn to Count. 2005. (SPA., Illus.). 22p. (J). bds. (978-970-718-250-9(4), Silver Dolphin en Español) Advanced Marketing, S. de R. L. de C. V.

—Disney Serie Aprendizaje: Disney Princesses Learn to Write. 2005. (SPA., Illus.). 22p. (J). bds. (978-970-718-248-6(2), Silver Dolphin en Español) Advanced Marketing, S. de R. L. de C. V.

—Disney Serie Aprendizaje: Disney Winnie the Pooh Learning Shapes. 2005. (SPA., Illus.). 22p. (J). bds. (978-970-718-249-3(0), Silver Dolphin en Español) Advanced Marketing, S. de R. L. de C. V.

Silver Dragon Books Staff, et al. Jump Start. 2012. (ENG., Illus.). 80p. pap., act. bk. ed. 5.99 (978-0-9830404-7-7(8), 9780983040477) Zenescope Entertainment.

Silvestri, Marc & Hawkins, Matt. Cyber Force Rebirth, Vol. 1. 2013. (ENG., Illus.). 160p. (YA). pap. 9.99 (978-1-60706-671-2(8), 9781607066712) Image Comics.

Simmonds, Posy. Lulu & the Chocolate Wedding. 2016. (ENG., Illus.). 32p. (J). (-k). pap. 12.99 (978-1-78344-407-6(X)) Andersen Pr. GBR. Dist: Independent Pubs. Group.

Simmons, Alex. Scooby-Doo in Dead & Let Spy, 1 vol. Pope, Robert, illus. 2010. (Scooby-Doo Graphic Novels Ser.: No. 1). (ENG.). 24p. (J). (gr. 2-5). 24.21 (978-1-59961-692-6(0)) Spotlight.

Simmons, Andrew & Averdonz, N. R. I Was an Eighth-Grade Ninja, 1 vol. Padilla, Ariel, illus. 2007. (Z Graphic Novels / Tomo Ser.). (ENG.). 160p. (J). (gr. 3-7). pap. 6.99 (978-0-310-71300-5(5)) Zondervan.

Simon, Jenne. Double Trouble. 2014. (Illus.). 32p. (J). (978-1-4844-2319-6(4)) Scholastic, Inc.

Simon, Kristen Koerner. Jack's Knack: Book Three of the Blue Forest Series: Book Three of the Blue Forest Series. 2010. (Illus.). 32p. (J). 12.99 (978-1-60706-190-8(2)) Image Comics.

Simonson, Louise. The Death of Balder. Garcia, Eduardo, illus. 2016. (Norse Myths: a Viking Graphic Novel Ser.). (ENG.). 56p. (gr. 3-4). lib. bdg. 27.99 (978-1-4965-3488-0(3)) Stone Arch Bks.

—Lex Luthor's Power Grab! Vecchio, Luciano, illus. 2015. (Superman: Comic Chapter Bks.). (ENG.). 88p. (gr. 3-7). lib. bdg. 21.32 (978-1-4965-0508-8(5)) Stone Arch Bks.

—Monster Magic, 1 vol. Schoening, Dan, illus. (Wonder Woman Ser.). (ENG.). 56p. (gr. 2-3). 2013. pap. 4.95 (978-1-4342-2260-2(8)) 2010. lib. bdg. 26.65 (978-1-4342-1884-1(8)) Stone Arch Bks. (DC Super Heroes).

—Snow White & the Seven Robots. Sanchez, Jimena, illus. 2015. (Far Out Fairy Tales Ser.). (ENG.). 40p. (gr. 3-4). lib. bdg. 25.32 (978-1-4342-9648-1(2)) Stone Arch Bks.

Simonson, Louise, et al. Far Out Fairy Tales. Frampton, Otis et al, illus. 2016. (Far Out Fairy Tales Ser.). (ENG.). 176p. (gr. 3-4). pap. 12.95 (978-1-4965-2511-6(6), Far Out Fairy Tales) Stone Arch Bks.

Simonson, Walter. Jurassic Park: Danger: Vol. 1, 1 vol. 2013. (Jurassic Park Ser.). (ENG.). 32p. (J). (gr. 4-8). lib. bdg. 24.21 (978-1-61479-183-6(X)) Spotlight.

—Jurassic Park: Don't Move!: Vol. 3, 1 vol. 2013. (Jurassic Park Ser.). (ENG.). 32p. (J). (gr. 4-8). lib. bdg. 24.21 (978-1-61479-185-0(6)) Spotlight.

—Jurassic Park: Leaving Jurassic Park: Vol. 4, 1 vol. 2013. (Jurassic Park Ser.). (ENG.). 32p. (J). (gr. 4-8). lib. bdg. 24.21 (978-1-61479-186-7(4)) Spotlight.

—Jurassic Park: The Miracle of Cloning: Vol. 2, 1 vol. 2013. (Jurassic Park Ser.). (ENG.). 32p. (J). (gr. 4-8). lib. bdg. 24.21 (978-1-61479-184-3(8)) Spotlight.

—Meltdown, 3 vols. Simonson, Louise et al, illus. 2003. (Wolverine Legends Ser.: Vol. 2). 200p. (YA). pap. 19.99 (978-0-7851-1048-4(8)) Marvel Worldwide, Inc.

—Thor by Walter Simonson Volume 3. 2013. (ENG., Illus.). 264p. (J). (gr. 4-17). pap. 29.99 (978-0-7851-8462-1(7)) Marvel Worldwide, Inc.

Simonson, Walter & Englehart, Steve. Jurassic Park. 2013. (Jurassic Park Ser.: 10). 32p. (J). (gr. 4-8). lib. bdg. 242.10 (978-1-61479-182-9(1)) Spotlight.

Simonson, Walter, et al. Fantastic Four Epic Collection: Into the Timestream. Buckler, Rich et al, illus. 2014. (ENG.). 504p. (J). (gr. 4-17). pap. 39.99 (978-0-7851-8895-7(9)) Marvel Worldwide, Inc.

Simpson, D. C. Closer to the Void: Ozy & Millie 2006-2007. 2008. 127p. pap. 12.45 (978-1-4357-0504-3(1)) Lulu Pr., Inc.

Simpson, Dana. Phoebe & Her Unicorn: A Heavenly Nostrils Chronicle. 2014. (Phoebe & Her Unicorn Ser.: 1). (Illus.). 222p. (J). lib. bdg. 20.85 (978-0-606-36144-6(8)) Turtleback Bks.

—Unicorn on a Roll. 2015. (Phoebe & Her Unicorn Ser.: 2). lib. bdg. 20.85 (978-0-606-36985-5(6)) Turtleback Bks.

—Unicorn on a Roll: Another Heavenly Nostrils Chronicle. 2015. (Phoebe & Her Unicorn Ser.: 2). (ENG., Illus.). 224p. (J). pap. 9.99 (978-1-4494-7076-0(9)) Andrews McMeel Publishing.

Sims, Chris & Bowers, Chad. Down Set Fight. 2014. (ENG., Illus.). 144p. (YA). pap. 19.99 (978-1-62010-116-2(5), 9781620101162) Oni Pr., Inc.

Sims, Guy A. & Myers, Walter Dean. Monster. Anyabwile, Dawud, illus. 2015. (Monster Ser.). (ENG.). 160p. (YA). (gr. 8). pap. 9.99 (978-0-06-227499-1(6)) HarperCollins Pubs.

Singley, George. Mutation. 2007. (Illus.). 144p. (YA). pap. 14.99 (978-0-9738388-6-2(8)) Speakeasy Comics CAN. Dist: Diamond Bk. Distributors.

Singley, George T. Silent Ghost. 2006. (Illus.). 136p. (YA). pap. 14.99 (978-0-9738388-8-6(4)) Speakeasy Comics CAN. Dist: Diamond Bk. Distributors.

Slavin, Bill & Melo, Esperanca. Big Top Otto. Slavin, Bill, illus. 2013. (Elephants Never Forget Ser.). (ENG., Illus.). 88p. (J). (gr. 3-6). 16.95 (978-1-55453-806-5(8)); Vol. 2. pap. 7.95 (978-1-55453-807-2(6)) Kids Can Pr., Ltd. CAN. Dist: Hachette Bk. Group.

Slingerland, Janet. Werewolves & States of Matter, 1 vol. Mosquito, Angel, illus. 2011. (Monster Science Ser.). (ENG.). 32p. (gr. 3-4). pap. 8.10 (978-1-4296-7333-4(8)); pap. 47.70 (978-1-4296-7334-1(6)); lib. bdg. 30.65 (978-1-4296-6578-0(5)) Capstone Press of Coughlan Cos. (Graphic Library).

Slott, Dan & Busiek, Kurt. Spider-Man - Lizard: No Turning Back. Frenz, Ron, illus. 2013. (ENG.). 112p. (J). (gr. 4-17). pap. 16.99 (978-0-7851-6008-3(6), Marvel Pr.) Disney Publishing Worldwide.

Slott, Dan & Caselli, Stefano. Ends of the Earth. Silas, Thony et al, illus. 2013. (ENG.). 192p. (J). (gr. 4-17). pap. 24.99 (978-0-7851-6006-9(X)) Marvel Worldwide, Inc.

Slott, Dan & Templeton, Ty. Batman Adventures. Templeton, Ty, illus. 2013. (Batman Adventures Ser.). (ENG., Illus.). 32p. (gr. 2-3). 158.20 (978-1-4342-8837-0(4)) Stone Arch Bks.

Slott, Dan & Waid, Mark. The Amazing Spider-Man - Flying Blind. Camuncoli, Giuseppe et al, illus. 2012. (ENG.). 120p. (J). (gr. 4-17). pap. 16.99 (978-0-7851-6002-1(7)) Marvel Worldwide, Inc.

Slott, Dan, et al. Masquerade in Red!, 1 vol. 2013. (Batman Adventures Ser.). (ENG.). 32p. (gr. 2-3). 22.60 (978-1-4342-6036-9(4)) Stone Arch Bks.

—Phantasm Strikes!, 1 vol. Burchett, Rick, illus. 2013. (Batman Adventures Ser.). (ENG.). 32p. (gr. 2-3). 22.60 (978-1-4342-6035-2(6)) Stone Arch Bks.

—Playing with Matches, 1 vol. Burchett, Rick, illus. 2013. (Batman Adventures Ser.). (ENG.). 32p. (gr. 2-3). 22.60 (978-1-4342-6034-5(8)) Stone Arch Bks.

—Target: Deadshot!, 1 vol. Templeton, Ty, illus. 2013. (Batman Adventures Ser.). (ENG.). 32p. (gr. 2-3). 22.60 (978-1-4342-6033-8(X)) Stone Arch Bks.

Smart, Jamie. Bear, Vol. 1. 2004. (ENG., Illus.). 144p. pap. 14.95 (978-1-59362-001-1(2), 9781593620011) Slave Labor Bks.

—Bunny vs. Monkey. Smart, Jamie, illus. 2016. (ENG., Illus.). 64p. (J). (gr. 2-5). pap. 7.99 (978-0-545-86184-7(5), Graphix) Scholastic, Inc.

The Smartest Thing. 2004. (YA). (978-0-9762904-8-3(0)) Layne Morgan Media, Inc.

Smarto, Luke, illus. A Donde Te Vas? 2003. 16p. (J). per. 0.75 (978-0-930201-05-0(1)) Frontline Pr.

Smibert, Angie. Memento Nora, 0 vols. 2013. (Memento Nora Ser.: 1). (ENG.). 192p. (J). (gr. 7-10). pap. 9.99 (978-1-4778-1624-0(0), 9781477816240, Amazon Children's Publishing) Amazon Publishing.

Smiley, Jess Smart. Upside down: a Vampire Tale: A Vampire Tale. 2012. (ENG., Illus.). 144p. (J). (gr. 2-5). pap. 9.95 (978-1-60309-088-9(6), 9781603090889) Top Shelf Productions.

Smith, Andrea P. Daniel Boone. 2012. (Illus.). 24p. (J). 63.60 (978-1-4488-5227-7(7)); pap. 10.60 (978-1-4488-5226-0(9)); lib. bdg. 25.25 (978-1-4488-5194-2(7)) Rosen Publishing Group, Inc., The. (PowerKids Pr.).

—Davy Crockett. 2012. (Illus.). 24p. (J). 63.60 (978-1-4488-5223-9(4)); pap. 10.60 (978-1-4488-5222-2(6)); lib. bdg. 25.25 (978-1-4488-5192-8(0)) Rosen Publishing Group, Inc., The. (PowerKids Pr.).

—The First Thanksgiving. 2012. (Illus.). 24p. (J). 63.60 (978-1-4488-5213-0(7)); pap. 10.60 (978-1-4488-5212-3(9)); lib. bdg. 25.25 (978-1-4488-5187-4(4)) Rosen Publishing Group, Inc., The. (PowerKids Pr.).

—Jim Bowie. 2012. (Illus.). 24p. (J). 63.60 (978-1-4488-5231-4(5)); pap. 10.60 (978-1-4488-5230-7(7)); lib. bdg. 25.25 (978-1-4488-5196-6(3)) Rosen Publishing Group, Inc., The. (PowerKids Pr.).

—The Journey of the Mayflower. 2012. (Illus.). 24p. (J). 63.60 (978-1-4488-5211-6(0)); pap. 10.60 (978-1-4488-5210-9(2)); lib. bdg. 25.25 (978-1-4488-5186-7(6)) Rosen Publishing Group, Inc., The. (PowerKids Pr.).

—The Mystery of Roanoke, the Lost Colony. 2012. (Illus.). 24p. (J). 63.60 (978-1-4488-5209-3(9)); pap. 10.60 (978-1-4488-5208-6(0)); lib. bdg. 25.25 (978-1-4488-5185-0(8)) Rosen Publishing Group, Inc., The. (PowerKids Pr.).

—Paul Bunyan. 2012. (Illus.). 24p. (J). 63.60 (978-1-4488-5221-5(8)); pap. 10.60 (978-1-4488-5220-8(X)); lib. bdg. 25.25 (978-1-4488-5191-1(2)) Rosen Publishing Group, Inc., The. (PowerKids Pr.).

—Pocahontas & John Smith. 2012. (Illus.). 24p. (J). 63.60 (978-1-4488-5219-2(6)); pap. 10.60 (978-1-4488-5218-5(8));

lib. bdg. 25.25 *(978-1-4488-5190-4(4))* Rosen Publishing Group, Inc., The. (PowerKids Pr.).

Smith, Anne Collins, et al. The Planet of Music. 2012. (Little Prince Ser.: 3). (ENG., Illus.). 56p. (J). (gr. 4-8). lib. bdg. 26.60 *(978-0-7613-8753-4(6)*, Graphic Universe™) Lerner Publishing Group.

Smith, Brian. The Intrepid EscapeGoat: Curse of the Buddha's Tooth. Conkling, Jon & DeVito, Michael A., eds. 2012. (ENG., Illus.). 96p. pap. 12.95 *(978-0-9832161-3-1(4)*, 9780983216131) Th3rd World Studios.

Smith, Brian W. Tree Mail. 2016. (ENG., Illus.). 120p. (J). (gr. 3-7). pap. 12.99 *(978-1-5067-0096-0(9))* Dark Horse Comics.

Smith, Bruce L. Song of Life. Lt. ed. 2006. (Illus.). 32p. (J). lib. bdg. *(978-1-934190-08-1(X))* Ocean Front Bk. Publishing, Inc.

Smith, Don. Political Power: Richard Nixon. 2012. (ENG.). 32p. pap. 3.99 *(978-0-9855911-3-7(7))* Bluewater Productions, Inc.

Smith-Henderson, Susie. The Adventures of Snorro & the Keepers from Sleep. 2009. 32p. pap. 14.18 *(978-0-557-08682-5(5))* Lulu Pr., Inc.

Smith, Ian. Emily & the Intergalactic Lemonade Stand. 2004. (ENG., Illus.). 96p. (gr. 1-18). pap. 12.95 *(978-0-943151-96-0(1)*, 9780943151960) Slave Labor Bks.

Smith, Jeff. Ghost Circles. Smith, Jeff & Hamaker, Steve, illus. 2008. (Bone Ser.: 7). (ENG.). 160p. (J). (gr. 4-7). 26.99 *(978-0-439-70629-2(7)*, Graphix) Scholastic, Inc.

—The Graphix Collection, 3 bks., Set. Smith, Jeff, illus. Incl. Great Cow Race. Hamaker, Steve, illus. (gr. 4-7). 26.99 *(978-0-439-70624-7(6))*; Out from Boneville. pap. 26.99 *(978-0-439-70623-0(8))*; (Illus.). 144p. (J). 2005. 2006. 54.89 *(978-0-439-79840-2(X)*, Graphix) Scholastic, Inc.

—The Great Cow Race. Smith, Jeff & Hamaker, Steve, illus. 2005. (Bone Ser.: 2). (ENG.). 144p. (J). (gr. 4-7). pap. 12.99 *(978-0-439-70639-1(4)*, Graphix) Scholastic, Inc.

—Little Mouse Gets Ready. 2009. (ENG., Illus.). 32p. (J). (gr. -1-3). 12.95 *(978-1-935179-01-6(2))* TOON Books / RAW Junior, LLC.

—Little Mouse Gets Ready. 2013. (Toon Books Level 1 Ser.). lib. bdg. 14.75 *(978-0-606-31593-7(4)*, Turtleback) Turtleback Bks.

—Little Mouse Gets Ready, Level 1. 2013. (ENG., Illus.). 32p. (J). (gr. -1-3). pap. 6.99 *(978-1-935179-24-5(1))* TOON Books / RAW Junior, LLC.

—Out from Boneville. Smith, Jeff, illus. 2005. (Bone Ser.: 1). (ENG., Illus.). 144p. (J). pap. 26.99 *(978-0-439-70623-0(8)*, Graphix) Scholastic, Inc.

Smith, Jeff & Sniegoski, Tom. Tall Tales. Smith, Jeff, illus. 2010. (Bone Ser.). (ENG., Illus.). 128p. (J). (gr. 4-7). pap. 12.99 *(978-0-545-14096-6(X)*, Graphix) Scholastic, Inc.

Smith, Matt. Barbarian Lord. Smith, Matt, illus. 2014. (ENG., Illus.). 176p. (YA). (gr. 7-12). 17.99 *(978-0-547-85906-4(6))* Houghton Mifflin Harcourt Publishing Co.

Smith, Paul, et al, illus. Avengers: Falcon. 2014. (ENG.). 216p. (J). (gr. 4-17). pap. 24.99 *(978-0-7851-8826-1(6))* Marvel Worldwide, Inc.

Smith, Shane W. The Lesser Evil, Book 3 Comic Book. Smith, Shane W., illus. 2012. (Illus.). 114p. pap. *(978-1-927384-04-6(4))* Zeta Comics.

Smith, Tod, ed. The Legend of Sleepy Hollow, 1 vol. 2007. (Graphic Horror Ser.). (ENG., Illus.). 32p. (gr. 5-8). 28.50 *(978-1-60270-060-4(5)*, Graphic Planet- Fiction) ABDO Publishing Co.

Smith, Tod G., contrib. by. Graphic Expeditions, 10 vols., Set. Incl. Getting to the Bottom of Global Warming: An Isabel Soto Investigation. Collins, Terry. Schulz, Barbara, illus. lib. bdg. 30.65 *(978-1-4296-3972-9(5))*; Mesa Verde Cliff Dwellers: An Isabel Soto Archaeology Adventure. Collins, Terry. Anderson, Bill, illus. lib. bdg. 30.65 *(978-1-4296-3971-2(7))*; Searching for UFOs: An Isabel Soto Investigation. Sautter, Aaron. lib. bdg. 30.65 *(978-1-4296-3974-3(1))*; Secrets of Martial Arts: An Isabel Soto History Adventure. Harbo, Christopher L. lib. bdg. 30.65 *(978-1-4296-3973-6(3))*; (gr. 3-4). (Graphic Expeditions Ser.). (ENG.). 32p. 2010. Set lib. bdg. 306.50 o.p. *(978-1-4296-4449-5(4)*, Graphic Library) Capstone Press of Coughlan Cos.

Smyth, Jimmy. Causeway Coast. 2013. 34p. pap. *(978-0-9569314-6-7(4))* Smith, Jimmy.

—Titanic the Untold Story. 2013. 34p. pap. *(978-0-9569314-4-3(8))* Smith, Jimmy.

Sneaks Q1 2003. 2003. (YA). pap. *(978-1-59182-405-3(2))* TOKYOPOP, Inc.

Sneaks Q2 2003. 2003. (YA). pap. *(978-1-59182-406-0(0))* TOKYOPOP, Inc.

Sneaks Q4 2003. 2003. (YA). pap. *(978-1-59182-408-4(7))* TOKYOPOP, Inc.

Snider, Brandon T. Slice of Life with Pizza Steve. 2015. (Uncle Grandpa Ser.). (ENG., Illus.). 80p. (J). (gr. 3-7). pap. 8.99 *(978-0-8431-8314-6(4)*, Cartoon Network Books) Penguin Young Readers Group.

Snider, Jesse Blaze. Muppet Snow White. Paroline, Shelli, illus. 2010. (Muppet Show Ser.). 112p. (J). (gr. 3-6). pap. 9.99 *(978-1-60886-574-1(6))* Boom! Studios.

—Return of Buzz Lightyear, Vol. 2. Watson, Nathan, illus. 2010. (Toy Story Ser.). (ENG.). 112p. (J). pap. 9.99 *(978-1-60886-557-4(6))* Boom! Studios.

—Return of Buzz Lightyear Vol. 2. Watson, Nathan, illus. 2010. (Toy Story Ser.). (ENG.). 112p. (J). 24.99 *(978-1-60886-558-1(4))* Boom! Studios.

—Toy Story: Some Assembly Required. Watson, Nathan, illus. 2010. (Toy Story Ser.). 112p. (J). pap. 9.99 *(978-1-60886-570-3(3))* Boom! Studios.

Sniegoski, Tom & Smith, Jeff. Tall Tales. Smith, Jeff, illus. 2010. (Bone Ser.). (ENG., Illus.). 128p. (J). (gr. 4-7). 26.99 *(978-0-545-14095-9(1)*, Graphix) Scholastic, Inc.

Soda, Masahito. Firefighter! Vol. 10: Daigo of Fire Company M. Soda, Masahito, illus. 2005. (Firefighter Ser.: Vol. 10). (ENG., Illus.). 208p. pap. 9.95 *(978-1-59116-635-1(7))* Viz Media.

—Firefighter! Vol. 14. 2006. (Firefighter Ser.). (ENG., Illus.). 208p. pap. 9.95 *(978-1-4215-0318-9(2))* Viz Media.

Sohmer, Ryan. Gutters, Vol. 2. 2012. (ENG., Illus.). 136p. (YA). 39.95 *(978-1-926838-15-1(7)*, 9781926838151, Dynamite Entertainment) Dynamic Forces, Inc.

—Least I Could Do Beginnings Volume 1: Look at Me: Look at Me. 2010. 32p. 19.95 *(978-0-9812163-3-1(1))* Blind Ferret Entertainment CAN. Dist: Diamond Bk. Distributors.

Sohn, Emily & Barnett III, Charles. A Crash Course in Forces & Motion with Max Axiom, Super Scientist. Erwin, Steve, illus. 2016. (Graphic Science Ser.). (ENG.). 32p. (gr. 3-4). pap. 8.10 *(978-1-5157-4638-6(0)*, Graphic Library) Capstone Press of Coughlan Cos.

Sohn, Emily & Timmons, Anne. Adventures in Sound with Max Axiom, Super Scientist, 1 vol. Martin, Cynthia, illus. 2007. (Graphic Science Ser.). (ENG.). 32p. (gr. 3-4). per. 8.10 *(978-0-7368-7889-0(0)*, Graphic Library) Capstone Press of Coughlan Cos.

Soileau, Hodges, illus. The Comic Book Mystery. 2003. (Boxcar Children Ser.). 106p. (gr. 4-7). 15.00 *(978-0-7569-1611-4(9))* Perfection Learning Corp.

Soley, Liesel. Can You Be an Artist? Soley, Liesel, illus. 2011. (Illus.). 28p. (J). (gr. -1-3). 16.95 *(978-1-935359-69-2(X))* Book Pubs. Network.

Solomon, Chad. Adventures of Rabbit & Bear Paws: The Voyageurs. 2008. (ENG.). 32p. pap. *(978-0-9739906-2-1(7))* Little Spirit Bear Productions CAN. Dist: Lone Pine Publishing.

Solomons, David. My Brother Is a Superhero. 2017. lib. bdg. 18.40 ***(978-0-606-39790-2(6))*** Turtleback Bks.

Solomons, David. My Gym Teacher Is an Alien Overlord. Ferguson, Laura Ellen, illus. 2016. (ENG.). 288p. (J). (gr. 3-7). 16.99 *(978-0-451-47494-0(5)*, Viking Books for Young Readers) Penguin Young Readers Group.

Song-i, Yoon. Saint Teresa of Avila, God's Troublemaker. 2014. (ENG., Illus.). 208p. (J). pap. 14.95 *(978-0-8198-9038-2(3))* Pauline Bks. & Media.

Sonishi, Kenji. Leave It to PET!, Vol. 4. Sonishi, Kenji, illus. 2010. (ENG., Illus.). 192p. (J). pap. 7.99 *(978-1-4215-2652-2(2))* Viz Media.

Sonneborn, Scott. Attack of the Zom-Bees! Esparza, Andres et al, illus. 2013. (Tiger Moth Ser.). (ENG.). 48p. (gr. 1-3). pap. 6.19 *(978-1-4342-3871-9(7))* Stone Arch Bks.

—Beware Our Power!, 1 vol. Schoening, Dan, illus. 2011. (Green Lantern Ser.). (ENG.). 56p. (gr. 2-3). pap. 4.95 *(978-1-4342-3086-7(4)*, DC Super Heroes) Stone Arch Bks.

—The Good, the Bad, & the Monkeys, 1 vol. Bradley, Jessica, illus. 2013. (Comics Land Ser.). (ENG.). 32p. (gr. k-2). 7.95 *(978-1-4342-6283-7(9))*; lib. bdg. 25.32 *(978-1-4342-4945-6(X))* Stone Arch Bks.

—Pete Bogg: King of the Frogs. Aburtov, illus. 2013. (Pete Bogg Ser.). (ENG.). 48p. (gr. 1-3). pap. 5.95 *(978-1-4342-3872-6(5))*; lib. bdg. 23.99 *(978-1-4342-3284-7(0))* Stone Arch Bks.

—Prisoner of the Penguin!, 1 vol. Vecchio, Luciano, illus. 2014. (Batman: Comic Chapter Bks.). (ENG.). 88p. (gr. 3-7). 21.32 *(978-1-4342-9131-8(6))* Stone Arch Bks.

—Tiger Moth: Attack of the Zom-Bees!, 1 vol. Esparza, Andres, illus. 2013. (Tiger Moth Ser.). (ENG.). 48p. (gr. 1-3). lib. bdg. 23.99 *(978-1-4342-3283-0(2))* Stone Arch Bks.

Sonneborn, Scott, et al. Killer Croc Hunter, 1 vol. (Batman Ser.). (ENG., Illus.). 56p. (gr. 2-3). 2013. pap. 4.95 *(978-1-4342-2258-9(6))* 2010. lib. bdg. 26.65 *(978-1-4342-1876-6(7))* Stone Arch Bks. (DC Super Heroes).

—Shell Shocker, 1 vol. Doescher, Erik, illus. 2011. (Flash Ser.). (ENG.). 56p. (gr. 2-3). pap. 4.95 *(978-1-4342-3092-8(9)*, DC Super Heroes) Stone Arch Bks.

Sonoda, Hideki. Pokémon: Zoroark: Master of Illusions. 2011. (ENG.). 192p. (J). pap. 7.99 *(978-1-4215-4221-8(8))* Viz Media.

Soo, Kean. Jellaby, 1 vol. 2014. (Jellaby Ser.). (ENG.). 184p. (gr. 4-6). 55.98 *(978-1-4342-9601-6(6))* Stone Arch Bks.

—The Lost Monster. 2014. (Jellaby Ser.). (ENG.). 160p. (gr. 4-8). 27.99 *(978-1-4342-9195-0(2))* Stone Arch Bks.

—Monster in the City. 2014. (Jellaby Ser.). (ENG., Illus.). 184p. (gr. 4-8). pap. 12.95 *(978-1-4342-6421-3(1))* Stone Arch Bks.

Soo, Kean, illus. The Baker's Run. 2015. (March Grand Prix Ser.). (ENG.). 48p. (gr. 1-3). lib. bdg. 33.32 *(978-1-4342-9640-5(7))* Capstone Young Readers of Coughlan Cos.

—The Great Desert Rally. 2015. (March Grand Prix Ser.). (ENG.). 48p. (gr. 1-3). lib. bdg. 33.32 *(978-1-4342-9641-2(5))* Capstone Young Readers of Coughlan Cos.

—March Grand Prix: The Fast & the Furriest. 2015. (March Grand Prix Ser.). (ENG.). 144p. (gr. 1-3). pap. 14.95 *(978-1-62370-171-0(6))* Capstone Young Readers of Coughlan Cos.

—The Race at Harewood. 2015. (March Grand Prix Ser.). (ENG.). 48p. (gr. 1-3). lib. bdg. 33.32 *(978-1-4342-9639-9(3))* Capstone Young Readers of Coughlan Cos.

Sophie-chan. The Ocean of Secrets, Vol. 1. 2017. (ENG., Illus.). 176p. (YA). pap. 10.99 ***(978-1-4278-5714-9(8)***, 9781427857149) TOKYOPOP, Inc.

Soundprints Staff. Old MacDonald: And Other Favorites. 2005. (Meet Mother Goose Ser.). (ENG., Illus.). 36p. (J). 10.95 *(978-1-931465-30-4(4))* Soundprints.

Southey, Robert. Goldilocks & the Three Bears. 2005. (Classics Illustrated Junior Ser.). (Illus.). 32p. per. 5.99 *(978-1-894998-21-5(9))* Lake, Jack Productions, Inc. CAN. Dist: Hushion Hse. Publishing, Ltd.

Spanish Graphic Novels, 6 vols., Set. 2010. (Graphic Spin Ser.). (SPA., Illus.). 40p. 151.92 *(978-1-4342-2100-1(8))* Capstone Press of Coughlan Cos.

Spears, Rick. Black Metal Volume 3: Darkness Enthroned: Darkness Enthroned. 2014. (ENG., Illus.). 160p. (YA). pap. 11.99 *(978-1-934964-82-8(4)*, 9781934964828) Oni Pr., Inc.

Specter, Baron. Chasing Whales Aboard the Charles W. Morgan, 1 vol., Bk. 2. Evans, Dustin, illus. 2010. (Ghostly Graphic Adventures Ser.). (ENG.). 32p. (gr. 4-6). 28.50 *(978-1-60270-771-9(5)*, Graphic Planet- Fiction) ABDO Publishing Co.

—Dodging Danger on the Dartmouth, 1 vol., Bk. 1. Evans, Dustin, illus. 2010. (Ghostly Graphic Adventures Ser.). (ENG.). 32p. (J). (gr. 3-6). 28.50 *(978-1-60270-770-2(7))* ABDO Publishing Co.

—Drama at Dungeon Rock: #6, 1 vol. Evans, Dustin, illus. 2010. (Ghostly Graphic Adventures Ser.). (ENG.). 32p. (J). (gr. 3-6). 28.50 *(978-1-60270-775-7(8))* ABDO Publishing Co.

—The Lighthouse of Terror, 1 vol., Bk. 3. Evans, Dustin, illus. 2010. (Ghostly Graphic Adventures Ser.). (ENG.). 32p. (J). (gr. 3-6). 28.50 *(978-1-60270-772-6(3))* ABDO Publishing Co.

—The Spooky Short Sands Shipwreck: #4, 1 vol. Evans, Dustin, illus. 2010. (Ghostly Graphic Adventures Ser.). (ENG.). 32p. (J). (gr. 3-6). 28.50 *(978-1-60270-773-3(1))* ABDO Publishing Co.

—The Star Island Spirits: #5, 1 vol. Evans, Dustin, illus. 2010. (Ghostly Graphic Adventures Ser.). (ENG.). 32p. (J). (gr. 3-6). 28.50 *(978-1-60270-774-0(X))* ABDO Publishing Co.

Spencer, Nick. Morning Glories, Vol. 4. 2013. (ENG., Illus.). 216p. pap. 14.99 *(978-1-60706-727-6(7)*, 9781607067276) Image Comics.

Spencer, Nick & Hickman, Jonathan. Avengers - Prelude to Infinity, Vol. 3. Caselli, Stefano, illus. 2014. (ENG.). 152p. (YA). (gr. 8-17). pap. 19.99 *(978-0-7851-6654-2(8))* Marvel Worldwide, Inc.

Spider-Man & Friends. 2003. (J). per. *(978-1-57657-858-2(5))* Paradise Pr., Inc.

Spiegelman, Art. Jack & the Box, 1 vol. 2013. (Toon Bks). (ENG.). 36p. (J). (gr. k-1). lib. bdg. 27.07 *(978-1-61479-151-5(1))* Spotlight.

—Jack & the Box. Hayes, Geoffrey, illus. 2008. (ENG.). 32p. (J). (gr. -1-3). 12.95 *(978-0-9799238-3-8(2))* TOON Books / RAW Junior, LLC.

Spiegelman, Art & Mouly, Françoise. It Was a Dark & Silly Night... Spiegelman, Art & Mouly, Françoise, illus. 2003. (Little Lit Ser.: Vol. 3). (Illus.). 48p. (J). (gr. 1-18). 19.99 *(978-0-06-028628-6(8))* HarperCollins Pubs.

Spiegelman, Nadja. Zig & Wikki in Something Ate My Homework. Loeffler, Trade, illus. 2013. (ENG.). 40p. (J). (gr. -1-3). pap. 6.99 *(978-1-935179-38-2(1))* TOON Books / RAW Junior, LLC.

—Zig & Wikki in the Cow. Loeffler, Trade, illus. 2012. (ENG.). 40p. (J). (gr. -1-3). 12.95 *(978-1-935179-15-3(2))* TOON Books / RAW Junior, LLC.

Spiegelman, Nadja & Loeffler, Trade. Zig & Wikki in Something Ate My Homework, 1 vol. 2013. (Toon Bks). (ENG.). 40p. (J). (gr. 2-3). lib. bdg. 27.07 *(978-1-61479-157-7(0))* Spotlight.

—Zig & Wikki in Something Ate My Homework. 2013. (Toon Books Level 3 Ser.). lib. bdg. 14.75 *(978-0-606-32252-2(3)*, Turtleback) Turtleback Bks.

Spiewak, Chet. Vinney the Bug Man: The Journey Begins. 2007. (Illus.). 80p. (J). per. 9.95 *(978-0-9785827-1-5(3))* CWS Studios, Inc.

Spiotto, Joey. Firefly: Back from the Black. 2017. (ENG., Illus.). 160p. 14.95 ***(978-1-78565-375-9(X)***, Titan Bks.) Titan Bks. Ltd. GBR. Dist: Penguin Random Hse. LLC.

Spires, Ashley. Binky: License to Scratch. Spires, Ashley, illus. 2013. (Binky Adventure Ser.). (ENG., Illus.). 64p. (J). (gr. 2-5). 16.95 *(978-1-55453-963-5(3))*; pap. 7.95 *(978-1-55453-964-2(1))* Kids Can Pr., Ltd. CAN. Dist: Hachette Bk. Group.

—Binky Takes Charge. Spires, Ashley, illus. 2012. (Binky Adventure Ser.: 4). (ENG., Illus.). 64p. (J). (gr. 2-5). 7.95 *(978-1-55453-768-6(1))*; 16.95 *(978-1-55453-703-7(7))* Kids Can Pr., Ltd. CAN. Dist: Hachette Bk. Group.

SpongeBob Squarepants WOW! Scratchers. 2005. 4p. (J). 6.99 *(978-1-59524-031-6(4))* Giddy Up, LLC.

SpongeBob WOW Paper Scribble & Giggle Pad. 2004. 36p. (J). 7.99 *(978-1-59524-006-4(3))* Giddy Up, LLC.

SpongeBob WOW! Surprise & Shine. 2005. 4p. (J). 6.99 *(978-1-59524-049-1(7))* Giddy Up, LLC.

Sports Illustrated Kids Graphic Novels, 6 vols., Set. 2010. (Sports Illustrated Kids Graphic Novels Ser.). (ENG.). (gr. 3-8). pap. 41.70 *(978-1-4342-2483-5(X))* Stone Arch Bks.

Sports Illustrated Kids Graphic Novels Fall 2010 Set, 1 vol., Set. 2010. (Sports Illustrated Kids Graphic Novels Ser.). (ENG.). 56p. (gr. 2-3). 133.25 *(978-1-4342-2692-1(1))* Stone Arch Bks.

Spotlight Editors. Laugh with a Test Case. Gorelick, Victor, illus. 2007. (Archie Digest Library). (ENG.). 80p. (J). (gr. 3-6). 24.21 *(978-1-59961-284-3(4))* Spotlight.

—Quiet Please. 2007. (Archie Digest Library). (Illus.). 80p. (J). (gr. 3-6). 24.21 *(978-1-59961-260-7(7))* Spotlight.

St. Pierre, Joe, creator. Bold Blood. 2005. (YA). per. 5.95 *(978-0-9772727-0-9(2))* Astronaut Ink.

Stahlberg, L. R. The Three Musketeers. Cabrera, Eva, illus. 2016. (Graphic Revolve: Common Core Editions Ser.). (ENG.). 72p. (gr. 2-3). pap. 6.95 *(978-1-4965-3565-8(0)*, Graphic Revolve) Stone Arch Bks.

—The Three Musketeers. Cabrera, Eva, illus. 2016. (Graphic Revolve: Common Core Editions Ser.). (ENG.). 72p. (gr. 2-3). lib. bdg. 27.99 *(978-1-4965-3563-4(4)*, Graphic Revolve) Stone Arch Bks.

Stahlberg, L. R & Peters, Stephanie True. Graphic Revolve: Common Core Editions. Cabrera, Eva & Cano, Fern, illus. 2016. (Graphic Revolve: Common Core Editions Ser.). (ENG.). 72p. (gr. 2-3). 727.74 *(978-1-4965-3578-8(2)*, Graphic Revolve) Stone Arch Bks.

Stahnke, Rich. Furious Fist of the Drunken Monkey: Origin of the Species #3. 2007. (Illus.). 2.95 *(978-0-9791192-4-8(3))* Silent Devil Productions.

Stanley, John. Melvin Monster, 3 vols., Vol. 2. 2010. (John Stanley Library). (ENG., Illus.). 112p. 24.95 *(978-1-77046-003-4(9)*, 9781770460034) Drawn & Quarterly Pubns. CAN. Dist: Macmillan.

—Melvin Monster: The John Stanley Library, 3 vols. 2011. (John Stanley Library). (ENG., Illus.). 112p. 24.95 *(978-1-77046-030-0(6)*, 9781770460300) Drawn & Quarterly Pubns. CAN. Dist: Macmillan.

Staub, Rusty. Hello, Mr. Met. Moore, Danny, illus. 2006. 24p. (J). lib. bdg. 17.95 *(978-1-932888-82-9(9))* Mascot Bks., Inc.

Stauffacher, Sue & Love, Comfort. Wireman. 2007. (Illus.). 159p. (J). pap. *(978-0-9709811-4-1(7))* Grand Valley State Univ.

Steele, Michael A. High-Tech Terror, 1 vol. Schoening, Dan, illus. 2011. (Green Lantern Ser.). (ENG.). 56p. (gr. 2-3). pap. 4.95 *(978-1-4342-3084-3(8))*; lib. bdg. 26.65 *(978-1-4342-2609-9(3))* Stone Arch Bks. (DC Super Heroes).

Steinberg, D. J. Mac Attack! Smith, Brian, illus. 2008. (Daniel Boom Aka Loud Boy Ser.: 2). (ENG.). 96p. (J). (gr. 1-4). pap. 6.99 *(978-0-448-44699-8(5)*, Grosset & Dunlap) Penguin Young Readers Group.

Stephens, Sarah Hines. Creature of Chaos. Schoening, Dan, illus. 2013. (Wonder Woman Ser.). (ENG.). 56p. (gr. 2-3). pap. 4.95 *(978-1-4342-2256-5(X)*, DC Super Heroes) Stone Arch Bks.

—Superman Classic: Superman & the Mayhem of Metallo. Mada Design Staff, illus. 2010. (Superman Classics). (ENG.). 24p. (J). (gr. -1-3). pap. 3.99 *(978-0-06-188529-7(0)*, HarperFestival) HarperCollins Pubs.

Stern, Roger. Avengers: Absolute Vision. Akin, Ian et al, illus. 2014. (ENG.). 392p. (J). (gr. 4-17). pap. 39.99 *(978-0-7851-8535-2(6))* Marvel Worldwide, Inc.

Stern, Roger & Defalco, Tom. Avengers Epic Collection: Judgement Day. Pollard, Keith et al, illus. 2014. (ENG.). 464p. (J). (gr. 4-17). pap. 34.99 *(978-0-7851-8894-0(0))* Marvel Worldwide, Inc.

Sternin, Joshua & Ventimilia, J. R. Teenage Mutant Ninja Turtles Animated Volume 3: the Showdown: The Showdown. 2014. (Teenage Mutant Ninja Turtles Ser.). (ENG., Illus.). 132p. (J). (gr. 2-5). pap. 7.99 *(978-1-61377-833-3(3)*, 9781613778333) Idea & Design Works, LLC.

Stevens, Cara J. The Ender Eye Prophecy: An Unofficial Graphic Novel for Minecrafters, #3. Norgren, David & Norgren, Elias, illus. 2016. (Unofficial Graphic Novel for Minecrafters Ser.: 3). (ENG.). 192p. (J). (gr. 2-7). pap. 11.99 *(978-1-5107-1483-0(9)*, Sky Pony Pr.) Skyhorse Publishing Co., Inc.

Stevens, Eric & Fuentes, Benny. Skateboard Sonar, 1 vol. Sandoval, Gerardo, illus. 2010. (Sports Illustrated Kids Graphic Novels Ser.). (ENG.). 56p. (gr. 2-3). pap. 7.19 *(978-1-4342-2295-4(0))*; 26.65 *(978-1-4342-1910-7(0))* Stone Arch Bks.

Stevens, Eric, et al. The Menace of Metallo, 1 vol. 2013. (Superman Ser.). (ENG., Illus.). 56p. (gr. 2-3). pap. 4.95 *(978-1-4342-1371-6(4)*, DC Super Heroes) Stone Arch Bks.

—The Revenge of Clayface, 1 vol. Schigiel, Gregg, illus. (Batman Ser.). (ENG.). 56p. (gr. 2-3). 2013. pap. 4.95 *(978-1-4342-1369-3(2))* 2009. lib. bdg. 26.65 *(978-1-4342-1149-1(5))* Stone Arch Bks. (DC Super Heroes).

Stevens, R. Bacon Is a Vegetable, Coffee Is a Vitamin, Vol. 2. 2014. (ENG., Illus.). 136p. (YA). pap. 19.99 *(978-1-62010-091-2(6)*, 9781620100912) Oni Pr., Inc.

—Diesel Sweeties: I'M a Rocker, I Rock Out. 2013. (ENG., Illus.). 136p. (YA). pap. 19.99 *(978-1-62010-090-5(8)*, 9781620100905) Oni Pr., Inc.

Stevens, Terry. The Battle at Longshore Causeway. 2006. 64p. pap. *(978-1-84401-751-5(6))* Athena Pr.

Stevenson, James. El Tiovivo de Don Ramiro. (Coleccion el Faro Azul). (SPA., Illus.). (J). 8.95 *(978-84-348-1852-1(3)*, SM005) SM Ediciones ESP. Dist: Continental Bk. Co., Inc.

Stevenson, Robert Louis. Classics Illustrated #7: Dr. Jekyll & Mr. Hyde. 2009. (Classics Illustrated Graphic Novels Ser.). (ENG., Illus.). 56p. (J). (gr. 3-9). 9.95 *(978-1-59707-171-0(4)*, 9781597071710) Papercutz.

—Kidnapped. Kennedy, Cam, illus. 2007. (ENG.). 64p. (YA). (gr. 5). pap. 11.95 *(978-0-88776-843-9(1)*, Tundra Bks.) Tundra Bks. CAN. Dist: Penguin Random Hse. LLC.

—Kidnapped. 2006. (Classics Ser.). (Illus.). 80p. (YA). (gr. 4-7). per. 8.95 *(978-1-56254-873-5(5))* Saddleback Educational Publishing, Inc.

—Treasure Island. 2014. (Graphic Classics Ser.). 48p. (gr. 3-6). 37.10 *(978-1-908973-91-7(9))* Book Hse. GBR. Dist: Black Rabbit Bks.

—Treasure Island. Stevenson, Robert Louis & Hamilton, Tim, illus. 2005. (ENG.). 176p. (J). (gr. 3-7). 10.99 *(978-0-14-240470-6(5)*, Puffin Books) Penguin Young Readers Group.

Stewart, Yale. The Amazing Adventures of Superman! Stewart, Yale, illus. 2014. (Amazing Adventures of Superman! Ser.). (ENG., Illus.). 32p. (gr. k-2). 101.28 *(978-1-4795-5816-2(8)*, DC Super Heroes) Stone Arch Bks.

—Battle of the Super Heroes!, 1 vol. Stewart, Yale, illus. 2014. (Amazing Adventures of Superman! Ser.). (ENG., Illus.). 32p. (gr. k-2). 25.32 *(978-1-4795-5731-8(5)*, DC Super Heroes) Stone Arch Bks.

Stilton, Geronimo. Dinosaurs in Action. Cooper-McGuinness, Nanette, tr. from ITA. 2011. (Geronimo Stilton Graphic Novels Ser.). (ENG., Illus.). 56p. (J). (gr. 2-6). 9.99 *(978-1-59707-239-7(7)*, 9781597072397) Papercutz.

—The First Samurai. Cooper-McGuinness, Nanette, tr. from ITA. 2013. (Geronimo Stilton Graphic Novels Ser.). (ENG., Illus.). 56p. (J). (gr. 2-6). 9.99 *(978-1-59707-385-1(7)*, 9781597073851) Papercutz.

—Following the Trail of Marco Polo, No. 4. Cooper-McGuinness, Nanette, tr. 2010. (Geronimo Stilton Graphic Novels Ser.). (ENG., Illus.). 56p. (J). (gr. 2-6). 9.99 *(978-1-59707-188-8(9)*, 9781597071888) Papercutz.

—Geronimo Stilton Boxed Set: Vol. #4 - 6. 2011. (Geronimo Stilton Graphic Novels Ser.). (ENG., Illus.). 168p. (J). (gr. 2-6). 29.99 *(978-1-59707-271-7(0)*, 9781597072717) Papercutz.

—Geronimo Stilton Boxed Set Vol. #7-9. 2012. (Geronimo Stilton Graphic Novels Ser.). (ENG., Illus.). 168p. (J). (gr. 2-6). 29.99 *(978-1-59707-344-8(X)*, 9781597073448) Papercutz.

—Geronimo Stilton Saves the Olympics. Cooper-McGuinness, Nanette, tr. from ITA. 10th ed. 2012. (Geronimo Stilton Graphic Novels Ser.). (ENG., Illus.). 56p. (J). (gr. 2-6). 9.99 *(978-1-59707-319-6(9)*, 9781597073196) Papercutz.

—The Great Ice Age. Cooper-McGuinness, Nanette, tr. 2010. (Geronimo Stilton Graphic Novels Ser.). (ENG., Illus.). 56p. (J). (gr. 2-6). 9.99 *(978-1-59707-202-1(8)*, 9781597072021) Papercutz.

—Play It Again, Mozart! Cooper-McGuinness, Nanette, tr. 2011. (Geronimo Stilton Graphic Novels Ser.). (ENG., Illus.). 56p. (J). (gr. 2-6). 9.99 *(978-1-59707-276-2(1)*, 9781597072762) Papercutz.

—The Weird Book Machine. Cooper-McGuinness, Nanette, tr. from ITA. 2012. (Geronimo Stilton Graphic Novels Ser.). (ENG., Illus.). 56p. (J). (gr. 2-6). 9.99 *(978-1-59707-295-3(8)*, 9781597072953) Papercutz.

—We'll Always Have Paris. Cooper-McGuinness, Nanette, tr. from ITA. 2012. (Geronimo Stilton Graphic Novels Ser.). (ENG., Illus.). 56p. (J). (gr. 2-6). 9.99 *(978-1-59707-347-9(4)*, 9781597073479) Papercutz.

—Who Stole the Mona Lisa? Cooper-McGuinness, Nanette, tr. 2010. (Geronimo Stilton Graphic Novels Ser.). (ENG., Illus.).

C
D

56p. (J). (gr. 2-6). 9.99 *(978-1-59707-221-2(4),* 9781597072212) Papercutz.

Stilton, Thea. Revenge of the Lizard Club. Cooper-McGuinness, Nanette, tr. from ITA. 2013. (Thea Stilton Graphic Novels Ser.). (ENG., Illus.). 56p. (J). (gr. 1-5). 9.99 *(978-1-59707-430-8(6),* 9781597074308) Papercutz.

—The Secret of Whale Island, No. 1. Cooper-McGuinness, Nanette, tr. from ITA. 2013. (Thea Stilton Graphic Novels Ser.). (ENG., Illus.). 56p. (J). (gr. 1-5). 9.99 *(978-1-59707-403-2(9),* 9781597074032) Papercutz.

Stine, R. L. Creepy Creatures. Hernandez, Gabriel et al, illus. 2006. (Goosebumps Graphix Ser.: 1). (ENG.). 144p. (J). (gr. 3-7). pap. 9.99 *(978-0-439-84125-2(9),* Graphix) Scholastic, Inc.

—Dr. Maniac vs. Robby Schwartz. 2008. (Goosebumps HorrorLand Ser.: No. 5). (J). 34.99 *(978-1-60640-953-4(0))* Findaway World, LLC.

—Dr. Maniac Will See You Now. 2013. (Goosebumps Most Wanted Ser.: 5). (ENG.). 160p. (J). (gr. 3-7). pap. 6.99 *(978-0-545-41802-7(X),* Scholastic Paperbacks) Scholastic, Inc.

—Dr. Maniac Will See You Now. 2013. (Goosebumps Most Wanted Ser.: 5). lib. bdg. 17.20 *(978-0-606-32376-5(7),* Turtleback) Turtleback Bks.

—Slappy's Tales of Horror (Goosebumps Graphix) Roman, Dave et al, illus. 2015. (Goosebumps Graphix Ser.). (ENG.). 176p. (J). (gr. 3-7). pap. 12.99 *(978-0-545-83595-4(X),* Graphix) Scholastic, Inc.

—The Werewolf of Fever Swamp. 2009. (Goosebumps Ser.: 11). lib. bdg. 17.20 *(978-0-606-00241-7(3),* Turtleback) Turtleback Bks.

Stoker, Bram. Dracula. Williams, Anthony, illus. 2014. (ENG.). 32p. 8.95 *(978-1-78404-355-1(9))* Arcturus Publishing GBR. Dist: Bookmasters Distribution.

—Dracula. DiTerlizzi, Tony, illus. 2009. (Puffin Classics Ser.). (ENG.). 640p. (J). (gr. 5-7). 6.99 *(978-0-14-132566-8(6),* Puffin Books) Penguin Young Readers Group.

—Mummy, 1 vol. Miroglio, Brian, illus. 2007. (Graphic Horror Ser.). (ENG.). 32p. (gr. 3-7). 28.50 *(978-1-60270-061-1(3),* Graphic Planet- Fiction) ABDO Publishing Co.

Stone, Adam. The Apollo 13 Mission. 2014. (Disaster Stories Ser.). (ENG., Illus.). 24p. (J). (gr. 3-8). 29.95 *(978-1-62617-149-7(1),* Black Sheep) Bellwether Media.

Stone Arch Books. April Showers & Cinco de Mayo, 1 vol. Nguyen, Dustin, illus. 2014. (Batman: Li'l Gotham Ser.). (ENG.). 32p. (gr. 2-3). 22.60 *(978-1-4342-9220-9(7))* Stone Arch Bks.

—Batman: Li'l Gotham, 1 vol. Nguyen, Dustin Tri, illus. 2014. (Batman: Li'l Gotham Ser.). (ENG.). 32p. (gr. 2-3). 135.60 *(978-1-4342-9529-3(X))* Stone Arch Bks.

—Christmas & New Year's Eve, 1 vol. Nguyen, Dustin, illus. 2014. (Batman: Li'l Gotham Ser.). (ENG.). 32p. (gr. 2-3). 22.60 *(978-1-4342-9217-9(7))* Stone Arch Bks.

—Halloween & Thanksgiving, 1 vol. Nguyen, Dustin, illus. 2014. (Batman: Li'l Gotham Ser.). (ENG.). 32p. (gr. 2-3). 22.60 *(978-1-4342-9208-7(8))* Stone Arch Bks.

—Mother's Day & Father's Day, 1 vol. Nguyen, Dustin, illus. 2014. (Batman: Li'l Gotham Ser.). (ENG.). 32p. (gr. 2-3). 22.60 *(978-1-4342-9221-6(5))* Stone Arch Bks.

—St. Patrick's Day & Easter, 1 vol. Nguyen, Dustin, illus. 2014. (Batman: Li'l Gotham Ser.). (ENG.). 32p. (gr. 2-3). 22.60 *(978-1-4342-9219-3(3))* Stone Arch Bks.

—Valentine's Day & the Lunar New Year, 1 vol. Nguyen, Dustin, illus. 2014. (Batman: Li'l Gotham Ser.). (ENG.). 32p. (gr. 2-3). 22.60 *(978-1-4342-9218-6(5))* Stone Arch Bks.

Stone Arch Books & Fisch, Sholly. DC Super Friends, 1 vol. 2014. (DC Super Friends Ser.). (ENG.). 32p. (gr. 1-2). 90.40 *(978-1-4342-9526-2(5))* Stone Arch Bks.

Stone Arch Books (Firm: Afton, Minn.) Staff. Hansel & Gretel: The Graphic Novel, 1 vol. Dietrich, Sean, illus. 2008. (Graphic Spin Ser.). (ENG.). 40p. (gr. 1-3). pap. 5.95 *(978-1-4342-0863-7(X),* Graphic Revolve) Stone Arch Bks.

Stone Arch Books Staff. Beauty & the Beast: The Graphic Novel, 1 vol. Feldman, Luke, illus. 2008. (Graphic Spin Ser.). (ENG.). 40p. (gr. 1-3). pap. 5.95 *(978-1-4342-0861-3(3),* Graphic Revolve) Stone Arch Bks.

—Cinderella: The Graphic Novel, 1 vol. Timmins, Jeffrey Stewart, illus. 2008. (Graphic Spin Ser.). (ENG.). 40p. (gr. 1-3). pap. 5.95 *(978-1-4342-0860-6(5),* Graphic Revolve) Stone Arch Bks.

—Jack & the Beanstalk: The Graphic Novel, 1 vol. Tercio, Ricardo, illus. 2008. (Graphic Spin Ser.). (ENG.). 40p. (gr. 1-3). pap. 5.95 *(978-1-4342-0862-0(1),* Graphic Revolve) Stone Arch Bks.

—John Henry - Hammerin' Hero. Evergreen, Nelson, illus. 2010. (Graphic Spin Ser.). (ENG.). 40p. (gr. 1-3). pap. 5.95 *(978-1-4342-2265-7(9),* Graphic Revolve) Stone Arch Bks.

—The Legend of Johnny Appleseed. Lamoreaux, M. A. & Lamoreaux, Michelle, illus. 2010. (Graphic Spin Ser.). (ENG.). 40p. (gr. 1-3). pap. 5.95 *(978-1-4342-2266-4(7),* Graphic Revolve) Stone Arch Bks.

—Pecos Bill: Colossal Cowboy. Weber, Lisa K., illus. 2010. (Graphic Spin Ser.). (ENG.). 40p. (gr. 1-3). pap. 5.95 *(978-1-4342-2267-1(5),* Graphic Revolve) Stone Arch Bks.

—Red Riding Hood: The Graphic Novel, 1 vol. Rivas, Victor, illus. 2008. (Graphic Spin Ser.). (ENG.). 40p. (gr. 1-3). pap. 5.95 *(978-1-4342-0865-1(6),* Graphic Revolve) Stone Arch Bks.

—Robin Hood, 1 vol. Tobon, Sara, tr. Tanner, Jennifer, illus. 2010. (Classic Fiction Ser.). (ENG & SPA.). 72p. (gr. 2-3). pap. 7.15 *(978-1-4342-2275-6(6),* Graphic Revolve en Español) Stone Arch Bks.

—Rumpelstiltskin: The Graphic Novel, 1 vol. Alanis, Erik Valdez Y., illus. 2008. (Graphic Spin Ser.). (ENG.). 40p. (gr. 1-3). pap. 5.95 *(978-1-4342-0864-4(8),* Graphic Revolve) Stone Arch Bks.

—The Tall Tale of Paul Bunyan. Blecha, Aaron, illus. 2010. (Graphic Spin Ser.). (ENG.). 40p. (gr. 1-3). pap. 5.95 *(978-1-4342-2268-8(3),* Graphic Revolve) Stone Arch Bks.

Stone Arch Books Staff & Sutton, Laurie S. Superman: Comic Chapter Books, 1 vol. Vecchio, Luciano, illus. 2014. (Superman: Comic Chapter Bks.). (ENG.). 88p. (gr. 3-7). 42.64 *(978-1-4342-9378-7(5),* DC Super Heroes) Stone Arch Bks.

Stone Arch Books Staff, et al. Batman: Comic Chapter Books, 1 vol. Vecchio, Luciano, illus. 2014. (Batman: Comic Chapter Bks.). (ENG.). 32p. (gr. k-2). 42.64 *(978-1-4342-9377-0(7),* DC Super Heroes) Stone Arch Bks.

Storck, Patrick. Dreamworks Shrek Comics Collection. 2016. (J). lib. bdg. 20.85 *(978-0-606-39427-7(3))* Turtleback Bks.

Storck, Patrick & Rik Hoskin. Dreamworks Madagascar Comics Collection. 2017. (J). lib. bdg. 20.85 *(978-0-606-39426-0(5))* Turtleback Bks.

Storrie, Paul D. Beowulf: Monster Slayer. Randall, Ron, illus. 2008. (Graphic Myths & Legends Ser.). (ENG.). 48p. (gr. 4-8). pap. 8.95 *(978-0-8225-8512-1(X))* Lerner Publishing Group.

—Beowulf: Monster Slayer [a British Legend]. Randall, Ron, illus. 2015. (Graphic Myths & Legends Ser.). (ENG.). 48p. (gr. 4-8). 21.32 *(978-1-4677-5980-9(5),* Lerner Digital) Lerner Publishing Group.

—Made for Each Other, 2 vols. Cowgur, Eldon, illus. 2011. (My Boyfriend Is a Monster Ser.: 2). (ENG.). 128p. (YA). (gr. 7-12). 29.27 *(978-0-7613-5601-1(0))* Lerner Publishing Group.

—Nightmare on Zombie Island. Witt, David, illus. 2008. (Twisted Journeys (r) Ser.: 5). (ENG.). 112p. (J). (gr. 4-7). per. 7.95 *(978-0-8225-6200-9(6))* Lerner Publishing Group.

—Peril at Summerland Park. Carruthers, Sandy, illus. 2012. (Twisted Journeys Ser.: 20). (ENG.). 112p. (J). (gr. 4-7). pap. 45.32 *(978-0-7613-9290-3(4));* pap. 7.95 *(978-0-7613-8551-6(7));* lib. bdg. 27.93 *(978-0-7613-4935-8(9))* Lerner Publishing Group. (Graphic Universe™).

—Robin Hood: Outlaw of Sherwood Forest. Yeates, Thomas, illus. 2007. (Graphic Myths & Legends Ser.). (ENG.). 48p. (J). (gr. 4-8). lib. bdg. 27.93 *(978-0-8225-5964-1(1))* Lerner Publishing Group.

—Robin Hood: Outlaw of Sherwood Forest, an English Legend. Yeates, Thomas, illus. 2008. (Graphic Myths & Legends Ser.). 48p. (J). (gr. 3-7). per. 8.95 *(978-0-8225-6572-7(2))* Lerner Publishing Group.

—Terror in Ghost Mansion. Carruthers, Sandy, illus. 2007. (Twisted Journeys (r) Ser.: 3). (ENG.). 112p. (J). (gr. 4-7). per. 7.95 *(978-0-8225-6778-3(4),* Twenty-First Century Bks.) Lerner Publishing Group.

—#02 Made for Each Other. Cowgur, Eldon, illus. 2011. (My Boyfriend Is a Monster Ser.). 128p. (YA). pap. 56.72 *(978-0-7613-7604-0(6),* Graphic Universe™) Lerner Publishing Group.

Storrie, Paul D., et al. Twisted Journeys(r): Spring 2012 New Releases. 2012. (Twisted Journeys Ser.). (Illus.). 112p. (J). (gr. 4-7). lib. bdg. 55.86 *(978-0-7613-8910-1(5),* Graphic Universe™) Lerner Publishing Group.

Straczynski, J. Michael. Ten Grand Volume 1. 2014. (ENG., Illus.). 160p. pap. 12.99 *(978-1-60706-831-0(1),* 9781607068310) Image Comics.

Strom, Frank. Scooby-Doo & the Mystery Date, 1 vol. Deporter, Vincent, illus. 2010. (Scooby-Doo Graphic Novels Ser.: No. 1). (ENG.). 24p. (J). (gr. 2-5). 24.21 *(978-1-59961-689-6(0))* Spotlight.

The Strongest of Them All. 2003. (J). per. *(978-1-57657-862-9(3))* Paradise Pr., Inc.

Sturm, James. Ape & Armadillo Take over the World: Toon Level 340. 2016. (ENG., Illus.). 40p. (J). (gr. k-4). 12.95 *(978-1-943145-09-6(1))* TOON Books / RAW Junior, LLC.

—Fantastic Four: Unstable Molecules. Davis, Guy & Sikoryak, Bob, illus. 2003. (Fantastic Four Legends Ser.: Vol. 1). 128p. (YA). pap. 13.99 *(978-0-7851-1112-2(3))* Marvel Worldwide, Inc.

Sturm, James, illus. Birdsong: a Story in Pictures: TOON Level 1. 2016. (ENG.). 60p. (J). (gr. k). 12.95 *(978-1-935179-94-8(2))* TOON Books / RAW Junior, LLC.

Sturm, James, et al. Characters in Action! Sturm, James, illus. 2013. (Adventures in Cartooning Ser.). (ENG., Illus.). 64p. (J). (gr. 1-5). pap. 10.99 *(978-1-59643-732-6(4),* 9781596437326, First Second Bks.) Roaring Brook Pr.

—Gryphons Aren't So Great. 2015. (Adventures in Cartooning Ser.). (ENG., Illus.). 40p. (J). (gr. -1-k). 14.99 *(978-1-59643-652-7(2),* 9781596436527, First Second Bks.) Roaring Brook Pr.

—Sleepless Knight. 2015. (Adventures in Cartooning Ser.). (ENG., Illus.). 40p. (J). (gr. -1-k). 14.99 *(978-1-59643-651-0(4),* 9781596436510, First Second Bks.) Roaring Brook Pr.

Sudduth, Brent & Meredith Books Staff. Doom in a Box. Panosian, Dan, illus. 2008. 22p. (J). pap. 3.99 *(978-0-696-23956-4(6))* Meredith Bks.

—Heads or Tails. Mada Design Staff, illus. 2008. 20p. (J). pap. 3.99 *(978-0-696-23959-5(0))* Meredith Bks.

Suggs, Rob. Comic Book Bible. 2009. (ENG.). 264p. (J). pap. 5.99 *(978-1-60260-685-2(4),* Barbour Bks.) Barbour Publishing, Inc.

Sullivan, Mary. Ball. 2013. (ENG., Illus.). 40p. (J). (gr. -1-3). lib. bdg. 12.99 *(978-0-547-75936-4(3))* Houghton Mifflin Harcourt Publishing Co.

Sumerak, Marc. Ororo: Before the Storm. Barberi, Carlo, illus. 2012. (Ororo: Before the Storm Ser.). 24p. (J). (gr. 2-6). lib. bdg. 24.21 *(978-1-61479-024-2(8));* lib. bdg. 24.21 *(978-1-61479-025-9(6));* lib. bdg. 24.21 *(978-1-61479-027-3(2));* lib. bdg. 24.21 *(978-1-61479-026-6(4))* Spotlight.

Superman Adventures. 2013. (Superman Adventures Ser.). (ENG.). 32p. (gr. 1-2). 180.80 *(978-1-4342-4860-2(7))* Stone Arch Bks.

Superman: Comic Chapter Books, 1 vol. 2014. (Superman: Comic Chapter Bks.). (ENG.). 88p. (gr. 3-7). pap. 11.90 *(978-1-4342-9535-4(4),* DC Super Heroes) Stone Arch Bks.

Sutton, Laurie S. The Dark Side of the Apokolips. Vecchio, Luciano, illus. 2015. (Superman: Comic Chapter Bks.). (ENG.). 88p. (gr. 3-7). lib. bdg. 21.32 *(978-1-4965-0509-5(3))* Stone Arch Bks.

—Goldilocks & the Three Vampires: A Graphic Novel. Jennings, C. S., illus. 2016. (Far Out Fairy Tales Ser.). (ENG.). 40p. (gr. 3-4). lib. bdg. 25.32 *(978-1-4965-3783-6(1),* Far Out Fairy Tales) Stone Arch Bks.

—The Light King Strikes!, 1 vol. Schoening, Dan, illus. 2011. (Green Lantern Ser.). (ENG.). 56p. (gr. 2-3). pap. 4.95 *(978-1-4342-3083-6(X));* lib. bdg. 26.65 *(978-1-4342-2610-5(7))* Stone Arch Bks. (DC Super Heroes).

—The Planet Collector, 1 vol. Vecchio, Luciano, illus. 2014. (Superman: Comic Chapter Bks.). (ENG.). 88p. (gr. 3-7). 21.32 *(978-1-4342-9133-2(2))* Stone Arch Bks.

—The Real Man of Steel, 1 vol. Vecchio, Luciano, illus. 2014. (Superman: Comic Chapter Bks.). (ENG.). 88p. (gr. 3-7). 21.32 *(978-1-4342-9134-9(0))* Stone Arch Bks.

Sutton, Laurie S., et al. The Dark Knight. 2013. (Dark Knight Ser.). (ENG.). 88p. (gr. 2-3). 106.60 *(978-1-4342-4810-7(0));* 213.20 *(978-1-4342-4809-1(7));* pap. 23.80 *(978-1-4342-4861-9(5));* pap. 47.60 *(978-1-4342-4862-6(3))* Stone Arch Bks. (DC Super Heroes).

—Gorilla Warfare, 1 vol. Doescher, Erik, illus. 2011. (Flash Ser.). (ENG.). 56p. (gr. 2-3). pap. 4.95 *(978-1-4342-3087-4(2),* DC Super Heroes) Stone Arch Bks.

Swartz, Patricia. Pig-A-Poo Moves to the Zoo. 2009. (Illus.). 28p. pap. 14.99 *(978-1-4490-4616-3(9))* AuthorHouse.

Sylvander, Matthieu. The Battle of the Vegetables. Barrier, Perceval, illus. 2016. (ENG.). 48p. (J). (gr. 1-4). 15.99 *(978-0-544-35942-0(9),* Clarion Bks.) Houghton Mifflin Harcourt Trade & Reference Pubs.

Sylvester, Kevin. Neil Flambé & the Tokyo Treasure. Sylvester, Kevin, illus. 2014. (Neil Flambe Capers Ser.: 4). (ENG., Illus.). 368p. (J). (gr. 3-7). pap. 7.99 *(978-1-4424-4289-4(1),* Simon & Schuster Bks. For Young Readers) Simon & Schuster Bks. For Young Readers.

Tadano, Kazuko. Kazuko Tadano Portfolio. 2004. (Illus.). 80p. (YA). pap. 14.99 *(978-4-7661-1468-3(X))* Graphic-Sha JPN. Dist: Diamond Bk. Distributors.

Takahashi, Hiroshi. Worst, Vol. 1. 2004. (ENG., Illus.). 208p. pap. 12.95 *(978-1-56970-983-2(1),* 9781569709832) Digital Manga Publishing.

Takahashi, Kazuki. Yu-Gi-Oh!: Duelist, Vol. 2. Takahashi, Kazuki, illus. 2005. (ENG., Illus.). 208p. pap. 9.99 *(978-1-59116-716-7(7))* Viz Media.

—Yu-Gi-Oh!: Duelist, Vol. 3. Takahashi, Kazuki, illus. 2005. (ENG., Illus.). 216p. (gr. 8-13). pap. 9.99 *(978-1-59116-771-6(X))* Viz Media.

—Yu-Gi-Oh!: Duelist, Vol. 8. Takahashi, Kazuki, illus. 2005. (ENG., Illus.). 224p. pap. 9.99 *(978-1-59116-998-7(4))* Viz Media.

—Yu-Gi-Oh!: Millennium World, Vol. 3. Takahashi, Kazuki, illus. 2006. (ENG., Illus.). 208p. pap. 9.99 *(978-1-4215-0409-4(X))* Viz Media.

—Yu-Gi-Oh!, Vol. 3. Sengupta, Anita, tr. Takahashi, Kazuki, illus. 2003. (ENG., Illus.). 216p. pap. 9.99 *(978-1-59116-179-0(7))* Viz Media.

Takahashi, Rumiko. Inuyasha Vol. 19: Demon Box Set. 2004. (Inuyasha Ser.). (ENG., Illus.). 192p. pap. 24.99 *(978-1-59116-725-9(6))* Viz Media.

—Inuyasha Ani-Manga. (Inuyasha Ser.: 15). (ENG., Illus.). Vol. 15. 2006. 208p. pap. 11.99 *(978-1-4215-0482-7(0))* Vol. 20. 2007. 216p. pap. 11.99 *(978-1-4215-0904-4(0))* Viz Media.

—Maison Ikkoku. Takahashi, Rumiko, illus. 2nd ed. 2005. (Maison Ikkoku Ser.: 10). (ENG., Illus.). Vol. 10. 248p. pap. 9.95 *(978-1-59116-729-7(9))* Vol. 14. 240p. pap. 9.95 *(978-1-4215-0142-0(2))* Viz Media.

Takaya, Natsuki. Fruits Basket Collector's Edition, Vol. 11. 2017. (Fruits Basket Collector's Edition Ser.: 11). (ENG., Illus.). 384p. (gr. 8-17). pap. 20.00 *(978-0-316-50168-2(9),* Yen Pr.) Orbit.

—Fruits Basket Collector's Edition, Vol. 7. 2016. (Fruits Basket Collector's Edition Ser.: 7). (ENG., Illus.). 384p. (gr. 8-17). pap. 20.00 *(978-0-316-36072-2(4),* Yen Pr.) Orbit.

—Fruits Basket Collector's Edition, Vol. 8. 2016. (Fruits Basket Collector's Edition Ser.: 8). (ENG., Illus.). 384p. (gr. 8-17). pap. 20.00 *(978-0-316-36073-9(2),* Yen Pr.) Orbit.

—Fruits Basket Collector's Edition, Vol. 9. 2017. (Fruits Basket Collector's Edition Ser.: 9). (ENG., Illus.). 384p. (gr. 8-17). pap. 20.00 *(978-0-316-50162-0(X),* Yen Pr.) Orbit.

Takemoto, Novala. Kamikaze Girls. Kanesata, Yukio, illus. 2006. (Kamikaze Girls Ser.). (ENG.). 208p. pap. 8.99 *(978-1-4215-0268-7(2))* Viz Media.

Tallarico, Tony. How Fire Came to the Indians. 2005. (Classics Illustrated Junior Ser.). 32p. 5.99 *(978-1-894998-18-5(9))* Lake, Jack Productions, Inc. CAN. Dist: Hushion Hse. Publishing, Ltd.

Tamura, Mitsuhisa & Fujita, Kazuhiro. BakéGyamon, Vol. 1. 2009. (ENG.). 200p. (J). pap. 7.99 *(978-1-4215-1793-3(0))* Viz Media.

—BakéGyamon, Vol. 2. 2009. (ENG.). 200p. (J). pap. 7.99 *(978-1-4215-1794-0(9))* Viz Media.

Tamura, Yumi. Wild Com. Tamura, Yumi, illus. 2004. (Wild Com Ser.). (ENG., Illus.). 192p. (YA). pap. 9.95 *(978-1-59116-559-0(8))* Viz Media.

Tanabe, Yellow. Kekkaishi, Vol. 22. Tanabe, Yellow, illus. 2010. (ENG., Illus.). 192p. pap. 9.99 *(978-1-4215-3069-7(4))* Viz Media.

—Kekkaishi, Vol. 23. Tanabe, Yellow, illus. 2010. (ENG., Illus.). 192p. pap. 9.99 *(978-1-4215-3200-4(X))* Viz Media.

—Kekkaishi, Vol. 3. Tanabe, Yellow, illus. 2005. (ENG., Illus.). 200p. pap. 9.99 *(978-1-4215-0067-6(1))* Viz Media.

—Kekkaishi, Vol. 6. Tanabe, Yellow, illus. 2006. (ENG., Illus.). 208p. pap. 9.99 *(978-1-4215-0487-2(1))* Viz Media.

Tanaka, Rika. Kilala Princess, Vol. 1. 2016. (ENG., Illus.). 208p. (J). pap. 10.99 *(978-1-4278-5661-6(3),* 9781427856616) TOKYOPOP, Inc.

Taneja, Sweta. Krishna - Defender of Dharma. Nagulakonda, Rajesh, illus. 2013. (Campfire Graphic Novels Ser.). (ENG.). 152p. (YA). (gr. 5-12). pap. 14.99 *(978-93-80741-12-3(X),* Campfire) Steerforth Pr.

Tanemura, Arina. O Sagashite Vol. 6, 7 vols. Tanemura, Arina, illus. 2006. (Full Moon Ser.: 6). (ENG., Illus.). 208p. pap. 8.99 *(978-1-4215-0397-4(2))* Viz Media.

Tanguay, Dave. Come Together! Vaughns, Byron, illus. 2015. (Billy Batson & the Magic of Shazam! Ser.). (ENG.). 32p. (gr. 2-3). lib. bdg. 22.60 *(978-1-4342-9744-0(6))* Stone Arch Bks.

—Deception Reception! Vaughns, Byron, illus. 2015. (Billy Batson & the Magic of Shazam! Ser.). (ENG.). 32p. (gr. 2-3). lib. bdg. 22.60 *(978-1-4342-9742-6(X))* Stone Arch Bks.

—Fire Fire Everywhere! Vaughns, Byron, illus. 2015. (Billy Batson & the Magic of Shazam! Ser.). (ENG.). 32p. (gr. 2-3). lib. bdg. 22.60 *(978-1-4342-9745-7(4))* Stone Arch Bks.

—The Legacy of Mr. Banjo! Vaughns, Byron, illus. 2015. (Billy Batson & the Magic of Shazam! Ser.). (ENG.). 32p. (gr. 2-3). lib. bdg. 22.60 *(978-1-4342-9746-4(2))* Stone Arch Bks.

—To Be King! DeStefano, Stephen, illus. 2015. (Billy Batson & the Magic of Shazam! Ser.). (ENG.). 32p. (gr. 2-3). lib. bdg. 22.60 *(978-1-4342-9657-3(1))* Stone Arch Bks.

Tanigawa, Nagaru, et al. The Melancholy of Suzumiya Haruhi-Chan. 2012. (Melancholy of Suzumiya Haruhi-Chan Ser.: 6). (ENG., Illus.). 160p. (gr. 11-17). pap. 11.99 *(978-0-316-22914-2(8),* Yen Pr.) Orbit.

Tanner, Jennifer, illus. Robin Hood. 2010. (Classic Fiction Ser.). 72p. lib. bdg. 4.95 *(978-1-4342-2604-4(2),* Graphic Revolve) Stone Arch Bks.

Tatchell, Judy. How to Draw Cartoons & Caricatures. Round, Graham et al, illus. 2007. 40p. (J). (gr. 4). lib. bdg. 13.99 *(978-1-58086-895-2(9),* Usborne) EDC Publishing.

Tatsuyama, Sayuri. Happy Happy Clover, Vol. 4. Tatsuyama, Sayuri, illus. 2010. (ENG., Illus.). 192p. (J). pap. 7.99 *(978-1-4215-2735-2(9))* Viz Media.

Tatulli, Mark. Daydreaming. 2016. (ENG., Illus.). 40p. (J). 17.99 *(978-1-62672-354-2(0),* 9781626723542) Roaring Brook Pr.

—Desmond Pucket Makes Monster Magic. 2015. (Desmond Pucket Ser.: 1). lib. bdg. 20.85 *(978-0-606-38231-1(3))* Turtleback Bks.

Tatulli, Mark, et al. Lio: Making Friends. 2013. (Lio Ser.: 8). (ENG., Illus.). 224p. (J). pap. 9.99 *(978-1-4494-2558-6(5))* Andrews McMeel Publishing.

—Lio: "There's a Monster in My Socks" 2012. (Lio Ser.: 7). (ENG., Illus.). 224p. (J). pap. 9.99 *(978-1-4494-2304-9(3))* Andrews McMeel Publishing.

Taylor, Corey. House of Gold & Bones. Hahn, Sierra, ed. 2013. (ENG., Illus.). 104p. pap. 14.99 *(978-1-61655-287-9(5))* Dark Horse Comics.

Taylor, Drew Hayden. The Night Wanderer: A Graphic Novel. Wyatt, Michael, illus. 2013. (ENG.). 104p. (YA). (gr. 7-12). 24.95 *(978-1-55451-573-8(4),* 9781554515738); pap. 14.95 *(978-1-55451-572-1(6),* 9781554515721) Annick Pr., Ltd. CAN. Dist: Publishers Group West (PGW).

Taylor, Trace. Dogtown #5. 2010. (Dogtown Comics Ser.). 24p. (J). pap. 6.95 *(978-1-61541-142-9(9))* American Reading Co.

—Dogtown #6. 2010. (Dogtown Comics Ser.). 24p. (J). pap. 6.95 *(978-1-61541-144-3(5))* American Reading Co.

—Dogtown Diner. 2010. pap. 39.62 *(978-1-61541-088-0(0))* American Reading Co.

—Dogtown's Got Talent. 2010. pap. 39.62 *(978-1-61541-137-5(2))* American Reading Co.

—Flying over Dogtown. 2010. pap. 39.62 *(978-1-61541-141-2(0))* American Reading Co.

—Hair Day in Dogtown. 2010. pap. 39.62 *(978-1-61541-143-6(7))* American Reading Co.

—Happy Birthday Dogtown. 2010. pap. 39.62 *(978-1-61541-139-9(9))* American Reading Co.

—Wedding Day in Dogtown. 2010. pap. 39.62 *(978-1-61541-145-0(3))* American Reading Co.

—Who Took That Dog? Taylor, Trace, illus. 2008. (1B Graphic Novels Ser.). (ENG., Illus.). 32p. (J). (gr. k-2). pap. 5.99 *(978-1-59301-757-6(X))* American Reading Co.

Teer, Samuel. Veda: Assembly Required. Park, Hyeondo, illus. 2015. (ENG.). 144p. (J). (gr. 7). pap. 14.99 *(978-1-61655-497-2(5))* Dark Horse Comics.

Teitelbaum, Michael. I Am Superman. 2009. (Justice League Classic: I Can Read! Ser.). (J). lib. bdg. 13.55 *(978-0-606-06951-9(8),* Turtleback) Turtleback Bks.

—Meet the Super Heroes. 2009. (Justice League Classic: I Can Read! Ser.). (J). lib. bdg. 13.55 *(978-0-606-06941-0(0),* Turtleback) Turtleback Bks.

Telgemeier, Raina. Drama. 2012. lib. bdg. 22.10 *(978-0-606-26738-0(7),* Turtleback) Turtleback Bks.

Temple, Bob. The Day Mom Finally Snapped, 1 vol. Harpster, Steve, illus. 2006. (Graphic Sparks Ser.). (ENG.). 40p. (gr. 1-3). 23.99 *(978-1-59889-038-9(7),* Graphic Sparks) Stone Arch Bks.

—A Nose for Danger. Harpster, Steve, illus. 2006. (Graphic Sparks Ser.). (ENG.). 40p. (gr. 1-3). per. 5.95 *(978-1-59889-171-3(5),* Graphic Sparks) Stone Arch Bks.

Templeton, Ty & Slott, Dan. Free Man, 1 vol. Templeton, Ty, illus. 2012. (Batman Adventures Ser.). (ENG., Illus.). 32p. (gr. 2-3). lib. bdg. 22.60 *(978-1-4342-4558-8(6))* Stone Arch Bks.

—My Boyfriend's Back, 1 vol. Templeton, Ty, illus. 2012. (Batman Adventures Ser.). (ENG., Illus.). 32p. (gr. 2-3). lib. bdg. 22.60 *(978-1-4342-4559-5(4))* Stone Arch Bks.

—Need to Know, 1 vol. Templeton, Ty, illus. 2012. (Batman Adventures Ser.). (ENG., Illus.). 32p. (gr. 2-3). lib. bdg. 22.60 *(978-1-4342-4560-1(8))* Stone Arch Bks.

—No Asylum, 1 vol. Templeton, Ty, illus. 2012. (Batman Adventures Ser.). (ENG., Illus.). 32p. (gr. 2-3). lib. bdg. 22.60 *(978-1-4342-4557-1(8))* Stone Arch Bks.

Tennapel, Doug. Cardboard. 2012. lib. bdg. 24.50 *(978-0-606-26212-5(1),* Turtleback) Turtleback Bks.

TenNapel, Doug. Escape from the Lizzarks. 2015. (Nnewts Ser.: 1). (ENG., Illus.). 192p. (J). (gr. 3-7). pap. 10.99 *(978-0-545-67646-5(0),* Graphix) Scholastic, Inc.

—The Rise of Herk. 2016. (Nnewts Ser.: 2). (ENG.). 208p. (J). (gr. 3-7). 19.99 *(978-0-545-67652-6(5),* Graphix) Scholastic, Inc.

Tercio, Ricardo, illus. Jack & the Beanstalk: The Graphic Novel. 2008. (Graphic Spin Ser.). (ENG.). 40p. (gr. 1-3). 25.32 *(978-1-4342-0766-1(8),* Graphic Revolve) Stone Arch Bks.

Terrell, Brandon. Daydream Receiver. 2017. (Jake Maddox Graphic Novels Ser.). (ENG., Illus.). 72p. (gr. 2-5). lib. bdg. 26.65 *(978-1-4965-3702-7(5))* Stone Arch Bks.

—Double Scribble. 2017. (Jake Maddox Graphic Novels Ser.). (ENG., Illus.). 72p. (gr. 2-5). lib. bdg. 26.65 *(978-1-4965-3701-0(7))* Stone Arch Bks.

—Sports Illustrated Kids Graphic Novels, 1 vol. Ferrara, Eduardo, illus. 2014. (Sports Illustrated Kids Graphic Novels Ser.). (ENG.). 72p. (gr. 2-5). 106.60 *(978-1-4342-9528-6(1))* Stone Arch Bks.

—8-Bit Baseball, 1 vol. Ferrara, Eduardo, illus. 2014. (Sports Illustrated Kids Graphic Novels Ser.). (ENG.). 72p. (gr. 2-5). 26.65 *(978-1-4342-4164-1(5))* Stone Arch Bks.

Terrell, Brandon & Fuentes, Benny. Quarterback Scramble, 1 vol. Sandoval, Gerardo, illus. 2011. (Sports Illustrated Kids Graphic Novels Ser.). (ENG.). 56p. (gr. 2-3). pap. 7.19 *(978-1-4342-3070-6(8));* lib. bdg. 26.65 *(978-1-4342-2220-6(9))* Stone Arch Bks.

Terrell, Brandon, et al. Riptide Pride, 1 vol. 2011. (Sports Illustrated Kids Graphic Novels Ser.). (ENG., Illus.). 56p. (gr.

2-3). pap. 7.19 *(978-1-4342-3399-8(5))*; lib. bdg. 26.65 *(978-1-4342-2238-1(1))* Stone Arch Bks.

Tezuka, Osamu. Astro Boy, Vol. 20. Tezuka, Osamu, illus. 2003. (ENG., Illus.). 224p. pap. 9.95 *(978-1-56971-901-5(2))* Dark Horse Comics.

—Nextworld, Vol. 1. Tezuka, Osamu, illus. 2003. (ENG., Illus.). 168p. pap. 13.95 *(978-1-56971-866-7(0))* Dark Horse Comics.

—Nostalgia, Vol. 6. 2006. (Phoenix Ser.). (ENG., Illus.). 208p. pap. 16.99 *(978-1-4215-0258-8(5))* Viz Media.

—Phoenix, Vol. 1. Tezuka, Osamu, illus. 2003. (ENG., Illus.). 344p. pap. 15.95 *(978-1-56931-868-3(9))* Viz Media.

—Phoenix, Vol. 7. 2006. (ENG., Illus.). 208p. pap. 15.99 *(978-1-4215-0517-6(7))* Viz Media.

—Yamato/Space, Vol. 3. Tezuka, Osamu, illus. 2003. (Phoenix Ser.). (ENG., Illus.). 336p. pap. 15.95 *(978-1-59116-100-4(2))* Viz Media.

Thielbar, Melinda. The Ancient Formula: A Mystery with Fractions. Pantoja, Tintin, illus. 2011. (Manga Math Mysteries Ser.: 5). (ENG.). 46p. (gr. 3-5). pap. 6.95 *(978-0-7613-8134-1(1)*, Graphic Universe™) Lerner Publishing Group.

—The Ancient Formula No. 5: A Mystery with Fractions. Pantoja, Tintin, illus. 2010. (Manga Math Mysteries Ser.: 5). (ENG.). 48p. (gr. 3-5). 29.27 *(978-0-7613-4907-5(3))* Lerner Publishing Group.

—The Book Bandit: A Mystery with Geometry. Grandt, Eve et al, illus. 2010. (Manga Math Mysteries Ser.: 7). (ENG.). 48p. (gr. 3-5). 29.27 *(978-0-7613-4909-9(X))* Lerner Publishing Group.

—The Book Bandit No. 7: A Mystery with Geometry. Lee, Jenn Manley & Chow, Candice, illus. 2011. (Manga Math Mysteries Ser.: 7). (ENG.). 48p. (gr. 3-5). pap. 6.95 *(978-0-7613-8136-5(8)*, Graphic Universe™) Lerner Publishing Group.

—The Fishy Fountain. Lin, Yali, illus. 2010. (Manga Math Mysteries Ser.: 6). (ENG.). 48p. (gr. 3-5). 29.27 *(978-0-7613-4908-2(1))* Lerner Publishing Group.

—The Fishy Fountain: A Mystery with Multiplication & Division. Lin, Yali, illus. 2011. (Manga Math Mysteries Ser.: 6). (ENG.). 48p. (gr. 3-5). pap. 6.95 *(978-0-7613-8135-8(X)*, Graphic Universe™) Lerner Publishing Group.

—The Hundred-Dollar Robber. Pantoja, Tintin, illus. 2010. (Manga Math Mysteries Ser.: 2). (ENG.). 48p. (gr. 3-5). pap. 6.95 *(978-0-7613-5243-3(0)*, Graphic Universe™) Lerner Publishing Group.

—The Hundred-Dollar Robber: A Mystery with Money. Pantoja, Maria Kristina, illus. 2009. (Manga Math Mysteries Ser.: 2). (ENG.). 48p. (gr. 3-5). 29.27 *(978-0-7613-3854-3(3))* Lerner Publishing Group.

—The Kung Fu Puzzle: A Mystery with Time & Temperature. Ota, Yuko & Helmer, Der-Shing, illus. 2009. (Manga Math Mysteries Ser.: No. 4). 48p. (J). (gr. 2-5). 29.27 *(978-0-7613-3856-7(X))* Lerner Publishing Group.

—The Lost Key. Pantoja, Tintin, illus. 2010. (Manga Math Mysteries Ser.: 1). (ENG.). 45p. (gr. 3-5). pap. 6.95 *(978-0-7613-5244-0(9)*, Graphic Universe™) Lerner Publishing Group.

—The Secret Ghost: A Mystery with Distance & Measurement. Ota, Yuko, illus. 2010. (Manga Math Mysteries Ser.: 3). (ENG.). 46p. (gr. 3-5). pap. 6.95 *(978-0-7613-5245-7(7)*, Graphic Universe™) Lerner Publishing Group.

—#5 the Ancient Formula: A Mystery with Fractions. Pantoja, Tintin, illus. 2011. (Manga Math Mysteries Set II Ser.). pap. 39.62 *(978-0-7613-8362-8(X)*, Graphic Universe™) Lerner Publishing Group.

—#6 the Fishy Fountain: A Mystery with Multiplication & Division. Lin, Yali, illus. 2011. (Manga Math Mysteries Set II Ser.). pap. 39.62 *(978-0-7613-8363-5(8)*, Graphic Universe™) Lerner Publishing Group.

—#7 the Book Bandit: A Mystery with Geometry. Lee, Jenn Manley & Chow, Candice, illus. 2011. (Manga Math Mysteries Set II Ser.). pap. 39.62 *(978-0-7613-8364-2(6)*, Graphic Universe™) Lerner Publishing Group.

Thomas, Cynthia. Little Mountain Princess. 2008. 32p. pap. 12.95 *(978-1-933912-84-4(7))* Westview Publishing Co., Inc.

Thomas, John Ira. Zoo Force: Dear Eniko. Smith, Jeremy, illus. 2003. 68p. per. 6.95 *(978-0-9743147-1-6(4))* Candle Light Pr.

Thomas Nelson. Supersqueak Comics: the Mystery of the Missing Cheese. 2016. (ENG.). 12p. (gr. -1-2). bds. *(978-1-78598-653-6(8))* Make Believe Ideas.

Thomas, Rich, Jr. The Avengers: An Origin Story. Olliffe, Pat, illus. 2nd ed. 2013. (Origin Story Ser.). (ENG.). 48p. (J). (gr. 1-3). 8.99 *(978-1-4231-8308-2(8))* Marvel Worldwide, Inc.

Thomas, Rich. The Courageous Captain America: An Origin Story, 1 vol. Semeiks, Val, illus. 2012. (Marvel Origins Ser.). (ENG.). 48p. (J). (gr. -1-4). lib. bdg. 24.21 *(978-1-61479-008-2(6))* Spotlight.

—The Incredible Hulk: An Origin Story, 1 vol. Semeiks, Val, illus. 2012. (Marvel Origins Ser.). (ENG.). 48p. (J). (gr. -1-4). lib. bdg. 24.21 *(978-1-61479-009-9(4))* Spotlight.

—The Invincible Iron Man: An Origin Story, 1 vol. Rousseau, Craig, illus. 2012. (Marvel Origins Ser.). (ENG.). 48p. (J). (gr. -1-4). lib. bdg. 24.21 *(978-1-61479-010-5(8))* Spotlight.

—The Mighty Avengers: An Origin Story. Olliffe, Pat, illus. 2012. (Origin Story Ser.). (ENG.). 48p. (J). (gr. 1-3). 8.99 *(978-1-4231-4841-8(X)*, Marvel Pr.) Disney Publishing Worldwide.

—The Mighty Thor: An Origin Story, 1 vol. Clark, Jeff, illus. 2012. (Marvel Origins Ser.). (ENG.). 48p. (J). (gr. -1-4). lib. bdg. 24.21 *(978-1-61479-011-2(6))* Spotlight.

Thomas, Rich, Jr. Spider-Man: An Origin Story. Olliffe, Pat et al, illus. 2nd ed. 2013. (ENG.). 48p. (J). (gr. 1-3). 8.99 *(978-1-4231-8306-8(1))* Marvel Worldwide, Inc.

Thomas, Rich, Jr. & Siglain, Michael. Captain America: The Tomorrow Army. Disney Book Group Staff et al, illus. 2014. (Mighty Marvel Chapter Book Ser.: 2). (ENG.). 144p. (J). (gr. 1-3). pap. 5.99 *(978-1-4231-4303-1(5)*, Marvel Pr.) Disney Publishing Worldwide.

Thomas, Roy, text. Dracula. 2010. (ENG., Illus.). 208p. (gr. 10-17). 19.99 *(978-0-7851-4905-7(8))* Marvel Worldwide, Inc.

Thomas, Roy & Stevenson, Robert Louis. Death in the Forest, 1 vol., Vol. 4. Gully, Mario, illus. 2011. (Kidnapped! Ser.). (ENG.). 24p. (J). (gr. 5-9). 24.21 *(978-1-59961-784-8(6))* Spotlight.

—The End of the Quest, 1 vol., Vol. 5. Gully, Mario, illus. 2011. (Kidnapped! Ser.). (ENG.). 24p. (YA). (gr. 5-9). 24.21 *(978-1-59961-785-5(4))* Spotlight.

—I Go to Sea, 1 vol., Vol. 2. Gully, Mario, illus. 2011. (Kidnapped! Ser.). (ENG.). 24p. (J). (gr. 5-9). 24.21 *(978-1-59961-782-4(X))* Spotlight.

—The Loss of the Brig, 1 vol., Vol. 3. Gully, Mario, illus. 2011. (Kidnapped! Ser.). (ENG.). 24p. (YA). (gr. 5-9). 24.21 *(978-1-59961-783-1(8))* Spotlight.

Thompson, Jill. Magic Trixie. Thompson, Jill, illus. 2008. (ENG., Illus.). 96p. (J). (gr. 3-7). pap. 8.99 *(978-0-06-117045-4(3))* HarperCollins Pubs.

—Magic Trixie & the Dragon. Thompson, Jill, illus. 2009. (ENG., Illus.). 96p. (J). (gr. 3-7). pap. 7.99 *(978-0-06-117050-8(X))* HarperCollins Pubs.

—The Revenge of Jimmy. 2006. (Illus.). 48p. pap. 9.95 *(978-1-57989-071-1(7))* Sirius Entertainment, Inc.

—Scary Godmother. 2005. (Illus.). 48p. pap. 9.95 *(978-1-57989-070-4(9))* Sirius Entertainment, Inc.

—Scary Godmother Comic Book Stories. 2011. (ENG., Illus.). 312p. (J). (gr. 5). pap. 24.99 *(978-1-59582-723-4(4))* Dark Horse Comics.

Thompson, Jill, creator. Scary Godmother: The Mystery Date. 2004. (Illus.). 48p. pap. 9.95 *(978-1-57989-072-8(5))* Sirius Entertainment, Inc.

Thompson, Richard. Mighty Alice Goes Round & Round: A Cul de Sac Book. (Cul de Sac Ser.: Vol. 6). (ENG., Illus.). (J). 2016. (gr. 3-6). 37.99 ***(978-1-4494-7387-7(3))*** 2013. 224p. pap. 9.99 *(978-1-4494-3721-3(4))* Andrews McMeel Publishing.

Thompson, Vinny. Vinny & Bud Comix Book II. 2012. 44p. pap. 21.99 *(978-1-4772-4071-7(3))* AuthorHouse.

Thorne, Frank. Prodigal: Egg of First Light: Egg of First Light. 2012. (ENG., Illus.). 96p. (YA). pap. 12.95 *(978-1-934944-14-1(9)*, 9781934944141) Ape Entertainment.

Thoughts Staff. Police Stories: the fight Call. 2005. 16p. 8.99 *(978-1-4116-2267-8(7))* Lulu Pr., Inc.

Thrash, Maggie. Honor Girl. Thrash, Maggie, illus. 2017. (ENG., Illus.). 272p. (YA). (gr. 9). pap. 14.99 *(978-0-7636-8755-7(3))* Candlewick Pr.

Thrash, Maggie. Honor Girl: A Graphic Memoir. 2017. lib. bdg. 26.95 ***(978-0-606-39843-5(0))*** Turtleback Bks.

Thung, Diana. Captain Long Ears. 2010. (ENG., Illus.). 168p. (J). pap. 12.95 *(978-1-59362-187-2(6)*, 9781593621872) Slave Labor Bks.

Tieri, Frank. Weapon X: The Underground, Vol. 2. Youngquist, Jeff, ed. Jeanty, Georges, illus. 2004. (X-Men Ser.). 184p. pap. 19.99 *(978-0-7851-1253-2(7))* Marvel Worldwide, Inc.

Tiger Moth. 2013. (Tiger Moth Ser.). (ENG.). (gr. 1-3). 119.95 *(978-1-4342-5629-4(4))* Stone Arch Bks.

Tillworth, Mary. Cupcake Challenge! (Barbie: Life in the Dreamhouse) 2015. (Step into Reading Ser.). (ENG., Illus.). 48p. (J). (gr. k-3). 3.99 *(978-0-553-50745-4(1)*, Random Hse. Bks. for Young Readers) Random Hse. Children's Bks.

—Licensed to Drive. 2014. (Barbie Step into Reading Level 3 Ser.). lib. bdg. 13.55 *(978-0-606-35992-4(3))* Turtleback Bks.

Timmins, Jeffrey Stewart, illus. Cinderella: The Graphic Novel, 1 vol. 2008. (Graphic Spin Ser.). (ENG.). 40p. (gr. 1-3). 25.32 *(978-1-4342-0764-7(1)*, Graphic Revolve) Stone Arch Bks.

Timmons, Anne. Pigling: A Cinderella Story: A Korean Tale. 2008. (Graphic Myths & Legends Ser.). (Illus.). 48p. (J). (gr. 4-8). 27.93 *(978-0-8225-7174-2(9)*, Graphic Universe™) Lerner Publishing Group.

Tipton, Scott. Teenage Mutant Ninja Turtles: New Animated Adventures: Volume 3, 1 vol. 2016. (Teenage Mutant Ninja Turtles: New Animated Adventures Ser.). (ENG.). 24p. (J). lib. bdg. 24.21 *(978-1-61479-461-5(8)*, Graphic Planet) Magic Wagon.

Tipton, Scott, et al. Best of Klingons. Messina, David et al, illus. 2013. (Star Trek Ser.). (ENG.). 234p. pap. 24.99 *(978-1-61377-725-1(6)*, 9781613777251) Idea & Design Works, LLC.

Titan Books Staff, et al. Monsters vs. Aliens: the M Files. Dalton, Alex & Laguna, Fabio, illus. 2009. (ENG.). 48p. pap. 4.95 *(978-1-84856-281-3(0)*, Titan Bks.) Titan Bks. Ltd. GBR. Dist: Penguin Random Hse. LLC.

Titan Comics Staff. Penguins of Madagascar, Vol. 3. 2016. (ENG., Illus.). 64p. (gr. 1-4). pap. 6.99 *(978-1-78276-253-9(1))* Titan Bks. Ltd. GBR. Dist: Penguin Random Hse. LLC.

—Underworld, Vol. 6. 2015. (Riders of Berk Ser.). (ENG., Illus.). 64p. (J). (gr. 3-7). pap. 6.99 *(978-1-78276-081-8(4))* Titan Bks. Ltd. GBR. Dist: Penguin Random Hse. LLC.

Titan Comics Staff & Furman, Simon. Dangers of the Deep, Vol. 2. Max, Iman, illus. 2014. (Riders of Berk Ser.). (ENG.). 64p. (J). (gr. 3-7). pap. 6.99 *(978-1-78276-077-1(6))* Titan Bks. Ltd. GBR. Dist: Penguin Random Hse. LLC.

—Dragon Down, Vol. 1. Nazif, Iwan, illus. 2014. (Riders of Berk Ser.). (ENG.). 64p. (J). (gr. 3-7). pap. 6.99 *(978-1-78276-076-4(8))* Titan Bks. Ltd. GBR. Dist: Penguin Random Hse. LLC.

Titan Comics, Titan. The Ice Castle, Vol. 3. Lawrence, Jack, illus. 2015. (Riders of Berk Ser.). (ENG.). 64p. (J). (gr. 3-7). pap. 6.99 *(978-1-78276-078-8(4))* Titan Bks. Ltd. GBR. Dist: Penguin Random Hse. LLC.

Titan Comics, Titan & Ah-Koon, Didier. Minions, Vol. 1. 2015. (ENG., Illus.). 48p. (J). (gr. 1-4). 14.99 *(978-1-78276-557-8(3))* Titan Bks. Ltd. GBR. Dist: Penguin Random Hse. LLC.

To Wait Is to Win. 2004. (J). *(978-0-9762904-7-6(2))* Layne Morgan Media, Inc.

The Tobacco Temptation. (J). 39.50 *(978-1-56230-082-1(2))* Syndistar, Inc.

Tofield, Simon, creator. Simon's Cat off to the Vet ... & Other Adventures. 2015. (ENG., Illus.). 240p. 27.95 *(978-1-61775-402-9(1))* Akashic Bks.

Tokyopop and Art Impression Staff & Peymani, Christine. Skelanimals Vol. 1: It's a Wonderful Afterlife. 2011. (Illus.). 36p. 9.99 *(978-1-4278-3255-9(2))* TOKYOPOP, Inc.

Tokyopop Staff, illus. Rave Master: The Sound of Thunder, Vol. 3. 2005. 96p. (J). pap. 7.99 *(978-1-59532-791-8(6))* TOKYOPOP, Inc.

Tolkien, J. R. R., et al. El Hobbit. Diaz, Lorenzo, tr. from ENG. 2004. (SPA., Illus.). 136p. 19.95 *(978-1-59497-071-9(8))* Public Square Bks.

Tome. Spirou & Fantasio in New York. Janry, illus. 2011. (Spirou & Fantasio Ser.: 2). (ENG.). 48p. (J). (gr. 3-17). pap. 11.95 *(978-1-84918-054-2(7))* CineBook GBR. Dist: National Bk. Network.

Tomori, Miyoshi. Devil & Her Love Song, Vol. 13. 2014. (ENG., Illus.). 232p. pap. 9.99 *(978-1-4215-5136-4(5))* Viz Media.

Tong, Andie, illus. Justice League Reading Collection. 2017. (I Can Read Level 2 Ser.). (ENG.). 160p. (J). (gr. -1-3). pap. 16.99 *(978-0-06-229187-5(4))* HarperCollins Pubs.

Tonka Let's Go! 2004. (J). *(978-0-9767179-0-4(5))* ABC Development, Inc.

Tony's Sobering Lesson. (J). 39.50 *(978-1-56230-075-3(X))* Syndistar, Inc.

Toole, Anne. Crystal Cadets. Staffaroni, Adam, ed. 2016. (ENG., Illus.). 128p. (J). pap. 12.99 *(978-1-941302-16-3(5)*, 9781941302163) Lion Forge, LLC, The.

Toriyama, Akira. Dragon Ball (3-in-1 Edition), Vol. 4, 3 in 1 vols. 2014. (ENG., Illus.). 576p. (Orig.). pap. 14.99 *(978-1-4215-5612-3(X))* Viz Media.

—Dragon Ball: Chapter Book, Vol. 9. Toriyama, Akira, illus. 2010. (ENG., Illus.). 80p. (J). pap. 4.99 *(978-1-4215-3125-0(9))* Viz Media.

—Dragon Ball Full Color Freeza Arc, Volume 1. 2016. (Dragon Ball Freeza Ser.: 1). lib. bdg. 33.05 *(978-0-606-38706-4(4))* Turtleback Bks.

—Dragon Ball Full Color Freeza Arc, Volume 2. 2016. (Dragon Ball Freeza Ser.: 2). lib. bdg. 33.05 *(978-0-606-38934-1(2))* Turtleback Bks.

—Dragon Ball Full Color, Vol. 1. 2014. (ENG., Illus.). 248p. pap. 19.99 *(978-1-4215-6592-7(7))* Viz Media.

—Dragon Ball Full Color, Vol. 2. 2014. (ENG., Illus.). 248p. pap. 19.99 *(978-1-4215-6593-4(5))* Viz Media.

—Dragon Ball Z, Vol. 26. Toriyama, Akira, illus. 2006. (ENG., Illus.). 208p. pap. 9.99 *(978-1-4215-0636-4(X))* Viz Media.

—Dragon Ball Z, Vol. 8 (VIZBIG Edition) Toriyama, Akira, illus. 2010. (ENG., Illus.). 560p. pap. 19.99 *(978-1-4215-2071-1(0))* Viz Media.

—Fight to the Finish! Toriyama, Akira, illus. 2010. (Dragon Ball Ser.: 8). (ENG., Illus.). 80p. (J). pap. 4.99 *(978-1-4215-3124-3(0))* Viz Media.

—Let the Tournament Begin! Toriyama, Akira, illus. 2010. (Dragon Ball Ser.: 7). (ENG., Illus.). 80p. (J). pap. 4.99 *(978-1-4215-3123-6(2))* Viz Media.

—Strongest under the Heavens. Toriyama, Akira, illus. 2010. (Dragon Ball Ser.: 10). (ENG., Illus.). 80p. (J). pap. 4.99 *(978-1-4215-3126-7(7))* Viz Media.

Toriyama, Akira & Jones, Gerard. Dragon Ball Z, Vol. 20. Toriyama, Akira, illus. 2005. (ENG., Illus.). 192p. pap. 9.99 *(978-1-59116-808-9(2))* Viz Media.

Torres, Daniel. Tom Vol. 1: Las Aventuras de Tom. 2004. (SPA., Illus.). 48p. 19.95 *(978-1-59497-068-9(8))* Public Square Bks.

Torres, J. Batman: the Brave & the Bold. Beatty, Terry et al, illus. 2013. (Batman: the Brave & the Bold Ser.). (ENG.). 32p. (gr. 2-3). 180.80 *(978-1-4342-4858-9(5))*; 90.40 *(978-1-4342-4857-2(7))* Stone Arch Bks.

—Batman Versus the Yeti!, 1 vol. Barberi, Carlo & Beatty, Terry, illus. 2013. (Batman: the Brave & the Bold Ser.). (ENG.). 32p. (gr. 2-3). 22.60 *(978-1-4342-4708-7(2))* Stone Arch Bks.

—The Case of the Fractured Fairy Tale, 1 vol. Barberi, Carlo & Beatty, Terry, illus. 2013. (Batman: the Brave & the Bold Ser.). (ENG.). 32p. (gr. 2-3). 22.60 *(978-1-4342-4705-6(8))* Stone Arch Bks.

—The Collected Alison Dare Little Miss Adventures. Bone, J., illus. 2005. (J). *(978-1-4156-1359-7(1))* Oni Pr., Inc.

—Degrassi the Next Generation Extra Credit Suddenly, Last Summer. Northcott, Ed, illus. 2nd ed. 2006. (Degrassi the Next Generation Ser.). (ENG.). 128p. (J). pap. *(978-1-55168-320-1(2))* Fenn, H. B. & Co., Ltd.

—In My House. Rolston, Steve, illus. 4th ed. 2007. (Degrassi the Next Generation Ser.). (ENG.). 120p. (J). pap. *(978-1-55168-303-4(2))* Fenn, H. B. & Co., Ltd.

—Into the Woods. Hicks, Faith Erin, illus. 2012. (Bigfoot Boy Ser.: 1). (ENG.). 100p. (J). (gr. 2-5). 17.95 *(978-1-55453-711-2(8))*; pap. 9.95 *(978-1-55453-712-9(6))* Kids Can Pr., Ltd. CAN. Dist: Hachette Bk. Group.

—Jinx: Little Miss Steps. Burchett, Rick & Austin, Terry, illus. 2013. (Jinx Ser.: 2). (ENG.). (YA). (gr. 5). 114p. 16.99 *(978-1-936975-42-6(4))*; 112p. pap. 9.99 *(978-1-936975-41-9(6))* Archie Comic Pubns., Inc.

—Power Lunch Book 1: First Course: First Course. 2011. (ENG., Illus.). 40p. (J). 12.99 *(978-1-934964-70-5(0)*, 9781934964705) Oni Pr., Inc.

—Power Lunch Book 2: Seconds. 2014. (ENG., Illus.). 40p. (J). 12.99 *(978-1-62010-011-0(8)*, 9781620100110) Oni Pr., Inc.

—The Secret of the Doomsday Design!, 1 vol. Bone, J., illus. 2013. (Batman: the Brave & the Bold Ser.). (ENG.). 32p. (gr. 2-3). 22.60 *(978-1-4342-4707-0(4))* Stone Arch Bks.

—The Sound of Thunder. Hicks, Faith Erin, illus. 2014. (Bigfoot Boy Ser.). (ENG.). 100p. (J). (gr. 2-5). 17.95 *(978-1-894786-58-4(0))*; pap. 9.95 *(978-1-894786-59-1(9))* Kids Can Pr., Ltd. CAN. Dist: Hachette Bk. Group.

—Teen Titans Go! Bring It On. 2016. (ENG., Illus.). 136p. (gr. 2-5). pap. 12.99 *(978-1-4012-6468-0(9))* DC Comics.

—Titans Together. 2014. (ENG., Illus.). 144p. (J). (gr. 2-5). pap. 12.99 *(978-1-4012-5367-7(9))* DC Comics.

Torres, J. & Kim, Eric. Missing You. 3rd ed. 2007. (Degrassi the Next Generation Ser.). (ENG., Illus.). 120p. (J). pap. *(978-1-55168-301-0(6))* Fenn, H. B. & Co., Ltd.

Torres, J., et al. The Beast Boy Who Cried Wolf, 1 vol. 2014. (Teen Titans GO! Ser.). (ENG., Illus.). 32p. (gr. 2-3). 22.60 *(978-1-4342-6433-6(5))* Stone Arch Bks.

—Blackfire's Back!, 1 vol. 2014. (Teen Titans GO! Ser.). (ENG., Illus.). 32p. (gr. 2-3). 22.60 *(978-1-4342-9215-5(0))* Stone Arch Bks.

—Demo, 1 vol. 2014. (Teen Titans GO! Ser.). (ENG., Illus.). 32p. (gr. 2-3). 22.60 *(978-1-4342-4789-6(9))* Stone Arch Bks.

—Lame, 1 vol. 2014. (Teen Titans GO! Ser.). (ENG., Illus.). 32p. (gr. 2-3). 22.60 *(978-1-4342-6467-1(X))* Stone Arch Bks.

—Monster Zit!, 1 vol. 2014. (Teen Titans GO! Ser.). (ENG., Illus.). 32p. (gr. 2-3). 22.60 *(978-1-4342-9213-1(4))* Stone Arch Bks.

—My Crummy Valentine, 1 vol. 2014. (Teen Titans GO! Ser.). (ENG., Illus.). 32p. (gr. 2-3). 22.60 *(978-1-4342-6468-8(8))* Stone Arch Bks.

—Teen Titans GO!, 1 vol. 2014. (Teen Titans GO! Ser.). (ENG., Illus.). 32p. (gr. 2-3). 67.80 *(978-1-4342-9516-3(8))*; 90.40 *(978-1-4342-8765-6(3))* Stone Arch Bks.

—Teen Titans Go!: Ready for Action. 2017. (ENG., Illus.). (gr. 2-5). pap. 12.99 *(978-1-4012-6899-2(4))* DC Comics.

—Thunder & Lightning Strike!, 1 vol. 2014. (Teen Titans GO! Ser.). (ENG., Illus.). 32p. (gr. 2-3). 22.60 *(978-1-4342-9214-8(2))* Stone Arch Bks.

Torseter, Øyvind. The Heartless Troll. Torseter, Øyvind, illus. 2016. (ENG., Illus.). 120p. (J). (gr. 1-9). 19.95 *(978-1-59270-193-3(0))* Enchanted Lion Bks., LLC.

Torseter, Øyvind, creator. The Hole. 2013. (ENG., Illus.). 64p. (J). (gr. k). 22.95 *(978-1-59270-143-8(4))* Enchanted Lion Bks., LLC.

Tourville, Amanda Doering. Transportation in the City, 1 vol. Thompson, Jeffrey, illus. 2010. (First Graphics: My Community Ser.). (ENG.). 24p. (gr. 1-2). lib. bdg. 23.99 *(978-1-4296-5370-1(1))* Capstone Press of Coughlan Cos.

Townsend, Michael. Where Do Presidents Come From? And Other Presidential Stuff of Super Great Importance. 2012. (ENG.). 160p. (J). (gr. 3-7). 14.99 *(978-0-8037-3748-8(3)*, Dial Bks) Penguin Young Readers Group.

ToyBox Innovations, creator. Dead Man's Chest. 2006. (Pirates of the Caribbean Ser.). (ENG., Illus.). 24p. (J). (gr. -1-3). pap. *(978-0-7634-2177-9(4))* Walt Disney Records.

—Deep in the Jungle. abr. ed. 2006. (Disney's Read along Collection). (ENG.). (J). (gr. -1-3). pap. *(978-0-7634-2182-3(0))* Walt Disney Records.

—Disney Pixar's Toy Story: Read-along. 2006. (Disney's Read Along Ser.). (ENG., Illus.). 24p. (J). (gr. -1-3). pap. *(978-0-7634-2179-3(0))* Walt Disney Records.

—Disney's Chicken Little Read-along. 2006. (Disney's Read Along Ser.). (ENG., Illus.). 24p. (J). pap. *(978-0-7634-2170-0(7))* Walt Disney Records.

—Disney's Finding Nemo Read-along. 2006. (Disney's Read Along Ser.). (ENG., Illus.). 24p. (J). pap. *(978-0-7634-2172-4(3))* Walt Disney Records.

—Disney's Monsters, Inc. Read-along. 2006. (Disney's Read Along Ser.). (ENG., Illus.). 24p. (J). pap. *(978-0-7634-2175-5(8))* Walt Disney Records.

—Disney's the Little Mermaid: Read-along. 2006. (Disney's Read Along Ser.). (ENG., Illus.). 24p. (J). pap. *(978-0-7634-2174-8(X))* Walt Disney Records.

—Disney's Winnie the Pooh: Winnie the Pooh Springtime with Roo/Pooh's Heffalump Movie/Piglet's Big Movie. unabr. ed. 2005. (Disney's Read along Collection Ser.). (ENG.). (J). pap. *(978-0-7634-1147-3(7))* Walt Disney Records.

ToyBox Innovations & Walt Disney Records Staff, creators. Disney's Lilo & Stitch: Read-along. 2006. (Disney's Read Along Ser.). (ENG., Illus.). 24p. (J). pap. *(978-0-7634-2173-1(1))* Walt Disney Records.

Tra, Frank. Spy School. O'Reilly, Sean Patrick, ed. 2011. (Illus.). 76p. (YA). pap. 14.95 *(978-1-926914-27-5(9))* Arcana Studio, Inc.

The Transformation. 2003. (J). per. *(978-1-57657-863-6(1))* Paradise Pr., Inc.

Trembath, Brent. Scruggy Puppies Book. 2012. (ENG.). pap. 10.00 *(978-1-4675-2260-1(0))* Independent Pub.

Trillo, Carlos. Bird. Bobillo, Juan, illus. 2003. 48p. (YA). (gr. 11-18). 12.95 *(978-1-931724-22-7(9))* Diamond Select Toys & Collectibles.

Trine, Greg. The Brotherhood of the Traveling Underpants. Montijo, Rhode, illus. 7th ed. 2009. (Melvin Beederman, Superhero Ser.: 7). (ENG.). 144p. (J). (gr. 2-5). pap. 8.99 *(978-0-8050-8163-3(1)*, 9780805081633) Square Fish.

Trudell, Devin, illus. 3 Stories. Trudell, Devin, . 2007. (YA). 10.00 *(978-0-9794004-0-7(6))* Art Night Bks.

Trumbauer, Lisa. Standoff: Remembering the Alamo, 1 vol. Schoonover, Brent, illus. 2008. (Historical Fiction Ser.). (ENG.). 56p. (gr. 2-3). pap. 6.25 *(978-1-4342-0849-1(4)*, Graphic Flash) Stone Arch Bks.

Tsang, Evonne. I Love Him to Pieces. Görrissen, Janina, illus. 2011. (My Boyfriend Is a Monster Ser.: 1). (ENG.). 128p. (YA). (gr. 7-12). 29.27 *(978-0-7613-6004-9(2))* Lerner Publishing Group.

—Kung Fu Masters, No. 12. Martinez, Alitha E., illus. 2009. (Twisted Journeys (r) Ser.: 12). (ENG.). 112p. (J). (gr. 4-7). 27.93 *(978-0-8225-8878-8(1)*, Graphic Universe™) Lerner Publishing Group.

—#01 I Love Him to Pieces. Görrissen, Janina, illus. 2011. (My Boyfriend Is a Monster Ser.). 128p. (YA). pap. 56.72 *(978-0-7613-7602-6(X)*, Graphic Universe™) Lerner Publishing Group.

Tsang, Evonne & Jimenez, Adan. Hero City. BaróN, Lara & Torres, German, illus. 2012. (Twisted Journeys (r) Ser.: 22). (ENG.). 112p. (J). (gr. 4-7). pap. 7.95 *(978-1-57505-945-7(2)*, Graphic Universe™) Lerner Publishing Group.

—Hero City. Barón, Lara & Torres, German, illus. 2012. (Twisted Journeys (r) Ser.: 22). (ENG.). 112p. (J). (gr. 4-7). lib. bdg. 27.93 *(978-0-7613-4595-4(7)*, Graphic Universe™) Lerner Publishing Group.

Tsukirino, Yumi. Stitch! (ENG., 176p. (J). Vol. 1. 2016. Illus.). pap. 10.99 *(978-1-4278-5673-9(7)*, 9781427856739) Vol. 2. 2017. pap. 10.99 *(978-1-4278-5675-3(3)*, 9781427856753) TOKYOPOP, Inc.

Tsunetomo, Yamamoto & Wilson, William Scott. Hagakure: The Code of the Samurai, 1 vol. Kutsuwada, Chie, illus. 2011. (ENG.). 144p. pap. 14.95 *(978-4-7700-3120-4(3))* Kodansha America, Inc.

Tucker, Mark. Super Phil. Petete, Christine, illus. 2003. (J). 4.50 *(978-1-882440-00-9(5))* God's World Pubns. Inc.

Tulien, Sean. Super Billy Goats Gruff. Cano, Fernando, illus. 2015. (Far Out Fairy Tales Ser.). (ENG.). 40p. (gr. 3-4). lib. bdg. 25.32 *(978-1-4342-9649-8(0))* Stone Arch Bks.

Tulien, Sean & Maese, Fares. Paintball Punk, 1 vol. Aburto, Jesus & Esparza, Andres, illus. 2010. (Sports Illustrated Kids Graphic Novels Ser.). (ENG.). 56p. (gr. 2-3). 26.65 *(978-1-4342-2219-0(5))*; pap. 7.19 *(978-1-4342-2788-1(X))* Stone Arch Bks.

Tulien, Sean & Poe, Edgar Allen. The Pit & the Pendulum, 1 vol. Fabul, J. C. & Calero, Dennis, illus. 2013. (Edgar Allan Poe Graphic Novels Ser.). (ENG.). 72p. (gr. 2-3). pap. 6.10 *(978-1-4342-4260-0(9))*; lib. bdg. 27.99 *(978-1-4342-4024-8(X))* Stone Arch Bks.

Tulien, Sean & Simonson, Louise. Far Out Fairy Tales. Cano, Fern & Sanchez S., Jimena, illus. 2016. (Far Out Fairy Tales

C
D

Ser.). (ENG.). 40p. (gr. 3-4). 151.92 *(978-1-4965-2515-4(9),* Far Out Fairy Tales) Stone Arch Bks.

Tulien, Sean, et al. Shadow of the Sun, 1 vol. 2011. (Flash Ser.). (ENG., Illus.). 56p. (gr. 2-3). pap. 4.95 *(978-1-4342-3088-1(0),* DC Super Heroes) Stone Arch Bks.

Tulsidas. Sundarkaand: Triumph of Hanuman. Nagar, Sachin, illus. 2013. (Campfire Graphic Novels Ser.). (ENG.). 72p. (YA). (gr. 5-12). pap. 9.99 *(978-93-80741-70-3(7),* Campfire) Steerforth Pr.

Turk, Judy Vanslyke, et al. Laughing Thief. 2007. (Clifton Ser.: 2). (ENG., Illus.). 48p. (J). (gr. 4-7). per. 9.99 *(978-1-905460-07-6(4))* CineBook GBR. Dist: National Bk. Network.

—My Dear Wilkinson. 2007. (Clifton Ser.: 1). (ENG., Illus.). 48p. (J). (gr. 4-7). per. 11.95 *(978-1-905460-06-9(6))* CineBook GBR. Dist: National Bk. Network.

Turner, Tracey & Kindberg, Sally. The Comic Strip Big Fat Book of Knowledge. 2012. (ENG., Illus.). 288p. (J). (gr. 6-9). pap. 18.99 *(978-1-4088-0824-5(2),* 9781408808245, Bloomsbury USA Childrens) Bloomsbury Publishing USA.

Uderzo, Albert. EL ADIVINO. 2009. (SPA., Illus.). 48p. 19.95 *(978-84-345-6737-5(7))* Grupo Anaya, S.A. ESP. Dist: Baker & Taylor Bks.

—ASTÉRIX EN HISPANIA. 2009. (SPA., Illus.). 48p. 19.95 *(978-84-345-6732-0(6))* Grupo Anaya, S.A. ESP. Dist: Baker & Taylor Bks.

—ASTÉRIX Y CLEOPATRA. 2009. (SPA., Illus.). 50p. 19.95 *(978-84-345-6724-5(5))* Grupo Anaya, S.A. ESP. Dist: Baker & Taylor Bks.

—ASTÉRIX Y EL CALDERO. 2009. (SPA., Illus.). 48p. 19.95 *(978-84-345-6731-3(8))* Grupo Anaya, S.A. ESP. Dist: Baker & Taylor Bks.

—ASTÉRIX Y LOS GODOS. 2009. (SPA., Illus.). 52p. 19.95 *(978-84-345-6721-4(0))* Grupo Anaya, S.A. ESP. Dist: Baker & Taylor Bks.

—EL COMBATE DE LOS JEFES. 2009. (SPA., Illus.). 48p. 19.95 *(978-84-345-6725-2(3))* Grupo Anaya, S.A. ESP. Dist: Baker & Taylor Bks.

—LOS LAURELES DEL CÉSAR. 2009. (SPA., Illus.). 50p. 19.95 *(978-84-345-6736-8(9))* Grupo Anaya, S.A. ESP. Dist: Baker & Taylor Bks.

—LA VUELTA A LA GALIA DE ASTÉRIX. 2009. (SPA., Illus.). 48p. 19.95 *(978-84-345-6723-8(7))* Grupo Anaya, S.A. ESP. Dist: Baker & Taylor Bks.

Uderzo, Albert & Goscinny, René. Asterix & the Falling Sky. Bell, Anthea & Hockridge, Derek, trs. from FRE. Uderzo, Albert, illus. (ENG., Illus.). 48p. 2006. pap. 12.99 *(978-0-7528-7548-4(5))* 2005. 17.99 *(978-0-7528-7301-5(6))* Orion Publishing Group, Ltd. GBR. (Orion). Dist: Hachette Bk. Group.

—Asterix Omnibus 4: Includes Asterix the Legionary #10, Asterix & the Chieftain's Shield #11, & Asterix at the Olympic Games #12. 2011. (ENG., Illus.). 144p. (J). (gr. 4-6). 29.99 *(978-1-4440-0428-1(X),* Orion) Orion Publishing Group, Ltd. GBR. Dist: Hachette Bk. Group.

Ueda, Rinko. Tail of the Moon, Vol. 4. Ueda, Rinko, illus. 2007. (ENG., Illus.). 200p. (gr. 11). pap. 8.99 *(978-1-4215-0816-0(8))* Viz Media.

Ueyama, Michiro. Chaotic Century. Ueyama, Michiro, illus. (Zoids Ser.). (ENG., Illus.). Vol. 11. 2004. 82p. pap. 5.95 *(978-1-56931-858-4(1))* Vol. 12. 2003. 72p. pap. 5.95 *(978-1-56931-867-6(0))* Viz Media.

Umezu, Kazuo. The Drifting Classroom. Roman, Annette, ed. Umezu, Kazuo, illus. 2007. (Drifting Classroom Ser.: 9). (ENG., Illus.). 192p. pap. 9.99 *(978-1-4215-0961-7(X))*; pap. 9.99 *(978-1-4215-0960-0(1))* Viz Media.

Up in Smoke. 2004. (J). *(978-0-9762904-9-0(9))* Layne Morgan Media, Inc.

Urrea, Lourdes. Athon Labar. rev. ed. 2006. (Ediciones Castillo Castillo Del Terror Ser.). (SPA & ENG.). 136p. (J). (gr. 6-9). pap. 6.95 *(978-970-20-0309-0(1))* Castillo, Ediciones, S. A. de C. V. MEX. Dist: Macmillan.

Urrea, Lourdes, et al. El Dragon Jines. 2005. (Ediciones Castillo Castillo Del Terror Ser.). (SPA.). (J). (gr. 2-6). pap. 7.95 *(978-970-20-0357-1(1))* Castillo, Ediciones, S. A. de C. V. MEX. Dist: Iaconi, Mariuccia Bk. Imports.

—En Busca de Dracu. 2005. (Ediciones Castillo Castillo Del Terror Ser.).Tr. of Looking for Dracu. (SPA.). (J). (gr. 2-6). pap. 7.95 *(978-970-20-0339-7(3))* Castillo, Ediciones, S. A. de C. V. MEX. Dist: Iaconi, Mariuccia Bk. Imports.

—Piel de Gallina. 2005. (Ediciones Castillo Castillo Del Terror Ser.).Tr. of Chicken Bumps. (SPA.). (J). (gr. 2-6). pap. 7.95 *(978-970-20-0292-5(3))* Castillo, Ediciones, S. A. de C. V. MEX. Dist: Iaconi, Mariuccia Bk. Imports.

—El Secreto Gitano. 2005. (Ediciones Castillo Castillo Del Terror Ser.).Tr. of Gypsy Secret. (SPA.). (J). (gr. 2-6). pap. 7.95 *(978-970-20-0310-6(5))* Castillo, Ediciones, S. A. de C. V. MEX. Dist: Iaconi, Mariuccia Bk. Imports.

Usual Gang of Idiots Staff. Totally Useless MAD. 2013. (ENG., Illus.). 128p. pap. 12.99 *(978-1-4012-3911-4(0),* MAD) DC Comics.

Valdez Y Alanis, Erik, illus. Rumpelstiltskin: The Graphic Novel. 2008. (Graphic Spin Ser.). (ENG.). 40p. (gr. 1-3). 25.32 *(978-1-4342-0768-5(4),* Graphic Revolve) Stone Arch Bks.

Van Camp, Katie. Harry & Horsie. Agnew, Lincoln, illus. 2009. (Harry & Horsie Adventures Ser.: 1). (ENG.). 32p. (J). (gr. -1-1). 16.99 *(978-0-06-175598-9(2))* HarperCollins Pubs.

Van Hamme, Jean. Beyond the Shadows. Rosinski, Grzegorz, illus. 2008. (Thorgal Ser.: 3). (ENG.). 96p. pap. 19.95 *(978-1-905460-45-8(7))* CineBook GBR. Dist: National Bk. Network.

—The Brand of the Exiles. Rosinski, Grzegorz, illus. 2013. (Thorgal Ser.: 12). (ENG.). 48p. (J). (gr. 7-12). pap. 11.95 *(978-1-84918-136-5(5))* CineBook GBR. Dist: National Bk. Network.

—The Cage, Vol. 15. Rosinski, Grzegorz, illus. 2014. (Thorgal Ser.: 15). (ENG.). 48p. pap. 11.95 *(978-1-84918-186-0(1))* CineBook GBR. Dist: National Bk. Network.

—The Curse of the 30 Pieces of Silver, Vol. 14, Pt. 2. Shreder, Etienne & Aubin, Antoine, illus. 2012. (Blake & Mortimer Ser.: 14). (ENG.). 64p. (J). (gr. 5-12). pap. 15.95 *(978-1-84918-130-3(6))* CineBook GBR. Dist: National Bk. Network.

—The Heir. Francq, Philippe, illus. 2008. (Largo Winch Ser.: 1). (ENG.). 96p. pap. 19.95 *(978-1-905460-48-9(1))* CineBook GBR. Dist: National Bk. Network.

—The Invisible Fortress. Rosinski, Grzegorz, illus. 2012. (Thorgal Ser.: 11). (ENG.). 48p. (YA). (gr. 6-17). pap. 11.95 *(978-1-84918-103-7(9))* CineBook GBR. Dist: National Bk. Network.

—Ogotai's Crown. Rosinski, Grzegorz, illus. 2013. (Thorgal Ser.: 13). (ENG.). 48p. pap. 11.95 *(978-1-84918-142-6(X))* CineBook GBR. Dist: National Bk. Network.

—The Strange Encounter, Vol. 5. 2009. (Blake & Mortimer Ser.: 5). (ENG., Illus.). 66p. pap. 15.95 *(978-1-905460-75-5(9))* CineBook GBR. Dist: National Bk. Network.

—Thorgal: La Maga Traicionada. Rosinski, Grzegorz, illus. 2004. Orig. Title: Thorgal vol. 1: la Magicienne Trahie. (SPA.). 48p. pap. 16.95 *(978-1-59497-006-1(8))* Public Square Bks.

—The Three Elders of Aran. Rosinski, illus. 2007. (Thorgal Ser.: 2). (ENG.). 48p. (J). (gr. 4-7). pap. 14.99 *(978-1-905460-31-1(7))* CineBook GBR. Dist: National Bk. Network.

—Los Tres Ancianos del pais de Aran, Vol. 3. Roskinski, Grzegorz, illus. 2004. Orig. Title: Thorgal Vol. 3: les Trois Vieillards du Pays d'Aran. (SPA.). 48p. pap. 16.95 *(978-1-59497-008-5(4))* Public Square Bks.

Van Horn, William & Rosa, Don. Walt Disney's Comics, No. 663. Clark, John, ed. 2005. (ENG., Illus.). 64p. (YA). pap. 6.95 *(978-1-888472-03-5(0),* 9781888472035) Gemstone Publishing, Inc.

Van Horn, William, et al. Walt Disney's Comics. Clark, John, ed. 2006. (ENG., Illus.). 64p. Vol. 664. pap. 6.95 *(978-1-888472-17-2(0),* 9781888472172) Vol. 665. pap. 6.95 *(978-1-888472-18-9(9),* 9781888472189) Vol. 667. pap. 6.95 *(978-1-888472-20-2(0),* 9781888472202) Gemstone Publishing, Inc.

Van Lente, Fred. The Creeping Doom. Cliquet, Ronan, illus. 2009. (Iron Man Ser.: No. 1). 24p. (J). (gr. 2-5). 24.21 *(978-1-59961-551-6(7),* 1284980) Spotlight.

—Enter the Dragon. Cordeiro, James, illus. 2009. (Iron Man Ser.: No. 1). 24p. (J). (gr. 2-5). 24.21 *(978-1-59961-552-3(5),* 1284981) Spotlight.

—Heart of Steel. Cordeiro, James, illus. 2009. (Iron Man Ser.: No. 1). 24p. (J). (gr. 2-5). 24.21 *(978-1-59961-553-0(3),* 1284982) Spotlight.

—Hostile Takeover. Cordeiro, James, illus. 2009. (Iron Man Ser.: No. 1). 24p. (J). (gr. 2-5). 24.21 *(978-1-59961-554-7(1),* 1284983) Spotlight.

—The Pack: Part 1. 2013. (Wolverine First Class Set 2 Ser.). (Illus.). 24p. (J). (gr. 2-6). lib. bdg. 24.21 *(978-1-61479-178-2(3))* Spotlight.

—The Pack: Part 2. 2013. (Wolverine First Class Set 2 Ser.). (Illus.). 24p. (J). (gr. 2-6). lib. bdg. 24.21 *(978-1-61479-179-9(1))* Spotlight.

—Substitute. 2013. (Wolverine First Class Set 2 Ser.). (Illus.). 24p. (J). (gr. 2-6). lib. bdg. 24.21 *(978-1-61479-181-2(3))* Spotlight.

Van Lente, Fred, et al. Tales from the Crypt. Todd, Mort et al, illus. 2009. (Tales from the Crypt Graphic Novels Ser.: 6). (ENG.). 96p. (J). (gr. 5-12). 12.95 *(978-1-59707-137-6(4),* 9781597071376) Papercutz.

—Yabba Dabba Voodoo. Mannion, Steve et al, illus. 2009. (Tales from the Crypt Graphic Novels Ser.: 5). (ENG.). 96p. (J). (gr. 5-12). 12.95 *(978-1-59707-117-8(X),* 9781597071178) Papercutz.

Vanholme, Virginie. Malevolence & Mandrake. 2nd ed. 2009. (Scared to Death Ser.: 2). (ENG., Illus.). 48p. (gr. 3-17). pap. 11.95 *(978-1-905460-77-9(5))* CineBook GBR. Dist: National Bk. Network.

—The Vampire from the Marshes. Mauricet, illus. 2008. (Scared to Death Ser.: 1). (ENG.). 46p. pap. 11.95 *(978-1-905460-47-2(3))* CineBook GBR. Dist: National Bk. Network.

Vansant, Wayne. The Battle of the Bulge: A Graphic History of Allied Victory in the Ardennes 1944-1945. Vansant, Wayne, illus. 2015. (Graphic Histories Ser.). (ENG., Illus.). 104p. (J). (gr. 8-12). 34.65 *(978-1-939581-75-4(3))* Quarto Publishing Group USA.

—Grant vs. Lee: The Graphic History of the Civil War's Greatest Rivals During the Last Year of the War. Vansant, Wayne, illus. 2015. (Graphic Histories Ser.). (ENG., Illus.). 104p. (J). (gr. 8-12). 34.65 *(978-1-939581-78-5(8))* Quarto Publishing Group USA.

—Grant vs. Lee: The Graphic History of the Civil War's Greatest Rivals During the Last Year of the War. 2013. (Zenith Graphic Histories Ser.). (ENG., Illus.). 104p. pap. 19.99 *(978-0-7603-4531-3(7),* 0760345317, Zenith Pr.) Quarto Publishing Group USA.

—The Red Baron: The Graphic History of Richthofen's Flying Circus & the Air War in WWI. Vansant, Wayne, illus. 2015. (Graphic Histories Ser.). (ENG., Illus.). 104p. (J). (gr. 8-12). 34.65 *(978-1-939581-80-8(X))* Quarto Publishing Group USA.

Various. DC Super Hero Girls. 2017. (ENG.). 64p. (gr. 3-7). pap. 7.99 ***(978-1-4012-7458-0(7))*** DC Comics.

Various Authors Staff. Fable Comics. Duffy, Chris, ed. 2015. (ENG., Illus.). 128p. (J). (gr. 1-7). 19.99 *(978-1-62672-107-4(6),* 9781626721074, First Second Bks.) Roaring Brook Pr.

Varon, Sara. Bake Sale. Varon, Sara, illus. 2011. (ENG., Illus.). 160p. (J). (gr. 3-7). 19.99 *(978-1-59643-740-1(5),* 9781596437401); pap. 17.99 *(978-1-59643-419-6(8),* 9781596434196) Roaring Brook Pr. (First Second Bks.).

—Robot Dreams. Varon, Sara, illus. 2007. (ENG., Illus.). 208p. (J). (gr. 3-7). pap. 17.99 *(978-1-59643-108-9(3),* 9781596431089, First Second Bks.) Roaring Brook Pr.

—Robot Dreams. Varon, Sara, illus. 2016. (ENG., Illus.). 224p. (J). pap. 9.99 *(978-1-250-07350-1(2),* 9781250073501) Square Fish.

—Sweaterweather & Other Short Stories. 2016. (ENG., Illus.). 128p. (J). 19.99 *(978-1-62672-118-0(1),* 9781626721180, First Second Bks.) Roaring Brook Pr.

Venable, Colleen A. F. And Then There Were Gnomes. Yue, Stephanie, illus. 2010. (Guinea Pig, Pet Shop Private Eye Ser.: 2). (ENG.). 48p. (J). (gr. 2-5). pap. 6.95 *(978-0-7613-5480-2(8))*; lib. bdg. 27.93 *(978-0-7613-4599-2(X))* Lerner Publishing Group.

—The Ferret's a Foot, 3 vols. Yue, Stephanie, illus. 2011. (Guinea Pig, Pet Shop Private Eye Ser.: 3). (ENG.). 48p. (J). (gr. 2-5). 27.93 *(978-0-7613-5223-5(6))*; pap. 6.95 *(978-0-7613-5629-5(0))* Lerner Publishing Group.

—Fish You Were Here, No. 4. Yue, Stephanie, illus. 2011. (Guinea Pig, Pet Shop Private Eye Ser.: 4). (ENG.). 48p. (J). (gr. 2-5). pap. 6.95 *(978-0-7613-5630-1(4))*; lib. bdg. 27.93 *(978-0-7613-5224-2(4))* Lerner Publishing Group.

—Going, Going, Dragon! 2013. 48p. pap. 14.95 *(978-1-4677-0973-6(5))* Lerner Publishing Group.

—Going, Going, Dragon! Yue, Stephanie, illus. 2013. (Guinea Pig, Pet Shop Private Eye Ser.: 6). (ENG.). 48p. (J). (gr. 2-5). pap. 6.95 *(978-1-4677-0726-8(0))*; lib. bdg. 27.93 *(978-0-7613-6009-4(3))* Lerner Publishing Group.

—Hamster & Cheese. Yue, Stephanie, illus. 2010. (Guinea Pig, Pet Shop Private Eye Ser.: 1). (ENG.). 48p. (J). (gr. 2-5). pap. 6.95 *(978-0-7613-5479-6(4))*; lib. bdg. 27.93 *(978-0-7613-4598-5(1))* Lerner Publishing Group.

—Raining Cats & Detectives. Yue, Stephanie, illus. 2012. (Guinea Pig, Pet Shop Private Eye Ser.: 5). (ENG.). 48p. (J). (gr. 2-5). pap. 6.95 *(978-0-7613-8541-7(X))*; lib. bdg. 27.93 *(978-0-7613-6008-7(5))* Lerner Publishing Group.

—Raining Cats & Detectives. Yue, Stephanie, illus. 2012. (Guinea Pig, Pet Shop Private Eye Ser.: 5). lib. bdg. 17.15 *(978-0-606-26631-4(3),* Turtleback) Turtleback Bks.

Verano, Vladimir, illus. The Prince, the Demon King, & the Monkey Warrior. 2011. (ENG.). 96p. (J). (gr. 3-6). pap. 9.95 *(978-1-934159-30-9(1))* ThingsAsian Pr.

Verne, Jules. Around the World in 80 Days. Soleilhac, Aude, illus. 2011. (Classics Illustrated Deluxe Graphic Nove Ser.). (ENG.). 144p. (J). (gr. 3-9). 17.99 *(978-1-59707-284-7(2),* 9781597072847) Papercutz.

Verne, Jules & Lokus, Rex. Around the World in 80 Days. Smith, Tod G., illus. 2015. (Graphic Revolve: Common Core Editions Ser.). (ENG.). 72p. (gr. 2-3). pap. 6.95 *(978-1-4965-0381-7(3))* Stone Arch Bks.

Veronique, Catel. Bluesy Lucy - the Existential Chronicles of a Thirtysomething. 2013. (Bluesy Lucy - the Existential Chronicles of a Thirtysomething Ser.). (ENG., Illus.). 120p. 24.95 *(978-1-59465-048-2(9),* 9781594650482) Humanoids, Inc.

Vincent, Eric. Aesop's Fables. 2013. (Classics Illustrated Graphic Novels Ser.). (ENG., Illus.). 56p. (J). (gr. 5-9). 9.99 *(978-1-59707-441-4(1),* 9781597074414) Papercutz.

Vivat, Booki. Frazzled #2: Ordinary Mishaps & Inevitable Catastrophes. Vivat, Booki, illus. 2017. (Illus.). 224p. (J). (gr. 3-7). 12.99 ***(978-0-06-239881-9(4))*** HarperCollins Pubs.

Vivès, Bastien, et al. The Chase. 2015. (Last Man Ser.: 3). (ENG., Illus.). 208p. (gr. 9). pap. 9.99 *(978-1-62672-048-0(7),* 9781626720480, First Second Bks.) Roaring Brook Pr.

—The Royal Cup. 2015. (Last Man Ser.: 2). (ENG., Illus.). 208p. (gr. 9). pap. 9.99 *(978-1-62672-047-3(9),* 9781626720473, First Second Bks.) Roaring Brook Pr.

Viz Media. Fairy Dreams. 2013. (Winx Club Ser.: 5). lib. bdg. 17.20 *(978-0-606-26987-2(8),* Turtleback) Turtleback Bks.

VIZ Media, . & Straffi, Iginio. WINX Club, Vol. 7. 2013. (ENG.). 96p. (J). pap. 6.99 *(978-1-4215-4204-1(8))* Viz Media.

—WINX Club, Vol. 8. 2013. (ENG.). 96p. (J). pap. 6.99 *(978-1-4215-4205-8(6))* Viz Media.

Viz Media Staff. Meet Mameshiba! 2011. (ENG.). 96p. (J). pap. 6.99 *(978-1-4215-3972-0(1))* Viz Media.

VIZ Media Staff & Straffi, Iginio. WINX Club, Vol. 5. 2013. (ENG.). 96p. (J). pap. 6.99 *(978-1-4215-4163-1(7))* Viz Media.

VIZ Media Staff & Straffi, Iginio. WINX Club, Vol. 6. 2013. (ENG.). 96p. (J). pap. 6.99 *(978-1-4215-4203-4(X))* Viz Media.

Volozova, Olga, illus. The Airy Tales. 2008. (ENG.). 128p. (gr. 8). pap. 15.00 *(978-0-9797465-6-7(6))* Sparkplug Bks.

Wade, Mary Dodson. Christopher Columbus: Famous Explorer, 1 vol. Whigham, Rod & Barnett, Charles, III, illus. 2007. (Graphic Biographies Ser.). (ENG.). 32p. (gr. 3-4). per. 8.10 *(978-0-7368-7905-7(6),* 1264941, Graphic Library) Capstone Press of Coughlan Cos.

Wagner, John. Banzai Battalion: Just Another Bug Hunt. Bolland, Brian et al, illus. 2014. (ENG.). 160p. pap. 19.99 *(978-1-78108-218-8(9),* 2000 AD) Rebellion GBR. Dist: Simon & Schuster, Inc.

Wagner, Matt. The Demon - From the Darkness. 2014. (ENG., Illus.). 128p. pap. 14.99 *(978-1-4012-4250-3(2))* DC Comics.

Waid, Mark. City of Incredibles, Vol. 2. Takara, Marcio, illus. 2010. (Incredibles Ser.). (ENG.). 112p. (J). 24.99 *(978-1-60886-529-1(0))* Boom! Studios.

—Enter the Detective. Guice, Butch & Perkins, Mike, illus. 2003. (Ruse Traveler Ser.: Vol. 1). 192p. (YA). (gr. 7-18). pap. 9.95 *(978-1-59314-012-0(6))* CrossGeneration Comics, Inc.

—Imaginauts. Wieringo, Mike, illus. 2003. (Fantastic Four Ser.: Vol. 1). 144p. (YA). pap. 12.99 *(978-0-7851-1063-7(1))* Marvel Worldwide, Inc.

—Incorruptible. Takara, Marcio, illus. 2012. (ENG.). 128p. Vol. 6. (Incorruptible Ser.: 6). (gr. 10). pap. 16.99 *(978-1-60886-084-5(1))* Vol. 7. (gr. 9). pap. 16.99 *(978-1-60886-085-2(X))* Boom! Studios.

—The Incredibles: City of Incredibles, Vol. 2. Takara, Marcio, illus. 2010. (Incredibles Ser.). (ENG.). 112p. (J). pap. 9.99 *(978-1-60886-503-1(7))* Boom! Studios.

Waid, Mark & Haspiel, Dean. The Fox - Freak Magnet. Haspiel, Dean, illus. 2014. (Fox Ser.). (ENG., Illus.). 144p. pap. 14.99 *(978-1-936975-93-8(9),* Dark Circle Comics) Archie Comic Pubns., Inc.

Waid, Mark & Walker, Landry. Revenge from Below. Takara, Marcio, illus. 2010. (Incredibles Ser.). (ENG.). 112p. (J). (gr. 3-6). pap. 9.99 *(978-1-60886-518-5(5))* Boom! Studios.

Walker, Landry. Little Gloomy Super Scary Monster Show Volume 1. 2008. (ENG., Illus.). 104p. pap. 9.95 *(978-1-59362-103-2(5),* 9781593621032) Slave Labor Bks.

—Secrets & Lies. Takara, Marcio, illus. 2010. (Incredibles Ser.). 112p. (J). (gr. 3-8). pap. 9.99 *(978-1-60886-583-3(5))* Boom! Studios.

—Supergirl: Cosmic Adventures of the 8th Grade. 2016. lib. bdg. 24.50 *(978-0-606-38776-7(5))* Turtleback Bks.

Walker, Landry Q. Danger Club Vol. 1: Death. 2012. (ENG., Illus.). 102p. (YA). pap. 9.99 *(978-1-60706-634-7(3),* 9781607066347) Image Comics.

—Secret Entity! #4, 1 vol. Jones, Eric, illus. 2013. (Supergirl: Cosmic Adventures in the 8th Grade Ser.). (ENG.). 32p. (gr. 2-3). 22.60 *(978-1-4342-4720-9(1))* Stone Arch Bks.

—Super Hero School: #3, 1 vol. Jones, Eric, illus. 2013. (Supergirl: Cosmic Adventures in the 8th Grade Ser.). (ENG.). 32p. (gr. 2-3). 22.60 *(978-1-4342-4719-3(8))* Stone Arch Bks.

—Supergirl: Cosmic Adventures in the 8th Grade. Jones, Eric, illus. 2013. (Supergirl: Cosmic Adventures in the 8th Grade Ser.). (ENG.). 32p. (gr. 2-3). lib. bdg. 135.60 *(978-1-4342-8830-1(7))*; lib. bdg. 45.20 *(978-1-4342-8831-8(5))*; lib. bdg. 45.20 *(978-1-4342-4367-6(2))* Stone Arch Bks.

Walker, Landry Q. & Mason, Joey. Evil in a Skirt! #5, 1 vol. Jones, Eric, illus. 2013. (Supergirl: Cosmic Adventures in the 8th Grade Ser.). (ENG.). 32p. (gr. 2-3). 22.60 *(978-1-4342-6045-1(3))* Stone Arch Bks.

—Her First Extra-Ordinary Adventure! #1, 1 vol. Jones, Eric, illus. 2013. (Supergirl: Cosmic Adventures in the 8th Grade Ser.). (ENG.). 32p. (gr. 2-3). 22.60 *(978-1-4342-4717-9(1))* Stone Arch Bks.

—My Own Best Frenemy: #2, 1 vol. Jones, Eric, illus. 2013. (Supergirl: Cosmic Adventures in the 8th Grade Ser.). (ENG.). 32p. (gr. 2-3). 22.60 *(978-1-4342-4718-6(X))* Stone Arch Bks.

—Off to Save the Day..., No. 6. Jones, Eric, illus. 2013. (Supergirl: Cosmic Adventures in the 8th Grade Ser.). (ENG.). 32p. (gr. 2-3). 22.60 *(978-1-4342-6046-8(1))* Stone Arch Bks.

Walker, Landry Quinn. Supergirl Cosmic Adventures of the 8th Grade. 2016. (ENG., Illus.). 144p. (J). (gr. 4-7). pap. 12.99 *(978-1-4012-6320-1(8))* DC Comics.

Walter, Dan. Hello, Willie! 2007. (J). 14.95 *(978-1-932888-52-2(7))* Mascot Bks., Inc.

Walter Foster Creative Team. Learn to Draw Disney Minnie & Daisy Best Friends Forever Fabulous Fashions. Disney Storybook Artists Staff, illus. 2014. 64p. (J). (gr. 3-5). 33.27 *(978-1-939581-32-7(X))* Quarto Publishing Group USA.

Walter Foster Creative Team, ed. How to Draw Transformers. 2008. 32p. pap. 5.95 *(978-1-60058-119-9(6))* Quarto Publishing Group USA.

Waltz, Tom & Eastman, Kevin B. Teenage Mutant Ninja Turtles Volume 3: Shadows of the Past: Shadows of the Past. Duncan, Dan, illus. 2016. (Teenage Mutant Ninja Turtles Ser.). (ENG.). 104p. pap. 17.99 *(978-1-61377-405-2(2),* 9781613774052) Idea & Design Works, LLC.

—Teenage Mutant Ninja Turtles Volume 5: Krang War: Krang War. Bates, Ben, illus. 2013. (Teenage Mutant Ninja Turtles Ser.). (ENG.). 104p. pap. 17.99 *(978-1-61377-640-7(3),* 9781613776407) Idea & Design Works, LLC.

Waltz, Tom, et al. Teenage Mutant Ninja Turtles Volume 1: Change Is Constant Deluxe Edition: Change Is Constant Deluxe Edition. Duncan, Dan, illus. 2012. (Teenage Mutant Ninja Turtles Ser.). (ENG.). 192p. 49.99 *(978-1-61377-233-1(5),* 9781613772331) Idea & Design Works, LLC.

Ward, Nick. The Naughty Fairy's Naughty Surprise! 2008. 24p. (J). 15.99 *(978-1-60010-269-1(7))* Diamond Bk. Distributors.

Warner, Gertrude Chandler. Boxcar Children Graphic Novels, 6 vols., Set 2. Incl. Amusement Park Mystery. Denton, Shannon Eric. Dubisch, Mike, illus. 28.50 *(978-1-60270-718-4(9))*; Castle Mystery. Denton, Shannon Eric. Dubisch, Mike, illus. 28.50 *(978-1-60270-720-7(0))*; Haunted Cabin Mystery. Bloodworth, Mark, illus. 28.50 *(978-1-60270-717-7(0))*; Pizza Mystery. Worley, Rob M. Dubisch, Mike, illus. 28.50 *(978-1-60270-719-1(7))*; Snowbound Mystery. Dubisch, Mike, illus. 28.50 *(978-1-60270-715-3(4))*; Tree House Mystery. Long, Christopher E. Bloodworth, Mark, illus. 28.50 *(978-1-60270-716-0(2))*; (J). (gr. 2-5). (Boxcar Children Graphic Novels Ser.). 32p. 2010. 171.00 *(978-1-60270-714-6(6),* Graphic Planet- Fiction) ABDO Publishing Co.

—Boxcar Children Graphic Novels, 6 vols., Set 3. Dunn, Ben, illus. Incl. Bk. 13. Woodshed Mystery. Dunn, Joeming. 28.50 *(978-1-61641-121-3(X))*; Bk. 14. Lighthouse Mystery. Dunn, Joeming. 28.50 *(978-1-61641-122-0(8))*; Bk. 15. Mountain Top Mystery. Dunn, Joeming. 28.50 *(978-1-61641-123-7(6))*; Bk. 16. Houseboat Mystery. Dunn, Joeming W., illus. & adapted by. 28.50 *(978-1-61641-124-4(4))*; Bk. 17. Bicycle Mystery. Dunn, Joeming W., illus. & adapted by. 28.50 *(978-1-61641-125-1(2))*; Bk. 18. Mystery in the Sand. Dunn, Joeming. 28.50 *(978-1-61641-126-8(0))*; (J). (gr. 2-5). (Boxcar Children Graphic Novels Ser.). (Illus.). 32p. 2011. 171.00 *(978-1-61641-120-6(1),* Graphic Planet- Fiction) ABDO Publishing Co.

Watari, Wataru. My Youth Romantic Comedy Is Wrong, as I Expected. 2016. (My Youth Romantic Comedy Is Wrong, As I Expected Ser.: 1). (ENG.). 240p. (gr. 8-17). pap. 14.00 *(978-0-316-31229-5(0),* Yen Pr.) Orbit.

Watase, Yû. Bandit, 4. Watase, Yû, illus. 2nd ed. 2004. (Fushigi Yugi Ser.). (ENG., Illus.). 200p. (YA). pap. 9.95 *(978-1-56931-993-2(6))* Viz Media.

Watase, Yuu. Absolute Boyfriend, Vol. 3, 6 vols. 2007. (ENG., Illus.). 200p. pap. 9.99 *(978-1-4215-1003-3(0))* Viz Media.

—Alice 19th, Vol. 6, 7 vols. Watase, Yuu, illus. 2004. (ENG., Illus.). 200p. pap. 9.99 *(978-1-59116-243-8(2))* Viz Media.

—Arata: The Legend, Vol. 17. Watase, Yuu, illus. 2014. (ENG., Illus.). 192p. pap. 9.99 *(978-1-4215-5876-9(9))* Viz Media.

—Ceres: Celestial Legend, Vol. 8, 14 vols. Watase, Yuu, illus. 2004. (ENG., Illus.). 200p. pap. 9.95 *(978-1-59116-260-5(2))* Viz Media.

—Fushigi Yûgi: Genbu Kaiden, Vol. 12. Watase, Yuu, illus. 2014. (ENG., Illus.). 192p. pap. 9.99 *(978-1-4215-6434-0(3))* Viz Media.

—Fushigi Yûgi: Genbu Kaiden, Vol. 4. Watase, Yuu, illus. 2006. (ENG., Illus.). 208p. pap. 8.99 *(978-1-4215-0579-4(7))* Viz Media.

Watase, Yuu & Caselman, Lance. Alice 19th, Vol. 1, 7 vols. Watase, Yuu, illus. 2003. (ENG., Illus.). 192p. pap. 9.95 *(978-1-59116-215-5(7))* Viz Media.

—Alice 19th, Vol. 2, 7 vols. JN Productions Staff, tr. from JPN. Watase, Yuu, illus. 2003. (ENG., Illus.). 200p. pap. 9.95 *(978-1-59116-229-2(7))* Viz Media.

—The Lost Word, 7 vols. Watase, Yuu, illus. 2004. (Alice 19th Ser.). (ENG., Illus.). 200p. pap. 9.99 *(978-1-59116-244-5(0))* Viz Media.

Water Goes Round, 4 vols. Incl. Eggs, Legs, Wings: A Butterfly Life Cycle. Knudsen, Shannon. Smith, Simon, illus. lib. bdg. 23.99 *(978-1-4296-5367-1(1))*; Hide & Seek Moon: The

Moon Phases. Koontz, Robin Michal. Davidson, Chris, illus. 23.99 *(978-1-4296-5365-7(5))*; Water Goes Round: The Water Cycle. Koontz, Robin Michal. Davidson, Chris, illus. lib. bdg. 23.99 *(978-1-4296-5364-0(7))*; (gr. 1-2). (First Graphics: Nature Cycles Ser.). (ENG.). 24p. 2010. Set lib. bdg. 71.97 *(978-1-4296-5368-8(X))* Capstone Press of Coughlan Cos.

Watson, Andi. Princess Decomposia & Count Spatula. 2015. (ENG., Illus.). 176p. (YA). (gr. 8). 19.99 *(978-1-62672-275-0(7)*, 9781626722750, First Second Bks.) Roaring Brook Pr.

Watson Dubisch, Carolyn. The Horribles. 2010. 73p. pap. 16.96 *(978-0-557-35938-7(4))* Lulu Pr., Inc.

Watson, Tom. Stick Dog Craves Candy. 2017. (Stick Dog Ser.: 7). 224p. (J). (gr. 3-7). 12.99 ***(978-0-06-241094-8(6))*** HarperCollins Pubs.

Watsuki, Nobuhiro. Busou Renkin. (JPN., Illus.). (YA). Vol. 1. 188p. pap. *(978-4-08-873557-3(9))* Vol. 3. 182p. pap. *(978-4-08-873630-3(3))* Vol. 4. 204p. pap. *(978-4-08-873651-8(6))* Vol. 5. 185p. pap. *(978-4-08-873670-9(2))* Shuei-Sha.

—Busou Renkin Vol. 2: Fade to Black. (Illus.). 203p. (YA). pap. *(978-4-08-873587-0(0))* Shuei-Sha.

Watters, Shannon, ed. Adventure Time - Cover Gallery, Vol. 1. 2013. (ENG., Illus.). 128p. (J). (gr. 4). 24.99 *(978-1-60886-343-3(3))* Boom! Studios.

Watterson, William. Achtung, Fertig, Los! Goetting, Waltraud, tr. from ENG. (Calvin & Hobbes Ser.: Vol. 8). (GER., Illus.). 64p. (J). pap. *(978-3-8105-0336-7(3))* Kruger, Wolfgang Verlag, GmbH DEU. Dist: International Bk. Import Service, Inc.

—Alles unter Kontrolle. Goetting, Waltraud, tr. from ENG. (Calvin & Hobbes Ser.: Vol. 3). (GER., Illus.). 64p. (J). pap. *(978-3-8105-0330-5(4))* Kruger, Wolfgang Verlag, GmbH DEU. Dist: International Bk. Import Service, Inc.

—Auf dem Sprung. Goetting, Waltraud, tr. from ENG. (Calvin & Hobbes Ser.: Bk. 1). (GER., Illus.). 96p. (J). pap. *(978-3-8105-0320-6(7))* Kruger, Wolfgang Verlag, GmbH DEU. Dist: International Bk. Import Service, Inc.

—Bloss nicht Aergern. Goetting, Waltraud, tr. from ENG. (Calvin & Hobbes Ser.: Bk. 3). (GER., Illus.). 96p. (J). pap. *(978-3-8105-0322-0(3))* Kruger, Wolfgang Verlag, GmbH DEU. Dist: International Bk. Import Service, Inc.

—Calvin & Hobbes: Das Jubilaumsalbum, 10 vols. Bartoszko, Alexandra, tr. from ENG. (Calvin & Hobbes Ser.). (GER., Illus.). 208p. (J). *(978-3-8105-0370-1(3))* Kruger, Wolfgang Verlag, GmbH DEU. Dist: International Bk. Import Service, Inc.

—Einfach Umwerfend. Goetting, Waltraud, tr. from ENG. (Calvin & Hobbes Ser.: Vol. 13). (GER., Illus.). 48p. (J). pap. *(978-3-8105-0350-3(9))* Kruger, Wolfgang Verlag, GmbH DEU. Dist: International Bk. Import Service, Inc.

—Enorm in Form. Goetting, Waltraud, tr. from ENG. (Calvin & Hobbes Ser.: Vol. 9). (GER., Illus.). 64p. (J). pap. *(978-3-8105-0340-4(1))* Kruger, Wolfgang Verlag, GmbH DEU. Dist: International Bk. Import Service, Inc.

—Feine Freunde. Goetting, Waltraud, tr. from ENG. (Calvin & Hobbes Ser.: Vol. 15). (GER., Illus.). 80p. (J). pap. *(978-3-8105-0353-4(3))* Kruger, Wolfgang Verlag, GmbH DEU. Dist: International Bk. Import Service, Inc.

—Fix & Fertig. Goetting, Waltraud, tr. from ENG. (Calvin & Hobbes Ser.: Bk. 2). (GER., Illus.). 96p. (J). pap. *(978-3-8105-0321-3(5))* Kruger, Wolfgang Verlag, GmbH DEU. Dist: International Bk. Import Service, Inc.

—Ganz schoen Daneben. Goetting, Waltraud, tr. from ENG. (Calvin & Hobbes Ser.: Vol. 7). (GER., Illus.). 64p. (J). pap. *(978-3-8105-0335-0(5))* Kruger, Wolfgang Verlag, GmbH DEU. Dist: International Bk. Import Service, Inc.

—Immer mit der Ruhe. Goetting, Waltraud, tr. from ENG. (Calvin & Hobbes Ser.: Vol. 4). (GER., Illus.). 64p. (J). pap. *(978-3-8105-0331-2(2))* Kruger, Wolfgang Verlag, GmbH DEU. Dist: International Bk. Import Service, Inc.

—Immer Voll Drauf. Goetting, Waltraud, tr. from ENG. (Calvin & Hobbes Ser.: Vol. 5). (GER., Illus.). 64p. (J). pap. *(978-3-8105-0332-9(0))* Kruger, Wolfgang Verlag, GmbH DEU. Dist: International Bk. Import Service, Inc.

—Jetzt Erst Recht. Goetting, Waltraud, tr. from ENG. (Calvin & Hobbes Ser.: Vol. 10). (GER., Illus.). 64p. (J). pap. *(978-3-8105-0339-8(8))* Kruger, Wolfgang Verlag, GmbH DEU. Dist: International Bk. Import Service, Inc.

—Jetzt geht's Rund. Goetting, Waltraud, tr. from ENG. (Calvin & Hobbes Ser.: Vol. 1). (GER., Illus.). 64p. (J). pap. *(978-3-8105-0328-2(2))* Kruger, Wolfgang Verlag, GmbH DEU. Dist: International Bk. Import Service, Inc.

—Mach mir den Tiger. Goetting, Waltraud, tr. from ENG. (Calvin & Hobbes Ser.: Vol. 11). (GER., Illus.). 64p. (J). pap. *(978-3-8105-0341-1(X))* Kruger, Wolfgang Verlag, GmbH DEU. Dist: International Bk. Import Service, Inc.

—Die Phantastischen Zwei. Goetting, Waltraud, tr. from ENG. (Calvin & Hobbes Ser.: Vol. 14). (GER., Illus.). 80p. (J). pap. *(978-3-8105-0351-0(7))* Kruger, Wolfgang Verlag, GmbH DEU. Dist: International Bk. Import Service, Inc.

—Steil nach Oben. Goetting, Waltraud, tr. from ENG. (Calvin & Hobbes Ser.: Vol. 6). (GER., Illus.). 64p. (J). pap. *(978-3-8105-0333-6(9))* Kruger, Wolfgang Verlag, GmbH DEU. Dist: International Bk. Import Service, Inc.

—Tierisch Lyrisch. Goetting, Waltraud, tr. from ENG. (Calvin & Hobbes Ser.: Vol. 12). (GER., Illus.). 64p. (J). pap. *(978-3-8105-0349-7(5))* Kruger, Wolfgang Verlag, GmbH DEU. Dist: International Bk. Import Service, Inc.

—Die Welt der Wunder. Bartoszko, Alexandra, tr. from ENG. (Calvin & Hobbes Ser.: Vol. 16). (GER., Illus.). 64p. (J). pap. *(978-3-8105-0365-7(7))* Kruger, Wolfgang Verlag, GmbH DEU. Dist: International Bk. Import Service, Inc.

Watts, Irene. Seeking Refuge, 1 vol. Shoemaker, Kathryn, illus. 2017. (ENG.). 128p. (J). (gr. 3-6). pap. 15.95 *(978-1-926890-02-9(7))* Tradewind Bks. CAN. Dist: Orca Bk. Pubs. USA.

Wax, Wendy. Phonics Comics: Clara the Klutz - Level 2. Sullivan, Mary, illus. 2007. (ENG.). 24p. (J). (gr. 1-17). per. 3.99 *(978-1-58476-565-3(8))* Innovative Kids.

Wax, Wendy & Weiss, Bobbi. A Tale of Too Many Cities - Egypt. Vargus, Nanci, ed. Slocum, Bradley, illus. 2008. (ENG.). 24p. (J). (gr. 1-17). pap. 3.99 *(978-1-58476-722-0(7))* Innovative Kids.

Way, Daniel. Sabretooth: Open Season. Sears, Bart, illus. 2005. (Wolverine Ser.). 96p. pap. 9.99 *(978-0-7851-1507-6(2))* Marvel Worldwide, Inc.

Wayne, Matt. Attack of the Virtual Villains. Moy, Philip, illus. 2012. (Batman: the Brave & the Bold Ser.). (ENG.). 32p. (gr. 2-3). lib. bdg. 22.60 *(978-1-4342-4546-5(2))* Stone Arch Bks.

—Menace of the Time Thief, 1 vol. Suriano, Andy & Davis, Dan W., illus. 2012. (Batman: the Brave & the Bold Ser.). (ENG.). 32p. (gr. 2-3). lib. bdg. 22.60 *(978-1-4342-4548-9(9))* Stone Arch Bks.

—Panic of the Composite Creatures. Suriano, Andy & Davis, Dan W., illus. 2012. (Batman: the Brave & the Bold Ser.). (ENG.). 32p. (gr. 2-3). lib. bdg. 22.60 *(978-1-4342-4545-8(4))* Stone Arch Bks.

—President Batman, 1 vol. Suriano, Andy & Davis, Dan W., illus. 2012. (Batman: the Brave & the Bold Ser.). (ENG.). 32p. (gr. 2-3). lib. bdg. 22.60 *(978-1-4342-4547-2(0))* Stone Arch Bks.

Weakland, Mark. Zombies & Electricity, 1 vol. Jok, Diego, illus. 2013. (Monster Science Ser.). (ENG.). 32p. (gr. 3-4). pap. 8.10 *(978-1-62065-822-2(4)*, Graphic Library) Capstone Press of Coughlan Cos.

—Zombies & Electricity, 6 vols. Jok, illus. 2013. (Monster Science Ser.). (ENG.). 32p. (gr. 3-4). 47.70 *(978-1-62065-823-9(2)*, Graphic Library) Capstone Press of Coughlan Cos.

Weakland, Mark, retold by. The Adventures of Perseus: A Graphic Retelling. 2015. (Ancient Myths Ser.). (ENG., Illus.). 32p. (gr. 3-4). lib. bdg. 30.65 *(978-1-4914-2073-7(1)*, Graphic Library) Capstone Press of Coughlan Cos.

Webb, Mack H., Jr. Danny & the Detention Demons. Espinola, Nicole & Nealon, Eve, illus. l.t. ed. 2007. 52p. (J). per. 15.95 *(978-0-9779576-2-0(4))* Pilinut Pr., Inc.

Weber, Bob. Oh, Brother! Brat Attack! Stephens, Jay, illus. 2015. (ENG.). 176p. (J). pap. 9.99 *(978-1-4494-7225-2(7))* Andrews McMeel Publishing.

Webster, Christy. Brave Batgirl! (DC Super Friends) Doescher, Erik, illus. 2017. (Step into Reading Ser.). (ENG.). 24p. (J). (gr. -1-1). pap. 4.99 ***(978-1-5247-1711-7(8))***; lib. bdg. 12.99 ***(978-1-5247-1712-4(6))*** Random Hse. Children's Bks. (Random Hse. Bks. for Young Readers).

Weiser, Joey. Mermin Book Two: The Big Catch, Softcover Edition. 2016. (ENG., Illus.). 144p. (J). pap. 12.99 *(978-1-62010-354-8(0)*, 9781620103548) Oni Pr., Inc.

—The Ride Home. 2007. (ENG., Illus.). 168p. pap. 8.95 *(978-0-9770304-4-6(X)*, 9780977030446) AdHouse Bks.

Weisman, Greg. Gargoyles #1. 2006. (Illus.). 24p. (YA). pap. 3.50 *(978-1-59362-040-0(3)*, Slave Labor Graphics) Slave Labor Bks.

Weisman, Greg, et al. Rabbit Holes, 1 vol. Davis, Dan, illus. 2013. (Young Justice Ser.). (ENG.). 32p. (gr. 2-3). 22.60 *(978-1-4342-6039-0(9))* Stone Arch Bks.

—Wonderland, 1 vol. Jones, Christopher, illus. 2013. (Young Justice Ser.). (ENG.). 32p. (gr. 2-3). 22.60 *(978-1-4342-6040-6(2))* Stone Arch Bks.

Weiss, Bobbi & Weiss, David. Hiro Dragon Warrior: Battle at Mount Kamado. Short, Robbie, illus. 2008. (ENG.). 24p. (J). (gr. 1-17). pap. 3.99 *(978-1-58476-721-3(9))* Innovative Kids.

—Twisted Tales II, Vol. 7. 2009. (ENG., Illus.). 24p. (J). (gr. 1-17). pap. 3.99 *(978-1-58476-815-9(0))* Innovative Kids.

Weiss, Bobbi Jg & Weiss, David Cody. Phonic Comics - Hiro Dragon Warrior: Fight or Flight Level 2, Issue 3. 2011. (ENG., Illus.). 24p. (J). (gr. 1-17). pap. 3.99 *(978-1-60169-111-8(4))* Innovative Kids.

Weiss, Lynne. The Voyage of Odysseus, 1 vol., 1. 2014. (Jr. Graphic Myths: Greek Heroes Ser.). (ENG., Illus.). 24p. (J). (gr. 3-6). 26.25 *(978-1-4777-6244-8(2)*, PowerKids Pr.) Rosen Publishing Group, Inc., The.

Weiss, Sam. Jess Plays the Catskills. 2004. 96p. per. 11.95 *(978-0-9754699-0-3(8))* Gross, H. H.

Wells, H. G. The Invisible Man. Calero, Dennis, illus. (Classic Fiction Ser.). 72p. 2010. pap. 0.60 *(978-1-4342-3208-3(5))* 2007. (ENG.). (gr. 2-3). lib. bdg. 27.99 *(978-1-59889-831-6(0))* Stone Arch Bks. (Graphic Revolve).

—The Invisible Man, 1 vol. Calero, Dennis, illus. 2007. (Classic Fiction Ser.). (ENG.). 72p. (gr. 2-3). per. 7.15 *(978-1-59889-887-3(6)*, Graphic Revolve) Stone Arch Bks.

—The Time Machine, 1 vol. Dunn, Ben, illus. 2007. (Graphic Classics). (ENG.). 32p. (gr. 4-7). 28.50 *(978-1-60270-054-3(0)*, Graphic Planet- Fiction) ABDO Publishing Co.

West, Tracey, adapted by. Robotic Fish Gone Wild! 2005. (Illus.). 30p. (J). pap. *(978-0-439-76833-7(0))* Scholastic, Inc.

Westerfeld, Scott & Grayson, Devin. Shay's Story. 2012. (Uglies Graphic Novel Ser.: 1). lib. bdg. 24.50 *(978-0-606-26475-4(2)*, Turtleback) Turtleback Bks.

Weston Woods Staff, creator. All the Colors of the Earth. 2004. (J). 38.75 *(978-1-55592-627-4(4))*; 18.95 *(978-1-55592-100-2(0))* Weston Woods Studios, Inc.

Wetterer, Margaret K. The Midnight Adventure of Kate Shelley, Train Rescuer. Trover, Zachary, illus. 2010. (History's Kid Heroes Ser.). (ENG.). 32p. (gr. 3-5). 26.60 *(978-0-7613-6173-2(1))*; pap. 8.95 *(978-0-7613-6192-3(8)*, Graphic Universe™) Lerner Publishing Group.

Wetterer, Margaret K. & Wetterer, Charles M. The Snowshoeing Adventure of Milton Daub, Blizzard Trekker. Trover, Zachary, illus. 2010. (History's Kid Heroes Ser.). (ENG.). 32p. (gr. 3-5). pap. 8.95 *(978-0-7613-6194-7(4)*, Graphic Universe™); lib. bdg. 26.60 *(978-0-7613-6175-6(8))* Lerner Publishing Group.

Wheeler, Ron. Stinky Stevens: Escape from Aunt Smoochie-Kiss (Book 4) 2012. 114p. pap. 6.95 *(978-0-9829377-7-8(6))* Written World Communications.

—Stinky Stevens: The Missing Soggy Soccer Shoe (Book 3) 2012. 114p. pap. 6.95 *(978-0-9829377-6-1(8))* Written World Communications.

Wheeler, Shannon & Torres, J. Wall E Vol. 1: Recharge. Luthi, Morgan, illus. 2010. (ENG.). 112p. (J). 24.99 *(978-1-60886-554-3(1))* Boom! Studios.

Wheeler, Shannon, et al. Wall-E Vol. 1: Recharge. Luthi, Morgan & Barks, Carl, illus. 2010. (ENG.). 112p. (J). pap. 9.99 *(978-1-60886-512-3(6))* Boom! Studios.

Wheeler-Toppen, Jodi. Ghosts & Atoms, 1 vol. Haus, Estudio, illus. 2011. (Monster Science Ser.). (ENG.). 32p. (gr. 3-4). pap. 8.10 *(978-1-4296-7329-7(X))*; pap. 47.70 *(978-1-4296-7330-3(3))* Capstone Press of Coughlan Cos. (Graphic Library).

Whelon, Chuck. Word Play - Write Your Own Crazy Comics, No. 1. 2013. (BOOST Educational Ser.). (ENG.). 64p. (J). (gr. 3-5). pap. 5.99 *(978-0-486-49441-8(1))* Dover Pubns., Inc.

When Kingdoms Collide Part 2. 2005. (SPA, JPN, RUS, CHI & HEB.). (YA). 2.50 *(978-0-9762842-1-5(9))* Fantasy Prone Comics.

Wheres Lily? 2006. (Illus.). (J). per. 8.95 *(978-0-9786404-0-8(3))* Damiano Sara, Janeen.

White, Paul. Jungle Doctor Meets a Lion. 2011. (Flamingo Fiction 9-13s Ser.). (ENG., Illus.). 176p. (J). 8.99 *(978-1-84550-392-5(9)*, 9781845503925) Christian Focus Pubns. GBR. Dist: Bookmasters Distribution.

White, Tracy. How I Made It to Eighteen: A Mostly True Story. White, Tracy, illus. 2010. (ENG., Illus.). 160p. (YA). (gr. 9-13). 23.99 *(978-1-59643-454-7(6)*, 9781596434547) Roaring Brook Pr.

White, Vernon. Birdhouse. 2010. (ENG., Illus.). 136p. (YA). pap. 10.95 *(978-1-59362-185-8(X)*, 9781593621858) Slave Labor Bks.

Whitley, Jeremy. Cutie Mark Crusaders & Discord, 1 vol. Fleecs, Tony, illus. 2016. (ENG.). 24p. (J). *(978-1-61479-506-3(1))* Spotlight.

—Pinkie Pie & Princess Luna, 1 vol. Fleecs, Tony, illus. 2016. (ENG.). 24p. (J). *(978-1-61479-509-4(6))* Spotlight.

Wiebe, Kurtis J. Peter Panzerfaust Deluxe Edition Volume 1 HC. 2013. (Illus.). 364p. (YA). 39.99 *(978-1-60706-778-8(1))* Image Comics.

Wilde, Oscar. Fairy Tales of Oscar Wilde: the Complete Hardcover Set 1-5. Russell, P. Craig, illus. 2014. (Fairy Tales of Oscar Wilde Ser.). (ENG.). 192p. (J). (gr. 4-7). 79.99 *(978-1-56163-890-1(0))* NBM Publishing Co.

—The Fairy Tales of Oscar Wilde: the Happy Prince Signed & Numbered. Russell, P. Craig, illus. 2012. (Fairy Tales of Oscar Wilde Ser.). (ENG.). 32p. (J). (gr. 4-7). 50.00 *(978-1-56163-629-7(0))*; 49.99 *(978-1-56163-687-7(8))* NBM Publishing Co.

—The Happy Prince. Russell, P. Craig, illus. 5th ed. 2012. (Fairy Tales of Oscar Wilde Ser.: 5). (ENG.). 32p. (J). (gr. 4-7). 16.99 *(978-1-56163-626-6(6))* NBM Publishing Co.

—The Importance of Being Earnest the Graphic Novel Quick Text: (American English) Stokes, John, illus. 2012. 144p. (J). pap. *(978-1-907127-32-8(1)*, Classical Comics, Ltd.) Classical Comics.

Wigus, Alison. Science Comics: Flying Machines: How the Wright Brothers Soared. Brooks, Molly, illus. 2017. (Science Comics Ser.). (ENG.). 128p. (J). pap. 12.99 *(978-1-62672-139-5(4)*, 9781626721395, First Second Bks.) Roaring Brook Pr.

Wilkerson, L. Kobie, 3rd, reader. Fred & Mary. 2008. (Illus.). 32p. (J). 24.95 incl. DVD, audio compact disk *(978-0-9796679-0-9(9))* Love II Learn Bks.

Williams, Anthony. Creating Superhero Comics, 1 vol. 2015. (Creating Comics Ser.). (ENG.). 32p. (J). 27.50 *(978-1-4777-5934-9(4)*, PowerKids Pr.) Rosen Publishing Group, Inc., The.

Williams, Anthony, illus. The Hound of the Baskervilles. 2014. (ENG.). 32p. pap. 8.95 *(978-1-78404-357-5(5))* Arcturus Publishing GBR. Dist: Bookmasters Distribution.

Williams, Marcia. Greek Myths. Williams, Marcia, illus. 2011. (ENG., Illus.). 40p. (J). (gr. k-4). pap. 8.99 *(978-0-7636-5384-2(5))* Candlewick Pr.

—The Tudors: Kings, Queens, Scribes, & Ferrets! Williams, Marcia, illus. 2016. (ENG., Illus.). 48p. (J). (gr. 3-7). 17.99 *(978-0-7636-8122-7(9))* Candlewick Pr.

Williamson, Joshua. Sketch Monsters Book 1: Escape of the Scribbles: Escape of the Scribbles. 2011. (ENG., Illus.). 40p. 12.99 *(978-1-934964-69-9(7)*, 9781934964699) Oni Pr., Inc.

Willis, Jeanne. Penguin Pandemonium. 2013. (Awesome Animals Ser.). (ENG., Illus.). 192p. (J). (gr. 2-7). pap. 6.99 *(978-1-4380-0301-6(3))* Barron's Educational Series, Inc.

Wilson, Matthew. Scrooge & Santa GN. 2011. (Illus.). 100p. pap. 14.95 *(978-1-897548-98-1(2))* Arcana Studio, Inc.

Wilson, Sean Michael & Dickson, Benjamin. Fight the Power! A Visual History of Protest among the English Speaking Peoples. Emerson, Hunt et al, illus. 2013. (ENG.). 192p. pap. 19.95 *(978-1-60980-492-3(9))* Seven Stories Pr.

Wingerter, Linda. Home on the Range. 2010. 32p. (J). (gr. -1-3). 14.95 *(978-0-316-83202-1(2)*, Tingley, Megan Bks.) Little, Brown Bks. for Young Readers.

Winick, Judd. Pedro & Me: Friendship, Loss, & What I Learned. 2009. (ENG., Illus.). 192p. (YA). (gr. 9-13). pap. 19.99 *(978-0-8050-8964-6(0)*, 9780805089646) Square Fish.

Winnick, Judd. Pedro & Me. 2011. 14.10 *(978-0-7848-3537-1(3)*, Everbind) Marco Bk. Co.

Wohl, David, et al. Top Cow's Best of Michael Turner. 2006. (ENG., Illus.). 240p. (YA). pap. 24.99 *(978-1-58240-544-5(1)*, 9781582405445) Image Comics.

Wolfman, Marv. Nova Classic Volume 3. Buscema, John et al, illus. 2014. (ENG.). 304p. (J). (gr. 4-17). pap. 34.99 *(978-0-7851-8552-9(6))* Marvel Worldwide, Inc.

Wong, Clarissa. S Is for Super Hero. Pierfederici, Mirco, illus. 2016. (ENG.). 26p. (J). (gr. -1-k). bds. 12.99 *(978-1-4847-2358-6(9)*, Marvel Pr.) Disney Publishing Worldwide.

Wong, Clarissa S. World of Reading: Black Widow This Is Black Widow. Di Vito, Andrea, illus. 2015. (World of Reading Ser.). (ENG.). 32p. (J). (gr. 1-3). pap. 3.99 *(978-1-4847-2517-7(4)*, Marvel Pr.) Disney Publishing Worldwide.

Wong, Clarissa S. & Lambert, Nancy R. Ant-Man - A Growing Hero, Level 2. Lim, Ron & Rosenberg, Rachelle, illus. 2015. (World of Reading Ser.). (ENG.). 32p. (J). (gr. 1-3). pap. 3.99 *(978-1-4847-3130-7(1)*, Marvel Pr.) Disney Publishing Worldwide.

Wood, Brian. Mara TP. 2013. (ENG., Illus.). 136p. (YA). pap. 12.99 *(978-1-60706-810-5(9)*, 9781607068105) Image Comics.

—Star Wars, 1 vol. D'Anda, Carlos, illus. 2014. (Star Wars: in the Shadow of Yavin Ser.: Vol. 1). (ENG.). 24p. (J). (gr. 9-14). 24.21 *(978-1-61479-286-4(0))* Spotlight.

Wood, Dick. Boris Karloff Tales of Mystery Archives Volume 5. 2011. (ENG., Illus.). 232p. 49.99 *(978-1-59582-615-2(7))* Dark Horse Comics.

Wooding, Chris. Havoc. 2010. (Malice Ser.: 2). (ENG., Illus.). 400p. (J). (gr. 3-7). 16.99 *(978-0-545-16045-2(6)*, Scholastic Pr.) Scholastic, Inc.

—Malice, Bk. 1. Chemett, Dan, illus. 2009. (Malice Ser.: 1). (ENG.). 384p. (J). (gr. 7-12). 14.99 *(978-0-545-16043-8(X))* Scholastic, Inc.

—Malice #2: Havoc. 2012. (Malice Ser.: 2). (ENG.). 400p. (J). (gr. 3-7). pap. 9.99 *(978-0-545-16046-9(4)*, Scholastic Pr.) Scholastic, Inc.

Word of Life Press, creator. Manga Bible Story. 2006. (JPN., Illus.). 879p. (J). (gr. 4-7). 78.00 *(978-4-264-01798-1(X))* Word of Life Press Ministries JPN. Dist: Send The Light Distribution LLC.

World Almanac Editors, creator. Great Stories of Courage: The Call of the Wild, the Red Badge of Courage, Treasure Island. 2007. (Bank Street Graphic Novels Ser.). (Illus.). 56p. (gr. 5-8). pap. 14.05 *(978-0-8368-7933-9(1))* Stevens, Gareth Publishing LLLP.

World Almanac Editors, et al. Historical Adventure: A Connecticut Yankee in King Arthur's Court/ Around the World in 80 Days/the Prisoner of Zenda. 2007. (Bank Street Graphic Novels Ser.). (Illus.). 56p. (gr. 5-8). lib. bdg. 31.00 *(978-0-8368-7927-8(9))* Stevens, Gareth Publishing LLLP.

World Book, Inc Staff, contrib. by. Fractions. 2012. (J). *(978-0-7166-1434-0(0))*; pap. *(978-0-7166-1475-3(8))* World Bk., Inc.

—Numbers. 2012. (J). *(978-0-7166-1436-4(7))*; pap. *(978-0-7166-1477-7(4))* World Bk., Inc.

Wrecks, Billy. Batman: Adventures of the Dark Knight. 2016. (DK Adventures Ser.). lib. bdg. 16.00 *(978-0-606-38229-8(1))* Turtleback Bks.

—Big Heroes! (DC Super Friends) Golden Books Staff, illus. 2011. (Little Golden Book Ser.). (ENG.). 24p. (J). (gr. -1-2). 4.99 *(978-0-375-87237-2(X)*, Golden Bks.) Random Hse. Children's Bks.

—Bizarro Day! 2013. (Step into Reading Level 2 Ser.). lib. bdg. 13.55 *(978-0-606-26971-1(1)*, Turtleback) Turtleback Bks.

—Bizarro Day! (DC Super Friends) Legramandi, Francesco, illus. 2013. (Step into Reading Ser.). (ENG.). 32p. (J). (gr. k-3). pap. 3.99 *(978-0-307-98119-6(3)*, Random Hse. Bks. for Young Readers) Random Hse. Children's Bks.

—Catch Catwoman! DeCarlo, Mike & Tanguay, David D., illus. 2013. (Step into Reading Ser.). (ENG.). 32p. (J). (gr. -1-1). 3.99 *(978-0-449-81616-5(8)*, Random Hse. Bks. for Young Readers) Random Hse. Children's Bks.

—Catch Catwoman! 2013. (Step into Reading Level 2 Ser.). lib. bdg. 13.55 *(978-0-606-32196-9(9)*, Turtleback) Turtleback Bks.

—The Courageous Captain America. Golden Books Staff, illus. 2016. (Little Golden Book Ser.). (ENG.). 24p. (J). (gr. -1-k). 4.99 *(978-0-307-93050-7(5)*, Golden Bks.) Random Hse. Children's Bks.

—DK Adventures: DC Comics: Batman: Adventures of the Dark Knight. 2016. (DK Adventures Ser.). (ENG., Illus.). 96p. (J). (gr. 3-7). 16.99 *(978-1-4654-4608-4(7)*, DK Children) Dorling Kindersley Publishing, Inc.

—The Mighty Thor. Golden Books Staff, illus. 2016. (Little Golden Book Ser.). (ENG.). 24p. (J). (gr. -1-k). 4.99 *(978-0-307-93051-4(3)*, Golden Bks.) Random Hse. Children's Bks.

—Reptile Rumble! Doescher, Erik, illus. 2014. (Step into Reading Ser.). (ENG.). 32p. (J). (gr. -1-1). 3.99 *(978-0-385-37403-3(8)*, Random Hse. Bks. for Young Readers) Random Hse. Children's Bks.

—Reptile Rumble! 2014. (Step into Reading Level 2 Ser.). lib. bdg. 13.55 *(978-0-606-35541-4(3))* Turtleback Bks.

—Wonder Woman & Her Super Friends! (DC Super Friends) Random House, illus. 2016. (Tabbed Board Book Ser.). (ENG.). 16p. (J). (-k). bds. 7.99 *(978-1-101-93992-5(3)*, Random Hse. Bks. for Young Readers) Random Hse. Children's Bks.

Wright, Bill, et al. Mickey Mouse: Timeless Tales Volume 1: Timeless Tales Volume 1. Murry, Paul, illus. 2016. (Mickey Mouse Ser.). (ENG.). 260p. 29.99 *(978-1-63140-580-8(2)*, 9781631405808) Idea & Design Works, LLC.

Wullie, Oor. Oor Wullie Colouring Book. 2017. (ENG.). 64p. (J). (gr. 3). pap. 12.99 ***(978-1-910230-44-2(8))*** Black and White Publishing Ltd. GBR. Dist: Independent Pubs. Group.

Wyatt, Chris. Star-Lord - Knowhere to Run. Lim, Ron & Troy, Andy, illus. 2014. (ENG.). 128p. (J). (gr. 3-7). pap. 5.99 *(978-1-4847-1269-6(2)*, Marvel Pr.) Disney Publishing Worldwide.

—World of Reading: Ant-Man This Is Ant-Man: Level 1. Lim, Ron & Rosenberg, Rachelle, illus. 2015. (World of Reading Ser.). (ENG.). 32p. (J). (gr. -1-k). pap. 3.99 *(978-1-4847-1455-3(5)*, Marvel Pr.) Disney Publishing Worldwide.

Wyre, Yvonne. The Adventures of Cuthbert the Coal Lorry. 2005. 160p. pap. *(978-1-84401-500-9(9))* Athena Pr.

Yadate, Hajime. Cowboy Bebop, 2 vols. Kuga, Cain, illus. 2003. pap. 44.99 *(978-1-59182-590-6(3))* TOKYOPOP, Inc.

Yagami, Yu & Yugami, Yu. Those Who Hunt Elves, Vol. 6. 2004. (Illus.). 202p. (YA). pap. 9.99 *(978-1-4139-0098-9(4))* ADV Manga.

Yamada, Masaki. Innocence: After the Long Goodbye. Oniki, Yuji & Horn, Carl Gustav, trs. from JPN. 2005. (Ghost in the Shell Novel Ser.: Vol. 1). (ENG., Illus.). 264p. 19.99 *(978-1-4215-0156-7(2))* Viz Media.

Yamamoto, Satoshi, illus. Pokemon Omega Ruby Alpha Sapphire, Vol. 1. 2016. (Pokemon Ser.: 1). (ENG.). 96p. (J). pap. 4.99 *(978-1-4215-9070-7(0))* Viz Media.

—Pokémon Omega Ruby Alpha Sapphire, Vol. 3. 2017. (Pokemon Ser.: 3). (ENG.). 96p. (J). pap. 4.99 *(978-1-4215-9156-8(1))* Viz Media.

—Pokemon Omega Ruby & Alpha Sapphire, Vol. 4. 2017. (Pokemon Ser.: 4). (ENG.). 96p. (J). pap. 4.99 ***(978-1-4215-9223-7(1))*** Viz Media.

—Pokémon X*y, Vol. 10. 2017. (Pokemon Ser.: 10). (ENG.). 112p. (J). pap. 4.99 *(978-1-4215-9164-3(2))* Viz Media.

Yamamoto, Satoshi, illus. Pokémon X*y, Vol. 11. 2017. (Pokemon Ser.: 11). (ENG.). 96p. (J). pap. 4.99 ***(978-1-4215-9066-0(2))*** Viz Media.

Yan, Wing & Tung, King. King of Fighters 2003, Vol. 4. 2008. (ENG., Illus.). 140p. (YA). pap. 13.95 *(978-1-59796-010-6(1))* DrMaster Pubns. Inc.

C
D

Yan, Wing Tung, et al. King of Fighters 2003, Vol. 5. 2008. (ENG., Illus.). 140p. (YA). pap. 13.95 *(978-1-59796-011-3(X))* DrMaster Pubns. Inc.

Yang, Gene Luen. Animal Crackers: A Gene Luen Yang Collection. 2012. (ENG., Illus.). 216p. (YA). pap. 14.95 *(978-1-59362-183-4(3),* 9781593621834) Slave Labor Bks.

—Secrets & Sequences. Holmes, Mike, illus. 2017. (Secret Coders Ser.: 3). (ENG.). 112p. (J). pap. 10.99 *(978-1-62672-077-0(0),* 9781626720770, First Second Bks.) Roaring Brook Pr.

—Secrets & Sequences. 2017. (Secret Coders Ser.: 3). (J). lib. bdg. 22.10 ***(978-0-606-40345-0(0))*** Turtleback Bks.

Yang, Gene Luen & Holmes, Mike. Secret Coders. 2015. (Secret Coders Ser.: 1). (J). lib. bdg. 20.85 *(978-0-606-37803-1(0))* Turtleback Bks.

Yang, Gene Luen & Pham, Thien. Level Up. 2016. (YA). lib. bdg. 20.85 *(978-0-606-38563-3(0))* Turtleback Bks.

Yasuda, Anita. Big City Sights, 1 vol. Harpster, Steve, illus. 2011. (My First Graphic Novel Ser.). (ENG.). 32p. (gr. k-2). pap. 6.25 *(978-1-4342-3060-7(0));* lib. bdg. 24.65 *(978-1-4342-2515-3(1))* Stone Arch Bks. (My First Graphic Novel).

—Dino Detectives. Harpster, Steve, illus. 2013. (Dino Detectives Ser.). (ENG.). 32p. (gr. 1-2). pap. 23.80 *(978-1-4342-3937-2(3))* Stone Arch Bks.

—The Swim Race, 1 vol. Harpster, Steve, illus. 2012. (My First Graphic Novel Ser.). (ENG.). 32p. (gr. k-2). pap. 6.25 *(978-1-4342-3864-1(4));* lib. bdg. 24.65 *(978-1-4342-3280-9(8))* Stone Arch Bks. (My First Graphic Novel).

Yazawa, Nao. Moon & Blood, Vol. 1. 2011. (ENG., Illus.). 72p. (YA). pap. 6.95 *(978-1-56970-207-9(1),* 9781569702079) Digital Manga Publishing.

Yee, Lisa. DC Super Hero Girls Books, 2 vols. Random House Staff, illus. 2016. (ENG.). 240p. (J). (gr. 3-7). 27.98 *(978-1-5247-1631-8(6),* Random Hse. Bks. for Young Readers) Random Hse. Children's Bks.

—Katana at Super Hero High (DC Super Hero Girls) Random House, illus. 2017. (ENG.). 240p. (J). (gr. 4-7). 13.99 ***(978-1-101-94068-6(9));*** lib. bdg. 16.99 ***(978-1-101-94069-3(7))*** Random Hse. Children's Bks. (Random Hse. Bks. for Young Readers).

Yee, Lisa. Wonder Woman at Super Hero High. Random House Disney Staff, illus. 2016. (ENG.). 240p. (J). (gr. 3-7). 13.99 *(978-1-101-94059-4(X),* Random Hse. Bks. for Young Readers) Random Hse. Children's Bks.

Yeh, Julie. Poppie's Adventures: Serpents in Paradise. Hsu, Jack, illus. 2003. 48p. (J). per. *(978-0-9742386-0-9(0))* Way Out Comics.

Yoe, Craig, et al. Felix the Cat Paintings. Ollerenshaw, Rod, ed. 2014. (ENG., Illus.). 168p. 34.99 *(978-1-61377-839-5(2),* 9781613778395) Idea & Design Works, LLC.

Yolen, Jane. Curses! Foiled Again. Cavallaro, Mike, illus. 2013. (ENG.). 176p. (J). (gr. 6-9). pap. 15.99 *(978-1-59643-619-0(0),* 9781596436190, First Second Bks.) Roaring Brook Pr.

—Foiled. Cavallaro, Mike, illus. 2010. (ENG.). 160p. (J). (gr. 6-9). pap. 17.99 *(978-1-59643-279-6(9),* 9781596432796, First Second Bks.) Roaring Brook Pr.

—Foiled. 2010. (J). lib. bdg. 30.60 *(978-0-606-14452-0(8),* Turtleback) Turtleback Bks.

—The Last Dragon. Guay, Rebecca, illus. 2011. (ENG.). 144p. (J). (gr. 7-7). pap. 29.99 *(978-1-59582-798-2(6))* Dark Horse Comics.

Yolen, Jane & Stemple, Adam. Stone Cold. Zangara, Orion, illus. 2016. (Stone Man Mysteries Ser.: 1). (ENG.). 80p. (J). (gr. 7-12). lib. bdg. 29.32 *(978-1-4677-4196-5(5));* E-Book 21.99 *(978-1-5124-0903-1(0),* 9781512409031) Lerner Publishing Group. (Graphic Universe™).

Yomtov, Nel. Adventures in Science. O'Neill, Sean et al, illus. 2012. (Adventures in Science Ser.). (ENG.). 32p. (gr. 3-4). pap. 31.80 *(978-1-4296-8469-9(0));* pap. 190.80 *(978-1-4296-8470-5(4))* Capstone Press of Coughlan Cos. (Graphic Library).

—The Apollo 11 Moon Landing: July 20 1969, 1 vol. 2014. (24-Hour History Ser.). (ENG., Illus.). 48p. (gr. 3-5). lib. bdg. 33.32 *(978-1-4329-9292-7(9),* NA-h) Heinemann-Raintree.

—The Attack on Pearl Harbor: December 7 1941, 1 vol. 2014. (24-Hour History Ser.). (ENG., Illus.). 48p. (gr. 3-5). lib. bdg. 33.32 *(978-1-4329-9293-4(7),* NA-h) Heinemann-Raintree.

—Death Camp Uprising: The Escape from Sobibor Concentration Camp. Tortosa, Wilson & Bartolo, Michael, illus. 2017. (Great Escapes of World War II Ser.). (ENG.). 32p. (gr. 3-4). lib. bdg. 30.65 *(978-1-5157-3532-8(X),* Graphic Library) Capstone Press of Coughlan Cos.

—Defend until Death! Nickolas Flux & the Battle of the Alamo, 1 vol. Ginevra, Dante, illus. 2014. (Nickolas Flux History Chronicles Ser.). (ENG.). 32p. (gr. 3-4). lib. bdg. 30.65 *(978-1-4765-3945-4(6),* Graphic Library) Capstone Press of Coughlan Cos.

—How to Write a Comic Book. Petelinsek, Kathleen, illus. 2013. (Explorer Junior Library: How to Write Ser.). (ENG.). 24p. (J). (gr. 1-4). pap. 12.79 *(978-1-62431-319-6(1),* 203074) Cherry Lake Publishing.

—Rocks & the People Who Love Them, 1 vol. Foss, Timothy, illus. 2012. (Adventures in Science Ser.). (ENG.). 32p. (gr. 3-4). pap. 8.10 *(978-1-4296-7988-6(3));* pap. 47.70 *(978-1-4296-8466-8(6))* Capstone Press of Coughlan Cos. (Graphic Library).

—Sarah Palin: Political Rebel, 1 vol. D'Ottavi, Francesca, illus. 2011. (American Graphic Ser.). (ENG.). 32p. (gr. 3-4). pap. 8.10 *(978-1-4296-7341-9(9));* pap. 47.70 *(978-1-4296-7342-6(7))* Capstone Press of Coughlan Cos. (Graphic Library).

—True Stories of the Civil War. Molinari, Carlo, illus. 2012. (Stories of War Ser.). (ENG.). 32p. (gr. 3-4). pap. 47.70 *(978-1-4296-9341-7(X),* Graphic Library) Capstone Press of Coughlan Cos.

—True Stories of World War I. Proctor, Jon, illus. 2012. (Stories of War Ser.). (ENG.). 32p. (gr. 3-4). pap. 47.70 *(978-1-4296-9345-5(2),* Graphic Library) Capstone Press of Coughlan Cos.

—Tunnelling to Freedom: The Great Escape from Stalag Luft III. Valdrighi, Alessandro, illus. 2017. (Great Escapes of World War II Ser.). (ENG.). 32p. (gr. 3-4). pap. 7.95 *(978-1-5157-3536-6(2));* lib. bdg. 30.65 *(978-1-5157-3531-1(1))* Capstone Press of Coughlan Cos. (Graphic Library).

Yomtov, Nel & Biskup, Agnieszka. American Graphic Fall 2011. 2011. (American Graphic Ser.). (ENG.). 32p. (gr. 3-4). lib. bdg. 61.30 *(978-1-4296-6584-1(X),* Graphic Library) Capstone Press of Coughlan Cos.

Yomtov, Nel & Fuentes, Benny. Reality Check, 1 vol. Sandoval, Gerardo, illus. 2010. (Sports Illustrated Kids Graphic Novels Ser.). (ENG.). 56p. (gr. 2-3). pap. 7.19 *(978-1-4342-2294-7(2));* 26.65 *(978-1-4342-1912-1(7))* Stone Arch Bks.

Yomtov, Nel, et al. Adventures in Science. O'Neill, Sean et al, illus. 2012. (Adventures in Science Ser.). (ENG.). 32p. (gr. 3-4). lib. bdg. 91.95 *(978-1-4296-8172-8(1),* Graphic Library) Capstone Press of Coughlan Cos.

—Jason & the Golden Fleece, 1 vol. Sandoval, Gerardo, illus. 2009. (Mythology Ser.). (ENG.). 72p. (gr. 2-3). pap. 7.15 *(978-1-4342-1385-3(4));* lib. bdg. 27.99 *(978-1-4342-1172-9(X))* Stone Arch Bks. (Graphic Revolve).

—Nickolas Flux History Chronicles, 1 vol. Ginevra, Dante, illus. 2014. (Nickolas Flux History Chronicles Ser.). (ENG.). 32p. (gr. 3-4). lib. bdg. 122.60 *(978-1-4765-7310-6(7),* Graphic Library) Capstone Press of Coughlan Cos.

—Stories of War. 2012. (Stories of War Ser.). (ENG.). 32p. (gr. 3-4). pap. 190.80 *(978-1-4296-9349-3(5));* pap. 31.80 *(978-1-4296-9348-6(7))* Capstone Press of Coughlan Cos. (Graphic Library).

—Theseus & the Minotaur, 1 vol. Smith, Tod G., illus. (Mythology Ser.). (ENG.). 72p. (gr. 2-3). 2010. pap. 7.15 *(978-1-4342-1387-7(0))* 2009. lib. bdg. 27.99 *(978-1-4342-1171-2(1))* Stone Arch Bks. (Graphic Revolve).

Yomtov, Nelson. Sarah Palin: Political Rebel, 1 vol. D'Ottavi, Francesca, illus. 2011. (American Graphic Ser.). (ENG.). 32p. (gr. 3-4). lib. bdg. 30.65 *(978-1-4296-6018-1(X),* Graphic Library) Capstone Press of Coughlan Cos.

—Trapped in Antarctica! Nickolas Flux & the Shackleton Expedition. Simmons, Mark, illus. 2015. (Nickolas Flux History Chronicles Ser.). (ENG.). 32p. (gr. 3-4). lib. bdg. 30.65 *(978-1-4914-2069-0(3),* Graphic Library) Capstone Press of Coughlan Cos.

—True Stories of the Civil War, 1 vol. Molinari, Carlo, illus. 2012. (Stories of War Ser.). (ENG.). 32p. (gr. 3-4). pap. 8.10 *(978-1-4296-9340-0(1));* lib. bdg. 30.65 *(978-1-4296-8624-2(3))* Capstone Press of Coughlan Cos. (Graphic Library).

Yonebayashi, Hiromasa & Miyazaki, Hayao. The Secret World of Arrietty (Film Comic), Vol. 1. 2012. (ENG., Illus.). 272p. pap. 16.99 *(978-1-4215-4116-7(5))* Viz Media.

—The Secret World of Arrietty (Film Comic), Vol. 2. 2012. (ENG.). 336p. pap. 16.99 *(978-1-4215-4117-4(3))* Viz Media.

Yorinks, Arthur. Making Scents. Lamb, Braden & Paroline, Shelli, illus. 2017. (ENG.). 112p. (J). 15.99 *(978-1-59643-452-3(X),* 9781596434523, First Second Bks.) Roaring Brook Pr.

Young, J. E. Horror in Space. Huddleston, Courtney, illus. 2011. (Twisted Journeys Ser.: 18). (ENG.). 112p. (J). (gr. 4-7). pap. 45.32 *(978-0-7613-7614-9(3));* pap. 7.95 *(978-0-8225-9273-0(8))* Lerner Publishing Group. (Graphic Universe™).

YoYo. Vermonia 7: Battle for the Turtle Realm. 1. 2014. (Vermonia Ser.). (ENG.). 208p. (J). (gr. 3-6). pap. 11.75 *(978-1-61533-651-7(6),* Windmill Bks.) Rosen Publishing Group, Inc., The.

Yuki, Kaori. Alice in Murderland, Vol. 5. 2017. (Alice in Murderland Ser.: 5). (ENG., Illus.). 176p. (gr. 11-17). 17.00 *(978-0-316-50279-5(0),* Yen Pr.) Orbit.

—Demon from Afar. 2015. (Demon from Afar Ser.: 5). (ENG., Illus.). 176p. (gr. 11-17). 18.00 *(978-0-316-34579-8(2),* Yen Pr.) Orbit.

—Godchild. 2007. (GodChild Ser.: 4). (ENG., Illus.). 200p. pap. 8.99 *(978-1-4215-0478-0(2))* Viz Media.

—The Sound of a Boy Hatching. Yuki, Kaori, illus. 2006. (Cain Saga Ser.: 2). (ENG., Illus.). 208p. pap. 8.99 *(978-1-59116-977-2(1))* Viz Media.

Yun, Mi-Kyung. Bride of the Water God Volume 14. Simon, Philip, ed. Yun, Mi-Kyung, illus. 2013. (ENG., Illus.). 168p. pap. 9.99 *(978-1-61655-187-2(9))* Dark Horse Comics.

Yung, Kao & Liang, Kuan. Magic Lover's Tower, Vol. 2. 2008. (Magic Lover's Tower Ser.). (ENG., Illus.). 176p. (YA). (gr. 8). pap. 9.95 *(978-1-59796-154-7(X))* DrMaster Pubns. Inc.

Zahler, Thom. Fluttershy & Zecora, 1 vol. Fleecs, Tony, illus. 2016. (ENG.). 24p. (J). *(978-1-61479-507-0(X))* Spotlight.

—Rainbow Dash & Trixie, 1 vol. Garbowska, Agnes, illus. 2016. (ENG.). 24p. (J). *(978-1-61479-511-7(8))* Spotlight.

Zahler, Thomas F., illus. Twilight Sparkle, 1 vol. 2015. (ENG.). 24p. (J). *(978-1-61479-336-6(0))* Spotlight.

Zahler, Thomas F., et al. Pony Tales, Vol. 1. Curnow, Bobby, illus. 2013. (My Little Pony Ser.). (ENG.). 152p. pap. 19.99 *(978-1-61377-740-4(X),* 9781613777404) Idea & Design Works, LLC.

Zdunich, Terrance. The Molting: Issue #1 Guilty Susie. 2009. pap. 7.99 *(978-1-61623-120-0(3))* Independent Pub.

Zellers, Michelle. Maya's Magic Carpet. 2006. (J). per. 11.95 *(978-1-889743-48-6(8))* Robbie Dean Pr.

Zenescope Entertainment Staff. Discovery Channel's Great White Sharks. 2014. (ENG., Illus.). 120p. (J). pap. 9.99 *(978-1-937068-39-4(0),* 9781937068394) Zenescope Entertainment.

—Discovery Channel's Megalodon & Prehistoric Sharks. 2013. (ENG., Illus.). 120p. pap. 9.99 *(978-1-937068-38-7(2),* 9781937068387) Zenescope Entertainment.

Zenescope Entertainment Staff & Brusha, Joe. Sci-Fi & Fantasy: The Perfect Mate. 2012. (Illus.). 168p. (YA). pap. 15.99 *(978-1-937068-91-2(9))* Zenescope Entertainment.

Zenescope Entertainment Staff, et al. Mankind Vol. 1: The Story of All of Us. 2012. (ENG., Illus.). 120p. (J). pap. 14.99 *(978-1-937068-68-4(4),* 9781937068684) Zenescope Entertainment.

—Mankind Vol. 2: The Story of All of Us. 2012. (ENG., Illus.). 120p. (J). pap. 14.99 *(978-1-937068-69-1(2),* 9781937068691) Zenescope Entertainment.

—Never Underestimate a Hermit Crab. 2014. (ENG., Illus.). 48p. (J). pap. 9.99 *(978-1-939683-25-0(4),* 9781939683250) Zenescope Entertainment.

Zhao, Yun & I-Haun. Real Fake Princess, Vol. 1. 2006. (Real/Fake Princess Ser.). (ENG., Illus.). 200p. (YA). pap. 9.95 *(978-1-59796-079-3(9))* DrMaster Pubns. Inc.

Zidrou. Ducoboo: In the Corner! Godi, illus. 2007. (Ducoboo Ser.: 2). (ENG.). 48p. (J). (gr. 4-7). pap. 9.99 *(978-1-905460-26-7(0))* CineBook GBR. Dist: National Bk. Network.

—Ducoboo: The Class Struggle. Spear, Luke, tr. from FRE. Godi & Grobet, Veronique, illus. 2010. (Ducoboo Ser.: 4). (ENG.). 46p. (J). (gr. 3-17). pap. 11.95 *(978-1-84918-031-3(8))* CineBook GBR. Dist: National Bk. Network.

—Ducoboo No. 3: Your Answers or Your Life! Godi, illus. 2008. (Ducoboo Ser.: 3). (ENG.). 48p. pap. 11.95 *(978-1-905460-28-1(7))* CineBook GBR. Dist: National Bk. Network.

Zircher, Patrick, et al, illus. Captain America by Ed Brubaker - Volume 3. 2013. (ENG.). 125p. (J). (gr. 4-17). pap. 19.99 *(978-0-7851-6076-2(0),* Marvel Pr.) Disney Publishing Worldwide.

Zoo Animals for Kids: Amazing Pictures & Fun Fact Children Book. 2013. 32p. pap. 9.97 *(978-1-63022-042-6(6))* Speedy Publishing LLC.

Zornow, Jeff. Werewolf, 1 vol. Zornow, Jeff, illus. 2007. (Graphic Horror Ser.). (ENG., Illus.). 32p. (gr. 3-7). 28.50 *(978-1-60270-062-8(1),* Graphic Planet- Fiction) ABDO Publishing Co.

Zub, Jim. Figment: Journey into Imagination. 2016. (Figment: Journey into Imagination Ser.: 5). (ENG.). 24p. (J). (gr. k-5). lib. bdg. 121.05 *(978-1-61479-444-8(8),* Graphic Planet) Magic Wagon.

—Figment: Journey into Imagination: Volume 1, 1 vol. 2016. (Figment: Journey into Imagination Ser.). (ENG., Illus.). 24p. (J). (gr. k-5). lib. bdg. 24.21 *(978-1-61479-445-5(6),* Graphic Planet) Magic Wagon.

—Figment: Journey into Imagination: Volume 2, 1 vol. 2016. (Figment: Journey into Imagination Ser.). (ENG., Illus.). 24p. (J). (gr. k-5). lib. bdg. 24.21 *(978-1-61479-446-2(4),* Graphic Planet) Magic Wagon.

—Figment: Journey into Imagination: Volume 3, 1 vol. 2016. (Figment: Journey into Imagination Ser.). (ENG., Illus.). 24p. (J). (gr. k-5). lib. bdg. 24.21 *(978-1-61479-447-9(2),* Graphic Planet) Magic Wagon.

—Figment: Journey into Imagination: Volume 4, 1 vol. 2016. (Figment: Journey into Imagination Ser.). (ENG., Illus.). 24p. (J). (gr. k-5). lib. bdg. 24.21 *(978-1-61479-448-6(0),* Graphic Planet) Magic Wagon.

—Figment: Journey into Imagination: Volume 5, 1 vol. 2016. (Figment: Journey into Imagination Ser.). (ENG., Illus.). 24p. (J). (gr. k-5). lib. bdg. 24.21 *(978-1-61479-449-3(9),* Graphic Planet) Magic Wagon.

60 Years of the Dandy & the Beano 2004. 2003rd ed. 2003. (Illus.). 144p. *(978-0-85116-808-1(6))* Thomson, D.C. & Co., Ltd. GBR. Dist: APG Sales & Distribution Services.

CARVER, GEORGE WASHINGTON, 1864?-1943

Abrams, Dennis. George Washington Carver: Scientist & Educator. 2008. (Black Americans of Achievement Ser.). (Illus.). 119p. (gr. 6-12). lib. bdg. 35.00 *(978-0-7910-9717-5(X),* Chelsea Hse.) Facts On File, Inc.

Adler, David A. A Picture Book of George Washington Carver. Brown, Dan, illus. 2008. (Picture Book Biography Ser.). (J). (gr. -1-2). 28.95 incl. audio compact disk *(978-1-4301-0348-6(5))* Live Oak Media.

Benge, Janet. George Washington Carver: What Do You See?, 1bk. James, Kennon, illus. 2003. (Another Great Achiever Ser.). (J). lib. bdg. 23.95 incl. audio *(978-1-57537-792-6(6))* Advance Publishing, Inc.

Carter, Andy & Saller, Carol. George Washington Carver. Paladino, Lance, illus. 2006. (Yo Solo Biografías Ser.). 48p. (J). (gr. 2-5). lib. bdg. 23.93 *(978-0-8225-6258-0(8),* Ediciones Lerner) Lerner Publishing Group.

Collins, Luke. George Washington Carver, 1 vol. 2014. (Great African-Americans Ser.). (ENG.). 24p. (gr. k-1). lib. bdg. 21.99 *(978-1-4765-3957-7(X),* Pebble Bks.) Capstone Press of Coughlan Cos.

Doeden, Matt. George Washington Carver. 2008. pap. 52.95 *(978-0-8225-9390-4(4))* Lerner Publishing Group.

—George Washington Carver. Butler, Tad, illus. 2007. (History Maker Biographies Ser.). 48p. (J). (gr. 3-7). lib. bdg. 26.60 *(978-0-8225-7605-1(8),* Lerner Pubns.) Lerner Publishing Group.

Driscoll, Laura. George Washington Carver: The Peanut Wizard. Weber, Jill, illus. 2003. (Smart about History Ser.). (ENG.). 32p. (J). (gr. k-4). mass mkt. 5.99 *(978-0-448-43243-4(9),* Grosset & Dunlap) Penguin Young Readers Group.

Dunn, Joeming W. George Washington Carver, 1 vol. Allen, Chris, illus. 2008. (Bio-Graphics Ser.). (ENG.). 32p. 28.50 *(978-1-60270-171-7(7),* Graphic Planet- Nonfiction) ABDO Publishing Co.

Edwards, Linda McMurry. George Washington Carver: The Life of the Great American Agriculturist. 2009. (Library of American Lives & Times Ser.). 112p. (gr. 5-5). 69.20 *(978-1-60853-485-2(5))* Rosen Publishing Group, Inc., The.

Feinstein, Stephen. Read about George Washington Carver. 2006. (I Like Biographies! Ser.). (Illus.). 24p. (J). (gr. 1-3). lib. bdg. 22.60 *(978-0-7660-2597-4(7),* Enslow Elementary) Enslow Pubs., Inc.

George Washington Carver. 2006. (J). pap. 6.95 *(978-0-8225-6625-0(7),* Ediciones Lerner) Lerner Publishing Group.

Gomez, Rebecca. George Washington Carver, 1 vol. 2003. (First Biographies Ser.). (ENG., Illus.). 32p. (gr. k-4). 27.07 *(978-1-57765-944-0(9),* Buddy Bks.) ABDO Publishing Co.

Gould, Jane H. George Washington Carver. 2013. (Jr. Graphic American Inventors Ser.). (ENG., Illus.). 24p. (J). (gr. 3-6). pap. 10.60 *(978-1-4777-0141-6(9));* lib. bdg. 25.25 *(978-1-4777-0078-5(1))* Rosen Publishing Group, Inc., The. (PowerKids Pr.).

Jones, Natalya. George Washington Carver: Peanut Scientist. 2009. (Real Life Readers Ser.). 16p. (gr. 2-3). pap. 7.05 *(978-1-4358-0085-4(0),* Rosen Classroom) Rosen Publishing Group, Inc., The.

Jovin, Michelle. Fantastic Kids: George Washington Carver (Level 2) 2017. (Exploring Reading Ser.). (Illus.). 28p. (gr. 2-2). pap. 7.99 ***(978-1-4258-4961-0(X))*** Teacher Created Materials, Inc.

Kittinger, Jo S. George Washington Carver. 2005. (Scholastic News Nonfiction Readers Ser.). (Illus.). 24p. (J). pap. 6.95 *(978-0-516-24782-3(4),* Children's Pr.) Scholastic Library Publishing.

Kramer, Barbara. The Life of George Washington Carver: Inventor & Scientist. 2015. (Legendary African Americans Ser.). 96p. (J). (gr. 6-12). 27.94 *(978-0-7660-6270-2(8));* pap. 10.95 *(978-0-7660-6271-9(6))* Enslow Pubs., Inc.

Labrecque, Ellen. George Washington Carver, 1 vol. 2014. (Science Biographies Ser.). (ENG.). 32p. (gr. 2-4). lib. bdg. 30.65 *(978-1-4109-6240-9(7),* Raintree Perspectives) Heinemann-Raintree.

Leavitt, Amie Jane. George Washington Carver. 2007. (What's So Great About... ? Ser.). (Illus.). 32p. (YA). (gr. 2-4). lib. bdg. 25.70 *(978-1-58415-580-5(9))* Mitchell Lane Pubs., Inc.

Macceca, Stephanie. George Washington Carver: Agriculture Pioneer, 1 vol. 2007. (Science Readers Ser.). (ENG.). 32p. (J). (gr. 3-3). pap. 8.99 *(978-0-7439-0590-9(3))* Shell Educational Publishing.

MacLeod, Elizabeth. George Washington Carver: An Innovative Life. 2007. (Snapshots: Images of People & Places in History Ser.). (ENG., Illus.). 32p. (J). (gr. 3-7). 6.95 *(978-1-55337-907-2(1));* 14.95 *(978-1-55337-906-5(3))* Kids Can Pr., Ltd. CAN. Dist: Hachette Bk. Group.

Marzollo, Jean. The Little Plant Doctor: The Story of George Washington Carver. Wilson-Max, Ken, illus. 2011. (ENG.). 32p. (J). (gr. -1-3). 16.95 *(978-0-8234-2325-5(5))* Holiday Hse., Inc.

McKissack, Patricia C. & McKissack, Fredrick L. George Washington Carver: Scientist & Inventor. 2013. (Famous African Americans Ser.). 24p. (J). (gr. k-3). pap. 7.95 *(978-1-4644-0197-8(7));* (Illus.). lib. bdg. 22.60 *(978-0-7660-4102-8(6))* Enslow Pubs., Inc. (Enslow Elementary).

McMurry Edwards, Linda. George Washington Carver: The Life of the Great American Agriculturist. 2005. (Library of American Lives & Times). (Illus.). 112p. (J). (gr. 4-8). lib. bdg. 34.60 *(978-0-8239-6633-2(X))* Rosen Publishing Group, Inc., The.

Meachen Rau, Dana. George Washington Carver. 2014. (Rookie Biographies(r) Ser.). (ENG.). 32p. (J). lib. bdg. 23.00 *(978-0-531-21061-1(8))* Scholastic Library Publishing.

Miller, Barbara Kiely. George Washington Carver. 2007. (Great Americans Ser.). 24p. (gr. 1-4). pap. 8.15 *(978-0-8368-8320-6(9));* lib. bdg. 22.00 *(978-0-8368-8313-8(6));* (SPA., Illus.). pap. 8.15 *(978-0-8368-8334-3(9));* (SPA., Illus.). lib. bdg. 22.00 *(978-0-8368-8327-5(6))* Stevens, Gareth Publishing LLLP. (Weekly Reader Leveled Readers).

National Geographic Kids & Kitson, Jazynka. George Washington Carver. 2016. (Readers Bios Ser.). (ENG.). 32p. (J). (gr. -1-1). lib. bdg. 13.90 *(978-1-4263-2286-0(0),* National Geographic Children's Bks.) National Geographic Society.

National Geographic Kids Staff & Jazynka, Kitson. George Washington Carver. 2016. (Readers Bios Ser.). (ENG., Illus.). 32p. (J). (gr. -1-1). pap. 3.99 *(978-1-4263-2285-3(2),* National Geographic Children's Bks.) National Geographic Society.

Nelson, Robin. George Washington Carver: A Life of Devotion. (Pull Ahead Books-Biographies Ser.). 32p. 2007. (ENG.). (gr. k-3). pap. 7.95 *(978-0-8225-6455-3(6))* 2006. (Illus.). (J). (gr. 3-7). lib. bdg. 22.60 *(978-0-8225-6461-4(0),* Lerner Pubns.) Lerner Publishing Group.

Olson, Nathan. George Washington Carver: Ingenious Inventor, 1 vol. Tucker, Keith, illus. 2006. (Graphic Biographies Ser.). (ENG.). 32p. (gr. 3-4). 30.65 *(978-0-7368-5484-9(3),* Graphic Library) Capstone Press of Coughlan Cos.

Riley, John B. George Washington Carver: A Photo Biography. l.t. ed. 2004. (First Biographies Ser.). (Illus.). 24p. (YA). (gr. 5-18). 16.95 *(978-1-883846-62-6(5),* First Biographies) Reynolds, Morgan Inc.

Schier, Helga. George Washington Carver: Agricultural Innovator, 1 vol. 2008. (Essential Lives Set 2 Ser.). (ENG., Illus.). 112p. (J). (gr. 6-12). lib. bdg. 35.64 *(978-1-60453-035-3(9))* ABDO Publishing Co.

Scraper, Katherine. George Washington Carver. 2011. (Early Connections Ser.). (J). *(978-1-61672-551-8(6))* Benchmark Education Co.

Wheeler, Jill C. George Washington Carver. 2003. (Breaking Barriers Ser.). 64p. (gr. 3-8). 27.07 *(978-1-57765-904-4(X),* Abdo & Daughters) ABDO Publishing Co.

CARVER, GEORGE WASHINGTON, 1864?-1943—FICTION

Andrews, Andy. The Kid Who Changed the World, 1 vol. 2014. (ENG.). 40p. (J). 14.99 *(978-1-4003-2433-0(5))* Nelson, Thomas Inc.

Grigsby, Susan. In the Garden with Dr. Carver. Tadgell, Nicole, illus. 2012. (J). *(978-1-61913-157-6(9))* Weigl Pubs., Inc.

—In the Garden with Dr. Carver. Tadgell, Nicole, illus. 2010. (ENG.). 32p. (J). (gr. 2-3). 16.99 *(978-0-8075-3630-8(X))* Whitman, Albert & Co.

CARVING, WOOD

see Wood-Carving

CASH, JOHNNY, 1932-2003

Neimark, Anne E. Johnny Cash. 2008. (Up Close Ser.). (ENG., Illus.). 208p. (YA). (gr. 7-18). 7.99 *(978-0-14-241047-9(0),* Puffin Books) Penguin Young Readers Group.

—Johnny Cash: A Twentieth-Century Life. 2007. (Up Close Ser.). (Illus.). 207p. (J). *(978-1-4287-3958-1(0),* Viking Adult) Penguin Publishing Group.

Willett, Edward. Johnny Cash: "The Man in Black" 2010. (American Rebels Ser.). 160p. (YA). (gr. 7-12). 35.94 *(978-0-7660-3386-3(4))* Enslow Pubs., Inc.

CASSATT, MARY, 1845-1926

Casey, Carolyn. Mary Cassatt: The Life of an Artist. 2004. (Artist Biographies Ser.). (Illus.). 48p. (J). lib. bdg. 25.27 *(978-0-7660-2093-1(2))* Enslow Pubs., Inc.

Cernak, Linda. Mary Cassatt. Morrow, J. T., illus. 2014. (World's Greatest Artists Ser.). (ENG.). 24p. (J). (gr. 2-5). 28.50 *(978-1-62687-350-6(X),* 207190) Child's World, Inc., The.

Ferrara, Cos. Mary Cassatt: The Life & Art of a Genteel Rebel. 2004. (Girls Explore, Reach for the Stars Ser.). (Illus.). 101p. (J). 20.00 *(978-0-9749456-3-7(3),* Girls Explore) Girls Explore LLC.

Harris, Lois V. Mary Cassatt: Impressionist Painter, 1 vol. Cassatt, Mary, illus. 2007. (ENG.). 32p. (J). (gr. k-3). 16.99 *(978-1-58980-452-4(X))* Pelican Publishing Co., Inc.

Herkert, Barbara. Mary Cassatt: Extraordinary Impressionist Painter. Swiatkowska, Gabi, illus. 2015. (ENG.). 32p. (J). (gr. -1-3). 17.99 *(978-1-62779-016-1(0)*, 9781627790161, Holt, Henry & Co. Bks. For Young Readers) Holt, Henry & Co.

Mattern, Joanne. Mary Cassatt, 1 vol. 2005. (Great Artists Set 1 Ser.). (ENG., Illus.). 32p. (gr. k-6). 27.07 *(978-1-59197-840-4(8)*, Checkerboard Library) ABDO Publishing Co.

O'Connor, Jane. Mary Cassatt: Family Pictures. Kalis, Jennifer, illus. 2003. (Smart about Art Ser.). (ENG.). 32p. (J). (gr. k-4). mass mkt. 5.99 *(978-0-448-43152-9(1)*, Grosset & Dunlap) Penguin Young Readers Group.

Taylor, Charlotte. Get to Know Mary Cassatt. 2016. (Famous Artists Ser.). (ENG., Illus.). 48p. (J). (gr. 3-4). 27.93 *(978-0-7660-7234-3(7))* Enslow Pubs., Inc.

Venezia, Mike. Mary Cassatt. Venezia, Mike, illus. rev. ed. 2015. (Getting to Know the World's Greatest Artists Ser.). (ENG., Illus.). 40p. (J). pap. 7.95 *(978-0-531-21292-9(0))* Scholastic Library Publishing.

Zaczek, Iain. Mary Cassatt. 2014. (Great Artists Ser.). 32p. (J). (gr. 3-6). pap. 10.50 *(978-1-4824-1219-2(5))* Stevens, Gareth Publishing LLLP.

CASTLE OF SEVEN TOWERS (IMAGINARY PLACE)—FICTION

Nix, Garth. Aenir. 2004. (Seventh Tower Ser.). 233p. (gr. 3-7). 18.00 *(978-0-7569-3525-2(3))* Perfection Learning Corp.

—The Violet Keystone. 2004. (Seventh Tower Ser.: Bk. 6). 233p. (gr. 4-7). 17.00 *(978-0-7569-3506-1(7))* Perfection Learning Corp.

CASTLES

Anderson, Scoular. Castles & Cannons. 2017. (Early Reader Non Fiction Ser.). (ENG., Illus.). 64p. (J). (gr. k-3). pap. 6.99 *(978-1-4440-1564-5(8)*, Orion Children's Bks.) Hachette Children's Group GBR. Dist: Hachette Bk. Group.

Arlon, Penelope & Gordon-Harris, Tory. Knights & Castles: A LEGO Adventure in the Real World. 2016. (Illus.). 64p. (J). ***(978-1-4844-8524-8(6))*** Scholastic, Inc.

Arnold, Tedd. Castles. 2017. (Fly Guy Presents Ser.). lib. bdg. 13.55 ***(978-0-606-39716-2(7))*** Turtleback Bks.

Arnold, Tedd. Fly Guy Presents: Castles (Scholastic Reader, Level 2) 2017. (Scholastic Reader, Level 2 Ser.). (ENG.). 32p. (J). (gr. k-2). pap. 3.99 *(978-0-545-91738-4(7))* Scholastic, Inc.

Ball, Jacqueline A. Himeji Castle: Japan's Samurai Past. 2005. (Castles, Palaces, & Tombs Ser.). 32p. (J). lib. bdg. 25.27 *(978-1-59716-001-8(6))* Bearport Publishing Co., Inc.

Baum, Margaux & Hilliam, David. Castles & Cathedrals. 2016. (Life in the Middle Ages Ser.). 00064p. (J). (gr. 5-5). 34.45 *(978-1-5081-7318-2(4))* Rosen Publishing Group, Inc., The.

Bingham, Jane. Great Castle Search. 2005. 32p. (J). pap. 7.95 *(978-0-7945-0998-9(3)*, Usborne) EDC Publishing.

Bodden, Valerie. Castles. 2007. (Built to Last Ser.). (Illus.). 24p. (J). (gr. 3-7). lib. bdg. 24.25 *(978-1-58341-561-0(0)*, Creative Education) Creative Co., The.

Bow, James. Your Guide to Castles & Medieval Warfare. 2017. (Destination: Middle Ages Ser.). (ENG., Illus.). 32p. (J). ***(978-0-7787-2994-5(X))***; pap. ***(978-0-7787-3000-2(X))*** Crabtree Publishing Co.

Boyer, Crispin. National Geographic Kids Everything Castles: Capture These Facts, Photos, & Fun to Be King of the Castle! 2011. (National Geographic Kids Everything Ser.). (ENG., Illus.). 64p. (J). (gr. 3-7). 25.90 *(978-1-4263-0804-8(3))*; pap. 12.95 *(978-1-4263-0803-1(5))* National Geographic Society. (National Geographic Children's Bks.).

Bruce, Julia. Siege! Can You Capture a Castle? Dennis, Peter, illus. 2009. (Step into History Ser.). 32p. (J). (gr. 2-5). lib. bdg. 23.94 *(978-0-7660-3475-4(5))* Enslow Pubs., Inc.

Chambers, Catherine. A King's Guide. Pentney, Ryan, illus. 2017. (How-To Guides for Fiendish Rulers Ser.). (ENG.). 32p. (J). (gr. 3-6). lib. bdg. 26.65 *(978-1-5124-1550-6(2))*; 7.99 ***(978-1-5124-3624-2(0))***; 39.99 ***(978-1-5124-2706-6(3))***; 39.99 ***(978-1-5124-3623-5(2))*** Lerner Publishing Group.

Clements, Gillian. Medieval Castle. 2009. (Building History Ser.). (Illus.). 32p. (J). (gr. 3-5). 27.10 *(978-1-59771-145-6(4))* Sea-To-Sea Pubns.

Cohn, Jessica. 10 Fascinating Facts about Castles. 2017. (Rookie Star — Fact Finder Ser.). (ENG., Illus.). 32p. (J). lib. bdg. 25.00 *(978-0-531-22259-1(4)*, Children's Pr.) Scholastic Library Publishing.

Coombs, Rachel. A Year in a Castle. (Time Goes By Ser.). (gr. k-3). 2009. (ENG.). pap. 39.62 *(978-0-7613-4715-6(1))* 2008. (Illus.). 24p. (J). lib. bdg. 22.60 *(978-1-58013-550-4(1))* Lerner Publishing Group.

Cox, Phil Roxbee. What Were Castles For? rev. ed. 2004. (Starting Point History Ser.). (Illus.). (J). (ENG.). 1p. pap. 4.99 *(978-0-7945-0178-5(8)*, Usborne); 32p. lib. bdg. 12.95 *(978-1-58086-396-4(5))* EDC Publishing.

Crosbie, Duncan. Life in an Irish Castle: The Journal of a 17th Century Castles in Times of Peace & War. Dixey, Kay, illus. 2007. (ENG.). 19p. (J). 37.95 *(978-0-7171-4273-6(6))* M.H. Gill & Co. U. C. IRL. Dist: Dufour Editions, Inc.

Dargie, Richard. Castles under Siege. 2008. (Age of Castles Ser.). (Illus.). 48p. (J). (gr. 3-7). lib. bdg. 29.25 *(978-1-4042-4294-4(5)*, PowerKids Pr.) Rosen Publishing Group, Inc., The.

—Knights & Castles. 2008. (Age of Castles Ser.). (Illus.). 48p. (J). (gr. 4-8). lib. bdg. 29.25 *(978-1-4042-4295-1(3)*, PowerKids Pr.) Rosen Publishing Group, Inc., The.

Daynes, Katie. See inside Castles. Hancock, David, illus. 2005. 16p. (J). 12.95 *(978-0-7945-1022-0(1)*, Usborne) EDC Publishing.

Dennis, Peter, illus. Castle. 2006. (Leap Through Time Ser.). 31p. (J). *(978-0-7607-7523-3(0))* backpackbook.

Dixon, Philip. Knights & Castles. 2007. (Insiders Ser.). (ENG., Illus.). 64p. (J). (gr. 3-7). 17.99 *(978-1-4169-3864-4(8)*, Simon & Schuster Bks. For Young Readers) Simon & Schuster Bks. For Young Readers.

Doeden, Matt. Edinburgh Castle: A Chilling Interactive Adventure. 2017. (You Choose: Haunted Places Ser.). (ENG., Illus.). 112p. (gr. 3-4). lib. bdg. 31.99 *(978-1-5157-3648-6(2)*, You Choose Bks.) Capstone Press of Coughlan Cos.

Dorling Kindersley Publishing Staff. Castles & Knights. 2014. (Eye Wonder Ser.). (ENG.). 56p. (J). (gr. k-4). 10.99 *(978-1-4654-1562-2(9)*, DK Children) Dorling Kindersley Publishing, Inc.

Dorling Kindersley Publishing Staff & Matthews, Rupert. Knights & Castles. 2016. (DK Readers Ser.). (ENG., Illus.). 64p. (J). (gr. 2-4). pap. 3.99 *(978-1-4654-5393-8(8)*, DK Children) Dorling Kindersley Publishing, Inc.

Duke, Nell K., et al. All about Castles. SanGiacomo, Scott, illus. 2016. 32p. (J). *(978-0-87659-687-6(1))* Gryphon Hse., Inc.

Eastwood, Kay. Life in a Castle. 2004. (Medieval World Ser.). (ENG., Illus.). 32p. (J). (gr. 5). pap. *(978-0-7787-1375-3(X))* Crabtree Publishing Co.

Freeman, Maggie. Castles. 2005. (Big Cat Ser.). pap. 6.50 *(978-1-60457-093-9(8))* Pacific Learning, Inc.

Ganeri, Anita. How to Live Like a Medieval Knight. Epelbaum, Mariano, illus. 2015. (How to Live Like... Ser.). (ENG.). 32p. (J). (gr. 3-6). lib. bdg. 26.65 *(978-1-4677-6353-0(5))* Lerner Publishing Group.

Gilkerson, Patricia. My Adventure in a Castle. 2006. 44p. (J). 8.99 *(978-1-59092-271-2(9))* Blue Forge Pr.

Giulieri, Anne. The Castle, 1 vol. Kreinberg, Sylvia, photos by. 2012. (Engage Literacy Magenta Ser.). (ENG., Illus.). 32p. (gr. k-2). pap. 5.99 *(978-1-4296-8872-7(6)*, Engage Literacy) Capstone Press of Coughlan Cos.

Gravett, Christopher. Castle. 2008. (DK Eyewitness Bks.). (ENG.). 72p. (J). (gr. 3-7). 16.99 *(978-0-7566-3769-9(4)*, DK Children) Dorling Kindersley Publishing, Inc.

Gregory, Josh. If You Were a Kid in a Medieval Castle. 2017. (If You Were a Kid Ser.). (ENG.). 32p. (J). lib. bdg. 26.00 *(978-0-531-22385-7(X)*, Children's Pr.) Scholastic Library Publishing.

Hamilton, John. Castles & Dungeons, 1 vol. 2006. (Fantasy & Folklore Ser.). (ENG., Illus.). 32p. (gr. 5-8). 27.07 *(978-1-59679-335-4(X)*, Abdo & Daughters) ABDO Publishing Co.

Harris, Nicholas. Let's Explore a Castle. Lee, Brian, illus. 2010. 36p. (J). (gr. k-3). 13.99 *(978-0-8437-1395-4(X))* Hammond World Atlas Corp.

Harris, Nicolas. Castles Through Time. 2009. (Fast Forward Ser.). 32p. (YA). (gr. 2-5). lib. bdg. 25.25 *(978-1-4358-2798-1(8))* Rosen Publishing Group, Inc., The.

Haunted! Edinburgh Castle. 2013. (History's Most Haunted Ser.). 32p. (J). (gr. 3-6). pap. 63.00 *(978-1-4339-9255-1(8))* Stevens, Gareth Publishing LLLP.

Hicks, Peter. How Castles Were Built. 2008. (Age of Castles Ser.). (Illus.). 48p. (J). (gr. 3-7). lib. bdg. 29.25 *(978-1-4042-4293-7(7)*, PowerKids Pr.) Rosen Publishing Group, Inc., The.

Hilliam, David. Castles & Cathedrals. 2004. (Library of the Middle Ages Ser.). (Illus.). 64p. (YA). (gr. 5-9). lib. bdg. 31.95 *(978-0-8239-3990-9(1))* Rosen Publishing Group, Inc., The.

—Castles & Cathedrals: The Great Buildings of Medieval Times. 2009. (Library of the Middle Ages Ser.). 64p. (gr. 5-8). 58.50 *(978-1-60853-896-6(6)*, Rosen Reference) Rosen Publishing Group, Inc., The.

Hindley, J. Knights & Castles. rev. ed. 2004. (Time Traveler Ser.). (Illus.). 32p. (J). pap. 6.95 *(978-0-7945-0335-2(7))* EDC Publishing.

Hindley, Judy. Knights & Castles. Wheatley, Abigail, ed. Goffe, Toni, illus. 2006. (Time Traveler Ser.). 32p. (J). (gr. 3). lib. bdg. 14.95 *(978-1-58086-554-8(2))* EDC Publishing.

Hoggard, Brian. Crusader Castles: Christian Fortresses in the Middle East. (Library of the Middle Ages Ser.). 64p. (gr. 5-8). 2009. 58.50 *(978-1-60853-897-3(4)*, Rosen Reference) 2004. (Illus.). (YA). lib. bdg. 31.95 *(978-0-8239-4212-1(0))* Rosen Publishing Group, Inc., The.

Howse, Jennifer. Neuschwanstein Castle. 2015. (Illus.). 24p. (J). *(978-1-4896-3396-5(0))* Weigl Pubs., Inc.

Ives, Rob. Castle Attack: Make Your Own Medieval Battlefield. De Quay, John Paul, illus. 2016. (Tabletop Wars Ser.). (ENG.). 32p. (J). (gr. 3-6). 26.65 *(978-1-5124-0639-9(2))* Lerner Publishing Group.

Jeffrey, Gary. Castles. 2014. (ENG., Illus.). 48p. (J). *(978-0-7787-0396-9(7))* Crabtree Publishing Co.

Kenney, Sean. Cool Castles. 2012. (ENG., Illus.). 32p. (J). (gr. -1-3). 12.99 *(978-0-8050-9539-5(X)*, 9780805095395, Holt, Henry & Co. Bks. For Young Readers) Holt, Henry & Co.

Key Porter Books Staff. Gymboree in a Princess Castle. rev. ed. 2007. (ENG., Illus.). 1p. (J). *(978-1-55263-923-8(1))* Magma.

Knox, Barbara. Edinburgh Castle: Scotland's Haunted Fortress. 2006. (Castles, Palaces, & Tombs Ser.). (Illus.). 32p. (YA). (gr. 2-5). lib. bdg. 25.27 *(978-1-59716-248-7(5))* Bearport Publishing Co., Inc.

Knox, Barbara J. Castle Dracula: Romania's Vampire Home. 2005. (Castles, Palaces, & Tombs Ser.). (Illus.). 32p. (J). (gr. 2-5). lib. bdg. 25.27 *(978-1-59716-000-1(8))* Bearport Publishing Co., Inc.

Leavitt, Amie Jane. My Home Is My Castle Windsor Castle: Windsor Castle. 2015. (ENG., Illus.). 48p. (J). 29.95 *(978-1-62469-142-3(0))* Purple Toad Publishing, Inc.

Lee, Brian, illus. A Castle. 2005. (What's Inside? Ser.). (J). *(978-0-7607-6568-5(5))* backpackbook.

Lee, Sally. Castles & Palaces, 1 vol. 2013. (Royalty Ser.). (ENG.). 24p. (gr. k-1). lib. bdg. 26.65 *(978-1-62065-121-6(1)*, Pebble Plus) Capstone Press of Coughlan Cos.

Macaulay, David. Castle: Revised & in Full Color. 2013. (ENG., Illus.). 80p. (J). (gr. 5-7). 19.99 *(978-0-544-10226-2(6))* Houghton Mifflin Harcourt Publishing Co.

Macaulay, David & Keenan, Sheila. Castle: How It Works. 2015. (ENG., Illus.). 32p. (J). (gr. 1-4). 17.99 *(978-1-62672-208-8(0)*, 9781626722088, Macaulay, David Studio) Roaring Brook Pr.

MacDonald, Fiona. Knights & Castles. 2009. (History Explorers Ser.). (ENG.). 24p. (J). (gr. k-2). pap. 5.95 *(978-1-84696-215-8(3)*, TickTock Books) Octopus Publishing Group GBR. Dist: Independent Pubs. Group.

—Knights, Castles, & Warfare in the Middle Ages. 2005. (World Almanac Library of the Middle Ages). (Illus.). 48p. (gr. 5-12). lib. bdg. 31.00 *(978-0-8368-5895-2(6)*, Gareth Stevens Secondary Library) Stevens, Gareth Publishing LLLP.

Macdonald, Fiona. The Medieval Chronicles: Vikings, Knights, & Castles. Antram, David, illus. 2013. 92p. (J). *(978-1-4351-5067-6(8))* Barnes & Noble, Inc.

—You Wouldn't Want to Be in a Medieval Dungeon! Prisoners You'd Rather Not Meet. Antram, David, illus. 2013. (You Wouldn't Want to... Ser.). (ENG.). (J). 40p. pap. 9.95 *(978-0-531-24504-0(7))*; 32p. 29.00 *(978-0-531-25948-1(X))* Scholastic Library Publishing. (Watts, Franklin).

—You Wouldn't Want to Be in a Medieval Dungeon! Prisoners You'd Rather Not Meet. 2013. (You Wouldn't Want To... Ser.). lib. bdg. 20.80 *(978-0-606-31629-3(9)*, Turtleback) Turtleback Bks.

Matthews, Rupert. Battle at the Castle. 2014. (DK Readers Ser.). (ENG., Illus.). 32p. (J). (gr. 1-3). 14.99 *(978-1-4654-2004-6(5)*, DK Children) Dorling Kindersley Publishing, Inc.

Matthews, Rupert & Dorling Kindersley Publishing Staff. Battle at the Castle. 2014. (DK Readers Ser.). (ENG., Illus.). 32p. (J). (gr. 1-3). pap. 3.99 *(978-1-4654-2005-3(3)*, DK Children) Dorling Kindersley Publishing, Inc.

Mayer, Cassie. Knights & Castles. 2012. (Illus.). 64p. (J). pap. 12.99 *(978-1-62267-007-9(8))* Bright Connections Media.

Meachen Rau, Dana. Bookworms: The Inside Story, 6 bks., Set. Incl. Castle. 32p. (gr. k-2). lib. bdg. 15.95 *(978-0-7614-2272-3(2))*; Igloo. 32p. (gr. k-2). lib. bdg. 15.95 *(978-0-7614-2273-0(0))*; Log Cabin. 31p. (J). (gr. -1-3). lib. bdg. 22.79 *(978-0-7614-2274-7(9))*; Pyramid. 32p. (gr. k-2). lib. bdg. 15.95 *(978-0-7614-2275-4(7))*; Skyscraper. 32p. (gr. k-2). lib. bdg. 15.95 *(978-0-7614-2276-1(5))*; Tepee. 31p. (J). (gr. -1-3). lib. bdg. 22.79 *(978-0-7614-2277-8(3))*; (Illus.). 2006. 2006. Set lib. bdg. 136.71 *(978-0-7614-2271-6(4)*, Benchmark Bks.) Marshall Cavendish Corp.

—Castle. 2006. (Bookworms Ser.). (Illus.). 32p. (gr. k-2). lib. bdg. 15.95 *(978-0-7614-2272-3(2)*, Benchmark Bks.) Marshall Cavendish Corp.

Media, Cont. Knights & Castles. 2008. (ENG., Illus.). 48p. (YA). 12.99 *(978-1-931703-24-6(8))* Crosby Advanced Medical Systems Inc.

Morley, Jacqueline. Live in a Medieval Castle! A Home You'D Rather Not Inhabit. Antram, David, illus. 2008. (You Wouldn't Want to...: History of the World Ser.). (ENG.). 32p. (J). 29.00 *(978-0-531-20703-1(X)*, Watts, Franklin) Scholastic Library Publishing.

Murrell, Deborah Jane. Castles. 2008. (Medieval Warfare Ser.). 32p. (gr. 5-8). (J). lib. bdg. 26.00 *(978-0-8368-9208-6(9)*, Gareth Stevens Secondary Library); pap. 10.50 *(978-0-8368-9335-9(2))* Stevens, Gareth Publishing LLLP.

Nagelhout, Ryan. Haunted! Edinburgh Castle. 2013. 32p. (J). (gr. 3-6). 26.60 *(978-1-4339-9253-7(1))* Stevens, Gareth Publishing LLLP.

Nishida, Masaki. Drawing Manga Medieval Castles & Knights. 2007. (How to Draw Manga Ser.: Vol. 4). (Illus.). 24p. (J). (gr. 4-7). lib. bdg. 25.25 *(978-1-4042-3849-7(2))* Rosen Publishing Group, Inc., The.

Page, Jason. Castles & Dungeons. 2008. (Factastic Journey Ser.). (Illus.). 32p. (J). (gr. k-7). pap. 8.95 *(978-1-59905-239-7(3))* Saddleback Educational Publishing, Inc.

Parvis, Sarah. Creepy Castles. (Scary Places Ser.). 32p. (gr. 4-8). 2017. (ENG.). (J). 8.95 ***(978-1-68402-609-8(1))*** 2008. (Illus.). (YA). lib. bdg. 25.27 *(978-1-59716-576-1(X))* Bearport Publishing Co., Inc.

Pipe, Jim. Castle Sticker Book: Complete Your Own Mighty, Medieval Fortress! Taylor, Maria, illus. 2014. (ENG.). 40p. (J). (gr. 1). pap. 9.95 *(978-1-78312-013-0(4))* Carlton Bks., Ltd. GBR. Dist: Sterling Publishing Co., Inc.

—Lift, Look & Learn Castle: Uncover the Secrets of a Medieval Fortress. Taylor, Maria, illus. 2014. (ENG.). 24p. (J). (gr. 1). 19.95 *(978-1-78312-081-9(9))* Carlton Bks., Ltd. GBR. Dist: Sterling Publishing Co., Inc.

Platt, Richard & Biesty, Stephen. Castle. (Illus.). 32p. (J). pap. 21.95 *(978-0-590-24346-9(2))* Scholastic, Inc.

Pratt, Leonie. Knights & Castles Things to Make & Do. Thompson, Josephine Et Al, illus. 2006. 32p. (J). pap. 6.99 *(978-0-7945-1355-9(7)*, Usborne) EDC Publishing.

Rau, Dana Meachen. Building Sandcastles. 2012. (How-To Library). (ENG.). 32p. (gr. 3-6). 28.50 *(978-1-61080-468-4(6)*, 202078); pap. 14.21 *(978-1-61080-642-8(5)*, 202252) Cherry Lake Publishing.

—Castle. 2007. (J). pap. 6.99 *(978-0-7614-3297-5(3))* Marshall Cavendish Corp.

Reid, Struan. Castle Life. 2008. (Age of Castles Ser.). (Illus.). 48p. (J). (gr. 4-8). lib. bdg. 29.25 *(978-1-4042-4292-0(9)*, PowerKids Pr.) Rosen Publishing Group, Inc., The.

Riggs, Kate. Enchanted Castles. 2013. (Illus.). 24p. (J). 25.65 *(978-1-60818-240-4(1)*, Creative Education) Creative Co., The.

Rothrock, Megan H. The LEGO Adventure Book Vol. 2: Spaceships, Pirates, Dragons & More! 2013. (ENG., Illus.). 196p. (gr. 5). 24.95 *(978-1-59327-512-9(9)*, 9781593275129) No Starch Pr., Inc.

Scholastic, Inc. Staff. Knights & Castles: A LEGO(r) Adventure in the Real World. 2016. (LEGO Nonfiction Ser.). (ENG., Illus.). 64p. (J). (gr. 1-3). pap. 8.99 *(978-0-545-94767-1(7))* Scholastic, Inc.

Simon, Seymour. Knights & Castles. 2006. (SeeMore Readers Ser.: SEMR). (ENG., Illus.). 40p. (J). (gr. 3-5). pap. 3.95 *(978-0-8118-5409-2(4))* Chronicle Bks. LLC.

Sims, L. Castles. 2004. (SPA., Illus.). 104p. (J). (gr. 4). pap. 14.95 *(978-0-7945-0144-0(3)*, Usborne); lib. bdg. 22.95 *(978-1-58086-425-1(2))* EDC Publishing.

Sims, Lesley. The Story of Castles. Gower, Teri, illus. 2004. (Young Reading Ser.: Vol. 2). 64p. (J). (gr. 2-18). lib. bdg. 13.95 *(978-1-58086-701-6(4)*, Usborne) EDC Publishing.

Snedden, Robert. Castles & Fortresses. 2016. (Engineering Eurekas Ser.). 00032p. (J). (gr. 3-4). pap. 10.00 *(978-1-4994-3093-6(0)*, PowerKids Pr.) Rosen Publishing Group, Inc., The.

Stadler, Charlotte. Building a Castle. 2011. (Early Connections Ser.). (J). *(978-1-61672-628-7(8))* Benchmark Education Co.

Stewart, David. You Wouldn't Want to Be in a Medieval Dungeon! Antram, David, illus. rev. ed. 2013. (You Wouldn't Want to... Ser.). (ENG.). 32p. (J). 29.00 *(978-0-531-25949-8(8)*, Watts, Franklin) Scholastic Library Publishing.

Stiefel, Chana. Ye Castle Stinketh: Could You Survive Living in a Castle? Kelley, Gerald, illus. 2011. (Ye Yucky Middle Ages Ser.). 48p. (J). (gr. 5-18). pap. 8.95 *(978-1-59845-374-4(2))*; (gr. 7-12). lib. bdg. 25.27 *(978-0-7660-3786-1(X))* Enslow Pubs., Inc.

Taylor, Barbara. The Amazing History of Castles & Knights. 2016. (ENG., Illus.). 64p. (J). (gr. -1-12). 12.99 *(978-1-86147-717-0(1)*, Armadillo) Anness Publishing GBR. Dist: National Bk. Network.

—The Amazing World Of: Castles. 2008. (ENG., Illus.). 64p. (J). (gr. 4-7). pap. 12.99 *(978-1-84476-599-7(7))* Anness Publishing GBR. Dist: National Bk. Network.

Turnbull, S. Castles. 2004. (Beginners Ser.). 32p. (J). (gr. 1-18). (ENG.). pap. 4.95 *(978-0-7945-0320-8(9))*; lib. bdg. 12.95 *(978-1-58086-481-7(3))* EDC Publishing.

Turnbull, Stephanie. Castles: Information for Young Readers - Level 1. King, Colin, illus. 2007. (Usborne Beginners Ser.). 32p. (J). 4.99 *(978-0-7945-1335-1(2)*, Usborne) EDC Publishing.

—Castles IR (Rev Cover) 2015. (Beginners Ser.). (ENG.). 32p. (J). (gr. k-5). 4.99 *(978-0-7945-3568-1(2)*, Usborne) EDC Publishing.

Walker, Jane. Knights & Castles. 2013. (Illus.). 48p. (J). *(978-1-4351-5093-5(7))* Barnes & Noble, Inc.

—100 Things You Should Know about Knights & Castles. 2008. (Illus.). 64p. *(978-1-84236-002-6(7))* Miles Kelly Publishing, Ltd.

Watson, Danielle. The Castle in Medieval Europe. 2016. (Life in Medieval Europe Ser.). (Illus.). 80p. (J). (gr. 6-6). 35.64 *(978-1-5026-1878-8(8))* Cavendish Square Publishing.

Weil, Ann. The World's Most Amazing Castles, 1 vol. 2011. (Landmark Top Tens Ser.). (ENG.). 32p. (gr. 3-5). pap. 8.29 *(978-1-4109-4252-4(X))*; 30.65 *(978-1-4109-4241-8(4))* Heinemann-Raintree. (Raintree Perspectives).

Wilson, Phil, illus. Medieval Castle: A Three Dimensional. 2004. (ENG.). (J). 22.00 *(978-1-58117-365-9(2)*, Intervisual/Piggy Toes) Bendon, Inc.

World Book, Inc Staff, contrib. by. The Age of Knights & Castles. 2011. (J). *(978-0-7166-1787-7(0))* World Bk., Inc.

CASTLES—FICTION

Abbott, Tony. The Riddle of Zorfendorf Castle. Merrell, David, illus. 2005. (Secrets of Droon Ser.: No. 25). 124p. (J). lib. bdg. 15.38 *(978-1-4242-0310-9(4))* Fitzgerald Bks.

Arrigan, Mary. Milo & the Pirate Sisters. 2015. (ENG., Illus.). 176p. (J). pap. 13.00 *(978-1-84717-562-5(7))* O'Brien Pr., Ltd., The IRL. Dist: Dufour Editions, Inc.

Ballou, Kathy. The Tracks Out Back. l.t. ed. 2005. (Illus.). 24p. (J). per. 10.00 *(978-1-932338-50-8(0))* Lifevest Publishing, Inc.

Barbera, Katia. Iron Horse, 1 vol. 2010. 16p. 24.95 *(978-1-4489-4634-1(4))* PublishAmerica, Inc.

Bartow, Philip. T & the Jello Castle-Book 1. 2013. 252p. (J). pap. 13.30 *(978-0-9835176-2-7(2))* Institute For Outdoor Awareness, Inc.

Bishop, Phyllis. Tommy Minor & Tiny Major Danger. l.t. ed. 2005. (Illus.). 36p. (J). per. 9.99 *(978-1-59879-028-3(5))* Lifevest Publishing, Inc.

Bloodworth, Mark, illus. The Castle Mystery. 2010. (Boxcar Children Graphic Novels Ser.: 12). (ENG.). 32p. (J). (gr. 1-5). pap. 6.99 *(978-0-8075-1080-3(7))* Whitman, Albert & Co.

Brege, K. B. Ghost Board Posse London Screaming! 2008. (Ghost Board Posse Ser.: No. 1). (Illus.). 207p. (YA). pap. 6.99 *(978-0-9774119-6-2(6))* Team B Creative LLC.

Brocklehurst, Ruth & Doherty, Gillian. Illustrated Grimm's Fairy Tales. 2011. (Illustrated Stories Ser.). 303p. (J). ring bd. 19.99 *(978-0-7945-2409-8(5)*, Usborne) EDC Publishing.

Buckey, Sarah Masters. Clue in the Castle Tower: A Samantha Mystery. Ross, Peg, ed. Giovine, Sergio, illus. 2011. (ENG.). 184p. (YA). (gr. 4-18). pap. 6.95 *(978-1-59369-752-5(X))* American Girl Publishing, Inc.

Buckmaster, Heath L. Box of Hair: A Fairy Tale, 3 bks., Bk. 1. (Illus.). (YA). 2007. 102p. pap. 12.99 *(978-0-9771802-5-7(5))* 2008. 108p. lib. bdg. 25.00 *(978-0-9771802-4-0(7))* Transaltar Publishing.

Caballero, Erica. Mount Mole. 2006. pap. 10.00 *(978-1-4257-2301-9(2))* Xlibris Corp.

Carroll, Jacquie Lund. The Queen's Jewels. Gillen, Rosemarie, illus. 2013. 26p. pap. 9.99 *(978-1-61286-147-0(4))* Avid Readers Publishing Group.

Clark, CoraMarie. Emily's Magical Journey with Toothena the Tooth Fairy. Lawton, Val, illus. 2007. (ENG.). 32p. (J). *(978-0-9783779-0-8(7))* Strategix Ltd.

Cook, Sherry & Johnson, Terri. Quincy Quake, 26. Kuhn, Jesse, illus. l.t. ed. 2006. (Quirkles — Exploring Phonics through Science Ser.: 17). 32p. (J). 7.99 *(978-1-933815-16-9(7)*, Quirkles, The) Creative 3, LLC.

Coomber, Suzanne. The Magic Sandcastle. 2011. 16p. 8.32 *(978-1-4520-9612-4(0))* AuthorHouse.

Coombs, Rachel. A Year in a Castle. 2009. (Time Goes By Ser.). (ENG.). 24p. (gr. k-3). pap. 6.95 *(978-1-58013-796-6(2)*, First Avenue Editions) Lerner Publishing Group.

Côté, Geneviève. Mr. King's Castle. Côté, Geneviève, illus. 2013. (Mr. King Ser.). (ENG., Illus.). 32p. (J). (gr. -1-2). 16.95 *(978-1-55453-972-7(2))* Kids Can Pr., Ltd. CAN. Dist: Hachette Bk. Group.

Coulton, Mia. Danny's Castle. Coulton, Mia, photos by. 2005. (ENG., Illus.). 16p. pap. 5.35 *(978-1-933624-00-6(0))* Maryruth Bks., Inc.

Davis, Tony. Roland Wright: at the Joust. Rogers, Gregory, illus. 2011. (ENG.). 144p. (J). (gr. 1-4). 6.99 *(978-0-375-87328-7(7)*, Yearling) Random Hse. Children's Bks.

—Roland Wright: Brand-New Page. Rogers, Gregory, illus. 2011. (Roland Wright Ser.). (ENG.). 144p. (J). (gr. 1-4). 6.99 *(978-0-385-73803-3(X)*, Yearling) Random Hse. Children's Bks.

Disney Book Group. Beauty & the Beast: The Story of Belle. Disney Storybook Art Team, illus. 2016. (ENG.). 112p. (J). (gr. -1-k). 12.99 *(978-1-4847-6720-7(9))* Disney Pr.

Disney Press Editors. Chaos at the Castle. 2016. (Star Wars: World of Reading Ser.). (J). lib. bdg. 13.55 *(978-0-606-38340-0(9))* Turtleback Bks.

Disney Princess, Disney. Disney Princess Once upon a Castle: Hidden Stories. 2014. (Hidden Stories Ser.: 4). (ENG.). 10p. (J). (gr. -1-1). 15.99 *(978-0-7944-3107-5(0))* Reader's Digest Assn., Inc., The.

Dower, Laura. Sunny & the Secret Passage. 2013. (Palace Puppies Ser.: 4). (J). lib. bdg. 14.75 *(978-0-606-35108-9(6)*, Turtleback) Turtleback Bks.

Doyle, Malachy & Parsons, Garry. The Football Ghosts. 2007. (Red Bananas Ser.). (ENG., Illus.). 48p. (J). (gr. k-2). pap.

5.99 *(978-1-4052-2749-0(4))* Egmont Bks., Ltd. GBR. Dist: Independent Pubs. Group.
Duey, Kathleen. Castle Avamir. Rayyan, Omar, illus. 2005. 76p. (J). lib. bdg. 15.00 *(978-1-59054-899-8(X))* Fitzgerald Bks.
—Castle Avamir. Rayyan, Omar, illus. 2004. (Unicorn's Secret Ser.). 73p. (gr. 2-5). 15.00 *(978-0-7569-3357-9(9))* Perfection Learning Corp.
Ephron, Amy. The Castle in the Mist. 2017. (ENG.). 192p. (J). (gr. 3-7). 16.99 *(978-0-399-54698-3(7),* Philomel Bks.) Penguin Young Readers Group.
Evatt, Harriet. The Mystery of the Alpine Castle. 2011. 242p. 46.95 *(978-1-258-08839-2(8))* Literary Licensing, LLC.
Fairy Tales- Jack & the Beanstalk. 2005. (J). bds. *(978-1-4194-0040-7(1))* Paradise Pr., Inc.
Fast, David R. Doctor Dave's Dragon Tales. Ciesinska, Izabela, illus. 2007. 160p. (J). per. 13.95 *(978-0-9793944-8-5(1))* Digi-Tall Media.
Fischel, Ana. The Twelve Quests - Book 4, Rapunzel's Hair. 2009. 158p. pap. *(978-1-84923-876-2(6))* YouWriteOn.
Ford, Jayme. The Adventures of Glop-A-Lopikins & the Pink Castle. 2013. 28p. pap. 24.95 *(978-1-62709-206-7(4))* America Star Bks.
Fox, Janet. The Charmed Children of Rookskill Castle. (ENG.). 400p. (J). (gr. 5). 2017. 8.99 *(978-0-14-751713-5(3),* Puffin Books) 2016. (Illus.). 16.99 *(978-0-451-47633-3(6),* Viking Books for Young Readers) Penguin Young Readers Group.
Gayzagian, Doris K. One White Wishing Stone: A Beach Day Counting Book. Swarner, Kristina, illus. 2006. (ENG.). 32p. (J). (gr. -1-2). 16.95 *(978-0-7922-5110-1(5));* 25.90 *(978-0-7922-5573-4(9))* National Geographic Society. (National Geographic Children's Bks.).
George, Jessica Day. Fridays with the Wizards. (Tuesdays at the Castle Ser.). (ENG.). 2017. 256p. (J). pap. 7.99 *(978-1-68119-204-8(7),* 9781681192048) 2016. 240p. (YA). 16.99 *(978-1-61963-429-9(5),* 9781619634299) Bloomsbury Publishing USA. (Bloomsbury USA Childrens).
—Saturdays at Sea. 2017. (Tuesdays at the Castle Ser.). (ENG.). 272p. (J). 16.99 *(978-1-61963-957-7(2),* 9781619639577, Bloomsbury USA Childrens) Bloomsbury Publishing USA.
—Thursdays with the Crown. (Tuesdays at the Castle Ser.). (ENG.). 2017. 240p. (J). pap. 7.99 *(978-1-68119-221-5(7),* 9781681192215) 2016. 240p. (J). pap. 7.99 *(978-1-61963-796-2(0),* 9781619637962) 2014. 224p. (YA). (gr. 3-6). 16.99 *(978-1-61963-299-8(3),* 9781619632998) Bloomsbury Publishing USA. (Bloomsbury USA Childrens).
—Tuesdays at the Castle. 2011. (Tuesdays at the Castle Ser.: 1). (ENG.). 240p. (YA). (gr. 3-12). 16.99 *(978-1-59990-644-7(9),* 9781599906447, Bloomsbury USA Childrens) Bloomsbury Publishing USA.
—Wednesdays in the Tower. 2017. (Tuesdays at the Castle Ser.). (ENG.). 256p. (J). pap. 7.99 *(978-1-68119-219-2(5),* 9781681192192, Bloomsbury USA Childrens) 2014. (Tuesdays at the Castle Ser.: 2). (ENG.). 256p. (YA). (gr. 3-6). pap. 7.99 *(978-1-61963-265-3(9),* 9781619632653, Bloomsbury USA Childrens) 2013. 240p. E-Book 16.99 *(978-1-61963-051-2(6))* 2013. (Tuesdays at the Castle Ser.: 2). (ENG.). 240p. (YA). (gr. 3-6). 16.99 *(978-1-59990-645-4(7),* 9781599906454, Bloomsbury USA Childrens) Bloomsbury Publishing USA.
Giulieri, Anne. My Big Sandcastle, 1 vol. Boyer, Susy, illus. 2012. (Engage Literacy Magenta Ser.). (ENG.). 32p. (gr. k-2). pap. 5.99 *(978-1-4296-8870-3(X),* Engage Literacy) Capstone Press of Coughlan Cos.
Grindley, Sally. Shhh! 2008. (ENG.). 32p. (J). (gr. -1-3). 16.95 *(978-1-933718-19-4(6))* Tanglewood Pr.
Grogan, John. Marley Learns a Lesson. Cowdrey, Richard, illus. 2013. (I Can Read Level 2 Ser.). (ENG.). 32p. (J). (gr. -1-3). 16.99 *(978-0-06-207487-4(3))* HarperCollins Pubs.
H & T Imaginations Unlimited, Inc. Sand Castles with Professor Woodpecker. 2009. 12p. pap. 8.49 *(978-1-4389-7262-6(8))* AuthorHouse.
Hamlin, Robyn Maria. Polly Dactyl's Magic Castle Missions. 2011. 64p. pap. 31.99 *(978-1-4628-5146-1(0))* Xlibris Corp.
Hapka, Cathy, pseud. Disney Sofia the First - Sofia's Magical World: The First Hidden Stories. 2015. (Hidden Stories Ser.: 2). (ENG.). 10p. (J). (gr. -1-1). 15.99 *(978-0-7944-3201-0(8),* Reader's Digest Children's Bks.) Studio Fun International.
Haskell, Merrie. The Castle Behind Thorns. 2014. (J). (ENG.). 336p. (gr. 3-7). 16.99 *(978-0-06-200819-0(6),* Tegen, Katherine Bks); 327p. *(978-0-06-200820-6(X))* HarperCollins Pubs.
Hawkins, Loreatha V. The Prince & the Musical Castle. 2009. 32p. pap. 14.49 *(978-1-4389-7678-5(X))* AuthorHouse.
Holub, Joan. The Knights Before Christmas. Magoon, Scott, illus. 2015. (ENG.). 32p. (J). (gr. k-3). 16.99 *(978-0-8050-9932-4(8),* 9780805099324, Holt, Henry & Co. Bks. For Young Readers) Holt, Henry & Co.
Hope, Kathleen. Isiah Thomas & the Mysterious Castle Mcscary. 2012. (Illus.). 44p. pap. 24.40 *(978-1-4685-0496-5(7))* AuthorHouse.
Howard, Kate. Hotel of Horrors. 2012. (Scooby Doo 8X8 Ser.). lib. bdg. 14.75 *(978-0-606-31559-3(4),* Turtleback) Turtleback Bks.
Hunter, Donna K. Hunterston Happenings: Kilts, Casts & Castles. 2013. (Illus.). 60p. pap. 24.99 *(978-1-4772-2400-7(9))* AuthorHouse.
Johnson, Anne E. Trouble at the Scriptorium. 2012. (ENG., Illus.). 144p. (YA). (gr. 7-13). pap. 9.99 *(978-0-88092-392-7(X))* Royal Fireworks Publishing Co.
Johnson, James Ray. Timmy Wee Pee & Castle Friends. 2009. 28p. pap. 24.95 *(978-1-60836-886-0(6))* America Star Bks.
Johnson, Shane L., illus. Princess for a Day: A Pop-Up Storybook. 2011. (Olivia TV Tie-In Ser.). (ENG.). 12p. (J). (gr. -1-1). 17.99 *(978-1-4424-3141-6(5),* Simon Spotlight) Simon Spotlight.
Jones, Janey Louise. Cloudberry Castle, 1 vol. 2010. (ENG., Illus.). 176p. (J). (gr. 2-5). 11.95 *(978-0-86315-765-3(3))* Floris Bks. GBR. Dist: SteinerBooks, Inc.
Katz, Bebe Weinberg. A Best Friend for Claudia. 2008. 77p. pap. 19.95 *(978-1-60563-485-2(9))* America Star Bks.
Keeney, Stephen S. Spencer the Adventurer & the Castle of Bran. 2009. (ENG.). 256p. (J). pap. 14.99 *(978-1-934135-31-0(3),* Zumaya Thresholds) Zumaya Pubns. LLC.
Kelly, Allison, et al. The Castle That Jack Built. import ed. 2007. (ENG., Illus.). 48p. *(978-0-7460-7709-2(2),* Usborne) EDC Publishing.
Kent, Gabrielle. The Secrets of Hexbridge Castle. 2016. (ENG.). 336p. (J). (gr. 3-7). 16.99 *(978-0-545-86929-4(3),* Scholastic Pr.) Scholastic, Inc.
Kilgore, Lee. Widga's Quest, 1 vol. 2009. 48p. pap. 16.95 *(978-1-4489-2517-9(7))* America Star Bks.
Kindl, Patrice. Keeping the Castle. 2013. (ENG.). 304p. (YA). (gr. 7). pap. 10.99 *(978-0-14-242655-5(5),* Speak) Penguin Young Readers Group.
Lacek, Carolyn. Destiny Awakened. 2009. 52p. pap. 18.25 *(978-1-60860-736-5(4),* Eloquent Bks.) Strategic Book Publishing & Rights Agency (SBPRA).
Lamere, Jill. The King's Crown. 2007. (Illus.). 5p. (J). (gr. -1). vinyl bd. 14.95 *(978-0-9772320-2-4(6))* Minikin Pr.
Langrish, Katherine. The Shadow Hunt. 2010. 322p. lib. bdg. *(978-0-06-111678-0(5))* HarperCollins Pubs.
Lester, Anna. Stories of Fairytale Castles. Lo Cascio, Maria Cristina, illus. 2007. (Young Reading Series 1 Gift Bks). 48p. (J). (gr. 4-7). 8.99 *(978-0-7945-1679-6(3),* Usborne) EDC Publishing.
Leung, Julie. A Tail of Camelot. Carr, Lindsey, illus. 2016. (Mice of the Round Table Ser.: 1). 304p. (J). (gr. 3-7). 16.99 *(978-0-06-240399-5(0))* HarperCollins Pubs.
Linke, Uwe. Knights of the Castle. Muller, Daniel, illus. 2008. (ENG.). 24p. (J). (gr. -1-3). 11.95 *(978-0-7358-2201-6(8))* North-South Bks., Inc.
Lonni, Andrea. Spooky Castle. 2014. (ENG.). 8p. (J). (gr. -1-k). bds. 6.99 *(978-0-7641-6734-8(0))* Barron's Educational Series, Inc.
Lynn, Kelly. The Princess Transformation, 1 vol. 2010. 132p. pap. 24.95 *(978-1-4512-1417-8(0))* America Star Bks.
Lyons, Maggie. Dewi & the Seeds of Doom. 2012. 70p. pap. 9.99 *(978-1-61244-094-1(0))* Halo Publishing International.
Man-Kong, Mary. Barbie & the Diamond Castle. Rainmaker Entertainment Staff & Rainmaker Entertainment, illus. 2008. (Little Golden Book Ser.). (ENG.). 24p. (J). (gr. -1-2). 3.99 *(978-0-375-87508-3(5),* Golden Bks.) Random Hse. Children's Bks.
—Barbie & the Diamond Castle: A Storybook. Golden Books Staff, illus. 2008. (Pictureback(R) Ser.). (ENG.). 24p. (J). (gr. -1-2). pap. 3.99 *(978-0-375-87505-2(0),* Golden Bks.) Random Hse. Children's Bks.
Marsh, Carole. The Mystery of the Crystal Castle: Bavaria, Germany. 2009. (Around the World in 80 Mysteries Ser.). 133p. (J). 18.99 *(978-0-635-07041-8(3),* Marsh, Carole Mysteries) Gallopade International.
Marshall, Natalie, illus. Seaside Sandcastle! 2014. (J). *(978-1-4351-5505-3(X))* Barnes & Noble, Inc.
Martin, J. P. Uncle. Blake, Quentin, illus. 2017. (ENG.). 176p. (J). (gr. 4-7). pap. 9.99 ***(978-1-68137-185-6(5),*** NYRB Kids) New York Review of Bks., Inc., The.
Martin, J. P. Uncle Cleans Up. Blake, Quentin, illus. 2008. (ENG.). 184p. (J). (gr. 4-7). 17.95 *(978-1-59017-276-6(0),* NYR Children's Collection) New York Review of Bks., Inc., The.
McCusker, Tammy. Move over! Princess Coming Through!, 1 vol. Greve, Hannah K., illus. 2009. 34p. pap. 24.95 *(978-1-60749-803-2(0))* America Star Bks.
Meadows, Daisy. Flora the Dress-Up Fairy. 2010. (Rainbow Magic Ser.). (ENG., Illus.). 192p. (J). (gr. 2-5). 6.99 *(978-0-545-22176-4(5),* Scholastic Paperbacks) Scholastic, Inc.
Milbourne, Anna. In the Castle. Davies, Benji, illus. 2006. (English Heritage Ser.). 24p. (J). (gr. -1-3). 9.99 *(978-0-7945-1243-9(7),* Usborne) EDC Publishing.
Miles, Cindy. Forevermore. 2013. (ENG.). 288p. (J). (gr. 7). pap. 9.99 *(978-0-545-42622-0(7))* Scholastic, Inc.
Militzer, Jill. Kizzy's Castle. 2005. 35p. 13.24 *(978-1-4116-5538-6(9))* Lulu Pr., Inc.
Miller, Eileen Rudisill. Princess Super. 2011. (Dover Sticker Bks.). (ENG., Illus.). 8p. (J). (gr. k-5). 7.99 *(978-0-486-48382-5(7))* Dover Pubns., Inc.
Miyazaki, Hayao. The Art of Howl's Moving Castle. Miyazaki, Hayao, illus. 2005. (ENG., Illus.). 256p. 34.99 *(978-1-4215-0049-2(3))* Viz Media.
—Howls Moving Castle Picture Book. Miyazaki, Hayao, illus. 2005. (ENG., Illus.). 184p. 19.99 *(978-1-4215-0090-4(6))* Viz Media.
Munsch, Robert. The Sandcastle Contest. 2007. 15.00 *(978-0-7569-7690-3(1))* Perfection Learning Corp.
The Mysterious Castle. 80p. (YA). (gr. 6-12). pap. 10.95 *(978-0-8224-3942-4(5))* Globe Fearon Educational Publishing.
Nesbit, E. The Enchanted Castle. (gr. -1-7). 2006. 168p. per. 13.95 *(978-1-59818-831-8(3))* 2005. 256p. 26.95 *(978-1-59818-173-9(4))* Aegypan.
Osborne, Mary Pope. El Caballero Del Alba. 2004. (Casa del Arbol Ser.: 2). (SPA.). (J). pap. 5.99 *(978-1-930332-50-8(5))* Lectorum Pubns., Inc.
—Haunted Castle on Hallows Eve. Murdocca, Sal, illus. 2010. (Magic Tree House Merlin Mission Ser.: 2). (ENG.). 144p. (J). (gr. 2-5). pap. 5.99 *(978-0-375-86090-4(8),* Random Hse. Bks. for Young Readers) Random Hse. Children's Bks.
—Haunted Castle on Hallows Eve. 2010. (Magic Tree House Merlin Missions Ser.: 2). lib. bdg. 16.00 *(978-0-606-13992-2(3),* Turtleback) Turtleback Bks.
—The Knight at Dawn. unabr. ed. 2004. (Magic Tree House Ser.: No. 2). 66p. (J). (gr. k-3). pap. 17.00 incl. audio *(978-0-8072-0331-6(9),* Listening Library) Random Hse. Audio Publishing Group.
—The Knight at Dawn. Murdocca, Sal, illus. 20th anniv. ed. 2013. (Magic Tree House Ser.). (ENG.). 96p. (J). (gr. 1-4). 14.99 *(978-0-449-81822-0(5),* Random Hse. Bks. for Young Readers) Random Hse. Children's Bks.
Packard, Edward. The Forbidden Castle. Willis, Drew, illus. 2013. (U-Ventures Ser.). (ENG.). 192p. (J). (gr. 3-7). pap. 5.99 *(978-1-4424-3428-8(7),* Simon & Schuster Bks. For Young Readers) Simon & Schuster Bks. For Young Readers.
Parkinson, Curtis. The Castle on Deadman's Island. 2009. (ENG.). 224p. (YA). (gr. 5-9). pap. 12.95 *(978-0-88776-893-4(8),* Tundra Bks.) Tundra Bks. CAN. Dist: Penguin Random Hse. LLC.
Perrotti, P. J. Jason & the Enchanted Forest. 2004. 48p. pap. 16.95 *(978-1-4137-4593-1(8))* America Star Bks.
Poltera, Anne. Castle Magic & the Sinister Encroaching Fir Wood. 2012. (Illus.). 256p. (-18). pap. 19.76 *(978-1-4772-3943-8(X))* AuthorHouse.
Priddy, Roger. My Fairytale Castle. 2015. (Let's Pretend Ser.). (ENG.). 72p. (J). (gr. -1-1). pap., act. bk. ed. 5.99 *(978-0-312-51842-4(0),* 9780312518424, Priddy Bks.) St. Martin's Pr.
Prins, Piet. The Haunted Castle. 2006. (Illus.). 139p. (J). pap. *(978-1-894666-44-2(5))* Inheritance Pubns.
—The Treasure of Rodensteyn Castle. Kramer, Jaap, illus. 2006. 132p. (J). pap. *(978-1-894666-47-3(X))* Inheritance Pubns.
Reinhart, Matthew. My Little Pony: the Castles of Equestria: An Enchanted My Little Pony Pop-Up Book. 2015. (ENG., Illus.). 10p. (J). (gr. 1-17). 24.99 *(978-0-316-18832-6(8))* Little, Brown Bks. for Young Readers.
Rodriguez, Marisol. The Princess & the Chocolate Castle. 2012. 24p. pap. 17.99 *(978-1-4685-4911-9(1))* AuthorHouse.
Rogers, Jewels. The Princess & the Parakeet. 2011. 28p. pap. 12.50 *(978-1-4567-5170-8(0))* AuthorHouse.
Rouncville, Bibi. Castle at Trail's End. 2008. 52p. pap. 9.50 *(978-1-4357-3967-3(1))* Lulu Pr., Inc.
Rouzer, Walter. Rebel Stone & the Ghost Whisperers. 2009. 304p. 28.95 *(978-0-595-51192-1(9));* pap. 18.95 *(978-0-595-52313-9(7))* iUniverse, Inc.
Roy, Ron. A to Z Mysteries Collection, No. 1. Gurney, John Steven, illus. 2010. (to Z Mysteries Ser.: Nos. 1-4). (ENG.). 384p. (J). (gr. 1-4). 9.99 *(978-0-375-85946-5(2),* Random Hse. Bks. for Young Readers) Random Hse. Children's Bks.
Russell, P. Craig. Fairy Tales of Oscar Wilde: The Selfish Giant & the Star Child, Vol. 1. Russell, P. Craig, illus. 2003. (Fairy Tales of Oscar Wilde Ser.: 1). (ENG., Illus.). 1111p. pap. 9.99 *(978-1-56163-375-3(5))* NBM Publishing Co.
Sagar, Marie. Princess Samantha? 2009. 20p. pap. 12.49 *(978-1-4389-5297-0(X))* AuthorHouse.
Sanders, Roy E. Land of Pink. Patzelt, Kasie, illus. 2007. (Not So Far Ago Ser.). 37p. (J). (gr. -1-3). 19.99 *(978-1-59879-327-7(6))* Lifevest Publishing, Inc.
Santillo, LuAnn. I Have Fun. Santillo, LuAnn, ed. 2003. (Half-Pint Kids Readers Ser.). (Illus.). 7p. (J). (gr. -1-1). pap. 1.00 *(978-1-59256-055-4(5))* Half-Pint Kids, Inc.
Schmid, Susan Maupin. Ghost of a Chance. Marlin, Lissy, illus. 2017. (100 Dresses Ser.: 2). (ENG.). 320p. (J). (gr. 3-7). 16.99 *(978-0-553-53373-6(8),* Random Hse. Bks. for Young Readers) Random Hse. Children's Bks.
Scotton, Rob. On with the Show. Scotton, Rob, illus. 2013. (Splat the Cat Ser.). (ENG., Illus.). 24p. (J). (gr. -1-3). pap. 3.99 *(978-0-06-209010-2(0),* HarperFestival) HarperCollins Pubs.
Seabrooke, Brenda. Stonewolf. 2004. (ENG.). 240p. (J). (gr. 7-18). tchr. ed. 16.95 *(978-0-8234-1848-0(0))* Holiday Hse., Inc.
Shapiro D., Brian. Plaquetooth. 2008. 28p. pap. 13.99 *(978-1-4343-8913-8(8))* AuthorHouse.
Sharma, Shivan. The Castle, Dragons & a Cricket Ball. 2009. 76p. pap. *(978-1-84549-415-5(6),* Swirl) arima publishing.
Sims, Lesley. The Castle That Jack Built. Gordon, Mike, illus. 2007. (Usborne First Reading: Level 3 Ser.). 48p. (J). (gr. -1-3). 8.99 *(978-0-7945-1599-7(1),* Usborne) EDC Publishing.
—The Enchanted Castle. Marks, Alan, illus. 2007. (Young Reading Series 2 Gift Bks). 62p. (J). (gr. 4-7). 8.99 *(978-0-7945-1347-4(6),* Usborne) EDC Publishing.
—The Story of Castles. 2004. (Young Reading Series Two Ser.). (Illus.). 64p. (J). (gr. 2-18). pap. 5.95 *(978-0-7945-0756-5(5),* Usborne) EDC Publishing.
Spohn, Kate. Turtle & Snake's Day at the Beach. Spohn, Kate, illus. 2004. (Puffin Easy-to-Read Ser.). (Illus.). 32p. (gr. k-3). 14.00 *(978-0-7569-2826-1(5))* Perfection Learning Corp.
Starwolf. Where Sand Castles Go. 2010. 36p. pap. 19.95 *(978-1-4269-3821-4(7))* Trafford Publishing.
Stilton, Geronimo. Cat & Mouse in a Haunted House. Wolf, Matt & Keys, Larry, illus. 2004. (Geronimo Stilton Ser.: 3). (ENG.). 128p. (J). (gr. -1-3). pap. 7.99 *(978-0-439-55965-2(0),* Scholastic Paperbacks) Scholastic, Inc.
—Cat & Mouse in a Haunted House. 2004. (Geronimo Stilton Ser.: 3). (gr. 3-6). lib. bdg. 18.40 *(978-0-613-72224-7(8),* Turtleback) Turtleback Bks.
—The Haunted Castle. 2011. (ENG.). 128p. (J). (gr. 2-5). pap. 7.99 *(978-0-545-10374-9(6),* Scholastic Paperbacks) Scholastic, Inc.
—The Stinky Cheese Vacation. 2014. (Geronimo Stilton Ser.: 57). lib. bdg. 18.40 *(978-0-606-35843-9(9))* Turtleback Bks.
Stine, Faye. The Golden Goblet: 200 Years in a Medieval Castle. 2013. (ENG.). 169p. (YA). pap. 12.95 *(978-1-4787-1063-9(2))* Outskirts Pr., Inc.
Stockton, Frank Richard. Ting-a-Ling Tales. 2008. 88p. pap. 8.95 *(978-1-60664-056-2(9))* Aegypan.
Sturm auf die Burg. (GER.). *(978-3-411-09321-2(8))* Bibliographisches Institut & F. A. Brockhaus AG DEU. Dist: i. b. d., Ltd.
Thomas, Micahla F. Anna & Jasmine & the Tale of the Gateway Castle. 2004. (J). 5.99 *(978-0-9719727-0-4(2))* Honorable Pr.
Thompson, Colin. Castles. 2006. (Illus.). 32p. (J). (gr. k-2). *(978-0-09-188486-4(1),* Hutchinson) Random Hse.
—Castles. Thompson, Colin, illus. 2007. (ENG., Illus.). 32p. (J). (gr. k-2). pap. 15.99 *(978-0-09-943942-4(5),* Red Fox) Random House Children's Books GBR. Dist: Independent Pubs. Group.
Top That. Press Out & Play Magic Castle. 2008. *(978-1-84666-600-1(7))* Top That! Publishing PLC.
—Press Out & Play Princess Castle. 2008. *(978-1-84666-611-7(2))* Top That! Publishing PLC.
Tub Tales: The Castle. 2003. (Illus.). 10p. (J). 6.00 *(978-0-9713507-0-0(1),* 841) Panline U.S.A., Inc.
Tudhope, Simon & Cox, Phil Roxbee. Slot-Together Castle with an Usborne Book. 2015. (Slot-Together Castle with an Usborne Book Ser.). (ENG.). 90 press-out pp. (J). (gr. k-5). 41.99 *(978-0-7945-3441-7(4),* Usborne) EDC Publishing.
Tyler, Jenny & Doherty, Gillian, eds. Usborne Stories for Little Boys. 2008. (Picture Books Ser.). (Illus.). 135p. (J). (gr. -1-3). 18.99 *(978-0-7945-1973-5(3),* Usborne) EDC Publishing.
Vargo, Tim. Unbound: A Tale of Temptation & Terror. 2003. 242p. pap. 12.95 *(978-1-930008-04-5(X))* Willowgate Pr.
Vernon, Ursula. Castle Hangnail. 2016. lib. bdg. 19.65 *(978-0-606-38388-2(3))* Turtleback Bks.
Warner, Gertrude Chandler, creator. The Legend of the Irish Castle. 2016. (Boxcar Children Mysteries Ser.: 142). (ENG., Illus.). 128p. (J). (gr. 1-5). 15.99 *(978-0-8075-0705-6(9))* Whitman, Albert & Co.
White, Vernon. Birdhouse. 2010. (ENG., Illus.). 136p. (YA). pap. 10.95 *(978-1-59362-185-8(X),* 9781593621858) Slave Labor Bks.
The Windsor Caper. 2013. (Illus.). 258p. pap. *(978-0-9576554-0-9(1))* Good, Martin.
Winthrop, Elizabeth. The Battle for the Castle. 211p. (J). pap. 5.50 *(978-0-8072-1501-2(5),* Listening Library) Random Hse. Audio Publishing Group.
Wright, Betty Ren. Crandalls' Castle. 2005. (ENG.). 184p. (J). pap. 6.95 *(978-0-8234-1978-4(9))* Holiday Hse., Inc.
Young, Annemarie. Our Castle. Redshaw, Louise, illus. 2013. (Start Reading Ser.). (ENG.). 24p. (gr. k-1). pap. 41.94 *(978-1-4765-3228-8(1));* pap. 7.95 *(978-1-4765-3194-6(3))* Capstone Press of Coughlan Cos.

CASTRO, FIDEL, 1927-2016

Butts, Ellen R. & Schwartz, Joyce R. Fidel Castro. 2005. (Biography Ser.). (Illus.). 112p. (J). 29.27 *(978-0-8225-2371-0(X),* Lerner Pubns.); (gr. 6-18). pap. 7.95 *(978-0-8225-9524-3(9))* Lerner Publishing Group.
Fabiny, Sarah. Who Was Fidel Castro? Hammond, Ted, illus. 2017. (Who Was? Ser.). (ENG.). 112p. (J). (gr. 3-7). 5.99 ***(978-0-451-53333-3(X));*** lib. bdg. 15.99 ***(978-0-451-53335-7(6))*** Penguin Young Readers Group. (Penguin Workshop).
January, Brendan. Fidel Castro: Cuban Revolutionary. 2003. (Book Report Biographies Ser.). (ENG., Illus.). 112p. (J). 30.50 *(978-0-531-11676-0(X),* Watts, Franklin) Scholastic Library Publishing.
Markel, Rita J. Fidel Castro's Cuba. 2007. (Dictatorships Ser.). (ENG., Illus.). 160p. (J). (gr. 9-12). lib. bdg. 38.60 *(978-0-8225-7284-8(2))* Lerner Publishing Group.
Marsico, Katie. Fidel Castro: Cuban President & Revolutionary, 1 vol. 2009. (Essential Lives Set 3 Ser.). (ENG., Illus.). 112p. (J). (gr. 6-12). lib. bdg. 35.64 *(978-1-60453-522-8(9))* ABDO Publishing Co.
Naden, Corinne J. & Blue, Rose. Fidel Castro & the Cuban Revolution. 2006. (World Leaders Ser.). (Illus.). 144p. (J). (gr. 3-7). lib. bdg. 27.95 *(978-1-59935-029-5(7))* Reynolds, Morgan Inc.
Prentzas, G. S. The Cuban Revolution. 2011. (Milestones in Modern World History Ser.). (Illus.). 144p. (J). (gr. 9). 35.00 *(978-1-60413-921-1(8),* Chelsea Hse.) Facts On File, Inc.
Uschan, Michael V. Fidel Castro. 2008. (Twentieth Century's Most Influencial Hispanics Ser.). (ENG., Illus.). 104p. (J). (gr. 7-10). lib. bdg. 33.45 *(978-1-4205-0059-2(7),* LML02109-240047, Lucent Bks.) Cengage Gale.

CAT

see Cats

CAT FAMILY (MAMMALS)

see also Cheetah; Jaguar; Leopard; Lion; Lynx; Panthers; Puma; Tiger

ABDO Publishing Company Staff & Archer, Claire. Big Cats. 2014. (Big Cats Ser.: 6). (ENG.). 24p. (J). (gr. 4-8). lib. bdg. 171.00 *(978-1-62970-000-7(2))* ABDO Publishing Co.
Bailey, Gerry. Sabre-Tooth Tiger. Reaveley, Trevor, illus. 2011. (Smithsonian Prehistoric Zone Ser.). (ENG.). 32p. (J). (gr. k-3). *(978-0-7787-1801-7(8));* pap. *(978-0-7787-1814-7(X))* Crabtree Publishing Co.
Becker, John. Wild Cats: Past & Present. Hallett, Mark, illus. 2008. (Darby Creek Exceptional Titles Ser.). (ENG.). 80p. (gr. 6-12). 18.95 *(978-1-58196-052-5(2),* Darby Creek) Lerner Publishing Group.
Big Cats. 2014. (Animal Q & A Ser.). (Illus.). 24p. (J). (gr. k-3). lib. bdg. 23.60 *(978-1-4777-9182-0(5))* Windmill Bks.
Big Cats Are Not Pets! 2013. (When Pets Attack! Ser.). 32p. (J). (gr. 3-6). pap. 63.00 *(978-1-4339-9275-9(2))* Stevens, Gareth Publishing LLLP.
Blake, Carly. Why Why Why... Are Lions Crazy? 2010. (Why Why Why Ser.). 32p. (J). (gr. 1-3). lib. bdg. 18.95 *(978-1-4222-1569-2(5))* Mason Crest.
Bowman, Donna H. Big Cats. Wald, Christina, illus. 2008. (ENG.). 24p. (J). (gr. 3-18). 19.95 *(978-1-58117-781-7(X),* Intervisual/Piggy Toes) Bendon, Inc.
Carney, Elizabeth. Big Cats: Pictures to Purr about & Info to Make You Roar! 2011. (National Geographic Kids Everything Ser.). (ENG., Illus.). 64p. (J). (gr. 3-7). 25.90 *(978-1-4263-0806-2(X),* National Geographic Children's Bks.) National Geographic Society.
—Wild Cats. 2017. (Readers Ser.). (ENG., Illus.). 32p. (J). (gr. -1-1). pap. 3.99 *(978-1-4263-2677-6(7),* National Geographic Children's Bks.) National Geographic Society.
Clutton-Brock, Juliet. DK Eyewitness Books: Cat: Cat. 2014. (DK Eyewitness Bks.). (ENG.). 72p. (J). (gr. 3-7). pap. 9.99 *(978-1-4654-2050-3(9),* DK Children) Dorling Kindersley Publishing, Inc.
Corwin, Jeff & Kavanagh, James. The World of Wild Cats. 2014. (Jeff Corwin's Explorer Ser.). (ENG., Illus.). 12p. 7.95 *(978-1-58355-817-1(9))* Western National Parks Assn.
Coupe, Robert. Cats of the Wild. 2014. (Discovery Education: Animals Ser.). 32p. (J). (gr. 3-6). 26.25 *(978-1-4777-6944-7(7));* pap. 10.00 *(978-1-4777-6945-4(5))* Rosen Publishing Group, Inc., The. (PowerKids Pr.).
De la Bédoyère, Camilla. Big Cats. 2010. (Remarkable Man & Beast Ser.). (Illus.). 48p. (J). (gr. 3-18). lib. bdg. 19.95 *(978-1-4222-1965-2(8))* Mason Crest.
—The Wild Life of Big Cats, 1 vol. 2015. (ENG., Illus.). 24p. (J). lib. bdg. 23.60 *(978-1-4777-5490-0(3),* Windmill Bks.) Rosen Publishing Group, Inc., The.
Dorling Kindersley Publishing Staff & Walker, Sarah. Big Cats. 2014. (Eye Wonder Ser.). (ENG.). 56p. (J). (gr. k-4). 10.99 *(978-1-4654-1561-5(0),* DK Children) Dorling Kindersley Publishing, Inc.
Eppard, Jon. Big Cats. 2012. (ENG., Illus.). 24p. (J). pap. *(978-1-60014-854-5(9));* (gr. 3-8). 25.95 *(978-1-60014-809-5(3),* Express Bks.) Bellwether Media.
Goldish, Meish. Bobcat. 2015. (Desert Animals Searchin' for Shade Ser.). (ENG.). 24p. (J). (gr. -1-3). lib. bdg. 23.93 *(978-1-62724-538-8(3))* Bearport Publishing Co., Inc.

Group/McGraw-Hill, Wright. Cougar Level: Wildcats Cougar Complete Kit. (Wildcats Ser.). (gr. 2-8). 599.95 *(978-0-322-06680-9(8))* Wright Group/McGraw-Hill.
—Cougar Level Set: Adventure Journal. (Wildcats Ser.). (gr. 2-8). 31.95 *(978-0-322-05788-3(4))* Wright Group/McGraw-Hill.
—Creature Talk, 6 vols. (Wildcats Ser.). 32p. (gr. 2-8). *(978-0-322-05860-6(0))* Wright Group/McGraw-Hill.
—Panther Level: Adventure Journal Set. (Wildcats Ser.). (gr. 2-8). 31.95 *(978-0-322-05793-7(0))* Wright Group/McGraw-Hill.
Guillain, Charlotte. Cats. Elsom, Clare, illus. 2013. (Animal Family Albums Ser.). (ENG.). 32p. (gr. 2-4). pap. 8.29 *(978-1-4109-4940-0(0))*; 30.65 *(978-1-4109-4935-6(4))* Heinemann-Raintree. (Raintree Perspectives).
Hamilton, S. L. Big Cats. 2010. (Xtreme Predators Ser.). 32p. (gr. 3-9). 27.07 *(978-1-60453-991-2(7),* A&D Xtreme) ABDO Publishing Co.
Harrison, Paul. The Brilliant Book of 3D Thrillers: Get Ready for the Ultimate 3d Adventure! 2012. (ENG., Illus.). 96p. (J). pap. 9.95 *(978-1-84837-875-9(0))* Arcturus Publishing GBR. Dist: Bookmasters Distribution.
Hodge, Deborah. Looking at Wild Cats. Ogle, Nancy Gray, illus. 2008. (Kids Can Read Ser.). (ENG.). 32p. (J). (gr. k-1). pap. 3.95 *(978-1-55453-285-8(X))* Kids Can Pr., Ltd. CAN. Dist: Hachette Bk. Group.
Huggins-Cooper, Lynn. Big Cats. 2006. (Killer Nature! Ser.). (Illus.). 32p. (J). (gr. 4-7). lib. bdg. 28.50 *(978-1-58340-931-2(9))* Black Rabbit Bks.
Ireland, Kenneth. Big Cats. 2009. (Wild Reads Ser.). (ENG., Illus.). 32p. (Orig.). (YA). (gr. k). pap. 4.95 *(978-0-19-911925-7(2))* Oxford Univ. Pr., Inc.
Johnson, Bruce. We Read Phonics-Big Cats (Nonfiction) 2010. (ENG., Illus.). 32p. (J). 9.95 *(978-1-60115-313-5(9))*; pap. 4.99 *(978-1-60115-314-2(7))* Treasure Bay, Inc.
Kenan, Tessa. Es un Jaguar! 2017. (Bumba Books (tm) en Español — Animales de la Selva Tropical (Rain Forest Animals) Ser.). (SPA., Illus.). 24p. (J). (gr. -1-1). 25.32 ***(978-1-5124-4130-7(9))*** Lerner Publishing Group.
Klepeis, Alicia. The Language of Cats & Other Felines. 2016. (Call of the Wild Ser.). (ENG., Illus.). 32p. (J). (gr. 3-3). 28.50 *(978-1-5026-1724-8(2))* Cavendish Square Publishing.
Klevansky, Rhonda. Big Cats. 2015. (ENG., Illus.). 64p. (J). (gr. -1-k). 12.99 *(978-1-86147-406-3(7),* Armadillo) Anness Publishing GBR. Dist: National Bk. Network.
Landau, Elaine. Big Cats: Hunters of the Night. 2007. (Animals after Dark Ser.). (Illus.). 32p. (J). (gr. 2-4). lib. bdg. 23.94 *(978-0-7660-2770-1(8),* Enslow Elementary) Enslow Pubs., Inc.
Leapfrog Learners - Big Cats. 2004. (J). per. 4.99 *(978-1-933581-21-7(2))* Byeway Bks.
Leapfrog Learners - Big Cats. 2004. (Explorasaws Ser.). (Illus.). 48p. (J). pap. *(978-1-84229-758-2(9))* Top That! Publishing PLC.
Lynch, Annabelle. Big Cats, 01 vols., 1. 2016. (Nature Explorers Ser.). (ENG.). 24p. (J). pap. 8.25 *(978-1-5081-9053-0(4),* Windmill Bks.) Rosen Publishing Group, Inc., The.
Marsico, Katie. Big Cats. 2017. (True Book(tm) — The Most Endangered Ser.). (ENG., Illus.). 48p. (J). lib. bdg. 31.00 *(978-0-531-22726-8(X),* Children's Pr.) Scholastic Library Publishing.
Marzolf, Julie. Big Cats Are Not Pets! 2013. 32p. (J). (gr. 3-6). 26.60 *(978-1-4339-9273-5(6))*; pap. 10.50 *(978-1-4339-9274-2(4))* Stevens, Gareth Publishing LLLP.
Mattern, Joanne. Cats Are Night Animals. 2007. (Night Animals Ser.). (Illus.). 24p. (gr. k-3). lib. bdg. 22.00 *(978-0-8368-7846-2(9),* Weekly Reader Leveled Readers) Stevens, Gareth Publishing LLLP.
—Cats Are Night Animals (Los Felinos Son Animales Nocturnos) 2007. (Night Animals/ Animales Nocturnos Ser.). (ENG & SPA., Illus.). 24p. (gr. k-3). pap. 8.15 *(978-0-8368-8050-2(1))*; lib. bdg. 22.00 *(978-0-8368-8043-4(9))* Stevens, Gareth Publishing LLLP. (Weekly Reader Leveled Readers).
McKay, Sindy. We Both Read-Big Cats, Little Cats. ed. 2015. (We Both Read Ser.). (ENG., Illus.). 44p. (J). (gr. -1-1). pap. 4.99 *(978-1-60115-276-3(0))* Treasure Bay, Inc.
Morgan, Sally. Small Cats. 2004. (J). lib. bdg. *(978-1-59389-176-3(8))* Cherrytree Bks.
National Geographic Kids Staff. Big Cats - National Geographic Kids. 2017. (Look & Learn Ser.). (ENG., Illus.). 24p. (J). (-k). bds. 6.99 *(978-1-4263-2701-8(3),* National Geographic Children's Bks.) National Geographic Society.
O'Shaughnessy, Ruth. Big Cats after Dark. 2015. (Animals of the Night Ser.). (ENG.). 32p. (J). (gr. 3-4). pap. 10.52 *(978-0-7660-7044-8(1))*; (Illus.). 25.27 *(978-0-7660-7046-2(8))* Enslow Pubs., Inc.
Owen, Ruth. Carnivorous Big Cats. 2012. (Eye to Eye with Animals Ser.). (ENG., Illus.). 32p. (J). (gr. k-5). 25.25 *(978-1-4488-8069-0(6))*; pap. 10.00 *(978-1-4488-8105-5(6))* Windmill Bks.
Parker, Steve. Big Cats. Jackson, Ian, illus. 2010. (I Love Animals Ser.). (ENG.). 24p. (J). (gr. 1-5). pap. 8.15 *(978-1-61533-251-9(0))*; lib. bdg. 22.60 *(978-1-61533-245-8(6))* Windmill Bks.
Rabinowitz, Alan. A Boy & a Jaguar. Chien, Catia, illus. 2014. (ENG.). 32p. (J). (gr. -1-3). 17.99 *(978-0-547-87507-1(X),* HMH Books For Young Readers) Houghton Mifflin Harcourt Publishing Co.
Regan, Lisa. Big Cat, Little Cat. 2012. (ENG., Illus.). 24p. (J). (gr. -1-3). 15.00 *(978-1-4081-6401-3(9),* 9781408164013, Bloomsbury USA Childrens) Bloomsbury USA Publishing USA.
Riggs, Kate. Amazing Animals: Cougars. 2014. (Amazing Animals Ser.). (ENG.). 24p. (J). (gr. 1-3). pap. 8.99 *(978-0-89812-926-7(5),* Creative Paperbacks) Creative Co., The.
Scott, Johnathan & Scott, Angela. Big Cat Babies. Scott, Jonathan, illus. 2005. (Collins Big Cat Ser.). (ENG.). 48p. (J). (gr. k-1). pap. 6.99 *(978-0-00-718594-8(4))* HarperCollins Pubs. Ltd. GBR. Dist: Independent Pubs. Group.
Sengupta, Monalisa. Discover Big Cats. 2008. (Discover Animals Ser.). (Illus.). 48p. (J). (gr. 5-9). lib. bdg. 25.27 *(978-0-7660-3473-0(9))* Enslow Pubs., Inc.
Shea, Therese. Wild Cats. (Big Bad Biters Ser.). 24p. 2009. (gr. 2-3). 42.50 *(978-1-61511-566-2(8))* 2006. (Illus.). (J). (gr. 3-7). lib. bdg. 22.60 *(978-1-4042-3522-9(1))* Rosen Publishing Group, Inc., The. (PowerKids Pr.).
Sheikh-Miller, J. & Turnbull, S. Big Cats. 2004. (Discovery Program Ser.). (Illus.). 48p. (J). lib. bdg. 16.95 *(978-1-58086-467-1(8))* EDC Publishing.
Sheikh-Miller, Jonathan. Big Cats II. 2010. (Discovery Nature Ser.). 48p. (J). 8.99 *(978-0-7945-2243-8(2),* Usborne) EDC Publishing.
Shores, Erika L. Canada Lynx. 1 vol. 2010. (Wildcats Ser.). (ENG.). 24p. (gr. k-1). lib. bdg. 26.65 *(978-1-4296-4484-6(2),* Pebble Plus) Capstone Press of Coughlan Cos.
Simon, Seymour. Big Cats. 2015. 40p. pap. 7.00 *(978-1-61003-599-6(2))* Center for the Collaborative Classroom.
Simpson, Phillip. Big Cats Head to Head: A Compare & Contrast Text. 1 vol. 2014. (Text Structures Ser.). (ENG.). 32p. (gr. 1-3). pap. 7.99 *(978-1-4846-0414-4(8),* Heinemann First Library) Heinemann-Raintree.
Smith, Ben. Where Do Big Cats Live? 2014. (Little Books of Answers: Level B Ser.). (Illus.). 16p. (gr. k-2). pap. 7.95 *(978-1-927136-17-1(2))* Three Crows Media NZL. Dist: RiverStream Publishing.
Steffora, Tracey. Comparing with Cats. 1 vol. 2013. (Animal Math Ser.). (ENG.). 24p. (gr. -1-1). 22.65 *(978-1-4329-7559-3(5))*; pap. 6.95 *(978-1-4329-7566-1(8))* Heinemann-Raintree. (NA-h).
Twine, Alice. Cats of the Wild. 2009. (Baby Animals Ser.). 24p. (gr. 1-1). 42.50 *(978-1-61511-488-7(2),* PowerKids Pr.) Rosen Publishing Group, Inc., The.
—Cats of the Wild/Gatos Salvajes. 2009. (Baby Animals/Animales bebé Ser.). (ENG & SPA.). 24p. (gr. 1-1). 42.50 *(978-1-61511-499-3(8),* Editorial Buenas Letras) Rosen Publishing Group, Inc., The.
—Cats of the Wild/Gatos Salvajes. Obregon, Jose Maria, tr. 2007. (Baby Animals / Animales Bebé Ser.). (ENG & SPA., Illus.). 24p. (J). (gr. -1-3). lib. bdg. 22.60 *(978-1-4042-7631-4(9),* Editorial Buenas Letras) Rosen Publishing Group, Inc., The.
Wexo, John Bonnett. Big Cats. rev. ed. 2003. (Illus.). 24p. (J). 10.95 *(978-1-888153-91-0(1),* Zoo Bks.) Wildlife Education, Ltd.
Wiseman, Blaine. Lynxes. 2010. (Backyard Animals Ser.). (Illus.). 24p. (gr. 2-4). (J). pap. 11.95 *(978-1-60596-944-2(3))*; (YA). lib. bdg. 25.70 *(978-1-60596-943-5(5))* Weigl Pubs., Inc.

CAT FAMILY (MAMMALS)—FICTION

Fields, Jan. Hunt the Ozark Howler. 1 vol. Brundage, Scott, illus. 2016. (ENG.). 80p. (J). lib. bdg. *(978-1-62402-152-7(2))* Magic Wagon.
Sargent, Dave & Sargent, Pat. Bobby Bobcat: Be a Friend. 15 vols., Vol. 10. Huff, Jeane, illus. 2nd rev. ed. 2003. (Animal Pride Ser.: No. 10). 42p. (J). pap. 6.95 *(978-1-56763-778-6(7))*; lib. bdg. 20.95 *(978-1-56763-777-9(9))* Ozark Publishing.
—Dike the Wolf: Teamwork. 56 vols., Vol. 5. Huff, Jeane, illus. 2nd rev. ed. 2003. (Animal Pride Ser.: Vol. 15). 42p. (J). lib. bdg. 20.95 *(978-1-56763-767-0(1))* Ozark Publishing.

CAT IN THE HAT (FICTITIOUS CHARACTER)—FICTION

Condenzio, John. Cocoa the Witch Cat. 2013. 20p. pap. 24.95 *(978-1-62709-264-7(1))* America Star Bks.
Golden Books. I See Seeds! Ruiz, Aristides, illus. 2013. (Color Plus Chunky Crayons Ser.). (ENG.). 48p. (J). (gr. -1-2). pap. 3.99 *(978-0-307-98209-4(2),* Golden Bks.) Random Hse. Children's Bks.
McCann, Jesse Leon. The Cat in the Hat. 2003. (Illus.). 24p. (J). (gr. k-k). 0.33 *(978-0-375-82780-8(3),* Golden Bks.) Random Hse. Children's Bks.
Moonah, Karen. Spring into Summer! 2012. (Cat in the Hat Knows a Lot about That Ser.). lib. bdg. 14.75 *(978-0-606-23849-6(2),* Turtleback) Turtleback Bks.
Rabe, Tish. The Cat in the Hat Knows a Lot about Christmas! (Dr. Seuss/Cat in the Hat) Mathieu, Joe, illus. 2013. (Big Golden Book Ser.). (ENG.). 48p. (J). (gr. -1-1). 9.99 *(978-0-449-81495-6(5),* Golden Bks.) Random Hse. Children's Bks.
—The Chocolate Voyage. Aikins, Dave, illus. 2013. (Little Golden Book Ser.). (ENG.). 24p. (J). (-k). 3.99 *(978-0-307-98023-6(5),* Golden Bks.) Random Hse. Children's Bks.
—Night Lights. 2014. (Cat in the Hat Knows a Lot about That Ser.). lib. bdg. 14.75 *(978-0-606-35537-7(5))* Turtleback Bks.
—Night Lights (Dr. Seuss/Cat in the Hat) Ruiz, Aristides & Mathieu, Joe, illus. 2014. (Pictureback(R) Ser.). (ENG.). 16p. (J). (gr. -1-2). pap. 4.99 *(978-0-385-37116-2(0),* Random Hse. Bks. for Young Readers) Random Hse. Children's Bks.
—A Reindeer's First Christmas / New Friends for Christmas. 2012. (Cat in the Hat Knows a Lot about That Ser.). lib. bdg. 14.75 *(978-0-606-26787-8(5),* Turtleback) Turtleback Bks.
—Thump!/The Lost Egg (Cat in the Hat/Seuss) Ruiz, Aristides & Mathieu, Joe, illus. 2013. (Pictureback(R) Ser.). (ENG.). 32p. (J). (gr. -1-2). pap. 4.99 *(978-0-307-98063-2(4),* Random Hse. Bks. for Young Readers) Random Hse. Children's Bks.
—The Tree Doctor. 2013. (Step into Reading Level 2 Ser.). lib. bdg. 13.55 *(978-0-606-26965-0(7),* Turtleback) Turtleback Bks.
—What Cat Is That? All about Cats. Ruiz, Aristides & Mathieu, Joe, illus. 2013. (Cat in the Hat's Learning Library). (ENG.). 48p. (J). (gr. k-3). 9.99 *(978-0-375-86640-1(X),* Random Hse. Bks. for Young Readers) Random Hse. Children's Bks.
Seuss, Dr. The Cat in the Hat. 2010. (ENG., Illus.). 64p. pap. *(978-0-00-734869-5(X),* HarperCollins Children's Bks.) HarperCollins Pubs. Ltd.
—The Cat in the Hat's. Ruiz, Aristides, illus. 2014. (Great Big Board Book Ser.). (ENG.). 12p. (J). (gr. k — 1). bds. 12.99 *(978-0-679-89360-8(1),* Random Hse. Bks. for Young Readers) Random Hse. Children's Bks.
Universal Dreamworks Pictures Staff & Greenberg, James. Cat in the Hat. 2003. (ENG., Illus.). 128p. pap. 12.95 *(978-1-57243-609-1(3),* 53846352) Triumph Bks.

CATASTROPHES

see Disasters

CATERPILLARS

see also Butterflies; Moths

Barry, Frances. Caterpillar to Butterfly. 2010. (J). *(978-0-7636-4261-7(4))* Candlewick Pr.
Berger, Melvin & Berger, Gilda. A Caterpillar Grows Up. 2008. (Illus.). 32p. (J). *(978-0-439-02527-0(3))* Scholastic, Inc.
Bishop, Celeste. Creepy Caterpillars. 2015. (Icky Animals! Small & Gross Ser.). (ENG.). 24p. (J). (gr. 1-1). pap. 8.25 *(978-1-4994-0698-6(3),* PowerKids Pr.) Rosen Publishing Group, Inc., The.
Butterfly & Caterpillar. 2003. 38.95 *(978-0-8136-4171-3(3))* Modern Curriculum Pr.
Calder, Joan Z. Airplanes in the Garden: Monarch Butterflies Take Flight. l.t. alt. ed. 2014. (ENG., Illus.). 32p. (J). 16.95 *(978-0-9832962-1-8(9))* Willow Creek Pr., Inc.
Dibble, Traci. Caterpillars Love to Eat. 2015. (1G Bugs Ser.). (ENG., Illus.). 20p. (J). pap. 5.99 *(978-1-63437-087-5(2))* American Reading Co.
Drew, David. Caterpillar Diary. 2007. (Informazing Ser.). (Illus.). 17p. (J). (gr. -1). pap. *(978-0-947328-54-2(8),* Rigby) Pearson Education Australia.
Earley, Chris G. Caterpillars: Find - Identify - Raise Your Own. 2013. (ENG., Illus.). 32p. (J). (gr. 3-6). 19.95 *(978-1-77085-182-5(8),* 9781770851825); pap. 6.95 *(978-1-77085-183-2(6),* 9781770851832) Firefly Bks., Ltd.
Engle, Margarita. Summer Birds: The Butterflies of Maria Merian. Paschkis, Julie, illus. 2010. (ENG.). 32p. (J). (gr. k-3). 17.99 *(978-0-8050-8937-0(3),* 9780805089370, Holt, Henry & Co. Bks. For Young Readers) Holt, Henry & Co.
Fiedler, Heidi. Butterflies: A Close-Up Photographic Look Inside Your World. 2017. (Up Close Ser.). (ENG., Illus.). (J). (gr. k-6). lib. bdg. 27.99 ***(978-1-942875-37-6(1),*** Walter Foster Jr) Quarto Publishing Group USA.
French, Vivian. Caterpillar Caterpillar: Read & Wonder. Voake, Charlotte, illus. 2009. (Read & Wonder Ser.). (ENG.). 32p. (J). (gr. -1-3). pap. 6.99 *(978-0-7636-4263-1(0))* Candlewick Pr.
Ganeri, Anita. Butterflies & Caterpillars. Axworthy, Ann, illus. 2012. (Animal Families Ser.). 24p. (J). (gr. -1-k). 12.79 *(978-1-60753-097-8(X))* Amicus Publishing.
—Butterflies & Caterpillars. Axworthy, Ani, illus. 2010. (Animal Families Ser.). (ENG.). 14p. (J). bds. 10.99 *(978-1-84089-641-1(8))* Evans Brothers, Ltd. GBR. Dist: Independent Pubs. Group.
Hayes, Amy. A Caterpillar Becomes a Butterfly. 2016. (Transformations in Nature Ser.). (ENG., Illus.). 24p. (J). (gr. 1-1). pap. 8.22 *(978-1-5026-0822-2(7))* Cavendish Square Publishing.
Heiligman, Deborah. From Caterpillar to Butterfly Big Book. Weissman, Bari, illus. 2008. (Let's-Read-And-Find-Out Science 1 Ser.). (ENG.). 32p. (J). (gr. -1-3). pap. 24.99 *(978-0-06-111975-0(X),* Collins) HarperCollins Pubs.
Herrington, Lisa M. Caterpillar to Butterfly. 2014. (Rookie Read-About(r) Science - Life Cycles Ser.). (ENG.). 32p. (J). lib. bdg. 23.00 *(978-0-531-21055-0(3))* Scholastic Library Publishing.
Kalman, Bobbie. Caterpillars to Butterflies. 2008. (It's Fun to Learn about Baby Animals Ser.). (ENG., Illus.). 24p. (J). (gr. k-3). pap. *(978-0-7787-3974-6(0),* 1294250) Crabtree Publishing Co.
—The Life Cycle of a Butterfly. 2007. (ENG.). 32p. (J). *(978-0-7787-7700-7(6))* Crabtree Publishing Co.
Kant, Tanya. How a Caterpillar Grows into a Butterfly. Franklin, Carolyn, illus. 2008. (Amaze Ser.). (ENG.). 32p. (J). 27.00 *(978-0-531-24046-5(0))*; (gr. -1-3). pap. 8.95 *(978-0-531-23800-4(8))* Scholastic Library Publishing. (Children's Pr.).
Kay, Jill. Caterpillars & Butterflies. 2013. (InfoMax Readers Ser.). (ENG.). 24p. (J). (gr. 2-3). pap. 8.25 *(978-1-4777-2263-3(7))*; pap. 49.50 *(978-1-4777-2264-0(5))* Rosen Publishing Group, Inc., The. (Rosen Classroom).
Leigh, Autumn. From Caterpillar to Butterfly: A Life Cycle. 2009. (Real Life Readers Ser.). 16p. (gr. 2-3). pap. 7.05 *(978-1-4358-0223-0(3),* Rosen Classroom) Rosen Publishing Group, Inc., The.
Linde, Barbara M. Tent Caterpillars. 2014. (Animals of Mass Destruction Ser.). 32p. (J). (gr. 2-5). 25.25 *(978-1-4824-1056-3(7))* Stevens, Gareth Publishing LLLP.
Lord, Pia. Cato the Caterpillar. 2011. 28p. pap. 24.95 *(978-1-4626-3239-8(4))* America Star Bks.
Marsh, Laura. National Geographic Readers: Caterpillar to Butterfly. 2012. (Readers Ser.). (ENG., Illus.). 32p. (J). (gr. -1-1). lib. bdg. 13.90 *(978-1-4263-0921-2(X),* National Geographic Children's Bks.) National Geographic Society.
Merritt, Robin. The Life Cycle of a Butterfly. 2011. (Life Cycles Ser.). (ENG., Illus.). 32p. (J). (gr. k-3). lib. bdg. 29.93 *(978-1-60973-143-4(3),* 201168) Child's World, Inc., The.
Mikus, Paul. Wow, I've Changed! 2008. 32p. pap. 14.49 *(978-1-4389-0145-9(3))* AuthorHouse.
Mitchell, Melanie S. Butterflies. 2003. (First Step Nonfiction - Animal Life Cycles Ser.). (ENG., Illus.). 24p. (gr. k-2). pap. 6.95 *(978-0-8225-4599-6(3),* Lerner Pubns.); lib. bdg. 23.93 *(978-0-8225-4598-9(5))* Lerner Publishing Group.
Murawski, Darlyne. Face to Face with Caterpillars. 2009. (Face to Face with Animals Ser.). (ENG., Illus.). 32p. (J). (gr. 2-5). 6.95 *(978-1-4263-0473-6(0),* National Geographic Children's Bks.) National Geographic Society.
Murawski, Darlyne A. Face to Face with Caterpillars. Murawski, Darlyne A., illus. 2007. (Face to Face with Animals Ser.). (ENG., Illus.). 32p. (J). (gr. 2-5). 16.95 *(978-1-4263-0052-3(2))*; lib. bdg. 25.90 *(978-1-4263-0053-0(0))* National Geographic Society. (National Geographic Children's Bks.).
Nagle, Frances. Zombie Caterpillars. 2015. (Zombie Animals: Parasites Take Control! Ser.). (ENG., Illus.). 24p. (J). (gr. 2-3). pap. 8.15 *(978-1-4824-2832-2(6))* Stevens, Gareth Publishing LLLP.
Nelson, Robin. Creeping Caterpillars. 2016. (First Step Nonfiction — Backyard Critters Ser.). (ENG., Illus.). 24p. (J). (gr. k-2). 23.99 *(978-1-5124-0880-5(8))* Lerner Publishing Group.
Peters, Elisa. It's a Caterpillar! 2009. (Everyday Wonders Ser.). 24p. (gr. 1-1). 42.50 *(978-1-61512-322-3(9),* PowerKids Pr.); (Illus.). (J). lib. bdg. 22.60 *(978-1-4042-4459-7(X))* Rosen Publishing Group, Inc., The.
—It's a Caterpillar! Aes una Oruga! 2009. (Everyday Wonders / Maravillas de Todos Los días Ser.). (SPA & ENG.). 24p. (J). lib. bdg. 22.60 *(978-1-4358-2524-6(1),* PowerKids Pr.) Rosen Publishing Group, Inc., The.
—It's a Caterpillar! / ¡Es una Oruga! 2009. (Everyday Wonders / Maravillas de todos los días Ser.). (ENG & SPA.). 24p. (gr. 1-1). 42.50 *(978-1-61512-328-5(8),* Editorial Buenas Letras) Rosen Publishing Group, Inc., The.
Pringle, Laurence. The Secret Life of the Woolly Bear Caterpillar. Paley, Joan, illus. 2014. (ENG.). 32p. (J). (gr. k-2). 16.95 *(978-1-62091-000-9(4))* Boyds Mills Pr.
Reid, Barbara. Caterpillar to Butterfly. braille ed. 2004. (J). (gr. 1). spiral bd., bds. *(978-0-616-03086-8(X))* Canadian National Institute for the Blind/Institut National Canadien pour les Aveugles.
Reinke, Beth Bence. Where Did the Caterpillar Go? 2016. (Everyday Earth Science Ser.). (ENG.). 24p. (J). (gr. k-3). 27.07 *(978-1-5038-0793-8(2),* 210632) Child's World, Inc., The.
Rissman, Rebecca. Caterpillars, 1 vol. 2012. (Creepy Critters Ser.). (ENG.). 24p. (gr. -1-k). pap. 9.95 *(978-1-4109-4817-5(X))*; lib. bdg. 25.32 *(978-1-4109-4804-5(8))* Heinemann-Raintree.
Ross, Michael Elsohn. Caterpillarology. Erickson, Darren, illus. Grogan, Brian, photos by. 2003. (Backyard Buddies Ser.). 48p. (YA). (gr. 3-5). 6.95 *(978-1-57505-434-6(5),* Carolrhoda Bks.) Lerner Publishing Group.
Scholastic, Inc. Staff, contrib. by. Is That a Caterpillar? 2016. (Rookie Toddler(tm) Ser.). (ENG., Illus.). 12p. (J). bds. 6.95 *(978-0-531-22698-8(0),* Children's Pr.) Scholastic Library Publishing.
Singer, Marilyn. Caterpillars. 2011. (ENG., Illus.). 40p. (J). (gr. -1-3). 14.95 *(978-0-9797455-7-7(8))* EarlyLight Bks., Inc.
Stewart, Melissa & American Museum of Natural History. Caterpillar to Butterfly. 2016. (Science for Toddlers Ser.). (ENG., Illus.). 24p. (J). (gr. -1 — 1). bds. 7.95 *(978-1-4549-1406-8(8))* Sterling Publishing Co., Inc.
Tomblin, Mark. The Itchy-Scratchy Caterpillar. Jones, Doug, illus. 2010. 16p. (J). *(978-0-545-24822-8(1))* Scholastic, Inc.
Trueit, Trudi Strain. Caterpillars. 2009. (Benchmark Rebus Ser.). 24p. (gr. k-1). 15.95 *(978-0-7614-3963-9(3))* Marshall Cavendish Corp.
—Caterpillars & Butterflies. 2011. (Backyard Safari Ser.). 32p. (gr. 3). 28.50 *(978-1-60870-243-5(X))* Marshall Cavendish GBR. Dist: Marshall Cavendish Corp.
Turnbull, S. Caterpillars & Butterflies. 2004. (Beginners Ser.). 32p. (J). (gr. 1-18). (ENG.). pap. 4.95 *(978-0-7945-0378-9(0))*; lib. bdg. 12.95 *(978-1-58086-506-7(2))* EDC Publishing.
Turnbull, Stephanie. Caterpillars & Butterflies. Guille, Rosanne & Mayer, Uwe, illus. 2007. (Usborne Beginners Ser.). 32p. (J). (gr. -1-3). 4.99 *(978-0-7945-1337-5(9),* Usborne) EDC Publishing.
Twinn, M. Metamorphoses: Butterfly. 2006. (Metamorphoses Ser.). (ENG., Illus.). 16p. (J). (gr. 1-5). bds. *(978-1-84643-013-8(5))* Child's Play International Ltd.
Werner, Cherie. New Life in Jesus! 2008. (Illus.). (J). pap. *(978-1-933234-54-0(7))* CTA.

CATERPILLARS—FICTION

Alders, Willa. Leafy Finds a Home. Burns, Sandra, illus. 2013. 24p. pap. 8.99 *(978-1-938768-13-2(2))* Gypsy Pubns.
Anderson, Kathy Archibald. Max the Happy Caterpillar. 2010. 36p. pap. 16.99 *(978-1-4520-8888-4(8))* AuthorHouse.
Barton, Renee, illus. Amagestic: A Caterpillar's Journey. 2005. Orig. Title: Amagestic. (J). per. 7.99 *(978-0-9741864-2-9(2),* 1) NT Publishing, L.L.C.
Bell, Patricia A. Timothy Caterpillar Gets New Shoes. 2012. 24p. 24.95 *(978-1-62709-669-0(8))* America Star Bks.
Bickford, Janette. Vern's Vacation. 2012. 16p. pap. 12.68 *(978-1-4669-2311-9(3))* Trafford Publishing.
Birkenstock, Michelle M. Harry the Caterpillar. 2010. 20p. pap. 10.95 *(978-1-60911-250-9(4),* Eloquent Bks.) Strategic Book Publishing & Rights Agency (SBPRA).
Blocker, Adam P. Joshua & the Spider. Taylor, Josh, illus. 2013. (ENG.). 72p. 17.99 *(978-1-939418-08-1(9))* Writer of the Round Table Pr.
Branch, Dianne. Logan's Caterpillar. 2011. 28p. pap. 12.03 *(978-1-4567-9952-6(5))* AuthorHouse.
Broberg, Janel. Catie the Cute, Curious & Sometimes Crooked Caterpillar. 2012. 24p. pap. 12.00 *(978-1-61170-073-2(6))* Robertson Publishing.
Bruel, Robert O. Bob & Otto. Bruel, Nick, illus. 2007. (ENG.). 32p. (J). (gr. -1-3). 17.99 *(978-1-59643-203-1(9),* 9781596432031) Roaring Brook Pr.
Cain, Sheridan. The Crunching Munching Caterpillar. Tickle, Jack, illus. (J). 2013. (ENG.). 20p. (gr. -1). 9.99 *(978-1-58925-616-3(6))* 2005. 18p. bds. 6.95 *(978-1-58925-757-3(X))* Tiger Tales.
—Crunching Munching Caterpillar. Tickle, Jack, illus. 2003. 32p. (J). tchr. ed. 15.95 *(978-1-58925-025-3(7))* Tiger Tales.
—The Crunching Munching Caterpillar Pop-up. Tickle, Jack, illus. 2006. 16p. (J). 15.95 *(978-1-58925-771-9(5))* Tiger Tales.
Capucilli, Alyssa Satin & Cole, Henry. Katy Duck Is a Caterpillar. 2009. (Katy Duck Ser.). (ENG., Illus.). 32p. (J). (gr. -1-k). 14.99 *(978-1-4169-6061-4(9),* Little Simon) Little Simon.
Carbonell, Paula. BUTTERFLY TRIP. 2007. (ENG., Illus.). 48p. (J). 18.95 *(978-84-96788-85-5(7))* OQO, Editora ESP. Dist: Baker & Taylor Bks.
Carle, Eric. Chenille Qui Fait des Trous.Tr. of Very Hungry Caterpillar. (FRE.). pap. 18.95 *(978-2-87142-174-0(9))* Mijade Editions BEL. Dist: Distribooks, Inc.
—Count with the Very Hungry Caterpillar. Carle, Eric, illus. 2006. (World of Eric Carle Ser.). (ENG., Illus.). 16p. (J). (gr. -1-k). pap. 6.99 *(978-0-448-44420-8(8),* Grosset & Dunlap) Penguin Young Readers Group.
—Die kleine Raupe Nimmersatt: Ein Bilderbuch.Tr. of Very Hungry Caterpillar. (GER., Illus.). 17p. pap. 16.95 *(978-3-423-07922-8(3))* Deutscher Taschenbuch Verlag GmbH & Co KG DEU. Dist: Distribooks, Inc.
—Love from the Very Hungry Caterpillar. 2015. (ENG.). 32p. (J). (-k). 8.99 *(978-0-448-48932-2(5),* Grosset & Dunlap) Penguin Young Readers Group.
—My Own Very Hungry Caterpillar. Carle, Eric, illus. 2003. (ENG., Illus.). 32p. (J). (gr. -1-k). 5.99 *(978-0-399-24207-6(4),* Philomel Bks.) Penguin Young Readers Group.
—The Very Hungry Caterpillar. Carle, Eric, illus. 2011. (ENG & SPA., Illus.). 32p. (J). (gr. -1-k). 21.99 *(978-0-399-25604-2(0),* Philomel Bks.) Penguin Young Readers Group.
—The Very Hungry Caterpillar. 2004. (J). (gr. -1-2). spiral bd. *(978-0-616-01611-4(5))*; spiral bd. *(978-0-616-01610-7(7))*

C D

Canadian National Institute for the Blind/Institut National Canadien pour les Aveugles.
—The Very Hungry Caterpillar. 2004. (Illus.). 23p. (J). (978-1-85269-127-1(1)) Mantra Lingua.
—The Very Hungry Caterpillar. Carle, Eric, illus. 2004. (ENG & BEN., Illus.). 20p. (J). pap. (978-1-85269-125-7(5)) Mantra Lingua.
—The Very Hungry Caterpillar. 2004. (ENG & SOM., Illus.). 19p. (J). pap. (978-1-85269-128-8(X)) Mantra Lingua.
—The Very Hungry Caterpillar. Carle, Eric, illus. 2004. (Illus.). 20p. (J). (ENG & URD.). pap. (978-1-85269-129-5(8)); (ENG & CHI., (gr. -1-2). pap. (978-1-85269-126-4(3)); (ARA & ENG., (gr. -1-5). pap. (978-1-85269-124-0(7)) Mantra Lingua.
—The Very Hungry Caterpillar. 2008. (CHI., Illus.). 32p. (978-7-5332-5673-9(5)) Mingtian Chubanshe.
—The Very Hungry Caterpillar. Carle, Eric, illus. 2007. (ENG., Illus.). 24p. (J). (gr. -1 — 1). bds., bds. 15.99 (978-0-399-24745-3(9), Philomel Bks.) Penguin Young Readers Group.
—The Very Hungry Caterpillar (La Oruga Muy Hambrienta) Carle, Eric, illus. 2011. (SPA & ENG., Illus.). 24p. (J). (gr. -1 — 1). bds. 10.99 (978-0-399-25605-9(9), Philomel Bks.) Penguin Young Readers Group.
—The Very Hungry Caterpillar's Christmas 123. Carle, Eric, illus. 2015. (ENG., Illus.). 18p. (J). (— 1). bds. 8.99 (978-0-448-49009-0(9), Grosset & Dunlap) Penguin Young Readers Group.
—The Very Hungry Caterpillar's Finger Puppet Book. 2011. (World of Eric Carle Ser.). (ENG.). 7p. (J). (gr. -1-k). bds. 12.99 (978-0-448-45597-6(8), Grosset & Dunlap) Penguin Young Readers Group.
Carle, Eric, illus. I Love Mom with the Very Hungry Caterpillar. 2017. (World of Eric Carle Ser.). (ENG.). 32p. (J). (-k). 8.99 (978-0-451-53346-3(1), Grosset & Dunlap) Penguin Young Readers Group.
Carle, Eric & Chronicle Books Staff. String-Alongs. 2012. (ENG., Illus.). 10p. (J). (gr. -1-17). 18.99 (978-1-4521-0515-4(4)) Chronicle Bks. LLC.
—The World of Eric Carle the Very Hungry Caterpillar Flash Cards. 2014. (ENG., Illus.). 22p. (J). (gr. -1 — 1). 14.99 (978-1-4521-3190-0(2)) Chronicle Bks. LLC.
Carle, Eric & Mack, Jeff. The Very Hungry Caterpillar. Carle, Eric, illus. 2015. (ENG., Illus.). 24p. (J). (gr. -1-k). bds. 19.99 (978-0-399-17317-2(X), Philomel Bks.) Penguin Young Readers Group.
Caterpillar Hides Away. 2003. (Daisy Board Books Ser.). 10p. (J). bds. 9.95 (978-0-7525-8298-6(4)) Parragon, Inc.
Clarke, Wanda Marie. The Butterfly Ball. 2012. 32p. pap. 13.95 (978-1-4497-2211-1(3), WestBow Pr.) Author Solutions, Inc.
Colon, Danny. The Little Caterpillar Who Dreams to Fly. 2012. 40p. pap. 15.99 (978-1-4624-0377-6(8), Inspiring Voices) Author Solutions, Inc.
Cooper, Afua. The Red Caterpillar on College Street. Martin, Stephanie, illus. Date not set. 400p. (J). (gr. -1-3). pap. (978-0-920813-87-4(9)) Sister Vision Pr.
Creepy Crawly Caterpillar. 2005. (J). bds. 7.99 (978-1-933200-16-3(2)) Family Bks. at Home.
Dahms, Theresa V. Pookie, the Little Caterpillar. 2009. 20p. pap. 10.49 (978-1-4389-6049-4(2)) AuthorHouse.
Dexter & Milly the Caterpillar. 2004. (J). per. 15.99 (978-0-9753533-4-9(9)) Golden Eagle Publishing Hse., Inc.
Dhar, Lisa Jane. Aisha Goes in Search of Colour. Zulkifi, Azhari, illus. 2009. (ENG.). 32p. (J). (gr. k-2). 6.95 (978-0-86037-472-5(6)) Kube Publishing Ltd. GBR. Dist: Consortium Bk. Sales & Distribution.
DiMarco, Carol. Alchemy. 2007. 44p. (J). 8.99 (978-1-59092-219-4(0)) Blue Forge Pr.
Dontell, Susan L. Sassafras in What Is Metamorphosis? Andrews, Luke, illus. 2008. 36p. pap. 24.95 (978-1-60441-776-0(5)) America Star Bks.
Dychtwald, Ken, et al. Gideon's Dream: A Tale of New Beginnings. Zaboski, Dave, illus. 2008. 40p. (J). (gr. -1-3). lib. bdg. 17.89 (978-0-06-143498-3(1)) HarperCollins Pubs.
Edwards, Pamela Duncan. Clara Caterpillar. Cole, Henry, illus. 2004. (ENG.). 40p. (J). (gr. -1-1). reprint ed. pap. 6.99 (978-0-06-443691-5(8)) HarperCollins Pubs.
Elwell, Susan. Madigan's Discoveries: Book One - the Magic of Transformation. 2009. 106p. pap. 12.95 (978-1-933063-22-5(X)) Global Partnership, LLC.
Fieber, Valerie. Three Caterpillars & a Lost Toy. 2012. 24p. pap. 14.93 (978-1-4669-5573-8(2)) Trafford Publishing.
Fontenot, Mary Alice. Clovis Crawfish & Petit Papillon, 1 vol. Graves, Keith, illus. 2009. (Clovis Crawfish Ser.). (ENG.). 32p. (J). (gr. k-3). 16.99 (978-1-58980-772-3(3)) Pelican Publishing Co., Inc.
Frazier, Laverne & Bishop, Elaine. Where Are My Wings? 2009. 28p. pap. 13.99 (978-1-4389-9295-2(5)) AuthorHouse.
G & G Wilcox. Tex, the Little Caterpillar from Texas. 2009. 68p. pap. 41.99 (978-1-4363-6494-2(9)) Xlibris Corp.
Galjanic, Lisa. When Caterpillars Grow Up. Hope, Michelle, illus. 2007. (J). 9.95 (978-1-933532-03-5(3)) LSG Pubns.
—When Series 6 Volume Set. 6. 2007. (Illus.). 100p. (J). 34.95 (978-1-933532-06-6(8)) LSG Pubns.
Garnett, Jana. How the Caterpillar Got Its Wings: (How Acknowledging Your Feelings Can Give You Flight) 2003. (Illus.). (J). spiral bd. 19.95 (978-0-9728716-7-9(5)) Journey Pubns., LLC.
Gawade, Akansha A. This Is Who I Am. 2006. (J). pap. 8.00 (978-0-8059-6886-6(5)) Dorrance Publishing Co., Inc.
A Gift for Roo. 2013. (Illus.). 24p. pap. 10.95 (978-1-61633-441-3(X)) Guardian Angel Publishing, Inc.
Giulieri, Anne. Sleepy Little Caterpillar, 1 vol. Florian, Mélanie, illus. 2012. (Engage Literacy Red Ser.). (ENG.). 32p. (gr. k-2). pap. 5.99 (978-1-4296-8932-8(3), Engage Literacy) Capstone Press of Coughlan Cos.
Grateful Steps Publishing & Tipton, Angela. Butterflies Don't Crawl. Irvine, Wil, illus. 2009. 32p. (J). 16.95 (978-1-935130-14-7(5)) Grateful Steps.
Guerrera, Debra. The Adventures of Baby Caterpillar & His Traveling Butterfly Family. 2011. 28p. pap. 15.99 (978-1-4628-9982-1(X)) Xlibris Corp.
Hardy, Edward. Where Is Fred? Pye, Ali, illus. 2013. (ENG.). 32p. (J). (gr. -1-k). pap. 9.99 (978-1-4052-5403-8(3)) Egmont Bks., Ltd. GBR. Dist: Independent Pubs. Group.
Hatch, Justina. Charlie the Caterpillar, 1 vol. 2010. 44p. pap. 24.95 (978-1-4489-9256-0(7)) PublishAmerica, Inc.
Heinz, Renata Perpetua. Nali's Life. 2008. 17p. pap. 24.95 (978-1-4241-9245-8(5)) America Star Bks.
Hinkler Books Staff, ed. Casper the Caterpillar. 2009. (ENG.). 12p. (J). bds. 12.99 (978-1-74183-541-0(0), Ideal Pubns.) Worthy Publishing.
Hood, Susan. Caterpillar Spring, Butterfly Summer: 10th Anniversary Edition. Gevry, Claudine, illus. 2014. (ENG.). 12p. (J). (gr. -1-k). 12.99 (978-0-7944-3038-2(4)) Reader's Digest Assn., Inc., The.
House, Darrell. Miller the Green Caterpillar. Argoff, Patti, illus. l.t. ed. 2005. 32p. 16.95 (978-0-9663276-9-4(1)) Red Engine Pr.
Hover Get's His Wings. 2004.Tr. of Cometin recibe sus alas. (SPA.). 24p. 10.99 (978-1-59185-422-7(9), Casa Creacion) Charisma Media.
Huck, Jeremy. Charlie, the Christmas Caterpillar. 2011. 20p. pap. 24.95 (978-1-4560-4972-0(0)) America Star Bks.
—Charlie, the Christmas Caterpillar, & Marvin Mouse. 2013. 16p. pap. 24.95 (978-1-62709-632-4(9)) America Star Bks.
Human, Deborah. Pinky Promise. 2009. 40p. (J). pap. 11.99 (978-0-9818374-0-6(9)) Writing Bench LLC., The.
I Wish I Could Fly: Lonely Caterpillar/the Lonely Butterfly. l.t. ed. 2006. (Illus.). 60p. (J). (gr. -1-3). per. 17.99 (978-1-59879-196-9(6)) Lifevest Publishing, Inc.
Irwin, Gerald. Harry the Spider & His Friend Charlie. 2012. 28p. pap. 19.99 (978-1-4772-6620-5(8)) AuthorHouse.
Jefferson, E. Louis. The Little Caterpillar-A Story of Kindness. 2012. 38p. pap. 17.00 (978-1-105-76076-1(6)) Lulu Pr., Inc.
—The Little Caterpillar-A Story of Kindness-Companion Coloring Book. 2012. 52p. pap. 8.00 (978-1-105-92194-0(8)) Lulu Pr., Inc.
Jett, Cindy. Harry the Happy Caterpillar Grows: Helping Children Adjust to Change. Voerg, Kathy, illus. 2010. (Let's Talk Ser.). (ENG.). 48p. (J). (gr. -1-4). pap. 8.95 (978-0-88282-316-4(7)) New Horizon Pr. Pubs., Inc.
Jewell, Laura. Ty Gets His Wings. 2012. (ENG.). (J). pap. 18.00 (978-1-4675-4702-4(6)) Independent Pub.
Juarbe, Cynthia. Callie the Caterpillar Collects Coins. 2011. 24p. pap. 13.50 (978-1-4520-5641-8(2)) AuthorHouse.
Kann, Victoria. Pinkalicious & the Little Butterfly. Kann, Victoria, illus. 2016. (Pinkalicious Ser.). (Illus.). 24p. (J). (gr. -1-3). pap. 4.99 (978-0-06-241071-9(7), HarperFestival) HarperCollins Pubs.
Keller, Holly. Farfallina & Marcel. Keller, Holly, illus. 2005. (ENG., Illus.). 32p. (J). (gr. -1-4). reprint ed. pap. 6.99 (978-0-06-443872-8(4), Greenwillow Bks.) HarperCollins Pubs.
—Farfallina & Marcel. Keller, Holly, illus. 2005. (Illus.). (gr. -1-3). 17.00 (978-0-7569-5785-8(0)) Perfection Learning Corp.
King, Zola. Whatever Became of Charlie Caterpillar? 2011. 44p. pap. 16.59 (978-1-4634-7441-6(5)) AuthorHouse.
Kirouac Bn, Nicole. I Am Unique. 2013. 32p. pap. 13.99 (978-1-4525-7594-0(0), Balboa Pr.) Author Solutions, Inc.
Kompelien, Tracy. Monarch Butterfly, 1 vol. Chawla, Neena, illus. 2007. (Critter Chronicles Ser.). (ENG.). 24p. (J). (gr. k-3). lib. bdg. 24.21 (978-1-59928-454-5(5), SandCastle) ABDO Publishing Co.
Kubler, Annie, illus. The Mixed up Caterpillar. 2006. (Finger Puppet Bks.). (ENG.). 24p. (J). (gr. 1-1). (978-1-84643-026-8(7)) Child's Play International Ltd.
Lal, Ranjit. Caterpillar Who Went on a Diet & Other Stories. 2004. (Illus.). 188p. (J). pap. (978-0-14-333593-1(6), Puffin) Penguin Publishing Group.
Lallouz, Michele. The Adventures of Cali. Nielson, Ginger, illus. 2007. 32p. (J). pap. 9.95 (978-0-9793004-0-0(1)) Cali Publishing.
Lamont, Tracey. The Adventures of Speedy & Creedy: Mrs. Smith's Kitchen. 2008. (ENG.). 32p. 14.49 (978-1-4389-3043-5(7)) AuthorHouse.
Lehnert, R. B. The Adventures of Billy Butterfly. Garcia, Marc Khayam, illus. 2003. (J). per. (978-0-9747628-2-1(2)) BKB Group, Inc., The.
Lei, Vicki. Creepy Caterpillar. 2011. 24p. pap. 15.99 (978-1-4568-5591-8(3)) Xlibris Corp.
Lewis, Kelly. Katie the Caterpillar. 2016. (Spring Forward Ser.). (J). (gr. 2). (978-1-4900-3732-5(2)) Benchmark Education Co.
Libby, Lori Ann. The Adventures of Henry Hamper & the Flying Fish. Lee, Tricia Ting, illus. 2010. 34p. pap. 13.95 (978-1-60911-493-0(0), Eloquent Bks.) Strategic Book Publishing & Rights Agency (SBPRA).
Lionni, Leo. Inch by Inch. (ENG.). 32p. (J). (gr. -1-2). 2012. bds. 7.99 (978-0-307-93125-2(0)) 2010. 16.99 (978-0-375-85764-5(8)) Random Hse. Children's Bks. (Knopf Bks. for Young Readers).
—Inch by Inch. Lionni, Leo, illus. unabr. ed. 2006. (Illus.). (J). (gr. -1-1). 18.95 (978-0-439-90585-5(0), WPCD699) Weston Woods Studios, Inc.
Lucado, Max, creator. Hermie: A Common Caterpillar. 2005. 32p. (J). pap. 3.99 (978-1-4003-0663-3(9)) Nelson, Thomas Inc.
Lucado, Max & Smith, Brian. Turn: Remembering Our Foundations. 2005. (ENG., Illus.). 160p. 12.99 (978-1-59052-450-3(0), Multnomah) Doubleday Religious Publishing Group, The.
MacKinnon, Mary & Berg, N. Erpill the Caterpillar. 2011. 12p. pap. 8.32 (978-1-4520-8263-9(4)) AuthorHouse.
Macri, Rebecca. Pip: A Very Special Little Caterpillar. 2010. 32p. (J). 16.95 (978-1-886057-61-6(3)) Warren Publishing, Inc.
Mann, Gerre. Cora the Caterpillar. Brody, Joyce, illus. 2012. 20p. pap. 14.99 (978-1-61170-088-6(4)) Robertson Publishing.
Martin, Anne E. Spike the Friendly Caterpillar. McCabb, Jamie, illus. l.t. ed. 2006. 53p. (J). per. 9.99 (978-1-59879-127-3(3)) Lifevest Publishing, Inc.
Martin, Bill, Jr. Ten Little Caterpillars. Ehlert, Lois, illus. 2011. (ENG.). 40p. (J). (gr. -1-3). 17.99 (978-1-4424-3385-4(X), Beach Lane Bks.) Beach Lane Bks.
McConville, Alexandra. The Adventures of Sass-O-Frask: A Tale of Kindness. 2012. 32p. pap. 19.99 (978-1-4772-6006-7(4)) AuthorHouse.
McFarland, Clive. Caterpillar Dreams. McFarland, Clive, illus. 2017. (Illus.). 32p. (J). (gr. -1-3). 17.99 (978-0-06-238636-6(0)) HarperCollins Pubs.
McNamara, Margaret. Butterfly Garden. Gordon, Mike, illus. 2012. (Robin Hill School Ser.). (ENG.). 32p. (J). (gr. -1-1). 15.99 (978-1-4424-3643-5(3)); pap. 3.99 (978-1-4424-3642-8(5)) Simon Spotlight. (Simon Spotlight).
—Butterfly Garden. 2012. (Robin Hill School Ready-To-Read Ser.). lib. bdg. 13.55 (978-0-606-23694-2(5), Turtleback) Turtleback Bks.
McNamee, Barbara Oakley. Kelsey & Seattle. 2007. (J). pap. 15.00 (978-0-8059-7428-7(8)) Dorrance Publishing Co., Inc.
Mescall, Ron. The Adventures of Goo Goo Malou: A Parent's Guide for Teaching Values. 2009. 24p. pap. 10.96 (978-1-4269-0836-1(9)) Trafford Publishing.
Moran, Kelly. The Tiny Caterpillar & the Great Big Tree. 2009. 50p. pap. 19.50 (978-0-557-09498-1(4)) Lulu Pr., Inc.
Mullins, Allene. Katie's Wish. 2012. 16p. pap. 15.99 (978-1-4772-6811-7(1)) AuthorHouse.
Murray, Cassie. Olivia, the Olive Bug. 2009. 24p. pap. 15.99 (978-1-4415-1966-5(1)) Xlibris Corp.
The Mysterious Secret. 2013. (Illus.). 30p. pap. 14.99 (978-1-940426-03-7(0)) Love Ink LLC.
Notarfrancesco, Lisa Christiano & Padovano, Chris. Catherine the Caterpillar & Friends Coloring Book: A Children's Guide to Autism. 2014. (ENG.). 72p. pap. 1.95 (978-1-63443-539-0(7)) Primedia eLaunch LLC.
O'Callahan, Jay. Herman & Marguerite: An Earth Story, 1 vol. O'Callahan, Laura, illus. 2003. (ENG.). 36p. (J). (gr. k-3). pap. 7.95 (978-1-56145-283-5(1)) Peachtree Pubs.
Ogunsuyi, Melissa. The Grumpy Caterpillar. 2010. 28p. pap. 14.99 (978-1-4520-4613-6(1)) AuthorHouse.
O'Neal, Kerry. I Wish I Could Fly/I Can Fly! The Lonely Caterpillar BOOK I & the Lonely Butterfly BOOK II. O'Neal, Kerry, illus. l.t. ed. 2006. (Illus.). 60p. (J). 29.99 (978-1-59879-197-6(4)) Lifevest Publishing, Inc.
Paourou, Maria. Bubblebea Wants to Be a Hero. 2009. (Illus.). 40p. pap. 16.99 (978-1-4343-7330-4(4)) AuthorHouse.
Parker, Emma. Cecil the Caterpillar. 2010. (Illus.). pap. (978-1-877547-95-9(6)) First Edition Ltd.
Phillips, Gina & Martin, Stuart. Ants & Caterpillars. 2003. (Busy Bugs Ser.). 12p. (J). bds. 14.95 (978-1-74047-240-1(3)) Book Co. Publishing Pty, Ltd., The AUS. Dist: Penton Overseas, Inc.
Posner-Sanchez, Andrea. Ariel's Dolphin Adventure - Snow White's New Friend, 2 bks. in 1. Random House Disney Staff, illus. 2010. (Pictureback(R) Ser.). (ENG.). 32p. (J). (gr. -1-2). pap. 4.99 (978-0-7364-2654-1(X), RH/Disney) Random Hse. Children's Bks.
Potts, Christiane Elenes. Lola & the Caterpillar. 2011. 28p. pap. 13.99 (978-1-4520-2563-6(0)) AuthorHouse.
Pova, Rosie. Ladybug & Caterpillar: The Way to Friendship. 2008. 16p. pap. 24.95 (978-1-60474-950-2(4)) America Star Bks.
Powers, David M. F. Ein Schmetterling Ohne Flügel. Vail, Sue, tr. Nesterova, Natalia, illus. 2013. 42p. pap. 9.99 (978-0-9860373-7-3(8)) Pants On Fire Pr.
Puzzi, Jessica. Rosy & Simon's Front Yard Adventure, 1 vol. 2010. 18p. pap. 24.95 (978-1-4489-2601-5(7)) PublishAmerica, Inc.
Randolph, Joanne. Bella: A Butterfly's Story. 2009. (Nature Stories Ser.). (Illus.). 24p. (J). (gr. -1-2). pap. 8.15 (978-1-60754-099-1(1)); lib. bdg. 22.60 (978-1-60754-098-4(3)) Windmill Bks.
Ray, See. Caterpillar Stickers: Be Yourself & Be Butterfly Beautiful! 2012. 28p. pap. 16.99 (978-1-4772-6864-3(2)) AuthorHouse.
Reihs, Linda. The Adventures of Maddy Morphis. 2012. 34p. pap. 9.99 (978-0-9819648-1-2(8)) Mindstir Media.
Roderick, Judith A. Connie the Caterpillar: Connie Teaches Others a Lesson of True Beauty. 2011. 20p. pap. 11.50 (978-1-4634-3357-4(3)) AuthorHouse.
Rodriguez, AJ. Cycle of Life. 2009. 20p. pap. 12.49 (978-1-4389-5528-5(6)) AuthorHouse.
Rose, Jasmine. The Last Caterpillar Princess. 2011. 16p. pap. 8.64 (978-1-4634-1953-0(8)) AuthorHouse.
Sawyer, J. Scott. The Broccoli Bush. Bozeman, Gary, illus. 2012. 36p. pap. 24.95 (978-1-4626-2501-7(0)) America Star Bks.
Scaglione, Joanne & Small, Gail. Life's Little Lessons: An Inch-by-Inch Tale of Success. 2006. (ENG., Illus.). 64p. pap. 21.00 (978-1-57886-336-5(8)) Rowman & Littlefield Publishers, Inc.
Schield, Allie Schield. Solomon & Lily. Jerome, Barb, illus. 2003. 34p. (J). per. 11.99 (978-0-9743948-0-0(7)) One Little Miracle.
Schmauss, Judy Kentor. The Caterpillar. Collier, Mary, illus. 2006. (Reader's Clubhouse Level 1 Reader Ser.). (ENG.). 24p. (J). (gr. 1-4). pap. 4.99 (978-0-7641-3286-5(5)) Barron's Educational Series, Inc.
Segvic-Boudreaux, Ivana. Desperately Seeking Talent: A Puppy's Journey. 2010. 108p. pap. 13.95 (978-1-4327-6112-7(9)) Outskirts Pr., Inc.
Shemayne S. A Place Called There. 2011. 20p. pap. 10.95 (978-1-4497-1611-0(3), WestBow Pr.) Author Solutions, Inc.
Slusher, Randall. A Day in the Life. 2004. 8p. (J). pap. 6.98 (978-1-4116-1237-2(X)) Lulu Pr., Inc.
Sommer, Carl. The Ugly Caterpillar. 2003. (Another Sommer-Time Story Ser.). (Illus.). 48p. (J). (gr. 1-4). 16.95 incl. audio (978-1-57537-564-9(8)) Advance Publishing, Inc.
—The Ugly Caterpillar. Budwine, Greg, illus. 2003. (Another Sommer-Time Story Ser.). 48p. (J). (gr. 1-4). 16.95 incl. audio compact disk (978-1-57537-515-1(X)) Advance Publishing, Inc.
—The Ugly Caterpillar Read-along 2003. (Another Sommer-Time Story Ser.). (Illus.). (J). lib. bdg. 23.95 incl. audio (978-1-57537-765-0(9)) Advance Publishing, Inc.
—The Ugly Caterpillar Read-along. Budwine, Greg, illus. 2003. (Another Sommer-Time Story Ser.). (ENG.). 48p. (J). lib. bdg. 23.95 incl. audio compact disk (978-1-57537-715-5(2)) Advance Publishing, Inc.
Southard, Ashley. Maddie. 2006. 10p. 8.01 (978-1-4116-8318-1(8)) Lulu Pr., Inc.
Stave, Mel. How Harry Found the Meaning of Friendship. 2010. (Illus.). 40p. pap. 14.95 (978-1-60911-147-2(8), Eloquent Bks.) Strategic Book Publishing & Rights Agency (SBPRA).
Steuerwald, Shannon B. From Scrawny to Brawny. 2006. (J). per. 9.95 (978-1-931787-19-2(0)) Fundamental Christian Endeavors.
Sullivan, Melody. Lillibit's Dream. Grof, Stanislav, illus. 2011. (ENG.). 32p. (J). 19.95 (978-1-59275-000-9(1)) Hanford Mead Pubs., Inc.
Swope, Sam. Gotta Go! Gotta Go! Riddle, Sue, illus. 2004. (ENG.). 32p. (J). (gr. -1-1). reprint ed. pap. 8.99 (978-0-374-42786-3(0), 9780374427863) Square Fish.
Tandy, Clive. Quarry Grove. 2008. 60p. per. 11.59 (978-1-4251-4974-1(X)) Trafford Publishing.
Tarbett, Debbie. Ten Wriggly Wiggly Caterpillars. (Illus.). 24p. (J). bds. 19.95 (978-1-84506-027-5(X)) Little Tiger Pr.
Taylor, Betty Ann. Mari's Miracle. 2013. 32p. pap. 16.99 (978-1-4808-0230-8(1)) Archway Publishing.
Thompson, Holly Sue. Molly, the Good Furry Friend. Thompson, Kristi June, illus. 2011. 36p. pap. 14.75 (978-1-60911-431-2(0), Eloquent Bks.) Strategic Book Publishing & Rights Agency (SBPRA).
Thompson, Susan A. Katie the Christian Caterpillar: The Loss of a Loved One. 2012. 20p. pap. 10.99 (978-1-4624-0223-6(2), Inspiring Voices) Author Solutions, Inc.
Thottam, Meena. The Do or Die Caterpillar. 2006. (J). 3.95 (978-0-9776917-1-5(3), Curcumin Bks.) Davlaw Press.
Timmis, Jeff. You'd Have Wings If You'd Just Said No. 2012. 28p. pap. 19.99 (978-1-4772-7604-4(1)) AuthorHouse.
Truchses, Susan Ruth. A Time to Be. 2012. 24p. pap. 17.99 (978-1-4685-6446-4(3)) AuthorHouse.
University Games Staff. Very Hungrey Caterpillar. 2006. 24p. (J). (978-1-57528-891-8(5)) Univ. Games.
Volta, A. Patulous, the Different Caterpillar. 2008. (Illus.). 28p. (J). 17.99 (978-0-9711040-0-6(X)) Working Parents, LLC.
Watson, Kenneth C. The Big Yellow Butterfly. 2010. 36p. 15.69 (978-1-4490-5974-3(0)) AuthorHouse.
Wendling, Peter. Caterpillars Never Lie, 1 vol. 2010. 26p. pap. 24.95 (978-1-4489-4676-1(X)) PublishAmerica, Inc.
Wenger, Shaunda. Caterpillar Can't Wait! 2006. (Early Explorers Ser.). (J). pap. (978-1-4108-6101-6(5)) Benchmark Education Co.
Weston Woods Staff, creator. The Caterpillar & the Polliwog. 2011. 38.75 (978-0-439-73154-6(2)); 18.95 (978-0-439-73152-2(6)) Weston Woods Studios, Inc.
—Inch by Inch. 2011. 38.75 (978-0-439-90543-5(5)) Weston Woods Studios, Inc.
Wheelwright, Ryan. Olivar & the Forbidden Plum Patch. 2011. 21p. (J). pap. 11.95 (978-1-4327-6689-4(9)) Outskirts Pr., Inc.
Willett, Christie. Isabella. 2011. 52p. (gr. -1). pap. 19.39 (978-1-4269-6387-2(4)) Trafford Publishing.
Willis, Jeanne. Caterpillar Dreams. Ross, Tony, illus. 2013. (ENG.). 32p. (J). (gr. -1-k). pap. 8.99 (978-1-84939-025-5(8)) Andersen Pr. GBR. Dist: Independent Pubs. Group.
Wilson, George H. The Perils of Cory the Caterpillar. 2010. (Illus.). 50p. (J). 15.00 (978-0-9778477-0-9(5)) A Story Plus Children Bks.
Wilson, Steve. Hedgehugs & the Hattiepillar. Tapper, Lucy, illus. 2016. (Hedgehugs Ser.). (ENG.). 32p. (J). 16.99 (978-1-62779-414-5(X), 9781627794145, Holt, Henry & Co. Bks. For Young Readers) Holt, Henry & Co.
Zabriskie, Cindy. The Daily Adventures of Ruckus & Otis. Benger, Chelsi L., illus. 2008. 24p. pap. 24.95 (978-1-60672-829-1(6)) America Star Bks.

CATHEDRALS

Baum, Margaux & Hilliam, David. Castles & Cathedrals. 2016. (Life in the Middle Ages Ser.). 0064p. (J). (gr. 5-5). 34.45 (978-1-5081-7318-2(4)) Rosen Publishing Group, Inc., The.
Green, John. Cathedrals of the World Coloring Book. 2013. (Dover Coloring Bks.). (ENG., Illus.). 48p. (gr. 3-12). pap. 4.99 (978-0-486-28339-5(9)) Dover Pubns., Inc.
Gregory, Joy. St. Patrick's Cathedral. 2014. (J). (978-1-4896-2610-3(7)) Weigl Pubs., Inc.
Hilliam, David. Castles & Cathedrals. 2004. (Library of the Middle Ages Ser.). (Illus.). 64p. (YA). (gr. 5-9). lib. bdg. 31.95 (978-0-8239-3990-9(1)) Rosen Publishing Group, Inc., The.
—Castles & Cathedrals: The Great Buildings of Medieval Times. 2009. (Library of the Middle Ages Ser.). 64p. (gr. 5-8). 58.50 (978-1-60853-896-6(6), Rosen Reference) Rosen Publishing Group, Inc., The.
Jovinelly, Joann. The Crafts & Culture of a Medieval Cathedral. 2009. (Crafts & Cultures of the Middle Ages Ser.). 48p. (gr. 5-5). 58.50 (978-1-61512-054-3(8), Rosen Reference) Rosen Publishing Group, Inc., The.
Jovinelly, Joann & Netelkos, Jason. The Crafts & Culture of a Medieval Cathedral. 2006. (Crafts & Cultures of the Middle Ages Ser.). (Illus.). 48p. (J). (gr. 3-7). lib. bdg. 29.25 (978-1-4042-0758-5(9)) Rosen Publishing Group, Inc., The.
Macaulay, David. Cathedral: The Story of Its Construction. rev. ed. 2013. (ENG., Illus.). 80p. (J). (gr. 5-7). 19.99 (978-0-544-10000-8(X)) Houghton Mifflin Harcourt Publishing Co.
Macdonald, Fiona. You Wouldn't Want to Work on a Medieval Cathedral! A Difficult Job That Never Ends. 2010. (You Wouldn't Want to... Ser.). 32p. (J). 29.00 (978-0-531-20504-4(5), Watts, Franklin) Scholastic Library Publishing.
MacDonald, Fiona. You Wouldn't Want to Work on a Medieval Cathedral! A Difficult Job That Never Ends. 2010. (You Wouldn't Want to... Ser.). (ENG., Illus.). 32p. (J). (gr. 3-18). pap. 9.95 (978-0-531-13784-0(8), Watts, Franklin) Scholastic Library Publishing.
Nanji, Shenaaz. Notre Dame. 2014. (J). (978-1-4896-1146-8(0)) Weigl Pubs., Inc.

CATHER, WILLA, 1873-1947

Ehrlich, Amy. Willa: The Story of Willa Cather, an American Writer. Minor, Wendell, illus. 2016. (ENG.). 72p. (J). (gr. 2-5). 16.99 (978-0-689-86573-2(2), Simon & Schuster Bks. For Young Readers) Simon & Schuster Bks. For Young Readers.
Meltzer, Milton. Willa Cather: A Biography. 2008. (Literary Greats Ser.). (ENG., Illus.). 160p. (gr. 7-12). lib. bdg. 33.26 (978-0-8225-7604-4(X)) Lerner Publishing Group.

CATHERINE DE MEDICIS, QUEEN, CONSORT OF HENRY II, KING OF FRANCE, 1519-1589

Havemeyer, Janie. Catherine de' Medici: "The Black Queen" Malone, Peter, illus. 2011. (Thinking Girl's Treasury of Dastardly Dames Ser.). (ENG.). 32p. (J). (gr. 3-8). 18.95 (978-0-9834256-3-2(9)) Goosebottom Bks. LLC.

Whitelaw, Nancy. Catherine de Medici & the Protestant Reformation. 2004. (World Leaders Ser.). (Illus.). 160p. (YA). (gr. 6-12). lib. bdg. 26.95 *(978-1-931798-26-6(5))* Reynolds, Morgan Inc.

CATHERINE II, EMPRESS OF RUSSIA, 1729-1796

Catherine the Great & the Enlightenment in Russia. 2005. (World Leaders Ser.). (Illus.). 160p. (gr. 6-12). lib. bdg. 28.95 *(978-1-931798-27-3(3))* Reynolds, Morgan Inc.

Gibson, Karen Bush. The Life & Times of Catherine the Great. 2005. (Biography from Ancient Civilizations Ser.). (Illus.). 48p. (J). (gr. 4-7). lib. bdg. 29.95 *(978-1-58415-347-4(4))* Mitchell Lane Pubs., Inc.

Rozett, Louise. Ice Queen: Catherine the Great Seizes Power in Russia. 2011. (J). pap. *(978-0-545-32946-0(9))* Scholastic, Inc.

Vincent, Zu. Catherine the Great: Empress of Russia. 2009. (Wicked History Ser.). (ENG.). 128p. (J). (gr. 6-12). pap. 5.95 *(978-0-531-20738-3(2))*; (Illus.). 31.00 *(978-0-531-21802-0(3))* Scholastic Library Publishing. (Watts, Franklin).

CATHERINE, THE GREAT, 1729-1796

see Catherine II, Empress of Russia, 1729-1796

CATHOLIC CHURCH

Cannizzo, Karen, ed. Mass Prayers: For Young Catholics. 2006. (Illus.). 31p. (J). (gr. -1-2). per. 2.25 *(978-1-933178-40-0(X))* Pflaum Publishing Group.

Daughters of St. Paul Staff, contrib. by. Prayers for Young Catholics. 2014. (ENG., Illus.). 192p. (J). 14.95 *(978-0-8198-5995-2(8))* Pauline Bks. & Media.

DeDomenico, Elizabeth Marie. Saint John Vianney: A Priest for All People. Hatke, Ben, illus. 2008. (Encounter the Saints Ser.). 122p. (J). (gr. 4-7). pap. 7.95 *(978-0-8198-7115-2(X))* Pauline Bks. & Media.

Faith First Development Team, creator. Faith First Grade 6. 2006. (Illus.). 336p. per. 12.50 *(978-0-7829-0928-9(0))* RCL Benziger Publishing.

Ficocelli, Elizabeth. Child's Guide to Reconciliation. Blake, Anne Catharine, tr. Blake, Anne Catharine, illus. 2004. 32p. 9.95 *(978-0-8091-6709-8(3)*, 6709-3) Paulist Pr.

Flatt, Lizann. Religion in the Renaissance. 2009. (ENG., Illus.). 32p. (J). (gr. 5-7). *(978-0-7787-4597-6(X))*; (gr. 6-9). pap. *(978-0-7787-4617-1(8))* Crabtree Publishing Co.

Howell, Maria L. Catholicism. 2007. (Religions & Religious Movements Ser.). (ENG.). 224p. (gr. 10-12). lib. bdg. 46.40 *(978-0-7377-3511-6(2)*, Greenhaven Pr., Inc.) Cengage Gale.

Hunt, Jeanne. Celebrating Saints & Seasons: Hundreds of Activities for Catholic Children. 2010. (ENG.). 192p. pap. 12.99 *(978-0-86716-959-1(1))* Franciscan Media.

Hunt, Marigold. A Life of Our Lord for Children. 2003. (Illus.). v, 189p. (J). pap. 14.95 *(978-1-928832-64-5(4))* Sophia Institute Pr.

Keane, Michael. What You Will See Inside a Catholic Church. 2003.Tr. of Lo Que Se Puede Ver Dentro de una Iglesia Catolica. (Illus.). 32p. *(978-2-89507-357-4(0))* Novalis Publishing.

Kolka, Diane & Clarke, Steve. Roman Catholic Christianity. 2011. (Religions to Inspire for KS3 Ser.). (Illus.). 88p. pap. 29.50 *(978-1-4441-2218-3(5))* Hodder Education Group GBR. Dist: Trans-Atlantic Pubns., Inc.

Lynch, Diane M., ed. & compiled by. Between You & Me, God: Prayers by Catholic Kids. Lynch, Diane M., compiled by. 2008. 144p. (J). (gr. 5-8). pap. 9.95 *(978-0-8198-1171-4(8))* Pauline Bks. & Media.

Lynch, Kelly Ann. He Said Yes: The Story of Father Mychal Judge. Oatman, M. Scott, illus. 2007. 32p. (J). (gr. -1-3). 12.95 *(978-0-8091-6740-1(9)*, 6740-1) Paulist Pr.

McEntee, Sean & Breen, Michael, eds. The Columba Lectionary for Masses with Children Year C. 2010. (ENG.). 186p. pap. 44.95 *(978-1-85607-676-0(8))* Columba Pr. IRL. Dist: Dufour Editions, Inc.

Questions for God Series. 2006. (J). 54.95 *(978-0-9779497-0-0(2))* VirTru Powers.

Richards, Virginia Helen & Halpin, D. Thomas, illus. Blessed Miguel Pro. 2011. (J). pap. 2.95 *(978-0-8198-1192-9(0))* Pauline Bks. & Media.

Sisters of Notre Dame, Chardon, Ohio. God Cares for Us: Grade 2. 2008. (Christ Our Life 2009 Ser.). (ENG.). 222p. (gr. 1-8). pap., stu. ed. 15.20 *(978-0-8294-2407-2(5))* Loyola Pr.

—We Believe: Grade 3. 2008. (Christ Our Life 2009 Ser.). (ENG.). 252p. (gr. 1-8). pap., stu. ed. 15.20 *(978-0-8294-2410-2(5))* Loyola Pr.

Skinner, Christine Way. Jesus Invites Me to the Feast: My First Eucharist Journal. 2011. (J). *(978-0-7648-1998-8(4))* Liguori Pubns.

Spinner, Stephanie. Who Is Pope Francis? Putra, Dede, illus. 2017. (Who Was? Ser.). (ENG.). 112p. (J). (gr. 3-7). 5.99 ***(978-0-451-53336-4(4))***; lib. bdg. 15.99 ***(978-0-451-53338-8(0))*** Penguin Young Readers Group. (Penguin Workshop).

Stotts, Stuart. Father Groppi: Marching for Civil Rights. 2013. (Badger Biographies Ser.). (ENG., Illus.). 160p. (J). pap. 12.95 *(978-0-87020-575-0(7))* Wisconsin Historical Society.

Synder, Bernadette. 131 Fun-Damental Facts for Catholic Kids: Liturgy, Litanies, Rituals, Rosaries, Symbols, Sacraments & Sacred Scripture. Sharp, Chris, illus. 2006. (Liguori's Fun Facts Ser.). 144p. (J). (gr. 3-7). per. 12.99 *(978-0-7648-1502-7(4))* Liguori Pubns.

Vecchini, Silvia. The Beatitudes Explained. Vincenti, Antonio, illus. 2017. (J). pap. ***(978-0-8198-1238-4(2))*** Pauline Bks. & Media.

Walsh, Alison. Hugh O'Flaherty: His Wartime Adventures. 2011. (ENG., Illus.). 114p. (J). pap. 4.99 *(978-1-84889-058-9(3))* Collins Pr., The IRL. Dist: Vearsa.

White, Bender Richardson, et al. Catholicism & Orthodox Christianity. 3rd rev. ed. 2009. (World Religions Ser.). (Illus.). 144p. (gr. 6-12). 40.00 *(978-1-60413-106-2(3)*, Chelsea Hse.) Facts On File, Inc.

William H. Sadlier, Inc Staff, contrib. by. We Believe & Pray: Prayers & Practices for Young Catholics. 2008. 64p. (J). pap. *(978-0-8215-5700-6(9))* Sadlier, William H. Inc.

Windeatt, Mary F. Pauline Jaricot: Foundress of the Living Rosary & the Society for the Propagation of the Faith. Grout, Paul A., illus. 2009. (ENG.). 256p. (J). (gr. 3-9). reprint ed. pap. 15.95 *(978-0-89555-425-3(9))* TAN Bks.

With Jesus Always. 2006. (Illus.). 29p. (J). pap. *(978-0-8215-5729-7(7))* Sadlier, William H. Inc.

Wood Lake Books Staff & Novalis Staff. Your Child's Baptism: Roman Catholic. Date not set. 16p. (Orig.). (J). pap. 2.50 *(978-2-89088-669-8(7))* Logos Productions, Inc.

Worth, Richard. Pope Francis: The People's Pope. 2016. (Influential Latinos Ser.). (ENG., Illus.). 128p. (J). (gr. 7-8). 37.27 *(978-0-7660-7328-9(9))* Enslow Pubs., Inc.

CATHOLIC CHURCH—DICTIONARIES

Alampi, Janet L. Look It Up! Over 600 Definitions for Catholic Kids & Their Parents & Teachers. 2008. (Illus.). 87p. (J). pap. *(978-0-8198-4523-8(X))* Pauline Bks. & Media.

The Catholic Connections Handbook for Middle Schoolers, Second Edition. rev. ed. 2014. (ENG.). (gr. 5-8). pap. 24.95 *(978-1-59982-331-7(4))* St. Mary's Pr. of MN.

Hunt, Marigold. St. Patrick's Summer: A Children's Adventure Catechism. 2006. (Illus.). 279p. (J). (gr. 3-7). per. *(978-1-928832-92-8(X))* Sophia Institute Pr.

CATHOLIC CHURCH—DOCTRINES

Ascension Press, creator. Theology of the Body for Teens Student Workbook: Discovering God's Plan for Love & Life. 2006. (Illus.). 210p. per. 14.95 *(978-1-932927-86-3(7))* Ascension Pr.

Berlatsky, Noah. The Catholic Church. 2010. (Opposing Viewpoints Ser.). (ENG.). 240p. 42.95 *(978-0-7377-5104-8(5))*; 224p. (gr. 10-12). pap. 33.80 *(978-0-7377-5105-5(3))* Cengage Gale. (Greenhaven Pr., Inc.).

Claussen, Janet, et al. The Catholic Connections Handbook for Middle Schoolers. 2009. (Illus.). 552p. (YA). (gr. 5-9). pap. 20.95 *(978-0-88489-994-5(2))* St. Mary's Pr. of MN.

Donaghy, Thomas J. New Catholic Children's Bible. 2006. (Illus.). 214p. (J). (gr. -1). 11.95 *(978-0-89942-644-0(1))* Catholic Bk. Publishing Corp.

Ellis, Colette. Credo: I Believe. Avakoff, Caroline, ed. Pelicano, Christopher J., illus. 2009. (Faith & Life Ser.). 121p. (J). pap. 7.95 *(978-0-89870-898-1(2))* Ignatius Pr.

Jenkins, Diana R. Goodness Graces! Ten Short Stories about the Sacraments. 2010. (J). (gr. 3-6). pap. 7.95 *(978-0-8198-3110-1(7))* Pauline Bks. & Media.

Knowing Our Catholic Faith: 26 Lessons. 2004. *(978-0-8294-1129-4(1))*; Vol. 2. *(978-0-8294-1130-0(5))*; Vol. 3. *(978-0-8294-1131-7(3))* Loyola Pr.

Knowing Our Catholic Faith: 32 Lessons. 2004. Vol. 4. *(978-0-8294-1132-4(1))* Vol. 5. *(978-0-8294-1134-8(8))* Vol. 6. *(978-0-8294-1135-5(6))* Loyola Pr.

Knowing Our Catholic Faith: 38 Lessons. 2004. Vol. 7. *(978-0-8294-1136-2(4))* Vol. 8. *(978-0-8294-1137-9(2))* Loyola Pr.

Knowing Our Catholic Faith: Complete Set, 8 vols. 2004. *(978-0-8294-1508-7(4))* Loyola Pr.

Knowlton, Laurie Lazzaro, et al. Catholic Book of Bible Stories, 1 vol. Ettlinger, Doris, illus. 2004. (ENG.). 224p. (J). 16.99 *(978-0-310-70505-5(3))* Zonderkidz.

Lockman, Vic. Catechism for Young Children Coloring Book. Lockman, Vic, illus. 2003. (Illus.). 24p. (J). (gr. -1-3). *(978-0-936175-41-6(9))* Lockman, Vic.

Rabideau, Lacy. A Picture Book of the Mass: Illustrated by the Masters. 2012. (ENG.). pap. *(978-1-4675-2533-6(2))* Independent Pub.

Vecchini, Silvia. The 10 Commandments Explained. Vincenti, Antonio, illus. 2015. (J). 6.95 *(978-0-8198-7523-5(6))* Pauline Bks. & Media.

Vecchini, Silvia & Daughters of St. Paul Staff. The Creed Explained. Vincenti, Antonio, illus. 2015. (J). 6.95 *(978-0-8198-7519-8(8))* Pauline Bks. & Media.

Wright, Melissa & Curelli, Augusta. My Bible: The Story of God's Love. Curreli, Augusta, illus. 2004. 236p. (J). 24.95 *(978-0-8198-4834-5(4)*, 332-223) Pauline Bks. & Media.

CATHOLIC CHURCH—FICTION

Casanova, Mary. Curse of a Winter Moon. 2014. (ENG.). 144p. pap. 9.95 *(978-0-8166-9207-1(6))* Univ. of Minnesota Pr.

Durango, Julia. The Walls of Cartagena. Pohrt, Tom, illus. 2008. (ENG.). 160p. (J). (gr. 3-7). 15.99 *(978-1-4169-4102-6(9)*, Simon & Schuster Bks. For Young Readers) Simon & Schuster Bks. For Young Readers.

Hurley, Tonya. The Blessed. Watkins, Abbey, illus. 2012. (Blessed Ser.). (ENG.). 416p. (YA). (gr. 9). 17.99 *(978-1-4424-2951-2(8)*, Simon & Schuster Bks. For Young Readers) Simon & Schuster Bks. For Young Readers.

—Passionaries. (Blessed Ser.). (ENG., Illus.). 368p. (YA). (gr. 9). 2015. pap. 12.99 *(978-1-4424-2955-0(0))* 2014. 17.99 *(978-1-4424-2954-3(2))* Simon & Schuster Bks. For Young Readers. (Simon & Schuster Bks. For Young Readers).

—Precious Blood. Watkins, Abbey, illus. 2013. (Blessed Ser.). (ENG.). 432p. (YA). (gr. 9). pap. 9.99 *(978-1-4424-2952-9(6)*, Simon & Schuster Bks. For Young Readers) Simon & Schuster Bks. For Young Readers.

Jacobson, Jennifer Richard. Stained. 2005. (ENG., Illus.). 208p. (YA). (gr. 8-18). 16.95 *(978-0-689-86745-3(X)*, Atheneum/Richard Jackson Bks.) Simon & Schuster Children's Publishing.

Littman, Sarah Darer. Confessions of a Closet Catholic. 2006. (ENG.). 208p. (J). (gr. 5-18). reprint ed. 7.99 *(978-0-14-240597-0(3)*, Puffin Books) Penguin Young Readers Group.

Nobisso, Josephine. El Peso de Una Misa: Un Relato de fe. Szegedi, Katalin, illus. 2003. Orig. Title: The Weight of a Mass a Tale of Faith. (SPA.). 32p. (J). (gr. k-2). pap. 9.95 *(978-0-940112-17-9(5))* Gingerbread Hse.

—El Peso de Una Misa: Un Relato de Fe. Szegedi, Katalin, illus. 2003. Orig. Title: The Weight of a Mass a Tale of Faith. (SPA.). 32p. (J). (gr. k-2). 17.95 *(978-0-940112-15-5(9))* Gingerbread Hse.

Perego, Jeanne. Joseph & Chico: The Life of Pope Benedict XVI as Told by a Cat. Matt, Andrew, tr. from ITA. Casagrande, Donata Dal Molin, illus. 2008. 36p. (J). (gr. k-7). 17.95 *(978-1-58617-252-7(2))* Ignatius Pr.

Riordan, Robert. Medicine for Wildcat: A Story of the Friendship between a Menominee Indian & Frontier Priest Samuel Mazzuchelli. 2006. (Illus.). 132p. (YA). per. 14.95 *(978-0-9774934-0-1(7))* Sinsinawa Dominicans, Inc.

CATHOLIC CHURCH—HISTORY

Bartolotta, Kenneth L. The Inquisition: The Quest for Absolute Religious Power. 2017. (World History Ser.). 104p. (YA). (gr. 7-7). lib. bdg. 39.90 ***(978-1-5345-6049-9(1)***, Lucent Pr.) Greenhaven Publishing LLC.

Faith Handed On. 2004. (Effective Dre Ser.). pap. *(978-0-8294-1497-4(5))* Loyola Pr.

Hill, Mary Lea. The Church Rocks! A History of the Catholic Church for Kids & Their Parents & Teachers. 2017. (J). pap. ***(978-0-8198-1657-3(4))*** Pauline Bks. & Media.

Kramer, Barbara. National Geographic Readers: Pope Francis. 2015. (Readers Bios Ser.). (ENG.). 32p. (J). (gr. -1-1). pap. 3.99 *(978-1-4263-2253-2(4)*, National Geographic Children's Bks.) National Geographic Society.

Reformation DBA. 2003. spiral bd. 16.95 *(978-1-56004-167-2(6))* Social Studies Schl. Service.

Stanton, Sue. Great Women of Faith: Inspiration for Action. 2003. (Illus.). 128p. (J). 12.95 *(978-0-8091-4123-4(X)*, 4123-x) Paulist Pr.

Welborn, Amy. Loyola Kids Book of Heroes: Stories of Catholic Heroes & Saints Throughout History. Konstantinov, Vitali, illus. 2003. (ENG.). 208p. (J). (gr. 3-7). 17.95 *(978-0-8294-1584-1(X))* Loyola Pr.

CATHOLIC LITERATURE

John Paul II, Pope, pseud. My Dear Young Friends: Pope John Paul II Speaks to Youth on Life, Love, & Courage. Vitek, John, ed. 2003. (Illus.). 144p. (YA). pap., pap. 9.95 *(978-0-88489-748-4(6))* St. Mary's Pr. of MN.

Singer-Towns, Brian, ed. Catholic Youth Bible: Pray It, Study It, Live It. rev. ed. 2003. (Illus.). 1576p. (YA). (gr. 7-12). 37.95 *(978-0-88489-667-8(6))*; pap. 27.95 *(978-0-88489-489-6(4))* St. Mary's Pr. of MN.

CATLIN, GEORGE, 1796-1872

Reich, Susanna. Painting the Wild Frontier: The Art & Adventures of George Catlin. 2008. (ENG., Illus.). 176p. (J). (gr. 5-7). 22.00 *(978-0-618-71470-4(7))* Houghton Mifflin Harcourt Publishing Co.

Worth, Richard. George Catlin: Painter of Indian Life. 2009. (ENG., Illus.). 80p. (C). (gr. 6-18). lib. bdg. 158.00 *(978-0-7656-8152-2(8)*, Y182314) Routledge.

CATS

ABDO Publishing Company Staff. Cat Craze Set 2, 1 vol. 2011. (Cat Craze Set 2 Ser.). (ENG., Illus.). 24p. 153.90 *(978-1-61714-828-6(8)*, Super SandCastle) ABDO Publishing Co.

—Cats Set 2 *2015. 2014. (Cats Set 2 Ser.: 6). (ENG.). 24p. (gr. 8-12). lib. bdg. 153.90 *(978-1-62403-320-9(2)*, Checkerboard Library) ABDO Publishing Co.

Adelman, Beth. Cool Cats. 2007. (Reading Rocks! Ser.). (ENG., Illus.). 32p. (J). (gr. 2-5). 28.50 *(978-1-59296-865-7(1)*, 200742) Child's World, Inc., The.

Alderton, David. How to Look after Your Pet Cat: A Practical Guide to Caring for Your Pet, in Step-By-Step Photographs. 2013. (ENG., Illus.). 20p. (J). (gr. -1-12). 8.99 *(978-1-84322-732-8(0)*, Armadillo) Anness Publishing GBR. Dist: National Bk. Network.

All about Cats. 2010. (All about Cats Ser.). (ENG.). 32p. (gr. 3-4). lib. bdg. 251.91 *(978-1-4296-5458-6(9)*, Edge Bks.) Capstone Press of Coughlan Cos.

Alley Cats. (Sails Literacy Ser.). 24p. (gr. 2-18). 27.00 *(978-0-7635-6996-9(8))*;Pack. 57.00 *(978-0-7578-3211-6(3))* Rigby Education.

Anonymous & Laughing Elephant Staff. Kitty's A. B. C. Shape Book. 2011. (Shape Bks.). (ENG., Illus.). 16p. (J). (gr. -1-k). pap. 9.95 *(978-1-59583-448-5(6)*, Green Tiger Pr.) Laughing Elephant.

Armadillo. Kittens. 2015. (ENG., Illus.). 24p. bds. 6.99 *(978-1-86147-645-6(0)*, Armadillo) Anness Publishing GBR. Dist: National Bk. Network.

Armstrong, Yvette. My Curious Kitty. 2010. 20p. 10.49 *(978-1-4520-1741-9(7))* AuthorHouse.

Bacon, Carly J. Cat Care: Nutrition, Exercise, Grooming, & More. 2016. (Cats Rule! Ser.). (ENG., Illus.). 32p. (gr. 3-4). lib. bdg. 27.99 *(978-1-4914-8399-2(7)*, Snap Bks.) Capstone Press of Coughlan Cos.

Bacon, Carly J. & Webster, Maureen. Cat Rule! 2016. (Cats Rule! Ser.). (ENG.). 32p. (gr. 3-4). 111.96 *(978-1-4914-8419-7(5)*, Snap Bks.) Capstone Press of Coughlan Cos.

Barnes, Julia. Pet Cats. 2006. (Pet Pals Ser.). (Illus.). 32p. (gr. 2-6). lib. bdg. 26.00 *(978-0-8368-6776-3(9)*, Gareth Stevens Learning Library) Stevens, Gareth Publishing LLLP.

Barnes, L. Cats & Kittens: Learning the Hard C & K Sound. 2009. (PowerPhonics Ser.). 24p. (gr. 1-1). 39.90 *(978-1-60851-437-3(4)*, PowerKids Pr.) Rosen Publishing Group, Inc., The.

Batten, Mary. Wild Cats. Rowe, Michael Langham, illus. 2004. (Step into Reading Ser.). (ENG.). 48p. (J). (gr. 2-4). pap. 3.99 *(978-0-375-82551-4(7)*, Random Hse. Bks. for Young Readers) Random Hse. Children's Bks.

Baumbusch, Brigitte. Cats in Art. 2005. (What Makes a Masterpiece? Ser.). (Illus.). 32p. (gr. 1-4). lib. bdg. 23.00 *(978-0-8368-4444-3(0)*, Gareth Stevens Learning Library) Stevens, Gareth Publishing LLLP.

Bearce, Stephanie. Care for a Kitten. 2009. (How to Convince Your Parents You Can ... Ser.). 32p. (J). (gr. 1-4). 25.70 *(978-1-58415-803-5(4))* Mitchell Lane Pubs., Inc.

Beck, Isabel L., et al. Trophies Kindergarten: Little Cat, Big Cat. 2003. (Trophies Ser.). (gr. k-6). 13.80 *(978-0-15-329552-2(X))* Harcourt Schl. Pubs.

Bendon Publishing International Staff. Hello Kitty Sticker W/Poster Book #1705. 2004. 3.99 *(978-1-59394-355-4(5))* Bendon, Inc.

Bicknell, Joanna. Touch & Feel Noisy Kitten. 2006. (Touch & Feel Noisy Ser.). (Illus.). 12p. (gr. -1). per., bds. *(978-1-84610-284-4(7))* Make Believe Ideas.

Big Cats: An Amazing Discovery Book. 2009. (Amazing Animal Discovery Bks.). (ENG.). 12p. (J). (gr. -1). 5.95 *(978-1-58117-847-0(6)*, Intervisual/Piggy Toes) Bendon, Inc.

Birchall, Mark. Copy Cat. 2010. (Child's Play Library). (ENG., Illus.). 32p. (J). (gr. 1-2). *(978-1-84643-367-2(3))* Child's Play International Ltd.

Bistline, Lesley. Hairballs in the Morning. 2008. 56p. pap. 9.95 *(978-1-4327-2007-0(4))* Outskirts Pr., Inc.

Bledsoe, Michele. Kitty Treats Cookbook. Rupert, Chris et al, illus. 2010. (ENG.). 15p. (gr. 6). bds. 10.95 *(978-0-9753883-8-9(X))* Come & Get It Publishing.

Bodden, Valerie. Cats. (My First Look At Ser.). 24p. (J). 2011. (ENG.). (gr. 1-17). pap. 7.99 *(978-1-926722-39-9(6)*, Creative Paperbacks) 2006. (Illus.). (gr. -1-3). lib. bdg. 15.95 *(978-1-58341-457-6(6)*, Creative Education) Creative Co., The.

Borgert-Spaniol, Megan. Bobcats. 2014. (Backyard Wildlife Ser.). (ENG., Illus.). 24p. (J). (gr. k-3). lib. bdg. 25.95 *(978-1-62617-062-9(2)*, Blastoff! Readers) Bellwether Media.

Bozzo, Linda. Mi Primer Gato. 2008. (My First Pet Bilingual Library from the American Humane Association Ser.).Tr. of My First Cat. (ENG & SPA., Illus.). 32p. (J). (gr. 1-3). lib. bdg. 23.94 *(978-0-7660-3033-6(4))* Enslow Pubs., Inc.

—My First Cat. 2007. (My First Pet Library from the American Humane Association Ser.). (Illus.). 32p. (J). (gr. 1-2). lib. bdg. 23.94 *(978-0-7660-2750-3(3)*, Enslow Elementary) Enslow Pubs., Inc.

Brecke, Nicole & Stockland, Patricia M. Cats You Can Draw. Brecke, Nicole, illus. 2009. (Ready, Set, Draw! Ser.). (ENG., Illus.). 32p. (gr. 2-4). lib. bdg. 25.26 *(978-0-7613-4161-1(7)*, Millbrook Pr.) Lerner Publishing Group.

Brett, Flora. A Cat's View of the World. 2015. (Pet Perspectives Ser.). (ENG., Illus.). 24p. (gr. 1-2). lib. bdg. 25.32 *(978-1-4914-5050-5(9)*, First Facts) Capstone Press of Coughlan Cos.

Britton, Tamara L. Abyssinian Cats, 1 vol. 2011. (Cats Set 1 *2011 Ser.). (ENG.). 24p. (J). (gr. 2-5). 25.65 *(978-1-61613-397-9(X))* ABDO Publishing Co.

—Maine Coon Cats, 1 vol. 2011. (Cats Set 1 *2011 Ser.). (ENG., Illus.). 24p. 25.65 *(978-1-61613-398-6(8)*, Checkerboard Library) ABDO Publishing Co.

—Manx Cats, 1 vol. 2011. (Cats Set 1 *2011 Ser.). (ENG., Illus.). 24p. 25.65 *(978-1-61613-399-3(6)*, Checkerboard Library) ABDO Publishing Co.

—Persian Cats, 1 vol. 2011. (Cats Set 1 *2011 Ser.). (ENG.). 24p. 25.65 *(978-1-61613-400-6(3)*, Checkerboard Library) ABDO Publishing Co.

—Siamese Cats, 1 vol. 2011. (Cats Set 1 *2011 Ser.). (ENG.). 24p. 25.65 *(978-1-61613-401-3(1)*, Checkerboard Library) ABDO Publishing Co.

—Tabby Cats, 1 vol. 2011. (Cats Set 1 *2011 Ser.). (ENG.). 24p. 25.65 *(978-1-61613-402-0(X)*, Checkerboard Library) ABDO Publishing Co.

Bronson, Wilfrid S., illus. Cats. 2008. 84p. (J). per. 18.95 *(978-0-86534-645-1(3))* Sunstone Pr.

Brown, Domini. Egyptian Maus. 2016. (Cool Cats Ser.). (ENG., Illus.). 24p. (J). (gr. k-3). lib. bdg. 25.95 *(978-1-62617-310-1(9)*, Blastoff! Readers) Bellwether Media.

—Exotics. 2016. (Cool Cats Ser.). (ENG., Illus.). 24p. (J). (gr. k-3). lib. bdg. 25.95 *(978-1-62617-311-8(7)*, Blastoff! Readers) Bellwether Media.

—Norwegian Forest Cats. 2016. (Cool Cats Ser.). (ENG., Illus.). 24p. (J). (gr. k-3). 25.95 *(978-1-62617-397-2(4)*, Blastoff! Readers) Bellwether Media.

—Orientals. 2016. (Cool Cats Ser.). (ENG., Illus.). 24p. (J). (gr. k-3). lib. bdg. 25.95 *(978-1-62617-313-2(3)*, Blastoff! Readers) Bellwether Media.

—Russian Blues. 2016. (Cool Cats Ser.). (ENG., Illus.). 24p. (J). (gr. k-3). 25.95 *(978-1-62617-398-9(2)*, Blastoff! Readers) Bellwether Media.

Brydon, Irene M. Fluffy's Story. 2009. (Illus.). 56p. pap. *(978-1-84748-492-5(1))* Athena Pr.

Bugbird, Tim. Charm Books Kittens. 2007. (Illus.). 64p. (J). (gr. 4-7). *(978-1-84610-648-4(6))* Make Believe Ideas.

—Charm Books Kittens Poly Bag. 2007. (Illus.). 64p. (J). (gr. -1-3). *(978-1-84610-705-4(9))* Make Believe Ideas.

—Charm Books Kittens/Puppies Clip Strip. 2007. (Illus.). 64p. (J). (gr. -1-3). *(978-1-84610-702-3(4))* Make Believe Ideas.

—Charm Books Kittens/Puppies Pos Rack. 2007. (Illus.). 64p. (J). (gr. -1-3). *(978-1-84610-706-1(7))* Make Believe Ideas.

Calenda, Kristen. Nubian: A True Story about a Very Special Kitty. 2012. 40p. pap. 20.99 *(978-1-4772-1988-1(9))* AuthorHouse.

Capstone Press. Strange but True. 2010. (Strange but True Ser.). (ENG.). 32p. lib. bdg. 101.28 *(978-1-4296-5909-3(2)*, Blazers) Capstone Press of Coughlan Cos.

—Wildcats. 2010. (Wildcats Ser.). (ENG.). 32p. lib. bdg. 143.94 *(978-1-4296-5903-1(3)*, Pebble Plus) Capstone Press of Coughlan Cos.

Carney, Elizabeth. Big Cats: Pictures to Purr about & Info to Make You Roar! 2011. (National Geographic Kids Everything Ser.). (ENG., Illus.). 64p. (J). (gr. 3-7). pap. 12.95 *(978-1-4263-0805-5(1)*, National Geographic Children's Bks.) National Geographic Society.

—Cats vs. Dogs. 2011. (Readers Ser.). (ENG., Illus.). 48p. (J). (gr. 1-4). pap. 3.99 *(978-1-4263-0755-3(1))*; lib. bdg. 13.90 *(978-1-4263-0756-0(X))* National Geographic Society. (National Geographic Children's Bks.).

Carr, Aaron. Bobcats. 2014. (J). *(978-1-4896-2938-8(6))* Weigl Pubs., Inc.

—Cat. 2011. (J). *(978-1-61690-566-8(2))*; *(978-1-61690-920-8(X))* Weigl Pubs., Inc.

—El Gato. 2012. (J). *(978-1-61913-181-1(1))* Weigl Pubs., Inc.

Carrell, Elizabeth. A Cat Named Romeo. 2011. 28p. pap. 12.03 *(978-1-4670-2559-1(3))* AuthorHouse.

Cashford, Brenda. Bobbins Story: The Little Cat That Touched So Many Lives. 2013. (Illus.). 34p. pap. *(978-1-907163-34-0(4))* Coast and Country Productions, Ltd.

Cass, Liz. Ouisa & the Big People. 2012. (ENG., Illus.). 77p. *(978-1-907629-35-8(1))* ShieldCrest.

The Cat: Individual Title-Six Packs. (Chiquilibros Ser.). (gr. k-1). 23.00 *(978-0-7635-0456-4(4))* Rigby Education.

A Cat Book. 2007. 224p. *(978-1-4075-0584-8(X))* Parragon, Inc.

Cat Chat. (Little Book Practice Reader). (J). *(978-0-8136-2066-4(X))* Modern Curriculum Pr.

Cat-Ographies, 6 vols., Set. Incl. Abyssinians: Egyptian Royalty? Oldfield, Dawn Bluemel. (J). lib. bdg. 22.61 *(978-1-61772-145-8(X))*; American Shorthairs: Pioneers. Rudolph, Jessica. (YA). lib. bdg. 22.61 *(978-1-61772-143-4(3))*; Maine Coons: Super Big. White, Nancy. (J). lib. bdg. 22.61 *(978-1-61772-142-7(5))*; Persians: Long-Haired Friends. Markovics, Joyce L. (YA). lib. bdg. 22.61 *(978-1-61772-141-0(7))*; Ragdolls: Alien Cats. Stamper, Judith Bauer. (YA). lib. bdg. 22.61 *(978-1-61772-146-5(8))*; Siamese: Talk to Me! White, Nancy. (J). lib. bdg. 22.61 *(978-1-61772-144-1(1))*; (gr. 2-5). 24p. 2011. Set lib. bdg. 135.66 *(978-1-61772-140-3(9))* Bearport Publishing Co., Inc.

C D

Cats. (Eyes on Nature Ser.). 32p. (J). (gr. 1). pap. *(978-1-882210-52-7(2))* Action Publishing, Inc.

Cats. (Eyes on Nature Ser.). (Illus.). 32p. (J). (gr. 1-18). 7.95 *(978-1-56156-419-4(2))* Kidsbooks, LLC.

Cats. 2007. (Nonfiction Collection). (J). 8.00 *(978-1-60343-030-2(X))* Pioneer Valley Bks.

Cats & Dogs (Gr. PreK-5) 2003. (J). *(978-1-58232-018-2(7))* ECS Learning Systems, Inc.

Cats & Kittens Kid Kit. 2003. (Illus.). 32p. 13.95 *(978-1-58086-526-5(7))* EDC Publishing.

Cats Are Cool. 2013. (Cats Are Cool Ser.). 32p. (J). (gr. k-5). 151.50 *(978-1-4777-1538-3(X))*; pap. 360.00 *(978-1-4777-2696-9(9))*; pap. 60.00 *(978-1-4777-2695-2(0))* Rosen Publishing Group, Inc., The. (PowerKids Pr.).

Chin, Amanda. Pet's Playground: Playing Safe in a Dog-And-Cat World. Feldman, Luke, illus. 2009. 104p. (J). pap. 11.95 *(978-1-58326-115-6(X))* American Animal Hospital Assn. Pr.

Claire Horton-Bussey. Cats, Vol. 12. 2016. (Understanding & Caring for Your Pet Ser.: Vol. 12). (ENG., Illus.). 128p. (J). (gr. 5-8). 25.95 *(978-1-4222-3693-2(5))* Mason Crest.

—Kittens, Vol. 12. 2016. (Understanding & Caring for Your Pet Ser.: Vol. 12). (ENG., Illus.). 128p. (J). (gr. 5-8). 25.95 *(978-1-4222-3700-7(1))* Mason Crest.

Clutton-Brock, Juliet. DK Eyewitness Books: Cat: Cat. 2014. (DK Eyewitness Bks.). (ENG.). 72p. (J). (gr. 3-7). pap. 9.99 *(978-1-4654-2050-3(9))*, DK Children) Dorling Kindersley Publishing, Inc.

Cohn, Scotti. Big Cat, Little Kitty, 1 vol. Detwiler, Susan, illus. 2011. (ENG.). 32p. (J). (gr. -1-3). 16.95 *(978-1-60718-124-8(X))*; pap. 8.95 *(978-1-60718-134-7(7))* Arbordale Publishing.

Colson, Mary. The Truth about Cats: What Cats Do When You're Not Looking. 2017. (Pets Undercover! Ser.). (ENG., Illus.). 32p. (gr. 2-4). lib. bdg. 29.99 *(978-1-4109-8605-4(5)*, Read Me!) Heinemann-Raintree.

Conley, Kate. Cats Set 9. 2015. (Cats Set 9 Ser.: Vol. 6). (ENG.). 24p. (J). (gr. -1-3). lib. bdg. 153.90 *(978-1-62403-809-9(3))* ABDO Publishing Co.

Conley, Kate A. Burmilla Cats, 1 vol. 2016. (ENG., Illus.). 24p. (J). *(978-1-62403-810-5(7))* ABDO Publishing Co.

—Siberian Cats, 1 vol. 2016. (ENG., Illus.). 24p. (J). *(978-1-62403-814-3(X))* ABDO Publishing Co.

—Turkish Van Cats, 1 vol. 2016. (ENG., Illus.). 24p. (J). *(978-1-62403-815-0(8))* ABDO Publishing Co.

Connelly, Claire K. Moxie. Jacobs, Joyce M., illus. 2010. 84p. pap. 10.49 *(978-1-4520-7634-8(0))* AuthorHouse.

Coppendale, Jean. Kitten. 2004. (QEB You & Your Pet Ser.). (Illus.). 32p. (J). lib. bdg. 18.95 *(978-1-59566-050-3(X))* QEB Publishing Inc.

Coulton, Mia. The Cat Wants to Play. Campbell, D. B., illus. 2011. (ENG.). 12p. (J). pap. 5.35 *(978-1-933624-74-7(4))* Maryruth Bks., Inc.

Creese, Sarah. Mad about Perfect Puppies & Cute Kittens. 2009. (Mad About Ser.). (ENG., Illus.). 24p. (J). (gr. -1-3). pap. 3.99 *(978-1-84879-006-3(6))* Make Believe Ideas GBR. Dist: Nelson, Thomas Inc.

Crisp, Marty. Everything Cat: What Kids Really Want to Know about Cats. 2003. (Kids Faqs Ser.). (ENG., Illus.). 64p. (J). (gr. 3-6). pap. 7.95 *(978-1-55971-865-3(X))* Cooper Square Publishing Llc.

Dahlen, Noelle. Spark - Cool Cats Coloring Book. 2015. (Dover Coloring Bks.). (ENG., Illus.). 64p. (J). (gr. 1-4). pap. 5.99 *(978-0-486-80058-5(X))* Dover Pubns., Inc.

Daily, Don. The Twelve Days of Christmas Cats. Daily, Don, illus. 2014. (ENG., Illus.). 40p. (J). 18.95 *(978-1-60433-495-1(9)*, Applesauce Pr.) Cider Mill Pr. Bk. Pubs., LLC.

Dalton, Kippy. Kitten Looks for Mom. 2016. (Spring Forward Ser.). (J). (gr. 2). *(978-1-4900-6016-3(2))* Benchmark Education Co.

Dash, Meredith. Calico Cats, 1 vol. 2014. (Cats Ser.). (ENG.). 24p. (J). (gr. 4-8). lib. bdg. 28.50 *(978-1-62970-008-3(8))* ABDO Publishing Co.

—El Gato Siamés, 1 vol. 2014. (Gatos Ser.). (SPA., Illus.). 24p. (J). (gr. 4-8). lib. bdg. 28.50 *(978-1-62970-307-7(9)*, 1377526) ABDO Publishing Co.

—Maine Coon Cats, 1 vol. 2014. (Cats Ser.). (ENG.). 24p. (J). (gr. 4-8). lib. bdg. 28.50 *(978-1-62970-009-0(6))* ABDO Publishing Co.

—Manx Cats, 1 vol. 2014. (Cats Ser.). (ENG.). 24p. (J). (gr. 4-8). lib. bdg. 28.50 *(978-1-62970-010-6(X))* ABDO Publishing Co.

—Persian Cats, 1 vol. 2014. (Cats Ser.). (ENG.). 24p. (J). (gr. 4-8). lib. bdg. 28.50 *(978-1-62970-011-3(8))* ABDO Publishing Co.

—Scottish Fold Cats, 1 vol. 2014. (Cats Ser.). (ENG.). 24p. (J). (gr. 4-8). lib. bdg. 28.50 *(978-1-62970-012-0(6))* ABDO Publishing Co.

—Siamese Cats, 1 vol. 2014. (Cats Ser.). (ENG.). 24p. (J). (gr. 4-8). lib. bdg. 28.50 *(978-1-62970-013-7(4))* ABDO Publishing Co.

Dewin, Howard, told to. The Dog: Dogs Rule Cats Drool. 2007. (Artist Collection). (Illus.). 31p. pap. *(978-0-545-01196-9(5))* Scholastic, Inc.

Dora Blat's Cat, 6 vols. 8p. (gr. k-1). 21.50 *(978-0-322-02066-5(2))* Wright Group/McGraw-Hill.

Dorling Kindersley Publishing Staff. Baby Touch & Feel: Kittens. 2017. (Baby Touch & Feel Ser.). (ENG.). 14p. (J). (— 1). bds. 5.99 *(978-1-4654-5622-9(8)*, DK Children) Dorling Kindersley Publishing, Inc.

—Cat. 2006. (Ultimate Sticker Bks.). (ENG., Illus.). 16p. (J). (gr. k-4). pap. 6.99 *(978-0-7566-2097-4(X)*, DK Children) Dorling Kindersley Publishing, Inc.

—Pop-Up Peekaboo! - Meow! 2012. (ENG., Illus.). 12p. (J). (gr. -1 — 1). bds. 9.99 *(978-0-7566-9309-1(8)*, DK Children) Dorling Kindersley Publishing, Inc.

—Puppies & Kittens. 2008. (Baby Touch & Feel Ser.). (ENG., Illus.). 14p. (J). (gr. -1 — 1). bds. 5.99 *(978-0-7566-3835-1(6)*, DK Children) Dorling Kindersley Publishing, Inc.

Dorling Kindersley Publishing Staff, creator. Kitten: More Than 60 Reusable Full Colos Stickers. 2006. (Ultimate Sticker Bks.). (ENG., Illus.). 16p. (J). (gr. k-3). pap. 6.99 *(978-0-7566-2101-8(1)*, DK Children) Dorling Kindersley Publishing, Inc.

Doucet, Bob, illus. Cat Craze, 6 vols., Set. Incl. Awesome Abyssinians. Hanson, Anders. 25.65 *(978-1-60453-721-5(3))*; Hip Himalayans. Hengel, Katherine. 25.65 *(978-1-60453-722-2(1))*; Marvelous Maine Coons. Scheunemann, Pam. 25.65 *(978-1-60453-723-9(X))*; Popular Persians. Scheunemann, Pam. 25.65 *(978-1-60453-724-6(8))*; Sleek Siamese. Hanson, Anders. 25.65 *(978-1-60453-725-3(6))*; Smooth Sphynx. Hengel, Katherine. 25.65 *(978-1-60453-726-0(4))*; (J). (gr. k-3). (Cat Craze Ser.). (Illus.). 24p. 2009. 153.90 *(978-1-60453-720-8(5)*, Super SandCastle) ABDO Publishing Co.

Elig, Jennifer. A Cat's Life: La Vida de un Gato. 2012. 20p. pap. 10.95 *(978-1-4497-4469-4(9)*, WestBow Pr.) Author Solutions, Inc.

Elora, Grace. Kittens. 2011. (Cute & Cuddly: Baby Animals Ser.). (Illus.). 24p. (gr. k-2). 69.20 *(978-1-4339-6151-9(2))*; (J). lib. bdg. 22.60 *(978-1-4339-4511-3(8))* Stevens, Gareth Publishing LLLP.

Endres, Hollie. Cats. 2007. (Farm Animals Ser.). (ENG., Illus.). 24p. (J). (gr. k-3). lib. bdg. 25.95 *(978-1-60014-111-9(0))* Bellwether Media.

Fact Atlas: Cats. 2009. (FACT ATLAS Ser.). 72p. (J). 14.95 *(978-0-8437-1851-5(X))* Hammond World Atlas Corp.

Fahiner, Paul. Dog & Cat. Chambliss, Maxie, illus. 2004. (My First Reader Ser.). (ENG.). 32p. (J). (gr. k-1). pap. 3.95 *(978-0-516-24626-0(7)*, Children's Pr.) Scholastic Library Publishing.

Felix, Rebecca. Abyssinians. 2015. (Cool Cats Ser.). (ENG., Illus.). 24p. (J). (gr. k-3). lib. bdg. 25.95 *(978-1-62617-229-6(3)*, Blastoff! Readers) Bellwether Media.

—Maine Coons. 2015. (Cool Cats Ser.). (ENG., Illus.). 24p. (J). (gr. k-3). lib. bdg. 25.95 *(978-1-62617-232-6(3)*, Blastoff! Readers) Bellwether Media.

—Persians. 2015. (Cool Cats Ser.). (ENG., Illus.). 24p. (J). (gr. k-3). lib. bdg. 25.95 *(978-1-62617-233-3(1)*, Blastoff! Readers) Bellwether Media.

—Ragdolls. 2015. (Cool Cats Ser.). (ENG., Illus.). 24p. (J). (gr. k-3). lib. bdg. 25.95 *(978-1-62617-234-0(X)*, Blastoff! Readers) Bellwether Media.

—Siamese. 2015. (Cool Cats Ser.). (ENG., Illus.). 24p. (J). (gr. k-3). lib. bdg. 25.95 *(978-1-62617-235-7(8)*, Blastoff! Readers) Bellwether Media.

—Sphynx. 2015. (Cool Cats Ser.). (ENG., Illus.). 24p. (J). (gr. k-3). lib. bdg. 25.95 *(978-1-62617-236-4(6)*, Blastoff! Readers) Bellwether Media.

Finne, Stephanie. American Curl Cats, 1 vol. 2014. (Cats Set 2 Ser.). (ENG.). 24p. (gr. 8-12). lib. bdg. 25.65 *(978-1-62403-321-6(0)*, Checkerboard Library) ABDO Publishing Co.

—Balinese Cats, 1 vol. 2014. (Cats Set 2 Ser.). (ENG.). 24p. (gr. 8-12). lib. bdg. 25.65 *(978-1-62403-322-3(9)*, Checkerboard Library) ABDO Publishing Co.

—Devon Rex Cats, 1 vol. 2014. (Cats Set 2 Ser.). (ENG.). 24p. (gr. 8-12). lib. bdg. 25.65 *(978-1-62403-323-0(7)*, Checkerboard Library) ABDO Publishing Co.

—Exotic Shorthair Cats, 1 vol. 2014. (Cats Set 2 Ser.). (ENG.). 24p. (gr. 8-12). lib. bdg. 25.65 *(978-1-62403-324-7(5)*, Checkerboard Library) ABDO Publishing Co.

—Oriental Shorthair Cats, 1 vol. 2014. (Cats Set 2 Ser.). (ENG., Illus.). 24p. (J). (gr. 8-12). lib. bdg. 25.65 *(978-1-62403-325-4(3)*, Checkerboard Library) ABDO Publishing Co.

—Russian Blue Cats, 1 vol. 2014. (Cats Set 2 Ser.). (ENG.). 24p. (gr. 8-12). lib. bdg. 25.65 *(978-1-62403-326-1(1)*, Checkerboard Library) ABDO Publishing Co.

Flanagan, Alice K. Cats: The Sound of Short A. 2015. (Long & Short Vowels Ser.). (ENG.). 24p. (J). (gr. -1-2). 25.64 *(978-1-63407-020-1(8)*, 208855) Child's World, Inc., The.

Fleury, Rick & Staehr, Linda. Rainbows for Buckeroo. 2013. 24p. pap. 10.95 *(978-1-4497-8775-2(4)*, WestBow Pr.) Author Solutions, Inc.

Fordham, Kate. Me & My Kitten. 2006. (Illus.). 80p. (J). *(978-0-439-89293-3(7))* Scholastic, Inc.

Franklin, Carolyn. Big Cats. 2009. (How to Draw Ser.). (Illus.). 32p. (J). lib. bdg. 26.50 *(978-1-4358-2516-1(0)*, PowerKids Pr.) Rosen Publishing Group, Inc., The.

Fraser, Tara Lynn. My Kitty. 2011. 16p. 10.99 *(978-1-4269-4865-7(4))* Trafford Publishing.

Frattini, Stephane. Face-to-Face with the Cat. Klein, Jean-Louis & Hubert, Marie-Luce, illus. 2004. (Face to Face Ser.). 28p. (J). 9.95 *(978-1-57091-454-6(0))* Charlesbridge Publishing, Inc.

Furstinger, Nancy. American Shorthair Cats, 1 vol. 2006. (Cats Set 4 Ser.). (ENG., Illus.). 24p. (gr. k-6). 25.65 *(978-1-59679-264-7(7)*, Checkerboard Library) ABDO Publishing Co.

—American Shorthair Cats. 2014. (Domestic Cats Ser.). (ENG.). 24p. (J). (gr. 2-5). 28.50 *(978-1-62687-381-0(X)*, 207114) Child's World, Inc., The.

—American Shorthair Cats. 2016. (J). ***(978-1-4896-5620-9(0))*** Weigl Pubs., Inc.

—Calico Cats, 1 vol. 2006. (Cats Set 4 Ser.). (ENG., Illus.). 24p. (gr. k-6). 25.65 *(978-1-59679-265-4(5)*, Checkerboard Library) ABDO Publishing Co.

—Himalayan Cats, 1 vol. 2006. (Cats Set 4 Ser.). (ENG., Illus.). 24p. (gr. k-6). 25.65 *(978-1-59679-266-1(3)*, Checkerboard Library) ABDO Publishing Co.

—Maine Coon Cats. 2014. (Domestic Cats Ser.). (ENG.). 24p. (J). (gr. 2-5). 28.50 *(978-1-62687-382-7(8)*, 207115) Child's World, Inc., The.

—Maine Coon Cats. 2016. (J). ***(978-1-4896-5623-0(5))*** Weigl Pubs., Inc.

—Norwegian Forest Cats, 1 vol. 2006. (Cats Set 4 Ser.). (ENG., Illus.). 24p. (gr. k-6). 25.65 *(978-1-59679-267-8(1)*, Checkerboard Library) ABDO Publishing Co.

—Siamese Cats. 2014. (Domestic Cats Ser.). (ENG.). 24p. (J). (gr. 2-5). 28.50 *(978-1-62687-387-2(9)*, 207119) Child's World, Inc., The.

—Siamese Cats. 2016. (J). ***(978-1-4896-5635-3(9))*** Weigl Pubs., Inc.

—Somali Cats, 1 vol. 2006. (Cats Set 4 Ser.). (ENG., Illus.). 24p. (gr. k-6). 25.65 *(978-1-59679-268-5(X)*, Checkerboard Library) ABDO Publishing Co.

—Sphynx Cats, 1 vol. 2006. (Cats Set 4 Ser.). (ENG., Illus.). 24p. (J). (gr. k-6). 25.65 *(978-1-59679-269-2(8)*, Checkerboard Library) ABDO Publishing Co.

—Sphynx Cats. 2014. (Domestic Cats Ser.). (ENG.). 24p. (J). (gr. 2-5). 28.50 *(978-1-62687-388-9(7)*, 207120) Child's World, Inc., The.

—Sphynx Cats. 2016. (J). ***(978-1-4896-5638-4(3))*** Weigl Pubs., Inc.

Gagne, Tammy. Abyssinian Cats. 2014. (Domestic Cats Ser.). (ENG.). 24p. (J). (gr. 2-5). 28.50 *(978-1-62687-385-8(2)*, 207113) Child's World, Inc., The.

—Abyssinian Cats. 2016. (J). ***(978-1-4896-5617-9(0))*** Weigl Pubs., Inc.

—Manx Cats. 2014. (Domestic Cats Ser.). (ENG.). 24p. (J). (gr. 2-5). 28.50 *(978-1-62687-383-4(6)*, 207116) Child's World, Inc., The.

—Manx Cats. 2016. (J). ***(978-1-4896-5626-1(X))*** Weigl Pubs., Inc.

—Persian Cats. 2014. (Domestic Cats Ser.). (ENG.). 24p. (J). (gr. 2-5). 28.50 *(978-1-62687-384-1(4)*, 207117) Child's World, Inc., The.

—Persian Cats. 2016. (J). ***(978-1-4896-5629-2(4))*** Weigl Pubs., Inc.

—Scottish Fold Cats. 2014. (Domestic Cats Ser.). (ENG.). 24p. (J). (gr. 2-5). 28.50 *(978-1-62687-386-5(0)*, 207118) Child's World, Inc., The.

—Scottish Fold Cats. 2016. (J). ***(978-1-4896-5632-2(4))*** Weigl Pubs., Inc.

Galat, Joan & National Geographic Kids Staff. Cats, Level 1. 2017. (Readers Ser.). (ENG., Illus.). 48p. (J). (-k). pap. 4.99 ***(978-1-4263-2883-1(4)***, National Geographic Children's Bks.) National Geographic Society.

Galeron, Henri & De Bourgoing, Pascale. Cats. Galeron, Henri, illus. 2006. (ENG., Illus.). 32p. (J). (gr. k-3). pap. 11.99 *(978-1-85103-084-2(0))* Moonlight Publishing, Ltd. GBR. Dist: Independent Pubs. Group.

Ganeri, Anita. Kitty's Guide to Caring for Your Cat, 1 vol. Peterson, Rick, illus. 2013. (Pets' Guides). (ENG.). 32p. (gr. 1-3). pap. 8.29 *(978-1-4329-7137-3(9))*; lib. bdg. 27.32 *(978-1-4329-7130-4(1))* Heinemann-Raintree. (Heinemann First Library).

Ganeri, Anita & Heinemann Library Staff. Cats, 1 vol. 2nd ed. 2009. (Pet's Life Ser.). (ENG.). 32p. (gr. 1-3). pap. 7.99 *(978-1-4329-3396-8(5)*, Heinemann First Library) Heinemann-Raintree.

Gardeski, Christina Mia. Cat Care. 2016. (Cats, Cats, Cats Ser.). (ENG., Illus.). 24p. (gr. k-1). lib. bdg. 26.65 *(978-1-5157-0957-2(4)*, Pebble Plus) Capstone Press of Coughlan Cos.

—Cats: Questions & Answers. 2016. (Pet Questions & Answers Ser.). (ENG., Illus.). 24p. (gr. k-1). lib. bdg. 26.65 *(978-1-5157-0356-3(8)*, Pebble Plus) Capstone Press of Coughlan Cos.

—Cats, Cats, Cats. 2016. (Cats, Cats, Cats Ser.). (ENG.). 24p. (gr. k-1). 106.60 *(978-1-5157-1365-4(2)*, Pebble Plus) Capstone Press of Coughlan Cos.

—Long-Haired Cat Breeds. (Illus.). 24p. 2017. (J). pap. *(978-1-5157-1125-4(0))* 2016. (ENG., lib. bdg. 26.65 *(978-1-5157-0959-6(0)*, Pebble Plus) Capstone Press of Coughlan Cos.

—Short-Haired Cat Breeds. 2016. (Cats, Cats, Cats Ser.). (ENG., Illus.). 24p. (gr. k-1). lib. bdg. 26.65 *(978-1-5157-0958-9(2)*, Pebble Plus) Capstone Press of Coughlan Cos.

Gatitos: Individual Title Six-Packs. (Literatura 2000 Ser.). (SPA.). (gr. -1-1). 28.00 *(978-0-7635-1195-1(1))* Rigby Education.

Gay, Marie-Louise. Caramba, 1 vol. 2013. (ENG., Illus.). 40p. (J). (-k). 14.95 *(978-1-55498-390-2(8))* Groundwood Bks. CAN. Dist: Publishers Group West (PGW).

Ghigna, Charles. A Carnival of Cats, 1 vol. Bridgeman, Kristi, illus. 2015. (ENG.). 26p. (J). (gr. -1-k). bds. 9.95 *(978-1-4598-0686-3(7))* Orca Bk. Pubs. USA.

Gigi. The Adventures of Simsim: Based on a True Story. Alvarado, Eladia, illus. 2010. 60p. pap. 12.99 *(978-1-4490-6524-9(4))* AuthorHouse.

Glaser, Rebecca. Kittens Pounce. 2017. (Amicus Ink Board Bks.). (ENG., Illus.). 14p. (J). (gr. -1 — 1). bds. 7.99 ***(978-1-68152-197-8(0))*** Amicus.

Goecke, Michael P. Scimitar Cat, 1 vol. 2003. (Prehistoric Animals Set II Ser.). (ENG.). 24p. (gr. k-4). 25.65 *(978-1-57765-977-8(5)*, Buddy Bks.) ABDO Publishing Co.

Goodbody, Slim & Burstein, John. Cats. McGinnis, Ben, illus. 2008. (Slim Goodbody's Inside Guide to Pets Ser.). 32p. (gr. 2-6). lib. bdg. 26.00 *(978-0-8368-8954-3(1)*, Gareth Stevens Learning Library) Stevens, Gareth Publishing LLLP.

Gordon, Emily. The Kitty Book. Cagle, Terry R., illus. 2011. 32p. (J). 14.95 *(978-1-930076-12-9(6)*, New Leaf Bks.) WigWam Publishing Co.

Graubart, Norman D. Mi Gato / My Cat, 1 vol., 1. 2014. (¡Las Mascotas Son Geniales! / Pets Are Awesome! Ser.). (SPA & BYN.). 24p. (J). (gr. k-2). 23.60 *(978-1-4777-3304-2(3)*, PowerKids Pr.) Rosen Publishing Group, Inc., The.

—My Cat, 1 vol., 1. 2014. (Pets Are Awesome! Ser.). (ENG.). 24p. (J). (gr. k-2). 23.60 *(978-1-4777-2865-9(1)*, PowerKids Pr.) Rosen Publishing Group, Inc., The.

Grimm, Hannelore. Kittens: Keeping & Caring for Your Pet. 2013. (Keeping & Caring for Your Pet Ser.). 72p. (J). lib. bdg. 29.27 *(978-0-7660-4186-8(7))*; (gr. 6-12). pap. 8.95 *(978-1-4644-0303-3(1))* Enslow Pubs., Inc.

Grumpy Cat, Grumpy. Grumpy Cat Coloring Book. 2014. (ENG.). 64p. (J). (gr. 6-12). pap. 5.99 *(978-0-486-79163-0(7))* Dover Pubns., Inc.

—Grumpy Cat Stickers. 2014. (ENG.). 4p. (J). (gr. k-3). pap. 1.99 *(978-0-486-79164-7(5))* Dover Pubns., Inc.

—Grumpy Cat Tattoos. 2014. (ENG.). 2p. (J). (gr. 1-4). pap. 1.99 *(978-0-486-79165-4(3))* Dover Pubns., Inc.

Guillain, Charlotte. Cats. Elsom, Clare, illus. 2013. (Animal Family Albums Ser.). (ENG.). 32p. (gr. 2-4). pap. 8.29 *(978-1-4109-4940-0(0))*; 30.65 *(978-1-4109-4935-6(4))* Heinemann-Raintree. (Raintree Perspectives).

Gunzi, Christiane. Furry Kittens. 2005. (Feels Real Bks.). (ENG., Illus.). 10p. (J). bds. 6.99 *(978-0-7641-5854-4(6))* Barron's Educational Series, Inc.

—Let's Count Noisy Kittens. 2015. (ENG., Illus.). 10p. (J). 9.99 *(978-1-905503-19-3(9))* Award Pubns. Ltd. GBR. Dist: Parkwest Pubns., Inc.

Hamilton, S. L. Cats. 2013. (Xtreme Pets Ser.). (Illus.). 32p. (J). (gr. 3-9). lib. bdg. 27.07 *(978-1-61783-971-9(X)*, Abdo & Daughters) ABDO Publishing Co.

Hanson, Anders. Awesome Abyssinians, 1 vol. Doucet, Bob, illus. 2009. (Cat Craze Ser.). (ENG.). 24p. (J). (gr. k-3). 25.65 *(978-1-60453-721-5(3))* ABDO Publishing Co.

—Cuddly Cats, 1 vol. 2007. (Perfect Pets Ser.). (ENG., Illus.). 24p. (J). (gr. k-3). lib. bdg. 24.21 *(978-1-59928-745-4(5)*, SandCastle) ABDO Publishing Co.

—Sleek Siamese, 1 vol. Doucet, Bob, illus. 2009. (Cat Craze Ser.). (ENG.). 24p. (J). (gr. k-3). 25.65 *(978-1-60453-725-3(6))* ABDO Publishing Co.

Hart, Joyce. Cats. 2007. (Great Pets Ser.). (Illus.). 48p. (gr. 3-7). lib. bdg. 29.93 *(978-0-7614-2710-0(4)*, Benchmark Bks.) Marshall Cavendish Corp.

Hartman, Eve & Meshbesher, Wendy. Animal Classification: Do Cats Have Family Trees?, 1 vol. 2014. (Show Me Science Ser.). (ENG.). 32p. (gr. 3-5). lib. bdg. 30.65 *(978-1-4329-8752-7(6)*, Raintree Perspectives) Heinemann-Raintree.

Head, Honor. Cats. 2012. (Pets Plus Ser.). (Illus.). 32p. (gr. 3-6). lib. bdg. 31.35 *(978-1-59920-698-1(6))* Black Rabbit Bks.

—Cats & Kittens. 2007. (QEB Know Your Pet Ser.). (Illus.). 32p. lib. bdg. 19.95 *(978-1-59566-217-0(0))* QEB Publishing Inc.

Hendrickson, Terry D. What Is Choo-Choo? Choo Choo Is A Cat. 2010. 40p. pap. 20.99 *(978-1-4490-9026-5(5))* AuthorHouse.

Heneghan, Judith. Love Your Cat. 2013. (Your Perfect Pet Ser.). (ENG., Illus.). 32p. (gr. k-5). 25.25 *(978-1-4777-0184-3(2))*; pap. 10.00 *(978-1-4777-0196-6(6))* Windmill Bks.

Hengel, Katherine. Delightful Devon Rexes, 1 vol. Doucet, Bob, illus. 2011. (Cat Craze Set 2 Ser.). (ENG.). 24p. (J). (gr. k-3). 25.65 *(978-1-61714-830-9(X))* ABDO Publishing Co.

—Hip Himalayans, 1 vol. Doucet, Bob, illus. 2009. (Cat Craze Ser.). (ENG.). 24p. (J). (gr. k-3). 25.65 *(978-1-60453-722-2(1))* ABDO Publishing Co.

—Outgoing Oriental Shorthairs, 1 vol. Doucet, Bob, illus. 2011. (Cat Craze Set 2 Ser.). (ENG.). 24p. (J). (gr. k-3). 25.65 *(978-1-61714-831-6(8))* ABDO Publishing Co.

—Smooth Sphynx, 1 vol. Doucet, Bob, illus. 2009. (Cat Craze Ser.). (ENG.). 24p. (J). (gr. k-3). 25.65 *(978-1-60453-726-0(4))* ABDO Publishing Co.

—Sweet Scottish Folds, 1 vol. Doucet, Bob, illus. 2011. (Cat Craze Set 2 Ser.). (ENG.). 24p. (J). (gr. k-3). 25.65 *(978-1-61714-833-0(4))* ABDO Publishing Co.

—Terrific Tabbies, 1 vol. Doucet, Bob, illus. 2011. (Cat Craze Set 2 Ser.). (ENG.). 24p. (J). (gr. k-3). 25.65 *(978-1-61714-834-7(2))* ABDO Publishing Co.

Hensler, Sue. Cage Fight. 2009. 24p. pap. 12.49 *(978-1-4490-1163-5(2))* AuthorHouse.

Heos, Bridget. Do You Really Want a Cat? Longhi, Katya, illus. 2013. (Do You Really Want a Pet? Ser.). (ENG.). 24p. (gr. 1-4). 27.10 *(978-1-60753-203-3(4))* Amicus Publishing.

Herlihy, Angela. My First Cat Book: Simple & Fun Ways to Care for Your Feline Friend for Kids Aged 7+ 2016. (ENG., Illus.). 128p. (J). (gr. 7-11). pap. 14.95 *(978-1-78249-380-8(8)*, 1782493808, CICO Books) Ryland Peters & Small GBR. Dist: WIPRO.

Hill, JoAnn. Missy's Babies. 2013. 36p. pap. 15.95 *(978-1-4624-0647-0(5)*, Inspiring Voices) Author Solutions, Inc.

Hoare, Ben. Cat. 2008. (Owning a Pet Ser.). (Illus.). 32p. (YA). (gr. 2-5). lib. bdg. 28.50 *(978-1-59771-053-4(9))* Sea-To-Sea Pubns.

Holland, Gini. American Shorthairs. 2013. (Cats Are Cool Ser.). 32p. (J). (gr. k-5). pap. 60.00 *(978-1-4777-1349-5(2))*; pap. 10.00 *(978-1-4777-1342-6(5))*; (ENG., Illus.). lib. bdg. 25.25 *(978-1-4777-1277-1(1))* Rosen Publishing Group, Inc., The. (PowerKids Pr.).

—Ragdolls. 2013. (Cats Are Cool Ser.). 32p. (J). (gr. k-5). pap. 10.00 *(978-1-4777-1340-2(9))*; (ENG., Illus.). lib. bdg. 25.25 *(978-1-4777-1276-4(3))* Rosen Publishing Group, Inc., The. (PowerKids Pr.).

Holmen, Lene. Kittens. 2006. (Touch & Sparkle Ser.). (Illus.). 12p. (gr. -1). per., bds. *(978-1-84610-077-2(1))* Make Believe Ideas.

Holt, Carmen & Jim. Betun: The Story of a Rascalero As Told by His Companeros. 2012. 28p. pap. 19.99 *(978-1-4772-6665-6(8))* AuthorHouse.

Honders, Christine. How Cats & Other Animals See at Night. 2015. (Superior Animal Senses Ser.). (ENG., Illus.). 24p. (J). (gr. 3-4). pap. 8.25 *(978-1-4994-0989-5(3)*, PowerKids Pr.) Rosen Publishing Group, Inc., The.

Hosley, Maria. Cats, 1 vol. 2007. (First Drawings Ser.). (ENG., Illus.). 24p. (gr. -1-3). 25.65 *(978-1-59679-801-4(7)*, Buddy Bks.) ABDO Publishing Co.

Hubbard, Ben. Caring for Cats & Kittens. 2016. (Battersea Dogs & Cats Home Pet Care Guides). (ENG., Illus.). 64p. (J). (gr. 2-4). pap. 6.99 *(978-1-4451-2780-4(6)*, Franklin Watts) Hachette Children's Group GBR. Dist: Hachette Bk. Group.

Husar, Lisa & Husar, Mike, photos by. Bobcat Babies. 2013. (Illus.). 26p. (J). 8.95 *(978-1-56037-133-5(1))* Farcountry Pr.

Huseby, Victoria. Cat. 2008. (J). 25.65 *(978-1-59920-177-1(1))* Black Rabbit Bks.

Hutmacher, Kimberly M. I Want a Cat, 1 vol. 2012. (I Want a Pet Ser.). (ENG.). 24p. (gr. k-1). lib. bdg. 26.65 *(978-1-4296-7596-3(9)*, Pebble Plus) Capstone Press of Coughlan Cos.

Ireland, Charles E. Toolbox. Diienno, Trish, illus. 2006. (J). *(978-1-892142-30-6(9))* Cedar Tree Bks.

Jackson, Shelley. Mimi's Dada Catifesto. Jackson, Shelley, illus. 2010. (ENG., Illus.). 48p. (J). (gr. 1-4). 17.00 *(978-0-547-12681-4(6))* Houghton Mifflin Harcourt Publishing Co.

Jacobs, Pat. Cat Pals. 2017. 32p. (J). ***(978-0-7787-3550-2(8))*** Crabtree Publishing Co.

Jeffrey, Laura S. Cats: How to Choose & Care for a Cat. 2004. (American Humane Pet Care Library). (Illus.). 48p. (J). lib. bdg. 25.27 *(978-0-7660-2516-5(0))* Enslow Pubs., Inc.

—Choosing a Cat: How to Choose & Care for a Cat. 2013. (American Humane Association Pet Care Ser.). 48p. (J). (gr. 3-18). lib. bdg. 25.27 *(978-0-7660-4079-3(8))*; pap. 8.95 *(978-1-4644-0214-2(0)*, Enslow Elementary) Enslow Pubs., Inc.

Jenkins, Steve. Dogs & Cats. 2012. lib. bdg. 18.40 *(978-0-606-26606-2(2)*, Turtleback) Turtleback Bks.

Johnson, Jinny. Kitten. 2014. (My New Pet Ser.). 24p. (Orig.). (gr. k-3). lib. bdg. 28.50 *(978-1-62588-026-0(X))* Black Rabbit Bks.

—Kitten. 2014. (My New Pet Ser.). (ENG., Illus.). 24p. (Orig.). (J). (gr. -1-3). pap. 8.95 *(978-1-77092-208-2(3))* Saunders Bk. Co. CAN. Dist: RiverStream Publishing.

Jordan, Apple. The Cat: Why Do Cats Purr? & Other True Facts. 2007. (Illus.). 30p. (J). pap. *(978-0-545-00088-8(2))* Scholastic, Inc.

Kaelberer, Angie Peterson. Favorite Cat Breeds: Persians, Abyssinians, Siamese, Sphynx, & All the Breeds In-Between. 2016. (Cats Rule! Ser.). (ENG., Illus.). 32p. (gr. 3-4). lib. bdg. 27.99 *(978-1-4914-8402-9(0)*, Snap Bks.) Capstone Press of Coughlan Cos.

Kahn, Sarah. Little Book of Cats & Kittens: Internet-Linked. 2009. (Miniature Editions Ser.). 64p. (YA). (gr. 3-18). 6.99 *(978-0-7945-2299-5(8)*, Usborne) EDC Publishing.

Kalman, Bobbie. Baby Cats. 2008. (It's Fun to Learn about Baby Animals Ser.). (ENG., Illus.). 24p. (J). (gr. 3-7). pap. *(978-0-7787-3970-8(8))* Crabtree Publishing Co.

—My Funny Cat. 2010. (My World Ser.). (ENG.). 16p. (J). (gr. k-3). *(978-0-7787-9500-1(4))*; pap. *(978-0-7787-9525-4(X))* Crabtree Publishing Co.

Kalman, Bobbie & Bishop, Amanda. Les Félins. 2003. (Petit Monde Vivant Ser.). (FRE., Illus.). 32p. (J). pap. 9.95 *(978-2-89579-006-8(X))* Bayard Canada Livres CAN. Dist: Crabtree Publishing Co.

Kawa, Katie. Curious Cats. 2011. (Pet Corner Ser.). (Illus.). 24p. (gr. k-2). (J). pap. 8.15 *(978-1-4339-5588-4(1))*; (J). lib. bdg. 22.60 *(978-1-4339-5586-0(5))*; 69.20 *(978-1-4339-6880-8(0))* Stevens, Gareth Publishing LLLP.

—Curious Cats: Gatos Curiosos. 2011. (Pet Corner / RincóN de Las Mascotas Ser.). (SPA & ENG., Illus.). 24p. (J). (gr. k-3). lib. bdg. 22.60 *(978-1-4339-5590-7(3))* Stevens, Gareth Publishing LLLP.

Kellen, Susan. My Name Is Ed or Betty. 2010. 28p. pap. 14.50 *(978-1-4490-7149-3(X))* AuthorHouse.

Kimiko. EL GATO. (SPA.). 10p. *(978-84-95150-52-3(2))* Corimbo, Editorial S.L.

King, Emmett. A Kitten Grows. 2007. (Illus.). 8p. pap. 4.75 *(978-0-15-377221-4(2))* Harcourt Schl. Pubs.

The Kittens: KinderConcepts Individual Title Six-Packs. (Kinderstarters Ser.). 8p. (gr. -1-1). 21.00 *(978-0-7635-8717-8(6))* Rigby Education.

Kramer, Mark. Santa Claws: A True Story. 2009. (Illus.). 25p. (J). pap. 15.95 *(978-1-4327-4793-0(2))* Outskirts Pr., Inc.

Kuntz, Doug & Shrodes, Amy. Lost & Found Cat: The True Story of Kunkush's Incredible Journey. Cornelison, Sue, illus. 2017. (ENG.). 48p. (J). (gr. -1-3). lib. bdg. 20.99 *(978-1-5247-1548-9(4)*, Crown Books For Young Readers) Random Hse. Children's Bks.

Laidlaw, Rob. Cat Champions: Caring for Our Feline Friends. (ENG., Illus.). 64p. (J). (gr. 3-7). 2015. pap. 11.95 *(978-1-927485-54-5(1))* 2014. 15.95 *(978-1-927485-31-6(2))* Pajama Pr. CAN. Dist: Ingram Publisher Services.

Landau, Elaine. American Shorthairs Are the Best! 2011. (Best Cats Ever Ser.). (ENG., Illus.). 32p. (gr. 2-4). 25.26 *(978-0-7613-6430-6(7)*, Lerner Pubns.) Lerner Publishing Group.

—Egyptian Maus Are the Best! 2011. (Best Cats Ever Ser.). (ENG.). 32p. (gr. 2-4). lib. bdg. 25.26 *(978-0-7613-6431-3(5)*, Lerner Pubns.) Lerner Publishing Group.

—Manx Are the Best! 2011. (Best Cats Ever Ser.). (ENG.). 32p. (gr. 2-4). 25.26 *(978-0-7613-6432-0(3)*, Lerner Pubns.) Lerner Publishing Group.

—Ragdolls Are the Best! 2011. (Best Cats Ever Ser.). (ENG., Illus.). 32p. (gr. 2-4). lib. bdg. 25.26 *(978-0-7613-6428-3(5)*, Lerner Pubns.) Lerner Publishing Group.

—Siamese Are the Best! 2011. (Best Cats Ever Ser.). (ENG., Illus.). 32p. (gr. 2-4). 25.26 *(978-0-7613-6427-6(7)*, Lerner Pubns.) Lerner Publishing Group.

—Sphynx Are the Best! 2011. (Best Cats Ever Ser.). (ENG.). 32p. (gr. 2-4). 25.26 *(978-0-7613-6429-0(3)*, Lerner Pubns.) Lerner Publishing Group.

—Your Pet Cat. Landau, Elaine, illus. rev. ed. 2007. (True Bks.). (ENG., Illus.). 48p. (J). (gr. 3-5). pap. 6.95 *(978-0-531-15464-9(5)*, Children's Pr.) Scholastic Library Publishing.

Larson, Kirby & Nethery, Mary. Two Bobbies. Cassels, Jean, illus. 2015. 36p. pap. 8.00 *(978-1-61003-411-1(2))* Center for the Collaborative Classroom.

—Two Bobbies: A True Story of Hurricane Katrina, Friendship, & Survival. Cassels, Jean, illus. 2008. (ENG.). 32p. (J). (gr. k-3). 16.99 *(978-0-8027-9754-4(7)*, 9780802797544, Bloomsbury USA Childrens) Bloomsbury Publishing USA.

Lassieur, Allison. Meats & Proteins. 2015. (Illus.). 32p. (J). lib. bdg. 28.50 *(978-1-60753-498-3(3))* Amicus Publishing.

Leaf, Christina. American Shorthairs. 2015. (Cool Cats Ser.). (ENG., Illus.). 24p. (J). (gr. k-3). lib. bdg. 25.95 *(978-1-62617-230-2(7)*, Blastoff! Readers) Bellwether Media.

—Birmans. 2015. (Cool Cats Ser.). (ENG., Illus.). 24p. (J). (gr. k-3). lib. bdg. 25.95 *(978-1-62617-231-9(5)*, Blastoff! Readers) Bellwether Media.

—Devon Rexes. 2016. (Cool Cats Ser.). (ENG., Illus.). 24p. (J). (gr. k-3). lib. bdg. 25.95 *(978-1-62617-309-5(5)*, Blastoff! Readers) Bellwether Media.

—Manx. 2016. (Cool Cats Ser.). (ENG., Illus.). 24p. (J). (gr. k-3). lib. bdg. 25.95 *(978-1-62617-312-5(5)*, Blastoff! Readers) Bellwether Media.

—Scottish Folds. 2016. (Cool Cats Ser.). (ENG., Illus.). 24p. (J). (gr. k-3). lib. bdg. 25.95 *(978-1-62617-314-9(1)*, Blastoff! Readers) Bellwether Media.

Leighton, Christina. Bobcats. 2017. (North American Animals Ser.). (ENG., Illus.). 24p. (J). (gr. k-3). lib. bdg. 25.95 *(978-1-62617-565-5(9)*, Blastoff! Readers) Bellwether Media.

—British Shorthairs. 2016. (Cool Cats Ser.). (ENG., Illus.). 24p. (J). (gr. k-3). 25.95 *(978-1-62617-395-8(8)*, Blastoff! Readers) Bellwether Media.

—Cornish Rexes. 2016. (Cool Cats Ser.). (ENG., Illus.). 24p. (J). (gr. k-3). 25.95 *(978-1-62617-396-5(6)*, Blastoff! Readers) Bellwether Media.

Lodien, Jennie, des. Cat Tales. 2004. (Illus.). 48p. (YA). ring bd. 16.95 *(978-0-9746341-8-0(2))* Chin & A Pr.

Loewen, Nancy. Scarlett the Cat to the Rescue: Fire Hero, 1 vol. Sorra, Kristin, illus. 2014. (Animal Heroes Ser.). (ENG.). 32p. (gr. k-2). 28.65 *(978-1-4795-5464-5(2))* Picture Window Bks.

Loxton, Howard. Cats: An Eyewitness 3-D Book. 2004. (Illus.). 58p. (YA). reprint ed. 17.00 *(978-0-7567-7414-1(4))* DIANE Publishing Co.

Lucky (The Cat). My 9 8 7 6 5 4 3 2 1 Lives: A Cat's Tail of Her near Death & Life Experiences. 2009. 52p. pap. 22.49 *(978-1-4490-0076-9(2))* AuthorHouse.

Lynch, Annabelle. Cats & Kittens. 2017. (Animals & Their Babies Ser.). (Illus.). 24p. (gr. k-3). 28.50 ***(978-1-62588-415-2(X)***, Smart Apple Media) Black Rabbit Bks.

Macken, JoAnn Early. Kittens. 2003. (Weekly Reader Early Learning Library). (Illus.). 24p. (gr. k-3). pap. 8.15 *(978-0-8368-3846-6(7)*, Weekly Reader Leveled Readers) Stevens, Gareth Publishing LLLP.

MacLeod, Elizabeth. Why Do Cats Have Whiskers? 2008. (ENG., Illus.). 64p. (J). (gr. 3-7). 14.95 *(978-1-55453-196-7(9))* Kids Can Pr., Ltd. CAN. Dist: Hachette Bk. Group.

Magellan, Marta. Those Colossal Cats. Weaver, Steve, illus. 2009. (Those Amazing Animals Ser.). (ENG.). 55p. (J). (gr. k-4). 14.95 *(978-1-56164-457-5(9))*; pap. 8.95 *(978-1-56164-458-2(7))* Pineapple Pr., Inc.

Mansfield, Carol M. Jake & Jebadiah Visit the Veterinarian, 1 vol. 2010. 22p. pap. 24.95 *(978-1-4489-2548-3(7))* PublishAmerica, Inc.

Mara, Wil. What Should I Do? If I See a Stray Animal. 2011. (Community Connections: What Should I Do? Ser.). (ENG., Illus.). 24p. (J). (gr. 2-5). lib. bdg. 25.64 *(978-1-61080-050-1(8)*, 1330905) Cherry Lake Publishing.

Marina J. Royer. Kitten Velvetiz Volume I the Fish & Veggies Eater - Economical Guide for Bringing up Your First Kitten. 2011. (FRE & ENG., Illus.). 174p. pap. *(978-1-907011-20-7(X))* Esteemworld Pubns.

Markovics, Joyce L. Jaguarundi: Otter Cat. 2012. (America's Hidden Animal Treasures Ser.). 32p. (J). (gr. 2-7). lib. bdg. 26.60 *(978-1-61772-579-1(X))* Bearport Publishing Co., Inc.

—Persians: Long-Haired Friends. 2011. (Cat-Ographies Ser.). 24p. (YA). (gr. 2-5). lib. bdg. 22.61 *(978-1-61772-141-0(7))* Bearport Publishing Co., Inc.

Marks, Jennifer L. Bobcats, 1 vol. 2010. (Wildcats Ser.). (ENG.). 24p. (gr. k-1). lib. bdg. 26.65 *(978-1-4296-4480-8(X)*, Pebble Plus) Capstone Press of Coughlan Cos.

Mataya, Marybeth. Are You My Cat?, 1 vol. Williams, Matthew, illus. 2008. (Are You My Pet? Ser.). (ENG.). 32p. (J). (gr. 1-4). 28.50 *(978-1-60270-242-4(X))* Magic Wagon.

Mattern, Joanne. Abyssinian Cats, 1 vol. 2011. (All about Cats Ser.). (ENG.). 32p. (gr. 3-4). lib. bdg. 27.99 *(978-1-4296-6865-1(2)*, Edge Bks.) Capstone Press of Coughlan Cos.

—All about Cats. 2011. (All about Cats Ser.). (ENG.). 32p. (gr. 3-4). lib. bdg. 83.97 *(978-1-4296-6868-2(7)*, Edge Bks.) Capstone Press of Coughlan Cos.

—All about Cats, 12 vols., Set. Incl. Abyssinian Cats. 2011. lib. bdg. 27.99 *(978-1-4296-6865-1(2))*; American Shorthair Cats. 2010. lib. bdg. 27.99 *(978-1-4296-6628-2(5))*; Birman Cats. 2010. lib. bdg. 27.99 *(978-1-4296-6629-9(3))*; Exotic Cats. 2010. lib. bdg. 27.99 *(978-1-4296-6630-5(7))*; Maine Coon Cats. 2010. lib. bdg. 27.99 *(978-1-4296-6631-2(5))*; Manx Cats. 2010. lib. bdg. 27.99 *(978-1-4296-6632-9(3))*; Ocicats. 2010. lib. bdg. 27.99 *(978-1-4296-6633-6(1))*; Oriental Cats. (Illus.). 2011. lib. bdg. 27.99 *(978-1-4296-6866-8(0))*; Persian Cats. 2010. lib. bdg. 27.99 *(978-1-4296-6634-3(X))*; Ragdoll Cats. 2011. lib. bdg. 27.99 *(978-1-4296-6867-5(9))*; Siamese Cats. 2010. lib. bdg. 27.99 *(978-1-4296-6635-0(8))*; Sphynx Cats. 2010. lib. bdg. 27.99 *(978-1-4296-6636-7(6))*; (gr. 3-4). (All about Cats Ser.). (ENG.). 32p. 2011. Set lib. bdg. 335.88 *(978-1-4296-6869-9(5)*, Edge Bks.) Capstone Press of Coughlan Cos.

—American Shorthair Cats, 1 vol. 2010. (All about Cats Ser.). (ENG.). 32p. (gr. 3-4). lib. bdg. 27.99 *(978-1-4296-6628-2(5)*, Edge Bks.) Capstone Press of Coughlan Cos.

—Birman Cats, 1 vol. 2010. (All about Cats Ser.). (ENG.). 32p. (gr. 3-4). lib. bdg. 27.99 *(978-1-4296-6629-9(3)*, Edge Bks.) Capstone Press of Coughlan Cos.

—Exotic Cats, 1 vol. 2010. (All about Cats Ser.). (ENG.). 32p. (gr. 3-4). lib. bdg. 27.99 *(978-1-4296-6630-5(7)*, Edge Bks.) Capstone Press of Coughlan Cos.

—Maine Coon Cats, 1 vol. 2010. (All about Cats Ser.). (ENG.). 32p. (gr. 3-4). lib. bdg. 27.99 *(978-1-4296-6631-2(5)*, Edge Bks.) Capstone Press of Coughlan Cos.

—Manx Cats, 1 vol. 2010. (All about Cats Ser.). (ENG.). 32p. (gr. 3-4). lib. bdg. 27.99 *(978-1-4296-6632-9(3)*, Edge Bks.) Capstone Press of Coughlan Cos.

—Ocicats, 1 vol. 2010. (All about Cats Ser.). (ENG.). 32p. (gr. 3-4). lib. bdg. 27.99 *(978-1-4296-6633-6(1)*, Edge Bks.) Capstone Press of Coughlan Cos.

—Oriental Cats, 1 vol. 2011. (All about Cats Ser.). (ENG., Illus.). 32p. (gr. 3-4). lib. bdg. 27.99 *(978-1-4296-6866-8(0)*, Edge Bks.) Capstone Press of Coughlan Cos.

—Persian Cats, 1 vol. 2010. (All about Cats Ser.). (ENG.). 32p. (gr. 3-4). lib. bdg. 27.99 *(978-1-4296-6634-3(X)*, Edge Bks.) Capstone Press of Coughlan Cos.

—Ragdoll Cats, 1 vol. 2011. (All about Cats Ser.). (ENG.). 32p. (gr. 3-4). lib. bdg. 27.99 *(978-1-4296-6867-5(9)*, Edge Bks.) Capstone Press of Coughlan Cos.

—Siamese Cats, 1 vol. 2010. (All about Cats Ser.). (ENG.). 32p. (gr. 3-4). lib. bdg. 27.99 *(978-1-4296-6635-0(8)*, Edge Bks.) Capstone Press of Coughlan Cos.

—Sphynx Cats, 1 vol. 2010. (All about Cats Ser.). (ENG.). 32p. (gr. 3-4). lib. bdg. 27.99 *(978-1-4296-6636-7(6)*, Edge Bks.) Capstone Press of Coughlan Cos.

McAneney, Caitie. Bobcats. 2016. (Creatures of the Forest Habitat Ser.). 00024p. (J). (gr. 3-3). 23.60 *(978-1-4994-2930-5(4))*; pap. 8.25 *(978-1-4994-2710-3(7))* Rosen Publishing Group, Inc., The. (PowerKids Pr.).

McCreary, Candace. Meki & the Three Cockers. 2012. (ENG.). 24p. (J). pap. 12.95 *(978-1-4787-1952-6(4))* Outskirts Pr., Inc.

McCuin, Sam. The Story of Camo Kitty. 2013. 32p. pap. 16.99 *(978-1-4624-0693-7(9)*, Inspiring Voices) Author Solutions, Inc.

McDonnell, Patrick. The Mutts Diaries. 2014. (Mutts Kids Ser.: 1). (ENG., Illus.). 224p. (J). pap. 9.99 *(978-1-4494-5870-6(X))* Andrews McMeel Publishing.

McGrath Avery, Pat. Famous Dogs & a Cat. 2013. 94p. pap. 7.99 *(978-1-937958-34-3(5))* Red Engine Pr.

—15 Dogs & a Cat Speak Out: Interviews by Luke the Detective Dog. 2012. 119p. pap. 6.99 *(978-1-937958-11-4(6))* Red Engine Pr.

McKay, Sindy. Too Many Cats: Demasiados Gatos. 2010. (SPA., Illus.). 41p. (J). *(978-1-60115-039-4(3))* Treasure Bay, Inc.

—We Both Read-Big Cats, Little Cats. ed. 2015. (We Both Read Ser.). (ENG., Illus.). 44p. (J). (gr. -1-1). pap. 4.99 *(978-1-60115-276-3(0))* Treasure Bay, Inc.

—We Both Read Bilingual Edition-Too Many Cats/Demasiados Gatos. Johnson, Meredith, illus. 2011. (ENG & SPA.). 44p. (J). pap. 4.99 *(978-1-60115-040-0(7))* Treasure Bay, Inc.

Meachen Rau, Dana. Adivina Quién Ronronea. 2008. (Adivina Quién Ser.). (SPA.). 32p. (gr. k-2). lib. bdg. 15.95 *(978-0-7614-3454-2(2)*, Benchmark Bks.) Marshall Cavendish Corp.

—Purrs: Ronronea. 2007. (Bookworms — Bilingual Editions: Guess Who/Adivina Quien 3 Ser.). (SPA.). 32p. (gr. k-2). 15.95 *(978-0-7614-3480-1(1))* Marshall Cavendish Corp.

—Top 10 Cats for Kids. 2008. (Top Pets for Kids with American Humane Ser.). (Illus.). 48p. (J). (gr. 2-5). lib. bdg. 25.27 *(978-0-7660-3071-8(7))* Enslow Pubs., Inc.

Meister, Cari. Cats. 2014. (Illus.). 24p. (J). lib. bdg. 25.65 *(978-1-62031-121-9(6)*, Bullfrog Bks.) Jump! Inc.

Metz, Gabriele. Get to Know Cat Breeds: Over 40 Best-Known Breeds. 2014. (Get to Know Cat, Dog, & Horse Breeds Ser.). 128p. (J). lib. bdg. 33.27 *(978-0-7660-4260-5(X))* Enslow Pubs., Inc.

Micco, Trudy. Discover Abyssinian Cats. 2012. (Discover Cats with the Cat Fanciers' Association Ser.). (Illus.). 24p. (J). (gr. k-3). pap. 7.95 *(978-1-4644-0112-1(8))*; 22.60 *(978-0-7660-3856-1(4))* Enslow Pubs., Inc. (Enslow Elementary).

—Discover Maine Coon Cats. 2012. (Discover Cats with the Cat Fanciers' Association Ser.). 24p. (J). (gr. k-3). (Illus.). pap. 7.95 *(978-1-4644-0117-6(9))*; 22.60 *(978-0-7660-3852-3(1))* Enslow Pubs., Inc. (Enslow Elementary).

—Discover Mixed-Breed Cats. 2012. (Discover Cats with the Cat Fanciers' Association Ser.). 24p. (J). (gr. k-3). (Illus.). pap. 7.95 *(978-1-4644-0116-9(0))*; 22.60 *(978-0-7660-3851-6(3))* Enslow Pubs., Inc. (Enslow Elementary).

—Discover Oriental Shorthair Cats. 2012. (Discover Cats with the Cat Fanciers' Association Ser.). (Illus.). 24p. (J). (gr. k-3). pap. 7.95 *(978-1-4644-0115-2(2))*; 22.60 *(978-0-7660-3853-0(X))* Enslow Pubs., Inc. (Enslow Elementary).

—Discover Persian Cats. 2012. (Discover Cats with the Cat Fanciers' Association Ser.). 24p. (J). (gr. k-3). (Illus.). pap. 7.95 *(978-1-4644-0114-5(4))*; 22.60 *(978-0-7660-3854-7(8))* Enslow Pubs., Inc. (Enslow Elementary).

—Discover Ragdoll Cats. 2012. (Discover Cats with the Cat Fanciers' Association Ser.). 24p. (J). (gr. k-3). (Illus.). pap. 7.95 *(978-1-4644-0113-8(6))*; 22.60 *(978-0-7660-3855-4(6))* Enslow Pubs., Inc. (Enslow Elementary).

Michele, Tracey. Big Cats, Little Cats. 2011. (Learn-Abouts Ser.). (Illus.). 16p. (J). pap. 7.95 *(978-1-59920-595-3(5))* Black Rabbit Bks.

Milanowski, Lorraine. Holly the Lucky Little Kitten. 2009. 20p. pap. 10.49 *(978-1-4490-0380-7(X))* AuthorHouse.

Milbourne, Anna. Cats. Donaera, Patrizia, illus. 2006. (Beginners Nature: Level 1 Ser.). 32p. (J). (gr. k-2). 4.99 *(978-0-7945-1394-8(8)*, Usborne) EDC Publishing.

—Cats. Donaera, Patrizia & Fox, Christyan, illus. 2006. (Usborne Beginners Ser.). 32p. (J). (gr. 1). lib. bdg. 12.99 *(978-1-58086-942-3(4)*, Usborne) EDC Publishing.

Miles, Ellen. Kitty Corner: Guide to Kittens. 2013. (Kitty Corner Ser.). lib. bdg. 16.00 *(978-0-606-31502-9(0)*, Turtleback) Turtleback Bks.

—Kitty Corner: Guide to Kittens. 2013. (Kitty Corner Ser.). (ENG.). 80p. (J). (gr. 2-5). pap. 5.99 *(978-0-545-48434-3(0)*, Scholastic Paperbacks) Scholastic, Inc.

Minden, Cecilia. Kittens Grow up to Be Cats. 2010. (21st Century Basic Skills Library: Animals Grow Up Ser.). (ENG.). 24p. (gr. k-3). lib. bdg. 22.79 *(978-1-60279-852-6(4)*, 200570) Cherry Lake Publishing.

Montardre, Hélène. Little Cats. 2006. (Born to Be Wild Ser.). (Illus.). 24p. (gr. k-3). lib. bdg. 23.00 *(978-0-8368-6162-4(0)*, Gareth Stevens Learning Library) Stevens, Gareth Publishing LLLP.

Morita, Yoneo. Tiny Cat. 2016. (ENG., Illus.). 72p. 9.95 *(978-1-4521-4975-2(5))* Chronicle Bks. LLC.

Moser, Chris & Moser, Liz. The Discoveries of Shuggs, A Curious Cat. Moser, Chris & Moser, Liz, illus. 2011. (Illus.). (J). pap. 10.95 *(978-0-9842881-9-9(8))* Capital City Bks. LLC.

Murray, Julie. American Curl Cats, 1 vol. 2005. (Animal Kingdom Set Ii Ser.). (ENG., Illus.). 24p. (gr. k-4). 25.65 *(978-1-59197-301-0(5)*, Buddy Bks.) ABDO Publishing Co.

—Bombay Cats, 1 vol. 2003. (Cats Set 3 Ser.). (ENG.). 24p. (J). (gr. 2-5). 25.65 *(978-1-57765-862-7(0))* ABDO Publishing Co.

—Burmese Cats, 1 vol. 2003. (Cats Set 3 Ser.). (ENG.). 24p. (J). (gr. 2-5). 25.65 *(978-1-57765-865-8(5))* ABDO Publishing Co.

—Cats, 1 vol. 2015. (ENG., Illus.). 24p. (J). 27.07 *(978-1-62970-899-7(2)*, 1391169) ABDO Publishing Co.

—Cornish Rex Cats, 1 vol. 2003. (Cats Set 3 Ser.). (ENG.). 24p. (J). (gr. 2-5). 25.65 *(978-1-57765-863-4(9))* ABDO Publishing Co.

—Korat Cats, 1 vol. 2003. (Cats Set 3 Ser.). (ENG.). 24p. (gr. k-6). 25.65 *(978-1-57765-864-1(7)*, Checkerboard Library) ABDO Publishing Co.

—Ocicat Cats, 1 vol. 2003. (Cats Set 3 Ser.). (ENG.). 24p. (gr. k-6). 25.65 *(978-1-57765-866-5(3)*, Checkerboard Library) ABDO Publishing Co.

—Persian Cats, 1 vol. 2005. (Animal Kingdom Set Ii Ser.). (ENG., Illus.). 24p. (gr. k-4). 25.65 *(978-1-59197-330-0(9)*, Buddy Bks.) ABDO Publishing Co.

—Scottish Fold Cats, 1 vol. 2003. (Cats Set 3 Ser.). (ENG.). 24p. (gr. k-6). 25.65 *(978-1-57765-867-2(1)*, Checkerboard Library) ABDO Publishing Co.

—Siamese Cats, 1 vol. 2003. (Animal Kingdom Ser.). (ENG.). 24p. (gr. k-4). 25.65 *(978-1-57765-644-9(X)*, Buddy Bks.) ABDO Publishing Co.

—Tabby Cats, 1 vol. 2003. (Animal Kingdom Ser.). (ENG.). 24p. (gr. k-4). 25.65 *(978-1-57765-645-6(8)*, Buddy Bks.) ABDO Publishing Co.

Myron, Vicki & Witter, Bret. Dewey: There's a Cat in the Library! James, Steve, illus. 2009. (ENG.). 40p. (J). (gr. -1-3). 16.99 *(978-0-316-06874-1(8))* Little, Brown Bks. for Young Readers.

—Dewey the Library Cat. 2011. (ENG., Illus.). 224p. (J). (gr. 3-7). pap. 8.99 *(978-0-316-06870-3(5))* Little, Brown Bks. for Young Readers.

National Geographic Kids. National Geographic Kids Cats Sticker Activity Book. 2017. (NG Sticker Activity Bks.). (ENG.). 56p. (J). (gr. -1-3). pap. 6.99 ***(978-1-4263-2800-8(1)***, National Geographic Children's Bks.) National Geographic Society.

National Geographic Kids Staff & Evans, Shira. Play, Kitty! 2016. (Readers Ser.). (ENG.). 24p. (J). (-k). pap. 3.99 *(978-1-4263-2409-3(X)*, National Geographic Children's Bks.) National Geographic Society.

Newbery, L. Azul, el Gato de Humo. (Raton de Biblioteca Coleccion). (SPA.). 80p. (J). (gr. 3). 7.95 *(978-84-88061-73-7(0))* Serres, Ediciones, S. L. ESP. Dist: Lectorum Pubns., Inc.

Newhouse Jr., Quentin. Hope, the Big Headed Cat: Not Just Another Animal Story. 2011. 68p. (gr. -1). pap. 9.95 *(978-1-4497-2313-2(6)*, WestBow Pr.) Author Solutions, Inc.

Newman, Aline Alexander. Cat Tales: True Stories of Kindness & Companionship with Kitties. 2017. (ENG., Illus.). 160p. (J). (gr. k-12). 12.99 *(978-1-4263-2734-6(X)*, National Geographic Children's Bks.) National Geographic Society.

Niehaus, Rebecca. The Birth of a Kitten. 2011. 48p. pap. 19.99 *(978-1-4567-6556-9(6))* AuthorHouse.

Niven, Felicia Lowenstein. Learning to Care for a Cat. 2010. (Beginning Pet Care with American Humane Ser.). 48p. (J). 25.27 *(978-0-7660-3191-3(8)*, Enslow Elementary) Enslow Pubs., Inc.

Niver, Heather Moore. When Cats Get Angry. 2017. (Animal Emotions Ser.). 32p. (J). (gr. 3-3). pap. 10.52 ***(978-0-7660-8865-8(0))*** Enslow Pubs., Inc.

Noe, Tristan. Cats from Head to Tail. 2016. (Animals from Head to Tail Ser.). (Illus.). 24p. (J). (gr. k-k). lib. bdg. 22.60 *(978-1-4824-4536-7(0))* Stevens, Gareth Publishing LLLP.

Norman, Kim & Ogden, Betina. Storytime Stickers: All Kinds of Kittens. 2010. (Storytime Stickers Ser.). (ENG., Illus.). 16p. (J). (gr. k-2). pap. 5.95 *(978-1-4027-7464-5(8))* Sterling Publishing Co., Inc.

Norris, A. Smokey the Kitten - A True Story. 2007. 264p. pap. 4.95 *(978-1-4184-7028-9(7))* AuthorHouse.

Old Cat, New Cat: Level I, 6 vols. (Wonder Worldtm Ser.). 16p. 29.95 *(978-0-7802-4591-4(1))* Wright Group/McGraw-Hill.

Oldfield, Dawn Bluemel. Abyssinians: Egyptian Royalty? 2011. (Cat-Ographies Ser.). 24p. (J). (gr. 2-5). lib. bdg. 22.61 *(978-1-61772-145-8(X))* Bearport Publishing Co., Inc.

Olson, Bethany. Baby Cats. 2013. (Super Cute! Ser.). (ENG., Illus.). 24p. (J). (gr. k-3). lib. bdg. 25.95 *(978-1-60014-923-8(5)*, Blastoff! Readers) Bellwether Media.

Olson, Gillia M. Pet Cats up Close. (Pets up Close Ser.). (ENG.). 24p. (gr. k-1). 2015. pap. 6.95 *(978-1-4914-7764-9(4))* 2014. 26.65 *(978-1-4914-0582-6(1))* Capstone Press of Coughlan Cos. (Pebble Plus).

Owen, Ruth. American Longhairs. 2013. (Cats Are Cool Ser.). 32p. (J). (gr. k-5). pap. 60.00 *(978-1-4777-1350-1(6))*; pap. 10.00 *(978-1-4777-1343-3(3))*; lib. bdg. 25.25 *(978-1-4777-1278-8(X))* Rosen Publishing Group, Inc., The. (PowerKids Pr.).

—Persians. 2013. (Cats Are Cool Ser.). (Illus.). 32p. (J). (gr. k-5). pap. 60.00 *(978-1-4777-1345-7(X))*; pap. 10.00 *(978-1-4777-1344-0(1))*; lib. bdg. 25.25 *(978-1-4777-1279-5(8))* Rosen Publishing Group, Inc., The. (PowerKids Pr.).

—Ragdolls. 2013. (Cats Are Cool Ser.). 32p. (J). (gr. k-5). pap. 60.00 *(978-1-4777-1341-9(7)*, PowerKids Pr.) Rosen Publishing Group, Inc., The.

—Siamese. 2013. (Cats Are Cool Ser.). (Illus.). 32p. (J). (gr. k-5). pap. 10.00 *(978-1-4777-1346-4(8))*; pap. 60.00 *(978-1-4777-1347-1(6))*; lib. bdg. 25.25 *(978-1-4777-1280-1(1))* Rosen Publishing Group, Inc., The. (PowerKids Pr.).

—Sphynx. 2013. (Cats Are Cool Ser.). 32p. (J). (gr. k-5). pap. 60.00 *(978-1-4777-1351-8(4))*; pap. 10.00 *(978-1-4777-1348-8(4))*; lib. bdg. 25.25 *(978-1-4777-1281-8(X))* Rosen Publishing Group, Inc., The. (PowerKids Pr.).

—Your Cat's Superhero Skills. 2015. (It's a Fact Ser.). (ENG.). 32p. (J). (gr. 3-6). lib. bdg. 26.60 *(978-1-909673-88-5(9))* Bearport Publishing Co., Inc.

Palmer, Andrea. Cats & Dogs! 2017. (Animals in My World Ser.). 24p. (gr. 4-6). pap. 8.25 ***(978-1-5383-2189-8(0)***, PowerKids Pr.) Rosen Publishing Group, Inc., The.

Parker, Steve. Cats & Kittens. 2010. (Mosaic of Magical Information Ser.). (Illus.). 48p. (YA). (gr. 3-18). 19.95 *(978-1-4222-1987-4(9))* Mason Crest.

—10 Things You Should Know about Big Cats. Borton, Paula, ed. Jackson, Ian, illus. 2004. (Things You Should Know about Ser.). 24p. (J). 6.99 *(978-1-84236-119-1(8))* Miles Kelly Publishing, Ltd. GBR. Dist: Independent Pubs. Group.

Peterson, Megan Cooley & Rustad, Martha E. H. Black Cats, 1 vol. 2013. (Halloween Fun Ser.). (ENG.). 24p. (gr. k-1). lib. bdg. 26.65 *(978-1-4765-2181-7(6)*, Pebble Plus) Capstone Press of Coughlan Cos.

Petrie, Kristin. American Bobtail Cats, 1 vol. 2013. (Cats Set 7 Ser.). (ENG.). 24p. (J). (gr. 3-6). lib. bdg. 25.65 *(978-1-61783-863-7(2)*, Checkerboard Library) ABDO Publishing Co.

—Birman Cats, 1 vol. 2013. (Cats Set 7 Ser.). (ENG.). 24p. (J). (gr. 3-6). lib. bdg. 25.65 *(978-1-61783-864-4(0)*, Checkerboard Library) ABDO Publishing Co.

—Chartreux Cats, 1 vol. 2013. (Cats Set 7 Ser.). (ENG.). 24p. (J). (gr. 3-6). lib. bdg. 25.65 *(978-1-61783-865-1(9)*, Checkerboard Library) ABDO Publishing Co.

—Selkirk Rex Cats, 1 vol. 2013. (Cats Set 7 Ser.). (ENG.). 24p. (J). (gr. 3-6). lib. bdg. 25.65 *(978-1-61783-866-8(7)*, Checkerboard Library) ABDO Publishing Co.

—Singapura Cats, 1 vol. 2013. (Cats Set 7 Ser.). (ENG.). 24p. (J). (gr. 3-6). lib. bdg. 25.65 *(978-1-61783-867-5(5)*, Checkerboard Library) ABDO Publishing Co.

—Turkish Angora Cats, 1 vol. 2013. (Cats Set 7 Ser.). (ENG.). 24p. (J). (gr. 3-6). lib. bdg. 25.65 (978-1-61783-868-2(3), Checkerboard Library) ABDO Publishing Co.
Phillips, Marie. Memoirs of a Feline Heroine. 2010. 196p. pap. (978-1-907211-87-4(X)) Grosvenor Hse. Publishing Ltd.
Pickett, Robert & Pickett, Justine, illus. Cat. Pickett, Robert & Pickett, Justine, photos by. 2004. 32p. (J). lib. bdg. 27.10 (978-1-58340-431-7(7)) Black Rabbit Bks.
Piggy Toes Press, creator. Pop & Touch Kittens. 2008. (ENG., Illus.). 12p. (J). 10.95 (978-1-58117-675-9(9), Intervisual/Piggy Toes) Bendon, Inc.
Price, Pamela S. Cool Pet Treats: Easy Recipes for Kids to Bake, 1 vol. 2010. (Cool Baking Ser.). (ENG.). 32p. (gr. 3-6). 28.50 (978-1-60453-777-2(9), Checkerboard Library) ABDO Publishing Co.
Priddy, Roger. Kittens. 2005. (ENG.). 12p. (J). 0.97 (978-0-312-49615-9(X), Priddy Bks.) St. Martin's Pr.
Pugliano-Martin, Carol. Cats of the Serengeti. 2011. (Early Connections Ser.). (J). (978-1-61672-575-4(3)) Benchmark Education Co.
—Cats of the Serengeti: Set Of 6. 2011. (Early Connections Ser.). (J). pap. 37.00 net. (978-1-4108-1068-7(2)) Benchmark Education Co.
Quinton, Sasha. Rat-A-Tat: A Phonics Reader. 2009. (Illus.). pap. (978-1-936199-04-4(1)) Book Shop, Ltd., The.
Randall, Henry. Bobcats. 2011. (Cats of the Wild Ser.). (ENG.). 24p. (J). pap. 8.25 (978-1-4488-2625-4(X)); lib. bdg. 22.60 (978-1-4488-2520-2(2)) Rosen Publishing Group, Inc., The. (PowerKids Pr.).
—Bobcats: Linces Rojos. 2011. (Cats of the Wild / Felinos Salvajes Ser.). (SPA & ENG., Illus.). 24p. lib. bdg. 22.60 (978-1-4488-3132-6(6), PowerKids Pr.) Rosen Publishing Group, Inc., The.
—Wildcats. 2011. (Cats of the Wild Ser.). (ENG.). 24p. (J). pap. 8.25 (978-1-4488-2627-8(6)); lib. bdg. 22.60 (978-1-4488-2521-9(0)) Rosen Publishing Group, Inc., The. (PowerKids Pr.).
Rath, Tom. Kittencat Adventures for a Special Person. 2012. 40p. pap. (978-0-9866065-4-0(5)) Wood Islands Prints.
Rathburn, Betsy. American Curls. 2017. (Cool Cats Ser.). (ENG., Illus.). 24p. (J). (gr. k-3). lib. bdg. 25.95 **(978-1-62617-625-6(6)**, Blastoff! Readers) Bellwether Media.
—Balinese. 2017. (Cool Cats Ser.). (ENG., Illus.). 24p. (J). (gr. k-3). lib. bdg. 25.95 **(978-1-62617-626-3(4)**, Blastoff! Readers) Bellwether Media.
—Burmese. 2017. (Cool Cats Ser.). (ENG., Illus.). 24p. (J). (gr. k-3). lib. bdg. 25.95 (978-1-62617-561-7(6), Blastoff! Readers) Bellwether Media.
—Japanese Bobtails. 2017. (Cool Cats Ser.). (ENG., Illus.). 24p. (J). (gr. k-3). lib. bdg. 25.95 (978-1-62617-562-4(4), Blastoff! Readers) Bellwether Media.
—Ocicats. 2017. (Cool Cats Ser.). (ENG., Illus.). 24p. (J). (gr. k-3). lib. bdg. 25.95 (978-1-62617-563-1(2), Blastoff! Readers) Bellwether Media.
—RagaMuffins. 2017. (Cool Cats Ser.). (ENG., Illus.). 24p. (J). (gr. k-3). lib. bdg. 25.95 **(978-1-62617-627-0(2)**, Blastoff! Readers) Bellwether Media.
—Selkirk Rexes. 2017. (Cool Cats Ser.). (ENG., Illus.). 24p. (J). (gr. k-3). lib. bdg. 25.95 (978-1-62617-564-8(0), Blastoff! Readers) Bellwether Media.
Rathburn, Betsy. Siberians. 2017. (Cool Cats Ser.). (ENG., Illus.). 24p. (J). (gr. k-3). lib. bdg. 25.95 **(978-1-62617-628-7(0)**, Blastoff! Readers) Bellwether Media.
Rau, Harry the Cat. 2009. 28p. pap. 15.99 (978-1-4389-3876-9(4)) AuthorHouse.
Rau, Dana Meachen. Kids Top 10 Pet Cats. 2015. (American Humane Association Top 10 Pets for Kids Ser.). 48p. (J). (gr. 3-4). 25.27 (978-0-7660-6630-4(4)); pap. 8.95 (978-0-7660-6631-1(2), Enslow Elementary) Enslow Pubs., Inc.
Rayner, Matthew & BVetMed MRCVS Staff. Cat. Burton, Jane & Greenaway, Frank, photos by. 2004. (I Am Your Pet Ser.). (Illus.). 32p. (gr. k-4). lib. bdg. 26.00 (978-0-8368-4102-2(6), Gareth Stevens Learning Library) Stevens, Gareth Publishing LLLP.
Rayyan, Omar, illus. My Kitten's First Year. 2008. (ENG.). 24p. (J). (gr. -1-3). 12.99 (978-0-8249-5572-4(2), Ideal Pubns.) Worthy Publishing.
Rebman, Renee C. Cats. 2009. (Animals Animals 10 Ser.). 48p. (gr. 3). 29.93 (978-0-7614-3975-2(7)) Marshall Cavendish GBR. Dist: Marshall Cavendish Corp.
Reed, Cristie. Ferret. 2015. (ENG.). 32p. (gr. 3-6). 32.79 (978-1-63430-432-0(2)) Rourke Educational Media.
Rees, Gwyneth. Cosmo & the Magic Sneeze, 1. Hearn, Samuel, illus. 3rd unabr. ed. 2005. (Cosmo Ser.: 1). (ENG.). 256p. (J). (gr. 2-4). pap. 8.99 (978-0-330-43729-5(1)) Macmillan Pubs., Ltd. GBR. Dist: Independent Pubs. Group.
Regan, Lisa. Big Cat, Little Cat. 2012. (ENG., Illus.). 24p. (J). (gr. -1-3). 15.00 (978-1-4081-6401-3(9), 9781408164013, Bloomsbury USA Childrens) Bloomsbury Publishing USA.
Richter, Ian. Chloe the Cat. 2013. 24p. pap. 12.45 (978-1-4525-8111-8(8), Balboa Pr.) Author Solutions, Inc.
Ring, Susan. Caring for Your Cat. Kissock, Heather & Marshall, Diana, eds. 2003. (Caring for Your Pet Ser.). (Illus.). 32p. (J). pap. 9.95 (978-1-59036-062-0(1)) Weigl Pubs., Inc.
—Caring for Your Cat. 2003. (Caring for Your Pet Ser.). (Illus.). 32p. (J). (gr. -1-3). lib. bdg. 26.00 (978-1-59036-032-3(X)) Weigl Pubs., Inc.
—Cat. 2008. (My Pet Ser.). (Illus.). 32p. (J). (gr. 3-5). pap. 9.95 (978-1-59036-899-2(1)); lib. bdg. 26.00 (978-1-59036-898-5(3)) Weigl Pubs., Inc.
Ringstad, Arnold. Bobcats. 2014. (Illus.). 24p. (J). 27.10 (978-1-60753-598-0(X)) Amicus Publishing.
Rissman, Rebecca. Cat Shows: Competing for Top Prize. 2016. (Cats Rule! Ser.). (ENG., Illus.). 32p. (gr. 3-4). lib. bdg. 27.99 (978-1-4914-8401-2(2), Snap Bks.) Capstone Press of Coughlan Cos.
Robb, Jackie & Stringle, Berny. The Story of Cat. Duncan, Karen & Stringle, Sam, illus. 2004. (Bang on the Door Ser.). 32p. (YA). pap. (978-1-85602-314-6(1), Pavilion Children's Books) Pavilion Bks.
Rober, Harold T. I Love Cats. 2016. (Bumba Books (tm) — Pets Are the Best Ser.). (ENG., Illus.). 24p. (J). (gr. -1-1). 25.32 (978-1-5124-1413-4(1)) Lerner Publishing Group.
Robins, Sandy. For the Love of Cats: An A-to-Z Primer for Cat Lovers of All Ages. Anderson, Mark, illus. 2011. (For the Love Of... Ser.). (ENG.). 48p. 16.95 (978-1-60078-581-8(6)) Triumph Bks.
Rockwell, Anne F. How Kittens Grow. Date not set. 40p. (J). (gr. -1-1). pap. 4.99 (978-0-06-445219-9(0)); pap. 15.99 (978-0-06-029103-7(6)); lib. bdg. 16.89 (978-0-06-029104-4(4)) HarperCollins Pubs.
Roytman, Arkady. Maneki Neko Lucky Cat Coloring Book. 2015. (Dover Clip Art Design Tools Ser.). (ENG., Illus.). 32p. (J). (gr. 2-5). pap. 3.99 (978-0-486-79930-8(1)) Dover Pubns., Inc.
Roza, Greg. Your Neighbor the Alley Cat. 2011. (City Critters Ser.). (ENG., Illus.). 24p. (J). (gr. k-5). pap. 8.25 (978-1-4488-5127-0(0)); lib. bdg. 22.60 (978-1-4488-4999-4(3)) Windmill Bks.
Rudolph, Jessica. American Shorthairs: Pioneers. 2011. (Cat-Ographies Ser.). 24p. (YA). (gr. 2-5). lib. bdg. 22.61 (978-1-61772-143-4(3)) Bearport Publishing Co., Inc.
Ruffin, Fran. Cats. 2009. (My World of Animals Ser.). 24p. (gr. 1-1). 37.50 (978-1-61514-711-3(X), PowerKids Pr.) Rosen Publishing Group, Inc., The.
Saltzberg, Barney. I Love Cats. 2006. 20p. pap. 8.99 (978-0-7636-3318-9(6)) Four Blocks.
Salzmann, Mary Elizabeth. Alley to Zippy: Cats from A to Z, 1 vol. 2009. (Let's Learn A to Z Ser.). (ENG., Illus.). 32p. (J). (gr. -1-2). 27.07 (978-1-60453-493-1(1)) ABDO Publishing Co.
Satkamp, Diana. The Woodpile Kitty. 2011. 28p. pap. 13.54 (978-1-4634-4386-3(2)) AuthorHouse.
Save A Gato, as told by. Old San Juan Cat Tales: Cuentos de Gatos del Viejo San Juan. 2007.Tr. of Cuentos de Gatos del Viejo San Juan. (ENG & SPA., Illus.). 24p. (J). 24.00 (978-0-9791782-0-7(7)) ALVARADOPLUS.
Schaefer, Peggy. More Stories of Cats. 2005. (Illus.). 208p. 12.95 (978-0-8249-4638-8(3), Ideal Pubns.) Worthy Publishing.
Scheunemann, Pam. Cats Meow!, 1 vol. 2009. (Animal Sounds Set 1 Ser.). (ENG., Illus.). 24p. (J). (gr. k-3). lib. bdg. 24.21 (978-1-60453-568-6(7), SandCastle) ABDO Publishing Co.
—Marvelous Maine Coons, 1 vol. Doucet, Bob, illus. 2009. (Cat Craze Ser.). (ENG.). 24p. (J). (gr. k-3). 25.65 (978-1-60453-723-9(X)) ABDO Publishing Co.
—Popular Persians, 1 vol. Doucet, Bob, illus. 2009. (Cat Craze Ser.). (ENG.). 24p. (J). (gr. k-3). 25.65 (978-1-60453-724-6(8)) ABDO Publishing Co.
Schuh, Mari C. Abyssinians. 2017. (Favorite Cat Breeds Ser.). (ENG., Illus.). 24p. (J). (gr. k-2). pap. 8.99 (978-1-68152-095-7(8)) Amicus.
—Abyssinians. 2016. (ENG., Illus.). 24p. (J). (gr. 1-4). 20.95 (978-1-60753-966-7(7)) Amicus Publishing.
—American Shorthair Cats. 2017. (Favorite Cat Breeds Ser.). (ENG., Illus.). 24p. (J). (gr. k-2). pap. 8.99 (978-1-68152-096-4(6)) Amicus.
—American Shorthair Cats. 2016. (Favorite Cat Breeds Ser.). (ENG., Illus.). 24p. (J). (gr. 1-4). 20.95 (978-1-60753-967-4(5)) Amicus Publishing.
—Birman Cats. 2016. (Favorite Cat Breeds Ser.). (ENG., Illus.). 24p. (J). (gr. 1-4). 20.95 (978-1-60753-968-1(3)) Amicus Publishing.
—Maine Coon Cats. 2017. (Favorite Cat Breeds Ser.). (ENG., Illus.). 24p. (J). (gr. k-2). pap. 8.99 (978-1-68152-098-8(2)) Amicus.
—Maine Coon Cats. 2016. (Favorite Cat Breeds Ser.). (ENG., Illus.). 24p. (J). (gr. 1-4). 20.95 (978-1-60753-969-8(1)) Amicus Publishing.
—Persian Cats. 2017. (Favorite Cat Breeds Ser.). (ENG., Illus.). 24p. (J). (gr. k-2). pap. 8.99 (978-1-68152-099-5(0)) Amicus.
—Persian Cats. 2016. (Favorite Cat Breeds Ser.). (ENG., Illus.). 24p. (J). (gr. 1-4). 20.95 (978-1-60753-970-4(5)) Amicus Publishing.
—Ragdoll Cats. 2017. (Favorite Cat Breeds Ser.). (ENG., Illus.). 24p. (J). (gr. k-2). pap. 8.99 (978-1-68152-100-8(8)) Amicus.
—Ragdoll Cats. 2016. (Favorite Cat Breeds Ser.). (ENG., Illus.). 24p. (J). (gr. 1-4). 20.95 (978-1-60753-971-1(3)) Amicus Publishing.
—Siamese Cats. 2017. (Favorite Cat Breeds Ser.). (ENG., Illus.). 24p. (J). (gr. k-2). pap. 8.99 (978-1-68152-101-5(6)) Amicus.
—Siamese Cats. 2016. (Favorite Cat Breeds Ser.). (ENG., Illus.). 24p. (J). (gr. 1-4). 20.95 (978-1-60753-972-8(1)) Amicus Publishing.
—Sphynx Cats. 2017. (Favorite Cat Breeds Ser.). (ENG., Illus.). 24p. (J). (gr. k-2). pap. 8.99 (978-1-68152-102-2(4)) Amicus.
—Sphynx Cats. 2016. (Favorite Cat Breeds Ser.). (ENG., Illus.). 24p. (J). (gr. 1-4). 20.95 (978-1-60753-973-5(X)) Amicus Publishing.
Scollen, Chris. Busy Kids Kittens & Puppies Sb. 2008. (Busy Kids Ser.). (Illus.). 20p. (J). (gr. -1-3). 4.99 (978-1-84610-632-3(X)) Make Believe Ideas GBR. Dist: Nelson, Thomas Inc.
Sexton, Colleen. Kittens. 2008. (Watch Animals Grow Ser.). (ENG., Illus.). 24p. (J). (gr. k-3). lib. bdg. 25.95 (978-1-60014-168-3(4)) Bellwether Media.
—The Life Cycle of a Cat. 2010. (Life Cycles Ser.). (ENG., Illus.). 24p. (J). (gr. k-3). lib. bdg. 25.95 (978-1-60014-449-3(7), Blastoff! Readers) Bellwether Media.
Sheikh-Miller, Jonathan. Big Cats II. 2010. (Discovery Nature Ser.). 48p. (J). 8.99 (978-0-7945-2243-8(2), Usborne) EDC Publishing.
Silverstein, Alvin, et al. Curious Cats. 2003. (What a Pet! Ser.). (ENG., Illus.). 48p. (gr. 3-6). lib. bdg. 23.93 (978-0-7613-2512-3(3), Millbrook Pr.) Lerner Publishing Group.
—Hairless Cats: Cool Pets! Kelley, Gerald, illus. 2011. (Far-Out & Unusual Pets Ser.). 48p. (J). (gr. 3-5). lib. bdg. 25.27 (978-0-7660-3688-8(X), Enslow Elementary) Enslow Pubs., Inc.
Simon, Seymour. Big Cats (revised Edition) 2017. 40p. (J). (gr. 1-5). pap. 6.99 **(978-0-06-247035-5(3))** HarperCollins Pubs.
Simon, Seymour. Cats. Simon, Seymour, illus. (Illus.). (J). 2009. (ENG.). 32p. (gr. k-4). pap. 6.99 (978-0-06-446254-9(4)) 2004. 40p. (gr. -1-3). lib. bdg. 17.89 (978-0-06-028941-6(4)) HarperCollins Pubs.
Skiles, Janet & Coloring Books Staff. How to Care for Your Cat: A Color & Learn Guide for Kids. 2011. (Dover Children's Activity Bks.). (ENG., Illus.). 32p. (J). (gr. -1-3). pap. 3.99 (978-0-486-48148-7(4)) Dover Pubns., Inc.
Soffer, Ruth. Cats Stained Glass Coloring Book. 2009. (Dover Nature Stained Glass Coloring Book Ser.). (ENG., Illus.). 32p. (gr. -1-8). pap. 7.99 (978-0-486-46994-2(8)) Dover Pubns., Inc.
Spaht-Gill, Janie. Socks. Lambson, Elizabeth, illus. (J). 5.95 (978-0-89868-301-1(7)) ARO Publishing Co.
Squadrito, Vanessa. The Girl & Her Cat. Iwanaga, Kent, illus. 2011. 24p. 12.56 (978-1-4269-5531-0(6)) Trafford Publishing.
Squire, Ann O. Bobcats. 2005. (True Bks.). (ENG., Illus.). 48p. (J). (gr. 3-5). per. 6.95 (978-0-516-27931-2(9), Children's Pr.) Scholastic Library Publishing.
Stamper, Judith Bauer. Ragdolls: Alien Cats. 2011. (Cat-Ographies Ser.). 24p. (YA). (gr. 2-5). lib. bdg. 22.61 (978-1-61772-146-5(8)) Bearport Publishing Co., Inc.
Standley, Andrew. My Old Cat. 2003. (Illus.). 8p. (J). (978-1-888223-48-4(0)) McMillen Publishing.
Starke, Katherine. Cats & Kittens. rev. ed. 2005. 32p. (J). (gr. 1-18). pap. 5.95 (978-0-7945-0798-5(0), Usborne) EDC Publishing.
Starke, Katherine & Watt, Fiona. Cats & Kittens. Fox, Christyan, illus. Burton, Jane, photos by. 2006. 30p. (J). pap. (978-0-439-78492-4(1)) Scholastic, Inc.
Steffora, Tracey. Animal Math: Comparing & Measuring, 1 vol. 2014. (Animal Math Ser.). (ENG.). 32p. (gr. -1-1). 29.99 (978-1-4846-0062-7(2), NA-h) Heinemann-Raintree.
—Comparing with Cats, 1 vol. 2013. (Animal Math Ser.). (ENG.). 24p. (gr. -1-1). 22.65 (978-1-4329-7559-3(5)); pap. 6.95 (978-1-4329-7566-1(8)) Heinemann-Raintree. (NA-h).
Sterling Publishing Co., Inc. Begin Smart(tm) Meow. 2016. (Begin Smart(tm) Ser.). (ENG., Illus.). 14p. (J). (— 1). bds. 8.95 (978-1-4549-1877-6(2)) Sterling Publishing Co., Inc.
Stevens, Kathryn. Cats. 2015. (Pet Care Ser.). (ENG.). 24p. (J). (gr. -1-2). 25.64 (978-1-63143-726-7(7), 208543) Child's World, Inc., The.
Stevenson, Sharry. Gibby's Story. 2012. 36p. pap. 18.41 (978-1-4669-3322-4(4)) Trafford Publishing.
Steward, Martha. Bangle Bear: The Tale of a Tailless Cat. 2011. 28p. pap. 15.47 (978-1-4520-0694-9(6)) AuthorHouse.
Stoltman, Joan. My First Cat. 2017. (Let's Get a Pet! Ser.). 24p. (gr. 1-2). pap. 8.15 **(978-1-4824-6445-0(4))** Stevens, Gareth Publishing LLLP.
Stone, Lynn M. Exotic Cats. 2009. (Illus.). 24p. (J). lib. bdg. 27.07 (978-1-60694-336-6(7)) Rourke Educational Media.
Strange but True, 1 vol. 2010. (Strange but True Ser.). (ENG.). 32p. (gr. 1-2). lib. bdg. 106.60 (978-1-4296-4554-6(7), Blazers) Capstone Press of Coughlan Cos.
Submarine Cat. (Buggy Buddies with Flaps Ser.). (Illus.). (YA). bds. 3.00 net. (978-1-56021-391-8(4)) W.J. Fantasy, Inc.
Summers, Alex. Rescue & Shelter Cats. 2015. (ENG.). 24p. (gr. 1-4). 28.50 (978-1-63430-065-0(3)) Rourke Educational Media.
Swensen, C. Cats. 2016. (In the Barnyard Ser.). (ENG.). 24p. (J). (gr. k-3). 27.07 (978-1-5038-0823-2(8), 210667) Child's World, Inc., The.
Swigelson, Kayce M. The Grand Adventures of Petit Louis. Swigelson, Kayce M., illus. 2013. (Illus.). 54p. 24.95 (978-0-9889643-1-0(7)) MathisJones Communications, LLC.
Tait, Leia. Little Draggin' Bear. 2008. (Inspiring Animals Ser.). (Illus.). 24p. (J). (gr. 2-4). pap. 8.95 (978-1-59036-861-9(4)); lib. bdg. 24.45 (978-1-59036-860-2(6)) Weigl Pubs., Inc.
Taylor, Trace. Cats. 2010. pap. 39.62 (978-1-61541-094-1(5)) American Reading Co.
Thomson, Ruth. The Life Cycle of a Cat. 2007. (Learning about Life Cycles Ser.). (Illus.). 24p. (J). (gr. 4-7). lib. bdg. 22.60 (978-1-4042-3710-0(0), PowerKids Pr.) Rosen Publishing Group, Inc., The.
Tiger Tales, ed. & compiled by. Kittens. Tiger Tales, compiled by. 2014. (My First Touch & Feel Ser.). (ENG.). 10p. (J). (gr. -1 — 1). bds. 8.99 (978-1-58925-563-0(1)) Tiger Tales.
Top That Publishing Staff, ed. Kittens & Cats. 2005. (Illus.). 24p. (978-1-84510-538-9(9)) Top That! Publishing PLC.
Tuxworth, Nicole. Kittens. 2015. (ENG., Illus.). 20p. (J). (gr. -1 — 1). bds. 6.99 (978-1-86147-384-4(2), Armadillo) Anness Publishing GBR. Dist: National Bk. Network.
Tweedy, Bonnie. Grandma Bonnie's Cats: In Love Again. 2011. 28p. pap. 12.98 (978-1-4520-1150-9(8)) AuthorHouse.
Twine, Alice. Cats of the Wild. 2007. (Baby Animals Ser.). (Illus.). 24p. (J). (gr. -1-3). lib. bdg. 22.60 (978-1-4042-3772-8(0), PowerKids Pr.) Rosen Publishing Group, Inc., The.
—Kittens. (Baby Animals Ser.). 24p. 2009. (gr. 1-1). 42.50 (978-1-61511-492-4(0)) 2008. (Illus.). (J). (gr. 3-7). lib. bdg. 22.60 (978-1-4042-4144-2(2)) Rosen Publishing Group, Inc., The. (PowerKids Pr.).
—Kittens/Gatitos. 2009. (Baby Animals/Animales bebé Ser.). (ENG & SPA.). 24p. (gr. 1-1). 42.50 (978-1-61511-504-4(8), Editorial Buenas Letras) Rosen Publishing Group, Inc., The.
—Kittens/Gatitos. Obregon, Jose Maria, tr. from ENG. 2008. (Baby Animals / Animales Bebé Ser.). (SPA., Illus.). 24p. (J). (gr. k-3). lib. bdg. 22.60 (978-1-4042-7685-7(8)) Rosen Publishing Group, Inc., The.
Ventura, Marne. Kunkush: The True Story of a Refugee Cat. Guo, Beidi, illus. 2017. (Encounter: Narrative Nonfiction Picture Bks.). (ENG.). 32p. (gr. 3-4). lib. bdg. 28.65 **(978-1-5157-7319-1(1))** Encounter Bks.
Walker, Kathryn. See How Cats Grow. 2009. (See How They Grow Ser.). (J). lib. bdg. 22.60 (978-1-4358-2829-2(1), PowerKids Pr.) Rosen Publishing Group, Inc., The.
Walker, Niki & Kalman, Bobbie. Los Gatitos. Crabtree, Marc, photos by. 2006. (Cuidado de las Mascotas Ser.). (SPA., Illus.). 32p. (J). (gr. 3-7). pap. (978-0-7787-8476-0(2)); lib. bdg. (978-0-7787-8454-8(1)) Crabtree Publishing Co.
—Kittens. 2014. 32p. pap. 9.00 (978-1-61003-354-1(X)) Center for the Collaborative Classroom.
—Kittens. 2003. (Pet Care Ser.). (ENG., Illus.). 32p. (J). pap. (978-0-7787-1762-9(8)) Crabtree Publishing Co.
Walker, Niki, et al. Les Chatons. 2010. (Petit Monde Vivant Ser.). (FRE., Illus.). 32p. (J). pap. 9.95 (978-2-89579-325-0(5)) Bayard Canada Livres CAN. Dist: Crabtree Publishing Co.
Wheeler, Jill C. American Wirehair Cats, 1 vol. 2012. (Cats Set 6 Ser.). (ENG.). 24p. (J). (gr. 2-5). 25.65 (978-1-61783-238-3(3)) ABDO Publishing Co.
—Bengal Cats, 1 vol. 2011. (Cats Set 5: Designer Cats Ser.). (ENG., Illus.). 24p. (J). (gr. 2-5). 25.65 (978-1-60453-728-4(0)) ABDO Publishing Co.
—British Shorthair Cats, 1 vol. 2012. (Cats Set 6 Ser.). (ENG.). 24p. (J). (gr. 2-5). 25.65 (978-1-61783-239-0(1)) ABDO Publishing Co.
—Chausie Cats, 1 vol. 2011. (Cats Set 5: Designer Cats Ser.). (ENG., Illus.). 24p. (J). (gr. 2-5). 25.65 (978-1-60453-729-1(9)) ABDO Publishing Co.
—Egyptian Mau Cats, 1 vol. 2012. (Cats Set 6 Ser.). (ENG.). 24p. (J). (gr. 2-5). 25.65 (978-1-61783-240-6(5)) ABDO Publishing Co.
—Havana Brown Cats, 1 vol. 2012. (Cats Set 6 Ser.). (ENG.). 24p. (J). (gr. 2-5). 25.65 (978-1-61783-241-3(3)) ABDO Publishing Co.
—Japanese Bobtail Cats, 1 vol. 2012. (Cats Set 6 Ser.). (ENG.). 24p. (J). (gr. 2-5). 25.65 (978-1-61783-242-0(1)) ABDO Publishing Co.
—Pixiebob Cats, 1 vol. 2011. (Cats Set 5: Designer Cats Ser.). (ENG., Illus.). 24p. (J). (gr. 2-5). 25.65 (978-1-60453-730-7(2)) ABDO Publishing Co.
—Ragdoll Cats, 1 vol. 2012. (Cats Set 6 Ser.). (ENG.). 24p. (J). (gr. 2-5). 25.65 (978-1-61783-243-7(X)) ABDO Publishing Co.
—Safari Cats, 1 vol. 2011. (Cats Set 5: Designer Cats Ser.). (ENG., Illus.). 24p. (J). (gr. 2-5). 25.65 (978-1-60453-731-4(0)) ABDO Publishing Co.
—Savannah Cats, 1 vol. 2011. (Cats Set 5: Designer Cats Ser.). (ENG., Illus.). 24p. (J). (gr. 2-5). 25.65 (978-1-60453-732-1(9)) ABDO Publishing Co.
—Toyger Cats, 1 vol. 2011. (Cats Set 5: Designer Cats Ser.). (ENG., Illus.). 24p. (J). (gr. 2-5). 25.65 (978-1-60453-733-8(7)) ABDO Publishing Co.
White, Nancy. Maine Coons: Super Big. 2011. (Cat-Ographies Ser.). 24p. (J). (gr. 2-5). lib. bdg. 22.61 (978-1-61772-142-7(5)) Bearport Publishing Co., Inc.
—Siamese: Talk to Me! 2011. (Cat-Ographies Ser.). 24p. (J). (gr. 2-5). lib. bdg. 22.61 (978-1-61772-144-1(1)) Bearport Publishing Co., Inc.
Wilbur, Helen L. M Is for Meow: A Cat Alphabet. Papp, Robert, illus. rev. ed. 2006. (ENG.). 40p. (J). (gr. k-6). 17.95 (978-1-58536-304-9(9)) Sleeping Bear Pr.
Wildcats, 1 vol. 2010. (Wildcats Ser.). (ENG.). 24p. (gr. k-1). lib. bdg. 159.90 (978-1-4296-4486-0(9)); lib. bdg. 106.60 (978-1-4296-5691-7(3)) Capstone Press of Coughlan Cos. (Pebble Plus).
William H. Sadlier Staff. Cats! Cats! Cats!, Vol. 2. 2005. (Emergent Library: Vol. 1). (gr. -1-1). 24.00 net. (978-0-8215-8908-3(3)) Sadlier, William H. Inc.
Wilsdon, Christina. Cats. 2009. (Amazing Animals Ser.). 48p. (gr. 2-6). pap. 10.50 (978-1-4339-2022-6(0), Gareth Stevens Learning Library); (J). (gr. 3-6). lib. bdg. 28.00 (978-0-8368-9105-8(8)) Stevens, Gareth Publishing LLLP.
—Cats. 2007. (J). (978-1-59939-128-1(7), Reader's Digest Young Families, Inc.) Studio Fun International.
Winters, Kari, told to. Princess Fiona: My Purrsonal Story. 2003. (YA). pap. 14.95 (978-0-9740980-0-5(0)) shelterpetsink.
Wolf, Clarissa. Cat, Cat, Feral Cat. Messer, Corey, illus. 2009. 28p. pap. 9.99 (978-1-935105-26-8(4)) Avid Readers Publishing Group.
Wood, Mandy. My First Kitty. 2013. (ENG.). 24p. (J). (gr. 1-6). pap. 8.95 (978-1-61448-533-9(X)) Morgan James Publishing.
World Book, Inc. Staff, contrib. by. Persians & Other Long-Haired Cats. 2009. (J). (978-0-7166-1375-6(1)) World Bk., Inc.
World Book, Inc Staff, contrib. by. Siamese & Other Short-Haired Cats. 2007. (World Book's Animals of the World Ser.). (Illus.). 64p. (J). (978-0-7166-1335-0(2)) World Bk., Inc.
Wyrwas, Kim. The Lonely Cat. 2012. 30p. 24.95 (978-1-4626-6459-7(8)) America Star Bks.
Zobel, Derek. Caring for Your Cat. 2010. (Pet Care Library). (ENG., Illus.). 24p. (J). (gr. 2-5). lib. bdg. 25.95 (978-1-60014-465-3(9), Blastoff! Readers) Bellwether Media.
Zuffi, Stefano. The Cat in Art. Jones, Simon, tr. 2007. (ENG., Illus.). 360p. (gr. 8-17). 40.00 (978-0-8109-9328-0(7)) Abrams, Inc.

CATS—FICTION

Aalborg, Gordon. Cat Tracks. l.t. ed. 2005. pap. 13.95 (978-0-9765185-0-1(3), 800-431-1579) Delphi Bks.
Aardvark, D. Punkin's upside down Day. l.t. ed. 2004. (Illus.). 40p. (J). per. 10.95 (978-0-9755567-0-2(3)) Aardvark's Weedpatch Pr.
Abbott, D. K. Mrs. Potter's Cat. McKenzie, Josie, illus. 2007. 28p. per. 24.95 (978-1-4241-8345-6(6)) America Star Bks.
Abel, Melanie. Kitten up a Tree. Lederhos, Anne, illus. 2008. 24p. (J). pap. 15.95 (978-0-9791606-4-6(2)) E & E Publishing.
Abley, Mark. Ghost Cat. Reczuch, Karen, illus. 2004. (J). (gr. k-3). spiral bd. (978-0-616-11091-1(X)); spiral bd. (978-0-616-11092-8(8)) Canadian National Institute for the Blind/Institut National Canadien pour les Aveugles.
Ackerman, Jill. Hey, Diddle Diddle! Berg, Michelle, illus. 2011. (Little Scholastic Ser.). (ENG.). 6p. (J). (gr. k — 1). 12.99 (978-0-545-35113-3(8), Cartwheel Bks.) Scholastic, Inc.
Adam, Sally. The Adventures of Rex Adam. 2011. 28p. pap. 14.00 (978-1-4567-1721-6(9)) AuthorHouse.
—The Cats of Ellis Island. 2009. 28p. pap. 12.50 (978-1-4389-6012-8(3)) AuthorHouse.
Adams, Ann. Moppet the Hero. 2012. (Illus.). 54p. pap. 6.00 (978-1-78035-372-2(3), Fastprint Publishing) Upfront Publishing Ltd. GBR. Dist: Printondemand-worldwide.com.
Adams, Sandi. Watch What You Wish: Kajsa Conquers Her World. 2009. 36p. pap. 15.49 (978-1-4490-3513-6(2)) AuthorHouse.
Adler, David A. Young Cam Jansen & the Spotted Cat Mystery, No. 12. Natti, Susanna & Natti, S., illus. 2007. (Young Cam Jansen Ser.: 12). (ENG.). 32p. (J). (gr. 1-3). pap. 3.99 (978-0-14-241012-7(8), Penguin Young Readers) Penguin Young Readers Group.
—Young Cam Jansen & the Spotted Cat Mystery. Natti, Susanna, illus. 2007. (Young Cam Jansen (prebound) Ser.).

31p. (gr. -1-3). 14.00 *(978-0-7569-8155-6(7))* Perfection Learning Corp.
Aiken, Joan. El Gato Mog.Tr. of Necklace of Raindrops. (SPA.). 104p. (J). 5.95 *(978-84-348-1275-8(4))* SM Ediciones ESP. Dist: AIMS International Bks., Inc.
Albee, Sarah. Hello, Cat, Hello, Dog. Leigh, Tom, illus. 2006. (Step-By-Step Readers Ser.). (J). pap. *(978-1-59939-054-3(X)*, Reader's Digest Young Families, Inc.) Studio Fun International.
Aldrich, Thomas Bailey. The Story of a Cat. 2006. (Illus.). pap. 19.95 *(978-1-4254-9049-2(2))* Kessinger Publishing, LLC.
Aldrick, Shirley H. F. Gordon, the Great Gobbley Grasshopper. 2011. 32p. pap. 13.00 *(978-1-60976-643-6(1)*, Strategic Bk. Publishing) Strategic Book Publishing & Rights Agency (SBPRA).
Alexander, John. The Adventures of Thunder & Avalanche: Up & Away. Alexander, John, illus. 2013. (Illus.). 48p. 15.99 *(978-0-9887625-1-0(X))* Mountain Thunder Publishing.
Alexander, Lestat. The Blue-Eyed Alligator. 2011. 24p. pap. 12.56 *(978-1-4269-5467-2(0))* Trafford Publishing.
Alexander, Lloyd. The Cat Who Wished to Be a Man. 107p. (J). pap. 3.99 *(978-0-8072-1505-0(8)*, Listening Library) Random Hse. Audio Publishing Group.
—Dream-of-Jade: The Emperor's Cat. Burkett, D. Brent, illus. 2005. (ENG.). 48p. (J). (gr. 3-7). 17.95 *(978-0-8126-2736-7(9))* Cricket Bks.
—Time Cat: The Remarkable Journeys of Jason & Gareth. 2012. (ENG., Illus.). 240p. (J). (gr. 3-7). pap. 7.99 *(978-0-312-63213-7(4)*, 9780312632137) Square Fish.
Alexander, R. C. Unfamiliar Magic. 2011. (ENG.). 368p. (J). (gr. 3-7). pap. 8.99 *(978-0-375-85855-0(5)*, Yearling) Random Hse. Children's Bks.
Alexander, Troas. A Cat's Tale. Roberts, Ramona, illus. 2007. 36p. per. 14.95 *(978-1-59858-371-7(9))* Dog Ear Publishing, LLC.
Alexander, Troas James. Stray's Great Adventure. Mitchell Jr., Leonard, illus. 2010. 40p. pap. 15.95 *(978-1-60844-200-3(4))* Dog Ear Publishing, LLC.
Alfonso, Velia De Guevara. Sandy Comes Home. 2011. 28p. pap. 12.50 *(978-1-60976-467-8(6)*, Eloquent Bks.) Strategic Book Publishing & Rights Agency (SBPRA).
Allegri, Natasha. Fionna & Cake Mathematical. Allegri, Natasha, illus. 2014. (Adventure Time Ser.: 1). (ENG., Illus.). 192p. (J). (gr. 4). 39.99 *(978-1-60886-391-4(3))* Boom! Studios.
Allegri, Natasha, illus. Adventure Time - Fionna & Cake. Allegri, Natasha, . 2013. (ENG.). 176p. (J). (gr. 4). pap. 19.99 *(978-1-60886-338-9(7))* Boom! Studios.
Allen, Debbie. Winker & the Kitten. 2009. 28p. pap. 13.99 *(978-1-4389-8266-3(6))* AuthorHouse.
Allen, J. J. Hello Kitty's Fun Friend Day! 2003. (Illus.). 32p. (J). pap. *(978-0-439-44917-5(0))* Scholastic, Inc.
Allen, Jonathan. Is That My Cat? 2014. (ENG., Illus.). 32p. (J). (gr. -1-k). 16.95 *(978-1-907967-74-0(5))* Boxer Bks., Ltd. GBR. Dist: Sterling Publishing Co., Inc.
Alligator Books Staff & Fabiny, Sarah. Katie Kitten Finds a Friend. Hughes, Cathy, illus. 2012. (Squeaky Board Bks.). (ENG.). 20p. (J). bds. 4.99 *(978-0-7641-6481-1(3))* Barron's Educational Series, Inc.
Allman-Varty, Faye. The Kitten Tales of Pumpkin & Parsnip 'Fairy Fields. Knott, Stephen, illus. 2008. 20p. pap. *(978-1-905553-28-0(5))* BookPublishingWorld.
Allyson, Libby. Scottie Rides the Bus. 2004. 27p. pap. 24.95 *(978-1-4137-3298-6(4))* PublishAmerica, Inc.
Alter, Anna. Francine's Day. Alter, Anna, illus. 2003. (Illus.). 32p. (J). lib. bdg. 16.89 *(978-0-06-623937-8(0))* HarperCollins Pubs.
Alumenda, Stephen. Toko & the Lost Kittens. 2004. (Illus.). 24p. pap. *(978-9966-25-170-1(7))* Heinemann Kenya, Limited (East African Educational Publishers Ltd E.A.E.P.) KEN. Dist: Michigan State Univ. Pr.
Ammirato, Lidia. Why Does the Dog Chase the Cat & the Cat Chase the Mouse? 2012. 24p. pap. 15.99 *(978-1-4771-0651-8(0))* Xlibris Corp.
Anderson, Airlie. Cat's Colors. Anderson, Airlie, illus. 2016. (Child's Play Library). (ENG., Illus.). 32p. (J). (gr. k-2). *(978-1-84643-761-8(X))* Child's Play International Ltd.
Anderson, Alice. Penny's Love for Cats. 2012. 20p. pap. 17.99 *(978-1-4772-9245-7(4))* AuthorHouse.
Anderson, Laurie Halse. Homeless. 2007. (Vet Volunteers Ser.: 2). (ENG.). 160p. (J). (gr. 3-7). 6.99 *(978-0-14-240863-6(8)*, Puffin Books) Penguin Young Readers Group.
—Masks, 11 vols. 2012. (Vet Volunteers Ser.: 11). (ENG.). 128p. (J). (gr. 3-7). 6.99 *(978-0-14-241257-2(0)*, Puffin Books) Penguin Young Readers Group.
Anderson, Trey. Jesse & Midnight. 2007. 56p. per. 16.95 *(978-1-60474-062-2(0))* America Star Bks.
Andrea, Leona. El Club de Las Siete Gatas. 2004.Tr. of Seven Kittens Club. (SPA., Illus.). 176p. 13.95 *(978-84-95618-73-3(7)*, Umbriel) Ediciones Urano S. A. ESP. Dist: Spanish Pubs., LLC.
Andrews, Alexa. Cat Days. John and Wendy, illus. 2012. (Penguin Young Readers, Level 1 Ser.). (ENG.). 32p. (J). (gr. k-1). pap. 3.99 *(978-0-448-46305-6(9)*, Penguin Young Readers) Penguin Young Readers Group.
—Cat Days. 2012. (Penguin Young Readers Level 1 Ser.). lib. bdg. 13.55 *(978-0-606-26638-3(0)*, Turtleback) Turtleback Bks.
Andrews, Jackie. Three Little Kittens. Smith, Lesley, illus. 2012. (ENG.). 32p. (J). pap. 6.50 *(978-1-84135-197-1(0))* Award Pubns. Ltd. GBR. Dist: Parkwest Pubns., Inc.
Andrews, Julie. Little Bo: The Story of Bonnie Boadicea, No. 2. 2011. (Illus.). (J). lib. bdg. 18.89 *(978-0-06-008912-2(1))* HarperCollins Pubs.
Andrews, Julie & Edwards, Julie Andrews. Little Bo in Italy: The Continued Adventures of Bonnie Boadicea. Cole, Henry, illus. 2010. (ENG.). 112p. (J). (gr. 1-4). 19.99 *(978-0-06-008908-5(3))* HarperCollins Pubs.
Andrews McMeel Publishing Staff & Vasan, Gandee. Crazy Cats. 2009. (ENG.). 10p. (J). (gr. -1). bds. 7.99 *(978-0-7407-8111-7(1))* Andrews McMeel Publishing.
Ann, Melissa. Redfish, Goldfish. 2012. 24p. 24.95 *(978-1-4626-5772-8(9))* America Star Bks.
Antiporda, Enrico. The Adventures of Jimbo, the Homeless Cat. Antiporda, Enrico, illus. 2013. (Illus.). 66p. pap. 14.95 *(978-0-9672793-5-0(6))* Blue Owl Editions.
Antonia, Miller, illus. Baby's Very First Little Book of Kittens. 2011. (Baby's Very First Board Bks). 10p. (J). ring bd. 6.99 *(978-0-7945-2956-7(9)*, Usborne) EDC Publishing.
Anzalone, Karen. Time in a Bottle. 2003. 100p. (YA). pap. 9.00 *(978-0-7599-3840-3(7))* Hard Shell Word Factory.
Appelt, Kathi. The Underneath. Small, David, illus. 2010. (KOR.). 395p. (YA). pap. *(978-89-527-5767-8(X))* Sigongsa Co., Ltd.
—The Underneath. Small, David, illus. (ENG.). (J). (gr. 5-9). 2010. 336p. pap. 8.99 *(978-1-4169-5059-2(1))* 2008. 320p. 17.99 *(978-1-4169-5058-5(3))* Simon & Schuster Children's Publishing. (Atheneum Bks. for Young Readers).
—The Underneath. 2010. lib. bdg. 19.65 *(978-0-606-14504-6(4)*, Turtleback) Turtleback Bks.
Applegate, Katherine. Crenshaw. 2015. (ENG.). 256p. (J). (gr. 5-9). 16.99 *(978-1-250-04323-8(9)*, 9781250043238) Feiwel & Friends.
—Crenshaw. 2017. (ENG.). 272p. (J). pap. 7.99 ***(978-1-250-09166-6(7)**, 9781250091666)* Square Fish.
—Crenshaw. 2017. (J). lib. bdg. 18.40 ***(978-0-606-40539-3(9))*** Turtleback Bks.
—Crenshaw. 2016. (SPA.). 192p. (J). (gr. 5-8). pap. 13.99 *(978-987-747-067-3(5))* V&R Editoras.
—Never Race a Runaway Pumpkin. Biggs, Brian, illus. 2009. (Roscoe Riley Rules Ser.: 7). (ENG.). 96p. (J). (gr. 1-5). 15.99 *(978-0-06-178372-2(2))*; pap. 4.99 *(978-0-06-178370-8(6))* HarperCollins Pubs.
—Never Race a Runaway Pumpkin. 2009. (Roscoe Riley Rules Ser.: 7). (J). lib. bdg. 14.75 *(978-0-606-06090-5(1)*, Turtleback) Turtleback Bks.
Archambault, John. Boom Chicka Rock. Chitwood, Suzanne Tanner & Chitwood, Suzanne, illus. 2004. (ENG.). 32p. (J). (gr. -1-k). 16.99 *(978-0-399-23587-0(6)*, Philomel Bks.) Penguin Young Readers Group.
—Cat in the Tree. Cooper, Stephanie, illus. 2007. (J). *(978-1-58669-230-8(5))* Childcraft Education Corp.
Archibald, Laura. The Cats of Grand Central. Beckett, Garner, illus. 2004. 30p. 16.95 *(978-0-9730951-0-4(5))* Solomon's Signature CAN. Dist: Hushion Hse. Publishing, Ltd.
Aristocats. (Disney Read-Alongs Ser.). (J). 7.99 incl. audio *(978-1-55723-022-5(6))* Walt Disney Home Video.
Arkell, O. E. The Adventures of Munchkin-Patch Tabby: How Munchkin Patch-Tabby Got His Name. 2009. 16p. pap. 15.95 *(978-1-4389-4273-5(7))* AuthorHouse.
Armstrong, Alan W. Whittington. Schindler, S. D., illus. 2007. 191p. (gr. 3-7). 17.00 *(978-0-7569-7768-9(1))* Perfection Learning Corp.
—Whittington. 2006. (ENG., Illus.). 208p. (J). (gr. 3-7). 7.99 *(978-0-375-82865-2(6)*, Yearling) Random Hse. Children's Bks.
Armstrong, Kate. David & the Mittens Kitten Stories. 2006. (J). 15.00 net. *(978-0-9790205-0-6(6))* Cedar Creek Publishing.
Arnold, Barbara Studebaker. Marmalade. 2011. 32p. pap. 21.99 *(978-1-4568-9609-6(1))* Xlibris Corp.
Arnold, George. Pharaohs' Follies: Kits of the CIA Adventures in Egypt. Kablaoui, Rasmia, tr. Eckhardt, Jason C., illus. 2016. (Cats of the CIA Ser.). (ENG.). (YA). (gr. 7-12). pap. 19.95 ***(978-1-68179-074-9(2)**, Eakin Pr.)* Eakin Pr.
Arreola, Perla. Weenz the Cat: What about Me? Arreola, Manuel, illus. 2013. 30p. 14.99 *(978-0-9859298-7-9(1))* Dream&Achieve Bks.
Aryal, Aimee. Hello Wildcat! Cooper, Blair, illus. 2004. 24p. (J). 19.95 *(978-1-932888-33-1(0))* Mascot Bks., Inc.
As Orange As Marmalade: Tan naranja como Mermelada. 2007. (ENG & SPA.). (J). per. 10.00 *(978-0-9749876-8-2(9))* Journey of a Dream Pr.
Asch, Frank. Here Comes the Cat! Vagin, Vladimir, illus. 25th ed. 2011. (ENG & RUS.). 32p. (J). (gr. -1-3). 12.95 *(978-1-936365-41-8(3))* McSweeney's Publishing.
—Here Comes the Cat! Vagin, Vladimir, illus. 2004. (Bookshelf Ser.). (J). pap. 5.99 *(978-0-439-66942-9(1))* Scholastic, Inc.
—Monsieur Saguette & His Baguette. Asch, Frank, illus. 2006. (ENG., Illus.). 32p. (J). (gr. -1-2). 6.95 *(978-1-55337-978-2(0))* Kids Can Pr., Ltd. CAN. Dist: Hachette Bk. Group.
—Mr. Maxwell's Mouse, 0 vols. Asch, Devin, illus. 2014. (ENG.). 32p. (J). (gr. k-4). pap. 8.95 *(978-1-77138-117-8(5))* Kids Can Pr., Ltd. CAN. Dist: Hachette Bk. Group.
—Mrs. Marlowe's Mice. Asch, Devin, illus. 2007. (ENG.). 32p. (J). (gr. k-4). 17.95 *(978-1-55453-022-9(9))* Kids Can Pr., Ltd. CAN. Dist: Hachette Bk. Group.
Asch, Frank & Asch, Devin. Mr. Maxwell's Mouse. Asch, Frank & Asch, Devin, illus. 2004. (ENG., Illus.). 32p. (J). (gr. k-4). 18.95 *(978-1-55337-486-2(X))* Kids Can Pr., Ltd. CAN. Dist: Hachette Bk. Group.
Ashby, Mandy Anne. Mindy's Adventure with the Pussycat Witches: Playing in the Rain. 2011. (Illus.). 28p. pap. 20.66 *(978-1-4567-8788-2(8))* AuthorHouse.
Asnong, Jocey, illus. Nuptse & Lohtse Go to the Rockies, 1 vol. 2014. (ENG.). 40p. (J). (gr. k). pap. 12.00 *(978-1-77160-019-4(5))* Road West Publishing Co.
Atchison, David. The Adventures of Black Bart: the Lone Stranger. 2009. 84p. pap. 8.95 *(978-0-578-02511-7(6))* Black Bart Bks.
Atchison, David C. The Adventures of Black Bart: an Encounter with Regret. 2008. 84p. pap. 7.94 *(978-0-615-23723-7(1))* Black Bart Bks.
—The Adventures of Black Bart: Dry Bones. 2008. 84p. pap. 7.94 *(978-0-615-20238-9(1))* Black Bart Bks.
Aubuchon, Hope L. Tiger, Ruler of the Universe. 2009. 48p. pap. 24.95 *(978-1-60749-896-4(0))* America Star Bks.
Auerbach, Annie. Meet Boulder the Construction-Bot. 2013. (Transformers Passport to Reading Ser.). (J). lib. bdg. 13.55 *(978-0-606-32274-4(4)*, Turtleback) Turtleback Bks.
Austen, Catherine. My Cat Isis. Egger, Virginie, illus. 2011. (ENG.). 32p. (J). (gr. -1-2). 16.95 *(978-1-55453-413-5(5))* Kids Can Pr., Ltd. CAN. Dist: Hachette Bk. Group.
Averill, Esther. Captains of the City Streets. Averill, Esther, illus. 2005. (New York Review Children's Collection Ser.). (ENG., Illus.). 164p. (J). (gr. 4-7). 18.95 *(978-1-59017-174-5(8)*, NYR Children's Collection) New York Review of Bks., Inc., The.
—The Hotel Cat. Averill, Esther, illus. 2005. (New York Review Children's Collection Ser.). (ENG., Illus.). 180p. (J). (gr. k-4). 17.95 *(978-1-59017-159-2(4)*, NYR Children's Collection) New York Review of Bks., Inc., The.
—Jenny Goes to Sea. Averill, Esther, illus. 2005. (New York Review Children's Collection). (ENG., Illus.). 140p. (J). (gr. k-4). reprint ed. 17.95 *(978-1-59017-155-4(1)*, NYR Children's Collection) New York Review of Bks., Inc., The.
—Jenny's Birthday Book. Averill, Esther, illus. 2005. (New York Review Children's Collection). (ENG., Illus.). 44p. (J). (gr. -1-2). reprint ed. 15.95 *(978-1-59017-154-7(3)*, NYR Children's Collection) New York Review of Bks., Inc., The.
—Jenny's Moonlight Adventure. 32p. (J). pap. 12.95 *(978-0-553-15145-9(2))* Random House Publishing Group.
—Jenny's Moonlight Adventure: A Jenny's Cat Club Book. Averill, Esther, illus. 2005. (New York Review Children's Collection). (ENG., Illus.). 32p. (J). (gr. -1-2). 14.00 *(978-1-59017-160-8(8)*, NYR Children's Collection) New York Review of Bks., Inc., The.
—The School for Cats. Averill, Esther, illus. 2005. (New York Review Children's Collection Ser.). (ENG., Illus.). 32p. (J). (gr. -1-2). 14.00 *(978-1-59017-173-8(X)*, NYR Children's Collection) New York Review of Bks., Inc., The.
Averill, Esther H. Jenny & the Cat Club: A Collection of Favorite Stories about Jenny Linsky. Averill, Esther H., illus. 2003. (New York Review Children's Collection Ser.). (ENG., Illus.). 176p. (J). (gr. k-4). 16.95 *(978-1-59017-047-2(4)*, NYR Children's Collection) New York Review of Bks., Inc., The.
Avery, Tammy. Molly's Kat Tales, 1 vol. 2009. 17p. pap. 24.95 *(978-1-60836-474-9(7))* America Star Bks.
Avi. Ragweed. Howard, E., ed. Floca, Brian, illus. 2006. (Poppy Stories Ser.). (ENG.). 224p. (J). (gr. 3-7). pap. 6.99 *(978-0-380-80167-1(1))* HarperCollins Pubs.
Aviation Book Company Staff. Ragweed. 2006. (Poppy Stories Ser.: 1). (J). (gr. 3-6). lib. bdg. 17.20 *(978-0-613-26699-4(4)*, Turtleback) Turtleback Bks.
Award, Anna. The Story of Puss in Boots: See the Picture & Say the Word. 2012. (ENG.). 24p. (J). pap. 9.95 *(978-1-84135-512-2(7))* Award Pubns. Ltd. GBR. Dist: Parkwest Pubns., Inc.
Ayme, Marcel. Los Cuentos Del Gato Encaramado, No. 1. 2006. (la Orilla del Viento Ser.). (SPA.). 192p. (J). pap. 8.50 *(978-968-16-7060-3(4))* Fondo de Cultura Economica USA.
AZ Books, creator. Kitten Searches for a Friend. 2012. (Plush Baby Ser.). (ENG., Illus.). 10p. (J). (gr. -1 — 1). bds. 11.95 *(978-1-61889-219-5(3))* AZ Bks. LLC.
Babbitt, Natalie. Elsie Times Eight. Babbitt, Natalie, illus. 2005. (Illus.). 26p. (J). (gr. k-4). reprint ed. 16.00 *(978-0-7567-9640-2(7))* DIANE Publishing Co.
Backer, Charles. Fireclaw. 2010. 288p. pap. 15.49 *(978-1-4520-1229-2(6))* AuthorHouse.
Bagdanov, Patricia. The Adventures of Charlie & a Dragon Named Trevor. 2013. 26p. pap. 16.95 *(978-1-63004-985-0(9))* PublishAmerica, Inc.
Baglio, Ben M. Kitty in the Candy Hearts. 2007. (Illus.). 147p. (J). pap. *(978-0-439-87119-8(0))* Scholastic, Inc.
—Runaway Rascal. 2006. (Illus.). 157p. (J). *(978-0-439-79250-9(9))* Scholastic, Inc.
Baglio, Ben M. & Lasher, Mary Ann. Tabby under the Tree. Baum, Ann, illus. 2007. 145p. (J). *(978-0-439-02532-4(X))* Scholastic, Inc.
Bagwell, Angela. The King of Gran Lala's Cats. 2013. 28p. pap. 19.99 *(978-1-4772-8716-3(7))* AuthorHouse.
Bail, Mina Mauerstein. Max & Voltaire Getting to Know You. Choquette, Gabriel, illus. 2015. 66p. (J). pap. 16.95 *(978-1-59095-151-4(4))* TotalRecall Pubns.
Bailey, Vicki. Catland Adventures. 2009. 32p. pap. 9.96 *(978-0-557-06543-1(7))* Lulu Pr., Inc.
Baker, Barbara. Digby & Kate & the Beautiful Day. Winborn, Marsha, illus. 2004. (Puffin Easy-to-Read Ser.). 48p. (J). (gr. 1-4). 11.65 *(978-0-7569-2959-6(8))* Perfection Learning Corp.
Baker, Ed. The Story of Kitten Cuckoo. Baker, Ed, illus. 2007. (ENG., Illus.). 32p. (J). (gr. -1-17). 15.95 *(978-1-933572-04-8(3))* Centro Bks., LLC.
Balestrino, Jerry. Pumpkin the Angel Cat: Pumpkins 1st Mission. 2009. 32p. pap. 13.99 *(978-1-4343-7105-8(0))* AuthorHouse.
Ballard, George Anne & Bolton, Georgia Helen. The Trouble with Cats. Aguilar, Arelys, illus. 2012. 24p. pap. 12.00 *(978-0-9855312-1-8(5))* Bolton Publishing LLC.
Ballock-Dixon, Saige J. & Medina, Sylvia M. Chilean Mines. Eagle, Joy, illus. 2013. 36p. pap. 11.49 *(978-1-939871-00-8(X))* Green Kids Club, Inc.
Baltazar, Art & Aureliani, Franco. Aw Yeah Comics! and... Action!, Vol. 1. Baltazar, Art, illus. 2014. (ENG., Illus.). 152p. (J). (gr. 3-7). pap. 12.99 *(978-1-61655-558-0(0))* Dark Horse Comics.
Banerjee, Timir. The Cat & the Kids of Millbrae. Dickman, Michael, illus. 2011. 24p. pap. 24.95 *(978-1-4560-9721-9(0))* America Star Bks.
Banks, Kate. The Cat Who Walked Across France. Hallensleben, Georg, illus. 2004. (ENG.). 40p. (J). (gr. -1-2). 18.99 *(978-0-374-39968-9(9)*, 9780374399689, Farrar, Straus & Giroux (BYR)) Farrar, Straus & Giroux.
—City Cat. Castillo, Lauren, illus. 2013. (ENG.). 48p. (J). (gr. -1-2). 17.99 *(978-0-374-31321-0(0)*, 9780374313210, Farrar, Straus & Giroux (BYR)) Farrar, Straus & Giroux.
Banks, Robin Washington. Big Boy. Morgan, Vincent, illus. 2011. 20p. pap. 24.95 *(978-1-4560-7068-7(1))* PublishAmerica, Inc.
Bannister, Bram. Rupert, the Alien & the Bank Robbery. 2007. 56p. per. 8.95 *(978-0-595-44839-5(9))* iUniverse, Inc.
Baraba, Joseph Frank. Dusty. 2006. 59p. pap. 16.95 *(978-1-4241-2018-5(7))* PublishAmerica, Inc.
Baratz-Logsted, Lauren. Georgia's Greatness. 2009. (Sisters Eight Ser.: 3). (ENG., Illus.). 128p. (J). (gr. 1-4). pap. 5.99 *(978-0-547-05340-0(1))*;Bk. 3. 15.00 *(978-0-547-16699-5(0))* Houghton Mifflin Harcourt Publishing Co.
Barbaresi, Nina, illus. The Tale of Tom Kitten: A Story about Good Behavior. 2006. (J). 6.99 *(978-1-59939-002-4(7))* Cornerstone Pr.
Barbante, Lynn. Kitty Heaven's in the Sky! 2004. (J). 8.95 *(978-0-9791362-1-4(0))* Tony Tales.
Barbo, Maria S. Catnapped Caper, 1 vol. 2013. (Scooby-Doo! Picture Clue Bks.). (ENG.). 24p. (J). (gr. -1-1). lib. bdg. 24.21 *(978-1-61479-035-8(3)*, Essential Library) ABDO Publishing Co.
—Hello Kitty, Ice-Skating Princess. 2005. 32p. *(978-0-439-68070-7(0))* Scholastic, Inc.
Barbre, Mark. A Cat Named Friend. Smith, Brody, illus. 2008. 18p. (J). pap. 9.95 *(978-0-615-20414-7(7))* Edgar Road Publishing.
Bardhan-Quallen, Sudipta. Purrmaids #1: the Scaredy Cat. 2017. (Purrmaids Ser.: 1). (ENG.). 96p. (J). (gr. 1-4). lib. bdg. 12.99 ***(978-1-5247-0162-8(9))***; (Illus.). 4.99 ***(978-1-5247-0161-1(0))*** Random Hse. Children's Bks. (Random Hse. Bks. for Young Readers).
—Purrmaids #2: the Catfish Club. 2017. (Purrmaids Ser.: 2). (ENG.). 96p. (J). (gr. 1-4). lib. bdg. 12.99 ***(978-1-5247-0165-9(3))***; (Illus.). 4.99 ***(978-1-5247-0164-2(5))*** Random Hse. Children's Bks. (Random Hse. Bks. for Young Readers).
Barfield, Asia. My Inspiration. 2009. 14p. 10.70 *(978-0-557-05867-9(8))* Lulu Pr., Inc.
Bargellini, Demetrio & Stilton, Geronimo. The Coliseum Con. Cooper-McGuinness, Nanette, tr. 2009. (Geronimo Stilton Graphic Novels Ser.). (ENG., Illus.). 56p. (J). (gr. 2-6). 9.99 *(978-1-59707-172-7(2)*, 9781597071727) Papercutz.
Bargellini, Demetrio, et al. The Secret of the Sphinx. Cooper-McGuinness, Nanette, tr. 2009. (Geronimo Stilton Graphic Novels Ser.). (ENG., Illus.). 56p. (J). (gr. 2-6). 9.99 *(978-1-59707-159-8(5)*, 9781597071598) Papercutz.
Barker, Cordell. The Cat Came Back. 2017. (ENG., Illus.). 48p. (J). (gr. k-3). 19.95 ***(978-1-77085-929-6(2)**, 9781770859296)* Firefly Bks., Ltd.
Barr, Mary. The Trouble with Filly Tucker. 2010. 112p. (gr. 4-6). 20.95 *(978-1-4502-3517-4(4))*; pap. 10.95 *(978-1-4502-3515-0(8))* iUniverse, Inc.
Barrett, Audrey & Vogt, Denis. The Adventures of Audrey the Cat. 2008. 28p. pap. 14.95 *(978-1-4389-1228-8(5))* AuthorHouse.
Barrett, Ms S. Moe. Mangoe & Marlie: Mangoe Takes Care of Marlie. 2013. 56p. pap. 11.93 *(978-0-9701289-5-9(9))* Moselle Productions, Inc.
Barrett, Ron. Cats Get Famous. Barrett, Ron, illus. 2015. (ENG., Illus.). 32p. (J). (gr. -1-3). 17.99 *(978-1-4424-9453-4(0)*, Simon & Schuster Bks. For Young Readers) Simon & Schuster Bks. For Young Readers.
Barrows, Robert. Milestones - the Sixth World. 2009. 312p. pap. 16.98 *(978-0-557-02589-3(3))* Lulu Pr., Inc.
Barsy, Kalman. Los Tres Naufragos. Perez-Moliere, Marnie, illus. 2004. (Orange Ser.). (SPA.). 40p. (J). (gr. 3-5). pap. 5.95 *(978-1-57581-469-8(2))* Santillana USA Publishing Co., Inc.
Bartlett, Brittany D. Cooper the Curious: And the First Snowfall. 2012. 40p. pap. 19.57 *(978-1-4669-2869-5(7))* Trafford Publishing.
Barton, Byron. My House. Barton, Byron, illus. 2016. (Illus.). 40p. (J). (gr. -1-3). 16.99 *(978-0-06-233703-0(3)*, Greenwillow Bks.) HarperCollins Pubs.
Basore, Polly M. Santa's Stray. Williams, Carlene H., illus. 2004. 32p. (J). per. *(978-0-9771749-2-8(1))* AngelBooks.
Bassett, Madge A. At Bumblebee Farm. Bassett, Madge A., illus. 2009. (Illus.). 20p. pap. 13.46 *(978-1-4251-9230-3(0))* Trafford Publishing.
Bastet - Evaluation Guide: Evaluation Guide. 2006. (J). *(978-1-55942-400-4(1))* Witcher Productions.
Bauer, Linda. Fruits & Flowers & Footprints OH MY!!! 2007. (Illus.). 29p. (J). 13.99 *(978-0-9798146-0-0(X))* Bauer, Linda.
Bauer, Marion Dane. Christmas in the Forest. Hearn, Diane Dawson, illus. (Holiday House Reader Ser.). (ENG.). 48p. (J). (gr. k-3). tchr. ed. 15.95 *(978-0-8234-1371-3(3))* Holiday Hse., Inc.
—Little Cat's Luck. Bell, Jennifer A., illus. 2016. (ENG.). 224p. (J). (gr. 3-7). 17.99 *(978-1-4814-2488-2(2)*, Simon & Schuster Bks. For Young Readers) Simon & Schuster Bks. For Young Readers.
—Little Cat's Luck. 2017. lib. bdg. 18.40 ***(978-0-606-39746-9(9))*** Turtleback Bks.
Baum, Lonna. Monty the Menace: Understanding Differences. Messing, Dave, illus. 2012. (ENG.). 32p. (J). 16.95 *(978-0-9839373-0-2(3))* Baum & Baum, LLC.
Baxter, Anne M. Everybody Needs a Name: The Adventures of Maybe, Book 1. 2009. 40p. pap. 18.49 *(978-1-4389-5816-3(1))* AuthorHouse.
—Maybe Wins!, Bk. 1. 2011. 32p. pap. 14.39 *(978-1-4389-5843-9(9))* AuthorHouse.
Beardsley, Martyn. Five Naughty Kittens. East, Jacqueline, illus. 2005. (Reading Corner Ser.). 24p. (J). (gr. k-3). lib. bdg. 22.80 *(978-1-59771-006-0(7))* Sea-To-Sea Pubns.
Bechtold, Lisze. Buster the Very Shy Dog Finds a Kitten. 2015. (Green Light Readers Level 3 Ser.). (ENG., Illus.). 32p. (J). (gr. 1-4). pap. 3.99 *(978-0-544-33605-6(4)*, HMH Books For Young Readers) Houghton Mifflin Harcourt Publishing Co.
Beck, Carolyn. Wellington's Rainy Day, 1 vol. Kerrigan, Brooke, illus. 2011. (ENG.). 32p. (J). (gr. -1-3). 19.95 *(978-1-55469-284-2(9))* Orca Bk. Pubs. USA.
Beck, Rachel. Bella & the Little Gray Kitten. 2011. 40p. (gr. -1). pap. 18.50 *(978-1-4567-3365-0(6))* AuthorHouse.
Becker, Helaine. Juba This, Juba That. Lightburn, Ron, illus. 2011. (ENG.). 24p. (J). (gr. k-k). 17.95 *(978-0-88776-975-7(6)*, Tundra Bks.) Tundra Bks. CAN. Dist: Penguin Random Hse. LLC.
Bedell, Lorraine Frances. The Christmas Cat Story, 1 vol. 2010. 48p. pap. 16.95 *(978-1-4512-0249-6(0))* America Star Bks.
Bednar, Martin. Sandy's Vision. 2006. (J). lib. bdg. 19.95 *(978-1-933732-15-2(6))* Big Ransom Studio.
Beharrell, Gayle. The Adventures of Charlie. 2008. 36p. pap. 16.99 *(978-1-4389-2546-2(8))* AuthorHouse.
Bell, Michael D. Lantern Sam & the Blue Streak Bandits. (ENG., Illus.). 288p. (J). (gr. 3-7). 2015. pap. 7.99 *(978-0-385-75320-3(9)*, Yearling) 2014. 15.99 *(978-0-385-75317-3(9)*, Knopf Bks. for Young Readers) Random Hse. Children's Bks.
Bell, Anthea, ed. & tr. The Bremen Town Musicians. Bell, Anthea, tr. Lai, Hsin-Shih, illus. 2007. 32p. (J). (gr. -1-3). 17.95 *(978-0-88010-583-5(6)*, Bell Pond Bks.) SteinerBooks, Inc.
Bell, Clare. Clan Ground. 2010. (Named Ser.: Bk. 2). (ENG.). 307p. (YA). pap. 14.95 *(978-0-9745603-7-3(5))* Imaginator Pr.
—Ratha's Challenge. 2011. (Named Ser.: Bk. 4). (ENG.). 252p. (YA). pap. 14.95 *(978-0-9745603-9-7(1))* Imaginator Pr.
—Ratha's Creature. 2011. (Named Ser.: Bk. 1). (ENG.). 296p. (YA). pap. 14.95 *(978-1-936917-01-3(7))* Imaginator Pr.
Bell, Karen. Cookie's Victorian. 2010. 84p. pap. 31.95 *(978-1-4497-0558-9(8)*, WestBow Pr.) Author Solutions, Inc.

C
D

Bell, Philip. Kurt the Dog & His Friend Lisa the Cat. 2012. 20p. pap. 24.95 *(978-1-4626-8140-2(9))* America Star Bks.

Belshaw, Yvonne & Sheldon, Tamia. Toby the Flying Cat. 2013. 24p. pap. 9.99 *(978-1-62395-495-6(9))* Xist Publishing.

Benator, Eileen B. A Ballet for Bobcat. Benator, Seth, illus. l.t. ed. 2005. 32p. (J). (gr. -1-2). 15.95 *(978-0-9748478-7-0(9))* Lion's Tale Pr., LLC.

Benchmark Education Co., LLC. Where Is Moggie? Big Book. 2014. (Shared Reading Foundations Ser.). (J). (gr. -1). *(978-1-4509-9429-3(6))* Benchmark Education Co.

Benjamin, Amanda. Journey Through Jerusalem. Blumenfeld, Tamar, illus. 2016. (J). *(978-1-68115-531-9(1))* Behrman Hse., Inc.

Bennett, Marcia. Backpack Cat. Bennett, Michele & Dunlap, Joan, illus. 2004. 124p. 19.95 *(978-1-932196-50-4(1))* WordWright.biz, Inc.

—Backpack Cat. 2004. 124p. pap. 12.95 *(978-1-932196-37-5(4))* WordWright.biz, Inc.

Bennett, Marian. God Made Kittens. Marlin, Kathryn, illus. 2015. (Faith That Sticks Bks.). (ENG.). 30p. (J). pap. 3.99 *(978-1-4964-0319-3(3))* Tyndale Hse. Pubs.

Bentley, Sue. A Christmas Surprise. Swan, Angela & Farley, Andrew, illus. 2008. (Magic Kitten Ser.). (ENG.). 128p. (J). (gr. 1-3). pap. 5.99 *(978-0-448-45001-8(1)*, Grosset & Dunlap) Penguin Young Readers Group.

—A Circus Wish. 2009. (Magic Kitten Ser.: 6). lib. bdg. 14.75 *(978-0-606-06970-0(4)*, Turtleback) Turtleback Bks.

—A Circus Wish #6, 6 vols. Farley, Andrew & Swan, Angela, illus. 2009. (Magic Kitten Ser.: 6). (ENG.). 128p. (J). (gr. 1-3). pap. 5.99 *(978-0-448-45062-9(3)*, Grosset & Dunlap) Penguin Young Readers Group.

—Classroom Chaos, 2 vols. Swan, Angela & Farley, Andrew, illus. 2008. (Magic Kitten Ser.: 2). (ENG.). 128p. (J). (gr. 1-3). pap. 5.99 *(978-0-448-44999-9(4)*, Grosset & Dunlap) Penguin Young Readers Group.

—Double Trouble, 4 vols. Farley, Andrew & Swan, Angela, illus. 2009. (Magic Kitten Ser.: 4). (ENG.). 128p. (J). (gr. 1-3). pap. 5.99 *(978-0-448-45060-5(7)*, Grosset & Dunlap) Penguin Young Readers Group.

—Double Trouble. 2009. (Magic Kitten Ser.: 4). lib. bdg. 16.00 *(978-0-606-06004-2(9)*, Turtleback) Turtleback Bks.

—Firelight Friends. 2014. (Magic Kitten Ser.: 10). lib. bdg. 14.75 *(978-0-606-34136-3(6)*, Turtleback) Turtleback Bks.

—Firelight Friends #10. Swan, Angela, illus. 2014. (Magic Kitten Ser.: 10). (ENG.). 128p. (J). (gr. 1-3). 5.99 *(978-0-448-46788-7(7)*, Grosset & Dunlap) Penguin Young Readers Group.

—A Glittering Gallop, No. 8. Swan, Angela, illus. 2013. (Magic Kitten Ser.: 8). (ENG.). 128p. (J). (gr. 1-3). 5.99 *(978-0-448-46730-6(5)*, Grosset & Dunlap) Penguin Young Readers Group.

—A Glittering Gallop. 2013. (Magic Kitten Ser.: 8). lib. bdg. 16.00 *(978-0-606-32120-4(9)*, Turtleback) Turtleback Bks.

—Moonlight Mischief. 2009. (Magic Kitten Ser.: 5). lib. bdg. 14.75 *(978-0-606-06016-5(2)*, Turtleback) Turtleback Bks.

—Moonlight Mischief #5, 5 vols. Swan, Angela & Farley, Andrew, illus. 2009. (Magic Kitten Ser.: 5). (ENG.). 128p. (J). (gr. 1-3). pap. 4.99 *(978-0-448-45061-2(5)*, Grosset & Dunlap) Penguin Young Readers Group.

—Picture Perfect. 2014. (Magic Kitten Ser.: 13). lib. bdg. 14.75 *(978-0-606-35683-1(5))* Turtleback Bks.

—Picture Perfect #13. Swan, Angela & Farley, Andrew, illus. 2014. (Magic Kitten Ser.: 13). (ENG.). 128p. (J). (gr. 1-3). 4.99 *(978-0-448-46796-2(8)*, Grosset & Dunlap) Penguin Young Readers Group.

—A Puzzle of Paws. 2014. (Magic Kitten Ser.: 12). lib. bdg. 14.75 *(978-0-606-35682-4(7))* Turtleback Bks.

—A Puzzle of Paws #12. Swan, Angela & Farley, Andrew, illus. 2014. (Magic Kitten Ser.: 12). (ENG.). 128p. (J). (gr. 1-3). 4.99 *(978-0-448-46795-5(X)*, Grosset & Dunlap) Penguin Young Readers Group.

—Seaside Mystery. 2013. (Magic Kitten Ser.: 9). lib. bdg. 16.00 *(978-0-606-32121-1(7)*, Turtleback) Turtleback Bks.

—Seaside Mystery #9. Swan, Angela, illus. 2013. (Magic Kitten Ser.: 9). (ENG.). 128p. (J). (gr. 1-3). 5.99 *(978-0-448-46731-3(3)*, Grosset & Dunlap) Penguin Young Readers Group.

—A Shimmering Splash. 2014. (Magic Kitten Ser.: 11). lib. bdg. 14.75 *(978-0-606-34137-0(4)*, Turtleback) Turtleback Bks.

—A Shimmering Splash #11. Swan, Angela & Farley, Andrew, illus. 2014. (Magic Kitten Ser.: 11). (ENG.). 128p. (J). (gr. 1-3). 4.99 *(978-0-448-46789-4(5)*, Grosset & Dunlap) Penguin Young Readers Group.

—Sparkling Steps. 7th ed. 2007. (ENG., Illus.). 128p. (J). pap. *(978-0-14-132155-4(5)*, Puffin) Penguin Publishing Group.

—Sparkling Steps #7, 7 vols. Farley, Andrew & Swan, Angela, illus. 2009. (Magic Kitten Ser.: 7). (ENG.). 128p. (J). (gr. 1-3). pap. 5.99 *(978-0-448-45063-6(1)*, Grosset & Dunlap) Penguin Young Readers Group.

—A Splash of Forever. 2014. (Magic Kitten Ser.: 14). lib. bdg. 16.00 *(978-0-606-35684-8(3))* Turtleback Bks.

—A Splash of Forever #14. Swan, Angela & Farley, Andrew, illus. 2014. (Magic Kitten Ser.: 14). (ENG.). 128p. (J). (gr. 1-3). 5.99 *(978-0-448-46797-9(6)*, Grosset & Dunlap) Penguin Young Readers Group.

—Star Dreams, 3 vols. Swan, Angela & Farley, Andrew, illus. 2008. (Magic Kitten Ser.: 3). (ENG.). 128p. (J). (gr. 1-3). pap. 5.99 *(978-0-448-45000-1(3)*, Grosset & Dunlap) Penguin Young Readers Group.

—A Summer Spell. Swan, Angela & Farley, Andrew, illus. 2008. (Magic Kitten Ser.: 1). (ENG.). 128p. (J). (gr. 1-3). pap. 5.99 *(978-0-448-44998-2(6)*, Grosset & Dunlap) Penguin Young Readers Group.

Bently, Peter. The Cat, the Mouse, & the Runaway Train. Cox, Steve, illus. 2013. (J). *(978-1-4351-4968-7(8))* Barnes & Noble, Inc.

Benton, Jim. Robot Kitties: An up & down Book. 2015. (ENG.). 16p. (J). (— 1). bds. 5.99 *(978-0-545-64786-1(X)*, Cartwheel Bks.) Scholastic, Inc.

Beraducci, Deborah. Tyler's Halloween Horror, 1 vol. Eyre, Jane, illus. 2009. 22p. pap. 24.95 *(978-1-4489-2133-1(3))* America Star Bks.

Berenstain, Jan & Berenstain, Mike. Kitten Rescue, 1 vol. 2011. (I Can Read! / Berenstain Bears / Good Deed Scouts / Living Lights Ser.). (ENG.). 32p. (J). (gr. -1-2). pap. 3.99 *(978-0-310-72097-3(4))* Zonderkidz.

Berenstain, Jan, et al. The Berenstain Bears' New Kitten. Berenstain, Jan et al, illus. 2007. (I Can Read Level 1 Ser.). (ENG.). 32p. (J). (gr. k-3). 16.99 *(978-0-06-058356-9(8))*; pap. 3.99 *(978-0-06-058357-6(6))* HarperCollins Pubs.

Berg-Seuffert, Barbara. Good Heaven - Eleven! A Tail of Many Cats. 2009. 28p. pap. 12.99 *(978-1-4490-3044-5(0))* AuthorHouse.

Bergeron, Joe. Cosmic Cat. 2005. 50p. pap. 14.99 *(978-1-4116-6246-9(6))* Lulu Pr., Inc.

Bergner, Bobby. Why kitty Is afraid of Poo: A cautionary Tale. Bergner, Bobby, illus. 2008. (Illus.). 20p. 12.99 *(978-0-615-21301-9(4))* Bergner, Bobby.

Berkowitz, Barbara. A Mouse in the House. 2009. 32p. pap. 14.49 *(978-1-4490-4258-5(9))* AuthorHouse.

Berquist, Nita G. The Song of Pounce: Homestead Harmonies. 2012. (ENG.). 203p. pap. 14.95 *(978-1-4327-8346-4(7))* Outskirts Pr., Inc.

Berry, Lynne. The Curious Demise of a Contrary Cat. LaMarca, Luke, illus. 2006. (ENG.). 40p. (J). (gr. -1-3). 17.99 *(978-1-4169-0211-9(2)*, Simon & Schuster Bks. For Young Readers) Simon & Schuster Bks. For Young Readers.

Bersson, Robert & Shoup, Dolores. Stripes & Stars. Bersson, Robert & Trobaugh, Scott, illus. l.t. ed. 2003. 40p. (J). (gr. 1-4). per. 16.95 *(978-0-9740585-0-4(5))* Legacy Group Productions, LLC.

Betterton, Jerry W. The Adventures of Hot Rolls. 2013. 44p. pap. 24.99 *(978-1-4797-8184-3(3))* Xlibris Corp.

Beware of the Cat! 3-in-1 Package. (Sails Literacy Ser.). 24p. (gr. 1-18). 57.00 *(978-0-7578-3204-8(0))* Rigby Education.

Beware of the Cat! Big Book Only. (Sails Literacy Ser.). 24p. (gr. 1-18). 27.00 *(978-0-7635-5927-4(X))* Rigby Education.

Big Davie. The Lady & Her Cat As Told by Bigdavie: A simple easy reading bedtime story that will leave children with delightful images while drifting off to S. 2009. (Illus.). 28p. pap. 12.49 *(978-1-4389-3124-1(7))* AuthorHouse.

Bilichniansky, Theodore. The Adventures of Little Tommy Cabin Part Ii: Tom Cabin Meets Mittens. 2012. (Illus.). 40p. pap. 21.99 *(978-1-4797-5374-1(2))* Xlibris Corp.

Biller, Maxim. Poppy's Biggest Wish. 2006. (ENG., Illus.). 32p. (J). (gr. -1-k). 17.99 *(978-0-7475-8236-6(X)*, Bloomsbury Childrens) Bloomsbury Publishing Plc GBR. Dist: Independent Pubs. Group.

Bird, Benjamin. A Cat Is Chasing Me Through This Book!, 1 vol. Pérez, Carmen, illus. 2014. (Tom & Jerry Ser.). (ENG.). 32p. (gr. -1-2). 22.65 *(978-1-4795-5229-0(1))* Picture Window Bks.

—Don't Give This Book a Bowl of Milk!, 1 vol. Pérez, Carmen, illus. 2014. (Tom & Jerry Ser.). (ENG.). 32p. (gr. -1-2). 22.65 *(978-1-4795-5230-6(5))* Picture Window Bks.

—This Book Is Not a Piece of Cheese!, 1 vol. Pérez, Carmen, illus. 2014. (Tom & Jerry Ser.). (ENG.). 32p. (gr. -1-2). 22.65 *(978-1-4795-5231-3(3))* Picture Window Bks.

Birnbaum, A. Green Eyes. Birnbaum, A., illus. 2011. (Family Storytime Ser.). (ENG., Illus.). 48p. (J). (gr. -1-2). pap. 7.99 *(978-0-375-86201-4(3)*, Dragonfly Bks.) Random Hse. Children's Bks.

Bise, Sharon. The Story of Katu. 2013. 32p. pap. 17.25 *(978-1-4907-0724-2(7))* Trafford Publishing.

Bistricean, Karen. The Adventures of Fergus & Lady: Home Sweet Home. Bistricean, Claudius, illus. 2006. (J). *(978-0-9786975-1-8(0))* Fergus & Lady Publishing.

—The Adventures of Fergus & Lady: The Beginning. Bistricean, Claudius, illus. 2006. (J). *(978-0-9786975-0-1(2))* Fergus & Lady Publishing.

Bixley, Donovan. Dogfight. 2016. (Flying Furballs Ser.: 1). (ENG., Illus.). 112p. (J). (gr. 2-4). pap. 8.99 *(978-1-927262-53-5(4))* Upstart Pr. NZL. Dist: Independent Pubs. Group.

Bixley, Donovan. Hot Air. Bixley, Donovan, illus. 2017. (Flying Furballs Ser.: 2). (ENG., Illus.). 112p. (J). (gr. 2-4). pap. 8.99 ***(978-1-927262-54-2(2))*** Upstart Pr. NZL. Dist: Independent Pubs. Group.

Blace, Maria. Lunie Balloonies. Swope, Brenda, illus. 2011. 24p. pap. 24.95 *(978-1-4560-0947-2(8))* America Star Bks.

Blackmon, Rodney Allan. A Kitten Named Buddy: Buddy Goes Outside. 2013. 20p. pap. 24.95 *(978-1-62709-677-5(9))* America Star Bks.

—A Kitten Named Buddy: Buddy Makes a Friend. 2013. 24p. pap. 24.95 *(978-1-62709-676-8(0))* America Star Bks.

—A Kitten Named Buddy: Buddy Stays Clean. 2013. 20p. pap. 24.95 *(978-1-62709-675-1(2))* America Star Bks.

—A Kitten Named Buddy, Buddy's Circus. 2013. 20p. pap. 24.95 *(978-1-62709-674-4(4))* America Star Bks.

Blackstone, Stella. Cleo & Caspar. Mockford, Caroline, illus. 2013. (ENG.). 24p. (J). 6.99 *(978-1-78285-053-3(8))* Barefoot Bks., Inc.

—Cleo in the Snow. Mockford, Caroline, illus. 2013. (ENG.). 24p. (J). 6.99 *(978-1-78285-054-0(6))*; 6.99 *(978-1-78285-055-7(4))* Barefoot Bks., Inc.

—Cleo on the Move. Mockford, Caroline, illus. 2013. (ENG.). 24p. (J). 6.99 *(978-1-78285-056-4(2))* Barefoot Bks., Inc.

—Cleo the Cat. Mockford, Caroline, illus. 2013. (ENG.). 24p. (J). (gr. -1-k). pap. 6.99 *(978-1-78285-051-9(1))* Barefoot Bks., Inc.

—Cleo's Color Book. Mockford, Caroline, illus. 2006. 0032p. (J). 15.99 *(978-1-905236-30-5(1))* Barefoot Bks., Inc.

—Come Here, Cleo! Mockford, Caroline, illus. 2013. (ENG.). 24p. (J). (gr. -1-k). pap. 6.99 *(978-1-84148-330-6(3))* Barefoot Bks., Inc.

—Where's the Cat? Harter, Debbie, illus. 2003. (ENG.). 24p. (J). (gr. k-2). bds. 6.99 *(978-1-84148-607-9(8))* Barefoot Bks., Inc.

Blackstone, Stella & Mockford, Caroline. Cleo's Alphabet Book. 2003. (Cleo the Cat Ser.). (ENG., Illus.). 32p. (J). 15.99 *(978-1-84148-008-4(8))*; pap. 6.99 *(978-1-84148-165-4(3))* Barefoot Bks., Inc.

Blaine, John. The Egyptian Cat Mystery: A Rick Brant Science Adventure Story. 2011. 192p. 42.95 *(978-1-258-09449-2(5))* Literary Licensing, LLC.

Blair, Eric. Belling the Cat: A Retelling of Aesop's Fable, 1 vol. Silverman, Dianne, illus. 2013. (My First Classic Story Ser.). (ENG.). 24p. (gr. k-3). pap. 7.10 *(978-1-4795-1854-8(9))*, My First Classic Story) Picture Window Bks.

Blair, Eric & Aesop Enterprise Inc. Staff. Belling the Cat: A Retelling of Aesop's Fable, 1 vol. Silverman, Dianne, illus. 2011. (My First Classic Story Ser.). (ENG.). 24p. (gr. k-3). lib. bdg. 22.65 *(978-1-4048-6504-4(7))*, My First Classic Story) Picture Window Bks.

Blake, Kendare. Anna Dressed in Blood. 2012. (Anna Dressed in Blood Ser.: 1). (YA). lib. bdg. 22.10 *(978-0-606-26252-1(0)*, Turtleback) Turtleback Bks.

—Girl of Nightmares. (Anna Dressed in Blood Ser.: 2). (ENG.). 336p. (YA). (gr. 8). 2014. pap. 9.99 *(978-0-7653-2868-7(2)*, 9780765328687) 2012. 17.99 *(978-0-7653-2866-3(6)*, 9780765328663) Doherty, Tom Assocs., LLC. (Tor Teen).

—Girl of Nightmares. l.t. ed. 2012. (ENG.). 412p. 23.99 *(978-1-4104-5206-1(9))* Thorndike Pr.

Blatchford, David. The Story of Mr Tomkins. 2012. (Illus.). 50p. pap. *(978-1-908773-29-6(4))* Iponymous Publishing, Ltd.

Blevins, Wiley. A New Friend. 2013. (Penguin Young Readers, Level 1 Ser.). (ENG.). 32p. (J). (gr. k-1). 14.99 *(978-0-448-46572-2(8))*; pap. 3.99 *(978-0-448-46180-9(3))* Penguin Young Readers Group. (Penguin Young Readers).

—A New Friend. 2013. (Penguin Young Readers Level 1 Ser.). lib. bdg. 13.55 *(978-0-606-31705-4(8)*, Turtleback) Turtleback Bks.

Blissman, Rodger J. Spookster the Halloween Cat. 2004. 85p. (J). (gr. 3-7). pap. 5.99 *(978-0-9745895-0-3(0))* Oxfordshire Publishing Co.

Bliven, Jeremy. Captain Stumpy the Pirate Cat. 2004. (ENG., Illus.). 44p. (J). pap. *(978-0-9713890-8-3(X))* Outer Banks Pr.

Blunt, Edna M. Margie the Cat. pap. 6.95 *(978-0-681-02740-4(1))* Booklines Hawaii, Ltd.

Blyton, Enid. Birthday Kitten. (Illus.). (J). 192p. pap. 5.95 *(978-0-09-977930-8(7))*; 95p. pap. 4.95 *(978-0-09-924100-3(5))* Random Hse. GBR. Dist: Trafalgar Square Publishing.

—Mr Pink-Whistle Interferes. (ENG., Illus.). 112p. (J). pap. 7.99 *(978-0-7475-3859-2(X))* Bloomsbury Publishing Plc GBR. Dist: Trafalgar Square Publishing.

Boehm, Patricia. Does Noah's Kitten Have Autism Too? Kelly, Robert, illus. 2013. 16p. pap. 24.95 *(978-1-62709-877-9(1))* America Star Bks.

Boelts, Maribeth. Sleeping Bootsie. Cantor, Patricia, illus. 2011. (Step into Reading Ser.). (ENG.). 48p. (J). (gr. k-3). pap. 3.99 *(978-0-375-86678-4(7)*, Random Hse. Bks. for Young Readers) Random Hse. Children's Bks.

Bogart, Jo Ellen. The White Cat & the Monk: A Retelling of the Poem Pangur Bán, 1 vol. Smith, Sydney, illus. 2016. (ENG.). 32p. (J). (gr. -1-3). 18.95 *(978-1-55498-780-1(6))* Groundwood Bks. CAN. Dist: Publishers Group West (PGW).

Bolander, Sharon Miller. At the Stroke of Midnight. 2012. 40p. pap. 24.95 *(978-1-4626-8905-7(1))* America Star Bks.

Bolton, Robin. Sunny Goes Out to Play. 2011. 28p. pap. 12.03 *(978-1-4634-2530-2(9))* AuthorHouse.

Bonnell, Kris. The Big Hungry Cat. 2006. (J). pap. 5.95 *(978-1-933727-33-2(0))* Reading Reading Bks., LLC.

—Where Can Louis Sleep? 2007. (J). pap. 5.95 *(978-1-933727-57-8(8))* Reading Reading Bks., LLC.

—Where Is the Big Cat? 2007. (J). pap. 6.95 *(978-1-933727-62-2(4))* Reading Reading Bks., LLC.

Booth, Crystal. Introducing Tucker. 2005. 49p. pap. 16.95 *(978-1-4137-8934-8(X))* PublishAmerica, Inc.

Borando, Silvia. Black Cat, White Cat. 2015. (Minibombo Ser.). (ENG., Illus.). 48p. (J). (-k). 14.00 *(978-0-7636-8106-7(7))* Candlewick Pr.

—The Cat Book: A Minibombo Book. Borando, Silvia, illus. 2017. (Minibombo Ser.). (ENG., Illus.). 32p. (J). (-k). 9.99 *(978-0-7636-9472-2(X))* Candlewick Pr.

Borando, Silvia, et al. The White Book. 2015. (Minibombo Ser.). (ENG., Illus.). 48p. (J). (gr. -1-k). 14.00 *(978-0-7636-8107-4(5))* Candlewick Pr.

Borchini, Ernest. Three Stories about Jonathan, the Computer, & Little Kitty: Three Short Stories about a Boy & His Magic Cat. 2013. 36p. (gr. -1). pap. 15.49 *(978-1-4669-6636-9(X))* Trafford Publishing.

Bottner, Barbara. The Scaredy Cats. Chess, Victoria, illus. 2013. (ENG.). 32p. (J). (gr. -1-3). 16.99 *(978-1-4814-2166-9(2)*, Simon & Schuster Bks. For Young Readers) Simon & Schuster Bks. For Young Readers.

Bouchard, Linda. Sunny the Day Care Cat. 2012. 32p. *(978-1-105-61170-4(1))* Lulu.com.

Bow, Erin. Plain Kate. (ENG.). 320p. (J). (gr. 7-7). 2012. pap. 9.99 *(978-0-545-16665-2(9))* 2010. 17.99 *(978-0-545-16664-5(0))* Scholastic, Inc. (Levine, Arthur A. Bks.).

Bowater, Alan. A Pig Called Pete Meets a Cat Called Kitty. Pascoe, Pete, illus. 2009. (Pig Called Pete Ser.). 32p. (J). (gr. -1-2). 22.60 *(978-1-60754-561-3(6))*; pap. 10.55 *(978-1-60754-562-0(4))* Windmill Bks.

Bowlby, Linda S. How Amazon Got Her Name. Helms, Dana, illus. 2008. 30p. (J). pap. 9.95 *(978-0-9779993-7-8(8))* Red Earth Publishing.

Bowman, Crystal. Little David's Brave Day, 1 vol. Hartung, Susan Kathleen & Endersly, Frank, illus. 2010. (I Can Read! / Little David Ser.). (ENG.). 32p. (J). pap. 3.99 *(978-0-310-71709-6(4))* Zonderkidz.

—Thank You, God, for This Day. Fletcher, Rusty, illus. 2014. (Happy Day Ser.). (ENG.). 16p. (J). pap. 2.49 *(978-1-4143-9486-2(1))* Tyndale Hse. Pubs.

Bowman, Patty. The Amazing Hamweenie Escapes! Bowman, Patty, illus. 2015. (Amazing Hamweenie Ser.: 2). (ENG., Illus.). 32p. (J). (gr. k-3). 16.99 *(978-0-399-25689-9(X)*, Philomel Bks.) Penguin Young Readers Group.

Boyer, Cécile, illus. Woof Meow Tweet-Tweet. 2011. (ENG.). 48p. (J). (gr. -1). 15.95 *(978-1-934734-60-5(8))* Seven Footer Pr.

Boyle, Karen Cother. Butterhead & the tired Lamb. 2010. 251p. pap. 19.50 *(978-0-557-54126-3(3))* Lulu Pr., Inc.

—Butterhead's Dream. 2010. 152p. pap. 15.49 *(978-0-557-53742-6(8))* Lulu Pr., Inc.

Boyle, Keri Claiborne. Teddy the Dog: Be Your Own Dog. Sneider, Jonathan, illus. 2016. (Teddy the Dog Ser.: 1). 32p. (J). (gr. -1-3). 17.99 *(978-0-06-238283-2(7))* HarperCollins Pubs.

—Teddy the Dog: (Almost) Best in Show. Sneider, Jonathan, illus. 2017. (Teddy the Dog Ser.). 32p. (J). (gr. -1-3). 17.99 *(978-0-06-238284-9(5))* HarperCollins Pubs.

Boynton, Sandra. Tickle Time! 2012. (ENG., Illus.). 24p. (J). (gr. k-1). bds. 6.95 *(978-0-7611-6883-6(4)*, 16883) Workman Publishing Co., Inc.

Bradley, Matthew J. Oi! Who Ate My Dinner! & Other Colin the Cat Stories. 2010. (ENG., Illus.). 98p. pap. *(978-1-84748-766-7(1))* Athena Pr.

Braeuner, Shellie. The Great Dog Wash. Neubecker, Robert, illus. 2009. (ENG.). 32p. (J). (gr. -1-1). 15.99 *(978-1-4169-7116-0(5)*, Simon & Schuster Bks. For Young Readers) Simon & Schuster Bks. For Young Readers.

Bramsen, Carin. Hey, Duck! 2013. (ENG., Illus.). 40p. (J). (gr. -1-2). 17.99 *(978-0-375-86990-7(5)*, Random Hse. Bks. for Young Readers) Random Hse. Children's Bks.

—Just a Duck? 2015. (ENG., Illus.). 40p. (J). (gr. -1-2). 17.99 *(978-0-385-38415-5(7)*, Random Hse. Bks. for Young Readers) Random Hse. Children's Bks.

Brand, Mary. Aspen Cat: Adventurer Extraordinaire. Roberts, Tempie, illus. 2009. 44p. pap. 24.95 *(978-1-60749-165-1(6))* America Star Bks.

Breathed, Berkeley. The Bill the Cat Story: A Bloom County Epic. Breathed, Berkeley, illus. 2016. (ENG., Illus.). 40p. (J). (gr. -1-3). 18.99 *(978-0-399-54662-4(6)*, Philomel Bks.) Penguin Young Readers Group.

Breckenridge, Bill. Bernie Bolts Bergen. 2010. 176p. pap. 13.95 *(978-1-4461-5870-8(5))* Lulu Pr., Inc.

Brett, Jan. Annie & the Wild Animals. (ENG., Illus.). 32p. (J). (gr. -1-3). 2012. audio compact disk 10.99 *(978-0-547-85082-5(4))* 2006. bds. 7.95 *(978-0-618-74786-3(9))* Houghton Mifflin Harcourt Publishing Co.

—Annie & the Wild Animals. Brett, Jan, illus. 2012. (ENG., Illus.). 32p. (J). (gr. -1-k). 17.99 *(978-0-399-16104-9(X)*, G.P. Putnam's Sons Books for Young Readers) Penguin Young Readers Group.

—Annie & the Wild Animals Send-A-Story. 2011. (Send a Story Ser.). (ENG., Illus.). 32p. (J). (gr. -1-3). pap. 4.99 *(978-0-547-56692-4(1))* Houghton Mifflin Harcourt Publishing Co.

Brian, Janeen. Cat-Astrophe at the Opera, 1 vol. rev. ed. 2013. (Fiction Readers Ser.). (ENG., Illus.). 28p. (J). (gr. 3-3). pap. 8.99 *(978-1-4333-5597-4(3))* Shell Educational Publishing.

—Cat-Astrpohe at the Opera. rev. ed. 2013. (Fiction Readers Ser.). (ENG., Illus.). 28p. (gr. 3-3). pap. 19.96 *(978-1-4807-1719-0(3))* Teacher Created Materials, Inc.

Brisebois, Ro. Sherlock & Elf: The Mystery of the Thicket Behind the Shed. 2008. 100p. pap. 12.99 *(978-1-4343-9987-8(7))* AuthorHouse.

Brisland, Toni. DemiChat & the Lost Mummy. de los reyes Cruz, Cheryl, illus. 2013. 142p. (J). pap. 14.95 *(978-1-60131-173-3(7))* Big Tent Bks.

Broad, Michael. Ghost Diamond!, No. 1. Broad, Michael, illus. 2011. (Agent Amelia Ser.: 1). (ENG., Illus.). 144p. (J). (gr. 2-5). pap. 5.95 *(978-0-7613-8060-3(4)*, Darby Creek); lib. bdg. 22.60 *(978-0-7613-8056-6(6))* Lerner Publishing Group.

—#1 Ghost Diamond! 2011. (Agent Amelia Ser.). pap. 33.92 *(978-0-7613-8341-3(7)*, Darby Creek) Lerner Publishing Group.

Brockington, Drew. CatStronauts: Mission Moon. 2017. (CatStronauts Ser.: 1). (ENG., Illus.). 160p. (J). (gr. 1-5). 16.99 *(978-0-316-30747-5(5))*; pap. 7.99 *(978-0-316-30745-1(9))* Little Brown & Co.

—CatStronauts: Race to Mars. 2017. (CatStronauts Ser.: 2). (ENG.). 184p. (J). (gr. 1-5). 16.99 *(978-0-316-30748-2(3))* Little, Brown Bks. for Young Readers.

Brodsky, Irene. The Adventures of Silly Kitty, Princess Jasmine & First Puppy. 2010. (Illus.). 44p. (J). pap. 23.95 *(978-1-4327-5552-2(8))* Outskirts Pr., Inc.

Brodsky, Kathy. A CatFish Tale. Bennett, Cameron, illus. 2012. (ENG.). (J). 19.99 *(978-0-9828529-3-4(2))* Helpingwords.

Bronstein, S. N. Private Eye Cats: Book One: the Case of the Neighborhood Burglars. 2012. 108p. (gr. 4-6). 23.99 *(978-1-4685-4557-9(4))*; pap. 14.95 *(978-1-4685-4558-6(2))* AuthorHouse.

Brooke, Samantha. Unikitty - A Cuckoo Adventure. 2014. (LEGO: the LEGO Movie Ser.). (ENG., Illus.). 24p. (J). (gr. -1-3). pap. 3.99 *(978-0-545-79541-8(9))* Scholastic, Inc.

Brooke, Susan Rich & Seuss, Dr. The Cat in the Hat Flips His Lid. Enik, Ted, illus. 2003. (J). *(978-0-7853-8446-5(4))* Publications International, Ltd.

Brooks, Dawn Marie. Cat-Ice. 2004. 175p. pap. 13.95 *(978-0-7414-2240-8(9))* Infinity Publishing.

Brooks, Felicity & Litchfield, Jo. The Missing Cat. 2004. (Easy Reading Ser.). (Illus.). 96p. (J). (gr. -1-3). lib. bdg. 13.95 *(978-1-58086-226-4(8))* EDC Publishing.

Broughton, Theresa. Three Amazing Farm Animals. 2008. 12p. pap. 24.95 *(978-1-60474-545-0(2))* America Star Bks.

Brouwer, Sigmund. Justine Mckeen, Eat Your Beets, 1 vol. Whamond, Dave, illus. 2013. (Orca Echoes Ser.). (ENG.). 64p. (J). (gr. 2-3). pap. 6.95 *(978-1-55469-933-9(9))* Orca Bk. Pubs. USA.

Brown, Celease N. & Mubarak, Enoch. The Color Orange. 2004. (Illus.). 32p. *(978-1-55306-742-9(8)*, Guardian Bks.) Essence Publishing.

Brown, Elizabeth Rhea. Sweet Maneuvers. 2013. 36p. pap. 24.95 *(978-1-4626-8977-4(9))* America Star Bks.

Brown Lcsw, Jennifer. La Informacion Disexpectad: La historia de Star se permite a los ninos, padres, y profesionales del salud mental al explorer los emociones e Acciones. 2012. 32p. pap. 15.99 *(978-1-4678-5801-4(3))* AuthorHouse.

Brown, Margaret Wise. The Color Kittens. Provensen, Alice & Provensen, Martin, illus. 2003. (Little Golden Book Ser.). (ENG.). 24p. (J). (gr. -1-2). 4.99 *(978-0-307-02141-0(6)*, Golden Bks.) Random Hse. Children's Bks.

—Little Golden Book Kitten Tales. Williams, Garth et al, illus. 2017. (Little Golden Book Favorites Ser.). (ENG.). 80p. (J). (-k). 7.99 *(978-0-399-55501-5(3)*, Golden Bks.) Random Hse. Children's Bks.

—A Pussycat's Christmas. Mortimer, Anne, illus. 2009. (ENG.). 32p. (J). (gr. k-4). 9.99 *(978-0-06-186978-5(3)*, Tegen, Katherine Bks) HarperCollins Pubs.

Brown, Monica. Lola Levine Meets Jelly & Bean. 2017. (Lola Levine Ser.: 4). (ENG., Illus.). 96p. (J). (gr. 1-5). pap. 5.99 *(978-0-316-25850-0(4))* Little, Brown Bks. for Young Readers.

—Lola Levine Meets Jelly & Bean. 2017. (Lola Levine Ser.: 4). (J). lib. bdg. 16.00 ***(978-0-606-40221-7(7))*** Turtleback Bks.

Brown, Pauline A. Cat Tales. Burke, Ruth Anne, illus. 2013. 146p. (J). pap. 9.99 *(978-0-9838653-2-2(9))* Doorlight Pubns.

Brown, Ruth. Gracie, the Lighthouse Cat. Brown, Ruth, illus. 2011. (Andersen Press Picture Bks). (ENG., Illus.). 32p. (J). (gr. -1-3). 16.95 (978-0-7613-7454-1(X)) Lerner Publishing Group.

Brown, Tricia. Groucho's Eyebrows: An Alaskan Cat Tale. Lavallee, Barbara, illus. 2012. (ENG.). 32p. (J). (gr. -1-1). pap. 9.99 (978-0-88240-892-7(5), Alaska Northwest Bks.) Graphic Arts Ctr. Publishing Co.

Browne, Anthony. Little Beauty. Browne, Anthony, illus. 2010. (ENG., Illus.). 32p. (J). (gr. -1-2). pap. 6.99 (978-0-7636-4967-8(8)) Candlewick Pr.

—Little Beauty. 2010. lib. bdg. 17.20 (978-0-606-14714-9(4), Turtleback) Turtleback Bks.

Bruel, Nick. Bad Kitty. Bruel, Nick, illus. (Bad Kitty Ser.). (ENG., Illus.). 40p. (J). (gr. -1-3). 2nd ed. 2007. 17.99 (978-1-59643-299-4(3), 9781596432994) 10th anniv. ed. 2015. 16.99 (978-1-62672-245-3(5), 9781626722453) Roaring Brook Pr.

—A Bad Kitty Christmas. Bruel, Nick, illus. 2011. (Bad Kitty Ser.). (ENG., Illus.). 40p. (J). (gr. -1-3). 16.99 (978-1-59643-668-8(9), 9781596436688) Roaring Brook Pr.

—Bad Kitty Christmas Storytime Set. unabr. ed. 2014. (ENG.). (J). 12.99 (978-1-4272-5230-2(0), 9781427252302) Macmillan Audio.

—Bad Kitty Does Not Like Candy. 2015. (Bad Kitty Ser.). (ENG., Illus.). 24p. (J). (gr. -1-k). 4.99 (978-1-62672-230-9(7), 9781626722309) Square Fish.

—Bad Kitty Does Not Like Candy. 2015. (Bad Kitty Picture Bks.). (J). lib. bdg. 14.75 (978-0-606-37274-9(1)) Turtleback Bks.

—Bad Kitty Does Not Like Dogs. 2015. (Bad Kitty Picture Bks.). (J). lib. bdg. 14.75 (978-0-606-37275-6(X)) Turtleback Bks.

—Bad Kitty Does Not Like Snow. 2016. (Bad Kitty Ser.). (ENG., Illus.). 24p. (J). pap. 4.99 (978-1-62672-581-2(0), 9781626725812) Roaring Brook Pr.

—Bad Kitty Does Not Like Snow. 2016. (Bad Kitty Picture Bks.). (ENG.). 24p. (J). (gr. -1-k). 14.75 (978-0-606-39296-9(3)) Turtleback Bks.

—Bad Kitty Does Not Like Video Games. 2016. (Bad Kitty Ser.). (ENG., Illus.). 24p. (J). pap. 4.99 (978-1-62672-582-9(9), 9781626725829) Roaring Brook Pr.

—Bad Kitty Does Not Like Video Games. 2016. (Bad Kitty Picture Bks.). (ENG.). 24p. (J). (gr. -1-k). 14.75 (978-0-606-39297-6(1)) Turtleback Bks.

—Bad Kitty Drawn to Trouble. 2014. (Bad Kitty Ser.). (ENG., Illus.). 128p. (J). (gr. 2-5). 13.99 (978-1-59643-671-8(9), 9781596436718) Roaring Brook Pr.

—Bad Kitty for President. 2012. (Bad Kitty Ser.). (ENG., Illus.). 144p. (J). (gr. 2-5). 15.99 (978-1-59643-669-5(7), 9781596436695) Roaring Brook Pr.

—Bad Kitty for President. 2012. (Bad Kitty Ser.). (ENG., Illus.). 160p. (J). (gr. 2-5). pap. 6.99 (978-1-250-01016-2(0), 9781250010162) Square Fish.

—Bad Kitty for President. 2012. (Bad Kitty Chapter Bks.). (J). lib. bdg. 17.20 (978-0-606-26568-3(6), Turtleback) Turtleback Bks.

—Bad Kitty Gets a Bath. Bruel, Nick, illus. 2008. (Bad Kitty Ser.). (ENG., Illus.). 128p. (J). (gr. 2-5). 15.99 (978-1-59643-341-0(8), 9781596433410) Roaring Brook Pr.

—Bad Kitty Gets a Bath. Bruel, Nick, illus. 2009. (Bad Kitty Ser.). (ENG., Illus.). 144p. (J). (gr. 2-5). pap. 6.99 (978-0-312-58138-1(6), 9780312581381) Square Fish.

—Bad Kitty Goes to the Vet. 2017. (Bad Kitty Chapter Bks.). (J). lib. bdg. 17.20 **(978-0-606-39582-3(2))** Turtleback Bks.

—Bad Kitty Makes Comics. 2015. (Bad Kitty Chapter Bks.). (J). lib. bdg. 24.50 (978-0-606-37120-9(6)) Turtleback Bks.

—Bad Kitty Meets the Baby. Bruel, Nick, illus. 2011. (Bad Kitty Ser.). (ENG., Illus.). 144p. (J). (gr. 2-5). 14.99 (978-1-59643-597-1(6), 9781596435971) Roaring Brook Pr.

—Bad Kitty Meets the Baby. Bruel, Nick, illus. 2012. (Bad Kitty Ser.). (ENG., Illus.). 160p. (J). (gr. 2-5). pap. 6.99 (978-0-312-64121-4(4), 9780312641214) Square Fish.

—Bad Kitty Meets the Baby. 2012. (Bad Kitty Chapter Bks.). (J). lib. bdg. 17.20 (978-0-606-23754-3(2), Turtleback) Turtleback Bks.

—Bad Kitty Scaredy-Cat. 2016. (Bad Kitty Ser.). (ENG., Illus.). 32p. (J). 16.99 (978-1-59643-978-8(5), 9781596439788) Roaring Brook Pr.

—Bad Kitty School Daze. 2013. (Bad Kitty Ser.). (ENG., Illus.). 160p. (J). (gr. 2-5). 13.99 (978-1-59643-670-1(0), 9781596436701) Roaring Brook Pr.

—Bad Kitty School Daze. 2014. (Bad Kitty Ser.). (ENG., Illus.). 176p. (J). (gr. 2-5). pap. 6.99 (978-1-250-03947-7(9), 9781250039477) Square Fish.

—Bad Kitty School Daze. 2014. (Bad Kitty Chapter Bks.). (J). lib. bdg. 17.20 (978-0-606-34010-6(6), Turtleback) Turtleback Bks.

—Bad Kitty Storytime Set. unabr. ed. 2014. (ENG.). (J). 12.99 (978-1-4272-3178-9(8), 9781427231789) Macmillan Audio.

—Bad Kitty Takes a Test. 2017. (Bad Kitty Ser.). (ENG., Illus.). 144p. (J). 13.99 (978-1-62672-589-8(6), 9781626725898) Roaring Brook Pr.

—Bad Kitty vs. Uncle Murray. Bruel, Nick, illus. 2011. (Bad Kitty Ser.). (ENG., Illus.). 176p. (J). (gr. 2-5). pap. 6.99 (978-0-312-67483-0(X), 9780312674830) Square Fish.

—Bad Kitty vs. Uncle Murray. 2011. (Bad Kitty Chapter Bks.). (J). lib. bdg. 17.20 (978-0-606-23753-6(4), Turtleback) Turtleback Bks.

—Bad Kitty vs. Uncle Murray: The Uproar at the Front Door. Bruel, Nick, illus. 2010. (Bad Kitty Ser.). (ENG., Illus.). 160p. (J). (gr. 2-5). 14.99 (978-1-59643-596-4(8), 9781596435964) Roaring Brook Pr.

—Bad Kitty's Tasty Treats. 2014. (Slide & Find Ser.). (ENG., Illus.). 16p. (J). (gr. -1 — 1). bds. 12.99 (978-0-312-51723-6(8), 9780312517236) Roaring Brook Pr.

—Does Not Like Dogs, 2 vols. 2015. (Bad Kitty Ser.). (ENG., Illus.). 24p. (J). (gr. -1-k). 4.99 (978-1-62672-231-6(5), 9781626722316) Square Fish.

—Drawn to Trouble. 2015. (Bad Kitty Chapter Bks.). (J). lib. bdg. 17.20 (978-0-606-36446-1(3)) Turtleback Bks.

—Happy Birthday, Bad Kitty. Bruel, Nick, illus. 2009. (Bad Kitty Ser.). (ENG., Illus.). 160p. (J). (gr. 2-5). 15.99 (978-1-59643-342-7(6), 9781596433427) Roaring Brook Pr.

—Happy Birthday, Bad Kitty. Bruel, Nick, illus. 2010. (Bad Kitty Ser.). (ENG., Illus.). 176p. (J). (gr. 2-5). pap. 6.99 (978-0-312-62902-1(8), 9780312629021) Square Fish.

—Poor Puppy & Bad Kitty. Bruel, Nick, illus. 2012. (Bad Kitty Ser.). (ENG., Illus.). 40p. (J). (gr. -1-3). 17.99 (978-1-59643-844-6(4), 9781596438446) Roaring Brook Pr.

—Puppy's Big Day. Bruel, Nick, illus. 2015. (Bad Kitty Ser.). (ENG., Illus.). 160p. (J). (gr. 2-5). 13.99 (978-1-59643-976-4(9), 9781596439764) Roaring Brook Pr.

Brundage, Frances. The Cats' Pajamas. Brundage, Frances, illus. 2006. (Shape Bks.). (ENG., Illus.). 16p. (J). (gr. -1-3). 9.95 (978-1-59583-054-8(5), 9781595830548) Laughing Elephant.

Brutton, Elizabeth. Tabbies & Tigers in Provence. 2009. (Illus.). 112p. pap. 12.49 (978-1-4490-2104-7(2)) AuthorHouse.

Bruzzone, Catherine. Lucy the Cat at the Farm: Lucie le Chat a la Ferme. Beaton, Clare, illus. 2005. (Lucy Cat Ser.). (ENG & FRE.). 24p. (J). (gr. -1-1). pap. 7.99 (978-1-902915-11-1(9)) B Small Publishing GBR. Dist: Independent Pubs. Group.

—Lucy the Cat in Town: Lucie le Chat en Ville. Beaton, Clare, illus. 2005. (Lucy Cat Ser.). (ENG & FRE.). 24p. (J). (gr. -1-1). pap. 7.99 (978-1-902915-15-9(1)) B Small Publishing GBR. Dist: Independent Pubs. Group.

Bryan, Alexandra Faer. Green Kitty. 2010. 88p. pap. 27.49 (978-1-4520-1736-5(0)) AuthorHouse.

Bryan, Jennifer Liu. The Different Dragon. Hosler, Danamarie, illus. 2006. (J). pap. 12.95 (978-0-9674468-6-8(4)) Two Lives Publishing.

Bryan, Suzanne. Bonkers Finds His Way Home. 2008. 45p. pap. 7.54 (978-1-4357-4461-5(6)) Lulu Pr., Inc.

Bryant, Ann. The Lost Broomstick. 2011. (Tadpoles Ser.: No. 37). (ENG., Illus.). 24p. (J). (gr. k-3). pap. (978-0-7787-0594-9(3)) Crabtree Publishing Co.

Bryant, Annie. Charlotte in Paris. 2008. (Beacon Street Girls Ser.: No. 1). (ENG.). 224p. (J). (gr. 5-8). pap. 8.99 (978-1-4169-6428-5(2), Aladdin) Simon & Schuster Children's Publishing.

Buckeridge, Anthony. Just Like Jennings. 2008. (Jennings Ser.: 12). (ENG.). 184p. (J). (gr. -1-12). pap. 12.95 (978-0-7551-0170-2(7)) House of Stratus, Inc. GBR. Dist: Gardners Bks. Ltd.

Bug. Patty Cat & the Woong: An I've Got Feelings! Feel Better Book. 2010. 48p. pap. 18.49 (978-1-4520-5270-0(0)) AuthorHouse.

Bunting, Eve. Ghost Cat. Barry, Kevin M., illus. 2017. (ENG.). 32p. (J). (gr. k-2). 16.99 **(978-1-58536-993-5(4)**, 204323) Sleeping Bear Pr.

Bunting, Eve. Scary, Scary Halloween, 1 vol. Brett, Jan, illus. 2013. (ENG.). 40p. (J). (gr. -1-3). audio compact disk 10.99 (978-0-544-11114-1(1)) Houghton Mifflin Harcourt Publishing Co.

Burgess, B. L. Finding Hartagetu. 2009. 84p. pap. 10.59 (978-1-4389-7741-6(7)) AuthorHouse.

Burke, Linda. Knood the Cat. 2008. 24p. pap. 13.50 (978-1-60693-449-4(X), Eloquent Bks.) Strategic Book Publishing & Rights Agency (SBPRA).

Burks, James. Bird & Squirrel on the Run! 2012. (Bird & Squirrel Ser.). (ENG., Illus.). 128p. (J). (gr. 2-5). pap. 8.99 (978-0-545-31283-7(3), Graphix) Scholastic, Inc.

—Bird & Squirrel on the Run! 2012. (Bird Squirrel Ser.). (Illus.). 125p. (J). lib. bdg. 19.65 (978-0-606-26211-8(3), Turtleback) Turtleback Bks.

Burnford, Sheila. The Incredible Journey. unabr. ed. 2004. 145p. (J). (gr. 5-9). pap. 29.00 incl. audio (978-0-8072-8322-6(3), YA162SP, Listening Library) Random Hse. Audio Publishing Group.

Burningham, John. It's a Secret! Burningham, John, illus. 2009. (ENG., Illus.). 56p. (J). (gr. -1-2). 16.99 (978-0-7636-4275-4(4)) Candlewick Pr.

Burrows, Christopher. Alley Cats. 2012. 104p. pap. 19.95 (978-1-4626-9874-5(3)) America Star Bks.

Burstein, Chaya M. Hanukkah Cat. Henn, Judy Hanks, illus. 2003. 32p. (J). (gr. -1-3). pap. 6.95 (978-1-58013-029-5(1), Kar-Ben Publishing) Lerner Publishing Group.

Burton, Bria & burton, brain. Lance & Ringo Tails: The Wild Adventures of a Dog & a Cat As Told by Their Human. 2013. 134p. pap. 9.99 (978-1-939181-45-9(3)) Soul Attitude Press.

Busby, Cylin. The Nine Lives of Jacob Tibbs. Kelly, Gerald, illus. 2016. (ENG.). 272p. (J). (gr. 3-7). 16.99 (978-0-553-51123-9(8), Knopf Bks. for Young Readers) Random Hse. Children's Bks.

—The Nine Lives of Jacob Tibbs. 2017. lib. bdg. 17.20 **(978-0-606-39874-9(0))** Turtleback Bks.

Busch, Miriam. Lion, Lion. Day, Larry, illus. 2014. (ENG.). 32p. (J). (gr. -1-3). 17.99 (978-0-06-227104-4(0)) HarperCollins Pubs.

Bush, Randall. The Caterbury Tails. Watson, Ben, illus. 2013. 60p. pap. 13.99 (978-1-936670-75-8(5)) BorderStone Pr., LLC.

Butterworth, Nick. Jingle Bells. 2014. (ENG.). 32p. (J). 9.99 (978-0-00-758399-7(0), HarperCollins Children's Bks.) HarperCollins Pubs. Ltd. GBR. Dist: HarperCollins Pubs.

—Q Pootle 5. Butterworth, Nick, illus. 2009. (ENG., Illus.). 32p. (J). (gr. -1-k). pap. 11.95 (978-0-00-717235-1(4), HarperCollins Children's Bks.) HarperCollins Pubs. Ltd. GBR. Dist: HarperCollins Pubs.

—Tiger. 2009. (ENG., Illus.). 32p. 10.95 (978-0-00-725772-0(4)) HarperCollins Pubs. Ltd. GBR. Dist: Independent Pubs. Group.

—Tiger. Butterworth, Nick, illus. 2006. (ENG., Illus.). 32p. (J). (gr. k — 1). pap. 7.95 (978-0-00-711975-2(5), HarperCollins Children's Bks.) HarperCollins Pubs. Ltd. GBR. Dist: HarperCollins Pubs.

—The Whisperer. Butterworth, Nick, illus. 2005. (ENG., Illus.). 32p. (J). (gr. k-3). pap. 15.95 (978-0-00-712018-5(4), HarperCollins Children's Bks.) HarperCollins Pubs. Ltd. GBR. Dist: HarperCollins Pubs.

Byrd, Michael. The Adventures of Banter & Jafar: Spoiled Rotten, 1 vol. Bai, Jenny, illus. 2009. 36p. pap. 24.95 (978-1-60836-131-1(4)) America Star Bks.

Byrne, John Patrick. Donald & Benoit. Byrne, John Patrick, illus. 2011. (ENG., Illus.). 64p. (J). (gr. 2-5). 17.95 (978-0-7893-2084-1(3)) Universe Publishing.

Cabrera, Jane. Cat's Colors. 2015. 32p. pap. 8.00 (978-1-61003-526-2(7)) Center for the Collaborative Classroom.

—Kitty's Cuddles. 2007. (ENG., Illus.). 32p. (J). (gr. -1-k). 16.95 (978-0-8234-2066-7(3)) Holiday Hse., Inc.

Caim, Barbara. Gatsby's Grand Adventure: Book 2 Renoir's the Apple Seller. Ruble, Eugene, illus. 2013. 16p. pap. 9.95 (978-1-61633-387-4(1)) Guardian Angel Publishing, Inc.

Cairns, Barbara. Gatsby's Grand Adventures: Book 1 Winslow Homer's Snap the Whip. Ruble, Eugene, illus. 2012. 16p. pap. 9.95 (978-1-61633-350-8(2)) Guardian Angel Publishing, Inc.

Callen, Sharon. How to Be a Kitten, 1 vol. rev. ed. 2013. (Fiction Readers Ser.). (ENG., Illus.). 12p. (J). (gr. 1-1). pap. 12.96 (978-1-4807-1136-5(5)); pap. 4.99 (978-1-4333-5457-1(8)) Shell Educational Publishing.

Cameron, Ann. Spunky Tells All. Castillo, Lauren, illus. 2011. (ENG.). 112p. (J). (gr. 3-6). 16.99 (978-0-374-38000-7(7), 9780374380007, Farrar, Straus & Giroux (BYR)) Farrar, Straus & Giroux.

Cameron, Jill. Miffy, the Crooked-Eyed Cat. 2009. 28p. pap. 12.99 (978-1-60860-353-4(9), Eloquent Bks.) Strategic Book Publishing & Rights Agency (SBPRA).

Cameron, Kathleen. The Chicken Without a Coop. 2003. (Night Before Christmas Ser.). (Illus.). (J). 0.85 (978-1-882897-71-1(4)) Pelican Publishing Co., Inc.

Cammilleri, Johnathon. The White Cat of Big Pine Hills. 2008. (Illus.). 24p. (gr. k-12). 47.00 (978-0-615-25933-8(2)) Cammilleri Productions.

Campbell, Mari & Jennings, Randy. Maggiemoosetracks: Christmas Star. 2013. 106p. pap. 21.00 (978-0-9895205-4-6(4)) MaggieMooseTracks.

Candelario, Margo. Looking to the Clouds for Daddy. Craft, Jerry, illus. 2009. (J). (978-0-9820221-7-7(4)) Hunter, Karen Media.

Canning, Seán. The Cat That Loves to Eat. Canning, Erin, ed. Canning, Seán, illus. 2005. (Illus.). (J). 9.95 (978-0-9773134-0-2(9)) SP Family Productions, LLC.

Capatti, Bérénice. Klimt & His Cat. Monaco, Octavia, illus. 2004. (ENG.). 40p. (J). 20.00 (978-0-8028-5282-3(3)) Eerdmans, William B. Publishing Co.

Caple, Kathy. Hillary to the Rescue. Caple, Kathy, illus. 2003. (Picture Bks.). (Illus.). 32p. (J). (gr. -1-3). 15.95 (978-1-57505-420-9(5), Carolrhoda Bks.) Lerner Publishing Group.

—Starring Hillary. Caple, Kathy, illus. 2003. (Picture Bks.). (Illus.). 28p. (J). (gr. -1-3). 15.95 (978-1-57505-261-8(X), Carolrhoda Bks.) Lerner Publishing Group.

Capucilli, Alyssa Satin. Mrs. McTats & Her Houseful of Cats. Rankin, Joan E. & Rankin, Joan, illus. 2004. (ENG.). 32p. (J). (gr. -1-3). 7.99 (978-0-689-86991-4(6), Aladdin) Simon & Schuster Children's Publishing.

—My Mom & Me. Mitchell, Susan, illus. 2009. (ENG.). 16p. (J). (gr. -1-1). 7.99 (978-1-4169-5829-1(0), Little Simon) Little Simon.

—Scat, Cat! Meisel, Paul, illus. 2010. (My First I Can Read Ser.). (ENG.). 32p. (J). (gr. -1 — 1). 16.99 (978-0-06-117754-5(7)); pap. 3.99 (978-0-06-117756-9(3)) HarperCollins Pubs.

Carey-Costa, Denise. Lucky. Sjostrom, Nicole & Iseminger, Jonathan, illus. 2011. 34p. pap. 12.99 (978-1-61170-035-0(3)) Robertson Publishing.

Carey, Kathleen. Jack Kat Had a Day, 1 vol. Carey, Joseph, illus. 2009. 21p. pap. 24.95 (978-1-60836-314-8(7)) America Star Bks.

Carle, Eric. Have You Seen My Cat? Carle, Eric, illus. 2009. (World of Eric Carle Ser.). (ENG., Illus.). 16p. (J). bds. 7.99 (978-1-4169-8514-3(X), Little Simon) Little Simon.

—Have You Seen My Cat? Carle, Eric, illus. 2012. (World of Eric Carle Ser.). (ENG., Illus.). 24p. (J). (gr. -1-k). 16.99 (978-1-4424-4575-8(0)); pap. 3.99 (978-1-4424-4574-1(2)) Simon Spotlight. (Simon Spotlight).

—Have You Seen My Cat? 2012. (Eric Carle Ready-To-Read Ser.). lib. bdg. 13.55 (978-0-606-26356-6(X), Turtleback) Turtleback Bks.

—Rooster Is off to See the World. 2013. (Eric Carle Ready-To-Read Ser.). lib. bdg. 13.55 (978-0-606-32063-4(6), Turtleback) Turtleback Bks.

Carlow, Emma & Bradman, Tony. Flora the Fairy. Carlow, Emma, illus. 2005. (Green Bananas Ser.). (ENG., Illus.). 48p. (J). lib. bdg. (978-0-7787-1022-6(X)) Crabtree Publishing Co.

Carlson, Nancy. Arnie & the Skateboard Gang. Carlson, Nancy, illus. 2012. (Nancy Carlson Picture Bks). (Illus.). 32p. (J). (gr. k-2). (ENG.). 9.95 (978-0-7613-8948-4(2)); 56.72 (978-0-7613-9303-0(X)) Lerner Publishing Group. (Carolrhoda Bks.).

—Arnie Goes to Camp. Carlson, Nancy, illus. 2012. (Nancy Carlson Picture Bks). (Illus.). 32p. (J). (gr. k-2). (ENG.). 9.95 (978-0-7613-8947-7(4)); 56.72 (978-0-7613-9302-3(1)) Lerner Publishing Group. (Carolrhoda Bks.).

Carman, Debby. I'm Gronk & I'm Green. Carman, Debby, illus. 2007. (Illus.). 28p. (J). (gr. -1-1). 14.99 (978-0-9777340-0-9(5)) Faux Paw Media Group.

—I'm Maximum Cat, That's a Fact! 2007. (Illus.). 28p. (J). 14.99 (978-0-9777340-2-3(1)) Faux Paw Media Group.

—Kittywimpuss Got Game. Carman, Debby, illus. 2007. (Illus.). 28p. (J). (gr. -1-1). 14.99 (978-0-9777340-4-7(8)) Faux Paw Media Group.

—The Nutcracker Cats of the Kremlin. Carman, Debby, illus. 2007. (Illus.). 80p. (J). (gr. 1-7). 28.99 (978-0-9777340-7-8(2)) Faux Paw Media Group.

—Purrlonia's Lullaby. Carman, Debby, illus. 2008. (Illus.). 28p. (J). (gr. -1-1). 14.99 (978-0-9777340-1-6(3)) Faux Paw Media Group.

Carmichael, Clay. Wild Things. (ENG.). (J). 2012. 184p. (gr. 5-8). pap. 9.95 (978-1-59078-914-8(8)) 2009. 248p. (gr. 4-6). 18.95 (978-1-59078-627-7(0), Front Street) Boyds Mills Pr.

—Wild Things, 6 vols. 2010. (J). 77.75 (978-1-4498-0632-3(5)) Recorded Bks., Inc.

Carmichael, Heather. Ellie Finds a New Home. McFarland, Shea, illus. 2008. (ENG.). 36p. pap. 16.99 (978-1-4389-2976-7(5)) AuthorHouse.

Carpenter, Christopher, illus. Lilly's Heart: The Veterinary Clinic Cases Series. 2006. 32p. (J). per. 9.95 (978-0-9766641-0-9(0)) Ichabod Ink.

Carpenter, Gloria. Prissy the Persnickety Cat. 2008. 20p. pap. 24.95 (978-1-4241-9394-3(X)) America Star Bks.

Cartwright, Stephen, illus. Find the Kitten. 2007. (Find-its Board Bks). 12p. (J). (gr. -1-k). bds. 6.99 (978-0-7945-1803-5(6), Usborne) EDC Publishing.

Carty, Hilda. Catventure. 2009. (Illus.). 40p. pap. 18.49 (978-1-4389-4659-7(7)) AuthorHouse.

Casanova, Mary. Some Cat! Hoyt, Ard, illus. 2012. (ENG.). 40p. (J). (gr. -1-k). 17.99 (978-0-374-37123-4(7), 9780374371234, Farrar, Straus & Giroux (BYR)) Farrar, Straus & Giroux.

Cash, John Carter. The Cat in the Rhinestone Suit. Nash, Scott, illus. 2012. (ENG.). 32p. (J). (gr. -1-3). 17.99 (978-1-4169-7483-3(0), Little Simon Inspirations) Little Simon Inspirations.

Cash, M. A. Edward of Canterbury & the King of Red. Adams, Craig, illus. 2003. (J). (978-0-9772711-0-8(2)) Jama Kids.

Cassidy, Sara. Seeing Orange, 1 vol. Meissner, Amy, illus. 2012. (Orca Echoes Ser.). (ENG.). 64p. (J). (gr. 2-3). pap. 6.95 (978-1-55469-991-9(6)) Orca Bk. Pubs. USA.

Castelli, Jeanette. Los Gatos en la Luna/the Cats on the Moon. Santana, Andrea, illus. 2005. (Bilingual Collection). (SPA.). 51p. (J). (gr. k-2). (978-958-30-1767-4(1)) Panamericana Editorial.

Castro, Giovanni & Chabot, Jacob. It's about Time. 2015. (Hello Kitty Graphic Novel Ser.). lib. bdg. 18.40 (978-0-606-37243-5(1)) Turtleback Bks.

Castro, Shirley. The Pelican Family Series — Telly's Story. Castro, Christopher, illus. 2008. 36p. (J). 15.00 (978-0-9790307-1-0(4)) Castro, Shirley.

Cat Concert: Individual Title Six-Packs. (Literatura 2000 Ser.). (gr. 2-3). 33.00 (978-0-7635-0163-1(8)) Rigby Education.

The Cat-Flap Trap: Individual Title Six-Packs. (Story Steps Ser.). (gr. k-2). 32.00 (978-0-7635-9824-2(0)) Rigby Education.

Cat in the Hen House: KinderConcepts Individual Title Six-Packs. (Kinderstarters Ser.). 8p. (gr. -1-1). 21.00 (978-0-7635-8728-4(1)) Rigby Education.

Catalanotto, Peter. Kitten Red, Yellow, Blue. Catalanotto, Peter, illus. 2005. (ENG., Illus.). 32p. (J). (gr. -1-k). 18.99 (978-0-689-86562-6(7), Atheneum/Richard Jackson Bks.) Simon & Schuster Children's Publishing.

Cater, Angela. The Adventures of Sailor Sam. Cater, Angela, illus. 2007. (ENG., Illus.). 32p. (J). pap. (978-0-9555725-0-0(9)) Tabby Cat Pr.

Cats & Other Stories: Individual Title Six-Pack. (Story Steps Ser.). (gr. k-2). 48.00 (978-0-7635-9848-8(8)) Rigby Education.

Cats Got Talent. 2014. (ENG., Illus.). 32p. (J). (gr. -1-3). 17.99 (978-1-4424-9451-0(4), Simon & Schuster/Paula Wiseman Bks.) Simon & Schuster/Paula Wiseman Bks.

Cecil, Laura. Cunning Cat Tales. Chichester Clark, Emma, illus. 2006. 71p. (J). (gr. k-4). reprint ed. pap. 17.00 (978-1-4223-5013-3(4)) DIANE Publishing Co.

Cerino, Ann. Carmella the Cat. 2013. 36p. pap. 12.95 (978-1-4787-2389-9(0)) Outskirts Pr., Inc.

Cerulli, Claudia. Ottavia e I Gatti Di Roma - Octavia & the Cats of Rome: A Bilingual Picture Book in Italian & English. Lätti, Leo, illus. 2013. 40p. pap. (978-1-938712-11-1(0)) Roxby Media Ltd.

Cesak, Jerry. My Personal Panther. Naughton, Terry, illus. 2012. (J). (978-0-578-10507-9(1)) U. S. ISBN Agency.

Cesmat, Sheryl. Adopted Kitty from the City. 2013. 36p. pap. 18.41 (978-1-4669-8285-7(3)) Trafford Publishing.

Chabot, Jacob. Fashion Music Wonderland. 2015. (Hello Kitty Graphic Novel Ser.). lib. bdg. 17.20 (978-0-606-37245-9(8)) Turtleback Bks.

—Hello Kitty: Work of Art. 2014. lib. bdg. 18.40 (978-0-606-36123-1(5)) Turtleback Bks.

—Hello Kitty - It's about Time. McGinty, Ian et al, illus. 2015. (ENG.). 64p. (J). pap. 7.99 (978-1-4215-7769-2(0)) Viz Media.

—Hello Kitty: Work of Art. McGinty, Ian et al, illus. 2014. (ENG.). 64p. (J). pap. 7.99 (978-1-4215-7542-1(6)) Viz Media.

Chamberlin, Ann. Dumpling. 2012. (Illus.). 32p. pap. 21.99 (978-1-4691-6313-0(6)) Xlibris Corp.

Chambers, Jerry. The Cat Who Became a Teacher. 2013. 40p. pap. 24.95 (978-1-63000-040-0(X)) America Star Bks.

Chan, Marty. True Story. Bennett, Lorna, illus. 2009. (ENG.). 32p. (J). 9.95 (978-0-9810449-0-3(5)) Ink Jockey, Inc. CAN. Dist: Univ. of Toronto Pr.

Chandler, Jeff. The New Kitten: A Story about a Foster Puppy, 1 vol. 2009. 48p. pap. 24.95 (978-1-61546-176-9(0)) America Star Bks.

Chandler, Joan. Cat Tales. 2013. 64p. pap. 9.99 (978-1-62697-511-8(6)) Salem Author Services.

Charara, Hayan & Brown, Monica. The Three Lucys, 1 vol. Kahn, Sara & Palacios, Sara, illus. 2016. (ENG.). 40p. (J). 18.95 (978-1-60060-998-5(8)) Lee & Low Bks., Inc.

Charlie & the Kitten. 2006. (Charlie's Great Adventures: 5). (Illus.). 96p. (J). per. 5.95 (978-0-9702546-6-5(0)) GoodyGoody Bks.

Le Chat Botte.Tr. of Puss in Boots. (FRE.). 48p. pap. 12.95 incl. audio compact disk (978-2-89558-062-1(6)) Coffragants CAN. Dist: Penton Overseas, Inc.

Cherna. Patch's Country Quilt. Cherna, illus. 2013. (Illus.). 54p. 25.95 (978-1-60571-188-1(8)); 50p. pap. 17.95 (978-1-60571-187-4(X)) Northshire Pr.

The Cheshire Cheese Cat, 1 vol. 2014. (ENG., Illus.). 234p. (J). (gr. 3-6). pap. 8.95 (978-1-56145-810-3(4)) Peachtree Pubs.

Chessa, Francesca. Holly's Red Boots. Chessa, Francesca, illus. 2008. (ENG., Illus.). 32p. (J). (gr. -1-1). 16.95 (978-0-8234-2158-9(9)) Holiday Hse., Inc.

Chew, Ruth. The Wednesday Witch. 2015. (Matter-Of-Fact Magic Book Ser.). (ENG., Illus.). 144p. (J). (gr. 2-5). pap. 5.99 (978-0-449-81556-4(0), Random Hse. Bks. for Young Readers) Random Hse. Children's Bks.

Chichester Clark, Emma. Plenty of Love to Go Around. Chichester Clark, Emma, illus. 2016. (ENG., Illus.). 32p. (J). (-k). 17.99 (978-0-399-54666-2(9), Nancy Paulsen Books) Penguin Young Readers Group.

Chichester Clark, Emma, illus. Cunning Cat Tales. 2003. (ENG.). 80p. (J). (gr. k-2). 24.00 (978-1-86205-376-2(6), Pavilion) Pavilion Bks. GBR. Dist: Independent Pubs. Group.

Child, Jeremy. Kitty. Davies, Caroline, illus. 2013. (Rock & Rattle Bks.). (ENG.). 8p. (J). (gr. -1 — 1). bds. 3.99 (978-0-7641-6590-0(9)) Barron's Educational Series, Inc.

Children's Press, contrib. by. The Three Little Kittens Get Dressed. 2009. (Rookie Preschool-NEW Ser.). (ENG.). 24p. (J). pap. 6.95 (978-0-531-24579-8(9), Children's Pr.) Scholastic Library Publishing.

Chin, Oliver Clyde. Harriet's Hairballs. Crawford, Gregory, tr. Crawford, Gregory, illus. 2003. 32p. (J). 15.95 (978-1-58394-078-5(2), Frog Ltd.) North Atlantic Bks.

Chriss, Granddad. The Adventures of Barazaburg. 2011. 54p. 24.99 (978-1-4568-7988-4(X)); pap. 15.99 (978-1-4568-7987-7(1)) Xlibris Corp.

Christensen-Hall, Nancy. Good Night, Little Kitten. Hockerman, Dennis, illus. 2004. (My First Reader Ser.). (ENG.). 32p. (J). (gr. k-1). pap. 3.95 (978-0-516-24628-4(3), Children's Pr.) Scholastic Library Publishing.

Christian, Cheryl. Where's the Kitten? (Haitian Creole/English), 1 vol. Dwight, Laura, photos by. 2005. (Photoflaps Ser.). (HAT & ENG., Illus.). 12p. (J). (gr. -1). 5.95 (978-1-59572-028-3(6)) Star Bright Bks., Inc.

—Where's the Kitten? (Korean), 1 vol. Choi, Jin, tr. Dwight, Laura, photos by. 2004. (KOR & ENG., Illus.). 12p. (J). 5.95 (978-1-932065-78-7(4)) Star Bright Bks., Inc.

—Where's the Kitten? (Russian/English), 1 vol. Dwight, Laura, photos by. 2004. (RUS & ENG., Illus.). 12p. (J). 5.95 (978-1-932065-84-8(9)) Star Bright Bks., Inc.

—Where's the Kitten? (Simplified Mandarin) Dwight, Laura, photos by. 2004. (CHI., Illus.). 12p. (J). bds. 5.95 (978-1-932065-66-4(0)) Star Bright Bks., Inc.

—Where's the Kitten? (Spanish/English) Bilingual Edition, 1 vol. Fiol, Maria A., tr. Dwight, Laura, photos by. 2004. (SPA & ENG., Illus.). 32p. (J). bds. 5.50 (978-1-932065-54-1(7), 718-784-9112) Star Bright Bks., Inc.

—Where's the Kitten? (Traditional Cantonese), 1 vol. Dwight, Laura, photos by. 2004. (CHI & ENG., Illus.). 12p. (J). 5.95 (978-1-932065-60-2(1)) Star Bright Bks., Inc.

—Where's the Kitten? (Vietnamese) Dwight, Laura, photos by. 2004. (VIE., Illus.). 12p. (J). bds. 5.95 (978-1-932065-72-5(5)) Star Bright Bks., Inc.

Chronicle Books Staff & Image Books Staff. Little Cat: Finger Puppet Book. Put, Klaartje van der, illus. 2014. (Little Finger Puppet Board Bks.). (ENG.). 12p. (J). (gr. -1 — 1). bds. 6.99 (978-1-4521-2916-7(9)) Chronicle Bks. LLC.

Claire, Black. Puss in Boots. Eric, Kincaid, illus. 2004. 30p. pap. (978-1-84577-074-7(9)) Berryland Bks.

Clairmont, Patsy. 5 Cheesy Stories: About Friendship, Bravery, Bullying, & More, 1 vol. Oeltjenbruns, Joni, illus. 2007. (Tails from the Pantry Ser.). (ENG.). 144p. (gr. -1-2). 15.99 (978-1-4003-1042-5(3)) Nelson, Thomas Inc.

Clanchy, Kate. Our Cat Henry Comes to the Swings. Bird, Jemima, illus. 2007. 32p. (J). (gr. -1-1). 16.00 (978-1-56148-563-5(2), Good Bks.) Skyhorse Publishing Co., Inc.

Clark, L. D. The World According to Coho. 2009. 36p. pap. 16.99 (978-1-4490-2393-5(2)) AuthorHouse.

Clark, Pat. Katz & Dogz Rule. 2013. 48p. pap. 12.99 (978-1-935711-32-2(6)) Peak City Publishing, LLC.

Clark, Seneca & Giardi, Sandy. Frankie Goes to Fenway: The Tale of the Faithful, Red Sox-Loving Mouse. Decedue, Julie, illus. 2008. 56p. (J). 18.95 (978-0-9767276-3-7(3)) Three Bean Pr.

—The Yellowest Yellow Lab. Decedue, Julie, illus. 2005. 30p. (J). 11.95 (978-0-9767276-2-0(5)) Three Bean Pr.

Clarke, Jane. Chewy Hughie. McConnell, Sarah, illus. 2006. (Collins Big Cat Ser.). (ENG.). 136p. (J). (gr. 2-2). pap. 6.99 (978-0-00-718692-1(4)) HarperCollins Pubs. Ltd. GBR. Dist: Independent Pubs. Group.

—Clover the Bunny. 2016. (Dr. KittyCat Ser.: 2). (ENG.). 96p. (J). (gr. 2-5). pap. 4.99 (978-0-545-87336-9(3), Scholastic Paperbacks) Scholastic, Inc.

—Daisy the Kitten. 2016. (Dr. KittyCat Ser.: 3). (ENG.). 96p. (J). (gr. 2-5). pap. 4.99 (978-0-545-87343-7(6), Scholastic Paperbacks) Scholastic, Inc.

—Posy the Puppy. 2016. (Dr. KittyCat Ser.: 1). (ENG.). 96p. (J). (gr. 2-5). pap. 4.99 (978-0-545-87333-8(9), Scholastic Paperbacks) Scholastic, Inc.

Cleary, Beverly. Socks. Darwin, Beatrice et al, illus. 2008. (ENG.). 160p. (J). (gr. 3-7). 16.99 (978-0-688-20067-1(2)) HarperCollins Pubs.

Clineff, Jeff. Too Many Kitties. Movshina, Marina, illus. 2007. 22p. (J). E-Book 9.95 incl. cd-rom (978-1-933090-45-0(6)) Guardian Angel Publishing, Inc.

—Too Many Kitties. Movshina, Marina, illus. 2007. (ESK.). 24p. (J). 9.95 (978-1-933090-10-8(3)) Guardian Angel Publishing, Inc.

Coan, S. M. Crawlspace Charlie. 2011. 50p. pap. 24.95 (978-1-4560-6931-5(4)) America Star Bks.

Coatsworth, Elizabeth. The Cat Who Went to Heaven. 2011. 7.64 (978-0-7848-3455-8(5), Everbind) Marco Bk. Co.

—The Cat Who Went to Heaven. Vitale, Raoul, illus. 2008. (ENG.). 96p. (J). (gr. 3-7). pap. 6.99 (978-1-4169-4973-2(9), Simon & Schuster/Paula Wiseman Bks.) Simon & Schuster/Paula Wiseman Bks.

—Gata Que Se Fue para el Cielo. 2011. (SPA.). 104p. (gr. 5-8). pap. 12.99 (978-958-04-1530-5(7), NR4853) Norma S.A. COL. Dist: Lectorum Pubns., Inc.

Coblentz, Catherine Cate. The Blue Cat of Castle Town. Holland, Janice, illus. 2017. (ENG.). 128p. pap. 5.95 (978-0-486-81527-5(7)) Dover Pubns., Inc.

Coffey, Ethel. How Meg Changed Her Mind. Schweitzer-Johnson, Betty, illus. 2014. (ENG.). 32p. pap. 11.95 (978-1-4525-8377-8(3), Balboa Pr.) Author Solutions, Inc.

Cole, Henry. Spot, the Cat. Cole, Henry, illus. 2016. (ENG., Illus.). 32p. (J). (gr. -1-3). 17.99 (978-1-4814-4225-1(2), Little Simon) Little Simon.

Cole, Molly. Joe & His Strong Purr. 2012. 26p. 24.95 (978-1-4626-6149-7(1)) America Star Bks.

Coleman, William L. Oscar: A Cat's Tale. Amatisto, Brandi, illus. 2012. 38p. pap. 16.97 (978-1-61204-750-8(5), Strategic Bk. Publishing) Strategic Book Publishing & Rights Agency (SBPRA).

Collins, C. B. Where's My Face? A Simon-the-Cat Tale. Holgren, Anna C., illus. 2008. 36p. pap. 24.95 (978-1-60441-009-9(4)) America Star Bks.

Collins, Sheila. Truffles' Diary: The Encore. 2007. (Illus.). 76p. pap. (978-1-906358-13-6(3)) Apex Publishing Ltd., Essex.

Collins, Stephan. The Chronicles of Timothy Tabbis. 2009. 45p. pap. 8.55 (978-0-557-09266-6(3)) Lulu Pr., Inc.

Collins UK. My Balcony Oasis: Level 10. 2016. (Collins Big Cat Arabic Ser.). (ENG.). 24p. (J). pap. 5.99 (978-0-00-818582-4(4)) HarperCollins Pubs. Ltd. GBR. Dist: Independent Pubs. Group.

Colorado, Papa. Nui & Kiwi's Fantastic Adventures. 2011. 70p. pap. 19.95 (978-1-4626-2806-3(0)) PublishAmerica, Inc.

Colors All Day. (J). 26.20 (978-0-8136-8399-7(8)); (gr. -1-3). 59.50 (978-0-8136-7918-1(4)) Modern Curriculum Pr.

Colwell, Emerson/Mylon, Jr. The Fisher Cat. Colwell, Emerson/Mylon, Jr., illus. 2009. (ENG., Illus.). 36p. (J). pap. 14.95 (978-0-9840916-1-4(0)) TINK INK Publishing.

Comfort, Ray. Scratch & Sniff. Hohnstadt, Cedric, illus. 2007. (Creation for Kids Ser.). 24p. (gr. -1-5). 14.99 (978-0-88270-328-2(5)) Bridge-Logos, Inc.

Compagnucci, Veronica M. Emily Finds Her Voice. 2013. 40p. pap. 24.95 (978-1-63004-288-2(9)) America Star Bks.

Condenzio, John. Cocoa the Witch Cat. 2013. 20p. pap. 24.95 (978-1-62709-264-7(1)) America Star Bks.

Coniglio, John. The Cat Who Slept All Day: What Happens While the Cat Sleeps. Key, Pamela, illus. 2006. 24p. (J). per. 2.99 (978-1-59958-004-3(7)) Journey Stone Creations, LLC.

Conlin, Judy. Crissy,the Cross-Eyed Cat. 2012. 28p. pap. 19.99 (978-1-4685-0789-8(3)) AuthorHouse.

Connolly, Timothy. Joy's Journey Home. Sullivan, Mary, illus. 2012. (ENG.). 92p. (J). 17.95 (978-0-9859986-2-2(8)); pap. 8.95 (978-0-9859986-1-5(X)) Nectar Pubns.

Connors, Jerrold. Now, Louie! Connors, Jerrold, illus. 2006. (Illus.). 40p. (J). 12.99 (978-0-9721416-1-1(8)) Alligator Boogaloo.

Cooke, Bev. Feral, 1 vol. 2008. (ENG.). 208p. (YA). (gr. 7-12). pap. 9.95 (978-1-55143-747-7(3)) Orca Bk. Pubs. USA.

Coons, Susan Anderson. Lighthouse Mouse Meets Simon the Cat. Sanne, Don, illus. 2012. 52p. pap. 10.03 (978-1-4669-1223-6(5)) Trafford Publishing.

Cooper, Diana. Tara & Her Talking Kitten Meet a Mermaid. Shannon, Kate, illus. 2012. (Tara & Ash-ting Ser.). (ENG.). 80p. (J). (gr. k-4). (978-1-84409-580-3(0)) Me to We.

—Tara & the Talking Kitten Meet a Unicorn. Shannon, Kate, illus. 2011. (Tara & Ash-ting Ser.). (ENG.). 80p. (J). (gr. k-4). 8.95 (978-1-84409-557-5(6)) Innovation Pr., The.

—Tara & the Talking Kitten Meet Angels & Fairies. Shannon, Kate, illus. 2011. (Tara & Ash-ting Ser.). (ENG.). 80p. (J). (gr. k-4). 8.95 (978-1-84409-551-3(7)) Innovation Pr., The.

Cooper, Elisha. Big Cat, Little Cat. 2017. (ENG., Illus.). 40p. (J). 16.99 (978-1-62672-371-9(0), 9781626723719) Roaring Brook Pr.

Cooper, Helen S. Delicious! Cooper, Helen S., illus. 2007. (ENG., Illus.). 32p. (J). (gr. -1-3). 16.99 (978-0-374-31756-0(9), 9780374317560, Farrar, Straus & Giroux (BYR)) Farrar, Straus & Giroux.

—Pumpkin Soup, Set. unabr. ed. 2009. (ENG., Illus.). 32p. (J). (gr. -1-3). 9.99 (978-1-4272-0740-1(2), 9781427207401) Macmillan Audio.

Cooper, Polly. The Adventures of Sir George & His Friends. 2008. (Illus.). 48p. pap. 17.49 (978-1-4343-4057-3(0)) AuthorHouse.

Cope-Robinson, Lyn. Cat Tails. Cope-Robinson, Lyn, illus. l.t. ed. 2003. (Illus.). 32p. (J). lib. bdg. (978-1-887774-14-7(9), Wynden) Canmore Pr.

Coppel, Chris. Far from Burden Dell. 2005. 286p. (J). (gr. 6-16). per. 4.95 (978-0-9746481-6-3(7)) Brown Barn Bks.

Corder, Zizou. Lion Boy - The Chase. 2005. (ENG., Illus.). 288p. (J). (gr. 3-7). 8.99 (978-0-14-240454-6(3), Puffin Books) Penguin Young Readers Group.

—Lionboy. 2004. (ENG., Illus.). 304p. (J). (gr. 3-7). reprint ed. pap. 8.99 (978-0-14-240226-9(5), Puffin Books) Penguin Young Readers Group.

—Lionboy: The Truth. 2006. (ENG., Illus.). 240p. (J). (gr. 3-7). 7.99 (978-0-14-240705-9(4), Puffin Books) Penguin Young Readers Group.

Cordone Warner, Debra. Henry's Daily Walk. 2010. 56p. pap. 24.99 (978-0-557-60667-2(5)) Lulu Pr., Inc.

Corrado, Diane. I Wanna Be Purr-Fect! ShowCat. Kanarek, Michael, illus. 2006. 48p. (J). 14.95 incl. audio compact disk (978-0-9795049-2-1(9)) Kidz Entertainment, Inc.

Cosgrove, Stephen. Wheedle & the Noodle. James, Robin, illus. 2011. (ENG.). 32p. (J). (gr. -1-2). 16.99 (978-1-57061-730-0(9), Little Bigfoot) Sasquatch Bks.

Cosy Cat. 2005. (J). bds. 6.99 (978-0-9753127-5-9(8)) Family Bks. at Home.

Cote, Genevieve & Côté, Geneviève. Mr. King's Machine. Cote, Genevieve & Côté, Geneviève, illus. 2016. (Mr. King Ser.). (ENG., Illus.). 32p. (J). (gr. -1-2). 16.95 (978-1-77138-021-8(7)) Kids Can Pr., Ltd. CAN. Dist: Hachette Bk. Group.

County Studio Staff. Katie: The Mischievous Kitten. 16p. (J). bds. (978-0-7554-1095-8(5)) Grandreams Bks., Inc.

Cousineau-Peiffer, Trisha. Have You Ever Heard of a Rainbow Farm. Everett-Hawkes, Bonnie, illus. 2006. 32p. (J). 12.95 (978-0-9792084-1-6(6)) Dream Ridge Pr.

—Have You Ever Heard of a Rainbow Farm: The Missing Color Kittens. Everett-Hawkes, Bonnie, illus. 2007. 48p. (J). per. 15.95 (978-0-9792084-2-3(4)) Dream Ridge Pr.

Cowhard, Patricia Ann. B J 's Underground Adventure. 2011. 28p. pap. 15.99 (978-1-4628-5577-3(6)) Xlibris Corp.

Cowlard, Irene. Moriarty's Dream. 2007. (Illus.). 52p. per. (978-1-84748-062-0(4)) Athena Pr.

Cox, Judy. One Is a Feast for Mouse: A Thanksgiving Tale. Ebbeler, Jeffrey, illus. 2009. (ENG.). 32p. (J). (gr. -1-3). pap. 7.99 (978-0-8234-2231-9(3)) Holiday Hse., Inc.

Cox, Katherine. Scholastic Reader Level 2: Katie Fry, Private Eye #1: the Lost Kitten. Newton, Vanessa Brantley, illus. 2015. (Scholastic Reader Level 2 Ser.). (ENG.). 32p. (J). (gr. 1-3). pap. 3.99 (978-0-545-66672-5(4)) Scholastic, Inc.

Cox, Phil Roxbee. Fat Cat on a Mat. Tyler, Jenny, ed. Cartwright, Stephen, illus. rev. ed. 2006. (Phonics Readers Ser.). 16p. (J). (gr. -1-3). pap. 6.99 (978-0-7945-1502-7(9), Usborne) EDC Publishing.

Cox, Phil Roxbee & Cartwright, S. Fat Cat on a Mat. 2004. (Phonics Board Bks.). 10p. (J). 4.95 (978-0-7945-0059-7(5), Usborne) EDC Publishing.

—Ted's Shed, Toad Makes a Road, Fat Cat on a Mat & Sam Sheep Can't Sleep. 2004. (Easy Words to Read Ser.). (Illus.). 16p. (J). (gr. 1-18). pap. 9.95 (978-0-7945-0245-4(8), Usborne) EDC Publishing.

Coxon, Michele. The Cat Who Found His Way Home. 2005. (Illus.). 32p. (J). (gr. -1 — 1). pap. (978-1-903285-21-3(6)) Happy Cat Bks.

—Have You Fed the Cat?, 1 vol. Coxon, Michele, illus. 2004. (ENG., Illus.). 32p. (J). 15.95 (978-1-932065-90-9(3)) Star Bright Bks., Inc.

—Have You Fed the Cat? 2004. (ENG., Illus.). 32p. (J). pap. 5.95 (978-1-932065-91-6(1)) Star Bright Bks., Inc.

—Have You Fed the Cat? (Spanish/English) Coxon, Michele, illus. 2004. (SPA & ENG., Illus.). 32p. (J). 15.95 (978-1-59572-001-6(4)); pap. 5.95 (978-1-59572-002-3(2)) Star Bright Bks., Inc.

—Kitten's Adventure (Portuguese/English), 1 vol. 2006. (POR, ABK, ACE & ENG., Illus.). 12p. (J). (gr. -1-k). pap. 6.00 (978-1-59572-047-4(2)) Star Bright Bks., Inc.

—Kitten's Adventure (Spanish/English), 1 vol. Coxon, Michele, illus. 2006. (SPA., Illus.). 32p. (J). (gr. -1-k). pap. 5.95 (978-1-59572-048-1(0)) Star Bright Bks., Inc.

—Kitten's Adventure (Vietnamese/English), 1 vol. 2008. (ENG & VIE., Illus.). 32p. (J). (gr. -1-k). pap. 6.00 (978-1-59572-157-0(6)) Star Bright Bks., Inc.

—Where's My Kitten? (Illus.). 16p. (J). pap. 5.95 (978-1-903285-02-2(X)) Happy Cat Bks. GBR. Dist: Star Bright Bks., Inc.

Craig-Gaddis, Lora. Elsie & Pooka Stories of the Sabbats & Seasons. 2008. 126p. pap. 43.18 (978-0-557-01530-6(8)) Lulu Pr., Inc.

Crawford, Deborah & Crawford, Ryan. Pity's Porch. Ballard, Merry, illus. 2012. 24p. pap. 11.50 (978-1-60976-796-9(9), Strategic Bk. Publishing) Strategic Book Publishing & Rights Agency (SBPRA).

Crawford, Deborah Kay. Pity & the Princess. Turner, Aubrey, illus. 2013. 40p. pap. 24.95 (978-1-62709-695-9(7)) America Star Bks.

Cray, Ronda. What's the Matter Cat? 2008. 24p. pap. 24.95 (978-1-60672-674-7(9)) America Star Bks.

Crebbin, June. A Cat for Tom. 2005. (ENG.). 32p. pap. 9.50 (978-0-521-67471-3(9)) Cambridge Univ. Pr.

Creech, Sharon. Hate That Cat. (ENG.). (J). (gr. 3-7). 2010. 176p. pap. 6.99 (978-0-06-143094-7(3)) 2008. 160p. 16.99 (978-0-06-143092-3(7)) HarperCollins Pubs.

Crisp, Marty. Titanicat. Papp, Robert, illus. 2008. (ENG.). 40p. (J). (gr. k-6). 17.95 (978-1-58536-355-1(3)) Sleeping Bear Pr.

Crofoot, Nancy. Sandy & Mitzi: Their First Adventure, 1 vol. Rawat, Tania, illus. 2009. 31p. pap. 24.95 (978-1-60836-707-8(X)) America Star Bks.

Croteau, Marie-Danielle. Fred & the Mysterious Letter, 1 vol. Cummins, Sarah, tr. from FRE. St-Aubin, Bruno, illus. 2005. (Formac First Novels Ser.). (ENG.). 64p. (J). (gr. 2-5). 4.95 (978-0-88780-688-9(0), 9780887806889) Formac Publishing Co., Ltd. CAN. Dist: Casemate Pubs. & Bk. Distributors, LLC.

Crotty, Martha. Hong Kong Kitty. Thum, Gwen & Thum, David Ryan, illus. 2005. (J). per. 14.00 (978-0-9766017-0-8(2)) Ironcreek Pr.

Crow, Kristyn. Skeleton Cat. Krall, Dan, illus. 2012. (ENG.). 32p. (J). (gr. -1-3). pap. 6.99 (978-0-545-15385-0(9), Scholastic Pr.) Scholastic, Inc.

—Skeleton Cat. 2012. lib. bdg. 17.20 (978-0-606-26209-5(1), Turtleback) Turtleback Bks.

Crow, Marilee & Snider, K. C. Alleycat. 2008. 24p. pap. 10.95 (978-1-935137-65-8(4)) Guardian Angel Publishing, Inc.

Crow, Stanford. Lazy Hero Cat of Egypt. Hemmingson, Nancy S., illus. 2013. 24p. 24.00 (978-1-940021-01-0(4)) Bliss Group.

Crowell, Marcia. The Adventures of Little Blackie & Friends. 2009. 36p. pap. 15.99 (978-1-4389-0386-6(3)) AuthorHouse.

Curry, Peter. Millie at Home. 2004. (First Words with Millie Ser.). (Illus.). 12p. (J). bds. 3.99 (978-1-85854-508-0(0)) Brimax Books Ltd. GBR. Dist: Byeway Bks.

—Millie Goes Driving. 2004. (First Words with Millie Ser.). (Illus.). 12p. (J). bds. 3.99 (978-1-85854-506-6(4)) Brimax Books Ltd. GBR. Dist: Byeway Bks.

—Millie Goes Shopping. 2004. (First Words with Millie Ser.). (Illus.). 12p. (J). bds. 3.99 (978-1-85854-505-9(6)) Brimax Books Ltd. GBR. Dist: Byeway Bks.

—Millie in the Garden. 2004. (First Words with Millie Ser.). (Illus.). 12p. (J). bds. 3.99 (978-1-85854-507-3(2)) Brimax Books Ltd. GBR. Dist: Byeway Bks.

Curtiss, A. B. & Curtiss, A. B. Hanner & the Bullies. Brown, Jason, illus. 2012. 140p. pap. 9.99 (978-0-932529-63-3(1)) Oldcastle Publishing.

Cusack, Dale. Grace & the Drawl. 2008. (Illus.). 169p. pap. 11.95 (978-1-4357-0926-3(8)) Lulu Pr., Inc.

—Grace & the Revenge of the Drawl. 2009. (Illus.). 154p. pap. 10.95 (978-1-4357-1792-3(9)) Lulu Pr., Inc.

Cushman, Doug. Space Cat. Cushman, Doug, illus. 2006. (I Can Read Level 1 Ser.). (ENG., Illus.). 32p. (J). (gr. -1-3). pap. 3.99 (978-0-06-008967-2(9)) HarperCollins Pubs.

—Space Cat. Cushman, Doug, illus. 2006. (I Can Read Bks.). (Illus.). 32p. (gr. -1-3). 14.00 (978-0-7569-6977-6(8)) Perfection Learning Corp.

Cutchin, Marcia, illus. Feathers: A Jewish Tale from Eastern Europe. 2005. (ENG.). 32p. (J). (gr. k-3). 16.95 (978-0-87483-755-1(3), 1249133) August Hse. Pubs., Inc.

Czekaj, Jef. Cat Secrets. Czekaj, Jef, illus. 2011. (ENG., Illus.). 32p. (J). (gr. -1-3). 16.99 (978-0-06-192088-2(6)) HarperCollins Pubs.

D. The City Kittens & the Old House Cat. 2013. 34p. 29.99 (978-1-4575-1682-5(9)); pap. 19.99 (978-1-4575-1619-1(5)) Dog Ear Publishing, LLC.

D' Almfras, Pauline H. Pisi the Cat & His Adventures. 2009. 16p. pap. 12.95 (978-1-60860-111-0(0), Strategic Bk. Publishing) Strategic Book Publishing & Rights Agency (SBPRA).

Dahl, Michael. Me & My Cat. Persico, Zoe, illus. 2016. (Me & My Pet Ser.). (ENG.). 24p. (gr. 1-2). lib. bdg. 22.65 (978-1-5158-0239-6(6), Fiction Picture Bks.) Picture Window Bks.

—Me & My Cat. Persico, Zoe, illus. 2016. (Me & My Pet Ser.). (ENG.). 24p. (gr. 1-2). 6.95 (978-1-62370-794-1(3)) Capstone Young Readers of Coughlan Cos.

—Nap Time for Kitty, 1 vol. Vidal, Oriol, illus. 2011. (Hello Genius Ser.). (ENG.). 20p. (gr. 1-2). bds. 7.99 (978-1-4048-5216-7(6)) Picture Window Bks.

Dahlstrom, Halene. Raven Cove Mystery: A Rennie of Alaska Mystery. 2003. (YA). pap. 12.95 (978-1-59433-001-8(8)) Publication Consultants.

Daines, McKay. The Cats of Storm Mountain. Daines, Cameron, illus. 2003. 294p. (YA). 28.95 (978-0-9749467-1-9(0)); pap. 17.99 (978-0-9749467-0-2(2)) Shine Publishing Hse.

Dalmatian Press Staff. To the Rescue! 2008. (ENG.). 6p. bds. 4.95 (978-1-58117-724-4(0), Intervisual/Piggy Toes) Bendon, Inc.

Dalton, Kippy. Cat & Squirrel. 2016. (Spring Forward Ser.). (J). (gr. 1). (978-1-4900-3714-1(4)) Benchmark Education Co.

Dane Rehagen. How Katie Got Her Meow. 2010. 42p. pap. 15.00 (978-1-4251-8664-7(5)) Trafford Publishing.

Daniel, Beverly. The Adventures of Madilyn Millicent Middleton-Mew. Daniel, Cindy, ed. Daniel, Beverly, illus. 2013. (Illus.). 64p. pap. 8.95 (978-0-9789429-6-0(5)) Batelier Publishing.

Daniel, Liesle. Mittens: A Kitten in Search of Hope. 2011. 48p. pap. 9.95 (978-1-4497-1314-0(9), WestBow Pr.) Author Solutions, Inc.

DANOWSKI, Sonja. Night Cat. 2016. (ENG., Illus.). 48p. 19.95 (978-0-7358-4266-3(3)) North-South Bks., Inc.

Darby Hall. The Adventures of Tigeret S Meow. 2011. (Illus.). 24p. (gr. -1-3). pap. 15.99 (978-1-4568-9086-5(7)) Xlibris Corp.

D'Aulaire, Ingri & D'Aulaire, Edgar Parin. Too Big. 2008. (New York Review Children's Collection). (ENG., Illus.). 40p. (J). (gr. k-k). 14.95 (978-1-59017-291-9(4), NYR Children's Collection) New York Review of Bks., Inc., The.

Davey, Keith Peter. Squeaks Narrow Squeaks. Frost, Justine, illus. 2009. 32p. pap. 14.62 (978-1-4120-4402-8(2)) Trafford Publishing.

Davies, Becky. Three Little Pugs & the Big Bad Cat. Attia, Caron, illus. 2017. (ENG.). 32p. (J). (gr. -1-2). 16.99 **(978-1-68010-043-3(2))** Tiger Tales.

Davies, Katie. The Great Cat Conspiracy. Shaw, Hannah, illus. 2012. (Great Critter Capers Ser.). (ENG.). 224p. (J). (gr. 3-7). 12.99 (978-1-4424-4513-0(0), Beach Lane Bks.) Beach Lane Bks.

Davies, Peter. Molly's Magic Pencil: The Blue Genie. 2011. 28p. (gr. 1-2). 14.99 (978-1-4567-3018-5(5)) AuthorHouse.

Davis, Anne. Bud & Gabby. Davis, Anne, illus. 2006. (Illus.). 32p. (J). (gr. -1-2). lib. bdg. 16.89 (978-0-06-075351-1(X)) HarperCollins Pubs.

—No Dogs Allowed!, No. 1. Davis, Anne, illus. 2011. (ENG., Illus.). 32p. (J). (gr. -1-3). 16.99 (978-0-06-075353-5(6)) HarperCollins Pubs.

Davis, Bertha. Jay's Friend Kitty Brew Jumbo Coloring & Activity Book. Bowman, Todd A., illus. 2013. 26p. pap. 9.99 (978-0-9899472-1-3(1)) Kids At Heart Publishing, LLC.

Davis, Bertha M. Jay's Friend Kitty Brew. Bowman, Todd A., illus. 2013. 28p. pap. 14.99 (978-0-9886360-5-7(0)) Kids At Heart Publishing, LLC.

Davis, Jim. Fat Cat, No.1. 2003. (Garfield Ser.). (gr. 5-8). lib. bdg. 29.40 (978-0-613-68581-8(4), Turtleback) Turtleback Bks.

—Garfield: Sticht Zu. Goetting, Waltraud & Bartoszko, Alexandra, trs. from ENG. (Garfield Ser.: Vol. 10). (GER., Illus.). 128p. (J). pap. 10.95 (978-3-8105-0754-9(7)) Kruger, Wolfgang Verlag, GmbH DEU. Dist: Distribooks, Inc.

—Garfield & Co. Boxed Set Vol. #1-4. 2012. (Garfield Graphic Novels Ser.). (ENG., Illus.). 128p. (J). (gr. 1-6). 29.99 (978-1-59707-342-4(3), 9781597073424) Papercutz.

—Garfield Benimmt sich Daneben. Goetting, Waltraud & Bartoszko, Alexandra, trs. from ENG. (GER., Illus.). 128p. (J). pap. (978-3-8105-0890-4(X)) Kruger, Wolfgang Verlag, GmbH DEU. Dist: International Bk. Import Service, Inc.

—Garfield Blast sich Auf. Goetting, Waltraud & Bartoszko, Alexandra, trs. from ENG. (Garfield Ser.: Vol. 20). (GER., Illus.). 128p. (J). pap. (978-3-8105-0884-3(5)) Kruger, Wolfgang Verlag, GmbH DEU. Dist: International Bk. Import Service, Inc.

—Garfield Bleibt sich Treu. Goetting, Waltraud & Bartoszko, Alexandra, trs. from ENG. (Garfield Ser.: Vol.19). (GER., Illus.). 128p. (J). pap. (978-3-8105-0880-5(2)) Kruger, Wolfgang Verlag, GmbH DEU. Dist: International Bk. Import Service, Inc.

—Garfield Caution - Wide Load. 2013. (Garfield Ser.: 56). (ENG., Illus.). 96p. pap. 14.00 (978-0-345-52596-3(5), Ballantine Bks.) Random House Publishing Group.

—Garfield Dreht Durch. Goetting, Waltraud & Bartoszko, Alexandra, trs. from ENG. (Garfield Ser.: Vol. 22). (GER., Illus.). 128p. (J). pap. (978-3-8105-0886-7(1)) Kruger, Wolfgang Verlag, GmbH DEU. Dist: International Bk. Import Service, Inc.

—Garfield Fat Cat 3-Pack #9. 2015. (Garfield Ser.). lib. bdg. 29.40 (978-0-606-37256-5(3)) Turtleback Bks.

—Garfield Gets in a Pickle. 2012. (Garfield Ser.: 54). lib. bdg. 25.75 (978-0-606-26835-6(9), Turtleback) Turtleback Bks.

—Garfield Halt die Ohren Steif. Goetting, Waltraud & Bartoszko, Alexandra, trs. from ENG. (Garfield Ser.: Vol. 23). (GER., Illus.). 128p. (J). pap. (978-3-8105-0889-8(6)) Kruger, Wolfgang Verlag, GmbH DEU. Dist: International Bk. Import Service, Inc.

—Garfield Hangt Ab. Bartoszko, Alexandra, tr. from ENG. (Garfield Ser.: Vol. 32). (GER., Illus.). 128p. (J). pap. (978-3-8105-0918-5(3)) Kruger, Wolfgang Verlag, GmbH DEU. Dist: International Bk. Import Service, Inc.

—Garfield Hat Genug. Goetting, Waltraud & Bartoszko, Alexandra, trs. from ENG. (Garfield Ser.: Vol. 18). (GER., Illus.). 128p. (J). pap. (978-3-8105-0833-1(0)) Kruger, Wolfgang Verlag, GmbH DEU. Dist: International Bk. Import Service, Inc.

—Garfield Hat Schwein. Bartoszko, Alexandra, tr. from ENG. (Garfield Ser.: Vol. 31). (GER., Illus.). 128p. (J). pap. (978-3-8105-0897-3(7)) Kruger, Wolfgang Verlag, GmbH DEU. Dist: International Bk. Import Service, Inc.

—Garfield Hebt Ab. Goetting, Waltraud & Bartoszko, Alexandra, trs. from ENG. (Garfield Ser.: Vol. 16). (GER., Illus.). 128p. (J). pap. (978-3-8105-0776-1(8)) Kruger, Wolfgang Verlag, GmbH DEU. Dist: International Bk. Import Service, Inc.

—Garfield ist Spitze. Goetting, Waltraud & Bartoszko, Alexandra, trs. from ENG. (Garfield Ser.: Vol. 11). (GER., Illus.). 128p. (J). pap. (978-3-8105-0757-0(1)) Kruger, Wolfgang Verlag, GmbH DEU. Dist: International Bk. Import Service, Inc.

—Garfield Kratzt die Kurve. Goetting, Waltraud & Bartoszko, Alexandra, trs. from ENG. (Garfield Ser.: Vol. 28). (GER., Illus.). 128p. (J). pap. (978-3-8105-0894-2(2)) Kruger, Wolfgang Verlag, GmbH DEU. Dist: International Bk. Import Service, Inc.

—Garfield Lasst nicht Locker. Goetting, Waltraud & Bartoszko, Alexandra, trs. from ENG. (Garfield Ser.: Vol. 14). (GER., Illus.). 128p. (J). pap. (978-3-8105-0771-6(7)) Kruger, Wolfgang Verlag, GmbH DEU. Dist: International Bk. Import Service, Inc.

—Garfield Legts Drauf An. Goetting, Waltraud & Bartoszko, Alexandra, trs. from ENG. (Garfield Ser.: Vol. 25). (GER.). 128p. (J). pap. (978-3-8105-0891-1(8)) Kruger, Wolfgang Verlag, GmbH DEU. Dist: International Bk. Import Service, Inc.

—Garfield Nimmt den Mund Voll. Goetting, Waltraud & Bartoszko, Alexandra, trs. from ENG. (Garfield Ser.: Vol. 21). (GER., Illus.). 128p. (J). pap. (978-3-8105-0885-0(3)) Kruger, Wolfgang Verlag, GmbH DEU. Dist: International Bk. Import Service, Inc.

—Garfield Nimmt's Leicht. Bartoszko, Alexandra, tr. from ENG. (Garfield Ser.: Vol. 29). (GER., Illus.). 128p. (J). pap. (978-3-8105-0895-9(0)) Kruger, Wolfgang Verlag, GmbH DEU. Dist: International Bk. Import Service, Inc.

—Garfield Platzt aus allen Naehten. Bartoszko, Alexandra, tr. from ENG. (Garfield Ser.: Vol. 33). (GER., Illus.). 128p. (J). pap. (978-3-8105-0919-2(1)) Kruger, Wolfgang Verlag, GmbH DEU. Dist: International Bk. Import Service, Inc.

—Garfield Riecht den Braten. Bartoszko, Alexandra, tr. from ENG. (Garfield Ser.: Vol. 34). (GER., Illus.). 128p. (J). pap. (978-3-8105-0920-8(5)) Kruger, Wolfgang Verlag, GmbH DEU. Dist: International Bk. Import Service, Inc.

—Garfield Spielt auf Zeit. Goetting, Waltraud & Bartoszko, Alexandra, trs. from ENG. (Garfield Ser.: Vol. 13). (GER., Illus.). 128p. (J). pap. (978-3-8105-0759-4(8)) Kruger, Wolfgang Verlag, GmbH DEU. Dist: International Bk. Import Service, Inc.

—Garfield Streicht Ein. Goetting, Waltraud & Bartoszko, Alexandra, trs. from ENG. (Garfield Ser.: Vol. 12). (GER., Illus.). 128p. (J). pap. (978-3-8105-0758-7(X)) Kruger, Wolfgang Verlag, GmbH DEU. Dist: International Bk. Import Service, Inc.

—Garfield Waechst & Gegeiht. Bartoszko, Alexandra, tr. from ENG. (Garfield Ser.: Vol. 30). (GER., Illus.). 128p. (J). pap. (978-3-8105-0896-6(9)) Kruger, Wolfgang Verlag, GmbH DEU. Dist: International Bk. Import Service, Inc.

—Garfield Will es Wissen. Goetting, Waltraud & Bartoszko, Alexandra, trs. from ENG. (Garfield Ser.: Vol. 26). (GER., Illus.). 128p. (J). pap. (978-3-8105-0892-8(6)) Kruger, Wolfgang Verlag, GmbH DEU. Dist: International Bk. Import Service, Inc.

—Garfield Zeigt die Krallen. Goetting, Waltraud & Bartoszko, Alexandra, trs. from ENG. (Garfield Ser.: Vol. 27). (GER., Illus.). 128p. (J). pap. (978-3-8105-0893-5(4)) Kruger, Wolfgang Verlag, GmbH DEU. Dist: International Bk. Import Service, Inc.

Davis, Jim & Evanier, Mark. Catzilla. Ellipsanime Staff & Dargaud Media, illus. 2011. (Garfield Graphic Novels Ser.). (ENG.). 32p. (J). (gr. 1-6). 7.99 (978-1-59707-278-6(8), 9781597072786) Papercutz.

—Garfield & Co. #7: Home for the Holidays. Ellipsanime Staff & Dargaud Media, illus. 2012. (Garfield Graphic Novels Ser.). (ENG.). 32p. (J). (gr. 1-6). 7.99 (978-1-59707-370-7(9), 9781597073707) Papercutz.

Davis, Jim & Michiels, Cedric. Unfair Weather. Dargaud Media Staff & Ellipsanime Staff, illus. 2013. (Garfield Show Ser.). (ENG.). 64p. (J). (gr. 1-5). 11.99 (978-1-59707-433-9(0), 9781597074339) Papercutz.

Davis, Jim, et al. A Game of Cat & Mouse. Dargaud Media Staff & Ellipsanime Staff, illus. 2012. (Garfield Graphic Novels Ser.). (ENG.). 32p. (J). (gr. 1-6). 7.99 (978-1-59707-300-4(8), 9781597073004) Papercutz.

—Garfield & Co. #6: Mother Garfield. Ellipsanime Staff, illus. 2012. (Garfield Graphic Novels Ser.). (ENG.). 32p. (J). (gr. 1-6). 7.99 (978-1-59707-318-9(0), 9781597073189) Papercutz.

Day, Alexandra. Carl & the Kitten. 2011. (My Readers Ser.). (ENG., Illus.). 32p. (J). (gr. -1-1). pap. 4.99 (978-0-312-68197-5(6), 9780312681975) Square Fish.

de Lint, Charles. The Cats of Tanglewood Forest. Vess, Charles, illus. 2014. (ENG.). 320p. (J). (gr. 3-7). pap. 11.99 (978-0-316-05359-4(7)) Little, Brown Bks. for Young Readers.

—The Cats of Tanglewood Forest. 2014. (J). lib. bdg. 22.10 (978-0-606-36532-1(X)) Turtleback Bks.

Dean, James. Cavecat Pete. Dean, James, illus. 2015. (Pete the Cat Ser.). (ENG., Illus.). 24p. (J). (gr. -1-3). pap. 4.99 (978-0-06-219863-1(7), HarperFestival) HarperCollins Pubs.

—Cavecat Pete. 2015. (Pete the Cat (HarperCollins) Ser.). (J). lib. bdg. 14.75 (978-0-606-36465-2(X)) Turtleback Bks.

—Construction Destruction. Dean, James, illus. 2015. (Pete the Cat Ser.). (ENG., Illus.). 24p. (J). (gr. -1-3). pap. 4.99 (978-0-06-219861-7(0), HarperFestival) HarperCollins Pubs.

—Construction Destruction. 2015. (Pete the Cat (HarperCollins) Ser.). (J). lib. bdg. 14.75 (978-0-606-36489-8(7)) Turtleback Bks.

—Five Little Pumpkins. Dean, James, illus. 2015. (Pete the Cat Ser.). (ENG., Illus.). 32p. (J). (gr. -1-3). 9.99 (978-0-06-230418-6(6)) HarperCollins Pubs.

—Go, Pete, Go! Dean, James, illus. 2016. (Pete the Cat Ser.). (Illus.). 24p. (J). (gr. -1-3). pap. 4.99 (978-0-06-240439-8(3), HarperFestival) HarperCollins Pubs.

—Go, Pete, Go. 2016. (Pete the Cat (HarperCollins) Ser.). (J). lib. bdg. 14.75 (978-0-606-38759-0(5)) Turtleback Bks.

—Old MacDonald Had a Farm. Dean, James, illus. 2014. (Pete the Cat Ser.). (ENG., Illus.). 32p. (J). (gr. -1-3). 9.99 (978-0-06-219873-0(4)) HarperCollins Pubs.

—Out of This World. 2017. (Pete the Cat (HarperCollins) Ser.). lib. bdg. 14.75 **(978-0-606-40077-0(X))** Turtleback Bks.

—Pete at the Beach. Dean, James, illus. 2013. (My First I Can Read Ser.). (ENG., Illus.). 32p. (J). (gr. -1-3). 16.99 (978-0-06-211073-2(X)) HarperCollins Pubs.

—Pete at the Beach. 2013. (Pete the Cat I Can Read Ser.). (J). lib. bdg. 13.55 (978-0-606-31810-5(0), Turtleback) Turtleback Bks.

—Pete the Cat - Robo-Pete. Dean, James, illus. 2015. (Pete the Cat Ser.). (ENG., Illus.). 24p. (J). (gr. -1-3). pap. 4.99 (978-0-06-230427-8(5), HarperFestival) HarperCollins Pubs.

—Pete the Cat: 5-Minute Pete the Cat Stories. Dean, James, illus. 2017. (Pete the Cat Ser.). (Illus.). 192p. (J). (gr. -1-3). 12.99 (978-0-06-247019-5(1), HarperFestival) HarperCollins Pubs.

—Pete the Cat & the Bad Banana. Dean, James, illus. 2014. (My First I Can Read Ser.). (ENG., Illus.). 32p. (J). (gr. -1-3). pap. 3.99 (978-0-06-230382-0(1)) HarperCollins Pubs.

—Pete the Cat & the Lost Tooth. Dean, James, illus. 2017. (My First I Can Read Ser.). (Illus.). 32p. (J). (gr. -1-3). pap. 3.99 **(978-0-06-267518-7(4))** HarperCollins Pubs.

—Pete the Cat & the Surprise Teacher. Dean, James, illus. 2017. (My First I Can Read Ser.). (Illus.). 32p. (J). (gr. -1-3). 3.99 (978-0-06-240428-2(8)) HarperCollins Pubs.

—Pete the Cat & the Surprise Teacher. 2017. (Pete the Cat I Can Read Ser.). (J). lib. bdg. 13.55 **(978-0-606-39628-8(4))** Turtleback Bks.

—Pete the Cat & the Tip-Top Tree House (backpack Special Edition) Dean, James, illus. 2017. (My First I Can Read Ser.). (Illus.). 32p. (J). (gr. -1-3). 4.50 **(978-0-06-274847-8(5))** HarperCollins Pubs.

—Pete the Cat & the Treasure Map. Dean, James, illus. 2017. (Pete the Cat Ser.). (Illus.). 24p. (J). (gr. -1-3). pap. 4.99 (978-0-06-240441-1(5), HarperFestival) HarperCollins Pubs.

—Pete the Cat: Five Little Ducks. Dean, James, illus. 2017. (Pete the Cat Ser.). (Illus.). 32p. (J). (gr. -1-3). 9.99 (978-0-06-240448-0(2)) HarperCollins Pubs.

—Pete the Cat Giant Sticker Book. Dean, James, illus. 2016. (Pete the Cat Ser.). (Illus.). 100p. (J). (gr. -1-3). pap. 12.99 (978-0-06-230423-0(2), HarperFestival) HarperCollins Pubs.

—Pete the Cat: Meet Pete. Dean, James, illus. 2017. (Pete the Cat Ser.). (Illus.). 18p. (J). (gr. -1 — 1). bds. 8.99 **(978-0-06-267517-0(6)**, HarperFestival) HarperCollins Pubs.

—Pete the Cat: Old MacDonald Had a Farm Board Book. Dean, James, illus. 2016. (Pete the Cat Ser.). (Illus.). 32p. (J). (gr. -1 — 1). bds. 7.99 (978-0-06-238160-6(1), HarperFestival) HarperCollins Pubs.

—Pete the Cat: Out of This World. Dean, James, illus. 2017. (Pete the Cat Ser.). (Illus.). 24p. (J). (gr. -1-3). pap. 4.99 (978-0-06-240443-5(1), HarperFestival) HarperCollins Pubs.

—Pete the Cat Phonics Box. Dean, James & Dean, Josh, illus. 2017. (My First I Can Read Ser.). 144p. (J). (gr. -1-3). pap. 12.99 (978-0-06-240452-7(0)) HarperCollins Pubs.

—Pete the Cat: Scuba-Cat. Dean, James, illus. 2016. (My First I Can Read Ser.). (Illus.). 32p. (J). (gr. -1-3). pap. 3.99 (978-0-06-230388-2(0)) HarperCollins Pubs.

—Pete the Cat: Sir Pete the Brave. Dean, James, illus. 2016. (My First I Can Read Ser.). (Illus.). 32p. (J). (gr. -1-3). pap. 3.99 (978-0-06-240421-3(0)) HarperCollins Pubs.

—Pete the Cat: Snow Daze. Dean, James, illus. 2016. (My First I Can Read Ser.). (Illus.). 32p. (J). (gr. -1-3). 16.99 (978-0-06-240425-1(3)) HarperCollins Pubs.

—Pete the Cat Storybook Collection. Dean, James, illus. 2016. (Pete the Cat Ser.). (Illus.). 192p. (J). (gr. -1-3). 11.99 (978-0-06-230425-4(9)) HarperCollins Pubs.

—Pete the Cat Take-Along Storybook Set: 5-Book 8x8 Set. Dean, James, illus. 2017. (Pete the Cat Ser.). (Illus.). 120p. (J). (gr. -1-3). pap. 11.99 **(978-0-06-240447-3(4)**, HarperFestival) HarperCollins Pubs.

—Pete the Cat: Trick or Pete. Dean, James, illus. 2017. (Pete the Cat Ser.). (ENG., Illus.). 16p. (J). (gr. -1-3). pap. 6.99 **(978-0-06-219870-9(X)**, HarperFestival) HarperCollins Pubs.

—Pete the Cat: Twinkle, Twinkle, Little Star Board Book. Dean, James, illus. 2016. (Pete the Cat Ser.). (Illus.). 32p. (J). (gr. -1 — 1). bds. 7.99 (978-0-06-238161-3(X), HarperFestival) HarperCollins Pubs.

—Pete the Cat's Got Class. Dean, James, illus. 2016. (Pete the Cat Ser.). (Illus.). 24p. (J). (gr. -1-3). 9.99 (978-0-06-230410-0(0)) HarperCollins Pubs.

—Pete the Cat's Super Cool Reading Collection. Dean, James, illus. 2014. (My First I Can Read Ser.). (ENG., Illus.). 32p. (J). (gr. -1-3). pap. 16.99 (978-0-06-230424-7(0)) HarperCollins Pubs.

—Pete the Cat's Train Trip. Dean, James, illus. 2015. (My First I Can Read Ser.). (ENG., Illus.). 32p. (J). (gr. -1-3). pap. 3.99 (978-0-06-230385-1(6)) HarperCollins Pubs.

—Pete's Big Lunch. Dean, James, illus. 2013. (My First I Can Read Ser.). (ENG., Illus.). 32p. (J). (gr. -1-3). 16.99 (978-0-06-211070-1(5)) HarperCollins Pubs.

—Pete's Big Lunch. 2013. (Pete the Cat I Can Read Ser.). (J). lib. bdg. 13.55 (978-0-606-27146-2(5), Turtleback) Turtleback Bks.

—Play Ball! Dean, James, illus. 2013. (My First I Can Read Ser.). (ENG., Illus.). 32p. (J). (gr. -1-3). 16.99 (978-0-06-211067-1(5)) HarperCollins Pubs.

—Play Ball! 2013. (Pete the Cat I Can Read Ser.). (J). lib. bdg. 13.55 (978-0-606-27145-5(7), Turtleback) Turtleback Bks.

—Rock On, Mom & Dad! Dean, James, illus. 2015. (Pete the Cat Ser.). (ENG., Illus.). 24p. (J). (gr. -1-3). pap. 6.99 (978-0-06-230408-7(9), HarperFestival) HarperCollins Pubs.

—Rock on, Mom & Dad! Dean, James, illus. 2015. (Pete the Cat (HarperCollins) Ser.). (Illus.). (J). lib. bdg. 17.20 (978-0-606-36490-4(0)) Turtleback Bks.

—Scuba-Cat. 2016. (Pete the Cat I Can Read Ser.). (J). lib. bdg. 13.55 (978-0-606-38156-7(2)) Turtleback Bks.

—Sing-Along Story Collection. Dean, James, illus. 2014. (Pete the Cat Ser.). (ENG., Illus.). 96p. (J). (gr. -1-3). 19.99 (978-0-06-230420-9(8)) HarperCollins Pubs.

—Too Cool for School. 2014. (Pete the Cat I Can Read Ser.). (J). lib. bdg. 13.55 (978-0-606-35062-4(4), Turtleback) Turtleback Bks.

—Twinkle, Twinkle, Little Star. Dean, James, illus. 2014. (Pete the Cat Ser.). (ENG., Illus.). 32p. (J). (gr. -1-3). 9.99 (978-0-06-230416-2(X)) HarperCollins Pubs.

Dean, James, illus. I Love My White Shoes. 2010. (Pete the Cat Ser.). (J). lib. bdg. (978-0-06-107623-7(6)) HarperCollins Pubs.

—Pete the Cat: Scuba-Cat. 2016. 31p. (J). (978-1-4844-7052-7(4)) Harper & Row Ltd.

—Sir Pete the Brave. 2016. 32p. (J). **(978-1-5182-0881-2(9))** Harper & Row Ltd.

Dean, James, illus. Valentine's Day Is Cool. 2013. (Pete the Cat Ser.). (ENG.). 24p. (J). (gr. -1-3). 9.99 (978-0-06-219865-5(3), HarperFestival) HarperCollins Pubs.

Dean, James & Dean, Kimberly. Big Easter Adventure. Dean, James & Dean, Kimberly, illus. 2014. (Pete the Cat Ser.). (ENG., Illus.). 24p. (J). (gr. -1-3). 9.99 (978-0-06-219867-9(X)) HarperCollins Pubs.

—The First Thanksgiving. Dean, James, illus. 2013. (Pete the Cat Ser.). (ENG., Illus.). 16p. (J). (gr. -1-3). 6.99 (978-0-06-219869-3(6), HarperFestival) HarperCollins Pubs.

—A Pet for Pete. Dean, James, illus. 2014. (My First I Can Read Ser.). (ENG., Illus.). 32p. (J). (gr. -1-3). pap. 3.99 (978-0-06-230379-0(1)) HarperCollins Pubs.

—Pete the Cat & His Magic Sunglasses. Dean, James, illus. 2013. (Pete the Cat Ser.). (Illus.). 40p. (J). (gr. -1-3). (ENG.). 17.99 (978-0-06-227556-1(9)); lib. bdg. 18.89 (978-0-06-227557-8(7)) HarperCollins Pubs.

—Pete the Cat & the Bedtime Blues. Dean, James, illus. 2015. (Pete the Cat Ser.). (Illus.). 40p. (J). (gr. -1-3). (ENG.). 17.99 (978-0-06-230430-8(5)); lib. bdg. 18.89 (978-0-06-230431-5(3)) HarperCollins Pubs.

—Pete the Cat & the Cool Cat Boogie. Dean, James, illus. 2017. (Pete the Cat Ser.). (Illus.). 40p. (J). (gr. -1-3). (ENG.). 17.99 (978-0-06-240434-3(2)); lib. bdg. 18.89 (978-0-06-240909-6(3)) HarperCollins Pubs.

—Pete the Cat & the Missing Cupcakes. Dean, James, illus. 2016. (Pete the Cat Ser.). (Illus.). 40p. (J). (gr. -1-3). 17.99 (978-0-06-230434-6(8)); lib. bdg. 18.89 (978-0-06-230435-3(6)) HarperCollins Pubs.

—Pete the Cat & the New Guy. Dean, James, illus. 2014. (Pete the Cat Ser.). (ENG., Illus.). 40p. (J). (gr. -1-3). 17.99 (978-0-06-227560-8(7)); lib. bdg. 18.89 (978-0-06-227561-5(5)) HarperCollins Pubs.

—Too Cool for School. Dean, James & Dean, Kimberly, illus. 2014. (My First I Can Read Ser.). (ENG., Illus.). 32p. (J). (gr. -1-3). 16.99 (978-0-06-211076-3(4)); pap. 3.99 (978-0-06-211075-6(6)) HarperCollins Pubs.

Dean, Kim & Dean, James. Big Easter Adventure. 2014. (Pete the Cat Ser.). (Illus.). (J). (978-1-4844-1829-1(8)) HarperCollins Pubs.

Deane, Nancy Lou. Meg's Secret. 2011. 148p. (gr. 4-6). pap. 14.69 (978-1-4567-8884-1(1)) AuthorHouse.

Deedy, Carmen Agra & Wright, Randall. The Cheshire Cheese Cat: A Dickens of a Tale, 1 vol. Moser, Barry, illus. 2011. (ENG.). 256p. (J). 16.95 (978-1-56145-595-9(4)) Peachtree Pubs.

Deeley, Patrick. Snobby Cat. Feeney, Tatyana, illus. 2005. (Pandas Ser.: 32). (ENG.). 64p. (J). pap. 9.95 (978-0-86278-946-6(X)) O'Brien Pr., Ltd., The IRL. Dist: Dufour Editions, Inc.

Del Toro, Gladys. The Mutation of Black Cat, 1 vol. 2009. 76p. pap. 16.95 (978-1-61546-487-6(5)) PublishAmerica, Inc.

Delmain, Judy. Andy Beane & the Catkins' Tale. 2012. 192p. pap. 12.99 (978-0-9857420-0-3(3)) Shadow Canyon Graphics.

DeMaio, Alison. Tyler, the tiniest Tiger. 2010. 21p. 12.21 (978-0-557-19780-4(5)) Lulu Pr., Inc.

Demas, Corinne. Here Comes Trouble! Jones, Noah, illus. 2013. (J). (978-0-545-55449-7(7), Scholastic Pr.) Scholastic, Inc.

Demers, Karen. The Adventuresome Antics of Taf, Tif, Tobe, Tiggy, Princess & Toby. 2012. 24p. pap. 15.99 (978-1-4797-0699-0(X)) Xlibris Corp.

Denton, P. J. Girls Against Boys. Denos, Julia, illus. 2013. (Sleepover Squad Ser.: 7). (ENG.). 96p. (J). (gr. 1-4). pap. 4.99 (978-1-4169-5933-5(5), Simon & Schuster/Paula Wiseman Bks.) Simon & Schuster/Paula Wiseman Bks.

Depken, Kristen L. & Schurr, Cathleen. The Shy Little Kitten. DiCicco, Sue, illus. 2015. (Step into Reading Ser.). (ENG.). 32p. (J). (gr. -1-1). 12.99 (978-0-375-97377-2(X), Random Hse. Bks. for Young Readers) Random Hse. Children's Bks.

DePrisco, Dorothea. Willie & Buster Take the Train. Ansley, Frank, illus. 2003. (Stories to Share Ser.). 10p. (J). 10.95 (978-1-58117-183-9(8), Intervisual/Piggy Toes) Bendon, Inc.

DeRosier, Cher. The Plight of the Jelly Bean. Contreras, Gilbert, illus. 2005. (J). (978-1-891685-50-7(3)) Dearborn Publishing.

Des Fosses, John. The Cat Lottery. 2013. 148p. pap. (978-1-61950-071-6(X)) Roxby Media Ltd.

Desch, Sandra Lee. Erika Flowers. Seeds of Grace. Phipps, Catherine Wood, illus. 2013. 80p. pap. 10.00 (978-1-61170-144-9(9)) Robertson Publishing.

DeSpain, Pleasant. Tales of Cats. 2016. (ENG., Illus.). 80p. (J). (gr. 3-4). pap. 9.95 (978-1-941460-36-8(4)) August Hse. Pubs., Inc.

Devine, Robert. Barney of the Serengeti. 2006. 22p. 9.99 (978-1-4116-7294-9(1)) Lulu Pr., Inc.

Dexter & Missy the Kitten. 2004. (J). per. 15.99 (978-0-9753533-1-8(4)) Golden Eagle Publishing Hse., Inc.

Diagana, Susan. Princess Aminata & the Apple Tree. 2013. 40p. pap. 20.99 (978-1-4772-7910-6(5)) AuthorHouse.

Diamand, Emily. Raiders' Ransom. 2009. (Raiders' Ransom Ser.: 1). (ENG.). 368p. (J). (gr. 3-7). 17.99 (978-0-545-14297-7(0)) Scholastic, Inc.

Diederich, Ellen Jean. Where's Petunia? 2003. (Illus.). 32p. (J). per. 18.99 (978-0-9728654-0-1(3)) Givinity Pr.

Disney Book Group. Doc Mcstuffins Smitten with a Kitten. Disney Storybook Art Team, illus. 2016. (ENG.). 24p. (J). (gr. -1-k). pap. 4.99 (978-1-4847-6203-5(7)) Disney Pr.

—Sheriff Callie's Wild West Sparky's Lucky Day. Disney Storybook Art Team, illus. 2016. (ENG.). 24p. (J). (gr. -1-k). pap. 4.99 (978-1-4847-1927-5(1)) Disney Pr.

—World of Reading: Sheriff Callie's Wild West Callie Asks for Help: Level Pre-1. Disney Storybook Art Team, illus. 2015. (World of Reading Ser.). (ENG.). 32p. (J). (gr. -1-k). pap. 3.99 (978-1-4847-1631-1(0)) Disney Pr.

Disney Book Group Staff. Royal Kittens: A Palace Pets Book & Magnetic Play Set. 2015. (ENG.). 32p. (J). (gr. -1-k). 14.99 (978-1-4847-0512-4(2)) Disney Pr.

—Sheriff Callie's Wild West - The Cat Who Tamed the West. Disney Storybook Art Team, illus. 2015. (ENG.). 40p. (J). (gr. -1-k). 8.99 (978-1-4847-1495-9(4)) Disney Pr.

—Sheriff Callie's Wild West Toby Braves the Bully. Disney Storybook Art Team, illus. 2015. (ENG.). 16p. (J). (gr. -1-k). pap. 6.99 (978-1-4847-1562-8(4)) Disney Pr.

Distler, Christine A. Pegasus: The Introduction. 2005. 84p. pap. 11.95 (978-1-59113-763-4(2)) Booklocker.com, Inc.

Dixon, Joyce Ann. The Witches' Cat, 1 vol. 2010. 48p. pap. 16.95 (978-1-4489-7030-8(X)) America Star Bks.

Dodd, Lynley. Hairy Maclary's Caterwaul Caper. Dodd, Lynley, illus. 2009. (Hairy Maclary & Friends Ser.). (ENG., Illus.). 32p. (J). (gr. -1-2). pap. 6.99 (978-1-58246-307-0(7), Tricycle Pr.) Random Hse. Children's Bks.

Dodd, Susan. Dreaming the Dreams That Only Cats Can Dream. 2013. 150p. pap. (978-1-78148-654-2(9)) Grosvenor Hse. Publishing Ltd.

Dodson, Emma. The Very Important Idea. Dodson, Emma, illus. 2006. (ENG., Illus.). 32p. (J). (gr. -1-k). 19.99 (978-0-340-87808-8(8)) Hachette Children's Group GBR. Dist: Hachette Bk. Group.

Doe, Cheyenne. Kitty Kats. 2012. 264p. 27.95 (978-1-4626-7201-1(9)) America Star Bks.

Dolan, Penny. The Egyptian Cat Mystery. 2015. (Race Further with Reading Ser.). (ENG., Illus.). 48p. (J). (978-0-7787-2060-7(8)) Crabtree Publishing Co.

Dolheguy, Heather. Meg & Mr Biggs - the Magic Cat. 2008. 64p. 32.78 (978-1-4092-2382-5(5)) Lulu Pr., Inc.

Doll, Nancy L. Buddee the Bugger & Me: Told by Mac, 1 vol. 2009. 48p. pap. 24.95 (978-1-60749-979-4(7)) America Star Bks.

Donaldson, Julia. The Further Adventures of the Owl & the Pussy-Cat. Voake, Charlotte, illus. 2017. (ENG.). 32p. (J). (gr. -1-2). 16.99 (978-0-7636-9081-6(3)) Candlewick Pr.

—Tabby McTat: The Musical Cat. Scheffler, Axel, illus. 2012. (ENG.). 32p. (J). (gr. -1-3). 17.99 (978-0-545-45168-0(X), Levine, Arthur A. Bks.) Scholastic, Inc.

Donlon, Diane Youngblood. Like a Cat: Creep, Sleep, Pounce, & Peek. . . Suhr, James W., illus. 2003. 32p. (J). 16.95 (978-0-9720427-2-7(5)) OLLY Publishing Co.

Dormer, Frank W. Click! Dormer, Frank W., illus. 2016. (ENG., Illus.). 38p. (J). (-k). 17.99 (978-0-451-47644-9(1), Viking Books for Young Readers) Penguin Young Readers Group.

Domer, Nancy L. Crackerjack the Christmas Cat. Alphenaar, Pamela L., illus. 2008. 40p. pap. 16.95 (978-0-9818488-0-8(X)) Ajoyin Publishing, Inc.

Dorsey, Angela. The Time Thief. 2011. (ENG.). 144p. (YA). (gr. 6). pap. 9.99 (978-1-926607-27-6(9), Napoleon & Co.) Dundum CAN. Dist: Ingram Publisher Services.

Dow, Carrie. Morning, Miss Moo: (story of an omery Cat) 2009. 16p. pap. 14.99 (978-1-4269-1879-7(8)) Trafford Publishing.

Downey, Glen. Ice Journey. Brucker, Glenn, illus. 2007. 48p. (J). lib. bdg. 23.08 (978-1-4242-1618-5(4)) Fitzgerald Bks.

Dreher, Gidge. Gus, Scruffy, Clara & Friends. 2007. 80p. per. 9.95 (978-1-933912-24-0(3)) Westview Publishing Co., Inc.

Drinnon, Sheila. Cuddles. 2008. 24p. pap. 24.95 (978-1-60474-857-4(5)) America Star Bks.

Drogo, Susette. Five Blessings. Lukas, Mary, illus. 2008. 24p. (J). pap. 15.00 (978-0-9800611-8-5(0)) Orr Bks.

Drummond, Ree. Charlie & the Christmas Kitty. deGroat, Diane, illus. 2012. (Charlie the Ranch Dog Ser.). (ENG.). 40p. (J). (gr. -1-3). 17.99 (978-0-06-199657-3(2)) HarperCollins Pubs.

Dubuc, Marianne. The Sea. 2012. (ENG., Illus.). 92p. 19.95 (978-88-89854-85-3(5)) Officina Libraria srl ITA. Dist: National Bk. Network.

Duckers, John. The Amazing Adventures of the Silly Six. 2013. (Illus.). 188p. pap. (978-1-78148-626-9(3)) Grosvenor Hse. Publishing Ltd.

Duff, Ms. Michelle Ann. Five Cats, One Dog, a Motorcycle & a Lady in a Hot Pink Jacket. 2012. 146p. pap. (978-0-9685706-7-8(4)) Mad8 Publishing.

Duggan, Olive. Spy Kitties Create a Better World. 2013. 158p. pap. 7.95 (978-1-62137-257-8(X)) Virtualbookworm.com Publishing, Inc.

Dultz, Dorothy. Stories for Dreamers. Margolis, Al, illus. 2013. 68p. (J). pap. 9.95 (978-1-61863-425-2(9)) Bookstand Publishing.

Dupree, J. And S. Cat Tales: The Travel Adventures of Blue Boo & Sambootoo. 2008. 164p. pap. 10.95 (978-1-4327-3243-1(9)) Outskirts Pr., Inc.

Duthie, Marion. The Adventures of Pussy Whoosie. 2013. 72p. pap. 21.50 (978-1-62212-614-9(9), Strategic Bk. Publishing) Strategic Book Publishing & Rights Agency (SBPRA).

Duvall, Deborah L. Rabbit Goes to Kansas. Jacob, Murv, illus. 2007. (ENG.). 32p. (J). (gr. 1-18). 16.95 (978-0-8263-4181-5(0)) Univ. of New Mexico Pr.

Dyan, Penelope. Blake the Cat & His Very Loose Tooth! Dyan, Penelope, illus. 2011. (Illus.). 34p. pap. 10.95 (978-1-935630-77-7(6)) Bellissima Publishing, LLC.

—The Cat Named Blake. Weigand, John D., photos by. 2013. (Illus.). 76p. pap. 8.95 (978-1-61477-110-4(3)) Bellissima Publishing, LLC.

—Vita Mccafee Mckay, Cat Rescuer. Dyan, Penelope, illus. 2009. (Illus.). 44p. pap. 11.95 (978-1-935118-53-4(6)) Bellissima Publishing, LLC.

—Where Is Lucy? Dyan, Penelope, illus. 2013. (Illus.). 34p. pap. 11.95 (978-1-61477-120-3(0)) Bellissima Publishing, LLC.

Dyas, Amy. The Robins of St Lawrence Church. 2009. 128p. pap. 29.96 (978-0-9786567-8-2(4)) Parson Place Pr., LLC.

Dybacz, Carol. Tanner, 1 vol. 2009. 20p. pap. 24.95 (978-1-61546-588-0(X)) America Star Bks.

Dynamo. Googly Eyes: Fluffy Kitten Goes Exploring! 2014. (ENG., Illus.). 12p. (J). (gr. 3-2). bds. 6.99 (978-1-84322-880-6(7), Armadillo) Anness Publishing GBR. Dist: National Bk. Network.

Eagle, Rita. Farina & the Baby. 2011. 44p. pap. 17.99 (978-1-4568-5917-6(X)) Xlibris Corp.

East, Bob. Tommy Cat & the Giant Chickens. East, Matt, illus. 2008. 24p. per. 24.95 (978-1-4241-9242-7(0)) America Star Bks.

—Tommy Cat & the Haunted Well, 1 vol. 2009. 42p. pap. 24.95 (978-1-60703-754-5(8)) America Star Bks.

Eaton, Jason Carter. The Catawampus Cat. Gordon, Gus, illus. 2017. (ENG.). 32p. (J). (gr. -1-3). 16.99 (978-0-553-50971-7(3), Crown Books For Young Readers) Random Hse. Children's Bks.

Eaton, Kelly Toole. Kitten Trouble. 2011. 36p. pap. 21.99 (978-1-4568-8937-1(0)) Xlibris Corp.

Ebl, Donna. The Adventures of Salamander Sam. 2004. (J). pap. 9.00 (978-0-8059-6165-2(8)) Dorrance Publishing Co., Inc.

Eddy, Claudia. Boone: The Cat Who Could Stand on His Head. 2013. 20p. pap. 24.95 (978-1-63000-663-1(7)) America Star Bks.

Edgar, Amy. Here, Kitty, Kitty. Tejido, Jomike, illus. 2017. (Scholastic Reader, Level 2 Ser.). (ENG.). 32p. (J). (gr. k-2). pap. 5.99 **(978-1-338-04591-8(1))** Scholastic, Inc.

Edmonds, Wayne. Mi Gato. 2010. 40p. 16.99 (978-1-4520-7253-1(1)) AuthorHouse.

Edwards, Jamee-Marie. But I Am a Cat! 2013. 44p. pap. 20.00 (978-1-4772-8231-1(9)) AuthorHouse.

Edwards, Julie Andrews. Little Bo in London, No. 2. Cole, Henry, illus. 2012. (ENG.). 112p. (J). (gr. 1-4). 19.99 *(978-0-06-008911-5(3))* HarperCollins Pubs.

Edwards, Leo. Jerry Todd & the Rose-Colored Cat. 2007. 264p. 29.95 *(978-1-4344-9192-3(7))*; per. 19.95 *(978-1-4344-9098-8(X))* Wildside Pr., LLC.

Edwards, Linda M. Emma & Topsy's Story: The Art of Loving & Letting Go. Maher, Bob, illus. 2010. 20p. pap. 10.95 *(978-1-60911-808-2(1),* Eloquent Bks.) Strategic Book Publishing & Rights Agency (SBPRA).

Edwards, Marnie. Pets & Parties. Hodgkinson, Leigh, illus. 2013. (Magical Mix-Ups Ser.). (ENG.). 96p. (J). (gr. 2-5). pap. 6.99 *(978-0-7636-6371-1(9),* Nosy Crow) Candlewick Pr.

Edwards, Wayne. Ali & the Magic Ball. Golden, Rayna, illus. 2009. 24p. pap. 12.50 *(978-1-60860-367-1(9),* Eloquent Bks.) Strategic Book Publishing & Rights Agency (SBPRA).

Egea, Marcelo. Sobe, the Cat That Thinks He's a Dog. 2012. 24p. pap. 15.99 *(978-1-4691-5925-6(2))* Xlibris Corp.

Eggleton, Jill. Crumpet, the Cat: 3-in-1 Package. Hawley, Kelvin, illus. (Sails Literacy Ser.). 24p. (gr. 1-18). 57.00 *(978-0-7578-8619-5(1))* Rigby Education.

—Crumpet, the Cat: Big Book Only. Hawley, Kelvin, illus. (Sails Literacy Ser.). 24p. (gr. 1-18). 27.00 *(978-0-7578-6203-8(9))* Rigby Education.

Egielski, Richard. Slim & Jim. Egielski, Richard, illus. 2005. (Illus.). 37p. (J). (gr. k-4). reprint ed. 16.00 *(978-0-7567-8936-7(2))* DIANE Publishing Co.

Ehlert, Lois. Boo to You! Ehlert, Lois, illus. 2009. (ENG., Illus.). 42p. (J). (gr. -1-2). 17.99 *(978-1-4169-8625-6(1),* Beach Lane Bks.) Beach Lane Bks.

Eichler, Darlene. Where's the Kitty. Wyles, Betty, illus. 2013. 52p. pap. 18.95 *(978-0-9893063-1-7(3))* ProsePress.

Einhorn, Edward. A Very Improbable Story. Gustavson, Adam, illus. 2008. (ENG.). 32p. (J). (gr. 2-5). pap. 7.95 *(978-1-57091-872-8(4))* Charlesbridge Publishing, Inc.

Elchgar, Yasmin. Noonoo the Doctor. 2013. 20p. pap. 13.77 *(978-1-4907-1037-2(X))* Trafford Publishing.

Eldridge, Les. Santa's Cat. Eldridge, Les & Casey, James, illus. 2003. 24p. (J). *(978-1-877338-03-8(6))* Steele Roberts Aotearoa Ltd.

Eliot, Margaret. Cat & Tiger Go to the Seaside. 2012. 24p. pap. 28.03 *(978-1-4691-7674-1(2))* Xlibris Corp.

Eliot, T. S. Macavity: The Mystery Cat. Robins, Arthur, illus. 75th ed. 2016. (Old Possum Picture Bks.). (ENG.). 32p. (J). (-k). pap. 9.95 *(978-0-571-30813-2(9))* Faber & Faber, Inc.

Elliott, John C. Ri Ra: An Adventure Begins. 2006. 48p. pap. 16.95 *(978-1-4241-2771-9(8))* PublishAmerica, Inc.

Ellis, Deborah. The Cat at the Wall, 1 vol. (ENG., Illus.). (J). 2015. 152p. pap. 9.95 *(978-1-55498-707-8(5))* 2014. 144p. (gr. 3-7). 16.95 *(978-1-55498-491-6(2))* Groundwood Bks. CAN. Dist: Publishers Group West (PGW).

Ellis, Mary. Dick & His Cat. 2007. (Illus.). 48p. per. *(978-1-4065-3442-9(0))* Dodo Pr.

Emberley, Rebecca & Emberley, Ed. Mice on Ice. 2013. (I Like to Read(r) Ser.). (ENG.). 24p. (J). (gr. -1-3). pap. 6.99 *(978-0-8234-2908-0(3))* Holiday Hse., Inc.

Emberley, Rebecca & Emberley, Edward R. Mice on Ice. Emberley, Rebecca & Emberley, Edward R., illus. 2012. (I Like to Read(r) Ser.). (ENG., Illus.). 24p. (J). (gr. -1-3). 14.95 *(978-0-8234-2576-1(2))* Holiday Hse., Inc.

Emch, Christiana M. Donut Cat's Bakery. 2010. 16p. pap. 9.30 *(978-1-935125-67-9(2))* Robertson Publishing.

—Rainbow Girl, Make a Joyful Noise. 2010. 16p. pap. 9.30 *(978-1-935125-66-2(4))* Robertson Publishing.

Emm, David. Madison Meets the Minister. Bedrick, Jeff, illus. 2010. (ENG.). 48p. (J). 12.95 *(978-1-889658-42-1(1))* New Canaan Publishing Co. LLC.

Enderle, Dotti. Clawed! An Up2U Horror Adventure, 1 vol. To, Vivienne, illus. 2013. (Up2U Adventures Ser.). (ENG.). 80p. (J). (gr. 2-5). lib. bdg. 27.07 *(978-1-61641-965-3(2),* Calico Chapter Bks) Magic Wagon.

Enders, Genie. Don't Call Me Hefty Holly. 2010. 103p. pap. 10.95 *(978-1-4327-4751-0(7))* Outskirts Pr., Inc.

Epperson, Kathy. Belly Thumpers. 2012. 24p. pap. 24.95 *(978-1-4626-9251-4(6))* America Star Bks.

Epstein, Adam Jay & Jacobson, Andrew. The Familiars. 2011. (Familiars Ser.: 1). (ENG.). 384p. (J). (gr. 3-7). pap. 6.99 *(978-0-06-196110-6(8))* HarperCollins Pubs.

Erickson, John R. The Case of the Falling Sky. Holmes, Gerald L., illus. 2011. (Hank the Cowdog Ser.: No. 45). (ENG.). 129p. (J). (gr. 3-6). pap. 5.99 *(978-1-59188-145-2(5))* Maverick Bks., Inc.

—The Case of the Haystack Kitties. Holmes, Gerald L., illus. 2011. (Hank the Cowdog Ser.). (ENG.). 123p. (J). (gr. 3-6). pap. 5.99 *(978-1-59188-130-8(7))* Maverick Bks., Inc.

—The Case of the Missing Cat. Holmes, Gerald L., illus. 2011. (Hank the Cowdog Ser.: No. 15). (ENG.). 114p. (J). (gr. 3-6). pap. 5.99 *(978-1-59188-115-5(3))* Maverick Bks., Inc.

—The Case of the Twisted Kitty. Holmes, Gerald L., illus. 2004. (Hank the Cowdog Ser.: No. 43). 131p. (J). lib. bdg. 17.00 *(978-1-4242-1600-0(1))* Fitzgerald Bks.

—The Case of the Twisted Kitty. Holmes, Gerald L., illus. 2011. (Hank the Cowdog Ser.). (ENG.). 131p. (J). (gr. 3-6). pap. 5.99 *(978-1-59188-143-8(9))* Maverick Bks., Inc.

—The Case of the Vampire Cat. Holmes, Gerald L., illus. 2011. (Hank the Cowdog Ser.). (ENG.). 115p. (J). (gr. 3-6). pap. 5.99 *(978-1-59188-121-6(8))* Maverick Bks., Inc.

Esbaum, Jill. Tom's Tweet. Stone, Kyle M. & Santat, Dan, illus. 2011. (ENG.). 32p. (J). (gr. -1-2). 16.99 *(978-0-375-85171-1(2),* Knopf Bks. for Young Readers) Random Hse. Children's Bks.

Espinoza, Olivia G. Jay-Dylan's Cat & Fish. 2011. 24p. (gr. -1). pap. 14.39 *(978-1-4567-5119-7(0))* AuthorHouse.

Essence, Angel. The Amazing Adventures of Callie the Cat: The Long Night. 2012. 28p. pap. 19.99 *(978-1-4772-9907-4(6))* AuthorHouse.

Estes, Eleanor. Miranda the Great. Ardizzone, Edward, illus. 2005. (ENG.). 96p. (J). (gr. 2-5). pap. 7.95 *(978-0-15-205411-3(1))* Houghton Mifflin Harcourt Publishing Co.

Eubank, Patricia Reeder. The Leprechaun's Big Pot of Gold. Eubank, Patricia Reeder, illus. 2012. (Illus.). 20p. (J). bds. 6.99 *(978-0-8249-1877-4(0),* Ideal Pubns.) Worthy Publishing.

Evanier, Mark. Garfield, Vol. 1. Barker, Gary, illus. 2012. (Garfield Ser.). (ENG.). 112p. (J). (gr. 2). pap. 13.99 *(978-1-60886-287-0(9))* Boom! Studios.

Evans, Betty J. Three Young Wild Cats. Bucher, Barbara Latini, illus. 2008. 20p. pap. 24.95 *(978-1-60610-809-3(3))* America Star Bks.

Evans, Michelle D. I Don't Belong in the Jungle. 2011. 20p. pap. 24.95 *(978-1-4626-1382-3(9))* America Star Bks.

Ewert, Marcus. Mummy Cat. Brown, Lisa, illus. 2015. (ENG.). 48p. (J). (gr. 1-4). 16.99 *(978-0-544-34082-4(5),* Clarion Bks.) Houghton Mifflin Harcourt Trade & Reference Pubs.

Faber, Jules, illus. Cat Stories. 2017. (ENG.). 208p. (J). (gr. 1-4). 12.99 ***(978-0-14-378099-1(9))*** Random Hse. Australia AUS. Dist: Independent Pubs. Group.

Fairhurst, Joanne. Archie & the Red Wool. Fairhurst, Joanne, illus. 2011. (Illus.). 16p. pap. *(978-1-908341-21-1(1))* Paragon Publishing, Rothersthorpe.

Falsetto, Rita. A Cat's Furry Tale. 2011. 60p. pap. 31.99 *(978-1-4568-4802-6(X))* Xlibris Corp.

Fantich, Susanna. A Cat's Tale. 2012. 210p. 33.99 *(978-1-4582-0527-8(4))*; pap. 15.99 *(978-1-4582-0525-4(8))* Author Solutions, Inc. (Abbott Pr.).

Farber, Erica. Richard Scarry's Readers (Level 2): One, Two, AH-CHOO! Scarry, Huck, illus. 2014. (Richard Scarry's Great Big Schoolhouse Ser.). (ENG.). 24p. (J). (gr. k-1). 12.95 *(978-1-4549-0380-2(5))* Sterling Publishing Co., Inc.

Farley, Jan. Griffin & Griseld: Book 3 in the Fleur Series. 2011. 84p. pap. 19.95 *(978-1-4626-3592-4(X))* America Star Bks.

Farley, Robin. Adventures of MIA. Ivanov, A. & Ivanov, O., illus. 2013. 158p. (J). *(978-1-4351-5061-4(9))* Barnes & Noble, Inc.

—Mia & the Big Sister Ballet. Ivanov, Olga & Ivanov, Aleksey, illus. 2012. (My First I Can Read Ser.). (ENG.). 32p. (J). (gr. -1-3). pap. 3.99 *(978-0-06-173307-9(5))* HarperCollins Pubs.

—Mia & the Big Sister Ballet. 2012. (Mia I Can Read Bks.). (J). lib. bdg. 13.55 *(978-0-606-26282-8(2),* Turtleback) Turtleback Bks.

—Mia & the Daisy Dance. Ivanov, Olga & Ivanov, Aleksey, illus. 2012. (My First I Can Read Ser.). (ENG.). 32p. (J). (gr. -1-3). 16.99 *(978-0-06-173306-2(7))*; pap. 3.99 *(978-0-06-173305-5(9))* HarperCollins Pubs.

—Mia & the Daisy Dance. 2012. (Mia I Can Read Bks.). (J). lib. bdg. 13.55 *(978-0-606-23595-2(7),* Turtleback) Turtleback Bks.

—Mia & the Girl with a Twirl. Ivanov, Olga & Ivanov, Aleksey, illus. 2013. (My First I Can Read Ser.). (ENG.). 32p. (J). (gr. -1-3). 16.99 *(978-0-06-208689-1(8))*; pap. 3.99 *(978-0-06-208688-4(X))* HarperCollins Pubs.

—Mia & the Girl with a Twirl. 2013. (Mia I Can Read Bks.). (J). lib. bdg. 13.55 *(978-0-606-31811-2(9),* Turtleback) Turtleback Bks.

—Mia & the Tiny Toe Shoes. Ivanov, Aleksey & Ivanov, Olga, illus. 2012. (My First I Can Read Ser.). (ENG.). 32p. (J). (gr. -1-3). 16.99 *(978-0-06-208683-9(9))*; pap. 3.99 *(978-0-06-208682-2(0))* HarperCollins Pubs.

—Mia & the Tiny Toe Shoes. 2012. (Mia I Can Read Bks.). (J). lib. bdg. 13.55 *(978-0-606-26863-9(4),* Turtleback) Turtleback Bks.

—Mia & the Too Big Tutu. Ivanov, Aleksey & Ivanov, Olga, illus. 2010. (My First I Can Read Ser.). (ENG.). 32p. (J). (gr. -1-3). 16.99 *(978-0-06-173302-4(4))*; pap. 3.99 *(978-0-06-173301-7(6))* HarperCollins Pubs.

—Mia Dances Back to School! Ivanov, Olga & Ivanov, Aleksey, illus. 2013. (Mia Ser.). (ENG.). 24p. (J). (gr. -1-3). pap. 4.99 *(978-0-06-210014-6(9),* HarperFestival) HarperCollins Pubs.

—Mia Jazzes It Up! Ivanov, Olga & Ivanov, Aleksey, illus. 2013. (My First I Can Read Ser.). (ENG.). 32p. (J). (gr. -1-3). 16.99 *(978-0-06-208692-1(8))*; pap. 3.99 *(978-0-06-208691-4(X))* HarperCollins Pubs.

—Mia Jazzes It Up! 2013. (Mia I Can Read Bks.). (J). lib. bdg. 13.55 *(978-0-606-32164-8(0),* Turtleback) Turtleback Bks.

—Mia Sets the Stage. Ivanov, Olga & Ivanov, Aleksey, illus. 2013. (My First I Can Read Ser.). (ENG.). 32p. (J). (gr. -1-3). pap. 3.99 *(978-0-06-208685-3(5))* HarperCollins Pubs.

—Mia's Nutcracker Ballet. Ivanov, Olga & Ivanov, Aleksey, illus. 2013. (Mia Ser.). (ENG.). 32p. (J). (gr. -1-3). 9.99 *(978-0-06-223830-6(2))* HarperCollins Pubs.

—The Sweetest Valentine. Ivanov, Aleksey & Ivanov, Olga, illus. 2012. (Mia Ser.). (ENG.). 24p. (J). (gr. -1-3). pap. 4.99 *(978-0-06-210012-2(2),* HarperFestival) HarperCollins Pubs.

Farnsley, Kathleen. This Little Piggy Named Pony. 2008. 24p. pap. 12.99 *(978-1-4389-2659-9(6))* AuthorHouse.

Favretto, Robert. Cat-Astrophe. 2012. 40p. pap. *(978-0-9859147-9-0(3))* Morris Publishing Australia.

Fearnley, Jan. Billy Tibble Moves Out! Fearnley, Jan, illus. 2006. (Illus.). 29p. (J). (gr. k-4). reprint ed. 16.00 *(978-1-4223-5557-2(8))* DIANE Publishing Co.

Feder, Jane. A Little Kitty. Schwartz, Amy, illus. 2009. (ENG.). 14p. (J). (— 1). bds. 4.99 *(978-0-7636-2650-1(3))* Candlewick Pr.

Feiffer, Jules. Rupert Can Dance. Feiffer, Jules, illus. 2014. (ENG., Illus.). 32p. (J). (gr. -1-1). 17.95 *(978-0-374-36363-5(3),* 9780374363635, Farrar, Straus & Giroux (BYR)) Farrar, Straus & Giroux.

Feldman, Thea. Hello Kitty Movie Theater Storybook & Movie Projector. 2015. (Movie Theater Ser.). (ENG.). 32p. (J). (gr. -1-1). 19.99 *(978-0-7944-3510-3(6))* Reader's Digest Assn., Inc., The.

Fenn, G. Manville. Brownsmith's Boy. 2008. 260p. pap. 15.95 *(978-1-60664-154-5(9))* Aegypan.

Ferchaud, Steve, illus. The Man Who Spoke with Cats. 2006. (ENG.). 48p. (J). 18.95 *(978-1-58478-019-9(3),* Highland Children's Pr.) Heather & Highlands Publishing.

Fernandes, Eugenie. Kitten's Autumn. Fernandes, Eugenie, illus. 2010. (ENG., Illus.). 24p. (J). (gr. -1 — 1). 14.95 *(978-1-55453-341-1(4))* Kids Can Pr., Ltd. CAN. Dist: Hachette Bk. Group.

—Kitten's Summer. Fernandes, Eugenie, illus. (ENG., Illus.). 24p. (J). (gr. -1 — 1). 2013. bds. 7.95 *(978-1-55453-721-1(5))* 2011. 14.95 *(978-1-55453-342-8(2))* Kids Can Pr., Ltd. CAN. Dist: Hachette Bk. Group.

—Kitten's Winter. Fernandes, Eugenie, illus. 2011. (ENG., Illus.). 24p. (J). (gr. -1 — 1). 14.95 *(978-1-55453-343-5(0))* Kids Can Pr., Ltd. CAN. Dist: Hachette Bk. Group.

Fernandez, Joyce & Marsh, Laura. Eins und Zwei are One & Two. 2009. 22p. 15.95 *(978-0-578-00208-8(6))* My Second Language Publishing, USA.

—Un et Deux are One & Two. 2009. 22p. 15.95 *(978-0-615-26239-0(2))* My Second Language Publishing, USA.

—Un Is One. 2009. 21p. 15.95 *(978-0-615-26238-3(4))* My Second Language Publishing, USA.

—Uno Is One. 2009. 22p. 15.95 *(978-0-615-24460-0(2))* My Second Language Publishing, USA.

—Um Is One. 2009. 22p. 15.95 *(978-0-557-05629-3(2))* Lulu Pr., Inc.

Ferro, Ursula. Tanny's Meow. Huff, Ariella, illus. 2005. 51p. (J). pap. 12.95 *(978-0-9766006-0-2(9))* Marti Bks.

Fiani, M. A Cat Named Monkey. 2008. 24p. pap. 14.99 *(978-1-4389-1966-9(2))* AuthorHouse.

Fiedler, Lisa. Hopper's Destiny. To, Vivienne, illus. 2016. (Mouseheart Ser.: 2). (ENG.). 368p. (J). (gr. 3-7). pap. 7.99 *(978-1-4814-2090-7(9),* McElderry, Margaret K. Bks.) McElderry, Margaret K. Bks.

—Mouseheart. To, Vivienne, illus. (Mouseheart Ser.: 1). (ENG.). (J). (gr. 3-7). 2015. 336p. pap. 7.99 *(978-1-4424-8783-3(6))* 2014. 320p. 16.99 *(978-1-4424-8781-9(X))* McElderry, Margaret K. Bks. (McElderry, Margaret K. Bks.).

—Mouseheart. 2015. (Mouseheart Ser.: 1). lib. bdg. 18.40 *(978-0-606-37132-2(X))* Turtleback Bks.

Fielder, Barbara L. Missy, the Kitty, Plays Hide & Go Seek. (Illus.). 17p. (J). 6.95 *(978-0-9639986-5-1(X))* Fielder Group.

—Missy, the Kitty, Visits the Veterinarian. (Illus.). 15p. (J). 6.95 *(978-0-9639986-7-5(6))* Fielder Group.

—Treats for Missy, the Kitty. (Illus.). 13p. (J). 6.95 *(978-0-9639986-4-4(1))* Fielder Group.

Fielder, Barbara L. & Broady, Brianna. Missy, the Kitty, Learns about Sharing. (Illus.). 13p. (J). 6.95 *(978-0-9639986-2-0(5))* Fielder Group.

—Missy, the Mischievous Kitty. (Illus.). 17p. (J). 6.95 *(978-0-9639986-3-7(3))* Fielder Group.

—Missy, the Patriotic Kitty. (Illus.). 11p. (J). 6.95 *(978-0-9639986-1-3(7))* Fielder Group.

Filipina, Monika. All about Cats. Filipina, Monika, illus. 2017. (Child's Play Library). (ENG., Illus.). 32p. (J). pap. *(978-1-84643-933-9(7))* Child's Play International Ltd.

Finch, Kate. A Big Surprise. 2013. (Pet Hotel Ser.: 2). lib. bdg. 14.75 *(978-0-606-31985-0(9),* Turtleback) Turtleback Bks.

—On with the Show! Gurney, John Steven, illus. 2014. 76p. (J). *(978-1-4242-5954-0(1))* Scholastic, Inc.

—On with the Show! 2014. (Pet Hotel Ser.: 4). lib. bdg. 14.75 *(978-0-606-35201-7(5))* Turtleback Bks.

—Pet Hotel #4: on with the Show! Gurney, John Steven & Jessell, Tim, illus. 2014. (Pet Hotel Ser.: 4). (ENG.). 96p. (J). (gr. 2-5). pap. 4.99 *(978-0-545-50184-2(9),* Scholastic Paperbacks) Scholastic, Inc.

Finch, Keith. Poppy Cat's Garden. Jones, Lara, illus. 2008. (ENG.). 8p. (J). (gr. 3-6). bds. 16.95 *(978-0-230-01715-3(0),* Macmillan) Pan Macmillan GBR. Dist: Trans-Atlantic Pubns., Inc.

Finkbeiner, Betty Ladley. Pepper's Forever Home. 2013. 24p. pap. 15.99 *(978-1-4797-6982-7(7))* Xlibris Corp.

Finn McCool The Magic Leprechaun Cat. Irish Holiday Fairy Tales: Volume 1. 2012. 44p. pap. 19.95 *(978-1-4772-1331-5(7))* AuthorHouse.

Firth, Norma. Tasha a Fraidy Cat. 2012. 28p. pap. 15.99 *(978-1-4685-6079-4(4))* AuthorHouse.

Fischer, Hans. Pitschi. 2010. (ENG., Illus.). 32p. (J). (gr. -1-3). 16.95 *(978-0-7358-2278-8(6))* North-South Bks., Inc.

Fish, Mister, illus. Snerfy Cat Meets Prancy Finch. Fish, Mister, . 2007. 80p. (J). 14.99 *(978-0-9794753-0-6(9))* Children's Classic Book Pubs.

Fisher, Karianne Marie. In a Land Called Hogeye, 1 vol. 2010. 24p. pap. 24.95 *(978-1-4489-8798-6(9))* PublishAmerica, Inc.

Flambaum, Victor & Flambaum, Andrew. How to Make a Big Bang: A Cosmic Journey. 2012. (ENG.). 226p. (J). (gr. 7-10). pap. 14.95 *(978-1-936782-72-7(3))* Salem Author Services.

Flamburis, Georgia M. How Karis' Kitten Got Its Name. 2012. 34p. pap. 9.99 *(978-0-615-47908-8(1))* Flamburis, Georgia.

The Flat Hat: KinderReaders Individual Title Six-Packs. (Kinderstarters Ser.). 8p. (gr. -1-1). 21.00 *(978-0-7635-8662-1(5))* Rigby Education.

Flemming, Denise. Buster. 2007. (J). (gr. k-3). 29.95 incl. audio compact disk *(978-0-8045-4182-4(5))*; 27.95 incl. audio *(978-0-8045-6959-0(2))* Spoken Arts, Inc.

Flener, Bettie D. Sidney's Bedtime Stories. Flener, Sheila S., illus. 2011. 44p. pap. 24.95 *(978-1-4560-3226-5(7))* America Star Bks.

Fletcher, Ashlee. My Dog, My Cat. 2012. (ENG., Illus.). 16p. (J). (gr. k — 1). bds. 7.99 *(978-1-933718-81-1(1))* Tanglewood Pr.

—My Dog, My Cat. Fletcher, Ashlee, illus. 2011. (ENG., Illus.). 32p. (J). (gr. -1-3). 13.95 *(978-1-933718-22-4(6))* Tanglewood Pr.

Flickinger, Joie & Flickinger, Amanda. Clutch the Trucking Cat. 2007. 236p. per. 24.95 *(978-1-4241-9535-0(7))* America Star Bks.

Flor Ada, Alma. Celebrate Kwanzaa with Boots & Her Kittens. Docampo, Valeria, illus. 2007. (Cuentos para Celebrar / Stories to Celebrate Ser.). 30p. (gr. k-6). per. 11.95 *(978-1-59820-135-2(2))* Santillana USA Publishing Co., Inc.

Florek, Amy. Silly Beulah! l.t. ed. 2006. (Illus.). 21p. (J). 15.95 *(978-1-59879-158-7(3))*; per. 9.99 *(978-1-59879-138-9(9))* Lifevest Publishing, Inc.

Flynn, S. E. That Night. 2009. 24p. pap. 11.95 *(978-1-4389-6699-1(7))* AuthorHouse.

Follow the Paw Prints: Small Book. (Pebble Soup Explorations Ser.). 16p. (gr. -1-18). 5.00 *(978-0-7635-7042-2(7))* Rigby Education.

Ford, Sandy Lee, illus. Gullah, the Nawleans Cat Meets Katrina. 2007. 32p. (J). *(978-0-9793637-0-2(5))* Hart Street Pubs.

Foreman, Michael. Cat & Canary. 2004. (ENG., Illus.). 32p. (J). pap. 8.99 *(978-1-84270-287-1(4))* Andersen Pr. GBR. Dist: Trafalgar Square Publishing.

—Cat & Dog. Foreman, Michael, illus. 2014. (ENG., Illus.). 32p. (J). (gr. -1-3). 16.95 *(978-1-4677-5124-7(3))* Lerner Publishing Group.

—Friends. Foreman, Michael, illus. 2012. (Andersen Press Picture Bks). (ENG., Illus.). 32p. (J). (gr. -1-3). 16.95 *(978-1-4677-0317-8(6))* Lerner Publishing Group.

Forrester, Margaret. The Cat Who Decided: The Almost True Story of an Edinburgh Cat, 1 vol. Klaassen, Sandra, illus. 2007. (Young Kelpies Ser.). (ENG.). 112p. (J). per. *(978-0-86315-612-0(6))* Floris Bks.

Forward, Toby. The Quayside Cat. Brown, Ruth, illus. 2014. (ENG.). 32p. (J). (gr. -1-3). 16.95 *(978-1-4677-3452-3(7))* Lerner Publishing Group.

Fosburgh. Bella Arabella. 2010. (ENG.). 112p. (J). (gr. 4-6). pap. 6.99 *(978-1-4424-1351-1(4),* Simon & Schuster Bks. For Young Readers) Simon & Schuster Bks. For Young Readers.

Fosha, Kent. The Cat Who Wanted to Moo. 2008. 20p. pap. 24.95 *(978-1-60474-125-4(2))* America Star Bks.

Fosina, Mickie. The Kitten Girls Are Scaredy Cats. 2012. 24p. pap. 15.99 *(978-1-4691-8172-1(X))* Xlibris Corp.

Fotso, Serge. The Hungry Little Cat. Woods, Michele, illus. 2011. 32p. pap. 24.95 *(978-1-4626-1805-7(7))* America Star Bks.

Fox, Diane. The Cat, the Dog, Little Red, the Exploding Eggs, the Wolf, & Grandma. Fox, Christyan, illus. 2014. (ENG.). 32p. (J). (gr. -1-3). 16.99 *(978-0-545-69481-0(7),* Scholastic Pr.) Scholastic, Inc.

Francesa. The Coming of Amber: The Story of a Stray. 2016. (ENG., Illus.). pap. ***(978-1-925590-09-8(7))*** Vivid Publishing.

Franciosi, Pete. Dusty Wants A Kitty. 2011. 23p. 14.95 *(978-1-4327-7596-4(0))* Outskirts Pr., Inc.

Francois, Betsy. The Horse Who Thinks She's a Cat. 2011. 24p. pap. 15.99 *(978-1-4653-4322-2(9))* Xlibris Corp.

Frank, Lucy. Just Ask Iris. 2003. (ENG., Illus.). 224p. (J). (gr. 5-9). pap. 10.99 *(978-0-689-84454-6(9),* Atheneum Bks. for Young Readers) Simon & Schuster Children's Publishing.

Frankford, Marilyn. My Tiger Cat. Kaeden Corp. Staff, ed. Dragony, Barbara, illus. 2006. (ENG.). 12p. (gr. k-2). pap. 7.95 *(978-1-879835-52-8(5),* Kaeden Bks.) Kaeden Corp.

Fraser, P. J. The Mouse with the Torch, 1 vol. 2009. 48p. pap. 16.95 *(978-1-4489-2080-8(9))* America Star Bks.

Frasier, Debra. Spike: Ugliest Dog in the Universe. Frasier, Debra, illus. 2013. (ENG., Illus.). 40p. (J). (gr. -1-3). 16.99 *(978-1-4424-1452-5(9),* Beach Lane Bks.) Beach Lane Bks.

Frederick, H. J. Timber Howligan Secret Agent Cat. Wilkins, Wendy H., illus. 2015. (J). pap. 8.99 *(978-0-9964246-9-1(5))* Lionheart Pr.

Freed, marie. Kitty Cat Kids. 2012. (ENG.). (J). pap. *(978-1-4675-1591-7(4))* Independent Pub.

Freeman, Kathie. Catwalk: A Feline Odyyssey. 2003. 236p. per. 11.95 *(978-0-9742062-3-3(7))* McPugh, Kathleen.

Freeman, Martha. Mrs. Wow Never Wanted a Cow. Salerno, Steven, illus. 2006. (Beginner Books(R) Ser.). (ENG.). 48p. (J). (gr. -1-2). 9.99 *(978-0-375-83418-9(4),* Random Hse. Bks. for Young Readers) Random Hse. Children's Bks.

—Who Is Stealing the 12 Days of Christmas? 2008. (ENG., Illus.). 200p. (J). (gr. 3-7). pap. 7.95 *(978-0-8234-2167-1(8))* Holiday Hse., Inc.

—Who Stole Halloween? 2005. (Chickadee Court Mystery Ser.). (ENG.). 224p. (J). (gr. 3-7). 16.95 *(978-0-8234-1962-3(2))* Holiday Hse., Inc.

—Who Stole Uncle Sam? 2008. (Chickadee Court Mystery Ser.). (ENG., Illus.). 128p. (J). (gr. 3-7). 16.95 *(978-0-8234-2091-9(4))* Holiday Hse., Inc.

Freeman, Meryl. The Voyages of Galley Cat. 2008. 36p. pap. 24.95 *(978-1-60474-632-7(7))* America Star Bks.

Frees, Jessie Lynch. Jackie Winquackey & Her 43 Cats Go to Hollywood. Gebr, Jaroslav, illus. 2005. 32p. (J). 14.99 *(978-0-9760553-0-3(9))* Tizbit Books, LLC.

French, Vivian. The Kitten with No Name. Young, Selina, illus. 2011. (ENG.). 96p. (J). (gr. -1-k). 7.99 *(978-1-4440-0078-8(0),* Orion Children's Bks.) Hachette Children's Group GBR. Dist: Hachette Bk. Group.

—The Kitten with No Name. Young, Selina, illus. 2010. (ENG.). 112p. 14.99 *(978-1-4440-0077-1(2))* Orion Publishing Group, Ltd. GBR. Dist: Hachette Bk. Group.

—Morris & the Cat Flap. Villet, Olivia, illus. 2011. (ENG.). 64p. (J). (gr. 2-4). pap. 5.99 *(978-0-00-714161-6(0),* HarperCollins Children's Bks.) HarperCollins Pubs. Ltd. GBR. Dist: HarperCollins Pubs.

—Morris the Mouse Hunter. Villet, Olivia, illus. 2011. (ENG.). 64p. (J). (gr. 2-4). pap. 5.99 *(978-0-00-714732-8(5))* HarperCollins Pubs. Ltd. GBR. Dist: HarperCollins Pubs.

Frenkel, Yetti. Libby & the Cat. Frenkel, Yetti, illus. 2005. (Illus.). 32p. (J). 16.95 *(978-0-9749006-2-9(1))* Snow Tree Bks.

—Trudy & the Captain's Cat. Frenkel, Yetti, illus. 2005. (Illus.). 32p. (J). 16.95 *(978-0-9749006-1-2(3))* Snow Tree Bks.

Frey, Cathy. Muttin's Puttins. 2010. 24p. pap. 13.99 *(978-1-4490-6753-3(0))* AuthorHouse.

Friday, Stormy. Signal's Airport Adventure. Saroff, Phyllis, illus. 2006. (J). 14.95 *(978-0-9717047-5-6(9))* Bay Media, Inc.

Friebert, Judith M. The Flying Cats: Oliver & Jimmy. 2003. (Illus.). 16p. (Orig.). (J). (gr. -1-6). pap. *(978-0-9744852-0-1(9))* Sandner-Petersen International Bks.

Friedman, Carol. Nicky the Jazz Cat. 2004. (Illus.). 32p. (J). (gr. -1-3). 16.95 *(978-0-9726092-0-3(2))* Dominick Pictures.

Friedman, Laurie. Ruby Valentine & the Sweet Surprise. Avril, Lynne, illus. 2014. (ENG.). 32p. (J). (gr. k-3). 16.95 *(978-0-7613-8873-9(7),* Carolrhoda Bks.) Lerner Publishing Group.

Friedman, Mel, et al. Un Castillo para Gatitos. Adams, Lynn, illus. 2008. (SPA.). (J). *(978-1-57565-275-7(7))* Kane Press, Inc.

Friend, Shirley. Lucy a Special Ragdoll. 2011. 28p. pap. 15.99 *(978-1-4628-6669-4(7))* Xlibris Corp.

Froeb, Lori. I Am Daisy. Lemay, Violet, illus. 2015. (ENG.). 32p. (J). (gr. 1-3). pap. 3.99 *(978-0-7944-3311-6(1),* Reader's Digest Children's Bks.) Studio Fun International.

Fruchter, Jason, illus. Friends Help Each Other. 2014. (Daniel Tiger's Neighborhood Ser.). (ENG.). 32p. (J). (gr. -1-k). pap. 3.99 *(978-1-4814-0366-5(4),* Simon Spotlight) Simon Spotlight.

Fuentes, Peggy Jo. Boogoos, the Calico Kitty. 2009. 16p. pap. 24.95 *(978-1-60836-914-0(5))* America Star Bks.

Fujikawa, Brian. The Adventures of Bibole, Rivol & Michelle: The French Fry Caper. 2013. 72p. pap. 24.27 *(978-1-4907-0954-3(1))* Trafford Publishing.

Fuks, Menuhah & Tager, Gavriella. Smile with Avigayil #2: Avigayil & the Black Cat. Haas, Esti, illus. 2006. (ENG.). 64p. (J). 12.95 *(978-1-932443-58-5(4))* Judaica Pr., Inc., The.

Fuller, Niki. The Cat from M-31. 2009. 24p. pap. 15.99 *(978-1-4415-3826-0(7))* Xlibris Corp.

Fuller, Sandy Ferguson. My Cat, Coon Cat, 1 vol. Brett, Jeannie, illus. 2011. (ENG.). 36p. (J). 17.95 *(978-1-934031-32-2(1),*

4251474a-88ba-4ed7-90df-8651e2bedb12) Islandport Pr., Inc.

Futterer, Kurt. Emile. Gray, Bronwen et al, trs. from GER. Futterer, Ralf, illus. 2004. (ENG.). 32p. (J). (978-1-931561-95-2(8)) MacAdam/Cage Publishing, Inc.

Fuzz & the Glass Eye: Individual Title Six-Packs. (Action Packs Ser.). 120p. (gr. 3-5). 44.00 (978-0-7635-8421-4(5)) Rigby Education.

Gág, Wanda. Millions of Cats. Gág, Wanda, illus. gif. ed. 2006. (ENG., Illus.). 32p. (J). (gr. -1-k). pap. 7.99 (978-0-14-240708-0(9), Puffin Books) Penguin Young Readers Group.

—Millions of Cats. Gág, Wanda, illus. 2006. (Illus.). (gr. -1-3). 18.00 (978-0-7569-6785-7(6)) Perfection Learning Corp.

Gaichies, Sarah. Mirabelle the Lost Kitten. 2010. (Illus.). 76p. pap. 24.99 (978-1-4490-5593-6(1)) AuthorHouse.

Galer, Chris. Ross Gang. 2006. 136p. per. (978-1-905529-84-1(8)) Grosvenor Hse. Publishing Ltd.

Gall, Chris. Dog vs. Cat. 2014. (ENG., Illus.). 32p. (J). (gr. -1-3). 17.99 (978-0-316-23801-4(5)) Little, Brown Bks. for Young Readers.

Gallagher, Diana G. The Great Kitten Challenge, 1 vol. Juarez, Adriana & Puglisi, Adriana, illus. 2013. (Pet Friends Forever Ser.). (ENG.). 88p. (gr. 1-3). pap. 5.95 (978-1-4795-1864-7(6)); lib. bdg. 25.32 (978-1-4048-7501-2(8)) Picture Window Bks.

Gallico, Paul. The Abandoned. 2013. (ENG.). 320p. (J). (gr. 4-7). 15.95 (978-1-59017-626-9(X), NYR Children's Collection) New York Review of Bks., Inc., The.

Gantos, Jack. Best in Show for Rotten Ralph. Rubel, Nicole, illus. 2008. (Rotten Ralph Rotten Readers Ser.). (J). 28.95 incl. audio compact disk (978-1-4301-0451-3(1)); 25.95 incl. audio (978-1-4301-0448-3(1)) Live Oak Media.

—Practice Makes Perfect for Rotten Ralph. Rubel, Nicole, illus. 2009. (Rotten Ralph Rotten Readers Ser.: 2). (ENG.). 48p. (J). (gr. 1-3). pap. 8.99 (978-0-374-40002-6(4), 9780374400026) Square Fish.

—Rotten Ralph Feels Rotten. Rubel, Nicole, tr. Rubel, Nicole, illus. 2004. (Rotten Ralph Rotten Readers Ser.: 3). (ENG.). 48p. (J). (gr. 1-3). 16.99 (978-0-374-36357-4(9), 9780374363574, Farrar, Straus & Giroux (BYR)) Farrar, Straus & Giroux.

—Rotten Ralph Feels Rotten. Rubel, Nicole, illus. 2007. (Rotten Ralph Ser.). (J). (gr. -1-3). 28.95 incl. audio compact disk (978-1-4301-0098-0(2)) Live Oak Media.

—Rotten Ralph Helps Out. Rubel, Nicole, illus. unabr. ed. 2006. (Readalongs for Beginning Readers Ser.). (J). (gr. -1-3). 24.95 incl. audio (978-1-59519-678-1(1)); 28.95 incl. audio compact disk (978-1-59519-679-8(X)) Live Oak Media.

—Rotten Ralph Helps Out, 4 bks., Set. unabr. ed. 2006. (Readalongs for Beginning Readers Ser.). (Illus.). (J). (gr. -1-3). pap. 29.95 incl. audio (978-1-59519-676-7(5)); pap. 31.95 incl. audio compact disk (978-1-59519-677-4(3)) Live Oak Media.

—Rotten Ralph Helps Out. Rubel, Nicole, illus. (Rotten Ralph Rotten Readers Ser.: 1). (ENG.). 48p. (J). (gr. 1-3). 2012. 15.99 (978-0-312-64172-6(9), 9780312641726) 2012. pap. 3.99 (978-0-312-67281-2(0), 9780312672812) 2004. pap. 6.99 (978-0-374-46355-7(7), 9780374463557) Square Fish.

—Rotten Ralph's Rotten Family. Rubel, Nicole, illus. 2014. (Rotten Ralph Rotten Readers Ser.: 6). (ENG.). 48p. (J). (gr. 1-3). 16.99 (978-0-374-36353-6(6), 9780374363536, Farrar, Straus & Giroux (BYR)) Farrar, Straus & Giroux.

—Three Strikes for Rotten Ralph. Rubel, Nicole, illus. 2011. (Rotten Ralph Rotten Readers Ser.: 5). (ENG.). 48p. (J). (gr. 1-3). 16.99 (978-0-374-36354-3(4), 9780374363543, Farrar, Straus & Giroux (BYR)) Farrar, Straus & Giroux.

Garcia, Alice Cook. Bella's Dreams. 2011. 16p. pap. 8.32 (978-1-4634-3485-4(5)) AuthorHouse.

Gardiner, C. Pirate Betty of Wigan. 2013. 12p. pap. 10.60 (978-1-291-30672-9(2)) Lulu Pr., Inc.

Gardner, Sally. Operation Bunny. Roberts, David, illus. 2014. (Wings & Co Ser.: 1). (ENG.). 192p. (J). (gr. 2-5). 12.99 (978-0-8050-9892-1(5), 9780805098921, Holt, Henry & Co. Bks. For Young Readers) Holt, Henry & Co.

—Operation Bunny. Roberts, David, illus. 2014. (Wings & Co Ser.: 1). (ENG.). 208p. (J). (gr. 2-5). pap. 6.99 (978-1-250-05053-3(7), 9781250050533) Square Fish.

—The Vanishing of Billy Buckle. Roberts, David, illus. 2015. (Wings & Co Ser.: 3). (ENG.). 240p. (J). (gr. 2-5). 13.99 (978-0-8050-9915-7(8), 9780805099157, Holt, Henry & Co. Bks. For Young Readers) Holt, Henry & Co.

Garis, Howard R. The Curlytops & Their Pets. 2009. 120p. 22.95 (978-1-60664-609-0(5)); pap. 10.95 (978-1-60664-341-9(X)) Rodgers, Alan Bks.

Garralon, Claire. Black Cat & White Cat. 2016. (ENG.). 30p. (J). bds. 7.99 (978-1-4926-3781-3(5), 9781492637813, Sourcebooks Jabberwocky) Sourcebooks, Inc.

Garretson, Jerri. Kansas Tall Tales: Tenth Anniversary Anthology. Garretson, Jerri & Dollar, Diane A., illus. 2008. 106p. (J). pap. 19.95 (978-0-9659712-7-0(9)) Ravenstone Pr.

Garrow, Rhonda. Michaela & the Christmas Village. 2011. 24p. pap. 11.32 (978-1-4634-8751-5(7)) AuthorHouse.

—Saber & the Onion. 2011. 24p. pap. 11.32 (978-1-4634-1525-9(7)) AuthorHouse.

El Gato, 6 Packs. (Chiquilibros Ser.). (SPA.). (gr. k-1). 23.00 (978-0-7635-8622-5(6)) Rigby Education.

Gay, Delmas Levi. The Ears at the Top of the Stairs. 2008. 56p. per. 15.99 (978-1-4363-0273-9(0)) Xlibris Corp.

Gay, Marie-Louise. Caramba & Henry. 2011. (ENG., Illus.). 40p. (J). (gr. k-k). 17.95 (978-1-55498-097-0(6)) Groundwood Bks. CAN. Dist: Publishers Group West (PGW).

Gee, Randi. Everybody Has a Cat Named Molly. 2010. 32p. pap. 15.50 (978-0-557-27671-4(3)) Lulu Pr., Inc.

Gentry, Jennifer Mills. Maria the Cat, 1 vol. 2010. 24p. pap. 24.95 (978-1-4489-7748-2(7)) PublishAmerica, Inc.

George, Olivia. Copy Cat. Hudson, Brett, illus. 2004. (My First Reader Ser.). (J). 18.50 (978-0-516-24679-6(8), Children's Pr.) Scholastic Library Publishing.

Gerowin, Sean. Catte au Lait & the Big Hurricane. 2005. 36p. (J). 8.99 (978-1-4116-5157-9(X)) Lulu Pr., Inc.

Gerstein, Mordicai. The Night World. 2015. (ENG., Illus.). 40p. (J). (gr. -1-3). 18.00 (978-0-316-18822-7(0)) Little Brown & Co.

Gerstein, Mordicai, illus. Three Samurai Cats: A Story from Japan. 2004. (ENG.). 32p. (J). (gr. k-3). 6.95 (978-0-8234-1877-0(4)) Holiday Hse., Inc.

—Three Samurai Cats: A Story from Japan. 2004. (J). (978-0-439-69256-4(3)) Scholastic, Inc.

Ghahremani, Susie. Stack the Cats. 2017. (ENG., Illus.). 32p. (J). (gr. -1-k). 14.95 (978-1-4197-2349-0(9), Abrams Appleseed) Abrams, Inc.

Gianferrari, Maria. Officer Katz & Houndini: A Tale of Two Tails. Chatzikonstantinou, Danny, illus. 2016. (ENG.). 32p. (J). (gr. -1-2). 17.99 (978-1-4814-2265-9(0), Aladdin) Simon & Schuster Children's Publishing.

Gibbs, Jon. Barnum's Revenge. 2013. 246p. pap. 12.99 (978-1-59080-722-4(7)) Echelon Press Publishing.

Giles, Susan. Caribbean Cats. Giles, Susan, illus. 2003. (Meet the Author Ser.). (ENG., Illus.). 16p. (J). pap. 5.75 net. (978-1-57274-662-6(9), 2728, Bks. for Young Learners) Owen, Richard C. Pubs., Inc.

Gilgen, Paula L. C a T. 2012. 120p. pap. 14.95 (978-0-9851416-1-5(1)) Oak Ridge Publishing.

Gill, Amber. Joseph's Summer. 2006. 71p. pap. 16.95 (978-1-4241-0122-1(0)) PublishAmerica, Inc.

Gill, Janet. Basket Weaver & Catches Many Mice. Choi, Yangsook, illus. 2005. 30p. (J). (gr. k-4). reprint ed. 19.00 (978-0-7567-9420-0(X)) DIANE Publishing Co.

Glass, Calliope. Disney Tails Figaro's Halloween Surprise. Disney Storybook Art Team, illus. 2015. (Disney Tails Ser.). (ENG.). 10p. (J). (gr. -1 — 1). bds. 6.99 (978-1-4847-1372-3(9), 1392357) Disney Pr.

—Disney Tails We Love Marie. Disney Storybook Art Team, illus. 2015. (Disney Tails Ser.). (ENG.). 10p. (J). (gr. -1 — 1). bds. 6.99 (978-1-4847-1373-0(7)) Disney Pr.

Gleasner, Diana C. Popoki, the Hawaiian Cat: An Amazing Adventure with the Whale. Winton, Andrea Evans, illus. 2004. (J). (978-0-9651185-7-6(6)) Gleasner, Bill & Diana Inc.

Glessner, Gordon. Water Wars, Secrets Revealed. 2012. 24p. 12.00 (978-0-9859603-0-8(2)) Laughing Rhino Bks.

Glover, Darryl. The Pirate Kitty. Austin, Britta, ed. Kosir, Ana, illus. 2008. 24p. (J). 16.95 (978-0-9821387-0-0(9)) MagicStar Inc.

Glover, Dennis W. The Cat in the Woods. 2010. 20p. pap. 10.49 (978-1-4389-8492-6(8)) AuthorHouse.

Go, Wildcats! 2009. 24p. pap. 3.99 (978-1-4231-2273-9(9)) Disney Pr.

Gobo Books, creator. My Magnetic Shapes & Colors: Flo & Zip's Busy Day. 2007. (Magnix Learning Fun Ser.). (Illus.). 8p. (J). (gr. -1-3). bds. 9.95 (978-1-932915-38-9(9)) Sandvik Innovations, LLC.

Godwin, Laura. One Moon, Two Cats. Tanaka, Yoko, illus. 2011. (ENG.). 32p. (J). (gr. -1-1). 16.99 (978-1-4424-1202-6(X), Atheneum Bks. for Young Readers) Simon & Schuster Children's Publishing.

Goebel, Jenny. Fortune Falls. (ENG.). 208p. (J). (gr. 3-7). 2017. pap. 6.99 **(978-1-338-13470-4(1))** 2016. 16.99 (978-0-545-81190-3(2), Scholastic Pr.) Scholastic, Inc.

Goguen, Martha. Sissy Goes to Washington. Fowler, Faith, illus. 2013. 36p. pap. (978-1-897435-59-5(2)) Agio Publishing Hse.

Going, K. L. Dog in Charge. Santat, Dan, illus. 2012. (ENG.). 40p. (J). (gr. -1-k). 16.99 (978-0-8037-3479-1(4), Dial Bks) Penguin Young Readers Group.

Goldberg, Whoopi. Sugar Plum to the Rescue! Roos, Maryn, illus. 2011. (ENG.). 160p. (J). (gr. 1-5). pap. 4.99 (978-0-7868-5264-2(X), Jump at the Sun) Hyperion Bks. for Children.

Golden Books. From Army Ants to Zebrafish: Animals That Hop, Fly & Swish! (Dr. Seuss/Cat in the Hat) Ruiz, Aristides, illus. 2013. (Deluxe Stickerific Ser.). (ENG.). 64p. (J). (gr. -1-2). pap. 5.99 (978-0-449-81432-1(7), Golden Bks.) Random Hse. Children's Bks.

—Happy Holi-Doodles! Moroney, Christopher, illus. 2012. (Doodle Book Ser.). (ENG.). 128p. (J). (gr. -1-2). pap. 5.99 (978-0-307-93198-6(6), Golden Bks.) Random Hse. Children's Bks.

—The Little Grumpy Cat That Wouldn't (Grumpy Cat) Golden Books, illus. 2016. (Little Golden Book Ser.). (ENG., Illus.). 24p. (J). (gr. -1-1). 4.99 (978-0-399-55354-7(1), Golden Bks.) Random Hse. Children's Bks.

—My Book of Kittens. 2016. (Little Golden Book Ser.). (ENG., Illus.). 24p. (J). (gr. -1-k). 4.99 (978-0-553-53919-6(1), Golden Bks.) Random Hse. Children's Bks.

Golden Books. Puss in Boots. Nedelcu, Ovi, illus. 2017. (Little Golden Book Ser.). (ENG.). 24p. (J). (-k). 4.99 **(978-1-5247-6766-2(2)**, Golden Bks.) Random Hse. Children's Bks.

Golden Books Staff. The Itty-Bitty Kitty Rescue (Paw Patrol) Golden Books Staff & Petrossi, Fabrizio, illus. 2014. (Little Golden Book Ser.). (ENG.). 24p. (J). (-k). 4.99 (978-0-553-50884-0(9), Golden Bks.) Random Hse. Children's Bks.

—Oh, the Things Spring Brings! Ruiz, Aristides, illus. 2013. (Color Plus Stencil Ser.). (ENG.). 64p. (J). (-k). pap. 5.99 (978-0-307-98123-3(1), Golden Bks.) Random Hse. Children's Bks.

—Pat the Bunny: At the Apple Orchard. Vilela, Luiz, illus. 2015. (ENG.). 24p. (J). (— 1). bds. 6.99 (978-0-553-51205-2(6), Golden Bks.) Random Hse. Children's Bks.

Goldsberry, Booty. Scaredy-Cat, I'm Not. 2007. (ENG., Illus.). 40p. (gr. 4-7). pap. 9.95 (978-0-9792875-0-3(2)) Goldsberry, Booty.

Gollub, Matthew. The Twenty-Five Mixtec Cats. Martinez, Leovigildo, illus. 2004. (J). 32p. pap. 6.95 (978-1-889910-29-1(5)); (978-1-889910-30-7(9)) Tortuga Pr.

Gollub, Matthew W. The Twenty-five Mixtec Cats. Martinez, Leovigildo, illus. rev. ed. 2004. 32p. (J). 15.95 (978-1-889910-28-4(7)) Tortuga Pr.

Gomez, Rebecca. Happy Easter, Hello Kitty! 2005. (Illus.). 32p. (978-0-439-67637-3(1)) Scholastic, Inc.

Goodhart, Pippa. Big Cat. 2011. (Tadpoles Ser.: No. 28). (ENG., Illus.). 24p. (J). (gr. k-3). pap. (978-0-7787-0585-7(4)) Crabtree Publishing Co.

—Fire Cat. 2005. (Red Go Bananas Ser.). (ENG., Illus.). 48p. (J). (gr. 2-3). lib. bdg. (978-0-7787-2675-3(4)) Crabtree Publishing Co.

Gopigian, Susan Kadian. Gadoo the Cat: An Armenian Folktale. Bolt, Susan Collier, illus. 2008. 39p. 16.95 (978-0-9801453-0-4(9)) Wayne State Univ. Pr.

Gorbachev, Valeri. The Best Cat. Gorbachev, Valeri, illus. 2010. (ENG., Illus.). 32p. (J). (gr. -1-2). 15.99 (978-0-7636-3675-3(4)) Candlewick Pr.

—Cats Are Cats. Gorbachev, Valeri, illus. 2014. (ENG., Illus.). 32p. (J). (gr. -1-3). 16.95 (978-0-8234-3052-9(9)) Holiday Hse., Inc.

—Catty Jane Who Hated the Rain. Gorbachev, Valeri, illus. 2012. (ENG., Illus.). 32p. (J). (gr. -1-3). 16.95 (978-1-59078-700-7(5)) Boyds Mills Pr.

Gordon, Danielle. Garage Cat. 2012. (ENG.). pap. (978-1-4675-1344-9(X)) Independent Pub.

Gordon, Judy Ann. Grammie's Magical Garden: Beyond the Gate. 2012. 68p. pap. 28.99 (978-1-4772-7973-1(3)) AuthorHouse.

Gordon, Sylvia. Further Adventures of the Potty Wizard & His Cat, Muddles. 2009. (Illus.). 60p. pap. 10.49 (978-1-4389-6819-3(1)) AuthorHouse.

Gorey, Edward & Chess, Victoria. Fletcher & Zenobia. Chess, Victoria, illus. 2016. (ENG., Illus.). 72p. (J). (gr. k-2). 14.95 (978-1-59017-963-5(3), NYR Children's Collection) New York Review of Bks., Inc., The.

Gottesfeld, Jeff. The Cat Whisperer, 1 vol. 2015. (Red Rhino Ser.). (ENG.). 72p. (J). (gr. 3-6). mass mkt. 7.95 (978-1-62250-955-3(2)) Saddleback Educational Publishing, Inc.

Grabo, Carl. The Cat in Grandfather's House. 2008. 120p. 23.95 (978-1-60664-842-1(X)); pap. 10.95 (978-1-60664-087-6(9)) Aegypan.

Graham-Barber, Lynda. KokoCat, Inside & Out. Lane, Nancy, illus. 2012. (ENG.). 24p. (J). (gr. k). 16.95 (978-0-940719-12-5(6)) Gryphon Pr., The.

Grant, Jacob. Cat Knit. 2016. (ENG., Illus.). 40p. (J). 16.99 (978-1-250-05150-9(9), 9781250051509) Feiwel & Friends.

Grant, Joan. Cat & Fish. Curtis, Neil, illus. 2005. (ENG.). 32p. (J). (gr. k-3). 16.95 (978-1-894965-14-9(0)) Simply Read Bks. CAN. Dist: Ingram Publisher Services.

—Cat & Fish Go to See. Curtis, Neil, illus. 2006. (ENG.). 32p. (J). (gr. -1-3). 16.95 (978-1-894965-39-2(6)) Simply Read Bks. CAN. Dist: Ingram Publisher Services.

Gravdahl, John. Curious Catwalk. 2003. (Illus.). (J). (gr. k-5). 16.95 (978-0-9678577-8-7(3)) Propeller Pr.

Graves, Damien. The Cat Lady. 2007. (Midnight Library). (Illus.). 168p. (J). (gr. 4-7). 13.65 (978-0-7569-8324-6(X)) Perfection Learning Corp.

Gravett, Emily. Matilda's Cat. Gravett, Emily, illus. 2014. (ENG., Illus.). 32p. (J). (gr. -1-3). 16.99 (978-1-4424-7527-4(7), Simon & Schuster Bks. For Young Readers) Simon & Schuster Bks. For Young Readers.

Gray, Amy. It's Good to Give. 2011. 28p. pap. 15.99 (978-1-4653-3670-5(2)) Xlibris Corp.

Gray, Jennifer. Atticus Claw on the Misty Moor. Ecob, Mark, illus. 2017. (Atticus Claw Ser.). (ENG.). 256p. (gr. 1-4). 7.95 (978-0-571-31710-3(3)) Faber & Faber, Inc.

Gray, Kes. Daisy & the Trouble with Kittens. Sharratt, Nick & Parsons, Garry, illus. 2010. (Daisy Ser.). (ENG.). 256p. (J). (gr. 2-4). pap. 11.99 (978-1-86230-834-3(9), Red Fox) Random House Children's Books GBR. Dist: Independent Pubs. Group.

—Frog on a Log? Field, Jim, illus. 2015. (ENG.). 32p. (J). (gr. -1-k). 16.99 (978-0-545-68791-1(8), Scholastic Pr.) Scholastic, Inc.

Gray, Shelly. A Cat Called Spot. 2011. 24p. pap. 24.95 (978-1-4626-0346-6(7)) America Star Bks.

Graziani, Maria. A Black Cat on Halloween: Un Gato Negro en Dia de Brujas. Elejalde, Eliana, illus. l.t. ed. 2004. (SPA.). 23p. (J). 7.00 (978-0-9762361-1-5(7)) Ed. Acespanish S.A.C.- Lima, Peru.

Green, Jonathan, illus. Amadeus, the Leghorn Rooster. 2004. (J). 17.95 (978-0-87844-174-7(3)) Sandlapper Publishing Co., Inc.

Green, Teri & Taylor, Sue. The Littlest Soldier, 1 vol. 2009. 94p. pap. 19.95 (978-1-4489-2714-2(5)) America Star Bks.

Greene, Carol. The Cat & the Bear. 2005. 32p. (J). pap. (978-0-7868-1175-5(7)) Hyperion Bks. for Children.

Griffiths, Andy. The Cat, the Rat, & the Baseball Bat. Denton, Terry, illus. 2013. (My Readers Ser.). (ENG.). 32p. (J). (gr. -1-1). pap. 3.99 (978-1-250-02774-0(8), 9781250027740) Square Fish.

Grime, L. L. The Make up Story. 2007. 36p. 17.50 (978-1-4357-0585-2(8)) Lulu Pr., Inc.

Grinti, Mike & Grinti, Rachel. Claws. 2012. (J). (978-0-545-43314-3(2)); (ENG.). 256p. (gr. 5-9). 16.99 (978-0-545-43313-6(4)) Scholastic, Inc. (Chicken Hse., The).

Groce, Michelle. Jasper. Duis, Laura, illus. 2003. 174p. (J). 17.95 (978-0-9708972-6-8(X)) Novello Festival Pr.

Grogan, John. Marley & the Kittens. Cowdrey, Richard, illus. 2010. (Marley Ser.). 40p. (J). (gr. -1-3). (ENG.). 17.99 (978-0-06-171486-3(0)); lib. bdg. 18.89 (978-0-06-171487-0(9)) HarperCollins Pubs.

—Marley Learns a Lesson. Cowdrey, Richard, illus. 2013. (I Can Read Level 2 Ser.). (ENG.). 32p. (J). (gr. -1-3). 16.99 (978-0-06-207487-4(3)) HarperCollins Pubs.

Group/McGraw-Hill, Wright. The Klutzy Cat: Level N, 6 vols. 128p. (gr. 3-6). 36.95 (978-0-322-05882-8(1)) Wright Group/McGraw-Hill.

Gudeon, Adam. Me & Meow. Gudeon, Adam, illus. 2011. (ENG., Illus.). 32p. (J). (gr. -1-k). 12.99 (978-0-06-199821-8(4)) HarperCollins Pubs.

Guibert, Emmanuel. A Nasty Cat. 2015. (Ariol Ser.: 6). (J). lib. bdg. 24.50 (978-0-606-36453-9(6)) Turtleback Bks.

Guillain, Charlotte. Cat & the Beanstalk, 1 vol. Beacon, Dawn, illus. 2014. (Animal Fairy Tales Ser.). (ENG.). 24p. (gr. 1-2). lib. bdg. 23.99 (978-1-4109-6113-6(3), NA-r) Heinemann-Raintree.

—The Kitten Who Cried Dog, 1 vol. Beacon, Dawn, illus. 2013. (Animal Fairy Tales Ser.). (ENG.). 24p. (gr. -1-2). pap. 6.49 (978-1-4109-5029-1(8)); lib. bdg. 23.99 (978-1-4109-5023-9(9)) Heinemann-Raintree. (NA-r).

—Ratpunzel, 1 vol. Beacon, Dawn, illus. 2014. (Animal Fairy Tales Ser.). (ENG.). 24p. (gr. 1-2). lib. bdg. 23.99 (978-1-4109-6112-9(5), NA-r) Heinemann-Raintree.

Guillain, Charlotte & Aesop. The Kitten Who Cried Dog. Beacon, Dawn, illus. 2013. (Animal Fairy Tales Ser.). (ENG.). 24p. (gr. -1-2). 26.00 (978-1-4109-5041-3(7), NA-r) Heinemann-Raintree.

Guin, Anatoly. Smart Tales from Brainy the Cat. 2010. 84p. pap. 29.95 (978-1-4327-6147-9(1)) Outskirts Pr., Inc.

Gulack, Robin. Root Beer Cats. 2009. 28p. pap. 15.49 (978-1-4343-9628-0(2)) AuthorHouse.

Hacker, Erin. Harley's Tale. 2011. 48p. pap. 24.95 (978-1-4560-4063-5(4)) America Star Bks.

Hahn, Mary Downing. Witch Catcher. (ENG.). 240p. (J). (gr. 5-7). 2011. pap. 7.99 (978-0-547-57714-2(1)) 2006. (Illus.). 16.00 (978-0-618-50457-2(5)) Houghton Mifflin Harcourt Publishing Co.

Haig, Matt. To Be a Cat. Curtis, Stacy, illus. (ENG.). 304p. (J). (gr. 3-7). 2014. pap. 8.99 (978-1-4424-5406-4(7)) 2013. 16.99 (978-1-4424-5405-7(9)) Simon & Schuster Children's Publishing.

Haines, Genny, illus. Five Cute Kittens. 2016. (ENG.). 10p. (J). (gr. -1 — 1). bds. 8.99 (978-1-4998-0218-4(8)) Little Bee Books Inc.

Hale, Bruce. Fat Cat of Underwhere. Hillman, Shane, illus. 2009. (Underwhere Ser.). 176p. (J). pap. 5.99 (978-0-06-085135-4(X)) HarperCollins Pubs.

—Pirates of Underwhere. Hillman, Shane, illus. (Underwhere Ser.: 2). (J). (gr. 3-7). 2009. (ENG.). 176p. pap. 6.99 (978-0-06-085129-3(5)) 2008. 164p. lib. bdg. 16.89 (978-0-06-085128-6(7)) HarperCollins Pubs.

—Prince of Underwhere. Hillman, Shane, illus. 2009. (Underwhere Ser.: 1). (ENG.). 176p. (J). (gr. 3-7). pap. 5.99 (978-0-06-085126-2(0)) HarperCollins Pubs.

Hall, Caroline V. Rhett & Abby: Abby's New Home. 2011. 40p. pap. 15.95 (978-1-4497-1887-9(6), WestBow Pr.) Author Solutions, Inc.

Hall, Michael. Cat Tale. Hall, Michael, illus. 2012. (ENG., Illus.). 40p. (J). (gr. -1-k). 16.99 (978-0-06-191516-1(5), Greenwillow Bks.) HarperCollins Pubs.

Hall, Raelene. The New Puppy. Collier, Kevin Scott & LeBlanc, Giselle, illus. 2013. 16p. pap. 9.95 (978-1-61633-415-4(0)) Guardian Angel Publishing, Inc.

Halstead, Jayce N. The True Legend of White Crow: Adventures of the Fudge Sisters. Twomey-Lange, Marianna, photos by. 2004. (Illus.). 80p. (J). per. 7.95 (978-0-9749046-3-4(5)) Aarow Pr.

Hamilton, Elizabeth L. Christopher Cat's Character Club. 2003. (Character Critters Ser.: No. 1). (Illus.). 32p. (J). (gr. -1-3). per. 5.95 (978-0-9713749-2-8(9), Character-in-Action) Quiet Impact, Inc.

Hamilton, Pat. Peaches the Private Eye Poodle: The Missing Muffin Caper. 2008. 32p. pap. 13.50 (978-1-60693-277-3(2), Eloquent Bks.) Strategic Book Publishing & Rights Agency (SBPRA).

Hamilton, S. J. The Cat's Eye View. 2012. 186p. pap. 24.95 (978-1-4626-6056-8(8)) America Star Bks.

Hancocks, Helen. Penguin in Peril. Hancocks, Helen, illus. 2014. (ENG., Illus.). 32p. (J). (gr. -1-2). 15.99 (978-0-7636-7159-4(2), Templar) Candlewick Pr.

Hanes, Rosann. Diamond H Ranch: Told by: Val - Loyal Ranch Dog. 2010. 28p. pap. 13.99 (978-1-4490-7714-3(5)) AuthorHouse.

Hannam, John-Pierre M., Sr. Uncle Jake's Hat. 2009. 43p. pap. 20.00 (978-0-557-02568-8(0)) Lulu Pr., Inc.

Hannan, Peter. Petlandia. Hannan, Peter, illus. 2015. (ENG., Illus.). 144p. (J). (gr. 2-5). 8.99 (978-0-545-16211-1(4), Scholastic Pr.) Scholastic, Inc.

Hansen, Kate. Spike the Sewer Cat. Illustrations byVoigt, Karen S., illus. 2008. 27p. pap. 24.95 (978-1-60474-094-3(9)) America Star Bks.

Hansen, Roland. Tim the Cat. Jackson, Brittany Janay, illus. 2008. (ARA.). 28p. per. 8.85 (978-0-9814650-0-5(5)) G Publishing LLC.

—Tim the Cat. 2007. (Illus.). 28p. (J). 8.95 (978-0-9796978-0-7(8)) G Publishing LLC.

Hanson, Mary. How to Save Your Tail: If You Are a Rat Nabbed by Cats Who Really Like Stories about Magic Spoons, Wolves with Snout-Warts, Big, Hairy Chimney Trolls ... & Cookies, Too. 2008. (ENG., Illus.). 112p. (J). (gr. 1-4). 5.99 (978-0-440-42228-0(0), Yearling) Random Hse. Children's Bks.

Hapka, Catherine, pseud. No Time for Hallie. Regan, Dana, illus. 2015. (Pet Rescue Club Ser.: 2). (ENG.). 128p. (J). (gr. 1-3). lib. bdg. 16.99 (978-0-7944-3352-9(9)) Reader's Digest Assn., Inc., The.

—No Time for Hallie. Regan, Dana, illus. 2015. (Pet Rescue Club Ser.: 2). (ENG.). 128p. (J). (gr. 1-3). pap. 5.99 (978-0-7944-3313-0(8)) Studio Fun International.

Happel-Holtz, Ruby H. Kool Kat Charlie of Cocoa Beach. 2011. 72p. pap. (978-1-4269-9484-5(2)) Trafford Publishing (UK) Ltd.

The Happy Tale of Two Cats. 2012. 38p. pap. 12.95 (978-0-9853752-1-8(3)) Pet Pundit Publishing.

Harder, Linda Janet. Kittens in the Classroom. 2011. 40p. (gr. -1). pap. 16.59 (978-1-4567-6414-2(4)) AuthorHouse.

Harnett, Katie, illus. Archie Snufflekins Oliver Valentine Cupcake Tiberius Cat. 2016. (ENG.). 32p. (J). (gr. -1-k). 16.95 (978-1-909263-37-6(0)) Flying Eye Bks. GBR. Dist: Consortium Bk. Sales & Distribution.

Harpan, Gaile. The Ballad of Calvin the Cat. Reddy, Sneha, illus. 2008. 24p. pap. 12.95 (978-0-9817572-6-1(X)) Peppertree Pr., The.

—The Ballad of Omar the Cat. Reddy, Sneha, illus. 2008. 28p. pap. 12.95 (978-0-9820479-1-0(6)) Peppertree Pr., The.

—The Ballad of Snowball the Cat. Reddy, Sneha, illus. 2009. 24p. pap. 12.95 (978-1-936051-25-0(7)) Peppertree Pr., The.

—The Ballad of Victor the Cat. Reddy, Sneha, illus. 2008. 20p. pap. 12.95 (978-0-9814894-4-5(3)) Peppertree Pr., The.

Harper, Anita. It's Not Fair. McQuillan, Mary, illus. 2007. (ENG.). 32p. (J). (gr. -1-3). 16.95 (978-0-8234-2094-0(9)) Holiday Hse., Inc.

Harper, Charise Mericle. Crafty Cat. 2017. (Crafty Cat Ser.: 1). (ENG., Illus.). 128p. (J). 13.99 (978-1-62672-486-0(5), 9781626724860, First Second Bks.) Roaring Brook Pr.

—Just Grace. 2008. (Just Grace Ser.: 1). (ENG., Illus.). 144p. (J). (gr. 1-4). pap. 5.99 (978-0-547-01440-1(6)) Houghton Mifflin Harcourt Publishing Co.

Harper, Eleanor. Honey & Harebell. 2010. 64p. pap. 11.95 (978-0-9818092-7-4(8)) Illumina Publishing.

Harries, Tony. Zeegpaw & the Cat Cult. 2008. 304p. pap. 18.95 (978-1-4357-0754-2(0)) Lulu Pr., Inc.

Harris, David. Pussy Footin' 2010. 190p. pap. 26.50 (978-1-4457-8092-4(5)) Lulu Pr., Inc.

Harris, Marian. Ten Little Kittens. Harris, Jim, illus. 2010. (ENG.). 28p. (J). (gr. k). 15.99 *(978-0-7407-9197-0(4))* Andrews McMeel Publishing.

Harris, Marian & Harris, Jim. Ten Little Kittens. 2011. (ENG., Illus.). 26p. (J). (gr. -1-k). bds. 9.99 *(978-1-4494-0175-7(9))* Andrews McMeel Publishing.

Harris, Patricia. The Cat & the Dog. 2017. (Farmyard Tales Ser.). 24p. (gr. 4-6). pap. 8.25 ***(978-1-5383-2178-2(5)***, PowerKids Pr.) Rosen Publishing Group, Inc., The.

Harris, Rita & Long, Paul. The 19 Cats of Alabama. 2004. (ENG.). 35p. 24.95 *(978-1-4137-3006-7(X))* America Star Bks.

Harris, Trudy. Tally Cat Keeps Track. Harris, Andrew, illus. 2010. (Math Is Fun! Ser.). (ENG.). 32p. (gr. k-2). lib. bdg. 22.60 *(978-0-7613-4451-3(9)*, Millbrook Pr.) Lerner Publishing Group.

Harrison, Hannah E. Bernice Gets Carried Away. 2015. (ENG., Illus.). 32p. (J). (gr. -1-k). 16.99 *(978-0-8037-3916-1(8)*, Dial Bks) Penguin Young Readers Group.

Harrison, Marie P. Sir Jack Cat & Friends. 2007. 50p. pap. 16.95 *(978-1-4241-6577-3(6))* America Star Bks.

Harrison, Megan Bernadette. The Adventures of Kitty Tom & Blossom: Book One. 2009. 36p. pap. 24.95 *(978-1-60749-257-3(1))* America Star Bks.

Harrison, Paul. The Elves Help Puss in Boots. Sutcliffe, Tim, illus. 2016. (Fairy Tale Mix-Ups Ser.). (ENG.). 24p. (gr. k-2). lib. bdg. 23.32 *(978-1-4109-8303-9(X))* Heinemann-Raintree.

Hart, Charlie. Once upon a Time in Elmore: the Story Behind the Watterson House. Johnson, Shane L., illus. 2016. (Amazing World of Gumball Ser.). (ENG.). 80p. (J). (gr. 3-7). 5.99 *(978-0-8431-8346-7(2)*, Cartoon Network Books) Penguin Young Readers Group.

Hartmann, Jennifer. Kristofur Kitty: Crossing the Street. 2003. (J). pap. 8.00 *(978-0-8059-5388-6(4))* Dorrance Publishing Co., Inc.

Hartwell, Joe. Hunted Down. 2005. 204p. pap. 14.95 *(978-1-4208-1841-3(4))* AuthorHouse.

Harvey, Jayne. Cat Show. Petrosino, Tamara, illus. 2003. (Penguin Young Readers, Level 2 Ser.). (ENG.). 32p. (J). (gr. 1-2). mass mkt. 3.99 *(978-0-448-43112-3(2)*, Penguin Young Readers) Penguin Young Readers Group.

Harvey, Keith. Tiberius Meets Sneaky Cat. Hickman, Paula, illus. 2010. (Tiberius Tales Ser.). 24p. (J). (gr. -1-2). pap. 8.15 *(978-1-60754-835-5(6))*; lib. bdg. 22.60 *(978-1-60754-831-7(3))* Windmill Bks.

Hasbro & O'Ryan, Ellie. Littlest Pet Shop - Terriers & Tiara Reunion: Starring Zoe Trent! 2015. (ENG.). 160p. (J). (gr. 3-7). pap. 5.99 *(978-0-316-30136-7(1))* Little, Brown Bks. for Young Readers.

Hawkins, Wanda. Geronimo Discovers Faith. 2007. (Illus.). 24p. (J). per. 12.99 *(978-1-59879-336-9(5))* Lifevest Publishing, Inc.

Haworth, Margaret. Jarry, Garry Palas: Cat Tail Stories. Haworth, Margaret, photos by. l.t. ed. 2003. (Books That Help Ser.: Vol. 3). (Illus.). 34p. (J). (gr. 1-6). pap. 9.95 *(978-0-9740313-5-4(6))* Haworth, Margaret.

—Oh Holly Dallig: Cat Tail Stories. Haworth, Margaret, photos by. l.t. ed. 2003. (Books That Help Ser.: Vol. 3). (Illus.). 34p. (J). (gr. 1-6). pap. 9.95 *(978-0-9740313-4-7(8))* Haworth, Margaret.

Hay, Sam. Revenge of the Phantom Furball. Cooper, Simon, illus. 2014. (Undead Pets Ser.: 2). (ENG.). 112p. (J). (gr. 1-3). 5.99 *(978-0-448-47796-1(3)*, Grosset & Dunlap) Penguin Young Readers Group.

Hayatian, MaryAnn. Cookie, a cat's Tale. 2010. 32p. pap. 20.00 *(978-0-557-70819-2(2))* Lulu Pr., Inc.

Haydel, Catherine. Uno the Cat & Hurricane Katrina. 2006. 18.00 *(978-0-8059-7341-9(9))* Dorrance Publishing Co., Inc.

Haynes, Natalie. The Great Escape. 2014. (ENG.). 288p. (J). pap. 8.99 *(978-1-4711-2184-5(4)*, Simon & Schuster Children's) Simon & Schuster, Ltd. GBR. Dist: Simon & Schuster, Inc.

HB Staff. Davy Crockett & the Wild Cat. 97th ed. 2003. (Signatures Ser.). (gr. 1-18). pap. 19.20 *(978-0-15-308172-9(4))* Harcourt Schl. Pubs.

—Every Cat. 97th ed. 2003. (Signatures Ser.). (gr. 1-18). pap. 19.20 *(978-0-15-308173-6(2))* Harcourt Schl. Pubs.

Head, Mat. Warduff & the Corn Cob Caper. Head, Mat, illus. 2011. (Andersen Press Picture Books Ser.). (Illus.). 16.95 *(978-0-7613-8095-5(7))* Andersen Pr. GBR. Dist: Lerner Publishing Group.

Hearn, Michael Patrick. The Porcelain Cat. Dillon, Leo & Dillon, Diane, illus. 2004. (ENG.). 32p. (J). (gr. 4-7). 16.95 *(978-1-59687-175-5(X))* IBks., Inc.

—The Porcelain Cat. Dillon, Leo & Dillon, Diane, illus. 2004. 32p. (J). (gr. -1). 16.95 *(978-0-689-03592-0(6)*, Milk & Cookies) ibooks, Inc.

Heflick, LaMonte. The Story of Ninja Cat. 2004. 64p. pap. 3.99 *(978-1-56175-905-7(8))* Remedia Pubns.

Hegarty, Patricia. Five Black Cats. Woolf, Julia, illus. 2013. (ENG.). 22p. (J). (gr. -1). bds. 8.95 *(978-1-58925-611-8(5))* Tiger Tales.

Heiden, Gina. Zippy, Lolly & Surfer Dude. 2009. 28p. pap. 16.50 *(978-1-60693-172-1(5)*, Eloquent Bks.) Strategic Book Publishing & Rights Agency (SBPRA).

Heimerl, Kristen. Inspector Dewey. 2015. (ENG., Illus.). (J). 19.99 *(978-1-939710-27-7(8))* Orange Frazer Pr.

Heinz, Brian J. The Barnyard Cat. l.t. ed. 2003. (Illus.). 32p. (J). pap. 6.96 *(978-0-936335-07-0(6))* Ballyhoo BookWorks, Inc.

Hello Kitty: Fashion Music Wonderland. 2015. (ENG.). 48p. (J). pap. 6.99 *(978-1-4215-5903-2(X))* Viz Media.

Helmer, Marilyn. Fog Cat. 2004. (Illus.). (J). (gr. k-3). spiral bd. *(978-0-616-03039-4(8))* Canadian National Institute for the Blind/Institut National Canadien pour les Aveugles.

—Sharing Snowy, 1 vol. Charko, Kasia, illus. 2008. (Orca Echoes Ser.). (ENG.). 64p. (J). (gr. 2-3). pap. 6.95 *(978-1-55469-021-3(8))* Orca Bk. Pubs. USA.

Hench, Larry. Boing-Boing the Bionic Cat & the Jewel Thief. Steed, Tobias, ed. Lear, Ruth, illus. 2004. (Boing-Boing the Bionic Cat Ser.: 2). (ENG.). 60p. (J). (gr. 2-4). pap. 7.99 *(978-1-904872-01-6(8)*, Can of Worms Kids Pr.) Can of Worms Pr. GBR. Dist: Independent Pubs. Group.

—Boing-Boing the Bionic Cat & the Space Station. Morgan-Jones, Tom, illus. 2011. (Boing-Boing the Bionic Cat Ser.: 5). (ENG.). 96p. (J). (gr. 2-4). pap. 8.99 *(978-1-904872-07-8(7)*, Can of Worms Kids Pr.) Can of Worms Pr. GBR. Dist: Independent Pubs. Group.

Henderson, Kathy. Tabby Cat's Secret. 2003. (Illus.). 36p. pap. *(978-0-7112-1883-3(8))* ReiseArt Buchhandlung GmbH.

Henderson, Virginia. Zippy the Dreamer. 2010. 20p. 13.77 *(978-1-4269-3448-3(3))* Trafford Publishing.

Henkes, Kevin. Kitten's First Full Moon. Henkes, Kevin, illus. 2004. (ENG., Illus.). 40p. (J). (gr. -1-3). 17.99 *(978-0-06-058828-1(4)*, Greenwillow Bks.) HarperCollins Pubs.

—La Primera Luna Llena de Gatita, 1 vol. Henkes, Kevin, illus. 2006. Orig. Title: Kitten's First Full Moon. (SPA., Illus.). 40p. (J). (gr. -1-2). 17.99 *(978-0-06-087223-6(3))* HarperCollins Pubs.

Henley, Ivan. Kitty Milo Says the Alphabet (A Read-Aloud Book for Children) 2008. 68p. pap. 34.50 *(978-1-4357-1423-6(7))* Lulu Pr., Inc.

Henrichs, Wendy. I Am Tama, Lucky Cat: A Japanese Legend, 1 vol. Jaeggi, Yoshiko, illus. (ENG.). 32p. (J). (gr. k-3). 2016. pap. 7.95 *(978-1-56145-916-2(X))* 2011. 16.95 *(978-1-56145-589-8(X)*, Peachtree Junior) Peachtree Pubs.

Henry, Marguerite. Benjamin West & His Cat Grimalkin. Dennis, Wesley, illus. 2014. (ENG.). 160p. (J). (gr. 3-7). pap. 7.99 *(978-1-4814-0394-8(X)*, Aladdin) Simon & Schuster Children's Publishing.

—The Marguerite Henry Complete Collection: Benjamin West & His Cat Grimalkin; Black Gold; Born to Trot; Brighty; Brown Sunshine; Cinnabar; Gaudenzia; Justin Morgan; King of the Wind; Misty of Chincoteague; Misty's Twilight; Mustang; Sea Star; Stormy; San Domingo; White Stallion of Lipizza. 2014. (ENG., Illus.). 3056p. (J). (gr. 3-7). pap. 99.99 *(978-1-4814-2299-4(5)*, Simon & Schuster/Paula Wiseman Bks.) Simon & Schuster/Paula Wiseman Bks.

Henry, Steve. Cat Got a Lot. 2015. (I Like to Read(r) Ser.). (ENG., Illus.). 24p. (J). (gr. -1-2). 14.95 *(978-0-8234-3385-8(4))* Holiday Hse., Inc.

—Happy Cat. Henry, Steve, illus. 2014. (I Like to Read(r) Ser.). (ENG., Illus.). 24p. (J). (gr. -1-3). 6.99 *(978-0-8234-3177-9(0))* Holiday Hse., Inc.

—Happy Cat. 2013. (I Like to Read(r) Ser.). (ENG., Illus.). 24p. (J). (gr. -1-3). 14.95 *(978-0-8234-2659-1(9))* Holiday Hse., Inc.

Henry, T. K. Rickey & Rachel, the Cats without Tails & Their Awesome Adventure. 2007. 40p. (J). pap. 8.00 *(978-0-8059-7224-5(2))* Dorrance Publishing Co., Inc.

Hesse, Karen. The Cats in Krasinski Square. Watson, Wendy, illus. 2004. (ENG.). 32p. (J). (gr. 2-5). 18.99 *(978-0-439-43540-6(4)*, Scholastic Pr.) Scholastic, Inc.

Hewett, Katherine. Magic Bubble Bath. 2012. 40p. pap. 25.10 *(978-0-578-09202-7(6))* Hewett, Katherine J.E.

Hickman, B. Jo. Old Cat, Fat Rat, & Boo. 2011. 28p. pap. 15.99 *(978-1-4653-3615-6(X))* Xlibris Corp.

Hiebert, Elfrieda H. & Juel, Connie. The Cat That Broke the Rules. (Little Book Practice Reader Ser.). (J). *(978-0-8136-0967-6(4))* Modern Curriculum Pr.

—That Cat. (Little Book Practice Reader Ser.). (J). *(978-0-8136-0941-6(0))* Modern Curriculum Pr.

Hietpas, Polly. Hello Rosie Cat. 2009. 16p. pap. 8.49 *(978-1-4490-0283-1(8))* AuthorHouse.

—Rosie Cat's Bad Fur Day. 2009. 20p. pap. 10.49 *(978-1-4490-0777-5(5))* AuthorHouse.

Hiiragi, Aoi. Baron: The Cat Returns. Hiiragi, Aoi, illus. 2005. (Baron Ser.). (ENG., Illus.). 224p. pap. 9.99 *(978-1-59116-956-7(9))* Viz Media.

Hileman, Jane & Pitt, Marilyn. Come with Me. Bianchi, John, illus. 2011. (Power 50 - Potato Chip Bks). 12p. pap. 33.92 *(978-1-61541-163-4(1))* American Reading Co.

—Home Alone. Bianchi, John, illus. 2011. (Power 50 - Potato Chip Bks). 12p. pap. 33.92 *(978-1-61541-408-6(8))* American Reading Co.

Hill, Karen. Cat Tails. 2010. 24p. 14.99 *(978-1-4567-0049-2(9))* AuthorHouse.

Hill, Merle Roddy. Kitty Goes Splash. Diez-Luckie, Cathy, illus. 2005. (ENG.). 12p. (J). 5.75 *(978-1-57274-823-1(0)*, 2171, Bks. for Young Learners) Owen, Richard C. Pubs., Inc.

Hillert, Margaret. The Little Runaway. Dumm, Brian, illus. 2016. (BeginningtoRead Ser.). (ENG.). 32p. (J). (gr. -1-2). pap. 11.94 *(978-1-60357-942-1(7))*; (gr. k-2). 22.60 *(978-1-59953-801-3(6))* Norwood Hse. Pr.

—The No-Tail Cat or, I Like What I Am: For the Earliest Reader, 5 bks. Starfall Education, illus. 2005. (ENG.). 32p. (J). 6.95 *(978-1-59577-024-0(0))*; pap. *(978-1-59577-025-7(9))* Starfall Education.

Hillert, Margaret. Who Feels Happy, Dear Dragon? Pullan, Jack, illus. 2017. (BeginningtoRead Ser.). (ENG.). 32p. (J). (-2). 22.60 ***(978-1-59953-824-2(5))***; pap. 11.94 ***(978-1-68404-002-5(7))*** Norwood Hse. Pr.

Himmelman, John. Katie Loves the Kittens. Himmelman, John, illus. 2008. (ENG., Illus.). 32p. (J). (gr. -1-3). 18.99 *(978-0-8050-8682-9(X)*, 9780805086829, Holt, Henry & Co. Bks. For Young Readers) Holt, Henry & Co.

Hinkes, Enid. Police Cat. 2015. (Illus.). 32p. (J). *(978-1-4896-3873-1(3))* Weigl Pubs., Inc.

Hitschler, Cynthia, illus. Gleb... the Terrible! 2004. 36p. pap. *(978-0-9761041-1-7(3)*, 1239008) Celstumo Publishing.

—The Perils of Pink Cat. 2004. 36p. (J). pap. *(978-0-9761041-2-4(1)*, 1239009) Celstumo Publishing.

—The World of Jacky Blue & Other Cats. 2004. 40p. (J). pap. *(978-0-9761041-0-0(5)*, 1239007) Celstumo Publishing.

Hlad, Carole. Daisy's Dance Party: (from the Amanda's Cats Series) 2011. 24p. pap. 15.99 *(978-1-4628-8006-5(1))* Xlibris Corp.

Hliva, Diana. My Pet Lunecat. 2010. 36p. pap. 18.41 *(978-1-4269-3208-3(1))* Trafford Publishing.

Hobbie, Holly. A Cat Named Swan. 2017. (ENG., Illus.). 32p. (J). (gr. -1-2). 17.99 *(978-0-553-53744-4(X)*, Random Hse. Bks. for Young Readers) Random Hse. Children's Bks.

Hobbs, Leigh. Old Tom, Man of Mystery, 1 vol. Hobbs, Leigh, illus. 2005. (ENG., Illus.). 32p. (J). (gr. -1-3). 16.95 *(978-1-56145-346-7(3))* Peachtree Pubs.

—Old Tom's Holiday. Hobbs, Leigh, illus. 2004. (ENG., Illus.). 32p. (J). 16.95 *(978-1-56145-316-0(1))* Peachtree Pubs.

Hochenauer, Mary & Hochenauer-Fox, Lois. Sunny & Wondrous, Cat Cousins. 2007. (ENG.). 32p. (J). 16.95 *(978-0-9778005-0-6(4))* Gnatcatcher Children'S Bks.

Hodgkinson, Leigh. Boris & the Snoozebox. Hodgkinson, Leigh, illus. 2008. (Tiger Tales Ser.). (Illus.). 40p. (J). (gr. -1-3). 15.95 *(978-1-58925-071-0(0))* Tiger Tales.

—Boris & the Wrong Shadow. 2012. (ENG.). 32p. (J). pap. *(978-1-58925-434-3(1))* Tiger Tales.

Hodgman, Ann. Do Touch! Don't Touch! Barnard, Lucy, illus. 2012. (ENG.). 18p. (J). bds. *(978-1-58925-867-9(3))* Tiger Tales.

—Uh-Oh! Oh No! Barnard, Lucy, illus. 2012. (Into-Everything Baby Stages Ser.). (ENG.). 18p. (gr. -1). bds. 7.95 *(978-1-58925-866-2(5))* Tiger Tales.

Hogan, Anne Harmon. The Three Amigos. 2011. 26p. pap. 14.95 *(978-1-61434-276-2(8))* Booklocker.com, Inc.

Hoh, Molly. Creating the Purrfect Tale. 2004. 179p. pap. 24.95 *(978-1-4137-4443-9(5))* America Star Bks.

Holden, Pam. Presents for Grace, 6 pack. Hawley, Kelvin, illus. 2009. (Red Rocket Readers Ser.). (ENG.). 16p. (gr. 2-2). pap. *(978-1-877363-61-0(8)*, Red Rocket Readers) Flying Start Bks.

Holm, Jennifer L. & Hamel, Jonathan. The Postman Always Brings Mice. Weinman, Brad, illus. 2005. (Stink Files Ser.: No. 1). 129p. (J). 12.65 *(978-0-7569-6529-7(2))* Perfection Learning Corp.

—To Scratch a Thief. Weinman, Brad, illus. (Stink Files Ser.: No. 2). 144p. 2005. pap. 4.99 *(978-0-06-052984-0(9)*, Harper Trophy) 2004. (J). 14.99 *(978-0-06-052982-6(2))* 2004. (J). lib. bdg. 15.89 *(978-0-06-052983-3(0))* HarperCollins Pubs.

Holmes, S. D. The Adventures of Mister. 2009. 56p. pap. 23.99 *(978-1-4389-3786-1(5))* AuthorHouse.

Holub, Joan. Itty Bitty Kitty. Burks, James, illus. 2015. (ENG.). 32p. (J). (gr. -1-3). 17.99 *(978-0-06-232219-7(2))* HarperCollins Pubs.

—Itty Bitty Kitty & the Rainy Play Day. Burks, James, illus. 2016. 32p. (J). (gr. -1-3). 17.99 *(978-0-06-232220-3(6))* HarperCollins Pubs.

—Itty Bitty Kitty: Firehouse Fun. Burks, James, illus. 2016. (My First I Can Read Ser.). 32p. (J). (gr. -1-3). pap. 3.99 *(978-0-06-232221-0(4))* HarperCollins Pubs.

—Shampoodle. Bowers, Tim, illus. 2009. (Step into Reading Ser.). (ENG.). 32p. (J). (gr. -1-1). pap. 3.99 *(978-0-375-85576-4(9)*, Random Hse. Bks. for Young Readers) Random Hse. Children's Bks.

Hooker, Adele. Sailor the Cat. Gwinner, Patricia, illus. 2011. 24p. pap. 24.95 *(978-1-4560-8026-6(1))* America Star Bks.

Hooks, Gwendolyn. Find the Cat! A Pet Club Story. Byrne, Mike, illus. 2010. (Pet Club Ser.). (ENG.). 32p. (gr. 1-2). pap. 6.25 *(978-1-4342-2795-9(2))* Stone Arch Bks.

Hooper, Carrie Lynn. Harley & the Hummingbird. 2011. 24p. pap. 11.32 *(978-1-4634-4686-4(1))* AuthorHouse.

Hoover, Laney Laube. The Tale of the Tailless Cat. 2007. (ENG.). 90p. pap. 7.99 *(978-1-4196-7441-9(2))* CreateSpace Independent Publishing Platform.

Hope, Laura Lee. Freddie & Flossie & the Train Ride. Pyle, Chuck, illus. 2005. (Bobbsey Twins Ser.). (ENG.). 32p. (J). (gr. -1-k). pap. 13.99 *(978-1-4169-0269-0(4)*, Simon Spotlight) Simon Spotlight.

Hope, Lauryne. Little Kitty. 2012. 24p. pap. 15.99 *(978-1-4771-3097-1(7))* Xlibris Corp.

Hord, Colleen. Keep Your Chin Up. Dufalla, Anita, illus. 2012. (ENG.). 24p. (gr. 1-2). pap. 8.95 *(978-1-61810-315-4(6))* Rourke Educational Media.

Horn, Emily. Excuse Me... Are You a Witch? Pawlak, Pawel, illus. 2004. (ENG.). 32p. (J). (gr. -1-2). pap. 7.95 *(978-1-58089-103-5(9))* Charlesbridge Publishing, Inc.

Hosta, Dar. Mavis & Her Marvelous Mooncakes. 2006. (Illus.). (J). (gr. -1-1). lib. bdg. 17.95 *(978-0-9721967-2-7(2))* Brown Dog Bks.

Houran, Lori Haskins. Too Many Cats. Mathieu, Joe, illus. 2009. (Step into Reading Ser.). (ENG.). 32p. (J). (gr. -1-1). pap. 3.99 *(978-0-375-85197-1(6)*, Random Hse. Bks. for Young Readers) Random Hse. Children's Bks.

Houston, Rebecca. Cat's Visitors. 2012. 24p. pap. 24.95 *(978-1-4626-7672-9(3))* America Star Bks.

Hovaguimian, Vroni. Deep in the Woods. 2011. 32p. pap. 13.00 *(978-0-557-70332-6(8))* Lulu Pr., Inc.

Howe, Deborah & Howe, James. A Rabbit-Tale of Mystery. unabr. ed. 2004. (Bunnicula Ser.). 98p. (J). (gr. 3-7). pap. 29.00 incl. audio *(978-0-8072-8204-5(9)*, YYA139SP, Listening Library) Random Hse. Audio Publishing Group.

Howe, James. Bunnicula Strikes Again! 2004. (Bunnicula Ser.). 116p. (J). (gr. 3-7). pap. 29.00 incl. audio *(978-0-8072-8213-7(8)*, Listening Library) Random Hse. Audio Publishing Group.

—Bunnicula Strikes Again! Daniel, Alan, illus. 2007. (Bunnicula & Friends Ser.). (ENG.). 144p. (J). (gr. 3-7). pap. 6.99 *(978-1-4169-3968-9(7)*, Atheneum Bks. for Young Readers) Simon & Schuster Children's Publishing.

—The Celery Stalks at Midnight. unabr. ed. 2004. (Bunnicula Ser.). 111p. (J). (gr. 3-7). pap. 29.00 incl. audio *(978-0-8072-8357-8(6)*, YA173SP, Listening Library) Random Hse. Audio Publishing Group.

—The Celery Stalks at Midnight. Morrill, Leslie H., illus. 2006. (Bunnicula & Friends Ser.). (ENG.). 144p. (J). (gr. 3-7). pap. 6.99 *(978-1-4169-2814-0(6)*, Atheneum Bks. for Young Readers) Simon & Schuster Children's Publishing.

—Hot Fudge. Mack, Jeff, illus. 2006. (Bunnicula & Friends Ser.). 42p. (gr. k-4). 14.00 *(978-0-7569-7224-0(8))* Perfection Learning Corp.

—Hot Fudge. Mack, Jeff, tr. Mack, Jeff, illus. 2004. (Bunnicula & Friends Ser.: 2). (ENG.). 48p. (J). (gr. 1-3). 16.99 *(978-0-689-85725-6(X)*, Atheneum Bks. for Young Readers) Simon & Schuster Children's Publishing.

—Hot Fudge. Mack, Jeff, illus. 2006. (Bunnicula & Friends Ser.: 2). (ENG.). 48p. (J). (gr. 1-3). pap. 3.99 *(978-0-689-85750-8(0)*, Simon Spotlight) Simon Spotlight.

—Houndsley & Catina. Gay, Marie-Louise, illus. (ENG.). 40p. (J). (gr. k-4). 2013. (Candlewick Sparks Ser.). pap. 3.99 *(978-0-7636-6638-5(6))* 2006. (Houndsley & Catina Ser.: 1). 15.99 *(978-0-7636-2404-0(7))* Candlewick Pr.

—Houndsley & Catina. Gay, Marie-Louise, illus. 2007. 36p. (J). (gr. k-2). lib. bdg. 12.65 *(978-0-7569-8141-9(7))* Perfection Learning Corp.

—Houndsley & Catina. 2013. (Candlewick Sparks Ser.). lib. bdg. 13.55 *(978-0-606-31608-8(6)*, Turtleback) Turtleback Bks.

—Houndsley & Catina & the Birthday Surprise. Gay, Marie-Louise, illus. (ENG.). 48p. (J). (gr. k-4). 2013. (Candlewick Sparks Ser.). pap. 3.99 *(978-0-7636-6639-2(4))* 2006. (Houndsley & Catina Ser.: 2). 15.99 *(978-0-7636-2405-7(5))* Candlewick Pr.

—Houndsley & Catina & the Quiet Time. Gay, Marie-Louise, illus. (ENG.). 48p. (J). (gr. k-4). 2013. (Candlewick Sparks Ser.). pap. 3.99 *(978-0-7636-6863-1(X))* 2008. (Houndsley & Catina Ser.: 3). 15.99 *(978-0-7636-3384-4(4))* Candlewick Pr.

—Houndsley & Catina Plink & Plunk. Gay, Marie-Louise, illus. 2013. (Candlewick Sparks Ser.). (ENG.). 48p. (J). (gr. k-4). pap. 3.99 *(978-0-7636-6640-8(8))* Candlewick Pr.

—Howliday Inn. Munsinger, Lynn, illus. 2006. 195p. (gr. 3-7). 16.00 *(978-0-7569-6807-6(0))* Perfection Learning Corp.

—Howliday Inn. Munsinger, Lynn, illus. 2nd ed. 2006. (Bunnicula & Friends Ser.). (ENG.). 224p. (J). (gr. 3-7). pap. 7.99 *(978-1-4169-2815-7(4)*, Atheneum Bks. for Young Readers) Simon & Schuster Children's Publishing.

—Nighty-Nightmare. unabr. ed. 2004. (Bunnicula Ser.). 128p. (J). (gr. 3-7). pap. 29.00 incl. audio *(978-0-8072-8397-4(5)*, YA201SP, Listening Library) Random Hse. Audio Publishing Group.

—Nighty-Nightmare. Morrill, Leslie, illus. 2007. (Bunnicula & Friends Ser.). (ENG.). 144p. (J). (gr. 3-7). pap. 6.99 *(978-1-4169-3966-5(0)*, Atheneum Bks. for Young Readers) Simon & Schuster Children's Publishing.

—Plink & Plunk. Gay, Marie-Louise, illus. 2009. (Houndsley & Catina Ser.). (ENG.). 48p. (J). (gr. k-4). 15.99 *(978-0-7636-3385-1(2))* Candlewick Pr.

—Rabbit-Cadabra! Mack, Jeff, illus. (Bunnicula & Friends Ser.: 4). (ENG.). 48p. (J). (gr. 1-3). 2007. pap. 3.99 *(978-0-689-85752-2(7))* 2006. 16.99 *(978-0-689-85727-0(6))* Simon Spotlight. (Simon Spotlight).

—Return to Howliday Inn. Daniel, Alan, illus. 2007. (Bunnicula & Friends Ser.). (ENG.). 192p. (J). (gr. 3-7). pap. 6.99 *(978-1-4169-3967-2(9)*, Atheneum Bks. for Young Readers) Simon & Schuster Children's Publishing.

—Return to Howliday Inn. Daniel, Alan, illus. 2007. (Bunnicula Ser.: 5). (gr. 4-7). lib. bdg. 17.20 *(978-1-4177-9044-9(X)*, Turtleback) Turtleback Bks.

—Scared Silly. Mack, Jeff, illus. 2006. (Bunnicula & Friends Ser.). 42p. (gr. 1-3). 14.00 *(978-0-7569-7225-7(6))* Perfection Learning Corp.

—Scared Silly. Mack, Jeff, illus. 2005. (Bunnicula & Friends Ser.: 3). (ENG.). 48p. (J). (gr. 1-3). 16.99 *(978-0-689-85726-3(8)*, Atheneum Bks. for Young Readers) Simon & Schuster Children's Publishing.

—Scared Silly. Mack, Jeff, illus. 2006. (Bunnicula & Friends Ser.: 3). (ENG.). 48p. (J). (gr. 1-3). pap. 3.99 *(978-0-689-85751-5(9)*, Simon Spotlight) Simon Spotlight.

—The Vampire Bunny. Mack, Jeff, illus. 2005. (Bunnicula & Friends Ser.: 1). (ENG.). 48p. (J). (gr. 1-3). pap. 3.99 *(978-0-689-85749-2(7)*, Simon Spotlight) Simon Spotlight.

Howell, Hayley L. Sammy's Two Left Feet: Groovin' with Mr. Smooth: Discovering How to Believe in Yourself. 2010. 32p. pap. 15.95 *(978-1-4520-5733-0(8))* AuthorHouse.

Hsu, Stacey W. Old Mo. Ritter, Adam, illus. 2011. (Rookie Ready to Learn — Animals Ser.). 40p. (J). (gr. -1-k). lib. bdg. 25.00 *(978-0-531-26418-8(1))*; pap. 5.95 *(978-0-531-26699-1(0))* Scholastic Library Publishing. (Children's Pr.).

Hubbard, Ben. My Very Own Kitten. Guile, Gill, illus. 2014. (ENG.). 12p. (J). (gr. -1). *(978-1-78244-602-6(8))* Top That! Publishing PLC.

Huchel, Gerald. She-Devil the Sassy Kitten. 2012. 28p. pap. 16.95 *(978-1-4626-8825-8(X))* America Star Bks.

Huizenga, Nathaniel. Justice in Winter: Justice the Dog Series. 2009. 28p. pap. 13.99 *(978-1-4389-7361-6(6))* AuthorHouse.

Hulst, W. G. van de & Hulst, Willem G. van de, illus. The Black Kitten. 2014. (J). *(978-1-928136-07-1(9))* Inheritance Pubns.

—Kittens, Kittens Everywhere. 2014. (J). *(978-1-928136-20-0(6))* Inheritance Pubns.

Hult, Gene & Bright, J. E. Cat Commander. Vecchio, Luciano, illus. (Dark Knight Ser.). (ENG.). 88p. (gr. 2-3). 2013. pap. 5.95 *(978-1-4342-4214-3(5))* 2012. 26.65 *(978-1-4342-4088-0(6))* Stone Arch Bks.

Humphrey, 6 Packs. (Action Packs Ser.). 104p. (gr. 3-5). 44.00 *(978-0-7635-8403-0(7))* Rigby Education.

Humphreys, Patrick B. 1-2-3 Kitties: A Cat Counting Book. 2008. 25p. pap. 24.95 *(978-1-60610-804-8(2))* America Star Bks.

Hunter, Erin. After the Flood. Barry, James L. & Hunt, John, illus. 2012. (Warriors Manga Ser.: 3). (ENG.). 112p. (J). (gr. 3-7). pap. 7.99 *(978-0-06-200838-1(2))* HarperCollins Pubs.

—After the Flood. 2012. (Warriors — SkyClan & the Stranger Ser.: 3). (J). lib. bdg. 17.20 *(978-0-606-23597-6(3)*, Turtleback) Turtleback Bks.

—The Apprentice's Quest. 2017. (Warriors — a Vision of Shadows Ser.: 1). (J). lib. bdg. 18.40 ***(978-0-606-39643-1(8))*** Turtleback Bks.

—Battles of the Clans. 2010. (Warriors Field Guide Ser.). 208p. (J). (gr. 3-7). (ENG.). 16.99 *(978-0-06-170230-3(7))*; lib. bdg. 17.89 *(978-0-06-170231-0(5))* HarperCollins Pubs.

—Beyond the Code. Barry, James L., illus. 2011. (Warriors Manga Ser.: 2). (ENG.). 112p. (J). (gr. 3-7). pap. 6.99 *(978-0-06-200837-4(4))* HarperCollins Pubs.

—The Blazing Star. 2014. (Warriors Ser.: Bk. 4). (ENG., Illus.). 320p. (J). 16.99 *(978-0-06-206358-8(8))* HarperCollins Pubs.

—Bluestar's Prophecy. McLoughlin, Wayne, illus. (Warriors Super Edition Ser.: 2). (ENG.). (J). (gr. 3-7). 2010. 560p. pap. 7.99 *(978-0-06-158250-9(6))* 2009. 544p. 17.99 *(978-0-06-158247-9(6))* HarperCollins Pubs.

—Cats of the Clans. McLoughlin, Wayne, illus. 2008. (Warriors Field Guide Ser.: No. 2). (ENG.). 112p. (J). (gr. 3-7). 16.99 *(978-0-06-145856-9(2))* HarperCollins Pubs.

—Code of the Clans. McLoughlin, Wayne, illus. 2009. (Warriors Field Guide Ser.: No. 3). 176p. (J). (gr. 3-7). (ENG.). 16.99 *(978-0-06-166009-2(6))*; lib. bdg. 17.89 *(978-0-06-166010-8(8))* HarperCollins Pubs.

—Crookedstar's Promise. (Warriors Super Edition Ser.: 4). 528p. (J). (gr. 3-7). 2012. (ENG.). pap. 7.99 *(978-0-06-198099-2(4))* 2011. (ENG.). 17.99 *(978-0-06-198097-8(8))* 2011. lib. bdg. 18.89 *(978-0-06-198098-5(6))* HarperCollins Pubs.

—Crookedstar's Promise. 2012. (Warriors Ser.: No. 4). (J). lib. bdg. 18.40 *(978-0-606-26263-7(6)*, Turtleback) Turtleback Bks.

—A Dangerous Path. Richardson, Owen & Stevenson, Dave, illus. 2015. (Warriors: the Prophecies Begin Ser.: 5). (ENG.). 368p. (J). (gr. 3-7). pap. 7.99 *(978-0-06-236700-6(5))* HarperCollins Pubs.

—A Dangerous Path. Stevenson, Dave, illus. 2004. (Warriors: the Prophecies Begin Ser.: 5). (ENG.). 336p. (J). (gr. 3-7). 16.99 *(978-0-06-000006-6(6))* HarperCollins Pubs.

—A Dangerous Path. 2015. (Warriors Ser.: 5). (J). lib. bdg. 18.40 *(978-0-606-36498-0(6))* Turtleback Bks.

—Dark River. (Warriors: Power of Three Ser.: 2). (ENG.). (J). (gr. 3-7). 2015. 368p. pap. 7.99 *(978-0-06-236709-9(9))* 2008. 368p. pap. 6.99 *(978-0-06-089207-4(2))* 2007. (Illus.). 352p. 16.99 *(978-0-06-089205-0(6))* HarperCollins Pubs.

—The Darkest Hour. Richardson, Owen & Stevenson, Dave, illus. 2015. (Warriors: the Prophecies Begin Ser.: 6). (ENG.). 368p. (J). (gr. 3-7). pap. 7.99 *(978-0-06-236701-3(3))* HarperCollins Pubs.

—The Darkest Hour. Stevenson, Dave, illus. (Warriors: the Prophecies Begin Ser.: 6). (ENG.). 336p. (J). (gr. 3-7). 2005. pap. 6.99 *(978-0-06-052585-9(1))* 2004. 17.99 *(978-0-06-000007-3(4))* HarperCollins Pubs.

—Dawn. Richardson, Owen & Stevenson, Dave, illus. 2015. (Warriors: the New Prophecy Ser.: 3). (ENG.). 400p. (J). (gr. 3-7). pap. 7.99 *(978-0-06-236704-4(8))* HarperCollins Pubs.

—Dawn. Stevenson, Dave, illus. (Warriors: the New Prophecy Ser.: 3). (ENG.). 352p. (J). (gr. 3-7). 2006. pap. 6.99 *(978-0-06-074457-1(X))* 2005. 16.99 *(978-0-06-074455-7(3))* HarperCollins Pubs.

—Eclipse. (Warriors: Power of Three Ser.: 4). (ENG.). (J). (gr. 3-7). 2015. 368p. pap. 7.99 *(978-0-06-236711-2(0))* 2009. 336p. pap. 7.99 *(978-0-06-089213-5(7))* 2008. (Illus.). 336p. 16.99 *(978-0-06-089211-1(0))* HarperCollins Pubs.

—Enter the Clans. 2012. (Warriors Field Guide Ser.: Nos. 1-2). (ENG.). 400p. (J). (gr. 3-7). pap. 7.99 *(978-0-06-210239-3(7))* HarperCollins Pubs.

—Enter the Clans. 2012. (Warriors Ser.). (J). lib. bdg. 18.40 *(978-0-606-26296-5(2)*, Turtleback) Turtleback Bks.

—Fading Echoes. Richardson, Owen & Douglas, Allen, illus. (Warriors: Omen of the Stars Ser.: 2). (ENG.). (J). (gr. 3-7). 2011. 368p. pap. 6.99 *(978-0-06-155514-5(2))* 2010. 352p. 16.99 *(978-0-06-155512-1(6))* HarperCollins Pubs.

—Fading Echoes. 2015. (Warriors — Omen of the Stars Ser.: 2). (J). lib. bdg. 18.40 *(978-0-606-37723-2(9))* Turtleback Bks.

—Fire & Ice. Richardson, Owen & Stevenson, Dave, illus. 2015. (Warriors: the Prophecies Begin Ser.: 2). (ENG.). 368p. (J). (gr. 3-7). pap. 7.99 *(978-0-06-236697-9(1))* HarperCollins Pubs.

—Fire & Ice. Stevenson, Dave, illus. (Warriors: the Prophecies Begin Ser.: 2). (ENG.). 336p. (J). (gr. 3-7). 2004. pap. 6.99 *(978-0-06-052559-0(2))* 2003. 16.99 *(978-0-06-000003-5(1))* HarperCollins Pubs.

—Fire & Ice. 2015. (Warriors Ser.: 2). (J). lib. bdg. 18.40 *(978-0-606-36495-9(1))* Turtleback Bks.

—Fire in the Sky. 2010. (Seekers Ser.: 5). (ENG.). 272p. (J). (gr. 3-7). 16.99 *(978-0-06-087134-5(2))* HarperCollins Pubs.

—Firestar's Quest. Chalk, Gary, illus. 2008. (Warriors Super Edition Ser.: 1). (ENG.). 544p. (J). (gr. 3-7). pap. 7.99 *(978-0-06-113167-7(9))* HarperCollins Pubs.

—Firestar's Quest. 2007. (Warriors Super Edition Ser.: 1). (ENG., Illus.). 528p. (J). (gr. 3-7). 17.99 *(978-0-06-113164-6(4))* HarperCollins Pubs.

—The First Battle. McLoughlin, Wayne & Douglas, Allen, illus. 2015. (Warriors: Dawn of the Clans Ser.: 3). (ENG.). 352p. (J). (gr. 3-7). pap. 6.99 *(978-0-06-206356-4(1))* HarperCollins Pubs.

—The First Battle. 2016. (Warriors — Dawn of the Clans Ser.: 3). (J). lib. bdg. 18.40 *(978-0-606-38163-5(5))* Turtleback Bks.

—A Forest Divided. McLoughlin, Wayne & Douglas, Allen, illus. 2015. (Warriors Ser.: Bk. 5). (ENG.). 384p. (J). (gr. 3-7). 16.99 *(978-0-06-206352-6(5))* HarperCollins Pubs.

—Forest of Secrets. Richardson, Owen & Stevenson, Dave, illus. 2015. (Warriors: the Prophecies Begin Ser.: 3). (ENG.). 368p. (J). (gr. 3-7). pap. 7.99 *(978-0-06-236698-6(X))* HarperCollins Pubs.

—Forest of Secrets. Stevenson, Dave, illus. (Warriors: the Prophecies Begin Ser.: 3). 336p. (J). (gr. 3-7). 2004. (ENG.). pap. 6.99 *(978-0-06-052561-3(4))* 2003. (ENG.). 16.99 *(978-0-06-000004-2(X))* 2003. lib. bdg. 17.89 *(978-0-06-052560-6(6))* HarperCollins Pubs.

—Forest of Secrets. 2015. (Warriors Ser.: 3). (J). lib. bdg. 18.40 *(978-0-606-36496-6(X))* Turtleback Bks.

—The Forgotten Warrior. Richardson, Owen & Douglas, Allen, illus. (Warriors: Omen of the Stars Ser.: 5). (ENG.). (J). (gr. 3-7). 2012. 384p. pap. 6.99 *(978-0-06-155526-8(6))* 2011. 368p. 16.99 *(978-0-06-155522-0(3))* HarperCollins Pubs.

—The Fourth Apprentice. Richardson, Owen & Douglas, Allen, illus. (Warriors: Omen of the Stars Ser.: 1). (ENG.). (J). (gr. 3-7). 2010. 368p. pap. 7.99 *(978-0-06-155511-4(8))* 2009. 352p. 16.99 *(978-0-06-155509-1(6))* HarperCollins Pubs.

—The Fourth Apprentice. 2015. (Warriors — Omen of the Stars Ser.: 1). (J). lib. bdg. 18.40 *(978-0-606-37728-7(X))* Turtleback Bks.

—Hawkwing's Journey. Barry, James L., illus. 2016. (Warriors Super Edition Ser.: 9). 480p. (J). (gr. 3-7). 18.99 *(978-0-06-246768-3(9))* HarperCollins Pubs.

—The Heart of a Warrior. Barry, James L., illus. 2010. (Warriors Manga Ser.: 3). (ENG.). 112p. (J). (gr. 3-7). pap. 6.99 *(978-0-06-168867-6(3))* HarperCollins Pubs.

—Into the Wild. Richardson, Owen & Stevenson, Dave, illus. 2015. (Warriors: the Prophecies Begin Ser.: 1). (ENG.). 320p. (J). (gr. 3-7). pap. 7.99 *(978-0-06-236696-2(3))* HarperCollins Pubs.

—Into the Wild. Stevenson, Dave, illus. 2003. (Warriors: the Prophecies Begin Ser.: 1). (ENG.). 288p. (J). (gr. 3-7). 16.99 *(978-0-06-000002-8(3))* HarperCollins Pubs.

—Into the Wild. 2015. (Warriors Ser.: 1). (J). lib. bdg. 18.40 *(978-0-606-36494-2(3))* Turtleback Bks.

—Into the Woods. Hudson, Don, illus. 2008. (Warriors Manga Ser.: 1). (ENG.). 112p. (J). (gr. 3-7). pap. 7.99 *(978-0-06-154792-8(1))* HarperCollins Pubs.

—The Last Hope. Richardson, Owen & Douglas, Allen, illus. (Warriors: Omen of the Stars Ser.: 6). (ENG.). (J). (gr. 3-7). 2013. 400p. pap. 7.99 *(978-0-06-155529-9(0))* 2012. 384p. 16.99 *(978-0-06-155527-5(4))* HarperCollins Pubs.

—Legends of the Clans. 2017. (Warriors Ser.). (J). lib. bdg. 18.40 ***(978-0-606-39642-4(X))*** Turtleback Bks.

—Long Shadows. (Warriors: Power of Three Ser.: 5). (ENG.). (J). (gr. 3-7). 2015. 368p. pap. 7.99 *(978-0-06-236712-9(9))* 2009. 352p. pap. 7.99 *(978-0-06-089216-6(1))* 2008. 336p. 16.99 *(978-0-06-089214-2(5))* HarperCollins Pubs.

—The Lost Warrior, 3 vols. 2007. (Warriors Manga Ser.: No. 1). (ENG., Illus.). 112p. (J). (gr. 3-7). pap. 6.99 *(978-0-06-124020-1(6))* HarperCollins Pubs.

—Midnight. Richardson, Owen & Stevenson, Dave, illus. 2015. (Warriors: the New Prophecy Ser.: 1). (ENG.). 352p. (J). (gr. 3-7). pap. 7.99 *(978-0-06-236702-0(1))* HarperCollins Pubs.

—Midnight. Stevenson, Dave, illus. 2006. (Warriors: the New Prophecy Ser.: 1). (ENG.). 336p. (J). (gr. 3-7). pap. 6.99 *(978-0-06-074451-9(0))* HarperCollins Pubs.

—Midnight. 2005. (Warriors Ser.: Bk. 1). (Illus.). 320p. (J). (gr. 5-18). lib. bdg. 17.89 *(978-0-06-074450-2(2))* HarperCollins Pubs.

—Midnight. Stevenson, Dave, illus. 2005. (Warriors: the New Prophecy Ser.: 1). (ENG.). 320p. (J). (gr. 3-7). 16.99 *(978-0-06-074449-6(9))* HarperCollins Pubs.

—Moonrise. Richardson, Owen & Stevenson, Dave, illus. 2015. (Warriors: the New Prophecy Ser.: 2). (ENG.). 336p. (J). (gr. 3-7). pap. 7.99 *(978-0-06-236703-7(X))* HarperCollins Pubs.

—Moonrise. Stevenson, Dave, illus. (Warriors: the New Prophecy Ser.: 2). (ENG.). (J). (gr. 3-7). 2006. 320p. pap. 6.99 *(978-0-06-074454-0(5))* 2005. 304p. 16.99 *(978-0-06-074452-6(9))* HarperCollins Pubs.

—Moonrise. 2015. (Warriors — the New Prophecy Ser.: 2). (J). lib. bdg. 18.40 *(978-0-606-36501-7(X))* Turtleback Bks.

—The New Prophecy, Vols. 1-6. 2008. (Warriors: the New Prophecy Ser.: Bks. 1-6). (J). (gr. 3-7). pap. 36.99 *(978-0-06-144898-0(2))* HarperCollins Pubs.

—Night Whispers. Richardson, Owen & Douglas, Allen, illus. (Warriors: Omen of the Stars Ser.: 3). (ENG.). (J). (gr. 3-7). 2011. 368p. pap. 6.99 *(978-0-06-155517-6(7))* 2010. 352p. 16.99 *(978-0-06-155515-2(0))* HarperCollins Pubs.

—Outcast. (Warriors: Power of Three Ser.: 3). (ENG.). (J). (gr. 3-7). 2015. 368p. pap. 7.99 *(978-0-06-236710-5(2))* 2008. (Illus.). 352p. 16.99 *(978-0-06-089208-1(0))* HarperCollins Pubs.

—A Pack Divided. 2016. (Survivors Gathering Darkness Ser.: 1). (J). lib. bdg. 18.40 *(978-0-606-38767-5(6))* Turtleback Bks.

—The Rescue. Barry, James L., illus. 2011. (Warriors Manga Ser.: 1). (ENG.). 112p. (J). (gr. 3-7). pap. 6.99 *(978-0-06-200836-7(6))* HarperCollins Pubs.

—Return to the Clans. Hudson, Don, illus. 2009. (Warriors Manga Ser.: 3). (ENG.). 112p. (J). (gr. 3-7). pap. 6.99 *(978-0-06-154794-2(8))* HarperCollins Pubs.

—The Rise of Scourge. Kurkoski, Bettina M., illus. 2008. (Warriors Manga Ser.: No. 3). (ENG.). 112p. (J). (gr. 3-7). pap. 6.99 *(978-0-06-147867-3(9))* HarperCollins Pubs.

—Rising Storm. Richardson, Owen & Stevenson, Dave, illus. 2015. (Warriors: the Prophecies Begin Ser.: 4). (ENG.). 368p. (J). (gr. 3-7). pap. 7.99 *(978-0-06-236699-3(8))* HarperCollins Pubs.

—Rising Storm. Stevenson, Dave, illus. (Warriors: the Prophecies Begin Ser.: 4). (ENG.). 336p. (J). (gr. 3-7). 2005. pap. 6.99 *(978-0-06-052563-7(0))* 2004. 16.99 *(978-0-06-000005-9(8))* HarperCollins Pubs.

—Rising Storm. 2015. (Warriors Ser.: 4). (J). lib. bdg. 18.40 *(978-0-606-36497-3(8))* Turtleback Bks.

—Secrets of the Clans. McLoughlin, Wayne, illus. 2007. (Warriors Field Guide Ser.: No. 1). 176p. (J). (gr. 3-7). (ENG.). 16.99 *(978-0-06-123903-8(8))*; lib. bdg. 16.89 *(978-0-06-123904-5(6))* HarperCollins Pubs.

—The Sight. (Warriors: Power of Three Ser.: 1). (ENG.). (J). (gr. 3-7). 2015. 416p. pap. 7.99 *(978-0-06-236708-2(0))* 2008. (Illus.). 336p. pap. 7.99 *(978-0-06-089204-3(8))* 2007. (Illus.). 384p. 16.99 *(978-0-06-089201-2(3))* HarperCollins Pubs.

—Sign of the Moon. Richardson, Owen & Douglas, Allen, illus. (Warriors: Omen of the Stars Ser.: 4). (J). (gr. 3-7). 2011. (ENG.). 352p. 16.99 *(978-0-06-155518-3(5))* 2011. 352p. lib. bdg. 17.89 *(978-0-06-155520-6(7))*No. 4. 2012. (ENG.). 368p. pap. 6.99 *(978-0-06-155521-3(5))* HarperCollins Pubs.

—Skyclan's Destiny. McLoughlin, Wayne, illus. (Warriors Super Edition Ser.: 3). (ENG.). 528p. (J). (gr. 3-7). 2011. pap. 7.99 *(978-0-06-169996-2(9))* 2010. 17.99 *(978-0-06-169994-8(2))* HarperCollins Pubs.

—Starlight. Richardson, Owen & Stevenson, Dave, illus. 2015. (Warriors: the New Prophecy Ser.: 4). (ENG.). 368p. (J). (gr. 3-7). pap. 7.99 *(978-0-06-236705-1(6))* HarperCollins Pubs.

—Starlight. Stevenson, Dave, illus. 2006. (Warriors: the New Prophecy Ser.: 4). (ENG.). 336p. (J). (gr. 3-7). 16.99 *(978-0-06-082758-8(0))* HarperCollins Pubs.

—Starlight. 2015. (Warriors — the New Prophecy Ser.: 4). (J). lib. bdg. 18.40 *(978-0-606-36503-1(6))* Turtleback Bks.

—The Sun Trail. McLoughlin, Wayne & Douglas, Allen, illus. (Warriors: Dawn of the Clans Ser.: 1). (ENG.). (J). (gr. 3-7). 2014. 368p. pap. 7.99 *(978-0-06-206348-9(0))* 2013. 352p. 16.99 *(978-0-06-206346-5(4))* HarperCollins Pubs.

—The Sun Trail. 2016. (Warriors — Dawn of the Clans Ser.: 1). (J). lib. bdg. 18.40 *(978-0-606-38161-1(9))* Turtleback Bks.

—Sunrise. 2010. (Warriors: Power of Three Ser.: 6). (ENG.). 368p. (J). (gr. 3-7). pap. 7.99 *(978-0-06-089219-7(6))* HarperCollins Pubs.

—Sunset. Richardson, Owen & Stevenson, Dave, illus. 2015. (Warriors: the New Prophecy Ser.: 6). (ENG.). 352p. (J). (gr. 3-7). pap. 7.99 *(978-0-06-236707-5(2))* HarperCollins Pubs.

—Sunset. Stevenson, Dave, illus. 2006. (Warriors: the New Prophecy Ser.: 6). (ENG.). 320p. (J). (gr. 3-7). 16.99 *(978-0-06-082769-4(6))* HarperCollins Pubs.

—Tales from the Clans. 2014. (Warriors Ser.). (J). lib. bdg. 17.20 *(978-0-606-35970-2(2))* Turtleback Bks.

—Tallstar's Revenge. Barry, James L., illus. 2014. (Warriors Super Edition Ser.: 6). (ENG.). 560p. (J). (gr. 3-7). pap. 7.99 *(978-0-06-221806-3(9))* HarperCollins Pubs.

—Tallstar's Revenge. 2014. (Warriors Super Edition Ser.). (J). lib. bdg. 18.40 *(978-0-606-35954-2(0))* Turtleback Bks.

—Thunder & Shadow. 2016. (Illus.). 376p. (J). ***(978-0-06-257415-2(9))*** Harper & Row Ltd.

—Thunder Rising. 2016. (Warriors — Dawn of the Clans Ser.: 2). (J). lib. bdg. 18.40 *(978-0-606-38162-8(7))* Turtleback Bks.

—Twilight. Richardson, Owen & Stevenson, Dave, illus. 2015. (Warriors: the New Prophecy Ser.: 5). (ENG.). 368p. (J). (gr. 3-7). pap. 7.99 *(978-0-06-236706-8(4))* HarperCollins Pubs.

—Twilight. Stevenson, Dave, illus. (Warriors: the New Prophecy Ser.: 5). (ENG.). (J). (gr. 3-7). 2007. 352p. pap. 6.99 *(978-0-06-082767-0(X))* 2006. 336p. 16.99 *(978-0-06-082764-9(5))* HarperCollins Pubs.

—Twilight. 2015. (Warriors — the New Prophecy Ser.: 5). (J). lib. bdg. 18.40 *(978-0-606-36506-2(0))* Turtleback Bks.

—The Untold Stories. McLoughlin, Wayne, illus. 2013. (Warriors Ser.). (ENG.). 320p. (J). (gr. 3-7). pap. 6.99 *(978-0-06-223292-2(4))* HarperCollins Pubs.

—Warriors, 6. (J). (gr. 3-7). Set. 2007. (Warriors Ser.: Bks. 1-6). 2112p. pap. 36.99 *(978-0-06-147793-5(1))*Vols. 1-6. 2015. (Warriors: the Prophecies Begin Ser.). (ENG.). 2112p. pap. 42.99 *(978-0-06-236714-3(5))*Vols. 1 to 6. 2015. (Warriors: Power of Three Ser.). (ENG.). 2256p. pap. 44.99 *(978-0-06-236716-7(1))* HarperCollins Pubs.

—Warriors: Into the Wild, Fire & Ice, Forest of Secrets. 2015. (Warriors: the Prophecies Begin Ser.). (ENG.). 1056p. (J). (gr. 3-7). pap. 19.99 *(978-0-06-237329-8(3))* HarperCollins Pubs.

—Warriors: The First Battle. 2014. (Warriors: Dawn of the Clans Ser.: 3). (ENG., Illus.). 352p. (J). (gr. 3-7). 16.99 *(978-0-06-206353-3(7))* HarperCollins Pubs.

—Warriors - Sunrise. 2015. (Warriors: Power of Three Ser.: 6). (ENG.). 368p. (J). (gr. 3-7). pap. 7.99 *(978-0-06-236713-6(7))* HarperCollins Pubs.

—Warriors - The New Prophecy, Vol. 1-6. Richardson, Owen, illus. 2015. (Warriors: the New Prophecy Ser.). (ENG.). 2176p. (J). (gr. 3-7). pap. 44.99 *(978-0-06-236715-0(3))* HarperCollins Pubs.

—Warriors: a Vision of Shadows #1: the Apprentice's Quest. (Warriors: a Vision of Shadows Ser.: 1). (J). (gr. 3-7). 2017. 352p. pap. 7.99 *(978-0-06-238639-7(5))* 2016. (ENG., Illus.). 336p. 16.99 *(978-0-06-238637-3(9))* 2016. (Illus.). 336p. lib. bdg. 17.89 *(978-0-06-238638-0(7))* HarperCollins Pubs.

—Warriors: a Vision of Shadows #2: Thunder & Shadow. (Warriors: a Vision of Shadows Ser.: 2). (J). (gr. 3-7). 2017. 416p. pap. 7.99 ***(978-0-06-238643-4(3))*** 2016. (Illus.). 400p. 16.99 *(978-0-06-238641-0(7))* 2016. (Illus.). 400p. lib. bdg. 17.89 *(978-0-06-238642-7(5))* HarperCollins Pubs.

—Warriors: a Vision of Shadows #3: Shattered Sky. 2017. (Warriors: a Vision of Shadows Ser.: 3). 320p. (J). (gr. 3-7). 16.99 *(978-0-06-238645-8(X))*; lib. bdg. 17.89 *(978-0-06-238646-5(8))* HarperCollins Pubs.

—Warriors: a Vision of Shadows #4: Darkest Night. 2017. (Warriors: a Vision of Shadows Ser.: 4). 336p. (J). (gr. 3-7). 16.99 ***(978-0-06-238649-6(2))***; (ENG.). lib. bdg. 17.89 ***(978-0-06-238650-2(6))*** HarperCollins Pubs.

—Warriors Boxed Set: Rising Storm; A Dangerous Path; The Darkest Hour. 2007. (Warriors Ser.: Nos. 4-6). (J). pap. 19.99 *(978-0-06-128452-6(1)*, Harper Trophy) HarperCollins Pubs.

—Warriors: Dawn of the Clans #2: Thunder Rising. McLoughlin, Wayne & Douglas, Allen, illus. 2016. (Warriors: Dawn of the Clans Ser.: 2). 368p. (J). (gr. 3-7). pap. 7.99 *(978-0-06-241001-6(6))* HarperCollins Pubs.

—Warriors: Dawn of the Clans #3: the First Battle. McLoughlin, Wayne & Douglas, Allen, illus. 2016. (Warriors: Dawn of the Clans Ser.: 3). 352p. (J). (gr. 3-7). pap. 7.99 *(978-0-06-241002-3(4))* HarperCollins Pubs.

—Warriors: Dawn of the Clans #6: Path of Stars. McLoughlin, Wayne & Douglas, Allen, illus. 2015. (Warriors: Dawn of the Clans Ser.: 6). (ENG.). 352p. (J). (gr. 3-7). 16.99 *(978-0-06-206366-3(9))* HarperCollins Pubs.

—Warriors: Dawn of the Clans Box Set: Volumes 1 To 3. McLoughlin, Wayne, illus. 2016. (Warriors: Dawn of the Clans Ser.). 1088p. (J). (gr. 3-7). pap. 20.97 *(978-0-06-234325-3(4))* HarperCollins Pubs.

—Warriors: Graystripe's Adventure: The Lost Warrior, Warrior's Refuge, Warrior's Return. Barry, James L., illus. 2017. (Warriors Manga Ser.). 272p. (J). (gr. 3-7). pap. 12.99 ***(978-0-06-257300-1(4))*** HarperCollins Pubs.

—Warriors Manga - Graystripe's Adventure, 3 vols., Set. Barry, James, illus. 2009. (Warriors Manga Ser.). 336p. (J). (gr. 3-7). pap. 16.99 *(978-0-06-178228-2(9))* HarperCollins Pubs.

—Warriors: Omen of the Stars #2: Fading Echoes. Richardson, Owen & Douglas, Allen, illus. 2015. (Warriors: Omen of the Stars Ser.: 2). (ENG.). 384p. (J). (gr. 3-7). pap. 7.99 *(978-0-06-238259-7(4))* HarperCollins Pubs.

—Warriors: Omen of the Stars Box Set: Volumes 1 To 6. 2013. (Warriors: Omen of the Stars Ser.). (ENG.). 2256p. (J). (gr. 3-7). pap. 36.99 *(978-0-06-226887-7(2))* HarperCollins Pubs.

—Warriors Super Edition: Bramblestar's Storm. 2014. (Warriors Ser.). (ENG., Illus.). 512p. (J). (gr. 3-7). 18.99 *(978-0-06-229143-1(2))* HarperCollins Pubs.

—Warriors Super Edition: Moth Flight's Vision. Barry, James L. & Richardson, Owen, illus. 2016. (Warriors Super Edition Ser.: 8). 544p. (J). (gr. 3-7). pap. 7.99 *(978-0-06-229149-3(1))* HarperCollins Pubs.

—Warriors Super Edition: Tigerheart's Shadow. Barry, James L., illus. 2017. (Warriors Super Edition Ser.: 10). 464p. (J). (gr. 3-7). 18.99 ***(978-0-06-246772-0(7))*** HarperCollins Pubs.

Hunter, Erin. Yellowfang's Secret. Barry, James L., illus. (Warriors Super Edition Ser.: 5). (J). (gr. 3-7). 2014. (ENG.). 544p. pap. 7.99 *(978-0-06-208216-9(7))* 2012. (ENG.). 528p. 18.99 *(978-0-06-208214-5(0))* 2012. 528p. lib. bdg. 19.89 *(978-0-06-208215-2(9))* HarperCollins Pubs.

—Yellowfang's Secret. 2014. (Warriors Super Edition Ser.). (J). lib. bdg. 18.40 *(978-0-606-35074-7(8)*, Turtleback) Turtleback Bks.

Hunter, Erin & Jolley, Dan. Escape from the Forest. Hudson, Don, illus. 2008. (Warriors Manga Ser.: 2). (ENG.). 112p. (J). (gr. 3-7). pap. 7.99 *(978-0-06-154793-5(X))* HarperCollins Pubs.

—Warrior's Return, 3 vols. Barry, James L., illus. 2008. (Warriors Manga Ser.: No. 3). (ENG.). 112p. (J). (gr. 3-7). pap. 6.99 *(978-0-06-125233-4(6))* HarperCollins Pubs.

Hunter, Erin, et al. Moth Flight's Vision. Barry, James L. & Richardson, Owen, illus. 2015. (Warriors Super Edition Ser.: 8). (ENG.). 528p. (J). (gr. 3-7). 18.99 *(978-0-06-229147-9(5))* HarperCollins Pubs.

Hurd, Thacher. Cat's Pajamas. 2015. (ENG., Illus.). 16p. (J). (gr. -1-k). 9.95 *(978-1-63076-030-4(7))* Taylor Trade Publishing.

Hurtado, Patricia. The Magical Feline & the White Haven. 2009. 142p. pap. 10.95 *(978-1-60594-325-1(8)*, Llumina Pr.) Aeon Publishing Inc.

Hurwitz, Johanna. Ethan Out & about Big Book: Brand New Readers. Floca, Brian, illus. 2010. (Brand New Readers Ser.). (ENG.). 48p. (J). (gr. -1-3). pap. 24.99 *(978-0-7636-4811-4(6))* Candlewick Pr.

Husar, Stephane. Cat & Mouse Come to My House! Mehee, Loic, illus. 2015. (Av2 Fiction Readalong 2016 Ser.). (ENG.). (J). lib. bdg. 34.28 *(978-1-4896-3804-5(0)*, AV2 by Weigl) Weigl Pubs., Inc.

—Cat & Mouse Eat Good Food! Mehee, Loic, illus. 2015. (Av2 Fiction Readalong 2016 Ser.). (ENG.). (J). lib. bdg. 34.28 *(978-1-4896-3807-6(5)*, AV2 by Weigl) Weigl Pubs., Inc.

—Cat & Mouse Feelings. Mehee, Loic, illus. 2015. (Av2 Fiction Readalong 2016 Ser.). (ENG.). (J). lib. bdg. 34.28 *(978-1-4896-3810-6(5)*, AV2 by Weigl) Weigl Pubs., Inc.

—Cat & Mouse Let's Go Shopping! Mehee, Loic, illus. 2015. (Av2 Fiction Readalong 2016 Ser.). (ENG.). (J). lib. bdg. 34.28 *(978-1-4896-3816-8(4)*, AV2 by Weigl) Weigl Pubs., Inc.

—Cat & Mouse Meet the Animals! Mehee, Loic, illus. 2015. (Av2 Fiction Readalong 2016 Ser.). (ENG.). (J). lib. bdg. 34.28 *(978-1-4896-3819-9(9)*, AV2 by Weigl) Weigl Pubs., Inc.

Ice, Rod. The Cat & the Strat. 2007. 32p. per. 24.95 *(978-1-4241-8646-4(3))* America Star Bks.

Immonen, Laurel. Werepuppy. 2013. 24p. pap. 24.95 *(978-1-63000-774-4(9))* America Star Bks.

Inches, Alison. My Visit with Periwinkle. Levy, David B., illus. 2003. (Blue's Clues Ser.). (ENG.). 24p. (J). pap. 3.99 *(978-0-689-85230-5(4)*, Simon Spotlight/Nickelodeon) Simon Spotlight/Nickelodeon.

Inez, Peggy. The Gully. 2007. 140p. per. 7.95 *(978-1-59858-400-4(6))* Dog Ear Publishing, LLC.

Ingman, Bruce. When Martha's Away. 2010. (ENG., Illus.). 32p. (J). (gr. -1-2). 16.99 *(978-0-7636-5135-0(4))* Candlewick Pr.

Inkpen, Mick. Rollo & Ruff & the Little Fluffy Bird. Inkpen, Mick, illus. 2011. (ENG., Illus.). 32p. (J). (gr. k-2). pap. 9.99 *(978-0-340-98959-3(9))* Hodder & Stoughton GBR. Dist: Hachette Bk. Group.

Inkpen, Mick & Butterworth, Nick. Just Like Jasper! 2008. (ENG., Illus.). 32p. (J). (gr. -1-k). pap. 9.99 *(978-0-340-94510-0(9))* Hodder & Stoughton GBR. Dist: Hachette Bk. Group.

Ioan, Elwyn. Ici'r Ddôl A'r Cathod Nadolig. 2005. (WEL., Illus.). 36p. pap. *(978-0-86243-361-1(4))* Y Lolfa.

Iriyama, Satoshi. Good Night, Chirp. 2015. (Chirp the Chick Ser.). (ENG., Illus.). 36p. (J). (— 1). 8.99 *(978-0-544-35994-9(1)*, HMH Books For Young Readers) Houghton Mifflin Harcourt Publishing Co.

Irvin, Juanita. Zack the Cool Cat. 2011. 16p. 9.99 *(978-1-4567-4615-5(4))* AuthorHouse.

Isaac, Lowell. Mr. Cat & the End of the World. 2013. 36p. pap. 20.99 *(978-1-4817-0297-3(1))* AuthorHouse.

Israelievitch, Gabrielle. Where's Home? 2011. (Illus.). 64p. (J). pap. 15.95 *(978-0-937404-72-0(1))* Triad Publishing Co.

Ives, Bob. The Three Ants & the Cat. Fairy, Meg, illus. 2003. 40p. (J). *(978-1-920832-07-0(6))* Four Heads Publishing Group Pty, Ltd.

Jachimczyk, Victoria. Max's Tale: Home Sweet Home. 2012. 24p. pap. 17.99 *(978-1-4772-2115-0(8))* AuthorHouse.

Jack Stanley. The Coaster Cats Go to the Amusement Park. Breuer, Paul, illus. 2006. 19p. (J). pap. 5.99 *(978-0-9776284-0-7(X))* Forbes Literary Ltd. Inc.

Jackson, Leona Novy. The Littlest Christmas Kitten. Dupre, Kelly, illus. 2005. 32p. (J). 16.00 *(978-0-930643-18-8(6)*, 1250560) Images Unlimited Publishing.

Jacobsen, Annie. The Terrible Troll Cat. Hanson, Susan Jo, illus. (J). 2012. 32p. 9.98 *(978-0-9778276-4-0(X))* 2006. 16.95 *(978-0-9778276-0-2(7))* Pickled Herring Pr.

Jaffe, Michele. Bad Kitty. 2007. (Bad Kitty Ser.: 1). (ENG., Illus.). 304p. (YA). (gr. 8-12). pap. 9.99 *(978-0-06-078110-1(6)*, HarperTeen) HarperCollins Pubs.

James, D. B. That Cat Is a Brat! 2013. 24p. pap. 17.99 *(978-1-4817-0342-0(0))* AuthorHouse.

James, Rosalind. Bertie Rides Again. 2012. (Illus.). 126p. 29.99 *(978-1-4771-2272-3(9))* Xlibris Corp.

Jameson, Rosemary. Mortimer & Teasdale's Adventures. 2009. 44p. pap. 14.50 *(978-1-60693-441-8(4)*, Eloquent Bks.) Strategic Book Publishing & Rights Agency (SBPRA).

Janjua, Sajid. Dusty the Kitten. 2012. (Illus.). 20p. pap. 19.82 *(978-1-4772-2225-6(1))* AuthorHouse.

Jankowski, Susan. Say No to a Bully. 2012. 24p. pap. 15.99 *(978-1-4797-2139-9(5))* Xlibris Corp.

Janovitz, Marilyn. We Love School (¡Nos Encanta la Escuela!) Janovitz, Marilyn, illus. 2009. (ENG & SPA., Illus.). 32p. (J). (gr. -1-k). 7.95 *(978-0-7358-2246-7(8))* North-South Bks., Inc.

Janowski, Alice. The Adventures of Inka the Feline. Smith, Jerry, illus. 2010. 36p. pap. 14.00 *(978-1-60844-576-9(3))* Dog Ear Publishing, LLC.

Janowski, Alice & Boyer, Colleen McKinnon. Dakota & the Magical Gardens. 2008. 28p. pap. 12.95 *(978-1-59858-711-1(0))* Dog Ear Publishing, LLC.

Jarman, Julia. The Time-Travelling Cat & the Aztec Sacrifice. 2006. (Time-Travelling Cat Ser.). (ENG., Illus.). 160p. (J). (gr. 3-6). pap. 12.99 *(978-1-84270-516-2(4))* Andersen Pr. GBR. Dist: Independent Pubs. Group.

—The Time-Travelling Cat & the Egyptian Goddess. 2007. (Time-Travelling Cat Ser.: 1). (ENG.). 128p. (J). (gr. 4-7). per. 12.99 *(978-1-84270-521-6(0))* Andersen Pr. GBR. Dist: Independent Pubs. Group.

—The Time-Travelling Cat & the Roman Eagle. (Illus.). (J). 128p. 16.95 *(978-0-86264-861-9(0))*; 2008. (Time-Travelling Cat Ser.: 3). (ENG., 156p. (gr. 4-7). pap. 13.99 *(978-1-84270-617-6(9))* Andersen Pr. GBR. Dist: Trafalgar Square Publishing, Independent Pubs. Group.

—The Time-Travelling Cat & the Viking Terror. 2008. (Time-Travelling Cat Ser.: 4). (ENG., Illus.). 176p. (J). (gr. 4-7). pap. 11.99 *(978-1-84270-686-2(1))* Andersen Pr. GBR. Dist: Independent Pubs. Group.

Jasper the Cat. 2003. (Chunky Animal Shaped Boards Ser.). (J). 10p. bds. 9.95 *(978-0-7525-7854-5(5))*; (Illus.). bds. 1.98 *(978-0-7525-7775-3(1))* Parragon, Inc.

Jasper the Cat Chapter Set 1. 2004. (J). (978-1-58453-287-3(4)) Pioneer Valley Bks.

Jazz. Gizmo & Scatz: A Tail of Friendship. 2012. (Illus.). 16p. pap. 17.55 (978-1-4678-8267-5(4)) AuthorHouse.

Jeffries, Alison. Sam & the Bag. Andreasen, Dan, illus. 2004. (Green Light Readers Level 1 Ser.). (ENG.). 24p. (J). (gr. -1-3). pap. 3.95 (978-0-15-205151-8(1)) Houghton Mifflin Harcourt Publishing Co.

—Sam & the Bag. Andreasen, Dan, illus. 2004. (Green Light Readers Level 1 Ser.). (gr. -1-1). 13.95 (978-0-7569-4331-8(0)) Perfection Learning Corp.

Jenkins, Emily. Cinco Criaturas. Cortes, Eunice, tr. Bogacki, Tomek, illus. 2003. (Picture Bks.).Tr. of Five Creatures. (SPA.). (J). (978-970-690-648-9(7)) Planeta Mexicana Editorial S. A. de C. V.

—Five Creatures. Bogacki, Tomek, illus. 2005. (ENG.). 32p. (J). (gr. -1-1). reprint ed. per. 8.99 (978-0-374-42328-5(8), 9780374423285) Square Fish.

—Princessland. Tanaka, Yoko, illus. 2017. (ENG.). 32p. (J). 16.99 (978-0-374-36115-0(0), 9780374361150, Farrar, Straus & Giroux (BYR)) Farrar, Straus & Giroux.

Jennings, Patrick. Hissy Fitz. Austin, Michael, illus. 2017. (ENG.). 128p. (gr. 2-4). 7.99 (978-1-5124-4145-1(7), Carolrhoda Bks.) Lerner Publishing Group.

—Hissy Fitz. Allen, Michael, illus. 2015. (ENG.). 128p. (J). (gr. 2-4). 14.99 (978-1-5124-0137-0(4), Carolrhoda Bks.) Lerner Publishing Group.

—Hissy Fitz. Austin, Michael Allen, illus. 2015. (ENG.). 128p. (gr. 2-4). 14.99 (978-1-60684-596-7(9), Carolrhoda Bks.) Lerner Publishing Group.

Jepsen, D. R. Fabulous Fred Gets the Cheese. 2007. 16p. per. 24.95 (978-1-4241-8456-9(8)) America Star Bks.

Jerome, Kate Boehm. Miniature Golf Madness. 2005. (Illus.). 32p. (J). 15.95 (978-0-9769087-3-9(5)) Vertical Connect Pr.

Jin, Chris & Trimmer, Christian. Simon's New Bed. Van der Paardt, Melissa, illus. 2015. (ENG.). 32p. (J). (gr. -1-3). 17.99 (978-1-4814-3019-7(X)) Simon & Schuster Children's Publishing.

Jjdenson. Kitty Crunch & Doggy Chow. 2011. 32p. pap. 21.99 (978-1-4500-7383-7(2)) Xlibris Corp.

Joe & Trish. The Adventures of Sasha, the Six-Fingered Cat. 2010. 36p. pap. 16.99 (978-1-4520-8406-0(8)) AuthorHouse.

Johnson, David. The Boy Who Drew Cats, 1 vol. Johnson, David, illus. 2007. (Rabbit Ears: A Classic Tale Ser.). (ENG., Illus.). 36p. (gr. -1-3). 25.65 (978-1-59961-305-5(0)) Spotlight.

Johnson, Jane. Legends of the Shadow World: The Secret Country; the Shadow World; Dragon's Fire. Stower, Adam, illus. 2010. (ENG.). 1120p. (J). (gr. 3-7). pap. 14.99 (978-1-4169-9082-6(8), Simon & Schuster Bks. For Young Readers) Simon & Schuster Bks. For Young Readers.

—The Secret Country. Stower, Adam, illus. 2007. (Eidolon Chronicles Ser.: 1). (ENG.). 336p. (J). (gr. 3-7). per. 15.99 (978-1-4169-3815-6(X), Simon & Schuster Bks. For Young Readers) Simon & Schuster Bks. For Young Readers.

Johnson, Kimberly P. Not Again, Mr. Cat! Smith, Landa, illus. 2003. 36p. (J). (gr. k-3). 14.95 (978-1-57197-362-7(1), Ivy House Publishing Group) Pentland Pr., Inc.

Johnson, Linda Rene'. Prissy, Where Are You? 2004. 37p. pap. 24.95 (978-1-4137-3009-8(4)) PublishAmerica, Inc.

Johnson, Margaret. Selfish & the Blue Box. 2008. 28p. pap. 24.95 (978-1-60563-992-5(3)) America Star Bks.

Johnson, Michael E. Barley & Betsy: Journey #1 A cat & dog's great adventure to the Mall. Atchley, Kendra, illus. 2011. 36p. pap. 24.95 (978-1-4560-4077-2(4)) America Star Bks.

Johnson, Rebecca. Cat Show Queen. 2015. (Juliet, Nearly a Vet Ser.: 10). (ENG., Illus.). 96p. (J). (gr. 3-5). 8.99 (978-0-14-330872-0(6)) Penguin Books Australia AUS. Dist: Independent Pubs. Group.

Johnson, Sandi. Cats on Vacation. Durant, Sybrina, ed. Brundige, Britt & Sturgeon, Bobbi, illus. 2014. (ENG.). 12p. (J). (gr. -1-6). pap. 12.99 (978-1-929063-46-8(6), 146) Moons & Stars Publishing For Children.

—Dingbat: El Gato Voluntario. Johnson, Britt, ed. Short, Elizabeth, tr. from ENG. Trevinio, Juan, illus. l.t. ed. 2003. Orig. Title: Dingbat the Wayward Cat. (SPA.). 14p. (J). (gr. k-5). spiral bd. 4.99 (978-1-929063-85-7(7), 326) Moons & Stars Publishing For Children.

Johnson, Shane L., illus. OLIVIA Trains Her Cat. (Olivia TV Tie-In Ser.). (ENG.). 24p. (J). (gr. -1-1). 2010. 16.99 (978-1-4424-1383-2(2)) 2009. pap. 3.99 (978-1-4169-8296-8(5)) Simon Spotlight. (Simon Spotlight).

Johnston, Jan. Amélie the Most Amazing Butterfly: I Do So Love Being a Butterfly ... 2013. (Illus.). 24p. pap. 17.99 (978-1-4817-8018-6(2)) AuthorHouse.

—Lisa Finds a Playful Tree Elf: No! I Am Not a Fairy! 2013. (Illus.). 24p. pap. 17.99 (978-1-4817-8020-9(4)) AuthorHouse.

—Ruby - the Naughty Little Black Kitten: Hello! My Name Is Ruby ... 2013. (Illus.). 24p. pap. 17.99 (978-1-4817-8023-0(9)) AuthorHouse.

Johnston, Tony. The Cat with Seven Names. Davenier, Christine, illus. 2013. (ENG.). 40p. (J). (gr. k-3). 16.95 (978-1-58089-381-7(3)) Charlesbridge Publishing, Inc.

Jolley, Dan & Hunter, Erin. The Rise of Scourge. Kurkoski, Bettina, illus. 2008. (Warriors Manga Ser.: 4). 82p. (J). (gr. 3-7). lib. bdg. 17.20 (978-1-4178-3120-3(0), Turtleback) Turtleback Bks.

Jonell, Lynne. The Sign of the Cat. 2015. (ENG., Illus.). 368p. (J). (gr. 3-7). 16.99 (978-0-8050-9683-5(3), 9780805096835, Holt, Henry & Co. Bks. For Young Readers) Holt, Henry & Co.

—The Sign of the Cat. 2016. (J). lib. bdg. 18.40 (978-0-606-39559-5(8)) Turtleback Bks.

Jones, Bryan E. Somebody Stole My Yawn! Embry, Stacey, illus. 2009. 28p. pap. 24.95 (978-1-60749-877-3(4)) America Star Bks.

Jones, C. B. The Cats' Meow. Green, Chris, illus. 2017. (Bog Hollow Boys Ser.). (ENG.). 72p. (gr. 4-5). lib. bdg. 25.32 (978-1-4965-4057-7(3)) Stone Arch Bks.

Jones, Carl L., Sr. Joint Jerome Jones. 2004. (Illus.). 56p. (YA). pap. 12.99 (978-0-9748266-0-8(X)) Grampa Jones's Publishing Co.

Jones, Diana Wynne. Earwig & the Witch. Zelinsky, Paul O., illus. 2012. 128p. (J). (gr. 3-7). 15.99 (978-0-06-207511-6(X), Greenwillow Bks.) HarperCollins Pubs.

Jones, Diana Wynne & Jones, Ursula. The Islands of Chaldea. 368p. (J). (gr. 3-7). 2015. pap. 9.99 (978-0-06-229508-8(X)) 2014. 17.99 (978-0-06-229507-1(1)) HarperCollins Pubs. (Greenwillow Bks.).

Jones, Lara. All Aboard! 2015. (Poppy Cat Ser.). (ENG., Illus.). 18p. (J). (gr. -1-k). bds. 7.99 (978-0-230-75400-3(7)) Pan Macmillan GBR. Dist: Independent Pubs. Group.

—Blast Off! 2015. (Poppy Cat Ser.). (ENG., Illus.). 18p. (J). (gr. -1-k). bds. 7.99 (978-0-230-75399-0(X)) Pan Macmillan GBR. Dist: Independent Pubs. Group.

Jones, Nancy. The Grandpaws. 2005. 57p. pap. 16.95 (978-1-4137-4778-2(7)) America Star Bks.

Jones, Stephen B. Scratch the Boatyard Cat. 2004. (Illus.). 56p. (J). pap. 18.95 (978-0-9718303-9-4(8)) Flat Hammock Pr.

Joy, Angelica. My Cat Merigold. Bolle, Frank, illus. 2008. 56p. pap. 19.95 (978-1-59858-591-9(6)) Dog Ear Publishing, LLC.

Joyce, James. The Cats of Copenhagen. Sorrow, Casey, illus. 2012. (ENG.). 32p. 19.99 (978-1-4767-0894-2(0), Scribner) Scribner.

Jude, Tracey. Mr. Topaz Takes a Walk. 2005. 43p. (J). spiral bd. 16.99 (978-1-4116-5691-8(1)) Lulu Pr., Inc.

Judith Anne Moody. Golden Eye & the Killer Cat. 2009. 248p. pap. 19.49 (978-1-4251-7684-6(4)) Trafford Publishing.

Jules, Jacqueline. Abuela's Birthday. Smith, Kim, illus. 2015. (Sofia Martinez Ser.). (ENG.). 32p. (gr. k-2). lib. bdg. 21.32 (978-1-4795-5775-2(7), Sofia Martinez) Picture Window Bks.

June-Bug. Sweetbread & Tattletale. 2012. 32p. 24.95 (978-1-4626-6040-7(1)) America Star Bks.

Justice, W. Shelton. Miss Fluffy a Special Cat. 2008. 24p. pap. 13.95 (978-1-4327-3296-7(X)) Outskirts Pr., Inc.

Kanata, Konami. Chi's Sweet Home, Vol. 11. 2014. (Chi's Sweet Home Ser.). (ENG., Illus.). 152p. (gr. k-12). pap. 13.95 (978-1-939130-51-8(4), Vertical) Vertical, Inc.

—Chi's Sweet Home 11. 2014. (Chi's Sweet Home Ser.: 11). lib. bdg. 25.70 (978-0-606-35893-4(5)) Turtleback Bks.

—Chi's Sweet Home, Volume 12. 2015. (Chi's Sweet Home Ser.). (ENG., Illus.). 176p. (J). (gr. 2-5). pap. 13.95 (978-1-941220-25-2(8), Vertical) Kodansha America, Inc.

Kang, A. N. Papillon, Book 2 Papillon Goes to the Vet. Kang, A. N., illus. 2017. (Papillon Ser.). (ENG., Illus.). 40p. (J). (gr. -1-k). 16.99 **(978-1-4847-2881-9(5))** Hyperion Bks. for Children.

Kang, A. N. The Very Fluffy Kitty, Papillon. Kang, A. N., illus. 2016. (Papillon Ser.). (ENG., Illus.). 40p. (J). (gr. -1-k). 16.99 (978-1-4847-1798-1(8)) Disney Pr.

Kaputa, Christine C. Bad Kitty! 2007. 16p. per. 9.95 (978-1-59858-478-3(2)) Dog Ear Publishing, LLC.

Kawamura, Yayo. A Day with Pepe & Milli. Kawamura, Yayo, illus. 2017. (Pepe & Millie Ser.). (ENG., Illus.). 16p. (J). (gr. -1 — 1). bds. 9.99 **(978-0-8075-6481-3(8))** Whitman, Albert & Co.

Kay, Karin. Floppy Cat. 2009. (J). 16.95 (978-0-9823818-0-9(8)) Floppy Cat Co.

Kaye, Danny. Danny Kaye's Stories from Far Away Places. Bevans Marks And Barrow, illus. 2011. 30p. 35.95 (978-1-258-00232-9(9)) Literary Licensing, LLC.

Keats, Ezra Jack. Kitten for a Day. 2008. (Illus.). lib. bdg. 17.00 (978-0-7569-9008-4(4)) Perfection Learning Corp.

Keegan, Anne. A Cat for Claire. 2008. 28p. pap. 15.00 (978-1-4389-2737-4(1)) AuthorHouse.

Keep, Richard. A Thump from Upstairs: Starring Mr. Boo & Max, 1 vol. Keep, Richard, illus. 2005. (ENG., Illus.). 36p. (J). (gr. -1-3). 15.95 (978-1-56145-348-1(X)) Peachtree Pubs.

Kehret, Peg & the Cat, Pete. Spy Cat. 2008. (Pete the Cat Ser.). (ENG.). 192p. (J). (gr. 3-7). 5.99 (978-0-14-241219-0(8), Puffin Books) Penguin Young Readers Group.

—The Stranger Next Door. 2008. (Pete the Cat Ser.). (ENG.). 176p. (J). (gr. 3-7). 5.99 (978-0-14-241248-0(1), Puffin Books) Penguin Young Readers Group.

—Trapped! 2008. (Pete the Cat Ser.). (ENG.). 192p. (J). (gr. 3-7). 5.99 (978-0-14-241189-6(2), Puffin Books) Penguin Young Readers Group.

Keller, Holly. A Bed Full of Cats. 2003. (Green Light Readers Level 2 Ser.). (ENG., Illus.). 24p. (J). (gr. -1-3). pap. 3.95 (978-0-15-204836-5(7)) Houghton Mifflin Harcourt Publishing Co.

—A Bed Full of Cats. 2003. (Green Light Readers — Level 2 Ser.). (Illus.). 20p. (J). (gr. k-2). lib. bdg. 13.50 (978-0-613-99759-1(X), Turtleback) Turtleback Bks.

Kelly, Kathy & Feder, Debbie. Jelly Bean's Art Museum Adventure. 2012. 40p. pap. 20.99 (978-1-4772-4828-7(5)) AuthorHouse.

Kelly, Martin & Adamac, Matt. Three Little Kittens. (Illus.). 6p. (J). 4.95 (978-1-929766-24-6(6)) Handprint Bks.

Kelsey, Annie. Love & Chicken Nuggets. 2016. (Pippa Morgan's Diary Ser.: 2). (ENG.). 176p. (J). (gr. 3-7). 12.99 (978-1-4926-3141-5(8), 9781492631415, Sourcebooks Jabberwocky) Sourcebooks, Inc.

Kenah, Katharine. Ferry Tail. Wong, Nicole, illus. 2014. (ENG.). 32p. (J). (gr. k-3). 16.99 (978-1-58536-829-7(6), 203011) Sleeping Bear Pr.

Kendall, Bridget. Bond & the Big Green Hill. 2009. 28p. pap. 13.99 (978-1-4490-1458-2(5)) AuthorHouse.

Kennedy, Laura. Pat's Vat Goes Splat: A Lesson in Honesty. 2013. 12p. pap. 10.99 (978-0-9836230-1-4(5)) Kennedy Enterprises, LLC.

Kent, Derek Taylor. El Perro con Sombrero: A Bilingual Doggy Tale. Henry, Jed, illus. 2015. (ENG & SPA.). 40p. (J). (gr. -1-2). 17.99 (978-0-8050-9989-8(1), 9780805099898, Holt, Henry & Co. Bks. For Young Readers) Holt, Henry & Co.

Keough, Kevin. Snoozy Dog: And Curly Cat Too! 2011. 24p. (gr. -1). pap. 12.98 (978-1-4389-4794-5(1)) AuthorHouse.

Kerr, Judith. Goodbye Mog. Kerr, Judith, illus. 2003. (ENG., Illus.). 32p. (J). (gr. k-2). pap. 9.99 (978-0-00-714969-8(7), HarperCollins Children's Bks.) HarperCollins Pubs. Ltd. GBR. Dist: HarperCollins Pubs.

—Mog & Bunny. Kerr, Judith, illus. 2005. (Mog Ser.). (ENG., Illus.). 32p. (J). (gr. k-2). pap. 10.99 (978-0-00-717130-9(7)) HarperCollins Pubs. Ltd. GBR. Dist: Independent Pubs. Group.

—Mog & the Baby. Kerr, Judith, illus. 2005. (ENG., Illus.). 32p. (J). (gr. k-2). pap. 11.95 (978-0-00-717132-3(3), HarperCollins Children's Bks.) HarperCollins Pubs. Ltd. GBR. Dist: HarperCollins Pubs.

—Mog & the Granny. (Illus.). (J). (ENG.). 100p. 17.99 (978-0-00-198176-8(5)); 32p. pap. 9.99 (978-0-00-664592-4(5)) HarperCollins Pubs. Ltd. GBR. Dist: Trafalgar Square Publishing.

—MOG & the V. E. T. Kerr, Judith, illus. 2005. (ENG., Illus.). 32p. (J). (gr. k-2). pap. 9.99 (978-0-00-717128-6(5), HarperCollins Children's Bks.) HarperCollins Pubs. Ltd. GBR. Dist: HarperCollins Pubs.

—Mog & the Vet. (ENG., Illus.). (J). 34p. 19.99 (978-0-00-198211-6(7)); 32p. pap. 9.99 (978-0-00-664620-4(4)) HarperCollins Pubs. Ltd. GBR. Dist: Trafalgar Square Publishing.

—Mog in the Dark. (ENG., Illus.). 48p. (J). pap. 9.99 (978-0-00-662774-6(9)) HarperCollins Pubs. Ltd. GBR. Dist: Trafalgar Square Publishing.

—Mog in the Dark. Kerr, Judith, illus. 2006. (ENG., Illus.). 48p. (J). (gr. k-2). pap. 9.99 (978-0-00-717133-0(1), HarperCollins Children's Bks.) HarperCollins Pubs. Ltd. GBR. Dist: HarperCollins Pubs.

—Mog on Fox Night. (ENG., Illus.). 32p. (J). pap. 9.99 (978-0-00-664501-6(1)) HarperCollins Pubs. Ltd. GBR. Dist: Trafalgar Square Publishing.

—Mog on Fox Night. Kerr, Judith, illus. 2004. (ENG., Illus.). 32p. (J). (gr. k-2). pap. 12.95 (978-0-00-717136-1(6), HarperCollins Children's Bks.) HarperCollins Pubs. Ltd. GBR. Dist: HarperCollins Pubs.

—Mog the Forgetful Cat. Kerr, Judith, illus. 2006. (ENG., Illus.). 40p. (J). (gr. -1-2). bds. 7.99 (978-0-00-722895-9(3), HarperCollins Children's Bks.) HarperCollins Pubs. Ltd. GBR. Dist: HarperCollins Pubs.

—Mog's ABC. Kerr, Judith, illus. 2005. (ENG., Illus.). 48p. (J). (gr. -1-k). pap. 8.99 (978-0-00-717131-6(5), HarperCollins Children's Bks.) HarperCollins Pubs. Ltd. GBR. Dist: HarperCollins Pubs.

—Mog's Bad Thing. 2004. (Mog Ser.). (ENG., Illus.). 32p. (J). (gr. k-2). pap. 9.99 (978-0-00-664755-3(3), HarperSport) HarperCollins Pubs. Ltd. GBR. Dist: Independent Pubs. Group.

—Mog's Christmas. unabr. ed. 2005. (ENG., Illus.). 32p. (J). pap. 14.00 incl. audio compact disk (978-0-00-719366-0(1)) HarperCollins Pubs.

—Twinkles, Arthur & Puss. Kerr, Judith, illus. 2008. (ENG., Illus.). 40p. (J). (gr. k-2). pap. 9.95 (978-0-00-725447-7(4)) HarperCollins Pubs. Ltd. GBR. Dist: Independent Pubs. Group.

—Twinkles, Arthur & Puss. 2007. (ENG., Illus.). 40p. (J). (gr. k-2). 22.95 (978-0-00-725446-0(6)) HarperCollins Pubs. Ltd. GBR. Dist: Independent Pubs. Group.

Kessler, Liz. Poppy the Pirate Dog & the Missing Treasure. Phillips, Mike, illus. (Candlewick Sparks Ser.). (ENG.). 64p. (J). (gr. k-4). 2016. pap. 3.99 (978-0-7636-8772-4(3)) 2015. 14.99 (978-0-7636-7497-7(4)) Candlewick Pr.

Key, Pamela Marie. Kitty Fantastic in Monroe's Art Adventure. 2006. (Illus.). 40p. (J). (gr. -1-3). per. 17.95 (978-0-9771971-1-8(5)) Brass Frog Bookworks.

Khan, Hana. Taylor's Birthday Party. Kemble, Mai S., illus. 2008. (J). (978-1-60108-048-6(4)) Red Cygnet Pr.

Kiick, Lisa. Bailey & Friends. Stouch, Ryan, illus. 2008. 40p. pap. 14.95 (978-1-59858-743-2(9)) Dog Ear Publishing, LLC.

Kim, Aram. Cat on the Bus. Kim, Aram, illus. 2016. (ENG., Illus.). 32p. (J). (gr. -1-1). 16.95 (978-0-8234-3647-7(0)) Holiday Hse., Inc.

King, Clive. The Town That Went South. 2014. (ENG., Illus.). 128p. (J). (gr. 3-7). pap. 13.99 (978-1-4814-4487-3(5), Atheneum Bks. for Young Readers) Simon & Schuster Children's Publishing.

King, Julia. Bingo Explores the Farm. (ENG., Illus.). 46p. (J). 2012. pap. 8.99 (978-0-9839827-1-5(6)) 2011. lib. bdg. 15.99 (978-0-9839827-0-8(8)) King, Julia.

—Bingo's Big Adventure: A Cat's Tale. 2010. (ENG., Illus.). 36p. (J). pap. 8.99 (978-0-615-37032-3(2)) King, Julia.

King-smith, Dick. The Catlady. Eastwood, John, illus. 2007. (ENG.). 80p. (J). (gr. 1-4). 5.99 (978-0-440-42031-6(8), Yearling) Random Hse. Children's Bks.

—Three Terrible Trins. 105p. (J). pap. 4.99 (978-0-8072-1482-4(5), Listening Library) Random Hse. Audio Publishing Group.

King, Zelda. Where's That Cat? 2006. (Neighborhood Readers Ser.). (ENG.). 12p. (gr. 1-3). pap. 5.90 (978-1-4042-6851-7(0), Rosen Classroom) Rosen Publishing Group, Inc., The.

Kinsman, Josephine. Ginger's New Tail. 2011. 40p. pap. 24.95 (978-1-4626-1184-3(2)) America Star Bks.

Kirby, Ruth M. Claudius Saves the Pumpkin Patch. Larson, Lisa K., illus. 2008. 20p. pap. 24.95 (978-1-60703-827-6(7)) America Star Bks.

Kirby, Stan. Captain Awesome & the New Kid. O'Connor, George, illus. 2012. (Captain Awesome Ser.: 3). (ENG.). 128p. (J). (gr. k-4). 16.99 (978-1-4424-4200-9(X)); pap. 5.99 (978-1-4424-4199-6(2)) Little Simon. (Little Simon).

—Captain Awesome & the New Kid. 2012. (Captain Awesome Ser.: 3). lib. bdg. 16.00 (978-0-606-26324-5(1), Turtleback) Turtleback Bks.

Kitten. (Buggy Buddies Ser.). (Illus.). (J). (gr. -1). bds. (978-1-56021-350-5(7), 201) W.J. Fantasy, Inc.

Kitten chased a Fly 6 Packs. Individual Title. (gr. 1-2). 22.00 (978-0-7635-9163-2(7)) Rigby Education.

Kittens: Individual Title Six-Packs. (Literatura 2000 Ser.). (gr. -1-1). 28.00 (978-0-7635-0033-7(X)) Rigby Education.

Kitten's House. Date not set. (Illus.). (J). bds. 4.98 (978-1-4054-0786-1(7)) Parragon, Inc.

The Kitty with the Racoon Tail. 2006. (J). per. (978-0-9772425-7-3(9)) BLPH, Inc.

Klimpton, Diana. Amy Wild, Animal Talker - the Musical Mouse. 2013. pap. 4.99 (978-0-7945-3145-4(8), Usborne) EDC Publishing.

Kline, Suzy. Horrible Harry & the Goog. Remkiewicz, Frank & Frank, Remkiewicz, illus. 2006. (Horrible Harry Ser.). (ENG.). 64p. (J). (gr. 2-4). pap. 4.99 (978-0-14-240728-8(3), Puffin Books) Penguin Young Readers Group.

—Horrible Harry & the Goog. Remkiewicz, Frank, illus. 2006. (Horrible Harry Ser.). 56p. (gr. 2-5). 14.00 (978-0-7569-6948-6(4)) Perfection Learning Corp.

Knight, Chris. Piggy's Party. 2011. (Illus.). 36p. (gr. 1-2). pap. 17.07 (978-1-4520-9585-1(X)) AuthorHouse.

Kochalka, James. Dragon Puncher Book 1. 2010. (Dragon Puncher Ser.: 1). (ENG., Illus.). 40p. (J). (gr. 2-5). 9.95 (978-1-60309-057-5(6), 9781603090575) Top Shelf Productions.

—Dragon Puncher Book 2: Dragon Puncher Island: Dragon Puncher Island. 2011. (Dragon Puncher Ser.: 2). (ENG., Illus.). 40p. (J). (gr. 2-5). 9.95 (978-1-60309-085-8(1), 9781603090858) Top Shelf Productions.

Korte, Steve. The Cat Crime Club, 1 vol. Baltazar, Art, illus. 2012. (DC Super-Pets Ser.). (ENG.). 56p. (gr. 2-2). pap. 4.95 (978-1-4048-7665-1(0)); 23.99 (978-1-4048-6493-1(8)) Picture Window Bks. (DC Super-Pets).

Koubena, Elizabeth. The Trouble with Harry. 2005. (Illus.). 20p. (J). 11.00 (978-1-4120-4075-4(2)) Trafford Publishing.

Kouris, Kiki. Kittens of Color. 2011. 28p. pap. 15.99 (978-1-4568-3238-4(7)) Xlibris Corp.

Krailing, Tessa. El Ladron de Gatos. (Club de las Mascotas Coleccion). (SPA.). 96p. (J). (gr. 3). (978-84-88061-89-8(7)) Serres, Ediciones, S. L. ESP. Dist: Lectorum Pubns., Inc.

Krasnesky, Thad. That Cat Can't Stay. Parkins, David, illus. 2010. (ENG.). 32p. (J). (gr. k-2). 16.95 (978-0-9799746-5-6(8)) Flashlight Pr.

Kredensor, Diane. Ollie & Moon: Aloha! 2013. (Step into Reading Ser.). (ENG., Illus.). 48p. (J). (gr. 1-4). 3.99 (978-0-307-97950-6(4), Random Hse. Bks. for Young Readers) Random Hse. Children's Bks.

Krejewski, Sandra. Kitty Kitty. 2009. 16p. (J). 12.50 (978-1-60695-038-8(X)) Callanish Pr.

Kreloff, Elliot, illus. No More TV, Sleepy Cat. 2005. (I'm Going to Read(r) Ser.). (ENG.). 28p. (J). (gr. -1-k). pap. 3.95 (978-1-4027-2508-1(6)) Sterling Publishing Co., Inc.

Krensky, Stephen. Fraidy Cats. Lewin, Betsy, illus. 2015. (Scholastic Reader, Level 2 Ser.). (ENG.). 32p. (J). (gr. -1-3). pap. 3.99 (978-0-545-79966-9(X), Cartwheel Bks.) Scholastic, Inc.

—Fraidy Cats. 2015. (Scholastic Reader Level 2 Ser.). lib. bdg. 13.55 (978-0-606-37747-8(6)) Turtleback Bks.

—Malarkey & the Big Trap. Shortley, Michele, illus. 2011. 29p. (J). pap. (978-0-7680-3487-5(6)) SAE Intl.

—Snack Attack. Curtis, Stacy, illus. 2008. (Ready-To-Reads Ser.). (ENG.). 32p. (J). (gr. -1-1). pap. 3.99 (978-1-4169-0238-6(4), Simon Spotlight) Simon Spotlight.

Kristen, Judith. My Name Is Henley: My life & times as a rescued Dog. 2007. 150p. (J). per. 11.95 (978-0-9800448-0-5(4)) Aquinas & Krone Publishing, LLC.

Krivinskas, Carol Italiano. Barnyard Babies to the Rescue. 2008. 20p. pap. 13.95 (978-1-4327-2183-1(6)) Outskirts Pr., Inc.

Kroll, Jeri. A Coat of Cats. James, Ann, illus. 32p. pap. (978-0-7344-0118-2(3), Lothian Children's Bks.) Hachette Australia.

Kroll, Jeri & James, Ann. A Coat of Cats. (Illus.). 32p. (978-0-85091-953-0(3), Lothian Children's Bks.) Hachette Australia.

Krosoczka, Jarrett J. Ollie the Purple Elephant. 2011. (ENG.). 40p. (J). (gr. -1-2). 16.99 (978-0-375-86654-8(X), Knopf Bks. for Young Readers) Random Hse. Children's Bks.

Krulik, Nancy. Follow That Furball. Braun, Sebastien, illus. 2013. (Magic Bone Ser.: 3). (ENG.). 128p. (J). (gr. 1-3). 5.99 (978-0-448-46445-9(4), Grosset & Dunlap) Penguin Young Readers Group.

—Follow That Furball. 2013. (Magic Bone Ser.: 3). lib. bdg. 16.00 (978-0-606-32127-3(6), Turtleback) Turtleback Bks.

Kunhardt, Dorothy. Pat the Bunny: First Books for Baby, 3 vols. 2015. (Touch-And-Feel Ser.). (ENG., Illus.). 20p. (J). (— 1). pap. 29.99 (978-0-553-50838-3(5), Golden Bks.) Random Hse. Children's Bks.

Kuntz, Doug & Shrodes, Amy. Lost & Found Cat: The True Story of Kunkush's Incredible Journey. Cornelison, Sue, illus. 2017. (ENG.). 48p. (J). (gr. -1-3). 17.99 (978-1-5247-1547-2(6), Crown Books For Young Readers) Random Hse. Children's Bks.

Kuskin, Karla. So, What's It Like to Be a Cat? Lewin, Betsy, illus. (ENG.). (J). (gr. -1-3). 2008. 40p. 7.99 (978-0-689-85930-4(9)) 2005. 32p. 17.99 (978-0-689-84733-2(5)) Simon & Schuster Children's Publishing. (Atheneum Bks. for Young Readers).

Laaker, Terry, illus. Charlie the Spy: Charlie's Great Adventure #6. 2008. 104p. (J). pap. 5.95 (978-0-9702546-7-2(9)) GoodyGoody Bks.

Lachenmeyer, Nathaniel. Scarlatti's Cat. Beccia, Carlyn, illus. 2014. (ENG.). 32p. (J). (gr. -1-3). 16.95 (978-0-7613-5472-7(7), Carolrhoda Bks.) Lerner Publishing Group.

Lal, Neeta. The Whisker Cats: Life on the Farm. 2012. 16p. pap. 15.99 (978-1-4772-3706-9(2)) AuthorHouse.

Lambe, Mona. Yintin Tales. 2013. (Illus.). 60p. pap. (978-0-9576015-0-5(6)) Moyin Bks.

Lamuth, Nancy. Lucky & Me. Thomas, Richard A., illus. 2012. 20p. pap. 24.95 (978-1-4626-0665-8(2)) America Star Bks.

Landstrom, Olof, et al. Boo & Baa Have Company. Sandin, Joan, tr. from SWE. 2006. (Illus.). 40p. (J). (gr. -1-1). 15.00 (978-91-29-66546-8(9)) R & S Bks. SWE. Dist: Macmillan.

Lane, M. j. & Lane, M. J. Where in the World Is Snickers? 2011. 42p. pap. 19.99 (978-0-557-81843-3(5)) Lulu Pr., Inc.

Lane, Nathan & Elliott, Devlin. Naughty Mabel. Krall, Dan, illus. 2015. (Naughty Mabel Ser.). (ENG.). 48p. (J). (gr. -1-3). 17.99 (978-1-4814-3022-7(X), Simon & Schuster Bks. For Young Readers) Simon & Schuster Bks. For Young Readers.

Lang, Valerie E. Jet's Day: A Whisker Team Story. 2011. 32p. pap. 13.00 (978-1-61204-178-0(7), Strategic Bk. Publishing) Strategic Book Publishing & Rights Agency (SBPRA).

Langford, Virginia. Monty Says Mice Are Nice. 2009. 20p. pap. 12.95 (978-1-4389-3429-7(7)) AuthorHouse.

LaRochelle, David. This Is Not a Cat. Wohnoutka, Mike, illus. 2016. (ENG.). 40p. (J). (gr. -1). 14.95 (978-1-4549-1574-4(9)) Sterling Publishing Co., Inc.

Larson, Kirby. Audacity Jones Steals the Show (Audacity Jones #2) 2017. (Audacity Jones Ser.: 2). (ENG.). 192p. (J). (gr. 3-7). 16.99 (978-0-545-84065-1(1), Scholastic Pr.) Scholastic, Inc.

Larwick, Valerie. A Cat Named Frenchy Blue: Arrow Yellow Dog of the great Northwest. 2011. 60p. pap. 23.88 (978-1-4634-0868-8(4)) AuthorHouse.

Lashley, Beverly. One Can Never Have Too Many Cats!! Morrow, Jason, illus. 2006. (J). *(978-0-9786835-0-4(1))* Two Tired Teachers Connection, Inc., The.

Lasota, Mary. Kitty Piper Angel Cat: I Almost Lost My Best Friend. 2009. 36p. pap. 16.99 *(978-1-4490-2012-5(7))* AuthorHouse.

—Kitty Piper, Angel Cat, Book: A tribute to Scooter. 2011. 32p. pap. 14.39 *(978-1-4634-4750-2(7))* AuthorHouse.

—Kitty Piper Angel Cat, Book: Sweet Lucy. 2012. 40p. pap. 20.99 *(978-1-4772-6076-0(5))* AuthorHouse.

—Kitty Piper, Angel Cat, Book 2: The Venusians Have Landed. 2010. 40p. pap. 18.46 *(978-1-4520-8823-5(3))* AuthorHouse.

Lathan, Betty Jean. Sierra, the Unwanted Cat. 2011. 28p. pap. 13.59 *(978-1-4567-3297-4(8))* AuthorHouse.

LaTondre, Richard. Grandpa's Cat. 2006. 9.00 *(978-0-8059-7343-3(5))* Dorrance Publishing Co., Inc.

Laughing Elephant Staff, creator. Cats' Christmas ABC. 2012. (Christmas Ser.). (Illus.). 54p. pap. 4.95 *(978-1-59583-393-8(5)*, 9781595833938) Laughing Elephant.

The Laughing Lavender Field. 2005. (J). 5.00 *(978-0-9765731-0-4(5))* DTJ, LLC.

Laura Beth. Two Girls 2 Cats: A Magical Mystery, 1 vol. 2010. 130p. pap. 24.95 *(978-1-4489-4235-0(7))* PublishAmerica, Inc.

Laurie, Peter. Mauby & the Hurricane. 2007. (Illus.). 56p. pap. 16.00 *(978-1-4050-7718-7(2))* Macmillan Caribbean GBR. Dist: Interlink Publishing Group, Inc.

Laurin, Anthony. Mally. 2011. 28p. pap. 24.95 *(978-1-4626-3672-3(1))* America Star Bks.

Laverty, Neil. Bebe's Big Adventure: A Bebe & Muckle Book. Diana Cox, illus. 2013. 44p. pap. 17.97 *(978-1-62212-612-5(2)*, Strategic Bk. Publishing) Strategic Book Publishing & Rights Agency (SBPRA).

Lawson, Jessica. Sharing & Making Friends. 2010. 20p. pap. 10.00 *(978-1-60911-707-8(7)*, Eloquent Bks.) Strategic Book Publishing & Rights Agency (SBPRA).

Lawson, Julie. The Klondike Cat. Mombourquette, Paul, illus. 2004. (ENG.). 32p. (J). (gr. k-4). 5.95 *(978-1-55337-766-5(4))* Kids Can Pr., Ltd. CAN. Dist: Hachette Bk. Group.

Layton, Roxanne A. Eddie Saves Cats. 2012. 26p. 24.95 *(978-1-4626-6193-0(9))* America Star Bks.

—Keep Goin' Owen! 2012. 24p. pap. 24.95 *(978-1-4626-6599-0(3))* America Star Bks.

Le Gall, Frank. Freedom! Balthazar, Flore, illus. 2012. (Miss Annie Ser.). 48p. (J). (gr. 2-4). pap. 39.62 *(978-0-7613-9281-1(5))*; (ENG.). lib. bdg. 29.27 *(978-0-7613-7884-6(7))* Lerner Publishing Group. (Graphic Universe™).

—Miss Annie. Balthazar, Flore, illus. 2012. (Miss Annie Ser.). 48p. (J). (gr. 2-4). lib. bdg. 58.54 *(978-0-7613-8902-6(4)*, Graphic Universe™) Lerner Publishing Group.

—Miss Annie: 6Pack Set. Balthazar, Flore, illus. 2012. (Miss Annie Ser.). 48p. (J). (gr. 2-4). pap. 79.23 *(978-0-7613-9284-2(X)*, Graphic Universe™) Lerner Publishing Group.

—Miss Annie: Single Copy Set. Balthazar, Flore, illus. 2012. (Miss Annie Ser.). 48p. (J). (gr. 2-4). pap. 13.21 *(978-0-7613-9283-5(1)*, Graphic Universe™) Lerner Publishing Group.

—Rooftop Cat. Balthazar, Flore, illus. 2012. (Miss Annie Ser.). 48p. (J). (gr. 2-4). pap. 39.62 *(978-0-7613-9282-8(3))*; (ENG.). lib. bdg. 29.27 *(978-0-7613-7885-3(5))* Lerner Publishing Group. (Graphic Universe™).

Le Gall, Frank & Doo, Robin. Freedom! Balthazar, Flore, illus. 2012. (Miss Annie Ser.: 1). (ENG.). 48p. (J). (gr. 2-4). pap. 6.95 *(978-0-7613-8546-2(0)*, Graphic Universe™) Lerner Publishing Group.

Le Guin, Ursula K. Catwings. 2003. (Catwings Ser.: 1). (gr. 3-6). lib. bdg. 16.00 *(978-0-613-70842-5(3)*, Turtleback) Turtleback Bks.

—Catwings Return. 2003. (Catwings Ser.: 2). (gr. 3-6). lib. bdg. 16.00 *(978-0-613-65072-4(7)*, Turtleback) Turtleback Bks.

Lear, Edward. Buho y la Gatita.Tr. of Owl & the Cat. (SPA., Illus.). 32p. (J). 14.95 *(978-84-261-3023-5(2))* Juventud, Editorial ESP. Dist: AIMS International Bks., Inc.

—The Owl & the Pussy-Cat & Other Stories. 2012. (ENG., Illus.). 80p. (J). (gr. 2). 12.99 *(978-0-7123-5876-7(5))* British Library, The GBR. Dist: Independent Pubs. Group.

Leatham, Alan D. Four Cats, Five Monkeys, Absurd Birds & Other Fanciful Stuff. 2006. 108p. pap. 19.95 *(978-1-4241-0692-9(3))* America Star Bks.

Leathers, Philippa. How to Catch a Mouse. Leathers, Philippa, illus. 2015. (ENG., Illus.). 40p. (J). (gr. -1-2). 15.99 *(978-0-7636-6912-6(1))* Candlewick Pr.

LeBaron, Cecilia. The Map. 2007. (Illus.). 16p. (J). 5.95 *(978-0-9798869-1-1(0))* Crush Publishing.

—Nat & Tab. 2007. (Illus.). 16p. (J). 5.95 *(978-0-9798869-0-4(2))* Crush Publishing.

—Sam & Val. 2007. (Illus.). 16p. (J). 5.95 *(978-0-9798869-3-5(7))* Crush Publishing.

Lee, G. I Want My Kitty Cat Tv! Scott, E., illus. 2012. 24p. pap. 24.95 *(978-1-4626-6610-2(8))* America Star Bks.

Lee, Ingrid. Cat Found. 2013. (ENG.). 176p. (J). (gr. 3-7). pap. 6.99 *(978-0-545-35108-9(1)*, Chicken Hse., The) Scholastic, Inc.

Lee, Lee. The Lost Kitten. Sakai, Komako, illus. 2017. (ENG.). 32p. (gr. -1-k). 16.99 *(978-1-77657-126-0(6))* Gecko Pr. NZL. Dist: Lerner Publishing Group.

Lefèvre, A. M. Pws Esgid Uchel. 2005. (WEL., Illus.). 10p. *(978-0-86381-647-5(9))* Gwasg Carreg Gwalch.

Lehman, Jacques. The Adventures of Pepe Pandejo. 2007. 64p. per. 16.95 *(978-1-4241-4980-3(0))* PublishAmerica, Inc.

Lemaster, Karen Frisbie. Little Bill the Bengal Kitten: The Black Smoke Kitten. 2013. 36p. pap. 20.99 *(978-1-4772-9981-4(5))* AuthorHouse.

Lement, Wendy. Keri Tarr - Cat Detective. Burrows, Jeffrey Scott, illus. 2004. (ENG.). 80p. (J). pap. 9.95 *(978-1-891369-52-0(0))* Breakaway Bks.

Lendroth, Susan. Maneki Neko: The Tale of the Beckoning Cat. Otoshi, Kathryn, illus. 2010. (J). *(978-1-885008-39-8(2)*, Shen's Bks.) Lee & Low Bks., Inc.

LenKaitis-Thompson, Kristen. Momo Kitty, Maddy Girl, & the Strange Little Creature, 1 vol. 2010. 16p. pap. 24.95 *(978-1-4489-8976-8(0))* PublishAmerica, Inc.

Levandowski, Barbara. The Adventures of Muffin & Alexander: A New Home, a New Beginning. 2011. (SPA.). 28p. pap. 16.95 *(978-1-4269-5917-2(6))* Trafford Publishing.

—The Adventures of Muffin & Alexander: Let the Explorations Begin. 2011. 36p. pap. *(978-1-4269-8746-5(3))* Trafford Publishing (UK) Ltd.

—The Adventures of Muffin & Alexander: The Please & Thank You Tea Party. 2012. 36p. pap. 18.41 *(978-1-4669-6246-0(1))* Trafford Publishing.

Lewin, Betsy. Thumpy Feet. Lewin, Betsy, illus. 2014. (ENG., Illus.). 32p. (J). (gr. -1-1). 6.99 *(978-0-8234-3174-8(6))* Holiday Hse., Inc.

—Where Is Tippy Toes? Lewin, Betsy, illus. 2010. (ENG., Illus.). 32p. (J). (gr. -1-2). 16.99 *(978-1-4169-3808-8(7)*, Atheneum Bks. for Young Readers) Simon & Schuster Children's Publishing.

Lewis. Want to Trade Two Brothers for a Cat? 2008. (ENG.). 112p. (YA). (gr. 7). pap. 7.95 *(978-1-4169-7538-0(1)*, Simon Pulse) Simon Pulse.

Lewis, Lorinne. Junior & Callie's Awesome Adventure. 2012. 36p. pap. 16.95 *(978-1-62709-269-2(2))* America Star Bks.

Lewis, Melinda. Bulls-Eye Bob & the Backyard Buddies. 2008. 68p. pap. 15.99 *(978-1-4363-3109-8(9))* Xlibris Corp.

Lightfoot, Joanne. The Cat & the Fat Suit. 2012. (Illus.). 32p. pap. 21.35 *(978-1-4678-9080-9(4))* AuthorHouse.

Limon, Cyndi. Hello, My Name Is Boots. 2011. 20p. pap. 10.50 *(978-1-4634-3670-4(X))* AuthorHouse.

Lindbergh, Reeve. Homer: The Library Cat. Wilsdorf, Anne, illus. 2011. (ENG.). 32p. (J). (gr. -1-3). 16.99 *(978-0-7636-3448-3(4))* Candlewick Pr.

Lindemann, Lindy. A Cat's Tale, One Cat's Search for the Meaning of Life. Wheeler, Jody, illus. 2007. 28p. per. 12.95 *(978-1-934246-03-0(4))* Peppertree Pr., The.

Lindman. Flicka, Ricka, Dicka & the Three Kittens. Lindman, illus. 2013. (Flicka, Ricka, Dicka Ser.). (ENG., Illus.). 32p. (J). (gr. k-3). 9.99 *(978-0-8075-2515-9(4))* Whitman, Albert & Co.

Lisi, Charlotte. I Am Special. Ortega, David, illus. 2006. 16p. (J). 9.99 *(978-1-4120-8911-1(5))* Trafford Publishing.

Lisle, Janet Taylor. Highway Cats. 2009. (ENG.). 128p. (J). (gr. 3-7). 6.99 *(978-0-14-241485-9(9)*, Puffin Books) Penguin Young Readers Group.

Little, Jean. The Birthday Girl. Lawrason, June, illus. 2004. 64p. (J). lib. bdg. 20.00 *(978-1-4242-1256-9(1))* Fitzgerald Bks.

Little Kitten. 2003. (Goodnight Mr. Moon Ser.). (Illus.). (J). bds. 2.98 *(978-0-7525-4743-5(7))* Parragon, Inc.

Littlewolf, Grandmother. Mr. Feathers & the Geow-Lud-Mo-Sis-Eg. 2013. 16p. pap. 10.00 *(978-1-62212-968-3(7)*, Strategic Bk. Publishing) Strategic Book Publishing & Rights Agency (SBPRA).

Litwin, Eric. I Love My White Shoes. Dean, James, illus. 2010. (Pete the Cat Ser.). 40p. (J). (gr. -1-3). (ENG.). 17.99 *(978-0-06-190622-0(0))*; lib. bdg. 17.89 *(978-0-06-190623-7(9))* HarperCollins Pubs.

—Pete the Cat & His Four Groovy Buttons. 2013. (CHI & ENG.). (J). (gr. -1-2). ***(978-957-570-982-2(9))*** Eastern Publishing Co., Ltd., The.

—Pete the Cat & His Four Groovy Buttons. Dean, James, illus. 2012. (Pete the Cat Ser.). 40p. (J). (gr. -1-2). (ENG.). 17.99 *(978-0-06-211058-9(6))*; lib. bdg. 17.89 *(978-0-06-211059-6(4))* HarperCollins Pubs.

—Pete the Cat Saves Christmas. Dean, James, illus. (Pete the Cat Ser.). 40p. (J). (gr. -1-3). 2014. (ENG.). 17.99 *(978-0-06-211062-6(4))* 2012. lib. bdg. 18.89 *(978-0-06-211063-3(2))* HarperCollins Pubs.

—Rocking in My School Shoes. Dean, James, illus. 2011. (Pete the Cat Ser.). 40p. (J). (gr. -1-3). (ENG.). 17.99 *(978-0-06-191024-1(4))*; lib. bdg. 17.89 *(978-0-06-191025-8(2))* HarperCollins Pubs.

Litwin, Eric, ed. Rocking in My School Shoes. 2011. *(978-0-545-50106-4(7))* Scholastic, Inc.

Litwin, Eric & Dean, James. I Love My White Shoes. 2010. (Pete the Cat Ser.). pap. *(978-0-545-41966-6(2))* Scholastic, Inc.

Lively, Deborah Dreher. Hateya Sam. 2009. 32p. pap. 13.75 *(978-1-60860-029-8(7)*, Eloquent Bks.) Strategic Book Publishing & Rights Agency (SBPRA).

Llewellyn, Claire. Cat Nap, 1 vol. East, Jacqueline, illus. 2013. (Start Reading Ser.). (ENG.). 24p. (gr. k-1). pap. 7.95 *(978-1-4765-4087-0(X))* Capstone Press of Coughlan Cos.

Lloyd, Sam R. & Lloyd, Sam. Mr. Pusskins: A Love Story. Lloyd, Sam R. & Lloyd, Sam, illus. 2006. (ENG., Illus.). 32p. (J). (gr. -1-3). 17.99 *(978-1-4169-2517-0(1)*, Atheneum Bks. for Young Readers) Simon & Schuster Children's Publishing.

—Mr. Pusskins & Little Whiskers: Another Love Story. Lloyd, Sam R. & Lloyd, Sam, illus. 2008. (ENG., Illus.). 32p. (J). (gr. -1-3). 17.99 *(978-1-4169-5796-6(0)*, Atheneum Bks. for Young Readers) Simon & Schuster Children's Publishing.

Lochhead, Joyce N. The Adventures of Mr Figaro Tailhead. 2008. 172p. pap. 11.99 *(978-1-4389-0790-1(7))* AuthorHouse.

Lockwood, Penny. Boo's Bad Day. Johnson, Deborah C., illus. 2013. 32p. pap. 11.99 *(978-0-9852661-5-8(5))* 4RV Publishing, LLC.

Lodge, Jo, illus. Pounce! Little Kitten. 2017. (Little Movers Ser.). (ENG.). 10p. (J). (gr. -1-k). bds. 9.99 ***(978-1-5098-0669-0(5))*** Pan Macmillan GBR. Dist: Independent Pubs. Group.

Lomas, Graham. Smoky the Mischievous Kitten. 2012. 24p. pap. 28.03 *(978-1-4691-6973-6(8))* Xlibris Corp.

Lombardi, Kristine A. Mr. Biddles. Lombardi, Kristine A., illus. 2017. (Illus.). 40p. (J). (gr. -1-3). 17.99 ***(978-0-06-244114-0(0))*** HarperCollins Pubs.

Lombardo, Constance. Mr. Puffball: Stunt Cat Across America. Lombardo, Constance, illus. 2016. (Mr. Puffball Ser.: 2). (Illus.). 240p. (J). (gr. 3-7). 12.99 *(978-0-06-232068-1(8)*, Tegen, Katherine Bks) HarperCollins Pubs.

—Stunt Cat to the Stars. Lombardo, Constance, illus. 2015. (Mr. Puffball Ser.: 1). (ENG., Illus.). 240p. (J). (gr. 3-7). 12.99 *(978-0-06-232065-0(3))* HarperCollins Pubs.

Long, Angela Pullam. Salvador the Spy in the Case of the Missing Cats. 2008. 32p. pap. 24.95 *(978-1-60672-724-9(9))* America Star Bks.

Long, Ethan. Big Cat. Long, Ethan, illus. 2016. (I Like to Read(r) Ser.). (ENG., Illus.). 24p. (J). (gr. -1-3). 6.99 *(978-0-8234-3539-5(3))*; 14.95 *(978-0-8234-3538-8(5))* Holiday Hse., Inc.

Long, Olivia. Too Many Kittens. Long, Olivia, illus. Date not set. (Pets & Their People Ser.). (Illus.). 32p. (J). (gr. -1-4). *(978-1-880042-09-0(6))* Shelf-Life Bks.

Lopresti, Tony. My Cat. Johnson, Deborah C., illus. 2012. 24p. pap. 13.99 *(978-0-9838018-6-3(X))* 4RV Publishing, LLC.

Loran. My Friends Call Me Rocky: Book I Rocky's Rescue Book Ii Runaway Rocky. 2003. 108p. pap. 13.95 *(978-1-4140-3116-3(5))* AuthorHouse.

Lord, Janet. Where Is Catkin?, 1 vol. Paschkis, Julie, illus. (ENG.). 32p. (J). (gr. -1-1). 2013. 7.95 *(978-1-56145-684-0(5))* 2010. 16.95 *(978-1-56145-523-2(7))* Peachtree Pubs.

Lotorto-Soroka, Mary. Memoirs of a Cat: Interpreted for Humans Too! 2011. 32p. (gr. 1-2). 14.50 *(978-1-4567-4323-9(6))* AuthorHouse.

Lowery, Mike. The Rise of the Rusty Robo-Cat! 2017. (Doodle Adventures Ser.). (ENG., Illus.). 112p. (J). (gr. 2). 12.95 *(978-0-7611-8721-9(9))* Workman Publishing Co., Inc.

Lowthert, Carrie. Minkie & Emily. 2007. 66p. pap. 11.95 *(978-1-4303-2576-5(3))* Lulu Pr., Inc.

Lucero, Erik Kristofer. Ki-Ky the Cat. 2011. 24p. pap. 24.95 *(978-1-4560-3761-1(7))* America Star Bks.

Luciani, Brigitte. A Hubbub. Gauvin, Edward, tr. from FRE. Tharlet, Eve, illus. 2010. (Mr. Badger & Mrs. Fox Ser.: 2). (ENG.). 32p. (J). (gr. k-3). pap. 6.95 *(978-0-7613-5632-5(0)*, Graphic Universe™);Bk. 2. 25.26 *(978-0-7613-5626-4(6))* Lerner Publishing Group.

Lueck, Andrew M. Chicabee. 2006. (Illus.). 32p. (gr. -1-3). 16.95 *(978-0-9774547-0-9(3))* Lueck Studios.

Lukesh, Jean A. My Favorite Dog & Cat Story: My Favorite Dog Story/My Favorite Cat Story. Lukesh, Ronald E., illus. 2013. 38p. (J). pap. 14.95 *(978-0-9888021-0-0(4))* Field Mouse Productions.

Lundquist, Mary. Cat & Bunny. Lundquist, Mary, illus. 2015. (ENG., Illus.). 32p. (J). (gr. -1-3). 17.99 *(978-0-06-228780-9(X))* HarperCollins Pubs.

Lundy, Charlotte. Thank You, Jesus. Waldrep, Evelyn L., ed. Claremont, Heather, illus. 2003. 32p. (gr. k-3). 15.95 *(978-0-9670280-1-9(9))* Bay Light Publishing.

Luper, Eric. Gumball's Summer Journal That He Definitely Finished All on His Own. Reed, Stephen, illus. 2015. (Amazing World of Gumball Ser.). (ENG.). 112p. (J). (gr. 3-7). 8.99 *(978-0-8431-8282-8(2)*, Cartoon Network Books) Penguin Young Readers Group.

Lutz, Barbara. My Cat. 2011. 28p. pap. 15.99 *(978-1-4628-4512-5(6))* Xlibris Corp.

Lutz Ii, William. Prisoner of Castle Windward. 2007. 232p. pap. 14.95 *(978-1-4116-9260-2(8))* Lulu Pr., Inc.

Lyle-Soffe, Shari. Shoo Cat. Foster, Jack, illus. 2010. 16p. pap. 9.95 *(978-1-61633-033-0(3))* Guardian Angel Publishing, Inc.

Lynch, Jay. Otto's Backwards Day. Cammuso, Frank, illus. 2013. (ENG.). 32p. (J). (gr. -1-3). 12.95 *(978-1-935179-33-7(0))* TOON Books / RAW Junior, LLC.

—Otto's Orange Day. Cammuso, Frank, illus. 2013. (ENG.). 40p. (J). (gr. -1-3). pap. 4.99 *(978-1-935179-27-6(6))* TOON Books / RAW Junior, LLC.

—Otto's Orange Day. Mouly, Francoise, ed. Cammuso, Frank, illus. 2008. (ENG.). 40p. (J). (gr. -1-3). 12.95 *(978-0-9799238-2-1(4))* TOON Books / RAW Junior, LLC.

Lynch, Jay & Cammuso, Frank. Otto's Orange Day, 1 vol. 2013. (Toon Bks). (ENG.). 36p. (J). (gr. 2-3). lib. bdg. 27.07 *(978-1-61479-154-6(6))* Spotlight.

—Otto's Orange Day. 2013. (Toon Books Level 3 Ser.). lib. bdg. 14.75 *(978-0-606-32103-7(9)*, Turtleback) Turtleback Bks.

Lynne, Kimberlee, illus. The Frog & the Mouse. 2011. (First Steps in Music Ser.). (ENG.). 32p. (J). (gr. k-2). 16.95 *(978-1-57999-802-8(X))* G I A Pubns., Inc.

MacDonald, Alan. Scaredy Mouse. Warnes, Tim, illus. 2007. (Storytime Board Bks.). 16p. (J). (gr. -1-k). bds. 6.95 *(978-1-58925-827-3(4))* Tiger Tales.

MacDonald, Maryann. The Christmas Cat. Bates, Amy June, illus. 2013. (ENG.). 32p. (J). (gr. -1-k). 16.99 *(978-0-8037-3498-2(0)*, Dial Bks) Penguin Young Readers Group.

MacFarlane, Stuart & MacFarlane, Linda. The Secret Diary of Adrian Cat. 2006. (ENG.). 286p. (J). (gr. 4-8). *(978-1-933255-23-1(4))* DNA Pr.

Mack, Phillip. Missy Finds a Home. 2005. v, 93p. pap. 14.00 *(978-1-4120-6681-5(6))* Trafford Publishing.

Mackall, Dandi Daley. Wild Cat. 2009. (Starlight Animal Rescue Ser.: 3). (ENG.). 224p. (J). (gr. 3-7). mass mkt. 5.99 *(978-1-4143-1270-5(9)*, Tyndale Kids) Tyndale Hse. Pubs.

MacLachlan, Patricia. Waiting for the Magic. Bates, Amy June, illus. (ENG.). (J). (gr. 3-7). 2012. 176p. pap. 6.99 *(978-1-4169-2746-4(8))* 2011. 160p. 16.99 *(978-1-4169-2745-7(X))* Simon & Schuster Children's Publishing. (Atheneum Bks. for Young Readers).

MacLean, Heather. The Mousecat & the Moonicorns on Halloween Night. 2013. 40p. pap. 16.95 *(978-1-4525-7617-6(3)*, Balboa Pr.) Author Solutions, Inc.

Macmillan, Sue. Racing, Chasing Kitten. Ward, Sarah, illus. 2014. (Cheery Chasers Ser.). (ENG.). 8p. (J). (gr. -1 — 1). bds. 4.99 *(978-0-7641-6701-0(4))* Barron's Educational Series, Inc.

Madaras, Diana. Kitty Humbug's Christmas Tail. Madaras, Diana & Nielsen, Ric, illus. 2009. 24p. 17.99 *(978-1-892344-56-4(4))* Palomino Publishing.

Madel, Dan. Cracker the Cat, Almost Caught. 2008. 24p. pap. 24.95 *(978-1-4241-9252-6(8))* America Star Bks.

Mader, C. Roger. Lost Cat. Mader, C. Roger, illus. 2013. (ENG., Illus.). 32p. (J). (gr. -1-3). 17.99 *(978-0-547-97458-3(2))* Houghton Mifflin Harcourt Publishing Co.

Mader, C. Roger, illus. Stowaway in a Sleigh. 2016. (ENG.). 32p. (J). (gr. -1-3). 17.99 *(978-0-544-48174-9(7)*, HMH Books For Young Readers) Houghton Mifflin Harcourt Publishing Co.

Magellan, Mauro. Max the Apartment Cat. Magellan, Mauro, illus. 2013. (Illus.). 36p. pap. 12.95 *(978-0-89334-887-8(2))* Green Dragon Bks.

Magnat, Julien, et al. The Curse of the Cat People. Ellipsanime Staff & Dargaud Media Staff, illus. 2011. (Garfield Graphic Novels Ser.). (ENG.). 32p. (J). (gr. 1-6). 7.99 *(978-1-59707-267-0(2)*, 9781597072670) Papercutz.

Make Believe Ideas. Cuddle Buddies Cat. 2014. (ENG.). 8p. (J). 12.99 *(978-1-78235-959-3(1))* Make Believe Ideas GBR. Dist: Nelson, Thomas Inc.

Malbrough, Mike. Marigold Bakes a Cake. Malbrough, Mike, illus. 2017. (ENG., Illus.). 40p. (J). (gr. -1-2). 17.99 ***(978-1-5247-3738-2(0)***, Philomel Bks.) Penguin Young Readers Group.

Malnor, Carol L. & Hunner, Trina L. Molly's Organic Farm. Hunner, Trina L., illus. 2012. (ENG., Illus.). 32p. (J). (gr. k-4). 16.95 *(978-1-58469-166-2(2))*; pap. 8.95 *(978-1-58469-167-9(0))* Dawn Pubns.

Maltbie, P. I. Bambino & Mr. Twain. Miyares, Daniel, illus. 2012. (ENG.). 40p. (J). (gr. k-3). 15.95 *(978-1-58089-272-8(8))* Charlesbridge Publishing, Inc.

Maltbie, Priscilla. Bambino & Mr. Twain. 2012. 40p. 29.95 *(978-0-8045-4237-1(6))* Spoken Arts, Inc.

Manley, Curtis. The Summer Nick Taught His Cats to Read. Berube, Kate, illus. 2016. (ENG.). 32p. (J). (gr. -1-3). 17.99 *(978-1-4814-3569-7(8)*, Simon & Schuster Bks. For Young Readers) Simon & Schuster Bks. For Young Readers.

Manlove, FionaCarding. The Cat Sat on the Mat. Carding, Hannah, illus. 2011. (ENG.). 32p. (J). (gr. -1-k). pap. 9.99 ***(978-1-85714-373-7(6))*** Ragged Bears USA.

Manning, Jane. Cat Nights. Manning, Jane, illus. 2008. (Illus.). 32p. (J). lib. bdg. 17.89 *(978-0-06-113889-8(4)*, Greenwillow Bks.) HarperCollins Pubs.

Manzak, Bonnie. The Big Red Cat. 2011. 32p. pap. 21.99 *(978-1-4568-6607-5(9))* Xlibris Corp.

Marano, John. Kody the Kid Cop: And the Case of the Missing Cat. 2012. 20p. pap. 17.99 *(978-1-4685-9555-0(5))* AuthorHouse.

Marchi, C. You Can Grow Old with Me: A True Story. 2011. 24p. (gr. -1). pap. 12.95 *(978-1-4520-3716-5(7))* AuthorHouse.

Marciano, John Bemelmans. Madeline & the Cats of Rome. 2008. (Madeline Ser.). (ENG.). 48p. (J). (gr. 1-3). 17.99 *(978-0-670-06297-3(9)*, Viking Books for Young Readers) Penguin Young Readers Group.

—The Nine Lives of Alexander Baddenfield. Blackall, Sophie, illus. 2013. (ENG.). 144p. (J). (gr. 5). 16.99 *(978-0-670-01406-4(0)*, Viking Books for Young Readers) Penguin Young Readers Group.

Marinaro, Stacy. The Cat who rules the Star Mice. 2009. 32p. pap. 15.95 *(978-0-557-08180-6(7))* Lulu Pr., Inc.

Mariolle, Mathieu. Even for a Dreamer Like Me. MiniKim et al, illus. 2010. (Nola's Worlds Ser.: 3). (ENG.). 128p. (J). (gr. 6-9). 30.60 *(978-0-7613-6505-1(2))* Lerner Publishing Group.

—Even for a Dreamer Like Me. Jeffrey, Erica Olson, tr. from FRE. MiniKim et al, illus. 2010. (Nola's Worlds Ser.: 3). (ENG.). 136p. (J). (gr. 6-9). pap. 9.95 *(978-0-7613-6541-9(9)*, Graphic Universe™) Lerner Publishing Group.

—Ferrets & Ferreting Out. Buffiere, Mélanie & Lajic, Maïté, illus. 2010. (Nola's Worlds Ser.: 2). (ENG.). 136p. (J). (gr. 6-9). pap. 9.95 *(978-0-7613-6542-6(7)*, Graphic Universe™) Lerner Publishing Group.

—Ferrets & Ferreting Out. MiniKim et al, illus. 2010. (Nola's Worlds Ser.: 2). (ENG.). 136p. (J). (gr. 6-9). 30.60 *(978-0-7613-6504-4(4))* Lerner Publishing Group.

Marlow, Herb. The Lost Kitten. Head, Pat, illus. 2003. 16p. (J). 19.95 *(978-1-893595-34-7(X))* Four Seasons Bks., Inc.

Marlow, Layn. The Witch with a Twitch. Dreidemy, Joëlle, illus. (Tiger Tales Ser.). (J). (gr. -1-2). 2006. 28p. pap. 6.95 *(978-1-58925-400-8(7))* 2005. 32p. 15.95 *(978-1-58925-052-9(4))* Tiger Tales.

Marois, Andri. Le Chat Botti New York. 2004. (FRE., Illus.). (J). (gr. k-3). spiral bd. *(978-0-616-07263-9(5))* Canadian National Institute for the Blind/Institut National Canadien pour les Aveugles.

Marr, Ella J. The Adventures of Curtis & Grammy. 2006. 57p. pap. 16.95 *(978-1-4241-4743-4(3))* PublishAmerica, Inc.

Marrero, Carla. The Magical Cat. 2006. (ENG., Illus.). 28p. (J). 16.95 *(978-1-59299-232-4(3))* Inkwater Pr.

Marsh, Kay. The Story of Bleulatoo: The Cat That Could Rhyme. 2012. (ENG.). 20p. (J). pap. 11.95 *(978-1-4327-8678-6(4))* Outskirts Pr., Inc.

Martin, Anne E. A Tail & Two Kitties. Martin, Anne E., illus. 2007. (Illus.). 40p. (J). (gr. -1-3). per. 13.99 *(978-1-59879-340-6(3))* Lifevest Publishing, Inc.

Martin, Bill, Jr. & Sampson, Michael. Kitty Cat, Kitty Cat, Are You Going to School?, 0 vols. Bryant, Laura J., illus. 2013. (ENG.). 24p. (J). (gr. -1-2). 16.99 *(978-1-4778-1722-3(0)*, 9781477817223, Amazon Children's Publishing) Amazon Publishing.

—Kitty Cat, Kitty Cat, Are You Going to Sleep?, 0 vols. Bryant, Laura J., illus. 2011. (ENG.). 24p. (J). (gr. -1-3). 15.99 *(978-0-7614-5946-0(4)*, 9780761459460, Amazon Children's Publishing) Amazon Publishing.

—Kitty Cat, Kitty Cat, Are You Waking Up?, 0 vols. Bryant, Laura J., illus. 2011. (ENG.). 26p. (J). (gr. -1-1). pap. 6.99 *(978-0-7614-5841-8(7)*, 9780761458418, Amazon Children's Publishing) Amazon Publishing.

Martin, David Lozell. All for Pie, Pie for All. Gorbachev, Valeri, illus. 2008. (ENG.). 32p. (J). (gr. -1-2). pap. 6.99 *(978-0-7636-3891-7(9))* Candlewick Pr.

Martin, Lisa & Martin, Valerie. Anton & Cecil, Book 2: Cats on Track. Murphy, Kelly, illus. (Anton & Cecil Ser.: 2). (ENG.). 272p. (J). (gr. 3-7). 2016. pap. 6.95 *(978-1-61620-638-3(1))* 2015. 16.95 *(978-1-61620-419-8(2))* Algonquin Bks. of Chapel Hill.

—Cats at Sea. 2013. (Anton & Cecil Ser.: 1). (ENG., Illus.). 256p. (J). (gr. 3-7). 16.95 *(978-1-61620-246-0(7)*, 73246) Algonquin Bks. of Chapel Hill.

Mary, Agnes. The Story of Sammie. 2011. 28p. pap. 15.99 *(978-1-4568-7771-2(2))* Xlibris Corp.

Mary Barr. The Ditch Dog the Hedge Cat. 2009. 108p. 20.95 *(978-1-4401-5560-4(7))*; pap. 10.95 *(978-1-4401-5558-1(5))* iUniverse, Inc.

Mary John Lewis. Pookie in Paris. 2009. 24p. pap. 12.49 *(978-1-4389-6514-7(1))* AuthorHouse.

Mary, Mize. Letters from Scamper. Shirley, Hoskins, illus. 2012. 32p. pap. 10.00 *(978-0-9832514-3-9(6))* Gypsy Heart Pr.

Mason, Jane B. Super Hero Splash Down, 1 vol. Baltazar, Art, illus. 2011. (DC Super-Pets Ser.). (ENG.). 56p. (gr. 2-2). pap. 4.95 *(978-1-4048-6624-9(8))*; lib. bdg. 23.99

(978-1-4048-6357-6(5)) Picture Window Bks. (DC Super-Pets).
Mass, Wendy. A Mango-Shaped Space. 2005. (ENG.). 240p. (YA). (gr. 3-7). per. 8.99 (978-0-316-05825-4(4)) Little, Brown Bks. for Young Readers.
Masson, J. Moussaieff. The Cat Who Came in from the Cold: A Fable. 2004. 107p. (978-0-345-47867-2(3), Ballantine Bks.) Random House Publishing Group.
Master, Angel Michael. She Is a Gift from Jah. 2003. (Illus.). pap. 13.00 (978-0-8059-5967-3(X)) Dorrance Publishing Co., Inc.
Masters, Jane E. Indy. 2013. 40p. pap. 9.99 (978-1-62839-260-9(6)) Salem Author Services.
Masterson, Madeline Ann. Wonka's Christmas Story. 2015. (ENG.). 36p. (J). (gr. 2-3). mass mkt. 11.95 (978-1-78612-086-1(0), 470e8853-74bf-4cb8-9970-ad8b75618e44) Austin, Stan AUS. Dist: Bookmasters Distribution.
Masurel, Claire. A Cat & a Dog. Kolar, Bob, illus. 2003. (Cheshire Studio Book Ser.). (ENG.). 32p. (J). (gr. -1). 7.95 (978-0-7358-1780-7(4)) North-South Bks., Inc.
Matchett, Gillian. The Adventures of Weston Super Cat with Activities. 2009. (Illus.). 92p. pap. 30.49 (978-1-4389-2241-6(8)) AuthorHouse.
Matison, Jimbo. I'm Going to Catch My Tail! 2014. (ENG., Illus.). 40p. (J). (gr. k-2). 14.95 (978-1-4197-1382-8(5), Abrams Bks. for Young Readers) Abrams, Inc.
Matson, Laurie. Jaz-O & 'G' in Key West. Matson, Laurie, illus. l.t. ed. 2003. (Illus.). (J). 4.95 (978-0-9673704-5-3(0)) Seastory Pr.
Matsutani, Miyoko. Peek-A-Boo. Segawa, Yasuo, illus. 2006. 20p. (J). (gr. -1). 10.95 (978-1-74126-047-2(7)) R.I.C. Pubns. AUS. Dist: SCB Distributors.
Mayer, Mercer. What a Good Kitty. Mayer, Mercer, illus. 2012. (My First I Can Read Ser.). (ENG., Illus.). 32p. (J). (gr. -1-3). 16.99 (978-0-06-083566-8(4)); pap. 3.99 (978-0-06-083565-1(6)) HarperCollins Pubs.
—What a Good Kitty! 2012. (Little Critter: I Can Read! Ser.). (J). lib. bdg. 13.55 (978-0-606-26261-3(X), Turtleback) Turtleback Bks.
Mayerhofer, Felix. Horace the Great Harmonica King. MacFarlane, John, illus. 2006. 31p. (J). (gr. -1-7). per. 16.95 (978-1-60002-255-5(3), 4313) Mountain Valley Publishing, LLC.
Mazula, Derek. A Drifen's Tale. 2009. 48p. pap. 24.99 (978-1-4490-2782-7(2)) AuthorHouse.
McAneney, Caitie. Koko the Cat. 2017. (Pet Tales! Ser.). 24p. (J). (gr. 4-6). pap. 8.25 (**978-1-5081-5675-8(1)**, PowerKids Pr.) Rosen Publishing Group, Inc., The.
McBride, Anthony & McBride, Autumn. The Lost Cat. 2007. (Illus.). pap. 11.00 (978-1-56411-540-9(2), CB Publishing & Design) UBUS Communications Systems.
McCallister, Colleen. Boaz the Ginger Cat & the Mysterious Mishap of the Kitchen Sponge. 2013. 36p. pap. 12.59 (978-0-9787336-9-8(X)) CMC Publishing.
McCann, Jesse L., et al. Bad Moon Rising. 1 vol. 2014. (Krypto the Superdog Ser.). (ENG., Illus.). 32p. (gr. 1-2). 22.60 (978-1-4342-6475-6(0)) Stone Arch Bks.
—The Purr-Fect Crime. 1 vol. 2014. (Krypto the Superdog Ser.). (ENG., Illus.). 32p. (gr. 1-2). 22.60 (978-1-4342-6474-9(2)) Stone Arch Bks.
McCann, Jesse Leon. The Cat in the Hat. 2003. (Illus.). 24p. (J). (gr. k-k). 0.33 (978-0-375-82780-8(3), Golden Bks.) Random Hse. Children's Bks.
McCarthy, Margaret. The Cat Did Not Know. Molloy, Sophie, illus. 2006. (ENG.). 36p. (J). pap. 14.95 (978-1-85390-923-8(8)) Veritas Pubns. IRL. Dist: Dufour Editions, Inc.
McCarty, Peter. Fabian Escapes. McCarty, Peter, illus. rev. ed. 2007. (ENG., Illus.). 40p. (J). (gr. -1-1). 21.99 (978-0-8050-7713-1(8), 9780805077131, Holt, Henry & Co. Bks. For Young Readers) Holt, Henry & Co.
—Hondo & Fabian. McCarty, Peter, illus. 2007. (ENG., Illus.). 40p. (J). (gr. -1-1). per. 8.99 (978-0-312-36747-3(3), 9780312367473) Square Fish.
—Hondo & Fabian. unabr. ed. 2006. (Illus.). (J). (gr. -1-3). 29.95 (978-0-439-84906-7(3), WHCD688) Weston Woods Studios, Inc.
McClure, Nikki. How to Be a Cat. 2013. (ENG., Illus.). 40p. (J). (gr. -1-k). 16.95 (978-1-4197-0528-1(8), Abrams Bks. for Young Readers) Abrams, Inc.
Mccormick, Scott. Camping Catastrophe! Lazzell, R. H., illus. 2016. (Mr. Pants Ser.: 4). (ENG.). 128p. (J). (gr. k-3). 12.99 (978-0-525-42812-1(7), Dial Bks) Penguin Young Readers Group.
McCormick, Scott. It's Go Time! Lazzell, R. H., illus. 2014. (Mr. Pants Ser.: 1). (ENG.). 128p. (J). (gr. 1-3). 14.99 (978-0-8037-4007-5(7), Dial Bks) Penguin Young Readers Group.
Mccormick, Scott. It's Go Time! Lazzell, R. H., illus. 2015. (Mr. Pants Ser.: 1). (ENG.). 128p. (J). (gr. 1-3). 7.99 (978-0-14-751710-4(9), Puffin Books) Penguin Young Readers Group.
McCormick, Scott. Slacks, Camera, Action! Lazzell, R. H., illus. 2015. (Mr. Pants Ser.: 2). (ENG.). 128p. (J). (gr. k-3). 14.99 (978-0-8037-4009-9(3), Dial Bks) Penguin Young Readers Group.
Mccormick, Scott. Slacks, Camera, Action! Lazzell, R. H., illus. 2015. (Mr. Pants Ser.: 2). (ENG.). 128p. (J). (gr. k-3). 7.99 (978-0-14-751711-1(7), Puffin Books) Penguin Young Readers Group.
McCormick, Scott. Trick or Feet! Lazzell, R. H., illus. 2015. (Mr. Pants Ser.: 3). (ENG.). 128p. (J). (gr. k-3). 12.99 (978-0-525-42811-4(9), Dial Bks) Penguin Young Readers Group.
McCoy, Allen. The Cat That Was Elected President. 2012. 42p. pap. 6.95 (978-1-61286-121-0(0)) Avid Readers Publishing Group.
McDonald, Fiona. Ghost Doll & Jasper. 2012. (ENG., Illus.). 112p. (J). (gr. 2-7). 12.95 (978-1-62087-174-4(2), 620174, Sky Pony Pr.) Skyhorse Publishing Co., Inc.
McDonald, Kirsten. The Nighttime Noise. 1 vol. Meza, Erika, illus. 2016. (Carlos & Carmen Ser.). (ENG.). 32p. (J). (gr. k-3). 27.07 (978-1-62402-139-8(5)) Magic Wagon.
McDonald, Kirsten. The Pet Show Problem. 2016. (Carlos & Carmen Set 3 Ser.). (ENG., Illus.). (J). (gr. -1-3). lib. bdg. 27.07 (**978-1-62402-184-8(0)**) ABDO Publishing Co.
McDonnell, Patrick. The Gift of Nothing. (ENG., Illus.). 56p. (gr. -1-3). 2005. (J). 15.99 (978-0-316-11488-2(X)) 2009. 19.99 (978-0-316-05441-6(0)) Little, Brown Bks. for Young Readers.
—Hug Time. (ENG., Illus.). (J). (gr. -1 — 1). 2012. 30p. bds. 6.99 (978-0-316-18295-9(8)) 2007. 48p. 14.99 (978-0-316-11494-3(4)) Little, Brown Bks. for Young Readers.
—I Want to Be the Kitty, Vol. 8. 2003. (Mutts Ser.: 10). (ENG., Illus.). 128p. pap. 12.99 (978-0-7407-3305-5(2)) Andrews McMeel Publishing.
—The Little Gift of Nothing. 2016. (ENG., Illus.). 30p. (J). (gr. -1 — 1). bds. 7.99 (978-0-316-39473-4(4)) Little, Brown Bks. for Young Readers.
—The Little Red Cat Who Ran Away & Learned His ABC's (the Hard Way) 2017. (ENG.). 48p. (J). (gr. -1-1). 17.99 (**978-0-316-50246-7(4)**) Little, Brown Bks. for Young Readers.
—The Mutts Autumn Diaries. 2016. (Mutts Kids Ser.: Vol. 3). (ENG., Illus.). (J). (gr. 4-6). 33.99 (**978-1-4494-8500-9(6)**) Andrews McMeel Publishing.
—The Mutts Autumn Diaries. 2016. (Mutts for Kids Ser.). lib. bdg. 20.85 (978-0-606-39181-8(9)) Turtleback Bks.
—The Mutts Diaries. 2016. (ENG., Illus.). 226p. (J). (gr. 3-7). 29.99 (978-1-4494-7380-8(6)) Andrews McMeel Publishing.
—Wag! 2009. (ENG., Illus.). 40p. (J). (gr. -1-3). 17.00 (978-0-316-04548-3(9)) Little, Brown Bks. for Young Readers.
McDonnell, Patrick & Mystery Writers of America Staff. South. 2008. (ENG., Illus.). 48p. (J). (gr. -1-3). 16.99 (978-0-316-00509-8(6)) Little Brown & Co.
McDonough, Yona Zeldis. The Cats in the Doll Shop. Maione, Heather, illus. 2012. (ENG.). 160p. (J). (gr. 3-7). pap. 5.99 (978-0-14-242198-7(7), Puffin Books) Penguin Young Readers Group.
McElroy, Roland. Jibicle & Cokie: Friends at Last. 2006. (J). pap. 9.95 (978-0-9673917-1-7(7)) McElroy & Assocs.
McFadden, Jennifer. Rusty My Playful Cat. 2010. 24p. pap. 11.49 (978-1-4490-5101-3(4)) AuthorHouse.
McFarland, Lyn Rossiter. Widget. McFarland, Jim, illus. 2004. (J). (gr. -1-k). spiral bd. (978-0-616-11122-2(3)); spiral bd. (978-0-616-11121-5(5)) Canadian National Institute for the Blind/Institut National Canadien pour les Aveugles.
—Widget. McFarland, Jim, illus. 2006. (ENG.). 32p. (J). (gr. -1-1). per. 8.99 (978-0-374-48386-9(8), 9780374483869) Square Fish.
McGonagle, Joanne L. The Tiniest Tiger. 2008. (ENG.). 52p. pap. 15.00 (978-1-4196-8467-8(1)) CreateSpace Independent Publishing Platform.
McGrath, Maureen Julie. The Tale of the Cat with the Crooked Tail. 2013. 24p. pap. 13.50 (978-1-62516-859-7(4), Strategic Bk. Publishing) Strategic Book Publishing & Rights Agency (SBPRA).
McGraw, Royal, et al. Grumpy Cat & Pokey. 2016. (ENG., Illus.). 104p. (J). 12.99 (978-1-5241-0004-9(8), 9781524100049, Dynamite Entertainment) Dynamic Forces, Inc.
McGuinness-Kelly, Tracy-Lee. Bad Cat. McGuinness-Kelly, Tracy-Lee, illus. 2006. (Illus.). 29p. (J). (gr. k-4). reprint ed. 16.00 (978-0-7567-9823-9(X)) DIANE Publishing Co.
McKain, Susan & Swann, Sandy. Tugger & Mini-Mew. 2011. 32p. pap. 15.95 (978-1-4634-4920-9(8)) AuthorHouse.
McKay, Hilary. Lulu & the Cat in the Bag. Lamont, Priscilla, illus. (Lulu Ser.: 3). (ENG.). 112p. (J). (gr. 1-5). 2014. pap. 4.99 (978-0-8075-4805-9(7)) 2013. 13.99 (978-0-8075-4804-2(9)) Whitman, Albert & Co.
McKay, Sindy. We Both Read-Too Many Cats. Johnson, Meredith, illus. 2003. (We Both Read Ser.). 44p. (J). (gr. k-18). 7.99 (978-1-891327-49-0(6)); pap. 4.99 (978-1-891327-50-6(X)) Treasure Bay, Inc.
McKendry, Sam. Curious Kitties: A Color Book. Mitchell, Melanie, illus. 2007. (ENG.). 14p. (J). (gr. -1-3). bds. 5.95 (978-1-58117-554-7(X), Intervisual/Piggy Toes) Bendon, Inc.
—Curious Kitties: A Colors Book. Mitchell, Melanie, illus. 2005. (ENG.). 16p. (J). bds. 9.95 (978-1-58117-417-5(9), Intervisual/Piggy Toes) Bendon, Inc.
McKimmie, Chris. Lara of Newtown. 2016. (ENG.). 32p. (J). (gr. -1-3). 19.99 (978-1-76011-232-5(1)) Allen & Unwin AUS. Dist: Independent Pubs. Group.
McKinlay, Penny. Flabby Tabby. Teckentrup, Britta, illus. 2009. (ENG.). 32p. (J). (gr. -1-2). pap. 7.95 (978-1-84507-565-1(X), Frances Lincoln) Quarto Publishing Group UK GBR. Dist: Hachette Bk. Group.
McLean, Linda. The Adventures of Simba the Frisky Feline. Faschi, Silvia, illus. 2012. (J). 14.95 (978-1-937406-24-0(5)) Mascot Bks., Inc.
McLoughlin Brothers, creator. Snowflake Stories. 2011. (American Antiquarian Society Ser.). (ENG., Illus.). 16p. (gr. 1). 24.95 (978-1-4290-9735-2(3)) Applewood Bks.
McLoughlin, Wayne, illus. Warriors - Tales from the Clans. 2014. (Warriors Novella Ser.). (ENG.). 320p. (J). (gr. 3-7). pap. 6.99 (978-0-06-229085-4(1)) HarperCollins Pubs.
McMahon, Kara. Friday the Scaredy Cat. McClellan, Maddy, illus. 2011. (Friday the Scaredy Cat Ser.). (ENG.). 24p. (J). (gr. -1-1). 15.99 (978-1-4424-3612-1(3)); pap. 3.99 (978-1-4424-2293-3(9)) Simon Spotlight. (Simon Spotlight).
—Playdates Are Not Scary! McClellan, Maddy, illus. 2015. (Friday the Scaredy Cat Ser.). (ENG.). 24p. (J). (gr. -1-1). pap. 3.99 (978-1-4814-3591-8(4), Simon Spotlight) Simon Spotlight.
—The Scariest Day Ever ... So Far. McClellan, Maddy, illus. 2013. (Friday the Scaredy Cat Ser.). (ENG.). 24p. (J). (gr. -1-1). 16.99 (978-1-4424-6694-4(4), Simon Spotlight) Simon Spotlight.
—The Scariest Day Ever... So Far. McClellan, Maddy, illus. 2013. (Friday the Scaredy Cat Ser.). (ENG.). 24p. (J). (gr. -1-1). pap. 3.99 (978-1-4424-6693-7(6), Simon Spotlight) Simon Spotlight.
McMahon, Kathleen A. Mister Pudge. McMahon, James P., illus. 2009. 20p. pap. 8.50 (978-1-4251-8704-0(8)) Trafford Publishing.
—Mister Pudge Meets Baby Beth. 2011. 44p. 22.00 (978-1-4269-5800-7(5)) Trafford Publishing.
McMullan, Kate. The Amazing Adventures of Supercat! Making the World Safe for Blankies. Lemaître, Pascal, illus. 2011. (ENG.). 40p. (J). (gr. k — 1). 7.95 (978-0-7611-6320-6(4), 16320) Workman Publishing Co., Inc.
—Supercat to the Rescue. Lemaître, Pascal, illus. (ENG.). 1p. (J). bds. 55.60 (978-0-7611-3234-9(1), 23234) Workman Publishing Co., Inc.
MCP Staff. The Big Cat, 6 bks., set, Level 4, Bk. 2. 2003. (J). (gr. -1-3). 24.50 (978-0-8136-2373-3(1)) Modern Curriculum Pr.
McPhail, David. Crash! the Cat. McPhail, David, illus. 2016. (ENG., Illus.). 32p. (J). (gr. -1-2). 16.95 (978-0-8234-3649-1(7)) Holiday Hse., Inc.
McPherson, Christopher. Mama Cat. 2003. (J). per. 9.99 (978-1-932205-79-4(9)) Word Association Pubs.
McPherson, Dottie. Kizzi's Special Friends. 2003. (Illus.). (J). 14.95 (978-0-9724979-0-9(0), Advocate Hse.) A Cappela Publishing.
McQuinn, Anna. Lola Gets a Cat. Beardshaw, Rosalind, illus. 2017. (ENG.). 28p. (J). (-k). lib. bdg. 15.99 (978-1-58089-736-5(3)) Charlesbridge Publishing, Inc.
McVeigh, Mark. Hello Kitty: Superterrific Sleepover! 2004. pap. (978-0-439-67634-2(7)) Scholastic, Inc.
Mcwethy, Betty. That Fat White Cat & the Missing Socks. 2012. 40p. pap. 24.95 (978-1-4626-2209-2(7)) PublishAmerica, Inc.
Meachen Rau, Dana. Sweet Pea: Escape in the Garden. Hannon, Holly, illus. 2006. (J). (978-1-58987-200-4(2)) Kindermusik International.
Meadows, Daisy. Amelia Sparklepaw's Party Problem. 2016. (Magic Animal Friends Special Edition Ser.). (ENG.). 176p. (J). (gr. 2-5). pap. 6.99 (978-0-545-94080-1(X), Scholastic Pr.) Scholastic, Inc.
—Bella Tabbypaw in Trouble. 2015. (Magic Animal Friends Ser.: 4). (ENG., Illus.). 112p. (J). (gr. 2-5). pap. 4.99 (978-0-545-68648-8(2), Scholastic Paperbacks) Scholastic, Inc.
—Grace Woollyhop's Musical Mystery. 2016. (Magic Animal Friends Ser.: 12). lib. bdg. 14.75 (978-0-606-38802-3(8)) Turtleback Bks.
—Grace Woollyhop's Musical Mystery (Magic Animal Friends #12) 2016. (Magic Animal Friends Ser.: 12). (ENG., Illus.). 112p. (J). (gr. 2-5). pap. 4.99 (978-0-545-94079-5(6), Scholastic Paperbacks) Scholastic, Inc.
—Katie the Kitten Fairy. Ripper, Georgie, illus. 2008. (J). (Pet Fairies Ser.: 1). (ENG.). 80p. (gr. -1-3). pap. 4.99 (978-0-545-02816-5(7), Scholastic Paperbacks); 65p. pap. (978-0-545-13320-3(3)) Scholastic, Inc.
—Katie the Kitten Fairy. Ripper, Georgie, illus. 2008. (Rainbow Magic — the Pet Fairies Ser.). 65p. (gr. 1-4). lib. bdg. 14.75 (978-1-4178-2999-6(0), Turtleback) Turtleback Bks.
—Lara the Black Cat Fairy. 2012. (Illus.). 65p. (J). (978-0-545-42596-4(4)) Scholastic, Inc.
Meadows, Daisy & Scott, Lisa Ann. Amelia Sparklepaw's Party Problem. 2016. (Magic Animal Friends Ser.). (ENG.). 176p. (J). (gr. 2-5). 17.20 (978-0-606-39140-5(1)) Turtleback Bks.
Meister, Cari. Tiny Goes to the Movies. 2016. (Penguin Young Readers Level 2 Ser.). lib. bdg. 13.55 (978-0-606-38851-1(6)) Turtleback Bks.
Mellor, Jodie. Missing! Dann, Penny, illus. 2010. (Mystery Pups Ser.). (ENG.). 112p. (J). (gr. k-2). pap. 6.99 (978-1-84738-226-9(6)) Simon & Schuster, Ltd. GBR. Dist: Independent Pubs. Group.
Merboth, Natalie. Blessing the Cat: A Newfound Family. 2013. 16p. pap. 7.95 (978-1-4908-1262-5(8), WestBow Pr.) Author Solutions, Inc.
Metcalf, Dan. The Curse of the Cairo Cat: A Lottie Lipton Adventure. Panagarry, Rachelle, illus. 2017. (Adventures of Lottie Lipton Ser.). (ENG.). (J). (gr. 2-5). 80p. pap. 6.99 (**978-1-5124-8186-0(6)**); lib. bdg. 25.32 (**978-1-5124-8179-2(3)**) Lerner Publishing Group. (Darby Creek).
Metzger, Steve. Princess Kitty. Okstad, Ella, illus. 2017. 32p. (J). (gr. -1-3). 17.99 (978-0-06-230662-3(6)) HarperCollins Pubs.
Meyer, Ronald. Casey Cougar. 2007. (Illus.). 32p. (J). 19.95 (978-0-9754701-2-1(4)) Natures Beauty Publishing.
Middlebrook, Amy. Meet My Cat. 2011. 28p. pap. 12.50 (978-1-61204-513-9(8), Strategic Bk. Publishing) Strategic Book Publishing & Rights Agency (SBPRA).
Middleton, Sydney Elise. Green Dog & Red Cat. 2011. 12p. 8.79 (978-1-4567-2736-9(2)) AuthorHouse.
Miles, Ellen. Maggie & Max. 2008. (Puppy Place Ser.: 10). (ENG.). 96p. (J). (gr. 2-5). 4.99 (978-0-545-03456-2(6), Scholastic Paperbacks) Scholastic, Inc.
Miller, Debra Warren. Grandpa Popsicle. 2013. 28p. pap. 13.99 (978-1-4624-0205-2(4), Inspiring Voices) Author Solutions, Inc.
Miller, Jay. Opal, Herby, & Squeaky. 2008. 44p. pap. 18.99 (978-1-4389-1808-2(9)) AuthorHouse.
Miller, Nathan. The Official Librarian: Bessy's Back! 2009. 124p. pap. 12.49 (978-1-4490-2391-1(6)) AuthorHouse.
Min, Laura. Las Gallinas de la Senora Sato, Level 1. Flor Ada, Alma, tr. Huang, Benrei, illus. 2003. (Dejame Leer Ser.). (SPA.). 8p. (J). (gr. -1-3). 6.50 (978-0-673-36298-8(1), Good Year Bks.) Celebration Pr.
Minarik, Else Holmelund. Cat & Dog. Siebel, Fritz, illus. 2017. (My First I Can Read Ser.). 40p. (J). (gr. -1-3). 9.99 (978-0-06-265174-7(9)) HarperCollins Pubs.
—Cat & Dog. Langdo, Bryan, illus. 2005. (My First I Can Read Ser.). (ENG.). 32p. (J). (gr. -1 — 1). 16.99 (978-0-06-074247-8(X)) HarperCollins Pubs.
Minolli Skupinski, Teresa. The Courtship of Leonora: A Fable about Gentle Hearts & Timeless Values. 2005. (Illus.). 88p. (J). spiral bd. 19.95 (978-0-9753326-0-3(0)) Drago, Vincent.
Minou: Evaluation Guide. 2006. (J). (978-1-55942-416-5(8)) Witcher Productions.
Mockford, Caroline. What's This? A Seed's Story. Mockford, Caroline, illus. 2007. (ENG., Illus.). 32p. (J). (gr. -1-2). pap. 7.99 (978-1-84686-071-3(7)) Barefoot Bks., Inc.
Mockford, Caroline, illus. Cleo the Cat. (J). 12.99 (978-1-84148-458-7(X)) Barefoot Bks., Inc.
Mockford, Caroline & Blackstone, Stella. Cleo's Alphabet Book. 2007. (Cleo Ser.). (ENG., Illus.). 24p. (J). (gr. -1-k). bds. 7.99 (978-1-84686-046-1(6)) Barefoot Bks., Inc.
—Cleo's Color Book. Mockford, Caroline, illus. 2007. (Cleo Ser.). (ENG., Illus.). 24p. (J). (gr. -1-k). bds. 6.99 (978-1-84686-060-7(1)) Barefoot Bks., Inc.
Moggie, Felix. Living with the Mach Factor: Four Paws. 2005. (Illus.). 336p. pap. (978-1-84401-529-0(7)) Athena Pr.
Moglia, Amy. Alfalfa Kitty. 20th ed. 2003. (Illus.). 30p. (J). spiral bd. 12.95 (978-0-9622500-3-3(1)) Clements, Jehan.
Mohd Salleh, Muhammad Ashraf. Tubby the Tabby. 2013. 28p. pap. 23.35 (978-1-4669-3218-0(X)) Trafford Publishing.
Moncomble, Gerard & Arinouchkine, Andrei. The Nine Lives of the Cat. 2005. (Illus.). 32p. (J). 16.95 (978-0-689-04637-7(5), Milk & Cookies) ibooks, Inc.
Monlongo, Jorge & Chabot, Jacob. Hello Kitty: Just Imagine. Monlongo, Jorge, illus. 2014. (ENG., Illus.). 64p. (J). pap. 7.99 (978-1-4215-7362-5(8)) Viz Media.
Montana, Scarlett. Lunch with a Blue Kitty. Montana, Scarlett, illus. 2007. (Illus.). 41p. (J). pap. (978-0-9796814-0-0(5)) Blue Kitty, The.
Montardre, Hélène. The Cat & the Dog. 2003. (Illus.). 8p. (J). bds. 7.95 (978-1-58728-483-0(9), Two-Can Publishing) T&N Children's Publishing.
Montelongo, Monica. The Adventures of Roxy & Mozart. 2009. 28p. pap. 14.50 (978-1-60860-458-6(6), Eloquent Bks.) Strategic Book Publishing & Rights Agency (SBPRA).
Moon, Catherine R. & Everette, Maureen C. The Adventures of NanaCat & Her Children: Someone New. Richardson, Kara, illus. 2004. 32p. (J). per. 6.95 (978-0-930507-02-2(9)) GRAND Media, LLC.
Moon, Josephine. The Tale of the Lucky Cat. Seki, Sunny, illus. 2008. (KOR & ENG.). 32p. (J). (978-0-9799339-1-2(9)) East West Discovery Pr.
Moore, Inga. Captain Cat. Moore, Inga, illus. 2013. (ENG., Illus.). 48p. (J). (gr. -1-2). 15.99 (978-0-7636-6151-9(1)) Candlewick Pr.
Moore, Leslie. A Day in the Life of Whiskers. 2008. 16p. 15.95 (978-1-4357-1383-3(4)) Lulu Pr., Inc.
Moore, Stephen. Skin & Bone. mass mkt. 8.99 (978-0-340-70455-4(1)) Hodder & Stoughton GBR. Dist: Trafalgar Square Publishing.
Moore, Suzi. Whoops! Ayto, Russell, illus. 2016. (ENG.). 32p. (J). (gr. -1-2). 16.99 (978-0-7636-8180-7(6), Templar) Candlewick Pr.
Moore, Thomas. Zoe & the Back Yard Boys: The Magic Garden Haunted House Adventure. 2012. 24p. pap. 17.99 (978-1-4772-9086-6(9)) AuthorHouse.
Mora, Pat. Una Cesta de Cumpleanos para Tia Abuela. Lang, Cecily, illus. (SPA.). (J). (gr. k-2). pap. 3.16 net. (978-0-395-78817-2(X), HMS088) Houghton Mifflin Harcourt Publishing Co.
—Here, Kitty, Kitty! (Ven, Gatita, Ven!) Suarez, Maribel, illus. 2008. (My Family: Mi Familia Ser.). (SPA & ENG.). 24p. (J). (gr. 4-7). lib. bdg. 15.89 (978-0-06-085045-6(0), Rayo) HarperCollins Pubs.
—Here Kitty Kitty!/Ven Gatita Ven! Suarez, Maribel, illus. 2008. (My Family: Mi Familia Ser.). (SPA & ENG.). 24p. (J). (gr. -1-1). 14.99 (978-0-06-085044-9(2), Rayo) HarperCollins Pubs.
Moran, Alex. Come Here, Tiger! Ernst, Lisa Campbell, illus. 2003. (Green Light Readers Level 1 Ser.). (ENG.). 24p. (J). (gr. -1-3). pap. 3.95 (978-0-15-204860-0(X)) Houghton Mifflin Harcourt Publishing Co.
—Come Here, Tiger! 2003. (Green Light Readers — Level 1 Ser.). (gr. -1-2). lib. bdg. 13.50 (978-0-613-64473-0(5), Turtleback) Turtleback Bks.
Morgan, Derek T. Cats Tails. 2011. 378p. pap. 20.95 (978-1-60976-729-7(2), Eloquent Bks.) Strategic Book Publishing & Rights Agency (SBPRA).
Morita, Hiroyuki. The Cat Returns Picture Book. Searleman, Eric, ed. Hiiragi, Aoi, illus. 2007. (Cat Returns Ser.: 1). (ENG.). 112p. (J). (gr. -1). 14.99 (978-1-4215-1498-7(2)) Viz Media.
Moroney, Trace, creator. The Owl & the Pussy Cat. 2008. (Illus.). 10p. (gr. -1-1). bds. 4.99 (978-1-74178-515-9(4)) Gardner Pubns.
Morpurgo, Michael. Kaspar the Titanic Cat. Foreman, Michael, illus. 2012. 208p. (J). (gr. 3-7). 16.99 (978-0-06-200618-9(5)) HarperCollins Pubs.
Morris, Ashara. Let's Find Lucy! 2008. (Illus.). 32p. pap. 17.95 (978-1-4327-3221-9(8)) Outskirts Pr., Inc.
Morris, Jackie & Quarto Generic Staff. I Am Cat. 2013. (ENG., Illus.). 32p. (J). (gr. k-3). 17.99 (978-1-84780-135-7(8), Frances Lincoln) Quarto Publishing Group UK GBR. Dist: Hachette Bk. Group.
Morris, M. R. Midnight's Court. 2012. 60p. pap. 24.99 (978-1-4685-9548-2(2)) AuthorHouse.
Morrison, Anna C. & Movshina, Marina. Silly Moments. 2010. 16p. pap. 9.95 (978-1-61633-039-2(2)) Guardian Angel Publishing, Inc.
Morrison, Kenny. Sevenlives & the Woof Pack. 2011. (Illus.). 104p. pap. 13.32 (978-1-4567-8595-6(8)) AuthorHouse.
Morrow, Dj. Charlie & Joe. 2013. 28p. pap. 24.95 (978-1-62709-833-5(X)) America Star Bks.
Morse, William A. Bip & the Bulb. 2009. 64p. pap. 23.49 (978-1-4490-2498-7(X)) AuthorHouse.
Mortensen, Lori. The Cat That Disappeared. 1 vol. Simard, Remy, illus. 2010. (My First Graphic Novel Ser.). (ENG.). 32p. (gr. k-2). pap. 6.25 (978-1-4342-2282-4(9)); lib. bdg. 24.65 (978-1-4342-1887-2(2)) Stone Arch Bks. (My First Graphic Novel).
—Mousequerade Ball: A Counting Tale. Lewin, Betsy, illus. 2016. (ENG.). 32p. (J). 16.99 (978-1-61963-422-0(8), 9781619634220, Bloomsbury USA Childrens) Bloomsbury Publishing USA.
Mortimer, Anne. Pumpkin Cat. Mortimer, Anne, illus. 2011. (ENG., Illus.). 24p. (J). (gr. -1-2). 14.99 (978-0-06-187485-7(X), Tegen, Katherine Bks) HarperCollins Pubs.
Moses, Anne E. Gatos Musikos: A Secret Told by the Moon. 2013. (Illus.). 58p. 24.95 (978-1-4575-2189-8(X)) Dog Ear Publishing, LLC.
Moses, Will. Raining Cats & Dogs: A Collection of Irresistible Idioms & Illustrations to Tickle the Funny Bones. Moses, Will, illus. 2008. (ENG., Illus.). 40p. (J). (gr. k-3). 17.99 (978-0-399-24233-5(3), Philomel Bks.) Penguin Young Readers Group.
Mosesson, Connie. Lovey Dovey & the Makeover Mistake. 2008. 40p. pap. 16.50 (978-1-60693-275-9(6), Eloquent Bks.) Strategic Book Publishing & Rights Agency (SBPRA).

Moss, Barbara E. The Adventures of Sir Goblin, the Feline Knight. Houx, Emily Marie Cornell du, illus. 2009. 336p. pap. 15.95 *(978-1-882190-03-4(3))* Porcupine Communications.

Moss, Miriam. Matty Takes Off! Simmons, Jane, illus. 2008. (Matty & Milly Ser.). (ENG.). 32p. (J). (gr. -1-k). 19.95 *(978-1-84270-701-2(9))* Andersen Pr. GBR. Dist: Independent Pubs. Group.

Mother Goose. The Three Little Kittens. Winter, Milo, illus. 2009. (Shape Bks.). (ENG.). 16p. (J). (gr. -1-1). pap. 9.95 *(978-1-59583-374-7(9),* 9781595833747, Green Tiger Pr.) Laughing Elephant.

Mowery, Julia M. Chester the Cat. 2013. 36p. pap. 7.95 *(978-0-9710529-1-8(3))* Mowery, Julia.

Mudaly, Jessica. And That's Just the Trouble with Cats! 2011. 116p. pap. 10.95 *(978-1-61204-186-5(8),* Eloquent Bks.) Strategic Book Publishing & Rights Agency (SBPRA).

—Cats Can Be So Cattish! 2013. 116p. pap. 10.95 *(978-1-62212-084-0(1),* Strategic Bk. Publishing) Strategic Book Publishing & Rights Agency (SBPRA).

Mulligan, Frank. Cookie & Curley. Myler, Terry, illus. 2003. (Chimps Ser.: 2). (ENG.). 64p. (J). (gr. k-18). pap. 9.95 *(978-1-901737-38-7(1))* Anvil Bks., Ltd. IRL. Dist: Dufour Editions, Inc.

Muncaster, Harriet. Happy Halloween, Witch's Cat! Muncaster, Harriet, illus. 2015. (ENG., Illus.). 32p. (J). (gr. -1-3). 15.99 *(978-0-06-222916-8(8))* HarperCollins Pubs.

—I Am a Witch's Cat. Muncaster, Harriet, illus. 2014. (ENG., Illus.). 32p. (J). (gr. -1-3). 15.99 *(978-0-06-222914-4(1))* HarperCollins Pubs.

Munoz, Isabel. Where Is Eric? (¿Donde Está Eric?) Mazali, Gustavo, illus. 2006. (Eric & Julieta Ser.). (ENG & SPA.). 24p. (J). (gr. -1-3). pap. 3.99 *(978-0-439-78371-2(2))* Scholastic, Inc.

Murdock, Catherine Gilbert. Wisdom's Kiss. 2013. (ENG.). 320p. (YA). (gr. 7). pap. 8.99 *(978-0-547-85540-0(0))* Houghton Mifflin Harcourt Publishing Co.

—Wisdom's Kiss: A Thrilling & Romantic Adventure, Incorporating Magic, Villany, & a Cat. 2011. (ENG.). 304p. (YA). (gr. 7). 16.99 *(978-0-547-56687-0(5))* Houghton Mifflin Harcourt Publishing Co.

Murphy, Shirley Rousseau & Murphy, Pat J. J. The Cat, the Devil, the Last Escape: A Novel. 2015. (ENG., Illus.). 320p. 24.99 *(978-0-06-226910-2(0),* Morrow, William & Co.) HarperCollins Pubs.

Murphy, Steve & Murphy, Sonia. The Secret. Ostrom, Bob, illus. 2004. (Teenage Mutant Ninja Turtles Ser.). 32p. (J). (gr. k-2). 11.65 *(978-0-7569-5401-7(0))* Perfection Learning Corp.

Murphy, Stuart J. Freda Organiza una Merienda. 2011. (I See I Learn Ser.). (SPA & ENG., Illus.). 32p. (J). (-k). 14.95 *(978-1-58089-488-3(7));* pap. 6.95 *(978-1-58089-489-0(5))* Charlesbridge Publishing, Inc.

—Freda Says Please. Jones, Tim, illus. 2013. (I See I Learn Ser.). (ENG.). 32p. (J). (-k). pap. 6.95 *(978-1-58089-475-3(5))* Charlesbridge Publishing, Inc.

—Freda Says Please. Jones, Tim, illus. 2013. (I See I Learn Ser.). (ENG.). 32p. (J). (-k). lib. bdg. 14.95 *(978-1-58089-474-6(7))* Charlesbridge Publishing, Inc.

—Freda Stops a Bully. Jones, Tim, illus. 2012. (I See I Learn Ser.). (ENG.). 32p. (J). (-k). 14.95 *(978-1-58089-466-1(6));* pap. 6.95 *(978-1-58089-467-8(4))* Charlesbridge Publishing, Inc.

Murray, Alison. The House That Zack Built. Murray, Alison, illus. 2016. (ENG., Illus.). 32p. (J). (-k). 16.99 *(978-0-7636-7844-9(9))* Candlewick Pr.

Murray, Rosalie. Bobby & Bun Bun's Afternoon Adventure. Swope, Brenda, illus. 2012. 32p. pap. 24.95 *(978-1-4560-5090-0(7))* America Star Bks.

—Breakfast for Two. Balogh, Jared, illus. 2013. 32p. pap. 24.95 *(978-1-4560-7051-9(7))* America Star Bks.

Mustaine Hettinger, Cynthia. Boomerang, the Farm Cat. Ramsey, Jayne, illus. 2004. (Electra's Acres Ser.: 4). 32p. (J). per. 14.95 *(978-0-9746330-5-3(4))* Anton Berkshire Publishing.

My Cat Sam Set B: Individual Title Six-Packs. (Supersonic Phonics Ser.). (gr. k-3). 29.00 *(978-0-7635-0535-6(8))* Rigby Education.

My Crazy Christmas Catastrophe Cat. 2003. (Illus.). 22p. (J). 9.95 *(978-0-9744751-1-0(4))* Timothy Lane Pr.

My Name Is Boots: A Cat's Tale. 2003. (Illus.). 55p. (J). *(978-0-9742277-0-2(6))* Hargroves Publishing Co.

Myers, Tim & Myers, Tim J. Looking for Luna, 0 vols. Reed, Mike, illus. 2009. (ENG.). 32p. (J). (gr. -1-3). 17.99 *(978-0-7614-5564-6(7),* 9780761455646, Amazon Children's Publishing) Amazon Publishing.

Nadimi, Suzan. The Hungry Cat Downie, Christopher, illus. l.t. ed. 2005. (PER.). 32p. 5.95 net. *(978-0-9764947-0-6(1))* Nur Pubns.

Nagda, Ann Whitehead. The Perfect Cat-Sitter. Roth, Stephanie, illus. 2007. (ENG.). 96p. (J). (gr. 4-7). 15.95 *(978-0-8234-2112-1(0))* Holiday Hse., Inc.

—The Valentine Cat. Roth, Stephanie, illus. 2008. (ENG.). 32p. (J). (gr. 2-5). 16.95 *(978-0-8234-2123-7(6))* Holiday Hse., Inc.

Nana, Old. The Girl Who Converses with Butterflies. 2012. 24p. pap. 11.50 *(978-1-61204-972-4(9),* Strategic Bk. Publishing) Strategic Book Publishing & Rights Agency (SBPRA).

Nanette. Tootie the Green Kitten. 2004. (Life on Granny's Farm Ser.). (J). 12.95 *(978-0-9741269-7-5(7))* St. Bernard Publishing, LLC.

Napthine, Margaret. The Kittens Thomas & Tut. Lovejoy, Brenda, illus. 2006. (J). per. 16.00 *(978-0-9763993-2-2(6),* Ithaca Pr.) Authors & Artists Publishers of New York, Inc.

Nash, Margaret. Sammy's Secret. Axworthy, Anni, illus. 2008. (Tadpoles Ser.). (ENG.). 24p. (J). (gr. -1-3). pap. *(978-0-7787-3894-7(9));* lib. bdg. *(978-0-7787-3863-3(9))* Crabtree Publishing Co.

Nastari, Nadine, illus. Mr. TLC (Three-Legged Cat) 2007. 36p. (J). spiral bd. 14.95 *(978-0-9798387-5-0(4))* Nastari, Nadine.

Natasha & David Breen. The Feisty Cats. 2011. 28p. pap. 15.99 *(978-1-4568-3272-8(7))* Xlibris Corp.

Nation, Kay. Jamie Learns to Love. 2006. pap. 10.00 *(978-1-4257-0534-3(0))* Xlibris Corp.

Naughty Kitten: Set B Individual Title, 6 Packs. (Smart Start Ser.). (gr. k-1). 23.00 *(978-0-7635-0420-5(3))* Rigby Education.

Naylor, Phyllis Reynolds. The Grand Escape. Daniel, Alan, illus. 2005. (ENG.). 160p. (J). (gr. 3-7). pap. 7.99 *(978-0-689-87407-9(3),* Atheneum Bks. for Young Readers) Simon & Schuster Children's Publishing.

—The Healing of Texas Jake. Daniel, Alan, illus. 2005. (ENG.). 128p. (J). (gr. 3-7). pap. 6.99 *(978-0-689-87406-2(5),* Atheneum Bks. for Young Readers) Simon & Schuster Children's Publishing.

—Patches & Scratches, 0 vols. Ramsey, Marcy, illus. 2010. (Simply Sarah Ser.: 0). (ENG.). 80p. (J). (gr. 2-6). pap. 6.99 *(978-0-7614-5731-2(3),* 9780761457312, Amazon Children's Publishing) Amazon Publishing.

—Polo's Mother. Daniel, Alan, illus. 2006. (ENG.). 176p. (J). (gr. 3-7). pap. 6.99 *(978-0-689-87404-8(9),* Atheneum Bks. for Young Readers) Simon & Schuster Children's Publishing.

Needham, T. L. Kitty Claus. 2012. (ENG.). 27p. (J). (-18). pap. 19.95 *(978-1-4787-1788-1(2))* Outskirts Pr., Inc.

Neer, P. J. Cats Can't Fly: Teaching Children to Value New Friendships. Gazsi, Benjamin, illus. 2012. (Let's Talk Ser.). (ENG.). 48p. (J). (gr. -1-2). pap. 9.95 *(978-0-88282-381-2(7))* New Horizon Pr. Pubs., Inc.

Nelson-Schmidt, Michelle. Cats, Cats! Nelson-Schmidt, Michelle, illus. 2011. (ENG., Illus.). 32p. (J). pap. 5.99 *(978-1-61067-042-5(6))* Kane Miller.

Nesbit, Edith. Pussy & Doggy Tales. 2011. 106p. 22.95 *(978-1-4638-9856-4(8));* pap. 9.95 *(978-1-4638-0127-4(0))* Rodgers, Alan Bks.

Nettles Jr, J. H. Hit Em' with Words, 1 vol. Jones, Joff, illus. 2010. 22p. 24.95 *(978-1-4489-4102-5(4))* PublishAmerica, Inc.

Neubeck, Jon. The Quest. 2009. 47p. pap. 23.10 *(978-0-557-07108-1(9))* Lulu Pr., Inc.

Neuschwander, Angel & Johnston, Becky. Gretchen Asks, How Do Cars Work? 2009. 24p. pap. 12.99 *(978-1-4389-2886-9(6))* AuthorHouse.

Nevis, Lance. Animal Rain. Laible MBA, Steve William, ed. Piper, Tom, illus. 2012. 36p. pap. 10.99 *(978-0-9850142-7-8(X))* Kodel Group, LLC, The.

Newberry, Clare Turlay. Marshmallow. Newberry, Clare Turlay, illus. 2008. (ENG., Illus.). 32p. (J). (gr. -1-1). 16.99 *(978-0-06-072486-3(2))* HarperCollins Pubs.

Newbery, Linda. Posy. Rayner, Catherine, illus. 2008. (ENG.). 32p. (J). (gr. -1-k). 16.99 *(978-1-4169-7112-2(2),* Atheneum Bks. for Young Readers) Simon & Schuster Children's Publishing.

Newell, Jeff. Skimper-Scamper. Hranilovich, Barbara, illus. 2005. (Green Light Readers Level 2 Ser.). (J). (gr. k-2). 11.60 *(978-0-7569-5244-0(1))* Perfection Learning Corp.

Newman, Lesléa. The Best Cat in the World. Himler, Ronald, illus. 2004. 32p. (J). (gr. 1-4). 16.00 *(978-0-8028-5252-6(1));* (gr. -1-3). 8.00 *(978-0-8028-5294-6(7),* Eerdmans Bks For Young Readers) Eerdmans, William B. Publishing Co.

—Cats, Cats, Cats! Oller, Erika, illus. 2004. (ENG.). 32p. (J). (gr. -1-3). reprint ed. 7.99 *(978-0-689-86697-5(6),* Simon & Schuster Bks. For Young Readers) Simon & Schuster Bks. For Young Readers.

—Ketzel, the Cat Who Composed. Bates, Amy June, illus. 2015. (ENG.). 40p. (J). (gr. k-3). 16.99 *(978-0-7636-6555-5(X))* Candlewick Pr.

Newton, Dan. The Wildcat. 2010. 28p. pap. 13.99 *(978-1-4520-2370-0(0))* AuthorHouse.

Ní Mhurchú, Caitríona & Feeney, Tatyana. An Run Mor. 2007. (Sraith Sos Ser.: 14). (ENG, GLE & IRI., Illus.). 64p. (J). pap. 9.95 *(978-1-84717-016-3(1))* O'Brien Pr., Ltd., The IRL. Dist: Dufour Editions, Inc.

Nickel, Scott. Monster Trouble. Fentz, Mike, illus. 2004. (Scholastic Reader Ser.). 22p. (J). pap. *(978-0-439-66977-1(4))* Scholastic, Inc.

Nightingale, Clare Theresa. The Adventures of Fishkins & Pepperjacket. 2011. (Illus.). 220p. pap. 56.49 *(978-1-4520-8803-7(9))* AuthorHouse.

Nishimura, Kae. Dinah! 2004. 32p. 14.00 *(978-0-618-33613-5(3),* Clarion Bks.) Houghton Mifflin Harcourt Trade & Reference Pubs.

Nodset, Joan L. Come Back, Cat. Kellogg, Steven, illus. 2008. 40p. (J). (gr. -1-3). lib. bdg. 17.89 *(978-0-06-028082-6(4))* HarperCollins Pubs.

Nolan, Tina. Charlie, the Home-Alone Kitten. Rentta, Sharon, illus. 2008. 96p. (J). (gr. 1-5). 3.99 *(978-1-56148-648-9(5),* Good Bks.) Skyhorse Publishing Co., Inc.

—The Home Alone Kitten. Chernyshova, Anna, illus. 2016. (Animal Rescue Center Ser.). (ENG.). 112p. (J). (gr. 1-3). pap. 4.99 *(978-1-58925-493-0(7))* Tiger Tales.

Nolan, Tina. The Injured Fox Kit. Chernyshova, Anna, illus. 2017. (Animal Rescue Center Ser.). (ENG.). 112p. (J). (gr. 1-3). pap. 4.99 ***(978-1-58925-499-2(6))*** Tiger Tales.

Nolen, Jerdine, et al. Bradford Street Buddies: Backyard Camp-Out. Henninger, Michelle, illus. 2015. (Green Light Readers Level 3 Ser.). (ENG.). 48p. (J). (gr. 1-4). pap. 3.99 *(978-0-544-36844-6(4),* HMH Books For Young Readers) Houghton Mifflin Harcourt Publishing Co.

—Bradford Street Buddies: Backyard Camp-Out. Henninger, Michelle, illus. 2015. (Green Light Readers Level 3 Ser.). (ENG.). 48p. (J). (gr. 1-4). 12.99 *(978-0-544-36843-9(6),* HMH Books For Young Readers) Houghton Mifflin Harcourt Publishing Co.

Nordling, Lee. BirdCatDog. Bosch, Meritxell, illus. 2014. (J). lib. bdg. 25.32 *(978-1-4677-4522-2(7),* Graphic Universe™) Lerner Publishing Group.

—BirdCatDog. 2014. (ENG.). 32p. pap. 6.95 *(978-1-4677-4523-9(5))* Lerner Publishing Group.

Nordqvist, Sven. The Birthday Cake: The Adventures of Pettson & Findus. 2015. (Adventures of Pettson & Findus Ser.). (ENG., Illus.). 32p. (J). 17.95 *(978-0-7358-4203-8(5))* North-South Bks., Inc.

—Findus Disappears! 2014. (Adventures of Pettson & Findus Ser.). (ENG., Illus.). 32p. (J). 17.95 *(978-0-7358-4184-0(5))* North-South Bks., Inc.

—Pancakes for Findus. Nordqvist, Sven, illus. 2008. (Findus & Pettson Ser.). (ENG., Illus.). 28p. (J). *(978-1-903458-79-2(X))* Hawthorn Pr.

Norrie, Louise Rosalyn. The Adventures of Flat Cat. 2011. 144p. 29.99 *(978-1-4628-9397-3(X));* pap. 19.99 *(978-1-4628-9396-6(1))* Xlibris Corp.

Norris, L. Wayne. The Adventures of Ricky Raccoon & Jodi the Cat with Boomer. l.t. ed. 2003. (Illus.). 36p. (J). pap. *(978-0-9709408-1-0(5))* Pinetree Pubns.

Norton Kreider, Barbara. The Surprise Party. Dimbylow, Jube, illus. 2013. 30p. pap. *(978-1-921883-37-8(5),* MBS Pr.) Pick-a-Woo Woo Pubs.

Norton, Miriam. The Kitten Who Thought He Was a Mouse. Williams, Garth, illus. 2008. (Little Golden Book Ser.). (ENG.). 24p. (J). (gr. -1-2). 4.99 *(978-0-375-84822-3(3),* Golden Bks.) Random Hse. Children's Bks.

Nosy Crow Staff. Princess Penelope & the Runaway Kitten. Murray, Alison, illus. 2013. (ENG.). 32p. (J). (gr. -1-2). 15.99 *(978-0-7636-6952-2(0),* Nosy Crow) Candlewick Pr.

Novesky, Amy. Cat's Not-So-Perfect Sandcastle. Wakiyama, Hanako, illus. 2012. (ENG.). 28p. (J). (gr. -1-3). 14.95 *(978-0-9837668-2-7(7))* Plushy Feely Corp.

Nowiki, Boszenna. Why Some Cats Are Rascals: Book 1. 2007. (Illus.). 140p. (J). (gr. 4-7). per. 8.95 *(978-0-9727328-2-6(9))* Healthy Life Pr., Inc.

—Why Some Cats Are Rascals: Book 3, No. 3. 2007. 207p. (J). (gr. 4-7). per. 9.95 *(978-0-9727328-6-4(1))* Healthy Life Pr., Inc.

—Why Some Cats Are Rascals: Book 2, No. 2. 2006. 224p. (J). (gr. 4-7). per. 9.95 *(978-0-9727328-5-7(3))* Healthy Life Pr., Inc.

Noyes, Kristie Spangler. Mr. Daisy. 2008. 40p. pap. 24.95 *(978-1-60474-276-3(3))* America Star Bks.

Noyes, William H., Jr. Mittens. 2008. 36p. pap. 24.95 *(978-1-4241-9440-7(7))* America Star Bks.

Numeroff, Laura Joffe. Happy Valentine's Day, Mouse! Bond, Felicia, illus. 2009. (If You Give... Ser.). (ENG.). 24p. (J). (gr. -1-3). bds. 6.99 *(978-0-06-180432-8(0))* HarperCollins Pubs.

—If You Give a Cat a Cupcake. Bond, Felicia, illus. 2008. (If You Give... Ser.). 32p. (J). (gr. -1-3). lib. bdg. 17.89 *(978-0-06-028325-4(4))* HarperCollins Pubs.

—If You Give a Cat a Cupcake. Bond, Felicia, illus. 2008. (If You Give... Ser.). (ENG.). 32p. (J). (gr. -1-3). 17.99 *(978-0-06-028324-7(6))* HarperCollins Pubs.

—If You Give a Cat a Cupcake: Book & Doll. Bond, Felicia, illus. Date not set. (If You Give... Ser.). (J). 19.99 *(978-0-694-01431-6(1))* HarperCollins Pubs.

—Si le das un Pastelito a un Gato, 1 vol. Bond, Felicia, illus. 2010. (If You Give... Ser.). (SPA & ENG.). 32p. (J). (gr. -1-2). 16.99 *(978-0-06-180431-1(2))* HarperCollins Pubs.

—What Puppies Do Best. Munsinger, Lynn, illus. 2011. (ENG.). 32p. (J). (gr. -1-2). 14.99 *(978-0-8118-6601-9(7))* Chronicle Bks. LLC.

Nunes, Lygia Bojunga. El Sofa Estampado. (SPA.). 184p. (YA). (gr. 5-8). *(978-84-239-2748-7(2),* EC2752) Espasa Calpe, S.A. ESP. Dist: Lectorum Pubns., Inc.

Nurston, Nicholas. The Adventures of Smoky: (It's a Cat's Life) 2012. (Illus.). 44p. pap. 21.99 *(978-1-4797-3585-3(X))* Xlibris Corp.

Oakes, Krista Ralston. Jake the Puppy & Emma the Cat. Fuhriman, Raphael Scott, illus. 2012. 36p. (J). 19.99 *(978-0-9838321-2-6(9))* Higher Ground Pr.

Oates, Joyce Carol. Naughty Cherie! Graham, Mark, illus. 2008. 32p. (J). (gr. -1-3). lib. bdg. 17.89 *(978-0-06-074359-8(X))* HarperCollins Pubs.

—Where Is Little Reynard? Graham, Mark, illus. 2003. 32p. (J). 16.89 *(978-0-06-029583-7(X))* HarperCollins Pubs.

Ocker, Christa Holder. Smitten the Kitten. 2006. (J). per. *(978-1-59872-713-5(3))* Instant Pub.

O'Connell, Isabel. Gypsy. Scott, Susan, illus. 2012. 24p. pap. 12.99 *(978-0-9855202-8-1(0))* Kids At Heart Publishing, LLC.

Odgers, Darrel & Odgers, Sally. Cranky Paws. Dawson, Janine, illus. 2009. (Pet Vet Ser.: 1). 96p. (J). (gr. 2-6). pap. 4.99 *(978-1-935279-01-3(7))* Kane Miller.

Odierno, Lisa. Kitten & Her Sister. 2009. (ENG.). 16p. (J). 6.95 *(978-1-60727-000-3(5))* Soundprints.

O'Donnell, Liam. Baxter Needs a Home. Hynes, Robert, illus. 2005. (Pet Tales Ser.). (ENG.). 32p. (J). (gr. -1-2). 2.95 *(978-1-59249-298-5(3),* 1B015); 9.95 *(978-1-59249-320-3(3),* 1B016) Soundprints.

—Baxter Needs a Home. Hynes, Robert, illus. 2004. (ENG.). 32p. (J). (gr. -1-2). 4.95 *(978-1-59249-297-8(5),* 1B013) Soundprints.

—Lucy & the Busy Boat. Hynes, Robert, illus. (Pet Tales Ser.). (ENG.). 32p. (J). (gr. -1-2). 2005. 2.95 *(978-1-59249-296-1(7),* 1B021) 2004. 4.95 *(978-1-59249-295-4(9),* 1B019) 2004. 9.95 *(978-1-59249-319-7(X),* 1B022) Soundprints.

Oelschlager, Vanita. Carrot. Blackwood, Kristin, illus. 2011. (ENG.). 44p. (gr. -1-3). (J). pap. 8.95 *(978-0-9826366-0-2(1));* 15.95 *(978-0-9819714-9-0(0))* VanitaBooks.

Oh, Jiwon. Mr. Monkey's Classroom. Oh, Jiwon, illus. 2005. (Illus.). 32p. (J). (gr. -1-2). lib. bdg. 15.89 *(978-0-06-055722-5(2))* HarperCollins Pubs.

O'Herron, Mary. A Letter from Marty: Grandma & Grandpa's Cat. O'Herron, Mary, illus. 2004. (Illus.). 32p. (J). (gr. -1-1). pap. 8.95 *(978-0-9664732-4-7(8))* Countinghouse Pr., Inc.

Okugas, Juanaiga. The tales of Mew the Cat. 2011. 92p. pap. 35.30 *(978-1-4567-3480-0(6))* AuthorHouse.

Old Cat & the Kitten. 2014. (ENG., Illus.). 128p. (J). (gr. 3-7). pap. 6.99 *(978-1-4814-1938-3(2),* Aladdin) Simon & Schuster Children's Publishing.

Oldfield, Jenny. Home Farm Twins Christmas Special. (Illus.). 124p. (J). pap. 8.99 *(978-0-340-72682-2(2))* Hodder & Stoughton GBR. Dist: Trafalgar Square Publishing.

Olek, Lisa B. The Naked Cat With The Velvet Paws. Gruenfelder, Robin, illus. 2011. 40p. (J). 18.95 *(978-1-60131-092-7(7))* Big Tent Bks.

Olien, Jessica. Shark Detective! Olien, Jessica, illus. 2015. (ENG., Illus.). 32p. (J). (gr. -1-3). 17.99 *(978-0-06-235714-4(X))* HarperCollins Pubs.

Oliver, Amanda Eaddy. Cheyenne the Cat. 2010. 28p. 13.99 *(978-1-4520-6218-1(8))* AuthorHouse.

Ollweiler, Angela Messina. The Strange Wish. Ollweiler, D. R., illus. 2010. 112p. pap. 10.95 *(978-1-60844-274-4(8))* Dog Ear Publishing, LLC.

O'Malley, Kevin. Herbert Fieldmouse, Secret Agent. 2003. (Illus.). 32p. (J). pap. *(978-1-59336-043-6(6));* (gr. 1-6). 15.95 *(978-1-59336-042-9(8))* Mondo Publishing.

Oram, Hiawyn. My Unwilling Witch Gets a Makeover. Warburton, Sarah, illus. 2010. (Rumblewick's Diary Ser.: 4). (ENG.). 112p. (J). (gr. 1-4). 7.99 *(978-0-316-03462-3(2))* Little, Brown Bks. for Young Readers.

—My Unwilling Witch Goes to Ballet School. Warburton, Sarah, illus. 2009. (Rumblewick's Diary Ser.: 1). (ENG.). 112p. (J). (gr. 1-4). 7.99 *(978-0-316-03472-2(X))* Little, Brown Bks. for Young Readers.

O'Rourke, Ryan. Bella Lost & Found. O'Rourke, Ryan, illus. 2014. (ENG., Illus.). 40p. (J). (gr. -1-3). 17.99 *(978-0-06-221861-2(1))* HarperCollins Pubs.

—Bella, Up, Up & Away. O'Rourke, Ryan, illus. 2016. (Illus.). 40p. (J). (gr. -1-3). 17.99 *(978-0-06-221863-6(8))* HarperCollins Pubs.

Orr, Wendy. Missing! - A Cat Called Buster. Boase, Susan, illus. 2011. (Rainbow Street Shelter Ser.: 2). (ENG.). 128p. (J). (gr. 2-5). 15.99 *(978-0-8050-8932-5(2),* 9780805089325, Holt, Henry & Co. Bks. For Young Readers) Holt, Henry & Co.

Ottolenghi, Carol. Puss in Boots. 2009. (Keepsake Stories Ser.). (ENG.). 32p. (gr. -1-3). pap. 3.99 *(978-0-7696-5867-4(9),* Brighter Child) Carson-Dellosa Publishing, LLC.

—Puss in Boots (El Gato con Botas) 2009. (Keepsake Stories Ser.). (ENG & SPA.). 32p. (gr. -1-2). pap. 3.99 *(978-0-7696-5863-6(6),* Brighter Child) Carson-Dellosa Publishing, LLC.

P. Cats & Cows & Moos & Meows. 2011. 28p. (gr. -1). pap. 13.50 *(978-1-4567-3464-0(4))* AuthorHouse.

Pack, Sherri. Little Cat, 1 vol. 2009. 20p. pap. 24.95 *(978-1-60813-706-0(6))* America Star Bks.

Packard, Debbie. Smokey's Silly Christmas Adventures, 1 vol. 2010. 26p. 24.95 *(978-1-4512-0080-5(3))* PublishAmerica, Inc.

Page, Gail. How to Be a Good Cat. 2011. (ENG., Illus.). 32p. (J). 16.99 *(978-1-59990-474-0(8),* 9781599904740, Bloomsbury USA Childrens) Bloomsbury Publishing USA.

—How to Be a Good Cat. Page, Gail, illus. 2011. (ENG., Illus.). 32p. (J). (gr. -1-1). 17.89 *(978-1-59990-475-7(6),* 9781599904757, Bloomsbury USA Childrens) Bloomsbury Publishing USA.

—How to Be a Good Dog. Page, Gail, illus. (ENG., Illus.). 32p. (J). (gr. -1-3). 2007. pap. 7.99 *(978-1-59990-151-0(X),* 9781599901510) 2006. 15.95 *(978-1-58234-683-0(6),* 9781582346830) Bloomsbury Publishing USA. (Bloomsbury USA Childrens).

Palatini, Margie. Cats Hanukkah. 2006. *(978-0-06-052637-5(8));* lib. bdg. *(978-0-06-052638-2(6))* HarperCollins Canada, Ltd.

Palmer, Barbara A. Finding Fido the Feline: Flip Book with American Sign Language. Palmer, Barbara A., illus. 2004. (Illus.). (J). bds. 11.99 *(978-0-9728228-1-7(X))* Palmer, Barbara A.

—The Journey of Cattail. Palmer, Barbara A., illus. 2004. (Illus.). 26p. (J). 16.95 *(978-0-9728228-0-0(1))* Palmer, Barbara A.

Palmer, Barbara A., illus. The Journey of Cattail. 2012. 26p. (J). *(978-0-9728228-4-8(4))* Palmer, Barbara A.

Pankhurst, Kate. Mariella Mystery Investigates a Kitty Calamity. 2015. (Mariella Mysteries Ser.). (ENG., Illus.). 176p. (J). (gr. 2-6). pap. 5.99 *(978-1-4380-0704-5(3))* Barron's Educational Series, Inc.

Panks, Kristin & Harpan, Gaile. The Ballad of Furrio the Cat. Reddy, Sneha, illus. 2008. 24p. pap. 12.95 *(978-0-9822540-4-2(0))* Peppertree Pr., The.

Papa Piccolo: Evaluation Guide. 2006. (J). 17.95 *(978-1-55942-419-6(2))* Witcher Productions.

Paquet, Claudine, et al. Antonio, Plumero y Manchitas. 2006. (SPA., Illus.). 110p. (J). pap. *(978-958-30-2016-2(8))* Panamericana Editorial.

Paquette, Ammi-Joan. Petey & Pru & the Hullabaloo. Ang, Joy, illus. 2013. (ENG.). 40p. (J). (gr. -1-3). 16.99 *(978-0-544-03888-2(6))* Houghton Mifflin Harcourt Publishing Co.

Parish, Herman. Amelia Bedelia & the Cat. Sweat, Lynn, illus. (I Can Read Level 2 Ser.). (ENG.). 48p. (J). (gr. k-3). 2009. pap. 3.99 *(978-0-06-084351-9(9))* 2008. 16.99 *(978-0-06-084349-6(7))* HarperCollins Pubs. (Greenwillow Bks.).

Parker, Emma. Cat on the High Seas. 2010. (Illus.). 16p. pap. *(978-1-877561-75-7(4))* First Edition Ltd.

—Sooty the Stink Bomb. 2010. (Illus.). pap. *(978-1-877561-15-3(0))* First Edition Ltd.

Parker, Marjorie Blain. I Love You near & Far. Henry, Jed, illus. 2015. (Snuggle Time Stories Ser.). (ENG.). 24p. (J). (gr. -1-1). 9.95 *(978-1-4549-0507-3(7))* Sterling Publishing Co., Inc.

Parr, Garnet A. Mosey. 2012. 60p. pap. 31.99 *(978-1-4691-7928-5(8))* Xlibris Corp.

Parvela, Timo. Bicycling to the Moon. Talvitie, Virpi, illus. 2016. (ENG.). 128p. (gr. k-5). 16.99 *(978-1-77657-031-7(6));* 16.99 *(978-1-77657-080-5(4));* 16.99 *(978-1-77657-091-1(X));* 9.99 *(978-1-77657-078-2(2))* Gecko Pr. NZL. Dist: Lerner Publishing Group.

Pasnak, William. The Ginger Princess, 1 vol. 2006. (Lorimer Streetlights Ser.). (ENG.). 96p. (J). (gr. 2-5). 7.95 *(978-1-55028-952-7(7),* 9781550289527) Lorimer, James & Co., Ltd., Pubs. CAN. Dist: Casemate Pubs. & Bk. Distributors, LLC.

Pasqualini, Rosie. Nantarctica: Twilight-Water. 2008. 62p. pap. 6.98 *(978-0-557-00921-3(9))* Lulu Pr., Inc.

Passey, Joel. Treween. 2011. 24p. pap. 15.99 *(978-1-4653-5551-5(0))* Xlibris Corp.

Pastis, Stephan. Timmy Failure: the Cat Stole My Pants. Pastis, Stephan, illus. 2017. (Timmy Failure Ser.: 6). (ENG., Illus.). 288p. (J). (gr. 3-7). 14.99 *(978-0-7636-9733-4(8))* Candlewick Pr.

Patton, Julia. Drat That Fat Cat! Patton, Julia, illus. 2016. (ENG., Illus.). 32p. (J). (gr. -1-3). 16.99 *(978-0-8075-1713-0(5))* Whitman, Albert & Co.

Paul. Best Friends. 2012. 24p. pap. 17.99 *(978-1-4772-0755-0(4))* AuthorHouse.

Paul, Cinco & Daurio, Ken. Sleepy Kittens. Guillon, Eric, illus. 2010. (Despicable Me Ser.). (ENG.). 10p. (J). (gr. -1 — 1). bds. 8.99 *(978-0-316-08381-2(X),* L,B Kids) Hachette Bk. Group.

Paula, Cristina De. Sweet Pomchu. 2011. 28p. pap. 15.99 *(978-1-4568-5816-2(5))* Xlibris Corp.

Pauley, Kimberly. Cat Girl's Day Off, 1 vol. 2012. (ENG.). 336p. (YA). 17.95 *(978-1-60060-883-4(3),* Tu Bks.) Lee & Low Bks., Inc.

Paull, John W. The Great Stampede: A Jimmy James Story. 2010. 28p. 16.09 (978-1-4269-4698-1(8)) Trafford Publishing.

Peachey, Ann. The Adventures of a Greek Cat Called Mani. 2012. (Illus.). 44p. pap. 24.40 (978-1-4685-8206-2(2)) AuthorHouse.

Pearce, Margaret. A Belinda Robinson Novel Book 1: Belinda & the Witch's Cat. 2013. 82p. pap. (978-1-922066-58-9(3)) Writers Exchange E-Publishing.

—A Belinda Robinson Novel Book 2: Belinda & the Holidays It Rained. 2013. 78p. pap. (978-1-922233-22-6(6)) Writers Exchange E-Publishing.

—A Belinda Robinson Novel Book 3: Belinda & the Missing Will. 2013. 80p. pap. (978-1-922233-23-3(4)) Writers Exchange E-Publishing.

Pelletier, Jennifer. The Wonderful Imagination of Alish. 2011. 32p. pap. 24.95 (978-1-4626-2613-7(0)) America Star Bks.

Pelley, Kathleen T. Raj the Bookstore Tiger. Keiser, Paige, illus. 2011. (ENG.). 32p. (J). (gr. -1-3). 15.95 (978-1-58089-230-8(2)) Charlesbridge Publishing, Inc.

Pennypacker, Sara. Clementine, Friend of the Week. Frazee, Marla, illus. (Clementine Book Ser.). (ENG.). 176p. (J). 2011. (gr. 1-3). pap. 5.99 (978-1-4231-1560-1(0)) 2010. (gr. 2-5). 14.99 (978-1-4231-1355-3(1)) Hyperion Pr.

Perego, Jeanne. Joseph & Chico: The Life of Pope Benedict XVI as Told by a Cat. Matt, Andrew, tr. from ITA. Casagrande, Donata Dal Molin, illus. 2008. 36p. (J). (gr. k-7). 17.95 (978-1-58617-252-7(2)) Ignatius Pr.

Perez, Vivian. Stolen Stories for My Nieces. 2007. (ENG.). 68p. per. 19.95 (978-1-4241-6679-4(9)) America Star Bks.

Perrault, Charles. Puss in Boots (El Gato Con Botas) Merino, Jose Luis, illus. 2004. (Bilingual Fairy Tales Ser.: BILI). (ENG & SPA.). 32p. (J). (gr. -1-7). pap. 6.99 (978-0-8118-3924-2(9)) Chronicle Bks. LLC.

Perritano, John. The Comet of Doom, 1 vol. Laughead, Mike, illus. 2014. (Kid Squad Saves the World Ser.). (ENG.). 112p. (J). (gr. 8-12). 27.07 (978-1-62402-038-4(0)) Magic Wagon.

—The Egyptian Prophecy, 1 vol. Laughead, Mike, illus. 2014. (Kid Squad Saves the World Ser.). (ENG.). 112p. (J). (gr. 8-12). 27.07 (978-1-62402-039-1(9)) Magic Wagon.

Peschke, Marci. Spelling Queen, 1 vol. Mourning, Tuesday, illus. 2012. (Kylie Jean Ser.). (ENG.). 112p. (gr. 2-3). pap. 5.95 (978-1-4048-7212-7(4)); lib. bdg. 22.65 (978-1-4048-6801-4(1)) Picture Window Bks. (Kylie Jean).

Peters, Lisa Westberg. Frankie Works the Night Shift. Taylor, Jennifer, illus. 2010. (ENG.). 32p. (J). (gr. -1-k). 16.99 (978-0-06-009095-1(2), Greenwillow Bks.) HarperCollins Pubs.

Peterson, Jim. Kitten Tales. 2006. (ENG.). 76p. per. 16.95 (978-1-4241-4448-8(5)) PublishAmerica, Inc.

—Kittens in the Mall. 2006. 76p. pap. 16.95 (978-1-4241-2604-0(5)) PublishAmerica, Inc.

—The Summer House Kitten. 2007. 48p. pap. 16.95 (978-1-60441-914-6(8)) America Star Bks.

Petrarca, Natalie. Stinky the Cat. 2009. 24p. pap. 13.95 (978-1-4327-1184-9(9)) Outskirts Pr., Inc.

Pevear, Ted F. & Pevear, Linda W. The Date in the Junk Yard. 2012. 28p. 24.95 (978-1-62709-781-9(3)) America Star Bks.

Pez, Christine & Duggins, Shirley. Casey & the Junkyard Cats: Pudgy's New Hero. 2010. 16p. 10.99 (978-1-4520-8518-0(8)) AuthorHouse.

Philip, Simon. I Don't Know What to Call My Cat. Bailey, Ella, illus. 2017. (ENG.). 32p. (J). (gr. -1-3). 16.99 (978-0-544-97143-1(4), HMH Books For Young Readers) Houghton Mifflin Harcourt Publishing Co.

Phillipps, J. C. Monkey Ono. 2013. (ENG., Illus.). 40p. (J). (gr. -1-k). 16.99 (978-0-670-78505-6(9), Viking Books for Young Readers) Penguin Young Readers Group.

Phillips, Azelin. Quicksilver. 2010. 32p. pap. 14.49 (978-1-4490-4522-7(7)) AuthorHouse.

Phillips, Dee & Ticktock Media, Ltd. Staff. What Do Cats Do? 2009. (What Do Animals Do? Ser.). (ENG.). 5p. (J). (gr. k—1). bds. 4.95 (978-1-84696-958-4(1), TickTock Books) Octopus Publishing Group GBR. Dist: Independent Pubs. Group.

Piantedosi, John J. The Cat That Purred. Maglio-Macullar, Andrea, illus. 2014. (ENG.). (J). pap. 11.95 (978-1-56548-540-2(8)) New City Press of the Focolare.

Picayo, Mario. A Very Smart Cat: Una Gata Muy Inteligente. Fundora, Yolanda V., illus. 2008. (SPA & ENG.). 32p. (J). (978-1-934370-00-1(2)) Editorial Campana.

Pike, Christopher, pseud. The Wicked Cat. 2015. (Spooksville Ser.: 10). (ENG., Illus.). 128p. (J). (gr. 3-7). pap. 6.99 (978-1-4814-1086-1(5), Aladdin) Simon & Schuster Children's Publishing.

—The Wicked Cat. 2015. (Spooksville Ser.: 10). lib. bdg. 17.20 (978-0-606-37851-2(0)) Turtleback Bks.

Pilkey, Dav. Dog Man. Pilkey, Dav, illus. 2016. (Dog Man Ser.: 1). (ENG., Illus.). 240p. (J). (gr. 2). 9.99 (978-0-545-58160-8(5), Graphix) Scholastic, Inc.

—Dog Man Unleashed. 2016. (Dog Man Ser.: 2). (ENG., Illus.). 224p. (J). (gr. 2-7). 9.99 (978-0-545-93520-3(2), Graphix) Scholastic, Inc.

—Dog Man Unleashed. 2016. (Dog Man Ser.: 2). (ENG.). (J). (gr. 2). lib. bdg. 20.85 **(978-0-606-39709-4(4))**; 240p. 20.85 (978-0-606-39115-3(0)) Turtleback Bks.

—Dragon's Fat Cat. 2008. (Illus.). 48p. (gr. -1-3). 16.00 (978-0-7569-8835-7(7)) Perfection Learning Corp.

—Kat Kong. 2003. (ENG., Illus.). 32p. (J). pap. 5.95 (978-0-15-204950-8(9)) Houghton Mifflin Harcourt Publishing Co.

—Kat Kong. 2003. (gr. k-3). lib. bdg. 15.95 (978-0-613-71635-2(3), Turtleback) Turtleback Bks.

Pilkey, Dav. A Tale of Two Kitties. 2017. (Dog Man Ser.: bk.3). (ENG., Illus.). 256p. (J). (gr. 2-5). 9.99 **(978-0-545-93521-0(0)**, Graphix) Scholastic, Inc.

—A Tale of Two Kitties. 2017. (Dog Man Ser.: 3). lib. bdg. 20.85 **(978-0-606-40547-8(X))** Turtleback Bks.

Pinkwater, Daniel M. Adventures of a Cat-Whiskered Girl. 2011. (ENG., Illus.). 288p. (J). (gr. 5-7). pap. 16.95 (978-0-547-55002-2(2)) Houghton Mifflin Harcourt Publishing Co.

—Beautiful Yetta's Hanukkah Kitten. Pinkwater, Jill, illus. 2014. (ENG.). 32p. (J). (gr. -1-2). 17.99 (978-0-312-62134-6(5), 9780312621346) Feiwel & Friends.

—Mrs. Noodlekugel. Stower, Adam, illus. 2013. (Mrs. Noodlekugel Ser.). (ENG.). 80p. (J). (gr. k-4). pap. 5.99 (978-0-7636-6452-7(9)) Candlewick Pr.

—Mrs. Noodlekugel & Four Blind Mice. Stower, Adam, illus. 2013. (Mrs. Noodlekugel Ser.). (ENG.). 96p. (J). (gr. k-4). 14.99 (978-0-7636-5054-4(4)) Candlewick Pr.

Pitt, Marilyn & Hileman, Jane. My Babies. 2010. pap. 39.62 (978-1-61541-066-8(X)) American Reading Co.

—Pretty Cat. 2010. pap. 39.62 (978-1-61541-068-2(6)) American Reading Co.

—Pretty Cat. Bianchi, John, illus. 2010. (1G Potato Chip Bks.). (ENG.). 12p. (J). (gr. k-1). pap. 5.99 (978-1-61541-067-5(8)) American Reading Co.

Pitt, Marilyn & Sánchez, Lucía M. Solos en Casa. Bianchi, John, illus. 2011. (1G Libros Papas Fritas Ser.).Tr. of Home Alone. (SPA.). 12p. (J). (gr. k-1). pap. 6.99 (978-1-61541-409-3(6)) American Reading Co.

Pitts, Constance. Chulita the Blind Cat. 2007. (Illus.). 48p. (J). (978-0-9652902-2-7(0)) Beevinwood, Inc.

Pizzoli, Greg. Templeton Gets His Wish. Pizzoli, Greg, illus. 2015. (ENG., Illus.). 48p. (J). (gr. -1-k). 16.99 (978-1-4847-1274-0(9)) Disney Pr.

The Playful Kitten. 2003. (J). per. (978-1-57657-888-9(7)) Paradise Pr., Inc.

Pliszka, Jodi. Bella & Gizmo's Adventures — the Hairless Sphynx Cats. 2005. (Illus.). 30p. (J). per. 18.95 (978-1-933449-27-2(6)) Nightengale Pr.

Plumides, Damon & Boerke, Arthur Mark. The Adventures of Caterwaul the Cat: Feline Pie. 2011. (ENG., Illus.). 226p. (J). (gr. 4-7). pap. 17.95 (978-1-937084-19-6(1)) Boutique of Quality Books Publishing Co., Inc.

Plunkett, Windyann. Fiddle Me a Riddle & Bring Me the Moon. Davidson, Mary, illus. 2011. 24p. pap. 24.95 (978-1-4626-3920-5(8)) America Star Bks.

Polacco, Patricia, illus. Because of Thursday. 2016. (ENG.). 40p. (J). (gr. -1-3). 17.99 (978-1-4814-2140-9(9), Simon & Schuster Bks. For Young Readers) Simon & Schuster Bks. For Young Readers.

Polan, Alex. Following Meowth's Footprints: PokéStop Stories, Book Two. 2016. (ENG.). 112p. (J). (gr. 1-7). pap. 7.99 (978-1-5107-2158-6(4), Sky Pony Pr.) Skyhorse Publishing Co., Inc.

Pollack, Pamela. Spy Cats: Revenge of the Robot Rats. 2004. (Illus.). 57p. (978-0-439-56603-2(7)) Scholastic, Inc.

Pollitz, Edith Elizabeth. Carrie. 2004. (ENG.). 44p. 24.95 (978-1-4137-3355-6(7)) America Star Bks.

Popsicle, Patty. Crack-A-Doodle Horse Tales: A Tale about Scratching. 2011. 24p. pap. 12.99 (978-1-4520-6094-1(0)) AuthorHouse.

Posner-Sanchez, Andrea. Time to Fly! (Disney Junior: Sheriff Callie's Wild West) Fruchter, Jason, illus. 2015. (Little Golden Book Ser.). (ENG.). 24p. (J). (-k). 4.99 (978-0-7364-3362-4(7), Golden/Disney) Random Hse. Children's Bks.

Posner-Sanchez, Andrea & Lagonegro, Melissa. Callie's Cowgirl Twirl (Disney Junior: Sheriff Callie's Wild West) Fruchter, Jason, illus. 2016. (Little Golden Book Ser.). (ENG.). 24p. (J). (-k). 4.99 (978-0-7364-3442-3(9), Golden/Disney) Random Hse. Children's Bks.

Potter, Alicia. Miss Hazeltine's Home for Shy & Fearful Cats. Sif, Birgitta, illus. 2015. (ENG.). 40p. (J). (gr. k-3). 16.99 (978-0-385-75334-0(9)); lib. bdg. 19.99 (978-0-385-75335-7(7)) Random Hse. Children's Bks. (Knopf Bks. for Young Readers).

Potter, Beatrix. Conte de Tom Chaton. pap. 18.95 (978-2-07-054700-5(0)) Gallimard, Editions FRA. Dist: Distribooks, Inc.

—The Tale of Kitty in Boots. Blake, Quentin, illus. 2016. (Peter Rabbit Ser.). (ENG.). 72p. (J). (gr. -1-2). 20.00 (978-0-241-24944-4(9), Warne) Penguin Young Readers Group.

—The Tale of Tom Kitten. (Illus.). 12p. 4.95 (978-1-58989-273-6(9)) Thurman Hse., LLC.

Poulin, Stephane. Peux-Tu Attraper Josephine? 2003. (FRE & SPA., Illus.). 24p. (J). (gr. k-3). pap. 6.95 (978-0-88776-643-5(9)) Tundra Bks. CAN. Dist: Penguin Random Hse. LLC.

Powell, Anthony. Our Cat Hogan - Could He Be Part Dog? Stodden, Lindsay, illus. 2012. 24p. (J). 19.95 (978-1-61863-358-3(9)) Bookstand Publishing.

Powell, Gail. The Adventures of Harold J. Kat. 2008. 40p. pap. 16.99 (978-1-4259-6334-7(X)) AuthorHouse.

Powell, Richard. Kitty's Tail. Davis, Caroline, illus. 2003. (Animal Tails Ser.). 10p. (J). 3.95 (978-1-58925-673-6(5)) Tiger Tales.

Pratchett, Terry. The Amazing Maurice & His Educated Rodents. 2008. (Discworld Novels Ser.). 368p. (YA). (gr. 8-18). pap. 8.99 (978-0-06-001235-9(8)) HarperCollins Pubs.

—The Amazing Maurice & His Educated Rodents. 2003. (ENG.). 340p. (gr. 7). 19.00 (978-0-7569-1458-5(2)) Perfection Learning Corp.

—The Amazing Maurice & His Educated Rodents. 2008. (Discworld Ser.: 33). (YA). (gr. 5-8). 19.65 (978-0-613-65757-0(8), Turtleback) Turtleback Bks.

Prentice, Amy. Mouser Cats' Story. 2004. reprint ed. pap. 15.95 (978-1-4191-3542-2(2)); pap. 1.99 (978-1-4192-3542-9(7)) Kessinger Publishing, LLC.

Preston-Gannon, Frann. Pepper & Poe. 2015. (ENG., Illus.). 32p. (J). (gr. -1-k). 16.99 (978-0-545-68357-9(2), Orchard Bks.) Scholastic, Inc.

Preston, Mary Lou. Do You Know What Wildcats Do at School in P. E. Class? Wildcat's First Day in Class. 2006. (J). pap. 8.00 (978-0-8059-7013-5(4)) Dorrance Publishing Co., Inc.

Prevost, Jeanne. It's Raining Cats & Cats! Hansen, Amelia, illus. 2008. (ENG.). 24p. (J). (gr. k-2). 16.95 (978-0-940719-06-4(1)) Gryphon Pr., The.

Prevost, Pamela Ms Ed. The Adventures of Charlie: The Curious Cat & Me. 2012. 32p. (-18). pap. 21.99 (978-1-4797-4280-6(5)) Xlibris Corp.

Price, Mathew. Gatito. Goldman, Judy, tr. Kemp, Moira, illus. 2010. (SPA & ENG.). 10p. bds. 5.99 (978-1-935021-99-5(0)) Price, Mathew Ltd.

Priddy, Roger. Hello Friends. 2014. (Little Friends Ser.). (ENG.). 24p. (J). (gr. -1 — 1). bds. 5.99 (978-0-312-51684-0(3), 9780312516840, Priddy Bks.) St. Martin's Pr.

—Hello Kitty - Chalk Fun. 2014. (Hello Kitty Ser.). (ENG.). 16p. (J). (gr. -1-1). bds. 8.99 (978-0-312-51767-0(X), 9780312517670, Priddy Bks.) St. Martin's Pr.

—Hello Kitty - My Home. 2014. (Lift-The-Flap Tab Bks.). (ENG.). 16p. (J). (gr. -1-1). bds. 8.99 (978-0-312-51768-7(8), 9780312517687, Priddy Bks.) St. Martin's Pr.

—Hello Kitty: Giant Sticker Book. 2015. (Hello Kitty Ser.). (ENG.). 128p. (J). (gr. -1-1). pap. 12.99 (978-0-312-51838-7(2), 9780312518387, Priddy Bks.) St. Martin's Pr.

—My World. 2015. (Hello Kitty Ser.). (ENG.). 16p. (J). (gr. -1-1). bds. 12.99 (978-0-312-51817-2(X), 9780312518172, Priddy Bks.) St. Martin's Pr.

—Tea Party Set. 2014. (Hello Kitty Ser.). (ENG.). 8p. (J). (gr. -1-1). bds. 14.99 (978-0-312-51766-3(1), 9780312517663, Priddy Bks.) St. Martin's Pr.

Prisant, Guillermo Murray. Que Miedo! rev. ed. 2006. (Castillo del Terror Ser.). (SPA & ENG.). 112p. (J). (gr. 6-9). pap. 6.95 (978-970-20-0338-0(5)) Castillo, Ediciones, S. A. de C. V. MEX. Dist: Macmillan.

Pruitt, Kat. Si Si the Circus Cat. Griftner, Rebecca, illus. 2011. (ENG.). 24p. (J). pap. 12.95 (978-0-9844037-2-1(8)) Pruggus Publishing.

Pryor, Bonnie. Mr. Munday & the Rustlers. 2013. (ENG.). 32p. (J). (gr. -1-3). 16.99 (978-1-4424-8876-2(X), Atheneum Bks. for Young Readers) Simon & Schuster Children's Publishing.

Publications International Ltd. Staff, ed. First Look & Find Hello Kitty. 2013. (gr. -1-1). bds. 7.98 (978-1-4508-6378-0(7), 900f7270-d27c-4dbf-8614-52373c31c3df) Phoenix International Publications, Inc.

—Hello Kitty: My Friend Hello Kitty: Play-A-Sound Book & Cuddly Hello Kitty. 2013. (J). (gr. -1-4). bds. 13.99 (978-1-4508-1181-1(7), 21ea0785-0317-4c86-b812-bf2727f2df16) Phoenix International Publications, Inc.

—Rainbow Kittens A Colorful Tale. 2010. (J). bds. 7.98 (978-1-60553-434-3(X)) Phoenix International Publications, Inc.

—Wonder Pets: Save the Baby Kitten. 2008. (J). bds. 10.98 (978-1-4127-9198-4(7)) Publications International, Ltd.

Pueppke, M. D. Even Fuzzier Logic: Fuzzy the Cat Digs Deeper. 2004. (Illus.). 166p. (YA). per. (978-0-9678352-3-5(2)) MD Pueppke.

Pugliano-Martin, Carol. Little Cat Goes Fast. 2011. (Early Connections Ser.). (J). (978-1-61672-358-3(0)) Benchmark Education Co.

Pulford, Elizabeth. Billy Brown's Cat, 1 vol. Brown, Daniel J., illus. 2012. (Engage Literacy Green Ser.). (ENG.). 32p. (gr. k-2). pap. 5.99 (978-1-4296-8838-3(6), Engage Literacy) Capstone Press of Coughlan Cos.

Punter, Russell. Scaredy Cat. 2009. 48p. 19.99 (978-0-7945-2281-0(5)) EDC Publishing.

—There Was a Crooked Man. Semple, David, illus. 2010. (First Reading Level 2 Ser.). 32p. (J). 6.99 (978-0-7945-2682-5(9), Usborne) EDC Publishing.

Purkiss, Cathy. Flat on Top. 2012. 16p. pap. 24.95 (978-1-62709-347-7(8)) America Star Bks.

Quail, Annette. Lucy & Coco. 2008. 44p. pap. 24.95 (978-1-60441-854-5(0)) America Star Bks.

Quinones, Juan Carlos. La Pandilla Bajo el Arbol. Ortiz Montanez, Nivea, illus. 2004. (Purple Ser.). (SPA.). 44p. (J). (gr. 3-5). pap. 5.95 (978-1-57581-439-1(0)) Santillana USA Publishing Co., Inc.

Quintero, Isabel. Ugly Cat & Pablo. Knight, Tom, illus. 2017. (ENG.). 112p. (J). (gr. 2-5). pap. 6.99 **(978-0-545-94091-7(5)**, Scholastic Pr.) Scholastic, Inc.

Quinton, Sasha. Eek-A-Squeak: A Phonics Reader. 2009. (Illus.). pap. (978-1-936199-05-1(X)) Book Shop, Ltd., The.

Quiroga, Luis Alberto. Chiquita. (SPA.). pap. 8.95 (978-950-07-1987-2(8)) Editorial Sudamericana S.A. ARG. Dist: Distribooks, Inc.

Rabe, Tish. Chasing Rainbows. Ruiz, Aristides & Mathieu, Joe, illus. 2012. (Pictureback(R) Ser.). (ENG.). 16p. (J). (gr. -1-2). pap. 4.99 (978-0-375-87124-5(1), Random Hse. Bks. for Young Readers) Random Hse. Children's Bks.

—Home for Christmas. Brannon, Tom, illus. 2012. (Step into Reading Ser.). (ENG.). 48p. (J). (gr. k-3). pap. 3.99 (978-0-307-97625-3(4), Random Hse. Bks. for Young Readers) Random Hse. Children's Bks.

—I Love the Nightlife! Ruiz, Aristides & Mathieu, Joe, illus. 2010. (Pictureback Ser.). (ENG.). 16p. (J). (gr. -1-2). pap. 3.99 (978-0-375-86354-7(0), Random Hse. Bks. for Young Readers) Random Hse. Children's Bks.

—Spring into Summer! Mathieu, Joe & Ruiz, Aristides, illus. 2012. (Pictureback(R) Ser.). (ENG.). 32p. (J). (gr. -1-2). pap. 4.99 (978-0-307-93057-6(2), Random Hse. Bks. for Young Readers) Random Hse. Children's Bks.

—The Thinga-Ma-Jigger Is Coming Today! Moroney, Christopher, illus. 2010. (Little Golden Book Ser.). (ENG.). 24p. (J). (gr. -1-2). 4.99 (978-0-375-85927-4(6), Golden Bks.) Random Hse. Children's Bks.

—Trick-or-Treat!/Aye-Aye! Ruiz, Aristides & Mathieu, Joe, illus. 2012. (Pictureback(R) Ser.). (ENG.). 32p. (J). (gr. -1-2). pap. 4.99 (978-0-307-93056-9(4), Random Hse. Bks. for Young Readers) Random Hse. Children's Bks.

Radzinski, Kandy. What Cats Want for Christmas. Radzinski, Kandy, illus. rev. ed. 2007. (ENG., Illus.). 32p. (J). (gr. k-6). 16.95 (978-1-58536-340-7(5)) Sleeping Bear Pr.

—Where to Sleep. 2010. (ENG.). 22p. (J). 9.95 (978-1-58536-535-7(1)) Sleeping Bear Pr.

—Where to Sleep. Radzinski, Kandy, illus. 2009. (ENG., Illus.). 32p. (J). (gr. k-6). 15.95 (978-1-58536-436-7(3)) Sleeping Bear Pr.

Raglin, Tim. The Curse of Catunkhamun. 2007. (Illus.). (J). (978-0-9788969-0-4(4), Exhibit A) TR Bks.

Raines, Gary. My Brother's Blue. 2009. 32p. pap. 14.49 (978-1-4490-4185-4(X)) AuthorHouse.

Rainey, L. E. Sad Sam, Glad Sam. 2006. (Illus.). 32p. (J). 16.95 (978-0-9785521-0-7(5)) Shoetree Publishers, Inc.

Ralston, Carole. Light in the Forest. 2012. 24p. 24.95 (978-1-4626-6283-8(8)) America Star Bks.

Ramski, Mitch. Firehouse Cat: How Cinder Became a Firehouse Cat. 2011. 28p. (gr. -1). pap. 12.75 (978-1-4490-8661-9(6)) AuthorHouse.

Randall, Dennis E. Those Darn Cats Patchie & Teddy: Having Fun & Making Friends. 2012. 44p. pap. 21.99 (978-1-4685-8535-3(5)) AuthorHouse.

Randall, Marilyn Mae. The Three Wives of Hero the Second. Heavner, Jodi, illus. 2004. (J). per. 14.99 (978-0-9713589-7-3(4)) Ubaviel's Gifts.

Randolph, Robert. Ben Goes to the Farmer's Market, 1 vol. 2009. 37p. pap. 24.95 (978-1-4489-1934-5(7)) PublishAmerica, Inc.

—Ben the Flying Cat, 1 vol. Sappington, Ray, illus. 2009. 30p. pap. 24.95 (978-1-60749-088-3(9)) America Star Bks.

Random House. Save the Kitten!/Buster's Big Day (Team Umizoomi) Ostrom, Bob, illus. 2014. (Pictureback(R) Ser.). (ENG.). 32p. (J). (gr. -1-2). 4.99 (978-0-385-37520-7(4), Random Hse. Bks. for Young Readers) Random Hse. Children's Bks.

Random House Disney Staff. Go for the Gold! Random House Disney Staff & Petrossi, Fabrizio, illus. 2016. (Pictureback(R) Ser.). (ENG.). 16p. (J). (gr. -1-2). pap. 4.99 (978-0-399-55595-4(1), Random Hse. Bks. for Young Readers) Random Hse. Children's Bks.

Rankin, H. L. Chaya & the Spider Gem. White, Siobhán, illus. 2011. 152p. (YA). pap. 9.95 (978-2-930583-10-5(X)) White & MacLean Publishing BEL. Dist: Gardners Bks. Ltd.

Ransom, Jeanie Franz. There's a Cat in Our Class! A Tale about Getting Along. Langdo, Bryan, illus. 2016. 32p. (J). (978-1-4338-2262-9(8), Magination Pr.) American Psychological Assn.

Rea, Monique. Toulouse the Moose. 2003. (J). 3.50 (978-1-891030-30-7(2)) Paragon Agency, The.

—Toulouse the Moose & the Mystery Guests. 2012. 34p. pap. 13.99 (978-0-9788926-4-7(X)) Trails of Discovery.

Rea, Monique F. The Original Story of Toulouse the Moose & His Friends: Book & CD. 2007. (J). (978-0-9788926-2-3(3)) Trails of Discovery.

Rearick, Nancy. Life Through a Kitten's Eyes. 2010. 24p. (J). pap. 14.99 (978-1-4520-2841-5(9)) AuthorHouse.

Reasoner, Charles & Wood, Steven. Scaredy Cat. 2015. (Charles Reasoner Halloween Bks.). (ENG., Illus.). 12p. (gr. -1 — 1). bds. 5.99 (978-1-4795-8501-4(7)) Picture Window Bks.

Red Fox Picture Books Staff & Transworld Publishing Staff. Better Play Times. 2006. (ENG., Illus.). 24p. (J). (gr. k-k). pap. 7.95 (978-1-86230-164-1(6), Red Fox) Random House Children's Books GBR. Dist: Independent Pubs. Group.

Redbank, Tennant. Beauty: Aurora's Sleepy Kitten. Random House Disney Staff, illus. 2014. (Stepping Stone Book Ser.). (ENG.). 64p. (J). (gr. 2-5). 5.99 (978-0-7364-3266-5(3), RH/Disney) Random Hse. Children's Bks.

—Beauty the Sleepiest Kitty. Random House Disney Staff, illus. 2014. (Stepping Stone Book(TM) Ser.). (ENG.). 64p. (J). (gr. 1-4). lib. bdg. 12.99 (978-0-7364-8163-2(X), RH/Disney) Random Hse. Children's Bks.

—The Kitchen Catastrophe. The Disney Storybook Art Team & Batson, Alan, illus. 2016. (Disney Chapters Ser.). (ENG.). 64p. (J). (gr. 1-4). 5.99 (978-0-7364-3643-4(X), RH/Disney) Random Hse. Children's Bks.

—Lily: Tiana's Helpful Kitten (Disney Princess: Palace Pets) Random House Disney Staff & Matta, Gabriella, illus. 2016. (Stepping Stone Book(TM) Ser.). (ENG.). 64p. (J). (gr. 1-4). 5.99 (978-0-7364-3393-8(7), RH/Disney) Random Hse. Children's Bks.

—Treasure: Ariel's Curious Kitten. 2015. (Disney Princess Palace Pets Ser.). lib. bdg. 16.00 (978-0-606-36392-1(0)) Turtleback Bks.

—Treasure: Ariel's Curious Kitten (Disney Princess: Palace Pets) RH Disney Staff et al, illus. 2015. (Stepping Stone Book(TM) Ser.). (ENG.). 64p. (J). (gr. 1-4). 5.99 (978-0-7364-3346-4(5), RH/Disney) Random Hse. Children's Bks.

Redd, Faye V. Mia & Her Kitten Sophie. 2008. 24p. pap. 11.49 (978-1-4343-9835-2(8)) AuthorHouse.

Redman-Waldeyer, Christine. Around the World with Rosalie. Adams, Marcella Ryan, illus. 2003. pap. 9.00 (978-0-8059-6185-0(2)) Dorrance Publishing Co., Inc.

Reed, Emma & Reed, Jennifer. Romeo's Rescue. Movshina, Marina, illus. 2012. 24p. pap. 10.95 (978-1-61633-247-1(6)) Guardian Angel Publishing, Inc.

Reed, Joel B. Grandpa's New Kitty. Reed, Joel B., illus. 2008. (Illus.). 28p. pap. 12.95 (978-1-933482-65-1(6)) White Turtle Bks.

Reeg, Cynthia. Kitty Kerplunking: Preposition Fun. Movshina, Marina, illus. 2006. 24p. (J). E-Book 9.95 incl. cd-rom (978-1-933090-27-6(8)) Guardian Angel Publishing, Inc.

—Kitty Kerplunking: Preposition Fun. l.t. ed. 2006. (ENG., Illus.). 24p. (J). 11.95 (978-1-933090-29-0(4)) Guardian Angel Publishing, Inc.

Rees, Gwyneth. Cosmo & the Secret Spell, 1. Hearn, Samuel, illus. unabr. ed. 2010. (Cosmo Ser.: 3). (ENG.). 208p. (J). (gr. 2-4). pap. 7.99 (978-0-330-44216-9(3)) Macmillan Pubs., Ltd. GBR. Dist: Independent Pubs. Group.

Reeves, Claire. Adventures of Boots the One Eyed Cat 2003. (Illus.). 32p. (J). 15.95 (978-0-9743048-1-6(6)) LTI Publishing.

Reeves, Thomas. I Had a Cat. 2013. (ENG., Illus.). 32p. (J). (gr. -1-3). 16.99 (978-1-4814-2129-4(8), Simon & Schuster Bks. For Young Readers) Simon & Schuster Bks. For Young Readers.

Reher, Matt. Dan Gets a Cat. 2015. (1B Fiction Ser.). (ENG., Illus.). 12p. (J). pap. 5.99 (978-1-63437-176-6(3)) American Reading Co.

Reibold, Mary. Ninya's Great Adventure: A Cat's Tale. 2007. 96p. per. 19.95 (978-1-4241-7135-4(0)) America Star Bks.

Reibstein, Mark. Wabi Sabi. Young, Ed, illus. 2008. (ENG.). 40p. (J). (gr. -1-3). 18.99 (978-0-316-11825-5(7)) Little Brown & Co.

—Wabi Sabi. 2009. (J). 192.75 (978-1-4407-1919-6(5)); 39.75 (978-1-4407-1922-6(5)); 37.75 (978-1-4407-1920-2(9)); 1.25 (978-1-4407-1925-7(X)); 37.75 (978-1-4407-1924-0(1)); 39.75 (978-1-4407-1918-9(7)) Recorded Bks., Inc.

Reich, Susanna. Minette's Feast: The Delicious Story of Julia Child & Her Cat. Bates, Amy, illus. 2012. (ENG.). 40p. (J). (gr. -1-k). 17.95 (978-1-4197-0177-1(0), Abrams Bks. for Young Readers) Abrams, Inc.

Reiff, Lauren & Geiser, Christina. Meows-Key Motel: A Great Vacation Spot for Hip Cats. 2009. 12p. pap. 8.95 (978-1-4389-8801-6(X)) AuthorHouse.

Reinhardt, Jennifer Black. Blue Ethel. Reinhardt, Jennifer Black, illus. 2017. (ENG., Illus.). 40p. (J). 17.99

(978-0-374-30382-2(7), 9780374303822, Farrar, Straus & Giroux (BYR)) Farrar, Straus & Giroux.

Renek, Nava. Venice Is for Cats. 2013. (Illus.). pap. 20.00 (978-0-989389-53-6(9)) Spuyten Duyvil Publishing.

Rey, H. A. & Rey, Margret. Circus Act. 2008. (Curious George Ser.). (ENG., Illus.). 16p. (J). (gr. -1-3). 5.99 (978-0-618-99909-5(4)) Houghton Mifflin Harcourt Publishing Co.

Reynolds, Alison. A New Friend for Marmalade. McKenzie, Heath, illus. 2014. (ENG.). 40p. (J). (gr. -1-1). 15.99 (978-1-4814-2046-4(1), Little Simon) Little Simon.

—A Year with Marmalade. McKenzie, Heath, illus. 2013. (ENG.). 40p. (J). (gr. -1-1). 15.99 (978-1-4424-8105-3(6), Little Simon) Little Simon.

RH Disney Staff & Posner-Sanchez, Andrea. Treasure's Day at Sea (Disney Princess: Palace Pets) RH Disney Staff & DiCicco, Sue, illus. 2015. (Little Golden Book Ser.). (ENG.). 24p. (J). (-k). 4.99 (978-0-7364-3335-8(X), Golden/Disney) Random Hse. Children's Bks.

Riad, Hala. Twinkie Has a New Home. 2011. 24p. pap. 14.93 (978-1-4269-7120-4(6)) Trafford Publishing.

Ribble, S. A Child's Book of Kitty-cat & Puppy-dog Tales. 2007. (Illus.). 72p. per. (978-1-84401-961-8(6)) Athena Pr.

Richards, Chuck. Catch That Cat! A Chase up & down & Through M.C. Escher's Art. 2016. (J). (978-0-553-53562-4(5)) Bantam Doubleday Dell Large Print Group, Inc.

Richardson, Michelle Y. Kaito: Shedding Tears. 2010. 104p. (J). pap. 9.95 (978-1-4502-5267-6(2)) iUniverse, Inc.

Richemont, Enid. The Night of the Were-Boy. 2015. (Race Further with Reading Ser.). (ENG., Illus.). 48p. (J). (978-0-7787-2087-4(X)) Crabtree Publishing Co.

Richter, Jutta. The Cat: Or, How I Lost Eternity. Brailovsky, Anna, tr. from GER. Berner, Rotraut Susanne, illus. 2007. (ENG.). 80p. (J). (gr. 1-6). 14.00 (978-1-57131-676-9(0)) Milkweed Editions.

Riddle, Peter H. The Painted Ponies of Partequineus & the Summer of the Kittens: Two Novels for Young Readers. 2009. (Illus.). 260p. (J). pap. (978-1-926585-19-2(4), CCB Publishing) CCB Publishing.

Ridell, Chris. Ottoline y la gata amarilla/ Ottolina & the Yellow Cat. 2008. (SPA.). 172p. (J). 13.95 (978-84-263-6832-4(8)) Vives, Luis Editorial (Edelvives) ESP. Dist: Baker & Taylor Bks.

Rieser, Karen. A Cat with Three Tales. 2013. 48p. pap. 8.95 (978-1-937260-93-4(3)) Sleepytown Pr.

Rifkin, L. Life Four. 2008. (Nine Lives of Romeo Crumb Ser.). (Illus.). 201p. (gr. 6-8). per. 8.95 (978-0-9743221-9-3(9)) Sunrise Publishing Co.

—Life One. Hartman, Kurt, illus. 2007. (Nine Lives of Romeo Crumb Ser.). 311p. (J). (gr. 6-8). per. 8.95 (978-0-9743221-3-1(X)) Sunrise Publishing Co.

—The Nine Lives of Romeo Crumb: Life 6. Hartman, Kurt, illus. 2010. 246p. (YA). pap. 8.95 (978-0-9743221-8-6(0)) Sunrise Publishing Co.

—The Nine Lives of Romeo Crumb: Life One. 2005. (Illus.). 311p. (J). (gr. 6-8). 16.95 (978-0-9743221-0-0(5)) Sunrise Publishing Co.

—The Nine Lives of Romeo Crumb: Life Seven. 2011. 218p. (J). pap. 8.95 (978-0-9835480-0-3(5)) Sunrise Publishing Co.

Rifkin, L. (Lauren). The Nine Lives of Romeo Crumb: Life Five. Hartman, Kurt, illus. 2009. 169p. (YA). pap. 8.95 (978-0-9743221-7-9(2)) Sunrise Publishing Co.

Rifkin, Lauren I. The Nine Lives of Romeo Crumb: Life Eight. 2013. (ENG.). 224p. (YA). pap. 8.95 (978-0-9886853-8-3(8)) Sunrise Publishing Co.

RIGBY. Little Kitten, Big Cat: First Grade Big Books. 2003. (Rigby on Our Way to English Ser.). (ENG.). 24p. (gr. 1-1). pap. 50.70 (978-0-7578-1511-9(1)) Rigby Education.

Rigby Education Staff. Cargo Cat. (Sails Literacy Ser.). (Illus.). 16p. (gr. 1-2). 27.00 (978-0-7635-9915-7(8), 699158C99) Rigby Education.

—Cat's Diary. (Sails Literacy Ser.). (Illus.). 16p. (gr. 2-3). 27.00 (978-0-7635-9937-9(9), 699379C99) Rigby Education.

—Custard's Cat Flap. (Sails Literacy Ser.). (Illus.). 16p. (gr. 1-2). 27.00 (978-0-7635-9903-4(4), 699034C99) Rigby Education.

—The Daily Meow. (Sails Literacy Ser.). (Illus.). 16p. (gr. 2-3). 27.00 (978-0-7635-9940-9(9), 699740C99) Rigby Education.

—The Happy House. (Sails Literacy Ser.). (Illus.). 16p. (gr. 1-2). 27.00 (978-0-7635-9908-9(5), 699085C99) Rigby Education.

—McGinty's Friend. (Sails Literacy Ser.). (Illus.). 16p. (gr. 2-3). 27.00 (978-0-7635-9947-8(6), 699476C99) Rigby Education.

—The Space Cat. (Sails Literacy Ser.). (Illus.). 16p. (gr. 2-3). 27.00 (978-0-7635-9949-2(2), 699492C99) Rigby Education.

Rigo, L. Little Kitten. 2012. (Look at Me Bks.). (ENG., Illus.). 10p. (J). bds. 7.99 (978-0-7641-6523-8(2)) Barron's Educational Series, Inc.

Rimland, Mark, illus. The Secret Night World of Cats. 2008. 32p. (YA). 15.00 (978-0-9740360-6-9(4)) Autism Research Institute.

Risselada, Melissa. Seven Cats & the Big Gray Fence. Kalpart, illus. 2013. 28p. pap. 12.50 (978-1-62516-777-4(6), Strategic Bk. Publishing) Strategic Book Publishing & Rights Agency (SBPRA).

Rissi, Anica Mrose. Anna, Banana, & the Little Lost Kitten. Park, Meg, illus. 2017. (Anna, Banana Ser.: 5). (ENG.). 144p. (J). (gr. 1-5). 16.99 **(978-1-4814-8669-9(1)**, Simon & Schuster Bks. For Young Readers) Simon & Schuster Bks. For Young Readers.

Rissman, Rebecca. A Cat's Day, 1 vol. Moor, Becka, illus. 2014. (ENG.). 32p. (gr. 1-2). 26.65 (978-1-4846-0396-3(6)) Heinemann-Raintree.

Ritchey, Carmil White. The Adventures of Pine Cone the Cat. 2012. 24p. pap. 17.99 (978-1-4685-9470-6(2)) AuthorHouse.

Ritz, Karen. Windows with Birds. 2010. (ENG., Illus.). 32p. (J). (gr. k-2). 16.95 (978-1-59078-656-7(4)) Boyds Mills Pr.

Roberts, Bethany. Halloween Mice! Cushman, Doug, illus. 2011. (ENG.). 28p. (J). (gr. k — 1). bds. 5.99 (978-0-547-57573-5(4)) Houghton Mifflin Harcourt Publishing Co.

Roberts, Courtney. Uh-Oh! Cat. 2009. 40p. pap. 18.99 (978-1-4389-7705-8(0)) AuthorHouse.

Roberts, Dina. Thirty Cats. 2003. 162p. (YA). pap. 12.95 (978-0-595-29775-7(7)) iUniverse, Inc.

Robeson, K. S. Chloe, Bia & the Little People: Tales from Wind Creek Book Three. 2003. (Tales from Wind Creek Ser.: 3). 104p. (J). pap. 8.95 (978-0-9723530-4-5(6)) Falcor Bks.

Robinson, Hilary. Over the Moon. Abbott, Jane, illus. 2009. (Tadpoles Ser.). (ENG.). 24p. (J). (gr. k-2). pap. (978-0-7787-3899-2(X)); lib. bdg. (978-0-7787-3868-8(X)) Crabtree Publishing Co.

Robison, Peggy. Prince Cody Meets A Monster. Clay, Doris, illus. 2004. 40p. pap. 9.95 (978-0-9708395-7-2(X)) Legacy Publishing Services, Inc.

—Prince Cody Runs Ahead of the Hurricane. Clay, Doris, illus. 2005. 64p. per. 9.95 (978-0-9764982-7-8(8)) Legacy Publishing Services, Inc.

Robson, Samantha Eliza. Jack & the Cats. 2011. 24p. pap. 16.95 (978-1-4475-0178-7(0)) Lulu Pr., Inc.

Robyck, Michael. Where Is Lauren's Cat, Chaulky? 2011. 28p. pap. 15.99 (978-1-4568-8797-1(1)) Xlibris Corp.

Rochkind, Pat. McGooster & Mcgyman Begin Their Adventures. Wozniak, Patricia A., illus. 2008. 144p. (J). (gr. 4-7). per. 12.95 (978-0-9792430-1-1(7)) Wing Lane Pr.

Rocklin, Joanne. The Five Lives of Our Cat Zook. (ENG.). 240p. (J). (gr. 3-7). 2013. pap. 7.95 (978-1-4197-0525-0(3)) 2012. 17.95 (978-1-4197-0192-4(4)) Abrams, Inc. (Amulet Bks.).

Rockwell, Anne F. Katie Catz Makes a Splash. Meisel, Paul, illus. 2003. (Good Sports Ser.). 40p. (J). (gr. -1-1). 15.99 (978-0-06-028441-1(2)) HarperCollins Pubs.

Roderick, Judith A. Charlie the Cat: Charlie Teaches Others a Lesson about Honesty. 2011. 24p. pap. 11.60 (978-1-4634-1920-2(1)) AuthorHouse.

Roe, E. T. Fun & Frolic. 2004. reprint ed. pap. 1.99 (978-1-4192-2129-3(9)) Kessinger Publishing, LLC.

Roesser, Griffin. Digger Makes a Friend. 2006. (Neighborhood Readers Ser.). (ENG.). 8p. (gr. -1-3). pap. 5.15 (978-1-4042-5774-0(8), Rosen Classroom) Rosen Publishing Group, Inc., The.

Rogers, Anne. Sooty Wooty Is a Cat. 2008. 32p. pap. 23.95 (978-1-4092-2565-2(8)) Lulu Pr., Inc.

Rogers, Tony. Molly's Cat. 2013. 24p. pap. 12.99 (978-1-4525-7595-7(9), Balboa Pr.) Author Solutions, Inc.

Rohmann, Eric. A Kitten Tale. 2012. (ENG.). 32p. (J). (gr. -1-2). pap. 7.99 (978-0-307-97774-8(9), Dragonfly Bks.) Random Hse. Children's Bks.

Root, Phyllis. Scrawny Cat. Friend, Alison, illus. 2011. (ENG.). 40p. (J). (gr. -1-3). 16.99 (978-0-7636-4164-1(2)) Candlewick Pr.

Rosario, Joann. Puddy Cat & the Chick Muck. Rosario, Joann, illus. 2004. (Illus.). 15p. (J). (gr. -1-5). pap. 10.00 (978-0-9758746-3-9(2), 1246169) J.G.R. Enterprises.

Rosebrock, Katie. Tabitha & Dundee: A Story of Friendship. 2013. 16p. pap. 15.99 (978-1-4817-1257-6(8)) AuthorHouse.

Rosen, Michael & Quarto Generic Staff. Lovely Old Roly. Lamont, Priscilla, illus. 2004. (ENG.). 32p. (J). (gr. -1-2). pap. 7.95 (978-1-84507-144-8(1), Frances Lincoln) Quarto Publishing Group UK GBR. Dist: Hachette Bk. Group.

Rosenthal, Eileen. Bobo the Sailor Man! Rosenthal, Marc, illus. 2013. (ENG.). 40p. (J). (gr. -1-1). 15.99 (978-1-4424-4443-0(6)) Simon & Schuster Children's Publishing.

—I Must Have Bobo! Rosenthal, Marc, illus. 2011. (ENG.). 40p. (J). (gr. -1-1). 14.99 (978-1-4424-0377-2(2), Atheneum Bks. for Young Readers) Simon & Schuster Children's Publishing.

—I'll Save You Bobo! Rosenthal, Marc, illus. 2012. (ENG.). 40p. (J). (gr. -1-1). 14.99 (978-1-4424-0378-9(0), Atheneum Bks. for Young Readers) Simon & Schuster Children's Publishing.

Ross, Darien. The Carr House Cats at Christmas. 2012. 36p. pap. 18.41 (978-1-4669-4794-8(2)) Trafford Publishing.

Ross, Tony. I Want a Cat! Ross, Tony, illus. 2008. (ENG., Illus.). 32p. (J). (gr. -1-k). pap. 12.99 (978-1-84270-691-6(8)) Andersen Pr. GBR. Dist: Independent Pubs. Group.

—Quiero un Gato (I Want a Cat) (SPA.). 28p. (J). 17.95 (978-84-233-1999-2(7)) Ediciones Destino ESP. Dist: AIMS International Bks., Inc.

Rossitto, Tamara. Alura. 2007. 127p. pap. 10.95 (978-1-4357-0421-3(5)) Lulu Pr., Inc.

Rostoker-Gruber, Karen. Ferret Fun, 0 vols. De Tagyos, Paul Rátz, illus. 2011. (ENG.). 32p. (J). (gr. k-3). 17.99 (978-0-7614-5817-3(4), 9780761458173, Amazon Children's Publishing) Amazon Publishing.

Rotter, Laura. Terratorv. 2009. 32p. pap. 12.99 (978-1-4490-3092-6(0)) AuthorHouse.

Roudon Jr., James. The Adventures of Ratsy & Kitten: Which Way Is Home? 2007. 56p. per. 16.95 (978-1-4241-8549-8(1)) America Star Bks.

Roundtree, Beth. Wilhamina Constance Winston Churchill Ingersol & the Cat. 2012. 24p. pap. 10.99 (978-1-4624-0389-9(1), Inspiring Voices) Author Solutions, Inc.

Rouse, Walt. The Adventures of Clever Kitty. Bowker, Margie, illus. 2013. 56p. pap. (978-1-4602-1254-7(1)) FriesenPress.

Rovan, Joan. Patches the Cow-Cat. 2008. 32p. pap. 16.50 (978-1-4357-3480-7(7)) Lulu Pr., Inc.

Rowland, Patty. Marvelous Max, the Mansion Mouse. Rasmussen, Wendy, tr. Rasmussen, Wendy, illus. 2003. 32p. (J). 17.95 (978-0-9649934-4-0(9)) Norfleet Pr., Inc.

Rowland, Wickie. Good Morning, Strawberry Banke. 2010. (ENG.). 40p. (J). (gr. -1-5). pap. 12.95 (978-1-935557-62-3(9)) PublishingWorks.

Roy, Claude. Chat qui parlait malgre Lui. pap. 14.95 (978-2-07-051422-9(6)) Gallimard, Editions FRA. Dist: Distribooks, Inc.

Royther, Chris. Zippy's Christmas Tree. 2011. 36p. pap. 24.95 (978-1-4560-9864-3(0)) America Star Bks.

Rsm Ma, Anne Frances Pulling. Tales from the Pumpkin Patch Spooky: Kitten Who Wanted to Fly. 2012. 24p. pap. 12.99 (978-1-4653-8747-9(1)) Xlibris Corp.

Rubin, Adam. Those Darn Squirrels! Salmieri, Daniel, illus. 2011. (ENG.). 32p. (J). (gr. -1-3). pap. 7.99 (978-0-547-57681-7(1)) Houghton Mifflin Harcourt Publishing Co.

—Those Darn Squirrels & the Cat Next Door. Salmieri, Daniel, illus. 2011. (ENG.). 32p. (J). (gr. -1-3). 17.99 (978-0-547-42922-9(3)) Houghton Mifflin Harcourt Publishing Co.

Rubinger, Ami. Big Cat, Small Cat. Baitner, Ray, tr. from HEB. Rubinger, Ami, illus. 2009. (ENG., Illus.). 28p. (J). (gr. -1-k). 13.95 (978-0-7892-1029-6(0), Abbeville Kids) Abbeville Pr., Inc.

Ruelle, Karen Gray. April Fool! (ENG., Illus.). 32p. (J). (gr. k-3). 4.95 (978-0-8234-1780-3(8)) Holiday Hse., Inc.

—Dear Tooth Fairy. Ruelle, Karen Gray, illus. 2006. (Harry & Emily Adventure Ser.). (ENG., Illus.). 32p. (J). (gr. k-3). 4.95 (978-0-8234-1984-5(3)) Holiday Hse., Inc.

—Dear Tooth Fairy: A Harry & Emily Adventure. Ruelle, Karen Gray, illus. 2006. (Holiday House Readers: Level 2 Ser.). (ENG., Illus.). 32p. (J). (gr. 5-8). 14.95 (978-0-8234-1929-6(0)) Holiday Hse., Inc.

—Easter Egg Disaster: A Harry & Emily Adventure. Ruelle, Karen Gray, illus. 2003. (Holiday House Readers Ser.). (ENG., Illus.). 32p. (J). (gr. k-3). pap. 4.95 (978-0-8234-1823-7(5)) Holiday Hse., Inc.

—Easter Egg Disaster: A Harry & Emily Adventure. 2003. (ENG., Illus.). 32p. (J). (gr. k-3). tchr. ed. 14.95 (978-0-8234-1806-0(5)) Holiday Hse., Inc.

—Just in Time for New Year's! 2004. (ENG., Illus.). 32p. (J). tchr. ed. 14.95 (978-0-8234-1841-1(3)) Holiday Hse., Inc.

—Just in Time for New Year's! A Harry & Emily Adventure. Ruelle, Karen Gray, illus. 2004. (Holiday House Readers Ser.). (ENG., Illus.). 32p. (J). pap. 4.95 (978-0-8234-1842-8(1)) Holiday Hse., Inc.

Russell, Ann. Little Truff & the Siamese Cat. Morris, Adrienne, ed. 2nd ed. 2013. 144p. pap. (978-0-473-26077-4(8)) Bellbird Pubns.

Russell, John. Sam & Socrates. 2012. 60p. (gr. 4-6). pap. 8.95 (978-1-4620-6830-2(8)) iUniverse, Inc.

Rylant, Cynthia. Brownie & Pearl Get Dolled Up. Biggs, Brian, illus. 2010. (Brownie & Pearl Ser.). (ENG.). 24p. (J). (gr. -1-3). 14.99 (978-1-4169-8631-7(6), Beach Lane Bks.) Beach Lane Bks.

—Brownie & Pearl Get Dolled Up. Biggs, Brian, illus. 2014. (Brownie & Pearl Ser.). (ENG.). 24p. (J). (gr. -1-k). 16.99 (978-1-4424-9568-5(5)); pap. 3.99 (978-1-4424-9567-8(7)) Simon Spotlight. (Simon Spotlight).

—Brownie & Pearl Go for a Spin. Biggs, Brian, illus. 2012. (Brownie & Pearl Ser.). (ENG.). 24p. (J). (gr. -1-3). 14.99 (978-1-4169-8633-1(2), Beach Lane Bks.) Beach Lane Bks.

—Brownie & Pearl Go for a Spin. Biggs, Brian, illus. 2015. (Brownie & Pearl Ser.). (ENG.). 24p. (J). (gr. -1-k). pap. 3.99 (978-1-4814-2570-4(6), Simon Spotlight) Simon Spotlight.

—Brownie & Pearl Grab a Bite. Biggs, Brian, illus. 2011. (Brownie & Pearl Ser.). (ENG.). 24p. (J). (gr. -1-k). 13.99 (978-1-4169-8634-8(0), Beach Lane Bks.) Beach Lane Bks.

—Brownie & Pearl Grab a Bite. Biggs, Brian, illus. 2014. (Brownie & Pearl Ser.). (ENG.). 24p. (J). (gr. -1-k). 16.99 (978-1-4814-1717-4(7)); pap. 3.99 (978-1-4814-1715-0(0)) Simon Spotlight. (Simon Spotlight).

—Brownie & Pearl Hit the Hay. Biggs, Brian, illus. 2011. (Brownie & Pearl Ser.). (ENG.). 24p. (J). (gr. -1-k). 13.99 (978-1-4169-8635-5(9), Beach Lane Bks.) Beach Lane Bks.

—Brownie & Pearl Hit the Hay. Biggs, Brian, illus. 2013. (Brownie & Pearl Ser.). (ENG.). 24p. (J). (gr. -1-k). 16.99 (978-1-4424-8742-0(9)); pap. 3.99 (978-1-4424-8741-3(0)) Simon Spotlight. (Simon Spotlight).

—Brownie & Pearl Make Good. Biggs, Brian, illus. 2012. (Brownie & Pearl Ser.). (ENG.). 24p. (J). (gr. -1-k). 13.99 (978-1-4169-8636-2(7), Beach Lane Bks.) Beach Lane Bks.

—Brownie & Pearl See the Sights. Biggs, Brian, illus. 2010. (Brownie & Pearl Ser.). (ENG.). 24p. (J). (gr. -1-k). 14.99 (978-1-4169-8637-9(5), Beach Lane Bks.) Beach Lane Bks.

—Brownie & Pearl See the Sights. Biggs, Brian, illus. 2013. (Brownie & Pearl Ser.). (ENG.). 24p. (J). (gr. -1-k). 16.99 (978-1-4424-8744-4(5)); pap. 3.99 (978-1-4424-8743-7(7)) Simon Spotlight. (Simon Spotlight).

—Brownie & Pearl Step Out. Biggs, Brian, illus. 2009. (Brownie & Pearl Ser.). (ENG.). 24p. (J). (gr. -1-3). 14.99 (978-1-4169-8632-4(4), Beach Lane Bks.) Beach Lane Bks.

—Brownie & Pearl Step Out. Biggs, Brian, illus. 2014. (Brownie & Pearl Ser.). (ENG.). 24p. (J). (gr. -1-k). 16.99 (978-1-4814-0314-6(1)); pap. 3.99 (978-1-4814-0313-9(3)) Simon Spotlight. (Simon Spotlight).

—Brownie & Pearl Take a Dip. Biggs, Brian, illus. 2011. (Brownie & Pearl Ser.). (ENG.). 24p. (J). (gr. -1-3). 14.99 (978-1-4169-8638-6(3), Beach Lane Bks.) Beach Lane Bks.

—El Caso del Gato Escalador.Tr. of Case of the Climbing Cat. (SPA.). (J). 7.95 (978-958-04-7076-2(6)) Norma S.A. COL. Dist: Distribuidora Norma, Inc.

—The Eagle. McDaniels, Preston, illus. 2004. (Lighthouse Family Ser.: 3). (ENG.). 64p. (J). (gr. 1-5). 15.99 (978-0-689-86243-4(1), Simon & Schuster Bks. For Young Readers) Simon & Schuster Bks. For Young Readers.

—The Eagle. McDaniels, Preston, illus. 2005. (Lighthouse Family Ser.: 3). (ENG.). 64p. (J). (gr. 1-5). pap. 5.99 (978-0-689-86311-0(X), Simon & Schuster Bks. For Young Readers) Simon & Schuster Bks. For Young Readers.

—Moonlight: The Halloween Cat. Sweet, Melissa, illus. (ENG.). 32p. (J). (gr. -1-3). 2009. pap. 6.99 (978-0-06-443814-8(7)) 2003. 17.99 (978-0-06-029711-4(5)) HarperCollins Pubs.

—Mr. Putter & Tabby Dance the Dance. Howard, Arthur, illus. 2012. (Mr. Putter & Tabby Ser.: 21). (ENG.). 40p. (J). (gr. 1-4). 14.99 (978-0-15-206415-0(X)) Houghton Mifflin Harcourt Publishing Co.

—Mr. Putter & Tabby Dance the Dance. 2013. (Mr. Putter & Tabby Ser.). lib. bdg. 16.00 (978-0-606-32338-3(4), Turtleback) Turtleback Bks.

—Mr. Putter & Tabby Drop the Ball. Howard, Arthur, illus. (Mr. Putter & Tabby Ser.). (ENG.). 44p. (J). (gr. 1-4). 2014. pap. 5.99 (978-0-544-34115-9(5), HMH Books For Young Readers) 2013. 14.99 (978-0-15-205072-6(8)) Houghton Mifflin Harcourt Publishing Co.

—Mr. Putter & Tabby Drop the Ball. 2014. (Mr. Putter & Tabby Ser.). lib. bdg. 16.00 (978-0-606-35985-6(0)) Turtleback Bks.

—Mr. Putter & Tabby Feed the Fish. Howard, Arthur, illus. 2007. (Mr. Putter & Tabby Ser.). pap. 7.93 (978-1-4189-5238-9(9)) Houghton Mifflin Harcourt Supplemental Pubs.

—Mr. Putter & Tabby Hit the Slope. Howard, Arthur, illus. 2016. (Mr. Putter & Tabby Ser.). (ENG.). 40p. (J). (gr. 1-4). 14.99 (978-0-15-206427-3(3), HMH Books For Young Readers) Houghton Mifflin Harcourt Publishing Co.

—Mr. Putter & Tabby Make a Wish. Howard, Arthur, illus. 2006. (Mr. Putter & Tabby Ser.). (ENG.). 44p. (J). (gr. -1-3). pap. 5.99 (978-0-15-205443-4(X)) Houghton Mifflin Harcourt Publishing Co.

—Mr. Putter & Tabby Make a Wish. Howard, Arthur, illus. 2006. (Mr. Putter & Tabby Ser.). (gr. 1-4). 16.00 (978-0-7569-6892-2(5)) Perfection Learning Corp.

—Mr. Putter & Tabby Ring the Bell. Howard, Arthur, illus. (Mr. Putter & Tabby Ser.). (ENG.). 44p. (J). (gr. 1-4). 2012. pap. 5.99 (978-0-547-85075-7(1)) 2011. 14.99 (978-0-15-205071-9(X)) Houghton Mifflin Harcourt Publishing Co.

—Mr. Putter & Tabby Ring the Bell. Howard, Arthur, illus. 2012. (Mr. Putter & Tabby Ser.). lib. bdg. 16.00 (978-0-606-26614-7(3), Turtleback) Turtleback Bks.

—Mr. Putter & Tabby Run the Race. Howard, Arthur, illus. 2010. (Mr. Putter & Tabby Ser.). (ENG.). 44p. (J). (gr. 1-4). pap. 5.99 (978-0-547-24824-0(5)) Houghton Mifflin Harcourt Publishing Co.

—Mr. Putter & Tabby See the Stars. Howard, Arthur, illus. 2008. (Mr. Putter & Tabby Ser.). (ENG.). 44p. (J). (gr. 1-4). pap. 5.99 (978-0-15-206366-5(8)) Houghton Mifflin Harcourt Publishing Co.

—Mr. Putter & Tabby Smell the Roses. Howard, Arthur, illus. (Mr. Putter & Tabby Ser.: 24). (ENG.). 40p. (J). (gr. 1-4). 2016. pap. 5.99 (978-0-544-80907-9(6)) 2015. 14.99 (978-0-15-206081-7(2)) Houghton Mifflin Harcourt Publishing Co. (HMH Books For Young Readers).

—Mr. Putter & Tabby Spill the Beans. Howard, Arthur, illus. 2010. (Mr. Putter & Tabby Ser.). (ENG.). 44p. (J). (gr. 1-4). pap. 5.99 (978-0-547-41433-1(1)) Houghton Mifflin Harcourt Publishing Co.

—Mr. Putter & Tabby Spin the Yarn. Howard, Arthur, illus. 2007. (Mr. Putter & Tabby Ser.). (ENG.). 44p. (J). (gr. 1-4). pap. 5.99 (978-0-15-206095-4(2)) Houghton Mifflin Harcourt Publishing Co.

—Mr. Putter & Tabby Spin the Yarn. Howard, Arthur, illus. 2007. (Mr. Putter & Tabby Ser.). (gr. 1-4). lib. bdg. 16.00 (978-0-7569-8062-7(3)) Perfection Learning Corp.

—Mr. Putter & Tabby Stir the Soup. Howard, Arthur, illus. 2004. (Mr. Putter & Tabby Ser.). (ENG.). 44p. (J). (gr. 1-4). pap. 5.99 (978-0-15-205058-0(2)) Houghton Mifflin Harcourt Publishing Co.

—Mr. Putter & Tabby Stir the Soup. Howard, Arthur, illus. 2004. (Mr. Putter & Tabby Ser.). (gr. 1-4). 16.00 (978-0-7569-3915-1(1)) Perfection Learning Corp.

—Mr. Putter & Tabby Turn the Page. Howard, Arthur, illus. (Mr. Putter & Tabby Ser.). (ENG.). 40p. (J). (gr. 1-4). 2015. pap. 5.99 (978-0-544-58232-3(2)) 2014. 14.99 (978-0-15-206063-3(4)) Houghton Mifflin Harcourt Publishing Co. (HMH Books For Young Readers).

—Mr. Putter & Tabby Turn the Page. 2015. (Mr. Putter & Tabby Ser.). lib. bdg. 16.00 (978-0-606-37453-8(1)) Turtleback Bks.

—Mr. Putter & Tabby Walk the Dog. Howard, Arthur, illus. 2007. (Mr. Putter & Tabby Ser.). pap. 7.93 (978-1-4189-5209-9(5)) Houghton Mifflin Harcourt Trade & Reference Pubs.

—Mr. Putter & Tabby Write the Book. Howard, Arthur, illus. 2005. (Mr. Putter & Tabby Ser.). (ENG.). 44p. (J). (gr. 1-4). pap. 5.99 (978-0-15-200242-8(1)) Houghton Mifflin Harcourt Publishing Co.

—Mr. Putter & Tabby Write the Book. Howard, Arthur, illus. 2005. (Mr. Putter & Tabby Ser.). 36p. (J). (gr. 1-4). 13.60 (978-0-7569-5446-8(0)) Perfection Learning Corp.

—The Storm. McDaniels, Preston, illus. 2003. (Lighthouse Family Ser.: 1). (ENG.). 80p. (J). (gr. 1-5). pap. 5.99 (978-0-689-84882-7(X), Simon & Schuster Bks. For Young Readers) Simon & Schuster Bks. For Young Readers.

Rylant, Cynthia & Howard, Arthur. Mr. Putter & Tabby Catch the Cold. Howard, Arthur, illus. 2003. (Mr. Putter & Tabby Ser.). (ENG., Illus.). 44p. (J). (gr. 1-4). pap. 5.99 (978-0-15-204760-3(3)) Houghton Mifflin Harcourt Publishing Co.

—Mr. Putter & Tabby Dance the Dance. Howard, Arthur, illus. 2013. (Mr. Putter & Tabby Ser.). (ENG., Illus.). 40p. (J). (gr. 1-4). pap. 5.99 (978-0-544-10496-9(X)) Houghton Mifflin Harcourt Publishing Co.

Rymas-Loomis, Cathy. Calamity Clancey: The Calamity Cat from Kalvesta Kansas. 2007. 40p. per. 12.97 (978-1-932344-85-1(3)) Thornton Publishing, Inc.

Saab, Julie. Little Lola. Gothard, David, illus. 2014. (ENG.). 32p. (J). (gr. -1-3). 16.99 (978-0-06-227457-1(0), Greenwillow Bks.) HarperCollins Pubs.

—Little Lola Saves the Show. Gothard, David, illus. 2016. 32p. (J). (gr. -1-3). 17.99 (978-0-06-227453-3(8), Greenwillow Bks.) HarperCollins Pubs.

Sagara, Sou & Okomeken. The Hentai Prince & the Stony Cat. 2012. (ENG., Illus.). 200p. (YA). pap. 12.95 (978-1-56970-285-7(3), 9781569702857) Digital Manga Publishing.

Sakmar-Sullivan, Eva M. Willie the Taxi Cat, 1 vol. 2013. (ENG., Illus.). 32p. (J). 16.99 (978-0-7643-4436-7(6), 9780764344367) Schiffer Publishing, Ltd.

Salamon, Julie. Cat in the City. Weber, Jill, illus. 2014. (ENG.). 208p. (J). (gr. 3-7). 16.99 (978-0-8037-4056-3(5), Dial Bks) Penguin Young Readers Group.

Salmassian, Jennifer. Sally Saves the Mice. 2007. (J). per. 0.01 net. (978-1-60402-115-8(2)) Independent Pub.

—Sally the Firefighter. 2007. (J). per. 0.01 net. (978-1-60402-164-6(0)) Independent Pub.

Salten, Felix. Djibi. Levin, Raya, tr. 2016. (Bambi's Classic Animal Tales Ser.). (ENG., Illus.). 192p. (J). (gr. 3-7). pap. 8.99 (978-1-4424-8764-2(X), Aladdin) Simon & Schuster Children's Publishing.

Salter, Michelle Lewis. The Kitty Who Found His Meeooww. Stone, Jonny, illus. 2011. 40p. pap. 24.95 (978-1-4560-5953-8(X)) America Star Bks.

Samarrippas, Gloria. In Search for Lucky's Lost Toys. 2006. 17.00 (978-0-8059-7329-7(X)) Dorrance Publishing Co., Inc.

Samuels, Barbara. The Trucker. Samuels, Barbara, illus. 2010. (ENG., Illus.). 40p. (J). (gr. -1-1). 16.99 (978-0-374-37804-2(5), 9780374378042, Farrar, Straus & Giroux (BYR)) Farrar, Straus & Giroux.

Sanchez, Kevin & Sanchez, Laura. Nikki's Hurricane Adventure. 2011. 24p. pap. 11.32 (978-1-4567-1452-9(X)) AuthorHouse.

C
D

Sanders, D. m. & Sanders, D. M. Fin the Godsend. 2010. 36p. pap. 25.49 *(978-1-4343-7864-4(0))* AuthorHouse.
Sanders, Stephanie & Pauling, Galen T. Q. T. Pie's Rescue Adventure. 2003. (Illus.). 36p. (J). (gr. -1-6). mass mkt. 4.99 *(978-0-9670875-3-5(8),* 313-533-7383) SanPaul Group, LLC, The.
Sanderson, Ruth. A Castle Full of Cats. 2015. (ENG., Illus.). 40p. (J). (gr. -1-2). lib. bdg. 19.99 *(978-0-375-97154-9(8),* Random Hse. Bks. for Young Readers) Random Hse. Children's Bks.
Sang, Franchesca Ho, compiled by. Wisdom of Kittens. 2006. (Wisdom of Animals Ser.). (Illus.). 120p. (J). (gr. k). *(978-1-59258-252-5(4))* Hylas Publishing.
Sanrio. Best Friends: Hello Kitty & Me. 2014. (ENG., Illus.). 32p. (J). (-2). 9.99 *(978-1-4022-9645-1(2),* Sourcebooks Jabberwocky) Sourcebooks, Inc.
—Easter Bonnet Surprise. 2013. (ENG., Illus.). 24p. (J). (gr. k-2). pap. 6.99 *(978-1-4197-0910-4(0),* Abrams Bks. for Young Readers) Abrams, Inc.
—Hello Kitty Goes to Camp. 2015. (Hello Kitty Ser.). (J). lib. bdg. 17.15 *(978-0-606-37240-4(7))* Turtleback Bks.
—Hello Kitty, Hello Halloween! 2014. (ENG., Illus.). 24p. (J). (gr. k-2). 6.95 *(978-1-4197-1375-0(2),* Abrams Bks. for Young Readers) Abrams, Inc.
—Hello Kitty, Hello Love! 2014. (ENG., Illus.). 24p. (J). (gr. k-2). pap. 6.99 *(978-1-4197-1249-4(7),* Abrams Bks. for Young Readers) Abrams, Inc.
—Hello Kitty Storybook Collection. 2014. (ENG., Illus.). 176p. (J). (gr. k-2). 12.95 *(978-1-4197-1248-7(9),* Abrams Bks. for Young Readers) Abrams, Inc.
—Hello Kitty: What Will You Be a to Z? 2013. (ENG., Illus.). 32p. (J). (gr. k-2). 12.95 *(978-1-4197-0911-1(9),* Abrams Bks. for Young Readers) Abrams, Inc.
—Hugs: Hello Kitty & Me. 2014. (ENG.). 32p. (J). (-2). 9.99 *(978-1-4022-9640-6(1),* Sourcebooks Jabberwocky) Sourcebooks, Inc.
—Let's Go to School. 2014. (ENG.). 32p. (J). (-2). 9.99 *(978-1-4022-9660-4(6),* Sourcebooks Jabberwocky) Sourcebooks, Inc.
—Trick or Treat: Hello Kitty & Me. 2014. (ENG.). 32p. (J). (-2). 9.99 *(978-1-4022-9665-9(7),* 9781402296659) Sourcebooks, Inc.
Sanrio & Kabushiki, Kaisha. A Day of Thanks. 2015. (Hello Kitty Ser.). (J). lib. bdg. 17.15 *(978-0-606-37417-0(5))* Turtleback Bks.
Sanrio Company, LTD. Hello Kitty a Day of Thanks. 2015. (ENG., Illus.). 24p. (J). (gr. -1-1). 6.95 *(978-1-4197-1842-7(8),* Abrams Bks. for Young Readers) Abrams, Inc.
—Hello Kitty, Hello Winter! Hirashima, Jean, illus. 2013. (ENG.). 14p. (J). (gr. -1 — 1). bds. 7.95 *(978-1-4197-0797-1(3),* Abrams Appleseed) Abrams, Inc.
—Hello Kitty Presents the Storybook Collection: Thumbelina. 2017. (Hello Kitty Storybook Ser.). (ENG., Illus.). 32p. (J). (gr. -1-k). pap. 6.95 *(978-1-4197-2489-3(4),* Abrams Appleseed) Abrams, Inc.
Sanrio Company, Ltd. Staff. Happy Birthday, Hello Kitty. 2014. (ENG., Illus.). 24p. (J). (gr. k-2). 6.95 *(978-1-4197-1466-5(X),* Abrams Bks. for Young Readers) Abrams, Inc.
—Hello Kitty, Hello Fall! Hirashima, Jean, illus. 2013. (ENG.). 14p. (J). (gr. -1 — 1). bds. 7.95 *(978-1-4197-0799-5(X),* Abrams Appleseed) Abrams, Inc.
—Hello Kitty, Hello New York! Hirashima, Jean, illus. 2014. (ENG.). 16p. (J). (gr. -1 — 1). bds. 7.95 *(978-1-4197-1096-4(6),* Abrams Appleseed) Abrams, Inc.
—Hello Kitty, Hello Spring! Hirashima, Jean, illus. 2013. (ENG.). 14p. (J). (gr. -1 — 1). bds. 7.95 *(978-1-4197-0688-2(8),* Abrams Appleseed) Abrams, Inc.
—Hello Kitty, Hello Summer! Hirashima, Jean, illus. 2013. (ENG.). 14p. (J). (gr. -1 — 1). bds. 7.95 *(978-1-4197-0687-5(X),* Abrams Appleseed) Abrams, Inc.
Santillo, LuAnn. The Cat. Santillo, LuAnn, ed. 2003. (Half-Pint Kids Readers Ser.). (Illus.). 7p. (J). (gr. -1-1). pap. 1.00 *(978-1-59256-066-0(0))* Half-Pint Kids, Inc.
Santomero, Angela C. The Baby Is Here! 2015. (Daniel Tiger's Neighborhood 8X8 Ser.). (Illus.). (J). lib. bdg. 13.55 *(978-0-606-36314-3(9))* Turtleback Bks.
Santoro, Scott. Farm-Fresh Cats. 2006. (Illus.). 32p. (J). (gr. -1-2). 16.89 *(978-0-06-078179-8(3))* HarperCollins Pubs.
Sarduy, Severo. Gatico-Gatico. Gomez, Patricio, illus. (Literary Encounters Ser.). (SPA.). (J). (gr. 3-5). pap. *(978-968-494-062-8(9),* CI1124) Centro de Informacion y Desarrollo de la Comunicacion y la Literatura MEX. Dist: Lectorum Pubns., Inc.
Sargeant, Glen. Finders Keepers. 1 vol. 2009. 142p. pap. 24.95 *(978-1-61582-202-7(X))* America Star Bks.
Sargent, Dave & Sargent, David, Jr. Tin Wren: Be Nice, 19 vols., Vol. 19. Lenoir, Jane, illus. 2003. (Feather Tales Ser.: No. 19). 42p. (J). pap. 10.95 *(978-1-56763-756-4(6))* Ozark Publishing.
—Tom Turkey: Don't Bully, 19, 20. Lenoir, Jane, illus. 2003. (Feather Tales Ser.: 20). 42p. (J). pap. 6.95 *(978-1-56763-758-8(2))* Ozark Publishing.
Sargent, Dave & Sargent, Pat. Cat Who Barked, 10 vols., Vol. 18. Robinson, Laura, illus. 2004. (Learn to Read Ser.: 10). 18p. (J). pap. 10.95 *(978-1-56763-832-5(5));* lib. bdg. 20.95 *(978-1-56763-831-8(7))* Ozark Publishing.
—Cat Who Barked/el gato que Ladró, 10. Robinson, Laura, illus. 2004. (Learn to Read Ser.: 10). (ENG & SPA.). 18p. (J). 18. pap. 9.95 *(978-1-56763-996-4(8))* Vol. 18. lib. bdg. 20.95 *(978-1-56763-995-7(X))* Ozark Publishing.
—Little Big Cat, 10 vols., Vol. 16. Robinson, Laura, illus. 2004. (Learn to Read Ser.: 10). 18p. (J). pap. 10.95 *(978-1-56763-828-8(7));* lib. bdg. 20.95 *(978-1-56763-827-1(9))* Ozark Publishing.
—Little Big Cat/Gato pequeño y Grande, 10 vols., Vol. 16. Robinson, Laura, illus. 2004. (Learn to Read Ser.: 10). (ENG & SPA.). 18p. (J). pap. 10.95 *(978-1-56763-992-6(5))* Ozark Publishing.
—Little Big Cat/Gato Pequeño y Grande, 10 vols., Vol. 16. Robinson, Laura, illus. 2004. (Learn to Read Ser.: 10).Tr. of Gato Pequeno y Grande. (ENG & SPA.). 18p. (J). (gr. k-2). lib. bdg. 20.95 *(978-1-56763-991-9(7))* Ozark Publishing.
Sarnella, Jeanette. Santini's Magic Castle. 2010. 28p. 15.49 *(978-1-4520-4908-3(4))* AuthorHouse.
Saunders, Kate. The Curse of the Chocolate Phoenix: A Companion to the Whizz Pop Chocolate Shop. 2015. (ENG.). 272p. (J). (gr. 5). 19.99 *(978-0-375-99183-7(2),* Delacorte Bks. for Young Readers) Random Hse. Children's Bks.
—The Whizz Pop Chocolate Shop. (ENG.). 304p. (J). (gr. 5). 2014. 7.99 *(978-0-385-74302-0(5),* Yearling) 2013. 16.99 *(978-0-385-74301-3(7),* Delacorte Bks. for Young Readers) Random Hse. Children's Bks.
Saunders, Marshall. Pussy BlackFace or the Story of A Kitten. 2006. (Illus.). pap. 31.95 *(978-1-4254-9478-0(1))* Kessinger Publishing, LLC.
Savage, Derek. Cool Cat Loves Biodiesel. 2010. (Cool Cat Ser.: Vol. 1).Tr. of Cool Cat le gusta Biodiesel. (ENG & SPA., Illus.). 32p. (J). 7.95 *(978-0-9673000-3-0(7))* Blue Thunder Bks.
—Cool Cat Loves Going Green. 2010. (Cool Cat Ser.: Vol. 2).Tr. of Cool Cat le gusta Cuidar el Medio Ambiente. (ENG & SPA., Illus.). 32p. (J). 7.95 *(978-0-9673000-4-7(5))* Blue Thunder Bks.
Sawyer, J. Scott. The Broccoli Bush. Bozeman, Gary, illus. 2012. 36p. pap. 24.95 *(978-1-4626-2501-7(0))* America Star Bks.
Sazaklis, John. Barnyard Brainwash, 1 vol. Baltazar, Art, illus. 2012. (DC Super-Pets Ser.). (ENG.). 56p. (gr. 2-2). pap. 4.95 *(978-1-4048-7213-4(2));* lib. bdg. 23.99 *(978-1-4048-6483-2(0))* Picture Window Bks. (DC Super-Pets).
—Royal Rodent Rescue, 1 vol. Baltazar, Art, illus. 2011. (DC Super-Pets Ser.). (ENG.). 56p. (gr. 2-2). pap. 4.95 *(978-1-4048-6622-5(1));* lib. bdg. 23.99 *(978-1-4048-6307-1(9))* Picture Window Bks. (DC Super-Pets).
Scarry, Richard. Richard Scarry's All the Colors of Busytown. 2013. (Richard Scarry's Concept Bks.). (ENG.). 18p. (J). (gr. -1 — 1). bds. 7.99 *(978-0-7641-6601-3(8))* Barron's Educational Series, Inc.
—Richard Scarry's Best Little Word Book Ever! Scarry, Richard, illus. 2016. (Pictureback(R) Ser.). (ENG., Illus.). 24p. (J). (-k). pap. 4.99 *(978-0-385-39271-6(0),* Random Hse. Bks. for Young Readers) Random Hse. Children's Bks.
—Richard Scarry's Great Big Schoolhouse. 2008. (ENG., Illus.). 72p. (J). (gr. -1-2). 14.95 *(978-1-4027-5820-1(0))* Sterling Publishing Co., Inc.
Schachner, Judy. Bits & Pieces. 2013. (ENG.). 32p. (J). (gr. -1-k). 17.99 *(978-0-8037-3788-4(2),* Dial Bks) Penguin Young Readers Group.
—Color Crazy. Schachner, Judy, illus. 2007. (Skippyjon Jones Ser.). (ENG., Illus.). 12p. (J). (gr. -1 — 1). bds. 6.99 *(978-0-525-47782-2(9),* Dutton Books for Young Readers) Penguin Young Readers Group.
—The Doghouse. 2008. (Skippyjon Jones Ser.). (ENG., Illus.). 32p. (J). (gr. -1-k). 10.99 *(978-0-14-241041-7(1),* Puffin Books) Penguin Young Readers Group.
—The Grannyman. 2003. (ENG., Illus.). 32p. (J). (gr. -1-2). 6.99 *(978-0-14-250062-0(3),* Puffin Books) Penguin Young Readers Group.
—The Great Bean Caper. 2009. (Skippyjon Jones Ser.). (ENG.). 32p. (J). (gr. -1-k). mass mkt. 3.99 *(978-0-448-45167-1(0),* Grosset & Dunlap) Penguin Young Readers Group.
—Puffin Storytime. 2007. (Skippyjon Jones Ser.). (ENG., Illus.). 32p. (J). (gr. -1-k). 10.99 *(978-0-14-240872-8(7),* Puffin Books) Penguin Young Readers Group.
—Skippyjon Jones. Schachner, Judy, illus. 2005. (Skippyjon Jones Ser.). (ENG., Illus.). 32p. (J). (gr. k-k). reprint ed. pap. 6.99 *(978-0-14-240403-4(9),* Puffin Books) Penguin Young Readers Group.
—Skippyjon Jones. 2009. (Illus.). 32p. 17.00 *(978-1-60686-417-3(3))* Perfection Learning Corp.
—Skippyjon Jones & the Big Bones. 2007. (Skippyjon Jones Ser.). (ENG.). 40p. (J). (gr. -1-k). 17.99 *(978-0-525-47864-3(1),* Dutton Books for Young Readers) Penguin Young Readers Group.
—Skippyjon Jones Book & Toy Set, Set. Schachner, Judy, illus. 2007. (Skippyjon Jones Ser.). (ENG., Illus.). 32p. (J). (gr. -1-k). 16.99 *(978-0-525-47774-7(8),* Dutton Books for Young Readers) Penguin Young Readers Group.
—Skippyjon Jones Cirque de Ole. 2012. (Skippyjon Jones Ser.). (ENG.). 32p. (J). (gr. -1-k). 17.99 *(978-0-8037-3782-2(3),* Dial Bks) Penguin Young Readers Group.
—Skippyjon Jones, Class Action. (Skippyjon Jones Ser.). (ENG.). (J). 2017. (-k). pap. 8.99 ***(978-0-425-28892-4(7),*** Puffin Books) 2011. 32p. (gr. -1-k). 17.99 *(978-0-525-42228-0(5),* Dutton Books for Young Readers) Penguin Young Readers Group.
—Skippyjon Jones in Mummy Trouble. 2008. (Skippyjon Jones Ser.). (ENG.). 32p. (J). (gr. -1-k). pap. 6.99 *(978-0-14-241211-4(2),* Puffin Books) Penguin Young Readers Group.
—Skippyjon Jones in Mummy Trouble. Schachner, Judy, illus. 2006. (Skippyjon Jones Ser.). (ENG., Illus.). 32p. (J). (gr. -1-k). 17.99 *(978-0-525-47754-9(3),* Dutton Books for Young Readers) Penguin Young Readers Group.
—Skippyjon Jones in Mummy Trouble. 2009. (Skippyjon Jones Ser.). 17.00 *(978-1-60686-418-0(1))* Perfection Learning Corp.
—Skippyjon Jones in the Doghouse. Schachner, Judy, illus. 2007. (Skippyjon Jones Ser.). (ENG., Illus.). 32p. (J). (gr. -1-k). pap. 6.99 *(978-0-14-240749-3(6),* Puffin Books) Penguin Young Readers Group.
—Skippyjon Jones in the Doghouse. Wilhelm, James J., ed. Schachner, Judy, illus. 2005. (Skippyjon Jones Ser.). (ENG., Illus.). 32p. (J). (gr. -1-18). 16.99 *(978-0-525-47297-1(5),* Dutton Books for Young Readers) Penguin Young Readers Group.
—Skippyjon Jones in the Doghouse. 2009. (Illus.). 32p. 17.00 *(978-1-60686-419-7(X))* Perfection Learning Corp.
—Skippyjon Jones, Lost in Spice. Schachner, Judy, illus. 2009. (Skippyjon Jones Ser.). (ENG., Illus.). 32p. (J). (gr. -1-k). 17.99 *(978-0-525-47965-9(1),* Dutton Books for Young Readers) Penguin Young Readers Group.
—Skippyjon Jones, Lost in Spice, 2 vols. 2009. (Skippyjon Jones Ser.). (J). 192.75 *(978-1-4407-6557-5(X));* 37.75 *(978-1-4407-6558-2(8));* 1.25 *(978-1-4407-6563-6(4))* Recorded Bks., Inc.
—Skippyjon Jones Presto-Change-O. 2010. (Skippyjon Jones Ser.). (ENG.). 32p. (J). (gr. -1-k). 17.99 *(978-0-525-42358-4(3),* Dutton Books for Young Readers) Penguin Young Readers Group.
—Skippyjon Jones Snow What. 2014. (Skippyjon Jones Ser.). (ENG., Illus.). 32p. (J). (gr. -1-k). 17.99 *(978-0-8037-3789-1(0),* Dial Bks) Penguin Publishing Group.
—A Surprise for Mama. 2008. (Skippyjon Jones Ser.). (ENG., Illus.). 16p. (J). (gr. -1-k). pap. 5.99 *(978-0-448-44816-9(5),* Grosset & Dunlap) Penguin Young Readers Group.
—Up & Down. Schachner, Judy, illus. 2007. (Skippyjon Jones Ser.). (ENG., Illus.). 12p. (J). (gr. -1 — 1). bds. 6.99 *(978-0-525-47807-2(8),* Dutton Books for Young Readers) Penguin Young Readers Group.
Schaefer, Lola M. Follow Me, Mittens. Hartung, Susan Kathleen, illus. (My First I Can Read Ser.). 32p. (J). (gr. -1 — 1). 2008. (ENG.). pap. 3.99 *(978-0-06-054667-0(0))* 2007. (ENG.). 15.99 *(978-0-06-054665-6(4))* 2007. lib. bdg. 16.89 *(978-0-06-054666-3(2))* HarperCollins Pubs.
—Happy Halloween, Mittens. Hartung, Susan Kathleen, illus. 2010. (My First I Can Read Ser.). (ENG.). 32p. (J). (gr. -1-3). 16.99 *(978-0-06-170222-8(6));* pap. 3.99 *(978-0-06-170221-1(8))* HarperCollins Pubs.
—Mittens. Hartung, Susan Kathleen, illus. 2007. (My First I Can Read Ser.). (ENG.). 32p. (J). (gr. -1-3). pap. 3.99 *(978-0-06-054661-8(1))* HarperCollins Pubs.
—Mittens. Hartung, Susan Kathleen, illus. 2007. (I Can Read Bks.). 25p. (gr. -1-k). 14.00 *(978-0-7569-8104-4(2))* Perfection Learning Corp.
—Mittens. 2007. (My First I Can Read Ser.). (J). lib. bdg. 13.55 *(978-1-4178-1001-7(7),* Turtleback) Turtleback Bks.
—Mittens at School. Hartung, Susan Kathleen, illus. 2012. (My First I Can Read Ser.). (ENG.). 32p. (J). (gr. -1-3). 16.99 *(978-0-06-170224-2(2));* pap. 3.99 *(978-0-06-170223-5(4))* HarperCollins Pubs.
—Mittens at School. 2012. (My First I Can Read Ser.). (J). lib. bdg. 13.55 *(978-0-606-26292-7(X),* Turtleback) Turtleback Bks.
—Mittens, Where Is Max? Hartung, Susan Kathleen, illus. 2011. (My First I Can Read Ser.). (ENG.). 32p. (J). (gr. -1 — 1). 16.99 *(978-0-06-170227-3(7));* pap. 3.99 *(978-0-06-170226-6(9))* HarperCollins Pubs.
—What's That, Mittens? Hartung, Susan Kathleen, illus. 2009. (My First I Can Read Ser.). (ENG.). 32p. (J). (gr. -1 — 1). pap. 3.99 *(978-0-06-054664-9(6))* HarperCollins Pubs.
Schaenen, Inda. All the Cats of Cairo. 2007. 225p. (J). (gr. -1-10). per. 8.95 *(978-0-9768126-5-4(7))* Brown Barn Bks.
Schauer, Tosca M. J. J. Bear. 2013. 28p. pap. 16.99 *(978-1-4582-0783-8(8),* Abbott Pr.) Author Solutions, Inc.
Scheffler, Axel, illus. Katie the Kitten. (Buggy Buddies Ser.). (ENG.). 12p. (J). (— 1). 2015. bds. 7.99 *(978-0-230-75615-1(8))* 2014. 13.99 *(978-1-4472-6805-5(9))* Pan Macmillan GBR. Dist: Independent Pubs. Group.
Scheidies, Carolyn R. WHERE IS CAT? She's Obviously Been Here! 2007. 50p. pap. 14.88 *(978-0-615-16673-5(3))* C R Pubns.
Scheunemann, Pam. Cat Tails, 1 vol. Chawla, Neena, illus. 2006. (Animal Tales Ser.). 24p. (J). (gr. k-3). (ENG.). lib. bdg. 24.21 *(978-1-59679-927-1(7),* SandCastle); pap. 48.42 *(978-1-59679-928-8(5))* ABDO Publishing Co.
Schindel, John. Busy Kitties. Franzen, Sean, photos by. 2004. (Busy Book Ser.). (ENG., Illus.). 20p. (J). (— 1). bds. 6.99 *(978-1-58246-130-4(9),* Knopf Bks. for Young Readers) Random Hse. Children's Bks.
Schindler, Holly. Feral. 2014. (ENG.). 432p. (YA). (gr. 8). 17.99 *(978-0-06-222020-2(9),* HarperTeen) HarperCollins Pubs.
Schirmer, Jodi L. Dear Deer Friend. 2008. 24p. pap. 11.95 *(978-1-4327-2540-2(8))* Outskirts Pr., Inc.
—It Is a Good Day: Clay. 2009. 23p. (J). pap. 11.95 *(978-1-4327-4018-4(0))* Outskirts Pr., Inc.
Schmidt, Annie M. G. The Cat Who Came in off the Roof. Colmer, David, tr. from DUT. 2016. (ENG.). 160p. (J). (gr. 5). 14.99 *(978-0-553-53500-6(5),* Delacorte Bks. for Young Readers) Random Hse. Children's Bks.
—Miaou. 2004. (FRE.). 224p. (J). pap. *(978-2-89021-705-8(1))* Diffusion du livre Mirabel (DLM).
Schoedl, Mark A. It's a New Day. 2012. 16p. pap. 12.68 *(978-1-4669-4835-8(3))* Trafford Publishing.
Schoenherr, Ian. Cat & Mouse. Schoenherr, Ian, illus. 2008. (Illus.). 40p. (J). (gr. -1). lib. bdg. 17.89 *(978-0-06-136314-6(6),* Greenwillow Bks.) HarperCollins Pubs.
Schofield, Brent R. Hairballs & Sticky Things. 2003. 120p. pap. 10.95 *(978-0-595-27470-3(6),* Writer's Showcase Pr.) iUniverse, Inc.
Scholastic Library Publishing. The Three Little Kittens Get Dressed. 2009. (Rookie Preschool Ser.). 24p. (J). (gr. -1). lib. bdg. 23.00 *(978-0-531-24404-3(0),* Children's Pr.) Scholastic Library Publishing.
Schoombee, Cherese. Frilly Lilly. 2009. 28p. 16.95 *(978-1-84799-435-6(0))* Lulu Pr., Inc.
Schoonmaker, Elizabeth. Square Cat. Schoonmaker, Elizabeth, illus. 2011. (ENG., Illus.). 32p. (J). (gr. -1-3). 16.99 *(978-1-4424-0619-3(4),* Aladdin) Simon & Schuster Children's Publishing.
Schubert, Ingrid & Schubert, Dieter. My Hero. 2005. (ENG., Illus.). 32p. (J). (gr. -1-3). 16.95 *(978-1-932425-10-9(1),* 9781932425109) Lemniscaat USA.
Schuepbach, Lynnette. Cat Time. 2006. 28p. pap. 12.95 *(978-0-9759613-2-2(2))* Creative Sources.
Schulz, Hal. Dak's Country Visit: The Painter & His Cat. 2011. 32p. pap. *(978-1-4269-6743-6(8))* Trafford Publishing (UK) Ltd.
Schurr, Cathleen. The Shy Little Kitten. Tenggren, Gustaf, illus. deluxe ed. Date not set. (J). (gr. -1-2). reprint ed. *(978-1-929566-57-0(3))* Cronies.
—The Shy Little Kitten: Classic Edition. Tenggren, Gustaf, illus. Date not set. (J). (gr. -1-1). reprint ed. *(978-1-929566-51-8(4))* Cronies.
Schwaeber, Barbie H. Princess: A Lucky Kitten. Huerta, Catherine, illus. 2007. (Pet Tales Ser.). (ENG.). 32p. (J). per. 2.95 *(978-1-59249-676-1(8))* Soundprints.
Schwaeber, Barbie Heit. Princess: A Lucky Kitten. Huerta, Catherine, illus. 2007. (Pet Tales Ser.). (ENG.). 32p. (J). 4.95 *(978-1-59249-675-4(X))* Soundprints.
—Princess a Lucky Kitten. Huerta, Catherine, illus. 2007. (ENG.). 32p. (J). 9.95 *(978-1-59249-677-8(6))* Soundprints.
Schwarz, Viviane. Is There a Dog in This Book? Schwarz, Viviane, illus. 2014. (ENG., Illus.). 32p. (J). (gr. -1-2). 16.99 *(978-0-7636-6991-1(1))* Candlewick Pr.
Scillian, Devin. Memoirs of a Hamster. Bowers, Tim, illus. 2013. (ENG.). 32p. (J). (gr. -1-2). 15.99 *(978-1-58536-831-0(8),* 202365) Sleeping Bear Pr.
Scoon, Saska. Miss Rosie's Academy of Ballet. 2016. (ENG., Illus.). 64p. (J). (gr. 1-2). 14.99 *(978-1-74257-811-8(X))* New Holland Pubs. Pty, Ltd. AUS. Dist: Midpoint Trade Bks., Inc.
Scotton, Rob. And the Snowy Day Surprise. Scotton, Rob, illus. 2014. (Splat the Cat Ser.). (ENG., Illus.). 16p. (J). (gr. -1-3). pap. 6.99 *(978-0-06-197864-7(7),* HarperFestival) HarperCollins Pubs.
—The Big Helper. Scotton, Rob, illus. 2015. (Splat the Cat Ser.). (ENG., Illus.). 24p. (J). (gr. -1-3). pap. 3.99 *(978-0-06-229427-2(X),* HarperFestival) HarperCollins Pubs.
—The Big Helper. 2015. (Splat the Cat 8X8 Ser.). (J). lib. bdg. 13.55 *(978-0-606-36491-1(9))* Turtleback Bks.
—Blow, Snow, Blow. Scotton, Rob, illus. 2013. (I Can Read Level 1 Ser.). (ENG., Illus.). 32p. (J). (gr. -1-3). pap. 3.99 *(978-0-06-209027-0(5))* HarperCollins Pubs.
—Blow, Snow, Blow. 2013. (Splat the Cat: I Can Read Ser.). (J). lib. bdg. 13.55 *(978-0-606-32160-0(8),* Turtleback) Turtleback Bks.
—Christmas Countdown. Scotton, Rob, illus. 2015. (Splat the Cat Ser.). (ENG., Illus.). 12p. (J). (gr. -1 — 1). bds. 6.99 *(978-0-06-197865-4(5),* HarperFestival) HarperCollins Pubs.
—Fishy Tales. Scotton, Rob, illus. 2012. (Splat the Cat Ser.). (ENG., Illus.). 24p. (J). (gr. -1-3). pap. 3.99 *(978-0-06-197852-4(3),* HarperFestival) HarperCollins Pubs.
—Funny Valentine. Scotton, Rob, illus. 2012. (Splat the Cat Ser.). (ENG., Illus.). 16p. (J). (gr. -1-3). pap. 6.99 *(978-0-06-197862-3(0),* HarperFestival) HarperCollins Pubs.
—Good Night, Sleep Tight. Scotton, Rob & Eberz, Robert, illus. 2011. (I Can Read Level 1 Ser.). (ENG.). 32p. (J). (gr. -1-3). pap. 3.99 *(978-0-06-197855-5(8))* HarperCollins Pubs.
—I Scream for Ice Cream. Scotton, Rob, illus. 2015. (I Can Read Level 1 Ser.). (ENG., Illus.). 32p. (J). (gr. -1-3). 16.99 *(978-0-06-229419-7(9))* HarperCollins Pubs.
—Love, Splat. Scotton, Rob, illus. (Splat the Cat Ser.). (ENG., Illus.). 40p. (J). (gr. -1-2). 2011. 9.99 *(978-0-06-207776-9(7))* 2008. 16.99 *(978-0-06-083157-8(X))* HarperCollins Pubs.
—Merry Christmas, Splat. Scotton, Rob, illus. (Splat the Cat Ser.). (ENG., Illus.). 40p. (J). (gr. -1-2). 2013. 9.99 *(978-0-06-212450-0(1))* 2009. 16.99 *(978-0-06-083160-8(X))* HarperCollins Pubs.
—The Name of the Game. Scotton, Rob, illus. 2012. (I Can Read Level 1 Ser.). (ENG., Illus.). 32p. (J). (gr. -1-3). 16.99 *(978-0-06-209015-7(1))* HarperCollins Pubs.
—The Name of the Game. 2012. (Splat the Cat: I Can Read Ser.). (J). lib. bdg. 13.55 *(978-0-606-26281-1(4),* Turtleback) Turtleback Bks.
—On with the Show. Scotton, Rob, illus. 2013. (Splat the Cat Ser.). (ENG., Illus.). 24p. (J). (gr. -1-3). pap. 3.99 *(978-0-06-209010-2(0),* HarperFestival) HarperCollins Pubs.
—On with the Snow. 2013. (Splat the Cat 8X8 Ser.). (J). lib. bdg. 13.55 *(978-0-606-27152-3(X),* Turtleback) Turtleback Bks.
—Oopsie-Daisy. Scotton, Rob, illus. 2014. (Splat the Cat Ser.). (ENG., Illus.). 24p. (J). (gr. -1-3). pap. 4.99 *(978-0-06-211585-0(5),* HarperFestival) HarperCollins Pubs.
—The Perfect Present for Mom & Dad. Scotton, Rob, illus. 2012. (Splat the Cat Ser.). (ENG., Illus.). 24p. (J). (gr. k-3). pap. 4.99 *(978-0-06-210009-2(2),* HarperFestival) HarperCollins Pubs.
—The Perfect Present for Mom & Dad. 2012. (Splat the Cat 8X8 Ser.). (J). lib. bdg. 14.75 *(978-0-606-23579-2(5),* Turtleback) Turtleback Bks.
—The Rain Is a Pain. Scotton, Rob, illus. 2012. (I Can Read Level 1 Ser.). (ENG., Illus.). 32p. (J). (gr. -1-3). pap. 3.99 *(978-0-06-209017-1(8))* HarperCollins Pubs.
—The Rain Is a Pain. 2012. (Splat the Cat: I Can Read Ser.). (J). lib. bdg. 13.55 *(978-0-606-26861-5(8),* Turtleback) Turtleback Bks.
—Scaredy-Cat, Splat! Scotton, Rob, illus. (Splat the Cat Ser.). (Illus.). 40p. (J). (gr. -1-3). 2015. (ENG.). 9.99 *(978-0-06-236897-3(4))* 2010. (ENG.). 16.99 *(978-0-06-117760-6(1))* 2010. lib. bdg. 17.89 *(978-0-06-117761-3(X))* HarperCollins Pubs.
—Secret Agent Splat! Scotton, Rob, illus. 2012. (Splat the Cat Ser.). (Illus.). 40p. (J). (gr. -1-2). (ENG.). 16.99 *(978-0-06-197871-5(X));* lib. bdg. 17.89 *(978-0-06-197872-2(8))* HarperCollins Pubs.
—Sings Flat. Scotton, Rob, illus. 2011. (I Can Read Level 1 Ser.). (ENG., Illus.). 32p. (J). (gr. -1-3). 16.99 *(978-0-06-197854-8(X))* HarperCollins Pubs.
—Splat & Seymour, Best Friends Forevermore. 2014. (Splat the Cat: I Can Read Ser.). (J). lib. bdg. 13.55 *(978-0-606-35960-3(5))* Turtleback Bks.
—Splat & the Cool School Trip. Scotton, Rob, illus. 2013. (Splat the Cat Ser.). (ENG., Illus.). 40p. (J). (gr. -1-3). 17.99 *(978-0-06-213386-1(1))* HarperCollins Pubs.
—Splat Says Thank You! Scotton, Rob, illus. 2012. (Splat the Cat Ser.). (ENG., Illus.). 40p. (J). (gr. -1-3). 16.99 *(978-0-06-197874-6(4))* HarperCollins Pubs.
—Splat the Cat. Scotton, Rob, illus. (Splat the Cat Ser.). (Illus.). (J). (gr. -1-3). 2013. (ENG.). 100p. pap. 12.99 *(978-0-06-211594-2(4),* HarperFestival) 2008. (ENG., 40p. 17.99 *(978-0-06-083154-7(5))* 2008. 40p. lib. bdg. 17.89 *(978-0-06-083155-4(3))* HarperCollins Pubs.
—Splat the Cat. 2011. (J). (gr. -1-2). 29.95 *(978-0-545-23794-9(7))* Weston Woods Studios, Inc.
—Splat the Cat: A Whale of a Tale. Scotton, Rob, illus. 2013. (I Can Read Level 1 Ser.). (ENG., Illus.). 32p. (J). (gr. -1-3). 16.99 *(978-0-06-209024-9(0))* HarperCollins Pubs.
—Splat the Cat: Big Reading Collection. Scotton, Rob, illus. 2012. (I Can Read Level 1 Ser.). (ENG., Illus.). 100p. (J). (gr. k-3). pap. 16.99 *(978-0-06-209029-4(1))* HarperCollins Pubs.
—Splat the Cat: Blow, Snow, Blow. Scotton, Rob, illus. 2013. (I Can Read Level 1 Ser.). (ENG., Illus.). 32p. (J). (gr. -1-3). 16.99 *(978-0-06-209026-3(7))* HarperCollins Pubs.
—Splat the Cat: Good Night, Sleep Tight. Scotton, Rob & Eberz, Robert, illus. 2011. (I Can Read Level 1 Ser.). (ENG.). 32p. (J). (gr. -1-3). 16.99 *(978-0-06-197856-2(6))* HarperCollins Pubs.
—Splat the Cat: Splat & Seymour, Best Friends Forevermore. Scotton, Rob, illus. 2014. (I Can Read Level 1 Ser.). (ENG.,

Illus.). 32p. (J). (gr. -1-3). pap. 3.99 (978-0-06-211601-7(0)) HarperCollins Pubs.

—Splat the Cat: Twice the Mice. Scotton, Rob, illus. 2015. (I Can Read Level 1 Ser.). (ENG., Illus.). 32p. (J). (gr. -1-3). pap. 3.99 (978-0-06-229421-0(0)) HarperCollins Pubs.

—Splat the Cat: What Was That? Scotton, Rob, illus. deluxe ed. 2013. (Splat the Cat Ser.). (ENG., Illus.). 16p. (J). (gr. k-3). pap. 6.99 (978-0-06-197863-0(9), HarperFestival) HarperCollins Pubs.

—Splat the Cat - I Scream for Ice Cream. Scotton, Rob, illus. 2015. (I Can Read Level 1 Ser.). (ENG., Illus.). 32p. (J). (gr. -1-3). pap. 3.99 (978-0-06-229418-0(0)) HarperCollins Pubs.

—Splat the Cat - The Rain Is a Pain. Scotton, Rob, illus. 2012. (I Can Read Level 1 Ser.). (ENG., Illus.). 32p. (J). (gr. -1-3). 16.99 (978-0-06-209018-8(6)) HarperCollins Pubs.

—Splat the Cat - Twice the Mice. Scotton, Rob, illus. 2015. (I Can Read Level 1 Ser.). (ENG., Illus.). 32p. (J). (gr. -1-3). 16.99 (978-0-06-229422-7(9)) HarperCollins Pubs.

—Splat the Cat & the Big Secret. Scotton, Rob, illus. 2016. (Splat the Cat Ser.). (Illus.). 24p. (J). (gr. -1-3). pap. 3.99 (978-0-06-229431-9(8), HarperFestival) HarperCollins Pubs.

—Splat the Cat & the Big Secret. Farley, Rick & Eberz, Robert, illus. 2016. (J). **(978-1-4844-8600-9(5))** Publishers Quality Library Service.

—Splat the Cat & the Big Secret. 2016. (Splat the Cat 8X8 Ser.). (Illus.). (J). lib. bdg. 13.55 (978-0-606-38770-5(6)) Turtleback Bks.

—Splat the Cat & the Duck with No Quack. Scotton, Rob, illus. 2011. (I Can Read Level 1 Ser.). (ENG., Illus.). 32p. (J). (gr. k-3). pap. 3.99 (978-0-06-197857-9(4)) HarperCollins Pubs.

—Splat the Cat & the Hotshot. Scotton, Rob, illus. 2015. (I Can Read Level 1 Ser.). (ENG., Illus.). 32p. (J). (gr. -1-3). pap. 3.99 (978-0-06-229415-9(6)) HarperCollins Pubs.

—Splat the Cat & the Late Library Book. Scotton, Rob, illus. 2016. (Splat the Cat Ser.). (Illus.). 24p. (J). (gr. -1-3). pap. 3.99 (978-0-06-229429-6(6), HarperFestival) HarperCollins Pubs.

—Splat the Cat & the Pumpkin-Picking Plan. Scotton, Rob, illus. 2014. (Splat the Cat Ser.). (ENG., Illus.). 24p. (J). (gr. -1-3). pap. 4.99 (978-0-06-211586-7(3)) HarperCollins Pubs.

—Splat the Cat & the Quick Chicks. Scotton, Rob, illus. 2016. (I Can Read Level 1 Ser.). (Illus.). 32p. (J). (gr. -1-3). pap. 3.99 (978-0-06-229424-1(5)) HarperCollins Pubs.

—Splat the Cat & the Quick Chicks. Eberz, Robert, illus. 2016. 30p. (J). **(978-1-4844-7139-5(3))** Harper & Row Ltd.

—Splat the Cat Board Book. Scotton, Rob, illus. 2016. (Splat the Cat Ser.). (Illus.). 34p. (J). (gr. -1 — 1). bds. 7.99 (978-0-06-229436-4(9), HarperFestival) HarperCollins Pubs.

—Splat the Cat Dreams Big. Scotton, Rob, illus. 2013. (Splat the Cat Ser.). (ENG., Illus.). 24p. (J). (gr. -1-3). pap. 3.99 (978-0-06-209012-6(7), HarperFestival) HarperCollins Pubs.

—Splat the Cat for President. Scotton, Rob, illus. 2016. (Splat the Cat Ser.). (Illus.). 24p. (J). (gr. -1-3). pap. 3.99 (978-0-06-229433-3(4), HarperFestival) HarperCollins Pubs.

—Splat the Cat for President. 2016. (Splat the Cat 8X8 Ser.). (J). lib. bdg. 13.55 **(978-0-606-40003-9(6))** Turtleback Bks.

—Splat the Cat Goes to the Doctor. Scotton, Rob, illus. 2014. (Splat the Cat Ser.). (ENG., Illus.). 24p. (J). (gr. -1-3). pap. 4.99 (978-0-06-211588-1(X), HarperFestival) HarperCollins Pubs.

—Splat the Cat Makes Dad Glad. Scotton, Rob, illus. 2014. (I Can Read Level 1 Ser.). (ENG., Illus.). 32p. (J). (gr. -1-3). 16.99 (978-0-06-211599-7(5)); pap. 3.99 (978-0-06-211597-3(9)) HarperCollins Pubs.

—Splat the Cat Makes Dad Glad. 2014. (Splat the Cat: I Can Read Ser.). (J). lib. bdg. 13.55 (978-0-606-35475-2(1)) Turtleback Bks.

—Splat the Cat Sings Flat. Scotton, Rob, illus. 2011. (I Can Read Level 1 Ser.). (ENG., Illus.). 32p. (J). (gr. -1-3). pap. 3.99 (978-0-06-197853-1(1)) HarperCollins Pubs.

—Splat the Cat Storybook Collection. Scotton, Rob, illus. 2013. (Splat the Cat Ser.). (ENG., Illus.). 192p. (J). (gr. -1-3). 11.99 (978-0-06-213383-0(7)) HarperCollins Pubs.

—Splat the Cat Takes the Cake. Scotton, Rob, illus. 2012. (I Can Read Level 1 Ser.). (ENG., Illus.). 32p. (J). (gr. k-3). 16.99 (978-0-06-197860-9(4)); pap. 3.99 (978-0-06-197859-3(0)) HarperCollins Pubs.

—Splat the Cat Treasure Box. Scotton, Rob, illus. 2011. (Splat the Cat Ser.). (ENG., Illus.). (J). (gr. k-3). pap. 15.99 (978-0-06-210010-8(6)) HarperCollins Pubs.

—Splat the Cat with a Bang & a Clang. Scotton, Rob, illus. 2013. (I Can Read Level 1 Ser.). (ENG., Illus.). 32p. (J). (gr. -1-3). 16.99 (978-0-06-209021-8(6)) HarperCollins Pubs.

—Splat the Cat with a Bang & a Clang. 2013. (Splat the Cat: I Can Read Ser.). (J). lib. bdg. 13.55 (978-0-606-27148-6(1), Turtleback) Turtleback Bks.

—Splish, Splash, Splat! Scotton, Rob, illus. 2011. (Splat the Cat Ser.). (ENG., Illus.). 40p. (J). (gr. -1-3). 16.99 (978-0-06-197868-5(X)) HarperCollins Pubs.

—Splish, Splash, Splat! Board Book. Scotton, Rob, illus. 2016. (Splat the Cat Ser.). (Illus.). 36p. (J). (gr. -1 — 1). bds. 7.99 (978-0-06-229438-8(5), HarperFestival) HarperCollins Pubs.

—Up in the Air at the Fair. Scotton, Rob, illus. 2014. (I Can Read Level 1 Ser.). (ENG., Illus.). 32p. (J). (gr. -1-3). 16.99 (978-0-06-211596-6(0)); pap. 3.99 (978-0-06-211595-9(2)) HarperCollins Pubs.

—Up in the Air at the Fair. 2014. (Splat the Cat: I Can Read Ser.). (J). lib. bdg. 13.55 (978-0-606-35059-4(4), Turtleback) Turtleback Bks.

—A Whale of a Tale. Scotton, Rob, illus. 2013. (I Can Read Level 1 Ser.). (ENG., Illus.). 32p. (J). (gr. -1-3). pap. 3.99 (978-0-06-209022-5(4)) HarperCollins Pubs.

—A Whale of a Tale. 2013. (Splat the Cat: I Can Read Ser.). (J). lib. bdg. 13.55 (978-0-606-31814-3(3), Turtleback) Turtleback Bks.

—Where's the Easter Bunny? Scotton, Rob, illus. 2011. (Splat the Cat Ser.). (ENG., Illus.). 16p. (J). (gr. -1-1). pap. 6.99 (978-0-06-197861-6(2), HarperFestival) HarperCollins Pubs.

Scotton, Rob & Driscoll, Laura. I Scream for Ice Cream. 2015. (Splat the Cat: I Can Read Ser.). (J). lib. bdg. 13.55 (978-0-606-36948-0(1)) Turtleback Bks.

Second and Fourth Grade Franklin Elementary. The Cat Has Class! 2007. (Illus.). 32p. (J). (gr. k-10). 16.95 (978-0-929915-71-5(2)) Headline Bks., Inc.

Seda, Gus. Prohex the Cat. 2012. 44p. pap. 24.95 (978-1-4626-7704-7(5)) America Star Bks.

Seddon, Jane. Tales of Bermy Wood, 1 vol. 2010. 64p. pap. 19.95 (978-1-4489-2195-9(3)) America Star Bks.

Segal, Lore. The Story of Mrs. Lovewright & Purrless Her Cat. Zelinsky, Paul O., illus. 2005. (ENG.). 40p. (J). (gr. -1-3). reprint ed. 17.99 (978-0-689-87327-0(1), Atheneum/Anne Schwartz Bks.) Simon & Schuster Children's Publishing.

Segvic-Boudreaux, Ivana. Desperately Seeking Talent: A Puppy's Journey. 2010. 108p. pap. 13.95 (978-1-4327-6112-7(9)) Outskirts Pr., Inc.

Seidler, Tor. Toes. Beddows, Eric, illus. 2004. 176p. (J). (gr. 3-18). (ENG.). 15.99 (978-0-06-054099-9(0)); lib. bdg. 16.89 (978-0-06-054100-2(8)) HarperCollins Pubs. (Geringer, Laura Book).

Seki, Sunny. The Tale of the Lucky Cat. Seki, Sunny, illus. 2008. (ENG & SPA., Illus.). 32p. (J). 18.95 (978-0-9669437-9-5(1)) East West Discovery Pr.

Seki, Sunny, illus. & retold by. The Tale of the Lucky Cat. Seki, Sunny, retold by. 32p. (J). 2008. (978-0-9669437-6-4(7)) 2007. (JPN & ENG.). 18.95 (978-0-9669437-5-7(9)) East West Discovery Pr.

Selden, George. The Cricket in Times Square. Williams, Garth, illus. 2008. (Chester Cricket & His Friends Ser.: 1). (ENG.). 144p. (J). (gr. 1-4). pap. 6.99 (978-0-312-38003-8(8), 9780312380038) Square Fish.

—Harry Kitten & Tucker Mouse. Williams, Garth, illus. 2009. (Chester Cricket & His Friends Ser.). (ENG.). 144p. (J). (gr. 1-4). pap. 8.99 (978-0-312-58248-7(X), 9780312582487) Square Fish.

—Tucker's Countryside. Williams, Garth, illus. 2012. (ENG.). 192p. (J). (gr. 3-7). pap. 7.99 (978-1-250-00256-3(7), 9781250002563) Square Fish.

Senior, Patricia. Pip & the Magic Flute. 2008. (Illus.). 40p. pap. 18.49 (978-1-4389-0023-0(6)) AuthorHouse.

Sepe, Kim A. Crouching Cat, Hidden Kitten. 2012. 36p. pap. 18.41 (978-1-4669-6259-0(3)) Trafford Publishing.

Sepulveda, Luis. Gaviota y del Gato. 9th ed. 2003. (SPA.). 144p. (978-968-7723-11-2(4), 6020) Tusquests Editores Mexico, S.A. de C.V.

Sermons, Faye. No Ordinary Cat. Becket, Nancy, illus. 2009. 40p. pap. 16.99 (978-1-4389-6242-9(8)) AuthorHouse.

Serpa, Dylon J. Moosey's Adventures: The Way Home. 2013. 28p. pap. 24.95 (978-1-62709-256-2(0)) America Star Bks.

Serrano, Pet. Best Friends No Matter What. 2007. (Illus.). 32p. (J). pap. (978-0-9770497-9-0(5), Itty Bitty Kitty) Singing Moon Pr.

Seuss, Dr. The Cat in the Hat. 2010. (ENG., Illus.). 64p. pap. (978-0-00-734869-5(X), HarperCollins Children's Bks.) HarperCollins Pubs. Ltd.

—The Cat in the Hat. (Beginner Books(R) Ser.). (ENG.). (J). 2012. 72p. (gr. k-3). 17.99 (978-0-449-81086-6(0)) 2005. (Illus.). 64p. (gr. -1-2). 9.95 (978-0-375-83492-9(3)) Random Hse. Children's Bks. (Random Hse. Bks. for Young Readers).

—The Cat in the Hat Book & Hat. 2012. (Beginner Books Ser.). (ENG.). 72p. (J). (gr. k-3). 24.99 (978-0-307-93044-6(0), Random Hse. Bks. for Young Readers) Random Hse. Children's Bks.

—The Cat in the Hat Cloth Book. 2015. (Bright & Early Cloth Book Ser.). (ENG., Illus.). 8p. (J). (— 1). 14.99 (978-0-385-39268-6(0), Random Hse. Bks. for Young Readers) Random Hse. Children's Bks.

—The Cat in the Hat/el Gato Ensombrerado: Bilingual Edition. 2015. (Classic Seuss Ser.). (ENG & SPA.). 72p. (J). (gr. -1-2). 15.00 (978-0-553-52443-7(7), Random Hse. Bks. for Young Readers) Random Hse. Children's Bks.

—The Cat in the Hat's. Ruiz, Aristides, illus. 2014. (Great Big Board Book Ser.). (ENG.). 12p. (J). (gr. k — 1). bds. 12.99 (978-0-679-89360-8(1), Random Hse. Bks. for Young Readers) Random Hse. Children's Bks.

—El Gato con Sombrero Viene de Nuevo! Canetti, Yanitzia, tr. from ENG. 2004.Tr. of Cat in the Hat Comes Back. (SPA., Illus.). 63p. (gr. -1-1). 8.99 (978-1-930332-43-0(2)) Lectorum Pubns., Inc.

—El Gato Ensombrerado. 2015. (Beginner Books(R) Ser.). (ENG & SPA., Illus.). 72p. (J). (gr. -1-2). lib. bdg. 13.99 (978-0-553-50980-9(2), Random Hse. Bks. for Young Readers) Random Hse. Children's Bks.

—Gatola da Cartola. pap. 23.95 (978-85-7406-085-9(2)) Schwarcz, Editora Ltda, Companhia das Letrinhas BRA. Dist: Distribooks, Inc.

Seymour, Jane & Keach, James. And Then There Were Three. Planer, Geoffrey, illus. 2003. (This One & That One Ser.: Vol. 5). (ENG.). 32p. (J). (gr. -1-3). 12.99 (978-1-932431-09-4(8)) Left Field,Angel Gate.

—Boing! No Bouncing on the Bed. Planer, Geoffrey, illus. 2003. (This One & That One Ser.: Vol. 1). (ENG.). 32p. (J). (gr. -1-3). 12.99 (978-1-932431-06-3(3)) Left Field,Angel Gate.

—Fried Pies & Roast Cake. Planer, Geoffrey, illus. 2003. (This One & That One Ser.: Vol. 5). (ENG.). 32p. (J). (gr. -1-3). 12.99 (978-1-932431-10-0(1)) Left Field,Angel Gate.

—Splat! The Tale of a Colorful Cat. Planer, Geoffrey, illus. 2003. (This One & That One Ser.: Vol. 2.). (ENG.). 32p. (J). (gr. -1-3). 12.99 (978-1-932431-07-0(1)) Left Field,Angel Gate.

—Yum! A Tale of Two Cookies. Planer, Geoffrey, illus. 2nd ed. 2003. (This One & That One Ser.: Vol. 3). (ENG.). 32p. (J). (gr. -1-3). 12.99 (978-1-932431-08-7(X)) Left Field,Angel Gate.

Shah, Indries. The Farmer's Wife/la Esposa Del Granjero. Santiago, Rose Mary, illus. 2003. (SPA & ENG.). (J). 6.95 (978-1-883536-34-3(0), FAWI3, Hoopoe Bks.) I S H K.

Shahan, Sherry. Cool Cats Counting. Barragán, Paula, illus. (ENG.). (J). (gr. -1-2). 2016. 28p. pap. 8.95 (978-1-941460-42-9(9)) 2005. 24p. 16.95 (978-0-87483-757-5(X)) August Hse. Pubs., Inc.

Shanklin, Sandra, told to. Tales of Cat Canyon. 2005. (Illus.). 143p. pap. 12.95 (978-0-9632459-2-2(9)) Great Plains Pr.

Sharp, Margery. The Rescuers. Williams, Garth, illus. 2016. (ENG.). 160p. (J). (gr. 4-7). pap. 9.99 (978-1-68137-007-1(7), NYRB Kids) New York Review of Bks., Inc., The.

Shaw, Chrysie. The Cat & the Goldfish. 2013. 20p. pap. 9.99 (978-1-4575-2451-6(1)) Dog Ear Publishing, LLC.

Shea, Bob. Ballet Cat: The Totally Secret Secret. Shea, Bob, illus. (Ballet Cat Ser.). (ENG., Illus.). 56p. (J). (gr. 1-3). 2016. bds. 9.99 (978-1-4847-1379-2(6)) 2015. 9.99 (978-1-4847-1378-5(8)) Disney Pr.

—Cheetah Can't Lose. Shea, Bob, illus. 2013. (ENG., Illus.). 40p. (J). (gr. -1-3). 17.99 (978-0-06-173083-2(1)) HarperCollins Pubs.

—What's Your Favorite Favorite? Shea, Bob, illus. 2017. (Ballet Cat Ser.). (ENG., Illus.). 56p. (J). (gr. 1-3). 9.99 (978-1-4847-7809-8(X)) Disney Pr.

Sheehan, Linda Clarke. The Chronicles of Mr. Kitty Mozart. 2011. 28p. (gr. -1 — 1). pap. 16.09 (978-1-4269-5571-6(5)) Trafford Publishing.

Sheen, C. D. McKnight. Morphani: And the Valley of the Coloured Doorway's. 2012. 76p. 37.37 (978-1-4691-7680-2(7)); pap. 18.68 (978-1-4691-7679-6(3)) Xlibris Corp.

Shell, S. E. Coffee with Orange Sherbert: Friendship Can Be Found Where Eyes & Hearts Are Open. Smith, Mary Elizabeth, illus. 2012. (ENG.). 42p. (J). pap. 14.99 (978-0-9885461-2-7(4)) Osherbert Bks., LLC.

Shepard, Aaron. King o' the Cats. Sorra, Kristin, illus. 2010. (ENG.). 32p. (J). (gr. -1-3). 11.99 (978-1-4424-1256-9(9), Atheneum Bks. for Young Readers) Simon & Schuster Children's Publishing.

Shepherd, Wilf. Behind the Whiskers: Tales for the Young at Heart. 2012. 282p. pap. 28.03 (978-1-4797-0473-6(3)) Xlibris Corp.

Shoo, Shoo, Shoo! & Other Stories, 6 Packs. (Story Steps Ser.). (gr. k-2). 48.00 (978-0-7635-9604-0(3)) Rigby Education.

Short, Carol. Todd's Nine Lives. 2009. 28p. pap. 12.49 (978-1-4389-3893-6(4)) AuthorHouse.

Shortridge, Retha. Baby & Meow. 2004. 42p. per. 12.83 (978-1-4116-1085-9(7)) Lulu Pr., Inc.

Shulman, Mark. Big Cat. Chambers, Sally, illus. 2004. 8p. (J). bds. 6.95 (978-1-58925-737-5(5)) Tiger Tales.

Sickler, Jonas, illus. Hey Diddle Diddle: Hey Baby Look at the Cat & His Fiddle - in New Orleans! 2010. (Indestructibles Ser.). (ENG.). 12p. (J). (gr. k — 1). pap. 5.95 (978-0-7611-5862-2(6), 15862) Workman Publishing Co., Inc.

Sicks, Linda. How Different Is Good: Nick the Wise Old Cat. Messing, Dave, illus. 2010. (Importance of Friendship Ser.). 40p. (J). 18.95 (978-1-936193-04-2(3)) Nick The Cat, LLC.

—Nick the Wise Old Cat: How I Found My Family. Messing, Dave, illus. 2010. (ENG.). 40p. (J). 18.95 (978-1-936193-00-4(0)) Nick The Cat, LLC.

—Nick the Wise Old Cat How I Found My Family. Messing, Dave, illus. 2009. 32p. (J). 17.95 (978-1-934878-63-7(4)) Mascot Bks., Inc.

—Nick's Holiday Celebration. Messing, Dave, illus. 2010. (Importance of Family Ser.). 40p. (J). 18.95 (978-1-936193-05-9(1)) Nick The Cat, LLC.

Silver, Pattie, illus. Kitty's Barn. 2005. 12p. (J). bds. 9.95 (978-1-58117-385-7(7), Intervisual/Piggy Toes) Bendon, Inc.

Silverman, Erica. Mrs. Peachtree & the Eighth Avenue Cat. Beier, Ellen, illus. 2011. (ENG.). 32p. (J). (gr. -1-3). pap. 16.99 (978-1-4424-4340-2(5), Simon & Schuster Bks. For Young Readers) Simon & Schuster Bks. For Young Readers.

Simmonds, Posy. Baker Cat. Simmonds, Posy, illus. 2015. (ENG., Illus.). 32p. (J). (gr. -1-k). pap. 11.99 (978-1-78344-105-1(4)) Andersen Pr. GBR. Dist: Independent Pubs. Group.

—Fred. 2014. (ENG., Illus.). 32p. (J). (-k). pap. 9.99 (978-1-78344-029-0(5)) Andersen Pr. GBR. Dist: Independent Pubs. Group.

Simmons Bell, Linda. Kylie & Mr Whiskers. 2009. 20p. pap. 13.00 (978-1-4389-3555-3(2)) AuthorHouse.

Simmons, Jane. Ship's Cat Doris. Simmons, Jane, illus. 2011. (ENG., Illus.). 176p. (J). (gr. k-2). pap. 8.99 (978-1-4083-0896-7(7)) Hodder & Stoughton GBR. Dist: Hachette Bk. Group.

Simon, Charnan. Luna the Wake-Up Cat. Huang, Benrei, illus. 2011. (Rookie Ready to Learn — Animals Ser.). 40p. (J). (gr. -1-k). lib. bdg. 25.00 (978-0-531-26414-0(9)); (ENG.). pap. 5.95 (978-0-531-26695-3(8)) Scholastic Library Publishing. (Children's Pr.).

Simon, Francesca. Higgledy Piggledy the Hen Who Loved to Dance. Moseng, Elisabeth, illus. 2016. (ENG.). 32p. (J). 17.99 (978-0-00-813946-9(6), HarperCollins Children's Bks.) HarperCollins Pubs. Ltd. GBR. Dist: HarperCollins Pubs.

—Yum Yum. Bolam, Emily, illus. 2012. (ENG.). 80p. (J). (gr. -1-k). 7.99 (978-1-4440-0200-3(7), Orion Children's Bks.) Hachette Children's Group GBR. Dist: Hachette Bk. Group.

Simonson, Audrey. Where Is Your Mousey? 2006. (ENG.). 40p. per. 22.65 (978-1-4134-0270-4(4)) Xlibris Corp.

Sims, Lori. Starvin' Marvin & Skinny Minnie Shake up San Francisco. 2009. 78p. (YA). pap. 9.95 (978-1-4327-3651-4(5)) Outskirts Pr., Inc.

Singleton, Linda Joy. Cash Kat, 1 vol. Wald, Christina, illus. 2016. (ENG & SPA.). 32p. (J). (gr. k-3). 17.95 (978-1-62855-728-2(1)) Arbordale Publishing.

—A Cat Is Better. Martin, Jorge, illus. 2017. (ENG.). 32p. (J). (gr. -1-3). 16.99 (978-1-4998-0278-8(1)) Little Bee Books Inc.

—Elena Efectivo, 1 vol. Wald, Christina, illus. 2016. (SPA.). 32p. (J). (gr. k-3). pap. 9.95 (978-1-62855-742-8(7)) Arbordale Publishing.

Sisco, Joann Ellen. The Story of Many Blankets: 3. 2012. 96p. pap. 13.95 (978-1-4772-5895-8(7)) AuthorHouse.

Sivier, Janet. Charlotte & Jackson: The Butterfly. 2012. 28p. pap. 16.09 (978-1-4669-4555-5(9)) Trafford Publishing.

—Charlotte & Jackson: The Strange Flowers. 2012. 16p. pap. 12.68 (978-1-4669-3965-3(6)) Trafford Publishing.

Skafish, Brad. Outnumbered! the Bad Cats Learn about Numbers. 2011. 20p. pap. 12.95 (978-1-61434-290-8(3)) Booklocker.com, Inc.

—Red Letter Day: The Bad Cats Learn about Letters! 2012. 20p. pap. 11.95 (978-1-62141-260-1(1)) Booklocker.com, Inc.

Skotnicki, Jill. Ham & Beans: Have You Seen the Color Green? 2010. 28p. pap. 12.49 (978-1-4520-6452-9(0)) AuthorHouse.

Sky Koster, Amy. Cute, Sweet, & Petite! (Disney Princess: Palace Pets) Random House Disney Staff, illus. 2015. (Big Golden Book Ser.). (ENG.). 64p. (J). (gr. -1-2). 9.99 (978-0-7364-3412-6(7), Golden/Disney) Random Hse. Children's Bks.

Sleigh, Barbara. Carbonel: The King of the Cats. Drummond, V. H., illus. 2004. (ENG.). 216p. (J). (gr. 4-7). reprint ed. 16.95 (978-1-59017-126-4(8), NYR Children's Collection) New York Review of Bks., Inc., The.

—Carbonel & Calidor: Being the Further Adventures of a Royal Cat. Front, Charles, illus. 2009. (ENG.). 224p. (J). (gr. 4-7). 17.95 (978-1-59017-333-6(3), NYR Children's Collection) New York Review of Bks., Inc., The.

—The Kingdom of Carbonel. Kennedy, Richard, illus. 2009. (ENG.). 240p. (J). (gr. 4-7). 17.95 (978-1-59017-315-2(5), NYR Children's Collection) New York Review of Bks., Inc., The.

Sloan, William. Of Bees & Bats of Crocodiles & Cats. 2009. 73p. pap. 14.95 (978-1-4092-9470-2(6)) Lulu Pr., Inc.

Small, Lily. Chloe the Kitten. 2015. (Fairy Animals of Misty Wood Ser.: 1). (ENG., Illus.). 144p. (J). (gr. k-3). pap. 5.99 (978-1-62779-141-0(8), 9781627791410, Holt, Henry & Co. Bks. For Young Readers) Holt, Henry & Co.

Small, Lily. Kylie the Kitten. 2017. (Fairy Animals of Misty Wood Ser.). (ENG., Illus.). 144p. (J). pap. 5.99 **(978-1-250-12698-6(3)**, 9781250126986, Holt, Henry & Co. Bks. For Young Readers) Holt, Henry & Co.

Smalley, Roger. Big Cat Trouble. Shaw, Charles, illus. 2005. (J). (978-1-933248-13-4(0)) World Quest Learning.

Smith, Craig. Remarkably Rexy. 2016. (ENG., Illus.). 32p. (J). (gr. -1-2). 17.99 (978-1-76011-394-0(8)) Allen & Unwin AUS. Dist: Independent Pubs. Group.

Smith, David, told to. The Cart. 2003. (J). pap. 8.00 (978-0-8059-5745-7(6)) Dorrance Publishing Co., Inc.

Smith, Jay F. A Day to Remember: A Sam & Coco Story. Smith, Jay F., illus. 2005. (Illus.). 32p. (J). (978-0-9764719-0-5(6)) MiceWorks.

Smith, Jill & Diller, Howard. Nat the Fat Cat. 2006. (Illus.). 91p. (J). pap. (978-1-933873-00-8(0)) Read Well Publishing Inc.

—Nat the Fat Cat: Workbook. 2006. (Illus.). 80p. (J). pap. (978-1-933873-01-5(9)) Read Well Publishing Inc.

Smith, Joy V. Why Won't Anyone Play with Me? 2007. 20p. per. 24.95 (978-1-4241-8634-1(X)) America Star Bks.

Smith, Leone. Jasmine Finds a Doctor. Smith, Marcelle, illus. 2011. 30p. pap. 12.50 (978-1-61204-042-4(X), Strategic Bk. Publishing) Strategic Book Publishing & Rights Agency (SBPRA).

Smith, Linda. Mrs. Crump's Cat. Roberts, David, illus. 2006. 32p. (J). (gr. -1-3). 17.89 (978-0-06-443551-2(2)) HarperCollins Pubs.

Smith, Louise C. Mr. Stubbs: Autobiography of a Clever Cat. 2008. pap. 9.00 (978-0-8059-8691-4(X)) Dorrance Publishing Co., Inc.

Smith, Maggie Caldwell. Tommy Wilson, Junior Veterinarian: The Case of the Orphaned Bobcat. Heyer, Carol & White, Charlotte L., illus. 2006. (J). per. 7.95 (978-0-9788391-1-6(0)) Magpie Pr., Pine Mountain Club, CA.

Smith-Mansell, Dana. The Smith Family's New Puppy: Helping Children Cope with a New Family Member. Voerg, Kathy, illus. 2008. (Let's Talk Ser.). (ENG.). 48p. (J). (gr. -1-4). pap. 8.95 (978-0-88282-327-0(2)) New Horizon Pr. Pubs., Inc.

Smith Novelty Company Staff. Clyde the Cable Car. 2006. (J). pap. 9.95 (978-1-59099-076-6(5)) Smith Novelty Co., Inc.

Smith, S. Hey Silly Cat! Dont Tease the Dog! 2010. (Illus.). 32p. (J). 17.99 (978-0-9842632-9-5(2)) Scandora.

Smith, Sindy. Mr. Minko. Smith, Sindy, illus. 2012. (Illus.). 38p. 29.95 (978-1-4626-9863-9(8)) America Star Bks.

Smith, Yeardley. I, Lorelei. 2009. 352p. (J). (gr. 3-7). lib. bdg. 17.89 (978-0-06-149345-4(7), Geringer, Laura Book) HarperCollins Pubs.

Snyder, Zilpha Keatley. The Witches of Worm. 2009. 9.00 (978-0-7848-3612-5(4), Everbind) Marco Bk. Co.

—The Witches of Worm. Raible, Alton, illus. 2009. (ENG.). (J). (gr. 3-7). 192p. 16.99 (978-1-4169-9531-9(5)); 208p. pap. 7.99 (978-1-4169-9053-6(4)) Simon & Schuster Children's Publishing. (Atheneum Bks. for Young Readers).

—The Witches of Worm. 2006. 22.75 (978-0-8446-7290-8(4)) Smith, Peter Pub., Inc.

Soderberg, Erin. Catnapped! 2016. (Puppy Pirates Ser.). (ENG., Illus.). 96p. (J). (gr. 1-4). lib. bdg. 12.99 (978-0-553-51174-1(2), Random Hse. Bks. for Young Readers) Random Hse. Children's Bks.

—Puppy Pirates #5: Search for the Sea Monster. 2016. (Puppy Pirates Ser.). (ENG., Illus.). 96p. (J). (gr. 1-4). 4.99 (978-1-101-93776-1(9), Random Hse. Bks. for Young Readers) Random Hse. Children's Bks.

Soenen, Chantal. Sally: And the Wheel of the Year. 2012. (Illus.). 124p. (gr. 4-6). 27.45 (978-1-4772-3038-1(6)); pap. 15.18 (978-1-4772-3037-4(8)) AuthorHouse.

Sokol, Dawn DeVries. Here, Kitty Kitty, 1 vol. 2017. (ENG., Illus.). 22p. bds. 9.99 (978-1-4236-4704-1(1)) Gibbs Smith, Publisher.

Sommer, Carl. If Only I Were. . . 2003. (Another Sommer-Time Story Ser.). (Illus.). 48p. (J). (gr. 1-4). 16.95 incl. audio (978-1-57537-551-9(6)) Advance Publishing, Inc.

—If Only I Were. . . James, Kennon, illus. 2003. (Another Sommer-Time Story Ser.). (ENG.). 48p. (J). 16.95 incl. audio compact disk (978-1-57537-502-1(8)) Advance Publishing, Inc.

Song, Mika. Tea with Oliver. Song, Mika, illus. 2017. (Illus.). 40p. (J). (gr. -1-3). 17.99 **(978-0-06-242948-3(5))** HarperCollins Pubs.

Sonneborn, Scott. Attack of the Invisible Cats, 1 vol. Baltazar, Art, illus. 2011. (DC Super-Pets Ser.). (ENG.). 56p. (gr. 2-2). pap. 4.95 (978-1-4048-6847-2(X)); lib. bdg. 23.99 (978-1-4048-6481-8(4)) Picture Window Bks. (DC Super-Pets).

Soto, Gary. Chato & the Party Animals. Guevara, Susan, illus. (Chato Ser.). 28.95 incl. audio compact disk (978-1-59112-920-2(6)); 25.95 incl. audio (978-1-59112-460-3(3)); 25.95 incl. audio (978-1-59112-460-3(3)); pap. 37.95 incl. audio (978-1-59112-461-0(1)); pap. 39.95 incl. audio compact disk (978-1-59112-921-9(4)); pap. 37.95 incl. audio (978-1-59112-461-0(1)); pap. 39.95 incl. audio compact disk (978-1-59112-921-9(4)) Live Oak Media.

—Chato & the Party Animals. Guevara, Susan, illus. 2004. (Chato Ser.). (ENG.). 32p. (J). (gr. -1-3). reprint ed. pap. 7.99 (978-0-14-240032-6(7), Puffin Books) Penguin Young Readers Group.

—Chato & the Party Animals. Guevara, Susan, illus. 2004. (Chato Ser.). (gr. -1-3). 17.00 *(978-0-7569-2921-3(0))* Perfection Learning Corp.
—Chato Goes Cruisin' Guevara, Susan, illus. 2008. (Chato Ser.). (J). 25.95 incl. audio *(978-1-59519-906-5(3))*; pap. 16.95 *(978-1-59519-905-8(5))* Live Oak Media.
—Chato's Kitchen. Guevara, Susan, illus. 2003. (Chato Ser.). (J). (gr. -1-2). pap. 39.95 *(978-1-59112-527-3(8))* Live Oak Media.
Spedding, Steven. Boriscat & the Quest for the Golden Carp. 2010. 136p. pap. 10.99 *(978-1-4520-5759-0(1))* AuthorHouse.
Spellmeyer, William. Ick-N-Pog: The Encounter Book 2. 2012. 104p. (gr. 2-4). pap. 12.81 *(978-1-4251-9237-2(8))* Trafford Publishing.
Spencer, Debbie. Monty & His Amazing Adventures at Christmas. 2015. (ENG.). 25p. (J). (gr. 2-3). mass mkt. 13.95 *(978-1-78554-708-9(9)*, c404417d-e519-44a9-b243-445d307c70e4) Austin, Stan AUS. Dist: Bookmasters Distribution.
Spicer, Lin. Faerie Baby. 2006. 148p. pap. 13.50 *(978-1-84426-384-4(3))* Upfront Publishing Ltd. GBR. Dist: Printondemand-worldwide.com.
Spinelli, Eileen. Do You Have a Cat? Valério, Geraldo, illus. 2010. (ENG.). 32p. (J). (gr. -1-3). 16.00 *(978-0-8028-5351-6(X)*, Eerdmans Bks For Young Readers) Eerdmans, William B. Publishing Co.
—Hero Cat, 0 vols. Stammen, Jo Ellen McAllister, illus. 2011. (ENG.). 32p. (J). (gr. -1-3). pap. 9.99 *(978-0-7614-5837-1(9)*, 9780761458371, Amazon Children's Publishing) Amazon Publishing.
Spires, Ashley. Binky: License to Scratch. Spires, Ashley, illus. 2013. (Binky Adventure Ser.). (ENG., Illus.). 64p. (J). (gr. 2-5). pap. 7.95 *(978-1-55453-964-2(1))* Kids Can Pr., Ltd. CAN. Dist: Hachette Bk. Group.
—Binky Takes Charge. Spires, Ashley, illus. 2012. (Binky Adventure Ser.: 4). (ENG., Illus.). 64p. (J). (gr. 2-5). 7.95 *(978-1-55453-768-6(1))*; 16.95 *(978-1-55453-703-7(7))* Kids Can Pr., Ltd. CAN. Dist: Hachette Bk. Group.
—Binky the Space Cat. Spires, Ashley, illus. 2009. (Binky Adventure Ser.). (ENG., Illus.). 64p. (J). (gr. 2-5). 16.95 *(978-1-55453-309-1(0))* Kids Can Pr., Ltd. CAN. Dist: Hachette Bk. Group.
—Binky to the Rescue. Spires, Ashley, illus. 2010. (Binky Adventure Ser.). (ENG., Illus.). 64p. (J). (gr. 2-5). 7.95 *(978-1-55453-597-2(2))* Kids Can Pr., Ltd. CAN. Dist: Hachette Bk. Group.
Spradlin, Joe. Sugar. 2007. 48p. per. 14.95 *(978-1-4327-0200-7(9))* Outskirts Pr., Inc.
Sprague, Howard Lee. Snowflake's Vacation. Borrajero, Judy, illus. 2011. 40p. pap. 9.95 *(978-1-881276-16-6(3))* Serey/Jones Pubs.
Spurgeon, S. The Great Kitten Mystery. 2008. 73p. pap. 19.95 *(978-1-60610-798-0(4))* America Star Bks.
Square Cat ABC. 2014. (ENG., Illus.). 32p. (J). (gr. -1-3). 15.99 *(978-1-4424-9895-2(1)*, Aladdin) Simon & Schuster Children's Publishing.
St. John, Patricia. Friska My Friend & the Other Kitten. 2003. (Illus.). 192p. 6.49 *(978-1-85999-312-5(5))* Scripture Union GBR. Dist: Gabriel Resources.
Stadler, John. Catilda. Stadler, John, illus. 2010. (ENG., Illus.). 32p. (J). (gr. -1-k). 16.99 *(978-1-4424-2939-0(9)*, Atheneum Bks. for Young Readers) Simon & Schuster Children's Publishing.
—The Cats of Mrs. Calamari, 1 vol. 2011. (ENG., Illus.). 32p. (J). pap. 6.95 *(978-1-59572-257-7(2))* Star Bright Bks., Inc.
Stafford, Jean. Elephi: The Cat with the High IQ. Blegvad, Erik, illus. 2017. (ENG.). 80p. (gr. 1-3). pap. 6.95 *(978-0-486-81426-1(2))* Dover Pubns., Inc.
Stafford, Jean & Van Draanen, Wendelin. Villain's Lair. Blegvad, Erik & Gilpin, Stephen, illus. 2011. (Gecko & Sticky Ser.: Bk. 2). (ENG.). 208p. (J). (gr. 3-7). pap. 7.99 *(978-0-440-42242-6(6)*, Yearling) Random Hse. Children's Bks.
Stahl, Mary L. Accumulating Cats. (Illus.). 56p. (J). (gr. k-6). *(978-1-886075-09-2(3))* Grass Root Enterprises.
Stainton, Sue. The Chocolate Cat. Mortimer, Anne, illus. 2007. 32p. (J). (gr. -1-3). 17.89 *(978-0-06-057246-4(9))* HarperCollins Pubs.
—The Lighthouse Cat. Mortimer, Anne, illus. 2004. (ENG.). 32p. (J). (gr. -1-2). 16.99 *(978-0-06-009604-5(7)*, Tegen, Katherine Bks) HarperCollins Pubs.
Staman, A. Louise. Rupert & the Bag. Adams, Rich, illus. 2006. (J). 11.99 *(978-0-9787263-0-0(8))* Tiger Iron Pr.
Stampler, Ann Redisch. The Cats on Ben Yehuda Street. Carabelli, Francesca, illus. 2013. (Israel Ser.). (ENG.). 32p. (J). (gr. -1-2). 7.95 *(978-0-7613-8124-2(4))*; lib. bdg. 16.95 *(978-0-7613-8123-5(6))* Lerner Publishing Group. (Kar-Ben Publishing).
Stanek, Gerald. Sarah 'n' Dippity. Stanek, Joyce Huntington, illus. 2004. (ENG.). 28p. (J). 14.95 *(978-0-9747417-0-3(1))* Shiver Hill Bks.
Starling, Landa. If You Sleep with a Cat on Your Head. Formelio, Lorri, illus. 2008. 27p. pap. 24.95 *(978-1-60703-318-9(6))* America Star Bks.
Starobinets, Anna. Catlantis. Bugaeva, Jane, tr. from RUS. Klimowski, Andrzej, illus. 2016. (ENG.). 136p. (J). (gr. 3-7). 16.95 *(978-1-68137-000-2(X)*, NYR Children's Collection) New York Review of Bks., Inc., The.
Steffen, Tim & Thornton, Susan. The Adventures of Baby Cat in Cherry Grove: Home Sweet Home. 2006. (Illus.). (J). per. 15.00 *(978-0-9779518-0-2(4))* Cardinal Pr.
Steffen, Tim & Thornton, Susan Ann. The Adventures of Baby Cat in Cherry Grove: Finding Faith. Thornton, Susan Ann, illus. 2007. (Illus.). 50p. (J). per. 12.00 *(978-0-9779518-1-9(2))* Cardinal Pr.
—The Golden Dragonfly: The Adventures of Baby Cat in Cherry Grove. Thornton, Susan Ann, illus. 2009. (Illus.). 76p. pap. 8.95 *(978-1-4401-4804-0(X))* iUniverse, Inc.
Stepanian, Isabel H. Cat Paws Through History: Ko-Ko the Cat Meets Napoleon Bonaparte. 2011. 292p. (gr. -1). 28.00 *(978-1-4389-5811-8(0))*; pap. 18.00 *(978-1-4389-5810-1(2))* AuthorHouse.
Stephens, Sarah Hines. Catwoman's Purrfect Plot. Vecchio, Luciano, illus. 2017. (Batman & Robin Adventures Ser.). (ENG.). 88p. (gr. 2-3). lib. bdg. 26.65 ***(978-1-4965-5349-2(7)***, DC Super Heroes) Stone Arch Bks.
—Sleepy Time Crime, 1 vol. Baltazar, Art, illus. 2012. (DC Super-Pets Ser.). (ENG.). 56p. (gr. 2-2). pap. 4.95 *(978-1-4048-7215-8(9))*; lib. bdg. 23.99 *(978-1-4048-6485-6(7))* Picture Window Bks. (DC Super-Pets).
—Superpowered Pony, 1 vol. Baltazar, Art, illus. 2011. (DC Super-Pets Ser.). (ENG.). 56p. (gr. 2-2). pap. 4.95 *(978-1-4048-6846-5(1))*; lib. bdg. 23.99 *(978-1-4048-6479-5(2))* Picture Window Bks. (DC Super-Pets).
Stephenson, Nancy. The Three Little Kittens. Faris, Eva, illus. l.t. ed. 2003. 30p. (J). per. 7.99 *(978-1-932338-13-3(6))* Lifevest Publishing, Inc.
Stephenson, Susan. Monster Maddie. Snider, K. C., illus. 2010. 20p. pap. 10.95 *(978-1-61633-027-9(9))* Guardian Angel Publishing, Inc.
Sterling Children's, Sterling, ed. Sleepy Kitty. 2015. (ENG., Illus.). 22p. (J). (— 1). bds. 6.95 *(978-1-4549-1464-8(5))* Sterling Publishing Co., Inc.
Stern, A. J. Doggy Day Care, 2 vols. Marts, Doreen Mulryan, illus. 2010. (Frankly, Frannie Ser.: 2). (ENG.). 128p. (J). (gr. 1-3). pap. 4.99 *(978-0-448-45350-7(9)*, Grosset & Dunlap) Penguin Young Readers Group.
Stern, Beth. Yoda: The Story of a Cat & His Kittens. Crane, Devin, illus. 2014. (ENG.). 32p. (J). (gr. -1-3). 17.99 *(978-1-4814-4407-1(7)*, Aladdin) Simon & Schuster Children's Publishing.
—Yoda Gets a Buddy. Crane, Devin, illus. 2015. (ENG.). 32p. (J). (gr. -1-3). 17.99 *(978-1-4814-6969-2(X)*, Aladdin) Simon & Schuster Children's Publishing.
Sternberg, Demetria. Hey, What's Going on down There? 2005. 23p. pap. 24.95 *(978-1-4137-3806-3(0))* PublishAmerica, Inc.
Stevens, Janet & Stevens Crummel, Susan. My Big Dog. Stevens, Janet, illus. 2009. (Golden Classic Ser.). (ENG., Illus.). 32p. (J). (gr. -1-2). pap. 7.99 *(978-0-375-85103-2(8)*, Dragonfly Bks.) Random Hse. Children's Bks.
Stevens, Jon Ellis. Old Softy & Angel, 1 vol. 2017. (Old Softy & Angel Ser.). (ENG.). 40p. (J). 34.99 *(978-1-4512-0551-0(1))* America Star Bks.
Stewart, Linda. The Great Catsby: A Sam the Cat Mystery. 2013. 4. (ENG.). 152p. (J). pap. 10.95 *(978-0-9675073-6-1(7))* Cheshire House Bks.
Stilton, Geronimo. Cat & Mouse in a Haunted House. 2004. (Geronimo Stilton Ser.: 3). (gr. 3-6). lib. bdg. 18.40 *(978-0-613-72224-7(8)*, Turtleback) Turtleback Bks.
—The Golden Statue Plot. 2013. (ENG.). 128p. (J). (gr. 2-5). pap. 7.99 *(978-0-545-55629-3(5)*, Scholastic Paperbacks) Scholastic, Inc.
Stine, R. L. Claws! 2011. (Goosebumps Hall of Horrors Ser.: 1). (ENG.). 160p. (J). (gr. 3-7). pap. 6.99 *(978-0-545-28933-7(5)*, Scholastic Paperbacks) Scholastic, Inc.
—Night of the Werecat. 2011. (R. L. Stine's Ghosts of Fear Street Ser.). (ENG.). 128p. (J). (gr. 3-7). pap. 4.99 *(978-1-4424-2698-6(5)*, Aladdin) Simon & Schuster Children's Publishing.
Stinson, June. Yellow Kitty Rags. 2013. 24p. pap. 24.95 *(978-1-4626-8191-4(3))* America Star Bks.
Stockham, Jess, illus. Puss in Boots. 2012. (Classic Fairy Tales Ser.). (ENG.). 24p. (J). *(978-1-84643-441-9(6))* Child's Play International Ltd.
Stokes, Carolyn Ashe. Multy: The Search to Belong . . . a Story of Hope. 2003. pap. 9.00 *(978-0-8059-5679-5(4))* Dorrance Publishing Co., Inc.
Storer, June. Kip, Brenda & Emong's Adventure. 2013. 164p. pap. *(978-0-9923603-1-3(5))* BWM Bks.
Stower, Adam. Naughty Kitty! Stower, Adam, illus. 2014. (ENG., Illus.). 40p. (J). (gr. -1-k). 16.99 *(978-0-545-57604-8(0)*, Orchard Bks.) Scholastic, Inc.
Strange, Jason. Strays, 1 vol. Evergreen, Nelson & Kendall, Bradford, illus. 2012. (Jason Strange Ser.). (ENG.). 72p. (gr. 2-3). pap. 6.25 *(978-1-4342-3883-2(0))*; lib. bdg. 25.32 *(978-1-4342-3295-3(6))* Stone Arch Bks.
Strong, Frances Dinkins. Pat, the Cat. Lee, Linda, illus. 2003. 24p. (J). pap. *(978-0-9720267-1-0(1))* Learning Abilities Bks.
Stuart, Lisa Marie. The Little Cat, the Wonderful Witch, & the Clever Mouse. Potter, Lori, illus. 2008. 60p. pap. 21.95 *(978-1-59858-691-6(2))* Dog Ear Publishing, LLC.
Stuart, Wrigley. Who'd Have Thunk It? 2014. (Amazing World of Gumball Ser.). (ENG., Illus.). 208p. (J). (gr. 3-7). pap. 9.99 *(978-0-8431-8106-7(0)*, Price Stern Sloan) Penguin Young Readers Group.
Studer, Diana. The Tabby's Gift. 2009. 24p. pap. 12.55 *(978-1-4389-5582-7(0))* AuthorHouse.
Stutson, Caroline. Cats' Night Out. Klassen, Jon, illus. 2010. (ENG.). 32p. (J). (gr. -1-3). 17.99 *(978-1-4169-4005-0(7)*, Simon & Schuster/Paula Wiseman Bks.) Simon & Schuster/Paula Wiseman Bks.
Su, Lucy. Make a Picnic. Su, Lucy, illus. 2003. (Kitten & Baby Kitten Ser.). (Illus.). 32p. (YA). *(978-1-85602-445-7(8)*, Pavilion Children's Books) Pavilion Bks.
—Make Cards. Su, Lucy, illus. 2003. (Kitten & Baby Kitten Ser.). (Illus.). 32p. (YA). *(978-1-85602-446-4(6)*, Pavilion Children's Books) Pavilion Bks.
—Play Dressing Up. Su, Lucy, illus. 2003. (Kitten & Baby Kitten Ser.). (Illus.). 24p. (J). bds. *(978-1-85602-463-1(6)*, Pavilion Children's Books) Pavilion Bks.
—Play Hide & Seek. Su, Lucy, illus. 2003. (Kitten & Baby Kitten Ser.). (Illus.). 42p. (J). pap. *(978-1-85602-538-6(1)*, Pavilion Children's Books) Pavilion Bks.
—Say Good Morning. Su, Lucy, illus. 2003. (Kitten & Baby Kitten Ser.). (Illus.). 42p. (J). bds. *(978-1-85602-466-2(0)*, Pavilion Children's Books) Pavilion Bks.
—Say Good Night. Su, Lucy, illus. 2003. (Kitten & Baby Kitten Ser.). (Illus.). 42p. (J). bds. *(978-1-85602-537-9(3)*, Pavilion Children's Books) Pavilion Bks.
Suchowacki, William. The Adventures of Maggie & Mikey. 2013. 20p. pap. 10.99 *(978-1-4582-1113-2(4)*, Abbott Pr.) Author Solutions, Inc.
Suedkamp, Shirley M. The Cat Who Lost His Meow. 2013. 16p. pap. 12.99 *(978-1-62839-466-5(8))* Salem Author Services.
Suggs, Dona. The Adventures of Ms Dee & Misti the Kitten. 2010. 19p. pap. 13.95 *(978-1-4327-6514-9(0))* Outskirts Pr., Inc.
Surovec, Yasmine. A Bed for Kitty. Surovec, Yasmine, illus. 2014. (ENG., Illus.). 40p. (J). (gr. -1-1). 16.99 *(978-1-59643-863-7(0)*, 9781596438637) Roaring Brook Pr.
—My Pet Human. 2015. (My Pet Human Ser.). (ENG., Illus.). 112p. (J). (gr. 1-5). 13.99 *(978-1-62672-073-2(8)*, 9781626720732) Roaring Brook Pr.
Suzuki, Genevieve A. The Original Poi Cats on Oahu. 2005. 40p. 13.95 *(978-1-56647-718-5(2))* Mutual Publishing LLC.
Sweeny, Vell. Second Hand Cat. Sweeny, Elizabeth Mifflin, illus. 2013. (ENG.). 48p. (J). (gr. -1-6). 14.95 *(978-0-9816360-2-3(0))* Pink Pig Pr.
Sykes, Julie. Bella at the Ball. Morgan, Richard, illus. 2014. 119p. (J). pap. *(978-0-545-69221-2(0))* Scholastic, Inc.
Talbott, Hudson. It's All about Me-Ow. Talbott, Hudson, illus. 2012. (ENG., Illus.). 32p. (J). (gr. -1-2). 16.99 *(978-0-399-25403-1(X)*, Nancy Paulsen Books) Penguin Young Readers Group.
Tapley-Milton, Katherine. The Adventures of Sir Lancelot the Cat. 2013. 16p. pap. 7.99 *(978-1-4497-8838-4(6)*, WestBow Pr.) Author Solutions, Inc.
Tarter, Mildred. Alexis Sets up Search Groups. 2013. 26p. pap. 16.49 *(978-1-4389-6881-0(7))* AuthorHouse.
Tattum, Stephan. The Mad Cat. 2nd ed. 2005. (J). 4.95 *(978-1-59792-001-8(0))* F.A.S.T. Learning LLC.
Tavener, Carys. The Adventures of T. C & Friends. 2011. (Illus.). 132p. pap. 38.72 *(978-1-4567-7096-9(9))* AuthorHouse.
Taylor, Celestine. Just Another Life. 2004. (Illus.). 88p. pap. *(978-1-84401-051-6(1))* Athena Pr.
Taylor, Di. Lost Kitten. 2010. (ENG., Illus.). 20p. 4.81 *(978-0-19-440086-2(7))* Oxford Univ. Pr., Inc.
Teague, Mark. Detective LaRue: Letters from the Investigation. Teague, Mark, illus. 2004. (LaRue Bks.). (ENG., Illus.). 32p. (J). (gr. -1-3). 17.99 *(978-0-439-45868-9(4)*, Scholastic Pr.) Scholastic, Inc.
Teckentrup, Britta. Grumpy Cat. 2013. (ENG., Illus.). 26p. (J). (— 1). bds. 6.95 *(978-1-907967-48-1(6))* Boxer Bks., Ltd. GBR. Dist: Sterling Publishing Co., Inc.
Ted in a Red Bed Kid Kit. 2004. (Kid Kits Ser.). (Illus.). 10p. (J). bds. 9.95 *(978-1-58086-404-6(X))* EDC Publishing.
Teitelbaum, Michael. Garfield & the Santa Spy. Fentz, Mike, illus. 2004. 92p. (J). *(978-0-439-70543-1(6))* Scholastic, Inc.
Tenbeth, Kate. Burly & Grum & the Secret City. Jones, Rob, illus. 2012. 108p. pap. *(978-0-9572119-5-7(3))* Magic Toy Bks.
Terada, Junzo. Animal Friends: Barnyard Jamboree! 2017. (ENG., Illus.). 10p. (J). bds. 9.99 *(978-1-4521-5189-2(X))* Chronicle Bks. LLC.
Terango, Christine. Teddy's Surprise Adventure. 2011. 24p. 12.95 *(978-1-4567-4069-6(5))* AuthorHouse.
Ternes, Caroline. Will You Be My Friend? The Prancer & Button Story. 2010. 20p. 14.99 *(978-1-4490-7731-0(5))* AuthorHouse.
Testa, Joseph Anthony. Are Cat Ears Made of Chocolate? A Children's Rhyme. 2012. 28p. pap. 17.99 *(978-1-4772-7977-9(6))* AuthorHouse.
Testa, Susan L. Myra the House Cat & the Garbage Can Monster. 2011. 44p. pap. 24.95 *(978-1-4560-4887-7(2))* America Star Bks.
Theis, Patricia & Theis, Matthew. Clarabelle the Cat Loses Her Hair. Norhelm, Karen, illus. 2008. 24p. pap. 12.95 *(978-1-59858-865-1(6))* Dog Ear Publishing, LLC.
Thereza, Rowe & Rowe, Thereza. Mister Pip. 2016. (ENG., Illus.). 32p. (J). (gr. -1-k). 16.95 *(978-1-84976-382-0(8))* Tate Publishing, Ltd. GBR. Dist: Abrams, Inc.
Thieme-Baeseman, Rebecca. Miller: The Mostly Misunderstood Mischief-Maker Who Went Missing. Konecny, John, illus. 2012. 24p. pap. 9.99 *(978-1-937165-32-1(9))* Orange Hat Publishing.
Thiruppathi, Shanthi. The Tales of Tiggy & Tobias: Brotherly Love. 2012. 28p. 18.95 *(978-1-4575-1703-7(5))*; pap. 12.95 *(978-1-4575-1600-9(4))* Dog Ear Publishing, LLC.
Thomas, Jan. Here Comes the Big, Mean Dust Bunny! Thomas, Jan, illus. 2009. (ENG., Illus.). 40p. (J). (gr. -1-3). 15.99 *(978-1-4169-9150-2(6)*, Beach Lane Bks.) Beach Lane Bks.
—What Will Fat Cat Sit On? 2007. (ENG., Illus.). 40p. (J). (gr. -1-k). 12.95 *(978-0-15-206051-0(0))* Houghton Mifflin Harcourt Publishing Co.
Thomas, Linda. The Cats of Dogwood Lane: Daisy Finds a Home. 2009. 28p. pap. 15.00 *(978-1-4389-3831-8(4))* AuthorHouse.
Thomas Nelson. Playdate Pals Kitten Learns to Listen. 2016. (ENG.). 24p. (J). (gr. -1-7). pap. *(978-1-78598-479-2(9))* Make Believe Ideas.
—Posie the Kitten in Pink. 2016. (ENG., Illus.). 32p. (J). (gr. -1-7). pap. *(978-1-78598-142-5(0))* Make Believe Ideas.
Thomas, P. J. The Cloud & the Cat. 2012. 52p. pap. 24.95 *(978-1-4626-7211-0(6))* America Star Bks.
Thomas, Patricia. Mouse's Christmas Cookie, 0 vols. Nez, Jon, illus. 2013. (ENG.). 24p. (J). (gr. -1-2). 14.99 *(978-1-4778-4704-6(9)*, 9781477847046, Amazon Children's Publishing) Amazon Publishing.
Thomas, Shelley Moore. No, No, Kitten! Nichols, Lori, illus. 2015. (ENG.). 40p. (J). (gr. -1-2). 16.95 *(978-1-62091-631-5(2))* Boyds Mills Pr.
Thompson, Debra. The Crumb Snatchers. Dennis, Tammy D., illus. 2012. 24p. pap. 12.95 *(978-1-61493-037-2(6))* Peppertree Pr., The.
Thompson, Elissa. Tryin' Ryan. 2006. (J). 15.00 *(978-0-9787341-0-7(6))* Aidan's Butterfly Pubns.
Thompson, Kate. I'm Just a Little Kitten. Green, Barry, illus. 2016. (Googley-Eye Bks.). (ENG.). 12p. (J). (gr. -1-k). bds. 7.99 *(978-1-78445-861-4(9))* Top That! Publishing PLC GBR. Dist: Independent Pubs. Group.
Thompson, Patricia Parrott. Chocolate & Her Meow. 2003. pap. 12.00 *(978-0-8059-5774-7(X))* Dorrance Publishing Co., Inc.
Thomson, Pat. It's So Unfair! Allen, Jonathan, illus. 2007. (ENG.). 32p. (J). (gr. k-2). pap. 10.99 *(978-1-84270-594-0(6))* Andersen Pr. GBR. Dist: Independent Pubs. Group.
Thorneycroft, Berni. Nap Sack Cat Tales. 2009. 28p. pap. 13.99 *(978-1-4389-0298-2(0))* AuthorHouse.
Tillman, Nancy. Tumford the Terrible. Tillman, Nancy, illus. 2011. (Tumford Ser.). (ENG., Illus.). 32p. (J). (gr. -1-1). 16.99 *(978-0-312-36840-1(2)*, 9780312368401) Feiwel & Friends.
—Tumford's Rude Noises. Tillman, Nancy, illus. 2012. (Tumford Ser.). (ENG., Illus.). 32p. (J). (gr. -1-1). 16.99 *(978-0-312-36841-8(0)*, 9780312368418) Feiwel & Friends.
Timbers, James. Salmon & Fuzz in Helping a Friend. 2004. 30p. pap. 24.95 *(978-1-4137-2602-2(X))* PublishAmerica, Inc.
Timmy: Individual Title Six-Packs. (Literatura 2000 Ser.). (gr. 1-2). 28.00 *(978-0-7635-0067-2(4))* Rigby Education.
Tirado, Raquel. That Sticky Cat. 2012. 20p. pap. 17.99 *(978-1-4685-8857-6(5))* AuthorHouse.
Tirgari, Simin. Color of the Heart. 2011. 84p. pap. 8.95 *(978-1-4620-4966-0(4))* iUniverse, Inc.
Tisha Admire Duncan. My Dirty Cat Mutt. 2009. 28p. pap. 17.99 *(978-1-4389-5684-8(3))* AuthorHouse.
Titus, Eve. Anatole & the Cat. 2010. (ENG., Illus.). 32p. (J). (gr. k-3). pap. 7.99 *(978-0-375-85547-4(5)*, Dragonfly Bks.) Random Hse. Children's Bks.
—Basil & the Cave of Cats. Galdone, Paul, illus. 2016. (Great Mouse Detective Ser.: 2). (ENG.). 112p. (J). (gr. 1-4). pap. 5.99 *(978-1-4814-6404-8(3)*, Aladdin) Simon & Schuster Children's Publishing.
Tobin, Paul. How to Capture an Invisible Cat. 2017. (Genius Factor Ser.: 1). (J). lib. bdg. 18.40 ***(978-0-606-39596-0(2))*** Turtleback Bks.
Tocher, Timothy. Bill Pennant, Babe Ruth, & Me. 2009. (ENG.). 184p. (J). (gr. 3-7). 17.95 *(978-0-8126-2755-8(5))* Cricket Bks.
Todd, Ruthven. Space Cat. 2008. (J). (gr. k-4). 27.50 *(978-0-8446-6561-0(4))* Smith, Peter Pub., Inc.
Tofield, Simon, creator. Simon's Cat off to the Vet . . & Other Adventures. 2015. (ENG., Illus.). 240p. 27.95 *(978-1-61775-402-9(1))* Akashic Bks.
Toft, Julie. Blot on the Landscape. 2010. (Illus.). 48p. pap. 10.49 *(978-1-4490-6453-2(1))* AuthorHouse.
Tomaszewski, Suzanne Lyon. Samuel's Exeter Walkabout. Dionne, Nina, illus. 2003. 37p. (J). *(978-0-9744855-0-8(0))* Gold Charm Publishing, LLC.
Tomonari, Itsuko. The Adventures of Meow Meow & Friends. 2003. (Illus.). 82p. per. 15.95 *(978-1-59405-012-1(0))* New Age World Publishing.
Tomos, Angharad. Diwrnod Golchi. 2005. (WEL., Illus.). 48p. pap. *(978-0-86243-115-0(8))* Y Lolfa.
—Jam Poeth. 2005. (WEL., Illus.). 48p. pap. *(978-0-86243-145-7(X))* Y Lolfa.
—Mali Meipen. 6th ed. 2005. (WEL., Illus.). 48p. pap. *(978-0-86243-104-4(2))* Y Lolfa.
Tóth-Jones, Dee S. The Street Cats of Marrakech. Stevenson, Seline, illus. 2013. 34p. pap. *(978-1-908794-08-6(9))* Chiaroscuro Bks.
Townsend, Michael. Cute & Cuter. 2013. (ENG., Illus.). 40p. (J). (gr. k-3). lib. bdg. 18.99 *(978-0-375-95718-5(9)*, Knopf Bks. for Young Readers) Random Hse. Children's Bks.
Townsend, Tamela Ann. Finding Pumpkin, 1 vol. 2010. 48p. pap. 16.95 *(978-1-4489-5983-9(7))* America Star Bks.
Tracy, Louis. The Black Cat. 2011. 318p. 50.95 *(978-1-258-09467-6(3))* Literary Licensing, LLC.
Trafford, Adrienne. SPARK Cat & Dog Around the World Coloring Book. 2017. (Dover Coloring Bks.). (ENG.). 64p. (J). (gr. 1-4). pap. 5.99 *(978-0-486-81433-9(5))* Dover Pubns., Inc.
Trail, George. Moby & Family. 2009. 103p. pap. 20.95 *(978-0-9559927-0-4(2))* Trail, George GBR. Dist: Lulu Pr., Inc.
Travers, James A. Kitten & the Barn. 2008. 44p. pap. 24.95 *(978-1-4241-8771-3(0))* America Star Bks.
Trites, Judy. Charlie's Challenge. 2011. 24p. pap. 15.99 *(978-1-4628-4568-2(1))* Xlibris Corp.
Troyer, Gloria Irene. Beatrice & the Snow People. 2013. 114p. pap. 14.95 *(978-1-62646-481-0(2))* Booklocker.com, Inc.
Truesdell, Charlotte White. Steinway Kitty. 2010. 16p. 8.49 *(978-1-4490-5922-4(8))* AuthorHouse.
Tucker, Ellen. Cats in the Belfry. 2004. (YA). per. *(978-1-932496-21-5(1))* Penman Publishing, Inc.
Tucker, Sally A. Leo & Apollo: The Forbidden Land. 2012. 28p. pap. 15.00 *(978-1-105-60121-7(8))* Lulu Pr., Inc.
Tukan, Jaytoe Anthony, Sr. Kitty cat had a Dream: Kingdom without a King. 2005. (Illus.). 124p. (J). per. 19.95 *(978-0-9665909-7-5(X))* Kalawantis Publishing Services, Inc.
Tulani, K. Todd & Ricca: The Pepperoni Pizza. 2011. 24p. 11.32 *(978-1-4567-0188-8(6))* AuthorHouse.
Turner, Ann Warren. Pumpkin Cat. Bates, Amy, illus. 2004. (ENG.). 32p. (gr. -1-2). 15.99 *(978-0-7868-0494-8(7))* Hyperion Pr.
Turner, Dona. Ella Minnow Pea. Turner, Dona, illus. 2008. (ENG., Illus.). 32p. (J). *(978-1-59692-229-7(X))* MacAdam/Cage Publishing, Inc.
Turner, Dona & Dunn, Mark. Ella Minnow Pea. Turner, Dona & Brennan, Tim, illus. gif. ed. 2009. (ENG.). 225p. *(978-1-59692-299-0(0))* MacAdam/Cage Publishing, Inc.
Tuttle, Lucia. There's a Mouse in the House. 2008. 36p. pap. 19.99 *(978-1-4363-4000-7(4))* Xlibris Corp.
Tweedy, Bonnie. Grandma Bonnie's Cats: A Happy Place. 2009. 28p. pap. 12.98 *(978-1-4343-8793-6(3))* AuthorHouse.
Twisdale, Monica. Old Man Goes to Show & Tell. 2012. 24p. pap. 15.99 *(978-1-4797-1173-4(X))* Xlibris Corp.
The Two Foolish Cats: Individual Title Six-Packs. (Literatura 2000 Ser.). (gr. 2-3). 33.00 *(978-0-7635-0190-7(5))* Rigby Education.
Tylicki, Gene J. & Tylicki, Jo. Lonesome George: The First Three Weeks, 1 vol. 2009. 16p. pap. 24.95 *(978-1-60749-330-3(6))* America Star Bks.
—More Cat Tails As Told by George to Guy: A Lonesome George Work. 2013. 36p. pap. 24.95 *(978-1-63004-047-5(9))* America Star Bks.
—The Saga Continues As Told by George to Guy: A Lonesome George Work. 2011. 36p. pap. 24.95 *(978-1-4560-5068-9(0))* America Star Bks.
Typaldos, Melanie. Celeste & the Adorable Kitten. Tayts, Alexandra, illus. 2013. 244p. 14.99 *(978-0-9899847-0-6(2))* Capybara Madness.
Ulkutay Design Group Staff & Random House Children's Books Staff, contrib. by. My Book of Kittens. 2016. (Illus.). (J). *(978-0-8066-9710-2(9)*, Golden Bks.) Random Hse. Children's Bks.
Underwood, Deborah. Here Comes Teacher Cat. Rueda, Claudia, illus. 2017. (ENG.). 88p. (J). (-k). 16.99

(978-0-399-53905-3(0), Dial Bks) Penguin Young Readers Group.
—Here Comes the Easter Cat. Rueda, Claudia, illus. 2014. (ENG.). 80p. (J). (gr. -1-k). 16.99 (978-0-8037-3939-0(7), Dial Bks) Penguin Publishing Group.
—Here Comes the Tooth Fairy Cat. Rueda, Claudia, illus. 2015. (ENG.). 96p. (J). (gr. -1-k). 16.99 (978-0-525-42774-2(0), Dial Bks) Penguin Young Readers Group.
—Here Comes Valentine Cat. Rueda, Claudia, illus. 2015. (ENG.). 88p. (J). (-k). 16.99 (978-0-525-42915-9(8), Dial Bks) Penguin Young Readers Group.
Universal Dreamworks Pictures Staff & Greenberg, James. Cat in the Hat. 2003. (ENG., Illus.). 128p. pap. 12.95 (978-1-57243-609-1(3), 53846352) Triumph Bks.
Unser, Virginia. The Night Before Cat-Mas. Anagost, Karen, illus. 2007. (Petite Plush Kit Ser.). 64p. (J). (gr. -1-3). 9.95 (978-1-59359-882-2(3)) Peter Pauper Pr. Inc.
Untermeyer, Louis. One & One & One. Jones, Robert, illus. 2016. (ENG.). 64p. (gr. k-3). pap. 9.99 (978-0-486-81065-2(8)) Dover Pubns., Inc.
Ure, Jean. Ice Lolly. 2010. (ENG., Illus.). 208p. (J). (gr. 4-7). 9.99 (978-0-00-728173-2(0), HarperCollins Children's Bks.) HarperCollins Pubs. Ltd. GBR. Dist: HarperCollins Pubs.
Valko, Danna. Dee & Maya Are Best Friends. 2013. (Illus.). (978-1-62563-112-1(X)); (978-1-62510-726-8(9)) Tate Publishing, Ltd.
Van Draanen, Wendelin. Sammy Keyes & the Psycho Kitty Queen. 2008. (Sammy Keyes Ser.: Bk. 9). (J). 64.99 (978-1-60640-643-4(4)) Findaway World, LLC.
—Sammy Keyes & the Psycho Kitty Queen. 2006. (Sammy Keyes Ser.: Bk. 9). (J). pap. 36.95 incl. audio (978-1-59519-774-0(5)); pap. 54.95 incl. audio compact disk (978-1-59519-775-7(3)) Live Oak Media.
—Sammy Keyes & the Psycho Kitty Queen. 2006. (Sammy Keyes Ser.: 9). (ENG., Illus.). 320p. (J). (gr. 5-7). 7.99 (978-0-440-41910-5(7), Yearling) Random Hse. Children's Bks.
Van Fleet, Matthew. Cat. Stanton, Brian, photos by. 2009. (ENG., Illus.). 20p. (J). (gr. -1-2). 18.99 (978-1-4169-7800-8(3), Simon & Schuster/Paula Wiseman Bks.) Simon & Schuster/Paula Wiseman Bks.
Vaniko, K. L. Why the Dog Chases the Cat & the Cat Chases the Mouse. 2006. 189p. 30.99 (978-1-59926-863-7(9)) Xlibris Corp.
Vant, Jeanie. The Witch's Cat. Vant, Tim, illus. 2010. 24p. pap. 11.50 (978-1-60976-051-9(4), Eloquent Bks.) Strategic Book Publishing & Rights Agency (SBPRA).
Velasquez, Crystal. The Circle of Lies. 2016. (Hunters of Chaos Ser.: 2). (ENG., Illus.). 240p. (J). (gr. 3-7). pap. 7.99 (978-1-4814-2456-1(4), Aladdin) Simon & Schuster Children's Publishing.
Veldkamp, Debby. Quake! Six Point Five: The Cat Survived. Van Den Berg, Helen, illus. 2004. (J). lib. bdg. 16.95 (978-1-930401-25-9(6)) Central Coast Bks./Pr.
Ventura, Antonio. Lucas y el Ruisenor. Angela-Lago, illus. 2005. (SPA.). 24p. (J). (gr. 1-3). pap., pap. 6.99 (978-980-257-285-4(3)) Ekare, Ediciones VEN. Dist: Lectorum Pubns., Inc.
Verde, Susan. You & Me. Reynolds, Peter H., illus. 2015. (ENG.). 32p. (J). (gr. k-2). 14.95 (978-1-4197-1197-8(0), Abrams Bks. for Young Readers) Abrams, Inc.
Vere, Ed. Max at Night. 2016. (Max Ser.: 2). (ENG.). 32p. (J). (-2). 16.99 (978-1-4926-3296-2(1), 9781492632962, Sourcebooks Jabberwocky) Sourcebooks, Inc.
—Max el Valiente. 2014. (SPA.). 36p. (gr. k-2). 20.99 (978-84-261-4071-5(8)) Juventud, Editorial ESP. Dist: Lectorum Pubns., Inc.
Vere, Ed. Max the Brave. (ENG.). (J). 2017. 30p. bds. 7.99 **(978-1-4926-5706-4(9))** 2015. (Max Ser.: 1). 32p. 16.99 (978-1-4926-1651-1(6), 9781492616511) Sourcebooks, Inc. (Sourcebooks Jabberwocky).
Villar Liébana, Luisa. El Misterio de la Gata Maga. 2005. (Investigator Big Ears Ser.). (SPA., Illus.). 72p. (J). (gr. 2-3). 8.95 (978-84-348-9423-5(8)) SM Ediciones ESP. Dist: Iaconi, Mariuccia Bk. Imports.
Villiers, Alan. Joey Goes to Sea. Dowling, Victor J., illus. 2005. (Maritime Ser.). (ENG.). 70p. (J). (gr. 4-7). pap. 9.95 (978-0-939511-10-5(X)) Mystic Seaport Museum, Inc.
Vincenza. My Name Is Mollie. 2009. 36p. pap. 16.99 (978-1-4389-5160-7(4)) AuthorHouse.
Viscardi, Dolly. All Around Cats, Brooks, David, illus. 2004. (ENG.). 32p. (J). (gr. k-3). 15.95 (978-1-55971-072-5(1)) Cooper Square Publishing Llc.
Vischer, Frans. Fuddles. Vischer, Frans, illus. 2011. (ENG., Illus.). 32p. (J). (gr. -1-2). 17.99 (978-1-4169-9155-7(7), Aladdin) Simon & Schuster Children's Publishing.
—Fuddles & Puddles. Vischer, Frans, illus. 2016. (ENG., Illus.). 32p. (J). (gr. -1-3). 17.99 (978-1-4814-3839-1(5), Aladdin) Simon & Schuster Children's Publishing.
—A Very Fuddles Christmas. Vischer, Frans, illus. 2013. (ENG., Illus.). 32p. (J). (gr. -1-2). 15.99 (978-1-4169-9156-4(5), Aladdin) Simon & Schuster Children's Publishing.
Voigt, Cynthia. Young Fredle. Yates, Louise, illus. 2011. (ENG.). 240p. (J). (gr. 3-7). 16.99 (978-0-375-86457-5(1), Knopf Bks. for Young Readers) Random Hse. Children's Bks.
Volz, Carole A. Tiggy Finds a Home. Volz, Katie, illus. 2013. 44p. (J). 18.95 (978-1-62287-445-3(5)) First Edition Design eBook Publishing.
Von Buhler, Cynthia. But Who Will Bell the Cats? Von Buhler, Cynthia, illus. 2009. (ENG., Illus.). 32p. (J). (gr. -1-3). 17.00 (978-0-618-99718-3(0)) Houghton Mifflin Harcourt Publishing Co.
Von Kanel, Liz. The Search for Cuddles & Jonathan's Dream. 2012. 40p. pap. (978-1-77097-158-5(0)) FriesenPress.
Wade, Barbara. Smokey Gets His Christmas Wish. 2010. (Illus.). 24p. pap. 12.99 (978-1-4520-0164-7(2)) AuthorHouse.
Wade, Taylor. The Magical Well. 2008. 33p. pap. 12.95 (978-1-4357-5175-0(2)) Lulu Pr., Inc.
Wagner, Fiona. The Little Cat. 2005. 15p. (J). 9.99 (978-1-4116-5568-3(0)) Lulu Pr., Inc.
Walker, Landry Q. Secret Entity! #4, 1 vol. Jones, Eric, illus. 2013. (Supergirl: Cosmic Adventures in the 8th Grade Ser.). (ENG.). 32p. (gr. 2-3). 22.60 (978-1-4342-4720-9(1)) Stone Arch Bks.
Walko. Amigos: Friends Forever. 2012. (ENG., Illus.). 28p. (J). (gr. -1-k). 16.95 (978-1-61608-388-5(3), 608388, Sky Pony Pr.) Skyhorse Publishing Co., Inc.
Wallace, Bill. Goosed! Rogers, Jacqueline, illus. 2004. (ENG.). 128p. (J). (gr. 2-4). pap. 6.99 (978-0-689-86681-4(X), Aladdin) Simon & Schuster Children's Publishing.
—Snot Stew. McCue, Lisa, illus. 2nd ed. 2008. (ENG.). 96p. (J). (gr. 3-7). pap. 6.99 (978-1-4169-5804-8(5), Aladdin) Simon & Schuster Children's Publishing.
—Totally Disgusting! Morrill, Leslie, illus. 2008. (ENG.). 144p. (J). (gr. 3-7). pap. 5.99 (978-1-4169-5805-5(3), Simon & Schuster/Paula Wiseman Bks.) Simon & Schuster/Paula Wiseman Bks.
Wallace, Daniel. The Cat's Pajamas. 2014. (ENG., Illus.). 32p. (J). (gr. -1-3). 18.00 (978-1-941758-00-7(2)) Inkshares.
Wallace, Karen. Detective Derek. Blake, Beccy, illus. 2009. (Go! Readers Ser.). 48p. (J). (gr. 2-5). pap. 12.85 (978-1-60754-276-6(5)); lib. bdg. 29.25 (978-1-60754-275-9(7)) Windmill Bks.
Wallace, Nancy K. The Christmas Cats, 1 vol. Housley, Cathren, illus. 2011. (ENG.). 32p. (J). (gr. k-3). 16.99 (978-1-58980-979-6(3)) Pelican Publishing Co., Inc.
Walls, Sarah. Christmas Kitten: Special Delivery. 2010. 20p. 10.49 (978-1-4490-9750-9(2)) AuthorHouse.
Walsh, Franny. Who Cat: A Louisiana Tale. 2013. (ENG.). 32p. (J). pap. 16.95 (978-1-4787-0280-1(X)) Outskirts Pr., Inc.
Walter, Judy S. The Grey & White Stranger. 2012. 96p. pap. 9.95 (978-0-578-10299-3(4)) Sluser Publishing.
Walters, Eric. Hunter, 1 vol. 2012. (ENG.). 208p. (J). (gr. 4-7). pap. 9.95 (978-1-4598-0157-8(1)) Orca Bk. Pubs. USA.
Wang, Michael. A Stray. 2016. (ENG.). 40p. 10.00 (978-981-4751-30-8(8)) Marshall Cavendish International (Asia) Private Ltd. SGP. Dist: National Bk. Network.
Ward, B. J. Farty Marty. Kellogg, Steven, illus. 2013. (ENG.). 32p. (J). (gr. -1-3). 16.99 (978-1-4424-3901-6(7), Simon & Schuster Bks. For Young Readers) Simon & Schuster Bks. For Young Readers.
Ward, Cindy. Cookie's Week. dePaola, Tomie, illus. 2015. 32p. pap. 7.00 (978-1-61003-528-6(3)) Center for the Collaborative Classroom.
Ward, Greta. Pinkie the Cat Gets a Baby Sister. 2007. (Illus.). 44p. (J). pap. 9.95 (978-0-9798346-0-8(0)) P.M. Publishing.
Wardlaw, Lee. Won Ton: A Cat Tale Told in Haiku. Yelchin, Eugene, illus. 2011. (ENG.). 40p. (J). (gr. -1-3). 17.99 (978-0-8050-8995-0(0), 9780805089950, Holt, Henry & Co. Bks. For Young Readers) Holt, Henry & Co.
—Won Ton & Chopstick. Yelchin, Eugene, illus. 2015. (ENG.). 40p. (J). (gr. -1-3). 17.99 (978-0-8050-9987-4(5), 9780805099874, Holt, Henry & Co. Bks. For Young Readers) Holt, Henry & Co.
Warhola, James. Uncle Andy's Cats. Warhola, James, illus. 2009. (ENG., Illus.). 32p. (J). (gr. k-3). 16.99 (978-0-399-25180-1(4), G.P. Putnam's Sons Books for Young Readers) Penguin Young Readers Group.
Waring, Geoff. Oscar & the Bat: A Book about Sound. Waring, Geoff, illus. 2009. (Start with Science Ser.). (ENG., Illus.). 32p. (J). (gr. -1-3). pap. 6.99 (978-0-7636-4513-7(3)) Candlewick Pr.
—Oscar & the Bird: A Book about Electricity. Waring, Geoff, illus. 2011. (Start with Science Ser.). (ENG., Illus.). 32p. (J). (gr. -1-3). pap. 6.99 (978-0-7636-5302-6(0)) Candlewick Pr.
—Oscar & the Cricket: A Book about Moving & Rolling. Waring, Geoff, illus. 2009. (Start with Science Ser.). (ENG., Illus.). 32p. (J). (gr. -1-3). pap. 6.99 (978-0-7636-4512-0(5)) Candlewick Pr.
—Oscar & the Frog: A Book about Growing. Waring, Geoff, illus. (Start with Science Ser.). (ENG., Illus.). 32p. (J). (gr. -1-3). 2008. pap. 6.99 (978-0-7636-4030-9(1)) 2007. 11.99 (978-0-7636-3558-9(8)) Candlewick Pr.
—Oscar & the Moth: A Book about Light & Dark. Waring, Geoff, illus. 2008. (Start with Science Ser.). (ENG., Illus.). 32p. (J). (gr. -1-3). pap. 6.99 (978-0-7636-4031-6(X)) Candlewick Pr.
—Oscar & the Snail: A Book about Things That We Use. Waring, Geoff, illus. (Start with Science Ser.). (ENG., Illus.). 32p. (J). (gr. -1-3). 2011. pap. 6.99 (978-0-7636-5303-3(9)) 2009. 14.99 (978-0-7636-4039-2(5)) Candlewick Pr.
Warner, Emilia & Garland, Peter. Micia. 2007. (ENG.). 56p. 20.25 (978-1-905299-39-3(7), Stacey International) Stacey Publishing GBR. Dist: Casemate Pubs. & Bk. Distributors, LLC.
Warner, Gertrude Chandler, creator. The Celebrity Cat Caper. 2016. (Boxcar Children Mysteries Ser.: 143). (ENG., Illus.). 128p. (J). (gr. 1-5). 15.99 (978-0-8075-0711-7(3)) Whitman, Albert & Co.
Warner, Jodi. Shia's Tail 2. 2012. 24p. pap. 10.95 (978-1-4624-0369-1(7), Inspiring Voices) Author Solutions, Inc.
Waters, Michael. Dumdickle & Tweedy: A Tail of Two Cats. 2006. 16p. (J). 10.30 (978-1-4116-6734-1(4)) Lulu Pr., Inc.
—Tommy & his Flying Saucer of Milk. 2009. 32p. 18.95 (978-1-4092-8450-5(6)); pap. 16.95 (978-1-4357-4802-6(6)) Lulu Pr., Inc.
Watson, Jacqueline. Mattie-Jo-Calico. 2003. 109p. pap. 19.95 (978-1-59286-920-6(3)) America Star Bks.
Watson, Tom. Cats in the City. 2017. (Stick Cat Ser.: 2). 224p. (J). (gr. 3-7). 12.99 (978-0-06-241102-0(0)) HarperCollins Pubs.
—Stick Cat. 2016. (Stick Cat Ser.: 1). (Illus.). 208p. (J). (gr. 3-7). 12.99 (978-0-06-241100-6(4)) HarperCollins Pubs.
Watson, Tom. Stick Cat: Two Catch a Thief. Long, Ethan, illus. 2017. (Stick Cat Ser.: 3). 240p. (J). (gr. 3-7). 12.99 **(978-0-06-241104-4(7))** HarperCollins Pubs.
Watt, Fiona. That's Not My Kitten. Wells, Rachel, illus. rev. ed. 2006. (Touchy-Feely Board Bks.). 10p. (J). (gr. -1-k). bds. 7.99 (978-0-7945-1266-8(6), Usborne) EDC Publishing.
Watt, Mélanie. Chester. Watt, Mélanie, illus. (Chester Ser.). (ENG., Illus.). 32p. (J). (gr. -1-3). 2009. pap. 8.95 (978-1-55453-460-9(7)) 2007. 18.95 (978-1-55453-140-0(3)) Kids Can Pr., Ltd. CAN. Dist: Hachette Bk. Group.
—Chester's Back! Watt, Mélanie, illus. (Chester Ser.). (ENG., Illus.). 32p. (J). (gr. -1-3). 2013. 8.95 (978-1-55453-461-6(5)) 2008. 18.95 (978-1-55453-287-2(6)) Kids Can Pr., Ltd. CAN. Dist: Hachette Bk. Group.
—Chester's Masterpiece. Watt, Mélanie, illus. 2010. (Chester Ser.). (ENG., Illus.). 32p. (J). (gr. -1-3). 18.95 (978-1-55453-566-8(2)) Kids Can Pr., Ltd. CAN. Dist: Hachette Bk. Group.
Weaver, A. J. Big Cats, Little Cats. Budgen, Tim, illus. 2013. 32p. pap. (978-1-909423-03-9(3)) Bks. to Treasure.
Weaver, Jack W. Cat & Dog Breath Meet the Last Pirates: How to Fly a Basset Hound. 2012. 164p. 24.95 (978-1-4626-6652-2(3)) America Star Bks.
Webb, Holly. The Brave Kitten. Williams, Sophy, illus. 2016. (Pet Rescue Adventures Ser.). (ENG.). 128p. (J). (gr. 2-6). 4.99 (978-1-58925-480-0(5)) Tiger Tales.
—The Case of the Phantom Cat. Lindsay, Marion, illus. (Mysteries of Maisie Hitchins Ser.: 3). (ENG.). 176p. (J). (gr. 2-5). 2016. pap. 5.99 (978-0-544-81084-6(8)) 2015. 15.99 (978-0-544-58243-9(8)) Houghton Mifflin Harcourt Publishing Co. (HMH Books For Young Readers).
—Kitten Nobody Wanted. Williams, Sophy, illus. 2015. (Pet Rescue Adventures Ser.). (ENG.). 128p. (J). (gr. 2-6). lib. bdg. 19.99 (978-1-58925-182-3(2)) Tiger Tales.
—Lost in the Snow. Williams, Sophy, illus. 2008. 96p. (J). (gr. 1-5). 3.99 (978-1-56148-650-2(7), Good Bks.) Skyhorse Publishing Co., Inc.
—Lost in the Snow. Williams, Sophy, illus. 2015. (Pet Rescue Adventures Ser.). (ENG.). 128p. (J). (gr. 2-6). pap. 4.99 (978-1-58925-472-5(4)); lib. bdg. 19.99 (978-1-68010-004-4(1)) Tiger Tales.
—The Missing Kitten. Williams, Sophy, illus. 2016. (Pet Rescue Adventures Ser.). (ENG.). 128p. (J). (gr. 2-6). pap. 4.99 (978-1-58925-488-6(0)) Tiger Tales.
—Misty the Abandoned Kitten. Williams, Sophy, illus. 2016. (Pet Rescue Adventures Ser.). (ENG.). 128p. (J). (gr. 2-6). pap. 4.99 (978-1-58925-489-3(9)) Tiger Tales.
—Sammy the Shy Kitten. Williams, Sophy, illus. 2017. (Pet Rescue Adventures Ser.). (ENG.). 128p. (J). (gr. 2-6). 19.99 **(978-1-68010-050-1(5))** Tiger Tales.
—The Secret Kitten. Williams, Sophy, illus. 2017. (Pet Rescue Adventures Ser.). (ENG.). 128p. (J). (gr. 2-6). 19.99 **(978-1-68010-049-5(1))** Tiger Tales.
Webb, Holly. Sky the Unwanted Kitten. Williams, Sophy, illus. 2016. (Pet Rescue Adventures Ser.). (ENG.). 128p. (J). (gr. 2-6). 4.99 (978-1-58925-481-7(3)) Tiger Tales.
Webb, James, Jr. They Call Me Giz. 2012. 72p. pap. 28.99 (978-1-4772-3761-8(5)) AuthorHouse.
Webb, Melissa & Webb, Lexy. Zoe the Earless Kitten: Zoe Meets the Family. 2011. 40p. pap. 21.99 (978-1-4628-8462-9(8)) Xlibris Corp.
Webb, Steve. City Kitty Cat. Le Huche, Magali, illus. 2015. (ENG.). 32p. (J). (gr. -1-3). 17.99 (978-1-4814-4331-9(3), Simon & Schuster Bks. For Young Readers) Simon & Schuster Bks. For Young Readers.
Webster, Christy. Grumpy Cat Little Golden Book #2 (Grumpy Cat) Golden Books, illus. 2017. (Little Golden Book Ser.). (ENG.). 24p. (J). (gr. -1-1). 4.99 (978-0-399-55783-5(0), Golden Bks.) Random Hse. Children's Bks.
Weeks, Sarah. Glamourpuss. Small, David, illus. 2015. (ENG.). 40p. (J). (gr. -1-1). 16.99 (978-0-545-60954-8(2), Scholastic Pr.) Scholastic, Inc.
—Mac & Cheese. Manning, Jane K., illus. 2010. (I Can Read Level 1 Ser.). (ENG.). 32p. (J). (gr. -1-3). 16.99 (978-0-06-117079-9(8)); pap. 3.99 (978-0-06-117081-2(X)) HarperCollins Pubs.
—Mac & Cheese & the Perfect Plan. Manning, Jane, illus. 2012. 32p. (J). lib. bdg. 17.89 (978-0-06-117083-6(6)); (ENG.). 16.99 (978-0-06-117082-9(8)); (ENG.). pap. 3.99 (978-0-06-117084-3(4)) HarperCollins Pubs.
—Pie. 2011. (ENG.). 192p. (J). (gr. 4-7). 16.99 (978-0-545-27011-3(1), Scholastic Pr.) Scholastic, Inc.
Weiskal, N. j. & Weiskal, N. J. The Skittery Kitten & the Scaredy Cat. Weiskal, N. J., illus. 2009. (Illus.). 36p. pap. 8.00 (978-1-935125-59-4(1)) Robertson Publishing.
Weisner, David. Mr. Wuffles! Weisner, David, illus. 2013. (Illus.). 14.99 (978-0-9777098-8-5(4)); 49.99 (978-0-9777098-7-8(6)) Dreamscape Media, LLC.
Weiss, Ellen & Friedman, Mel. Porky & Bess. Winborn, Marsha, illus. 2011. (Step into Reading Ser.). (ENG.). 48p. (J). (gr. 2-4). pap. 3.99 (978-0-375-86113-0(0), Random Hse. Bks. for Young Readers) Random Hse. Children's Bks.
Wejrmeijer, Annelien. Mason & Buddy. van de Liejgraaf, Deborah, illus. 2013. (My Best Friend & Me Ser.). (ENG.). 10p. (J). (gr. -1 — 1). bds. 6.99 (978-0-7641-6637-2(9)) Barron's Educational Series, Inc.
Welling, Peter. Joe Van der Katt & the Great Picket Fence, 1 vol. Welling, Peter, illus. 2005. (ENG., Illus.). 32p. (J). (gr. k-3). 16.99 (978-1-58980-281-0(0)) Pelican Publishing Co., Inc.
Welling, Peter J. Darlene Halloween & the Great Chicago Fire, 1 vol. Welling, Peter J., illus. 2007. (ENG., Illus.). 32p. (J). (gr. k-3). 16.99 (978-1-58980-479-1(1)) Pelican Publishing Co., Inc.
Wells, Rachel. Alfie Cat in Trouble. 2016. (ENG., Illus.). 144p. (J). 5.99 (978-0-00-817208-4(0), HarperCollins Children's Bks.) HarperCollins Pubs. Ltd. GBR. Dist: HarperCollins Pubs.
Wells, Rosemary. Yoko. Wells, Rosemary, illus. 2009. (ENG., Illus.). 32p. (J). (gr. -1-1). pap. 6.99 (978-1-4231-1983-8(5)) Hyperion Pr.
—Yoko Finds Her Way. 2014. (Yoko Book Ser.). (ENG.). 32p. (J). (gr. -1-k). 16.99 (978-1-4231-6512-5(8)) Hyperion Pr.
Wells, Vivi. Whispers: The Cat with Nine Lives. 2010. (Illus.). 88p. pap. 10.49 (978-1-4490-5629-2(6)) AuthorHouse.
Wendling, Peter. The Magic of the Dark Ravine. Durie, Sally, illus. 2011. 36p. pap. 13.95 (978-1-60976-933-8(3), Eloquent Bks.) Strategic Book Publishing & Rights Agency (SBPRA).
Wenzel, Brendan. They All Saw a Cat. Wenzel, Brendan, illus. 2016. (Illus.). 44p. pap. 16.99 (978-1-4521-8805-8(X)); (ENG., (J). (gr. -1-k). 16.99 (978-1-4521-5013-0(3)) Chronicle Bks. LLC.
West, Colin. Marmaduke the Magic Cat. (Illus.). 64p. (J). pap. (978-0-340-66094-2(5)) Hodder & Stoughton.
West, Jacqueline. The Shadows. 2011. (Books of Elsewhere Ser.: 1). (ENG.). 272p. (J). (gr. 5-7). 7.99 (978-0-14-241872-7(2), Puffin Books) Penguin Young Readers Group.
—The Shadows. Bernatene, Poly, illus. 2010. (Books of Elsewhere Ser.: 1). (ENG.). 256p. (J). (gr. 5-18). 16.99 (978-0-8037-3440-1(9), Dial Bks) Penguin Young Readers Group.
—The Shadows. l.t. ed. 2010. (Books of Elsewhere Ser.: Vol. 1). (ENG.). 268p. 23.99 (978-1-4104-3139-4(8)) Thorndike Pr.
—The Shadows. 2011. (Books of Elsewhere Ser.: 1). lib. bdg. 17.20 (978-0-606-23070-4(X), Turtleback) Turtleback Bks.
—Spellbound, 2 vols. (Books of Elsewhere Ser.: 2). (ENG.). (J). (gr. 5-18). 2012. 320p. pap. 7.99 (978-0-14-242102-4(2), Puffin Books) Vol. 2. 2011. (Illus.). 304p. 16.99 (978-0-8037-3441-8(7), Dial Bks) Penguin Young Readers Group.
West, Judy. Do You Have My Purr? Warnes, Tim, illus. 2014. (My First Storybook Ser.). (ENG.). 32p. (J). (gr. -1-1). 6.99 (978-1-58925-511-1(9)) Tiger Tales.
West, Tracey. Me & My Robot. Revell, Cindy, illus. 2003. (Penguin Young Readers, Level 2 Ser.). (ENG.). 32p. (J). (gr. 1-2). mass mkt. 3.99 (978-0-448-42895-6(4), Penguin Young Readers) Penguin Young Readers Group.
—Me & My Robot No.2: The Show-and-Tell Show-Off. 2003. (Penguin Young Readers Level 2 Ser.). (gr. k-3). lib. bdg. 13.55 (978-0-613-64065-7(9), Turtleback) Turtleback Bks.
Westall, Robert. Blitzcat. 2015. (ENG.). 240p. (J). (gr. 4-6). pap. 8.99 (978-1-4472-8460-4(7)) Pan Macmillan GBR. Dist: Independent Pubs. Group.
Westling, Vicki Diane. Cats Keep Out: Sam & Friends. 2009. 40p. pap. 16.99 (978-1-4490-3623-2(6)) AuthorHouse.
—Hannibal Breaks His Promise: Sam & Friends. 2009. 32p. pap. 15.99 (978-1-4490-4711-5(4)) AuthorHouse.
Weston, Martha. Cats Are Like That. Weston, Martha, illus. (Holiday House Reader Ser.). (ENG., Illus.). 32p. (J). (gr. k-3). tchr. ed. 15.95 (978-0-8234-1419-2(1)) Holiday Hse., Inc.
Weston Woods Staff, creator. Chato & the Party Animals. 2011. 38.75 (978-0-439-84581-6(5)) 2011. 18.95 (978-0-439-73984-9(5)) 2004. 29.95 (978-1-55592-703-5(3)) 2004. 29.95 (978-1-55592-703-5(3)) Weston Woods Studios, Inc.
—Chato's Kitchen. 2004. (J). 18.95 (978-1-55592-386-0(0)); 38.75 (978-1-55592-388-4(7)) Weston Woods Studios, Inc.
—A Dark, Dark Tale. 2004. (J). 38.75 (978-1-55592-821-6(8)); 18.95 (978-1-55592-804-9(8)) Weston Woods Studios, Inc.
—Five Creatures. 2011. 18.95 (978-0-439-80441-7(8)); 38.75 (978-0-439-80444-8(2)) Weston Woods Studios, Inc.
—Hondo & Fabian. 2011. 18.95 (978-0-545-14958-7(4)); 38.75 (978-0-545-14959-4(2)) Weston Woods Studios, Inc.
—Kitten's First Full Moon. 2011. 29.95 (978-0-545-37422-4(7)) Weston Woods Studios, Inc.
—Millions of Cats Weston Woods. 2011. 29.95 (978-0-439-73496-7(7)); 18.95 (978-0-439-72840-9(1)); 38.75 (978-0-439-72842-3(8)) Weston Woods Studios, Inc.
Wexler, Django. The Forbidden Library. 2015. (ENG., Illus.). 400p. (J). (gr. 5). 8.99 (978-0-14-242681-4(4), Puffin Books) Penguin Young Readers Group.
—The Mad Apprentice. Jansson, Alexander, illus. 2015. (Forbidden Library). (ENG.). 352p. (J). (gr. 5). 16.99 (978-0-8037-3976-5(1), Kathy Dawson Books) Penguin Young Readers Group.
What Bird? 2006. (Illus.). 30p. (J). 14.95 (978-1-934138-00-7(2), 459-007) Bouncing Ball Bks., Inc.
What Tommy Did: Individual Title, 6 packs. (Literatura 2000 Ser.). (gr. 1-2). 28.00 (978-0-7635-0152-5(2)) Rigby Education.
Wheeler, Lisa. Castaway Cats. Goembel, Ponder, illus. 2006. (ENG.). 32p. (J). (gr. -1-2). 17.99 (978-0-689-86232-8(6), Atheneum/Richard Jackson Bks.) Simon & Schuster Children's Publishing.
White, A. Rose. Just the Way I Am. 2012. 16p. pap. 12.99 (978-1-62230-382-3(2)) Salem Author Services.
White, Ellen Emerson. Webster: Tale of an Outlaw. 2015. (ENG., Illus.). 256p. (J). (gr. 3-7). 17.99 (978-1-4814-2201-7(4), Aladdin) Simon & Schuster Children's Publishing.
White, J. Scratch & Sniff: The Case of the Stuck Seagull. 2013. 32p. pap. (978-1-4602-0552-5(9)) FriesenPress.
White, Margaret (Kintner). 18 Lives: The Adventures of Sam & Emil. 2008. 84p. pap. 8.95 (978-0-595-46521-7(8)) iUniverse, Inc.
White, Steve. Cleo the Curious Cat. 2009. 32p. pap. 19.98 (978-1-4092-5464-5(X)) Lulu Pr., Inc.
Whitmore, Gary. Prince Luna & the Space Dreamers. 2011. (ENG.). 204p. pap. 8.50 (978-1-4565-8438-2(3)) CreateSpace Independent Publishing Platform.
Wicke, Ed. Nicklus. 2011. 184p. (J). per. 9.99 (978-0-9677652-4-2(2), BlacknBlue Pr. UK) Blacknblue Pr.
Wiesner, David. Mr. Wuffles! 2013. (CHI.). 40p. (J). (978-986-189-418-8(7)) Grimm Cultural Ent., Co., Ltd.
—Mr. Wuffles! 2013. (ENG., Illus.). 32p. (J). (gr. -1-3). 17.99 (978-0-618-75661-2(2), Clarion Bks.) Houghton Mifflin Harcourt Publishing Co.
Wilcox, Jean A. Diary of Sir Winston Loki, 1 vol. 2010. 34p. 24.95 (978-1-4512-1813-8(3)) PublishAmerica, Inc.
Wilkerson, Alison. The Adventures of Tabby Cat. 2009. (Illus.). 104p. pap. 12.49 (978-1-4389-6695-3(4)) AuthorHouse.
Willems, Mo. Cat the Cat Who Is That? Willems, Mo, illus. 2010. (Illus.). 32p. (J). (gr. -1-3). (ENG.). 10.99 (978-0-06-172840-2(3)); lib. bdg. 14.89 (978-0-06-172841-9(1)) HarperCollins Pubs.
—Let's Say Hi to Friends Who Fly! Willems, Mo, illus. 2010. (Illus.). 32p. (J). (gr. -1-3). (ENG.). 10.99 (978-0-06-172842-6(X)); lib. bdg. 14.89 (978-0-06-172846-4(2)) HarperCollins Pubs.
—The Story of Diva & Flea. DiTerlizzi, Tony, illus. 2015. (ENG.). 80p. (J). (gr. 1-3). 14.99 (978-1-4847-2284-8(1)) Disney Pr.
—Time to Sleep, Sheep the Sheep! Willems, Mo, illus. 2010. (Illus.). 32p. (J). (gr. -1-3). (ENG.). 10.99 (978-0-06-172847-1(0)); lib. bdg. 14.89 (978-0-06-172848-8(9)) HarperCollins Pubs.
—Who Flies, Cat the Cat? Willems, Mo, illus. 2014. (ENG., Illus.). 22p. (J). (gr. -1 — 1). bds. 6.99 (978-0-06-230652-4(9)) HarperCollins Pubs.
—Who Is That, Cat the Cat? Willems, Mo, illus. 2014. (ENG., Illus.). 22p. (J). (gr. -1 — 1). bds. 6.99 (978-0-06-230653-1(7)) HarperCollins Pubs.
—Who Says That, Cat the Cat? Willems, Mo, illus. 2014. (ENG., Illus.). 22p. (J). (gr. -1 — 1). bds. 6.99 (978-0-06-230654-8(5)) HarperCollins Pubs.

—Who Sleeps, Cat the Cat? Willems, Mo, illus. 2014. (ENG., Illus.). 22p. (J). (gr. -1 — 1). bds. 6.99 *(978-0-06-230655-5(3))* HarperCollins Pubs.
Willett, Frances. Tropper's Tale. 2007. (Illus.). 84p. per. *(978-1-84401-914-4(4))* Athena Pr.
Williams, Alison. Pink Cat Blue Cat. 2009. (Illus.). 32p. pap. 14.49 *(978-1-4389-4623-8(6))* AuthorHouse.
Williams, Brenda May. The Unusual Pet Shop. Williams, Raymond, illus. 2012. 24p. pap. 11.50 *(978-1-61897-798-4(9)*, Strategic Bk. Publishing) Strategic Book Publishing & Rights Agency (SBPRA).
Williams, Jan. An Amazing Storytelling Cat. Peecock, Simon & McKissock, Charmaine, illus. 2013. 120p. pap. *(978-0-9568146-6-9(7))* Swift Publishing.
Williams, John. Smokie Forever. 2003. 74p. (J). pap. 8.95 *(978-0-595-29340-7(9))* iUniverse, Inc.
Williams, Lee. Seaweed, the Purrfect Cat. Johnson, Tamaris, illus. 2013. 36p. (J). 9.99 *(978-1-937493-47-9(4))* Dancing Moon Pr.
Williams, Rozanne Lanczak. Cat Can't Write: A Cat & Dog Story. Leary, Catherine, illus. (Learn to Write Ser.). 16p. (J). 2007. (gr. -1-3). pap. 8.99 *(978-1-59198-344-6(4))* 2006. (gr. k-2). pap. 3.49 *(978-1-59198-293-7(6)*, 6187) Creative Teaching Pr., Inc.
—Cat's Fairy Tale: A Cat & Dog Story. Leary, Catherine, illus. 2006. (Learn to Write Ser.). 16p. (J). (gr. k-2). pap. 3.49 *(978-1-59198-294-4(4)*, 6191) Creative Teaching Pr., Inc.
—Cat's Fairy Tale: A Cat & Dog Story. Maio, Barbara, ed. Leary, Catherine, illus. 2006. (J). per. 8.99 *(978-1-59198-348-4(7))* Creative Teaching Pr., Inc.
Willis, Jeanne. Dr Xargle's Book of Earth Tiggers. Ross, Tony, illus. 2012. (ENG.). 28p. (J). (gr. -1-k). pap. 11.99 *(978-1-84939-297-6(8))* Andersen Pr. GBR. Dist: Independent Pubs. Group.
—Flabby Cat & Slobby Dog. Ross, Tony, illus. 2009. (Andersen Press Picture Bks). (ENG.). 32p. (J). (gr. -1-3). 16.95 *(978-0-7613-5151-1(5)*, Carolrhoda Bks.) Lerner Publishing Group.
—Supercat vs the Party Pooper (Supercat, Book 2) 2015. (Supercat Ser.: 2). (ENG.). 208p. (J). 5.99 *(978-0-00-811040-6(9)*, HarperCollins Children's Bks.) HarperCollins Pubs. Ltd. GBR. Dist: HarperCollins Pubs.
Wilson, Alexandria M. Happy Birthday Gideon. 2013. 24p. pap. 24.95 *(978-1-62709-808-3(9))* America Star Bks.
Wilson, Anna. Kitten Catastrophe. 2016. (Kitten Chaos Ser.: 3). (ENG., Illus.). 304p. (J). (gr. 4-7). pap. 9.99 *(978-1-5098-0466-5(8))* Pan Macmillan GBR. Dist: Independent Pubs. Group.
—The Kitten Hunt. 2016. (Kitten Chaos Ser.: 1). (ENG., Illus.). 304p. (J). (gr. 4-7). pap. 9.99 *(978-1-5098-0462-7(5))* Pan Macmillan GBR. Dist: Independent Pubs. Group.
—Kitten Wars. 2016. (Kitten Chaos Ser.: 2). (ENG.). 288p. (J). (gr. 4-7). pap. 9.99 *(978-1-5098-0464-1(1))* Pan Macmillan GBR. Dist: Independent Pubs. Group.
Wilson, Barbara. Milly & Her Kittens. Fine, Aron, illus. 2012. (ENG.). 16p. (gr. k-3). pap. 9.00 *(978-1-56778-542-5(5))* Wilson Language Training.
Wilson, Karma. Sleepyhead. Segal, John, illus. 2012. (Classic Board Bks.). (ENG.). 32p. (J). (gr. -1 — 1). bds. 7.99 *(978-1-4424-3433-2(3)*, Little Simon) Little Simon.
—Sleepyhead. Segal, John, illus. 2006. (ENG.). 32p. (J). (gr. -1-2). 16.99 *(978-1-4169-1241-5(X)*, McElderry, Margaret K. Bks.) McElderry, Margaret K. Bks.
—Trick or Treat, Calico! Erdogan, Buket, illus. 2014. (J). *(978-1-4351-5610-4(2)*, Little Simon) Little Simon.
Wilson-Max, Ken. Happy Cat, Me! A Slide-the-Spot Book of Animals. Stojic, Manya & Hamilton, Allen, illus. 2005. 10p. (J). (gr. k-4). reprint ed. 10.00 *(978-0-7567-9364-7(5))* DIANE Publishing Co.
Wilson, Nicole. The Callie Gang: Who Said Cats Don't Talk? 2010. 264p. pap. 15.50 *(978-1-60911-323-0(3)*, Eloquent Bks.) Strategic Book Publishing & Rights Agency (SBPRA).
Winbolt-Lewis, Martin. The Soggy Saga of Samuel Sprat. Mason, Abi, illus. 2013. 24p. pap. *(978-1-78222-152-4(2))* Paragon Publishing, Rothersthorpe.
Windolph, Maria Theresa. Sugar Bear. 2008. 16p. pap. 24.95 *(978-1-60474-813-0(3))* America Star Bks.
Wingfield, Hayley. Little Johnny's Book of Wild & Crazy Friends. 2011. 28p. pap. 24.95 *(978-1-4626-2801-8(X))* America Star Bks.
Wise, D. Rudd & Wise, Rachel. The Three Little Orphan Kittens. Gottschalk, Deana, illus. 2006. (J). 15.95 *(978-0-9786276-0-7(1))* Mentzer Printing Ink.
Witthaus, A. S. Princess Sach. 2011. 28p. pap. 24.95 *(978-1-4626-4482-7(1))* America Star Bks.
Wiviott, Meg. Benno & the Night of Broken Glass. Bisaillon, Josée, illus. 2010. (ENG.). 32p. (J). (gr. 2-5). pap. 7.95 *(978-0-8225-9975-3(9))*; lib. bdg. 17.95 *(978-0-8225-9929-6(5))* Lerner Publishing Group. (Kar-Ben Publishing).
Wohlford, Martha Crikelair. Splash: The Staniel Cay Cat. 2006. (Illus.). (J). per. 21.95 *(978-0-9787981-0-9(4))* Serenity Pr.
Wojtusik, Elizabeth. Kitty Up! Yoshikawa, Sachiko, illus. 2008. (J). *(978-0-8037-3045-8(4)*, Dial) Penguin Publishing Group.
Wolczyk, Deborah R. Maisie - the Dress up Cat. 2010. 76p. pap. 24.99 *(978-1-4520-7681-2(2))* AuthorHouse.
Wolf, Clarissa. Orange Fizz. Wolf, Myron, photos by. 2009. (Illus.). 32p. pap. 9.99 *(978-1-935105-39-8(6))* Avid Readers Publishing Group.
Wolf, Linda. Cozy Kitty, 1 vol. 2009. 43p. pap. 24.95 *(978-1-61546-636-8(3))* America Star Bks.
Wolfe, Jane. Happy Cat. Benham, Tors, illus. 2016. (ENG.). 8p. bds. 6.99 *(978-1-84322-720-5(7)*, Armadillo) Anness Publishing GBR. Dist: National Bk. Network.
Wong, Liz. Quackers. 2016. (ENG.). 40p. (J). (gr. -1-2). 15.99 *(978-0-553-51154-3(8)*, Knopf Bks. for Young Readers) Random Hse. Children's Bks.
Wood, A. J. Slide & Play: Curious Kitten. Pledger, Maurice, illus. 2016. (Slide & Play Ser.). (ENG.). 16p. (J). (gr. -1). bds. 14.99 *(978-1-62686-574-7(4)*, Silver Dolphin Bks.) Readerlink Distribution Services, LLC.
Wood, Audrey. Princess, the Dragon & Scaredy Cats. (J). audio *(978-0-85953-375-1(1))* Child's Play International Ltd.
—Scaredy Cats. Wood, Audrey, illus. 2005. (Child's Play Library). (ENG., Illus.). 32p. (J). pap. *(978-1-904550-48-8(7))* Child's Play International Ltd.
Wood, Franklin. Teddy the Cat That Barks. 2011. 24p. pap. 15.99 *(978-1-4628-7908-3(X))* Xlibris Corp.
Wood, Gary. Bertrand - The Story of a Cat. 2008. 80p. pap. 16.95 *(978-1-60703-744-6(0))* PublishAmerica, Inc.
Wood, Steve & Fox, Woody. Courageous Cats Compete. 2006. (ENG., Illus.). 174p. (J). (gr. 2-4). pap. 8.99 *(978-0-7459-6011-1(1))* Lion Hudson PLC GBR. Dist: Independent Pubs. Group.
Woodbridge, Nancy Garfield. A Bouquet of Fairy Tales. 2012. 108p. 24.99 *(978-1-4771-4493-0(5))*; pap. 15.99 *(978-1-4771-4492-3(7))* Xlibris Corp.
Woodrow, Allan. The Pet War. 2015. (ENG.). 272p. (J). (gr. 3-7). pap. 6.99 *(978-0-545-51320-3(0)*, Scholastic Paperbacks) Scholastic, Inc.
Worth, Bonnie. The Cat in the Hat - Cooking with the Cat. Moroney, Christopher, illus. 2003. (Step into Reading Ser.). (ENG.). 32p. (J). (gr. -1-1). pap. 3.99 *(978-0-375-82494-4(4)*, 53560581, Random Hse. Bks. for Young Readers) Random Hse. Children's Bks.
—Oh, the Places on Earth! A Cat in the Hat's Learning Library Collection, 4 vols. 2012. (ENG., Illus.). 48p. (J). (gr. k-3). 39.96 *(978-0-307-93139-9(0)*, Random Hse. Bks. for Young Readers) Random Hse. Children's Bks.
Wozniak, Patricia. McGooster & Mcgyman Begin Their Adventures. 2008. (Illus.). 144p. (J). 16.95 *(978-0-9792430-0-4(9))* Wing Lane Pr.
Wrecks, Billy. Catch Catwoman! DeCarlo, Mike & Tanguay, David D., illus. 2013. (Step into Reading Ser.). (ENG.). 32p. (J). (gr. -1-1). 3.99 *(978-0-449-81616-5(8)*, Random Hse. Bks. for Young Readers) Random Hse. Children's Bks.
Wynne-Jones, Tim. Zoom, 1 vol. Beddows, Eric, illus. 2009. (ENG.). 96p. (J). (gr. -1-2). 25.00 *(978-0-88899-936-8(4))* Groundwood Bks. CAN. Dist: Publishers Group West (PGW).
—Zoom at Sea, 1 vol. Beddows, Eric, illus. 2013. (ENG.). 32p. (J). (gr. -1-2). 14.95 *(978-1-55498-391-9(6))* Groundwood Bks. CAN. Dist: Publishers Group West (PGW).
Wynne-Jones, Tim & Tapia, Alfredo. Pounce de Leon, 1 vol. 2009. (ENG., Illus.). 32p. (J). (gr. -1-3). 18.95 *(978-0-88995-375-8(9))* Red Deer Pr. CAN. Dist: Ingram Publisher Services.
Yamada, Shale. Rainbow Kitty Saves the Day. Riedler, Amelia, ed. 2013. (Story Lines Ser.). (ENG.). 24p. (J). (gr. -1-3). 9.95 *(978-1-935414-92-6(5))* Compendium, Inc., Publishing & Communications.
Yeoman, John. Mouse Trouble. Blake, Quentin, illus. 2011. (ENG.). 32p. (J). (gr. -1-k). pap. 12.99 *(978-1-84939-201-3(3))* Andersen Pr. GBR. Dist: Independent Pubs. Group.
Ying, Victoria. Meow! Ying, Victoria, illus. 2017. (Illus.). 32p. (J). (gr. -1-3). 15.99 ***(978-0-06-244096-9(9))*** HarperCollins Pubs.
Yokococo. Matilda & Hans. Yokococo, illus. 2013. (ENG., Illus.). 32p. (J). (gr. -1-2). 16.99 *(978-0-7636-6434-3(0)*, Templar) Candlewick Pr.
Yolen, Jane. How Do Dinosaurs Love Their Cats? Teague, Mark, illus. 2010. (How Do Dinosaurs...? Ser.). (ENG.). 6p. (J). (gr. -1-k). bds. 6.99 *(978-0-545-15354-6(9))* Scholastic, Inc.
Yoon, Salina. Where's Boo? 2013. (ENG., Illus.). 18p. (J). (— 1). bds. 6.99 *(978-0-307-97808-0(7)*, Random Hse. Bks. for Young Readers) Random Hse. Children's Bks.
Yost-Filgate, Susan. A Good Day for Abbey. Filgate, Leonard, illus. 2009. (ENG.). 12p. (J). (gr. -1-12). 6.99 *(978-1-934960-45-6(4)*, Raven Tree Pr.,Csi) Continental Sales, Inc.
—Rip Squeak & His Friends. Filgate, Leonard, illus. 2009. (ENG.). 32p. (J). (gr. -1-3). 16.95 *(978-1-934960-40-0(3)*, Raven Tree Pr.,Csi) Continental Sales, Inc.
—The Treasure. 2009. (ENG.). 32p. (J). (gr. -1-3). 16.95 *(978-1-934960-41-7(1)*, Raven Tree Pr.,Csi) Continental Sales, Inc.
Young, Caroline. Grubby Finn Robinson. 2009. 52p. pap. 10.55 *(978-1-4251-3002-2(X))* Trafford Publishing.
Young, Ed & Mack, Jeff. The Cat from Hunger Mountain. Young, Ed, illus. 2016. (ENG., Illus.). 32p. (J). (gr. -1-3). bds. 17.99 *(978-0-399-17278-6(5)*, Philomel Bks.) Penguin Young Readers Group.
Young, Jeanna Stolle & Johnson, Jacqueline Kinney. Princess Grace & the Little Lost Kitten, 1 vol. Aranda, Omar, illus. 2011. (Princess Parables Ser.). (ENG.). 32p. (J). (gr. -1-2). 14.99 *(978-0-310-71640-2(3))* Zonderkidz.
Young, Jessica. Pet-Rified. Secheret, Jessica, illus. 2017. (Finley Flowers Ser.). (ENG.). 128p. (gr. 2-3). lib. bdg. 25.32 ***(978-1-4795-9805-2(4)***, Finley Flowers) Picture Window Bks.
Young, Norene. Cathy, the Castaway Cat. Woodyard, Sandy Lilly, illus. 2012. 34p. 24.95 *(978-1-4626-6111-4(4))* America Star Bks.
Young, Scott Alexander. The Wild Cats of Piran. Christe, Moreno, illus. 2014. (Young Europe Bks.). (ENG.). 124p. (YA). (gr. 5). pap. 10.99 *(978-0-9900043-0-1(9)*, Young Europe Bks.) Steerforth Pr.
Your Purrr-Fect Birthday. 2007. (Dragonlarks Ser.). (Illus.). 64p. (J). (gr. k-3). per. 7.99 *(978-1-933390-55-0(7))* Chooseco LLC.
Yuly, Toni. Cat Nap. (ENG., Illus.). (J). 2017. 32p. bds. 7.99 *(978-1-250-11261-3(3)*, 9781250112613) 2016. 40p. 16.99 *(978-1-250-05458-6(3)*, 9781250054586) Feiwel & Friends.
Zabrosky, Joseph. Rudy Cazootie, 3 vols., 4 bks. Lt. ed. 2005. (Illus.). 32p. (J). per. *(978-0-9768831-2-8(0))* Elohim Bks.
Zahnow, Vicki. My Little Kitten, Patch. 2012. 24p. pap. 9.99 *(978-0-9885180-3-2(1))* Mindstir Media.
Zaikine, Zak. A Mother's Love. Zaikine, Zak & O'Keefe, Karin, eds. deluxe ed. 2005. (Illus.). 42p. (J). 24.95 *(978-0-934290-01-2(6))* Moon Valley Productions.
Zalme, Ron, illus. Sunny Day Tales. 2009. (J). *(978-1-59078-735-9(8))* Highlights for Children.
Zangrillo, Marguerite Rochelle. Calli the Cat. 2009. 28p. pap. 15.99 *(978-1-4363-8939-6(9))* Xlibris Corp.
Zera, Annette & Szekeres, Vivienne. Grandma Gets a Visitor. 2013. (Illus.). 20p. pap. 9.50 *(978-1-78035-633-4(1)*, Fastprint Publishing) Upfront Publishing Ltd. GBR. Dist: Printondemand-worldwide.com.
Zoellick, Todd. Daniel Harrington Fairbanks the Third & a Day on the Farm. 2012. 40p. pap. 18.58 *(978-1-4772-8408-7(7))* AuthorHouse.
Zuhdi, Darla. A South Sea Adventure, Vol. 4. 2005. (Cat Detectives Present Ser.: 4). (Illus.). 104p. (J). per. 6.99 *(978-0-9706062-6-6(5))* catBOX Entertainment, Inc.

CATS—HABITS AND BEHAVIOR

Arlon, Penelope. Puppies & Kittens. 2013. (Scholastic Discover More Ser.). (ENG., Illus.). 32p. (J). (gr. -1-3). 7.99 *(978-0-545-49566-0(0)*, Scholastic Reference) Scholastic, Inc.
Bader, Bonnie. Kit-Kit-Kittens. 2015. (Penguin Young Readers, Level 2 Ser.). (ENG., Illus.). 32p. (J). (gr. 1-2). pap. 3.99 *(978-0-448-48443-3(9)*, Penguin Young Readers) Penguin Young Readers Group.
Brooks, Linda. Wait for Me!!!!!!!! The Misadventures of Smokie & Leroy. 2009. 28p. pap. 12.49 *(978-1-4490-1503-9(4))* AuthorHouse.
Gardeski, Christina Mia. Cat Behavior. 2016. (Cats, Cats, Cats Ser.). (ENG., Illus.). 24p. (gr. k-1). lib. bdg. 26.65 *(978-1-5157-0956-5(6)*, Pebble Plus) Capstone Press of Coughlan Cos.
George, Jean Craighead. How to Talk to Your Cat. Truesdell, Sue & Meisel, Paul, illus. 2003. (ENG.). 40p. (J). (gr. 1-4). pap. 6.99 *(978-0-06-000622-8(6))* HarperCollins Pubs.
Hibbert, Clare. If You Were a Cat. 2013. (If You Were A... Ser.). (Illus.). 32p. (gr. 2-5). lib. bdg. 31.35 *(978-1-59920-959-3(4))* Black Rabbit Bks.
Michelon, Laura. Lari, Layne, & the Cat Colony. 2009. 36p. pap. 15.49 *(978-1-4490-1751-4(7))* AuthorHouse.
Newman, Aline Alexander & Weitzman, Gary. How to Speak Cat: A Guide to Decoding Cat Language. 2015. (ENG., Illus.). 176p. (J). (gr. 3-7). pap. 12.99 *(978-1-4263-1863-4(4)*, National Geographic Children's Bks.) National Geographic Society.
Rogala, Jennifer. My Cat at Home in the Wild. 2007. 32p. (J). per. 12.95 *(978-1-58939-962-4(5))* Virtualbookworm.com Publishing, Inc.
Von Zumbusch, Amelie. Dangerous Cats, 6 bks., Set. Incl. Cheetahs: World's Fastest Cats. lib. bdg. 22.60 *(978-1-4042-3630-1(9)*, PowerKids Pr.); Jaguars: World's Strongest Cats. lib. bdg. 22.60 *(978-1-4042-3628-8(7)*, PowerKids Pr.); Leopards: Silent Stalkers. lib. bdg. 22.60 *(978-1-4042-3633-2(3)*, PowerKids Pr.); Lions: King of the Beasts. lib. bdg. 22.60 *(978-1-4042-3631-8(7))*; Tigers: World's Largest Cats. lib. bdg. 22.60 *(978-1-4042-3632-5(5))*; (Illus.). 24p. (J). (gr. 3-7). 2007. 2007. Set lib. bdg. 127.50 *(978-1-4042-3600-4(7))* Rosen Publishing Group, Inc., The.
Webster, Maureen. Cat Speak: Revealing Answers to the Strangest Cat Behaviors. 2016. (Cats Rule! Ser.). (ENG., Illus.). 32p. (gr. 3-4). lib. bdg. 27.99 *(978-1-4914-8400-5(4)*, Snap Bks.) Capstone Press of Coughlan Cos.

CATS—HISTORY

Fineran, John J., 3rd, ed. The Traditional Siamese & Classic Siamese Cat: A Complete History of the Breed 2003. (Illus.). 980p. per. 85.00 *(978-0-9746554-0-6(6)*, 1) Tullycrine, LLC.

CATS—PICTORIAL WORKS

Aigner-Clark, Julie. Gatos. 2004. (Baby Einstein Ser.). (SPA., Illus.). 20p. (J). bds. *(978-970-718-157-1(5)*, Silver Dolphin en Español) Advanced Marketing, S. de R. L. de C. V.
Butterworth, Nick. Tiger in the Snow! 2008. (ENG., Illus.). 32p. (J). (gr. k — 1). pap. 7.95 *(978-0-00-711969-1(0))* HarperCollins Pubs. Ltd. GBR. Dist: Independent Pubs. Group.
Cats & Kittens Sticker Activity Book. (My Sticker Activity Ser.). (Illus.). 12p. (J). *(978-1-4054-1178-3(3))* Parragon, Inc.
Creative Team at Walter Foster Publishing Staff. I Love Cats! Activity Book: Meow-velous stickers, trivia, step-by-step drawing projects, & more for the cat lover in You! Fisher, Diana, illus. 2011. (I Love Activity Bks.). (ENG.). 112p. (J). (gr. 1-3). pap. 9.95 *(978-1-60058-224-0(9)*, 1600582249) Quarto Publishing Group USA.
Dean, James. Pete the Cat's Big Doodle & Draw Book. Dean, James, illus. 2015. (Pete the Cat Ser.). (ENG., Illus.). 128p. (J). (gr. -1-3). pap. 12.99 *(978-0-06-230442-1(9)*, HarperFestival) HarperCollins Pubs.
Dorling Kindersley Publishing Staff. Kitten. 2011. (Touch & Feel Ser.). (ENG.). 12p. (J). (gr. -1-k). bds. 6.99 *(978-0-7566-9165-3(6)*, DK Children) Dorling Kindersley Publishing, Inc.
Foster, Walter, ed. Cats & Kittens. Fisher, Diana, illus. 2004. (Learn to Draw Ser.). (ENG.). 40p. (J). (gr. 1-3). pap. 4.95 *(978-1-56010-844-3(4)*, 1560108444) Quarto Publishing Group USA.
Gottlieb, Wendy Ruth. Purr-Im Cat. 2008. (Illus.). 32p. (J). 16.95 *(978-1-932687-91-0(2)*, Devora Publishing) Simcha Media Group.
Green, John. World of Cats to Paint or Color. 2007. (Dover Art Coloring Book Ser.). (ENG., Illus.). 48p. (gr. 3-8). 5.99 *(978-0-486-46233-2(1))* Dover Pubns., Inc.
Harris, John & Lorenz, Catherine. Cats. 2009. (ENG., Illus.). 24p. (gr. -1). 4.95 *(978-0-89236-951-5(5))* Oxford Univ. Pr., Inc.
Innovative Kids Staff, creator. Soft Shapes Photo Books: Kittens. 2011. (ENG.). 8p. (J). (gr. -1 — 1). 10.99 *(978-1-60169-155-2(6))* Innovative Kids.
Peterson, Ltc Roy E. Albert: The Cat That Thought He Could Fly. 2011. 40p. pap. 17.99 *(978-1-4634-1293-7(2))* AuthorHouse.
Piven, Hanoch. What Cats Are Made of. Piven, Hanoch, illus. 2009. (ENG., Illus.). 40p. (J). (gr. -1-3). 16.99 *(978-1-4169-1531-7(1)*, Atheneum Bks. for Young Readers) Simon & Schuster Children's Publishing.
Rausch, Kathy. King Louis: The Sun Cat! 2012. 32p. pap. 19.99 *(978-1-4772-7791-1(9))* AuthorHouse.
Rosen, Michael J., ed. Purr: Children's Book Illustrators Brag about Their Cats. 2003. (Illus.). 42p. (J). (gr. 3-7). reprint ed. 22.00 *(978-0-7567-6794-5(6))* DIANE Publishing Co.
Soffer, Ruth. The Cat Lovers. 2007. (Dover Nature Coloring Book Ser.). (ENG., Illus.). 32p. (gr. 3-5). 3.99 *(978-0-486-46200-4(5))* Dover Pubns., Inc.
Walter Foster Creative Team. Learn to Draw Cats & Kittens: Step-By-Step Instructions for More Than 25 Favorite Feline Friends. Cuddy, Robbin, illus. 2015. (Learn to Draw: Expanded Edition Ser.). (ENG.). 64p. (J). (gr. 3-5). 33.32 *(978-1-939581-66-2(4))* Quarto Publishing Group USA.
Watt, Fiona & Wells, Rachel. Gatitos. 2004. (SPA.). 10p. (J). 11.95 *(978-0-7460-5091-0(7))* EDC Publishing.

CATS—POETRY

Bixley, Donovan, illus. Pussycat, Pussycat: Purrfect Nursery Rhymes. 2016. (ENG.). 24p. (J). (— 1). pap. 9.99 *(978-1-927262-28-3(3))* Upstart Pr. NZL. Dist: Independent Pubs. Group.
Chambers, Karen. Cats in Flats. 2011. 24p. pap. *(978-1-4269-5939-4(7))* Trafford Publishing (UK) Ltd.
Dean, James. Twinkle, Twinkle, Little Star. 2014. (Pete the Cat Ser.). (ENG.). 32p. (J). *(978-0-06-235967-4(3))* Harper & Row Ltd.
Florian, Douglas. Mammalabilia. 2004. (ENG., Illus.). 48p. (J). (gr. 1-4). reprint ed. pap. 7.99 *(978-0-15-205024-5(8))* Houghton Mifflin Harcourt Publishing Co.
Galdone, Paul. Three Little Kittens. (Paul Galdone Classics Ser.). (ENG., Illus.). (J). (gr. -1-3). 2013. 32p. 26.99 *(978-0-547-99480-2(X))* 2011. 40p. 8.99 *(978-0-547-57575-9(0))* Houghton Mifflin Harcourt Publishing Co.
—Three Little Kittens, 1 vol. Galdone, Paul, illus. 2007. (Paul Galdone Classics Ser.). (ENG., Illus.). 32p. (J). (gr. -1-3). audio compact disk 10.99 *(978-0-618-85285-7(9))* Houghton Mifflin Harcourt Publishing Co.
Humphreys, Sandra Ann. Kittens Have the Smallest Chins. 2013. 24p. pap. 24.95 *(978-1-4626-9430-3(6))* America Star Bks.
Johnston, Tony. Cat, What Is That? Minor, Wendell, illus. 2008. (ENG.). 32p. (J). pap. 10.95 *(978-1-56792-351-3(8))* Godine, David R. Pub.
Lee, Dennis. The Cat & the Wizard. Johnson, Gillian, illus. 2013. (ENG.). 32p. (J). 15.99 *(978-1-4434-1175-2(2))* HarperCollins Pubs.
Melia, John. The Casebook of Mysterious Morris. 2010. 48p. pap. 10.49 *(978-1-4520-1809-6(X))* AuthorHouse.
Rosen, Michael J. The Maine Coon's Haiku: And Other Poems for Cat Lovers. White, Lee, illus. 2015. (ENG.). 56p. (J). (gr. 1-4). 17.99 *(978-0-7636-6492-3(8))* Candlewick Pr.

CATS—TRAINING

Ewing, Susan. Cats! Train Your Owner! Cider Mill Press Staff, ed. Mullen, Lana, illus. 2008. (My-T-Smart(tm) Flash Cards Ser.). (ENG.). 32p. 14.95 *(978-1-933662-77-0(8))* Cider Mill Pr. Bk. Pubs., LLC.
Miles, Ellen. Kitty Corner: Guide to Kittens. 2013. (Kitty Corner Ser.). lib. bdg. 16.00 *(978-0-606-31502-9(0)*, Turtleback) Turtleback Bks.

CATTLE

see also Cows; Dairying; Livestock; Veterinary Medicine

Elston, Heidi M. D. Buffaloes Eat & Grow: Level 2. Keimig, Candice, illus. 2014. (Magic Readers Ser.). (ENG.). 24p. (J). (gr. 5-9). 24.21 *(978-1-62402-061-2(5))* ABDO Publishing Co.
Gartland, Robert A. Cowboys & Cattle. 2011. 50p. 35.95 *(978-1-258-06963-6(6))* Literary Licensing, LLC.
Graubart, Norman D. Cattle in American History. 2014. (How Animals Shaped History Ser.). (Illus.). 24p. (J). (gr. k-5). pap. 8.25 *(978-1-4777-6766-5(5)*, PowerKids Pr.) Rosen Publishing Group, Inc., The.
Hudak, Heather C. Cattle. 2006. (Farm Animals Ser.). (Illus.). 24p. (J). (gr. 3-7). per. 8.95 *(978-1-59036-429-1(5))* Weigl Pubs., Inc.
Kuskowski, Alex. Calves, 1 vol. 2013. (Baby Animals Set 1 Ser.). (ENG.). 24p. (J). (gr. k-3). lib. bdg. 24.21 *(978-1-61783-836-1(5)*, SandCastle) ABDO Publishing Co.
Macken, JoAnn Early. Cows. 2nd rev. ed. 2009. (Animals That Live on the Farm Ser.). (ENG.). 24p. (J). (gr. -1-3). pap. 8.15 *(978-1-4339-2465-1(X))*; lib. bdg. 22.60 *(978-1-4339-2396-8(3))* Stevens, Gareth Publishing LLLP. (Weekly Reader Leveled Readers).
Metz, Lorijo. Cattle: Cows, Bulls, & Calves. 2010. (On the Farm Ser.). (Illus.). 24p. (J). 22.60 *(978-1-4488-0687-4(9))*; pap. 8.25 *(978-1-4488-1335-3(2))* Rosen Publishing Group, Inc., The. (PowerKids Pr.).
Oatman, Eric. Cowboys & Cattle Drives: Life on the Western Trail. 2007. (Reading Expeditions Ser.). (ENG., Illus.). 40p. (J). pap. 19.95 *(978-0-7922-4550-6(4))* CENGAGE Learning.
Olson, Tod. How to Get Rich on a Texas Cattle Drive: In Which I Tell the Honest Truth about Rampaging Rustlers, Stampeding Steers & Other Fateful Hazards on the Wild Chisolm Trail. Allred, Scott & Proch, Gregory, illus. 2010. (How to Get Rich Ser.). (ENG.). 48p. (J). (gr. 3-7). 27.90 *(978-1-4263-0525-2(7))*; 18.95 *(978-1-4263-0524-5(9))* National Geographic Society. (National Geographic Children's Bks.).
Peterson, Cris. Amazing Grazing. Upitis, Alvis, photos by. 2011. (ENG., Illus.). 32p. (J). (gr. k-2). pap. 10.95 *(978-1-59078-868-4(0))* Boyds Mills Pr.
Schuetz, Kari. Baby Cows. 2013. (Super Cute! Ser.). (ENG., Illus.). 24p. (J). (gr. -1-3). lib. bdg. 25.95 *(978-1-60014-924-5(3)*, Blastoff! Readers) Bellwether Media.
Schwartz, Heather. War, Cattle, & Cowboys: Texas as a Young State, 1 vol. 2012. (Primary Source Readers Ser.). (ENG.). 32p. (J). (gr. 4-4). pap. 8.99 *(978-1-4333-5050-4(5))* Teacher Created Materials, Inc.
Stockland, Patricia M. In the Cattle Yard, 1 vol. Ouren, Todd, illus. 2007. (Barnyard Buddies Ser.). (ENG.). 24p. (gr. -1-2). 27.07 *(978-1-60270-022-2(2)*, Looking Glass Library-Nonfiction) Magic Wagon.
Top That Publishing Staff, ed. Wacky Bull. 2004. (Wacky Animals Ser.). (Illus.). 10p. (J). pap. *(978-1-84510-085-8(9))* Top That! Publishing PLC.
Webber, Desiree Morrison. Bone Head: Story of the Longhorn. Shropshire, Sandy, illus. 2003. 74p. (J). 16.95 *(978-1-57168-763-0(7))*; pap. 9.95 *(978-1-57168-750-0(5))* Eakin Pr. (Eakin Pr.).
West, David. Lots of Things You Want to Know about Cowboys: ... & Some You Don't! 2015. (Lots of Things You Want to Know About Ser.). (Illus.). 24p. (J). 28.50 *(978-1-62588-089-5(8))* Black Rabbit Bks.
Wolfman, Judy. Life on a Cattle Farm. Winston, David Lorenz, photos by. 2005. (Life on a Farm Ser.). (Illus.). 48p. (gr. 2-5). lib. bdg. 23.93 *(978-1-57505-516-9(3))* Lerner Publishing Group.

CATTLE—FICTION

Allan, Jo. Hungry Hettie, 1 vol. 2010. (ENG., Illus.). 24p. (J). (gr. -1-1). 11.95 *(978-0-86315-779-0(3))* Floris Bks. GBR. Dist: SteinerBooks, Inc.

Bester, Maryanne. The Cool Nguni. Bester, Shayle, illus. 2007. (Cool Nguni Ser.). (ENG.). 24p. (J). (gr. k-2). 12.00 *(978-1-77009-264-8(1))* Jacana Media ZAF. Dist: Independent Pubs. Group.

—I Know That! Bester, Shayle, illus. 2015. (ENG.). 32p. (J). (gr. -1-k). pap. 9.95 *(978-1-4314-0491-9(8))* Jacana Media ZAF. Dist: Independent Pubs. Group.

—The Missing Ball. Bester, Shayle, illus. 2010. (Cool Nguni Ser.: 4). (ENG.). 32p. (J). (gr. k-2). 12.00 *(978-1-77009-704-9(X))* Jacana Media ZAF. Dist: Independent Pubs. Group.

Cazet, Denys. Wanted Dead or Alive. 2008. (Minnie & Moo Ser.). (J). (gr. k-2). 25.95 incl. audio *(978-1-4301-0472-8(4))* Live Oak Media.

Chambers, Linda Kandelin. The Littlest Bull. 2009. 48p. pap. 25.32 *(978-1-4363-7450-7(2))* Xlibris Corp.

Clegg, Maryanne & Bester, Maryanne. Why Dog Is Afraid of Storms. Bester, Shayle, illus. 2012. (ENG.). 32p. (J). (gr. -1-k). pap. 12.95 *(978-1-4314-0219-9(2))* Jacana Media ZAF. Dist: Independent Pubs. Group.

Davis, David. Texas Zeke & the Longhorn, 1 vol. Stacy, Alan, illus. 2006. (ENG.). 32p. (J). (gr. k-3). 16.99 *(978-1-58980-348-0(5))* Pelican Publishing Co., Inc.

Davison, Ann-Marie. Harold & Walnut. 2016. (ENG., Illus.). 36p. (J). pap. 34.51 ***(978-1-4990-9869-3(3))*** Xlibris Corp.

Derubertis, Barbara. Xavier Ox's Xylophone Experiment. Alley, R. W., illus. 2011. (Animal Antics A to Z Set III Ser.). pap. 45.32 *(978-0-7613-8433-5(2))* Kane Press, Inc.

Fletcher, B. R. The Long Haired Yellow Bellies. 2008. 76p. pap. 24.99 *(978-1-4389-1519-7(5))* AuthorHouse.

Heard, Foreman. Tales of Pinkie Posie. 2008. 76p. pap. 15.90 *(978-1-4357-3292-6(8))* Lulu Pr., Inc.

Hedrick, Helen Groves. Tails, Trails & Pies: An Appalachian Cattle Drive. Spiker, Sue Ann Maxwell, illus. 2008. 32p. 15.95 *(978-0-929915-87-6(9))* Headline Bks., Inc.

Horowitz, Dave. Little Big Horse. 2014. (Scholastic Reader Level 1 Ser.). lib. bdg. 13.55 *(978-0-606-35375-5(5))* Turtleback Bks.

Houts, Michelle. The Beef Princess of Practical County. 2010. (ENG.). 240p. (J). (gr. 3-7). 7.99 *(978-0-440-42270-9(1),* Yearling) Random Hse. Children's Bks.

Johnson, Carolyn W. Sano Comes to the Farm, 1 vol. 2009. 13p. pap. 24.95 *(978-1-61546-091-5(8))* America Star Bks.

Kamau, G. Why Beetles Roll Cowdung. 2004. 22p. pap. *(978-9966-25-167-1(7))* Heinemann Kenya, Limited (East African Educational Publishers Ltd E.A.E.P.) KEN. Dist: Michigan State Univ. Pr.

Lindgren, Astrid. A Calf for Christmas, 1 vol. Lawson, Polly, tr. from SWE. Törnqvist, Marit, illus. 2010. (ENG.). 36p. (J). (gr. -1-2). 17.95 *(978-0-86315-785-1(8))* Floris Bks. GBR. Dist: SteinerBooks, Inc.

Murphy, Mel. The Barnyard Bully. 2013. (Illus.). 20p. pap. 10.95 *(978-1-4624-0589-3(4),* Inspiring Voices) Author Solutions, Inc.

Roach, Joyce Gibson. Horned Toad Canyon. Shaw, Charles, illus. 2003. (ENG.). 48p. (J). (gr. 2-4). 17.95 *(978-1-931721-01-1(7),* c2d211ff-dcbc-4d55-8600-9edaa91d316d) Bright Sky Pr.

Rodman, Dennis & Warburton, Dustin. Dennis the Wild Bull. 2013. (ENG.). 32p. (J). (gr. -1-5). pap. 16.00 *(978-0-615-75249-5(7))* Neighborhood Pubs.

Sandall, Ellie. Daisy Plays Hide-and-Seek. Sandall, Ellie, illus. (ENG., Illus.). 32p. (J). (gr. -1-k). 2012. pap. 8.99 *(978-1-4052-5457-1(2))* 2011. 17.99 *(978-1-4052-5419-9(X))* Egmont Bks., Ltd. GBR. Dist: Independent Pubs. Group.

Toska, Mary Lou. Ernest's Dream: A Young Boy Wanting to Spend the Summer in the High Alps. 2012. 20p. pap. 24.95 *(978-1-4626-8662-9(1))* America Star Bks.

Wallace, Bill. That Doggone Calf. Wallace, Carol, illus. 2010. (ENG.). 160p. (J). (gr. 3-7). pap. 6.95 *(978-0-8234-2303-3(4))* Holiday Hse., Inc.

Wolfe, Jane. Crazy Cow. Benham, Tors, illus. 2013. (ENG.). 8p. (J). (gr. -1-k). bds. 6.99 *(978-1-84322-775-5(4),* Armadillo) Anness Publishing GBR. Dist: National Bk. Network.

CAVE-DRAWINGS

see Cave Paintings

CAVE DWELLERS—FICTION

Barnett, Mac. Oh No! Not Again! Or How I Built a Time Machine to Save History - Or at Least My History Grade. Santat, Dan, illus. 2012. (Oh No! Picture Book Ser.). (ENG.). 40p. (J). (gr. -1-k). 17.99 *(978-1-4231-4912-5(2))* Hyperion Pr.

dePaola, Tomie. Little Grunt & the Big Egg: A Prehistoric Fairy Tale. dePaola, Tomie, illus. 2008. (ENG., Illus.). 32p. (J). (gr. -1-3). pap. 6.99 *(978-0-14-241143-8(4),* Puffin Books) Penguin Young Readers Group.

—Little Grunt & the Big Egg: A Prehistoric Fairy Tale. 2007. 29.95 incl. audio compact disk *(978-0-8045-4158-9(2))* Spoken Arts, Inc.

French, Vivian. Cave-Baby & the Mammoth. Williams, Lisa, illus. 2010. 32p. pap. *(978-1-84089-635-0(3))* Zero to Ten, Ltd.

Gerstein, Mordicai. The First Drawing. 2013. (ENG., Illus.). 40p. (J). (gr. -1-3). 18.99 *(978-0-316-20478-1(1))* Little, Brown Bks. for Young Readers.

Perkins, Lucy Fitch. The Cave Twins. (J). 19.95 *(978-0-89190-467-0(0))* Amereon Ltd.

Sauer, Tammi. Me Want Pet! Shea, Bob, illus. 2012. (ENG.). 40p. (J). (gr. -1-3). 17.99 *(978-1-4424-0810-4(3),* Simon & Schuster/Paula Wiseman Bks.) Simon & Schuster/Paula Wiseman Bks.

Temple, Valerie. Mud Witch Boy of Ghost Canyon. 2009. 113p. pap. 10.95 *(978-1-4327-3103-8(3))* Outskirts Pr., Inc.

CAVE PAINTINGS

Burnham, Brad. Cave of Lascaux: The Cave of Prehistoric Wall Paintings. 2009. (Famous Caves of the World Ser.). 24p. (gr. 3-4). 42.50 *(978-1-61512-495-4(0),* PowerKids Pr.) Rosen Publishing Group, Inc., The.

Harris, Nathaniel. Stories Behind the Art: Wall Paintings. 2016. (Stories in Art Ser.). (ENG., Illus.). 32p. (J). (gr. 2-4). pap. 11.99 *(978-0-7502-9446-1(9),* Wayland) Hachette Children's Group GBR. Dist: Hachette Bk. Group.

—Wall Paintings. 2009. (Stories in Art Ser.). (Illus.). 30p. (J). (gr. 4-8). lib. bdg. 26.50 *(978-1-4042-4440-5(9),* PowerKids Pr.) Rosen Publishing Group, Inc., The.

Howard, Nancy Shroyer. Mischief in Tuscany: Running Wild in a Famous Italian Painting. 2008. (ENG., Illus.). 48p. 17.95 *(978-88-7461-094-5(7))* Mandragora ITA. Dist: National Bk. Network.

Lauber, Patricia. Painters of the Caves. 2005. (Reader's Workshop Ser.). (ENG., Illus.). 48p. (C). pap. 21.95 *(978-0-7362-2807-7(1))* CENGAGE Learning.

Litwin, Laura Baskes. Diego Rivera: Legendary Mexican Painter. 2005. (Latino Biography Library). (Illus.). 128p. (J). (gr. 6-13). lib. bdg. 33.27 *(978-0-7660-2486-1(5))* Enslow Pubs., Inc.

The Mural, 6 vols. (Multicultural Programs Ser.). 16p. (gr. 1-3). 24.95 *(978-0-7802-9207-9(3))* Wright Group/McGraw-Hill.

Price, Justine. The Class Mural: Reason with Shapes & Their Attributes. 2014. (Math Masters: Geometry Ser.). 24p. (J). (gr. 2-3). 23.60 *(978-1-4777-6443-5(7));* (ENG.). pap. 8.25 *(978-1-4777-4903-6(9))* Rosen Publishing Group, Inc., The. (Rosen Classroom).

CAVELL, EDITH LOUISA, 1865-1915

Batten, Jack. Silent in an Evil Time: The Brave War of Edith Cavell. 2007. (ENG., Illus.). 144p. (J). (gr. 5-18). pap. 16.95 *(978-0-88776-737-1(0),* Tundra Bks.) Tundra Bks. CAN. Dist: Penguin Random Hse. LLC.

Guillain, Charlotte. Brave Nurses. 2015. (Collins Big Cat Ser.). (ENG.). 32p. (J). (gr. 2-2). pap. 7.95 *(978-0-00-759124-4(1))* HarperCollins Pubs. Ltd. GBR. Dist: Independent Pubs. Group.

Howell, Izzi. Edith Cavell. 2016. (Fact Cat: History Ser.). (ENG., Illus.). 24p. (J). (gr. k-2). 14.99 *(978-0-7502-9772-1(7),* Wayland) Hachette Children's Group GBR. Dist: Hachette Bk. Group.

CAVELL, EDITH LOUISA, 1865-1915—FICTION

Farenhorst, Christine. A Cup of Cold Water: The Compassion of Nurse Edith Cavell. 2007. 222p. (J). (gr. 3-7). per. 11.99 *(978-1-59638-026-4(8))* P & R Publishing.

CAVES

Alien Cave Explorers: Meet NASA Inventor William "Red" Whittaker & His Team's. 2017. (J). ***(978-0-7166-6163-4(2))*** World Bk., Inc.

Allman, Toney. Life in a Cave. 2004. (Ecosystems Ser.). (Illus.). 48p. (J). (gr. 4-7). 29.15 *(978-0-7377-3014-2(5),* Greenhaven Pr., Inc.) Cengage Gale.

Banting, Erinn. Caves. 2006. (J). 9.95 *(978-1-59036-437-6(6))* Weigl Pubs., Inc.

Best, B. J. How Are Caves Formed? 2017. (J). ***(978-1-5026-2533-5(4))*** Cavendish Square Publishing.

Blaisdell, Molly. Caves. 2008. (Discovering & Exploring Science Ser.). (Illus.). 16p. (J). (gr. -1-3). lib. bdg. 12.95 *(978-0-7569-8427-4(0))* Perfection Learning Corp.

Bodden, Valerie. Caves. 2017. (J). *(978-1-60818-805-5(1),* Creative Education) Creative Co., The.

Burnham, Brad. Caves of the Thousand Buddhas: Treasure House of Chinese Art. 2009. (Famous Caves of the World Ser.). 24p. (gr. 3-4). 42.50 *(978-1-61512-496-1(9),* PowerKids Pr.) Rosen Publishing Group, Inc., The.

—Kazumura Cave: The World's Longest Lava Tube. (Famous Caves of the World Ser.). 24p. 2009. (gr. 3-4). 42.50 *(978-1-61512-497-8(7))* 2003. (Illus.). (J). lib. bdg. 22.60 *(978-0-8239-6261-7(X))* Rosen Publishing Group, Inc., The. (PowerKids Pr.).

—Mammoth Cave: The World's Longest Cave System. 2009. (Famous Caves of the World Ser.). 24p. (gr. 3-4). 42.50 *(978-1-61512-498-5(5),* PowerKids Pr.) Rosen Publishing Group, Inc., The.

—Qumran Caves: Hiding Place for the Dead Sea Scrolls. 2003. (Famous Caves of the World Ser.). (Illus.). 24p. (J). lib. bdg. 22.60 *(978-0-8239-6259-4(8),* PowerKids Pr.) Rosen Publishing Group, Inc., The.

Cates, Darrin. A Look Inside Caves. 2013. (Rosen Readers Ser.). (ENG.). 24p. (J). (gr. 2-3). pap. 49.50 *(978-1-4777-2338-8(2));* pap. 8.25 *(978-1-4777-2337-1(4))* Rosen Publishing Group, Inc., The. (Rosen Classroom).

Champion, Neil. Wild Underground: Caves & Caving. 2013. (Illus.). 32p. (J). lib. bdg. 28.50 *(978-1-59920-810-7(5))* Black Rabbit Bks.

Chapman, David E. Daddy & I Explore... the Caves! 2012. (ENG.). pap. 15.00 *(978-1-4675-3249-5(5))* Independent Pub.

Claybourne, Anna. Caves. HL Studios Staff, illus. 2013. (Explorer Travel Guides). (ENG.). 48p. (gr. 3-6). pap. 8.95 *(978-1-4109-5435-0(8),* NA-r) Heinemann-Raintree.

Costain, Meredith. Into the Earth: The Story of Caves. 2006. (Science Chapters Ser.). (ENG., Illus.). 48p. (J). (gr. 1-4). lib. bdg. 17.90 *(978-0-7922-5950-3(5),* National Geographic Children's Bks.) National Geographic Society.

Creature Color & Discover Cave Life. (Illus.). 28p. (J). (gr. 1-8). reprint ed. *(978-1-881469-41-4(7))* Safari, Ltd.

Crowther, Robert. Deep down under Ground: A Pop-up Book of Amazing Facts & Feats. Crowther, Robert, illus. 2004. (Illus.). 18p. (J). (gr. 3-8). reprint ed. pap. 22.00 *(978-0-7567-7179-9(X))* DIANE Publishing Co.

Las Cuevas. (Coleccion Tierra Viva).Tr. of Caves. (SPA.). (YA). (gr. 5-8). pap. *(978-84-348-3264-0(X))* SM Ediciones.

David, Jack. Caving. 2008. (Action Sports Ser.). (ENG., Illus.). 24p. (J). (gr. 3-7). lib. bdg. 25.95 *(978-1-60014-199-7(4))* Bellwether Media.

Devillers, Carole. L' Histoire des Grottes D'Haïti: Racontée Par la Petite Goutte D'eau. 2014.Tr. of Story of the Caves of Haiti, Told by the Little Water Drop. (FRE & ENG., Illus.). 61p. (J). pap. 17.50 *(978-1-62632-220-2(1))* Educa Vision Inc.

Dubowski, Mark. Discovery in the Cave. Barnard, Bryn, illus. 2010. (Step into Reading Ser.). (ENG.). 48p. (J). (gr. 2-4). pap. 3.99 *(978-0-375-85893-2(8),* Random Hse. Bks. for Young Readers) Random Hse. Children's Bks.

Famous Caves of the World. (Illus.). (J). (gr. k-5). 112.50 *(978-0-8239-7264-7(X))* Rosen Publishing Group, Inc., The.

Fay, Keith. What's in a Cave? 2013. (InfoMax Readers Ser.). (ENG.). 24p. (J). (gr. 2-3). pap. 49.50 *(978-1-4777-2322-7(6));* (Illus.). pap. 8.25 *(978-1-4777-2321-0(8))* Rosen Publishing Group, Inc., The. (Rosen Classroom).

Goodman, Michael E. Dark Labyrinths. (Scary Places Ser.). 32p. (gr. 4-8). 2017. (ENG.). (J). 8.95 ***(978-1-68402-607-4(5))*** 2010. (Illus.). (YA). lib. bdg. 25.27 *(978-1-936087-56-3(1))* Bearport Publishing Co., Inc.

Hanson, Jeanne K. Caves. 2007. (Extreme Earth Ser.). (Illus.). 142p. (YA). (gr. 7-12). 35.00 *(978-0-8160-5917-1(9))* Facts On File, Inc.

Harrod-Eagles, Cynthia. Cave Homes. 2007. (Illus.). 16p. (J). *(978-0-545-00712-2(7))* Scholastic, Inc.

Henson, Heather. Lift Your Light a Little Higher: The Story of Stephen Bishop: Slave-Explorer. Collier, Bryan, illus. 2016. (ENG.). 32p. (J). (gr. -1-3). 17.99 *(978-1-4814-2095-2(X),* Atheneum/Caitlyn Dlouhy Books) Simon & Schuster Children's Publishing.

Honders, Christine. Cave Geologists, 01 vols., 1. 2016. (Out of the Lab: Extreme Jobs in Science Ser.). (ENG., Illus.). 32p. (J). pap. 10.00 *(978-1-5081-4513-4(X),* PowerKids Pr.) Rosen Publishing Group, Inc., The.

Johnson, Rebecca L. & National Geographic Learning Staff. Peering into Darkness. 2007. (Reading Expeditions Ser.). (ENG., Illus.). 32p. (J). pap. 17.95 *(978-0-7922-8451-2(8))* CENGAGE Learning.

Kuskowski, Alex. Biggest, Baddest Book of Caves, 1 vol. 2014. (Biggest, Baddest Books Set 2 Ser.). (ENG.). 24p. (gr. k-4). 25.65 *(978-1-62403-514-2(0))* ABDO Publishing Co.

Labrecque, Ellen. Caves, 1 vol. 2014. (Learning about Landforms Ser.). (ENG., Illus.). 32p. (gr. 1-3). lib. bdg. 27.32 *(978-1-4329-9533-1(2),* Heinemann First Library) Heinemann-Raintree.

Lauber, Patricia. Painters of the Caves. 2005. (Reader's Workshop Ser.). (ENG., Illus.). 48p. (C). pap. 21.95 *(978-0-7362-2807-7(1))* CENGAGE Learning.

Lindop, Laurie. Cave Sleuths. 2005. (Science on the Edge Ser.). (ENG., Illus.). 80p. (gr. 5-12). 27.93 *(978-0-7613-2702-8(9))* Lerner Publishing Group.

Lunis, Natalie. Haunted Caves. 2012. (Scary Places Ser.). 32p. (J). (gr. 4-8). lib. bdg. 25.27 *(978-1-61772-456-5(4))* Bearport Publishing Co., Inc.

Lynette, Rachel. Caves. 2005. (Wonders of the World Ser.). (ENG., Illus.). 48p. (J). (gr. 4-8). 27.50 *(978-0-7377-2645-9(8),* Greenhaven Pr., Inc.) Cengage Gale.

—Who Lives in a Deep, Dark Cave? 2010. (Exploring Habitats Ser.). (ENG.). 24p. (J). pap. 8.25 *(978-1-4488-1277-6(1));* lib. bdg. 22.60 *(978-1-4488-0676-8(3))* Rosen Publishing Group, Inc., The. (PowerKids Pr.).

MacDonald, Margaret. Caves. 2011. (Learn-Abouts Ser.). (Illus.). 16p. (J). pap. 7.95 *(978-1-59920-633-2(1))* Black Rabbit Bks.

MacLeod, Elizabeth. Secrets Underground: North America's Buried Past. 2014. (ENG., Illus.). 96p. (YA). (gr. 5-12). 24.95 *(978-1-55451-631-5(5),* 9781554516315); pap. 14.95 *(978-1-55451-630-8(7),* 9781554516308) Annick Pr., Ltd. CAN. Dist: Publishers Group West (PGW).

McFall, Christie. America Underground. McFall, Christie, illus. 2004. (Illus.). 80p. (J). (gr. 4-8). reprint ed. 14.00 *(978-0-7567-7712-8(7))* DIANE Publishing Co.

Meachen Rau, Dana. Caves. 2007. (Wonders of Nature Ser.). (SPA & ENG.). 32p. (gr. 1-2). lib. bdg. 15.95 *(978-0-7614-2665-3(5),* Benchmark Bks.) Marshall Cavendish Corp.

—Caves/Las Cuevas. 2007. (Wonders of Nature/Maravillas de la Naturaleza Ser.). (SPA & ENG., Illus.). 32p. (gr. 1-2). lib. bdg. 15.95 *(978-0-7614-2828-2(3),* Benchmark Bks.) Marshall Cavendish Corp.

—Las Cuevas. 2007. (Maravillas de la Naturaleza Ser.). (SPA & ENG., Illus.). 32p. (gr. 1-2). lib. bdg. 15.95 *(978-0-7614-2804-6(6),* Benchmark Bks.) Marshall Cavendish Corp.

Mills, J. Elizabeth. The Creation of Caves. 2009. (Illus.). 64p. (J). 77.70 *(978-1-4358-5593-9(0));* (ENG., (YA). pap. 12.95 *(978-1-4358-5592-2(2));* (ENG., (YA). (gr. 5-9). lib. bdg. 31.95 *(978-1-4358-5297-6(4))* Rosen Publishing Group, Inc., The.

Mis, Melody S. Exploring Caves. 2009. (Geography Zone: Landforms Ser.). (Illus.). 24p. (J). (gr. 2-4). pap. 8.25 *(978-1-4358-3111-7(X));* 24p. (gr. 2-3). 42.50 *(978-1-61512-695-8(3));* (J). lib. bdg. 22.60 *(978-1-4358-2713-4(9))* Rosen Publishing Group, Inc., The. (PowerKids Pr.).

Nadeau, Isaac. Caves. 2009. (Library of Landforms Ser.). 24p. (gr. 3-4). 42.50 *(978-1-60853-725-9(0),* PowerKids Pr.) Rosen Publishing Group, Inc., The.

Rodríguez, Ana María. Vampire Bats, Giant Insects, & Other Mysterious Animals of the Darkest Caves. 2012. (Extreme Animals in Extreme Environments Ser.). (Illus.). 48p. (J). (gr. 5-18). pap. 8.95 *(978-1-4644-0018-6(0))* Enslow Pubs., Inc.

Rosenberg, Pam. Cave Crawlers, 1 vol. 2011. (Landform Adventurers Ser.). (ENG.). 32p. (gr. 1-2). pap. 8.29 *(978-1-4109-4144-2(2));* 29.99 *(978-1-4109-4137-4(X))* Heinemann-Raintree. (Read Me!).

Rustad, Martha E. H. What's in a Cave? 2015. (What's in There? Ser.). (ENG., Illus.). 24p. (gr. k-1). lib. bdg. 21.99 *(978-1-4914-6009-2(1),* Pebble Bks.) Capstone Press of Coughlan Cos.

Silverstru, Emil. The Cave Book. 2008. 80p. (J). 15.99 *(978-0-89051-496-2(8))* Master Bks.

Sisk, Maeve T. Caving. 2012. (Great Outdoors Ser.). (Illus.). 24p. (J). (gr. 2-5). pap. 8.15 *(978-1-4339-7092-4(9));* lib. bdg. 22.60 *(978-1-4339-7091-7(0))* Stevens, Gareth Publishing LLLP.

Stamper, Judith Bauer. Caves. 2010. (Illus.). 32p. (J). pap. *(978-0-545-28545-2(3))* Scholastic, Inc.

Taylor, Peter Lane. The Secret of Priest's Grotto: A Holocaust Survival Story. 2007. (Holocaust Ser.). (Illus.). 64p. (J). (gr. 3-7). lib. bdg. 18.95 *(978-1-58013-260-2(X),* Kar-Ben Publishing) Lerner Publishing Group.

Taylor, Peter Lane & Nicola, Christos. The Secret of Priest's Grotto: A Holocaust Survival Story. 2007. (Holocaust Ser.). (ENG., Illus.). 64p. (YA). (gr. 5-12). per. 8.95 *(978-1-58013-261-9(8),* Kar-Ben Publishing) Lerner Publishing Group.

Turnbull, Stephanie. Caving. 2016. (Adventure Sports Ser.). 24p. (gr. 2-6). 28.50 *(978-1-62588-383-4(8),* Smart Apple Media) Black Rabbit Bks.

Walker, Sally M. Caves. 2008. pap. 52.95 *(978-0-8225-9335-5(1))* 2007. (ENG., Illus.). 48p. (gr. 2-5). lib. bdg. 26.60 *(978-0-8225-6734-9(2),* Lerner Pubns.) Lerner Publishing Group.

Weber, Valerie J. Por Qué Algunos Animales Viven en Cuevas. 2008. (Donde viven los animales (Where Animals Live) Ser.). (SPA., Illus.). 24p. (J). (gr. 1-4). pap. 8.15 *(978-0-8368-8815-7(4),* Weekly Reader Leveled Readers) Stevens, Gareth Publishing LLLP.

—Por Qué Algunos Animales Viven en Cuevas. 2008. (Donde viven los animales (Where Animals Live) Ser.). (SPA., Illus.). 24p. (J). (gr. 1-4). lib. bdg. 22.00 *(978-0-8368-8808-9(1),* Weekly Reader Leveled Readers) Stevens, Gareth Publishing LLLP.

—Why Animals Live in Caves. 2008. (Where Animals Live Ser.). 24p. (gr. 1-4). pap. 8.15 *(978-0-8368-8801-0(4));* (Illus.). lib. bdg. 22.00 *(978-0-8368-8794-5(8))* Stevens, Gareth Publishing LLLP. (Weekly Reader Leveled Readers).

Whiting, Jim. Caving. 2017. (J). *(978-1-60818-690-7(3),* Creative Education) Creative Co., The.

World Book, Inc Staff, contrib. by. Worlds Beneath Our Feet. 2017. (J). ***(978-0-7166-3371-6(X))*** World Bk., Inc.

Zappa, Marcia. Caves, 1 vol. 2010. (Big Buddy Bks.). (ENG.). 32p. (J). (gr. 2-5). 28.50 *(978-1-61613-490-7(9))* ABDO Publishing Co.

CAVES—FICTION

Abbott, Tony. In the Ice Caves of Krog. Adams, Gil & Jessell, Tim, illus. 2003. (Secrets of Droon Ser.: No. 20). 114p. (J). (gr. 2-5). 12.65 *(978-0-7569-3940-3(2))* Perfection Learning Corp.

Anderson, Max Elliott. Secret of Abbott's Cave. 2004. (Tweener Press Adventure Ser.). 127p. (J). (gr. 3). per. 10.95 *(978-0-9752880-0-9(8))* Baker Trittin Pr.

Anzai, Nobuyuki. Flame of Recca. 2007. (Flame of Recca Ser.: 22). (ENG., Illus.). 192p. pap. 9.99 *(978-1-4215-0893-1(1))* Viz Media.

Appleton, Victor. Tom Swift Omnibus #3: Tom Swift among the Diamond Makers, Tom Swift in the Caves of Ice, Tom Swift & His Sky Racer. 2007. 296p. per. 12.99 *(978-1-60459-101-9(3));* per. 12.99 *(978-1-60459-102-6(1))* Wilder Pubns., Corp.

Avlon And Matt. Bronsky the Bat. 2013. (Illus.). 24p. pap. 19.82 *(978-1-4817-8333-0(5))* AuthorHouse.

Behrens, Kathryn J. Breakdown. 2016. (Atlas of Cursed Places Ser.). (ENG.). 96p. (YA). (gr. 6-12). lib. bdg. 26.65 *(978-1-5124-1323-6(2),* Darby Creek) Lerner Publishing Group.

Black, Holly & DiTerlizzi, Tony. The Ironwood Tree. DiTerlizzi, Tony, illus. 2013. (Spiderwick Chronicles Ser.: 4). (ENG., Illus.). (J). (gr. 1-5). 128p. 15.99 *(978-1-4424-8702-4(X));* 144p. pap. 7.99 *(978-1-4424-8701-7(1))* Simon & Schuster Bks. For Young Readers. (Simon & Schuster Bks. For Young Readers).

Blue, Sebastien. Liquid Diamond. 2013. 176p. pap. *(978-1-4602-3346-7(8))* FriesenPress.

Bowman, Robert. The Three Vests: The New Brilliants. 2003. 224p. (J). pap. 7.95 *(978-0-9713530-2-2(6))* Smart & Smarter Publishing.

Brezenoff, Steve. The Cave That Shouldn't Collapse, 1 vol. Calo, Marcos, illus. 2011. (Field Trip Mysteries Ser.). (ENG.). 88p. (gr. 2-3). pap. 6.10 *(978-1-4342-3430-8(4));* lib. bdg. 25.32 *(978-1-4342-3227-4(1))* Stone Arch Bks.

Bullock, Rob. Noah Ramsbottom & the Cave Elves. 2009. 48p. pap. 12.25 *(978-1-60860-335-0(0),* Strategic Bk. Publishing) Strategic Book Publishing & Rights Agency (SBPRA).

Clark, Malcolm. Bounty's Cave. 2007. (ENG.). 156p. per. 19.95 *(978-1-932762-82-2(5))* Elderberry Press, Inc.

Deal, Paul. Lighting Candles. 2003. 122p. (YA). 20.95 *(978-0-595-65804-6(0));* pap. 10.95 *(978-0-595-28457-3(4))* iUniverse, Inc.

DiTerlizzi, Tony & Black, Holly. The Ironwood Tree. DiTerlizzi, Tony, illus. 4th ed. 2004. (Spiderwick Chronicles Ser.: 4). (ENG., Illus.). 128p. (J). (gr. 2-6). 10.99 *(978-0-689-85939-7(2),* Simon & Schuster Bks. For Young Readers) Simon & Schuster Bks. For Young Readers.

—The Ironwood Tree. l.t. ed. 2006. (Spiderwick Chronicles: Bk. 4). 90p. (YA). (gr. 2-18). 23.95 *(978-0-7862-8583-9(4))* Thorndike Pr.

Dreyer, Ellen. The Glow Stone, 1 vol. 2006. (ENG.). 224p. (YA). (gr. 7-18). 15.95 *(978-1-56145-370-2(6))* Peachtree Pubs.

Eaton, Anthony. The Girl in the Cave. Danalis, John, illus. 2004. 128p. (J). pap. *(978-0-7022-3437-8(0))* Univ. of Queensland Pr.

Edward S. Ellis. The Cave in the Mountain: A Sequel to in the Pecos Country by Lieut. R. H. J. l.t. ed. 2007. (ENG.). 186p. pap. 21.99 *(978-1-4264-8202-1(7))* Creative Media Partners, LLC.

Fogg, K. L. Diamondback Cave: A Novel. 2008. 377p. (J). *(978-1-59811-512-3(X))* Covenant Communications.

Fox, Gaines. Go Fly a Kite: A Juvenile Adventure Novel. 2008. 200p. pap. 24.95 *(978-1-60703-573-2(1))* America Star Bks.

Freeman, Martha. The Spy Wore Shades. Date not set. 160p. (YA). (gr. 3-18). pap. 4.99 *(978-0-06-440957-5(0))* HarperCollins Pubs.

Gosine, Aarti. The Magic Cave: A Cascade Children's Book. 2011. (Illus.). 100p. pap. 12.52 *(978-1-4567-7050-1(0))* AuthorHouse.

Hays, Anna Jane. The Secret of the Circle-K Cave. Smath, Jerry, illus. 2006. (Science Solves It! Ser.). 32p. (J). (gr. -1-3). pap. 5.95 *(978-1-57565-189-7(0))* Kane Press, Inc.

Higman, Anita. The Living Darkness: Texas Caves. 2nd ed. 2003. (Illus.). xiii, 93p. (J). *(978-1-57168-783-8(1),* Eakin Pr.) Eakin Pr.

Hobbs, Will & Hobbs, William. Wild Man Island. 2003. (ENG.). 192p. (J). (gr. 5-18). pap. 5.99 *(978-0-380-73310-1(2))* HarperCollins Pubs.

The Ice Cave: Level 3, 6 vols. (Fluency Strand Ser.). (gr. 4-8). 45.00 *(978-1-4045-1220-7(9))* Wright Group/McGraw-Hill.

Kirby, Matthew J. Cave of Wonders. 2015. (Infinity Ring Ser.: 5). (ENG.). 192p. (J). (gr. 3-7). pap. 6.99 *(978-0-545-90120-8(0),* Scholastic Pr.) Scholastic, Inc.

Knight, Andrew. Dead Beckoning. (Thumbprint Mysteries Ser.). 32.86 *(978-0-8092-0421-2(5))* McGraw-Hill/Contemporary.

Kuykendoll, Kim. The Adventures of the Coral Way Gang. 2008. 160p. pap. 13.99 *(978-1-60477-840-3(7))* Salem Author Services.

Landers, Ace. Cave Race! White, Dave, illus. 2010. 32p. (J). *(978-0-545-20871-0(8))* Scholastic, Inc.

Leveen, Tom. Hellworld. 2017. (ENG., Illus.). 304p. (YA). (gr. 9). 17.99 *(978-1-4814-6633-2(X),* Simon Pulse) Simon Pulse.

The Lotus Caves. 2014. (ENG., Illus.). 288p. (J). (gr. 4-8). pap. 7.99 (978-1-4814-1837-9(8), Aladdin) Simon & Schuster Children's Publishing.
The Lotus Caves. 2014. (ENG., Illus.). 288p. (J). (gr. 4-8). 17.99 (978-1-4814-1838-6(6), Simon & Schuster/Paula Wiseman Bks.) Simon & Schuster/Paula Wiseman Bks.
Marsh, Carole. Dear Bats: The Creepy Cave Caper Mystery. 2007. (Postcard Mysteries Ser.). (Illus.). 115p. (J). (gr. 2-9). per. 5.99 (978-0-635-06342-7(5)) Gallopade International.
Martone, Ginny. Trapped in Dead Man's Cave. 2007. 61p. pap. 19.95 (978-1-60474-227-5(5)) America Star Bks.
McCune, Susan. Yun Explores a Cave, 01 vols., 1. 2016. (Rosen REAL Readers: STEM & STEAM Collection). (ENG.). 12p. (J). pap. 6.33 (978-1-5081-1608-0(3), Rosen Classroom) Rosen Publishing Group, Inc., The.
McMullan, Kate. Class Trip to the Cave of Doom, 3 vols. Basso, Bill, illus. 2003. (Dragon Slayers' Academy Ser.: 3). (ENG.). 112p. (J). (gr. 2-5). pap. 5.99 (978-0-448-43110-9(6), Grosset & Dunlap) Penguin Young Readers Group.
—Class Trip to the Cave of Doom, 1 vol. Basso, Bill, illus. 2006. (Dragon Slayers' Academy Ser.: No. 3). (ENG.). 112p. (gr. 1-7). 24.21 (978-1-59961-123-5(6)) Spotlight.
Meister, Cari. Buzz Beaker & the Cave Creatures. McGuire, Bill, illus. 2010. (Buzz Beaker Bks.). (ENG.). 32p. (gr. 2-3). pap. 6.25 (978-1-4342-2797-3(9)); 22.65 (978-1-4342-2060-8(5)) Stone Arch Bks.
Montes, Hugo & Montes, Michelle. Young Eagles Armor Academy: The Whispering Cave, V03. 2010. 76p. (J). pap. 5.99 (978-1-60683-023-9(6)) Harrison House Pubs.
Nash, Tim. The Club. 2009. 112p. pap. 12.49 (978-1-4490-2087-3(9)) AuthorHouse.
Nesbit, Troy. Diamond Cave Mystery. 2013. (Wilderness Mystery Ser.). (ENG., Illus.). 280p. (J). (gr. 3-7). pap. 12.95 (978-1-58979-809-0(0)) Taylor Trade Publishing.
Palmer, Bernard. Danny & Ron Orlis in the Sacred Cave. 2011. 130p. 40.95 (978-1-258-08134-8(2)) Literary Licensing, LLC.
Parnell, Paul. Talking Rocks. 2009. 52p. pap. 16.95 (978-1-61546-651-1(7)) America Star Bks.
Pike, Christopher, pseud. The Haunted Cave. 2014. (Spooksville Ser.: 3). (ENG., Illus.). 128p. (J). (gr. 3-7). pap. 6.99 (978-1-4814-1055-7(5), Aladdin) Simon & Schuster Children's Publishing.
Power, Nicholas D. Paudie's Magical Adventures. 2009. 236p. 24.75 (978-1-60693-534-7(8), Strategic Bk. Publishing) Strategic Book Publishing & Rights Agency (SBPRA).
Ragan, Lyn. Berc's Inner Voice. 2013. 24p. 21.95 (978-0-9860205-4-4(0)) HourGlass Publishing.
—Berc's Inner Voice. Meyer, Alison, illus. 2013. 24p. pap. 14.95 (978-0-9860205-3-7(2)) HourGlass Publishing.
Ransom, Candice. The Underground Adventure of Arly Dunbar, Cave Explorer. Hammond, Ted & Carbajal, Richard Pimentel, illus. 2011. (History's Kid Heroes Set III Ser.). pap. 51.02 (978-0-7613-7640-8(2), Graphic Universe™) Lerner Publishing Group.
—The Underground Adventure of Arly Dunbar, Cave Explorer. Hammond, Ted & Carbajal, Richard, illus. 2011. (History's Kid Heroes Ser.). (ENG.). 32p. (gr. 3-5). (J). 26.60 (978-0-7613-6182-4(0)); pap. 8.95 (978-0-7613-7074-1(9), Graphic Universe™) Lerner Publishing Group.
Sell, Jeff. The Quarry Cave. 2006. 51p. pap. 16.95 (978-1-4241-1188-6(9)) PublishAmerica, Inc.
Sheard, Jean. A Chinese Fantasy - Cave in a Casket. 2007. 128p. 34.95 (978-1-84753-349-4(3)); (Illus.). pap. 10.50 (978-1-84753-249-7(7)) Lulu Pr., Inc.
Siler, D. Danger Cave. 2006. 76p. pap. 16.95 (978-1-4241-4335-1(7)) PublishAmerica, Inc.
Taitano, Janice G. The Legend of Lutung. 2006. 260p. pap. 29.00 (978-1-59752-482-7(4), Resource Pubns.(OR)) Wipf & Stock Pubs.
Teitelbaum, Michael. The Cave of No Return. 2015. (Cold Whispers Ser.). (ENG., Illus.). 32p. (J). (gr. 2-6). lib. bdg. 26.60 (978-1-62724-812-9(9)) Bearport Publishing Co., Inc.
VanNuys, Elroy. The Mysterious Cave. 2010. 108p. 24.49 (978-1-4490-9224-5(1)); pap. 13.99 (978-1-4490-9223-8(3)) AuthorHouse.
Watson, J. R. Wizard down Under. 2009. 160p. 23.50 (978-1-60860-138-7(2), Eloquent Bks.) Strategic Book Publishing & Rights Agency (SBPRA).
Watson, Richard A. & National Geographic Learning Staff. In the Dark Cave. Norman, Dean, illus. 2010. (Rise & Shine Ser.). (ENG.). 40p. (C). (gr. -1-2). 9.95 (978-1-59572-038-2(3)) National Geographic School Publishing, Inc.
Wilson, N. D. Leepike Ridge. 2008. (ENG., Illus.). 256p. (J). (gr. 3-7). 6.99 (978-0-375-83874-3(0), Yearling) Random Hse. Children's Bks.
Wormell, Chris. The Wild Girl. Wormell, Chris, illus. 2006. (Illus.). 32p. (J). (gr. -1). 17.00 (978-0-8028-5311-0(0), Eerdmans Bks For Young Readers) Eerdmans, William B. Publishing Co.
Young, Eileen Parrigin. The Cousins & the Cave of Fire, 1 vol. 2010. 204p. pap. 24.95 (978-1-4489-4858-1(4)) America Star Bks.

CAXTON, WILLIAM, APPROXIMATELY 1422-1491 OR 1492

Guillain, Charlotte. Spreading the Word. 2015. (Collins Big Cat Ser.). (ENG.). 32p. (J). (gr. 2-2). pap. 7.95 (978-0-00-759127-5(6)) HarperCollins Pubs. Ltd. GBR. Dist: Independent Pubs. Group.

CD-ROMS

Cole, John O. Plugged in to English: English & Language Arts Activities for the Computer Lab. 2003. (ENG., Illus.). 144p. pap. 28.95 (978-1-877673-60-3(9), PI-BWK03) Cottonwood Pr., Inc.

CELEBRITIES

Berlatsky, Noah. Celebrity Culture. 2015. (Opposing Viewpoints Ser.). (ENG.). 224p. (J). (gr. 10-12). 48.80 (978-0-7377-7246-3(8), Greenhaven Pr., Inc.) Cengage Gale.
Bragg, Georgia. How They Choked: Failures, Flops, & Flaws of the Awfully Famous. O'Malley, Kevin, illus. 2016. (ENG.). 208p. (J). pap. 9.99 (978-1-68119-216-1(0), 9781681192161, Bloomsbury USA Childrens) Bloomsbury Publishing USA.
The Britannica Guide to the World's Most Influential People: Set 2, 1 vol., 1. 2016. (Britannica Guide to the World's Most Influential People Ser.). (ENG.). 224p. (YA). (gr. 10-10). 270.00 (978-1-68048-223-2(8), Britannica Educational Publishing) Rosen Publishing Group, Inc., The.
Celebrity Chefs: Set 2. 2016. (Celebrity Chefs Ser.). 128p. (gr. 6-6). lib. bdg. 149.08 (978-0-7660-7509-2(5)) Enslow Pubs., Inc.
Croll, Jennifer. Bad Girls of Fashion: Style Rebels Through the Ages. Buchholc, Ada, illus. 2016. (ENG.). 208p. (J). pap. 14.95 (978-1-55451-785-5(0)) Annick Pr., Ltd. CAN. Dist: Publishers Group West (PGW).
Dorling Kindersley Publishing Staff. DK Readers L4: Amazing Women. 2017. (DK Readers Ser.). (ENG., Illus.). 96p. (J). (gr. 4-7). pap. 3.99 (978-1-4654-5768-4(2), DK Children) Dorling Kindersley Publishing, Inc.
—100 Women Who Made History. 2017. (ENG., Illus.). 128p. (J). (gr. 3-7). 16.99 (978-1-4654-5688-5(0), DK Children) Dorling Kindersley Publishing, Inc.
Ganchinello, Sheena. Tim Westergren & Pandora. 2013. (Internet Biographies Ser.). (ENG., Illus.). 128p. (YA). (gr. 7-12). lib. bdg. 34.60 (978-1-4488-9526-7(X), Rosen Classroom) Rosen Publishing Group, Inc., The.
Hollander, Barbara Gottfried. Ellen DeGeneres: Television's Funniest Host, 1 vol. 2015. (ENG.). 112p. (YA). 35.60 (978-1-4777-7895-1(0), Rosen Young Adult) Rosen Publishing Group, Inc., The.
Lawley, Kian & Caylen, JC. Don't Try This at Home! 2016. (Illus.). 224p. (YA). (gr. 8). pap. 15.99 (978-0-06-243716-7(X)) HarperCollins Pubs.
Little Bee Books Staff. The Vloggers Yearbook. 2015. (ENG., Illus.). 64p. (J). (gr. 4-9). pap. 9.99 (978-1-4998-0230-6(7)) Little Bee Books Inc.
Making a Difference. 2014. (Making a Difference Ser.). 48p. (YA). (gr. 5-8). 310.20 (978-1-62275-538-7(3)) Rosen Publishing Group, Inc., The.
Making a Difference: Leaders Who Are Changing the World. 2014. (Making a Difference: Leaders Who Are Changing the World Ser.). 48p. (YA). (gr. 5-8). 155.10 (978-1-62275-455-7(7)) Rosen Publishing Group, Inc., The.
Meet the Greats. 2016. (Meet the Greats Ser.). 00048p. (J). lib. bdg. 191.70 **(978-1-4824-5854-1(3))** Stevens, Gareth Publishing LLLP.
Nagle, Jeanne. Gordon Ramsay. 2016. (Celebrity Chefs Ser.). (ENG.). 128p. (J). (gr. 7-8). lib. bdg. 37.27 (978-0-7660-7246-6(0)) Enslow Pubs., Inc.
Raij, Emily. Ghosts of the Rich & Famous. 2015. (Spooked Ser.). (ENG.). 32p. (gr. 1-2). lib. bdg. 26.65 (978-1-4914-4079-7(1)) Capstone Press of Coughlan Cos.
Rauf, Don. Jamie Oliver. 2016. (Celebrity Chefs Ser.). (Illus.). 128p. (J). (gr. 6-6). 37.27 (978-0-7660-7760-7(8)) Enslow Pubs., Inc.
Schwartz, Heather E. & Meinking, Mary. Star Biographies. 2016. (Star Biographies Ser.). (ENG.). 32p. (gr. 3-4). lib. bdg. 139.95 (978-1-5157-4033-9(1), Snap Bks.) Capstone Press of Coughlan Cos.
Swartz, Clay. Who Wins? 100 Historical Figures Go Head-to-Head & You Decide the Winner! Booth, Tom, illus. 2016. (Who Wins? Ser.). (ENG.). 104p. (J). (gr. 3-6). spiral bd. 14.95 (978-0-7611-8544-4(5)) Workman Publishing Co., Inc.
Weakland, Mark. Leaders Doing Headstands. Grvina, Oksana et al, illus. 2016. (Leaders Doing Headstands Ser.). (ENG.). 32p. (gr. 2-3). 111.96 (978-1-4795-9687-4(6)) Picture Window Bks.
Wooten, Sara McIntosh. Donald Trump: Real Estate Mogul & President. 2017. (Influential Lives Ser.). 128p. (J). (gr. 7-8). lib. bdg. 37.27 **(978-0-7660-8499-5(X))** Enslow Pubs., Inc.

CELEBRITIES—FICTION

Bankes, Liz. Undeniable. 2015. (ENG.). 256p. (YA). (gr. 9). 17.99 (978-0-8027-3623-9(8), 9780802736239, Bloomsbury USA Childrens) Bloomsbury Publishing USA.
Baratz-Logsted, Lauren. Red Girl, Blue Boy: An If Only Novel. 2015. (If Only... Ser.). (ENG.). 304p. (YA). (gr. 7). pap. 9.99 (978-1-61963-685-9(9), 9781619636859, Bloomsbury USA Childrens) Bloomsbury Publishing USA.
Benincasa, Sara. Great. 2014. (ENG.). 272p. (YA). (gr. 9). 17.99 (978-0-06-222269-5(4), HarperTeen) HarperCollins Pubs.
Brown, Jeff. Showdown at the Alamo. 2013. (Flat Stanley's Worldwide Adventures Ser.: 10). (J). lib. bdg. 14.75 (978-0-606-35046-4(2), Turtleback) Turtleback Bks.
Colasanti, Susane. Now & Forever. 2014. (ENG.). 272p. (YA). (gr. 7). 17.99 (978-0-670-01424-8(9), Viking Books for Young Readers) Penguin Young Readers Group.
Costain, Meredith. Dreams Come True. McDonald, Danielle, illus. 2017. (Ella Diaries Ser.: 4). 144p. (J). pap. 5.99 (978-1-61067-523-9(1)) Kane Miller.
Cotler, Steve. Cheesie Mack Is Not Exactly Famous. Holgate, Douglas, illus. 2014. (Cheesie Mack Ser.). (ENG.). 256p. (J). (gr. 3-7). 15.99 (978-0-385-36984-8(0), Random Hse. Bks. for Young Readers) Random Hse. Children's Bks.
Daly, Niki. A Song for Jamela. Daly, Niki, illus. 2014. (ENG., Illus.). 36p. (J). (gr. -1-2). pap. 8.99 (978-1-84780-429-7(2), Frances Lincoln) Quarto Publishing Group UK GBR. Dist: Hachette Bk. Group.
Dimopoulos, Elaine. Material Girls. 2015. (ENG.). 336p. (YA). (gr. 9-12). 17.99 (978-0-544-38850-5(X), HMH Books For Young Readers) Houghton Mifflin Harcourt Publishing Co.
Duff, Hilary. True: An Elixir Novel. 2014. (Elixir Ser.). (ENG., Illus.). 304p. (YA). (gr. 7). pap. 9.99 (978-1-4424-0858-6(8), Simon & Schuster Bks. For Young Readers) Simon & Schuster Bks. For Young Readers.
Foreman, Matthew Sinclair. Disney Descendants - Secrets Revealed. 2016. (ENG.). 20p. (J). (gr. 3-6). 16.99 (978-0-7944-3750-3(8), Reader's Digest Children's Bks.) Studio Fun International.
Laybourne, Emmy. Sweet. 2015. (ENG.). 288p. (YA). (gr. 8). 17.99 (978-1-250-05519-4(9)) Feiwel & Friends.
Lee, Honest & Gilbert, Matthew J. The Fantastic & Terrible Fame of Classroom 13. 2018. (Classroom 13 Ser.: 3). (J). lib. bdg. 16.00 **(978-0-606-40639-0(5))** Turtleback Bks.
Locklear, Morgan & Locklear, Jennifer. Exposure. 2014. (ENG.). 271p. pap. 19.99 (978-1-62342-121-2(7)) Omnific Publishing.
Marciniak, Christine. Lights, Camera, All! 2013. 232p. pap. 13.99 (978-1-61271-214-7(2)) Zumaya Pubns. LLC.
Simon, Coco. Emma: Lights! Camera! Cupcakes! Halpin, Abigail, illus. 2014. (Cupcake Diaries: 19). (ENG.). 160p. (J). (gr. 3-7). pap. 6.99 (978-1-4424-9930-0(3), Simon Spotlight) Simon Spotlight.
You Came for Me. 2013. (ENG.). 240p. pap. 14.99 (978-1-60861-221-5(X)) Covenant Communications, Inc.

CELLS

see also DNA; Embryology; Protozoa

Abramovitz, Melissa. Stem Cells. 2012. (Hot Topics Ser.). (ENG., Illus.). 128p. (gr. 7-10). lib. bdg. 39.40 (978-1-4205-0748-5(6), Lucent Bks.) Cengage Gale.
Allman, Toney. Stem Cells. 2005. (Great Medical Discoveries Ser.). (ENG., Illus.). 128p. (YA). (gr. 7-10). lib. bdg. 30.85 (978-1-59018-772-2(5), Lucent Bks.) Cengage Gale.
Anders, Mason. Animal Cells. 2017. (Genetics Ser.). (ENG.). 32p. (gr. 3-4). lib. bdg. 27.32 **(978-1-5157-7259-0(4)**, Fact Finders) Capstone Press of Coughlan Cos.
Arato, Rona. Protists. 2010. (Class of Their Own Ser.). (ENG., Illus.). 48p. (J). (gr. 5-8). pap. (978-0-7787-5391-9(3)); lib. bdg. (978-0-7787-5377-3(8)) Crabtree Publishing Co.
Ballard, Carol. Cells & Cell Function. 2016. (Living Processes Ser.). (ENG., Illus.). 48p. (J). (gr. 7-11). pap. 11.99 (978-0-7502-9641-0(0), Wayland) Hachette Children's Group GBR. Dist: Hachette Bk. Group.
—Cells & Cell Function. 2010. (Living Processes Ser.). (Illus.). 48p. (J). pap. 11.75 (978-1-61532-349-4(X), 1306852); 48p. (YA). (gr. 5-8). lib. bdg. 29.25 (978-1-61532-342-5(2), 1306852); 46p. (J). 70.50 (978-1-61532-355-5(4), 1306852) Rosen Publishing Group, Inc., The. (Rosen Reference).
Belval, Brian, ed. Critical Perspectives on Stem Cell Research. (Critical Anthologies of Nonfiction Writing Ser.). 176p. 2009. (gr. 8-8). 63.90 (978-1-61512-080-2(7)) 2005. (YA). (gr. 7-12). lib. bdg. 37.95 (978-1-4042-0540-6(3)) Rosen Publishing Group, Inc., The.
Benchmark Education Company, LLC Staff. Cells Teacher's Guide. 2004. (978-1-4108-2584-1(1)) Benchmark Education Co.
Biskup, Agnieszka. Vampires & Cells, 1 vol. Jok, Diego, illus. 2011. (Monster Science Ser.). (ENG.). 32p. (gr. 3-4). pap. 8.10 (978-1-4296-7331-0(1), Graphic Library) Capstone Press of Coughlan Cos.
—Vampires & Cells. Jok, illus. 2011. (Monster Science Ser.). (ENG.). 32p. (gr. 3-4). pap. 47.70 (978-1-4296-7332-7(X), Graphic Library) Capstone Press of Coughlan Cos.
—Vampires & Cells, 1 vol. Jok, Diego, illus. 2011. (Monster Science Ser.). (ENG.). 32p. (gr. 3-4). lib. bdg. 30.65 (978-1-4296-6582-7(3), Graphic Library) Capstone Press of Coughlan Cos.
Black, Laura. The Stem Cell Debate: The Ethics & Science Behind the Research. 2006. (Issues in Focus Today Ser.). (Illus.). 128p. (J). (gr. 6). lib. bdg. 31.93 (978-0-7660-2545-5(4)) Enslow Pubs., Inc.
Building Blocks of Science: Understanding Cells & DNA Teacher's Guide (Firsthand Learning) 2007. ring bd. (978-0-89278-338-0(9)) Carolina Biological Supply Co.
Building Blocks of Science: Understanding Cells & DNA Unit Kit (Firsthand Learning) 2007. ring bd. (978-0-89278-433-2(4)) Carolina Biological Supply Co.
Canavan, Thomas. How Many Cells Are in Your Body? Questions about Cells & Systems. 2016. (Human Body FAQ Ser.). 00032p. (J). (gr. 3-3). pap. 10.00 (978-1-4994-3165-0(1), PowerKids Pr.) Rosen Publishing Group, Inc., The.
Cell Biology. 2011. (Science Made Simple Ser.). (ENG.). 64p. (YA). pap. 12.95 (978-1-4488-2241-6(6)) Rosen Publishing Group, Inc., The.
La Celula, el Origen de la Vida. (Coleccion Mundo Invisible). (SPA.). (YA). (gr. 5-8). pap. 8.00 (978-958-04-3223-4(6)) Norma S.A. COL. Dist: Distribuidora Norma, Inc.
Cobb, Allan B. Cell Theory. 2011. (Science Foundations Ser.). (Illus.). 104p. (gr. 6-12). 35.00 (978-1-60413-058-4(X), Chelsea Hse.) Facts On File, Inc.
Cohen, Marina. Cells. 2009. (Let's Relate to Genetics Ser.). (ENG., Illus.). 48p. (J). (gr. 5-8). lib. bdg. (978-0-7787-4945-5(2)); (gr. 6-9). pap. (978-0-7787-4962-2(2)) Crabtree Publishing Co.
—What Is Cell Theory? 2010. (Shaping Modern Science Ser.). (ENG.). 64p. (J). (gr. 5-8). pap. (978-0-7787-7206-4(3)); lib. bdg. (978-0-7787-7199-9(7)) Crabtree Publishing Co.
Coots, Catherine & Viegas, Jennifer. How Cells Function, 1 vol. 2015. (ENG.). 64p. (YA). 31.70 (978-1-62275-810-4(2), Britannica Educational Publishing) Rosen Publishing Group, Inc., The.
Cregan, Elizabeth R. C. All about Mitosis & Meiosis, 1 vol. 2007. (Science Readers Ser.). (SPA & ENG.). 32p. (J). (gr. 4-4). pap. 8.99 (978-0-7439-0585-5(7)) Shell Educational Publishing.
Design Cell Guide. 3rd rev. ed. 2004. 178p. pap. (978-0-86657-505-8(7)) Lab-Volt Systems, Inc.
Dowdy, Penny. Plant Cells. 2009. (Let's Relate to Genetics Ser.). (ENG., Illus.). 48p. (J). (gr. 6-9). pap. (978-0-7787-4963-9(0)) Crabtree Publishing Co.
Eaton, Louise & Rogers, Kara. Examining Cells. 2017. (J). lib. bdg. **(978-1-5383-0007-7(9))** Rosen Publishing Group, Inc., The.
Ellis, Catherine. Cars & Trucks. 2007. (Mega Military Machines Ser.). (Illus.). 24p. (J). (gr. 3-7). lib. bdg. 22.60 (978-1-4042-3669-1(4)) Rosen Publishing Group, Inc., The.
Favor, Lesli J. Eukaryotic & Prokaryotic Cell Structures: Understanding Cells with & Without a Nucleus. (Library of Cells Ser.). 48p. 2009. (gr. 5-5). 53.00 (978-1-60853-571-2(1)) 2004. (Illus.). (YA). lib. bdg. 29.25 (978-1-4042-0323-5(0)) Rosen Publishing Group, Inc., The.
Forman, Lillian. Stem Cell Research, 1 vol. 2007. (Essential Viewpoints Set 1 Ser.). (ENG., Illus.). 112p. (J). (gr. 6-12). lib. bdg. 35.64 (978-1-59928-864-2(8)) ABDO Publishing Co.
Freedman, Jeri. America Debates Stem Cell Research. (America Debates Ser.). 64p. (gr. 5-6). 2009. 58.50 (978-1-61511-334-7(7), Rosen Reference) 2007. (Illus.). (YA). lib. bdg. 31.95 (978-1-4042-1928-1(5)) Rosen Publishing Group, Inc., The.
—Ovarian Cancer: Current & Emerging Trends in Detection & Treatment. 2009. (Cancer & Modern Science Ser.). (J). lib. bdg. 31.95 (978-1-4358-5006-4(8)) Rosen Publishing Group, Inc., The.
French, Cathy. Cells & Las Células: 6 English, 6 Spanish Adaptations. 2011. (ENG & SPA.). (J). 101.00 net. (978-1-4108-5726-2(3)) Benchmark Education Co.
French, Kathy. Cells: Set Of 6. 2011. (Navigators Ser.). (J). pap. 50.00 net. (978-1-4108-2569-8(8)) Benchmark Education Co.
Friedman, Lauri S. Stem Cell Research. 2009. (Introducing Issues with Opposing Viewpoints Ser.). (ENG., Illus.). 144p. (gr. 7-10). 36.95 (978-0-7377-4175-9(9), Greenhaven Pr., Inc.) Cengage Gale.
Friedman, Lauri S., ed. Stem Cell Research. 2012. (Introducing Issues with Opposing Viewpoints Ser.). (ENG., Illus.). 144p. (gr. 7-10). lib. bdg. 36.95 (978-0-7377-6282-2(9), Greenhaven Pr., Inc.) Cengage Gale.
Friedman, Michael. Cell Communication: Understanding How Information Is Stored & Used in Cells. 2009. (Library of Cells Ser.). 48p. (gr. 5-5). 53.00 (978-1-60853-567-5(3)) Rosen Publishing Group, Inc., The.
GIANTmicrobes(r). GIANTmicrobes — Cells Coloring Book. Cutting, David, illus. 2014. (ENG.). 32p. (J). (gr. k-5). pap. 3.99 (978-0-486-78017-7(1)) Dover Pubns., Inc.
Green, Jen. Inside Animals. 2010. (Invisible Worlds Ser.). 48p. (gr. 4). 28.50 (978-0-7614-4195-3(6)) Marshall Cavendish Corp.
Hollar, Sherman. A Closer Look at Biology, Microbiology, & the Cell. 2011. (J). lib. bdg. 31.70 (978-1-61530-514-8(9)) Rosen Publishing Group, Inc., The.
Holt, Rinehart and Winston Staff. Holt Science & Technology Chapter 3: Life Science: Cells - Basic Units. 5th ed. 2004. (Illus.). pap. 12.86 (978-0-03-030171-1(8)) Holt McDougal.
—Holt Science & Technology Chapter 4: Life Science: The Cell in Action. 5th ed. 2004. (Illus.). pap. 12.86 (978-0-03-030176-6(9)) Holt McDougal.
Johnson, Rebecca L. Mighty Animal Cells. 2008. pap. 52.95 (978-0-8225-9382-9(3)) Lerner Publishing Group.
—Mighty Animal Cells. Desrocher, Jack & Fairman, Jennifer, illus. 2007. (Microquests Ser.). (ENG.). 48p. (gr. 3-5). lib. bdg. 29.27 (978-0-8225-7137-7(4), Millbrook Pr.) Lerner Publishing Group.
Johnson, Rebecca L. & National Geographic Learning Staff. Looking at Cells. 2007. (Nonfiction Reading & Writing Workshops Ser.). (ENG., Illus.). 32p. (J). pap. 17.95 (978-0-7922-8868-8(8)) CENGAGE Learning.
Johnson, Rebecca L. & Schifini, Alfredo. From Cells to Systems. 2007. (Avenues Ser.). (ENG., Illus.). 36p. (J). pap. 18.95 (978-0-7922-5410-2(4)) CENGAGE Learning.
Kaspar, Anna & Yablonski, Judy. How Plant & Animal Cells Differ, 1 vol. 2015. (ENG.). 64p. (YA). 31.70 (978-1-62275-804-3(8), Britannica Educational Publishing) Rosen Publishing Group, Inc., The.
Keyser, Amber J., et al. The Basics of Cell Life with Max Axiom, Super Scientist, 1 vol. 2009. (Graphic Science Ser.). (ENG., Illus.). 32p. (gr. 3-4). lib. bdg. 30.65 (978-1-4296-3414-4(6)); pap. 8.10 (978-1-4296-3904-0(0)) Capstone Press of Coughlan Cos. (Graphic Library).
Langwith, Jacqueline, ed. Stem Cells. 2011. (Opposing Viewpoints Ser.). (Illus.). 240p. pap. 29.45 (978-0-7377-5760-6(4), Greenhaven Pr., Inc.); (YA). (gr. 9-12). 42.95 (978-0-7377-5759-0(0)) Cengage Gale.
Lee, Kimberly Fekany. Looking Inside Cells, 1 vol. 2007. (Science Readers Ser.). (SPA & ENG.). 32p. (J). (gr. 4-4). pap. 8.99 (978-0-7439-0583-1(0)) Shell Educational Publishing.
The Library of Cells, 6 bk. set. 2005. (YA). (gr. 7-12). lib. bdg. 151.50 (978-1-4042-0379-2(6)) Rosen Publishing Group, Inc., The.
Lokere, Jillian. Cells: An Anthology of Current Thought. 2005. (Contemporary Discourse in the Field of Biology Ser.). (Illus.). 224p. (YA). (gr. 7-12). lib. bdg. 35.95 (978-1-4042-0398-3(2)) Rosen Publishing Group, Inc., The.
Lokere, Jillian, ed. Cells: An Anthology of Current Thought. 2009. (Contemporary Discourse in the Field of Biology Ser.). 224p. (gr. 10-12). 63.90 (978-1-61511-910-3(8)) Rosen Publishing Group, Inc., The.
Lomberg, Michelle. Animal Cells. 2016. (Illus.). 32p. (J). (978-1-5105-1184-2(9)) SmartBook Media, Inc.
Mangor, Jodie. Cells: Constructing Living Things. 2016. (Let's Explore Science Ser.). (ENG., Illus.). 48p. (gr. 5-8). 35.64 (978-1-68191-397-1(6)) Rourke Educational Media.
Marzilli, Alan. Stem Cell Research & Cloning. 2006. (Point/Counterpoint Ser.). (Illus.). 144p. (YA). (gr. 9-12). lib. bdg. 35.00 (978-0-7910-9230-9(5)) Facts On File, Inc.
McDougal-Littell Publishing Staff. Modules: Physical Science; Cells & Heredity Unit. 2004. (McDougal Littell Science Ser.). (ENG.). 64p. (gr. 6-8). pap., lab manual ed. 15.30 (978-0-618-43722-1(3), 2-01215) Great Source Education Group, Inc.
McLaughlin, Marc, et al. How Cells Send, Receive, & Process Information, 1 vol. 2015. (ENG.). 64p. (YA). 31.70 (978-1-62275-800-5(5), Britannica Educational Publishing) Rosen Publishing Group, Inc., The.
McManus, Lori. Cell Systems, 1 vol. 2010. (Investigating Cells Ser.). (ENG., Illus.). 48p. (gr. 3-6). 33.32 (978-1-4329-3879-6(7), Heinemann InfoSearch) Heinemann-Raintree.
Merchant, Raina G. & Favor, Lesli J. How Eukaryotic & Prokaryotic Cells Differ, 1 vol. 2015. (ENG.). 64p. (YA). 31.70 (978-1-62275-806-7(4), Britannica Educational Publishing) Rosen Publishing Group, Inc., The.
Moore, Pete. Stem Cell Research. 2011. (Ethical Debates Ser.). (ENG., Illus.). 48p. (YA). (gr. 5-8). pap. 11.75 (978-1-4488-7015-8(1)); lib. bdg. 29.25 (978-1-4488-6021-0(0)) Rosen Publishing Group, Inc., The. (Rosen Reference).
Mullins, Matt. Super Cool Science Experiments: Cells. 2009. (Explorer Library: Science Explorer Ser.). (ENG.). 32p. (gr. 4-8). lib. bdg. 28.50 (978-1-60279-517-4(7), 200287); (Illus.). pap. 14.21 (978-1-60279-596-9(7), 200882) Cherry Lake Publishing.
Nelson, Maria. Cells up Close. 2013. (Under the Microscope Ser.). 32p. (J). (gr. 4-6). pap. 70.20 (978-1-4339-8340-5(0)); (Illus.). 26.60 (978-1-4339-8338-2(9)); (Illus.). pap. 11.70 (978-1-4339-8339-9(7)) Stevens, Gareth Publishing LLLP.
Orr, Tamra. Ovarian Tumors & Cysts. 2009. (Library of Sexual Health Ser.). (YA). (gr. 7-12). lib. bdg. 31.95 (978-1-4358-5060-6(2)) Rosen Publishing Group, Inc., The.
Panno, Joseph. The Cell: Nature's First Life-Form. 2nd rev. ed. 2010. (New Biology Ser.). 304p. (gr. 6-12). 40.00 (978-0-8160-6849-4(6)) Facts On File, Inc.

Paris, Stephanie Herweck. Cells. 2015. (Science Readers: Content & Literacy Ser.). (Illus.). 32p. (gr. 5-5). pap. 8.99 (978-1-4807-4718-0(1)) Teacher Created Materials, Inc.

Rainis, Kenneth G. Cell & Microbe Science Fair Projects. rev. exp. ed. 2010. (Biology Science Projects Using the Scientific Method Ser.). (Illus.). 160p. (J). (gr. 5-18). 35.94 (978-0-7660-3420-4(8)) Enslow Pubs., Inc.

—Cell & Microbe Science Fair Projects: Using Microscopes, Mold, & More. 2005. (Biology! Best Science Projects Ser.). (Illus.). 128p. (J). (gr. 6-12). lib. bdg. 27.94 (978-0-7660-2369-7(9)) Enslow Pubs., Inc.

Rand, Casey. DNA & Heredity, 1 vol. 2010. (Investigating Cells Ser.). (ENG., Illus.). 48p. (gr. 3-6). 33.32 (978-1-4329-3880-2(0), Heinemann InfoSearch) Heinemann-Raintree.

Romano, Amy. Cell Specialization & Reproduction: Understanding How Cells Divide & Differentiate. (Library of Cells Ser.). 48p. 2009. (gr. 5-5). 53.00 (978-1-60853-570-5(3)) 2004. (Illus.). lib. bdg. 29.25 (978-1-4042-0322-8(2)) Rosen Publishing Group, Inc., The.

Rosen Publishing Staff. The Britannica Guide to Cell Biology, 1 vol. 2015. (Britannica Guide to Cell Biology Ser.). (ENG.). 64p. (YA). 190.20 (978-1-62275-812-8(9), Britannica Educational Publishing) Rosen Publishing Group, Inc., The.

Rushworth, Gary. Body Systems Human Cells: Set Of 6. 2011. (Navigators Ser.). (J). pap. 48.00 net. (978-1-4108-5086-7(2)) Benchmark Education Co.

Sakany, Lois. Cell Regulation: Understanding How Cell Functions, Growth, & Division Are Regulated. 2009. (Library of Cells Ser.). 48p. (gr. 5-5). 53.00 (978-1-60853-569-9(X)) Rosen Publishing Group, Inc., The.

—Cell Regulation: Understanding How Cell Functions. Growth, & Division are Regulated. 2004. (Library of Cells Ser.). (Illus.). 48p. (J). lib. bdg. 29.25 (978-1-4042-0321-1(4)) Rosen Publishing Group, Inc., The.

Sherman, Josepha. How Do We Know the Nature of the Cell. (Great Scientific Questions & the Scientists Who Answered Them Ser.). 112p. (gr. 7-12). 2009. 63.90 (978-1-61513-203-4(1)) 2005. (Illus.). (J). lib. bdg. 34.60 (978-1-4042-0072-2(X)) Rosen Publishing Group, Inc., The.

Silverstein, Alvin, et al. Cells. rev. ed. 2009. (Science Concepts, Second Ser.). (ENG.). 112p. (gr. 6-8). 31.93 (978-0-7613-3934-2(5)) Lerner Publishing Group.

Simon, Alyssa & Romano, Amy. How Cells Divide, Reproduce, & Specialize, 1 vol. 2015. (ENG.). 64p. (YA). 31.70 (978-1-62275-802-9(1), Britannica Educational Publishing) Rosen Publishing Group, Inc., The.

Somervill, Barbara A. Animal Cells & Life Processes, 1 vol. 2010. (Investigating Cells Ser.). (ENG., Illus.). 48p. (gr. 3-6). 33.32 (978-1-4329-3877-2(0), Heinemann InfoSearch) Heinemann-Raintree.

—Plant Cells & Life Processes, 1 vol. 2010. (Investigating Cells Ser.). (ENG.). 48p. (gr. 3-6). 33.32 (978-1-4329-3878-9(9), Heinemann InfoSearch) Heinemann-Raintree.

Spilsbury, Louise & Spilsbury, Richard. Cells, 1 vol. 2013. (Essential Life Science Ser.). (ENG.). 48p. (gr. 4-6). 33.32 (978-1-4329-7807-5(1), Heinemann InfoSearch) Heinemann-Raintree.

Stewart, Melissa. Cell Biology. 2007. (Great Ideas of Science Ser.). (Illus.). 80p. (YA). (gr. 9-12). lib. bdg. 27.93 (978-0-8225-6603-8(6)) Twenty First Century Bks.

Stille, Darlene R. Cells. 2007. (Gareth Stevens Vital Science-Life Science Ser.). 48p. (gr. 5-12). pap. 14.05 (978-0-8368-8446-3(9), Gareth Stevens Secondary Library) Stevens, Gareth Publishing LLLP.

Stille, Darlene R. & Ryback, Carol. Cells. 2007. (Gareth Stevens Vital Science- Life Science Ser.). (Illus.). 48p. (gr. 5-12). lib. bdg. 27.00 (978-0-8368-8437-1(X), Gareth Stevens Secondary Library) Stevens, Gareth Publishing LLLP.

Stimola, Aubrey. Cell Biology. 2011. (Science Made Simple Ser.). (Illus.). 64p. (YA). (gr. 5-8). lib. bdg. 31.95 (978-1-4488-1234-9(8)) Rosen Publishing Group, Inc., The.

Thomas, Isabel. What Is the Controversy over Stem Cell Research?, 1 vol. 2012. (Sci-Hi: Science Issues Ser.). (ENG.). 48p. (gr. 4-4). pap. 9.95 (978-1-4109-4474-0(3)); lib. bdg. 33.32 (978-1-4109-4467-2(0)) Heinemann-Raintree. (Sci-Hi).

Trefil, James, et al. Cells & Heredity. 2004. (McDougal Littell Middle School Science Ser.). (ENG., Illus.). 80p. (gr. 6-8). 21.80 (978-0-618-33427-8(0), 2-01015) Great Source Education Group, Inc.

Tucker, Clementine & Sakany, Lois. How Cell Processes Are Regulated, 1 vol. 2015. (ENG.). 64p. (YA). 31.70 (978-1-62275-809-8(9), Britannica Educational Publishing) Rosen Publishing Group, Inc., The.

Vescia, Monique, et al. What You Can Do about Sickle Cell Disease. 2015. (Contemporary Diseases & Disorders Ser.). (ENG., Illus.). 128p. (J). (gr. 7-7). 37.27 (978-0-7660-7040-0(9)) Enslow Pubs., Inc.

Wells, Robert E. What's Smaller Than a Pygmy Shrew? 2012. (J). (978-1-61913-158-3(7)) Weigl Pubs., Inc.

World Book, Inc Staff, contrib. by. The Cell Cycle. 2014. (J). (978-0-7166-2828-6(7)) World Bk., Inc.

World Book Staff. The Circulatory System. 2014. 32p. (978-0-7166-1841-6(9)) World Bk., Inc.

CELLS, ELECTRIC

see Electric Batteries

CELTIC LEGENDS

see Celts—Folklore; Legends—Ireland

CELTS

Bernard, Catherine. Celtic Mythology Rocks! Bock, William Sauts, illus. 2011. (Mythology Rocks! Ser.). 104p. (J). (gr. 6-18). lib. bdg. 33.27 (978-0-7660-3895-0(5)) Enslow Pubs., Inc.

Brezina, Corona. Celtic Mythology. 2009. (Mythology Around the World Ser.). 64p. (gr. 5-5). 58.50 (978-1-61514-748-9(9), Rosen Reference) Rosen Publishing Group, Inc., The.

Callery, Sean. The Celts. 2015. (Collins Big Cat Ser.). (ENG., Illus.). 48p. (J). (gr. 3-4). pap. 9.95 (978-0-00-812782-4(4)) HarperCollins Pubs. Ltd. GBR. Dist: Independent Pubs. Group.

Dougherty, Martin J. The Untold History of the Celts. 2016. (History Exposed Ser.). (ENG.). 224p. (YA). (gr. 9-9). 55.00 (978-1-5026-1900-6(8)) Cavendish Square Publishing.

Gagne, Tammy. The Celts of the British Isles. 2012. (Explore Ancient Worlds Ser.). (Illus.). 48p. (J). (gr. 3-6). lib. bdg. 29.95 (978-1-61228-283-1(0)) Mitchell Lane Pubs., Inc.

Gerace, Frank E. & Leslie, Clare Walker. The Ancient Celtic Festivals: And How We Celebrate Them Today. 2nd ed. 2008. (ENG., Illus.). 64p. (J). (gr. 4-7). pap. 12.95 (978-1-59477-256-6(8)) Inner Traditions International, Ltd.

Grant, Neil. Everyday Life of the Celts. Cappon, Manuela, illus. 2004. (Uncovering History Ser.). 46p. (J). (gr. 4-7). lib. bdg. 19.95 (978-1-58340-252-8(7)) Black Rabbit Bks.

Green, Jen. Ancient Celts: Archaeology Unlocks the Secrets of the Celts' Past. 2008. (National Geographic Investigates Ser.). (ENG., Illus.). 64p. (J). (gr. 5). lib. bdg. 27.90 (978-1-4263-0226-8(6), National Geographic Children's Bks.) National Geographic Society.

—The Celts & the Iron Age. 2016. (Discover Through Craft Ser.). (ENG., Illus.). 32p. (J). (gr. 2-4). pap. 12.99 (978-1-4451-3749-0(6), Franklin Watts) Hachette Children's Group GBR. Dist: Hachette Bk. Group.

Green, Jen & National Geographic Kids Staff. Ancient Celts: Archaeology Unlocks the Secrets of the Celts' Past. 2008. (National Geographic Investigates Ser.). (ENG., Illus.). 64p. (J). (gr. 5). 17.95 (978-1-4263-0225-1(8), National Geographic Children's Bks.) National Geographic Society.

Hinds, Kathryn. Ancient Celts: Europe's Tribal Ancestors. 2009. (Barbarians! Ser.). 80p. (gr. 6-8). 35.64 (978-0-7614-4062-8(3)) Marshall Cavendish Corp.

Leavy, Una. Magical Celtic Tales. O'Connor, Fergal, illus. 2017. (ENG.). 96p. (J). 21.00 **(978-1-84717-546-5(5))** O'Brien Pr., Ltd., The IRL. Dist: Dufour Editions, Inc.

Light, Douglas B. Cells, Tissues, & Skin. 2009. (Human Body: How It Works Ser.). (Illus.). 160p. (C). (gr. 9-18). 35.00 (978-1-60413-370-7(8), Chelsea Hse.) Facts On File, Inc.

MacDonald, Fiona. Hands-On History! the Celts: Step into the World of the Celtic Peoples, with 15 Step-By-Step Projects & over 400 Exciting Pictures. 2014. (ENG., Illus.). 64p. (J). (gr. 1-8). 12.99 (978-1-84322-993-3(5), Armadillo) Anness Publishing GBR. Dist: National Bk. Network.

Nelson, Jo. The Top Ten Britons. 2017. (ENG., Illus.). 48p. (J). pap. 8.99 **(978-0-00-820888-2(3))** HarperCollins Pubs. Ltd. GBR. Dist: Independent Pubs. Group.

Newland, Sonya. Celts. 2017. (Explore! Ser.). (ENG., Illus.). 32p. (J). (gr. 4-6). pap. 12.99 **(978-0-7502-9735-6(2)**, Wayland) Hachette Children's Group GBR. Dist: Hachette Bk. Group.

Pratt, Leonie. Celts: Information for Young Readers - Level 2. McKenna, Terry, illus. 2007. (Usborne Beginners Ser.). 32p. (J). 4.99 (978-0-7945-1580-5(0), Usborne) EDC Publishing.

Steele, Philip & MacDonald, Fiona. The Vikings & the Celts: Ancient Warriors & Raiders. 2010. (ENG., Illus.). 128p. (J). (gr. -1-12). pap. 17.99 (978-1-84476-878-3(3)) Anness Publishing GBR. Dist: National Bk. Network.

Taylor, Dereen. Celts. 2009. (Illus.). 48p. (YA). pap. 11.75 (978-1-4358-5517-5(5), 1300547, PowerKids Pr.); (gr. 3-6). 29.25 (978-1-4358-5516-8(7)) Rosen Publishing Group, Inc., The.

Wayland Publishers & Newland, Sonya. Celts. 2016. (ENG., Illus.). 32p. (J). (gr. 4-6). 17.99 (978-0-7502-9550-5(3), Wayland) Hachette Children's Group GBR. Dist: Hachette Bk. Group.

CELTS—FOLKLORE

Leonard, Scott A. Myths & Legends of Ancient Britain & Ireland. 2015. (Illus.). 64p. (J). (978-0-7166-2637-4(3)) World Bk., Inc.

Matthews, Caitlín. Celtic Memories. Whelan, Olwyn, illus. 2003. 80p. (J). 19.99 (978-1-84148-097-8(5)) Barefoot Bks., Inc.

CEMETERIES

Allen, Judy. Ghostly Graveyards. 2016. (Scary Places Ser.). (ENG., Illus.). 32p. (J). (gr. 4-8). 19.95 (978-1-943553-08-2(4)) Bearport Publishing Co., Inc.

Bodden, Valerie. Cemeteries. 2017. (J). (978-1-60818-806-2(X), Creative Education) Creative Co., The.

Burrows, Jennifer. Arlington National Cemetery. 2009. (War Memorials Ser.). (Illus.). 32p. (YA). (gr. 3-6). lib. bdg. 29.95 (978-1-60694-425-7(8)) Rourke Educational Media.

Demarest, Chris L. Arlington: The Story of Our Nation's Cemetery. Demarest, Chris L., illus. 2010. (ENG., Illus.). 32p. (J). (gr. 1-5). 18.99 (978-1-59643-517-9(8), 9781596435179) Roaring Brook Pr.

Ferut, Michael. St. Louis Cemetery No. 1. 2014. (Scariest Places on Earth Ser.). (ENG., Illus.). 24p. (J). (gr. 3-7). lib. bdg. 25.95 (978-1-60014-997-9(9), Torque Bks.) Bellwether Media.

George, Enzo. The Roman Catacombs. 2017. (Crypts, Tombs, & Secret Rooms Ser.). 48p. (gr. 4-5). pap. 84.30 **(978-1-5382-0643-0(9))** Stevens, Gareth Publishing LLLP.

Greene, Meg. Rest in Peace: A History of American Cemeteries. 2008. (People's History Ser.). (ENG., Illus.). 112p. (gr. 5-12). lib. bdg. 33.26 (978-0-8225-3414-3(2)) Lerner Publishing Group.

Huey, Lois Miner. Forgotten Bones: Uncovering a Slave Cemetery. 2015. (ENG., Illus.). 56p. (gr. 4-8). (J). lib. bdg. 30.65 (978-1-4677-3393-9(8)); 30.65 (978-1-4677-6300-4(4)) Lerner Publishing Group. (Millbrook Pr.).

Klepeis, Alicia Z. Haunted Cemeteries Around the World. 2017. (It's Haunted! Ser.). (ENG., Illus.). 32p. (gr. 3-4). lib. bdg. 27.99 (978-1-5157-3861-9(2), Snap Bks.) Capstone Press of Coughlan Cos.

Lynette, Rachel. Burial Grounds. 2009. (Mysterious Encounters Ser.). (ENG., Illus.). 48p. (gr. 4-8). 33.60 (978-0-7377-4411-8(1), Kidhaven) Cengage Gale.

Malam, John. Burial Places: Discover Stone, Bronze & Iron Age Britain. 2017. (Prehistoric Adventures Ser.). (ENG., Illus.). 32p. (J). (gr. 2-4). 17.99 (978-0-7502-9594-9(5), Wayland) Hachette Children's Group GBR. Dist: Hachette Bk. Group.

Markovics, Joyce L. Chilling Cemeteries. 2017. (Tiptoe into Scary Places Ser.). (ENG., Illus.). 24p. (J). (gr. k-3). 18.95 (978-1-68402-048-5(4)) Bearport Publishing Co., Inc.

Nagelhout, Ryan. Preserving the Dead. 2014. (Digging up the Dead Ser.). 32p. (J). (gr. 4-6). pap. 63.00 (978-1-4824-1234-5(9)) Stevens, Gareth Publishing LLLP.

Owings, Lisa. Ghosts in Cemeteries. 2016. (Ghost Stories Ser.). (ENG., Illus.). 24p. (J). (gr. 3-7). 25.95 (978-1-62617-427-6(X), Epic Bks.) Bellwether Media.

Rajczak, Kristen. Famous Graveyards. 2014. (Digging up the Dead Ser.). (Illus.). 32p. (J). (gr. 4-6). pap. 63.00 (978-1-4824-1232-1(2)) Stevens, Gareth Publishing LLLP.

Shea, Therese. The African Burial Ground. 2016. (Hidden History Ser.). 00032p. (J). pap. 10.50 (978-1-4824-5787-2(3)) Stevens, Gareth Publishing LLLP.

Williams, Dinah. Spooky Cemeteries. 2008. (Scary Places Ser.). (Illus.). 32p. (YA). (gr. 4-7). lib. bdg. 25.27 (978-1-59716-562-4(X)) Bearport Publishing Co., Inc.

Wood, Alix. Creepy Cemeteries. 2016. (World's Scariest Places Ser.). 00032p. (J). pap. 10.50 **(978-1-4824-5901-2(9))** Stevens, Gareth Publishing LLLP.

CEMETERIES—FICTION

Breslin, Theresa. Whispers in the Graveyard. 2004. (ENG.). 128p. (J). pap. 8.99 (978-0-7497-4480-9(4)) Egmont Bks., Ltd. GBR. Dist: Trafalgar Square Publishing.

Callaghan, Cindy. Sydney Mackenzie Knocks 'Em Dead. 2017. (ENG., Illus.). 256p. (J). (gr. 4-8). 17.99 (978-1-4814-6569-4(4), Simon & Schuster/Paula Wiseman Bks.) Simon & Schuster/Paula Wiseman Bks.

Charest, Jocelyne. La Loi du Talion. Fil & Julie, illus. 2004. (FRE.). 145p. (YA). 8.95 (978-2-922565-85-0(8)) Editions de la Paix CAN. Dist: World of Reading, Ltd.

Crawford, Clint. The Rag Tag Gang, 1 vol. 2009. 83p. pap. 19.95 (978-1-4489-9697-1(X)) America Star Bks.

Duckworth, Michael. Voodoo Island. Oxford University Press Staff & Bassett, Jennifer, eds. 3rd ed. 2008. (ENG., Illus.). 64p. 10.00 (978-0-19-479075-8(4)) Oxford Univ. Pr., Inc.

Enderle, Dotti. Beyond the Grave: An Up2U Mystery Adventure, 1 vol. Uhles, Mary, illus. 2013. (Up2U Adventures Ser.). (ENG.). 80p. (J). (gr. 2-5). 27.07 (978-1-61641-964-6(4), Calico Chapter Bks) Magic Wagon.

Etshied, Karl Jeffrey. Eggplant Rufus: Amused Indifference on a Stupid Planet. 2008. 158p. pap. (978-0-9814627-3-8(1)) Great American Pr., The.

Fleming, Candace. On the Day I Died: Stories from the Grave. 2012. (ENG.). 208p. (J). (gr. 5-9). 16.99 (978-0-375-86781-1(3), Schwartz & Wade Bks.) Random Hse. Children's Bks.

Gaiman, NEil. The Graveyard Book. McKean, Dave, illus. (J). 2014. (ENG.). 352p. (gr. 5-7). pap. 9.99 (978-0-06-234918-7(X)) 2010. (ENG.). 352p. (gr. 5). pap. 8.99 (978-0-06-053094-5(4)) 2008. 552p. pap. 17.99 (978-0-06-170912-8(3)) 2008. (ENG.). 320p. (gr. 5-7). 17.99 (978-0-06-053092-1(8)) 2008. 320p. (gr. 5-7). lib. bdg. 18.89 (978-0-06-053093-8(6)) HarperCollins Pubs.

—The Graveyard Book. 2009. 19.00 (978-1-60686-823-2(3)) Perfection Learning Corp.

—The Graveyard Book. 2011. (Literature Kit Ser.). (ENG., Illus.). 55p. pap. 12.95 (978-1-55319-559-7(0), Classroom Complete Pr.) Rainbow Horizons Publishing, Inc.

—The Graveyard Book, 7 vols. 2008. (J). 100.75 (978-1-4361-5887-9(7)); 256.75 (978-1-4361-5882-4(6)) Recorded Bks., Inc.

—The Graveyard Book. l.t. ed. 2009. (ENG.). 373p. (YA). 23.95 (978-1-4104-1441-0(8)) Thorndike Pr.

—The Graveyard Book. 2010. (J). lib. bdg. 19.65 (978-0-606-14883-2(3), Turtleback) Turtleback Bks.

—EL LIBRO DEL CEMENTERIO. (SPA.). 2010. 256p. pap. 20.95 (978-84-9918-146-2(5)) 2009. 306p. (YA). 20.95 (978-84-9918-030-4(2)) Roca Editorial ESP. Dist: Spanish Pubs., LLC.

Gaiman, NEil & Russell, P. Craig. The Graveyard Book Graphic Novel. Russell, P. Craig, illus. 2014. (ENG., Illus.). (J). (gr. 3-7). Vol. 1. 192p. 19.99 (978-0-06-219481-7(X)) Vol. 2. 176p. 19.99 (978-0-06-219483-1(6)) HarperCollins Pubs.

Huehner, Mariah. The First Day of the Rest of Her Life, Vol. 1. 2017. (Stitched Ser.: 1). (J). lib. bdg. 20.85 **(978-0-606-39878-7(3))** Turtleback Bks.

Jessell, Tim, illus. The Return of the Graveyard Ghost. 2013. (Boxcar Children Mysteries Ser.: 133). (ENG.). 128p. (J). (gr. 1-5). 5.99 (978-0-8075-6936-8(4)); 15.99 (978-0-8075-6935-1(6)) Whitman, Albert & Co.

Keith, David. Hands Across Time. 2010. 129p. pap. 10.98 (978-0-557-27121-4(5)) Lulu Pr., Inc.

Kerrin, Jessica Scott. The Spotted Dog Last Seen, 1 vol. 2013. (ENG.). 196p. (J). 14.95 (978-1-55498-387-2(8)) Groundwood Bks. CAN. Dist: Publishers Group West (PGW).

Longo, Jennifer. Six Feet over It. 2014. (ENG.). 352p. (YA). (gr. 7). 17.99 (978-0-449-81871-8(3), Random Hse. Bks. for Young Readers) Random Hse. Children's Bks.

McChiller, BBH. Monster Moon: Curse of Zala Manor. 2009. 192p. (J). (gr. 3-6). 15.95 (978-1-933277-10-3(6)) Stargazer Publishing Co.

Pavanello, Roberto. Treasure in the Graveyard, 1 vol. Zeni, Marco, tr. from ITA. Pisapia, Blasco & Brughera, Pamela, illus. 2012. (Echo & the Bat Pack Ser.). (ENG.). 128p. (gr. 2-3). 9.95 (978-1-4342-4248-8(X)) Stone Arch Bks.

Pratchett, Terry. Johnny & the Dead. 2006. (Johnny Maxwell Trilogy). 213p. (J). (gr. 3-7). 15.99 (978-0-06-054188-0(1)); lib. bdg. 16.89 (978-0-06-054189-7(X)) HarperCollins Pubs.

Price, Charlie. Dead Connection. 2008. (ENG.). 240p. (YA). (gr. 7). pap. 10.99 (978-0-312-37966-7(8), 9780312379667) Square Fish.

—Dead Investigation. 2015. (ENG.). 336p. (YA). (gr. 7). 18.99 (978-0-374-30227-6(8), 9780374302276, Farrar, Straus & Giroux (BYR)) Farrar, Straus & Giroux.

Ray, Delia. Here Lies Linc. (ENG.). 320p. (J). (gr. 3-7). 2012. 7.99 (978-0-375-86538-1(1), Yearling) 2011. 16.99 (978-0-375-86757-6(0), Knopf Bks. for Young Readers) Random Hse. Children's Bks.

Roy, Ron. The Zombie Zone. Gurney, John Steven, illus. 2005. (to Z Mysteries Ser.: 26). (ENG.). 96p. (J). (gr. 1-4). pap. 4.99 (978-0-375-82483-8(9), Random Hse. Bks. for Young Readers) Random Hse. Children's Bks.

Specter, Baron. All in a Night's Work, 1 vol. Kneupper, Setch, illus. 2012. (Graveyard Diaries Ser.). (ENG.). 128p. (J). (gr. 3-8). 27.07 (978-1-61641-903-5(2)) Magic Wagon.

—How Not to Be Killed by a Zombie, 1 vol. Kneupper, Setch, illus. 2012. (Graveyard Diaries Ser.). (ENG.). 128p. (J). (gr. 3-8). 27.07 (978-1-61641-900-4(8)) Magic Wagon.

—To Werewolf or Not to Werewolf, 1 vol. Kneupper, Setch, illus. 2012. (Graveyard Diaries Ser.). (ENG.). 128p. (J). (gr. 3-8). 27.07 (978-1-61641-901-1(6)) Magic Wagon.

—Vampires Are Not Your Friends, 1 vol. Kneupper, Setch, illus. 2012. (Graveyard Diaries Ser.). (ENG.). 128p. (J). (gr. 3-8). 27.07 (978-1-61641-902-8(4)) Magic Wagon.

Spector, Baron. Approaching the Undead, 1 vol. Kneupper, Setch, illus. 2012. (Graveyard Diaries Ser.). (ENG.). 128p. (J). (gr. 3-8). lib. bdg. 27.07 (978-1-61641-899-1(0), Calico Chapter Bks) Magic Wagon.

—Tracking Your Nightmare, 1 vol. Kneupper, Setch, illus. 2012. (Graveyard Diaries Ser.). (ENG.). 128p. (J). (gr. 3-8). lib. bdg. 27.07 (978-1-61641-898-4(2), Calico Chapter Bks) Magic Wagon.

Stine, R. L. The Attack of the Aqua Apes & Nightmare in 3-D: Twice Terrifying Tales. 2009. (R. L. Stine's Ghosts of Fear Street Ser.). (ENG.). 272p. (J). (gr. 3-7). pap. 12.99 (978-1-4169-9136-6(0), Aladdin) Simon & Schuster Children's Publishing.

—Hide & Shriek & Who's Been Sleeping in My Grave? Twice Terrifying Tales. 2009. (R. L. Stine's Ghosts of Fear Street Ser.). (ENG.). 256p. (J). (gr. 3-7). pap. 7.99 (978-1-4169-9134-2(4), Aladdin) Simon & Schuster Children's Publishing.

Strange, Jason. The Graveyard Plot, 1 vol. Evergreen, Nelson & Kendall, Bradford, illus. 2012. (Jason Strange Ser.). (ENG.). 72p. (gr. 2-3). pap. 6.25 (978-1-4342-3886-3(5)) Stone Arch Bks.

Teitelbaum, Michael. Night of the Gravedigger. 2015. (Cold Whispers Ser.). (ENG., Illus.). 32p. (J). (gr. 2-6). lib. bdg. 26.60 (978-1-62724-805-1(6)) Bearport Publishing Co., Inc.

Thomas, Deborah Kadiar. Cemetery Jamboree, 1 vol. Thomas, Deborah Kadiar, illus. 2016. (ENG., Illus.). 32p. (J). (gr. k-5). pap. 9.95 (978-1-4556-2239-9(7)) Pelican Publishing Co., Inc.

CENSORSHIP

Abdo Publishing. Hot Topics in Media, 1 vol. 2013. (Hot Topics in Media Ser.: 6). (ENG.). 48p. (J). (gr. 3-6). lib. bdg. 196.74 (978-1-61783-730-2(X)) ABDO Publishing Co.

Barbour, William. Censorship. 2010. (Opposing Viewpoints Ser.). (Illus.). 240p. (J). pap. 29.45 (978-0-7377-4762-1(5), Greenhaven Pr., Inc.) Cengage Gale.

Bily, Cynthia A., ed. Banned Books. 2012. (Introducing Issues with Opposing Viewpoints Ser.). (ENG., Illus.). 144p. (J). (gr. 7-10). lib. bdg. 36.95 (978-0-7377-5671-5(3), Greenhaven Pr., Inc.) Cengage Gale.

Harris, Ashley Rae. Graphic Novels, 1 vol. 2013. (Hot Topics in Media Ser.). (ENG.). 48p. (J). (gr. 3-6). lib. bdg. 32.79 (978-1-61783-733-3(4)); (Illus.). pap. 15.64 (978-1-61783-783-8(0)) ABDO Publishing Co.

Herda, D. J. Fighting Censorship: New York Times V. United States. 2016. (US Supreme Court Landmark Cases Ser.). (Illus.). 128p. (J). 37.27 (978-0-7660-8432-2(9)) Enslow Pubs., Inc.

Hinds, Maurene J. John Steinbeck: Banned, Challenged, & Censored. 2008. (Authors of Banned Bks). (Illus.). 160p. (YA). (gr. 3-7). lib. bdg. 35.94 (978-0-7660-2688-9(4)) Enslow Pubs., Inc.

Houle, Michelle M. Mark Twain: Banned, Challenged, & Censored. 2008. (Authors of Banned Bks). (Illus.). 160p. (YA). (gr. 4-7). lib. bdg. 35.94 (978-0-7660-2689-6(2)) Enslow Pubs., Inc.

Lankford, Ronnie D. Censorship. 2010. (Issues That Concern You Ser.). (Illus.). 144p. (J). 36.95 (978-0-7377-4744-7(7)) Cengage Gale.

Lusted, Marcia Amidon. Banned Books. 2013. (ENG.). 48p. (J). pap. 15.64 (978-1-61783-781-4(4)); (gr. 3-6). lib. bdg. 32.79 (978-1-61783-731-9(8)) ABDO Publishing Co.

Magoon, Kekla. Media Censorship, 1 vol. 2009. (Essential Viewpoints Set 4 Ser.). (ENG., Illus.). 112p. (J). (gr. 6-12). lib. bdg. 35.64 (978-1-60453-533-4(4)) ABDO Publishing Co.

McClellan, Marilyn. Madeleine L'Engle: Banned, Challenged, & Censored. 2008. (Authors of Banned Bks). (Illus.). 160p. (YA). (gr. 4-7). lib. bdg. 35.94 (978-0-7660-2708-4(2)) Enslow Pubs., Inc.

Merino, Noël. Censorship. 2010. (Introducing Issues with Opposing Viewpoints Ser.). (Illus.). 144p. (J). 36.95 (978-0-7377-4731-7(5), Greenhaven Pr., Inc.) Cengage Gale.

Otfinoski, Steven. Classic Books. 2009. (Our Freedom to Read Ser.). 144p. (gr. 5-8). 40.00 (978-1-60413-029-4(6), Chelsea Hse.) Facts On File, Inc.

—Coming-of-Age Fiction. 2009. (Freedom to Read Ser.). 144p. (gr. 5-8). 40.00 (978-1-60413-030-0(X), Chelsea Hse.) Facts On File, Inc.

Riggs, Thomas. Book Banning. 2011. (At Issue Ser.). (ENG.). 128p. (gr. 10-12). 39.40 (978-0-7377-5554-1(7)); pap. 27.80 (978-0-7377-5555-8(5), Greenhaven Pr., Inc.) Cengage Gale.

Vos MacDonald, Joan. J. K. Rowling: Banned, Challenged, & Censored. 2008. (Authors of Banned Bks). (Illus.). 160p. (YA). (gr. 3-7). lib. bdg. 35.94 (978-0-7660-2687-2(6)) Enslow Pubs., Inc.

CENSORSHIP—FICTION

Crutcher, Chris. The Sledding Hill. 2006. (ENG.). 256p. (YA). (gr. 8-12). pap. 9.99 (978-0-06-050245-4(2), Greenwillow Bks.) HarperCollins Pubs.

Downey, Jen Swann. The Ninja Librarians: The Accidental Keyhand. 2015. (Ninja Librarians Ser.: 1). (ENG.). 400p. (J). (gr. 4-7). pap. 8.99 (978-1-4926-0180-7(2), Sourcebooks Jabberwocky) Sourcebooks, Inc.

Grabenstein, Chris. Mr. Lemoncello's Library Olympics. (ENG., (J). (gr. 3-7). 2017. Illus.). 320p. 7.99 **(978-0-553-51042-3(8)**, Yearling) 2016. 288p. 16.99 (978-0-553-51040-9(1), Random Hse. Bks. for Young Readers) 2016. 288p. lib. bdg. 19.99 (978-0-553-51041-6(X), Random Hse. Bks. for Young Readers) Random Hse. Children's Bks.

—Mr. Lemoncello's Library Olympics. 2017. lib. bdg. 18.40 **(978-0-606-39875-6(9))** Turtleback Bks.

Reed, M. K. Americus. Hill, Jonathan David, illus. 2011. (ENG.). 224p. (YA). (gr. 7). pap. 16.99 (978-1-59643-601-5(8), 9781596436015, First Second Bks.) Roaring Brook Pr.

CENTIPEDES

Amstutz, Lisa J. Centipedes, 1 vol. 2013. (Creepy Crawlers Ser.). (ENG., Illus.). 24p. (gr. k-1). lib. bdg. 26.65

(978-1-4765-2053-7(4), Pebble Plus) Capstone Press of Coughlan Cos.

Bishop, Celeste. Crawling Centipedes. 2015. (Icky Animals! Small & Gross Ser.). (ENG.). 24p. (J). (gr. 1-1). pap. 8.25 *(978-1-4994-0692-4(4)*, PowerKids Pr.) Rosen Publishing Group, Inc., The.

Bodden, Valerie. Centipedes. 2011. (Creepy Creatures Ser.). 24p. (J). (gr. 1-3). (ENG.). pap. 7.99 *(978-0-89812-565-8(0)*, Creative Paperbacks); 24.25 *(978-1-58341-992-2(6)*, Creative Education) Creative Co., The.

—Centipedes. 2010. (Illus.). 24p. (J). 8.95 *(978-1-926853-72-7(5))* Saunders Bk. Co. CAN. Dist: Creative Co., The.

Clark, Willow & Rockwood, Leigh. Centipedes & Millipedes Are Gross! 2010. (Creepy Crawlies Ser.). 24p. (J). (ENG.). pap. 8.25 *(978-1-4488-1363-6(8)*, PowerKids Pr.); (Illus.). lib. bdg. 22.60 *(978-1-4488-0701-7(8))* Rosen Publishing Group, Inc., The.

Dahl, Michael. ¡Córrele, Córrele Ciempiés! Cuenta de Diez en Diez. Trover, Zachary, illus. 2010. (Apréndete Tus Números/Know Your Numbers Ser.).Tr. of Speed, Speed Centipede! - Counting by Tens. (SPA & MUL.). 24p. (gr. -1-2). lib. bdg. 26.65 *(978-1-4048-6299-9(4))* Picture Window Bks.

Elkin, Matthew. 20 Fun Facts about Centipedes. 2013. (Fun Fact File: Bugs! Ser.). (Illus.). 32p. (J). (gr. 2-5). pap. 10.50 *(978-1-4339-8231-6(5))*; lib. bdg. 25.25 *(978-1-4339-8230-9(7))* Stevens, Gareth Publishing LLLP.

Feltes Taylor, Kimberly. Scorpion vs. Centipede: Duel to the Death. 2016. (Bug Wars Ser.). (ENG., Illus.). 32p. (gr. 3-4). lib. bdg. 27.99 *(978-1-4914-8066-3(1)*, Edge Bks.) Capstone Press of Coughlan Cos.

Gates, Margo. Centipedes. (Illus.). 24p. (J). 2014. *(978-0-531-28476-6(X))* 2013. (ENG., lib. bdg. 25.95 *(978-1-60014-918-4(9)*, Blastoff! Readers) Bellwether Media.

Hartley, Karen, et al. Centipede. (Bug Bks.). 32p. pap. 6.95 *(978-1-4034-3323-7(2))* Heinemann-Raintree.

Lunis, Natalie. Leggy Centipedes. 2009. (No Backbone! Ser.). (Illus.). 24p. (J). (gr. k-3). lib. bdg. 21.28 *(978-1-59716-752-9(5))* Bearport Publishing Co., Inc.

Mitchell, Susan K. Biggest vs. Smallest Creepy, Crawly Creatures. 2010. (Biggest vs. Smallest Animals Ser.). (Illus.). 24p. (J). 22.60 *(978-0-7660-3581-2(6)*, Enslow Elementary) Enslow Pubs., Inc.

Petrie, Kristin. Centipedes, 1 vol. 2009. (Bugs! Ser.). (ENG.). 32p. (gr. 3-6). 27.07 *(978-1-60453-065-0(0)*, Checkerboard Library) ABDO Publishing Co.

Rissman, Rebecca. Centipedes, 1 vol. 2012. (Creepy Critters Ser.). (ENG., Illus.). 24p. (gr. -1-k). lib. bdg. 25.32 *(978-1-4109-4805-2(6))* Heinemann-Raintree.

Schuetz, Kari. Centipedes. 2015. (Creepy Crawlies Ser.). (ENG., Illus.). 24p. (J). (gr. k-3). lib. bdg. 25.95 *(978-1-62617-221-0(8)*, Blastoff! Readers) Bellwether Media.

Slade, Suzanne. Do All Bugs Have Wings? And Other Questions Kids Have about Bugs, 1 vol. Pillo, Cary, illus. 2010. (Kids' Questions Ser.). (ENG.). 24p. (gr. 1-2). lib. bdg. 26.65 *(978-1-4048-5761-2(3))* Picture Window Bks.

CENTIPEDES—FICTION

Banks, Lynne Reid. Harry the Poisonous Centipede: A Story to Make You Squirm. 118p. (J). (gr. 1-3). pap. 4.50 *(978-0-8072-1523-4(6)*, Listening Library) Random Hse. Audio Publishing Group.

—Harry the Poisonous Centipede Goes to Sea. Ross, Tony, illus. 2006. 203p. (J). (gr. 3-7). lib. bdg. 16.89 *(978-0-06-077549-0(1))* HarperCollins Pubs.

Dixon, Dallas L. Shelby's Collection Day. Williams, Nancy E., ed. Forrest, Grace Metzger, illus. 2013. 24p. (J). pap. 12.98 *(978-1-938526-54-1(6))* Laurus Bks.

Itoh, Shimpei. Hyper Dolls, Vol. 5. 2003. (Illus.). 208p. pap. 15.95 *(978-1-929090-67-9(6))* International Comics & Entertainment L.L.C.

Ogle, Bonnie. Arthur the Arthropod. 2012. 28p. pap. 15.99 *(978-1-4771-1424-7(6))* Xlibris Corp.

Ramsay, Betsy. Cecil Centipede's Career. Christman, Therese, illus. 2005. 25p. (J). per. 19.99 *(978-1-4208-7870-7(0))* AuthorHouse.

Ross, Tony. Centipede's One Hundred Shoes. Ross, Tony, illus. rev. ed. 2003. (ENG., Illus.). 32p. (J). (gr. -1-3). 18.99 *(978-0-8050-7298-3(5)*, 9780805072983, Holt, Henry & Co. Bks. For Young Readers) Holt, Henry & Co.

Snyder, Susan. The Very Stubborn Centipede. Johanson, Anna, illus. 2005. 24p. (J). (gr. 2-4). 9.95 *(978-0-9767163-0-3(5))* Kotzig Publishing, Inc.

Top That Publishing Staff, ed. Millie the Millipede: Collects Colors as She Munches Her Way Through the Pages. Elliott, Rebecca, illus. 2007. (Story Book Ser.). 20p. (J). (gr. -1). bds. *(978-1-84666-274-4(5)*, Tide Mill Pr.) Top That! Publishing PLC.

Williams, Dawn. Cyril T. Centipede Looks for New Shoes, 1. Chou, Joey, illus. 2006. 48p. (J). (gr. -1-3). 15.00 *(978-0-9770783-0-1(2))* SunriseHouse Pubs.

CENTRAL AMERICA

Cammarata, Jan. Karli's Kritters. 2009. 20p. pap. 12.00 *(978-1-4389-6726-4(8))* AuthorHouse.

Cox, Vicki. Oscar Arias Sanchez: Bringing Peace to Central America. 2007. (Modern Peacemakers Ser.). (Illus.). 118p. (YA). (gr. 9-12). lib. bdg. 30.00 *(978-0-7910-8999-6(1))* Facts On File, Inc.

Keedle, Jayne. Americans from the Caribbean & Central America. 2009. (New Americans Ser.). 80p. (gr. 5-8). 35.64 *(978-0-7614-4302-5(9))* Marshall Cavendish Corp.

Malam, John. Pyramids. 2010. (100 Things You Should Know About Ser.). (Illus.). 32p. (YA). (gr. 4-6). lib. bdg. 19.95 *(978-1-4222-1525-8(3))* Mason Crest.

McGaffey, Leta & Spilling, Michael. Honduras. 2nd rev. ed. 2009. (Cultures of the World 18 Ser.). 144p. (gr. 6). 42.79 *(978-0-7614-4848-8(9))* Marshall Cavendish Corp.

Miller, Debra A. Belize. 2005. (Modern Nations of the World Ser.). (ENG., Illus.). 112p. (YA). (gr. 7-10). lib. bdg. 30.85 *(978-1-59018-726-5(1)*, Lucent Bks.) Cengage Gale.

Putnam, James. Pyramid. 2011. (DK Eyewitness Bks.). (ENG.). 72p. (J). (gr. 3-7). 16.99 *(978-0-7566-5832-8(2)*, DK Children) Dorling Kindersley Publishing, Inc.

Schwartz, Eric. Central American Immigrants to the United States: Refugees from Unrest. 2007. (Hispanic Heritage Ser.). (Illus.). 112p. (YA). (gr. 4-7). lib. bdg. 22.95 *(978-1-59084-929-3(9))* Mason Crest.

Streissguth, Tom. Belize in Pictures. 2009. (Visual Geography Series, Second Ser.). (ENG.). 80p. (gr. 5-12). 31.93 *(978-1-57505-958-7(4)*, Twenty-First Century Bks.) Lerner Publishing Group.

Woods, Michael & Woods, Mary B. Seven Natural Wonders of Central & South America. 2009. (Seven Wonders Ser.). (Illus.). 80p. (YA). (gr. 5-9). lib. bdg. 33.26 *(978-0-8225-9070-5(0))* Twenty First Century Bks.

CENTRAL AMERICA—ANTIQUITIES

Hofer, Charles. Ancient Maya Technology. 2016. (Spotlight on the Maya, Aztec, & Inca Civilizations Ser.). (Illus.). 32p. (J). (gr. 6-4). 26.25 *(978-1-4994-1983-2(X)*, PowerKids Pr.) Rosen Publishing Group, Inc., The.

Weil, Ann. The World's Most Amazing Pyramids, 1 vol. 2011. (Landmark Top Tens Ser.). (ENG., Illus.). 32p. (gr. 3-5). 30.65 *(978-1-4109-4240-1(6)*, Raintree Perspectives) Heinemann-Raintree.

Woods, Michael & Woods, Mary B. Seven Wonders of Ancient Central & South America. 2008. (Seven Wonders Ser.). (ENG., Illus.). 80p. (gr. 5-8). lib. bdg. 33.26 *(978-0-8225-7570-2(1))* Lerner Publishing Group.

CENTRAL AMERICA—HISTORY

Benchmark Education Co., LLC. Ancient Cultures of Mesoamerica. 2014. (PRIME Ser.). (J). (gr. 6-8). pap. *(978-1-4509-9484-2(9))* Benchmark Education Co.

Boyd, Judy. Central America & the Caribbean, Vol. 10. 2016. (Social Progress & Sustainability Ser.). (Illus.). 80p. (J). (gr. 7). 24.95 *(978-1-4222-3493-8(2))* Mason Crest.

DePietro, Frank. Central American Immigrants. 2012. (J). pap. *(978-1-4222-2334-5(5))* Mason Crest.

—Central American Immigrants. Limón, José E., ed. 2012. (Hispanic Americans: Major Minority Ser.). 64p. (J). (gr. 4). 22.95 *(978-1-4222-2317-8(5))* Mason Crest.

Frazel, Ellen. Honduras. 2013. (Exploring Countries Ser.). (ENG., Illus.). 32p. (J). (gr. 3-7). lib. bdg. 26.95 *(978-1-60014-860-6(3)*, Blastoff! Readers) Bellwether Media.

George, Charles & George, Linda. Mayan Civilization. 2010. (World History Ser.). (Illus.). 128p. (J). 34.95 *(978-1-4205-0240-4(9)*, Lucent Bks.) Cengage Gale.

Hernandez, Romel. Immigration from Central America. 2005. (Changing Face of North America Ser.). (Illus.). 112p. (YA). lib. bdg. 24.95 *(978-1-59084-688-9(5))* Mason Crest.

Jermyn, Leslie & Yong, Jui Lin. Belize. 2nd rev. ed. 2010. (Cultures of the World 22 Ser.). 144p. (gr. 6). 42.79 *(978-1-60870-452-1(1))* Marshall Cavendish Corp.

Kennedy, Mike & Stewart, Mark. Soccer in Central America. 2011. (Smart about Soccer Ser.). 24p. (J). (gr. k-3). lib. bdg. 22.60 *(978-1-59953-443-5(6))* Norwood Hse. Pr.

Kuskowski, Alex. Super Simple South & Central American Art: Fun & Easy Art from Around the World, 1 vol. 2012. (ENG.). 32p. 27.07 *(978-1-61783-215-4(4)*, Super SandCastle) ABDO Publishing Co.

Malam, John. Pyramids. 2015. (100 Facts You Should Know Ser.). (ENG., Illus.). 48p. (J). (gr. 4-5). lib. bdg. 31.95 *(978-1-4824-2185-9(2))* Stevens, Gareth Publishing LLLP.

Maloy, Jackie. The Ancient Maya. (True Book(tm), a — Ancient Civilizations Ser.). (ENG.). 48p. (J). 2009. (gr. 2-5). 31.00 *(978-0-531-25229-1(9))* 2010. (Illus.). (gr. 3-5). pap. 6.95 *(978-0-531-24110-3(6))* Scholastic Library Publishing.

Nicaragua. 2010. (Modern World Nations Ser.). (Illus.). 128p. (J). (gr. 6-12). 35.00 *(978-1-60413-619-7(7)*, Chelsea Hse.) Facts On File, Inc.

Patkau, Karen. Who Needs a Jungle? 2012. (Ecosystem Ser.). (ENG., Illus.). 32p. (J). (gr. 2-5). 17.95 *(978-0-88776-992-4(6)*, Tundra Bks.) Tundra Bks. CAN. Dist: Penguin Random Hse. LLC.

Scholl, Elizabeth J. The Mayan Civilization. 2009. (How'd They Do That? Ser.). (Illus.). 64p. (J). (gr. 4-8). lib. bdg. 33.95 *(978-1-58415-822-6(0))* Mitchell Lane Pubs., Inc.

Shields, Charles J. Belize. 2010. (Central America Today Ser.). 63p. (YA). (gr. 7-18). pap. 9.95 *(978-1-4222-0711-6(0))*; (Illus.). (gr. 9-12). 21.95 *(978-1-4222-0644-7(0))* Mason Crest.

—Belize, Vol. 8. Henderson, James D., ed. 2015. (Discovering Central America: History, Politics, & Culture Ser.). (Illus.). 64p. (J). (gr. 7). lib. bdg. 22.95 *(978-1-4222-3285-9(9))* Mason Crest.

—Central America: Facts & Figures. 2010. (Central America Today Ser.). (YA). 63p. (YA). (gr. 7-18). pap. 9.95 *(978-1-4222-0712-3(9))*; (Illus.). 64p. (gr. 9-12). 21.95 *(978-1-4222-0645-4(9))* Mason Crest.

—Central America: Facts & Figures, Vol. 8. Henderson, James D., ed. 2015. (Discovering Central America: History, Politics, & Culture Ser.). (Illus.). 64p. (J). (gr. 7). lib. bdg. 22.95 *(978-1-4222-3286-6(7))* Mason Crest.

Somervill, Barbara A. Ancient Maya. 2012. (Ancient World Ser.). (ENG.). 112p. (J). pap. 9.95 *(978-0-531-25981-8(1))*; (gr. 6-9). lib. bdg. 34.00 *(978-0-531-25181-2(0))* Scholastic Library Publishing.

Torres, John Albert. The Guatemalan Genocide of the Maya People. 2017. (J). ***(978-1-5081-7736-4(8))*** Rosen Publishing Group, Inc., The.

VanVoorst, Jennifer Fretland. The Ancient Maya, 1 vol. 2012. (Exploring the Ancient World Ser.). (ENG., Illus.). 48p. (gr. 5-6). 29.32 *(978-0-7565-4564-2(1))* Compass Point Bks.

—The Ancient Maya, 1 vol. 2012. (Exploring the Ancient World Ser.). (ENG., Illus.). 48p. (gr. 5-6). pap. 9.10 *(978-0-7565-4584-0(6))* Compass Point Bks.

CENTRAL EUROPE

see Europe, Central

CENTRAL STATES

see Middle West

CEREBRAL PALSY

Bjarnadottir, Hildur. The Triplets. 2011. 24p. 14.93 *(978-1-4269-5284-5(8))* Trafford Publishing.

Bjorklund, Ruth. Cerebral Palsy. 2006. (Health Alert Ser.). (Illus.). 64p. (gr. 4-7). lib. bdg. 32.79 *(978-0-7614-2209-9(9)*, Benchmark Bks.) Marshall Cavendish Corp.

Busby, Barbara Sheen. Cerebral Palsy. Kling, Andrew A., ed. 2012. (Diseases & Disorders Ser.). (ENG.). 128p. (gr. 7-10). lib. bdg. 39.90 *(978-1-4205-0836-9(9)*, Lucent Bks.) Cengage Gale.

Curran, Abbey & Kaye, Elizabeth. The Courage to Compete: Living with Cerebral Palsy & Following My Dreams. 2015. (ENG., Illus.). 272p. (YA). (gr. 8-7). 17.99 *(978-0-06-236391-6(3))* HarperCollins Pubs.

Gilman, Laura Anne. Coping with Cerebral Palsy. (Coping Ser.). 192p. (gr. 7-12). 2009. 63.90 *(978-1-61511-994-3(9))* 2005. (Illus.). (J). lib. bdg. 34.60 *(978-0-8239-3150-7(1))* Rosen Publishing Group, Inc., The.

Levete, Sarah. Explaining Cerebral Palsy. 2009. (Explaining... Ser.). 48p. (gr. 7-12). 37.10 *(978-1-59920-311-9(1))* Black Rabbit Bks.

Levine, Michelle. Cerebral Palsy. 2015. (Living With... Ser.). (Illus.). 32p. (J). 28.50 *(978-1-60753-482-2(7))* Amicus Publishing.

Ninteau, Sherrie. Rick's Story-the Story of Rick Hoyt. 2009. (J). 14.95 *(978-1-934878-87-3(1))* Mascot Bks., Inc.

Philip, Aaron & Bolden, Tonya. This Kid Can Fly: It's about Ability (NOT Disability) 2016. (Illus.). 192p. (J). (gr. 3-7). 16.99 *(978-0-06-240354-4(0))* HarperCollins Pubs.

Pincus, Dion. Everything You Need to Know about Cerebral Palsy. 2005. (Need to Know Library). (Illus.). 64p. (YA). (gr. 7-12). lib. bdg. 31.95 *(978-0-8239-2960-3(4)*, NTCEPA) Rosen Publishing Group, Inc., The.

Sheen, Barbara. Cerebral Palsy. 2003. (Diseases & Disorders Ser.). (ENG., Illus.). 96p. (J). 33.45 *(978-1-59018-038-9(0)*, Lucent Bks.) Cengage Gale.

Ziemer, Laura. Deena, My Best Friend. 2012. 28p. pap. 10.95 *(978-1-4626-6765-9(1))* America Star Bks.

CEREBRAL PALSY—FICTION

Abdullah, Shaila & Abdullah, Aanyah. My Friend Suhana: A Story of Friendship & Cerebral Palsy. 2014. 30p. pap. 14.95 *(978-1-61599-211-9(1))* Loving Healing Pr., Inc.

Burkhart, Alma J. If You Could See Her Smile. Burns, Sandra, illus. 2013. 24p. pap. 8.99 *(978-1-938768-32-3(9))* Gypsy Pubns.

Draper, Sharon M. Out of My Mind. 2009. 9.00 *(978-0-7848-3780-1(5)*, Everbind) Marco Bk. Co.

—Out of My Mind. (ENG., Illus.). (J). (gr. 5). 2012. 320p. pap. 9.99 *(978-1-4169-7171-9(8))* 2010. 304p. 18.99 *(978-1-4169-7170-2(X))* Simon & Schuster Children's Publishing. (Atheneum Bks. for Young Readers).

—Out of My Mind. 2012. lib. bdg. 20.85 *(978-0-606-25672-8(5)*, Turtleback) Turtleback Bks.

Hiner, Danielle E. Mommy Can I Play with Tommy? Based on Joseph Hiner, a boy with Cerebral Palsy. 2004. 25p. pap. 24.95 *(978-1-4137-2677-0(1))* America Star Bks.

Johnson, Harriet McBryde. Accidents of Nature. rev. ed. 2006. (ENG.). 240p. (YA). (gr. 7-12). 19.99 *(978-0-8050-7634-9(4)*, Holt, Henry & Co. Bks. For Young Readers) Holt, Henry & Co.

—Accidents of Nature. rev. l.t. ed. 2007. (Thorndike Literacy Bridge Ser.). 273p. (YA). (gr. 7-12). 22.95 *(978-0-7862-9182-3(6))* Thorndike Pr.

Kamata, Suzanne. Gadget Girl: The Art of Being Invisible. 2013. (ENG., Illus.). 256p. (YA). pap. 14.95 *(978-1-936846-38-2(1))* GemmaMedia.

Kinra, Richa, illus. The Princess Panda Tea Party: A Cerebral Palsy Fairy Tale. 2014. 45p. (J). pap. 14.95 *(978-1-61599-219-5(7))* Loving Healing Pr., Inc.

Koertge, Ron. Now Playing: Stoner & Spaz II. 2011. (ENG., Illus.). 224p. (YA). (gr. 9-18). 16.99 *(978-0-7636-5081-0(1))* Candlewick Pr.

—Stoner & Spaz. 2011. (ENG., Illus.). 192p. (YA). (gr. 9). pap. 7.99 *(978-0-7636-5757-4(3))* Candlewick Pr.

McGovern, Cammie. Say What You Will. 2015. (ENG.). 368p. (YA). (gr. 9). pap. 9.99 *(978-0-06-227111-2(3)*, HarperTeen) HarperCollins Pubs.

Metzger, Haley & Banks, Rayelynn. I Am Not Weird, 1 vol. 2010. 22p. pap. 24.95 *(978-1-4489-7001-8(6))* PublishAmerica, Inc.

Mikaelsen, Ben. Petey. 2010. (ENG.). 256p. (J). (gr. 3-7). pap. 6.99 *(978-1-4231-3174-8(6))* Hyperion Pr.

—Petey. 2011. 8.32 *(978-0-7848-3604-0(3)*, Everbind) Marco Bk. Co.

Roesti, Delores. Mareena Maree Mulligan & the Flying Wheel Chair: Book 1: School Days. 2007. 81p. pap. 9.95 *(978-0-7414-4048-8(2))* Infinity Publishing.

—Mareena Maree Mulligan & the Flying Wheelchair: Book 2: The Busybodies. 2008. 102p. pap. 10.95 *(978-0-7414-4477-6(1))* Infinity Publishing.

Sachar, Louis. Small Steps. 2008. (Readers Circle Ser.). 257p. (gr. 5-9). 20.00 *(978-0-7569-9130-2(7))* Perfection Learning Corp.

—Small Steps. 2008. (ENG.). 288p. (YA). (gr. 7-9). pap. 9.99 *(978-0-385-73315-1(1)*, Ember) Random Hse. Children's Bks.

—Small Steps. rev. l.t. ed. 2006. 339p. 23.95 *(978-0-7862-8297-5(5))* Thorndike Pr.

Stenton, Murray. My Brother Is Special: A Cerebral Palsy Story. Stenton, Murray, illus. 2017. (ENG., Illus.). (J). (gr. k-2). 27.95 ***(978-1-61599-326-0(6))*** Loving Healing Pr., Inc.

Terry, Trueman & Trueman. Stuck in Neutral. 2014. (ENG.). 128p. (J). (gr. 8-12). 13.24 *(978-1-63245-299-3(5))* Lectorum Pubns., Inc.

Trueman, Terry & Trueman. Stuck in Neutral. 2012. (Stuck in Neutral Ser.: 1). (ENG.). 144p. (YA). (gr. 8-18). pap. 9.99 *(978-0-06-447213-5(2)*, HarperTeen) HarperCollins Pubs.

White, Andrea. Window Boy. 2008. (ENG.). 256p. (J). (gr. 4-7). 17.95 *(978-1-933979-14-4(3)*, 9781933979144) Bright Sky Pr.

Willis, Wren. Why Is My Name September? 2005. 155p. pap. 11.39 *(978-1-4116-6534-7(1))* Lulu Pr., Inc.

CEREMONIES

see Etiquette; Manners and Customs; Rites and Ceremonies

CERTAINTY

see Belief and Doubt; Probabilities

CERVANTES SAAVEDRA, MIGUEL DE, 1547-1616

Aller, Eduardo Murias, et al. Cervantes: Un Escritor en Busca de la Libertad. 2006. (SPA., Illus.). (J). (gr. 6-8). 9.60 *(978-84-316-7840-1(2)*, W33552) Vicens-Vives, Editorial, S.A. ESP. Dist: Lectorum Pubns., Inc.

Iturralde, Edna. Conoce a Miguel de Cervantes: Get to Know Miguel de Cervantes. 2014. (Personajes Del Mundo Hispnico Ser.). (ENG & SPA., Illus.). 32p. (J). (gr. -1-3). 15.95 *(978-1-61435-352-2(2)*, Alfaguara) Santillana USA Publishing Co., Inc.

Parker, Barbara Keevil & Parker, Duane F. Miguel de Cervantes. 2003. (Great Hispanic Heritage Ser.). (Illus.). 112p. (gr. 6-12). 35.00 *(978-0-7910-7252-3(5)*, Chelsea Hse.) Facts On File, Inc.

CEYLON

see Sri Lanka

CEZANNE, PAUL, 1839-1906

Brooks, Susie. Paul Cezanne, 01 vols., 1. 2016. (Inspiring Artists Ser.). (ENG.). 48p. (J). 30.25 *(978-1-5081-7062-4(2)*, Rosen Young Adult) Rosen Publishing Group, Inc., The.

Hardy, Rachael. Cézanne, Vol. 7. 2015. (Great Artists Collection). (Illus.). 64p. (J). (gr. 7). lib. bdg. 23.95 *(978-1-4222-3257-6(3))* Mason Crest.

Harris, Nathaniel. Paul Cézanne. 2003. (Artists in Their Time Ser.). (ENG., Illus.). 48p. (J). 24.00 *(978-0-531-12242-6(5)*, Watts, Franklin) Scholastic Library Publishing.

Mis, Melody S. Paul Cezanne. (Meet the Artist Ser.). 24p. (gr. 2-3). 2009. 42.50 *(978-1-61514-631-4(8)*, PowerKids Pr.) 2007. (Illus.). (YA). lib. bdg. 22.60 *(978-1-4042-3842-8(5))* Rosen Publishing Group, Inc., The.

Soni, Jaymee & Schubert, Charles. A Kid at Art - Paul Cezanne. 2003. (J). pap. 14.99 *(978-0-9743760-0-4(0))* Little Noggin LLC.

Tracy, Kathleen. Paul Cezanne. 2007. (Art Profiles for Kids Ser.). (Illus.). 48p. (YA). (gr. 4-7). lib. bdg. 29.95 *(978-1-58415-565-2(5))* Mitchell Lane Pubs., Inc.

Venezia, Mike. Paul Cezanne. 2016. (Getting to Know the World's Greatest Artists Ser.). (ENG., Illus.). 40p. (J). pap. 7.95 *(978-0-531-22108-2(3)*, Children's Pr.) Scholastic Library Publishing.

—Paul Cezanne (Revised Edition) 2016. (Getting to Know the World's Greatest Artists Ser.). (ENG., Illus.). 40p. (J). lib. bdg. 29.00 *(978-0-531-21669-9(1)*, Children's Pr.) Scholastic Library Publishing.

Wood, Alix. Paul Cézanne. 2013. (Artists Through the Ages Ser.). (ENG., Illus.). 32p. (J). (gr. 3-6). pap. 10.00 *(978-1-61533-625-8(7))*; lib. bdg. 25.25 *(978-1-61533-619-7(2))* Windmill Bks.

Zaczek, Iain. Paul Cézanne. 2014. (Great Artists Ser.). 32p. (J). (gr. 3-6). pap. 10.50 *(978-1-4824-1216-1(0))* Stevens, Gareth Publishing LLLP.

CHAGALL, MARC, 1887-1985

Anholt, Laurence. Papa Chagall, Tell Us a Story. 2014. (ENG.). 32p. (J). (gr. -1-3). 16.99 *(978-0-7641-6644-0(1))* Barron's Educational Series, Inc.

Emert, Phyllis Raybin. Marc Chagall. Greenhaven Press Editors, ed. 2014. (Eye on Art Ser.). (ENG., Illus.). 128p. (gr. 7-10). lib. bdg. 39.40 *(978-1-4205-0916-8(0)*, Lucent Bks.) Cengage Gale.

Landmann, Bimba. I Am Marc Chagall. Landmann, Bimba, illus. 2006. (Eerdmans Books for Young Readers). (ENG., Illus.). 34p. (J). (gr. 2). 18.00 *(978-0-8028-5305-9(6)*, Eerdmans Bks For Young Readers) Eerdmans, William B. Publishing Co.

Mason, Antony. Marc Chagall. 2004. (Lives of the Artists Ser.). (Illus.). 48p. (gr. 5-12). pap. 14.05 *(978-0-8368-5654-5(6))*; lib. bdg. 31.00 *(978-0-8368-5649-1(X))* Stevens, Gareth Publishing LLLP. (Gareth Stevens Secondary Library).

Mattern, Joanne. Marc Chagall, 1 vol. 2005. (Great Artists Set 1 Ser.). (ENG., Illus.). 32p. (gr. k-6). 27.07 *(978-1-59197-841-1(6)*, Checkerboard Library) ABDO Publishing Co.

Welton, Jude. Marc Chagall. 2003. (Artists in Their Time Ser.). (ENG., Illus.). 48p. (J). 24.00 *(978-0-531-12235-8(2))*; (gr. 5-7). pap. 6.95 *(978-0-531-16645-1(7))* Scholastic Library Publishing. (Watts, Franklin).

CHAIRS

Cappetta, Cynthia. Chairs, Chairs, Chairs! Stromoski, Rick, illus. 2004. (Rookie Readers Ser.). 31p. (gr. k-3). 14.95 *(978-0-7569-3639-6(X))* Perfection Learning Corp.

Moscattini, Alexander. The Classroom Chair: A True Story. 2007. 22p. pap. 24.95 *(978-1-4241-9225-0(0))* America Star Bks.

Ridley, Sarah. A Wooden Chair. 2006. (How It's Made Ser.). (Illus.). 32p. (gr. 1-4). lib. bdg. 26.00 *(978-0-8368-6296-6(1)*, Gareth Stevens Learning Library) Stevens, Gareth Publishing LLLP.

CHAIRS—FICTION

Babcock, Allison. Braxton's Potty Chair. 2011. (Illus.). 12p. pap. 12.95 *(978-1-257-20963-7(9))* Lulu Pr., Inc.

Barulich-Liederbach, Terri & Liederbach, Tom. The Memory Chair. 2010. 48p. pap. 19.49 *(978-1-4520-5672-2(2))* AuthorHouse.

Bertram, Debbie & Bloom, Susan. The Best Place to Read. 2007. lib. bdg. 18.40 *(978-1-4177-9097-5(0)*, Turtleback) Turtleback Bks.

Bloom, Susan & Bertram, Debbie. The Best Place to Read. Garland, Michael, illus. 2007. (ENG.). 32p. (J). (gr. -1-2). pap. 7.99 *(978-0-375-83757-9(4)*, Dragonfly Bks.) Random Hse. Children's Bks.

Clyde, Addie Mae. Charlie the Chair. 2006. (J). per. 10.95 *(978-1-59872-694-7(3))* Instant Pub.

Jack, Keats Ezra. Peter's Chair. 2014. (ENG.). 40p. (J). (gr. k-k). 11.24 *(978-1-63245-276-4(6))* Lectorum Pubns., Inc.

Keats, Ezra Jack. Peter's Chair. 2015. 40p. pap. 7.00 *(978-1-61003-534-7(8))* Center for the Collaborative Classroom.

—Peter's Chair. Keats, Ezra Jack, illus. 2006. (ENG., Illus.). 32p. (J). (gr. -1 — 1). bds. 6.99 *(978-0-670-06190-7(5)*, Viking Books for Young Readers) Penguin Young Readers Group.

—Peter's Chair. (J). (gr. -1-3). pap. 12.95 incl. audio Weston Woods Studios, Inc.

Keffer, Ann. The Seventh Chair. 2007. 76p. (J). per. 8.95 *(978-0-595-45917-9(X))* iUniverse, Inc.

Magoun, James. There's a Bear in My Chair. Magnuson, Diana, illus. 2004. (ENG.). 20p. (gr. k-2). pap. 8.95 *(978-1-57874-080-2(0)*, Kaeden Bks.) Kaeden Corp.

Morábito, Fabio. Gerardo y la Cama. Cardemil, Carmen, illus. 2003. (SPA.). *(978-968-494-087-1(4)*, CI31141) Centro de Informacion y Desarrollo de la Comunicacion y la Literatura MEX. Dist: Lectorum Pubns., Inc.

Niland, Deborah. Annie's Chair. Niland, Deborah, illus. 2005. (Illus.). 32p. (J). *(978-0-670-04249-4(8))* Penguin Books Australia.

Pak, Jiyeon. My Grandpa's Chair. 2017. (ENG.). 32p. (J). (gr. -1-2). 17.99 ***(978-1-5247-0075-1(4))***; lib. bdg. 20.99

(978-1-5247-0076-8(2)) Random Hse. Children's Bks. (Knopf Bks. for Young Readers).
Patterson, Ann Elizabeth. Rocking Chair Bear. 2009. 32p. pap. 12.99 *(978-1-4343-9331-9(3))* AuthorHouse.
Perret, Delphine. Pablo & His Chair. 2016. (ENG., Illus.). 32p. (J). (gr. -1-3). 17.95 *(978-1-61689-490-0(3))* Princeton Architectural Pr.
Rivera, Lassen. Mi Silla de Ruedas. Alvarez, Mrinali, illus. 2006. (SPA.). 28p. 8.95 *(978-0-8477-1568-8(X))* Univ. of Puerto Rico Pr.
Santucci, Barbara. Abby's Chairs. Santini, Debrah L., illus. 2004. 32p. 16.00 *(978-0-8028-5205-2(X))* Eerdmans, William B. Publishing Co.
Suen, Anastasia. Helping Sophia, 1 vol. Ebbeler, Jeffrey, illus. 2007. (Main Street School - Kids with Character Ser.). (ENG.). 32p. (gr. -1-4). 28.50 *(978-1-60270-030-7(3),* Looking Glass Library) ABDO Publishing Co.
Vendlinger, Joan. The Littlest Chair. 2012. 24p. 24.95 *(978-1-4626-6070-4(3))* America Star Bks.
Weston Woods Staff, creator. Peter's Chair. 2011. 29.95 *(978-0-439-76006-5(2))* Weston Woods Studios, Inc.
Williams, Vera B. A Chair for Always. Williams, Vera B., illus. 2009. (SPA & ENG., Illus.). 40p. (J). (gr. -1-3). 16.99 *(978-0-06-172279-0(0),* Greenwillow Bks.) HarperCollins Pubs.
—A Chair for My Mother. Williams, Vera B., illus. 25th anniv. ed. 2007. (Reading Rainbow Bks.). (ENG., Illus.). 32p. (J). (gr. -1-3). pap. 7.99 *(978-0-688-04074-1(8),* Greenwillow Bks.) HarperCollins Pubs.
—A Chair for My Mother. 2014. (Reading Rainbow Bks). (ENG.). 32p. (J). (gr. k-3). 11.24 *(978-1-63245-340-2(1))* Lectorum Pubns., Inc.
—A Chair for My Mother. 2007. (Reading Rainbow Bks.). (Illus.). 32p. (J). (gr. -1-3). 18.40 *(978-0-8085-3385-6(1),* Turtleback) Turtleback Bks.
—Un Sillón para Siempre, 1 vol. Williams, Vera B., illus. 2009.Tr. of Chair for Always. (SPA & ENG., Illus.). 40p. (J). (gr. -1-3). 17.99 *(978-0-06-172283-7(9),* Greenwillow Bks.) HarperCollins Pubs.

CHAMBERLAIN, WILT, 1936-1999

Doeden, Matt. Wilt Chamberlain. 2010. (Sports Heroes & Legends Ser.). (ENG.). 120p. (gr. 5-12). lib. bdg. 30.60 *(978-0-7613-5369-0(0))* Lerner Publishing Group.
Greenberger, Robert. Wilt Chamberlain. 2009. (Basketball Hall of Famers Ser.). 112p. (gr. 5-8). 63.90 *(978-1-61511-536-5(6),* Rosen Reference) Rosen Publishing Group, Inc., The.

CHAMELEONS

Berne, Emma Carlson. Chameleons. 2013. (Animal Superpowers Ser.). 24p. (J). (gr. k-5). pap. 8.25 *(978-1-4777-0835-4(9),* PowerKids Pr.) Rosen Publishing Group, Inc., The.
Berne, Emma Carlson & Carlson Berne, Emma. Chameleons. 2013. 24p. (J). (gr. k-5). 22.60 *(978-1-4777-0747-0(6),* PowerKids Pr.) Rosen Publishing Group, Inc., The.
Bishop, Nic, illus. & photos by. Chameleon! Bishop, Nic, photos by. 2005. (J). pap. *(978-0-439-78111-4(6),* Scholastic Pr.) Scholastic, Inc.
Bodden, Valerie. Chameleons. 2016. (Amazing Animals Ser.). 24p. (J). (ENG.). (gr. 1-3). pap. 8.99 *(978-1-62832-215-6(2),* Creative Paperbacks); (Illus.). 28.50 *(978-1-60818-609-9(1),* Creative Education) Creative Co., The.
Brett, Flora. Get to Know Chameleons. 2015. (Get to Know Reptiles Ser.). (ENG.). 24p. (gr. 1-2). lib. bdg. 25.32 *(978-1-4914-2059-1(6))* Capstone Press of Coughlan Cos.
Calhoun, Kelly. Colas Reviradas. 2016. (Adivina (Guess What) Ser.). (SPA., Illus.). 24p. (J). (gr. k-2). 28.50 *(978-1-63471-453-2(9),* 208875) Cherry Lake Publishing.
—Twisty Tails: Chameleon. 2015. (Guess What Ser.). (ENG., Illus.). 24p. (J). (gr. k-2). 28.50 *(978-1-63362-628-7(8),* 206708) Cherry Lake Publishing.
Carlson Berne, Emma. Chameleons: Masters of Disguise! 2013. (Animal Superpowers Ser.). 24p. (J). (gr. k-5). pap. 49.50 *(978-1-4777-0836-1(7),* PowerKids Pr.) Rosen Publishing Group, Inc., The.
Carr, Aaron. Chameleon. 2014. (J). *(978-1-4896-2625-7(5))* Weigl Pubs., Inc.
Connors, Kathleen. Chameleons. 2013. (Really Wild Reptiles Ser.). (Illus.). 24p. (J). (gr. 2-5). pap. 8.15 *(978-1-4339-8360-3(5));* lib. bdg. 22.60 *(978-1-4339-8359-7(1))* Stevens, Gareth Publishing LLLP.
Devillier, Christy. Chameleons, 1 vol. 2014. (Amazing Reptiles Ser.). (ENG.). 48p. (gr. 8-12). lib. bdg. 32.79 *(978-1-62403-370-4(9))* ABDO Publishing Co.
Gish, Melissa. Chameleons. 2013. (Illus.). 48p. (J). 35.65 *(978-1-60818-285-5(1),* Creative Education) Creative Co., The.
—Living Wild: Chameleons. 2014. (Living Wild Ser.). (ENG., Illus.). 48p. (J). (gr. 4-7). pap. 12.00 *(978-0-89812-838-3(2),* Creative Paperbacks) Creative Co., The.
Hansen, Grace. Chameleons, 1 vol. 2014. (Reptiles Ser.). (ENG.). 24p. (J). (gr. 4-8). lib. bdg. 28.50 *(978-1-62970-058-8(4))* ABDO Publishing Co.
Hansen, Grace, et al. Camaleones. 2015. (Reptiles Ser.). (SPA., Illus.). 24p. (J). (gr. k-1). pap. 7.95 *(978-1-4966-0501-6(2))* Capstone Classroom.
Hirsch, Rebecca E. Panther Chameleons: Color-Changing Reptiles. 2015. (ENG., Illus.). 32p. (J). (gr. 2-4). 26.65 *(978-1-4677-7978-4(4),* Lerner Pubns.) Lerner Publishing Group.
Jenkins, Martin. Chameleons Are Cool. Shields, Sue, illus. 2015. 32p. pap. 7.00 *(978-1-61003-406-7(6))* Center for the Collaborative Classroom.
Kenan, Tessa. Es un Camaleón! 2017. (Bumba Books (tm) en Español — Animales de la Selva Tropical (Rain Forest Animals) Ser.). (SPA., Illus.). 24p. (J). (gr. -1-1). pap. 6.99 ***(978-1-5124-5408-6(7))*** Lerner Publishing Group.
—It's a Chameleon! 2017. (Bumba Books (tm) — Rain Forest Animals Ser.). (ENG.). 24p. (J). (gr. -1-1). 12.99 ***(978-1-5124-3750-8(6),*** Lerner Pubns.); 38.65 ***(978-1-5124-3749-2(2),*** Lerner Pubns.); 38.65 ***(978-1-5124-2758-5(6),*** Lerner Pubns.); (Illus.). 25.32 *(978-1-5124-2568-0(0))* Lerner Publishing Group.
Labella, Susan. Chameleons & Other Animals with Amazing Skin. 2005. (Scholastic News Nonfiction Readers Ser.). (ENG., Illus.). 24p. (J). (gr. 1-2). lib. bdg. 22.00 *(978-0-516-24925-4(8))* Scholastic Library Publishing.
Lawrence, Ellen. A Chameleon's Life. 2012. (Science Slam: Animal Diaries-Life Cycles Ser.). 24p. (J). (gr. -1-3). lib. bdg. 23.93 *(978-1-61772-596-8(X))* Bearport Publishing Co., Inc.
Macejko, Jeanne Anne, illus. A Million Chameleons. 2004. (J). pap. 10.95 *(978-1-888836-13-4(X))* Shenango River Bks.
Marsico, Katie. Chameleons Change Color. 2015. (Tell Me Why Library). (ENG., Illus.). 24p. (J). (gr. 2-5). pap. 12.79 *(978-1-63362-699-7(7),* 206621) Cherry Lake Publishing.
Meister, Cari. Chameleons. 2015. (Illus.). 24p. (J). lib. bdg. *(978-1-62031-194-3(1),* Bullfrog Bks.) Jump! Inc.
Miller, Jake. The Chameleon. (Lizard Library). 24p. 2009. (gr. 3-3). 42.50 *(978-1-60854-012-9(X))* 2003. (Illus.). (J). lib. bdg. 22.60 *(978-0-8239-6417-8(5))* Rosen Publishing Group, Inc., The. (PowerKids Pr.).
Murray, Peter. Chameleons. 2015. (Animals of the Rain Forest Ser.). (ENG.). 24p. (J). (gr. 2-5). 27.07 *(978-1-63143-703-8(8),* 208516) Child's World, Inc., The.
Petrie, Kristin. Chameleons, 1 vol. 2012. (Unique Pets Ser.). (ENG.). 24p. (J). (gr. 3-6). lib. bdg. 25.65 *(978-1-61783-439-4(4),* Checkerboard Library) ABDO Publishing Co.
Raum, Elizabeth. Chameleons. 2015. (Lizards Ser.). (Illus.). 32p. (J). 28.50 *(978-1-60753-484-6(3))* Amicus Publishing.
Schuetz, Kari. Chameleons. 2014. (Animal Safari Ser.). (ENG., Illus.). 24p. (J). (gr. k-3). lib. bdg. 25.95 *(978-1-62617-056-8(8),* Blastoff! Readers) Bellwether Media.
Whiting, Jim. Care for a Pet Chameleon. 2007. (How to Convince Your Parents You Can ... Ser.). (Illus.). 32p. (YA). (gr. 1-4). lib. bdg. 25.70 *(978-1-58415-605-5(8))* Mitchell Lane Pubs., Inc.
Yates, Gene. The Chameleon Colors Book. 2004. (Illus.). (J). *(978-1-58865-182-2(7))* Kidsbooks, LLC.

CHAMPLAIN, SAMUEL DE, 1567-1635

Anderson, Zachary. Samuel de Champlain: Exploring the Great Lakes. 2015. (J). lib. bdg. *(978-1-62713-423-1(9))* Cavendish Square Publishing.
Faber, Harold. Samuel de Champlain, Explorer of Canada. 2003. (Great Explorations Ser.). (J). 34.21 *(978-0-7614-1608-1(0),* Benchmark Bks.) Marshall Cavendish Corp.
Fryer, Mary Beacock. Champlain: Peacemaker & Explorer. 2011. (ENG., Illus.). 152p. (YA). (gr. 6). pap. 19.99 *(978-1-55488-940-2(5))* Dundurn CAN. Dist: Ingram Publisher Services.
MacLeod, Elizabeth. Samuel de Champlain. Mantha, John, illus. 2008. (Kids Can Read Ser.). (ENG.). 32p. (J). (gr. 1-3). 14.95 *(978-1-55453-049-6(0));* pap. 3.95 *(978-1-55453-050-2(4))* Kids Can Pr., Ltd. CAN. Dist: Hachette Bk. Group.
Morganelli, Adrianna. Samuel de Champlain: From New France to Cape Cod. 2005. (In the Footsteps of Explorers Ser.). (ENG., Illus.). 32p. (J). (gr. 4-5). pap. *(978-0-7787-2450-6(6))* Crabtree Publishing Co.
O'Brien, Cynthia. Explore with Samuel de Champlain. 2014. (ENG., Illus.). 32p. (J). *(978-0-7787-1256-5(7));* pap. *(978-0-7787-1260-2(5))* Crabtree Publishing Co.
Pelleschi, Andrea. Samuel de Champlain. 2013. (Jr. Graphic Famous Explorers Ser.). (ENG., Illus.). 24p. (J). (gr. 3-6). pap. 10.60 *(978-1-4777-0133-1(8));* lib. bdg. 25.25 *(978-1-4777-0074-7(9))* Rosen Publishing Group, Inc., The. (PowerKids Pr.).
Sherman, Josepha. Samuel de Champlain: Explorer of the Great Lakes Region & Founder of Quebec. (Library of Explorers & Exploration Ser.). 112p. (gr. 5-8). 2009. 66.50 *(978-1-60853-611-5(4))* 2003. (Illus.). (J). lib. bdg. 34.60 *(978-0-8239-3629-8(5))* Rosen Publishing Group, Inc., The. (Rosen Reference).
Whiting, Jim. The Life & Times of Samuel de Champlain. 2007. (Profiles in American History Ser.). (J). lib. bdg. *(978-1-58415-432-7(2))* Mitchell Lane Pubs., Inc.

CHAMPLAIN, SAMUEL DE, 1567-1635—FICTION

Messner, Kate. Champlain & the Silent One. Gulley, Martha, illus. 2008. (J). *(978-1-59531-050-7(9))* North Country Bks., Inc.
Taylor, Cora. Champlain & Cartier, 1 vol. 2004. (Ghost Voyages Ser.: No. 4). (ENG., Illus.). 128p. (J). (gr. 3-6). pap. 7.95 *(978-1-55050-374-6(X))* Coteau Bks. CAN. Dist: Orca Bk. Pubs. USA.

CHAMPLAIN, LAKE—FICTION

Altsheler, Joseph A. The Rulers of the Lakes: A Story of George & Champlain. 2006. (French & Indian War Ser.: Vol. 3). 300p. (J). reprint ed. 29.95 *(978-1-4218-1778-1(0));* pap. 14.95 *(978-1-4218-1878-8(7))* 1st World Publishing, Inc. (1st World Library - Literary Society).
—The Rulers of the Lakes: A Story of George & Champlain. (French & Indian War Ser.: Vol. 3). (J). reprint ed. 25.95 *(978-0-8488-0906-5(8))* Amereon Ltd.
—The Rulers of the Lakes: A Story of George & Champlain. 2008. (French & Indian War Ser.: Vol. 3). 272p. (J). 25.99 *(978-0-554-34451-5(3))* 2008. (French & Indian War Ser.: Vol. 3). 272p. (J). 28.99 *(978-0-554-25148-6(5))* 2007. (ENG.). 268p. reprint ed. pap. 23.99 *(978-1-4264-8309-7(0))* 2010. (French & Indian War Ser.: Vol. 3). (ENG.). 370p. (J). (gr. 4-7). reprint ed. pap. 32.75 *(978-1-177-56810-4(1))* Creative Media Partners, LLC.
—The Rulers of the Lakes: A Story of George & Champlain. Henry, J., illus. 2007. (French & Indian War Ser.: Vol. 3). 214p. (J). reprint ed. pap. 20.99 *(978-1-4264-8272-4(8))* Creative Media Partners, LLC.
—The Rulers of the Lakes: A Story of George & Champlain. 2006. (French & Indian War Ser.: Vol. 3). (J). reprint ed. pap. *(978-1-4065-0819-2(5))* Dodo Pr.
—The Rulers of the Lakes: A Story of George & Champlain. 2010. 166p. pap. 24.67 *(978-1-152-80290-2(9));* (French & Indian War Ser.: Vol. 3). (Illus.). 160p. (J). (gr. 4-7). reprint ed. pap. 19.99 *(978-1-153-71979-7(7))* General Bks. LLC.
—The Rulers of the Lakes: A Story of George & Champlain. reprint ed. 2010. 366p. 39.16 *(978-1-163-74095-8(0))* 2010. 366p. pap. 27.16 *(978-1-163-71977-0(3))* 2007. (French & Indian War Ser.: Vol. 3). 368p. (J). 48.95 *(978-0-548-43205-1(8))* 2007. (French & Indian War Ser.: Vol. 3). 368p. (J). pap. 33.95 *(978-0-548-40955-8(2))* Kessinger Publishing, LLC.
—The Rulers of the Lakes: A Story of George & Champlain. 2011. (French & Indian War Ser.: Vol. 3). 272p. (J). (gr. 4-7). reprint ed. pap. *(978-3-8424-7701-8(5))* Tredition GmbH.
Gilligan, Shannon. The Lake Monster Mystery. Newton, Keith, illus. 2009. (Dragonlarks Ser.). 80p. (J). (gr. k-3). pap. 7.99 *(978-1-933390-60-4(3))* Chooseco LLC.
LaFaye, A. Water Steps. 2009. (ENG., Illus.). 208p. (J). (gr. 2-7). 16.95 *(978-1-57131-687-5(6));* pap. 6.95 *(978-1-57131-686-8(8))* Milkweed Editions.
Messner, Kate. Spitfire. 2007. (J). *(978-1-59531-018-7(5))* North Country Bks., Inc.
Montgomery, R. A. Island of Time. Louie, Wes & Cannella, Marco, illus. 2008. 144p. (J). (gr. 2-7). pap. 6.99 *(978-1-933390-28-4(X))* Chooseco LLC.
Optic, Oliver, pseud. Haste & Waste; or, the Young Pilot of Lake Champlain. 2007. 112p. (gr. 4-7). per. *(978-1-4068-3636-3(2))* Echo Library.

CHAMPOLLION, JEAN FRANCOIS, 1790-1832

Rumford, James. Seeker of Knowledge: The Man Who Deciphered Egyptian Hieroglyphs. 2003. (Rise & Shine Ser.). (ENG., Illus.). 32p. (C). (gr. -1-3). pap. 11.95 *(978-0-618-33345-5(2))* National Geographic School Publishing, Inc.

CHANGE, SOCIAL

see Social Change

CHAPLIN, CHARLIE, 1889-1977

Demuth, Patricia Brennan. Who Was Charlie Chaplin? Copeland, Gregory, illus. 2016. (Who Was? Ser.). (ENG.). 112p. (J). (gr. 3-7). lib. bdg. 15.99 *(978-0-399-54241-1(8),* Grosset & Dunlap) Penguin Young Readers Group.
Fleischman, Sid. Sir Charlie: Chaplin, the Funniest Man in the World. 2010. (ENG.). 288p. (J). (gr. 4-18). 19.99 *(978-0-06-189640-8(3),* Greenwillow Bks.) HarperCollins Pubs.

CHAPMAN, JOHN, 1774-1845

see Appleseed, Johnny, 1774-1845

CHARACTER EDUCATION

see Moral Education

CHARACTERS AND CHARACTERISTICS IN LITERATURE

see also African Americans in Art

Anton, Carrie & Falligant, Erin. American Girl Character Encyclopedia. 2017. (ENG.). 208p. (J). (gr. 2). 16.99 ***(978-1-4654-6079-0(9),*** DK Children) Dorling Kindersley Publishing, Inc.
Bodden, Valerie. Dialogue & Characterization. 2016. (Illus.). 80p. (J). *(978-1-60818-727-0(6),* Creative Education) Creative Co., The.
Card, Orson Scott, et al. Great Snape Debate: Is Snape Innocent or Guilty? 2007. (ENG.). 192p. (J). (gr. 7). pap. *(978-1-933771-35-9(6))* BenBella Bks.
Curto, Rosa M. Fun & Easy Drawing Storybook Characters. 2013. (Fun & Easy Drawing Ser.). 36p. (J). lib. bdg. 23.94 *(978-0-7660-6043-2(8));* pap. 7.95 *(978-0-7660-6044-9(6))* Enslow Pubs., Inc. (Enslow Elementary).
Disney Princess Enchanted Character Guide. 2014. (ENG., Illus.). 144p. (J). (gr. 2-5). 16.99 *(978-1-4654-1569-1(6),* DK Children) Dorling Kindersley Publishing, Inc.
Dorling Kindersley Publishing Staff & Manning, Matthew. Iron Man: The Ultimate Guide to the Armored Super Hero. 2010. (ENG., Illus.). 200p. (J). (gr. 3-7). 24.99 *(978-0-7566-5749-9(0),* DK Children) Dorling Kindersley Publishing, Inc.
Garbot, Dave. Crazy, Zany Cartoon Characters: Learn to Draw 20 Weird, Wacky Characters! 2014. (Cartooning for Kids Ser.). (ENG., Illus.). 64p. (J). (gr. 1-3). pap. 8.95 *(978-1-60058-385-8(7),* 1600583857) Quarto Publishing Group USA.
Hamilton, Sue L. The Incredible Hulk. 2006. 48.42 *(978-1-59679-981-3(1))* ABDO Publishing Co.
hirschmann, kris. Frankenstein. 2011. (Monsters & Mythical Creatures Ser.). (Illus.). 80p. (J). (gr. 7-12). lib. bdg. 27.95 *(978-1-60152-180-4(4))* ReferencePoint Pr., Inc.
How Much Wood Could a Woodchuck Chuck? unabr. ed. 2007. (J). (gr. -1-k). 17.00 incl. audio compact disk *(978-0-9705773-4-4(6))* Kids At Our House, Inc., The.
Pow! 2014. (Peanuts Kids Ser.: 3). (ENG., Illus.). 224p. (J). 9.99 *(978-1-4494-5826-3(2))* Andrews McMeel Publishing.

CHARITY

Craats, Rennay. The United Way. 2003. (International Organizations Ser.). (Illus.). 32p. (J). (gr. 4-7). lib. bdg. 26.00 *(978-1-59036-022-4(2))* Weigl Pubs., Inc.
Friedman, Michael. Settlement Houses: Improving the Social Welfare of America's Immigrants. 2009. (Progressive Movement 1900-1920: Efforts to Reform America's New Industrial Society Ser.). 32p. (gr. 3-4). 47.90 *(978-1-60854-170-6(3))* Rosen Publishing Group, Inc., The.
Minden, Cecilia. Giving Back. 2015. (21st Century Skills Library: Real World Math Ser.). (ENG., Illus.). 32p. (J). (gr. 4-7). 29.93 *(978-1-63362-570-9(2),* 206464) Cherry Lake Publishing.
Nault, Jennifer. Save the Children. 2003. (International Organizations Ser.). (Illus.). 32p. (J). (gr. 4-7). lib. bdg. 26.00 *(978-1-59036-021-7(4))* Weigl Pubs., Inc.
Organizaciones de Ayuda Series, 6 bks., Set. 2003. (Organizaciones de Ayuda Ser.). (SPA & ENG., Illus.). (J). 103.50 *(978-0-8239-6918-0(5),* Editorial Buenas Letras) Rosen Publishing Group, Inc., The.
St. Germain, Mark. Three Cups: Teaching Children How to Save, Spend & Be Charitable with Money Is As Easy As 1, 2, 3. Willy, April, illus. 2007. (ENG.). 28p. (J). pap. 10.00 *(978-0-9794563-0-5(4))* Three Cups, LLC.
Sullivan, Erin Ash. Communities Helping Communities: Text Pairs. 2008. (Bridges/Navigators Ser.). (J). (gr. 3). 94.00 *(978-1-4108-8355-1(8))* Benchmark Education Co.
Trussell-Cullen, Alan. Mother Teresa. 2009. pap. 13.25 *(978-1-60559-066-0(5))* Hameray Publishing Group, Inc.
Uschan, Michael V. Matt Dalio: China Care Founder. 2007. (Young Heroes Ser.). (ENG., Illus.). 64p. (gr. 4-8). lib. bdg. 35.70 *(978-0-7377-3670-0(4),* Kidhaven) Cengage Gale.
Zeiler, Freddi. A Kids Guide to Giving. Schumaker, Ward, illus. 2006. (ENG.). 208p. (J). (gr. 7-17). 9.99 *(978-1-58476-489-2(9),* IKIDS) Innovative Kids.

CHARLEMAGNE, EMPEROR, 742-814

Bhote, Themina. Charlemagne: Life & Times of an Early Medieval Emperor. 2004. (Leaders of the Middle Ages Ser.). (Illus.). 112p. (YA). (gr. 5-9). lib. bdg. 34.60 *(978-1-4042-0161-3(0))* Rosen Publishing Group, Inc., The.
Gagne, Tammy. Charlemagne. 2017. (Junior Biography From Ancient Civilization Ser.). (gr. 4-6). 29.95 *(978-1-68020-020-1(8))* Mitchell Lane Pubs., Inc.
Gelfand, Dale Evva. Charlemagne. 2003. (Ancient World Leaders Ser.). (Illus.). 112p. (gr. 6-12). 30.00 *(978-0-7910-7224-0(X),* Chelsea Hse.) Facts On File, Inc.
Schlesinger, Arthur M., Jr., intro. Ancient World Leaders. (Illus.). (gr. 6-12). lib. bdg. *(978-0-7910-8056-6(0),* Chelsea Hse.) Facts On File, Inc.
Whiting, Jim. The Life & Times of Charlemagne. 2005. (Biography from Ancient Civilizations Ser.). (Illus.). 48p. (J). (gr. 4-8). lib. bdg. 29.95 *(978-1-58415-346-7(6))* Mitchell Lane Pubs., Inc.

CHARLEMAGNE, EMPEROR, 742-814—FICTION

Holmes, Mary Tavener & Harris, John. The Elephant from Baghdad, 0 vols. Cannell, Jon, illus. 2012. (ENG.). 40p. (J). (gr. k-3). 17.99 *(978-0-7614-6111-1(6),* 9780761461111, Amazon Children's Publishing) Amazon Publishing.

CHARLES I, KING OF ENGLAND 1600-1649

Abbott, Jacob. History of King Charles the Second of en. 2006. pap. *(978-1-4065-0357-9(6))* Dodo Pr.

CHARLES II, KING OF ENGLAND, 1630-1685

Abbot, Jacob. History of King Charles the Second of England. 2005. 204p. pap. 12.95 *(978-1-4218-0152-0(3));* 27.95 *(978-1-4218-0052-3(7))* 1st World Publishing, Inc. (1st World Library - Literary Society).

CHARLESTON (S.C.)

Baldwin, William. Charleston My Picture Guide to a Holy City. Baldwin, Aaron et al, eds. 2003. per. 24.95 *(978-0-9740091-1-7(3))* Village Museum.
Colbert, Nancy A. The Firing on Fort Sumter: A Splintered Nation Goes to War. 2004. (First Battles Ser.). (Illus.). 112p. (J). (gr. 6-12). 23.95 *(978-1-883846-51-0(X),* First Biographies) Reynolds, Morgan Inc.
Crewe, Sabrina & Uschan, Michael V. Fort Sumter: The Civil War Begins. 2005. (Events That Shaped America Ser.). (Illus.). 32p. (gr. 3-6). lib. bdg. 26.00 *(978-0-8368-3414-7(3),* Gareth Stevens Learning Library) Stevens, Gareth Publishing LLLP.
Jerome, Kate Boehm. Charleston, SC: Cool Stuff Every Kid Should Know. 2008. (Arcadia Kids Ser.). (ENG., Illus.). 48p. (J). pap. 9.99 *(978-1-4396-0001-6(5))* Arcadia Publishing.
Maynard, Charles W. Fort Sumter. 2009. (Famous Forts Throughout American History Ser.). 24p. (gr. 3-4). 42.50 *(978-1-61512-520-3(5),* PowerKids Pr.) Rosen Publishing Group, Inc., The.
Samuels, Charlie. The Attack on Fort Sumter, Vol. 1. 2014. (Turning Points in US Military History Ser.). (ENG.). 48p. (J). (gr. 5-6). 31.95 *(978-1-4824-0401-2(X))* Stevens, Gareth Publishing LLLP.
Vierow, Wendy. Shots Fired at Fort Sumter. 2004. (Headlines from History Ser.). (Illus.). 24p. (J). lib. bdg. 22.60 *(978-0-8239-6220-4(2))* Rosen Publishing Group, Inc., The.
—Shots Fired at Fort Sumter: Civil War Breaks Out! 2009. (Headlines from History Ser.). 24p. (gr. 3-3). 42.50 *(978-1-61513-238-6(4),* PowerKids Pr.) Rosen Publishing Group, Inc., The.
Walker, Sally M. Shipwreck Search: Discovery of the H. L. Hunley. Verstraete, Elaine, illus. (On My Own Science Ser.). (ENG.). 48p. (gr. 2-4). 2007. per. 6.95 *(978-0-8225-6449-2(1),* First Avenue Editions) 2006. lib. bdg. 25.26 *(978-1-57505-878-8(2),* Millbrook Pr.) Lerner Publishing Group.

CHARLESTON (S.C.)—FICTION

Cadell, Ava. NeuroLoveology: The Power to Mindful Love & Sex. 2014. (ENG.). 310p. pap. 14.99 *(978-1-4976-6112-7(9))* Open Road Integrated Media, Inc.
Curtis, Alice Turner. A Yankee Girl at Fort Sumter. 2005. 26.95 *(978-1-4218-0301-2(1));* 180p. pap. 11.95 *(978-1-4218-0401-9(8))* 1st World Publishing, Inc. (1st World Library - Literary Society).
—Yankee Girl at Fort Sumter. 2004. reprint ed. pap. 19.95 *(978-1-4191-9516-7(6));* pap. 1.99 *(978-1-4192-9516-4(0))* Kessinger Publishing, LLC.
Gunderson, Jessica. A Rebel among Redcoats: A Revolutionary War Novel. 2015. (Revolutionary War Ser.). (ENG., Illus.). 96p. (gr. 4-4). lib. bdg. 26.65 *(978-1-4342-9701-3(2))* Stone Arch Bks.
Hogan, Stephen. Johnny Lynch: Patriot Drummerboy. rev. ed. 2007. (J). *(978-0-9795474-0-9(7))* KAM Publishing.
—Johnny Lynch: Road to Camden. 2007. (J). *(978-0-9795474-1-6(5))* KAM Publishing.
Jacobs, Lily. The Littlest Bunny in Charleston: An Easter Adventure. 2015. (ENG.). 32p. (J). (-3). 9.99 *(978-1-4926-1048-9(8),* Sourcebooks Jabberwocky) Sourcebooks, Inc.
James, Eric. A Halloween Scare in Charleston. Le Ray, Marina, illus. 2015. (ENG.). 32p. (J). (-5). 9.99 *(978-1-4926-2368-7(7),* 9781492623687, Sourcebooks Jabberwocky) Sourcebooks, Inc.
—Santa's Sleigh Is on Its Way to Charleston: A Christmas Adventure. Dunn, Robert, illus. 2016. (ENG.). 32p. (J). (-2). 12.99 *(978-1-4926-4322-7(X),* 9781492643227, Sourcebooks Jabberwocky) Sourcebooks, Inc.
Jasper, Mark. Good Night Charleston. Kelly, Cooper, illus. 2007. (Good Night Our World Ser.). (ENG.). 20p. (J). (gr. k — 1). bds. 9.95 *(978-1-60219-022-1(4))* Good Night Bks.
Lavender, William. Just Jane: A Daughter of England Caught in the Struggle of the American Revolution. 2005. (Great Episodes Ser.). (ENG.). 336p. (YA). (gr. 7-12). pap. 15.95 *(978-0-15-205472-4(3))* Houghton Mifflin Harcourt Publishing Co.
Lewis, Amey. Nipper of Drayton Hall. McElroy, Gerry, illus. 2015. (Young Palmetto Bks.). (ENG.). 40p. (J). (gr. 5-5). 19.95 *(978-1-61117-625-4(5))* Univ. of South Carolina Pr.
McClure, Beverly Stowe. Listen to the Ghost. 2005. (J). per. 16.95 *(978-1-933353-51-7(1),* Paladin Timeless) Twilight Times Bks.
McDavid-Jones, Elizabeth. Mystery on Skull Island. 2009. (Mysteries Through Time Ser.). 192p. (YA). (gr. 4-8). 31.95 *(978-1-60754-286-5(2));* pap. 15.25 *(978-1-60754-302-2(8))* Windmill Bks.
Reichs, Kathy & Reichs, Brendan. Seizure. 2013. (Virals Ser.: 2). (ENG.). 512p. (J). (gr. 5). pap. 9.99 *(978-1-59514-486-7(2),* Puffin Books) Penguin Young Readers Group.

C
D

—Seizure. 2013. (Virals Ser.: 2). lib. bdg. 20.85 *(978-0-606-30050-6(3),* Turtleback) Turtleback Bks.

Silvano, Wendi. Love Is All Around Charleston. Czernichowska, Joanna, illus. 2016. (ENG.). 32p. (J). (-6). 12.99 *(978-1-4926-2911-5(1),* Sourcebooks Jabberwocky) Sourcebooks, Inc.

Smallman, Steve. Santa Is Coming to Charleston. Dunn, Robert, illus. 2013. (ENG.). 32p. (J). (-3). 9.99 *(978-1-4022-8985-9(5),* Sourcebooks Jabberwocky) Sourcebooks, Inc.

Stroll with Mr. Emmett: A Walk Through Charleston. 2004. (J). lib. bdg. 15.95 *(978-0-9759346-0-9(0))* Mr. Emmett Publishing.

Thompson, J. E. Disappearance at Hangman's Bluff. (Felony Bay Mysteries Ser.: 2). (ENG.). 336p. (J). (gr. 3-7). 2015. pap. 6.99 *(978-0-06-210450-2(0))* 2014. (Illus.). 16.99 *(978-0-06-210449-6(7))* HarperCollins Pubs. (Waldon Pond Pr.).

—The Girl from Felony Bay. 2014. (Felony Bay Mysteries Ser.: 1). (ENG.). 400p. (J). (gr. 3-7). pap. 6.99 *(978-0-06-210447-2(0),* Waldon Pond Pr.) HarperCollins Pubs.

Verrico, Susan. The Privateer's Apprentice, 1 vol. 2012. (ENG.). 224p. (J). 15.95 *(978-1-56145-633-8(0))* Peachtree Pubs.

Walker, Melissa. Ashes to Ashes. 2013. (ENG.). 336p. (YA). (gr. 8). 17.99 *(978-0-06-207734-9(1),* Tegen, Katherine Bks) HarperCollins Pubs.

—Dust to Dust. 320p. (YA). (gr. 8). 2016. pap. 9.99 *(978-0-06-207738-7(4))* 2015. (ENG.). 17.99 *(978-0-06-207737-0(6))* HarperCollins Pubs. (Tegen, Katherine Bks).

CHARMS

Riggs, Kate. Spells & Potions. 2013. (Illus.). 24p. (J). 25.65 *(978-1-60818-244-2(4),* Creative Education) Creative Co., The.

CHARTOGRAPHY

see Map Drawing; Maps

CHATEAUX

see Castles

CHAUCER, GEOFFREY, -1400

Hubbard-Brown, Janet. Chaucer: Celebrated Poet & Author. 2005. (Makers of the Middle Ages & Renaissance Ser.). (Illus.). 144p. (gr. 5-8). 32.95 *(978-0-7910-8635-3(6),* Chelsea Hse.) Facts On File, Inc.

Mattern, Joanne. Geoffrey Chaucer: Medieval Writer, 1 vol. 2012. (Primary Source Readers Ser.). (ENG.). 32p. (J). (gr. 4-4). pap. 8.99 *(978-1-4333-5006-1(8))* Teacher Created Materials, Inc.

CHAVEZ, CESAR, 1927-1993

Adler, David A. & Adler, Michael S. A Picture Book of Cesar Chavez. Olofsdotter, Marie, illus. (ENG.). 32p. (J). 2011. pap. 7.99 *(978-0-8234-2383-5(2))* 2010. (gr. -1-3). 17.95 *(978-0-8234-2202-9(X))* Holiday Hse., Inc.

Apte, Sunita. Cesar Chavez: We Can Do It! 2005. (Defining Moments Ser.). (Illus.). 32p. (J). (gr. 2-5). lib. bdg. 25.27 *(978-1-59716-073-5(3))* Bearport Publishing Co., Inc.

Auster, Michael A. They Led the Way. 2005. (Yellow Umbrella Fluent Level Ser.). (ENG.). 16p. (gr. k-1). pap. 35.70 *(978-0-7368-5315-6(4),* Yellow Umbrella Bks.) Capstone Press of Coughlan Cos.

Baughan, Brian. Cesar Chavez. 2009. (Sharing the American Dream Ser.). (Illus.). 64p. (YA). (gr. 7-12). 22.95 *(978-1-4222-0582-2(7))* Mason Crest.

Berne, Emma Carlson. What's Your Story, Cesar Chavez? 2015. (ENG.). 32p. (J). (gr. k-3). 26.65 *(978-1-4677-7967-8(9))* Lerner Publishing Group.

Braun, Eric. Cesar Chavez: Fighting for Farmworkers, 1 vol. Roland, Harry et al, illus. 2005. (Graphic Biographies Ser.). (ENG.). 32p. (gr. 3-4). 30.65 *(978-0-7368-4631-8(X),* Graphic Library) Capstone Press of Coughlan Cos.

Brimner, Larry Dane. Strike! The Farm Workers' Fight for Their Rights. 2014. (ENG., Illus.). 172p. (J). (gr. 5). 16.95 *(978-1-59078-997-1(0),* Calkins Creek) Boyds Mills Pr.

Brown, Jonatha A. César Chávez. (People We Should Know Ser.). 2005. (SPA.). 24p. (gr. 1-4). pap. 8.15 *(978-0-8368-4766-6(0),* Weekly Reader Leveled Readers) 2005. (SPA., Illus.). 24p. (gr. 1-4). lib. bdg. 22.00 *(978-0-8368-4759-8(8),* Weekly Reader Leveled Readers) 2005. (Illus.). 24p. (gr. 1-4). lib. bdg. 22.00 *(978-0-8368-4745-1(8),* Weekly Reader Leveled Readers) 2004. (Illus.). 48p. (gr. 5-12). pap. 14.05 *(978-0-8368-5257-8(5),* Gareth Stevens Secondary Library) 2004. (Illus.). 48p. (gr. 5-12). lib. bdg. 31.00 *(978-0-8368-5097-0(1),* Gareth Stevens Secondary Library) Stevens, Gareth Publishing LLLP.

Brown, Jonatha A., et al. César Chávez. McHargue, D., illus. 2007. (Biografias Graficas (Graphic Biographies) Ser.). (SPA.). 32p. (gr. 5-8). lib. bdg. 27.00 *(978-0-8368-7879-0(5))* Stevens, Gareth Publishing LLLP.

Brown, Monica. Lado a Lado: La Historia de Dolores Huerta y Cesar Chavez. Cepeda, Joe, illus. 2010.Tr. of Side by Side - The Story of Dolores Huerta & Cesar Chavez. (SPA & ENG.). 32p. (J). (gr. -1-3). 16.99 *(978-0-06-122781-3(1),* Rayo) HarperCollins Pubs.

Cesar Chavez, Lider Laboral. 2003. pap. 48.95 *(978-0-8136-9205-0(9))* Modern Curriculum Pr.

Charlesworth, Eric. Easy Reader Biographies: Cesar Chavez: A Leader for Change. 2007. (ENG.). 16p. pap. 2.99 *(978-0-439-77416-1(0),* Teaching Resources) Scholastic, Inc.

Collard, Sneed B., III. American Heroes, 6 vols., Group 3. Incl. Cesar Chavez: The Farm Workers' Best Friend. 29.93 *(978-0-7614-4055-0(0));* George Washington: Our First President. 29.93 *(978-0-7614-4060-4(7));* Jacob Lawrence: A Painter's Story. 29.93 *(978-0-7614-4058-1(5));* Lady Bird Johnson: Keeping America Green. 29.93 *(978-0-7614-4056-7(9));* Phillis Wheatley: She Loved Words. 29.93 *(978-0-7614-4057-4(7));* Sitting Bull: Tatanka-Iyotake. 29.93 *(978-0-7614-4059-8(3));* 48p. (gr. 3-18). (American Heroes 3 Ser.). 2009. Set lib. bdg. 179.57 o.p. *(978-0-7614-4054-3(2))* Marshall Cavendish Corp.

—Cesar Chavez: The Farm Workers' Best Friend. 2009. (American Heroes Ser.). 48p. (gr. 3-18). 29.93 *(978-0-7614-4055-0(0))* Marshall Cavendish Corp.

Collins, David R. Cesar Chavez. 2005. (Just the Facts Biographies Ser.). (Illus.). 112p. (J). (gr. 6-12). 27.93 *(978-0-8225-2248-5(9))* Lerner Publishing Group.

Cruz, Bàrbara C. Cesar Chavez: A Voice for Farmworkers. 2005. (Latino Biography Library). (Illus.). 128p. (J). (gr. 6-13). lib. bdg. 33.27 *(978-0-7660-2489-2(X))* Enslow Pubs., Inc.

Cruz, Bárbara C. César Chávez: Civil Rights Activist. 2016. (Influential Latinos Ser.). (ENG.). 128p. (J). (gr. 7-8). lib. bdg. 37.27 *(978-0-7660-7179-7(0))* Enslow Pubs., Inc.

Cuesta, Vivian. It Can Be Done: The Life & Legacy of César Chávez. 2003. (ENG., Illus.). 32p. (J). (gr. 6-8). pap. 8.47 net. *(978-0-7652-3271-7(5),* Celebration Pr.) Pearson Schl.

Domblewski, Carol. Citizens Who Made a Difference: Set Of 6. 2011. (Navigators Ser.). (J). pap. 44.00 net. *(978-1-4108-5097-3(8))* Benchmark Education Co.

Dunn, Joeming W. Cesar Chavez, 1 vol. Espinosa, Rod, illus. 2008. (Bio-Graphics Ser.). (ENG.). 32p. (gr. 3-5). 28.50 *(978-1-60270-172-4(5),* Graphic Planet- Nonfiction) ABDO Publishing Co.

Ebon Research Systems Staff. Dare to Be... A Hero Vol. 3: Cesar Chavez. l.t. ed. 2003.Tr. of Atrevete Ser... Un Heroe Cesar Chavez. (ENG & SPA., Illus.). 16p. (J). 3.99 *(978-0-9648313-6-0(8))* Ebon Research Systems Publishing, LLC.

Eddy, Susan & National Geographic Learning Staff. Cesar Chavez. 2010. (Rise & Shine Ser.). (ENG., Illus.). 32p. (C). (gr. 1-2). pap. 7.95 *(978-0-516-27923-7(8))* National Geographic School Publishing, Inc.

Feinstein, Stephen. Lee Sobre Cesar Chavez. 2006. (I Like Biographies! Bilingual Ser.).Tr. of Read about Cesar Chavez. (ENG & SPA., Illus.). 24p. (J). (gr. -1-3). lib. bdg. 22.60 *(978-0-7660-2744-2(9),* Enslow Elementary) Enslow Pubs., Inc.

—Read about Cesar Chavez. 2004. (I Like Biographies! Ser.). (Illus.). 24p. (J). lib. bdg. 22.60 *(978-0-7660-2296-6(X))* Enslow Pubs., Inc.

Frey, Wendy. Citizen Heroes. 2007. (Illus.). 68p. (J). *(978-1-4105-0888-1(9)); (978-1-4105-0887-4(0))* Johnston, Don Inc.

Gay, Kathlyn. César Chávez: Fighting for Migrant Farmworkers. 2017. (Rebels with a Cause Ser.). 128p. (J). (gr. 8-8). lib. bdg. 37.27 ***(978-0-7660-8951-8(7))*** Enslow Pubs., Inc.

Gotsch, Patrice. Cesar Chavez: Changing Lives. Arreola, Gil, illus. 2006. 19p. pap. 6.30 *(978-1-55501-780-4(0))* Ballard & Tighe Pubs.

Gregory, Josh. Cesar Chavez. 2015. (True Book & Trade; & Mdash;Biographies Ser.). (ENG., Illus.). 48p. (J). pap. 6.95 *(978-0-531-21210-3(6))* Scholastic Library Publishing.

Griswold del Castillo, Richard. Cesar Chavez: The Struggle for Justice/la Lucha Por la Justicia. Colin, Jose Juan, tr. Accardo, Anthony, illus. 2008. (Hispanic Civil Rights Ser.). (SPA & ENG.). 32p. (J). (gr. -1-3). pap. 7.95 *(978-1-55885-424-6(X),* Piñata Books) Arte Publico Pr.

Guzman, Lila & Guzman, Rick. Cesar Chavez: Fighting for Fairness. 2006. (Famous Latinos Ser.). (Illus.). 32p. (J). (gr. 3-7). lib. bdg. 22.60 *(978-0-7660-2370-3(2),* Enslow Elementary) Enslow Pubs., Inc.

—Cesar Chavez: La Lucha Por lo Justo. 2007. (Latinos Famosos Ser.). (SPA., Illus.). 32p. (J). (gr. 3-7). lib. bdg. 22.60 *(978-0-7660-2679-7(5),* Enslow Elementary) Enslow Pubs., Inc.

Guzmán, Lila & Guzmán, Rick. César Chávez: La Lucha Por lo Justo. 2014. (Latinos Famosos Ser.). 32p. (gr. 2). pap. 7.95 *(978-0-7660-5443-1(8))* Enslow Pubs., Inc.

Hile, Kevin. Cesar Chavez. 2008. (Twentieth Century's Most Influential Hispanics Ser.). (ENG., Illus.). 96-128p. (gr. 7-10). 34.80 *(978-1-4205-0094-3(5),* Lucent Bks.) Cengage Gale.

Houle, Michelle E., ed. Cesar Chavez. 2003. (People Who Made History Ser.). (ENG., Illus.). 186p. (YA). (gr. 10-12). 26.50 *(978-0-7377-1299-5(6),* Greenhaven Pr., Inc.) Cengage Gale.

Hudson Goff, Elizabeth, et al. César Chávez. 2007. (Biografias Graficas (Graphic Biographies) Ser.). (SPA.). 32p. (gr. 5-8). pap. 10.50 *(978-0-8368-7886-8(8))* Stevens, Gareth Publishing LLLP.

Juarez, Christine. Cesar Chavez. 2016. (Great Hispanic & Latino Americans Ser.). (ENG.). 24p. (gr. k-1). lib. bdg. 21.99 *(978-1-5157-1892-5(1),* Pebble Bks.) Capstone Press of Coughlan Cos.

Krull, Kathleen. Cosechando Esperanza: La Historia de César Chávez. Campoy, F. Isabel & Flor Ada, Alma, trs. Morales, Yuyi, illus. 2004. (SPA & ENG.). 48p. (J). (gr. -1-3). pap. 7.99 *(978-0-15-205169-3(4))* Houghton Mifflin Harcourt Publishing Co.

—Harvesting Hope: The Story of Cesar Chavez. Morales, Yuyi, illus. 2003. (ENG.). 48p. (J). (gr. -1-3). 17.99 *(978-0-15-201437-7(3))* Houghton Mifflin Harcourt Publishing Co.

Magoon, Kekla. Cesar Chavez: Crusader for Labor Rights, 1 vol. 2010. (Essential Lives Set 5 Ser.). (ENG., Illus.). 112p. (J). (gr. 6-12). lib. bdg. 35.64 *(978-1-61613-512-6(3))* ABDO Publishing Co.

Miklowitz, Gloria. Cesar Chavez. 2009. pap. 13.25 *(978-1-60559-056-1(8))* Hameray Publishing Group, Inc.

Miklowitz, Gloria D. César Chávez. 2004. (ENG., Illus.). 29p. (J). (gr. 2-5). pap. 5.97 net. *(978-0-7685-1215-1(8),* Dominie Elementary) Pearson Schl.

Rau, Dana Meachen. Who Was Cesar Chavez? 2017. (Who Was... ? Ser.). lib. bdg. 16.00 ***(978-0-606-39780-3(9))*** Turtleback Bks.

Rinaldo, Denise. Cesar Chavez: With a Discussion of Compassion. 2003. (Values in Action Ser.). (J). *(978-1-59203-064-4(5))* Learning Challenge, Inc.

Roome, Anne Ross & Mattern, Joanne. Cesar Chavez. 2016. (Rookie Biographies(tm) Ser.). (ENG., Illus.). 32p. (J). lib. bdg. 25.00 *(978-0-531-22546-2(1),* Children's Pr.) Scholastic Library Publishing.

Seidman, David. Cesar Chavez: Labor Leader. 2004. (Great Life Stories Ser.). (ENG., Illus.). 127p. (J). 30.50 *(978-0-531-12319-5(7),* Watts, Franklin) Scholastic Library Publishing.

Soto, Gary. Cesar Chavez: A Hero for Everyone. Lohstoeter, Lori, illus. 2003. (Milestone Ser.). (ENG.). 80p. (J). (gr. 2-5). pap. 6.99 *(978-0-689-85922-9(8),* Simon & Schuster/Paula Wiseman Bks.) Simon & Schuster/Paula Wiseman Bks.

Thompson, E. L. Cesar Chavez, with Profiles of Terence V. Powderly & Dolores Huerta. 2006. (Biographical Connections Ser.). (Illus.). 112p. (J). *(978-0-7166-1827-0(3))* World Bk., Inc.

Wadsworth, Ginger. Cesar Chavez. Schroeder, Mark, illus. 2005. (Yo Solo - Biografias (on My Own - Biographies) Ser.). (SPA.). 48p. (J). (gr. 2-4). per. 6.95 *(978-0-8225-3125-8(9))* Lerner Publishing Group.

—Cesar Chavez. 2005. (On My Own Biography Ser.). (Illus.). 48p. (J). 25.26 *(978-1-57505-652-4(6),* Carolrhoda Bks.) Lerner Publishing Group.

—Cesar Chavez. Schroder, Mark, illus. 2005. (On My Own Biography Ser.). (ENG.). 48p. (gr. 2-4). pap. 6.95 *(978-1-57505-826-9(X))* Lerner Publishing Group.

—César Chávez. Fitzpatrick, Julia, tr. from ENG. Schroder, Mark, illus. 2005. (Yo Solo: Biografías (on My Own Biographies) Ser.). (SPA.). 48p. (gr. 2-4). lib. bdg. 25.26 *(978-0-8225-3124-1(0),* Ediciones Lerner) Lerner Publishing Group.

Wheeler, Jill C. Cesar Chavez. 2003. (Breaking Barriers Ser.). 64p. (gr. 3-8). 27.07 *(978-1-57765-905-1(8),* Abdo & Daughters) ABDO Publishing Co.

Young, Jeff C. Cesar Chavez. 2007. (American Workers Ser.). (Illus.). 160p. (J). (gr. 3-7). lib. bdg. 27.95 *(978-1-59935-036-3(X))* Reynolds, Morgan Inc.

CHECKERS

Alvarez, Michel J., creator. WonderCheckers - Checkers Kit for Kids: Featuring Unique Prize-fillable Pieces, Incentive Charts & Motivational Stickers - plus 3D Tic-Tac-Toe. 2005. (J). 17.95 *(978-0-9771787-2-8(2))* Wonder Chess LLC.

Cardie, John P. How to Beat Granddad at Checkers. Murr, Bob, illus. 2007. 62p. per. 15.95 *(978-1-59879-390-1(X))* Lifevest Publishing, Inc.

CHEERLEADING

ABDO Publishing. Cheerleading. 2016. (Cheerleading Ser.: 6). (ENG.). 32p. (J). (gr. 3-6). lib. bdg. 162.42 *(978-1-62403-980-5(4),* SportsZone) ABDO Publishing Co.

Cecchetti, Diane. Cheerleading Skills: How to Cheer Like a Champ. 2008. (How to Play Like a Pro Ser.). (Illus.). 48p. (J). (gr. 3-6). lib. bdg. 25.27 *(978-0-7660-3208-8(6))* Enslow Pubs., Inc.

Cheerleading Rules! 2005. (J). per. *(978-1-932855-36-4(X))* becker&mayer! books.

Crabtree Editors & Webb, Margaret. Pump It up Cheerleading. 2012. (Sports Starters Ser.). (ENG., Illus.). 32p. (J). (gr. 1-4). lib. bdg. *(978-0-7787-3149-8(9))* Crabtree Publishing Co.

Crossingham, John. Le Cheerleading. 2010. (FRE., Illus.). 32p. (J). pap. 9.95 *(978-2-89579-290-1(9))* Bayard Canada Livres CAN. Dist: Crabtree Publishing Co.

—Porristas en Acción. Rouse, Bonna, illus. Crabtree, Marc, photos by. 2005. (Deportes en Acción Ser.). (SPA & ENG.). 32p. (J). (gr. 3-4). lib. bdg. *(978-0-7787-8575-0(0));* (gr. 6-9). pap. *(978-0-7787-8621-4(8))* Crabtree Publishing Co.

Crossingham, John & Rouse, Bonna. Cheerleading in Action. 2003. (Sports in Action Ser.). (ENG., Illus.). 32p. (J). (gr. 1-4). pap. *(978-0-7787-0353-2(3))* Crabtree Publishing Co.

Douglas, Peter. Cheerleading: Techniques for Performing. 2017. (Preparing for Game Day Ser.: Vol. 10). (ENG.). (YA). (gr. 7-12). 24.95 ***(978-1-4222-3915-5(2))*** Mason Crest.

—Track & Field: Conditioning for Greatness. 2017. (J). ***(978-1-4222-3912-4(8))*** Mason Crest.

Emmer, Rae. Cheerleading: Porristas. 2004. (School Activities / Actividades Escolares Ser.). (SPA & ENG., Illus.). 24p. (J). (gr. 1-4). lib. bdg. 22.60 *(978-0-8239-6899-2(5))* Rosen Publishing Group, Inc., The.

—Cheerleading / Porristas. 2009. (School Activities / Actividades escolares Ser.). (SPA.). 24p. (gr. 1-2). 42.50 *(978-1-60853-001-4(9),* Editorial Buenas Letras) Rosen Publishing Group, Inc., The.

Gitlin, Marty. Girls Play to Win Cheerleading. 2011. (Girls Play to Win Ser.). 64p. (J). (gr. 3-6). lib. bdg. 27.93 *(978-1-59953-462-6(2))* Norwood Hse. Pr.

Green, Sara. Cheerleading. 2011. (My First Sports Ser.). (ENG., Illus.). 24p. (J). (gr. 2-5). lib. bdg. 25.95 *(978-1-60014-568-1(X),* Blastoff! Readers) Bellwether Media.

—Cheerleading. 2011. pap. *(978-0-531-20634-8(3))* Grolier Publishing.

—Cheerleading Basics. 2011. (Kick, Jump, Cheer! Ser.). (ENG., Illus.). 24p. (J). (gr. 3-8). lib. bdg. 25.95 *(978-1-60014-646-6(5),* Pilot Bks.) Bellwether Media.

—Cheerleading Camp. 2011. (Kick, Jump, Cheer! Ser.). (ENG., Illus.). 24p. (J). (gr. 3-8). lib. bdg. 25.95 *(978-1-60014-647-3(3),* Pilot Bks.) Bellwether Media.

—Cheerleading Competitions. 2011. (Kick, Jump, Cheer! Ser.). (ENG., Illus.). 24p. (YA). (gr. 3-8). lib. bdg. 25.95 *(978-1-60014-648-0(1),* Pilot Bks.) Bellwether Media.

—Cheerleading Professionals. 2011. (Kick, Jump, Cheer! Ser.). (ENG., Illus.). 24p. (YA). (gr. 3-8). lib. bdg. 25.95 *(978-1-60014-649-7(X),* Pilot Bks.) Bellwether Media.

—Cheerleading Squads. 2011. (Kick, Jump, Cheer! Ser.). (ENG., Illus.). 24p. (YA). (gr. 3-8). lib. bdg. 25.95 *(978-1-60014-650-3(3),* Pilot Bks.) Bellwether Media.

—Cheerleading Tryouts. 2011. (Kick, Jump, Cheer! Ser.). (ENG., Illus.). 24p. (J). (gr. 3-8). lib. bdg. 25.95 *(978-1-60014-651-0(1),* Pilot Bks.) Bellwether Media.

Greenhaven Press Editors & Schwartz, Heather E. Cheerleading. 2012. (Science Behind Sports Ser.). (ENG., Illus.). 128p. (gr. 7-10). lib. bdg. 39.40 *(978-1-4205-0818-5(0),* Lucent Bks.) Cengage Gale.

Hunt, Sara R. You've Got Spirit! Cheers, Chants, Tips, & Tricks Every Cheerleader Needs to Know. Perrett, Lisa, illus. (ENG.). 48p. (gr. 3-6). 2015. 34.65 *(978-1-4677-5991-5(0),* Lerner Digital) 2013. lib. bdg. 30.60 *(978-0-7613-8634-6(3),* Millbrook Pr.) Lerner Publishing Group.

Jaworowicz, Grace. Chelsea's Cheerleading Squad: Add Within 20. 2014. (Rosen Common Core Math Readers Ser.). (ENG.). 24p. (J). (gr. 2-3). pap. 8.25 *(978-1-4777-4636-3(6),* Rosen Classroom) Rosen Publishing Group, Inc., The.

Jones, Jen. Cheer Skills, 1 vol. 2010. (Cheerleading Ser.). (ENG.). 24p. (gr. k-1). lib. bdg. 26.65 *(978-1-4296-5276-6(4),* Pebble Plus) Capstone Press of Coughlan Cos.

—Cheerleading, 4 vols., Set. Incl. Cheer Skills. (ENG.). 24p. (gr. k-1). 2010. lib. bdg. 26.65 *(978-1-4296-5276-6(4),* Pebble Plus); (Cheerleading Ser.). (ENG.). 24p. 2010. Set lib. bdg. 53.30 o.p. *(978-1-4296-5277-3(2),* Pebble Plus) Capstone Press of Coughlan Cos.

Kenney, Karen Latchana. Cool School Cheerleading: Fun Ideas & Activities to Build School Spirit, 1 vol. 2011. (Cool School Spirit Ser.). (ENG., Illus.). 32p. (J). (gr. 3-6). 28.50 *(978-1-61714-665-7(X),* Checkerboard Library) ABDO Publishing Co.

Maurer, Tracy Nelson. The Cheerleaders. 2005. (Jump & Shout Ser.). (Illus.). 48p. (J). (gr. 4-8). lib. bdg. 31.36 *(978-1-59515-498-9(1))* Rourke Educational Media.

—Competitive Cheerleading. 2005. (Jump & Shout Ser.). (Illus.). 48p. (J). (gr. 4-8). lib. bdg. 31.36 *(978-1-59515-501-6(5))* Rourke Educational Media.

McCoy, Lisa. Cheerleading. 2005. (Sports Injuries Ser.). (Illus.). 64p. (YA). lib. bdg. 19.95 *(978-1-59084-628-5(1))* Mason Crest.

Mullarkey, Lisa. Cheerleading Basics. 2010. (Ready, Set, Cheer! Ser.). (Illus.). 48p. (J). 25.27 *(978-0-7660-3536-2(0));* pap. 8.95 *(978-1-59845-198-6(7))* Enslow Pubs., Inc.

—Cheerleading Spirit. 2010. (Ready, Set, Cheer! Ser.). 48p. (J). 25.27 *(978-0-7660-3538-6(7));* (Illus.). pap. 8.95 *(978-1-59845-199-3(5))* Enslow Pubs., Inc.

—Cheerleading Stunts & Tumbling. 2010. (Ready, Set, Cheer! Ser.). (Illus.). 48p. (J). pap. 8.95 *(978-1-59845-200-6(2))* Enslow Pubs., Inc.

—Cheerleading Tryouts & Competitions. 2010. (Ready, Set, Cheer! Ser.). 48p. (J). 25.27 *(978-0-7660-3539-3(5));* (Illus.). pap. 8.95 *(978-1-59845-201-3(0))* Enslow Pubs., Inc.

Mullarkey, Lisa & Library. Cheerleading Stunts & Tumbling. 2010. (Ready, Set, Cheer! Ser.). (Illus.). 48p. (J). lib. bdg. 25.27 *(978-0-7660-3537-9(9))* Enslow Pubs., Inc.

Peters, Craig. Chants, Cheers, & Jumps. 2004. (Let's Go Team Ser.). (Illus.). 64p. (YA). (gr. 5-18). lib. bdg. 19.95 *(978-1-59084-535-6(8))* Mason Crest.

—Cheerleading Stars. 2004. (Let's Go Team Ser.). (Illus.). 64p. (YA). (gr. 5-18). lib. bdg. 19.95 *(978-1-59084-533-2(1))* Mason Crest.

—Competitive Cheerleading. 2004. (Let's Go Team Ser.). (Illus.). 64p. (YA). (gr. 5-18). lib. bdg. 19.95 *(978-1-59084-532-5(3))* Mason Crest.

—Techniques of Cheerleading. 2003. (Let's Go Team Ser.). (Illus.). 64p. (J). (gr. 5-18). lib. bdg. *(978-1-59084-530-1(7))* Mason Crest.

—Techniques of Dance for Cheerleading. 2003. (Let's Go Team Ser.). (Illus.). 64p. (J). (gr. 5-18). lib. bdg. *(978-1-59084-531-8(5))* Mason Crest.

Rissman, Rebecca. Cheer Spirit. 2015. (Cheer Spirit Ser.). (ENG.). 32p. (gr. 3-4). 111.96 *(978-1-4914-6958-3(7),* Snap Bks.) Capstone Press of Coughlan Cos.

—Jump, Tuck, Flip: Mastering Cheerleading Skills & Stunts. 2015. (Cheer Spirit Ser.). (ENG., Illus.). 32p. (gr. 3-4). lib. bdg. 27.99 *(978-1-4914-5203-5(X),* Snap Bks.) Capstone Press of Coughlan Cos.

—Make Some Noise: Chants & Cheers That Fire up the Crowd. 2015. (Cheer Spirit Ser.). (ENG., Illus.). 32p. (gr. 3-4). lib. bdg. 27.99 *(978-1-4914-5204-2(8),* Snap Bks.) Capstone Press of Coughlan Cos.

—Quest for the Best: Conquering Cheerleading Tryouts & Competitions. 2015. (Cheer Spirit Ser.). (ENG., Illus.). 32p. (gr. 3-4). lib. bdg. 27.99 *(978-1-4914-5205-9(6),* Snap Bks.) Capstone Press of Coughlan Cos.

—Show Your Spirit: Cheerleading Basics You Need to Know. 2015. (Cheer Spirit Ser.). (ENG., Illus.). 32p. (gr. 3-4). lib. bdg. 27.99 *(978-1-4914-5214-1(5),* Snap Bks.) Capstone Press of Coughlan Cos.

Thomas, Patsy E. A Camp Carrot Cheer for Good Nutrition. 2011. 16p. (gr. 2-4). pap. 10.67 *(978-1-4269-6200-4(2))* Trafford Publishing.

Valliant, Doris. The History of Cheerleading. 2004. (Let's Go Team Ser.). (Illus.). 64p. (YA). (gr. 5-18). lib. bdg. 19.95 *(978-1-59084-534-9(X))* Mason Crest.

Vanderhoof, Gabrielle. Cheerleading. 2010. (Getting the Edge Ser.). 96p. (YA). lib. bdg. 24.95 *(978-1-4222-1732-0(9))* Mason Crest.

Webb, Margaret. Pump It up Cheerleading. 2012. (ENG., Illus.). 32p. (J). pap. *(978-0-7787-3160-3(X))* Crabtree Publishing Co.

Wells, Don. Cheerleading. (In the Zone Ser.). (Illus.). (J). 2010. 32p. (gr. 3-5). pap. 11.95 *(978-1-60596-896-4(X))* 2010. 32p. (gr. 3-5). lib. bdg. 25.70 *(978-1-60596-895-7(1))* 2005. 24p. (gr. 4-6). lib. bdg. 24.45 *(978-1-59036-295-2(0))* Weigl Pubs., Inc.

Yomtov, Nelson. Being Your Best at Cheerleading. 2016. (True Book(tm), a — Sports & Entertainment Ser.). (ENG., Illus.). 48p. (J). lib. bdg. 31.00 *(978-0-531-23265-1(4),* Children's Pr.) Scholastic Library Publishing.

101 Best Cheers. 2004. (J). per. 4.95 *(978-1-932855-06-7(8))* becker&mayer! books.

CHEETAH

Albee, Sarah & Delaney, Kate. Cheetahs. 2010. (Amazing Animals Ser.). (ENG.). 48p. (J). (gr. 2-6). pap. 10.50 *(978-1-4339-4011-8(6));* lib. bdg. 28.00 *(978-1-4339-4010-1(8))* Stevens, Gareth Publishing LLLP. (Gareth Stevens Learning Library).

—Cheetahs. 2007. (J). *(978-1-59939-118-2(X),* Reader's Digest Young Families, Inc.) Studio Fun International.

Archer, Claire. Cheetahs, 1 vol. 2014. (Big Cats Ser.). (ENG.). 24p. (J). (gr. 4-8). lib. bdg. 28.50 *(978-1-62970-001-4(0),* Abdo Kids) ABDO Publishing Co.

Archer, Claire, et al. Guepardos. 2015. (Grandes Felinos Ser.). (SPA., Illus.). 24p. (gr. k-1). pap. 7.95 *(978-1-4966-0457-6(1))* Capstone Classroom.

Becker, John E. Frenemies for Life: Cheetahs & Anatolian Shepherd Dogs. 2010. 56p. (YA). (gr. 5-8). pap. 8.95 *(978-0-9841554-1-5(4));* lib. bdg. 18.95 *(978-0-9841554-0-8(6))* Columbus Zoo & Aquarium, The.

Borgert-Spaniol, Megan. Cheetahs. 2012. (Animal Safari Ser.). (ENG., Illus.). 24p. (J). (gr. k-3). lib. bdg. 25.95 *(978-1-60014-716-6(X),* Blastoff! Readers) Bellwether Media.

Bowman, Donna H. Big Cats. Wald, Christina, illus. 2008. (ENG.). 24p. (J). (gr. 3-18). 19.95 *(978-1-58117-781-7(X),* Intervisual/Piggy Toes) Bendon, Inc.

Clarke, Ginjer L. Cheetah Cubs. Washburn, Lucia, illus. 2007. (All Aboard Science Reader Ser.). 48p. (gr. 1-3). 14.00 *(978-0-7569-8169-3(7))* Perfection Learning Corp.

—Cheetah Cubs, Level 3. Washburn, Lucia, illus. 2007. (Penguin Young Readers, Level 3 Ser.). (ENG.). 48p. (J). (gr.

1-3). mass mkt. 3.99 *(978-0-448-44361-4(9),* Penguin Young Readers) Penguin Young Readers Group.

Costain, Meredith. Cheetah. Posen, Mick, illus. 2016. (Wild World Ser.). 00032p. (J). (gr. 1-2). pap. 10.00 *(978-1-4994-8203-4(5),* Windmill Bks.) Rosen Publishing Group, Inc., The.

Denis-Huot, Christine & Denis-Huot, Michel. The Cheetah. 2004. (Animal Close-Ups Ser.). (Illus.). 28p. (J). pap. 6.95 *(978-1-57091-626-7(8))* Charlesbridge Publishing, Inc.

Doudna, Kelly. It's a Baby Cheetah!, 1 vol. 2009. (Baby African Animals Ser.). (ENG., Illus.). 24p. (J). (gr. k-3). lib. bdg. 24.21 *(978-1-60453-151-0(7),* SandCastle) ABDO Publishing Co.

Eckart, Edana. Cheetah. 2005. (Animals of the World Ser.). (ENG., Illus.). 24p. (gr. -1-2). 19.00 *(978-0-516-25052-6(3),* Children's Pr.) Scholastic Library Publishing.

Eszterhas, Suzi. Eye on the Wild: Cheetah. 2012. (Eye on the Wild Ser.). (Illus.). 32p. (J). *(978-1-84780-204-0(4),* Frances Lincoln) Quarto Publishing Group UK.

Gagne, Tammy. Cheetahs, 1 vol. 2012. (Big Cats Ser.). (ENG.). 32p. (gr. 3-4). lib. bdg. 27.99 *(978-1-4296-7641-0(8),* Edge Bks.) Capstone Press of Coughlan Cos.

Goldsworthy, Steve. Cheetahs. 2014. (J). *(978-1-4896-0910-6(5))* Weigl Pubs., Inc.

Grucella, Ethan. Cheetahs. 2010. (Animals That Live in the Grasslands Ser.). (ENG.). 24p. (J). (gr. -1-3). pap. 8.15 *(978-1-4339-3864-1(2));* lib. bdg. 22.60 *(978-1-4339-3863-4(4))* Stevens, Gareth Publishing LLLP.

Guillain, Charlotte. Cheetahs, 1 vol. 2014. (Living in the Wild: Big Cats Ser.). (ENG.). 48p. (gr. 3-6). lib. bdg. 33.32 *(978-1-4329-8105-1(6),* Heinemann InfoSearch) Heinemann-Raintree.

Guillain, Charlotte, et al. Living in the Wild: Big Cats, 1 vol. 2014. (Living in the Wild: Big Cats Ser.). (ENG.). 48p. (gr. 3-6). lib. bdg. 199.92 *(978-1-4329-8111-2(0),* Heinemann InfoSearch) Heinemann-Raintree.

Hanel, Rachael. Cheetahs. 2009. (Living Wild Ser.). (Illus.). 48p. (J). 22.95 *(978-1-58341-737-9(0),* Creative Education) Creative Co., The.

Harasymiw, R. P. Cheetahs. 2012. (Killer Cats Ser.). (Illus.). 24p. (J). (gr. 2-5). pap. 8.15 *(978-1-4339-7000-9(7));* lib. bdg. 22.60 *(978-1-4339-6999-7(8))* Stevens, Gareth Publishing LLLP.

Harkrader, Lisa. The Cheetah: A MyReportLinks. com Book. 2005. (Endangered & Threatened Animals Ser.). (Illus.). 48p. (J). lib. bdg. 25.26 *(978-0-7660-5065-5(3),* MyReportLinks.com Bks.) Enslow Pubs., Inc.

Herrington, Lisa M. Cheetahs & Leopards. 2015. (Rookie Read-About(tm) Science: What's the Difference? Ser.). (ENG., Illus.). 32p. (J). lib. bdg. 25.00 *(978-0-531-21481-7(8),* Children's Pr.) Scholastic Library Publishing.

Herriott, Charlotte. Cheetah vs. Ostrich. 2015. (Bizarre Beast Battles Ser.). (ENG., Illus.). 24p. (J). (gr. 2-3). pap. 8.15 *(978-1-4824-2784-4(2))* Stevens, Gareth Publishing LLLP.

Johns, Chris & Carney, Elizabeth. Face to Face with Cheetahs. 2008. (Face to Face with Animals Ser.). (ENG., Illus.). 32p. (J). (gr. 2-5). 25.90 *(978-1-4263-0324-1(6));* 16.95 *(978-1-4263-0323-4(8))* National Geographic Society. (National Geographic Children's Bks.).

Latta, Jan. Charlie the Cheetah. 2007. (Wild Animal Families Ser.). (Illus.). 24p. (gr. 1-4). pap. 8.15 *(978-0-8368-7774-8(8));* lib. bdg. 24.00 *(978-0-8368-7767-0(5))* Stevens, Gareth Publishing LLLP. (Gareth Stevens Learning Library).

—Gerardo el Guepardo. 2007. (Familias de animales salvajes (Wild Animal Families) Ser.). (SPA., Illus.). 24p. (gr. 1-4). lib. bdg. 24.00 *(978-0-8368-7967-4(8),* Gareth Stevens Learning Library) Stevens, Gareth Publishing LLLP.

Leaf, Christina. Baby Cheetahs. 2015. (Super Cute! Ser.). (ENG., Illus.). 24p. (J). (gr. k-3). lib. bdg. 25.95 *(978-1-62617-168-8(8),* Blastoff! Readers) Bellwether Media.

Levine, Michelle. Speedy Cheetahs. 2006. (Pull Ahead Books-Animals Ser.). (ENG., Illus.). 32p. (gr. k-3). lib. bdg. 22.60 *(978-0-8225-5933-7(1),* Lerner Pubns.); per. 7.95 *(978-0-8225-6510-9(2),* First Avenue Editions) Lerner Publishing Group.

Lunis, Natalie. Cheetah: Speed Demon! 2010. (Blink of an Eye: Superfast Animals Ser.). 24p. (J). (gr. k-3). lib. bdg. 22.61 *(978-1-936087-89-1(8))* Bearport Publishing Co., Inc.

MacMillan, Dianne M. Cheetahs. rev. ed. 2009. (Nature Watch Ser.). (ENG.). 48p. (gr. 4-8). 27.93 *(978-0-8225-9417-8(X))* Lerner Publishing Group.

Marsh, Laura. Cheetahs. 2011. (Readers Ser.). (ENG., Illus.). 32p. (J). (gr. 1-4). pap. 3.99 *(978-1-4263-0855-0(8),* National Geographic Children's Bks.) National Geographic Society.

—Cheetahs (1 Hardcover/1 CD) 2017. (National Geographic Kids Ser.). (ENG.). (J). 29.95 ***(978-1-4301-2673-7(6))*** Live Oak Media.

—Cheetahs (1 Paperback/1 CD) 2017. (National Geographic Kids Ser.). (ENG.). (J). pap. 19.95 ***(978-1-4301-2672-0(8))*** Live Oak Media.

—Cheetahs (4 Paperbacks/1 CD) 2017. (National Geographic Kids Ser.). (ENG.). (J). pap. 31.95 ***(978-1-4301-2674-4(4))*** Live Oak Media.

Marsh, Laura. National Geographic Readers: Cheetahs. 2011. (Readers Ser.). (ENG., Illus.). 32p. (J). (gr. 1-4). lib. bdg. 13.90 *(978-1-4263-0856-7(6),* National Geographic Children's Bks.) National Geographic Society.

Marsico, Katie. Cheetahs. 2012. (21st Century Basic Skills Library: Baby Zoo Animals Ser.). (ENG.). 24p. (gr. k-3). 22.79 *(978-1-61080-453-0(8),* 202063); pap. 12.79 *(978-1-61080-627-5(1),* 202237) Cherry Lake Publishing.

—Cheetahs. 2013. (Nature's Children Ser.). (ENG., Illus.). 48p. (J). pap. 6.95 *(978-0-531-24302-2(8));* lib. bdg. 28.00 *(978-0-531-20976-9(8))* Scholastic Library Publishing.

Montgomery, Sy. Chasing Cheetahs: The Race to Save Africa's Fastest Cats. Bishop, Nic, illus. Bishop, Nic, photos by. 2014. (Scientists in the Field Ser.). (ENG.). 80p. (J). (gr. 5-7). 18.99 *(978-0-547-81549-7(2),* HMH Books For Young Readers) Houghton Mifflin Harcourt Publishing Co.

Morgan, Sally. Cheetahs. 2015. (ENG.). 24p. (J). (gr. 3-5). 23.99 *(978-1-939581-87-7(7))* QEB Publishing Inc.

—Cheetahs: Animal Lives Series. 2008. 32p. (J). lib. bdg. 18.95 *(978-1-59566-536-2(6))* QEB Publishing Inc.

Murray, Julie. Cheetahs, 1 vol. (ENG.). 2012. 32p. 28.50 *(978-1-61783-217-8(0),* Big Buddy Bks.) 2005. (Illus.). 24p. 25.65 *(978-1-59197-305-8(8),* Buddy Bks.) ABDO Publishing Co.

Nagda, Ann Whitehead. Cheetah Math: Learning about Division from Baby Cheetahs. rev. ed. 2007. (ENG., Illus.). 32p. (J). (gr. 2-5). 18.99 *(978-0-8050-7645-5(X),* 9780805076455, Holt, Henry & Co. Bks. For Young Readers) Holt, Henry & Co.

National Geographic Editors. Favorite Animals Collection. 2013. (Readers Ser.). (ENG., Illus.). 128p. (J). (gr. -1-1). pap. 7.99 *(978-1-4263-1333-2(0),* National Geographic Children's Bks.) National Geographic Society.

Nuzzolo, Deborah. Cheetahs. (African Animals Ser.). (ENG.). 24p. 2016. pap. 7.29 *(978-1-5157-6195-2(9))* 2010. pap. 41.70 *(978-1-4296-5078-6(8))* Capstone Press of Coughlan Cos. (Pebble Plus).

—Cheetahs [Scholastic]. 2010. (African Animals Ser.). 24p. pap. 0.49 *(978-1-4296-5790-7(1),* Pebble Plus) Capstone Press of Coughlan Cos.

Parker, Barbara Keevil. Cheetahs. 2005. (Early Bird Nature Bks.). (Illus.). 48p. (J). (gr. 2-4). lib. bdg. 25.26 *(978-0-8225-3053-4(8))* Lerner Publishing Group.

Pohl, Kathleen. Cheetahs. 2007. (Animals I See at the Zoo Ser.). 24p. (gr. k-3). pap. 8.15 *(978-0-8368-8225-4(3));* (Illus.). lib. bdg. 22.00 *(978-0-8368-8218-6(0))* Stevens, Gareth Publishing LLLP. (Weekly Reader Leveled Readers).

—Cheetahs/Guepardos. 2007. (Animals I See at the Zoo/Animales que Veo en el Zoológico Ser.). (SPA & ENG., Illus.). 24p. (gr. k-3). lib. bdg. 22.00 *(978-0-8368-8232-2(6),* Weekly Reader Leveled Readers) Stevens, Gareth Publishing LLLP.

Randall, Henry. Cheetahs. 2011. (Cats of the Wild Ser.). (ENG.). 24p. (J). pap. 8.25 *(978-1-4488-2621-6(7));* lib. bdg. 22.60 *(978-1-4488-2518-9(0))* Rosen Publishing Group, Inc., The. (PowerKids Pr.).

—Cheetahs: Guepardos. 2011. (Cats of the Wild / Felinos Salvajes Ser.). (SPA & ENG., Illus.). 24p. lib. bdg. 22.60 *(978-1-4488-3130-2(X),* PowerKids Pr.) Rosen Publishing Group, Inc., The.

Reade, Clara. Cheetahs. 2012. (PowerKids Readers: Safari Animals Ser.). (ENG., Illus.). 24p. (J). (gr. k-2). pap. 8.25 *(978-1-4488-7471-2(8));* lib. bdg. 22.60 *(978-1-4488-7464-4(5))* Rosen Publishing Group, Inc., The. (PowerKids Pr.).

Riggs, Kate. Amazing Animals - Cheetahs. 2011. (Amazing Animals Ser.). (J). (gr. 2-5). 24.25 *(978-1-58341-988-5(8))* Creative Co., The.

—Cheetahs. (J). 2014. *(978-1-60818-452-1(8),* Creative Education) 2011. (ENG.). 24p. (gr. 1-3). pap. 8.99 *(978-0-89812-561-0(8),* Creative Paperbacks) Creative Co., The.

—Seedlings: Cheetahs. 2015. (Seedlings Ser.). (ENG.). 24p. (J). (gr. -1-1). pap. 7.99 *(978-1-62832-040-4(0),* Creative Paperbacks) Creative Co., The.

Ringstad, Arnold. Cheetahs. 2014. (Wild Cats Ser.). (Illus.). 24p. (J). 27.10 *(978-1-60753-599-7(8))* Amicus Publishing.

Silverman, Buffy. Can You Tell a Cheetah from a Leopard? 2011. (Animal Look-Alikes Ser.). pap. 45.32 *(978-0-7613-8384-0(0));* (ENG.). 32p. pap. 7.95 *(978-0-7613-7847-1(2));* (ENG., Illus.). 32p. lib. bdg. 26.60 *(978-0-7613-6735-2(7))* Lerner Publishing Group.

Simpson, Phillip. How Can We Save the Cheetah? A Problem & Solution Text, 1 vol. 2014. (Text Structures Ser.). (ENG.). 32p. (gr. 1-3). pap. 7.99 *(978-1-4846-0415-1(6),* Heinemann First Library) Heinemann-Raintree.

Spilsbury, Louise. Save the Cheetah, 1. 2014. (Animal SOS! Ser.). (ENG.). 32p. (J). (gr. k-5). 26.25 *(978-1-4777-6033-8(4),* Windmill Bks.) Rosen Publishing Group, Inc., The.

Squire, Ann O. Cheetahs. 2005. (True Bks.). (ENG., Illus.). 48p. (J). (gr. 3-5). per. 6.95 *(978-0-516-27932-9(7),* Children's Pr.) Scholastic Library Publishing.

Vogel, Elizabeth. Cheetahs. 2009. (Big Cats (Powerkids Readers) Ser.). 24p. (gr. 1-1). 37.50 *(978-1-61511-567-9(6),* PowerKids Pr.) Rosen Publishing Group, Inc., The.

Von Zumbusch, Amelie. Cheetahs. 2007. (Safari Animals Ser.). (Illus.). 24p. (J). (gr. 3-7). lib. bdg. 22.60 *(978-1-4042-3614-1(7),* 1266066, PowerKids Pr.) Rosen Publishing Group, Inc., The.

von Zumbusch, Amelie. Cheetahs. 2009. (Safari Animals Ser.). 24p. (gr. 1-1). 42.50 *(978-1-60852-949-0(5),* PowerKids Pr.) Rosen Publishing Group, Inc., The.

Von Zumbusch, Amelie. Cheetahs: World's Fastest Cats. 2007. (Dangerous Cats Ser.). (Illus.). 24p. (J). (gr. 3-7). lib. bdg. 22.60 *(978-1-4042-3630-1(9),* PowerKids Pr.) Rosen Publishing Group, Inc., The.

von Zumbusch, Amelie. Cheetahs: World's Fastest Cats. 2009. (Dangerous Cats Ser.). 24p. (gr. 2-3). 42.50 *(978-1-61512-126-7(9),* PowerKids Pr.) Rosen Publishing Group, Inc., The.

Von Zumbusch, Amelie. Cheetahs/Guepardos. Sanz, Pilar, tr. from ENG. 2007. (Safari Animals / Animales de Safari Ser.). (SPA & ENG., Illus.). 24p. (J). (gr. k-3). lib. bdg. 22.60 *(978-1-4042-7604-8(1))* Rosen Publishing Group, Inc., The.

von Zumbusch, Amelie. Cheetahs/Guepardos. 2009. (Safari Animals/Animales de safari Ser.). (ENG & SPA.). 24p. (gr. 1-1). 42.50 *(978-1-60852-970-4(3),* Editorial Buenas Letras) Rosen Publishing Group, Inc., The.

Waldendorf, Kurt. How Fast Is a Cheetah? 2017. (Comparison Fun Ser.). (ENG.). 24p. (J). (gr. -1-2). lib. bdg. 27.07 *(978-1-5038-1678-7(8),* 211513) Child's World, Inc., The.

CHEETAHS

see Cheetah

CHEMICAL ANALYSIS

see Chemistry, Analytic

CHEMICAL BONDS

Cesa, Irene, ed. Chemical Bonding, 24 vols., Vol. 5. 2004. (ChemTopic Labs Ser.: 5). (Illus.). (YA). per. 12.95 *(978-1-877991-73-8(2))* Flinn Scientific, Inc.

Holt, Rinehart and Winston Staff. Holt Science & Technology Chapter 13: Physical Science: Chemical Bonding. 5th ed. 2004. (Illus.). pap. 12.86 *(978-0-03-030406-4(7))* Holt McDougal.

Manning, Phillip. Chemical Bonds. 2009. (Essential Chemistry Ser.). 144p. (YA). (gr. 7-12). 35.00 *(978-0-7910-9740-3(4))* Facts On File, Inc.

CHEMICAL ELEMENTS

see also Periodic Law

Adair, Rick. Boron. 2007. 52p. (gr. 4-7). pap. 26.50 *(978-1-4358-3781-2(9))* Rosen Publishing Group, Inc., The.

Arbuthnott, Gill. Your Guide to the Periodic Table. Mones, Marc, illus. 2016. (ENG.). 64p. (J). lib. bdg. *(978-0-7787-2245-8(7))* Crabtree Publishing Co.

Basher, Simon & Dingle, Adrian. The Periodic Table: Elements with Style! Basher, Simon, illus. 2010. (Basher Science Ser.). (ENG., Illus.). 128p. (J). (gr. 5-9). 14.99 *(978-0-7534-6613-1(9),* 9780753466131, Kingfisher) Roaring Brook Pr.

Brandolini, Anita J. Fizz, Bubble & Flash! Element Explorations & Atom Adventures for Hands-On Science Fun! 2004. (Kids Can Bks.). (ENG., Illus.). 128p. (J). pap. 14.25 *(978-1-885593-83-2(X),* Ideal Pubns.) Worthy Publishing.

Burt, Judith. The 10 Most Valuable Elements. 2008. 14.99 *(978-1-55448-540-6(1))* Scholastic Library Publishing.

Challoner, Jack. Exploring the Mysteries of the Elements. 2016. (STEM Guide to the Universe Ser.). (ENG.). 160p. (YA). (gr. 9-9). lib. bdg. 46.10 *(978-1-4994-6409-2(6))* Rosen Publishing Group, Inc., The.

Cobb, Allan B. The Basics of Nonmetals. 2013. (Core Concepts Ser.). 96p. (YA). (gr. 7-12). 34.60 *(978-1-4777-2711-9(6))* Rosen Publishing Group, Inc., The.

Cooper, Chris. Arsenic. 2006. (Elements Ser.). (Illus.). 32p. (J). (gr. 3-7). lib. bdg. 28.50 *(978-0-7614-2203-7(X),* Benchmark Bks.) Marshall Cavendish Corp.

Crabtree Publishing Company Staff & Montgomerie, Adrienne. Non-Metals. 2012. (ENG., Illus.). 32p. (J). *(978-0-7787-4232-6(6));* pap. *(978-0-7787-4236-4(9))* Crabtree Publishing Co.

Dingle, Adrian. How to Make a Universe with 92 Ingredients: An Electrifying Guide to the Elements. 2013. (ENG., Illus.). 96p. (J). (gr. 7-9). 18.95 *(978-1-77147-008-7(9))* Owlkids Bks. Inc. CAN. Dist: Publishers Group West (PGW).

Dingle, Adrian & Basher, Simon. The Periodic Table: Elements with Style! Basher, Simon, illus. 2007. (Basher Science Ser.). (ENG., Illus.). 128p. (J). (gr. 5-9). pap. 8.99 *(978-0-7534-6085-6(8),* 9780753460856, Kingfisher) Roaring Brook Pr.

Dingle, Adrian, et al. Basher Science: the Complete Periodic Table: All the Elements with Style! Basher, Simon, illus. 2015. (Basher Science Ser.). (ENG.). 192p. (J). (gr. 5-9). pap. 11.99 *(978-0-7534-7197-5(3),* 9780753471975, Kingfisher) Roaring Brook Pr.

The Elements, 4 bks., Gorup 8. Incl. Boron. Beatty, Richard. lib. bdg. 28.50 *(978-0-7614-1921-1(7));* Chromium. Lepora, Nathan. lib. bdg. 28.50 *(978-0-7614-1920-4(9));* Radioactive Elements. Jackson, Tom. lib. bdg. 28.50 *(978-0-7614-1923-5(3));* Zinc. Gray, Leon. lib. bdg. 28.50 *(978-0-7614-1922-8(5));* (Illus.). (gr. 4-7). (Elements 8 Ser.). 32p. 2005. 114.00 *(978-0-7614-1919-8(5),* Benchmark Bks.) Marshall Cavendish Corp.

The Elements - Group 7, 4 Bks, Set. 2004. (J). 102.57 *(978-0-7614-1810-8(5))* Marshall Cavendish Corp.

The Elements Group 9, 4 bks., Set. Incl. Arsenic. Cooper, Chris. (J). (gr. 3-7). lib. bdg. 28.50 *(978-0-7614-2203-7(X));* Cobalt. Watt, Susan. (gr. 4-7). lib. bdg. 28.50 *(978-0-7614-2200-6(5));* Lithium. Jackson, Tom. (gr. 4-7). lib. bdg. 28.50 *(978-0-7614-2199-3(8));* Molybdenum. Lepora, Nathan. (gr. 4-7). lib. bdg. 28.50 *(978-0-7614-2201-3(3));* (Illus.). 32p. 2006. 2007. Set lib. bdg. 114.00 *(978-0-7614-2197-9(1),* Benchmark Bks.) Marshall Cavendish Corp.

Gray, Leon. The Basics of the Periodic Table. 2013. (Core Concepts Ser.). 96p. (YA). (gr. 7-12). 34.60 *(978-1-4777-2712-6(4))* Rosen Publishing Group, Inc., The.

Green, Dan. The Elements. 2012. (Scholastic Discover More Ser.). (ENG.). 112p. (J). (gr. 5-9). 15.99 *(978-0-545-33019-0(X),* Scholastic Reference) Scholastic, Inc.

Green, Joey. The Electric Pickle: 50 Experiments from the Periodic Table, from Aluminum to Zinc. 2017. (ENG.). 272p. pap. 19.99 ***(978-1-61373-959-4(1))*** Chicago Review Pr., Inc.

Halka, Monica & Nordstrom, Brian. Periodic Table of the Elements, 6 vols., Set. 2011. (Periodic Table of the Elements Ser.). (C). (gr. 9). 240.00 *(978-0-8160-8299-5(5))* Facts On File, Inc.

Hasan, Heather. Aluminum. 2009. (Understanding the Elements of the Periodic Table Ser.). 48p. (gr. 6-6). 53.00 *(978-1-60854-629-9(2),* Rosen Reference) Rosen Publishing Group, Inc., The.

—Fluorine. 2007. (Understanding the Elements of the Periodic Table Ser.). (Illus.). 48p. (YA). (gr. 5-9). lib. bdg. 29.25 *(978-1-4042-1005-9(9))* Rosen Publishing Group, Inc., The.

—Nitrogen. 2009. (Understanding the Elements of the Periodic Table Ser.). 48p. (gr. 6-6). 53.00 *(978-1-60854-673-2(X),* Rosen Reference) Rosen Publishing Group, Inc., The.

Jackson, Tom. Lithium. 2006. (Elements Ser.). (Illus.). 32p. (gr. 4-7). lib. bdg. 28.50 *(978-0-7614-2199-3(8),* Benchmark Bks.) Marshall Cavendish Corp.

—Radioactive Elements. 2005. (Elements Ser.). (Illus.). 32p. (gr. 4-7). lib. bdg. 28.50 *(978-0-7614-1923-5(3),* Benchmark Bks.) Marshall Cavendish Corp.

Johanson, Paula. Cobalt. (Understanding the Elements of the Periodic Table Ser.). 48p. 2009. (gr. 6-6). 53.00 *(978-1-60854-645-9(4),* Rosen Reference) 2008. (Illus.). (YA). (gr. 5-9). lib. bdg. 29.25 *(978-1-4042-1410-1(0))* Rosen Publishing Group, Inc., The.

—Lithium. 2007. 52p. (gr. 4-7). pap. 26.50 *(978-1-4358-3776-8(2))* Rosen Publishing Group, Inc., The.

Kjelle, Marylou Morano. The Properties of Salts. (Library of Physical Science Ser.). 24p. (gr. 4-4). 2009. 42.50 *(978-1-60853-793-8(5),* PowerKids Pr.) 2007. (ENG., Illus.). pap. 7.05 *(978-1-4042-2172-7(7),* PowerKids Pr.) 2006. (Illus.). (YA). lib. bdg. 22.60 *(978-1-4042-3425-3(X))* Rosen Publishing Group, Inc., The.

Krouti Artists, creator. The Elements & Their Electron Configurations: Build the Atoms from Actinum to Zirconium. 2004. (Illus.). 144p. per. 24.95 *(978-1-932689-01-3(X))* EDGEucation Publishing.

Kukla, Lauren & Craig, Diane. Elements at Work, 1 vol. 2016. (ENG., Illus.). 24p. (J). *(978-1-68078-140-3(5))* ABDO Publishing Co.

Lepora, Nathan. Molybdenum. 2006. (Elements Ser.). (Illus.). 32p. (gr. 4-7). lib. bdg. 28.50 *(978-0-7614-2201-3(3),* Benchmark Bks.) Marshall Cavendish Corp.

Lew, Kristi. Argon. (Understanding the Elements of the Periodic Table Ser.). 48p. 2009. (gr. 6-6). 53.00 *(978-1-60854-632-9(2),* Rosen Reference) 2008. (Illus.). (YA). (gr. 5-9). lib. bdg. 29.25 *(978-1-4042-1409-5(7))* Rosen Publishing Group, Inc., The.

—Iodine. 2009. (Understanding the Elements of the Periodic Table Ser.). 48p. (gr. 6-6). 53.00 *(978-1-60854-657-2(8),* Rosen Reference); (YA). (gr. 5-9). lib. bdg. 29.25 *(978-1-4358-5071-2(8))* Rosen Publishing Group, Inc., The.

Miller, Ron. The Elements: What You Really Want to Know. 2005. (Worlds Beyond Ser.). (ENG., Illus.). 128p. (gr. 7-12). 29.27 *(978-0-7613-2794-3(0))* Lerner Publishing Group.

Mullins, Matt. The Elements. 2011. (True Bk Ser.). (ENG., Illus.). 48p. (J). pap. 6.95 *(978-0-531-26585-7(4));* lib. bdg. 29.00 *(978-0-531-26323-5(1))* Scholastic Library Publishing. (Children's Pr.).

Polinsky, Paige V. Super Simple Experiments with Elements: Fun & Innovative Science Projects. 2016. (ENG., Illus.). 32p. (J). 27.07 *(978-1-68078-168-7(5))* ABDO Publishing Co.

Roza, Greg. Arsenic. (Understanding the Elements of the Periodic Table Ser.). 48p. 2009. (gr. 6-6). 53.00 *(978-1-60854-633-6(0),* Rosen Reference) 2008. (Illus.). (YA). (gr. 5-9). lib. bdg. 29.25 *(978-1-4042-1782-9(7))* Rosen Publishing Group, Inc., The.

—Calcium. (Understanding the Elements of the Periodic Table Ser.). 48p. 2009. (gr. 6-6). 53.00 *(978-1-60854-641-1(1),* Rosen Reference) 2007. (Illus.). (YA). (gr. 5-9). lib. bdg. 29.25 *(978-1-4042-1963-2(3))* Rosen Publishing Group, Inc., The.

—Potassium. 2009. (Understanding the Elements of the Periodic Table Ser.). 48p. (gr. 6-6). 53.00 *(978-1-60854-678-7(0),* Rosen Reference) Rosen Publishing Group, Inc., The.

—Zirconium. 2009. (Understanding the Elements of the Periodic Table Ser.). 48p. (gr. 6-6). 53.00 *(978-1-60854-690-9(X),* Rosen Reference); (YA). (gr. 5-9). lib. bdg. 29.25 *(978-1-4358-5070-5(X))* Rosen Publishing Group, Inc., The.

Saucerman, Linda. Chlorine. 2009. (Understanding the Elements of the Periodic Table Ser.). 48p. (gr. 6-6). 53.00 *(978-1-60854-643-5(8),* Rosen Reference) Rosen Publishing Group, Inc., The.

—Hydrogen: The Fuel for Life. 2005. (Understanding the Elements of the Periodic Table Ser.). (Illus.). 48p. (J). (gr. 5-8). lib. bdg. 29.25 *(978-1-4042-0156-9(4))* Rosen Publishing Group, Inc., The.

Slade, Suzanne. Elements, 1 vol., 1. 2014. (Ultimate Science: Physical Science Ser.). (ENG.). 24p. (gr. 3-6). 23.60 *(978-1-4777-6085-7(7),* PowerKids Pr.) Rosen Publishing Group, Inc., The.

—Elements & the Periodic Table. (Library of Physical Science Ser.). 24p. (gr. 4-4). 2009. 42.50 *(978-1-60853-781-5(1),* PowerKids Pr.) 2007. (ENG., Illus.). pap. 7.05 *(978-1-4042-2165-9(4),* PowerKids Pr.) 2006. (Illus.). (YA). lib. bdg. 22.60 *(978-1-4042-3418-5(7))* Rosen Publishing Group, Inc., The.

—The Elements Common to Most Living Organisms. 2007. (Library of Physical Sciences). (ENG., Illus.). 24p. (gr. 4-8). pap. 7.05 *(978-1-4042-2171-0(9),* PowerKids Pr.) Rosen Publishing Group, Inc., The.

—Elements in Living Organisms. (Library of Physical Science Ser.). 24p. 2009. (gr. 4-4). 42.50 *(978-1-60853-782-2(X))* 2006. (Illus.). (J). (gr. 3-7). lib. bdg. 21.25 *(978-1-4042-3424-6(1))* Rosen Publishing Group, Inc., The. (PowerKids Pr.).

—The Nitrogen Cycle. 2009. (Cycles in Nature Ser.). 24p. (gr. 3-3). 42.50 *(978-1-61512-114-4(5),* PowerKids Pr.) Rosen Publishing Group, Inc., The.

Sommers, Michael. Silicon. 2009. (Understanding the Elements of the Periodic Table Ser.). 48p. (gr. 6-6). 53.00 *(978-1-60854-681-7(0),* Rosen Reference) Rosen Publishing Group, Inc., The.

Stefoff, Rebecca. The Four Elements & the Periodic Table. 2014. 48p. pap. 29.93 *(978-1-62712-518-5(3))* Cavendish Square Publishing.

Tocci, Salvatore. Chlorine. (True Bks.). (ENG., Illus.). 48p. (J). (gr. 3-7). 2006. per. 6.95 *(978-0-516-25574-3(6))* 2005. lib. bdg. 25.00 *(978-0-516-23698-8(9))* Scholastic Library Publishing. (Children's Pr.).

—Silicon. 2005. (True Bks.). (ENG., Illus.). 48p. (J). (gr. 3-7). lib. bdg. 25.00 *(978-0-516-23701-5(2),* Children's Pr.) Scholastic Library Publishing.

—Sodium. 2005. (True Bks.). (ENG., Illus.). 48p. (J). (gr. 3-7). lib. bdg. 25.00 *(978-0-516-23702-2(0),* Children's Pr.) Scholastic Library Publishing.

—Zinc. 2006. (True Bks.). (ENG., Illus.). 48p. (J). (gr. 3-7). per. 6.95 *(978-0-516-25579-8(7),* Children's Pr.) Scholastic Library Publishing.

Van Gorp, Lynn. The World of Elements & Their Properties, 1 vol. 2007. (Science Readers Ser.). (ENG.). 32p. (J). (gr. 4-4). pap. 8.99 *(978-0-7439-0581-7(4))* Shell Educational Publishing.

Watt, Susan. Cobalt. 2006. (Elements Ser.). (Illus.). 32p. (gr. 4-7). lib. bdg. 28.50 *(978-0-7614-2200-6(5),* Benchmark Bks.) Marshall Cavendish Corp.

—Zirconium. 2007. (Elements Ser.). (Illus.). 32p. (J). (gr. 4-7). lib. bdg. 28.50 *(978-0-7614-2688-2(4),* Benchmark Bks.) Marshall Cavendish Corp.

Weir, Kirsten & Brent, Lynnette. Elements & Compounds. 2008. (Why Chemistry Matters Ser.). (ENG., Illus.). 32p. (J). (gr. 3-7). pap. *(978-0-7787-4249-4(0))* Crabtree Publishing Co.

Willett, Edward. Magnesium. 2009. (Understanding the Elements of the Periodic Table Ser.). 48p. (gr. 6-6). 53.00 *(978-1-60854-664-0(0),* Rosen Reference) Rosen Publishing Group, Inc., The.

—Neon. 2007. 52p. (gr. 3-7). pap. 26.50 *(978-1-4358-3783-6(5))* Rosen Publishing Group, Inc., The.

Zannos, Susan. Dmitri Mendeleyev & the Periodic Table. 2004. (Uncharted, Unexplored, & Unexplained Ser.). (Illus.). 48p. (J). (gr. 4-8). lib. bdg. 29.95 *(978-1-58415-267-5(2))* Mitchell Lane Pubs., Inc.

CHEMICAL ENGINEERING

see also Biotechnology; Chemistry, Technical

C
D

Biskup, Agnieszka, et al. The Dynamic World of Chemical Reactions with Max Axiom. 2010. (Graphic Science Ser.). (ENG., Illus.). 32p. (gr. 3-4). pap. 8.10 (978-1-4296-5635-1(2), Graphic Library) Capstone Press of Coughlan Cos.

Cooper, Chris. The Basics of Energy & Reactions. 2013. (Core Concepts Ser.). 96p. (YA). (gr. 7-12). 34.60 (978-1-4777-2710-2(8)) Rosen Publishing Group, Inc., The.

Hoffman, Mary Ann. Scientific Inquiry in Action: Chemical Reaction! 2009. (Real Life Readers Ser.). (J). (ENG., Illus.). 32p. (gr. 5-6). pap. 10.00 (978-1-4358-0187-5(3), 1291698); lib. bdg. 25.25 (978-1-4358-3012-7(1)) Rosen Publishing Group, Inc., The. (PowerKids Pr.).

Judson, Karen. Biological & Chemical Warfare. 2003. (Open for Debate Ser.). (Illus.). 128p. (gr. 7-18). lib. bdg. 42.79 (978-0-7614-1585-5(8), Benchmark Bks.) Marshall Cavendish Corp.

Oxlade, Chris. Mezclar y Separar, 1 vol. 2010. (Materiales Cambiantes Ser.). (SPA.). 32p. (gr. 1-3). 27.32 (978-1-4329-4431-5(2)); pap. 8.95 (978-1-4329-4436-0(3)) Heinemann-Raintree.

Rauf, Don. Solving Real World Problems with Chemical Engineering, 01 vols., 1. 2016. (Let's Find Out! Ser.). (ENG., Illus.). 32p. (J). 23.45 (978-1-68048-265-2(3), Britannica Educational Publishing) Rosen Publishing Group, Inc., The.

Richards, Jon. Chemicals & Reactions. 2009. (Science Factory Ser.). 32p. (gr. 4-5). 50.50 (978-1-60853-019-9(1), PowerKids Pr.) Rosen Publishing Group, Inc., The.

Simon, Chaman. Super Cool Science Experiments: Compounds & Mixtures. 2009. (Explorer Library: Science Explorer Ser.). (ENG., Illus.). 32p. (gr. 4-8). lib. bdg. 28.50 (978-1-60279-536-5(3), 200288) Cherry Lake Publishing.

Snedden, Robert. Chemical Engineering & Chain Reactions. 2013. (ENG.). 32p. (J). (978-0-7787-1197-1(8)); (Illus.). pap. (978-0-7787-1230-5(3)) Crabtree Publishing Co.

CHEMICAL TECHNOLOGY

see Chemistry, Technical

CHEMICALS

see also Chemistry, Technical

Carlson Berne, Emma. Hazmat: Disposing Toxic Materials. 2014. (ENG.). 32p. (gr. 4-8). 32.79 (978-1-62717-658-3(6)) Rourke Educational Media.

Field, Jon Eben. Cleaning Chemistry. 2011. (Chemtastrophe! Ser.). (ENG.). 32p. (J). (gr. 5-8). pap. (978-0-7787-5301-8(8)) Crabtree Publishing Co.

Haynes, Danielle. Chemical Catastrophes. 2017. (Unnatural Disasters Ser.). 32p. (J). (gr. 4-5). pap. 63.00 (978-1-5382-0417-7(7)) Stevens, Gareth Publishing LLLP.

—Lethal Leaks & Spills. 2017. (Unnatural Disasters Ser.). 32p. (gr. 4-5). pap. 10.50 (978-1-5382-0440-5(1)) Stevens, Gareth Publishing LLLP.

Kerrigan, Michael. Biological & Germ Warfare Protection. 2004. (Rescue & Prevention Ser.). (Illus.). 96p. (YA). (gr. 7-18). lib. bdg. 22.95 (978-1-59084-411-3(4)) Mason Crest.

Mara, Wil. Hazmat Removal Worker. 2015. (21st Century Skills Library: Cool STEAM Careers Ser.). (ENG.). 32p. (J). (gr. 4-7). 29.93 (978-1-63362-004-9(2), 205928) Cherry Lake Publishing.

Martin, Bobi. The Nitrogen Cycle. 2017. (J). pap. (978-1-68048-826-5(0)) Rosen Publishing Group, Inc., The.

Ollhoff, Jim. Hazmat. 2012. (Emergency Workers Ser.). 32p. (J). (gr. 5-9). lib. bdg. 27.07 (978-1-61783-514-8(5), Abdo & Daughters) ABDO Publishing Co.

Petersen, Justin. HAZMAT Teams: Disposing Dangerous Materials. 2016. (Emergency! Ser.). (ENG., Illus.). 32p. (gr. 3-4). lib. bdg. 27.99 (978-1-4914-8029-8(7), Edge Bks.) Capstone Press of Coughlan Cos.

Richards, Jon. Chemicals & Reactions. (Science Factory Ser.). 32p. (gr. 4-5). 2009. 50.50 (978-1-60853-019-9(1), PowerKids Pr.) 2008. (Illus.). (YA). lib. bdg. 26.50 (978-1-4042-3906-7(5)) Rosen Publishing Group, Inc., The.

Roza, Greg. Bromine. 2009. (Understanding the Elements of the Periodic Table Ser.). 48p. (gr. 6-6). 53.00 (978-1-60854-640-4(3), Rosen Reference) Rosen Publishing Group, Inc., The.

Spilsbury, Richard. Chemical Reactions: Investigating an Industrial Accident, 1 vol. 2013. (Anatomy of an Investigation Ser.). (ENG.). 56p. (gr. 7-8). 34.65 (978-1-4329-7600-2(1)); pap. 9.95 (978-1-4329-7606-4(0)) Heinemann-Raintree.

CHEMISTRY

see also Alchemy; Biochemistry; Color; Explosives; Fire; Pharmacy; Poisons

also headings beginning with the word Chemical

Ace Academics, ed. Chemistry: A Whole Course in a Box! 2007. (Exambusters Ser.). 384p. (gr. 7-18). 12.95 (978-1-881374-93-0(9), Exambusters) Ace Academics, Inc.

Allgemeine Chemie. 2nd ed. (Duden Abiturhilfen Ser.). (GER.). 112p. (YA). (gr. 12-13). (978-3-411-04622-5(8)) Bibliographisches Institut & F. A. Brockhaus AG DEU. Dist: International Bk. Import Service, Inc.

Aloian, Molly. Different Kinds of Soil. 2010. (Everybody Digs Soil Ser.). (ENG., Illus.). 32p. (J). (gr. 3-6). pap. (978-0-7787-5413-8(8)); lib. bdg. (978-0-7787-5400-8(6)) Crabtree Publishing Co.

—Mixtures & Solutions. 2008. (Why Chemistry Matters Ser.). (ENG., Illus.). 32p. (J). (gr. 3-7). pap. (978-0-7787-4250-0(4)) Crabtree Publishing Co.

Barber, Jacqueline. Of Cabbages & Chemistry. Bergman Publishing Co. Staff & Fairwell, Kay, eds. Bevilacqua, Carol & Klofkorn, Lisa, illus. Hoyt, Richard, photos by. rev. ed. 2003. (Great Explorations in Math & Science Ser.). 80p. (J). (gr. 4-8). pap., tchr. ed. 10.50 (978-0-924886-28-7(5), GEMS) Univ. of California, Berkeley, Lawrence Hall of Science.

Basher, Simon & Green, Dan. Chemistry: Getting a Big Reaction! Basher, Simon, illus. 2010. (Basher Science Ser.). (ENG., Illus.). 128p. (J). (gr. 5-9). pap. 8.99 (978-0-7534-6413-7(6), 9780753464137, Kingfisher) Roaring Brook Pr.

Beatty, Richard. Boron. 2005. (Elements Ser.). (Illus.). 32p. (gr. 4-7). lib. bdg. 28.50 (978-0-7614-1921-1(7), Benchmark Bks.) Marshall Cavendish Corp.

Beech, Linda Ward. The Magic School Bus Gets Baked in a Cake: A Book about Kitchen Chemistry. Duchesne, Lucie, tr. from ENG. Degen, Bruce, illus. (Magic School Bus Ser.). (FRE.). 32p. (J). (gr. 1-4). pap. 5.99 (978-0-590-24660-6(7)) Scholastic, Inc.

Bell, Suzanne. Drugs, Poisons, & Chemistry. 2008. (Essentials of Forensic Science Ser.). (Illus.). 124p. (gr. 6-12). 35.00 (978-0-8160-5510-4(6)) Facts On File, Inc.

Benchmark Education Company, LLC Staff, compiled by. Chemistry: Theme Set. 2006. (J). 173.00 (978-1-4108-7134-3(7)) Benchmark Education Co.

Brent, Lynette & Brent, Lynnette. Acids & Bases. 2008. (Why Chemistry Matters Ser.). (ENG., Illus.). 32p. (J). (gr. 3-7). pap. (978-0-7787-4246-3(6)) Crabtree Publishing Co.

—Chemical Changes. 2008. (Why Chemistry Matters Ser.). (ENG., Illus.). 32p. (J). (gr. 3-7). pap. (978-0-7787-4248-7(2)); lib. bdg. (978-0-7787-4241-8(5)) Crabtree Publishing Co.

—Why Chemistry Matters, 6 vols., Set. Incl. Chemical Changes. (ENG., Illus.). 32p. (J). (gr. 3-7). 2008. lib. bdg. (978-0-7787-4241-8(5)); (ENG.). 32p. 2011. Set lib. bdg. (978-0-7787-4238-8(5)) Crabtree Publishing Co.

Brian, Sarah Jane. Forensics Chemistry & Crime: Set Of 6. 2010. (Navigators Ser.). (J). pap. 48.00 net. (978-1-4108-6234-1(8)) Benchmark Education Co.

Cardenas, Ernesto & Saavedra, Patricia. El laboratorio de Ciencias. l.t. ed. 2006. (SPA., Illus.). 16p. pap. 4.95 (978-1-933668-24-6(5)) Milo Educational Bks. & Resources.

Cesa, Irene, ed. Chemical Bonding, 24 vols., Vol. 5. 2004. (ChemTopic Labs Ser.: 5). (Illus.). (YA). per. 12.95 (978-1-877991-73-8(2)) Flinn Scientific, Inc.

—Chemical Reactions. 2004. (ChemTopic Labs Ser.: 6). (YA). per. 12.95 (978-1-877991-74-5(0)) Flinn Scientific, Inc.

—Solubility & Solutions. 2004. (ChemTopic Labs Ser.: No. 12). (YA). per. 12.95 (978-1-877991-80-6(5)) Flinn Scientific, Inc.

A Chef's Laboratory: Individual Title Six-Packs. (Bookweb Ser.). 32p. (gr. 6-18). 34.00 (978-0-7578-0912-5(X)) Rigby Education.

Chemical Reactions. 2011. (Science Made Simple Ser.). (ENG.). 64p. (YA). pap. 12.95 (978-1-4488-2242-3(4), Rosen Reference) Rosen Publishing Group, Inc., The.

Chemie: Formeln, Gesetze und Fachbegriffe. Mit vielen Beispielen im handlichen Pocketformat. (Duden-Schuelerduden Ser.). (GER., Illus.). 442p. (YA). (978-3-411-05383-4(6)) Bibliographisches Institut & F. A. Brockhaus AG DEU. Dist: International Bk. Import Service, Inc.

Chemist. (Science Ser.). (J). incl. audio NewSound, LLC.

Chemistry at Work. (YA). (gr. 9-12). (978-0-669-30704-7(1)) Houghton Mifflin Harcourt School Pubs.

Cleary, Brian P. Oils (Just a Bit) to Keep Your Body Fit: What Are Oils? Goneau, Martin, illus. 2011. (Food Is CATegorical Ser.). (ENG.). 32p. (gr. k-3). pap. 7.95 (978-0-7613-6389-7(0)) Lerner Publishing Group.

Cleary, Brian P. & Goneau, Martin. Oils (Just A Bit) to Keep Your Body Fit: What Are Oils? 2011. (Food Is CATegorical Ser.). pap. 45.32 (978-0-7613-8352-9(2), Millbrook Pr.) Lerner Publishing Group.

Cobb, Allan. Cadmium. 2007. (Elements Ser.). (Illus.). 32p. (J). (gr. 4-7). lib. bdg. 28.50 (978-0-7614-2686-8(8), Benchmark Bks.) Marshall Cavendish Corp.

Cobb, Allan B. The Basics of Chemistry. 2013. (Core Concepts Ser.). 96p. (YA). (gr. 7-12). 34.60 (978-1-4777-2716-4(7)) Rosen Publishing Group, Inc., The.

Conoley, Chris. A Level Chemistry: Strengthen Your Science, Maths & Written Communication Skills. 2014. (Science Skills Ser.). (ENG., Illus.). 16p. (YA). (gr. 12). pap. 15.99 (978-0-00-755464-5(8)) HarperCollins Pubs. Ltd. GBR. Dist: Independent Pubs. Group.

Cooke, Andy & Martin, Jean Ami. Spectrum Chemistry. 2004. (Spectrum Key Stage 3 Science Ser.). (ENG., Illus.). 181p. pap. 15.00 (978-0-521-54922-6(1)) Cambridge Univ. Pr.

Corrick, James A. & Lew, Kristi. Acids & Bases. 2008. (Essential Chemistry Ser.). (Illus.). 128p. (YA). (gr. 7-12). 35.00 (978-0-7910-9783-0(8)) Facts On File, Inc.

Coulter, Shirley. Chemistry. Date not set. (Science Fair Ser.). 48p. (J). (gr. 3-6). lib. bdg. 22.60 (978-1-57103-427-4(7)) Rourke Educational Media.

Csiszar, John. Aluminum. 2017. (Chemistry of Everyday Elements Ser.). (ENG.). (YA). (gr. 7-12). 23.95 (978-1-4222-3838-7(5)) Mason Crest.

de Pinna, Simon. Chemical Reactions. 2007. (Gareth Stevens Vital Science: Physical Science Ser.). (Illus.). 48p. (gr. 5-12). pap. 14.05 (978-0-8368-8093-9(5)); lib. bdg. 27.00 (978-0-8368-8084-7(6)) Stevens, Gareth Publishing LLLP. (Gareth Stevens Secondary Library).

Diagram Group Staff. Chemistry: An Illustrated Guide to Science. 2006. (Science Visual Resources Ser.). (Illus.). 208p. (gr. 6-12). 49.50 (978-0-8160-6163-1(7)) Facts On File, Inc.

Discovering French, Nouveau! Blanc: Activites Pour Tous, Level 2. 2003. (978-0-618-29912-6(2)) Holt McDougal.

Eagen, Rachel. Environmental Chemistry. 2011. (Chemtastrophe! Ser.). (ENG.). 32p. (J). (gr. 5-8). pap. (978-0-7787-5302-5(6)); lib. bdg. (978-0-7787-5285-1(2)) Crabtree Publishing Co.

Fabre, Jean Henri. The Wonder Book of Chemistry. 2009. 392p. pap. 14.95 (978-1-59915-253-0(3)) Yesterday's Classics.

Farndon, John & Graham, Ian. Discovering Science. 2010. (Science Library). 40p. (J). (gr. 3-18). lib. bdg. 19.95 (978-1-4222-1548-7(2)) Mason Crest.

Fluids & Solutions Chemistry: Integrated Physics & Chemistry /Algebra I Insturctional Unit. 2003. (Region IV ESC Resources for Mathematics & Science Ser.). stu. ed., per. (978-1-932524-71-0(1)) Region IV Education Service Ctr.

The Four Elements. 2014. (Four Elements Ser.). 32p. (J). (gr. k-3). 105.00 (978-1-4777-9114-1(0)) Windmill Bks.

Gaddi, Rosalie. A Day at Work with a Chemist, 01 vols., 1. 2016. (Super STEM Careers Ser.). (ENG., Illus.). 24p. (J). pap. 8.25 (978-1-5081-4402-1(8), PowerKids Pr.) Rosen Publishing Group, Inc., The.

Gardner, Jane P. Helium. 2017. (Chemistry of Everyday Elements Ser.: Vol. 10). (ENG.). (YA). (gr. 7-12). 23.95 (978-1-4222-3841-7(5)) Mason Crest.

—Silicon. 2017. (Chemistry of Everyday Elements Ser.: Vol. 10). (ENG.). (YA). (gr. 7-12). 23.95 (978-1-4222-3844-8(X)) Mason Crest.

—Understanding the Periodic Table. 2017. (Chemistry of Everyday Elements Ser.: Vol. 10). (ENG.). (YA). (gr. 7-12). 23.95 (978-1-4222-3846-2(6)) Mason Crest.

Gray, Leon. Zinc. 2005. (Elements Ser.). (Illus.). 32p. (gr. 4-7). lib. bdg. 28.50 (978-0-7614-1922-8(5), Benchmark Bks.) Marshall Cavendish Corp.

Grundlagen der Chemie. (Duden-Schuelerhilfen Ser.). (GER.). 109p. (YA). (gr. 8-10). (978-3-411-05931-7(1)) Bibliographisches Institut & F. A. Brockhaus AG DEU. Dist: International Bk. Import Service, Inc.

Hall, Derek. Chemistry, Earth, & Space Sciences. 2010. (Facts at Your Fingertips Ser.). (YA). (gr. 7-12). 35.65 (978-1-933834-47-4(1)) Brown Bear Books.

Hall, James W. & Zumdahl, Steven S. Introductory Chemistry: A Foundation. 5th ed. 2003. (ENG.). 688p. (C). (gr. 6-12). 120.00 (978-0-618-38803-5(6), 370781) Brooks/Cole.

Holt, Rinehart and Winston Staff. Chemistry: Chapter Resource File. 6th ed. 2006. No. 1. pap. 11.73 (978-0-03-041432-9(6))No. 2. pap. 11.73 (978-0-03-041433-6(4))No. 3. pap. 11.73 (978-0-03-041434-3(2))No. 4. pap. 11.73 (978-0-03-041437-4(7))No. 5. pap. 11.73 (978-0-03-041438-1(5))No. 6. pap. 11.73 (978-0-03-041439-8(3))No. 7. pap. 11.73 (978-0-03-041442-8(3))No. 8. pap. 11.73 (978-0-03-041443-5(1))No. 9. pap. 11.73 (978-0-03-041444-2(X))No. 10. pap. 11.73 (978-0-03-041447-3(4))No. 11. pap. 11.73 (978-0-03-041448-0(2))No. 12. pap. 11.73 (978-0-03-041449-7(0))No. 13. pap. 11.73 (978-0-03-041452-7(0))No. 14. pap. 11.73 (978-0-03-041453-4(9))No. 15. pap. 11.73 (978-0-03-041454-1(7))No. 16. pap. 11.73 (978-0-03-041457-2(1))No. 17. pap. 11.73 (978-0-03-041458-9(X))No. 18. pap. 11.73 (978-0-03-041459-6(8))No. 19. pap. 11.73 (978-0-03-041462-6(8))No. 20. pap. 11.73 (978-0-03-041463-3(6)) Harcourt Schl. Pubs.

—Holt Chemistry: Enhanced Online Edition. 4th ed. 2004. 17.26 (978-0-03-037154-7(6)) Holt McDougal.

—Holt Chemistry: Strategies & Practice for Reading: New York Edition. 5th ed. Date not set. (Chemistry Ser.). pap. 12.80 (978-0-03-074139-5(4)) Holt McDougal.

—Holt Chemistry Chptr. 5: Ionic Compounds. 4th ed. Date not set. pap. 11.20 (978-0-03-068127-1(8)) Holt McDougal.

—Holt Chemistry Chptr. 6: Covalent Bonds. 4th ed. Date not set. pap. 11.20 (978-0-03-068128-8(6)) Holt McDougal.

—Holt Chemistry Chptr. 7: Molecules/Chemical Compositions. 4th ed. Date not set. pap. 11.20 (978-0-03-068131-8(6)) Holt McDougal.

—Holt Chemistry Chptr. 8: Chemical Equations/Reactions. 4th ed. Date not set. pap. 11.20 (978-0-03-068132-5(4)) Holt McDougal.

—Holt Chemistry Chptr. 10: Causes of Change. 4th ed. Date not set. pap. 11.20 (978-0-03-068134-9(0)) Holt McDougal.

—Holt Chemistry Chptr. 11: States of Matter & Forces. 4th ed. Date not set. pap. 11.20 (978-0-03-068136-3(7)) Holt McDougal.

—Holt Chemistry Chptr. 13: Solutions. 4th ed. Date not set. pap. 11.20 (978-0-03-068138-7(3)) Holt McDougal.

—Holt Chemistry Chptr. 14: Chemical Equilibrium. 4th ed. Date not set. pap. 11.20 (978-0-03-068139-4(1)) Holt McDougal.

—Holt Chemistry Chptr. 16: Reaction Rates. 4th ed. Date not set. pap. 11.20 (978-0-03-068142-4(1)) Holt McDougal.

—Holt Chemistry Chptr. 17: Oxidation/Reduction. 4th ed. Date not set. pap. 11.20 (978-0-03-068143-1(X)) Holt McDougal.

—Holt Chemistry Chptr. 18: Nuclear Chemistry. 4th ed. Date not set. pap. 11.20 (978-0-03-068144-8(8)) Holt McDougal.

—Holt Chemistry 2 Chptr. 3: Atoms & Molecules. 4th ed. Date not set. pap. 11.20 (978-0-03-068124-0(3)) Holt McDougal.

—Holt Chemistry 2 Chptr. 4: The Periodic Table. 4th ed. Date not set. pap. 11.20 (978-0-03-068126-4(X)) Holt McDougal.

—Holt Chemistry 2 Chptr. 9: Stoichiometry. 4th ed. Date not set. pap. 11.20 (978-0-03-068133-2(2)) Holt McDougal.

—Holt Science & Technology Chapter 14: Physical Science: Chemical Reactions. 5th ed. 2004. (Illus.). pap. 12.86 (978-0-03-030411-8(3)) Holt McDougal.

—Holt Science & Technology Chapter 15: Physical Science: Chemical Compounds. 5th ed. 2004. (Illus.). pap. 12.86 (978-0-03-030412-5(1)) Holt McDougal.

Howell, Sara. Chemists at Work. 2017. (Scientists at Work Ser.). 32p. (J). (gr. 6-8). pap. 12.90 (978-1-68048-753-4(1), Britannica Educational Publishing) Rosen Publishing Group, Inc., The.

Hulick, Kathryn. Hydrogen. 2017. (Chemistry of Everyday Elements Ser.: Vol. 10). (ENG.). (YA). (gr. 7-12). 23.95 (978-1-4222-3842-4(3)) Mason Crest.

Husting, Chad. Chemistry Student Lab Manual. 2003. (Illus.). stu. ed., per., wbk. ed. (978-1-931680-32-5(9), Expert Systems for Teachers) Teaching Point, Inc.

Integrated Physics & Chemistry, Chapter 1, Activities. 2005. (Illus.). 22p. (YA). pap. 5.00 (978-1-59476-173-7(6)) Paradigm Accelerated Curriculum.

Integrated Physics & Chemistry Chapter 1, Text. 2005. Orig. Title: (Key Topics. (Illus.). 34p. (YA). pap. 7.00 (978-1-59476-161-4(2)) Paradigm Accelerated Curriculum.

Integrated Physics & Chemistry, Chapter 10, Activities. 2005. (Illus.). 32p. (YA). pap. 5.00 (978-1-59476-182-9(5)) Paradigm Accelerated Curriculum.

Integrated Physics & Chemistry, Chapter 10, Text. 2005. (Illus.). 68p. (YA). pap. 7.00 (978-1-59476-170-6(1)) Paradigm Accelerated Curriculum.

Integrated Physics & Chemistry, Chapter 11, Activities. 2005. (Illus.). 40p. (YA). pap. 5.00 (978-1-59476-183-6(3)) Paradigm Accelerated Curriculum.

Integrated Physics & Chemistry, Chapter 11, Text. 2005. (Illus.). 64p. (YA). pap. 7.00 (978-1-59476-171-3(X)) Paradigm Accelerated Curriculum.

Integrated Physics & Chemistry, Chapter 12, Activities. 2005. (Illus.). 32p. (YA). pap. 5.00 (978-1-59476-184-3(1)) Paradigm Accelerated Curriculum.

Integrated Physics & Chemistry, Chapter 12, Text. 2005. (Illus.). 66p. (YA). pap. 7.00 (978-1-59476-172-0(8)) Paradigm Accelerated Curriculum.

Integrated Physics & Chemistry, Chapter 2, Activities. 2005. (Illus.). 42p. (YA). pap. 5.00 (978-1-59476-174-4(4)) Paradigm Accelerated Curriculum.

Integrated Physics & Chemistry, Chapter 2, Text. 2005. (Illus.). 66p. (YA). pap. 7.00 (978-1-59476-162-1(0)) Paradigm Accelerated Curriculum.

Integrated Physics & Chemistry, Chapter 3 Activities. 2005. (Illus.). 32p. (YA). pap. 5.00 (978-1-59476-175-1(2)) Paradigm Accelerated Curriculum.

Integrated Physics & Chemistry, Chapter 3, Text. 2005. (Illus.). 66p. (YA). pap. 7.00 (978-1-59476-163-8(9)) Paradigm Accelerated Curriculum.

Integrated Physics & Chemistry, Chapter 4, Text. 2005. (Illus.). 64p. (YA). pap. 7.00 (978-1-59476-164-5(7)) Paradigm Accelerated Curriculum.

Integrated Physics & Chemistry, Chapter 5, Activities. 2005. (Illus.). 32p. (YA). pap. 5.00 (978-1-59476-177-5(9)) Paradigm Accelerated Curriculum.

Integrated Physics & Chemistry, Chapter 5, Text. 2005. (Illus.). 64p. (YA). pap. 7.00 (978-1-59476-165-2(5)) Paradigm Accelerated Curriculum.

Integrated Physics & Chemistry, Chapter 6, Activities. 2005. (Illus.). 32p. (YA). pap. 5.00 (978-1-59476-178-2(7)) Paradigm Accelerated Curriculum.

Integrated Physics & Chemistry, Chapter 6, Text. 2005. (Illus.). 64p. (YA). pap. 7.00 (978-1-59476-166-9(3)) Paradigm Accelerated Curriculum.

Integrated Physics & Chemistry, Chapter 7, Activities. 2005. (Illus.). 32p. (YA). pap. 5.00 (978-1-59476-179-9(5)) Paradigm Accelerated Curriculum.

Integrated Physics & Chemistry, Chapter 7, Text. 2005. (Illus.). 66p. (YA). pap. 7.00 (978-1-59476-167-6(1)) Paradigm Accelerated Curriculum.

Integrated Physics & Chemistry, Chapter 8, Activities. 2005. (Illus.). 32p. (YA). pap. 5.00 (978-1-59476-180-5(9)) Paradigm Accelerated Curriculum.

Integrated Physics & Chemistry, Chapter 8, Text. 2005. (Illus.). 64p. (YA). pap. 7.00 (978-1-59476-168-3(X)) Paradigm Accelerated Curriculum.

Integrated Physics & Chemistry, Chapter 9, Activities. 2005. (Illus.). 32p. (YA). pap. 5.00 (978-1-59476-181-2(7)) Paradigm Accelerated Curriculum.

Integrated Physics & Chemistry, Chapter 9, Text. 2005. (Illus.). 68p. (YA). pap. 7.00 (978-1-59476-169-0(8)) Paradigm Accelerated Curriculum.

Integrated Physics & Chemistry, Full Course Kit, 25 bks. 2005. (Illus.). 7969p. (YA). 169.00 (978-1-59476-187-4(6)) Paradigm Accelerated Curriculum.

Integrated Physics & Chemistry, Teacher's Resource Kit with CD. 2005. (Illus.). 439p. (YA). pap. 25.00 (978-1-59476-185-0(X)) Paradigm Accelerated Curriculum.

Introductory Chemistry: Complete Solutions Guide. 5th ed. 2004. (ENG.). 544p. (gr. 6-12). pap. (978-0-618-30532-2(7), 3-70778) CENGAGE Learning.

Introductory Chemistry: Test Item File. 5th ed. 2004. (ENG.). 272p. (gr. 6-12). pap. (978-0-618-30535-3(1), 3-70780) CENGAGE Learning.

Jackson, Tom. Radioactive Elements. 2005. (Elements Ser.). (Illus.). 32p. (gr. 4-7). lib. bdg. 28.50 (978-0-7614-1923-5(3), Benchmark Bks.) Marshall Cavendish Corp.

Johnson, Rebecca L. Acids & Bases. 2007. (Reading Expeditions Ser.). (ENG., Illus.). 32p. (J). pap. 17.95 (978-0-7922-4582-7(2)) CENGAGE Learning.

—Chemical Changes. 2007. (Reading Expeditions Ser.). (ENG., Illus.). 32p. (J). pap. 17.95 (978-0-7922-4583-4(0)) CENGAGE Learning.

Keller, Rebecca W. Real Science-4-kids Chemistry Level I Student Textbook. l.t. ed. 2005. (Real Science-4-Kids Ser.). (ENG., Illus.). 64p. (gr. 3-6). 32.95 (978-0-9749149-0-9(8)) Gravitas Pubns., Inc.

Kuhtz, Russell, ed. Chemistry: Understanding Substance & Matter. 2014. (Study of Science Ser.). 160p. (YA). (gr. 7-12). 35.25 (978-1-62275-415-1(8)) Rosen Publishing Group, Inc., The.

Lepora, Nathan. Chromium. 2005. (Elements Ser.). (Illus.). 32p. (gr. 4-7). lib. bdg. 28.50 (978-0-7614-1920-4(9), Benchmark Bks.) Marshall Cavendish Corp.

Lew, Kristi. Chemical Reactions. 2008. (Essential Chemistry Ser.). (Illus.). 114p. (YA). (gr. 7-12). 35.00 (978-0-7910-9531-7(2)) Facts On File, Inc.

Mahase, Compton & Morris, Mark. Chemistry. 2nd rev. ed. 2007. (ENG.). 84p. pap. 9.50 (978-0-521-69296-0(2)) Cambridge Univ. Pr.

Marsico, Katie. Key Discoveries in Physical Science. 2015. (Science Discovery Timelines Ser.). (ENG., Illus.). 48p. (J). (gr. 6-8). pap. 8.99 (978-1-4677-6160-4(5)); lib. bdg. 30.65 (978-1-4677-5785-0(3)) Lerner Publishing Group. (Lerner Pubns.).

Maurer, Tracy Nelson. Mix It up! Solution or Mixture? 2012. (ENG.). 24p. (gr. 3-4). pap. 8.95 (978-1-61810-227-0(3)) Rourke Educational Media.

McDougal-Littell Publishing Staff. Chemical Interactions. 2004. (McDougal Littell Middle School Science Ser.). (ENG., Illus.). 64p. (gr. 6-8). lib. bdg. 21.80 (978-0-618-33438-4(6), 2-01025) Great Source Education Group, Inc.

—Modules: Physical Science - Chemical Interactions. 2004. (McDougal Littell Science Ser.). (ENG.). 64p. (gr. 6-8). pap., lab manual ed. 15.30 (978-0-618-43723-8(1), 2-01216) Great Source Education Group, Inc.

McGraw-Hill Staff. Chemistry: Concepts & Applications. 2004. stu. ed. 95.96 (978-0-07-861798-0(7), 9780078617980) Glencoe/McGraw-Hill.

McNeil, Niki, et al. Foundations for Chemistry. 2007. (In the Hands of a Child: Custom Designed Project Pack Ser.). (Illus.). 52p. spiral bd. 23.00 (978-1-60308-109-2(7)) In the Hands of a Child.

Mitchell, David. The Wonders of Waldorf Chemistry: Notes from a Teacher's Notebook. Odermatt, Brian, illus. 2004. (ENG.). 250p. (gr. 7-9). per. 22.00 (978-1-888365-16-0(1)) Waldorf Publications.

Mooney, Carla. Chemistry: Investigate the Matter That Makes up Your World. Carbaugh, Samuel, illus. 2016. (Inquire & Investigate Ser.). (ENG.). 128p. (gr. 6-10). 22.95 (978-1-61930-361-4(2), 1405466) Open City Bks.

Murphy, Brian, et al. Chemistry 2014. 2014. (IB Diploma Program Ser.). (ENG., Illus.). 1p. 82.00 (978-0-19-830775-4(6)) Oxford Univ. Pr., Inc.

Myers. Holt Chemistry: Premier Online Edition. 6th ed. 2005. 19.93 (978-0-03-040067-4(8)) Holt McDougal.

Newmark, Ann & Dorling Kindersley Publishing Staff. Chemistry. 2005. (DK Eyewitness Bks.). (ENG., Illus.). 72p. (J). (gr. 3-7). 16.99 *(978-0-7566-1385-3(X)*, DK Children) Dorling Kindersley Publishing, Inc.

Newton, David E. Chemistry of the Environment. 2007. (New Chemistry Ser.). (Illus.). 240p. (gr. 6-12). 35.00 *(978-0-8160-5273-8(5))* Facts On File, Inc.

—The New Chemistry Set. 2007. (New Chemistry Ser.). 192p. (gr. 6-12). 210.00 *(978-0-8160-5272-1(7))* Facts On File, Inc.

Norman, Penny. Science One Two Three Chemistry. Einstein, Ann, ed. 2005. 15.95 *(978-1-886978-66-9(2))* Norman & Globus, Inc.

Owen, Steve, et al. Chemistry for the IB Diploma. 2nd rev. ed. 2014. (IB Diploma Ser.). (ENG.). 600p. pap. 64.94 *(978-1-107-62270-8(0))* Cambridge Univ. Pr.

Oxlade, Chris, et al, eds. The Usborne Illustrated Dictionary of Chemistry. 2nd rev. ed. 2004. (Illustrated Dictionaries Ser.). (ENG., Illus.). 1p. (J). (gr. 7-18). pap. 12.95 *(978-0-7460-3794-2(5))* EDC Publishing.

Parker, Steve. Crackling Chemistry. 2011. (Science Crackers Ser.). (ENG.). 32p. (J). (gr. 4-7). lib. bdg. 17.99 *(978-1-60992-038-8(4))* QEB Publishing Inc.

Peterson, Megan Cooley. Scooby-Doo! a Science of Chemical Reactions Mystery: The over-Reacting Ghost. Brizuela, Dario, illus. 2017. (Scooby-Doo Solves It with S. T. E. M. Ser.). (ENG.). 32p. (gr. 3-4). pap. 7.95 *(978-1-5157-3701-8(2))* Capstone Press of Coughlan Cos.

Phelan, Gary. Chemistry in the Kitchen: Set Of 6. 2010. (Navigators Ser.). (J). pap. 48.00 net. *(978-1-4108-6232-7(1))* Benchmark Education Co.

Regan, Lisa. Chemistry Is Explosive. 2016. (Amazing World of Science & Math Ser.). 48p. (gr. 5-5). pap. 14.05 *(978-1-4824-4990-7(0))* Stevens, Gareth Publishing LLLP.

Rich, Mari. Oxygen. 2017. (Chemistry of Everyday Elements Ser.: Vol. 10). (ENG.). (YA). (gr. 7-12). 23.95 ***(978-1-4222-3843-1(1))*** Mason Crest.

—Silver. 2017. (Chemistry of Everyday Elements Ser.). (ENG.). (YA). (gr. 7-12). 23.95 ***(978-1-4222-3845-5(8))*** Mason Crest.

Riley, Peter D. Checkpoint Chemistry. 2005. (Illus.). 192p. pap., stu. ed. 47.50 *(978-0-7195-8065-9(X))* Hodder Education Group GBR. Dist: Trans-Atlantic Pubns., Inc.

Romero, Libby. Discover Forensic Chemistry. 2006. (J). pap. *(978-1-4108-6503-8(7))* Benchmark Education Co.

—Forensic Chemistry. 2006. (J). pap. *(978-1-4108-6500-7(2))* Benchmark Education Co.

—Kitchen Chemistry. 2006. (J). pap. *(978-1-4108-6498-7(7))* Benchmark Education Co.

Ryan, Lawrie, et al. Chemistry. 2003. (ENG., Illus.). 72p. pap. *(978-0-7487-6800-4(9))* Nelson Thornes Ltd.

Saunders, Nigel. Exploring Chemical Reactions. 2007. (Exploring Physical Science Ser.). (Illus.). 48p. (J). (gr. 4-7). lib. bdg. 26.50 *(978-1-4042-3751-3(8))* Rosen Publishing Group, Inc., The.

Science Stories Foss Spanish Mixtures & Solutions EA CR05. 2005. (J). *(978-1-59242-594-5(1))* Delta Education, LLC.

Sganga, Francis T. Essential Chemistry for Gifted Students: Preparation for High School Chemistry, Grades 4-8. 2003. (Illus.). 75p. spiral bd. 18.00 net. *(978-0-910609-44-9(6))* Gifted Education Pr.

Slade, Suzanne. Elements, 1 vol., 1. 2014. (Ultimate Science: Physical Science Ser.). (ENG.). 24p. (gr. 3-6). 23.60 *(978-1-4777-6085-7(7)*, PowerKids Pr.) Rosen Publishing Group, Inc., The.

—The Nitrogen Cycle. 2007. (Cycles in Nature Ser.). (Illus.). 24p. (J). (gr. 3-7). lib. bdg. 21.25 *(978-1-4042-3491-8(8)*, PowerKids Pr.) Rosen Publishing Group, Inc., The.

Smith, A. & Clarke, P. Mixtures & Compounds. 2004. (Library of Science Ser.). 64p. (J). lib. bdg. 17.95 *(978-1-58086-377-3(9))* EDC Publishing.

Snedden, Robert. Chemical Engineering & Chain Reactions. 2013. (ENG.). 32p. (J). *(978-0-7787-1197-1(8))*; (Illus.). pap. *(978-0-7787-1230-5(3))* Crabtree Publishing Co.

Sohn, Emily & Brennan, Joseph. Mixtures & Solutions: The Sugar in the Tea. 2011. (IScience Readers Ser.). 48p. (J). (gr. 5-6). lib. bdg. 23.94 *(978-1-59953-428-2(2))* Norwood Hse. Pr.

Solway, Andrew. Chemistry. 2010. (CC: 21st Century Science Ser.). 112p. (gr. 6-12). 42.80 *(978-1-933834-71-9(4))* Brown Bear Bks.

Sootin, Harry. Robert Boyle, Founder of Modern Chemistry. Schrotter, Gustav, illus. 2011. 142p. 40.95 *(978-1-258-00545-0(X))* Literary Licensing, LLC.

Tocci, Salvatore. Chlorine. (True Bks.). (ENG., Illus.). 48p. (J). (gr. 3-7). 2006. per. 6.95 *(978-0-516-25574-3(6))* 2005. lib. bdg. 25.00 *(978-0-516-23698-8(9))* Scholastic Library Publishing. (Children's Pr.).

Trout, Laura. POGIL Activities for High School Chemistry. 2012. spiral bd. 49.95 *(978-1-933709-36-9(7))* Flinn Scientific, Inc.

U.S. Defense Dept. & Defense Department Staff, eds. Julie & the Atom. 2013. (ENG., Illus.). 32p. 4.50 *(978-0-16-091707-3(7)*, Defense Dept.) United States Government Printing Office.

Weakland, Mark. Kaboom! Wile E. Coyote Experiments with Chemical Reactions. Billiau, Loic, illus. 2017. (Wile E. Coyote, Physical Science Genius Ser.). (ENG.). 32p. (gr. 3-5). lib. bdg. 30.65 *(978-1-5157-3733-9(0))* Capstone Press of Coughlan Cos.

Weir, Kirsten & Brent, Lynnette. Elements & Compounds. 2008. (Why Chemistry Matters Ser.). (ENG., Illus.). 32p. (J). (gr. 3-7). pap. *(978-0-7787-4249-4(0))* Crabtree Publishing Co.

—States of Matter. 2008. (Why Chemistry Matters Ser.). (ENG., Illus.). 32p. (J). (gr. 3-7). pap. *(978-0-7787-4251-7(2))* Crabtree Publishing Co.

Westrup, Hugh. Mixtures & Solutions. 2015. (Science Readers: Content & Literacy Ser.). (Illus.). 32p. (J). (gr. 5-5). pap. 8.99 *(978-1-4807-4721-0(1))* Teacher Created Materials, Inc.

Why Chemistry Matters, 6 vols., Set. Incl. Acids & Bases. Brent, Lynette & Brent, Lynnette. pap. *(978-0-7787-4246-3(6))*; Atoms & Molecules. Aloian, Molly. pap. *(978-0-7787-4247-0(4))*; Chemical Changes. Brent, Lynette & Brent, Lynnette. pap. *(978-0-7787-4248-7(2))*; Elements & Compounds. Weir, Kirsten & Brent, Lynnette. pap. *(978-0-7787-4249-4(0))*; Mixtures & Solutions. Aloian, Molly. pap. *(978-0-7787-4250-0(4))*; States of Matter. Weir, Kirsten & Brent, Lynnette. pap. *(978-0-7787-4251-7(2))*; (Illus.). (J). (gr. 3-7). 2008. (ENG.). 32p. 2011. Set pap. *(978-0-7787-4245-6(8))* Crabtree Publishing Co.

Winston, Robert. It's Elementary! How Chemistry Rocks Our World. 2016. (Big Questions Ser.). (ENG., Illus.). 96p. (J). (gr. 3-7). pap. 9.99 *(978-1-4654-4001-3(1)*, DK Children) Dorling Kindersley Publishing, Inc.

Winterberg, Jenna. Chemical Reactions. 2015. (Science Readers: Content & Literacy Ser.). (Illus.). 32p. (gr. 5-5). pap. 8.99 *(978-1-4807-4724-1(6))* Teacher Created Materials, Inc.

Wolny, Philip. Chemical Reactions. 2011. (Science Made Simple Ser.). (Illus.). 64p. (YA). (gr. 5-8). lib. bdg. 31.95 *(978-1-4488-1235-6(6)*, Rosen Reference) Rosen Publishing Group, Inc., The.

Young, June. Look How It Changes! 2006. (Rookie Read-About Science Ser.). (ENG., Illus.). 32p. (J). (gr. 1-2). pap. 4.95 *(978-0-516-28178-0(X)*, Children's Pr.) Scholastic Library Publishing.

CHEMISTRY, ANALYTIC

Oxlade, Chris. Mezclar y Separar, 1 vol. 2010. (Materiales Cambiantes Ser.). (SPA.). 32p. (gr. 1-3). 27.32 *(978-1-4329-4431-5(2))*; pap. 8.95 *(978-1-4329-4436-0(3))* Heinemann-Raintree.

Shores, Lori. How to Make Slime, 1 vol. 2010. (Hands-On Science Fun Ser.). (ENG.). 24p. (gr. k-1). 26.65 *(978-1-4296-4492-1(3)*, Pebble Plus) Capstone Press of Coughlan Cos.

CHEMISTRY, BIOLOGICAL

see Biochemistry

CHEMISTRY—DICTIONARIES

Usborne Books Staff, ed. Illustrated Dictionary of Chemistry. rev. ed. 2004. (Illustrated Dictionaries Ser.). (Illus.). 128p. (J). (gr. 7-18). lib. bdg. 20.95 *(978-1-58086-282-0(9))* EDC Publishing.

CHEMISTRY—EXPERIMENTS

Arnold, Nick & De Saulles, Tony. Esa Caotica Quimica. De Saulles, Tony, tr. 2003. (Coleccion Esa Horrible Ciencia). (SPA., Illus.). 158p. (YA). *(978-84-272-2052-2(9)*, ML8312) Molino, Editorial ESP. Dist: Lectorum Pubns., Inc.

Bateman, Graham, ed. Chemical Reactions. 2011. (Facts at Your Fingertips: Introducing Chemistry Ser.). 64p. (YA). (gr. 7-12). lib. bdg. 35.65 *(978-1-936333-11-0(2))* Brown Bear Bks.

Biskup, Agnieszka. Super Cool Chemical Reaction Activities with Max Axiom. Baez, Marcelo, illus. 2015. (Max Axiom Science & Engineering Activities Ser.). (ENG.). 32p. (gr. 3-4). lib. bdg. 30.65 *(978-1-4914-2077-5(4)*, Graphic Library) Capstone Press of Coughlan Cos.

Brown, Cynthia Light. Amazing Kitchen Chemistry Projects. Shedd, Blair, illus. 2008. (Build It Yourself Ser.). (ENG.). 128p. (J). (gr. 3-7). 21.95 *(978-1-934670-06-4(5))* Octavio Publishing.

Coelho, Alexa & Field, Simon Quellen. Why Is Milk White? & 200 Other Curious Chemistry Questions. 2013. (ENG., Illus.). 288p. (J). (gr. 4). pap. 14.95 *(978-1-61374-452-9(8))* Chicago Review Pr., Inc.

Dingle, Adrian. How to Make a Universe with 92 Ingredients: An Electrifying Guide to the Elements. 2013. (ENG., Illus.). 96p. (J). (gr. 7-9). 18.95 *(978-1-77147-008-7(9))* Owlkids Bks. Inc. CAN. Dist: Publishers Group West (PGW).

Eagen, Rachel. Body Care Chemistry. 2011. (Chemtastrophe! Ser.). (ENG.). 32p. (J). (gr. 5-8). pap. *(978-0-7787-5288-2(7))*; lib. bdg. *(978-0-7787-5282-0(8))* Crabtree Publishing Co.

Farndon, John. Experimenting with Chemistry. 2008. (Experimenting with Science Ser.). 104p. (gr. 4-18). lib. bdg. 24.95 *(978-0-7614-3928-8(5)*, Benchmark Bks.) Marshall Cavendish Corp.

Field, Jon Eben. Cleaning Chemistry. 2011. (Chemtastrophe! Ser.). (ENG.). 32p. (J). (gr. 5-8). pap. *(978-0-7787-5301-8(8))*; lib. bdg. *(978-0-7787-5284-4(4))* Crabtree Publishing Co.

—Kitchen Chemistry. 2011. (Chemtastrophe! Ser.). (ENG.). 32p. (J). (gr. 5-8). pap. *(978-0-7787-5303-2(4))*; lib. bdg. *(978-0-7787-5286-8(0))* Crabtree Publishing Co.

—Medicine Cabinet Chemistry. 2011. (Chemtastrophe! Ser.). (ENG.). 32p. (J). (gr. 5-8). pap. *(978-0-7787-5304-9(2))*; lib. bdg. *(978-0-7787-5287-5(9))* Crabtree Publishing Co.

Firth, Alex. What's Chemistry All About? 2010. (Science Stories Ser.). 96p. (YA). (gr. 3-18). pap. 10.99 *(978-0-7945-2108-0(8)*, Usborne) EDC Publishing.

Gardner, Robert. Ace Your Science Project Using Chemistry Magic & Toys: Great Science Fair Ideas. 2009. (Ace Your Science Project Ser.). (Illus.). 128p. (J). (gr. 5-9). lib. bdg. 33.27 *(978-0-7660-3226-2(4))* Enslow Pubs., Inc.

—Chemistry Experiments in Your Own Laboratory. 2015. (Design, Build, Experiment Ser.). (ENG.). 128p. (J). (gr. 7-7). lib. bdg. 37.27 *(978-0-7660-6953-4(2))* Enslow Pubs., Inc.

—Chemistry Projects with a Laboratory You Can Build. 2007. (Build-A-Lab! Science Experiments Ser.). (Illus.). 128p. (J). (gr. 3-7). lib. bdg. 33.27 *(978-0-7660-2805-0(4))* Enslow Pubs., Inc.

—Chemistry Science Fair Projects Using Acids, Bases, Metals, Salts, & Inorganic Stuff. 2004. (Chemistry! Best Science Projects Ser.). (Illus.). 128p. (J). lib. bdg. 27.94 *(978-0-7660-2210-2(2))* Enslow Pubs., Inc.

—Chemistry Science Fair Projects Using Inorganic Stuff. LaBaff, Tom & LaBaff, Stephanie, illus. rev. exp. ed. 2010. (Chemistry Science Projects Using the Scientific Method Ser.). 160p. (J). (gr. 5-18). 35.94 *(978-0-7660-3413-6(5))* Enslow Pubs., Inc.

—Easy Genius Science Projects with Chemistry: Great Experiments & Ideas. 2008. (Easy Genius Science Projects Ser.). (Illus.). 112p. (J). (gr. 5-9). lib. bdg. 33.27 *(978-0-7660-2925-5(5))* Enslow Pubs., Inc.

Gardner, Robert. Experiments with Chemistry. 2017. (Science Whiz Experiments Ser.). 128p. (gr. 5-5). lib. bdg. 37.27 ***(978-0-7660-8676-0(3))*** Enslow Pubs., Inc.

Gardner, Robert & Conklin, Barbara Gardner. Chemistry Science Fair Projects Using French Fries, Gumdrops, Soap, & Other Organic Stuff. 2004. (Chemistry! Best Science Projects Ser.). (Illus.). 128p. (J). lib. bdg. 27.94 *(978-0-7660-2211-9(0))* Enslow Pubs., Inc.

Gardner, Robert & Conklin, Joshua. Experiments for Future Chemists. 2016. (Experiments for Future STEM Professionals Ser.). 128p. (J). (gr. 6-6). lib. bdg. 37.27 *(978-0-7660-7856-7(6))* Enslow Pubs., Inc.

Gardner, Robert, et al. Ace Your Chemistry Science Project: Great Science Fair Ideas. 2009. (Ace Your Science Project Ser.). (Illus.). 112p. (J). (gr. 5-9). mass mkt. 33.27 *(978-0-7660-3227-9(2))* Enslow Pubs., Inc.

Green, Joey. The Electric Pickle: 50 Experiments from the Periodic Table, from Aluminum to Zinc. 2017. (ENG.). 272p. pap. 19.99 ***(978-1-61373-959-4(1))*** Chicago Review Pr., Inc.

Hoffman, Mary Ann. Scientific Inquiry in Action: Chemical Reaction! 2009. (Real Life Readers Ser.). (ENG., Illus.). 32p. (J). (gr. 5-6). pap. 10.00 *(978-1-4358-0187-5(3)*, 1291698); 32p. (gr. 5-5). 47.90 *(978-1-60853-056-4(6))*; (J). lib. bdg. 25.25 *(978-1-4358-3012-7(1))*; (Illus.). 32p. (J). 60.00 *(978-1-4358-0188-2(1)*, 1291698) Rosen Publishing Group, Inc., The. (PowerKids Pr.).

Knight, Erin. Chemistry Around the House. 2011. (Chemtastrophe! Ser.). (ENG.). 32p. (J). (gr. 5-8). pap. *(978-0-7787-5300-1(X))*; lib. bdg. *(978-0-7787-5283-7(6))* Crabtree Publishing Co.

Light Brown, Cynthia. Amazing Kitchen Chemistry Projects. Shedd, Blair D., illus. 2008. (Build It Yourself Ser.). (ENG.). 128p. (J). (gr. 3-7). pap. 15.95 *(978-0-9792268-2-3(1))* Octavio Publishing.

Low, A. M. Popular Scientific Recreations - Science. 2006. 292p. per. *(978-1-4067-9717-6(0)*, Hesperides Pr.) Read Bks.

Marks, Jennifer L. How to Make a Bouncing Egg. (Hands-On Science Fun Ser.). (ENG.). 24p. (gr. k-1). 2011. pap. 41.70 *(978-1-4296-6384-7(7))* 2010. lib. bdg. 26.65 *(978-1-4296-5291-9(8))* Capstone Press of Coughlan Cos. (Pebble Plus).

Mercer, Bobby. Junk Drawer Chemistry: 50 Awesome Experiments That Don't Cost a Thing. 2015. (Junk Drawer Science Ser.). (ENG., Illus.). 224p. (J). (gr. 4). pap. 14.95 *(978-1-61373-179-6(5))* Chicago Review Pr., Inc.

Navarro, Paula & Jimenez, Angels. Incredible Experiments with Chemical Reactions & Mixtures. Cuxart, Bernadette, illus. 2014. (Magic Science Ser.). (ENG.). 36p. (J). (gr. 1-6). pap. 7.99 *(978-1-4380-0427-3(3))* Barron's Educational Series, Inc.

Nsrc, prod. Science & Technology for Children BOOKS: Chemical Tests. 2008. (Illus.). 64p. (J). *(978-1-933008-41-7(5)*, Science and Technology Concepts (STC)) Smithsonian Science Education Ctr. (SSEC).

O'Neal, Claire. A Project Guide to Matter. 2011. (Physical Science Projects for Kids Ser.). (Illus.). 48p. (J). (gr. 3-6). lib. bdg. 29.95 *(978-1-58415-967-4(7))* Mitchell Lane Pubs., Inc.

Oxlade, Chris. Changing Materials. 2007. (Working with Materials Ser.). (ENG., Illus.). 32p. (J). (gr. -1-3). pap. *(978-0-7787-3648-6(2))* Crabtree Publishing Co.

—Joining Materials. 2007. (Working with Materials Ser.). (ENG.). 32p. (J). pap. *(978-0-7787-3649-3(0))* Crabtree Publishing Co.

—Mixing & Separating. 2007. (ENG., Illus.). 32p. (J). (gr. -1-3). pap. *(978-0-7787-3650-9(4))* Crabtree Publishing Co.

—Shaping Materials. 2007. (Working with Materials Ser.). (ENG., Illus.). 32p. (J). (gr. -1-3). pap. *(978-0-7787-3651-6(2))* Crabtree Publishing Co.

Perchyonok, Tamara. Chemistry & Fun for Kids of All Ages: Bilingual Book. 2007. pap. 9.00 *(978-0-8059-8606-8(5))* Dorrance Publishing Co., Inc.

Phelan, Glen. Chemistry in the Kitchen: Text Pairs. 2008. (Bridges/Navigators Ser.). (J). (gr. 5). 94.00 *(978-1-4108-8411-4(2))* Benchmark Education Co.

VanCleave, Janice. More of Janice VanCleave's Wild, Wacky, & Weird Chemistry Experiments. 2016. (Janice VanCleave's Wild, Wacky, & Weird Science Experiments Ser.). 00064p. (J). (gr. 5-5). pap. 12.95 *(978-1-4994-6545-7(9)*, Rosen Young Adult) Rosen Publishing Group, Inc., The.

—Step-by-Step Science Experiments in Chemistry. 2012. (Janice VanCleave's First-Place Science Fair Projects Ser.). (ENG., Illus.). 80p. (J). (gr. 5-8). 33.25 *(978-1-4488-6981-7(1))*; pap. 14.15 *(978-1-4488-8465-0(9))* Rosen Publishing Group, Inc., The. (Rosen Reference).

VanCleave, Janice Pratt. Even More of Janice VanCleave's Wild, Wacky, & Weird Chemistry Experiments. 2017. (Janice VanCleave's Wild, Wacky, & Weird Science Experiments Ser.). 64p. (J). (gr. 10-10). 34.45 ***(978-1-4994-6688-1(9)***, Rosen Central) Rosen Publishing Group, Inc., The.

—Janice VanCleave's Wild, Wacky, & Weird Chemistry Experiments. 2016. (Janice VanCleave's Wild, Wacky, & Weird Science Experiments Ser.). 64p. (YA). (gr. 5-5). pap. 12.95 *(978-1-4777-8969-8(3)*, Rosen Reference) Rosen Publishing Group, Inc., The.

VanCleave, Janice Pratt. Many More of Janice VanCleave's Wild, Wacky, & Weird Chemistry Experiments. 2017. (J). ***(978-1-4994-3947-2(4)***, Rosen Reference) Rosen Publishing Group, Inc., The.

Walker, Pamela & Wood, Elaine. Chemistry Experiments. 2010. (Facts on File Science Experiments Ser.). (Illus.). 177p. (gr. 6-12). 40.00 *(978-0-8160-8172-1(7))* Facts On File, Inc.

Wheeler-Toppen, Jodi. Cool Chemistry Activities for Girls, 1 vol. 2012. (Girls Science Club Ser.). (ENG., 32p. (gr. 3-4). Illus.). pap. 8.19 *(978-1-4296-8020-2(2))*; pap. 47.70 *(978-1-4296-8518-4(2))*; (Illus.). lib. bdg. 27.99 *(978-1-4296-7674-8(4))* Capstone Press of Coughlan Cos. (Snap Bks.).

CHEMISTRY—HISTORY

Burling, Alexis. Robert Boyle. 2017. (Leaders of the Scientific Revolution Ser.). 112p. (gr. 12-13). 37.10 ***(978-1-5081-7476-9(8)***, Rosen Young Adult) Rosen Publishing Group, Inc., The.

Hall, Derek. Physical Sciences. 2009. (FAYFT: Great Scientists Ser.). 64p. (gr. 4-10). 39.95 *(978-1-933834-46-7(3))* Brown Bear Bks.

Johnson, Rose. Discoveries in Chemistry That Changed the World, 1 vol. 2015. (ENG.). 48p. (J). 30.25 *(978-1-4777-8605-5(8)*, Rosen Reference) Rosen Publishing Group, Inc., The.

Kjelle, Marylou. Antoine Lavoisier: Father of Modern Chemistry. 2004. (Uncharted, Unexplored, & Unexplained Ser.). (Illus.). 48p. (J). (gr. 4-8). lib. bdg. 29.95 *(978-1-58415-309-2(1))* Mitchell Lane Pubs., Inc.

Ripley, Tim. Smoke Screens & Gas Masks: Chemistry Goes to War. 2017. (STEM on the Battlefield Ser.). (ENG.). 48p. (J). (gr. 4-6). 31.99 ***(978-1-5124-3925-0(8))*** Lerner Publishing Group.

Stefoff, Rebecca. Alchemy & Chemistry. 2014. 48p. pap. 29.93 *(978-1-62712-509-3(4))* Cavendish Square Publishing.

CHEMISTRY, INDUSTRIAL

see Chemical Engineering; Chemistry, Technical

CHEMISTRY, INORGANIC

see also Metals

Thomas, Michelle. Sodium. 2005. (Understanding the Elements of the Periodic Table Ser.). (Illus.). 48p. (J). (gr. 5-8). lib. bdg. 29.25 *(978-1-4042-0160-6(2))* Rosen Publishing Group, Inc., The.

CHEMISTRY, MEDICAL AND PHARMACEUTICAL

see Pharmaceutical Chemistry

CHEMISTRY, ORGANIC

Gardner, Jane P. Carbon. 2017. (Chemistry of Everyday Elements Ser.). (ENG.). (YA). (gr. 7-12). 23.95 ***(978-1-4222-3839-4(3))*** Mason Crest.

Gardner, Robert & Conklin, Barbara Gardner. Organic Chemistry Science Fair Projects, Revised & Expanded Using the Scientific Method. LaBaff, Tom & LaBaff, Stephanie, illus. 2010. (Chemistry Science Projects Using the Scientific Method Ser.). 160p. (J). (gr. 5-18). 35.94 *(978-0-7660-3414-3(3))* Enslow Pubs., Inc.

Hart, Harold. Organische Chemie. 2nd ed. (Duden Abiturhilfen Ser.). (GER.). 112p. (YA). (gr. 12-13). *(978-3-411-70862-8(X))* Bibliographisches Institut & F. A. Brockhaus AG DEU. Dist: International Bk. Import Service, Inc.

Hart Organic Chemistry: A Short Course. 11th ed. 2003. (gr. 6-12). *(978-0-618-21546-1(8)*, 3-22519) CENGAGE Learning.

Holt, Rinehart and Winston Staff. Holt Chemistry Chptr. 19: Carbon & Organics. 4th ed. Date not set. pap. 11.20 *(978-0-03-068129-5(4))* Holt McDougal.

Kunststoffe, Farbstoffe, Waschmittel. (Duden Abiturhilfen Ser.). (GER.). 96p. (YA). (gr. 12-13). *(978-3-411-04511-2(6))* Bibliographisches Institut & F. A. Brockhaus AG DEU. Dist: International Bk. Import Service, Inc.

Nam, Elain, et al. Organic Chemistry with Vernier. 2012. (C). spiral bd. 48.00 *(978-1-929075-89-8(8))* Vernier Software & Technology.

Simon, Charnan. Super Cool Science Experiments: Compounds & Mixtures. 2009. (Explorer Library: Science Explorer Ser.). (ENG., Illus.). 32p. (gr. 4-8). lib. bdg. 28.50 *(978-1-60279-536-5(3)*, 200288) Cherry Lake Publishing.

CHEMISTRY, PHARMACEUTICAL

see Pharmaceutical Chemistry

CHEMISTRY, PHYSICAL AND THEORETICAL

see also Atoms; Crystallography; Electrochemistry; Molecules; Nuclear Physics; Periodic Law; Polymers; Radiochemistry; Thermodynamics

Atomic & Molecular Structure. 2011. (Science Made Simple Ser.). (ENG.). 64p. (YA). pap. 12.95 *(978-1-4488-2238-6(6)*, Rosen Reference) Rosen Publishing Group, Inc., The.

Chaffee, Joel. Atomic & Molecular Structure. 2011. (Science Made Simple Ser.). (Illus.). 64p. (YA). (gr. 5-8). lib. bdg. 31.95 *(978-1-4488-1230-1(5)*, Rosen Reference) Rosen Publishing Group, Inc., The.

Gases & Their Properties. 2011. (Science Made Simple Ser.). (ENG.). 64p. (YA). pap. 12.95 *(978-1-4488-2243-0(2)*, Rosen Reference) Rosen Publishing Group, Inc., The.

Holt, Rinehart and Winston Staff. Holt Science & Technology Chapter 4: Physical Science: Elements, Compounds, & Mixtures. 5th ed. 2004. (Illus.). pap. 12.86 *(978-0-03-030371-5(0))* Holt McDougal.

Kjelle, Marylou Morano. Mixtures & Compounds. (Library of Physical Science Ser.). 24p. (gr. 4-4). 2009. 42.50 *(978-1-60853-785-3(4)*, PowerKids Pr.) 2007. (ENG., Illus.). pap. 7.05 *(978-1-4042-2167-3(0)*, PowerKids Pr.) 2006. (Illus.). (YA). lib. bdg. 22.60 *(978-1-4042-3420-8(9))* Rosen Publishing Group, Inc., The.

McLean, Adam. What Is Atomic Theory? 2010. (Shaping Modern Science Ser.). (ENG.). 64p. (J). (gr. 5-8). pap. *(978-0-7787-7204-0(7))* Crabtree Publishing Co.

Meyer, Susan. Gases & Their Properties. 2011. (Science Made Simple Ser.). (Illus.). 64p. (YA). (gr. 5-8). lib. bdg. 31.95 *(978-1-4488-1233-2(X)*, Rosen Reference) Rosen Publishing Group, Inc., The.

Sabean, Maurice. Atomic Structure. 2011. (Science Foundations Ser.). (Illus.). 108p. (gr. 6-12). lib. bdg. 35.00 *(978-1-60413-342-4(2)*, Chelsea Hse.) Facts On File, Inc.

CHEMISTRY, PHYSIOLOGICAL

see Biochemistry

CHEMISTRY, TECHNICAL

see also Alloys; Canning and Preserving; Chemical Engineering; Chemicals; Dyes and Dyeing; Electrochemistry; Synthetic Products; Waste Products also names of specific industries and products, e.g. Clay Industries

Cardenas, Ernesto A. Mixtures & Solutions. 2009. 23.95 *(978-1-60698-044-6(0))*; pap. 4.95 *(978-1-60698-042-2(4))* Milo Educational Bks. & Resources.

Carlson Berne, Emma. Transforming! Chemical Energy. 2013. (Energy Everywhere Ser.). (ENG., Illus.). 24p. (J). (gr. 3-6). 22.60 *(978-1-4488-9652-3(5))*; pap. 8.25 *(978-1-4488-9762-9(9))* Rosen Publishing Group, Inc., The. (PowerKids Pr.).

Field, Jon Eben. Kitchen Chemistry. 2011. (Chemtastrophe! Ser.). (ENG.). 32p. (J). (gr. 5-8). pap. *(978-0-7787-5303-2(4))*; lib. bdg. *(978-0-7787-5286-8(0))* Crabtree Publishing Co.

Martineau, Susan. Fizz in the Kitchen. Noyes, Leighton, illus. 2011. (Everyday Science Experiments Ser.). (ENG.). 24p. (J). (gr. 3-6). pap. 10.60 *(978-1-61533-411-7(4)*, 1328714); lib. bdg. 25.25 *(978-1-61533-373-8(8)*, 1328714) Windmill Bks.

CHEMISTRY—VOCATIONAL GUIDANCE

Cohen, Judith Love. You Can Be A Chemist. Katz, David A., illus. l.t. ed. 2005. Orig. Title: You Can Be A Woman Chemist. 40p. (J). per. 7.00 *(978-1-880599-71-6(6))* Cascade Pass, Inc.

—You Can Be A Woman Chemist. Katz, David A., illus. l.t. ed. 2005. 40p. (J). 13.95 *(978-1-880599-72-3(4))* Cascade Pass, Inc.

Etingoff, Kim. Women in Chemistry. Lee-Karlon, Ann, ed. 2013. (Major Women in Science Ser.: 10). 64p. (J). (gr. 7-18). 22.95 *(978-1-4222-2925-5(4))* Mason Crest.

Infobase Publishing Staff, creator. Chemistry. 2008. (Careers in Focus Ser.). (Illus.). 201p. (gr. 6-12). 32.95 *(978-0-8160-7279-8(5),* Ferguson Publishing Co.) Facts On File, Inc.

CHEMISTS

see also Chemistry—Vocational Guidance

Borzendowski, Janice. Marie Curie: Mother of Modern Physics. 2009. (Sterling Biographies(r) Ser.). (ENG., Illus.). 128p. (J). (gr. 5-18). pap. 5.95 *(978-1-4027-5318-3(7))* Sterling Publishing Co., Inc.

Cobb, Vicki & Dorling Kindersley Publishing Staff. Marie Curie. 2008. (DK Biography Ser.). (ENG., Illus.). 128p. (J). (gr. 5-12). pap. 6.99 *(978-0-7566-3831-3(3),* DK Children) Dorling Kindersley Publishing, Inc.

Conley, Kate A. Joseph Priestly & the Discovery of Oxygen. 2005. (Uncharted, Unexplored, & Unexplained Ser.). (Illus.). 48p. (J). (gr. 4-8). lib. bdg. 29.95 *(978-1-58415-367-2(9))* Mitchell Lane Pubs., Inc.

Cregan, Elizabeth R. C. Marie Curie: Pioneering Physicist, 1 vol. 2007. (Science Readers Ser.). (ENG., Illus.). 32p. (J). (gr. 3-3). pap. 8.99 *(978-0-7439-0570-1(9))* Shell Educational Publishing.

Edison, Erin. Marie Curie, 1 vol. 2014. (Great Women in History Ser.). (ENG.). 24p. (gr. k-1). lib. bdg. 21.99 *(978-1-4765-4216-4(3),* Pebble Bks.) Capstone Press of Coughlan Cos.

Etingoff, Kim. Women in Chemistry. Lee-Karlon, Ann, ed. 2013. (Major Women in Science Ser.: 10). 64p. (J). (gr. 7-18). 22.95 *(978-1-4222-2925-5(4))* Mason Crest.

Gaddi, Rosalie. A Day at Work with a Chemist, 01 vols., 1. 2016. (Super STEM Careers Ser.). (ENG., Illus.). 24p. (J). pap. 8.25 *(978-1-5081-4402-1(8),* PowerKids Pr.) Rosen Publishing Group, Inc., The.

Gordon, Fernando. Marie Curie, 1 vol. 2016. (ENG., Illus.). 24p. (J). 25.65 *(978-1-68078-154-0(5))* ABDO Publishing Co.

Hall, Derek. Chemistry, Earth, & Space Sciences. 2010. (Facts at Your Fingertips Ser.). (YA). (gr. 7-12). 35.65 *(978-1-933834-47-4(1))* Brown Bear Books.

Hardyman, Robyn. Pierre & Marie Curie. 2014. (Dynamic Duos of Science Ser.). 48p. (YA). (gr. 5-8). pap. 84.30 *(978-1-4824-1287-1(X))* Stevens, Gareth Publishing LLLP.

Healy, Nick. Marie Curie. 2005. (Genius Ser.). (Illus.). 48p. (J). (gr. 5-9). lib. bdg. 21.95 *(978-1-58341-332-6(4),* Creative Education) Creative Co., The.

Howell, Sara. Chemists at Work. 2017. (Scientists at Work Ser.). 32p. (J). (gr. 6-8). pap. 12.90 ***(978-1-68048-753-4(1),*** Britannica Educational Publishing) Rosen Publishing Group, Inc., The.

Jane Gardner. Black Achievement in Science: Chemistry, Vol. 10. Pouson, Mel, ed. 2016. (Black Achievement in Science Ser.: Vol. 10). (ENG., Illus.). 64p. (J). (gr. 7-12). 23.95 *(978-1-4222-3556-0(4))* Mason Crest.

Kepnes, Caroline. Stephen Crane. 2004. (Classic Storytellers Ser.). (Illus.). 48p. (J). (gr. 4-8). lib. bdg. 29.95 *(978-1-58415-272-9(9))* Mitchell Lane Pubs., Inc.

Kjelle, Marylou. Antoine Lavoisier: Father of Modern Chemistry. 2004. (Uncharted, Unexplored, & Unexplained Ser.). (Illus.). 48p. (J). (gr. 4-8). lib. bdg. 29.95 *(978-1-58415-309-2(1))* Mitchell Lane Pubs., Inc.

—John Dalton & the Atomic Theory. 2004. (Uncharted, Unexplored, & Unexplained Ser.). (Illus.). 48p. (J). (gr. 4-8). lib. bdg. 29.95 *(978-1-58415-308-5(3))* Mitchell Lane Pubs., Inc.

Koestler-Grack, Rachel A. Marie Curie: Scientist. 2009. (Women of Achievement Ser.). (Illus.). 136p. (gr. 6-12). 35.00 *(978-1-60413-086-7(5),* Chelsea Hse.) Facts On File, Inc.

Krieg, Katherine. Marie Curie: Physics & Chemistry Pioneer, 1 vol. 2014. (Great Minds of Science Ser.). (ENG., Illus.). 48p. (J). (gr. 8-12). lib. bdg. 32.79 *(978-1-62403-377-3(6))* ABDO Publishing Co.

Krull, Kathleen. Marie Curie. 2009. (Giants of Science Ser.). (ENG.). 144p. (J). (gr. 3-7). pap. 7.99 *(978-0-14-241265-7(1),* Puffin Books) Penguin Young Readers Group.

Labrecque, Ellen. Stephanie Kwolek & Bulletproof Material. 2017. (21st Century Junior Library: Women Innovators Ser.). (ENG., Illus.). 24p. (J). (gr. 2-5). lib. bdg. 27.07 *(978-1-63472-183-7(7),* 209304) Cherry Lake Publishing.

Lin, Yoming S. The Curies & Radioactivity. 2012. (Eureka! Ser.). (Illus.). 24p. (YA). (gr. 3-6). lib. bdg. 22.60 *(978-1-4488-5033-4(9))* Rosen Publishing Group, Inc., The.

Lindeen, Mary. Marie Curie: Scientist, 1 vol. Soud, illus. 2008. (Beginner Biographies Ser.). (ENG.). 32p. (gr. -1-3). 28.50 *(978-1-60270-248-6(9),* Looking Glass Library- Nonfiction) Magic Wagon.

MacBain, Jennifer. Gertrude Elion: Nobel Prize Winner in Physiology & Medicine. 2009. (Women Hall of Famers in Mathematics & Science Ser.). 112p. (gr. 5-8). 63.90 *(978-1-60854-811-8(2),* Rosen Reference) Rosen Publishing Group, Inc., The.

MacLeod, Elizabeth. Marie Curie. Mantha, John, illus. 2009. (Kids Can Read Ser.). (ENG.). 32p. (J). (gr. 1-3). 3.95 *(978-1-55453-297-1(3));* 14.95 *(978-1-55453-296-4(5))* Kids Can Pr., Ltd. CAN. Dist: Hachette Bk. Group.

—Marie Curie: A Brilliant Life. 2004. (Snapshots: Images of People & Places in History Ser.). (ENG., Illus.). 32p. (J). (gr. 3-7). 7.95 *(978-1-55337-571-5(8))* Kids Can Pr., Ltd. CAN. Dist: Hachette Bk. Group.

Marsh, Carole. Marie Curie, Nobel Prize Winning Scientist. 2004. 12p. (gr. k-4). 2.95 *(978-0-635-02374-2(1))* Gallopade International.

Mattern, Joanne & Brandt, Keith. Marie Curie, Brave Scientist. Dugan, Karen, illus. 2005. 45p. (J). *(978-0-439-80153-9(2))* Scholastic, Inc.

McKown, Robin. Marie Curie. Rethi, Lili, illus. 2012. 128p. *40.95 (978-1-258-23532-1(3)); pap. 25.95 (978-1-258-24675-4(9))* Literary Licensing, LLC.

Miller, Connie Colwell. Marie Curie & Radioactivity, 1 vol. Larson, Scott & Heike, Mark, illus. 2006. (Inventions & Discovery Ser.). (ENG.). 32p. (gr. 3-4). 30.65 *(978-0-7368-6486-2(5),* Graphic Library) Capstone Press of Coughlan Cos.

Mortensen, Lori. Marie Curie: Prize-Winning Scientist, 1 vol. Jaekel, Susan, illus. 2008. (Biographies Ser.). (ENG.). 24p. (gr. k-3). lib. bdg. 26.65 *(978-1-4048-3731-7(0))* Picture Window Bks.

Ogilvie, Marilyn Bailey. Marie Curie: A Biography, 1 vol. 2004. (Greenwood Biographies Ser.). (Illus.). 184p. (C). 43.00 *(978-0-313-32529-8(4),* GR2529, Greenwood) ABC-CLIO, LLC.

O'Quinn, Amy M. Marie Curie for Kids: Her Life & Scientific Discoveries, with 21 Activities & Experiments. 2016. (For Kids Ser.). (ENG.). 144p. (J). (gr. 4). pap. 16.99 *(978-1-61373-320-2(8))* Chicago Review Pr., Inc.

Orr, Tamra. Marie Curie. 2003. (World Was Never the Same Ser.). (J). pap. *(978-1-58417-263-5(0));* lib. bdg. *(978-1-58417-262-8(2))* Lake Street Pubs.

Pasachoff, Naomi E. Linus Pauling: Advancing Science, Advocating Peace. 2004. (Nobel Prize-Winning Scientists Ser.). (Illus.). 128p. (J). lib. bdg. 26.60 *(978-0-7660-2130-3(0))* Enslow Pubs., Inc.

Poynter, Margaret. Marie Curie: Discoverer of Radium. rev. ed. 2007. (Great Minds of Science Ser.). (Illus.). 112p. (J). (gr. 4-10). lib. bdg. 33.27 *(978-0-7660-2795-4(3))* Enslow Pubs., Inc.

—Marie Curie: Genius Researcher of Radioactivity. 2015. (Genius Scientists & Their Genius Ideas Ser.). 96p. (J). (gr. 5-12). 27.94 *(978-0-7660-6580-2(4));* pap. 10.95 *(978-0-7660-6581-9(2))* Enslow Pubs., Inc.

Sherman, Josepha. Henry Cavendish & the Discovery of Hydrogen. 2005. (Uncharted, Unexplored, & Unexplained Ser.). (Illus.). 48p. (J). (gr. 4-8). lib. bdg. 29.95 *(978-1-58415-368-9(7))* Mitchell Lane Pubs., Inc.

Stewart, Gail B. Stephanie Kwolek: Creator of Kevlar. 2008. (Innovators Ser.). (ENG., Illus.). 48p. (J). (gr. 4-8). lib. bdg. 29.95 *(978-0-7377-4040-0(X),* LML02109-239897, Kidhaven) Cengage Gale.

Stine, Megan. Who Was Marie Curie? Hammond, Ted & Harrison, Nancy, illus. 2014. (Who Was? Ser.). (ENG.). 112p. (J). (gr. 3-7). 5.99 *(978-0-448-47896-8(X),* Grosset & Dunlap) Penguin Young Readers Group.

Thiel, Kristin. Dorothy Hodgkin: Biochemist & Developer of Protein Crystallography. 2016. (Women in Science Ser.). 128p. (J). lib. bdg. 45.64 *(978-1-5026-2313-3(7))* Cavendish Square Publishing.

Throp, Claire. Marie Curie. 2015. (Against the Odds Biographies Ser.). (ENG., Illus.). 48p. (gr. 3-6). 33.32 *(978-1-4846-2467-8(X))* Heinemann-Raintree.

Tracy, Kathleen. Pierre & Marie Curie & the Discovery of Radium. 2004. (Uncharted, Unexplored, & Unexplained Ser.). (Illus.). 48p. (J). (gr. 4-8). lib. bdg. 29.95 *(978-1-58415-310-8(5))* Mitchell Lane Pubs., Inc.

Venezia, Mike. Marie Curie: Scientist Who Made Glowing Discoveries. Venezia, Mike, illus. (Getting to Know the World's Greatest Inventors & Scientists Ser.). (ENG., Illus.). 32p. (J). 2009. (gr. 3-4). pap. 6.95 *(978-0-531-22208-9(X),* Children's Pr.) 2008. (gr. 2-5). 28.00 *(978-0-531-14977-5(3))* Scholastic Library Publishing.

Waxman, Laura Hamilton. Marie Curie. 2003. (History Maker Biographies Ser.). (ENG., Illus.). 48p. (gr. 3-6). 27.93 *(978-0-8225-0300-2(X),* Lerner Pubns.) Lerner Publishing Group.

Wheeler, Jill C. Hayat Sindi: Brilliant Biochemist, 1 vol. 2012. (Women in Science Ser.). (ENG., Illus.). 32p. (J). (gr. 3-6). lib. bdg. 27.07 *(978-1-61783-450-9(5),* Checkerboard Library) ABDO Publishing Co.

Whiting, Jim. Otto Hahn & the Story of Nuclear Fission. 2003. (Unlocking the Secrets of Science Ser.). (Illus.). 56p. (gr. 4-10). lib. bdg. 25.70 *(978-1-58415-204-0(4))* Mitchell Lane Pubs., Inc.

Wyckoff, Edwin Brit. The Woman Who Invented the Thread That Stops Bullets: The Genius of Stephanie Kwolek. 2013. (Genius Inventors & Their Great Ideas Ser.). 48p. (J). (gr. 3-4). pap. 8.95 *(978-1-4644-0211-1(6),* Enslow Elementary); (Illus.). 25.27 *(978-0-7660-4141-7(7))* Enslow Pubs., Inc.

Yount, Lisa. Antoine Lavoisier: Founder of Modern Chemistry. rev. ed. 2008. (Great Minds of Science Ser.). (Illus.). 128p. (J). (gr. k-5). lib. bdg. 33.27 *(978-0-7660-3011-4(3))* Enslow Pubs., Inc.

—Antoine Lavoisier: Genius of Modern Chemistry. 2015. (Genius Scientists & Their Genius Ideas Ser.). 96p. (J). (gr. 5-12). 27.94 *(978-0-7660-6520-8(0));* pap. 10.95 *(978-0-7660-6521-5(9))* Enslow Pubs., Inc.

Zannos, Susan. Dmitri Mendeleyev & the Periodic Table. 2004. (Uncharted, Unexplored, & Unexplained Ser.). (Illus.). 48p. (J). (gr. 4-8). lib. bdg. 29.95 *(978-1-58415-267-5(2))* Mitchell Lane Pubs., Inc.

—Linus Pauling & the Chemical Bond. 2003. (Unlocking the Secrets of Science Ser.). (Illus.). 56p. (gr. 4-10). lib. bdg. 25.70 *(978-1-58415-123-4(4))* Mitchell Lane Pubs., Inc.

CHEMOTHERAPY

see also Antibiotics

Bonnice, Sherry. Drug Therapy & Premenstrual Disorders. 2004. (Encyclopedia of Psychiatric Drugs & Their Disorders Ser.). (Illus.). 128p. (YA). lib. bdg. 24.95 *(978-1-59084-572-1(2))* Mason Crest.

Bonnice, Sherry & Hoard, Carolyn. Drug Therapy & Cognitive Disorders. 2004. (Encyclopedia of Psychiatric Drugs & Their Disorders Ser.). (Illus.). 128p. (YA). lib. bdg. 24.95 *(978-1-59084-562-2(5))* Mason Crest.

Brent, Mary & Caitlin, Knutsson. Chemo to the Rescue: A Children's Book about Leukemia. 2008. 48p. pap. 17.49 *(978-1-4343-9720-1(3))* AuthorHouse.

Brinkerhoff, Shirley. Childhood & Adolescent Disorders. McDonnell, Mary Ann & Esherick, Donald, eds. 2013. (State of Mental Illness & Its Therapy Ser.: 19). 128p. (J). (gr. 7-18). 24.95 *(978-1-4222-2822-7(3))* Mason Crest.

—Drug Therapy & Anxiety Disorders. 2004. (Encyclopedia of Psychiatric Drugs & Their Disorders Ser.). (Illus.). 128p. (YA). lib. bdg. 24.95 *(978-1-59084-561-5(7))* Mason Crest.

—Drug Therapy & Childhood & Adolescent Disorders. 2004. (Encyclopedia of Psychiatric Drugs & Their Disorders Ser.). (Illus.). 128p. (YA). lib. bdg. 24.95 *(978-1-59084-563-9(3))* Mason Crest.

—Drug Therapy & Eating Disorders. (Encyclopedia of Psychiatric Drugs & Their Disorders Ser.). (Illus.). (YA). 2004. 128p. lib. bdg. 24.95 *(978-1-59084-565-3(X))* 2003. 124p. (gr. 7-12). pap. 14.95 *(978-1-4222-0389-7(1))* Mason Crest.

—Drug Therapy & Obsessive-Compulsive Disorders. 2004. (Encyclopedia of Psychiatric Drugs & Their Disorders Ser.). (Illus.). 128p. (YA). lib. bdg. 24.95 *(978-1-59084-569-1(2))* Mason Crest.

—Drug Therapy & Personality Disorders. (Encyclopedia of Psychiatric Drugs & Their Disorders Ser.). (Illus.). (YA). 2004. 128p. lib. bdg. 24.95 *(978-1-59084-571-4(4))* 2003. 126p. (gr. 4-7). pap. 14.95 *(978-1-4222-0394-1(8))* Mason Crest.

—Drug Therapy & Schizophrenia. 2004. (Encyclopedia of Psychiatric Drugs & Their Disorders Ser.). (Illus.). 128p. (YA). lib. bdg. 24.95 *(978-1-59084-574-5(9))* Mason Crest.

—Drug Therapy & Substance-Related Disorders. 2004. (Encyclopedia of Psychiatric Drugs & Their Disorders Ser.). (Illus.). 128p. (YA). lib. bdg. 24.95 *(978-1-59084-577-6(3))* Mason Crest.

Esherick, Joan. Drug Therapy & Mood Disorders. 2004. (Encyclopedia of Psychiatric Drugs & Their Disorders Ser.). (Illus.). 128p. (YA). lib. bdg. 24.95 *(978-1-59084-568-4(4))* Mason Crest.

Esherick, Joan, frwd. Drug Therapy & Sleep Disorders. 2004. (Encyclopedia of Psychiatric Drugs & Their Disorders Ser.). (Illus.). 128p. (YA). lib. bdg. 24.95 *(978-1-59084-576-9(5))* Mason Crest.

Giddens, Sandra. Coping with Chemotherapy. 2009. (Coping Ser.). 192p. (gr. 7-12). 63.90 *(978-1-61511-995-0(7))* Rosen Publishing Group, Inc., The.

Giddens, Sandra & Giddens, Owen. Coping with Chemotherapy. 2005. (Coping Ser.). (Illus.). 192p. (YA). (gr. 7-12). lib. bdg. 34.60 *(978-0-8239-3361-7(X))* Rosen Publishing Group, Inc., The.

Libal, Autumn. Drug Therapy & Dissociative Disorders. 2004. (Encyclopedia of Psychiatric Drugs & Their Disorders Ser.). (Illus.). 128p. (YA). lib. bdg. 24.95 *(978-1-59084-564-6(1))* Mason Crest.

—Drug Therapy & Impulse Control Disorders. 2004. (Encyclopedia of Psychiatric Drugs & Their Disorders Ser.). (Illus.). 128p. (YA). lib. bdg. 24.95 *(978-1-59084-566-0(8))* Mason Crest.

Libal, Joyce. Drug Therapy for Mental Disorders Caused by a Medical Condition. 2004. (Encyclopedia of Psychiatric Drugs & Their Disorders Ser.). (Illus.). 128p. (YA). lib. bdg. 24.95 *(978-1-59084-567-7(6))* Mason Crest.

Meyers, Barbara & Mays, Lydia. The Long & the Short of It: A Tale about Hair. Bersani, Shennen, illus. 2011. (ENG.). 32p. (J). (gr. 2-4). 14.95 *(978-1-60443-017-2(6))* American Cancer Society, Inc.

Vitale, Ann E. Drug Therapy & Sexual Disorders. 2004. (Encyclopedia of Psychiatric Drugs & Their Disorders Ser.). (Illus.). 128p. (YA). lib. bdg. 24.95 *(978-1-59084-575-2(7))* Mason Crest.

CHESS

Alvarez, Michel J. WonderChess - Chess Kit for Kids: Featuring unique, prize-fillable pieces & 3D illustrated lesson Book. Scauzillo, Tony, illus. Thyrion, Marie-Noelle, photos by. 2004. 54p. (J). pap. 19.95 *(978-0-9771787-0-4(6))* Wonder Chess LLC.

—WonderChess - Chess Kit for Kids - Deluxe Edition in Tin: Featuring, unique prize fillable pieces & 3D illustrated lesson Book, 1. Scauzillo, Tony, illus. Thyrion, Marie-Noelle, photos by. 2005. 54p. (J). 29.95 *(978-0-9771787-1-1(4))* Wonder Chess LLC.

Basman, Michael & Ling, Mary. Chess for Kids. 2006. (ENG., Illus.). 48p. (J). (gr. 3-7). pap. 7.99 *(978-0-7566-1807-0(X),* DK Children) Dorling Kindersley Publishing, Inc.

Breutigam-Duden, Martin. Schachturnier: Knifflige Situationen aus Beruehmten Partien. (Pocket-Quizspiel Ser.). (Illus.). 56p. bds. *(978-3-411-09411-0(7))* Bibliographisches Institut & F. A. Brockhaus AG DEU. Dist: i. b. d., Ltd.

Castor, H. Starting Chess. 2004. (First Skills Ser.). (Illus.). 32p. (J). (gr. k-3). pap. 4.95 *(978-0-7945-0115-0(X),* Usborne); lthr. 12.95 *(978-1-58086-435-0(X))* EDC Publishing.

Chandler, Murray. Chess Puzzles for Kids. 2012. (ENG.). 128p. 16.95 *(978-1-906454-40-1(X))* Gambit Pubns., Ltd. GBR. Dist: Two Rivers Distribution.

—Chess Tactics for Kids. 2005. (ENG., Illus.). 128p. reprint ed. 16.95 *(978-1-901983-99-9(4))* Gambit Pubns., Ltd. GBR. Dist: Two Rivers Distribution.

Chandler, Murray & Milligan, Helen. Chess for Children. McCluskey, Cindy, illus. 2004. (ENG.). 96p. 16.95 *(978-1-904600-06-0(9))* Gambit Pubns., Ltd. GBR. Dist: Two Rivers Distribution.

Chess Attack. 2004. (Formula Fun Ser.). (Illus.). 48p. (J). pap. *(978-1-84229-582-3(9))* Top That! Publishing PLC.

Chess Book (was Chess Activity Book) IR (consignment) 2017. (Chess Ser.). (ENG.). (J). spiral bd. 9.99 ***(978-0-7945-3732-6(4),*** Usborne) EDC Publishing.

Chevannes, Sabrina. The Batsford Book of Chess for Children. 2014. (ENG., Illus.). 128p. (J). (gr. 2). 14.95 *(978-1-84994-069-6(X),* Batsford) Pavilion Bks. GBR. Dist: Sterling Publishing Co., Inc.

—Chess for Children. 2015. (ENG., Illus.). 120p. (J). (gr. 2). pap., act. bk. ed. 12.95 *(978-1-84994-284-3(6),* Batsford) Pavilion Bks. GBR. Dist: Sterling Publishing Co., Inc.

Dalby, Elizabeth. The Complete Book of Chess. Le Rolland, Leonard, illus. 2006. (Chess Guides). 96p. (J). (gr. 5). lib. bdg., act. bk. ed. 25.95 *(978-1-58086-517-3(8))* EDC Publishing.

—Complete Book of Chess (Reduced Format) - Internet Linked. 2008. (Chess Guides). 96p. (J). pap. 12.99 *(978-0-7945-2420-3(6),* Usborne) EDC Publishing.

—The Usborne Internet-Linked Complete Book of Chess. 2005. (Illus.). 96p. (J). pap. *(978-0-439-78711-6(4))* Scholastic, Inc.

Hertan, Charles. Power Chess for Kids: Learn How to Think Ahead & Become One of the Best Players in Your School. 2011. (ENG.). 144p. pap. 16.95 *(978-90-5691-330-4(1),* New in Chess) Continental Sales, Inc.

—Power Chess for Kids: More Ways to Think Ahead & Become One of the Best Players in Your School, Volume 2. 2013. (ENG.). 160p. pap. 16.95 *(978-90-5691-433-2(2),* New In Chess,Csi) Continental Sales, Inc.

Khmelnitsky, Igor. Chess Exam & Training Guide: Rate yourself & learn how to Improve. 2004. (Chess Exams Ser.). (ENG., Illus.). 320p. per. 24.95 *(978-0-9754761-2-3(2))* IamCoach.com Publishing.

Kidder, Harvey. Ajedrez Infantil: Diviertete Con el Juego Mas Inteligente! Osorio, Sergio, illus. 2005.Tr. of Chess for Children. (SPA.). 128p. (YA). (gr. 2). pap. *(978-968-403-315-3(X))* Selector, S.A. de C.V.

Linder, Kevin. Get into Chess. 2016. (Get-Into-It Guides). (ENG., Illus.). 32p. (J). (gr. 3-6). *(978-0-7787-2639-5(8))* Crabtree Publishing Co.

Reppen, Ellisiv. Chess: Be the King! Hartberg, Flu, illus. 2016. (ENG.). 176p. (J). (gr. 6). pap. 14.99 *(978-1-63450-160-6(8),* Sky Pony Pr.) Skyhorse Publishing Co., Inc.

Roza, Greg. Checkmate! the Game of Chess: Applying Strategies from Simple to Complex Problems. (PowerMath: Proficiency Ser.). 32p. (gr. 4-5). 2009. 47.90 *(978-1-60851-392-5(0),* PowerKids Pr.) 2004. (ENG.). 47.50 *(978-0-8239-7648-5(3))* Rosen Publishing Group, Inc., The.

—Checkmate! The Game of Chess: Applying Strategies from Simpler Problems to Complex Problems. 2004. (PowerMath: Proficiency Ser.). (Illus.). 32p. (YA). (gr. 5-9). lib. bdg. 25.25 *(978-0-8239-8996-6(8))* Rosen Publishing Group, Inc., The.

—The Game of Chess: Applying Strategies from Simple to Complex Problems. 2009. (PowerMath Ser.). (Illus.). 32p. (gr. 4-5). pap. 10.00 *(978-0-8239-8925-6(9),* PowerKids Pr.) Rosen Publishing Group, Inc., The.

Schneider, Stephen A. Chess Basics. 2005. (ENG.). (J). per. 22.50 *(978-0-9729456-6-0(0))* Championship Chess.

—Endgame Strategies 1. 2003. (Illus.). per. 22.50 *(978-0-9729456-4-6(4))* Championship Chess.

—Endgame Strategies 1: 2nd Edition. 2nd ed. 2005. 195p. (J). per., act. bk. ed. 24.50 *(978-0-9729456-7-7(9))* Championship Chess.

Snyder, Robert M. Unbeatable Chess Lessons for Juniors. 2003. (McKay Chess Library for Kids). (Illus.). 272p. 15.95 *(978-0-8129-3511-0(X),* Random Hse. Puzzles & Games) Random Hse. Information Group.

—Winning Chess Tournaments for Juniors. 2004. (Illus.). 208p. pap. 14.95 *(978-0-8129-3635-3(3),* Random Hse. Puzzles & Games) Random Hse. Information Group.

Storey, Charles H. The National Chess Syllabus Featuring the Bandana Martial Art Exam System. 2005. (Illus.). 240p. 48.42 *(978-1-4120-4542-1(8))* Trafford Publishing.

Sukhin, Igor. Gary's Adventures in Chess Country. 2009. (ENG., Illus.). 152p. (J). (gr. -1-12). 23.95 *(978-0-9791482-2-4(7))* Mongoose Pr.

Watson, John & Burgess, Graham. Chess Openings for Kids. 2011. (ENG.). 128p. 16.95 *(978-1-906454-26-5(4))* Gambit Pubns., Ltd. GBR. Dist: Two Rivers Distribution.

Watt, Fiona. Complete Book of Chess. 2004. (Chess Guides). (ENG., Illus.). 96p. (J). act. bk. ed. 17.95 *(978-0-7945-0371-0(3),* Usborne) EDC Publishing.

CHESS—FICTION

Blackwood, Gary. Curiosity. 2015. (ENG.). 336p. (J). (gr. 4-7). 8.99 *(978-0-14-242448-3(X),* Puffin Books) Penguin Young Readers Group.

Bontempelli, Massimo. The Chess Set in the Mirror. Gilson, Estelle, tr. from ITA. sto, illus. 2007. (Nautilus Ser.). (ENG.). 114p. (J). (gr. 7-9). per. 9.95 *(978-1-58988-031-3(5))* Dry, Paul Bks., Inc.

DeLaCroix, Alice. How to Survive a Totally Boring Summer. Fisher, Cynthia, illus. 2007. (ENG.). 96p. (J). (gr. 1-4). 16.95 *(978-0-8234-2024-7(8))* Holiday Hse., Inc.

Dion. Chess with Butterflies. 2006. (Illus.). 65p. (J). (gr. 4). pap. 4.95 *(978-1-881929-43-7(4))* Oxton Hse., Pubs.

Ellington, Kyseme Ali & Crawford, Bobby. I'mpossible: ChessLife Strategies for Children & Young Adults. 2010. 108p. pap. 32.95 *(978-1-4490-6741-0(7))* AuthorHouse.

Fairchild-Lenyo, Mary. When Winston Wins. Vigil, Cristina, illus. 2007. 36p. per. 14.95 *(978-1-59858-405-9(7))* Dog Ear Publishing, LLC.

Klass, David. Grandmaster. 2014. (ENG.). 240p. (YA). (gr. 7). 16.99 *(978-0-374-32771-2(8),* 9780374327712, Farrar, Straus & Giroux (BYR)) Farrar, Straus & Giroux.

Neri, G. Chess Rumble. Watson, Jesse Joshua, illus. 2007. (ENG.). 64p. (J). (gr. 3-7). 18.95 *(978-1-58430-279-7(8))* Lee & Low Bks., Inc.

Porter, Duane. Charlie & the Chess Set. 2012. 88p. pap. 12.99 *(978-0-9800993-4-8(X))* Buried Treasure Publishing.

Sawaski, James H. The Next Chess Team: A Novel. 2012. 120p. (gr. 10-12). pap. 10.95 *(978-1-4759-2425-1(9))* iUniverse, Inc.

Wong, Janet S. Alex & the Wednesday Chess Club. Schuett, Stacey, illus. 2004. (ENG.). 40p. (J). (gr. -1-3). 17.99 *(978-0-689-85890-1(6),* McElderry, Margaret K. Bks.) McElderry, Margaret K. Bks.

CHESTER CRICKET (FICTITIOUS CHARACTER)—FICTION

Selden, George. The Cricket in Times Square. Williams, Garth, illus. (Chester Cricket Ser.). 151p. (J). (gr. 3-6). pap. 5.50 *(978-0-8072-8311-0(8),* Listening Library) Random Hse. Audio Publishing Group.

—The Cricket in Times Square. unabr. ed. 2004. (Chester Cricket Ser.). 151p. (J). (gr. 3-7). pap. 29.00 incl. audio *(978-0-8072-8310-3(X),* S YA 158 SP, Listening Library) Random Hse. Audio Publishing Group.

CHET GECKO (FICTITIOUS CHARACTER)—FICTION

Hale, Bruce. Farewell, My Lunchbag. 2009. (Chet Gecko Ser.: 3). (ENG., Illus.). 128p. (J). (gr. 2-5). pap. 6.99 *(978-0-15-202629-5(0))* Houghton Mifflin Harcourt Publishing Co.

—Give My Regrets to Broadway. 2005. (Chet Gecko Mystery Ser.). (Illus.). 115p. (gr. 3-7). 16.00 *(978-0-7569-5247-1(6))* Perfection Learning Corp.

—The Hamster of the Baskervilles. 2003. (Chet Gecko Ser.: 5). (ENG., Illus.). 144p. (J). (gr. 2-5). pap. 6.99 *(978-0-15-202509-0(X))* Houghton Mifflin Harcourt Publishing Co.

—The Malted Falcon. 2007. (Chet Gecko Mystery Ser.). (Illus.). 107p. (J). (gr. 4-7). pap. 6.60 *(978-1-4189-5239-6(7))* Harcourt Trade Pubs.

—The Malted Falcon. 2008. (Chet Gecko Ser.: 7). (ENG., Illus.). 128p. (J). (gr. 2-5). pap. 5.99 *(978-0-15-216712-7(9))* Houghton Mifflin Harcourt Publishing Co.

—Murder, My Tweet. 2005. (Chet Gecko Ser.: 10). (ENG., Illus.). 144p. (J). (gr. 2-5). pap. 5.99 *(978-0-15-205219-5(4))* Houghton Mifflin Harcourt Publishing Co.

—This Gum for Hire. 2003. (Chet Gecko Ser.: 6). (ENG., Illus.). 144p. (J). (gr. 2-5). pap. 5.99 *(978-0-15-202497-0(2))* Houghton Mifflin Harcourt Publishing Co.

CHICAGO (ILL.)

Adams, Colleen. A Weekend in the City: Adding & Subtracting Times to the Nearest Minute. 2009. (PowerMath Ser.). (ENG., Illus.). 24p. (gr. 3-4). pap. 8.25 *(978-0-8239-8897-6(X)*, PowerKids Pr.) Rosen Publishing Group, Inc., The.

Carole Marsh. Chicago Coloring & Activity Book. 2004. (City Bks.). 24p. (gr. k-5). pap. 3.95 *(978-0-635-02227-1(3))* Gallopade International.

Endsley, Kezia. Michelle Obama: 44th First Lady & Health & Education Advocate. 2014. (Leading Women Ser.). 112p. (YA). (gr. 7-11). lib. bdg. 39.93 *(978-1-62712-975-6(8))* Cavendish Square Publishing.

Fishman, Jon M. Anthony Davis. 2015. (ENG., Illus.). 32p. (gr. 2-5). (J). 26.65 *(978-1-4677-9367-4(1)*, Lerner Pubns.); pap. 7.95 *(978-1-4677-9369-8(8))* Lerner Publishing Group.

Furstinger, Nancy. Chicago, 1 vol. 2005. (Cities Set 1 Ser.). (ENG., Illus.). 32p. (gr. k-6). 27.07 *(978-1-59197-857-2(2)*, Checkerboard Library) ABDO Publishing Co.

Gamble, Adam. Good Night Chicago. Veno, Joe, illus. 2006. (Good Night Our World Ser.). (ENG.). 20p. (J). (gr. k — 1). bds. 9.95 *(978-0-9777979-2-9(9))* Good Night Bks.

Grambo, Ashleigh Deese. C Is for Chicago. 2009. 32p. pap. 12.99 *(978-1-4389-4095-3(5))* AuthorHouse.

Laforest, Carine. Chicago Monsters. Mackay, Stephanie & Drouot, Lucile Danis, illus. 2017. (ENG.). 22p. (J). (gr. -1). bds. 9.99 **(978-2-924734-01-8(0))** City Monsters Bks. CAN. Dist: Publishers Group West (PGW).

Murray, Julie. Sears Tower, 1 vol. 2005. (Buddy Book Ser.). (ENG., Illus.). 24p. (gr. k-4). 25.65 *(978-1-59197-508-3(5)*, Buddy Bks.) ABDO Publishing Co.

Puck. 123 Chicago. Somers, Kevin, illus. 2009. (Cool Counting Bks.). (ENG.). 22p. (J). (gr. k — 1). bds. 8.95 *(978-0-9796213-5-2(6))* Duo Pr. LLC.

Segal, Robin. ABC in Chicago. 2007. (All 'Bout Cities Ser.). (ENG.). 32p. (J). (gr. -1-k). *(978-0-9719697-8-0(7))* Murray Hill Bks., LLC.

Stein, R. Conrad. The Great Chicago Fire. 2005. (Cornerstones of Freedom Ser.). (ENG., Illus.). 48p. (J). 26.00 *(978-0-516-23640-7(7)*, Children's Pr.) Scholastic Library Publishing.

Stine, Megan. Who Is Michelle Obama? O'brien, John & Harrison, Nancy, illus. 2013. (Who Was? Ser.). (ENG.). 112p. (J). (gr. 3-7). 5.99 *(978-0-448-47863-0(3)*, Grosset & Dunlap) Penguin Young Readers Group.

CHICAGO (ILL.)—FICTION

Aldis, Dorothy Keeley. We're Going to Town! Gehr, Mary, illus. 2011. 58p. 36.95 *(978-1-258-08388-5(4))* Literary Licensing, LLC.

Andracki, Zenon. Dear Ashley: A Middle Grade Novel. 2006. (ENG.). 84p. per. 19.95 *(978-1-4241-6168-3(1))* America Star Bks.

Andrews, Randall. The Last Guardian of Magic. 2008. 448p. (YA). per. 23.95 *(978-0-595-47345-8(8))* iUniverse, Inc.

Askew, Kim & Helmes, Amy. Anyone but You. 2014. (Twisted Lit Ser.). (ENG.). 224p. (YA). 17.99 *(978-1-4405-7001-8(9)*, Simon Pulse) Simon Pulse.

Augustyn, Heather. Chi-Town Coyote. 2005. 215p. pap. 12.59 *(978-1-4116-3365-0(2))* Lulu Pr., Inc.

Avasthi, Swati. Chasing Shadows. Phillips, Craig, illus. (ENG.). (YA). (gr. 9). 2015. 336p. pap. 10.99 *(978-0-375-86343-1(5)*, Ember) 2013. 320p. 17.99 *(978-0-375-86342-4(7)*, Knopf Bks. for Young Readers) 2013. 320p. lib. bdg. 20.99 *(978-0-375-96341-4(3)*, Knopf Bks. for Young Readers) Random Hse. Children's Bks.

Balliett, Blue. Hold Fast. 2015. (ENG.). 288p. (J). (gr. 3-7). pap. 6.99 *(978-0-545-29989-3(6)*, Scholastic Paperbacks) Scholastic, Inc.

—Pieces & Players. 2015. (ENG., Illus.). 320p. (J). (gr. 3-7). 17.99 *(978-0-545-29990-9(X)*, Scholastic Pr.) Scholastic, Inc.

—The Wright 3. Helquist, Brett, illus. 2008. 318p. (gr. 4-7). 18.00 *(978-0-7569-8942-2(6))* Perfection Learning Corp.

—The Wright 3. Helquist, Brett, illus. 2007. (ENG.). 352p. (J). (gr. 3-7). pap. 7.99 *(978-0-439-69368-4(3)*, Scholastic Paperbacks) Scholastic, Inc.

Bastian, Kimberlee Ann. The Orphan, the Soulcatcher, & the Black Blizzard. 2012. 258p. pap. 22.50 *(978-1-105-06633-7(9))* Lulu.com GBR. Dist: Lulu Pr., Inc.

Binns, B. A. Pull. 2010. 310p. (YA). (gr. 9-18). 16.95 *(978-1-934813-43-0(5))* Westside Bks.

Blejwas, Emily. Once You Know This. 2017. (ENG.). 240p. (J). (gr. 4-7). 16.99 **(978-1-5247-0097-3(5))**; lib. bdg. 19.99 **(978-1-5247-0098-0(3))** Random Hse. Children's Bks. (Delacorte Bks. for Young Readers).

Bloch, Robert. The Crowded Earth. 2009. 112p. 22.95 *(978-1-60664-648-9(6))*; pap. 9.95 *(978-1-60664-273-3(1))* Rodgers, Alan Bks.

Bowen, Fred. Playoff Dreams, 1 vol. 2009. (All-Star Sports Story Ser.). (ENG., Illus.). 112p. (J). pap. 5.95 *(978-1-56145-507-2(5))* Peachtree Pubs.

Burgess, B. L. Finding Hartagetu. 2009. 84p. pap. 10.59 *(978-1-4389-7741-6(7))* AuthorHouse.

Carlin, Pat. Cow Visits Chicago. 2010. 32p. 17.25 *(978-1-4269-2841-3(6))* Trafford Publishing.

Cast, P. C. & Cast, Kristin. Neferet's Curse. 2013. (House of Night Novellas Ser.: 3). (ENG., Illus.). 160p. (YA). (gr. 7). 12.99 *(978-1-250-00025-5(4)*, 9781250000255, St. Martin's Griffin) St. Martin's Pr.

Center for Learning Network Staff. The House on Mango Street: Curriculum Unit. 2005. (Novel Ser.). (YA). tchr. ed., spiral bd. 19.95 *(978-1-56077-783-0(4))* Center for Learning, The.

Cestari, Crystal. The Best Kind of Magic. 2017. (Windy City Magic Ser.). (ENG.). 336p. (YA). (gr. 7-12). 17.99 *(978-1-4847-5272-2(4))* Hyperion Bks. for Children.

Chapman, Fern Schumer. Is It Night or Day? 2010. (ENG.). 224p. (J). (gr. 5-9). 17.99 *(978-0-374-17744-7(9)*, 9780374177447, Farrar, Straus & Giroux (BYR)) Farrar, Straus & Giroux.

Codell, Esmé Raji. Sahara Special. 2003. (ENG., Illus.). 208p. (J). (gr. 3-7). pap. 16.49 *(978-0-7868-2627-8(4))* Hyperion Bks. for Children.

—Sahara Special. 2004. (ENG.). 192p. (J). (gr. 3-7). pap. 6.99 *(978-0-7868-1611-8(2))* Hyperion Pr.

—Vive la Paris. 2006. (ENG.). 224p. (gr. 4-7). 15.99 *(978-0-7868-5124-9(4))* Hyperion Pr.

Crawford, Laura. Postcards from Chicago/Postales Desde Chicago. de La Vega, Eida, tr. Adamson, Bonnie, illus. 2008. (Traveling with Anna Ser.). (ENG.). 32p. (J). (gr. 4-7). 16.95 *(978-0-9795477-4-4(1)*, Raven Tree Pr.,Csi) Continental Sales, Inc.

Dachman, Adam. The Player Piano Mouse. Julich, Jenniffer, illus. 2008. 32p. (J). 14.99 *(978-0-9797794-0-4(5))* Player Piano Mouse Productions (PPMP).

Deaver, Julie Reece. The Night I Disappeared. 2012. (ENG.). 256p. (YA). (gr. 7). pap. 12.99 *(978-1-4424-7298-3(7)*, Simon Pulse) Simon Pulse.

Dorr, Shay. Khloe Dutch! 2011. 48p. pap. 8.95 *(978-1-4502-8332-8(2))* iUniverse, Inc.

Du Jardin, Rosamond. Young & Fair. 2003. (YA). pap. 12.95 *(978-1-930009-79-0(8)*, 800-691-7779) Image Cascade Publishing.

Duey, Kathleen & Bale, Karen A. Fire: Chicago 1871. 2014. (Survivors Ser.). (ENG., Illus.). 176p. (J). (gr. 3-7). pap. 6.99 *(978-1-4424-9054-3(3)*, Aladdin) Simon & Schuster Children's Publishing.

—Fire: Chicago 1871. 2014. (Survivors Ser.). (ENG., Illus.). 176p. (J). (gr. 3-7). 16.99 *(978-1-4424-9055-0(1)*, Simon & Schuster/Paula Wiseman Bks.) Simon & Schuster/Paula Wiseman Bks.

Elkeles, Simone. How to Ruin a Summer Vacation. 2006. (How to Ruin a Summer Vacation Novel Ser.: 1). (ENG.). 240p. (YA). (gr. 8-12). per. 9.95 *(978-0-7387-0961-1(1)*, Flux) North Star Editions.

Ellen, Raskin. The Westing Game. 2014. (Puffin Modern Classics Ser.). (ENG.). 192p. (J). (gr. 5-12). 12.24 *(978-1-63245-142-2(5))* Lectorum Pubns., Inc.

Finley, Martha. Elsie at the World's Fair. 2007. (ENG.). 156p. pap. 19.99 *(978-1-4346-2508-3(7))* Creative Media Partners, LLC.

—Elsie at the Worlds Fair. 2006. 27.95 *(978-1-4218-2991-3(6))*; pap. 12.95 *(978-1-4218-3091-9(4))* 1st World Publishing, Inc.

—Elsie at the World's Fair. Lt. ed. 2007. 172p. pap. 21.99 *(978-1-4346-2550-2(8))* Creative Media Partners, LLC.

Flor Ada, Alma & Zubizarreta, Gabriel M. Con Cariño, Amalia. (SPA., Illus.). (J). (gr. 3-7). 2013. 160p. pap. 6.99 *(978-1-4424-2406-7(0))* 2012. 144p. 15.99 *(978-1-4424-2405-0(2)*, Atheneum Bks. for Young Readers) Simon & Schuster Children's Publishing.

—Love, Amalia. (ENG., Illus.). (J). (gr. 3-7). 2013. 160p. pap. 6.99 *(978-1-4424-2403-6(6))* 2012. 144p. 15.99 *(978-1-4424-2402-9(8))* Simon & Schuster Children's Publishing. (Atheneum Bks. for Young Readers).

Foley, Jessie Ann. Neighborhood Girls. 2017. 368p. (YA). (gr. 9). 17.99 **(978-0-06-257185-4(0)**, HarperTeen) HarperCollins Pubs.

Galang, M. Evelina. Angel de la Luna & the 5th Glorious Mystery. 2013. (ENG.). 304p. (J). (gr. 6). pap. 12.00 *(978-1-56689-333-6(X))* Coffee Hse. Pr.

Galbraith, Bree. Once upon a Balloon, 1 vol. Malenfant, Isabelle, illus. 2013. (ENG.). 32p. (J). (gr. -1-3). 19.95 *(978-1-4598-0324-4(8))* Orca Bk. Pubs. USA.

Goeglein, T. M. Cold Fury. 2013. (Cold Fury Novel Ser.: 1). (ENG.). 336p. (YA). (gr. 7). pap. 9.99 *(978-0-14-242631-9(8)*, Speak) Penguin Young Readers Group.

—Flicker & Burn. 2014. (Cold Fury Novel Ser.: 2). (ENG.). 368p. (YA). (gr. 7). pap. 9.99 *(978-0-14-751141-6(0)*, Speak) Penguin Young Readers Group.

Gottesfeld, Jeff. Xo Ronette. 2013. (Campus Confessions Ser.). (ENG.). 160p. (YA). (gr. 9-12). pap. 9.95 *(978-1-62250-701-6(0))* Saddleback Educational Publishing, Inc.

—Xo Ronette. 2013. (Campus Confessions Ser.: 1). (ENG.). 158p. (YA). (gr. 9-12). lib. bdg. 20.80 *(978-0-606-33998-8(1)*, Turtleback) Turtleback Bks.

Green, John. Will Grayson, Will Grayson. 2011. lib. bdg. 22.10 *(978-0-606-15358-4(6)*, Turtleback) Turtleback Bks.

Green, John & Levithan, David. Will Grayson, Will Grayson. 2015. (SPA.). 336p. (YA). (gr. 7). pap. 12.95 *(978-1-101-91070-2(4)*, Vintage Espanol) Knopf Doubleday Publishing Group.

—Will Grayson, Will Grayson. (ENG., (YA). (gr. 9-18). 2011. Illus.). 352p. 10.99 *(978-0-14-241847-5(1)*, Speak) 2010. 320p. 17.99 *(978-0-525-42158-0(0)*, Dutton Books for Young Readers) Penguin Young Readers Group.

Greenberg, Doris & Shandley, Pandré. The Legend of L'Esprit: Dance Legacy Series. 2011. 272p. pap. 15.95 *(978-1-4634-1800-7(0))* AuthorHouse.

Greg, Neri. Yummy: The Last Days of a Southside Shorty. 2014. (ENG.). 94p. (YA). (gr. k-3). 21.20 *(978-1-63245-250-4(2))* Lectorum Pubns., Inc.

Haesche, Richard, Sr. The Mystery of Monster Manor. 2007. (ENG.). 306p. (YA). 11.99 *(978-0-9798536-6-1(4))* Kreative X-Pressions Pubns.

Hamilton, Kersten. When the Stars Threw down Their Spears. 2014. (ENG.). 400p. (YA). (gr. 7). pap. 8.99 *(978-0-544-22771-2(9)*, HMH Books For Young Readers) Houghton Mifflin Harcourt Publishing Co.

Hannigan, Kate. The Detective's Assistant. 2015. (ENG.). 368p. (J). (gr. 3-7). 17.00 *(978-0-316-40351-1(2))* Little Brown & Co.

Harlow, Joan Hiatt. Firestorm! (ENG.). 336p. (J). (gr. 3-7). 2011. pap. 7.99 *(978-1-4169-8486-3(0))* 2010. (Illus.). 16.99 *(978-1-4169-8485-6(2))* McElderry, Margaret K. Bks. (McElderry, Margaret K. Bks.).

Hawley, Richard. Paul & Juliana: A Novel. 2003. 188p. (YA). 19.95 *(978-1-890862-33-6(9))* Bancroft Pr.

Hechtman, Betty Jacobson. Blue Schwartz & Nefertiti's Necklace: A Mystery with Recipes. 2006. 152p. (J). (gr. 5-9). per. 8.95 *(978-0-9768126-3-0(0))* Brown Barn Bks.

Herman, Charlotte. My Chocolate Year: A Novel with 12 Recipes. Pham, LeUyen, illus. 2008. (ENG.). 176p. (J). (gr. 3-7). 15.99 *(978-1-4169-3341-0(7)*, Simon & Schuster Bks. For Young Readers) Simon & Schuster Bks. For Young Readers.

Jacobs, Lily. The Littlest Bunny in Chicago: An Easter Adventure. 2015. (ENG.). 32p. (J). (-3). 9.99 *(978-1-4926-1051-9(8)*, Sourcebooks Jabberwocky) Sourcebooks, Inc.

James, Eric. A Halloween Scare in Chicago. Le Ray, Marina, illus. 2014. (ENG.). 32p. (J). (-5). 9.99 *(978-1-4926-0579-9(4)*, 9781492605799, Sourcebooks Jabberwocky) Sourcebooks, Inc.

—Santa's Sleigh Is on Its Way to Chicago: A Christmas Adventure. Dunn, Robert, illus. 2016. (ENG.). 32p. (J). (-2). 12.99 *(978-1-4926-4323-4(8)*, 9781492643234, Sourcebooks Jabberwocky) Sourcebooks, Inc.

Jenkins, Jerry B. & Fabry, Chris. Windy City Danger. 2006. (Red Rock Mysteries Ser.: 11). (ENG.). 246p. (YA). (gr. 8-12). per. 6.99 *(978-1-4143-0150-1(2)*, Tyndale Kids) Tyndale Hse. Pubs.

Jitchotvisut, Donna M. Mittens for Christmas. 2009. 376p. 31.95 *(978-1-4401-0372-8(0))*; pap. 21.95 *(978-1-4401-0370-4(4))* iUniverse, Inc.

Kelly, David A. The Wrigley Riddle. Meyers, Mark, illus. 2013. (Ballpark Mysteries Ser.: Bk. 6). (ENG.). 112p. (J). (gr. 1-4). pap. 4.99 *(978-0-307-97776-2(5)*, Random Hse. Bks. for Young Readers) Random Hse. Children's Bks.

—The Wrigley Riddle. 2013. (Ballpark Mysteries Ser.: Bk. 6). lib. bdg. 14.75 *(978-0-606-26998-8(3)*, Turtleback) Turtleback Bks.

Kimpton, Paul & Kimpton, Ann Kaczkowski. Summer of Firsts: WWII Is Ending, but the Music Adventures Are Just Beginning. 2013. (Adventures with Music Ser.: 3). (ENG., Illus.). 288p. (J). (gr. 4-7). pap. 8.95 *(978-1-57999-972-8(7))* G I A Pubns., Inc.

King, Deja. Ride Wit' Me: A Novel. 2009. 151p. (YA). pap. *(978-0-9755811-9-3(8))* King Production, A.

King, Katina. Ride Wit' Me: A Young Adult Urban Tale. 2006. 144p. (J). per. 12.00 *(978-0-9724003-8-1(9))* Power Play Media.

Klimo, Kate. Cinders. Sanderson, Ruth, illus. 2016. (Horse Diaries). (ENG.). 176p. (J). (gr. 3-7). pap. 7.99 *(978-1-101-93690-0(8)*, Random Hse. Bks. for Young Readers) Random Hse. Children's Bks.

—Sparky. Jessell, Tim, illus. 2016. (Dog Diaries: 9). (ENG.). 160p. (J). (gr. 2-5). pap. 7.99 *(978-0-553-53493-1(9)*, Random Hse. Bks. for Young Readers) Random Hse. Children's Bks.

Klise, James. The Art of Secrets. 2014. (ENG.). 272p. (YA). (gr. 7-10). 16.95 *(978-1-61620-195-1(9)*, 73195) Algonquin Bks. of Chapel Hill.

Laberje, Reji. Max Explores Chicago. Fenech, Liza, illus. 2014. (Max Explores Ser.). (ENG.). 20p. (J). (— 1). bds. 9.95 *(978-1-62937-003-3(7))* Triumph Bks.

Larkin, Jillian. Vixen. 2011. (Flappers Ser.). (ENG.). 448p. (YA). (gr. 7). pap. 9.99 *(978-0-385-74035-7(2)*, Ember) Random Hse. Children's Bks.

Lockwood, Cara. Wuthering High: At Boarding School, No One Can Hear Your Scream. 2006. (Bard Academy Ser.: 1). (ENG.). 272p. (gr. 8-12). pap. 17.99 *(978-1-4165-2475-5(4)*, MTV Bks.) MTV Books.

Lollino, Jessica. Little Lily Mays & the Daddy Dilemma. Kendrick-TaZiyah, Brandi, illus. 2006. (Little Lily Mays Ser.: vol. 1). 32p. (J). per. 20.00 *(978-0-9712383-1-2(6))* Culturatti Ink.

Long, Loren & Bildner, Phil. Great Balls of Fire. Long, Loren, illus. 2009. (Sluggers Ser.: 3). (ENG., Illus.). 224p. (J). (gr. 3-7). pap. 7.99 *(978-1-4169-1889-9(2)*, Simon & Schuster Bks. For Young Readers) Simon & Schuster Bks. For Young Readers.

Lyons, Stefanie. Dating Down. 2015. (ENG., Illus.). 312p. (YA). pap. 9.99 *(978-0-7387-4337-0(2)*, Flux) North Star Editions.

Magoon, Kekla. Fire in the Streets. 2013. (ENG., Illus.). 352p. (J). (gr. 5-9). pap. 7.99 *(978-1-4424-2231-5(9)*, Aladdin) Simon & Schuster Children's Publishing.

Magoon, Kekla & Keene, Carolyn. Strangers on a Train. 2013. (Nancy Drew Diaries: 2). (ENG.). 208p. (J). (gr. 3-7). pap. 6.99 *(978-1-4169-9073-4(9)*, Aladdin) Simon & Schuster Children's Publishing.

Malone, Marianne. Stealing Magic. Call, Greg, illus. 2012. (Sixty-Eight Rooms Adventures Ser.). (ENG.). 256p. (J). (gr. 3-7). 16.99 *(978-0-375-86819-1(4)*, Random Hse. Bks. for Young Readers) Random Hse. Children's Bks.

Mantell, Paul & Christopher, Matt. Snowboard Champ. 2005. (Matt Christopher Sports Ser.). 146p. (gr. 3-7). 16.00 *(978-0-7569-5198-6(4))* Perfection Learning Corp.

Margo's Magic Trunk. 2006. (Illus.). 32p. (J). pap. 6.95 *(978-0-9789016-0-8(6))* Jodaviste Publishing.

Marsh, Carole. The Mystery of the Missing Dinosaurs. 2009. (Real Kids, Real Places Ser.). 146p. (J). 18.99 *(978-0-635-06995-5(4)*, Marsh, Carole Mysteries) Gallopade International.

—The Mystery of the Missing Dinosaurs (Hardcover) 2003. 160p. (gr. 2-8). 14.95 *(978-0-635-01662-1(1))* Gallopade International.

Martinez, Claudia Guadalupe. Pig Park. 2014. (ENG.). 248p. (J). 15.95 *(978-1-935955-76-4(4))* Cinco Puntos Pr.

Martinez, Jessica. Virtuosity. (ENG.). (YA). (gr. 9). 2012. 320p. pap. 9.99 *(978-1-4424-2053-3(7))* 2011. 304p. 16.99 *(978-1-4424-2052-6(9))* Simon Pulse. (Simon Pulse).

Matthews, Curtis. Boots Meets the Grizzly Bears. 2007. 164p. per. 13.95 *(978-1-4343-3372-8(8))* AuthorHouse.

McMann, Lisa. Bang. (Visions Ser.: 2). (ENG., (YA). (gr. 9). 2014. Illus.). 272p. pap. 9.99 *(978-1-4424-6628-9(6))* 2013. 256p. 16.99 *(978-1-4424-6625-8(1))* Simon Pulse. (Simon Pulse).

Meyerhoff, Jenny. Green Thumbs-Up! Chatelain, Éva, illus. 2015. (Friendship Garden Ser.: 1). (ENG.). 176p. (J). (gr. 2-5). pap. 5.99 *(978-1-4814-3904-6(9)*, Aladdin) Simon & Schuster Children's Publishing.

—Sweet Peas & Honeybees. 2016. (Friendship Garden Ser.: 4). lib. bdg. 16.00 *(978-0-606-38978-5(4))* Turtleback Bks.

Monsell, Mary Elise. A Fish Named Yum Vol. IV: MR. PIN. 2007. 72p. (gr. 1-4). per. 8.95 *(978-0-595-47246-8(X)*, Backinprint.com) iUniverse, Inc.

—The Spy Who Came North from the Pole. 2007. 68p. (gr. -1-3). per. 8.95 *(978-0-595-47248-2(6)*, Backinprint.com) iUniverse, Inc.

Mosley, Walter. When the Thrill Is Gone, 3 vols. 2012. (Leonid McGill Mystery Ser.: Bk. 3). (ENG.). 384p. (gr. 12). 16.00 *(978-0-451-23565-7(7)*, Berkley) Penguin Publishing Group.

Mula, Tom. The Hackers of Oz. 2012. 272p. (-18). 21.95 *(978-1-4575-1562-0(8))*; pap. 14.99 *(978-1-4575-1564-4(4))* Dog Ear Publishing, LLC.

Naylor, Phyllis Reynolds. Cuckoo Feathers, 0 vols. Ramsey, Marcy, illus. 2009. (Simply Sarah Ser.: 0). (ENG.). 96p. (J). (gr. 2-5). pap. 6.99 *(978-0-7614-5541-7(8)*, 9780761455417, Amazon Children's Publishing) Amazon Publishing.

Neill, Chloe. Charmfall. 2012. (Dark Elite Ser.: 3). (ENG.). 288p. (YA). (gr. 9). 9.99 *(978-0-451-23080-5(9)*, Berkley) Penguin Publishing Group.

—Firespell: A Novel of the Dark Elite. 2010. (Dark Elite Ser.: 1). (ENG.). 256p. (YA). (gr. 9-18). 6.99 *(978-0-451-22886-4(3)*, Berkley) Penguin Publishing Group.

Pauley, Kimberly. Cat Girl's Day Off, 1 vol. 2012. (ENG.). 336p. (YA). 17.95 *(978-1-60060-883-4(3)*, Tu Bks.) Lee & Low Bks., Inc.

Pearsall, Shelley. All Shook Up. 2009. (ENG.). 272p. (J). (gr. 3-7). 6.99 *(978-0-440-42139-9(X)*, Yearling) Random Hse. Children's Bks.

Peck, Richard. Fair Weather. 2003. (Illus.). 146p. (gr. 4-7). 17.00 *(978-0-7569-1376-2(4))* Perfection Learning Corp.

—Fair Weather. 2004. 146p. (J). (gr. 5-9). pap. 36.00 incl. audio *(978-0-8072-2038-2(8)*, Listening Library) Random Hse. Audio Publishing Group.

Pinkwater, Daniel M. The Education of Robert Nifkin. 2005. (ENG.). 192p. (YA). (gr. 7). pap. 12.95 *(978-0-618-55208-5(1))* Houghton Mifflin Harcourt Publishing Co.

Polacco, Patricia. Fiona's Lace. Polacco, Patricia, illus. 2014. (ENG., Illus.). 48p. (J). (gr. -1-3). 17.99 *(978-1-4424-8724-6(0)*, Simon & Schuster/Paula Wiseman Bks.) Simon & Schuster/Paula Wiseman Bks.

Polikoff, Barbara Garland. Her Mother's Secret. 2012. (ENG.). 184p. (YA). pap. 14.99 *(978-0-9831938-7-6(8))* Allium Pr. of Chicago.

Powell, Maud Macrory. City of Grit & Gold. 2017. (ENG.). 164p. (J). (gr. 4-6). pap. 16.99 **(978-0-9967558-5-6(3))** Allium Pr. of Chicago.

Poyner, James R. Toy-Maker's Apprentice. 2006. 67p. per. 12.00 *(978-1-60002-282-1(0)*, 4145) Mountain Valley Publishing, LLC.

Raskin, Ellen. The Westing Game. 2003. 182p. (J). lib. bdg. 15.00 *(978-1-4242-2271-1(0))* Fitzgerald Bks.

Robbins, Trina. The Maltese Mummy. Page, Tyler, illus. 2011. (Chicagoland Detective Agency Ser.: 2). (ENG.). 64p. (gr. 4-8). 29.27 *(978-0-7613-4615-9(5))* Lerner Publishing Group.

—A Midterm Night's Scheme. Page, Tyler, illus. 2014. (Chicagoland Detective Agency Ser.: 6). (ENG.). 64p. (gr. 4-8). lib. bdg. 29.27 *(978-0-7613-8167-9(8)*, Graphic Universe™) Lerner Publishing Group.

Robinet, Harriette Gillem. Missing from Haymarket Square. 2003. (ENG., Illus.). 142p. (J). (gr. 4-7). pap. 8.99 *(978-0-689-85490-3(0)*, Simon & Schuster/Paula Wiseman Bks.) Simon & Schuster/Paula Wiseman Bks.

Rosebrock, Katie. Tabitha & Dundee: A Story of Friendship. 2013. 16p. pap. 15.99 *(978-1-4817-1257-6(8))* AuthorHouse.

Roth, Veronica. Divergent. 2014. (Divergent Ser.). (ENG.). 496p. (J). 14.24 *(978-1-63245-208-5(1))* Lectorum Pubns., Inc.

Schomer-Wendel, Gretchen & Schomer, Adam Anthony. Becka Goes to Chicago. 2009. (Becka & the Big Bubble Ser.). (Illus.). 32p. (J). (gr. -1-2). 22.60 *(978-1-60754-119-6(X))*; pap. 10.55 *(978-1-60754-120-2(3))* Windmill Bks.

Selzer, Adam. Just Kill Me. 2016. (ENG., Illus.). 336p. (YA). (gr. 9). 17.99 *(978-1-4814-3494-2(2)*, Simon & Schuster Bks. For Young Readers) Simon & Schuster Bks. For Young Readers.

Silvano, Wendi. Love Is All Around Chicago. Czernichowska, Joanna, illus. 2016. (ENG.). 32p. (J). (-6). 12.99 *(978-1-4926-2912-2(X)*, Sourcebooks Jabberwocky) Sourcebooks, Inc.

Sinclair, Upton, et al. The Jungle. (Classics Illustrated Ser.). (Illus.). 52p. (YA). pap. 4.95 *(978-1-57209-025-5(1))* Classics International Entertainment, Inc.

Skewes, John & Mullin, Michael. Larry Gets Lost in Chicago. Skewes, John, illus. 2010. (Larry Gets Lost Ser.). (ENG., Illus.). 32p. (J). (gr. -1-2). 16.99 *(978-1-57061-619-8(1)*, Little Bigfoot) Sasquatch Bks.

Smallman, Steve. Santa Is Coming to Chicago. Dunn, Robert, illus. 2012. (ENG.). 32p. (J). (-3). 9.99 *(978-1-4022-7509-8(9)*, Sourcebooks Jabberwocky) Sourcebooks, Inc.

—Santa Is Coming to Naperville. Dunn, Robert, illus. 2013. (ENG.). 32p. (J). (-3). 9.99 *(978-1-4022-9063-3(2)*, Sourcebooks Jabberwocky) Sourcebooks, Inc.

Smith, Jennifer E. The Comeback Season. 2008. (ENG.). 256p. (YA). (gr. 8). 15.99 *(978-1-4169-3847-7(8)*, Simon & Schuster Bks. For Young Readers) Simon & Schuster Bks. For Young Readers.

Smith, Roland & Spradlin, Michael P. The Windy City, Bk.5. 2014. (I, Q Ser.). (ENG.). 240p. (YA). (gr. 5-7). 9.99 *(978-1-58536-823-5(7)*, 202902) Sleeping Bear Pr.

Springer, Kristina. The Espressologist. 2011. (ENG.). 208p. (YA). (gr. 7-12). pap. 15.99 *(978-0-312-65923-3(7))* Square Fish.

Stein, R. Conrad. Someone Talked! 2011. (ENG.). 146p. (J). pap. 8.95 *(978-1-935178-17-0(2)*, ChironBooks) Coleman/Perrin.

Stevens, Charles McCellan. The Adventures of Uncle Jeremiah & Family at the Great Fair: Their Observations & Triumphs. 2007. (ENG.). 186p. pap. 19.99 *(978-1-4346-5343-7(9))*; 212p. pap. 22.99 *(978-1-4346-5344-4(7))* Creative Media Partners, LLC.

Stokes, Jordan & Belinkie, Matt. Gilded Delirium. 2007. (YA). pap. *(978-1-4114-9670-5(1)*, Spark Publishing Group) Sterling Publishing Co., Inc.

Stoklasa, JoAnne. Oliver & I: The Long Way Home. 2012. 20p. pap. 11.59 *(978-1-4669-5287-4(3))* Trafford Publishing.

Sully, Katherine. Night-Night Chicago. Kolanovic, Dubravka & Poole, Helen, illus. 2016. (ENG.). 20p. (J). (-1). bds. 9.99 *(978-1-4926-3935-0(4)*, 9781492639350, Sourcebooks Jabberwocky) Sourcebooks, Inc.

Tarshis, Lauren. I Survived the Great Chicago Fire 1871. 2015. (I Survived Ser.: 11). (ENG., Illus.). 112p. (J). (gr. 2-5). pap. 4.99 *(978-0-545-65846-1(2))* Scholastic, Inc.

Thill, Mary Kay. Wablenica: The Tale of a Lakotah Orphan. 2004. 240p. (J). per. *(978-0-9743908-0-2(1)*, 1232791) Balance Bks., Inc.

C D

Tibensky, Arlaina. And Then Things Fall Apart. 2011. (ENG.). 272p. (YA). (gr. 9). pap. 9.99 (978-1-4424-1323-8(9), Simon Pulse) Simon Pulse.

TJ & the Mysterious Stranger. 2004. (J). bds. 16.95 (978-0-9710487-2-0(X)) Highlights of Chicago Pr.

Trees, Annie Mae. The Old Apartment Building: A Tale from the Trees. 2012. 24p. 24.95 (978-1-4626-6093-3(2)) America Star Bks.

Tubb, Kristin O'Donnell. Selling Hope. 2010. (ENG.). 224p. (YA). (gr. 5-9). 29.99 (978-0-312-61122-4(6), 9780312611224) Feiwel & Friends.

Walsh, Alice. Pomiuk, Prince of the North. Whitehead, Jerry, illus. 2006. (ENG.). 64p. (J). (gr. 3). pap., tchr. ed. 6.95 (978-0-88878-447-6(3)) Dundurn CAN. Dist: Ingram Publisher Services.

Wartik, David J. The Vonnesta Project. 2006. 140p. (J). (gr. 3-6). pap. 12.95 (978-1-59113-938-6(4)) Booklocker.com, Inc.

Welling, Peter J. Darlene Halloween & the Great Chicago Fire, 1 vol. Welling, Peter J., illus. 2007. (ENG., Illus.). 32p. (J). (gr. k-3). 16.99 (978-1-58980-479-1(1)) Pelican Publishing Co., Inc.

Wendel, Gretchen Schomer & Schomer, Adam Anthony. Becka Goes to Chicago. Renthrope, Damon, illus. 2008. (ENG.). 36p. (J). (gr. -1-3). 11.99 (978-1-933754-52-9(4)) Waterside Publishing.

Woodson, J. L. The Things I Could Tell You! Malone, Susan Mary et al, eds. collector's ed. 2003. 206p. pap. 14.95 (978-0-9702699-6-6(X)) Macro Publishing Group.

Yaroslavskaya, Lyudmila. The Great Lakes Legends & Fairy Tales. 2006. (ENG & RUS., Illus.). (J). per. (978-0-9791248-0-8(8)) Yaroslavskaya, Lyudmila.

Zettel, Sarah. Bad Luck Girl. 2014. (American Fairy Trilogy Ser.: Bk. 3). (ENG.). 368p. (YA). (gr. 7). 17.99 (978-0-375-86940-2(9), Random Hse. Bks. for Young Readers) Random Hse. Children's Bks.

CHICAGO (ILL.)—HISTORY

Andrews McMeel Publishing LLC Staff. Chicago. 2014. (ENG.). 12p. (J). bds. 12.99 (978-1-4494-6028-0(3)) Andrews McMeel Publishing.

Bartlett, Karen T. A Kid's Guide to Chicago. Brown, Don, illus. 2010. 64p. pap. 16.95 (978-1-934907-03-0(0)) Twin Lights Pubs., Inc.

Bennie, Paul. The Great Chicago Fire Of 1871. 2008. (Great Historic Disasters Ser.). (Illus.). 128p. (gr. 5-8). lib. bdg. 35.00 (978-0-7910-9638-3(6), Chelsea Hse.) Facts On File, Inc.

Boehm Jerome, Kate. Chicago & the State of Illinois: Cool Stuff Every Kid Should Know. 2011. (Arcadia Kids Ser.). (ENG., Illus.). 48p. (J). (gr. 3-6). pap. 9.99 (978-1-4396-0100-6(3)) Arcadia Publishing.

Brexel, Bernadette. The Knights of Labor & the Haymarket Riot: The Fight for an Eight-Hour Workday. 2004. (America's Industrial Society in the 19th Century Ser.). (ENG., Illus.). 32p. (gr. 5-8). pap. 10.00 (978-0-8239-4283-1(X)) Rosen Publishing Group, Inc., The.

Cleland, JoAnn. Surviving the Great Chicago Fire. 2009. (ENG., Illus.). 32p. (gr. 4-8). pap. 9.95 (978-1-60694-549-0(1)) Rourke Educational Media.

Dell, Pamela. Chicago City of Big Shoulders. 2016. (Spring Forward Ser.). (J). (gr. 2). (978-1-4900-9460-1(1)) Benchmark Education Co.

Diemer, Lauren. Sears Tower. 2009. (Structural Wonders Ser.). (Illus.). 32p. (J). (gr. 4-6). 9.95 (978-1-60596-139-2(6)); lib. bdg. 26.00 (978-1-60596-138-5(8)) Weigl Pubs., Inc.

Dybwad, G. L. & Bliss, Joy V. White City Recollections: The Illustrated 1893 Diary of Friend Pitts Williams' Trip to the World's Columbian Exposition. 2nd ed. 2003. (Illus.). 180p. per. 18.95 (978-0-9631612-2-2(9)) Bk. Stops Here.

Epstein, Brad M. Chicago 101: My First City-Board-book. l.t. ed. 2009. (101 — My First Text-Board Books). (Illus.). 24p. (J). (978-1-60730-001-4(X), 101 Bk.) Michaelson Entertainment.

—Chicago Bears 101. 2010. (Illus.). 28p. (J). bds. (978-1-60730-105-9(9), 101 Bk.) Michaelson Entertainment.

Herzog, Brad. W Is for Wrigley: A Friendly Confines Alphabet. Hanley, John, illus. 2013. (ENG.). (J). (978-1-58536-816-7(4)) Sleeping Bear Pr.

Hurd, Owen. Chicago History for Kids: Triumphs & Tragedies of the Windy City Includes 21 Activities. 2007. (For Kids Ser.). (ENG., Illus.). 192p. (J). (gr. 4-7). pap. 16.95 (978-1-55652-654-1(7)) Chicago Review Pr., Inc.

Johnson, Robin. The Great Chicago Fire. 2016. (ENG., Illus.). 48p. (J). pap. (978-0-7787-2235-9(X)) Crabtree Publishing Co.

Layne, Steven, et al. W Is for Windy City: A Chicago City Alphabet. Hays, Michael, illus. 2010. (Sleeping Bear City Alphabet Ser.). (ENG.). 40p. (J). 17.95 (978-1-58536-420-6(7)) Sleeping Bear Pr.

Lewis, Anna. City Doodles - Chicago, 1 vol. Chaffin, Daniel, illus. 2013. (ENG.). 240p. (J). pap. 9.99 (978-1-4236-3479-9(9)) Gibbs Smith, Publisher.

Marx, Christy. The Great Chicago Fire of 1871. 2004. (Tragic Fires Throughout History Ser.). (Illus.). 48p. (gr. 5-8). lib. bdg. 29.25 (978-0-8239-4487-3(5), Rosen Reference) Rosen Publishing Group, Inc., The.

—The Great Chicago Fire Of 1871. 2009. (Tragic Fires Throughout History Ser.). 48p. (gr. 5-8). 53.00 (978-1-60854-582-7(2), Rosen Reference) Rosen Publishing Group, Inc., The.

Matthews, Rupert. You Wouldn't Want to Be a Chicago Gangster! Some Dangerous Characters You'd Better Avoid. Bergin, Mark, illus. 2010. (You Wouldn't Want to Ser.). (ENG.). 32p. (J). (gr. 3-18). pap. 9.95 (978-0-531-22825-8(8)) Scholastic Library Publishing.

Matthews, Rupert & Salariya, David. You Wouldn't Want to Be a Chicago Gangster! Some Dangerous Characters You'd Better Avoid. Bergin, Mark, illus. 2010. (You Wouldn't Want to Ser.). (ENG.). 32p. (J). 29.00 (978-0-531-20470-2(7)) Scholastic Library Publishing.

McHugh, Janet. The Great Chicago Fire. 2007. (Code Red Ser.). (Illus.). 32p. (YA). (gr. 2-5). lib. bdg. 25.27 (978-1-59716-360-6(0)) Bearport Publishing Co., Inc.

Murphy, Jim. The Great Fire. 2006. (Illus.). 144p. (gr. 4-7). 23.00 (978-0-7569-6632-4(9)) Perfection Learning Corp.

—The Great Fire. 2006. (ENG., Illus.). 144p. (J). (gr. 4-7). pap. 12.99 (978-0-439-20307-4(4), Scholastic Paperbacks) Scholastic, Inc.

Ogintz, Eileen. Kid's Guide to Chicago. 2013. (Kid's Guides Ser.). (ENG., Illus.). 160p. pap. 12.95 (978-0-7627-9231-3(0)) Globe Pequot Pr., The.

O'Neal, Claire. Chicago. 2010. (Class Trip Ser.). (Illus.). 48p. (J). (gr. 2-5). lib. bdg. 29.95 (978-1-58415-881-3(6)) Mitchell Lane Pubs., Inc.

Owens, L. L. The Great Chicago Fire, 1 vol. 2007. (Essential Events Set 1 Ser.). (ENG., Illus.). 112p. (J). (gr. 6-12). lib. bdg. 35.64 (978-1-59928-851-2(6)) ABDO Publishing Co.

Pascal, Janet. What Was the Great Chicago Fire? 2016. (What Was? Ser.). (ENG., Illus.). 112p. (J). (gr. 3-7). 5.99 (978-0-399-54158-2(6), Penguin Workshop); lib. bdg. 15.99 (978-0-399-54238-1(8), Grosset & Dunlap) Penguin Young Readers Group.

—What Was the Great Chicago Fire? 2016. (What Was... ? Ser.). (ENG.). 112p. (J). (gr. 3-7). 16.00 (978-0-606-39318-8(8)) Turtleback Bks.

Publications International Ltd. Staff. Yesterday & Today Chicago. 2008. 192p. 24.95 (978-1-4127-1574-4(1)) Publications International, Ltd.

Regan, Michael. The Great Chicago Fire: A Cause-And-Effect Investigation. 2016. (Cause-And-Effect Disasters Ser.). (ENG., Illus.). 40p. (J). (gr. 4-6). 30.65 (978-1-5124-1120-1(5)); 46.65 (978-1-5124-1130-0(2), Lerner Pubns.) Lerner Publishing Group.

Rudolph, Jessica. Chicago. 2017. (Citified! Ser.). (ENG.). 24p. (J). (gr. k-3). 17.95 **(978-1-68402-234-2(7))** Bearport Publishing Co., Inc.

Skewes, John. Chicago ABC. 2016. (Larry Gets Lost Ser.). (ENG., Illus.). 32p. (J). (-k). 14.99 (978-1-57061-993-9(X), Little Bigfoot) Sasquatch Bks.

—Larry Loves Chicago! Skewes, John, illus. 2014. (Larry Gets Lost Ser.). (ENG., Illus.). 20p. (J). (— 1). bds. 9.99 (978-1-57061-913-7(1), Little Bigfoot) Sasquatch Bks.

Staton, Hilarie. Chicago. 2016. (Dropping in On Ser.). (ENG., Illus.). 32p. (gr. 2-4). 32.79 (978-1-68191-406-0(9)) Rourke Educational Media.

Stine, Megan. Who Is Michelle Obama? 2013. (Who Is... ? Ser.). lib. bdg. 14.75 (978-0-606-32131-0(4), Turtleback) Turtleback Bks.

Turner, Bernard. Our Chicago — People & Places. 2006. pap. 5.95 (978-0-9710487-1-3(1)) Highlights of Chicago Pr.

Yancey, Diane. Al Capone's Chicago. 2003. (Travel Guide to Ser.). (ENG., Illus.). 112p. (J). 30.85 (978-1-59018-248-2(0), Lucent Bks.) Cengage Gale.

Zable, Stacey. City by the Lake. 2011. (Early Connections Ser.). (J). (978-1-61672-659-1(8)) Benchmark Education Co.

Zourelias, Diana. All Around Chicago Mini Coloring Book. 2015. (Dover Little Activity Bks.). (ENG.). 64p. (J). (gr. k-3). pap. 1.99 (978-0-486-79750-2(3)) Dover Pubns., Inc.

Zschock, Martha Day. Hello, Chicago! 2013. (Hello! Ser.). (ENG., Illus.). 16p. (J). (gr. -1-k). bds. 9.95 (978-1-933212-72-2(1), Commonwealth Editions) Applewood Bks.

CHICAGO BEARS (FOOTBALL TEAM)

Burgess, Zack. Meet the Chicago Bears. 2016. (Big Picture Sports Ser.). (ENG., Illus.). 24p. (J). (gr. k-3). lib. bdg. 22.60 (978-1-59953-723-8(0)) Norwood Hse. Pr.

Frisch, Aaron. Chicago Bears. (Super Bowl Champions Ser.). (J). (gr. 1-3). 2011. 24.25 (978-1-60818-015-8(8)) 2005. (Illus.). 24p. lib. bdg. 16.95 (978-1-58341-381-4(2), Creative Education) Creative Co., The.

—Chicago Bears. 2014. (Illus.). 24p. (J). (978-1-60818-373-9(4), Creative Education) Creative Co., The.

—The History of the Chicago Bears. 2004. (NFL Today Ser.). (Illus.). 32p. (YA). (gr. 5-9). 18.95 (978-1-58341-291-6(3)) Creative Co., The.

Holmes, Parker. Packers vs. Bears. 2014. (J). (978-1-4777-2791-1(4), PowerKids Pr.) Rosen Publishing Group, Inc., The.

Howell, Brian. Chicago Bears. 2015. (Insider's Guide to Pro Football Ser.). (ENG.). 32p. (J). (gr. k-3). 28.50 (978-1-63407-007-2(0), 208842) Child's World, Inc., The.

LeBoutillier, Nate. The Story of the Chicago Bears. 2009. (NFL Today Ser.). 48p. (YA). (gr. 5-9). 22.95 (978-1-58341-750-8(8)) Creative Co., The.

MacRae, Sloan. The Chicago Bears. 2011. (America's Greatest Teams Ser.). (Illus.). 24p. (J). pap. 8.25 (978-1-4488-2749-7(3)); lib. bdg. 22.60 (978-1-4488-2580-6(6)) Rosen Publishing Group, Inc., The. (PowerKids Pr.).

Morey, Allan. The Chicago Bears Story. 2016. (NFL Teams Ser.). (ENG., Illus.). 32p. (J). (gr. 3-7). lib. bdg. 26.95 (978-1-62617-360-6(5), Torque Bks.) Bellwether Media.

Publications International Ltd. Staff. Yesterday & Today Nfl Chicago Bears. 2009. 160p. 9.95 (978-1-4127-6117-8(4)) Publications International, Ltd.

Stewart, Mark. The Chicago Bears. rev. ed. 2012. (Team Spirit Ser.). (ENG.). 48p. (J). (gr. 3-6). lib. bdg. 29.27 (978-1-59953-517-3(3)) Norwood Hse. Pr.

Uschan, Michael V. Brian Urlacher. (Superstars of Pro Football Ser.). 64p. (YA). (gr. 7-12). 2009. (Illus.). lib. bdg. 22.95 (978-1-4222-0555-6(X)) 2007. pap. 9.95 (978-1-4222-0838-0(9)) Mason Crest.

Whiting, Jim. NFL Today: Chicago Bears. 2013. (NFL Today Ser.). (ENG., Illus.). 48p. (J). (gr. 4-7). pap. 12.00 (978-0-89812-850-5(1), Creative Paperbacks) Creative Co., The.

—The Story of the Chicago Bears. 2013. (Illus.). 48p. (J). 35.65 (978-1-60818-297-8(5), Creative Education) Creative Co., The.

Wyner, Zach. Chicago Bears. 2015. (Illus.). 32p. (J). (978-1-4896-0802-4(8)) Weigl Pubs., Inc.

Zappa, Marcia. Chicago Bears, 1 vol. 2014. (NFL's Greatest Teams Ser.). (ENG.). 32p. (gr. 7-11). lib. bdg. 28.50 (978-1-62403-359-9(8), Big Buddy Bks.) ABDO Publishing Co.

CHICAGO CUBS (BASEBALL TEAM)

Castle, George. Chicago Cubs, 1 vol. (Inside MLB Ser.). (ENG., Illus.). 48p. (gr. 3-6). 2011. (YA). lib. bdg. 32.79 (978-1-61714-038-9(4)) 2014. (J). lib. bdg. 32.79 (978-1-62403-464-0(0), SportsZone) ABDO Publishing Co.

Connery-Boyd, Peg. Chicago Cubs. 2016. (Hawk's Nest Activity Bks.: 0). (ENG.). 64p. (J). (gr. k-3). pap., act. bk. ed. 8.99 (978-1-4926-3364-8(X), 9781492633648) Sourcebooks, Inc.

Gilbert, Sara. Chicago Cubs. 2013. (Illus.). 24p. (J). 25.65 (978-1-60818-261-9(4), Creative Education) Creative Co., The.

—The Story of the Chicago Cubs. 2011. (J). 35.65 (978-1-60818-035-6(2), Creative Education) Creative Co., The.

—World Series Champs: Chicago Cubs. 2013. (World Series Champions Ser.). (ENG.). 24p. (J). (gr. 1-3). pap. 7.99 (978-0-89812-812-3(9), Creative Paperbacks) Creative Co., The.

Hammer, Max. Superstars of the Chicago Cubs. 2014. (Pro Sports Superstars Ser.). 24p. (J). 27.10 (978-1-60753-592-8(0)) Amicus Publishing.

Kelley, K. C. Chicago Cubs. 2016. (J). **(978-1-4896-5938-5(2)**, AV2 by Weigl) Weigl Pubs., Inc.

Kennedy, Mike & Stewart, Mark. Meet the Cubs. 2010. (Smart about Sports Ser.). (Illus.). 24p. (J). (gr. k-3). lib. bdg. 22.60 (978-1-59953-369-8(3)) Norwood Hse. Pr.

Omoth, Tyler. The Story of the Chicago Cubs. 2007. (Baseball, the Great American Game Ser.). (Illus.). 48p. (J). (gr. 4-7). lib. bdg. 32.80 (978-1-58341-482-8(7)) Creative Co., The.

Stewart, Mark. The Chicago Cubs. 2012. (Team Spirit Ser.). 48p. (J). (gr. 3-6). 29.27 (978-1-59953-476-3(2)) Norwood Hse. Pr.

CHICAGO WHITE SOX (BASEBALL TEAM)

Castle, George. Chicago White Sox, 1 vol. (Inside MLB Ser.). (ENG., Illus.). 48p. (gr. 3-6). 2011. (YA). lib. bdg. 32.79 (978-1-61714-039-6(2)) 2014. (J). lib. bdg. 32.79 (978-1-62403-465-7(9), SportsZone) ABDO Publishing Co.

Connery-Boyd, Peg. Chicago White Sox. 2016. (Hawk's Nest Activity Bks.: 0). (ENG.). 64p. (J). (gr. k-3). pap., act. bk. ed. 8.99 (978-1-4926-3363-1(1)) Sourcebooks, Inc.

Elish, Dan. The Black Sox Scandal of 1919. 2008. (Cornerstones of Freedom Ser.). (ENG.). 48p. (J). pap. 5.95 (978-0-531-20828-1(1), Children's Pr.) Scholastic Library Publishing.

Epstein, Brad. Chicago White Sox 101. 2013. (My First Team-Board-Book Ser.). (ENG., Illus.). 24p. (J). bds. (978-1-60730-298-8(5), 101 Bk.) Michaelson Entertainment.

—Chicago White Sox ABC. 2013. (My First Alphabet Books (Michaelson Entertainment) Ser.). (ENG., Illus.). (J). bds. 11.95 (978-1-60730-204-9(7)) Michaelson Entertainment.

Frisch, Aaron. Chicago White Sox. 2009. (World Series Champions Ser.). 23p. (J). (gr. 2-3). 24.25 (978-1-58341-696-9(X), Creative Education) Creative Co., The.

Gilbert, Sara. Chicago White Sox. 2013. (Illus.). 24p. (J). 25.65 (978-1-60818-262-6(2), Creative Education) Creative Co., The.

—World Series Champs: Chicago White Sox. 2013. (World Series Champions Ser.). (ENG.). 24p. (J). (gr. 1-3). pap. 7.99 (978-0-89812-813-0(7), Creative Paperbacks) Creative Co., The.

LeBoutillier, Nate. The Story of the Chicago White Sox. 2011. (J). 35.65 (978-1-60818-036-3(0), Creative Education) Creative Co., The.

O'Hearn, Michael. The Story of the Chicago White Sox. 2007. (Baseball, the Great American Game Ser.). (Illus.). 48p. (YA). (gr. 4-7). lib. bdg. 32.80 (978-1-58341-483-5(5)) Creative Co., The.

Pellowski, Michael J. The Chicago Black Sox Baseball Scandal. 2003. (Headline Court Cases Ser.). (Illus.). 128p. (J). (gr. 6-12). lib. bdg. 26.60 (978-0-7660-2044-3(4)) Enslow Pubs., Inc.

Sandler, Michael. Jermaine Dye & the Chicago White Sox: 2005 World Series. 2008. (World Series Superstars). (Illus.). 24p. (J). (gr. 1-4). lib. bdg. 22.61 (978-1-59716-637-9(5)) Bearport Publishing Co., Inc.

Stewart, Mark. The Chicago White Sox. 2012. (Team Spirit Ser.). 48p. (J). (gr. 3-6). lib. bdg. 29.27 (978-1-59953-477-0(0)) Norwood Hse. Pr.

—Los White Sox de Chicago. Kalmanovitz, Manuel, tr. from ENG. 2007. (Espíritu de Equipo Ser.). (SPA.). 48p. (J). (gr. 3-6). lib. bdg. 26.60 (978-1-59953-101-4(1)) Norwood Hse. Pr.

CHICKEN POX

Gosman, Gillian. I Have Chicken Pox. 2012. (Get Well Soon! Ser.). (ENG., Illus.). 24p. (J). (gr. 1-3). 22.60 (978-1-4488-7411-8(4), PowerKids Pr.) Rosen Publishing Group, Inc., The.

Guilfoile, Patrick. Chicken Pox. 2009. (Deadly Diseases & Epidemics Ser.). (Illus.). 112p. (C). (gr. 9-18). 34.95 (978-1-60413-227-4(2), Chelsea Hse.) Facts On File, Inc.

Hoffmann, Gretchen. Chickenpox. 2008. (Health Alert Ser.). 64p. (gr. 4-18). lib. bdg. 32.79 (978-0-7614-2916-6(6), Benchmark Bks.) Marshall Cavendish Corp.

Landau, Elaine. Chickenpox. 2009. (Head-to-Toe Health Ser.). 32p. (gr. 2-3). 28.50 (978-0-7614-3498-6(4)) Marshall Cavendish Corp.

Plumb, Jennifer. Everything You Need to Know about Chicken Pox & Shingles. 2009. (Need to Know Library). 64p. (gr. 5-5). 58.50 (978-1-60854-057-0(X)) Rosen Publishing Group, Inc., The.

Powell, Jillian. Chicken Pox. Chambers, Mark A., illus. 2013. (Start Reading Ser.). (ENG.). 24p. (gr. k-1). pap. 7.95 (978-1-4765-4089-4(6)) Capstone Press of Coughlan Cos.

Sévigny, Eric, illus. Caillou Is Sick. 2012. (Clubhouse Ser.).Tr. of Caillou Est Malade. (ENG.). 24p. (J). (gr. -1-1). pap. 3.99 (978-2-89450-865-7(4)) Caillouet, Gerry.

CHICKEN POX—FICTION

Aber, Linda Williams. Quien Tiene Manchas; Who's Got Spots? 2008. pap. 34.95 (978-1-58013-759-1(8)) Kane Press, Inc.

Barber, Tiki & Barber, Ronde. Red Zone. (Barber Game Time Bks.). (ENG., 176p. (J). (gr. 3-7). 2013. Illus.). pap. 7.99 (978-1-4169-6861-0(X)) 2010. 15.99 (978-1-4169-6860-3(1)) Simon & Schuster/Paula Wiseman Bks. (Simon & Schuster/Paula Wiseman Bks.).

Byrne, Richard. Spotty Lottie & Me. Byrne, Richard, illus. (ENG., Illus.). 32p. (J). (-k). 2016. pap. 12.99 (978-1-78344-206-5(9)) 2015. 22.99 (978-1-78344-117-4(8)) Andersen Pr. GBR. Dist: Independent Pubs. Group.

Cazet, Denys. Grandpa Spanielson's Chicken Pox Stories No. 1: The Octopus. Cazet, Denys, illus. 2005. (I Can Read Bks.). (Illus.). 48p. (J). (gr. -1-3). lib. bdg. 16.89 (978-0-06-051089-3(7)) HarperCollins Pubs.

—The Octopus. Cazet, Denys, illus. 2008. (Grandpa Spanielson's Chicken Pox Stories Ser.). (Illus.). (J). (gr. -1-3). pap. 16.95 incl. audio (978-1-4301-0455-1(4));Set. pap. 31.95 incl. audio compact disk (978-1-4301-0460-5(0));Set. pap. 29.95 incl. audio (978-1-4301-0457-5(0)) Live Oak Media.

—The Shrunken Head. 2007. (I Can Read Bks.: No. 3). (Illus.). 48p. (J). (gr. -1-3). lib. bdg. 16.89 (978-0-06-073014-7(5)) HarperCollins Pubs.

Danziger, Paula. You Can't Eat Your Chicken Pox, Amber Brown. Ross, Tony, illus. 2006. (Amber Brown Ser.: No. 2). 100p. (gr. 2-5). 15.00 (978-0-7569-6756-7(2)) Perfection Learning Corp.

—You Can't Eat Your Chicken Pox, Amber Brown. (Amber Brown Ser.: No. 2). 101p. (J). (gr. 3-6). pap. 3.50 (978-0-8072-1290-5(3), Listening Library) Random Hse. Audio Publishing Group.

—You Can't Eat Your Chicken Pox, Amber Brown. Ross, Tony, illus. 2006. (Amber Brown Ser.: 2). (ENG.). 128p. (J). (gr. 2-5). 5.99 (978-0-14-240629-8(5), Puffin Books) Penguin Young Readers Group.

Deacon, Melissa. Chicken Pox? 2011. 20p. pap. 24.95 (978-1-4626-0528-6(1)) America Star Bks.

Dealey, Erin. Goldie Locks Has Chicken Pox. 2004. (Illus.). (J). (gr. k-3). spiral bd. (978-0-616-14573-9(X)); spiral bd. (978-0-616-14572-2(1)) Canadian National Institute for the Blind/Institut National Canadien pour les Aveugles.

—Goldie Locks Has Chicken Pox. Wakiyama, Hanako, illus. 2005. (ENG.). 40p. (J). (gr. -1-2). reprint ed. 8.99 (978-0-689-87610-3(6), Aladdin) Simon & Schuster Children's Publishing.

Gorgas, Paula Blais. The Perfect Purple Present. 2007. (Illus.). 20p. (J). per. 11.99 (978-0-9797574-4-0(4)) Dragonfly Publishing, Inc.

MacDonald, Alan. Germs!, 1 vol. Roberts, David, illus. 2012. (Dirty Bertie Ser.). (ENG.). 112p. (gr. 1-3). pap. 4.95 (978-1-4342-4266-2(8)); 25.32 (978-1-4342-4600-4(0)) Stone Arch Bks.

Messenger, Stephanie. Melanie's Marvelous Measles. 2012. 40p. pap. 19.57 (978-1-4669-3889-2(7)) Trafford Publishing.

Montano, Josie. Chicken Pox. . . Yuck! 2005. (Illus.). 160p. pap. (978-0-7344-0335-3(6), Lothian Children's Bks.) Hachette Australia.

Rippin, Sally. The Spotty Vacation. Fukuoka, Aki, illus. 2013. 43p. (J). (978-1-61067-233-7(X)) Kane Miller.

—The Spotty Vacation: Billie B. Brown. Fukuoka, Aki, illus. 2014. (ENG.). 48p. (J). pap. 4.99 (978-1-61067-183-5(X)) Kane Miller.

Shank, Cheryl. And God Said, Let There Be Chickenpox . 2013. 28p. pap. 12.45 (978-1-4908-1285-4(7), WestBow Pr.) Author Solutions, Inc.

Townsend, Amber C. Once upon a Time. 2007. (J). 7.95 (978-0-9796978-6-9(7)) G Publishing LLC.

Williams Aber, Linda. Quien Tiene Manchas? Fiammenghi, Gioia, illus. 2007. (Math Matters Ser.). (SPA.). 32p. (J). (gr. -1-3). pap. 5.95 (978-1-57565-251-1(X)) Kane Press, Inc.

CHICKENPOX

see Chicken Pox

CHICKENS

Amoroso, Cynthia & Noyed, Bob. Chickens. 2016. (In the Barnyard Ser.). (ENG.). 24p. (J). (gr. k-3). 27.07 (978-1-5038-0824-9(6), 210668) Child's World, Inc., The.

Arnold, Caroline. Hatching Chicks in Room 6. 2017. (ENG., Illus.). 40p. (J). (gr. -1-2). lib. bdg. 16.99 (978-1-58089-735-8(5)) Charlesbridge Publishing, Inc.

Asim, Jabari. Preaching to the Chickens: The Story of Young John Lewis. Lewis, E. B., illus. 2016. (ENG.). 32p. (J). (gr. k-3). 17.99 (978-0-399-16856-7(7), Nancy Paulsen Books) Penguin Young Readers Group.

Barbe-Julien, Colette. Little Chickens. 2006. (Born to Be Wild Ser.). (Illus.). 24p. (gr. k-3). lib. bdg. 23.00 (978-0-8368-6163-1(9), Gareth Stevens Learning Library) Stevens, Gareth Publishing LLLP.

Barnes, J. Chicks & Chickens: Learning the CH Sound. 2009. (PowerPhonics Ser.). 24p. (gr. 1-1). 39.90 (978-1-60851-438-0(2), PowerKids Pr.) Rosen Publishing Group, Inc., The.

Black, Vickie. Young Chicken Farmers: Tips for Kids Raising Backyard Chickens. 2012. (J). 16.95 (978-1-59298-555-5(6)) Beaver's Pond Pr., Inc.

Borgert-Spaniol, Megan. Baby Chickens. 2016. (Super Cute! Ser.). (ENG., Illus.). 24p. (J). (gr. k-3). 25.95 (978-1-62617-388-0(5), Blastoff! Readers) Bellwether Media.

Carraway, Rose. Chickens on the Farm. 2012. (Farm Animals Ser.). (Illus.). 24p. (gr. k-2). 69.20 (978-1-4339-8052-7(5)); (J). 22.60 (978-1-4339-7344-4(8)); (J). pap. 8.15 (978-1-4339-7345-1(6)) Stevens, Gareth Publishing LLLP.

—Chickens on the Farm / Pollos de Granja. 2012. (Farm Animals / Animales de granja Ser.). (SPA & ENG., Illus.). 24p. (J). (gr. k-2). 22.60 (978-1-4339-7394-9(4)) Stevens, Gareth Publishing LLLP.

Caughey, Melissa. A Kid's Guide to Keeping Chickens: Best Breeds, Creating a Home, Care & Handling, Outdoor Fun, Crafts & Recipes. 2015. (ENG., Illus.). 144p. (J). (gr. 2-8). pap. 16.95 (978-1-61212-418-6(6), 622418) Storey Publishing, LLC.

—A Kid's Guide to Keeping Chickens: Best Breeds, Creating a Home, Care & Handling, Outdoor Fun, Crafts & Treats. 2015. (ENG., Illus.). 144p. (J). (gr. 2-8). 26.95 (978-1-61212-648-7(0)) Storey Publishing, LLC.

Chicken & Egg. 2003. (J). 36.95 (978-0-8136-9274-6(1)); 38.95 (978-0-8136-4195-9(0)) Modern Curriculum Pr.

Chicks. 2003. (Three Minute Tales Ser.). 32p. (J). 7.95 (978-0-7525-4759-6(3)); 5.98 (978-0-7525-8915-2(6)) Parragon, Inc.

Clay, Kathryn. Chickens, 1 vol. 2012. (Farm Animals Ser.). (ENG., Illus.). 24p. (gr. k-1). lib. bdg. 26.65 (978-1-4296-8650-1(2), Pebble Plus) Capstone Press of Coughlan Cos.

De la Bédoyère, Camilla. Lifecycles Egg to Chicken ScholBC SS. 2009. 24p. (J). (978-1-59566-708-3(3)) QEB Publishing Inc.

Dicker, Katie. Chickens. 2014. (Farm Animals Ser.). (Illus.). 24p. (gr. 2-5). 28.50 (978-1-62588-018-5(9)) Black Rabbit Bks.

Dickmann, Nancy. A Chicken's Life, 1 vol. 2010. (Watch It Grow Ser.). (ENG., Illus.). 24p. (gr. -1-1). pap. 6.29 *(978-1-4329-4148-2(8),* Acorn) Heinemann-Raintree.

—La Vida del Pollo. 2011. (¡Mira Cómo Crece! Ser.). (Illus.). 24p. (gr. -1-1). (SPA & ENG.). 22.65 *(978-1-4329-5272-3(2));* (ENG & SPA., pap. 6.29 *(978-1-4329-5284-6(6))* Heinemann-Raintree. (Bellota).

DiSiena, Laura Lyn & Eliot, Hannah. Chickens Don't Fly: And Other Fun Facts. Oswald, Pete, illus. 2014. (Did You Know? Ser.). (ENG.). 32p. (J). (gr. -1-3). 17.99 *(978-1-4424-9353-7(4));* pap. 6.99 *(978-1-4424-9326-1(7))* Little Simon. (Little Simon).

Dolphin, Colleen. Clucky Chickens, 1 vol. 2011. (Farm Pets Ser.). (ENG., Illus.). 24p. (J). (gr. k-3). lib. bdg. 24.21 *(978-1-61613-370-2(8))* ABDO Publishing Co.

Doubleday Entertainment USA - Chickens: Down on the Farm. 2006. (J). per. 6.95 *(978-1-59566-226-2(X))* QEB Publishing Inc.

Gibbons, Gail. Chicks & Chickens. 2005. (ENG., Illus.). 32p. (J). (gr. k-3). pap. 7.99 *(978-0-8234-1939-5(8))* Holiday Hse., Inc.

Gibbs, Maddie. Chickens, 1 vol. 2015. (ENG., Illus.). 24p. (J). lib. bdg. 23.60 *(978-1-4994-0064-9(0),* PowerKids Pr.) Rosen Publishing Group, Inc., The.

Godwin, Sam. The Hen Can't Help It: A First Look at the Life Cycle of a Chicken. Abel, Simone, illus. 2004. (First Look: Science Ser.). (ENG.). 32p. (gr. -1-2). 26.65 *(978-1-4048-0653-5(9))* Picture Window Bks.

Green, Emily K. Chickens. 2007. (Farm Animals Ser.). (ENG., Illus.). 24p. (J). (gr. k-3). lib. bdg. 25.95 *(978-1-60014-064-8(5))* Bellwether Media.

Havard, Christian. Face-to-Face with the Chicken. 2004. (Face-to-Face Ser.). (Illus.). 28p. (J). 9.95 *(978-1-57091-455-3(9))* Charlesbridge Publishing, Inc.

Hendrix, Emilia. Chickens & Chicks. 2016. (Animal Family Ser.). (ENG., Illus.). 24p. (J). (gr. k-k). pap. 8.15 *(978-1-4824-3771-3(6))* Stevens, Gareth Publishing LLLP.

Heppermann, Christine. City Chickens. 2015. (ENG., Illus.). 64p. (J). (gr. 1-4). pap. 8.99 *(978-0-544-45593-1(2),* HMH Books For Young Readers) Houghton Mifflin Harcourt Publishing Co.

Hudak, Heather C. Chickens. 2006. (Farm Animals Ser.). (Illus.). 24p. (J). (gr. 3-7). lib. bdg. 24.45 *(978-1-59036-423-9(6));* per. 8.95 *(978-1-59036-430-7(9))* Weigl Pubs., Inc.

Huseby, Victoria. Chicken. 2008. (J). 25.65 *(978-1-59920-175-7(5))* Black Rabbit Bks.

Janney, Connie. The Most Extraordinary Farm. 2012. 30p. (-18). pap. 13.99 *(978-1-4525-6213-1(X))* Balboa Pr.

Kant, Tanya. How an Egg Grows into a Chicken. Franklin, Carolyn, illus. 2008. (Amaze Ser.). (ENG.). 32p. (J). (gr. -1-3). pap. 8.95 *(978-0-531-23801-1(6));* (gr. k-3). 27.00 *(978-0-531-20447-2(9))* Scholastic Library Publishing. (Children's Pr.).

Kishel, Ann-Marie. Chickens & Chicks. 2006. (First Step Nonfiction - Animal Families Ser.). (ENG., Illus.). 8p. (gr. -1-1). pap. 4.95 *(978-0-8225-5648-0(0),* Lerner Pubns.) Lerner Publishing Group.

Kopp, Megan. Chickens. 2012. (J). 12.95 *(978-1-61913-279-5(6));* 27.13 *(978-1-61913-275-7(3))* Weigl Pubs., Inc.

—Gallinas. 2013. (Animales en la Granja Ser.). (SPA., Illus.). 24p. (J). (gr. -1-3). lib. bdg. 27.13 *(978-1-62127-585-5(X),* AV2 by Weigl) Weigl Pubs., Inc.

Macken, JoAnn Early. Chickens. 2nd rev. ed. 2009. (Animals That Live on the Farm Ser.). (ENG.). 24p. (J). (gr. -1-3). pap. 8.15 *(978-1-4339-2464-4(1));* lib. bdg. 22.60 *(978-1-4339-2395-1(5))* Stevens, Gareth Publishing LLLP. (Weekly Reader Leveled Readers).

—Chickens;Las Gallinas. 2nd rev. ed. 2009. (Animals That Live on the Farm/Animales que viven en la granja Ser.). (ENG & SPA.). 24p. (J). (gr. -1-3). pap. 8.15 *(978-1-4339-2471-2(4));* lib. bdg. 22.60 *(978-1-4339-2427-9(7))* Stevens, Gareth Publishing LLLP. (Weekly Reader Leveled Readers).

Madian. Bald-Headed Chicken. (J). (gr. k-2). 75.00 *(978-0-669-13449-0(X))* Houghton Mifflin Harcourt School Pubs.

Markovics, Joyce L. Chicken. 2017. (See Them Grow Ser.). (ENG., Illus.). 24p. (J). (gr. -1-3). 17.95 ***(978-1-68402-042-3(5))*** Bearport Publishing Co., Inc.

—Polish Chicken. 2017. (Weirder & Cuter Ser.). (ENG.). 24p. (J). (gr. -1-3). 17.95 ***(978-1-68402-262-5(2))*** Bearport Publishing Co., Inc.

Meister, Cari. Chickens. 2012. (ENG., Illus.). 24p. (J). lib. bdg. 25.65 *(978-1-62031-000-7(7))* Jump! Inc.

Mercer, Abbie. Chickens on a Farm. (Barnyard Animals Ser.). (J). 2010. 49.50 *(978-1-4042-8064-9(2))* 2009. (ENG.). 24p. pap. 8.25 *(978-1-4042-8063-2(4))* Rosen Publishing Group, Inc., The. (PowerKids Pr.).

Merritt, Robin. The Life Cycle of a Chicken. 2011. (Life Cycles Ser.). (ENG., Illus.). 32p. (J). (gr. k-3). lib. bdg. 29.93 *(978-1-60973-144-1(1),* 201169) Child's World, Inc., The.

Metz, Lorijo. Chickens: Hens, Roosters, & Chicks. 2010. (On the Farm Ser.). (ENG.). 24p. (J). pap. 8.25 *(978-1-4488-1343-8(3));* lib. bdg. 22.60 *(978-1-4488-0691-1(7))* Rosen Publishing Group, Inc., The. (PowerKids Pr.).

Minden, Cecilia. Farm Animals: Chickens. 2009. (21st Century Junior Library: Farm Animals Ser.). (ENG., Illus.). 24p. (gr. 2-4). lib. bdg. 27.07 *(978-1-60279-545-7(2),* 200270) Cherry Lake Publishing.

Murray, Julie. Chickens, 1 vol. (ENG., 24p. 2015. Illus.). (J). 27.07 *(978-1-62970-938-3(7),* 1391176) 2007. (gr. -1-3). 25.65 *(978-1-59928-704-1(8),* Buddy Bks.) 2003. (J). (gr. 1-4). 25.65 *(978-1-57765-649-4(0))* ABDO Publishing Co.

Nelson, Robin. Chickens. 2009. pap. 34.95 *(978-0-7613-4090-4(4));* (ENG.). 24p. 23.93 *(978-0-7613-4060-7(2),* Lerner Pubns.) Lerner Publishing Group.

—From Egg to Chicken. 2003. (Start to Finish Ser.). (ENG., Illus.). 24p. (gr. k-3). lib. bdg. 19.93 *(978-0-8225-4662-7(0))* Lerner Publishing Group.

Owen, Ruth. Eggs! Life on a Chicken Farm. 2012. (Food from Farmers Ser.). (ENG., Illus.). 32p. (J). (gr. k-3). pap. 11.75 *(978-1-61533-536-7(6));* lib. bdg. 26.50 *(978-1-61533-529-9(3))* Windmill Bks.

Patchett, Fiona. Eggs & Chicks. Kushii, Tetsuo & Wray, Zoe, illus. 2007. (Usborne Beginners Ser.). 32p. (J). (gr. -1). 4.99 *(978-0-7945-1342-9(5),* Usborne) EDC Publishing.

—Eggs & Chicks. 2004. (Beginners Ser.). (Illus.). 32p. (J). (gr. 1-18). (ENG.). pap. 4.95 *(978-0-7945-0166-2(4),* Usborne); lib. bdg. 12.95 *(978-1-58086-482-4(1))* EDC Publishing.

Los Pollitos Dicen Pio. 2005. 5.99 *(978-84-263-4738-1(X))* Vives, Luis Editorial (Edelvives) ESP. Dist: Lectorum Pubns., Inc.

Ray, Hannah. Chickens. 2008. (Down on the Farm (N.Y.) Ser.). (ENG., Illus.). 24p. (J). (gr. 3-7). pap. *(978-0-7787-4050-6(1))* Crabtree Publishing Co.

Reynolds, Shaye. The Life Cycle of a Chicken. 2015. (Watch Them Grow! Ser.). (ENG., Illus.). 24p. (J). (gr. 1-1). pap. 8.25 *(978-1-4994-0664-1(9),* PowerKids Pr.) Rosen Publishing Group, Inc., The.

Riggs, Kate. Seedlings: Chickens. 2017. (Seedlings Ser.). (ENG., Illus.). 24p. (J). (gr. -1-1). pap. 7.99 ***(978-1-62832-391-7(4),*** Creative Paperbacks) Creative Co., The.

Schindel, John & Holt, Steven. Busy Chickens. Holt, Steven, photos by. 2009. (Busy Book Ser.). (ENG., Illus.). 20p. (J). (gr. -1 — 1). bds. 6.99 *(978-1-58246-275-2(5),* Knopf Bks. for Young Readers) Random Hse. Children's Bks.

Sexton, Colleen. The Life Cycle of a Chicken. 2010. (Life Cycles Ser.). (ENG., Illus.). 24p. (J). (gr. k-3). lib. bdg. 25.95 *(978-1-60014-450-9(0),* Blastoff! Readers) Bellwether Media.

Silverman, Buffy. Meet a Baby Chicken. 2016. (Lightning Bolt Books (tm) — Baby Farm Animals Ser.). (ENG., Illus.). 32p. (J). (gr. 1-3). 26.65 *(978-1-5124-0803-4(4));* 39.99 *(978-1-5124-1025-9(X),* Lerner Pubns.) Lerner Publishing Group.

Sklansky, Amy E. Where Do Chicks Come From? Paparone, Pam, illus. 2005. (Let's-Read-and-Find-Out-Science Ser.). 40p. (J). (gr. -1-1). (ENG.). 15.99 *(978-0-06-028892-1(2));* lib. bdg. 16.89 *(978-0-06-028893-8(0))* HarperCollins Pubs.

—Where Do Chicks Come From? Paparone, Pamela, illus. 2005. (Let's-Read-And-Find-Out Science 1 Ser.). (ENG.). 40p. (J). (gr. -1-3). pap. 5.99 *(978-0-06-445212-0(3))* HarperCollins Pubs.

Stiefel, Chana. Chickens on the Family Farm. 2013. (Animals on the Family Farm Ser.). 24p. (J). (gr. k-3). pap. 7.95 *(978-1-4644-0351-4(1),* Enslow Elementary); lib. bdg. 22.60 *(978-0-7660-4204-9(9))* Enslow Pubs., Inc.

Stockland, Patricia M. In the Chicken Coop, 1 vol. Ouren, Todd, illus. 2007. (Barnyard Buddies Ser.). (ENG.). 24p. (gr. -1-2). 27.07 *(978-1-60270-023-9(0),* Looking Glass Library-Nonfiction) Magic Wagon.

Thomas, Isabel. Henrietta's Guide to Caring for Your Chickens, 1 vol. Peterson, Rick, illus. 2014. (Pets' Guides). (ENG.). 32p. (gr. 1-3). pap. 8.29 *(978-1-4846-0269-0(2));* 27.32 *(978-1-4846-0262-1(5))* Heinemann-Raintree. (Heinemann First Library).

Thomson, Ruth. A Chicken's Life Cycle. 2010. (Let's Look at Life Cycles Ser.). 24p. (J). (ENG.). pap. 8.25 *(978-1-61532-222-0(1),* PowerKids Pr.); lib. bdg., E-Book 42.50 *(978-1-4488-0356-9(X));* (Illus.). 49.50 *(978-1-61532-223-7(X),* PowerKids Pr.); (Illus.). lib. bdg. 22.60 *(978-1-61532-217-6(5),* PowerKids Pr.) Rosen Publishing Group, Inc., The.

—The Life Cycle of a Chicken. 2007. (Learning about Life Cycles Ser.). (Illus.). 24p. (J). (gr. 4-7). lib. bdg. 22.60 *(978-1-4042-3715-5(1),* PowerKids Pr.) Rosen Publishing Group, Inc., The.

Wearing, Judy. Chickens. 2010. pap. 9.95 *(978-1-60596-914-5(1));* 24p. (J). (gr. 2-4). lib. bdg. 25.70 *(978-1-60596-913-8(3))* Weigl Pubs., Inc.

Wight, Milan E. & Bratton, Chris. Chickens Are Our Friends. 2011. 24p. 15.00 *(978-1-4269-5238-8(4))* Trafford Publishing.

Wolfman, Judy. Life on a Chicken Farm. Winston, David Lorenz, illus. Winston, David Lorenz, photos by. 2004. (Life on a Farm Ser.). (ENG.). 48p. (gr. 2-5). lib. bdg. 23.93 *(978-1-57505-191-8(5))* Lerner Publishing Group.

Zollman, Pam. Cómo Crece un Pollito. 2008. (Scholastic News Nonfiction Readers en Espanol Ser.). 24p. (J). pap. 6.95 *(978-0-531-20640-9(8))* Scholastic Library Publishing.

CHICKENS—FICTION

Adams, Jesse. Farmer Dillo Counts His Chickens. Speer, Julie & Rogers, David, illus. 2008. 22p. (gr. -1-1). pap. 7.99 *(978-1-59166-868-8(9))* BJU Pr.

Airgood, Ellen. Prairie Evers. (ENG.). 224p. (J). (gr. 3-7). 2014. pap. 7.99 *(978-0-14-242668-5(7),* Puffin Books) 2012. 15.99 *(978-0-399-25691-2(1),* Nancy Paulsen Books) Penguin Young Readers Group.

Alafaci, Marie. Zelda's Big Adventure. McG, Shane, illus. 2017. (ENG.). 32p. (J). (gr. -1-3). 16.99 ***(978-1-328-66081-7(8),*** Clarion Bks.) Houghton Mifflin Harcourt Trade & Reference Pubs.

Alakija, Polly. Counting Chickens. 2014. (ENG., Illus.). 32p. (J). (gr. -1-1). 17.99 *(978-1-84780-437-2(3),* Frances Lincoln) Quarto Publishing Group UK GBR. Dist: Hachette Bk. Group.

Alborough, Jez. Six Little Chicks. 2013. (ENG.). 32p. (J). (gr. -1-1). pap. 6.99 *(978-1-4380-0181-4(9))* Barron's Educational Series, Inc.

Allen, Jonathan. I'm Not Reading! 2013. (Baby Owl Ser.). (ENG., Illus.). 32p. (J). (gr. -1-k). 16.95 *(978-1-907967-44-3(3))* Boxer Bks., Ltd. GBR. Dist: Sterling Publishing Co., Inc.

Allen, Pat. The Field by the Sea. 2010. 20p. 21.50 *(978-1-4457-3405-7(2))* Lulu Pr., Inc.

Andersen, Hans Christian. For Sure! for Sure! White, Mus, tr. from DAN. Czernecki, Stefan, illus. 2006. 29p. (J). (gr. k-4). reprint ed. 17.00 *(978-1-4223-5208-3(0))* DIANE Publishing Co.

Andrews, Jackie. Little Red Hen & the Wheat. Smith, Lesley, illus. 2012. (ENG.). 32p. pap. 6.50 *(978-1-84135-190-2(3))* Award Pubns. Ltd. GBR. Dist: Parkwest Pubns., Inc.

Appleton-Smith, Laura. Oh My, It Must Be the Sky! Neel, Preston, illus. 2004. (Book to Remember Ser.). (ENG.). 52p. pap. 8.95 *(978-1-929262-21-2(3),* Books To Remember) Flyleaf Publishing.

Argueta, Jorge. La Gallinita en la Ciudad: The Little Hen in the City. Castro, Mima, illus. 2006. (Bilingual Bks). 32p. (gr. 3-5). 15.95 *(978-1-59820-093-5(3),* Alfaguara) Santillana USA Publishing Co., Inc.

Aronson, Billy & Oxley, Jennifer. The Chicken Problem. 2012. (ENG., Illus.). 32p. (J). (gr. -1-2). 16.99 *(978-0-375-86989-1(1),* Random Hse. Bks. for Young Readers) Random Hse. Children's Bks.

Artful Doodlers Limited Staff, illus. It's Absolutely True. 2006. (Famous Fables Ser.). (J). 6.99 *(978-1-59939-029-1(9))* Cornerstone Pr.

Artzi, Yocheved. Freedom Chickens: The Story of Lonely Chicken. 2011. 34p. pap. 13.50 *(978-1-61204-265-7(1),* Strategic Bk. Publishing) Strategic Book Publishing & Rights Agency (SBPRA).

Asher, Sandy. Chicken Story Time. Fearing, Mark, illus. 2016. (ENG.). 40p. (J). (-k). 17.99 *(978-0-8037-3944-4(3),* Dial Bks) Penguin Young Readers Group.

Atherton, Isabel & Straker, Bethany. Springy Chicken. Straker, Bethany, illus. 2014. (ENG., Illus.). 32p. (J). (gr. -1-k). 14.95 *(978-1-62636-161-4(4),* Sky Pony Pr.) Skyhorse Publishing Co., Inc.

Attema, Martha. The Paper Wagon. Ross, Graham, illus. 2005. 61p. (J). lib. bdg. 20.00 *(978-1-4242-1260-6(X))* Fitzgerald Bks.

—The Paper Wagon, 1 vol. Ross, Graham, illus. 2005. (Orca Echoes Ser.). (ENG.). 64p. (J). (gr. 2-3). per. 6.95 *(978-1-55143-356-1(7))* Orca Bk. Pubs. USA.

Auch, Mary Jane. Beauty & the Beaks: A Turkey's Cautionary Tale. Auch, Herm & Auch, Mary Jane, illus. 2007. (ENG.). 32p. (J). (gr. -1-3). 17.95 *(978-0-8234-1990-6(8))* Holiday Hse., Inc.

—Chickerella. Auch, Herm, tr. Auch, Herm, illus. 2005. (ENG.). 32p. (J). 17.95 *(978-0-8234-1804-6(9))* Holiday Hse., Inc.

—I Was a Third Grade Bodyguard. Auch, Herm, illus. 2003. (ENG.). 73p. (J). (gr. 4-6). tchr. ed. 16.95 *(978-0-8234-1775-9(1))* Holiday Hse., Inc.

—The Plot Chickens. Auch, Mary Jane & Auch, Herm, illus. (ENG.). 32p. (J). (gr. -1-3). 2010. pap. 7.99 *(978-0-8234-2307-1(7))* 2009. 17.95 *(978-0-8234-2087-2(6))* Holiday Hse., Inc.

—Souperchicken. Auch, Herm, illus. 2004. (ENG.). 32p. (J). (gr. -1-3). reprint ed. pap. 6.95 *(978-0-8234-1829-9(4))* Holiday Hse., Inc.

Auch, Mary Jane & Auch, Herm. The Buk Buk Buk Festival. 2015. (ENG., Illus.). 32p. (J). (gr. -1-3). 16.95 *(978-0-8234-3201-1(7))* Holiday Hse., Inc.

Aunt Judy. Chickens in the Know! Chickens of Different Occupations. Aunt Judy, illus. 2007. (Illus.). 40p. (J). pap. 7.00 *(978-0-9780693-1-5(5))* McEwen, Judith A.

—Chickens on the Go! Chickens from different locations around the World. Aunt Judy, illus. 2nd ed. 2006. (Illus.). 40p. (J). pap. 7.00 *(978-0-9780693-0-8(7))* McEwen, Judith A.

Baker, Keith. Big Fat Hen Big Book. Baker, Keith, illus. 2010. (ENG., Illus.). 32p. (J). (gr. -1-3). 26.99 *(978-0-547-32859-1(1))* Houghton Mifflin Harcourt Publishing Co.

Bald-Headed Chicken. (J). (gr. k-2). pap. 9.90 *(978-0-669-15613-3(2));* pap. 9.90 *(978-0-669-15896-0(8))* Houghton Mifflin Harcourt School Pubs.

Baniti, Nailah. Nana's Sweetie-Pie-Chicken. 2012. 32p. pap. 9.99 *(978-0-9853574-1-2(X))* Mountan Creek Pubns.

Barbot, Daniel. Rosaura en Bicicleta. Fuenmayor, Morella, illus. 2005. (SPA.). 23p. (J). (gr. -1-2). reprint ed. pap. 14.00 *(978-0-7567-8947-3(8))* DIANE Publishing Co.

Bardhan-Quallen, Sudipta. Chicks Run Wild. Jenkins, Ward, illus. 2011. (ENG.). 32p. (J). (gr. -1-1). 15.99 *(978-1-4424-0673-5(9),* Simon & Schuster Bks. For Young Readers) Simon & Schuster Bks. For Young Readers.

Barkaw, Henriette. Don't Cry Sly: Big Book English Only. Johnson, Richard, illus. 2004. (J). *(978-1-85269-999-4(X))* Mantra Lingua.

Barkow, Henriette. Don't Cry, Sly! Johnson, Richard, illus. 2004. 32p. (J). (ENG & TAM.). pap. *(978-1-85269-663-4(X));* (ENG & PAN.). pap. *(978-1-85269-658-0(3));* (ENG.). pap. *(978-1-85269-660-3(5));* (ENG & ITA.). pap. *(978-1-85269-657-3(5));* (ENG & GUJ.). pap. *(978-1-85269-656-6(7));* (GER & ENG.). pap. *(978-1-85269-655-9(9));* (ENG & CZE.). pap. *(978-1-85269-652-8(4));* (ENG & CHI.). pap. *(978-1-85269-651-1(6));* (ENG & BEN.). pap. *(978-1-85269-650-4(8));* (ENG & SOM.). pap. *(978-1-85269-661-0(3));* (ENG & TUR.). pap. *(978-1-85269-670-2(2));* (ENG & POL.). pap. *(978-1-85269-813-3(6));* (ENG & URD.). pap. *(978-1-85269-671-9(0))* Mantra Lingua.

Baxter, Nicola. The Little Red Hen. Howarth, Daniel, illus. 2015. (ENG.). 24p. pap. 6.99 *(978-1-86147-653-1(1),* Armadillo) Anness Publishing GBR. Dist: National Bk. Network.

Berggren, Jeff. Chicken Cherries. Hansen, Tammy A., ed. Berggren, Jeff, illus. l.t. ed. 2005. (Illus.). 32p. (J). per. 14.95 *(978-0-9755033-0-0(8))* Deep Dish Design.

Bertha Bantam. 2003. (J). 9.99 *(978-0-9740847-7-0(8))* GiGi Bks.

Bidelman, Jeff. The Adventures of Mr. Chicken Butt. Mozi, Jennifer, illus. 2013. (ENG.). (J). 14.95 *(978-1-62086-354-1(5))* Mascot Bks., Inc.

Binks. Don't Be a Chicken. Begonia, Ruby, illus. 2013. 32p. 15.95 *(978-1-935448-22-8(6))* Lost Coast Pr.

Blabey, Aaron. The Bad Guys. 2017. (Bad Guys Ser.: 2). (ENG.). 144p. (J). (gr. 2-5). pap. 5.99 *(978-0-545-91241-9(5),* Scholastic Pr.) Scholastic, Inc.

Blabey, Aaron. Mission Unpluckable. 2017. (Bad Guys Ser.: 2). lib. bdg. 16.00 ***(978-0-606-40154-8(7))*** Turtleback Bks.

Black Literary. The Chicken Coopers. 2008. (Illus.). 18p. (J). pap. 8.95 *(978-0-615-22609-5(4))* Black Literary, Inc.

Blakeney, Crystal Denise. Paradise & Cove Counts Feathered Friends. 2012. 16p. pap. 15.99 *(978-1-4772-5962-7(7))* AuthorHouse.

—Paradise & Cove Go Camping. 2012. 20p. pap. 17.99 *(978-1-4772-7587-0(8))* AuthorHouse.

Blanc, Esther Silverstein & Eagle, Godeane. Long Johns for a Small Chicken. Dixon, Tennessee, illus. 2003. (J). 16.95 *(978-1-884244-23-0(8))* volcano pr.

Blevins, Wiley & Bader, Bonnie. Max Finds an Egg. Clanton, Ben, illus. 2015. (Penguin Young Readers, Level 1 Ser.). (ENG.). 32p. (J). (gr. k-1). 3.99 *(978-0-448-47993-4(1),* Penguin Young Readers) Penguin Young Readers Group.

Bobo, W. L. Chickendoodle! Where Are You? 2011. 28p. pap. 21.95 *(978-1-4269-5742-0(4))* Trafford Publishing.

Bodach, Vijaya. Ten Easter Eggs. Logan, Laura, illus. 2015. (ENG.). 22p. (J). (gr. -1-k). bds. 8.99 *(978-0-545-74730-1(9),* Cartwheel Bks.) Scholastic, Inc.

Bolton, Robin. Roo-Star, the Smartest Chicken in the Coop. 2013. 28p. pap. 13.99 *(978-1-4624-0585-5(1),* Inspiring Voices) Author Solutions, Inc.

Book Company Staff. Who Am I: Chick. 2003. (Board Bks.). (Illus.). (J). bds. 10.95 *(978-1-74047-307-1(8))* Book Co. Publishing Pty, Ltd., The AUS. Dist: Penton Overseas, Inc.

Bowles, Paula. Scary Mary. 2012. (ENG., Illus.). 24p. (J). *(978-1-58925-110-6(5))* Tiger Tales.

Boynton, Sandra. Eek! Halloween! 2016. (ENG., Illus.). 24p. (J). bds. 6.95 *(978-0-7611-9300-5(6))* Workman Publishing Co., Inc.

Braffet, Mary. Maile & the Huli Hula Chicken. Braffet, Holly, illus. 2010. 32p. (J). 12.95 *(978-1-56647-925-7(8))* Mutual Publishing LLC.

Branford, Henrietta. Six Chicks. Elfezzani, Thierry, illus. 2004. (ENG.). 32p. (J). (gr. k-k). pap. 8.99 *(978-0-00-664767-6(7),* HarperCollins Children's Bks.) HarperCollins Pubs. Ltd. GBR. Dist: Independent Pubs. Group.

Bray, Sorcha. The Adventures of Powerpup & Wonderboy & the Case of the Wicked Chickens. 2010. 48p. pap. 19.75 *(978-1-4490-7133-2(3))* AuthorHouse.

Brett, Jan. Cinders: A Chicken Cinderella. Brett, Jan, illus. 2013. (ENG., Illus.). 32p. (J). (gr. k). 17.99 *(978-0-399-25783-4(7),* G.P. Putnam's Sons Books for Young Readers) Penguin Publishing Group.

—Daisy Comes Home. Brett, Jan, illus. 2005. (ENG., Illus.). 32p. (J). (gr. k-3). reprint ed. pap. 6.99 *(978-0-14-240270-2(2),* Puffin Books) Penguin Young Readers Group.

Brezenoff, Steve. Dinosaur That Disappeared. 2013. (Field Trip Mysteries Ser.). (ENG.). 88p. (gr. 2-3). pap. 35.70 *(978-1-4342-6233-2(2))* Stone Arch Bks.

—The Dinosaur That Disappeared, 1 vol. Calo, Marcos, illus. 2013. (Field Trip Mysteries Ser.). (ENG.). 88p. (gr. 2-3). pap. 6.10 *(978-1-4342-6213-4(8));* lib. bdg. 25.32 *(978-1-4342-5980-6(3))* Stone Arch Bks.

Briers, Erica. Runaway Chick. Boey, Stephanie, illus. 2006. (ENG.). 24p. (J). *(978-1-55168-314-0(8))* Fenn, H. B. & Co., Ltd.

Briggs-Anderson, Naomi. Mattie & Percy: The Story of a Chicken & a Duck. Wooten, Vernon Lee, illus. 2011. 32p. pap. 24.95 *(978-1-4560-5319-2(1))* America Star Bks.

Brigham, Anthea. Henrietta, World War II Hen: This Is a True Story. Brigham, Anthea, illus. 2008. (ENG., Illus.). 28p. (J). 7.00 *(978-0-9740778-2-6(8))* Whale's Jaw Publishing.

Broadbent, Tom & Kosmo, Lisa. Henrietta. 2009. pap. *(978-1-61623-033-3(9))* Independent Pub.

Brown, Jo. Hoppity Skip Little Chick. 2005. (Illus.). 32p. (J). 15.95 *(978-1-58925-045-1(1))* Tiger Tales.

Brown, Ken. The Scarecrow's Hat, 1 vol. Brown, Ken, illus. 2011. (ENG., Illus.). 32p. (J). (gr. -1-1). pap. 7.95 *(978-1-56145-570-6(9))* Peachtree Pubs.

Browne, Eileen. Handa's Hen. 2011. (ENG., Illus.). 32p. (J). (gr. -1-2). pap. 6.99 *(978-0-7636-5361-3(6))* Candlewick Pr.

Buchholz, Erwin. Born under a Star, 1 vol. Legg, Barbara, illus. 2009. 44p. pap. 24.95 *(978-1-61546-130-1(2))* America Star Bks.

Bunting, Eve. Hurry! Hurry! Mack, Jeff, illus. (ENG.). (J). 2009. 32p. (gr. k — 1). bds. 6.99 *(978-0-15-206686-4(1))* 2007. 40p. (gr. -1-3). 16.99 *(978-0-15-205410-6(3))* Houghton Mifflin Harcourt Publishing Co.

Bush, Rosetta Bowman. Chicken Every Sunday. 2013. 24p. pap. 24.95 *(978-1-63004-065-9(7))* America Star Bks.

Butler, Dori. Detective Cluck & the Missing Hens. 2005. (J). pap. *(978-1-4108-4192-6(8))* Benchmark Education Co.

Byrd, Robert. Brave Chicken Little. Byrd, Robert, illus. 2014. (ENG., Illus.). 40p. (J). (gr. -1-3). 17.99 *(978-0-670-78616-9(0),* Viking Books for Young Readers) Penguin Young Readers Group.

Caleca, James Renny. Hope, the Wonder Chicken. 2003. (J). 18.00 *(978-0-8059-5028-1(1))* Dorrance Publishing Co., Inc.

Cameron, Kathleen. The Chicken Without a Coop. 2003. (Night Before Christmas Ser.). (Illus.). (J). 0.85 *(978-1-882897-71-1(4))* Pelican Publishing Co., Inc.

Carsonie, Diane Lynn. Little Red Chicken, 1 vol. Bullen, Marjorie J., illus. 2009. 17p. pap. 24.95 *(978-1-60813-495-3(4))* America Star Bks.

Caruso, Barbara, reader. Elvis the Rooster Almost Goes to Heaven, 4 bks., Set. unabr. ed. 2006. (Readalongs for Beginning Readers Ser.). (Illus.). (J). (gr. -1-3). pap. 29.95 incl. audio *(978-1-59519-684-2(6));* pap. 31.95 incl. audio compact disk *(978-1-59519-685-9(4))* Live Oak Media.

The Case of the Weird Blue Chicken: The Next Misadventure. 2014. (Chicken Squad Ser.: 2). (ENG., Illus.). 112p. (J). (gr. 2-5). 12.99 *(978-1-4424-9679-8(7),* Atheneum Bks. for Young Readers) Simon & Schuster Children's Publishing.

Cazet, Denys. Minnie & Moo: The Night Before Christmas. Cazet, Denys, illus. 2004. (Readalongs for Beginning Readers Ser.). (Illus.). 25.95 incl. audio *(978-1-59112-884-7(6))* Live Oak Media.

Chaconas, Dori. Coriander the Contrary Hen. Carrington, Marsha Gray, illus. 2007. (Carolrhoda Picture Bks.). (ENG.). 32p. (J). (gr. k-3). lib. bdg. 16.95 *(978-1-57505-749-1(2),* Carolrhoda Bks.) Lerner Publishing Group.

Charlesworth, Liza. Six Silly Chicks: An Animal Friends Reader. Smith, Ian, illus. 2015. 16p. (J). pap. ***(978-0-545-85966-0(2))*** Scholastic, Inc.

Charlie Chicken goes to Playgroup. 2004. (Play Pals Ser.). (Illus.). 12p. (J). bds. *(978-1-84229-639-4(6))* Top That! Publishing PLC.

Chick & Go. 2004. (J). per. *(978-1-57657-516-1(0))* Paradise Pr., Inc.

Chicken Licken: Set C Individual Title Six-Packs. (Supersonic Phonics Ser.). (gr. k-3). 29.00 *(978-0-7635-0541-7(2))* Rigby Education.

Clark, Leslie Ann. Peepsqueak! Clark, Leslie Ann, illus. 2012. (ENG., Illus.). 32p. (J). (gr. -1-k). 12.99 *(978-0-06-207801-8(1))* HarperCollins Pubs.

—Peepsqueak Wants a Friend! Clark, Leslie Ann, illus. 2013. (ENG., Illus.). 32p. (J). (gr. -1-3). 15.99 *(978-0-06-207804-9(6))* HarperCollins Pubs.

Clynes, Kate. Little Red Hen & Wheat. 2004. (Illus.). 32p. (J). *(978-1-84444-058-0(3))* Mantra Lingua.

C
D

Cobb, Shawna. Little Sticker. 2012. 32p. pap. 24.95 *(978-1-62709-940-0(9))* America Star Bks.

Coerr, Eleanor. The Josefina Story Quilt. Degen, Bruce, illus. 2003. (I Can Read! Level 3 Ser.). 64p. (J). (gr. 2-4). lib. bdg. 13.55 *(978-0-8335-2723-3(1),* Turtleback) Turtleback Bks.

Colandro, Lucille. There Was an Old Lady Who Swallowed a Chick! Lee, Jared, illus. 2011. (ENG.). (J). (gr. -1-k). pap. 18.99 incl. audio compact disk *(978-0-545-27369-5(2))* Scholastic, Inc.

Conrad, Liz, illus. Little Chick. 2009. (My Sparkling Springtime Friends Ser.). (ENG.). 10p. (J). bds. 3.95 *(978-1-58117-866-1(2),* Intervisual/Piggy Toes) Bendon, Inc.

Costain, Meredith. Stella & the Pet Parade. McGowan, Shane, illus. 2015. (Legends in Their Own Lunchbox Ser.). (ENG.). 48p. (gr. 1-2). pap. 7.99 *(978-1-4966-0243-5(9),* Legends in Their Own Lunchbox) Capstone Classroom.

—Stella's Got Talent. McGowan, Shane, illus. 2015. (Legends in Their Own Lunchbox Ser.). (ENG.). 48p. (gr. 1-2). pap. 7.99 *(978-1-4966-0249-7(8),* Legends in Their Own Lunchbox) Capstone Classroom.

Cousins, Lucy. Count with Maisy, Cheep, Cheep, Cheep! Cousins, Lucy, illus. 2015. (Maisy Ser.). (ENG., Illus.). 32p. (J). (-k). 15.99 *(978-0-7636-7643-8(8))* Candlewick Pr.

Cox, Judy. The Secret Chicken Society. Haley, Amanda, illus. (ENG.). 96p. (J). 2013. pap. 5.99 *(978-0-8234-2765-9(X))* 2012. 15.95 *(978-0-8234-2372-9(7))* Holiday Hse., Inc.

Cox, Phil Roxbee. Hen's Pens. Tyler, Jenny, ed. Cartwright, Stephen, illus. rev. ed. 2006. (Phonics Readers Ser.). 16p. (J). (gr. -1-3). pap. 6.99 *(978-0-7945-1506-5(1),* Usborne) EDC Publishing.

Cox, Phil Roxbee & Cartwright, Stephen. Hen's Pens. 2004. (Easy Words to Read Ser.). (Illus.). 16p. (J). (gr. 1-18). pap. 6.95 *(978-0-7945-0113-6(3),* Usborne) EDC Publishing.

—Ted's Shed. 2004. (Phonics Board Bks.). (Illus.). 10p. (J). 4.95 *(978-0-7945-0304-8(7),* Usborne) EDC Publishing.

Crimi, Carolyn. Henry & the Crazed Chicken Pirates. Manders, John, illus. 2010. (ENG.). 40p. (J). (gr. -1-3). pap. 7.99 *(978-0-7636-4999-9(6))* Candlewick Pr.

Cronin, Doreen. The Case of the Weird Blue Chicken. 2016. (Chicken Squad Ser.: 2). lib. bdg. 16.00 *(978-0-606-38495-7(2))* Turtleback Bks.

—The Case of the Weird Blue Chicken: The Next Misadventure. 2015. (Chicken Squad Ser.: 2). 35.75 *(978-1-4906-4049-5(5))* Recorded Bks., Inc.

—The Chicken Squad. Cornell, Kevin, illus. 2014. 92p. (J). ***(978-0-605-90609-9(2))*** Simon & Schuster Children's Publishing.

—The Chicken Squad: The First Misadventure. 2014. (Chicken Squad Ser.: 1). 1.25 *(978-1-4906-2066-4(4));* 33.75 *(978-1-4906-2064-0(8));* 35.75 *(978-1-4906-2065-7(6))* Recorded Bks., Inc.

—The Chicken Squad: The First Misadventure. Cornell, Kevin, illus. (Chicken Squad Ser.: 1). (ENG.). 112p. (J). (gr. 2-5). 2015. pap. 6.99 *(978-1-4424-9677-4(0))* 2014. 12.99 *(978-1-4424-9676-7(2))* Simon & Schuster Children's Publishing. (Atheneum Bks. for Young Readers).

—The Chicken Squad: The First Misadventure. 2015. (Chicken Squad Ser.: 1). lib. bdg. 17.20 *(978-0-606-37884-0(7))* Turtleback Bks.

—Dark Shadows: Yes, Another Misadventure. Gilpin, Stephen, illus. 2017. (Chicken Squad Ser.: 4). (ENG.). 128p. (J). (gr. 2-5). 12.99 *(978-1-4814-5049-2(2),* Atheneum/Caitlyn Dlouhy Books) Simon & Schuster Children's Publishing.

—Into the Wild. 2017. (Chicken Squad Ser.: 3). lib. bdg. 17.20 ***(978-0-606-40204-0(7))*** Turtleback Bks.

—Into the Wild: Yet Another Misadventure. Warrick, Jessica & Gilpin, Stephen, illus. 2017. (Chicken Squad Ser.: 3). (ENG.). 112p. (J). (gr. 2-5). pap. 6.99 *(978-1-4814-5047-8(6))* Simon & Schuster Children's Publishing.

—Into the Wild: Yet Another Misdventure. Gilpin, Stephen, illus. 2016. (Chicken Squad Ser.: 3). (ENG.). 112p. (J). (gr. 2-5). 12.99 *(978-1-4814-5046-1(8),* Atheneum/Caitlyn Dlouhy Books) Simon & Schuster Children's Publishing.

—Smick! Medina, Juana, illus. 2015. (ENG.). 34p. (J). (gr. -1-k). 16.99 *(978-0-670-78578-0(4),* Viking Books for Young Readers) Penguin Young Readers Group.

—The Trouble with Chickens. Cornell, Kevin, illus. (J). (gr. 1-5). 2012. (ENG.). 144p. pap. 5.99 *(978-0-06-121534-6(1))* 2011. (ENG.). 128p. 14.99 *(978-0-06-121532-2(5))* 2011. 128p. lib. bdg. 15.89 *(978-0-06-121533-9(3))* HarperCollins Pubs.

Cutler, Betty Jackson. The Flight of SaraJane. 2008. 29p. pap. 24.95 *(978-1-60672-025-7(2))* America Star Bks.

—The Flight of SaraJane, 1 vol. 2010. 30p. 24.95 *(978-1-4512-1018-7(3))* PublishAmerica, Inc.

Cuyler, Margery. Purim Chicken. Pinillos, Puy, illus. 2017. (ENG.). 32p. (J). (gr. -1-3). 16.99 *(978-0-8075-3381-9(5))* Whitman, Albert & Co.

Daniel, Claire & Ernst, Lisa Campbell. El Pollito Que No Quería Salir del Huevo. Flor Ada, Alma & Campoy, F. Isabel, trs. from ENG. Ernst, Lisa Campbell, illus. 2009. (Green Light Readers Level 2 Ser.).Tr. of Chick That Wouldn't Hatch. (SPA & ENG., Illus.). 28p. (J). (gr. -1-3). pap. 3.99 *(978-0-15-206446-4(X))* Houghton Mifflin Harcourt Publishing Co.

David, Lawrence, ed. Chicken Run: Action-Packed Storybook. Barnes, Tom, photos by. 2005. (Illus.). 48p. (gr. k-4). reprint ed. pap. 8.00 *(978-0-7567-9472-9(2))* DIANE Publishing Co.

Davies, Gill & Freeman, Tina. Happy Hen. 2004. (Tales from Yellow Barn Farm Ser.). (Illus.). 24p. (J). 3.99 *(978-1-85854-323-9(1))* Brimax Books Ltd. GBR. Dist: Byeway Bks.

Davies, Rob. Henhouse High Jinx: Mr. Stevens & Friends. 2013. 176p. 21.99 *(978-1-4669-9492-8(4));* pap. 11.99 *(978-1-4669-9491-1(6))* Trafford Publishing.

Daviess, Maria Thompson. The Golden Bird. 2007. 92p. per. *(978-1-4068-1853-6(4))* Echo Library.

Davis, Jerry & Davis, Katie. Little Chicken's Big Day. Davis, Katie, illus. 2011. (ENG., Illus.). 40p. (J). (gr. -1 — 1). 14.99 *(978-1-4424-1401-3(4),* McElderry, Margaret K. Bks.) McElderry, Margaret K. Bks.

Day, Sunnie. Sunnie & Her Peeps. 2011. 46p. pap. 16.95 *(978-1-4626-4092-8(3))* America Star Bks.

De La Garza, David. The Great, Great, Great Chicken War. 2007. (Illus.). 48p. (J). (gr. -1-3). 15.95 *(978-0-9795266-0-2(4))* Anchorage Foundation Pr.

de Las Casas, Dianne. Madame Poulet & Monsieur Roach, 1 vol. Gentry, Marita, illus. 2009. (ENG.). 32p. (J). (gr. k-3). 16.99 *(978-1-58980-686-3(7))* Pelican Publishing Co., Inc.

Delena Deatherage. The Beginning of People's Chicken. Joe Kent, illus. 2009. 40p. pap. 18.95 *(978-1-4208-9094-5(8))* AuthorHouse.

Dempsey, Kristy. Surfer Chick. Cole, Henry, illus. 2012. (ENG.). 32p. (J). (gr. -1-k). 16.95 *(978-1-4197-0188-7(6),* Abrams Bks. for Young Readers) Abrams, Inc.

deRubertis, Barbara. Hanna Hippo's Horrible Hiccups. Alley, R. W., illus. 2010. (Animal Antics A to Z Ser.). 32p. (J). (gr. -1-3). pap. 7.95 *(978-1-57565-312-9(5));* lib. bdg. 22.60 *(978-1-57565-319-8(2))* Kane Press, Inc.

deRubertis, Barbara & DeRubertis, Barbara. Hanna Hippo's Horrible Hiccups. Alley, R. W., illus. 2012. (Animal Antics A to Z Ser.). 32p. (J). (gr. 2 — 1). cd-rom 7.95 *(978-1-57565-401-0(6))* Kane Press, Inc.

Dewolfe, Jeannee'. The Adventures of Billy Chicken Toes & the Wolf: Add Your Own Art Children's Books. 2012. 56p. pap. 11.97 *(978-1-61204-921-2(4),* Strategic Bk. Publishing) Strategic Book Publishing & Rights Agency (SBPRA).

DiCamillo, Kate. Louise, the Adventures of a Chicken. Bliss, Harry, illus. 2008. (ENG.). 56p. (J). (gr. -1-3). 17.99 *(978-0-06-075554-6(7))* HarperCollins Pubs.

—Louise, the Adventures of a Chicken. Bliss, Harry, illus. 2009. (J). (gr. -1-2). 29.95 incl. audio compact disk *(978-1-4301-0688-3(3))* Live Oak Media.

Dillard, Sarah. Extraordinary Warren: A Super Chicken. Dillard, Sarah, illus. 2014. (Pix Ser.). (ENG., Illus.). 64p. (J). (gr. 1-4). 12.99 *(978-1-4424-5340-1(0),* Aladdin) Simon & Schuster Children's Publishing.

Doan, Janet Mailan. A Monster Stole My Chickens! 2012. 28p. pap. 16.09 *(978-1-4669-6468-6(5))* Trafford Publishing.

Don't Cry Sly. 2004. (J). E-Book incl. cd-rom *(978-1-84444-457-1(0))* Mantra Lingua.

Dorros, Arthur. City Chicken. Date not set. 40p. (J). (gr. -1-1). pap. 5.99 *(978-0-06-443587-1(3))* HarperCollins Pubs.

—City Chicken. Cole, Henry, illus. 2003. 40p. (J). (gr. -1-3). 16.89 *(978-0-06-028483-1(8))* HarperCollins Pubs.

Doudna, Kelly. El Peinado Del Gallo, 1 vol. Haberstroh, Anne, illus. 2007. (Cuentos de Animales Ser.).Tr. of Rooster Combs. (SPA & ENG.). 24p. (J). (gr. k-3). lib. bdg. 24.21 *(978-1-59928-663-1(7),* SandCastle) ABDO Publishing Co.

—Rooster Combs, 1 vol. Haberstroh, Anne, illus. 2006. (Animal Tales Ser.). 24p. (J). (gr. k-3). (ENG.). lib. bdg. 24.21 *(978-1-59679-965-3(X),* SandCastle); pap. 48.42 *(978-1-59679-966-0(8))* ABDO Publishing Co.

Dowell, Frances O'Roark. Chicken Boy. Krause, George, photos by. 2007. (ENG., Illus.). 224p. (J). (gr. 5-9). pap. 6.99 *(978-1-4169-3482-0(0),* Atheneum Bks. for Young Readers) Simon & Schuster Children's Publishing.

—Chicken Boy. 2005. (ENG., Illus.). 208p. (J). (gr. 5-9). 17.99 *(978-0-689-85816-1(7),* Atheneum Bks. for Young Readers) Simon & Schuster Children's Publishing.

—Sam the Man & the Chicken Plan. Bates, Amy June, illus. 2017. (Sam the Man Ser.: 1). (ENG.). 144p. (J). (gr. 1-4). pap. 6.99 *(978-1-4814-4067-7(5))* Simon & Schuster Children's Publishing.

—Sam the Man & the Chicken Plan. 2016. (Sam the Man Ser.: 1). (ENG., Illus.). 128p. (J). (gr. 1-4). 15.99 *(978-1-4814-4066-0(7))* Simon & Schuster Children's Publishing.

Downard, Barry. Carla's Famous Traveling Feather & Fur Show. Downard, Barry, illus. 2006. (ENG., Illus.). 32p. (J). (gr. 4-7). 16.95 *(978-1-59687-171-7(7))* IBks., Inc.

Dunbar, Joyce. A Chick Called Saturday. Granström, Brita, illus. 2004. 32p. (J). 16.00 *(978-0-8028-5260-1(2))* Eerdmans, William B. Publishing Co.

East, Bob. Tommy Cat & the Giant Chickens. East, Matt, illus. 2008. 24p. per. 24.95 *(978-1-4241-9242-7(0))* America Star Bks.

Educa Vision, Inc., Staff. Papiyon. (CRP., Illus.). 21p. (YA). (gr. 3-18). pap. 7.50 *(978-1-58432-059-3(1))* Educa Vision Inc.

Edwards, Michelle. Chicken Man. 2008. (J). *(978-1-58838-237-5(0));* 3rd ed. (Illus.). 32p. 16.95 *(978-1-58838-223-8(0))* NewSouth, Inc. (Junebug Bks.).

Elliott, David. One Little Chicken: A Counting Book. Long, Ethan, illus. 2007. (ENG.). 24p. (J). (gr. -1-3). 16.95 *(978-0-8234-1983-8(5))* Holiday Hse., Inc.

Emberley, Ed & Emberley, Rebecca. Red Hen. Emberley, Ed, illus. 2010. (ENG., Illus.). 32p. (J). (gr. -1-2). 18.99 *(978-1-59643-492-9(9),* 9781596434929) Roaring Brook Pr.

Emberley, Rebecca & Emberley, Ed. Chicken Little. 2011. (Illus.). (J). (gr. -1-2). 29.95 *(978-0-545-29673-1(0))* Weston Woods Studios, Inc.

Erickson, John R. The Case of the Tender Cheeping Chickies. Holmes, Gerald L., illus. 2011. (Hank the Cowdog Ser.). (ENG.). 129p. (J). (gr. 3-6). pap. 5.99 *(978-1-59188-147-6(1))* Maverick Bks., Inc.

Ethier, Vicki. Papa & the Hen. Ethier, Vicki, illus. 2004. (Illus.). 36p. (J). 7.00 *(978-1-928972-12-9(8))* Critter Pubns.

Extraordinary Warren Saves the Day. 2014. (Pix Ser.). (ENG., Illus.). 64p. (J). (gr. 1-4). 12.99 *(978-1-4814-0352-8(4),* Aladdin) Simon & Schuster Children's Publishing.

Fenton, Tanya. Three Silly Chickens. Fenton, Tanya, illus. 2015. (ENG., Illus.). 32p. (J). (gr. -1-1). pap. 8.99 *(978-1-907432-11-8(6))* Hogs Back Bks. GBR. Dist: Independent Pubs. Group.

Finkelstein, Ruth. The Thankyou Twins. Rubenstein, Reva, illus. 2006. 24p. (J). *(978-0-9628157-5-1(6))* Finkelstein, Ruth.

First Chick Stories. Date not set. (Illus.). (J). bds. 9.98 *(978-0-7525-9171-1(1))* Parragon, Inc.

Fitzpatrick, Heather. Chuck: The Chicken That Thought He Was a Duck. 2012. 24p. pap. 17.99 *(978-1-4772-6012-8(9))* AuthorHouse.

Fleming, Maria & Charlesworth, Liza. Chicken in the City. Kennedy, Kelly, illus. 2004. (Grammar Tales Ser.). (ENG.). 16p. (J). (gr. 3-7). pap. 3.25 *(978-0-439-45816-0(1))* Scholastic, Inc.

Flor Ada, Alma. Daniel y Su Mascota. Karas, G. Brian, illus. 2008. (Green Light Readers Level 1 Ser.).Tr. of Daniel's Pet. (SPA & ENG.). 28p. (J). (gr. -1-3). pap. 3.95 *(978-0-15-206243-9(2))* Houghton Mifflin Harcourt Publishing Co.

—Daniel's Pet. Karas, G. Brian, illus. 2010. (Rise & Shine Ser.). (ENG.). 24p. (C). (gr. -1-3). pap. 6.95 *(978-0-15-204865-5(0))* National Geographic School Publishing, Inc.

—Daniel's Pet. 2003. (Green Light Readers — Level 1 Ser.). (gr. -1-2). 13.50 *(978-0-613-64481-5(6),* Turtleback) Turtleback Bks.

Foreman, Michael. Chicken Licken. (Illus.). 32p. (J). 19.95 *(978-0-86264-847-3(5))* Andersen Pr. GBR. Dist: Trafalgar Square Publishing.

Franceschelli, Christopher. Oliver. 2011. (ENG., Illus.). 16p. (J). (gr. -1). 12.95 *(978-1-935954-01-9(6),* 9781935954019) Lemniscaat USA.

Frank Alvarado Madrigal. Las Increíbles Aventuras Del Pollito Pío Pío: The Incredible Adventures of Pew Pew, the Little Chicken. 2010. 32p. pap. *(978-1-4269-2520-7(4))* Trafford Publishing (UK) Ltd.

Freedman, Deborah. Blue Chicken. 2011. (ENG.). 40p. (J). (gr. -1-k). 15.99 *(978-0-670-01293-0(9),* Viking Books for Young Readers) Penguin Young Readers Group.

Gaber, Susan, illus. The Little Red Hen: An Old Fable. 2015. (ENG.). 32p. (J). (gr. -1-3). pap. 8.95 *(978-1-939160-97-3(9))* August Hse. Pubs., Inc.

Galdone, Paul. The Little Red Hen. 2006. (Paul Galdone Classics Ser.). (ENG., Illus.). (J). (gr. -1-3). 40p. 26.99 *(978-0-618-83684-0(5));* 48p. audio compact disk 10.99 *(978-0-618-75250-8(1))* Houghton Mifflin Harcourt Publishing Co.

—The Little Red Hen. Galdone, Paul, illus. (J). (gr. -1-k). pap. 12.95 incl. audio Weston Woods Studios, Inc.

Garland, Betsy. The Golden Rule. 2012. 28p. pap. 16.99 *(978-1-4624-0172-7(4),* Inspiring Voices) Author Solutions, Inc.

Garrett, Lisa. Four Little Chicks. 2009. 24p. pap. 14.99 *(978-1-4490-5032-0(8))* AuthorHouse.

Gehl, Laura. I'm Not Hatching. Wan, Joyce, illus. 2016. (Peep & Egg Ser.). (ENG.). 40p. (J). 16.99 *(978-0-374-30121-7(2),* 9780374301217, Farrar, Straus & Giroux (BYR)) Farrar, Straus & Giroux.

—I'm Not Trick-Or-Treating. Wan, Joyce, illus. 2016. (Peep & Egg Ser.). (ENG.). 40p. (J). 16.99 *(978-0-374-30122-4(0),* 9780374301224, Farrar, Straus & Giroux (BYR)) Farrar, Straus & Giroux.

Gernhart, Cyndi. The Adventures of Gertrude Mccluck, Chicken in Charge Vol. 1: The Missing Eggs, 4 vols. Gernhart, Carlie, illus. l.t. ed. 2005. 32p. (J). 8.00 *(978-0-9778240-1-4(2))* Prairie Winds Publishing.

—The Adventures of Gertrude Mccluck, Chicken in Charge Vol. 2: The Great Crate Mystery, 4 vols. Gernhart, Carlie, illus. l.t. ed. 2005. 40p. (J). 8.00 *(978-0-9778240-2-1(0))* Prairie Winds Publishing.

—The Adventures of Gertrude Mccluck, Chicken in Charge Vol. 3: The Yellow-Eyed Pond Monster, 4 vols. Gernhart, Carlie, illus. l.t. ed. 2005. 52p. (J). 8.00 *(978-0-9778240-3-8(9))* Prairie Winds Publishing.

—The Adventures of Gertrude Mccluck, Chicken in Charge Vol. 4: A Midwinter Light's Dream, 4 vols. Gernhart, Carlie, illus. l.t. ed. 2006. 52p. (J). 8.00 *(978-0-9778240-4-5(7))* Prairie Winds Publishing.

—Gertrude Sees... On the Farm. Gernhart, Cyndi et al, illus. l.t. ed. 2006. 20p. (J). 8.00 *(978-0-9778240-0-7(4))* Prairie Winds Publishing.

Giacomo, Renee San. Lily's Rainbow. Fernandez, Carina, illus. 2013. 28p. pap. 24.95 *(978-1-63004-174-8(2))* America Star Bks.

Ginsburg, Mirra. The Chick & the Duckling. Russian of V. Ésuteyev Publishing Staff, tr. Aruego, Jose & Dewey, Ariane, illus. 2010. (Rise & Shine Ser.). (ENG.). 32p. (C). (gr. -1-3). reprint ed. 11.95 *(978-0-689-71226-5(X))* National Geographic School Publishing, Inc.

Godby, Giovanna. Quaddles, Dwaddles, & Elizabeth: The Tale of a Very Confused Chicken. 2013. 40p. (J). (gr. -1-3). pap. 12.95 *(978-0-9890975-0-5(1))* Caledonia Pr., LLC.

Gomi, Taro. Mommy! Mommy! 2013. (ENG., Illus.). 22p. (J). (gr. -1 — 1). bds. 6.99 *(978-1-4521-0834-6(X))* Chronicle Bks. LLC.

Goodnight, Little Bug & Where's the Chick? 2005. (J). bds. 19.99 *(978-0-9767325-8-7(0))* Toy Quest.

Gorbachev, Valeri. Two Little Chicks Go to School. 2011. (ENG., Illus.). 28p. (J). (gr. -1-3). 6.95 *(978-0-7358-4027-0(X))* North-South Bks., Inc.

Grant, Judyann. Chicken Said, "Cluck!" Truesdell, Sue, illus. 2008. (My First I Can Read Bks.). 32p. (J). (gr. -1-3). lib. bdg. 16.89 *(978-0-06-028724-5(1))* HarperCollins Pubs.

Grant, Judyann Ackerman. Chicken Said, "Cluck!" Truesdell, Sue, illus. 2010. (My First I Can Read Ser.). (ENG.). 32p. (J). (gr. -1-3). pap. 3.99 *(978-0-06-444276-3(4))* HarperCollins Pubs.

—Chicken Said, "Cluck!" Truesdell, Sue, illus. 2008. (My First I Can Read Ser.). (ENG.). 32p. (J). (gr. -1-3). 16.99 *(978-0-06-028723-8(3))* HarperCollins Pubs.

Graves, Keith. Chicken Big. 2010. (ENG., Illus.). 40p. (J). (gr. -1-3). 16.99 *(978-0-8118-7237-9(8))* Chronicle Bks. LLC.

Gray, Kes. Cluck O'Clock. McQuillan, Mary, tr. McQuillan, Mary, illus. 2004. (ENG.). 32p. (J). (gr. k-3). tchr. ed. 17.95 *(978-0-8234-1809-1(X))* Holiday Hse., Inc.

Green, Kate. A Number of Animals. Wormell, Christopher, illus. 2012. (ENG.). 32p. (J). (gr. -1-k). 15.99 *(978-1-56846-222-6(0),* Creative Editions) Creative Co., The.

Griffin, Adele & Sheinmel, Courtney. Agnes & Clarabelle. Palacios, Sara, illus. 2017. (Agnes & Clarabelle Ser.). (ENG.). 80p. (J). 9.99 *(978-1-61963-137-3(7),* 9781619631373, Bloomsbury USA Childrens) Bloomsbury Publishing USA.

Grogan, John. Marley - Not a Peep! Cowdrey, Richard & Whipple, Rick, illus. 2012. (I Can Read Level 2 Ser.). (ENG.). 32p. (J). (gr. k-3). pap. 3.99 *(978-0-06-207477-5(6))* HarperCollins Pubs.

—Not a Peep! Cowdrey, Richard & Whipple, Rick, illus. 2012. (I Can Read Level 2 Ser.). (ENG.). 32p. (J). (gr. k-3). 16.99 *(978-0-06-207478-2(4))* HarperCollins Pubs.

Guatemala, Anne. The Story of Señor Pico. Frazao, Catia, illus. 2007.Tr. of Historia del Señor Pico. (ENG & SPA.). 32p. (J). pap. 17.00 *(978-0-8059-7818-6(6))* Dorrance Publishing Co., Inc.

Gudeon, Adam. Peep & Zeep. 2017. (I Like to Read(r) Ser.). (ENG.). 24p. (J). (gr. -1-3). 14.95 *(978-0-8234-3674-3(8))* Holiday Hse., Inc.

—Peeper & Zeep. 2017. (I Like to Read(r) Ser.). (ENG.). 24p. (J). (gr. -1-3). 6.99 *(978-0-8234-3779-5(5))* Holiday Hse., Inc.

Hagemann, Bernhard. Charlie Gallina Ciega. (Torre de Papel Ser.). (SPA., Illus.). (J). 7.95 *(978-958-04-5032-0(3))* Norma S.A. COL. Dist: Distribuidora Norma, Inc.

Hale, Aaron. Addy Gets Made. 2008. 27p. pap. 24.95 *(978-1-60610-339-5(3))* America Star Bks.

Hansen, Alli. Huevos Rancheros. 2008. 32p. pap. 24.95 *(978-1-60672-993-9(4))* PublishAmerica, Inc.

Happy Hen. 2006. (J). per. 3.99 *(978-1-934004-15-9(4))* Byeway Bks.

Harchy, Atelier Philippe, illus. Chicken Little: A Tale about Common Sense. 2006. (J). 6.99 *(978-1-59939-019-2(1))* Cornerstone Pr.

Harrington, Janice N. Busy-Busy Little Chick. Pinkney, Brian, illus. 2013. (ENG.). 32p. (J). (gr. -1-1). 15.99 *(978-0-374-34746-8(8),* 9780374347468, Farrar, Straus & Giroux (BYR)) Farrar, Straus & Giroux.

Harris, Diane Banks. The Eagle & the Chickens. 2008. 13p. pap. 24.95 *(978-1-60703-092-8(6))* PublishAmerica, Inc.

Hazel Bell. When Fred the Rooster Crowed. 2012. 20p. pap. 24.95 *(978-1-4137-9659-9(1))* America Star Bks.

HB Staff. The Little Chicks Sing. 97th ed. 2003. (Signatures Ser.). (gr. 1-18). pap. 16.50 *(978-0-15-308159-0(7))* Harcourt Schl. Pubs.

Hege, Lynnita. The Little Black Hen. Keyes, Tina Misrasi, illus. 2013. 208p. (J). *(978-0-7399-2465-5(6))* Rod & Staff Pubs., Inc.

Helakoski, Leslie. Big Chickens. Cole, Henry, illus. 2008. (ENG.). 32p. (J). (gr. -1-k). pap. 6.99 *(978-0-14-241057-8(8),* Puffin Books) Penguin Young Readers Group.

—Big Chickens. Cole, Henry, illus. 2008. (J). (gr. -1-3). lib. bdg. 14.65 *(978-0-7569-8913-2(2))* Perfection Learning Corp.

—Big Chickens Fly the Coop. Cole, Henry, illus. 2010. (ENG.). 32p. (J). (gr. -1-k). pap. 6.99 *(978-0-14-241464-4(6),* Puffin Books) Penguin Young Readers Group.

Henderson, Barbara. Down in Mr Brown's Garden. 2009. 40p. pap. 14.75 *(978-1-60860-703-7(8),* Strategic Bk. Publishing) Strategic Book Publishing & Rights Agency (SBPRA).

Hendricks, Linda K. The Rainbow Egg. 2012. 26p. pap. 12.95 *(978-1-4497-7539-1(X),* WestBow Pr.) Author Solutions, Inc.

Hest, Amy. Little Chick: Three Little Stories. 2012. (ENG.). (J). (gr. -1-k). bds. 9.99 *(978-0-7636-5480-1(9))* Candlewick Pr.

Himmelman, John. Chickens to the Rescue. Himmelman, John, illus. 2006. (Barnyard Rescue Ser.). (ENG., Illus.). 32p. (J). (gr. -1-3). 17.99 *(978-0-8050-7951-7(3),* 9780805079517, Holt, Henry & Co. Bks. For Young Readers) Holt, Henry & Co.

Hirschmann, Kris. Triple Trouble Time. 2014. (Tickety Toc Ser.). (ENG.). 32p. (J). (gr. -1-k). pap. 3.99 *(978-0-545-61473-3(2))* Scholastic, Inc.

Hoadley, Jo. Miss Creant: The Adventures of a little Red Hen. l.t. ed. 2004. (Illus.). 127p. (J). per. 15.99 *(978-0-9765088-0-9(X))* Billy Jo Bks.

Hoff, Syd. Henrietta, the Early Bird Treasury. 2016. (ENG.). 144p. (J). (gr. k-5). pap. 14.99 *(978-0-486-80025-7(3))* Dover Pubns., Inc.

Hoffman, Cj. The Dragons & the Simmies: A Friendly Story. 2008. 20p. pap. 10.49 *(978-1-4389-1452-7(0))* AuthorHouse.

Holmes, Guy D. The Chicken Froze His Little Toes. 2011. 28p. pap. 14.99 *(978-1-4567-3819-8(4))* AuthorHouse.

Holmes, Harold H. The Tale of the Purple Chicken & Orange Frog. 2010. 26p. pap. 12.00 *(978-1-60911-653-8(4),* Eloquent Bks.) Strategic Book Publishing & Rights Agency (SBPRA).

Honsinger, Linda. Leonard Lou: Beautiful, Brave, Strong, & True. Honsinger, Alise, illus. 2012. 38p. 24.95 *(978-1-4626-6872-4(0))* America Star Bks.

Hopkins, Jackie Mims. Prairie Chicken Little, 1 vol. Cole, Henry, illus. 2015. (ENG.). 32p. (J). (gr. 1-3). pap. 7.95 *(978-1-56145-834-9(1))* Peachtree Pubs.

Horning, Sandra. Chicks! Goodell, Jon, illus. 2013. (Step into Reading Ser.). (ENG.). 32p. (J). (gr. -1-1). pap. 3.99 *(978-0-307-93221-1(4));* lib. bdg. 12.99 *(978-0-375-97117-4(3))* Random Hse. Children's Bks. (Random Hse. Bks. for Young Readers).

Horstman, Lisa. Squawking Matilda, 0 vols. 2013. (ENG.). 40p. (J). (gr. -1-3). pap. 9.99 *(978-1-4778-1664-6(X),* 9781477816646, Amazon Children's Publishing) Amazon Publishing.

How the Chick Tricked the Fox. (Little Book Practice Reader Ser.). (J). *(978-0-8136-0821-1(X))* Modern Curriculum Pr.

Hubble, Miles & Bryant, Justin. Bob & the Fowl War: Book One in the Poultry Series. 2008. 140p. pap. 11.95 *(978-1-4401-0857-0(9))* iUniverse, Inc.

Hudson, Katy. The Runaway Egg. 2017. (ENG., Illus.). 32p. (J). (gr. -1-2). 16.99 *(978-0-553-52319-5(8),* Random Hse. Bks. for Young Readers) Random Hse. Children's Bks.

The Hungry Chickens: Individual Title Six-Packs. (Literatura 2000 Ser.). (gr. 1-2). 28.00 *(978-0-7635-0136-5(0))* Rigby Education.

Hutchins, Pat. Rosie's Walk. 2009. 9.00 *(978-0-7848-2915-8(2),* Everbind) Marco Bk. Co.

—Where, Oh Where, Is Rosie's Chick? 2016. (ENG., Illus.). 32p. (J). (gr. -1-3). 17.99 *(978-1-4814-6071-2(4),* Simon & Schuster Bks. For Young Readers) Simon & Schuster Bks. For Young Readers.

Hwang, Sun-mi. The Hen Who Dreamed She Could Fly. 2013. lib. bdg. 28.20 *(978-0-606-35094-5(2),* Turtleback) Turtleback Bks.

Image Books Staff. Little Chick: Finger Puppet Book. Put, Klaartje van der, illus. 2015. (ENG.). 12p. (J). (gr. -1 — 1). bds. 6.99 *(978-1-4521-2917-4(7))* Chronicle Bks. LLC.

—Little Chicken. Put, Klaartje van der, illus. 2012. (Little Finger Puppet Board Bks.: FING). (ENG.). 12p. (J). (gr. -1 — 1). bds. 6.99 *(978-1-4521-0811-7(0))* Chronicle Bks. LLC.

Iwamura, Kazuo. Hooray for Spring! Iwamura, Kazuo, illus. 2009. (ENG., Illus.). 32p. (J). (gr. -1-3). 16.95 *(978-0-7358-2228-3(X))* North-South Bks., Inc.

Jadoul, Émile. Good Night, Chickie. 2010. (ENG.). 26p. (J). (gr. -1-k). 14.00 *(978-0-8028-5378-3(1),* Eerdmans Bks For Young Readers) Eerdmans, William B. Publishing Co.

Jennewein, Lenore. Chick-O-Saurus Rex. Jennewein, Daniel, illus. 2013. (ENG.). 32p. (J). (gr. -1-3). 16.99 *(978-1-4424-5186-5(6),* Simon & Schuster Bks. For Young Readers) Simon & Schuster Bks. For Young Readers.

Johansen, Hanna. Henrietta & the Golden Eggs. Barrett, John S., tr. from GER. 2004. (ENG., Illus.). 64p. (J). pap. 9.95 *(978-1-56792-288-2(0))* Godine, David R. Pub.

Johnson, Gerald J. J. Officer Buck MacDuck. Miltenberger, Dave & Jeri, illus. 2013. 24p. pap. 24.95 *(978-1-62709-429-0(6))* America Star Bks.

Johnson, Richard. Little Red Hen & the Grains of Wheat: Big Book English Only. 2004. (Illus.). (J). *(978-1-84444-298-0(5))* Mantra Lingua.

Johnson, Richard, illus. Don't Cry, Sly! 2004. 32p. (J). (ENG & POR.). pap. *(978-1-85269-659-7(1))*; (SPA & ENG.). pap. *(978-1-85269-662-7(1))*; (ENG, ARA & BEN.). pap. *(978-1-85269-649-8(4))*; (ENG & PER.). pap. *(978-1-85269-653-5(2))* Mantra Lingua.

Johnson, Richard & Barkow, Henriette. Little Red Hen & the Grains of Wheat. Jago, illus. 2005. (KOR & ENG.). 32p. (J). pap. *(978-1-84444-210-2(1))* Mantra Lingua.

Jones, Christianne C. Chicken Little, 1 vol. Hermanson, Kyle, illus. (My First Classic Story Ser.). (ENG.). 32p. (gr. k-3). 2011. pap. 7.10 *(978-1-4048-7355-1(4))* 2010. lib. bdg. 22.65 *(978-1-4048-6072-8(X))* Picture Window Bks. (My First Classic Story).

—La Gallinita Roja, 1 vol. Abello, Patricia, tr. from ENG. Magnuson, Natalie, illus. 2006. (Read-It! Readers en Español: Cuentos Folclóricos Ser.).Tr. of Little Red Hen. (SPA.). 32p. (gr. k-3). 21.32 *(978-1-4048-1650-3(X)*, Easy Readers) Picture Window Bks.

—The Little Red Hen, 1 vol. Magnuson, Natalie, illus. 2010. (My First Classic Story Ser.). (ENG.). 32p. (gr. k-3). lib. bdg. 22.65 *(978-1-4048-6073-5(8)*, My First Classic Story) Picture Window Bks.

Jones, Kelly. Unusual Chickens for the Exceptional Poultry Farmer. Kath, Katie, illus. 2015. (ENG.). 224p. (J). (gr. 3-7). 16.99 *(978-0-385-75552-8(X)*, Knopf Bks. for Young Readers) Random Hse. Children's Bks.

Joosse, Barbara M. Higgledy-Piggledy Chicks. Chrustowski, Rick, illus. 2010. 40p. (J). (gr. -1-k). (ENG.). 16.99 *(978-0-06-075042-8(1))*; lib. bdg. 17.89 *(978-0-06-075043-5(X))* HarperCollins Pubs. (Greenwillow Bks.).

Jumbo & Mrs. Hen's Eggs. 2004. (J). per. 15.99 *(978-0-9744205-1-6(4))* Golden Eagle Publishing Hse., Inc.

Justice, Robert H. Rainbow Chicken Feed. 2012. 32p. pap. *(978-1-77097-121-9(1))* FriesenPress.

Keene, Carolyn. Chick-Napped! Pamintuan, Macky, illus. 13th ed. 2008. (Nancy Drew & the Clue Crew Ser.: 13). (ENG.). 96p. (J). (gr. 1-4). pap. 5.99 *(978-1-4169-5522-1(4)*, Aladdin) Simon & Schuster Children's Publishing.

King-smith, Dick. Funny Frank. Eastwood, John, illus. 2003. (ENG.). 112p. (J). (gr. 1-4). 5.99 *(978-0-440-41880-1(1)*, Yearling) Random Hse. Children's Bks.

Knudsen, Michelle. Argus. Wesson, Andrea, illus. 2011. (ENG.). 32p. (J). (gr. -1-3). 15.99 *(978-0-7636-3790-3(4))* Candlewick Pr.

Kok, Gemma. Scribble (Printed in black & White) 2008. 42p. pap. 7.96 *(978-1-4092-2531-7(3))* Lulu Pr., Inc.

Kruse, Donald W. Cluck, Cluck, Cluck Splash! Crank, Donny, illus. 2012. 48p. pap. 12.95 *(978-1-59663-856-3(7)*, Castle Keep Pr.) Rock, James A. & Co. Pubs.

Krystosek, Richard. Chicken Scratch. 2013. 36p. pap. 24.95 *(978-1-63000-536-8(3))* America Star Bks.

Laiz, Jana. Thomas & Autumn. Lamb, Melody, illus. 2013. 40p. (J). 14.95 *(978-0-9814910-9-7(X))* Crow Flies Pr.

Lamb, Lenny. Facing Your Fears: Greener Grass Volume 4. 2012. 48p. pap. 24.95 *(978-1-4626-5398-0(7))* America Star Bks.

—The Truth about Lying: Greener Grass Volume 3. 2012. 48p. 24.95 *(978-1-4626-5046-0(5))* America Star Bks.

Lambert, Patricia. The Blue Ribbon Chicken. 2005. 36p. (J). pap. 14.93 *(978-1-4116-6163-9(X))* Lulu Pr., Inc.

Laminack, Lester. Three Hens & a Peacock, 1 vol. Cole, Henry, illus. 2014. (ENG.). 32p. (J). (gr. -1-3). pap. 7.95 *(978-1-56145-726-7(4))* Peachtree Pubs.

Laminack, Lester L. Three Hens & a Peacock, 1 vol. Cole, Henry, illus. 2011. (ENG.). 32p. (J). (gr. -1-3). 15.95 *(978-1-56145-564-5(4))* Peachtree Pubs.

Landstrom, Lena. Four Hens & a Rooster. Sandin, Joan, tr. from SWE. Landstrom, Olof, illus. 2005. 28p. (J). (gr. -1-3). 16.00 *(978-91-29-66336-5(9))* R & S Bks. SWE. Dist: Macmillan.

Lane, Jessica E. Fletcher: The Quickest Chicken Catcher. 2009. 52p. pap. 31.99 *(978-1-4415-3461-3(X))* Xlibris Corp.

Laurent, Karine. Coo Is in Love, 1 vol. Alastra, Stephanie, illus. 2012. (My Little Picture Book Ser.). (ENG.). 32p. (J). (gr. -1). pap. 6.95 *(978-2-7338-1244-0(0))* Auzou, Philippe Editions FRA. Dist: Consortium Bk. Sales & Distribution.

Lawrence, John. This Little Chick. Lawrence, John, illus. 2013. (ENG., Illus.). 32p. (J). (gr. -1-k). 4.99 *(978-0-7636-6350-6(6))* Candlewick Pr.

—This Little Chick. 2013. lib. bdg. 14.75 *(978-0-606-31599-9(3)*, Turtleback) Turtleback Bks.

Lawson, Barbara Spilman. Ozzy & Rudy. 2016. (Spring Forward Ser.). (J). (gr. 1). *(978-1-4900-9386-4(9))* Benchmark Education Co.

Lehrhaupt, Adam. Chicken in School. Kober, Shahar, illus. 2017. 40p. (J). (gr. -1-3). 17.99 *(978-0-06-236413-5(8))* HarperCollins Pubs.

—Chicken in Space. Kober, Shahar, illus. 2016. 40p. (J). (gr. -1-3). 17.99 *(978-0-06-236412-8(X))* HarperCollins Pubs.

Leland, Debbie. The Little Prairie Hen. Ann Hollis Rife, illus. 2003. 32p. (J). lib. bdg. 14.95 *(978-0-9667086-3-9(6))* Wildflower Run.

Levey, Emma, illus. Hattie Peck. 2016. (ENG.). 32p. (J). (gr. -1-k). 16.99 *(978-1-63450-170-5(5)*, Sky Pony Pr.) Skyhorse Publishing Co., Inc.

Lihou, Gavin. Revenge of the Cannibal Chickens. Ross Kennedy, illus. 2013. 74p. pap. 10.50 *(978-1-62212-484-8(7)*, Strategic Bk. Publishing) Strategic Book Publishing & Rights Agency (SBPRA).

The Little Red Hen. (Ladybird Bks.). (ARA., Illus.). 52p. (J). 4.95 *(978-0-86685-203-6(4)*, LDL158) International Bk. Ctr., Inc.

The Little Red Hen. (Ladybird Bks.). (ARA., Illus.). 14.95 incl. audio *(978-0-86685-211-1(5)*, LDL122C) Librairie du Liban Pubns. FRA. Dist: International Bk. Ctr., Inc.

Little Red Hen & the Grains of Wheat. 2004. (J). (ENG & TUR.). *(978-1-84444-618-6(2))*; (ENG & TAM.). *(978-1-84444-617-9(4))*; (ENG & TAG.). *(978-1-84444-616-2(6))*; (ENG & SPA.). *(978-1-84444-615-5(8))*; (ENG & SOM.). *(978-1-84444-614-8(X))*; (ENG & RUS.). *(978-1-84444-613-1(1))*; (ENG & POR.). *(978-1-84444-612-4(3))*; (ENG & POL.). *(978-1-84444-610-0(7))*; (ENG & PAN.). *(978-1-84444-609-4(3))*; (ENG & KUR.). *(978-1-84444-608-7(5))*; (ENG & KOR.). *(978-1-84444-607-0(7))*; (ENG & JPN.). *(978-1-84444-606-3(9))*; (ENG & ITA.). *(978-1-84444-605-6(0))*; (ENG & HIN.). *(978-1-84444-604-9(2))*; (ENG & GUJ.). *(978-1-84444-603-2(4))*; (ENG & GRE.). *(978-1-84444-602-5(6))*; (ENG & FRE.). *(978-1-84444-601-8(8))*; (ENG & PER.). *(978-1-84444-600-1(X))*; (CRO & ENG.). *(978-1-84444-599-8(2))*; (CHI & ENG.). *(978-1-84444-598-1(4))*; (CHI & ENG.). *(978-1-84444-597-4(6))*; (BEN & ENG.). *(978-1-84444-596-7(8))*; (ARA & ENG.). *(978-1-84444-595-0(X))*; (ALB & ENG.). *(978-1-84444-594-3(1))*; (ENG & VIE.). *(978-1-84444-620-9(4))*; (ENG & URD.). *(978-1-84444-619-3(0))* Mantra Lingua.

Little Red HenGrains. 2004. (J). cd-rom *(978-1-84444-462-5(7))* Mantra Lingua.

Lodge, Jo. Oops! Little Chick. 2013. (Push, Pull, Pop! Bks.). (ENG., Illus.). 10p. (J). (gr. -1 — 1). 6.99 *(978-0-7641-6633-4(6))* Barron's Educational Series, Inc.

Lozzi, Annette. The Mystery of the Vanishing Chickens. Storey, Lela Belle, illus. 2013. 32p. pap. *(978-1-922120-68-7(5))* Interactive Pubns. Pty, Ltd.

Lustig, Loretta, illus. The Little Red Hen: A Tale about Cooperation. 2006. (J). 6.99 *(978-1-59939-018-5(3))* Cornerstone Pr.

MacLachlan, Patricia. Nora's Chicks. Brown, Kathryn, illus. 2013. (ENG.). 40p. (J). (gr. -1-2). 15.99 *(978-0-7636-4753-7(5))* Candlewick Pr.

Mancil, Julie A. Anna's Decision. 2011. 68p. (gr. 4-6). pap. 9.95 *(978-1-4497-1694-3(6)*, WestBow Pr.) Author Solutions, Inc.

Marchini, Tracy. Chicken Wants a Nap. Felix, Monique, illus. 2017. (ENG.). 24p. (J). (gr. 1-3). 17.99 ***(978-1-56846-308-7(1)***, Creative Editions) Creative Co., The.

Marko, Cyndi. The Birdy Snatchers. 2014. (Kung Pow Chicken Ser.: 3). (ENG.). 80p. (J). (gr. k-2). 15.99 *(978-0-545-61072-8(9))* Scholastic, Inc.

—The Birdy Snatchers. Marko, Cyndi, illus. 2014. (Kung Pow Chicken Ser.: 3). (ENG., Illus.). 80p. (J). (gr. k-2). pap. 4.99 *(978-0-545-61068-1(0))* Scholastic, Inc.

—The Birdy Snatchers. 2014. (Kung Pow Chicken Ser.: 3). lib. bdg. 14.75 *(978-0-606-35358-8(5))* Turtleback Bks.

—Bok! Bok! Boom! Marko, Cyndi, illus. 2014. (Kung Pow Chicken Ser.: 2). (ENG., Illus.). 80p. (J). (gr. k-2). 15.99 *(978-0-545-61064-3(8))*; pap. 4.99 *(978-0-545-61063-6(X))* Scholastic, Inc.

—Heroes on the Side. Marko, Cyndi, illus. 2014. (Kung Pow Chicken Ser.: 4). (ENG., Illus.). 80p. (J). (gr. k-2). 15.99 *(978-0-545-61077-3(X))*; pap. 4.99 *(978-0-545-61074-2(5))* Scholastic, Inc.

—Heroes on the Side. 2014. (Kung Pow Chicken Ser.: 4). lib. bdg. 14.75 *(978-0-606-36049-4(2))* Turtleback Bks.

—Let's Get Cracking! Marko, Cyndi, illus. 2014. (Kung Pow Chicken Ser.: 1). (ENG., Illus.). 80p. (J). (gr. k-2). 15.99 *(978-0-545-61062-9(1))*; pap. 4.99 *(978-0-545-61061-2(3))* Scholastic, Inc.

Marshall, James & Marshall, James. Wings: A Tale of Two Chickens. 2003. (ENG., Illus.). 32p. (J). (gr. -1-3). 6.95 *(978-0-618-31659-5(0))* Houghton Mifflin Harcourt Publishing Co.

Martin, David. Peep & Ducky. Walker, David, illus. (ENG.). (J). (— 1). 2015. 24p. bds. 6.99 *(978-0-7636-7243-0(2))* 2013. 32p. 14.99 *(978-0-7636-5039-1(0))* Candlewick Pr.

—Peep & Ducky Rainy Day. Walker, David, illus. 2015. (ENG.). 32p. (J). (— 1). 14.99 *(978-0-7636-6884-6(2))* Candlewick Pr.

Mattingly, Robin. Chicken Church. Swope, Brenda, illus. 2011. 28p. pap. 24.95 *(978-1-4560-0962-5(1))* America Star Bks.

Maxwell, Andre L. & Maxwell, Amanda L. The Great Chicken Caper. Carter, Jill, illus. 2012. 34p. (-18). 18.00 *(978-0-9881811-1-3(8))* Maxwell, Andre.

McBride M. D., Mark A., et al. The Chickens & the Ice Cream. 2010. 28p. pap. 12.99 *(978-1-4490-9172-9(5))* AuthorHouse.

McBrier, Page. The Chicken & the Worm. Peterson, Rick, illus. 2008. 36p. (J). *(978-0-9798439-2-1(8))* Heifer Project International.

McDonald, Jody. Who Is in the Egg? 2010. 28p. pap. 28.03 *(978-1-4500-8840-4(6))* Xlibris Corp.

McDonald, Megan. Hen Hears Gossip. Kim, Joung Un, illus. 2008. 32p. (J). (gr. -1-k). lib. bdg. 17.89 *(978-0-06-113877-5(0))*; (ENG.). 17.99 *(978-0-06-113876-8(2))* HarperCollins Pubs. (Greenwillow Bks.).

McGee, Rick, illus. Eleven Chickens in a Boat: A Story of Faith, Fear, & Feathers! 2013. (J). *(978-1-56722-974-5(3))* Word Aflame Pr.

McLellan, Sean. The Red Booted Chicken. 2009. 48p. (J). pap. 17.49 *(978-1-4389-5610-7(X))* AuthorHouse.

McNamee, Kevin. My Brother the Frog. Morris, Alexander, illus. 2011. 24p. 19.95 *(978-1-61633-167-2(4))*; pap. 10.95 *(978-1-61633-159-7(3))* Guardian Angel Publishing, Inc.

McOmber, Rachel B., ed. McOmber Phonics Storybooks: A Red Hen. rev. ed. (Illus.). (J). *(978-0-944991-25-1(4))* Swift Learning Resources.

—McOmber Phonics Storybooks: Hen Pox. rev. ed. (Illus.). (J). *(978-0-944991-28-2(9))* Swift Learning Resources.

McQueen, Lucinda. The Little Red Hen. McQueen, Lucinda, illus. abr. ed. 2007. (ENG., Illus.). (J). (gr. -1-3). 18.95 *(978-0-545-00511-1(6))* Scholastic, Inc.

Metzger, Steve. The Amazing Turkey Rescue. Paillot, Jim, illus. 2007. (J). ***(978-0-545-01420-5(4))*** Scholastic, Inc.

Meyer, Lisa O. The Sheep & the Chicken. Winward, Makenzie, illus. 2011. 16p. pap. 24.95 *(978-1-4626-0478-4(1))* America Star Bks.

Meyerhoff, Jenny. Project Peep. Chatelain, Éva, illus. 2016. (Friendship Garden Ser.: 3). (ENG.). 144p. (J). (gr. 2-5). pap. 5.99 *(978-1-4814-3913-8(8)*, Aladdin) Simon & Schuster Children's Publishing.

—Project Peep. 2016. (Friendship Garden Ser.: 3). lib. bdg. 16.00 *(978-0-606-38264-9(X))* Turtleback Bks.

Miles, Brenda & Sweet, Susan D. Chicken or Egg: Who Comes First? 2017. (J). ***(978-1-4338-2719-8(0))*** American Psychological Assn.

Mitchell, Malinda. Spencer the Spring Chicken & Other Stories. Schandy, Rosita & Wooten, Neal, illus. 2007. 88p. pap. 23.95 *(978-0-9800675-0-7(2))* Mirror Publishing.

Montanari, Susan McElroy. My Dog's a Chicken. Wilsdorf, Anne, illus. 2016. (ENG.). 40p. (J). (gr. -1-3). 16.99 *(978-0-385-38490-2(4)*, Schwartz & Wade Bks.) Random Hse. Children's Bks.

Morales, Rose. Mary's Egg, 1 vol. 2009. 13p. pap. 24.95 *(978-1-61546-912-3(5))* America Star Bks.

Mortensen, Lori. Chicken Lily. Crittenden, Nina Victor, illus. 2016. (ENG.). 40p. (J). 16.99 *(978-1-62779-120-5(5)*, 9781627791205, Holt, Henry & Co. Bks. For Young Readers) Holt, Henry & Co.

Moss, Yvonne. The Green Eyed Chick. 2011. 20p. (gr. 1-2). pap. 12.99 *(978-1-4634-0051-4(9))* AuthorHouse.

The Mother Goose Caper. 2005. (Georgie Giraffe Chapter Ser.). (J). 7.67 *(978-1-932570-46-5(2))* Pioneer Valley Bks.

Munté, Marta. KUKU AND MWEWE: A SWAHILI FOLKTALE. 2013. (ENG., Illus.). 30p. (J). (gr. -1-k). 16.95 *(978-84-15619-97-0(9))* Eastern National.

Nanette. Little Red. 2004. (Life on Granny's Farm Ser.). (J). 12.95 *(978-0-9741269-1-3(8))* St. Bernard Publishing, LLC.

Nash, Margaret. Hetty's New Hat. Impey, Martin, illus. 2005. (Reading Corner Ser.). 24p. (J). (gr. k-3). lib. bdg. 22.80 *(978-1-59771-007-7(5))* Sea-To-Sea Pubns.

Nelson, Sue Ellen. The Missing Easter Bunny. 2010. 36p. pap. 15.00 *(978-1-60844-439-7(2))* Dog Ear Publishing, LLC.

Nöstlinger, Christine. Juanito Habichuela y Otros Cuentos. (Torre de Papel Ser.). (SPA.). (J). (gr. 4-18). 8.95 *(978-958-04-4533-3(8))* Norma S.A. COL. Dist: Distribuidora Norma, Inc.

Numeroff, Laura Joffe. The Chicken Sisters. Collicott, Sharleen, illus. abr. ed. 2003. (J). (gr. -1-2). 28.95 incl. audio compact disk *(978-1-59112-533-4(2))* Live Oak Media.

Nunez, Marisa. The Featherless Chicken. Thomassen, Hellen, illus. 2003. 32p. (J). 14.95 *(978-84-95730-36-7(7))* Kalandraka Catalunya, Edicions, S.L. ESP. Dist: Independent Pubs. Group.

Nwapa-Ibuaka, Njideka. Tales from Animal Kingdom. unabr. ed. 2003. (Illus.). 40p. (gr. 2-5). pap. 7.95 *(978-0-9661598-4-4(5))* Ekwike Bks. & Publishing.

Odin, Jey. Chicken Fighter. 2011. (ENG.). 128p. (YA). pap., pap. 14.95 *(978-0-9831823-5-1(3)*, 9780983182351) Antarctic Pr., Inc.

Odle, Ingrid. The Case of the Missing Abacus. 2012. 16p. pap. 15.99 *(978-1-4772-5612-1(1))* AuthorHouse.

Ohi, Ruth. Chicken, Pig, Cow & the Purple Problem. Ohi, Ruth, illus. 2010. (Chicken, Pig, Cow Ser.). (ENG., Illus.). 32p. (J). (gr. -1-k). 19.95 *(978-1-55451-219-5(0)*, 9781554512195); 2nd ed. pap. 6.95 *(978-1-55451-218-8(2)*, 9781554512188) Annick Pr., Ltd. CAN. Dist: Publishers Group West (PGW).

—Chicken, Pig, Cow Horse Around. Ohi, Ruth, illus. 2010. (Chicken, Pig, Cow Ser.). (ENG., Illus.). 32p. (J). (gr. -1-k). 19.95 *(978-1-55451-245-4(X)*, 9781554512454) Annick Pr., Ltd. CAN. Dist: Publishers Group West (PGW).

—Chicken, Pig, Cow on the Move. Ohi, Ruth, illus. 3rd ed. 2009. (Chicken, Pig, Cow Ser.). (ENG., Illus.). 32p. (J). (gr. -1-k). 19.95 *(978-1-55451-194-5(1)*, 9781554511945); pap. 6.95 *(978-1-55451-193-8(3)*, 9781554511938) Annick Pr., Ltd. CAN. Dist: Publishers Group West (PGW).

Ohi, Ruth, illus. Chicken, Pig, Cow Horse Around. 3rd ed. 2010. (Chicken, Pig, Cow Ser.). (ENG.). 32p. (J). (gr. -1-k). pap. 6.95 *(978-1-55451-244-7(1)*, 9781554512447) Annick Pr., Ltd. CAN. Dist: Publishers Group West (PGW).

Okereke, Laurence. Barry & Big Joe. 2007. (ENG., Illus.). 20p. (J). *(978-0-9795739-0-3(4))* Dion's Pubn.

Once upon a Time Spanish Version-Chicken Little. 2005. (J). *(978-1-57022-558-1(3))* ECS Learning Systems, Inc.

Once upon a Time Spanish Version-the Little Red Hen. 2005. (J). *(978-1-57022-561-1(3))* ECS Learning Systems, Inc.

Oppenlander, Meredith. In the Hen House. Gedeon, Gloria, illus. l.t. ed. 2006. (ENG.). 12p. (gr. k-2). pap. 7.95 *(978-1-57874-003-1(7)*, Kaeden Bks.) Kaeden Corp.

Orford, Margie. The Little Red Hen. Lilje, Karen, illus. 2011. (Best Loved Tales for Africa Ser.). (ENG.). 32p. (J). (gr. k-2). pap. 10.95 *(978-1-77009-821-3(6))* Jacana Media ZAF. Dist: Independent Pubs. Group.

Pakkala, Christine. Last-But-Not-Least Lola & the Wild Chicken. Hoppe, Paul, illus. 2014. (Last-But-Not-Least Lola Ser.). (ENG.). 216p. (J). (gr. 2-5). 15.95 *(978-1-59078-983-4(0))* Boyds Mills Pr.

Palatini, Margie. Bad Boys Get Henpecked! Cole, Henry, illus. 2009. (ENG.). 32p. (J). (gr. -1-2). 17.99 *(978-0-06-074433-5(2)*, Tegen, Katherine Bks) HarperCollins Pubs.

Park, Barbara. Junie B. Jones Has a Peep in Her Pocket. unabr. ed. 2004. (Junie B. Jones Ser.: No. 15). 80p. (J). (gr. k-3). pap. 17.00 incl. audio *(978-0-8072-0336-1(X)*, Listening Library) Random Hse. Audio Publishing Group.

Parker, Emma. The Fluffiest Chicken. 2010. (Illus.). pap. *(978-1-877561-13-9(4))* First Edition Ltd.

Paschkis, Julie. P. Zonka Lays an Egg, 1 vol. Paschkis, Julie, illus. 2015. (ENG., Illus.). 32p. (J). (gr. 1-3). 16.95 *(978-1-56145-819-6(8))* Peachtree Pubs.

Pasquali, Elena & Vagnozzi, Barbara. Run Little Chicken Run! 2010. (Finger-Trail Animal Tales Ser.). (ENG., Illus.). 10p. (J). (gr. -1-k). bds. 7.99 *(978-0-7459-6173-6(8))* Lion Hudson PLC GBR. Dist: Independent Pubs. Group.

Pavón, Mar. Clucky & the Magic Kettle. 2013. (ENG., Illus.). 30p. (J). (gr. -1-k). 15.95 *(978-84-15619-44-4(8))* Eastern National.

—Clucky in the Garden of Mirrors. 2011. (Clucky Ser.). (ENG., Illus.). 44p. (J). (gr. k-2). *(978-84-15241-04-1(6))* D P & G Military Pubs.

—Clucky the Hen. 2011. (Clucky Ser.). (ENG., Illus.). 32p. (J). (gr. -1-k). *(978-84-15241-08-9(9))* D P & G Military Pubs.

Paye, Won-Ldy & Lippert, Margaret H. Mrs. Chicken & the Hungry Crocodile. Paschkis, Julie, illus. 2014. (ENG.). 32p. (J). (gr. -1-2). pap. 7.99 *(978-1-250-04673-4(4)*, 9781250046734) Square Fish.

Pérez, Amada Irma. Nana's Big Surprise. Gonzalez, Maya Christina, illus. 2013.Tr. of Nana, ¡Qué Sorpresa! (ENG & SPA.). 32p. (J). pap. 9.95 *(978-0-89239-307-7(6)*, Children's Book Press) Lee & Low Bks., Inc.

Perez, Amada Irma & Children's Book Press Staff. Nana, Que Sorpresa! Gonzalez, Maya Christina, illus. 2007.Tr. of Nana's Big Surprise. (ENG & SPA.). 32p. (J). (gr. k-2). lib. bdg. 16.95 *(978-0-89239-190-5(1))* Lee & Low Bks., Inc.

Perl, Erica S. Chicken Butt! Cole, Henry, illus. 2009. (ENG.). 32p. (J). (gr. -1-k). 13.95 *(978-0-8109-8325-0(7)*, Abrams Bks. for Young Readers) Abrams, Inc.

—Chicken Butt's Back! Cole, Henry, illus. 2011. (ENG.). 32p. (J). (gr. -1-k). 13.95 *(978-0-8109-9729-5(0)*, Abrams Bks. for Young Readers) Abrams, Inc.

Petre, Wanda E. The Watch Chicken: The Legend of Russell the Rooster & His Friend Hortense. 2006. 36p. (J). pap. 9.93 *(978-1-4116-9990-8(4))* Lulu Pr., Inc.

Pilney, Dovie. Charlie the Cocky Rooster. 2010. 44p. pap. 18.49 *(978-1-4490-9806-3(1))* AuthorHouse.

Pinkney, Jerry. The Little Red Hen. Pinkney, Jerry, illus. 2006. (ENG., Illus.). 32p. (J). (gr. -1-3). 17.99 *(978-0-8037-2935-3(9)*, Dial Bks) Penguin Young Readers Group.

Pinkwater, Daniel M. Beautiful Yetta: The Yiddish Chicken. Pinkwater, Jill, illus. 2010. (ENG.). 32p. (J). (gr. -1-2). 17.99 *(978-0-312-55824-6(4)*, 9780312558246) Feiwel & Friends.

—Beautiful Yetta's Hanukkah Kitten. Pinkwater, Jill, illus. 2014. (ENG.). 32p. (J). (gr. -1-2). 17.99 *(978-0-312-62134-6(5)*, 9780312621346) Feiwel & Friends.

—The Hoboken Chicken Emergency. Auth, Tony, illus. 2007. (ENG.). 112p. (J). (gr. 1-4). pap. 5.99 *(978-1-4169-2810-2(3)*, Aladdin) Simon & Schuster Children's Publishing.

Pollack, Pam & Belviso, Meg. Gallinas de Aqui para Alla. Adams, Lynn, illus. 2008. (Math Matters en Espanol Ser.). (SPA.). 32p. (J). (gr. -1-3). pap. 5.95 *(978-1-57565-268-9(4))* Kane Press, Inc.

—Gallinas de Aqui para Alla; Chickens on the Move. 2008. pap. 34.95 *(978-1-58013-784-3(9))* Kane Press, Inc.

Ponti, Claude. Chick & Chickie Play All Day! 2013. (Toon Books Level 1 Ser.). lib. bdg. 14.75 *(978-0-606-31595-1(0)*, Turtleback) Turtleback Bks.

—Chick & Chickie Play All Day!, 1 vol. 2013. (Toon Bks). (ENG.). 36p. (J). (gr. k-1). lib. bdg. 27.07 *(978-1-61479-150-8(3))* Spotlight.

—Chick & Chickie Play All Day! Ponti, Claude, illus. 2012. (ENG., Illus.). 36p. (J). (gr. -1-3). 12.95 *(978-1-935179-14-6(4))* TOON Books / RAW Junior, LLC.

Popsicle, Patty. Crack-A-Doodle Horse Tales: A Tale about Scratching. 2011. 24p. pap. 12.99 *(978-1-4520-6094-1(0))* AuthorHouse.

Porter, Harry. Wolf. Stites, Theresa, illus. 2012. 28p. pap. 14.99 *(978-0-9838018-5-6(1))* 4RV Publishing, LLC.

Poskitt, Kjartan & Hargis, Wes. Agatha Parrot & the Thirteenth Chicken. 2017. (Agatha Parrot Ser.). (ENG., Illus.). 160p. (J). (gr. 2-5). 16.99 *(978-0-544-50909-2(9))* Houghton Mifflin Harcourt Publishing Co.

Postgate, Daniel, illus. The Little Red Hen. 2006. (First Reading Level 3 Ser.). 48p. (J). (gr. 1-4). 8.99 *(978-0-7945-1375-7(1)*, Usborne) EDC Publishing.

Price, Hugh. The Truth at Last about the Little Red Hen. Lowe, Isabel, illus. 2003. 16p. (J). pap. *(978-1-877228-19-3(2))* Steele Roberts Aotearoa Ltd.

Price, Mathew. Pollito. Goldman, Judy, tr. Kemp, Moira, illus. 2010. (SPA & ENG.). 10p. bds. 5.99 *(978-1-935021-59-9(1))* Price, Mathew Ltd.

Priddy, Roger. Fluffy Chick & Friends. 2015. (Touch & Feel Cloth Bks.). (ENG.). 6p. (J). (gr. -1 — 1). 12.99 *(978-0-312-51892-9(7)*, 9780312518929, Priddy Bks.) St. Martin's Pr.

Pritchett, Andy. Stick! 2013. (ENG., Illus.). 32p. (J). (gr. -1-2). 15.99 *(978-0-7636-6616-3(5))* Candlewick Pr.

Reasoner, Charles, illus. Peep! Peep! 2015. (J). *(978-1-4795-5943-5(1))* Picture Window Bks.

Rees, Douglas. Tyrannosaurus Rex vs. Edna, the Very First Chicken. Henry, Jed, illus. 2017. (ENG.). 40p. (J). 17.99 ***(978-1-62779-510-4(3)***, 9781627795104, Holt, Henry & Co. Bks. For Young Readers) Holt, Henry & Co.

Reynolds, Aaron. Chicks & Salsa. Bogan, Paulette, illus. 2007. (ENG.). 32p. (J). (gr. 1-3). pap. 7.99 *(978-1-59990-099-5(8)*, 9781599900995, Bloomsbury USA Childrens) Bloomsbury Publishing USA.

Rhoda, the Run Away Chicken. 2006. (J). per. 14.95 *(978-0-9754591-1-9(2))* Cubby Hole Tales.

Rigby Education Staff. Everything Changes: Little Red Riding Hood. (Pebble Soup Explorations Ser.). 16p. (gr. -1-18). 5.00 *(978-0-7635-7051-4(6))* Rigby Education.

Rodriguez, Béatrice. The Chicken Thief. 2010. (Stories Without Words Ser.).Tr. of Voleur de Poule. (ENG., Illus.). 32p. (J). (gr. -1-2). 14.95 *(978-1-59270-092-9(6))* Enchanted Lion Bks., LLC.

Rodriguez, Béatrice, illus. Fox & Hen Together. 2011. (Stories Without Words Ser.). (ENG.). 32p. (J). (gr. -1-3). 14.95 *(978-1-59270-109-4(4))* Enchanted Lion Bks., LLC.

Rosa-Mendoza, Gladys. Lola. 2007. (Englishspanish Story Book Ser.). (ENG & SPA., Illus.). 32p. (J). (gr. -1-3). 13.95 *(978-1-931398-51-0(8))* Me+Mi Publishing.

Rosado, Maribel. Little Red Hen Is a Good Hen. 2017. (Text Connections Guided Close Reading Ser.). (J). (gr. 1). *(978-1-4900-1804-1(2))* Benchmark Education Co.

Rosario, Joann. Puddy Cat & the Chick Muck. Rosario, Joann, illus. 2004. (Illus.). 15p. (J). (gr. -1-5). pap. 10.00 *(978-0-9758746-3-9(2)*, 1246169) J.G.R. Enterprises.

Rubio, Antonio. El Pollito de la Avellaneda. 2006. (SPA., Illus.). 32p. (J). (gr. 5-7). 15.99 *(978-84-96388-12-3(3))* Lectorum Pubns., Inc.

Sansone, V. K. Heavenly Hannah's Little Black Hat. 2009. 32p. pap. 14.98 *(978-0-557-07065-7(1))* Lulu Pr., Inc.

Santillo, LuAnn. The Chick. Santillo, LuAnn, ed. 2003. (Half-Pint Kids Readers Ser.). (Illus.). 7p. (J). (gr. -1-1). pap. 1.00 *(978-1-59256-059-2(8))* Half-Pint Kids, Inc.

Sarfatti, Esther, tr. from ENG. La Lechera. Pierola, Mabel, illus. 2006. (Bilingual Tales Ser.). (SPA.). 24p. (J). (gr. -1-3). pap. 3.99 *(978-0-439-77377-5(6)*, Scholastic en Espanol) Scholastic, Inc.

Sauer, Tammi. Chicken Dance. Santat, Dan, illus. (ENG.). 40p. (J). (gr. -1-2). 2015. pap. 6.95 *(978-1-4549-1477-8(7))* 2009. 14.95 *(978-1-4027-5366-4(7))* Sterling Publishing Co., Inc.

C
D

Scarry, Richard. Egg in the Hole. Golden Books Staff, illus. 2011. (Shaped Board Book Ser.). (ENG.). 20p. (J). (gr. k — 1). bds. 8.99 *(978-0-375-86291-5(9)*, Golden Bks.) Random Hse. Children's Bks.

Schuler, Christoph. Kiki. Eisenring, Rahel Nicole, illus. 2009. (ENG.). 32p. (J). (gr. -1-3). 14.95 *(978-0-7358-2202-3(6))* North-South Bks., Inc.

Schwartz, Corey Rosen & Gomez, Rebecca J. Hensel & Gretel, Ninja Chicks. Santat, Dan, illus. 2016. (ENG.). 40p. (J). (gr. k-3). 17.99 *(978-0-399-17626-5(8)*, G.P. Putnam's Sons Books for Young Readers) Penguin Young Readers Group.

Scotton, Rob. Splat the Cat & the Quick Chicks. Scotton, Rob, illus. 2016. (I Can Read Level 1 Ser.). (Illus.). 32p. (J). (gr. -1-3). pap. 3.99 *(978-0-06-229424-1(5))* HarperCollins Pubs.

Scotton, Rob. Splat the Cat & the Quick Chicks. Eberz, Robert, illus. 2016. 30p. (J). ***(978-1-4844-7139-5(3))*** Harper & Row Ltd.

Sedrak, Asham. The Santa Claus Fox. 2011. 28p. pap. 13.59 *(978-1-4670-2484-6(8))* AuthorHouse.

Senkungu, Dinah. The Wishing Needle. 2011. 40p. pap. 17.04 *(978-1-4520-7108-4(X))* AuthorHouse.

Shah, Idries. The Silly Chicken. Jackson, Jeff, illus. 2005. 32p. (J). pap., pap. 6.99 *(978-1-883536-50-3(2)*, Hoopoe Bks.) I S H K.

—The Silly Chicken/el Pollo Bobo. Wirkala, Rita, tr. Jackson, Jeff, illus. 2005. 32p. (J). (gr. -1-3). 18.00 *(978-1-883536-37-4(5)*, Hoopoe Bks.) I S H K.

Shannon, George. Tippy-Toe Chick, Go! Dronzek, Laura, illus. 2003. (ENG.). 32p. (J). (gr. -1-3). 17.99 *(978-0-06-029823-4(5)*, Greenwillow Bks.) HarperCollins Pubs.

Shoo, Shoo, Shoo! & Other Stories, 6 Packs. (Story Steps Ser.). (gr. k-2). 48.00 *(978-0-7635-9604-0(3))* Rigby Education.

Silver Dolphin en Español Editors. Magical Magnets: Chicken Little. 2006. (SPA., Illus.). 8p. (J). bds. 12.95 *(978-970-718-318-6(7))* Readerlink Distribution Services, LLC.

Sly Fox & Red Hen, Level 2. 2016. (Ladybird Readers Ser.). (ENG.). 48p. (J). (gr. 2-4). pap. 9.99 *(978-0-241-25443-1(4))* Penguin Bks., Ltd. GBR. Dist: Independent Pubs. Group.

Smith, Carrie. Chicken Little: Classic Tales Series. Harpster, Steve, illus. 2011. (Classic Tales Ser.). (J). *(978-1-936258-74-1(9))* Benchmark Education Co.

—The Little Red Hen: Classic Tales Series. Palmer, James, illus. 2011. (Classic Tales Ser.). (J). *(978-1-936258-66-6(8))* Benchmark Education Co.

Smith, Margie Fulton. Chicken Kate's Visit to Church. 2006. 9.00 *(978-0-8059-9071-3(2))* Dorrance Publishing Co., Inc.

Smith, Sindy. Little Lucy Lou. Smith, Sindy, illus. 2012. (Illus.). 38p. 29.95 *(978-1-4489-3350-1(1))* America Star Bks.

Sommer, Carl. The Eagle & the Chickens. Noé, illus. 2016. (J). *(978-1-57537-945-6(7))* Advance Publishing, Inc.

—Proud Rooster & Little Hen. 2003. (Another Sommer-Time Story Ser.). (Illus.). 48p. (J). (gr. 1-4). 16.95 incl. audio *(978-1-57537-559-5(1))* Advance Publishing, Inc.

—Proud Rooster & Little Hen. Budwine, Greg, illus. 2003. (Another Sommer-Time Story Ser.). (ENG.). 48p. (J). (gr. 1-4). 16.95 incl. audio compact disk *(978-1-57537-510-6(9))* Advance Publishing, Inc.

—The Sly Fox & the Chicks. James, Kennon, illus. 2014. (J). pap. *(978-1-57537-966-1(X))* Advance Publishing, Inc.

—The Sly Fox & the Chicks. 2003. (Another Sommer-Time Story Ser.). (Illus.). 48p. (J). (gr. 1-4). 16.95 incl. audio *(978-1-57537-553-3(2))* Advance Publishing, Inc.

—The Sly Fox & the Chicks. James, Kennon, illus. 2003. (Another Sommer-Time Story Ser.). (ENG.). 48p. (J). 16.95 incl. audio compact disk *(978-1-57537-504-5(4))* Advance Publishing, Inc.

—The Sly Fox & the Chicks(El Zorro Astuto y los Pollitos) James, Kennon, illus. 2009. (Another Sommer-Time Story Bilingual Ser.). (SPA & ENG.). 48p. (J). lib. bdg. 16.95 *(978-1-57537-166-5(9))* Advance Publishing, Inc.

Sommer, Sharon. The Adventures of Summer Hills: Rowdy Red's Lesson. 2008. 28p. per. 24.95 *(978-1-4241-9374-5(5))* America Star Bks.

Sophie's Chicken: 6 Small Books. (gr. k-3). 24.00 *(978-0-7635-6232-8(7))* Rigby Education.

Speceal, Edetha. The Lost Egg & Other Stories. 2006. (Illus.). 144p. pap. *(978-1-84401-644-0(7))* Athena Pr.

Sperling, Thomas, illus. Chicken Licken. 2005. (J). *(978-0-7664-1050-3(1))* Abrams, Inc.

—The Little Red Hen. 2005. (J). *(978-0-7664-1052-7(8))* Abrams, Inc.

St. Jean, Alan. The Legend of OinkADoodleMoo. St. Jean, Alan, ed. Krock, Libby Carruth, illus. 2013. 32p. 19.95 *(978-0-9777272-9-2(7))* Oren Village, LLC.

Stanley, David J. A Lovely Day for Knitting. 2010. 28p. pap. 12.50 *(978-1-60911-773-3(5)*, Eloquent Bks.) Strategic Book Publishing & Rights Agency (SBPRA).

Stanton, Elizabeth Rose. Henny. Stanton, Elizabeth Rose, illus. 2014. (ENG., Illus.). 40p. (J). (gr. -1-3). 17.99 *(978-1-4424-8436-8(5)*, Simon & Schuster/Paula Wiseman Bks.) Simon & Schuster/Paula Wiseman Bks.

Starfall Education. Peg the Hen. Starfall Education, ed. 2004. (ENG., Illus.). 8p. (J). pap. *(978-1-59577-002-8(X))* Starfall Education.

Steers, Billy. Lift-The-Flap Tab: Tractor Mac: Friends on the Farm. 2015. (Lift-The-Flap Tab Bks.). (ENG., Illus.). 16p. (J). (gr. -1-k). bds. 8.99 *(978-0-374-30168-2(9)*, 9780374301682) Square Fish.

Stein, David Ezra. Interrupting Chicken. Stein, David Ezra, illus. (ENG., Illus.). 40p. (J). (gr. -1-3). 2016. 7.99 *(978-0-7636-8903-2(3))* 2010. 16.99 *(978-0-7636-4168-9(5))* Candlewick Pr.

—Interrupting Chicken. (J). 1.25 *(978-1-4498-6832-1(0))*; 2011. 37.75 *(978-1-4498-6828-4(2))*; 2011. 39.75 *(978-1-4498-6829-1(0))*; 2011. 37.75 *(978-1-4498-6831-4(2))* Recorded Bks., Inc.

—Interrupting Chicken. Stein, David Ezra, illus. 2016. (ENG., Illus.). 40p. (J). (gr. -1-3). 18.40 *(978-0-606-39099-6(5))* Turtleback Bks.

Stewart, Maddie. Bertie Rooster. Aggs, Patrice, tr. Aggs, Patrice, illus. 2007. (Panda Cubs Ser.: 02). (ENG.). 48p. (J). pap. 9.95 *(978-0-86278-798-1(X))* O'Brien Pr., Ltd., The IRL. Dist: Dufour Editions, Inc.

Stockham, Jess, illus. The Cockerel, the Mouse & the Little Red Hen. (Flip-Up Fairy Tales Ser.). (ENG.). 24p. (J). 2007. (gr. -1-2). audio compact disk *(978-1-84643-092-3(5))* 2006. (gr. 2-2). *(978-1-904550-75-4(4))* Child's Play International Ltd.

Stoeke, Janet Morgan. The Loopy Coop Hens. 2013. (Penguin Young Readers Level 2 Ser.). lib. bdg. 13.55 *(978-0-606-28751-7(5)*, Turtleback) Turtleback Bks.

—Minerva Louise on Christmas Eve. Stoeke, Janet Morgan, illus. 2009. (ENG., Illus.). 32p. (J). (gr. -1-k). pap. 6.99 *(978-0-14-241449-1(2)*, Puffin Books) Penguin Young Readers Group.

—Pip's Trip. Stoeke, Janet Morgan, illus. 2014. (Loopy Coop Hens Ser.). (ENG., Illus.). 32p. (J). (gr. 1-2). pap. 3.99 *(978-0-448-48133-3(2)*, Penguin Young Readers) Penguin Young Readers Group.

—Snow Hens. 2016. (Loopy Coop Hens Ser.). (ENG., Illus.). 32p. (J). (gr. 1-2). pap. 3.99 *(978-0-448-48843-1(4)*, Penguin Young Readers) Penguin Young Readers Group.

Stoeke, Janet Morgan & Bader, Bonnie. Letting Go. Stoeke, Janet Morgan, illus. 2015. (Loopy Coop Hens Ser.). (ENG., Illus.). 32p. (J). (gr. 1-2). 3.99 *(978-0-448-48458-7(7)*, Penguin Young Readers) Penguin Young Readers Group.

Stout, Shawn K. Don't Chicken Out. Ying, Victoria, illus. 2013. (Not-So-Ordinary Girl Ser.: 3). (ENG.). 176p. (J). (gr. 1-5). pap. 5.99 *(978-1-4169-7111-5(4)*, Aladdin) Simon & Schuster Children's Publishing.

—Don't Chicken Out. Ying, Victoria, illus. 2013. (Not-So-Ordinary Girl Ser.: 3). (ENG.). 176p. (J). (gr. 1-5). 15.99 *(978-1-4169-7929-6(8)*, Simon & Schuster/Paula Wiseman Bks.) Simon & Schuster/Paula Wiseman Bks.

Strader, Irm. What Came First. 2012. 32p. pap. *(978-1-77067-828-6(X))* FriesenPress.

Strong, Jeremy. Chicken Licken. Blundell, Tony, illus. 2007. (Collins Big Cat Ser.). (ENG.). 136p. (J). (gr. 1-2). pap. 7.99 *(978-0-00-718672-3(X))* HarperCollins Pubs. Ltd. GBR. Dist: Independent Pubs. Group.

Stuchner, Joan Betty. Can Hens Give Milk?, 1 vol. Weissmann, Joe, illus. 2013. (ENG.). 32p. (J). (gr. -1-3). 9.95 *(978-1-4598-0427-2(9))* Orca Bk. Pubs. USA.

Sutton, Jane. What's up with This Chicken?, 1 vol. Welling, Peter, illus. 2015. (ENG.). 32p. (J). (gr. k-3). 16.99 *(978-1-4556-2085-2(8))* Pelican Publishing Co., Inc.

Sykes, Julie. Dora's Chicks. Chapman, Jane, illus. 2004. 32p. (J). pap. 6.95 *(978-1-58925-386-5(8))*; (gr. -1-2). 14.95 *(978-1-58925-015-4(X))* Tiger Tales.

—Dora's Eggs. Chapman, Jane, illus. 2007. (Storytime Board Bks.). (J). (gr. -1-3). bds. 6.95 *(978-1-58925-801-3(0))* Tiger Tales.

Tafuri, Nancy. Five Little Chicks. Tafuri, Nancy, illus. 2011. (Classic Board Bks.). (ENG., Illus.). 34p. (J). (gr. -1 — 1). bds. 7.99 *(978-1-4424-0722-0(0)*, Little Simon) Little Simon.

—Five Little Chicks. Tafuri, Nancy, illus. 2006. (ENG., Illus.). 32p. (J). (gr. -1-3). 16.99 *(978-0-689-87342-3(5)*, Simon & Schuster Bks. For Young Readers) Simon & Schuster Bks. For Young Readers.

Teague, Mark. The Sky Is Falling! 2015. (ENG., Illus.). 32p. (J). (gr. -1-k). 16.99 *(978-0-545-63217-1(X))* Scholastic, Inc.

Thomas, Dylan. Iona'r lâr. 2005. (WEL., Illus.). 33p. *(978-0-86243-434-2(3))* Y Lolfa.

Thomas, Jan. Is Everyone Ready for Fun? Thomas, Jan, illus. 2011. (ENG., Illus.). 40p. (J). (gr. -1-3). 14.99 *(978-1-4424-2364-0(1)*, Beach Lane Bks.) Beach Lane Bks.

Thompson, Lauren. Little Chick. Butler, John, illus. 2014. (ENG.). 30p. (J). (gr. -1-k). bds. 5.99 *(978-1-4424-9311-7(9)*, Little Simon) Little Simon.

—Little Chick. Butler, John, illus. 2014. (J). *(978-1-4351-5351-6(0)*, Simon & Schuster Bks. For Young Readers) Simon & Schuster Bks. For Young Readers.

—Little Chick/Little Bunny Vertical 2-Pack. Butler, John, illus. 2014. (ENG.). 60p. (J). (gr. -1-k). bds. 11.98 *(978-1-4814-1876-8(9)*, Little Simon) Little Simon.

—Wee Little Chick. Butler, John, illus. 2008. (Wee Little Ser.). (ENG.). 32p. (J). (gr. -1-1). 15.99 *(978-1-4169-3468-4(5)*, Simon & Schuster Bks. For Young Readers) Simon & Schuster Bks. For Young Readers.

Thompson, Mike. Chicken Boy & the Wrath of Dr. Dimwad. Thompson, Mike, illus. 2008. (Illus.). 102p. (J). per. 9.95 *(978-0-9799216-0-5(0))* Thompson Original Productions LLC.

Tiger Tales, ed. Chicken Little. East, Nick, illus. 2016. (My First Fairy Tales Ser.). (ENG.). 32p. (J). (gr. -1-2). pap. 7.99 *(978-1-58925-476-3(7))* Tiger Tales.

Tomlinson, Jill. The Hen Who Wouldn't Give Up. Howard, Paul, illus. 2014. (ENG.). 112p. (J). (gr. -1-2). pap. 9.99 *(978-1-4052-7193-6(0))* Egmont Bks., Ltd. GBR. Dist: Independent Pubs. Group.

Top That, ed. Cock a Doodle Boo. 2008. (Story Book Ser.). 22p. (J). (gr. -1). *(978-1-84666-559-2(0)*, Tide Mill Pr.) Top That! Publishing PLC.

Townsend, Amber C. The Hungry Chickens. 2007. (Illus.). (J). per. 7.95 *(978-0-9801297-4-8(5))* G Publishing LLC.

ToyBox Innovations, creator. Disney's Chicken Little Read-along. 2006. (Disney's Read Along Ser.). (ENG., Illus.). 24p. (J). pap. *(978-0-7634-2170-0(7))* Walt Disney Records.

—Disney's Instant Classics: Chicken Little/Lilo & Stitch/Brother Bear. unabr. abr. ed. 2005. (Disney's Read along Collection). (ENG., Illus.). (J). pap. *(978-0-7634-1148-0(5))* Walt Disney Records.

Trasler, Janee. Dinnertime for Chickies. Trasler, Janee, illus. 2014. (Chickies Ser.). (ENG., Illus.). 24p. (J). (gr. -1 — 1). bds. 8.99 *(978-0-06-227470-0(8)*, HarperFestival) HarperCollins Pubs.

—A New Chick for Chickies. Trasler, Janee, illus. 2014. (Chickies Ser.). (ENG., Illus.). 24p. (J). (gr. -1 — 1). bds. 8.99 *(978-0-06-227471-7(6)*, HarperFestival) HarperCollins Pubs.

Trout Fishing in America Staff, et al. My Name Is Chicken Joe. Jorisch, Stéphane, illus. 2009. (ENG.). 50p. (J). (gr. -1-2). 16.95 *(978-2-923163-49-9(4))* La Montagne Secrete CAN. Dist: Independent Pubs. Group.

Two Little Chicks: KinderReaders, 6 Packs. (Kinderstarters Ser.). 8p. (gr. -1-1). 21.00 *(978-0-7635-8646-1(3))* Rigby Education.

Valdez, Joseph G. Lean on Me, Lee. Martinez, Gayle Denise, illus. 2012. 24p. pap. *(978-1-77067-670-1(8))* FriesenPress.

Valentina, Marina. Lost in the Roses. 2008. (Illus.). 24p. (J). pap. 5.95 *(978-1-60108-024-0(7))* Red Cygnet Pr.

—Lost in the Roses. Valentina, Marina, illus. 2007. (Illus.). 24p. (J). (gr. -1-1). 14.95 *(978-1-60108-014-1(X))* Red Cygnet Pr.

Van Leeuwen, Jean. Chicken Soup. Gavril, David, illus. 2009. (ENG.). 40p. (J). (gr. k-2). 16.95 *(978-0-8109-8326-7(5)*, Abrams Bks. for Young Readers) Abrams, Inc.

Vitale, Jill. Freddie: The Free-Range Chicken. 2007. (ENG., Illus.). 28p. (J). (gr. 1-2). 15.95 *(978-0-9767269-6-8(3))* WND Bks, Inc.

—Freddie the Free-Range Chicken. 2006. (J). 12.95 *(978-0-9767269-5-1(5)*, Kids Ahead Bks.) WND Bks, Inc.

Vokey, Jessica. Chester the Easter Chicken. 2012. 28p. pap. 15.99 *(978-1-4771-4276-9(2))* Xlibris Corp.

Vue, Jeng Tong & Vue, See. Baby Chick & the Fox. 2009. 44p. pap. 9.95 *(978-1-936107-27-8(9))* Salem Author Services.

Wahl, Phoebe. Sonya's Chickens. 2015. (ENG., Illus.). 32p. (J). (gr. -1-3). 17.99 *(978-1-77049-789-4(7)*, Tundra Bks.) Tundra Bks. CAN. Dist: Penguin Random Hse. LLC.

Walker, Anna. Peggy: A Brave Chicken on a Big Adventure. (ENG., Illus.). 32p. (J). (gr. -1-3). 2017. pap. 6.99 *(978-0-544-92819-0(9)*, HMH Books For Young Readers) 2014. 16.99 *(978-0-544-25900-3(9))* Houghton Mifflin Harcourt Publishing Co.

—Peggy: A Brave Chicken on a Big Adventure. 2017. (ENG.). (J). (gr. -1-3). lib. bdg. 17.20 ***(978-0-606-39828-2(7))*** Turtleback Bks.

Wallen, Virginia. Amanda: Duck or Chicken? 2007. 17.00 *(978-0-8059-8828-4(9))* Dorrance Publishing Co., Inc.

Waltz, Michael. The Hen & I. 2012. (ENG.). pap. 15.00 *(978-1-4675-5236-3(4))* Independent Pub.

Waring, Richard & Jayne, Waring -. La Gallina Hambrienta. Church, Caroline Jayne, illus. 2003. (SPA.). 28p. (J). (gr. k-2). 17.99 *(978-84-261-3339-7(8))* Juventud, Editorial ESP. Dist: Lectorum Pubns., Inc.

Weber, Elka. One Little Chicken. Kleven, Elisa, illus. 2011. (ENG.). 32p. (J). (gr. -1-2). 16.99 *(978-1-58246-374-2(3)*, Tricycle Pr.) Random Hse. Children's Bks.

Weston Woods Staff, creator. Chicken Little. 2004. (J). 38.75 *(978-1-55592-392-1(5))*; 18.95 *(978-1-55592-391-4(7))* Weston Woods Studios, Inc.

—Wings: A Tale of Two Chickens. 2011. 18.95 *(978-0-439-72920-8(3))*; 38.75 *(978-0-439-72921-5(1))* Weston Woods Studios, Inc.

When Aunt Mattie Got Her Wings. 2014. (ENG., Illus.). 32p. (J). (gr. -1-3). 17.99 *(978-1-4814-1044-1(X)*, Beach Lane Bks.) Beach Lane Bks.

Whiten, Jan. Chooky-Doodle-Doo. Hanley, Sinéad, illus. 2015. (ENG.). 32p. (J). (-k). 12.99 *(978-0-7636-7327-7(7))* Candlewick Pr.

Wiggin, Kate Douglas. A Village Stradivarius. 2004. reprint ed. pap. 1.99 *(978-1-4179-9941-5(1))* Kessinger Publishing, LLC.

Wiles, Deborah. Love, Ruby Lavender. 2005. (ENG., Illus.). 240p. (J). (gr. 2-5). reprint ed. pap. 7.99 *(978-0-15-205478-6(2))* Houghton Mifflin Harcourt Publishing Co.

—Love, Ruby Lavender. 2004. 216p. (J). (gr. 3-7). pap. 36.00 incl. audio *(978-0-8072-2096-2(5)*, Listening Library) Random Hse. Audio Publishing Group.

Williams, Brenda. Millie's Chickens. Cis, Valeria, illus. 2014. 40p. (J). 16.99 *(978-1-78285-082-3(1))* Barefoot Bks., Inc.

Williams, Greg. Puggley Wuggley & the Three-Legged Chicken. 2011. 40p. pap. 19.00 *(978-1-60746-233-0(8))* FastPrncil, Inc.

Williams, Randy. A Hero Named Herman. 2007. 21p. pap. 24.95 *(978-1-4241-8648-8(X))* PublishAmerica, Inc.

Willis, Jeanne. Chicken Clicking. Ross, Tony, illus. 2015. (ENG.). 32p. (J). (gr. -1-k). pap. 9.99 *(978-1-78344-161-7(5))* Andersen Pr. GBR. Dist: Independent Pubs. Group.

Wilson, Barbara. Mrs. Hen & Her Six Chicks. Fine, Aron, illus. 2012. (ENG.). 16p. (gr. k-3). pap. 9.00 *(978-1-56778-543-2(3))* Wilson Language Training.

Wolff, Ashley. The Baby Chicks Are Singing: Sing along in English & Spanish! Wolff, Ashley, illus. 2005. (ENG., Illus.). 22p. (J). (gr. -1 — 1). bds. 7.99 *(978-0-316-06732-4(6))* Little, Brown Bks. for Young Readers.

Woodson, Rick. Poodles & Thunderchicken. 2012. 40p. pap. 24.95 *(978-1-4626-7531-9(X))* America Star Bks.

Wormell, Chris. A Number of Animals. 2003. (Illus.). 24p. (J). (gr. -1-3). pap. 7.95 *(978-0-89812-384-5(4)*, Creative Paperbacks) Creative Co., The.

Yashar, Michael. The Chickadee Story. 2008. 15p. pap. 24.95 *(978-1-60813-032-0(0))* America Star Bks.

Yoon, Salina. Penguin Goes to the Farm! Yoon, Salina, illus. 2010. (Illus.). 10p. bds. 7.95 *(978-1-60747-752-5(1)*, Pickwick Pr.) Phoenix Bks., Inc.

Young-Robinson, Christine. Chicken Wing 2nd ed. 2005. (Illus.). 32p. (J). per. 9.95 *(978-0-9706985-1-3(8))* Young-Robinson, Christine.

Zephaniah, Benjamin. Funky Chickens. (ENG., Illus.). 96p. (J). 9.95 *(978-0-14-037945-7(2))* Penguin Bks., Ltd. GBR. Dist: Trafalgar Square Publishing.

Zilis, Tom, illus. The Little Red Hen: Read Well Level K Unit 20 Storybook. 2003. (Read Well Level K Ser.). 20p. (J). *(978-1-57035-691-9(2)*, 55600) Cambium Education, Inc.

Zschock, Martha Day. Hello, Rhode Island! 2011. (Hello! Ser.). (ENG., Illus.). 16p. (J). (gr. -1-k). bds. 9.95 *(978-1-933212-62-3(4)*, Commonwealth Editions) Applewood Bks.

CHIEF JUSTICES

see Judges

CHIHUAHUA (DOG BREED)

Hengel, Katherine. Chipper Chihuahuas, 1 vol. Doucet, Bob, illus. 2010. (Super SandCastle Ser.). (ENG.). 24p. 25.65 *(978-1-61613-377-1(5)*, Super SandCastle) ABDO Publishing Co.

Lunis, Natalie. Chihuahua: Señor Tiny. (Little Dogs Rock! Ser.). 32p. (gr. 2-7). 2016. (ENG.). (J). pap. 8.95 *(978-1-944998-46-2(2))* 2009. (Illus.). (YA). lib. bdg. 25.27 *(978-1-59716-743-7(6))* Bearport Publishing Co., Inc.

Shores, Erika L. All about Chihuahuas, 1 vol. 2012. (Dogs, Dogs, Dogs Ser.). (ENG., Illus.). 24p. (gr. k-1). lib. bdg. 26.65 *(978-1-4296-8724-9(X)*, Pebble Plus) Capstone Press of Coughlan Cos.

CHILD, LYDIA MARIA, 1802-1880

Jackson, Constance L. Over the River: Life of Lydia Maria Child, Abolitionist for Freedom, 1802-1880. 2008. (Illus.). 160p. pap. 18.95 *(978-0-9818204-0-8(9))* Permanent Productions Publishing.

CHILD ABUSE

see also Child Sexual Abuse

Becker, Jacalyn D. I Am No One's Little Girl but God's Own Child, 1 vol. 2010. 56p. pap. 16.95 *(978-1-4489-4954-0(8))* America Star Bks.

Bollen, Dan. The Mother! Secrets of the House. 2011. 62p. pap. 15.99 *(978-1-4568-8005-7(5))* Xlibris Corp.

Burns, Cheryl Am. A-B-Used Me. 2011. 20p. 11.99 *(978-1-4567-4205-8(1))* AuthorHouse.

Cavaciuti, Susan. Someone Hurt Me. Cavaciuti, Susan, illus. 2004. (Illus.). 222p. pap. 8.95 *(978-1-890995-20-1(7)*, Vital Health Publishing) Square One Pubs.

Child Abuse. 2007. (Social Issues Firsthand Ser.). (Illus.). 120p. (YA). (gr. 8-12). lib. bdg. 28.70 *(978-0-7377-3835-3(9)*, Greenhaven Pr., Inc.) Cengage Gale.

Gerrits, Julie & Newton, Sydney. Child Abuse. 2010. (ENG.). 48p. (J). pap. *(978-0-7787-2134-5(5))*; lib. bdg. *(978-0-7787-2127-7(2))* Crabtree Publishing Co.

Giacabello, John. You & Violence in Your Family. 2009. (Family Matters Ser.). 48p. (gr. 5-8). 53.00 *(978-1-61512-484-8(5)*, Rosen Reference) Rosen Publishing Group, Inc., The.

Giacobello, John. You & Violence in Your Family. 2005. (Family Matters Ser.). (Illus.). 48p. (J). (gr. 5-8). lib. bdg. 29.25 *(978-0-8239-3353-2(9))* Rosen Publishing Group, Inc., The.

Gordon, Sherri Mabry & Mabry-Gordon, Sherri. Are You Being Abused? 2015. (Got Issues? Ser.). (ENG.). 128p. (J). (gr. 7-7). 37.27 *(978-0-7660-6979-4(6))* Enslow Pubs., Inc.

Hall, Shyima. Hidden Girl: The True Story of a Modern-Day Child Slave. 2014. (ENG., Illus.). 240p. (YA). (gr. 9). 18.99 *(978-1-4424-8168-8(4)*, Simon & Schuster Bks. For Young Readers) Simon & Schuster Bks. For Young Readers.

Honowitz, Stacey. My Privates Are Private. 2012. 24p. 19.95 *(978-1-4575-1327-5(7))* Dog Ear Publishing, LLC.

J'Lynn. Who's Your Daddy, 1 vol. 2010. 64p. pap. 19.95 *(978-1-4489-9515-8(9))* America Star Bks.

Libal, Joyce. A House Between Homes: Youth in the Foster Care System. 2003. (Youth with Special Needs Ser.). (Illus.). 127p. (YA). pap. 14.95 *(978-1-4222-0419-1(7))* Mason Crest.

—Protective Services. Albers, Lisa et al, eds. 2014. (Living with a Special Need Ser.: 16). 128p. (J). (gr. 7-18). 25.95 *(978-1-4222-3042-8(2))* Mason Crest.

—Somebody Hear Me Crying: Youth in Protective Services. 2003. (Youth with Special Needs Ser.). (Illus.). 127p. (YA). pap. 14.95 *(978-1-4222-0430-6(8))* Mason Crest.

McKinnon, Margie. Repair for Teens: A Program for Recovery from Incest & Childhood Sexual Abuse. Splho, Michal, illus. 2012. 138p. (J). 28.95 *(978-1-61599-127-3(1))*; pap. 16.95 *(978-1-61599-126-6(3))* Loving Healing Pr., Inc.

Miller, Susan B. When Parents Have Problems: A Book for Teens & Older Children Who Have a Disturbed or Difficult Parent. 2nd ed. 2012. xiv, 105p. (J). pap. 19.95 *(978-0-398-08713-5(X))* Thomas, Charles C. Pub., Ltd.

Penney, Betty. Tell Your Mother. 2004. (Illus.). 32p. (J). pap. 8.95 *(978-0-9631975-4-2(1))* Morgan, E. A.

Rankin, Renee. Miss Lantz & Sadey: First in the Series of Little Sunshines Life Journey. 2013. 44p. pap. 16.95 *(978-1-63000-412-5(X))* America Star Bks.

Rogers, Barbara. Screams from Childhood 2004. 272p. per. 19.95 *(978-0-9719097-2-4(5))* Barabara Pr.

Stevens, Dylan. Wooded Sanctuary. 2004. 136p. (YA). pap. 13.95 *(978-0-595-31093-7(1))* iUniverse, Inc.

Stewart, Sheila. When Daddy Hit Mommy. (Kids Have Troubles Too Ser.). 48p. (YA). (gr. 5-18). 2010. lib. bdg. 19.95 *(978-1-4222-1696-5(9))* 2009. pap. 7.95 *(978-1-4222-1909-6(7))* Mason Crest.

Wood, Ira. How to Stay Safe at Home & On-line. 2009. (Reading Room Collection 2 Ser.). 24p. (gr. 3-4). 42.50 *(978-1-60851-972-9(4)*, PowerKids Pr.) Rosen Publishing Group, Inc., The.

CHILD ABUSE—FICTION

The adventures of officer Byrd. 2007. (J). 16.99 *(978-0-9787322-0-2(0))* Officer Byrd Publishing Co.

Alexander, Tonia. Sometimes I Forget to Breathe. 2nd ed. 2005. (YA). *(978-0-9770550-0-5(0))* Head On Dialogue Publishing.

Alger, Horatio. Phil the Fiddler. 2006. pap. *(978-1-4068-0667-0(6))* Echo Library.

Alphin, Elaine Marie. Counterfeit Son. 2010. (ENG., Illus.). 192p. (YA). (gr. 9). pap. 7.99 *(978-0-547-25853-9(4))* Houghton Mifflin Harcourt Publishing Co.

Anjelais, M. Breaking Butterflies. 2014. (ENG.). 272p. (J). (gr. 9). 17.99 *(978-0-545-66766-1(6)*, Chicken Hse., The) Scholastic, Inc.

Avasthi, Swati. Split. 2012. (ENG.). 288p. (YA). (gr. 9). pap. 9.99 *(978-0-375-86341-7(9)*, Ember) Random Hse. Children's Bks.

Banting, Celia. I Only Said I Had No Choice. 2006. (I Only Said Ser.). (Illus.). 202p. (YA). pap. 14.99 *(978-0-9786648-0-0(9))* Wighita Pr.

Barcellona, Kelley Powell. The Hive. 2009. 92p. 14.95 *(978-0-9824095-1-0(6))* Pegasus Bks. for Children.

Barker, M. P. Mending Horses. 2014. (ENG.). 320p. (J). (gr. 5). 17.95 *(978-0-8234-2948-6(2))* Holiday Hse., Inc.

Beard, Sarah. Porcelain Keys. 2014. pap. 15.99 *(978-1-4621-1396-5(6)*, Horizon Pubs.) Cedar Fort, Inc./CFI Distribution.

Beauty of the Broken. 2014. (ENG., Illus.). 368p. (YA). (gr. 9). 17.99 *(978-1-4814-0709-0(0)*, Simon Pulse) Simon Pulse.

Ben, Mikaelsen. Touching Spirit Bear. 2014. (ENG.). 256p. (J). 11.24 *(978-1-63245-157-6(3))* Lectorum Pubns., Inc.

Brouwer, Sigmund. Unleashed, 1 vol. 2015. (Retribution Ser.). (ENG.). 168p. (YA). (gr. 8-12). pap. 9.95 *(978-1-4598-0730-3(8))* Orca Bk. Pubs. USA.

Burgess, Melvin. Nicholas Dane. 2013. (ENG.). 432p. (YA). (gr. 9-13). pap. 9.99 *(978-0-312-55146-9(0)*, 9780312551469) Square Fish.

Cassidy, Anne. Looking for JJ. 2009. (ENG., Illus.). 336p. (J). (gr. 7). pap. 20.95 *(978-0-15-206638-3(1))* Houghton Mifflin Harcourt Publishing Co.

Chaltas, Thalia. Because I Am Furniture. 2010. (ENG.). 368p. (YA). (gr. 7-18). 8.99 (978-0-14-241510-8(3), Speak) Penguin Young Readers Group.
Crosby, Sarah. Cindy's Story, 1 vol. Hare, Mary Alyce, illus. 2009. 47p. pap. 24.95 (978-1-60749-608-3(9)) America Star Bks.
Crutcher, Chris. Chinese Handcuffs. 2004. (ENG.). 304p. (YA). (gr. 9). pap. 9.99 (978-0-06-059839-6(5), Greenwillow Bks.) HarperCollins Pubs.
Cummins, Maria S. The Lamplighter. 2011. 308p. pap. 16.99 (978-1-61203-228-3(1)) Bottom of the Hill Publishing.
D'Adamo, Francesco. Iqbal. Leonori, Ann, tr. from ITA. 2005. (ENG., Illus.). 128p. (J). (gr. 3-7). reprint ed. pap. 6.99 (978-1-4169-0329-1(1), Aladdin) Simon & Schuster Children's Publishing.
—Iqbal Vol. 5: A Novel. Leonori, Ann, tr. 2003. (ENG., Illus.). 128p. (J). (gr. 3-7). 17.99 (978-0-689-85445-3(5), Atheneum Bks. for Young Readers) Simon & Schuster Children's Publishing.
Deans, Sis Boulos. Racing the Past. 2005. (ENG.). 160p. (J). (gr. 3-7). reprint ed. 5.99 (978-0-14-240308-2(3), Puffin Books) Penguin Young Readers Group.
—Racing the Past. 2005. 151p. (J). (gr. 5-9). 13.65 (978-0-7569-5068-2(6)) Perfection Learning Corp.
DeFelice, Cynthia C. Signal. 2011. (ENG.). 176p. (J). (gr. 5-8). pap. 8.99 (978-0-312-61776-9(3), 9780312617769) Square Fish.
Dessen, Sarah. Lock & Key. 2009. (ENG.). 448p. (YA). (gr. 7-18). 10.99 (978-0-14-241472-9(7), Speak) Penguin Young Readers Group.
—Lock & Key. 2009. lib. bdg. 22.10 (978-0-606-14396-7(3), Turtleback) Turtleback Bks.
Donohoe, Helen. Birdy Flynn. 2017. (ENG.). 384p. pap. 11.99 (978-1-78074-939-6(2)) Oneworld Pubns. GBR. Dist: Publishers Group West (PGW).
Donovan, Rebecca. Barely Breathing, 0 vols. unabr. ed. 2013. (Breathing Ser.: 2). (ENG.). 512p. (YA). (gr. 10-12). pap. 9.99 (978-1-4778-1717-9(4), 9781477817179, Amazon Children's Publishing) Amazon Publishing.
—The Breathing Series: Books 1 And 2, 0 vols. 2013. (Breathing Ser.). (ENG.). 978p. (YA). (gr. 10-12). pap. 12.99 (978-1-4778-1695-0(X), 9781477816950, Skyscape) Amazon Publishing.
—Reason to Breathe, 0 vols. 2013. (Breathing Ser.: 1). (ENG.). 466p. (YA). (gr. 10-12). pap. 9.99 (978-1-4778-1714-8(X), 9781477817148, Amazon Children's Publishing) Amazon Publishing.
Draper, Sharon M. Forged by Fire. 2013. (Hazelwood High Trilogy Ser.: 2). (ENG., Illus.). 176p. (YA). (gr. 7). pap. 9.99 (978-1-4424-8914-1(6), Atheneum Bks. for Young Readers) Simon & Schuster Children's Publishing.
—Forged by Fire. 2013. (Hazelwood High Trilogy Ser.: 2). lib. bdg. 20.85 (978-0-606-32333-8(3), Turtleback) Turtleback Bks.
Dunbar, Helene. These Gentle Wounds. 2014. (ENG.). 312p. (YA). pap. 11.99 (978-0-7387-4027-0(6), Flux) North Star Editions.
Ellis, Ann Dee. This Is What I Did. 2009. (ENG.). 176p. (J). (gr. 7-17). pap. 7.99 (978-0-316-01362-8(5)) Little, Brown Bks. for Young Readers.
Felin, M. Sindy. Touching Snow. (ENG., Illus.). 240p. (YA). (gr. 7). 2011. pap. 11.99 (978-1-4424-1735-9(8)) 2007. 16.99 (978-1-4169-1795-3(0)) Simon & Schuster Children's Publishing. (Atheneum Bks. for Young Readers).
Fine, Anne. Blood Family. 2017. (ENG., Illus.). 304p. (YA). (gr. 9). 17.99 (978-1-4814-7773-4(0), Simon & Schuster Bks. For Young Readers) Simon & Schuster Bks. For Young Readers.
Flinn, Alex. Breathing Underwater. unabr. ed. 2004. (Young Adult Cassette Librarieslm Ser.). 272p. (J). (gr. 7-18). pap. 36.00 incl. audio (978-0-8072-0992-9(9), S YA 346 SP, Listening Library) Random Hse. Audio Publishing Group.
—Nothing to Lose. 2004. 288p. (J). 16.99 (978-0-06-051750-2(6), HarperTeen) HarperCollins Pubs.
Francesco, D'Adamo. Iqbal. 2014. (ENG.). 128p. (J). (gr. 3-7). 11.24 (978-1-63245-261-0(8)) Lectorum Pubns., Inc.
Haddix, Margaret Peterson. Don't You Dare Read This, Mrs. Dunphrey. 2012. (ENG.). 128p. (YA). (gr. 7-7). pap. 9.99 (978-1-4424-4315-0(4), Simon & Schuster Bks. For Young Readers) Simon & Schuster Bks. For Young Readers.
Heathfield, Lisa. Paper Butterflies. 2017. (ENG.). 272p. (YA). (gr. 7-12). 18.99 **(978-1-5124-8241-6(2)**, Carolrhoda Bks.) Lerner Publishing Group.
Hernandez, David. Suckerpunch. 2007. (ENG.). 224p. (YA). (gr. 9-18). 17.99 (978-0-06-117330-1(4), HarperTeen) HarperCollins Pubs.
Hopkinson, Deborah. A Bandit's Tale: The Muddled Misadventures of a Pickpocket. 2016. (ENG.). 304p. (J). (gr. 3-7). lib. bdg. 19.99 (978-0-385-75500-9(7), Knopf Bks. for Young Readers) Random Hse. Children's Bks.
Hulet, Debra. Independence Rock. 2011. 208p. pap. 13.99 (978-1-59955-441-9(0), Bonneville Bks.) Cedar Fort, Inc./CFI Distribution.
Jacobson, Jennifer Richard. Stained. (ENG.). 208p. (YA). (gr. 8). 2012. pap. 10.99 (978-1-4424-8565-5(5), Atheneum Bks. for Young Readers) 2005. (Illus.). 16.95 (978-0-689-86745-3(X), Atheneum/Richard Jackson Bks.) Simon & Schuster Children's Publishing.
Johansson, J. R. Cut Me Free. 2015. (ENG.). 304p. (YA). (gr. 9-16). 17.99 (978-0-374-30023-4(2), 9780374300234, Farrar, Straus & Giroux (BYR)) Farrar, Straus & Giroux.
Johnson, D. C. & Turner, Sandra. Let's Be Friends. Johnson, D. C. & Johnson, Darnell, illus. 2007. (J). per. 9.95 (978-1-933556-66-6(8)) Publishers' Graphics, L.L.C.
Klass, David. You Don't Know Me. 2010. (ENG.). 288p. (YA). (gr. 9-12). pap. 9.99 (978-0-312-65302-6(6)) Square Fish.
Kreller, Susan. You Can't See the Elephants. Gaffney, Elizabeth, tr. from GER. 2015. (ENG.). 192p. (J). (gr. 5-7). 16.99 (978-0-399-17209-0(2), G.P. Putnam's Sons Books for Young Readers) Penguin Young Readers Group.
Lew, Craig. Breath to Breath. Dryden, Emma, ed. 2015. (ENG.). 448p. (J). (gr. 9). 19.95 (978-1-939775-08-5(6)) March 4th, Inc.
Lewis, Beverly. SummerHill Secrets, Vol. 1. 2007. (Summerhill Secrets Ser.: Vols. 1-5). (ENG.). 560p. (gr. 6-9). pap. 17.00 (978-0-7642-0445-6(9)) Bethany Hse. Pubs.
Lois, Lowry. Gossamer. 2006. (ENG.). 144p. (J). (gr. 5-7). 17.99 (978-0-618-68550-9(2)) Houghton Mifflin Harcourt Publishing Co.
—Gossamer. 2008. (ENG.). 176p. (J). (gr. 3-7). 6.99 (978-0-385-73416-5(6), Yearling) Random Hse. Children's Bks.
MacLean, Jill. Home Truths, 1 vol. 2016. (ENG.). 224p. (YA). (gr. 6-10). 14.95 (978-1-897151-96-9(9), Dancing Cat Bks.) Cormorant Bks. Inc. CAN. Dist: Orca Bk. Pubs. USA.
Miller, Mary Beth. Aimee. 2005. 276p. (gr. 9-12). 17.00 (978-0-7569-6303-3(6)) Perfection Learning Corp.
Murdoch, Emily. If You Find Me. (ENG.). (YA). (gr. 7). 2014. 288p. pap. 10.99 (978-1-250-03327-7(6), 9781250033277) 2013. 256p. 17.99 (978-1-250-02152-6(9), 9781250021526) St. Martin's Pr. (St. Martin's Griffin).
Olson, Gretchen. Call Me Hope. 2008. (ENG.). 288p. (J). (gr. 3-7). pap. 5.99 (978-0-316-01239-3(4)) Little, Brown Bks. for Young Readers.
Parner, Rosey. Para el Abuso: La palabra asociada al Abuso. 2006. 17.00 (978-0-8059-7330-3(3)) Dorrance Publishing Co., Inc.
Parker, Robert B. Chasing the Bear. 2010. (ENG.). 176p. (YA). (gr. 7-18). 8.99 (978-0-14-241573-3(1), Speak) Penguin Young Readers Group.
Parsons, Ash. Still Waters. 2015. (ENG.). 320p. (YA). (gr. 9). 17.99 (978-0-399-16847-5(8), Philomel Bks.) Penguin Young Readers Group.
Perry, Jolene. Stronger Than You Know. 2014. (ENG.). 256p. (YA). (gr. 8-12). 16.99 (978-0-8075-3155-6(3)) Whitman, Albert & Co.
Peters, Julie Anne. Rage: A Love Story. 2010. (ENG.). 306p. (YA). (gr. 9). pap. 9.99 (978-0-375-84411-9(2), Knopf Bks. for Young Readers) Random Hse. Children's Bks.
Pokeberry, P. J. The Huckenpuck Papers: The Tales of a Family's Secret & a Young Girls Search for Self-Esteem. 2003. (Illus.). 87p. (J). pap. 8.95 (978-0-943962-03-0(X)) Viewpoint Pr.
Roe, Robin. A List of Cages. 2017. (ENG.). 320p. (YA). (gr. 7-12). 17.99 (978-1-4847-6380-3(7)) Hyperion Bks. for Children.
Rosas, Marcelino. Afuera: A Young Latino's Journey. 2013. 226p. (YA). pap. 12.99 (978-0-9859437-0-7(X)) Proud Peacock Publishing.
Rottman, S. L. Hero, 1 vol. 2007. (ENG.). 144p. (YA). (gr. 7-18). (978-1-56145-427-3(3)) Peachtree Pubs.
—Out of the Blue, 1 vol. (ENG.). 288p. (gr. 7-12). 2014. (J). pap. 9.95 (978-1-56145-786-1(8)) 2009. (YA). 16.95 (978-1-56145-499-0(0)) Peachtree Pubs.
Schmidt, Gary D. Orbiting Jupiter. (ENG.). 192p. (gr. 7). 2017. (YA). pap. 9.99 (978-0-544-93839-7(9), HMH Books For Young Readers) 2015. (J). 17.99 (978-0-544-46222-9(X), Clarion Bks.) Houghton Mifflin Harcourt Publishing Co.
—Orbiting Jupiter. 2017. (ENG.). (YA). (gr. 7). lib. bdg. 20.85 **(978-0-606-39818-3(X))** Turtleback Bks.
Shaw, Susan. The Boy from the Basement. 2006. (ENG.). 208p. (YA). (gr. 7-18). 6.99 (978-0-14-240546-8(9), Speak) Penguin Young Readers Group.
Shea, Pegi Deitz & Deitz Shea, Pegi. The Carpet Boy's Gift, 1 vol. Morin, Leane, illus. 2005. (ENG.). 40p. (J). (gr. 3-6). 16.95 (978-0-88448-248-2(0)) Tilbury Hse. Pubs.
Shusterman, Neal. Bruiser. 2010. (ENG.). 336p. (YA). (gr. 9-18). 17.99 (978-0-06-113408-1(2), HarperTeen) HarperCollins Pubs.
Stahler, David, Jr. Doppelganger. (YA). 2008. (ENG.). 272p. (gr. 8). pap. 8.99 (978-0-06-087234-2(9), HarperTeen) 2006. (Illus.). 272p. (gr. 7-12). 16.99 (978-0-06-087232-8(2)) 2006. (Illus.). 258p. (gr. 7-12). lib. bdg. 17.89 (978-0-06-087233-5(0)) HarperCollins Pubs.
Straus, Susan Farber. Somebody Cares: A Guide for Kids Who Have Experienced Neglect. Keay, Claire, illus. 2016. 32p. (J). (978-1-4338-2109-7(5), Magination Pr.) American Psychological Assn.
Swindells, Robert. Abomination. 2008. (ENG.). 208p. (YA). (gr. 7). per. 12.95 (978-0-552-55588-3(6)) Transworld Publishers Ltd. GBR. Dist: Independent Pubs. Group.
Tamanini, Kara T. I Promised Not to Tell. 2009. 44p. pap. 18.50 (978-1-60860-470-8(5), Eloquent Bks.) Strategic Book Publishing & Rights Agency (SBPRA).
Vigilante, Danette. The Trouble with Half a Moon. 2015. (ENG.). 208p. (J). (gr. 5). 7.99 (978-0-14-751550-6(5), Puffin Books) Penguin Young Readers Group.
Warwick, J. M. An Open Vein. 2007. (YA). per. 12.95 (978-1-933963-96-9(4)) Grove Creek Publishing, LLC.
Waters, Tawni. Beauty of the Broken. 2014. 368p. 17.99 (978-1-4814-1857-7(2)) Simon & Schuster, Inc.
Werlin, Nancy. The Rules of Survival. 2008. (ENG.). 304p. (YA). (gr. 7-18). 8.99 (978-0-14-241071-4(3), Speak) Penguin Young Readers Group.
Wright, Julie. My Not-So-Fairytale Life. 2005. 256p. (YA). pap. 15.95 (978-1-59038-476-3(8)) Deseret Bk. Co.
Wynne-Jones, Tim. The Maestro. l.t. ed. 2013. 304p. pap. (978-1-4596-6503-3(1)) ReadHowYouWant.com, Ltd.

CHILD AND PARENT

see Parent and Child

CHILD AUTHORS

Here are entered works on children as authors and works written by children.

Loewen, Nancy. Make Me Giggle: Writing Your Own Silly Story, 1 vol. Doerrfeld, Cori & Lyles, Christopher, illus. 2009. (Writer's Toolbox Ser.). (ENG.). 32p. (gr. 2-4). pap. 8.95 (978-1-4048-5704-9(4)) Picture Window Bks.
McCurry, Kristen. Pick a Picture, Write a Story!, 1 vol. 2014. (Little Scribe Ser.). (ENG.). 32p. (gr. 1-2). lib. bdg. 27.32 (978-1-4765-4238-6(4), Aplus Bks.) Capstone Press of Coughlan Cos.
Owen, James A., ed. Secrets of the Dragon Riders: Your Favorite Authors on Christopher Paolini's Inheritance Cycle: Completely Unauthorized. 2010. (ENG., Illus.). 192p. (J). (gr. 7-11). pap. 12.95 (978-1-933771-97-7(6)) BenBella Bks.
Thomson, Rachel Starr & Currey, Carolyn Joy. Tales of the Heartily Homeschooled. 2008. 216p. pap. (978-0-9739591-7-8(7)) Little Dozen Press.

CHILD BIRTH

see Childbirth

CHILD DEVELOPMENT

see also Child Psychology; Child Rearing; Children—Growth

Anderson, Nancy. My Dad Takes a Train to Work. 2016. (Rosen REAL Readers: Social Studies Nonfiction / Fiction: Family, Community, & the World Ser.). 8p. (gr. 1-k). pap. 5.46 (978-1-5081-2278-4(4), Rosen Classroom) Rosen Publishing Group, Inc., The.
—My Family's Famous Pizza. 2016. (Rosen REAL Readers: Social Studies Nonfiction / Fiction: Family, Community, & the World Ser.). 12p. (gr. 1-k). pap. 6.33 (978-1-5081-2559-4(7), Rosen Classroom) Rosen Publishing Group, Inc., The.
—My Mother Helps Me with Homework. 2016. (Rosen REAL Readers: Social Studies Nonfiction / Fiction: Family, Community, & the World Ser.). 8p. (gr. 1-k). pap. 5.46 (978-1-5081-2284-5(9), Rosen Classroom) Rosen Publishing Group, Inc., The.
Bartholomew, Andrew & Bartholomew, Hailey. Ruby Who? Zinn, Alarna, illus. 2012. 40p. pap. (978-0-9876653-0-0(8)) Pause for Effect Ltd.
Brignaud, Pierre, illus. Caillou - Toddler Essentials: 5 Books about Growing. 2015. (ENG.). 120p. (J). (gr. -1-k). 12.99 (978-2-89718-171-0(0)) Caillouet, Gerry.
Chamberlain, Catherine. Basic Concept Workbook. 2006. (Illus.). 168p. (J). per. 34.95 (978-0-7606-0655-1(2)) LinguiSystems, Inc.
Cloyd, Nancy J. & Wach, Delia Bowman. Teddy Bear's Favorite Pictures: A Quiet Time Sharing Book. Wach, Delia Bowman, illus. 2007. (Illus.). 32p. (J). (gr. -1). 15.95 (978-0-929915-75-3(5)) Headline Bks., Inc.
Coldwell, Lamar. Mr. Adams Shows Us Vibration. 2016. (Rosen REAL Readers: STEM & STEAM Collection). 12p. (gr. 1-k). pap. 6.33 (978-1-5081-2643-0(7), Rosen Classroom) Rosen Publishing Group, Inc., The.
Conigliaro, Phil & Yu, Tae-Won. My First Baby Signs. 2017. (ENG., Illus.). 20p. (J). 15.95 (978-0-7611-8948-0(3)) Workman Publishing Co., Inc.
Dahl, Regina. When Butterflies Fly. 2013. 24p. pap. 10.95 (978-1-4497-8095-1(4), WestBow Pr.) Author Solutions, Inc.
Ford, Jean. Growth & Development. Forman, Sara, ed. 2013. (Young Adult's Guide to the Science of Health Ser.: 15). 128p. (J). (gr. 7-18). 24.95 (978-1-4222-2810-4(X)) Mason Crest.
Gray, Virginia Butler. My Magic Glasses. 2012. 20p. pap. 12.99 (978-1-4525-6031-1(5)) Balboa Pr.
Hack, Brittany. American Sign Language, Counting with Sea Creatures. 2012. 28p. pap. 24.95 (978-1-4626-8930-9(2)) America Star Bks.
Halpin, Mikki. It's Your World - If You Don't Like It, Change It: Activism for Teenagers. 2004. (ENG.). 304p. (YA). (gr. 7). pap. 14.99 (978-0-689-87448-2(0), Simon Pulse) Simon Pulse.
Hardy, Sherrie. Just Say No. 2012. 16p. pap. 15.99 (978-1-4772-5316-8(5)) AuthorHouse.
Helen, Grace. Ms. Marpoli Always Says: (Small Experiences) 2012. 36p. 24.95 (978-1-4512-3026-0(5)) America Star Bks.
Hirose, George, photos by. I Catch My Moment: Art & Writing by Children on the Life of Play. 2008. (Illus.). 56p. (J). (gr. -1-3). pap. 10.00 (978-1-929299-06-5(0)) Touchstone Ctr. Pubns.
Hotchkins, Dewayne. Looking at My Grandmother's Old Letters. 2016. (Rosen REAL Readers: Social Studies Nonfiction / Fiction: Family, Community, & the World Ser.). 8p. (gr. 1-k). pap. 5.46 (978-1-5081-2308-8(X), Rosen Classroom) Rosen Publishing Group, Inc., The.
Iverson, Jenna. A Smile a Day: A Child's Daily Journal. 2011. 372p. 30.74 (978-1-4269-5188-6(4)); pap. 20.74 (978-1-4269-5187-9(6)) Trafford Publishing.
James, Wayan. Map Tools Help Us Move from Place to Place. 2016. (Rosen REAL Readers: Social Studies Nonfiction / Fiction: Family, Community, & the World Ser.). 12p. (gr. 1-k). pap. 6.33 (978-1-5081-2356-9(X), Rosen Classroom) Rosen Publishing Group, Inc., The.
—Playing with Marbles. 2016. (Rosen REAL Readers: STEM & STEAM Collection). 8p. (gr. 1-k). pap. 5.46 (978-1-5081-2368-2(3), Rosen Classroom) Rosen Publishing Group, Inc., The.
Johnson, Ali C. My Two Little Hands Book. 2012. 32p. pap. 13.95 (978-1-4497-6071-7(6), WestBow Pr.) Author Solutions, Inc.
Kiers, Erin L. I Have Chakras Just Like You. 2012. 24p. pap. (978-1-4602-0343-9(7)) FriesenPress.
Lauren, Jessica. Piggy Wiggy, Yum Yum: My Healthy Future! 2012. 28p. pap. 19.99 (978-1-4772-2045-0(3)) AuthorHouse.
Markova, Dawna. Como Desarrollar la Inteligencia de Sus Hijos. 2010.Tr. of How to Develop Your Child's. (SPA.). (J). 9.95 (978-968-403-887-5(9)) Selector, S.A. de C.V. MEX. Dist: AIMS International Bks., Inc.
McAlpine, Margaret. Working with Children. 2004. (My Future Career Ser.). (Illus.). 64p. (gr. 3-7). lib. bdg. 27.00 (978-0-8368-4241-8(3), Gareth Stevens Learning Library) Stevens, Gareth Publishing LLLP.
McLachlan, Joni. Twilla & the Fuzzy Finger. McLachlan, J. P., illus. 2012. 20p. pap. (978-0-9878035-2-8(2)) Insomniac Pr.
Mokhemar, Mary Ann. Just for Kids Interactive Auditory Processing Pictures Manual. 2006. (J). 0.00 (978-0-7606-0665-0(X)) LinguiSystems, Inc.
Monds, Pirkko. Thanks Series Edition: Therapeutic Healing & Nurturing Kid's Stories. 2012. 48p. pap. 20.45 (978-1-4525-0599-2(3)) Balboa Pr.
Mulstay, Linda Muratore. Autism & PDD Answering Questions, Level 1. 2006. (J). per. 29.95 (978-0-7606-0673-5(0)) LinguiSystems, Inc.
Muratore, Linda Mulstay. Autism & PDD Answering Questions, Level 2. 2006. (J). per. 29.95 (978-0-7606-0674-2(9)) LinguiSystems, Inc.
Murphy, John Paul. Watt's Special Purpose. 2012. 20p. pap. 17.99 (978-1-4685-5344-4(5)) AuthorHouse.
Myers, Douglas E. Pivot-Point: The Beginning of Your Financial Journey. 2012. 96p. pap. 13.95 (978-1-4772-4154-7(X)) AuthorHouse.
Paderewski, Elliot. My Father Was Born in the United States. 2016. (Rosen REAL Readers: Social Studies Nonfiction / Fiction: Family, Community, & the World Ser.). 8p. (gr. 1-k). pap. 5.46 (978-1-5081-2290-6(3), Rosen Classroom) Rosen Publishing Group, Inc., The.
—My Mom Takes a Bus to Work. 2016. (Rosen REAL Readers: Social Studies Nonfiction / Fiction: Family, Community, & the World Ser.). 8p. (gr. 1-k). pap. 5.46 (978-1-5081-2272-2(5), Rosen Classroom) Rosen Publishing Group, Inc., The.
—My Mom's Magic Bus. 2016. (Rosen REAL Readers: Social Studies Nonfiction / Fiction: Family, Community, & the World Ser.). 8p. (gr. 1-k). pap. 5.46 (978-1-5081-2488-7(4), Rosen Classroom) Rosen Publishing Group, Inc., The.
—My Teacher Was a Marine. 2016. (Rosen REAL Readers: Social Studies Nonfiction / Fiction: Family, Community, & the World Ser.). 8p. (gr. 1-k). pap. 5.46 (978-1-5081-2512-9(0), Rosen Classroom) Rosen Publishing Group, Inc., The.
Paonessa, Mary. Growth & Development with Friends, 8 vols. 3rd rev. ed. 2003. (Human Growth & Development Ser.). (Illus.). 41p. (J). (gr. 5-18). pap. 9.00 (978-0-9711721-0-4(2), 388) Paon Pubns.
—Growth & Development with Friends & Family, 8 vols. 3rd rev. ed. 2003. (Human Growth & Development Ser.). (Illus.). 64p. (J). (gr. 6-18). pap. 11.00 (978-0-9711721-2-8(9), 390) Paon Pubns.
Preparing for School Success. 2017. **(978-1-59723-348-4(X))** Active Parenting Pubs.
Ramirez, Lasean. Push & Pull. 2016. (Rosen REAL Readers: STEM & STEAM Collection). 8p. (gr. 1-k). pap. 5.46 (978-1-5081-2365-1(9), Rosen Classroom) Rosen Publishing Group, Inc., The.
Robertson, Charmaine. My Mother Was Born in Mexico. 2016. (Rosen REAL Readers: Social Studies Nonfiction / Fiction: Family, Community, & the World Ser.). 8p. (gr. 1-k). pap. 5.46 (978-1-5081-2281-4(4), Rosen Classroom) Rosen Publishing Group, Inc., The.
—Ramon's Town Tour. 2016. (Rosen REAL Readers: Social Studies Nonfiction / Fiction: Family, Community, & the World Ser.). 8p. (gr. 1-k). pap. 5.46 (978-1-5081-2485-6(X), Rosen Classroom) Rosen Publishing Group, Inc., The.
Rothenberg, Annye. Why Do I Have To? Wenzel, David T., illus. 2009. 40p. (J). pap. 9.95 (978-0-9790420-1-0(1)) Perfecting Parenting Pr.
Saffer, Sally. A Friend in Need Is a Friend Indeed: A Lesson Within a Story from the Series, Learning to Be Wise. 2012. (ENG.). 30p. (J). pap. 13.95 (978-1-4787-2040-9(9)) Outskirts Pr., Inc.
Saffter, Sally. Every Cloud Has a Silver Lining: A Lesson Within a Story from the Series Learning to Be Wise. 2012. (ENG.). 28p. (J). pap. 16.95 (978-1-4327-9322-7(5)) Outskirts Pr., Inc.
Sample, Vincent W. Reach to Your Youth Mentor Project Vol. 1: Reaching Your Potential Student's Workbook. 2007. 216p. per. 24.95 (978-0-595-46531-6(5)) iUniverse, Inc.
Schmidt, Mollie. Children of Courage. 2013. 70p. (J). pap. 12.95 (978-1-59713-143-8(1)) Goose River Pr.
Sévigny, Eric, illus. Caillou & the Rain. 2012. (Clubhouse Ser.). (ENG.). 24p. (J). (gr. -1-1). pap. 3.99 (978-2-89450-870-1(0)) Caillouet, Gerry.
Shakarian, Lorraine & Huggins, Pat. Helping Kids Handle Conflict (Intermediate Version) Teaching Self-control. 2003. (ASSIST Program Ser.). (Illus.). 564p. (gr. 4-6). pap. 54.95 (978-1-57035-818-0(4), 235 CONINT) Cambium Education, Inc.
Steps to Healthy Touching: Activities to Help Kids Understand & Control Their Problems with Touching. 2nd ed. 2003. (Illus.). 128p. (J). per., wbk. ed. 14.95 (978-1-55864-138-9(6)) JIST Publishing.
Taylor, Chad. Mountain Man Malik. 2016. (Rosen REAL Readers: Social Studies Nonfiction / Fiction: Family, Community, & the World Ser.). 8p. (gr. 1-k). pap. 5.46 (978-1-5081-2515-0(5), Rosen Classroom) Rosen Publishing Group, Inc., The.
Teal, Marion. I Like Me. 2012. 28p. pap. 12.99 (978-1-4525-5460-0(9)) Balboa Pr.
Todd, Heather. Tapping Away My Worries: A Book for Children, Parents, & Teachers. 2012. 32p. pap. 14.75 (978-1-4251-4313-8(X)) Trafford Publishing.
Traugh, Steven & Traugh, Susan. Mother Goose Brain Boost: Using Music & Movement to Teach Cognitive Skills. 2006. (Early Learning Ser.). (Illus.). 80p. (J). (gr. -1-1). pap. 19.99 incl. audio compact disk (978-1-59198-234-0(0), 2224) Creative Teaching Pr., Inc.
Walker, Alcee Howard. The Substitute #8. 2012. 82p. pap. 17.95 (978-1-4626-8271-3(5)) America Star Bks.
The Weaver Curriculum. 2004. (gr. k-12). Vol. 1. 145.00 (978-1-58095-842-4(7), WV001, Weaver) Vol. 2. 145.00 (978-1-58095-843-1(5), WV002, Weaver) Vol. 3. 145.00 (978-1-58095-844-8(3), WV003, Lifepac) Vol. 4. 145.00 (978-1-58095-845-5(1), WV004, Lifepac) Vol. 5. 145.00 (978-1-58095-846-2(X), WV005, Weaver) Alpha Omega Pubns., Inc.
Whitcombe, Renee Raab. Look Who's Going to Be a Big Brother. 2003. (Illus.). 24p. (J). 24.95 (978-0-9741882-1-8(2)) Budding Family Publishing.
—Look Who's Going to Be a Big Sister. 2003. (Illus.). 24p. (J). 24.95 (978-0-9741882-0-1(4)) Budding Family Publishing.
White, Ted. My Ride to Daycare. 2013. (I Love My Daycare Ser.). (ENG.). 24p. (J). pap. 9.95 (978-1-4787-1248-0(1)) Outskirts Pr., Inc.
Willard, Renee. Memommy's Miracles. 2013. 32p. pap. 24.95 (978-1-63000-644-0(0)) America Star Bks.
2003 (Guide) Book for Starlight Bands & Sunshine Bands. pap. (978-1-58942-115-8(9)) R.H. Boyd Publishing Corp.

CHILD LABOR

Bartoletti, Susan Campbell. Kids on Strike! 2003. (ENG., Illus.). 208p. (J). (gr. 5-7). pap. 9.95 (978-0-618-36923-2(6)) Houghton Mifflin Harcourt Publishing Co.
Burgan, Michael. Breaker Boys: How a Photograph Helped End Child Labor, 1 vol. 2011. (Captured History Ser.). (ENG.). 64p. (gr. 5-7). pap. 9.10 (978-0-7565-4510-9(2), CPB Grades 4-8) Compass Point Bks.
Child Labor in America. (Teaching with Primary Sources Ser.: Vol. 3). (YA). (gr. 4-9). ring bd. 28.95 (978-0-942389-23-4(9)) Cobblestone Publishing Co.
Coil, Suzanne M. Struggle for Child Labor Laws. (Liberty & Justice For All Ser.). (Illus.). 64p. (J). (gr. 5-8). lib. bdg. 15.98 (978-0-8050-2986-4(9), Twenty-First Century Bks.) Lerner Publishing Group.
Farrell, Courtney. Children's Rights, 1 vol. 2010. (Essential Issues Set 1 Ser.). (ENG.). 112p. (J). (gr. 6-12). lib. bdg.

C D

35.64 *(978-1-60453-952-3(6)*, Essential Library) ABDO Publishing Co.
Gifford, Clive. Child Labor. 2010. (Voices Ser.). (YA). (gr. 5-9). 34.25 *(978-1-59920-279-2(4))* Black Rabbit Bks.
Greenwood, Barbara. Factory Girl. 2007. (ENG., Illus.). 136p. (J). (gr. 4-9). 16.95 *(978-1-55337-649-1(8))*; 19.95 *(978-1-55337-648-4(X))* Kids Can Pr., Ltd. CAN. Dist: Hachette Bk. Group.
Herumin, Wendy. Child Labor Today: A Human Rights Issue. 2007. (Issues in Focus Today Ser.). (Illus.). 112p. (J). (gr. 3-7). lib. bdg. 33.27 *(978-0-7660-2682-7(5))* Enslow Pubs., Inc.
Miller, Connie Colwell. Mother Jones: Labor Leader. Erwin, Steve & Barnett, Charles, III, illus. 2006. (Graphic Biographies Ser.). (ENG.). 32p. (gr. 3-4). 30.65 *(978-0-7368-5487-0(8)*, Graphic Library) Capstone Press of Coughlan Cos.
—Mother Jones: Labor Leader, 1 vol. Erwin, Steve & Barnett, Charles, III, illus. 2006. (Graphic Biographies Ser.). (ENG.). 32p. (gr. 3-4). per. 8.10 *(978-0-7368-9662-7(7)*, Graphic Library) Capstone Press of Coughlan Cos.
Miller, Raymond H. Jhalak Man Tamang: Slave Labor Whistleblower. 2006. (Young Heroes Ser.). (ENG., Illus.). 48p. (J). (gr. 3-7). lib. bdg. 30.50 *(978-0-7377-3616-8(X)*, Kidhaven) Cengage Gale.
Otfinoski, Steven. The Child Labor Reform Movement: An Interactive History Adventure. 2013. (You Choose: History Ser.). (ENG.). 112p. (gr. 3-4). pap. 6.95 *(978-1-4765-3608-8(2))*; 31.99 *(978-1-4765-0255-7(2))* Capstone Press of Coughlan Cos. (You Choose Bks.).
Reynolds, Mattie. Kids Making Money: An Introduction to Financial Literacy. 2013. (Start Smart: Money Ser.). (Illus.). 24p. (gr. k-2). (J). lib. bdg. 17.95 net. *(978-1-937529-41-3(X))*; (ENG., pap. 5.95 *(978-1-937529-37-6(1))* Red Chair Pr.
Scott, Janine. Kids Have Rights Too! 2007. (Shockwave: the Human Experience Ser.). (ENG., Illus.). 36p. (J). (gr. 4-6). lib. bdg. 25.00 *(978-0-531-17763-1(7)*, Children's Pr.) Scholastic Library Publishing.
Worth, Richard. Lewis Hine: Photographer of Americans at Work. 2009. (ENG., Illus.). 83p. (C). (gr. 6-18). lib. bdg. 158.00 *(978-0-7656-8153-9(6)*, Y182862) Routledge.

CHILD MOLESTING
see Child Sexual Abuse

CHILD PSYCHOLOGY
see also Child Rearing

Adams, Alison. Citizenship. 2017. (Text Connections Guided Close Reading Ser.). (J). (gr. 1). *(978-1-4900-1815-7(8))* Benchmark Education Co.
Adams, Rodney & Adams, Eunice. Ooooooooo, You Said A Bad Wooord! How A Group of Young People Outgrew 'Adult' Language. 2010. 45p. pap. 11.95 *(978-1-4327-4252-2(3))* Outskirts Pr., Inc.
Allen, Kathy, et al. Tech Safety Smarts. 2013. (Tech Safety Smarts Ser.). (ENG.). 32p. (gr. 3-4). lib. bdg. 109.28 *(978-1-4296-9947-1(7)*, Fact Finders) Capstone Press of Coughlan Cos.
Alter, Robin & Clarke, Crystal. The Anxiety Workbook for Kids: Take Charge of Fears & Worries Using the Gift of Imagination. Burns, Oliver, illus. 2016. (ENG.). 136p. (J). (gr. k-5). pap. 16.95 *(978-1-62625-477-0(X))* New Harbinger Pubns.
An, Vickie. Just Right Words: Fighting Fair (Level 3) 2017. (Exploring Reading Ser.). (Illus.). 32p. (J). (gr. 3-3). pap. 8.99 ***(978-1-4258-4975-7(X))*** Teacher Created Materials, Inc.
Andersen, Jill. Resolving Conflicts at School. 2016. (Rosen REAL Readers: Social Studies Nonfiction / Fiction: Family, Community, & the World Ser.). 12p. (gr. 1-k). pap. 6.33 *(978-1-5081-2317-0(9)*, Rosen Classroom) Rosen Publishing Group, Inc., The.
Andrews, Beth. I Miss You! A Military Kid's Book about Deployment. Wright, Hawley, illus. 2007. (ENG.). 56p. (J). (-k). per. 12.99 *(978-1-59102-534-4(6))* Prometheus Bks., Pubs.
Annunziata, Jane & Nemiroff, Marc. Sometimes I'm Scared. Langdo, Bryan, illus. 2009. 32p. (J). (gr. -1-3). 14.95 *(978-1-4338-0449-6(2)*, Magination Pr.) American Psychological Assn.
Apel, Melanie Ann. Let's Talk about Feeling Defeated. 2009. (Let's Talk Library). 24p. (gr. 2-3). 42.50 *(978-1-60853-440-1(5)*, PowerKids Pr.) Rosen Publishing Group, Inc., The.
—Let's Talk about When You Think Nobody Likes You. 2009. (Let's Talk Library). 24p. (gr. 2-3). 42.50 *(978-1-60853-449-4(9)*, PowerKids Pr.) Rosen Publishing Group, Inc., The.
Armstrong, Thomas. You're Smarter Than You Think: A Kid's Guide to Multiple Intelligences. 2nd rev. ed. 2014. (ENG., Illus.). 192p. (J). (gr. 4-8). pap. 15.99 *(978-1-57542-431-6(2))* Free Spirit Publishing, Inc.
Bennett, Howard J. Max Archer, Kid Detective: The Case of the Wet Bed. Gerrell, Spike, illus. 2011. 48p. (J). (gr. 1-5). 14.95 *(978-1-4338-0953-8(2))*; pap. 9.95 *(978-1-4338-0954-5(0))* American Psychological Assn. (Magination Pr.).
Berry, Joy. Help Me Be Good about Overdoing It. 2009. (Help Me Be Good Ser.). 32p. pap. 7.95 *(978-1-60577-106-9(6))* Berry, Joy Enterprises.
—Tough Situations. 2005. (Winning skills series, get over it! Ser.). (ENG., Illus.). 48p. (J). pap. 3.95 *(978-1-57687-279-6(3)*, PowerHouse Kids) powerHouse Cultural Entertainment, Inc.
Berry, Joy Wilt. A Book about Interrupting. 2005. (Illus.). (J). *(978-0-7172-8599-0(5))* Scholastic, Inc.
Birtha, Becky. Far Apart, Close in Heart. Kastelic, Maja, illus. 2017. (ENG.). 32p. (J). (gr. -1-3). 16.99 *(978-0-8075-1275-3(3))* Whitman, Albert & Co.
Boswell, Kelly. Displaying Information. 2013. (Displaying Information Ser.). (ENG.). 32p. (gr. 1-2). 109.28 *(978-1-4765-0317-2(6))*; pap. 31.80 *(978-1-4765-3618-7(X))* Capstone Press of Coughlan Cos. (Aplus Bks.).
Brinkerhoff, Shirley. Childhood & Adolescent Disorders. McDonnell, Mary Ann & Esherick, Donald, eds. 2013. (State of Mental Illness & Its Therapy Ser.: 19). 128p. (J). (gr. 7-18). 24.95 *(978-1-4222-2822-7(3))* Mason Crest.
Brukner, Lauren. How to Be a Superhero Called Self-Control! Super Powers to Help Younger Children to Regulate Their Emotions & Senses. Phillips-Smith, Anthony & Apsley House, London Staff, illus. 2015. (ENG.). 112p. 19.95 *(978-1-84905-717-2(6)*, 8140) Kingsley, Jessica Pubs. GBR. Dist: Macmillan Distribution Ltd.
—The Keep-Calm Guru's Guide to Staying Awesome & in Control. Phillips-Smith, Anthony & Apsley House, London Staff, illus. 2016. (ENG.). 136p. 19.95 *(978-1-78592-714-0(0)*, 8410) Kingsley, Jessica Pubs. GBR. Dist: Macmillan Distribution Ltd.
—The Kids' Guide to Staying Awesome & in Control: Simple Stuff to Help Children Regulate Their Emotions & Senses. Apsley, illus. 2014. (ENG.). 112p. 19.95 *(978-1-84905-997-8(7)*, 1656) Kingsley, Jessica Pubs. GBR. Dist: Macmillan Distribution Ltd.
Brukner, Lauren. Self-Control to the Rescue! Super Powers to Help Kids Through the Tough Stuff in Everyday Life. Apsley, illus. 2017. (ENG.). 112p. 19.95 ***(978-1-78592-759-1(0)***, 9279) Kingsley, Jessica Pubs. GBR. Dist: Macmillan Distribution Ltd.
Burton, Margie, et al. Our Class Survey. 2011. (Early Connections Ser.). (J). *(978-1-61672-530-3(3))* Benchmark Education Co.
Callahan, Timothy & Isler, Claudia. A Teen's Guide to Custody. 2016. (Divorce & Your Family Ser.). 64p. (J). (gr. 7-7). 34.45 *(978-1-5081-7130-0(0))* Rosen Publishing Group, Inc., The.
Callier, Marie-Isabelle. No, No, No! Masson, Annick, illus. 2013. 32p. pap. 9.95 *(978-1-4338-1312-2(2))*; (J). *(978-1-4338-1311-5(4))* American Psychological Assn. (Magination Pr.).
Canetti, Yanitzia. Casos y cosas que dan Risa. 2010. (SPA.). 32p. (J). pap. *(978-1-59835-252-8(0)*, BrickHouse Education) Cambridge BrickHouse, Inc.
—Could It Be? 2010. 32p. (J). pap. 8.99 *(978-1-59835-253-5(9)*, BrickHouse Education) Cambridge BrickHouse, Inc.
—No somos tan Diferentes: La alegria de estar Juntos. 2010. 24p. (J). pap. 5.99 *(978-1-59835-121-7(4)*, BrickHouse Education) Cambridge BrickHouse, Inc.
—Not So Different. 2010. 24p. (J). pap. 5.99 *(978-1-59835-120-0(6)*, BrickHouse Education) Cambridge BrickHouse, Inc.
—Que le Dijo? Bate, bate, Disparates. 2010. (J). pap. 8.99 *(978-1-59835-254-2(7)*, BrickHouse Education) Cambridge BrickHouse, Inc.
—Say What? 2010. 32p. 8.99 *(978-1-59835-255-9(5)*, BrickHouse Education) Cambridge BrickHouse, Inc.
—What They Can Do, We Can Too! Curl Up. 2010. 24p. (J). 5.99 *(978-1-59835-227-6(X)*, BrickHouse Education) Cambridge BrickHouse, Inc.
Chara, Kathleen A. & Lehner, Tasha. Caleb Finds Out about Attachment. 2016. (ENG., Illus.). 144p. pap. 19.95 *(978-1-78592-702-7(7)*, 8250) Kingsley, Jessica Pubs. GBR. Dist: Macmillan Distribution Ltd.
Chuta, Edith N. Straight Talk to Troubled Kids: Finding Wisdom Underneath Our Pains. 2007. 76p. per. 10.95 *(978-0-595-43778-8(8))* iUniverse, Inc.
Clark, Rosalyn. Feeling Angry. 2017. (Bumba Books (tm) — Feelings Matter Ser.). (ENG.). (J). (gr. -1-1). pap. 6.99 ***(978-1-5124-5546-5(6))***; (Illus.). lib. bdg. 25.32 ***(978-1-5124-3370-8(5))*** Lerner Publishing Group.
Collins-Donnelly, Kate. Banish Your Body Image Thief: A Cognitive Behavioural Therapy Workbook on Building Positive Body Image for Young People. 2014. (Gremlin & Thief CBT Workbooks Ser.). (ENG., Illus.). 240p. pap. 24.95 *(978-1-84905-463-8(0)*, 1957) Kingsley, Jessica Pubs. GBR. Dist: Macmillan Distribution Ltd.
—Starving the Stress Gremlin: A Cognitive Behavioural Therapy Workbook on Stress Management for Young People. 2013. (Gremlin & Thief CBT Workbooks Ser.). (ENG., Illus.). 136p. (C). pap. 19.95 *(978-1-84905-340-2(5)*, 1993) Kingsley, Jessica Pubs. GBR. Dist: Macmillan Distribution Ltd.
Comprendiendo las Diferencias. 2010. (Comprendiendo Las Diferencias/Understanding Differences Ser.).Tr. of Understanding Differences. (MUL & ENG.). 24p. lib. bdg. 65.97 *(978-1-4296-4607-9(1))* Capstone Press of Coughlan Cos.
Connors, Kathleen. Saying I'm Sorry. 2015. (J). pap. 8.15 *(978-1-4824-1723-4(5))* Stevens, Gareth Publishing LLLP.
Craig, Dave. Bad Attitude: A Sure Way to Look Rather Silly! 2005. (Illus.). 44p. (YA). spiral bd. 7.50 *(978-1-59721-003-4(X))* Paperbacks for Educators.
—Cheating: A Sure Way to Become Untrustworthy! 2005. (Illus.). 44p. (YA). spiral bd. 7.50 *(978-1-59721-002-7(1))* Paperbacks for Educators.
—Lying: A Sure Way to Destroy Your Credibility! 2005. (J). spiral bd. 7.50 *(978-1-59721-001-0(3))* Paperbacks for Educators.
—Stealing: A Sure Way to Make Life Miserable! 2005. (YA). spiral bd. 7.50 *(978-1-59721-000-3(5))* Paperbacks for Educators.
Craver, Marcella Marino. Chillax! How Ernie Learns to Chill Out, Relax, & Take Charge of His Anger. Pinelli, Amerigo, illus. 2011. 64p. (J). pap. 9.95 *(978-1-4338-1037-4(9)*, Magination Pr.) American Psychological Assn.
De la Bédoyère, Camilla. Balancing Work & Play. 2010. (Healthy Lifestyles Ser.). 48p. (J). 35.65 *(978-1-60753-083-1(X))* Amicus Publishing.
Deen, Marilyn. Share & Be Fair, 1 vol. 2012. (Wonder Readers: Mathematics Ser.). (ENG.). 20p. (gr. -1-2). lib. bdg. 22.65 *(978-1-4296-9609-8(5)*, Wonder Readers) Capstone Press of Coughlan Cos.
Do, Elisa Shipon-Blum. Understanding Katie: A Day in the Life Of. Salus, Diane, illus. 2003. 28p. (J). (gr. -1-18). pap. *(978-0-9714800-3-2(6))* Selective Mutism Anxiety Research & Treatment Ctr.
Donaghey, Reese. Telling the Truth. 2015. (Illus.). 23p. (J). lib. bdg. *(978-1-4824-1730-2(8))* Stevens, Gareth Publishing LLLP.
Donovan, Sandy. How Can I Deal with Bullying? A Book about Respect. 2014. (Show Your Character Ser.). (ENG., Illus.). 32p. (gr. 1-3). lib. bdg. 26.60 *(978-1-4677-1362-7(7)*, Lerner Pubns.) Lerner Publishing Group.
Eason, Sarah. Chin up, Charlie: Be Brave. 2013. (You Choose Ser.). (Illus.). 32p. (J). lib. bdg. 23.94 *(978-0-7660-4305-3(3)*, Enslow Elementary) Enslow Pubs., Inc.
—Come Clean, Carlos: Tell the Truth. 2013. (You Choose Ser.). (Illus.). 32p. (J). lib. bdg. 23.94 *(978-0-7660-4306-0(1)*, Enslow Elementary) Enslow Pubs., Inc.
Edwards, Hazel & Alexander, Goldie. Talking about the Dangers of Taking Risks. 2010. (Healthy Living Ser.). (Illus.). 32p. (YA). (gr. 3-6). lib. bdg. 26.00 *(978-1-4339-3659-3(3))* Stevens, Gareth Publishing LLLP.
Espejo, Roman. Behavioral Disorders. Greenhaven Press Editors & Gale Editors, eds. 2014. (Opposing Viewpoints Ser.). (ENG., Illus.). 224p. (gr. 7-12). pap. 33.80 *(978-0-7377-6950-0(5))*; lib. bdg. 48.80 *(978-0-7377-6949-4(1))* Cengage Gale. (Greenhaven Pr., Inc.).
Evans, Jane. Little Meerkat's Big Panic: A Story about Learning New Ways to Feel Calm. Bean, Izzy, illus. 2016. (ENG.). 48p. 16.95 *(978-1-78592-703-4(5)*, 8251) Kingsley, Jessica Pubs. GBR. Dist: Macmillan Distribution Ltd.
Fargo, Donna. You Are in My Thoughts & Prayers. 2008. (ENG.). pap. 12.95 *(978-1-59842-352-5(5))* Blue Mountain Arts Inc.
Ferguson, Addy. Are You a Bully? 2013. (Stand up: Bullying Prevention Ser.). (ENG., Illus.). 24p. (J). (gr. 3-6). pap. 8.25 *(978-1-4488-9790-2(4))*; lib. bdg. 22.60 *(978-1-4488-9666-0(5))* Rosen Publishing Group, Inc., The. (PowerKids Pr.).
—Bullying with Words: Teasing, Name-Calling, & Rumors. 2013. (Stand up: Bullying Prevention Ser.). (ENG., Illus.). 24p. (J). (gr. 3-6). pap. 8.25 *(978-1-4488-9798-8(X))*; lib. bdg. 22.60 *(978-1-4488-9670-7(3))* Rosen Publishing Group, Inc., The. (PowerKids Pr.).
—What You Can Do to Stop Bullying. 2013. (Stand up: Bullying Prevention Ser.). (ENG., Illus.). 24p. (J). (gr. 3-6). pap. 8.25 *(978-1-4488-9792-6(0))*; lib. bdg. 22.60 *(978-1-4488-9667-7(3))* Rosen Publishing Group, Inc., The. (PowerKids Pr.).
Ferguson, Olivia & Haugen, Hayley Mitchell. Is Childhood Becoming Too Sexualized? 2010. (At Issue Ser.). (ENG.). 114p. pap. 24.45 *(978-0-7377-4885-7(0)*, Greenhaven Pr., Inc.) Cengage Gale.
Ferguson, Olivia, et al. Is Childhood Becoming Too Sexualized? 2010. (At Issue Ser.). (ENG.). 128p. (gr. 10-12). 39.40 *(978-0-7377-4884-0(2))* Cengage Gale.
Ford, Jean. Growth & Development. Forman, Sara, ed. 2013. (Young Adult's Guide to the Science of Health Ser.: 15). 128p. (J). (gr. 7-18). 24.95 *(978-1-4222-2810-4(X))* Mason Crest.
Ford, Vikke. Angel Anya's Adventures: Anya's Magic Heart. 2009. 28p. pap. 15.95 *(978-1-4490-0698-3(1))* AuthorHouse.
Fortuna, Lois. Helping a Friend. 2016. (We Can Do It! Ser.). (ENG.). 24p. (J). (gr. k-k). pap. 8.15 *(978-1-4824-3807-9(0))* Stevens, Gareth Publishing LLLP.
Francis, Amy. Has Child Behavior Worsened? Greenhaven Press Editors, ed. 2013. (At Issue Ser.). (ENG.). 128p. (gr. 10-12). pap. 27.80 *(978-0-7377-6835-0(5))*; lib. bdg. 39.40 *(978-0-7377-6834-3(7))* Cengage Gale. (Greenhaven Pr., Inc.).
Francis, Suzanne, et al. Spy by Night: Stealth & Secrets after Dark. 2007. (Illus.). 32p. (J). pap. *(978-0-545-01557-8(X))* Scholastic, Inc.
Freedman, Jeri. Step-By-Step Guide to Becoming a Leader at School & on the Job. 2014. (Winning at Work Readiness Ser.). 64p. (YA). (gr. 9-12). 32.95 *(978-1-4777-7778-7(4))* Rosen Publishing Group, Inc., The.
Freeland, Claire A.B. & Toner, Jacqueline B. What to Do When Mistakes Make You Quake: A Kid's Guide to Accepting Imperfection. McDonnell, Janet, illus. 2015. 96p. (J). *(978-1-4338-1930-8(9)*, Magination Pr.) American Psychological Assn.
—What to Do When You Feel Too Shy: A Kid's Guide to Overcoming Social Anxiety. McDonnell, Janet, illus. 2016. 80p. (J). pap. *(978-1-4338-2276-6(8)*, Magination Pr.) American Psychological Assn.
Frisch-Schmoll, Joy. Top & Bottom. 2013. (Exploring Opposites Ser.). (ENG.). 24p. (gr. k-1). pap. 41.70 *(978-1-62065-902-1(6)*, Pebble Plus) Capstone Press of Coughlan Cos.
Gainer, Cindy. I'm Like You, You're Like Me: A Book about Understanding & Appreciating Each Other. Sakamoto, Miki, illus. 2016. (ENG & SPA.). 36p. (J). (gr. -1-2). pap. 9.99 *(978-1-63198-123-4(4))* Free Spirit Publishing, Inc.
Garstecki, Julia & Benchmark Education Co. Staff. Childhood in Different Times & Places. 2014. (Text Connections Ser.). (J). (gr. 6). *(978-1-4900-1515-6(9))* Benchmark Education Co.
George, Liz. Conflict Resolution: When Friends Fight. 2015. (Rookie Talk about It(tm) Ser.). (ENG.). 32p. (J). pap. 5.95 *(978-0-531-21381-0(1)*, Children's Pr.) Scholastic Library Publishing.
Gerber, Larry. Step-By-Step Guide to Problem Solving at School & Work. 2014. (Winning at Work Readiness Ser.). 64p. (J). (gr. 9-12). 32.95 *(978-1-4777-7782-4(2))* Rosen Publishing Group, Inc., The.
Gerry, Lisa M. 100 Things to Know Before You Grow Up. 2016. (ENG., Illus.). 256p. (J). (gr. 4-7). pap. 9.99 *(978-1-4263-2316-4(6)*, National Geographic Children's Bks.) National Geographic Society.
Giroux, Lindsay Nina. We Are Problem Solvers. Archer, Micha, illus. 2016. (J). *(978-0-87659-715-6(0))* Gryphon Hse., Inc.
Glasser, Judith M. Learning to Feel Good & Stay Cool: Emotional Regulation Tools for Kids with AD/HD. 2013. (Illus.). 127p. 14.95 *(978-1-4338-1342-9(4))* American Psychological Assn.
—Learning to Feel Good & Stay Cool: Emotional Regulation Tools for Kids with ADHD. 2013. (Illus.). 127p. 14.95 *(978-1-4338-1343-6(2))* American Psychological Assn.
Greven, Alec. How to Talk to Girls. Acedera, Kei, illus. 2008. (ENG.). 48p. (J). (gr. 1-5). 9.99 *(978-0-06-170999-9(9)*, Collins) HarperCollins Pubs.
Haisha, Lisa. Whispers from Children's Hearts. 2005. *(978-0-9771404-0-4(7))* Risa Publications.
Hall, Petisamara G. Why Grandmas Go to Heaven. 2009. 24p. pap. 11.49 *(978-1-4490-4962-1(1))* AuthorHouse.
Hamod, Rania. I Am Lovable. 2012. 52p. pap. 20.95 *(978-1-4525-5838-7(8))* Balboa Pr.
Hanson, Anders. No Bullies Allowed! The Kids' Book of Dealing with Bullies, 1 vol. 2014. (What We Stand For Ser.). (ENG.). 24p. (gr. 5-10). lib. bdg. 25.65 *(978-1-62403-296-7(6)*, Super SandCastle) ABDO Publishing Co.
—Stand up for Yourself: The Kids' Book of Courage, 1 vol. 2014. (What We Stand For Ser.). (ENG.). 24p. (gr. 5-10). lib. bdg. 25.65 *(978-1-62403-297-4(4)*, Super SandCastle) ABDO Publishing Co.
Hardyman, Robyn. Relationships. 2010. (Being Healthy, Feeling Great Ser.). (ENG.). 32p. (J). pap. 10.60 *(978-1-61532-380-7(5)*, PowerKids Pr.); (gr. 3-6). lib. bdg. 26.50 *(978-1-61532-371-5(6))* Rosen Publishing Group, Inc., The.
—Safe & Healthy. 2012. (Healthy & Happy Ser.). (Illus.). 32p. (J). (gr. 1-4). lib. bdg. 26.50 *(978-1-4488-5278-9(1))* Rosen Publishing Group, Inc., The.
Harr, Alexandra, illus. Make a Stand: When Life Gives You Lemons, Change the World! 2014. (ENG.). (J). (gr. -1-3). 18.99 *(978-0-9911314-0-2(1))* Chocolate Sauce.
Harrison, Anne-Marie. Babies Are Noisy: A Book for Big Brothers & Sisters Including Those on the Autism Spectrum. Byrne, Beth, illus. 2013. (ENG.). 40p. (J). 15.95 *(978-1-84905-459-1(2)*, 4085) Kingsley, Jessica Pubs. GBR. Dist: Macmillan Distribution Ltd.
Helen, Grace. Ms. Marpol Always Says: (Small Experiences) 2012. 36p. 24.95 *(978-1-4512-3026-0(5))* America Star Bks.
Henig, Sherry. Group Rules! The Social Skills & Ground Rules for Children's Groups. 2008. (Illus.). 32p. (J). pap. *(978-0-9777203-5-4(7))* Brenner Publishing, LLC.
Hertzog, Nancy, et al. Around My House! rev. ed. 2015. (Smart Start Ser.: 1). (ENG.). 16p. (J). 10.95 *(978-1-61821-449-2(7))* Prufrock Pr.
—Let's Go to the Market! rev. ed. 2015. (Smart Start Ser.: 3). (ENG.). 16p. (J). 10.95 *(978-1-61821-451-5(9))* Prufrock Pr.
—Let's Play! rev. ed. 2015. (Smart Start Ser.: 2). (ENG.). 16p. (J). 10.95 *(978-1-61821-450-8(0))* Prufrock Pr.
Hicks, Kelli L. Honesty. 2012. (ENG., Illus.). 24p. (gr. k-2). pap. 8.95 *(978-1-61810-265-2(6))* Rourke Educational Media.
—Responsibility. 2012. (ENG.). 24p. (gr. k-2). pap. 8.95 *(978-1-61810-263-8(X))* Rourke Educational Media.
Higginbotham, Anastasia, illus. Tell Me about Sex, Grandma. 2017. (Ordinary Terrible Things Ser.). (ENG.). 64p. (J). (gr. -1-3). 17.95 *(978-1-55861-419-2(2))* Feminist Pr. at The City Univ. of New York.
Higgins, Melissa. We All Look Different, 1 vol. 2012. (Celebrating Differences Ser.). (ENG.). 24p. (gr. k-1). 26.65 *(978-1-4296-7576-5(4))*; pap. 7.29 *(978-1-4296-7890-2(9))* Capstone Press of Coughlan Cos. (Pebble Plus).
Howard Ed.D., Tequila E. All about Me! 2013. 48p. pap. 21.88 *(978-1-4669-8957-3(2))* Trafford Publishing.
Humphrey, Sandra McLeod. Hot Issues, Cool Choices: Facing Bullies, Peer Pressure, Popularity, & Put-Downs. 2007. (ENG., Illus.). 133p. (J). (gr. 4-7). per. 14.99 *(978-1-59102-569-6(9))* Prometheus Bks., Pubs.
Hyde, Margaret O. & Forsyth, Elizabeth H. Stress 101: An Overview for Teens. 2008. (Teen Overviews Ser.). (ENG., Illus.). 120p. (gr. 7-12). lib. bdg. 27.93 *(978-0-8225-6788-2(1))* Lerner Publishing Group.
Jackson, Wayne P. Don't Let the Spoon Get Taken Out of Your Mouth, 1 vol. 2010. 48p. pap. 16.95 *(978-1-4489-5268-7(9))* America Star Bks.
Johansen, Heidi. What I Look Like When I am Angry / Cómo me veo cuando estoy Enojado. 2009. (Let's Look at Feelings / un vistazo a los sentimientos Ser.). (ENG & SPA.). 24p. (gr. k-1). 42.50 *(978-1-61514-245-3(2)*, Editorial Buenas Letras) Rosen Publishing Group, Inc., The.
Jones, Ashton & Gangemi, Alicia. I Am Special: Daily Gratitude & Affirmations for Children. 2012. 28p. pap. 13.95 *(978-1-4525-6189-9(3))* Balboa Pr.
Kalman, Bobbie. Are You Like Me? 2010. (My World Ser.). (ENG.). 16p. (J). (gr. k-3). *(978-0-7787-9508-7(X))*; pap. *(978-0-7787-9533-9(0))* Crabtree Publishing Co.
—These Are My Friends. 2010. (My World Ser.). (ENG., Illus.). 16p. (J). (gr. k-2). *(978-0-7787-9439-4(3))*; pap. *(978-0-7787-9483-7(0))* Crabtree Publishing Co.
Kanji, Sheneeza. Amazing Canadian Kids! What They're Doing to Make A Difference & How You Can Too! 2012. 88p. (gr. 4-6). pap. 12.95 *(978-1-4634-2060-4(9))* AuthorHouse.
Kawa, Katie. I Feel Happy. 2013. (How Do I Feel? Ser.). (Illus.). 24p. (J). (gr. k-2). pap. 8.15 *(978-1-4339-8108-1(4))*; lib. bdg. 22.60 *(978-1-4339-8107-4(6))* Stevens, Gareth Publishing LLLP.
—I Feel Lonely. 2013. (How Do I Feel? Ser.). (Illus.). 24p. (J). (gr. k-2). pap. 8.15 *(978-1-4339-8112-8(2))*; lib. bdg. 22.60 *(978-1-4339-8111-1(4))* Stevens, Gareth Publishing LLLP.
—I Feel Mad. 2013. (How Do I Feel? Ser.). (Illus.). 24p. (J). (gr. k-2). pap. 8.15 *(978-1-4339-8116-6(5))*; lib. bdg. 22.60 *(978-1-4339-8115-9(7))* Stevens, Gareth Publishing LLLP.
—I Feel Sad. 2013. (How Do I Feel? Ser.). (Illus.). 24p. (J). (gr. k-2). pap. 8.15 *(978-1-4339-8120-3(3))*; lib. bdg. 22.60 *(978-1-4339-8119-7(X))* Stevens, Gareth Publishing LLLP.
—I Feel Scared. 2013. (How Do I Feel? Ser.). (Illus.). 24p. (J). (gr. k-2). pap. 8.15 *(978-1-4339-8124-1(6))*; lib. bdg. 22.60 *(978-1-4339-8123-4(8))* Stevens, Gareth Publishing LLLP.
—I Feel Worried. 2013. (How Do I Feel? Ser.). (Illus.). 24p. (J). (gr. k-2). pap. 8.15 *(978-1-4339-8128-9(9))*; lib. bdg. 22.60 *(978-1-4339-8127-2(0))* Stevens, Gareth Publishing LLLP.
Kemper, Bitsy. Teens & Phobias. 2017. (ENG.). 80p. (J). (gr. 5-12). *(978-1-68282-128-2(5))* ReferencePoint Pr., Inc.
Kennedy-Moore, Eileen & McLaughlin, Christine. Growing Friendships: A Kid's Guide to Making & Keeping Friends. 2017. (ENG., Illus.). 192p. (J). (gr. 1-4). pap. 14.99 *(978-1-58270-588-0(7))* Aladdin/Beyond Words.
Kerstein, Lauren H. A Week of Switching, Shifting, & Stretching: How to Make My Thinking More Flexible. 2013. (ENG., Illus.). 57p. (J). (gr. -1-5). pap. 18.00 *(978-1-937473-89-1(9))* Autism Asperger Publishing Co.
Kidde, Rita & Wilson, Antoine. Mourning a Death in the Family, 01 vols., 1. 2016. (Family Issues & You Ser.). (ENG.). 48p. (J). pap. 11.75 *(978-1-4994-3689-1(0)*, Rosen Central) Rosen Publishing Group, Inc., The.
Kim, Young-Ah. So Lonely. Shin, Ji-Soo, illus. 2012. 32p. (J). *(978-1-4338-1287-3(8))*; pap. *(978-1-4338-1288-0(6))* American Psychological Assn. (Magination Pr.).
Knutson, Eric. I Never Get Scared. Stensen, Cindy, illus. 2010. (J). *(978-1-930596-99-3(5))* Amherst Pr.
Kravetz, Jonathan. How to Deal with Fighting. 2009. (Let's Work It Out Ser.). 24p. (gr. 2-3). 42.50

(978-1-61514-261-3(4), PowerKids Pr.) Rosen Publishing Group, Inc., The.

Langdown, Leanne Shea. My Happy Gift. McKay, Traci, illus. 2011. 26p. pap. 6.99 *(978-1-61667-300-0(1))* Raider Publishing International.

Langensiepen, Julia. Deeno's Dream Journeys in the Big Blue Bubble: A Relaxation Programme to Help Children Manage Their Emotions. 2009. (ENG., Illus.). 128p. pap. 28.95 ***(978-1-84905-039-5(2)***, 3581) Kingsley, Jessica Pubs. GBR. Dist: Macmillan Distribution Ltd.

Lavallee, Kristen & Schneider, Silvia. What to Do When You Don't Want to Be Apart: A Kid's Guide to Overcoming Separation Anxiety. McDonnell, Janet, illus. 2017. (J). pap. ***(978-1-4338-2713-6(1)***, Magination Pr.) American Psychological Assn.

Lewis, Barbara A. What Do You Stand for? a Kid's Guide ToBuilding Character. 2014. 30.00 *(978-1-63419-753-3(4))* Perfection Learning Corp.

Libal, Autumn. Emotional Disturbance. Albers, Lisa et al, eds. 2014. (Living with a Special Need Ser.: 16). 128p. (J). (gr. 7-18). 25.95 *(978-1-4222-3034-3(1))* Mason Crest.

Lissberger, Susan. Aa You Are Amazing Zz You Are Zzzzzzz Best. 2012. 32p. pap. 21.99 *(978-1-4691-9203-1(9))* Xlibris Corp.

Living with Peer Pressure & Bullying. 2010. (Teen's Guides). (Illus.). 176p. (gr. 6-12). pap. 14.95 *(978-0-8160-7915-5(3)*, Checkmark Bks.) Facts On File, Inc.

Lupton, David, illus. Goodbye Brecken. 2012. 32p. (J). *(978-1-4338-1289-7(4))*; pap. *(978-1-4338-1290-3(8))* American Psychological Assn. (Magination Pr.).

Lynch, Christopher. Totally Chill: A Stress Management Workbook for Kids with Social, Emotional, or Sensory Sensitivities: My Complete Guide to Staying Cool. 2012. (ENG., Illus.). 135p. (J). pap. 21.95 *(978-1-937473-04-4(X))* Autism Asperger Publishing Co.

Lynette, Rachel. How to Deal with Secrets. 2009. (Let's Work It Out Ser.). 24p. (gr. 2-3). 42.50 *(978-1-61514-266-8(5)*, PowerKids Pr.) Rosen Publishing Group, Inc., The.

Mandel, Joey. Anxiety: Deal with It Before It Ties You up in Knots. Heeley, Ted, illus. 2014. (Lorimer Deal with It Ser.). (ENG.). 32p. (YA). (gr. 4-6). pap. 12.95 *(978-1-4594-0709-1(1)*, 9781459407091) Lorimer, James & Co., Ltd., Pubs. CAN. Dist: Casemate Pubs. & Bk. Distributors, LLC.

Marvel, Robin. Awakening Consciousness: A Boy's Guide! 2009. (J). pap. 17.95 *(978-1-932690-91-0(3))* Loving Healing Pr., Inc.

—Awakening Consciousness: A Girl's Guide. 2009. (J). pap. 16.95 *(978-1-932690-80-4(8))* Loving Healing Pr., Inc.

Mathis, Rev. Catherine. It's Your Big Day. 2013. 16p. pap. 10.70 *(978-1-4669-6573-7(8))* Trafford Publishing.

Mcaneney, Caitie. Let's Talk about It, 1 vol. 2015. (Let's Talk about It Ser.). (ENG.). 24p. (J). 49.50 *(978-1-4994-0322-0(4)*, PowerKids Pr.) Rosen Publishing Group, Inc., The.

McPherson, Stephanie Sammartino. Are You Stressed Out in School? 2015. (Got Issues? Ser.). (ENG., Illus.). 128p. (J). (gr. 7-7). 37.27 *(978-0-7660-6983-1(4))* Enslow Pubs., Inc.

Miller, Connie Colwell. Happy Is... 2011. (Know Your Emotions Ser.). (ENG.). 24p. (gr. 1-2). pap. 47.70 *(978-1-4296-7058-6(4)*, Aplus Bks.) Capstone Press of Coughlan Cos.

—Happy Is ... 2011. (Know Your Emotions Ser.). (ENG.). 24p. (gr. 1-2). pap. 8.10 *(978-1-4296-7051-7(7)*, Aplus Bks.) Capstone Press of Coughlan Cos.

—You Can Listen to Directions: Stop or Go? Victoria Assanelli, illus. 2017. (Making Good Choices Ser.). (ENG.). 24p. (J). (gr. 1-4). 20.95 ***(978-1-68151-166-5(5)***, Amicus Illustrated) Amicus Publishing.

—You Can Stay in Control: Wild or Calm? Victoria Assanelli, illus. 2017. (Making Good Choices Ser.). (ENG.). 24p. (J). (gr. 1-4). 20.95 ***(978-1-68151-165-8(7)***, Amicus Illustrated) Amicus Publishing.

—You're Angry: Throw a Fit or Talk It Out? Victoria Assanelli, illus. 2017. (Making Good Choices Ser.). (ENG.). 24p. (J). (gr. 1-4). 20.95 ***(978-1-68151-164-1(9)***, Amicus Illustrated) Amicus Publishing.

Miller, Tiwana Mutch. Positive Outweighs Negative. 2007. (J). per. 10.00 *(978-0-9788937-1-2(9))* Amani Publishing, LLC.

Moses, Melissa. Alex & the Scary Things: A Story for Children Who Have Experienced Scary Things. MacEachern, Alison, illus. 2015. (ENG.). 40p. (J). 17.95 *(978-1-84905-793-6(1)*, 4189) Kingsley, Jessica Pubs. GBR. Dist: Macmillan Distribution Ltd.

Moss, Wendy. Bounce Back: How to Be a Resilient Kid. 2015. (Illus.). 112p. (J). *(978-1-4338-1921-6(X)*, Magination Pr.) American Psychological Assn.

Mullen, Jodi Ann. Naughty No More: A Workbook for Children Who Want to Make Good Decisions. 2013. 56p. pap. 8.99 *(978-1-4525-6716-7(6))* Balboa Pr.

Nadeau, Kathleen G. Learning to Plan & Be Organized: Enhancing Executive Function Skills in Kids with AD/HD. Beyl, Charles, illus. 2016. 120p. (J). pap. *(978-1-4338-2213-1(X)*, Magination Pr.) American Psychological Assn.

Nelson, Robin. Can People Count on Me? A Book about Responsibility. 2014. (Show Your Character Ser.). (ENG., Illus.). 32p. (gr. 1-3). lib. bdg. 26.60 *(978-1-4677-1363-4(5)*, Lerner Pubns.) Lerner Publishing Group.

Nichols, Cheyenne. Tristeza Es... Strictly Spanish LLC. Staff, tr. from ENG. 2013. (Reconoce Tus Emociones/Know Your Emotions Ser.). Tr. of Sad Is.... (ENG, SPA & MUL.). 24p. (gr. 1-2). lib. bdg. 27.32 *(978-1-62065-152-0(1))* Capstone Press of Coughlan Cos.

Orr, Tamra. Combatting Body Shaming. 2016. (Combatting Shaming & Toxic Communities Ser.). 64p. (J). (gr. 7-7). 34.45 *(978-1-5081-7114-0(9))* Rosen Publishing Group, Inc., The.

Palser, Barb. Selling Ourselves: Marketing Body Images, 1 vol. 2012. (Exploring Media Literacy Ser.). (ENG., Illus.). 80p. (gr. 6-7). pap. 9.10 *(978-0-7565-4534-5(X))*; lib. bdg. 34.65 *(978-0-7565-4519-2(6))* Compass Point Bks. (CPB Grades 4-8).

Park, Angeland. Wherever I Am, I Am Home. 2011. 20p. pap. 24.95 *(978-1-4560-7725-9(2))* America Star Bks.

Peltier, Sylvia M. Nanny & I. Peltier, Sylvia M., illus. 2003. (Illus.). 32p. (YA). (gr. -1-18). 16.95 *(978-0-9724394-0-4(4))* Sylables.

Peters, Daniel B., et al. The Warrior Workbook: A Guide for Conquering Your Worry Monster. 2017. (Illus.). vii, 96p. (J). pap. 16.95 *(978-1-935067-44-3(3))* Great Potential Pr., Inc.

Peters, Diane. Procrastination: Deal with It All in Good Time, 1 vol. Tankard, Jeremy, illus. 2006. (Lorimer Deal with It Ser.). (ENG.). 32p. (J). (gr. 4-6). pap. 12.95 *(978-1-55028-947-3(0)*, 9781550289473) Lorimer, James & Co., Ltd., Pubs. CAN. Dist: Casemate Pubs. & Bk. Distributors, LLC.

Poltarnees, Welleran. Hooray for Babies. 2010. (ENG., Illus.). 72p. pap. 15.95 *(978-1-59583-389-1(7)*, 9781595833891) Laughing Elephant.

Poole, H. W. Depression, Vol. 13. Walters, Anne S., ed. 2015. (Mental Illnesses & Disorders: Awareness & Understanding Ser.). (Illus.). 48p. (J). (gr. 5). 20.95 *(978-1-4222-3370-2(7))* Mason Crest.

—Disruptive Behavior Disorders, Vol. 13. Walters, Anne S., ed. 2015. (Mental Illnesses & Disorders: Awareness & Understanding Ser.). (Illus.). 48p. (J). (gr. 5). 20.95 *(978-1-4222-3368-9(5))* Mason Crest.

Poole, Hilary W. Phobias. 2017. (J). ***(978-1-4222-3728-1(1))*** Mason Crest.

Poole, Hilary W. & Walters, Anne S. Medical Fears. 2017. (J). ***(978-1-4222-3726-7(5))*** Mason Crest.

—Social Fears. 2017. (J). ***(978-1-4222-3731-1(1))*** Mason Crest.

Potts, Kimberly. What's Your Mood? A Good Day, Bad Day, In-Between Day Book. 2005. (ENG., Illus.). 176p. pap. 8.95 *(978-1-59337-217-0(5))* Adams Media Corp.

Powell, Jillian. My New Babysitter. 2012. (New Beginnings Ser.). (ENG., Illus.). 24p. (J). (gr. k-3). 21.25 *(978-1-4488-6636-6(7)*, PowerKids Pr.) Rosen Publishing Group, Inc., The.

Price, Elizabeth. Divorce & Teens: When a Family Splits Apart. 2004. (Teen Issues Ser.). (Illus.). 64p. (J). lib. bdg. 22.60 *(978-0-7660-1670-5(6))* Enslow Pubs., Inc.

Pryor, Kimberley Jane. Responsibility. 2010. (Values 2 Ser.). 32p. (gr. 1). 18.56 *(978-1-60870-146-9(8))* Marshall Cavendish Corp.

Purcell, Mark C. & Murphy, Jason R. Mindfulness for Teen Anger: A Workbook to Overcome Anger & Aggression Using MBSR & DBT Skills. 2014. (ENG.). 152p. (YA). (gr. 6-12). pap. 16.95 *(978-1-60882-916-3(2)*, 1369797) New Harbinger Pubns.

Randolph, Joanne. What I Look Like When I Am Sad. 2009. (Let's Look at Feelings Ser.). 24p. (gr. k-1). 42.50 *(978-1-61514-241-5(X)*, PowerKids Pr.) Rosen Publishing Group, Inc., The.

—What I Look Like When I am Sad / Cómo me veo cuando estoy Triste. 2009. (Let's Look at Feelings / un vistazo a los sentimientos Ser.). (ENG & SPA.). 24p. (gr. k-1). 42.50 *(978-1-61514-247-7(9)*, Editorial Buenas Letras) Rosen Publishing Group, Inc., The.

Reed, Cristie. Problem Solving. 2012. (ENG., Illus.). 24p. (gr. k-2). pap. 8.95 *(978-1-61810-266-9(4))* Rourke Educational Media.

Regan, Lisa. Don't Get Angry, Annie: Stay Calm. 2017. (You Choose Ser.). 32p. (J). (gr. 2-2). lib. bdg. 25.27 ***(978-0-7660-8700-2(X))*** Enslow Pubs., Inc.

Rice, Dona Herweck. Esta Soy Yo, 1 vol. 2nd rev. ed. 2011. (Nonfiction Readers Ser.). (SPA.). 12p. (J). (gr. 1-1). pap. 4.99 *(978-1-4333-4407-7(6))* Teacher Created Materials, Inc.

—This Is Me, 1 vol. 2nd rev. ed. 2011. (Nonfiction Readers Ser.). (ENG.). 12p. (J). (gr. 1-1). pap. 4.99 *(978-1-4333-3568-6(9))* Teacher Created Materials, Inc.

Robbins, Lynette. How to Deal with Autism. 2010. (Illus.). 24p. (J). 49.50 *(978-1-4358-3422-4(4)*, 1300434, PowerKids Pr.) Rosen Publishing Group, Inc., The.

Robinson, Beth. Where Will I Grow Up? Green, Noel, illus. 2013. 20p. (J). mass mkt. 8.99 *(978-0-9799092-6-9(0))* Robinson, Beth.

Rosen Publishing Staff. Let's Talk about It, 1 vol. 2015. (Let's Talk about It Ser.). (ENG.). 24p. (J). 141.60 *(978-1-4777-5732-1(5)*, PowerKids Pr.) Rosen Publishing Group, Inc., The.

Rothenberg, Annye. Why Do I Have To? Wenzel, David T., illus. 2009. 40p. (J). pap. 9.95 *(978-0-9790420-1-0(1))* Perfecting Parenting Pr.

Rutledge, Jill Zimmerman. Picture Perfect: What You Need to Feel Better about Your Body. 2007. (ENG.). 240p. (gr. 8-12). pap. 14.95 *(978-0-7573-0607-5(1))* Health Communications, Inc.

Schrier, Allyson Valentine, et al. Tech Safety Smarts. 2013. (Tech Safety Smarts Ser.). (ENG.). 32p. (gr. 3-4). pap. 190.80 *(978-1-62065-805-5(4)*, Fact Finders) Capstone Press of Coughlan Cos.

Schwartz, Heather E. Stress Less: Your Guide to Managing Stress. 2011. (Healthy Me Ser.). (ENG.). 32p. (gr. 3-4). pap. 47.70 *(978-1-4296-7298-6(6)*, Snap Bks.) Capstone Press of Coughlan Cos.

Shepherd, Joanne. What I Look Like When I Am Scared. 2009. (Let's Look at Feelings Ser.). 24p. (gr. k-1). 42.50 *(978-1-61514-242-2(8)*, PowerKids Pr.) Rosen Publishing Group, Inc., The.

—What I Look Like When I am Scared / Cómo me veo cuando estoy Asustado. 2009. (Let's Look at Feelings / un vistazo a los sentimientos Ser.). (ENG & SPA.). 24p. (gr. k-1). 42.50 *(978-1-61514-248-4(7)*, Editorial Buenas Letras) Rosen Publishing Group, Inc., The.

—What I Look Like When I Am Surprised. 2009. (Let's Look at Feelings Ser.). 24p. (gr. k-1). 42.50 *(978-1-61514-243-9(6)*, PowerKids Pr.) Rosen Publishing Group, Inc., The.

—What I Look Like When I am Surprised / Cómo me veo cuando estoy Sorprendido. 2009. (Let's Look at Feelings / un vistazo a los sentimientos Ser.). (ENG & SPA.). 24p. (gr. k-1). 42.50 *(978-1-61514-249-1(5)*, Editorial Buenas Letras) Rosen Publishing Group, Inc., The.

Shumsky, Ron, et al. The Survival Guide for School Success: Use Your Brain's Built-In Apps to Sharpen Attention, Battle Boredom, & Build Mental Muscle. 2014. (ENG., Illus.). 128p. (J). (gr. 5-8). pap. 14.99 *(978-1-57542-482-8(7))* Free Spirit Publishing, Inc.

Siddoway, Ramona. Self-Control. 2013. (7 Character Strengths of Highly Successful Students Ser.). 64p. (J). (gr. 5-8). pap. 77.70 *(978-1-4488-9564-9(2))*; (ENG., Illus.). pap. 12.95 *(978-1-4488-9563-2(4)*, Rosen Classroom); (ENG., Illus.). lib. bdg. 31.95 *(978-1-4488-9543-4(X)*, Rosen Classroom) Rosen Publishing Group, Inc., The.

Simon, Mary Manz. First Feelings (padded Cover) Twelve Stories for Toddlers. Stott, Dorothy, illus. rev. ed. 2017. (ENG.). 256p. (J). (gr. -1-k). 12.99 *(978-1-4336-4384-2(7)*, B&H Kids) B&H Publishing Group.

Sjonger, Rebecca. Stress Less! A Kid's Guide to Managing Emotions. 2015. (ENG., Illus.). 24p. (J). *(978-0-7787-1882-6(4))* Crabtree Publishing Co.

Solomon, Andrew. Far from the Tree: Young Adult Edition. 2017. (ENG., Illus.). 464p. (YA). (gr. 9). 18.99 *(978-1-4814-4090-5(X)*, Simon & Schuster Bks. For Young Readers) Simon & Schuster Bks. For Young Readers.

Stewart, Sheila. I Don't Keep Secrets. (Kids Have Troubles Too Ser.). 48p. (YA). (gr. 5-18). 2010. lib. bdg. 19.95 *(978-1-4222-1698-9(5))* 2009. pap. 7.95 *(978-1-4222-1911-9(9))* Mason Crest.

—When Life Makes Me Mad. (Kids Have Troubles Too Ser.). 48p. (YA). (gr. 5-18). 2010. lib. bdg. 19.95 *(978-1-4222-1700-9(0))* 2009. pap. 7.95 *(978-1-4222-1913-3(5))* Mason Crest.

Strayer, Troy & Strayer, Beverly. Check-In Assessments for Differentiated Lessons: Quick, Engaging Activities That Help You Find Out What Students Know at the Beginning & End of Your Lessons So You Can Plan Your Next Instructional Steps. 2012. (ENG.). 96p. (gr. 5-5). pap. 16.99 *(978-0-545-29682-3(X)*, Teaching Resources) Scholastic, Inc.

Stutz, David. Hydraulics on My Stroller! 2012. 16p. pap. 12.68 *(978-1-4669-3856-4(0))* Trafford Publishing.

Tarshis, Thomas Paul. Living with Peer Pressure & Bullying. 2010. (Teen's Guides). (Illus.). 176p. (gr. 6-12). 34.95 *(978-0-8160-7914-8(5))* Facts On File, Inc.

Thomas, Christina L. Dear Little One. 2013. 20p. pap. 12.70 *(978-1-4669-9265-8(4))* Trafford Publishing.

Thomas, Isabel. Dealing with Feeling... Angry. 2013. (Dealing with Feeling... Ser.). (ENG.). 24p. (gr. 1-2). pap. 6.79 *(978-1-4329-7112-0(3)*, Heinemann Read & Learn) Heinemann-Raintree.

—Dealing with Feeling... Caring. 2013. (Dealing with Feeling... Ser.). (ENG.). 24p. (gr. 1-2). pap. 6.79 *(978-1-4329-7113-7(1))*; lib. bdg. 23.32 *(978-1-4329-7104-5(2))* Heinemann-Raintree. (Heinemann Read & Learn).

—Dealing with Feeling... Sad. 2013. (Dealing with Feeling... Ser.). (ENG.). 24p. (gr. 1-2). pap. 6.79 *(978-1-4329-7117-5(4))*; lib. bdg. 23.32 *(978-1-4329-7108-3(5))* Heinemann-Raintree. (Heinemann Read & Learn).

—Dealing with Feeling... Worried. 2013. (Dealing with Feeling... Ser.). (ENG.). 24p. (gr. 1-2). pap. 6.79 *(978-1-4329-7119-9(0))*; lib. bdg. 23.32 *(978-1-4329-7110-6(7))* Heinemann-Raintree. (Heinemann Read & Learn).

Tourville, Amanda Doering & Sorra, Kristin. Mi Amigo Tiene Autismo. Translations.com Staff, tr. from ENG. Sorra, Kristin, illus. 2012. (Amigos con Discapacidades/Friends with Disabilities Ser.). Tr. of My Friend Has Autism. (MUL, SPA & ENG., Illus.). 24p. (gr. k-3). lib. bdg. 25.99 *(978-1-4048-7312-4(0))* Picture Window Bks.

Verdick, Elizabeth. Calm-Down Time. Heinlen, Marieka, illus. 2010. (Toddler Tools Ser.). (ENG.). 24p. (J). (gr. -1). 7.95 *(978-1-57542-316-6(2))* Free Spirit Publishing, Inc.

—Don't Behave Like You Live in a Cave. Mark, Steve, illus. 2010. (Laugh & Learn Ser.). (ENG.). 128p. (J). (gr. 3-7). pap. 8.95 *(978-1-57542-353-1(7))* Free Spirit Publishing, Inc.

—Naptime. Heinlen, Marieka, illus. 2008. (Toddler Tools Ser.). (ENG.). 24p. (J). (gr. k — 1). bds. 7.95 *(978-1-57542-300-5(6)*, 1285965) Free Spirit Publishing, Inc.

—Voices Are Not for Yelling. Heinlen, Marieka, illus. 2015. (Best Behavior Ser.). (ENG.). (J). 24p. bds. 7.95 *(978-1-57542-500-9(9))*; 40p. (gr. -1-2). pap. 11.95 *(978-1-57542-501-6(7))* Free Spirit Publishing, Inc.

Verdick, Elizabeth. Voices Are Not for Yelling / la Voz No Es para Gritar. Heinlen, Marieka, illus. 2017. (Best Behavior Ser.). (ENG & SPA.). (J). 24p. bds. 7.95 ***(978-1-63198-194-4(3))***; 40p. (gr. -1-2). pap. 11.95 ***(978-1-63198-191-3(9))*** Free Spirit Publishing, Inc.

Verdick, Elizabeth & Lisovskis, Marjorie. How to Take the Grrr Out of Anger. 2nd rev. ed. 2015. (Laugh & Learn(r) Ser.). (ENG., Illus.). 128p. (J). (gr. 3-7). pap. 8.95 *(978-1-57542-494-1(0))* Free Spirit Publishing, Inc.

Waddington, Emma. Why Don't We All Live Together Anymore? Big Issues for Little People after a Family Break-Up. Thomas, Louis & Thomas, Louis, illus. 2016. (Life & Soul Library). (ENG.). 32p. (J). (gr. -1-3). 12.99 ***(978-1-84780-867-7(0)***, Frances Lincoln Children's Bks.) Quarto Publishing Group UK GBR. Dist: Hachette Bk. Group.

Wagner, Aureen Pinto. Up & down the Worry Hill: A Children's Book about Obsessive-Compulsive Disorder & Its Treatment. 3rd rev. ed. 2013. (ENG.). 48p. pap. 19.95 *(978-0-9795392-5-1(0))* Lighthouse Pr., Inc.

Williams, Sam. Are You a Bully? 2012. (ENG., Illus.). 24p. (gr. k-2). pap. 8.95 *(978-1-61810-267-6(2))* Rourke Educational Media.

WJW. Leroy & Cheryl's Adventure. 2013. 60p. pap. 10.30 *(978-1-4669-9368-6(5))* Trafford Publishing.

You Choose: Set 2. 2017. (You Choose Ser.). 32p. (gr. 2-2). pap. 42.08 ***(978-0-7660-8899-3(5))***; lib. bdg. 101.08 ***(978-0-7660-8076-8(5))*** Enslow Pubs., Inc.

CHILD REARING

Here are entered works on the principles and techniques of raising children. Works on the psycho-social interaction between parents and their minor children are under Parent and Child.

see also Babysitters; Moral Education; Problem Children

Berry, Joy Wilt. A Children's Book about Disobeying. 2005. (Illus.). (J). *(978-0-7172-8593-8(6))* Scholastic, Inc.

Curatilo Zieminski, D. Stumbling but Not Falling. 2007. 32p. per. 24.95 *(978-1-4241-8340-1(5))* America Star Bks.

DeGaetano, Gloria. Parenting Well in a Media Age: Keeping Our Kids Human. 2004. (ENG.). 272p. pap. 18.95 *(978-1-932181-12-8(1))* Personhood Pr.

Duhaime, Edmund. Discipline Required. 2004. 56p. (J). per. 9.95 *(978-1-151-67843-0(0))* American Literary Pr.

Haugen, David M. Parenting. Greenhaven Press Editors, ed. 2014. (Teen Rights & Freedoms Ser.). (ENG., Illus.). 176p. (gr. 10-12). lib. bdg. 42.00 *(978-0-7377-7001-8(5)*, Greenhaven Pr., Inc.) Cengage Gale.

Henry, Debra. Best Behavior: A Celebration of Good Manners for Our African-American Children. Deal, David, photos by. 2004. (Illus.). (J). per. 15.00 *(978-0-9758611-0-3(7))* Black Society Pages, Inc.

Hurt, Laurie S. What I Think I Want to Be. (J). (gr. k-3). 14.95 *(978-0-9729403-0-6(8))* Marshall, George Publishing.

Lindeen, Mary. Getting Ready for Bed. 2015. (BeginningtoRead Ser.). (ENG.). 32p. (J). (gr. k-2). pap. 11.94 *(978-1-60357-761-8(0))*; (Illus.). lib. bdg. 22.60 *(978-1-59953-701-6(X))* Norwood Hse. Pr.

Lyons, Shelly. Safety in My Neighborhood. 2013. (My Neighborhood Ser.). (ENG.). 24p. (gr. k-1). pap. 41.70 *(978-1-62065-888-8(7))*; pap. 7.29 *(978-1-62065-887-1(9))*; lib. bdg. 26.65 *(978-1-62065-102-5(5))* Capstone Press of Coughlan Cos. (Pebble Plus).

O'Donoghue, Chris. Charlie's Reading Rescue: Improve an Older Child's Reading. 2011. (Illus.). 188p. pap. 10.50 *(978-1-60976-573-6(7)*, Eloquent Bks.) Strategic Book Publishing & Rights Agency (SBPRA).

Phelan,, Thomas W. & Lee, Tracy M. 1-2-3 Magic for Kids: Helping Your Kids Understand the New Rules. 2nd ed. 2017. (ENG., Illus.). 128p. pap. 9.99 *(978-1-4926-4786-7(1)*, 9781492647867) Sourcebooks, Inc.

Rosenthal, Beth. Gay Parenting. 2012. (Opposing Viewpoints Ser.). (ENG., Illus.). 224p. (gr. 10-12). lib. bdg. 48.80 *(978-0-7377-6422-2(8)*, Greenhaven Pr., Inc.) Cengage Gale.

Rosenthal, Beth, ed. Gay Parenting. 2012. (Opposing Viewpoints Ser.). (ENG., Illus.). 240p. (gr. 10-12). pap. 29.45 *(978-0-7377-6423-9(6)*, Greenhaven Pr., Inc.) Cengage Gale.

Sévigny, Eric, illus. Caillou Puts Away His Toys. 3rd ed. 2012. (Clubhouse Ser.). (ENG.). 24p. (J). (gr. -1-1). pap. 3.99 *(978-2-89450-938-8(3))* Caillouet, Gerry.

Simons, Rae. Grandparents Raising Kids. 2010. (Changing Face of Modern Families Ser.). (Illus.). 64p. (YA). (gr. 6-18). lib. bdg. 22.95 *(978-1-4222-1496-1(6))* Mason Crest.

Summer Rogers Martin. Kaylea Grows Up: Mommy & Me Days. Debi Rogers, illus. 2009. 20p. pap. 10.99 *(978-1-4389-5908-5(7))* AuthorHouse.

Verdick, Elizabeth. Bedtime. Heinlen, Marieka, illus. 2010. (Toddler Tools Ser.). (ENG.). 24p. (J). (gr. -1). 7.95 *(978-1-57542-315-9(4))* Free Spirit Publishing, Inc.

—Sharing Time. Heinlen, Marieka, illus. 2009. (Toddler Tools Ser.). (ENG.). 24p. (J). (gr. -1). 7.95 *(978-1-57542-314-2(6))* Free Spirit Publishing, Inc.

—Sharing Time/Tiempo para Compartir. Heinlen, Marieka, illus. 2016. (Toddler Tools Ser.). (SPA, ENG & MUL.). 24p. (J). 7.95 *(978-1-63198-096-1(3))* Free Spirit Publishing, Inc.

CHILD REARING—FICTION

Alvarez, Miguel, et al. Why, Mommy!!, 1 vol. Pastrovicchio, Lorenzo, illus. 2009. 17p. pap. 24.95 *(978-1-60749-429-4(9))* America Star Bks.

Galassi, Isabel. I Want, 1 vol. 2009. 12p. pap. 24.95 *(978-1-61546-535-4(9))* America Star Bks.

Rosanbalm, Sunny, illus. A Gift for Baby. 2009. (SPA & ENG.). *(978-0-9685754-7-5(1))* Natural Child Project Society, The.

Splawn, "E". Planting Fruitful Seeds. 2011. 32p. pap. 12.77 *(978-1-4567-3896-9(8))* AuthorHouse.

Tiller, Amy. My Sister Is Like a Baby Bird. Tiller, Amy, illus. 2009. (ENG., Illus.). 26p. (J). 12.95 *(978-1-935130-02-4(1))* Grateful Steps.

Walsh, Aly. My Mum Says Blah Blah Blah. Walsh, Marilyn, illus. 2012. 26p. pap. 15.97 *(978-1-61204-854-3(4)*, Strategic Bk. Publishing) Strategic Book Publishing & Rights Agency (SBPRA).

CHILD SEXUAL ABUSE

Farrell, Courtney. Children's Rights, 1 vol. 2010. (Essential Issues Set 1 Ser.). (ENG.). 112p. (J). (gr. 6-12). lib. bdg. 35.64 *(978-1-60453-952-3(6)*, Essential Library) ABDO Publishing Co.

Foltz, Linda Lee. Kids Helping Kids Break the Silence of Sexual Abuse. 2003. 144p. (J). 21.95 *(978-0-9637966-8-4(2))*; (YA). pap. 14.95 *(978-0-9637966-9-1(0))* Lighthouse Point Pr.

Honowitz, Stacey. My Privates Are Private. 2012. 24p. 19.95 *(978-1-4575-1327-5(7))* Dog Ear Publishing, LLC.

International Center for Assault Prevention Staff & Pro Familia, Deutsche Gesellschaft für Sexualberatung und Familienplanung Staff. My Body Belongs to Me from My Head to My Toes. Geisler, Dagmar, illus. 2014. (ENG.). 36p. (J). (gr. -1-k). 16.95 *(978-1-62636-345-8(5)*, 263345, Sky Pony Pr.) Skyhorse Publishing Co., Inc.

Kats, Jewel. Reena's Bollywood Dream: A Story about Sexual Abuse. 2010. (Illus.). 20p. (J). pap. *(978-1-61599-014-6(3))* Loving Healing Pr., Inc.

Mcdonald, P. J. A Cry for Help No One Heard. 2011. 148p. (gr. 10-12). pap. 14.95 *(978-1-4670-7105-6(5))* AuthorHouse.

McDowell, Josh & Stewart, Ed. Past Sexual Abuse. 2009. (Project 17:17 Ser.). (ENG.). 64p. (J). mass mkt. 4.99 *(978-1-84550-443-4(7)*, 9781845504434) Christian Focus Pubns. GBR. Dist: Bookmasters Distribution.

McKinnon, Margie & McKinnon, Tom W. Repair for Kids: A Children's Program for Recovery from Incest & Childhood Sexual Abuse. McKinnon, Margie & McKinnon, Tom W., illus. 2008. (Illus.). 92p. (J). pap. 34.95 *(978-1-932690-57-6(3))* Loving Healing Pr., Inc.

Nelson, Sara. Stay Safe! How You Can Keep Out of Harm's Way. 2009. pap. 52.95 *(978-0-7613-4688-3(0))* Lerner Publishing Group.

Nelson, Sara Kirsten. Stay Safe! How You Can Keep Out of Harm's Way. Desrocher, Jack, illus. 2008. (Health Zone Ser.). (ENG.). 64p. (gr. 4-7). lib. bdg. 30.60 *(978-0-8225-7551-1(5))* Lerner Publishing Group.

Starishevsky, Jill. My Body Belongs to Me: A Book about Body Safety. Padrón, Angela, illus. 2014. (ENG.). 32p. (J). (gr. -1-3). 12.99 *(978-1-57542-461-3(4))* Free Spirit Publishing, Inc.

CHILD SEXUAL ABUSE—FICTION

Brown, Linnet. Secrets Can Be Told. 2013. 74p. pap. 10.99 *(978-1-62697-265-0(6))* Salem Author Services.

C
D

Cumbie, Patricia. Where People Like Us Live. 2008. 224p. (YA). (gr. 7-18). lib. bdg. 17.89 *(978-0-06-137598-9(5),* Geringer, Laura Book) HarperCollins Pubs.

Fluttert, Pam. Until Today, 1 vol. 2013. (ENG.). 200p. (YA). (gr. 8-12). pap. 12.95 *(978-1-927583-16-6(0))* Second Story Pr. CAN. Dist: Orca Bk. Pubs. USA.

Frank, E. R. Friction. 2015. (ENG., Illus.). 240p. (YA). (gr. 9). pap. 9.99 *(978-1-4814-4810-9(2),* Atheneum Bks. for Young Readers) Simon & Schuster Children's Publishing.

Garner, Linda. Some Secrets Hurt: A Story of Healing. Speth, Brandilyn, illus. 2009. 64p. (J). (gr. 1). 15.95 *(978-1-60641-135-3(7))* Deseret Bk. Co.

Glasgow, Kathleen. Girl in Pieces. 2016. (ENG.). 416p. (YA). (gr. 9). lib. bdg. 21.99 *(978-1-101-93473-9(5),* Delacorte Pr.) Random House Publishing Group.

—Girl in Pieces. 2016. (ENG.). 416p. (YA). (gr. 9). 18.99 *(978-1-101-93471-5(9),* Delacorte Pr.) Random Hse. Children's Bks.

Horowitz, Stacey & Brenner, Jordyn. My Privates Are Private. 2009. 24p. pap. 12.95 *(978-1-60844-281-2(0))* Dog Ear Publishing, LLC.

Hopkins, Ellen. Identical. (ENG.). (YA). (gr. 9-18). 2010. 592p. pap. 12.99 *(978-1-4169-5006-6(0))* 2008. 576p. 17.99 *(978-1-4169-5005-9(2))* McElderry, Margaret K. Bks. (McElderry, Margaret K. Bks.).

Kennedy, Tammy Helena. Jingles Lost Her Jingle. 2nd ed. 2013. 128p. pap. 14.95 *(978-0-9910841-0-4(1))* King's Treasure Box Ministries, The.

Lyga, Barry. Boy Toy. 2009. (ENG.). 416p. (YA). (gr. 9). pap. 9.99 *(978-0-547-07634-8(7))* Houghton Mifflin Harcourt Publishing Co.

Marsh, Carole. The Colonial Caper Mystery at Williamsburg. 2009. (Real Kids, Real Places Ser.). (Illus.). 143p. (J). (gr. 4-7). pap. 7.99 *(978-0-635-06826-2(5),* Marsh, Carole Bks.) Gallopade International.

McDaniel-Sanderson, Lynne. Mattie Tells Her Secret. 2012. 16p. pap. 15.99 *(978-1-4772-5610-7(5))* AuthorHouse.

McMann, Lisa. Fade. (Wake Ser.: Bk. 2). (ENG.). (YA). (gr. 9-18). 2010. Illus.). 272p. pap. 10.99 *(978-1-4169-7448-2(2))* 2009. 256p. 17.99 *(978-1-4169-5358-6(2))* Simon Pulse. (Simon Pulse).

Mi-Leing. Chrystal's Castle. 2007. 40p. 18.50 *(978-1-4303-2242-9(X))* Lulu Pr., Inc.

Nathanson, Laura. El Problema de los Miercoles. (SPA.). 160p. (YA). (gr. 5-8). *(978-84-279-3181-7(6),* NG3677) Noguer y Caralt Editores, S. A. ESP. Dist: Lectorum Pubns., Inc.

Ramsey, Jo. Work Boots & Tees. (YA). 2016. (ENG., Illus.). (gr. 9-12). 24.99 ***(978-1-63477-997-5(5),*** Harmony Ink Pr.) 2015. 156p. *(978-1-61372-834-5(4))* Dreamspinner Pr.

Rapp, Adam. 33 Snowfish. Ering, Timothy Basil, illus. 2006. (ENG.). 192p. (YA). (gr. 9-12). per. 7.99 *(978-0-7636-2917-5(0))* Candlewick Pr.

Schamburg, Tracy M. Catie the Caterpillar: A Story to Help Break the Silence of Sexual Abuse. Riley, Melanie Ellis, illus. 2006. 31p. (J). (gr. -1). pap. 6.95 *(978-0-7648-1434-1(6))* Liguori Pubns.

Smith, Al. Koala & Bunny: Instilling Protective Behaviours in Children. 2011. 38p. pap. 14.50 *(978-1-61204-102-5(7),* Eloquent Bks.) Strategic Book Publishing & Rights Agency (SBPRA).

Waldorf, Heather. Leftovers, 1 vol. 2009. (ENG.). 208p. (YA). (gr. 7-12). pap. 12.95 *(978-1-55143-937-2(9))* Orca Bk. Pubs. USA.

Weeks, Sarah. Jumping the Scratch. (J). (gr. 5-9). 2007. (ENG.). 192p. pap. 6.99 *(978-0-06-054111-8(3))* 2006. (Illus.). 167p. lib. bdg. 16.89 *(978-0-06-054110-1(5),* Geringer, Laura Book) HarperCollins Pubs.

CHILD STUDY

see Child Development; Child Psychology

CHILD WELFARE

Here are entered works on the aid, support, and protection of children, by the state or by private welfare organizations.

see also Child Labor; Children—Health and Hygiene; Foster Home Care; Juvenile Delinquency; Playgrounds

Bryfonski, Dedria. Child Custody. 2011. (Opposing Viewpoints Ser.). 240p. pap. 29.45 *(978-0-7377-5218-2(1));* (ENG.). 224p. (gr. 12-12). lib. bdg. 48.80 *(978-0-7377-5217-5(3))* Cengage Gale. (Greenhaven Pr., Inc.).

Currie-McGhee, Leanne. Foster Youth. 2016. (ENG.). 80p. (J). (gr. 5-12). *(978-1-60152-976-3(7))* ReferencePoint Pr., Inc.

Duckworth, Katie. Health. 2004. (Children's Rights Ser.). (J). lib. bdg. 27.10 *(978-1-58340-420-1(1))* Black Rabbit Bks.

Libal, Joyce. Protective Services. Albers, Lisa et al, eds. 2014. (Living with a Special Need Ser.: 16). 128p. (J). (gr. 7-18). 25.95 *(978-1-4222-3042-8(2))* Mason Crest.

—Somebody Hear Me Crying: Youth in Protective Services. 2004. (Youth with Special Needs Ser.). (Illus.). 128p. (YA). lib. bdg. 24.95 *(978-1-59084-739-8(3))* Mason Crest.

Malarek, Victor. Hey Malarek! The True Story of a Street Kid Who Made It. 2nd ed. 2012. (ENG.). 244p. pap. 22.95 *(978-1-4594-0047-4(X),* 9781459400474) Lorimer, James & Co., Ltd., Pubs. CAN. Dist: Casemate Pubs. & Bk. Distributors, LLC.

Marsico, Katie. The Texas Polygamist Raid: Religious Freedom Versus Child Welfare. 2011. (Perspectives on 3 Ser.). 112p. (gr. 7). 39.93 *(978-1-60870-449-1(1))* Marshall Cavendish Corp.

Morris, Kimberly & Burke, Kathleen. Just for Now: Kids & the People of the Court. Sansevero, Tony, illus. 2007. 48p. (J). (gr. k-4). 16.95 *(978-0-9754959-1-9(0))* Child Advocates, Inc.

Parry, Ann. Save the Children. 2005. (Humanitarian Organizations Ser.). (Illus.). 32p. (gr. 5-8). lib. bdg. 25.00 *(978-0-7910-8816-6(2),* Chelsea Hse.) Facts On File, Inc.

Spilsbury, Louise. Protecting & Caring for Children, 1 vol. 2012. (Charities in Action Ser.). (ENG.). 64p. (gr. 6-10). pap. 10.95 *(978-1-4329-6394-1(5));* lib. bdg. 35.99 *(978-1-4329-6387-3(2))* Heinemann-Raintree.

Strom, Laura Layton. Don't Try This at Home: The Science of Extreme Behaviors. 2007. (Shockwave: Science in Practice Ser.). (ENG., Illus.). 36p. (J). (gr. 4-6). lib. bdg. 25.00 *(978-0-531-17573-6(1),* Children's Pr.) Scholastic Library Publishing.

Weekley, Randy/ J. Strangers Bullies Safety & More... A How to Guide to Child Safety. 2nd ed. 2007. (Illus.). 48p. (J). per. 9.99 *(978-0-9777457-9-1(1))* Privacy Trust Group, The.

CHILD WELFARE—FICTION

Bauer, A. C. E. & Shakespeare, William. Come Fall. 2011. (ENG.). 240p. (J). (gr. 3-7). pap. 6.99 *(978-0-375-85826-0(1),* Yearling) Random Hse. Children's Bks.

Robe, Adam D. Moving to Another Foster Home. Robe, Kim A., ed. Gavet, Nathalie, illus. 2009. 16p. pap. 11.99 *(978-0-9817403-4-8(0))* Robe Communications, Inc.

—Wanting to Belong. Robe, Kim A., ed. Gavet, Nathalie, illus. 2009. 16p. pap. 11.99 *(978-0-9817403-6-2(7))* Robe Communications, Inc.

CHILDBIRTH

see also Pregnancy

Bailey, Jacqui. What Happens When You Are Born & Grow? (gr. k-5). 2009. 32p. pap. 10.60 *(978-1-4358-2615-1(9),* Rosen Classroom) 2008. (Illus.). 30p. (J). lib. bdg. 26.50 *(978-1-4042-4425-2(5),* PowerKids Pr.) Rosen Publishing Group, Inc., The.

bint Robert, Na'ima. Welcome to the World, Baby. 2004. (J). (BEN & ENG.). 16.95 *(978-1-84444-623-0(9));* (CHI & ENG.). 16.95 *(978-1-84444-624-7(7));* (ENG & RUS.). 16.95 *(978-1-84444-638-4(7));* (ENG & VIE.). 16.95 *(978-1-84444-644-5(1))* Mantra Lingua GBR. Dist: Chinasprout, Inc.

¿De Donde Vienen los Bebes? (Coleccion Primeros Pasos en la Ciencia). (SPA., Illus.). (J). (gr. 1-3). pap. *(978-950-724-218-2(X),* LMA8221) Lumen ARG. Dist: Lectorum Pubns., Inc.

Fields, J. Choosing a Career as a Nurse-Midwife. 2009. (World of Work Ser.). 64p. (gr. 5-5). 58.50 *(978-1-60854-323-6(4))* Rosen Publishing Group, Inc., The.

Fields, Jennifer. Choosing a Career as a Nurse-Midwife. 2005. (World of Work Ser.). (Illus.). 64p. (YA). (gr. 7-12). lib. bdg. 31.95 *(978-0-8239-3293-1(1))* Rosen Publishing Group, Inc., The.

Ganeri, Anita. Celebrating Birth Around the World. 2015. (Cultures & Customs Ser.). (ENG., Illus.). 32p. (gr. 3-3). pap. 7.99 *(978-1-4109-8020-5(0),* Raintree Perspectives) Heinemann-Raintree.

Gordon, Elaine R. Mommy, Did I Grow in Your Tummy? Where Some Babies Come From. Clo, Kathy, illus. Date not set. 28p. (Orig.). (J). (gr. -1-4). pap. 9.95 *(978-0-9634561-0-6(5))* EM Greenberg Pr., Inc.

Harris, Robie H. It's Not the Stork! A Book about Girls, Boys, Babies, Bodies, Families & Friends. Emberley, Michael, illus. (Family Library). (ENG.). 64p. (J). (gr. -1-3). 2008. pap. 11.99 *(978-0-7636-3331-8(3))* 2006. 16.99 *(978-0-7636-0047-1(4))* Candlewick Pr.

Harrison, Anne-Marie. Babies Are Noisy: A Book for Big Brothers & Sisters Including Those on the Autism Spectrum. Byrne, Beth, illus. 2013. (ENG.). 40p. (J). 15.95 *(978-1-84905-459-1(2),* 4085) Kingsley, Jessica Pubs. GBR. Dist: Macmillan Distribution Ltd.

Hernandez, Jewel. Being Born: The Doula's Role. Mithuna, R. Michael, illus. 2008. (ENG.). 32p. (J). pap. 9.95 *(978-1-890772-83-3(6))* Hohm Pr.

Hernandez, Jewel & Mithuna, R. Michael. El Nacimiento: El Papel de una Doula = Being Born: The Doula's Role. Mithuna, R. Michael, illus. 2009. (SPA & ENG., Illus.). (J). pap. *(978-1-890772-91-8(7))* Hohm Pr.

Maravilla de la Vida. (SPA.). 266p. (J). 10.00 *(978-84-342-1466-8(0))* Parramon Ediciones S.A. ESP. Dist: Distribuidora Norma, Inc.

Merritt, Robin. The Life Cycle of a Human. 2011. (Life Cycles Ser.). (ENG., Illus.). 32p. (J). (gr. k-3). lib. bdg. 29.93 *(978-1-60973-147-2(6),* 201174) Child's World, Inc., The.

Meyer, Brian E. What You Mean to Me. 2010. 20p. 11.99 *(978-1-4520-8170-0(0))* AuthorHouse.

Nixon, Joan Lowery. Before You Were Born. Heaston, Rebecca J., illus. 2nd sensomatic ed. 2006. 31p. pap. 10.95 *(978-1-59276-219-4(0))* Our Sunday Visitor, Publishing Div.

Nystrom, Carolyn. Before I Was Born. Speidel, Sandra, illus. rev. ed. 2007. (God's Design for Sex Ser.: 2). (ENG.). 40p. pap. 10.99 *(978-1-60006-014-4(5))* NavPress Publishing Group.

Robert, Na'ima Bint. Welcome to the World Baby. Brazell, Derek, illus. 2005. 32p. (J). (ENG & GER.). pap. *(978-1-84444-276-8(4));* (FRE & ENG.). pap. *(978-1-84444-275-1(6));* (ENG & PER.). pap. *(978-1-84444-274-4(8));* (ENG & GUJ.). pap. *(978-1-84444-278-2(0));* (ENG & HIN.). pap. *(978-1-84444-279-9(9));* (ENG & ITA.). pap. *(978-1-84444-280-5(2));* (JPN & ENG.). pap. *(978-1-84444-281-2(0));* (ENG & KOR.). pap. *(978-1-84444-282-9(9));* (ENG & PAN.). pap. *(978-1-84444-283-6(7));* (POL & ENG.). pap. *(978-1-84444-284-3(5));* (ENG & POR.). pap. *(978-1-84444-285-0(3));* (ENG & ALB.). pap. *(978-1-84444-268-3(3));* (ENG & ARA.). pap. *(978-1-84444-269-0(1));* (ENG & BEN.). pap. *(978-1-84444-270-6(5));* (ENG & CHI.). pap. *(978-1-84444-271-3(3));* (SPA & ENG.). pap. *(978-1-84444-289-8(6));* (ENG & SOM.). pap. *(978-1-84444-288-1(8));* (ENG & RUS.). pap. *(978-1-84444-287-4(X));* (ENG & CHI.). pap. *(978-1-84444-272-0(1));* (ENG, HRV & SER.). pap. *(978-1-84444-273-7(X));* (WEL, ENG, KOR & KUR.). pap. *(978-1-84444-633-9(6));* (ENG & SNA.). pap. *(978-1-84444-450-2(3));* (YOR & ENG.). pap. *(978-1-84444-297-3(7));* (ENG & VIE.). pap. *(978-1-84444-296-6(9));* (ENG & URD.). pap. *(978-1-84444-295-9(0));* (TUR & ENG.). pap. *(978-1-84444-293-5(4));* (ENG & SWA.). pap. *(978-1-84444-290-4(X));* (ENG & RUM.). pap. *(978-1-84444-286-7(1))* Mantra Lingua.

Robert, Na'ima Bint & Petrova-Browning, Nina. Welcome to the World Baby. Brazell, Derek, illus. 2005. (ENG & BUL.). 32p. (J). pap. *(978-1-84444-721-3(9))* Mantra Lingua.

Roberts, Jillian. Where Do Babies Come From? Our First Talk about Birth, 1 vol. Revell, Cindy, illus. 2015. (Just Enough Ser.). (ENG.). 32p. (J). (gr. k-1). 19.95 *(978-1-4598-0942-0(4))* Orca Bk. Pubs. USA.

Showers, Paul. How a Baby Begins. Date not set. 40p. (J). (gr. k-4). lib. bdg. 16.89 *(978-0-06-025413-1(0))* HarperCollins Pubs.

Silverberg, Cory. What Makes a Baby. 2013. (ENG., Illus.). 36p. (J). (gr. -1-2). 16.95 *(978-1-60980-485-5(6),* Triangle Square) Seven Stories Pr.

Welcome to the World, Baby. 2004. (J). (ENG & GRE.). *(978-1-84444-628-5(X));* (ENG & FRE.). *(978-1-84444-645-2(X));* (ENG & PER.). *(978-1-84444-627-8(1));* (CRO & ENG.). *(978-1-84444-626-1(3));* (CHI & ENG.). *(978-1-84444-625-4(5));* (ARA & ENG.). *(978-1-84444-622-3(0));* (ALB & ENG.). *(978-1-84444-621-6(2));* (ENG & URD.). *(978-1-84444-643-8(3));* (ENG & TUR.). *(978-1-84444-642-1(5));* (ENG & TAM.). *(978-1-84444-641-4(7));* (ENG & SPA.). *(978-1-84444-640-7(9));* (ENG & SOM.). *(978-1-84444-639-1(5));* (ENG & POR.). *(978-1-84444-637-7(9));* (ENG & POL.). *(978-1-84444-636-0(0));* (ENG & PAN.). *(978-1-84444-635-3(2));* (ENG & KUR.). *(978-1-84444-634-6(4));* (ENG & JPN.). *(978-1-84444-632-2(8));* (ENG & ITA.). *(978-1-84444-631-5(X));* (ENG & HIN.). *(978-1-84444-630-8(1));* (ENG & GUJ.). *(978-1-84444-629-2(8))* Mantra Lingua.

White, Mia. On the day you were Born Everything that has Breath: Dr. Mia White. 2006. (Illus.). per. 20.00 *(978-0-9703419-2-1(X))* Belle Media International, Inc. Div of True News.

X. Before You Were Born - Our Wish for A Baby - IVF: Version 1: in Vitro Fertilization. 2004. (ENG., Illus.). 16p. (J). pap. 17.95 *(978-0-9755028-0-8(8))* X, Y, & Me LLC.

CHILDBIRTH—FICTION

Brott, Ardyth. Here I Am!, 1 vol. Miladovich, Dragana, illus. 2012. (ENG.). 32p. (J). (gr. k-7). pap. 14.95 *(978-0-88962-938-7(2),* 9780889629387) Mosaic Pr. CAN. Dist: Independent Pubs. Group.

Butler, Dori Hillestad. Alexandra Hopewell, Labor Coach. 2005. 136p. (J). (gr. 3-6). 15.99 *(978-0-8075-0242-6(1))* Whitman, Albert & Co.

Calaf, Monica. How You Were Born. Fuentes, Mikel, illus. 2014. (ENG.). 48p. (J). (gr. -1-3). 9.99 *(978-1-78066-125-4(8))* Pinter & Martin Ltd. GBR. Dist: National Bk. Network.

Doman, Regina. Mi Angelito en Las Aguas. Hatke, Ben, illus. 2006. (SPA.). 40p. (J). (gr. -1-3). pap. 6.95 *(978-1-933184-22-7(1))* Sophia Institute Pr.

Feiffer, Kate. The Wild, Wild Inside: A View from Mommy's Tummy! Huliska-Beith, Laura, illus. 2010. (ENG.). 32p. (J). (gr. -1-3). 15.99 *(978-1-4169-4099-9(5),* Simon & Schuster/Paula Wiseman Bks.) Simon & Schuster/Paula Wiseman Bks.

Galloway, Teresa A. The Tiny Star Birth of a Soul. 2009. 36p. pap. 15.95 *(978-1-4389-3857-8(8))* AuthorHouse.

Holt, Sharon. Did My Mother Do That? Lovelock, Brian, illus. 2010. (ENG.). 32p. (J). (gr. -1-2). 15.99 *(978-0-7636-4685-1(7))* Candlewick Pr.

Morgan, Cythia. The Day I Met You & You Met Me! Cable, Annette, illus. 2008. 32p. pap. 5.95 *(978-0-9802497-0-5(8))* King'S Land Pr. Inc.

Moss, Maureen. God's Promise. Purnell, Gerald, illus. 2008. 30p. (J). (gr. -1-3). 15.95 *(978-0-9740190-7-9(0))* Illumination Arts Publishing Co., Inc.

O'Leary, Sara. Where You Came From. Morstad, Julie, illus. 2008. (ENG.). 32p. (J). (gr. -1-3). 16.95 *(978-1-894965-46-0(9))* Simply Read Bks. CAN. Dist: Ingram Publisher Services.

Paulsen, Gary. The Quilt. 2005. 83p. (gr. 3-7). 16.00 *(978-0-7569-4781-1(2))* Perfection Learning Corp.

—The Quilt. 2005. (ENG., Illus.). 96p. (J). (gr. 3-7). 6.99 *(978-0-440-22936-0(7),* Yearling) Random Hse. Children's Bks.

CHILDREN

see also Child Development

Alexander, Florence & Alexander, Stanley. Come with Me & See... Children of the World. l.t. ed. 2003. (ENG & SPA., Illus.). 32p. (J). 9.99 *(978-0-9648313-9-1(2))* Ebon Research Systems Publishing, LLC.

Allman, Toney. Food in Schools. rev. ed. 2014. (Matters of Opinion Ser.). (ENG.). 64p. (J). (gr. 4-6). lib. bdg. 27.93 *(978-1-59953-604-0(8))* Norwood Hse. Pr.

Amoroso, Cynthia. Tolerance. 2013. (Values to Live By Ser.). (ENG.). 24p. (J). (gr. -1-2). 25.64 *(978-1-62323-527-7(8),* 206298) Child's World, Inc., The.

Bai, Durga, illus. The Churki-Burki Book of Rhyme. 2010. (ENG.). 24p. (J). (gr. -1-3). *(978-93-80340-06-7(0))* Tara Publishing.

Barakat, Ibtisam. Tasting the Sky: A Palestinian Childhood. 2007. (ENG., Illus.). 192p. (YA). (gr. 6-10). 17.99 *(978-0-374-35733-7(1),* 9780374357337, Farrar, Straus & Giroux (BYR)) Farrar, Straus & Giroux.

BeaverSimon. SAVED! HEROES IN EVERYDAY LIFE BEGINNING BOOK WITH ONLINE ACCESS. 2014. (ENG., Illus.). 24p. pap. 7.50 *(978-1-107-64705-3(3))* Cambridge Univ. Pr.

Bekele, Aregash, tr. Carry Me (Amharic/English), 1 vol. 2010. (Babies Everywhere Ser.). (ENG., Illus.). 20p. (J). 6.95 *(978-1-59572-260-7(2))* Star Bright Bks., Inc.

Bennett, Howard J. Lions Aren't Scared of Shots: A Story for Children about Visiting the Doctor. Weber, M. S., illus. 2006. 32p. (J). (gr. -1-3). 14.95 *(978-1-59147-473-9(6),* 441A473); per. 9.95 *(978-1-59147-474-6(4),* 441A474) American Psychological Assn. (Magination Pr.).

Bily, Cynthia A., ed. Banned Books. 2012. (Introducing Issues with Opposing Viewpoints Ser.). (ENG., Illus.). 144p. (J). (gr. 7-10). lib. bdg. 36.95 *(978-0-7377-5671-5(3),* Greenhaven Pr., Inc.) Cengage Gale.

Bingham, Jane. Courageous Children, 1 vol. 2011. (War Stories Ser.). (ENG.). 32p. (gr. 3-6). 30.65 *(978-1-4329-4836-8(9),* NA-h) Heinemann-Raintree.

Bottoms, James. Kid Ethics 2: From A to Z. 2007. (Illus.). 59p. (J). per. 12.95 *(978-0-9794863-1-9(9))* Summerland Publishing.

Bowman, Crystal & Taylor, Christy Lee. Devotions for Beginning Readers, 1 vol. 2014. (ENG.). 240p. (J). 14.99 *(978-0-529-10401-4(6))* Nelson, Thomas Inc.

Boyer, Marilyn. Character Trails: Learning to Walk in Paths of Righteousness. 2011. 168p. *(978-0-9777685-3-0(8))* Learning Parent, The.

Brandeis, Madeline. Little Tony of Italy. 2011. 160p. 41.95 *(978-1-258-09804-9(0))* Literary Licensing, LLC.

Branon, Dave. Heads Up! Sports Devotions for All-Star Kids, 1 vol. rev. ed. 2012. (ENG.). 346p. (J). pap. 9.99 *(978-0-310-72544-2(5))* Zondervan.

Canfield, Jack, et al. Chicken Soup for the Child's Soul: Character-Building Stories to Read with Kids Ages 5-8. 2012. (ENG.). 400p. pap. 14.95 *(978-1-62361-115-6(6),* CSS Backlist) Chicken Soup for the Soul Publishing, LLC.

Castle, Caroline. For Every Child: The UN Convention on the Rights of the Child in Words & Pictures. 2004. (J). (gr. k-3). spiral bd. *(978-0-616-14618-7(3));* spiral bd. *(978-0-616-14617-0(5))* Canadian National Institute for the Blind/Institut National Canadien pour les Aveugles.

Champion, Gina. Anna & Her Mommy. Mitchell, Nanci, illus. 2005. 36p. (J). (gr. k-6). pap. 10.00 *(978-1-884363-20-7(2))* Odenwald Pr.

Children around the World. 2005. (J). per. 8.95 *(978-1-59566-138-8(7))* QEB Publishing Inc.

Coster, Patience. My Life in Brazil. 2015. (Children of the World Ser.). (ENG.). 32p. (J). (gr. 5-5). pap. 10.58 *(978-1-5026-0041-7(2))* Cavendish Square Publishing.

—My Life in France. 2015. (J). pap. *(978-1-62713-332-6(1))* Cavendish Square Publishing.

—My Life in Jamaica. 2015. (Children of the World Ser.). (ENG.). 32p. (J). (gr. 5-5). pap. 10.58 *(978-1-5026-0054-7(4))* Cavendish Square Publishing.

Cricket Books Staff & Cobblestone Publishing, Inc. Staff. If I Were a Kid in Ancient Rome: Children of the Ancient World. Sheldon, Ken, ed. 2007. (If I Were a Kid In... Ser.). (ENG., Illus.). 32p. (J). (gr. 1-5). 17.95 *(978-0-8126-7930-4(X))* Cricket Bks.

Crockett, Kyle A. Nutrition for Achievement in Sports & Academics. Borus, Joshua, ed. 2013. (Understanding Nutrition: a Gateway to Physical & Mental Health Ser.). (Illus.). 48p. (J). (gr. 5-18). pap. 9.95 *(978-1-4222-2990-3(4))* Mason Crest.

de Las Casas, Dianne & Eliana, Kid. Cool Kids Cook: Fresh & Fit, 1 vol. Lisette, Soleil, illus. 2014. (ENG.). 64p. (J). (gr. 3-7). 14.95 *(978-1-4556-1892-7(6))* Pelican Publishing Co., Inc.

DeMocker, Michael. Long Ago & Far Away Ancient Rome: Ancient Rome. 2015. (ENG., Illus.). 32p. (J). 26.50 *(978-1-62469-128-7(5))* Purple Toad Publishing, Inc.

Dorling Kindersley Publishing Staff. A Life Like Mine: How Children Live Around the World. 2005. (ENG., Illus.). 128p. (J). (gr. 2-5). pap. 12.99 *(978-0-7566-1803-2(7),* DK Children) Dorling Kindersley Publishing, Inc.

Elliott, Lynne. Children & Games in the Middle Ages. 2004. (Medieval World Ser.). (ENG., Illus.). 32p. (J). pap. *(978-0-7787-1381-4(4));* lib. bdg. *(978-0-7787-1349-4(0))* Crabtree Publishing Co.

Ellis, Deborah. Kids of Kabul: Living Bravely Through a Never-Ending War, 1 vol. 2012. (ENG., Illus.). 128p. (J). (gr. 6). 15.95 *(978-1-55498-181-6(6))* Groundwood Bks. CAN. Dist: Publishers Group West (PGW).

Etingoff, Kim. Decisions, Decisions: Vegetarianism, Breakfasts, & Beyond. Borus, Joshua, ed. 2013. (Understanding Nutrition: a Gateway to Physical & Mental Health Ser.: 11). (Illus.). 48p. (J). (gr. 5-18). 19.95 *(978-1-4222-2875-3(4))* Mason Crest.

—Drugs & Alcohol. Stephens, Ronald, ed. 2014. (Safety First Ser.: 11). 48p. (J). (gr. 5-18). 20.95 *(978-1-4222-3046-6(5))* Mason Crest.

—Healthy Alternatives to Sweets & Snacks. Borus, Joshua, ed. 2013. (Understanding Nutrition: a Gateway to Physical & Mental Health Ser.). (Illus.). 48p. (J). (gr. 5-18). pap. 9.95 *(978-1-4222-2992-7(0))* Mason Crest.

Farndon, John. How to Live Like an Egyptian Mummy Maker. Campidelli, Maurizio, illus. 2016. (How to Live Like... Ser.). (ENG.). 32p. (J). (gr. 3-6). 26.65 *(978-1-5124-0629-0(5))* Lerner Publishing Group.

Fields, Julianna. Kids Growing up Without a Home. 2010. (Changing Face of Modern Families Ser.). (Illus.). 64p. (YA). (gr. 5-18). lib. bdg. 22.95 *(978-1-4222-1498-5(2))* Mason Crest.

Fiol, Maria A., tr. Llevame, 1 vol. 2010. (Bebes Por Dondequiera Ser.).Tr. of Carry Me. (SPA., Illus.). 20p. (J). bds. 6.95 *(978-1-59572-223-2(8))* Star Bright Bks., Inc.

Fontes, Justine. Rude Ralph: A Rookie Reader. Jordan, Charles, illus. 2011. (Rookie Ready to Learn Ser.). 40p. (J). pap. 5.95 *(978-0-531-26711-0(3));* (gr. -1-k). lib. bdg. 23.00 *(978-0-531-26529-1(3))* Scholastic Library Publishing. (Children's Pr.).

Garrett, Winston. Let's Ride the School Bus! 2014. (Public Transportation Ser.). 24p. (J). (gr. k-2). pap. 49.50 *(978-1-4777-6517-3(4),* PowerKids Pr.) Rosen Publishing Group, Inc., The.

Gordon, Sharon. We Share. 2007. (J). pap. 6.99 *(978-0-7614-3276-0(0))* Marshall Cavendish Corp.

—We Tell the Truth. 2007. (J). pap. 6.99 *(978-0-7614-3277-7(9))* Marshall Cavendish Corp.

Graham, Billy. Hope for Each Day: 365 Devotions for Kids, 1 vol. 2017. (ENG.). 400p. (J). 15.99 *(978-0-7180-8617-6(1))* Nelson, Thomas Inc.

Graves, Sue. I Don't Want to Be Nice! A Book about Showing Kindness. Carletti, Emanuela & Guicciardini, Desideria, illus. 2017. (Our Emotions & Behavior Ser.). (ENG.). 28p. (J). (gr. -1-3). 12.99 ***(978-1-63198-132-6(3))*** Free Spirit Publishing, Inc.

Hall, Kirsten. Kids in Sports. 2005. (True Tales Ser.). (ENG., Illus.). 48p. (J). (gr. 2-4). pap. 4.95 *(978-0-516-24685-7(2),* Children's Pr.) Scholastic Library Publishing.

Hamod, Rania. I Am Good. 2012. 52p. (-18). pap. 20.95 *(978-1-4525-0807-8(0))* Balboa Pr.

Hardyman, Robyn. Relationships. 2010. (Being Healthy, Feeling Great Ser.). (ENG.). 32p. (J). pap. 10.60 *(978-1-61532-380-7(5),* PowerKids Pr.); (gr. 3-6). lib. bdg. 26.50 *(978-1-61532-371-5(6))* Rosen Publishing Group, Inc., The.

Harry-Jennings, Pamela. This Is Who I Am. 2008. 20p. pap. 24.95 *(978-1-60813-166-2(1))* America Star Bks.

Hauser, Jill Frankel. The Kid's Guide to Becoming the Best You Can Be! Developing 5 Traits You Need to Achieve Your Personal Best. Kline, Michael, illus. (ENG.). 128p. (J). (gr. 3-7). 2008. pap. 14.25 *(978-0-8249-6788-8(7))* 2006. 16.95 *(978-0-8249-6789-5(5))* Worthy Publishing. (Ideal Pubns.).

Hess, Ingrid. Sleep in Peace. 2007. (ENG., Illus.). 40p. (J). (gr. 3-7). per. 12.99 *(978-0-8361-9381-7(4))* Herald Pr.

Hinds, Maurene J. Do You Know Your Rights? 2016. (Got Issues? Ser.). (ENG., Illus.). 112p. (J). (gr. 7-8). 37.27 *(978-0-7660-7193-3(6))* Enslow Pubs., Inc.

Hong, Chen Jiang. Mao & Me. Bedrick, Claudia Z., tr. from FRE. 2008. (ENG., Illus.). 96p. (J). (gr. 3-5). 19.95 *(978-1-59270-079-0(9))* Enchanted Lion Bks., LLC.

Huey, Lois Miner. Children of the Past: Archaeology & the Lives of Kids. 2017. (Nonfiction — Grades 4-8 Ser.). (ENG.). 56p. (J). (gr. 4-8). 16.99 ***(978-1-5124-3878-9(2))***; 47.99 ***(978-1-5124-2843-8(4))***; 47.99 ***(978-1-5124-3879-6(0))***; (Illus.). 31.99 *(978-1-5124-1316-8(X))* Lerner Publishing Group. (Millbrook Pr.).

Humphrey, Sandra McLeod. Hot Issues, Cool Choices: Facing Bullies, Peer Pressure, Popularity, & Put-Downs. 2007. (ENG., Illus.). 133p. (J). (gr. 4-7). per. 14.99 *(978-1-59102-569-6(9))* Prometheus Bks., Pubs.

Hunter, Rebecca & Walker, Kathryn. Growing up in the Forties. 2003. (Illus.). 32p. pap. *(978-0-7502-3434-4(2)*, Wayland) Hachette Children's Group.

—Growing up in the Thirties. 2003. (Illus.). 32p. pap. *(978-0-7502-3433-7(4)*, Wayland) Hachette Children's Group.

Jackson, Ellen B. Turn of the Century: Eleven Centuries of Children & Change. Ellis, Jan Davey, illus. 2003. (ENG.). 32p. (J). (gr. k-3). pap. 8.95 *(978-0-88106-370-7(3))* Charlesbridge Publishing, Inc.

Kallmeyer-Mehlhorn, Margarete. The Wondrous Ball of Yarn: A Facsimile of the Previously Unpublished Manuscript. 2008.Tr. of Wunderknaul. (ENG & GER., Illus.). 40p. 41.00 *(978-0-9745168-2-0(1))* Cotsen Occasional Pr.

Kawa, Katie. My First Trip to the Dentist. Livingston, Jessica, illus. 2012. (My First Adventures Ser.). (ENG.). 24p. (J). (gr. k-2). pap. 8.15 *(978-1-4339-6243-1(8))*; lib. bdg. 22.60 *(978-1-4339-6241-7(1))* Stevens, Gareth Publishing LLLP.

—My First Trip to the Doctor. Livingston, Jessica, illus. 2012. (My First Adventures Ser.). (ENG.). 24p. (J). (gr. k-2). pap. 8.15 *(978-1-4339-6247-9(0))*; lib. bdg. 22.60 *(978-1-4339-6245-5(4))* Stevens, Gareth Publishing LLLP.

Kelley, Michelle. Just Like You. 2006. (ENG., Illus.). 8p. (gr. -1-k). pap. 5.95 *(978-1-59515-934-2(7))* Rourke Educational Media.

Keogh, Josie. A Trip to the Hospital. 2012. (PowerKids Readers: My Community Ser.). (ENG., Illus.). 24p. (J). (gr. k-2). pap. 8.25 *(978-1-4488-7486-6(9))*; lib. bdg. 22.60 *(978-1-4488-7407-1(6))* Rosen Publishing Group, Inc., The. (PowerKids Pr.).

—A Trip to the Hospital / de visita en el Hospital. Alamán, Eduardo, tr. from ENG. 2012. (PowerKids Readers: My Community / Mi comunidad Ser.). (ENG & SPA., Illus.). 24p. (J). (gr. k-2). 22.60 *(978-1-4488-7831-4(4)*, Editorial Buenas Letras) Rosen Publishing Group, Inc., The.

Kerley, Barbara & National Geographic Kids Staff. Brave Like Me. 2016. (ENG., Illus.). 48p. (J). (gr. -1-3). 17.99 *(978-1-4263-2360-7(3)*, National Geographic Children's Bks.) National Geographic Society.

Kid Ethics: From A to Z. 2006. (Illus.). 56p. (J). (gr. -1-3). per. 12.95 *(978-0-9794863-0-2(0))* Summerland Publishing.

Kielburger, Craig. Lessons from a Street Kid, 1 vol. Antonello, Marisa & Laidley, Victoria, illus. 2012. (ENG.). 40p. (J). (gr. k-5). 19.95 *(978-1-55365-865-8(5)*, Greystone Bks.) Greystone Books Ltd. CAN. Dist: Publishers Group West (PGW).

Lamothe, Matt. This Is How We Do It. 2017. (ENG., Illus.). 52p. (J). 17.99 *(978-1-4521-5018-5(4))* Chronicle Bks. LLC.

Lebovics, Dania. Baby Chronicles: My Very Own Story: From Pre-Natal to Pre-School. Quach, Lam, illus. 2007. (ENG.). 72p. spiral bd. 19.95 *(978-0-9699203-7-3(7)*, 9780969920373) Kiddy Chronicles Publishing CAN. Dist: Firefly Bks., Ltd.

Loewen, Nancy. Save, Spend, or Donate? A Book about Managing Money. Fitzpatrick, Brad & Jensen, Brian, illus. 2005. (Money Matters Ser.). (ENG.). 24p. (gr. 1-3). 25.99 *(978-1-4048-0952-9(X)*, Nonfiction Picture Bks.) Picture Window Bks.

Mackall, Dandi Daley. Kids' Rules for Life: A Guide to Life's Journey from Those Just Starting Out. 2003. (Illus.). 176p. pap. 8.95 *(978-1-57071-909-7(8))* Sourcebooks, Inc.

Mahmout, Ulfet & Thompson, Alan. My Life Story. 2004. (Illus.). 34p. (J). *(978-1-85269-840-9(3))*; *(978-1-85269-895-9(0))*; *(978-1-85269-890-4(X))*; *(978-1-85269-880-5(2))*; *(978-1-85269-875-1(6))*; *(978-1-85269-870-6(5))*; *(978-1-85269-860-7(8))*; *(978-1-85269-855-3(1))*; *(978-1-85269-845-4(4))*; (ENG & BEN., pap. *(978-1-85269-850-8(0))* Mantra Lingua.

Mara, Wil. If You Were a Kid During the American Revolution. 2016. (If You Were a Kid Ser.). (ENG., Illus.). 32p. (J). lib. bdg. 26.00 *(978-0-531-21971-3(2)*, Children's Pr.) Scholastic Library Publishing.

Marcovitz, Hal. Teens & Cheating. Developed in Association with the Gallup Organization Staff, ed. 2013. (Gallup Youth Survey: Major Issues & Trends Ser.: 14). 112p. (J). (gr. 7-18). 24.95 *(978-1-4222-2951-4(3))* Mason Crest.

Marks, Jennifer L. Children. rev. ed. 2009. (People Ser.). (ENG.). 24p. (gr. k-1). lib. bdg. 21.99 *(978-1-4296-2237-0(7)*, Pebble Bks.) Capstone Press of Coughlan Cos.

—Children, 1 vol. rev. ed. 2009. (People Ser.). (ENG.). 24p. (gr. k-1). pap. 6.29 *(978-1-4296-3460-1(X)*, Pebble Bks.) Capstone Press of Coughlan Cos.

Marsico, Katie. Plan Ahead! 2012. (21st Century Basic Skills Library: Kids Can Make Manners Count Ser.). (ENG.). 24p. (gr. k-3). 22.79 *(978-1-61080-436-3(8)*, 202046); pap. 12.79 *(978-1-61080-610-7(7)*, 202220) Cherry Lake Publishing.

Mather, Anne D. & Weldon, Louise B. Character Building Day by Day: 180 Quick Read-Alouds for Elementary School & Home. Braun, Eric, ed. 2006. (ENG.). 240p. (gr. 3-6). pap. 15.99 *(978-1-57542-178-0(X))* Free Spirit Publishing, Inc.

Mattern, Joanne. Eating Lunch at School (El Almuerzo en la Escuela) 2006. (My Day at School/ Mi dia en la escuela Ser.). (SPA., Illus.). 24p. (gr. k-3). lib. bdg. 22.00 *(978-0-8368-7358-0(0)*, Weekly Reader Leveled Readers) Stevens, Gareth Publishing LLLP.

—Getting Ready for School (Me Preparo para Ir a la Escuela) 2006. (My Day at School/ Mi dia en la escuela Ser.). (ENG & SPA., Illus.). 24p. (gr. k-3). pap. 8.15 *(978-0-8368-7366-5(1)*, Weekly Reader Leveled Readers) Stevens, Gareth Publishing LLLP.

—Going to School/de camino a la Escuela. 2006. (My Day at School/ Mi dia en la escuela Ser.). (SPA., Illus.). 24p. (gr. k-3). lib. bdg. 22.00 *(978-0-8368-7360-3(2)*, Weekly Reader Leveled Readers) Stevens, Gareth Publishing LLLP.

—Me Preparo para IR a la Escuela (Getting Ready for School) 2006. (My Day at School/ Mi dia en la escuela Ser.). (ENG & SPA., Illus.). 24p. (gr. k-3). lib. bdg. 22.00 *(978-0-8368-7359-7(9)*, Weekly Reader Leveled Readers) Stevens, Gareth Publishing LLLP.

—Playing at School: Juego en la Escuela. 2006. (My Day at School/ Mi dia en la escuela Ser.). (ENG & SPA., Illus.). 24p. (gr. k-3). pap. 8.15 *(978-0-8368-7369-6(6)*, Weekly Reader Leveled Readers) Stevens, Gareth Publishing LLLP.

—Playing at School (Juego en la Escuela) 2006. (My Day at School/ Mi dia en la escuela Ser.). (SPA., Illus.). 24p. (gr. k-3). lib. bdg. 22.00 *(978-0-8368-7362-7(9)*, Weekly Reader Leveled Readers) Stevens, Gareth Publishing LLLP.

—Staying Safe on the School Bus. 2007. (Safety First Ser.). (Illus.). 24p. (gr. k-3). pap. 8.15 *(978-0-8368-7802-8(7))*; lib. bdg. 22.00 *(978-0-8368-7795-3(0))* Stevens, Gareth Publishing LLLP. (Weekly Reader Leveled Readers).

—Staying Safe on the School Bus/La Seguridad en el Autobús Escol Ar. 2007. (Safety First / la Seguridad Es lo Primero Ser.). (SPA., Illus.). 24p. (gr. k-3). lib. bdg. 22.00 *(978-0-8368-8060-1(9)*, Weekly Reader Leveled Readers) Stevens, Gareth Publishing LLLP.

McCarney, Rosemary. Where Will I Live?, 1 vol. United Nations High Commissioner for Refugees (Islamabad, Pakistan) Staff, photos by. 2017. (ENG., Illus.). 24p. (J). (gr. 1-5). 19.95 *(978-1-77260-028-5(8))* Second Story Pr. CAN. Dist: Orca Bk. Pubs. USA.

Miller, Jake. Who's Who in a Rural Community. 2005. (Communities at Work Ser.). (Illus.). 24p. (J). (gr. 2-4). lib. bdg. 22.60 *(978-1-4042-2787-3(3)*, PowerKids Pr.) Rosen Publishing Group, Inc., The.

Minden, Cecilia. Giving Back. 2009. (21st Century Skills Library: Real World Math Ser.). (ENG.). 32p. (gr. 4-8). lib. bdg. 28.50 *(978-1-60279-314-9(X)*, 200210) Cherry Lake Publishing.

—Investing: Making Your Money Work for You. 2007. (21st Century Skills Library: Real World Math Ser.). (ENG., Illus.). 32p. (gr. 4-8). lib. bdg. 28.50 *(978-1-60279-003-2(5)*, 200069) Cherry Lake Publishing.

Moss, Marissa. Amelia's School Survival Guide. Moss, Marissa, illus. 2006. (Amelia Ser.). (ENG., Illus.). 64p. (J). (gr. 2-5). 12.99 *(978-1-4169-0915-6(X)*, Simon & Schuster/Paula Wiseman Bks.) Simon & Schuster/Paula Wiseman Bks.

Ogburn, Jacqueline. Little Treasures: Endearments from Around the World. Raschka, Chris, illus. 2012. (ENG.). 32p. (J). (gr. -1-3). 16.99 *(978-0-547-42862-8(6))* Houghton Mifflin Harcourt Publishing Co.

Olson, Karen W. Healthy Choices, Healthy Lives. Hamelin, Marie-Micheline, illus. 2005. (ENG.). 20p. (J). pap. 10.95 *(978-1-894778-31-2(6))* Theytus Bks., Ltd. CAN. Dist: Univ. of Toronto Pr.

Pitzer, Marjorie. Animal Fun for Everyone! 2014. (ENG., Illus.). 14p. (J). pap. 12.95 *(978-1-60613-188-6(5))* Woodbine Hse.

Pryor, Kimberley Jane. Fairness. 2010. (Values 2 Ser.). 32p. (gr. 1). 18.56 *(978-1-60870-143-8(3))* Marshall Cavendish Corp.

Reimer, Jackie. No Thanks, but I'd Love to Dance! Choosing to Live Smoke Free. Reimer, Jackie, illus. 2010. (ENG., Illus.). 32p. (J). (gr. 2-4). 14.95 *(978-1-60443-027-1(3))* American Cancer Society, Inc.

Reynolds, Mattie. Kids Making Money: An Introduction to Financial Literacy. 2013. (Start Smart: Money Ser.). (Illus.). 24p. (J). (gr. k-2). lib. bdg. 17.95 net. *(978-1-937529-41-3(X))* Red Chair Pr.

—Saving for the Future: An Introduction to Financial Literacy. 2013. (Start Smart: Money Ser.). (Illus.). 24p. (gr. k-2). (J). lib. bdg. 17.95 net. *(978-1-937529-42-0(8))*; (ENG., pap. 5.95 *(978-1-937529-38-3(X))* Red Chair Pr.

—Sharing with Others: An Introduction to Financial Literacy. 2013. (Start Smart: Money Ser.). (Illus.). 24p. (J). (gr. k-2). (ENG.). pap. 5.95 *(978-1-937529-40-6(1))*; lib. bdg. 23.93 *(978-1-937529-44-4(4))* Red Chair Pr.

—Super-Smart Shopping: An Introduction to Financial Literacy. 2013. (Start Smart: Money Ser.). (Illus.). 24p. (gr. k-2). (J). lib. bdg. 17.95 net. *(978-1-937529-43-7(6))*; (ENG., pap. 5.95 *(978-1-937529-39-0(8))* Red Chair Pr.

Rice, Dona Herweck. This Is Me, 1 vol. 2nd rev. ed. 2013. (Nonfiction Readers Ser.). (ENG., Illus.). 12p. (J). (gr. 1-1). pap. 15.96 *(978-1-4807-1007-8(5))* Shell Educational Publishing.

Robberecht, Thierry. I Can't Do Anything! Masson, Annick, illus. 2013. 32p. (J). ***(978-1-4338-1309-2(2))*** American Psychological Assn.

Rosen Publishing Staff. How Kids Lived, 1 vol. 2015. (How Kids Lived Ser.). (ENG.). 24p. (J). 141.60 *(978-1-4777-5733-8(3)*, PowerKids Pr.) Rosen Publishing Group, Inc., The.

Ross, Michael & Ross, Christopher. Finding Faith in a Minecrafty World: 80 a-To-Z (Kid Only) Survival Secrets [an Unofficial Guide]. 2017. (ENG., Illus.). 256p. (J). pap. 14.99 *(978-0-7369-7085-3(1))* Harvest Hse. Pubs.

Rotner, Shelley. Different Kinds of Good-Byes. 2013. (Shelley Rotner's World Ser.). (ENG.). 32p. (gr. 1-2). pap. 47.70 *(978-1-62065-751-5(1)*, Aplus Bks.) Capstone Press of Coughlan Cos.

—Different Kinds of Good-Byes, 1 vol. Rotner, Shelley, photos by. 2013. (Shelley Rotner's World Ser.). (ENG., Illus.). 32p. (gr. 1-2). pap. 8.10 *(978-1-62065-750-8(3))*; lib. bdg. 27.32 *(978-1-62065-066-0(5))* Capstone Press of Coughlan Cos.

Rotner, Shelley & Kelly, Sheila M. Yummy! Rotner, Shelley, photos by. 2013. (ENG., Illus.). 32p. (J). (gr. -1-1). 16.95 *(978-0-8234-2426-9(X))* Holiday Hse., Inc.

Ruurs, Margriet. Families Around the World. Gordon, Jessica Rae, illus. 2017. (Around the World Ser.). (ENG.). 40p. (J). (gr. -1-2). pap. 8.95 *(978-1-77138-807-8(2))* Kids Can Pr., Ltd. CAN. Dist: Hachette Bk. Group.

Sawyer, Judith L. This Is How I Pray. Sawyer, Judith L., illus. 2008. (Illus.). 24p. (J). pap. *(978-1-926585-11-6(9)*, CCB Publishing) CCB Publishing.

Schaefer, Peggy. Bob & Larry's Book of Prayers. Reed, Lisa, illus. 2014. (VeggieTales Bk Ser.). 32p. (J). bds. 10.99 *(978-0-8249-1929-0(7)*, Ideal Pubns.) Worthy Publishing.

Schuette, Sarah L. Foster Families, 1 vol. 2010. (My Family Ser.). (ENG.). 24p. (gr. k-1). lib. bdg. 21.99 *(978-1-4296-3979-8(2)*, Pebble Bks.) Capstone Press of Coughlan Cos.

Sheen, Barbara. Growing up in Mexico. 2017. (Growing up Around the World Ser.). (ENG.). 80p. (YA). (gr. 5-12). ***(978-1-68282-221-0(4))*** ReferencePoint Pr., Inc.

Shivers, Holly Hawkins. I Can Learn the Bible: The Joshua Code for Kids: 52 Scriptures Every Kid Should Know, 1 vol. 2014. (ENG.). 224p. (J). 14.99 *(978-0-529-10899-9(2))* Nelson, Thomas Inc.

Smith, David J. This Child, Every Child: A Book about the World's Children. Armstrong, Shelagh, illus. 2011. (CitizenKid Ser.). (ENG.). 36p. (J). (gr. 3-7). 18.95 *(978-1-55453-466-1(6))* Kids Can Pr., Ltd. CAN. Dist: Hachette Bk. Group.

Spivet, Bonnie. Protecting Your Privacy Online. 2011. (CyberSmarts: Staying Safe Online Ser.). (ENG.). 24p. (J). (gr. 4-6). pap. 10.00 *(978-1-4488-6418-8(6))*; lib. bdg. 21.25 *(978-1-4488-6412-6(7))* Rosen Publishing Group, Inc., The. (PowerKids Pr.).

—Stopping Cyberbullying. 2011. (CyberSmarts: Staying Safe Online Ser.). (ENG.). 24p. (J). (gr. 4-6). pap. 10.00 *(978-1-4488-6420-1(8))*; lib. bdg. 21.25 *(978-1-4488-6413-3(5))* Rosen Publishing Group, Inc., The. (PowerKids Pr.).

Sterling Children's, Sterling. M. A. S. H. What Does Your Future Hold? 2017. (ENG., Illus.). 96p. (J). (gr. 2-6). pap. 6.95 ***(978-1-4549-2278-0(8))*** Sterling Publishing Co., Inc.

Sundem, Garth. Real Kids, Real Stories, Real Change: Courageous Actions Around the World. 2010. (ENG.). 176p. (J). (gr. 4-8). pap. 9.99 *(978-1-57542-350-0(2))* Free Spirit Publishing, Inc.

—Real Kids, Real Stories, Real Character: Choices That Matter Around the World. 2016. (ENG., Illus.). 176p. (J). (gr. 3-8). pap. 9.99 *(978-1-63198-026-8(2))* Free Spirit Publishing, Inc.

Tiehel, Amy. Long Ago & Far Away Ancient Egypt: Ancient Egypt. 2015. (ENG., Illus.). 32p. (J). 26.50 *(978-1-62469-126-3(9))* Purple Toad Publishing, Inc.

Tuyl, Christine Van & Merino, Noël. Media Violence. 2010. (OPPOSING VIEWPOINTS VISUALS Ser.). (Illus.). 128p. (YA). (gr. 7-12). 36.95 *(978-0-7377-4480-4(4))* Cengage Gale.

Verdick, Elizabeth. Bedtime. Heinlen, Marieka, illus. 2010. (Toddler Tools Ser.). (ENG.). 24p. (J). (gr. -1). 7.95 *(978-1-57542-315-9(4))* Free Spirit Publishing, Inc.

Waryncia, Lou. Young Heroes of the North & South. Hale, Sarah Elder, ed. 2005. (ENG., Illus.). 48p. (J). (gr. 3-9). 17.95 *(978-0-8126-7901-4(6))* Cobblestone Publishing Co.

Weber, Rebecca. Safety Basics. 2012. (Health & Your Body Ser.). (ENG.). 24p. (gr. k-1). pap. 41.70 *(978-1-4296-8346-3(5))*; lib. bdg. 26.65 *(978-1-4296-7694-6(9))* Capstone Press of Coughlan Cos. (Pebble Plus).

Wilkins, Verna. Children Around the World. 2004. (QEB Start Reading Ser.). (Illus.). 24p. (J). lib. bdg. 15.95 *(978-1-59566-010-7(0))* QEB Publishing Inc.

Wilson, Janet. Our Heroes: How Kids Are Making a Difference, 1 vol. 2014. (ENG., Illus.). 32p. (J). (gr. 3-8). 18.95 *(978-1-927583-41-8(1))* Second Story Pr. CAN. Dist: Orca Bk. Pubs. USA.

Wilson, Todd. Investigating Childhood in Tudor England. (Illus.). 32p. (J). pap. 8.95 *(978-0-7078-0335-7(7))* National Trust, Aylesbury GBR. Dist: Trafalgar Square Publishing.

Wood, Ira. How to Stay Safe at Home & On-line. 2009. (Reading Room Collection 2 Ser.). 24p. (gr. 3-4). 42.50 *(978-1-60851-972-9(4)*, PowerKids Pr.) Rosen Publishing Group, Inc., The.

Woolf, Alex. My Life in India. 2015. (Children of the World Ser.). (ENG., Illus.). 32p. (J). (gr. 5-5). pap. 10.58 *(978-1-5026-0049-3(8))* Cavendish Square Publishing.

—My Life in Indonesia. 2015. (J). lib. bdg. *(978-1-62713-337-1(2))*; (ENG., Illus.). 32p. (gr. 5-5). pap. 10.58 *(978-1-5026-0278-7(4))* Cavendish Square Publishing.

—My Life in Kenya. 2015. (Children of the World Ser.). (ENG., Illus.). 32p. (J). (gr. 5-5). pap. 10.58 *(978-1-5026-0055-4(2))* Cavendish Square Publishing.

Wrazen, Nicholas. Don't Talk to Strangers. 2008. (Real Readers - Upper Emergent Ser.). (ENG., Illus.). 12p. (gr. 1-2). pap. 5.90 *(978-0-8239-8192-2(4))* Rosen Publishing Group, Inc., The.

Wroble, Lisa A. Kids in Ancient Egypt. 2004. (Kids Throughout History Ser.). 24p. (J). 22.60 *(978-0-8239-6931-9(2)*, PowerKids Pr.) Rosen Publishing Group, Inc., The.

Yonge, Charlotte M. Little Lucy's Wonderful Globe. 2004. reprint ed. pap. 1.99 *(978-1-4192-3079-0(4))* Kessinger Publishing, LLC.

—Little Lucy's Wonderful Globe. 2008. 160p. pap. *(978-1-4097-0614-4(1))* Read Bks.

Zullo, Allan. The Rescuers: Kids Who Risked Everything to Save Others. 2006. 135p. pap. *(978-0-439-85483-2(0))* Scholastic, Inc.

CHILDREN—ADOPTION

see Adoption

CHILDREN—AFRICA

Cricket Books Staff & Cobblestone Publishing, Inc. Staff. If I Were a Kid in Ancient Egypt: Children of the Ancient World. Sheldon, Ken, ed. 2007. (If I Were a Kid In... Ser.). (ENG., Illus.). 32p. (J). (gr. 1-5). 17.95 *(978-0-8126-7932-8(6))* Cricket Bks.

Humphreys, Jessica Dee & Chikwanine, Michel. Child Soldier: When Boys & Girls Are Used in War. Dávila, Claudia, illus. 2015. (CitizenKid Ser.). (ENG.). 48p. (J). (gr. 5-9). 17.95 *(978-1-77138-126-0(4))* Kids Can Pr., Ltd. CAN. Dist: Hachette Bk. Group.

Kabana, Joni. Torina's World: A Child's Life in Madagascar. 2nd ed. 2007. (ENG., Illus.). 52p. (J). 14.95 *(978-0-9794771-4-0(X))* ACS, LLC Amica Creative Services.

Macdonald, Fiona. The Egyptians. 2011. (Children in History Ser.). (Illus.). 32p. (YA). (gr. 4-7). lib. bdg. 28.50 *(978-1-59771-269-9(8)*, 1324614) Sea-To-Sea Pubns.

Robinson, Anthony, et al. Street Children. Robinson, Anthony, photos by. 2016. (ENG., Illus.). 40p. (J). (gr. 4-7). pap. 10.99 *(978-1-84780-598-0(1)*, Frances Lincoln) Quarto Publishing Group UK GBR. Dist: Littlehampton Bk Services, Ltd.

Shoveller, Herb. Ryan & Jimmy: And the Well in Africa That Brought Them Together. (CitizenKid Ser.). (ENG., Illus.). 56p. (J). (gr. 3-7). 2008. pap. 9.95 *(978-1-55453-271-1(X))* 2006. 16.95 *(978-1-55337-967-6(5))* Kids Can Pr., Ltd. CAN. Dist: Hachette Bk. Group.

CHILDREN—ASIA

Brooks, Susie. India. 2006. (Our Lives, Our World Ser.). (Illus.). (J). *(978-1-59389-288-3(8))* Chrysalis Education.

Nagara, Innosanto. My Night in the Planetarium. 2016. (ENG., Illus.). 24p. (J). (gr. 1-4). 17.95 *(978-1-60980-700-9(6)*, Triangle Square) Seven Stories Pr.

Yousafzai, Malala. I Am Malala: The Girl Who Stood up for Education & Was Shot by the Taliban. (ENG.). (J). 2016. 256p. 98.91 *(978-0-316-30398-9(4))* 2016. (Illus.). 256p. (gr. 5-17). pap. 10.99 *(978-0-316-32791-6(3))* 2014. 256p. 153.00 *(978-0-316-33917-9(2))* 2014. (Illus.). 240p. (gr. 5-17). 17.99 *(978-0-316-32793-0(X))* 2015. 240p. (gr. 5-17). 17.00 *(978-0-316-31119-9(7))* Little, Brown Bks. for Young Readers.

—I Am Malala: The Girl Who Stood up for Education & Was Shot by the Taliban. 2016. (J). lib. bdg. 22.10 *(978-0-606-37164-3(8))* Turtleback Bks.

Yousafzai, Malala & McCormick, Patricia. I Am Malala: The Girl Who Stood up for Education & Was Shot by the Taliban. l.t. ed. 2017. (ENG., Illus.). 302p. 22.99 ***(978-1-4104-9916-5(2))*** Cengage Gale.

CHILDREN—BOOKS AND READING

Here are entered works on the reading interests of children, or lists of books read by or recommended for children. Collections of works published for children are entered under Children's Literature.

Adamson, Lynda G. Literature Links to World History, K-12: Resources to Enhance & Entice, 1 vol. 2010. (Children's & Young Adult Literature Reference Ser.). 684p. (C). 70.00 *(978-1-59158-470-4(1)*, LU4701, Libraries Unlimited) ABC-CLIO, LLC.

Andersen, Hans Christian. The Constant Tin Soldier. (World of Words Ser.). (J). (gr. k-3). pap. 10.00 incl. audio Spoken Arts, Inc.

Briefing Associates Staff. This Is BRIEF! Or Starting Preschool & Homeschool Children Reading Naturally - at Once. Khaiphus, Kosta Demetrius, ed. Brown, Linnea, illus. 2004. 136p. (gr. -1-1). pap. 24.95 *(978-0-9706105-0-8(5))* BR:IEFing Assocs. of New England.

Castellano Boyum, Marie. More Simply Super Storytimes: Programming Ideas for Ages 3-6. 2006. (Illus.). 172p. (J). (gr. -1-1). per. 16.95 *(978-1-932146-29-5(6)*, Upstart Bks.) Highsmith Inc.

Collins, Carolyn Strom & Eriksson, Christina Wyss. Inside the Secret Garden: A Treasury of Crafts, Recipes, & Activities. Tudor, Tasha, illus. 2004. 130p. (J). (gr. 2-8). reprint ed. 25.00 *(978-0-7567-7630-5(9))* DIANE Publishing Co.

Gayle-Evans, Guda. An Annotated Bibliography of Multi-Cultural Literature for Children Three to Ten Years. 2004. (Mellen Studies in Children's Literature: Vol. 6). (Illus.). 204p. 109.95 *(978-0-7734-6474-2(3))* Mellen, Edwin Pr., The.

Harcourt School Publishers Staff. Changing Patterns Level 3-1. 3rd ed. 2003. (Harcourt School Publishers Trophies Ser.). (ENG., Illus.). 448p. (gr. 3-3). pupil's gde. ed. 60.35 *(978-0-15-322476-8(2))* Harcourt Schl. Pubs.

Harris, Julie, reader. Puss in Boots. unabr. ed. (World of Words Ser.). (J). (gr. k-3). pap. 10.00 incl. audio *(978-0-8045-6604-9(6)*, SAC 6500D) Spoken Arts, Inc.

Luna Rising Editors. The Great Southwest Activity Book. 2004. (ENG., Illus.). 56p. (J). (gr. 1-5). pap., act. bk. ed. 9.95 *(978-0-87358-844-7(4))* Cooper Square Publishing Llc.

Nagle, Jeanne, ed. Great Authors of Children's Books. 2013. (Essential Authors for Children & Teens Ser.). (YA). (gr. 7-12). 45.00 *(978-1-62275-096-2(9))* Rosen Publishing Group, Inc., The.

Northland Editors. The Great Yellowstone Grand Teton Glacier Activity Book. 2004. (ENG., Illus.). 56p. (J). (gr. 1-5). pap., act. bk. ed. 7.95 *(978-0-87358-860-7(6))* Cooper Square Publishing Llc.

Oliver, Patrick M., ed. Turn the Page & You Don't Stop: Sharing Successful Chapters in Our Lives with Youth. 2006. (Illus.). 156p. pap. 12.00 *(978-0-9779499-0-8(7))* Say It Loud! Readers & Writers Series.

Perera, Hilda & Fraga, Mana F. La Pata Pita Vuelve. (SPA.). (J). 7.95 *(978-0-8056-0140-4(6))* Minerva Bks., Ltd.

Reid, Rob. Storytime Slam: 15 Lesson Plans for Preschool & Primary Story Programs. 2006. (Illus.). 85p. per. 16.95 *(978-1-932146-52-3(0)*, Upstart Bks.) Highsmith Inc.

Responding to Literature. 912p. (YA). (gr. 8). 52.95 *(978-0-8219-1364-2(6)*, 35456) EMC/Paradigm Publishing.

Roberts, Russell. John Newbery & the Story of the Newbery Medal. 2003. (Great Achiever Awards Ser.). (Illus.). 48p. (J). (gr. 4-8). lib. bdg. 29.95 *(978-1-58415-201-9(X))* Mitchell Lane Pubs., Inc.

Sanrio Company, Ltd. Staff. I Heart Hello Kitty Activity Book: Read, Write, Count, & Draw with Hello Kitty & Friends! 2012. (ENG.). 224p. (J). (gr. k-2). pap. 10.95 *(978-1-4197-0551-9(2)*, Abrams Bks. for Young Readers) Abrams, Inc.

Schulze, Bianca. 101 Books to Read Before You Grow Up. 2017. (101 Ser.). (ENG., Illus.). 144p. (J). (gr. 3-5). lib. bdg. 33.32 ***(978-1-942875-17-8(7)***, Walter Foster Jr) Quarto Publishing Group USA.

Schulze, Bianca. 101 Books to Read Before You Grow Up: The Must-Read Book List for Kids. 2016. (101 Series for Kids Ser.). (ENG., Illus.). 144p. (J). (gr. 3-7). 12.95 *(978-1-63322-169-7(5)*, Walter Foster Jr) Quarto Publishing Group USA.

World Book, Inc. Staff, contrib. by. Baby's First Book: A Book of Learning: Featuring Selections from Childcraft — the How & Why Library. 2003. (Illus.). 95p. (J). *(978-0-7166-0364-1(0))* World Bk., Inc.

CHILDREN—CANADA

Ellis, Deborah. Looks Like Daylight, 1 vol. 2013. (ENG., Illus.). 256p. (J). (gr. 6). 15.95 (978-1-55498-120-5(4)) Groundwood Bks. CAN. Dist: Publishers Group West (PGW).

—Off to War: Voices of Soldiers' Children, 1 vol. 2010. (ENG., Illus.). 176p. (J). (gr. 3). pap. 9.95 (978-0-88899-895-8(3)) Groundwood Bks. CAN. Dist: Publishers Group West (PGW).

Goyette, Linda. Northern Kids. 2010. (Courageous Kids Ser.). (ENG., Illus.). 240p. (J). pap. (978-1-897142-49-3(8)) Brindle & Glass Publishing.

Kanji, Sheneeza. Amazing Canadian Kids! What They're Doing to Make A Difference & How You Can Too! 2012. 88p. (gr. 4-6). pap. 12.95 (978-1-4634-2060-4(9)) AuthorHouse.

Pezzi, Bryan. Craig Kielburger: Ma Vie. Karvonen, Tanjah, tr. from ENG. 2011. (FRE., Illus.). 24p. (YA). (gr. 2-4). (978-1-77071-428-1(6)) Weigl Educational Pubs. Ltd.

CHILDREN—CARE AND HYGIENE

see Children—Health and Hygiene

CHILDREN—CHARITIES, PROTECTION, ETC.

see Child Welfare

CHILDREN—CHINA

Waryncia, Lou, et al. If I Were a Kid in Ancient China: Children of the Ancient World. 2007. (If I Were a Kid In... Ser.). (ENG., Illus.). 32p. (J). (gr. 1-5). 17.95 (978-0-8126-7931-1(8)) Cricket Bks.

CHILDREN, DELINQUENT

see Juvenile Delinquency

CHILDREN—DISCIPLINE

see Child Rearing

CHILDREN—DISEASES

Allen, Sue. Can I Tell You about Sensory Processing Difficulties? A Guide for Friends, Family & Professionals. 2015. (Can I Tell You About... ? Ser.).Tr. of 56. (ENG., Illus.). 56p. pap. 14.95 (978-1-84905-640-3(4), 7884) Kingsley, Jessica Pubs. GBR. Dist: Macmillan Distribution Ltd.

Bennett, Howard J. It Hurts When I Poop! A Story for Children Who Are Scared to Use the Potty. Weber, M. S., illus. 2007. 32p. (J). (gr. -1-1). 14.95 (978-1-4338-0130-3(2), 4418001); pap. 9.95 (978-1-4338-0131-0(0), 4418002) American Psychological Assn. (Magination Pr.).

Bowman-Kruhm, Mary. Everything You Need to Know about Down Syndrome. rev. ed. 2005. (Need to Know Library). (Illus.). 64p. (YA). (gr. 4-6). lib. bdg. 31.95 (978-0-8239-3767-7(4)) Rosen Publishing Group, Inc., The.

Carlson, Geri L. Andrew Goes to the Chiropractor. Kiel, Casey K., illus. 2007. (J). 21.99 (978-1-59879-432-8(9)); per. 15.99 (978-1-59879-467-0(1)) Lifevest Publishing, Inc. (Lifevest).

Chara, Kathleen A., et al. Allergy Busters: A Story for Children with Autism or Related Spectrum Disorders Struggling with Allergies. Berns, J. M., illus. 2004. (ENG.). 48p. pap. 18.95 (978-1-84310-782-8(1), 1788) Kingsley, Jessica Pubs. GBR. Dist: Macmillan Distribution Ltd.

Chastain, Zachary. Sick All the Time: Kids with Chronic Illness. 2009. (Kids with Special Needs Ser.). 48p. (YA). (gr. 5-18). pap. 7.95 (978-1-4222-1922-5(4)) Mason Crest.

Chastain, Zachary & Flath, Camden. Sick All the Time: Kids with Chronic Illness. 2010. (Kids with Special Needs Ser.). 48p. (YA). (gr. 5-18). lib. bdg. 19.95 (978-1-4222-1719-1(1)) Mason Crest.

Chastain, Zachary & Livingston, Phyllis. Youth with Asperger's Syndrome: A Different Drummer. 2007. (Helping Youth with Mental, Physical, & Social Challenges Ser.). (Illus.). 128p. (YA). pap. 14.95 (978-1-4222-0437-5(5)) Mason Crest.

Chilman-Blair, Kim & Deloache, Shawn. Medikidz Explain Depression. 2010. (Superheroes on a Medical Mission Ser.). (Illus.). 40p. (YA). pap. 11.75 (978-1-4488-1837-2(0)); (gr. 5-8). lib. bdg. 29.25 (978-1-4358-9455-6(3)) Rosen Publishing Group, Inc., The. (Rosen Reference).

—Medikidz Explain Sleep Apnea. 2010. (Superheroes on a Medical Mission Ser.). 40p. (YA). (ENG.). pap. 11.75 (978-1-4488-1841-9(9)); (Illus.). (gr. 5-8). lib. bdg. 29.25 (978-1-4358-9459-4(6)) Rosen Publishing Group, Inc., The. (Rosen Reference).

Chilman-Blair, Kim & Taddeo, John. Medikidz Explain Autism. 2010. (Superheroes on a Medical Mission Ser.). (Illus.). 40p. (YA). pap. 11.75 (978-1-4488-1835-8(4)); (gr. 5-8). lib. bdg. 29.25 (978-1-4358-9460-0(X)) Rosen Publishing Group, Inc., The. (Rosen Reference).

Chilman-Blair, Kim, et al. Medikidz Explain Scoliosis: What's up with John? 2010. (Illus.). 32p. (J). pap. (978-1-906935-04-7(1)) Medikidz Ltd.

Edwards, Hazel & Alexander, Goldie. Talking about Illnesses. 2010. (Healthy Living Ser.). (Illus.). 32p. (YA). (gr. 3-6). lib. bdg. 26.00 (978-1-4339-3657-9(7)) Stevens, Gareth Publishing LLLP.

Esherick, Joan. Brain Injury. Albers, Lisa et al, eds. 2014. (Living with a Special Need Ser.: 16). 128p. (J). (gr. 7-18). 25.95 (978-1-4222-3031-2(7)) Mason Crest.

Fall, Guy. Everything You Need to Know about Juvenile Arthritis. 2005. (Need to Know Library). (Illus.). 64p. (YA). (gr. 4-6). lib. bdg. 31.95 (978-0-8239-3614-4(7)) Rosen Publishing Group, Inc., The.

French, Deborah. The Cookbook for Children with Special Needs: Learning a Life Skill with Fun, Tasty, Healthy Recipes. Ehrlich, Leah, illus. 2015. (ENG.). 200p. 24.95 (978-1-84905-538-3(6), 3467) Kingsley, Jessica Pubs. GBR. Dist: Macmillan Distribution Ltd.

Gagne, Tammy. Ways to Help Chronically Ill Children: A Guide to Giving Back. 2010. (How to Help Ser.). (Illus.). 48p. (J). (gr. 4-8). lib. bdg. 29.95 (978-1-58415-919-3(7)) Mitchell Lane Pubs., Inc.

Gilman, Laura Anne. Coping with Cerebral Palsy. 2009. (Coping Ser.). 192p. (gr. 7-12). 63.90 (978-1-61511-994-3(9)) Rosen Publishing Group, Inc., The.

Goodbody, Slim. Staying Well. McGinnis, Ben, illus. Pinchbeck, Chris, photos by. 2007. (Slim Goodbody's Good Health Guides Ser.). 32p. (J). (gr. 2-6). lib. bdg. 26.00 (978-0-8368-7744-1(6), Gareth Stevens Learning Library) Stevens, Gareth Publishing LLLP.

Gosman, Gillian. I Have an Ear Infection. 2012. (Get Well Soon! Ser.). (ENG., Illus.). 24p. (J). (gr. 1-3). lib. bdg. 22.60 (978-1-4488-7413-2(0), PowerKids Pr.) Rosen Publishing Group, Inc., The.

Hood, Korey K. Type 1 Teens: A Guide to Managing Your Diabetes. Ishe, Bryan, illus. 2010. 112p. (YA). (gr. 7-18). pap. 14.95 (978-1-4338-0788-6(2), Magination Pr.) American Psychological Assn.

Huebner, Dawn. What to Do When You Dread Your Bed: A Kid's Guide to Overcoming Problems with Sleep. Matthews, Bonnie, illus. 2008. (What to Do Guides for Kids Ser.). 93p. (J). (gr. 1-7). per. 15.95 (978-1-4338-0318-5(6), Magination Pr.) American Psychological Assn.

Huffman, Beth. Awesome Andrea. 2012. (ENG.). (J). pap. 10.00 (978-1-4675-1086-8(6)) Independent Pub.

Hunter, David & Livingston, Phyllis. Youth with Bipolar Disorder: Achieving Stability. 2007. (Helping Youth with Mental, Physical, & Social Challenges Ser.). (Illus.). 128p. (YA). pap. 14.95 (978-1-4222-0438-2(3)) Mason Crest.

Jangjiravat, Somjai. Who Is Mr Piggy Pig? 2011. 48p. pap. 21.99 (978-1-4653-3850-1(0)) Xlibris Corp.

Juettner, Bonnie. Childhood Obesity. 2009. (In Controversy Ser.). (YA). (gr. 7-12). 25.95 (978-1-60152-083-8(2)) ReferencePoint Pr., Inc.

Kelly, P. Coping with Diabetes. 2009. (Coping Ser.). 192p. (gr. 7-12). 63.90 (978-1-61511-998-1(1)) Rosen Publishing Group, Inc., The.

Laird, Chynna T. Don't Rush Me! For Siblings of Children with Sensory Processing Disorder (SPD) 2015. (J). pap. (978-1-61599-264-5(2)) Loving Healing Pr., Inc.

—I'm Not Weird, I Have Sensory Processing Disorder (SPD) Alexandra's Journey. 2nd ed. 2012. (J). 24p. 29.95 (978-1-61599-159-4(X)); (Illus.). 22p. pap. (978-1-61599-158-7(1)) Loving Healing Pr., Inc.

Landau, Elaine. Bumps, Bruises, & Scrapes. 2008. (Head-to-Toe Health Ser.). 32p. (gr. 2-7). lib. bdg. 28.50 (978-0-7614-2849-7(6), Benchmark Bks.) Marshall Cavendish Corp.

—Earaches. 2010. (Head-to Toe Health 3 Ser.). 32p. (gr. 2). 28.50 (978-0-7614-4831-0(4)) Marshall Cavendish Corp.

Libal, Autumn. Chained: Youth with Chronic Illness. 2003. (Youth with Special Needs Ser.). (Illus.). 127p. (YA). (gr. 4-7). pap. 14.95 (978-1-4222-0421-4(9)) Mason Crest.

—Chronic Illness. Albers, Lisa et al, eds. 2014. (Living with a Special Need Ser.: 16). 128p. (J). (gr. 7-18). 25.95 (978-1-4222-3032-9(5)) Mason Crest.

Liddle, Sharon. Eli - the Bi-Polar Bear. Maximilian Press Staff, ed. Garnvin, Rebecka, illus. deluxe ed. 2003. 76p. (J). (gr. 1-4). 29.95 (978-1-930211-49-0(X)) Maximilian Pr. Pubs.

Mosca, Isabelle. Adventure to Autism Planet. 2011. (ENG., Illus.). 32p. (YA). 15.00 (978-1-935232-36-0(3)) ComteQ Publishing.

Perry, Mignon Marie, text. Look at Me I Had Surgery, A Child's Personalized Guide Through the Perioperative Process. 2006. 28p. (J). 3.00 (978-1-59971-891-0(X)) Aardvark Global Publishing.

Phillips, Jennifer. Tucker's Strength. 2008. 28p. pap. 24.95 (978-1-60813-376-5(1)) America Star Bks.

Robbins, Lynette. How to Deal with Allergies. 2009. (Kids' Health Ser.). (Illus.). 24p. (YA). (gr. 2-5). lib. bdg. 22.60 (978-1-4042-8139-4(8)) Rosen Publishing Group, Inc., The.

—How to Deal with Diabetes. 2009. (Kids' Health Ser.). (Illus.). 24p. (J). pap. 8.25 (978-1-4358-3425-5(9), PowerKids Pr.); (YA). (gr. 2-5). lib. bdg. 22.60 (978-1-4042-8144-8(4)) Rosen Publishing Group, Inc., The.

—How to Deal with Obesity. 2009. (Kids' Health Ser.). 24p. (ENG.). (J). pap. 8.25 (978-1-4358-3423-1(2), PowerKids Pr.); (Illus.). (YA). (gr. 2-5). lib. bdg. 22.60 (978-1-4042-8143-1(6)) Rosen Publishing Group, Inc., The.

Rocha, Toni L. Coping When Someone in Your Family Has Cancer. 2009. (Coping Ser.). 192p. (gr. 7-12). 63.90 (978-1-61511-988-2(4)) Rosen Publishing Group, Inc., The.

Rosaler, Maxine. Cystic Fibrosis. 2006. (Genetic Diseases & Disorders Ser.). (Illus.). 64p. (YA). (gr. 5-9). lib. bdg. 31.95 (978-1-4042-0696-0(5)) Rosen Publishing Group, Inc., The.

Schaefer, Lola M. Some Kids Wear Leg Braces, 1 vol. 2007. (Understanding Differences Ser.). (ENG., Illus.). 24p. (gr. k-1). 21.99 (978-1-4296-0813-8(7), Pebble Bks.) Capstone Press of Coughlan Cos.

Sévigny, Eric, illus. Caillou Is Sick. 2012. (Clubhouse Ser.).Tr. of Caillou Est Malade. (ENG.). 24p. (J). (gr. -1-1). pap. 3.99 (978-2-89450-865-7(4)) Caillouet, Gerry.

Shaul, Joel. Our Brains Are Like Computers! Exploring Social Skills & Social Cause & Effect with Children on the Autism Spectrum. 2016. (ENG., Illus.). 80p. (J). 24.95 (978-1-84905-716-5(8), 8164) Kingsley, Jessica Pubs. GBR. Dist: Macmillan Distribution Ltd.

Stewart, Sheila & Flath, Camden. Finding My Voice: Kids with Speech Impairment. 2010. (Kids with Special Needs Ser.). (Illus.). 48p. (YA). (gr. 5-18). lib. bdg. 19.95 (978-1-4222-1722-1(1)) Mason Crest.

Sutherland, Joe. The Broken Egg: A story to help children cope with the loss of a younger Sibling. 2010. (Illus.). 24p. 11.99 (978-1-4490-8347-2(1)) AuthorHouse.

Therrien, Patricia. An Enemy Within: Overcoming Cancer & Other Life-Threatening Diseases. 2009. (J). pap. 24.95 (978-1-4222-1463-3(X)) Mason Crest.

Welton, Jude. Can I Tell You about Asperger Syndrome? A Guide for Friends & Family. Telford, Jane, illus. 2003. (Can I Tell You About... ? Ser.). (ENG.). 48p. pap. 13.95 (978-1-84310-206-9(4), 5357) Kingsley, Jessica Pubs. GBR. Dist: Macmillan Distribution Ltd.

CHILDREN—DISEASES—FICTION

Bateman, Claire Boudreaux. This Little Light of Mine. Alexander, Katie Norwood, illus. 2005. 32p. (J). per. 18.50 (978-0-9706732-2-0(1)) Shell Beach Publishing, LLC.

Benz, Suzanne. Harry's Last Wish: A Story about Forever. Alvarado, Carol, illus. 2007. (ENG.). 32p. (J). 24.95 (978-0-944963-23-4(4)) Glastonbury Pr.

Blume, Judy. Deenie. 143p. (YA). (gr. 7-18). pap. 3.99 (978-0-8072-1360-5(8), Listening Library) Random Hse. Audio Publishing Group.

Bray, Libba. Going Bovine. 2010. (ENG.). 496p. (YA). (gr. 9). pap. 10.99 (978-0-385-73398-4(4), Ember) Random Hse. Children's Bks.

Gabolinscy, Jack & Harrison, Brian. Not Again. 2008. (Rigby Focus Forward: Level P Ser.). (Illus.). 24p. (J). (gr. 4-7). pap. (978-1-4190-3859-4(1), Rigby) Pearson Education Australia.

Gaynor, Kate. The Bravest Girl in School. Murphy, Aileen, illus. 2013. 20p. pap. (978-0-9555787-4-8(4)) Special Stories Publishing.

Grimshaw, Luke. Sniffle, Sneeze, Cough Back Off! Brzozowski, Christina, illus. 2008. 24p. pap. 24.95 (978-1-60703-607-4(X)) America Star Bks.

Hamilton, Patricia Birdsong. Why do you Walk Funny? l.t. ed. 2006. (Ataxia: A Lifestyle Change). 38p. (J). 16.95 (978-1-889826-91-2(X)) Scripts Publishing.

Hessman, Amy. Understanding Special Needs Kids: Seizures. 2012. 36p. pap. 20.99 (978-1-4685-4384-1(9)) AuthorHouse.

Holliman, Lynn. The Best Day Ever!, 1 vol. 2009. 18p. pap. 24.95 (978-1-60836-731-3(2)) America Star Bks.

Howe, Katherine. Conversion. (ENG.). 432p. (YA). (gr. 7). 2015. pap. 10.99 (978-0-14-751155-3(0), Speak) 2014. 18.99 (978-0-399-16777-5(3), G.P. Putnam's Sons Books for Young Readers) Penguin Young Readers Group.

Hull, Maureen. The View from a Kite, 1 vol. 2007. (ENG., Illus.). 320p. (YA). (gr. 8-12). pap. 15.95 (978-1-55109-591-2(2), Vagrant Pr.) Nimbus Publishing, Ltd. CAN. Dist: Orca Bk. Pubs. USA.

Jay, Gina & Beattie, Julie. Hope the Hip Hippo. Turner, Cherie, illus. 2012. 48p. pap. (978-1-4602-0062-9(4)) FriesenPress.

Kelley, Ann. The Burying Beetle. 2005. (ENG.). 208p. (gr. 7-9). per. 19.95 (978-1-84282-099-5(0), 9781842820995) Luath Pr. Ltd. GBR. Dist: Midpoint Trade Bks., Inc.

Krumrey, Melanie. Bagels, Buddy, & Me: A Story about Gluten Intolerance & Celiac Disease. 2007. (Illus.). 40p. (J). per. 14.95 (978-0-9797703-0-2(0)) Mustard Seed Pr.

Laietta, Luann. Tonka the Special Puppy. 2011. 24p. pap. 15.99 (978-1-4628-5263-5(7)) Xlibris Corp.

Laird, Elizabeth & Davison, Roz. Jungle School. Sim, David, illus. 2006. (Green Bananas Ser.). (ENG.). 48p. (J). (gr. -1-3). lib. bdg. (978-0-7787-1026-4(2)) Crabtree Publishing Co.

Lennard, Daric. My Name Is Berta. 2008. 48p. pap. 16.95 (978-1-60672-036-3(8)) America Star Bks.

Levine, Karen Rae. All about Color Blindness. 2012. 32p. pap. (978-0-557-43852-5(7)) Lulu.com.

Meunier, Sylvain. Raffi's Animal Rescue, 1 vol. Cummins, Sarah, tr. from FRE. Eudes-Pascal, Elisabeth, illus. 2007. (Formac First Novels Ser.). (ENG.). 64p. (J). (gr. 2-5). 4.95 (978-0-88780-740-4(2), 9780887807404) Formac Publishing Co., Ltd. CAN. Dist: Casemate Pubs. & Bk. Distributors, LLC.

Nolt, Debbie. Love for Lyndon. 2011. (Illus.). 62p. (J). (gr. 3-6). 3.40 (978-0-7399-2430-3(3)) Rod & Staff Pubs., Inc.

O'Neill, Ian. Jimmy First & Destiny's Watch. 2011. 122p. pap. (978-0-7552-0675-9(4)) Authors OnLine, Ltd.

Price, Rebecca. Toby & the Flood, 1 vol. 2008. (ENG., Illus.). 32p. (J). pap. (978-0-86315-635-9(5)) Floris Bks.

Richards, Laura Elizabeth Howe. Queen Hildegarde. 2007. 92p. per. (978-1-4068-3867-1(5)) Echo Library.

Romansky, Sally Rosenberg. Invincible. Ott, Margot Janet, illus. 2006. (J). pap. 8.95 (978-0-9723729-4-7(6)) Imagination Stage, Inc.

Roth-Fisch, Marla. Sensitive Sam: Sam's Sensory Adventure Has a Happy Ending! 2009. (ENG., Illus.). 29p. (J). pap. 9.95 (978-1-932565-86-7(8)) Future Horizons, Inc.

Stark, Teri. Alison's Helmet. 2005. (J). per. 12.50 (978-1-933570-46-4(6)) Aardvark Global Publishing.

CHILDREN—EDUCATION

see Education, Elementary

CHILDREN, EMOTIONALLY DISTURBED

see Problem Children

CHILDREN—EMPLOYMENT

see Child Labor

CHILDREN—EUROPE

Altman, Linda Jacobs. Escape-Teens on the Run: Primary Sources from the Holocaust. 2010. (True Stories of Teens in the Holocaust Ser.). (Illus.). 128p. (YA). (gr. 9-12). 33.27 (978-0-7660-3270-5(1)) Enslow Pubs., Inc.

Bedford, Kate. Greeks. 2011. (Children in History Ser.). 32p. (YA). (gr. 4-7). lib. bdg. 28.50 (978-1-59771-270-5(1)) Sea-To-Sea Pubns.

Bensinger, Henry. Ancient Greek Daily Life. 2013. (Spotlight on Ancient Civilizations: Greece Ser.). (ENG., Illus.). 24p. (J). (gr. 3-4). pap. 10.00 (978-1-4777-0877-4(4)); lib. bdg. 23.60 (978-1-4777-0772-2(7)) Rosen Publishing Group, Inc., The. (PowerKids Pr.).

Brooks, Susie. Greece. 2006. (Our Lives, Our World Ser.). (J). (978-1-59389-287-6(X)) Chrysalis Education.

Cricket Books Staff & Cobblestone Publishing Staff. If I Were a Kid in Ancient Greece: Children of the Ancient World. Sheldon, Ken, ed. 2007. (If I Were a Kid In... Ser.). (ENG., Illus.). 32p. (J). (gr. 1-5). 17.95 (978-0-8126-7929-8(6)) Cricket Bks.

Macdonald, Fiona. Romans. 2011. (Children in History Ser.). (Illus.). 32p. (YA). (gr. 4-7). lib. bdg. 28.50 (978-1-59771-271-2(X)) Sea-To-Sea Pubns.

Wroble, Lisa A. Kids in the Middle Ages. (Kids Throughout History Ser.). 24p. 2009. (gr. 3-3). 42.50 (978-1-61513-895-1(1)) 2004. (J). 22.60 (978-1-4042-2666-1(4)) Rosen Publishing Group, Inc., The. (PowerKids Pr.).

CHILDREN—FICTION

A. L. O. E. The Triumph over Midian. 2006. 344p. per. 23.99 (978-1-4255-3466-0(X)) Michigan Publishing.

Abbott, Jacob. Aunt Margaret; or, How John True Kept His Resolutions. 2013. 160p. pap. 19.95 (978-1-4455-2937-0(8)) Research Pr.

Alcott, Louisa May. Under the Lilacs. 2007. 296p. per. 13.45 (978-1-59462-879-5(3), Book Jungle) Standard Pubns., Inc.

Alger, Horatio. Paul the Peddler. rev. ed. 2006. (ENG.). 232p. 27.95 (978-1-4218-2090-3(0), 1st World Library - Literary Society) 1st World Publishing, Inc.

Alger Jr. Horatio Staff. Herbert Carter's Legacy. rev. ed. 2006. 264p. 28.95 (978-1-4218-1756-9(X)); pap. 13.95 (978-1-4218-1856-6(6)) 1st World Publishing, Inc. (1st World Library - Literary Society).

Allen, Constance. Shake a Leg! Swanson, Maggie, illus. 2010. (Big Bird's Favorites Board Bks.). (ENG.). 24p. (J). (gr. k — 1). bds. 4.99 (978-0-375-85424-8(X), Random Hse. Bks. for Young Readers) Random Hse. Children's Bks.

Andrews, Jane. Young Reader's Series: The stories mother nature told her Children. 2009. 156p. pap. 16.95 (978-1-60444-036-2(8)) IndoEuropeanPublishing.com.

Anh, Nguyen Nhat. Ticket to Childhood. Naythons, Will, tr. from VIE. 2014. (ENG.). 160p. (gr. 12). 21.95 (978-1-4683-0959-1(5), 460959) Overlook Pr., The.

Annie S. Swan. Thankful Rest. 2007. 98p. pap. 16.99 (978-1-4346-1978-5(8)); (ENG.). 102p. pap. 19.99 (978-1-4346-1888-7(9)) Creative Media Partners, LLC.

Atkins, Jeannine. Preparadas... Listas... Ya! 2004. (SPA., Illus.). (J). (gr. k-3). spiral bd. (978-0-616-07274-5(0)) Canadian National Institute for the Blind/Institut National Canadien pour les Aveugles.

Bannerman, Helen. The Story of Little Black Mingo & the Story of Little Black Sambo. 2010. 92p. pap. 34.50 (978-1-4452-8667-9(X)) Lulu Pr., Inc.

Barbarite, Lynn. Kitty Heaven's in the Sky! 2004. (J). 8.95 (978-0-9791362-1-4(0)) Tony Tales.

Barkow, Henriette. That's My Mum. Brazell, Derek, illus. 2004. (J). 24p. (978-1-85269-604-7(4)); (ENG & SPA.). 28p. pap. (978-1-85269-606-1(0)); (ENG & CZE.). 28p. pap. (978-1-85269-628-3(1)); (ENG & VIE.). 28p. pap. (978-1-85269-802-7(0)); (GER & ENG.). 28p. pap. (978-1-85269-803-4(9)); (ENG & ITA.). 28p. pap. (978-1-85269-804-1(7)); (ENG & SOM.). 28p. pap. (978-1-85269-605-4(2)); (ENG & TUR.). 28p. pap. (978-1-85269-608-5(7)); (ENG & PER.). 28p. pap. (978-1-85269-599-6(4)); (ENG & URD.). 28p. pap. (978-1-85269-609-2(5)); (ENG & CHI.). 28p. pap. (978-1-85269-598-9(6)); (ENG & BEN.). 28p. pap. (978-1-85269-597-2(8)); (ENG & GUJ.). 28p. pap. (978-1-85269-601-6(X)); (ENG & POR.). 28p. pap. (978-1-85269-603-0(6)); (ENG & PAN.). 28p. pap. (978-1-85269-602-3(8)) Mantra Lingua.

—That's My Mum: Ajo Eshte Nena Ime. Brazell, Derek, illus. 2004. (ENG & ARA.). 28p. (J). pap. (978-1-85269-596-5(X)) Mantra Lingua.

Beaumont, Karen. Move over, Rover! Dyer, Jane, illus. 2006. (ENG.). 40p. (J). (gr. -1-3). 16.99 (978-0-15-201979-2(0)) Houghton Mifflin Harcourt Publishing Co.

Benenfeld, Rikki. I Go to the Doctor. Benenfeld, Rikki, illus. 2004. (Toddler Experience Ser.). (Illus.). (J). lib. bdg. 10.95 (978-1-929628-15-5(3)) Hachai Publishing.

Big Davie. The Lady & Her Cat As Told by Bigdavie: A simple easy reading bedtime story that will leave children with delightful images while drifting off to S. 2009. (Illus.). 28p. pap. 12.49 (978-1-4389-3124-1(7)) AuthorHouse.

Blitz, Shmuel. The Adventures of Aliza & Dovid: Holidays at the Farm. Katz, Tova, illus. 2005. (ArtScroll Youth Ser.). 48p. (J). (978-1-4226-0021-4(1)) Mesorah Pubns., Ltd.

Boone, Sheila. Free As a Butterfly. Knox, Susi Grell, illus. 2003. 32p. (J). (gr. -1-3). pap. 7.95 (978-1-891577-80-2(8)) Image Pr., Inc.

Boullosa, Carmen. Solo para Muchachos. Martinez, Enrique, illus. 2003. (SPA.). 60p. (J). (gr. 4-7). 11.95 (978-968-19-0325-1(0)) Aguilar, Altea, Taurus, Alfaguara, S.A. de C.V MEX. Dist: Santillana USA Publishing Co., Inc.

Boynton, Sandra. The Going to Bed Book. Boynton, Sandra, illus. 2006. (ENG., Illus.). 14p. (J). bds. 12.95 (978-1-4169-2794-5(8), Little Simon) Little Simon.

Bradman, Tony. The Sandal. Dupasquier, Philippe, illus. 32p. (J). (gr. 1-3). pap. 9.99 (978-0-86264-843-5(2)) Andersen Pr. GBR. Dist: Trafalgar Square Publishing.

Brown, Margaret Wise & Brown. Another Important Book. Raschka, Chris, illus. 2006. (ENG.). 32p. (J). (gr. -1-k). reprint ed. pap. 6.99 (978-0-06-443785-1(X)) HarperCollins Pubs.

Byars, Betsy. Bingo Brown y el Lenguaje del Amor. 2003. (Survival Ser.).Tr. of Bingo Brown & the Language of Love. (SPA.). (J). (gr. 4-5). pap. 10.95 (978-84-239-7152-7(X), EC5211) Espasa Calpe, S.A. ESP. Dist: Planeta Publishing Corp.

—Las Preguntas de Bingo Brown. Gatagan, T., illus. 2nd ed. 2003. (Espasa Juvenil Ser.: Vol. 15).Tr. of Burning Questions of Bingo Brown. (SPA.). 186p. (J). (gr. 7-18). (978-84-239-8862-4(7), EC4398) Espasa Calpe, S.A. ESP. Dist: Lectorum Pubns., Inc.

Castlemon, Harry. No Moss; or, the Career of a Rolling Stone, by Harry Castlemon [Pseud.]. 2006. 328p. per. 23.99 (978-1-4255-3290-1(X)) Michigan Publishing.

Chilman-Blair, Kim & DeLoache, Shawn. Medikidz Explain Having an Operation. 2012. (Illus.). 16p. (J). pap. (978-1-906935-82-5(3)) Medikidz Ltd.

Cleary, Beverly. Henry & Beezus. Darling, Louis et al, illus. 2014. (Henry Huggins Ser.: 2). (ENG.). 224p. (J). (gr. 3-7). 16.99 (978-0-688-21383-1(9)) HarperCollins Pubs.

Collura, Mary-Ellen Lang. Winners, 1 vol. Ehrlemark, Anna, illus. 2014. (ENG.). 144p. (J). pap. 12.95 (978-1-55054-223-3(0), Greystone Bks.) Greystone Books Ltd. CAN. Dist: Publishers Group West (PGW).

Cook, Julia. I Can't Believe You Said That! De Weerd, Kelsey, illus. 2014. (ENG.). 32p. (J). pap. 10.95 (978-1-934490-67-9(9)) Boys Town Pr.

Cook, Julia. The Procrastinator, no. 5. DuFalla, Anita, illus. 2017. (Responsible Me! Ser.: 5). (ENG.). 32p. (J). pap. 10.95 **(978-1-944882-09-9(X))** Boys Town Pr.

Davies, Rocky. Harvey Happy Bee. 2005. (Bee Attitude Board Books). (Illus.). (J). (978-1-59156-775-2(0)) Covenant Communications.

Dawson, Eugene T. Little Valerie Wants to Grow Taller. 2009. 24p. pap. 14.95 (978-1-4389-7002-8(1)) AuthorHouse.

De Aragon, Ray J. Dodo the Bird & Other Stories. Calles, Rosa M., illus. 105p. (Orig.). (J). (gr. 1-12). pap. 5.95 (978-0-932906-21-2(4)) Pan-American Publishing Co.

Degen, Bruce. Snow Joke. Degen, Bruce, illus. 2014. (I Like to Read(r) Ser.). (ENG., Illus.). 24p. (J). (gr. -1-3). 14.95 (978-0-8234-3065-9(0)) Holiday Hse., Inc.

Derrick, Patricia. Farley the Ferret of Farkleberry Farm. Martinez, J-P Loppo, illus. 2007. 32p. (J). (gr. -1-3). 18.95 incl. audio compact disk (978-1-933818-12-2(3)) Animalations.

Doggy Heaven's in the Sky! 2004. (J). 4.95 (978-0-9791362-0-7(2)) Tony Tales.

Duchesne, Christiane. Edmond et Amandine. 2004. (FRE., Illus.). (J). (gr. -1-3). spiral bd. (978-0-616-11143-7(6)) Canadian National Institute for the Blind/Institut National Canadien pour les Aveugles.

Edwards, Richard. The Forest Child. Malone, Peter, illus. 2004. 28p. (J). reprint ed. (978-0-7567-7850-7(6)) DIANE Publishing Co.

Ende, Michael. Momo. Brownjohn, Maxwell J., tr. from GER. 2009. (ENG.). 240p. pap. **(978-0-14-031753-4(8)**, Puffin) Penguin Bks., Ltd.

—Momo. Ende, Michael, illus. 2004. (SPA., Illus.). 256p. (YA). (gr. 8-12). pap. 10.95 *(978-968-19-0255-1(6))* Santillana USA Publishing Co., Inc.

Ewing, Juliana Horatia. A Great Emergency & Other Tales. 2007. 188p. per. *(978-1-4065-2525-0(1))* Dodo Pr.

Finley, Martha. Elsie's Children, Vol. 6. 320p. (gr. 7-12). pap. 5.95 *(978-1-58182-069-0(0)*, Cumberland Hse.) Sourcebooks, Inc.

—Elsie's Young Folks, Vol. 25. 320p. (gr. 4-7). pap. 5.95 *(978-1-58182-180-2(8)*, Cumberland Hse.) Sourcebooks, Inc.

Flam, Chanie. By Myself. (Goldie Gold Board Book Ser.: Vol. 5). (Illus.). (J). (gr. -1-1). bds. 4.95 *(978-1-58330-029-9(5))* Feldheim Pubs.

Fluharty, Jeff & McAndrew, Kelly. I Can't Talk Now, I'm Busy Writing Nothing. 2003. 123p. (J). (gr. 2-6). pap. 9.95 *(978-1-878044-60-0(5))* Mayhaven Publishing, Inc.

Funke, Cornelia. Thief Lord. Birmingham, Christian, illus. 2010. (ENG.). 376p. (J). (gr. 3-7). 7.99 *(978-0-545-22770-4(4)*, Chicken Hse., The) Scholastic, Inc.

Gill, Janie S. Just Like You. Lambson, Elizabeth, illus. Date not set. pap. 3.95 *(978-0-89868-429-2(3))* ARO Publishing Co.

Greene, Bette. Philip Hall Likes Me, I Reckon Maybe. l.t. ed. 2003. (Children's Large Print Ser.). (J). 28.95 *(978-1-58118-107-4(8))* LRS.

Griggs, Terry. Nieve. L'Hirondelle, Cheryl, illus. 2010. (ENG.). 264p. (J). (gr. 4-10). pap. 14.95 *(978-1-897231-87-6(3))* Biblioasis CAN. Dist: Consortium Bk. Sales & Distribution.

Hall, Frostie. Dread Champions of the King: The Humble Beginning. 2004. (Dread Champions of the King Ser.: Bk. 1). 96p. (J). per. *(978-1-55306-836-5(X))* Essence Publishing.

Hallinan, P. K. I'm Thankful Each Day. 2003. (ENG.). 24p. (J). bds. 6.95 *(978-0-8249-4238-0(8)*, Ideal Pubns.) Worthy Publishing.

Harris, Isobel. Little Boy Brown. François, André, illus. 2013. (ENG.). 48p. (J). (gr. -1-3). 15.95 *(978-1-59270-135-3(3))* Enchanted Lion Bks., LLC.

Hirschmann, Kris & Langdo, Bryan, illus. We're Going on a Ghost Hunt. 2011. (J). *(978-0-545-34173-8(6))* Scholastic, Inc.

Hobbs, Constance. Dreamers. 2007. 436p. pap. 35.95 *(978-0-9556783-0-1(7))* Hobbs, Constance GBR. Dist: Lulu Pr., Inc.

Hofmeister, Alan, et al. The Bat. (Reading for All Learners Ser.). (Illus.). (J). *(978-1-56861-126-6(9))* Swift Learning Resources.

—Meet Mit. (Reading for All Learners Ser.). (Illus.). (J). pap. *(978-1-56861-079-5(3))* Swift Learning Resources.

—The Men. (Reading for All Learners Ser.). (Illus.). (J). pap. *(978-1-56861-116-7(1))* Swift Learning Resources.

—Mit Is Wet. (Reading for All Learners Ser.). (Illus.). (J). pap. *(978-1-56861-108-2(0))* Swift Learning Resources.

—Sam Is Mad. (Reading for All Learners Ser.). (Illus.). (J). pap. *(978-1-56861-087-0(4))* Swift Learning Resources.

—See It. (Reading for All Learners Ser.). (Illus.). (J). pap. *(978-1-56861-080-1(7))* Swift Learning Resources.

—See Mat. (Reading for All Learners Ser.). (Illus.). (J). pap. *(978-1-56861-078-8(5))* Swift Learning Resources.

—See Them. (Reading for All Learners Ser.). (Illus.). (J). pap. *(978-1-56861-107-5(2))* Swift Learning Resources.

—Sell the Shell. (Reading for All Learners Ser.). (Illus.). (J). pap. *(978-1-56861-104-4(8))* Swift Learning Resources.

—Sid. (Reading for All Learners Ser.). (Illus.). (J). pap. *(978-1-56861-088-7(2))* Swift Learning Resources.

—Sit on It. (Reading for All Learners Ser.). (Illus.). (J). pap. *(978-1-56861-081-8(5))* Swift Learning Resources.

—Smash It. (Reading for All Learners Ser.). (Illus.). (J). *(978-1-56861-136-5(6))* Swift Learning Resources.

—To the Den. (Reading for All Learners Ser.). (Illus.). (J). *(978-1-56861-138-9(2))* Swift Learning Resources.

—Up the Path. (Reading for All Learners Ser.). (Illus.). (J). pap. *(978-1-56861-134-1(X))* Swift Learning Resources.

—Up We Go. (Reading for All Learners Ser.). (Illus.). (J). pap. *(978-1-56861-129-7(3))* Swift Learning Resources.

—Was It Wet? (Reading for All Learners Ser.). (Illus.). (J). pap. *(978-1-56861-114-3(5))* Swift Learning Resources.

—We Will See. (Reading for All Learners Ser.). (Illus.). (J). pap. *(978-1-56861-089-4(0))* Swift Learning Resources.

—Who Am I? (Reading for All Learners Ser.). (Illus.). (J). *(978-1-56861-096-2(3))* Swift Learning Resources.

Ihebereme, Chidozie . N. Dad Says Write. 2007. per. *(978-1-59872-954-2(3))* Instant Pub.

Jenkins, Steve. Looking Down. 2003. (ENG., Illus.). 32p. (J). (gr. -1-3). pap. 7.99 *(978-0-618-31098-2(3))* Houghton Mifflin Harcourt Publishing Co.

—Looking Down. 2003. (gr. k-3). 17.15 *(978-0-613-60775-9(9)*, Turtleback) Turtleback Bks.

Karp, Ken, illus. Will You Wear a Blue Hat? 2009. (Rookie Toddler: Sing along Toddler Ser.). (ENG.). 12p. (J). (gr. -1). bds. 6.95 *(978-0-531-24549-1(7))* Scholastic Library Publishing.

Kidd, Pennie. Oops! Beardshaw, Rosalind, illus. 2011. (ENG.). 32p. (J). (gr. -1-k). pap. 8.99 *(978-0-7459-4892-8(8))* Lion Hudson PLC GBR. Dist: Independent Pubs. Group.

kieliszewski, sheila. Superhero. 2009. 24p. 13.70 *(978-0-578-00002-2(4))* Kieliszewski, Sheila.

King, Frank. Tee Tee Peetum. 2003. (ENG., Illus.). 48p. (J). pap. 14.95 *(978-1-878044-65-5(6))* Mayhaven Publishing, Inc.

Kipling, Rudyard. The Jungle Book. Daily, Don, illus. 2014. (ENG.). 68p. (J). (gr. -1). 18.95 *(978-1-60433-475-3(4))* Cider Mill Pr. Bk. Pubs., LLC.

Knight, Jovannah. A Heavenly Message. 2011. 20p. pap. 16.95 *(978-1-61204-430-9(1)*, Strategic Bk. Publishing) Strategic Book Publishing & Rights Agency (SBPRA).

Knights, Harry B. Angel's Star. 2006. (J). lib. bdg. 20.00 *(978-0-9632248-8-0(3))* Synergetic Pubns., Inc.

Kroll, Virginia. On the Way to Kindergarten. Schlossberg, Elizabeth, illus. 2008. (ENG.). 32p. (J). (gr. -1-k). pap. 6.99 *(978-0-14-241144-5(2)*, Puffin Books) Penguin Young Readers Group.

Lambert, Martha. I Won't Get Lost. (Illus.). 32p. (J). (gr. -1-2). Date not set. 5.99 *(978-0-06-443679-3(9))* 2003. lib. bdg. 16.89 *(978-0-06-028961-4(9))* HarperCollins Pubs.

Langley, Noel. The Land of Green Ginger. Ardizzone, Edward, illus. 2007. (ENG.). 149p. (J). (gr. 3-7). per. 11.95 *(978-1-56792-333-9(X))* Godine, David R. Pub.

Leslie, Emma. For Merrie England: A Tale of the Weavers of Norfolk. Taylor, R., illus. 2010. 168p. 20.95 *(978-1-934671-38-2(X))*; pap. 10.95 *(978-1-934671-39-9(8))* Salem Ridge Press LLC.

Levine, Gail Carson. The Wish. unabr. ed. 2004. 208p. (J). (gr. 3-7). pap. 36.00 incl. audio *(978-0-8072-8747-7(4)*, Listening Library) Random Hse. Audio Publishing Group.

Lichtenheld, Tom. What Are You So Grumpy About? Lichtenheld, Tom, illus. 2007. (ENG., Illus.). 40p. (J). (gr. -1-3). 7.99 *(978-0-316-06589-4(7))* Little, Brown Bks. for Young Readers.

Madison, Ron. Ned & the General: A Lesson about Deployment. Covolo, David, illus. 2004. 26p. (J). (gr. -1-3). *(978-1-887206-25-9(6))* Ned's Head Productions.

Maloney, Peter & Zekauskas, Felicia. Lose That Tooth! 2005. (Illus.). 32p. (J). *(978-0-439-67639-7(8))* Scholastic, Inc.

Masino, Brian. Cabbage Patch Kids: We Are All Best Friends. Karl, Linda, illus. 2006. (J). pap. *(978-0-439-76820-7(9))* Scholastic, Inc.

Matcheck, Diane. Untitled Novel. 2009. *(978-0-374-38041-0(4)*, Farrar, Straus & Giroux (BYR)) Farrar, Straus & Giroux.

Matsuura, Richard & Matsuura, Ruth. Kalani & Primo. Chao, Linus, illus. (J). 8.95 *(978-1-887916-03-5(2))* Orchid Isle Publishing Co.

McCue, Lisa. My First Mother Goose. 2009. (Carry along Bks.). (ENG., Illus.). 20p. (J). (gr. -1-k). bds. 14.99 *(978-0-7944-1931-8(3)*, Reader's Digest Children's Bks.) Studio Fun International.

McDaniel, Lurlene. If I Should Die Before I Wake. 2004. (ENG., Illus.). 128p. (YA). (gr. 7-12). pap. 4.99 *(978-1-58196-009-9(3))* Lerner Publishing Group.

McIntyre, Gary P. Little People up Jump. 2009. 24p. pap. 14.49 *(978-1-4389-8002-7(7))* AuthorHouse.

Miller, Margaret. Now I'm Big. Date not set. (Illus.). 32p. (YA). (gr. 5-18). pap. 5.95 *(978-0-06-050299-7(1))* HarperCollins Pubs.

Moncure, Jane Belk. What Do You Say When a Monkey Acts This Way? A Book about Manners. Gallagher-Cole, Mernie, illus. 2013. (Magic Castle Readers Ser.). (ENG.). 32p. (J). (gr. -1-2). 25.64 *(978-1-62323-590-1(1)*, 206325) Child's World, Inc., The.

Moreton, Clara. Frank & Fanny: A Rural Story. 2007. (ENG.). 66p. per. 16.99 *(978-1-4346-2717-9(9))*; per. 18.99 *(978-1-4346-2723-0(3))* Creative Media Partners, LLC.

Morphew, Chris. The Phoenix Files, Arrival. 2013. 304p. (J). pap. 6.99 *(978-1-61067-091-3(4))* Kane Miller.

Myers, Benjamin J. Blood Alchemy. 2010. (ENG.). 384p. *(978-1-84255-641-2(X))* Orion Publishing Group, Ltd. GBR. Dist: Hachette Bk. Group.

Nadin, Joanna. Penny Dreadful Causes a Kerfuffle. 2015. (Penny Dreadful Ser.). (ENG.). 139p. (J). (gr. k-5). pap. 5.99 *(978-0-7945-2305-3(6)*, Usborne) EDC Publishing.

—Penny Dreadful Is a Complete Catastrophe. 2015. (Penny Dreadful Ser.). (ENG.). 144p. (J). (gr. k-5). pap. 5.99 *(978-0-7945-3020-4(6)*, Usborne) EDC Publishing.

—Penny Dreadful Is a Magnet for Disaster. 2015. (Penny Dreadful Ser.). (ENG.). 141p. (J). (gr. k-5). pap. 5.99 *(978-0-7945-2325-1(0)*, Usborne) EDC Publishing.

Napoli, Donna Jo. The King of Mulberry Street. 2007. 245p. (gr. 3-7). 17.00 *(978-0-7569-7945-4(5))* Perfection Learning Corp.

Norman, Tyler & Perez, Jose S. The Banjoman/El Hombre del Banjo. Perez, Jose S., illus. 2004. (ENG & SPA., Illus.). 32p. (J). 12.95 *(978-1-57072-292-9(7))* Overmountain Pr.

O'Brien, Frances. Sheer Bliss: Confessions of a (Reluctant) Celebrity Spawn. 2006. (ENG.). 144p. *(978-1-905886-32-6(2))* Troubador Publishing Ltd.

Offill, Jenny. 11 Experiments That Failed. Carpenter, Nancy, illus. 2011. (ENG.). 40p. (J). (gr. -1-3). 17.99 *(978-0-375-84762-2(6)*, Schwartz & Wade Bks.) Random Hse. Children's Bks.

Parker, David. I Am Creative! Durrell, Julie, illus. 2005. (J). *(978-0-439-73586-5(6))* Scholastic, Inc.

Pausacker, Jenny. Get a Life. (Livewire Ser.). 126p. (YA). (gr. 6-9). pap. 8.99 *(978-0-7043-4925-4(6))* Women's Pr., Ltd., The GBR. Dist: Trafalgar Square Publishing.

Peanuts. Date not set. 5.95 *(978-0-89868-353-0(X))* ARO Publishing Co.

Piano, Maureen. When Flamingos Fly: Discovering the Wonders of the World. 2006. (Illus.). 44p. (J). (gr. -1-3). pap. 12.99 incl. audio compact disk *(978-1-59092-362-7(6))* Blue Forge Pr.

Rausin, K. D. Elle & Buddy. Ulasowski, Muza, illus. 2015. (ENG.). 32p. (J). pap. 13.95 *(978-1-942155-00-3(X))* Randall, Peter E. Pub.

Ready Reader Staff. Just Like Us: Short U, 6 bks., set, Level A. 2003. (J). (gr. -1-3). 24.50 *(978-0-8136-2023-7(6))* Modern Curriculum Pr.

Renee Daeumler Thompson. I Made a Bad Choice. 2009. 16p. pap. 8.49 *(978-1-4389-7561-0(9))* AuthorHouse.

Roberts, Ken. Hiccup Champion of the World, 1 vol. (ENG.). 96p. (J). pap. 595.00 *(978-0-88899-233-8(5))* Groundwood Bks. CAN. Dist: Publishers Group West (PGW).

Romeu, Emma. Gregorio y el Mar. 2003.Tr. of Gregory & the Sea. (SPA., Illus.). 151p. (J). (gr. 5-8). pap. 15.95 *(978-968-19-0316-9(1))* Santillana USA Publishing Co., Inc.

Rosen, Michael. You Wait till I'm Older Than You! Rayner, Shoo, illus. (ENG.). 128p. (J). 7.95 *(978-0-14-038014-9(0))* Penguin Bks., Ltd. GBR. Dist: Trafalgar Square Publishing.

Ruurs, Margriet. Families Around the World. Gordon, Jessica Rae, illus. 2014. (Around the World Ser.). (ENG.). 40p. (J). (gr. -1-2). 18.95 *(978-1-894786-57-7(2))* Kids Can Pr., Ltd. CAN. Dist: Hachette Bk. Group.

Sanders, Cecilia. The Tale of the Perfect Whitetails. 2008. 36p. pap. 17.98 *(978-1-4389-0644-7(7))* AuthorHouse.

Sari. Jeanne-Marie Goes to Market: A Story of the West Indies. 2011. 26p. 35.95 *(978-1-258-10346-0(X))* Literary Licensing, LLC.

Scimone, Diana. Adventures with Pawpaw: China. Wiedemer, Leah, illus. 2003. 32p. (J). 8.95 *(978-0-9729507-0-1(2))* Peapod Publishing, Inc.

The Seven Little Kids. 2005. (Folk Tales Set 2 Ser.). (J). 5.33 *(978-1-58453-305-4(6))* Pioneer Valley Bks.

Sidney, Margaret & Sidney, James. Five Little Peppers & How They Grew. 2007. (ENG.). 420p. (gr. 4-7). 24.95 *(978-1-55709-591-6(4))* Applewood Bks.

Simonson, Lona Marie. Grandma Lucy Feeds the Birds, 1 vol. Herges, Connie, illus. 2009. 44p. pap. 24.95 *(978-1-60836-732-0(0))* America Star Bks.

Skrypuch, Marsha Forchuk. Making Bombs for Hitler. 2017. (ENG.). 240p. (J). (gr. 3-7). 17.99 *(978-0-545-93191-5(6)*, Scholastic Pr.) Scholastic, Inc.

Smith, Cleveland W. Billabongo. 2008. 172p. pap. *(978-1-84923-100-8(1))* YouWriteOn.

Smith, Darshiel & Haddi, Javon. Introducing the Rollies. 2013. 28p. pap. 24.95 *(978-1-63000-582-5(7))* America Star Bks.

Smith, Doris Buchanan. A Taste of Blackberries. 74p. (J). pap. 4.95 *(978-0-8072-1266-0(0)*, Listening Library) Random Hse. Audio Publishing Group.

Sommer, Carl. Light Your Candle. 2003. (Another Sommer-Time Story Ser.). (Illus.). 48p. (J). (gr. k-4). lib. bdg. 23.95 incl. audio compact disk *(978-1-57537-768-1(3))*; 16.95 incl. audio *(978-1-57537-567-0(2))* Advance Publishing, Inc.

—Light Your Candle. James, Kennon, illus. 2003. (Another Sommer-Time Story Ser.). 48p. (J). (ENG.). 16.95 incl. audio compact disk *(978-1-57537-518-2(4))*; lib. bdg. 23.95 incl. audio compact disk *(978-1-57537-718-6(7))* Advance Publishing, Inc.

Sprecher, John. Eric & the Angrrry Frog, Vol. 2. Forrest, James, illus. l.t. ed. Date not set. (Special Kids "Special Message" Book Ser.). 32p. (J). (gr. k-4). pap. 10.00 *(978-1-892186-01-0(2))* Anythings Possible, Inc.

Stoehr, Shelley. Weird on the Outside. 2003. 224p. (YA). pap. 16.95 *(978-0-595-26953-2(2)*, Writers Club Pr.) iUniverse, Inc.

Stone, Susheila. Eid Ul-Fitr. 2004. (ENG., Illus.). 32p. pap. 4.95 *(978-0-7136-4083-0(9)*, 93344, A&C Black) Bloomsbury Publishing Plc GBR. Dist: Consortium Bk. Sales & Distribution.

Strasser, Todd. Can't Get There from Here. 2004. (ENG.). 208p. (YA). (gr. 7-7). 17.99 *(978-0-689-84169-9(8)*, Simon & Schuster Bks. For Young Readers) Simon & Schuster Bks. For Young Readers.

—Can't Get There from Here. 2005. (ENG.). 208p. (YA). (gr. 7-12). mass mkt. 7.99 *(978-0-689-84170-5(1)*, Simon Pulse) Simon Pulse.

Superle, Michelle. Black Dog Dream Dog, 1 vol. Balance, Millie, illus. 2011. (ENG.). 143p. (J). (gr. 3-6). pap. 12.95 *(978-1-896580-34-0(3))* Tradewind Bks. CAN. Dist: Orca Bk. Pubs. USA.

Swan, Richard. The Listeners. 2009. (Illus.). 64p. pap. 10.49 *(978-1-4389-6224-5(X))* AuthorHouse.

Taylor, Jeannie. You Wouldnt Love Me If You Kne. 2009. 32p. (J). pap. 10.99 *(978-0-687-65786-5(5))* Abingdon Pr.

Tillman, Nancy. On the Night You Were Born, 1. l.t. ed. 2005. (Illus.). 32p. (J). 17.95 *(978-0-9765761-0-5(4))* Darling Pr. LLC.

Troughton, Joanna. The Tiger Child: A Folk Tale from India. Troughton, Joanna, illus. (ENG., Illus.). 32p. (J). pap. 11.95 *(978-0-14-038238-9(0))* Penguin Bks., Ltd. GBR. Dist: Trafalgar Square Publishing.

Ursu, Anne. Breadcrumbs. 2013. (J). lib. bdg. 17.20 *(978-0-606-27130-1(9)*, Turtleback) Turtleback Bks.

Vail, Emily Blake. The Grey Ghost of the Pharaoh. Barbra K. Mudd, illus. 2004. 176p. (YA). per. 8.99 *(978-0-935087-27-7(3))* Wright Publishing, Inc.

Viorst, Judith. Super-Completely & Totally the Messiest. Glasser, Robin Preiss, illus. 2004. (ENG.). 32p. (J). (gr. -1-2). 7.99 *(978-0-689-86617-3(8)*, Atheneum Bks. for Young Readers) Simon & Schuster Children's Publishing.

Whitby, Adele. Camille's Story 1910. 2015. (Secrets of the Manor Ser.: 7). (ENG., Illus.). 160p. (J). (gr. 3-7). pap. 6.99 *(978-1-4814-3988-6(X)*, Simon Spotlight) Simon Spotlight.

Wilhelm, Hans. Chico Valiente Como Yo. (SPA.). 32p. (J). 13.95 *(978-84-261-2658-0(8))* Juventud, Editorial ESP. Dist: AIMS International Bks., Inc.

Wood, Maryrose. The Mysterious Howling, Bk. I. Klassen, Jon, illus. 2010. (Incorrigible Children of Ashton Place Ser.: 1). (ENG.). 272p. (J). (gr. 3-7). 16.99 *(978-0-06-179105-5(9))* HarperCollins Pubs.

Zadunajsky, Donna M. Tayla's First Day of School. Bicking, Judith, illus. 2013. (ENG.). 26p. pap. 9.15 *(978-1-938037-35-1(9))* Zadunajsky, Donna M.

Zidrou. Ducoboo: In the Corner! Godi, illus. 2007. (Ducoboo Ser.: 2). (ENG.). 48p. (J). (gr. 4-7). pap. 9.99 *(978-1-905460-26-7(0))* CineBook GBR. Dist: National Bk. Network.

CHILDREN—FOREIGN COUNTRIES

Hollyer, Beatrice. Let's Eat: What Children Eat Around the World. rev. ed. 2004. (ENG., Illus.). 48p. (J). (gr. k-4). 18.99 *(978-0-8050-7322-5(1)*, 9780805073225, Holt, Henry & Co. Bks. For Young Readers) Holt, Henry & Co.

Kaltenhauser, Bettina & van Swol-Ulbrich, Hilly. When Abroad - Do As the Local Children Do: Ori's Guide for Young Expats. 2004. (ENG., Illus.). 112p. (J). pap. *(978-90-5594-262-6(6))* Cyan Communications GBR. Dist: Independent Pubs. Group.

Rice, Dona Herweck. Kids Around the World, 1 vol. 2nd rev. ed. 2011. (TIME for KIDS(r) Nonfiction Readers Ser.). (ENG.). 20p. (J). (gr. 1-1). 4.99 *(978-1-4333-3599-0(9))* Teacher Created Materials, Inc.

—Niños Alrededor del Mundo, 1 vol. 2nd rev. ed. 2012. (Nonfiction Readers Ser.). (SPA.). 20p. (J). (gr. 1-1). pap. 4.99 *(978-1-4333-4432-9(7))* Teacher Created Materials, Inc.

CHILDREN—FOREIGN COUNTRIES—FICTION

Gavilanes, Enrique & Inniss, Michelle. Global Language Detective. 2005. (ENG., Illus.). 40p. pap. 7.95 *(978-1-84059-318-1(0))* Milet Publishing.

CHILDREN—GREAT BRITAIN

Barber, Jill. Children in Victorian Times. 2013. (Step up History Ser.). (ENG., Illus.). 32p. (J). (gr. 2-6). pap. 12.99 *(978-0-237-54381-5(8))* Evans Brothers, Ltd. GBR. Dist: Independent Pubs. Group.

Power, Rhoda & Power, Eileen. Boys & Girls of History. 2012. (ENG.). 360p. pap. 35.99 *(978-0-521-23606-5(1))* Cambridge Univ. Pr.

CHILDREN—GREAT BRITAIN—FICTION

Malley, Gemma. The Declaration. 2008. (Declaration Ser.). (ENG., Illus.). 320p. (YA). (gr. 7). 10.99 *(978-1-59990-295-1(8)*, 9781599902951, Bloomsbury USA Childrens) Bloomsbury Publishing USA.

—The Declaration, 7 vols. (YA). 2008. 119.75 *(978-1-4281-7284-5(X))* 2007. 91.75 *(978-1-4281-7278-4(5))* 2007. 89.75 *(978-1-4281-7280-7(7))* 2007. 121.75 *(978-1-4281-7282-1(3))* 2007. 245.75 *(978-1-4281-7279-1(3))* 2007. 1.25 *(978-1-4281-7275-3(0))* Recorded Bks., Inc.

Meade, L. T. The Children's Pilgrimage. 2007. (ENG.). 254p. pap. 21.99 *(978-1-4346-4863-1(X))*; 280p. pap. 23.99 *(978-1-4346-4864-8(8))* Creative Media Partners, LLC.

CHILDREN—GROWTH

Cameron, Milissa. Faster, Daddy! 2009. 16p. pap. 8.49 *(978-1-4389-2646-9(4))* AuthorHouse.

Douglas, Ann. Baby Science: How Babies Really Work! Desputeaux, Helene, illus. 2004. 32p. (J). (gr. k-4). reprint ed. pap. 7.00 *(978-0-7567-8455-3(7))* DIANE Publishing Co.

Kalman, Bobbie. Crezco y Cambio. 2010. (SPA.). 16p. (J). pap. *(978-0-7787-8582-8(3))* Crabtree Publishing Co.

—I Am Growing & Changing. 2010. (ENG., Illus.). 16p. (J). (gr. k-2). *(978-0-7787-9422-6(9))*; pap. *(978-0-7787-9466-0(0))* Crabtree Publishing Co.

Madaras, Lynda & Davick, Linda. Ready, Set, Grow! A What's Happening to My Body? Book for Younger Girls. 2003. (What's Happening to My Body? Ser.). (ENG., Illus.). 128p. (gr. 4-6). pap. 12.99 *(978-1-55704-565-2(8)*, William Morrow Paperbacks) HarperCollins Pubs.

Madaras, Lynda & Gilligan, Paul. On Your Mark, Get Set, Grow! 2008. (What's Happening to My Body? Ser.). (ENG., Illus.). 123p. (gr. 3-4). 22.00 *(978-1-55704-780-9(4)*, Morrow, William & Co.) HarperCollins Pubs.

—On Your Mark, Get Set, Grow! A What's Happening to My Body? Book for Younger Boys. 2008. (What's Happening to My Body? Ser.). (ENG., Illus.). 128p. (gr. 3-4). pap. 12.00 *(978-1-55704-781-6(2)*, William Morrow Paperbacks) HarperCollins Pubs.

McManus, Valerie Rainon. A Look in the Mirror: Freeing Yourself from the Body Image Blues. 2004. 110p. pap. 14.95 *(978-0-87868-897-5(8)*, 8978, Child & Family Pr.) Child Welfare League of America, Inc.

Meredith, Susan. Growing Up. 2004. (Facts of Life Ser.). 56p. (J). pap. 7.95 *(978-0-7945-0764-0(6)*, Usborne) EDC Publishing.

Parker, Steve. Tell Me How Does My Body Fit Together? And More about the Human Body. 2004. (Illus.). 32p. (J). pap. *(978-1-84458-058-3(X)*, Pavilion Children's Books) Pavilion Bks.

Spearman, David. What Will I Grow up to Be?, 1 vol. Spearman, Davidx & Spearman, Terry, illus. 2009. 34p. pap. 24.95 *(978-1-60749-728-8(X))* America Star Bks.

Thomasson, Merry F. Hey, Look at Me! Baby Days. Kopald, Sue-Anne, illus. (Hey, Look at Me! Ser.). (J). *(978-1-882607-06-8(6))* Merrybooks & More.

CHILDREN—HEALTH AND HYGIENE

Here are entered general works on the physical care of children. Works limited to their physical care in school are entered under School Hygiene.

see also Babysitters; Children—Diseases; Health Education; School Nursing

Acosta, Jamey & Apodaca, Blanca. Miss Molly's Dolly, 1 vol. 2010. (Early Childhood Themes Ser.). (ENG., Illus.). 16p. (J). (gr. -1-2). pap. 19.99 *(978-1-4333-1813-9(X))*; pap. 6.99 *(978-1-4333-1812-2(1))* Shell Educational Publishing.

Ajmera, Maya, et al. Healthy Kids. 2013. (ENG., Illus.). 32p. (J). (gr. -1-3). pap. 7.95 *(978-1-58089-437-1(2))*; lib. bdg. 17.95 *(978-1-58089-436-4(4))* Charlesbridge Publishing, Inc.

Amos, Janine. Going to the Hospital. 2009. (Changes Ser.). (Illus.). 32p. (J). (gr. k-2). 22.60 *(978-1-60754-484-5(9))*; (gr. 2-5). pap. 10.55 *(978-1-60754-486-9(5))* Windmill Bks.

Ann Chambers Bsdh Ms. Monty Molar & Friends. 2008. 64p. pap. 31.99 *(978-1-4363-0764-2(3))* Xlibris Corp.

Barber, Nicola. Going to the Hospital. 2009. (Big Day! Ser.). 24p. (J). (gr. k-2). (ENG., Illus.). pap. 8.25 *(978-1-4358-2896-4(8))*; lib. bdg. 22.60 *(978-1-4358-2840-7(2))* Rosen Publishing Group, Inc., The. (PowerKids Pr.).

Barnes, Mary K. Is Today A Stay at Home Day? 2010. 30p. 14.99 *(978-0-557-46691-7(1))* Lulu Pr., Inc.

Becker, Lynne, creator. Me Too Mommy. 2004. (J). spiral bd. 11.95 *(978-0-9748889-0-3(7))* Lynne Ellen, Inc.

Benett, Janet M. IJustWantTo SLEEP for KIDS. Kater, Mary, ed. Linke, Donald Q., Jr., illus. 2005. (J). 56.97 net. *(978-0-9744357-0-1(8))* IJustWantToSleep, Inc.

Bennett, Howard J. Harry Goes to the Hospital: A Story for Children about What It's Like to Be in the Hospital. Weber, M. S., illus. 2008. 32p. (J). (gr. -1-3). 14.95 *(978-1-4338-0319-2(4))*; pap. 9.95 *(978-1-4338-0320-8(8))* American Psychological Assn. (Magination Pr.).

Berry, Joy. Illness. 2009. (ENG.). 40p. (J). (gr. k — 1). bds. 7.95 *(978-1-60577-012-3(4))* Berry, Joy Enterprises.

—Teach Me about Bathtime. 2009. (ENG.). 40p. (J). (gr. k — 1). bds. 7.95 *(978-1-60577-008-6(6))* Berry, Joy Enterprises.

Birch, Ann. Head Lice up Close 6 Pack. 2004. pap. 40.50 *(978-1-4109-1154-4(3))* Harcourt Schl. Pubs.

A Boy's Guide to Growing up. 2005. (Illus.). tchr. ed. 22.95 *(978-1-55942-210-9(6))* Witcher Productions.

Brew Ed.D., Ranelle L. Healthy Days. 2013. 24p. pap. 10.96 *(978-1-4669-6005-3(1))* Trafford Publishing.

Cider Mill Press Staff & Copeland, Cynthia L. Secrets of Middle School: Everything You Need to Succeed. 2010. (ENG.). 144p. (J). pap. 12.95 *(978-1-60433-195-0(X)*, Applesauce Pr.) Cider Mill Pr. Bk. Pubs., LLC.

Cleland, Jo. Clean Hands, Dirty Hands. 2012. (ENG.). 24p. (gr. k-2). pap. 8.95 *(978-1-61810-213-3(3))* Rourke Educational Media.

—Clean Teeth, Dirty Teeth. 2012. (ENG.). 24p. (gr. k-2). pap. 8.95 *(978-1-61810-215-7(X))* Rourke Educational Media.

—Fabulous Food. 2012. (ENG.). 24p. (gr. k-2). pap. 8.95 *(978-1-61810-217-1(6))* Rourke Educational Media.

Cox, Judith. The Wellness Tree. Rogers, Denny, illus. 2003. (ENG.). 32p. (J). (gr. k-4). 19.95 *(978-1-878044-29-7(X))* Mayhaven Publishing, Inc.

Desalle, Nicole. I Am Clean, Healthy. 2011. pap. 39.95 *(978-0-7664-3748-7(5))* Abrams & Co. Pubs., Inc.

Duckworth, Katie. Health. 2004. (Children's Rights Ser.). (J). lib. bdg. 27.10 *(978-1-58340-420-1(1))* Black Rabbit Bks.

Dunham, Kelli. The Boy's Body Book. 4th rev. ed. 2017. (ENG.). 148p. (J). pap. 12.95 ***(978-1-60433-713-6(3)***, Applesauce Pr.) Cider Mill Pr. Bk. Pubs., LLC.

Edwards, Hazel & Alexander, Goldie. Talking about the Dangers of Taking Risks. 2010. (Healthy Living Ser.). (Illus.). 32p. (YA). (gr. 3-6). lib. bdg. 26.00 *(978-1-4339-3659-3(3))* Stevens, Gareth Publishing LLLP.

Eneas, Celeste. My Body, My Temple. 2012. 22p. pap. 17.99 *(978-1-62230-590-2(6))* Salem Author Services.

Etingoff, Kim. Healthy Alternatives to Sweets & Snacks. Borus, Joshua, ed. 2013. (Understanding Nutrition: a Gateway to Physical & Mental Health Ser.: 11). (Illus.). 48p. (J). (gr. 5-18). 19.95 *(978-1-4222-2878-4(9))* Mason Crest.

—Healthy Fast Foods. Borus, Joshua, ed. 2013. (Understanding Nutrition: a Gateway to Physical & Mental Health Ser.: 11). (Illus.). 48p. (J). (gr. 5-18). 19.95 *(978-1-4222-2879-1(7))* Mason Crest.

Fretland VanVoorst, Jenny. Therapy Cats, Dogs, & Rabbits. 2013. (We Work! Animals with Jobs Ser.). 24p. (J). (gr. -1-3). lib. bdg. 21.32 *(978-1-61772-895-2(0))* Bearport Publishing Co., Inc.

Galvin, Matthew. Clouds & Clocks: A Story for Children Who Soil. 2nd ed. 2007. (Illus.). 32p. (J). (gr. 3-7). 14.95 *(978-1-59147-733-4(6))*; per. 9.95 *(978-1-59147-734-1(4))* American Psychological Assn. (Magination Pr.).

Giles, Sophie. The Children's Book of Healthy Habits. Davies, Kate, illus. 2014. (ENG.). 40p. (J). pap. 10.00 *(978-1-84135-972-4(6))* Award Pubns. Ltd. GBR. Dist: Parkwest Pubns., Inc.

Gogerly, Liz. Looking after Me. Gordon, Mike, illus. 2008. (ENG.). 32p. (J). (gr. -1-3). *(978-0-7787-4109-1(5))* Crabtree Publishing Co.

—Teeth. Gordon, Mike, illus. 2008. (Looking after Me Ser.). (ENG.). 32p. (J). (gr. -1-3). pap. *(978-0-7787-4122-0(2))*; lib. bdg. *(978-0-7787-4115-2(X))* Crabtree Publishing Co.

Green, Tammy L., et al. Ruby Explores the World of Wellnss. 2005. (ENG., Illus.). 88p. (gr. k-5). stu. ed. 20.00 *(978-0-7360-6229-9(7))* Human Kinetics Pubs.

—Ruby Learns about the World of Wellness. 2005. (ENG., Illus.). 88p. (gr. k-5). stu. ed. 20.00 *(978-0-7360-6228-2(9))* Human Kinetics Pubs.

—Sydney Travels Through the World of Wellness. 2005. (ENG., Illus.). 88p. (gr. k-5). stu. ed. 20.00 *(978-0-7360-6232-9(7))* Human Kinetics Pubs.

—T. J.'s Adventures in the World of Wellness. 2005. (ENG., Illus.). 88p. (gr. k-5). stu. ed. 20.00 *(978-0-7360-6231-2(9))* Human Kinetics Pubs.

Health Watch, 14 bks., Set. Incl. Alzheimer's Disease. Gold, Susan Dudley. (YA). 2000. lib. bdg. 23.93 *(978-0-7660-1650-7(1))*; Arthritis. Gold, Susan Dudley. (YA). 2001. lib. bdg. 23.93 *(978-0-7660-1659-0(5))*; Asthma. Gold, Susan Dudley. (J). 2000. lib. bdg. 23.93 *(978-0-7660-1656-9(0))*; Attention Deficit Disorder. Gold, Susan Dudley. (YA). 2000. lib. bdg. 23.93 *(978-0-7660-1657-6(9))*; Bipolar Disorder & Depression. Gold, Susan Dudley. (J). 2000. lib. bdg. 25.27 *(978-0-7660-1654-5(4))*; Cancer. Gold, John Coopersmith. (YA). 2001. lib. bdg. 23.93 *(978-0-7660-1652-1(8))*; Cerebral Palsy. Gold, John Coopersmith. (YA). 2001. lib. bdg. 23.93 *(978-0-7660-1663-7(3))*; Cystic Fibrosis. Gold, Susan Dudley. (YA). 2000. lib. bdg. 23.93 *(978-0-7660-1655-2(2))*; Diabetes. Semple, Carol McCormick. (YA). 2000. lib. bdg. 23.93 *(978-0-7660-1660-6(9))*; Epilepsy. Dudley, Mark Edward. (YA). 2001. lib. bdg. 23.93 *(978-0-7660-1661-3(7))*; Heart Disease. Gold, John Coopersmith. (YA). 2000. lib. bdg. 23.93 *(978-0-7660-1653-8(6))*; Multiple Sclerosis. Gold, Susan Dudley. (YA). 2001. lib. bdg. 23.93 *(978-0-7660-1658-3(7))*; Muscular Dystrophy. Burnett, Gail Lemley. (YA). 2000. lib. bdg. 23.93 *(978-0-7660-1651-4(X))*; Sickle Cell Disease. Gold, Susan Dudley. (YA). 2001. lib. bdg. 23.93 *(978-0-7660-1662-0(5))*; 48p. (gr. 4-10). (Illus.). Set lib. bdg. 265.30 *(978-0-7660-1606-4(4))* Enslow Pubs., Inc.

Himmelreich, Cheri. Does It Hurt? 2013. 56p. (J). pap. 14.99 *(978-1-59713-114-8(8))* Goose River Pr.

Holness, Allison. Bath Time. 2009. 16p. pap. 9.49 *(978-1-4389-8283-0(6))* AuthorHouse.

Hulme, Janet A. Bladder & Bowel Issues for Kids: A Handy Guide for Kids Ages 4-12. 2003. (Illus.). 92p. pap. 14.95 *(978-1-928812-05-0(8)*, 4000-07) Phoenix Publishing.

Kalman, Bobbie. Mi Cuerpo Sano. 2010. (SPA & ENG.). 16p. (J). pap. *(978-0-7787-8583-5(1))*; lib. bdg. *(978-0-7787-8557-6(2))* Crabtree Publishing Co.

—My Healthy Body. 2010. (My World Ser.). (ENG., Illus.). 16p. (J). (gr. k-2). pap. *(978-0-7787-9471-4(7))* Crabtree Publishing Co.

Keeping Healthy. 2010. (Keeping Healthy Ser.). 24p. lib. bdg. 95.96 *(978-1-4296-5194-3(6)*, Pebble Plus) Capstone Press of Coughlan Cos.

Kern, Merilee A. Making Healthy Choices: A Story to Inspire Fit, Weight-Wise Kids (Boys' Edition) 2007. (J). pap. 11.95 *(978-1-58736-742-7(4))* Wheatmark, Inc.

—Making Healthy Choices: A Story to Inspire Fit, Weight-Wise Kids (Girls' Edition) 2007. (J). pap. 11.95 *(978-1-58736-743-4(2))* Wheatmark, Inc.

Lanser, Amanda. School Lunches: Healthy Choices vs. Crowd Pleasers. 2015. (Perspectives Flip Books: Issues Ser.). (ENG.). 64p. (gr. 5-6). 33.99 *(978-0-7565-4993-0(0))* Compass Point Bks.

Leaf, Munro. Brushing Your Teeth Can Be Fun: And Lots of Other Good Ideas for How to Grow up Healthy, Strong, & Smart. 2008. (ENG., Illus.). 56p. (J). (gr. k-4). 14.95 *(978-0-7893-1594-6(7))* Universe Publishing.

Lorig, Steffanie. Oodles de Doodles. 2005. Orig. Title: Oodles of Doodles. (SPA., Illus.). 48p. (YA). (gr. 2-18). 10.95 *(978-0-9715240-3-3(3))* Art With Heart Press.

Lynette, Rachel. What to Do When Your Family Can't Afford Health Care. 2010. (Let's Work It Out Ser.). 24p. (ENG.). (J). pap. 8.25 *(978-1-4358-9772-4(2)*, PowerKids Pr.); (Illus.). (YA). (gr. 2-5). lib. bdg. 22.60 *(978-1-4358-9342-9(5))* Rosen Publishing Group, Inc., The.

Marsico, Katie. Visit the Doctor! 2015. (21st Century Junior Library: Your Healthy Body Ser.). (ENG., Illus.). 24p. (J). (gr. 2-5). 27.07 *(978-1-63188-985-1(0)*, 205852) Cherry Lake Publishing.

Mattern, Joanne. Eating Lunch at School. 2006. (My Day at School Ser.). 24p. (gr. k-3). pap. 8.15 *(978-0-8368-6791-6(2))*; (Illus.). lib. bdg. 22.00 *(978-0-8368-6784-8(X))* Stevens, Gareth Publishing LLLP. (Weekly Reader Leveled Readers).

McAlpine, Margaret. Working with Children. 2004. (My Future Career Ser.). (Illus.). 64p. (gr. 3-7). lib. bdg. 27.00 *(978-0-8368-4241-8(3)*, Gareth Stevens Learning Library) Stevens, Gareth Publishing LLLP.

Miller, Edward. The Tooth Book: A Guide to Healthy Teeth & Gums. Miller, Edward, illus. 2009. (ENG., Illus.). 32p. (J). (gr. -1-3). pap. 7.99 *(978-0-8234-2206-7(2))* Holiday Hse., Inc.

Mills Inc. Letters to Antonio Andrew Anderson from His Mother. Steinhardt, Marge, illus. 2011. 36p. pap. 35.95 *(978-1-258-10331-6(1))* Literary Licensing, LLC.

Minden, Cecilia. Lunch by the Numbers. 2007. (21st Century Skills Library: Real World Math Ser.). (ENG., Illus.). 32p. (gr. 4-8). lib. bdg. 28.50 *(978-1-60279-012-4(4)*, 200066) Cherry Lake Publishing.

MINJA, ADVELINE J. A Clean Kid Is A Healthier Kid. 2007. 56p. pap. 22.95 *(978-1-4357-0392-6(8))* Lulu Pr., Inc.

Montanari, Donata. Children Around the World. Montanari, Donata, illus. 2004. (Around the World Ser.). (ENG., Illus.). 32p. (J). (gr. -1-2). pap. 8.99 *(978-1-55337-684-2(6))* Kids Can Pr., Ltd. CAN. Dist: Hachette Bk. Group.

Nelson, Robin. Staying Safe in Emergencies. 2006. (Pull Ahead Books: Health Ser.). (ENG., Illus.). 32p. (gr. k-3). lib. bdg. 22.60 *(978-0-8225-3391-7(X))* Lerner Publishing Group.

Nygard, Bonnie K., et al. Cody Investigates the World of Wellness. 2005. (ENG., Illus.). 88p. (gr. k-5). stu. ed. 20.00 *(978-0-7360-6230-5(0))* Human Kinetics Pubs.

—WOW! Sydney Travels Through the World of Wellness. 2005. (ENG., Illus.). 88p. (gr. k-5). pap., stu. ed. 12.00 *(978-0-7360-5580-2(0))* Human Kinetics Pubs.

Petrikowski, Nicki Peter. Teen Life 411: Set 3. 2015. (Teen Life 411 Ser.). (ENG.). 112p. (J). (gr. 6-7). 213.60 *(978-1-4994-6190-9(9)*, Rosen Young Adult) Rosen Publishing Group, Inc., The.

Phillips, Jennifer. Tucker's Strength. 2008. 28p. pap. 24.95 *(978-1-60813-376-5(1))* America Star Bks.

Rabe, Tish. Oh, the Things You Can Do That Are Good for You! All about Staying Healthy. Ruiz, Aristides, illus. 2015. (Cat in the Hat's Learning Library). (ENG.). 64p. (J). (gr. k-3). lib. bdg. 13.99 *(978-0-375-91098-2(0)*, Random Hse. Bks. for Young Readers) Random Hse. Children's Bks.

Rosa-Mendoza, Gladys. I Take Care of Myself!/Me Se Cuidar! Powell, Luciana Navarro, illus. 2007. (English Spanish Foundations Ser.). (ENG & SPA.). 20p. (J). (gr. -1-k). bds. 6.95 *(978-1-931398-22-0(4))* Me+Mi Publishing.

Rosen Publishing Staff. Teen Life 411: Set 2, 1 vol. 2015. (Teen Life 411 Ser.). (ENG.). 112p. (YA). 284.80 *(978-1-4777-7988-0(4)*, Rosen Young Adult) Rosen Publishing Group, Inc., The.

Rothenberg, Annye. I Like to Eat Treats. Wenzel, David T., illus. 2010. 48p. (J). pap. 9.95 *(978-0-9790420-2-7(X))* Perfecting Parenting Pr.

Salzmann, Mary Elizabeth. Healthy Habits. 2004. (Healthy Habits Ser.: 5). (ENG., Illus.). 24p. (J). (gr. k-3). lib. bdg. 121.05 *(978-1-59197-549-6(2)*, SandCastle) ABDO Publishing Co.

Schaefer, Adam. Mantenerse Sano, 1 vol. 2010. (Salud y el Estado Fisico Ser.). (SPA.). 32p. (gr. 1-3). 27.32 *(978-1-4329-4445-2(2))*; pap. 8.29 *(978-1-4329-4450-6(9))* Heinemann-Raintree.

Scheunemann, Pam. Cool Jobs for Kids Who Like Kids: Ways to Make Money Working with Children, 1 vol. 2011. (Cool Kid Jobs Ser.). (ENG.). 32p. (gr. 3-6). 28.50 *(978-1-61613-196-8(9)*, Checkerboard Library) ABDO Publishing Co.

Sharma, Kavita. Healthy Happy Me: Easy-Peasy Guide to Awesome Health. 2016. (ENG.). 28p. pap. *(978-81-7993-368-8(7))* Energy and Resources Institute, The IND. Dist: Motilal (UK) Bks. of India.

SHARP Literacy, compiled by. Growing up Strong: Healthy Children can Change the World. 2010. 130p. (J). pap. 18.00 *(978-0-9770816-8-4(0))* SHARP Literacy, Inc.

Shoveller, Herb. Ryan & Jimmy: And the Well in Africa That Brought Them Together. 2008. (CitizenKid Ser.). (ENG., Illus.). 56p. (J). (gr. 3-7). pap. 9.95 *(978-1-55453-271-1(X))* Kids Can Pr., Ltd. CAN. Dist: Hachette Bk. Group.

Sjonger, Rebecca. Stress Less! A Kid's Guide to Managing Emotions. 2015. (ENG., Illus.). 24p. (J). *(978-0-7787-1882-6(4))* Crabtree Publishing Co.

—You Need Rest to Be at Your Best! 2015. (ENG., Illus.). 24p. (J). *(978-0-7787-1881-9(6))* Crabtree Publishing Co.

Suen, Anastasia. Getting a Job in Child Care. 2013. (Job Basics: Getting the Job You Need Ser.). 80p. (YA). (gr. 9-12). 33.25 *(978-1-4488-9612-7(6))* Rosen Publishing Group, Inc., The.

Take Care of Your Skin, Hair & Nails! With Annie Funelli & the Funsters. 2003. (Lessons for a Healthy Childhood Ser.). (J). (gr. k-3). instr.'s gde. ed. 69.95 *(978-1-55942-195-9(9)*, 9236V9) Witcher Productions.

Vestergaard, Hope. Potty Animals: What to Know When You've Gotta Go! Petrone, Valeria, illus. 2010. (ENG.). 32p. (J). (gr. -1-1). 14.95 *(978-1-4027-5996-3(7))* Sterling Publishing Co., Inc.

Vogel, Elizabeth. ¡A hacer ejercicio! (Let's Exercise) 2009. (Limpieza y salud todo el día (Clean & Healthy All Day Long) Ser.). (SPA.). 24p. (gr. 1-1). 37.50 *(978-1-61514-291-0(6)*, Editorial Buenas Letras) Rosen Publishing Group, Inc., The.

—¡A lavarse las manos! (Washing My Hands) 2009. (Limpieza y salud todo el día (Clean & Healthy All Day Long) Ser.). (SPA.). 24p. (gr. 1-1). 37.50 *(978-1-61514-292-7(4)*, Editorial Buenas Letras) Rosen Publishing Group, Inc., The.

—Let's Exercise = a Hacer Ejercicio. 2004. (Limpieza y salud todo el Día Ser.). (ENG & SPA., Illus.). 24p. (J). lib. bdg. 18.75 *(978-0-8239-6615-8(1)*, Editorial Buenas Letras) Rosen Publishing Group, Inc., The.

—Let's Exercise / ¡A hacer Ejercicio! 2009. (Clean & Healthy All Day Long / Limpieza y salud todo el día Ser.). (SPA.). 24p. (gr. 1-1). 37.50 *(978-1-61511-871-7(3)*, Editorial Buenas Letras) Rosen Publishing Group, Inc., The.

Weber, Rebecca. Healthy Habits, 1 vol. 2011. (Health & Your Body Ser.). (ENG.). 24p. (gr. k-1). pap. 7.29 *(978-1-4296-7127-9(0))*; pap. 41.70 *(978-1-4296-7133-0(5))* Capstone Press of Coughlan Cos. (Pebble Plus).

CHILDREN—MANAGEMENT

see Child Rearing

CHILDREN—NORTH AMERICA

Ellis, Deborah. Looks Like Daylight, 1 vol. 2013. (ENG., Illus.). 256p. (J). (gr. 6). 15.95 *(978-1-55498-120-5(4))* Groundwood Bks. CAN. Dist: Publishers Group West (PGW).

CHILDREN—PICTORIAL WORKS

Ajmera, Maya & Ivanko, John D. To Be a Kid. 2004. (ENG., Illus.). 26p. (J). (-k). bds. 7.95 *(978-1-57091-371-6(4))* Charlesbridge Publishing, Inc.

Brecon, Connah. Tomorrow. 2005. (Illus.). 32p. (J). (gr. -1-7). *(978-0-7344-0730-6(0)*, Lothian Children's Bks.) Hachette Australia.

Griffin, Starla. Girl, 13: A Global Snapshot of Generation E. 2004. (Illus.). 240p. (J). pap. *(978-1-59258-112-2(9))* Hylas Publishing.

Kerley, Barbara. One World, One Day. 2009. (Barbara Kerley Photo Inspirations Ser.). (ENG., Illus.). 48p. (J). (gr. -1-3). lib. bdg. 26.90 *(978-1-4263-0461-3(7)*, National Geographic Children's Bks.) National Geographic Society.

Kerley, Barbara & National Geographic Kids Staff. One World, One Day. 2009. (Barbara Kerley Photo Inspirations Ser.). (ENG., Illus.). 48p. (J). (gr. -1-3). 17.95 *(978-1-4263-0460-6(9)*, National Geographic Children's Bks.) National Geographic Society.

Popper, Garry. Winston in the Caribbean. Johnson, Andi, illus. 2004. 36p. (gr. -1-7). 4.00 *(978-1-84161-061-0(5))* Ravette Publishing, Ltd. GBR. Dist: Parkwest Pubns., Inc.

CHILDREN—PSYCHOLOGY

see Child Psychology

CHILDREN—RELIGIOUS LIFE

Adams, Michelle Medlock. Why I Trust You, God. Munger, Nancy, illus. 2006. 20p. (J). (gr. -1). bds. 5.49 *(978-0-7586-0913-7(2))* Concordia Publishing Hse.

Alexander, Pat & Box, Su. The Lion First Bible & Prayers, 2 vols. Baxter, Leon, illus. 2016. (ENG.). 608p. (J). (gr. k-3). 16.99 *(978-0-7459-6493-5(1))* Lion Hudson PLC GBR. Dist: Independent Pubs. Group.

Anthony, Michelle. The Big God Story, 1 vol. Godbey, Cory, illus. 2010. (ENG.). 36p. (J). 12.99 *(978-1-4347-6454-6(0))* Cook, David C.

B&H Kids Editorial Staff. 100 Galactic Devotions: Discovering the God of the Universe. 2017. (ENG.). 208p. (J). (gr. 1-7). pap. 9.99 ***(978-1-4336-4870-0(9)***, B&H Kids) B&H Publishing Group.

Bernice, Janet. Tiny Talks: I Will Follow God's Plan for Me, Vol. 5. 2004. (J). pap. 7.95 *(978-1-55517-815-4(4))* Cedar Fort, Inc./CFI Distribution.

Bird, Rebecca. My Sunday Quiet Book. 2017. (ENG.). (J). pap. 39.99 ***(978-1-4621-1936-3(0))*** Cedar Fort, Inc./CFI Distribution.

Brandt, Catharine. We Light the Candles: Devotions Related to Family Use of the Advent Wreath. 2004. 40p. 5.99 *(978-0-8066-1544-8(3)*, 10-15443, Augsburg Bks.) Augsburg Fortress, Pubs.

Bryant, Wanda. This Time & Place We Live, 1 vol. 2009. 48p. pap. 16.95 *(978-1-4489-8677-4(X))* America Star Bks.

Carlson, Amie. Manners Matter! 2016. (Lift-The-Flap Ser.). (ENG., Illus.). 16p. (J). pap. 7.99 *(978-1-4964-1580-6(9)*, Tyndale Kids) Tyndale Hse. Pubs.

Countryman, Jack & Parker, Amy. God's Promises for Boys, 1 vol. 2010. (ENG.). 128p. (gr. 1-5). 12.99 *(978-1-4003-1592-5(1))* Nelson, Thomas Inc.

—God's Promises for Girls, 1 vol. 2010. (ENG.). 128p. (gr. 1-5). 12.99 *(978-1-4003-1591-8(3))* Nelson, Thomas Inc.

David, Juliet. Candle Prayers for Toddlers & Candle Bible for Toddlers, 2 vols. Prole, Helen, illus. 2009. (Candle Bible for Toddlers Ser.). 528p. (J). 24.99 *(978-0-8254-7380-7(2)*, Candle Bks.) Lion Hudson PLC GBR. Dist: Kregel Pubns.

—99 Prayers for Children, 1 vol. Ellis, Elina, illus. 2015. (ENG.). 96p. (J). 9.99 *(978-1-78128-191-8(2)*, Candle Bks.) Lion Hudson PLC GBR. Dist: Kregel Pubns.

David, Juliet & Freedman, Claire. Candle Bible & Prayers for Kids, 1 vol. Parry, Jo, illus. 2016. (ENG.). 528p. (J). 24.99 *(978-1-78128-274-8(9)*, Candle Bks.) Lion Hudson PLC GBR. Dist: Kregel Pubns.

Demars, Sue. Jesus Loves You More. 2009. 20p. pap. 10.95 *(978-1-60860-695-5(3)*, Eloquent Bks.) Strategic Book Publishing & Rights Agency (SBPRA).

Demi. Talking to God: Prayers for Children from the World's Religions. 2017. (ENG., Illus.). 36p. (J). (gr. k-3). 17.95 ***(978-1-937786-69-4(2)***, Wisdom Tales) World Wisdom, Inc.

Donaghy, Thomas J. Joyful Prayers. 2009. (St. Joseph Board Bks.). (Illus.). 12p. bds. 5.95 *(978-0-89942-663-1(8))* Catholic Bk. Publishing Corp.

Doward, Jan S. Sweeeet! God's Awesome Plan for You. 2010. (J). pap. 15.99 *(978-0-8280-2510-2(X))* Review & Herald Publishing Assn.

Elkins, Stephen. Just Like Jesus Bible Storybook. 2015. (Wonder Kids Ser.). (ENG.). 176p. (J). 14.99 *(978-1-4964-0821-1(7))* Tyndale Hse. Pubs.

Elliott, Rebecca. God Bless This Starry Night. Elliott, Rebecca, illus. 2016. (ENG., Illus.). 5p. (J). (— 1). bds. 7.99 *(978-0-7459-6558-1(X))* Lion Hudson PLC GBR. Dist: Independent Pubs. Group.

—God Loves Little Me. Elliott, Rebecca, illus. 2016. (ENG., Illus.). 10p. (J). (— 1). bds. 7.99 *(978-0-7459-6559-8(8))* Lion Hudson PLC GBR. Dist: Independent Pubs. Group.

Ellis, Gwen. Our Daily Bread: Prayers, Graces, & Slices of Scripture. 2006. (ENG., Illus.). 10p. (J). (gr. -1-k). bds. 10.99 *(978-0-7847-1852-0(0)*, B&H Kids) B&H Publishing Group.

Ellis, Gwen & Cowman, L. B. Streams in the Desert(r) for Kids: 366 Devotions to Bring Comfort, 1 vol. 2009. (ENG.). 384p. (J). pap. 12.99 *(978-0-310-71600-6(4))* Zonderkidz.

Ennis, Pat. Becoming a Young Woman Who Pleases God: A Teen's Guide to Discovering Her Biblical Potential. 2009. (Illus.). 160p. pap. 14.99 *(978-1-59669-240-4(5))* New Hope Pubs.

Fernandez, Cecilia Fau. Dios Me Escucha: Oraciones en Rima para Ninos. Kroeger, Vanesa, illus. 2007. (SPA.). 48p. (J). lib. bdg. 8.99 *(978-0-7586-1248-9(6))* Concordia Publishing Hse.

Frazee, Randy. Believe Storybook: Think, Act, Be Like Jesus, 1 vol. Adams, Steve, illus. 2015. (ENG.). 256p. (J). 19.99 *(978-0-310-74590-7(X))* Zonderkidz.

Freedman, Claire. Candle Prayers for Kids, 1 vol. Parry, Jo, illus. 2014. (ENG.). 128p. (J). 12.99 *(978-1-78128-102-4(5)*, Candle Bks.) Lion Hudson PLC GBR. Dist: Kregel Pubns.

George, Jim. A Boy after God's Own Heart Action Devotional. 2017. (ENG.). 160p. (J). 9.99 *(978-0-7369-6751-8(6))* Harvest Hse. Pubs.

Glenn, Lauren J. Where Is God. 2005. (J). bds. 6.99 *(978-0-9772459-0-1(X))* Glenn, Lauren.

Godfrey, Jan, et al. Mi Biblia para la Hora de Dormir. Doherty, Paula, illus. 2015. (SPA.). 96p. (J). 14.99 *(978-1-4143-9874-7(3))* Tyndale Hse. Pubs.

Gudmundson, C. J. When I Take the Sacrament, I Remember Jesus. Tenney, Shawna J. C., illus. 2012. (J). *(978-1-62108-020-6(X))* Covenant Communications, Inc.

Hall, Annalisa. I Want to Be Baptized. Egbert, Corey, illus. 2014. 14.99 *(978-1-4621-1461-0(X))* Cedar Fort, Inc./CFI Distribution.

Halverson, Delia Touchton. Oak Street Chonicles & the Good News: Everyday Life & Christian Faith. Dotts, M. Franklin, ed. (Illus.). 48p. (Orig.). (J). pap., tchr. ed. 4.95 *(978-0-687-75340-6(6))* Abingdon Pr.

Henry, Deborah, ed. My Devotions: Fifty Years. 50th anniv. ed. 2008. 368p. (J). 12.99 *(978-0-7586-1593-0(0))* Concordia Publishing Hse.

Hill-Sullivan, Shunice. Son, Do You Know How Truly Blessed You Are? 2009. 24p. pap. 12.95 *(978-1-4490-0011-0(8))* AuthorHouse.

Holmes, Andy & Voltz, Ralph. Biblia para Mi, 1 vol. 2004.Tr. of Bible for Me. (SPA., Illus.). 48p. 12.99 *(978-0-88113-785-9(5))* Grupo Nelson.

Howell, Troy, illus. First Prayers: A Celebration of Faith & Love. 2012. (ENG.). 32p. (J). 12.95 *(978-1-4027-6454-7(5))* Sterling Publishing Co., Inc.

I Can Follow Jesus. 2014. (Happy Day Ser.). (ENG., Illus.). 16p. (J). pap. 2.49 *(978-1-4143-9419-0(5))* Tyndale Hse. Pubs.

Icilda. God Made Me Perfect & Wonderful: To Do What? 2009. 28p. pap. 13.99 *(978-1-4490-4545-6(6))* AuthorHouse.

Ingell, Jessica. Mommy Does God See Me? 2009. 28p. pap. 17.99 *(978-1-4490-3966-0(9))* AuthorHouse.

Kennedy, Pamela & Brady, Anne Kennedy. Five-Minute Bible Devotions for Children: Stories from the New Testament. Wummer, Amy, illus. 2012. 48p. (J). spiral bd. 15.99 *(978-0-8249-5644-8(3)*, Ideal Pubns.) Worthy Publishing.

MacKenzie, Erin. Promise Comics - Issue 1. Nummela, Pam, ed. Halbleib, Michael, illus. 2017. (ENG.). (J). pap. 1.49 ***(978-0-7586-5742-8(0))*** Concordia Publishing Hse.

McDowell, Josh & Johnson, Kevin. The Great Treasure Quest. Jones, Buck, illus. 2006. 103p. (J). (gr. 3-7). per. 10.99 *(978-1-932587-85-2(3))* Practical Christianity Foundation.

Merritt, James. 52 Weeks with Jesus for Kids: A Devotional for Tweens. 2016. (ENG.). 112p. (J). pap. 10.99 *(978-0-7369-6697-9(8))* Harvest Hse. Pubs.

Missions Moments. 2005. pap. 12.99 *(978-1-56309-943-4(8))* Woman's Missionary Union.

Monchamp, Genny. Shine: Choices to Make God Smile. Kaminski, Karol, illus. 2011. (J). 10.95 *(978-0-8198-7149-7(4))* Pauline Bks. & Media.

Nappa, Jon & Gosselin, Suzanne Hadley. God's Got an Answer for That Devotional. 2015. (ENG.). 96p. (J). pap. 9.99 *(978-0-7369-6123-3(2))* Harvest Hse. Pubs.

Nellist, Glenys. Snuggle Time Psalms, 1 vol. Biscoe, Cee, illus. 2016. (Snuggle Time Ser.). (ENG.). 30p. (J). bds. 9.99 *(978-0-310-74925-7(5))* Zonderkidz.

O'Brien, Kathryn. Be Still. Flint, Gillian, illus. 2016. (Sit for a Bit Ser.). (ENG.). 40p. (J). 14.99 *(978-1-4964-1116-7(1))* Tyndale Hse. Pubs.

—Give Thanks. Flint, Gillian, illus. 2016. (Sit for a Bit Ser.). (ENG.). 40p. (J). 14.99 *(978-1-4964-1118-1(8))* Tyndale Hse. Pubs.

—I Can. Flint, Gillian, illus. 2016. (Sit for a Bit Ser.). (ENG.). 40p. (J). 14.99 *(978-1-4964-1117-4(X))* Tyndale Hse. Pubs.

O'Keefe, Kathy Della Torre. Child's Guide to the Beatitudes. 2011. (Illus.). 32p. (J). *(978-0-8091-6756-2(5))* Paulist Pr.

Omartian, Stormie. The Power of a Praying Kid. 2015. (Power of a Praying Kid Ser.). (ENG.). 112p. (J). pap. 10.99 *(978-0-7369-6603-0(X))* Harvest Hse. Pubs.

Peckham, Lori, ed. Guide's Greatest Grace Stories. 2008. 160p. pap. 11.99 *(978-0-8280-2390-0(5))* Review & Herald Publishing Assn.

—Guide's Greatest Narrow Escape Stories. 2008. (Pathfinder Junior Book Club Ser.). 160p. (J). (gr. 5-9). pap. 11.99 *(978-0-8280-2040-4(X))* Review & Herald Publishing Assn.

Piper, Sophie. First Prayers for Baby. Spenceley, Annabel, illus. 2016. (ENG.). 48p. (J). (— 1). 12.99 *(978-0-7459-7665-5(4))* Lion Hudson PLC GBR. Dist: Independent Pubs. Group.

—Prayers & Verses for a Child's Baptism. Williams, Sophy, illus. 2016. (ENG.). 64p. (J). (-k). 14.99 *(978-0-7459-7615-0(8))* Lion Hudson PLC GBR. Dist: Independent Pubs. Group.

Power Twins Handbook Volume One. 2006. (J). spiral bd. *(978-0-9742355-1-6(2))* Brda, Tracy.

Publications International Ltd. Staff. Gilded Treasury Bible Stories. 2006. 320p. (J). 14.98 *(978-1-4127-6337-0(1))* Phoenix International Publications, Inc.

Redford, Marjorie. My Bible Says. Marlin, Kathryn, illus. 2013. (Happy Day Ser.). (ENG.). 16p. (J). pap. 2.49 *(978-1-4143-9301-8(6))* Tyndale Hse. Pubs.

—My Bible Says. Marlin, Kathryn, illus. 2013. (Happy Day Ser.). (ENG.). 18p. (J). bds. 4.99 *(978-1-4143-9291-2(5))* Tyndale Hse. Pubs.

Ritsi, Renee. Mwangi: A Young African Boy's Journey of Faith. Thorp, Cameron, illus. 2006. 32p. (J). 17.95 *(978-1-888212-67-9(5))* Ancient Faith Publishing.

Ritter, Helen E. And a Child Shall Lead Them... 2007. pap. 12.00 *(978-0-8059-8601-3(4))* Dorrance Publishing Co., Inc.

Seifert, Sheila & Naylor, Beth. Stepping up, Stepping Out. 2008. (DSJ Ser.). (Illus.). 112p. (J). (gr. 1-6). pap. 16.99 *(978-0-7814-4562-7(0))* Cook, David C.

Seifert, Sheila, et al. Lead the Way, Jesus. 2008. (DSJ Ser.). (Illus.). 112p. (J). (gr. 1-6). pap. 16.99 *(978-0-7814-4560-3(4))* Cook, David C.

Setzer, Lee Ann. Tiny Talks #6: I will Trust in Heavenly Father & His Son, Jesus Christ-Their Promises are Sure, Vol. 6.

2005. (J). pap. 7.99 *(978-1-55517-889-5(8))* Cedar Fort, Inc./CFI Distribution.
Shivers, Holly Hawkins. I Can Learn to Pray, 1 vol. 2016. (ENG., Illus.). 224p. (J). 14.99 *(978-0-7180-8169-0(2))* Nelson, Thomas Inc.
Simmons, Justine, et al. God, Can You Hear Me? 2007. (ENG., Illus.). 32p. (gr. -1-3). 16.99 *(978-0-06-115397-6(4),* Amistad) HarperCollins Pubs.
Southall, M. Renee. My Daddy Loves Me & He Can Do Anything. 2012. 28p. pap. 19.99 *(978-1-4772-8221-2(1))* AuthorHouse.
Southern, Randy, et al. Revolution Devotional: 90 Daily Devotions for Guys, 1 vol. 2006. (Invert Ser.). (ENG., Illus.). 224p. (YA). (gr. 4-7). pap. 12.99 *(978-0-310-26706-5(4))* Zondervan.
Stahl, Daniel. Who Knows What God Knows. 2009. 28p. pap. 9.50 *(978-1-4389-5723-4(8))* AuthorHouse.
Swaim, Colleen. Lleven Su Fuego Al Mundo: Jóvenes Que Alcanzaron la Santidad. 2012. (SPA.). (J). *(978-0-7648-2176-9(8))* Liguori Pubns.
Thurman, Debbie. Hold My Heart: A Teen's Journal for Healing & Personal Growth. 2004. 112p. pap. 10.95 *(978-0-9676289-2-9(X))* Cedar Hse. Pubs.
—Sheer Faith: A Teen's Journey to Godly Growth. 2004. 112p. pap. 10.95 *(978-0-9676289-3-6(8))* Cedar Hse. Pubs.
West, Mary. He Called, I Answered. 2009. 34p. 20.00 *(978-0-578-02740-1(2))* West, Mary.
With Jesus Always. 2006. (Illus.). 29p. (J). pap. *(978-0-8215-5729-7(7))* Sadlier, William H. Inc.
Wolfe, Jaymie Stuart. Adoring Jesus with the Holy Father. 2011. (J). pap. 9.95 *(978-0-8198-0802-8(4))* Pauline Bks. & Media.
Woolley, John. I Am with You: For Young People & for Those Young at Heart. 2012. (ENG.). 111p. pap. 6.95 *(978-1-78099-089-7(8),* O Bks.) Hunt, John Publishing Ltd. GBR. Dist: National Bk. Network.
World Book, Inc Staff, contrib. by. Birth & Growing up Celebrations. 2009. (Illus.). 46p. (J). *(978-0-7166-5044-7(4))* World Bk., Inc.
Zondervan Bible Publishers (Grand Rapids, Mich.) Staff, contrib. by. The Beginner's Bible Kid-Sized Devotions, 1 vol. rev. ed. 2015. (Beginner's Bible Ser.). (ENG., Illus.). 384p. (J). 9.99 *(978-0-310-75142-7(X))* Zonderkidz.
Zondervan Staff. Everyday with God Collection, 1 vol. 2010. (I Can Read! / Mothers of Preschoolers Ser.). (ENG.). 100p. (J). pap. 19.99 *(978-0-310-71996-0(8))* Zonderkidz.

CHILDREN—SOUTH AMERICA

Lynette, Rachel. Ana Dodson: Advocate for Peruvian Orphans. 2007. (Young Heroes Ser.). (ENG., Illus.). 48p. (J). (gr. 3-7). lib. bdg. 30.50 *(978-0-7377-3865-0(0),* Kidhaven) Cengage Gale.

CHILDREN—TRAINING

see Child Rearing

CHILDREN—UNITED STATES

Andrews, Beth. I Miss You! A Military Kid's Book about Deployment. Wright, Hawley, illus. 2007. (ENG.). 56p. (J). (-k). per. 12.99 *(978-1-59102-534-4(6))* Prometheus Bks., Pubs.
Botones para el General Washington (Buttons for General Washington) 2006. (J). pap. 6.95 *(978-0-8225-6617-5(6),* Ediciones Lerner) Lerner Publishing Group.
Clayton, Lawrence. Coping with a Drug-Abusing Parent. 2003. (C). per. 34.95 *(978-0-9709523-6-3(8))* Clayro Corp.
Cohen, Laura. The Gault Case & Young People's Rights: Debating Supreme Court Decisions. 2006. (Debating Supreme Court Decisions Ser.). (Illus.). 128p. (J). (gr. 7-12). lib. bdg. 27.94 *(978-0-7660-2476-2(8))* Enslow Pubs., Inc.
Ehrlich, Amy, ed. When I Was Your Age Vol. 2: Original Stories about Growing Up. 2006. (Illus.). 187p. (YA). (gr. 8-11). reprint ed. 17.00 *(978-1-4223-5199-4(8))* DIANE Publishing Co.
Freedman, Russell. Children of the Great Depression. 2010. (ENG., Illus.). 128p. (J). (gr. 5-7). pap. 10.99 *(978-0-547-48035-0(0))* Houghton Mifflin Harcourt Publishing Co.
Glasser, Debbie & Schenck, Emily. New Kid, New Scene: A Guide to Moving & Switching Schools. 2011. (Illus.). 112p. (J). pap. 9.95 *(978-1-4338-1038-1(7),* Magination Pr.) American Psychological Assn.
Gold, Susan Dudley. In Re Gault: Do Minors Have the Same Rights as Adults? 2007. (Supreme Court Milestones Ser.). (Illus.). 128p. (gr. 7-16). lib. bdg. 42.79 *(978-0-7614-2584-7(5),* Benchmark Bks.) Marshall Cavendish Corp.
Harness, Cheryl. Our Colonial Year. Harness, Cheryl, illus. 2005. (ENG., Illus.). 40p. (J). (gr. -1-3). 16.95 *(978-0-689-83479-0(9),* Simon & Schuster Bks. For Young Readers) Simon & Schuster Bks. For Young Readers.
Hemmel, David Lee & Knutson, Janette C. Alexis' Island: Growing up in the Tropical Paradise of Key West. 2006. (J). per. 14.95 *(978-0-9745637-2-5(2))* Duval Publishing.
Hooks, Gwendolyn. If You Were a Kid During the Civil Rights Movement. 2017. (If You Were a Kid Ser.). (ENG., Illus.). 32p. (J). lib. bdg. 26.00 *(978-0-531-22384-0(1),* Children's Pr.) Scholastic Library Publishing.
Kilgour, Mary Cameron. Me May Mary. 2004. 200p. (J). pap. 13.95 *(978-1-58760-018-0(8),* Child & Family Pr.) Child Welfare League of America, Inc.
Kule, Elaine A. Beginning Again: Immigrating to America. Thermes, Jennifer, illus. 2006. 40p. *(978-1-59137-473-2(1))* Options Publishing.
Lemke, Donald B. The Schoolchildren's Blizzard. 2007. (Disasters in History Ser.). (ENG., Illus.). 32p. (gr. 3-4). 30.65 *(978-1-4296-0157-3(4),* Graphic Library) Capstone Press of Coughlan Cos.
Libal, Joyce. Somebody Hear Me Crying: Youth in Protective Services. 2003. (Youth with Special Needs Ser.). (Illus.). 127p. (YA). pap. 14.95 *(978-1-4222-0430-6(8))* Mason Crest.
Lynette, Rachel. Ana Dodson: Advocate for Peruvian Orphans. 2007. (Young Heroes Ser.). (ENG., Illus.). 48p. (J). (gr. 3-7). lib. bdg. 30.50 *(978-0-7377-3865-0(0),* Kidhaven) Cengage Gale.
MacElroy, Mary H. Work & Play in Colonial Days. reprint ed. 150.00 *(978-0-7222-6600-7(6))* Library Reprints, Inc.
Machajewski, Sarah. A Kid's Life in Colonial America, 1 vol. 2015. (ENG., Illus.). 24p. (J). lib. bdg. 23.60 *(978-1-4994-0006-9(3),* PowerKids Pr.) Rosen Publishing Group, Inc., The.
Mara, Wil. If You Were a Kid During the Civil War. 2016. (If You Were a Kid Ser.). (ENG., Illus.). 32p. (J). lib. bdg. 26.00 *(978-0-531-21969-0(0),* Children's Pr.) Scholastic Library Publishing.
—If You Were a Kid in the Thirteen Colonies. Farré, Lluís, illus. 2016. (If You Were a Kid Ser.). (ENG.). 32p. (J). lib. bdg. 26.00 *(978-0-531-21972-0(0),* Children's Pr.) Scholastic Library Publishing.
Micklos, John. The Brave Women & Children of the American Revolution. 2008. (Revolutionary War Library). (Illus.). 48p. (J). (gr. 3-4). lib. bdg. 25.27 *(978-0-7660-3019-0(9),* Enslow Elementary) Enslow Pubs., Inc.
—Courageous Children & Women of the American Revolution: Through Primary Sources. 2013. (American Revolution Through Primary Sources Ser.). 48p. (J). (gr. 4-18). 25.27 *(978-0-7660-4131-8(X))* Enslow Pubs., Inc.
Miller, Brandon Marie. Growing up in Revolution & the New Nation, 1775 to 1800. 2003. (Our America Ser.). (Illus.). 64p. (J). (gr. 4-7). lib. bdg. 26.60 *(978-0-8225-0078-0(7))* Lerner Publishing Group.
Nelson, Julie. Families Change: A Book for Children Experiencing Termination of Parental Rights. Gallagher, Mary, illus. 2006. (Kids Are Important Ser.). (ENG.). 32p. (J). (gr. -1-5). pap. 9.99 *(978-1-57542-209-1(3))* Free Spirit Publishing, Inc.
—Kids Are Important: A Book for Young Children in Foster Care. 2003. (Illus.). (J). *(978-0-9743826-1-6(2))* Lifetrack Resources.
Rhodes-Courter, Ashley. Three Little Words: A Memoir. 2009. (ENG.). 336p. (YA). (gr. 9). pap. 12.99 *(978-1-4169-4807-0(4),* Atheneum Bks. for Young Readers) Simon & Schuster Children's Publishing.
Roop, Peter & Roop, Connie. Botones Para el General Washington. Hanson, Peter E., illus. 2006. (Yo Solo - Historia (on My Own - History) Ser.).Tr. of Buttons for General Washington. (SPA.). 48p. (gr. 2-4). lib. bdg. 25.26 *(978-0-8225-6261-0(8))* Lerner Publishing Group.
Smith, Charles R., Jr. & La Raso, Carlo. I Am America. 2010. (Rise & Shine Ser.). (ENG., Illus.). 32p. (C). (gr. k-3). 30.95 *(978-0-439-43179-8(4))* National Geographic School Publishing, Inc.
Smith, Debra. Young Heroes of the Confederacy, 1 vol. 2012. (ENG., Illus.). 128p. (J). (gr. 3-7). pap. 12.95 *(978-1-4556-1684-8(2))* Pelican Publishing Co., Inc.
Snyder, Gail. Malia. 2007. (Obamas Ser.). 64p. (YA). (gr. 3-6). pap. 9.95 *(978-1-4222-1486-2(9));* (gr. 4-7). lib. bdg. 19.95 *(978-1-4222-1479-4(6))* Mason Crest.
Stewart, Sheila. Kids Have Troubles Too, 13 vols., Set. Incl. House Between Homes: Kids in the Foster Care System. Flath, Camden, told to. pap. 7.95 *(978-1-4222-1905-8(4));* I Don't Keep Secrets. Simons, Rae, told to. pap. 7.95 *(978-1-4222-1911-9(9));* I Like Me. Simons, Rae, told to. pap. 7.95 *(978-1-4222-1912-6(7));* I Live in Two Homes: Adjusting to Divorce & Remarriage. Simons, Rae, told to. pap. 7.95 *(978-1-4222-1907-2(0));* Place Called Dead. Simons, Rae, told to. (Illus.). pap. 7.95 *(978-1-4222-1914-0(3));* Sometimes My Mom Drinks Too Much. Simons, Rae, told to. (Illus.). pap. 7.95 *(978-1-4222-1917-1(8));* What's Going to Happen Next? Kids in the Juvenile Court System. Flath, Camden. pap. 7.95 *(978-1-4222-1906-5(2));* When Daddy Hit Mommy. Simons, Rae, told to. pap. 7.95 *(978-1-4222-1909-6(7));* When Life Makes Me Mad. Simons, Rae, told to. pap. 7.95 *(978-1-4222-1913-3(5));* When My Brother Went to Prison. Simons, Rae, told to. (Illus.). pap. 7.95 *(978-1-4222-1908-9(9));* When My Dad Lost His Job. Simons, Rae, told to. (Illus.). pap. 7.95 *(978-1-4222-1916-4(X));* (YA). (gr. 5-18). 2009. (Illus.). 48p. 2011. Set pap. 103.35 *(978-1-4222-1904-1(6));* Set lib. bdg. 259.35 *(978-1-4222-1691-0(8))* Mason Crest.
Stewart, Sheila & Flath, Camden. What's Going to Happen Next? Kids in the Juvenile Court System. (Kids Have Troubles Too Ser.). 48p. (YA). (gr. 5-18). 2010. (Illus.). lib. bdg. 19.95 *(978-1-4222-1693-4(4))* 2009. pap. 7.95 *(978-1-4222-1906-5(2))* Mason Crest.
Strange, Matthew. Jump Ropes, Jacks, & Endless Chores: Children's Lives in The 1800s. 2009. (Daily Life in America in the 1800s Ser.). 64p. (YA). (gr. 7-18). pap. 9.95 *(978-1-4222-1855-6(4));* lib. bdg. 22.95 *(978-1-4222-1782-5(5))* Mason Crest.
Warren, Andrea. Under Siege! Three Children at the Civil War Battle for Vicksburg. 2009. (ENG., Illus.). 176p. (YA). (gr. 4-8). 21.95 *(978-0-374-31255-8(9),* 9780374312558, Farrar, Straus & Giroux (BYR)) Farrar, Straus & Giroux.
Watkins, Christine. Are Adoption Policies Fair? 2012. (At Issue Ser.). (ENG.). 128p. (gr. 10-12). pap. 27.80 *(978-0-7377-6148-1(2),* Greenhaven Pr., Inc.) Cengage Gale.
Watkins, Christine, ed. Are Adoption Policies Fair? 2012. (At Issue Ser.). (ENG.). 128p. (J). (gr. 10-12). lib. bdg. 34.45 *(978-0-7377-6147-4(4),* Greenhaven Pr., Inc.) Cengage Gale.

CHILDREN—UNITED STATES—FICTION

Curtis, Christopher Paul & Paul, Curtis Christopher. Elias de Buxton. 2008. (SPA.). 368p. (gr. 6-12). pap. 12.99 *(978-84-441-4101-5(1))* Everest Editora ESP. Dist: Lectorum Pubns., Inc.
Hope, Laura Lee. Six Little Bunkers at Cowboy Jack's. 2007. 180p. 25.96 *(978-1-4218-3888-5(5),* 1st World Library - Literary Society) 1st World Publishing, Inc.
—Six Little Bunkers at Grandpa Ford's. 2007. 188p. 25.96 *(978-1-4218-3889-2(3),* 1st World Library - Literary Society) 1st World Publishing, Inc.
Hope, Lee Laura. Six Little Bunkers at Aunt Jo's. 2007. (ENG.). 144p. pap. 18.99 *(978-1-4346-3234-0(2));* 156p. pap. 21.99 *(978-1-4346-3235-7(0))* Creative Media Partners, LLC.
—Six Little Bunkers at Cowboy Jack's. 2007. (ENG.). 138p. pap. 18.99 *(978-1-4346-3242-5(3));* 156p. pap. 21.99 *(978-1-4346-3243-2(1))* Creative Media Partners, LLC.
Laura Lee Hope. Six Little Bunkers at Cowboy Jack's. 2007. 180p. per. 11.95 *(978-1-4218-3988-2(1),* 1st World Library - Literary Society) 1st World Publishing, Inc.
—Six Little Bunkers at Grandma Bell's. l.t. ed. 2007. (ENG.). 162p. pap. 21.99 *(978-1-4264-8193-2(4))* Creative Media Partners, LLC.
—Six Little Bunkers at Grandpa Ford's. 2007. 188p. per. 11.95 *(978-1-4218-3989-9(X),* 1st World Library - Literary Society) 1st World Publishing, Inc.

CHILDREN IN ART

Anderson, Janice. Children in Art. 2017. (Art Collections: Vol. 7). (ENG., Illus.). (YA). (gr. 9-12). 26.95 **(978-1-4222-3933-9(0))** Mason Crest.

CHILDREN OF PRESIDENTS

Besel, Jennifer M. Malia & Sasha Obama. 2012. (Star Biographies Ser.). (ENG.). 32p. (gr. 3-4). pap. 47.70 *(978-1-4296-9463-6(7),* Snap Bks.) Capstone Press of Coughlan Cos.
Connors, Kathleen. What's It Like to Be the President's Kid? 2014. (White House Insiders Ser.). 24p. (J). (gr. 2-5). 22.60 *(978-1-4824-1100-3(8))* Stevens, Gareth Publishing LLLP.
Davis, Gibbs. First Kids. Comport, Sally Wern, illus. 2009. (Step into Reading Ser.). (ENG.). 48p. (J). (gr. 2-4). pap. 3.99 *(978-0-375-82218-6(6),* Random Hse. Bks. for Young Readers) Random Hse. Children's Bks.
Doeden, Matt. Ivanka Trump: A Brand of Her Own. 2017. (Gateway Biographies Ser.). (ENG., Illus.). (J). (gr. 4-8). lib. bdg. 26.65 **(978-1-5124-8624-7(8))** Lerner Publishing Group.
Hoffman, Megan Mills. Ivanka Trump: Businesswoman & First Daughter. 2017. (J). **(978-1-5026-2701-8(9))** Cavendish Square Publishing.
Jones, Brenn. Learning about Public Service from the Life of John F. Kennedy Jr. 2009. (Character Building Book Ser.). 24p. (gr. 2-3). 42.50 *(978-1-61511-002-5(X),* PowerKids Pr.) Rosen Publishing Group, Inc., The.
Marsh, Carole. The Obama Family - Life in the White House: President Barack Obama, First Lady Michelle Obama, First Children Malia & Sasha. 2008. (Here & Now Ser.). 32p. (J). (gr. 2-9). pap. 8.99 *(978-0-635-07051-7(0))* Gallopade International.
Snyder, Gail. Malia. 2007. (Obamas Ser.). 64p. (YA). (gr. 3-6). pap. 9.95 *(978-1-4222-1486-2(9));* (gr. 4-7). lib. bdg. 19.95 *(978-1-4222-1479-4(6))* Mason Crest.
—Sasha. 2007. (Obamas Ser.). (Illus.). 64p. (YA). (gr. 3-6). pap. 9.95 *(978-1-4222-1487-9(7));* (gr. 4-7). lib. bdg. 19.95 *(978-1-4222-1480-0(X))* Mason Crest.
Tieck, Sarah. Sasha & Malia Obama: Historic First Kids, 1 vol. 2009. (Big Buddy Biographies Set 3 Ser.). (ENG., Illus.). 32p. (J). (gr. 2-5). 28.50 *(978-1-60453-710-9(8))* ABDO Publishing Co.
—Sasha & Malia Obama: Historic First Kids CD & Book. 2010. (Big Buddy Biographies CD+Book Ser.). 32p. (gr. 2-5). audio compact disk 57.00 *(978-1-61613-310-8(4),* Big Buddy Bks.) ABDO Publishing Co.
—Sasha & Malia Obama: Historic First Kids Site CD & Book. 2010. (Big Buddy Biographies Site CD+Book Ser.). 32p. (gr. 2-5). cd-rom 85.57 *(978-1-61613-282-8(5),* Big Buddy Bks.) ABDO Publishing Co.

CHILDREN'S BOOKS

see Children's Literature

CHILDREN'S CRUSADE, 1212—FICTION

McDonnell, Kathleen. 1212: Year of the Journey, 1 vol. 2007. (ENG., Illus.). 240p. (YA). (gr. 8-12). pap. 9.95 *(978-1-897187-11-1(4))* Second Story Pr. CAN. Dist: Orca Bk. Pubs. USA.

CHILDREN'S DISEASES

see Children—Diseases

CHILDREN'S LIBRARIES

see also Children—Books and Reading; Children's Literature

Alexander, Linda B. & Kwon, Nahyun, eds. Multicultural Programs for Tweens & Teens. 2010. 216p. pap. 50.00 *(978-0-8389-3582-8(6))* American Library Assn.
Gillespie, John T. Historical Fiction for Young Readers (Grades 4-8) An Introduction, 1 vol. 2008. (Children's & Young Adult Literature Reference Ser.). 504p. (C). 70.00 *(978-1-59158-621-0(6),* LU8621, Libraries Unlimited) ABC-CLIO, LLC.
Naidoo, Jamie Campbell. Rainbow Family Collections: Selecting & Using Children's Books with Lesbian, Gay, Bisexual, Transgender, & Queer Content, 1 vol. 2012. (Children's & Young Adult Literature Reference Ser.). (Illus.). 260p. (C). 50.00 *(978-1-59884-960-8(3),* A3634C) Pearson Education GBR. Dist: ABC-CLIO, LLC.
Pinborough, Jan. Miss Moore Thought Otherwise: How Anne Carroll Moore Created Libraries for Children. Atwell, Debby, illus. 2013. (ENG.). 40p. (J). (gr. 1-4). 17.99 *(978-0-547-47105-1(X))* Houghton Mifflin Harcourt Publishing Co.
StJohn, Amanda. How a Library Works. Ostrom, Bob, illus. 2012. (Library Skills Ser.). (ENG.). 24p. (J). (gr. -1-2). 28.50 *(978-1-61473-247-1(7),* 204949) Child's World, Inc., The.
—How an e-Book Works. Ostrom, Bob, illus. 2012. (Library Skills Ser.). (ENG.). 24p. (J). (gr. -1-2). 28.50 *(978-1-61473-248-8(5),* 204950) Child's World, Inc., The.

CHILDREN'S LITERATURE

Here are entered collections of works of a cross-genre nature, e.g., Poetry and Prose. Works on the reading interests of children, and or lists of books read by or recommended for children are entered under Children—Books and Reading.

see also Caldecott Medal; Children—Books and Reading; Children's Literature; Fairy Tales; Picture Books; Plays; Poetry; Stories

Adams, David. One, Two, Three: A Collection of Songs, Verses, Riddles, & Stories for Children of Grades 1- 3. Mitchell, David, ed. 2003. (J). per. 14.95 *(978-1-888365-35-1(8))* Waldorf Publications.
Adil, Janeen R. Dr. Seuss. 2004. (Robbie Reader Ser.). (Illus.). 32p. (J). (gr. 1-4). lib. bdg. 25.70 *(978-1-58415-288-0(5))* Mitchell Lane Pubs., Inc.
Agnew, Kate, ed. War & Peace: A Collection of Classic Poetry & Prose. 2004. (ENG.). 176p. (J). (gr. 7). 9.95 *(978-1-84046-570-9(0),* Wizard Books) Icon Bks., Ltd. GBR. Dist: Publishers Group Canada.
Allyn, Pam. Pam Allyn's Best Books for Boys: How to Engage Boys in Reading in Ways That Will Change Their Lives. 2011. (ENG.). 176p. (gr. k-8). pap. 21.99 *(978-0-545-20455-2(0),* Teaching Resources) Scholastic, Inc.
Ancona, George. Self Portrait. Ancona, George, photos by. 2006. (Meet the Author Ser.). (Illus.). 32p. (J). 14.95 *(978-1-57274-860-6(5),* 733, Meet the Author) Owen, Richard C. Pubs., Inc.
Andersen, Hans Christian. Hans Christian Andersen: Illustrated Fairy Tales, Vol. 1. 2004. (ENG., Illus.). 416p. (J). (gr. -1-3). *(978-87-7247-279-9(0))* Scandinavia Publishing Hse.
Arnosky, James. Whole Days Outdoors: An Autobiographical Album. Arnosky, Deanna, photos by. 2006. (Meet the Author Ser.). (ENG., Illus.). 32p. (J). 14.95 *(978-1-57274-859-0(1),* 734, Meet the Author) Owen, Richard C. Pubs., Inc.
Banting, Erinn. Mary Pope Osbourne. 2006. (My Favorite Writer Ser.). (Illus.). 32p. (YA). (gr. 5-18). pap. 9.95 *(978-1-59036-483-3(X));* lib. bdg. 26.00 *(978-1-59036-482-6(1))* Weigl Pubs., Inc.
Berne, Emma Carlson. Laura Ingalls Wilder, 1 vol. 2007. (Essential Lives Set 1 Ser.). (ENG., Illus.). 112p. (J). (gr. 6-12). lib. bdg. 35.64 *(978-1-59928-843-7(5))* ABDO Publishing Co.
Betteridge, Barbara Dawson. Whittle Your Ears. Mitchell, David S., ed. 2005. (J). per. 12.00 *(978-1-888365-68-9(4))* Waldorf Publications.
Bradford, Jumanne. Preserving a Young Generation. 2005. Vol. 1. 87p. pap. 24.99 *(978-1-4116-4015-3(2))* Vol. 2. 94p. pap. 24.99 *(978-1-4116-4154-9(X))* Lulu Pr., Inc.
Brine, M. D. Our Little Ones. 2005. pap. 34.95 *(978-1-4179-9715-2(X))* Kessinger Publishing, LLC.
Buzzeo, Toni. R Is for Research. Wong, Nicole, illus. 2008. (J). (gr. 2-4). 17.95 *(978-1-60213-030-2(2),* Upstart Bks.) Highsmith Inc.
Carver Middle School & compiled by. Voices from the Middle: Stepping into the Real World. Carver Middle School, compiled by. 2004. 224p. (YA). per. 9.99 *(978-0-9749811-3-0(3),* Sonship Pr.) 21st Century Pr.
Christopher Paolini. 2010. (Who Wrote That? Ser.). (Illus.). 136p. (J). (gr. 6-12). 35.00 *(978-1-60413-727-9(4),* Chelsea Hse.) Facts On File, Inc.
Cole, Sonja. Booktalking Around the World: Great Global Reads for Ages 9-14. 2010. (ENG.). 178p. E-Book *(978-1-59884-614-0(0),* Libraries Unlimited) ABC-CLIO, LLC.
Corbett, Sue. Cornelia Funke. 2013. 48p. (J). (gr. 5-8). 29.93 *(978-1-60870-930-4(2))* Cavendish Square Publishing.
—Jeff Kinney. 2013. 48p. (J). (gr. 5-8). 29.93 *(978-1-60870-932-8(9))* Cavendish Square Publishing.
Coy, Steven & Dooda, Ian, eds. BOOM! for Real: Anthology of Poetry, Prose, & Pictures (Volume One 2005) 2005. (Illus.). 134p. (YA). per. 10.00 *(978-0-9743235-4-1(3))* Better Non Sequitur.
Dafydd, Myrddin ap. Syniad Da Iawn! Morris, Siân, illus. 2005. (WEL.). 196p. pap. *(978-0-86381-641-3(X))* Gwasg Carreg Gwalch.
David "Dav" Pilkey. 2010. (Who Wrote That? Ser.). (Illus.). 112p. (gr. 6-12). 35.00 *(978-1-60413-500-8(X),* Chelsea Hse.) Facts On File, Inc.
Doman, Mary Kate. Big Military Machines. 2011. (All about Big Machines Ser.). (Illus.). 24p. (J). (gr. k-3). lib. bdg. 22.60 *(978-0-7660-3932-2(3))* Enslow Pubs., Inc.
Draze, Dianne. Junior Literature Companion. 2005. 64p. (Orig.). 11.95 *(978-1-59363-084-3(0))* Prufrock Pr.
Flor Ada, Alma & Campoy, F. Isabel. Anton Pirulero. (Literature Collection of Puertas Al Sol Ser.). (SPA.). 32p. (J). (gr. k-6). pap. 12.95 *(978-1-59437-703-7(0))* Santillana USA Publishing Co., Inc.
Florian, Douglas. See for Your Self. Florian, Douglas & Taplinger, Lee, photos by. 2005. (Meet the Author Ser.). (ENG., Illus.). 32p. (J). 14.95 *(978-1-57274-821-7(4),* 731, Meet the Author) Owen, Richard C. Pubs., Inc.
Fluckiger, Kory. Mylands. 2010. pap. 9.95 *(978-0-615-15654-5(1))* Fluckiger, Kory.
Foran, Jill. Dr. Seuss. 2012. (J). 13.95 *(978-1-61913-059-3(9));* pap. 28.55 *(978-1-61913-595-6(7))* Weigl Pubs., Inc.
Freese, Susan M. Carrots to Cupcakes: Reading, Writing, & Reciting Poems about Food, 1 vol. Westberg, Jan, illus. 2008. (Poetry Power Ser.). (ENG.). 32p. (J). (gr. 1-4). 27.07 *(978-1-60453-003-2(0))* ABDO Publishing Co.
—Fireworks to Fruitcake: Reading, Writing, & Reciting Poems about Holidays, 1 vol. Westberg, Jan, illus. 2008. (Poetry Power Ser.). (ENG.). 32p. (J). (gr. 1-4). 27.07 *(978-1-60453-004-9(9))* ABDO Publishing Co.
Gage, Kathryn, illus. Wow, I'm a Big Brother. 2011. 48p. (J). spiral bd. 6.25 net. *(978-1-890703-44-8(3))* Penny Laine Papers, Inc.
Gamboa, Norma & Soberon, Cecilia. Literatura para el Jardin de Ninos (Literature for Young Children) (SPA., Illus.). 207p. (J). (gr. k-2). pap. 17.95 *(978-968-416-858-9(6),* 684B) Fernandez USA Publishing.
Gillespie, John T. Historical Fiction for Young Readers (Grades 4-8) An Introduction, 1 vol. 2008. (Children's & Young Adult Literature Reference Ser.). 504p. (C). 70.00 *(978-1-59158-621-0(6),* LU8621, Libraries Unlimited) ABC-CLIO, LLC.
Granahan, Shirley. John Newbery: Father of Children's Literature, 1 vol. 2009. (Publishing Pioneers Ser.). (ENG., Illus.). 112p. (J). (gr. 6-12). lib. bdg. 35.64 *(978-1-60453-764-2(7),* Essential Library) ABDO Publishing Co.
Green, Connie R. & Oldendorf, Sandra Brenneman. Religious Diversity & Children's Literature: Strategies & Resources. 2011. E-Book *(978-1-61735-398-7(1))* Information Age Publishing, Inc.
Guillain, Charlotte. Dr. Seuss, 1 vol. 2012. (Author Biographies Ser.). (ENG.). 24p. (gr. 1-2). 23.32 *(978-1-4329-5959-3(X));* pap. 6.79 *(978-1-4329-5965-4(4))* Heinemann-Raintree. (Heinemann Read & Learn).
Harris, Laurie Lanzen. Biography for Beginners: All Authors. 2005. (Illus.). 300p. (J). lib. bdg. 50.00 *(978-1-931360-31-9(6))* Favorable Impressions.
Holt, Rinehart and Winston Staff. Preparation & Construct Response: Elemental Literature. 3rd ed. 2003. (J). pap. 12.20 *(978-0-03-068278-0(9))* Holt, Rinehart & Winston of Canada, Ltd. CAN. Dist: Harcourt Canada, Ltd.
—Preparation & Construction Response: Elemental Literature. 3rd ed. 2003. (J). pap. 12.20 *(978-0-03-068277-3(0));* pap.

C
D

12.20 *(978-0-03-068281-0(9))* Holt, Rinehart & Winston of Canada, Ltd. CAN. Dist: Harcourt Canada, Ltd.

—Preparation & Constructive Response: Elemental Literature. 3rd ed. 2003. (J). pap. 12.20 *(978-0-03-068282-7(7))*; pap. 12.20 *(978-0-03-068283-4(5))* Holt, Rinehart & Winston of Canada, Ltd. CAN. Dist: Harcourt Canada, Ltd.

Hume, Lotta Carswell & Lo, Koon-Chiu. Favorite Children's Stories from China & Tibet. Koon-Chiu, Lo, illus. 2004. (ENG.). 112p. (J). (gr. k-8). 18.95 *(978-0-8048-3586-2(1))* Tuttle Publishing.

Kaur, Prabhjot. Daddoo's Day Out. 2004. (Illus.). 24p. (J). pap. *(978-81-87649-94-6(1))* Katha.

Kelley, True. Who Was Roald Dahl? Marchesi, Stephen & Harrison, Nancy, illus. 2012. (Who Was? Ser.). (ENG.). 112p. (J). (gr. 3-7). pap. 5.99 *(978-0-448-46146-5(3)*, Grosset & Dunlap) Penguin Young Readers Group.

—Who Was Roald Dahl? 2012. (Who Was... ? Ser.). lib. bdg. 16.00 *(978-0-606-26650-5(X)*, Turtleback) Turtleback Bks.

Kimmel, Eric A. Tuning Up: A Visit with Eric Kimmel. Childers, Basil, photos by. 2005. (Meet the Author Ser.). (ENG., Illus.). 32p. (J). 14.95 *(978-1-57274-822-4(2)*, 732, Meet the Author) Owen, Richard C. Pubs., Inc.

Krull, Kathleen. The Boy on Fairfield Street: How Ted Geisel Grew up to Become Dr. Seuss. Johnson, Steve & Fancher, Lou, illus. 2010. (ENG.). 48p. (J). (gr. k-4). pap. 7.99 *(978-0-375-85550-4(5)*, Dragonfly Bks.) Random Hse. Children's Bks.

Kurtz, Jane. Jane Kurtz & YOU, 1 vol. 2007. (Author & YOU Ser.: No. 8). (Illus.). 204p. (C). per. 35.00 *(978-1-59158-295-3(4)*, LU2954, Libraries Unlimited) ABC-CLIO, LLC.

Kutscher, Marc, ed. Revolution of the Undertones: A Teen Anthology 2004. 240p. (YA). per. 14.95 *(978-0-9745493-0-9(4))* Scrap Paper Pr.

Lappi, Megan. Will Hobbs. 2006. (My Favorite Writer Ser.). (Illus.). 32p. (J). (gr. 3-7). pap. 9.95 *(978-1-59036-489-5(9))*; lib. bdg. 26.00 *(978-1-59036-488-8(0))* Weigl Pubs., Inc.

Leaf, Christina. Rick Riordan. 2016. (Children's Storytellers Ser.). (ENG., Illus.). 24p. (J). (gr. 2-5). lib. bdg. 25.95 *(978-1-62617-342-2(7)*, Blastoff! Readers) Bellwether Media.

Lee, J. Marie. 4Jellybean Junction. 2003. 125p. (J). per. 19.95 *(978-1-59196-326-4(5))* Instant Pub.

Lindgren, Alan. The Courage of the Flame: Ballads, Sonnets & Other Gardens of Poetry with Prose Writings. Lindgren, Alan, ed. 2003. 196p. (YA). pap. 12.95 *(978-0-9721429-8-4(3))* Sun Sings Pubns.

Little Golden Books: Inspirational Stories, 5 vols. 2014. (ENG., Illus.). 24p. (J). (-k). 24.95 *(978-0-449-81484-0(X)*, Golden Bks.) Random Hse. Children's Bks.

Mandl, Dave & Wilson, Peter L., eds. Wild Children: A Zine for Kids. Date not set. (Illus.). 64p. 5.00 *(978-0-936756-83-7(7))* Autonomedia.

Marcovitz, Hal. Bruce Coville. 2005. (Who Wrote That? Ser.). (Illus.). 128p. (gr. 6-12). 35.00 *(978-0-7910-8656-8(9)*, Chelsea Hse.) Facts On File, Inc.

—Pat Mora. 2007. (Who Wrote That? Ser.). (Illus.). 135p. (gr. 6-12). lib. bdg. 35.00 *(978-0-7910-9528-7(2)*, Chelsea Hse.) Facts On File, Inc.

Marlin Elementary Students, creator. Marlin Anthology: Exploring Our Horizons as Writers. 2006. per. 19.95 *(978-0-9768391-8-7(0))* Pen & Publish Inc.

McGintry, Alice B. Cynthia Rylant. 2009. (Library of Author Biographies Ser.). 112p. (gr. 5-8). 63.90 *(978-1-60853-530-9(4)*, Rosen Reference) Rosen Publishing Group, Inc., The.

McGinty, Alice B. Meet Jane Yolen. 2009. (About the Author Ser.). 24p. (gr. 4-4). 42.50 *(978-1-61511-252-4(9)*, PowerKids Pr.) Rosen Publishing Group, Inc., The.

McHatton, Todd. Grass Stained Twilight. 2008. 184p. pap. 12.99 *(978-1-4357-1059-7(2))* Lulu Pr., Inc.

Mead, Wendy. Maurice Sendak. 2014. (Spotlight on Children's Authors Ser.). 48p. (J). (gr. 4-6). 29.93 *(978-1-62712-840-7(9))* Cavendish Square Publishing.

Mikiowitz, Gloria D. Dr. Seuss. 2004. (ENG., Illus.). 26p. (J). (gr. 2-5). pap. 7.33 *(978-0-7685-1217-5(4)*, Dominie Elementary) Pearson Schl.

Montgomery, Janice. Inside Stories Bk. 1: Study Guides for Children's Literature. 2005. 104p. stu. ed. 13.95 *(978-1-59363-077-5(8))* Prufrock Pr.

—Inside Stories Bk. 2: Study Guides for Children's Literature. 2005. 96p. stu. ed. 13.95 *(978-1-59363-078-2(6))* Prufrock Pr.

—Inside Stories Bk. 4: Study Guides for Children's Literature. 2005. 96p. 13.95 *(978-1-59363-080-5(8))* Prufrock Pr.

—Inside Stories Vol. 5: Study Guides for Children's Literature. 2005. 96p. stu. ed. 13.95 *(978-1-59363-081-2(6))* Prufrock Pr.

Murray, Jennifer. Twas a Dark & Stormy Night... Why Writers Write. 2007. (Shockwave: Life Stories Ser.). (ENG., Illus.). 36p. (J). (gr. 3-5). 25.00 *(978-0-531-17773-0(4)*, Children's Pr.) Scholastic Library Publishing.

Nagle, Jeanne, ed. Great Authors of Children's Books. 2013. (Essential Authors for Children & Teens Ser.). (YA). (gr. 7-12). 45.00 *(978-1-62275-096-2(9))* Rosen Publishing Group, Inc., The.

Pascal, Janet. Who Was Dr. Seuss? Harrison, Nancy, illus. 2011. (Who Was? Ser.). (ENG.). 112p. (J). (gr. 3-7). pap. 5.99 *(978-0-448-45585-3(4)*, Grosset & Dunlap) Penguin Young Readers Group.

Peterson-Hilleque, Victoria. J. K. Rowling: Extraordinary Author, 1 vol. 2010. (Essential Lives Set 5 Ser.). (ENG.). 112p. (J). (gr. 6-12). lib. bdg. 35.64 *(978-1-61613-517-1(4))* ABDO Publishing Co.

Phipps, Michael. Hi, My Name Is Book. 2011. 28p. pap. 13.99 *(978-1-4567-5285-9(5))* AuthorHouse.

Pinkney, Andrea Davis & Wells, Rosemary. A Poem for Peter: The Story of Ezra Jack Keats & the Creation of the Snowy Day. Johnson, Steve & Fancher, Lou, illus. 2016. (ENG.). 60p. (J). (gr. 2-5). bds. 18.99 *(978-0-425-28768-2(8)*, Viking Books for Young Readers) Penguin Young Readers Group.

Prudence Wickham Heston. Sadie Plants Hydrangeas. 2009. 44p. pap. 16.99 *(978-1-4389-5253-6(8))* AuthorHouse.

Purslow, Neil. R. L. Stine. 2006. (My Favorite Writer Ser.). (Illus.). 32p. (J). (gr. 3-7). pap. 9.95 *(978-1-59036-487-1(2))*; lib. bdg. 26.00 *(978-1-59036-486-4(4))* Weigl Pubs., Inc.

Purvis, Laura, ed. Falling for the Story. 2nd ed. 2004. (J). per. 9.95 *(978-0-9759524-0-5(4))* Northern Virginia Writing Project.

Reid, Rob. Storytime Slam: 15 Lesson Plans for Preschool & Primary Story Programs. 2006. (Illus.). 85p. per. 16.95 *(978-1-932146-52-3(0)*, Upstart Bks.) Highsmith Inc.

Risby, Bonnie. Literature Companion. 2005. 64p. 11.95 *(978-1-59363-086-7(7))* Prufrock Pr.

Schuller, Kathleen. How to Be a Heroine-For Girls: Inspiration from Classic Heroines. Bailey, Melissa, illus. 2013. 68p. 19.95 *(978-1-4575-1649-8(7))* Dog Ear Publishing, LLC.

Sierra, Judy. Imagine That! How Dr. Seuss Wrote the Cat in the Hat. Hawkes, Kevin, illus. 2017. (ENG.). 48p. (J). (gr. -1-2). lib. bdg. 20.99 *(978-0-375-97429-8(6)*, Random Hse. Bks. for Young Readers) Random Hse. Children's Bks.

Small, Roberta Lee. Down by the Pond. 2005. 116p. (J). pap. 9.95 *(978-1-4116-5949-0(X))* Lulu Pr., Inc.

Vaux, F. B. Domestic Pleasures or the Happy Fire Side Illustrated by Interesting Conversations. 2004. reprint ed. pap. 20.95 *(978-1-4191-1640-7(1))*; pap. 1.99 *(978-1-4192-1640-4(6))* Kessinger Publishing, LLC.

Wheeler, Jill C. Avi, 1 vol. 2009. (Children's Authors Set 5 Ser.). (ENG.). 24p. (J). (gr. 2-5). 25.65 *(978-1-60453-075-9(8))* ABDO Publishing Co.

—Mary Pope Osborne, 1 vol. 2007. (Children's Authors Set 4 Ser.). (ENG., Illus.). 24p. (YA). (gr. 2-5). 25.65 *(978-1-59679-764-2(9))* ABDO Publishing Co.

Wolny, Philip & Green, Meg. Louis Sachar, 01 vols., 1. 2016. (All about the Author Ser.). (ENG., Illus.). 112p. (J). 35.60 *(978-1-4994-6264-7(6)*, Rosen Young Adult) Rosen Publishing Group, Inc., The.

Wong, Janet S. Before It Wriggles Away. Lindsay, Anne, photos by. 2006. (Meet the Author Ser.). (ENG., Illus.). 32p. (J). 14.95 *(978-1-57274-861-3(3)*, 735, Meet the Author) Owen, Richard C. Pubs., Inc.

Young Scribes Staff. Unlock the Secrets of Exeter: The Young Scribes of Exeter, NH. l.t. ed. 2004. (Illus.). 172p. (J). pap. 15.00 *(978-0-9744803-9-8(8))* PublishingWorks.

Younge, Jewel Sophia, creator. Pg-13. 2006. (Illus.). 29p. (YA). 10.00 *(978-0-9788158-0-6(7))* Sweet Potato Brown.

Zimmer, Kyle, frwd. Jane Yolen. 2005. (Who Wrote That? Ser.). (Illus.). 128p. (gr. 6-12). lib. bdg. 35.00 *(978-0-7910-8660-5(7)*, Chelsea Hse.) Facts On File, Inc.

CHILDREN'S LITERATURE—BIBLIOGRAPHY

Crew, Hilary S. Women Engaged in War in Literature for Youth: A Guide to Resources for Children & Young Adults, Vol. . 2007. (Literature for Youth Ser.: 11). (ENG.). 324p. per. 75.00 *(978-0-8108-4929-7(1))* Scarecrow Pr., Inc.

Gayle-Evans, Guda. An Annotated Bibliography of Multi-Cultural Literature for Children Three to Ten Years. 2004. (Mellen Studies in Children's Literature: Vol. 6). (Illus.). 204p. 109.95 *(978-0-7734-6474-2(3))* Mellen, Edwin Pr., The.

Otfinoski, Steven. Classic Books. 2009. (Our Freedom to Read Ser.). 144p. (gr. 5-8). 40.00 *(978-1-60413-029-4(6)*, Chelsea Hse.) Facts On File, Inc.

—Coming-of-Age Fiction. 2009. (Freedom to Read Ser.). 144p. (gr. 5-8). 40.00 *(978-1-60413-030-0(X)*, Chelsea Hse.) Facts On File, Inc.

—Outsider Fiction. 2009. (Freedom to Read Ser.). 144p. (gr. 5-8). 40.00 *(978-1-60413-031-7(8)*, Chelsea Hse.) Facts On File, Inc.

Scarry, Richard. Best Picture Dictionary Ever. Scarry, Richard, illus. 2016. (Giant Little Golden Book Ser.). (ENG., Illus.). 128p. (J). (gr. -1-2). 15.99 *(978-0-307-15548-1(X)*, 15548, Golden Bks.) Random Hse. Children's Bks.

Schulze, Bianca. 101 Books to Read Before You Grow Up. 2017. (101 Ser.). (ENG., Illus.). 144p. (J). (gr. 3-5). lib. bdg. 33.32 ***(978-1-942875-17-8(7)***, Walter Foster Jr) Quarto Publishing Group USA.

CHILDREN'S LITERATURE—HISTORY AND CRITICISM

Bell, James Stuart, et al. Inside the Lion, the Witch & the Wardrobe: Myths, Mysteries, & Magic from the Chronicles of Narnia. 2005. (ENG., Illus.). 240p. (YA). (gr. 8-13). pap. 18.99 *(978-0-312-34744-4(8)*, 9780312347444, St. Martin's Griffin) St. Martin's Pr.

Hallett, Cynthia J. & Huey, Peggy J., eds. New Casebooks - J. K. Rowling: Harry Potter, 1 vol. 2012. (New Casebooks Ser.). (ENG., Illus.). 224p. (C). 85.00 *(978-0-230-00849-6(6)*, 9780230008496); pap. 29.00 *(978-0-230-00850-2(X)*, 9780230008502) Palgrave Macmillan.

Maristella. One Step to Freedom. 2010. 82p. pap. *(978-1-84748-756-8(4))* Athena Pr.

Morrissette, Cora. Life Stories in the World of Fiction. 2009. 104p. pap. 17.95 *(978-1-4327-3851-8(8))* Outskirts Pr., Inc.

Otfinoski, Steven. Science Fiction & Fantasy. 2009. (Freedom to Read Ser.). 152p. (gr. 5-8). 40.00 *(978-1-60413-032-4(6)*, Chelsea Hse.) Facts On File, Inc.

Riordan, Rick, ed. Demigods & Monsters: Your Favorite Authors on Rick Riordan's Percy Jackson & the Olympians Series. rev. ed. 2013. (ENG.). 288p. (J). (gr. 5). pap. 12.95 *(978-1-937856-36-6(4))* BenBella Bks.

Roberts, Russell. John Newbery & the Story of the Newbery Medal. 2003. (Great Achiever Awards Ser.). (Illus.). 48p. (J). (gr. 4-8). lib. bdg. 29.95 *(978-1-58415-201-9(X))* Mitchell Lane Pubs., Inc.

CHILDREN'S READING

see Children's Literature; Reading

CHILE

Aronson, Marc. Trapped: How the World Rescued 33 Miners from 2,000 Feet below the Chilean Desert. 2012. (ENG., Illus.). 144p. (J). pap. 6.99 *(978-1-4424-4025-8(2)*, Atheneum Bks. for Young Readers) Simon & Schuster Children's Publishing.

Blomquist, Christopher. A Primary Source Guide to Chile. (Countries of the World). 24p. 2009. (gr. 2-3). 42.50 *(978-1-61512-027-7(0))* 2005. (Illus.). lib. bdg. 22.60 *(978-1-4042-2751-4(2))* Rosen Publishing Group, Inc., The. (PowerKids Pr.).

Burgan, Michael. Chile. (Enchantment of the World(tm) Ser.). (ENG., 144p. (J). 2016. Illus.). lib. bdg. 40.00 *(978-0-531-21885-3(6)*, Children's Pr.) 2009. (gr. 5-9). 40.00 *(978-0-531-20650-8(5))* Scholastic Library Publishing.

Crooker, Richard A. Chile. 2004. (Modern World Nations Ser.). (Illus.). 144p. (gr. 6-12). 35.00 *(978-0-7910-7912-6(0)*, Chelsea Hse.) Facts On File, Inc.

DiPiazza, Francesca Davis. Chile in Pictures. 2nd ed. 2007. (Visual Geography Series, Second Ser.). (ENG., Illus.). 80p. (gr. 5-12). lib. bdg. 31.93 *(978-0-8225-6587-1(0))* Lerner Publishing Group.

Holiday, Jane. Exploring Chile with the Five Themes of Geography. (Library of the Western Hemisphere Ser.). 24p. 2009. (gr. 4-4). 42.50 *(978-1-60853-924-6(5)*, PowerKids Pr.) 2005. (Illus.). (J). (gr. 5-7). lib. bdg. 22.60 *(978-1-4042-2677-7(X)*, PowerKids Pr.) 2005. (ENG., Illus.). (gr. 3-8). pap. 8.25 *(978-0-8239-4637-2(1))* Rosen Publishing Group, Inc., The.

Lusted, Marcia Amidon. The Chilean Miners' Rescue, 1 vol. 2011. (Essential Events Set 7 Ser.). (ENG., Illus.). 112p. (J). (gr. 6-12). lib. bdg. 35.64 *(978-1-61783-097-6(6))* ABDO Publishing Co.

Marsico, Katie. The Wettest & the Driest. 2015. (True Book(tm), a — Extreme Places Ser.). (ENG., Illus.). 48p. (J). lib. bdg. 31.00 *(978-0-531-21847-1(3)*, Children's Pr.) Scholastic Library Publishing.

Meachen Rau, Dana. Chile. 2006. (Discovering Cultures Ser.). (Illus.). 48p. (J). (gr. 3-7). lib. bdg. 28.50 *(978-0-7614-1988-4(8)*, Benchmark Bks.) Marshall Cavendish Corp.

Miller, Jennifer A. Chile. 2010. pap. 51.02 *(978-0-7613-6972-1(4))*; (ENG.). 48p. (gr. 2-4). pap. 9.95 *(978-0-7613-6032-2(8))*; (ENG.). 48p. (gr. 2-4). lib. bdg. 29.27 *(978-0-7613-5319-5(4))* Lerner Publishing Group.

Morrison, Marion. Chile, 1 vol. 2011. (Countries Around the World Ser.). (ENG.). 48p. (gr. 3-6). pap. 9.95 *(978-1-4329-5222-6(6)*, NA-h) Heinemann-Raintree.

Naughton, Diane. Rescued. 2014. (ENG., Illus.). 28p. (J). pap. 9.50 *(978-1-107-65519-5(6))* Cambridge Univ. Pr.

Nelson, David E. Chile. Greenhaven Press Editors, ed. 2014. (Genocide & Persecution Ser.). (ENG., Illus.). 240p. (gr. 10-12). lib. bdg. 42.00 *(978-0-7377-6896-1(7)*, Greenhaven Pr., Inc.) Cengage Gale.

Orr, Tamra. We Visit Chile. 2010. (Your Land & My Land Ser.). (Illus.). 64p. (J). (gr. 3-6). lib. bdg. 33.95 *(978-1-58415-888-2(3))* Mitchell Lane Pubs., Inc.

Owings, Lisa. Chile. 2011. (Exploring Countries Ser.). (ENG., Illus.). 32p. (YA). (gr. 3-7). lib. bdg. 26.95 *(978-1-60014-617-6(1)*, Blastoff! Readers) Bellwether Media.

Peppas, Lynn. The Atacama Desert. 2012. (ENG.). 32p. (J). *(978-0-7787-0709-7(1))*; (Illus.). pap. *(978-0-7787-0717-2(2))* Crabtree Publishing Co.

Porterfield, Jason. Chile: A Primary Source Cultural Guide. 2009. (Primary Sources of World Cultures Ser.). 128p. (gr. 4-5). 79.90 *(978-1-60851-918-7(X))* Rosen Publishing Group, Inc., The.

Scott, Elaine. Buried Alive! How 33 Miners Survived 69 Days Deep under the Chilean Desert. 2012. (ENG., Illus.). 80p. (J). (gr. 5-7). 18.99 *(978-0-547-70778-5(9))* Houghton Mifflin Harcourt Publishing Co.

Shields, Charles J. Chile. (South America Today Ser.). 64p. 2009. (Illus.). (J). (gr. 4-7). 21.95 *(978-1-4222-0634-8(3))* 2007. (YA). (gr. 7-18). pap. 9.95 *(978-1-4222-0701-7(3))* Mason Crest.

—Chile, Vol. 13. Henderson, James D., ed. 2015. (Discovering South America: History, Politics, & Culture Ser.). (Illus.). 64p. (J). (gr. 7). lib. bdg. 22.95 *(978-1-4222-3297-2(2))* Mason Crest.

Weber, Valerie J. I Come from Chile. 2006. (This Is My Story Ser.). (Illus.). 24p. (gr. 1-4). lib. bdg. 22.00 *(978-0-8368-7234-7(7)*, Weekly Reader Leveled Readers) Stevens, Gareth Publishing LLLP.

—I Come from Chile. 2006. (This Is My Story Ser.). (Illus.). 24p. (gr. 1-4). pap. 8.15 *(978-0-8368-7241-5(X)*, Weekly Reader Leveled Readers) Stevens, Gareth Publishing LLLP.

CHILE—FICTION

Agosín, Marjorie. I Lived on Butterfly Hill. White, Lee, illus. 2014. (ENG.). 464p. (J). (gr. 5-9). 18.99 *(978-1-4169-5344-9(2)*, Atheneum Bks. for Young Readers) Simon & Schuster Children's Publishing.

Ballock-Dixon, Saige J. & Medina, Sylvia M. Chilean Mines. Eagle, Joy, illus. 2013. 36p. pap. 11.49 *(978-1-939871-00-8(X))* Green Kids Club, Inc.

Collingwood, Harry. Under the Chilean Flag. 2009. 184p. 26.95 *(978-1-60664-598-7(6))*; pap. 13.95 *(978-1-60664-330-3(4))* Rodgers, Alan Bks.

MacDonald, Margaret Read. Algarabía en la Granja. Fatus, Sophie, illus. 2009. (SPA.). (J). pap. 9.99 *(978-1-84686-282-3(5))* Barefoot Bks., Inc.

—The Farmyard Jamboree. Fatus, Sophie, illus. 2009. (ENG.). (J). 16.99 *(978-1-84686-290-8(6))* Barefoot Bks., Inc.

Miller-Lachmann, Lyn. Gringolandia. 2009. (ENG.). 288p. (YA). (gr. 9-18). 18.95 *(978-1-931896-49-8(6))* Curbstone Pr.

—Surviving Santiago. 2015. (ENG.). 320p. (YA). (gr. 7). 16.95 *(978-0-7624-5633-8(7)*, Running Pr. Kids) Running Pr. Bk. Pubs.

Ryan, Pam Muñoz. The Dreamer. Sís, Peter, illus. (ENG.). (J). (gr. 4-7). 2012. 400p. pap. 8.99 *(978-0-439-26998-8(9)*, Scholastic Paperbacks) 2010. 384p. 21.99 *(978-0-439-26970-4(9)*, Scholastic Pr.) Scholastic, Inc.

—The Dreamer. 2012. lib. bdg. 19.65 *(978-0-606-23940-0(5)*, Turtleback) Turtleback Bks.

Thomas, Maria Jose & Thomas, María José. !Bravo, Rosina! Muñoz, Claudio, illus. 2005. (SPA.). 48p. (J). (gr. -1-5). 10.40 *(978-980-257-242-7(X)*, EK33833) Ekare, Ediciones VEN. Dist: Lectorum Pubns., Inc.

Vasquez, Elisa Irene. My Little Piggy: A Bilingual English-Spanish Children's Book. 2010. 28p. 14.95 *(978-1-4490-8716-6(7))* AuthorHouse.

Vicuna, Claudio Orrego. The Surprising Adventures of Balthazar. 2011. (Peace, Justice, Human Rights, & Freedom in Latin America Ser.). (SPA & ENG.). 160p. 15.00 *(978-1-58966-218-6(0))* Univ. of Scranton Pr.

Vidali, Valerio & Uman, Jennifer. Jemmy Button. Vidali, Valerio & Uman, Jennifer, illus. 2013. (ENG., Illus.). 48p. (J). (gr. k-12). 16.99 *(978-0-7636-6487-9(1)*, Templar) Candlewick Pr.

CHILLS AND FEVER

see Malaria

CHIMES

see Bells

CHIMPANZEES

Albee, Sarah. Chimpanzees. 2009. (Amazing Animals Ser.). (ENG.). 48p. (J). (gr. 2-6). pap. 10.50 *(978-1-4339-2118-6(9)*, Gareth Stevens Learning Library); (gr. 3-6). lib. bdg. 28.00 *(978-0-8368-9114-0(7))* Stevens, Gareth Publishing LLLP.

—Chimpanzees. 2006. (Illus.). 45p. (J). *(978-1-59939-062-8(0))*, Reader's Digest Young Families, Inc.) Studio Fun International.

Antle, Bhagavan. The Tiger Cubs & the Chimp: The True Story of How Anjana the Chimp Helped Raise Two Baby Tigers. Antle, Bhagavan, illus. Bland, Barry, photos by. 2013. (ENG., Illus.). 32p. (J). (gr. -1-3). 16.99 *(978-0-8050-9319-3(2)*, 9780805093193, Holt, Henry & Co. Bks. For Young Readers) Holt, Henry & Co.

Bell, Samantha. Chimpanzee. 2015. (21st Century Skills Library: Exploring Our Rainforests Ser.). (ENG., Illus.). 32p. (J). (gr. 3-6). 29.93 *(978-1-63188-974-5(5)*, 205808) Cherry Lake Publishing.

Bow, Patricia. Chimpanzee Rescue: Changing the Future for Endangered Wildlife. 2004. (Firefly Animal Rescue Ser.). (ENG., Illus.). 64p. (J). (gr. 5-8). 19.95 *(978-1-55297-909-9(1)*, 9781552979099); pap. 9.95 *(978-1-55297-908-2(3)*, 9781552979082) Firefly Bks., Ltd.

Briscoe, Diana. Jane Goodall: Finding Hope in the Wilds of Africa. 2004. (High Five Reading - Purple Ser.). (ENG., Illus.). 64p. (gr. 3-4). per. 9.00 *(978-0-7368-3851-1(1)*, High Five Reading (RBL)) Capstone Press of Coughlan Cos.

Carr, Aaron. Chimpanzee. 2014. (Illus.). 24p. (J). *(978-1-62127-281-6(8))* Weigl Pubs., Inc.

Chambers, Catherine E. Ape Adventures, Level 3. 2013. (DK Readers Ser.). (ENG.). 48p. (J). (gr. 2-4). pap. 3.99 *(978-1-4654-0239-4(X)*, DK Children) Dorling Kindersley Publishing, Inc.

Chimps & Monkeys Are Not Pets! 2013. (When Pets Attack! Ser.). 32p. (J). (gr. 3-6). pap. 63.00 *(978-1-4339-9290-2(6))* Stevens, Gareth Publishing LLLP.

Cline, Gina. Chimps Use Sticks. Shusterman, Danielle, illus. 2014. (1B Animal Behaviors Ser.). (ENG.). 32p. (J). pap. 5.99 *(978-1-61406-689-7(2))* American Reading Co.

Coxon, Michele. Termites on a Stick: A Chimp Learns to Use a Tool, 1 vol. Coxon, Michele, illus. 2008. (ENG., Illus.). 32p. (J). (gr. -1-3). 17.95 *(978-1-59572-121-1(5))* Star Bright Bks., Inc.

—Termites on a Stick: A Chimpanzee Learns to Use a Tool, 1 vol. Coxon, Michele, illus. 2008. (ENG., Illus.). 32p. (J). pap. 7.95 *(978-1-59572-183-9(5))* Star Bright Bks., Inc.

Dennard, Deborah. Chimpanzees. McGee, John F., illus. 2003. (Our Wild World Ser.). (ENG.). 48p. (J). (gr. 2-5). 10.95 *(978-1-55971-846-2(3))* Cooper Square Publishing Llc.

Doak, Robin S. Jane Goodall: Chimpanzee Protector, 1 vol. 2014. (Women in Conservation Ser.). (ENG., Illus.). 48p. (gr. 3-6). 33.32 *(978-1-4846-0469-4(5))*; pap. 8.99 *(978-1-4846-0474-8(1))* Heinemann-Raintree. (Heinemann InfoSearch).

Dorman, Clive & Dorman, Helen. Okomi Enjoys His Outings, Vol. 5. Hutchings, Tony, illus. 2004. (Okomi Stories Ser.). 24p. (J). pap. 4.95 *(978-1-58469-055-9(0))* Dawn Pubns.

Doudna, Kelly. It's a Baby Chimpanzee!, 1 vol. 2009. (Baby African Animals Ser.). (ENG., Illus.). 24p. (J). (gr. k-3). lib. bdg. 24.21 *(978-1-60453-152-7(5)*, SandCastle) ABDO Publishing Co.

Edwards, Roberta. Who Is Jane Goodall? Marchesi, Stephen et al, illus. 2012. (Who Was? Ser.). (ENG.). 112p. (J). (gr. 3-7). 5.99 *(978-0-448-46192-2(7)*, Grosset & Dunlap) Penguin Young Readers Group.

—Who Is Jane Goodall? 2012. (Who Is... ? Ser.). lib. bdg. 16.00 *(978-0-606-26651-2(8)*, Turtleback) Turtleback Bks.

Eggleton. Sail Blu Nf Chimpanzees. 2004. (Rigby Sails Early Ser.). (ENG.). 16p. (gr. 1-2). pap. 6.95 *(978-0-7578-9960-7(9))* Rigby Education.

Feinstein, Stephen. The Chimpanzee: Help Save This Endangered Species! 2007. (Saving Endangered Species Ser.). (Illus.). 128p. (J). (gr. 5-9). lib. bdg. 34.60 *(978-1-59845-039-2(5)*, MyReportLinks.com Bks.) Enslow Pubs., Inc.

Fetty, Margaret. Chimpanzees. 2006. (Smart Animals! Ser.). (Illus.). 32p. (J). (gr. 2-5). lib. bdg. 25.27 *(978-1-59716-159-6(4))* Bearport Publishing Co., Inc.

French, Jess & The Born Free Foundation. Chimp Rescue: A True-Life Story. 2017. (Born Free... Bks.). (ENG.). 112p. (J). (gr. 2-6). pap. 6.99 *(978-1-4380-0985-8(2))* Barron's Educational Series, Inc.

Friesen, Helen Lepp. Chimpanzees. 2014. (Illus.). 24p. (J). *(978-1-4896-2870-1(3))* Weigl Pubs., Inc.

Frost, Helen. Chimpanzees [Scholastic]. 2011. (Rain Forest Animals Ser.). 24p. pap. 0.50 *(978-1-4296-6314-4(6)*, Pebble Bks.) Capstone Press of Coughlan Cos.

Gareth Stevens Publishing Staff, contrib. by. Chimpanzees. 2004. (All about Wild Animals Ser.). (Illus.). 32p. (gr. k-4). lib. bdg. 26.00 *(978-0-8368-4171-8(9)*, Gareth Stevens Learning Library) Stevens, Gareth Publishing LLLP.

Gish, Melissa. Chimpanzees. 2013. (Illus.). 46p. (J). 35.65 *(978-1-60818-286-2(X))* Creative Co., The.

—Living Wild: Chimpanzees. 2014. (Living Wild Ser.). (ENG., Illus.). 48p. (J). (gr. 4-7). pap. 12.00 *(978-0-89812-839-0(0)*, Creative Paperbacks) Creative Co., The.

Goodridge, Catherine. Jane Goodall (Spanish) 2011. (SPA.). (J). pap. 40.00 net. *(978-1-4108-2426-4(8)*, A24268) Benchmark Education Co.

Greenberg, Daniel A. & Wilsdon, Christina. Chimpanzees. 2009. (Benchmark Rockets Ser.). 24p. (gr. 1-18). lib. bdg. 24.21 *(978-0-7614-4341-4(X))* Marshall Cavendish Corp.

Guidi, Victoria. Who on Earth Is Jane Goodall? Champion for the Chimpanzees. 2009. (Scientists Saving the Earth Ser.). (Illus.). 112p. (J). (gr. 5-9). lib. bdg. 33.27 *(978-1-59845-119-1(7))* Enslow Pubs., Inc.

Hand, Carol. Jane Goodall. 2014. (Great Science Writers Ser.). (Illus.). 112p. (J). (gr. 7-12). 35.60 *(978-1-4777-7685-8(0))* Rosen Publishing Group, Inc., The.

Hansen, Grace. Chimpanzees, 1 vol. 2015. (ENG., Illus.). 24p. (J). 28.50 *(978-1-62970-892-8(5))* ABDO Publishing Co.

Harris, Tim. Chimpanzees. 2012. (Animal Families Ser.). (Illus.). 32p. (gr. 2-5). lib. bdg. 31.35 ***(978-1-78121-001-7(2))*** Brown Bear Bks.

Hustad, Douglas. Animal Scientist & Activist Jane Goodall. 2016. (STEM Trailblazer Bios Ser.). (ENG., Illus.). 32p. (J).

(gr. 2-5). 26.65 *(978-1-5124-0788-4(7))* Lerner Publishing Group.

Ingram, Doreen. My Sanctuary, a Place I Call Home. 2010. (Illus.). 54p. pap. 17.50 *(978-1-60911-480-0(9),* Eloquent Bks.) Strategic Book Publishing & Rights Agency (SBPRA).

Jacobs, Liza. Chimpanzees. 2003. (Wild Wild World Ser.). (Illus.). 24p. (J). 23.70 *(978-1-4103-0031-7(5),* Blackbirch Pr., Inc.) Cengage Gale.

Jankowski, Connie. Jane Goodall: Animal Scientist & Friend, 1 vol. 2007. (Science Readers Ser.). (SPA & ENG.). 32p. (J). (gr. 3-3). pap. 8.99 *(978-0-7439-0594-7(6))* Shell Educational Publishing.

Johnson, Jinny. Chimpanzee. Rosewarne, Graham, illus. 2007. (Zoo Animals in the Wild Ser.). 32p. (J). (gr. -1-3). lib. bdg. 28.50 *(978-1-58340-900-8(9))* Black Rabbit Bks.

Kalman, Bobbie & Dyer, Hadley. Les Chimpanzés. Briere, Marie-Josee, tr. from ENG. rev. ed. 2007. (Petit Monde Vivant Ser.). (FRE., Illus.). 32p. (J). (gr. 1-7). pap. 9.95 *(978-2-89579-128-7(7))* Bayard Canada Livres CAN. Dist: Crabtree Publishing Co.

—Endangered Chimpanzees. 2005. (Earth's Endangered Animals Ser.). (ENG., Illus.). 32p. (J). (gr. 1-5). pap. *(978-0-7787-1905-2(7));* (gr. 3-5). lib. bdg. *(978-0-7787-1859-8(X))* Crabtree Publishing Co.

Kane, Karen. Chimpanzees. Ellis, Gerry, illus. Ellis, Gerry, photos by. 2004. (Early Bird Nature Bks.). (ENG.). 48p. (gr. 2-5). 26.60 *(978-0-8225-2418-2(X),* Lerner Pubns.) Lerner Publishing Group.

Kenan, Tessa. Es un Chimpancé! 2017. (Bumba Books (tm) en Español — Animales de la Selva Tropical (Rain Forest Animals) Ser.). (SPA., Illus.). 24p. (J). (gr. -1-1). 25.32 ***(978-1-5124-4131-4(7));*** pap. 6.99 ***(978-1-5124-5409-3(5))*** Lerner Publishing Group.

—It's a Chimpanzee! 2017. (Bumba Books (tm) — Rain Forest Animals Ser.). (ENG.). 24p. (J). (gr. -1-1). 12.99 ***(978-1-5124-3753-9(0),*** Lerner Pubns.); 38.65 ***(978-1-5124-3752-2(2),*** Lerner Pubns.); 38.65 ***(978-1-5124-2759-2(4),*** Lerner Pubns.); (Illus.). 25.32 *(978-1-5124-2572-7(9))* Lerner Publishing Group.

Kittinger, Jo S. Jane Goodall. 2005. (Scholastic News Nonfiction Readers Ser.). (Illus.). 24p. pap. 6.95 *(978-0-516-24783-0(2),* Children's Pr.) Scholastic Library Publishing.

Krohn, Katherine. Jane Goodall: Animal Scientist, 1 vol. Martin, Cynthia & Timmons, Anne, illus. 2006. (Graphic Biographies Ser.). (ENG.). 32p. (gr. 3-4). 30.65 *(978-0-7368-5485-6(1),* Graphic Library) Capstone Press of Coughlan Cos.

Leavitt, Amie Jane. Care for a Pet Chimpanzee. 2007. (How to Convince Your Parents You Can ... Ser.). (Illus.). 32p. (J). (gr. 1-4). lib. bdg. 25.70 *(978-1-58415-607-9(4))* Mitchell Lane Pubs., Inc.

Levine, Mathea. I'm Lucy: A Day in the Life of a Young Bonobo. Brickner, Marian, illus. 2008. 32p. (gr. -1-3). 19.95 *(978-0-615-18110-3(4))* Blue Bark Pr.

Lindeen, Mary. Jane Goodall: Friend of the Apes, 1 vol. Soud, illus. 2008. (Beginner Biographies Ser.). (ENG.). 32p. (gr. -1-3). 28.50 *(978-1-60270-249-3(7),* Looking Glass Library-Nonfiction) Magic Wagon.

Llewellyn, Claire. Kingfisher Readers L2: Chimpanzees. 2015. (ENG., Illus.). 32p. (gr. k-3). 12.99 *(978-0-7534-7225-5(2),* 9780753472255, Kingfisher) Roaring Brook Pr.

Marsico, Katie. Chimpanzees. 2012. (21st Century Basic Skills Library: Baby Zoo Animals Ser.). (ENG.). 24p. (gr. k-3). 22.79 *(978-1-61080-455-4(4),* 202065); pap. 12.79 *(978-1-61080-629-9(8),* 202239) Cherry Lake Publishing.

—Chimpanzees. 2012. (Nature's Children Ser.). (ENG., Illus.). 48p. (J). pap. 6.95 *(978-0-531-21085-7(5));* (gr. 3-5). lib. bdg. 28.00 *(978-0-531-20910-3(5))* Scholastic Library Publishing. (Children's Pr.).

Meltzer, Brad. I Am Jane Goodall. Eliopoulos, Christopher, illus. 2016. (Ordinary People Change the World Ser.). (ENG.). 40p. (J). (gr. k-3). 14.99 *(978-0-525-42849-7(6),* Dial Bks) Penguin Young Readers Group.

Miklowitz, Gloria D. Jane Goodall. 2004. (ENG., Illus.). 28p. (J). (gr. 2-5). pap. 7.33 *(978-0-7685-1218-2(2),* Dominie Elementary) Pearson Schl.

Moore, Heidi. Chimpanzees, 1 vol. 2012. (Living in the Wild: Primates Ser.). (ENG.). 48p. (gr. 3-6). lib. bdg. 33.32 *(978-1-4329-5862-6(3),* Heinemann InfoSearch) Heinemann-Raintree.

Moore Niver, Heather. Chimps & Monkeys Are Not Pets! 2013. (When Pets Attack! Ser.). 32p. (J). (gr. 3-6). 26.60 *(978-1-4339-9288-9(4));* pap. 10.50 *(978-1-4339-9289-6(2))* Stevens, Gareth Publishing LLLP.

Murray, Julie. Chimpanzees, 1 vol. 2003. (Buddy Book Ser.). (ENG.). 24p. (J). (gr. 1-4). 25.65 *(978-1-57765-713-2(6))* ABDO Publishing Co.

Owen, Ruth. Chimpanzees. 2011. (World's Smartest Animals Ser.). (ENG., Illus.). 32p. (J). (gr. k-5). pap. 11.75 *(978-1-61533-417-9(3));* lib. bdg. 26.50 *(978-1-61533-380-6(0))* Windmill Bks.

Peterson, Megan Cooley & Rustad, Martha E. H. Chimpanzees Are Awesome! 2015. (Awesome African Animals! Ser.). (ENG.). 32p. (gr. 1-2). lib. bdg. 27.32 *(978-1-4914-1759-1(5))* Capstone Press of Coughlan Cos.

Pingry, Patricia A. & Sharp, Chris. Baby Chimpanzee. 2003. (San Diego Zoo Animal Library: Vol. 2). (ENG., Illus.). 24p. (J). bds. 6.95 *(978-0-8249-6530-3(2),* Ideal Pubns.) Worthy Publishing.

Polinsky, Paige V. Chimpanzee: Brainy Beast. 2016. (ENG., Illus.). 24p. (J). *(978-1-68078-147-2(2))* ABDO Publishing Co.

Pope, Kristen. Chimpanzees. 2015. (Endangered Animals Ser.). (ENG.). 24p. (J). (gr. 1-4). 27.07 *(978-1-63143-967-4(7),* 208802) Child's World, Inc., The.

Rice, William. Jane Goodall. 2017. (TIME for Kids en Español - Level 3 Ser.). (SPA.). 32p. (gr. 3-3). lib. bdg. 31.99 ***(978-1-5157-5191-5(0))*** Time for Kids Inc AUS. Dist: Capstone Pub.

Rice, William B. Jane Goodall, 1 vol. 2nd rev. ed. 2014. (TIME for KIDS(r) Nonfiction Readers Ser.). (ENG., Illus.). 32p. (J). (gr. 3-3). pap. 25.96 *(978-1-4807-1093-1(8))* Shell Educational Publishing.

Riggs, Kate. Chimpanzees. 2016. (Amazing Animals Ser.). (Illus.). 24p. (J). (ENG.). (gr. 1-3). pap. 8.99 *(978-1-62832-216-3(0),* Creative Paperbacks); 28.50 *(978-1-60818-610-5(5),* Creative Education) Creative Co., The.

Rockwood, Leigh. Chimpanzees Are Smart! 2010. (Super Smart Animals Ser.). (Illus.). 24p. (J). pap. 8.25 *(978-1-4358-9840-0(0),* PowerKids Pr.); (YA). (gr. 2-5). lib. bdg. 22.60 *(978-1-4358-9375-7(1))* Rosen Publishing Group, Inc., The.

Schuh, Mari C. Meet a Baby Chimpanzee. 2015. (ENG., Illus.). 32p. (J). (gr. k-2). 26.65 *(978-1-4677-7973-9(3),* Lerner Pubns.) Lerner Publishing Group.

Shea, Mary Molly. Menacing Chimpanzees. 2016. (Cutest Animals... That Could Kill You! Ser.). 24p. (J). (gr. 3-2). lib. bdg. 22.60 *(978-1-4824-4914-3(5))* Stevens, Gareth Publishing LLLP.

Shepherd, Jodie. Jane Goodall. 2015. (Rookie Biographies(tm) Ser.). (ENG.). 32p. (J). lib. bdg. 25.00 *(978-0-531-21413-8(3),* Children's Pr.) Scholastic Library Publishing.

Silvey, Anita & National Geographic Kids Staff. Untamed: The Wild Life of Jane Goodall. 2015. (ENG., Illus.). 96p. (J). (gr. 3-7). 18.99 *(978-1-4263-1518-3(X),* National Geographic Children's Bks.) National Geographic Society.

Spilsbury, Louise. Save the Chimpanzee, 1. 2014. (Animal SOS! Ser.). (ENG., Illus.). 32p. (J). (gr. k-5). pap. 10.00 *(978-1-4777-6036-9(9),* Windmill Bks.) Rosen Publishing Group, Inc., The.

Spilsbury, Louise & Spilsbury, Richard. Chimpanzee Troops. 2013. (Animal Armies Ser.). (ENG., Illus.). 32p. (J). (gr. k-5). pap. 10.00 *(978-1-4777-0328-1(4));* lib. bdg. 25.25 *(978-1-4777-0303-8(9))* Rosen Publishing Group, Inc., The. (PowerKids Pr.).

Spilsbury, Richard. A Troop of Chimpanzees: And Other Primate Groups, 1 vol. 2012. (Animals in Groups Ser.). (ENG.). 48p. (gr. 4-6). pap. 9.95 *(978-1-4329-6492-4(5));* lib. bdg. 33.32 *(978-1-4329-6485-6(2))* Heinemann-Raintree. (Heinemann InfoSearch).

Stefoff, Rebecca. Chimpanzees. 2003. (Animalways Ser.). (Illus.). 104p. (gr. 6-18). lib. bdg. 24.95 *(978-0-7614-1579-4(3),* Benchmark Bks.) Marshall Cavendish Corp.

Sweeney, Alyse. A Cheeky Chiller. 2010. (Zoo Animal Mysteries Ser.). (ENG.). 24p. (gr. k-1). lib. bdg. 26.65 *(978-1-4296-4499-0(0),* Pebble Plus) Capstone Press of Coughlan Cos.

Venezia, Mike. Jane Goodall: Researcher Who Champions Chimps. 2010. (Getting to Know the World's Greatest Inventors & Scientists Ser.). 32p. (J). (gr. 3-4). pap. 6.95 *(978-0-531-22352-9(3),* Children's Pr.) Scholastic Library Publishing.

—Jane Goodall: Researcher Who Champions Chimps. Venezia, Mike, illus. 2010. (Getting to Know the World's Greatest Inventors & Scientists Ser.). (ENG., Illus.). 32p. (J). (gr. 3-4). 28.00 *(978-0-531-23731-1(1))* Scholastic Library Publishing.

Welty, Tara. Jane Goodall. 2011. (Conservation Heroes Ser.). (Illus.). 128p. (gr. 6-12). 35.00 *(978-1-60413-952-5(8),* Chelsea Hse.) Facts On File, Inc.

Winter, Jeanette. The Watcher: Jane Goodall's Life with the Chimps. Winter, Jeanette, illus. 2011. (ENG., Illus.). 48p. (J). (gr. -1-3). 17.99 *(978-0-375-86774-3(0),* Schwartz & Wade Bks.) Random Hse. Children's Bks.

Zobel, Derek. Chimpanzees. 2011. (Animal Safari Ser.). (ENG., Illus.). 24p. (J). (gr. k-3). lib. bdg. 25.95 *(978-1-60014-602-2(3),* Blastoff! Readers) Bellwether Media.

CHIMPANZEES—FICTION

Alborough, Jez. Hug. Alborough, Jez, illus. (ENG., Illus.). 32p. (J). 2009. (gr. -1-k). pap. 3.99 *(978-0-7636-4510-6(9))* 2005. (— 1). bds. 11.99 *(978-0-7636-2893-2(X))* Candlewick Pr.

Anderson, Dawn. Chimpance, Como Yo ! 2006. (Illus.). (J). 15.95 *(978-0-9786570-1-7(2))* Opposable Thumb Pr.

—Chimpanzee, Like Me! 2006. (Illus.). (J). 15.95 *(978-0-9786570-0-0(4))* Opposable Thumb Pr.

Bently, Peter. Charlie & the Banana Monster: A Lift-the-Flap Story about Chimpanzees. 2013. (ENG.). 20p. (J). (gr. -1-2). bds. 9.99 *(978-1-4263-1097-3(8),* National Geographic Children's Bks.) National Geographic Society.

Browne, Anthony. How Do You Feel? Browne, Anthony, illus. 2012. (ENG., Illus.). 32p. (J). (gr. -1-2). 14.99 *(978-0-7636-5862-5(6))* Candlewick Pr.

—Things I Like. 2014. 24p. pap. 7.00 *(978-1-61003-372-5(8))* Center for the Collaborative Classroom.

—Willy's Stories. Browne, Anthony, illus. 2015. (ENG., Illus.). 32p. (J). (gr. k-3). 16.99 *(978-0-7636-7761-9(2))* Candlewick Pr.

Clenott, Peter. Devolution. 2013. 280p. pap. *(978-1-927792-14-8(2))* Imajin Bks.

Connelly, Peg. If the Forest Is Silent, Beware! 2007. 108p. pap. 19.95 *(978-1-60441-548-3(7))* America Star Bks.

DeLuise, Dom & Carter, Derek. Pouch Potato. 2007. 33p. pap. 9.95 *(978-0-9717952-0-4(7))* Bacchus Bks.

Dickinson, Peter. Eva. 2005. 220p. (YA). (gr. 7-12). 21.50 *(978-0-8446-7274-8(2),* 3589) Smith, Peter Pub., Inc.

Dorman, Clive & Dorman, Helen. Okomi Wakes up Early, Vol. 6. Hutchings, Tony, illus. 2004. (Sharing Nature with Children Book Ser.). 24p. (J). pap. 4.95 *(978-1-58469-056-6(9))* Dawn Pubns.

—Okomi Wanders Too Far, Vol. 8. Hutchings, Tony, illus. 2004. (Sharing Nature with Children Book Ser.). 24p. (J). pap. 4.95 *(978-1-58469-058-0(5))* Dawn Pubns.

Dorman, Helen & Dorman, Clive. Okomi & the Tickling Game, Vol. 2. Hutchings, Tony, illus. 2004. (Sharing Nature with Children Book Ser.: 2). 24p. (J). pap. 4.95 *(978-1-58469-046-7(1))* Dawn Pubns.

—Okomi Climbs a Tree, Vol. 4. Hutchings, Tony, illus. 2004. (Sharing Nature with Children Book Ser.: 4). 24p. (J). pap. 4.95 *(978-1-58469-045-0(3))* Dawn Pubns.

—Okomi Plays in the Leaves, Vol. 3. Hutchings, Tony, illus. 2004. (Sharing Nature with Children Book Ser.: 3). 24p. (J). pap. 4.95 *(978-1-58469-047-4(X))* Dawn Pubns.

—Okomi, the New Baby. Hutchings, Tony, illus. 2004. (Sharing Nature with Children Book Ser.: 1). 24p. (J). pap. 4.95 *(978-1-58469-044-3(5))* Dawn Pubns.

Duey, Kathleen. Korow: A Baby Chimpanzee's Story. Gurin, Lara, illus. 2008. (My Animal Family Ser.). (ENG.). 32p. (J). (gr. -1-3). 12.99 *(978-0-8249-1816-3(9),* Ideal Pubns.) Worthy Publishing.

Faulkner, Keith. Charlie Chimp's Christmas: A Pop-up Extravaganza of Festive Friends. Lambert, Jonathan, illus. 2006. 12p. (J). (gr. -1-3). reprint ed. 10.00 *(978-1-4223-5446-9(6))* DIANE Publishing Co.

Francois, Saragine. The White Gorilla & the Three Chimpanzees a Day from the Zoo. 2011. 28p. pap. 14.99 *(978-1-4520-3190-3(8))* AuthorHouse.

Knudtsen, Ken. My Monkey's Name Is Jennifer. 2003. (ENG., Illus.). 152p. (gr. 11-18). pap. 15.95 *(978-0-943151-71-7(6),* 9780943151717) Slave Labor Bks.

Martin, Carrie Waddington. Ham the Astrochimp: Anything Is Possible. 2012. 52p. (-18). pap. 24.99 *(978-1-4797-1059-1(8))* Xlibris Corp.

McGhee, Katie Mariah. The Case of the Missing Chimpanzee from Classroom C2. McGhee, Katie Mariah & Herrera, Aaron Jeremiah, illus. 2012. 28p. 24.95 *(978-1-4560-0039-4(X))* America Star Bks.

Nuckolls, Les. Chester the Chimpanzee. 2012. 14.99 *(978-1-4621-1131-2(9))* Cedar Fort, Inc./CFI Distribution.

Pepper, Lily. Bananas. 2012. (Illus.). 20p. pap. 19.82 *(978-1-4772-1964-5(1))* AuthorHouse.

Potter, Tracy. Charlie the Chimp's Day Out. 2013. 24p. pap. 24.95 *(978-1-63000-036-3(1))* America Star Bks.

Priddy, Roger. Charlie Champ Wins the Day. 2017. (Alphaprints Ser.). (ENG., Illus.). 32p. (J). 16.99 *(978-0-312-52177-6(4),* 9780312521776, Priddy Bks.) St. Martin's Pr.

Rey, H. A. & Rey, Margret. Curious George & the Birthday Surprise. Weston, Martha, illus. 2003. (Curious George Ser.). (ENG.). 24p. (J). (gr. -1-3). pap. 4.99 *(978-0-618-34687-5(2))* Houghton Mifflin Harcourt Publishing Co.

Schrefer, Eliot. Threatened. 2014. (ENG., Illus.). 288p. (J). (gr. 7). 17.99 *(978-0-545-55143-4(9),* Scholastic Pr.) Scholastic, Inc.

Stahnke, Rich. Furious Fist of the Drunken Monkey: Origin of the Species #3. 2007. (Illus.). 2.95 *(978-0-9791192-4-8(3))* Silent Devil Productions.

Stephens, Sarah. Midway Monkey Madness, 1 vol. Baltazar, Art, illus. 2011. (DC Super-Pets Ser.). (ENG.). 56p. (gr. 2-2). pap. 4.95 *(978-1-4048-6619-5(1));* lib. bdg. 23.99 *(978-1-4048-6305-7(2))* Picture Window Bks. (DC Super-Pets).

Young, Karen. A Chimpanzee Tale. 2009. (Illus.). 36p. pap. 16.99 *(978-1-4389-2448-9(8))* AuthorHouse.

Zakour, John. Baxter Moon Galactic Scout. 2008. 198p. (J). (gr. 5-10). per. 8.95 *(978-0-9768126-9-2(X))* Brown Barn Bks.

Zenz, Aaron. The Chimpansneeze. 2012. (Illus.). (J). *(978-0-545-51314-2(6));* pap. *(978-0-545-39870-1(3))* Scholastic, Inc.

CHINA

Amstutz, Lisa J. Chinese New Year. 2017. (Holidays Around the World Ser.). (ENG., Illus.). 24p. (gr. k-1). lib. bdg. 21.99 *(978-1-5157-4851-9(0),* Pebble Bks.) Capstone Press of Coughlan Cos.

Barcus, Dawn. Go2Guides China Ages 12+ Travel Guides for Kids Who Are Going Places. Dunlop-Kahren, Anne, ed. 2008. (Go2Guides Ser.). (Illus.). 8p. (J). 9.95 *(978-0-9800147-2-3(7))* GlobalVision Travel Resources, Inc.

—Go2Guides China Ages 5-7: Travel Guides for Kids Who Are Going Places. Dunlop-Kahren, Anne, ed. 2008. (Go2Guides Ser.). (Illus.). 8p. (J). 9.95 *(978-0-9800147-0-9(0))* GlobalVision Travel Resources, Inc.

—Go2Guides China Ages 8-11: Travel Guides for Kids Who Are Going Places. Dunlop-Kahren, Anne, ed. 2008. (Go2Guides Ser.). (Illus.). 8p. (J). 9.95 *(978-0-9800147-1-6(9))* GlobalVision Travel Resources, Inc.

Behnke, Alison. China in Pictures. 2nd rev. ed. 2003. (Visual Geography Ser.). (Illus.). 80p. (J). (gr. 5-12). 27.93 *(978-0-8225-0370-5(0))* Lerner Publishing Group.

Blevins, Wiley. China. 2017. (Follow Me Around Ser.). (ENG.). 32p. (J). lib. bdg. 27.00 ***(978-0-531-23707-6(9),*** Children's Pr.) Scholastic Library Publishing.

Bramwell, Neil D. Ancient China: A MyReportLinks. com Book. 2004. (Civilizations of the Ancient World Ser.). (Illus.). 48p. (J). lib. bdg. 25.26 *(978-0-7660-5184-3(6),* MyReportLinks.com Bks.) Enslow Pubs., Inc.

Burnham, Brad. Caves of the Thousand Buddhas: Treasure House of Chinese Art. 2009. (Famous Caves of the World Ser.). 24p. (gr. 3-4). 42.50 *(978-1-61512-496-1(9),* PowerKids Pr.) Rosen Publishing Group, Inc., The.

Caper, William. India & China: Set Of 6. 2010. (Navigators Ser.). (J). pap. 50.00 net. *(978-1-4108-5112-3(5))* Benchmark Education Co.

Chen, D. M. & Sun, Michelle. Tie a Wish with Bracelets: Easy & Fun Chinese Knotting. 2012. (ENG., Illus.). 71p. (J). (gr. 4). pap. 10.95 *(978-1-937489-01-4(9))* StoryRobin Co.

Chung, Liz. Life in China. 2012. (InfoMax Readers Ser.). (ENG., Illus.). 24p. (J). (gr. 1-2). pap. 8.25 *(978-1-4488-9025-5(X),* Rosen Classroom) Rosen Publishing Group, Inc., The.

Collier, Irene Dea. Chinese Mythology Rocks! Bock, William Sauts, illus. 2011. (Mythology Rocks! Ser.). 128p. (J). (gr. 6-18). pap. 10.95 *(978-1-59845-330-0(0))* Enslow Pubs., Inc.

Crean, Susan. Discover China. 2012. (Discover Countries Ser.). (YA). (gr. 4-7). lib. bdg. 26.50 *(978-1-4488-5266-6(8))* Rosen Publishing Group, Inc., The.

Deady, Kathleen W. & Dubois, Muriel L. Ancient China: Beyond the Great Wall. 2011. (Great Civilizations Ser.). (ENG.). 32p. (gr. 3-4). pap. 47.70 *(978-1-4296-7234-4(X),* Fact Finders) Capstone Press of Coughlan Cos.

Deasy, H. H. P. In Tibet & Chinese Turkestan: Being the Record of Three Years' Exploration. 2008. 95.00 *(978-1-57898-702-3(4));* pap. *(978-1-57898-703-0(2))* Martino Fine Bks.

Doeden, Matt. The Chinese: Life in China's Golden Age. Hiti, Sam, illus. 2009. (Life in Ancient Civilizations Ser.). (ENG.). 48p. (gr. 3-6). lib. bdg. 29.27 *(978-0-8225-8681-4(9),* Millbrook Pr.) Lerner Publishing Group.

Feinstein, Stephen. Marco Polo: Amazing Adventures in China. 2009. (Great Explorers of the World Ser.). (Illus.). 112p. (J). (gr. 7-12). lib. bdg. 33.27 *(978-1-59845-103-0(0))* Enslow Pubs., Inc.

Florence, Debbi Michiko. China: Over 40 Activities to Experience China - Past & Present. Caputo, Jim, illus. 2008. (ENG.). 96p. (J). (gr. 3-7). 16.99 *(978-0-8249-6813-7(1));* pap. 12.99 *(978-0-8249-6814-4(X))* Worthy Publishing. (Ideal Pubns.).

Friedman, Mel. China. 2008. (True Book(tm), A — Countries Ser.). (ENG., 48p. (J). (gr. 3-7). Illus.). 31.00 *(978-0-531-16852-3(2));* pap. 6.95 *(978-0-531-20726-0(9))* Scholastic Library Publishing. (Children's Pr.).

Goddard, Carole. China. 2004. (Countries of the World Ser.). (Illus.). 64p. (gr. 6-12). 30.00 *(978-0-8160-5506-7(8))* Facts On File, Inc.

Green, Jen. China. 2006. (Countries of the World Ser.). (ENG., Illus.). 64p. (J). (gr. 5-9). lib. bdg. 27.90 *(978-0-7922-6180-3(1),* National Geographic Children's Bks.) National Geographic Society.

—China - National Geographic. 2009. (Countries of the World Ser.). (ENG., Illus.). 64p. (J). (gr. 5). pap. 12.95 *(978-1-4263-0569-6(9),* National Geographic Children's Bks.) National Geographic Society.

Hardyman, Robyn. Celebrate: China. 2009. (Celebrate Country Ser.). 32p. (gr. 4-6). 28.00 *(978-1-60413-270-0(1),* Chelsea Clubhouse) Facts On File, Inc.

Hollihan-Elliot, Sheila. Art & Architecture of China. Wang, Jianwei, ed. 2012. (China: the Emerging Superpower Ser.). 120p. (J). (gr. 7). 24.95 *(978-1-4222-2155-6(5))* Mason Crest.

—Chinese Art & Architecture. 2011. (J). pap. *(978-1-4222-2166-2(0))* Mason Crest.

Huang, Chungliang Al. The Chinese Book of Animal Powers. 2011. (ENG., Illus.). 32p. 19.95 *(978-1-84819-066-5(2),* 3161, Singing Dragon) Kingsley, Jessica Pubs. GBR. Dist: Macmillan Distribution Ltd.

Jenner, Caryn. Welcome to China. 2008. (DK Readers Ser.). (ENG., Illus.). 48p. (J). (gr. 2-4). pap. 3.99 *(978-0-7566-3753-8(8),* DK Children) Dorling Kindersley Publishing, Inc.

Johnson, Robin & Kalman, Bobbie. Spotlight on China. 2008. (Spotlight on my Country Ser.). (ENG., Illus.). 32p. (J). (gr. 3-7). pap. *(978-0-7787-3480-2(3))* Crabtree Publishing Co.

Kalman, Bobbie. China: The Land. 3rd rev. ed. 2008. (Lands, Peoples & Cultures Ser.). (ENG., Illus.). 32p. (J). (gr. 3-7). lib. bdg. *(978-0-7787-9299-4(4))* Crabtree Publishing Co.

—China - The Culture. 3rd rev. ed. 2008. (Lands, Peoples & Cultures Ser.). (ENG., Illus.). 32p. (J). (gr. 3-7). pap. *(978-0-7787-9669-5(8));* lib. bdg. *(978-0-7787-9301-4(X))* Crabtree Publishing Co.

—China - The People. 3rd rev. ed. 2008. (Lands, Peoples & Cultures Ser.). (ENG., Illus.). 32p. (J). (gr. 3-9). pap. *(978-0-7787-9668-8(X))* Crabtree Publishing Co.

Liao, Yan. Food & Festivals of China. Wang, Jianwei, ed. 2012. (China: the Emerging Superpower Ser.). 120p. (J). (gr. 7). 24.95 *(978-1-4222-2159-4(8))* Mason Crest.

Litten, Kristyna. Hong Kong & Macau: a 3D Keepsake Cityscape. Litten, Kristyna, illus. 2013. (Panorama Pops Ser.). (ENG., Illus.). 30p. (J). (gr. k-4). 8.99 *(978-0-7636-6416-9(2))* Candlewick Pr.

Lu, Jia. The Geography of China. Wang, Jianwei, ed. 2012. (China: the Emerging Superpower Ser.). 112p. (J). (gr. 7). 24.95 *(978-1-4222-2160-0(1))* Mason Crest.

—The Geography of China. 2011. (J). pap. *(978-1-4222-2171-6(7))* Mason Crest.

Luh, Shu Shin. The Economy of China. Wang, Jianwei, ed. 2012. (China: the Emerging Superpower Ser.). 128p. (J). (gr. 7). 24.95 *(978-1-4222-2157-0(1))* Mason Crest.

—The Economy of China. 2011. (J). pap. *(978-1-4222-2168-6(7))* Mason Crest.

Lynch, Annabelle. Living in China. 2016. (Living In Ser.). (ENG., Illus.). 24p. (J). (gr. 1-3). 16.99 *(978-1-4451-4859-5(5),* Franklin Watts) Hachette Children's Group GBR. Dist: Hachette Bk. Group.

March, Michael. China. 2003. (Country Files Ser.). 32p. (J). lib. bdg. 24.25 *(978-1-58340-236-8(5))* Black Rabbit Bks.

Markle, Sandra. The Great Leopard Rescue: Saving the Amur Leopards. 2016. (ENG., Illus.). 48p. (J). (gr. 4-6). 30.65 *(978-1-4677-9247-9(0),* Millbrook Pr.) Lerner Publishing Group.

Marsh, Carole. China: A Great Wall Runs Thru It! 2009. (It's Your World Ser.). 48p. (J). (gr. 2-9). pap. 7.99 *(978-0-635-06812-5(5))* Gallopade International.

McNeil, Niki, et al. Ancient China. 2007. (In the Hands of a Child: Project Pack Continent Study Ser.). (Illus.). 64p. spiral bd. 20.00 *(978-1-60308-113-9(5))* In the Hands of a Child.

Michels, Dia L. Look What I See! Where Can I Be? Visiting China. Bowles, Michael J. N., photos by. 2005. (Look What I See! Where Can I Be? Ser.: Vol. 5). (ENG., Illus.). 32p. (J). (gr. -1-3). 9.95 *(978-1-930775-15-2(6))* Platypus Media, L.L.C.

Mis, Melody S. How to Draw China's Sights & Symbols. 2009. (Kid's Guide to Drawing the Countries of the World Ser.). 48p. (gr. 4-4). 53.00 *(978-1-61511-109-1(3),* PowerKids Pr.) Rosen Publishing Group, Inc., The.

Moon, Walt K. Let's Explore China. 2017. (Bumba Books (tm) — Let's Explore Countries Ser.). (ENG.). 24p. (J). (gr. -1-1). 12.99 ***(978-1-5124-3729-4(8),*** Lerner Pubns.); 38.65 ***(978-1-5124-3728-7(X),*** Lerner Pubns.); 38.65 ***(978-1-5124-3014-1(5),*** Lerner Pubns.); (Illus.). 25.32 *(978-1-5124-3004-2(8))* Lerner Publishing Group.

O'Connell, Kim A. China: A MyReportLinks. com Book. 2004. (Top Ten Countries of Recent Immigrants Ser.). (Illus.). 48p. (J). lib. bdg. 26.60 *(978-0-7660-5240-6(0),* MyReportLinks.com Bks.) Enslow Pubs., Inc.

Popper, Garry. Li & Lily May in China. Johnson, Andi, illus. 2004. 36p. (gr. -1-7). 4.00 *(978-1-84161-057-3(7))* Ravette Publishing, Ltd. GBR. Dist: Parkwest Pubns., Inc.

Powell, Jillian. Descubramos China. 2007. (Descubramos paises del mundo (Spanish- Looking at Countries) Ser.). (SPA.). 32p. (gr. 1-5). pap. 10.50 *(978-0-8368-8190-5(7),* Gareth Stevens Learning Library) Stevens, Gareth Publishing LLLP.

—Looking at China. 2007. (Looking at Countries Ser.). 32p. (gr. 1-5). pap. 10.50 *(978-0-8368-8176-9(1));* (Illus.). lib. bdg. 26.00 *(978-0-8368-8169-1(9))* Stevens, Gareth Publishing LLLP. (Gareth Stevens Learning Library).

Raatma, Lucia. China. 2010. (Explorer Library: Social Studies Explorer Ser.). (ENG.). 48p. (gr. 4-8). lib. bdg. 31.36 *(978-1-60279-823-6(0),* 200512) Cherry Lake Publishing.

Richardson, Adele. China. 2006. (My First Look at Countries Ser.). (Illus.). 24p. (J). (gr. -1-3). lib. bdg. 15.95

C
D

(978-1-58341-445-3(2), Creative Education) Creative Co., The.
—Great Wall of China. 2005. (Ancient Wonders of the World Ser.). (Illus.). 32p. (J). (gr. 4-7). lib. bdg. 18.95 *(978-1-58341-356-2(1),* Creative Education) Creative Co., The.
Riehecky, Janet. China. 2008. pap. 40.95 *(978-0-8225-9300-3(9))* 2007. (Illus.). 48p. (J). (gr. -1-3). lib. bdg. 27.93 *(978-0-8225-7129-2(3),* Lerner Pubns.) Lerner Publishing Group.
Roza, Greg. A Primary Source Guide to China. (Countries of the World). 24p. 2009. (gr. 2-3). 42.50 *(978-1-61512-028-4(9))* 2003. (ENG., Illus.). (gr. 3-6). pap. 8.25 *(978-0-8239-8075-8(8))* 2003. (Illus.). (J). lib. bdg. 22.60 *(978-0-8239-6591-5(0))* Rosen Publishing Group, Inc., The. (PowerKids Pr.).
Savery, Annabel. China. 2011. (ENG., Illus.). 32p. (J). pap. 10.95 *(978-1-77092-022-4(6))* Saunders Bk. Co. CAN. Dist: RiverStream Publishing.
Sebag-Montefiore, Hugh & Dorling Kindersley Publishing Staff. China. 2007. (DK Eyewitness Bks.). (ENG., Illus.). 72p. (J). (gr. 3-7). 16.99 *(978-0-7566-2976-2(4),* DK Children) Dorling Kindersley Publishing, Inc.
Sherman, Josepha. Your Travel Guide to Ancient China. 2003. (Passport to History Ser.). (ENG., Illus.). 80p. (gr. 5-9). 26.60 *(978-0-8225-3073-2(2))* Lerner Publishing Group.
Sonneborn, Liz. Ancient China. 2012. (ENG., Illus.). 112p. (J). lib. bdg. 34.00 *(978-0-531-25176-8(4))* Scholastic Library Publishing.
Sorensen, Launa. My Adventure in China. 2009. (ENG.). 44p. (J). 8.99 *(978-1-59092-425-9(8))* Blue Forge Pr.
Steloff, Rebecca. Asian Empires. 2004. (Illus.). 48p. (J). 31.36 *(978-0-7614-1643-2(9),* Benchmark Bks.) Marshall Cavendish Corp.
Streissguth, Tom. China in the 21st Century: A New World Power. 2008. (Issues in Focus Today Ser.). (Illus.). 112p. (J). (gr. 3-7). lib. bdg. 33.27 *(978-0-7660-2684-1(1))* Enslow Pubs., Inc.
Teacher Created Resources Staff. Travel Through - China: Come on a Journey of Discovery. 2008. (Travel Through Ser.). (ENG., Illus.). 32p. (gr. 4-7). pap. 7.99 *(978-1-4206-8280-9(6))* Teacher Created Resources, Inc.
Teichmann, Iris. China. 2007. (Countries in the News/Watts Ser.). (Illus.). 32p. (YA). (gr. 4-7). lib. bdg. 28.50 *(978-1-59920-015-6(5))* Black Rabbit Bks.
Tidey, John & Tidey, Jackie. Land & Climate. 2008. (China Ser.). 32p. (gr. 4-18). lib. bdg. 18.56 *(978-0-7614-3156-5(X),* Benchmark Bks.) Marshall Cavendish Corp.
Wang, Jianwei, ed. China, 10 vols. 2005. (Illus.). 112,144p. 249.50 *(978-1-59084-821-0(7))* Mason Crest.
Whitefield, Gary T. China. Gritzner, Charles F., ed. 2003. (Modern World Nations Ser.). (Illus.). 200p. (gr. 6-12). lib. bdg. 24.95 *(978-0-7910-6930-1(3),* Chelsea Hse.) Facts On File, Inc.
Yasuda, Anita. Dragon, the Phoenix, & the Beautiful Pearl: A Chinese Dragon Spirit Myth. 2014. (Short Tales Chinese Myths Ser.). 32p. (J). (gr. 3-6). lib. bdg. 24.21 *(978-1-62402-030-8(5),* Short Tales) Magic Wagon.
—Jade Emperor: A Chinese Zodiac Myth. 2014. (Short Tales Chinese Myths Ser.). 32p. (J). (gr. 3-6). lib. bdg. 24.21 *(978-1-62402-031-5(3),* Short Tales) Magic Wagon.

CHINA—BIOGRAPHY

Bernstein, Richard. A Girl Named Faithful Plum: The True Story of a Dancer from China & How She Achieved Her Dream. 2012. (ENG.). 288p. (J). (gr. 5-9). 7.99 *(978-0-375-87158-0(6),* Yearling) Random Hse. Children's Bks.
Chen, Da. China's Son: Growing up in the Cultural Revolution. 2004. (ENG.). 224p. (YA). (gr. 7-7). reprint ed. mass mkt. 6.99 *(978-0-440-22926-1(X),* Laurel Leaf) Random Hse. Children's Bks.
Clark, Travis. Yao Ming. 2010. (Modern Role Models Ser.). (Illus.). 64p. (YA). (gr. 7-12). lib. bdg. 22.95 *(978-1-4222-0484-9(7))* Mason Crest.
Cooper, Meghan. Sun Tzu. 2017. (J). ***(978-1-5026-2867-1(8))*** Cavendish Square Publishing.
Cunxin, Li. Mao's Last Dancer. movie tie-in ed. 2010. (ENG.). 528p. (gr. 12). 17.00 *(978-0-425-24030-4(4),* Berkley) Penguin Publishing Group.
Demi. The Great Voyages of Zheng He. 2012. (Illus.). (J). 21.95 *(978-1-885008-45-9(7),* Shen's Bks.) Lee & Low Bks., Inc.
—Su Dongpo: Chinese Genius. 2015. (ENG., Illus.). 56p. (J). pap. 12.95 *(978-1-62014-232-5(5))* Lee & Low Bks., Inc.
Demi & Demi Staff. Su Dongpo. 2006. (ENG., Illus.). 56p. (J). (gr. 2-5). 24.00 *(978-1-58430-256-8(9))* Lee & Low Bks., Inc.
Geyer, Flora. Mao Zedong: The Rebel Who Led a Revolution. 2007. (National Geographic World History Biographies Ser.). (ENG., Illus.). 64p. (J). (gr. 3-7). lib. bdg. 27.90 *(978-1-4263-0063-9(8),* National Geographic Children's Bks.) National Geographic Society.
Heuston, Kimberley. Mao Zedong. 2010. (Wicked History Ser.). (ENG.). 128p. (J). (gr. 6-12). pap. 5.95 *(978-0-531-22356-7(6),* Watts, Franklin) Scholastic Library Publishing.
Heuston, Kimberley Burton. Mao Zedong. 2010. (Wicked History Ser.). (ENG., Illus.). 128p. (J). (gr. 5-8). 31.00 *(978-0-531-20756-7(0))* Scholastic Library Publishing.
Jiang, Ji-Li. Red Scarf Girl: A Memoir of the Cultural Revolution. 2004. (ENG.). 320p. (J). (gr. 3-7). pap. 7.99 *(978-0-06-446208-2(0))* HarperCollins Pubs.
Krull, Kathleen. Kubla Khan: The Emperor of Everything. Byrd, Robert, illus. 2010. (ENG.). 48p. (J). (gr. 3-7). 17.99 *(978-0-670-01114-8(2),* Viking Books for Young Readers) Penguin Young Readers Group.
Leonard, Dion. Finding Gobi: The True Story of One Little Dog's Big Journey. 2017. (ENG.). 208p. (J). pap. 14.99 ***(978-0-7180-7531-6(5))*** Nelson, Thomas Inc.
Li, Richard T. The Golden Lotus: Life of a Bound-Feet Peasant Mother in the Chinese Cultural Revolution. 2004. (Illus.). 140p. (YA). pap. 7.95 *(978-0-9675988-3-3(4))* Li, Richard T.
Liao, Yan. Famous People of China. Wang, Jianwei, ed. 2012. (China: the Emerging Superpower Ser.). 120p. (J). (gr. 7). 24.95 *(978-1-4222-2158-7(X))* Mason Crest.
—Famous People of China. 2011. (J). *(978-1-4222-2169-3(5))* 2007. (Illus.). 119p. (YA). lib. bdg. 24.95 *(978-1-59084-826-5(8))* Mason Crest.
Luh, Shu Shin. The People of China. Wang, Jianwei, ed. 2012. (China: the Emerging Superpower Ser.). 128p. (J). (gr. 7). 24.95 *(978-1-4222-2163-1(6))* Mason Crest.
—The People of China. 2011. (J). pap. *(978-1-4222-2174-7(1))* Mason Crest.
MacDonald, Fiona & Geyer, Flora. Mao Zedong: The Rebel Who Led a Revolution. 2007. (National Geographic World History Biographies Ser.). (ENG., Illus.). 64p. (J). (gr. 3-7). 17.95 *(978-1-4263-0062-2(X),* National Geographic Children's Bks.) National Geographic Society.
Marx, Christy. Jet Li. (Martial Arts Masters Ser.). 112p. 2009. (gr. 5-5). 63.90 *(978-1-61514-374-0(2))* 2005. (Illus.). (YA). (gr. 7-12). lib. bdg. 34.60 *(978-0-8239-3519-2(1))* Rosen Publishing Group, Inc., The.
McCollum, Sean. The Chairman: Mao Unleashes Chaos in China. 2011. (J). pap. *(978-0-545-32936-4(3))* Scholastic, Inc.
Miller, Anna Carew & Carew-Miller, Anna. Confucius: Great Chinese Philosopher. 2013. (People of Importance Ser.: 21). (Illus.). 32p. (J). (gr. 4-18). 19.95 *(978-1-4222-2845-6(2))* Mason Crest.
Savage, Jeff. Yao Ming. rev. ed. 2009. (Amazing Athletes Ser.). (gr. 2-5). pap. 6.95 *(978-0-7613-3893-2(4),* Lerner Pubns.) Lerner Publishing Group.
Shea, Therese. Sharks. 2006. (Big Bad Biters Ser.). (Illus.). 24p. (J). (gr. 3-7). lib. bdg. 22.60 *(978-1-4042-3519-9(1))* Rosen Publishing Group, Inc., The.
—Yao Ming: International Basketball Star. 2006. (Tony Stead Nonfiction Independent Reading Collection). (ENG.). (gr. 3-6). pap. 8.85 *(978-1-4042-5538-8(9))* Rosen Publishing Group, Inc., The.
Smit, Anika. Taxi. 2006. (ENG.). 168p. per. 18.00 *(978-1-4251-0019-3(8))* Trafford Publishing.
Stone, Amy. Jackie Chan. 2007. (Today's Superstars). (Illus.). 32p. (gr. 5-8). lib. bdg. 31.95 *(978-0-8368-7648-2(2))* Stevens, Gareth Publishing LLLP.
Sullivan, Anne Marie. Dalai Lama: Spiritual Leader of Tibet. 2013. (People of Importance Ser.: 21). (Illus.). 32p. (J). (gr. 4-18). 19.95 *(978-1-4222-2846-3(0))* Mason Crest.
Twist, Clint. Marco Polo: History's Great Adventurer. 2011. (Historical Notebooks Ser.). (ENG., Illus.). 30p. (J). (gr. 3-7). 19.99 *(978-0-7636-5286-9(5),* Templar) Candlewick Pr.
Uschan, Michael V. Jet Li. 2011. (People in the News Ser.). (ENG., Illus.). 128p. (gr. 7-10). lib. bdg. 39.40 *(978-1-4205-0731-7(1))* Cengage Gale.
Vietze, Andrew. Zheng He: China's Greatest Navigator. 2017. (Spotlight on Explorers & Colonization Ser.). 48p. (gr. 10-11). pap. 11.75 ***(978-1-5081-7507-0(1),*** Rosen Young Adult) Rosen Publishing Group, Inc., The.
Yan, Ma. The Diary of Ma Yan: The Life of a Chinese School Girl. Haski, Pierre, ed. 2006. (Illus.). 208p. reprint ed. pap. 22.00 *(978-1-4223-5712-5(0))* DIANE Publishing Co.
Yim, Natasha. Cixi: "The Dragon Empress" Malone, Peter, illus. 2011. (Thinking Girl's Treasury of Dastardly Dames Ser.). (ENG.). 32p. (J). (gr. 3-8). 18.95 *(978-0-9834256-5-6(5))* Goosebottom Bks. LLC.
Young, Ed. The House Baba Built: An Artist's Childhood in China. 2011. (ENG.). 48p. (J). (gr. -1-3). 17.99 *(978-0-316-07628-9(7))* Little, Brown Bks. for Young Readers.

CHINA—FICTION

Ahern, Carolyn L. Tino Turtle Travels to Beijing, China. Burt-Sullivan, Neallia, illus. 2011. (ENG.). 56p. (J). (gr. -1-4). 19.95 incl. audio compact disk *(978-0-9793158-4-8(0))* Tino Turtle Travels, LLC.
Alexander, Lloyd. Dream-of-Jade: The Emperor's Cat. Burkett, D. Brent, illus. 2005. (ENG.). 48p. (J). (gr. 3-7). 17.95 *(978-0-8126-2736-7(9))* Cricket Bks.
Andersen, Hans Christian. The Nightingale. Oleynikov, Igor, illus. 2007.Tr. of Nattergalen. (ENG.). 40p. (J). (gr. k). lib. bdg. 16.50 *(978-1-933327-31-0(6));* (gr. 1). 15.95 *(978-1-933327-30-3(8))* Purple Bear Bks., Inc.
—El Ruisenor.Tr. of Nightingale. (SPA.). 32p. (J). (gr. 2-3). 12.95 *(978-84-233-1567-3(3))* Ediciones Destino ESP. Dist: Planeta Publishing Corp.
Anna, Jennifer. Year of the Dragon: The Complete Story Experience Edition. Brandon, Theresa, illus. 2nd exp. ed. 2005. (Turtle's Back Bks.). 100p. (J). (gr. -1-6). pap. 14.99 *(978-1-883573-18-8(1))* Blue Forge Pr.
Baccalario, Pierdomenico. Dragon of Seas. Janeczko, Leah D., tr. from ITA. 2013. (Century Ser.: 4). (ENG.). 320p. (J). (gr. 3-7). 7.99 *(978-0-375-85798-0(2),* Yearling) Random Hse. Children's Bks.
Barry, Nick. Escape of the Terra-Cotta Soldiers: An Ethan Sparks Adventure. 2008. 180p. 23.95 *(978-0-595-49365-4(3));* pap. 13.95 *(978-0-595-45413-6(5))* iUniverse, Inc.
Bouchard, David. The Great Race - The Legend of the Chinese Zodiac. 2004. (J). (gr. k-3). spiral bd. *(978-0-616-01430-1(9))* Canadian National Institute for the Blind/Institut National Canadien pour les Aveugles.
Brennan, Sarah. The Tale of a Dark Horse. 2013. (ENG., Illus.). 32p. (J). 24.95 *(978-1-937160-57-9(2))* Eliassen Creative.
Brennan, Sarah. The Tale of Rodney Ram. Harrison, Harry, illus. 2014. (J). ***(978-1-937160-60-9(2))*** Eliassen Creative.
Brett, Jan. Daisy Comes Home. Brett, Jan, illus. 2005. (ENG., Illus.). 32p. (J). (gr. k-3). reprint ed. pap. 6.99 *(978-0-14-240270-2(2),* Puffin Books) Penguin Young Readers Group.
Bridges, Shirin Yim. Ruby's Wish. 2015. (J). lib. bdg. 18.40 *(978-0-606-37443-9(4))* Turtleback Bks.
Buck, Pearl S. A House Divided. 2004. 304p. (C). reprint ed. pap. 12.95 *(978-1-55921-340-0(X))* Nodin Pr.
Burchett, Jan & Vogler, Sara. Earthquake Escape, 1 vol. Le Feyer, Diane, illus. 2012. (Wild Rescue Ser.). (ENG.). 152p. (gr. 3-6). lib. bdg. 25.32 *(978-1-4048-6891-5(7))* Picture Window Bks.
Capucilli, Alyssa Satin. Panda Kisses. Widdowson, Kay, illus. 2008. (Step into Reading Ser.). (ENG.). 32p. (J). (gr. -1-1). pap. 3.99 *(978-0-375-84562-8(3),* Random Hse. Bks. for Young Readers) Random Hse. Children's Bks.
Cardona, Jose. Mulan (Disney Princess) Golden Books, illus. 2013. (Little Golden Book Ser.). (ENG.). 24p. (J). (-k). 4.99 *(978-0-7364-3053-1(9),* Golden/Disney) Random Hse. Children's Bks.
Casey, Dawn. The Great Race: The Story of the Chinese Zodiac. Wilson, Anne, illus. 2008. (ENG.). 32p. (J). (gr. -1-2). 8.99 *(978-1-84686-202-1(7))* Barefoot Bks., Inc.
Chang, Grace. Jin Jin & Rain Wizard. Chang, Chong, illus. 2009. (ENG.). 48p. (J). (gr. -1-3). 16.95 *(978-1-59270-086-8(1))* Enchanted Lion Bks., LLC.
—Jin Jin the Dragon. Chang, Chong, illus. 2008. (ENG.). 48p. (J). (gr. -1-3). 16.95 *(978-1-59270-102-5(7))* Enchanted Lion Bks., LLC.
Chapman, Mary Beth & Chapman, Steven Curtis. Shaoey & Dot: A Trip to Dr. Betterbee. 2005. 20p. (J). 6.99 *(978-1-4003-0568-1(3))* Nelson, Thomas Inc.
—Shaoey & Dot: Back in a Bug's Blink. 2005. 20p. (J). 6.99 *(978-1-4003-0569-8(1))* Nelson, Thomas Inc.
—Shaoey & Dot: Thunder & Lightning Bugs. 2005. 20p. (J). 6.99 *(978-1-4003-0570-4(5))* Nelson, Thomas Inc.
Chen, Wei Dong. Blood & Renewal. Liang, Xiao Long, illus. 2015. (Outlaws of the Marsh Ser.). (ENG.). 176p. (YA). (gr. 6-12). pap. 9.99 *(978-89-98341-90-9(5))* Lerner Publishing Group.
—Etched in Blood. Long Liang, Xiao, illus. 2013. (Three Kingdoms Ser.: 5). 176p. (YA). (gr. 5-12). lib. bdg. 29.27 *(978-89-94208-98-5(4))* Lerner Publishing Group.
—The Expulsion of Sun Wu Kong. Peng, Chao, illus. 2013. (Monkey King Ser.: 7). 176p. (YA). (gr. 6-12). lib. bdg. 29.27 *(978-89-94208-75-6(5))* Lerner Publishing Group.
—The Family Plot. Long Liang, Xiao, illus. 2013. (Three Kingdoms Ser.: 2). 176p. (YA). (gr. 5-12). lib. bdg. 29.27 *(978-89-94208-92-3(5))* Lerner Publishing Group.
—Fight to the Death. Peng, Chao, illus. 2013. (Monkey King Ser.: 11). 176p. (YA). (gr. 6-12). lib. bdg. 29.27 *(978-89-94208-79-4(8))* Lerner Publishing Group.
—Heroes & Chaos. Long Liang, Xiao, illus. 2013. (Three Kingdoms Ser.: 1). 176p. (YA). (gr. 5-12). lib. bdg. 29.27 *(978-89-94208-90-9(9))* Lerner Publishing Group.
—The Lost Children. Peng, Chao, illus. 2013. (Monkey King Ser.: 12). 176p. (YA). (gr. 6-12). lib. bdg. 29.27 *(978-89-94208-80-0(1))* Lerner Publishing Group.
—Monkey King: Enemies & a New Friend. Peng, Chao, illus. 2012. (Monkey King Ser.: 4). (ENG.). 176p. (gr. 5-8). lib. bdg. 29.27 *(978-89-94208-72-5(0))* JR Comics KOR. Dist: Lerner Publishing Group.
—Monkey King: Journey to the West. Peng, Chao, illus. 2012. (Monkey King Ser.: 3). (ENG.). 176p. (gr. 5-8). lib. bdg. 29.27 *(978-89-94208-71-8(2))* JR Comics KOR. Dist: Lerner Publishing Group.
—Monkey King: The Bane of Heaven. Peng, Chao, illus. 2012. (Monkey King Ser.: 2). (ENG.). 176p. (gr. 5-8). lib. bdg. 29.27 *(978-89-94208-70-1(4))* JR Comics KOR. Dist: Lerner Publishing Group.
—Monkey King: The Sacred Tree. Peng, Chao, illus. 2012. (Monkey King Ser.: 6). (ENG.). 176p. (gr. 5-8). lib. bdg. 29.27 *(978-89-94208-74-9(7))* JR Comics KOR. Dist: Lerner Publishing Group.
—Monkey King: Three Trials. Peng, Chao, illus. 2012. (Monkey King Ser.: 5). (ENG.). 176p. (gr. 5-8). lib. bdg. 29.27 *(978-89-94208-73-2(9))* JR Comics KOR. Dist: Lerner Publishing Group.
—The Realm of the Infant King. Peng, Chao, illus. 2013. (Monkey King Ser.: 10). 176p. (YA). (gr. 6-12). lib. bdg. 29.27 *(978-89-94208-78-7(X))* Lerner Publishing Group.
—Revenge & Betrayal. Long Liang, Xiao, illus. 2013. (Three Kingdoms Ser.: 4). 176p. (YA). (gr. 5-12). lib. bdg. 29.27 *(978-89-94208-96-1(8))* Lerner Publishing Group.
—The Stolen Kingdom. Peng, Chao, illus. 2013. (Monkey King Ser.: 9). 176p. (YA). (gr. 6-12). lib. bdg. 29.27 *(978-89-94208-77-0(1))* Lerner Publishing Group.
—To Pledge Allegiance. Long Liang, Xiao, illus. 2013. (Three Kingdoms Ser.: 3). 176p. (YA). (gr. 5-12). lib. bdg. 29.27 *(978-89-94208-94-7(1))* Lerner Publishing Group.
—Treasures of the Mountain Kings. Peng, Chao, illus. 2013. (Monkey King Ser.: 8). 176p. (YA). (gr. 6-12). lib. bdg. 29.27 *(978-89-94208-76-3(3))* Lerner Publishing Group.
Chen, Wei Dong & Liang, Xiao Long. Blood & Honor, Vol. 6. 2013. (Three Kingdoms Ser.: 6). (ENG., Illus.). 176p. (gr. 5-12). pap. 8.95 *(978-89-94208-99-2(2))* JR Comics KOR. Dist: Lerner Publishing Group.
—The Brotherhood Restored, Vol. 7. Liang, Xiao Long, illus. 2013. (Three Kingdoms Ser.: 7). (ENG., Illus.). 176p. (gr. 5-12). pap. 9.99 *(978-89-94208-67-1(4))* JR Comics KOR. Dist: Lerner Publishing Group.
—Etched in Blood, Vol. 5. 2013. (Three Kingdoms Ser.: 5). (ENG., Illus.). 176p. (YA). (gr. 5-12). pap. 9.99 *(978-89-94208-97-8(6))* Lerner Publishing Group.
—The Family Plot, Vol. 2. 2013. (Three Kingdoms Ser.: 2). (ENG., Illus.). 176p. (YA). (gr. 5-12). pap. 9.99 *(978-89-94208-91-6(7))* Lerner Publishing Group.
—Revenge & Betrayal, Vol. 4. 2013. (Three Kingdoms Ser.: 4). (ENG., Illus.). 176p. (YA). (gr. 5-12). pap. 9.99 *(978-89-94208-95-4(X))* Lerner Publishing Group.
—Three Kingdoms, Vol. 9. Liang, Xiao Long, illus. 2013. (Three Kingdoms Ser.: 9). (ENG., Illus.). 176p. (gr. 5-12). pap. 9.99 *(978-89-98341-22-0(0))* JR Comics KOR. Dist: Lerner Publishing Group.
—To Pledge Allegiance, Vol. 3. 2013. (Three Kingdoms Ser.: 3). (ENG., Illus.). 176p. (YA). (gr. 5-12). pap. 9.99 *(978-89-94208-93-0(3))* Lerner Publishing Group.
Chen, Yong. A Gift. (ENG.). 32p. (J). (gr. k-2). 2011. pap. 6.95 *(978-1-59078-898-1(2))* 2009. 16.95 *(978-1-59078-610-9(6))* Boyds Mills Pr.
Cheng, Andrea. Shanghai Messenger, 1 vol. Young, Ed, illus. 2005. (ENG.). 40p. (J). (gr. 3-7). 17.95 *(978-1-58430-238-4(0))* Lee & Low Bks., Inc.
—The Year of the Fortune Cookie. Barton, Patrice, illus. 2014. (Anna Wang Novel Ser.: 3). (ENG.). 176p. (J). (gr. 1-4). 15.99 *(978-0-544-10519-5(2),* HMH Books For Young Readers) Houghton Mifflin Harcourt Publishing Co.
Cheng, Andrea & Young, Ed. Shanghai Messenger. 2015. (ENG.). 40p. (J). pap. 10.95 *(978-1-62014-230-1(9))* Lee & Low Bks., Inc.
Cheng'en, Wu. Journey to the West. Chiang, Shirley, illus. 2013. (Chinese Classics Ser.). (ENG.). 64p. pap. 6.95 *(978-1-906230-34-0(X))* Real Reads Ltd. GBR. Dist: Casemate Pubs. & Bk. Distributors, LLC.
Chin, Oliver. The Year of the Dragon: Tales from the Chinese Zodiac. 2012. (Tales from the Chinese Zodiac Ser.: 7). (ENG., Illus.). 36p. (J). (gr. -1-3). 15.95 *(978-1-59702-028-2(1))* Immedium.
—The Year of the Tiger: Tales from the Chinese Zodiac. Roth, Justin, illus. 2010. (Tales from the Chinese Zodiac Ser.). (ENG.). 36p. (J). (gr. -1-3). 15.95 *(978-1-59702-020-6(6))* Immedium.
Chin, Oliver, ed. The Year of the Snake: Tales from the Chinese Zodiac. Wood, Jennifer, illus. 2012. (Tales from the Chinese Zodiac Ser.: 8). (ENG.). 36p. (J). (gr. -1-3). 15.95 *(978-1-59702-038-1(9))* Immedium.
Chin, Oliver Clyde. The Year of the Rabbit: Tales from the Chinese Zodiac. Roth, Justin, illus. 2010. (Tales from the Chinese Zodiac Ser.). (ENG.). 36p. (J). (gr. -1-3). 15.95 *(978-1-59702-023-7(0))* Immedium.
—The Year of the Rat: Tales from the Chinese Zodiac. Alcorn, Miah, illus. 2008. (Tales from the Chinese Zodiac Ser.). (ENG.). 36p. (J). (gr. -1-k). 15.95 *(978-1-59702-011-4(7))* Immedium.
Chinese, the Singapore. Musical Adventures with Quek Quek: Discover the Sounds of the Chinese Orchestra. Fong, Lee Kow, illus. 2016. (ENG.). 96p. pap. 25.00 incl. cd-rom *(978-981-4677-23-3(X))* Marshall Cavendish International (Asia) Private Ltd. SGP. Dist: National Bk. Network.
Cleveland, Rob. The Archer & the Sun: A Tale from China. Hoffmire, Baird, illus. 2007. (Story Cove Ser.). (ENG.). 24p. (J). (gr. -1-3). pap. 3.95 *(978-0-87483-878-7(9))* August Hse. Pubs., Inc.
Colossal, Eric. Feasts of Fury. 2016. (Rutabaga the Adventure Chef Ser.: 2). (J). lib. bdg. 20.80 *(978-0-606-38205-2(4))* Turtleback Bks.
Compestine, Ying. The Story of Noodles: Amazing Chinese Inventions. Xuan, YongSheng, illus. 2016. (ENG & CHI.). 40p. (J). (gr. -1-3). 15.95 *(978-1-59702-121-0(0))* Immedium.
Compestine, Ying Chang. Boy Dumplings. Yamasaki, James, illus. 2009. (ENG.). 32p. (J). (gr. -1-3). 16.95 *(978-0-8234-1955-5(X))* Holiday Hse., Inc.
—Revolution Is Not a Dinner Party. 2009. (ENG.). 272p. (J). (gr. 5-9). pap. 9.99 *(978-0-312-58149-7(1),* 9780312581497) Square Fish.
—The Runaway Wok: A Chinese New Year Tale. Serra, Sebastia, illus. 2011. (ENG.). 32p. (J). (gr. 1-3). 16.99 *(978-0-525-42068-2(1),* Dutton Books for Young Readers) Penguin Young Readers Group.
Compestine, Ying Chang & Compestine, Vinson. Secrets of the Terra-Cotta Soldier. 2014. (ENG., Illus.). 240p. (YA). (gr. 3-7). 16.95 *(978-1-4197-0540-3(7),* Amulet Bks.) Abrams, Inc.
Converse, P. J. Subway Girl. 2011. (ENG.). 224p. (YA). (gr. 9-18). 16.99 *(978-0-06-157514-3(3),* HarperTeen) HarperCollins Pubs.
Dargaw, Kate. Who Came First. Oleynikov, Igor, illus. 2008. 32p. 15.95 *(978-1-933327-45-7(6))* Purple Bear Bks., Inc.
Demi. The Empty Pot. Demi, illus. 2007. (ENG., Illus.). 32p. (J). (gr. -1-3). pap. 25.99 *(978-0-8050-8227-2(1),* 9780805082272, Holt, Henry & Co. Bks. For Young Readers) Holt, Henry & Co.
—The Girl Who Drew a Phoenix. Demi, illus. 2008. (ENG., Illus.). 52p. (J). (gr. 2-5). 24.99 *(978-1-4169-5347-0(7),* McElderry, Margaret K. Bks.) McElderry, Margaret K. Bks.
—The Greatest Power. Demi, illus. 2004. (ENG., Illus.). 40p. (J). (gr. -1-3). 24.99 *(978-0-689-84503-1(0),* McElderry, Margaret K. Bks.) McElderry, Margaret K. Bks.
—The Magic Pillow. Demi, illus. 2008. (ENG., Illus.). 40p. (J). (gr. 2-5). 24.99 *(978-1-4169-2470-8(1),* McElderry, Margaret K. Bks.) McElderry, Margaret K. Bks.
—Marco Polo, 0 vols. 2008. (ENG., Illus.). 56p. (J). (gr. 4-7). 19.99 *(978-0-7614-5433-5(0),* 9780761454335, Amazon Children's Publishing) Amazon Publishing.
Dokey, Cameron. The Wild Orchid: A Retelling of the Ballad of Mulan. 2009. (Once upon a Time Ser.). (ENG.). 224p. (YA). (gr. 7-18). mass mkt. 7.99 *(978-1-4169-7168-9(8),* Simon Pulse) Simon Pulse.
Dong Chen, Wei. Band of Brothers. Peng, Chao, illus. 2013. (Monkey King Ser.: 18). (ENG.). 176p. (gr. 6-12). pap. 9.99 *(978-89-94208-63-3(1))* JR Comics KOR. Dist: Lerner Publishing Group.
—Battle of Red Cliffs. Liang, Xiao Long, illus. 2013. (Three Kingdoms Ser.: 11). (ENG.). 176p. (gr. 5-12). pap. 9.99 *(978-89-98341-24-4(7))* JR Comics KOR. Dist: Lerner Publishing Group.
—The Dual. Peng, Chao, illus. 2013. (Monkey King Ser.: 14). (ENG.). 176p. (gr. 6-12). pap. 9.99 *(978-89-94208-59-6(3))* JR Comics KOR. Dist: Lerner Publishing Group.
—Expulsion of Sun Wu. Peng, Chao, illus. 2013. (Monkey King Ser.: 7). (ENG.). 176p. (YA). (gr. 6-12). pap. 9.99 *(978-89-94208-51-0(8))* Lerner Publishing Group.
—Fanning the Flames. Peng, Chao, illus. 2013. (Monkey King Ser.: 15). (ENG.). 176p. (gr. 6-12). pap. 9.99 *(978-89-94208-60-2(7))* JR Comics KOR. Dist: Lerner Publishing Group.
—Fight to the Death. Peng, Chao, illus. 2013. (Monkey King Ser.: 11). (ENG.). 176p. (YA). (gr. 6-12). pap. 9.99 *(978-89-94208-56-5(9))* Lerner Publishing Group.
—The Fortunate Sons. Long Liang, Xiao, illus. 2013. (Three Kingdoms Ser.: 8). (ENG.). 176p. (gr. 5-12). pap. 9.99 *(978-89-98341-21-3(2))* JR Comics KOR. Dist: Lerner Publishing Group.
—Golden Temple. Peng, Chao, illus. 2013. (Monkey King Ser.: 16). (ENG.). 176p. (gr. 6-12). pap. 9.99 *(978-89-94208-61-9(5))* JR Comics KOR. Dist: Lerner Publishing Group.
—The Journey Ends. Peng, Chao, illus. 2013. (Monkey King Ser.: 20). (ENG.). 176p. (gr. 6-12). pap. 9.99 *(978-89-94208-65-7(8))* JR Comics KOR. Dist: Lerner Publishing Group.
—Lost Children. Peng, Chao, illus. 2013. (Monkey King Ser.: 12). (ENG.). 176p. (YA). (gr. 6-12). pap. 9.99 *(978-89-94208-57-2(7))* Lerner Publishing Group.
—Masters & Disciples. Peng, Chao, illus. 2013. (Monkey King Ser.: 19). (ENG.). 176p. (gr. 6-12). pap. 9.99 *(978-89-94208-64-0(X))* JR Comics KOR. Dist: Lerner Publishing Group.
—Realm of Infant King. Peng, Chao, illus. 2013. (Monkey King Ser.: 10). (ENG.). 176p. (YA). (gr. 6-12). pap. 9.99 *(978-89-94208-54-1(2))* Lerner Publishing Group.
—The Seven Sisters. Peng, Chao, illus. 2013. (Monkey King Ser.: 17). (ENG.). 176p. (gr. 6-12). pap. 9.99

(978-89-94208-62-6(3)) JR Comics KOR. Dist: Lerner Publishing Group.

—Stolen Kingdom. Peng, Chao, illus. 2013. (Monkey King Ser.: 9). (ENG.). 176p. (YA). (gr. 6-12). pap. 9.99 (978-89-94208-53-4(4)) Lerner Publishing Group.

—Treasures of the Mountain Kings. Peng, Chao, illus. 2013. (Monkey King Ser.: 8). (ENG.). 176p. (YA). (gr. 6-12). pap. 9.99 (978-89-94208-52-7(6)) Lerner Publishing Group.

—Trust & Temptation. Peng, Chao, illus. 2013. (Monkey King Ser.: 13). (ENG.). 176p. (gr. 6-12). pap. 9.99 (978-89-94208-58-9(5)) JR Comics KOR. Dist: Lerner Publishing Group.

—Wagers & Vows. Liang, Xiao Long, illus. 2013. (Three Kingdoms Ser.: 12). (ENG.). 176p. (gr. 5-12). pap. 9.99 (978-89-98341-25-1(5)) JR Comics KOR. Dist: Lerner Publishing Group.

—War of Words. Long Liang, Xiao, illus. 2013. (Three Kingdoms Ser.: 10). (ENG.). 176p. (gr. 5-12). pap. 9.99 (978-89-98341-23-7(9)) JR Comics KOR. Dist: Lerner Publishing Group.

Dong Chen, Wei & Peng, Chao. Bane of Heaven. 2012. (Monkey King Ser.: 2). (ENG., Illus.). 176p. (gr. 5-8). pap. 9.99 (978-89-94208-46-6(1)) JR Comics KOR. Dist: Lerner Publishing Group.

—Birth of Stone Monkey. 2012. (Monkey King Ser.: 1). (ENG., Illus.). 176p. (gr. 5-8). pap. 9.99 (978-89-94208-45-9(3)) JR Comics KOR. Dist: Lerner Publishing Group.

—Enemies & New Friend. 2012. (Monkey King Ser.: 4). (ENG., Illus.). 176p. (gr. 5-8). pap. 9.99 (978-89-94208-48-0(8)) JR Comics KOR. Dist: Lerner Publishing Group.

—Journey to the West. 2012. (Monkey King Ser.: 3). (ENG., Illus.). 176p. (gr. 5-8). pap. 9.99 (978-89-94208-47-3(X)) JR Comics KOR. Dist: Lerner Publishing Group.

—Sacred Tree. 2012. (Monkey King Ser.: 6). (ENG., Illus.). 176p. (gr. 5-8). pap. 9.99 (978-89-94208-50-3(X)) JR Comics KOR. Dist: Lerner Publishing Group.

—Three Trials. 2012. (Monkey King Ser.: 5). (ENG., Illus.). 176p. (gr. 5-8). pap. 9.99 (978-89-94208-49-7(6)) JR Comics KOR. Dist: Lerner Publishing Group.

Durkin, Mary Jane. The Shabby Little Princess. 2009. 24p. pap. 14.99 (978-1-4389-5115-7(9)) AuthorHouse.

Edwards, Hazel. Duty Free. 100p. (YA). pap. (978-0-7344-0334-6(8), Lothian Children's Bks.) Hachette Australia.

Folk Tales of the West Lake. 2007. 72p. per. 11.95 (978-1-59654-409-3(0)) Disruptive Publishing.

Forbes, Dillon. Careful Enough? 2008. (YA). 8.99 (978-1-59166-835-0(2)) BJU Pr.

Foster, Thomas. Travel Buddies: Robby & Sammy Visit China. 2006. (J). pap. 12.00 (978-1-890306-93-9(2)) Warwick Hse. Publishing.

Foutz, Ian. Year of the Dragon. Miller, Madeline, illus. 2014. (J). **(978-1-62086-634-4(X))** Mascot Bks., Inc.

Francia, Giada. Alex & Penny in China Jigsaw Book. 2011. (ENG., Illus.). 14p. 14.95 (978-88-544-0310-9(5)) White Star ITA. Dist: Random Hse., Inc.

Franco, Franco & Garcia, Eduardo. Dino-Mike & the Living Fossils. Franco, Franco, illus. 2016. (Dino-Mike! Ser.). (ENG., Illus.). 128p. (gr. 1-3). lib. bdg. 25.32 (978-1-4965-2489-8(6), Dino-Mike!) Stone Arch Bks.

Fritz, Jean. Homesick: My Own Story. Tomes, Margot, illus. 2007. (Puffin Modern Classics Ser.). (ENG.). 176p. (J). (gr. 3-7). 7.99 (978-0-14-240761-5(5), Puffin Books) Penguin Young Readers Group.

Fu, Shelley. Hoyi the Archer & other Classic Chinese Tales. Abboreno, Joseph F. & Fu, Sherwin, illus. 2005. 144p. (J). (gr. 4-8). reprint ed. 22.00 (978-0-7567-9713-3(6)) DIANE Publishing Co.

Fussell, Sandy. Samurai Kids #4: Monkey Fist. James, Rhian Nest, illus. 2012. (Samurai Kids Ser.: 4). (ENG.). 272p. (J). (gr. 4-7). pap. 6.99 (978-0-7636-5827-4(8)) Candlewick Pr.

—Shaolin Tiger. James, Rhian Nest, illus. 2011. (Samurai Kids Ser.: 3). (ENG.). 272p. (J). (gr. 4-7). pap. 6.99 (978-0-7636-5702-4(6)) Candlewick Pr.

Gallo, Tina, adapted by. The Po Who Cried Ghost. 2014. (Kung Fu Panda TV Ser.). (ENG., Illus.). 24p. (J). (gr. -1-2). pap. 3.99 (978-1-4814-0491-4(1), Simon Spotlight) Simon Spotlight.

Gilbert, Marcie. Zee: Adventure One: Borrowing China. Krebs, Patricia, illus. l.t. ed. 2006. 48p. (J). per. 16.99 (978-0-9771566-0-3(5)) Librujas.

Gill, Heidi. 2 Kurious Kids: China. Carter, Kris, illus. 2012. 38p. (J). 14.95 (978-1-936319-89-3(6)) Mascot Bks., Inc.

Goldish, Meish. The Empty Pot: A Chinese Legend. Treatner, Meryle, illus. 2005. 14p. pap. 6.00 (978-0-15-350582-9(6)) Harcourt Schl. Pubs.

Goldman Marshall, Lauren. My Beautiful Bow: An Adoption Story. Marschell, Hannah, illus. 2010. 36p. pap. 14.95 (978-1-60844-395-6(7)) Dog Ear Publishing, LLC.

Goodman, Alison. The Last Dragoneye. 2012. (ENG.). 672p. (YA). (gr. 7-18). 11.99 (978-0-14-242093-5(X), Firebird) Penguin Young Readers Group.

Gosline, Andrea & Alban, Andrea. Anya's War. 2011. (ENG.). 208p. (YA). (gr. 6-9). 16.99 (978-0-312-37093-0(8), 9780312370930) Feiwel & Friends.

Gower, Catherine & Zhihong, He. Long-Long's New Year. 2005. (ENG., Illus.). 32p. (J). (gr. k-3). 16.95 (978-0-8048-3666-1(3)) Tuttle Publishing.

Greenhut, Josh & Brown, Jeff. The Flying Chinese Wonders. Pamintuan, Macky, illus. 2011. (Flat Stanley's Worldwide Adventures Ser.: 7). (ENG.). 96p. (J). (gr. 1-5). 15.99 (978-0-06-143003-9(X)); pap. 4.99 (978-0-06-143002-2(1)) HarperCollins Pubs.

Guanzhong, Luo. The Three Kingdoms. Chiang, Shirley, illus. 2013. (Chinese Classics Ser.). (ENG.). 64p. pap. 6.95 (978-1-906230-35-7(8)) Real Reads Ltd. GBR. Dist: Casemate Pubs. & Bk. Distributors, LLC.

Hamel, Mike. Dragon's Lair, 5. 2007. (Matterhorn the Brave Ser.: 5). (ENG.). 192p. (J). (gr. 5-11). per. 9.99 (978-0-89957-837-8(3)) AMG Pubs.

Harvey, Jacqueline. Alice-Miranda in China. 2017. (Alice-Miranda Ser.: 14). (ENG.). 336p. (J). (gr. 3-7). pap. 9.99 (978-0-85798-520-0(5)) Random Hse. Australia AUS. Dist: Independent Pubs. Group.

Hathorn, Libby. The River. Wong, Stanley, illus. 2003. 40p. 28.95 (978-1-86366-516-2(1)) Education Services Australia Ltd. AUS. Dist: Cheng & Tsui Co.

Hergé. The Blue Lotus. (Illus.). (J). 19.95 (978-0-8288-5480-1(7)) French & European Pubns., Inc.

—The Blue Lotus. 2011. (Adventures of Tintin: Young Readers Edition Ser.). (ENG., Illus.). 96p. (J). (gr. 3-17). pap. 9.99 (978-0-316-13382-1(5)) Little, Brown Bks. for Young Readers.

—El Loto Azul.Tr. of Blue Lotus. (SPA., Illus.). 62p. (J). 19.95 (978-0-8288-5049-0(6)) French & European Pubns., Inc.

—El Loto Azul. (Tintin Ser.).Tr. of Blue Lotus. (SPA.). 64p. (J). 14.95 (978-84-261-1418-1(0)) Juventud, Editorial ESP. Dist: Distribooks, Inc.

—Le Lotus Bleu.Tr. of Blue Lotus. (FRE.). (J). (gr. 2-9). 19.95 (978-0-8288-5050-6(X)) French & European Pubns., Inc.

Holland, L. Tam. The Counterfeit Family Tree of Vee Crawford-Wong. (ENG.). 368p. (YA). (gr. 9). 2014. pap. 9.99 (978-1-4424-1265-1(8)) 2013. 17.99 (978-1-4424-1264-4(X)) Simon & Schuster Children's Publishing.

Holm, Kirsten C. Everyday Life in Ancient China. 2012. (Jr. Graphic Ancient Civilizations Ser.). (ENG.). 24p. (J). (gr. 3-6). pap. 10.60 (978-1-4488-6395-2(3)); lib. bdg. 25.25 (978-1-4488-6218-4(3)) Rosen Publishing Group, Inc., The. (PowerKids Pr.).

Hong, Chen Jian. La Leyenda De la Cometa. (SPA.). 32p. (978-84-95150-29-5(8)); (978-84-95150-39-4(5)) Corimbo, Editorial S.L.

Hood, Ann. Jewel of the East. Kwasny, Karl et al, illus. 2012. (Treasure Chest Ser.: 3). (ENG.). 208p. (J). (gr. 3-7). 15.99 (978-0-448-45473-3(4)); pap. 6.99 (978-0-448-45469-6(6)) Penguin Young Readers Group. (Grosset & Dunlap).

Hood, Douglas. The Stone Hat. Simonton, Tom, illus. 2005. (ENG.). 16p. (J). 5.75 (978-1-57274-754-8(4), 2784, Bks. for Young Learners) Owen, Richard C. Pubs., Inc.

Hope, Kathleen. Jack Eagle the Pirate & Other Mysterious Tales. 2012. (Illus.). 48p. pap. 24.40 (978-1-4678-9611-5(X)) AuthorHouse.

Hyde, Heidi Smith. Shanghai Sukkah. Tsong, Jing Jing, illus. 2015. (ENG.). 32p. (J). (gr. k-4). 17.99 (978-1-4677-3474-5(8)); pap. 7.99 (978-1-4677-3475-2(6)) Lerner Publishing Group. (Kar-Ben Publishing).

I-Haun. Real - Fake Princess. 2006. (Real/Fake Princess Ser.). (ENG., Illus.). 200p. (YA). pap. 9.95 (978-1-59796-080-9(2)) DrMaster Pubns. Inc.

—Real/Fake Princess, Vol. 4. Zhao, Yun, tr. 2007. (Real/Fake Princess Ser.). (ENG., Illus.). 200p. pap. 9.95 (978-1-59796-082-3(9)) DrMaster Pubns. Inc.

I-Huan. Real - Fake Princess, Set, Vols. 1-5. 2007. (ENG., Illus.). 200p. (YA). pap. 34.95 (978-1-59796-074-8(8)) DrMaster Pubns. Inc.

I-Huan & I-Haun. Real Fake Princess, Vol. 3. 2006. (Real/Fake Princess Ser.). (ENG., Illus.). 200p. (YA). pap. 9.95 (978-1-59796-081-6(0)) DrMaster Pubns. Inc.

Illek, Nuala. The Chinese Sausage Dog, the Panicky Porcupine & Mrs Shoo an Animal Tale of Friendship in Chin. 2009. 50p. pap. 9.99 (978-1-60860-781-5(X), Eloquent Bks.) Strategic Book Publishing & Rights Agency (SBPRA).

Jian, Li. The Horse & the Mysterious Drawing: A Story in English & Chinese. 2013. (ENG., Illus.). 42p. (J). (gr. -1-3). 16.95 (978-1-60220-984-8(7)) BetterLink Pr., Inc.

—Ming's Adventure with the Terracotta Army. Wert, Yijin, tr. 2013. (ENG & CHI., Illus.). 42p. (J). (gr. -1-3). 16.95 (978-1-60220-983-1(9)) BetterLink Pr., Inc.

Jiang, Ji-Li. Red Kite, Blue Kite. Ruth, Greg, illus. 2013. (ENG.). 32p. (J). (gr. 1-3). 17.99 (978-1-4231-2753-6(6)) Hyperion Pr.

Jolley, Dan. Guan Yu: Blood Brothers to the End [A Chinese Legend]. Randall, Ron, illus. 2009. (Graphic Myths & Legends Ser.). (ENG.). 48p. (gr. 4-8). pap. 8.95 (978-1-58013-890-1(X)) Lerner Publishing Group.

Jones Yang, Dori. Daughter of Xanadu. 2012. (ENG.). 352p. (YA). (gr. 7). pap. 9.99 (978-0-385-73924-5(9), Ember) Random Hse. Children's Bks.

Kacer, Kathy. Shanghai Escape, 1 vol. 2013. (Holocaust Remembrance Ser.). (ENG.). 204p. (J). (gr. 6-8). pap. 14.95 (978-1-927583-10-4(1)) Second Story Pr. CAN. Dist: Orca Bk. Pubs. USA.

Kang, Hildi. Chengli & the Silk Road Caravan. 2012. (ENG.). 176p. (J). (gr. 2-7). pap. 8.95 (978-1-933718-78-1(1)) Tanglewood Pr.

Kazeroid, Sibylle, tr. from FRE. Liu & the Bird: A Journey in Chinese Calligraphy. Louis, Catherine, illus. 2006. (FRE.). 40p. (J). (gr. -1-3). 16.95 (978-0-7358-2050-0(3)) North-South Bks., Inc.

Kendall, Carol & Li, Yao-Wen. Sweet & Sour: Tales from China. Felts, Shirley, illus. 2007. (ENG.). 114p. (J). (gr. 5-7). per. 8.95 (978-0-618-75245-4(5)) Houghton Mifflin Harcourt Publishing Co.

Kingsley, Salome. Two Wishes for Natty's Birthday. 2007. (Illus.). 54p. (J). pap. 15.00 (978-0-8059-7391-4(5)) Dorrance Publishing Co., Inc.

Korman, Gordon. The Summit. 2012. (Everest Ser.: 3). lib. bdg. 17.20 (978-0-606-23935-6(9), Turtleback) Turtleback Bks.

Krensky, Stephen. The Dragon Emperor: A Chinese Folktale. 2009. pap. 40.95 (978-0-7613-4817-7(4)) Lerner Publishing Group.

La Valley, Josanne. Factory Girl. 2017. (ENG.). 280p. (YA). (gr. 9). 17.99 (978-0-544-69947-2(5)) Houghton Mifflin Harcourt Publishing Co.

—The Vine Basket. 2015. (ENG.). 256p. (J). (gr. 5-7). pap. 7.99 (978-0-544-43939-9(2), HMH Books For Young Readers) Houghton Mifflin Harcourt Publishing Co.

Lane, Andrew. Snake Bite. 2014. (Sherlock Holmes: the Legend Begins Ser.: 5). (ENG.). 304p. (YA). (gr. 7-12). 17.99 (978-0-374-37090-9(7), 9780374370909, Farrar, Straus & Giroux (BYR)) Farrar, Straus & Giroux.

Lattimore, Eleanor Frances. Little Pear. Lattimore, Eleanor Frances, illus. 2006. (ENG., Illus.). 128p. (J). (gr. 1-4). pap. 5.95 (978-0-15-205502-8(9)) Houghton Mifflin Harcourt Publishing Co.

—Little Pear & His Friends. Lattimore, Eleanor Frances, illus. 2006. (ENG., Illus.). 144p. (J). (gr. 1-4). pap. 10.95 (978-0-15-205490-8(1)) Houghton Mifflin Harcourt Publishing Co.

Leblanc, André. The Red Piano. Werner, Justine, tr. from FRE. Barroux, illus. 2010.Tr. of Piano Rouge. (ENG.). 40p. (J). (gr. 2-4). 16.99 (978-0-9806070-1-7(9)) Wilkins Farago Pty, Ltd. AUS. Dist: Independent Pubs. Group.

Lee, Milly. Landed. Choi, Yangsook, illus. 2006. (ENG.). 40p. (J). (gr. 2-6). 17.99 (978-0-374-34314-9(4), 9780374343149, Farrar, Straus & Giroux (BYR)) Farrar, Straus & Giroux.

Levinson, Robin. Reyna & the Jade Star. 2006. (Illus.). (J). per. 12.00 (978-0-9773673-1-3(2)) Gali Girls, Inc.

Lewis, Elizabeth Foreman. Young Fu of the Upper Yangtze. Low, William & Cobalt Illustrations Studio Staff, illus. 2008. (ENG.). 320p. (YA). (gr. 5-9). pap. 8.99 (978-0-312-38007-6(0), 9780312380076) Square Fish.

Lewis, Rose & Zong, Grace. Orange Peel's Pocket. 2012. (ENG.). 32p. (J). (gr. -1-3). pap. 5.00 (978-1-4197-0293-8(9)) Abrams, Inc.

Li-Qiong, Yu. A New Year's Reunion: A Chinese Story. Cheng-Liang, Zhu, illus. 2013. (ENG.). 40p. (J). (gr. -1-2). 6.99 (978-0-7636-6748-1(X)) Candlewick Pr.

Lin, Chris. Mandy & Pandy Visit China. Villalta, Ingrid, illus. 2008. 20p. (J). (gr. -1-3). bds. 9.99 (978-0-9800156-6-9(9)) Mandy & Pandy Bks., LLC.

Lin, Grace. Kite Flying. 2004. (ENG., Illus.). 32p. (J). (gr. -1-2). pap. 7.99 (978-0-553-11254-2(6), Dragonfly Bks.) Random Hse. Children's Bks.

—Thanking the Moon: Celebrating the Mid-Autumn Moon Festival. 2010. (ENG.). 32p. (J). (gr. -1-2). 16.99 (978-0-375-86101-7(7), Knopf Bks. for Young Readers) Random Hse. Children's Bks.

—When the Sea Turned to Silver. (ENG.). (J). (gr. 3-7). 2017. 400p. pap. 9.99 **(978-0-316-12594-9(6))** 2016. (Illus.). 384p. 18.99 (978-0-316-12592-5(X)) Little, Brown Bks. for Young Readers.

—When the Sea Turned to Silver. 2017. (J). lib. bdg. 20.85 **(978-0-606-40629-1(8))** Turtleback Bks.

Litrel, Suzanne M. Jackie Tempo & the Emperor's Seal. 2007. 172p. (YA). per. 13.95 (978-0-595-46822-5(5)) iUniverse, Inc.

Liu, Na. Little White Duck: A Childhood in China. 2012. (Single Titles Ser.). (ENG., Illus.). 108p. (gr. 4-7). (J). lib. bdg. 29.27 (978-0-7613-6587-7(7)); pap. 9.95 (978-0-7613-8115-0(5)) Lerner Publishing Group. (Graphic Universe™).

Lloyd, Alison. Year of the Tiger. 2010. (ENG.). 228p. (YA). (gr. 5-18). pap. 16.95 (978-0-8234-2277-7(1)) Holiday Hse., Inc.

Lo, Rich. Father's Chinese Opera. Lo, Rich, illus. 2014. (ENG., Illus.). 40p. (J). (gr. -1-k). 16.95 (978-1-62873-610-6(0), Sky Pony Pr.) Skyhorse Publishing Co., Inc.

Look, Lenore. Alvin Ho: Allergic to the Great Wall, the Forbidden Palace, & Other Tourist Attractions. Pham, LeUyen, illus. 2014. (Alvin Ho Ser.). (ENG.). 176p. (J). (gr. 1-4). 15.99 (978-0-385-36972-5(7), Schwartz & Wade Bks.) Random Hse. Children's Bks.

—Brush of the Gods. So, Meilo, illus. 2013. (ENG.). 40p. (J). (gr. -1-3). 17.99 (978-0-375-87001-9(6), Schwartz & Wade Bks.) Random Hse. Children's Bks.

—Ruby Lu, Brave & True. Wilsdorf, Anne, illus. 2006. (Ruby Lu Ser.). 105p. (J). (gr. 1-5). 11.65 (978-0-7569-6553-2(5)) Perfection Learning Corp.

Lumry, Amanda & Hurwitz, Laura. Project Panda. 2008. (J). (978-1-60040-009-4(4)); (978-1-60040-008-7(6)) Eaglemont Pr.

Ma, Wing Shing. Storm Riders Vol. 1: Invading Sun. 2003. (Illus.). 128p. 9.95 (978-1-58899-359-5(0)) ComicsOne Corp./Dr. Masters.

MacKenzie, Catherine. Gladys Aylward - Are You Going to Stop? 2013. (Little Lights Ser.). (ENG., Illus.). 24p. (J). 7.99 (978-1-78191-161-7(4), cfd6d604-97c6-4c41-889d-ab61929b782a) Christian Focus Pubns. GBR. Dist: Bookmasters Distribution.

MacLean, Betty. Jiali's Traveling Heart. Kinra, Richa, illus. 2013. 34p. (J). 17.95 (978-1-60131-157-3(5), Castlebridge Bks.) Big Tent Bks.

MacLeod, Jean. At Home in This World: A China Adoption Story. Su, Qin, illus. 2nd ed. 2004. 32p. 15.95 (978-0-9726244-1-1(4)) EMK Pr.

Mah, Adeline Yen. Along the River: A Chinese Cinderella Novel. 2012. (ENG.). 216p. (YA). (gr. 7). pap. 7.99 (978-0-385-73896-5(X), Ember) Random Hse. Children's Bks.

—Chinese Cinderella & the Secret Dragon Society. 2006. (ENG., Illus.). 256p. (J). (gr. 5-9). pap. 7.99 (978-0-06-056736-1(8)) HarperCollins Pubs.

Marsh, Carole. The Mystery on the Great Wall of China. 2006. (Around the World in 80 Mysteries Ser.). (Illus.). 132p. (J). (gr. 3-5). per. 7.99 (978-0-635-06205-5(4)) Gallopade International.

—The Mystery on the Great Wall of China: Beijing, China. (Around the World in 80 Mysteries Ser.). (Illus.). 132p. (J). 2009. lib. bdg. 18.99 (978-0-635-07014-2(6), Marsh, Carole Mysteries) 2006. (gr. 3-5). 14.95 (978-0-635-06209-3(7)) Gallopade International.

Matott, Justin. When I Was a Boy... I Dreamed. Ludy, Mark, illus. 2004. (ENG.). 32p. (J). (gr. -1-4). (978-0-9664276-2-2(9)) Green Pastures Publishing, Inc.

McClintock, Barbara. Lost & Found: Adèle & Simon in China. 2016. (Adele & Simon Ser.). (ENG., Illus.). 40p. (J). 17.99 (978-0-374-39923-8(9), 9780374399238, Farrar, Straus & Giroux (BYR)) Farrar, Straus & Giroux.

McCloskey, John J. Warrior Ching. 2006. 179p. pap. 24.95 (978-1-4241-2389-6(5)) PublishAmerica, Inc.

McDougal-Littell Publishing Staff. Dragonwings. 2004. (McDougal Littell Literature Connections Ser.). (ENG.). 280p. (gr. 6-6). stu. ed. 16.90 (978-0-395-77136-5(6), 2-70214) Great Source Education Group, Inc.

McSween, Michele. Gordon & Li Li Count in Mandarin. Nam, Doan, illus. 2010. 32p. 9.99 (978-0-9820881-3-5(2)) McWong Ink.

—Gordon & Li Li Learn Animals in Mandarin. Nam, Doan, illus. 2010. 32p. 9.99 (978-0-9820881-2-8(4)) McWong Ink.

Meadows, Amy. Emma's American Chinese New Year. 2012. (ENG.). 31p. (J). pap. 12.95 (978-1-4327-8694-6(6)) Outskirts Pr., Inc.

Methods, Bryan. The Shanghai Incident. 2017. (Master Diplexito & Mr. Scant Ser.). (ENG.). 264p. (J). (gr. 5-8). 17.99 **(978-1-5124-0580-4(9)**, Carolrhoda Bks.) Lerner Publishing Group.

Millhouse, Jackie. The Tiger & the General. Girouard, Patrick, illus. 2007. (J). (978-1-932911-32-9(4)) World Tribune Pr.

Montgomery, R. A. Chinese Dragons. Semionov, Vladimir, illus. 2009. (Choose Your Own Adventure Ser.: No. 30). 144p. (J). (gr. 2-7). pap. 6.99 (978-1-933390-30-7(1)) Chooseco LLC.

Mosel, Arlene. Tikki Tikki Tembo. Lent, Blair, illus. 2008. (gr. k-2). 16.95 (978-0-7569-8457-1(2)) Perfection Learning Corp.

Mowll, Joshua. Operation Storm City, Bk. 3. 2009. (Guild of Specialists Ser.). (ENG., Illus.). 288p. (J). (gr. 5). 16.99 (978-0-7636-4224-2(X)) Candlewick Pr.

My Trip to China. 2004. (J). ring bd. 4.50 (978-0-9762740-6-3(X)) Smart Smiles Co., The.

Naian, Shi. The Water Margin. Chiang, Shirley, illus. 2013. (Chinese Classics Ser.). (ENG.). 64p. pap. 6.95 (978-1-906230-37-1(4)) Real Reads Ltd. GBR. Dist: Casemate Pubs. & Bk. Distributors, LLC.

Namioka, Lensey. Ties That Bind, Ties That Break: A Novel. 2006. (Reader's Workshop Ser.). (ENG.). 176p. (C). pap. 19.95 (978-0-7362-3149-7(8)) CENGAGE Learning.

Napoli, Donna Jo. Bound. 2006. (ENG., Illus.). 192p. (YA). (gr. 7-12). reprint ed. mass mkt. 7.99 (978-0-689-86178-9(8), Simon Pulse) Simon Pulse.

Nez, John, illus. The Dragon Painter. 2006. (First Reading Level 4 Ser.). 48p. (J). (gr. 1-4). 8.99 (978-0-7945-1275-0(5), Usborne) EDC Publishing.

Nohrden, Patrick. The Crystal Monkey. 2014. 286p. (YA). pap. 16.99 (978-1-4621-1481-8(4)) Cedar Fort, Inc./CFI Distribution.

Nona Theresa Perez - Bayanin. Nadia Mei's First Winter in the Forest & Meeting with First Friends. 2012. 28p. pap. 21.99 (978-1-4771-0596-2(4)) Xlibris Corp.

Oelschlager, Vanita. Made in China: A Story of Adoption. Blackwood, Kristin, illus. 2008. (ENG.). 32p. (J). (gr. -1-3). 17.95 (978-0-9800162-3-9(1)) VanitaBooks.

Osborne, Mary Pope. Day of the Dragon King. unabr. ed. 2004. (Magic Tree House Ser.: No. 14). 68p. (J). (gr. k-3). pap. 17.00 incl. audio (978-0-8072-0783-3(7), S FTR 242 SP, Listening Library) Random Hse. Audio Publishing Group.

—A Perfect Time for Pandas. Murdocca, Sal, illus. 2014. (Magic Tree House Merlin Mission Ser.: No. 20). (ENG.). 144p. (J). (gr. 2-5). pap. 5.99 (978-0-375-86798-9(8), Random Hse. Bks. for Young Readers) Random Hse. Children's Bks.

—A Perfect Time for Pandas. 2014. (Magic Tree House Merlin Missions Ser.: 20). lib. bdg. 16.00 (978-0-606-35564-3(2)) Turtleback Bks.

Ovani, Germano, illus. The Monkey King. 2007. (Young Reading Series 1 Gift Bks). 47p. (J). (gr. -1-3). 8.99 (978-0-7945-1593-5(2), Usborne) EDC Publishing.

Paris, Harper. The Mystery in the Forbidden City. Calo, Marcos, illus. 2014. (Greetings from Somewhere Ser.: 4). (ENG.). 128p. (J). (gr. k-2). pap. 5.99 (978-1-4814-0299-6(4), Little Simon) Little Simon.

Paterson, Katherine. Rebels of the Heavenly Kingdom. 2008. (ENG.). 176p. (J). (gr. 3-7). pap. 12.95 (978-0-88899-885-9(6)) Groundwood Bks. CAN. Dist: Publishers Group West (PGW).

Patterson, James & Grabenstein, Chris. Secret of the Forbidden City. Neufeld, Juliana, illus. 2015. (Treasure Hunters Ser.: 3). (ENG.). 448p. (J). (gr. 3-7). 14.99 (978-0-316-28480-6(7), Jimmy Patterson) Little Brown & Co.

Payne, Gregory. Chase to the Brazen Head. 2010. (ENG.). 228p. (YA). (gr. 4-7). pap. 11.95 (978-988-18094-6-9(0)) Haven Bks.

Peacock, Carol Antoinette. Red Thread Sisters. 2012. (ENG.). 240p. (J). (gr. 3-7). 15.99 (978-0-670-01386-9(2), Viking Books for Young Readers) Penguin Young Readers Group.

Pedraza, M. Eugenia Rueda. Nico's Voyage. 2013. 32p. pap. (978-1-4602-2360-4(8)) FriesenPress.

Penner, Stephen. Professor Barrister's Dinosaur Mysteries #4: The Case of the Colorful Caudipteryx. Penner, Stephen, illus. 2011. (Illus.). 62p. pap. 14.99 (978-1-60888-111-6(3)) Nimble Bks. LLC.

Philpot, Graham, illus. The Emperor & the Nightingale. 2007. (First Reading Level 4 Ser.). 48p. (J). (gr. -1-3). 8.99 (978-0-7945-1614-7(9), Usborne) EDC Publishing.

Pilegard, Virginia. The Emperor's Army, 1 vol. Tans, Adrian, illus. 2010. (ENG.). 32p. (J). (gr. k-3). 16.99 (978-1-58980-690-0(5)) Pelican Publishing Co., Inc.

Pilegard, Virginia Walton. The Warlord's Alarm, 1 vol. Debon, Nicolas, illus. 2006. (Warlord's Ser.). (ENG.). 32p. (J). (gr. k-3). 16.99 (978-1-58980-378-7(7)) Pelican Publishing Co., Inc.

—The Warlord's Kites, 1 vol. Debon, Nicolas, illus. 2004. (Warlord's Ser.). (ENG.). 32p. (J). (gr. k-3). 16.99 (978-1-58980-180-6(6)) Pelican Publishing Co., Inc.

—The Warlord's Messengers, 1 vol. Debon, Nicolas, illus. 2005. (Warlord's Ser.). (ENG.). 32p. (J). (gr. k-3). 16.99 (978-1-58980-271-1(3)) Pelican Publishing Co., Inc.

—The Warlord's Puppeteers, 1 vol. Debon, Nicolas, illus. 2003. (Warlord's Ser.: 4). (ENG.). 32p. (J). (gr. k-3). 16.99 (978-1-58980-077-9(X)) Pelican Publishing Co., Inc.

Pitman, Norman Hinsdale. The Chinese Wonder Book: A Classic Collection of Chinese Tales. Tang, Li Chu, illus. 2011. (ENG.). 96p. (J). (gr. 4-6). 16.95 (978-0-8048-4161-0(6)) Tuttle Publishing.

Pixton, Kaaren & Sickler, Jonas. Humpty Dumpty: Hey, Bay Look at the Humpty Dumpty - On the Great Wall of China! 2010. (Indestructibles Ser.). (ENG., Illus.). 12p. (J). (gr. k — 1). pap. 5.95 (978-0-7611-5861-5(8), 15861) Workman Publishing Co., Inc.

Polonsky, Ami. Threads. 2016. (ENG.). 256p. (J). (gr. 3-7). 16.99 (978-1-4847-4690-5(2)) Hyperion Bks. for Children.

Pon, Cindy. Silver Phoenix. (Silver Phoenix Ser.: 1). (ENG.). (YA). (gr. 9). 2011. 368p. pap. 8.99 (978-0-06-173024-5(6)) 2009. 352p. 17.99 (978-0-06-173021-4(1)) HarperCollins Pubs. (Greenwillow Bks.).

Poole, Amy Lowry, illus. & retold by. The Pea Blossom. Poole, Amy Lowry, retold by. 2006. (ENG.). 32p. (J). reprint ed. 6.95 (978-0-8234-2018-6(3)) Holiday Hse., Inc.

Poole, Amy Lowry & Andersen, Hans Christian. The Pea Blossom. 2005. (ENG., Illus.). 32p. (J). (gr. -1-3). 16.95 (978-0-8234-1864-0(2)) Holiday Hse., Inc.

Potter, Beatrix. Conte de Pierre Lapin. (FRE.). pap. 18.95 (978-2-07-054698-5(5)) Gallimard, Editions FRA. Dist: Distribooks, Inc.

Provensen, Alice. The Master Swordsman & the Magic Doorway: Two Legends from Ancient China. Provensen, Alice, illus. 2014. (ENG., Illus.). 40p. (J). (gr. k-3). 19.99 (978-1-4814-2874-3(8), Simon & Schuster Bks. For Young Readers) Simon & Schuster Bks. For Young Readers.

Prozeller, Ellen Lucey. 32 Days: A Story of Faith & Courage. 2016. (J). pap. *(978-0-8198-0657-4(9))* Pauline Bks. & Media.

Qu, Zhi. Little Sima & the Giant Bowl. Wang, Lin, illus. 2009. (On My Own Folklore Ser.). (ENG.). 48p. (gr. 2-4). pap. 6.95 *(978-1-58013-850-5(0),* First Avenue Editions) Lerner Publishing Group.

Quince, Lia. Abby & Jules. 2009. *(978-1-933791-14-2(4))* Finial Publishing.

Remza, Freddie. The Journey to Mei. 2007. 164p. (YA). per. 10.95 *(978-1-4327-0459-9(1))* Outskirts Pr., Inc.

Rideout, Henry. Dragons Blood. 2006. 144p. per. 11.95 *(978-1-59818-051-0(7)),* 24.95 *(978-1-59818-548-5(9))* Aegypan.

Ripley's Believe It Or Not! Staff. Running Wild. 2010. (Rbi Ser.: 3). (ENG.). 128p. (J). pap. 4.99 *(978-1-893951-55-6(3))* Ripley Entertainment, Inc.

Roberge, Tracy. Jacob & Alec Explore Shenzhen's Windows of the World. 2011. 40p. pap. 17.99 *(978-1-257-76087-9(4))* Lulu Pr., Inc.

Rosenberg, Michael. Chilly Goes to Hong Kong & China: Another Chilly the Toy Polar Bear Adventure. 2013. 36p. pap. 13.95 *(978-1-62212-841-9(9),* Strategic Bk. Publishing) Strategic Book Publishing & Rights Agency (SBPRA).

Ruby, Lois. Shanghai Shadows. 2006. (ENG.). 256p. (YA). 16.95 *(978-0-8234-1960-9(6))* Holiday Hse., Inc.

Sackstein, Starr. Simply May. 2009. 162p. pap. 19.99 *(978-0-557-13275-1(4))* Lulu Pr., Inc.

Samson, Lucretia. The Girl & the Waterfall: A Tale from China. Romanet, Caroline, illus. 2016. 24p. (J). pap. *(978-1-927244-61-6(7))* Flying Start Bks.

—The Girl & the Waterfall (Big Book Edition) A Tale from China. Romanet, Caroline, illus. 2016. 24p. (J). pap. *(978-1-927244-71-5(4))* Flying Start Bks.

Sander, Sonia. Chill Out, Scooby-Doo!, 1 vol. Duendes Del Sur Staff, illus. 2012. (Scooby-Doo! Set 2 Ser.: No. 2). (ENG.). 32p. (J). (gr. k-3). lib. bdg. 24.21 *(978-1-59961-865-4(6))* Spotlight.

Sarwari, Zohra. The Inheritance: A Journey to China (Book 1) 2013. 148p. pap. *(978-1-935948-30-8(X))* Roxby Media Ltd.

Sayer, Marjorie. The Girl Mechanic of Wanzhou. 2012. 186p. pap. 8.99 *(978-0-9882561-2-5(6))* Atelier Finwhale.

Sayle, Stephen. Cam & Zara the Travel Bugs. 2012. 20p. pap. 11.70 *(978-1-105-42214-0(3))* Lulu Pr., Inc.

Scherer, Catherine W. Simon & Barklee in China, Book 1 - the Southeast. 2007. (Another Country Calling Ser.). (J). per. 15.00 *(978-0-9714502-6-4(9),* Explorer Media) Simon & Barklee, Inc./ExplorerMedia.

—Simon & Barklee in China, Book 2 - the Mountains. 2008. (Another Country Calling Ser.). (J). per. 15.00 *(978-0-9714502-7-1(7),* Explorer Media) Simon & Barklee, Inc./ExplorerMedia.

—Simon & Barklee in China, Book 3 - the North. 2008. (Another Country Calling Ser.). (J). per. 15.00 *(978-0-9714502-8-8(5),* Explorer Media) Simon & Barklee, Inc./ExplorerMedia.

Schotz, Leo D. Rooftop. 2005. (Illus.). 32p. (J). 15.95 *(978-0-9741319-7-9(0))* 4N Publishing LLC.

Scieszka, Jon. Marco? Polo!, No. 16. McCauley, Adam, illus. 2008. (Time Warp Trio Ser.: 16). (ENG.). 96p. (J). (gr. 2-4). 5.99 *(978-0-14-241177-3(9),* Puffin Books) Penguin Young Readers Group.

—Marco? Polo! McCauley, Adam, illus. 2008. (Time Warp Trio Ser.: No. 16). 90p. (J). (gr. 4-6). 12.65 *(978-0-7569-8923-1(X))* Perfection Learning Corp.

Scimone, Diana. Adventures with Pawpaw: China. Wiedemer, Leah, illus. 2003. 32p. (J). 8.95 *(978-0-9729507-0-1(2))* Peapod Publishing, Inc.

Seaman, John E. On the Road with Ruben Doyle. 2010. 170p. 29.99 *(978-1-4500-3196-7(X));* pap. 19.99 *(978-1-4500-3195-0(1))* Xlibris Corp.

Sellier, Marie. Legend of the Chinese Dragon. Kazeroid, Sibylle, tr. from FRE. Louis, Catherine & Fei, Wang, illus. 2008. (ENG.). 40p. (J). (gr. -1-3). 15.95 *(978-0-7358-2152-1(6))* North-South Bks., Inc.

Shemin, Craig. Families Are Forever. McCoy, John, illus. 2006. 34p. (J). (gr. -1-2). 16.95 *(978-0-9728666-6-8(3))* As Simple As That Publishing.

Shen-Chow, Lulu. Silly Girl Adventures. 2011. 24p. pap. 15.99 *(978-1-4628-6478-2(3))* Xlibris Corp.

Shepard, Aaron. The Monkey King: A Superhero Tale of China, Retold from the Journey to the West. 2008. (Ancient Fantasy Ser.: 4). (J). 50p. lib. bdg. 15.00 *(978-0-938497-40-0(5));* 44p. lib. bdg. 6.00 *(978-0-938497-41-7(3))* Shepard Pubns. (Skyhook Pr.).

Shoushen, Jin. Beijing Legends. Yang, Gladys, tr. 2007. (Illus.). 124p. per. 11.95 *(978-1-59654-392-8(2))* Disruptive Publishing.

Silver Phoenix Staff & Pon, Cindy. Fury of the Phoenix. 2011. (Silver Phoenix Ser.: 2). (ENG.). 368p. (YA). (gr. 9-18). 17.99 *(978-0-06-173025-2(4),* Greenwillow Bks.) HarperCollins Pubs.

Simcox, Lorraine. A Single Red Thread. 2008. (J). 21.99 *(978-1-60131-024-8(2))* Big Tent Bks.

Slagle, Clark. Axel Cecil & the Rising Sun Adventures: the Janwah. 2009. 105p. pap. 9.95 *(978-0-615-24135-7(2))* Wold Creative Group.

Slinkard, Doreen. Wicky Wacky Farm Stories: Peppi Goes to China. 2012. 44p. pap. 14.97 *(978-1-60976-309-1(2),* Strategic Bk. Publishing) Strategic Book Publishing & Rights Agency (SBPRA).

Smith, Icy. Mystery of the Giant Mask of Sanxingdui. Roski, Gayle Garner, illus. 2015. (J). *(978-0-9913454-8-9(7))* East West Discovery Pr.

Snyder, Lavinia Branca. The Treasure of Lodian: The Kyss Family Mysteries. 2003. (Illus.). (J). mass mkt. *(978-1-932233-68-1(7))* Aurora Libris Corp.

Sonnichsen, A. L. Red Butterfly. Bates, Amy June, illus. 2015. (ENG.). 400p. (J). (gr. 3-7). 17.99 *(978-1-4814-1109-7(8))* Simon & Schuster, Inc.

Spangler, Jon. The Sky Princess. 2007. 24p. per. 10.95 *(978-1-4327-1557-1(7))* Outskirts Pr., Inc.

—The Sky Princess Moves to the Land of Peaches. 2009. 24p. pap. 11.95 *(978-1-4490-0015-8(0))* AuthorHouse.

Stilton, Geronimo. Valley of the Giant Skeletons. 2008. (Geronimo Stilton Ser.: 32). lib. bdg. 18.40 *(978-1-4364-2713-5(4))* Turtleback Bks.

Stilton, Geronimo & Stilton, Thea. Thea Stilton & the Ghost of the Shipwreck. 2010. (Thea Stilton Ser.: 3). (ENG., Illus.). 176p. (J). (gr. 2-5). mass mkt. 8.99 *(978-0-545-15059-0(0),* Scholastic Paperbacks) Scholastic, Inc.

Stone, Jeff. Five Ancestors Out of the Ashes: Phoenix. 2013. (Five Ancestors Out of the Ashes Ser.: 1). (ENG.). 304p. (J). (gr. 4-7). 6.99 *(978-0-375-87097-2(0),* Yearling) Random Hse. Children's Bks.

Stone, Kazuko G. & Keido, Ippo. The Butterfly's Dream: Children's Stories from China. 2003. (ENG., Illus.). 1p. 15.95 *(978-0-8048-3480-3(6))* Tuttle Publishing.

Style Guide Staff, illus. Good Po, Bad Po. 2014. (Kung Fu Panda TV Ser.). (ENG.). 24p. (J). (gr. -1-2). pap. 3.99 *(978-1-4814-0001-5(0),* Simon Spotlight) Simon Spotlight.

Tao, Ted. The Monkey King & the Book of Death. 2008. (ENG., Illus.). 200p. (YA). pap. 7.99 *(978-1-930655-01-0(0))* Golden Peach Publishing.

Thank You, Meiling: Evaluation Guide. 2006. (J). *(978-1-55942-423-3(0))* Witcher Productions.

Thong, Roseanne Greenfield. Noodle Magic. So, Meilo, illus. 2014. (ENG.). 32p. (J). (gr. -1-3). 17.99 *(978-0-545-52167-3(X))* Scholastic, Inc.

Top That Publishing Staff, ed. Chinese Myst. 2004. (Wicked Tattoos Ser.). (Illus.). 16p. (J). pap. *(978-1-84510-108-4(1))* Top That! Publishing PLC.

Torres, J. Batman Versus the Yeti!, 1 vol. Barberi, Carlo & Beatty, Terry, illus. 2013. (Batman: the Brave & the Bold Ser.). (ENG.). 32p. (gr. 2-3). 22.60 *(978-1-4342-4708-7(2))* Stone Arch Bks.

Trout, Richard. Sign of the Dragon, 1 vol. 2007. (MacGregor Family Adventure Ser.: 5). (ENG.). 272p. (YA). (gr. 5-12). 16.99 *(978-1-58980-476-0(7))* Pelican Publishing Co., Inc.

Tsang, Evonne. Kung Fu Masters, No. 12. Martinez, Alitha E., illus. 2009. (Twisted Journeys (r) Ser.: 12). (ENG.). 112p. (J). (gr. 4-7). 27.93 *(978-0-8225-8878-8(1),* Graphic Universe™) Lerner Publishing Group.

Tse, Brian. This Is the Greatest Place! A Palace Inspired by the World of Small Animals. Steinhardt, Nancy S., ed. Wang, Ben, tr. from CHI. Mak, Alice, illus. rev. ed. 2014. (ENG.). 44p. (J). (gr. -1-3). 12.95 *(978-0-9893776-2-1(8))* China Institute Gallery, China Institute in America.

Tucker, Kathy. The Seven Chinese Sisters. Lin, Grace, illus. 2003. (ENG.). 32p. (J). (gr. k-3). per. 6.99 *(978-0-8075-7310-5(8))* Whitman, Albert & Co.

Tucker, Kathy & Hong, Lily Toy. The Seven Chinese Sisters, Bk. 2. Hong, Lily Toy & Lin, Grace, illus. 2010. (Book & DVD Packages with Nutmeg Media Ser.). (ENG.). 4p. (J). (gr. -1-3). 69.95 *(978-0-8075-9984-6(0))* Whitman, Albert & Co.

Waller, Sharon Biggs. The Forbidden Orchid. 2016. (ENG., Illus.). 416p. (YA). (gr. 7). 18.99 *(978-0-451-47411-7(2),* Viking Books for Young Readers) Penguin Young Readers Group.

Walsh, Ann. By the Skin of His Teeth. 2005. (Illus.). 144p. (YA). pap., tchr. ed. 6.95 *(978-0-88878-448-3(1))* Beach Holme Pubs., Ltd. CAN. Dist: Literary Pr. Group of Canada.

Wang, Andrea. The Nian Monster. Chau, Alina, illus. 2016. (ENG.). 32p. (J). (gr. -1-3). 16.99 *(978-0-8075-5642-9(4))* Whitman, Albert & Co.

Wang, Gabrielle. The Race for the Chinese Zodiac. Rippin, Sally & Abos, Regine, illus. 2013. (ENG.). 32p. (J). (gr. k-4). 14.99 *(978-0-7636-6778-8(1))* Candlewick Pr.

Wang, Kateri. Wang Ming: The Greatest of the Great Pandas. 2012. 32p. pap. 19.99 *(978-1-4772-9042-2(7))* AuthorHouse.

Wang, Xiaohong. One Year in Beijing. Lin, Grace, illus. 2006. 32p. (J). (gr. -1-3). 16.95 *(978-0-9747302-5-7(4))* Chinasprout, Inc.

Wenxuan, Cao. Bronze & Sunflower. Wang, Helen, tr. So, Meilo, illus. 2017. (ENG.). 400p. (J). (gr. 4-7). 16.99 *(978-0-7636-8816-5(9))* Candlewick Pr.

What's in the Suitcase, Grandma? My Solar-Powered History, Book 3. 2013. (Illus.). 116p. pap. 12.99 *(978-1-937848-08-8(6))* Do Life Right, Inc.

Whelan, Gloria. Chu Ju's House. 240p. (J). (gr. 5-18). 2004. lib. bdg. 17.89 *(978-0-06-050725-1(X))* 2005. (ENG.). reprint ed. pap. 7.99 *(978-0-06-050726-8(8))* HarperCollins Pubs.

Wilhelm, Richard, ed. The Chinese Fairy Book. Martens, Frederick H., tr. from CHI. Hood, George W., illus. 2008. (Dover Children's Classics Ser.). (ENG.). 224p. (J). (gr. 4-7). pap. 10.95 *(978-0-486-45435-1(5))* Dover Pubns., Inc.

Williams, Brenda. Lin Yi's Lantern: A Moon Festival Tale. Lacombe, Benjamin, illus. 2009. (ENG.). 32p. (J). (gr. -1-5). 16.99 *(978-1-84686-147-5(0))* Barefoot Bks., Inc.

—Lin Yi's Lantern: A Moon Festival Tale. Tavares, Victor, illus. 2008. 32p. (J). *(978-1-84686-148-2(9))* Barefoot Bks., Inc.

Williams, David Morgan. Xcalibur, Merlin & the Teeth of the Dragon. 2015. (ENG.). 160p. (J). pap. 13.00 *(978-1-84771-823-5(X))* Y Lolfa GBR. Dist: Dufour Editions, Inc.

Williamson, Denise J. Silent Road to Rescue. 2008. (J). 8.99 *(978-1-59166-852-7(2))* BJU Pr.

Wilson, Barbara Ker & So, Meilo. Wishbones: A Folk Tale from China. (Illus.). 32p. (J). (gr. -1-2). pap. *(978-0-7112-1415-6(8))* ReiseArt Buchhandlung GmbH.

Xiong, Kim, illus. The Dragon Tribe. 2008. (ENG & CHI.). 33p. (J). 18.95 *(978-1-60603-000-4(0))* Better Chinese LLC.

—Kitchen God. 2008. 32p. (J). 18.95 *(978-1-60603-001-1(9))* Better Chinese LLC.

Xu, Lei. Cavern of the Blood Zombies. Mok, Kathy, tr. 2011. (Graver Robbers' Chronicles Ser.). (ENG.). 240p. pap. 9.95 *(978-1-934159-31-6(X))* ThingsAsian Pr.

Xueqin, Cao. Dream of the Red Chamber. Chiang, Shirley, illus. 2013. (Chinese Classics Ser.). (ENG.). 64p. pap. 6.95 *(978-1-906230-36-4(6))* Real Reads Ltd. GBR. Dist: Casemate Pubs. & Bk. Distributors, LLC.

Yang, Belle. Always Come Home to Me. Yang, Belle, illus. 2007. (ENG., Illus.). 32p. (J). (gr. -1-3). 16.99 *(978-0-7636-2899-4(9))* Candlewick Pr.

Yang, Belle & Williams, Marcia. Archie's War: My Scrapbook of the First World War. Williams, Marcia, illus. 2007. (ENG., Illus.). 48p. (J). (gr. 3-7). 18.99 *(978-0-7636-3532-9(4))* Candlewick Pr.

Yang, Gene Luen. Boxers & Saints Boxed Set. 2013. (Boxers & Saints Ser.: 1). (YA). lib. bdg. 31.80 *(978-0-606-32304-8(X),* Turtleback) Turtleback Bks.

—Saints. 2013. (Boxers & Saints Ser.: 2). (YA). lib. bdg. 28.15 *(978-0-606-32305-5(8),* Turtleback) Turtleback Bks.

Yang, Gene Luen & Pien, Lark. Boxers & Saints Boxed Set. Yang, Gene Luen, illus. 2013. (Boxers & Saints Ser.: 1). (ENG., Illus.). (YA). (gr. 7). 512p. 34.99 *(978-1-59643-924-5(6),* 9781596439245); 336p. pap. 18.99 *(978-1-59643-359-5(0),* 9781596433595) Roaring Brook Pr. (First Second Bks.).

—Saints. Yang, Gene Luen, illus. 2013. (Boxers & Saints Ser.: 2). (ENG., Illus.). 176p. (YA). (gr. 7). pap. 15.99 *(978-1-59643-689-3(1),* 9781596436893, First Second Bks.) Roaring Brook Pr.

Yardley, Liz. The Firefly Legacy - Book Vi. Yardley, Liz, illus. 2013. (Illus.). 336p. pap. *(978-0-9872013-1-7(X))* BlueFlower Bks.

Ye, Ting-Xing. Throwaway Daughter. 2004. (ENG.). 320p. (J). (gr. 7). mass mkt. 9.99 *(978-0-7704-2921-8(1),* Seal Bks.) Penguin Random House Canada Young Readers CAN. Dist: Penguin Random Hse. LLC.

Yee, Paul. The Jade Necklace. Lin, Grace, illus. 2006. 29p. (J). (gr. 4-8). reprint ed. 16.00 *(978-1-4223-5135-2(1))* DIANE Publishing Co.

Yen Mah, Adeline. Chinese Cinderella Boy Knight, Vol. 2. 2006. *(978-0-06-056737-8(6));* lib. bdg. *(978-0-06-056738-5(4))* HarperCollins Canada, Ltd.

—Chinese Cinderella: True Story of an Unwanted Daughter. 2011. 10.54 *(978-0-7848-3603-3(5),* Everbind) Marco Bk. Co.

Yep, Laurence & Yep, Kathleen S. The Dragon's Child: A Story of Angel Island. 2011. (ENG.). 160p. (J). (gr. 3-7). pap. 5.99 *(978-0-06-201815-1(9))* HarperCollins Pubs.

Yin. Coolies. Soentpiet, Chris K., illus. 2003. (ENG.). 40p. (J). (gr. 2-5). 7.99 *(978-0-14-250055-2(0),* Puffin Books) Penguin Young Readers Group.

Yip, Mingmei. Grandma Panda's China Storybook: Legends, Traditions & Fun. 2013. (ENG., Illus.). 32p. (J). (gr. -1-3). 15.95 *(978-0-8048-4149-8(7))* Tuttle Publishing.

Young, Ed & Adams, Tracey. The Lost Horse: A Chinese Folktale. 2004. (ENG., Illus.). 32p. (J). (gr. -1-3). pap. 7.00 *(978-0-15-205023-8(X))* Houghton Mifflin Harcourt Publishing Co.

Yu, Li Qiong. A New Year's Reunion: A Chinese Story. Liang, Zhu Chen, illus. 2011. (ENG.). 40p. (J). (gr. -1-2). 15.99 *(978-0-7636-5881-6(2))* Candlewick Pr.

Yue, Gui & Farrow, Clare. Little Leap Forward: A Boy in Beijing. Cann, Helen, illus. 2011. (ENG.). 120p. (J). (gr. 3-6). pap. 12.99 *(978-1-84686-539-8(5))* Barefoot Bks., Inc.

Yue, Guo & Farrow, Clare. Little Leap Forward: A Boy in Beijing. Cann, Helen, illus. 2008. (ENG.). 128p. (YA). (gr. 4-7). 16.99 *(978-1-84686-114-7(4))* Barefoot Bks., Inc.

Yun, Yeo-rim. Liang's Treasure: China. Cowley, Joy, ed. Choi, Yang-sook, illus. 2015. (Global Kids Storybooks Ser.). (ENG.). 32p. (gr. 1-4). 26.65 *(978-1-925246-05-6(1));* 7.99 *(978-1-925246-57-5(4));* 26.65 *(978-1-925246-31-5(0))* ChoiceMaker Pty. Ltd., The AUS. (Big and SMALL). Dist: Lerner Publishing Group.

—Liang's Treasure: China. Cowley, Joy, ed. Choi, Yang-sook, illus. 2015. (Global Kids Storybooks Ser.). (ENG.). 32p. (J). (gr. 1-4). pap. 7.99 *(978-1-925233-48-3(0))* Lerner Publishing Group.

Zaugg, Sandra L. The Man in the Blue Skirt. 2005. (Illus.). 95p. (J). pap. *(978-0-8163-2055-4(1))* Pacific Pr. Pubns.

—A Prayer for Mother. 2005. (Illus.). 95p. (J). *(978-0-8163-2056-1(X))* Pacific Pr. Pubns.

Zhang, Kat. The Emperor's Riddle. 2017. (ENG., Illus.). 256p. (J). (gr. 3-7). 16.99 ***(978-1-4814-7862-5(1),*** Aladdin) Simon & Schuster Children's Publishing.

Zhao, Yun & I-Haun. Real Fake Princess, Vol. 1. 2006. (Real/Fake Princess Ser.). (ENG., Illus.). 200p. (YA). pap. 9.95 *(978-1-59796-079-3(9))* DrMaster Pubns. Inc.

CHINA—FOREIGN RELATIONS

Abrams, Dennis. The Treaty of Nanking. 2011. (Milestones in Modern World History Ser.). (Illus.). 120p. (C). (gr. 9). 35.00 *(978-1-60413-495-7(X),* Chelsea Hse.) Facts On File, Inc.

Berlatsky, Noah. China. 2010. (Opposing Viewpoints Ser.). (Illus.). 240p. (J). 42.95 *(978-0-7377-4765-2(X),* 1304557); pap. 29.45 *(978-0-7377-4766-9(8),* 1304557) Cengage Gale. (Greenhaven Pr., Inc.).

Egendorf, Laura K. Should the U. S. Do Business with China? 2008. (At Issue Ser.). (ENG., Illus.). 128p. (gr. 10-12). 39.40 *(978-0-7377-4112-4(0));* pap. 27.80 *(978-0-7377-4113-1(9))* Cengage Gale. (Greenhaven Pr., Inc.).

CHINA—HISTORY

Abrams, Dennis. The Treaty of Nanking. 2011. (Milestones in Modern World History Ser.). (Illus.). 120p. (C). (gr. 9). 35.00 *(978-1-60413-495-7(X),* Chelsea Hse.) Facts On File, Inc.

Allan, Tony. Ancient China. 2007. (Cultural Atlas for Young People Ser.). (Illus.). 96p. (YA). (gr. 5-9). 35.00 *(978-0-8160-6827-2(5))* Facts On File, Inc.

Aloian, Molly. The Gobi Desert. 2012. (ENG.). 32p. (J). *(978-0-7787-0710-3(5));* (Illus.). pap. *(978-0-7787-0718-9(0))* Crabtree Publishing Co.

Anastasio, Dina. The Magic Turtle. 2011. (Early Connections Ser.). (J). *(978-1-61672-603-4(2))* Benchmark Education Co.

Anderson, Dale. Chinese Americans. 2006. (World Almanac Library of American Immigration). (Illus.). 48p. (gr. 5-12). pap. 14.05 *(978-0-8368-7321-4(1));* lib. bdg. 31.00 *(978-0-8368-7308-5(4))* Stevens, Gareth Publishing LLLP. (Gareth Stevens Secondary Library).

Atkins, Marcie Flinchum. Ancient China, 1 vol. 2014. (Ancient Civilizations Ser.). (ENG.). 112p. (J). (gr. 6-12). lib. bdg. 35.64 *(978-1-62403-536-4(1),* Essential Library) ABDO Publishing Co.

Bailey, Diane. Emperor Qin's Terra-Cotta Army, 1 vol. 2014. (Digging up the Past Ser.). (ENG.). 112p. (J). (gr. 6-12). lib. bdg. 35.64 *(978-1-62403-232-5(X),* Essential Library) ABDO Publishing Co.

Bailey, Linda. Adventures in Ancient China. Slavin, Bill, illus. 2008. (Good Times Travel Agency Ser.). (ENG.). 48p. (J). (gr. 4-6). 8.95 *(978-1-55337-454-1(1))* Kids Can Pr., Ltd. CAN. Dist: Hachette Bk. Group.

Ball, Jacqueline & Levey, Richard. National Geographic Investigates: Ancient China: Archaeology Unlocks the Secrets of China's Past. 2006. (National Geographic Investigates Ser.). (ENG., Illus.). 64p. (J). (gr. 3-7). 17.95 *(978-0-7922-7783-5(X),* National Geographic Children's Bks.) National Geographic Society.

Ball, Jacqueline & Levey, Richard H. National Geographic Investigates: Ancient China: Archaeology Unlocks the Secrets of China's Past. 2006. (National Geographic Investigates Ser.). (ENG., Illus.). 64p. (J). (gr. 4-7). lib. bdg. 27.90 *(978-0-7922-7856-6(9),* National Geographic Children's Bks.) National Geographic Society.

Benchmark Education Company. China Long Ago (Teacher Guide) 2005. *(978-1-4108-4668-6(7))* Benchmark Education Co.

Bjorklund, Ruth. China. 2015. (Exploring World Cultures Ser.). (ENG., Illus.). 32p. (J). (gr. 3-4). 28.50 *(978-1-5026-0592-4(9))* Cavendish Square Publishing.

—Projects about Ancient China. 2006. (Hands-On History Ser.). (Illus.). 48p. (gr. 3-7). lib. bdg. 21.95 *(978-0-7614-2257-0(9),* Benchmark Bks.) Marshall Cavendish Corp.

Bo, Zhiyue. The History of Modern China. Wang, Jianwei, ed. 2012. (China: the Emerging Superpower Ser.). 144p. (J). (gr. 7). 24.95 *(978-1-4222-2162-4(8))* Mason Crest.

—The History of Modern China. 2011. (J). pap. *(978-1-4222-2173-0(3))* Mason Crest.

Bradman, Tony. The Silk Road White Band. Cerisier, Emmanuel, illus. 2016. (Cambridge Reading Adventures Ser.). (ENG.). 15p. pap. 7.81 *(978-1-107-56232-5(5))* Cambridge Univ. Pr.

Bramwell, Neil D. Discover Ancient China. 2014. (Discover Ancient Civilizations Ser.). 104p. (J). pap. 10.95 *(978-1-4644-0331-6(7))* Enslow Pubs., Inc.

Brannon, Barbara. Discover Ancient China. 2005. (J). pap. *(978-1-4108-5162-8(1))* Benchmark Education Co.

Branscombe, Allison. All about China: Stories, Songs, Crafts & Games for Kids. Wang, Lin, illus. 2014. (ENG.). 64p. (J). (gr. 3-6). 16.95 *(978-0-8048-4121-4(7))* Tuttle Publishing.

Burnham, Brad. Caves of the Thousand Buddhas: Treasure House of Chinese Art. 2003. (Famous Caves of the World Ser.). (Illus.). 24p. (J). lib. bdg. 22.60 *(978-0-8239-6260-0(1))* Rosen Publishing Group, Inc., The.

Cain, Marie Mowery. George Takes a Road Trip, China. 2013. (Big Books, Red Ser.). (ENG & SPA., Illus.). 16p. pap. 33.00 *(978-1-59246-207-0(3))* Big Books, by George!

Campbell, Trenton, ed. Gods & Goddesses of Ancient China. 2014. (Gods & Goddesses of Mythology Ser.). 160p. (J). (gr. 9-12). 32.90 *(978-1-62275-393-2(3))* Rosen Publishing Group, Inc., The.

Campbell, Wallis. Angel Island. 2006. (Illus.). 48p. (J). pap. *(978-1-59034-808-6(7))* Mondo Publishing.

Caper, William. India & China: Text Pairs. 2008. (Bridges/Navigators Ser.). (J). (gr. 6). 94.00 *(978-1-4108-8441-1(4))* Benchmark Education Co.

Catel, Patrick. China, 1 vol. 2012. (Countries Around the World Ser.). (ENG.). 48p. (gr. 3-6). pap. 9.95 *(978-1-4329-6122-0(5));* lib. bdg. 33.32 *(978-1-4329-6096-4(2))* Heinemann-Raintree. (NA-h).

—What Did the Ancient Chinese Do for Me?, 1 vol. 2010. (Linking the Past & Present Ser.). (ENG.). 32p. (gr. 3-6). pap. 8.29 *(978-1-4329-3754-6(5),* Heinemann InfoSearch) Heinemann-Raintree.

Challen, Paul. Hail! Ancient Chinese. 2010. (ENG.). 32p. (J). *(978-0-7787-6621-6(7));* pap. *(978-0-7787-6628-5(4))* Crabtree Publishing Co.

Childress, Diana. Marco Polo's Journey to China. 2007. (Pivotal Moments in History Ser.). (ENG.). 160p. (gr. 9-12). lib. bdg. 38.60 *(978-0-8225-5903-0(X))* Lerner Publishing Group.

The Chinese Cultural Revolution. 2010. (Milestones in World History Ser.). (Illus.). 128p. (C). (gr. 9-18). 35.00 *(978-1-60413-278-6(7),* Chelsea Hse.) Facts On File, Inc.

Claybourne, Anna. The Shang Dynesty - Collins Big Cat. 2015. (Collins Big Cat Ser.). (ENG., Illus.). 56p. (J). (gr. 4-5). pap. 9.95 *(978-0-00-812790-9(5))* HarperCollins Pubs. Ltd. GBR. Dist: Independent Pubs. Group.

Cole, Forrest. Tiananmen Square Protests. 2012. (J). 35.00 *(978-1-60413-922-8(6),* Chelsea Hse.) Facts On File, Inc.

Collins, Terry. Ancient China: An Interactive History Adventure. 2012. (You Choose: Historical Eras Ser.). (ENG.). 112p. (gr. 3-4). pap. 41.70 *(978-1-4296-9473-5(4),* You Choose Bks.) Capstone Press of Coughlan Cos.

Collins, Terry, et al. Building the Great Wall of China: An Isabel Soto History Adventure. 2016. (Graphic Expeditions Ser.). (ENG., Illus.). 32p. pap. 8.10 *(978-1-5157-6156-3(8),* Graphic Library) Capstone Press of Coughlan Cos.

Conklin, Wendy. Ancient Civilizations - China - India - Africa - Mesopotamia: All-in-One Resource with Background Information, Map Activities, Simulations & Games, & a Read-Aloud Play to Support Comprehension & Critical Thinking in Social Studies, Grades 5 & Up. 2006. (Ancient Civilizations Ser.). (ENG., Illus.). 96p. (gr. 5). per. 14.99 *(978-0-439-53993-7(5),* Teaching Resources) Scholastic, Inc.

Cotterell, Arthur, et al. Eyewitness Travel Guide - Ancient China. Hills, Alan & Brightling, Geoff, photos by. 2005. (DK Eyewitness Bks.). (ENG., Illus.). 72p. (J). (gr. 3-7). 16.99 *(978-0-7566-1382-2(5),* DK Children) Dorling Kindersley Publishing, Inc.

Coupe, Robert. The Great Wall of China. 2013. (Discovery Education: Ancient Civilizations Ser.). (ENG., Illus.). 32p. (J). (gr. 3-6). pap. 10.00 *(978-1-4777-0085-3(4))* Rosen Publishing Group, Inc., The.

Crane, Carol. D Is for Dancing Dragon: A China Alphabet. 2016. (Av2 Fiction Readalong 2017 Ser.). (ENG.). (J). (gr. k-6). 34.28 ***(978-1-4896-5203-4(5),*** AV2 by Weigl) Weigl Pubs., Inc.

Crane, Carol. D Is for Dancing Dragon: A China Alphabet. Wang, Zong-Zhou, illus. rev. ed. 2006. (Discover the World Ser.). (ENG.). 48p. (J). (gr. -1-3). 17.95 *(978-1-58536-273-8(5))* Sleeping Bear Pr.

Culp, Jennifer. The Totally Gross History of Ancient China, 01 vols., 1. 2016. (Totally Gross History Ser.). (ENG.). 48p. (J). 30.25 *(978-1-4994-3758-4(7),* Rosen Central) Rosen Publishing Group, Inc., The.

Demuth, Patricia Brennan. Where Is the Great Wall? 2015. (Where Is... ? Ser.). lib. bdg. 16.00 *(978-0-606-36590-1(7))* Turtleback Bks.

Demuth, Patricia Brennan & dePaola, Tomie. Where Is the Great Wall? Groff, David & Hoare, Jerry, illus. 2015. (Where Is? Ser.). (ENG.). 112p. (J). (gr. 3-7). 5.99 *(978-0-448-48358-0(0),* Grosset & Dunlap) Penguin Young Readers Group.

Dramer, Kim. The Chinese. 2011. (Technology of the Ancients Ser.). 64p. (gr. 5). 32.79 *(978-1-60870-766-9(0))* Marshall Cavendish Corp.

DuTemple, Lesley A. The Great Wall of China. 2003. (Great Building Feats Ser.). (Illus.). 96p. (J). (gr. 5-9). 27.93 *(978-0-8225-0377-4(8))* Lerner Publishing Group.

Exploring China, 6 vols. (Book2WebTM Ser.). (gr. 4-8). 36.50 *(978-0-322-02991-0(0))* Wright Group/McGraw-Hill.

Franklin Watts & Scholastic, Inc. Staff, contrib. by. Population 1.3 Billion: China Becomes a Super Superpower. 2009. (24/7: Behind the Headlines Ser.). (ENG.). 64p. (J). (gr. 6-12). 29.00 *(978-0-531-21806-8(6))* Scholastic Library Publishing.

Friedman, Lauri S. China. 2009. (Introducing Issues with Opposing Viewpoints Ser.). (ENG.). 144p. (gr. 7-10). 36.95 *(978-0-7377-4335-7(2)*, Greenhaven Pr., Inc.) Cengage Gale.

Friedman, Mel. Ancient China. (True Book(tm), a — Ancient Civilizations Ser.). (ENG.). 48p. (J). 2009. (gr. 2-5). 31.00 *(978-0-531-25225-3(6))* 2010. (Illus.). (gr. 3-5). pap. 6.95 *(978-0-531-24106-6(8)*, Children's Pr.) Scholastic Library Publishing.

Ganeri, Anita. China: A Benjamin Blog & His Inquisitive Dog Guide, 1 vol. Isik, Semur, illus. 2014. (Country Guides, with Benjamin Blog & His Inquisitive Dog Ser.). (ENG.). 32p. (gr. 1-3). pap. 7.99 *(978-1-4109-6670-4(4)*, Read Me!) Heinemann-Raintree.

Gardner, April B. Mao: Boy of Stone. 2012. 24p. 24.95 *(978-1-4626-9867-7(0))*; pap. 24.95 *(978-1-4626-8244-7(8))* America Star Bks.

Gassós, Dolors. CHINA. 2006. (SPA.). 32p. (J). (gr. 6-8). 10.40 *(978-84-342-2737-8(1)*, PR33930) Parramon Ediciones S.A. ESP. Dist: Lectorum Pubns., Inc.

Gay, Kathlyn. The Aftermath of the Chinese Nationalist Revolution. 2008. (Aftermath of History Ser.). (ENG., Illus.). 160p. (J). (gr. 9-12). lib. bdg. 38.60 *(978-0-8225-7601-3(5))* Lerner Publishing Group.

—Mao Zedong's China. 2007. (Dictatorships Ser.). (ENG., Illus.). 160p. (gr. 9-12). lib. bdg. 38.60 *(978-0-8225-7285-5(0)*, Twenty-First Century Bks.) Lerner Publishing Group.

Gogerly, Liz & Hunt, Rob. China. 2016. (Journey Through Ser.). (ENG., Illus.). 32p. (J). (gr. 4-6). 16.99 *(978-1-4451-3681-3(3)*, Franklin Watts) Hachette Children's Group GBR. Dist: Hachette Bk. Group.

Goh, Sui Noi & Lim, Bee Ling. China. 2010. (Welcome to My Country Ser.). 48p. (gr. 3). 28.50 *(978-1-60870-151-3(4))* Marshall Cavendish Corp.

Goldsworthy, Steve. China. 2013. (J). *(978-1-62127-252-6(4))*; pap. *(978-1-62127-258-8(3))* Weigl Pubs., Inc.

The Great Wall of China. 2014. (Great Idea Ser.). (ENG.). 48p. (J). (gr. 4-6). lib. bdg. 26.60 *(978-1-59953-597-5(1))* Norwood Hse. Pr.

Greenberger, Robert. The Technology of Ancient China. (Technology of the Ancient World Ser.). 48p. 2009. (gr. 6-6). 61.20 *(978-1-60854-238-3(6)*, Rosen Reference) 2005. (Illus.). (J). (gr. 5-8). lib. bdg. 29.25 *(978-1-4042-0558-1(6))* Rosen Publishing Group, Inc., The.

Greenling, Jason. The Technology of Ancient China. 2016. (Ancient Innovations Ser.). 64p. (J). 34.21 *(978-1-5026-2235-8(1))* Cavendish Square Publishing.

Hamashita, Takeshi. China, East Asia & the Global Economy: Regional & Historical Perspectives. Grove, Linda & Selden, Mark, eds. 2008. (Asia's Transformations/Critical Asian Scholarship Ser.). (ENG., Illus.). 224p. (C). 50.95 *(978-0-415-46459-8(5)*, RU53282) Routledge.

—China, East Asia & the Global Economy: Regional & Historical Perspectives. Selden, Mark & Grove, Linda, eds. 2008. (Asia's Transformations/Critical Asian Scholarship Ser.). (ENG., Illus.). 224p. (C). 185.00 *(978-0-415-46458-1(7)*, RU53281) Routledge.

Hardwick, Susan. China: World-Wise Kids Guides. 2004. 96p. *(978-1-59258-094-1(7))* Hylas Publishing.

Harrison, Logan. What Was It Like in Ancient China? 2013. (InfoMax Readers Ser.). (ENG.). 24p. (J). (gr. 3-4). pap. 49.50 *(978-1-4777-2496-5(6)*, Rosen Classroom) Rosen Publishing Group, Inc., The.

Harrison, Lorraine & Harrison, Logan. What Was It Like in Ancient China? 2013. (InfoMax Readers Ser.). (ENG.). 24p. (J). (gr. 3-4). pap. 8.25 *(978-1-4777-2495-8(8)*, Rosen Classroom) Rosen Publishing Group, Inc., The.

Henzel, Cynthia Kennedy. Great Wall of China, 1 vol. 2011. (Troubled Treasures: World Heritage Sites Ser.). (ENG., Illus.). 32p. (YA). (gr. 3-6). 27.07 *(978-1-61613-565-2(4))* ABDO Publishing Co.

Herron, Pamela. Exploring Ancient China. 2017. (Exploring Ancient Civilizations Ser.). (ENG.). 32p. (gr. 2-7). pap. 9.95 ***(978-1-63235-526-3(4)**, 12-Story Library)* Pr. Room Editions LLC.

Hile, Lori. Daily Life in Shang Dynasty China. 2015. (Daily Life in Ancient Civilizations Ser.). (ENG., Illus.). 48p. (gr. 3-6). pap. 8.99 *(978-1-4846-2579-8(X))* Heinemann-Raintree.

Hinton, John. Ancient China. 2013. (Rosen Readers Ser.). (ENG.). 24p. (J). (gr. 3-4). pap. 49.50 *(978-1-4777-2484-2(2))*; pap. 8.25 *(978-1-4777-2483-5(4))* Rosen Publishing Group, Inc., The. (Rosen Classroom).

Hirsch, E. D., Jr., ed. Ancient China. 2003. tchr. ed. 9.95 *(978-0-7690-5044-7(1))*; stu. ed. 49.95 *(978-0-7690-2950-4(7))* Pearson Learning.

Hollihan-Elliot, Sheila. The Ancient History of China. Wang, Jianwei, ed. 2012. (China: the Emerging Superpower Ser.). 120p. (J). (gr. 7). 24.95 *(978-1-4222-2154-9(7))* Mason Crest.

—The Ancient History of China. 2011. (J). pap. *(978-1-4222-2165-5(2))* Mason Crest.

Hong, Chen Jiang. Mao & Me. Bedrick, Claudia Z., tr. from FRE. 2008. (ENG., Illus.). 96p. (J). (gr. 3-5). 19.95 *(978-1-59270-079-0(9))* Enchanted Lion Bks., LLC.

Howell, Izzi. Ancient China. 2016. (Explore! Ser.). (ENG., Illus.). 32p. (J). (gr. 4-6). 16.99 *(978-1-5263-0057-7(5)*, Wayland) Hachette Children's Group GBR. Dist: Hachette Bk. Group.

James, Oliver. China. 2010. (Countries in Our World Ser.). 32p. (gr. 4-7). 31.35 *(978-1-59920-440-6(1))* Black Rabbit Bks.

Jenson-Elliott, Cindy. Ancient Chinese Dynasties. 2014. (Understanding World History Ser.). (ENG., Illus.). 96p. (J). lib. bdg. *(978-1-60152-738-7(1))* ReferencePoint Pr., Inc.

Ji-Li, Jiang. Red Scarf Girl: A Memoir of the Cultural Revolution. 2014. (ENG.). 304p. (J). (gr. 12-12). 11.24 *(978-1-63245-134-7(4))* Lectorum Pubns., Inc.

Jiang, Ji-Li. Red Scarf Girl: A Memoir of the Cultural Revolution. (ENG.). 320p. (J). (gr. 3-7). 2008. pap. 8.99 *(978-0-06-166771-8(4))* 2004. pap. 7.99 *(978-0-06-446208-2(0))* HarperCollins Pubs.

Johnson, Robin & Kalman, Bobbie. Conoce China. 2009. (SPA.). 32p. (J). *(978-0-7787-8192-9(5))*; (gr. 2-5). pap. *(978-0-7787-8212-4(3))* Crabtree Publishing Co.

Juarez, Christine. China, 1 vol. 2013. (Countries Ser.). (ENG.). 24p. (gr. k-1). lib. bdg. 26.65 *(978-1-4765-3077-2(7)*, Pebble Plus) Capstone Press of Coughlan Cos.

—China, 1 vol. 2013. (Countries Ser.). (ENG.). 24p. (gr. k-1). pap. 6.95 *(978-1-4765-3517-3(5)*, Pebble Bks.) Capstone Press of Coughlan Cos.

Kallio, Jamie. Angel Island Immigration: A History Perspectives Book. 2014. (Perspectives Library). (ENG.). 32p. (J). (gr. 4-8). 28.50 *(978-1-63137-614-6(4)*, 205239) Cherry Lake Publishing.

Kaur, Ramandeep. The Bird's Nest. 2015. (How Did They Build That? Ser.). (ENG., Illus.). 32p. (gr. 3-8). 27.99 *(978-1-62920-560-1(5))* Scobre Pr. Corp.

Kenney, Karen Latchana. Mysteries of the Great Wall of China. 2017. (Ancient Mysteries Ser.). (ENG.). 32p. (J). (gr. 3-6). 27.99 ***(978-1-5124-4013-3(2))*** Lerner Publishing Group.

Kleeman, Terry & Barrett, Tracy. The Ancient Chinese World. 2005. (World in Ancient Times Ser.). (ENG., Illus.). 176p. (gr. 7-12). 36.95 *(978-0-19-517102-0(0))* Oxford Univ. Pr., Inc.

Kopp, Megan. Understanding Chinese Myths. 2012. (ENG.). 48p. (J). *(978-0-7787-4507-5(4))*; pap. *(978-0-7787-4512-9(0))* Crabtree Publishing Co.

Kramer, Lance. Great Ancient China Projects: You Can Build Yourself. Weinberg, Steven, illus. 2008. (Build It Yourself Ser.). (ENG.). 128p. (J). (gr. 3-7). pap. 21.95 *(978-1-934670-02-6(2))* Octavio Publishing.

Krebs, Laurie. We're Riding on a Caravan: An Adventure on the Silk Road. Cann, Helen, illus. 2005. (ENG.). 32p. (J). 16.99 *(978-1-84148-343-6(5))* Barefoot Bks., Inc.

Landau, Elaine. Exploring Ancient China with Elaine Landau. 2005. (Exploring Ancient Civilizations with Elaine Landau Ser.). (Illus.). 48p. (J). (gr. 4-7). lib. bdg. 25.27 *(978-0-7660-2338-3(9)*, Enslow Elementary) Enslow Pubs., Inc.

Lankford, Ronald D. Is China's Economic Growth a Threat to America? Greenhaven Press Editors, ed. 2013. (At Issue Ser.). (ENG.). 128p. (gr. 10-12). pap. 27.80 *(978-0-7377-6186-3(5))*; lib. bdg. 39.40 *(978-0-7377-6185-6(7))* Cengage Gale. (Greenhaven Pr., Inc.).

Lassieur, Allison. Building the Great Wall of China: An Interactive Engineering Adventure, 1 vol. 2014. (You Choose: Engineering Marvels Ser.). (ENG.). 112p. (gr. 3-4). lib. bdg. 31.99 *(978-1-4914-0399-0(3)*, You Choose Bks.) Capstone Press of Coughlan Cos.

Lee, Gisela. China, 1 vol. 2007. (Primary Source Readers Ser.). (ENG.). 32p. (J). (gr. 5-5). pap. 8.99 *(978-0-7439-0436-0(2))* Shell Educational Publishing.

Li, Moying. Snow Falling in Spring: Coming of Age in China During the Cultural Revolution. 2010. (ENG., Illus.). 192p. (YA). (gr. 7-12). pap. 9.99 *(978-0-312-60867-5(5)*, 9780312608675) Square Fish.

Lin, Zhimin. China under Reform. Wang, Jianwei, ed. 2012. (China: the Emerging Superpower Ser.). (Illus.). 120p. (J). (gr. 7). 24.95 *(978-1-4222-2156-3(3))* Mason Crest.

—China under Reform. (Illus.). 2011. 120p. (J). pap. *(978-1-4222-2167-9(9))* 2007. 144p. (YA). lib. bdg. 24.95 *(978-1-59084-823-4(3))* Mason Crest.

Liu-Perkins, Christine. At Home in Her Tomb: Lady Dai & the Ancient Chinese Treasures of Mawangdui. Brannen, Sarah S., illus. 2014. (ENG.). 80p. (J). (gr. 4-7). lib. bdg. 19.95 *(978-1-58089-370-1(8))* Charlesbridge Publishing, Inc.

—At Home in Her Tomb: Lady Dai & the Ancient Chinese Treasures of Mawangdui. 2014. 80p. pap. 19.95 *(978-1-60734-615-9(X))* Charlesbridge Publishing, Inc.

Lusted, Marcia Amidon. Tiananmen Square Protests, 1 vol. 2010. (Essential Events Set 5 Ser.). (ENG.). 112p. (J). (gr. 6-12). lib. bdg. 35.64 *(978-1-61613-686-4(3))* ABDO Publishing Co.

Lynette, Rachel. The Great Wall of China. 2004. (Great Structures in History Ser.). (Illus.). 48p. (J). (gr. 4-7). 26.20 *(978-0-7377-1558-3(8))* Cengage Gale.

Mah, Adeline Yen. China: Land of Dragons & Emperors. 2011. (ENG.). 256p. (YA). (gr. 7). pap. 8.99 *(978-0-385-73749-4(1)*, Ember) Random Hse. Children's Bks.

Malaspina, Ann. The Chinese Revolution & Mao Zedong in World History. 2004. (In World History Ser.). (Illus.). 128p. (J). lib. bdg. 27.94 *(978-0-7660-1935-5(7))* Enslow Pubs., Inc.

Mann, Elizabeth. The Great Wall: The Story of Thousands of Miles of Earth & Stone That Turned a Nation into a Fortress. Witschonke, Alan, illus. 2006. (Wonders of the World Book Ser.). (ENG.). 48p. (J). (gr. 4-8). pap. 12.95 *(978-1-931414-12-8(2)*, 9781931414128) Mikaya Pr.

Mara, Wil. People's Republic of China. 2011. (Enchantment of the World Ser.). (ENG., Illus.). 144p. (J). (gr. 5-9). lib. bdg. 40.00 *(978-0-531-25352-6(X))* Scholastic Library Publishing.

—The Tiananmen Square Massacre. 2013. (ENG.). 64p. (J). 30.00 *(978-0-531-28207-6(4))*; pap. 8.95 *(978-0-531-27672-3(4))* Scholastic Library Publishing.

Markovics, Joyce L. China. 2015. (Countries We Come From Ser.). (ENG., Illus.). 32p. (J). (gr. k-3). lib. bdg. 26.60 *(978-1-62724-858-7(7))* Bearport Publishing Co., Inc.

McMullan, James. Leaving China: An Artist Paints His World War II Childhood. 2014. (ENG., Illus.). 128p. (YA). (gr. 7-12). 19.95 *(978-1-61620-255-2(6)*, 73255) Algonquin Bks. of Chapel Hill.

Mills, Nathan & Li, John. I'm from China. 2012. (Rosen Readers Ser.). (ENG., Illus.). 24p. (J). (gr. 1-2). pap. 8.25 *(978-1-4488-8807-8(7)*, Rosen Classroom) Rosen Publishing Group, Inc., The.

Moon, Walt K. Exploremos China. 2017. (Bumba Books (tm) en Español — Exploremos Países (Let's Explore Countries) Ser.). (SPA.). 24p. (J). (gr. -1-1). lib. bdg. 25.32 ***(978-1-5124-4120-8(1))*** Lerner Publishing Group.

Morley, Jacqueline. You Wouldn't Want to Work on the Great Wall of China! Defenses You'd Rather Not Build. Antram, David, illus. 2006. (You Wouldn't Want to Ser.). (ENG.). 32p. (J). (gr. 2-5). 29.00 *(978-0-531-12424-6(X))*; pap. 9.95 *(978-0-531-12449-9(5)*, Watts, Franklin) Scholastic Library Publishing.

—You Wouldn't Want to Work on the Great Wall of China! (Revised Edition) 2017. (You Wouldn't Want to... History of the World Ser.). (ENG., Illus.). 32p. (J). lib. bdg. 29.00 *(978-0-531-23838-7(5)*, Watts, Franklin) Scholastic Library Publishing.

Murray, Julie. China, 1 vol. 2013. (Explore the Countries Ser.). (ENG.). 40p. (J). (gr. 2-5). lib. bdg. 29.93 *(978-1-61783-807-1(1)*, Big Buddy Bks.) ABDO Publishing Co.

Naden, Corinne J. Ancient Chinese & the Great Wall of China. 2003. (J). pap. *(978-1-58417-313-7(0))*; lib. bdg. *(978-1-58417-312-0(2))* Lake Street Pubs.

Oachs, Emily Rose. China. 2017. (Country Profiles Ser.). (ENG., Illus.). 32p. (J). (gr. 3-8). lib. bdg. 26.95 ***(978-1-62617-678-2(7)**, Blastoff! Discovery)* Bellwether Media.

O'Connor, Jane. Hidden Army: Clay Soldiers of Ancient China. 2011. (All Aboard Reading Ser.). (ENG.). 48p. (J). (gr. 1-3). mass mkt. 3.99 *(978-0-448-45580-8(3)*, Grosset & Dunlap) Penguin Young Readers Group.

O'Donnell, Kerri. The Great Wall of China. (Reading Room Collection 2 Ser.). 24p. 2009. (gr. 3-4). 42.50 *(978-1-60851-994-1(5)*, PowerKids Pr.) 2003. (Illus.). (J). lib. bdg. 22.60 *(978-0-8239-3715-8(1))* Rosen Publishing Group, Inc., The.

O'Neill, Joseph R. The Great Wall of China, 1 vol. 2009. (Essential Events Set 3 Ser.). (ENG., Illus.). 112p. (J). (gr. 6-12). lib. bdg. 35.64 *(978-1-60453-513-6(X))* ABDO Publishing Co.

Orr, Tamra. Meet Our New Student from China. 2008. (Meet Our New Student Ser.). (Illus.). 48p. (YA). (gr. 2-5). lib. bdg. 29.95 *(978-1-58415-647-5(3))* Mitchell Lane Pubs., Inc.

Osborne, Mary Pope & Boyce, Natalie Pope. China: Land of the Emperor's Great Wall. Murdocca, Sal & Molinari, Carlo, illus. 2014. (Magic Tree House - Fact Tracker Ser.: 31). (ENG.). 128p. (J). (gr. 2-5). pap. 6.99 *(978-0-385-38635-7(4)*, Random Hse. Bks. for Young Readers) Random Hse. Children's Bks.

Parley, Peter, pseud & Chubb, Andrew. Tales about China & the Chinese. 2011. (ENG.). 208p. pap. 14.99 *(978-988-19983-4-7(4))* Earnshaw Bks. HKG. Dist: Independent Pubs. Group.

Pelleschi, Andrea. China, 1 vol. 2011. (Countries of the World Set 1 Ser.). (ENG., Illus.). 144p. (J). (gr. 6-12). lib. bdg. 37.07 *(978-1-61783-107-2(7))* ABDO Publishing Co.

Perkins, Chloe. Living in ... China. Woolley, Tom, illus. 2016. (Living In... Ser.). (ENG.). 32p. (J). (gr. k-2). pap. 3.99 *(978-1-4814-6047-7(1)*, Simon Spotlight) Simon Spotlight.

Porterfield, Jason. Marco Polo. 2016. (Silk Road's Greatest Travelers Ser.). 112p. (gr. 6-6). 37.10 *(978-1-5081-7152-2(1))* Rosen Publishing Group, Inc., The.

Powell, Jillian. China. 2014. (My Country Ser.). 24p. (gr. k-3). lib. bdg. 28.50 *(978-1-59920-903-6(9))* Black Rabbit Bks.

—China. 2007. (Descubramos Países del Mundo (Looking at Countries) Ser.). (SPA., Illus.). 32p. (gr. 1-5). lib. bdg. 26.00 *(978-0-8368-8183-7(4)*, Gareth Stevens Learning Library) Stevens, Gareth Publishing LLLP.

Poynor, Alice Burnett. The Coming Day: A true Christmas story from China. 2011. 36p. pap. 13.95 *(978-1-4497-2002-5(1)*, WestBow Pr.) Author Solutions, Inc.

Pratt, Leonie. China (Level 2) - Internet Referenced. 2008. (Beginners Social Studies). 32p. (J). 4.99 *(978-0-7945-2127-1(4)*, Usborne) EDC Publishing.

Price, Sean Stewart & Price, Sean. Cixi: Evil Empress of China? 2009. (Wicked History Ser.). (ENG.). 128p. (J). (gr. 6-12). pap. 5.95 *(978-0-531-22171-6(7)*, Children's Pr.) Scholastic Library Publishing.

Qaiser, Annie. China. 2015. (One World, Many Countries Ser.). (ENG.). 32p. (J). (gr. 1-4). 28.50 *(978-1-63407-040-9(2)*, 208872) Child's World, Inc., The.

Randolph, Joanne, ed. Living & Working in Ancient China. 2017. (Back in Time Ser.). 48p. (gr. 5-6). pap. 11.70 ***(978-0-7660-8961-7(4))*** Enslow Pubs., Inc.

Raum, Elizabeth. Great Wall of China. 2015. (Ancient Wonders Ser.). (Illus.). 32p. (J). 28.50 *(978-1-60753-467-9(3))* Amicus Publishing.

Richardson, Adele. China. 2011. (My First Look At Ser.). (ENG.). 24p. (J). (gr. 1-17). pap. 7.99 *(978-1-926722-35-1(3)*, Creative Paperbacks) Creative Co., The.

Riggs, Kate. Great Wall of China. 2009. (Places of Old Ser.). 24p. (J). (gr. 1-5). lib. bdg. 24.25 *(978-1-58341-708-9(7)*, Creative Education) Creative Co., The.

Roberts, Russell. Ancient China. 2012. (Explore Ancient Worlds Ser.). (J). (gr. 3-6). lib. bdg. 29.95 *(978-1-61228-277-0(6))* Mitchell Lane Pubs., Inc.

Rose, Naomi C. Where Snow Leopard Prowls: Wild Animals of Tibet. Rose, Naomi C., illus. 2013. (ENG., Illus.). 32p. (J). 17.95 *(978-0-9836333-0-3(4))* Dancing Dakini Pr.

Rosen, Michael J. The Million Stories of Marco Polo. Pritelli, Maria Cristina, illus. 2016. (ENG.). 32p. (J). (gr. 1-3). 18.99 *(978-1-56846-290-5(5)*, Creative Editions) Creative Co., The.

Roxburgh, Ellis. The Chinese Empire. 2015. (Great Empires Ser.). (ENG., Illus.). 48p. (J). (gr. 7-7). 31.36 *(978-1-5026-0636-5(4))* Cavendish Square Publishing.

Ryall, Michael. China Long Ago. 2005. (J). pap. *(978-1-4108-4620-4(2))* Benchmark Education Co.

Salter, Christopher L. & Whiteford, Gary T. China. 2nd rev. ed. 2010. (Modern World Nations Ser.). (Illus.). 136p. (gr. 6-12). 35.00 *(978-1-60413-621-0(9)*, Chelsea Hse.) Facts On File, Inc.

Samuels, Charlie. Technology in Ancient China. 2013. 48p. (J). (gr. 4-6). pap. 14.05 *(978-1-4339-9625-2(1))*; pap. 84.30 *(978-1-4339-9626-9(X))*; (ENG., Illus.). lib. bdg. 31.95 *(978-1-4339-9624-5(3))* Stevens, Gareth Publishing LLLP.

Scholastic, Inc. Staff, contrib. by. Population 1.3 Billion: China Becomes a Super Superpower. 2009. (24/7: Behind the Headlines Ser.). (ENG.). 64p. (J). (gr. 6-18). pap. 7.95 *(978-0-531-22002-3(8)*, Children's Pr.) Scholastic Library Publishing.

Sexton, Colleen & Simmons, Walter. China. 2010. (Exploring Countries Ser.). (ENG., Illus.). 32p. (J). (gr. 3-7). lib. bdg. 26.95 *(978-1-60014-476-9(4)*, Blastoff! Readers) Bellwether Media.

Shuter, Jane. Ancient China. 2016. (Excavating the Past Ser.). (ENG.). 48p. (J). (gr. 4-6). pap. 8.99 *(978-1-4846-3645-9(7)*, NA-h) Heinemann-Raintree.

Slavicek, Louise Chipley. The Great Wall of China. 2004. (Arbitrary Borders Ser.). (Illus.). 120p. (C). (gr. 9-13). 35.00 *(978-0-7910-8019-1(6)*, Chelsea Hse.) Facts On File, Inc.

Smith, Tony. Shaolin Monks. 2012. (History's Greatest Warriors Ser.). (ENG., Illus.). 24p. (J). (gr. 3-7). lib. bdg. 25.95 *(978-1-60014-748-7(8)*, Torque Bks.) Bellwether Media.

Snedden, Robert. Ancient China. 2009. (Technology in Times Past Ser.). 32.80 *(978-1-59920-298-3(0))* Black Rabbit Bks.

—Ancient China. 2009. (Technology in Times Past Ser.). (Illus.). 46p. (J). (gr. 4-7). pap. *(978-1-897563-60-1(4))* Saunders Bk. Co.

Spilsbury, Louise. Ancient China. 2016. (History Hunters Ser.). (ENG.). 32p. (gr. 3-4). lib. bdg. 27.99 *(978-1-5157-2525-1(1)*, Edge Bks.) Capstone Press of Coughlan Cos.

Stanborough, Rebecca. Great Wall of China. 2016. (Engineering Wonders Ser.). (ENG., Illus.). 32p. (gr. 3-4). lib. bdg. 27.32 *(978-1-4914-8197-4(8)*, Fact Finders) Capstone Press of Coughlan Cos.

Steele, Philip. China. 2015. (Emerging Nations Ser.). (ENG., Illus.). 48p. (J). (gr. 4-9). 37.10 *(978-1-59920-987-6(X))* Black Rabbit Bks.

Steele, Phillip. Step Into: The Chinese Empire. 2008. (ENG., Illus.). 64p. (J). (gr. 4-7). pap. 12.99 *(978-1-84476-509-6(1))* Anness Publishing GBR. Dist: National Bk. Network.

Stewart, Gail B. The Han Dynasty. 2004. (Life During the Great Civilizations Ser.). (Illus.). 48p. (J). (gr. 3-5). 24.95 *(978-1-56711-737-0(6)*, Blackbirch Pr., Inc.) Cengage Gale.

Sylvester, Diane. Ancient China. Hillam, Corbin, illus. 2006. (Museum Ser.). 64p. (J). (gr. 5-8). per. 13.99 *(978-0-88160-389-7(9)*, LW444, Learning Works, The) Creative Teaching Pr., Inc.

Taylor, Trace. China. 2010. pap. 39.62 *(978-1-61541-129-0(1))* American Reading Co.

Taylor, Trace & Sánchez, Lucía M. China. 2010. (1Y Nuestro Mundo Ser.). (SPA.). 16p. (J). (gr. k-1). pap. 6.99 *(978-1-61541-151-1(8))* American Reading Co.

Taylor, Trace & SáNchez, LucíA M. China. 2010. pap. 39.62 *(978-1-61541-152-8(6))* American Reading Co.

Tidey, John & Tidey, Jackie. History & Government. 2008. (China Ser.). 32p. (gr. 4-18). lib. bdg. 18.56 *(978-0-7614-3155-8(1)*, Benchmark Bks.) Marshall Cavendish Corp.

—People & Cities. 2008. (China Ser.). 32p. (gr. 4-18). lib. bdg. 18.56 *(978-0-7614-3158-9(6)*, Benchmark Bks.) Marshall Cavendish Corp.

Timmons, Angie. The Nanjing Massacre. 2017. (J). ***(978-1-5081-7728-9(7))*** Rosen Publishing Group, Inc., The.

Ting, Renee. Chinese History Stories Vol. 1: Stories from the Zhou Dynasty. 2009. (Illus.). 110p. (YA). (gr. 5-9). 19.95 *(978-1-885008-37-4(6)*, Shen's Bks.) Lee & Low Bks., Inc.

—Chinese History Stories Vol. 2: Stories from the Imperial Era. 2009. (Illus.). 110p. (YA). (gr. 5-9). 19.95 *(978-1-885008-38-1(4)*, Shen's Bks.) Lee & Low Bks., Inc.

Tracy, Kathleen. The Life & Times of Confucius. 2004. (Biography from Ancient Civilizations Ser.). (Illus.). 48p. (J). (gr. 4-8). lib. bdg. 29.95 *(978-1-58415-246-0(X))* Mitchell Lane Pubs., Inc.

Webster, Christine. Great Wall of China. 2007. (Structural Wonders Ser.). (Illus.). 32p. (J). (gr. 4-7). lib. bdg. 26.00 *(978-1-59036-723-0(5))*; per. 9.95 *(978-1-59036-724-7(3))* Weigl Pubs., Inc.

Webster, Christine & Kissock, Heather. Great Wall of China. 2012. (J). pap. 11.95 *(978-1-61913-257-3(5))*; lib. bdg. 27.13 *(978-1-61913-251-1(6))* Weigl Pubs., Inc.

Weisberg, Ellen & Yoffe, Ken. All Across Chin. 2009. 84p. pap. *(978-1-84747-846-7(8))* Chipmunkapublishing.

Wilkinson, Philip. Chinese Myth: A Treasury of Legends, Art, & History. 2007. (Myth Ser.). (Illus.). 96p. (J). (gr. 4-7). pap. 7.99 *(978-0-7858-2348-3(4)*, Chartwell) Book Sales, Inc.

—Chinese Myth: A Treasury of Legends, Art, & History. 2007. (ENG., Illus.). 96p. (C). (gr. 6-18). lib. bdg. 158.00 *(978-0-7656-8103-4(X)*, Y181705) Routledge.

Williams, Suzanne. China's Daughters. MacLean, Amber, illus. 2011. (J). *(978-1-881896-34-0(X))* Pacific View Pr.

World Book, Inc Staff, contrib. by. Carved by Time. 2017. (J). ***(978-0-7166-3365-5(5))*** World Bk.-Childcraft International.

—Chinese of the Shang, Zhou, & Qin Dynasties. 2009. *(978-0-7166-2141-6(X))* World Bk., Inc.

—The Chinese Revolution. 2010. (J). *(978-0-7166-1503-3(7))* World Bk., Inc.

Ye, Ting-Xing. The Chinese Thought of It: Amazing Inventions & Innovations. 2009. (Jobs in History Ser.). (ENG., Illus.). 48p. (J). (gr. 5-7). 19.95 *(978-1-55451-196-9(8)*, 9781554511969); pap. 9.95 *(978-1-55451-195-2(X)*, 9781554511952) Annick Pr., Ltd. CAN. Dist: Publishers Group West (PGW).

Yomtov, Nelson. China. 2017. (Enchantment of the World Ser.). (ENG.). 144p. (J). lib. bdg. 40.00 ***(978-0-531-23571-3(8)**, Children's Pr.)* Scholastic Library Publishing.

Yu, Chun. Little Green: Growing up During the Chinese Cultural Revolution. 2005. (ENG., Illus.). 128p. (J). (gr. 5-9). 17.99 *(978-0-689-86943-3(6)*, Simon & Schuster/Paula Wiseman Bks.) Simon & Schuster/Paula Wiseman Bks.

Zhang, Ange. Red Land Yellow River: A Story from the Cultural Revolution, 1 vol. 2004. (ENG., Illus.). 56p. (J). 19.95 *(978-0-88899-489-9(3))* Groundwood Bks. CAN. Dist: Publishers Group West (PGW).

Zucker, Jonny. Lanterns & Firecrackers: A Chinese New Year Story. Cohen, Jan Barger, illus. 2014. (Festival Time Ser.). (ENG.). 24p. (J). (gr. -1-k). pap. 8.99 *(978-1-84507-076-2(3)*, Frances Lincoln) Quarto Publishing Group UK GBR. Dist: Hachette Bk. Group.

CHINA—HISTORY—BOXER REBELLION, 1899-1901

Zdrok, Jodie L. 1880-1900 (Events That Changed the World) 2004. (gr. 10-12). 22.45 *(978-0-7377-2038-9(7)*, Greenhaven Pr., Inc.) Cengage Gale.

CHINA—POLITICS AND GOVERNMENT

Berlatsky, Noah. China. 2010. (Opposing Viewpoints Ser.). (Illus.). 240p. (J). 42.95 *(978-0-7377-4765-2(X)*, 1304557); pap. 29.45 *(978-0-7377-4766-9(8)*, 1304557) Cengage Gale. (Greenhaven Pr., Inc.).

Burgan, Michael. Tank Man: How a Photograph Defined China's Protest Movement, 1 vol. 2014. (Captured World

C
D

History Ser.). (ENG.). 64p. (gr. 5-7). lib. bdg. 34.65 (978-0-7565-4731-8(8), CPB Grades 4-8) Compass Point Bks.

The Chinese Cultural Revolution. 2010. (Milestones in World History Ser.). (Illus.). 128p. (C). (gr. 9-18). 35.00 (978-1-60413-278-6(7), Chelsea Hse.) Facts On File, Inc.

Egendorf, Laura K. Should the U. S. Do Business with China? 2008. (At Issue Ser.). (ENG., Illus.). 128p. (gr. 10-12). 39.40 (978-0-7377-4112-4(0)); pap. 27.80 (978-0-7377-4113-1(9)) Cengage Gale. (Greenhaven Pr., Inc.).

Hurt, Avery. Ancient Chinese Government & Geography. 2016. (Spotlight on the Rise & Fall of Ancient Civilizations Ser.). 48p. (J). (gr. 6-6). pap. 11.75 (978-1-4777-8890-5(5)) Rosen Publishing Group, Inc., The.

Malaspina, Ann. Mao Zedong & the Chinese Revolution. 2016. (People & Events That Changed the World Ser.). (ENG., Illus.). 128p. (J). (gr. 7-8). lib. bdg. 37.27 (978-0-7660-7292-3(4)) Enslow Pubs., Inc.

Rice Jr., Earle. The Evolution of Government & Politics in China. 2014. 48p. (gr. 4-8). 29.95 (978-1-61228-581-8(3)) Mitchell Lane Pubs., Inc.

Tidey, John & Tidey, Jackie. History & Government. 2008. (China Ser.). 32p. (gr. 4-18). lib. bdg. 18.56 (978-0-7614-3155-8(1), Benchmark Bks.) Marshall Cavendish Corp.

Yu, Bin. Government of China. 2007. (History & Culture of China Ser.). (Illus.). 111p. (J). lib. bdg. 24.95 (978-1-59084-829-6(2)) Mason Crest.

—The Government of China. Wang, Jianwei, ed. 2012. (China: the Emerging Superpower Ser.). 112p. (J). (gr. 7). 24.95 (978-1-4222-2161-7(X)) Mason Crest.

—The Government of China. 2011. (J). pap. (978-1-4222-2172-3(5)) Mason Crest.

CHINA—SOCIAL LIFE AND CUSTOMS

Allen, John. Growing up in China. 2017. (Growing up Around the World Ser.). (ENG.). 80p. (YA). (gr. 5-12). **(978-1-68282-209-8(5))** ReferencePoint Pr., Inc.

Bingham, Jane & Sansom, Fiona. Chinese Myths. Kennedy, Graham, illus. 2009. (Myths from Many Lands Ser.). 48p. (YA). (gr. 2-6). pap. 12.85 (978-1-60754-219-3(6)); (gr. 4-7). 29.25 (978-1-60754-218-6(8)) Windmill Bks.

Bodden, Valerie. Ancient Civilization: China. 2015. (Ancient Civilization Ser.). (ENG.). 48p. (J). (gr. 5-8). pap. 12.00 (978-0-89812-978-6(8), Creative Paperbacks) Creative Co., The.

Bramwell, Neil D. Discover Ancient China. 2014. (Discover Ancient Civilizations Ser.). (Illus.). 104p. (J). (gr. 5-18). 33.27 (978-0-7660-4194-3(8)) Enslow Pubs., Inc.

Bullard, Lisa. Chelsea's Chinese New Year. Saunders, Katie, illus. 2012. (Holidays & Special Days Ser.). 24p. (gr. k-2). (J). pap. 39.62 (978-0-7613-9247-7(5), Millbrook Pr.); (ENG.). pap. 6.95 (978-0-7613-8579-0(7), Millbrook Pr.); (ENG.). lib. bdg. 23.93 (978-0-7613-5078-1(0)) Lerner Publishing Group.

Challen, Paul C. & Challen, Paul. Life in Ancient China. 2004. (Peoples of the Ancient World Ser.). (ENG., Illus.). 32p. (J). pap. (978-0-7787-2067-6(5)) Crabtree Publishing Co.

Chance, Robyn. C Is for Chin. Chance, Robyn, illus. 2012. (Illus.). 38p. 18.95 (978-1-936850-31-0(1)) Rhemalda Publishing.

Cheong, Colin. China. 2010. (Festivals of the World Ser.). 32p. (gr. 3). 28.50 (978-1-60870-096-7(8)) Marshall Cavendish Corp.

Clements, Jonathan. Chinese Life. 2006. (Illus.). 29p. (J). per. (978-1-59905-051-5(X)) Saddleback Educational Publishing, Inc.

Cohn, Jessica. The Ancient Chinese. 2012. (Crafts from the Past Ser.). (Illus.). 48p. (J). (gr. 4-6). pap. 14.05 (978-1-4339-7698-8(6)); lib. bdg. 31.95 (978-1-4339-7697-1(8)) Stevens, Gareth Publishing LLLP.

Collins, Terry. Ancient China: An Interactive History Adventure, 1 vol. 2012. (You Choose: Historical Eras Ser.). (ENG., Illus.). 112p. (gr. 3-4). pap. 6.95 (978-1-4296-9472-8(6)); lib. bdg. 31.99 (978-1-4296-4778-6(7)) Capstone Press of Coughlan Cos. (You Choose Bks.).

Colson, Mary. Chinese Culture, 1 vol. 2012. (Global Cultures Ser.). (ENG.). 48p. (gr. 4-6). pap. 9.95 (978-1-4329-6786-4(X)); 32.65 (978-1-4329-6777-2(0)) Heinemann-Raintree. (NA-h).

Culp, Jennifer. The Totally Gross History of Ancient China, 01 vols., 1. 2016. (Totally Gross History Ser.). (ENG.). 48p. (J). pap. 11.75 (978-1-4994-3756-0(0), Rosen Central) Rosen Publishing Group, Inc., The.

DeCristoforo, Jennifer. Lucky Bamboo Book of Crafts: Over 100 Projects & Ideas Celebrating Chinese Culture, vols. 2, vol. 101. DeCristoforo, Jennifer, illus. 2013. (ENG & CHI., Illus.). 136p. 26.99 (978-0-9884648-0-3(2)) Lucky Bamboo Crafts.

Demi Staff. Happy, Happy Chinese New Year! 2003. (ENG., Illus.). 24p. (J). (gr. -1-2). 8.99 (978-0-375-82642-9(4), Knopf Bks. for Young Readers) Random Hse. Children's Bks.

Dubois, Muriel L. & Deady, Kathleen W. Ancient China: Beyond the Great Wall, 1 vol. 2011. (Great Civilizations Ser.). (ENG.). 32p. (gr. 3-4). pap. 8.10 (978-1-4296-7233-7(1), Fact Finders) Capstone Press of Coughlan Cos.

Fullman, Joe. Ancient Chinese. 2011. (ENG., Illus.). 32p. (J). pap. 10.95 (978-1-926853-92-5(X)) Saunders Bk. Co. CAN. Dist: RiverStream Publishing.

Gleason, Carrie. Chinese New Year. 2008. (Celebrations in My World Ser.). (ENG., Illus.). 32p. (J). (gr. k-3). pap. (978-0-7787-4298-2(9)); lib. bdg. (978-0-7787-4280-7(6)) Crabtree Publishing Co.

Grack, Rachel. Chinese New Year. 2017. (Celebrating Holidays! Ser.). (ENG., Illus.). 24p. (J). (gr. k-3). lib. bdg. 25.95 (978-1-62617-591-4(8), Blastoff! Readers) Bellwether Media.

Greenblatt, Miriam. Han Wu Di & Ancient China. 2005. (Rulers & Their Times Ser.). (Illus.). 80p. (J). (gr. 3-7). lib. bdg. 29.93 (978-0-7614-1835-1(0), Benchmark Bks.) Marshall Cavendish Corp.

Hanson-Harding, Brian. Ancient Chinese Religion & Beliefs. 2016. (Spotlight on the Rise & Fall of Ancient Civilizations Ser.). 48p. (J). (gr. 6-6). pap. 11.75 (978-1-4777-8893-6(X)) Rosen Publishing Group, Inc., The.

Harrison, Logan. What Was It Like in Ancient China? 2013. (InfoMax Readers Ser.). (ENG.). 24p. (J). (gr. 3-4). pap. 49.50 (978-1-4777-2496-5(6), Rosen Classroom) Rosen Publishing Group, Inc., The.

Harrison, Lorraine & Harrison, Logan. What Was It Like in Ancient China? 2013. (InfoMax Readers Ser.). (ENG.). 24p. (J). (gr. 3-4). pap. 8.25 (978-1-4777-2495-8(8), Rosen Classroom) Rosen Publishing Group, Inc., The.

Hibbert, Clare. China. 2010. (World of Food Ser.). 32p. (YA). (gr. 4-7). lib. bdg. 24.95 (978-1-934545-09-6(0)) Oliver Pr., Inc.

Kalman, Bobbie. China: The Land. 3rd rev. ed. 2008. (Lands, Peoples & Cultures Ser.). (ENG., Illus.). 32p. (J). (gr. 3-7). pap. (978-0-7787-9667-1(1)) Crabtree Publishing Co.

Kelly, Tracey. The Culture & Recipes of China. 2016. (Let's Cook! Ser.). 00048p. (J). (gr. 4-4). pap. 11.75 (978-1-4994-3175-9(9), PowerKids Pr.) Rosen Publishing Group, Inc., The.

Kule, Elaine A. Celebrate Chinese New Year. 2006. (Celebrate Holidays Ser.). (Illus.). 112p. (J). (gr. 5-6). lib. bdg. 33.27 (978-0-7660-2577-6(2)) Enslow Pubs., Inc.

Kuskowski, Alex. Super Simple Chinese Art: Fun & Easy Art from Around the World, 1 vol. 2012. (ENG.). 32p. 27.07 (978-1-61783-212-3(X), Super SandCastle) ABDO Publishing Co.

Li, Richard T. The Golden Lotus: Life of a Bound-Feet Peasant Mother in the Chinese Cultural Revolution. 2004. (Illus.). 140p. (YA). pap. 7.95 (978-0-9675988-3-3(4)) Li, Richard T.

Lin, Zhimin. China under Reform. (Illus.). 2011. 120p. (J). pap. (978-1-4222-2167-9(9)) 2007. 144p. (YA). lib. bdg. 24.95 (978-1-59084-823-4(3)) Mason Crest.

Loh-Hagan, Virginia. PoPo's Lucky Chinese New Year. Benoit, Renné, illus. 2016. (ENG.). 32p. (J). (gr. 1-4). 16.99 (978-1-58536-978-2(0), 204113) Sleeping Bear Pr.

Mah, Adeline Yen. Chinese Cinderella. 2010. (ENG.). 240p. (YA). (gr. 7). pap. 9.99 (978-0-385-74007-4(7), Ember) Random Hse. Children's Bks.

Maher, Erin. Chinese Foods & Recipes. 2009. (Reading Room Collection 2 Ser.). 24p. (gr. 3-4). 42.50 (978-1-60851-961-3(9), PowerKids Pr.) Rosen Publishing Group, Inc., The.

Marsico, Katie. Chinese New Year, 1 vol. Conger, Holli, illus. 2009. (Cultural Holidays Ser.). (ENG.). 32p. (gr. -1-4). 28.50 (978-1-60270-600-2(X), Looking Glass Library- Nonfiction) Magic Wagon.

MoonRattles. Heritage Holiday Activity Guide: Mid Autumn Festival. 2007. (Illus.). 52p. (J). spiral bd. (978-0-9790920-8-4(6)) MoonRattles.

MoonRattles, compiled by. Heritage Holiday Activity Guide: Dragon Boat Festival. 2007. 52p. (J). spiral bd. 12.00 (978-0-9790920-4-6(3)) MoonRattles.

Morris, Ting. Arts & Crafts of Ancient China. Young, Emma, illus. 2006. (Arts & Crafts of Ser.). 32p. (J). lib. bdg. 27.10 (978-1-58340-914-5(9), 1262690) Black Rabbit Bks.

Orr, Tamra. The Food of China. 2011. (Flavors of the World Ser.). 64p. (gr. 4). 31.36 (978-1-60870-234-3(0)) Marshall Cavendish Corp.

Otto, Carolyn. Celebrate Chinese New Year: With Fireworks, Dragons, & Lanterns. (Holidays Around the World Ser.). (ENG., Illus.). 32p. (J). (gr. 1-4). 2015. pap. 7.99 (978-1-4263-2372-0(7)) 2009. lib. bdg. 23.90 (978-1-4263-0382-1(3)) National Geographic Society. (National Geographic Children's Bks.).

Otto, Carolyn & National Geographic Kids Staff. Celebrate Chinese New Year: With Fireworks, Dragons, & Lanterns. 2009. (Holidays Around the World Ser.). (ENG., Illus.). 32p. (J). (gr. 1-4). 15.95 (978-1-4263-0381-4(5), National Geographic Children's Bks.) National Geographic Society.

Peppas, Lynn. Cultural Traditions in China. 2012. (ENG.). 32p. (J). pap. (978-0-7787-7591-1(7)); lib. bdg. (978-0-7787-7584-3(4)) Crabtree Publishing Co.

Perritano, John. China, Vol. 12. 2015. (Major Nations in a Global World: Tradition, Culture, & Daily Life Ser.). 64p. (J). (gr. 7). 23.95 (978-1-4222-3342-9(1)) Mason Crest.

Pirotta, Saviour. Chinese New Year. 2007. (We Love Holidays Ser.). (Illus.). 24p. (J). (gr. 3-7). lib. bdg. 21.25 (978-1-4042-3709-4(7), PowerKids Pr.) Rosen Publishing Group, Inc., The.

Quan, Elizabeth. Beyond the Moongate: True Stories of 1920s China. 2013. (ENG., Illus.). 40p. (J). (gr. 1-4). 19.95 (978-1-77049-383-4(2), Tundra Bks.) Tundra Bks. CAN. Dist: Penguin Random Hse. LLC.

Randolph, Joanne, ed. Living & Working in Ancient China. 2017. (Back in Time Ser.). 48p. (gr. 5-6). pap. 11.70 **(978-0-7660-8961-7(4))** Enslow Pubs., Inc.

Ransom, Candice. Tools & Treasures of Ancient China. 2014. (Searchlight Books: What Can We Learn from Early Civilizations? Ser.). (ENG., Illus.). 40p. (gr. 3-5). lib. bdg. 27.93 (978-1-4677-1428-0(3), Lerner Pubns.) Lerner Publishing Group.

Robinson, Fay. Chinese New Year. 2016. (Story of Our Holidays Ser.). (Illus.). 32p. (J). pap. 10.52 (978-0-7660-8324-0(1)) Enslow Pubs., Inc.

Roholt, Christine VeLure. Foods of China. 2014. (Cook with Me Ser.). (ENG., Illus.). 24p. (J). (gr. 3-7). lib. bdg. 25.95 (978-1-62617-116-9(5), Express Bks.) Bellwether Media.

Rooney, Anne. China. 2008. (Costume Around the World Ser.). (Illus.). 32p. (J). (gr. 4-6). 28.00 (978-0-7910-9765-6(X), Chelsea Clubhouse) Facts On File, Inc.

Rosinsky, Natalie M. Ancient China, 1 vol. 2012. (Exploring the Ancient World Ser.). (ENG.). 48p. (J). (gr. 5-6). pap. 9.10 (978-0-7565-4578-9(1)) Compass Point Bks.

Sebra, Richard. It's Chinese New Year! 2016. (Bumba Books (tm) — It's a Holiday! Ser.). (ENG., Illus.). 24p. (J). (gr. -1-1). 25.32 (978-1-5124-1425-7(5)) Lerner Publishing Group.

Shaughnessy, Edward L. Exploring the Life, Myth, & Art of Ancient China. 2009. (Civilizations of the World Ser.). (Illus.). 144p. (J). (gr. 7-12). lib. bdg. 42.60 (978-1-4358-5617-2(1)) Rosen Publishing Group, Inc., The.

Shea, Therese. Foods of China. 2011. (Culture in the Kitchen Ser.). 24p. (J). (gr. 2-5). pap. 8.15 (978-1-4339-5704-8(3)); lib. bdg. 22.60 (978-1-4339-5702-4(7)) Stevens, Gareth Publishing LLLP. (Gareth Stevens Learning Library).

Sheen, Barbara. Foods of China. 2006. (Taste of Culture Ser.). (ENG., Illus.). 64p. (gr. 3-7). lib. bdg. 35.20 (978-0-7377-3031-9(5), Greenhaven Pr., Inc.) Cengage Gale.

Slepian, Curtis. You Are There! Ancient China 305 BC. 2016. (TIME for KIDS(r) Nonfiction Readers Ser.). (Illus.). 32p. (J). (gr. 6-6). pap. 8.99 (978-1-4938-3601-7(3)) Teacher Created Materials, Inc.

Slepian, Curtis. You Are There! Ancient China 305 BC. 2016. (Time for Kids Nonfiction Readers Ser.). (ENG.). (J). (gr. 5-8). lib. bdg. 19.65 **(978-0-606-39537-3(7))** Turtleback Bks.

Sonnebom, Liz. Ancient China. 2012. (Ancient World Ser.). (ENG., Illus.). 112p. (J). pap. 9.95 (978-0-531-25976-4(5)) Scholastic Library Publishing.

Spence, Kelly. Ancient China Inside Out. 2017. (Ancient Worlds Inside Out Ser.). (ENG.). 32p. (J). **(978-0-7787-2868-9(4))**; (Illus.). pap. **(978-0-7787-2875-7(7))** Crabtree Publishing Co.

Steele, Philip. The Chinese Empire. 2009. (Passport to the Past Ser.). (Illus.). 64p. (YA). (gr. 5-8). lib. bdg. 31.95 (978-1-4358-5174-0(9)) Rosen Publishing Group, Inc., The.

Steele, Phillip. Step Into: The Chinese Empire. 2008. (ENG., Illus.). 64p. (J). (gr. 4-7). pap. 12.99 (978-1-84476-509-6(1)) Anness Publishing GBR. Dist: National Bk. Network.

Stewart, Gail B. The Han Dynasty. 2004. (Life During the Great Civilizations Ser.). (Illus.). 48p. (J). (gr. 3-5). 24.95 (978-1-56711-737-0(6), Blackbirch Pr., Inc.) Cengage Gale.

Tang, Sanmu. Celebrating the Dragon Boat Festival. Tenison, Mina, tr. from CHI. 2010. (Chinese Festivals Ser.). (ENG., Illus.). 32p. (J). (gr. -1-3). pap. 4.95 (978-1-60220-968-8(5)) BetterLink Pr., Inc.

—Celebrating the Mid-Autumn Festival. Tenison, Mina, tr. from CHI. 2010. (Chinese Festivals Ser.). (ENG., Illus.). 32p. (J). (gr. -1-3). pap. 4.95 (978-1-60220-969-5(3)) BetterLink Pr., Inc.

Temko, Florence. Traditional Crafts from China. Gooch, Randall, illus. 2005. (Culture Crafts Ser.). 64p. (gr. 3-8). 23.93 (978-0-8225-2939-2(4)) Lerner Publishing Group.

Tidey, John & Tidey, Jackie. China: Land, Life, & Culture, 6 bks., Set. Incl. Arts & Culture. lib. bdg. 18.56 (978-0-7614-3154-1(3)); History & Government. lib. bdg. 18.56 (978-0-7614-3155-8(1)); Land & Climate. lib. bdg. 18.56 (978-0-7614-3156-5(X)); People & Cities. lib. bdg. 18.56 (978-0-7614-3158-9(6)); Plants. lib. bdg. 18.56 (978-0-7614-3159-6(4)); Wildlife. lib. bdg. 18.56 (978-0-7614-3161-9(6)); 32p. (gr. 4-18). (China: Land, Life, & Culture Ser.). 2008. Set lib. bdg. 111.36 (978-0-7614-3152-7(7), Benchmark Bks.) Marshall Cavendish Corp.

Warnycia, Lou, et al. If I Were a Kid in Ancient China: Children of the Ancient World. 2007. (If I Were a Kid In... Ser.). (ENG., Illus.). 32p. (J). (gr. 1-5). 17.95 (978-0-8126-7931-1(8)) Cricket Bks.

Whiting, Jim & Li, Shi Yu. My Teenage Life in China. 2017. (Illus.). 128p. (J). **(978-1-4222-3902-5(0))** Mason Crest.

Whittington, Thea. The Dragon's Back. 2010. (ENG., Illus.). 36p. (J). (gr. -1-3). pap. 9.95 (978-988-99799-5-9(0)) Blacksmith Bks. HKG. Dist: National Bk. Network.

Wiseman, Blaine. Chinese. 2016. (Illus.). 32p. (J). (978-1-5105-1096-8(6)) SmartBook Media, Inc.

Yu, Chun. Little Green: Growing up During the Chinese Cultural Revolution. 2005. (ENG., Illus.). 128p. (J). (gr. 5-9). 17.99 (978-0-689-86943-3(6), Simon & Schuster/Paula Wiseman Bks.) Simon & Schuster/Paula Wiseman Bks.

Zhang, Elizabeth Yuan. The Middle Kingdom As We Saw: My Journey to China In 2004. l.t. ed. 2005. (Illus.). 272p. (YA). 29.98 (978-1-933361-04-8(2)) Lexington Pubs.

Zocchi, Judy. On Chinese New Year. Wallis, Rebecca, illus. 2005. (Holiday Happenings Ser.). 32p. (J). pap. 10.95 (978-1-59646-188-8(8)); lib. bdg. 21.65 (978-1-891997-55-6(6)) Dingles & Co.

—On Chinese New Year/el Año Nuevo Chino. Wallis, Rebecca, illus. 2005. (Holiday Happenings Ser.).Tr. of Año Nuevo Chino. (ENG & SPA.). 32p. (J). pap. 10.95 (978-1-59646-190-1(X)); lib. bdg. 21.65 (978-1-891997-56-3(4)) Dingles & Co.

CHINA (PORCELAIN)

see Porcelain

CHINAWARE

see Porcelain

CHINCHILLAS

Doudna, Kelly. Cheeky Chinchillas, 1 vol. Nobens, C. A., illus. 2013. (Unusual Pets Ser.). (ENG.). 24p. (J). (gr. -1-3). 24.21 (978-1-61783-398-4(3)) ABDO Publishing Co.

Hudak, Heather C. Caring for Your Chinchilla. 2006. (Caring for Your Pet Ser.). (Illus.). 32p. (J). (gr. 3-7). per. 9.95 (978-1-59036-467-3(8)); lib. bdg. 26.00 (978-1-59036-466-6(X)) Weigl Pubs., Inc.

—Chinchilla. 2010. (J). pap. 9.95 (978-1-61690-068-7(7)); 32p. (gr. 3-5). lib. bdg. 27.13 (978-1-61690-067-0(9)) Weigl Pubs., Inc.

Leavitt, Amie Jane. Care for a Pet Chinchilla. 2009. (How to Convince Your Parents You Can ... Ser.). (Illus.). 32p. (J). (gr. 1-4). lib. bdg. 25.70 (978-1-58415-799-1(2)) Mitchell Lane Pubs., Inc.

CHINCHILLAS—FICTION

Gaidouk, Ekaterina. Adventures of Chi-Chi the Chinchill. 2012. 62p. pap. 29.99 (978-1-105-29529-4(X)) Lulu Pr., Inc.

CHINESE

Collier, Irene Dea. Chinese Mythology Rocks! Bock, William Sauts, illus. 2011. (Mythology Rocks! Ser.). 128p. (J). (gr. 6-18). lib. bdg. 33.27 (978-0-7660-3898-1(X)) Enslow Pubs., Inc.

The Origin of Chinese, 1. l.t. ed. 2004. (CHI., Illus.). 60p. (J). (978-0-9752775-1-5(0), 0-9752775-1-0) Unitrust Design.

CHINESE—CALIFORNIA—FICTION

Marlow, Susan K. Andrea Carter & the San Francisco Smugglers: A Novel, 1 vol. 2008. (Circle C Adventures Ser.). 144p. (J). pap. 7.99 (978-0-8254-3446-4(7)) Kregel Pubns.

CHINESE—UNITED STATES

Hoyt-Goldsmith, Diane. Celebrating Chinese New Year. Migdale, Lawrence, photos by. (ENG., Illus.). 32p. (J). (gr. 4-6). pap. 6.95 (978-0-8234-1520-5(1)) Holiday Hse., Inc.

CHINESE—UNITED STATES—FICTION

Blakeslee, Ann R. A Different Kind of Hero, 1 vol. 2005. (ENG.). 32p. (YA). pap. 5.95 (978-0-7614-5147-1(1)) Marshall Cavendish Corp.

Lo, Rich. New Year. 2016. (ENG., Illus.). 40p. (J). (gr. -1-k). 16.99 (978-1-5107-0723-8(9), Sky Pony Pr.) Skyhorse Publishing Co., Inc.

Waters, Kate. Lion Dancer: Ernie Wan's Chinese New Year. Cooper, Martha & Slovenz-Low, Madeline, illus. 2010. (Rise & Shine Ser.). (ENG.). 40p. (C). (gr. -1-3). pap. 9.95 (978-0-590-43047-0(5)) National Geographic School Publishing, Inc.

CHINESE AMERICANS

Abrams, Dennis. Maxine Hong Kingston. 2009. (Asian Americans of Achievement Ser.). (Illus.). 128p. (YA). (gr. 7-12). 35.00 (978-1-60413-568-8(9)) Facts On File, Inc.

Adler, Jack. Chinese Americans. (Successful Americans Ser.). 64p. (YA). 2009. (Illus.). (gr. 9-12). 22.95 (978-1-4222-0520-4(7)) 2007. (gr. 7-18). pap. 9.95 (978-1-4222-0855-7(9)) Mason Crest.

Anderson, Dale. Chinese Americans. 2006. (World Almanac Library of American Immigration). (Illus.). 48p. (gr. 5-12). pap. 14.05 (978-0-8368-7321-4(1)); lib. bdg. 31.00 (978-0-8368-7308-5(4)) Stevens, Gareth Publishing LLLP. (Gareth Stevens Secondary Library).

Angel, Ann. Amy Tan: Weaver of Asian-American Tales. 2009. (Authors Teens Love Ser.). (Illus.). 128p. (J). (gr. 6). lib. bdg. 33.27 (978-0-7660-2962-0(X)) Enslow Pubs., Inc.

Ashley, Susan. Yo-Yo Ma. 2004. (Trailblazers of the Modern World Ser.). (Illus.). 48p. (gr. 5-12). lib. bdg. 31.00 (978-0-8368-5497-8(7), Gareth Stevens Secondary Library) Stevens, Gareth Publishing LLLP.

Behnke, Alison. Chinese in America. 2004. (In America Ser.). (ENG., Illus.). 80p. (gr. 5-8). lib. bdg. 27.93 (978-0-8225-4695-5(7)) Lerner Publishing Group.

Bodden, Valerie. Nuclear Physicist Chien-Shiung Wu. 2016. (STEM Trailblazer Bios Ser.). (ENG., Illus.). 32p. (J). (gr. 2-5). 26.65 (978-1-5124-0786-0(0)) Lerner Publishing Group.

Boyer Binns, Tristan. Chinese Americans. 2003. (We Are America Ser.). (Illus.). 32p. (J). (gr. 2-4). lib. bdg. (978-1-4034-0162-5(4)) Heinemann-Raintree.

Brown, Tahiera Monique. Annihilator of Innocence: That Old Man. 2006. 271p. per. 19.95 (978-0-9713953-0-5(6)) Tavine'ra Publishing, LLC.

Bryan, Nichol. Chinese Americans, 1 vol. 2004. (One Nation Set 2 Ser.). (ENG.). 32p. (gr. k-6). 27.07 (978-1-59197-525-0(5), Checkerboard Library) ABDO Publishing Co.

Campbell, Wallis. Angel Island. 2006. (Illus.). 48p. (J). pap. (978-1-59034-808-6(7)) Mondo Publishing.

Caswell, Max. My Life As a Chinese Immigrant. 2017. (My Place in History Ser.). 24p. (J). (gr. 2-3). pap. 8.15 **(978-1-5382-0293-7(X))** Stevens, Gareth Publishing LLLP.

Chippendale, Lisa A. Yo-Yo Ma: A Cello Superstar Brings Music to the World. 2004. (People to Know Ser.). (Illus.). 112p. (J). lib. bdg. 26.60 (978-0-7660-2286-7(2)) Enslow Pubs., Inc.

Darraj, Susan Muaddi. Amy Tan. 2007. (Asian Americans of Achievement Ser.). 112p. (YA). (gr. 7-12). lib. bdg. 35.00 (978-0-7910-9269-9(0)) Facts On File, Inc.

Deiters, Erika & Deiters, Jim. The Chinese Community in America. 2003. (J). lib. bdg. (978-1-58417-027-3(1)) Lake Street Pubs.

Goodridge, Catherine. Michelle Kwan (Spanish) 2011. (SPA.). (J). pap. 40.00 net. (978-1-4108-2428-8(4), A24284) Benchmark Education Co.

Gustaitis, Joseph Alan. Chinese Americans. 2009. (New Americans Ser.). 80p. (gr. 5). 35.64 (978-0-7614-4303-2(7)) Marshall Cavendish Corp.

Harvey, Jeanne Walker. Maya Lin: Artist-Architect of Light & Lines. Phumiruk, Dow, illus. 2017. (ENG.). 32p. (J). 17.99 (978-1-250-11249-1(4), 9781250112491, Holt, Henry & Co. Bks. For Young Readers) Holt, Henry & Co.

Hill, Anne E. Michelle Kwan. 2004. (Sports Heroes & Legends Ser.). (ENG., Illus.). 112p. (J). (gr. 5-12). lib. bdg. 30.60 (978-0-8225-1795-5(7)) Lerner Publishing Group.

Kallio, Jamie. Angel Island Immigration: A History Perspectives Book. 2014. (Perspectives Library). (ENG.). 32p. (J). (gr. 4-8). 28.50 (978-1-63137-614-6(4), 205239) Cherry Lake Publishing.

Kaplan, Leslie C. Chinese New Year. (Library of Holidays Ser.). 24p. 2009. (gr. 2-3). 42.50 (978-1-60853-707-5(2)) 2004. (Illus.). (J). lib. bdg. 22.60 (978-0-8239-6658-5(5)) Rosen Publishing Group, Inc., The. (PowerKids Pr.).

Kite, Lorien. The Chinese: We Came to North America. 2006. (Illus.). 32p. (J). (gr. 4-8). reprint ed. 19.00 (978-0-7567-9904-5(X)) DIANE Publishing Co.

Lashnits, Tom. Maya Lin. 2007. (Asian Americans of Achievement Ser.). (Illus.). 128p. (J). (gr. 7-12). lib. bdg. 35.00 (978-0-7910-9268-2(2)) Facts On File, Inc.

Lawrence, Katherine. Laurence Yep. 2009. (Library of Author Biographies Ser.). 112p. (gr. 5-8). 63.90 (978-1-60853-542-2(8), Rosen Reference) Rosen Publishing Group, Inc., The.

Lawrence, Katherine Drobot. Laurence Yep. 2004. (Library of Author Biographies Ser.). 112p. (J). (gr. 5-8). lib. bdg. 34.60 (978-0-8239-4527-6(8), Rosen Reference) Rosen Publishing Group, Inc., The.

Lingen, Marissa. Chinese Immigration. 2005. (Changing Face of North America Ser.). (Illus.). 112p. (YA). lib. bdg. 24.95 (978-1-59084-694-0(X)) Mason Crest.

Louie, Ai-Ling. Yo-Yo & Yeou-Cheng Ma, Finding Their Way: Amazing Asian Americans. Peng, Cathy, illus. 2012. (Biographies of Amazing Asian Americans Ser.: 2). (ENG.). 48p. (J). pap. 16.99 (978-0-9787465-0-6(3)) Dragoneagle Pr.

MacMillan, Dianne M. Chinese New Year. rev. ed. 2008. (Best Holiday Bks.). (Illus.). 48p. (J). (gr. 3-4). lib. bdg. 25.27 (978-0-7660-3038-1(5)) Enslow Pubs., Inc.

Mah, Adeline Yen. Chinese Cinderella. 2010. (ENG.). 240p. (YA). (gr. 7). pap. 9.99 (978-0-385-74007-4(7), Ember) Random Hse. Children's Bks.

Martin, Michael. Chinese Americans. 2003. (Immigrants in America Ser.). (Illus.). 112p. (gr. 6-12). 30.00 (978-0-7910-7126-7(X), Chelsea Hse.) Facts On File, Inc.

McCormick, Patricia. Just Add One Chinese Sister (p) 2010. pap. 10.95 (978-1-59078-772-4(2)) Boyds Mills Pr.

McGinty, Alice B. Meet Laurence Yep. 2003. (About the Author Ser.). (Illus.). 24p. (J). lib. bdg. 22.60 (978-0-8239-6410-9(8), PowerKids Pr.) Rosen Publishing Group, Inc., The.

Miller, Raymond H. Michelle Kwan. 2003. (Stars of Sports Ser.). (ENG., Illus.). 48p. (J). 27.50 (978-0-7377-1540-8(5), Greenhaven Pr., Inc.) Cengage Gale.

Moreno, Barry. The Chinese Americans. 2007. (Major American Immigration Ser.). (YA). pap. 9.95 (978-1-4222-0672-0(6)) Mason Crest.

Moreno, Barry & Lingen, Marissa. The Chinese Americans. 2010. (Major American Immigration Ser.). (Illus.). 64p. (YA). (gr. 9-12). 22.95 *(978-1-4222-0605-8(X))* Mason Crest.

Mussari, Mark. Amy Tan. 2010. (Today's Writers & Their Works). 128p. (gr. 7-18). 42.79 *(978-0-7614-4127-4(1))* Marshall Cavendish Corp.

O'Connell, Kim A. China: A MyReportLinks. com Book. 2004. (Top Ten Countries of Recent Immigrants Ser.). (Illus.). 48p. (J). lib. bdg. 26.60 *(978-0-7660-5240-6(0),* MyReportLinks.com Bks.) Enslow Pubs., Inc.

O'Keefe, Sherry. From China to America: The Story of Amy Tan. 2011. (World Writers Ser.). 112p. (gr. 7-18). lib. bdg. 28.95 *(978-1-59935-138-4(2))* Reynolds, Morgan Inc.

Orr, Tamra. Amy Tan: Author Extraordinaire, 1 vol. 2009. (Essential Lives Set 4 Ser.). (ENG., Illus.). 112p. (J). (gr. 6-12). lib. bdg. 35.64 *(978-1-60453-705-5(1))* ABDO Publishing Co.

Pimental, Annette Bay & Lo, Rich. Mountain Chef: How One Man Lost His Groceries, Changed His Plans, & Helped Cook up the National Park Service. 2016. (ENG., Illus.). 40p. (J). (gr. 1-4). 16.95 *(978-1-58089-711-2(8))* Charlesbridge Publishing, Inc.

Slavicek, Louise Chipley. I. M. Pei. 2009. (Asian Americans of Achievement Ser.). (Illus.). 120p. (YA). (gr. 7-12). 35.00 *(978-1-60413-567-1(0))* Facts On File, Inc.

Teitlebaum, Michael. Chinese Immigrants. 2004. (Immigration to the United States Ser.). (Illus.). 96p. (gr. 4-9). 35.00 *(978-0-8160-5687-3(0))* Facts On File, Inc.

Thornton, Jeremy. The Gold Rush: Chinese Immigrants Come to America (1848-1882) (Primary Sources of Immigration & Migration in America Ser.). 24p. 2009. (gr. 3-4). 42.50 *(978-1-60851-784-8(5))* 2004. (Illus.). (J). lib. bdg. 22.60 *(978-0-8239-6833-6(2))* Rosen Publishing Group, Inc., The. (PowerKids Pr.).

—The Gold Rush: Chinese Immigrants Come to America, 1848-1882. 2004. (Primary Sources of Immigration & Migration in America Ser.). (ENG., Illus.). 24p. (gr. 4-8). pap. 9.40 *(978-0-8239-8959-1(3),* PowerKids Pr.) Rosen Publishing Group, Inc., The.

Wheeler, Jill C. Chien-Shiung Wu: Phenomenal Physicist, 1 vol. 2012. (Women in Science Ser.). (ENG., Illus.). 32p. (J). (gr. 3-6). lib. bdg. 27.07 *(978-1-61783-451-6(3),* Checkerboard Library) ABDO Publishing Co.

Wilson, Steve. The California Gold Rush: Chinese Laborers in America (1848-1882), 01 vols., 1. 2016. (Spotlight on Immigration & Migration Ser.). (ENG., Illus.). 24p. (J). pap. 10.00 *(978-1-5081-4061-0(8),* PowerKids Pr.) Rosen Publishing Group, Inc., The.

Wong, Li Keng. Good Fortune: My Journey to Gold Mountain, 1 vol. (ENG., Illus.). 144p. (J). (gr. 3-7). 2008. pap. 8.95 *(978-1-56145-464-8(8))* 2006. 14.95 *(978-1-56145-367-2(6))* Peachtree Pubs.

Worth, Richard. Vera Wang: Fashion Designer. 2016. (Influential Asians Ser.). 128p. (J). (gr. 7-6). 37.27 *(978-0-7660-7903-8(1))* Enslow Pubs., Inc.

Yoo, Paula & Wang, Lin. Shining Star: The Anna May Wong Story. 2016. (ENG., Illus.). 32p. (J). (gr. 1-4). pap. 9.95 *(978-1-62014-257-8(0))* Lee & Low Bks., Inc.

CHINESE AMERICANS—FICTION

Bjorkman, Lauren. Miss Fortune Cookie. 2012. (ENG.). 288p. (YA). (gr. 9-13). 16.99 *(978-0-8050-8951-6(9),* Holt, Henry & Co. Bks. For Young Readers) Holt, Henry & Co.

Cavanaugh, Nancy. Just Like Me. 2016. (ENG.). 256p. (J). (gr. 3-7). 16.99 *(978-1-4926-0427-3(5),* 9781492604273, Sourcebooks Jabberwocky) Sourcebooks, Inc.

Chang, Margaret. Celia's Robot. 2009. (ENG.). 208p. (J). (gr. 3-7). 16.95 *(978-0-8234-2181-7(3))* Holiday Hse., Inc.

Chen, Pauline W. Peiling & the Chicken-Fried Christmas. 2007. (ENG.). 144p. (YA). (gr. 3-6). 15.95 *(978-1-59990-122-0(6),* 9781599901220, Bloomsbury USA Childrens) Bloomsbury Publishing USA.

Chen, Shan-Shan & Goodman, Heidi. Mei-Mei's Lucky Birthday Noodles: A Loving Story of Adoption, Chinese Culture & a Special Birthday Treat. 2014. (ENG., Illus.). 32p. (J). (gr. -1-3). 13.95 *(978-0-8048-4461-1(5))* Tuttle Publishing.

Chen, Yong. A Gift. (ENG.). 32p. (J). (gr. k-2). 2011. pap. 6.95 *(978-1-59078-898-1(2))* 2009. 16.95 *(978-1-59078-610-9(6))* Boyds Mills Pr.

Cheng, Andrea. Goldfish & Chrysanthemums. Chang, Michelle, illus. 2003. (ENG.). 32p. (J). 16.95 *(978-1-58430-057-1(4))*; pap. 8.95 *(978-1-60060-889-6(2))* Lee & Low Bks., Inc.

—Shanghai Messenger, 1 vol. Young, Ed, illus. 2005. (ENG.). 40p. (J). (gr. 3-7). 17.95 *(978-1-58430-238-4(0))* Lee & Low Bks., Inc.

—The Year of the Baby. Barton, Patrice, illus. 2014. (Anna Wang Novel Ser.: 2). (ENG.). 176p. (J). (gr. 1-4). pap. 5.99 *(978-0-544-22525-1(2),* HMH Books For Young Readers) Houghton Mifflin Harcourt Publishing Co.

—The Year of the Book. Halpin, Abigail, illus. (Anna Wang Novel Ser.: 1). (ENG.). 160p. (J). (gr. 1-4). 2013. pap. 5.99 *(978-0-544-02263-8(7))* 2012. 16.99 *(978-0-547-68463-5(0))* Houghton Mifflin Harcourt Publishing Co.

—The Year of the Fortune Cookie. Barton, Patrice, illus. 2014. (Anna Wang Novel Ser.: 3). (ENG.). 176p. (J). (gr. 1-4). 15.99 *(978-0-544-10519-5(2),* HMH Books For Young Readers) Houghton Mifflin Harcourt Publishing Co.

—The Year of the Garden. Barton, Patrice, illus. 2017. (Anna Wang Novel Ser.: 5). (ENG.). 128p. (J). (gr. 1-4). 15.99 *(978-0-544-66444-9(2),* HMH Books For Young Readers) Houghton Mifflin Harcourt Publishing Co.

—The Year of the Three Sisters. Barton, Patrice, illus. (Anna Wang Novel Ser.: 4). (ENG.). 160p. (J). (gr. 1-4). 2016. pap. 5.99 *(978-0-544-66849-2(9))* 2015. 16.99 *(978-0-544-34427-3(8))* Houghton Mifflin Harcourt Publishing Co. (HMH Books For Young Readers).

Cheng, Andrea & Young, Ed. Shanghai Messenger. 2015. (ENG.). 40p. (J). pap. 10.95 *(978-1-62014-230-1(9))* Lee & Low Bks., Inc.

Chinn, Karen. Sam y el Dinero de la Suerte. Van Wright, Cornelius, illus. 2003.Tr. of Sam & the Lucky Money. (SPA.). (J). *(978-1-58430-167-7(8))* Lee & Low Bks., Inc.

—Sam y el Dinero de la Suerte. Van Wright, Cornelius & Hu, Ying-Hwa, illus. 2003.Tr. of Sam & the Lucky Money. (SPA.). 32p. (J). pap. 10.95 *(978-1-58430-168-4(6))* Lee & Low Bks., Inc.

Choldenko, Gennifer. Chasing Secrets. 2015. (ENG.). 288p. (J). (gr. 4-7). lib. bdg. 19.99 *(978-0-375-99063-2(1),* Lamb, Wendy Bks.) Random Hse. Children's Bks.

Clark, Henry. The Book That Proves Time Travel Happens. 2015. (ENG., Illus.). 416p. (J). (gr. 3-7). 17.00 *(978-0-316-40617-8(1))* Little Brown & Co.

Compestine, Ying Chang. Crouching Tiger. Nascimbene, Yan, illus. 2011. (ENG.). 40p. (J). (gr. 1-4). 16.99 *(978-0-7636-4642-4(3))* Candlewick Pr.

Currier, Katrina Saltonstall. Kai's Journey to Gold Mountain: An Angel Island Story. 2004. 40p. 16.95 *(978-0-9667352-7-7(7))*; (Illus.). 44p. (J). pap. 10.95 *(978-0-9667352-4-6(2))* Angel Island Assoc.

Fletcher, Susan. Walk Across the Sea. Jakesevic, Nenad, illus. 2003. (ENG.). 224p. (J). (gr. 4-8). pap. 11.95 *(978-0-689-85707-2(1),* Atheneum Bks. for Young Readers) Simon & Schuster Children's Publishing.

Flor Ada, Alma. Celebra el Ano Nuevo Chino con la Familia Fong. 2006. (Cuentos para Celebrar / Stories to Celebrate Ser.). (Illus.). 30p. (gr. k-6). per. 11.95 *(978-1-59820-114-7(X),* Alfaguara) Santillana USA Publishing Co., Inc.

—Celebrate Chinese New Year with the Fong Family. Castro, Mima, illus. 2006. (Cuentos para Celebrar / Stories to Celebrate Ser.). 30p. (gr. k-6). per. 11.95 *(978-1-59820-126-0(3))* Santillana USA Publishing Co., Inc.

Friedman, Darlene. Star of the Week: A Story of Love, Adoption, & Brownies with Sprinkles. Roth, Roger, illus. 2009. (ENG.). 32p. (J). (gr. k-3). 17.99 *(978-0-06-114136-2(4))* HarperCollins Pubs.

Gagnon, Mary. Are Those Your Shoes? 2008. 120p. pap. 11.95 *(978-1-4357-2942-1(0))* Lulu Pr., Inc.

Goldberg, Whoopi. Terrible Terrel. Roos, Maryn, illus. 2010. (ENG.). 160p. (J). (gr. 1-17). pap. 4.99 *(978-0-7868-5263-5(1),* Jump at the Sun) Hyperion Bks. for Children.

Grund, Carol A. Anna Mei, Blessing in Disguise. 2011. 181p. (J). pap. *(978-0-8198-0796-0(6))* Pauline Bks. & Media.

—Anna Mei, Cartoon Girl. 2010. 140p. (J). (gr. 4-7). pap. 8.95 *(978-0-8198-0788-5(5))* Pauline Bks. & Media.

—Anna Mei, Escape Artist. 2011. 168p. (J). (gr. 4-7). pap. 8.95 *(978-0-8198-0794-6(X))* Pauline Bks. & Media.

Hoena, Blake. Daring, 1 vol. Cano, Fernando, illus. 2014. (Tony Hawk: Live2Skate Ser.). (ENG.). 72p. (gr. 4-5). lib. bdg. 25.32 *(978-1-4342-9139-4(1))* Stone Arch Bks.

Hoena, Blake A. & Gonzalez, Jorge. Kickoff Blitz. Ruiz, Alfonso, illus. 2010. (Sports Illustrated Kids Graphic Novels Ser.). 56p. pap. 0.50 *(978-1-4342-3205-2(0))*; (ENG.). (gr. 2-3). pap. 7.19 *(978-1-4342-2292-3(6))*; (ENG.). (gr. 2-3). 26.65 *(978-1-4342-1909-1(7))* Stone Arch Bks.

Holland, L. Tam. The Counterfeit Family Tree of Vee Crawford-Wong. (ENG.). 368p. (YA). (gr. 9). 2014. pap. 9.99 *(978-1-4424-1265-1(8))* 2013. 17.99 *(978-1-4424-1264-4(X))* Simon & Schuster Children's Publishing.

Honeyman, Kay. The Fire Horse Girl. 2016. (ENG.). 336p. (J). (gr. 7). pap. 9.99 *(978-0-545-40311-5(1),* Levine, Arthur A. Bks.) Scholastic, Inc.

Ingold, Jeanette. Paper Daughter. 2013. (ENG.). 224p. (YA). (gr. 7). pap. 7.99 *(978-0-544-10484-6(6))* Houghton Mifflin Harcourt Publishing Co.

Isadora, Rachel. Happy Belly, Happy Smile. Isadora, Rachel, illus. 2009. (ENG., Illus.). 32p. (J). (gr. -1-3). 16.00 *(978-0-15-206546-1(6))* Houghton Mifflin Harcourt Publishing Co.

James, Helen Foster & Loh, Virginia Shin-Mui. Paper Son: Lee's Journey to America. Ong, Wilson, illus. 2013. (Tales of Young Americans Ser.). (ENG.). 32p. (J). (gr. 1-4). 16.99 *(978-1-58536-833-4(4),* 202366) Sleeping Bear Pr.

Jones, Patrick. The Gamble. 2014. (Bareknuckle Ser.). 104p. (YA). (gr. 6-12). lib. bdg. 27.93 *(978-1-4677-1462-4(3),* Darby Creek) Lerner Publishing Group.

Katz, Karen. My First Chinese New Year. Katz, Karen, illus. 2012. (My First Holiday Ser.). (ENG., Illus.). 32p. (J). (gr. -1-k). 6.99 *(978-1-250-01868-7(4),* 9781250018687) Square Fish.

Laurence, Yep. Dragonwings. 25th rev. ed. 2014. (Golden Mountain Chronicles Ser.). (ENG.). 336p. (J). (gr. 12-12). 11.24 *(978-1-63245-143-9(3))* Lectorum Pubns., Inc.

Lee, Milly. Landed. Choi, Yangsook, illus. 2006. (ENG.). 40p. (J). (gr. 2-6). 17.99 *(978-0-374-34314-9(4),* 9780374343149, Farrar, Straus & Giroux (BYR)) Farrar, Straus & Giroux.

Lee, Milly, et al. Earthquake. Choi, Yangsook, illus. 2003. (Avenues Ser.). (ENG.). 32p. (C). (gr. k-2). pap. 21.95 *(978-0-374-39964-1(6))* National Geographic School Publishing, Inc.

Lee, Stacey. Outrun the Moon. 2016. (ENG.). 400p. (YA). (gr. 7). 17.99 *(978-0-399-17541-1(5),* G.P. Putnam's Sons Books for Young Readers) Penguin Young Readers Group.

—Outrun the Moon. 2017. lib. bdg. 22.10 ***(978-0-606-40097-8(4))*** Turtleback Bks.

Lee, Stacey. Under a Painted Sky. 2015. (ENG.). 384p. (YA). (gr. 7). 16.99 *(978-0-399-16803-1(6),* G.P. Putnam's Sons Books for Young Readers) Penguin Young Readers Group.

—Under a Painted Sky. 2016. lib. bdg. 22.10 *(978-0-606-38391-2(3))* Turtleback Bks.

Lewis, Rose & Zong, Grace. Orange Peel's Pocket. 2012. (ENG.). 32p. (J). (gr. -1-3). pap. 5.00 *(978-1-4197-0293-8(9))* Abrams, Inc.

Lin, Grace. Bringing in the New Year. (ENG., (J). 2013. Illus.). 28p. (— 1). bds. 6.99 *(978-0-385-75365-4(9),* Knopf Bks. for Young Readers) 2010. 34p. (gr. -1-2). pap. 7.99 *(978-0-375-86605-0(1),* Dragonfly Bks.) 2008. (Illus.). 34p. (gr. -1-2). 15.99 *(978-0-375-83745-6(0),* Knopf Bks. for Young Readers) Random Hse. Children's Bks.

—Fortune Cookie Fortunes. Lin, Grace, illus. 2006. (ENG., Illus.). 32p. (J). (gr. -1-2). 7.99 *(978-0-440-42192-4(6),* Dragonfly Bks.) Random Hse. Children's Bks.

—Ling & Ting: Not Exactly the Same! (Passport to Reading Level 3 Ser.). (ENG.). 48p. (J). (gr. 1-4). 2011. pap. 3.99 *(978-0-316-02453-2(8))* 2010. (Illus.). 14.99 *(978-0-316-02452-5(X))* Little, Brown Bks. for Young Readers.

—Ling & Ting: Together in All Weather. 2015. (ENG., Illus.). 48p. (J). (gr. 1-4). 16.00 *(978-0-316-33549-2(5))* Little Brown & Co.

—Ling & Ting Share a Birthday. (ENG.). 48p. (J). (gr. 1-4). 2014. pap. 4.99 *(978-0-316-18404-5(7))* 2013. (Illus.). 15.00 *(978-0-316-18405-2(5))* Little, Brown Bks. for Young Readers.

—Ling & Ting Share a Birthday. 2014. (Passport to Reading Level 3 Ser.). (J). lib. bdg. 14.75 *(978-0-606-35932-0(X))* Turtleback Bks.

—Ling & Ting: Twice As Silly. 2014. (ENG., Illus.). 48p. (J). (gr. 1-4). 16.00 *(978-0-316-18402-1(0))* Little, Brown Bks. for Young Readers.

—Ugly Vegetables. 2014. 16.95 *(978-1-63419-748-9(8))* Perfection Learning Corp.

Lo, Ginnie & Lo, Beth. Auntie Yang's Great Soybean Picnic. 2012. (ENG., Illus.). 32p. (J). 18.95 *(978-1-60060-442-3(0))* Lee & Low Bks., Inc.

Look, Lenore. Alvin Ho: Allergic to Babies, Burglars, & Other Bumps in the Night. Pham, LeUyen, illus. 2013. (Alvin Ho Ser.). (ENG.). 192p. (J). (gr. 1-4). 15.99 *(978-0-375-87033-0(4),* Schwartz & Wade Bks.) Random Hse. Children's Bks.

—Alvin Ho: Allergic to Birthday Parties, Science Projects, & Other Man-Made Catastrophes. Pham, LeUyen, illus. 2011. (Alvin Ho Ser.). (ENG.). 192p. (J). (gr. 1-4). 6.99 *(978-0-375-87369-0(4),* Yearling) Random Hse. Children's Bks.

—Alvin Ho: Allergic to Camping, Hiking, & Other Natural Disasters. Pham, LeUyen, illus. 2010. (Alvin Ho Ser.). (ENG.). 192p. (J). (gr. 1-4). 6.99 *(978-0-375-85750-8(8),* Yearling) Random Hse. Children's Bks.

—Alvin Ho: Allergic to the Great Wall, the Forbidden Palace, & Other Tourist Attractions. Pham, LeUyen, illus. 2014. (Alvin Ho Ser.). (ENG.). 176p. (J). (gr. 1-4). 15.99 *(978-0-385-36972-5(7),* Schwartz & Wade Bks.) Random Hse. Children's Bks.

—Alvin Ho: Allergic to Babies, Burglars, & Other Bumps in the Night. Pham, LeUyen, illus. 2014. (Alvin Ho Ser.). (ENG.). 192p. (J). (gr. 1-4). 6.99 *(978-0-385-38600-5(1),* Yearling) Random Hse. Children's Bks.

—Alvin Ho: Allergic to Dead Bodies, Funerals, & Other Fatal Circumstances. Pham, LeUyen, illus. 2012. (Alvin Ho Ser.). (ENG.). 208p. (J). (gr. 1-4). 6.99 *(978-0-307-97695-6(5),* Yearling) Random Hse. Children's Bks.

—Ruby Lu, Brave & True. 2004. (Illus.). 104p. (J). lib. bdg. 15.00 *(978-1-4242-0914-9(5))* Fitzgerald Bks.

—Ruby Lu, Brave & True. Wilsdorf, Anne, illus. 2006. (ENG.). 112p. (J). (gr. 1-5). pap. 6.99 *(978-1-4169-1389-4(0),* Atheneum Bks. for Young Readers) Simon & Schuster Children's Publishing.

—Ruby Lu, Empress of Everything. Wilsdorf, Anne, illus. 2007. 164p. (gr. 1-5). 16.00 *(978-0-7569-8113-6(1))* Perfection Learning Corp.

—Ruby Lu, Empress of Everything. Wilsdorf, Anne, illus. 2007. (ENG.). 176p. (J). (gr. 1-5). pap. 5.99 *(978-1-4169-5003-5(6),* Atheneum Bks. for Young Readers) Simon & Schuster Children's Publishing.

—Ruby Lu, Star of the Show. Choi, Stef, illus. (ENG.). 144p. (J). (gr. 1-5). 2012. pap. 6.99 *(978-1-4169-1776-2(4))* 2011. 15.99 *(978-1-4169-1775-5(6))* Simon & Schuster Children's Publishing. (Atheneum Bks. for Young Readers).

—Uncle Peter's Amazing Chinese Wedding. Heo, Yumi, illus. 2006. (ENG.). 40p. (J). (gr. -1-3). 17.99 *(978-0-689-84458-4(1),* Atheneum Bks. for Young Readers) Simon & Schuster Children's Publishing.

Lord, Bette Bao. In the Year of the Boar & Jackie Robinson. Simont, Marc, illus. 2003. (ENG.). 176p. (J). (gr. 3-7). pap. 6.99 *(978-0-06-440175-3(8))* HarperCollins Pubs.

—In the Year of the Boar & Jackie Robinson. 2009. 8.32 *(978-0-7848-0826-9(0),* Everbind) Marco Bk. Co.

—In the Year of the Boar & Jackie Robinson. (J). 2008. 67.75 *(978-1-4281-8016-1(8))* 2004. 46.75 *(978-1-4025-9147-1(0))* Recorded Bks., Inc.

—In the Year of the Boar & Jackie Robinson. 2003. (J). (gr. 3-6). 16.00 *(978-0-8085-7599-3(6),* Turtleback) Turtleback Bks.

Louie, Therese On & Wang, Suling. Raymond's Perfect Present, 1 vol. 2015. (ENG.). 32p. (J). pap. 9.95 *(978-1-62014-229-5(5))* Lee & Low Bks., Inc.

Low, William. Chinatown. 2014. 32p. pap. 9.00 *(978-1-61003-224-7(1))* Center for the Collaborative Classroom.

Mak, Kam. My Chinatown. Mak, Kam, illus. 2016. (Illus.). 32p. (J). (gr. -1-3). pap. 6.99 *(978-0-06-443732-5(9))* HarperCollins Pubs.

Manushkin, Fran. Best Club. Lyon, Tammie, illus. 2016. (Katie Woo Ser.). (ENG.). 32p. (gr. k-2). lib. bdg. 21.32 *(978-1-4795-9639-3(6))* Picture Window Bks.

—Best Season Ever, 1 vol. Lyon, Tammie, illus. 2010. (Katie Woo Ser.). (ENG.). 32p. (gr. k-2). lib. bdg. 21.32 *(978-1-4048-5730-8(3))* Picture Window Bks.

—The Big Lie, 1 vol. Lyon, Tammie, illus. 2009. (Katie Woo Ser.). (ENG.). 32p. (gr. k-2). 21.32 *(978-1-4048-5497-0(5))* Picture Window Bks.

—Boo, Katie Woo!, 1 vol. Lyon, Tammie, illus. 2010. (Katie Woo Ser.). (ENG.). 32p. (gr. k-2). lib. bdg. 21.32 *(978-1-4048-5987-6(X))*; pap. 5.95 *(978-1-4048-6366-8(4))* Picture Window Bks.

—Boss of the World, 1 vol. Lyon, Tammie, illus. 2009. (Katie Woo Ser.). (ENG.). 32p. (gr. k-2). 21.32 *(978-1-4048-5493-2(2))* Picture Window Bks.

—Cartwheel Katie. Lyon, Tammie, illus. 2015. (Katie Woo Ser.). (ENG.). 32p. (gr. k-2). 21.32 *(978-1-4795-5894-0(X))* Picture Window Bks.

—Cowgirl Katie, 1 vol. Lyon, Tammie, illus. 2014. (Katie Woo Ser.). (ENG.). 32p. (gr. k-2). lib. bdg. 21.32 *(978-1-4795-2174-6(4))* Picture Window Bks.

—Fly High, Katie, 1 vol. Lyon, Tammie, illus. 2014. (Katie Woo Ser.). (ENG.). 32p. (gr. k-2). lib. bdg. 21.32 *(978-1-4795-2175-3(2))* Picture Window Bks.

—Goodbye to Goldie, 1 vol. Lyon, Tammie, illus. 2009. (Katie Woo Ser.). (ENG.). 32p. (gr. k-2). 21.32 *(978-1-4048-5495-6(9))* Picture Window Bks.

—A Happy Day, 1 vol. Lyon, Tammie, illus. 2009. (Katie Woo Ser.). (ENG.). 32p. (gr. k-2). 21.32 *(978-1-4048-5496-3(7))* Picture Window Bks.

—It Doesn't Need to Rhyme, Katie: Writing a Poem with Katie Woo, 1 vol. Lyon, Tammie, illus. 2013. (Katie Woo: Star Writer Ser.). (ENG.). 32p. (gr. k-2). pap. 6.95 *(978-1-4795-1923-1(5))*; lib. bdg. 20.65 *(978-1-4048-8128-0(X))* Picture Window Bks.

—Katie & the Class Pet, 1 vol. Lyon, Tammie, illus. 2011. (Katie Woo Ser.). (ENG.). 32p. (gr. k-2). pap. 5.95 *(978-1-4048-6856-4(9))*; lib. bdg. 21.32 *(978-1-4048-6520-4(9))* Picture Window Bks.

—Katie & the Fancy Substitute, 1 vol. 2014. (Katie Woo Ser.). (ENG.). 32p. (gr. k-2). 21.32 *(978-1-4795-5188-0(0))* Picture Window Bks.

—Katie Finds a Job, 1 vol. Lyon, Tammie, illus. 2011. (Katie Woo Ser.). (ENG.). 32p. (gr. k-2). pap. 5.95 *(978-1-4048-6614-0(0))*; lib. bdg. 21.32 *(978-1-4048-6513-6(6))* Picture Window Bks.

—Katie Goes Camping, 1 vol. Lyon, Tammie, illus. 2010. (Katie Woo Ser.). (ENG.). 32p. (gr. k-2). lib. bdg. 21.32 *(978-1-4048-5731-5(1))* Picture Window Bks.

—Katie in the Kitchen, 1 vol. Lyon, Tammie, illus. 2010. (Katie Woo Ser.). (ENG.). 32p. (gr. k-2). lib. bdg. 21.32 *(978-1-4048-5724-7(9))* Picture Window Bks.

—Katie Saves Thanksgiving, 1 vol. Lyon, Tammie, illus. 2010. (Katie Woo Ser.). (ENG.). 32p. (gr. k-2). lib. bdg. 21.32 *(978-1-4048-5988-3(8))*; pap. 5.95 *(978-1-4048-6367-5(2))* Picture Window Bks.

—Katie Saves the Earth, 1 vol. Lyon, Tammie, illus. 2013. (Katie Woo Ser.). (ENG.). 32p. (gr. k-2). pap. 5.95 *(978-1-4048-8046-7(1))*; lib. bdg. 21.32 *(978-1-4048-7652-1(9))* Picture Window Bks.

—Katie Woo, 1 vol. Lyon, Tammie, illus. (Katie Woo Ser.). (ENG.). 32p. (gr. k-2). 2014. lib. bdg. 639.60 *(978-1-4795-4813-2(8))* 2013. pap. 23.80 *(978-1-4048-8062-7(3))* 2013. pap. 130.90 *(978-1-4048-8063-4(1))* 2013. lib. bdg. 596.96 *(978-1-4048-8054-2(2))* 2013. lib. bdg. 85.28 *(978-1-4048-8055-9(0))* Picture Window Bks.

—Katie Woo & Friends, 1 vol. Lyon, Tammie, illus. 2012. (Katie Woo Ser.). (ENG.). 96p. (gr. k-2). pap. 4.95 *(978-1-4048-7909-6(9))* Picture Window Bks.

—Katie Woo & Her Big Ideas, 1 vol. Lyon, Tammie, illus. 2013. (Katie Woo Ser.). (ENG.). 96p. (gr. k-2). pap. 4.95 *(978-1-4795-2026-8(8))* Picture Window Bks.

—Katie Woo Celebrates, 1 vol. Lyon, Tammie, illus. 2013. (Katie Woo Ser.). (ENG.). 96p. (gr. k-2). pap. 4.95 *(978-1-4048-8100-6(X))* Picture Window Bks.

—Katie Woo, Don't Be Blue, 1 vol. Lyon, Tammie, illus. 2013. (Katie Woo Ser.). (ENG.). 96p. (gr. k-2). pap. 4.95 *(978-1-4048-8101-3(8))* Picture Window Bks.

—Katie Woo, Every Day's an Adventure, 1 vol. Lyon, Tammie, illus. 2014. (Katie Woo Ser.). (ENG.). 96p. (gr. k-2). pap. 4.95 *(978-1-4795-5211-5(9))* Picture Window Bks.

—Katie Woo Has the Flu, 1 vol. Lyon, Tammie, illus. 2011. (Katie Woo Ser.). (ENG.). 32p. (gr. k-2). pap. 5.95 *(978-1-4048-6854-0(2))*; lib. bdg. 21.32 *(978-1-4048-6518-1(7))* Picture Window Bks.

—Katie Woo Loves School, 1 vol. Lyon, Tammie, illus. 2013. (Katie Woo Ser.). (ENG.). 96p. (gr. k-2). pap. 4.95 *(978-1-4795-2027-5(6))* Picture Window Bks.

—Katie Woo Rules the School, 1 vol. Lyon, Tammie, illus. 2011. (Katie Woo Ser.). (ENG.). 96p. (gr. k-2). pap. 4.95 *(978-1-4048-7908-9(0))* Picture Window Bks.

—Katie Woo, Super Scout. Lyon, Tammie, illus. 2015. (Katie Woo Ser.). (ENG.). 32p. (gr. k-2). 21.32 *(978-1-4795-6178-0(9))* Picture Window Bks.

—Katie Woo Tries Something New. Lyon, Tammie, illus. 2015. (Katie Woo Ser.). (ENG.). 96p. (gr. k-2). pap. 4.95 *(978-1-4795-6182-7(7))* Picture Window Bks.

—Katie Woo, Where Are You?, 1 vol. Lyon, Tammie, illus. 2011. (Katie Woo Ser.). (ENG.). 32p. (gr. k-2). pap. 5.95 *(978-1-4048-6853-3(4))*; lib. bdg. 21.32 *(978-1-4048-6517-4(9))* Picture Window Bks.

—Katie's Happy Mother's Day. Lyon, Tammie, illus. 2015. (Katie Woo Ser.). (ENG.). 32p. (gr. k-2). 21.32 *(978-1-4795-6179-7(7))* Picture Window Bks.

—Katie's Lucky Birthday, 1 vol. Lyon, Tammie, illus. 2011. (Katie Woo Ser.). (ENG.). 32p. (gr. k-2). pap. 5.95 *(978-1-4048-6612-6(4))*; lib. bdg. 21.32 *(978-1-4048-6514-3(4))* Picture Window Bks.

—Katie's New Shoes, 1 vol. Lyon, Tammie, illus. 2011. (Katie Woo Ser.). (ENG.). 32p. (gr. k-2). pap. 5.95 *(978-1-4048-6855-7(0))*; lib. bdg. 21.32 *(978-1-4048-6519-8(5))* Picture Window Bks.

—Katie's Noisy Music. Lyon, Tammie, illus. 2015. (Katie Woo Ser.). (ENG.). 32p. (gr. k-2). 21.32 *(978-1-4795-5893-3(1))* Picture Window Bks.

—Katie's Spooky Sleepover. Lyon, Tammie, illus. 2016. (Katie Woo Ser.). (ENG.). 32p. (gr. k-2). lib. bdg. 21.32 *(978-1-4795-9640-9(X))* Picture Window Bks.

—Keep Dancing, Katie, 1 vol. 2014. (Katie Woo Ser.). (ENG.). 32p. (gr. k-2). 21.32 *(978-1-4795-5187-3(2))* Picture Window Bks.

—Look at You, Katie Woo!, 1 vol. Lyon, Tammie, illus. 2011. (Katie Woo Ser.). (ENG.). 112p. (gr. k-2). pap. 7.95 *(978-1-4048-6596-9(9))* Picture Window Bks.

—Moo, Katie Woo! Lyon, Tammie, illus. 2013. (J). pap. 35.70 *(978-1-4048-8093-1(3))*; (ENG.). 32p. pap. 5.95 *(978-1-4048-8047-4(X))*; (ENG.). 32p. lib. bdg. 21.32 *(978-1-4048-7653-8(7))* Picture Window Bks.

—A Nervous Night, 1 vol. Lyon, Tammie, illus. 2010. (Katie Woo Ser.). (ENG.). 32p. (gr. k-2). pap. 5.95 *(978-1-4048-6060-5(6))*; lib. bdg. 21.32 *(978-1-4048-5725-4(7))* Picture Window Bks.

—No More Teasing, 1 vol. Lyon, Tammie, illus. 2009. (Katie Woo Ser.). (ENG.). 32p. (gr. k-2). 21.32 *(978-1-4048-5492-5(4))* Picture Window Bks.

—No Valentines for Katie, 1 vol. Lyon, Tammie, illus. 2010. (Katie Woo Ser.). (ENG.). 32p. (gr. k-2). lib. bdg. 21.32 *(978-1-4048-5986-9(1))*; pap. 5.95 *(978-1-4048-6365-1(6))* Picture Window Bks.

—Piggy Bank Problems, 1 vol. Lyon, Tammie, illus. 2013. (Katie Woo Ser.). (ENG.). 32p. (gr. k-2). pap. 5.95 *(978-1-4048-8048-1(8))*; lib. bdg. 21.32 *(978-1-4048-7654-5(5))* Picture Window Bks.

—Red, White, & Blue & Katie Woo!, 1 vol. Lyon, Tammie, illus. 2010. (Katie Woo Ser.). (ENG.). 32p. (gr. k-2). lib. bdg. 21.32 *(978-1-4048-5985-2(3))*; pap. 5.95 *(978-1-4048-6364-4(8))* Picture Window Bks.

—Sincerely, Katie: Writing a Letter with Katie Woo, 1 vol. Lyon, Tammie, illus. 2013. (Katie Woo: Star Writer Ser.). (ENG.). 32p. (gr. k-2). pap. 6.95 *(978-1-4795-1921-7(9))*; lib. bdg. 20.65 *(978-1-4048-8126-6(3))* Picture Window Bks.

—Star of the Show, 1 vol. Lyon, Tammie, illus. 2011. (Katie Woo Ser.). (ENG.). 32p. (gr. k-2). pap. 5.95 (978-1-4048-6613-3(2)); lib. bdg. 21.32 (978-1-4048-6515-0(2)) Picture Window Bks.

—Stick to the Facts, Katie: Writing a Research Paper with Katie Woo, 1 vol. Lyon, Tammie, illus. 2013. (Katie Woo: Star Writer Ser.). (ENG.). 32p. (gr. k-2). pap. 6.95 (978-1-4795-1925-5(1)); lib. bdg. 20.65 (978-1-4048-8130-3(1)) Picture Window Bks.

—Too Much Rain, 1 vol. Lyon, Tammie, illus. 2009. (Katie Woo Ser.). (ENG.). 32p. (gr. k-2). 21.32 (978-1-4048-5494-9(0)) Picture Window Bks.

—The Tricky Tooth, 1 vol. Lyon, Tammie, illus. 2011. (Katie Woo Ser.). (ENG.). 32p. (gr. k-2). pap. 5.95 (978-1-4048-6611-9(6)); lib. bdg. 21.32 (978-1-4048-6516-7(0)) Picture Window Bks.

—What Do You Think, Katie? Writing an Opinion Piece with Katie Woo, 1 vol. Lyon, Tammie, illus. 2013. (Katie Woo: Star Writer Ser.). (ENG.). 32p. (gr. k-2). pap. 6.95 (978-1-4795-1926-2(X)); lib. bdg. 20.65 (978-1-4048-8131-0(X)) Picture Window Bks.

—What Happens Next, Katie? Writing a Narrative with Katie Woo, 1 vol. Lyon, Tammie, illus. 2013. (Katie Woo: Star Writer Ser.). (ENG.). 32p. (gr. k-2). pap. 6.95 (978-1-4795-1924-8(3)); lib. bdg. 20.65 (978-1-4048-8129-7(8)) Picture Window Bks.

—What's in Your Heart, Katie? Writing in a Journal with Katie Woo, 1 vol. Lyon, Tammie, illus. 2013. (Katie Woo: Star Writer Ser.). (ENG.). 32p. (gr. k-2). pap. 6.95 (978-1-4795-1922-4(7)); lib. bdg. 20.65 (978-1-4048-8127-3(1)) Picture Window Bks.

—Who Needs Glasses?, 1 vol. Lyon, Tammie, illus. 2013. (Katie Woo Ser.). (ENG.). 32p. (gr. k-2). pap. 5.95 (978-1-4048-8049-8(6)); lib. bdg. 21.32 (978-1-4048-7655-2(3)) Picture Window Bks.

Manushkin, Fran & Lyon, Tammie. Adiós a Goldie. Lyon, Tammie, illus. 2012. (Katie Woo en Español Ser.). (SPA., Illus.). 32p. (gr. k-2). pap. 6.95 (978-1-4048-7676-7(6)); lib. bdg. 21.32 (978-1-4048-7524-1(7)) Picture Window Bks.

—Basta de Burlas, 1 vol. Lyon, Tammie, illus. 2012. (Katie Woo en Español Ser.). (SPA., Illus.). 32p. (gr. k-2). pap. 6.95 (978-1-4048-7677-4(4)); lib. bdg. 21.32 (978-1-4048-7525-8(5)) Picture Window Bks.

—La Gran Mentira, 1 vol. Lyon, Tammie, illus. 2012. (Katie Woo en Español Ser.). (SPA., Illus.). 32p. (gr. k-2). pap. 6.95 (978-1-4048-7678-1(2)); lib. bdg. 21.32 (978-1-4048-7522-7(0)) Picture Window Bks.

—La Jefa Del Mundo, 1 vol. Lyon, Tammie, illus. 2012. (Katie Woo en Español Ser.). (SPA., Illus.). 32p. (gr. k-2). pap. 6.95 (978-1-4048-7679-8(0)); lib. bdg. 21.32 (978-1-4048-7523-4(9)) Picture Window Bks.

Mayer, Pamela. Chicken Soup, Chicken Soup. Melmon, Deborah, illus. 2016. (ENG.). 32p. (J). (gr. -1-3). 17.99 (978-1-4677-8934-9(8), Kar-Ben Publishing) Lerner Publishing Group.

McDonald, Megan. Happy New Year, Julie, Bk. 3. McAliley, Susan & Hunt, Robert, illus. 2007. (American Girl Ser.). (ENG.). 88p. (J). (gr. 3-7). 12.95 (978-1-59369-292-6(7)) American Girl Publishing, Inc.

McKernan, Victoria. Son of Fortune. 2015. (ENG.). 448p. (YA). (gr. 7). pap. 9.99 (978-0-375-85786-7(9), Ember) Random Hse. Children's Bks.

Messner, Kate. Escape from the Great Earthquake. McMorris, Kelley, illus. 2017. (Ranger in Time Ser.: 6). (ENG.). 160p. (J). (gr. 2-5). pap. 5.99 (978-0-545-90983-9(X)) Scholastic, Inc.

Namioka, Lensey. April & the Dragon Lady. 2007. (ENG., Illus.). 224p. (YA). (gr. 7-12). pap. 13.95 (978-0-15-205669-8(6)) Houghton Mifflin Harcourt Publishing Co.

—Half & Half. 2005. 136p. (gr. 3-7). 16.00 (978-0-7569-5680-6(3)) Perfection Learning Corp.

—Half & Half. 2004. (ENG.). 144p. (J). (gr. 3-7). 5.99 (978-0-440-41890-0(9), Yearling) Random Hse. Children's Bks.

Pryor, Bonnie. The Iron Dragon: The Courageous Story of Lee Chin. 2010. (Historical Fiction Adventures (HFA) Ser.). (Illus.). 160p. (J). (gr. 3-6). 29.27 (978-0-7660-3389-4(9)); (gr. 4-6). pap. 10.95 (978-1-59845-215-0(0)) Enslow Pubs., Inc.

Publications International Ltd. Staff, ed. Dragon Boat Festival. 2009. 9p. (J). bds. 10.98 (978-1-4127-7782-7(8), PIL Kids) Publications International, Ltd.

Rhodes, Jewell Parker. Sugar. 2013. (ENG.). 288p. (J). (gr. 3-7). 16.99 (978-0-316-04305-2(2)) Little, Brown Bks. for Young Readers.

Rose, Naomi C. Tashi & the Tibetan Flower Cure. 2016. (ENG.). 40p. (J). (gr. 1-6). pap. 10.95 (978-1-62014-318-6(6)) Lee & Low Bks., Inc.

Rosenberg, Madelyn & Shang, Wendy Wan-Long. This Is Just a Test: A Novel. 2017. (ENG.). 256p. (J). (gr. 3-7). 17.99 (978-1-338-03772-2(2), Scholastic Pr.) Scholastic, Inc.

Scattergood, Augusta. Making Friends with Billy Wong. 2016. (ENG.). 224p. (J). (gr. 3-7). 16.99 (978-0-545-92425-2(1), Scholastic Pr.) Scholastic, Inc.

Schroeder, Lisa. Keys to the City. 2017. (ENG.). 240p. (J). (gr. 3-7). 16.99 (978-0-545-90738-5(1), Scholastic Pr.) Scholastic, Inc.

Shang, Wendy Wan-Long. The Great Wall of Lucy Wu. 2013. (ENG.). 320p. (J). (gr. 3-7). pap. 7.99 (978-0-545-16216-6(5), Scholastic Paperbacks) Scholastic, Inc.

—The Way Home Looks Now. 2015. (ENG.). 272p. (J). (gr. 3-7). 16.99 (978-0-545-60956-2(9), Scholastic Pr.) Scholastic, Inc.

Shemin, Craig. Families Are Forever. McCoy, John, illus. l.t. ed. 2004. 34p. 9.95 (978-0-9728666-1-3(2), 1) As Simple As That Publishing.

Shinn, Sharon. Gateway. 2009. (ENG.). 288p. (YA). (gr. 7-18). 17.99 (978-0-670-01178-0(9), Viking Books for Young Readers) Penguin Young Readers Group.

Shirtliffe, Leanne. The Change Your Name Store. Kügler, Tina, illus. 2014. (ENG.). 32p. (J). (gr. -1-k). 16.95 (978-1-62873-608-3(9), Sky Pony Pr.) Skyhorse Publishing Co., Inc.

Smith, D. James. It Was September When We Ran Away the First Time. 2012. (ENG.). 240p. (J). (gr. 3-7). pap. 11.99 (978-1-4169-3810-1(9), Atheneum Bks. for Young Readers) Simon & Schuster Children's Publishing.

Stites, Clara. Lixia of Gold Mountain: A Story of Early California. 2015. (ENG., Illus.). 100p. (J). pap. 8.95 (978-1-56474-421-0(3), Fithian Pr) Daniel & Daniel, Pubs., Inc.

Stone, Jeff. Lion. 2013. (Five Ancestors Out of the Ashes Ser.). (ENG.). 240p. (J). (gr. 4-7). 16.99 (978-0-375-87019-4(9), Random Hse. Bks. for Young Readers) Random Hse. Children's Bks.

Stuber, Barbara. Girl in Reverse. 2014. (ENG., Illus.). 336p. (YA). (gr. 7). 17.99 (978-1-4424-9734-4(3), McElderry, Margaret K. Bks.) McElderry, Margaret K. Bks.

Tan, Susan. Cilla Lee-Jenkins: Future Author Extraordinaire. Wulfekotte, Dana, illus. 2017. (Cilla Lee-Jenkins Ser.). (ENG.). 256p. (J). 16.99 (978-1-62672-551-5(9), 9781626725515) Roaring Brook Pr.

Thong, Roseanne Greenfield. Gai See: What You Can See in Chinatown. Choi, Yangsook, illus. 2007. (ENG.). 40p. (J). (gr. 1-4). 16.95 (978-0-8109-9337-2(6), Abrams Bks. for Young Readers) Abrams, Inc.

—One Is a Drummer: A Book of Numbers. 2014. (Multicultural Shapes & Colors Ser.). (Illus.). 40p. (J). lib. bdg. 28.50 (978-1-60753-567-6(X)) Amicus Publishing.

—Red Is a Dragon. Lin, Grace, illus. 2014. 40p. pap. 7.00 (978-1-61003-333-6(7)) Center for the Collaborative Classroom.

—Red Is a Dragon: A Book of Colors. 2014. (Multicultural Shapes & Colors Ser.). (Illus.). 40p. (J). lib. bdg. 28.50 (978-1-60753-565-2(3)) Amicus Publishing.

—Red Is a Dragon: A Book of Colors. Lin, Grace, illus. 2008. (ENG.). 40p. (J). (gr. -1-17). pap. 7.99 (978-0-8118-6481-7(2)) Chronicle Bks. LLC.

—Round Is a Mooncake: A Book of Shapes. 2014. (Multicultural Shapes & Colors Ser.). (Illus.). 40p. (J). lib. bdg. 28.50 (978-1-60753-564-5(5)) Amicus Publishing.

Tsang, Evonne. I Love Him to Pieces. Görrissen, Janina, illus. 2011. (My Boyfriend Is a Monster Ser.: 1). (ENG.). 128p. (YA). (gr. 7-12). 29.27 (978-0-7613-6004-9(2)) Lerner Publishing Group.

—#01 I Love Him to Pieces. Görrissen, Janina, illus. 2011. (My Boyfriend Is a Monster Ser.). 128p. (YA). pap. 56.72 (978-0-7613-7602-6(X), Graphic Universe™) Lerner Publishing Group.

Wilson, Diane Lee. Tracks. (ENG., (J). (gr. 5-9). 2013. Illus.). 304p. pap. 6.99 (978-1-4424-2014-4(6)) 2012. 288p. 16.99 (978-1-4424-2013-7(8)) McElderry, Margaret K. Bks. (McElderry, Margaret K. Bks.).

Wong, Benedict Norbert. Lo & Behold. Wong, Benedict Norbert, illus. l.t. ed. 2003. (Illus.). 38p. (gr. 1-18). 16.95 (978-0-9728192-0-6(7), LOBE) Taiji Arts Publishing.

—Lo & Behold: A Boy & His Dragon. 2004. (Illus.). 44p. (J). (gr. 1-12). 8.95 (978-0-9728192-4-4(X)) Taiji Arts Publishing.

—Lo & Behold: Good Enough to Eat. Wong, Benedict Norbert, illus. l.t. ed. 2003. (Illus.). 40p. (J). (gr. 1-12). 16.95 (978-0-9728192-1-3(5), 1002LB) Taiji Arts Publishing.

—Lo & Behold: The Millennia Just Roll By. 2004. (Illus.). 40p. (J). (gr. 1-12). 16.95 (978-0-9728192-3-7(1)) Taiji Arts Publishing.

Wong, Janet S. Apple Pie Fourth of July. Chodos-Irvine, Margaret, illus. 2006. (ENG.). 40p. (J). (gr. -1-3). pap. 7.99 (978-0-15-205708-4(0)) Houghton Mifflin Harcourt Publishing Co.

Wong, Joyce Lee. Seeing Emily. 2005. (ENG., Illus.). 288p. (J). (gr. 7-11). 16.95 (978-0-8109-5757-2(4), Abrams Bks. for Young Readers) Abrams, Inc.

Yamada, Debbie Leung. Striking It Rich: Treasures from Gold Mountain. Tang, You-shan, illus. l.t. ed. 2004. 128p. (J). (gr. 4-8). pap. 13.95 (978-1-879965-21-8(6)) Polychrome Publishing Corp.

Yamate, Sandra S. & Yao, Carolina, illus. Char Siu Bao Boy. 2004. 32p. (J). (gr. k-3). pap. 15.95 (978-1-879965-19-5(4)) Polychrome Publishing Corp.

Yang, Belle. Hannah Is My Name. Yang, Belle, illus. 2007. (Illus.). (J). (gr. k-4). 14.65 (978-0-7569-8124-2(7)) Perfection Learning Corp.

—Hannah Is My Name: A Young Immigrant's Story. Yang, Belle, illus. 2007. (ENG., Illus.). 32p. (J). (gr. k-4). pap. 6.99 (978-0-7636-3521-3(9)) Candlewick Pr.

Yang, Gene Luen. American Born Chinese. 2011. 10.04 (978-0-7848-3435-0(0), Everbind) Marco Bk. Co.

—American Born Chinese. 2011. 20.00 (978-1-60686-920-8(5)) 2007. 29.00 (978-0-7569-7745-0(2)) Perfection Learning Corp.

—American Born Chinese. Yang, Gene Luen & Pien, Lark, illus. 2007. (ENG.). 240p. (YA). (gr. 7-18). 23.99 (978-1-59643-373-1(6), 9781596433731, First Second Bks.) Roaring Brook Pr.

—American Born Chinese. Yang, Gene Luen, illus. rev. ed. 2006. (ENG., Illus.). 240p. (YA). (gr. 7-12). pap. 18.99 (978-1-59643-152-2(0), 9781596431522, First Second Bks.) Roaring Brook Pr.

—American Born Chinese. Yang, Gene Luen, illus. 2008. (ENG., Illus.). 240p. (YA). (gr. 7-12). pap. 10.99 (978-0-312-38448-7(3), 9780312384487) Square Fish.

—American Born Chinese. 2008. (YA). lib. bdg. 22.10 (978-0-606-14484-1(6), Turtleback) Turtleback Bks.

—Animal Crackers: A Gene Luen Yang Collection. 2012. (ENG., Illus.). 216p. (YA). pap. 14.95 (978-1-59362-183-4(3), 9781593621834) Slave Labor Bks.

—Level Up. Pham, Thien, illus. 2011. (ENG.). 160p. (YA). (gr. 7). 19.99 (978-1-59643-714-2(6), 9781596437142, First Second Bks.) Roaring Brook Pr.

Yang, Gene Luen & Pham, Thien. Level Up. 2016. (YA). lib. bdg. 20.85 (978-0-606-38563-3(0)) Turtleback Bks.

Yee, Lisa. Millicent Min, Girl Genius. 2004. 248p. (gr. 3-7). 17.00 (978-0-7569-3919-9(4)) Perfection Learning Corp.

Yee, Paul. What Happened This Summer, 1 vol. 2006. (ENG., Illus.). 178p. (YA). (gr. 8-12). per. 10.95 (978-1-896580-88-3(2)) Tradewind Bks. CAN. Dist: Orca Bk. Pubs. USA.

Yep, Laurence. Child of the Owl. (Golden Mountain Chronicles). (J). pap., stu. ed. (978-0-13-053125-4(1)) Prentice Hall (Schl. Div.).

—The Earth Dragon Awakes: The San Francisco Earthquake of 1906. (ENG., Illus.). 128p. (J). (gr. 3-7). 2008. pap. 6.99 (978-0-06-000846-8(6)) 2006. 14.99 (978-0-06-027524-2(3)) HarperCollins Pubs.

—The Magic Paintbrush. Wang, Suling, illus. 2003. (ENG.). 96p. (J). (gr. 3-7). pap. 6.99 (978-0-06-440852-3(3)) HarperCollins Pubs.

—The Magic Paintbrush. Wang, Suling, illus. 2003. 89p. (J). (gr. 3-7). 12.65 (978-0-7569-1444-8(2)) Perfection Learning Corp.

—Skunk Scout. 2009. (Journeys Ser.). (ENG.). 192p. (gr. 5-5). pap. 7.45 (978-0-547-07397-2(6)) Houghton Mifflin Harcourt Publishing Co.

—The Tiger's Apprentice. 2005. (Tiger's Apprentice Ser.: Bk. 1). 184p. (J). lib. bdg. 24.62 (978-1-4242-0449-6(6)) Fitzgerald Bks.

—The Tiger's Apprentice. 2005. (Tiger's Apprentice (Tandem Library) Ser.). 184p. (gr. 5-9). 17.00 (978-0-7569-5074-3(0)) Perfection Learning Corp.

—Tiger's Blood. 2005. (Tiger's Apprentice Ser.: Bk. 2). (ENG.). 240p. (J). (gr. 5-18). 15.99 (978-0-06-001016-4(9)) HarperCollins Pubs.

—The Traitor. 2004. (Golden Mountain Chronicles). 310p. (J). (gr. 5). 14.65 (978-0-7569-3457-6(5)) Perfection Learning Corp.

—When the Circus Came to Town. Wang, Suling, illus. 2004. 112p. (J). (gr. 3-5). 13.65 (978-0-7569-2969-5(5)) Perfection Learning Corp.

Yep, Laurence & Yep, Kathleen S. The Dragon's Child: A Story of Angel Island. 2011. (ENG.). 160p. (J). (gr. 3-7). pap. 5.99 (978-0-06-201815-1(9)) HarperCollins Pubs.

Yin. Coolies. Soentpiet, Chris K., illus. 2003. (ENG.). 40p. (J). (gr. 2-5). 7.99 (978-0-14-250055-2(0), Puffin Books) Penguin Young Readers Group.

—Coolies. Soentpiet, Chris K., illus. 2003. (gr. k). 18.00 (978-0-7569-1545-2(7)) Perfection Learning Corp.

CHINESE LANGUAGE

Amery, Heather. First Hundred Words in Chinese. 2009. (First Hundred Words Ser.). 34p. (J). (gr. -1). pap. 6.99 (978-0-7945-2189-9(4), Usborne) EDC Publishing.

—First Hundred Words in Chinese II. 2015. (First Hundred Words Ser.). (ENG.). 32p. (J). pap. 6.99 (978-0-7945-3517-9(8), Usborne) EDC Publishing.

—First Thousand Words in Chinese: With Internet-Linked Pronunciation Guide. MacKinnon, Mairi, ed. Asian Absolute, tr. Cartwright, Stephen, illus. 2007. (Usborne Internet-Linked First Thousand Words Ser.). 63p. (J). 12.99 (978-0-7945-1550-8(9), Usborne) EDC Publishing.

Buddhist Text Translation Society Staff, contrib. by. Standards for Students: Instructions in Virtue from the Chinese Heritage = [Di Zi Gui]. 2003. (ENG & CHI., Illus.). 41p. (J). (978-0-88139-489-4(0)) Buddhist Text Translation Society.

Carole Marsh. Ho Lee Chow! Chinese for Kids. 2004. (Little Linguist Ser.). 32p. (gr. 2-6). pap. 5.95 (978-0-635-02435-0(7)) Gallopade International.

Chang, MacKerras, et al. Hanyu for Beginning Students. 2005. (CHI & ENG.). (YA). (gr. 7-9). tchr. ed., per. 22.50 (978-0-582-90869-7(8)); per. 22.50 (978-0-582-90870-3(1)) Pearson Education Australia AUS. Dist: Cheng & Tsui Co.

Chang, Nan, tr. Kids Stuff Chinese: Easy Chinese phrases for you & your Kids. 2007. (Bilingual Kids Ser.). (ENG & CHI., Illus.). 187p. (J). pap. 22.95 (978-0-9789152-1-6(6)) Chou Chou Pr.

Chang, Peter & Mackerras, Alyce. Hanyu for Beginning Students. 2005. (Illus.). (gr. 7-9). 184p. per. 46.95 (978-0-582-87003-1(8)); 96p. per., act. bk. ed. 27.95 (978-0-582-90868-0(X)) Pearson Education Australia AUS. Dist: Cheng & Tsui Co.

—Hanyu for Beginning Students Character Writing Book. 2005. (CHI & ENG., Illus.). 40p. (gr. 7-9). per., wbk. ed. 13.95 (978-0-582-91050-8(1)) Pearson Education Australia AUS. Dist: Cheng & Tsui Co.

—Hanyu for Intermediate Students, 4 vols. 2005. (CHI & ENG., Illus.). 120p. (gr. 10-12). per., act. bk. ed. 30.95 (978-0-7339-1368-6(7)); 216p. (gr. 7-10). per. 52.95 (978-0-582-80087-8(0)); 132p. (gr. 7-10). per., act. bk. ed. 33.95 (978-0-582-80086-1(2)) Pearson Education Australia AUS. Dist: Cheng & Tsui Co.

—Hanyu for Intermediate Students: Character Writing Book, 4 vols. 2005. (CHI & ENG., Illus.). 54p. (gr. 7-10). per., wbk. ed. 14.95 (978-0-582-80084-7(6)) Pearson Education Australia AUS. Dist: Cheng & Tsui Co.

Corbeil, Jean-Claude, et al. Milet Bilingual Visual Dictionary. 2005. (CHI & ENG., Illus.). 232p. (gr. 1-3). 29.95 (978-1-84059-258-0(3)) Milet Publishing.

Dong, Li. Tuttle Learner's Chinese-English Dictionary. 2005. (ENG & CHI., Illus.). 384p. pap. 29.95 (978-0-8048-3552-7(7)) Tuttle Publishing.

Fredlein, Shumang & Fredlein, Paul. Ni Hao. 2005. (C & T Asian Language Ser.). (CHI & ENG., Illus.). 3. 128p. (gr. 7-11). pap., tchr. ed. 59.95 (978-0-646-22330-8(5)) Vol. 1. 76p. (gr. 5-9). pap., tchr. ed. 59.95 (978-0-646-06658-5(7)) Cheng & Tsui Co.

Fuhua, Liu, et al. Chinese Paradise. 2005. (CHI & ENG.). (J). (gr. 4-6). 175p. tchr. ed. 17.95 incl. audio compact disk (978-7-5619-1441-0(5), CHPAI1); Vol. 1. 36p. stu. ed. 10.95 incl. audio compact disk (978-7-5619-1439-7(3), CHPA1A); Vol. 1. 26p. wbk. ed. 8.95 incl. audio compact disk (978-7-5619-1440-3(7), CHPAW1A); Vol. 2. 36p. stu. ed. 10.95 incl. audio compact disk (978-7-5619-1443-4(1), CHPA2A); Vol. 3. 42p. wbk. ed. 11.95 incl. audio compact disk (978-7-5619-1437-3(7), CHPAW3A) Beijing Language & Culture Univ. Pr., China CHN. Dist: China Books & Periodicals, Inc.

—Chinese Paradise 3, Vol. 3. 2005. (CHI & ENG.). 44p. (J). (gr. 4-6). stu. ed. 11.95 incl. audio compact disk (978-7-5619-1436-6(9), CHPA3A) Beijing Language & Culture Univ. Pr., China CHN. Dist: China Books & Periodicals, Inc.

Greenwood, Elinor & Dorling Kindersley Publishing Staff. Get Talking Chinese: Mandarin Chinese for Beginners. 2007. (ENG., Illus.). 128p. (J). (gr. 3-7). 14.99 (978-0-7566-2902-1(0), DK Children) Dorling Kindersley Publishing, Inc.

Gu, Licheng & Hambleton, Laura. Chinese with Lulu & Maomao. 2008. (Abby & Zak Ser.). (CHI & ENG., Illus.). 48p. (J). (gr. k-2). pap. 16.95 (978-1-84059-514-7(0)) Milet Publishing.

Hippocrene Books Staff, ed. Chinese Children's Picture Dictionary: English-Chinese/Chinese-English. 2006. (CHI & ENG., Illus.). 114p. pap. 14.95 (978-0-7818-1161-3(9)) Hippocrene Bks., Inc.

HOP, LLC. Hooked on Chinese. 2006. 99.99 (978-1-933863-86-3(2)) HOP, LLC.

Kalz, Jill. My First Mandarin Chinese Phrases, 1 vol. Advocate-Art Staff & Translations.com Staff, trs. Fabbri, Daniele, illus. 2012. (Speak Another Language! Ser.). (CHI & ENG.). 32p. (gr. 1-3). pap. 8.95 (978-1-4048-7246-2(9)) Picture Window Bks.

—My First Mandarin Chinese Phrases, 1 vol. Translations.com Staff, tr. Fabbri, Daniele, illus. 2012. (Speak Another Language! Ser.). (CHI & ENG.). 32p. (gr. 1-3). lib. bdg. 26.65 (978-1-4048-7155-7(1)) Picture Window Bks.

Karapetian, Marjam. Bilingual Content Dictionary: English to Mandarin Chinese. 2004. (CHI & ENG.). 4.95 (978-0-9768053-0-4(8)); 4.95 (978-0-9768053-1-1(6)); 15.95 (978-0-9768053-5-9(9)); 9.95 (978-0-9768053-2-8(4)); 13.95 (978-0-9768053-4-2(0)) WizdomInc.

—Bilingual Content Dictionary: English to Mandarin Chinese: Social Studies - American History Through 1776. 2004. (CHI & ENG.). 14.95 (978-0-9768053-3-5(2)) WizdomInc.

Kudela, Katy R. My First Book of Mandarin Chinese Words, 1 vol. 2009. (Bilingual Picture Dictionaries Ser.). (MUL, CHI, ENG & SPA., Illus.). 32p. (gr. 1-2). pap. 8.10 (978-1-4296-4371-9(4), Aplus Bks.) Capstone Press of Coughlan Cos.

Lin, Chris. Mandy & Pandy Play Let's Count. Villalta, Ingrid, illus. 2008. 18p. (J). (gr. -1-3). bds. 9.99 (978-0-9800156-5-2(0)) Mandy & Pandy Bks., LLC.

—Mandy & Pandy Say Ni Hao Ma? Villalta, Ingrid, illus. 2007. 18p. (J). (gr. -1-3). bds. 9.95 (978-0-9800156-4-5(2)) Mandy & Pandy Bks., LLC.

—Mandy & Pandy Say Ni Hao Ma? Teach Kids Chinese the Fun & Easy Way. 2007. 16p. (J). pap. 12.95 (978-0-9758805-7-9(8)) River Pointe Pubns.

Listen & Learn First Chinese Words. 2017. (Listen & Learn First Words Ser.). (ENG.). (J). bds. 19.99 (978-0-7945-3799-9(5), Usborne) EDC Publishing.

Ma, Yamin. Chinese Made Easy for Kids. (CHI & ENG.). 144p. 2004. pap., wbk. ed. 12.95 (978-962-04-2470-0(0), CMEKW1) Vol. 2. 2005. pap., wbk. ed. 12.95 (978-962-04-2499-1(9), CMEKW2) Vol. 3. 2006. pap., wbk. ed. 13.60 (978-962-04-2520-2(0), CMEKW3) Vol. 4. 2006. pap., wbk. ed. 13.60 (978-962-04-2524-0(3), CMEKW4) Joint Publishing Co. HKG. Dist: Chinasprout, Inc.

—Chinese Made Easy for Kids: Text Book. (CHI & ENG.). 128p. 2004. pap. 19.95 (978-962-04-2469-4(7), CMEKT1) Vol. 2. 2005. pap. 19.95 (978-962-04-2498-4(0), CMEKT2) Vol. 3. 2006. pap. 19.95 (978-962-04-2519-6(7), CMEKT3) Vol. 4. 2006. pap. 34.95 (978-962-04-2523-3(5), CMEKT4) Joint Publishing Co. HKG. Dist: Chinasprout, Inc.

Marsh, Carole. Ho Lee Chow! Chinese for Kids. Beard, Chad, ed. 2004. (Little Linguist Ser.). (Illus.). 32p. 29.95 (978-0-635-02443-5(8)) Gallopade International.

Milet Publishing Staff. Bilingual Visual Dictionary. 2011. (Milet Multimedia Ser.). (ENG & CHI., Illus.). 1p. (J). (gr. k-2). cd-rom 19.95 (978-1-84059-582-6(5)) Milet Publishing.

—Home. 2011. (My First Bilingual Book Ser.). (ENG., Illus.). 24p. (J). (gr. k — 1). bds. 7.99 (978-1-84059-642-7(2)) Milet Publishing.

—Milet Interactive for Kids - Chinese for English Speakers. 2012. (Milet Interactive for Kids Ser.). (ENG., Illus.). 1p. (J). (gr. k-2). cd-rom 24.95 (978-1-84059-676-2(7)) Milet Publishing.

—Milet Interactive for Kids - English for Chinese Speakers. 2012. (Milet Interactive for Kids Ser.). (ENG., Illus.). 1p. (J). (gr. k-2). cd-rom 24.95 (978-1-84059-672-4(4)) Milet Publishing.

—Music. 2012. (My First Bilingual Book Ser.). (ENG & CHI., Illus.). 24p. (J). (gr. k — 1). bds. 7.99 (978-1-84059-718-9(6)) Milet Publishing.

—My Bilingual Book - Smell. 2014. (My Bilingual Book Ser.). (ENG & CHI., Illus.). 28p. (J). (gr. -1-k). 9.95 (978-1-84059-806-3(9)) Milet Publishing.

—My Bilingual Book-Hearing. 2014. (My Bilingual Book Ser.). (ENG & CHI., Illus.). 28p. (J). (gr. -1-k). 9.95 (978-1-84059-774-5(7)) Milet Publishing.

—My Bilingual Book-Sight (English-Chinese) 2014. (My Bilingual Book Ser.). (ENG & CHI., Illus.). 28p. (J). (gr. -1-k). 9.95 (978-1-84059-790-5(9)) Milet Publishing.

—My Bilingual Book-Touch (English-Chinese) 2014. (My Bilingual Book Ser.). (ENG & CHI., Illus.). 28p. (J). (gr. -1-k). 9.95 (978-1-84059-838-4(7)) Milet Publishing.

—My First Bilingual Book - Animals. 2011. (My First Bilingual Book Ser.). (ENG., Illus.). 24p. (J). (gr. k — 1). bds. 8.99 (978-1-84059-610-6(4)) Milet Publishing.

—My First Bilingual Book - Colors. 2011. (My First Bilingual Book Ser.). (ENG.). 24p. (J). (gr. k — 1). bds. 7.99 (978-1-84059-598-7(1)) Milet Publishing.

—My First Bilingual Book - Fruit. 2011. (My First Bilingual Book Ser.). (ENG., Illus.). 24p. (J). (gr. k — 1). bds. 8.99 (978-1-84059-626-7(0)) Milet Publishing.

—My First Bilingual Book - Vegetables. 2011. (My First Bilingual Book Ser.). (ENG., Illus.). 24p. (J). (gr. k — 1). bds. 7.99 (978-1-84059-658-8(9)) Milet Publishing.

—My First Bilingual Book-Jobs (English-Chinese) 2012. (My First Bilingual Book Ser.). (ENG & CHI., Illus.). 24p. (J). (gr. k — 1). bds. 7.99 (978-1-84059-702-8(X)) Milet Publishing.

—My First Bilingual Book-Opposites. 2012. (My First Bilingual Book Ser.). (ENG & CHI., Illus.). 24p. (J). (gr. k — 1). bds. 7.99 (978-1-84059-734-9(8)) Milet Publishing.

—Sports. 2012. (My First Bilingual Book Ser.). (ENG & CHI., Illus.). 24p. (J). (gr. k — 1). bds. 7.99 (978-1-84059-750-9(X)) Milet Publishing.

National Taiwan Normal University Staff. Practical Audio-Visual Chinese Vol. 3: B. 2004. (CHI & ENG.). (gr. k-18). pap., tchr. ed. 12.95 (978-957-09-1244-9(8)) Cheng Chung Bk. Co., Ltd. TWN. Dist: Cheng & Tsui Co.

National Taiwan Normal University Staff, compiled by. A Practical Audio-Visual Chinese: A. 2004. (CHI & ENG.). (gr. k-18). pap. 35.00 (978-957-09-1238-8(3)) Cheng Chung Bk. Co., Ltd. TWN. Dist: Cheng & Tsui Co.

—Practical Audio-Visual Chinese Vol. 3: B. 2004. (gr. k-18). (CHI & ENG.). pap. 32.00 (978-957-09-1236-4(7)); (CHI & ENG.). pap. 35.00 (978-957-09-1239-5(1)); Vol. 2. (ENG &

CHI.). pap., tchr. ed. 14.95 *(978-957-09-1243-2(X))* Cheng Chung Bk. Co., Ltd. TWN. Dist: Cheng & Tsui Co.

Parnell, Declan. My Neighbor Speaks Chinese, 01 vols., 1. 2016. (Rosen REAL Readers: Social Studies Nonfiction / Fiction: Family, Community, & the World Ser.). (ENG.). 12p. (J). pap. 6.33 *(978-1-5081-1740-7(3),* Rosen Classroom) Rosen Publishing Group, Inc., The.

Peng, Tan Huay. PENG's Fun with Chinese Characters for Children: Help Your Child Learn Chinese the Fun Way! 2014. (ENG.). 144p. pap. 14.99 *(978-981-4561-14-3(2))* Marshall Cavendish International (Asia) Private Ltd. SGP. Dist: National Bk. Network.

Qing, Zheng. Find Out about China: Learn Chinese Words & Phrases & about Life in China. Hutchinson, Tim, illus. 2006. (Find Out about Bks.). (ENG.). 64p. (J). (gr. 3-18). 14.99 *(978-0-7641-5952-7(6))* Barron's Educational Series, Inc.

Reoch, Martin. Primary School Chinese: Book 3. 2013. (ENG.). 110p. pap. 22.00 *(978-0-9560526-2-9(2))* Cambridge Univ. Pr.

The Rosetta Stone Language Library: Chinese Level 2. 2005. (J). (gr. 1-18). cd-rom 239.00 *(978-1-883972-70-7(1))* Rosetta Stone Ltd.

Schumacher, Bev. Which Way? (Chinese-English) 2008. (CHI & ENG.). 20p. (J). lib. bdg. 9.95 *(978-1-935292-03-6(X))* Learning Props.

Shyu, Theresa. Bilingual Songs - English-Mandarin-Chinese, 2 vols., Vol. 1. 2009. (Bilingual Songs English Mandarin Ser.: 1). (MAN, ENG & CHI.). 48p. (J). 17.95 *(978-1-55386-107-2(8),* 1553861078) Jordan, Sara Publishing.

SISA CHINESE CULTURE CENTER, compiled by. Fun Chinese for Kids. 2004. (CHI & ENG.). 180p. 79.95 *(978-7-80052-929-0(0),* FUCHKI) Sinolingua CHN. Dist: China Books & Periodicals, Inc.

Tan, Huay Peng. Fun with Chinese Characters 1: The Straits Times Collection, 3 vols. 2003. (ENG & CHI., Illus.). 176p. 14.95 *(978-1-932457-00-1(3),* FUCHC1) China Language University Pr. CHN. Dist: China Books & Periodicals, Inc.

—Fun with Chinese Characters 2 Vol. 2: The Straits Times Collection, 3 vols., Vol. 2. 2003. (ENG & CHI., Illus.). 176p. 14.95 *(978-1-932457-01-8(1),* FUCHC2) China Language University Pr. CHN. Dist: China Books & Periodicals, Inc.

—Fun with Chinese Characters 3 Vol. 3: The Straits Times Collection, 3 vols., Vol. 3. 2003. (ENG & CHI., Illus.). 176p. 14.95 *(978-1-932457-02-5(X),* FUCHC3) People's Literature Publishing Hse. CHN. Dist: China Books & Periodicals, Inc.

Turhan, Sedat. New Bilingual Visual Dictionary (English-Chinese) 2nd ed. 2017. (New Bilingual Visual Dictionary Ser.). (ENG & CHI., Illus.). 144p. (J). (— 1). 19.95 ***(978-1-78508-883-4(1))*** Milet Publishing.

Tuttle Publishing Staff. More Chinese for Kids. 2008. (Tuttle Flash Cards Ser.). (ENG., Illus.). 1p. (J). (gr. 1-8). 19.95 *(978-0-8048-3939-6(5))* Tuttle Publishing.

—More Chinese for Kids: Traditional Character. 2008. (Tuttle Flash Cards Ser.). (ENG., Illus.). 1p. (J). (gr. 1-8). 19.95 *(978-0-8048-3938-9(7))* Tuttle Publishing.

Wu, Faye-Lynn. My First Book of Chinese Words: An ABC Rhyming Book. Padron, Aya, illus. 2013. (ENG & CHI.). 32p. (J). (gr. -1-3). 12.95 *(978-0-8048-4367-6(8))* Tuttle Publishing.

Yamin, M. & Xinying, L. Chinese Made Easy Bk. 1: Characters & Roman. 2004. (CHI & ENG.). 200p. pap., wbk. ed. 21.95 *(978-962-04-2041-2(1),* CMEW1) Joint Publishing Co. HKG. Dist: China Books & Periodicals, Inc.

Yang, Belle. A Nest in Springtime: A Bilingual Book of Numbers. Yang, Belle, illus. 2012. (CHI & ENG., Illus.). 24p. (J). (gr. k — 1). bds. 6.99 *(978-0-7636-5279-1(2))* Candlewick Pr.

Yao, Tao-chung, et al. Integrated Chinese. 2003. (CHI & ENG., Illus.). (gr. k-18). pap. 62.95 incl. audio compact disk *(978-0-88727-406-0(4))* Cheng & Tsui Co.

York, M. J. Learn Mandarin Chinese Words. Petelinsek, Kathleen, illus. 2014. (Foreign Language Basics Ser.). (ENG.). 24p. (J). (gr. 2-5). 27.07 *(978-1-62687-377-3(1),* 207124) Child's World, Inc., The.

Zeng, Sunny. Ni Hao Little Friends: Learn Chinese. 2003. (CHI & ENG.). (gr. -1-3). 24.95 *(978-0-9707332-0-7(8),* NIHALI1) Chinasprout, Inc.

—Ni Hao Little Friends 2: Chinese with Chinasprout, Vol. 2. 2003. (CHI & ENG.). (gr. -1-3). 24.95 *(978-0-9707332-4-5(0),* NIHALI2) Chinasprout, Inc.

CHIPMUNKS

Appleby, Alex. I See a Chipmunk. 2013. (In My Backyard Ser.). (Illus.). 24p. (J). (gr. k-2). pap. 8.15 *(978-1-4339-8548-5(9))*; lib. bdg. 22.60 *(978-1-4339-8547-8(0))* Stevens, Gareth Publishing LLLP.

—I See a Chipmunk: Puedo Ver una Ardilla Rayada. 2013. (In My Backyard / en Mi Jardín Ser.). (SPA & ENG., Illus.). 24p. (J). (gr. k-2). lib. bdg. 22.60 *(978-1-4339-8794-6(5))* Stevens, Gareth Publishing LLLP.

Beer, Amy-Jane. Chipmunks. 2008. (Nature's Children Ser.). (Illus.). 52p. (J). *(978-0-7172-6252-6(9))* Grolier, Ltd.

Berger, Melvin & Berger, Gilda. Chipmunks. 2010. (Illus.). 16p. (J). pap. *(978-0-545-24437-4(4))* Scholastic, Inc.

Bowman, Chris. Eastern Chipmunks. 2016. (North American Animals Ser.). (ENG., Illus.). 24p. (J). (gr. k-3). lib. bdg. 25.95 *(978-1-62617-335-4(4),* Blastoff! Readers) Bellwether Media.

Chipmunks. 2014. (ENG.). 48p. (J). lib. bdg. 28.00 *(978-0-531-20665-2(3))* Scholastic Library Publishing.

Kalman, Bobbie. Baby Chipmunks. 2010. (Fun to Learn about Baby Animals Ser.). (ENG.). 24p. (J). (gr. k-3). *(978-0-7787-4892-2(8))*; pap. *(978-0-7787-4897-7(9))* Crabtree Publishing Co.

Kalman, Bobbie, intro. Les Bébés Tamias. 2012. (FRE.). 24p. (J). pap. 9.95 *(978-2-89579-476-9(6))* Bayard Canada CAN. Dist: Crabtree Publishing Co.

O'Brien, Lindsy. Chipmunks. 2016. (Illus.). 24p. (J). *(978-1-60818-697-6(0),* Creative Education) Creative Co., The.

O'Brien, Lindsy J. Chipmunks. 2017. (In My Backyard Ser.). (ENG., Illus.). 24p. (J). (gr. 1-3). pap. 8.99 *(978-1-62832-293-4(4),* Creative Paperbacks) Creative Co., The.

Phillips, Dee. Chipmunk's Hole. 2012. (Hole Truth! Underground Animal Life Ser.). 24p. (J). (gr. -1-3). lib. bdg. 23.93 *(978-1-61772-407-7(6))* Bearport Publishing Co., Inc.

Piehl, Janet. Chattering Chipmunks. 2005. (Pull Ahead Bks.). (J). 22.60 *(978-0-8225-2420-5(1),* Lerner Pubns.) Lerner Publishing Group.

Schuh, Mari. Chipmunks. 2016. (My First Animal Library). 24p. (J). (gr. k-2). lib. bdg. 25.65 *(978-1-62031-288-9(3),* Bullfrog Bks.) Jump! Inc.

Schuh, Mari C. Chipmunks. 2015. (Backyard Animals Ser.). (ENG.). 24p. (gr. k-1). lib. bdg. 26.65 *(978-1-4914-2085-0(5),* Pebble Plus) Capstone Press of Coughlan Cos.

Sebastian, Emily. Chipmunks. 2012. (Illus.). 24p. (J). 49.50 *(978-1-4488-5059-4(2),* PowerKids Pr.); pap. 8.25 *(978-1-4488-5058-7(4),* PowerKids Pr.); lib. bdg. 22.60 *(978-1-4488-4954-3(3))* Rosen Publishing Group, Inc., The.

Sweeden, Staci. How the Chipmunk Got It's Stripes. 2004. (Reader's Theater Ser.). (J). pap. *(978-1-4108-0800-4(9))* Benchmark Education Co.

Wallace-Smith, Susan. The Chipmunk Adventure. 2011. 24p. pap. 11.32 *(978-1-4670-2473-0(2))* AuthorHouse.

Zobel, Derek. Chipmunks. 2010. (Backyard Wildlife Ser.). (ENG., Illus.). 24p. (J). (gr. k-3). lib. bdg. 25.95 *(978-1-60014-438-7(1),* Blastoff! Readers) Bellwether Media.

CHIPMUNKS—FICTION

Alvin & the Chipmunks. 2009. 64p. 4.99 *(978-0-06-184568-0(X))* HarperCollins Pubs.

Auerbach, Annie. The Squeakquel: Battle of the Bands. 2009. (Alvin & the Chipmunks Ser.). (ENG., Illus.). 24p. (J). (gr. -1-2). pap. 3.99 *(978-0-06-184565-9(5),* HarperFestival) HarperCollins Pubs.

Bailey, Arthur Scott. Sleepy-Time Tales: The Tale of Sandy Chi. 2006. pap. *(978-1-4065-0451-4(3))* Dodo Pr.

—The Tale of Sandy Chipmunk. 2004. reprint ed. pap. 1.99 *(978-1-4192-8480-9(0))*; pap. 15.95 *(978-1-4191-8480-2(6))* Kessinger Publishing, LLC.

Barclay. Chipmunk Joe Takes a Nap. 2009. 48p. pap. 11.50 *(978-1-60860-445-6(4),* Eloquent Bks.) Strategic Book Publishing & Rights Agency (SBPRA).

Berenstain, Stan & Berenstain, Jan. The Berenstain Bears & the Baby Chipmunk. Berenstain, Stan & Berenstain, Jan, illus. 2005. (I Can Read Level 1 Ser.). (ENG., Illus.). 32p. (J). (gr. k-3). pap. 3.99 *(978-0-06-058413-9(0))* HarperCollins Pubs.

Bright, J. E. Chipwrecked: Brittany Speaks! 2011. (Alvin & the Chipmunks Ser.). (ENG.). 24p. (J). (gr. -1-2). pap. 3.99 *(978-0-06-211907-0(9),* HarperFestival) HarperCollins Pubs.

—Chipwrecked: Castaway Critters. 2011. (Alvin & the Chipmunks Ser.). (ENG.). 24p. (J). (gr. -1-2). pap. 3.99 *(978-0-06-208655-6(3),* HarperFestival) HarperCollins Pubs.

—Chipwrecked: Too Cool for Rules. 2011. (I Can Read Level 2 Ser.). (ENG.). 32p. (J). (gr. k-3). pap. 3.99 *(978-0-06-208602-0(2))* HarperCollins Pubs.

Cole, Henry. Bayberry Island. Cole, Henry, illus. 2017. (Brambleheart Ser.: 2). (Illus.). 176p. (J). (gr. 3-7). 16.99 *(978-0-06-224551-9(1),* Tegen, Katherine Bks) HarperCollins Pubs.

—Brambleheart. Cole, Henry, illus. 2016. (Brambleheart Ser.: 1). (Illus.). 272p. (J). (gr. 3-7). 16.99 *(978-0-06-224546-5(5))* HarperCollins Pubs.

Finn, Perdita & HarperCollins Publishers Ltd. Staff. Alvin & the Chipmunks - The Squeakquel. 2009. (Alvin & the Chipmunks Ser.). (ENG., Illus.). 144p. (J). (gr. 3-7). pap. 5.99 *(978-0-06-184569-7(8),* HarperFestival) HarperCollins Pubs.

Frame, Andrew Graham. Ein Stein: The Chipmunk Who Became an Engineer. 2011. 32p. pap. 13.95 *(978-1-61204-009-7(8),* Eloquent Bks.) Strategic Book Publishing & Rights Agency (SBPRA).

—Ein Stein: The Chipmunk Who Succeeds by Brain Power. 2011. 52p. pap. 19.50 *(978-1-61204-416-3(6),* Strategic Bk. Publishing) Strategic Book Publishing & Rights Agency (SBPRA).

Gorbachev, Valeri. Me Too! Gorbachev, Valeri, illus. 2014. (I Like to Read(r) Ser.). (ENG., Illus.). 24p. (J). (gr. -1-3). 6.99 *(978-0-8234-3179-3(7))* Holiday Hse., Inc.

—Me Too! 2013. (I Like to Read(r) Ser.). (ENG., Illus.). 24p. (J). (gr. -1-3). 14.95 *(978-0-8234-2744-4(7))* Holiday Hse., Inc.

—Not Me! Gorbachev, Valeri, illus. 2016. (ENG., Illus.). 24p. (J). 14.95 *(978-0-8234-3546-3(6))*; pap. 6.99 *(978-0-8234-3547-0(4))* Holiday Hse., Inc.

Grossnickle, Mary. A Place in My Heart. Relyea, Alison, illus. 2014. (ENG.). 36p. 15.95 *(978-1-84905-771-4(0),* 3958) Kingsley, Jessica Pubs. GBR. Dist: Macmillan Distribution Ltd.

Harber Freeman, Anna. Love You More Than Anything. Henry, Jed, illus. 2014. (Snuggle Time Stories Ser.). (ENG.). 24p. (J). (gr. -1-k). 9.95 *(978-1-4549-0021-4(0))* Sterling Publishing Co., Inc.

Hayes, J. B. Freddy the Frog's First Christmas. 2012. 44p. pap. 21.99 *(978-1-4772-2870-8(5))* AuthorHouse.

Huang, Yu-Hsuan, illus. Baby Chipmunk: Finger Puppet Book. 2017. (ENG.). 12p. (J). (gr. -1 — 1). bds. 6.99 *(978-1-4521-5612-5(3))* Chronicle Bks. LLC.

Huelin, Jodi. Alvin & the Chipmunks: Alvin & the Big Art Show. Artful Doodlers Limited Staff, illus. 2013. (I Can Read Level 2 Ser.). (ENG.). 32p. (J). (gr. -1-3). pap. 3.99 *(978-0-06-225225-8(9),* HarperFestival) HarperCollins Pubs.

—Alvin & the Chipmunks: Alvin & the Substitute Teacher. Artful Doodlers Limited Staff, illus. 2013. (I Can Read Level 2 Ser.). (ENG.). 32p. (J). (gr. -1-3). pap. 3.99 *(978-0-06-225223-4(2),* HarperFestival) HarperCollins Pubs.

—Alvin & the Chipmunks: Alvin's Easter Break. Artful Doodlers Limited Staff & Carzon, Walter, illus. 2014. (ENG.). 24p. (J). (gr. -1-3). pap. 3.99 *(978-0-06-225222-7(4),* HarperFestival) HarperCollins Pubs.

—The Reason for the Season. Artful Doodlers Ltd Staff, illus. 2013. (Alvin & the Chipmunks Ser.). (ENG.). 24p. (J). (gr. -1-3). pap. 4.99 *(978-0-06-225221-0(6),* HarperFestival) HarperCollins Pubs.

Kirk, Trish. I Think There's a Bear Out There. 2009. 36p. pap. 16.99 *(978-1-4389-6097-5(2))* AuthorHouse.

Martin, Martha M. Chipper, the Heroic Chipmunk. Matzen, Deon C., illus. 2004. 32p. (J). (gr. -1-3). 16.95 *(978-0-9758580-0-4(9))* M & B Publishing.

Mayer, Kirsten. Alvin & the Chipmunks: Alvin Gets an A. Rogers, Jacqueline, illus. 2012. (I Can Read Level 2 Ser.). (ENG.). 32p. (J). (gr. -1-3). pap. 3.99 *(978-0-06-208603-7(0))* HarperCollins Pubs.

—A Chipmunk Valentine. 2011. (Alvin & the Chipmunks Ser.). (ENG.). 24p. (J). (gr. -1-3). pap. 3.99 *(978-0-06-208654-9(5),* HarperFestival) HarperCollins Pubs.

Michalak, Jamie. Larry & Rita. Newton, Jill, illus. 2007. (Brand New Readers Ser.). (ENG.). 48p. (J). (gr. -1-3). 14.99 *(978-0-7636-2963-2(4))* Candlewick Pr.

Middleton, William. The Chipmunk Jamboree. 2013. 24p. pap. 12.45 *(978-1-4624-0669-2(6),* Inspiring Voices) Author Solutions, Inc.

Miller, Kathy M. Chippy Chipmunk Parties in the Garden. Miller, Kathy M., photos by. 2009. (ENG., Illus.). 40p. (gr. 2-3). 19.95 *(978-0-9840893-0-7(6))* Celtic Sunrise.

Nana B. & Brittany. Forest Friends of Maine: The Chipmunks Have an Argument. 2010. 16p. pap. 8.49 *(978-1-4490-0647-1(7))* AuthorHouse.

Piehl, Janet. Chattering Chipmunks. 2005. (Pull Ahead Bks.). (Illus.). 32p. (J). (gr. k-2). per. 5.95 *(978-0-8225-2439-7(2))* Lerner Publishing Group.

Pinkney, Jerry. Twinkle, Twinkle, Little Star. 2016. (ENG., Illus.). 30p. (gr. -1 — 1). bds. 7.99 *(978-0-316-40693-2(7))* Little, Brown Bks. for Young Readers.

Rosen, Lucy, et al. The Squeakquel: Meet the 'Munks. 2009. (I Can Read Level 2 Ser.). (ENG., Illus.). 32p. (J). (gr. k-3). pap. 3.99 *(978-0-06-184566-6(3))* HarperCollins Pubs.

Rylant, Cynthia. Thimbleberry Stories. Kneen, Maggie, illus. 2006. (ENG.). 64p. (J). (gr. -1-3). reprint ed. pap. 8.99 *(978-0-15-205645-2(9))* Houghton Mifflin Harcourt Publishing Co.

Sauer, Tammi. Oh, Nuts! Krall, Dan, illus. 2012. (ENG.). 32p. (J). 17.89 *(978-1-59990-467-2(5),* 9781599904672); (gr. -1-6). 16.99 *(978-1-59990-466-5(7),* 9781599904665) Bloomsbury Publishing USA. (Bloomsbury USA Childrens).

Schade, Susan. Simon's Dream. Buller, Jon, illus. 2009. (Fog Mound Ser.: 3). (ENG.). 208p. (J). (gr. 3-7). pap. 12.99 *(978-0-689-87689-9(0),* Aladdin) Simon & Schuster Children's Publishing.

—Travels of Thelonious. Buller, Jon, illus. 2007. (Fog Mound Ser.: 1). (ENG.). 224p. (J). (gr. 3-7). pap. 11.99 *(978-0-689-87685-1(8),* Aladdin) Simon & Schuster Children's Publishing.

Schade, Susan & Buller, Jon. Faradawn. 2008. (Fog Mound Ser.: 2). (ENG., Illus.). 208p. (J). (gr. 3-7). pap. 12.99 *(978-0-689-87687-5(4),* Aladdin) Simon & Schuster Children's Publishing.

Scholastic, Inc. Staff & Howard, Kate. The Road Chip. 2015. (Alvin & the Chipmunks Ser.). (ENG.). 144p. (J). (gr. 2-5). pap. 5.99 *(978-0-545-93433-6(8))* Scholastic, Inc.

Schories, Pat. Jack Wants a Snack. 2008. (Jacks Ser.). (ENG.). 32p. (J). (gr. -1-1). 13.95 *(978-1-59078-546-1(0),* Front Street) Boyds Mills Pr.

Schories, Pat, illus. Jack Wants a Snack. 2015. (Jack Bks.). (ENG.). 32p. (J). (— 1). bds. 7.99 *(978-1-62979-406-8(6))* Boyds Mills Pr.

Sherrow, Victoria. Chipmunk at Hollow Tree Lane. Davis, Allen, illus. 2011. (Smithsonian's Backyard Ser.). (ENG.). 32p. (J). (gr. -1-3). 8.95 *(978-1-60727-635-7(6))*; 19.95 *(978-1-60727-634-0(8))* Soundprints.

Smith, Nicole. Chad the Allergic Chipmunk: A Children's Story of Nut Allergies. 2006. (Illus.). (J). per. 11.95 *(978-1-58628-054-3(6))* Allergic Child Publishing Group.

Smith, Sindy. Charlie the Chipmunk & the Lost Goldmine. Smith, Sindy, illus. 2012. (Illus.). 38p. 29.95 *(978-1-4626-9865-3(4))* America Star Bks.

—Charlie the Chipmunk & the Lost Goldmine. 2012. 40p. pap. 24.95 *(978-1-4626-8590-5(0))* America Star Bks.

Stevenski, Linda. Chetty T Chipmunk's Journey to Aunt Ella's. 2010. 24p. (J). pap. 12.99 *(978-1-4490-5448-9(X))* AuthorHouse.

Sullivan, Lauren M. & Lewis, Samantha. Chipwrecked. 2011. (Alvin & the Chipmunks Ser.). (ENG.). 12p. (J). (gr. -1-3). pap. 6.99 *(978-0-06-208656-3(1),* HarperFestival) HarperCollins Pubs.

Sweeden, Staci. Como la ardilla listada obruvo sus marcas & How the Chipmunk Got Its Stripes. 2005. spiral bd. 76.00 *(978-1-4108-5788-0(3))* Benchmark Education Co.

Vojtech, Anna. Surprise in the Meadow. Vojtech, Anna, illus. 2016. (ENG., Illus.). 32p. (J). 16.95 *(978-0-8234-3556-2(3))* Holiday Hse., Inc.

Vollmer, Howard R. Adventures of the Chipmunks Three. 2011. 60p. pap. 24.95 *(978-1-4567-3240-0(4))* AuthorHouse.

Windhorst, Brenda. Do You Want a Henry Story? 2011. 24p. pap. 15.99 *(978-1-4628-8796-5(1))* Xlibris Corp.

CHISHOLM, SHIRLEY, 1924-2005

Jackson, Garnet N. Shirley Chisholm, Congresswoman. 2012. (ENG., Illus.). (J). (gr. 1-4). pap. 7.47 net. *(978-0-8136-5247-4(2),* Modern Curriculum Pr.) Pearson Schl.

Raatma, Lucia. Shirley Chisholm. 2010. (Leading Women Ser.). 96p. (YA). (gr. 7-12). 39.93 *(978-0-7614-4953-9(1))* Marshall Cavendish Corp.

CHISHOLM TRAIL—FICTION

Dutton, Stella. Pinto the Chisholm Pony: 150th Chisholm Trail Edition. anniv. collector's ed. 2017. (ENG., Illus.). 62p. (J). (gr. -1-6). 39.99 *(978-0-9790832-9-7(X))* 405 Pubns.

CHIVALRY

see also Arthur, King; Civilization, Medieval; Crusades; Feudalism; Heraldry; Knights and Knighthood

Hopkins, Andrea. A Day in the Life of a Knight. 2009. (Day in the Life Ser.). 32p. (gr. 4-5). 47.90 *(978-1-61511-004-9(6),* PowerKids Pr.) Rosen Publishing Group, Inc., The.

Lee, Adrienne. Knights, 1 vol. Martin, Cynthia, illus. 2013. (Legendary Warriors Ser.). (ENG.). 32p. (gr. 1-2). 26.65 *(978-1-4765-3115-1(3),* Blazers) Capstone Press of Coughlan Cos.

Macdonald, Fiona. The Medieval Chronicles: Vikings, Knights, & Castles. Antram, David, illus. 2013. 92p. (J). *(978-1-4351-5067-6(8))* Barnes & Noble, Inc.

O'Brien, Cynthia. Your Guide to Knights & the Age of Chivalry. 2017. (Destination: Middle Ages Ser.). (ENG., Illus.). 32p. (J). ***(978-0-7787-2992-1(3))***; pap. ***(978-0-7787-2998-3(2))*** Crabtree Publishing Co.

West, David. Lots of Things You Want to Know about Knights: ... & Some You Don't! 2015. (Lots of Things You Want to Know About Ser.). (Illus.). 24p. (J). 28.50 *(978-1-62588-091-8(X))* Black Rabbit Bks.

CHIVALRY—FICTION

Greenwood, Grace. Stories from Famous Ballads for Children by Grace Greenwood [Pseud] with Illustrations by Billings. 2006. 160p. per. 18.99 *(978-1-4255-1221-7(6))* Michigan Publishing.

Oceanak, Karla. Kerfuffle: An Aldo Zelnick Comic Novel. Spanjer, Kendra, illus. 2016. (Aldo Zelnick Comic Novel Ser.: 11). (ENG.). 160p. (J). (gr. 1-8). pap. 8.95 *(978-1-934649-75-6(9))* Bailiwick Pr.

CHOCOLATE

see also Cocoa

Best, B. J. Cocoa to Chocolate. 2016. (How It Is Made Ser.). 24p. (J). pap. 8.22 *(978-1-5026-2130-6(4))* Cavendish Square Publishing.

Chocolate! Individual Title Six-Packs. (Action Packs Ser.). 120p. (gr. 3-5). 44.00 *(978-0-7635-8427-6(4))* Rigby Education.

Cooper, Sharon Katz. Milton Hershey's Sweet Idea: A Chocolate Kingdom. Lokus, Rex & Sánchez, Alvaro Iglesias, illus. 2015. (Story Behind the Name Ser.). (ENG.). 32p. (gr. 2-3). lib. bdg. 28.65 *(978-1-4795-7137-6(7))* Picture Window Bks.

Crump, A. K., ed. Chocolate French: Recipes, Language, & Directions to Francais Au Chocolat. 2004. (Illus.). 192p. (gr. 10). pap. *(978-0-9674898-4-1(9))* Temmen, Edition, Horst Temmen.

de Las Casas, Dianne. Blue Frog: The Legend of Chocolate, 1 vol. Stone-Barker, Holly, illus. 2011. (ENG.). 32p. (J). (gr. k-3). 16.99 *(978-1-4556-1459-2(9))* Pelican Publishing Co., Inc.

Frydenborg, Kay. Chocolate: Sweet Science & Dark Secrets of the World's Favorite Treat. 2015. (ENG., Illus.). 256p. (YA). (gr. 7). 18.99 *(978-0-544-17566-2(2),* HMH Books For Young Readers) Houghton Mifflin Harcourt Publishing Co.

Giulieri, Anne. Chocolate Banana Pops, 1 vol. Kreinberg, Sylvia, photos by. 2012. (Engage Literacy Yellow Ser.). (ENG., Illus.). 32p. (gr. k-2). pap. 5.99 *(978-1-4296-8836-9(X),* Engage Literacy) Capstone Press of Coughlan Cos.

Heos, Bridget. From Cocoa Beans to Chocolate. Coleman, Stephanie Fizer, illus. 2017. (Who Made My Lunch? Ser.). (ENG.). 24p. (gr. 1-4). 20.95 ***(978-1-68151-120-7(7))*** Amicus Publishing.

Herrington, Lisa M. Beans to Chocolate. 2013. (Rookie Read-About(r) Science Ser.). (ENG.). 32p. (J). pap. 5.95 *(978-0-531-24707-5(4))*; lib. bdg. 23.00 *(978-0-531-24741-9(4))* Scholastic Library Publishing.

Llewellyn, Claire. How Chocolate Is Made Turquoise Band. 2016. (Cambridge Reading Adventures Ser.). (ENG.). 24p. pap. 7.19 *(978-1-107-57616-2(4))* Cambridge Univ. Pr.

MacLeod, Elizabeth. Chock Full of Chocolate. Bradford, June, illus. 2005. (Kids Can Do It Ser.). (ENG.). 40p. (J). (gr. 3-7). 6.95 *(978-1-55337-763-4(X))* Kids Can Pr., Ltd. CAN. Dist: Hachette Bk. Group.

Malam, John. Journey of a Bar of Chocolate, 1 vol. 2012. (Journey of A... Ser.). (ENG.). 32p. (gr. 1-3). pap. 8.29 *(978-1-4329-6609-6(X))*; lib. bdg. 27.32 *(978-1-4329-6602-7(2))* Heinemann-Raintree. (Heinemann First Library).

Markle, Sandra. Chocolate: A Sweet History. Harper, Charise Mericle, illus. 2004. (Smart about History Ser.). (ENG.). 32p. (J). (gr. k-4). mass mkt. 5.99 *(978-0-448-43480-3(6),* Grosset & Dunlap) Penguin Young Readers Group.

Mattern, Joanne. The Mars Family: M&M Mars Candy Makers, 1 vol. 2011. (Food Dudes Ser.). (ENG., Illus.). 32p. (YA). (gr. 3-6). 27.07 *(978-1-61613-560-7(3))* ABDO Publishing Co.

—Milton Hershey: Hershey's Chocolate Creator, 1 vol. 2011. (Food Dudes Ser.). (ENG., Illus.). 32p. (J). (gr. 3-6). 27.07 *(978-1-61613-557-7(3))* ABDO Publishing Co.

McKinley, Herald P. Turning Beans into Chocolate. 2014. (Step-By-Step Transformations Ser.). 24p. (J). (gr. k-2). 24.21 *(978-1-62713-004-2(7))* Cavendish Square Publishing.

Morganelli, Adrianna. The Biography of Chocolate. 2005. (How did That Get There? Ser.). (ENG., Illus.). 32p. (J). (gr. 4-5). pap. *(978-0-7787-2517-6(0))* Crabtree Publishing Co.

Nelson, Robin. From Cocoa Bean to Chocolate. (Illus.). 24p. (gr. k-3). 2012. (Start to Finish, Second Series: Food Ser.: No. 2). (ENG.). pap. 6.95 *(978-1-58013-965-6(5))* 2012. (Start to Finish, Second Series: Food Ser.: No. 2). (ENG., lib. bdg. 23.93 *(978-0-7613-6560-0(5),* Lerner Pubns.) 2003. (Start to Finish Ser.). (J). lib. bdg. 18.60 *(978-0-8225-4665-8(5))* Lerner Publishing Group.

Newquist, H. P. The Book of Chocolate: The Amazing Story of the World's Favorite Candy. 2017. (ENG.). 160p. (J). (gr. 3-7). 17.99 *(978-0-670-01574-0(1),* Viking Books for Young Readers) Penguin Young Readers Group.

O'Donnell, Kerri. How Chocolate Is Made: From Natural Resource to Finished Product. 2009. (Real Life Readers Ser.). 24p. (gr. 3-4). pap. 8.25 *(978-1-4358-0227-8(6),* Rosen Classroom) Rosen Publishing Group, Inc., The.

Pellaton, Karen E., illus. The Official M&M's(r) Brand History of Chocolate. 2004. 32p. (J). (gr. 1-9). 16.95 *(978-1-57091-448-5(6))*; pap. 6.95 *(978-1-57091-449-2(4))* Charlesbridge Publishing, Inc.

Pirotta, Saviour. Chocolate. 2003. (Starters Ser.). 24p. (J). lib. bdg. 21.35 *(978-1-58340-264-1(0))* Black Rabbit Bks.

Polin, C. J. & Dorling Kindersley Publishing Staff. The Story of Chocolate. 2005. (DK Readers Ser.). (ENG.). 48p. (J). (gr. 2-4). pap. 3.99 *(978-0-7566-0992-4(5),* DK Children) Dorling Kindersley Publishing, Inc.

Sánchez, Lucía M. & Taylor, Trace. Chocolate (Spanish) Taylor, Trace, illus. 2012. (2G Necesidades Ser.). (SPA., Illus.). 24p. (J). pap. 6.99 *(978-1-61406-170-0(X))* American Reading Co.

Spielman, Madison. Make It Chocolate, 1 vol. 2nd rev. ed. 2014. (TIME for KIDS(r) Nonfiction Readers Ser.). (ENG., Illus.). 28p. (J). (gr. 2-2). pap. 23.96 *(978-1-4807-1048-1(2))* Shell Educational Publishing.

—Make It - Chocolate, 1 vol. 2nd rev. ed. 2011. (Nonfiction Readers Ser.). (ENG.). 28p. (J). (gr. 2-2). pap. 6.99 *(978-1-4333-3621-8(9))* Teacher Created Materials, Inc.

Stewart, Melissa & Young, Allen M. No Monkeys, No Chocolate. Wong, Nicole, illus. 2013. (ENG.). 32p. (J). (gr. k-3). 16.95 *(978-1-58089-287-2(6))* Charlesbridge Publishing, Inc.

Vaughn, Inés. Chocolate. 2009. (Native Foods of Latin America / Alimentos indígenas de Latino América Ser.).

C D

(ENG & SPA.). 24p. (gr. 2-3). 42.50 (978-1-61514-796-0(9), Editorial Buenas Letras); (SPA & ENG.). (J). 22.60 (978-1-4358-2726-4(0), PowerKids Pr.) Rosen Publishing Group, Inc., The.

Walker, Kathryn. See How Cats Grow. 2009. (See How They Grow Ser.). (SPA & ENG., Illus.). 24p. (J). (gr. k-3). pap. 8.25 (978-1-4358-2875-9(5), PowerKids Pr.) Rosen Publishing Group, Inc., The.

Woolf, Alex. The Story of Chocolate. 2016. (Story of Food Ser.). (ENG., Illus.). 32p. (J). (gr. 4-6). 16.99 (978-0-7502-9659-5(3), Wayland) Hachette Children's Group GBR. Dist: Hachette Bk. Group.

CHOICE OF BOOKS

see Books and Reading

CHOICE OF PROFESSION

see Vocational Guidance

CHOIRBOYS—FICTION

van de Ruit, John. Spud. 2005. 300p. pap. (978-0-14-302484-2(1)) Penguin Publishing Group.

—Spud. 2008. (ENG.). 336p. (YA). (gr. 7-18). 9.99 (978-1-59514-187-3(1), Razorbill) Penguin Young Readers Group.

Van De Ruit, John. Spud - The Madness Continues. 2009. (ENG.). 352p. (YA). (gr. 7-18). 9.99 (978-1-59514-245-0(2), Razorbill) Penguin Young Readers Group.

CHOPIN, FREDERIC, 1810-1849

Aljure, Luis Carlos. Frédéric Chopin -el Espíritu de la Música. 2005. (SPA.). 116p. (YA). (978-958-30-1722-3(1)) Panamericana Editorial.

Malaspina, Ann. Chopin's World. 2009. (Music Throughout History Ser.). 64p. (gr. 5-6). 58.50 (978-1-61514-683-3(0), Rosen Reference) Rosen Publishing Group, Inc., The.

Summerer, Eric Michael. Frederic Chopin. 2006. (Primary Source Library of Famous Composers Ser.). (Illus.). 32p. (J). (gr. -1-3). lib. bdg. 23.95 (978-1-4042-2769-9(5), PowerKids Pr.) Rosen Publishing Group, Inc., The.

—Frédéric Chopin. 2009. (Primary Source Library of Famous Composers Ser.). 32p. (gr. 4-4). 42.50 (978-1-60854-108-9(8), PowerKids Pr.) Rosen Publishing Group, Inc., The.

Venezia, Mike. Frederic Chopin (Revised Edition) 2017. (Getting to Know the World's Greatest Composers Ser.). (ENG.). 40p. (J). pap. 7.95 **(978-0-531-23035-0(X))**; lib. bdg. 29.00 **(978-0-531-22657-5(3))** Scholastic Library Publishing. (Children's Pr.).

Weill, Catherine. Frédéric Chopin. 2010. (Descubrimos a Los Músicos Ser.). (SPA., Illus.). 24p. (J). (gr. 2-4). 15.95 (978-84-9825-414-3(0)) Combel Editorial, S.A. ESP. Dist: Independent Pubs. Group.

Wheeler, Opal. Frederic Chopin, Son of Poland Later Years. Price, Christine, illus. 2007. 160p. (J). per. 12.95 (978-1-933573-09-0(0), 4717) Zeezok Publishing, LLC.

Wheeler, Opal. Frederic Chopin, Son of Poland, Early Years. Price, Christine, illus. 2007. 160p. (J). per. 12.95 (978-1-933573-11-3(2), 4716) Zeezok Publishing, LLC.

Whiting, Jim. The Life & Times of Frederic Chopin. 2004. (Masters of Music Ser.). (Illus.). 48p. (gr. 4-8). lib. bdg. 20.95 (978-1-58415-245-3(1)) Mitchell Lane Pubs., Inc.

Wilcox, Judy. Ferderic Chopin, Son of Poland, Early & Later Years Study Guide. 2007. (Illus.). 40p. (J). 9.95 (978-1-933573-12-0(0), 4718) Zeezok Publishing, LLC.

CHOREOGRAPHY

see Ballet; Dance

CHRIST

see Jesus Christ

CHRISTENING

see Baptism

CHRISTIAN ART AND SYMBOLISM

see also Bible—Pictorial Works; Church Architecture; Jesus Christ—Art

also subdivision Art under various subjects, e.g. Jesus Christ—Art

Jones, Lois S. The Development of Christian Symbolism, 4 vols.; set. Jones, Preston, ed. Date not set. (Development of Christian Symbolism Ser.). (YA). (gr. 10-12). pap. incl. VHS (978-1-882238-01-9(X)) Swan-Jones Production.

Nielsen, Pamela & Luhmann, Edward Q. Behold the Lamb: An Introduction to the Signs & Symbols of the Church. Kirchhoff, Art, illus. 2010. 48p. (J). 9.99 (978-0-7586-1550-3(7)) Concordia Publishing Hse.

Senker, Cath. Christianity: Signs, Symbols, Stories. 2009. (Religious Signs, Symbols, & Stories Ser.). (Illus.). 32p. (J). (ENG.). pap. 10.00 (978-1-4358-3045-5(8)); lib. bdg. 25.25 (978-1-4358-3037-0(7)) Rosen Publishing Group, Inc., The. (PowerKids Pr.).

CHRISTIAN BIOGRAPHY

see also Apostles; Clergy; Missionaries; Monasticism and Religious Orders; Pilgrims (New Plymouth Colony); Popes; Saints

Asim, Jabari. Preaching to the Chickens: The Story of Young John Lewis. Lewis, E. B., illus. 2016. (ENG.). 32p. (J). (gr. k-3). 17.99 (978-0-399-16856-7(7), Nancy Paulsen Books) Penguin Young Readers Group.

Benge, Janet & Benge, Geoff. Christian Heroes - Then & Now - Clarence Jones: Mr. Radio. 2005. (Christian Heroes Ser.). (ENG.). 200p. (YA). (gr. 4-7). pap. 9.99 (978-1-57658-343-2(0)) YWAM Publishing.

—Christian Heroes - Then & Now - Count Zinzendorf: First Fruit. 2006. (Christian Heroes Ser.). (ENG.). 183p. (YA). (gr. 5). pap. 9.99 (978-1-57658-262-6(0)) YWAM Publishing.

—Christian Heroes - Then & Now - Rachel Saint: A Star in the Jungle. 2004. (Christian Heroes Ser.). (ENG., Illus.). 208p. (YA). (gr. 4-7). pap. 9.99 (978-1-57658-337-1(6)) YWAM Publishing.

—Heroes Cristianos de Ayer y de Hoy - Buenas nuevas en todas las Lenguas: Cameron Townsend. 2004. Tr. of Christian Heroes: Then & Now - Cameron Townsend. (SPA.). 208p. pap. 6.99 (978-1-57658-308-1(2)) YWAM Publishing.

—Heroes Cristianos de Ayer y de Hoy - Peligro en la Selva: La Vida de Nate Saint. Editorial JUCUM, tr. 2005. (Heroes Cristianos de Ayer y Hoy Ser.). Tr. of Christian Heroes - Then & Now - Nate Saint. (SPA.). 189p. per. 6.99 (978-1-57658-317-3(1)) YWAM Publishing.

—Heroes Cristianos de Ayer y de Hoy - Persecucion en Holanda: La Vida de Corrie Ten Boom. 2005. (Christian Heroes Ser.). (SPA.). 208p. per. 6.99 (978-1-57658-338-8(4)) YWAM Publishing.

Bert, Ruth J. Everyone Called Her Sister Sarah. Westbeld, Kristine, illus. 2004. (ENG.). 32p. (J). (gr. -1-3). pap. 4.99 (978-1-928915-62-1(0)) Evangel Publishing Hse.

Bingham, Derick. Michael Faraday: Spiritual Dynamo. 2010. (Trailblazers Ser.). (ENG.). 176p. (J). pap. 8.99 (978-1-84550-156-3(X), 6da8f6db-c74f-4245-818d-6fca339103d3) Christian Focus Pubns. GBR. Dist: Bookmasters Distribution.

Bobb, Barry L. Hero of Faith - Johann Sebastian Bach. 2011. 64p. pap. 7.99 (978-0-7586-2829-9(3)) Concordia Publishing Hse.

C. S. Lewis. 2nd rev. ed. 2010. (Who Wrote That? Ser.). (Illus.). 136p. (gr. 6-12). 35.00 (978-1-60413-725-5(8), Chelsea Hse.) Facts On File, Inc.

C. S. Lewis: Twentieth Century Pilgrim. 2011. (World Writers Ser.). 128p. (gr. 7-9). lib. bdg. 28.95 (978-1-59935-112-4(9)) Reynolds, Morgan Inc.

Carolyn, Berg. Jesus Walks Away. Paris, Pat, illus. 2003. (Arch Bks.). 16p. (J). 2.49 (978-0-7586-0504-7(8)) Concordia Publishing Hse.

Carr, Simonetta. Augustine of Hippo. Lowe, Wes, illus. 2009. (ENG.). 62p. (J). 18.00 (978-1-60178-073-7(7)) Reformation Heritage Bks.

Dickens, Charles. The Life of Our Lord: Illustrated 200th Anniversary Edition. Dewey, Simon, illus. 2012. 17.99 (978-1-60907-185-1(9), Shadow Mountain) Shadow Mountain Publishing.

Dredge, Kath. Living 4 God: Learning from the Lives of William Tyndale, John Newton, David Brainerd, Eric Liddell. 2007. (Illus.). 80p. 7.00 (978-1-84625-034-7(X)) DayOne Pubns. GBR. Dist: Send The Light Distribution LLC.

Eddy, Susan. Mother Teresa. 2004. (Rookie Biographies Ser.). (ENG., Illus.). 32p. (J). (gr. 1-2). pap. 4.95 (978-0-516-27922-0(X), Children's Pr.) Scholastic Library Publishing.

Evangelical Press Staff & Scrimshire, Hazel. God's Little Giants: A Colouring Book. 2006. (Bible Art Ser.). (ENG.). 16p. (J). (gr. -1-3). pap., act. bk. ed. 1.99 (978-1-85792-306-3(5), a3f4817e-60d0-4585-b346-79ee9a9b7583) Christian Focus Pubns. GBR. Dist: Bookmasters Distribution.

Ferry, Therese. Feed My Lambs. 2014. (ENG.). 64p. (J). pap. 20.00 (978-1-78218-116-3(4)) Columba Pr. IRL. Dist: Dufour Editions, Inc.

Finlayson, Linda. Adventure & Faith: Volume 1. 2009. (Risktakers Ser.). (ENG., Illus.). 128p. (J). 8.99 (978-1-84550-491-5(7), 6cf822a4-86bc-44b2-afb7-4dd13268f24c) Christian Focus Pubns. GBR. Dist: Bookmasters Distribution.

Fowler, Ethan & Fowler, Mardene. Brushed Back: The Story of Trevor Bullock. 2009. 189p. (YA). pap. 14.99 (978-0-8280-2420-4(0)) Review & Herald Publishing Assn.

Gabourel, Harriet. True to Her Faith: A Story of France at the Time of the Huguenots. 2006. (ENG., Illus.). 224p. (J). per. 7.99 (978-1-84550-220-1(5), 9d879b33-bec0-477a-a976-afb79bfae58a) Christian Focus Pubns. GBR. Dist: Bookmasters Distribution.

Giraldo, Maria Loretta. Saints & Their Stories. Moran, Margaret Edward, tr. Bertelle, Nicoletta, illus. 2010. Tr. of I Santi: i miei primi Amici. 168p. (J). (gr. 2-5). 19.95 (978-0-8198-7134-3(6)) Pauline Bks. & Media.

Gormley, Beatrice. C. S. Lewis: The Man Behind Narnia. 2nd ed. 2005. (ENG., Illus.). 192p. (gr. 8-12). per. 14.00 (978-0-8028-5301-1(3), Eerdmans Bks For Young Readers) Eerdmans, William B. Publishing Co.

Granfield, Linda. Amazing Grace: The Story of the Hymn. braille ed. 2004. (Illus.). (J). (gr. 2-4). spiral bd. (978-0-616-01661-9(1)) Canadian National Institute for the Blind/Institut National Canadien pour les Aveugles.

Grube, George. The Church Fathers for Young People. Thomas, Michael, illus. 2007. (ENG.). 35p. (J). pap. 7.95 (978-1-933654-07-2(4)) Light & Life Publishing Co.

Hall, Ron & Moore, Denver. Same Kind of Different As Me for Kids, 1 vol. 2017. (ENG., Illus.). 32p. (J). 14.99 (978-0-7180-9179-8(5)) Nelson, Thomas Inc.

Hamilton, Bethany & Bundschuh, Rick. Soul Surfer: A True Story of Faith, Family, & Fighting to Get Back on the Board. 2006. (ENG., Illus.). 240p. pap. 15.00 (978-1-4165-0346-0(3), MTV Bks.) MTV Books.

Hartzler, Aaron. Rapture Practice: A True Story about Growing up Gay in an Evangelical Family. 2014. (ENG.). 416p. (YA). (gr. 10-17). pap. 11.99 (978-0-316-09464-1(1)) Little, Brown Bks. for Young Readers.

Here's My Heart Lord. 2003. (YA). per. (978-1-55630-522-1(2)) Brentwood Communications Group.

Hovland, Stephenie M. Heinrich Melchior Muhlenberg. Johnson, Larry, illus. 2012. (Hero of Faith Ser.). (ENG.). 58p. (J). pap. 7.99 (978-0-7586-3076-6(X)) Concordia Publishing Hse.

Howat, Irene. George Müller: The Children's Champion. 2013. (Trailblazers Ser.). (ENG.). 176p. (J). (gr. 4-7). pap. 8.99 (978-1-85792-549-4(1), 9781857925494) Christian Focus Pubns. GBR. Dist: Bookmasters Distribution.

—Ten Boys Who Used Their Talents. 2012. (Lightkeepers Ser.). (ENG., Illus.). 160p. (J). (gr. 3-7). per. 8.99 (978-1-84550-146-4(2), cd5b19a1-cb3e-4f1d-a5bc-00dec664cd78) Christian Focus Pubns. GBR. Dist: Bookmasters Distribution.

—Ten Girls Who Used Their Talents. 2014. (Lightkeepers Ser.). (ENG., Illus.). 160p. (J). (gr. 3-7). per. 8.99 (978-1-84550-147-1(0), de728062-6bc3-4bf7-87b9-a97ebd0810fb) Christian Focus Pubns. GBR. Dist: Bookmasters Distribution.

Hyde, Katherine. Lucia: Saint of Light. 2009. 32p. 18.50 (978-0-9822770-4-1(0)) Ancient Faith Publishing.

Kent, Deborah. Dorothy Day: Friend to the Forgotten. 2004. (Illus.). 187p. (J). pap. 12.00 (978-0-8028-5265-6(3)) Eerdmans, William B. Publishing Co.

Latham, Frank. Jed Smith: Trail Blazer of the West. McHugh, Michael J., ed. Murch, Frank, illus. 2003. 121p. pap. 6.95 (978-1-930367-86-9(4)) Christian Liberty Pr.

Liardon, Roberts & Goldberg, Olly. God's Generals for Kids, Volume 3: John Alexander Dowie. 2014. (ENG., Illus.). 176p. (J). (gr. 4-7). pap. 11.99 (978-1-61036-118-7(0)) Bridge-Logos, Inc.

MacKenzie, Catherine. Amy Carmichael - Can Brown Eyes Be Made Blue? Ammassari, Rita, illus. 2011. (Little Lights Ser.). (ENG.). 24p. (J). (gr. -1-2). 7.99 (978-1-84550-108-2(X), 91ca3a79-be4d-488e-9c3f-283c9f77bf68) Christian Focus Pubns. GBR. Dist: Bookmasters Distribution.

—Corrie Ten Boo - Are All of the Watches Safe? Ammassari, Rita, illus. 2011. (Little Lights Ser.). (ENG.). 24p. (J). (gr. -1-2). 7.99 (978-1-84550-109-9(8), 8f71ca06-a3ed-4fbd-93f4-7acda1909291) Christian Focus Pubns. GBR. Dist: Bookmasters Distribution.

McAdam, Claudia Cangilla. Kristoph & the First Christmas Tree: A Legend of St. Boniface. Hill, David, illus. 2015. (ENG.). 32p. (J). 16.99 (978-1-61261-630-8(5)) Paraclete Pr., Inc.

McDonald, Muriel. Muriel Remembers. 2011. (ENG., Illus.). 60p. pap. 9.95 (978-1-57258-648-2(6), Aspect Bk.) TEACH Services, Inc.

McKenzie, Janet P. Reading the Saints: Lists of Catholic Books for Children Plus Book Collecting Tips for the Home & School Library. 2nd ed. 2013. (ENG.). 278p. pap. 29.95 (978-1-934185-45-2(0)) Biblio Resource Pubns., Inc.

Meloche, Renee. Heroes for Young Readers - Cameron Townsend: Planting God's Word. Pollard, Bryan, illus. 2004. (Heroes for Young Readers Ser.). (ENG.). 32p. (J). 8.99 (978-1-57658-241-1(8)) YWAM Publishing.

—Heroes for Young Readers - Hudson Taylor: Friend of China. Pollard, Bryan, illus. 2004. (ENG.). 32p. (J). 8.99 (978-1-57658-234-3(5)) YWAM Publishing.

—Heroes for Young Readers - Jim Elliot: A Light for God. Pollard, Bryan, illus. 2004. (Heroes for Young Readers Ser.). (ENG.). 32p. (J). 8.99 (978-1-57658-235-0(3)) YWAM Publishing.

—Heroes for Young Readers - Jonathan Goforth: Never Give Up. Pollard, Bryan, illus. 2004. (Heroes for Young Readers Ser.). (ENG.). 32p. (J). 8.99 (978-1-57658-242-8(6)) YWAM Publishing.

—Heroes for Young Readers - Lottie Moon: A Generous Offering. Pollard, Bryan, illus. 2004. (Heroes for Young Readers Ser.). (ENG.). 32p. (J). 8.99 (978-1-57658-243-5(4)) YWAM Publishing.

Montemayor, Jerry & Montemayor, Sherry. From Sin to Serenity: My Father's Story. 2007. 96p. per. 14.95 (978-1-4327-0606-7(3)) Outskirts Pr., Inc.

Morrett, John J. Saints I Have Known & Known About. 2003. 117p. (YA). pap. 12.95 (978-0-7414-1435-9(X)) Infinity Publishing.

Muldoon, Kathleen M. Little Book of Saints, 2 bks. Mattozzi, Patricia R., illus. 2005. 24p. (J). Vol. 2. pap. 3.95 (978-0-8198-4511-5(6), 332-187) Vol. I. pap. 3.95 (978-0-8198-4510-8(8), 332-186) Pauline Bks. & Media.

Nichols, Stephen J. & Bustard, Ned. The Church History ABCs: Augustine & 25 Other Heroes of the Faith. 2010. 32p. (J). 16.99 (978-1-4335-1472-2(9)) Crossway.

Pagotto, Toni. Pope John Paul II. Toppi, Sergio, illus. 2006. (Comic Book Ser.). 64p. (J). pap. 7.95 (978-0-8198-5957-0(5)) Pauline Bks. & Media.

Peckham, Lori. Guide's Greatest Hero Stories. 2012. (ENG.). 144p. (J). pap. 11.99 (978-0-8280-2637-6(8)) Review & Herald Publishing Assn.

Pershbacher, Gerald. Hero of Faith - C.F.W. Walther. 2011. 64p. pap. 7.99 (978-0-7586-2828-2(5)) Concordia Publishing Hse.

Piper, Don & Murphey, Cecil. 90 Minutes in Heaven: My True Story, 1 vol. 2009. (ENG.). 160p. (J). pap. 9.99 (978-0-8007-3399-5(1)) Revell.

Robertson, Sadie. Live Original Devotional. 2016. (Live Original Ser.). (ENG., Illus.). 256p. (gr. 7). 16.99 (978-1-5011-2651-2(2), Howard Bks.) Howard Books.

Sanderson, Ruth. Saints: Lives & Illuminations. Sanderson, Ruth, illus. 2010. (ENG., Illus.). 160p. (J). (gr. 3-18). 16.00 (978-0-8028-5365-3(X), Eerdmans Bks For Young Readers) Eerdmans, William B. Publishing Co.

Shaw, Maura D. Dorothy Day: A Catholic Life of Action. Marchesi, Stephen, illus. 2004. (ENG.). 32p. (J). 12.99 (978-1-59473-011-5(3), 9781594730115, Skylight Paths Publishing) LongHill Partners, Inc.

Stiegemeyer, Julie. Dorothea Creamer. Martin, John, illus. 2012. (Hero of Faith Ser.). (ENG.). 47p. (J). pap. 7.99 (978-0-7586-3077-3(8)) Concordia Publishing Hse.

Tebow, Tim. Through My Eyes: A Quarterback's Journey, 1 vol. 2011. (ENG., Illus.). 216p. (YA). 16.99 (978-0-310-72345-5(0)) Zonderkidz.

—Through My Eyes: A Quarterback's Journey, 1 vol. 2013. (ENG.). 216p. (YA). pap. 12.99 (978-0-310-73291-4(3)) Zondervan.

Tinling, Christine I. Heroes of the Cross, All for Jesus, Vol. 8. (J). pap. 5.99 (978-0-88019-162-3(7)) Schmul Publishing Co., Inc.

Walsh, Kay. John Paton - South Sea Island Rescue. 2005. (Trailblazers Ser.). (ENG.). 160p. (J). mass mkt. 8.99 (978-1-85792-852-5(0), 19477cb3-06d2-420c-a2a4-07fe90bdf166) Christian Focus Pubns. GBR. Dist: Bookmasters Distribution.

Washburn, Kim. Beyond the Music: The Bono Story, 1 vol. rev. ed. 2013. (ZonderKidz Biography Ser.). (ENG.). 128p. (J). pap. 6.99 (978-0-310-73838-1(5)) Zonderkidz.

Watson, Jean. Corrie Ten Boom: The Watchmaker's Daughter. 2014. (Trailblazers Ser.). (ENG.). 192p. (J). (gr. 4-7). mass mkt. 8.99 (978-1-85792-116-8(X), 638cb23a-1df9-4470-b7bf-b3b8b247d85c) Christian Focus Pubns. GBR. Dist: Bookmasters Distribution.

Windeatt, Mary Fabyan & Ignatz, Marie. Vocabulary Quiz Workbook: Based on 6 Great Saints' Lives by Mary Fabyan Windeatt. Lester, Mary Frances, ed. 2004. (ENG.). 200p. (gr. 5-9). pap., wbk. ed. 21.95 (978-0-89555-743-8(6), 1841) TAN Bks.

Withrow, Brandon & Withrow, Mindy. Hearts & Hands: Chronicles of the Awakening Church. 2007. (History Lives Ser.). (ENG., Illus.). 224p. (J). (gr. 4-9). per. 9.99 (978-1-84550-288-1(4), 9781845502881) Christian Focus Pubns. GBR. Dist: Bookmasters Distribution.

—Monks & Mystics: Chronicles of the Medieval Church, Vol. 2. 2005. (History Lives Ser.). (ENG., Illus.). 224p. (J). (gr. 3-7). per. 9.99 (978-1-84550-083-2(0), 9781845500832) Christian Focus Pubns. GBR. Dist: Bookmasters Distribution.

—Peril & Peace: Chronicles of the Ancient Church, Vol. 1. 2014. (History Lives Ser.). (ENG., Illus.). 240p. (J). (gr. 3-7). per. 9.99 (978-1-84550-082-5(2), 9781845500825) Christian Focus Pubns. GBR. Dist: Bookmasters Distribution.

Withrow, Mindy & Withrow, Brandon. Courage & Conviction: Chronicles of the Reformation Church, Vol. 3. 2009. (History Lives Ser.). (ENG., Illus.). 256p. (J). per. 9.99 (978-1-84550-222-5(1), 9781845502225) Christian Focus Pubns. GBR. Dist: Bookmasters Distribution.

—Rescue & Redeem Vol. 5: Chronicles of the Modern Church. 2014. (History Lives Ser.). (ENG., Illus.). 256p. (J). 9.99 (978-1-84550-433-5(X), 9781845504335) Christian Focus Pubns. GBR. Dist: Bookmasters Distribution.

Wright, Chris. An Incubating Miracle Taylor, Minnie, ed. 2004. 107p. (J). per. 12.95 (978-1-930908-30-7(X), AGB/me) AGB Publishing.

Yolen, Jane. Friend: The Story of George Fox & the Quakers. 2nd ed. 2005. (Illus.). xii, 179p. (J). (978-1-888305-41-8(X)) QuakerPress.

CHRISTIAN DOCTRINE

see Theology

CHRISTIAN EDUCATION

see Religious Education

CHRISTIAN ETHICS

Birky, Joy. Bully Bill. Thompson, Chad, illus. 2007. 40p. (J). (gr. 3-7). per. 12.99 (978-0-8361-9382-4(2)) Herald Pr.

Carlson, Amie. My Princesses Learn to Share. Heyworth, Heather, illus. 2014. (ENG.). 24p. (J). 6.99 (978-1-4143-9662-0(7)) Tyndale Hse. Pubs.

Christian Morality. 2004. (Effective Dre Ser.). pap. (978-0-8294-1061-7(9)) Loyola Pr.

Jordan, Anne. Perspectives on Religious Issues. 2003. (ENG., Illus.). 160p. pap., stu. ed. (978-0-7487-7255-1(3)) Nelson Thornes Ltd.

Lessons in Responsibility for Boys: Level One. 2007. (YA). per. 18.95 (978-0-9792446-0-5(9)) Messiah Publishing - Pearables.

Lessons in Responsibility for boys Level Two. 2007. (YA). per. 18.95 (978-0-9792446-1-2(7)) Messiah Publishing - Pearables.

MacKenzie, Carine. My First Book of Christian Values. 2008. (My First Bks.). (ENG., Illus.). 64p. (J). (gr. -1-2). pap. 3.99 (978-1-84550-262-1(0), 7f7e41fe-7f77-4552-9163-a10f885274fd) Christian Focus Pubns. GBR. Dist: Bookmasters Distribution.

Wean, Sarah. Teach Them to Your Children: An Alphabet of Biblical Poems, Verses, & Stories. Sanford, Lori Hood, illus. 2006. 56p. (J). 17.00 (978-0-9787559-5-9(2)) Vision Forum, Inc., The.

White, Anne. Lessons in Responsibility for Girls: Level One. 2006. Orig. Title: Home Economics for Home Schoolers Level One. (J). per., pupil's gde. ed. 18.95 (978-0-9792446-2-9(5)) Messiah Publishing - Pearables.

—Lessons in Responsibility for Girls: Level Three, 3. 2005. Orig. Title: Home Economics for Home Schoolers Level Three. (J). per., pupil's gde. ed. (978-0-9792446-4-3(1)) Messiah Publishing - Pearables.

—Lessons in Responsibility for Girls: Level Two, 2. 2006. Orig. Title: Home Economics for Home Schoolers Level Two. (J). per., pupil's gde. ed. 18.95 (978-0-9792446-3-6(3)) Messiah Publishing - Pearables.

CHRISTIAN LIFE

see also Christian Ethics; Faith; Prayer; Religious Education; Spiritual Life

Abingdon. Promises for Girls Living Faithfully with God & Neighbor. 2006. 64p. 4.00 (978-0-687-49385-2(4)) Abingdon Pr.

Abingdon Press, creator. One Room Sunday School: Resource Kit. 2008. (Illus.). (J). pap. 56.00 incl. audio compact disk (978-0-687-03629-5(1)) Abingdon Pr.

Above & Beyond Quiet Time Guide. 2004. 1.95 (978-0-9743687-3-3(3)) Connection.

Abraham, Ken. Armed & Dangerous: Ephesians 6:11 Straight Answers from the Bible. 2003. (Value Book Ser.). 96p. (YA). pap. 0.99 (978-1-58660-733-3(2), Barbour Bks.) Barbour Publishing, Inc.

The Action Principles, Catholic Edition: Create a Life of Purpose, Passion, Prosperity & Peace. 2004. 144p. pap. 6.00 (978-1-884864-20-9(1)) American Success Institute, Inc.

Adams, M.H. Small Means & Great Ends (Illustrated. 2006. pap. (978-1-4065-0478-1(5)) Dodo Pr.

Adivina Lo Que Es: Individual 6-packs, Level 4. 2003. 23.95 (978-0-673-57868-6(2)) Celebration Pr.

Aguilera, Rich. Passport to Adventure: Daily Devotions for Juniors. 2016. 369p. (J). pap. (978-0-8163-6189-2(4)) Pacific Pr. Publishing Assn.

Alex, N. L. Smile All the While. I.t. ed. 2005. (Illus.). 16p. (J). 4.99 (978-0-9766080-0-4(6)) Joe Girl Ink.

Alley, R. W., illus. Making Christmas Count! A Kid's Guide to Keeping the Season Sacred. 2006. (Elf-Help Books for Kids Ser.). (AFA.). 32p. (J). (gr. -1-3). per. 7.95 (978-0-87029-401-3(6)) Abbey Pr.

Almquist, Beth, et al. Growing up in Jesus: Weekly Meeting Plans for Voyager Leaders. 2007. (J). 19.95 (978-0-9743503-5-6(4)) Pioneer Clubs.

American Tract Society Staff, compiled by. The Tract Primer: First Lessons in Sound Doctrine for Young Children. 2007. 112p. per. 11.00 (978-1-59925-130-1(2)) Solid Ground Christian Bks.

Anderson, Debby. Let's Talk about Heaven. 2003. (Illus.). 32p. (J). (gr. -1-2). 12.99 (978-0-7814-3077-7(1), 0781430771) Cook, David C.

Anderson, George William, ed. Achieving Success with Faith in God: The Concept of Faith - Based Perseverance. 2007. 128p. 15.95 (978-0-9786565-0-8(4)) Naypree Enterprises, LLC.

Anderson, John W. Straight the Highway: The Life Story of Petar & Hannah. 2007. 432p. per. 26.95 (978-0-595-43876-1(8)) iUniverse, Inc.

Anderson, Neil T. Beta Starter Kit. 2004. (Beta Discipleship Ser.). 99.99 (978-0-8307-3384-2(1), Gospel Light) Gospel Light Pubns.

Andrews, Pam. J-Force to the Rescue: A Kids' Musical Discovering the Ultimate Truth. 2004. (ENG., Illus.). 112p.

pap. 7.99 *(978-0-8341-7405-4(7)*, MB-935) Lillenas Publishing Co.

Anthony, Kitty. The King's Castles. 2004. 112p. (gr. -1-3). pap. 7.99 *(978-0-85151-777-3(3))* Banner of Truth, The.

Appelbaum, Barbara G. & Marchant, Peter, told to. Angie's Story. 2003. (YA). 25.95 *(978-0-9710686-4-3(X))*; per. 15.95 *(978-0-9710686-5-0(8))* Jewish Community Federation of Rochester, NY, Inc.

Armbrecht, Doug, compiled by. Quiet Time Prepack for Families (Quiet Time Devotionals), 21. 2006. (Illus.). (YA). per. 347.79 *(978-1-931235-53-2(8)*, gbookpack) Word of Life Fellowship, Inc.

Armstrong, Moses K. Orthodox Christian Alphabet Coloring Book. Date not set. 35p. (J). (gr. k-3). pap. 5.00 *(978-1-879038-45-5(5)*, 9013) Synaxis Pr.

Arthur, Kay & Arndt, Janna. Boy, Have I Got Problems. 2003. (Discover-4-Yourself for Kids Ser.). 140p. (J). pap. 8.99 *(978-1-888655-74-2(7))* Precept Ministries.

Ashour, Monica & Harrald-Pilz, Marilee. Everybody Has Something to Give. 2015. (Illus.). 29p. (J). pap. 12.95 *(978-0-8198-2389-2(9))* Pauline Bks. & Media.

Askew, Shirley. Jean's Magical Moments: Faith of a Child. 2010. 56p. pap. 14.95 *(978-1-4327-5168-5(9))* Outskirts Pr., Inc.

Auer, Jim. Handbook for Today's Catholic Teen. 2004. (YA). pap. 3.95 net. *(978-0-7648-1173-9(8))* Liguori Pubns.

AULT, Jane M., concept. Heart Connections: Finding Joy through Openness with God. 2003. (Illus.). 128p. (YA). 11.95 *(978-0-9708129-4-0(9)*, HC01012004-01) Franklin Publishing.

Aunt Harding's Keepsakes or the Two Bibles. 2004. reprint ed. pap. 15.95 *(978-1-4191-0822-8(0))*; pap. 1.99 *(978-1-4192-0822-5(5))* Kessinger Publishing, LLC.

Aventurate Dia A Dia. 2004. (SPA.). pap. 7.50 *(978-0-311-40067-6(1))* Casa Bautista de Publicaciones.

B&H Kids Editorial Staff. If You're Happy & You Know It, Sound Book. Conger, Holli, illus. 2016. (Little Words Matter(tm) Ser.). (ENG.). 12p. (J). (gr. -1 — 1). bds. 12.99 *(978-1-4336-8678-8(3)*, B&H Kids) B&H Publishing Group.

—In the Beginning/the Great Flood Flip-Over Book. McPherson, Heath, illus. 2016. (Big Picture Interactive / the Gospel Project Ser.). (ENG.). 32p. (J). (gr. -1-3). pap. 3.99 *(978-1-4336-4328-6(6)*, B&H Kids) B&H Publishing Group.

—Now I Lay Me down to Sleep, Sound Book. Conger, Holli, illus. 2016. (Little Words Matter(tm) Ser.). (ENG.). 12p. (J). (gr. -1 — 1). bds. 12.99 *(978-1-4336-8677-1(5)*, B&H Kids) B&H Publishing Group.

B&H Kids Editorial Staff & McPherson, Heath. Jesus Grows up/Jesus Teaches the People Flip-Over Book. 2016. (Big Picture Interactive / the Gospel Project Ser.). (ENG.). 32p. (J). (gr. -1-3). pap. 3.99 *(978-1-4336-4331-6(6)*, B&H Kids) B&H Publishing Group.

Baaumbach, Gerard F., creator. Sadlier We Believe. 2003. (Sadlier We Believe Religion Ser.). (J). per. *(978-0-8215-5500-2(6)*, Sadlier) Sadlier, William H. Inc.

Baby Blessings Staff. God Made Me Book W/Plush. 2006. 6p. 12.99 *(978-0-7847-1501-7(7)*, 04152) Standard Publishing.

Bagley, Val. My Little Book about Joseph. 2004. (Illus.). (J). bds. 9.95 *(978-1-57734-729-3(3))* Covenant Communications, Inc.

Balfour, R. C., III. Fishing for the Abundant Life 2 Journey to Faith. 2004. (gr. 9-18). 26.00 *(978-1-889574-21-9(X))* Sentry Pr., Inc.

Banks, Calvin J. Beginning Conversations with God: A Prayer & Spiritual Journal for Children. Hayden, Seito & Chandler, Alton, illus. (J). (gr. -1-3). pap. 14.95 *(978-1-877804-14-4(2))* Chandler/White Publishing Co.

Banks, Lois. Learn Your ABC's God's Way. 2006. (J). per. 9.95 *(978-1-933556-24-6(2))* Publishers' Graphics, L.L.C.

Barnes, Kathleen. Sacrament Time. 2009. 32p. pap. 9.95 *(978-1-60641-113-1(6))* Deseret Bk. Co.

Barnhill, Carla. The One Year Devotions for Preschoolers 2. Kucharik, Elena, illus. 2010. (Little Blessings Ser.). (ENG.). 384p. (J). 14.99 *(978-1-4143-3445-5(1)*, Tyndale Kids) Tyndale Hse. Pubs.

Bartel, Blaine. Little Black Book on Dreaming for Your Future. 2004. 80p. pap. 4.99 *(978-1-57794-627-4(8))* Harrison House Pubs.

—Little Black Book on How to Win a Friend to Christ. 2004. 80p. pap. 4.99 *(978-1-57794-628-1(6))* Harrison House Pubs.

Basic Friendship Curriculum: Year 1. (YA). (gr. 5-18). stu. ed. 13.25 *(978-1-56212-728-2(4)*, 300120) Faith Alive Christian Resources.

Basic Friendship Curriculum: Year 2. (YA). (gr. 5-18). stu. ed. 13.25 *(978-1-56212-733-6(0)*, 300220) Faith Alive Christian Resources.

Baumbach, Gerard F. Sadlier We Believe. 2003. (J). (gr. 1). per., tchr.'s training gde. ed. *(978-0-8215-5411-1(5))*; (gr. 2). per., tchr.'s training gde. ed. *(978-0-8215-5412-8(3))*; (gr. 3). per., tchr.'s training gde. ed. *(978-0-8215-5413-5(1))*; (gr. 4). per., tchr.'s training gde. ed. *(978-0-8215-5414-2(X))*; (gr. 6). per., tchr.'s training gde. ed. *(978-0-8215-5416-6(6))* Sadlier, William H. Inc. (Sadlier).

—Sadlier We Believe, Catechist's Guide. 2003. (J). (gr. 6). per. 42.75 *(978-0-8215-5516-3(2)*, Sadlier) Sadlier, William H. Inc.

—Sadlier We Believe, Parish Edition: God's Law Guides Us. 2003. (J). (gr. 4). per. *(978-0-8215-5504-0(9)*, Sadlier) Sadlier, William H. Inc.

—Sadlier We Believe, Parish Edition: Jesus Shares God's Life. 2003. (J). (gr. 2). per. *(978-0-8215-5502-6(2)*, Sadlier) Sadlier, William H. Inc.

—Sadlier We Believe, Parish Edition: We Are God's People. 2003. (J). (gr. 6). per. *(978-0-8215-5506-4(5)*, Sadlier) Sadlier, William H. Inc.

—Sadlier We Believe, School Edition: God Loves Us. 2003. (Sadlier We Believe Religion Ser.). (J). (gr. 1). per. *(978-0-8215-5401-2(8)*, Sadlier) Sadlier, William H. Inc.

—Sadlier We Believe, School Edition: We Are God's People. 2003. (J). (gr. 6). per. *(978-0-8215-5406-7(9)*, Sadlier) Sadlier, William H. Inc.

Baumbach, Gerard F., creator. Sadlier We Believe. 2003. (J). per., tchr.'s training gde. ed. *(978-0-8215-5410-4(7))*; (gr. 3). per., tchr.'s training gde. ed. *(978-0-8215-5503-3(0))*; (gr. 5). per., tchr.'s training gde. ed. *(978-0-8215-5415-9(8))* Sadlier, William H. Inc. (Sadlier).

—Sadlier We Believe, Catechist's Guide. 2003. (J). per. *(978-0-8215-5510-1(3))*; (gr. 2). per. *(978-0-8215-5512-5(X))*; (gr. 3). per. *(978-0-8215-5513-2(8))*; (gr. 4). per. *(978-0-8215-5514-9(6))*; (gr. 5). per. *(978-0-8215-5515-6(4))*; (gr. 6). per. *(978-0-8215-5405-0(0))* Sadlier, William H. Inc. (Sadlier).

—Sadlier We Believe, Parish Edition: God Loves Us. 2003. (J). (gr. 1). per. *(978-0-8215-5501-9(4)*, Sadlier) Sadlier, William H. Inc.

—Sadlier We Believe, Parish Edition: We Are the Church. 2003. (J). (gr. 3). per. *(978-0-8215-5403-6(4)*, Sadlier) Sadlier, William H. Inc.

—Sadlier We Believe, Parish Edition: We Meet Jesus in the Sacraments. 2003. (J). (gr. 5). per. *(978-0-8215-5505-7(7)*, Sadlier) Sadlier, William H. Inc.

—Sadlier We Believe, School Edition: God Loves Us. 2003. (J). (gr. 1). per. *(978-0-8215-5420-3(4)*, Sadlier) Sadlier, William H. Inc.

—Sadlier We Believe, School Edition: God's Law Guides Us. 2003. (J). (gr. 4). per. *(978-0-8215-5404-3(2)*, Sadlier) Sadlier, William H. Inc.

—Sadlier We Believe, School Edition: Jesus Shares God's Life. 2003. (J). (gr. 2). per. *(978-0-8215-5402-9(6)*, Sadlier) Sadlier, William H. Inc.

Becoming a Girl of Faith: According to God's Word. l.t. ed. 2004. 90p. (YA). 12.95 *(978-0-9764304-2-1(8))* Girls of Faith.

Beeke, Joel R. & Boorsma, Heidi. God's Alphabet for Life: Devotions for Young Children. 2nd ed. 2009. (Illus.). 80p. (J). pap. *(978-1-60178-068-3(0))* Reformation Heritage Bks.

Bell, Rob. Love Wins: For Teens. 2013. (ENG., Illus.). 160p. (YA). (gr. 8). 17.99 *(978-0-06-222187-2(6)*, Collins) HarperCollins Pubs.

Benjamin, M. A. Psalm 23: The Lord Is My Shepherd. 2011. 16p. (gr. -1). pap. 9.99 *(978-1-4567-5993-3(0))* AuthorHouse.

Berger, Mary J. Jesus Lives in Us: Activity Book. 96p. (J). (gr. 5). pap. 2.50 *(978-0-8198-3931-2(0))* Pauline Bks. & Media.

Berndt, Clarence, ed. Living in Christ. 2003. 80p. (gr. 4-6). pap., stu. ed., wbk. ed. 13.49 *(978-0-7586-0468-2(8))* Concordia Publishing Hse.

Betler, Jason. I Have Decided: Beginning Your New life with Jesus. 2004. 36p. *(978-0-9761415-0-1(7))* Nations Hope, Inc., The.

Beveridge, Amy. God Bless America. Fletcher, Rusty, illus. 2006. 16p. (J). pap. 1.99 *(978-0-7847-1509-3(2)*, 22136) Standard Publishing.

Bewes, Richard & Thompson, Ian. Top 100 Questions Remix: Spiritual Answers to Real Questions. 2010. (ENG.). 224p. (gr. 7-12). pap. 14.99 *(978-1-84550-191-4(8)*, 422120b2-6629-493b-8158-752e891c001a) Christian Focus Pubns. GBR. Dist: Bookmasters Distribution.

Bible Activities for Kids. 2004. pap. 1.50 *(978-0-87162-937-1(2))* Warner Pr., Inc.

Bible Visuals International Staff, compiled by. Be the One! the Todd Beamer Story. 2004. (Illus.). (J). cd-rom, audio compact disk *(978-1-932381-93-1(7)*, 5010-CD) Bible Visuals International, Inc.

—Discovering God's Ways Vol. 17: Old Testament. 2005. (Illus.). (J). pap. *(978-1-932381-77-1(5)*, 2017) Bible Visuals International, Inc.

—Living by Faith: New Testament Volume 38. 2006. (Illus.). (J). pap. *(978-1-932381-28-3(7)*, 1038) Bible Visuals International, Inc.

—Living the Christian Life Volume 23: New Testament. 2006. (Illus.). (J). pap. *(978-1-932381-52-8(X)*, 1023) Bible Visuals International, Inc.

Bick, Margaret & Ecker, Catherine. Alive in the Spirit. 2006. pap. 15.95 *(978-1-56854-604-9(1)*, AISCPL) Liturgy Training Pubns.

—Alive in the Spirit, Family Book. 2006. (YA). pap. 7.95 *(978-1-56854-603-2(3)*, AISCPF) Liturgy Training Pubns.

—Come, Spirit of God. 2006. pap. 15.95 *(978-1-56854-602-5(5)*, CSGCPL) Liturgy Training Pubns.

—Come, Spirit of God, Family Book. 2006. (J). pap. 7.95 *(978-1-56854-601-8(7)*, CSGCPF) Liturgy Training Pubns.

Biffi, Inos. An Illustrated Catechism: The Apostles' Creed, the Sacraments, the Ten Commandments, Prayer. Vignazia, Franco, illus. 2007. 141p. (J). (gr. 3). per. 19.95 *(978-1-56854-612-4(2))* Liturgy Training Pubns.

Big Idea, Inc. VeggieTales Kids' Worship! Getting to Know God: For Children's Church or Large-Group Programming, 0 vols. 2009. (J). 129.99 *(978-1-4003-1353-2(8))* Nelson, Thomas Inc.

—VeggieTales Kids' Worship! Unit 2 - Wild Bible Adventures: For Children's Church or Large-Group Programming, 0 vols. 2009. (J). 129.99 *(978-1-4003-1444-7(5))* Nelson, Thomas Inc.

Big Idea, Inc. Staff & Kenney, Cindy. God Loves You Very Much!, 1 vol. Ballinger, Bryan, illus. 2003. (Big Idea Books / VeggieTales Ser.). (ENG.). 18p. (J). bds. 7.99 *(978-0-310-70623-6(8))* Zonderkidz.

Biscontin, Chino. A Friend Named Jesus. (Illus.). 64p. 10.95 *(978-1-875570-66-9(7))* St Pauls Pubns. AUS. Dist: St Pauls/Alba Hse. Pubs.

Bishop, Jennie. Jesus Must Be Really Special. Wummer, Amy, illus. 2006. (Heritage Builders Ser.). 32p. (J). 14.99 *(978-0-7847-1379-2(0)*, 04029) Standard Publishing.

Bishop, Jennie & Henson, Susan. Life Lessons from the Squire & the Scroll: Battle Plans for a Pure Heart. 2006. (Revive Our Hearts Ser.). (ENG., Illus.). 65p. pap. 9.99 *(978-0-940110-67-0(9))* Life Action Inc.

Blake, D M. Achieving Success with Faith in God: The Concept of Faith-Based Perserverance. 2007. 128p. per. 13.95 *(978-0-9786565-1-5(2))* Naypree Enterprises, LLC.

Blake, Philip. We are Christians. 2016. (ENG., Illus.). 32p. (J). (gr. 4-6). pap. 11.99 *(978-1-4451-3825-1(5)*, Franklin Watts) Hachette Children's Group GBR. Dist: Hachette Bk. Group.

Blundell, Trevor, et al. On the Way, Bk. 3. 2008. (On the Way (11-14's) Ser.). (ENG.). 88p. (J). pap. 17.99 *(978-1-85792-706-1(0)*, 9781857927061) Christian Focus Pubns. GBR. Dist: Bookmasters Distribution.

—On the Way for 11 - 14's, Vol. 2. 2006. (On the Way (11-14's) Ser.). (ENG.). 96p. (J). pap. 17.99 *(978-1-85792-705-4(2)*, 9781857927054) Christian Focus Pubns. GBR. Dist: Bookmasters Distribution.

Boah, Ewuramma Hannah. Jehovah the Lifter of My Head. 2012. 94p. pap. 10.99 *(978-0-9849805-1-2(2))* Ewuramma.

Bohlmann, Katharine. Grandpa, Is There a Heaven? Erickson, David, illus. 2008. 32p. pap. 7.49 *(978-0-7586-1478-0(0))* Concordia Publishing Hse.

Borthwick, Paul, et al. Would Jesus Really Do That? 2004. (Custom Curriculum Ser.). (ENG., Illus.). 256p. (YA). per. 19.99 *(978-0-7814-4087-5(4)*, 0781440874) Cook, David C.

Bowen, Acton. Escape the Noise: A Thirty-Day Devotional Journey for Students. 2007. 196p. 26.95 *(978-0-595-70475-0(1))*; per. 16.95 *(978-0-595-46744-0(X))* iUniverse, Inc.

Bowman, Crystal & Taylor, Christy Lee. Devotions for Beginning Readers, 1 vol. 2014. (ENG.). 240p. (J). 14.99 *(978-0-529-10401-4(6))* Nelson, Thomas Inc.

Bradshaw, Frances C. F-A-i-t-h: Do You Have It ?? 2012. 28p. pap. 19.99 *(978-1-4772-9848-0(7))* AuthorHouse.

Braner, Andy. Duplicate This! Showing Your Friends How to Live Like Jesus, 1 vol. 2008. (Invert Ser.). (ENG.). 272p. (YA). (gr. 13). pap. 12.99 *(978-0-310-27754-5(X))* Zondervan.

Brewer, Michael. Gotta Have God 2: Ages 10-12. Heiser, Aline, illus. 2005. (Gotta Have God Ser.). 238p. (J). spiral bd. 12.99 *(978-1-58411-059-0(7)*, Legacy Pr.) Rainbow Pubs. & Legacy Pr.

Bright, et al. Building an Active Faith, Vol. 4. 2004. (ENG.). 192p. pap. 18.99 *(978-1-56399-154-7(3))* Campus Crusade for Christ.

Broslavick, Chris & Pichler, Tony. Totally Lent! A Teen's Journey to Easter 2007. 2006. (Illus.). 64p. pap. 5.95 *(978-1-933178-44-8(2))* Pflaum Publishing Group.

Brown, Mark. Tommy Books: Faith, 10 vols. Mekis, Pete, illus. l.t. ed. 2005. 24p. (J). 12.99 *(978-0-9762690-0-7(7))* Tommy Bks. Pubng.

—Tommy Books: Kings, 10 vols. Mekis, Pete, illus. l.t. ed. 2005. 24p. (J). 12.99 *(978-0-9762690-4-5(X))* Tommy Bks. Pubng.

—Tommy Books Vol. 2: Love, 10 vols. Mekis, Pete, illus. l.t. ed. 2005. 24p. (J). 12.99 *(978-0-9762690-1-4(5))* Tommy Bks. Pubng.

—Tommy Books Vol. 3: Too Busy, 10 vols. Mekis, Pete, illus. l.t. ed. 2005. 24p. (J). 12.99 *(978-0-9762690-2-1(3))* Tommy Bks. Pubng.

—Tommy Books Vol. 4: Praise, 10 vols. Mekis, Pete, illus. l.t. ed. 2005. 20p. (J). 12.99 *(978-0-9762690-3-8(1))* Tommy Bks. Pubng.

Brown, Tempe. The Little Dirt People. Brown, Tempe, illus. 2013. (Illus.). 50p. pap. 14.95 *(978-1-4507-3904-7(0))* Bush Publishing Inc.

Brundage, George. Vamos a la misa. 2006. pap. 4.75 *(978-0-89942-799-7(5))* Catholic Bk. Publishing Corp.

Bruno, Bonnie. God Thought of Everything Strange & Slimy. Brown, Kevin, illus. 2006. 128p. (YA). (gr. 3-6). pap. 8.99 *(978-0-7847-1448-5(7)*, 04084) Standard Publishing.

—God Thought of Everything Weird & Wacky. Brown, Kevin, illus. 2006. 128p. (YA). (gr. 3-6). pap. 8.99 *(978-0-7847-1447-8(9)*, 04083) Standard Publishing.

Brusselmans, Christiane, et al. Sunday: Book of Readings Adapted for Children Year C, Year C. 176p. (J). 49.95 *(978-0-929496-91-7(4))* Treehaus Communications, Inc.

Bryant, Stephen, et al. Has God Called You to Ministry? 2005. 107p. (gr. 9-18). pap. 5.95 *(978-1-885273-04-8(5))* First Century Publishing.

Buchanan, Colin. Super Saviour. 2009. (ENG., Illus.). 32p. (J). 14.99 *(978-1-84550-490-8(9)*, b43792bc-af9b-478f-8551-1c360ae64562) Christian Focus Pubns. GBR. Dist: Bookmasters Distribution.

Buchanan, Paul & Randall, Rod. The Misadventures of Willie Plummet Set. (Misadventures of Willie Plummet Ser.). (J). 114.99 *(978-0-7586-0012-7(7))* Concordia Publishing Hse.

Buell, Jean. Pray with Mary: A Child's Book of the Rosary. Larkin, Jean, ed. 2005. (Illus.). 32p. (J). pap. 3.95 *(978-1-933178-38-7(8))* Pflaum Publishing Group.

Bug House. 2009. (Vacation Bible School Ser.). (J). 17.99 *(978-1-4347-6459-1(1))* Cook, David C.

Burchett, Author Walter, BA. Christian children's fill in the blank Revised. 2009. 37p. pap. 14.48 *(978-0-557-08184-4(X))* Lulu Pr., Inc.

Burgdorf, Larry. Paul's Great Basket Caper. 2009. (Arch Bks.). 16p. (J). (gr. k-4). pap. 2.49 *(978-0-7586-1616-6(3))* Concordia Publishing Hse.

Burgen, Jim. What's the Big Deal about My Parents? Reeves, Dale, ed. 2006. (What's the Big Deal Ser.). 160p. (gr. 7-18). pap. 10.99 *(978-0-7847-1252-8(2)*, 23335) Standard Publishing.

Burns, Jim & DeVries, Mike. Fresh Ideas 11: Hot Topics. 136p. 17.99 *(978-0-8307-2921-0(6)*, Gospel Light) Gospel Light Pubns.

Burpo, Todd & Burpo, Sonja. Heaven Is for Real for Kids: A Little Boy's Astounding Story of His Trip to Heaven & Back, 1 vol. 2011. (ENG.). 32p. (J). 14.99 *(978-1-4003-1870-4(X))* Nelson, Thomas Inc.

Burpo, Todd & Vincent, Lynn. Heaven Is for Real for Kids: A Little Boy's Astounding Story of His Trip to Heaven & Back. 2011. (ENG.). 32p. (J). pap. 9.99 *(978-0-7852-3751-8(8))* Nelson, Thomas Inc.

Burton, Wade T. Tell Me the Old, Old Story... in a New Way. 2010. 32p. pap. 16.95 *(978-1-4497-0387-5(9)*, WestBow Pr.) Author Solutions, Inc.

Busch, Melinda Kay. God Calls Abraham... God Calls You! Dorenkamp, Michelle, illus. 2003. (Arch Bks.). (ENG.). 16p. (J). (gr. k-4). 1.99 *(978-0-7586-0502-3(1))* Concordia Publishing Hse.

Butcher, Sam, illus. Precious Moments: Angel Kisses & Snuggle Time Prayers with Dolly. 2003. 8.40 *(978-0-7180-0575-7(9))* Nelson, Thomas Inc.

—Precious Moments: Angel Kisses & Snuggle Time Prayers with Teddy Bear. 2003. 8.40 *(978-0-7180-0567-2(8))* Nelson, Thomas Inc.

—Precious Moments: Small Hands Bible with Lavender Bible Cover. 2003. 12.84 *(978-0-7180-0570-2(8))* Nelson, Thomas Inc.

Butler, Mary Ann. Protect Me Love My World! 2012. 70p. 19.95 *(978-1-4626-6213-5(7))* America Star Bks.

Bytheway, John. Are Your Standards Fences or Guardrails? 2003. (Illus.). xiv, 97p. (J). pap. *(978-1-57008-990-9(6))* Deseret Bk. Co.

Caduto, Michael J. A Child of God: Stories of Jesus & Stewardship Activities for Children. Tyrol, Adelaide, illus. 2005. 48p. (J). 16.95 *(978-0-8091-6726-5(3)*, 6726-3) Paulist Pr.

Cain, Dece. Seven Angels High. 2012. 30p. 25.99 *(978-1-62419-547-1(4))*; pap. 15.99 *(978-1-62419-546-4(6))* Salem Author Services.

Campbell, June M. & Campbell, Joe Bill. Thank You, God, for Who I Am. Date not set. (Illus.). viii, 36p. (J). 8.95 *(978-0-9665389-1-5(9))* Spring Hollow Bks., LLC.

Campbell, Patsy. Pray Work Win! 2004. 112p. pap. 7.99 *(978-0-89114-360-4(2))* Baptist Publishing Hse.

Campher, Jerome C. The Path of Purpose: Walking in God's Plan for Your Life. 2003. 36p. (YA). 6.95 *(978-0-9747956-4-5(X))* Greenwood, Lori Ministries, Inc.

Campolo, Tony. You Can Make a Difference, 1 vol. 2008. (ENG.). 144p. (gr. 8-12). per. 10.98 *(978-0-8499-1885-8(5))* Nelson, Thomas Inc.

Camps & Retreats to Go: Above & Beyond. 2004. spiral bd. 132.00 *(978-0-9743687-2-6(5))* Connection.

Canfield, Jack & Hansen, Mark Victor. Chicken Soup for the Tween's Soul Collection. 2005. (ENG.). 539p. (YA). pap. 19.95 *(978-0-7573-0386-9(2))* Health Communications, Inc.

Cannizzo, Karen, ed. Confirmation: Confirming My Commitment to Christ/Candidate Edition. 2003. (Hi-Time Ser.). (Illus.). 64p. (YA). pap. 7.95 *(978-0-89837-172-7(4)*, 1790) Pflaum Publishing Group.

Carlsen, Derek. Faith & Courage Commentary on Acts. 2004. 544p. per. 12.95 *(978-1-930367-98-2(8)*, CLP80091) Christian Liberty Pr.

Carmody, Michael A. Life with Jesus: Bible Study Workbook. 2003. 32p. (YA). pap. 10.00 *(978-0-910487-54-2(5))* Royalty Publishing Co.

Carper, Mary Ann. My Name Is Tiny: A Children's Devotional about Fitting In. 2011. 52p. pap. 23.95 *(978-1-4497-0931-0(1)*, WestBow Pr.) Author Solutions, Inc.

Carr, Dan. God I Need to Talk Hurting Oth. 2004. 16p. (J). 1.19 *(978-0-7586-0517-7(X))* Concordia Publishing Hse.

—God I Need to Talk Paying Atte. 2004. 16p. (J). 1.19 *(978-0-7586-0518-4(8))* Concordia Publishing Hse.

Carr, Josie. IGod: Prayers & Promises to Connect to You with Him. 2008. 86p. (YA). pap. 4.99 *(978-1-57794-885-8(8))* Harrison House Pubs.

Carroll, Michael & Carroll, Caroline. I Love God's Green Earth: Devotions for Kids Who Want to Take Care of God's Creation. 2010. (ENG.). 192p. (J). (gr. 3-7). pap. 12.99 *(978-1-4143-3179-9(7)*, Tyndale Kids) Tyndale Hse. Pubs.

Carson Sr., Johnny Lee. Cookies & Dreams. 2013. 40p. pap. 24.95 *(978-1-62709-682-9(5))* America Star Bks.

Cartwright, Deanna Vincent. Disciple's Diary Student Book. 2nd ed. 2004. (J). spiral bd. 14.99 *(978-0-9752605-1-7(0))* LOGOS System Assocs.

Cassel, Katrina. The Christian Girl's Guide to Being Your Best. 2004. (Illus.). 206p. (J). pap. 9.99 *(978-1-58411-035-4(X)*, Legacy Pr.) Rainbow Pubs. & Legacy Pr.

Catechism of Familiar Things. 2006. pap. *(978-1-4068-0491-1(6))* Echo Library.

Celee. My Life with God. 2008. 48p. pap. 17.49 *(978-1-4389-1196-0(3))* AuthorHouse.

Center for Learning Staff. Faith & Belief. 2007. (Religion Ser.). 124p. (YA). spiral bd. 18.95 *(978-1-56077-845-5(8))* Center for Learning, The.

—Justice & Peace. 2007. (Religion Ser.). 124p. (YA). spiral bd. 18.95 *(978-1-56077-795-3(8))* Center for Learning, The.

A Child's Book of Manners. 2014. (Happy Day Ser.). (ENG., Illus.). 16p. (J). pap. 2.49 *(978-1-4143-9462-6(4))* Tyndale Hse. Pubs.

A Child's Missal. 2004. per. 17.95 *(978-0-9741748-1-5(5))* Patmos, Inc.

Choices: On the Road. ldr.'s ed. (Ministry to Adolescent's Program Ser.). (Illus.). 72p. *(978-0-85910-804-1(X))* Openbook Publishers.

Christ Our Life: Confirmation-Confirmed in the Spirit; Parish-Catechist Manual. 2004. *(978-0-8294-0906-2(8))* Loyola Pr.

Christ Our Life: God Cares for Us. 2004. (gr. 2-18). stu. ed. *(978-0-8294-1655-8(2))* Loyola Pr.

Christ Our Life: God Cares for Us; Parish-Catechist Manual. 2004. (gr. 2-18). *(978-0-8294-1659-6(5))* Loyola Pr.

Christ Our Life: God Guides Us. 2004. (gr. 4-18). stu. ed. *(978-0-8294-1539-1(4))* Loyola Pr.

Christ Our Life: God Guides Us; Parish-Catechist Manual. 2004. (gr. 4-18). *(978-0-8294-1661-9(7))* Loyola Pr.

Christ Our Life: God Loves Us. 2004. (gr. k-18). stu. ed. *(978-0-8294-1656-5(0))* Loyola Pr.

Christ Our Life: God Loves Us; Parish-Catechist Manual. 2004. (gr. k-18). *(978-0-8294-1657-2(9))* Loyola Pr.

Christ Our Life: We Believe. 2004. (gr. 3-18). stu. ed. *(978-0-8294-1548-3(3))* Loyola Pr.

Christ Our Life: We Believe; Parish-Catechist Manual. 2004. (gr. 3-18). *(978-0-8294-1660-2(9))* Loyola Pr.

Christ Our Life: We Worship. 2004. (gr. 5-18). stu. ed. *(978-0-8294-1547-6(5))* Loyola Pr.

Christensen, Laurel. LYFSGUD: If God Sent You a Text Message. 2009. (J). *(978-1-60641-108-7(X))* Deseret Bk. Co.

Christian Belief Object Lessons: 14 True-to-the-Word Object Lessons also Includes Reproducible Pages & Music for "I Believe" Song. (J). (gr. -1-6). pap. 5.29 *(978-1-55976-165-9(2))* CEF Pr.

Christian Life & Work-Guide. 2003. (YA). pap. 4.99 *(978-1-56364-711-6(7))* Vision Video.

The Christian Soldier. (Pict-O-Graph Ser.). (Illus.). (J). 10.99 *(978-0-7847-1016-6(3)*, 02266) Standard Publishing.

The Christian Student Compass: KJV Monthly Version with Book of Proverbs. 2003. (YA). spiral bd. *(978-0-9725804-2-7(5))* Salt Pubs.

Christian Virtues Series Kindness, Contains Bible Based Activities, Puzzles, Raps, Poem. (J). (gr. -1). 4.95 *(978-0-382-30739-3(9))* Cobblestone Publishing Co.

Cintron, Carlos Juan, Sr., ed. Mis Primeros Pasos: Red de Niños. deluxe l.t. ed. 2005. (SPA., Illus.). 85p. (J). 12.00 *(978-0-9765828-5-4(6))* Editorial Vida Abundante.

Clark, Chap. Next Time I Fall in Love: How to Handle Sex, Intimacy, & Feelings in Dating Relationships. 2004. 144p. pap. 20.00 *(978-1-59244-684-1(1)*, Wipf and Stock) Wipf & Stock Pubs.

Clark, Jerusha. Inside a Cutter's Mind: Understanding & Helping Those Who Self-Injure. 2007. (ENG., Illus.). 240p.

(YA). per. 14.99 *(978-1-60006-054-0(4)*, Th1nk Bks.) NavPress Publishing Group.

Clarkson, Clay. Our 24 Family Ways Kids Color-In Book: Color-In Book. 2nd ed. 2014. (Illus.). 42p. pap. 5.99 *(978-1-888692-11-2(1)*, Whole Heart Pr.) Whole Heart Ministries.

Coblenz, John. Viata Familiei Crestine (Christian Family Living) Brinzei, Daniel, ed. Brinzei, Daniel, tr. from ENG. (SPA.). 272p. (YA). pap. *(978-1-885270-02-3(X))* Christian Aid Ministries.

Coleman, William L. The Big Book of Animal Devotions: 250 Daily Readings about God's Amazing Creation, 1 vol. 2009. (ENG.). 394p. (J). pap. 17.00 *(978-0-7642-0669-6(9))* Bethany Hse. Pubs.

Colkmire, Lance. Know It, Live It: Helping Kids Embrace Pentecostal Teachings. 2004. (Illus.). (J). per. 9.99 *(978-0-87148-468-0(4))* Pathway Pr.

Comfort, Ray. What Your Nose Shows. Hohnstadt, Cedric, illus. 2007. (Creation for Kids Ser.). 24p. (gr. -1-5). bds. 14.99 *(978-0-88270-326-8(9))* Bridge-Logos, Inc.

Comley, Kathlyn. My Sugar Bear. Piatt, Robert, illus. 2004. (J). bds. 9.99 *(978-1-4183-0001-2(2))* Christ Inspired, Inc.

Coniaris, Anthony M. The Nicene Creed for Young People. 2004. (ENG.). 106p. (J). (gr. 6-9). pap. 14.95 *(978-1-880971-91-8(7))* Light & Life Publishing Co.

Contagious Community: Living Beyond Yourself: Connect with God, Connect with Others, Connect with Life. 2008. 175p. pap. *(978-1-57494-431-0(2)*, Serendipity Hse.) LifeWay Christian Resources.

Cook, Billie Montgomery. The Real Deal: A Spiritual Guide for Black Teen Girls. 2004. 144p. pap. 14.00 *(978-0-8170-1458-2(6))* Judson Pr.

Cook, David Fuller, ed. A Balanced Approach to Long Life & Vitality for Christians: As Used in Fitness, Wellness, Clinical Weight Loss, & Cardiac Rehabilitation Programs. 2003. (Illus.). 105p. spiral bd. 33.95 *(978-0-9741629-4-2(9))* Cook, David.

Copeland, Gloria. Go with the Flow Booklet. 2004. pap. 1.00 *(978-1-57794-331-0(7))* Harrison House Pubs.

Cory, Diane. God & Me! 2: Ages 6-9, 3 vols. 2004. (Illus.). 238p. (J). spiral bd. 12.99 *(978-1-58411-055-2(4)*, Legacy Pr.) Rainbow Pubs. & Legacy Pr.

—Gotta Have God 2: Ages 6-9. Heiser, Aline, illus. 2005. (Gotta Have God Ser.). 238p. (J). spiral bd. 12.99 *(978-1-58411-058-3(9)*, Legacy Pr.) Rainbow Pubs. & Legacy Pr.

Courtney, Vicki. Reflect: Discovering the Beauty, Worth, & Wonderfulness of You. 2016. (ENG., Illus.). 208p. (J). (gr. 7-12). pap. 14.99 *(978-1-4336-9175-1(2)*, B&H Kids) B&H Publishing Group.

—Teenvirtue Confidential: Your Questions Answered about Guys, God, & Getting Older. 2007. (Illus.). 149p. (YA). per. 14.99 *(978-0-8054-4192-5(1)*, B&H Bks.) B&H Publishing Group.

Cousins, Kirk. Game Changer, 1 vol. 2014. (ENG.). 192p. (J). pap. 9.99 *(978-0-310-73905-0(5))* Zondervan.

Crain, Michael. What Catholic Teens Should Know about Retaliation. Larkin, Jean K., ed. 2004. (What Catholic Teens Should Know Ser.). (Illus.). 8p. (YA). 7.95 *(978-0-89837-238-0(0)*, 440910) Pflaum Publishing Group.

Crawford, Donald W. Is This a Test Lord? Prayers, Reflections & Celebrations of a Stroke Survivor, Offering Hope & Healing. 2004. per. 12.95 *(978-0-9763933-0-6(1))* Heartfelt Bks.

Creanga, Emil & Tudosa, Lucia. Studii Biblice Despre Valorile Crestine. 2013. 118p. pap. 11.95 *(978-1-936629-20-6(8))* Reflection Publishing.

Custom Curricul Staff. Can I Really Have a Relationship with God? 2004. (Custom Curriculum Ser.). 256p. pap., pap. 19.99 *(978-0-7814-4090-5(4)*, 0781440904) Cook, David C.

—Does God Love You No Matter What? 2004. (Custom Curriculum Ser.). 256p. pap., pap. 19.99 *(978-0-7814-4085-1(8)*, 0781440858) Cook, David C.

—Does the Bible Have Any Answers? 2004. (Custom Curriculum Ser.). 256p. pap., pap. 19.99 *(978-0-7814-4092-9(0)*, 0781440920) Cook, David C.

—What about Sex, Drugs, And... ? 2004. (Custom Curriculum Ser.). 256p. pap., pap. 19.99 *(978-0-7814-4093-6(9)*, 0781440939) Cook, David C.

—What, Me Holy? 2004. (Custom Curriculum Ser.). 256p. pap., pap. 19.99 *(978-0-7814-4091-2(2)*, 0781440912) Cook, David C.

Custom Curriculum Staff. Can I Really Know Jesus? 2004. (Custom Curriculum Ser.). 256p. pap., pap. 19.99 *(978-0-7814-4084-4(X)*, 078144084X) Cook, David C.

Daddy, Where Are You? 2005. (YA). per. 10.00 *(978-0-9773356-0-2(7))* Divine Ministry of North Florida, Inc.

Dahlstrom, Kathryn. Hate Fighters. Date not set. (Good News Club Ser.). (J). (gr. 4-11). pap. 4.99 *(978-1-55976-832-0(0))* CEF Pr.

Dall, Jeanette & Washington, Linda. God & Me! 2: Ages 10-12, 3 vols. 2004. (Illus.). 238p. (J). spiral bd. 12.99 *(978-1-58411-056-9(2)*, Legacy Pr.) Rainbow Pubs. & Legacy Pr.

Darcy-Bérubé, Françoise & Berube, John Paul. Growing up a Friend of Jesus: A Guide to Discipleship for Children. 2003. (Illus.). 128p. *(978-2-89507-041-2(5))* Novalis Publishing.

Darling, Sandra & Darling, Harold, eds. The Golden Rule. 2006. (ENG.). 48p. (J). (gr. 4-7). pap. 8.95 *(978-1-59583-057-9(X)*, 9781595830579) Laughing Elephant.

Dateno, Maria Grace. My First Missal. Esquinaldo, Virginia, illus. 2006. 48p. (J). pap. 3.95 *(978-0-8198-4842-0(5))* Pauline Bks. & Media.

David C. Cook Publishing Company Staff. God's Fruit. 2003. (My Jesus Pocket Bks.). (Illus.). 32p. (J). pap., pap. 8.90 *(978-1-55513-132-6(8)*, 1555131328) Cook, David C.

—Land of Milk & Honey. 2007. (LMH Ser.). 16p. (J). (gr. 1-3). Bk. 1. 6.99 *(978-0-7814-4524-5(8))*Bk. 2. 6.99 *(978-0-7814-4525-2(6))* Cook, David C.

—Let the Children Come 2009. (Pencil Fun Bks). 16p. (J). pap. 9.90 *(978-1-4347-6815-5(5))* Cook, David C.

Davis, Mary J. My Answer Journal: What Kids Wonder about God & the Bible. 2004. (Journals Just for Kids Ser.). (Illus.). 136p. (J). (gr. 4-7). pap. 9.99 *(978-1-885358-72-1(5)*, Legacy Pr.) Rainbow Pubs. & Legacy Pr.

A Day with Samuel. (Two Great Ways to Share God's Love Ser.). 16p. (gr. -1-k). 15.00 *(978-0-570-00313-7(X))* Concordia Publishing Hse.

Dayton, Howard & Dayton, Beverly. The Secret of Handling Money God's Way. 2003. (Leading Young Hearts & Minds to God Ser.). (ENG.). 112p. (J). pap. 14.99 *(978-0-8024-3154-7(2))* Moody Pubs.

De Sturtz, Mari. God Is. 2004. (ENG & SPA.). 32p. 1.99 *(978-0-7586-0292-3(8))* Concordia Publishing Hse.

Delgatto, Laurie, ed. Hey, God! What Now? Biblical Assurance for Life's Questions. 2003. 158p. (YA). per. 11.50 *(978-0-88489-793-4(1))* St. Mary's Pr. of MN.

Dellinger, Annetta. Adopted & Loved Forever. McDonnell, Janet, illus. 2nd ed. 2009. 32p. (J). 12.99 *(978-0-7586-1591-6(4))* Concordia Publishing Hse.

Dennis, Rainey. Passport 2 Purity. 2004. 29.99 *(978-1-57229-656-5(9))* FamilyLife.

Dent, Jenny. God Loves Us All. (Illus.). 32p. (J). (gr. k-9). 17.95 *(978-0-85487-051-6(2))* White Eagle Publishing Trust GBR. Dist: DeVorss & Co.

DeVries, Mike & Murphy, Troy. Exodus: The Sacred Journey. 2003. (No Limits Ser.). (ENG.). 112p. (J). (gr. 3-7). per. 12.99 *(978-0-8341-5005-8(0)*, 083-415-0050) Beacon Hill Pr. of Kansas City.

DeVries, Mike, et al. Acts: Face of the Fire. 2003. (No Limits Discipleship Ser.). (ENG.). 120p. (gr. 3-7). per. 12.99 *(978-0-8341-5006-5(9)*, 083-415-0069) Beacon Hill Pr. of Kansas City.

Diaz, Olimpia, ed. Oraciones y Guias: Para Jovenes Catolicos. 2005. (SPA., Illus.). 30p. per. 2.25 *(978-0-89837-197-0(X)*, 4659) Pflaum Publishing Group.

Dicker, Katie & Dilkes, Sam. I Belong to the Christian Faith. 2009. (I Belong Ser.). (Illus.). 24p. (J). (ENG.). pap. 8.25 *(978-1-4358-8618-6(6)*, PowerKids Pr.); (gr. 1-4). lib. bdg. 22.60 *(978-1-4358-3032-5(6))* Rosen Publishing Group, Inc., The.

Dickow, Cheryl. All Things Girl: Friends, Fashion & Faith Journal. 2013. 22p. pap. 12.99 *(978-1-936453-22-1(3))* Bezalel Bks.

DiMarco, Hayley. The God Girl Journey: A 30-Day Guide to a Deeper Faith. 2013. (ENG.). 176p. (YA). 14.99 *(978-0-8007-2067-4(9))* Revell.

Diocese of San Bernardino Staff. My Quinceanera Student Bk: Bilingual Formation Program & Remembrance Book. 120p. pap. 9.95 *(978-0-8198-4850-5(6)*, 332-228) Pauline Bks. & Media.

Disciple Helps: Spiritual Journal for Students. 2004. (J). (gr. 7-12). 2.25 *(978-0-633-19381-2(X))* LifeWay Christian Resources.

Disciple III, stu. ed. 30.00 *(978-0-687-76254-5(5))* Abingdon Pr.

Dobson, Danae. Let's Talk! Good Stuff for Girlfriends about God, Guys, & Growing Up. 2003. (ENG.). 204p. (YA). pap. 12.99 *(978-0-8423-0818-2(0))* Tyndale Hse. Pubs.

Dominic, Sister M. Little Nellie of Holy God 1903-1908. Vianney, M. John, illus. 2009. (ENG.). 32p. (J). (gr. 2-2). pap. 12.95 *(978-0-89555-834-3(3)*, 2120) TAN Bks.

Donaghy, Thomas J. Celebrating Mass. 2009. (St. Joseph Board Bks.). (Illus.). 12p. bds. 5.95 *(978-0-89942-662-4(X))* Catholic Bk. Publishing Corp.

Donahue, Laurie. God's Plan My Response. Rittenhouse, Ralph, ed. 2003. (Illus.). 100p. pap. 10.99 *(978-0-9718306-0-8(6))* LifeSong Pubs.

Doney. El Gorrion Muy Preocupado.Tr. of Very Worried Sparrow. (SPA.). (J). *(978-950-841-003-0(5))* Editorial Unilit.

Doney, Meryl. Whisker's Great Adventure. (Illus.). 32p. pap. *(978-0-340-60817-3(X))* Hodder & Stoughton.

Dotson, Jacob. React & Rise Up, 1 vol. 2010. 58p. pap. 16.95 *(978-1-4489-4168-1(7))* America Star Bks.

Dougherty, Chris. I Must Become Less: Making More Room in. 2006. 63p. pap. 16.95 *(978-1-4241-3393-2(9))* PublishAmerica, Inc.

Doxey, Heidi. Tiny Talks, Vol. 14. 2013. pap. 8.99 *(978-1-4621-1357-6(5)*, Horizon Pubs.) Cedar Fort, Inc./CFI Distribution.

—Tiny Talks, Volume 15. 2014. pap. 8.99 *(978-1-4621-1511-2(X)*, Horizon Pubs.) Cedar Fort, Inc./CFI Distribution.

Dredge, Kath. Living 4 God: Learning from the Lives of William Tyndale, John Newton, David Brainerd, Eric Liddell. 2007. (Illus.). 80p. 7.00 *(978-1-84625-034-7(X))* DayOne Pubns. GBR. Dist: Send The Light Distribution LLC.

Dreyer, Nicole. Easter Stranger. 2009. (Arch Bks.). (Illus.). 16p. (J). (gr. k-4). pap. 2.49 *(978-0-7586-1610-4(4))* Concordia Publishing Hse.

Duncan, George T., Jr. Walking with God, Intimately: As Your Father. 2004. (C). pap. 10.95 *(978-0-9752665-0-2(0))* Peace B Still Ministries Pr.

Dyrud, Loiell O. & Furman, Leola Dyrud. Each for the Other, All for Christ: Missionaries to Madagascar Rev. Amos & Ovidie Dyrud. 2004. (Illus.). 320p. per. 15.00 net. *(978-0-9759598-0-0(8))* Pony Rock Pr.

Eastman, Curtis. Extreme Talk Youth Devotional. 2004. pap. 9.99 *(978-1-57794-590-1(5))* Harrison House Pubs.

Editorial Portavoz Staff. Manual de Exploracion, Vol. 6. 2004. (Sabio Y Prudente Ser.).Tr. of Exploration Manual. (SPA.). 96p. (YA). (gr. 2-7). stu. ed. 3.99 *(978-0-8254-0943-1(8)*, Editorial Portavoz) Kregel Pubns.

Edwards-Wright, Tracy. Feasting on Fruit God's Way: The Fruit of the Spirit. 2012. (Illus.). 26p. 16.95 *(978-1-4560-2182-5(6))* America Star Bks.

Elkins, Stephen. Tell Me about Church. 2014. (Train 'Em Up Ser.). (ENG.). 24p. (J). pap. 4.99 *(978-1-4143-9681-1(3))* Tyndale Hse. Pubs.

—Tell Me about Faith. 2014. (Train 'Em Up Ser.). (ENG.). 24p. (J). pap. 4.99 *(978-1-4143-9675-0(9))* Tyndale Hse. Pubs.

—Tell Me about Grace. 2014. (Train 'Em Up Ser.). (ENG.). 24p. (J). pap. 4.99 *(978-1-4143-9678-1(3))* Tyndale Hse. Pubs.

—Tell Me about Praise & Worship. 2014. (Train 'Em Up Ser.). (ENG.). 24p. (J). pap. 4.99 *(978-1-4143-9676-7(7))* Tyndale Hse. Pubs.

—Tell Me about Prayer. 2014. (Train 'Em Up Ser.). (ENG.). 24p. (J). pap. 4.99 *(978-1-4143-9680-4(5))* Tyndale Hse. Pubs.

Ellis, Gwen. The Christmas Flower. Hansen, Clint, illus. 2005. 32p. (J). (gr. -1-3). 9.99 *(978-1-59185-728-0(7))* Charisma Media.

England, Don. God, Are You Really There? (YA). pap., stu. ed. 7.99 *(978-0-89098-105-4(1))* Twentieth Century Christian Bks.

Un Establo Prestado (A Borrowed Stable) (SPA.). (J). *(978-0-7899-0873-5(5)*, 496232) Editorial Unilit.

Evans, Tony. A Kid's Guide to the Armor of God. 2015. (ENG., Illus.). 112p. (J). pap. 10.99 *(978-0-7369-6056-4(2))* Harvest Hse. Pubs.

—Kingdom Quest - A Strategy Guide for Teens & Their Parents/Mentors: Taking Faith & Character to the Next Level, Ages 14+ 2015. (ENG., Illus.). 144p. pap. 10.99 *(978-1-58997-809-6(9))* Focus on the Family Publishing.

Every Day of Advent, Cycle C: A Book of Activites for Children. 2003. (J). pap. 2.95 net. *(978-0-7648-1081-7(2))* Liguori Pubns.

Every Day of Lent: A Book of Activities for Children, Cycle C. 2003. (J). pap. 3.95 net. *(978-0-7648-1080-0(4))* Liguori Pubns.

Fawcett, Cheryl & Newman, Robert C. Kids' Questions about Sin & Salvation. 2003. (Illus.). 61p. pap. *(978-1-59402-083-4(3))* Regular Baptist Pr.

FBS 1st & 2nd Graders Learner Guide. 2005. 1.70 *(978-0-633-17764-5(4))* 2005. 1.70 *(978-0-633-17566-5(8))* 2004. 1.70 *(978-0-633-17372-2(X))* 2004. 1.70 *(978-0-633-08316-8(X))* 2004. 1.70 *(978-0-633-08064-8(0))* 2003. 1.65 *(978-0-633-07691-7(0))* LifeWay Christian Resources.

Fears, Melissa. Thank God It's Sunday. 2004. (J). per. 6.95 *(978-0-89315-413-4(X))* Lambert Bk. Hse., Inc.

Feinberg, Margaret. Text Messages from God for Girls Only. 2007. (Instant Messages Ser.). 160p. (J). pap. 9.99 *(978-1-59379-038-7(4))* White Stone Bks.

Feinberg, Margaret & Gillespie, Natalie. Text Messages from God for Guys Only. 2007. (Instant Messages Ser.). 160p. (J). pap. 9.99 *(978-1-59379-039-4(2))* White Stone Bks.

Ferguson, Sinclair B. Big Book of Bible Truths, Vol. 1. Apps, Fred, illus. 2012. (ENG.). 64p. (J). pap. 14.99 *(978-1-84550-371-0(6)*, df9d28c0-46d4-40ea-9ab5-380c71e316dc) Christian Focus Pubns. GBR. Dist: Bookmasters Distribution.

—The Plan: How God Got the World Ready for Jesus. Ruta, Angelo, illus. 2009. (Colour Bks.). (ENG.). 40p. (J). 9.99 *(978-1-84550-451-9(8)*, 9781845504519) Christian Focus Pubns. GBR. Dist: Bookmasters Distribution.

Ficocelli, Elizabeth. Child's Guide to First Holy Communion. Blake, Anne Catharine, illus. 2003. 32p. 10.95 *(978-0-8091-6708-1(5)*, 3708-5) Paulist Pr.

—Child's Guide to the Seven Sacraments. Blake, Anne Catharine, illus. 2005. 32p. (J). *(978-0-8091-6723-4(9)*, 6723-9) Paulist Pr.

Fields, Doug. Creative Times with God: Discovering New Ways to Connect with the SAVIOR. 2009. (ENG.). 121p. pap. 9.99 *(978-0-7644-6298-6(9))* Group Publishing, Inc.

Fields, Doug & Eastman, Brett. Surrendering Your Life to Honor God, 1 vol. 2076. (Life Together Ser.). (ENG.). 144p. pap., stu. ed. 9.99 *(978-0-310-25338-9(1))* Zondervan.

Finlayson, Linda. Adventure & Faith: Volume 1. 2009. (Risktakers Ser.). (ENG., Illus.). 128p. (J). 8.99 *(978-1-84550-491-5(7)*, 6cf822a4-86bc-44b2-afb7-4dd13268f24c) Christian Focus Pubns. GBR. Dist: Bookmasters Distribution.

Firm Foundations Child Edition. 2004. 5.95 *(978-1-890040-03-1(7))*; 49.95 *(978-1-890040-02-4(9))* New Tribes Mission, Inc.

First Reconciliation: Activities for Primary Grades. 2005. (Illus.). 32p. pap. 9.95 *(978-1-933178-09-7(4)*, 3451) Pflaum Publishing Group.

Fischer, Carl. Days of Faith: Student Planner & Assignment Book/Intermediate Teacher Supplement. 2005. (J). *(978-1-933178-04-2(3))* Pflaum Publishing Group.

—Days of Faith Assignment Book & Student Planner. Homberg, Ansgar, illus. 2003. 108p. (J). spiral bd. 4.99 *(978-0-89837-232-8(1)*, 9804) Pflaum Publishing Group.

—Together in Jesus: First Eucharist Certificate. 2004. (Together in Jesus Ser.). (Illus.). (J). pap. 9.95 *(978-0-937997-74-1(9)*, 922110) Pflaum Publishing Group.

Fischer, Jean. 3-Minute Devotions for Little Hearts. 2017. (3-Minute Devotions Ser.). (ENG.). 192p. (J). pap. 7.99 **(978-1-68322-221-7(0)**, Barbour Bks.) Barbour Publishing, Inc.

Fisher, Patrica A. I Want to Live. Fisher, Patrica A., ed. Fisher, Patrica A., illus. 2004. (Illus.). 200p. (YA). 20.00 *(978-0-9677231-5-0(9))* ITSMEEE Industries.

FitzPatrick, Bill. The Catholic Action Principles: Creating Positive Conversations. 2004. 160p. pap. 20.00 *(978-1-884864-21-6(X))* American Success Institute, Inc.

Flanagan, Anne. Come to Jesus: A Kids' Book for Eucharistic Adoration. Cleary, Janice, illus. 2006. (J). 4.50 *(978-0-8198-1577-4(2))* Pauline Bks. & Media.

Flanagan, Anne J. Jesus Walks with Us: Activity Book. 85p. (J). (gr. 4). pap. 2.25 *(978-0-8198-3928-2(0))* Pauline Bks. & Media.

Flinn, Frank K. Encyclopedia of Catholicism. 2007. (Encyclopedia of World Religions Ser.). (Illus.). 704p. (C). (gr. 9). per. 21.95 *(978-0-8160-7335-1(X)*, Checkmark Bks.) Facts On File, Inc.

Flinn, Lisa & Younger, Barbara. Sharing God's Love in Children's Church: A Year's Worth of Programs for Children Ages 3-7. 2008. (Illus.). 136p. pap. 21.99 *(978-0-687-49165-0(7))* Abingdon Pr.

Florea, Jesse & Whiting, Karen. The One Year Devotions for Active Boys. 2014. (ENG.). 400p. (J). pap. 14.99 *(978-1-4143-9404-6(7))* Tyndale Hse. Pubs.

Fold 'n Tell, 3 vols. (Illus.). (gr. 1-4). Set 1. 6.00 *(978-0-570-05527-3(X)*, 54-1037)Set 2. 6.00 *(978-0-570-05528-0(8)*, 54-1038) Concordia Publishing Hse.

For Heaven's Sake: A Weekly Collection of Saintly Inspiration. 2004. (YA). 17.50 *(978-0-9752874-0-8(0))* Lange-Patton, Lorraine.

Francis. More Saints of the Eucharist. 2006. (J). 2.50 *(978-0-9778570-1-2(8))* MOS, Inc.

Franklin, Kirk. How Do Alligators Praise the Lord? Carrier, Jason, illus. 2005. 24p. (J). (gr. 4-7). 11.99 incl. audio compact disk *(978-1-59185-209-4(9)*, Charisma Kids) Charisma Media.

Frazee, Randy. A Believe Devotional for Kids: Think, Act, Be Like Jesus: 90 Devotions, 1 vol. Adams, Steve, illus. 2015. (ENG.). 192p. (J). 12.99 *(978-0-310-75202-8(7))* Zonderkidz.

Freeman, Emily. When Hope Is Gone. 2004. (YA). audio compact disk 6.95 *(978-1-887938-42-6(7))* Sound Concepts, Inc.

Freeman, Laurence. A Simple Way: The Path of Christian Meditation. 2004. 43p. (YA). pap. 9.95 *(978-0-9725627-6-8(1))* Medio Media Publishing.

Friedrich, Eliza. Play Pray & Hooray. 2004. 128p. 10.99 *(978-0-7586-0117-9(4))* Concordia Publishing Hse.

Friends: On the Road. ldr.'s ed. (Ministry to Adolescent's Program Ser.). (Illus.). 64p. *(978-0-85910-802-7(3)*, 23-0802) Openbook Publishers.

From Raindrops to Rainbows. 2004. (J). cd-rom 95.00 *(978-0-9745631-1-4(0))* Kremer Pubns, Inc.

Funkhouser, Sandi. The DoorKeeper: In the King's Presence. 2005. (YA). per. 9.95 *(978-0-9771204-0-6(6))* Three Sisters Communication, LLC.

G-Force. (J). (gr. 1-6). 2004. DVD, cd-rom 29.95 *(978-0-633-09412-6(9))* 2004. DVD, cd-rom 29.95 *(978-0-633-09499-7(4))* 2003. DVD, cd-rom 29.95 *(978-0-633-09406-5(4))* 2003. DVD, cd-rom 29.95 *(978-0-633-09935-0(X))* LifeWay Christian Resources.

G-Force Family. (J). (gr. 1-6). 2004. cd-rom 9.95 *(978-0-633-09409-6(9))* 2004. cd-rom 9.95 *(978-0-633-09411-9(0))* 2003. cd-rom 9.95 *(978-0-633-09410-2(2))* 2003. cd-rom 9.95 *(978-0-633-09125-5(1))* LifeWay Christian Resources.

G-Force Powercel Cards for Older Children. (J). (gr. 4-6). 2004. 10.95 *(978-0-633-09438-6(2))* 2004. 10.95 *(978-0-633-09433-1(1))* 2003. 10.95 *(978-0-633-09437-9(4))* 2003. 10.95 *(978-0-633-09122-4(7))* LifeWay Christian Resources.

G-Force Powercel Cards for Younger Children. (J). (gr. 1-3). 2004. 10.95 *(978-0-633-09434-8(X))* 2004. 10.95 *(978-0-633-09432-4(3))* 2003. 10.95 *(978-0-633-09436-2(6))* 2003. 10.95 *(978-0-633-09124-8(3))* LifeWay Christian Resources.

G-Force Visual Pack. (J). (gr. 1-6). 2004. 29.95 *(978-0-633-09408-9(0))* 2004. 29.95 *(978-0-633-09407-2(2))* 2003. 29.95 *(978-0-633-09405-8(6))* 2003. 29.95 *(978-0-633-09123-1(5))* LifeWay Christian Resources.

Gallery, Philip D. Can You Find Saints? Introducing Your Child to Holy Men & Women. Harlow, Janet L., tr. Harlow, Janet L., illus. 2003. (J). (ENG.). 41p. (gr. 2-4). 16.99 *(978-0-86716-487-9(5))*; 40p. *(978-2-89507-437-3(2))* Franciscan Media.

Ganeri, Anita. Christian Festivals Through the Year. 2003. (Year of Festivals Ser.). 30p. (J). lib. bdg. 24.25 *(978-1-58340-370-9(1))* Black Rabbit Bks.

Gangwer, Rosalie M. & Heffernan, Mary A., texts. Jesus Loves Us. 143p. (gr. 1). pap. 6.50 *(978-0-8198-3918-3(3))* Pauline Bks. & Media.

Gardiner, Lisa. Jesus Loves Me. Flowerpot Press, ed. 2012. (Illus.). 20p. (J). *(978-1-77093-415-3(4))* Flowerpot Children's Pr. Inc.

Gaskins, Renee Guerry. Kevin Blue Can't Moo: And He Doesn't Know What to Do! 2012. 28p. (-18). pap. 16.09 *(978-1-4669-6801-1(X))* Trafford Publishing.

Geisler, Ruth. It's a Great, Awful, In-Between Day: Devotions for Young Readers. 2003. (Illus.). 112p. (J). (gr. 1-4). 10.99 *(978-0-7586-0124-7(7))* Concordia Publishing Hse.

George, Elizabeth. Una Joven Conforme al Corazon de Dios. 2003. pap. 8.99 *(978-0-7899-1139-1(6))* Editorial Unilit.

George, Jim. A Boy after God's Own Heart Action Devotional. 2017. (ENG.). 160p. (J). 9.99 *(978-0-7369-6751-8(6))* Harvest Hse. Pubs.

Gerlitz, Menachem. Return to the Heavenly City. 91p. (YA). pap. 5.95 *(978-1-56062-085-3(4))* C I S Communications, Inc.

Gibbons, Casey Hartley. A Girl's Life with God. 2006. 160p. pap. 8.99 *(978-1-56309-757-7(5)*, N034115) New Hope Pubs.

Gibbons, Joyce. What God Has Made! Johnson, Donna T., illus. 2004. 36p. 24.95 *(978-1-4137-3566-6(5))* PublishAmerica, Inc.

Gibson, Cay. Catholic Mosaic: Living the Liturgical Year with Literature, an Illustrated Book Study for Children. Decaen, Rose, ed. 2006. (J). pap. 24.99 *(978-0-9766386-6-7(5))* Hillside Education.

Gibson, Roxie C. Hey, God! What Makes You Happy? Gibson, James C., illus. 2007. (ENG.). 64p. (J). 7.99 *(978-1-933725-78-9(8))* Premium Pr. America.

Gieser, Sherry. Opening Gifts: Marriage & Holy Orders. 2003. 32p. (J). per. *(978-1-931709-73-6(4))* Our Sunday Visitor, Publishing Div.

Giombi, Gary. Finding God in Prayer: A Backpack Journal for Teens. 2004. (Illus.). 48p. (YA). (gr. 8-12). pap. 6.95 *(978-0-89837-196-3(1)*, 3524) Pflaum Publishing Group.

God Guides Us. 2004. (gr. 4). suppl. ed. 1.75 *(978-0-8294-0852-2(5))*; suppl. ed. 1.75 *(978-0-8294-0857-7(6))* Loyola Pr.

God is Good. 2004. (gr. 1). suppl. ed. 1.75 *(978-0-8294-0850-8(9))* Loyola Pr.

God Made Me (for Three-Year-Olds) 2004. (gr. -1-18). 8.25 *(978-0-8294-0815-7(0))*; tchr. ed. 23.95 *(978-0-8294-0816-4(9))* Loyola Pr.

God's Good Plan for Joseph. (Two Great Ways to Share God's Love Ser.). 16p. (gr. -1-k). 15.00 *(978-0-570-00255-0(9))* Concordia Publishing Hse.

God's Promise to Every Boy & Girl. 2003. (J). 4.95 *(978-0-9745324-1-7(X))* Kingdom Publishing Group, Inc.

God's Ten Commandments. (Two Great Ways to Share God's Love Ser.). 16p. (gr. -1-k). 15.00 *(978-0-570-00257-4(5))* Concordia Publishing Hse.

God's Word on Giving. (YA). *(978-0-7673-9388-1(0))* LifeWay Christian Resources.

Goldsmith, Joel S. Class Lessons with Joel Goldsmith. 2008. 116p. pap. *(978-0-9793119-3-2(4))* Editorial Benei Noaj.

Goosen, Stephanie. Caleb's World. 2013. 26p. 19.99 *(978-0-578-11359-3(7))* Dog Ear Publishing, LLC.

Gorler, Rosemarie & Piscitelli, Donna. Just Like Mary. Sternhagen, Mimi, illus. 2003. 48p. (J). 5.95 *(978-1-931709-79-8(3))* Our Sunday Visitor, Publishing Div.

Gospel Light. Passport to Adventure: 13 Choices That Shape a Kid's Life. 2013. (13 Week Bible Curriculum Ser.). (ENG.).

256p. (J). (gr. -1-7). pap. 49.99 incl. audio compact disk *(978-0-8307-7059-5(3))* Gospel Light Pubns.
GP4U: God's Plan for You. (J). 16.00 *(978-0-8307-2406-2(0))* Gospel Light Pubns.
Graham, Billy. God's Good News Bible Storybook, 1 vol. 2015. (ENG., Illus.). 176p. (J). 19.99 *(978-0-7180-0630-3(5))* Nelson, Thomas Inc.
Grate, Gina. Project Noah. 2006. 32p. 4.50 *(978-0-8341-2231-4(6))* Nazarene Publishing Hse.
Greene, Carol. Why Boys & Girls Are Different. 2008. pap. 12.99 *(978-0-7586-1415-5(2))* Concordia Publishing Hse.
—Why Boys & Girls Are Different. Dorankamp, Michelle, illus. 2008. pap. 12.99 *(978-0-7586-1409-4(8))* Concordia Publishing Hse.
Greenwood, Lori. The Vision Link: 60 Keys to Fulfilling Your Future. 2003. (YA). 6.95 *(978-0-9747956-1-4(5))* Greenwood, Lori Ministries, Inc.
Gresh, Dannah. My Secret Keeper Girl(r) Diary. 2014. (ENG.). 160p. (J). 9.99 *(978-0-7369-6000-7(7))* Harvest Hse. Pubs.
Group Publishing Staff, creator. Grapple - Spring: Preteens' Toughest Questions. the Bible's Smartest Answers, 7 vols. 2013. (ENG.). 112p. (J). (gr. 4-6). pap. 69.99 *(978-1-4707-0469-8(2))* Group Publishing, Inc.
Growing up in Christ: 52 Bible Lessons from the New Testament. 2006. 320p. (YA). (gr. 3-7). 29.99 *(978-0-7847-1182-8(8)*, 42080) Standard Publishing.
Gustafon, Karen. Mongolia Cries Out for Prayer: Will You Be the One to Answer the Cry? 2004. 32p. (J). bds. 15.95 *(978-1-59298-080-2(5))* Beaver's Pond Pr., Inc.
Hakes, Matthew. What Catholic Teens Should Know about Ecstacy. Larkin, Jean, ed. 2003. (What Catholic Teens Should Know Ser.). (Illus.). 8p. (YA). 7.95 *(978-0-89837-188-6(0)*, 440110) Pflaum Publishing Group.
—What Catholic Teens Should Know about Going to War. Larkin, Jean, ed. 2003. (What Catholic Teens Should Know Ser.). (Illus.). 8p. (YA). 7.95 *(978-0-89837-190-1(2)*, 440310) Pflaum Publishing Group.
—What Catholic Teens Should Know about What Muslims Believe. Larkin, Jean K., ed. 2004. (What Catholic Teens Should Know Ser.). (Illus.). 8p. (YA). 7.95 *(978-0-89837-241-0(0)*, 440810) Pflaum Publishing Group.
—What Catholic Teens Should Know When Scandal Hits the Church. Larkin, Jean, ed. 2003. (What Catholic Teens Should Know Ser.). (Illus.). 8p. (YA). 7.95 *(978-0-89837-192-5(9)*, 440510) Pflaum Publishing Group.
Hall, Mark, et al. Thrive Student Edition: Digging Deep, Reaching Out, 1 vol. 2014. (ENG.). 240p. (YA). pap. 12.99 *(978-0-310-74757-4(0))* Zondervan.
Hall-Smith, Rachel. Tlk2me: God's Answer for Today. 2003. (ENG., Illus.). 32p. (J). pap. 1.50 *(978-1-85792-822-8(9)*, 9781857928228) Christian Focus Pubns. GBR. Dist: Bookmasters Distribution.
Halteman, Laverne K. Mommy Goes to Heaven. 2003. (Illus.). (J). *(978-0-87813-612-4(6))* Christian Light Pubns., Inc.
Ham, Ken. The Answers Book for Kids, Volume 4: 22 Questions from Kids on Sin, Salvation, & the Christian Life. 2009. (Answers Book for Kids Ser.). (Illus.). 48p. (J). (gr. 3-7). 7.99 *(978-0-89051-528-0(X))* Master Bks.
Hamilton, Dennis Stephen. Higher Ground. 2004. per. 12.95 *(978-0-9653904-6-0(2))* DCTS Publishing.
Hammari, Kimiko. Teeny Tiny Talks IV: My Eternal Family. Miller, Rebecca, illus. 2008. 116p. (J). pap. 12.99 *(978-1-59955-188-3(8))* Cedar Fort, Inc./CFI Distribution.
Hammond, Edward. Jesus the Way: The Child's Guide to Heav. 2005. pap. 10.99 *(978-1-59925-035-9(7))* Solid Ground Christian Bks.
Hare, Eric B. Clever Queen. 2011. 96p. reprint ed. pap. 10.95 *(978-1-57258-211-8(1))* TEACH Services, Inc.
Harper, Vicky. Selah, Vol. 1. 2003. pap. 10.00 *(978-0-9746997-0-7(5))* Little Bookstore Who Could, The.
Harrah, Judith. Jesus, I Believe. Kukreja, Julie, illus. 2012. 34p. (J). pap. 10.99 *(978-1-937331-10-8(5))* ShadeTree Publishing, LLC.
Harrast, Tracy. ¿Adivina Que? Historias de la Biblia, 1 vol. Sharp, Alice & Sharp, Paul, illus. 2005. (SPA.). 192p. (J). (gr. 1-5). 13.99 *(978-0-8297-4448-4(7))* Vida Pubs.
Hartley, Bob. Childrens Adoration Prayer Book. Clonts, E. M. M., illus. 2012. 114p. pap. 24.95 *(978-0-615-58840-7(9))* Deeper Waters.
Haskins, Amanda. God Is My Daddy. l.t. ed. 2006. (Illus.). 26p. (J). per. 11.99 *(978-1-59879-279-9(2))* Lifevest Publishing, Inc.
Hatfield, Ron. Love Notes from God. Boehm, Annette, ed. 2004. (YA). 7.95 *(978-0-9754117-0-4(5))* Butterfly Bk. Makers.
Hatfield, Tyrel & Hatfield, Justin. Righteous Roundup: Wanted: Righteous children of God. Hatfield, Tyrel, illus. 2008. (Illus.). (J). cd-rom 99.00 *(978-0-9766703-6-0(4))* Little Acorn LLC.
Hatfield, Tyrel S. & Hatfield, Justin R. Fix your eyes on Jesus. Hatfield, Tyrel S., illus. 2005. (Illus.). 108p. (J). spiral bd. 150.00 *(978-0-9766703-0-8(5))* Little Acorn LLC.
Heffernan, Eileen. Fifty-Seven Stories of Saints. Rizzo, Jerry, illus. 2003. (J). 552p. pap. 16.95 *(978-0-8198-2674-9(X)*, 332-094); 549p. *(978-0-8198-2675-6(8))* Pauline Bks. & Media.
Helms, Selah & Thompson, Susan. Small Talks on Big Questions Vol. 2: A Historical Companion to the Children's Catechism, 2 vols. Whitney, Caffy, illus. 2003. 192p. 26.99 *(978-1-894400-05-3(4))* Joshua Pr., Inc. CAN. Dist: Gabriel Resources.
Henderson, Susan & White, Emily. Raising the Roof: Destination Reality. 2003. (YA). pap. 14.99 *(978-0-89265-967-8(X))* Randall Hse. Pubns.
Henkel, Vernon & Tweed, Sean, illus. Esther Vol. 28: Old Testament Volume 28: Esther. 2003. (ENG.). 30p. (J). pap. *(978-1-932381-01-6(5)*, 2028) Bible Visuals International, Inc.
Henley, Karyn. God Is with Me All the Time. (Children's Ministry Folders). (Illus.). 8p. (gr. -1-k). 2.99 *(978-0-7847-0680-0(8)*, 42230) Standard Publishing.
—Hablame de Dios. Erickson, David L., illus. 2005. 20p. (J). (gr. 4-7). 8.99 *(978-1-59185-825-6(9)*, Charisma Kids) Charisma Media.
—I am Kind to My Friends. (Children's Ministry Folders). (Illus.). 8p. (gr. -1-k). 2.99 *(978-0-7847-0679-4(4)*, 42229) Standard Publishing.
—I Give. (Children's Ministry Folders). (Illus.). 8p. (gr. -1-k). 2.99 *(978-0-7847-0675-6(1)*, 42225) Standard Publishing.
—I Grow. (Children's Ministry Folders). (Illus.). 8p. (gr. -1-k). 2.99 *(978-0-7847-0662-6(X)*, 42212) Standard Publishing.
—I Help. (Children's Ministry Folders). (Illus.). 8p. (gr. -1-k). 2.99 *(978-0-7847-0666-4(2)*, 42216) Standard Publishing.
—I Listen. (Children's Ministry Folders). (Illus.). 8p. (gr. -1-k). 2.99 *(978-0-7847-0673-2(5)*, 42223) Standard Publishing.
—I Obey My Parents. (Children's Ministry Folders). (Illus.). 8p. (gr. -1-k). 2.99 *(978-0-7847-0664-0(6)*, 42214) Standard Publishing.
—I Praise God. (Children's Ministry Folders). (Illus.). 8p. (gr. -1-k). 2.99 *(978-0-7847-0661-9(1)*, 42211) Standard Publishing.
—I Pray. (Children's Ministry Folders). (Illus.). 8p. (gr. -1-k). 2.99 *(978-0-7847-0660-2(3)*, 42210) Standard Publishing.
—I Say Thank-You. (Children's Ministry Folders). (Illus.). 8p. (gr. -1-k). 2.99 *(978-0-7847-0674-9(3)*, 42224) Standard Publishing.
—I Share. (Children's Ministry Folders). (Illus.). 8p. (gr. -1-k). 2.99 *(978-0-7847-0665-7(4)*, 42215) Standard Publishing.
—I Take Care of My Body. (Children's Ministry Folders). (Illus.). 8p. (gr. -1-k). 2.99 *(978-0-7847-0663-3(8)*, 42213) Standard Publishing.
—I Take Care of My Pets. (Children's Ministry Folders). (Illus.). 8p. (gr. -1-k). 2.99 *(978-0-7847-0676-3(X)*, 42226) Standard Publishing.
—I Take Care of My Room. (Children's Ministry Folders). (Illus.). 8p. (gr. -1-k). 2.99 *(978-0-7847-0678-7(6)*, 42228) Standard Publishing.
—I Take Care of the Earth. (Children's Ministry Folders). (Illus.). 8p. (gr. -1-k). 2.99 *(978-0-7847-0677-0(8)*, 42227) Standard Publishing.
—I Trust God at Night. (Children's Ministry Folders). (Illus.). 8p. (gr. -1-k). 2.99 *(978-0-7847-0667-1(0)*, 42217) Standard Publishing.
—I Trust God When It Rains. (Children's Ministry Folders). (Illus.). 8p. (gr. -1-k). 2.99 *(978-0-7847-0668-8(9))* Standard Publishing.
—Tell Me about God. Erickson, David, illus. 2005. 24p. (J). 9.99 *(978-1-59185-616-0(7)*, Charisma Kids) Charisma Media.
Henley, Karyn F. Love Trumps Karma: Uncovering the Truth You Know You Know. 2005. 152p. (YA). per. 12.99 *(978-0-9743197-8-0(3)*, Karyn Henley Resources) Child Sensitive Communication, LLC.
Heroes for Today. 2006. 16p. (J). pap. 1.99 *(978-0-7847-1587-1(4)*, 22134) Standard Publishing.
Herrera, Erik, et al. Acquire the Fire: 40 Teen Devotionals, Vol. 1. Mauss, Doug, ed. 2006. (Teen Mania Ser.). (Illus.). 100p. (J). (gr. 4-7). per. 5.99 *(978-0-7814-4352-4(0)*, 0781443520) Cook, David C.
Hibschman, Barbara. 52 Ways to Teach Children to Share the Gospel. 2004. (Fifty-Two Ways Ser.). (Illus.). 64p. (J). (gr. -1-7). pap. 9.95 *(978-0-937282-00-7(6)*, RB36107) Rainbow Pubs. & Legacy Pr.
Higgs, Liz Curtis. The Pumpkin Patch Parable. (Parable Ser.). 2005. 32p. (J). pap. 3.99 *(978-1-4003-0668-8(X))* 2006. (ENG., Illus.). 36p. (gr. -1-2). 7.99 *(978-1-4003-0846-0(1))* Nelson, Thomas Inc.
Hill, Bartha. Kiwi Adventures. 2007. (Adventure Ser.). (ENG., Illus.). 96p. (J). per. 8.99 *(978-1-84550-282-9(5)*, bc2e1b1f-fc91-4f29-9bc6-4fd6af488a81) Christian Focus Pubns. GBR. Dist: Bookmasters Distribution.
Hill, Brenda. Messages of God Written in Rhyme. 2005. 57p. pap. 16.95 *(978-1-4137-9480-9(7))* PublishAmerica, Inc.
Hilton, John & Sweat, Anthony. How? Essential Skills for Living the Gospel. 2010. (Illus.). xii, 251p. (YA). 34.99 *(978-1-60641-789-8(4))* Deseret Bk. Co.
Hilton, Marilyn Copley. The Christian Girl's Guide to Your Mom. 2004. (Illus.). 176p. (J). pap. 9.99 *(978-1-58411-045-3(7)*, Legacy Pr.) Rainbow Pubs. & Legacy Pr.
Hinds Feet on High Places (Children's Version) Family Activity Guide. 2005. (J). per. 14.99 *(978-0-9772303-0-3(9))* A.I.M. Enterprises.
Hoard, Julia. God, What Is the Gift of Tongues? 2007. (ENG., Illus.). 32p. (gr. -1-3). 14.99 *(978-1-59979-076-3(9)*, Creation Hse.) Charisma Media.
Holl, Kristi. Girlz Rock: Devotions for Girls, 1 vol. 2005. (Faithgirlz Ser.). (ENG.). 192p. (J). pap. 9.99 *(978-0-310-70899-5(0))* Zonderkidz.
—What's a Girl to Do? Finding Faith in Everyday Life, 1 vol. 2007. (Faithgirlz Ser.). (ENG.). 192p. (J). (gr. 3-7). pap. 9.99 *(978-0-310-71348-7(X))* Zonderkidz.
Honoring God. 2003. per. *(978-1-55630-841-3(8))* Brentwood Communications Group.
Hook, Katie. Momma Loves You. Hook, Katie, illus. 2015. (ENG., Illus.). 32p. pap. 9.99 *(978-1-63047-495-9(9))* Morgan James Publishing.
Horne, Douglas V., ed. & compiled by. The Christian Leaders Home Discipleship Hymnbook. Horne, Douglas V., compiled by. 2004. 15.00 *(978-0-9753133-0-5(4))* Home Discipleship Pr.
Houser, Tina. God's Campground. 2008. 64p. (J). pap. 5.99 *(978-1-59317-341-8(5))* Warner Pr., Inc.
How the Church Grew: Student Guide. 80p. stu. ed. 10.95 *(978-0-7586-0472-9(6))* Concordia Publishing Hse.
Howat, Irene. Ten Boys Who Made History. 2012. (Lightkeepers Ser.). (ENG.). 160p. (J). pap. 8.99 *(978-1-85792-836-5(9)*, 27f2ee34-322e-4f55-9f50-39b1f77ab0c9) Christian Focus Pubns. GBR. Dist: Bookmasters Distribution.
—Ten Girls Who Made History. 2015. (Lightkeepers Ser.). (ENG.). 160p. (J). pap. 8.99 *(978-1-85792-837-2(7)*, 0745e90b-2eca-498b-bd1e-c9f553e4f9ac) Christian Focus Pubns. GBR. Dist: Bookmasters Distribution.
Howell, Brian. You Have Been Invited! Collins Powell, Judy, illus. 2012. (ENG.). 48p. 18.99 *(978-0-9882892-0-8(2))* Wheat State Media LLC.
Howver, Jen, et al. Wisdom on ... Getting along with Parents, 1 vol. 2008. (Wisdom Ser.). (ENG.). 144p. (YA). pap. 9.99 *(978-0-310-27929-7(1))* Zondervan.
Hubbard, Margaret Ann. Saint Louis & the Last Crusade. Barton, Harry, illus. 2013. (ENG.). 157p. pap. 9.95 *(978-1-58617-647-1(1))* Ignatius Pr.
Hudson. God Gave Me. pap. 1.59 *(978-0-687-05393-3(5))* Abingdon Pr.
Hudson, Wonderland D. The Believer under Fire 40-Day Devotional & Journal: Daily Inspiration for People Who Love Jesus That Are Going Through the Times of Fiery Trial & Testing. 2003. per. 14.99 *(978-0-9744733-4-5(0))* Good Works Publishing Hse.
Humphrey, Art & Humphrey, Pat. Don't Sweat It: Ask Art & Pat. Butler, Tad, illus. pap. 11.95 *(978-0-9712305-0-7(1))* Heart Path Publishing.
Hunt, E. Marlene. Every Apple. Hunt, E. Marlene, illus. l.t. ed. 2003. (Illus.). 12p. pap. 10.00 *(978-1-893555-45-7(3))* Grace Publishing.
Hunter, Zach. Generation Change: Roll up Your Sleeves & Change the World, 1 vol. 2013. (Invert Ser.). (ENG., Illus.). 176p. (YA). (gr. 8-11). pap. 12.99 *(978-0-310-28515-1(1))* Zondervan.
Hyles, Jack. Science of the Christian Life: Volume I, Vol. 1. 2003. per. *(978-0-9745499-5-8(9))* Hyles Pubns.
I Can Be More Like Jesus. 2006. 12.99 *(978-1-56309-916-8(0))* Woman's Missionary Union.
I Can Follow Jesus. 2014. (Happy Day Ser.). (ENG., Illus.). 16p. (J). pap. 2.49 *(978-1-4143-9419-0(5))* Tyndale Hse. Pubs.
I Can Honor God: 5 Lessons Explore the Rewards (Crowns) God Promises to Those Who Homor Him: Flannelgraph. (Biblegrams Bible Lesson Ser.). (J). (gr. -1). pap. 13.99 *(978-1-55976-077-5(X))* CEF Pr.
Ifrim, Clelia. Cui Apartine Ziua de Ieri? 2013. 94p. pap. 11.95 *(978-1-936629-19-0(4))* Reflection Publishing.
La Iglesia (The Church) Quarter 3, Level 3. (Caminando con Jesus (Walking with Jesus) Series A). (SPA.). (J). (gr. 3-4). stu. ed. 3.50 *(978-0-570-05151-0(7)*, 16-3813) Concordia Publishing Hse.
Invoke A Blessing Inc., Staff. The Uncommon Boy. 2012. (ENG., Illus.). 71p. pap. 10.00 *(978-0-9831902-6-4(7))* Invoke A Blessing Inc.
Irwin, James. Destination Moon. 15th anniv. ed. 2004. 52p. 16.00 *(978-1-929241-98-9(4))* Send The Light Distribution LLC.
Issues: On the Road. ldr.'s ed. (Ministry to Adolescent's Program Ser.). (Illus.). 72p. *(978-0-85910-798-3(1)*, 23-0798) Openbook Publishers.
Ives, Pastor Carla. Healed from the Inside Out! 2010. 32p. pap. 12.99 *(978-1-4490-3000-1(9))* AuthorHouse.
Jackson Black, Amy Sue. Mercy Said No. 2007. 13p. 7.90 *(978-0-615-16743-5(8))* Black, Amy Jackson.
Jackson, James, illus. Dancing with David. Date not set. 24p. (J). *(978-1-887399-02-9(X))* Colbert Hse., LLC, The.
Jackson, Vanessa Wyse. Recipes for Life: Fifty Ready-To-Use Spiritual Talks for Children. 2012. (ENG., Illus.). 134p. pap. 15.95 *(978-1-84730-360-8(9))* Veritas Pubns. IRL. Dist: Dufour Editions, Inc.
Jarrell, Jane & Saathoff, Deborah. Off to Work We Go. 2004. 50p. (gr. -1-18). pap., act. bk. ed. 6.99 *(978-0-8054-0823-2(1))* B&H Publishing Group.
Jeffery, P. Growing Up: Issues Ben Faces as a Christian Teenager. 2004. (Illus.). 48p. *(978-0-85234-528-3(3))* Evangelical Pr.
Jeffs, Stephanie & Tulip, Jenny. My First Find Out about Series. 2004. (gr. -1-18). *(978-0-8294-1735-7(4))* Loyola Pr.
Jensen, Rebecca Ridges, illus. My Heavenly Father Loves Me. 2015. (J). 10.99 *(978-1-4621-1564-8(0)*, Horizon Pubs.) Cedar Fort, Inc./CFI Distribution.
Jesus: On the Road. ldr.'s ed. (Ministry to Adolescent's Program Ser.). (Illus.). 64p. *(978-0-85910-800-3(7))* Openbook Publishers.
Jesus Company: Bible Time. 30p. (gr. 4-18). stu. ed. 10.50 *(978-0-570-00672-5(4)*, 22-2775) Concordia Publishing Hse.
Jesus Company: Bible Time, Grade 5. 30p. (gr. 5-18). stu. ed. 10.50 *(978-0-570-00678-7(3)*, 7.99) Concordia Publishing Hse.
Jesus Company: Worship, Friendship, Service & Witness, 4 bks., Set. (gr. 4-18). 45.00 *(978-0-570-00690-9(2)*, 22-2794); (gr. 5-18). 45.00 *(978-0-570-00691-6(0)*, 22-2795); (gr. 6-18). 45.00 *(978-0-570-00692-3(9)*, 22-2796) Concordia Publishing Hse.
Jesus, el Cristo (Jesus, the Christ) Quarter 2, Level 2. (Caminando con Jesus (Walking with Jesus) Series B). (SPA.). (J). (gr. 1-2). stu. ed. 3.50 *(978-0-570-05136-7(3)*, 16-2912) Concordia Publishing Hse.
A Jesus Kind of Life. 2004. (YA). per. 12.00 *(978-0-9747189-8-9(X))* LightHouse Pr.
Jesus Loves Me. 2006. (Illus.). 20p. (J). (gr. -1-3). bds. 5.49 *(978-0-7586-0914-4(0))* Concordia Publishing Hse.
Jesus' Message for the Church. 2003. (YA). lib. bdg. 7.99 *(978-0-9729477-1-8(X))* Morningstar Christian Chapel.
Jesus Te Ama Libro.Tr. of Jesus Loves You. (SPA.). (J). 1.69 *(978-0-7899-0532-1(9)*, 498795) Editorial Unilit.
Jingling, Kathy, ed. Barnabas & His Great Mission for Christ. Tobar, Malena, illus. 2011. (SPA.). 198p. (J). spiral bd. 7.00 *(978-1-931984-40-9(9)*, 2002-00E1) Faith & Action Team.
—Bernabe y su Gran Mision por Cristo. Oyola, Milta, tr. from ENG. Tobar, Malena, illus. 2011.Tr. of Barnabas & his Great Mission for Christ. (SPA.). 191p. (J). spiral bd. 7.00 *(978-1-931984-41-6(7)*, 2002-00S1) Faith & Action Team.
Johnson, Greg. If I Could Ask God Just One Question: 80 Answers to Teens' Most-Asked Questions. 2016. (ENG.). 192p. pap. 7.99 *(978-1-63058-351-4(0)*, Barbour Bks.) Barbour Publishing, Inc.
Johnson, Gregg. Bedroom Bible College Manual: BBC Manual. 2004. 123p. pap. 20.00 *(978-0-9766930-0-0(3))* Movement Makers International.
Johnson, Kevin. Pray: Talk to the King of the Universe, 1 vol. 2007. (Deeper Ser.). (ENG., Illus.). 112p. (gr. 13). pap. 7.99 *(978-0-310-27492-6(3))* Zondervan.
—Total Devotion: 365 Days to Hang Tight with Jesus. 2004. (ENG.). 374p. (YA). reprint ed. pap. 16.00 *(978-0-7642-2884-1(6))* Bethany Hse. Pubs.
Johnston, Kurt, et al. My School, 1 vol. 2007. (Middle School Survival Ser.). (ENG., Illus.). 192p. (YA). (gr. 7-9). pap. 9.99 *(978-0-310-27882-5(1))* Zondervan.
Jones, Jeremy V. The Keeper: The Tim Howard Story. 2010. (ZonderKidz Biography Ser.). (ENG.). 128p. (J). (gr. 4-7). pap. 6.99 *(978-0-310-72004-1(4))* Zonderkidz.
—Toward the Goal: The Kaká Story, 1 vol. 2010. (ZonderKidz Biography Ser.). (ENG.). 128p. (J). (gr. 4-7). pap. 6.99 *(978-0-310-72003-4(6))* Zonderkidz.
Jones, Stan & Jones, Brenna. The Story of Me. Spector, Joel, illus. 2007. (God's Design for Sex Ser.: 1). (ENG.). 48p. (Orig.). pap. 10.99 *(978-1-60006-013-7(7))* NavPress Publishing Group.
Jordan, Bernice. God Guides Us - Textbook: Footsteps of Faith - Old Testament Volume 4: Footsteps of Faith - Old Testament Volume 4. 2005. (ENG.). 180p. (J). pap. 14.99 *(978-0-86508-008-9(9))* BCM International Inc.
Joseph, E. T. Larry Light up Sneakers. 2004. 25p. pap. 24.95 *(978-1-4137-3335-8(2))* PublishAmerica, Inc.
Joseph-Samuel, Dennese H. God Is H. I. T. S. Happily Interested in Teenager's Services. 2004. (YA). per. 15.95 *(978-0-9747543-1-4(5))* Kids Children & Teens World 2000 & Beyond.
The Journey. 2004. (YA). pap., stu. ed. 5.00 *(978-0-9749186-1-7(X))* Revivalist Pr., The.
Kampakis, Kari. 10 Ultimate Truths Girls Should Know, 1 vol. 2014. (ENG.). 224p. (YA). pap. 14.99 *(978-0-529-11103-6(9))* Nelson, Thomas Inc.
Karr, Leona, compiled by. Make Way for Miracles. 2004. 140p. per. 14.95 *(978-0-9761694-0-6(1))* Venture Publishing.
Kaster, Jeffrey. What Catholic Teens Should Know about Homosexuality. Larking, Jean K., ed. 2004. (What Catholic Teens Should Know Ser.). (Illus.). 8p. (YA). 7.95 *(978-0-89837-236-6(4)*, 441010) Pflaum Publishing Group.
Kaster, Jeffrey & Kaster, Liz. What Catholic Teens Should Know about How Far to Go. Larkin, Jean, ed. 2003. (What Catholic Teens Should Know Ser.). (Illus.). 8p. (YA). 7.95 *(978-0-89837-191-8(0)*, 440410) Pflaum Publishing Group.
Kawasaki, Shauna Mooney, illus. My Family Can Be Forever: Sharing Time Activities. 2003. 62p. (J). pap. *(978-1-59038-232-5(3))* Deseret Bk. Co.
Kelley, Gail & Hershberger, Carol. Come Mime with Me: A Guide to Preparing Scriptural Dramas for Children. 2003. (Illus.). 104p. (YA). (gr. 1-18). 16.00 *(978-0-89390-089-2(3))* Resource Pubns., Inc.
Kelley, Matt. Crosswind: A Spirit-Driven Experience. 2007. (Illus.). 32p. (YA). (gr. 8-12). pap. 4.00 *(978-0-687-33457-5(8))* Abingdon Pr.
Kelly, Camryn, et al. Just Me & My Friends & Family. 2012. (Hot Chocolate with God Ser.: 2). (ENG.). 160p. (YA). (gr. 3-7). pap. 10.99 *(978-0-89296-844-2(3)*, Faithwords) Hachette Nashville.
Kenney, Cindy. God's World & Me: Boz's Big Book of Bible Fun. 2007. (Boz the Bear Ser.). (Illus.). 235p. (J). (gr. -1-3). pap. 14.99 *(978-0-7814-4544-3(2))* Cook, David C.
Kenney, Cindy, et al. Peas & Thank You!, 1 vol. 2003. (Big Idea Books / VeggieTales Ser.). (ENG.). 12p. (J). (gr. -1-1). bds. 4.99 *(978-0-310-70540-6(1))* Zonderkidz.
KID's Forecast for Life. 2005. 20.99 *(978-1-59781-647-2(7))* Salem Author Services.
The Kids Prayed & God Arrived. 2004. (YA). *(978-1-59581-083-0(8))* Brentwood Communications Group.
King, Clayton. True Love Project: How the Gospel Defines Your Purity. 2014. (True Love Project Ser.). (ENG.). 176p. (J). (gr. 7-12). pap. 12.99 *(978-1-4336-8433-3(0)*, B&H Kids) B&H Publishing Group.
—40 Days of Purity for Guys. 2014. (True Love Project Ser.). (ENG.). 176p. (J). (gr. 7-12). 9.99 *(978-1-4336-8435-7(7)*, B&H Kids) B&H Publishing Group.
King, Sharie. 40 Days of Purity for Girls. 2014. (True Love Project Ser.). (ENG.). 176p. (J). (gr. 7-12). 9.99 *(978-1-4336-8434-0(9)*, B&H Kids) B&H Publishing Group.
Kizer, Drew. Make Your Stand. 2004. (YA). per. 10.00 *(978-0-9725894-1-3(4))* Riddle Creek Publishing.
Klammer, Lynn. God & Me! 2: Ages 2-5, 3 vols. 2004. (Illus.). 238p. (J). spiral bd. 12.99 *(978-1-58411-054-5(6)*, Legacy Pr.) Rainbow Pubs. & Legacy Pr.
—Gotta Have God 2: Ages 2-5, 3. Heiser, Aline, illus. 2005. (Gotta Have God Ser.). 238p. (J). spiral bd. 12.99 *(978-1-58411-057-6(0)*, Legacy Pr.) Rainbow Pubs. & Legacy Pr.
Kline, Tom. God's Love in Action: The Amazing Gift of Jesus. Weber, Penny, illus. 2015. (ENG.). 62p. pap. 8.99 *(978-0-9863364-0-9(8))* Kline, Tom.
Knight 6 Personal Growth Planbook: Extreme Quest. 2003. (Illus.). 48p. (J). pap. 4.95 *(978-1-59312-047-4(8))* North American Mission Board, SBC.
Knowing Our Catholic Faith: 26 Lessons. 2004. *(978-0-8294-1129-4(1))*; Vol. 2. *(978-0-8294-1130-0(5))*; Vol. 3. *(978-0-8294-1131-7(3))* Loyola Pr.
Knowing Our Catholic Faith: 32 Lessons. 2004. Vol. 4. *(978-0-8294-1132-4(1))* Vol. 5. *(978-0-8294-1134-8(8))* Vol. 6. *(978-0-8294-1135-5(6))* Loyola Pr.
Knowing Our Catholic Faith: 38 Lessons. 2004. Vol. 7. *(978-0-8294-1136-2(4))* Vol. 8. *(978-0-8294-1137-9(2))* Loyola Pr.
Knowing Our Catholic Faith: Complete Set, 8 vols. 2004. *(978-0-8294-1508-7(4))* Loyola Pr.
Kunzinger, Bob. The Infant: A Tale from Prague. 2005. 85p. pap. 12.00 *(978-0-9725110-4-9(0))* All Nations Pr.
Lad 1 Personal Growth Planbook: Clue Chasers. 2003. (Illus.). 48p. (J). pap. 4.95 *(978-1-59312-042-9(7))* North American Mission Board, SBC.
Lad 2 Personal Growth Planbook: Everglade Explorers. 2003. (Illus.). 48p. (J). pap. 4.95 *(978-1-59312-043-6(5))* North American Mission Board, SBC.
Lad 3 Personal Growth Planbook: Rawhide Wranglers. 2003. (Illus.). 48p. (J). pap. 4.95 *(978-1-59312-044-3(3))* North American Mission Board, SBC.
Lagneau, Mary. Blessed Jacint: Patron for Children for Tummy Troubles. Gillen, Rosemarie, illus. 2012. 20p. pap. 7.50 *(978-1-61286-134-0(2))* Avid Readers Publishing Group.
Lamar, Melvin. The Call to Be Different. 2003. (YA). per. 12.99 *(978-0-9716068-2-1(X))* Lamar, Melvin Productions.
Lamplighter Staff. Boys of Grit Who Became Men Of. 2004. 16.00 *(978-1-58474-026-1(4))* Cornerstone Family Ministries/Lamplighter Publishing.
—Stephen Soldier of the Cross. 2004. 17.00 *(978-1-58474-032-2(9))* Cornerstone Family Ministries/Lamplighter Publishing.
Langford, Lynn F. God's Gals: Lessons in Forgiveness, Courage, Serving, & Sharing. 2013. 40p. pap. 16.95 *(978-1-4908-0368-5(8)*, WestBow Pr.) Author Solutions, Inc.
Larkin, Jean. Days of Faith: Student Planner & Assignment Book/Primary Teacher Supplement 2005-2006. 2005. (J). *(978-1-933178-06-6(X)*, 9816) Pflaum Publishing Group.

C
D

—Totally Lent! A Child's Journey to Easter 2007. 2006. (Illus.). 64p. pap. 5.95 *(978-1-933178-46-2(9))* Pflaum Publishing Group.

—Totally Lent! A Kid's Journey to Easter 2007. 2006. (Illus.). 64p. pap. 5.95 *(978-1-933178-45-5(0))* Pflaum Publishing Group.

Larkin, Jean, ed. First Eucharist: Activities for Primary Grades. 2005. (Illus.). 32p. pap. 9.95 *(978-1-933178-10-3(8)*, 3450) Pflaum Publishing Group.

Lawrence, Ava. A Button for a Crown. Ford, Christina, illus. I.t. ed. 2003. 84p. (J). 14.95 *(978-0-9651048-4-5(2))* Papillon Publishing.

Lawrence, David. The Chocolate Teapot: Surviving at School. 2004. (Illus.). 112p. pap. *(978-1-84427-051-4(3))* Scripture Union.

Lawson, Michael S. Grandpa Mike Talks about God. 2007. (ENG., Illus.). 112p. (J). (gr. -1-2). pap. 12.99 *(978-1-84550-250-8(7)*, 45f2618a-2b73-472b-b400-ad6436e5c5d1) Christian Focus Pubns. GBR. Dist: Bookmasters Distribution.

Lazurek, Michelle S. Daddy, Am I Beautiful? Stott, Apryl, illus. 2015. 24p. (J). pap. *(978-0-8198-1905-5(0))* Pauline Bks. & Media.

—Mommy, Am I Strong? Spinks, Scott, illus. 2015. 25p. (J). pap. *(978-0-8198-4948-9(0))* Pauline Bks. & Media.

Lechner, Diane, et al, texts. Jesus Comes to Us. 143p. (J). (gr. 2). pap. 6.50 *(978-0-8198-3921-3(3))* Pauline Bks. & Media.

Legacy. 7.50 *(978-0-8054-5927-2(8))* B&H Publishing Group.

Legacy Press Staff. God's Girls! Fun & Faith for Ages 9-12. 2004. (God's Girls Ser.: Vol. 1). (Illus.). (J). (gr. 4-7). 176p. pap. 12.99 *(978-1-58411-020-0(1))*; Vol. 2. 192p. pap. 12.99 *(978-1-58411-021-7(X))* Rainbow Pubs. & Legacy Pr. (Legacy Pr.).

—Gotta Have God: Devotions for Boys. 2004. (Gotta Have God Ser.). (Illus.). 238p. (J). (gr. -1-k). spiral bd. 12.99 *(978-1-885358-96-7(2))*; (gr. 1-4). spiral bd. 12.99 *(978-1-885358-97-4(0))*; (gr. 5-7). spiral bd. 12.99 *(978-1-885358-98-1(9))* Rainbow Pubs. & Legacy Pr. (Legacy Pr.).

Leichner, Jeannine Timko. Making Things Right: The Sacrament of Reconciliation. Davidson, Kevin, illus. 2005. 70p. pap. 6.95 *(978-1-59276-157-9(7))* Our Sunday Visitor, Publishing Div.

Leitch, Wayne. The Way of Assurance. 2006. pap. *(978-1-882701-99-5(2))* Gospel Folio Pr.

Lessons in Responsibility for Boys: Level One. 2007. (YA). per. 18.95 *(978-0-9792446-0-5(9))* Messiah Publishing - Pearables.

Lessons in Responsibility for boys Level Two. 2007. (YA). per. 18.95 *(978-0-9792446-1-2(7))* Messiah Publishing - Pearables.

Levey, Michael. The Book of the Holy Light. 2004. 204p. 17.95 *(978-1-59540-987-4(4)*, Sunstar Publishing) 1st World Publishing, Inc.

Lewellen, LaRose. A Grasp on Reality: Breaking It down for Our Teens. 2007. 124p. per. 12.95 *(978-0-595-43828-0(8))* iUniverse, Inc.

Lewis, Carole. First Place Group Starter Kit. 2004. 179.99 *(978-0-8307-3369-9(8)*, Gospel Light) Gospel Light Pubns.

—Life That Wins. 2004. (First Place Bible Studies). 224p. pap. 19.99 *(978-0-8307-2924-1(0)*, Gospel Light) Gospel Light Pubns.

—Life under Control. 2004. (First Place Bible Studies). 224p. pap. 19.99 *(978-0-8307-2930-2(5)*, Gospel Light) Gospel Light Pubns.

—Living the Legacy. 2004. (First Place Bible Studies). 240p. pap. 19.99 *(978-0-8307-2928-9(3)*, Gospel Light) Gospel Light Pubns.

—Making Wise Choices. 2004. (First Place Bible Studies). 208p. pap. 19.99 *(978-0-8307-3081-0(8)*, Gospel Light) Gospel Light Pubns.

—Seeking God's Best. 2004. (First Place Bible Studies). 208p. pap. 19.99 *(978-0-8307-2925-8(9)*, Gospel Light) Gospel Light Pubns.

Libro de Actividades. 2004. (Sabio Y Prudente Ser.).Tr. of Activity Book. (SPA.). 48p. (J). 3.25 *(978-0-8254-0924-0(1)*, Editorial Portavoz) Kregel Pubns.

The Life of Grace: Revised Grade 7. 2005. (J). pap., stu. ed. 12.95 *(978-0-89870-910-0(5))*; pap., act. bk. ed. 6.95 *(978-0-89870-900-1(8))* Ignatius Pr.

Life's Journey: A Clear Mind & A Clean Heart, 1 book. 2004. per. *(978-0-9752994-0-1(9))* Carroll, Sherry.

Lindsey, Brooklyn. Confessions of a Not-So-Supermodel: Faith, Friends, & Festival Queens, 1 vol. 2008. (Invert Ser.). (ENG., Illus.). 176p. (YA). (gr. 7-14). pap. 9.99 *(978-0-310-27753-8(1))* Zondervan.

Lingo, Susan L. Clip-n-Snip Object Talks for Kids! 25 Cool & Clever Messages Kids Snip from Paper! 2004. (ENG.). 64p. (J). (gr. k-5). pap. 14.99 *(978-0-7847-1604-5(8)*, 42082, B&H Kids) B&H Publishing Group.

—Fold-n-Hold Object Talks for Kids! 25 Cool & Clever Messages Kids Fold from Paper! 2004. (ENG.). 64p. (J). (gr. k-5). pap. 14.99 *(978-0-7847-1603-8(X)*, 42081, B&H Kids) B&H Publishing Group.

—Quick-Quiz Talk Starters: 30 Fast 'n Fun Quizzes - & More - to Get Kids Talking about God & Faith. 2006. 128p. (YA). (gr. 5-7). 15.99 *(978-0-7847-1370-9(7)*, 42100) Standard Publishing.

Litchford, David O. Nephi Was an Eagle. unabr. ed. 2004. (Illus.). 46p. (YA). (gr. 5-10). pap. 5.95 *(978-1-932280-60-9(X)*, 8060X) Granite Publishing & Distribution.

Living Christ's Passionate Life Guidebook. 2005. (YA). per. *(978-0-9772313-1-7(3))* The 101 Group, Inc.

Living for God. (Precious Moments Ser.). (J). 11.99 *(978-1-55976-181-9(4))* CEF Pr.

Living in Christ. 304p. stu. ed. 17.95 *(978-0-7586-0467-5(X))* Concordia Publishing Hse.

Living the Good News Staff. Growing a Grateful, Generous Heart Children's Papers Grades 3-4: Stewardship Resources for Children andTheir Families. 2003. (Illus.). 16p. 2.95 *(978-1-931960-19-9(4)*, Living the Good News) Church Publishing, Inc.

—Growing a Grateful, Generous Heart Children's Papers Grades 1-2: Stewardship Resources for Children & Their Families. 2003. (Illus.). 16p. 2.95 *(978-1-931960-18-2(6)*, Living the Good News) Church Publishing, Inc.

—Growing a Grateful, Generous Heart Children's Papers Grades 5-6: Stewardship Resources for Children & Their Families. 2003. (Illus.). 16p. 2.95 *(978-1-931960-20-5(8)*, Living the Good News) Church Publishing, Inc.

Living the Good News Staff, prod. First Eucharist & Beyond: Ongoing Initiation into Communion with Christ. rev. ed. 2013. 32p. pap. 6.25 *(978-1-931960-34-2(8)*, Living the Good News) Church Publishing, Inc.

Lord, Jill Roman. If Jesus Came to Visit Me. Graef, Renee, illus. 2006. (ENG.). 26p. (J). (gr. -1-k). 12.95 *(978-0-8249-6651-5(1)*, Ideal Pubns.) Worthy Publishing.

—If Jesus Lived Inside My Heart. Wummer, Amy, illus. 2014. (If Jesus Ser.). 22p. (J). bds. 6.99 *(978-0-8249-1937-5(8)*, Ideal Pubns.) Worthy Publishing.

Lotz, Louis. The Sweet Life: A Taste of God in the Ordinary. 2004. 139p. pap. *(978-0-916466-08-4(6))* Reformed Church Pr., Reformed Church in America.

Lucado, Max. En el Ojo de la Tormenta, 1 vol. 2003. (SPA.). 288p. pap. 13.99 *(978-0-88113-721-7(9))* Grupo Nelson.

—Every Day Deserves a Chance: Wake up & Live!, 1 vol. 2007. (ENG., Illus.). 164p. (gr. 7-12). pap. 12.99 *(978-1-4003-1077-7(6))* Nelson, Thomas Inc.

—Next Door Savior, 1 vol. 2008. (ENG.). 212p. pap. 13.99 *(978-1-4041-7544-0(X))* Nelson, Thomas Inc.

Lucas, Lawrence R. Purity. 2003. 56p. per. 5.95 *(978-0-9715916-1-5(X))* Lucas Co.

Lumpkin, Kenya. Quechning the Fire: Many Waters Cannont Quench Love. Lee, Mykle & Shefield, April, eds. 2007. (YA). 21.95 *(978-0-9744929-2-6(2))* Leeway Pubs.

Lynch, Fred D., et al. My Changes, 1 vol. 2008. (Middle School Survival Ser.). (ENG.). 192p. (YA). pap. 9.99 *(978-0-310-27883-2(X))* Zondervan.

Lynn, Debbie. Angel George Series James Needs a Miracle. Norberg, Ken, illus. 2006. (J). 15.95 *(978-0-9771318-9-1(0))* Hope Harvest Publishing.

MacDonald, Fiona. Religion. 2004. (Culture Encyclopedia Ser.). (Illus.). 40p. (YA). (gr. 5-18). lib. bdg. 19.95 *(978-1-59084-482-3(3))* Mason Crest.

MacDonald, Mindy. Jesus & the 12 Dudes Who Did. 2004. (GodCounts Ser.). (ENG.). 24p. bds. 14.99 *(978-1-59052-383-4(0)*, Multnomah Bks.) Crown Publishing Group.

—7 Days of Creation. 2004. (GodCounts Ser.). (ENG.). 24p. bds. 15.99 *(978-1-59052-408-4(X)*, Multnomah) Doubleday Religious Publishing Group, The.

—9 Fruits Alive. 2004. (GodCounts Ser.). (ENG., Illus.). 24p. bds. 14.99 *(978-1-59052-382-7(2)*, Multnomah) Doubleday Religious Publishing Group, The.

Mackall, Dandi Daley. Jesus lo Hizo por Mi. Petrov, Anton, illus. 2008. (SPA.). 28p. (J). (gr. -1). pap. 7.99 *(978-0-7586-1585-5(X))* Concordia Publishing Hse.

MacKenzie, Carine. Glorifying God: Obedient Lives from the Bible. 2013. (ENG., Illus.). 96p. (J). pap. 7.99 *(978-1-78191-124-2(X)*, 404a70e4-6acf-4784-85be-df8caceea0fa) Christian Focus Pubns. GBR. Dist: Bookmasters Distribution.

—God Is Everywhere. 2010. (Bible Art Ser.). (ENG.). 16p. (J). pap., act. bk. ed. 1.99 *(978-1-85792-637-8(4)*, 4642b1e9-4893-4848-af16-3e951df5c27a) Christian Focus Pubns. GBR. Dist: Bookmasters Distribution.

—God Is Faithful. 2006. (Bible Art Ser.). (ENG.). 16p. (J). pap., act. bk. ed. 1.99 *(978-1-85792-638-5(2)*, aae6f58c-dbca-4097-9d5e-2f5a431fdc09) Christian Focus Pubns. GBR. Dist: Bookmasters Distribution.

—God Knows Everything. 2010. (Bible Art Ser.). (ENG.). 16p. (J). pap., act. bk. ed. 1.99 *(978-1-85792-636-1(6)*, 85aaec2f-54d4-4638-b373-5432ebbedcfe) Christian Focus Pubns. GBR. Dist: Bookmasters Distribution.

—God Never Changes. 2010. (Bible Art Ser.). (ENG.). 16p. (J). pap., act. bk. ed. 1.99 *(978-1-85792-635-4(8)*, 4bc8cea6-2ef1-4aea-a0f0-7e1f0eccb8fd) Christian Focus Pubns. GBR. Dist: Bookmasters Distribution.

MacKenzie, Catherine. Could Somebody Pass the Salt? Ammassari, Rita, illus. 2012. (Little Lights Ser.). (ENG.). 24p. (J). (gr. 4-7). 7.99 *(978-1-84550-111-2(X)*, fc99de78-abc4-46d1-ad2d-579b7f21235e) Christian Focus Pubns. GBR. Dist: Bookmasters Distribution.

—Feelings. 2010. (Senses (Board Books) Ser.). (ENG.). 16p. (J). (gr. -1-3). bds. 3.99 *(978-1-85792-565-4(3)*, 9781857925654) Christian Focus Pubns. GBR. Dist: Bookmasters Distribution.

—George Müller: Does Money Grow on Trees? 2012. (Little Lights Ser.). (ENG., Illus.). 24p. (J). (gr. -1-3). 7.99 *(978-1-84550-110-5(1)*, af11d222-af25-41e4-93d0-1d014d537a0d) Christian Focus Pubns. GBR. Dist: Bookmasters Distribution.

—Hearing. 2010. (Senses (Board Books) Ser.). (ENG.). 16p. (J). (gr. -1-3). bds. 3.99 *(978-1-85792-563-0(7)*, 9781857925630) Christian Focus Pubns. GBR. Dist: Bookmasters Distribution.

Mackenzie, Catherine. I Can Say to God, Please. 2015. (Prayer (Board Books) Ser.). (ENG.). 10p. (J). bds. 3.99 *(978-1-85792-691-0(9)*, 4a46cdd3-be1d-48a9-bbee-7f9ad59ca112) Christian Focus Pubns. GBR. Dist: Bookmasters Distribution.

MacKenzie, Catherine. Jesus Finds His People. Apps, Fred, illus. 2008. (Sent to Save Ser.). (ENG.). 16p. (J). (gr. -1-3). bds. 3.99 *(978-1-84550-324-6(4)*, 9781845503246) Christian Focus Pubns. GBR. Dist: Bookmasters Distribution.

—Jesus Helps His People. Apps, Fred, illus. 2008. (Sent to Save Ser.). (ENG.). 16p. (J). (gr. -1-3). bds. 3.99 *(978-1-84550-322-2(8)*, 9781845503222) Christian Focus Pubns. GBR. Dist: Bookmasters Distribution.

—Jesus Rescues His People. Apps, Fred, illus. 2008. (Sent to Save Ser.). (ENG.). 16p. (J). (gr. 4-7). 3.99 *(978-1-84550-321-5(X)*, 9781845503215) Christian Focus Pubns. GBR. Dist: Bookmasters Distribution.

—Jesus Saves His People. Apps, Fred, illus. 2008. (Sent to Save Ser.). (ENG.). 16p. (J). (gr. -1-3). 3.99 *(978-1-84550-323-9(6)*, 9781845503239) Christian Focus Pubns. GBR. Dist: Bookmasters Distribution.

—Sight. 2010. (Senses (Board Books) Ser.). (ENG.). 16p. (J). (gr. -1-3). bds. 3.99 *(978-1-85792-562-3(9)*, 9781857925623) Christian Focus Pubns. GBR. Dist: Bookmasters Distribution.

—Touch. 2010. (Senses (Board Books) Ser.). (ENG.). 16p. (J). (gr. -1-3). bds. 3.99 *(978-1-85792-560-9(2)*, 9781857925609) Christian Focus Pubns. GBR. Dist: Bookmasters Distribution.

—What God Says: Creation. 2006. (Bible Art Ser.). (ENG.). 16p. (J). pap. 1.99 *(978-1-84550-219-5(1)*, 9781845502195) Christian Focus Pubns. GBR. Dist: Bookmasters Distribution.

—What God Says: Holiness. 2006. (Bible Art Ser.). (ENG.). 16p. (J). pap. 1.99 *(978-1-84550-214-0(0)*, b02e9199-6885-4e88-a17e-a6a1c0336f7f) Christian Focus Pubns. GBR. Dist: Bookmasters Distribution.

—What God Says: Redemption. 2006. (Bible Art Ser.). (ENG.). 16p. (J). pap. 1.99 *(978-1-84550-217-1(5)*, 8569bbc5-8685-4fb0-bdac-f94bc832dd0b) Christian Focus Pubns. GBR. Dist: Bookmasters Distribution.

—What God Says: Repenting. 2006. (Bible Art Ser.). (ENG.). 16p. (J). pap. 1.99 *(978-1-84550-216-4(7)*, a801aa9a-3026-4eb2-ba54-9b04f6b60757) Christian Focus Pubns. GBR. Dist: Bookmasters Distribution.

—What God Says: Resurrection. 2006. (Bible Art Ser.). (ENG.). 16p. (J). pap. 1.99 *(978-1-84550-218-8(3)*, e8deff6e-314a-430c-82a4-8f17c4d053fc) Christian Focus Pubns. GBR. Dist: Bookmasters Distribution.

—What God Says: Salvation. 2006. (Bible Art Ser.). (ENG.). 16p. (J). pap. 1.99 *(978-1-84550-215-7(9)*, e667eba6-d3ae-4232-b172-352a5debcd69) Christian Focus Pubns. GBR. Dist: Bookmasters Distribution.

Magee, Kanika A. M. Today I Got Saved, 1 book. Thomas, Sonya, illus. 2003. 20p. (J). 10.00 net. *(978-0-9748834-0-3(9))* Ebenezer A.M.E. Church.

Magnisi, Sabrina. Miss Sabrina's Learn the Hail Mary As You Color the Rosary: A Guide for Children 6 - 9 & Up! Magnisi, Sabrina & Magnisi, Angelica, illus. 2005. 104p. (J). per. *(978-1-933593-30-2(X))* Puarose Publishing.

Mahan, Asa & Hills, Aaron Merritt. Food for Lambs; Or, Leading Children to Christ. Friedrich, Richard, ed. 2003. 134p. per. 6.00 *(978-1-932370-03-4(X)*, 009) Alethea In Heart.

Mally, Sarah. Bright Lights Discipleship Notebook. 2003. (Illus.). (YA). ring bd. 50.00 net. *(978-0-9719405-1-2(7))* Tomorrow's Forefathers, Inc.

Malone, Tom. What's Important: A Roadmap for Loving God. 2004. 114p. (YA). 22.95 *(978-0-595-66316-3(8))* iUniverse, Inc.

Manousos, Demetrius. Know Your Mass. Burbank, Addison, illus. 2006. 96p. (YA). per. 14.95 *(978-1-892331-44-1(6))* Angelus Pr.

Marrying Right. 2003. (YA). *(978-0-9740142-0-3(6))* Five Star Christian Pubns.

Martin, Michael. TruthQuest Follywood VBS Kit. 2005. cd-rom 99.00 *(978-0-9709763-9-0(9))* Return To The Word.

Martin, Mildred A. Wisdom & the Millers: Proverbs for Children. Burkholder, Edith, illus. 2009. 159p. (J). *(978-1-884377-15-0(7))*; pap. *(978-1-884377-14-3(9))* Green Pastures Pr.

Martinez, Mary Ann. 6 Disciplinas Espirituales: Expande las dimensiones de tu relacion con Dios. 2005. (SPA.). 227p. per. 12.00 *(978-0-9763015-0-9(4))* Marcasa Bks.

Marxhausen, Joanne. Heaven is a Wonderful Place. Marxhausen, Ben & Koehler, Ed, illus. 2nd ed. 2004. 48p. (J). (gr. -1-4). 9.49 *(978-0-7586-0681-5(8))* Concordia Publishing Hse.

Mary Slessor. 2004. 174p. (J). pap. 6.99 *(978-1-932307-25-2(7)*, Ambassador-Emerald, International) Emerald Hse. Group, Inc.

Maselli, Christopher P. N. Secret of the Firm Foundations: 12 Mystery Stories to Solve Using the Foundations of Our Faith. 2006. (Sleuth-It-Yourself Mysteries Ser.). (Illus.). 48p. (J). (gr. 4-7). per. 9.99 *(978-1-59441-384-1(3))* Carson-Dellosa Publishing, LLC.

Mathews, Janice. Jack Gives Back. 2012. (J). 7.99 *(978-0-8280-2667-3(X))* Review & Herald Publishing Assn.

—Jack, Jake, Jacque, & Jodie: The Get-Along Doggies. 2015. (J). *(978-0-8163-5734-5(X))* Pacific Pr. Publishing Assn.

Matlock, Mark. Wisdom On... Friends, Dating, & Relationships, 1 vol. 2008. (Wisdom Ser.). (ENG.). 144p. (YA). (gr. 7-14). pap. 9.99 *(978-0-310-27927-3(5))* Zondervan.

—Wisdom On... Making Good Decisions, 1 vol. 2008. (Invert Ser.). (ENG.). 144p. (YA). (gr. 7-14). pap. 9.99 *(978-0-310-27926-6(7))* Zondervan.

McCarty, Diane Bischoff. My First Holy Communion: A non-Denominational Program for Preparing young Children to receive Communion for the first Time. 2006. (ENG., Illus.). 61p. (J). *(978-0-9712124-2-8(2))* Angel Heart Children's Pr.

McCaughrean, Geraldine. Dédalo e Icaro: El Rey Midas. Barroso, Paz, tr. Ross, Tony, illus. 2nd ed. 2005. (Mythology Series Collection Mitos Ser.).Tr. of Daedalus & Icarus (King Midas). (SPA.). 48p. (J). (gr. 2-3). 9.95 *(978-84-348-6431-3(2))* SM Ediciones ESP. Dist: Iaconi, Mariuccia Bk. Imports.

McCollum, Bobby. Must I Go to Church. 2012. (ENG.). (J). pap. *(978-1-4675-5460-2(X))* Independent Pub.

McConnell, Clem. I Speak to Myself: Encouraging Words for Children. McConnell, Clem, illus. 2007. (Illus.). 32p. (J). per. 5.00 *(978-0-9673490-0-8(1))* Positive Strokes.

McDonald, Arthur. Ye Must Be Born Again. 2004. 52p. *(978-0-9762892-0-3(2))* Bible Facts Pr.

McDowell, Josh & Bellis, Dave. Is the Bible Personally from God? The Real Truth about Living Like Jesus. 2006. (Illus.). 96p. per. 12.99 *(978-1-932587-94-4(2))* Practical Christianity Foundation.

McDowell, Josh & Stewart, Ed. Divorce of Parents. 2009. (Project 17:17 Ser.). (ENG.). 64p. (J). mass mkt. 4.99 *(978-1-84550-441-0(0)*, 9781845504410) Christian Focus Pubns. GBR. Dist: Bookmasters Distribution.

—My Friend Is Struggling with Unplanned Pregnancy. 2009. (Project 17:17 Ser.). (ENG.). 64p. (J). mass mkt. 4.99 *(978-1-84550-440-3(2)*, 088e0695-904e-407d-a6f0-b7042c01cae6) Christian Focus Pubns. GBR. Dist: Bookmasters Distribution.

—Past Sexual Abuse. 2009. (Project 17:17 Ser.). (ENG.). 64p. (J). mass mkt. 4.99 *(978-1-84550-443-4(7)*, 9781845504434) Christian Focus Pubns. GBR. Dist: Bookmasters Distribution.

McDowell, Sean. Ethix: Being Bold in a Whatever World. 2006. 163p. (YA). (gr. 8-13). per. 9.99 *(978-0-8054-4050-8(X))* B&H Publishing Group.

—Eti-k: En un Mundo Donde Todo Cuenta. 2007. 164p. per. 8.99 *(978-0-8054-4452-0(1)*, B&H Bks.) B&H Publishing Group.

McGrade, Francis & Juliana, M., Sr. I Believe: The Creed, Confession & the Ten Commandments for Children. 2013. (ENG., Illus.). 96p. (J). (gr. k-2). reprint ed. 16.95 *(978-1-930873-35-3(2)*, Neumann Pr.) TAN Bks.

McIntee, Ross. The WAY of Salvation. 2006. 12p. (J). pap. *(978-1-897117-12-5(4))* Gospel Folio Pr.

McKee, Jonathan. The Guy's Guide to God, Girls, & the Phone in Your Pocket: 101 Real-World Tips for Teenaged Guys. 2014. (ENG.). 224p. pap. 12.99 *(978-1-62416-990-8(2)*, Barbour Bks.) Barbour Publishing, Inc.

McNaney, Lowell & Lambert, Andy. Fuel for the Journey. 2003. (Illus.). (YA). pap. 15.00 *(978-1-930154-11-7(9))* Whitline Ink, Inc.

McQueen, David. The Mineral Book. 2014. 96p. 16.99 *(978-0-89051-802-1(5))* Master Bks.

Meadows, James L. God Speaks to Today's Teenagers. (YA). Vol. I. pap. 5.50 *(978-0-89098-375-1(5))* Vol. II. pap. 5.50 *(978-0-89098-376-8(3))* Twentieth Century Christian Bks.

Medina, Sarah. A Day to Remember. Brecknell, Annie, illus. 48p. pap. 8.99 *(978-0-7459-4770-9(0)*, Lion Books) Lion Hudson PLC GBR. Dist: Trafalgar Square Publishing.

Meet Herman. 2004. (J). 3.64 *(978-1-56870-508-8(5))* Hewell Publishing.

A Meeting in the Ladies Room: Life Lessons for My Little Sisters in Christ. 2004. (YA). *(978-0-9759008-0-2(3))* Nu-Nature.

Meister, Deborah. What Catholics Teens Should Know If Pregnant & Panicked. Larkin, Jean K., ed. 2004. (What Catholic Teens Should Know Ser.). (Illus.). 8p. (YA). 7.95 *(978-0-89837-237-3(2)*, 440710) Pflaum Publishing Group.

Menconi, Al. Full Tilt Media Challenge: 30 Day Devotional Guide. 2004. 200p. (YA). per. 20.00 *(978-0-942925-10-4(6))* New Song Publishing Co.

Mercadante, Frank. Positively Dangerous: Live Loud, Be Real, Change the World. 2003. 117p. (YA). pap. 11.50 *(978-0-88489-790-3(7))* St. Mary's Pr. of MN.

Metaxas, Eric. Amazing Grace: William Wilberforce & the Heroic Campaign to End Slavery. 2007. (ENG., Illus.). 304p. 23.99 *(978-0-06-117300-4(2)*, HarperOne) HarperCollins Pubs.

Meyer, Joyce. El Campo de Batalla de la Mente para Ninos. 2006. (SPA & ENG., Illus.). 176p. (gr. 5-9). per. 9.99 *(978-1-59185-475-3(X)*, Casa Creacion) Charisma Media.

Meyer, Joyce & Hafer, Todd. Battlefield of the Mind - For Teens: Winning the Battle in Your Mind. annot. ed. 2006. (ENG.). 176p. (YA). (gr. 8-17). per. 14.00 *(978-0-446-69764-4(8)*, Faithwords) Hachette Nashville.

Meyer, Joyce & Moore, Karen. Battlefield of the Mind for Kids. 2006. (ENG., Illus.). 192p. (J). (gr. 3-7). per. 12.00 *(978-0-446-69125-3(9)*, Faithwords) Hachette Nashville.

Mi Dios es Amor (My God Is Love) Quarter 2, Level 1. (Caminando con Jesus (Walking with Jesus) Series A). (SPA.). (J). (gr. -1-k). stu. ed. 3.50 *(978-0-570-05108-4(8)*, 16-1812) Concordia Publishing Hse.

Miller, Janet. Cut, Color & Paste: God's Creatures. 2004. (Illus.). 96p. (J). (gr. -1-2). 11.95 *(978-1-885358-81-3(4))* Rainbow Pubs. & Legacy Pr.

La Mision (The Mission) Quarter 2, Level 3. (Caminando con Jesus (Walking with Jesus) Series A). (SPA.). (J). stu. ed. 3.50 *(978-0-570-05150-3(9))* Concordia Publishing Hse.

Mitchell, Patricia. Saints Tell Their Stories. Casco, Maria Cristina Lo, illus. 2009. 62p. (J). (gr. k-5). 12.95 *(978-1-59325-161-1(0))* Word Among Us Pr.

Moerbe, Mary. How Can I Help? God's Calling for Kids - Mini Book. 2014. (ENG., Illus.). (J). pap. 2.49 *(978-0-7586-4972-0(X))* Concordia Publishing Hse.

Mommy Why? Collection: Stories that answer your kid's toughest Questions: Stories that answer your kid's toughest Questions. 2007. (Illus.). 277p. (J). pap. 17.99 *(978-0-7684-2507-9(7))* Destiny Image Pubs.

Mongtomery Gibson, Jane. In Olden Days. Mongtomery Gibson, Jane, illus. 2005. (Illus.). (YA). bds. 8.99 *(978-1-4183-0042-5(X))* Christ Inspired, Inc.

—My Heart Goes with You. Montgomery Gibson, Jane, illus. 2005. (Illus.). (J). bds. 8.99 *(978-1-4183-0029-6(2))* Christ Inspired, Inc.

Mongtomgery Gibson, Jane. Angels Long. Mongtomgery Gibson, Jane, illus. 2005. (Illus.). (YA). bds. 8.99 *(978-1-4183-0035-7(7))* Christ Inspired, Inc.

Montgomery Gibson, Jane. God's Little Boy. Montgomery Gibson, Jane, illus. 2005. (Illus.). (YA). bds. 8.99 *(978-1-4183-0034-0(9))* Christ Inspired, Inc.

—God's Little Girl. Montgomery Gibson, Jane, illus. 2005. (Illus.). (YA). bds. 8.99 *(978-1-4183-0045-6(4))* Christ Inspired, Inc.

—I Touched Jesus Today. Montgomery Gibson, Jane, illus. 2005. (Illus.). (YA). bds. 8.99 *(978-1-4183-0027-2(6))* Christ Inspired, Inc.

—I'll Tell You in Heaven. Montgomery Gibson, Jane, illus. 2005. (Illus.). (YA). bds. 8.99 *(978-1-4183-0043-2(8))* Christ Inspired, Inc.

—The Inner Soul. Montgomery Gibson, Jane, illus. 2005. (Illus.). (YA). bds. 8.99 *(978-1-4183-0049-4(7))* Christ Inspired, Inc.

—The Keeper of Lost & Found. Montgomery Gibson, Jane, illus. 2005. (Illus.). (YA). bds. 8.99 *(978-1-4183-0052-4(7))* Christ Inspired, Inc.

—A Little Bit Gone. Montgomery Gibson, Jane, illus. 2005. (Illus.). (YA). bds. 8.99 *(978-1-4183-0037-1(3))* Christ Inspired, Inc.

—Mama's Wings. Montgomery Gibson, Jane, illus. 2005. (Illus.). (YA). bds. 8.99 *(978-1-4183-0050-0(0))* Christ Inspired, Inc.

—Measure My Heart. Montgomery Gibson, Jane, illus. 2005. (Illus.). (YA). bds. 8.99 *(978-1-4183-0023-4(3))* Christ Inspired, Inc.

—Shiny Pants. Montgomery Gibson, Jane, illus. 2005. (Illus.). (YA). bds. 8.99 *(978-1-4183-0032-6(2))* Christ Inspired, Inc.

—Through Jesus Eyes. Montgomery Gibson, Jane, illus. 2005. (Illus.). (J). bds. 8.99 *(978-1-4183-0024-1(1))* Christ Inspired, Inc.

Moody, Dwight Lyman. President Lincoln Listened: A Story of Compassion. Bond, Bob, illus. 2006. (Story Time Ser.). (ENG.). 24p. (J). (gr. -1-4). 7.99 *(978-1-84550-115-0(2), 75397a47-48fa-498d-9c85-df9f190a384c)* Christian Focus Pubns. GBR. Dist: Bookmasters Distribution.

Moore, Beth, ed. A Heart for Jesus. 2004.Tr. of Un corazon para Jesus. (SPA.). 24p. 8.99 *(978-1-59185-420-3(2),* Casa Creacion) Charisma Media.

Moore, Karen. Hi God, Let's Talk about My Life. Wummer, Amy, illus. 2006. 128p. (YA). pap. 8.99 *(978-0-7847-1246-7(8),* 42173) Standard Publishing.

Moran, Mary Y. & Flanagan, Anne J. Jesus Comes to Us: Activity Book. 80p. (J). (gr. 2). pap. 2.25 *(978-0-8198-3922-0(1))* Pauline Bks. & Media.

—Jesus Loves Us: Activity Book. 80p. (J). (gr. 1). pap. 2.25 *(978-0-8198-3919-0(1))* Pauline Bks. & Media.

Morrison, Kevin. God's Garden: A story about What Happens When We Die. Bachoc, Patricia, illus. 2009. 32p. (J). pap. 9.95 *(978-0-8091-6741-8(7),* Ambassador Bks.) Paulist Pr.

Mothers. 7.50 *(978-0-8054-5972-2(3))* B&H Publishing Group.

Mueller, Marilyn J. Thank You God for Everything! Gracias a Dios por Todo. 2007. pap. 11.00 *(978-0-8059-8648-8(0))* Dorrance Publishing Co., Inc.

Mullins, Amy. I'm Reverent When- Bagley, Val Chadwick, illus. 2005. ("Move-About" Book Ser.). (J). *(978-1-59156-951-0(6))* Covenant Communications.

Munson, Jared. Courageous Witness: A Teenager Shares Jesus. 2003. (ENG., Illus.). 88p. pap. 8.95 *(978-0-8309-1069-4(7))* Herald Publishing Hse.

My Beloved. 7.50 *(978-0-8054-5913-5(8))* B&H Publishing Group.

Nalls, Charles. Prayer: A field Guide. 2008. 84p. pap. 10.95 *(978-0-595-49142-1(1))* iUniverse, Inc.

Nappa, Jon & Gosselin, Suzanne Hadley. Exploring the Great Bible Mysteries: A Devotional Adventure. 2015. (ENG., Illus.). 96p. (J). pap. 9.99 *(978-0-7369-6144-8(5))* Harvest Hse. Pubs.

Nardo, Don. Catholicism. 2006. (Religions of the World Ser.). (ENG., Illus.). 112p. (YA). (gr. 7-10). lib. bdg. 30.85 *(978-1-59018-632-9(X),* Lucent Bks.) Cengage Gale.

Naughton, Paul. Welcome to Ziklag. 2011. 72p. pap. *(978-1-908105-31-8(3))* Grosvenor Hse. Publishing Ltd.

Neuberger, Anne E. Blessed Kateria & the Cross in the Forest. 2003. (Saints for Children Ser.). 32p. (J). 7.95 *(978-1-931709-66-8(1))* Our Sunday Visitor, Publishing Div.

The New First Mass Book: Padded Girls Set. (J). 10.50 *(978-0-89942-756-0(1),* B808/42W, Resurrection Pr.) Catholic Bk. Publishing Corp.

The New My First Mass Book: Leatherette Boys Set. (J). lthr. 8.25 *(978-0-89942-755-3(3),* B808/67B, Resurrection Pr.) Catholic Bk. Publishing Corp.

The New My First Mass Book: Leatherette Girls Set. (J). lthr. 8.25 *(978-0-89942-754-6(5),* B808/67W, Resurrection Pr.) Catholic Bk. Publishing Corp.

The New Saint Joseph Children's Missal: Padded Girls Set. (J). 10.50 *(978-0-89942-742-3(1),* B806/42W, Resurrection Pr.) Catholic Bk. Publishing Corp.

Nicholas, Mother Andrea, compiled by. My Little Orthodox Christian Feast Days Activity Book. 2005. (J). spiral bd. 6.95 *(978-0-9773579-0-1(2))* St. Nicholas Monastery.

Noble, Alan R. Foundations of the Christian Faith. 2008. 160p. pap. 13.99 *(978-1-60477-694-2(3))* Salem Author Services.

Noonan, Robert, et al. Three Weavers Plus Companion: A Father's Guide to Guarding His Daughter's Purity. 2004. 120p. pap. 13.95 *(978-0-9700273-5-1(4))* Pumpkin Seed Pr.

Norris, David A. Lasting Success: Quality Decisions, Relationships & Untamed Emotions. 2003. (Illus.). 256p. per. *(978-0-943177-12-0(X),* 0-943177-12-x) Heartland Foundation, Inc.

Norvell, Walter. Fundamentals: Web Wise:-) (J). (gr. 6-18). *(978-0-633-05796-1(7))* LifeWay Christian Resources.

Nystrom, Carolyn. Before I Was Born. Speidel, Sandra, illus. rev. ed. 2007. (God's Design for Sex Ser.: 2). (ENG.). 40p. pap. 10.99 *(978-1-60006-014-4(5))* NavPress Publishing Group.

Nystrom, Jennifer. Favorite Bible Children: Grades 1 & 2. 2004. (Illus.). 96p. (J). (gr. 1-2). pap. 11.95 *(978-1-885358-77-6(6))* Rainbow Pubs. & Legacy Pr.

—Favorite Bible Children: Grades 3 & 4. 2004. (Illus.). 96p. (J). (gr. 3-4). pap. 11.95 *(978-1-885358-78-3(4))* Rainbow Pubs. & Legacy Pr.

Oaks, Robert C. Believe! Helping Youth Learn to Trust in the Lord. 2003. (Illus.). xiii, 126p. (J). pap. 14.95 *(978-1-59038-203-5(X))* Deseret Bk. Co.

O'Brien, Kathryn. Be Still. Flint, Gillian, illus. 2016. (Sit for a Bit Ser.). (ENG.). 40p. (J). 14.99 *(978-1-4964-1116-7(1))* Tyndale Hse. Pubs.

—Give Thanks. Flint, Gillian, illus. 2016. (Sit for a Bit Ser.). (ENG.). 40p. (J). 14.99 *(978-1-4964-1118-1(8))* Tyndale Hse. Pubs.

—I Can. Flint, Gillian, illus. 2016. (Sit for a Bit Ser.). (ENG.). 40p. (J). 14.99 *(978-1-4964-1117-4(X))* Tyndale Hse. Pubs.

O'Dell, Nicole. Girl Talk: a Journal: ... for Life's Ups, Downs, & In-Betweens. 2014. (ENG.). 176p. (YA). pap. 12.99 *(978-1-62416-848-2(5),* Barbour Bks.) Barbour Publishing, Inc.

Oestreicher, Mark, et al. My Faith, 1 vol. 2006. (Middle School Survival Ser.). (ENG., Illus.). 192p. (YA). (gr. 7-9). pap. 9.99 *(978-0-310-27382-0(X))* Zondervan.

—My Family, 1 vol. 2006. (Middle School Survival Ser.). (ENG., Illus.). 208p. (YA). (gr. 7-9). pap. 9.99 *(978-0-310-27430-8(3))* Zondervan.

Olla, Debbie. Retreats for Teens: Planning Strategies & Teen-Tested Models. Cannizzo, Karen A., ed. 2004. (Youth Ministry Resource Library). 96p. pap. 19.95 *(978-0-937997-78-9(1),* 797) Pflaum Publishing Group.

Omartian, Stormie. I Talk to God about How I Feel: Learning to Pray, Knowing He Cares. Warren, Shari, illus. 2010. (Power of a Praying Kid Ser.). (ENG.). 32p. (J). 14.99 *(978-0-7369-2685-0(2))* Harvest Hse. Pubs.

One Room Sunday School Fall: Resource Kit. (Illus.). 56.00 *(978-0-687-03622-6(4))* Abingdon Pr.

One Room Sunday School Winter: Resource Kit. (Illus.). 52.00 *(978-0-687-03619-6(4))* Abingdon Pr.

Osborne, Rick & Strauss, Ed. Angels & Demons, 1 vol. 2004. (2:52 Ser.). (ENG., Illus.). 112p. (J). pap. 7.99 *(978-0-310-70775-2(7))* Zonderkidz.

Osei-Bonsu, Patrick. Run to Win: Releasing the Champion Within You. 2004. (YA). 7.00 *(978-0-9747956-3-8(1))* Greenwood, Lori Ministries, Inc.

Our Goal & Our Guides. (YA). (gr. 9-12). 17.00 *(978-1-931555-41-8(9))* Our Lady of Victory Schl.

Our Life in the Church: Revised Grade 8 Activity Book. 2005. (J). pap. 6.95 *(978-0-89870-901-8(6))* Ignatius Pr.

Our Life in the Church: Revised Grade 8 Student Book. 2005. (J). pap. 12.95 *(978-0-89870-911-7(3))* Ignatius Pr.

Pablo y Silas. (Libros Arco Ser.).Tr. of Paul & Silas. (SPA.). 24p. (J). 2.49 *(978-0-7586-0496-5(3))* Concordia Publishing Hse.

Page 4 Personal Growth Planbook: Mission Max. 2003. (Illus.). 48p. (J). pap. 4.95 *(978-1-59312-045-0(1))* North American Mission Board, SBC.

Palmer, Alison. Walking the Path of Faith: More Fun Character-Building Activities for LDS Children - a Companion Volume to Planting Seeds of Faith. 2004. (J). per. 9.99 *(978-0-88290-764-2(6),* Horizon Pubs.) Cedar Fort, Inc./CFI Distribution.

Parker, Amy. The Plans I Have for You Journal, 1 vol. Brantley-Newton, Vanessa, illus. 2015. (ENG.). 208p. (J). pap. 12.99 *(978-0-310-72523-7(2))* Zonderkidz.

Parker, Sherri. Let's Seek God's Word Together. 2004. (J). spiral bd. 5.18 *(978-1-56870-544-6(1))* Hewell Publishing.

Parmer, Paul. Overcoming that "After-Camp Spiritual Dive" Date not set. 10p. (YA). (gr. 3-18). pap. *(978-1-884838-17-0(0))* Walterick Pubs., Inc.

Parry, L. Jesus Hace Amigos (Jesus Makes Friends) (SPA.). (J). 1.99 *(978-0-7899-0537-6(X),* 495666) Editorial Unilit.

—Jesus Llama a Sus Discipulos (Jesus Calls His Disciples) (SPA.). (J). 1.99 *(978-0-7899-0538-3(8),* 495665) Editorial Unilit.

Parry, L. & Parry, A. Siguiendo la Estrella Actividades.Tr. of Follow the Star Activity Book. (SPA.). (J). 9.99 *(978-1-56063-834-6(6),* 497746) Editorial Unilit.

Passey, Marion. My Tiny Book of Joseph Smith. 2004. (Illus.). (J). 5.95 *(978-1-59038-243-1(9))* Deseret Bk. Co.

Pastore, Vicki, illus. The Apostles' Creed. 2007. 32p. (J). (gr. -1-3). per. 7.95 *(978-0-8091-6738-8(7),* 6738-8) Paulist Pr.

Paterson, Katherine. Who Am I? Exploring What It Means to Be a Child of God. 2009. (ENG.). 92p. (J). pap. 10.00 *(978-0-8028-5361-5(7),* Eerdmans Bks For Young Readers) Eerdmans, William B. Publishing Co.

Peckham, Lori, ed. 60 Years of Guide: Anniversary Story Collection. 2013. 126p. pap. 13.99 *(978-0-8280-2730-4(7))* Review & Herald Publishing Assn.

Peckham, Lori. Guide's Greatest Amazing Rescue Stories. 2010. (J). *(978-0-8280-2559-1(2))* Review & Herald Publishing Assn.

—Guide's Greatest Mission Stories. 2009. (J). *(978-0-8280-2501-0(0))* Review & Herald Publishing Assn.

Peckham, Lori, ed. Guide's Greatest Narrow Escape Stories. 2008. (Pathfinder Junior Book Club Ser.). 160p. (J). (gr. 5-9). pap. 11.99 *(978-0-8280-2040-4(X))* Review & Herald Publishing Assn.

Pedersen, Mary Jo, et al. More Than Meets the Eye: Finding God in the Creases & Folds of Family Life. 2003. 160p. (YA). pap. 14.95 *(978-0-88489-594-7(7))* St. Mary's Pr. of MN.

Perkins, Greg. Un Ninito Los Guiara. Pomeroy, John, illus. 2005. 16p. (J). (gr. 4-7). 8.99 *(978-1-59185-826-3(7),* Charisma Kids) Charisma Media.

Perry, Janice Kapp. I'm Trying to Be Like Jesus. Abts, Stacey, illus. 2003. (J). *(978-1-57008-843-8(8),* Bookcraft, Inc.) Deseret Bk. Co.

Perry, Jason & Keels, Steve. You Are Not Your Own: Living Loud for God. 2004. (TruthQuest Ser.). 144p. (gr. 7-18). pap. 12.99 *(978-0-8054-2591-8(8))* B&H Publishing Group.

Perseghetti, Jackie & Perseghetti, Jonie. Faith Factor OT: Thru-the-Bible Devotions. 2007. (ENG., Illus.). 384p. (YA). (gr. 3-7). per. 16.99 *(978-0-7814-4458-3(6))* Cook, David C.

Petkau, Karen S. If Heaven Is So Great, Why Can't I Go Now? 2014. pap. *(978-1-4866-0026-7(3))* Word Alive Pr.

Pflaum Publishing Group, creator. Welcome Children! A Child's Mass Book. 2005. (Illus.). 32p. (J). (gr. -1-3). pap. 3.95 *(978-0-89837-174-1(0),* 3504) Pflaum Publishing Group.

Pingry, Patricia A. The Power of Faith for Teens: True Stories. 2004. (Illus.). 160p. pap. 9.95 *(978-0-8249-4622-7(7),* Ideal Pubns.) Worthy Publishing.

—The Story of the Lord's Prayer. Garvin, Elaine, illus. 2005. (ENG.). 26p. (J). (gr. -1-k). 9.95 *(978-0-8249-6637-9(6),* Ideal Pubns.) Worthy Publishing.

—The Story of the Star Spangled Banner. 2005. (ENG.). 28p. (J). bds. 7.69 *(978-0-8249-6567-9(1),* Ideal Pubns.) Worthy Publishing.

Pitts, Wynter. For Girls Like You: A Devotional for Tweens. 2015. (ENG.). 144p. (J). pap. 10.99 *(978-0-7369-6175-2(5))* Harvest Hse. Pubs.

Plans & Pluses, Vol. 5. 2003. (J). 19.95 *(978-0-633-09930-5(9))* LifeWay Christian Resources.

Plante, Patty. Joy for Jesus: Doing God's Word, 4. 2004. (Joy for Jesus Ser.: 4). 88p. (J). ring bd. 24.95 *(978-1-889723-42-6(8))* Family Harvest Church.

Plum, Joan. I Am Special Four Year Old Child's. 5th ed. 2003. 112p. (J). pap., act. bk. ed. 9.95 *(978-1-931709-20-0(3))* Our Sunday Visitor, Publishing Div.

Pohle & Dowley. Maqueta del Templo de Salomon. 2003.Tr. of Solomon's Temple Model. (SPA.). pap. 9.99 *(978-0-7899-1127-8(2))* Editorial Unilit.

Point Of Grace. Girls of Grace Journal. 2011. (ENG.). 124p. pap. 10.99 *(978-1-4516-4148-6(6),* Howard Bks.) Howard Books.

Pozdol, MaryBeth. Prison to Palace. Leonard, Erskine, illus. 2004. 189p. (J). ring bd. 29.95 *(978-1-889723-43-3(6))* Family Harvest Church.

Preston, Rhoda. Rock-a-Bye Toddlers & Two Leader's Guide (2009 - 2010) 2009. (Rockabye Ser.). 24.00 *(978-0-687-65534-2(X))* Abingdon Pr.

Priddy Books Staff. God Made Me & God Made Us, 2 bks. bds. 15.95 *(978-0-312-49161-1(1),* Priddy Bks.) St. Martin's Pr.

Primeros pasitos misioneros (First Steps, Spanish) 2004. pap. 12.99 *(978-1-56309-930-4(6))* Woman's Missionary Union.

Proclaiming Christ: 6 Lessons - Visuals. (Biblegrams Bible Lesson Ser.). (J). (gr. -1). pap. 18.00 *(978-1-55976-047-8(8))* CEF Pr.

Propes, Chrysti Carol. I Am. Bostrom, Laura, illus. 3rd ed. 2013. 40p. 24.95 *(978-0-9790791-8-4(7))* Fig & The Vine, LLC, The.

—I Am Here. Bostrom, Laura, illus. 3rd ed. 2013. 32p. 24.95 *(978-0-9790791-9-1(5))* Fig & The Vine, LLC, The.

Prosper, Tanzia. He Chose a Coat for Me! 2011. 44p. 17.95 *(978-1-4497-1316-4(5),* WestBow Pr.) Author Solutions, Inc.

Quantrell, Angie. I Can Do It! Lollar, Cathy, illus. 2003. 9.99 *(978-1-56309-626-6(9))* Woman's Missionary Union.

—I Can Give. 2003. 9.99 *(978-1-56309-625-9(0))* Woman's Missionary Union.

Rainbow Publishers Staff. Coloring Plus Activities: God's Promises. 2004. (Illus.). 64p. (J). (gr. -1-3). pap. 9.95 *(978-0-937282-49-6(9),* RB37165) Rainbow Pubs. & Legacy Pr.

—Coloring Plus Activities: Heroes of the Bible. 2004. (Illus.). 64p. (J). (gr. -1-3). pap. 9.95 *(978-0-937282-47-2(2),* RB37163) Rainbow Pubs. & Legacy Pr.

—Coloring Plus Activities: Living the Christian Life. 2004. (Illus.). 64p. (J). (gr. -1-3). pap. 9.95 *(978-0-937282-18-2(9),* RB37166) Rainbow Pubs. & Legacy Pr.

Ramshaw, Gail. Every Day & Sunday, Too. Jarret, Judy, illus. 2004. 44p. 15.99 *(978-0-8066-2334-4(9),* 10-23349, Augsburg Bks.) Augsburg Fortress, Pubs.

Rashad, Girmen. How Does God See Me? David, Amor, illus. 2008. (Little Christian Ser.). 24p. 9.99 *(978-0-9819100-0-0(9))* Elkarez Publishing Co.

Reams, Clyde. Stories by the Fire. 2006. 31p. 10.99 *(978-1-4116-7711-1(0))* Lulu Pr., Inc.

Redford, Marjorie. My Bible Says. Marlin, Kathryn, illus. 2013. (Happy Day Ser.). (ENG.). 16p. (J). pap. 2.49 *(978-1-4143-9301-8(6))* Tyndale Hse. Pubs.

—My Bible Says. Marlin, Kathryn, illus. 2013. (Happy Day Ser.). (ENG.). 18p. (J). bds. 4.99 *(978-1-4143-9291-2(5))* Tyndale Hse. Pubs.

Reeg, Cynthia. Gifts from God. Roberts, MarySue, photos by. 2007. (Illus.). (J). 28p. 10.95 *(978-1-933090-33-7(2));* 30p. E-Book 5.00 incl. cd-rom *(978-1-933090-34-4(0))* Guardian Angel Publishing, Inc.

Reeves. Day by Day Bible Daily Devotions for Reading with Children. 2005. 376p. pap. 16.95 *(978-1-56563-521-0(3))* Hendrickson Pubs. Marketing, LLC.

Reeves, Eira. Dios Te Ama.Tr. of God Loves You. (SPA.). (J). 1.89 *(978-0-7899-0477-5(2),* 498668) Editorial Unilit.

—Jesus & Me Every Day Book 1, 1 vol. 2009. (ENG., Illus.). 64p. (J). pap. *(978-1-85345-518-6(0))* Crusade for World Revival.

—Jesus & Me Every Day Book 2, 1 vol. 2009. (ENG., Illus.). 64p. (J). pap. *(978-1-85345-519-3(9))* Crusade for World Revival.

Relf, Sue. 100 Instant Children's Talks. 2007. (Illus.). 224p. pap. 13.99 *(978-0-85476-388-7(0))* Kingsway Pubns. GBR. Dist: Send The Light Distribution LLC.

Rise & Shine! the Early Church: 12 Instant Bible Lessons for Kids. 2006. (Pick up 'n' Do Ser.). (Illus.). 126p. pap., per. 19.99 *(978-0-7814-4376-0(8),* 0781443768) Cook, David C.

Ritter, Helen E. And a Child Shall Lead Them... 2007. pap. 12.00 *(978-0-8059-8601-3(4))* Dorrance Publishing Co., Inc.

Robertson, Korie & Howard, Chrys. Duck Commander Devotions for Kids, 1 vol. 2015. (ENG.). 224p. (J). 16.99 *(978-0-7180-2249-5(1))* Nelson, Thomas Inc.

Robins, Jeannie. College Roadmap: Your Guide to Becoming A Freshman in Life. Grimes, Liz & Lindemann, Kara, eds. 2004. (Illus.). 160p. (YA). pap. 14.95 *(978-0-9755370-0-8(8))* ReSource Guides, Inc.

Robinson, Helen Lee, ed. Guide's Greatest Sabbath Stories. 2004. (Review Kids Ser.). 144p. (J). pap. 10.99 *(978-0-8280-1814-2(6),* 79-978) Review & Herald Publishing Assn.

Rock, Lois. Al Final del Dia. Rawlings, Louise, illus. (Coleccion Luz de Noche). (SPA.). (J). (gr. k-3). *(978-84-236-5039-2(1))* Edebé ESP. Dist: Lectorum Pubns., Inc.

—La Gran Noticia. Rawlings, Louise, illus. (Coleccion Luz de Noche). (SPA.). (J). (gr. k-3). *(978-84-236-4917-4(2))* Edebé ESP. Dist: Lectorum Pubns., Inc.

—Todos los Dias Contigo. Rawlings, Louise, illus. (Coleccion Luz de Noche). (SPA.). (J). (gr. k-3). *(978-84-236-4916-7(4))* Edebé ESP. Dist: Lectorum Pubns., Inc.

Rock Solid Tween FaithZine Winter 2009-2010. 2009. (Efs Ser.). 5.20 *(978-0-687-65839-8(X),* Cokesbury) Abingdon Pr.

Rolling, Greg. The First Time I Heard the Gospel. Dotty, Zens, illus. 2012. 24p. pap. 11.99 *(978-0-9827446-9-7(2))* Quoir.

Rome, Jacqueline Thomas. Do I Have to Go to Church Today? Thomas, Pamela L., illus. 2010. 36p. pap. 14.95 *(978-0-9841899-6-0(3))* PearlStone Publishing, Inc.

Roseman, Kenneth D. Until the Messiah Comes. 2004. (Do-It-Yourself Jewish Adventure Ser.). (Illus.). 145p. (gr. 4-6). pap. 11.95 *(978-0-8074-0706-6(2),* 140073) URJ Pr.

Ross, Melanie H. & Guymon-King. Primary Partners. 2004. cd-rom 11.95 *(978-1-57734-691-3(2))* Covenant Communications, Inc.

—Super Little Singers. 2004. pap. 12.95 *(978-1-59156-163-7(9));* cd-rom 12.95 *(978-1-59156-164-4(7))* Covenant Communications, Inc.

Ross, Michael & Johnson, Greg. 10 Reasons to Stay Christian in High School: A Guide to Staying Sane When Everyone Else Has Jumped off the Deep End. 2015. (ENG.). 192p. (YA). pap. 7.99 *(978-1-63058-375-0(8),* GoTandem) Barbour Publishing, Inc.

Ross, Michael & Ross, Christopher. Finding Faith in a Minecrafty World: 80 a-To-Z (Kid Only) Survival Secrets [an Unofficial Guide]. 2017. (ENG., Illus.). 256p. (J). pap. 14.99 *(978-0-7369-7085-3(1))* Harvest Hse. Pubs.

Rottmann, Erik. A Meal for Many: My Gift for Jesus. Paris, Pat, illus. 2003. (Arch Bks.). (ENG.). 16p. (J). (gr. k-4). 1.99 *(978-0-7586-0377-7(0))* Concordia Publishing Hse.

Russell, Michael L. Lolabell, the Good Little Helper along with Patsy Poopoo & Friends. 2009. 49p. (J). pap. 13.95 *(978-1-4327-3344-5(3))* Outskirts Pr., Inc.

S. P. C. K. Stories from the History of Sweden. 2006. pap. 29.50 *(978-1-4101-0922-4(4))* Fredonia Bks.

Sadlier We Believe Review & Resource Book. 2003. (J). (gr. 1). per. *(978-0-8215-5421-0(2),* Sadlier) Sadlier, William H. Inc.

Savelle, Jerry. Don't Let Go of Your Dreams. Date not set. mass mkt. 3.99 *(978-0-88144-171-0(6))* Yorkshire Publishing Group.

Schalk, Anita. The Lost Sheep. 2015. (Bouncy Bible Buddies Ser.). (ENG.). 10p. (J). bds. 7.99 *(978-1-4964-1090-0(4))* Tyndale Hse. Pubs.

Schambach, R. W., frwd. This Charge, This Generation: Could This Be the Generation That Brings about Change in the Earth? 2005. 208p. per. 14.99 *(978-0-9763800-0-9(5),* 10) Orison Pubs.

Scherm, Deedra. Only One Me: A Sweet Little Rhyme to Help Your Light Shine. Dreyer, Laura, illus. 2008. (ENG.). 22p. (J). (gr. -1-3). 7.99 *(978-1-934789-02-5(X))* Lemon Vision Productions.

School of the Bible for Kids: The Most High God. 2003. (ENG & GER.). 238p. ring bd. 79.95 *(978-0-9767647-3-1(3))* Kids in Ministry International.

Schultz, Joani, et al. Easter Extras: Faith-Filled Ideas for Easter Week. Creyts, Patrick, illus. 2007. 24p. pap. 6.99 *(978-0-7644-3694-9(5))* Group Publishing, Inc.

Scott, Cassandra. Boys & Girls Are Created2Produce. 2013. 40p. pap. 17.99 *(978-0-9882936-2-5(5))* Scott, Cassandra Dr Ministries.

Scully, Michael & Donovan, Patrick. Reaching Teens Through Film, Vol. 11. Cannizzo, Karen A., ed. 2004. (Jesus in Modern Media Ser.: 11). 104p. (YA). per. 21.95 *(978-0-89837-195-6(3),* 3704) Pflaum Publishing Group.

Scully, Michael & Donovan, Patrick J. Reaching Teens Through Film, Vol. 10. Cannizzo, Karen, ed. 2003. (Jesus in the Media Ser.: 10). 88p. (YA). per. 19.95 *(978-0-89837-187-1(2),* 3703) Pflaum Publishing Group.

See, Sharon. God Gives Us Work. 2003. (Illus.). 32p. (gr. -1-5). 2.70 *(978-0-7399-2338-2(2),* 2773) Rod & Staff Pubs., Inc.

Seifert, Sheila & Naylor, Beth. And the Winner Is. 2007. (Discipleship Junction Ser.). (ENG., Illus.). 112p. (J). per. 19.99 *(978-0-7814-4512-2(4))* Cook, David C.

—Getting to Know God. 2006. (Dsj Ser.). (Illus.). 116p. pap., per. 19.99 *(978-0-7814-4322-7(9),* 0781443229) Cook, David C.

Seirei to Anata. 2004. (JPN.). (YA). ring bd. 14.00 *(978-0-9673342-5-7(X))* Saints Of Glory Church.

Sharp, Anna Layton. Taking Godly Care of My Money: Stewardship Lessons in Money Matters, Grades 2-5. Flint, Russ, illus. 2005. (Resource Bks.). 80p. (J). (gr. 2-5). per. 9.99 *(978-1-59441-082-6(8),* CD-204009) Carson-Dellosa Publishing, LLC.

Shaw, S. B. Children's Edition of Touching Incidents. 2005. pap. 15.95 *(978-1-59605-735-7(1),* Cosimo Classics) Cosimo, Inc.

Shellenberger, Susie & Weber, Kristin. The Smart Girl's Guide to God, Guys, & the Galaxy: Save the Drama! & 100 Other Practical Tips for Teens. 2014. (ENG., Illus.). 224p. pap. 12.99 *(978-1-62416-760-7(8),* Barbour Bks.) Barbour Publishing, Inc.

Shenton, Tim. The Life of Abraham: Faith, Courage, Children, God. 2003. (Daily Readings From Ser.). (Illus.). 76p. (J). (gr. -1-7). per. 7.99 *(978-1-903087-72-5(4))* DayOne Pubns. GBR. Dist: Send The Light Distribution LLC.

Shepherd, Sheri Rose. His Little Princess: Treasured Letters from Your King. Browning, Lisa Marie, illus. 2006. (His Princess Ser.). (ENG.). 128p. (gr. 4-7). 14.99 *(978-1-59052-601-9(5),* Multnomah Bks.) Crown Publishing Group.

Shivers, Holly Hawkins. I Can Learn the Bible: The Joshua Code for Kids: 52 Scriptures Every Kid Should Know, 1 vol. 2014. (ENG.). 224p. (J). 14.99 *(978-0-529-10899-9(2))* Nelson, Thomas Inc.

—I Can Learn to Pray, 1 vol. 2016. (ENG., Illus.). 224p. (J). 14.99 *(978-0-7180-8169-0(2))* Nelson, Thomas Inc.

Show Me the Road. 12.00 *(978-0-687-05431-2(1))* Abingdon Pr.

Silverthorne, Sandy. Surviving When You're Home Alone: How to Avoid Being Grounded for Life. Silverthorne, Sandy, illus. 2006. (Illus.). 96p. (YA). (gr. 3-6). pap. 5.99 *(978-0-7847-1434-8(7),* 42176) Standard Publishing.

Simon, Mary Manz. First Virtues (padded Cover) 12 Stories for Toddlers. rev. ed. 2016. (ENG.). 256p. (J). (gr. -1-k). 12.99 *(978-1-4336-8833-1(6),* B&H Kids) B&H Publishing Group.

Sirois, Celia M. Jesus Is the Promise, Vol. 6. 70p. (J). (gr. 6). 2.25 *(978-0-8198-3934-3(5))* Pauline Bks. & Media.

Slattery, Kathryn. If I Could Ask God Anything: Awesome Bible Answers for Curious Kids, 1 vol. 2nd ed. 2010. (ENG.). 224p. pap. 12.99 *(978-1-4003-1602-1(2))* Nelson, Thomas Inc.

Slaughter, Nathan E. & Lewis, Kevin. Clear Perceptions. 2nd ed. 2003. 118p. per. 9.00 *(978-0-9746463-2-9(6))* Sabyr Pr.

—Fresh Foundations. 3rd rev. ed. 2003. 116p. per. 9.00 *(978-0-9746463-1-2(8))* Sabyr Pr.

—Pure Reflections. 3rd ed. 2003. 116p. per. 9.00 *(978-0-9746463-3-6(4))* Sabyr Pr.

Smart Kids Publishing Staff, creator. God Loves.... 2006. (Rub a Dub Fun in the Tub Ser.). (ENG., Illus.). 10p. (J). (gr. -1-3). 8.95 *(978-0-8249-6682-9(1),* Ideal Pubns.) Worthy Publishing.

Smiley, Bob & Florea, Jesse. Devotions for Super Average Kids 2. 2014. (ENG.). 240p. (J). pap. 12.99 *(978-1-62405-131-9(6))* Tyndale Hse. Pubs.

Smith, Brenda J. Where Did Mommy Go? A Spiritual Tool to Help Children Grow from Grief to Peace. Smith, Brenda J. & Cloud, Olivia, eds. Smith, Brock R. & Smith, Raissa B., illus. 2004. Orig. Title: Listed Above. 52p. (gr. 3-12). pap. 16.95 *(978-0-9744549-0-0(7))* Tall Through Bks.

Smith, Hannah. The Christian's Secret of a Happy Life. 2017. (Read & Reflect with the Classics Ser.). (ENG.). 320p. 14.99 *(978-1-4336-4999-8(3),* B&H Bks.) B&H Publishing Group.

Smith, Louis. Sexual Sins of the Bible: Everything You Want to Know, but Wouldn't Ask! 2004. 200p. pap. 14.99 *(978-0-9744519-1-6(6))* Smith, Kasper.

Smith, Marilyn. Kingdom Lifestyles for Children: Kingdom Lifestyles for Successful Living. 2012. 28p. pap. 16.09 *(978-1-4669-3825-0(0))* Trafford Publishing.

So You Want to Be a Wise Guy. 136p. pap. 15.99 *(978-0-8307-2917-3(8),* Gospel Light) Gospel Light Pubns.

Solo Dios Salva (Only God Saves) Quarter 3, Level 3. (Caminando con Jesus (Walking with Jesus) Series B). (SPA.). (J). (gr. 3-4). stu. ed. 3.50 *(978-0-570-05154-1(1),* 16-3913) Concordia Publishing Hse.

Soul Survivor Guide to Service Projects. 2004. 96p. 19.99 *(978-0-8307-3529-7(1),* Gospel Light) Gospel Light Pubns.

Soul Survivor Guide to Youth Ministry. 2004. 96p. 19.99 *(978-0-8307-3530-3(5)*, Gospel Light) Gospel Light Pubns.

Soul Survivor Prayer Ministry How to Pray for Others. 2004. 72p. 5.99 *(978-0-8307-3527-3(5)*, Gospel Light) Gospel Light Pubns.

A Special Purpose. 2006. (Illus.). (J). ring bd. 9.99 net. *(978-0-9786031-5-1(X))* Hosannah Pubns.

Special Times. (Bulletin Board Jumbo Cutouts Ser.). (Illus.). 96p. (J). 9.99 *(978-0-7847-0553-7(4)*, 02590) Standard Publishing.

Spiritual Overcomers Series (SOS). 212 vols. 2005. (YA). per. 29.95 *(978-0-9772313-3-1(X))* The 101 Group, Inc.

Squire 5 Personal Growth Planbook: Daring Depths. 2003. (Illus.). 48p. (J). pap. 4.95 *(978-1-59312-046-7(X))* North American Mission Board, SBC.

St. James, Rebecca. 40 Days with God: A Devotional Journey. rev. ed. 2006. 112p. pap. 12.99 *(978-0-7847-1274-0(3)*, 23338) Standard Publishing.

St. John, Patricia. The Safe Place. 2003. (Colour Bks.). (ENG., Illus.). 24p. (J). 9.99 *(978-1-85792-779-5(6)*, 1a916922-68d2-476c-8878-b3256550b209) Christian Focus Pubns. GBR. Dist: Bookmasters Distribution.

Stanley, Barb. What Catholics Teens Should Know When Dating Turns Violent. Larkin, Jean K., ed. 2004. (What Catholic Teens Should Know Ser.). (Illus.). 8p. (YA). 7.95 *(978-0-89837-239-7(9)*, 441210) Pflaum Publishing Group.

Stanley, Mandy, illus. Lift & Look Daniel. 2005. 8p. (J). (gr. -1-k). 7.99 *(978-0-7847-1751-6(6)*, 04377) Standard Publishing.

Steele, Blake. Radical Forgiveness: A Handbook for Spiritual Growth. 2003. (Spiritual Vision Ser.). (Illus.). 112p. *(978-87-7247-263-8(4))* Scandinavia Publishing Hse.

Stenzel, Pam. Sex Has a Price Tag: Discussions about Sexuality, Spirituality, & Self-Respect. 1 vol. 2015. (ENG.). 144p. (YA). pap. 9.99 *(978-0-310-74885-4(2))* Zondervan.

Stevens, Margaret M. Stepping Stones for Boys & Girls. Stevens, David S., illus. 2003. 32p. (gr. 5-18). 5.95 *(978-0-87516-248-5(7))* DeVorss & Co.

Stewart, Ed & McDowell, Josh. Conflicts with Others. 2008. (Project 17:17 Ser.). (ENG.). 64p. (J). pap. 4.99 *(978-1-84550-354-3(6)*, fb41ae66-973d-4060-8e31-2a08e1f62976) Christian Focus Pubns. GBR. Dist: Bookmasters Distribution.

—Finding True Love. 2008. (Project 17:17 Ser.). (ENG.). 64p. (J). pap. 4.99 *(978-1-84550-356-7(2)*, d5fc11fa-99e7-4d6c-b4b5-7793875dbf44) Christian Focus Pubns. GBR. Dist: Bookmasters Distribution.

Stiegemeyer, Julie. Things I See in Church. Mitter, Kathy, illus. 2003. 20p. (J). bds. 5.49 *(978-0-7586-0357-9(6))* Concordia Publishing Hse.

Stiegemeyer, Julie & Mitter, Kathy. Things I Do in Church. 2003. (Illus.). 20p. (J). bds. 5.49 *(978-0-7586-0126-1(3))* Concordia Publishing Hse.

Stinnett, Leia A. In the Mirror I See, God's Reflection Within Me: A Workbook for Teenagers. Date not set. (Little Angel Bks.). (Illus.). (YA). (gr. 6-12). pap. *(978-1-880737-19-4(1))* Crystal Journeys Publishing.

Stohs, Anita. Here Is the Church. Mitter, Kathy, illus. 2009. 32p. (J). (gr. -1). 8.99 *(978-0-7586-1633-3(3))* Concordia Publishing Hse.

Stortz, Diane. Say & Pray Devotions. 1 vol. 2016. (ENG.). 40p. (J). bds. 9.99 *(978-0-7180-8691-6(0))* Nelson, Thomas Inc.

Stott, Darrel E. Gods Joy Can Make A Difference. l.t. ed. 2003. (Illus.). 52p. 5.00 *(978-0-9755564-1-2(X))* Stott, Darrel Ministry.

Strack, Jay. Identity Theft: The Thieves Who Want to Rob Your Future. 1 vol. 2006. (Student Leadership University Study Guide Ser.). (ENG.). 144p. per. 9.99 *(978-1-4185-0594-3(3))* Nelson, Thomas Inc.

Strack, Jay & Edwards, David. Life: How to Get There from Here. 1 vol. 2006. (Student Leadership University Study Guide Ser.). (ENG.). 144p. pap. 9.99 *(978-1-4185-0599-8(4))* Nelson, Thomas Inc.

Strack, Jay & Lucado, Max. Leadership Rocks: Becoming a Student of Influence. 1 vol. 2006. (Student Leadership University Study Guide Ser.). (ENG.). 144p. pap. 9.99 *(978-1-4185-0593-6(5))* Nelson, Thomas Inc.

Strickland, Della. Emma's Moments. 2008. 144p. pap. 10.99 *(978-1-58169-265-5(X))* Genesis Communications, Inc.

Stripling, Joe. See You in Heaven. Carroll, Joan, ed. Hunter, Charlene, illus. Date not set. (Sunday School Two Thousand Ser.). 38p. (J). pap. 12.95 *(978-1-881223-07-8(8))* Zulema Enterprises Publishing.

Strobel, Lee. The Case for Faith: A Journalist Investigates the Toughest Objections to Christianity. 1 vol. 2014. (Case for ... Series for Students Ser.). (ENG.). 112p. (YA). pap., stu. ed. 9.99 *(978-0-310-74542-6(X))* Zondervan.

—The Case for Faith for Kids. 1 vol. enl. ed. 2010. (Case for... Series for Kids Ser.). (ENG.). 144p. (J). pap. 7.99 *(978-0-310-71991-5(7))* Zonderkidz.

—Case for Grace for Kids. 1 vol. 2015. (ENG., Illus.). 176p. (J). pap. 7.99 *(978-0-310-73656-1(0))* Zonderkidz.

—The Case for the Real Jesus: A Journalist Investigates Current Challenges to Christianity. 1 vol. 2014. (Case for ... Series for Students Ser.). (ENG.). 208p. (YA). pap., stu. ed. 9.99 *(978-0-310-74567-9(5))* Zondervan.

Strobel, Lee, et al. Secret Survivors: Real-Life Stories to Give You Hope for Healing. 1 vol. 2008. (ENG.). 160p. (YA). pap. 12.99 *(978-0-310-28322-5(1))* Zondervan.

Strong, Terri. Wee Wisdom. 2007. 60p. per. 10.95 *(978-1-933912-69-1(3))* Westview Publishing Co., Inc.

Stuff to Know When Cults Come Knocking. (Other Beliefs Ser.). (YA). pap., stu. ed. 8.95 *(978-1-59255-196-5(3)*, 130530); pap. 16.50 *(978-1-59255-197-2(1)*, 130535) Faith Alive Christian Resources.

Sturtz, Maria. God Gave Me. 2004. 32p. (J). 1.79 *(978-0-7586-0105-6(0))* Concordia Publishing Hse.

—God Is. 2004. 32p. (J). 1.79 *(978-0-7586-0104-9(2))* Concordia Publishing Hse.

Sub FBS 1st-2Nd Graders Learner Guide. 9.15 *(978-0-633-05036-8(9))* LifeWay Christian Resources.

Sub FBS 1st & 2Nd Graders. ldr.'s ed. 18.95 *(978-0-633-05035-1(0))*; 79.35 *(978-0-633-05072-6(5))* LifeWay Christian Resources.

Sub FBS 3rd-4th Graders. ldr.'s ed. 18.95 *(978-0-633-05037-5(7))* LifeWay Christian Resources.

Sub FBS 3rd & 4th Graders. ldr.'s ed. 79.35 *(978-0-633-05074-0(1))* LifeWay Christian Resources.

Sub FBS 3rd & 4th Graders Learner Guide. 9.15 *(978-0-633-05038-2(5))* LifeWay Christian Resources.

Sub FBS Preschool Bible Fun. 8.28 *(978-0-633-05132-7(2))* LifeWay Christian Resources.

Sublett, Kit. After Camp: Beginning the Christian Adventure. 2003. (YA). pap. 3.95 *(978-0-9758577-0-0(3))* Whitecaps Media.

Suzanne, Rentz. Daughters of Heaven Devotional. 2004. pap. 12.99 *(978-1-57794-560-4(3))* Harrison House Pubs.

Swain, Claudia. What's a Girl to Do? 2004. 128p. pap. 6.99 *(978-1-56309-440-8(1))* New Hope Pubs.

A Sword in My Hand. 2004. (YA). 12.00 *(978-0-9747189-6-5(3))* LightHouse Pr.

Szabo, Grable. Holy Donuts: Impacting Schools for Christ. 2005. pap. 9.99 *(978-1-59781-155-2(6))* Salem Author Services.

Tameka Trask. Thank You Jesus: A Child's Everyday Book of Praise, & Song!!! 2012. 20p. pap. 17.99 *(978-1-4772-4468-5(9))* AuthorHouse.

Tangvald, Christine Harder. Playtime Devotions: Sharing Bible Moments with Your Baby or Toddler. Schmitz, Tamara, illus. 2006. (Heritage Builders Ser.). 36p. (J). 15.99 *(978-0-7847-1361-7(8)*, 04024) Standard Publishing.

Taylor, Carol & Taylor, Winford. Take Time to Know & Love Them. 2008. 296p. pap. 18.99 *(978-0-9818753-2-3(7))* Leading Lady Pubns.

Taylor, Caroline. Lord God Made Us All. Longfoot, Stephanie, illus. 2004. (My First Prayers Ser.). 10p. (J). bds. 3.99 *(978-1-85854-243-0(X))* Brimax Books Ltd. GBR. Dist: Byeway Bks.

Taylor, David A. Eternal Vision: Seeing Life from Heaven's Perspective. 2005. (Illus.). 341p. per. 12.00 *(978-0-9762933-0-9(7))* Taylor Publishing Grp.

Tebow, Tim. Shaken: Young Reader's Edition: Fighting to Stand Strong No Matter What Comes Your Way. 2017. (ENG.). 208p. (J). (gr. 5). 17.99 ***(978-0-7352-8996-3(4)***, WaterBrook Pr.) Crown Publishing Group.

Tenney, Tommy. God Chasers for Kids. 2005. (Illus.). 96p. (J). 11.99 *(978-0-7684-2165-1(9))* Destiny Image Pubs.

Thiele, Christine. What Catholic Teens Should Know about Suicide. Larkin, Jean K., ed. 2004. (What Catholic Teens Should Know Ser.). (Illus.). 8p. (YA). 7.95 *(978-0-89837-240-3(2)*, 441110) Pflaum Publishing Group.

Thomas, Daniel D. Prophecies of Life. 2004. (YA). per. 9.95 *(978-0-9761604-0-3(4))* Life Line Publishing.

Thomas, Danita & Thomas, John E. Inventos de Dimensiones Biblicas para Ninos. 2007. (Illus.). 78p. (J). per. 9.99 *(978-0-8054-4499-5(8)*, B&H Bks.) B&H Publishing Group.

Thomas, Erika & Treg, Mccoy, illus. Petey Yikes! A very, very true story about a homeless little blue bird in New York City. 2006. (J). *(978-0-9789642-0-7(9))* Petey, Rock & Roo Children's Pubns.

Thomas, Jerry D. What We Believe: Helping Children Understand the Beliefs of the Seventh-Day Adventist Church. 2006. (J). 11.99 *(978-0-8163-2167-4(1))* Pacific Pr. Publishing Assn.

Thomas, Jerry D. & Thomas, Kitty. Step by Step: Helping Children Understand the Principles of Steps to Christ. 2008. (J). pap. 11.99 *(978-0-8163-2277-0(5))* Pacific Pr. Publishing Assn.

Thomas, Mack. What Would Jesus Pray? A Story to Change the World. 2006. (ENG., Illus.). 160p. (J). (gr. 5-7). 12.99 *(978-1-59052-738-2(0)*, Multnomah) Doubleday Religious Publishing Group, The.

Thornborough, Tim. The Fright of Your Life. 25 vols. 2010. 6p. (J). *(978-1-906334-27-7(7))* Good Bk. Co.

Thorne, Rick. The Hidden Secrets of Jesus & Other Revelations. 2004. (Illus.). 268p. (YA). pap. 19.95 *(978-0-937327-04-3(2))* Soul Pubns.

Through God's Eyes. 2005. per. *(978-1-59581-169-1(9))* Brentwood Communications Group.

Through God's Eyes. 2004. spiral bd. 16.99 *(978-0-87808-359-6(6))* Carey, William Library Pubs.

Timothy Grows in God's Word. (Two Great Ways to Share God's Love Ser.). 16p. (gr. -1-k). 15.00 *(978-0-570-00314-4(8))* Concordia Publishing Hse.

Titles of the Triune God: Studies in Divine Self-Revelation. 2004. 190p. pap. 19.95 *(978-0-9752843-0-8(4))* Capstone Bks.

Tm412 All Terrain Student Book. 2004. (J). (gr. 7-12). 5.95 *(978-0-633-01998-3(4))* LifeWay Christian Resources.

TNT Ministries Staff. God's Miracle Maker: Elisha. 2007. (King of Clubs Ser.). (ENG.). 96p. (J). pap. 17.99 *(978-1-84550-291-1(4)*, 9781845502911) Christian Focus Pubns. GBR. Dist: Bookmasters Distribution.

Tnt Ministries Staff. On the Way 11 - 14's, Vol. 4. 2003. (On the Way (11-14's) Ser.). (ENG.). 96p. (J). pap. 17.99 *(978-1-85792-707-8(9)*, 9781857927078) Christian Focus Pubns. GBR. Dist: Bookmasters Distribution.

Todd, Richard E. Salvation: A Bible Study Wordbook for Kids. 2009. (Children's Wordbooks Ser.). (ENG., Illus.). 32p. (gr. 4-7). pap. 5.99 *(978-1-60066-198-3(X))* WingSpread Publishers.

Together in Jesus: Spanish First Eucharist Certificate. 2004. (SPA., Illus.). 1p. (J). pap. 9.95 *(978-0-89837-243-4(7)*, 972110) Pflaum Publishing Group.

Tomlinson, Elisa. True Reflection: A Girls' Guide to Identity in Christ. 2004. 96p. (YA). *(978-0-9758989-0-1(6))* Eternity Pr.

Tommy Books: Fear. 10 vols. l.t. ed. 2005. (Illus.). 24p. (J). 12.99 *(978-0-9762690-5-2(8))* Tommy Bks. Pubng.

Tommy Books: Forgiveness. 10 vols. l.t. ed. 2005. (Illus.). 24p. (J). 12.99 *(978-0-9762690-6-9(6))* Tommy Bks. Pubng.

Tommy Books: Grace & Mercy. 10 Vols. l.t. ed. 2005. (Illus.). 24p. (J). 12.99 *(978-0-9762690-8-3(2))* Tommy Bks. Pubng.

Tommy Books: Thank You. 10 vols. l.t. ed. 2005. (Illus.). 24p. (J). 12.99 *(978-0-9762690-9-0(0))* Tommy Bks. Pubng.

Tommy Books: Who Am I. 10 vols. l.t. ed. 2005. (Illus.). 24p. (J). 12.99 *(978-0-9762690-7-6(4))* Tommy Bks. Pubng.

Toms, Kate. God Knows All about Me. 2008. 26p. (J). bds. 7.99 *(978-1-4003-1275-7(2))* Nelson, Thomas Inc.

Topliff, Delores. Whoosh. l.t. ed. 2007. (Illus.). 34p. (J). 9.95 *(978-0-9769031-1-6(3))* Verona (Bk.) Publishing, Inc.

Totilo, Rebecca Park. The Christian Kids' Gardening Guide: Cool Stuff for You to Make & Grow. 2004. (Illus.). 168p. (J). pap. 12.99 *(978-1-58411-034-7(1)*, Legacy Pr.) Rainbow Pubs. & Legacy Pr.

Trebi-Ollennu, Flora. My Daily Walk: Discover the Life of Jesus. Barker, Peter, ed. 2005. 384p. *(978-1-894718-04-2(6))* Amerley Treb Bks.

Triplett, Donald & Eiland, Marie. Castle Club - Student Guide: Children Walking in the Way of the Lord. 2 vols., Vol. 22. Rdm, tr. 2011. Orig. Title: Club Castillo Manual del Estudiante. (SPA., Illus.). 82p. (J). spiral bd. 5.00 *(978-1-931984-78-2(6)*, 2004-00E1) Faith & Action Team.

—Castle Club Leader Manual: ... Children walking in the way of the Lord. 2 vols., Vol. 12. Rdm, tr. from SPA. 2011. Orig. Title: Club Castillo Manual del Maestro. (Illus.). 156p. spiral bd. 7.00 *(978-1-931984-93-5(X)*, 2003-00E1) Faith & Action Team.

Tripp, Terry. Growing in God's Word. 2004. (J). lib. bdg. *(978-0-9673093-4-7(4))* Song Revival Fellowship & Ministries.

Trock, Kathleen. Hiding Places. 2009.Tr. of Escondites. (Illus.). 64p. (J). 14.99 *(978-0-9821835-4-0(2))* This Joy Bks.

Troxell, Melanie. David Asks Why: Ellen G. White's Classic Steps to Christ Adapted to Children. 2009. (J). pap. 12.99 *(978-0-8163-2254-1(6))* Pacific Pr. Publishing Assn.

Trudgian, Sherri. Psalm 1 for Kidz: I'm So Happy I Want to Shout! Moreland Krass, Melanie, illus. 2013. 32p. (J). *(978-0-9779194-6-8(3))* Little Sprout Publishing Hse.

True God, True Man. 2004. (Effective Dre Ser.). pap. *(978-0-8294-1499-8(1))* Loyola Pr.

Trummel, D. Pauline. A Reformed Baptist Sunday School Curriculum: New Testament Survey, year 2 Semester 1. Nichols, Gregory G., ed. 2003. (Illus.). 160p. (J). ring bd. 25.00 *(978-1-889520-20-9(9))* Truth For Eternity Ministries.

—A Reformed Baptist Sunday School Curriculum: New Testament Survey, year 2 Semester 2. Nichols, Gregory G., ed. 2004. (Illus.). 160p. (J). ring bd. 25.00 *(978-1-889520-21-6(7))* Truth For Eternity Ministries.

Tween Time. 24.00 *(978-0-687-34263-1(5))* Abingdon Pr.

Ulmer, Louise. Good Friday. Sandland, Reg, illus. 2004. (Arch Bks.). (ENG.). 16p. (J). 1.99 *(978-0-7586-0638-9(9))* Concordia Publishing Hse.

Understanding the Gift in Your Pastor. 2005. per. 10.99 *(978-0-9765809-0-4(X))* Garing, Bernard.

Upthegrove, C. S. The Wait... the Power... the Evidence... Miracles That Followed the Angelic Visit 2003. 23.99 *(978-0-9716523-6-1(8))* Hope Harvest Publishing.

Valeri, Jennifer. God from A-Z: A Child's Guide to Learning about God. 2009. 32p. pap. 15.00 *(978-1-60860-761-7(5)*, Eloquent Bks.) Strategic Book Publishing & Rights Agency (SBPRA).

Van Dyke, Jan. Living Like a King's Kid. Van Order, Laura & VonSeggen, Jon, illus. rev. ed. 2003. 77p. (J). spiral bd. 30.00 *(978-1-58302-249-8(X))* One Way St., Inc.

Vamadeau, Jeni. Chikchat(r) Workshop Manual. 2005. 92p. pap. 12.00 *(978-0-9766634-7-8(3))* ChikChat(r) Ink.

Veerman, David. Ready for Life. 2008. 400p. (J). pap. 16.99 *(978-0-9724616-4-1(7))* Barton-Veerman Co.

Vidrine, Beverly Barras. Easter Day Alphabet. 1 vol. Lyne, Alison Davis, illus. 2003. (ENG.). 32p. (J). (gr. k-k). pap. 8.95 *(978-1-58980-076-2(1))* Pelican Publishing Co., Inc.

Vineyard Church of Columbus. Little Son Catchers Leader's Guide: Pre-school curriculum Fall Quarter, Year One. 2007. pap. 19.99 *(978-0-9786394-6-4(4))* Ampelon Publishing, LLC.

Vivian May Edwards. Creation's Praise: For little Ones. 2009. 20p. pap. 14.99 *(978-1-4389-5919-1(2))* AuthorHouse.

Viviendo como un Hijo del Rey. 2004. (SPA.). (J). spiral bd. 30.00 *(978-1-58302-255-9(4))* One Way St., Inc.

Wade, Connie Morgan. Bible Songs & Action Rhymes, Ages 3-6. 2016. (ENG., Illus.). 224p. (J). (gr. -1-3). per. 16.99 *(978-0-7847-1781-3(8)*, 24190) Standard Publishing.

Walker, Joni. Apostles Creed. Walker, Joni, illus. 2005. (Follow & Do Ser.). (Illus.). 32p. (J). 7.49 *(978-0-7586-0802-4(0))* Concordia Publishing Hse.

—Confession. 2005. (Follow & Do Ser.). (Illus.). 23p. (J). (gr. -1). 7.49 *(978-0-7586-0808-6(X))* Concordia Publishing Hse.

—Follow & Do Books: The Lord's Prayer. Walker, Joni, illus. 2004. (Follow & Do Ser.). (Illus.). 32p. (J). 7.49 *(978-0-7586-0678-5(8))* Concordia Publishing Hse.

—Jesus Knows Me. Walker, Joni, illus. 2003. (Illus.). 14p. (J). (gr. -1-k). bds. 5.49 *(978-0-7586-0507-8(2))* Concordia Publishing Hse.

—Lords Supper. Walker, Joni, illus. 2005. (Follow & Do Ser.). (Illus.). 23p. (J). (gr. -1-3). 7.49 *(978-0-7586-0801-7(2))* Concordia Publishing Hse.

Walsh, Sheila. You're Worth It for Girls: God Thinks You Rock! 2016. (ENG.). 112p. (J). 9.99 *(978-0-7369-6387-9(1))* Harvest Hse. Pubs.

Warlick, Sonya. A King's Love for His Daughter. 2010. 24p. pap. 7.99 *(978-0-88144-511-4(8)*, Thorncrown Publishing) Yorkshire Publishing Group.

Warren, Rick. The Lord's Prayer: Words of Hope & Happiness. 1 vol. Watson, Richard Jesse, illus. 2016. (ENG.). 32p. (J). 16.99 *(978-0-310-75755-9(X))* Zonderkidz.

Washington, L. Manners First - G I F T S. 2007. 88p. pap. 14.99 *(978-0-88144-273-1(9))* Yorkshire Publishing Group.

Washington, Linda & Dall, Jeanette. Favorite Bible Children: Ages 4 & 5. 2004. (Illus.). 96p. (J). pap. 11.95 *(978-1-885358-76-9(8))* Rainbow Pubs. & Legacy Pr.

Watson, Charles D. Christianity for Fools: A Simple Understanding of the Christian Faith. 2004. 143p. (YA). lib. bdg. 12.95 *(978-0-9678519-2-1(0))* Abounding Love Ministries, Inc.

Weaver, Roger. Holy Eucharist for the Children of God. 2003. pap. 8.95 *(978-0-9709575-5-9(6))* Singing River Pubns.

Weider, Nicole. Project Inspired: Tips & Tricks for Staying True to Who You Are. 1 vol. 2015. (ENG., Illus.). 168p. (YA). pap. 17.99 *(978-0-310-74939-4(5))* Zondervan.

Weiss, N. E. According to Plan. (YA). (gr. 7-8). 144p. stu. ed. *(978-0-85910-315-2(3)*, 23-0562); 65p. stu. ed., wbk. ed. *(978-0-85910-317-6(X)*, 23-0563) Openbook Publishers.

Welborn, Amy. Loyola Kids Book of Heroes: Stories of Catholic Heroes & Saints Throughout History. Konstantinov, Vitali, illus. 2003. (ENG.). 208p. (J). (gr. 3-7). 17.95 *(978-0-8294-1584-1(X))* Loyola Pr.

Welborn-Step-by-Step Childrens Church. (Illus.). (J). *(978-0-687-39335-0(3))* Abingdon Pr.

Welch, Michael, Sr. Why You Can Do God's Will. Butler, Latrica, ed. 2004. 108p. per. 12.99 *(978-0-9753773-0-7(2))* MCW Publishing.

Welch, Michael Eric, Sr. What the Devil Do Not Want You to Know... 2005. per. *(978-0-9753773-1-4(0))* MCW Publishing.

Welters, M. Andrine. My Confession Book: A Child's Preparation for the Sacrament of Penance. 2009. Orig. Title: Pax: A Preparation for the Sacrament of Penance for Children. (ENG., Illus.). 48p. (gr. 7-7). reprint ed. pap. 2.00 *(978-0-89555-600-4(6)*, 1505) TAN Bks.

Werner, Cherie. New Life in Jesus! 2008. (Illus.). (J). pap. *(978-1-933234-54-0(7))* CTA.

Wesbrooks, Linda. The New You: Lessons for Teenage Girls. (YA). pap. 7.99 *(978-0-89098-406-2(9))* Twentieth Century Christian Bks.

What Would Jesus Do? 2. (Illus.). 16p. (J). pap. 1.50 *(978-0-87162-806-0(6)*, E4511) Warner Pr., Inc.

What Would Jesus Do? An Activity Book about Biblical Values. (Illus.). 16p. (J). pap. 1.50 *(978-0-87162-700-1(0)*, E4509) Warner Pr., Inc.

Where Was God September 11? There Is an Answer. 2003. (YA). *(978-0-9740898-0-5(X))* Orchid Publishing Co.

White, Anne. Lessons in Responsibility for Girls: Level One. 2006. Orig. Title: Home Economics for Home Schoolers Level One. (J). per., pupil's gde. ed. 18.95 *(978-0-9792446-2-9(5))* Messiah Publishing - Pearables.

—Lessons in Responsibility for Girls: Level Three. 3. 2005. Orig. Title: Home Economics for Home Schoolers Level Three. (J). per., pupil's gde. ed. *(978-0-9792446-4-3(1))* Messiah Publishing - Pearables.

—Lessons in Responsibility for Girls: Level Two. 2. 2006. Orig. Title: Home Economics for Home Schoolers Level Two. (J). per., pupil's gde. ed. 18.95 *(978-0-9792446-3-6(3))* Messiah Publishing - Pearables.

White, Ellen Gould Harmon. Amazing Love. Vol. 1. 2nd ed. 2005. 96p. pap. 9.95 *(978-1-883012-79-3(1))* Remnant Pubns., Inc.

Whitfield, Laurie A. & Cammarata, Robert P. Taking Care of God's Gifts Stewardship: A Way of Life Grades 3-5. 2003. 48p. (J). pap. 2.95 *(978-1-59276-020-6(1))*; pap. 24.95 *(978-1-59276-040-4(6))* Our Sunday Visitor, Publishing Div.

—Taking Care of God's Gifts Stewardship: A Way of Life Grades K-2. 2003. 48p. (J). pap. 2.95 *(978-1-59276-019-0(8))*; pap. 24.95 *(978-1-59276-039-8(2))* Our Sunday Visitor, Publishing Div.

Wholistic Health Student. 1.25 *(978-0-687-37395-6(6))* Abingdon Pr.

Why Do Christians Do What They Do? 96p. (J). pap. 5.99 *(978-1-85792-782-5(6))* Christian Focus Pubns. GBR. Dist: Riverside.

Why I Believe in Jesus: A Finish-the-Picture Coloring Book. (Illus.). 16p. (J). pap. 1.50 *(978-0-87162-814-5(7)*, E6027) Warner Pr., Inc.

Widenhouse, Kathy. The Christian Girl's Guide to Friendship. 2004. (Illus.). 192p. (J). pap. 9.99 *(978-1-58411-043-9(0)*, Legacy Pr.) Rainbow Pubs. & Legacy Pr.

Wiliamson, Nancy. 52 Ideas for Special Days. 2004. (Fifty-Two Ways Ser.). (Illus.). 64p. (J). (gr. -1-7). pap. 9.95 *(978-0-937282-01-4(4)*, RB36108) Rainbow Pubs. & Legacy Pr.

Wilkinson, Bruce & Thomas, Mack. A Life God Rewards: Guys Only. ltd. ed. 2006. 96p. bds. 9.99 *(978-1-60142-002-2(1)*, Multnomah) Doubleday Religious Publishing Group, The.

Will, Julianne M. Stations of the Cross for Children. Mattozzi, Patricia, illus. 2005. 32p. (J). (gr. -1-3). pap. 3.95 *(978-1-59276-153-1(4))* Our Sunday Visitor, Publishing Div.

Williams, Alex. Holy Spy: Student Ministry in Eastern Europe. 2004. (Illus.). 208p. (J). pap. *(978-1-85792-906-5(3))* Christian Focus Pubns. GBR. Dist: Riverside.

Williams, Carla. Fold & Do. 2004. 54p. (gr. 2-4). 10.99 *(978-0-570-05287-6(4))* Concordia Publishing Hse.

—Little Hands Fold & Do. 2004. 54p. (gr. -1-1). 10.99 *(978-0-570-05286-9(6))* Concordia Publishing Hse.

Williamson, Wendy. Christian Martial Arts 101. 2004. (ENG.). 256p. per. 29.95 *(978-0-9721328-1-7(3))* Agapy LLC.

—Christian Martial Arts 101 (Instructor's Edition) 2004. (ENG.). 288p. per. 18.95 *(978-0-9721328-2-4(1))* Agapy LLC.

Wilson, Jacqui. Little Johnny's Faith Adventures: Our Beginnings. 2010. 68p. pap. 9.95 *(978-1-4497-0790-3(4)*, WestBow Pr.) Author Solutions, Inc.

Windle, Margaret. Assorted Saints & the Virtues. 2006. (Illus.). 64p. (J). 11.99 *(978-0-9798889-1-5(3))* Growing with the Saints, Inc.

—St Catherine Laboure. 2007. (Illus.). 53p. (J). 11.99 *(978-0-9798889-2-2(1))* Growing with the Saints, Inc.

Withers, Margaret. Welcome to the Lord's Table: A Practical Course for Preparing Children to Receive Holy Communion. 3rd rev. ed. 2013. (ENG., Illus.). 96p. pap. *(978-1-84101-734-1(5)*, Barnabas for Children) Bible Reading Fellowship.

Witherspoon Press Staff, contrib. by. Belonging to God: A First Catechism. 2003. (J). *(978-1-57153-036-3(3)*, Witherspoon Pr.) Curriculum Publishing, Presbyterian Church (U. S. A.).

Wood, Charles M., II. Living the Good Life: Surviving in the 21st Century. 2003. 160p. per. 13.95 *(978-0-9724867-0-5(4))* Woodland Pr., LLC.

Working with God. (Precious Moments Ser.). (J). 11.99 *(978-1-55976-183-3(0))*; pap. 9.99 *(978-1-55976-184-0(9))* CEF Pr.

Wright, Ben. Top Priority: Manna 2. 2003. (YA). ring bd. *(978-0-9719491-8-8(2))* Positive Action For Christ.

Written By Doretta Elaine Wilson; Illust. The Ultimate Heart. Baker, Jonathan, illus. 2011. 32p. pap. 24.95 *(978-1-4626-0684-9(9))* America Star Bks.

WWJD: What Would Jesus Do? (Illus.). 16p. (J). pap. 1.50 *(978-0-87162-833-6(3)*, E6021) Warner Pr., Inc.

Yaconelli, Mike. Devotion: A Raw-Truth Journal on Following Jesus. 1 vol. 2004. (Invert Ser.). (ENG., Illus.). 80p. (YA). pap. 10.99 *(978-0-310-25559-8(7))* Zondervan.

Yoshiike, Yoshitaka. A Christmas Interview: Reporting Live from Bethlehem! Tsuchiya, Fujio, illus. 2005. 32p. (J). (gr. -1-3). per. 7.95 *(978-0-8198-1572-9(1))* Pauline Bks. & Media.

You Can't Run Away from You: A Young Man's Journey to Himself. 2004. (Illus.). 188p. per. 15.00 *(978-0-9755616-0-7(X))* Darnell Publishing.

Young, Jeanna & Johnson, Jacqueline Kinney. Princess Prayers, 1 vol. Aranda, Omar, illus. 2017. (Princess Parables Ser.). (ENG.). 30p. (J). bds. 9.99 *(978-0-310-75869-3(6))* Zonderkidz.

Young, Sarah. Jesus Today Teen Cover: Experience Hope in His Presence, 1 vol. 2016. (ENG.). 384p. (YA). 16.99 *(978-0-7180-8681-7(3))* Nelson, Thomas Inc.

Youngs, Bettie B. Living the Ten Commandments in New Times: A Book for Teens. 2004. (ENG.). 304p. (YA). pap. 12.95 *(978-0-7573-0128-5(2),* Faith Communications) Health Communications, Inc.

Ytreeide, Arnold. Bartholomew's Passage. 2004. 168p. pap. 12.99 *(978-0-8307-3383-5(3),* Regal Bks.) Gospel Light Pubns.

—Jotham's Journey. 2004. 168p. pap. 12.99 *(978-0-8307-3448-1(1),* Regal Bks.) Gospel Light Pubns.

—Tabitha's Travels: A Family Story for Advent, 1 vol. 2010. (Illus.). 160p. (J). (gr. 7-18). pap. 15.99 *(978-0-8254-4172-1(2))* Kregel Pubns.

10 Mandamientos. 2004. 15.95 *(978-1-56814-614-0(0))* CCC of America.

50 Crosses Charted for Needlepoint: Christian Symbols Book II. 2004. spiral bd. 39.95 *(978-0-9760188-0-3(2))* Roberts, Michele.

100 Days with God. 2004. per. 7.00 *(978-0-9762014-0-3(2))* L'Edge Pr.

CHRISTIAN LIFE—FICTION

A. L. O. E. The Triumph over Midian. 2006. 344p. per. 23.99 *(978-1-4255-3466-0(X))* Michigan Publishing.

AB Publishing Staff. Peep Behind the Scenes. 2004. pap. 5.95 *(978-1-881545-95-8(4))* A B Publishing.

ABC of the New Testament. 2005. (J). bds. 8.95 *(978-0-9741748-4-6(X))* Patmos, Inc.

Alcock, Deborah. The King's Service: A Story of the Thirty Years' War. 2008. (YA). *(978-1-894666-06-0(2))* Inheritance Pubns.

Alden-Tirrill, Anna. The Alabaster Jar. 2013. 290p. pap. 14.95 *(978-1-885831-07-1(2))* Proclaim Publishing.

—The Promise Box. 2013. 284p. pap. 14.95 *(978-1-885831-05-7(6))* Proclaim Publishing.

Alsbrooks, Stephanie. The Ten Commandments. Meier, Paul, illus. 2005. (J). bds. 9.99 *(978-1-4183-0064-7(0))* Christ Inspired, Inc.

Alward, Diane. Pedals & Promises: An Adventure Devotional for Kids. 2013. 86p. pap. 9.95 *(978-1-4908-0512-2(5),* WestBow Pr.) Author Solutions, Inc.

Amado, Elisa. Primas, 1 vol. Iribarren, Elena & Iribarren, Leopoldo, trs. from ENG. Garay, Luis, illus. 2004. (SPA & ENG.). 32p. (J). 16.95 *(978-0-88899-548-3(2))* Groundwood Bks. CAN. Dist: Publishers Group West (PGW).

Anderson, Andrea Patrice. Heaven's Diary: Our Gift from God. 2006. 37.00 *(978-0-8059-8845-1(9))* Dorrance Publishing Co., Inc.

Anderson, Max Elliot. North Woods Poachers. 2004. 144p. pap. 10.95 *(978-0-9729256-8-6(6),* Tweener Pr.) Baker Trittin Pr.

Andrews, Andy. The Young Traveler's Gift, 1 vol. 2004. (ENG.). 160p. pap. 12.99 *(978-1-4003-0427-1(X))* Nelson, Thomas Inc.

Angeles: Redemption/Redencion. 2004. (Angeles Ser.).Tr. of Angels. (SPA., Illus.). 48p. pap. 4.99 *(978-0-8054-2839-1(9))* B&H Publishing Group.

Angeles: The Secret/el Secreto. 2004. (Angeles Ser.).Tr. of Angels. (SPA., Illus.). 48p. pap. 4.99 *(978-0-8054-2833-9(X))* B&H Publishing Group.

Angeles: The Sin/el Pecado. 2004. (Angeles Ser.).Tr. of Angels. (SPA., Illus.). 48p. pap. 4.99 *(978-0-8054-2838-4(0))* B&H Publishing Group.

Angler, Evan. Spark, 1 vol. 2013. (Swipe Ser.). (ENG.). 272p. (J). pap. 9.99 *(978-1-4003-2198-8(0))* Nelson, Thomas Inc.

Annie Hamilton, Donnell. Three Young Knights & Miss Theodosia's Heartstrings. 2007. (ENG.). 142p. pap. 18.99 *(978-1-4346-1511-4(1))* Creative Media Partners, LLC.

Annie, Johnston. Three Weavers. 2004. 11.00 *(978-1-58474-021-6(3))* Cornerstone Family Ministries/Lamplighter Publishing.

Annie S. Swan. Thankful Rest. 2007. 98p. pap. 16.99 *(978-1-4346-1978-5(8));* (ENG.). 102p. pap. 19.99 *(978-1-4346-1886-7(9))* Creative Media Partners, LLC.

Anya@Russia. Com. 2004. 32p. pap. 3.99 *(978-0-8341-2087-7(9))* Beacon Hill Pr. of Kansas City.

Archer, James. Travelling Light. 2005. 43p. spiral bd. 20.98 *(978-1-4116-4011-5(X))* Lulu Pr., Inc.

Arensen, Shel. The Poison Arrow Tree. 2003. (Rugendo Rhino Ser.). (Illus.). 128p. (J). pap. 5.99 *(978-0-8254-2041-2(5))* Kregel Pubns.

Arruda, Suzanne M. A Stocking for Jesus. Ogden, Betina, illus. 2005. (J). pap. 7.95 *(978-0-8198-7076-6(5),* 332-372) Pauline Bks. & Media.

Ascough, Deirdre Mary. My First Holy Communion. Brown, Lisa, illus. 2013. (ENG.). 72p. (J). 17.95 *(978-1-58617-708-9(7))* Ignatius Pr.

Auer, Chris. The Legend of the Sand Dollar, Newly Illustrated Edition: An Inspirational Story of Hope for Easter, 1 vol. Cowdrey, Richard, illus. 2017. (ENG.). 32p. (J). 16.99 *(978-0-310-74980-6(8))* Zonderkidz.

Avery, Ben & Zondervan Staff. Time Trap, 1 vol. Wong, Scott, illus. 2009. (Z Graphic Novels / TimeFlyz Ser.). (ENG.). 160p. (J). pap. 6.99 *(978-0-310-71366-1(8))* Zondervan.

B&H Kids Editorial Staff. Braving the Big Battle with the Baroness / Repelling the Ronin of Wrong, Flip-Over Book. 2016. (Bibleman Ser.). (ENG., Illus.). 32p. (J). (gr. -1-2). pap. 3.99 *(978-1-4336-4573-0(4),* B&H Kids) B&H Publishing Group.

—Dr. Fear's Almost Perfectly Disastrous Day / Clobbering the Crusher, Flip-Over Book. 2016. (Bibleman Ser.). (ENG., Illus.). 32p. (J). (gr. -1-2). pap. 3.99 *(978-1-4336-4574-7(2),* B&H Kids) B&H Publishing Group.

—Melting the Master of Mean / the Mayor of Maybe Doles Out Doubt, Flip-Over Book. 2016. (Bibleman Ser.). (ENG., Illus.). 32p. (J). (gr. -1-2). pap. 3.99 *(978-1-4336-4575-4(0),* B&H Kids) B&H Publishing Group.

Bacchus, Tamika D. Plain Jane Learns to Pray. 2011. 48p. pap. 19.99 *(978-1-61379-455-5(X))* Salem Author Services.

Balestrino, Jerry. Pumpkin the Angel Cat: Pumpkins 1st Mission. 2009. 32p. pap. 13.99 *(978-1-4343-7105-8(0))* AuthorHouse.

Ballantyne, R. M. The Crew of the Water Wagtail. 2011. 146p. 24.95 *(978-1-4638-9596-9(8))* Rodgers, Alan Bks.

—Red Rooney: Or, the Last of the Crew. 2007. (R. M. Ballantyne Collection). (Illus.). 408p. 22.00 *(978-1-934554-08-1(1))* Vision Forum, Inc., The.

Ballantyne, Robert Michael. My Doggie & I. 2007. 120p. pap. 18.99 *(978-1-4346-3682-9(8));* (ENG.). 130p. pap. 19.99 *(978-1-4346-3730-7(1))* Creative Media Partners, LLC.

—Red Rooney: The Last of the Crew. 2007. (ENG.). 270p. pap. 21.99 *(978-1-4346-3693-5(3));* 302p. pap. 24.99 *(978-1-4346-3741-3(7))* Creative Media Partners, LLC.

Ballard, Kim. Light at Summer's End. 2007. 116p. per. 15.95 *(978-1-60290-047-9(7))* OakTara Publishing Group LLC.

Barrett, Mary Brigid. Shoebox Sam, 1 vol. Morrison, Frank, illus. 2011. (ENG.). 32p. (J). 15.99 *(978-0-310-71549-8(0))* Zonderkidz.

Barry, Rick. Gunner's Run: A World War II Novel. 2007. 215p. (YA). (gr. 8-12). per. 8.99 *(978-1-59166-761-2(5))* BJU Pr.

Basham, Tom. Accidental Evie. Calvert, Lissa, illus. 2012. 120p. *(978-1-77097-373-2(7));* pap. *(978-1-77097-374-9(5))* FriesenPress.

Batson, Wayne Thomas. Isle of Fire, 1 vol. 2009. (ENG.). 352p. pap. 9.99 *(978-1-4003-1512-3(3))* Nelson, Thomas Inc.

—Isle of Swords, 1 vol. 2008. (ENG.). 352p. pap. 9.99 *(978-1-4003-1363-1(5))* Nelson, Thomas Inc.

Batson, Wayne Thomas & Hopper, Christopher. Curse of the Spider King: The Berinfell Prophecies Series - Book One. 2014. (ENG.). 384p. (J). pap. 14.99 *(978-0-7180-2987-6(9))* Nelson, Thomas Inc.

Batterson, Mark & Clark, Joel N. Jack Staples & the City of Shadows. 2015. (ENG.). 256p. (J). pap. 9.99 *(978-0-7814-1108-0(4))* Cook, David C.

Batterson, Mark, et al. Jack Staples & the Ring of Time. 2014. (ENG.). 240p. (J). pap. 9.99 *(978-0-7814-1107-3(6))* Cook, David C.

Beale, Fleur. I Am Not Esther. 2013. 246p. pap. *(978-1-4596-5748-9(9))* ReadHowYouWant.com, Ltd.

Beauty of the Broken. 2014. (ENG., Illus.). 368p. (YA). (gr. 9). 17.99 *(978-1-4814-0709-0(0),* Simon Pulse) Simon Pulse.

Beeke, Joel R. & Kleyn, Diana. How God Used a Thunderstorm. Anderson, Jeff, illus. 2007. (Building on the Rock Ser.). (ENG.). 176p. (J). pap. 8.99 *(978-1-85792-815-0(6),* 9781857928150, CF4Kids) Christian Focus Pubns. GBR. Dist: Bookmasters Distribution.

Bell, Lucy J. God Made Feelings. Rimmington, Natasha, illus. 2017. 10p. (J). 6.99 ***(978-1-5064-1782-0(5),*** Sparkhouse Family) Augsburg Fortress, Pubs.

—Rufus Loses His Cape. Garton, Michael, illus. 2017. (J). 12.99 ***(978-1-5064-1788-2(4),*** Sparkhouse Family) Augsburg Fortress, Pubs.

—Uri & the Busy Day. Garton, Michael, illus. 2017. (J). 12.99 ***(978-1-5064-1787-5(6),*** Sparkhouse Family) Augsburg Fortress, Pubs.

Bell, Shirley. Boys on the Make. 2007. 54p. 16.95 *(978-1-4241-6575-9(X))* America Star Bks.

Bender, Esther. Elisabeth & the Windmill. 2003. (ENG.). 112p. (J). (gr. 3-7). pap. 6.99 *(978-0-8361-9204-9(4))* Herald Pr.

Benintendi, Steve. Break Out: Operation: Ascent Part 3 Of 12. 2003. (Powermark Ser.). (Illus.). 32p. (J). pap. 2.95 *(978-0-9713412-4-1(9))* PowerMark Productions.

—Redemption. 2003. (Powermark Comics Ser.). (Illus.). 32p. (J). pap. 2.95 *(978-0-9713412-1-0(4))* PowerMark Productions.

—Sacrifice: Operation: Ascent Part 4 Of 12. 2003. (Powermark Ser.). (Illus.). 32p. (J). pap. 2.95 *(978-0-9713412-5-8(7))* PowerMark Productions.

—Sinister Plans: Operation: Ascent Part 2 Of 12. 2003. (Powermark Ser.). (Illus.). 32p. (J). pap. 2.95 *(978-0-9713412-3-4(0))* PowerMark Productions.

—Standing Tall: Operation: Ascent Part 1 Of 12. 2003. (Powermark Comics Ser.). (Illus.). 32p. (J). pap. 2.95 *(978-0-9713412-2-7(2))* PowerMark Productions.

—Trojan Horse. 2003. (Powermark Ser.). (Illus.). 32p. (J). pap. 2.95 *(978-0-9713412-0-3(6))* PowerMark Productions.

Bennett, James W. & Bennett, James. Faith Wish. 2003. (ENG.). 160p. (J). (gr. 7-18). tchr. ed. 16.95 *(978-0-8234-1778-0(6))* Holiday Hse., Inc.

Benson, Amber. Ghosts of Albion: Initiation. (J). 17.00 *(978-1-931555-18-0(4))* Our Lady of Victory Schl.

Benton, Ann. Ferdinand: The Engine That Went off the Rails. 2009. (Colour Bks.). (ENG., Illus.). 40p. (J). 7.99 *(978-1-84550-444-1(5),* 50636419-0f36-4fc3-909c-1010b7b811f6) Christian Focus Pubns. GBR. Dist: Bookmasters Distribution.

Berenstain, Jan & Berenstain, Mike. All Things Bright & Beautiful, 1 vol. 2012. (Berenstain Bears/Living Lights Ser.). (ENG., Illus.). 32p. (J). pap. 4.99 *(978-0-310-72088-1(5))* Zonderkidz.

—The Berenstain Bears & a Job Well Done, 1 vol. Berenstain, Stan, illus. 2010. (Berenstain Bears/Living Lights Ser.). (ENG.). 32p. (J). (gr. -1-2). pap. 3.99 *(978-0-310-71254-1(8))* Zonderkidz.

—Berenstain Bears & the Forgiving Tree, 1 vol. 2011. (Berenstain Bears/Living Lights Ser.). (ENG.). 32p. (J). pap. 3.99 *(978-0-310-72084-3(2))* Zonderkidz.

—Berenstain Bears & the Gift of Courage, 1 vol. Berenstain, Stan, illus. 2010. (Berenstain Bears/Living Lights Ser.). (ENG.). 32p. (J). (gr. -1-2). pap. 3.99 *(978-0-310-71256-5(4))* Zonderkidz.

—The Berenstain Bears & the Joy of Giving, 1 vol. 2010. (Berenstain Bears/Living Lights Ser.). (ENG.). 32p. (J). (gr. -1-2). pap. 3.99 *(978-0-310-71255-8(6))* Zonderkidz.

—The Berenstain Bears & the Little Lost Cub, 1 vol. 2011. (I Can Read! / Berenstain Bears / Good Deed Scouts / Living Lights Ser.). (ENG.). 32p. (J). pap. 3.99 *(978-0-310-72100-0(8))* Zonderkidz.

—The Berenstain Bears & the Trouble with Things, 1 vol. 2013. (Berenstain Bears/Living Lights Ser.). (ENG., Illus.). 32p. (J). pap. 4.99 *(978-0-310-72091-1(5))* Zonderkidz.

—The Berenstain Bears Bear Country Fun Sticker & Activity Book, 1 vol. 2016. (Berenstain Bears/Living Lights Ser.). (ENG., Illus.). 32p. (J). pap. 6.99 *(978-0-310-75336-0(8))* Zonderkidz.

—God Bless Our Home, 1 vol. 2012. (Berenstain Bears/Living Lights Ser.). (ENG., Illus.). 32p. (J). pap. 3.99 *(978-0-310-72089-8(3))* Zonderkidz.

—God Made the Colors, 1 vol. 2013. (I Can Read! / Berenstain Bears / Living Lights Ser.). (ENG.). 32p. (J). pap. 3.99 *(978-0-310-72507-7(0))* Zonderkidz.

—Help the Homeless, 1 vol. 2012. (I Can Read! / Berenstain Bears / Good Deed Scouts / Living Lights Ser.). (ENG., Illus.). 32p. (J). pap. 3.99 *(978-0-310-72102-4(4))* Zonderkidz.

—Honey Hunt Helpers, 1 vol. 2012. (I Can Read! / Berenstain Bears / Good Deed Scouts / Living Lights Ser.). (ENG., Illus.). 32p. (J). pap. 3.99 *(978-0-310-72101-7(6))* Zonderkidz.

—Kitten Rescue, 1 vol. 2011. (I Can Read! / Berenstain Bears / Good Deed Scouts / Living Lights Ser.). (ENG.). 32p. (J). (gr. -1-2). pap. 3.99 *(978-0-310-72097-3(4))* Zonderkidz.

—Let the Bible Be Your Guide. 2011. (Berenstain Bears/Living Lights Ser.). (ENG., Illus.). 40p. (J). 6.99 *(978-0-310-72714-9(6))* Zonderkidz.

—Mama's Helpers, 1 vol. 2011. (I Can Read! / Berenstain Bears / Good Deed Scouts / Living Lights Ser.). (ENG.). 32p. (J). pap. 3.99 *(978-0-310-72099-7(0))* Zonderkidz.

—A Neighbor in Need, 1 vol. 2011. (I Can Read! / Berenstain Bears / Good Deed Scouts / Living Lights Ser.). (ENG.). 32p. (J). (gr. -1-2). pap. 3.99 *(978-0-310-72098-0(2))* Zonderkidz.

Berenstain, Jan, et al. The Berenstain Bears Get Involved, 1 vol. 2012. (Berenstain Bears/Living Lights Ser.). (ENG.). 32p. (J). pap. 3.99 *(978-0-310-72090-4(7))* Zonderkidz.

—The Berenstain Bears Play a Good Game, 1 vol. 2009. (Berenstain Bears/Living Lights Ser.). (ENG., Illus.). 32p. (J). (gr. -1-2). pap. 3.99 *(978-0-310-71252-7(1))* Zonderkidz.

—Kindness Counts, 1 vol. 2010. (Berenstain Bears/Living Lights Ser.). (ENG.). 32p. (J). (gr. -1-2). pap. 3.99 *(978-0-310-71257-2(2))* Zonderkidz.

Berenstain, Mike. The Berenstain Bears & the Biggest Brag, 1 vol. 2014. (Berenstain Bears/Living Lights Ser.). (ENG.). 24p. (J). pap. 3.99 *(978-0-310-73479-6(7))* Zonderkidz.

—The Berenstain Bears & the Christmas Angel, 1 vol. 2016. (Berenstain Bears/Living Lights Ser.). (ENG.). 24p. (J). pap. 3.99 *(978-0-310-74924-0(7))* Zonderkidz.

—The Berenstain Bears Blessed Are the Peacemakers, 1 vol. 2014. (Berenstain Bears/Living Lights Ser.). (ENG.). 24p. (J). pap. 3.99 *(978-0-310-73481-9(9))* Zonderkidz.

—God Made You Special, 1 vol. 2014. (Berenstain Bears/Living Lights Ser.). (ENG.). 24p. (J). pap. 3.99 *(978-0-310-73483-3(5))* Zonderkidz.

Berenstain, Mike. Mother's Day Blessings. 2016. (Illus.). (J). ***(978-1-4844-6294-2(7))*** Zonderkidz.

Berenstain, Mike, illus. The Berenstain Bears: Easter Blessings. 2016. (J). *(978-0-8249-1967-2(X),* Ideal Pubns.) Worthy Publishing.

—The Berenstain Bears Love One Another. 2016. (J). *(978-0-8249-1963-2(1),* Ideal Pubns.) Worthy Publishing.

Berenstain, Mike & Berenstain, Jan. The Berenstain Bears Go to Sunday School, 1 vol. 2008. (Berenstain Bears/Living Lights Ser.). (ENG., Illus.). 32p. (J). (gr. -1-2). pap. 3.99 *(978-0-310-71248-0(3))* Zonderkidz.

—The Berenstain Bears Say Their Prayers, 1 vol. 2008. (Berenstain Bears/Living Lights Ser.). (ENG., Illus.). 32p. (J). (gr. -1-2). pap. 3.99 *(978-0-310-71246-6(7))* Zonderkidz.

Berenstain, Mike & Berenstain, Stan. The Berenstain Bears God Bless Our Country, 1 vol. 2015. (Berenstain Bears/Living Lights Ser.). (ENG.). 24p. (J). pap. 4.99 *(978-0-310-73485-7(1))* Zonderkidz.

Berenstain, Mike, et al. The Berenstain Bears & the Golden Rule, 1 vol. 2008. (Berenstain Bears/Living Lights Ser.). (ENG., Illus.). 32p. (J). (gr. -1-2). pap. 3.99 *(978-0-310-71247-3(5))* Zonderkidz.

—Faithful Friends, 1 vol. Berenstain, Stan, illus. 2009. (Berenstain Bears/Living Lights Ser.). (ENG.). 32p. (J). (gr. -1-2). pap. 3.99 *(978-0-310-71253-4(X))* Zonderkidz.

Berenstain, Stan, et al. The Berenstain Bears Discover God's Creation, 1 vol. 2010. (Berenstain Bears/Living Lights Ser.). (ENG.). 40p. (J). (gr. -1-2). 6.99 *(978-0-310-71936-6(4))* Zonderkidz.

—The Berenstain Bears Do Their Best, 1 vol. 2010. (Berenstain Bears/Living Lights Ser.). (ENG.). 40p. (J). (gr. -1-2). 6.99 *(978-0-310-71937-3(2))* Zonderkidz.

—The Berenstain Bears Learn to Share, 1 vol. 2010. (Berenstain Bears/Living Lights Ser.). (ENG.). 40p. (J). (gr. -1-2). 6.99 *(978-0-310-71939-7(9))* Zonderkidz.

—Do Not Fear, God Is Near, 1 vol. 2013. (I Can Read! / Berenstain Bears / Living Lights Ser.). (ENG.). 32p. (J). pap. 3.99 *(978-0-310-72511-4(9))* Zonderkidz.

—God Loves You!, 1 vol. 2008. (Berenstain Bears/Living Lights Ser.). (ENG., Illus.). 32p. (J). pap. 3.99 *(978-0-310-71250-3(5))* Zonderkidz.

Bergren, Lisa T. God Found Us You. Bryant, Laura J., illus. 2009. (J). lib. bdg. 3.99 *(978-0-06-113177-6(6))* HarperCollins Pubs.

—God Found Us You. Bryant, Laura J., illus. 2009. (HarperBlessings Ser.). (ENG.). 40p. (J). (gr. -1-2). 10.99 *(978-0-06-113176-9(8))* HarperCollins Pubs.

—God Gave Us Love. Bryant, Laura J., illus. 2011. (ENG.). 22p. (J). (gr. k — 1). bds. 6.99 *(978-0-307-73027-5(1),* WaterBrook Pr.) Crown Publishing Group.

—God Gave Us Love. 2009. (ENG., Illus.). 40p. (J). (gr. -1-2). 10.99 *(978-1-4000-7447-1(9),* WaterBrook Pr.) Crown Publishing Group.

—God Gave Us the World. Bryant, Laura J., illus. 2011. (ENG.). 40p. (J). (gr. -1-2). 10.99 *(978-1-4000-7448-8(7),* WaterBrook Pr.) Crown Publishing Group.

Bergren, Lisa Tawn. God Gave Us Heaven. 2008. (ENG., Illus.). 40p. (J). (gr. -1-2). 10.99 *(978-1-4000-7446-4(0),* WaterBrook Pr.) Crown Publishing Group.

—God Gave Us Sleep. Bryant, Laura J., illus. 2015. (ENG.). 40p. (J). (gr. -1-2). 10.99 *(978-1-60142-663-5(1),* WaterBrook Pr.) Crown Publishing Group.

—God Gave Us Thankful Hearts. Hohn, David, illus. 2016. (ENG.). 40p. (J). (gr. -1-2). 10.99 *(978-1-60142-874-5(X),* WaterBrook Pr.) Crown Publishing Group.

Bertola, Ann Marie, et al, contrib. by. Four in the Afternoon. 2003. 118p. pap. 11.99 *(978-0-9743661-0-4(2))* Circle Pr.

Bethers, Linda, retold by. Christmas Oranges. 2004. 13p. pap. 3.95 *(978-1-57734-546-6(0),* 01114387) Covenant Communications, Inc.

Bickle, Laura. The Outside. (ENG.). 320p. (YA). (gr. 7). 2014. pap. 8.99 *(978-0-544-33635-3(6),* HMH Books For Young Readers) 2013. 16.99 *(978-0-544-00013-1(7))* Houghton Mifflin Harcourt Publishing Co.

Big Idea Entertainment, LLC & B&H Kids Editorial Staff. VeggieTales: Whenever You Fear, God Is near, a Digital Pop-Up Book (padded) 2017. (VeggieTales Ser.). (ENG.). 20p. (J). (gr. -1-2). bds. 12.99 *(978-1-4336-9058-7(6),* B&H Kids) B&H Publishing Group.

Bigler, Ashley Hansen. Once upon a Time: An Adoption Story. Hintz, Amy, illus. 2010. (J). pap. 12.99 *(978-1-59955-310-8(4))* Cedar Fort, Inc./CFI Distribution.

Billingsley, ReShonda Tate. Friends 'Til the End. 2009. (Good Girlz Ser.: 6). (ENG., Illus.). 208p. pap. 11.00 *(978-1-4165-5877-4(2),* Gallery Bks.) Gallery Bks.

—Nothing but Drama. 2006. (Good Girlz Ser.: 1). (ENG., Illus.). 288p. pap. 12.99 *(978-1-4165-2560-8(2),* Gallery Bks.) Gallery Bks.

Birkas, Carol. Christmas Treena. 2009. 58p. pap. 23.95 *(978-1-4327-4107-5(1))* Outskirts Pr., Inc.

Birkholz, Gay Lyn. Veneti: Lake Michigan's Treasure. Williamson, Linda K., illus. 2010. 52p. pap. 17.00 *(978-1-60860-129-5(3),* Strategic Bk. Publishing) Strategic Book Publishing & Rights Agency (SBPRA).

Bishop, Jennie. The Squire & the Scroll Coloring Book. 2005. (J). pap. 1.79 *(978-1-59317-085-1(8))* Warner Pr., Inc.

Black, Chuck. Kingdom's Call. 2007. (Kingdom Ser.). (ENG., Illus.). 160p. (YA). (gr. 4-7). per. 9.99 *(978-1-59052-750-4(X),* Multnomah) Doubleday Religious Publishing Group, The.

—Kingdom's Dawn. 2006. (Kingdom Ser.: 1). (ENG., Illus.). 160p. (J). (gr. 4-7). per. 9.99 *(978-1-59052-679-8(1),* Multnomah) Doubleday Religious Publishing Group, The.

—Kingdom's Hope. 2006. (Kingdom Ser.: 2). (ENG., Illus.). 160p. (J). (gr. 4-7). per. 9.99 *(978-1-59052-680-4(5),* Multnomah) Doubleday Religious Publishing Group, The.

—Kingdom's Quest. 2007. (Kingdom Ser.). (ENG., Illus.). 176p. (YA). (gr. 4-7). per. 9.99 *(978-1-59052-749-8(6),* Multnomah Bks.) Crown Publishing Group.

—Kingdom's Reign. 2007. (Kingdom Ser.). (ENG.). 176p. (YA). (gr. 4-7). per. 9.99 *(978-1-59052-682-8(1),* Multnomah Bks.) Crown Publishing Group.

—Lady Carliss & the Waters of Moorue. 2010. (Knights of Arrethtrae Ser.). (ENG.). 208p. (YA). (gr. 5-7). pap. 9.99 *(978-1-60142-127-2(3),* Multnomah Bks.) Crown Publishing Group.

—The Light of the Last, Bk. 3. 2016. (Wars of the Realm Ser.). (ENG.). 368p. (YA). (gr. 7). pap. 11.99 *(978-1-60142-506-5(6),* Multnomah Bks.) Crown Publishing Group.

—Rise of the Fallen: Wars of the Realm, Book 2. 2015. (Wars of the Realm Ser.). (ENG.). 320p. (YA). (gr. 7). pap. 11.99 *(978-1-60142-504-1(X),* Multnomah Bks.) Crown Publishing Group.

—Sir Bentley & Holbrook Court. 2009. (Knights of Arrethtrae Ser.). (ENG., Illus.). 208p. (YA). (gr. 5-7). pap. 9.99 *(978-1-60142-125-8(7),* Multnomah Bks.) Crown Publishing Group.

—Sir Dalton & the Shadow Heart. 2009. (Knights of Arrethtrae Ser.). (ENG., Illus.). 176p. (YA). (gr. 7-9). pap. 9.99 *(978-1-60142-126-5(5),* Multnomah Bks.) Crown Publishing Group.

—Sir Quinlan & the Swords of Valor. 2010. (Knights of Arrethtrae Ser.). (ENG., Illus.). 208p. (YA). (gr. 4-7). pap. 9.99 *(978-1-60142-128-9(1),* Multnomah) Doubleday Religious Publishing Group, The.

Black, Cuyler. The Goat of Many Colors, 1 vol. 2010. (ENG.). 32p. (J). (gr. k-3). pap. 4.99 *(978-0-310-71634-1(9))* Zonderkidz.

Black, Kat. A Templar's Destiny. 2012. (Book of Tormod Ser.). (ENG.). 256p. (J). (gr. 7-7). 17.99 *(978-0-545-05677-9(2),* Scholastic Pr.) Scholastic, Inc.

—A Templar's Gifts. 2011. (Book of Tormod Ser.: 2). (ENG.). 272p. (J). (gr. 7-7). 17.99 *(978-0-545-05675-5(6),* Scholastic Pr.) Scholastic, Inc.

Blackaby, Tom & Osborne, Rick. Sammy Experiences Jesus. Kung, Isabella, illus. 2014. (Experiencing God at Home Ser.). (ENG.). 32p. (J). (gr. -1-3). 14.99 *(978-1-4336-7981-0(7),* B&H Kids) B&H Publishing Group.

Blake, Chris & Charismalife. Hover Get's His Wings. 2004. 24p. (J). (gr. k-3). 9.99 *(978-1-59185-452-4(0),* Charisma Kids) Charisma Media.

—I'm Just the Right Size. 2004. (Illus.). 24p. (J). (gr. k-3). 9.99 *(978-1-59185-461-6(X),* Charisma Kids) Charisma Media.

Bledsoe, Amanda. Chores S'mores, 1 vol. 2010. 26p. 24.95 *(978-1-4512-1507-6(X))* PublishAmerica, Inc.

Blosser, Connie S. Single White Feather. 2012. 28p. pap. 24.95 *(978-1-4626-9339-9(3))* America Star Bks.

Bly, Stephen A. The Secret of the Old Rifle. 2004. (Lewis & Clark Squad Adventure Ser.: No. 2). 160p. (gr. 4-9). 4.99 *(978-0-89107-940-8(8))* Crossway.

—Treachery at the River Canyon. 2004. (Lewis & Clark Squad Adventure Ser.: No. 3). 160p. (YA). (gr. 4-9). 4.99 *(978-0-89107-941-5(6))* Crossway.

Boger-Bass, Vallerie. The Mustard Seed: A Christian Promise. Boger-Bass, Vallerie, illus. 2003. (Illus.). 40p. pap. 10.00 *(978-0-8059-5640-5(9))* Dorrance Publishing Co., Inc.

Bollback, Anthony G. Capture of the Twin Dragon. 2012. 152p. pap. 8.99 *(978-0-9849359-1-8(6))* Finding the Cause, LLC.

—Hijacked. 2012. 176p. pap. 8.99 *(978-0-9849359-5-6(9))* Finding the Cause, LLC.

—Mystery of the Counterfeit Money. 2012. 170p. (gr. 4-7). pap. 8.99 *(978-0-9849359-2-5(4))* Finding the Cause, LLC.

—Rescue at Cripple Creek. 2012. 178p. pap. 8.99 *(978-0-9849359-3-2(2))* Finding the Cause, LLC.

—Smugglers in Hong Kong. 2012. 156p. pap. 8.99 *(978-0-9849359-0-1(8))* Finding the Cause, LLC.

—The Tiger Shark Strikes Again. 2012. 172p. pap. 8.99 *(978-0-9849359-4-9(0))* Finding the Cause, LLC.

Bond, Douglas. Guns of Providence. 2010. (J). pap. *(978-1-59638-156-8(6))* P & R Publishing.

—Guns of Thunder. 2007. (Faith & Freedom Ser.). (Illus.). 261p. (J). (gr. 4-7). per. 11.99 *(978-1-59638-013-4(6))* P & R Publishing.

—Hammer of the Huguenots. 2015. (Illus.). 226p. (J). pap. *(978-1-59638-763-8(7))* P & R Publishing.

—Hostage Lands. 2006. 234p. (YA). (gr. 7). per. 9.99 *(978-1-59638-027-1(6))* P & R Publishing.

C
D

—King's Arrow. Bird, Matthew, illus. 2003. (Crown & Covenant Ser.). 208p. (J). per. 10.99 (978-0-87552-743-7(4)) P & R Publishing.
—Rebel's Keep. Bird, Matthew, illus. 2004. (Crown & Covenant Ser.). 285p. (J). per. 9.99 (978-0-87552-744-4(2)) P & R Publishing.
Bond, Thomas A. Mill Creek Kids. 2009. 132p. pap. 14.99 (978-1-60791-634-5(7)) Salem Author Services.
Borntrager, Mary Christner. Polly. 2015. (ENG.). 176p. (YA). (gr. 4-7). pap. 9.99 (978-0-8361-3670-8(5)) Herald Pr.
Bostrom, Kathleen. The Secret of the Twelve Days of Christmas. Bostrom, Christopher, illus. 2005. 68p. (gr. -1-7). per. 10.95 (978-1-931195-74-4(9)) KiwE Publishing, Ltd.
Bower, Gary. Cody's Castle: Encouraging Others. Bower, Jan, illus. l.t. ed. 2004. (Thinking of Others: Vol. 4). 32p. (J). 16.95 (978-0-9704621-3-8(1)) Storybook Meadow Publishing.
—The Person I Marry. Bower, Jan, illus. 2008. 32p. (J). pap. 11.99 (978-0-9704621-7-6(4)) Storybook Meadow Publishing.
Bowman, Crystal. Jake's Brave Night, 1 vol. Maizel, Karen, illus. 2007. (I Can Read! / the Jake Ser.). (ENG.). 32p. (J). (gr. -1-3). pap. 3.99 (978-0-310-71456-9(7)) Zonderkidz.
—Little David & His Best Friend. Hartung, Susan Kathleen & Endersly, Frank, illus. 2010. (I Can Read! / Little David Ser.). (ENG.). 32p. (J). pap. 3.99 (978-0-310-71710-2(8)) Zonderkidz.
—Little David's Brave Day, 1 vol. Hartung, Susan Kathleen & Endersly, Frank, illus. 2010. (I Can Read! / Little David Ser.). (ENG.). 32p. (J). pap. 3.99 (978-0-310-71709-6(4)) Zonderkidz.
—Mommy, May I Hug the Fish?, 1 vol. Christensen, Donna, illus. 2009. (I Can Read! / ¡Yo Sé Leer! Ser.).Tr. of Mamá, Puedo Abrazar Al Pez? (ENG & SPA.). 32p. (J). pap. 3.99 (978-0-310-71868-0(6)) Vida Pubs.
—My Happy Pumpkin: God's Love Shining Through Me, 1 vol. 2014. (ENG.). 14p. (J). bds. 6.99 (978-0-310-73828-2(8)) Zonderkidz.
—The Story of the Resurrection Eggs, 1 vol. Johnson, Richard G., illus. 2013. (ENG.). 40p. (J). 7.99 (978-0-310-72595-4(X)) Zonderkidz.
Brammer, Deb. Moose. 2007. 132p. (YA). (gr. 8-12). per. 8.99 (978-1-59166-722-3(4)) BJU Pr.
—Two Sides to Everything. 2003. (Illus.). 151p. (J). (978-1-59166-166-5(8)) BJU Pr.
Brandenburg, Claire. The Monk Who Grew Prayer. Brandenburg, Claire, illus. 2003. (ENG., Illus.). 32p. (J). pap. 11.95 (978-1-888212-66-2(7)) Ancient Faith Publishing.
Brantley, Meg. Love Family Adventures. 2009. 116p. pap. 11.99 (978-1-60791-786-1(6)) Salem Author Services.
Breisacher, Cathy. Petunia Pepper's Picture Day. Elden, Christian, illus. 2010. 32p. (J). 14.99 (978-1-59317-397-5(0)) Warner Pr., Inc.
Brian's All-Star Day. 2004. 32p. pap. 3.99 (978-0-8341-2089-1(5)) Beacon Hill Pr. of Kansas City.
Bridges, Charlene. Tell me a Story. 2004. (J). per. 9.95 (978-1-59352-062-5(X)) Christian Services Publishing.
Bright, et al. Beginning the Christian Adventure, Vol. 1. 2004. (ENG.). 192p. pap. 18.99 (978-1-56399-151-6(9)) Campus Crusade for Christ.
—Discover Our Awesome God, Vol. 2. 2004. (ENG.). 192p. pap. 18.99 (978-1-56399-152-3(7)) Campus Crusade for Christ.
Brodeur, Tom. Regina Silsby's Phantom Militia. 2005. (Illus.). 267p. (J). (gr. 3-7). 7.49 (978-1-59166-385-0(7)) BJU Pr.
Brooks, Linda Grace. The Asquinn Twins & Where the Trail Forks. 2005. 119p. pap. 16.95 (978-0-7414-2445-7(2)) Infinity Publishing.
Brother Egbert's Christmas. 2015. (ENG., Illus.). 64p. (J). (gr. k-4). 17.99 (978-0-7459-6548-2(2)) Lion Hudson PLC GBR. Dist: Independent Pubs. Group.
Brouwer, Sigmund. Ambush. 2009. (Robot Wars Ser.: 3). (ENG.). 304p. (YA). pap. 7.99 (978-1-4143-2311-4(5), Tyndale Kids) Tyndale Hse. Pubs.
—Counterattack. 2009. (Robot Wars Ser.: 4). (ENG.). 304p. (YA). pap. 6.99 (978-1-4143-2312-1(3), Tyndale Kids) Tyndale Hse. Pubs.
—Final Battle. 2009. (Robot Wars Ser.: 5). (ENG.). 320p. (YA). pap. 7.99 (978-1-4143-2313-8(1), Tyndale Kids) Tyndale Hse. Pubs.
—Wings of an Angel. 2004. (Winds of Light Ser.). 214p. (YA). pap. 5.99 (978-1-55305-032-2(0)) Cygnet Publishing Group, Inc./Coolreading.com CAN. Dist: Orca Bk. Pubs. USA.
Bruner, Roger & Bruner, Kristi Rae. Found in Translation: An Unforgettable Mission Trip Where Faith, Obedience, & Forgiveness Intersect. 2011. (Altered Hearts Ser.: 1). (ENG.). 368p. (YA). (gr. 9-12). pap. 9.99 (978-1-60260-961-7(6), Barbour Bks.) Barbour Publishing, Inc.
Buchanan, Paul & Buchanan, P. The Last Place I Want to Be, 1 vol. 2009. 176p. (J). pap. 7.99 (978-0-8254-2408-3(9)) Kregel Pubns.
Buchanan, Sue, et al. Mud Pie Annie, 1 vol. Allen, Joy, illus. 2008. (I Can Read! Ser.). (ENG.). 32p. (J). (gr. -1-1). pap. 3.99 (978-0-310-71572-6(5)) Zonderkidz.
Bundschuh, Rick. Burned, 1 vol. 2014. (Faithgirlz / Soul Surfer Ser.). (ENG.). 128p. (J). pap. 7.99 (978-0-310-74555-6(1)) Zonderkidz.
—Clash, 1 vol. 2014. (Faithgirlz / Soul Surfer Ser.). (ENG.). 128p. (J). pap. 7.99 (978-0-310-74582-2(9)) Zonderkidz.
Bunyan, John. The Pilgrim's Progress, No. 1. 2004. pap. 9.99 (978-0-88270-938-3(0)) Bridge-Logos, Inc.
—The Pilgrim's Progress. 2013. (ENG., Illus.). 192p. (J). 17.99 (978-1-84550-102-0(0), 4e9114e8-e2b3-4cdb-80e0-08313f2cef6c, Christian Focus) Christian Focus Pubns. GBR. Dist: Bookmasters Distribution.
—Pilgrim's Progress 2: Christiana's Story. 2013. (ENG., Illus.). 176p. (J). 17.99 (978-1-84550-233-1(7), 727dca39-534d-4d30-b897-5c6d0c303b92) Christian Focus Pubns. GBR. Dist: Bookmasters Distribution.
—The Pilgrim's Progress from This World to That Which Is to Come;Delivered under the Similitude of a Dream. Barnard, Frederick & Linton, J. D., illus. 2012. 316p. (978-1-78139-097-9(5)) Benediction Classics.
Burch, Deborah, illus. God's Greatest Gift. 2007. 32p. (J). lib. bdg. 17.95 (978-0-9796477-7-2(0)) God's Greatest Gift, LLC.
Burkart, Jeff. Once Upon a Clear Dark Night. 2011. 16p. pap. 2.49 (978-0-7586-2579-3(0)) Concordia Publishing Hse.
Burkart, Jeffrey. The Hidden Prince. 2011. (YA). 16.95 (978-0-9825713-3-0(X)) Clifton Carriage House Pr.
Burkart, Jeffrey E., retold by. The Hidden Prince. 2003. (Illus.). 32p. (J). 9.99 incl. audio compact disk (978-0-570-07174-7(7)) Concordia Publishing Hse.
Burke, Ruth. Gowandale Adventure: And other stories for Boys. 2007. (Illus.). 96p. 9.00 (978-1-84625-070-5(6)) DayOne Pubns. GBR. Dist: Send The Light Distribution LLC.
Burkhart, Alma J. Little Witnesses. 2013. 32p. pap. 8.99 (978-1-938768-24-8(8)) Gypsy Pubns.
Burnett, Mark & Downey, Roma. A Story of God & All of Us Young Readers Edition. 2013. (ENG., Illus.). 224p. (J). (gr. 3-17). pap. 7.99 (978-0-316-24383-4(3)) Little, Brown Bks. for Young Readers.
Burney, Claudia Mair. Exorsistah, No. 1. 2008. (ENG.). 272p. (YA). pap. 9.95 (978-1-4165-6133-0(1), Gallery Bks.) Gallery Bks.
Burton, Jacky. The Other Stable. 2013. 32p. pap. 24.95 (978-1-62709-371-2(0)) America Star Bks.
Bush, Rosetta Bowman. Chicken Every Sunday. 2013. 24p. pap. 24.95 (978-1-63004-065-9(7)) America Star Bks.
Bushnell, Steven G. The Big Adventures of Little Church Mouse: The Parables of Jesus. 2009. 96p. pap. 31.99 (978-1-4490-0620-4(5)) AuthorHouse.
Butler, Heather. Ellie & the Clown Crisis. Buckley, Joel, illus. 2004. 64p. pap. (978-1-84427-023-1(8)) Scripture Union.
Byler, Linda. The Little Amish Matchmaker: A Christmas Romance. 2012. (ENG.). 187p. 14.95 (978-1-56148-776-9(7), Good Bks.) Skyhorse Publishing Co., Inc.
Cahill, Bear. We're Brothers & Sisters. Collier, Kevin Scott, illus. 2008. 20p. pap. 9.95 (978-1-933090-70-2(7)) Guardian Angel Publishing, Inc.
Campos Eichelberger, Misty. Who Is Santa? & Where Did He Come From? 2009. 16p. pap. 9.49 (978-1-4490-1857-3(2)) AuthorHouse.
The Captain, His Daughter, & Their Discovery. 2007. 48p. pap. 6.50 (978-0-8341-2296-3(0), 083-412-2960) Beacon Hill Pr. of Kansas City.
Carl And Betty Coggins. Mr Bowbow. 2009. 24p. pap. 12.99 (978-1-4490-1010-2(5)) AuthorHouse.
Carlson, Melody. Bad Connection. 2006. (Secret Life of Samantha Mcgregor Ser.: No. 1). (ENG.). 256p. (J). (gr. 7-12). per. 12.99 (978-1-59052-692-7(9), Multnomah) Doubleday Religious Publishing Group, The.
—Beyond Reach. 2007. (Secret Life of Samantha Mcgregor Ser.: No. 2). (ENG.). 256p. (J). (gr. 7-12). per. 14.99 (978-1-59052-693-4(7), Multnomah) Doubleday Religious Publishing Group, The.
—Bright Purple: Color Me Confused. 2006. (Truecolors Ser.: 10). (ENG.). 224p. (YA). (gr. 4-7). per. 14.99 (978-1-57683-950-8(8), Th1nk Bks.) NavPress Publishing Group.
—Dark Blue: Color Me Lonely. 2004. (Truecolors Ser.: 1). (ENG.). 208p. (YA). pap. 14.99 (978-1-57683-529-6(4), Th1nk Bks.) NavPress Publishing Group.
—Forgive Others. Reagan, Susan Joy, illus. 2004. (Just Like Jesus Said Ser.). 32p. (J). (gr. -1-5). 12.99 (978-0-8054-2385-3(0)) B&H Publishing Group.
—Goodnight, Angels, 1 vol. Allsopp, Sophie, illus. 2011. (ENG.). 32p. (J). 15.99 (978-0-310-71687-7(X)) Zonderkidz.
—Hi, I'm Blackbeary: The Fruit of the Spirit Is Peace. Mahan, Ben, illus. 2004. (Beary Patch Bears Ser.). 96p. bds. 6.99 (978-1-58134-182-9(2)) Crossway.
—Homecoming Queen, 1 vol. 2014. (Carter House Girls Ser.). (ENG.). 224p. (YA). pap. 9.99 (978-0-310-74725-3(2)) Zondervan.
—I Do! 2005. (Diary of a Teenage Girl Ser.: Bk. 9). (ENG.). 272p. (J). (gr. 7). pap. 14.99 (978-1-59052-320-9(2), Multnomah) Doubleday Religious Publishing Group, The.
—Ireland. 2006. (Notes from a Spinning Planet Ser.). (ENG.). 256p. (YA). (gr. 7-12). per. 12.99 (978-1-4000-7144-9(5), WaterBrook Pr.) Crown Publishing Group.
—It's a Green Thing. 2009. (Diary of a Teenage Girl Ser.: Bk. 15). (ENG.). 256p. pap. 14.99 (978-1-60142-118-0(4), Multnomah) Doubleday Religious Publishing Group, The.
—Last Dance, 1 vol. 2014. (Carter House Girls Ser.). (ENG.). 208p. (YA). pap. 9.99 (978-0-310-74900-4(X)) Zondervan.
—Lost in Las Vegas, 1 vol. 2014. (Carter House Girls Ser.). (ENG.). 208p. (YA). pap. 9.99 (978-0-310-74716-1(3)) Zondervan.
—Mixed Bags, 1 vol. 2014. (Carter House Girls Ser.). (ENG.). 224p. (YA). pap. 9.99 (978-0-310-74756-7(2)) Zondervan.
—New York Debut, 1 vol. 2014. (Carter House Girls Ser.). (ENG.). 224p. (YA). pap. 9.99 (978-0-310-74779-6(1)) Zondervan.
—A Not-So-Simple Life. 2008. (Diary of a Teenage Girl Ser.: Bk. 14). (ENG.). 256p. (YA). (gr. 7). pap. 14.99 (978-1-60142-117-3(6), Multnomah) Doubleday Religious Publishing Group, The.
—Notes from a Spinning Planet: Papua New Guinea. 2007. (Notes from a Spinning Planet Ser.: 2). (ENG.). 240p. (YA). (gr. 7-12). per. 12.99 (978-1-4000-7145-6(3), WaterBrook Pr.) Crown Publishing Group.
—Notes from a Spinning Planet - Mexico. 2007. (Notes from a Spinning Planet Ser.). (ENG.). 256p. (YA). (gr. 7). pap. 12.99 (978-1-4000-7146-3(1), WaterBrook Pr.) Crown Publishing Group.
—Payback. 2008. (Secret Life of Samantha Mcgregor Ser.: No. 4). (ENG.). 240p. (gr. 8-12). pap. 12.99 (978-1-59052-934-8(0), Multnomah) Doubleday Religious Publishing Group, The.
—Playing with Fire. 2007. (Secret Life of Samantha Mcgregor Ser.: No. 3). (ENG.). 256p. (YA). (gr. 7-12). per. 12.99 (978-1-59052-694-1(5), Multnomah Bks.) Crown Publishing Group.
—Road Trip. 2003. (Diary of a Teenage Girl Ser.: Bk. 7). (ENG.). 304p. (J). (gr. 7). pap. 14.99 (978-1-59052-142-7(0), Multnomah) Doubleday Religious Publishing Group, The.
—Sold Out. 2003. (Diary of a Teenage Girl Ser.: Bk. 6). (ENG.). 288p. (YA). (gr. 7). pap. 14.99 (978-1-59052-141-0(2), Multnomah Bks.) Crown Publishing Group.
—Spotlight, 1 vol. 2014. (On the Runway Ser.). (ENG.). 224p. (YA). pap. 9.99 (978-0-310-74821-2(6)) Zondervan.
—Spring Breakdown, 1 vol. 2014. (Carter House Girls Ser.). (ENG.). 208p. (YA). pap. 9.99 (978-0-310-74809-0(7)) Zondervan.
—Stealing Bradford, 1 vol. 2014. (Carter House Girls Ser.). (ENG.). 224p. (YA). pap. 9.99 (978-0-310-74654-6(X)) Zondervan.
—Viva Vermont!, 1 vol. 2014. (Carter House Girls Ser.). (ENG.). 224p. (YA). pap. 9.99 (978-0-310-74714-7(7)) Zondervan.
—What Matters Most. 2009. (Diary of a Teenage Girl Ser.: Bk. 3). (ENG.). 256p. pap. 13.99 (978-1-60142-119-7(2), Multnomah) Doubleday Religious Publishing Group, The.
—When the Creepy Things Come Out! Reagan, Susan Joy, illus. 2003. 32p. (J). (gr. -1-5). 12.99 (978-0-8054-2687-8(6)) B&H Publishing Group.
Carlstrom, Nancy White. This Is the Day!, 1 vol. Cowdrey, Richard, illus. 2009. (ENG.). 32p. (J). (gr. -1-2). 15.99 (978-0-310-71428-6(1)) Zonderkidz.
Carmouche, Angelica Drisana. A Mommy in Mind. 2012. 20p. pap. 24.95 (978-1-4626-8145-7(X)) America Star Bks.
Carnes, Daphane. Grace. 2009. 48p. (J). pap. 12.95 (978-1-4327-3380-3(X)) Outskirts Pr., Inc.
Caroll, Robin. Samantha Sanderson at the Movies, 1 vol. 2014. (FaithGirlz / Samantha Sanderson Ser.). (ENG.). 272p. (J). pap. 8.99 (978-0-310-74245-6(5)) Zonderkidz.
—Samantha Sanderson on the Scene, 1 vol. 2014. (FaithGirlz / Samantha Sanderson Ser.). (ENG.). 256p. (J). pap. 8.99 (978-0-310-74247-0(1)) Zonderkidz.
—Samantha Sanderson Without a Trace, 1 vol. 2016. (FaithGirlz / Samantha Sanderson Ser.). (ENG.). 224p. (J). pap. 8.99 (978-0-310-74251-7(X)) Zonderkidz.
Carr, Elías. Ava y el Picnic Raquítico. Garton, Michael, illus. 2016. (SPA.). (J). **(978-1-5064-2095-0(8))** Augsburg Fortress, Pubs.
—Hal y el Nuevo Compañero. Garton, Michael, illus. 2016. (SPA.). (J). **(978-1-5064-2098-1(2))** Augsburg Fortress, Pubs.
—Jo y la Sopa Lenta. Garton, Michael, illus. 2016. (SPA.). (J). **(978-1-5064-2097-4(4),** Sparkhouse Pr.) Spark Hse.
—Rufus y Su Cola Enojada. Garton, Michael, illus. 2016. (SPA.). (J). **(978-1-5064-2096-7(6))** Augsburg Fortress, Pubs.
Carr, Jon & Carr, Debra. Harry the Hippo. 2004. 6.00 (978-1-59089-724-9(2)) Creflo Dollar Ministries Pubns.
Carson, Diana Pastora. All the Muchos in the World: A Special Story about Love. Pruitt, Ginny, illus. 2006. 32p. (J). pap. 8.95 (978-0-8198-0779-3(6)) Pauline Bks. & Media.
Castle, Elizabeth. Because I Love You More Than All the Stars in Heaven. 2008. 21p. pap. 24.95 (978-1-4241-9395-0(8)) America Star Bks.
Castleberry, Stephen B., Sr. & Castleberry, Susie L. Weighty Matters. 2003. (Farm Mystery Ser.). 155p. (YA). per. 8.50 (978-1-891907-13-5(1)) Castleberry Farms Pr.
Celebrate God's Harvest. 28p. (J). 3.29 (978-0-7847-1022-7(8)) Standard Publishing.
Chambers, Aidan. Now I Know. 2009. (ENG.). 336p. (YA). (gr. 9-17). pap. 8.95 (978-0-8109-8353-3(2), Amulet Bks.) Abrams, Inc.
Chapman, Kelly. Princess with a Purpose. Lyon, Tammie, illus. 2010. (ENG.). 32p. (J). (gr. -1-4). 14.99 (978-0-7369-2435-1(3)) Harvest Hse. Pubs.
—A Warrior Prince for God. Ebbeler, Jeff, illus. 2010. (ENG.). 32p. (J). (gr. -1-4). 14.99 (978-0-7369-2895-3(2)) Harvest Hse. Pubs.
—A Warrior Prince for God Curriculum Leader's Guide. Ebbeler, Jeff, illus. 2009. pap. 12.99 (978-0-7369-2899-1(5)) Harvest Hse. Pubs.
Chapman, Steven Curtis. Cinderella: The Love of a Daddy & His Princess, 1 vol. 2008. (ENG., Illus.). 64p. 14.99 (978-1-4041-0522-5(0)) Nelson, Thomas Inc.
Chauvin, Belinda N. Megan... A Child of God I Am. Sun Star, Elan & Snyder, Diana, illus. 2008. 40p. (J). 14.75 (978-0-9801675-2-8(3)) Robertson Publishing.
Cheney, Roland. The Racing Angelettes. 2005. 25.50 (978-1-59330-290-0(8)) Aventine Pr.
Cherrington, Sharnett Felicia. Bitter Sweet. 2005. (YA). per. 12.95 (978-1-933570-70-9(9)) Aardvark Global Publishing.
Chidley, Howard J. FiftyTwo Story Talks to Boys & Girls D. 2007. pap. (978-1-4065-1446-9(2)) Dodo Pr.
Chief White Hair's Secret. 2004. 54p. pap. 6.99 (978-0-8341-2091-4(7)) Beacon Hill Pr. of Kansas City.
Ching, Lorilei. He Ping: An Orphan's Destiny. 2013. 32p. pap. 13.95 (978-1-4624-0807-8(9), Inspiring Voices) Author Solutions, Inc.
Chris, Wright. Pilgrim's Progress Puzzle Book. 2008. (YA). pap. 14.95 (978-0-9797863-3-4(9)) Lighthouse Publishing.
Chrisagis, Brian. Who & What Am I? Good News Gang. Chrisagis, Shawn, illus. 2006. 24p. (J). 9.99 (978-1-59958-014-2(4)) Journey Stone Creations, LLC.
Christensen, Catherine, told to. Blessing the Nephite Children. 2016. (ENG.). (J). bds. 10.99 (978-1-4621-1875-5(5)) Cedar Fort, Inc./CFI Distribution.
Christian, Focus & Tnt Ministries Staff. God's Zoo. Charnick, Tim, illus. 2005. (King of Clubs Ser.). (ENG.). 96p. (J). per. 17.99 (978-1-84550-069-6(5), 9781845500696) Christian Focus Pubns. GBR. Dist: Bookmasters Distribution.
Clark, Carol. Eternity Express. 2009. 32p. pap. 10.95 (978-0-9818488-6-0(9)) Ajoyin Publishing, Inc.
Claydon, Darlene. A Most Unusual Whale Tale: The Adventure Begins. 2012. 44p. pap. 24.95 (978-1-4626-8806-7(3)) America Star Bks.
Coach B. Kingdom College. 2009. 48p. pap. 19.49 (978-1-4389-5181-2(7)) AuthorHouse.
Cobblekids Staff. Making Melody W/Your Heart Pri. 2004. 11.95 (978-1-931737-01-2(0)) Lollipop Publishing, LLC.
Coelho, Paulo. Veronika beschließt zu sterben. (GER.). pap. 22.95 (978-3-257-23305-6(1)) Diogenes Verlag AG CHE. Dist: Distribooks, Inc.
Cole, Burton. Bash & the Chocolate Milk Cows. Lewis, Buddy, illus. 2015. (ENG.). 224p. (J). (gr. 3-7). pap. 8.99 (978-1-4336-8530-9(2), B&H Kids) B&H Publishing Group.
Cole, Hana. Hooray! I'm Catholic. Steege, Joanna, illus. 2010. 32p. (J). 14.95 (978-0-8091-6746-3(8), Ambassador Bks.) Paulist Pr.
Coleman, Charles G. The Shining Sword. 2006. (Illus.). 154p. (J). per. 14.95 (978-1-933573-05-2(8), 3372) Zeezok Publishing, LLC.
Collins, Amberly & Collins, Brandilyn. Final Touch, 1 vol. 2010. (Rayne Tour Ser.). (ENG.). 224p. (YA). (gr. 8-11). pap. 9.99 (978-0-310-71933-5(X)) Zondervan.
Collins, Brandilyn & Collins, Amberly. Always Watching, 1 vol. 2015. (Rayne Tour Ser.). (ENG.). 224p. (YA). pap. 9.99 (978-0-310-74918-9(2)) Zondervan.
—Final Touch, 1 vol. 2015. (Rayne Tour Ser.). (ENG.). 224p. (YA). pap. 9.99 (978-0-310-74959-2(X)) Zondervan.
Comfort, Ray. Scratch & Sniff. Hohnstadt, Cedric, illus. 2007. (Creation for Kids Ser.). 24p. (gr. -1-5). 14.99 (978-0-88270-328-2(5)) Bridge-Logos, Inc.
Comley, Kathryn. That's How I Found God. Lane, Ranae, illus. 2004. (J). bds. 9.99 (978-1-4183-0014-2(4)) Christ Inspired, Inc.
Comrie, Margaret S. The Heroes of Castle Bretten. 2003. (Illus.). 229p. (J). (978-1-894666-65-7(8)) Inheritance Pubns.
Condie, Ally. Yearbook. 2006. 208p. (YA). pap. 14.95 (978-1-59038-690-3(6)) Deseret Bk. Co.
Cook, Philip. Erden: Flame of the Creator. 2014. xiii, 259p. (YA). (978-1-4908-2033-0(7), WestBow Pr.) Author Solutions, Inc.
Cooney, Caroline B. A Friend at Midnight. 2008. (ENG.). 192p. (YA). (gr. 7). pap. 8.99 (978-1-4000-7209-5(3), WaterBrook Pr.) Crown Publishing Group.
—A Friend at Midnight. 2008. (ENG.). 192p. (YA). (gr. 7). pap. 8.99 (978-0-385-73327-4(5), Delacorte Bks. for Young Readers) Random Hse. Children's Bks.
Cooper, Christina. If I Only Had One Wish. 2008. 20p. pap. 12.50 (978-1-60693-304-6(3), Strategic Bk. Publishing) Strategic Book Publishing & Rights Agency (SBPRA).
Crane, Cheri J. Moment of Truth: A Novel. 2005. 238p. (YA). (978-1-59156-727-1(0)) Covenant Communications.
Cranse, Pratima. All the Major Constellations. 2015. (ENG.). 336p. (YA). (gr. 9). 17.99 (978-0-670-01645-7(4), Viking Books for Young Readers) Penguin Young Readers Group.
Crenshaw, Mills. The Christmas of 45. 2010. 176p. pap. 11.99 (978-1-59955-455-6(0)) Cedar Fort, Inc./CFI Distribution.
Crossley-Holland, Kevin. Crossing to Paradise. 2008. (J). pap. (978-0-545-05868-1(6), Levine, Arthur A. Bks.) Scholastic, Inc.
Crossno, Frances M. Cole's Perfect Puppy, Perfect Puppies Book One. 2016. (ENG., Illus.). 98p. (J). pap. 14.95 (978-1-5069-0168-8(9)) First Edition Design eBook Publishing.
Crouch, Cheryl. Troo Makes a Big Splash, 1 vol. Zimmer, Kevin, illus. 2011. (I Can Read! / Rainforest Friends Ser.). (ENG.). 32p. (J). (gr. -1-2). pap. 3.99 (978-0-310-71810-9(4)) Zonderkidz.
—Troo's Big Climb, 1 vol. Zimmer, Kevin, illus. 2011. (I Can Read! / Rainforest Friends Ser.). (ENG.). 32p. (J). (gr. -1-2). pap. 3.99 (978-0-310-71808-6(2)) Zonderkidz.
—Troo's Secret Clubhouse, 1 vol. Zimmer, Kevin, illus. 2011. (I Can Read! / Rainforest Friends Ser.). (ENG.). 32p. (J). (gr. -1-2). pap. 3.99 (978-0-310-71809-3(0)) Zonderkidz.
Crouch, Cheryl Lynne. Tennis Shoes Trouble. 2006. 48p. 6.50 (978-0-8341-2227-7(8)) Beacon Hill Pr. of Kansas City.
Cummins, Maria S. The Lamplighter. 2011. 308p. pap. 16.99 (978-1-61203-228-3(1)) Bottom of the Hill Publishing.
Cunning, Concord. Scripture Sleuth 3. 2004. pap. 8.95 (978-1-885904-39-3(8)) Focus Publishing.
Cunningham, Elaine. Missing in Madagascar. 2006. 32p. 4.50 (978-0-8341-2230-7(8)) Beacon Hill Pr. of Kansas City.
Curley, Marianne. Los Elegidos. 2003. (SPA.). 288p. (YA). 12.95 (978-84-7888-577-0(3), 1952) Publicaciones y Ediciones Salamandra, S.A. ESP. Dist: Spanish Pubs., LLC.
Cutrer, Elisabeth. Molly's Magic Smile. Sexton, Jessa R., ed. Williams, Jayne, illus. 2013. 38p. 17.00 (978-0-9860244-3-6(0)) O'More Publishing.
Dacey, Richard. Spinner McClock & the Christmas Visit. Gillett, Hallie, illus. 2004. 32p. (J). 13.95 (978-1-929039-24-1(7)) Ambassador Bks., Inc.
Dahlstrom, Kathryn. Peppy's Rescue. Date not set. (Good News Club Ser.). (J). (gr. 4-11). pap. 4.99 (978-1-55976-826-9(6)) CEF Pr.
Dahlstrom, S. J. The Elk Hunt: The Adventure Begins. 2013. (Adventures of Wilder Good Ser.). (ENG., Illus.). 110p. (J). (gr. 3). pap. 8.95 (978-1-58988-087-0(0)) Dry, Paul Bks., Inc.
—Texas Grit: the Adventures of Wilder Good #2. 2014. (Adventures of Wilder Good Ser.). (ENG.). 141p. (J). (gr. 3). pap. 7.95 (978-1-58988-094-8(3)) Dry, Paul Bks., Inc.
Daniels, Kimberly. Animal Bible Stories - AbraHAM, 1 vol. 2009. 20p. pap. 24.95 (978-1-60749-382-2(9)) America Star Bks.
Darden, Hunter. Pete's Angel. Vaca, Sally, illus. 2008. 44p. pap. 12.00 (978-1-60693-264-3(0), Strategic Bk. Publishing) Strategic Book Publishing & Rights Agency (SBPRA).
Dateno, Maria Grace. Braving the Storm, 6 vols., Vol. 2. Cunningham, Paul, illus. 2013. 70p. (J). pap. 5.95 (978-0-8198-1204-9(8)) Pauline Bks. & Media.
—Courageous Quest. Cunningham, Paul, illus. 2014. 81p. (J). pap. 5.95 (978-0-8198-1628-3(0)) Pauline Bks. & Media.
—Danger at Sea. Cunningham, Paul, illus. 2013. 80p. (J). pap. 5.95 (978-0-8198-1891-1(7)) Pauline Bks. & Media.
—Discovery at Dawn. Cunningham, Paul, illus. 2014. (ENG.). 79p. (J). pap. 5.95 (978-0-8198-1895-9(X)) Pauline Bks. & Media.
—Mystery of the Missing Jars. Cunningham, Paul, illus. 2014. 77p. (J). 5.95 (978-0-8198-4922-9(7)) Pauline Bks. & Media.
—Shepherds to the Rescue, 6 vols., Vol. 1. Cunningham, Paul, illus. 2013. 71p. (J). pap. 5.95 (978-0-8198-7251-7(2)) Pauline Bks. & Media.
David C. Cook Publishing Company Staff. The Beginning. 2003. (My Jesus Pocket Bks.). (Illus.). 32p. (J). pap., pap. 8.90 (978-1-55513-092-3(5), 1555130925) Cook, David C.
Davis, Bryan. From the Mouth of Elijah. 2012. (Children of the Bard Ser.: 2). (ENG.). 512p. (YA). (gr. 7). pap. 14.99 (978-0-89957-881-1(0)) AMG Pubs.
Davis, Dean. The Dangerous Journey of Sherman the Sheep. 2005. (Illus.). 160p. (J). per. 9.99 (978-0-9759619-2-6(6)) CLADACH Publishing.
Davis, Holly. Thankful Together. Sokolova, Valerie, illus. 2006. 36p. (J). 5.99 (978-0-7847-1436-2(3), 04077) Standard Publishing.
Davis, Susan. I'm Adopted, You're Adopted: Welcome to God's Family. 2007. (ENG.). 79p. (J). (gr. 1-4). per. 8.99 (978-0-8127-0434-1(7)) Autumn Hse. Publishing Co.

Davis, Susan Page. Sarah's Long Ride. 2007. (Piper Ranch Ser.). 173p. (J). (gr. 3-7). per. 8.99 *(978-1-59166-737-7(2))* BJU Pr.

Dawson, Christopher B. Treasure in the Mirror. 2007. (Illus.). 32p. (J). *(978-0-9796456-1-7(1))* Unlock A Bk. Pubs., LLC.

Degarmo, Serena. Penny Sue the Pure Hearted. De Marco, Arielle, illus. 2013. 30p. pap. 7.99 *(978-1-936341-55-9(7))* DeWard Publishing Co., Ltd.

Denham, Joyce. Study Guide for Dragon Slayers. 2011. (ENG.). 64p. (J). (gr. 3-8). pap. 6.99 *(978-1-61261-124-2(9))* Paraclete Pr., Inc.

Dennis, Sandra L. The King of New Hearts. 2012. 16p. pap. 24.95 *(978-1-4626-8907-1(8))* America Star Bks.

Deseret Book Company Staff, contrib. by. A Story to Tell: The Classic Book of Virtues for Children. 2nd ed. 2004. 508p. (J). 16.95 *(978-1-59038-359-9(1))* Deseret Bk. Co.

Despain, Bree. The Dark Divine. 2010. (ENG.). 384p. (gr. 7). pap. 9.99 *(978-1-60684-154-9(8)*, Carolrhoda Lab™) Lerner Publishing Group.

—The Lost Saint. 2011. (ENG.). 416p. (J). (gr. 7). pap. 9.99 *(978-1-60684-235-5(8)*, Carolrhoda Lab™) Lerner Publishing Group.

—The Savage Grace. 2013. (ENG.). 496p. (J). (gr. 7). pap. 9.99 *(978-1-60684-416-8(4)*, Carolrhoda Lab™) Lerner Publishing Group.

Devore, David Y. Tessie, ed. Happy Birthday to Me. 2004.Tr. of Feliz cumpleanos a mi! (SPA.). 24p. 8.99 *(978-1-59185-421-0(0)*, Casa Creacion) Charisma Media.

DeVries, Catherine. Let's Learn about Psalm 23. Jackson, Ryan, illus. 2016. (HeartSmart Ser.). (ENG.). 26p. (J). bds. 10.99 *(978-0-7814-1270-4(6))* Cook, David C.

Dewitt, Becky. Destiny's Closet. 2010. 64p. pap. 24.00 *(978-1-4490-8970-2(4))* AuthorHouse.

—Destiny's Closet: The Wonder School. 2012. 64p. pap. 24.99 *(978-1-4772-7222-0(4))* AuthorHouse.

Dickens, Charles, et al. A Budget of Christmas Tales. 2013. 228p. pap. 9.99 *(978-1-62755-450-3(5))* Wilder Pubns., Corp.

Dickerson, Melanie. The Huntress of Thornbeck Forest, 1 vol. 2015. (Medieval Fairy Tale Ser.: 1). (ENG.). 320p. pap. 15.99 *(978-0-7180-2624-0(1))* Nelson, Thomas Inc.

—The Noble Servant, 1 vol. 2017. (ENG.). 336p. (J). 14.99 *(978-0-7180-2660-8(8))* Nelson, Thomas Inc.

—The Princess Spy, 1 vol. 2014. (Fairy Tale Romance Ser.). (ENG.). 304p. (YA). pap. 12.99 *(978-0-310-73098-9(8))* Zondervan.

—The Silent Songbird, 1 vol. 2016. (ENG.). 304p. (YA). 14.99 *(978-0-7180-2631-8(4))* Nelson, Thomas Inc.

DiGuido, George. Commandment Eleven: The Most Important One of All. 2004. 188p. pap. 20.99 *(978-1-4134-5172-6(1))* Xlibris Corp.

A Dinosaur Goes to Church. 2013. (ENG., Illus.). 32p. (J). 14.99 *(978-1-62108-423-5(X))* Covenant Communications, Inc.

Dobinson, Tony. The Crossing. 2006. 158p. (YA). (gr. 8-12). per. 10.00 *(978-1-84427-003-3(3))* Send The Light Distribution LLC.

Dockery, Marie F. The Three Billy Goats Gruff Find Jesus & the Three Little Souls. 2008. 52p. pap. 12.99 *(978-1-60647-605-5(X))* Salem Author Services.

Domney, Alexis. Splish, Splat!, 1 vol. Crawford, Alice, illus. 2011. (ENG.). 24p. (J). (gr. 1-3). 15.95 *(978-1-897187-88-3(2))* Second Story Pr. CAN. Dist: Orca Bk. Pubs. USA.

Donahue, Laurie. Mr. Blue a Job for You. Bryan, Hintz, illus. 2010. 32p. (J). 15.95 *(978-0-9799116-2-0(1))* LifeSong Pubs.

Doney, Meryl. The Very Worried Sparrow. Hansen, Gaby, illus. 2008. (J). (gr. -1-3). 12.95 *(978-0-8198-8038-3(8))* Pauline Bks. & Media.

Donnell, Annie Hamilton. Three Young Knights & Miss Theodosia's Heartstrings. l.t. ed. 2007. (ENG.). 156p. pap. 21.99 *(978-1-4346-1605-0(3))* Creative Media Partners, LLC.

Don't Do That, Dexter! 2014. (Happy Day Ser.). (ENG., Illus.). 16p. (J). pap. 2.49 *(978-1-4143-9409-1(8))* Tyndale Hse. Pubs.

Doughtie, Patrick & Doughtie, Heather. Letters to God, 1 vol. Lyon, Tammie, illus. 2016. (Letters to God Ser.). (ENG.). 32p. (J). 16.99 *(978-0-310-75395-7(3))* Zonderkidz.

Douglas, Kathleen. Johnny, the Unaware Angel. 2007. 108p. per. 19.95 *(978-1-4241-9939-6(5))* PublishAmerica, Inc.

Dowley, Tim. Pilgrim's Progress, 1 vol. Smallman, Steve, illus. 2015. 80p. (J). pap. 7.99 *(978-1-78128-229-8(3)*, Candle Bks.) Lion Hudson PLC GBR. Dist: Kregel Pubns.

—El Viaje Especial del Burrito - Donkey's Special Ride. (Serie Libros de Carton - Board Bks.). pap. *(978-1-56063-956-5(3))* Editorial Unilit.

Doyle, Mary K. Saint Theodora & Her Promise to God. Velikan, Phil, illus. 2013. 34p. 16.99 *(978-0-9897397-0-2(8))* Sisters of Providence.

Drella, Michele. A Mazing Grace. 2012. 26p. pap. 13.95 *(978-1-4497-4781-7(7)*, WestBow Pr.) Author Solutions, Inc.

Dreyer, Nicole E. Joseph's Christmas Story. Ebert, Len, illus. 2004. (ENG.). 16p. (J). 1.99 *(978-0-570-07577-6(7))* Concordia Publishing Hse.

Drury, David. Duckville. Swartz, Daniel, illus. 2013. 32p. (J). *(978-0-89827-721-0(3))* Wesleyan Publishing Hse.

Dungy, Tony. You Can Do It! Bates, Amy June, illus. 2008. (ENG.). 32p. (J). (gr. -1-2). 17.99 *(978-1-4169-5461-3(9)*, Little Simon Inspirations) Little Simon Inspirations.

Dungy, Tony & Dungy, Lauren. You Can Be a Friend. Mazellan, Ron, illus. 2011. (ENG.). 32p. (J). (gr. -1-2). 16.99 *(978-1-4169-9771-9(7)*, Little Simon Inspirations) Little Simon Inspirations.

Dunham, Wendy. Hope Girl. 2016. (ENG.). 144p. (J). (gr. 2-7). pap. 7.99 *(978-0-7369-6495-1(9))* Harvest Hse. Pubs.

—My Name Is River. 2015. (ENG.). 144p. (J). (gr. 2-7). pap. 7.99 *(978-0-7369-6461-6(4))* Harvest Hse. Pubs.

Dunlop, Ed. Escape to Liechtenstein. 2003. (Young Refugees Ser.). 152p. (J). (gr. 3-7). per. 7.49 *(978-1-59166-013-2(0))* BJU Pr.

—The Incredible Rescues. Halverson, Tom, illus. 2003. 166p. (J). (gr. 4-7). 7.49 *(978-1-59166-012-5(2))* BJU Pr.

—The Search for the Silver Eagle. Halverson, Tom, illus. 2003. 159p. (J). (gr. 4-7). 7.49 *(978-1-59166-014-9(9))* BJU Pr.

—Sherlock Jones: The Assassination Plot. 2004. 116p. (J). 8.99 *(978-1-59166-315-7(6))* BJU Pr.

—Sherlock Jones: The Missing Diamond. 2005. (Sherlock Jones Ser.). 109p. (J). (gr. 3-7). per. 8.99 *(978-1-59166-316-4(4))* BJU Pr.

—Sherlock Jones: The Willoughby Bank Robbery. 2004. 96p. (J). 8.99 *(978-1-59166-314-0(8))* BJU Pr.

Durrant, George D. Sam's Christmas Wish. Burr, Dan, illus. 2014. (ENG.). 32p. (J). (gr. 3). 17.99 *(978-1-60907-606-1(0)*, Shadow Mountain) Shadow Mountain Publishing.

Eareckson Tada, Joni & Jensen, Steve. The Meanest Teacher. 2005. (Darcy & Friends Ser.). 144p. (gr. 3-6). pap. 5.99 *(978-1-58134-256-7(X)*, Crossway Bibles) Crossway.

—The Mission Adventure. 2005. (Darcy & Friends Ser.). 143p. (gr. 3-6). pap. 5.99 *(978-1-58134-257-4(8)*, Crossway Bibles) Crossway.

—Tell Me the Promises. DiCianni, Ron, illus. 2004. 48p. (gr. 5-7). 17.99 *(978-0-89107-904-0(1))* Crossway.

Eaton, Gordon J. Piebald & the Parade of Small Animals. 2009. 184p. pap. 14.99 *(978-1-60791-991-9(5))* Salem Author Services.

Eden, David. The Potter's Wheel Story & Activity Book. Eden, David, illus. 2011. (ENG., Illus.). 48p. (J). pap. 16.95 *(978-0-9841658-6-5(X)*, Ignition Pr.) Publishing Services @ Thomson-Shore.

Edgren, David. The Serpent Scroll. 2009. (J). 11.99 *(978-0-8163-2330-2(5))* Pacific Pr. Publishing Assn.

Edwards, Carol. Jacy Meets Betsy: Jacy's Search for Jesus Book 2. Frey, Daniel, illus. 2006. 32p. (J). 15.95 *(978-0-9755314-1-9(7))* Majestic Publishing, LLC.

Eglin, Lorna. A Boy of Two Worlds. 2014. (Flamingo Fiction 9-13s Ser.). (ENG., Illus.). 208p. (J). (gr. 4-7). per. 8.99 *(978-1-84550-126-6(8)*, 4efaf8ef-841a-4d73-b71e-3ed4bb7cb5a4) Christian Focus Pubns. GBR. Dist: Bookmasters Distribution.

Eileen, Pamela & Eileen, Angela. No Wrong Turns. 2004. (Illus.). 18p. (J). 18.25 *(978-0-9753902-0-7(1))* TYL Publishing.

Elkins, Stephen. Ebony & Ivory: Discovering 10 Keys to Racial Harmony. Reisch, Jessie, illus. 2003. 32p. (J). (gr. k-18). 14.99 incl. audio compact disk *(978-0-8054-2674-8(4))* B&H Publishing Group.

—Know God, No Fear. Reisch, Jessie, illus. 2003. 32p. (J). (gr. k-5). 14.99 *(978-0-8054-2658-8(2))* B&H Publishing Group.

Elliott, Ann. GypsyBridge Friends: The Vine. 2003. 40p. pap. 12.95 *(978-0-9721825-0-8(0))* Open Vision Entertainment Corp.

Ellis, Edward Sylvester. Through Forest & Fire. 2005. pap. 14.95 *(978-1-59224-221-4(9))* Wildside Pr., LLC.

Elmer, Robert. Beyond Corista, 1 vol. 2009. (Shadowside Trilogy Ser.). (ENG.). 320p. (YA). (gr. 8-11). pap. 9.99 *(978-0-310-71423-1(0))* Zondervan.

—Candy Bombers, 1 vol. 2006. (Wall Ser.: Bk. 1). (ENG.). 160p. (J). pap. 6.99 *(978-0-310-70943-5(1))* Zonderkidz.

Emm, David. Madison Meets the Minister. Bedrick, Jeff, illus. 2010. (ENG.). 48p. (J). 12.95 *(978-1-889658-42-1(1))* New Canaan Publishing Co. LLC.

Engelman, Stephanie. A Single Bead. 2016. 199p. (YA). pap. *(978-0-8198-9054-2(5))* Pauline Bks. & Media.

Erhard, Lorie. Mama's Many Hats. Kalis, Jennifer, illus. 2014. (ENG.). 32p. (J). 18.99 *(978-0-9914701-4-3(1))* Bumble Bee Bks.

Evangel - the Smallest Angel. 2006. (J). 14.95 *(978-0-9790210-0-8(6))* Evening Star Enterprise, Inc.

Evans, Alfreda. The Little Boy in Blue. 2009. 24p. pap. *(978-1-55452-399-3(0)*, Guardian Bks.) Essence Publishing.

Evans, Alfreda Lockett. The Little Boy in Blue. 2009. 24p. pap. *(978-1-55452-402-0(4))* Essence Publishing.

Evans, Cathy. Halo & the Rainbows. 2013. 36p. pap. 16.95 *(978-1-4624-0704-0(8)*, Inspiring Voices) Author Solutions, Inc.

Evans, Freddi Williams. Hush Harbor: Praying in Secret. Banks, Erin, illus. 2008. (ENG.). 32p. (J). (gr. k-3). 16.95 *(978-0-8225-7965-6(0)*, Carolrhoda Bks.) Lerner Publishing Group.

Evans, Loralee. The King's Heir. 2006. 287p. (YA). (gr. 8-12). per. 18.99 *(978-1-55517-865-9(0)*, Bonneville Bks.) Cedar Fort, Inc./CFI Distribution.

Evensen, Rachelle. Finn's Marching Band: A Story of Counting, Colors, & Playing Together. 2009. 32p. (J). 14.95 *(978-0-8091-6749-4(2)*, Ambassador Bks.) Paulist Pr.

Ewing, Juliana Horatia. The Brownies & Other Tales. 2007. 140p. per. *(978-1-4065-2523-6(5))* Dodo Pr.

—A Great Emergency & Other Tales. 2007. 188p. per. *(978-1-4065-2525-0(1))* Dodo Pr.

Faith in Children: Stories from Faith-Based Children's Centers. 2007. (Illus.). 246p. per. 34.95 *(978-1-57736-385-9(X))* Providence Hse Pubs.

Fanning, Kim M. Beyond the Island: The Journey of a Boy. 2012. 92p. pap. 10.99 *(978-1-62419-343-9(9))* Salem Author Services.

Farenhorst, Christine. A Cup of Cold Water: The Compassion of Nurse Edith Cavell. 2007. 222p. (J). (gr. 3-7). per. 11.99 *(978-1-59638-026-4(8))* P & R Publishing.

Fames, Catherine. The Slide. 2003. 128p. (J). 6.49 *(978-1-57924-967-0(1))* BJU Pr.

—Snowblind. 2004. 108p. (J). *(978-1-59166-329-4(6))* BJU Pr.

Fechner, Maggie. Growing Up Gracie. 2010. 240p. pap. 15.99 *(978-1-59955-453-2(4))* Cedar Fort, Inc./CFI Distribution.

Fehler, Gene. Never Blame the Umpire, 1 vol. 2010. (ENG.). 192p. (J). (gr. 4-7). 12.99 *(978-0-310-71941-0(0))* Zonderkidz.

Fehr, Sheryl. Luke Helps Out. 2013. 32p. pap. *(978-1-4602-2989-7(4))* FriesenPress.

Ferguson, Sinclair B. Big Book of Bible Truths 2. Apps, Fred, illus. 2008. (ENG.). 64p. (J). pap. 14.99 *(978-1-84550-372-7(4)*, 9781845503727) Christian Focus Pubns. GBR. Dist: Bookmasters Distribution.

The Fijiboat Adventure. 2004. 56p. pap. 6.99 *(978-0-8341-2092-1(5))* Beacon Hill Pr. of Kansas City.

Finley, Martha. Elsie & Her Loved Ones, Vol. 27. 320p. (gr. 4-7). pap. 5.95 *(978-1-58182-183-3(2)*, Cumberland Hse.) Sourcebooks, Inc.

—Elsie & Her Namesakes, Vol. 28. 320p. (gr. 4-7). pap. 5.95 *(978-1-58182-184-0(0)*, Cumberland Hse.) Sourcebooks, Inc.

—Elsie at Home. 2006. 27.95 *(978-1-4218-2989-0(4))*; pap. 12.95 *(978-1-4218-3089-6(2))* 1st World Publishing, Inc.

—Elsie at Home. 2007. (ENG.). 152p. pap. 19.99 *(978-1-4346-2866-4(3))*; 168p. pap. 21.99 *(978-1-4346-2901-2(5))* Creative Media Partners, LLC.

—Elsie at Ion, Vol. 19. 320p. (gr. 4-7). pap. 5.95 *(978-1-58182-171-0(9)*, Cumberland Hse.) Sourcebooks, Inc.

—Elsie at the World's Fair. 2007. (ENG.). 156p. pap. 19.99 *(978-1-4346-2508-3(7))* Creative Media Partners, LLC.

—Elsie at the Worlds Fair. 2006. 27.95 *(978-1-4218-2991-3(6))*; pap. 12.95 *(978-1-4218-3091-9(4))* 1st World Publishing, Inc.

—Elsie at the World's Fair. l.t. ed. 2007. 172p. pap. 21.99 *(978-1-4346-2550-2(8))* Creative Media Partners, LLC.

—Elsie at the World's Fair, Vol. 20. 320p. (gr. 4-7). pap. 5.95 *(978-1-58182-172-7(7)*, Cumberland Hse.) Sourcebooks, Inc.

—Elsie at Viamede, Vol. 18. 320p. (gr. 4-7). pap. 5.95 *(978-1-58182-114-7(X)*, Cumberland Hse.) Sourcebooks, Inc.

—Elsie Dinsmore. 2006. (ENG.). pap. 13.95 *(978-1-4218-3092-6(2))* 1st World Publishing, Inc.

—Elsie's Girlhood. 2006. 29.95 *(978-1-4218-2993-7(2))*; pap. 14.95 *(978-1-4218-3093-3(0))* 1st World Publishing, Inc.

—Elsie's Girlhood. l.t. ed. 2007. (ENG.). 254p. pap. 23.99 *(978-1-4264-3884-4(2))* Creative Media Partners, LLC.

—Elsie's Holiday at Roselands. 2009. (Original Elsie Classics Ser.). (Illus.). 284p. (YA). pap. 7.95 *(978-1-59856-401-3(3))* Hendrickson Pubs. Marketing, LLC.

—Elsie's Journey on Inland Waters, Vol. 21. 320p. (gr. 4-7). pap. 5.95 *(978-1-58182-174-1(3)*, Cumberland Hse.) Sourcebooks, Inc.

—Elsie's Kith & Kin. 2006. 28.95 *(978-1-4218-2994-4(0))*; pap. 13.95 *(978-1-4218-3094-0(9))* 1st World Publishing, Inc.

—Elsie's Kith & Kin, Vol. 12. 320p. (gr. 4-7). pap. 5.95 *(978-1-58182-105-5(0)*, Cumberland Hse.) Sourcebooks, Inc.

—Elsie's Motherhood. 2006. 29.95 *(978-1-4218-2995-1(9))*; pap. 14.95 *(978-1-4218-3095-7(7))* 1st World Publishing, Inc.

—Elsie's Motherhood. l.t. ed. 2007. 286p. pap. 23.99 *(978-1-4264-8102-4(0))* Creative Media Partners, LLC.

—Elsie's New Relations. 2006. 28.95 *(978-1-4218-2996-8(7))*; pap. 13.95 *(978-1-4218-3096-4(5))* 1st World Publishing, Inc.

—Elsie's New Relations. 2007. (ENG.). 200p. pap. 19.99 *(978-1-4346-2507-6(9))*; 224p. pap. 22.99 *(978-1-4346-2549-6(4))* Creative Media Partners, LLC.

—Elsie's New Relations, Vol. 9. 320p. (gr. 4-7). pap. 5.95 *(978-1-58182-101-7(8)*, Cumberland Hse.) Sourcebooks, Inc.

—Elsie's Vacation & after Events. 2006. 27.95 *(978-1-4218-2997-5(5))*; pap. 12.95 *(978-1-4218-3097-1(3))* 1st World Publishing, Inc.

—Elsie's Vacation & after Events, Vol. 17. 320p. (gr. 4-7). pap. 5.95 *(978-1-58182-113-0(1)*, Cumberland Hse.) Sourcebooks, Inc.

—Elsie's Womanhood. l.t. ed. 2007. 218p. pap. 23.99 *(978-1-4264-8300-4(7))* Creative Media Partners, LLC.

—Elsie's Young Folks. 2008. 296p. 34.99 *(978-1-58960-287-8(0))* Sovereign Grace Pubs., Inc.

—Holidays at Roselands. 2007. pap. 20.99 *(978-1-4346-2429-1(3))*; (ENG.). 274p. pap. 23.99 *(978-1-4346-2475-8(7))* Creative Media Partners, LLC.

—The Two Elsies. 2006. 27.95 *(978-1-4218-3000-1(0))*; pap. 12.95 *(978-1-4218-3100-8(7))* 1st World Publishing, Inc.

Fixmer, Elizabeth. Down from the Mountain. 2015. (ENG.). 288p. (YA). (gr. 8-12). 16.99 *(978-0-8075-8370-8(7))* Whitman, Albert & Co.

Fletcher, Susan. Walk Across the Sea. Jakesevic, Nenad, illus. 2003. (ENG.). 224p. (J). (gr. 4-8). pap. 11.95 *(978-0-689-85707-2(1)*, Atheneum Bks. for Young Readers) Simon & Schuster Children's Publishing.

Flora, B. David. An Angel's Day on Earth. Alexander, Johnna A., illus. 2011. 24p. pap. 24.95 *(978-1-4560-9851-3(9))* PublishAmerica, Inc.

Fluharty, Kristi & Fluharty, T. Lively. Fool Moon Rising. Fluharty, Kristi & Fluharty, T. Lively, illus. 2009. (Illus.). 40p. (J). 16.99 *(978-1-4335-0682-6(3))* Crossway.

Focus on the Family Staff & Hering, Marianne. Light in the Lions' Den. 2017. (AIO Imagination Station Bks.: 19). (ENG.). 144p. (J). pap. 4.99 *(978-1-58997-878-2(1))* Focus on the Family Publishing.

Forbes, Dillon. Careful Enough? 2008. (YA). 8.99 *(978-1-59166-835-0(2))* BJU Pr.

Fortner, Tama. God Is Always Good: Comfort for Kids Facing Grief, Fear, or Change, 1 vol. Vasylenko, Veronica, illus. 2014. (ENG.). 32p. (J). 12.99 *(978-0-7180-1145-1(7))* Nelson, Thomas Inc.

Foster, Lisa. 5 Little Tomatoes. 2008. 44p. pap. 17.95 *(978-1-4327-2306-4(5))* Outskirts Pr., Inc.

Foster, Ron, illus. I Like Snow! 2006. 28p. (J). (gr. -1-3). *(978-1-929039-37-1(9))* Ambassador Bks., Inc.

Fotheringham, Juanita. A Little Ranch on the Side. 2013. 38p. pap. 9.99 *(978-1-62697-215-5(X))* Salem Author Services.

Freedman, Georgene. The Olive Tree. 2nd num. ed. 2006. (J). per. 12.95 *(978-0-9771322-1-8(8))* Simpatico Bks.

Freeman, Chip. Why, Daddy, Why Are There Stars in the Sky? Perry, Lee Ann, illus. 2012. 20p. (-18). pap. 11.95 *(978-1-937770-23-5(0)*, SPC Bks.) RPJ & Co., Inc.

Friesen, Jonathan. Both of Me, 1 vol. 2016. (ENG.). 256p. (J). pap. 9.99 *(978-0-310-73187-0(9))* Blink.

Fruits from Faith. 2006. (Illus.). 24p. (J). 12.95 *(978-0-9777041-1-8(4))* Third Dimension Publishing.

Gaard, Betty. Jericho Ride. 2003. (Illus.). 165p. (J). pap. 8.99 *(978-1-57924-968-7(X))* BJU Pr.

Gaffney, Sean. Larryboy & the Sinister Snow Day, 1 vol. 2003. (Big Idea Books / LarryBoy Ser.). (ENG., Illus.). 96p. (J). pap. 4.99 *(978-0-310-70561-1(4))* Zonderkidz.

Gail, Cornelia. Juvey. 2015. 153p. (YA). per. 14.95 *(978-0-9674454-4-1(2))* Girls In Da Game Publishing.

Gamble, Shanae. God's Dogs go to Heaven: Christian myths & Fables. 2011. 28p. pap. 15.99 *(978-1-4520-5424-7(X))* AuthorHouse.

Garcia, Katherine. Jojo & the Tule Tree. 2013. 20p. pap. 9.95 *(978-1-935752-39-4(1))* Bryce Cullen Publishing.

Garza, Ray. Captain Christian. 2010. (ENG.). 32p. (J). pap. 9.95 *(978-0-9795680-3-9(X))* Believers Publishing.

Gatlin, Shawana. Now I Lay Me down to Sleep. 2011. 12p. 12.68 *(978-1-4269-5778-9(5))* Trafford Publishing.

Gendron, Elizabeth. In God's Playpen: For the Child in all of Us. 2011. 44p. 17.50 *(978-1-4269-6442-8(0))* Trafford Publishing.

Gerard, Justin, illus. The Lightlings. 2006. 40p. (J). (gr. -1-3). lib. bdg. *(978-1-56769-078-1(5))* Reformation Pubs.

Gibbons, Teresa Dominguez. The Greatest Gift. 2010. 26p. pap. 12.00 *(978-1-60911-666-8(6)*, Eloquent Bks.) Strategic Book Publishing & Rights Agency (SBPRA).

Gibson, Marley. Radiate. 2012. (ENG.). 416p. (YA). (gr. 7). pap. 21.99 *(978-0-547-61728-2(3))* Houghton Mifflin Harcourt Publishing Co.

God Made You Special. 2006. (Faith Discovery Ser.). (Illus.). 24p. (J). bds. 6.99 *(978-0-7847-1399-0(5)*, 04059) Standard Publishing.

Gollahon, Carleen Anderson. Sophie & the Mysterious Ring. 2012. 62p. (gr. 4-18). pap. 8.99 *(978-1-4624-0379-0(4)*, Inspiring Voices) Author Solutions, Inc.

Gomez, Sally. Too Many Freckles! Mitchell, Hazel, illus. 2008. (ENG.). 32p. pap. *(978-1-934363-32-4(4))* Zoe Life Publishing.

Good, Linnea, et al. Adventures of the God Detectives. 2006. (ENG., Illus.). 96p. (J). (gr. 10-10). per. 6.95 *(978-1-55145-542-6(0))* Wood Lake Publishing, Inc. CAN. Dist: Westminster John Knox Pr.

Goon, Geraldine. Grandma Tells Dozens of Stories. 2008. 64p. pap. *(978-1-84748-515-1(4))* Athena Pr.

Gorman, Patrick. Alicia & Policia, 1 vol. Gorman, Kyrsten, illus. 2010. 24p. 24.95 *(978-1-4489-6425-3(3))* PublishAmerica, Inc.

Gould, M&R. What Would Jesus Do? Purity of Intention. 2008. 35p. pap. 24.95 *(978-1-60672-675-4(7))* America Star Bks.

Goza, Shelly. Mr. Meme. Gil, Rodolpho, illus. 2005. (J). bds. 9.99 *(978-1-4183-0077-7(2))* Christ Inspired, Inc.

Graber, Lois, illus. A Song in the Storm. 2012. 32p. (J). *(978-0-7399-2445-7(1))* Rod & Staff Pubs., Inc.

Graceland Book Publishers, as told by. A Little Girl by Chinyere Nwakanma. 2nd ed. 2010. (Illus.). 32p. (J). *(978-0-9566210-0-9(7))* Graceland Book Publishing U.K.

Grant, Myrna. Ivan & the American Journey. 2006. (Flamingo Fiction 9-13s Ser.). (ENG., Illus.). 144p. (J). (gr. 4-7). per. 6.99 *(978-1-84550-131-0(4)*, 219b73c2-7f68-49a8-b40f-d5dbfb745039) Christian Focus Pubns. GBR. Dist: Bookmasters Distribution.

—Ivan & the Daring Escape. 2006. (Flamingo Fiction 9-13s Ser.). (ENG., Illus.). 144p. (J). (gr. 4-7). per. 6.99 *(978-1-84550-132-7(2)*, 24be2b87-de69-4377-8a1b-bc7b2ad8cd87) Christian Focus Pubns. GBR. Dist: Bookmasters Distribution.

—Ivan & the Hidden Bible. 2006. (Flamingo Fiction 9-13s Ser.). (ENG., Illus.). 144p. (J). (gr. 4-7). per. 6.99 *(978-1-84550-133-4(0)*, 9394aef3-942b-4824-b0b8-0ae3449d32e0) Christian Focus Pubns. GBR. Dist: Bookmasters Distribution.

—Ivan & the Informer. 2013. (Flamingo Fiction 9-13s Ser.). (ENG., Illus.). 128p. (J). (gr. 1-8). per. 6.99 *(978-1-84550-134-1(9)*, a4873bb8-0b7a-4393-a40a-6315d03042d2) Christian Focus Pubns. GBR. Dist: Bookmasters Distribution.

—Ivan & the Moscow Circus. 2006. (Flamingo Fiction 9-13s Ser.). (ENG., Illus.). 160p. (J). (gr. 4-7). per. 6.99 *(978-1-84550-135-8(7)*, 4a6719e2-1a18-4f7c-9b8f-fed8a960777e) Christian Focus Pubns. GBR. Dist: Bookmasters Distribution.

—Ivan & the Secret in the Suitcase. 2006. (Flamingo Fiction 9-13s Ser.). (ENG., Illus.). 144p. (J). (gr. 4-7). per. 6.99 *(978-1-84550-136-5(5)*, 90ba43f9-c4f3-4eac-aa9d-e552a2ffb74d) Christian Focus Pubns. GBR. Dist: Bookmasters Distribution.

Grant, Nancy. Maggie & the Backyard Helpers. 2006. (ENG.). 60p. per. 16.95 *(978-1-4241-4373-3(X))* PublishAmerica, Inc.

Grant, Natalie. The Miracle in Music City, 1 vol. 2016. (Faithgirlz / Glimmer Girls Ser.). (ENG.). 208p. (J). pap. 8.99 *(978-0-310-75250-9(7))* Zonderkidz.

Grant Sr, Hector J. Sybil: The Trials & Triumphs of a Jamaican Girl. 2008. 208p. per. 15.95 *(978-1-4327-1889-3(4))* Outskirts Pr., Inc.

Greene, Rhonda Gowler. Baa! Oink! Moo! God Made the Animals, 1 vol. Walker, David, illus. 2017. (ENG.). 26p. (J). bds. 9.99 *(978-0-310-75227-1(2))* Zonderkidz.

Greenwood, Diana. Insight, 1 vol. 2012. (ENG.). 224p. (YA). pap. 7.99 *(978-0-310-72315-8(9))* Zondervan.

Gregory, Philippa. Changeling. 10 vols. 2012. (Order of Darkness Ser.). (YA). 92.75 *(978-1-4640-4583-7(6))*; 90.75 *(978-1-4640-4587-5(9))*; 265.75 *(978-1-4640-4584-4(4))*; 90.75 *(978-1-4640-4586-8(0))* Recorded Bks., Inc.

—Changeling. van Deelen, Fred & Taylor, Sally, illus. 2013. (Order of Darkness Ser.: 1). (ENG.). 352p. (YA). (gr. 9). pap. 9.99 *(978-1-4424-5345-6(1)*, Simon Pulse) Simon Pulse.

—Changeling. Taylor, Sally & van Deelen, Fred, illus. 2012. (Order of Darkness Ser.: 1). (ENG.). 272p. (YA). (gr. 9). 18.99 *(978-1-4424-5344-9(3)*, Simon Pulse) Simon Pulse.

Gregory, Regina. Mollie & Ike Find Jesus in a Hotair Balloon? 2013. 24p. pap. 10.95 *(978-1-4908-0738-6(1)*, WestBow Pr.) Author Solutions, Inc.

Groom, Juliet. Because God Loves Me. Anderson, Laura Ellen, illus. 2016. (ENG.). 24p. (J). (gr. -1-k). bds. 8.99 *(978-1-58925-237-0(3))* Tiger Tales.

Gross, Carmen. Ryan Elias Finds: The Truth Behind Lying. Dixon, Nehemiah F., illus. 2008. 27p. pap. 24.95 *(978-1-60474-945-8(8))* America Star Bks.

Grovet, Heather. Beanie, the Horse That Wasn't a Horse. 2004. 95p. (J). 6.99 *(978-0-8163-2053-0(5))* Pacific Pr. Publishing Assn.

—Blondie's Big Ride. 2008. (Illus.). 95p. (J). pap. 5.97 *(978-0-8163-2225-1(2))* Pacific Pr. Publishing Assn.

—A Friend for Zipper. 2008. (J). pap. 5.97 *(978-0-8163-2226-8(0))* Pacific Pr. Publishing Assn.

—Super Star Problems. 2008. (J). pap. 5.97 *(978-0-8163-2255-8(4))* Pacific Pr. Publishing Assn.

Grund, Carol A. Anna Mei, Cartoon Girl. 2010. 140p. (J). (gr. 4-7). pap. 8.95 *(978-0-8198-0788-5(5))* Pauline Bks. & Media.

C D

Guffrey, Lindsey. A Psalm for the Solar System. 2013. 24p. pap. 9.00 *(978-0-9896518-0-6(0))* Yorkshire Publishing Group.

Gunn, Robin Jones. Christy Miller Collection, Vol. 2. 2006. (Christy Miller Collection: Bks. 4-6). (ENG.). 496p. (J). (gr. 7-12). 16.99 *(978-1-59052-585-2(X),* Multnomah Bks.) Crown Publishing Group.

—Christy Miller Collection Vol. 3, Vol. 3. 2006. (Christy Miller Collection: Bks. 7-9). (ENG.). 480p. (J). (gr. 7-12). 16.99 *(978-1-59052-586-9(8),* Multnomah) Doubleday Religious Publishing Group, The.

—Christy Miller Collection, Vol 1, Vol. 1. 2005. (Christy Miller Collection: Bks. 1-3). (ENG., Illus.). 496p. (J). (gr. 7-12). 16.99 *(978-1-59052-584-5(1),* Multnomah) Doubleday Religious Publishing Group, The.

—Christy Miller Collection, Vol 4, Vol. 4. 2006. (Christy Miller Collection: Bks. 10-12). (ENG.). 496p. (J). (gr. 7-12). 16.99 *(978-1-59052-587-6(6),* Multnomah) Doubleday Religious Publishing Group, The.

—Mrs. Rosey Posey & the Fine China Plate, 1 vol. Schofield, Christina Diane, illus. 2008. (I Can Read! Ser.). (ENG.). 32p. (J). (gr. -1-3). pap. 3.99 *(978-0-310-71578-8(4))* Zonderkidz.

—Open Your Heart Vol. 3, Vol. 3. 2006. (Sierra Jensen Collection: Bks. 7-9). (ENG.). 480p. (J). (gr. 7-12). 15.99 *(978-1-59052-590-6(6),* Multnomah) Doubleday Religious Publishing Group, The.

—Sierra Jensen Collection, Vol. 4. 2006. (Sierra Jensen Collection: Bks. 10-12). (ENG.). 464p. (J). (gr. 7-12). 15.99 *(978-1-59052-591-3(4),* Multnomah) Doubleday Religious Publishing Group, The.

—Sierra Jensen Collection, Vol 1, Vol. 1. 2006. (Sierra Jensen Collection: Bks. 1-3). (ENG.). 432p. (J). (gr. 7-12). 15.99 *(978-1-59052-588-3(4),* Multnomah) Doubleday Religious Publishing Group, The.

—Whispers. 2004. (Glenbrooke Ser.: Bk. 2). (ENG.). 288p. pap. 14.99 *(978-1-59052-192-2(7),* Multnomah) Doubleday Religious Publishing Group, The.

Haddix, Margaret Peterson. Leaving Fishers. 262p. (YA). (gr. k-18). pap. 4.50 *(978-0-8072-1541-8(4),* Listening Library) Random Hse. Audio Publishing Group.

—Leaving Fishers. 2012. (ENG.). 272p. (YA). (gr. 7). pap. 8.99 *(978-1-4424-4314-3(6),* Simon & Schuster Bks. For Young Readers) Simon & Schuster Bks. For Young Readers.

Hadley, Caroline. Woodside; or, Look, Listen & Learn. 2007. (ENG., Illus.). 80p. per. *(978-1-4065-1557-2(4))* Dodo Pr.

Hadnot, Victor. The Wheels of God. 2003. 140p. (YA). pap. 11.95 *(978-0-595-27507-6(9),* Writers Club Pr.) iUniverse, Inc.

Hagler, Liz & Hagler, Jack. Hooked on the Book: Patrick's Adventures Through the Books of the Bible. 2012. (ENG.). 96p. (J). (gr. 1-6). 19.95 *(978-1-61448-225-3(X))* Morgan James Publishing.

Hague, Michael. A Child's Book of Prayers. Hague, Michael, ed. 2010. (ENG., Illus.). 32p. (J). (gr. -1-k). pap. 6.99 *(978-0-312-64576-2(7),* 9780312645762) Square Fish.

Hale, Edward Everett. Margaret Percival in America; a Tale Ed by a New England Minister, a B Being a Sequel to Margaret Percival a Tale Ed by Rev William Sewell, B. 2006. 288p. per. 23.99 *(978-1-4255-2654-2(3))* Michigan Publishing.

Hall, Frostie. Dread Champions for the King, Book 2: For the King! 2006. 112p. per. *(978-1-55452-044-2(4))* Essence Publishing.

—Dread Champions of the King: The Humble Beginning. 2004. (Dread Champions of the King Ser.: Bk. 1). 96p. (J). per. *(978-1-55306-836-5(X))* Essence Publishing.

Hall, Hannah. God Bless My Friends, 1 vol. Whitlow, Steve, illus. 2016. (God Bless Book Ser.). (ENG.). 20p. (J). bds. 9.99 *(978-0-7180-8953-5(7))* Nelson, Thomas Inc.

Hall, Hannah C. God Bless Our Fall, 1 vol. Whitlow, Steve, illus. 2015. (God Bless Book Ser.). (ENG.). 20p. (J). bds. 9.99 *(978-0-529-12333-6(9))* Nelson, Thomas Inc.

Hall, Mark & West, Matthew. City on the Hill. Vania, Tatio, illus. 2014. (ENG.). 32p. (gr. -1-3). 16.99 *(978-1-4336-8231-5(1),* B&H Kids) B&H Publishing Group.

Hall, S.C. Turns of Fortune & Other Tales. 2007. (ENG.). 116p. per. *(978-1-4065-1586-2(8))* Dodo Pr.

Hallinan, P. K. Thank You, God. 2008. (ENG., Illus.). 28p. (J). (gr. -1-k). bds. 7.95 *(978-0-8249-5457-4(2),* Ideal Pubns.) Worthy Publishing.

Halverson, Mathew. Concord Cunningham Pursues the Clues: The Scripture Sleuth 5. 2008. (Mystery Ser.). (Illus.). 98p. (J). (gr. 4-7). pap. 8.95 *(978-1-885904-55-3(X))* Focus Publishing.

Hambrick, Sharon. Brain Games. 2009. (J). 8.99 *(978-1-59166-954-8(5))* BJU Pr.

Hamel, Mike. Dragon's Lair, 5. 2007. (Matterhorn the Brave Ser.: 5). (ENG.). 192p. (J). (gr. 5-11). per. 9.99 *(978-0-89957-837-8(3))* AMG Pubs.

—Jewel Heist, 4. 2007. (Matterhorn the Brave Ser.: 4). (ENG.). 192p. (gr. 8-7). per. 9.99 *(978-0-89957-836-1(5))* AMG Pubs.

—Pyramid Scheme. 2007. (Matterhorn the Brave Ser.: 3). (ENG.). 176p. (J). (gr. 5-7). per. 9.99 *(978-0-89957-835-4(7))* AMG Pubs.

—Rylan the Renegade, 6. 2007. (Matterhorn the Brave Ser.: 6). (ENG.). 192p. (J). (gr. 8-7). per. 9.99 *(978-0-89957-838-5(1))* AMG Pubs.

—The Sword & the Flute. 2007. (Matterhorn the Brave Ser.: 1). (ENG.). 176p. (J). (gr. 5-12). per. 9.99 *(978-0-89957-833-0(0))* AMG Pubs.

—Talis Hunters, Vol. 2. 2007. (Matterhorn the Brave Ser.: 2). (ENG.). 176p. (J). (gr. 5-12). per. 9.99 *(978-0-89957-834-7(9))* AMG Pubs.

Hansen, Eric. Great White Judgment. Moody, Julie, illus. 2005. (YA). bds. 9.99 *(978-1-4183-0059-3(4))* Christ Inspired, Inc.

Harder Tangvald, Christine. Someone I Love Died. 2003. (Please Help Me God Ser.). (Illus.). 24p. (J). (gr. -1-18). 9.99 *(978-1-55513-490-7(4),* 1555134904) Cook, David C.

Hardie, Jill. The Sparkle Box: The Story of a Very Special Christmas Gift. Komacki, Christine, illus. 2012. 32p. (J). 19.99 *(978-0-8249-5647-9(8),* Ideal Pubns.) Worthy Publishing.

—The Sparkle Egg. Komacki, Christine, illus. 2014. 32p. (J). 16.99 *(978-0-8249-5664-6(8),* Ideal Pubns.) Worthy Publishing.

Hardy, LeAnne. Between Two Worlds: A Novel. 2003. 160p. (J). pap. 7.99 *(978-0-8254-2793-0(2))* Kregel Pubns.

Hare, Eric B. Curse Proof. 2007. (Illus.). 95p. (J). 10.99 *(978-0-8163-2208-4(2))* Pacific Pr. Publishing Assn.

Hargis, Alvin. Kingdom of Mystique Series: Book 1. 2007. 25p. pap. 24.95 *(978-1-4241-8635-8(8))* PublishAmerica, Inc.

Harley, Jason. Journey to the Light. 2003. 270p. (J). 22.95 *(978-1-929642-47-2(4))* Literally Speaking Publishing Hse.

Harold & I. 2007. (ENG., Illus.). 291p. (J). (gr. 3-8). per. 13.99 *(978-0-7684-2432-4(1))* Send The Light Distribution LLC.

Harris, Robert E. The Rose That Grew Out the Concrete, 1 vol. 2010. 48p. pap. 16.95 *(978-1-4489-5811-5(3))* America Star Bks.

Harris, Virginia. Charlie's Cage. 2008. 28p. pap. 15.99 *(978-1-4343-6892-8(0))* AuthorHouse.

Harrod-Eagles, Cynthia. A Church Anniversary. 2011. 44p. pap. 18.46 *(978-1-4567-6493-7(4))* AuthorHouse.

Hartman, Bob. The Big Pig Stampede: And a Bunch More Amazing Miracles. 2015. (Goat Boy Chronicles Ser.). (ENG., Illus.). 192p. (J). 12.99 *(978-1-4964-0865-5(9))* Tyndale Hse. Pubs.

Haugaard, Erik Christian. Little Fishes. Johnson, Milton, illus. 2008. (J). (gr. 4-7). 23.00 *(978-0-8446-6245-9(3))* Smith, Peter Pub., Inc.

Hedlund, Jody. A Daring Sacrifice, 1 vol. 2016. (ENG.). 224p. (YA). pap. 12.99 *(978-0-310-74937-0(9))* Zondervan.

Heimerdinger, Chris. The Warriors of Cumorah, Vol. 8. 2004. (Tennis Shoes Adventure Ser.). xi, 394p. pap. 14.95 *(978-1-57734-922-8(9))* Covenant Communications, Inc.

The Hell House Experience. 2008. (ENG.). 70p. 14.99 *(978-0-9817520-8-2(X))* Torch Legacy Pubns.

Hemphill, Helen. Long Gone Daddy. (ENG.). 176p. 2014. (YA). (gr. 6). pap. 8.95 *(978-1-62091-737-4(8))* 2006. (J). (gr. 8-12). 16.95 *(978-1-932425-38-3(1),* Lemniscaat) Boyds Mills Pr.

Henderson, Patti & Golden Books Staff. A Blessing from Above. Edge, Elizabeth, illus. 2004. (Little Golden Book Ser.). (ENG.). 24p. (J). (gr. -1-2). 4.99 *(978-0-375-82866-9(4),* Golden Bks.) Random Hse. Children's Bks.

Henderson, Sara. Howie Finds a Hug, 1 vol. Zenz, Aaron, illus. 2008. (I Can Read! / Howie Ser.). (ENG.). 32p. (J). (gr. -1-3). pap. 3.99 *(978-0-310-71607-5(1))* Zonderkidz.

—Howie's Tea Party, 1 vol. Zenz, Aaron, illus. 2008. (I Can Read! / Howie Ser.). (ENG.). 32p. (J). (gr. -1-3). pap. 3.99 *(978-0-310-71605-1(5))* Zonderkidz.

Henderson, Sara & Zenz, Aaron. Howie Goes Shopping(Fido Va de Compras), 1 vol. Henderson, Sara & Zenz, Aaron, illus. 2009. (I Can Read! / Howie Series / ¡Yo Sé Leer! / Serie: Fido Ser.). (ENG., Illus.). 32p. (J). pap. 3.99 *(978-0-310-71874-1(0))* Zonderkidz.

—Howie Wants to Play, 1 vol. Henderson, Sara & Zenz, Aaron, illus. 2009. (I Can Read! / Howie Series / ¡Yo Sé Leer! / Serie: Fido Ser.). (ENG., Illus.). 32p. (J). pap. 3.99 *(978-0-310-71875-8(9))* Zonderkidz.

Hendey, Lisa M. The Whisper in the Ruins. Bower, Jenn, illus. 2016. (Chime Travelers Ser.: 3). (ENG.). 128p. (gr. 2-5). pap. 6.99 *(978-1-63253-036-3(8),* Servant Bks.) Franciscan Media.

Henley, Karyn. Marvy Gets the Thumps. 2004. 88p. (J). 10.99 *(978-1-4003-0389-2(3))* Nelson, Thomas Inc.

—Monday, Tuesday, Oopsday! 2004. 88p. (J). 10.99 *(978-1-4003-0294-9(3))* Nelson, Thomas Inc.

—Pot Luck Supper. 2004. 88p. (J). 10.99 *(978-1-4003-0388-5(5))* Nelson, Thomas Inc.

Hering, Marianne. In Fear of the Spear. 2016. (AIO Imagination Station Bks.: 17). (ENG.). 144p. (J). pap. 4.99 *(978-1-58997-804-1(8))* Focus on the Family Publishing.

—Trouble on the Orphan Train. 2016. (AIO Imagination Station Bks.: 18). (ENG.). 144p. (J). pap. 4.99 *(978-1-58997-805-8(6))* Focus on the Family Publishing.

Hering, Marianne & Sanders, Nancy I. Captured on the High Seas. 2014. (AIO Imagination Station Bks.: 14). (ENG.). 144p. (J). pap. 4.99 *(978-1-58997-775-4(0))* Tyndale Hse. Pubs.

Hering, Marianne, et al. Doomsday in Pompeii. 2015. (AIO Imagination Station Bks.: 16). (ENG., Illus.). 144p. (J). pap. 4.99 *(978-1-58997-803-4(X))* Focus on the Family Publishing.

Hernandez, David. Land of the Pharaohs, 1 vol. 2003. (Adventures of Toby Digz Ser.: 1). (ENG., Illus.). 96p. pap. 5.99 *(978-1-4003-0195-9(5))* Nelson, Thomas Inc.

—The Mighty Armor, 1 vol., Vol. 2. 2003. (Adventures of Toby Digz Ser.: 2). (ENG., Illus.). 96p. pap. 5.99 *(978-1-4003-0196-6(3))* Nelson, Thomas Inc.

Hervey, Cheston & Doane, Darren. Kill the Dragon, Get the Girl. 2017. (J). pap. ***(978-1-59128-188-7(1))*** Canon Pr.

Herzing, Nancy. The Night the Angels Came. 2012. 46p. pap. 19.99 *(978-1-62419-373-6(0))* Salem Author Services.

Hewlett, Stefanie & Foulk, Allison. Heart Stockings. McCann, Caroline, illus. 2015. (J). pap. 7.99 *(978-1-62972-159-0(X))* Deseret Bk. Co.

Heyne, Kara. The Locket's Secret. 2013. (ENG.). 162p. (J). pap. 8.95 *(978-0-8198-7484-9(1))* Pauline Bks. & Media.

Hickey, Sally. Empty Shoes. 2004. 139p. (YA). per. 7.95 *(978-1-931742-59-7(6),* MountainView) Treble Heart Bks.

Higgs, Liz Curtis. The Parable of the Lily, 1 vol. Munger, Nancy, illus. 10th anniv. ed. 2007. (Parable Ser.). (ENG.). 32p. (gr. -1-2). 7.99 *(978-1-4003-0844-6(5))* Nelson, Thomas Inc.

—The Pine Tree Parable. 2005. (Parable Ser.). 32p. (J). pap. 3.99 *(978-1-4003-0685-5(X))* Nelson, Thomas Inc.

Highstreet, Harry. Melanie Ann. 2005. 118p. pap. 19.95 *(978-1-4137-8946-1(3))* PublishAmerica, Inc.

Hildahl, Melita K. Life Is an Adventure with Emie. 2008. 156p. per. 15.99 *(978-1-60477-139-8(9))* Salem Author Services.

Hilmo, Tess. With a Name Like Love. 2013. (ENG.). 272p. (J). (gr. 5-9). pap. 10.99 *(978-1-250-02733-7(0),* 9781250027337) Square Fish.

Hinds, Ruth McNaughton. Puppy & I. 2006. (J). per. 7.95 *(978-0-9764232-2-5(7))* River City Pr.

Hodgson, Mona. The Princess Twins & the Puppy, 1 vol. Olson, Julie, illus. 2015. (I Can Read! / Princess Twins Ser.). (ENG.). 32p. (J). pap. 3.99 *(978-0-310-75064-2(4))* Zonderkidz.

—The Princess Twins Play in the Garden, 1 vol. Olson, Julie, illus. 2015. (I Can Read! / Princess Twins Ser.). (ENG.). 32p. (J). pap. 3.99 *(978-0-310-75050-5(4))* Zonderkidz.

Hodgson, Mona Gansberg. Desert Critter Friends Set, 12 vols. (Desert Critter Friends Ser.). (J). 54.99 *(978-0-7586-0007-3(0))* Concordia Publishing Hse.

—The Princess Twins & the Puppy, 1 vol. Hansen, Red, illus. 2011. (I Can Read! / Princess Twins Ser.). (ENG.). 32p. (J). pap. 3.99 *(978-0-310-72709-5(X))* Zonderkidz.

Holl, Kristi. Chat Freak. 2004. 128p. (J). pap. 5.99 *(978-1-4003-0326-7(5))* Nelson, Thomas Inc.

Holland, Gretchen. Because He Loves Me. 2005. (J). 8.99 *(978-0-9768340-0-7(6))* Holland, Gretchen.

Holm, H. R. Against an Amber Sky. 2007. 214p. (gr. 3-7). per. 14.99 *(978-1-55517-991-5(6))* Cedar Fort, Inc./CFI Distribution.

Holmes, Andy. Tipper Tells a Lie, 1 vol. de Giorgi, Sergio, illus. 2014. (ENG.). 22p. (J). bds. 9.99 *(978-0-529-11213-2(2))* Nelson, Thomas Inc.

Horrocks, Anita. Almost Eden. 2006. (ENG.). 288p. (J). (gr. 5-9). pap. 9.95 *(978-0-88776-742-5(7),* Tundra Bks.) Tundra Bks. CAN. Dist: Penguin Random Hse. LLC.

Horton, Jeanette. God's Alphabet. 2012. 82p. (gr. 4-6). pap. 14.95 *(978-1-4772-9730-8(8))* AuthorHouse.

Hotz, Donna. Aaron's Surprise! 2010. 32p. pap. 14.49 *(978-1-4520-4522-1(4))* AuthorHouse.

House, Catherine. Little Elephant. Whelan, Olwyn, illus. 2007. 32p. pap. 11.95 *(978-1-59325-093-5(2))* Word Among Us Pr.

House, Peggy. Prairie Anna. 2012. (J). *(978-1-60682-395-8(7))* BJU Pr.

Houselander, Caryll. Catholic Tales for Boys & Girls. 2003. Orig. Title: Terrible Farmer Timson (New York: Sheed & Ward, 1957). (Illus.). 160p. (J). pap. 11.95 *(978-1-928832-74-4(1))* Sophia Institute Pr.

—More Catholic Tales for Boys & Girls. 2003. Orig. Title: Inside the Ark: & Other Stories (New York: Sheed & Ward, 1956). (Illus.). v, 150p. (J). pap. 10.95 *(978-1-928832-84-3(9))* Sophia Institute Pr.

Hover Get's His Wings. 2004.Tr. of Cometin recibe sus alas. (SPA.). 24p. 10.99 *(978-1-59185-422-7(9),* Casa Creacion) Charisma Media.

Howell, David. Swan Songs-in Search of the Staffstone. 2005. per. 13.99 *(978-1-59781-002-9(9))* Salem Author Services.

Howerton-Willis, Deborah. Amos the Aardvark. 2012. 48p. pap. 24.99 *(978-1-62419-623-2(3))* Salem Author Services.

Howitt, Mary Botham. Strive & Thrive a Tale by Mary Howitt. 2006. 180p. per. 18.99 *(978-1-4255-1426-6(X))* Michigan Publishing.

Hronas, Georgia. Tell Us a Story, Grandma: More of Grandma's Orthodox Spiritual Stories. 2005. (ENG., Illus.). 114p. (gr. 3-7). pap. 13.95 *(978-1-880971-93-2(3))* Light & Life Publishing Co.

Hubler, Marsha. Blue Ribbon Champ, 1 vol. rev. ed. 2010. (Keystone Stables Ser.). (ENG.). 112p. (J). pap. 7.99 *(978-0-310-71797-3(3))* Zonderkidz.

—A Horse to Love, 1 vol. ed. 2009. (Keystone Stables Ser.). (ENG.). 144p. (J). pap. 4.99 *(978-0-310-71792-8(2))* Zonderkidz.

—Leading the Way, 1 vol. 2010. (Keystone Stables Ser.). (ENG.). 128p. (J). pap. 7.99 *(978-0-310-71796-6(5))* Zonderkidz.

—The Long Ride Home, 1 vol. 2010. (Keystone Stables Ser.). (ENG.). 144p. (J). pap. 7.99 *(978-0-310-71692-1(6))* Zonderkidz.

—On the Victory Trail, 1 vol. rev. ed. 2009. (Keystone Stables Ser.). (ENG.). 144p. (J). pap. 7.99 *(978-0-310-71793-5(0))* Zonderkidz.

—Southern Belle's Special Gift, 1 vol. 2009. (Keystone Stables Ser.). (ENG.). 128p. (J). pap. 7.99 *(978-0-310-71794-2(9))* Zonderkidz.

—Summer Camp Adventure, 1 vol. 2009. (Keystone Stables Ser.). (ENG.). 128p. (J). pap. 7.99 *(978-0-310-71795-9(7))* Zonderkidz.

—Whispering Hope, 1 vol., Bk. 7. 2010. (Keystone Stables Ser.). (ENG.). 144p. (J). pap. 7.99 *(978-0-310-71691-4(8))* Zonderkidz.

Hudson, Bonnie Rose. The Hidden Village. 2017. (J). ***(978-1-62856-311-5(7))*** BJU Pr.

Hudson, Lisa. Meet Lisa Jo: First Day of School & Words Can Hurt. 2013. 42p. pap. 17.45 *(978-1-4497-8463-8(1),* WestBow Pr.) Author Solutions, Inc.

Hudson, Wade. It's Church Going Time. 2008. (Illus.). 32p. (gr. -1-3). 16.95 *(978-1-60349-005-4(1),* Marimba Bks.) Hudson Publishing Group, The.

Hughes, Lynn Gordon. To Live a Truer Life: A Story of the Hopedale Community. Lindro, illus. 2003. 32p. (J). 10.00 *(978-0-9725017-2-9(X))* Blackstone Editions.

Hughes, Marilynn. The Former Angel - A Children's Tale. 2003. 22p. 9.94 *(978-1-4116-1712-4(6))* Lulu Pr., Inc.

Hulst, W. G. van de & Hulst, Willem G. van de, illus. The Search for Christmas. 2014. (J). *(978-1-928136-12-5(5))* Inheritance Pubns.

Hunt, Angela. The True Princess. 2005. (Illus.). 32p. (J). 9.99 *(978-1-59185-633-7(7))* Charisma Media.

Hunt, Susan. Sammy & His Shepherd. Godbey, Corey, illus. 2008. (J). *(978-1-56769-109-2(9))* Reformation Pubs.

Huskins, T. A. I Am a Whosoever. 2006. 62p. pap. 16.95 *(978-1-4241-0308-9(8))* PublishAmerica, Inc.

Hutton, Janice Turney. When My Shoes Aren't Cool. 2012. 16p. pap. 7.95 *(978-1-4497-4953-8(4),* WestBow Pr.) Author Solutions, Inc.

I Love Me Because God Made Me. 2011. 24p. pap. 15.99 *(978-1-4568-9408-5(0))* Xlibris Corp.

Iakovos-Dalalakis, Helen. Nicholas Wins the Prize 1: Young Nicholas Experiences the Sacrament of Confession. Gabrili, Alexandra, illus. 2003. (ENG.). 24p. (J). (gr. 2-6). 15.95 *(978-1-880971-82-6(8))* Light & Life Publishing Co.

I'm Just the Right Size. 2004.Tr. of Soy del tamano correcto! (SPA.). 24p. 8.99 *(978-1-59185-423-4(7),* Casa Creacion) Charisma Media.

Imbody, Amy E. & Imbody, Amy. Snug as a Bug, 1 vol. Gordon, Mike, illus. 2008. (I Can Read! Ser.). (ENG.). 32p. (J). (gr. -1-1). pap. 3.99 *(978-0-310-71575-7(X))* Zonderkidz.

Inny. Epiphany Rose-the Message. 2006. pap. 8.99 *(978-1-60034-097-0(0))* Salem Author Services.

Inslee, Francine. Charlie's Walk. 2004. (ENG.). (J). pap. 12.95 *(978-0-8309-1073-1(5))* Herald Publishing Hse.

Inthof, Marian. Our Friends at Farmer John's Meadow. 2008. 27p. pap. 24.95 *(978-1-60441-286-4(0))* America Star Bks.

Ireland, Mary E. & Brandstaedter, German H. Vacaciones de Eric,Las. Clingan, Darrell, tr. 2011.Tr. of Eric's Vacation. (Illus.). 237p. (YA). (gr. 11). pap. 7.25 *(978-0-7399-7766-8(0))* Rod & Staff Pubs., Inc.

It's Good Sunday. 2004. (J). bds. 15.95 *(978-0-9743394-1-2(5))* More Pr.

Jaden, Denise. Losing Faith. 2010. (ENG.). 400p. (YA). (gr. 9-18). pap. 9.99 *(978-1-4169-9609-5(5),* Simon Pulse) Simon Pulse.

Jakobitz, Marilee. Martha Lu & the Whobegots. 2008. 32p. pap. 24.95 *(978-1-60441-482-0(0))* America Star Bks.

James, Jake. Jake s Short Stories. 2010. 64p. pap. 10.99 *(978-1-60957-640-0(3))* Salem Author Services.

Jarwin. Love in the Springtime. 2012. 224p. 24.95 *(978-1-4626-6818-2(6))* America Star Bks.

Jelsma, Amber. Noah's Little Lamb, 1 vol. Pease, Tristyn, illus. 2010. 32p. pap. 24.95 *(978-1-4489-6068-2(1))* PublishAmerica, Inc.

Jenkins, Jerry B. Crash at Cannibal Valley, 1 vol. 2006. (AirQuest Adventures Ser.). (ENG.). 160p. (J). (gr. 3-7). pap. 6.99 *(978-0-310-71347-0(1))* Zonderkidz.

—Disaster in the Yukon, 1 vol. 2006. (AirQuest Adventures Ser.). (ENG., Illus.). 160p. (J). (gr. 3-7). pap. 6.99 *(978-0-310-71345-6(5))* Zonderkidz.

Jenkins, Jerry B. & Fabry, Chris. Canyon Echoes. 2005. (Red Rock Mysteries Ser.: 8). (ENG.). 234p. (YA). pap. 6.99 *(978-1-4143-0147-1(2),* Tyndale Kids) Tyndale Hse. Pubs.

—Dead End. 2006. (Red Rock Mysteries Ser.: 15). (ENG.). 248p. (YA). (gr. 3-7). per. 6.99 *(978-1-4143-0154-9(5),* Tyndale Kids) Tyndale Hse. Pubs.

—Double Fault. 2005. (Red Rock Mysteries Ser.: 7). (ENG.). 272p. (YA). pap. 6.99 *(978-1-4143-0146-4(4),* Tyndale Kids) Tyndale Hse. Pubs.

—Grave Shadows. 2005. (Red Rock Mysteries Ser.: 5). (ENG., Illus.). 240p. (YA). pap. 6.99 *(978-1-4143-0144-0(8),* Tyndale Kids) Tyndale Hse. Pubs.

—Hidden Riches. 2006. (Red Rock Mysteries Ser.: 13). (ENG.). 262p. (YA). (gr. 3-7). per. 6.99 *(978-1-4143-0152-5(9),* Tyndale Kids) Tyndale Hse. Pubs.

—Hollywood Holdup. 2006. (Red Rock Mysteries Ser.: 12). (ENG.). 224p. (YA). (gr. 8-12). per. 6.99 *(978-1-4143-0151-8(0),* Tyndale Kids) Tyndale Hse. Pubs.

—Instant Menace. 2006. (Red Rock Mysteries Ser.: 9). (ENG.). 256p. (YA). (gr. 3-7). per. 6.99 *(978-1-4143-0148-8(0),* Tyndale Kids) Tyndale Hse. Pubs.

—Missing Pieces. 2005. (Red Rock Mysteries Ser.: 3). (ENG., Illus.). 224p. (YA). (gr. -1-7). pap. 6.99 *(978-1-4143-0142-6(1),* Tyndale Kids) Tyndale Hse. Pubs.

—Phantom Writer. 2005. (Red Rock Mysteries Ser.: 6). (ENG.). 256p. (YA). pap. 5.99 *(978-1-4143-0145-7(6),* Tyndale Kids) Tyndale Hse. Pubs.

—Stolen Secrets. 2005. (Red Rock Mysteries Ser.: 2). (ENG., Illus.). 224p. (YA). (gr. -1-7). pap. 6.99 *(978-1-4143-0141-9(3),* Tyndale Kids) Tyndale Hse. Pubs.

—Wild Rescue. 2005. (Red Rock Mysteries Ser.: 4). (ENG.). 256p. (YA). (gr. -1-7). pap. 6.99 *(978-1-4143-0143-3(X),* Tyndale Kids) Tyndale Hse. Pubs.

—Wind Chill. 2006. (Red Rock Mysteries Ser.: 14). (ENG.). 240p. (YA). (gr. 3-7). per. 6.99 *(978-1-4143-0153-2(7),* Tyndale Kids) Tyndale Hse. Pubs.

—Windy City Danger. 2006. (Red Rock Mysteries Ser.: 11). (ENG.). 246p. (YA). (gr. 8-12). per. 6.99 *(978-1-4143-0150-1(2),* Tyndale Kids) Tyndale Hse. Pubs.

Jenkins, Jerry B. & LaHaye, Tim. Heat Wave: Surviving the Fourth Bowl Judgment. 2004. (Left Behind: the Kids Ser.: 37). (ENG.). 208p. (YA). mass mkt. 5.99 *(978-0-8423-8347-9(6))* Tyndale Hse. Pubs.

—The Perils of Love: Breaking Through the Darkness. 2004. (Left Behind: the Kids Ser.: 38). (ENG.). 208p. (YA). mass mkt. 5.99 *(978-0-8423-8348-6(4))* Tyndale Hse. Pubs.

—Pursued, Bk. 2. 2003. (ENG.). 400p. (YA). (gr. 5-8). 9.97 *(978-0-8423-8352-3(2))* Tyndale Hse. Pubs.

Jensen, Bonnie Rickner. God Loves Daddy & Me, 1 vol. 2017. (ENG., Illus.). 20p. (J). bds. 9.99 *(978-0-7180-9177-4(9))* Nelson, Thomas Inc.

—God Loves Mommy & Me, 1 vol. 2017. (ENG., Illus.). 20p. (J). bds. 9.99 *(978-0-7180-9178-1(7))* Nelson, Thomas Inc.

Jensen, Sydell A. Christian Alphabet. 2010. 32p. pap. 14.99 *(978-1-4490-0631-0(0))* AuthorHouse.

The Jesus Jeepney. 2007. 32p. pap. 4.50 *(978-0-8341-2276-5(6),* 083-412-2766) Beacon Hill Pr. of Kansas City.

Jin, Susie Lee, illus. It's Bedtime for Little Monkeys. 2010. (ENG.). 5p. (J). bds. 5.99 *(978-0-7369-2832-8(4))* Harvest Hse. Pubs.

John, P. El Lugar Seguro. 2004.Tr. of Safe Place. 8.99 *(978-0-7899-1181-0(7))* Editorial Unilit.

Johnson, C. M. Cjs' Bible Adventure: CJs' first Adventure. 2011. 24p. pap. 10.95 *(978-1-4497-2161-9(3),* WestBow Pr.) Author Solutions, Inc.

Johnson, Elizabeth. And Then Nicholas Sang: The Story of the Trisagion Hymn. Lobastov, Masha, illus. 2010. 32p. (J). 18.95 *(978-1-936270-05-7(6))* Ancient Faith Publishing.

Johnson, Jacqueline & Young, Jeanna Stolle. Princess Charity's Courageous Heart, 1 vol. Aranda, Omar, illus. 2012. (Princess Parables Ser.). (ENG.). 32p. (J). 14.99 *(978-0-310-72701-9(4))* Zonderkidz.

—Princess Faith's Mysterious Garden, 1 vol. Aranda, Omar, illus. 2012. (Princess Parables Ser.). (ENG.). 32p. (J). 14.99 *(978-0-310-72703-3(0))* Zonderkidz.

Johnson, Jacqueline Kinney & Young, Jeanna. Princess Grace & Poppy, 1 vol. 2012. (I Can Read! / Princess Parables Ser.). (ENG.). 32p. (J). pap. 3.99 *(978-0-310-72677-7(8))* Zonderkidz.

Johnson, Ken & Myers, Bill. The Big Lie: A Star in the Breaking / The Not-so-Great Escape. 2015. (McGee & Me! Ser.). (ENG.). 256p. (J). pap. 9.99 *(978-1-4964-0329-2(0))* Tyndale Hse. Pubs.

Johnson, Lois Walfrid. The Creeping Shadows. 2009. (Orig.). (J). 8.99 *(978-0-88062-277-6(6))* Mott Media.

—The Disappearing Stranger. 2009. (Orig.). (J). 8.99 *(978-0-88062-275-2(X))* Mott Media.

—Disaster on Windy Hill. 2009. (J). 8.99 *(978-0-88062-284-4(9))* Mott Media.

—Grandpa's Stolen Treasure. 2009. (Orig.). (J). 8.99 *(978-0-88062-281-3(4))* Mott Media.

—Heart of Courage. 2005. (Viking Quest Ser.: 4). (ENG., Illus.). 240p. (J). (gr. 3). pap. 8.99 (978-0-8024-3115-8(1)) Moody Pubs.

—The Hidden Message. 2009. (Orig.). (J). 8.99 (978-0-88062-276-9(8)) Mott Media.

—Mysterious Hideaway. 2009. (J). 8.99 (978-0-88062-280-6(6)) Mott Media.

—Mystery of the Silver Coins, Vol. 2. 2003. (Viking Quest Ser.: 2). (ENG., Illus.). 208p. (J). (gr. 3). pap. 8.99 (978-0-8024-3113-4(5)) Moody Pubs.

—Raiders from the Sea. 2003. (Viking Quest Ser.: 1). (ENG., Illus.). 208p. (J). (gr. 3-7). pap. 8.99 (978-0-8024-3112-7(7)) Moody Pubs.

—The Raider's Promise. 2006. (Viking Quest Ser.: 5). (ENG., Illus.). 304p. (J). (gr. 3-7). per. 8.99 (978-0-8024-3116-5(X)) Moody Pubs.

—The Runaway Clown. 2009. (Orig.). (J). 8.99 (978-0-88062-282-0(2)) Mott Media.

—Trouble at Wild River. 2009. (J). 8.99 (978-0-88062-279-0(2)) Mott Media.

—The Vanishing Footprints. 2009. (J). 8.99 (978-0-88062-278-3(4)) Mott Media.

Joiner, D. Wayne, Sr. Dudley Gloworm & the Saving Light. Joiner, D. Wayne, Sr., illus. 2006. (Illus.). (J). 25.00 (978-0-9785103-0-5(5)) Willy Waw wees, LLC.

Jones, Brenda. Kids Sunday Notes: I Will Follow God's Plan for Me. l.t. ed. 2004. 100p. (J). 7.95 (978-1-57636-168-9(3)) SunRise Publishing.

Jones, Jenny B. So Not Happening, 1 vol. 2009. (Charmed Life Ser.: 1). (ENG.). 336p. (YA). (gr. 7-18). pap. 12.99 (978-1-59554-541-1(7)) Nelson, Thomas Inc.

Jones, Katy Huth. Treachery & Truth: A Story of Sinners, Servants, & Saints. 2016. 163p. (YA). pap. (978-0-8198-7535-8(X)) Pauline Bks. & Media.

Jones, Nathan Smith. The Boy Who Ate America. Nelson, Casey, illus. 2007. 32p. (J). (gr. -1-3). 16.95 (978-1-59038-814-3(3), Shadow Mountain) Shadow Mountain Publishing.

Jordan, Stephanie. Is the Moon God's? Houston, Melissa, illus. 2005. (J). bds. 9.99 (978-1-4183-0062-3(4)) Christ Inspired, Inc.

Joseph, O'Day E. I Like Wind! Foster, Ron, illus. 2007. 28p. (J). (gr. -1-3). (978-1-929039-42-5(5)) Ambassador Bks., Inc.

Kaplan, Gloria. Ride the White Horse. 2004. (YA). per. 8.99 (978-1-889732-48-0(6), A & E Sivells Pubns.) Word For Word Publishing Co.

Karen, Frantz. Children's Parables: Earthly Stories with Heavenly Lessons for Children. 2013. 162p. pap. 13.95 (978-1-4908-1675-3(5), WestBow Pr.) Author Solutions, Inc.

Kaulen, Diane Bouman. In the Wake of Suicide: A Child's Journey. McAdoo, Grami & McAdoo, O'Pa, illus. 2008. (J). (gr. 3-5). 14.95 (978-0-9764026-5-7(3)) Longhorn Creek Pr.

Keeling, Annie E. Andrew Golding A Tale of the Great Plague. 2004. reprint ed. pap. 15.95 (978-1-4191-0694-1(5)); pap. 1.99 (978-1-4192-0694-8(X)) Kessinger Publishing, LLC.

Keith, Brooke. Chrissie's Shell. Bausman, Mary, illus. 2010. 32p. (J). 14.99 (978-1-59317-398-2(9)) Warner Pr., Inc.

Kelby, Tom. Nathaniel's Journey: The King's Armory. Yaeger, Mark, illus. 2003. (J). per. (978-1-930914-04-9(0)) Hands to the Plow, Inc.

Kellogg, Elijah. The Young Shipbuilders of Elm Island by Rev Elijah Kellogg. 2006. 316p. per. 23.99 (978-1-4255-3063-1(X)) Michigan Publishing.

Kelly, Stephen M. Symbala's River. 2006. (YA). lib. bdg. 6.99 (978-1-4276-0237-4(9)) Aardvark Global Publishing.

Kelly, Theresa. Aloha Cove Set, 7 vols. (Aloha Cove Ser.). (YA). 39.99 (978-0-7586-0005-9(4)) Concordia Publishing Hse.

Kenneally, Miranda. Things I Can't Forget. 2013. (Hundred Oaks Ser.: Bk. 3). (ENG.). 320p. (YA). (gr. 7-12). pap. 9.99 (978-1-4022-7190-8(5), 9781402271908) Sourcebooks, Inc.

Kennedy, Pamela. Moving Day for Sam: A Story about Change. Petrov, Anton, illus. 2007. 32p. (J). (gr. -1-3). 8.99 (978-0-8249-5558-8(7), Ideal Pubns.) Worthy Publishing.

Kenney, Cindy. Junior Asparagus. 2004. (ENG., Illus.). 100p. (J). pap. 3.99 (978-0-310-70722-6(6)) Zonderkidz.

—Laura Carrot. 2004. (ENG., Illus.). 100p. (J). pap. 3.99 (978-0-310-70723-3(4)) Zonderkidz.

—Where Is God When I'm Scared?, 1 vol. 2004. (Big Idea Bks.). (ENG., Illus.). 22p. (J). 4.99 (978-0-310-70784-4(6)) Zonderkidz.

Kenney, Rebecca. The Silent. 2009. (YA). 8.99 (978-1-60682-054-4(0), JourneyForth) BJU Pr.

Kenny, Cindy. Larry Cucumber: I Can. 2004. (ENG., Illus.). 100p. (J). pap. 3.99 (978-0-310-70721-9(8)) Zonderkidz.

Kent, Renee Holmes. Adventures in Misty Falls, Vol. 8. 2004. (Adventures in Misty Falls Ser.: Vol. 8). (Illus.). 100p. (gr. 4-7). pap. 4.99 (978-1-56309-456-9(8), N017104) Woman's Missionary Union.

—Best Friends Forever?, Vol. 2. 2004. (Adventures in Misty Falls Ser.: Bk. 2). (Illus.). 100p. (gr. 4-7). pap. 4.99 (978-1-56309-734-8(6), N007117) New Hope Pubs.

—Cassie, You're a Winner! 2004. (Adventures in Misty Falls Ser.: Vol. 1). (Illus.). 100p. (gr. 4-7). pap. 2.99 (978-1-56309-735-5(4), N007116) New Hope Pubs.

—Girl Talk, Vol. 7. 2004. (Adventures in Misty Falls Ser.: Vol. 7). (Illus.). 100p. (J). (gr. 4-7). pap. 4.99 (978-1-56309-455-2(X), N017103) New Hope Pubs.

—J. J. Navajo Princess, Vol. 3. 2004. (Adventures in Misty Falls Ser.: Vol. 3). (Illus.). 100p. (gr. 4-7). pap. 4.99 (978-1-56309-763-8(X), N007105) New Hope Pubs.

—Robyn to the Rescue, Vol. 5. 2004. (Adventures in Misty Falls Ser.: Vol. 5). (Illus.). 100p. (J). (gr. 4-7). pap. 4.99 (978-1-56309-451-4(7), N007109) New Hope Pubs.

—Tell the Truth, Cassie, Vol. 6. 2004. (Adventures in Misty Falls Ser.: Vol. 6). (Illus.). 100p. (J). (gr. 4-7). pap. 4.99 (978-1-56309-452-1(5), N007110) New Hope Pubs.

Keys, Demetria M. The Replacements. 2007. 68p. per. 7.95 (978-1-4327-0649-4(7)) Outskirts Pr., Inc.

Kieper, Rienhold Richard. Tomahawk. 2004. 19p. (J). pap. 10.00 (978-0-9719284-2-8(8)) Blue Thunder One, Inc.

Kimberly, Anne. Dark Well of Decision. 2007. 136p. per. 7.99 (978-0-9800356-5-0(1)) Highland Pr. Publishing.

Kimchi & Komoshins. 2004. 56p. pap. 6.99 (978-0-8341-2090-7(9)) Beacon Hill Pr. of Kansas City.

Kinde, Christa. The Hidden Deep, 1 vol. 2013. (Threshold Ser.). (ENG.). 272p. (J). 14.99 (978-0-310-72489-6(9)) Zonderkidz.

Kinder, Connie & Virden, Carole. Dash's Pause: An Adventure in Being Found. 2012. (Illus.). 40p. pap. 20.95 (978-1-4497-6981-9(0), WestBow Pr.) Author Solutions, Inc.

Kindig, Tess. Luv @ First Site. 2004. 128p. (J). pap. 5.99 (978-1-4003-0325-0(7)) Nelson, Thomas Inc.

Kindig, Tess Eileen. Slam Dunk Set, 8 vols. (Slam Dunk Ser.). (J). 38.99 (978-0-7586-0014-1(3)) Concordia Publishing Hse.

King, Kimberly. God Is in the Window. Jones, Erik, illus. 2007. 37p. (J). 18.95 (978-0-9771936-6-0(7)) InterWeave Corp.

Kingsbury, Karen. Always Daddy's Princess, 1 vol. Docampo, Valeria, illus. rev. ed. 2013. (ENG.). 32p. (J). 15.99 (978-0-310-71647-1(0)) Zonderkidz.

—Whatever You Grow up to Be, 1 vol. Docampo, Valeria, illus. rev. ed. 2014. (ENG.). 32p. (J). 15.99 (978-0-310-71646-4(2)) Zonderkidz.

Kirk, Janice. The Christmas Redwood. Kirk, Janice, illus. 2007. (Illus.). 56p. per. 18.95 (978-1-60290-147-6(3)) OakTara Publishing Group LLC.

Kirkman, Robert. Genesis, Vol. 1. 2009. (ENG., Illus.). 120p. pap. 14.99 (978-1-58240-572-8(7), 9781582405728) Image Comics.

Kjellberg, B. Apple Acres: The Farm. 2006. (J). per. 7.95 (978-0-912868-10-3(4)) Kjellberg, Inc.

Kjellberg Publishers. Courtnee: A Farm Girl, 6 vols., bk. 1. 2nd ed. 2005. (ENG., Illus.). 84p. (J). 7.95 (978-0-912868-06-6(6), Kjellberg Pubs.) Kjellberg, Inc.

—Sandy: A City Girl, 6 bks., bk. 1. 2nd ed. 2005. (ENG., Illus.). 94p. (J). 7.95 (978-0-912868-08-0(2), 8080, Kjellberg Pubs.) Kjellberg, Inc.

Kjellberg Publishing. Abe: A Farm Boy, 6 vols., vol. 1. 2nd l.t. ed. 2006. (Illus.). 96p. (J). 7.95 (978-0-912868-07-3(4), Kjellberg Pubs.) Kjellberg, Inc.

Klassen, Kirsten L. Katelyn's Affection. 2004. (ENG.). 280p. pap. 11.99 (978-0-8361-9281-0(8)) Herald Pr.

Klein, Jennifer. Sir Bumble. 2013. 32p. pap. 8.95 (978-1-4575-2096-9(6)) Dog Ear Publishing, LLC.

Klodt, Louise. Door to Kandalaura: Book One of the Kandalaura Chronicles. 2015. (ENG.). 112p. pap. 9.99 (978-1-62998-395-0(0), Creation Hse.) Charisma Media.

Knife, Ivan M. Uses the. Black Thursday. 2010. 108p. pap. 15.99 (978-1-4500-6311-1(X)) Xlibris Corp.

Knowlton, Laurie. N 2 Deep. 2004. 128p. (J). pap. 5.99 (978-1-4003-0327-4(3)) Nelson, Thomas Inc.

Koenig, Albert. Wood, Hay, & Pigs. Compton, Donna, illus. 2005. (J). 8.99 (978-1-4183-0078-4(0)) Christ Inspired, Inc.

Koertge, Ron. Coaltown Jesus. 2013. (ENG.). 128p. (YA). (gr. 9). 16.99 (978-0-7636-6228-8(3)) Candlewick Pr.

Kraai, David. Gesta De Salomon. 2008. 120p. pap. 19.95 (978-1-933916-25-5(7)) Nelson Publishing & Marketing.

—Solomons Quest. 2008. 120p. pap. 19.95 (978-1-933916-05-7(2)) Nelson Publishing & Marketing.

Krohn, Genendel. Who Is the Builder? Pelleg, Tirtsa, illus. 32p. 13.99 (978-1-58330-515-7(7)) Feldheim Pubs.

Krueger, Jim & Zondervan Staff. Betrayal of Trust, 1 vol. Rogers, Bud, ed. Padilla, Ariel, illus. 2009. (Z Graphic Novels / Tomo Ser.). (ENG.). 160p. (J). pap. 6.99 (978-0-310-71306-7(4)) Zondervan.

Kuhn, Tom B. Little Chick: Learns to Trust in the Lord, 1 vol. Kuhn, Douglas W., illus. 2009. 23p. pap. 24.95 (978-1-60836-929-4(3)) America Star Bks.

Kuijer, Guus & Nieuwenhuizen, John. The Book of Everything. 2006. ix, 101p. (J). 16.99 (978-0-439-74919-0(0), Levine, Arthur A. Bks.) Scholastic, Inc.

Kumara, Mark. The Tr-Youth Truth: Knowledge, Apprehens. 2005. (Illus.). 206p. pap. 24.75 (978-1-4120-6960-1(2)) Trafford Publishing.

Kuykendoll, Kim. The Adventures of the Coral Way Gang. 2008. 160p. pap. 13.99 (978-1-60477-840-3(7)) Salem Author Services.

Kwon, Min, illus. Snow Biz, Vol. 5. 2006. (Serenity Ser.: Vol. 5). 96p. (YA). (gr. 7-12). per. 7.97 (978-1-59310-874-8(5), Barbour Bks.) Barbour Publishing, Inc.

Kyle, Sherry. Love, Lexi: Letters to God. 2016. (ENG.). 224p. (YA). pap. 12.99 (978-1-4964-0963-8(9)) Tyndale Hse. Pubs.

Lagerlöf, Selma. Christ Legends: & Other Stories. 2010. 200p. pap. 44.50 (978-1-4092-0934-8(2)) Lulu Pr., Inc.

LaHaye, Tim & Jenkins, Jerry B. Dejados Atrás. 2003. (Left Behind Ser.).Tr. of Left Behind. (SPA., Illus.). 48p. 4.99 (978-0-8054-2843-8(7)); Vol. 2. pap. 4.99 (978-0-8054-2847-6(X)); Vol. 3. 4.99 (978-0-8054-2844-5(5)) B&H Publishing Group.

Lamplighter Staff. Tales of the Restoration. 2004. 20.00 (978-1-58474-056-8(6)) Cornerstone Family Ministries/Lamplighter Publishing.

—Teddys Button Hardcover. 2004. 15.00 (978-1-58474-027-8(2)) Cornerstone Family Ministries/Lamplighter Publishing.

—Tom Gillies. 2004. 16.00 (978-1-58474-048-3(5)) Cornerstone Family Ministries/Lamplighter Publishing.

—Tom Watkins Mistake. 2004. 15.00 (978-1-58474-034-6(5)) Cornerstone Family Ministries/Lamplighter Publishing.

Lane, L. E. The Mysterious Golden Seed. l.t. ed. 2004. 144p. (J). pap. (978-0-9746867-0-7(0)) Christian Visionary Communications.

Langstrom, Angela Chapman. And God Said See, I Told You So! A True Story of Faith & Adoption. 2008. 20p. per. 24.95 (978-1-4241-9195-6(5)) America Star Bks.

Larson, Heidi. Love the Lord Your God! 2012. 32p. pap. 13.99 (978-1-4624-0295-3(X), Inspiring Voices) Author Solutions, Inc.

Lash, Jill. He Knows You. 2007. (J). 15.99 (978-1-59955-089-3(X)) Cedar Fort, Inc./CFI Distribution.

Law, Jerel. Spirit Fighter, 1 vol. 2012. (Son of Angels, Jonah Stone Ser.). (ENG.). 256p. (J). pap. 9.99 (978-1-4003-1843-8(2)) Nelson, Thomas Inc.

—Truth Runner, 1 vol. 2013. (Son of Angels, Jonah Stone Ser.). (ENG.). 272p. (J). pap. 9.99 (978-1-4003-2287-9(1)) Nelson, Thomas Inc.

Lawhead, Stephen R. The Dragon King Trilogy: n the Hall of the Dragon King; The Warlords of Nin; The Sword & the Flame. 2008. (Dragon King Trilogy: Bks. 1-3). 1168p. 19.99 (978-1-59554-518-3(2)) Nelson, Thomas Inc.

Lawton, Wendy. A La Sombra de Su Mano, 1 vol. 2009. Orig. Title: Shadow of His Hand. (SPA.). 160p. pap. 4.99 (978-0-8254-1379-7(6), Editorial Portavoz) Kregel Pubns.

Lawton, Wendy G. Shadow of His Hand: A Story Based on the Life of Holocaust Survivor Anita Dittman. 2004. (Daughters of the Faith Ser.). (ENG.). 160p. (J). (gr. 3). pap. 7.99 (978-0-8024-4074-7(6)) Moody Pubs.

Layton, Dian. Armor of Light. 2003. (Illus.). vi, 58p. 4.99 (978-0-9707919-7-9(6)) Mercy Place, Inc.

—Rescued from the Dragon. 2005. (Illus.). 64p. (J). (gr. 2-5). pap. 4.99 (978-0-9677402-2-5(3)) Destiny Image Pubs.

—Seeker's Great Adventure. 2005. (Illus.). 64p. (J). (gr. 2-5). pap. 4.99 (978-0-9677402-1-8(5)) Destiny Image Pubs.

Le Feuvre, Amy. Harebell's Friend. 2004. (Golden Inheritance Ser.: Vol. 8). (Illus.). 140p. (J). pap. (978-0-921100-84-3(1)) Inheritance Pubns.

—His Big Opportunity. 2007. (Illus.). 148p. per. (978-1-4065-2382-9(8)) Dodo Pr.

—Teddy's Button. 2007. 92p. per. (978-1-4065-2383-6(6)) Dodo Pr.

—Teddy's Button. 2004. reprint ed. pap. 15.95 (978-1-4191-5094-4(4)); pap. 1.99 (978-1-4192-5094-1(9)) Kessinger Publishing, LLC.

Lecomte, Eva. Paula the Waldensian. 2004. reprint ed. pap. 1.99 (978-1-4192-4044-7(7)) Kessinger Publishing, LLC.

Lee, Helen. Guide's Greatest Escape from Crime Stories. 2003. (Pathfinder Junior Book Club Ser.). 141p. (J). pap. 10.99 (978-0-8280-1753-4(0), 79-967) Review & Herald Publishing Assn.

Lee, Janice G. The Adventures of Chewy & Tonk. 2003. (Illus.). 40p. (J). per. (978-1-55306-599-9(9), Guardian Bks.) Essence Publishing.

Lee, Jonathan. So I Could Fly Free. 2008. (ENG., Illus.). 32p. (J). (978-1-85345-434-9(6)) Crusade for World Revival.

Lee, Kathy. Hall of Mirrors. 2011. 144p. pap. (978-1-84427-506-9(X)) Scripture Union.

—No Means No. 2007. 143p. pap. (978-1-84427-253-2(2)) Scripture Union.

—River Rapids. 2011. 144p. pap. (978-1-84427-508-3(6)) Scripture Union.

—The Runaway Train. 2011. 144p. pap. (978-1-84427-505-2(1)) Scripture Union.

—Space Invaders. 2011. 144p. pap. (978-1-84427-507-6(8)) Scripture Union.

Lefeuvre, Amy. Probable Sons. 2004. reprint ed. pap. 15.95 (978-1-4191-4306-9(9)); pap. 1.99 (978-1-4192-4306-6(3)) Kessinger Publishing, LLC.

Leigh, Susan K. God I Need to Talk to you About Bedtime. 2011. 16p. pap. 1.19 (978-0-7586-2658-5(4)) Concordia Publishing Hse.

—God I Need to Talk to you About Homework. 2011. 16p. pap. 1.19 (978-0-7586-2657-8(6)) Concordia Publishing Hse.

—God I Need to Talk to you About Video Games. 2011. 16p. pap. 1.19 (978-0-7586-2659-2(2)) Concordia Publishing Hse.

—God I Need to Talt To you About Healthy Eating. 2011. 16p. pap. 1.19 (978-0-7586-2660-8(6)) Concordia Publishing Hse.

Lepp, Royden. Happy Birthday Barnabas, 1 vol. Lepp, Royden, illus. 2008. (I Can Read! / Barnabas Ser.). (ENG., Illus.). 32p. (J). (gr. -1-1). pap. 3.99 (978-0-310-71586-3(5)) Zonderkidz.

Leppard, Lois Gladys. The Mandie Collection. (ENG.). (J). (gr. 3-8). 2011. 368p. pap. 12.99 (978-0-7642-0932-1(9)) 2011. 384p. pap. 13.00 (978-0-7642-0878-2(0)) 2011. 368p. pap. 10.99 (978-0-7642-0689-4(3)) 2011. 368p. pap. 12.99 (978-0-7642-0877-5(2)) Vol. 1. 2007. 544p. pap. 15.99 (978-0-7642-0446-3(7)) Vol. 2. 2008. (Illus.). 576p. pap. 15.99 (978-0-7642-0538-5(2)) Bethany Hse. Pubs.

—Mandie Collection, Vol. 3. 2008. (ENG.). 608p. (J). pap. 15.99 (978-0-7642-0593-4(5)) Bethany Hse. Pubs.

—The Mysterious Teacher. 2003. 160p. (J). mass mkt. 4.99 (978-1-889893-98-3(6), Ambassador-Emerald, International) Emerald Hse. Group, Inc.

LeRoye, Dee. Crossfire. 2003. 137p. (YA). per. 5.99 (978-0-9727056-0-8(0)) Dakota Rose.

Leslie, Emma. For Merrie England: A Tale of the Weavers of Norfolk. Taylor, R., illus. 2010. 168p. 20.95 (978-1-934671-38-2(X)); pap. 10.95 (978-1-934671-39-9(8)) Salem Ridge Press LLC.

LeSourd, Nancy. Adventures in Jamestown, 1 vol. 2008. (Liberty Letters Ser.). (ENG.). 240p. (J). pap. 7.99 (978-0-310-71392-0(7)) Zonderkidz.

—Attack at Pearl Harbor, 1 vol. 2008. (Liberty Letters Ser.). (ENG.). 224p. (J). pap. 7.99 (978-0-310-71389-0(7)) Zonderkidz.

—Escape on the Underground Railroad, 1 vol. 2008. (Liberty Letters Ser.). (ENG.). 224p. (J). pap. 7.99 (978-0-310-71391-3(9)) Zonderkidz.

—Secrets of Civil War Spies, 1 vol. 2008. (Liberty Letters Ser.). (ENG.). 224p. (J). pap. 7.99 (978-0-310-71390-6(0)) Zonderkidz.

Lewin, Terry. God Remembered Us. Gumm, Susan Kathleen, illus. 2006. 36p. (J). per. 19.00 (978-0-9771482-1-9(1), Ithaca Pr.) Authors & Artists Publishers of New York, Inc.

Lewis, Beverly. Girls Only! 2008. (Girls Only (Go!) Ser.: Vols. 5-8). (ENG.). (J). (gr. 4-7). 510p. pap. 20.00 (978-0-7642-0462-3(9));Vols. 1-4. 512p. pap. 16.00 (978-0-7642-0461-6(0)) Bethany Hse. Pubs.

—In Jesse's Shoes: Appreciating Kids with Special Needs. Nikiel, Laura Gibbons, illus. 2007. (ENG.). 32p. (J). (gr. -1-4). 11.99 (978-0-7642-0313-8(4)) Bethany Hse. Pubs.

—SummerHill Secrets. 2007. (Summerhill Secrets Ser.: Vols. 1-5). (ENG.). Vol. 1. 560p. (gr. 6-9). pap. 17.00 (978-0-7642-0445-6(9)) Vol. 2. (Illus.). 544p. (gr. 11-12). pap. 17.00 (978-0-7642-0452-4(1)) Bethany Hse. Pubs.

Lewis, Beverly & Querin, Pamela. Annika's Secret Wish. 2006. (Illus.). 32p. (J). (gr. k-4). reprint ed. 15.00 (978-0-7567-9876-5(0)) DIANE Publishing Co.

Lewis, Kurt. The Improbable Barnsy & the Pocket Full of Teeth. 2009. 152p. pap. 12.96 (978-0-557-11956-1(1)) Lulu Pr., Inc.

Liebig, Nelda Johnson. Carrie & the Boarding House. 2005. 127p. (J). (gr. 3-7). 10.95 (978-1-883953-35-5(9)) Great Lakes Literary, LLC.

Lienas, Gemma. Callejon Slin Salida. 2003. (SPA.). 112p. (978-84-348-5285-3(3), SM7488) SM Ediciones ESP. Dist: Lectorum Pubns., Inc.

Lindquist, N. J. More Than a Friend. 2016. (Circle of Friends Ser.: Vol. 4). (ENG., Illus.). (YA). pap. **(978-1-927692-07-3(5))** That's Life! Communications.

—With Friends Like These. 2016. (Circle of Friends Ser.: Vol. 2). (ENG., Illus.). (YA). pap. **(978-1-927692-05-9(9))** That's Life! Communications.

Little Farm down the Lane, Bk. III. 2005. pap. 10.99 (978-1-59781-702-8(3)) Salem Author Services.

Little Lambs: Reproducible Student Materials. (Midweek Curriculum Ser.). 64p. (gr. -1-k). stu. ed. 17.95 (978-0-570-00791-3(7)) Concordia Publishing Hse.

Livingood, Allen. No Luck at All. 2012. 28p. pap. 19.99 (978-1-4772-5552-0(4)) AuthorHouse.

Llorente, Pilar Molina. Aura Gris. (SPA.). 192p. (YA). (gr. 5-8). (978-84-216-0993-4(9), BU3870) Bruño, Editorial ESP. Dist: Lectorum Pubns., Inc.

Loeffler, Sherry. The Guardian Angel. 2012. 70p. pap. 10.99 (978-1-62230-792-0(5)) Salem Author Services.

Loesch, Joe. Lions, Lions Everywhere: The Story of Daniel as told by God's Animals. Hutchinson, Cheryl, ed. Cox, Brain T., illus. 2004. (Bible Stories for Kids Ser.). 56p. (J). bds. 16.95 incl. audio compact disk (978-1-932332-24-7(3)) Toy Box Productions.

López, Diana. Ask My Mood Ring How I Feel. 2013. (ENG.). 336p. (J). (gr. 3-7). 17.00 (978-0-316-20996-0(1)) Little Brown & Co.

Lord, Jill Roman. If Jesus Walked Beside Me. Wummer, Amy, illus. 2014. (If Jesus Ser.). 22p. (J). bds. 6.99 (978-0-8249-1920-7(3), Ideal Pubns.) Worthy Publishing.

Lovett, Vienna. Mission from God. 2013. 256p. (978-1-77069-833-8(7)) Word Alive Pr.

Loyola, Mother Mary. The King of the Golden City: An Allegory for Children. Davis, John Watson, illus. 2nd ed. 2005. 128p. (J). per. (978-0-9764691-0-0(3)) Little Way Pr.

—The King of the Golden City Study Edition, an Allegory for Children. 2007. 180p. (J). per. 18.95 (978-1-934185-03-2(5)) Biblio Resource Pubns., Inc.

Lozano, Neal. Can God See Me in the Dark? Hatke, Ben, illus. 2007. (ENG.). 32p. (J). 16.95 (978-1-883551-45-2(5), Maple Corners Press) Attic Studio Publishing Hse.

Lucado, Max. Itsy Bitsy Christmas: You're Never Too Little for His Love, 1 vol. 2013. (ENG., Illus.). 32p. (J). 14.99 (978-1-4003-2262-6(6)) Nelson, Thomas Inc.

—Just in Case You Ever Wonder, 1 vol. 32p. 2011. (ENG.). (J). 16.99 (978-1-4003-1958-9(7)) 2009. (ENG.). (J). bds. 12.99 (978-1-4003-8531-7(8)) 2005. 9.99 (978-1-4003-0740-1(6)) Nelson, Thomas Inc.

—A Max Lucado Children's Treasury: A Child's First Collection, 1 vol. 2007. (ENG., Illus.). 144p. (gr. -1-3). 19.99 (978-1-4003-1048-7(2)) Nelson, Thomas Inc.

—The Oak Inside the Acorn, 1 vol. Angelini, George, illus. 2006. (ENG.). 48p. 16.99 (978-1-4003-0601-5(9)) Nelson, Thomas Inc.

—The Tallest of Smalls, 1 vol. Monescillo, Maria, illus. 2009. (ENG.). 32p. (gr. -1-2). 16.99 (978-1-4003-1514-7(X)) Nelson, Thomas Inc.

—Tell Me the Story: A Story for Eternity. DiCianni, Ron, illus. 2015. 48p. 19.99 (978-1-4335-4744-7(9)) Crossway.

—You Are Mine. Martinez, Sergio, illus. import ed. 2005. 28p. bds. (978-1-85985-546-1(6), Candle Bks.) Lion Hudson PLC.

—You Are Special. Martinez, Sergio, illus. rev. ed. 2007. 32p. (J). (gr. -1-3). 19.99 (978-1-58134-894-1(0)) Crossway.

Lucado, Max & Schmidt, Troy. Flo, the Lyin' Fly. 2005. 32p. (J). pap. 3.99 (978-1-4003-0664-0(7)) Nelson, Thomas Inc.

—Webster, the Scaredy Spider. 2005. 32p. (J). pap. 3.99 (978-1-4003-0665-7(5)) Nelson, Thomas Inc.

Luchsinger, Dena. Sometimes Smart Is Good/A Veces Es Bueno Ser Listo. Jerome, Karen A., illus. 2007. (SPA & ENG.). 32p. (J). (gr. -1). 16.00 (978-0-8028-5215-1(7), Eerdmans Bks For Young Readers) Eerdmans, William B. Publishing Co.

Lundy, Charlotte. Thank You, Ruth & Naomi. Waldrep, Evelyn L., ed. Sagasti, Miriam, illus. 2004. 32p. (J). (gr. k-4). 15.95 (978-0-9741817-0-7(6)) Bay Light Publishing.

Lynch, Diane M., ed. Family Ties: Thirteen Short Stories. 2010. 112p. (J). (gr. 4-7). pap. 7.95 (978-0-8198-2688-6(X)) Pauline Bks. & Media.

—Now You're Cooking! Ten Short Stories with Recipes. 2009. (J). (gr. 4-7). pap. 7.95 (978-0-8198-5167-3(1)) Pauline Bks. & Media.

MacDonald, George. The History of Gutta-Percha Willie. 2006. 116p. per. 9.95 (978-1-59818-578-2(0)) Aegypan.

—Ranald Bannermans Boyhood. 2006. 168p. per. 13.95 (978-1-59818-238-5(2)) Aegypan.

MacDonald, Mindy. My Bible Storybook. 2005. (GodCounts Ser.). (ENG., Illus.). 24p. (J). bds. 14.99 (978-1-59052-410-7(1), Multnomah Bks.) Crown Publishing Group.

Mackall, Dandi. The Super Gifts of Spring: Easter. 2015. (Seasons Ser.). (ENG., Illus.). 32p. (J). (gr. -1-3). 9.99 (978-1-4336-8233-9(8), B&H Kids) B&H Publishing Group.

Mackall, Dandi Daley. Bed Time Blessings. Kucharik, Elena, illus. 2012. (Little Blessings Ser.). (ENG.). 32p. (J). pap. 3.99 (978-1-4143-7528-1(X)) Tyndale Hse. Pubs.

—Bob's Great Escape, 1 vol. Wolf, Claudia, illus. 2011. (I Can Read! / a Horse Named Bob Ser.). (ENG.). 32p. (J). pap. 3.99 (978-0-310-71784-3(1)) Zonderkidz.

—Double Trouble, 1 vol. Wolf, Claudia, illus. 2011. (I Can Read! / a Horse Named Bob Ser.). (ENG.). 32p. (J). pap. 3.99 (978-0-310-71785-0(X)) Zonderkidz.

—A Horse Named Bob, 1 vol. Wolf, Claudia, illus. 2011. (I Can Read! / a Horse Named Bob Ser.). (ENG.). 32p. (J). pap. 3.99 (978-0-310-71782-9(5)) Zonderkidz.

—Horsefeathers Set, 8 vols. 2004. (YA). 44.99 (978-0-7586-0009-7(7)) Concordia Publishing Hse.

—The Legend of the Christmas Cookie, 1 vol. Cowdrey, Richard, illus. 2015. (ENG.). 32p. (J). 16.99 (978-0-310-74767-3(8)) Zonderkidz.

—The Legend of the Easter Robin: An Easter Story of Compassion & Faith, 1 vol. Cowdrey, Richard, illus. 2016. (ENG.). 30p. (J). 16.99 (978-0-310-74964-6(6)) Zonderkidz.

—Natalie: School's First Day of Me, 1 vol. Blakeslee, Lys, illus. 2009. (That's Nat! Ser.). (ENG.). 96p. (J). (gr. 1-4). pap. 4.99 (978-0-310-71568-9(7)) Zonderkidz.

—Natalie & the Bestest Friend Race, 1 vol. Blakeslee, Lys, illus. 2009. (That's Nat! Ser.). (ENG.). 96p. (J). (gr. 1-4). pap. 4.99 (978-0-310-71570-2(9)) Zonderkidz.

—Natalie & the Downside-Up Birthday, 1 vol. Blakeslee, Lys, illus. 2009. (That's Nat! Ser.). (ENG.). 96p. (J). (gr. 1-4). pap. 4.99 (978-0-310-71569-6(5)) Zonderkidz.

—Natalie & the One-of-a-Kind Wonderful Day!, 1 vol. Blakeslee, Lys, illus. 2009. (That's Nat! Ser.). (ENG.). 96p. (J). (gr. 1-4). pap. 4.99 (978-0-310-71566-5(0)) Zonderkidz.

—Natalie Really Very Much Wants to Be a Star, 1 vol. Blakeslee, Lys, illus. 2009. (That's Nat! Ser.). (ENG.). 96p. (J). (gr. 1-4). pap. 4.99 (978-0-310-71567-2(9)) Zonderkidz.

—Natalie Wants a Puppy, 1 vol. Blakeslee, Lys, illus. 2009. (That's Nat! Ser.). (ENG.). 96p. (J). (gr. 1-4). pap. 4.99 (978-0-310-71571-9(7)) Zonderkidz.

—A Perfect Pony, 1 vol. Wolf, Claudia, illus. 2011. (I Can Read! / a Horse Named Bob Ser.). (ENG.). 32p. (J). pap. 3.99 (978-0-310-71783-6(3)) Zonderkidz.

—Wild Cat. 2009. (Starlight Animal Rescue Ser.: 3). (ENG.). 224p. (J). (gr. 3-7). mass mkt. 5.99 (978-1-4143-1270-5(9), Tyndale Kids) Tyndale Hse. Pubs.

MacKenzie, Carine. How God Changes People: Conversion Stories from the Bible. 2012. (ENG., Illus.). 48p. (J). 9.99 (978-1-84550-822-7(X), e5e27b55-010c-4952-912d-4d962f516ac6) Christian Focus Pubns. GBR. Dist: Bookmasters Distribution.

MacKenzie, Catherine. Can You Imagine? 2013. (Little Lights Ser.). (ENG., Illus.). 24p. (J). 7.99 (978-1-78191-160-0(6), ca87b05f-1a2a-4100-ae57-2c04da6e7366) Christian Focus Pubns. GBR. Dist: Bookmasters Distribution.

—Gladys Aylward - Are You Going to Stop? 2013. (Little Lights Ser.). (ENG., Illus.). 24p. (J). 7.99 (978-1-78191-161-7(4), cfd6d604-97c6-4c41-889d-ab61929b782a) Christian Focus Pubns. GBR. Dist: Bookmasters Distribution.

Mackenzie, Catherine. I Can Say to God, I Love You. 2015. (Prayer (Board Books) Ser.). (ENG.). 10p. (J). bds. 3.99 (978-1-85792-692-7(7), b33d3726-4773-4ba6-8bac-974fdb2c47bd, Christian Focus) Christian Focus Pubns. GBR. Dist: Bookmasters Distribution.

MacKenzie, Catherine. I Can Say to God, I'm Sorry. 2015. (Prayer (Board Books) Ser.). (ENG.). 10p. (J). bds. 3.99 (978-1-85792-689-7(7), 4f5bf5e9-4426-4b31-bdc1-efb7d3818f6e) Christian Focus Pubns. GBR. Dist: Bookmasters Distribution.

—I Can Say to God, Thank You. 2015. (Prayer (Board Books) Ser.). (ENG.). 10p. (J). bds. 3.99 (978-1-85792-690-3(0), 3006ad76-458b-436e-875f-40775921841e, Christian Focus) Christian Focus Pubns. GBR. Dist: Bookmasters Distribution.

Magaro, Dan. The Adventures of Fred & Daisymae. 2010. 48p. pap. 10.99 (978-1-60957-407-9(9)) Salem Author Services.

Magness, Robert. Silent Knife, Holy Knife. Glon, Nancy, illus. 2003. 345p. 10.00 (978-0-9774577-0-0(2)) Magness, Robert Pubns., LLC.

Maines, David. Tales of the Resistance. 2004. 20.00 (978-1-58474-053-7(1)) Cornerstone Family Ministries/Lamplighter Publishing.

Malison, Anna. Through Thick & Thin. 2006. (ENG.). 136p. per. (978-1-897117-14-9(0)) Gospel Folio Pr.

Mancil, Julie A. Anna's Decision. 2011. 68p. (gr. 4-6). pap. 9.95 (978-1-4497-1694-3(6), WestBow Pr.) Author Solutions, Inc.

Mangum, Kay Lynn. When the Bough Breaks. 2007. 352p. (YA). pap. 15.95 (978-1-59038-748-1(1)) Deseret Bk. Co.

Marcos, Teri. Bethlehem's Gift. 2013. 24p. pap. 12.45 (978-1-4908-0901-4(5), WestBow Pr.) Author Solutions, Inc.

Margallo, Ramon. The MANGER, the CROSS, & the EMPTY TOMB Christian Apologetics for Young Readers: A Short Story. 2006. 108p. pap. 9.99 (978-1-4116-5751-9(9)) Lulu Pr., Inc.

Marie, Cynthia. Sister Aggie Goes Surfing. 2012. 50p. pap. 20.95 (978-1-4497-5404-4(X), WestBow Pr.) Author Solutions, Inc.

Marlow, Susan K. Andrea Carter & the Dangerous Decision, 1 vol. 2007. (Circle C Adventures Ser.). 144p. (J). pap. 7.99 (978-0-8254-3357-3(6)) Kregel Pubns.

—Andrea Carter & the Family Secret, 1 vol. 2008. (Circle C Adventures Ser.). 144p. (J). pap. 7.99 (978-0-8254-3365-8(7)) Kregel Pubns.

—Andrea Carter & the Price of Truth, 1 vol. 2017. (Circle C Adventures Ser.: 6). 144p. (J). pap. 8.99 **(978-0-8254-4505-7(1))** Kregel Pubns.

—Andrea Carter & the San Francisco Smugglers: A Novel, 1 vol. 2008. (Circle C Adventures Ser.). 144p. (J). pap. 7.99 (978-0-8254-3446-4(7)) Kregel Pubns.

—Andrea Carter's Tales from the Circle C Ranch, 1 vol. 2015. (Illus.). 160p. (J). pap. 7.99 (978-0-8254-4379-4(2)) Kregel Pubns.

—The Last Ride: An Andrea Carter Book, 1 vol. 2016. (Circle C Milestones Ser.: 3). 176p. (YA). pap. 9.99 (978-0-8254-4369-5(5)) Kregel Pubns.

—Thick As Thieves: An Andrea Carter Book, 1 vol. 2015. (Circle C Milestones Ser.: 1). 176p. (YA). pap. 9.99 (978-0-8254-4367-1(9)) Kregel Pubns.

Marston, Hope Irvin. Against the Tide: The Valor of Margaret Wilson. 2007. (Chosen Daughters Ser.). 219p. (J). (gr. 3-7). per. 11.99 (978-1-59638-061-5(6)) P & R Publishing.

Martin, Elaine S. Bowman. The Rooster's Fate: And Other Stories. Hackman, Evelyn, illus. 2014. 184p. (J). (978-0-7399-2481-5(8)) Rod & Staff Pubs., Inc.

Martin, Joan Watson. Inventing Chloe. 2008. 140p. 19.95 (978-1-934335-25-3(8)); pap. 9.95 (978-1-934335-24-6(X)) WordWright.biz, Inc. (One Night Bks.).

Martin, LaJoyce. The Silver Ghost. 2004. (Illus.). 161p. (J). pap. 9.99 (978-1-56722-643-0(4)) Word Aflame Pr.

Martin, Mildred A. Growing with the Millers. Burkholder, Edith, illus. 2012. 144p. (J). (978-1-884377-23-5(8)) Green Pastures Pr.

Martin, Rachael Lynn. McKenzie Drew: Adventures with David. 2008. 56p. pap. 16.95 (978-1-60610-389-0(X)) America Star Bks.

Martin, Rebecca. Blossoms on the Roof. 2015. (Amish Frontier Ser.). (ENG.). 160p. (J). (gr. 2-7). pap. 8.99 (978-0-7369-6367-1(7)) Harvest Hse. Pubs.

—The Treasure Hunt. 2015. (Amish Frontier Ser.). (ENG., Illus.). 160p. (J). (gr. 2-7). pap. 8.99 (978-0-7369-6369-5(3)) Harvest Hse. Pubs.

Martini, T. J. Christmas Lost & Found. Kiejna, Magdalenea, illus. 2017. (J). per. 15.99 (978-0-9705018-7-5(0)) Wings, Inc.

Martinusen-Coloma, Cindy. Ruby Unscripted, 1 vol. 2009. (ENG.). 272p. (YA). (gr. 7-18). pap. 12.99 (978-1-59554-356-1(2)) Nelson, Thomas Inc.

Maselli, Christopher P. N. Attack of the Tremendous Truth! 12 Mystery Stories to Solve Using the Teachings of Jesus. 2006. (Sleuth-It-Yourself Mysteries Ser.). (ENG., Illus.). 48p. (gr. 3-6). per. 9.99 (978-1-59441-385-8(1)) Carson-Dellosa Publishing, LLC.

—The Runaway Mission. 2004. 104p. 5.99 (978-1-57562-805-9(8)) Copeland, Kenneth Pubns.

Maselli, Christopher P. N. & Hoose, Bob. Jones & Parker Case Files. 2015. (Adventures in Odyssey Bks.). (ENG., Illus.). 128p. (J). pap. 9.99 (978-1-58997-806-5(4)) Focus on the Family Publishing.

Maslyn, Stacie K. B. & Maslyn, Stacie K. Mad Maddie Maxwell, 1 vol. Schettle, Jane, illus. 2007. (I Can Read! Ser.). (ENG.). 32p. (J). (gr. -1-1). pap. 3.99 (978-0-310-71467-5(2)) Zonderkidz.

Massachusetts Sabbath School Society Staff. Winnie Malone Written for the Mass S S Society, & Approved by the Committee of Publication. 2006. 144p. per. 18.99 (978-1-4255-1163-0(5)) Michigan Publishing.

Massop, Kimberley. Noah's Birds. Pereira, Kristin L., illus. 2017. (ENG.). 36p. (J). pap. 8.95 (978-1-68350-025-4(3)) Morgan James Publishing.

Mathieu, Jennifer. Devoted. 2015. (ENG.). 336p. (YA). (gr. 7). 16.99 (978-1-59643-911-5(4), 9781596439115) Roaring Brook Pr.

Mattucci, Sandra. Levi the Lightning Bug's Amazing Discovery. Mattucci, Sandra, illus. 2012. (Illus.). 36p. 19.99 (978-1-936453-08-5(8)) Bezalel Bks.

May, E. J. Louis' School Days: A Story for Boys. 2007. (ENG.). 242p. pap. 20.99 (978-1-4346-4563-0(0)); 274p. pap. 23.99 (978-1-4346-4564-7(9)) Creative Media Partners, LLC.

Mayer, Mercer. It's True, 1 vol. 2013. (ENG.). 24p. (J). pap. 3.99 (978-1-4003-2247-3(2)) Nelson, Thomas Inc.

—It's True!, 1 vol. 2013. (ENG., Illus.). 24p. (J). bds. 9.99 (978-1-4003-2246-6(4)) Nelson, Thomas Inc.

—Little Critters, 1 vol. 2014. (ENG., Illus.). 24p. (J). bds. 9.99 (978-1-4003-2250-3(2)) Nelson, Thomas Inc.

McCaughrean, Geraldine. Pilgrim's Progress. Cockcroft, Jason, illus. 112p. (J). pap. 16.99 (978-0-340-72754-6(3)) Hodder & Stoughton GBR. Dist: Trafalgar Square Publishing.

McClain, Jennie. Monday I Was a Monkey: A "Tale" of Reverence. Eichelberger, Jennifer, illus. 2011. (J). (978-1-60861-243-7(0)) Covenant Communications.

McCollon, Donell. When Fear Knocks at the Door. 2009. 28p. pap. 20.49 (978-1-4490-0226-8(9)) AuthorHouse.

McCorkle, Brent & Parker, Amy. Firebird: He Lived for the Sunshine. Corley, Rob & Vollmer, Chuck, illus. 2017. (ENG.). 32p. (J). (gr. -1-1). pap. 3.99 **(978-1-4627-4518-0(0)**, B&H Kids) B&H Publishing Group.

McCurry, Kristen & Hilton, Jennifer. Good Morning, World. Rimmington, Natasha, illus. 2017. (J). 6.99 **(978-1-5064-1785-1(X)**, Sparkhouse Family) Augsburg Fortress, Pubs.

McCusker, Paul. Danger Lies Ahead! 2006. (Adventures in Odyssey Bks.: No. 2). (ENG.). 336p. (J). (gr. 8-12). per. 15.99 (978-1-58997-329-9(1)) Tyndale Hse. Pubs.

—Memory's Gate, 1 vol. 2009. (Time Thriller Trilogy Ser.: Bk. 3). (ENG.). 208p. (YA). (gr. 8-11). pap. 9.99 (978-0-310-71438-5(9)) Zondervan.

—Out of Time, 1 vol. 2009. (Time Thriller Trilogy Ser.: Bk. 2). (ENG., Illus.). 240p. (YA). (gr. 8-11). pap. 9.99 (978-0-310-71437-8(0)) Zondervan.

—Point of No Return. 2006. (Adventures in Odyssey Bks.). (ENG.). 336p. (J). (gr. 3-7). per. 15.99 (978-1-58997-332-9(1)) Tyndale Hse. Pubs.

McDaniel, Lurlene. Raina's Story. 2006. (Angels in Pink Ser.). (ENG.). 208p. (YA). (gr. 7-12). mass mkt. 6.99 (978-0-440-23866-9(8), Laurel Leaf) Random Hse. Children's Bks.

McDowell, Josh & Hostetler, Bob. The Truth Twisters. 2006. (Illus.). 167p. (YA). (gr. 8-12). per. 11.99 (978-1-932587-84-5(5)) Practical Christianity Foundation.

McGee, Krista. Revolutionary, 1 vol. 2014. (Anomaly Ser.: 3). (ENG.). 320p. (YA). pap. 9.99 (978-1-4016-8876-9(4)) Nelson, Thomas Inc.

McGill, Debora J. Faith Journeys with Hope & Love: Short Stories of Inspiration. 2011. 114p. pap. 19.99 (978-1-4415-4203-8(5)) Xlibris Corp.

McKnight, Penny. Nix. 2006. (Illus.). 84p. (J). (gr. 3-7). per. 8.99 (978-1-59166-610-3(4)) BJU Pr.

McNicholas, Anne. The Sequel of Thank You Jesus. 2013. 304p. pap. 19.95 (978-1-4817-1022-0(2)) AuthorHouse.

McVoy, Terra Elan. Pure. (ENG.). (YA). 2010. 352p. (gr. 7). pap. 9.99 (978-1-4169-6748-4(6)) 2009. 336p. (gr. 9-18). 16.99 (978-1-4169-7872-5(0)) Simon Pulse. (Simon Pulse).

Meade, L. T. The Children's Pilgrimage. 2007. (ENG.). 254p. pap. 21.99 (978-1-4346-4863-1(X)); 280p. pap. 23.99 (978-1-4346-4864-8(8)) Creative Media Partners, LLC.

—Sue A Little Heroine. 2007. (ENG.). 222p. pap. 20.99 (978-1-4346-3546-4(5)); 244p. pap. 22.99 (978-1-4346-3547-1(3)) Creative Media Partners, LLC.

Meade, Starr, et al. Keeping Holiday. Gerard, Justin, illus. 2008. 192p. (gr. k). pap. 14.99 (978-1-4335-0142-5(2)) Crossway.

Merkel, Ruth Vitrano. Ann: 1833-1897. 2006. (Hannah's Girls Ser.). (Illus.). 112p. (J). (gr. 4-7). per. 9.99 (978-0-8280-1951-4(7)) Review & Herald Publishing Assn.

—Grace: 1890-1973, 6. 2006. (Hannah's Girls Ser.). (Illus.). 128p. (J). (gr. 4-7). per. 9.99 (978-0-8280-1953-8(3)) Review & Herald Publishing Assn.

—Hannah's Girls: Elaine. 2008. (Hannah's Girls Ser.: 5). (Illus.). 176p. (J). pap. 9.99 (978-0-8280-1955-2(X)) Review & Herald Publishing Assn.

—Hannah's Girls: Erin (Born 1988) 2009. (J). 9.99 (978-0-8280-1956-9(8)) Review & Herald Publishing Assn.

—Marilla 1851-1916, 6 bks. 2006. (Hannah's Girls Ser.). (Illus.). 144p. (J). (gr. 4-7). per. 9.99 (978-0-8280-1952-1(5)) Review & Herald Publishing Assn.

—Ruthie: Born 1931. 2007. (Hannah's Girls Ser.). (Illus.). 144p. (J). (gr. 4-7). per. 9.99 (978-0-8280-1954-5(1)) Review & Herald Publishing Assn.

Metallinos, Sophia. The Heavenly Place. l.t. ed. 2016. (ENG., Illus.). (J). pap. 9.99 **(978-1-58169-640-0(X)**, Axiom Pr.) Genesis Communications, Inc.

Metlen, Ryan W. & Metlen, Ryan. Ewe. 2009. (J). (978-1-58768-054-0(8), HiddenSpring) Paulist Pr.

Meyer, Jane G. The Man & the Vine. Gannon, Ned, illus. 2006. (ENG.). 32p. (J). 18.00 (978-0-88141-315-1(1)) St. Vladimir's Seminary Pr.

—The Suitcase: A Story to Learn How to Give. Pasqualotto, Chiara, illus. 2017. (ENG.). (J). (gr. -1). pap. 16.99 (978-1-61261-776-3(X)) Paraclete Pr., Inc.

Meyer, Jane G. & Gannon, Ned. The Woman & the Wheat. Meyer, Jane G. & Gannon, Ned, illus. 2009. (Illus.). 32p. (J). 18.00 (978-0-88141-059-4(4)) St. Vladimir's Seminary Pr.

Meyer, Karen. Conflict at Chillicothe. 2010. (ENG.). 132p. (J). pap. 9.99 (978-0-9766823-2-5(X)) Sable Creek Pr. LLC.

Michel, Becky. Miles of Smiles. 2013. 32p. pap. 13.99 (978-1-4908-0235-0(5), WestBow Pr.) Author Solutions, Inc.

Miller, David. Heat 16. 2003. 110p. (YA). pap. 9.95 (978-0-595-27424-6(2), Writers Club Pr.) iUniverse, Inc.

Miller, Gary & Miller, Lynda. The Adventures of Bob & Betty. 2006. (J). spiral bd. (978-1-933594-92-7(6)) FBC Pubns. & Printing.

Miller, Paula. One-Eyed Jack. Forrest, Chris, illus. (J). 2007. (ENG.). 133p. (gr. 2-7). pap. 8.95 (978-0-9769417-0-5(8)) 2006. 144p. 13.95 (978-0-9718348-8-0(1)) Blooming Tree Pr.

Millett, Melanie. CTR Boy. 2006. (Illus.). (J). (978-1-59811-062-3(4)) Covenant Communications.

Mills, Charles. The Bandit of Benson Park. 2003. (Honors Club Story Ser.: Vol. 1). 127p. (J). (978-0-8163-1977-0(4)) Pacific Pr. Pubns.

—The Great Sleepy-Time Stew Rescue. 2004. (Honors Club Story Ser.: Vol. 4). (Illus.). 127p. (J). 7.99 (978-0-8163-2009-7(8)) Pacific Pr. Publishing Assn.

—The Secret of Scarlett Cove. 2004. (Honors Club Story Ser.: Bk. 3). 127p. (J). 7.99 (978-0-8163-1999-2(5)) Pacific Pr. Publishing Assn.

—Storm on Shadow Mountain. 2003. 127p. (J). 7.99 (978-0-8163-1993-0(6)) Pacific Pr. Publishing Assn.

—Wings over Oshkosh. 2005. (Honors Club Story Ser.: Vol. 5). 127p. (J). 7.99 (978-0-8163-2089-9(6)) Pacific Pr. Publishing Assn.

Mishica, Claire. Superstar Charlie. 2014. (Happy Day Ser.). (ENG.). 16p. (J). pap. 2.49 (978-1-4143-9518-0(3)) Tyndale Hse. Pubs.

Mitchell, Racquel L. Penny Pincher Teaches: Tithing. 2011. 24p. pap. 16.99 (978-1-4670-2472-3(4)) AuthorHouse.

Mongtomery Gibson, Jane. Don't Renege! It's Just an Egg! Mongtomery Gibson, Jane, illus. 2005. (Illus.). (J). bds. 8.99 (978-1-4183-0036-4(5)) Christ Inspired, Inc.

—Jesus' Bread. Mongtomery Gibson, Jane, illus. 2005. (Illus.). (J). bds. 8.99 (978-1-4183-0028-9(4)) Christ Inspired, Inc.

Montgomery Gibson, Jane. Claire, Claire! Wash Your Hair! Montgomery Gibson, Jane, illus. 2005. (Illus.). (J). bds. 8.99 (978-1-4183-0044-9(6)) Christ Inspired, Inc.

—Gracie Got Glasses. Montgomery Gibson, Jane, illus. 2005. (Illus.). (J). bds. 8.99 (978-1-4183-0039-5(X)) Christ Inspired, Inc.

—How Do You Clean a Ballerina? Montgomery Gibson, Jane, illus. 2005. (Illus.). (J). bds. 8.99 (978-1-4183-0020-3(9)) Christ Inspired, Inc.

—Jesus Smith or Jones. Montgomery Gibson, Jane, illus. 2005. (Illus.). (YA). bds. 8.99 (978-1-4183-0031-9(4)) Christ Inspired, Inc.

—Mabel at the Table. Montgomery Gibson, Jane, illus. 2005. (Illus.). (J). bds. 8.99 (978-1-4183-0041-8(1)) Christ Inspired, Inc.

—Maggie Makeup. Montgomery Gibson, Jane, illus. 2005. (Illus.). (J). bds. 9.99 (978-1-4183-0030-2(6)) Christ Inspired, Inc.

—Pink Potatoes. Montgomery Gibson, Jane, illus. 2005. (Illus.). (J). bds. 8.99 (978-1-4183-0038-8(1)) Christ Inspired, Inc.

—Sit down, Clown! Montgomery Gibson, Jane, illus. 2005. (Illus.). (J). bds. 8.99 (978-1-4183-0040-1(3)) Christ Inspired, Inc.

Moore, Beth. My Child, My Princess: A Parable about the King. Warren, Beverly, illus. 2014. (ENG.). 32p. (J). (gr. -1-3). 9.99 (978-1-4336-8468-5(3), B&H Kids) B&H Publishing Group.

Moore, Karen. Everybody Counts. Reed, Lisa, illus. 2012. (Roma Downey's Little Angels Ser.). 24p. (J). bds. 7.99 (978-0-8249-5643-1(5), Ideal Pubns.) Worthy Publishing.

Moore, Ruth Nulton. The Christmas Surprise. Eitzen, Allan, illus. 2007. 160p. (gr. 4-7). pap. 20.00 (978-1-55635-418-2(5), Resource Pubns.(OR)) Wipf & Stock Pubs.

Moore, Stephanie Perry. Absolutely Worthy, Vol. 4. 2003. (Laurel Shadrach Ser.: 4). (ENG.). 192p. (YA). (gr. 8). pap. 7.99 (978-0-8024-4038-9(X)) Moody Pubs.

—Enjoying True Peace, 1 vol. 2010. (Yasmin Peace Ser.: 5). (ENG.). 176p. pap. 6.99 (978-0-8024-8606-6(1), Lift Every Voice) Moody Pubs.

—Equally Yoked, Vol. 3. 2003. (Laurel Shadrach Ser.: 3). (ENG.). 192p. (YA). (gr. 8). pap. 7.99 (978-0-8024-4037-2(1)) Moody Pubs.

—Experiencing the Joy, 1 vol. 2009. (Yasmin Peace Ser.: 3). (ENG.). 160p. (gr. 7-10). pap. 7.99 (978-0-8024-8604-2(5), Lift Every Voice) Moody Pubs.

—Finally Sure, Vol. 5. 2004. (Laurel Shadrach Ser.: 5). (ENG.). 176p. (YA). (gr. 8). pap. 7.99 (978-0-8024-4039-6(8)) Moody Pubs.

—Happy Princess. 2007. (Carmen Browne Ser.: 5). (ENG.). 128p. (gr. 4-7). per. 6.99 (978-0-8024-8171-9(X), Lift Every Voice) Moody Pubs.

—Perfect Joy. 2006. (Carmen Browne Ser.: 4). (ENG.). 112p. (gr. 4-7). per. 6.99 (978-0-8024-8170-2(1), Lift Every Voice) Moody Pubs.

—Prayed Up, 4 vols. 2008. (ENG., Illus.). 208p. (YA). (gr. 8-12). 15.00 (978-0-7582-2538-2(5), K-Teen/Dafina) Kensington Publishing Corp.

—True Friends. 2005. (Carmen Browne Ser.: 1). (ENG.). 128p. (YA). pap. 6.99 (978-0-8024-8172-6(8), Lift Every Voice) Moody Pubs.

—Turn up for Real. 2014. (Sharp Sisters Ser.: 3). (ENG.). 168p. (YA). (gr. 6-12). pap. 7.95 (978-1-4677-4490-4(5), Darby Creek); lib. bdg. 27.93 (978-1-4677-3726-5(7)) Lerner Publishing Group.

Moore, Stephanie Perry & Moody Publishing Staff. Believing in Hope. 2009. (Yasmin Peace Ser.: 2). (ENG.). 176p. (gr. 7-10). pap. 7.99 (978-0-8024-8603-5(7), Lift Every Voice) Moody Pubs.

—Finding Your Faith 2009. (Yasmin Peace Ser.: 1). (ENG.). 176p. (gr. 7-10). pap. 7.99 (978-0-8024-8602-8(9), Lift Every Voice) Moody Pubs.

Moores, Katie. The Land of Havala. Foote, Dan, illus. 2006. (ENG.). 64p. pap. 6.99 (978-1-59185-910-9(7), Creation Hse.) Charisma Media.

Morrison, Daequan T. What's the Spook? 2011. 28p. pap. 18.62 (978-1-4670-3887-4(3)) AuthorHouse.

Moses, Tammy. The Prophecy. 2006. 288p. per. 19.99 (978-1-58169-194-8(7)) Genesis Communications, Inc.

Mosher, Nancy & Turney, Maria. Fancy's Playground. 2010. 24p. 14.93 (978-1-4269-3613-5(3)) Trafford Publishing.

Mullican, Norma Waldon & Zivney, Missy Mullican. A Collection of Squirrel Tales: Something to Crow About. 2009. 84p. pap. 10.99 (978-1-60791-702-1(5)) Salem Author Services.

Murphy, Elspeth Campbell. God Makes It Right: Three Stories for Children Based on Favorite Bible Verses. Nelson, Jane E., illus. 72p. (J). (978-1-55513-109-8(3)) Cook, David C.

Murray, Mary. Larry Lights the Way, 1 vol. 2003. (Big Idea Books / VeggieTales Ser.). (ENG., Illus.). 40p. 9.99 (978-0-310-70674-8(2)) Zonderkidz.

Muschla, Gary Robert. Crusader. 2006. (YA). pap. (978-0-88092-491-7(8)) Royal Fireworks Publishing Co.

—The Sword & the Cross. 2009. (YA). lib. bdg. (978-0-88092-471-9(3)) Royal Fireworks Publishing Co.

Myers, Bill. Baseball for Breakfast: The Story of a Boy Who Hated to Wait. Riccio, Frank, illus. 2005. 29p. (J). (gr. 4-8). reprint ed. 15.00 (978-0-7567-9248-0(7)) DIANE Publishing Co.

—The Chamber of Lies, 1 vol. 2009. (Elijah Project Ser.). (ENG.). 128p. (J). (gr. 4-7). pap. 6.99 (978-0-310-71196-4(7)) Zonderkidz.

—The Enemy Closes In, 1 vol. 2009. (Elijah Project Ser.). (ENG.). 128p. (J). (gr. 4-7). pap. 6.99 (978-0-310-71194-0(0)) Zonderkidz.

—Invisible Terror Collection, 1 vol., Vol. 2. 2011. (Forbidden Doors Ser.). (ENG.). 368p. (YA). pap. 12.99 (978-0-310-72904-4(1)) Zondervan.

—My Life as a Haunted Hamburger, Hold the Pickles, 1 vol. 2006. (Incredible Worlds of Wally Mcdoogle Ser.: 27). (ENG., Illus.). 128p. (gr. 3-7). per. 6.99 (978-1-4003-0636-7(1)) Nelson, Thomas Inc.

—My Life as a Stupendously Stomped Soccer Star, 1 vol. 2006. (Incredible Worlds of Wally Mcdoogle Ser.: 26). (ENG.). 128p. (gr. 3-7). per. 6.99 (978-1-4003-0635-0(3)) Nelson, Thomas Inc.

—My Life as a Supersized Superhero... with Slobber, 1 vol. 2007. (Incredible Worlds of Wally Mcdoogle Ser.: 28). (ENG.). 128p. (gr. 3-7). per. 6.99 (978-1-4003-0637-4(X)) Nelson, Thomas Inc.

Myers, Bill & Riordan, James. On the Run, 1 vol. 2009. (Elijah Project Ser.). (ENG.). 128p. (J). (gr. 4-7). pap. 4.99 (978-0-310-71193-3(2)) Zonderkidz.

Myers, Bob. Trinity Goes to Soccer Camp. Bunker, Tom, illus. 2012. 36p. 24.95 (978-1-4560-2906-7(1)) America Star Bks.

Myers, Laurie. Escape by Night: A Civil War Adventure. Bates, Amy June, illus. 2011. (ENG.). 128p. (J). (gr. 3-7). 14.99 (978-0-8050-8825-0(3), 9780805088250, Holt, Henry & Co. Bks. For Young Readers) Holt, Henry & Co.

Myers, Martha. Nibbles, the Mostly Mischievous Monkey. 2003. (Julius & Friends Ser.: Vol. 10). (Illus.). 91p. (J). 6.99 (978-0-8163-1947-3(2)) Pacific Pr. Publishing Assn.

The Mystery of the Tiny Key. 2008. 32p. pap. 4.99 (978-0-8341-2351-9(7), 083-412-3517) Beacon Hill Pr. of Kansas City.

Naas, Katy Newton. Missing Max. 2017. (ENG.). 36p. (J). pap. 8.99 (978-1-68350-088-9(1)) Morgan James Publishing.

Naphot, John A. God Culture for Kids: Why Do People Die. 2015. (ENG., Illus.). 32p. (J). pap. 8.99 (978-1-63047-264-1(6)) Morgan James Publishing.

Narváez, Concha López. Endrina y el Secreto del Peregrino. (SPA.). 280p. (YA). (gr. 5-8). 7.60 (978-84-239-2785-2(7)); 16th ed. 2003. (Illus.). 206p. pap. (978-84-239-5899-3(X)) Espasa Calpe, S.A. ESP. Dist: Lectorum Pubns., Inc.

Nelson, Kadir. He's Got the Whole World in His Hands. Nelson, Kadir, illus. 2005. (ENG., Illus.). 32p. (J). (gr. -1-3). 17.99 (978-0-8037-2850-9(6), Dial Bks) Penguin Young Readers Group.

Nelson, Wendy Watson. The Not Even Once Club: My Promise to Heavenly Father. Dorman, Brandon, illus. 2013. 18.99 (978-1-60907-337-4(1)) Deseret Bk. Co.

Newbigin, Lesslie. Unfinished Agenda. 2012. (ENG.). 144p. (gr. k-5). pap. 15.00 (978-0-7152-0687-4(7)) Saint Andrew Pr., Ltd. GBR. Dist: Westminster John Knox Pr.

Newby-Tynes, Claudia. His Love Flows. 2012. 28p. pap. 24.95 (978-1-4626-8270-6(7)) America Star Bks.

Nobisso, Josephine. El Peso de Una Misa: Un Relato de fe. Szegedi, Katalin, illus. 2003. Orig. Title: The Weight of a Mass a Tale of Faith. (SPA.). 32p. (J). (gr. k-2). pap. 9.95 (978-0-940112-17-9(5)) Gingerbread Hse.

—El Peso de Una Misa: Un Relato de Fe. Szegedi, Katalin, illus. 2003. Orig. Title: The Weight of a Mass a Tale of Faith. (SPA.). 32p. (J). (gr. k-2). 17.95 (978-0-940112-15-5(9)) Gingerbread Hse.

—Take It to the Queen. 2009. 32p. 17.95 (978-0-8146-3288-8(2), Liturgical Pr. Bks.) Liturgical Pr.

—Take It to the Queen: A Tale of Hope. Szegedi, Katalin, illus. 2008. (ENG.). 32p. (J). (gr. k-2). 17.95 (978-0-940112-19-3(1)); pap. 9.95 (978-0-940112-21-6(3)) Gingerbread Hse.

Nolan, Allia Zobel. Fair & Squaresville: A Lesson in Playing Fair. Carter, Tod et al, illus. 2014. (VeggieTales (Big Idea) Ser.). (ENG.). 28p. (J). (gr. -1-3). pap. 6.99 incl. audio compact disk (978-1-61795-333-0(4)) Worthy Publishing.

Nolan, Han. If I Should Die Before I Wake. 2003. (ENG.). 320p. (YA). (gr. 7-12). pap. 9.99 *(978-0-15-204679-8(8))* Houghton Mifflin Harcourt Publishing Co.

—Send Me down a Miracle. 2003. (ENG.). 276p. (YA). (gr. 7-12). pap. 15.95 *(978-0-15-204680-4(1))* Houghton Mifflin Harcourt Publishing Co.

—When We Were Saints. 2005. (ENG.). 312p. (YA). (gr. 7-12). pap. 15.95 *(978-0-15-205322-2(0))* Houghton Mifflin Harcourt Publishing Co.

Norman, Thelma G. A Wife Called Tommie. 2005. 226p. per. 14.95 *(978-1-57258-295-8(2))* TEACH Services, Inc.

Ntihemuka, Patty Froese. Hyacinth Doesn't Go to Jail: And, Hyacinth Doesn't Miss Christmas. 2009. (J). pap. 10.99 *(978-0-8163-2372-2(0))* Pacific Pr. Publishing Assn.

—Hyacinth Doesn't Grow Up: And Hyacinth Doesn't Drown. 2010. (J). pap. 10.99 *(978-0-8163-2386-9(0))* Pacific Pr. Publishing Assn.

Nye, Julie & Nye, Julie. Scout: The Secret at les Cheneaux. 2007. (Illus.). 160p. (YA). per. *(978-0-9767762-1-5(9))* Fieldstone Hill Pr.

Nystrom, Carolyn, et al. The 5 Languages of Appreciation in the Workplace: Empowering Organizations by Encouraging People, 4 bks. Walles, Dwight, illus. 2012. (ENG.). 224p. (gr. -1-2). pap. 16.99 *(978-0-8024-6176-6(X))* Northfield Publishing.

Nyznyk, Darryl. Mary's Son: A Tale of Christmas. 2010. (ENG., Illus.). 176p. 15.95 *(978-0-9656513-5-6(5))* Cross Dove Publishing, LLC.

O'Day, Joseph E. I Like Sunshine! Foster, Ron, illus. 2007. (J). *(978-1-929039-41-8(7))* Ambassador Bks., Inc.

O'Donnell, Candy. Where Is God, Grandfather. Gillen, Rosemarie, illus. 2008. 28p. pap. 12.95 *(978-0-9814532-1-7(X))* Living Waters Publishing Co.

O'Hearn, Audrey. Me & Luke, 1 vol. 2005. (ENG.). 148p. (J). pap. 6.95 *(978-0-88899-066-2(9))* Groundwood Bks. CAN. Dist: Publishers Group West (PGW).

Oirich, Alan. The Amnesia Countdown. Randall, Ron, illus. 2003. (Jewish Hero Corps. Ser.: 1). 24p. (J). pap. 3.95 *(978-1-932443-06-6(1)*, JHC1, Shayach Comics) Judaica Pr., Inc., The.

Osborn, Susan Titus. Parables in Action Set, 8 vols. (Parables in Action Ser.). (J). 38.99 *(978-0-7586-0013-4(5))* Concordia Publishing Hse.

Osborne, Jill. Riley Mae & the Sole Fire Safari, 1 vol. 2014. (Faithgirlz / the Good News Shoes Ser.). (ENG.). 256p. (J). pap. 7.99 *(978-0-310-74283-8(8))* Zonderkidz.

Ostrowski, Jesse Feathers. God's Little Princess Warrior. 2013. 24p. pap. 12.95 *(978-1-4497-8552-9(2)*, WestBow Pr.) Author Solutions, Inc.

Out of the Blue. 2014. (J). pap. *(978-0-8163-5016-2(7))* Pacific Pr. Publishing Assn.

Owen, Linda. Robin's Song, 1 vol. 2009. (ENG.). 28p. (J). pap. *(978-1-85345-495-0(8))* Crusade for World Revival.

Owens, Jim. New Allegory. 2006. (J). per. 12.00 *(978-0-9769132-4-5(0))* Capri Publishing.

Pantelides, Sherry. It's Red Like Me! A Story about the Blood of Jesus. Perez, Debi, illus. 2007. (J). lib. bdg. 12.99 *(978-0-9771076-0-5(4))* Lacey Productions.

Parker, Amy. A Night Night Prayer, 1 vol. Pedler, Caroline, illus. 2014. (Night Night Ser.). (ENG.). 20p. (J). bds. 9.99 *(978-1-4003-2431-6(9))* Nelson, Thomas Inc.

—Thank You, God, for Grandma, 1 vol. 2017. (ENG., Illus.). 20p. (J). bds. 9.99 *(978-0-7180-8925-2(1))* Nelson, Thomas Inc.

—Thank You, God, for Grandpa, 1 vol. 2017. (ENG., Illus.). 20p. (J). bds. 9.99 *(978-0-7180-8929-0(4))* Nelson, Thomas Inc.

—Tiny Blessings: for All Seasons. Walsh, Sarah, illus. 2017. (ENG.). 10p. (J). (gr. -1 — 1). bds. 7.99 *(978-0-7624-6180-6(2)*, Running Pr.) Running Pr. Bk. Pubs.

Parker, Amy. Tiny Blessings: for Giving Thanks (large Trim) Walsh, Sarah, illus. 2017. (ENG.). 10p. (J). (gr. -1 — 1). bds. 9.95 ***(978-0-7624-6211-7(6)***, Running Pr.) Running Pr. Bk. Pubs.

Parker, Amy & Walsh, Sarah. Tiny Blessings: for Giving Thanks. Running Press Staff, ed. 2016. (ENG., Illus.). 10p. (J). (gr. -1-17). bds. 7.95 *(978-0-7624-5989-6(1)*, Running Pr. Kids) Running Pr. Bk. Pubs.

Parker, Claudia. Children's Church with a Preschool Pastor. 2012. 28p. pap. 21.99 *(978-1-4691-8213-1(0))* Xlibris Corp.

Parker, Donald James. Reforming the Potter's Clay. 2008. 220p. pap. 12.95 *(978-0-615-21223-4(9))* Sword of the Spirit Publishing.

Parra, Jen. Princess Shannon & the Yellow Moon. Meier, Paul, illus. 2004. (J). bds. 9.99 *(978-1-4183-0012-8(8))* Christ Inspired, Inc.

Parrott, Leslie. God Made You Nose to Toes, 1 vol. Corke, Estelle, illus. 2017. (ENG.). 18p. (J). bds. 9.99 *(978-0-310-75740-5(1))* Zonderkidz.

Parry, Rosanne. Heart of a Shepherd. 2010. (ENG.). 176p. (J). (gr. 3-7). pap. 7.99 *(978-0-375-84803-2(7)*, Yearling) Random Hse. Children's Bks.

Paterson, Katherine. Preacher's Boy. 2013. (ENG.). 176p. (J). (gr. 5-7). pap. 7.99 *(978-0-544-10490-7(0))* Houghton Mifflin Harcourt Publishing Co.

Patron, Susan. Lucky for Good. McGuire, Erin, illus. 2012. (ENG.). 224p. (J). (gr. 3-7). pap. 6.99 *(978-1-4169-9059-8(3)*, Atheneum Bks. for Young Readers) Simon & Schuster Children's Publishing.

—Lucky for Good. McGuire, Erin K., illus. 2011. (ENG.). 224p. (J). (gr. 3-7). 16.99 *(978-1-4169-9058-1(5)*, Atheneum Bks. for Young Readers) Simon & Schuster Children's Publishing.

Patterson, Sharon L. Where Is Happy? 2011. 48p. pap. 8.95 *(978-1-60594-755-6(5)*, Llumina Christian Bks.) Aeon Publishing Inc.

Patton, Donna Alice. The Gift of Summer Snow: A Tale from the Garden of Mysteries. 2010. (Illus.). ix, 133p. (J). *(978-0-9826867-3-7(0))* Philothea Pr.

Paul, Donita K. Two Renegade Realms, 1 vol. 2014. (Realm Walkers Ser.). (ENG.). 416p. (YA). pap. 13.99 *(978-0-310-73581-6(5))* Zondervan.

Pavlicin, Karen. Perch, Mrs. Sackets, & Crow's Nest. 2007. (J). (ENG.). 160p. 16.95 *(978-1-934617-00-7(8))*; pap. *(978-1-934617-01-4(6))* Elva Resa Publishing, LLC. (Alma Little).

—Summer of Courage. 2014. (ENG.). 160p. (J). pap. 12.95 *(978-1-934617-24-3(5)*, Alma Little) Elva Resa Publishing, LLC.

Payne, C. C. Something to Sing About. 2008. (ENG.). 167p. (J). (gr. 4-7). pap. 8.50 *(978-0-8028-5344-8(7))* Eerdmans, William B. Publishing Co.

Pearson, Carol Lynn. A Christmas Thief. 2008. 80p. 12.99 *(978-1-59955-184-5(5))* Cedar Fort, Inc./CFI Distribution.

—A Christmas Thief: A Novel. 2003. 67p. 14.95 *(978-0-8294-1764-7(8))* Loyola Pr.

Peck, Lisa J. A Challenge for Brittany: CTR Club - Book One, 4 bks. 2005. (J). pap. 6.95 *(978-0-9749241-5-1(6))* Golden Wings Enterprises.

Peckham, Lori, ed. Guide's Greatest Funny Stories. 2014. (ENG.). 160p. pap. 11.99 *(978-0-8280-2778-6(1))* Review & Herald Publishing Assn.

—Guide's Greatest Mystery Stories. 2007. 155p. per. 11.99 *(978-0-8280-2038-1(8))* Review & Herald Publishing Assn.

Peifer, Jane Hoober. The Family Song. Hess, Ingrid, illus. 2008. 64p. (J). (gr. -1-3). pap. 18.99 incl. audio compact disk *(978-0-8361-9414-2(4))* Herald Pr.

Pelton, Lisa. Logos & Adoption: Remi's Journey. 2012. 40p. pap. 14.95 *(978-1-4497-5378-8(7)*, WestBow Pr.) Author Solutions, Inc.

Penning, L. & Nelson, Marietjie. The Hero of Spionkop. 2006. (Illus.). 166p. (YA). pap. *(978-1-894666-92-3(5))* Inheritance Pubns.

—The Lion of Moddersprult. 2004. (Illus.). 142p. (YA). pap. *(978-1-894666-91-6(7))* Inheritance Pubns.

Penny, Agnes M. The Story of Our Lady of Victory. Penny, Agnes M., illus. 2008. (Illus.). 24p. (J). 4.50 *(978-0-9788687-2-7(2))* Requiem Pr.

Peoples, Alan, illus. James the Circus Boy. 2013. 80p. pap. 11.99 *(978-1-62839-474-0(9))* Salem Author Services.

Peretti, Frank E. The Deadly Curse of Toco-Rey, 1 vol. 2005. (Cooper Kids Adventure Ser.: 6). (ENG.). 160p. pap. 6.99 *(978-1-4003-0575-9(6))* Nelson, Thomas Inc.

—Hangman's Curse. 2008. 352p. (YA). mass mkt. 7.99 *(978-1-4003-1016-6(4))* Nelson, Thomas Inc.

—Nightmare Academy. 2008. 352p. (YA). mass mkt. 7.99 *(978-1-4003-1017-3(2))* Nelson, Thomas Inc.

Peretti, Frank E. & Thomas Nelson & Sons Staff. Mayday at Two Thousand Five Hundred, 1 vol. 2005. (Cooper Kids Adventure Ser.: 8). (ENG.). 160p. pap. 6.99 *(978-1-4003-0577-3(2))* Nelson, Thomas Inc.

—The Secret of the Desert Stone, 1 vol. 2005. (Cooper Kids Adventure Ser.: 5). (ENG.). 160p. pap. 6.99 *(978-1-4003-0574-2(8))* Nelson, Thomas Inc.

Peretz, I. L. The Seven Good Years: And Other Stories of I. L. Peretz. Hautzig, Esther, tr. Ray, Deborah Kogan, illus. 2004. (ENG & YID.). 96p. pap. 11.95 *(978-0-8276-0771-2(7))* Jewish Pubn. Society.

Perkins, John. Perceval: King Arthur's Knight of the Holy Grail, 1 vol. Spirin, Gennady, illus. 2007. (ENG.). 40p. (J). (gr. 3-7). 16.99 *(978-0-7614-5339-0(3))* Marshall Cavendish Corp.

Perrotti, P. Joseph & the Prodigal Son. 2005. 74p. pap. 19.95 *(978-1-4137-5491-9(0))* America Star Bks.

Perugini, Donna. Do Angels Go Camping? 2010. 32p. (Orig.). pap. 9.99 *(978-0-88144-536-7(3))* Yorkshire Publishing Group.

Peterson, Doug. In the Amazing Brain-Twister, 1 vol. 2003. (Big Idea Books / LarryBoy Ser.: Vol. 7). (ENG., Illus.). 96p. (J). pap. 4.99 *(978-0-310-70651-9(3))* Zonderkidz.

—Larryboy & the Abominable Trashman, 1 vol. 2003. (Big Idea Books / LarryBoy Ser.: Vol. 8). (ENG., Illus.). 96p. (J). pap. 4.99 *(978-0-310-70652-6(1))* Zonderkidz.

—LarryBoy Versus the Volcano, 1 vol., No. 9. 2004. (Big Idea Books / LarryBoy Ser.). (ENG., Illus.). 96p. (J). pap. 4.99 *(978-0-310-70728-8(5))* Zonderkidz.

Peterson, Esther Allen. The House That Cared. 2010. (J). pap. *(978-0-88092-505-1(1))* Royal Fireworks Publishing Co.

—Will Spring Come? 2009. (Illus.). 157p. (J). *(978-0-88092-768-0(2))* Royal Fireworks Publishing Co.

Peterson, Matt. The Epic Tales of a Misfit Hero. 2012. pap. 8.99 *(978-1-59955-999-5(4)*, Bonneville Bks.) Cedar Fort, Inc./CFI Distribution.

Phillips, Cynthia. The Way to Go! Emanuel, Effie Ann, illus. 2008. 17p. pap. 24.95 *(978-1-60610-455-2(1))* America Star Bks.

Phillips, Deborah. The Parable of the Princesses. 2008. 48p. (J). 19.99 *(978-1-59038-873-0(9))* Deseret Bk. Co.

Pierce, Seth J. Camporee of Doom. 2009. (J). pap. 12.99 *(978-0-8163-2364-7(X))* Pacific Pr. Publishing Assn.

—The Day the School Blew Up. 2009. (J). pap. 12.99 *(978-0-8163-2329-6(1))* Pacific Pr. Publishing Assn.

Piper, Noël. Most of All, Jesus Loves You! Anderson, Debby, illus. 2004. 24p. (J). 11.99 *(978-1-58134-630-5(1))* Crossway.

Pistole, Katy. Flying High. 2003. (Illus.). 126p. (J). 7.99 *(978-0-8163-1942-8(1))* Pacific Pr. Pubns.

Pitts, Daphne. What Makes God Laugh. 2012. 30p. 25.99 *(978-1-62419-299-9(8))*; pap. 15.99 *(978-1-62419-298-2(X))* Salem Author Services.

PM Seeker Series #8 Jesus, Someone Who Cares. 2005. (J). pap. 2.95 *(978-0-9749339-6-2(1))* PowerMark Productions.

Pogue, Carolyn & Price, Ian. After the Beginning. Kyle, Margaret, illus. 2006. (ENG.). 32p. 18.95 *(978-1-896836-83-6(6)*, Copperhouse) Wood Lake Publishing, Inc. CAN. Dist: Westminster John Knox Pr.

Polk, James. God Rules. 2003. pap. 11.00 *(978-0-8059-9231-1(6)*, RoseDog Bks.) Dorrance Publishing Co., Inc.

—Mr. & Mrs. Love & the Neighborhood Children. 2003. pap. 11.00 *(978-0-8059-9232-8(4)*, RoseDog Bks.) Dorrance Publishing Co., Inc.

Poole, Bud. Little Miss Muffet Gets Saved: A Christian Nursery Rhyme. 2012. 20p. pap. 7.95 *(978-1-4497-4170-9(3)*, WestBow Pr.) Author Solutions, Inc.

Popcorn, Socks, & Salvation. 2008. 32p. pap. 4.99 *(978-0-8341-2350-2(9)*, 083-412-3509) Beacon Hill Pr. of Kansas City.

Poteat, Bruce S. Evil Deception. 2013. 192p. (gr. 10-12). 30.95 *(978-1-4497-9565-8(X))*; pap. 13.95 *(978-1-4497-9570-2(6))* Author Solutions, Inc. (WestBow Pr.).

Poth, Karen. Listen up, Larry, 1 vol. 2013. (I Can Read! / Big Idea Books / VeggieTales Ser.). (ENG.). 32p. (J). pap. 3.99 *(978-0-310-73215-0(8))* Zonderkidz.

—Pirates, a Super Hero, & a Mess Detective, 1 vol. 2014. (I Can Read! / Big Idea Books / VeggieTales Ser.). (ENG.). 96p. (J). 9.99 *(978-0-310-74204-3(8))* Zonderkidz.

Potter, George. The Wisemen of Bountiful. Harmon, Glenn, illus. 2005. per. 11.99 *(978-1-55517-814-7(6))* Cedar Fort, Inc./CFI Distribution.

Powell, Kathy Bingham. Save the Seeds. 2010. (Illus.). 24p. pap. 14.99 *(978-1-4490-5936-1(8))* AuthorHouse.

Powell Smith, Brendan. Daniel in the Lions' Den: The Brick Bible for Kids. 2014. (Brick Bible for Kids Ser.). (ENG., Illus.). 32p. (J). (gr. -1-k). 12.95 *(978-1-62914-605-8(6)*, Sky Pony Pr.) Skyhorse Publishing Co., Inc.

Precious Moments, Precious. Precious Moments: Happy Harvest, 1 vol. 2016. (ENG., Illus.). 32p. (J). bds. 9.99 *(978-0-7180-3241-8(1))* Nelson, Thomas Inc.

Price, Gene. Lukas' Maiden Voyage. 2012. 108p. 28.95 *(978-1-4497-7753-1(8))*; (gr. 4-6). pap. 11.95 *(978-1-4497-7752-4(X))* Author Solutions, Inc. (WestBow Pr.).

Price, Matt. Out on a Limb. 2006. 32p. 4.50 *(978-0-8341-2229-1(4))* Beacon Hill Pr. of Kansas City.

Priebe, Trisha & Jenkins, Jerry B. The Paper Boat. 2017. (Thirteen Ser.). (ENG.). 240p. (J). 14.99 *(978-1-68322-178-4(8))* Barbour Publishing, Inc.

Prime, Derek. Sarah & Paul Go Back to School Bk. 1: Discover about God & the Bible. 2006. (Sarah & Paul Ser.). (ENG., Illus.). 128p. (J). (gr. 2-5). per. 6.99 *(978-1-84550-157-0(8)*, df1071c4-5480-4c1a-9480-a93d741bf494) Christian Focus Pubns. GBR. Dist: Bookmasters Distribution.

—Sarah & Paul Go on Holiday Again: Discover about Being a Christian. 2006. (Sarah & Paul Ser.). (ENG., Illus.). 128p. (J). per. 6.99 *(978-1-84550-162-4(4)*, 94175d0d-6922-46f5-bc95-9e8edf2f526c) Christian Focus Pubns. GBR. Dist: Bookmasters Distribution.

—Sarah & Paul Go to the Seaside. 2006. (Sarah & Paul Ser.). (ENG., Illus.). 128p. (J). (gr. 2-5). per. 6.99 *(978-1-84550-159-4(4)*, e21a5ea6-3d41-4387-977e-93990141367d) Christian Focus Pubns. GBR. Dist: Bookmasters Distribution.

—Sarah & Paul Make a Scrapbook. 2006. (Sarah & Paul Ser.). (ENG., Illus.). 128p. (J). (gr. 2-5). per. 6.99 *(978-1-84550-160-0(8)*, a9643561-9103-4038-81fa-3bbc6a03ab7a) Christian Focus Pubns. GBR. Dist: Bookmasters Distribution.

Prins, Piet. Stefan Derksen's Polar Adventure. 2004. (Illus.). 237p. (J). pap. *(978-1-894666-67-1(4))* Inheritance Pubns.

Prozeller, Ellen Lucey. 32 Days: A Story of Faith & Courage. 2016. (J). pap. *(978-0-8198-0657-4(9))* Pauline Bks. & Media.

Prus, Jennifer. A Toddler's Abc of Blessings. McIlhany, illus. 2012. 20p. pap. 9.95 *(978-1-61633-256-3(5))* Guardian Angel Publishing, Inc.

Puppets & Pockets from Paper Plates. (Illus.). 48p. (J). (gr. -1-5). pap. 5.95 *(978-0-87162-630-1(6)*, E4603) Warner Pr., Inc.

Pyrnelle, Louise Clarke. Diddie Dumps & Tot: Or, Plantation Child-life. 2007. 138p. pap. 18.99 *(978-1-4346-0721-8(6))*; (ENG.). 150p. pap. 19.99 *(978-1-4346-0781-2(X))* Creative Media Partners, LLC.

Rae, Kimberly. Seeking Mother. 2015. 168p. (YA). *(978-1-62856-028-2(2))* BJU Pr.

Rainey, Barbara. What God Wants for Christmas. Walker, John, illus. 2011. (J). (gr. 4-7). pap. 29.99 incl. audio compact disk *(978-1-60200-428-3(5))* FamilyLife.

Ramos, Peregrina. The Little Clay Jar: La Vasijita de Barro. Graham, Dennis, illus. 2006.Tr. of vasijita de Barro. (SPA & ENG.). (J). per. 15.95 *(978-0-9788381-0-2(6))* Word Gift Pubns.

Ranga, Katherine. Jesus Loves Me: A Bedtime Prayer. Ang, Selvi, illus. 2011. 26p. pap. 11.95 *(978-1-60976-989-5(9)*, Eloquent Bks.) Strategic Book Publishing & Rights Agency (SBPRA).

Rapp, Pat. Noisy Nativity. 2008. 24p. per. 24.95 *(978-1-4241-9866-5(6))* America Star Bks.

RealBuzz Studios Staff. Girl Overboard Frankensteins Monster: Life Camera Action Book 4. 2007. 128p. (YA). pap. 4.97 *(978-1-59789-580-4(6)*, Barbour Bks.) Barbour Publishing, Inc.

Redeker, Kent, et al. Larryboy in the Attack of Outback Jack, 1 vol., Bk. 6. 2003. (Big Idea Books / LarryBoy Ser.: Vol. 6). (ENG., Illus.). 96p. (J). pap. 4.99 *(978-0-310-70649-6(1))* Zonderkidz.

Redmond, Mark L. Arty's Long Day. Ury, Laura, illus. 2003. 102p. pap. *(978-0-87398-042-5(5))* Sword of the Lord Pubs.

Reece, Colleen L. Last Page in the Diary. 2011. 94p. pap. 8.95 *(978-1-61633-179-5(8))* Guardian Angel Publishing, Inc.

Reed, Lynn. Shannon's Search for the Lost Ark. 2010. 52p. pap. 22.99 *(978-1-4490-0392-0(3))* AuthorHouse.

Reed, Stephanie. The Light Across the River, 1 vol. 2008. (Illus.). 216p. (J). (gr. 4-7). pap. 10.99 *(978-0-8254-3574-4(9))* Kregel Pubns.

Reese, Erica, illus. My Almighty Daddy. 2007. 16p. (J). 10.00 *(978-0-9720773-3-0(2))* Christiangela Productions.

Reeve, Penny. God Made Something Beautiful. 2011. (Find the Animal Ser.). (ENG., Illus.). 16p. (J). pap. 4.99 *(978-1-85792-773-3(7)*, fd1b69a1-49ce-42a0-ad98-005844a05b04) Christian Focus Pubns. GBR. Dist: Bookmasters Distribution.

—God Made Something Clever. 2011. (Find the Animal Ser.). (ENG., Illus.). 16p. (J). pap. 4.99 *(978-1-85792-772-6(9)*, 35a2e541-8258-41d7-bf5e-37d06bf1ae40) Christian Focus Pubns. GBR. Dist: Bookmasters Distribution.

—God Made Something Strong. 2011. (Find the Animal Ser.). (ENG., Illus.). 16p. (J). pap. 4.99 *(978-1-85792-771-9(0)*, d0f5e64a-af70-4238-9b31-eaaa8ac3bf4a) Christian Focus Pubns. GBR. Dist: Bookmasters Distribution.

Reggie to the Rescue. 2004. 32p. pap. 3.99 *(978-0-8341-2088-4(7))* Beacon Hill Pr. of Kansas City.

Reiter, Douglas. Back to School in Cedar Heights. 2006. 79p. pap. 19.95 *(978-1-4137-9058-0(5))* America Star Bks.

Rennie, Cliff. Goal Behind the Curtain. 2011. (Freestyle Fiction 12+ Ser.). (ENG.). 176p. (J). mass mkt. 8.99 *(978-1-871676-47-1(9)*, df3a7515-5c5f-4709-ab1d-e32b03bb9c87) Christian Focus Pubns. GBR. Dist: Bookmasters Distribution.

—Offside in Ecuatina. 2011. (Freestyle Fiction 12+ Ser.). (ENG.). 176p. (J). (gr. 8-12). mass mkt. 8.99 *(978-1-871676-69-3(X)*, bbd7a9b0-91c7-42e1-a780-e99c2dd18085) Christian Focus Pubns. GBR. Dist: Bookmasters Distribution.

—True Gold. 2004. (Freestyle Fiction 12+ Ser.). (ENG.). 128p. (YA). mass mkt. 7.99 *(978-1-871676-90-7(8))* Christian Focus Pubns. GBR. Dist: Send The Light Distribution LLC.

Reynolds, Luke. The Looney Experiment, 1 vol. 2015. (ENG.). 208p. (J). 15.99 *(978-0-310-74642-3(6))* Blink.

Rhodes, Shayla. I Know Who I Am. 2012. 30p. pap. 15.00 *(978-0-9705008-7-8(4))* J & J Publishing Co.

Ricchiuti, Paul B. Treasure on Spyglass Hill. 2015. 143p. (J). pap. *(978-0-8163-5771-0(4))* Pacific Pr. Publishing Assn.

Rich, Juliann. Searching for Grace. 2014. (ENG.). 264p. (J). (gr. 7). pap. 11.95 *(978-1-62639-196-3(3))* Bold Strokes Bks.

Richardson, Arleta. Across the Border. 2016. (Beyond the Orphan Train Ser.: 4). (ENG.). 192p. (J). (gr. 3-6). pap. 7.99 *(978-0-7814-1358-9(3))* Cook, David C.

—Prairie Homestead. 2016. (Beyond the Orphan Train Ser.: 3). (ENG.). 192p. (J). pap. 7.99 *(978-0-7814-1357-2(5))* Cook, David C.

—Still More Stories from Grandma's Attic, 1. rev. ed. 2003. (Grandma's Attic Ser.). (Illus.). 144p. (J). (gr. 8-12). pap., pap. 8.99 *(978-0-7814-3270-2(7)*, 0781432707) Cook, David C.

—Treasures from Grandma. rev. ed. 2003. (Grandma's Attic Ser.). (Illus.). 144p. (J). (gr. 8-12). pap. 8.99 *(978-0-7814-3271-9(5)*, 0781432715) Cook, David C.

—Whistle Stop West. 2003. (Orphans' Journey Ser.: Vol. 2). 144p. (J). (gr. 3-7). pap., pap. 5.99 *(978-0-7814-3537-6(4)*, 0781435374) Cook, David C.

Richardson, Faith. Angel Walker. 2003. Orig. Title: The Sea, the Song & the Trumpetfish. (Illus.). 172p. (J). 19.95 *(978-0-9744989-2-8(0))*; pap. 12.95 *(978-0-9744989-3-5(9))* Fox Song Bks.

Richman, Karyn. The Land Where All Things Become Beautiful. 2011. 204p. pap. 15.99 *(978-1-61215-926-3(5))* Salem Author Services.

Rickman, Jeanie Parker. The Rising Star Ball. Taylor, Jennifer, illus. 2006. 32p. per. 17.95 *(978-1-59858-201-7(1))* Dog Ear Publishing, LLC.

Riordan, Betty J. The Imaginary Journeys of Bj & Dobbin. 2008. 108p. pap. 11.99 *(978-1-60647-432-7(4))* Salem Author Services.

Robertson, Dan. Zoe Pencarrow & the River of Life. 2013. 84p. pap. 10.99 *(978-1-62697-108-0(0))* Salem Author Services.

Robertson, Sadie. Life Just Got Real. 2016. (Live Original Fiction Ser.). (ENG.). 288p. (gr. 6-14). 17.99 *(978-1-5011-2646-8(6)*, Howard Bks.) Howard Books.

Robinson, Julie. Do Roosters Praise God. 2011. 20p. 10.03 *(978-1-4567-1987-6(4))* AuthorHouse.

Roddy, Lee. Case of the Dangerous Cruise. 2007. (Ladd Family Adventure Ser.: Vol. 11). (Illus.). 145p. (J). (gr. 3-7). per. 7.99 *(978-0-88062-260-8(1))* Mott Media.

—The City Bear's Adventures. 2008. (D. J. Dillon Adventure Ser.: No. 2). (J). 7.99 *(978-0-88062-266-0(0))* Mott Media.

—Dooger, the Grasshopper Hound. 2008. (D. J. Dillon Adventure Ser.: No. 3). (J). 7.99 *(978-0-88062-267-7(9))* Mott Media.

—Escape down the Raging Rapids. 2008. (D. J. Dillon Adventure Ser.: No. 10). (J). 7.99 *(978-0-88062-274-5(1))* Mott Media.

—Eye of the Hurricane. 2007. (Ladd Family Adventure Ser.: Vol. 9). (Illus.). 161p. (J). (gr. 3-7). per. 7.99 *(978-0-88062-258-5(X))* Mott Media.

—The Ghost Dog of Stoney Ridge. 2008. (D. J. Dillon Adventure Ser.: No. 4). (J). 7.99 *(978-0-88062-268-4(7))* Mott Media.

—Ghost of the Moaning Mansion. 2008. (D. J. Dillon Adventure Ser.: No. 8). (J). 7.99 *(978-0-88062-272-1(5))* Mott Media.

—The Hair-Pulling Bear Dog. 2008. (D. J. Dillon Adventure Ser.: No. 1). (J). 7.99 *(978-0-88062-265-3(2))* Mott Media.

—The Hermit of Mad River. 2008. (D. J. Dillon Adventure Ser.: No. 9). (J). 8.99 *(978-0-88062-273-8(3))* Mott Media.

—Hunted in the Alaskan Wilderness. 2008. (Ladd Family Adventure Ser.: Vol. 13). (Illus.). 149p. (Orig.). (J). (gr. 3-7). per. 7.99 *(978-0-88062-262-2(8))* Mott Media.

—The Legend of the White Raccoon. 2008. (D. J. Dillon Adventure Ser.: No. 6). (J). 7.99 *(978-0-88062-270-7(9))* Mott Media.

—Mad Dog of Lobo Mountain. 2008. (D. J. Dillon Adventure Ser.: No. 5). (J). 7.99 *(978-0-88062-269-1(5))* Mott Media.

—The Mystery of the Black Hole Mine. 2008. (D. J. Dillon Adventure Ser.: No. 7). (J). 8.99 *(978-0-88062-271-4(7))* Mott Media.

—The Mystery of the Wild Surfer. 2006. (Ladd Family Adventure Ser.: Vol. 6). (Illus.). 135p. (J). (gr. 4-7). per. 7.99 *(978-0-88062-255-4(5))* Mott Media.

—Night of the Vanishing Lights. 2007. (Ladd Family Adventure Ser.: Vol. 10). (Illus.). 159p. (J). (gr. 3-7). per. 7.99 *(978-0-88062-259-2(8))* Mott Media.

—Peril at Pirate's Point. 2006. (Ladd Family Adventure Ser.: Vol. 7). (Illus.). 153p. (J). (gr. 4-7). per. 7.99 *(978-0-88062-256-1(3))* Mott Media.

—Tracked by the Wolf Pack. 2006. (Ladd Family Adventure Ser.: Vol. 15). (J). 7.99 *(978-0-88062-264-6(4))* Mott Media.

Rodríguez, Orlando A. Valores Morales y Buenos Hábitos — Rangel, Mario Hugo, illus. (SPA.). 32p. (J). 2004. *(978-0-311-38597-3(4))* 2004. *(978-0-311-38596-6(6))* 2003. *(978-0-311-38595-9(8))* Baptist Spanish Publishing Hse./Casa Bavtista de Publicaciones: Mundo Hispano.

Rogers, Bud, et al. Truth Revealed, 1 vol. Padilla, Ariel, illus. 2009. (Z Graphic Novels / Tomo Ser.). (ENG.). 160p. (J). pap. 6.99 *(978-0-310-71305-0(6))* Zondervan.

Rosier, Joan. Christmas Stilts. 2008. (ENG.). 24p. 12.99 *(978-1-4389-3907-0(8))* AuthorHouse.

Rottmann, Erik. Barabbas Goes Free. Kitchel, JoAnn E., illus. 2003. (Arch Bks.). (ENG.). 16p. (J). 1.99 *(978-0-570-07582-0(3))* Concordia Publishing Hse.

Rousay II, Richard A. Choose the Right 'Walk with Alma' 2010. 94p. pap. 17.50 *(978-0-557-13491-5(9))* Lulu Pr., Inc.

Rowley, Deborah. The Miracle of the Wooden Shoes. 2008. 32p. (J). 18.95 *(978-1-59038-990-4(5))* Deseret Bk. Co.

Rowley, Deborah Pace. Easter Walk: A Treasure Hunt for the Real Meaning of Easter. Burr, Dan, illus. 2010. (J). *(978-1-60641-055-4(5))* Deseret Bk. Co.

Rue, Nancy. So Not Okay, 1 vol. 2014. (Mean Girl Makeover Ser.). (ENG.). 304p. (J). pap. 9.99 *(978-1-4003-2370-8(3))* Nelson, Thomas Inc.

—Sorry I'm Not Sorry: An Honest Look at Bullying from the Bully, 1 vol. 2015. (Mean Girl Makeover Ser.). (ENG.). 288p. (J). pap. 9.99 *(978-1-4003-2372-2(X))* Nelson, Thomas Inc.

—You Can't Sit with Us - Mean Girl Makeover, 1 vol. 2014. (Mean Girl Makeover Ser.). (ENG.). 224p. (J). pap. 9.99 *(978-1-4003-2371-5(1))* Nelson, Thomas Inc.

Rue, Nancy N. Lily's in London?!, 1 vol. 2003. (Lily Ser.). (ENG.). 192p. (J). pap. 6.99 *(978-0-310-70554-3(1))* Zonderkidz.

—Lily's Passport to Paris, 1 vol. 2003. (Lily Ser.). (ENG.). 160p. (J). pap. 6.99 *(978-0-310-70555-0(X))* Zonderkidz.

—Lucy Doesn't Wear Pink, 1 vol. 2016. (Faithgirlz / a Lucy Novel Ser.). (ENG.). 256p. (J). pap. 7.99 *(978-0-310-75442-8(9))* Zonderkidz.

—Lucy Finds Her Way, 1 vol. 2016. (Faithgirlz / a Lucy Novel Ser.). (ENG.). 192p. (J). pap. 7.99 *(978-0-310-75452-7(6))* Zonderkidz.

—Lucy's Perfect Summer, 1 vol. 2016. (Faithgirlz / a Lucy Novel Ser.). (ENG.). 192p. (J). pap. 7.99 *(978-0-310-75504-3(2))* Zonderkidz.

—Motorcycles, Sushi & One Strange Book, 1 vol. 2010. (Real Life Ser.). (ENG.). 224p. (YA). (gr. 8-11). pap. 9.99 *(978-0-310-71484-2(2))* Zondervan.

—Sophie Steps Up, 1 vol. 2009. (Faithgirlz! Ser.: No. 4). (ENG.). 128p. (J). pap. 6.99 *(978-0-310-71841-3(4))* Zonderkidz.

—Sophie's Drama, 1 vol. 2009. (Faithgirlz! Ser.: No. 11). (ENG.). 178p. (J). pap. 6.99 *(978-0-310-71844-4(9))* Zonderkidz.

—Sophie's Friendship Fiasco. 2009. (Faithgirlz! Ser.: No. 7). (ENG.). 128p. (J). pap. 6.99 *(978-0-310-71842-0(2))* Zonderkidz.

—Totally Unfair, 1 vol. 2005. ('Nama Beach High Ser.). (ENG.). 160p. (YA). pap. 6.99 *(978-0-310-25183-5(4))* Zondervan.

Rupp, Dain Chistopher. The Greatest Saint Stories A-Z: (Book 1 of 2: A-M) 2008. 32p. per. 24.95 *(978-1-60441-067-9(1))* America Star Bks.

Rupp, Rebecca. Octavia Boone's Big Questions about Life, the Universe & Everything. 2010. (ENG., Illus.). 192p. (J). (gr. 4-7). 15.99 *(978-0-7636-4491-8(9))* Candlewick Pr.

Sabatini, Kety. Joseph's Hands. Sabatini, Marie, illus. 2007. (ENG.). 36p. (J). per. 12.99 *(978-0-9792258-8-8(4))* Bezalel Bks.

Sabatini, Key. Isabel's Sister. 2008. (Illus.). 32p. per. 10.99 *(978-0-9794976-9-8(8))* Bezalel Bks.

Sanchez, Alex. The God Box. Del Rosario, Michael, ed. 2009. (ENG., Illus.). 272p. (YA). (gr. 7). pap. 10.99 *(978-1-4169-0900-2(1)*, Simon & Schuster Bks. For Young Readers) Simon & Schuster Bks. For Young Readers.

Sangster, Margaret. Splendid Times. 2007. 92p. per. 16.95 *(978-1-60466-008-1(2))* Capricorn Hse. Publishing.

Sarmiento, R. One Race Kids New Beginnings. 2010. 58p. pap. 27.99 *(978-1-60957-901-2(1))* Salem Author Services.

Sarmiento-Waring, D. Meet the One Race Kids. 2010. 20p. pap. 17.99 *(978-1-60957-899-2(6))* Salem Author Services.

—One Race Kids Fun Book. 2010. 58p. pap. 28.99 *(978-1-60957-902-9(X))* Salem Author Services.

Sassi, Laura. Goodnight, Ark, 1 vol. Chapman, Jane, illus. 2015. (ENG.). 24p. (J). bds. 8.99 *(978-0-310-74938-7(7))* Zonderkidz.

Saunders, Sara. Swirly. Pierce, Matthew, illus. 2012. 32p. (J). 7.99 *(978-0-8280-2681-9(5))* Review & Herald Publishing Assn.

Sawyer, Kim Vogel. Katy's Debate, 1 vol. 2015. (Katy Lambright Ser.). (ENG.). 208p. (YA). pap. 9.99 *(978-0-310-74755-0(4))* Zondervan.

—Katy's Homecoming, 1 vol. 2015. (Katy Lambright Ser.). (ENG.). 208p. (YA). pap. 9.99 *(978-0-310-74835-9(6))* Zondervan.

—Katy's New World, 1 vol. (Katy Lambright Ser.). (ENG.). 208p. (YA). 2015. pap. 9.99 *(978-0-310-74782-6(1))* 2010. (gr. 8-11). pap. 9.99 *(978-0-310-71924-3(0))* Zondervan.

Scanlon, Liz Garton. The Great Good Summer. 2015. (ENG., Illus.). 224p. (J). (gr. 3-7). 16.99 *(978-1-4814-1147-9(0)*, Beach Lane Bks.) Beach Lane Bks.

Scherm, Deedra. Cinco Panes y un Par de Peces: Una Historia de la Fe y de Dar. Dreyer, Laura, illus. 2008. (SPA.). 20p. (J). (gr. -1-3). bds. 7.99 *(978-1-934789-06-3(2))* Lemon Vision Productions.

—Solo uno Como Yo: Una Rima Dulce y Pequenita para Ayudar Hacer Brillar Tu Lucecita. Dreyer, Laura, illus. 2008. (SPA.). 22p. (J). (gr. -1-3). 7.99 *(978-1-934789-05-6(4))* Lemon Vision Productions.

Schmidt, Gary D. Pilgrim's Progress. Moser, Barry, illus. 2008. (ENG.). 189p. (J). (gr. 4-18). 16.50 *(978-0-8028-5346-2(3))* Eerdmans, William B. Publishing Co.

Schneider, Richard H. The Lighthouse Boy: A Story about Courage. Petrov, Anton, illus. 2007. (ENG.). 32p. (J). (gr. -1-3). pap. 8.99 *(978-0-8249-5557-1(9)*, Ideal Pubns.) Worthy Publishing.

—Why Christmas Trees Aren't Perfect. 2016. (ENG.). 32p. 12.99 *(978-1-5018-2583-5(6)*, Cokesbury) Abingdon Pr.

Schroder, Jennifer Michaels. Fish Food: Skimmer Catches His Spirit. 2010. 24p. pap. 14.49 *(978-1-4490-4784-9(X))* AuthorHouse.

Scott. Heinle Rdg Lib Ivanhoe. 2003. (Heinle Reading Library: Illustrated Classics Collection). (ENG.). 128p. (C). pap. 16.95 *(978-0-7593-9879-5(8)*, Cengage Learning) CENGAGE Learning.

Scott-Branagan, Browen. The Pandanuspeople. 2009. 32p. pap. 13.75 *(978-1-60860-006-9(8)*, Strategic Bk. Publishing) Strategic Book Publishing & Rights Agency (SBPRA).

Scott, Janice B. Children's Stories from the Village Shepherd. 2008. 172p. pap. 15.95 *(978-0-7880-2618-8(6))* CSS Publishing.

Scriber, Christian. The Adventures of Almighty Mouse: And Tales of His Friends. 2009. 112p. pap. 10.99 *(978-1-4389-4313-8(X))* AuthorHouse.

Scripture Teachers: Solomon & Friends Learn about Forgiveness. 2003. pap. *(978-0-9712894-1-3(7))* Lighthouse Christian Products Co.

Scripture Teachers: Solomon & Friends Learn about Prayer. 2003. pap. *(978-0-9712894-0-6(9))* Lighthouse Christian Products Co.

Scripture Teachers: Solomon & Friends Learn about Trusting God. 2003. pap. *(978-0-9712894-2-0(5))* Lighthouse Christian Products Co.

Seres, Frank & Seres, Nancy. The Jacob Series: Book #1 Fearfully & Wonderfully Made. 2009. 24p. (J). pap. 16.95 *(978-1-4327-3862-4(3))* Outskirts Pr., Inc.

Setzer, Lee Ann. Sarah McDuff: Primary Program Diva. Officer, Robyn, illus. 2004. 61p. (J). pap. 4.95 *(978-1-55517-786-7(7))* Cedar Fort, Inc./CFI Distribution.

Shank, Marilyn Sue. Child of the Mountains. 2013. (ENG.). 272p. (J). (gr. 4-7). 6.99 *(978-0-375-87331-7(7)*, Yearling) Random Hse. Children's Bks.

Shaw, Laura. Priscilla & the Big Red Ball, 1 vol. Shaw, Yvonne, illus. 2009. 19p. pap. 24.95 *(978-1-60749-523-9(6))* America Star Bks.

Shaw, Wendy M. How Much Do I Love You? Hemby, Margaret, illus. 2006. (J). 14.95 *(978-0-9788398-1-9(1))* Jostens Bks.

Shelton, Dierdre A. Angels Surrounding Me. 2009. 32p. pap. 16.49 *(978-1-4389-4407-4(1))* AuthorHouse.

Sherwood, Mary Marth. The History of Lucy Clare. 2004. reprint ed. pap. 15.95 *(978-1-4191-6620-4(4))* Kessinger Publishing, LLC.

Sherwood, Mary Martha. The History of Lucy Clare. 2004. reprint ed. pap. 1.99 *(978-1-4192-6620-1(9))* Kessinger Publishing, LLC.

Shimalla, Jen. Heaven Cent. 2013. 24p. pap. 10.95 *(978-1-4525-8042-5(1)*, Balboa Pr.) Author Solutions, Inc.

Shireman, Abbie. The Fish Tank. 2012. 20p. pap. 17.99 *(978-1-4772-8173-4(8))* AuthorHouse.

Shouse, Eric. The Good Shepherd. 2010. ring bd. 8.99 *(978-0-578-04648-8(2))* Everybody Run Music.

Siegrist, Bonnie. Little Farm down the Lane -Book IV. 2007. pap. 10.99 *(978-1-60034-912-6(9))* Salem Author Services.

Siegrist, Bonnie Bedi. Little Farm down the Lane Book V. 2008. 124p. pap. 11.99 *(978-1-60647-848-6(6))* Salem Author Services.

Simon, Mary Manz. Bear Obeys. Clearwater, Linda & Court, Kathy, illus. 2006. (First Virtues for Toddlers Ser.). 20p. (J). 5.99 *(978-0-7847-1416-4(9)*, 04068) Standard Publishing.

—God Made the Moon. Walkley, Lizzie, illus. 2016. (J). *(978-0-8249-1981-8(5)*, Ideal Pubns.) Worthy Publishing.

—God Made the Sun. Walkley, Lizzie, illus. 2016. (J). *(978-0-8249-1980-1(7)*, Ideal Pubns.) Worthy Publishing.

Skead, Robert A. & Skead, Robert J. Patriots, Redcoats & Spies, 1 vol. 2015. (American Revolutionary War Adventures Ser.). (ENG.). 192p. (J). 14.99 *(978-0-310-74841-0(0))* Zonderkidz.

Smiley, Jane. Gee Whiz. Clayton, Elaine, illus. 2013. (Horses of Oak Valley Ranch Ser.: Bk. 5). (ENG.). 272p. (J). (gr. 5). 16.99 *(978-0-375-86969-3(7)*, Knopf Bks. for Young Readers) Random Hse. Children's Bks.

—The Georges & the Jewels. 2010. (Horses of Oak Valley Ranch Ser.: Bk. 1). (ENG.). 240p. (J). (gr. 5). 6.99 *(978-0-375-86228-1(5)*, Yearling) Random Hse. Children's Bks.

—A Good Horse. 2011. (Horses of Oak Valley Ranch Ser.: Bk. 2). (ENG.). 256p. (J). (gr. 5). 6.99 *(978-0-375-86230-4(7)*, Yearling) Random Hse. Children's Bks.

—Pie in the Sky. 2013. (Horses of Oak Valley Ranch Ser.). (ENG.). 272p. (J). (gr. 5). 6.99 *(978-0-375-87131-3(4)*, Yearling) Random Hse. Children's Bks.

—True Blue. 2012. (Horses of Oak Valley Ranch Ser.: Bk. 3). (ENG.). 304p. (J). (gr. 5). 6.99 *(978-0-375-86232-8(3)*, Yearling) Random Hse. Children's Bks.

Smith, Debra. Hattie Marshall & the Dangerous Fire, 1 vol. 2007. (Hattie Marshall Ser.). (ENG.). 128p. (J). (gr. 3-6). per. 7.95 *(978-1-58980-492-0(9))* Pelican Publishing Co., Inc.

Smith, Debra West. Hattie Marshall & the Prowling Panther, 1 vol. 2005. (Hattie Marshall Ser.). (ENG.). 144p. (J). (gr. 4-6). pap. 7.95 *(978-1-56554-940-1(6))* Pelican Publishing Co., Inc.

Smith, Jada. Touched by an Angel. 2009. 76p. pap. 13.95 *(978-1-4251-8552-7(5))* Trafford Publishing.

Smith, Mary P. Wells. The Young Puritans in King Philip's War. Bridgman, L. J., illus. 2011. 396p. 54.95 *(978-1-258-05550-9(3))* Literary Licensing, LLC.

Smith, Sherry. The Wolf & the Shield: An Adventure with Saint Patrick. McNally, Nicholas, illus. 2016. 118p. (J). pap. *(978-0-8198-8356-8(5))* Pauline Bks. & Media.

Smith, Sherry Weaver. Search for the Hidden Garden: A Discovery with Saint Thérèse. Thornburgh, Rebecca McKillip, illus. 2016. 128p. (J). pap. 9.95 *(978-0-8198-9050-4(2))* Pauline Bks. & Media.

Smith, Stephanie Harms. For Everything There Is a Season in God's Time. 2007. 84p. per. 11.99 *(978-1-60477-224-1(7))* Salem Author Services.

Smith, Stephen. Game on Boxed Set Series for Boys. 2006. 512p. (J). 19.99 *(978-0-7847-1990-9(X))* Standard Publishing.

Snedeker, Caroline. Downright Dencey. Barney, Maginel Wright, illus. 2003. (Young Adult Library). 268p. (YA). pap. 12.95 *(978-1-883937-79-9(5))* Bethlehem Bks.

Snelling, Lauraine. Golden Filly, No. 1. 2009. (ENG.). 624p. (J). pap. 16.00 *(978-0-7642-0737-2(7))* Bethany Hse. Pubs.

—Golden Filly Collection 2. 2009. (ENG.). 624p. (J). pap. 16.00 *(978-0-7642-0738-9(5))* Bethany Hse. Pubs.

—What about Cimmaron? 2008. (J). 8.99 *(978-1-59166-872-5(7))* BJU Pr.

Snider, Cindy Gay. Finding Anna Bee. Chambers, Mary, illus. 2007. 163p. (J). (gr. 3-7). per. 9.99 *(978-0-8361-9392-3(X))* Herald Pr.

Snowballs & Coconuts. 2006. 56p. pap. 7.75 *(978-0-8341-2295-6(2)*, 083-412-2952) Beacon Hill Pr. of Kansas City.

Sowards, Ben, illus. Christmas Oranges. 2004. 32p. 17.95 *(978-1-59156-098-2(5))* Covenant Communications, Inc.

Spady, Angela & Thomas Nelson Publishing Staff. Channing O'Banning & the Rainforest Rescue, 1 vol. 2015. (ENG., Illus.). 112p. (J). pap. 6.99 *(978-0-7180-3262-3(4))* Nelson, Thomas Inc.

—Channing o'Banning & the Turquoise Trail, 1 vol. 2015. (ENG., Illus.). 128p. (J). pap. 6.99 *(978-0-7180-3236-4(5))* Nelson, Thomas Inc.

Spangenberg, Greg. A Christmas Eve Victory. Lodwick, Sarah, illus. I.t. ed. 2006. 32p. (J). 16.99 *(978-1-59879-140-2(0))* Lifevest Publishing, Inc.

Spangler, Paula Jeanne. Abigail's Christmas: Christmas Mom Reveals A Newborn. 2010. 48p. pap. 20.49 *(978-1-4490-8104-1(5))* AuthorHouse.

Spinelli, Eileen. Thankful, 1 vol. Preston, Archie, illus. (ENG.). (J). 2017. 20p. bds. 8.99 ***(978-0-310-76140-2(9))*** 2015. 32p. 16.99 *(978-0-310-00088-4(2))* Zonderkidz.

Spiritworks. Sleep, 1 vol. Foster, Jonathan, illus. 2010. 18p. 24.95 *(978-1-4489-4930-4(0))* PublishAmerica, Inc.

Spooner, F. M. Granny Spooner's Christian Bedtime Stories. 2010. (Illus.). 104p. pap. 11.74 *(978-1-4251-1390-2(7))* Trafford Publishing.

Sproul, R. C. The Barber Who Wanted to Pray. Fluharty, T. Lively, illus. 2011. 40p. (J). 17.99 *(978-1-4335-2703-6(0))* Crossway.

—The Priest with Dirty Clothes. Gerard, Justin, illus. 2nd ed. 2011. 45p. (J). *(978-1-56769-210-5(9))* Reformation Pubs.

—The Prince's Poison Cup. Gerard, Justin, illus. 2008. (J). *(978-1-56769-104-7(8))* Reformation Pubs.

Squiers, Connie. The Copper Colt. 2013. 94p. pap. 7.95 *(978-1-937829-78-0(2)*, Total Publishing & Media) Yorkshire Publishing Group.

St. John, Patricia. Friska My Friend & the Other Kitten. 2003. (Illus.). 192p. 6.49 *(978-1-85999-312-5(5))* Scripture Union GBR. Dist: Gabriel Resources.

—A Home for Virginia. Smith, Helen, illus. 2005. (ENG.). 24p. (J). (gr. 4-7). 9.99 *(978-1-85792-961-4(6)*, 61d6526b-9c8a-4a92-bdf8-4e663de02131) Christian Focus Pubns. GBR. Dist: Bookmasters Distribution.

St John, Patricia. Other Kitten. 2007. (Illus.). 96p. pap. *(978-1-84427-290-7(7))* Scripture Union.

St. John, Patricia. Secret of the Fourth Candle. rev. ed. 2003. (Illus.). 94p. 6.49 *(978-1-85999-511-2(X))* Scripture Union GBR. Dist: Gabriel Resources.

—The Victor. 2003. 176p. 6.49 *(978-0-86201-139-0(6))* Scripture Union GBR. Dist: Gabriel Resources.

St John, Patroca. Friska My Friend. 2007. (Illus.). 93p. pap. *(978-1-84427-289-1(3))* Scripture Union.

Stahl, Hilda. Big Trouble for Roxie. 2003. (Best Friends Ser.: No. 2). 160p. (YA). (gr. 4-7). pap. 4.99 *(978-0-89107-658-2(1))* Crossway.

Stanley, Andy. Go Fish: Because of What's on the Line. 2005. (North Point Resources Ser.). (ENG.). 96p. stu. ed., per., pupil's gde. ed. 9.99 *(978-1-59052-548-7(5)*, Multnomah Bks.) Crown Publishing Group.

Stannard, Russell. www.Here-I-Am. Pugh, Jonathan, illus. 2011. (ENG.). 160p. (YA). (gr. 5-8). pap. 9.95 *(978-1-890151-85-0(8))* Templeton Pr.

Stevens, Joy. Hugs in a Lunch Box. Stanley, Robin, ed. 2006. (Heritage Builders Ser.). 176p. (YA). pap. 8.99 *(978-0-7847-1363-1(4)*, 04023); (J). pap. 8.99 *(978-0-7847-1362-4(6)*, 04022) Standard Publishing.

Stewart, Maria. An Omelet Fit for a King. Cost, Steve, illus. 2013. 24p. pap. 14.99 *(978-1-936453-23-8(1))* Bezalel Bks.

Stewart, Willa. The Forever Bed. 2009. 28p. pap. 14.95 *(978-0-9822060-0-3(3))* Tree of Life Publishing Hse.

Stiegemeyer, Julie. Thanksgiving: A Harvest Celebration. Benoit, Renne, illus. 2006. 32p. (J). (gr. -1-3). per. 7.49 *(978-0-7586-0916-8(7))* Concordia Publishing Hse.

—Under the Baobab Tree, 1 vol. Lewis, E. B., illus. 2012. (ENG.). 32p. (J). 16.99 *(978-0-310-72561-9(5))* Zonderkidz.

Stortz, Diane. Adam Named the Animals from a to Z. Reed, Lisa, illus. 2012. (Roma Downey's Little Angels Ser.). 24p. (J). bds. 7.99 *(978-0-8249-5642-4(7)*, Ideal Pubns.) Worthy Publishing.

Stortz, Diane M. Baby, Baby! Busby, Allie, illus. 2016. (J). *(978-0-8249-1988-7(2)*, Ideal Pubns.) Worthy Publishing.

The Story of Christian. 2005. (Illus.). (J). per. 995.00 *(978-0-9762911-1-4(8)*, Ameeramac Bks.) Ameeramac Bks. Inc.

Strange, J. R. The Tree & the Light. Massivebrain.com, illus. 2013. 48p. pap. 11.99 *(978-0-9887214-0-1(6))* Firesidenook.

Stratemeyer, Edward. Richard Dare's Venture. 2007. 232p. 26.95 *(978-1-4218-4146-5(0))*; per. 11.95 *(978-1-4218-4244-8(0))* 1st World Publishing, Inc. (1st World Library - Literary Society).

Strauss, Ed. Devotions to Make You Stronger, 1 vol. 2007. (2:52 Ser.). (ENG., Illus.). 192p. (J). (gr. 3-7). pap. 9.99 *(978-0-310-71311-1(0))* Zonderkidz.

Streib, Sally. Octopus Encounter. 2007. (Illus.). 126p. (J). 6.97 *(978-0-8163-2210-7(4))* Pacific Pr. Publishing Assn.

Stretton, Hesba. Cassy. Hymper, W. & Stacey, W. S., illus. 2006. (Golden Inheritance Ser.: Vol. 9). 117p. (J). pap. *(978-0-921100-94-2(9))* Inheritance Pubns.

—Jessica's First Prayer. Doe, Charles J., ed. 2008. (ENG., Illus.). 54p. (YA). pap. 7.95 *(978-0-9817505-2-1(4))* Curiosmith.

—Jessica's First Prayer. 2004. reprint ed. pap. 15.95 *(978-1-4191-2751-9(9))*; pap. 1.99 *(978-1-4192-2751-6(3))* Kessinger Publishing, LLC.

—Jessica's First Prayer. 2006. 84p. pap. 9.95 *(978-1-59462-373-8(2)*, 409, Book Jungle) Standard Pubns., Inc.

—Lost Gip. 2003. (Golden Inheritance Ser.: Vol. 7). (Illus.). 121p. (J). *(978-0-921100-93-5(0))* Inheritance Pubns.

Stromberg, Ronica. Living It up to Live It Down. 2009. (J). lib. bdg. *(978-0-88092-752-9(6))* Royal Fireworks Publishing Co.

—A Shadow in the Dark. 2009. (J). pap. *(978-0-88092-751-2(8))*; lib. bdg. *(978-0-88092-750-5(X))* Royal Fireworks Publishing Co.

Sturgill, Jean A. Bouncing Beaver Discovers God: A Drew's Animals Book. 2007. (ENG.). 30p. pap. 15.99 *(978-1-4196-7822-6(1))* CreateSpace Independent Publishing Platform.

Sutton, Michelle. It's Not about Him. 2012. (Second Glances Ser.). (ENG.). 228p. pap. 12.99 *(978-0-9838836-0-9(2))* Sword of the Spirit Publishing.

—It's Not about Me. 2012. (Second Glances Ser.). (ENG.). 252p. pap. 12.99 *(978-0-9838836-9-2(6))* Sword of the Spirit Publishing.

Swinford, Betty. Secrets. 2006. (Freestyle Fiction 12+ Ser.). (ENG.). 176p. (J). (gr. 4-7). per. 6.99 *(978-1-84550-127-3(6)*, 2b7eb6f6-fcab-409d-af77-f07255764855) Christian Focus Pubns. GBR. Dist: Bookmasters Distribution.

Tagert-Paul, Kimberley. God's Ten Promises: Helping Children Understand the Ten Commandments. 2010. (J). 12.99 *(978-0-8163-2379-1(8))* Pacific Pr. Publishing Assn.

Tate, Andy. I Love My Church. Tate, Lizzy, illus. 2008. 16p. pap. 24.95 *(978-1-60441-419-6(7))* America Star Bks.

Taylor, Helen L. Little Pilgrim's Progress: From John Bunyan's Classic. 2006. (ENG., Illus.). 336p. (gr. -1-3). per. 8.99 *(978-0-8024-4924-5(7))* Moody Pubs.

Taylor, Jeannie. You Wouldnt Love Me If You Kne. 2009. 32p. (J). pap. 10.99 *(978-0-687-65786-5(5))* Abingdon Pr.

Teis, Sean P. After the Ark: Eli & Ella the Little Elephants - Children of the King! Boutheyette, Valerie, illus. 2013. 32p. pap. 14.99 *(978-1-937129-84-2(5))* Faithful Life Pubs.

Tell Me a Story III. 2005. (J). per. 9.95 *(978-1-59352-142-4(1))* Christian Services Publishing.

TerKeurst, Lysa. It Will Be Okay: Trusting God Through Fear & Change, 1 vol. 2014. (ENG., Illus.). 32p. (J). 14.99 *(978-1-4003-2419-4(X))* Nelson, Thomas Inc.

—Win or Lose, I Love You! Sometimes You Learn, 1 vol. 2015. (ENG., Illus.). 32p. (J). 15.99 *(978-0-529-10400-7(8))* Nelson, Thomas Inc.

Tessie & Devore, David. Happy Birthday to Me. 2005. (Charisma Kids Ser.). (Illus.). 24p. (J). (gr. k-3). 9.99 *(978-1-59185-207-0(2))* Charisma Media.

Tewkesbury, Alexa. Benny's Barmy Bits. 2007. (Topz Secret Diaries). (ENG., Illus.). 128p. (J). *(978-1-85345-431-8(1))* Crusade for World Revival.

—John's Jam-Packed Jottings, 1 vol. 2009. (Topz Secret Diaries). (ENG., Illus.). 128p. (J). pap. *(978-1-85345-503-2(2))* Crusade for World Revival.

—Josie's Jazzy Journal. 2008. (ENG., Illus.). 128p. (J). *(978-1-85345-457-8(5))* Crusade for World Revival.

—Paul's Potty Pages. 2008. (ENG., Illus.). 128p. (J). *(978-1-85345-456-1(7))* Crusade for World Revival.

—Sarah's Secret Scribblings. 2007. (ENG., Illus.). 128p. (J). *(978-1-85345-432-5(X))* Crusade for World Revival.

Thaler, Mike. Church Harvest Mess-Tivall, 1 vol. Lee, Jared, illus. 2010. (Tales from the Back Pew Ser.). (ENG.). 32p. (J). pap. 3.99 *(978-0-310-71595-5(4))* Zonderkidz.

—Church Summer Cramp, 1 vol. Lee, Jared, illus. 2009. (Tales from the Back Pew Ser.). (ENG.). 32p. (J). (gr. 1-4). pap. 3.99 *(978-0-310-71592-4(X))* Zonderkidz.

—Easter Egg Haunt, 1 vol. Lee, Jared, illus. 2009. (Tales from the Back Pew Ser.). (ENG.). 32p. (J). (gr. 1-4). pap. 3.99 *(978-0-310-71591-7(1))* Zonderkidz.

—Preacher Creature Strikes on Sunday, 1 vol. Lee, Jared, illus. 2009. (Tales from the Back Pew Ser.). (ENG.). 32p. (J). (gr. 1-4). pap. 3.99 *(978-0-310-71589-4(X))* Zonderkidz.

—The Three Wise Guys, 1 vol. Lee, Jared, illus. 2010. (Tales from the Back Pew Ser.). (ENG.). 32p. (J). (gr. 1-4). pap. 3.99 *(978-0-310-71593-1(8))* Zonderkidz.

The de Villiers Family Staff. The Long Shortcut. The de Villiers Family Staff, illus. 2006. (Sprout Growing with God Ser.). (ENG., Illus.). 40p. (J). (gr. -1-2). 9.99 *(978-1-4000-7195-1(X)*, WaterBrook Pr.) Crown Publishing Group.

The Man From A.N.K.L.E. Myles a Hedd. 2008. 76p. (gr. -1). pap. 8.95 *(978-0-595-51515-8(0))* iUniverse, Inc.

Theobald the Iron Hearted or Love to Ene. 2004. reprint ed. pap. 15.95 *(978-1-4191-8941-8(7))* Kessinger Publishing, LLC.

Thomas, Jacquelin. Divine Confidential. 2007. (ENG., Illus.). 272p. (gr. -1). pap. 17.99 *(978-1-4165-2719-0(2))* Pocket Books.

—It's a Curl Thing. 2009. (Divine & Friends Ser.). (ENG., Illus.). 288p. pap. 18.99 *(978-1-4165-9878-7(2))* Pocket Books.

—Split Ends. 2010. (ENG.). 272p. pap. 17.99 *(978-1-4165-9879-4(0))* Pocket Books.

Thomas, Jerry D. Shoebox Kids Bible Stories, Vol. 5. Justinen, Kim, illus. 2003. 128p. (J). 7.99 *(978-0-8163-1971-8(5))* Pacific Pr. Publishing Assn.

Thomas, Joan G. If Jesus Came to My House. McElrath-Eslick, Lori, illus. 2008. (HarperBlessings Ser.). (ENG.). 40p. (J). (gr. -1-3). 16.99 *(978-0-06-083942-0(2))* HarperCollins Pubs.

Thomas Nelson Community College Staff. God's Love in My Heart, 1 vol. 2014. (ENG.). 24p. bds. 9.99 *(978-0-529-11141-8(1))* Nelson, Thomas Inc.

Thomas Nelson Publishing Staff. Light Rangers: Mending the Maniac Madness: Protect the Children of Angeltown. 2008. cd-rom 19.95 *(978-0-9754280-5-4(5))* Nelson, Thomas Inc.

Thompson, Adria. Droves Cove. 2008. 72p. pap. 9.99 *(978-1-60477-653-9(6))* Salem Author Services.

Thompson, Michelle. Taming the Wind. 2010. 176p. pap. 12.99 *(978-1-59955-379-5(1))* Cedar Fort, Inc./CFI Distribution.

Thornburgh, Rebecca McKillip, illus. Rufus & Ryan Give Thanks. 2014. (Rufus & Ryan Ser.). 20p. (J). bds. 7.99 *(978-0-8249-1936-8(X)*, Ideal Pubns.) Worthy Publishing.

Threatt, Cedric Lanier, Sr. Different, but the Same. 2005. (J). 15.95 *(978-0-9720543-2-5(4))* Threatt, Cedric L.

Tietz, Heather. Yes, Jesus Loves You. Miller, Nancy, illus. 2009. 20p. (J). (gr. k-4). 14.95 *(978-0-8091-6743-2(3)*, Ambassador Bks.) Paulist Pr.

Tiger, Tales, ed. My Little Book of Bedtime Prayers. Jones, Anna, illus. 2016. (ENG.). 32p. (J). (gr. -1-2). mass mkt. 3.99 *(978-1-58925-486-2(4))* Tiger Tales.

Todd, John. Nuts for Boys to Crack: Earthly Stories with a Heavenly Meaning. 2009. 272p. pap. 20.00 *(978-1-59925-232-2(5))* Solid Ground Christian Bks.

Tomlin, Chris & Barrett, Pat. Good Good Father, 1 vol. 2016. (ENG.). 32p. (J). 16.99 *(978-0-7180-8695-4(3))* Nelson, Thomas Inc.

—Good Good Father for Little Ones, 1 vol. 2017. (ENG., Illus.). 24p. (J). bds. 9.99 *(978-0-7180-8697-8(X))* Nelson, Thomas Inc.

Torrance-Matthews, Armer, et al. Miss Bertha, the Talking Tree: A Delightful Story of a Talking Tree. 2010. 36p. pap. 18.95 *(978-1-4269-2051-6(2))* Trafford Publishing.

Tosh, Anita. The Zella Chronicles. 2016. (ENG., Illus.). 160p. (J). pap. 12.99 *(978-1-58169-610-3(8)*, Gazelle Pr.) Genesis Communications, Inc.

Tougas, Shelley. A Patron Saint for Junior Bridesmaids. 2016. (ENG.). 272p. (J). 16.99 *(978-1-62672-403-7(2)*, 9781626724037) Roaring Brook Pr.

Townsend, Diana. He Saw Their Faith. 2007. 25p. 21.50 *(978-0-615-16214-0(2))* Townsend, Diana.

Trachtman, Joseph, illus. & narrated by. Kosher Tales: Not So Grim Stories for Children. Trachtman, Joseph, narrated by.

2007.Tr. of Kosher Tales. (ENG & YID.). 86p. (J). pap. 25.00 *(978-0-9795170-0-6(1))* Trachtman, Joseph.
The Trail of the Wooden Horse. 2007. 32p. pap. 4.50 *(978-0-8341-2284-0(7)*, 083-412-2847) Beacon Hill Pr. of Kansas City.
Treasure Quest Guide. 2004. pap. 5.99 *(978-1-56309-913-7(6))* Woman's Missionary Union.
Trevor, Meriol. Sun Slower Sun Faster. Ardizzone, Edward, illus. 2nd ed. 2004. (Living History Library). 290p. (J). pap. 12.95 *(978-1-883937-41-6(8))* Bethlehem Bks.
Turner, Juliette. That's Not Hay in My Hair, 1 vol. 2016. (ENG.). 240p. (J). pap. 8.99 *(978-0-310-73244-0(1))* Zonderkidz.
Turner, Marie B. God Made the Animals. Romero, Naomi, illus. 2017. (J). 6.99 **(978-1-5064-2185-8(7)**, Sparkhouse Family) Augsburg Fortress, Pubs.
Twin Sisters(r) Staff, et al. Jonah & the Whale Padded Board Book & CD, 1 vol. 2014. (Let's Share a Story Ser.). 16p. (J). (-5). bds. 9.99 incl. audio compact disk *(978-1-63058-783-3(4))* Barbour Publishing, Inc.
Two Nisse in Santaland. 2004. (J). bds. 12.95 *(978-0-942684-21-6(4))* Wordshed.
Umina, Lisa. Milo & the Green Wagon. 2008. (Illus.). 32p. 15.95 *(978-0-9797429-4-1(3))* Halo Publishing International.
Valentin, Karen. What Did Abuela Say? 2010. 32p. (J). (gr. -1-3). 8.95 *(978-1-60349-016-0(7)*, Marimba Bks.) Hudson Publishing Group, The.
Van Dyke, Henry. The Mansion: 100th Anniversary Edition. 100th ed. 2011. 32p. (J). 18.99 *(978-1-60641-845-1(9)*, Shadow Mountain) Shadow Mountain Publishing.
Van Oss, Laura. Indigo's Gift: Does Indigo Have a Secret Gift? Wolf, Claudia, illus. 2006. 24p. (J). per. 2.99 *(978-1-59958-003-6(9))* Journey Stone Creations, LLC.
Vardamaskos, Angela. Everlasting Truth. Boumakis, Maria, illus. 2008. 48p. pap. 24.95 *(978-1-60610-950-2(2))* America Star Bks.
Vela, Eugenio H. Twinkle, Twinkle Little Harold. 2012. 28p. pap. 24.95 *(978-1-4560-0901-4(X))* America Star Bks.
Vera, J. The Mustard Seed Prayer. Brown, Kevin Christian, illus. 2012. 24p. 24.95 *(978-1-4626-5848-0(2))* America Star Bks.
Viguié, Debbie. The Spring of Candy Apples, 1 vol. 2009. (Sweet Seasons Novel Ser.). (ENG.). 208p. (YA). (gr. 8-11). pap. 9.99 *(978-0-310-71753-9(1))* Zondervan.
Vroom, Angela. Airplane Letters to God. l.t. ed. 2004. (Illus.). 24p. (J). pap. 8.50 *(978-0-9762935-0-7(1))* Perkins Crawford.
Waggoner, Sandra. Son of an Honest Man. 2013. 136p. (J). pap. 10.95 *(978-0-9890667-2-3(X))* Sable Creek Pr. LLC.
Wahl, Lesiea. The Perfect Blindside. 2015. 280p. (YA). pap. 10.95 *(978-0-8198-6013-2(1))* Pauline Bks. & Media.
Walker, Joni, illus. Jesus Hears Me. 2008. 20p. (J). (gr. -1). bds. 6.49 *(978-0-7586-1508-4(6))* Concordia Publishing Hse.
Walker, Melissa. Small Town Sinners. (ENG.). (YA). (gr. 9-12). 2013. 304p. pap. 9.99 *(978-1-59990-982-0(0)*, 9781599909820) 2011. 288p. 16.99 *(978-1-59990-527-3(2)*, 9781599905273) Bloomsbury Publishing USA. (Bloomsbury USA Childrens).
Walley, Keith. An Angel to Guide Me. 2012. 62p. pap. 12.99 *(978-1-105-68254-4(4))* Lulu Pr., Inc.
Walsh, Sheila. Gigi, God's Little Princess, 1 vol. Johnson, Meredith, illus. 2005. (Gigi, God's Little Princess Ser.: 1). (ENG.). 32p. 14.99 *(978-1-4003-0529-2(2))* Nelson, Thomas Inc.
—God's Little Princess Treasury, 1 vol. Johnson, Meredith, illus. 2009. (ENG.). 128p. (gr. -1-2). 19.99 *(978-1-4003-1472-0(0))* Nelson, Thomas Inc.
—Meet My Best Friend. 2015. (Bible Is My Best Friend Ser.). (ENG.). 32p. (J). (gr. -1-3). 14.99 *(978-1-4336-8805-8(0)*, B&H Kids) B&H Publishing Group.
Walters Iii, Harry C. Little Sam's Secret Place. Nicol, Brock, illus. 2012. 44p. 24.95 *(978-1-937763-41-1(2))*; pap. 14.95 *(978-1-937763-40-4(4))* Published by Westview, Inc.
Walton, O. F. Christie's Old Organ or Home, Sweet Home. 2005. reprint ed. pap. 22.95 *(978-0-7661-9430-4(2))* Kessinger Publishing, LLC.
—A Peep Behind the Scenes: A Little Girl's Journey of Discovery. 2015. (Classic Stories Ser.). (ENG.). 256p. (J). mass mkt. 8.99 *(978-1-85792-524-1(6)*, 37143942-7c21-48e0-b651-a53c9e09b36c, Christian Heritage) Christian Focus Pubns. GBR. Dist: Bookmasters Distribution.
—Saved at Sea: A Young Boy in a Dramatic Rescue. 2007. (Classic Stories Ser.). (ENG., Illus.). 144p. (J). mass mkt. 7.99 *(978-1-85792-795-5(8)*, 9781857927955) Christian Focus Pubns. GBR. Dist: Bookmasters Distribution.
Warburton, Carol. Edge of Night: A Novel. 2004. (Illus.). 278p. pap. 14.95 *(978-1-59156-013-5(6))* Covenant Communications, Inc.
Wargin, Kathy-jo. Frank & Beans, 1 vol. Lewis, Anthony, illus. 2010. (I Can Read! / Frank & Beans Ser.). (ENG.). 32p. (J). pap. 3.99 *(978-0-310-71847-5(3))* Zondervan.
—Frank & Beans & the Scary Campout, 1 vol. Lewis, Anthony, illus. 2010. (I Can Read! / Frank & Beans Ser.). (ENG.). 32p. (J). pap. 3.99 *(978-0-310-71850-5(3))* Zonderkidz.
Warner, Jodi. Shia's Tail 2. 2012. 24p. pap. 10.95 *(978-1-4624-0369-1(7)*, Inspiring Voices) Author Solutions, Inc.
Warner Press Staff. Divorce Comes to Our House. 2003. pap. *(978-1-59317-009-7(2))* Warner Pr., Inc.
Warner, Susan & Wetherell, Elizabeth. Daisy in the Field. 2011. 272p. 29.95 *(978-1-4638-9964-6(5))*; pap. 16.95 *(978-1-4638-0163-2(7))* Rodgers, Alan Bks.
Waters, Tawni. Beauty of the Broken. 2014. 368p. 17.99 *(978-1-4814-1857-7(2))* Simon & Schuster, Inc.
Watkins, Dawn L. Zoli's Legacy (Christian Fiction) 2003. (Illus.). 297p. (J). pap. 9.95 *(978-1-57924-763-8(6))* BJU Pr.
Watson, Casey. Dirty Heart Clean Heart. 2013. 30p. pap. 9.99 *(978-1-62509-564-0(3))* Salem Author Services.
Watson, Jean & Bunyan, John. The Family Pilgrim's Progress: Adapted from John Bunyan's Classic. 2013. (ENG., Illus.). 128p. (J). 17.99 *(978-1-84550-232-4(9)*, a27dc5b1-6b3c-43a6-ac3a-3756f774adec) Christian Focus Pubns. GBR. Dist: Bookmasters Distribution.
Watson, Renée. What Momma Left Me. (ENG.). 240p. (YA). 2012. pap. 7.99 *(978-1-59990-704-8(6)*, 9781599907048) 2010. (gr. 5-8). 16.99 *(978-1-59990-446-7(2)*, 9781599904467) Bloomsbury Publishing USA. (Bloomsbury USA Childrens).
Watt, J. S. The Hall of Sorrows. 2006. 67p. pap. 16.95 *(978-1-4241-2984-3(2))* PublishAmerica, Inc.
Weaver, Anna E. Stories From Grandma's Day. 2011. (Illus.). 285p. (YA). (gr. 4-9). pap. 8.90 *(978-0-7399-2426-6(5))* Rod & Staff Pubs., Inc.
Weaver, Lisa D. Praying with Our Feet. Hess, Ingrid, illus. 2005. 40p. (J). pap. 12.99 *(978-0-8361-9306-0(7))* Herald Pr.
Wehrheim, Carol A. The Word & Picture Books Set 2: For Year C/A, 6 vols. Incl. Baby for Sarah. Frank, Betsy, illus. bds. 4.95 *(978-0-8298-1197-1(4))*; God's Good World. Frank, Betsy, illus. bds. 4.95 *(978-0-8298-1196-4(6))*; Good News for Jesus' Friends. James, Betsy, illus. bds. 4.95 *(978-0-8298-1195-7(8))*; Jesus Visits Zacchaeus. James, Betsy, illus. bds. 4.95 *(978-0-8298-1193-3(1))*; Lost & Found. James, Betsy, illus. bds. 4.95 *(978-0-8298-1192-6(3))*; Three Visitors for Jesus. James, Betsy, illus. bds. 4.95 *(978-0-8298-1194-0(X))*; 12p. (J). (gr. -1). 1997. (Word & Picture Bks.). 29.70 *(978-0-8298-1191-9(5))* Pilgrim Pr., The/United Church Pr.
—The Word & Picture Books Set 3: For Year A/B, 6 vols. Incl. Boy Shares Food. James, Betsy, illus. bds. 4.95 *(978-0-8298-1229-9(6))*; Church People. Frank, Betsy, illus. bds. 4.95 *(978-0-8298-1228-2(8))*; God Is Our Home. Frank, Betsy, illus. bds. 4.95 *(978-0-8298-1199-5(0))*; Helping Others. Frank, Betsy, illus. bds. 4.95 *(978-0-8298-1225-1(3))*; Meet Simeon & Anna. Frank, Betsy, illus. bds. 4.95 *(978-0-8298-1226-8(1))*; Welcome Jesus! Frank, Betsy, illus. bds. 4.95 *(978-0-8298-1227-5(X))*; 12p. (J). (gr. -1). 1997. (Word & Picture Bks.). 29.70 *(978-0-8298-1198-8(2))* Pilgrim Pr., The/United Church Pr.
West, Gina. Pookie's New Faith, 1 vol. 2009. 11p. pap. 19.95 *(978-1-61582-311-6(5))* PublishAmerica, Inc.
Westlake, Courtney. That's How You Know. 2013. 24p. pap. 10.95 *(978-1-4908-1051-5(X)*, WestBow Pr.) Author Solutions, Inc.
Weyland, Jack. As Always, Dave. 2008. 320p. (YA). pap. 15.95 *(978-1-59038-849-5(6))* Deseret Bk. Co.
—Brianna, My Brother, & the Blog. 2009. (YA). *(978-1-60641-140-7(3))* Deseret Bk. Co.
When Quiet Comes. 2005. (YA). per. 14.95 *(978-0-9769815-0-3(5))* DesertStar Communications, LLC.
White, A. Rose. Just the Way I Am. 2012. 16p. pap. 12.99 *(978-1-62230-382-3(2))* Salem Author Services.
White, Paul. Jungle Doctor & the Whirlwind. 2015. (Flamingo Fiction 9-13s Ser.). (ENG., Illus.). 176p. (J). (gr. 5-7). pap. 8.99 *(978-1-84550-296-6(5)*, 635eeceb-43fd-433d-9826-6b2bf5273d01) Christian Focus Pubns. GBR. Dist: Bookmasters Distribution.
—Jungle Doctor on Safari. 2011. (Flamingo Fiction 9-13s Ser.). (ENG., Illus.). 144p. (J). 8.99 *(978-1-84550-391-8(0)*, 9781845503918) Christian Focus Pubns. GBR. Dist: Bookmasters Distribution.
—Jungle Doctor on the Hop. 2015. (Flamingo Fiction 9-13s Ser.). (ENG., Illus.). 160p. (J). (gr. 4-7). per. 8.99 *(978-1-84550-297-3(3)*, 941c8ee3-121e-4dda-84ae-b6809a4d4b39) Christian Focus Pubns. GBR. Dist: Bookmasters Distribution.
—Jungle Doctor's Crooked Dealings. 2011. (Flamingo Fiction 9-13s Ser.). (ENG., Illus.). 144p. (J). (gr. 5-7). pap. 8.99 *(978-1-84550-299-7(X)*, 9b21af6e-da89-4bc5-b0d9-5ce6419b0795) Christian Focus Pubns. GBR. Dist: Bookmasters Distribution.
—Jungle Doctor's Enemies. 2011. (Flamingo Fiction 9-13s Ser.). (ENG., Illus.). 160p. (J). (gr. 5-7). pap. 8.99 *(978-1-84550-300-0(7)*, c2552503-49be-450c-84cc-9ec522751da8) Christian Focus Pubns. GBR. Dist: Bookmasters Distribution.
White, Tim. A Single Heart. 2006. 193p. pap. 24.95 *(978-1-4137-9418-2(1))* PublishAmerica, Inc.
Whitney, A. D. T. Patience Strong's Outings by Mrs a D T Whitney. 2006. 236p. per. 20.99 *(978-1-4255-2007-6(3))* Michigan Publishing.
Wiggin, Kate Douglas. New Chronicles of Rebecc. 2008. 152p. (gr. 4-7). 24.95 *(978-1-60664-756-1(3))* Rodgers, Alan Bks.
Wilberforce, Samuel. Agathos the Rocky Island & Other Sunday Stories & Parables. 2013. (ENG.). 236p. pap. 30.99 *(978-1-107-67169-0(8))* Cambridge Univ. Pr.
Wilkinson, Lisa. Prickle Says I'm Sorry. McCord, Kathi, illus. 2015. (Faith That Sticks Bks.). (ENG.). 26p. (J). pap. 3.99 *(978-1-4964-0312-4(6))* Tyndale Hse. Pubs.
Williams, Dan. The Duck That Lost His Waddle. 2010. 40p. pap. 24.99 *(978-1-60957-538-0(5))* Salem Author Services.
Williams, M. C. No where to be Found: Time Is Short. l.t. ed. 2006. 38p. per. 3.65 *(978-1-59879-099-3(4))* Lifevest Publishing, Inc.
Williamson, Denise J. Forbidden Gates. 2008. (J). 8.99 *(978-1-59166-853-4(0))* BJU Pr.
—River of Danger. 2008. (J). 8.99 *(978-1-59166-854-1(9))* BJU Pr.
Wilson, Heather Gemmen. Lydia Barnes & the Blood Diamond Treasure. 2007. (Global Warning Ser.). 159p. (J). (gr. 3-7). per. 7.99 *(978-0-89827-350-2(1))* Wesleyan Publishing Hse.
—Lydia Barnes & the Escape from Shark Bay. 2008. 160p. (J). 9.99 *(978-0-89827-352-6(8))* Wesleyan Publishing Hse.
—Lydia Barnes & the Mystery of the Broken Cross. 2007. (Global Warning Ser.). 157p. (J). (gr. 3-7). per. 7.99 *(978-0-89827-351-9(X))* Wesleyan Publishing Hse.
Wilson, Jacqui. Little Johnny's Faith Adventures: Creation Curiosity! 2012. 30p. pap. 15.95 *(978-1-4497-5994-0(7)*, WestBow Pr.) Author Solutions, Inc.
Wilson, Ricky Derail. Mirror of Hope Mirror of Fame. 2007. 32p. per. 12.95 *(978-1-4327-1391-1(4))* Outskirts Pr., Inc.
Wimberley, Judy. The Jack Book: Who Can Help Him on Sunny Days & on Stormy Days? 2013. 40p. pap. 16.95 *(978-1-4497-8339-6(2)*, WestBow Pr.) Author Solutions, Inc.
Winegar, Tracy. Keeping Keller. 2008. 207p. pap. 14.99 *(978-1-59955-115-9(2))* Cedar Fort, Inc./CFI Distribution.
Witherow, Wendy. Bridget's Blog. Pulley, Kelly, illus. 2007. 95p. (J). pap. *(978-1-934306-09-3(6))* Mission City Pr., Inc.
—Miranda's Makeover. Pulley, Kelly, illus. 2007. 93p. (J). *(978-1-934306-11-6(8))* Mission City Pr., Inc.
Wofford, Delaney. For Courage. 2010. 229p. pap. 17.98 *(978-0-557-17045-6(1))* Lulu Pr., Inc.
Wolfe, Jaymie Stuart. Family Matters: Thirteen Short Stories. 2011. 126p. (J). pap. *(978-0-8198-2694-7(4))* Pauline Bks. & Media.
Wood, Holly J. Invaluable. 2011. (YA). pap. 14.99 *(978-1-60908-835-4(2))* Deseret Bk. Co.
Wood, Lena. Elijah Creek & the Armor of Gift Set. 2006. 576p. (J). Bks. 1-3. 17.99 *(978-0-7847-1966-4(7))*Bks. 4-6. 17.99 *(978-0-7847-1967-1(5))* Standard Publishing.
Wright, Caleb E. Marcus Blair A Story of Provincial Times. 2006. pap. 22.95 *(978-1-4286-6303-9(7))* Kessinger Publishing, LLC.
Wright, Julie. My Not-So-Fairytale Life. 2005. 256p. (YA). pap. 15.95 *(978-1-59038-476-3(8))* Deseret Bk. Co.
Yarber, Peggy Sue. Rocketships to Heaven & the Sos Fuel Station. 2009. 24p. pap. 11.50 *(978-1-60860-246-9(X)*, Eloquent Bks.) Strategic Book Publishing & Rights Agency (SBPRA).
Yates, Alma J. Sammy's Song: A Novel. 2005. 272p. (J). *(978-1-59156-945-9(1))* Covenant Communications.
Yi-K'lun, F. Los Cuatro Amigos. 2003. (SPA.). 24p. *(978-84-246-1923-7(4)*, GL30509) La Galera, S.A. Editorial ESP. Dist: Lectorum Pubns., Inc.
Young, Cleous. The Prophetic Artist. 2006. (J). per. 9.95 *(978-1-882185-75-7(7))* Cornerstone Publishing, Inc.
Young, Jeanna Stolle & Johnson, Jacqueline Kinney. Princess Grace & the Little Lost Kitten, 1 vol. Aranda, Omar, illus. 2011. (Princess Parables Ser.). (ENG.). 32p. (J). (gr. -1-2). 14.99 *(978-0-310-71640-2(3))* Zonderkidz.
—Princess Joy's Birthday Blessing, 1 vol. Aranda, Omar, illus. 2011. (Princess Parables Ser.). (ENG.). 32p. (J). (gr. -1-2). 14.99 *(978-0-310-71639-6(X))* Zonderkidz.
Young, T. M. Playing Church. Washington, Victoria, ed. Cromwell, Danielle, illus. 2012. 32p. pap. 24.95 *(978-1-4626-7883-9(1))* America Star Bks.
Youngberg, Norma R. Jungle Thorn. 2010. (Illus.). 132p. reprint ed. per. 11.95 *(978-1-57258-157-9(3)*, 945-6024) TEACH Services, Inc.
Youree, Barbara. Senegal Sleuths. 2006. 56p. 7.75 *(978-0-8341-2226-0(X))* Beacon Hill Pr. of Kansas City.
Yoxen, Jackie. Hannah's Sunday Hats. Francis, Lauren, illus. l.t. ed. 2006. 32p. (J). 19.95 *(978-1-59879-184-6(2))* Lifevest Publishing, Inc.
Yuen, Dan. Charlie the Chopper & the Greatest Toymaker. Davis, Tim, illus. 2010. 26p. (J). *(978-0-88144-480-3(4))* Yorkshire Publishing Group.
Zacharias, Ravi. The Merchant & the Thief: A Folktale from India, 1 vol. Fournier, Laure, illus. 2012. (ENG.). 32p. (J). 15.99 *(978-0-310-71636-5(5))* Zonderkidz.
Zaugg, Sandra L. Secret of the Desert Lights: A Story about Following God's Laws. 2009. (J). pap. 9.99 *(978-0-8163-2294-7(5))* Pacific Pr. Publishing Assn.
—Secret of the Yellow Van: A Book about Dealing with Loss. 2008. (J). pap. 8.99 *(978-0-8163-2246-6(5))* Pacific Pr. Publishing Assn.
Zimmerman, Leora. God Loves Me. 2003. (Illus.). 28p. (gr. -1-5). 2.70 *(978-0-7399-2342-9(0)*, 2786) Rod & Staff Pubs., Inc.
Zondervan Staff. A Dolphin Wish, 1 vol. 2016. (Faithgirlz / Glimmer Girls Ser.). (ENG.). 208p. (J). pap. 8.99 *(978-0-310-75253-0(1))* Zonderkidz.
Zondervan Staff & Grant, Natalie. A London Art Chase, 1 vol. 2016. (Faithgirlz / Glimmer Girls Ser.). (ENG., Illus.). 208p. (J). pap. 8.99 *(978-0-310-75265-3(5))* Zonderkidz.
Zondervan Staff & Lyons, P. J. Little Bunny's Bible, 1 vol. Mitchell, Melanie, illus. 2015. (ENG.). 16p. (J). bds. 15.99 *(978-0-310-74444-3(X))* Zonderkidz.
Zurcher, Corina. Growing up Claus. 2007. 188p. 21.99 *(978-1-60477-046-9(5))*; per. 13.99 *(978-1-60266-917-8(1))* Salem Author Services.

CHRISTIAN SCIENCE

Eddy, Mary Baker. Big with Blessings. 2007. (Illus.). (J). *(978-0-87952-331-2(X))* Eddy, The Writings of Mary Baker.
Ferguson, Isabel, et al. A World More Bright: The Life of Mary Baker Eddy. 2013. (Illus.). vi, 279p. (J). *(978-0-87510-494-2(0))* Christian Science Publishing Society.

CHRISTIAN SYMBOLISM

see Christian Art and Symbolism

CHRISTIANITY

see also Church; God; Jesus Christ; Missions; Protestantism; Reformation; Theology
also names of Christian churches and sects (e.g. Catholic church; Huguenots; etc.) and headings beginning with the words Christian and Church

Ahmedi, Waqar, et al. World Religions: Judaism, Christianity & Islam. 2017. (ENG.). 120p. (J). (gr. 6-9). pap. 29.99 **(978-0-00-822768-5(3))** HarperCollins Pubs. Ltd. GBR. Dist: Independent Pubs. Group.
Alcorn, Randy. Tell Me about Heaven. DiCianni, Ron, illus. 2007. 64p. (J). 19.99 *(978-1-58134-853-8(3)*, 1271662) Crossway.
Allen-Powell, Rebecca, et al. Pathfinder Handbook. 2006. (J). spiral bd. 9.50 *(978-0-9743503-9-4(7))* Pioneer Clubs.
Aman, Israa. The Monotheistic Faiths: Judaism, Christianity, & Islam, Vol. 8. Pecastaing, Camille, ed. 2016. (Understanding Islam Ser.: Vol. 8). (ENG., Illus.). 112p. (J). (gr. 7-12). 25.95 *(978-1-4222-3674-1(9))* Mason Crest.
Anderson, Carolyn B. Heaven Is a Real Place. 2007. 73p. per. 8.95 *(978-1-59824-512-7(0))* E-BookTime LLC.
Anglican Church of Canada Staff. The Gift of Life: Children's Book for the Eucharist from Life in the Eucharist Program. 56p. pap. 5.50 *(978-0-919891-62-3(4)*, 1275) Anglican Bk. Ctr. CAN. Dist: Forward Movement Pubns.
—Life in the Eucharist: A Communion Program for Children. 64p. pap., stu. ed. 12.95 *(978-0-919891-46-3(2)*, 1315) Forward Movement Pubns.
Ark & the Dove. (YA). (gr. 9-12). 19.00 *(978-1-931555-43-2(5))* Our Lady of Victory Schl.
Arthur, Kay. Lord, I Want to Know You. 2006. (Lord Ser.). 210p. (YA). pap. 13.99 *(978-1-888655-14-8(3))* Precept Ministries.
Baker, Rod. Real Healing for Kids: Knowing Jesus as Your Healer. 2005. (Real Life Ser.). (Illus.). 32p. (gr. 1-4). pap. 1.99 *(978-1-57794-708-0(8))* Harrison House Pubs.
—Real Power for Kids: Knowing the Holy Spirit as Your Friend. 2005. (Real Life Ser.). (Illus.). 28p. (gr. 1-4). pap. 1.99 *(978-1-57794-707-3(X))* Harrison House Pubs.
Barnabas Fund. Children of Courage: Raising Tomorrow's Church. 2013. (ENG., Illus.). 28p. 10.00 *(978-0-9892905-5-5(7))* Isaac Publishing.
Bauman, Carey. God Controls the Storm. Bauman, Carey, tr. 2007. (Little Jewel Book Ser.). (Illus.). 24p. (J). (gr. 2). pap. 2.70 *(978-0-7399-2396-2(X))* Rod & Staff Pubs., Inc.
Becky, Terri And Melissa. Garden Prayer for Little Farmers: Seeds of Evangelism Series (Book 1) 2013. 36p. pap. 15.49 *(978-1-4669-8787-6(1))* Trafford Publishing.
Benge, Janet. Richard Wurmbrand: Love Your Enemies. 2017. (J). pap. **(978-1-57658-987-8(0))** YWAM Publishing.
Benge, Janet & Benge, Geoff. Francis Asbury: Circuit Rider. 2013. (Christian Heroes: Then & Now Ser.). (ENG.). 189p. (YA). (gr. 3-7). pap. 9.99 *(978-1-57658-737-9(1))* YWAM Publishing.
Big Idea Entertainment, LLC. Veggies in Space: the Fennel Frontier. Jones, Cory, illus. 2016. (VeggieTales Ser.). (ENG.). 32p. (J). (gr. -1-3). pap. 3.99 *(978-1-4336-4352-1(9)*, B&H Kids) B&H Publishing Group.
Blake, Philip. We are Christians. 2016. (ENG., Illus.). 32p. (J). (gr. 4-6). pap. 11.99 *(978-1-4451-3825-1(5)*, Franklin Watts) Hachette Children's Group GBR. Dist: Hachette Bk. Group.
Blanck, Ryan. Engaging the Media: Equipping Young People to Think Critically & Make Biblical Decisions about Entertainment. 2003. 122p. (YA). pap. 12.95 *(978-0-595-30143-0(6))* iUniverse, Inc.
Bob, Schultz. Boyhood & Beyond. 2004. pap. 10.99 *(978-1-883934-09-5(5))* Great Expectations Bk. Co.
Boersma, Heather. Dream Big: 30 Days to Life Beyond All You Could Ask or Imagine. 2012. ix, 119p. *(978-1-77069-453-8(6))* Word Alive Pr.
Boshoff, Penny. God & Me: 365 Daily Devotions. 2005. (Illus.). 380p. (J). (gr. -1-7). 16.99 *(978-1-905051-78-6(6))* Make Believe Ideas GBR. Dist: Nelson, Thomas Inc.
Bowen, Aaron. Christianity. 2017. (J). **(978-1-4222-3817-2(2))** Mason Crest.
Bowman, Crystal & McKinley, Teri. Does God Take Naps? 2017. (I've Got Questions Ser.). (ENG.). 32p. (J). 9.99 *(978-1-4964-1741-1(0))* Tyndale Hse. Pubs.
Brannan, Dara, ed. ¡Vívelo al extremo! Nivel 1: Lecciones prácticas para aprender de Dios. Tobar, Malena, illus. 2011. 218p. (J). ring bd. 20.00 *(978-1-931984-36-2(0))* Faith & Action Team.
Bright, Brad, et al. Getting to Know Jesus for Little Ones: The Four Keys to Starting a Relationship with God. Bishop, Tracy, illus. 2015. (ENG.). 32p. (J). 12.99 *(978-0-7369-5401-3(5))* Harvest Hse. Pubs.
Brown, Alan. Christianity. (Illus.). 64p. (YA). (gr. 4-18). lib. bdg. 29.95 *(978-1-59389-131-2(8))* Chrysalis Education.
—Christianity. 2006. (QEB World of Faiths Ser.). (Illus.). 32p. (J). lib. bdg. 19.95 *(978-1-59566-207-1(3))* QEB Publishing Inc.
Catholic Book Publishing Staff, creator. Saints Teach Us. 2008. (St. Joseph Rattle Board Bks.). (Illus.). 14p. (gr. -1-k). bds. 4.95 *(978-0-89942-723-2(5))* Catholic Bk. Publishing Corp.
Christ Our Life: God Is Good. 2004. (gr. 1-18). stu. ed. *(978-0-8294-1549-0(1))* Loyola Pr.
Christ Our Life: God Is Good; Parish-Catechist Manual. 2004. (gr. 1-18). *(978-0-8294-1658-9(7))* Loyola Pr.
Christian Focus Publications (CFP) Staff & Tnt. Christmas Story, Preparation for Service & the Promised Messiah. 2014. (On the Way (3-9's) Ser.). (ENG.). 96p. (J). pap. 17.99 *(978-1-85792-327-8(8)*, 9781857923278) Christian Focus Pubns. GBR. Dist: Bookmasters Distribution.
Concordia Publishing House, creator. Happy Birthday: God's Blessings to You! 2007. (Illus.). 22p. (J). (gr. -1-k). bds. 6.49 *(978-0-7586-1331-8(8))* Concordia Publishing Hse.
Cram101 Textbook Reviews Staff. Studyguide for Jesus of History Christ of Faith by Zanzig, Isbn 9780884895305. 3rd ed. 2014. (ENG.). 184p. (C). pap. 30.95 *(978-1-61812-856-0(6))* Cram101 Inc.
Crouser, Brad. What's My Excuse for Not Being a Christian? 12 Myths of Christianity 12 Myths of Christianity. 2004. 160p. (YA). pap. 13.95 *(978-0-9724867-5-0(5))* Woodland Pr., LLC.
Cutrera, Melissa. God's Great Plan. Sample, Matthew II, illus. 2013. 28p. (J). *(978-1-936908-82-0(4))*; *(978-1-936908-83-7(2))*; *(978-1-936908-81-3(6))* Shepherd Pr. Inc.
Dagnino, Arianna. Jesus Christ Cyberstar. 2009. 92p. pap. *(978-88-95145-42-6(9))* Italian Paths of Culture.
Darcy-Bérubé, Françoise & Berube, John Paul. Growing up a Friend of Jesus: A Guide to Discipleship for Children. 2003. (Illus.). 128p. *(978-2-89507-041-2(5))* Novalis Publishing.
DeVries, Douglas. Enticed by Gold. 2005. 17.00 *(978-1-877721-07-6(7))*; pap. 12.00 *(978-1-877721-08-3(5))* Jade Ram Publishing.
Doerfler-Dall, Mary. Hands on Faith: 66 Projects, Activities & Crafts for Children. 2003. 128p. (gr. 2-6). tchr. ed., spiral bd. 17.95 *(978-0-87793-739-5(7))* Ave Maria Pr.
Donahue, Laurie & Phillips, Paul. The Lord's Supper... Let's Get Ready! Palmer, Scott, illus. 2005. 96p. per. 10.99 *(978-0-9718306-6-0(5))* LifeSong Pubs.
Dowley, Tim, et al. The Complete Collection, 1 vol. Reeves, Eira, illus. 2017. (ENG.). 168p. (J). pap. 12.99 *(978-1-78128-327-1(3)*, Candle Bks.) Lion Hudson PLC GBR. Dist: Kregel Pubns.
Doxey, Heidi. Tiny Talks, Vol 12. 2011. 96p. pap. 8.99 *(978-1-59955-931-5(5))* Cedar Fort, Inc./CFI Distribution.
Dudley, Cathy D. Toddler Theology: Childlike Faith for Everyone. 2012. 24p. pap. 13.99 *(978-1-4685-5728-2(9))* AuthorHouse.
Elkins, Stephen. First Steps in Faith: Beginning Lessons of God's Love. Colton, Ellie, illus. 2006. (First Steps in Faith Ser.). 25p. (J). (gr. -1-k). bds. 9.99 incl. audio compact disk *(978-0-8054-2662-5(0))* B&H Publishing Group.
—Tell Me about Salvation. 2014. (Train 'Em Up Ser.). (ENG.). 24p. (J). pap. 4.99 *(978-1-4143-9679-8(1))* Tyndale Hse. Pubs.
Ellis, Colette. Following Christ. 2004. (Illus.). 154p. *(978-0-89870-909-4(1))* Ignatius Pr.
Enloe, Tim & Enloe, Rochelle. (Bengali) Kid Power! the Holy Spirit's Super Power for Kids! 2011. (Illus.). (J). pap. *(978-0-9794331-4-6(2))* E M Pubns.
Foce, Natalia, tr. from ENG. Grandes Verdades para Niños Pequeños. 2004. Orig. Title: Great Truths for Little Children. (SPA., Illus.). 115p. (J). pap. *(978-1-932789-10-2(3))* Editorial Sendas Antiguas, LLC.

C D

Frazee, Randy. Believe - Kids' Edition: Think, Act, Be Like Jesus, 1 vol. 2015. (ENG.). 224p. (J). pap. 11.99 (978-0-310-74601-0(9)) Zonderkidz.

Friedl, Natalie. Help Me Pray Today. 2008. (Illus.). 32p. (J). (978-0-9797429-1-0(9)) Halo Publishing International.

Gallaudet, Thomas. The Child's Book on the Soul. 2007. 164p. per. 15.00 (978-1-59925-116-5(7)) Solid Ground Christian Bks.

Ganeri, Anita. Christian Stories. Phillips, Rachael, illus. 2014. (Storyteller Ser.). (ENG.). 32p. (J). (gr. 2-4). pap. 10.99 (978-1-78388-007-2(4)) Tulip Books GBR. Dist: Independent Pubs. Group.

Gortler, Rosemarie & Piscitelli, Donna. The Mass Book for Children. Sternhagen, Mimi, illus. 2004. 48p. per. 5.95 (978-1-59276-075-6(9)) Our Sunday Visitor, Publishing Div.

Grenfell, Susan. Religious Studies for Common Entrance. 2nd rev. ed. 2011. (Illus.). 168p. pap. 42.50 (978-1-4441-2425-5(0)) Hodder Education Group GBR. Dist: Trans-Atlantic Pubns., Inc.

Groenboom, Roger, et al. The Light of the World Is Jesus. (Walk with Me Ser.). (gr. k-8). 12.95 (978-1-59255-172-9(6), 017010) Faith Alive Christian Resources.

Guia Catolica Para Los Creyentes Mas Pequenos. 2003. (J). pap. 3.95 net. (978-0-7648-1042-8(1)) Liguori Pubns.

Guy, Only A. Hard Questions about Christianity. 2013. 150p. pap. 7.99 (978-1-939670-03-8(9)) VIP Ink Publishing, L.L.C.

—Hard Questions about the End Times. 2013. 80p. pap. 7.99 (978-1-939670-00-7(4)) VIP Ink Publishing, L.L.C.

Hallinan, P. K. A Love Letter from God. Watson, Laura, illus. 2014. 24p. (J). 12.99 (978-0-8249-5662-2(1), Ideal Pubns.) Worthy Publishing.

Hamilton, Bethany. Ask Bethany, 1 vol. rev. ed. 2014. (Faithgirlz / Soul Surfer Ser.). (ENG., Illus.). 192p. (J). pap. 9.99 (978-0-310-74572-3(1)) Zonderkidz.

—Ask Bethany: FAQs - Surfing, Faith & Friends, 1 vol. 2011. (Soul Surfer Ser.). (ENG.). 192p. (J). pap. 9.99 (978-0-310-72568-8(2)) Zonderkidz.

Hill, Karen. All God's Creatures. Fancher, Lou & Johnson, Steve, illus. 2005. (ENG.). 14p. (J). (gr. -1 — 1). 9.99 (978-0-689-87819-0(2), Little Simon) Little Simon.

Hilliam, David. Richard the Lionheart & the Third Crusade: The English King Confronts Saladin in AD 1191. 2009. (Library of the Middle Ages Ser.). 64p. (gr. 5-8). 58.50 (978-1-60853-902-4(4), Rosen Reference) Rosen Publishing Group, Inc., The.

Hipps, Amelia. Islam, Christianity, Judaism. 2005. (Introducing Islam Ser.). (Illus.). 112p. (J). lib. bdg. 24.95 (978-1-59084-698-8(2)) Mason Crest.

Hoehn, Roxy. God's Adventurers. 2006. pap. 7.99 (978-0-8163-2148-3(5)) Pacific Pr. Publishing Assn.

Hunt, Marigold. A Life of Our Lord for Children. 2003. (Illus.). v, 189p. (J). pap. 14.95 (978-1-928832-64-5(4)) Sophia Institute Pr.

Joslin, Mary. The Paraclete Treasury of Angel Stories. Temporin, Elena, illus. 2008. (ENG.). 48p. (J). (gr. -1-6). 18.95 (978-1-55725-572-3(5)) Paraclete Pr., Inc.

Kahrs, Evelyn. I Can Find God in My City. 2013. 36p. pap. 16.95 (978-1-4525-8506-2(7), Balboa Pr.) Author Solutions, Inc.

Kendall, R. T. Between the Times: Malachi: God's Last Prophet of the Old Testament. 2010. (ENG.). 208p. pap. 12.99 (978-1-85792-792-4(3), bf4d90e6-d439-4e58-93f9-ed6e19bc1571, Christian Focus) Christian Focus Pubns. GBR. Dist: Bookmasters Distribution.

Klenovsky, Daniel & Cabala, Edith. El Fruto del Espiritu: Mensajes para Ninos. 2008. (SPA., Illus.). 48p. (J). pap. 19.99 incl. audio compact disk (978-0-7586-1459-9(4)) Concordia Publishing Hse.

Kolka, Diane & Clarke, Steve. Christianity. 2011. (Illus.). 64p. pap., stu. ed. 29.50 (978-1-4441-2214-5(2)) Hodder Education Group GBR. Dist: Trans-Atlantic Pubns., Inc.

Lataif, Nicole. I Forgive You: Love We Can Hear, Ask for, & Give. Betz, Katy, illus. 2014. (ENG.). 40p. (J). 10.95 (978-0-8198-3726-4(1)) Pauline Bks. & Media.

Lee, Otha. Mrs. Lee's Stories about God's First People. 2013. 268p. pap. 19.95 (978-1-58427-387-5(9)) Guardian of Truth Foundation.

Leichner, Jeannine Timko. Joy Joy the Mass: Our Family Celebration. (Illus.). 30p. (J). (gr. 1-3). 5.95 (978-0-87973-350-6(0)) Our Sunday Visitor, Publishing Div.

Lesson in a Bag-Eucharist Lesson 10. 2012. (ENG.). 24.99 (978-1-59982-396-6(9)) St. Mary's Pr. of MN.

Lesson in a Bag-Eucharist Lesson 2. 2012. (ENG.). 24.99 (978-1-59982-388-1(8)) St. Mary's Pr. of MN.

Lesson in a Bag-Eucharist Lesson 3. 2012. (ENG.). (gr. 6-8). 24.99 (978-1-59982-389-8(6)) St. Mary's Pr. of MN.

Lesson in a Bag-Eucharist Lesson 4. 2012. (ENG.). 24.99 (978-1-59982-390-4(X)) St. Mary's Pr. of MN.

Lesson in a Bag-Eucharist Lesson 5. 2012. (ENG.). 24.99 (978-1-59982-391-1(8)) St. Mary's Pr. of MN.

Lesson in a Bag-Eucharist Lesson 6. 2012. (ENG.). 24.99 (978-1-59982-392-8(6)) St. Mary's Pr. of MN.

Lesson in a Bag-Eucharist Lesson 7. 2012. (ENG.). 24.99 (978-1-59982-393-5(4)) St. Mary's Pr. of MN.

Lesson in a Bag-Eucharist Lesson 8. 2012. (ENG.). 24.99 (978-1-59982-394-2(2)) St. Mary's Pr. of MN.

Lesson in a Bag-Eucharist Lesson 9. 2012. (ENG.). 24.99 (978-1-59982-395-9(0)) St. Mary's Pr. of MN.

Lesson in a Bag-Reconciliation Lesson 1. 2012. (ENG.). 24.99 (978-1-59982-398-0(5)) St. Mary's Pr. of MN.

Lesson in a Bag-Reconciliation Lesson 2. 2012. (ENG.). 24.99 (978-1-59982-399-7(3)) St. Mary's Pr. of MN.

Lesson in a Bag-Reconciliation Lesson 3. 2012. (ENG.). 24.99 (978-1-59982-400-0(0)) St. Mary's Pr. of MN.

Lesson in a Bag-Reconciliation Lesson 4. 2012. (ENG.). 24.99 (978-1-59982-401-7(9)) St. Mary's Pr. of MN.

Lesson in a Bag-Reconciliation Lesson 5. 2012. (ENG.). 24.99 (978-1-59982-402-4(7)) St. Mary's Pr. of MN.

Lesson in a Bag-Reconciliation Lesson 6. 2012. (ENG.). 24.99 (978-1-59982-403-1(5)) St. Mary's Pr. of MN.

Lesson in a Bag-Reconciliation Lesson 7. 2012. (ENG.). 24.99 (978-1-59982-404-8(3)) St. Mary's Pr. of MN.

Lesson in a Bag-Reconciliation Lesson 8. 2012. (ENG.). 24.99 (978-1-59982-405-5(1)) St. Mary's Pr. of MN.

Liardon, Roberts & Goldenberg, Olly. God's Generals for Kids, Volume 4: Maria Woodworth-Etter. 2014. (God's Generals for Kids Ser.: Vol. 4). (ENG., Illus.). 178p. (J). (gr. 4-7). pap. 13.99 (978-1-61036-122-4(9)) Bridge-Logos, Inc.

The Little Boys' Picnic. Date not set. pap. 5.95 (978-0-87162-985-2(2)) Warner Pr., Inc.

Little KidsTime 1: Bible Story Pictures. 2004. 104p. 19.99 (978-0-8307-2773-5(6), Gospel Light) Gospel Light Pubns.

Livingston, Joshua. Sun Rays: Tales for Children of Every Age. Roth, Judy Langemo, illus. 2011. 136p. pap. 19.00 (978-1-61097-261-1(9), Resource Pubns.(OR)) Wipf & Stock Pubs.

Lockwood, Barbara. Bible Crafts on a Shoestring Budget. 2004. (Illus.). 64p. (J). (gr. -1-k). pap. 9.95 (978-0-937282-09-0(X), RB36127) Rainbow Pubs. & Legacy Pr.

Lord Teach Me to Love. 2003. 101p. (YA). per. 16.95 (978-0-9716068-1-4(1)) Lamar, Melvin Productions.

The Lord's Lady Liberty (Children's Book) The Statue of Liberation Through Christ Helping America to Remember God. 2006. (J). pap. 7.00 (978-0-9749019-8-5(9)) Understanding For Life Ministries, Inc.

Lutz, A. Fowler. Stories of the Child Jesus from Many Lands. 2003. (Illus.). viii, 175p. (J). pap. 10.95 (978-1-928832-96-6(2)) Sophia Institute Pr.

MacDonald, Mindy. 7 Days of Creation. 2004. (GodCounts Ser.). (ENG.). 24p. bds. 15.99 (978-1-59052-408-4(X), Multnomah) Doubleday Religious Publishing Group, The.

Mackenzie, Catherine. God's Little Guidebooks - Creation: God Creates Light. 2003. (ENG., Illus.). 16p. (J). pap. 0.99 (978-1-85792-841-9(5), Christian Focus) Christian Focus Pubns. GBR. Dist: Send The Light Distribution LLC.

MacKenzie, Catherine. Mary Slessor: Servant to the Slave. Jones, Andrew Lloyd, illus. 2010. (Trailblazers Ser.). (ENG.). 192p. (J). per. 8.99 (978-1-85792-348-3(0), 0dc96f56-5f04-4d5c-a4fd-291f454b7f97) Christian Focus Pubns. GBR. Dist: Bookmasters Distribution.

Main, Judith Lang. A Is for Altar, B Is for Bible. 2003. (Illus.). 65p. (J). 10.00 (978-1-56854-458-8(8), Catechesis of the Good Shepherd) Liturgy Training Pubns.

Marsico, Katie. Christianity. 2017. (21st Century Skills Library: Global Citizens: World Religions Ser.). (ENG., Illus.). 32p. (J). (gr. 4-7). lib. bdg. 29.93 (978-1-63472-155-4(1), 209192) Cherry Lake Publishing.

Marxhausen, Joanne. El Cielo Es un Lugar Maravilloso. Marxhausen, Benjamin & Koehler, Ed, illus. 2008. (SPA.). 48p. (J). (gr. -1). pap. 7.99 (978-0-7586-1587-9(6)) Concordia Publishing Hse.

—3 In 1: A Picture of God. 2nd ed. 2004. (Illus.). 48p. (J). (gr. -1-4). 9.49 (978-0-7586-0680-8(X)) Concordia Publishing Hse.

Mathes, Ben & Clack, Karin. Rowvotions: The Devotional Book of Rivers of the World. 2008. 72p. pap. 8.95 (978-0-595-53519-4(4)) iUniverse, Inc.

Mathews, Janice. Jack's Hats. 2013. (Illus.). 31p. (J). (978-0-8280-2718-2(8)) Review & Herald Publishing Assn.

McDowell, Josh. Is Christ Really God? Grades 1-3. 2007. 48p. (J). wbk. ed. 5.99 (978-1-60098-004-6(X)) Practical Christianity Foundation.

—Is Christ Really God? Grades 3-6. 2007. 48p. (J). wbk. ed. 5.99 (978-1-60098-005-3(8)) Practical Christianity Foundation.

McDowell, Josh & Bellis, Dave. Is Christ Really God? Children's Workbook. ldr.'s ed. 2007. (True Foundations Ser.). (Illus.). 142p. per. 12.99 (978-1-60098-006-0(6)) Practical Christianity Foundation.

Mrowiec, Katia, et al. God, Yahweh, Allah. 2014. (Illus.). 192p. 19.95 (978-0-8091-6771-5(9)) Paulist Pr.

Mudge, Michael. Spiritual Warfare Basic Training. 2012. 44p. pap. 21.99 (978-1-4772-8539-8(3)) AuthorHouse.

My Story of Jesus. 2006. 32p. (J). pap. 2.89 (978-0-7847-1281-8(6), 22094) Standard Publishing.

Newry, Patricia. Like Jesus Did. 2012. 94p. pap. 8.99 (978-1-58169-420-8(2), Axiom Pr.) Genesis Communications, Inc.

Newton, Richard. The Safe Compass & How It Points. 2006. pap. 14.99 (978-1-59925-059-5(4)) Solid Ground Christian Bks.

Norsigian Rowles, Helen. Armenian History: A Journey for Children. 2009. 36p. pap. 17.99 (978-1-4389-4113-4(7)) AuthorHouse.

Nystrom, Carolyn. Preach, Paul! 2004. (Follow Me Bks.). 32p. (J). 10.99 (978-0-8254-3333-7(9)) Kregel Pubns.

—Sing, Mary! 2004. (Follow Me Bks.). 32p. (J). 10.99 (978-0-8254-3336-8(3)) Kregel Pubns.

Oaks, Kristen M. & Phillips, JoAnn. The Testimony Glove. Burr, Dan, illus. 2010. (J). (gr. -1-4). 17.99 (978-1-60641-151-3(9)) Deseret Bk. Co.

Oestreicher, Mark & Lindsey, Brooklyn. 99 Thoughts for Junior Highers: Biblical Truths in Bite-Size Pieces. 2013. (Simply for Students Ser.). (ENG.). 136p. (gr. 7-9). pap. 5.99 (978-1-4707-1028-6(5)) Group Publishing, Inc.

Ogunkoya, Olukayode. Godly Children, Praying Children. 2012. 52p. pap. 23.99 (978-1-61379-470-8(3)) Salem Author Services.

One of a Kind: A Study of Christian Identity. (Crossroads Ser.). (YA). (gr. 6-8). pap., tchr. ed. 14.50 (978-0-930265-73-1(4), 120035) Faith Alive Christian Resources.

O'Neal, Debbie Trafton. The Advent Wreath: A Light in the Darkness. 2004. 16p. 1.99 (978-0-8066-2375-7(6), 10-23756, Augsburg Bks.) Augsburg Fortress, Pubs.

Orme, Robert. Christianity. 2017. (ENG.). 40p. (J). (gr. 6-9). pap. 11.99 **(978-0-00-822770-8(5))** HarperCollins Pubs. Ltd. GBR. Dist: Independent Pubs. Group.

Pafford, John M. On the Solid Rock: Christianity & Public Policy. 2003. per. 10.99 (978-0-9745948-0-4(6), 5) Ctr. For Cultural Leadership.

Parker, Amy. How Far Is Faith? (padded Board Book) 2016. (Faith, Hope, Love Ser.). (ENG.). 24p. (J). (gr. -1-k). bds. 9.99 (978-1-4336-9040-2(3), B&H Kids) B&H Publishing Group.

Paterson, Katherine. Who Am I? 2004. 96p. (J). pap. 8.00 (978-0-8028-5270-0(X)) Eerdmans, William B. Publishing Co.

Payne, Kimberley J. Trees of the Book: Learning from God's Creation. 2013. 28p. pap. (978-1-896213-73-6(1)) Praise Publishing.

Peery, L. M. God's Eternal Gift of Learning for Children. 2009. 28p. pap. 15.99 (978-1-4415-1426-4(0)) Xlibris Corp.

Pelfrey, Wanda B. Bible Crafts on a Shoestring Budget. 2004. (Illus.). 64p. (J). (gr. -1 — 1). pap. 9.95 (978-0-937282-08-3(1), RB36126) Rainbow Pubs. & Legacy Pr.

Pien, Lark. The Rosary Comic Book. Yang, Gene Luen, illus. 2003. 56p. (J). mass mkt. 5.95 (978-0-8198-6479-6(X), 332-312) Pauline Bks. & Media.

Piper, Sophie. Bible Promises for Baby's Baptism. Woodward, Antonia, illus. 2015. (ENG.). 32p. (J). (— 1). 9.99 (978-0-7459-6554-3(7)) Lion Hudson PLC GBR. Dist: Independent Pubs. Group.

—Bible Promises for Baby's Christening. Woodward, Antonia, illus. 2015. (ENG.). 32p. (J). (— 1). 9.99 (978-0-7459-7620-4(4)) Lion Hudson PLC GBR. Dist: Independent Pubs. Group.

—Bible Promises for Baby's Dedication. Woodward, Antonia, illus. 2015. (ENG.). 32p. (J). (— 1). 9.99 (978-0-7459-7606-8(9)) Lion Hudson PLC GBR. Dist: Independent Pubs. Group.

Principles of Christian Faith. 2005. (YA). per. 6.50 (978-1-59872-115-7(1)) Instant Pub.

Rae, Kathryn. Always with You I Am. 2012. 24p. (gr. 2-4). pap. 12.45 (978-1-4497-4202-7(5), WestBow Pr.) Author Solutions, Inc.

Rahayu, Abigail. How Jesus Sees You ... 2013. 32p. pap. 13.95 (978-1-4908-0266-4(5), WestBow Pr.) Author Solutions, Inc.

Rainbow Publishers Staff. Coloring Plus Activities: Jesus Our Lord & Savior. 2004. (Illus.). 64p. (J). (gr. -1-3). pap. 9.95 (978-0-937282-17-5(0), RB37162) Rainbow Pubs. & Legacy Pr.

Redden, Vicki. Heroes in Training. 2004. 375p. (J). 13.99 (978-0-8280-1843-2(X), 84-980) Review & Herald Publishing Assn.

Roche, Maite. The Gospel for Little Ones. 2011. (ENG., Illus.). 32p. (J). (gr. -1-k). bds. 12.99 (978-1-58617-507-8(6)) Ignatius Pr.

Rock, Lois. Prayers & Verses for Your First Holy Communion. Jay, Alison, illus. 2016. (ENG.). 64p. (J). (gr. k-2). 16.99 (978-0-7459-7634-1(4)) Lion Hudson PLC GBR. Dist: Independent Pubs. Group.

Saints & Strangers - Guide. 2003. (YA). pap. 9.99 (978-1-56364-706-2(0)) Vision Video.

Sanders, Nancy I. Bible Crafts on a Shoestring Budget. 2004. (Illus.). 64p. (J). (gr. 3-4). pap. 9.95 (978-0-937282-11-3(1), RB36129) Rainbow Pubs. & Legacy Pr.

Sanna, Ellyn. Folk Religion. 2004. (North American Folklore Ser.). (Illus.). 112p. (YA). (gr. 7-18). lib. bdg. 22.95 (978-1-59084-348-2(7)) Mason Crest.

Savelle, Jerry. Don't Let Go of Your Dreams. Date not set. mass mkt. 3.99 (978-0-88144-171-0(6)) Yorkshire Publishing Group.

Saxon, Terrill. Now I Lay Me down to Sleep. 2006. (Baby Blessings Ser.). (Illus.). 12p. bds. 11.99 (978-0-7847-1241-2(7), 04053) Standard Publishing.

Seaman, Alison & Brown, Alan. My Christian Faith. (Illus.). 32p. (978-0-237-51895-0(3)) Evans Brothers, Ltd.

Self, David. Christianity. 2005. (Religions of the World Ser.). (Illus.). 48p. (gr. 5-12). pap. 14.05 (978-0-8368-5872-3(7)); lib. bdg. 31.00 (978-0-8368-5866-2(2)) Stevens, Gareth Publishing LLLP. (Gareth Stevens Secondary Library).

Senker, Cath. Christianity: Signs, Symbols, Stories. 2009. (Religious Signs, Symbols, & Stories Ser.). (Illus.). 32p. (J). (ENG.). pap. 10.00 (978-1-4358-3045-5(8)); lib. bdg. 25.25 (978-1-4358-3037-0(7)) Rosen Publishing Group, Inc., The. (PowerKids Pr.).

Setzer, LeeAnn. Tiny Talks 2009: My Eternal Family. Harmon, Glenn, illus. 2008. 114p. (J). pap. 8.99 (978-1-59955-210-1(8)) Cedar Fort, Inc./CFI Distribution.

Shepherd, Good. Our Almighty God: A Bible Study. 2008. 48p. pap. 13.49 (978-1-4389-1850-1(X)) AuthorHouse.

Sheriff, Marcia. God's Great Big Love. 2013. 24p. pap. 12.45 (978-1-4497-9288-6(X), WestBow Pr.) Author Solutions, Inc.

Slattery, Kathryn. If I Could Ask God Anything: Awesome Bible Answers for Curious Kids, 1 vol. 2nd ed. 2010. (ENG.). 224p. pap. 12.99 (978-1-4003-1602-1(2)) Nelson, Thomas Inc.

Smit, Nina. My First Book about God. 2013. (ENG.). 160p. pap. 9.95 (978-1-4153-1295-7(8)) Struik Christian Media ZAF. Dist: Casemate Pubs. & Bk. Distributors, LLC.

Snow, Eliza R. The Story of Jesus. 2011. (978-1-59955-940-7(4)) Cedar Fort, Inc./CFI Distribution.

SPCK. I Can Join in Common Worship: A Children's Communion Book. 2003. (Illus.). 24p. 5.00 (978-0-281-05568-5(8)) SPCK Publishing GBR. Dist: Pilgrim Pr., The/United Church Pr.

St. John, Patricia. A Young Person's Guide to Knowing God. 2014. (ENG.). 240p. (J). (gr. 8-13). pap. 10.99 (978-1-85792-558-6(0), 25eb103e-5706-4d05-ab4c-24ce869fd1b0) Christian Focus Pubns. GBR. Dist: Bookmasters Distribution.

Steer, Malcolm. A Christian's Evangelistic Pocket Guide to Islam. 2015. (ENG.). 80p. pap. 6.99 (978-1-85792-915-7(2), cfcf1379-a4b8-4893-9f7d-cc0543024c54, Christian Focus) Christian Focus Pubns. GBR. Dist: Bookmasters Distribution.

Stohs, Anita Reight. Manualidades Faciles con Vasos de Papel. Beckmann, Ewaldo, tr. Koehler, Ed, illus. 2008. 64p. (J). pap. 9.99 (978-0-7586-1586-2(8)) Concordia Publishing Hse.

Taylor, Ina, ed. Religion & Beliefs Christianity. 2006. (ENG., Illus.). 128p. (YA). pap., stu. ed. 32.50 (978-0-7487-9670-0(3)) Nelson Thornes Ltd. GBR. Dist: Trans-Atlantic Pubns., Inc.

Taylor, Jane, et al. God Made Colours. 2015. (Board Books God Made Ser.). (ENG.). 16p. (J). (gr. -1-k). bds. 3.99 (978-1-85792-291-2(3), 1461207d-807d-4ca1-bf12-8da7fc159297) Christian Focus Pubns. GBR. Dist: Bookmasters Distribution.

Thomas Nelson Publishing Staff. Faith Journal, 1 vol. 2013. (ENG.). 96p. (J). 9.99 (978-1-4003-2386-9(X)) Nelson, Thomas Inc.

—Joy Journal, 1 vol. 2013. (ENG.). 96p. (J). 9.99 (978-1-4003-2385-2(1)) Nelson, Thomas Inc.

Thornton, champ. The Radical Book for Kids: Exploring the Roots & Shoots of Faith. 2016. (Illus.). 253p. (J). 27.99 (978-1-942572-71-8(9)) New Growth Pr.

Toward Eternal Commencement. (YA). (gr. 9-12). 20.00 (978-1-931555-44-9(3)) Our Lady of Victory Schl.

Trudeau, Paul. Where Did We Come From? 2011. 20p. pap. 12.98 (978-1-4634-4222-4(X)) AuthorHouse.

Understanding Scripture: The Genesis Creation Story. 2004. (Our Catholic Tradition Handbooks Ser.). (978-0-8294-1044-0(9)) Loyola Pr.

Vaisey, Gill & Lewis, Siân. William Booth: Cristion Arbennig Iawn. 2005. (WEL., Illus.). 28p. pap. (978-1-85644-620-4(4)) CAA.

Vogel, Jane & Sytsma, Mary. Questions Worth Asking: A Study of the Heidelberg Catechism, Year 2. (Reformed Faith Ser.). (gr. 9-10). stu. ed. 18.50 (978-1-56212-838-8(8), 130160); 20.95 (978-1-56212-837-1(X), 130165) Faith Alive Christian Resources.

Wallace, J. Warner. Cold-Case Christianity for Kids: Investigate Jesus with a Real Detective. 2016. (ENG., Illus.). 128p. (J). pap. 9.99 (978-0-7814-1457-9(1)) Cook, David C.

Watson, Carol. Christian. (Beliefs & Cultures Ser.). (Illus.). 32p. (YA). (gr. 3-6). lib. bdg. 27.10 (978-1-932889-11-6(6)) Sea-To-Sea Pubns.

Wells, Elizabeth & Trout, Lisa. All Is Gift: Catholic Stewardship / Intermediates Grades. 2007. (Illus.). 32p. (J). (gr. 4-7). pap. 10.00 (978-1-893757-55-4(2), E T Nedder) Paulist Pr.

Wesemann, Tim. It's Your Birthday . . . Let's Celebrate! 2003. (J). 5.99 (978-0-9718985-9-2(6)) C T A, Inc.

Wezeman, Phyllis Vos, et al. Wipe the Tears: 30 Children's Sermons on Death. 2005. (New Brown Bag Ser.). (Illus.). 96p. 10.00 (978-0-8298-1520-7(1)) Pilgrim Pr., The/United Church Pr.

White, Bender Richardson, et al. Catholicism & Orthodox Christianity. 3rd rev. ed. 2009. (World Religions Ser.). (Illus.). 144p. (gr. 6-12). 40.00 (978-1-60413-106-2(3), Chelsea Hse.) Facts On File, Inc.

Wigger, J. Bradley. Thank You, God. Jago, illus. 2014. (ENG.). 26p. (J). 16.00 (978-0-8028-5424-7(9), Eerdmans Bks For Young Readers) Eerdmans, William B. Publishing Co.

Wilson, Nancy. Our Mother Tongue - Answer Key. 2004. (ENG.). 54p. pap. 5.00 (978-1-59128-016-3(8)) Canon Pr.

Wipperfurth, Jenny. God Made You Special: A Celebration of Uniqueness. 2010. 28p. 13.95 (978-1-4497-0442-1(5), WestBow Pr.) Author Solutions, Inc.

Zondervan Bibles Staff. Big Bugs, Little Bugs, 1 vol. 2011. (I Can Read! / Made by God Ser.). (ENG., Illus.). 32p. (J). (gr. -1-2). pap. 3.99 (978-0-310-72186-4(5)) Zonderkidz.

Zondervan Staff. Believe - Coloring Book: Think, Act, & Be Like Jesus, 1 vol. Pamintuan, Macky, illus. 2015. (ENG.). 64p. (J). pap. 4.99 (978-0-310-75222-6(1)) Zonderkidz.

—Our Feathered Friends, 1 vol. 2011. (I Can Read! / Made by God Ser.). (ENG.). 32p. (J). (gr. -1-2). pap. 3.99 (978-0-310-72184-0(9)) Zonderkidz.

—Rainforest Friends, 1 vol. 2011. (I Can Read! / Made by God Ser.). (ENG.). 32p. (J). pap. 3.99 (978-0-310-72182-6(2)) Zonderkidz.

CHRISTIANITY—HISTORY

see Church History

CHRISTIANITY AND SCIENCE

see Religion and Science

CHRISTMAS

see also Christmas—Fiction; Christmas—Poetry; Christmas Entertainments; Christmas Plays; Jesus Christ—Nativity; Santa Claus

Absolutely Advent! Day by Day to Christmas 2006. 2007. (J). 5.95 (978-1-933178-69-1(8)) Pflaum Publishing Group.

Absolutely Advent! Getting Ready for Christmas 2006 for Intermediate Grades. 2006. (J). 5.95 (978-1-933178-43-1(4)) Pflaum Publishing Group.

Absolutely Advent! Getting Ready for Christmas 2006 for Primary Grades. 2006. (J). 5.95 (978-1-933178-42-4(6)) Pflaum Publishing Group.

Accord Publishing Staff. Flip & Click Christmas Hangman. 2011. (ENG.). 72p. (J). pap. 4.99 (978-1-4494-0836-7(2)) Andrews McMeel Publishing.

Adams, Michelle Medlock. What Is Christmas? Wummer, Amy, illus. 2012. 24p. (J). bds. 6.99 (978-0-8249-1885-9(1), Ideal Pubns.) Worthy Publishing.

—What Is Christmas? 2008. (ENG., Illus.). 26p. (J). (gr. -1-k). bds. 6.95 (978-0-8249-6668-3(6), Ideal Pubns.) Worthy Publishing.

Aloian, Molly. Christmas. 2008. (Celebrations in My World Ser.). (ENG., Illus.). 32p. (J). (gr. k-3). pap. (978-0-7787-4305-7(5)); lib. bdg. (978-0-7787-4287-6(3)) Crabtree Publishing Co.

Alvarez, Lourdes. Reyes Magos. 2005. (SPA., Illus.). 29p. (J). bds. 12.95 (978-1-58173-258-0(9)) Sweetwater Pr.

Amery, Heather. Snowy Christmas Jigsaw Book. Cartwright, Stephen, illus. 2004. (Jigsaw Books Ser.). 14p. (J). 8.95 (978-0-7945-0768-8(9), Usborne) EDC Publishing.

Amery, Heather, illus. Christmas Treasury. gif. ed. 2004. (Christmas Treasury Ser.). 128p. (J). act. bk. ed. 7.95 incl. audio compact disk (978-0-7945-0224-9(5), Usborne) EDC Publishing.

Amstutz, Lisa J. Christmas. 2017. (Holidays Around the World Ser.). (ENG., Illus.). 24p. (gr. k-1). lib. bdg. 21.99 (978-1-5157-4852-6(9), Pebble Bks.) Capstone Press of Coughlan Cos.

Anglund, Joan Walsh. Little Angels' Book of Christmas. Anglund, Joan Walsh, illus. 2005. (ENG., Illus.). 32p. (J). (gr. -1-18). bds. 8.99 (978-1-4169-1003-9(4)) Simon & Schuster Children's Publishing.

Auerbach, Annie. Christmas Eve. 2017. (ENG.). 10p. (J). (gr. -1 — 1). bds. 6.99 **(978-0-7641-6896-3(7))** Barron's Educational Series, Inc.

B&H Kids Editorial Staff. Christmas (board Book) Conger, Holli, illus. 2016. (Little Words Matter(tm) Ser.). (ENG.). 24p. (J). (gr. -1 — 1). bds. 8.99 (978-1-4336-4454-2(1), B&H Kids) B&H Publishing Group.

Baby's Very First Touchy-Feely Christmas. 2015. (Baby's Very First Touchy-Feely Board Bks.). (ENG.). (J). 7.99 (978-0-7945-3629-9(8), Usborne) EDC Publishing.

Baggott, Stella. Baby's Very First Touchy-Feely Christmas Book. Baggott, Stella, illus. 2010. (Baby's Very First Board Bks). (Illus.). 10p. (J). bds. 6.99 (978-0-7945-2852-2(X), Usborne) EDC Publishing.

Baggott, Stella, illus. Advent Calendar to Color. 2011. (Coloring Bks). (J). ring bd. 7.99 *(978-0-7945-3136-2(9),* Usborne) EDC Publishing.
Baker, Robert C. What Happened to Merry Christmas? Hill, Dave, illus. 2007. 32p. (J). (gr. -1-3). 13.49 *(978-0-7586-1346-2(6))* Concordia Publishing Hse.
Barbaresi, Nina. Shiny Christmas Stickers. 2004. (Dover Little Activity Books Stickers Ser.). (ENG., Illus.). 2p. (J). (gr. 1-4). pap. 1.50 *(978-0-486-43533-6(4))* Dover Pubns., Inc.
Barton, Chris. The Nutcracker Comes to America: How Three Ballet-Loving Brothers Created a Holiday Tradition. Gendron, Cathy, illus. 2015. (ENG.). 36p. (J). (gr. 2-5). 19.99 *(978-1-4677-2151-6(4),* Millbrook Pr.) Lerner Publishing Group.
Bauchman, 'Della. The Many Faces of Sant. 2009. 24p. pap. 13.99 *(978-1-4490-4988-1(5))* AuthorHouse.
Beilenson, Evelyn. A Warm & Fuzzy Christmas. Giordano, illus. 2013. (ENG.). 80p. 5.95 *(978-1-4413-1358-4(3))* Peter Pauper Pr. Inc.
Berghof, Michael. The Story of Christmas: Carry-Me Puzzle Book. 2011. 8p. (J). 12.99 *(978-0-7586-2798-8(X))* Concordia Publishing Hse.
Beylon, Cathy. Christmas Family Fun Coloring Book. 2006. (Dover Holiday Coloring Book Ser.). (ENG., Illus.). 32p. (J). (gr. 1-5). 3.99 *(978-0-486-44749-0(9))* Dover Pubns., Inc.
Bickico Enterprises, concept. BabyKids: Christmas Book. 2005. 16p. (J). pap. 2.95 *(978-0-9746508-7-6(0))* Bickico Enterprises, Inc.
Big Picture Press, Big Picture. Walk This World at Christmastime. Powell, Debbie, illus. 2016. (ENG.). 24p. (J). (gr. k-3). 17.99 *(978-0-7636-8921-6(1),* Big Picture Press) Candlewick Pr.
Bixby, James F. The Mystery of the Christmas Dollhouse. 2010. 76p. pap. 11.95 *(978-1-4401-7141-3(6))* iUniverse, Inc.
Bloomsbury. Carry & Play: Christmas. 2016. (ENG.). 10p. (J). bds. 6.99 *(978-1-68119-095-2(8),* 9781681190952, Bloomsbury Activity Bks.) Bloomsbury Publishing USA.
Blundell, Trevor, et al. On the Way for 3 - 9's Vol. 2: The Christmas Story & Miracles of Jesus. 2006. (On the Way (3-9's) Ser.). (ENG.). 96p. (J). pap. 17.99 *(978-1-85792-319-3(7),* 9781857923193) Christian Focus Pubns. GBR. Dist: Bookmasters Distribution.
Bodleian Library Staff & F., Warner. Father Christmas' ABC: A Fascimile. 2005. (Illus.). 24p. (gr. -1-3). 11.99 *(978-1-85124-325-9(9))* Bodleian Library GBR. Dist: Chicago Distribution Ctr.
Bollow, Ludmilla. Lulu's Christmas Story: A True Story of Faith & Hope During the Great Depression. 2014. (ENG.). 256p. 22.95 *(978-0-9911938-5-1(7))* Titletown Publishing, LLC.
Bonnet, Rosalinde. Very First Words Christmas. 2011. (Very First Words Board Book Ser.). 24p. (J). ring bd. 6.99 *(978-0-7945-2937-6(2),* Usborne) EDC Publishing.
Bonnett, Rosalind, illus. Santa Flap Book. 2012. (Flap Bks). 10p. (J). bds. 7.99 *(978-0-7945-3316-8(7),* Usborne) EDC Publishing.
Bonnice, Sherry. Christmas & Santa Claus Folklore. 2004. (North American Folklore Ser.). (Illus.). 112p. (J). (gr. 7-18). lib. bdg. 22.95 *(978-1-59084-330-7(4))* Mason Crest.
Bowers, Annette. This Reminds Me of Christmas. 2011. (ENG.). 30p. pap. 12.00 *(978-1-4679-1559-5(9))* CreateSpace Independent Publishing Platform.
Bradford, Amy L. What God Wants for Christmas: Read along, Sing Along. Bogan, Lyuba, illus. 2006. 20p. (J). (gr. 4-7). 14.99 incl. audio compact disk *(978-1-57229-914-6(2))* FamilyLife.
Briggs, Betty. A Tuff-to-Beat Christmas, A New Edition 2004. (Illus.). 115p. (YA). per. 5.95 *(978-0-9656307-4-0(9))* Sunrise Selections.
Brooks, Felicity & Allen, Francesca. Baby's Christmas. Wells, Rachel, illus. 2005. (Baby's World (Usborne Board Books) Ser.). 10p. (J). (gr. -1-k). per., bds. 8.95 *(978-0-7945-1175-3(9),* Usborne) EDC Publishing.
Brown, Margaret. On Christmas Day. Harris, Phyllis, illus. 2011. (J). 12.99 *(978-1-882077-10-6(5))* WaterMark, Inc.
Browne, Yolanda. Getting Ready for Christmas. Girouard, Patrick, illus. 2005. 32p. (gr. -1-3). 7.49 *(978-0-7586-0860-4(8))* Concordia Publishing Hse.
Buck, Deanna Draper. My First Story of the First Christmas. Harston, Jerry, illus. 2016. (J). bds. 6.99 *(978-1-62972-240-5(5))* Deseret Bk. Co.
—My First Story of the First Christmas. 2010. 36p. pap. 8.99 *(978-1-60641-690-7(1))* Deseret Bk. Co.
—My First Story of the First Christmas. Harston, Jerry, illus. 2006. 24p. (J). 13.95 *(978-1-59038-635-4(3))* Deseret Bk. Co.
Bullard, Lisa. Carter's Christmas. Saunders, Katie, illus. 2012. (Cloverleaf Books (tm) — Fall & Winter Holidays Ser.). (ENG.). 24p. (J). (gr. k-2). 6.95 *(978-0-7613-8584-4(3));* lib. bdg. 23.93 *(978-0-7613-5074-3(8))* Lerner Publishing Group. (Millbrook Pr.).
California Classic Christmas Trivia. 2005. 32p. pap. 6.95 *(978-0-635-03357-4(7))* Gallopade International.
Chabot, Shersta. Stars, Stockings, & Shepherds. Egbert, Corey, illus. 2014. 14.99 *(978-1-4621-1462-7(8),* Horizon Pubs.) Cedar Fort, Inc./CFI Distribution.
Chandler, Michael. The Littlest Cowboy's Christmas, 2 vols. Jacobsen, Terry, illus. 2006. (ENG.). 32p. (J). (gr. k-3). 17.95 *(978-1-58980-381-7(7))* Pelican Publishing Co., Inc.
Chisholm, Jane. First Christmas. 2004. (First Christmas Ser.). 48p. (J). 13.95 *(978-0-7945-0832-6(4),* Usborne) EDC Publishing.
Christmas. (Illus.). (gr. 1-4). 3.00 *(978-0-570-05521-1(0),* 54-1031) Concordia Publishing Hse.
Christmas, 6, Set A, Pack. (Smart Start Ser.). (gr. k-1). 23.00 *(978-0-7635-0412-0(2))* Rigby Education.
Christmas Coloring Fun Santa Relaxing. 2004. (J). per. 6.95 *(978-1-885920-48-5(2))* Pyramid Publishing, Inc.
Christmas Coloring Fun Santa's New Sled. 2004. (J). per. 6.95 *(978-1-885920-88-1(1))* Pyramid Publishing, Inc.
Christmas Coloring Fun Snowman. 2004. (J). per. 6.95 *(978-1-885920-90-4(3))* Pyramid Publishing, Inc.
Christmas Dot to Dot: Santa's Big Dot to Dot. 2004. (J). per. 6.95 *(978-1-885920-89-8(X))* Pyramid Publishing, Inc.
Christmas Fun Coloring Book. 2006. 16p. (J). pap. 1.99 *(978-0-7847-1745-5(1),* 04371) Standard Publishing.
The Christmas Journey Storybook, 1 vol. 2014. (ENG., Illus.). 6p. (J). bds. 19.99 *(978-1-78128-139-0(4),* Candle Bks.) Lion Hudson PLC GBR. Dist: Kregel Pubns.
Christmas Programs for Children. annuals 2006. 48p. pap. 5.99 *(978-0-7847-1343-3(X),* 08604); 2003rd ed. pap. 5.99 *(978-0-7847-1308-2(1),* 08603) Standard Publishing.
Christmas Programs for the Church. annuals 2003rd ed. 2006. 48p. pap. 6.99 *(978-0-7847-1310-5(3),* 08623) Standard Publishing.
Christmas Sticker Scenes, 1 vol. 2014. (ENG., Illus.). 24p. (J). 11.99 *(978-1-78128-123-9(8),* Candle Bks.) Lion Hudson PLC GBR. Dist: Kregel Pubns.
Cirafesi-Keszczyk, Diane. Cloudy Christmas Myths to Clear Heavenly Beliefs: A Christian Analogy of the Christmas Season for All Who Are Ready to Learn the Truth about Santa Cla. 2012. 30p. pap. 13.99 *(978-1-4497-4820-3(1),* WestBow Pr.) Author Solutions, Inc.
Clibbon, Meg & Meg, Merry. Magical Christmas. Clibbon, Lucy, illus. 2008. (ENG.). 32p. (J). (gr. k-2). *(978-1-84089-377-9(X))* Zero to Ten, Ltd.
Color All About: Christmas: A Giant Coloring Book about Christmas. 2004. (SPA & ENG., Illus.). (J). *(978-0-9763307-7-6(6))* Food Marketing Consultants, Inc.
Concordia Publishing House. The Story of Christmas Coloring & Activity Book. 2015. (ENG.). 96p. (J). pap. 3.99 *(978-0-7586-5223-2(2))* Concordia Publishing Hse.
Crow, Nosy. The Coloring Book of Cards & Envelopes: Christmas. Jones, Rebecca, illus. 2016. (ENG.). 74p. (J). (gr. k-12). pap. 10.99 *(978-0-7636-9242-1(5),* Nosy Crow) Candlewick Pr.
Cuenta Regresiva de la Navidad.Tr. of Christmas Countdown. (SPA.). (J). 5.99 *(978-0-7899-0801-8(8),* 495057) Editorial Unilit.
Dahlen, Noelle. Merry Christmas Tattoos. 2011. (Dover Tattoos Ser.). (ENG., Illus.). 2p. (J). (gr. 1-4). pap. 1.50 *(978-0-486-48609-3(5))* Dover Pubns., Inc.
Danielle, Sara & James, Danielle. Where's Father Christmas? Find Father Christmas & His Festive Helpers in 15 Fun-Filled Puzzles. Bloom, Harry, illus. 2013. (ENG.). 42p. (J). (gr. 2-5). 16.99 *(978-1-78219-476-7(2))* Blake, John Publishing, Ltd. GBR. Dist: Independent Pubs. Group.
David, Juliet. The Busy Christmas Stable, 1 vol. Pitt, Sarah, illus. 2010. (Candle Peek-A-boo Ser.). (ENG.). 8p. (J). (gr. -1-2). bds. 11.99 *(978-1-85985-803-5(1),* Candle Bks.) Lion Hudson PLC GBR. Dist: Kregel Pubns.
—Puddle Pen Christmas, 1 vol. Poole, Helen, illus. 2010. (Candle Puddle Pen Ser.). (ENG.). 10p. (J). (gr. -1-k). bds. 12.99 *(978-1-85985-868-4(6),* Candle Bks.) Lion Hudson PLC GBR. Dist: Kregel Pubns.
—A Stable in Bethlehem. Denham, Gemma & Scott, Richard, illus. 2007. 14p. (J). (gr. -1-3). 16.99 *(978-0-8254-7341-8(1),* Candle Bks.) Lion Hudson PLC GBR. Dist: Kregel Pubns.
—The Very First Christmas, 1 vol. Prole, Helen, illus. 2007. (Candle Bible for Toddlers Ser.). 24p. (J). (gr. -1-k). act. bk. ed. 6.99 *(978-0-8254-7353-1(5),* Candle Bks.) Lion Hudson PLC GBR. Dist: Kregel Pubns.
—The Very First Christmas - Changing Pictures, 1 vol. Siewert, Pauline, illus. 2010. (ENG.). 14p. (J). 11.99 *(978-1-85985-870-7(8),* Candle Bks.) Lion Hudson PLC GBR. Dist: Kregel Pubns.
Davidson, Alice Joyce. Baby Blessings Christmas. 2009. (Baby Blessings Ser.). (ENG.). 18p. (J). (gr. -1-k). bds. 12.99 *(978-0-7847-2374-6(5),* B&H Kids) B&H Publishing Group.
De Graaf, A. M. La Primera Navidad (The First Christmas) (Divertidas Historias Biblicas para Ninos Ser.). (SPA.). (J). 3.49 *(978-0-7899-0526-0(4))* Editorial Unilit.
de Sturtz, Maria Ester H. & de Perez, Ursula S. Manos a la Obra: La Iglesia Celebra, Bilingual Level 1. (ENG & SPA.). 32p. (J). 6.99 *(978-0-7586-0645-7(1))* Concordia Publishing Hse.
—Manos a la Obra: La Iglesia Celebra, Bilingual Level 2. (ENG & SPA.). 32p. (J). 6.99 *(978-0-7586-0668-6(0))* Concordia Publishing Hse.
Dent, Jenny. Hoppy's Christmas Book. (Illus.). 16p. (J). (gr. k-3). 1.75 *(978-0-85487-061-5(X))* White Eagle Publishing Trust GBR. Dist: DeVorss & Co.
Dice, Elizabeth A. & Matters, Print. Christmas & Hanukkah. 2009. (Holidays & Celebration Ser.). (Illus.). 120p. (gr. 5-8). 40.00 *(978-1-60413-092-8(X),* Chelsea Hse.) Facts On File, Inc.
Dickens, Charles & Sims, Lesley. A Christmas Carol. gif. ed. 2004. 64p. (Orig.). (J). (gr. 2-18). 8.95 *(978-0-7945-0584-4(8),* Usborne) EDC Publishing.
Dickmann, Nancy. Christmas, 1 vol. 2010. (Holidays & Festivals Ser.). (ENG.). 24p. (gr. -1-1). 22.65 *(978-1-4329-4047-8(3));* pap. 6.29 *(978-1-4329-4066-9(X))* Heinemann-Raintree. (Acorn).
Dingles, Molly. On Christmas Eve. Wallis, Rebecca, illus. 2005. (Holiday Happenings Ser.). 32p. (J). per. 10.95 *(978-1-59646-225-0(6))* Dingles & Co.
Dittmer, Cherie Pless. Angel! Angel! 2004. (Illus.). 24p. (J). (gr. -1-k). bds. 7.49 *(978-0-7586-0687-7(7))* Concordia Publishing Hse.
Doherty, Gillian, ed. The Usborne Advent Nativity Book. Allman, Howard, photos by. 2006. (Illus.). 12p. (J). (gr. -1-3). bds. 14.99 *(978-0-7945-1174-6(0),* Usborne) EDC Publishing.
Dorling Kindersley Publishing Staff. Christmas. 2010. (Baby Touch & Feel Ser.). (ENG., Illus.). 14p. (J). (gr. -1 — 1). bds. 5.99 *(978-0-7566-6683-5(X),* DK Children) Dorling Kindersley Publishing, Inc.
—Christmas - Pop-Up Peekaboo! 2013. (ENG.). 12p. (J). (gr. -1 — 1). bds. 9.99 *(978-1-4654-0930-0(0),* DK Children) Dorling Kindersley Publishing, Inc.
—Christmas Peekaboo! 2008. (ENG.). 12p. (J). (gr. -1-k). bds. 9.99 *(978-0-7566-4022-4(9),* DK Children) Dorling Kindersley Publishing, Inc.
—Touch & Feel Christmas. 2014. (Touch & Feel Ser.). (ENG., Illus.). 12p. (J). (gr. -1-k). bds. 6.99 *(978-1-4654-2036-7(3),* DK Children) Dorling Kindersley Publishing, Inc.
Douglas, Bettye. Safari Oklahoma Presents: The Magic of Christmas Around the World. Douglas, Bettye, ed. Douglas, Punchye, illus. (Multicultural). 16p. (J). (gr. k-6). 5.00 *(978-0-9703183-4-3(0))* Douglas, Bettye Forum, Inc., The.
Douglas, Punchye, illus. Safari Oklahoma Presents Operation Safe 2000: Halloween Coloring Book. (Safari Oklahoma Presents). 16p. (J). (gr. k-6). 5.00 *(978-0-9703183-2-9(4))* Douglas, Bettye Forum, Inc., The.
Egmont Books. Christmas Doodle & Colouring Book. 2014. (ENG., Illus.). 128p. (J). (gr. -1). pap. 16.99 *(978-1-4052-7351-0(8))* Egmont Bks., Ltd. GBR. Dist: Independent Pubs. Group.
Ellis, Gwen. La Flor de Pascua. Hansen, Clint, illus. 2005. 32p. (J). (gr. -1-3). 8.99 *(978-1-59185-827-0(5),* Charisma Kids) Charisma Media.
Enderlein, Cheryl L. Christmas Around the World. 2013. (Christmas Around the World Ser.). (ENG.). 24p. (gr. 1-2). lib. bdg. 101.28 *(978-1-62065-142-1(4),* First Facts) Capstone Press of Coughlan Cos.
—Christmas in England, 1 vol. 2013. (Christmas Around the World Ser.). (ENG.). 24p. (gr. 1-2). lib. bdg. 25.32 *(978-1-62065-141-4(6))* Capstone Press of Coughlan Cos.
—Christmas in Mexico, 1 vol. 2013. (Christmas Around the World Ser.). (ENG.). 24p. (gr. 1-2). lib. bdg. 25.32 *(978-1-62065-138-4(6))* Capstone Press of Coughlan Cos.
—Christmas in Sweden, 1 vol. 2013. (Christmas Around the World Ser.). (ENG., Illus.). 24p. (gr. 1-2). lib. bdg. 25.32 *(978-1-62065-140-7(8))* Capstone Press of Coughlan Cos.
—Christmas in the Philippines, 1 vol. 2013. (Christmas Around the World Ser.). (ENG.). 24p. (gr. 1-2). lib. bdg. 25.32 *(978-1-62065-139-1(4))* Capstone Press of Coughlan Cos.
Enderlein, Cheryl L. & Manning, Jack. Christmas Around the World. 2013. (Christmas Around the World Ser.). (ENG.). 24p. (gr. 1-2). 202.56 *(978-1-4765-3651-4(1),* First Facts) Capstone Press of Coughlan Cos.
Engelbrecht, Edward A. & Pawlitz, Gail E., eds. The Christmas Story: Drawn Directly from the Bible. 2011. (Illus.). 32p. (J). 13.99 *(978-0-7586-1908-2(1))* Concordia Publishing Hse.
Equipo Staff & Joly, Dominique. La Montaña. (Coleccion Mundo Maravilloso). (SPA., Illus.). 32p. (J). (gr. 2-4). *(978-84-348-7227-1(7),* SM31364) SM Ediciones ESP. Dist: Lectorum Pubns., Inc.
Erickson, Jenny. My Favorite Advent & Christmas Activity Book. 2005. (Illus.). 66p. per. 14.95 *(978-1-58595-516-9(7))* Twenty-Third Pubns./Bayard.
FamilyLife Publishing, creator. What God Wants for Christmas. 2006. (J). (gr. 4-7). 17.99 *(978-1-57229-931-3(2))* FamilyLife.
Felix, Rebecca. We Celebrate Christmas in Winter. 2014. (21st Century Basic Skills Library: Let's Look at Winter Ser.). (ENG., Illus.). 24p. (J). (gr. k-3). 22.79 *(978-1-63137-609-2(8),* 205219) Cherry Lake Publishing.
Fincher, Kathy, illus. Baby's First Christmas. 2006. 8p. (gr. -1-k). bds. 7.95 *(978-0-88271-705-0(7))* Regina Pr., Malhame & Co.
First Christmas. 2003. (Illus.). 32p. (J). 4.98 *(978-1-4054-0981-0(9))* Parragon, Inc.
The First Christmas. 2003. (Illus.). (J). bds. 6.98 *(978-1-4054-0967-4(3))* Parragon, Inc.
The First Christmas. (Illus.). 12p. (J). 4.95 *(978-1-58969-102-9(3))* Thurman Hse., LLC.
Fischer, Jean & Brumbaugh, Renae'. Christmas Prayers & Stories for Bedtime. 2015. (ENG.). 384p. (J). 19.99 *(978-1-63409-032-2(2),* Barbour Bks.) Barbour Publishing, Inc.
Florida Classic Christmas Trivia. 2005. 32p. pap. 6.95 *(978-0-635-03356-7(9))* Gallopade International.
Fogle, Robin. Itty-bitty Bible Activity Book, the Legend of the Candy Cane. 2007. (Illus.). 48p. (J). pap. 1.49 *(978-1-59317-212-1(5))* Warner Pr., Inc.
Foran, Jill. Christmas. 2003. (Celebrating Cultures Ser.). (Illus.). 24p. (J). lib. bdg. 24.45 *(978-1-59036-091-0(5))* Weigl Pubs., Inc.
Foreman, Michael, illus. & compiled by. Classic Christmas Tales. Foreman, Michael, compiled by. 2014. (ENG.). 120p. (J). (gr. 3). 16.99 *(978-1-84365-266-3(8),* Pavilion) Pavilion Bks. GBR. Dist: Independent Pubs. Group.
Frisch, Aaron. Christmas. 2005. (My First Look at Holidays Ser.). (Illus.). 24p. (J). (gr. k-3). lib. bdg. 15.95 *(978-1-58341-366-1(9),* Creative Education) Creative Co., The.
Fyffe, Brian, illus. Christmas Counting: Count & Create with 42 Holiday Stickers. 2003. 10p. (J). (gr. -1-18). bds. 4.99 *(978-1-57151-722-7(7))* Playhouse Publishing.
Garris, Norma, illus. The Story of Christmas. 2013. (Happy Day Ser.). (ENG.). 16p. (J). pap. 2.49 *(978-1-4143-9524-1(8))* Tyndale Hse. Pubs.
Georgia Classic Christmas Trivia. 2005. 32p. pap. 6.95 *(978-0-635-03354-3(2))* Gallopade International.
Gibson, Roxie C. Hey God! What Is Christmas? Gibson, James C., illus. 2007. (ENG.). 64p. (J). (gr. 4-7). 7.99 *(978-1-887654-95-1(X))* Premium Pr. America.
Gillespie, Katie. Christmas. 2015. (Let's Celebrate American Holidays Ser.). (ENG.). (J). lib. bdg. 27.13 *(978-1-4896-3617-1(X),* AV2 by Weigl) Weigl Pubs., Inc.
Gilpen, Rebecca. Christmas Activity Book. 2012. (Activity Bks). 100p. (J). pap. 12.99 *(978-0-7945-3321-2(3),* Usborne) EDC Publishing.
Gittins, Sheri. The Christmas Journey. 2005. (J). pap. 1.79 *(978-1-59317-106-3(4))* Warner Pr., Inc.
Glaser, Rebecca. The Holy Moly Christmas Story. Ferenc, Bill, illus. 2015. (Holy Moly Bible Storybooks Ser.). (ENG.). 32p. (J). (gr. k-3). 12.99 *(978-1-5064-0257-4(7),* Sparkhouse Family) Augsburg Fortress, Pubs.
Godfrey, Jan. The Road to Christmas Day. Piwowarski, Marcin, illus. 2008. 32p. (J). (gr. -1-1). 14.95 *(978-0-8198-6487-1(0))* Pauline Bks. & Media.
Godwin, Laura. This First Christmas Night. Cobalt Illustrations Studio, Inc & Low, William, illus. 2016. (ENG.). 32p. (J). 16.99 *(978-1-250-08102-5(5),* 9781250081025) Feiwel & Friends.
Goeller, Dorothy. Christmas. 2010. (All about Holidays Ser.). (Illus.). 24p. (J). 22.60 *(978-0-7660-3805-9(X));* pap. 7.95 *(978-1-59845-174-0(X))* Enslow Pubs., Inc. (Enslow Elementary).
Gordon, Bob. Santa's Christmas. 2005. (Touch & Sparkle Ser.). (Illus.). 12p. (gr. -1-k). per., bds. *(978-1-905051-79-3(4))* Make Believe Ideas.
Gore, Teresa. Christmas on Cherrybrook Lane. 2012. 40p. pap. 13.95 *(978-1-4497-3180-9(5),* WestBow Pr.) Author Solutions, Inc.
Grack, Rachel. Christmas. 2017. (Christmas Ser.). 24p. (J). (gr. k-3). pap. 6.99 ***(978-1-61891-271-8(2));*** (ENG., Illus.). lib. bdg. 25.95 *(978-1-62617-592-1(6))* Bellwether Media. (Blastoff! Readers).
Green, John, et al. Merry Christmas! Stained Glass Coloring Book. 2008. (Holiday Stained Glass Coloring Book Ser.). (ENG., Illus.). 96p. (gr. 1-5). pap. 12.99 *(978-0-486-46944-7(1))* Dover Pubns., Inc.
Greenwell, Jessica. First Sticker Book Christmas. 2011. (First Sticker Bks). 16 + 8 stickerp. (J). pap. 6.99 *(978-0-7945-2658-0(6),* Usborne) EDC Publishing.
Group Publishing Staff. Christmas Extras! Faith-Filled Ideas for C elebrating Christmas. 2008. 24p. pap. 6.99 *(978-0-7644-3712-0(7))* Group Publishing, Inc.
Guess, Catherine Ritch. The Friendly Beasts. 2006. (ENG.). 256p. pap. 12.95 *(978-1-933341-17-0(3))* CRM.
Guess Who? Christmas: A Flip-The-Flap Book. 2015. (ENG., Illus.). 6p. (J). (— 1). bds. 9.99 *(978-0-7459-6408-9(7))* Lion Hudson PLC GBR. Dist: Independent Pubs. Group.
Hall, Francie. Appalachian Christmas ABCs. Oehm, Kent, illus. 2010. (ENG.). 53p. (J). 16.95 *(978-1-57072-328-5(1))* Overmountain Pr.
Hammond World Atlas Corporation Staff. Christmas. 2009. (Hammond Undercover Ser.). 72p. (J). (gr. 3-7). pap. 13.99 *(978-0-8416-1498-7(9))* Langenscheidt Publishing Group.
Hanegar, Renee. Activités de Noël. Bauer, Larry, illus. (FRE.). 16p. pap. 29.99 *(978-0-590-16904-2(1))* Scholastic Canada, Ltd.
Hansen, Janis. Jesus: The Birthday of the King, 5 vols. Francisco, Wendy, illus. 2003. (Bible Adventure Club Ser.). 36p. wbk. ed. 19.99 incl. audio, cd-rom *(978-1-58134-331-1(0))* Crossway.
Harmon, Ruth. The Christmas Story. Date not set. 4.95 *(978-0-88271-132-4(6),* 1415) Regina Pr., Malhame & Co.
Harper, Piers. Christmas Doodles: Over 100 Pictures to Complete & Create. 2014. (ENG.). 160p. (J). (gr. 1-17). pap. 12.95 *(978-0-7624-5656-7(6),* Running Pr. Kids) Running Pr. Bk. Pubs.
Harrast, Tracy. My Giant Fold-Out Book: Christmas. Doherty, Paula, illus. 2008. 10p. (J). (gr. -1). bds. 13.49 *(978-0-7586-1425-4(X))* Concordia Publishing Hse.
Haws, Dona. Angels Foretold of Baby Jesus. 2017. (ENG.). (J). (gr. k-3). 14.99 ***(978-1-4621-1987-5(5))*** Cedar Fort, Inc./CFI Distribution.
Heald, Glenn. Santa Talks! The Life Story of Saint Nicholas. 2013. 96p. pap. 11.95 *(978-1-4759-5069-4(1))* iUniverse, Inc.
Heiligman, Deborah. Celebrate Christmas: With Carols, Presents, & Peace. (Holidays Around the World Ser.). (ENG.). 32p. (J). (gr. 1-4). 2016. pap. 7.99 *(978-1-4263-2474-1(X))* 2007. (Illus.). 15.95 *(978-1-4263-0122-3(7))* 2007. (Illus.). lib. bdg. 23.90 *(978-1-4263-0123-0(5))* National Geographic Society. (National Geographic Children's Bks.).
—Celebremos la Navidad: Con Villancicos, Regalos y Paz. 2008. (Holidays Around the World Ser.). (SPA., Illus.). 32p. (J). (gr. 1-4). 15.95 *(978-1-4263-0453-8(6),* National Geographic Children's Bks.) National Geographic Society.
Henley, Karyn. Jesus Is God's Son: Christmas. (Children's Ministry Folders). (Illus.). 8p. (gr. -1-k). 2.99 *(978-0-7847-0670-1(0),* 42220) Standard Publishing.
Henning, Heather. Christmas. Bull, Nicola, ed. Chapman, Gillian, illus. 2007. (Touch & Feel Ser.). 14p. (J). (gr. -1-3). bds. 10.49 *(978-0-7586-1383-7(0))* Concordia Publishing Hse.
Heyer, Carol. The First Christmas. 2003. (ENG., Illus.). 30p. (J). 14.95 *(978-0-8249-5469-7(6),* Ideal Pubns.) Worthy Publishing.
Hinkler Studios Staff., ed. Baby's First Christmas. 2011. (Baby's First Ser.). 12p. (J). bds. 5.99 *(978-1-74184-699-7(4))* Hinkler Bks. Pty. Ltd. AUS. Dist: Ideals Pubns.
Hinman, Christmas. Christmas/Navidad. de la Vega, Eida, tr. from ENG. 2010. (Celebrate with Me/Celebra Conmigo Ser.). (ENG & SPA., Illus.). 32p. (J). (gr. -1-2). lib. bdg. 25.70 *(978-1-58415-864-6(6))* Mitchell Lane Pubs., Inc.
Hippie Bob. Jesus Believes in Santa Claus: A Christmas Dream... 2009. 40p. pap. 19.99 *(978-1-4389-7936-6(3))* AuthorHouse.
Hollihan, Kerrie Logan. Christmas Traditions in Latin America: Tradiciones Navidenas en Latinoamérica. Sanz, Ma Pilar, tr. 2010. (Latin American Celebrations & Festivals / Celebraciones y Festivales en Latinoamérica Ser.). (SPA & ENG., Illus.). 24p. (J). (gr. 2-5). lib. bdg. 22.60 *(978-1-4358-9365-8(4))* Rosen Publishing Group, Inc., The.
Houghton, Gillian. Christmas. 2009. (My Library of Holidays Ser.). 24p. (gr. 1-1). 37.50 *(978-1-61514-692-5(X),* PowerKids Pr.) Rosen Publishing Group, Inc., The.
Hyman, Corine & Bryant, Julie. Why We Give Gifts at Christmas Time. 2013. 34p. pap. 12.00 *(978-0-9855423-9-9(X))* Teaching Christ's Children Publishing.
Ingalls, Ann. Christmas Traditions Around the World. Chavarri, Elisa, illus. 2013. (World Traditions Ser.). (ENG.). 32p. (J). (gr. k-3). 28.50 *(978-1-61473-425-3(9),* 205130) Child's World, Inc., The.
Itty-Bitty Bible Activity Book: Christmas Edition. 2005. (J). pap. *(978-1-59317-015-8(7))* Warner Pr., Inc.
James, Bethan. The First Christmas Sticker Book. 2011. 14p. (J). pap. 6.99 *(978-0-7586-3060-5(3))* Concordia Publishing Hse.
James, Danielle & Green, Dan. Where's Rudolf? Find Rudolph & His Festive Helpers in 15 Fun-Filled Puzzles. 2015. (ENG., Illus.). 46p. (J). (gr. 2-5). 14.99 *(978-1-78418-016-4(5))* Blake, John Publishing, Ltd. GBR. Dist: Independent Pubs. Group.
Jaroszko, Mike, illus. Away in a Manger. 2008. 32p. (J). (gr. -1). 13.49 *(978-0-7586-1496-4(9))* Concordia Publishing Hse.
—Away in a Manger Devotional. 2008. pap. 2.29 *(978-0-7586-1449-0(7))* Concordia Publishing Hse.
Jensen, Bonnie Rickner. A Very Merry Christmas Prayer, 1 vol. 2015. (ENG., Illus.). 24p. (J). bds. 8.99 *(978-0-7180-3053-7(2))* Nelson, Thomas Inc.
Jesus Is Lord: Thematic Unit: Christmas. (Scripture Bites Ser.). (J). (gr. -1). pap. 1.99 *(978-0-7847-9085-4(X))* Standard Publishing.
Johnson, Florence. The Christmas ABC. Wilkin, Eloise, illus. 2015. (Big Golden Board Book Ser.). (ENG.). 24p. (J). (-k). bds. 10.99 *(978-0-553-52225-9(6),* Golden Bks.) Random Hse. Children's Bks.

C
D

Johnson, Jennifer Hunt & Hansen, Holly T. Christmas Memories, 915 vols. 2003. (Illus.). 26p. 9.95 (978-0-9729610-9-7(7), CMB09) Tapis & Assocs., Inc.

Jones, Bryony. Where's Santa? Whelon, Chuck, illus. 2015. (ENG.). 32p. (J). (gr. k-3). 12.99 (978-1-4814-0619-2(1), Aladdin) Simon & Schuster Children's Publishing.

Jumbo Christmas Coloring & Activity Book. (Illus.). 300p. (J). mass mkt. (978-0-87449-054-1(5)) Unisystems, Inc.

Kalman, Bobbie. A Visual Dictionary of Christmas Long Ago. 2010. (Crabtree Visual Dictionaries Ser.). (ENG.). 32p. (J). (gr. 1-7). pap. (978-0-7787-3526-7(5)); lib. bdg. (978-0-7787-3506-9(0)) Crabtree Publishing Co.

Kaplan, Richard, et al. Santa, NASA y el Hombre en la Luna. Palumbo, Debi, illus.Tr. of Santa, NASA & the Man in the Moon. (SPA.). (Orig.). (J). (gr. -1-5). pap. 14.95 (978-0-9649608-1-7(8)) Batyah Productions, Inc.

Kelley, Emily. Christmas Around the World. Oeltjenbruns, Joni, illus. rev. ed. (On My Own Holidays Ser.). 48p. (gr. 2-4). 2004. (J). lib. bdg. 25.26 (978-0-87614-915-7(8)) 2003. (ENG.). pap. 6.95 (978-1-57505-580-0(5)) Lerner Publishing Group.

—La Navidad Alrededor del Mundo. Oeltjenbruns, Joni, illus. 2005. (Yo Solo Festividades Ser.). (SPA.). 48p. (J). (gr. 2-4). per. 5.95 (978-0-8225-3117-3(8)) Lerner Publishing Group.

—La Navidad Alrededor del Mundo. Translations.com Staff, tr. Oeltjenbruns, Joni, illus. 2005. (Yo Solo - Festividades (on My Own - Holidays) Ser.). (SPA & ENG.). 48p. (gr. 2-4). lib. bdg. 25.26 (978-0-8225-3116-6(X)) Lerner Publishing Group.

Kenealy, Cindy Brouse. Away in a Manger: An ABC Book on the Birth of Jesus Christ. 2011. 36p. pap. 15.49 (978-1-4520-2293-2(3)) AuthorHouse.

Keogh, Josie. Christmas. 2013. (PowerKids Readers: Happy Holidays! Ser.). (ENG., Illus.). 24p. (J). (gr. k-2). pap. 8.25 (978-1-4488-9706-3(8)); lib. bdg. 22.60 (978-1-4488-9625-7(8)) Rosen Publishing Group, Inc., The. (PowerKids Pr.).

—Christmas: Navidad. Alamán, Eduardo, tr. from SPA. 2013. (PowerKids Readers: Happy Holidays! / !Felices Fiestas! Ser.). (ENG., Illus.). 24p. (gr. k-2). lib. bdg. 22.60 (978-1-4488-9968-5(0), PowerKids Pr.) Rosen Publishing Group, Inc., The.

KidsLabel Staff. Christmas. 2006. (Spot 7 Ser.: SPOT). (ENG., Illus.). 40p. (J). (gr. -1-17). 12.95 (978-0-8118-5323-1(3)) Chronicle Bks. LLC.

King James Bible Staff. Christmas Is Here. Castillo, Lauren, illus. 2010. (ENG.). 32p. (J). (gr. -1-2). 12.99 (978-1-4424-0822-7(7), Simon & Schuster Bks. For Young Readers) Simon & Schuster Bks. For Young Readers.

Kovacs, Victoria. Christmas/Easter Flip-Over Book. Krome, Mike, illus. 2015. (Little Bible Heroes(tm) Ser.). (ENG.). 32p. (J). (gr. k-2). pap. 3.99 (978-1-4336-8711-2(9), B&H Kids) B&H Publishing Group.

Kramer, Janice. The Christmas Baby. Rooney, Ronnie, illus. 2008. (Arch Bks.). 16p. (J). (gr. k-4). pap. 1.99 (978-0-7586-1454-4(3)) Concordia Publishing Hse.

Kramer, Mark. Santa Claws: A True Story. 2009. (Illus.). 25p. (J). pap. 15.95 (978-1-4327-4793-0(2)) Outskirts Pr., Inc.

Kurtz, John. Santa Claus Christmas Paper Dolls. 2013. (Dover Paper Dolls Ser.). (ENG.). 32p. (J). (gr. 1-5). pap. 9.99 (978-0-486-49424-1(1)) Dover Pubns., Inc.

Lacey, Minna & Gilpin, Rebecca. 50 Christmas Things to Make & Do. 2007. (50 Christmas Things to Make & Do Ser.). 104p. (J). spiral bd. 9.99 (978-0-7945-1837-0(0), Usborne) EDC Publishing.

Landau, Elaine. What Is Christmas? 2011. (I Like Holidays! Ser.). (Illus.). 24p. (J). (gr. k-18). pap. 7.95 (978-1-59845-295-2(9), Enslow Elementary); (gr. 1-4). lib. bdg. 22.60 (978-0-7660-3702-1(9)) Enslow Pubs., Inc.

—What Is Halloween? 2011. (I Like Holidays! Ser.). (Illus.). 24p. (J). (gr. k-18). pap. 7.95 (978-1-59845-293-8(2), Enslow Elementary) Enslow Pubs., Inc.

Lane, Leena. Christmas Fun: Bible Activity Book. Bishop, Roma, illus. 2015. (J). pap. 9.95 (978-0-8198-1651-1(5)) Pauline Bks. & Media.

Lang Books(Editors) Staff, ed. Christmas. gif. ed. 2004. 64p. 7.95 (978-0-8249-5866-4(7), Ideal Pubns.) Worthy Publishing.

—Christmas Ideals 2004, 61. 2004. (Illus.). 88p. pap. 5.95 (978-0-8249-1235-2(7), Ideal Pubns.) Worthy Publishing.

Larkin, Jean. Absolutely Advent! Getting Ready for Christmas 2007. 2007. (Illus.). 32p. pap. 5.95 (978-1-933178-68-4(X)) Pflaum Publishing Group.

Larkin, Jean K. Absolutely Advent! Getting Ready for Christmas 2005. l.t. ed. 2005. (Illus.). (J). 5.95 (978-1-933178-11-0(6), 3550) Pflaum Publishing Group.

Lawrence, Elizabeth. Celebrate Christmas. 2015. (Our Holidays Ser.). (ENG., Illus.). 24p. (J). (gr. 1-1). pap. 8.22 (978-1-5026-0406-4(X)) Cavendish Square Publishing.

Lee, Sally. A Short History of Christmas. 2015. (Holiday Histories Ser.). (ENG., Illus.). 24p. (gr. k-1). lib. bdg. 26.65 (978-1-4914-6095-5(4)) Capstone Press of Coughlan Cos.

Levivier, Juliette. Prayers Around the Crib. Gravier, Anne, illus. 2012. (ENG.). 46p. (J). (gr. -1-3). 9.99 (978-1-58617-773-7(7)) Ignatius Pr.

Liguori Publications, creator. Every Day of Advent & Christmas, Year C: A Book of Activities for Children. 2006. (Illus.). 31p. pap. 2.95 (978-0-7648-1541-6(5)) Liguori Pubns.

Lindeen, Mary. Christmas. 2015. (BeginningtoRead Ser.). (ENG.). 32p. (J). (gr. k-2). pap. 11.94 (978-1-60357-750-2(5)) Norwood Hse. Pr.

—Merry Christmas! 2015. (BeginningtoRead Ser.). (ENG., Illus.). 32p. (J). (gr. k-2). lib. bdg. 22.60 (978-1-59953-690-3(0)) Norwood Hse. Pr.

Litchfield, Jo. Christmas. Litchfield, Jo, illus. 2005. (Usborne Look & Say Ser.). (Illus.). 10p. (J). (gr. -1-k). bds. 9.95 (978-0-7945-1173-9(2), Usborne) EDC Publishing.

Locke, Ian. Cracking Christmas. Rowe, Alan, illus. 21st ed. 2003. (ENG.). 64p. (J). pap. 3.99 (978-0-330-37504-7(0), Pan) Pan Macmillan GBR. Dist: Trafalgar Square Publishing.

Lomax M.Ed., L. E. A Saint Called Nicholas: The Christmas Legends Series, Vol. I. 2012. 52p. pap. 23.99 (978-1-4582-0584-1(3), Abbott Pr.) Author Solutions, Inc.

Lorini, Andrea. The Christmas Stocking. Pagnoni, Roberta & Rigo, Laura, illus. 2016. (Little People Shape Bks.). (ENG.). 10p. (J). (gr. -1-k). bds. 7.99 (978-0-7641-6850-5(9)) Barron's Educational Series, Inc.

Lots of Things to Find & Color for Christmas. 2011. (Activity Bks). 96p. (J). pap. 12.99 (978-0-7945-3174-4(1), Usborne) EDC Publishing.

Lowery, Marie Hayes. Bruce & Swish: A Christmas Tale of Holiday Wishes & Dreams. 2012. 16p. pap. 15.99 (978-1-4772-5686-2(5)) AuthorHouse.

Lucado, Max. The Christmas Story for Children, 1 vol. 2014. (ENG.). 32p. (J). pap. 6.99 (978-0-310-73598-4(X)) Zonderkidz.

Mackall, Dandi Daley. The Wonder of Christmas. Hill, Dave, illus. 2008. 32p. (J). (gr. -1-3). 13.49 (978-0-7586-1499-5(3)) Concordia Publishing Hse.

Maier, Paul L. The Very First Christmas. 32p. (J). 9.99 (978-0-570-07186-0(0)) Concordia Publishing Hse.

—The Very First Christmas. Ordaz, Francisco, illus. 2004. 20p. (J). (gr. -1-k). bds. 7.49 (978-0-7586-0689-1(3)) Concordia Publishing Hse.

Manning, Jack. Christmas Around the World. 2013. (Christmas Around the World Ser.). (ENG.). 24p. (gr. 1-2). 101.28 (978-1-4765-3650-7(3), First Facts) Capstone Press of Coughlan Cos.

—Christmas in France, 1 vol. 2013. (Christmas Around the World Ser.). (ENG.). 24p. (gr. 1-2). 25.32 (978-1-4765-3102-1(1), First Facts) Capstone Press of Coughlan Cos.

—Christmas in Germany, 1 vol. 2013. (Christmas Around the World Ser.). (ENG.). 24p. (gr. 1-2). 25.32 (978-1-4765-3099-4(8), First Facts) Capstone Press of Coughlan Cos.

—Christmas in Italy, 1 vol. 2013. (Christmas Around the World Ser.). (ENG.). 24p. (gr. 1-2). 25.32 (978-1-4765-3100-7(5), First Facts) Capstone Press of Coughlan Cos.

—Christmas in Norway, 1 vol. 2013. (Christmas Around the World Ser.). (ENG.). 24p. (gr. 1-2). 25.32 (978-1-4765-3101-4(3), First Facts) Capstone Press of Coughlan Cos.

Marks, Anthony. Christmas Tunes - Internet Referenced. 2008. (Music Ser.). 64p. (J). spiral bd. 18.99 (978-0-7945-2256-8(4), Usborne) EDC Publishing.

Marsh, Carole. Christmas Traditions Around the World. 2003. 12p. (J). (gr. k-4). pap. 2.95 (978-0-635-02154-0(4)) Gallopade International.

—Michigan Classic Christmas Trivia. 2005. (Illus.). 32p. (J). (gr. 4-7). pap. 6.95 (978-0-635-03353-6(4)) Gallopade International.

—Ohio Classic Christmas Trivia. (Carole Marsh Ohio Bks.). (Illus.). 32p. lib. bdg. 21.95 (978-0-635-01597-6(8), 15978, Marsh, Carole Bks.); 2005. (J). (gr. 4-7). pap. 6.95 (978-0-635-03351-2(8)) Gallopade International.

—Virginia Classic Christmas Trivia. 2005. (Illus.). 32p. (J). (gr. 4-7). pap. 6.95 (978-0-635-03352-9(6)) Gallopade International.

—Why Do We Hang Christmas Stockings. 2003. 12p. (J). (gr. k-4). pap. 2.95 (978-0-635-02152-6(8)) Gallopade International.

Marzollo, Jean. A Christmas Tree. Wick, Walter, illus. 2010. (I Spy Ser.). (ENG.). 24p. (J). (gr. -1-3). 9.99 (978-0-545-22092-7(0), Cartwheel Bks.) Scholastic, Inc.

Mattern, Joanne. Celebrate Christmas. 2007. (Celebrate Holidays Ser.). (Illus.). 112p. (J). (gr. 5-9). lib. bdg. 33.27 (978-0-7660-2776-3(7)) Enslow Pubs., Inc.

Mazurkiewicz, Jessica. Santa's Busy Workshop Stained Glass Jr. Coloring Book. 2012. (Dover Stained Glass Coloring Book Ser.). (ENG.). 32p. (J). (gr. -1-5). pap. 3.99 (978-0-486-49870-6(0)) Dover Pubns., Inc.

—3-D Coloring Book — Crazy Christmas. 2011. (Dover 3-D Coloring Book Ser.). (ENG., Illus.). 32p. (J). (gr. 2-6). pap. 5.99 (978-0-486-48409-9(2)) Dover Pubns., Inc.

McGill, Jordan, ed. Christmas. 2011. (J). (gr. 3-5). pap. 12.95 (978-1-61690-685-6(5), AV2 by Weigl); (Illus.). 24p. (gr. 2-5). 27.13 (978-1-61690-679-5(0)) Weigl Pubs., Inc.

McGrath, Barbara Barbieri. Christmas Colors & Counting. Tagel, Peggy, illus. 2016. (First Celebrations Ser.). (ENG.). 12p. (J). (— 1). bds. 6.95 (978-1-58089-531-6(X)) Charlesbridge Publishing, Inc.

McKissack, Fredrick L. & McKissack, Lisa Beringer. Christmas. 2009. (Holidays—Count & Celebrate! Ser.). (Illus.). 32p. (J). (gr. k-3). lib. bdg. 23.94 (978-0-7660-3103-6(9)) Enslow Pubs., Inc.

McNeil, Niki, et al. HOCPP 1130 Christmas Cheer. 2006. spiral bd. 15.50 (978-1-60308-130-6(5)) In the Hands of a Child.

—HOCPP1021 Symbols of Christmas. 2004. spiral bd. 15.50 (978-1-60308-021-7(X)) In the Hands of a Child.

Medendorp, Donna & Medendorp, Nick. Keeping CHRIST in Christmas for Kids. 2004. (Illus.). 64p. (J). pap. 13.95 (978-0-9764433-0-8(9)) Kids 4 Ever.

Mercier, Johanne. Caillou - Merry Christmas! Brignaud, Pierre, illus. 2nd ed. 2012. (Confetti Ser.). (ENG.). 24p. (J). (gr. -1-1). pap. 4.99 (978-2-89718-020-1(X)) Caillouet, Gerry.

Meres, Jonathan. The Xmas Factor. 2012. (ENG., Illus.). 80p. (YA). (gr. 3-6). 10.99 (978-1-4081-8033-4(2), 9781408180334, Bloomsbury USA Childrens) Bloomsbury Publishing USA.

Merry Christmas, Dear. 4.95 (978-0-87895-623-4(9)) Modern Curriculum Pr.

Migliardo, Emiliano, illus. Seek & Find Christmas. 2017. (ENG.). 24p. (J). pap. 4.99 **(978-1-68119-542-1(9)**, 9781681195421, Bloomsbury Activity Bks.) Bloomsbury Publishing USA.

Miller, Claire. The Christmas Message. Dorenkamp, Michelle, illus. 2006. (Arch Bks.). 16p. (J). 1.99 (978-0-7586-0872-7(1)) Concordia Publishing Hse.

Monahan, Leo. The Twelve Days of Christmas. Monahan, Leo, illus. 2007. (ENG., Illus.). 24p. (J). 19.95 (978-1-58117-624-7(4), Intervisual/Piggy Toes) Bendon, Inc.

Montgomery Gibson, Jane. Go Find Christmas. Montgomery Gibson, Jane, illus. 2005. (Illus.). (YA). bds. 8.99 (978-1-4183-0025-8(X)) Christ Inspired, Inc.

Morrison, Jessica. Christmas. 2010. (Illus.). 24p. (978-1-55388-607-5(0)); pap. (978-1-55388-608-2(9)) Weigl Educational Pubs. Ltd.

Mullins, George. What Christmas Means to Me. 2006. (Illus.). 28p. per. 7.95 (978-1-59858-247-5(X)); per. 10.95 (978-1-59858-212-3(7)) Dog Ear Publishing, LLC.

Munro, Roxie. Christmastime in New York City. 2014. (ENG., Illus.). 32p. (J). (gr. -1-3). 14.95 (978-0-7893-2740-6(6)) Rizzoli International Pubns., Inc.

Murray, Julie. Christmas, 1 vol. 2003. (Holidays Ser.). (ENG.). 24p. (gr. k-4). 25.65 (978-1-57765-951-8(1), Buddy Bks.) ABDO Publishing Co.

My Nativity ABCs. 2017. (ENG.). (J). (gr. -1-k). 14.99 **(978-1-4621-2027-7(X))** Cedar Fort, Inc./CFI Distribution.

Navillus, Nell. Verdadero Cuento de Navidad. Alvarez, Lourdes, tr. Eitzen, Allan, illus. 2005. (SPA.). 28p. (J). 12.95 (978-1-58173-250-4(3)) Sweetwater Pr.

Nellist, Glenys. Christmas Love Letters from God: Bible Stories, 1 vol. Clowes, Rachel, illus. 2016. (Love Letters from God Ser.). (ENG.). 32p. (J). 16.99 (978-0-310-74824-3(0)) Zonderkidz.

New York Classic Christmas Trivia. 2005. 32p. pap. 6.95 (978-0-635-03355-0(0)) Gallopade International.

North, Merry. My Christmas: Picture, Play & Tote Book. 2003. (Illus.). 10p. (J). (gr. -1-18). bds. 5.99 (978-1-57151-717-3(0)) Playhouse Publishing.

Oakes, Loretta. A Peek-a-Boo Christmas! Hall, Mary, illus. 2010. 16p. (J). (gr. -1). pap. 9.95 (978-0-8091-6754-8(9), Ambassador Bks.) Paulist Pr.

O'Brien, Joan. Christmas Around the World Coloring Book. 2003. (Dover Holiday Coloring Book Ser.). (ENG., Illus.). 32p. (J). (gr. -1-5). pap. 3.99 (978-0-486-42651-8(3)) Dover Pubns., Inc.

Olive, Teresa, et al. Best-Loved Christmas Stories. Munger, Nancy et al, illus. 2014. (ENG.). 102p. (J). 9.99 (978-0-7586-4661-3(5)) Concordia Publishing Hse.

Olson, Barbara. Christmas in Gondar: Five Ethiopian Stories. 2010. 36p. pap. 15.49 (978-1-4520-3646-5(2)) AuthorHouse.

One Starry Night Coloring & Activity. 2005. mass mkt. 2.25 (978-1-59317-006-6(8)) Warner Pr., Inc.

Onyefulu, Ifeoma. An African Christmas. 2005. (ENG., Illus.). 32p. (J). (gr. -1-4). 15.95 (978-1-84507-387-9(8), Frances Lincoln Children's Bks.) Quarto Publishing Group UK GBR. Dist: Hachette Bk. Group.

Owens, L. L. Christmas, 1 vol. Conger, Holli, illus. 2009. (Cultural Holidays Ser.). (ENG.). 32p. (gr. -1-4). 28.50 (978-1-60270-601-9(8), Looking Glass Library- Nonfiction) Magic Wagon.

Pagnoni, Roberta & Rigo, Laura, illus. The Twelve Days of Christmas. 2013. (ENG.). 24p. (J). (gr. -1 — 1). bds. 10.99 (978-0-7641-6622-8(0)) Barron's Educational Series, Inc.

Palmer, Bill. And to All a Good Night: Christmas Folklore. 2013. (Illus.). 48p. (J). pap. (978-1-4222-2498-4(8)) Mason Crest.

—And to All a Good Night: Christmas Folklore. Jabbour, Alan, ed. 2012. (North American Folklore for Youth Ser.). (Illus.). 48p. (J). (gr. 4). 19.95 (978-1-4222-2487-8(2)) Mason Crest.

Papaw. Remembering A Child's Best Christmas. 2010. 48p. pap. 12.99 (978-1-4520-0080-0(8)) AuthorHouse.

Paradis, Anne. Caillou Waits for Santa: Christmas Special Edition with Advent Calendar. Sévigny, Éric, illus. 2015. (ENG.). 24p. (J). (gr. -1-k). 9.99 (978-2-89718-207-6(5)) Caillouet, Gerry.

Parton, Paula. We Love Christmas! Parton, Paula, illus. 2009. (Illus.). 30p. pap. 11.95 (978-1-935118-84-8(6)) Bellissima Publishing, LLC.

The Perfect Christmas. 2004. (J). mass mkt. 12.95 (978-0-9763223-0-6(7)) Wright, Robert.

Peter Pauper Press Staff, creator. Merry Christmas: An Art Activity Book. 2006. (Scratch & Sketch Ser.). (Illus.). 64p. (J). (gr. 4-7). 12.99 (978-1-59359-943-0(9)) Peter Pauper Pr. Inc.

Pettiford, Rebecca. Christmas. 2014. 24p. (J). lib. bdg. 25.65 (978-1-62031-128-8(3), Bullfrog Bks.) Jump! Inc.

Phillips, Dee. Colors. 2009. (Christmas Lift the Flap Ser.). (ENG.). 10p. (J). (gr. -1-k). bds. 5.95 (978-1-84696-966-9(2), TickTock Books) Octopus Publishing Group GBR. Dist: Independent Pubs. Group.

—First Addition. 2009. (Christmas Lift the Flap Ser.). (ENG.). 10p. (J). (gr. -1-k). bds. 5.95 (978-1-84696-967-6(0), TickTock Books) Octopus Publishing Group GBR. Dist: Independent Pubs. Group.

—First Words. 2009. (Christmas Lift the Flap Ser.). (ENG.). 10p. (J). (gr. -1-k). bds. 5.95 (978-1-84696-968-3(9), TickTock Books) Octopus Publishing Group GBR. Dist: Independent Pubs. Group.

—Numbers. 2009. (Christmas Lift the Flap Ser.). (ENG.). 10p. (J). (gr. -1-k). bds. 5.95 (978-1-84696-969-0(7), TickTock Books) Octopus Publishing Group GBR. Dist: Independent Pubs. Group.

Pingry, Patricia A. The Story of Christmas. Thornburgh, Rebecca, illus. 2012. 24p. (J). pap. 4.99 (978-0-8249-5645-5(1), Ideal Pubns.) Worthy Publishing.

—The Story of Christmas. 2010. (Illus.). 22p. (J). 6.99 (978-0-8249-1845-3(2), Ideal Pubns.) Worthy Publishing.

Pinnington, Andrea. Christmas Pocket Activity Fun & Games: Games, Puzzles, Fold-Out Scenes, Patterned Paper, Stickers! 2014. (Pocket Activity Fun & Games Ser.). (ENG.). 96p. (J). (gr. 1-5). pap. 7.99 (978-1-4380-0517-1(2)) Barron's Educational Series, Inc.

Pirotta, Saviour. Christmas. 2007. (We Love Holidays Ser.). (Illus.). 24p. (J). (gr. -1-3). lib. bdg. 22.60 (978-1-4042-3704-9(6), PowerKids Pr.) Rosen Publishing Group, Inc., The.

Pleau-Murissi, Marilyn. Happy Holidays! Sévigny, Eric, illus. 2008. (Caillou Ser.). (ENG.). 80p. (J). (gr. -1-1). 14.95 (978-2-89450-644-8(9)) Caillouet, Gerry.

Ponto, Joanna & Erlbach, Arlene. Christmas. 2016. (Story of Our Holidays Ser.). (Illus.). 32p. (J). (gr. 3-3). pap. 10.52 (978-0-7660-7617-4(2)) Enslow Pubs., Inc.

Poynor, Alice Burnett. The Coming Day: A true Christmas story from China. 2011. 36p. pap. 13.95 (978-1-4497-2002-5(1), WestBow Pr.) Author Solutions, Inc.

Priddy, Roger. Christmas Treasure Hunt. 2014. (ENG., Illus.). 16p. (J). (— 1). bds. 9.99 (978-0-312-51735-9(1), 9780312517359, Priddy Bks.) St. Martin's Pr.

—Merry Christmas. 2009. (Bright Baby Touch & Feel Ser.). (ENG.). 12p. (J). (gr. -1 — 1). bds. 4.95 (978-0-312-50652-0(X), 9780312506520, Priddy Bks.) St. Martin's Pr.

—Slide & Find Christmas. 2010. (Slide & Find Ser.). (ENG., Illus.). 10p. (J). (gr. -1 — 1). bds. 7.95 (978-0-312-50969-9(3), 9780312509699, Priddy Bks.) St. Martin's Pr.

—Sticker Friends: Christmas. 2016. (Sticker Friends Ser.). (ENG.). 24p. (J). pap. 4.99 (978-0-312-52050-2(6), 9780312520502, Priddy Bks.) St. Martin's Pr.

Publications International Ltd. Staff, ed. Rudolph the Red-Nosed Reindeer: My First Library. 2010. 10p. (J). bds. 12.98 (978-1-60553-819-8(1)) Phoenix International Publications, Inc.

—Rudolph the Red-Nosed Reindeer: Book & Cuddly Rudolph. 2010. (J). 5.98 (978-1-60553-750-4(0)) Phoenix International Publications, Inc.

—Rudolph the Red-Nosed Reindeer (Look & Find) 2010. 24p. (J). 7.98 (978-1-60553-958-4(9)) Phoenix International Publications, Inc.

Pulley, Kelly, illus. The Very First Christmas, 1 vol. 2008. (Beginner's Bible Ser.). (ENG.). 32p. (J). pap. 47.76 (978-0-310-71816-1(3)); pap. 1.99 (978-0-310-71826-0(0)) Zonderkidz.

Rauenhorst, Linda. Frohliche Weihnachten: Learning Songs & Traditions in German. Collier, Roberta, illus. 2007. (Teach Me Ser.). (GER & ENG.). 32p. (J). (gr. -1-3). 19.95 (978-1-59972-063-0(9)) Teach Me Tapes, Inc.

Reed, Jonathan. Christmas Surprise. Hale, Jenny, illus. 2011. (ENG.). 16p. (J). (gr. -1-k). 14.99 (978-1-921714-88-7(3)) Little Hare Bks. AUS. Dist: Independent Pubs. Group.

Reed, Jonathan & Hale, Jenny. Christmas Surprise. 2007. (Illus.). 16p. (978-1-921049-59-0(6)) Little Hare Bks. AUS. Dist: HarperCollins Pubs. Australia.

Reed, Phil. Extraordinary Grace. 2009. 56p. pap. 24.49 (978-1-4490-0429-3(6)) AuthorHouse.

Rees, Glyn, et al. Dolig Llawen! 2005. (WEL., Illus.). 48p. pap. (978-0-903131-20-9(X)) Urdd Gobaith Cymru.

Remson, Billie. A Mississippi Winter on Bluebird Hill: A True Story about Our Little Farm in the Hills of Southern Mississippi. Garraway, Kym, illus. 2004. (J). per. 12.95 (978-1-59571-044-4(2)) Word Association Pubs.

Renzi, Pam. The Global Christmas. 2012. 26p. pap. 15.95 (978-1-4525-5588-1(5)) Balboa Pr.

Richards, V. H. First Christmas Color Act Bk. 24p. pap. 1.25 (978-0-8198-2677-0(4), 332-096) Pauline Bks. & Media.

Richards, Virginia Helen & Halpin, D. Thomas, illus. My Christmas Picture Book. 2005. 14p. (J). 4.95 (978-0-8198-4829-1(8), 332-220) Pauline Bks. & Media.

Richterkessing, Suzanne. The Time of Christmas. 32p. (J). 7.99 (978-0-7586-0149-0(2)) Concordia Publishing Hse.

Rigby, Christopher & Sail, Nicola. Let's Have a Christmas: Flip Quiz. 2003. (Family Flip Quiz Ser.). (Illus.). 152p. (J). spiral bd. 12.95 (978-1-902947-96-9(7)) Miles Kelly Publishing, Ltd. GBR. Dist: Independent Pubs. Group.

Rivera Lassén, Carmen & Maldonado, Víctor. Los tres reyes a Caballo. Alvarez, Mrinali, illus. 2005. (SPA.). 28p. (J). 8.95 (978-0-8477-1552-7(3)) Univ. of Puerto Rico Pr.

Robertson, Brynn, compiled by. Standard Christmas Program Book: Poems & Programs for Christmas & Thanksgiving. 2006. (Illus.). 48p. pap. 6.99 (978-0-7847-1647-2(1)) Standard Publishing.

Robinson, Helen Lee, compiled by. Guide's Greatest Christmas Stories. 2003. (Pathfinder Junior Book Club Ser.). 144p. (J). pap. 10.99 (978-0-8280-1802-9(2)) Review & Herald Publishing Assn.

Roff, Don. Holiday Magic. 2012. (Illus.). 32p. (J). (978-0-545-52106-2(8)) Scholastic, Inc.

Rogers, Kirsteen. Christmas Coloring Book. 2009. (Coloring Bks). 34p. (J). pap. 5.99 (978-0-7945-2438-8(9), Usborne) EDC Publishing.

—Christmas Patterns Coloring Book. 2011. (Coloring Bks). 32p. (J). pap. 5.99 (978-0-7945-3184-3(9), Usborne) EDC Publishing.

Rustad, Martha E. H. All about Christmas. 2015. (Celebrate Winter Ser.). (ENG., Illus.). 24p. (gr. k-1). lib. bdg. 21.99 (978-1-4914-6006-1(7), Pebble Bks.) Capstone Press of Coughlan Cos.

Rydaker, Ewa. Lucia Morning in Sweden. Lewis, Anne Gillespie, ed. Stahlberg, Carina, illus. 2014. (ENG.). 35p. (J). (gr. -1-3). pap. 8.99 (978-1-935666-65-3(7)) Nodin Pr.

Salas, Laura Purdie. J Is for Jingle Bells: A Christmas Alphabet, 1 vol. 2010. (Alphabet Fun Ser.). (ENG & ABK.). 32p. (gr. 1-2). lib. bdg. 27.32 (978-1-4296-4463-1(X), Aplus Bks.) Capstone Press of Coughlan Cos.

Sanderson, CarolAnn. Two Nativities for Emilee: A Chronology of the Biblical Christmas Story. 2013. (Illus.). 24p. pap. 14.93 (978-1-4669-9314-3(6)) Trafford Publishing.

Santa Activity Book. 2007. (Shaped Christmas Activity Ser.). 64p. pap. (978-1-4075-0776-7(1)) Parragon, Inc.

Sapp, Karen, illus. Christmas Is... 2010. (ENG.). 24p. (J). (gr. -1-k). 8.99 (978-0-00-730375-5(0)) HarperCollins Pubs. Ltd. GBR. Dist: Independent Pubs. Group.

Saunders, Katie. Toddler Christmas: Activities, Games, & Stories for Excited Toddlers. 2013. (Toddler Bks.). (ENG.). 48p. (J). (gr. -1 — 1). 9.99 (978-0-7641-6631-0(X)) Barron's Educational Series, Inc.

Scheidies, Carolyn R. The heart of Christmas. 2005. 26p. 12.81 (978-1-4116-5925-4(2)) Lulu Pr., Inc.

Schlafer, Linda. A Gift for the Christ Child: A Christmas Folktale. Wilson, Anne, illus. 2004. 26p. (gr. -1-3). 15.95 (978-0-8294-1606-0(4)) Loyola Pr.

Schorr, Titus. We Celebrate Christmas, 01 vols., 1. 2016. (Rosen REAL Readers: Social Studies Nonfiction / Fiction: Family, Community, & the World Ser.). (ENG.). 8p. (J). pap. 5.46 (978-1-5081-1713-1(6), Rosen Classroom) Rosen Publishing Group, Inc., The.

Schroff, Laura & Tresniowski, Alex. An Invisible Thread Christmas Story. Root, Barry, illus. 2015. (ENG.). 32p. (J). (gr. -1-3). 17.99 (978-1-4814-1930-7(7), Little Simon) Little Simon.

Schuon, Catherine & Fitzgerald, Michael Oren, eds. King James Christmas: Biblical Selections with Illustrations from Around the World. 2012. (ENG., Illus.). 80p. (J). (gr. 3-7). 19.95 (978-1-937786-03-8(X)) World Wisdom, Inc.

Sebra, Richard. It's Christmas! 2016. (Bumba Books (tm) — It's a Holiday! Ser.). (ENG.). 24p. (J). (gr. -1-1). lib. bdg. 25.32 (978-1-5124-1426-4(3)) Lerner Publishing Group.

Sexton, Brenda & Sloan, Price Stern. Have a Crazy Christmas! Sexton, Brenda, illus. 2016. (Mad Libs Junior Ser.). (ENG., Illus.). 32p. (J). (gr. -1-k). bds., act. bk. ed. 7.99 (978-0-8431-8939-1(8), Mad Libs) Penguin Young Readers Group.

Shanddaramon. The 12 Days of Yule. 2008. 33p. 16.95 (978-0-615-26465-3(4)) Astor Pr.

Sibbett, Ed, Jr., et al. 3-D Coloring Book — Merry Christmas. 2011. (Dover 3-D Coloring Book Ser.). (ENG., Illus.). 32p. (J).

(gr. 2-6). pap. 5.99 *(978-0-486-48414-3(9))* Dover Pubns., Inc.

Sims, Lesley. Christmas Around the World. Ruta, Angelo et al, illus. 2006. (Young Reading Series 1 Gift Bks.). 47p. (J). (gr. -1-3). 8.99 *(978-0-7945-1132-6(5),* Usborne) EDC Publishing.

Sirett, Dawn & Dorling Kindersley Publishing Staff. My First Christmas Board Book. 2nd rev. ed. 2006. (My First Bks.). (ENG., Illus.). 36p. (J). (gr. -1 — 1). bds. 5.99 *(978-0-7566-0502-5(4),* DK Children) Dorling Kindersley Publishing, Inc.

Small World Creations. Chalkboard Christmas. 2016. (Chalkboard Bks.). (ENG.). 10p. (J). (gr. -1-2). bds. 7.99 *(978-0-7641-6869-7(X))* Barron's Educational Series, Inc.

Smith, Evans. The Christmas Angel. 2009. 40p. pap. 18.49 *(978-1-4490-4056-7(X))* AuthorHouse.

Smith, Martina. La Historia de la Navidad: Un Relato de la Biblia Chispita. Grosshauser, Peter & Temple, Ed, illus. 2016. (SPA.). (J). *(978-1-5064-2102-5(4))* Augsburg Fortress, Pubs.

—The Story of Christmas: A Spark Bible Story. Grosshauser, Peter, illus. 2015. (Spark Bible Stories Ser.). (ENG.). 32p. (J). (gr. -1-2). 12.99 *(978-1-5064-0224-6(0),* Sparkhouse Family) Augsburg Fortress, Pubs.

Spence, Christine, compiled by. Christmas Programs for Children. annuals 2005. (Illus.). 48p. per. 5.99 *(978-0-7847-1612-0(9),* 08605) Standard Publishing.

Staf, Edie. Christmas Novena: For Home or Classroom. 22p. (J). (gr. 2-8). pap. 1.50 *(978-0-8198-1456-2(3),* 332-032) Pauline Bks. & Media.

The Star, 1 vol. 2014. 12p. (J). bds. 5.99 *(978-0-8254-4207-0(9))* Kregel Pubns.

Star Chasers. 2006. (J). pap. 1.79 *(978-1-59317-170-4(6))* Warner Pr., Inc.

Starr, Debra, compiled by. The Book of Christmas: A Collection of Holiday Verse, Prose, & Carols. 128p. (J). *(978-0-681-22004-1(X))* Borders Group, Inc.

Stephens, Chris S. A Christmas Box. 2003. (ENG.). 48p. pap. 20.95 *(978-1-84323-306-0(1))* Beekman Bks., Inc.

Stiegemeyer, Julie. Fear Not, Joseph. Bladholm, Cheri, illus. 2008. 32p. (J). (gr. -1-3). 13.49 *(978-0-7586-1498-8(5))* Concordia Publishing Hse.

—Things I See at Christmas. Mitter, Kathryn, illus. 2005. 16p. (J). (gr. -1-17). bds. 5.49 *(978-0-7586-0809-3(8))* Concordia Publishing Hse.

Storey, Rita. The Christmas Book. 2014. (Seasonal Companions Ser.). (Illus.). 48p. (gr. 2-4). 37.10 *(978-1-59920-957-9(8))* Black Rabbit Bks.

The Story of Christmas. 2003. (J). per. *(978-1-57657-806-3(2))* Paradise Pr., Inc.

The Story of Christmas. Date not set. 4.99 *(978-0-88271-273-4(X),* 1440) Regina Pr., Malhame & Co.

Strain-Trueit, Trudi. Christmas. 2013. (ENG.). 32p. (J). 23.00 *(978-0-531-27202-2(8));* pap. 5.95 *(978-0-531-27352-4(0))* Scholastic Library Publishing.

Stump, Linda. The Empty Manger. 2012. 20p. pap. 10.95 *(978-1-4497-5303-0(5),* WestBow Pr.) Author Solutions, Inc.

Summerer, Marilyn. The First Christmas Present. van der Sterre, Johanna, illus. 2009. 32p. (J). (gr. -1). 14.99 *(978-0-7586-1663-0(5))* Concordia Publishing Hse.

Sundblom, Haddon H., illus. The Night Before Christmas: A Family Treasury of Songs, Poems, & Stories. 2007. 32p. (J). (gr. -1-3). 7.98 *(978-1-4127-8961-5(3))* Publications International, Ltd.

Swanson, Maggie. My First Christmas. Swanson, Maggie, illus. 2006. (Illus.). 10p. (gr. -1). bds. 7.95 *(978-0-88271-707-4(3))* Regina Pr., Malhame & Co.

Swanson, Tom, illus. Twas the Night Before Christmas. 2011. (Recordable Bks). 12p. (J). ring bd. 24.99 *(978-1-60130-261-8(4),* Usborne) EDC Publishing.

Taliaferro, Margaret. The Real Reason for Christmas: Letters to Children for the Twelve Nights of Christmas. (Illus.). 118p. (J). (gr. 1-7). reprint ed. pap. 6.95 *(978-0-9618730-0-4(0))* FEA Ministries.

Tanana, Mary. Christmas to Color. Tanana, Mary, illus. 2015. (Illus.). 96p. (J). (gr. -1). pap. 15.99 *(978-0-06-244379-3(8))* HarperCollins Pubs.

Taplin, Sam. Little Stories for Christmas. 2011. (Baby Board Bks). 12p. (J). ring bd. 12.99 *(978-0-7945-3183-6(0),* Usborne) EDC Publishing.

TerKeurst, Lysa. The Sweetest Story Ever Told Activity Kit. Sparks, Michal, illus. 2003. 14.99 *(978-0-8024-7093-5(9))* Moody Pubs.

Texas Classic Christmas Trivia. 2005. 32p. pap. 6.95 *(978-0-635-03350-5(X))* Gallopade International.

Thank You, God, for Christmas Coloring Book. 2006. 16p. (J). pap. 1.99 *(978-0-7847-1261-0(1),* 22119) Standard Publishing.

Thomas, Dylan. A Child's Christmas in Wales. Raskin, Ellen, illus. 2003. (New Directions Paperbook Ser.: Vol. 972). (ENG.). 32p. reprint ed. pap. 8.00 *(978-0-8112-1560-2(1))* New Directions Publishing Corp.

Thomas Nelson Publishing Staff. The Story of Christmas, 1 vol. 2013. (ENG.). 26p. (J). bds. 6.99 *(978-1-4003-2391-3(6))* Nelson, Thomas Inc.

Tiger Tales, ed. A Christmas Prayer. Rescek, Sanja, illus. 2014. (ENG.). 22p. (J). (gr. -1-k). bds. 8.95 *(978-1-58925-596-8(8))* Tiger Tales.

Tiger Tales, ed. & compiled by. Christmas Surprise. Tiger Tales, compiled by. 2014. (My First Lift & Learn Ser.). (ENG.). 10p. (J). (gr. -1 — 1). bds. 7.99 *(978-1-58925-577-7(1))* Tiger Tales.

Tiger Tales Staff. Christmas Holiday Fun. 2014. (My First Touch & Feel Ser.). (ENG.). 24p. (J). (gr. -1 — 1). bds. 12.99 *(978-1-58925-562-3(3))* Tiger Tales.

Traini, Agostino. Christmas Find & Color. 2009. (Dover Children's Activity Bks.). (ENG., Illus.). 48p. (J). (gr. -1-2). pap. 4.99 *(978-0-486-47112-9(8))* Dover Pubns., Inc.

Trueit, Trudi Strain. Christmas. 2010. (Benchmark Rebus Ser.). 24p. (gr. k-1). 15.95 *(978-0-7614-4885-3(3))* Marshall Cavendish Corp.

—Christmas. Bryan-Hunt, Jan, illus. 2013. (Holidays & Celebrations Ser.). (ENG.). 32p. (J). (gr. k-3). 27.07 *(978-1-62323-514-7(6),* 206276) Child's World, Inc., The.

Trunkhill, Brenda. Christmas Around the World. Carnehl, Jeff, illus. 2009. 32p. (J). (gr. k). 6.99 *(978-0-7586-1757-6(7))* Concordia Publishing Hse.

Turner, Patrenia. A Christmas Carol For Keeng Troyius. 2016. (Illus.). pap. *(978-0-578-18261-2(0))* Royalty Patrenia Turner Publications.

The Twelve Days of Christmas. 2003. (Traditional Christmas Stories Ser.). 32p. (J). 4.98 *(978-0-7525-8848-3(6))* Parragon, Inc.

Twin Sisters(r), et al. Christmas Joy Black & White Board Book. 2016. (Tell Me about God Board Bks.). (ENG.). 8p. (J). bds. 4.99 *(978-1-63409-802-1(1))* Barbour Publishing, Inc.

—My First Read-Along Christmas Story. 2016. (Let's Share a Story Ser.). (ENG.). 14p. (J). bds. 9.99 *(978-1-63409-899-1(4))* Barbour Publishing, Inc.

—The Story of Christmas: Coloring & Activity Book. 2016. (ENG.). 32p. (J). pap. 4.99 *(978-1-63409-801-4(3))* Barbour Publishing, Inc.

Twin Sisters(r) Staff. Jolly Old St.Nicholas. 2009. 16p. 4.99 *(978-1-59922-412-1(7))* Twin Sisters IP, LLC.

Tyrtania, Joachim & Hemrich-Skomer, Denise. Together Time: Cycle A. 2007. (Illus.). 80p. per. 10.95 *(978-0-9787087-2-6(5))* Bound by Grace Pr., LLC.

Van Leeuwen, Wendy. Itty-bitty Bible Activity Book, God's Big Christmas Plan. 2007. (Illus.). 48p. (J). pap. 1.49 *(978-1-59317-211-4(7))* Warner Pr., Inc.

Walsh, William S. The Story of Santa Klaus: Told for Children of All Ages from Six To. 2007. (ENG.). 216p. per. 24.95 *(978-1-4304-4232-5(8))* Kessinger Publishing, LLC.

Watt, Fiona. Christmas Baby Jigsaw Book. Wells, Rachel, illus. 2004. (Jigsaw Books Ser.). 14p. (J). 10.95 *(978-0-7945-0809-8(X),* Usborne) EDC Publishing.

—Christmas Doodles. 2009. (Activity Cards Ser.). 52p. (J). 9.99 *(978-0-7945-2435-7(4),* Usborne) EDC Publishing.

—Christmas Magic Painting Book. 2015. (Magic Painting Bks.). (ENG.). 32p. (J). (gr. k-5). pap. 9.99 *(978-0-7945-3577-3(1),* Usborne) EDC Publishing.

Watt, Fiona & Wells, Rachel. Christmas. 2004. (Illus.). 10p. (J). 12.95 *(978-0-7945-0498-4(1),* Usborne) EDC Publishing.

Wells, Rachel. That's Not My Christmas Coloring Book. 2011. (That's Not My... Coloring Book Ser.). 32p. (J). pap. 4.99 *(978-0-7945-3155-3(5),* Usborne) EDC Publishing.

Whelon, Chuck. What to Doodle? Christmas Creations! 2011. (Dover Doodle Bks.). (ENG., Illus.). 64p. (J). (gr. 2-5). pap. 5.99 *(978-0-486-48530-0(7))* Dover Pubns., Inc.

Wick, Walter. Can You See What I See? - Christmas Read-and-Seek. Wick, Walter, illus. 2008. (Scholastic Reader Level 1 Ser.). (ENG., Illus.). 32p. (J). (gr. -1-3). pap. 3.99 *(978-0-545-07887-0(3))* Scholastic, Inc.

Williams, Colleen Madonna Flood. My Adventure on Christmas. 2006. 44p. (J). 8.99 *(978-1-59092-545-4(9))* Blue Forge Pr.

Wood, Anita. Pocketdoodles for Christmas, 1 vol. Brockschmidt, Kev, illus. 2015. (ENG.). 240p. pap. 9.99 *(978-1-4236-4115-5(9))* Gibbs Smith, Publisher.

Workman Publishing, Workman. Eyelike Stickers: Christmas. 2nd rev. ed. 2015. (Eyelike Stickers Ser.). (ENG., Illus.). 12p. (J). 6.95 *(978-0-7611-8614-4(X),* Workman Publishing Co., Inc.

World Book, Inc. Staff. Christmas in Russia. 2004. (Christmas Around the World Ser.). 1760p. (gr. 2-8). 24.95 *(978-0-7166-0862-2(6))* World Bk., Inc.

World Book, Inc Staff, contrib. by. Christmas in America in the 1700's & 1800's. 2006. 80p. (J). *(978-0-7166-0808-0(1))* World Bk., Inc.

World Book, Inc. Staff, contrib. by. Christmas in Belgium. 2004. (Christmas Around the World from World Book Ser.). (Illus.). 1760p. (gr. 2-8). 24.95 *(978-0-7166-0864-6(2),* 20114) World Bk., Inc.

World Book, Inc Staff, contrib. by. A Christmas Train Across Canada. 2014. (J). *(978-0-7166-0828-8(6))* World Bk., Inc.

—!Feliz Navidad¡: Celebrating a Mexican Christmas. 2015. 80p. (J). *(978-0-7166-0830-1(8))* World Bk., Inc.

Yates, Irene. Christmas Activities for ks1 Maths. 2005. pap. *(978-1-903853-68-9(0))* Brilliant Pubns.

—Christmas Activities for Ks2 Maths. 2005. (Illus.). 64p. pap. *(978-1-903853-69-6(9))* Brilliant Pubns.

—Christmas Activities for Language & L. 2007. *(978-1-903853-67-2(2))* Brilliant Pubns.

Zenner, Dale M. 'Twas the Night Before Christmas: Yet Few People Knew. 2012. 24p. pap. 12.45 *(978-1-4497-5368-9(X),* WestBow Pr.) Author Solutions, Inc.

Zocchi, Judy. On Christmas Eve. Wallis, Rebecca, illus. 2005. (Holiday Happenings Ser.). 32p. (J). pap. 10.95 *(978-1-59646-224-3(8));* lib. bdg. 21.65 *(978-1-891997-47-1(5))* Dingles & Co.

—On Christmas Eve/la Nochebuena. Wallis, Rebecca, illus. 2005. (Holiday Happenings Ser.).Tr. of Nochebuena. 32p. (J). pap. 10.95 *(978-1-59646-226-7(4));* (ENG & SPA.). lib. bdg. 21.65 *(978-1-891997-48-8(3));* (ENG & SPA.). per. 10.95 *(978-1-59646-227-4(2))* Dingles & Co.

Zondervan. Ready, Set, Find Christmas, 1 vol. 2016. (Ready, Set, Find Ser.). (ENG.). 12p. (J). bds. 8.99 *(978-0-310-75766-5(5))* Zonderkidz.

Zondervan Staff. The Beginner's Bible a Christmas Celebration Sticker & Activity Book, 1 vol. 2015. (Beginner's Bible Ser.). (ENG.). 16p. (J). pap. 3.99 *(978-0-310-74670-6(1))* Zonderkidz.

—Jesus God's Great Gift, 1 vol. Jones, Dennis G., illus. 2010. (I Can Read! / Dennis Jones Ser.). (ENG.). 32p. (J). (gr. -1-2). pap. 3.99 *(978-0-310-71881-9(3))* Zonderkidz.

Zullo, Allan. Bad Pets Save Christmas! 2012. 139p. (J). pap. *(978-0-545-61229-6(2))* Scholastic, Inc.

CHRISTMAS—DRAMA

see Christmas Plays

CHRISTMAS—FICTION

Aardvark, D. Merry Kissmoose. Aardvark, D., illus. l.t. ed. 2005. (Illus.). 48p. (J). per. 12.95 *(978-0-9755567-2-6(X))* Aardvark's Weedpatch Pr.

Aboff, Marcie. Santa's Big Red Helper. Haefele, Steve, illus. 2005. (Clifford Ser.). (ENG.). 80p. (J). (gr. k — 1). 2.99 *(978-0-439-79150-2(2))* Scholastic, Inc.

Abramson, Jill & O'Connor, Jane. Holiday Helper. Melmon, Deborah, illus. 2014. (Penguin Young Readers, Level 2 Ser.). (ENG.). 32p. (J). (gr. 1-3). pap. 3.99 *(978-0-448-45677-5(X),* Penguin Young Readers) Penguin Young Readers Group.

Accord Publishing Staff. Oliver's First Christmas. Valiant, Kristi, illus. 2012. (ENG.). 14p. (J). (-k). bds. 5.99 *(978-1-4494-2245-5(4))* Andrews McMeel Publishing.

—Santa's Workshop: A Mini Animotion Book. Idle, Molly, illus. 2011. (ENG.). 12p. (J). 9.99 *(978-1-4494-0834-3(6))* Andrews McMeel Publishing.

—The Twelve Days of Christmas. Fang, Jade, illus. 2011. (ENG.). 26p. (J). 17.99 *(978-1-4494-0361-4(1))* Andrews McMeel Publishing.

Adair, Dick. The Story of Aloha Bear. Britt, Stephanie, illus. 2008. 24p. (J). 12.95 *(978-1-59700-492-3(8))* Island Heritage Publishing.

Adair, Tammi. The Heart of a Christmas Tree. Rudd, Benton, illus. 2013. 32p. 16.99 *(978-0-9886409-1-7(0))* Mindstir Media.

Adams, Adrienne. Christmas Party. 2017. (ENG.). 32p. (J). (gr. -1-3). 13.99 ***(978-1-5344-1244-6(1),*** Aladdin) Simon & Schuster Children's Publishing.

Adams-Cantrell, Renee. Peanut Bunny & the Christmas Lights. Daley-Prado, M. J., illus. 2009. 48p. pap. 24.95 *(978-1-60610-432-3(2))* America Star Bks.

Adams, Keith. The Tales of Henry Tuffin - Henry's Christmas. Geoff Hewitt, ed. Mawson, Alan, illus. 2013. 32p. pap. *(978-1-78222-172-2(7))* Paragon Publishing, Rothersthorpe.

Adams, Lisa. The Twelve Days of Christmas in New York City. Adams, Lisa, illus. 2009. (Twelve Days of Christmas in America Ser.). (ENG., Illus.). 40p. (J). (gr. k-3). 12.95 *(978-1-4027-6440-0(5))* Sterling Publishing Co., Inc.

Adams, Pam, illus. The First Day. 2009. 10p. (J). bds. *(978-0-85953-149-8(X))* Child's Play International Ltd.

The Adventures of Molly. 2004. pap. 13.95 *(978-1-59526-180-9(X))* Aeon Publishing Inc.

Aebersold, Carol V., et al. The Elf on the Shelf - Girl LT: Light Girl. 2012. (ENG.). 32p. (J). lib. bdg. 15.00 net. *(978-0-9769907-3-4(3))* CCA & B, LLC.

Agatha Jane. Ces Mignonnes Autres Créatures: L'Histoire de Ben. Mais Est-Elle Vraie ? 2012. 64p. (-18). pap. 27.45 *(978-1-4772-4306-0(2))* AuthorHouse.

—Those Sweet Other Beings: Ben's Story. 2012. (Illus.). 64p. pap. 27.45 *(978-1-4772-4693-1(2))* AuthorHouse.

Aguiar, Judy Lee. The Littlest Camel: And the Journey of the Three Kings. Rodriguez, Tom, illus. 2008. 176p. (J). per. *(978-0-9725231-2-7(X))* Turnapaige & Reed Moore.

Ahlstrom, Leonard. Christmas Shoes for Children. 2004. pap. 7.99 *(978-0-9714147-1-6(8))* Point To Point Publishing.

Akchurin, Sergo. Canadian Story. 2011. 16p. 12.99 *(978-1-4269-5215-9(5))* Trafford Publishing.

Albertson, Bernard. So, You Think There Is No Santa, Bk. 2. 2004. 96p. (J). pap. 7.95 *(978-0-87714-744-2(2))* i-5 Publishing LLC.

Albright, Ann. Samuel Sparrow & the Tree of Light. Albright, Ann, illus. 2nd ed. 2003. (ENG., Illus.). 28p. (J). pap. *(978-0-9715472-5-4(4))* Ascension Lutheran Church.

Alcott, Louisa May. The Louisa Alcott Reader: A Supplementar. 2006. pap. *(978-1-4065-0590-0(0))* Dodo Pr.

Alemagne, Beatrice. Bugs at Christmas. Gordon, Sam, tr. from FRE. 2013. (ENG., Illus.). 38p. 12.95 *(978-0-7148-6573-7(7))* Phaidon Pr., Inc.

Alexander, Annette M. Snow Magic & the Sad Little Christmas Tree. 2011. (Illus.). 32p. 14.66 *(978-1-4567-7182-9(5))* AuthorHouse.

Alexander, Marilee. The Wise Man's Last Wish: A Christmas Tale. Nash, Gisele, illus. 2012. (ENG.). 23p. (J). 23.95 *(978-1-4327-8307-5(6));* pap. 14.95 *(978-1-4327-8040-1(9))* Outskirts Pr., Inc.

Alko, Selina. Daddy Christmas & Hanukkah Mama. 2012. (ENG., Illus.). 32p. (J). (gr. k-3). 16.99 *(978-0-375-86093-5(2),* Knopf Bks. for Young Readers) Random Hse. Children's Bks.

All I Want for Christmas. 2003. (J). per. *(978-1-57657-707-3(4))* Paradise Pr., Inc.

Allan, Nicholas. Father Christmas Needs a Wee! Allan, Nicholas, illus. 2009. (ENG., Illus.). 32p. (J). (gr. -1-k). pap. 13.99 *(978-1-86230-825-1(X),* Red Fox) Random House Children's Books GBR. Dist: Independent Pubs. Group.

Allen, Eleanor. Mouse Monk in a Christmas Adventure. 2009. 36p. pap. 15.49 *(978-1-4490-2197-9(2))* AuthorHouse.

Allgeier, Steve. Christmas with Norky, the Adventure Begins... 2007. (Illus.). (J). per. 17.99 *(978-1-933156-25-5(2),* Visikid Bks.) GSVQ Publishing.

Alpert, Barbara. The True Meaning of Christmas, the Greatest Gift of All. Zamboni, David, illus. 2009. 24p. pap. 12.95 *(978-1-936051-18-2(4))* Peppertree Pr., The.

Amerikaner, Susan & Disney Book Group. Clubhouse Christmas. Loter Inc. Staff, illus. 2008. (ENG.). 12p. (J). (gr. -1-k). bds. 6.99 *(978-1-4231-1253-2(9))* Disney Pr.

Amery, Heather. Farmyard Tales Christmas Flap Bk And. 2006. 24p. 12.99 *(978-0-7945-0556-1(2),* Usborne) EDC Publishing.

Amy's Very Merry Christmas. 2014. (Critter Club Ser.: 9). (ENG., Illus.). 128p. (J). (gr. k-4). pap. 5.99 *(978-1-4424-9531-9(6),* Little Simon) Little Simon.

Anaya, Rudolfo A. The Santero's Miracle: A Bilingual Story. Lamadrid, Enrique R., tr. Córdova, Amy, illus. 2004. (ENG & SPA.). 32p. (J). 19.95 *(978-0-8263-2847-2(4))* Univ. of New Mexico Pr.

Andersen, Hans Christian. Little Match Girl. 2008. (ENG.). 31p. (J). 17.00 *(978-1-4379-5327-5(1))* DIANE Publishing Co.

Andersen-Murphy. If You Believe. 2004. (Illus.). 76p. pap. 14.95 *(978-0-9743580-8-6(8))* Brzamo Publishing.

Anderson, Derek. How the Easter Bunny Saved Christmas. Anderson, Derek, illus. 2006. (ENG., Illus.). 40p. (J). (gr. -1-3). 17.99 *(978-0-689-87634-9(3),* Simon & Schuster Bks. For Young Readers) Simon & Schuster Bks. For Young Readers.

Anderson, Rian B. A Christmas Prayer. 2004. pap. 2.95 *(978-1-57734-900-6(8))* Covenant Communications, Inc.

Andrews, Julie. Dumpy's Happy Holiday. Walton, Tony, illus. 2005. (Julie Andrews Collection). 32p. (J). lib. bdg. 16.89 *(978-0-06-052685-6(8),* Julie Andrews Collection) HarperCollins Pubs.

Andrews, Julie & Hamilton, Emma Walton. A Fairy Merry Christmas. Davenier, Christine, illus. 2012. (Passport to Reading Level 1 Ser.). (ENG.). 32p. (J). (gr. -1-3). pap. 4.99 *(978-0-316-21962-4(2))* Little, Brown Bks. for Young Readers.

—A Fairy Merry Christmas. 2012. (Passport to Reading Level 1 Ser.). (J). lib. bdg. 14.75 *(978-0-606-26692-5(5),* Turtleback) Turtleback Bks.

Andrews McMeel Publishing Staff. The Twelve Days of Christmas. Fang, Jade, illus. 2015. (ENG.). 24p. (J). bds. 9.99 *(978-1-4494-6001-3(1))* Andrews McMeel Publishing.

Andrews McMeel Publishing Staff & Moore, Clement C. Twas the Night Before Christmas. Goodell, Jon, illus. deluxe ed. 2009. (ENG.). 26p. (J). (gr. -1-3). 19.99 *(978-0-7407-8432-3(3))* Andrews McMeel Publishing.

Angel, Bruce. I Believe in Santa Claus. 2006. 121p. pap. 19.95 *(978-1-4241-1486-3(1))* PublishAmerica, Inc.

Anglund, Joan Walsh. The Cowboy's Christmas. Anglund, Joan Walsh, illus. 2004. (ENG., Illus.). 40p. (J). 8.95 *(978-0-7407-4675-8(8))* Andrews McMeel Publishing.

Anna. The Magic Money Tree. 2009. (Illus.). 20p. pap. 15.49 *(978-1-4389-0472-6(X))* AuthorHouse.

Anonymous. Rudolph the Red-Nosed Reindeer: Rudolph Saves the Day. 2014. (Rudolph the Red-Nosed Reindeer Ser.: 2). (ENG., Illus.). 24p. (J). (gr. -1-2). 4.99 *(978-1-250-05049-6(9),* 9781250050496) Square Fish.

Antoine, Leon. Santa's Destiny: A Legend Reborn, 1 vol. 2010. 48p. pap. 16.95 *(978-1-4512-9281-7(3))* America Star Bks.

Aoki, Hisako. Santa's Favorite Story: Santa Tells the Story of the First Christmas. Gantschev, Ivan, illus. 2007. (ENG.). 28p. (J). (gr. -1-3). 9.99 *(978-1-4169-5029-5(X),* Simon & Schuster Bks. For Young Readers) Simon & Schuster Bks. For Young Readers.

Apelian, Virginia. Aliens Celebrating CHRISTMAS. 2012. 30p. pap. 19.99 *(978-1-62419-384-2(6))* Salem Author Services.

Appel, Cindy. The Best Christmas Gift. Collier, Kevin Scott, illus. 2005. (J). E-Book 6.00 incl. cd-rom *(978-1-933090-19-1(7))* Guardian Angel Publishing, Inc.

Applegate, Katherine. Sun-Kissed Christmas. 2010. (Summer Ser.). (ENG.). 208p. (YA). (gr. 9-18). pap. 8.99 *(978-1-4169-9397-1(5),* Simon Pulse) Simon Pulse.

Arcturus Publishing Staff. Santa's Sleigh. 2013. (ENG., Illus.). 10p. (J). bds. 9.95 *(978-1-78212-186-2(2))* Arcturus Publishing GBR. Dist: Bookmasters Distribution.

Argenta, Joan. Santa Claus Comes to the Thomas Family. 2011. 16p. (gr. -1). pap. 8.43 *(978-1-4567-7846-0(3))* AuthorHouse.

Arnold, Tedd. Fly Guy's Ninja Christmas. Arnold, Tedd, illus. 2016. (Fly Guy Ser.: 16). (ENG., Illus.). 32p. (J). (gr. -1-3). 6.99 *(978-0-545-66277-2(X))* Scholastic, Inc.

Aronson, Jeff & Aronson, Miriam. Little Mike & Maddie's Christmas Book. Aronson, Jeff & Zephyr, Jay, illus. 2007. 32p. (J). 16.00 *(978-0-9795302-2-7(9),* CrumbGobbler Pr.) Downtown Wetmore Pr.

Arruda, Suzanne M. A Stocking for Jesus. Ogden, Betina, illus. 2005. (J). pap. 7.95 *(978-0-8198-7076-6(5),* 332-372) Pauline Bks. & Media.

Asbill, Annette. Mouse's Forever Christmas. Asbill, Annette, illus. 2012. (Illus.). 34p. pap. *(978-0-9860247-3-3(2))* Roxby Media Ltd.

Asher, Jay. What Light. 2016. (ENG.). 272p. (YA). (gr. 7). 18.99 *(978-1-59514-551-2(6),* Razorbill) Penguin Young Readers Group.

—What Light. 2017. lib. bdg. 22.10 ***(978-0-606-40488-4(0))*** Turtleback Bks.

Ashman, Linda. The Twelve Days of Christmas in Colorado. 2011. (Twelve Days of Christmas in America Ser.). (ENG., Illus.). 40p. (J). (gr. k-3). 12.95 *(978-1-4027-7463-8(X))* Sterling Publishing Co., Inc.

Atlas. The Antarctic Express. 2009. 32p. 19.95 *(978-1-58978-111-5(2),* Atlas Games) Trident, Inc.

Auch, Mary Jane. I Was a Third Grade Bodyguard. Auch, Herm, illus. 2003. (ENG.). 73p. (J). (gr. 4-6). tchr. ed. 16.95 *(978-0-8234-1775-9(1))* Holiday Hse., Inc.

Auerbach, Annie. Santa's Sleigh. Pagnoni, Roberta, illus. 2017. (ENG.). 12p. (J). (gr. -1-k). bds. 5.99 ***(978-1-4380-5000-3(3))*** Barron's Educational Series, Inc.

Augustine, Peggy. The Starlit Night. 2008. pap. 1.59 *(978-0-687-64736-1(3))* Abingdon Pr.

Awdry, W. Santa's Little Engine. 2014. (Thomas & Friends Step into Reading Ser.). lib. bdg. 13.55 *(978-0-606-36014-2(X))* Turtleback Bks.

—Thomas's Christmas Delivery. Stubbs, Tommy, illus. 2004. (Sparkle Storybook Ser.). (ENG.). 32p. (J). (gr. -1-2). 8.99 *(978-0-375-82877-5(X),* Random Hse. Bks. for Young Readers) Random Hse. Children's Bks.

Awdry, Wilbert V. Thomas' Christmas Star. Durk, Jim, illus. 2013. (Color Plus Card Stock Ser.). (ENG.). 48p. (J). (gr. -1-2). pap. 3.99 *(978-0-449-81880-0(2),* Golden Bks.) Random Hse. Children's Bks.

Ayasta, Ayasta. Star. 2007. 117p. 34.95 *(978-1-4303-1520-9(2));* pap. 17.96 *(978-1-4303-1809-5(0))* Lulu Pr., Inc.

Bach, Sherry. Abundant Christmas, 1 vol. 2009. 48p. pap. 16.95 *(978-1-4489-9120-4(X))* America Star Bks.

Badalamenti, Andrew. Around the World in One Night. Santa's Secrets Unwrapped! 2008. 28p. 14.50 *(978-0-615-25180-6(3))* Badalamenti, Andrew.

Baggott, Stella, illus. Baby's Very First Noisy Christmas. 2011. (Baby's Very First Noisy Book Ser.). 10p. (J). ring bd. 14.99 *(978-0-7945-3128-7(8),* Usborne) EDC Publishing.

Baglio, Ben M. Puupy in a Present. 2004. 139p. (J). *(978-0-439-68759-1(4))* Scholastic, Inc.

Bailey, Linda. When Santa Was a Baby. Godbout, Geneviève, illus. 2015. (ENG.). 36p. (J). (gr. -1-2). 16.99 *(978-1-77049-556-2(8),* Tundra Bks.) Tundra Bks. CAN. Dist: Penguin Random Hse. LLC.

Bailey, Tressie. The Little Box Kittens First Christmas. 2009. 41p. pap. 20.50 *(978-0-557-03166-5(4))* Lulu Pr., Inc.

Bainbridge, Bernadette. The Christmas Please & Thank You. 2011. (Illus.). 28p. pap. *(978-1-908447-82-1(6))* Grosvenor Hse. Publishing Ltd.

Baker, Adam. Maury C. Moose & the Forest Noel. 2014. (ENG., Illus.). 96p. (gr. 1-6). pap. 10.95 *(978-1-63047-054-8(6))* Morgan James Publishing.

Baker, Amanda, illus. The Cheesehead Night Before Christmas. 2007. 40p. (J). per. 19.95 *(978-0-9797781-0-0(7))* Dreams 2 Wings LLC.

Baker, Mary. Christmas Annie. 2009. 70p. pap. 7.96 *(978-0-557-17289-4(6))* Lulu Pr., Inc.

Baker, Tommy. Santa Claus, the Fourth Wise Man. 2012. (ENG.). 25p. (J). pap. 18.95 *(978-1-4327-9774-4(3))* Outskirts Pr., Inc.

Balducci, Rita. The Nutcracker. Beckett, Sheilah, illus. 2014. (Little Golden Book Ser.). (ENG.). 24p. (J). (-k). 4.99

C
D

(978-0-385-36993-0(X), Golden Bks.) Random Hse. Children's Bks.

Balian, Lorna. Bah! Humbug?, 1 vol. 2006. (ENG., Illus.). 32p. (J). (gr. -1-3). 15.95 (978-1-59572-036-8(7)) Star Bright Bks., Inc.

Ball, Marcia. Christmas Fals Do-Do. 2006. (Illus.). 36p. (J). per. 14.95 (978-1-58939-972-3(2)) Virtualbookworm.com Publishing, Inc.

Ballesteros, Jose Manuel & Manuel, Ballesteros Pastor José. La Foto de Navidad.Tr. of Christmas Picture. (SPA.). 63p. 6.00 (978-84-241-7717-1(7)) Everest Editora ESP. Dist: Lectorum Pubns., Inc.

Banda, Rey A. The Magical City of Northopolis; a Christmas Story. Patlan, Alyssa A., illus. 2012. 50p. (-18). pap. 16.95 (978-0-615-69125-1(0)) Northopolis.

Banks, Celia. Issy's Gift: A Story about Giving. 2006. (Illus.). 41p. 14.99 (978-0-9764460-7-1(3)) HonorNet.

Bannister, Barbara. The Christmas Train. Seiler, Jason & Farley, Jason, illus. 2007. 61p. (J). (gr. 3-7). per. 7.95 (978-0-940895-54-6(4)) Cornerstone Pr. Chicago.

Barbie: a Special Christmas. 2014. (ENG.). 16p. (J). (gr. -1-1). bds. 8.99 (978-0-7944-3231-7(X), Reader's Digest Children's Bks.) Studio Fun International.

Barbo, Maria S. The Velveteen Rabbit Christmas. Hague, Michael, illus. 2013. (My Readers Ser.). (ENG.). 32p. (J). (gr. -1-1). 15.99 (978-1-250-01768-0(8), 9781250017680) Square Fish.

Bardhan-Quallen, Sudipta. The Worst Twelve Days of Christmas. Wood, Ryan, illus. 2011. (ENG.). 32p. (J). (gr. k-2). 15.95 (978-1-4197-0033-0(2), Abrams Bks. for Young Readers) Abrams, Inc.

Barnes, Laura T. Ernest's Special Christmas. Camburn, Carol A., illus. 2003. (Ernest Ser.). 36p. (J). (gr. k-3). 17.95 (978-0-9674681-3-6(2)) Barnesyard Bks.

Barnett, Wm. Billy's Wish. Kiste, Tori Lynn, illus. 2008. 28p. pap. 24.95 (978-1-60563-330-5(5)) America Star Bks.

Baron, Michael & Aronica, Lou. A Winter Discovery. 2011. (ENG.). 60p. pap. 4.99 (978-1-61188-027-4(0)) Story Plant, The.

Barrett, Judi. Santa from Cincinnati. Hawkes, Kevin, illus. 2012. (ENG.). 48p. (J). (gr. -1-3). 16.99 (978-1-4424-2993-2(3), Atheneum Bks. for Young Readers) Simon & Schuster Children's Publishing.

Barrett, Robert, illus. The Other Wise Man. 32p. (J). pap. 6.95 (978-0-8249-5348-5(7), Ideal Pubns.) Worthy Publishing.

Barry, Robert. Mr. Willowby's Christmas Tree. Date not set. 32p. (J). 16.95 (978-0-8488-2206-4(4)) Amereon Ltd.

Barton, Zoe. Always Neverland. 2011. (ENG.). 320p. (J). (gr. 3-7). 16.99 (978-0-06-196325-4(9)) HarperCollins Pubs.

Basham, Tom. No Vacancy! 2013. 24p. (978-1-4602-0630-0(4)); pap. (978-1-4602-0629-4(0)) FriesenPress.

Basic, Zdenko, illus. Steampunk Charles Dickens' a Christmas Carol. 2014. (ENG.). 204p. (gr. 7). 18.95 (978-0-7624-5090-9(8), Running Pr. Kids) Running Pr. Bk. Pubs.

Basore, Polly M. Santa's Stray in A Piano for Christmas. Williams, Carlene H., illus. 2005. 32p. (J). per. (978-0-9771749-1-1(3)) AngelBooks.

Bastianich, Lidia Matticchio. Nonna Tell Me a Story: Lidia's Christmas Kitchen. Logan, Laura, illus. 2010. (ENG.). 56p. (J). (gr. -1-3). 15.95 (978-0-7624-3692-7(1)) Running Pr. Bk. Pubs.

Batchelor, Love. Mean Mo & the Christmas Star. 2013. (ENG., Illus.). (J). (gr. -1-3). pap. 9.95 (978-1-62086-461-6(4)) Mascot Bks., Inc.

Bateman, Teresa. The Christmas Pups. Kanzler, John, illus. 2012. (J). (978-1-61913-112-5(9)) Weigl Pubs., Inc.

Bates, Susan Welch. The Rag Picker's Christmas. 2008. 17p. pap. 24.95 (978-1-60672-967-0(5)) America Star Bks.

Bauer, Marion Dane. Christmas in the Forest. Hearn, Diane Dawson, illus. (Holiday House Reader Ser.). (ENG.). 48p. (J). (gr. k-3). tchr. ed. 15.95 (978-0-8234-1371-3(3)) Holiday Hse., Inc.

Bauer, Sepp. The Christmas Rose. Wenz-Vietor, Else, illus. 2008. 48p. (J). (gr. -1-3). 12.95 (978-1-58089-232-2(9)) Charlesbridge Publishing, Inc.

Baum, L. Frank. A Kidnapped Santa Claus. 2011. 24p. 12.95 (978-1-4638-9603-4(4)); pap. 6.95 (978-1-4638-0070-3(3)) Rodgers, Alan Bks.

—L Frank Baum's Book of Santa Claus. 2007. 84p. per. 7.99 (978-1-60459-118-7(8)) Wilder Pubns., Corp.

—The Life & Adventures of Santa Claus. 2007. 112p. 22.95 (978-1-60312-592-5(2)) Aegypan.

—The Life & Adventures of Santa Claus. 2008. (ENG.). 216p. pap. 24.95 (978-1-55709-180-2(3)) Applewood Bks.

—The Life & Adventures of Santa Claus. Clark, Mary Cowles, illus. 2011. 200p. (978-1-84902-560-7(6)) Benediction Classics.

—The Life & Adventures of Santa Claus. Clark, Mary, illus. 2007. 156p. (gr. 4-7). 23.95 (978-1-60206-778-3(3)); per. 9.95 (978-1-60206-777-6(5)) Cosimo, Inc.

—The Life & Adventures of Santa Claus. Clark, Mary Cowles, illus. 2015. (Penguin Christmas Classics Ser.). (ENG.). 176p. (gr. 12). 16.00 (978-0-14-312853-3(1), Penguin Classics) Penguin Publishing Group.

Baumgart, Klaus. Laura's Christmas Star. Waite, Judy, tr. from GER. 2003. (Illus.). 32p. (J). pap. 8.95 (978-1-58925-382-7(5)) Tiger Tales.

BBC Children's Books. Twelve Doctors of Christmas. 2016. (ENG., Illus.). 272p. (YA). 14.99 (978-1-4059-2895-3(6), 9781405928953) Penguin Bks., Ltd. GBR. Dist: Diamond Comic Distributors, Inc.

Beard, Lauren, illus. The Fairytale Hairdresser & Father Christmas. 2014. (Fairytale Hairdresser Ser.: 5). (ENG.). 32p. (J). (-k). pap. 9.99 (978-0-552-57052-7(4)) Transworld Publishers Ltd. GBR. Dist: Independent Pubs. Group.

Beam, Emily. Tumtum & Nutmeg: Adventures Beyond Nutmouse Hall. 2011. (Tumtum & Nutmeg Ser.: 1). (ENG., Illus.). 512p. (J). (gr. 3-7). pap. 10.00 (978-0-316-07574-9(4)) Little, Brown Bks. for Young Readers.

—Tumtum & Nutmeg: the Rose Cottage Adventures. Price, Nick, illus. 2013. (Tumtum & Nutmeg Ser.: 2). (ENG.). 416p. (J). (gr. 3-7). pap. 10.99 (978-0-316-08598-4(7)) Little, Brown Bks. for Young Readers.

Beck, Glenn, et al. The Christmas Sweater. Dorman, Brandon, illus. 2009. (ENG.). 40p. (J). (gr. -1-2). 17.99 (978-1-4169-9543-2(9), Aladdin) Simon & Schuster Children's Publishing.

Beck, Ian. The Christmas Story. 2005. (ENG., Illus.). 32p. (J). pap. 13.99 (978-0-552-54937-0(1)) Transworld Publishers Ltd. GBR. Dist: Independent Pubs. Group.

Becker, Curt. The Sad Sant. Fariss, Michelle, illus. 2009. 36p. pap. 14.95 (978-1-60844-161-7(X)) Dog Ear Publishing, LLC.

Beckley, N. K. Peggy. 2011. 78p. 24.99 (978-1-4568-6064-6(X)); pap. 15.99 (978-1-4568-6063-9(1)) Xlibris Corp.

A Bed for Baby Jesus. 2014. (Boardbooks - Board Book Ser.). (ENG., Illus.). 16p. (J). (gr. -1-k). bds. 9.99 (978-0-7944-3227-0(1)) Studio Fun International.

Bedell, Lorraine Frances. The Christmas Cat Story, 1 vol. 2010. 48p. pap. 16.95 (978-1-4512-0249-6(0)) America Star Bks.

Bedford, David. I've Seen Santa! Warnes, Tim, illus. 32p. 2008. pap. 6.95 (978-1-58925-411-4(2)) 2006. (J). (gr. -1-3). 15.95 (978-1-58925-058-1(3)) Tiger Tales.

Beedham, Edward. The Barking Family Christmas. 2015. (ENG.). 421p. (J). (gr. 4-6). mass mkt. 14.95 (978-1-78554-793-5(3), 170d87d7-898e-455e-98ef-fe5b792b577a) Austin, Stan AUS. Dist: Bookmasters Distribution.

Bell, Michael D. The Red Blazer Girls: the Secret Cellar. 2012. (Red Blazer Girls Ser.). (ENG., Illus.). 288p. (J). (gr. 5). 17.99 (978-0-375-86741-5(4), Knopf Bks. for Young Readers) Random Hse. Children's Bks.

—The Secret Cellar. 2013. (Red Blazer Girls Ser.). (ENG., Illus.). 288p. (J). (gr. 5). pap. 8.99 (978-0-375-86495-7(4), Yearling) Random Hse. Children's Bks.

Bell, Chanda & Aebersold, Carol. The Elf on the Shelf - a Christmas Tradition: Boy Light. Steinwart, Coe, illus. 2009. 32p. (J). lib. bdg. 29.95 (978-0-9769907-0-3(9)) CCA & B, LLC.

Bell, Jonas Fearon, des. Oh! Christmas Tree: A Fun-To-Find Lift-the-Flap Book. 2013. (ENG., Illus.). 20p. (gr. -1). bds. 8.99 (978-1-77093-498-6(7)) Flowerpot Pr.

Bellisario, Gina. The Twelve Days of Christmas in Illinois. Ebbeler, Jeffrey, illus. 2012. (Twelve Days of Christmas in America Ser.). (ENG.). 40p. (J). (gr. k-3). 12.95 (978-1-4027-9733-0(8)) Sterling Publishing Co., Inc.

Bemelmans, Ludwig. Madeline Christmas Activity Book. 2013. (Madeline Ser.). (ENG.). 16p. (J). (gr. -1-2). pap. 7.99 (978-0-670-01568-9(7), Viking Books for Young Readers) Penguin Young Readers Group.

—Madeline's Christmas, 1 vol. Bemelmans, Ludwig, illus. 2007. (Madeline Ser.). (ENG., Illus.). 15p. (J). (gr. -1-2). 9.99 (978-0-14-240897-1(2), Puffin Books) Penguin Young Readers Group.

Benedis-Grab, Daphne. The Angel Tree. 2014. (ENG.). 256p. (J). (gr. 3-7). 16.99 (978-0-545-61378-1(7), Scholastic Pr.) Scholastic, Inc.

—Clementine for Christmas. 2015. (ENG.). 256p. (J). (gr. 3-7). 16.99 (978-0-545-83951-8(3), Scholastic Pr.) Scholastic, Inc.

Bennett, Deborah. The Christmas Star. 2013. 24p. pap. 24.95 (978-1-63000-934-2(2)) America Star Bks.

Bennett, Marilyn J. The Poinsettia Adventure. 2010. 60p. pap. 21.99 (978-1-4490-7108-0(2)) AuthorHouse.

Benson, Julian. The Christmas Dog: Lc's Worst Day Ever! 2012. 20p. pap. 24.95 (978-1-4626-9816-5(6)) America Star Bks.

Benson, Nicky. The Spirit of Christmas: A Giving Tradition. Cockcroft, Jason, illus. 2014. (ENG.). 32p. (J). (gr. -1-3). 24.99 (978-1-58925-530-2(5)) Tiger Tales.

—The Spirit of Christmas: A Giving Tradition. 2014. 32p. 12.99 (978-1-58925-188-5(1)) Tiger Tales.

Benson, P. Bryn. Josefina, the Christmas Cow: A Tale of Hope & Faith. Cinelli, Lisa, illus. 2005. 35p. (J). (gr. -1-3). per. 9.95 (978-0-929636-47-4(3)) Syren Bk. Co.

Bentley, Sue. A Christmas Surprise. Swan, Angela & Farley, Andrew, illus. 2008. (Magic Kitten Ser.). (ENG.). 128p. (J). (gr. 1-3). pap. 5.99 (978-0-448-45001-8(1), Grosset & Dunlap) Penguin Young Readers Group.

Bently, Peter. The Tooth Fairy's Christmas. Parsons, Garry, illus. 2014. (J). (978-1-4351-5739-2(7)) Barnes & Noble, Inc.

Berenstain, Jan & Berenstain, Mike. The Berenstain Bears & the Joy of Giving, 1 vol. 2010. (Berenstain Bears/Living Lights Ser.). (ENG.). 32p. (J). (gr. -1-2). pap. 3.99 (978-0-310-71255-8(6)) Zonderkidz.

—The Berenstain Bears' Old-Fashioned Christmas. Berenstain, Jan & Berenstain, Mike, illus. 2012. (Berenstain Bears Ser.). (ENG., Illus.). 32p. (J). (gr. -1-3). 12.99 (978-0-06-057443-7(7)) HarperCollins Pubs.

—The Berenstain Bears, the Very First Christmas, 1 vol. 2015. (Berenstain Bears/Living Lights Ser.). (ENG., Illus.). 24p. (J). pap. 3.99 (978-0-310-75102-1(0)) Zonderkidz.

—The Berenstain Bears Trim the Tree. Berenstain, Jan & Berenstain, Mike, illus. 2007. (Berenstain Bears Ser.). (ENG., Illus.). 16p. (J). (gr. -1-1). pap. 6.99 (978-0-06-057417-8(8), HarperFestival) HarperCollins Pubs.

Berenstain, Jan, et al. The Berenstain Bears Save Christmas. Berenstain, Mike, illus. 2003. (Berenstain Bears Ser.). (ENG.). 48p. (J). (gr. -1-3). 14.99 (978-0-06-052670-2(X), HarperFestival) HarperCollins Pubs.

Berenstain, Mike. The Berenstain Bears & the Christmas Angel, 1 vol. 2016. (Berenstain Bears/Living Lights Ser.). (ENG.). 24p. (J). pap. 3.99 (978-0-310-74924-0(7)) Zonderkidz.

—The Berenstain Bears' Night Before Christmas. Berenstain, Mike, illus. 2013. (Berenstain Bears Ser.). (ENG., Illus.). 24p. (J). (gr. -1-3). pap. 3.99 (978-0-06-207553-6(5), HarperFestival) HarperCollins Pubs.

Berenstain, Stan & Berenstain, Jan. The Berenstain Bears Meet Santa Bear (Deluxe Edition) 2016. (First Time Books(R) Ser.). (ENG., Illus.). 32p. (J). (gr. -1-2). pap. 6.99 (978-0-399-55767-5(9), Random Hse. Bks. for Young Readers) Random Hse. Children's Bks.

—The Berenstain Bears Merry Christmas. 2013. (Illus.). (J). (978-0-375-97296-6(X)) Random Hse., Inc.

—The Berenstain Bears Save Christmas. Berenstain, Mike, illus. 2005. (Berenstain Bears Ser.). 48p. (J). (gr. -1-3). pap. 6.99 (978-0-06-052672-6(6), HarperFestival) HarperCollins Pubs.

Berenstain, Stan, et al. The Berenstain Bears' Christmas Tree, 1 vol. 2009. (Berenstain Bears/Living Lights Ser.). (ENG., Illus.). 72p. (J). (gr. -1-2). 9.99 (978-0-310-71940-3(2)) Zonderkidz.

—The Berenstain Bears Save Christmas. Berenstain, Stan et al, illus. 2003. (Berenstain Bears Ser.). (J). (gr. k-3). 129.90 (978-0-06-056995-2(6)) HarperCollins Pubs.

Beresford, Elisabeth. The Snow Womble. Price, Nick, illus. 2013. (Wombles Ser.). (ENG.). 32p. (J). pap. 12.99 (978-1-4088-3424-4(3), 9781408834244, Bloomsbury USA Childrens) Bloomsbury Publishing USA.

Bergeron, Joe. Cosmic Cat. 2005. 50p. pap. 14.99 (978-1-4116-6246-9(6)) Lulu Pr., Inc.

Bergren, Lisa T. God Gave Us Christmas. 2006. (God Gave Us Ser.). (ENG., Illus.). 40p. (J). (gr. -1-k). 10.99 (978-1-4000-7175-3(5), WaterBrook Pr.) Crown Publishing Group.

Berrios, Frank. A Monster Machine Christmas (Blaze & the Monster Machines) Dynamo Limited, illus. 2016. (Big Golden Book Ser.). (ENG.). 32p. (J). (gr. -1-2). 9.99 (978-0-399-55353-0(3), Golden Bks.) Random Hse. Children's Bks.

—A Very Mater Christmas (Disney/Pixar Cars) Random House Disney Staff, illus. 2011. (Glitter Board Book Ser.). (ENG.). 12p. (J). (— 1). bds. 6.99 (978-0-7364-2793-7(7), RH/Disney) Random Hse. Children's Bks.

Berry, Ron. We Wish You a Merry Christmas. Sharp, Chris, illus. 2011. 16p. (J). 10.99 (978-0-8249-1464-6(3), Ideal Pubns.) Worthy Publishing.

Berry, Ron & Mead, David. The Little Drummer Boy. Sharp, Chris, illus. 2009. (ENG.). 16p. 12.99 (978-0-8249-1429-5(5), Ideal Pubns.) Worthy Publishing.

Bertolet, J. Where Does Christmas Go? 2007. 32p. per. 12.95 (978-1-4327-0221-2(1)) Outskirts Pr., Inc.

Bethers, Linda, retold by. Christmas Oranges. 2004. 13p. pap. 3.95 (978-1-57734-546-6(0), 01114387) Covenant Communications, Inc.

Bevan, Sharon. Sparkles' First Christmas Eve. 2004. 28p. per. 17.32 (978-1-4134-5189-4(6)) Xlibris Corp.

Bickel, Karla. Surprise Christmas Birthday Party. Bickel, Karla, illus. l.t. ed. 2004. (Illus.). 16p. (J). (gr. -1-6). pap. 5.00 (978-1-891452-12-3(6), 3) Heart Arbor Bks.

Bieber, Hartmut. Busy Bear Celebrates Christmas. 2003. (Illus.). (J). 5.99 (978-1-59384-006-8(3)) Parklane Publishing.

Biedrzycki, David. Me & My Dragon: Christmas Spirit. Biedrzycki, David, illus. 2015. (ENG., Illus.). 40p. (J). (gr. -1-3). lib. bdg. 17.95 (978-1-58089-622-1(7)) Charlesbridge Publishing, Inc.

—Santa Retires. Biedrzycki, David, illus. 2012. (ENG., Illus.). 32p. (J). (gr. -1-3). 16.95 (978-1-58089-293-3(0)); pap. 7.95 (978-1-58089-294-0(9)) Charlesbridge Publishing, Inc.

—Santa's New Jet. Biedrzycki, David & Bonnet, Rosalinde, illus. 2011. (ENG.). 32p. (J). (gr. -1-2). 16.95 (978-1-58089-291-9(4)); pap. 7.95 (978-1-58089-292-6(2)) Charlesbridge Publishing, Inc.

—Santa's New Jet. 2007. (Illus.). (J). pap. (978-0-545-00238-7(9)) Scholastic, Inc.

Birch, Manuel James. Dudley the Angel & His Buddy Gabby the Elf. 2009. 40p. pap. 18.49 (978-1-4490-1704-0(5)) AuthorHouse.

Biro, Val. Gumdrop's Merry Christmas. (Illus.). 26p. (J). (978-0-340-71060-9(8)) Hodder & Stoughton.

—Merry Christmas. (Illus.). 26p. (J). pap. (978-0-340-71061-6(6)) Hodder & Stoughton.

Bishop, Brandy. The Christmas Mice, 1 vol. 2010. 30p. 24.95 (978-1-4489-4438-5(4)) PublishAmerica, Inc.

Bishop, Jennie. The Three Gifts of Christmas. McDaniels, Preston, illus. 2009. 32p. (J). (gr. 3-18). 15.99 incl. audio compact disk (978-1-59317-378-4(4)) Warner Pr., Inc.

Bishop, Karen C. The Christmas Lantern. Donahue, Jim, illus. 2008. 32p. (J). (978-0-615-20131-3(8)) Three River Rambler.

Bix, William T. Sometimes the Best Gets Picked Last. 2011. 24p. pap. 13.99 (978-1-4567-9646-4(1)) AuthorHouse.

Bizzarro, Grace. Christmas on the Internet. Bohart, Lisa, illus. 2013. 20p. pap. 12.95 (978-1-61493-197-3(6)) Peppertree Pr., The.

Bjornson, Nancy. Sleds, Skins & Snow. 2007. (J). (978-1-930596-83-2(9)) Amherst Pr.

Black, Birdie. Just Right for Christmas. Beardshaw, Rosalind, illus. 2014. (ENG.). 24p. (J). (-k). bds. 6.99 (978-0-7636-7563-9(6), Nosy Crow) Candlewick Pr.

Blackaby, Susan. The Twelve Days of Christmas in Oregon. Conahan, Carolyn Digby, illus. 2014. (Twelve Days of Christmas in America Ser.). (ENG.). 40p. (J). (gr. k). 12.95 (978-1-4549-0891-3(2)) Sterling Publishing Co., Inc.

Blackburn, C. Edward. The Stories of Christmas: As Told by a Little Lamb. Bishop, Megan, illus. l.t. ed. 2005. 24p. (J). 9.95 (978-0-9727440-3-4(7)) Redline Bks.

Blackburn, Richard & Carnahan, Rhonda. 'Twas, with a Twist! 2013. 36p. pap. 16.95 (978-1-4908-1292-2(X), WestBow Pr.) Author Solutions, Inc.

Blechman, R. O. The Juggler of Our Lady: The Classic Christmas Story. 2015. (Dover Graphic Novels Ser.). (ENG., Illus.). 144p. 16.95 (978-0-486-80030-1(X)) Dover Pubns., Inc.

Blowers, Norman. Christmas with Carly. 2008. 16p. pap. 11.50 (978-1-60693-337-4(X), Strategic Bk. Publishing) Strategic Book Publishing & Rights Agency (SBPRA).

Blyton, Enid. Family Christmas. (Illus.). 160p. (J). pap. 6.95 (978-0-09-987830-8(5)) Random Hse. GBR. Dist: Trafalgar Square Publishing.

Bobby Bright's Greatest Christmas Ever: The Story of the World's First Talking Christmas Tree Light Bulb. 2006. (Illus.). 133p. (J). lib. bdg. 16.95 (978-0-9788227-0-5(6)) Old Farm Pr.

Boehnert, Ernest. The Magic Christmas Train. 2010. 24p. 14.93 (978-1-4269-4447-5(0)) Trafford Publishing.

Boggs, Danielle. The Snow Globe. 2008. 55p. pap. 16.95 (978-1-60703-588-6(X)) America Star Bks.

Boggs, Garnett Reed. Totally Katy: Katy Is Always Planning, but Just How Well do Her Plans Work Out? 2011. 108p. (gr. 4-6). pap. 10.95 (978-1-4634-3233-1(X)) AuthorHouse.

Bolt, Bundy H. Christmas Island. 2004. 24p. (J). per. 6.95 (978-1-930648-95-1(2)) Goose River Pr.

Bolden-Fournier, Laura. An Orangutan's Night Before Christmas, 1 vol. Jaskiel, Stan, illus. 2016. (ENG.). 32p. (J). (gr. k-3). 16.99 (978-1-4556-2154-5(4)) Pelican Publishing Co., Inc.

Bond, Michael. Paddington & the Christmas Surprise. Alley, R. W., illus. (Paddington Ser.). (ENG.). 32p. (J). (gr. -1-3). 2015. 17.99 (978-0-06-231842-8(X)) 2008. 16.99 (978-0-06-168740-2(5)) HarperCollins Pubs.

Bosley, Judith A. Sing Christmas. Price, Susan D., illus. l.t. ed. Date not set. (J). (gr. -1-k). pap. 10.95 (978-0-930809-26-3(2)) Grand Bks., Inc.

Bostrom, Kathleen. The Secret of the Twelve Days of Christmas. Bostrom, Christopher, illus. 2005. 68p. (gr. -1-7). per. 10.95 (978-1-931195-74-4(9)) KiwE Publishing, Ltd.

Bour, Daniele. Petit ours brun aime Noel. pap. 12.95 (978-2-227-70915-7(4)) Bayard Editions FRA. Dist: Distribooks, Inc.

Bourgeois, Paulette. Franklin's Christmas: A Sticker Activity Book. Clark, Brenda, illus. 2003. (ENG.). 16p. (J). 6.95 (978-1-55337-561-6(0)); 6.95 (978-1-55337-506-7(8)) Kids Can Pr., Ltd. CAN. Dist: Hachette Bk. Group.

Bowen, Anne. Christmas Is Coming. Bogacki, Tomek, illus. 2007. (Carolrhoda Picture Bks.). 28p. (J). (gr. -1-3). 16.95 (978-1-57505-934-1(7), Carolrhoda Bks.) Lerner Publishing Group.

Bowman, Crystal. My Christmas Stocking: Filled with God's Love, 1 vol. Gevry, Claudine, illus. 2015. (ENG.). 14p. (J). bds. 6.99 (978-0-310-73823-7(7)) Zonderkidz.

Boyack, Merrilee. The Mismatched Nativity. Tenney, Shawna J. C., illus. 2016. (J). 18.99 (978-1-62972-239-9(1)) Deseret Bk. Co.

Boyd, Ken. Tinsel Tail Mouse. 2009. 48p. pap. 16.25 (978-1-60860-403-6(9), Eloquent Bks.) Strategic Book Publishing & Rights Agency (SBPRA).

Boynton, Sandra. Christmas Parade. Boynton, Sandra, illus. 2012. (ENG., Illus.). 32p. (J). (gr. -1-1). 14.99 (978-1-4424-6813-9(0), Little Simon) Little Simon.

Bragg, Jane. Teddy Bears Christmas Miracle. 2009. 49p. pap. 18.70 (978-0-557-22087-8(4)) Lulu Pr., Inc.

Brannon, Tom, illus. Elmo's Merry Christmas. 2011. (Lift-The-Flap Ser.). (ENG.). 10p. (J). (gr. -1-k). bds. 10.99 (978-0-7944-2326-1(4), Reader's Digest Children's Bks.) Studio Fun International.

Branson, Terri. A Very Dragon Christmas. 2007. (Illus.). 24p. (J). (978-0-9797574-0-2(1)); per. (978-0-9797574-1-9(X)) Dragonfly Publishing, Inc.

Bratun, Katy. Gingerbread Mouse. Bratun, Katy, illus. 2003. (Illus.). 32p. (J). (gr. -1-2). lib. bdg. 13.89 (978-0-06-009081-4(2)) HarperCollins Pubs.

Breeze, Johnny & Haws, Dallin. A Johnny Bugeyes Christmas. 2013. (ENG.). 46p. (J). pap. 9.99 (978-1-940745-05-3(5)) Telemachus Pr., LLC.

Brenner, Tom. And Then Comes Christmas. Christy, Jana, illus. 2014. (ENG.). 32p. (J). (gr. -1-3). 15.99 (978-0-7636-5342-2(X)) Candlewick Pr.

Brett, Jan. The Animals' Santa. Brett, Jan, illus. 2014. (ENG., Illus.). 32p. (J). (gr. -1-k). 17.99 (978-0-399-25784-1(5), G.P. Putnam's Sons Books for Young Readers) Penguin Young Readers Group.

—Gingerbread Baby. 2004. (J). (gr. k-3). spiral bd. (978-0-616-03025-7(8)); spiral bd. (978-0-616-04548-0(4)) Canadian National Institute for the Blind/Institut National Canadien pour les Aveugles.

—Gingerbread Christmas. Brett, Jan, illus. 2016. (ENG., Illus.). 32p. (J). (-k). 18.99 (978-0-399-17071-3(5), G.P. Putnam's Sons Books for Young Readers) Penguin Young Readers Group.

—Home for Christmas. Brett, Jan, illus. 2011. (ENG., Illus.). 32p. (J). (gr. -1-k). 17.99 (978-0-399-25653-0(9), G.P. Putnam's Sons Books for Young Readers) Penguin Young Readers Group.

—The Night Before Christmas. Brett, Jan, illus. 2011. (ENG., Illus.). 32p. (J). (gr. -1-k). 20.00 (978-0-399-25670-7(9), G.P. Putnam's Sons Books for Young Readers) Penguin Young Readers Group.

—The Twelve Days of Christmas. Brett, Jan, illus. 2004. (ENG., Illus.). 32p. (J). (gr. -1 — 1). bds. 7.99 (978-0-399-24329-5(1), G.P. Putnam's Sons Books for Young Readers) Penguin Young Readers Group.

Brian, Kate, pseud. Ex-Mas. 2009. (ENG., Illus.). 224p. (YA). (gr. 9-18). pap. 9.99 (978-1-4169-9151-9(4), Simon & Schuster Bks. For Young Readers) Simon & Schuster Bks. For Young Readers.

—Last Christmas: The Private Prequel. 2010. (Private Ser.). (ENG.). 288p. (YA). (gr. 9). pap. 9.99 (978-1-4169-1370-2(X), Simon & Schuster Bks. For Young Readers) Simon & Schuster Bks. For Young Readers.

Bridwell, Norman. Clifford's Christmas. Bridwell, Norman, illus. 2011. (Clifford 8x8 Ser.). (ENG., Illus.). 32p. (J). (gr. -1-k). pap. 3.99 (978-0-545-21596-1(X), Cartwheel Bks.) Scholastic, Inc.

—Clifford's Christmas Treasury. 2005. (Illus.). 96p. (gr. -1-3). pap. 10.99 (978-0-439-79137-3(5)) Scholastic, Inc.

—Clifford's First Christmas. (Clifford, the Big Red Dog Ser.). (FRE., Illus.). (J). (gr. k-2). pap. 5.99 (978-0-590-24374-2(8)) Scholastic, Inc.

—Clifford's First Christmas. Bridwell, Norman, illus. 2010. (Clifford Ser.). (ENG., Illus.). 20p. (J). (gr. k — 1). bds. 6.99 (978-0-545-21773-6(3), Cartwheel Bks.) Scholastic, Inc.

Briggs, Raymond. The Father Christmas: It's a Blooming Terrible Joke Book. (ENG., Illus.). 96p. (J). 5.95 (978-0-14-037354-7(3)) Penguin Bks., Ltd. GBR. Dist: Trafalgar Square Publishing.

Britland, Jan. The Adventures of Rodger Dodger Dog: A Christmas Story. Swaim, Michael, illus. 2009. 52p. pap. 18.95 (978-1-936051-48-9(6)) Peppertree Pr., The.

Brock Bryant, Anita. Abcs of Advent. 2009. 40p. pap. 16.99 (978-1-4490-3151-0(X)) AuthorHouse.

Broderick, Marian. The Lost Fairy. Caffrey, Aileen, illus. 2d rev. ed. 2015. (ENG.). 64p. (J). 9.00 (978-1-84717-739-1(5)) O'Brien Pr., Ltd., The IRL. Dist: Dufour Editions, Inc.

Bromley, Peter David. Aunty Liz the Lollipop Lady. 2004. 48p. pap. (978-0-7552-1013-8(1)) Authors OnLine, Ltd.

Bronson, Wilfrid S. Pinto's Journey. 2007. (ENG.). 64p. (J). per. 14.95 (978-0-86534-557-7(0)) Sunstone Pr.

Brooks, Felicity. Dress the Teddy Bears for Christmas. 2015. (Dress the Teddy Bears Sticker Bks.). (ENG.). 16+8p. (J). pap. 6.99 (978-0-7945-3585-8(2), Usborne) EDC Publishing.

—Musical Nativity. 2015. (Noisy Bks.). (ENG.). 10p. (J). 19.99 (978-0-7945-3582-7(8), Usborne) EDC Publishing.

Brother Egbert's Christmas. 2015. (ENG., Illus.). 64p. (J). (gr. k-4). 17.99 *(978-0-7459-6548-2(2))* Lion Hudson PLC GBR. Dist: Independent Pubs. Group.

Brown, Elizabeth Ferguson & Boyds Mills Press Staff. Coal Country Christmas. Stevenson, Harvey, illus. 2003. (ENG.). 32p. (J). (gr. 1-7). 15.95 *(978-1-59078-020-6(5))* Boyds Mills Pr.

Brown, Jeff. Stanley's Christmas Adventure. Nash, Scott & Pamintuan, Macky, illus. 2010. (Flat Stanley Ser.). (ENG.). 96p. (J). (gr. 2-5). pap. 4.99 *(978-0-06-442175-1(9))* HarperCollins Pubs.

—Stanley's Christmas Adventure. 2010. (Flat Stanley Ser.). (J). (gr. k-3). lib. bdg. 14.75 *(978-0-613-68466-8(4),* Turtleback) Turtleback Bks.

—The True Joy of Christmas. 2012. 28p. pap. 16.99 *(978-1-4624-0365-3(4),* Inspiring Voices) Author Solutions, Inc.

Brown, Marc. Arthur & the School Pet. 2005. (Step into Reading Sticker Bks.). (Illus.). 24p. 14.00 *(978-0-7569-5571-7(8))* Perfection Learning Corp.

—Arthur & the School Pet. 2003. (Step into Reading Ser.). (ENG., Illus.). 24p. (J). (gr. k-3). pap. 3.99 *(978-0-375-81001-5(3),* Random Hse. Bks. for Young Readers) Random Hse. Children's Bks.

—Arthur & the School Pet. 2003. (Arthur Step into Reading Ser.). (gr. -1-2). lib. bdg. 13.55 *(978-0-613-57492-1(3),* Turtleback) Turtleback Bks.

—Arthur's Perfect Christmas. 2004. (ENG., Illus.). 40p. (J). (gr. -1-1). pap. 6.99 *(978-0-316-00130-4(9),* Tingley, Megan Bks.) Little, Brown Bks. for Young Readers.

Brown, Marc & Sarfatti, Esther. Arturo y la Navidad. 2004. (SPA.). (J). pap. 6.95 *(978-1-930332-48-5(3))* Lectorum Pubns., Inc.

Brown, Margaret Wise. Christmas in the Barn. Dewdney, Anna, illus. 2016. 40p. (J). (gr. -1-3). 17.99 *(978-0-06-237986-3(0))* HarperCollins Pubs.

—Christmas in the Barn. Goode, Diane, illus. 2007. (ENG.). 32p. (J). (gr. -1-3). per. 7.99 *(978-0-06-052636-8(X))* HarperCollins Pubs.

—A Pussycat's Christmas. Mortimer, Anne, illus. 2009. (ENG.). 32p. (J). (gr. k-4). 9.99 *(978-0-06-186978-5(3),* Tegen, Katherine Bks) HarperCollins Pubs.

Brown, Margery W. Baby Jesus Like My Brother. 2008. (Illus.). 32p. 6.95 *(978-1-60349-000-9(0),* Marimba Bks.) Hudson Publishing Group, The.

Brown, Palmer. Something for Christmas. Brown, Palmer, illus. 2011. (ENG., Illus.). 40p. (J). (gr. -1-2). 12.95 *(978-1-59017-462-3(3),* NYR Children's Collection) New York Review of Bks., Inc., The.

Brown, Ruth, illus. The Christmas Mouse. 2013. (J). *(978-1-4351-5021-8(X))* Barnes & Noble, Inc.

Brown, Tricia. Musher's Night Before Christmas, 1 vol. Dubac, Debra, illus. 2011. (Night Before Christmas Ser.). (ENG.). 32p. (J). (gr. k-3). 16.99 *(978-1-58980-843-0(6))* Pelican Publishing Co., Inc.

Browning, Tom & Moore, Clement C. The Night Before Christmas. 2009. (ENG., Illus.). 48p. (J). (gr. k). 14.95 *(978-1-4027-5484-5(1),* Sterling Innovation) Sterling Publishing Co., Inc.

Broyles, Anne. Arturo & the Navidad Birds, 1 vol. Lewis, K. E., illus. 2013. (ENG & SPA.). 32p. (J). (gr. k-3). 16.99 *(978-1-4556-1801-9(2))* Pelican Publishing Co., Inc.

Bruel, Nick. A Bad Kitty Christmas. Bruel, Nick, illus. 2011. (Bad Kitty Ser.). (ENG., Illus.). 40p. (J). (gr. -1-3). 16.99 *(978-1-59643-668-8(9),* 9781596436688) Roaring Brook Pr.

—Bad Kitty Christmas Storytime Set. unabr. ed. 2014. (ENG.). (J). 12.99 *(978-1-4272-5230-2(0),* 9781427252302) Macmillan Audio.

Bryan, Ashley. Who Built the Stable? A Nativity Poem. Bryan, Ashley, illus. 2012. (ENG., Illus.). 40p. (J). (gr. -1-3). 16.99 *(978-1-4424-0934-7(7),* Atheneum Bks. for Young Readers) Simon & Schuster Children's Publishing.

Bryan, Jennifer Liu & Kendie, Hazel Cole. Cole Family Christmas. Julich, Jenniffer, illus. 2008. 80p. (J). (gr. 4-7). 17.95 *(978-0-9816265-0-5(5))* Next Chapter Pr.

Bryant, Ann. The Christmas Nutcracker. 2006. (Ballerina Dreams Ser.). (Illus.). 181p. (J). (gr. 5). lib. bdg. 12.99 *(978-1-58086-919-5(X),* Usborne) EDC Publishing.

Brzezinski, Kathleen. The Seed. 2009. 44p. pap. 17.95 *(978-0-557-19568-8(3))* Lulu Pr., Inc.

Buck, Angela R. Lily Elf. 2008. 73p. pap. 16.95 *(978-1-60672-881-9(4))* PublishAmerica, Inc.

Buckham, Derek. The Santa Stories. 2008. 81p. pap. 34.50 *(978-1-4092-4803-3(8))* Lulu Pr., Inc.

Buehner, Caralyn. Merry Christmas, Mr. Mouse. Buehner, Mark, illus. 2015. (ENG.). 40p. (J). (gr. -1-k). 17.99 *(978-0-8037-4010-5(7),* Dial Bks) Penguin Young Readers Group.

—Snowmen at Christmas. Buehner, Mark, illus. (ENG.). (J). (gr. -1-k). 2010. 28p. bds. 6.99 *(978-0-8037-3551-4(0))* 2005. 32p. 16.99 *(978-0-8037-2995-7(2))* Penguin Young Readers Group. (Dial Bks).

Bull, Jane. El Libro de la Navidad. Cortes, Eunice, tr. 2003. (SPA.). 48p. *(978-970-690-597-0(9))* Planeta Mexicana Editorial S. A. de C. V.

Bullard, Lisa. Not Enough Beds! A Christmas Alphabet Book. Oeltjenbruns, Joni, illus. 2004. (Picture Bks.). 32p. (J). (gr. -1-3). 15.95 *(978-1-57505-356-1(X),* Carolrhoda Bks.); per. 6.95 *(978-1-57505-797-2(2))* Lerner Publishing Group.

Bullman, Carol & Madsen, James. The Christmas House. Madsen, James, illus. 2009. (Illus.). 32p. (J). (gr. -1-3). 16.99 *(978-0-8249-5598-4(6),* Ideal Pubns.) Worthy Publishing.

Bunting, Eve. Frog & Friends Celebrate Thanksgiving, Christmas, & New Year's Eve. Masse, Josée, illus. 2015. (I AM a READER!: Frog & Friends Ser.). (ENG.). 40p. (J). (gr. 1-2). 9.99 *(978-1-58536-897-6(0),* 203949) Sleeping Bear Pr.

Burch, Genny. My Name Is Bobby Claus: A fictional Christmas story for Children. 2009. 36p. pap. 15.99 *(978-1-4490-4233-2(3))* AuthorHouse.

Burgess, Starr. Counselor Dynamite: Twas the Day Before Christmas Break. Guiza, Victor, illus. 2012. 28p. (J). 16.95 *(978-1-60131-118-4(4),* Castlebridge Bks.) Big Tent Bks.

Burkhart, Jessica. Home for Christmas. 2013. (Canterwood Crest Ser.). lib. bdg. 18.40 *(978-0-606-32322-2(8),* Turtleback) Turtleback Bks.

Burow, Ginger. The Night That Was Christmas, 1 vol. 2009. 21p. pap. 24.95 *(978-1-4489-9842-5(5))* America Star Bks.

Burton, Tim & Disney Book Group Staff. Nightmare Before Christmas. Burton, Tim, illus. 20th anniv. ed. 2013. (ENG., Illus.). 40p. (J). (gr. 1-3). 17.99 *(978-1-4231-7869-9(6))* Disney Pr.

Burton?s, Tim. PENGUIN ACTIVE READING 2: NIGHTMARE BEFORE CHRISTMAS BOOK AND CD-ROM PACK. 2008. (ENG.). pap. 17.32 *(978-1-4058-5210-4(0))* Pearson Education.

Bush, Leanne. A Very Special Christmas with Grandm. 2008. 18p. pap. 24.95 *(978-1-4241-9777-4(5))* America Star Bks.

Bush, Randall B. Gabriel's Magic Ornament. Schunemann, Ryan, illus. 2003. 120p. (gr. 5-8). pap. 11.95 *(978-0-9716633-0-5(0))* Pristine Pubs., Inc.

Butler, Craig. Possum's Christmas. 2009. 16p. pap. 11.50 *(978-1-60693-715-0(4),* Eloquent Bks.) Strategic Book Publishing & Rights Agency (SBPRA).

Butler, M. Christina. One Special Christmas. Macnaughton, Tina, illus. 2013. (ENG.). 32p. (J). *(978-1-58925-145-8(8))* Tiger Tales.

Butterworth, Nick. Jingle Bells. 2014. (ENG.). 32p. (J). 9.99 *(978-0-00-758399-7(0),* HarperCollins Children's Bks.) HarperCollins Pubs. Ltd. GBR. Dist: HarperCollins Pubs.

Buyske, Gail. How the Russian Snow Maiden Helped Santa Claus. Voronina, Natasha, illus. 2005. 32p. (J). 16.95 *(978-0-9725027-4-0(2))* Vernissage Pr., LLC.

Bynum, Janie. The Twelve Days of Christmas in Texas. 2016. (Twelve Days of Christmas in America Ser.). (ENG., Illus.). 22p. (J). (— 1). bds. 7.95 *(978-1-4549-2059-5(9))* Sterling Publishing Co., Inc.

—The Twelve Days of Christmas in Texas. Bynum, Janie, illus. 2009. (Twelve Days of Christmas in America Ser.). (ENG., Illus.). 40p. (J). (gr. k). 12.95 *(978-1-4027-6350-2(6))* Sterling Publishing Co., Inc.

Byrne, Barbara. The Magic Bell On. 2003. 13p. 12.66 *(978-1-4116-1078-1(4))* Lulu Pr., Inc.

Cabot, Meg. The Princess Present. 2004. (Princess Diaries: 6.5). (ENG.). 96p. (YA). (gr. 8-18). 12.99 *(978-0-06-075433-4(8),* HarperTeen) HarperCollins Pubs.

Cadwallader, Doris Jensen. Little Pine's Christmas Story. 2011. 24p. pap. 12.74 *(978-1-4634-1358-3(0))* AuthorHouse.

Caliri, Matt. The Gnome Exchange Program: North Pole Rescue. 2017. (ENG.). (J). (gr. 3-7). pap. 17.99 ***(978-1-4621-2012-3(1),*** Sweetwater Bks.) Cedar Fort, Inc./CFI Distribution.

Cameron, Harriet. Nomad's Joyous Christmas. 2012. (Illus.). 24p. 12.00 *(978-1-4251-2391-8(0))* Trafford Publishing.

Campbell, H. David. Stanley: The Littlest Elf. 2012. 48p. pap. 21.99 *(978-1-4685-6257-6(6))* AuthorHouse.

Campbell, Jeffrey. St. Francis & the Christmas Miracle of Greccio. Bianco, Francesca, illus. 2014. (ENG.). 28p. (J). 14.95 *(978-0-9796766-3-5(0),* Tau Publishing) Vesuvius Pr. Inc.

Campbell, Kathy. Down under Advent Calendar of Chrissy Stories: Great Activities for the 2013 Silly Season. 2013. 60p. pap. 23.95 *(978-1-4525-6540-8(6),* Balboa Pr.) Author Solutions, Inc.

Campbell, Mari & Jennings, Randy. Maggiemoosetracks: Christmas Star. 2013. 106p. pap. 21.00 *(978-0-9895205-4-6(4))* MaggieMooseTracks.

Campbell, Suzy. Pennies for Christmas, 1 vol. 2010. 24p. 24.95 *(978-1-4512-0553-4(8))* PublishAmerica, Inc.

Candlewick Press Staff. Peppa Pig & the Lost Christmas List. Ladybird Books Staff, illus. 2012. (Peppa Pig Ser.). (ENG.). 32p. (J). (gr. k-k). 12.99 *(978-0-7636-6276-9(3),* Candlewick Entertainment) Candlewick Pr.

Caple, Kathy. Duck & Company Christmas. Caple, Kathy, illus. 2011. (ENG., Illus.). 48p. (J). 15.95 *(978-0-8234-2239-5(9))* Holiday Hse., Inc.

Caprin, K. F. The Adventures of the Little Savages. 2009. (ENG.). 167p. pap. 16.95 *(978-1-4092-3379-4(0))* Lulu Pr., Inc.

Capstone Press. Jelly Bear Christmas Surprise, 1 vol. 2015. (Jelly Bear Ser.). (ENG.). 10p. (J). (gr. -1 — 1). bds. 12.99 *(978-1-62370-247-2(X))* Capstone Young Readers of Coughlan Cos.

Capucilli, Alyssa Satin. Biscuit's Christmas Eve. Schories, Pat, illus. 2007. (Biscuit Ser.). (ENG.). 20p. (J). (gr. -1-1). pap. 6.99 *(978-0-06-112836-3(8),* HarperFestival) HarperCollins Pubs.

—Biscuit's Christmas Storybook Collection. Schories, Pat, illus. 2013. (ENG.). 192p. (J). (gr. -1-3). 11.99 *(978-0-06-228842-4(3),* HarperFestival) HarperCollins Pubs.

—Biscuit's Pet & Play Christmas. Schories, Pat & Young, Mary O'Keefe, illus. 2006. (Biscuit Ser.). (ENG.). 12p. (J). (gr. -1-1). bds. 7.99 *(978-0-06-009470-6(2),* HarperFestival) HarperCollins Pubs.

Cardillo, Linda. The Smallest Christmas Tree. Cardillo, Linda & Albert, Dar, illus. 2013. 42p. pap. 9.49 *(978-0-9910861-0-8(4))* Bellastoria Pr.

Cardno, Anthony R. The Firflake: A Christmas Story. Cornue, Don, illus. 2008. 56p. pap. 8.95 *(978-0-595-52468-6(0))* iUniverse, Inc.

Carey, Mariah. All I Want for Christmas Is You. Madden, Colleen, illus. 2015. (ENG.). 32p. (J). (gr. -1-2). 17.99 *(978-0-399-55139-0(5),* Doubleday Bks. for Young Readers) Random Hse. Children's Bks.

Carle, Eric. Dream Snow. Carle, Eric, illus. 2015. (ENG., Illus.). 22p. (J). (gr. -1 — 1). bds. 9.99 *(978-0-399-17314-1(5),* Philomel Bks.) Penguin Young Readers Group.

—The Very Hungry Caterpillar's Christmas 123. Carle, Eric, illus. 2015. (ENG., Illus.). 18p. (J). (— 1). bds. 8.99 *(978-0-448-49009-0(9),* Grosset & Dunlap) Penguin Young Readers Group.

Carlson, Melody. 'Twas the Night: The Nativity Story. Reagan, Susan Joy, illus. 2005. 32p. (J). (gr. -1-4). 12.99 *(978-0-8054-2683-0(3))* B&H Publishing Group.

Carlson, Nancy. Harriet & George's Christmas Treat. Carlson, Nancy, illus. 2005. (Picture Bks.). (Illus.). 32p. (J). (gr. k-2). 15.95 *(978-1-57505-506-0(6))* Lerner Publishing Group.

—Harriet & George's Christmas Treat. 2003. (ENG., Illus.). 32p. (J). (gr. k-2). pap. 9.95 *(978-1-57505-639-5(9))* Lerner Publishing Group.

Carlstrom, Nancy White. Where Is Christmas, Jesse Bear? Degen, Bruce, illus. 2003. (ENG.). 32p. (J). (gr. -1-1). 13.99 *(978-0-689-86233-5(4),* Aladdin) Simon & Schuster Children's Publishing.

Carney, Larry, adapted by. The Three Bears Christmas. 2009. (ENG., Illus.). 24p. (J). 6.95 *(978-1-60072-112-0(5))* PC Treasures, Inc.

Caro, Joe. Santa's Christmas Train. Shih, Lin, illus. 2005. 32p. pap. *(978-0-9628078-2-4(6))* Cowboy Collector Pubns.

—Santa's Christmas Train Coloring Book. Shih, Lin, illus. 2005. 32p. pap. *(978-0-9628078-5-5(0))* Cowboy Collector Pubns.

Carothers, Nina. Red Ed & the True Meaning of Christmas. Nilsen, Richard J., ed. Padovano, Chris, illus. 2013. 32p. pap. 12.97 *(978-1-937376-27-7(3))* All Star Pr.

Carr, Karen. The Christmas Wishing Quilt. 2008. 24p. pap. 12.99 *(978-1-4389-1353-7(2))* AuthorHouse.

Carter, David A. Jingle Bugs: A Merry Pop-Up Book with Lights & Music! Carter, David A., illus. 2004. (David Carter's Bugs Ser.). (ENG., Illus.). 22p. (J). (gr. -1-2). 11.99 *(978-0-689-87416-1(2),* Little Simon) Little Simon.

—Merry Christmas, Bugs! Carter, David A., illus. 2014. (David Carter's Bugs Ser.). (ENG., Illus.). 24p. (J). (gr. -1-1). pap. 3.99 *(978-1-4424-9506-7(5),* Simon Spotlight) Simon Spotlight.

—The 12 Bugs of Christmas: A Pop-Up Christmas Counting Book. Carter, David A., illus. 2011. (David Carter's Bugs Ser.). (ENG., Illus.). 24p. (J). (gr. -1-1). 12.99 *(978-1-4424-2649-8(7),* Little Simon) Little Simon.

Casey, Dawn. Babushka. Hall, Amanda, illus. 2016. (ENG.). 32p. (J). (gr. -1-3). 16.99 *(978-1-68099-188-8(4),* Good Bks.) Skyhorse Publishing Co., Inc.

Casey, Grandpa. Meet the Müsh-Mice. 2008. 32p. per. 24.95 *(978-1-60441-061-7(2))* America Star Bks.

—The Trilogy: Three adventures of the Müsh-Mice. Brennan, Lisa, illus. 2011. 48p. pap. 24.95 *(978-1-4626-2095-1(7))* America Star Bks.

Casey, Sean. My Dad Cancelled Christmas! Casey, Quinn, illus. 2008. 25p. (J). 15.95 *(978-0-9797297-0-6(X))* Cool Kids Create.

Casten, Diane. The Christmas Doll. 2012. 46p. pap. 9.99 *(978-1-62419-021-6(9))* Salem Author Services.

Cavaliere, Wanda. Don't Be Afraid of the Dark: Nicky Moonbeam Saves Christmas. 2012. 24p. pap. 14.93 *(978-1-4669-0656-3(1))* Trafford Publishing.

Caviezel, Giovanni. The Christmas Star. Pagnoni, Roberta, illus. 2013. (ENG.). 10p. (J). (gr. -1 — 1). bds. 6.99 *(978-0-7641-6624-2(7))* Barron's Educational Series, Inc.

—Little Elf. Mesturini, Cristina, illus. 2012. (Mini People Shape Bks.). (ENG.). 10p. (J). bds. 4.99 *(978-0-7641-6577-1(1))* Barron's Educational Series, Inc.

—Little Gingerbread Man. Donati, Giuliana, illus. (Mini People Shape Bks.). (ENG.). 10p. (J). (gr. -1-2). 2014. bds. 4.99 *(978-0-7641-6735-5(9))* 2012. bds. 7.99 *(978-0-7641-6541-2(0))* Barron's Educational Series, Inc.

—Santa. Mesturini, Cristina, illus. 2012. (Mini People Shape Bks.). (ENG.). 10p. (J). bds. 4.99 *(978-0-7641-6578-8(X))* Barron's Educational Series, Inc.

—Santa's Toyshop. Rigo, Laura, illus. 2012. (ENG.). 10p. (J). (gr. -1-k). bds. 6.99 *(978-0-7641-6546-7(1))* Barron's Educational Series, Inc.

Cazet, Denys. Minnie & Moo: The Night Before Christmas. Cazet, Denys, illus. 2004. (Readalongs for Beginning Readers Ser.). (Illus.). 25.95 incl. audio *(978-1-59112-884-7(6))*; (J). pap. 31.95 incl. audio compact disk *(978-1-59112-889-2(7))*; (J). pap. 29.95 incl. audio *(978-1-59112-885-4(4))* Live Oak Media.

CC Claus: A Baseball Christmas Story. 2014. (ENG.). 40p. 16.99 *(978-0-06-231841-1(1),* Ecco) HarperCollins Pubs.

Chaconas, Dori. Merry Merry Holly Holly. McCue, Lisa, illus. 2015. (Cork & Fuzz Ser.: 11). (ENG.). 32p. (J). (gr. -1-k). 16.99 *(978-0-451-47501-5(1),* Viking Books for Young Readers) Penguin Young Readers Group.

Chand, Emlyn. Courtney Saves Christmas. Giffin, Noelle, illus. 2012. 60p. 21.95 *(978-1-62253-114-1(0))* Evolved Publishing.

Chandler, Jeffery. The Christmas Santa Overslept. 2008. 13p. pap. 24.95 *(978-1-60703-421-6(2))* America Star Bks.

Chandler, Samuel. Illustrated Stories for Christmas. Spatz, Caroline, ed. Luraschi, Anna, illus. 2010. (Illustrated Stories Ser.). 351p. (YA). (gr. 3-18). 14.99 *(978-0-7945-2687-0(X),* Usborne) EDC Publishing.

Chapman, Jane. Is It Christmas Yet? Chapman, Jane, illus. (ENG., Illus.). (J). 2015. 22p. (gr. -1-2). bds. 8.99 *(978-1-58925-553-1(4))* 2013. 32p. *(978-1-58925-149-6(0))* Tiger Tales.

Chartrand, Kenneth. A Martian's Dream of Christmas. 2006. 48p. pap. 16.95 *(978-1-4241-4123-4(0))* PublishAmerica, Inc.

Chase, Diana. Angel in a Gum Tree. 2006. 32p. pap. 13.50 *(978-1-921064-77-7(3))* Fremantle Pr. AUS. Dist: Independent Pubs. Group.

Chelkowski, Lisa. The Sisters' Christmas Tale. 2009. 44p. pap. 21.99 *(978-1-4415-3577-1(2))* Xlibris Corp.

Chen, Pauline W. Peiling & the Chicken-Fried Christmas. 2007. (ENG.). 144p. (YA). (gr. 3-6). 15.95 *(978-1-59990-122-0(6),* 9781599901220, Bloomsbury USA Childrens) Bloomsbury Publishing USA.

Cherry, Jason. Sassafras in the Window, 1 vol. 2009. 44p. pap. 24.95 *(978-1-61582-209-6(7))* America Star Bks.

Cheshire, Marc. Merry Christmas, Eloise! Bracken, Carolyn, illus. 2006. (Eloise Ser.). (ENG.). 18p. (J). (gr. -1-1). pap. 6.99 *(978-0-689-87155-9(4),* Little Simon) Little Simon.

Child, Jeremy. Santa. Leach, Emma, illus. 2010. (Snow Shakers Ser.). (ENG.). 8p. (J). (gr. -1-k). bds. 4.99 *(978-0-7641-6384-5(1))* Barron's Educational Series, Inc.

Chiodo, Stephen & Strain, Jim. Chiodo Bros.' Alien Xmas. Chiodo, Charles, illus. 2015. (ENG.). 100p. (J). (gr. -1). pap. 17.95 *(978-0-9729388-4-6(2))* Baby Tattoo Bks.

Choudhry, Fahima. The Snow Surprise. 2011. 24p. pap. 15.99 *(978-1-4653-4628-5(7))* Xlibris Corp.

Chrismer, Melanie. Phoebe Clappsaddle Has a Tumbleweed Christmas, 1 vol. Roeder, Virginia M., illus. 2004. (ENG.). 32p. (J). (gr. k-3). 16.99 *(978-1-58980-241-4(1))* Pelican Publishing Co., Inc.

Christensen, Catherine. Emily's Perfect Christmas Tree. 2015. (J). 14.99 *(978-1-4621-1750-5(3))* Cedar Fort, Inc./CFI Distribution.

Christensen, Evelyn B. The Twelve Days of Christmas in Kentucky. Culotta, Kent, illus. 2016. (Twelve Days of Christmas in America Ser.). (ENG.). 32p. (J). (gr. k). 12.95 *(978-1-4549-1959-9(0))* Sterling Publishing Co., Inc.

Christian, Norma. A Christmas Mouse. 2012. 32p. pap. 13.99 *(978-1-4624-0328-8(X),* Inspiring Voices) Author Solutions, Inc.

Christie, Gerschutz. Samuel the Camel & the Lone Star. 2006. (Eyes of the Stable Ser.). (ENG.). 128p. pap. 7.50 *(978-1-933341-19-4(X))* CRM.

Christmas. 2004. (J). mass mkt. 8.99 *(978-0-9741215-4-3(1))* Stories of My Life, The.

Christmas - All I Want. 2005. (J). bds. *(978-1-4194-0080-3(0))* Paradise Pr., Inc.

Christmas - Candy Canes. 2005. (J). *(978-1-4194-0081-0(9))* Paradise Pr., Inc.

Christmas - Cookies. 2005. (J). bds. *(978-1-4194-0083-4(5))* Paradise Pr., Inc.

Christmas - Stocking. 2005. (J). bds. *(978-1-4194-0082-7(7))* Paradise Pr., Inc.

Christmas Book. 2005. (J). bds. *(978-1-4194-0071-1(1))* Paradise Pr., Inc.

Christmas Book - Christmas Tree. 2005. (J). bds. *(978-1-4194-0073-5(8))* Paradise Pr., Inc.

Christmas Book - Santa Claus. 2005. (J). bds. *(978-1-4194-0074-2(6))* Paradise Pr., Inc.

Christmas book s/s - Presents. 2005. (J). bds. *(978-1-4194-0072-8(X))* Paradise Pr., Inc.

Christmas Book s/s - Snowman. 2005. (J). bds. *(978-1-4194-0075-9(4))* Paradise Pr., Inc.

Christmas Candy Canes. 2003. (J). per. *(978-1-57657-706-6(6))* Paradise Pr., Inc.

A Christmas Carol. 2004. (J). cd-rom 7.99 *(978-0-9740847-9-4(4))* GiGi Bks.

A Christmas Carol. 2003. (Illus.). 32p. (J). 4.98 *(978-1-4054-0980-3(0))*; 9.98 *(978-1-4054-0997-1(5))* Parragon, Inc.

The Christmas Chair l.t. ed. 2004. (Illus.). 27p. (J). 12.95 *(978-0-9763633-1-6(3))* Williams, Thomas.

Christmas in Bavaria. 2005. (YA). per. 16.95 *(978-0-9763572-7-8(5))* English Garden Talk Pr.

Christmas in Beartown. 2003. (J). bds. 4.99 *(978-1-59384-010-5(1))* Bk. Club of America.

Christmas Is Coming. 2003. (J). 6.99 *(978-1-59384-012-9(8))* Parklane Publishing.

A Christmas Prayer. 2003. (J). per. *(978-1-57657-805-6(4))* Paradise Pr., Inc.

The Christmas Rabbit. 2009. (J). per. 17.95 net. *(978-0-9749915-2-8(X))* Sawmill Publishing.

The Christmas Show. 2014. (ENG., Illus.). 32p. (J). (gr. -1-3). 14.99 *(978-1-4814-0114-2(9),* Simon & Schuster Bks. For Young Readers) Simon & Schuster Bks. For Young Readers.

Christmas Stocking. 2003. (J). per. *(978-1-57657-705-9(8))* Paradise Pr., Inc.

The Christmas Story. 2006. 16p. (J). pap. 1.99 *(978-0-7847-1389-1(8),* 22127) Standard Publishing.

The Christmas Story: From The Gospels of Luke. Date not set. (Illus.). 32p. (J). 5.99 *(978-0-06-443661-8(6))* HarperCollins Pubs.

A Christmas Surprise. 2003. (J). *(978-1-57657-928-2(X))* Paradise Pr., Inc.

A Christmas Tradition. 2007. 69p. pap. 16.26 *(978-1-4303-1458-5(3))* Lulu Pr., Inc.

Chronicle Books Staff, et al. Little Reindeer. 2006. (Little Finger Puppet Board Bks.: FING). (ENG., Illus.). 12p. (J). (gr. -1 — 1). bds. 6.99 *(978-0-8118-5457-3(4))* Chronicle Bks. LLC.

Church, Caroline Jayne. Here Comes Christmas! Church, Caroline Jayne, illus. 2010. (ENG., Illus.). 14p. (J). (gr. k — 1). bds. 7.99 *(978-0-545-11817-0(4),* Cartwheel Bks.) Scholastic, Inc.

Clark, Carol. The Christmas Tree. 2012. (Illus.). 32p. pap. 21.35 *(978-1-4772-2174-7(3))* AuthorHouse.

Clark, Debbie. Amberleigh's Christmas Angel: An Adolescent's Story of Love, Loss, & Renewed Hope for the Future. 2004. 48p. pap. 16.95 *(978-1-4137-4528-3(8))* America Star Bks.

Clark, Marilyn K. Mrs Cratchit's Christmas. 2012. (ENG.). 26p. pap. 11.95 *(978-1-4327-9567-2(8))* Outskirts Pr., Inc.

Clark, Mary Higgins. The Magical Christmas Horse. Minor, Wendell, illus. 2011. (ENG.). 40p. (J). (gr. -1-3). 17.99 *(978-1-4169-9478-7(5),* Simon & Schuster/Paula Wiseman Bks.) Simon & Schuster/Paula Wiseman Bks.

Clark, Ruth E. Florida Santa: Is He Real? How Do We Know It? Caterisano, Sarah, illus. 2008. (ENG.). 32p. (J). (gr. -1-3). 16.95 *(978-0-9792963-0-7(7))* Hibiscus Publishing.

Clarkson, Kelly. River Rose & the Magical Christmas. Fleming, Lucy, illus. 2017. (ENG.). 32p. (J). (gr. -1-3). 19.99 ***(978-0-06-269764-6(1))*** HarperCollins Pubs.

Claus, Nancy. Santa's Hat. Ferchaud, Steve, illus. 2006. (J). *(978-0-9746747-6-6(1))* Cypress Bay Publishing.

Claus, Santa. The Santa Legends Present: The Lost Button. 2005. (J). cd-rom 12.00 *(978-1-59971-079-2(X))* Aardvark Global Publishing.

Clayton, Irene Noda. A Hole in the Wall, a Christmas Tale. 2011. 32p. pap. 12.77 *(978-1-4634-3920-0(2))* AuthorHouse.

Cocca-Leffler, Maryann. A Homemade Together Christmas. Cocca-Leffler, Maryann, illus. 2015. (ENG., Illus.). 32p. (J). (gr. -1-3). 16.99 *(978-0-8075-3366-6(1))* Whitman, Albert & Co.

—What I Love about Christmas. 2016. (ENG., Illus.). 22p. (J). (gr. -1 — 1). bds. 12.95 *(978-1-4549-1820-2(9))* Sterling Publishing Co., Inc.

Coffelt, Soraya Diase. It's Not about You Mr. Santa Claus: A Love Letter about the True Meaning of Christmas. 2014. (Love Letters Book Ser.). (ENG., Illus.). 34p. pap. 8.99 *(978-1-63047-261-0(1))* Morgan James Publishing.

Coffin, Douglas. One Maine Christmas Eve, 1 vol. Coffin, Douglas, illus. 2015. (ENG., Illus.). 32p. (gr. -1-12). 16.95 *(978-0-88448-469-1(6),* 884469) Tilbury Hse. Pubs.

Colandro, Lucille. There Was an Old Lady Who Swallowed a Bell! Lee, Jared D., illus. 2016. (There Was an Old Lad Ser.). (ENG.). 32p. (J). bds. 6.99 *(978-0-545-94615-5(8),* Cartwheel Bks.) Scholastic, Inc.

—There Was an Old Lady Who Swallowed a Bell! Lee, Jared, illus. 2008. (ENG.). 32p. (J). (gr. -1-3). pap. 6.99 *(978-0-545-04361-8(1),* Cartwheel Bks.) Scholastic, Inc.

—There Was an Old Lady Who Swallowed a Turkey! Lee, Jared D., illus. 2016. (There Was an Old Lad Ser.). (ENG.).

C
D

32p. (J). (gr. -1-1). 6.99 (978-0-545-93190-8(8), Cartwheel Bks.) Scholastic, Inc.

Coldon, Christine. Emmalynn: Wondrously Magical Christmas Eve. 2012. 56p. pap. 24.99 (978-1-4685-8735-7(8)) AuthorHouse.

Coldwell, Lamar. Our Christmas Tree. 2016. (Rosen REAL Readers: STEM & STEAM Collection). 8p. (gr. 1-k). pap. 5.46 (978-1-5081-2598-3(8), Rosen Classroom) Rosen Publishing Group, Inc., The.

Cole, Brock. The Money We'll Save. Cole, Brock, illus. 2011. (ENG., Illus.). 40p. (J). (gr. -1-3). 16.99 (978-0-374-35011-6(6), 9780374350116, Farrar, Straus & Giroux (BYR)) Farrar, Straus & Giroux.

Cole, Bud. The Mystery of Little Bear. 2012. pap. 12.95 (978-0-7414-8106-1(5)) Infinity Publishing.

Cole, Henry. The Littlest Evergreen. Cole, Henry, illus. 2011. (ENG., Illus.). 32p. (J). (gr. -1-2). 16.99 (978-0-06-114619-0(6), Tegen, Katherine Bks) HarperCollins Pubs.

—The Littlest Evergreen. 2010. (J). lib. bdg. 18.89 (978-0-06-114620-6(X)) HarperCollins Pubs.

Cole, Joanne & Cole, Michael. Bod's Present. 2016. (Bod Ser.). (ENG., Illus.). 32p. (J). (gr. -1-1). 9.99 (978-1-4052-7754-9(8)) Egmont Bks., Ltd. GBR. Dist: Independent Pubs. Group.

Cole, Stacey. Fluffy's Very Special Christmas. 2010. (Illus.). 32p. (J). pap. 26.95 (978-1-4327-4569-1(7)) Outskirts Pr., Inc.

Coleman, Emily. Christmas with Mary, Mom, Dad, & Dee. 2009. 20p. pap. 10.49 (978-1-4490-4501-2(4)) AuthorHouse.

Coleman, Roger. The Pope & the Snowman: A Christmas Tale. 2009. (Illus.). 108p. 23.99 (978-1-4490-1128-4(4)); pap. 12.49 (978-1-4490-1127-7(6)) AuthorHouse.

Collett, Susan, illus. The Christmas Dragon. Collett, Susan, . 2007. 64p. (J). pap. 5.95 (978-0-9678115-1-2(1)) Dragonseed Pr.

Collict, Joan E. Robot Horse: A Christmas Tale. 2012. 20p. pap. 13.77 (978-1-4669-6318-4(2)) Trafford Publishing.

Collington, Peter. A Small Miracle. 2011. (ENG.). 32p. (J). (gr. k-12). pap. 7.99 (978-0-375-87150-4(0), Dragonfly Bks.) Random Hse. Children's Bks.

Collins, Rachel. Sidney Swallow's Christmas. 2010. 32p. pap. 16.95 (978-0-557-62625-0(0)) Lulu Pr., Inc.

Collins, Sonny. Mouse Tails. 2006. (ENG.). 52p. per. 16.95 (978-1-4241-4589-8(9)) PublishAmerica, Inc.

Color All About: Christmas: A Giant Coloring Book for Christmas. 2004. (Illus.). (J). (978-0-9763307-0-7(9)) Food Marketing Consultants, Inc.

Condenzio, Mary. The Mouse & the Star. Long, Paulette Rich, illus. 2008. 13p. pap. 24.95 (978-1-60441-449-3(9)) America Star Bks.

Conlon, Mara. Nutcracker Ballet: A Book, Theater, & Paper Doll Foldout Play Set. Gershman, Jo, illus. 2007. (Foldout Playset Ser.). 30p. (J). 17.99 (978-1-59359-885-3(8)) Peter Pauper Pr. Inc.

Connelly, Valerie. Arthur, the Christmas Elf: A Christmas Adventure. 2006. (Illus.). 60p. (J). per. 24.95 (978-1-933449-23-4(3)) Nightengale Pr.

Conners, Lauren. The Stuffed Frog in Santa's Sack. 2009. 28p. pap. 12.49 (978-1-4490-4623-1(1)) AuthorHouse.

Connick, Harry, Jr. The Happy Elf. Andreasen, Dan, illus. 2011. (ENG.). 32p. (J). (gr. -1-3). 17.99 (978-0-06-128879-1(9)) HarperCollins Pubs.

Connolly, Brian A. Allegheny River Christmas & Other Stories. 2007. 56p. per. 20.95 (978-1-58939-992-1(7)) Virtualbookworm.com Publishing, Inc.

Conroy, James F. Little Joe's Christmas. Berg, Elizabeth, illus. 2012. (ENG.). 44p. (J). pap. 17.95 (978-1-59299-846-3(1)) Inkwater Pr.

Cook, Gerri. Christmas in the Badlands. 2003. (Dinosaur Soup Ser.). (Illus.). 120p. (YA). (gr. 3-5). pap. 9.95 (978-1-895836-94-3(8)) River Bks. CAN. Dist: Fitzhenry & Whiteside, Ltd.

Cookie Jar Entertainment Inc Staff. It's a Happy Holiday! 2007. 32p. (J). mass mkt. 4.99 (978-1-60095-271-5(2), Doodlebops) Cookie Jar.

Cooper, Ilene. Lucy's Holiday Surprise. Fitzgerald, Royce, illus. 2015. (Lucy Ser.: 7). (ENG.). 112p. (J). (gr. 1-4). 12.99 (978-0-385-39131-3(5), Random Hse. Bks. for Young Readers) Random Hse. Children's Bks.

Cooper, Margaret. The Christmas Horse. Bohart, Lisa, illus. 2008. 32p. pap. 12.95 (978-0-9821654-9-2(8)) Peppertree Pr., The.

Corey, Shana. Milly & the Macy's Parade. Helquist, Brett, illus. 2006. 38p. (J). (gr. 4-8). reprint ed. 17.00 (978-1-4223-5174-1(2)) DIANE Publishing Co.

—Milly & the Macy's Parade. Helquist, Brett, illus. 2006. (Scholastic Bookshelf Ser.). (ENG.). 40p. (J). (gr. -1-3). pap. 6.99 (978-0-439-29755-4(9)) Scholastic, Inc.

Corey's Treasure. 2003. (978-0-9726114-1-1(X)) Scottish Christmas.

Corkran, Alice. Down the Snow Stairs: Or, from Goodnight to Goodmorning. Browne, Gordon, illus. 2012. 278p. pap. 14.95 (978-1-934671-12-2(6)) Salem Ridge Press LLC.

Cornelison, Sue F., illus. The Twelve Days of Christmas in Iowa. 2010. (Twelve Days of Christmas in America Ser.). (ENG.). 40p. (J). (gr. k). 12.95 (978-1-4027-6710-4(2)) Sterling Publishing Co., Inc.

Cornell-Castle, Violet R. Santa's Elves. 2008. 32p. pap. 18.65 (978-1-4363-5899-6(X)) Xlibris Corp.

Correa, Alvaro. Mountain Miracle: A Navtivity Story. Lorenzo, Gloria, illus. 2008. 94p. (J). (gr. -1). pap. 14.95 (978-1-933271-23-1(X)) Circle Pr.

Cotter, Bill. Don't Push the Button! A Christmas Adventure. 2017. (ENG.). 22p. (J). bds. 6.99 **(978-1-4926-5705-7(0))**; bds. 8.99 **(978-1-4926-5704-0(2))** Sourcebooks, Inc. (Sourcebooks Jabberwocky).

Cotter, Natasha. The Christmas Blessing. 2012. 24p. 24.95 (978-1-4626-6925-7(5)) America Star Bks.

Coudrille, Jonathon. Farmer Fisher's Russian Christmas. 2013. 42p. pap. (978-1-908867-20-9(5)) FootSteps Pr.

Couloumbis, Audrey. Jake. 2011. (ENG.). 176p. (J). (gr. 3-7). pap. 6.99 (978-0-375-85631-0(5), Yearling) Random Hse. Children's Bks.

Cousins, Lucy. Maisy's Christmas Presents. Cousins, Lucy, illus. 2016. (Maisy Ser.). (ENG., Illus.). 16p. (J). (-k). 14.99 (978-0-7636-9248-3(4)) Candlewick Pr.

—Maisy's Christmas Tree. Cousins, Lucy, illus. 2014. (Maisy Ser.). (ENG., Illus.). 16p. (J). (-k). bds. 6.99 (978-0-7636-7457-1(5)) Candlewick Pr.

Coven, Wanda. Heidi Heckelbeck & the Christmas Surprise. Burris, Priscilla, illus. 2013. (Heidi Heckelbeck Ser.: 9). (ENG.). 128p. (J). (gr. k-2). 16.99 (978-1-4424-8125-1(0)); pap. 4.99 (978-1-4424-8124-4(2)) Little Simon. (Little Simon).

—Heidi Heckelbeck & the Christmas Surprise. 2013. (Heidi Heckelbeck Ser.: 9). lib. bdg. 14.75 (978-0-606-32325-3(2), Turtleback) Turtleback Bks.

Covert, Ralph & Mills, G. Riley. A Nutty Nutcracker Christmas. Swain, Wilson, illus. 2009. (ENG.). 40p. (J). (gr. -1-2). 18.99 (978-0-8118-6111-3(2)) Chronicle Bks. LLC.

Craft, Mahlon. Christmas Moon. Craft, K. Y., illus. 2003. 32p. (J). 15.95 (978-1-58717-056-0(6)); lib. bdg. (978-1-58717-057-7(4)) Chronicle Bks. LLC. (SeaStar Bks.).

Crane, C. H. A Christmas Quest: A Young Boy's Unexpected Christmas Vacation. 2013. 122p. (gr. 4-6). 22.33 (978-1-4907-0807-2(3)); pap. 12.33 (978-1-4907-0808-9(1)) Trafford Publishing.

Creamer, Joan Klatil. The Magic Sceptre - the Legend of Blue Santa Claus. Creamer, Joan Klatil, illus. 2006. (Illus.). 32p. (J). 16.95 (978-0-9778476-3-1(2)) Silver Snowflake Publishing.

Creed, Elizabeth. Millie's Merry Christmas. 2011. 26p. (J). pap. 12.95 (978-1-4327-0580-0(6)) Outskirts Pr., Inc.

Crenshaw, Glenda. Friends of the Enchanted Forest: How they Save Christmas. 2011. 28p. pap. 15.47 (978-1-4520-0512-6(5)) AuthorHouse.

Crenshaw, Mills. The Christmas of 45. 2010. 176p. pap. 11.99 (978-1-59955-455-6(0)) Cedar Fort, Inc./CFI Distribution.

Crissey, Brian. The Loneliest Christmas Tree. Crissey, Noah, illus. 2004. 32p. (J). bds. 25.00 (978-1-893183-35-3(1), 598) Granite Publishing, LLC.

Crissey, Brian L. The Loneliest Christmas Tree. Crissey, Noah, illus. 2004. (J). (978-1-930724-12-9(8)); (978-1-930724-13-6(6)) Granite Publishing, LLC.

Crofoot, Nancy. Christmas in the Barn, 1 vol. Rawat, Tania, illus. 2009. 37p. pap. 24.95 (978-1-61582-585-1(1)) America Star Bks.

Croll, Carolyn, illus. The Story of Christmas. 2008. (ENG.). 96p. (gr. k-12). 16.95 (978-0-7611-5250-7(4), 15250) Workman Publishing Co., Inc.

Crompton, Richmal. Just William at Christmas. 2003. (ENG., Illus.). 200p. (J). pap. 6.95 (978-0-333-67104-7(X)) Macmillan Pubs., Ltd. GBR. Dist: Trafalgar Square Publishing.

Cronin, Doreen. Click, Clack, Ho! Ho! Ho! Lewin, Betsy, illus. 2015. (Click, Clack Book Ser.). (ENG.). 40p. (J). (gr. -1-2). 17.99 (978-1-4424-9673-6(8)) Simon & Schuster Children's Publishing.

Crow, A. D. Daisy & Her Shiny Heart. 2012. 20p. pap. 24.95 (978-1-4626-8039-9(9)) America Star Bks.

Crow, Nosy. Violet Rose & the Very Snowy Christmas. Ho, Jannie, illus. 2016. (ENG.). 52p. (J). (gr. -1-3). 8.99 (978-0-7636-9003-8(1), Nosy Crow) Candlewick Pr.

Crowson, Andrew. Flip Flap Christmas. Crowson, Andrew, illus. 2003. (Illus.). 12p. (J). bds. (978-1-85602-476-1(8), Pavilion Children's Books) Pavilion Bks.

Cruikshank, Fran. The Tale of the Not-So-Perfect Christmas Tree. Olson, Tom, illus. 2005. 17p. (J). 9.95 (978-1-59971-055-6(2)) Aardvark Global Publishing.

Cummings, David W. How Biddikins & Buddikins Made Santa Claus Work Fast! 2005. (J). pap. 15.00 (978-0-8059-6814-9(8)) Dorrance Publishing Co., Inc.

Cummings, Priscilla. Santa Claws: The Christmas Crab, 1 vol. Ramsey, Marcy Dunn, illus. 2009. (ENG.). 30p. (J). 10.50 (978-0-87033-576-1(6), 9780870335761, Cornell Maritime Pr./Tidewater Pubs.) Schiffer Publishing, Ltd.

Cummings, W. L. A Far West Texas Christmas, 1 vol. 2009. 25p. pap. 19.95 (978-1-4489-9402-1(0)) PublishAmerica, Inc.

Cunningham, Sarah. The Donkey in the Living Room: A Tradition That Celebrates the Real Meaning of Christmas. Foster, Michael K., illus. 2014. (ENG.). 32p. (J). (gr. -1-3). 14.99 (978-1-4336-8317-6(2), B&H Kids) B&H Publishing Group.

—The Donkey in the Living Room Nativity Set: A Tradition That Celebrates the True Meaning of Christmas. Foster, Michael K., illus. 2014. (ENG.). 32p. (J). (gr. -1-3). 29.99 (978-1-4336-8448-7(9), B&H Kids) B&H Publishing Group.

Curran, John. When I First Saw Santa. 2011. 20p. 10.03 (978-1-4567-2708-6(7)) AuthorHouse.

Currey, Anna. The Christmas Unicorn. 2013. (Illus.). (J). (978-1-4351-5017-1(1)) Barnes & Noble, Inc.

Currier Brileya, Elizabeth. Grandma B. 's Bedtime Stories. 2006. 68p. (J). pap. 8.39 (978-1-4116-9504-7(6)) Lulu Pr., Inc.

Curry, Kenneth. Priscilla & the Reindeer. 2007. (Illus.). 22p. (J). 10.95 (978-0-9798364-5-9(X)) Curry Brothers Publishing Group.

Curtiss, Phebe A. Christmas Stories & Legends. Curtiss, Phebe A., ed. 2011. 118p. 22.95 (978-1-4638-9660-7(3)) Rodgers, Alan Bks.

Curtiss, Phebe A., ed. Christmas Stories & Legends. 2009. 120p. pap. 10.95 (978-1-60664-397-6(5)) Rodgers, Alan Bks.

Curto Family, The & Fischer, Rusty. One Little Christmas Tree. 2012. 26p. pap. 9.99 (978-0-9840338-1-2(5)) Good Times at Home LLC.

Cusimano Love, Maryann & Ichikawa, Satomi. You Are My Miracle (Tú Eres Mi Milagro) 2016. (SPA & ENG., Illus.). 28p. (J). (— 1). bds. 7.99 (978-0-399-54734-8(7), Philomel Bks.) Penguin Young Readers Group.

Cuyler, Margery. The Christmas Snowman. Westerman, Johanna, illus. 2011. (ENG.). 32p. (J). (gr. k-2). 12.95 (978-1-61608-483-7(9), 608483, Sky Pony Pr.) Skyhorse Publishing Co., Inc.

Czajak, Paul. Monster Needs a Christmas Tree. Grieb, Wendy, illus. 2014. (Monster & Me Ser.). (ENG.). 32p. (J). (-k). 16.95 (978-1-938063-46-6(5), Mighty Media Kids) Mighty Media Pr.

Dahl, Michael. Christmas. Ho, Jannie, illus. 2015. (Baby Face Ser.). (ENG.). 10p. (gr. -1 — 1). bds. 7.99 (978-1-62370-292-2(5)) Capstone Young Readers of Coughlan Cos.

Dale, Jenny. Jingle Belle. Reid, Mick, illus. 2003. 107p. (J). (978-0-439-54366-8(5)) Scholastic, Inc.

—Little Star. Reid, Mick, illus. 2003. 109p. (J). (978-0-439-54363-7(0)) Scholastic, Inc.

—Snowy the Surprise Puppy. Hellard, Susan, illus. 2005. 60p. (J). pap. (978-0-439-79124-3(3)) Scholastic, Inc.

Daley, Pj. Roger & the Xmas Elf. 2012. 16p. pap. 12.69 (978-1-4669-7211-7(4)) Trafford Publishing.

Daley-Prado, M. The Super Heroes Save Christmas! 2007. 24p. per. 24.95 (978-1-4241-9123-9(8)) America Star Bks.

d'Allancé, Mireille. Dejame Decorar el Arbol de Navidad.Tr. of Let Me Decorate the Christmas Tree. (SPA.). 36p. (J). (gr. k-3). 9.20 (978-84-95150-26-4(3)) Corimbo, Editorial S.L. ESP. Dist: Lectorum Pubns., Inc.

Dalrymple, Lisa. If It's No Trouble... a Big Polar Bear, 1 vol. Pratt, Lizz, illus. 2012. (ENG.). 32p. (J). (gr. k-3). 12.95 (978-1-897174-95-1(0), Tuckamore Bks) Creative Bk. Publishing CAN. Dist: Orca Bk. Pubs. USA.

Dalton, Pamela, illus. A Village Christmas: 20 Exquisite Punch-Out Ornaments. 2015. (ENG.). 8p. (J). (gr. 1-4). 19.95 (978-1-4521-2746-0(8)) Chronicle Bks. LLC.

Daly, Jerald James. An Early Snow (the Visions Come) 2008. 180p. pap. 24.95 (978-1-60703-610-4(X)) America Star Bks.

Daniel, Noel, ed. A Treasury of Wintertime Tales. 2014. (ENG.). 324p. 39.99 (978-3-8365-4400-9(8)) TASCHEN DEU. Dist: Ingram Publisher Services.

Dannenbring, Cheryl. My Puppy Gave to Me, 1 vol. Kremsner, Cynthia, illus. 2014. (ENG.). 32p. (J). (gr. k-3). 16.99 (978-1-4556-1943-6(4)) Pelican Publishing Co., Inc.

Danowski, Jeffrey K. The Teddy Bear Necklace. 2012. 218p. 29.95 (978-1-4626-9762-5(3)) America Star Bks.

Danziger, Paula. Thames Doesn't Rhyme with James. (Remember Me to Harold Square Ser.: No. 2). 153p. (J). pap. 3.99 (978-0-8072-1473-2(6), Listening Library) Random Hse. Audio Publishing Group.

David, E. L. The Christmas Gift. 2011. 28p. pap. 14.99 (978-1-4634-2685-9(2)) AuthorHouse.

David, Erica. Christmas with Krabby Klaws. Martinez, Heather, illus. 2010. (SpongeBob SquarePants Ser.). (ENG.). 16p. (J). pap. 5.99 (978-1-4424-0805-0(7), Simon Spotlight/Nickelodeon) Simon Spotlight/Nickelodeon.

David, Juliet. The Christmas Story, 1 vol. Parry, Jo, illus. 2009. (Candle Read & Play Ser.). 12p. (J). bds. 11.99 (978-0-8254-7400-2(0), Candle Bks.) Lion Hudson PLC GBR. Dist: Kregel Pubns.

—The First Christmas, 1 vol. Denham, Gemma, illus. 2008. (Candle Playbook Ser.). 18p. (J). bds. 7.99 (978-0-8254-7377-7(2), Candle Bks.) Lion Hudson PLC GBR. Dist: Kregel Pubns.

—The Midnight Visitors, 1 vol. Parry, Jo, illus. 2015. 32p. (J). 14.99 (978-1-78128-233-5(1), Candle Bks.) Lion Hudson PLC GBR. Dist: Kregel Pubns.

—My Very First Story of Christmas, 1 vol. Prole, Helen, illus. 2016. (Candle Bible for Toddlers Ser.). (ENG.). 24p. (J). pap. 4.99 (978-1-78128-285-4(4), Candle Bks.) Lion Hudson PLC GBR. Dist: Kregel Pubns.

Davies, Margo. Do You Believe in Santa Claus? 2003. (J). 6.00 (978-0-9708959-7-4(6), Accent Pubns.) Ajoyin Publishing, Inc.

Davis, Anne Shirley. No Red Suit for Santa? 2008. 16p. pap. 8.49 (978-1-4389-2418-2(6)) AuthorHouse.

Davis, Chip, concept. Mannheim Steamroller - the Christmas Angel Davis, Chip, . 2004. (Illus.). 22p. per. 14.95 (978-0-9754149-1-0(7)) Mannheim Steamroller L.L.C.

Davis, Dan. An Orphan's Promise: A Christmas Story. Davis, Jan, ed. Siravo, Christina E., illus. 2006. 96p. (J). 14.95 (978-0-9725977-5-3(1)) Second Star Creations.

Davis, Dan T. The Blacksmith's Gift: A Christmas Story. Davis, Jan, ed. Armstrong, Matthew S., illus. 2004. 64p. (J). 14.95 (978-0-9725977-4-6(3)) Second Star Creations.

Davis, David. Nurse's Night Before Christmas, 1 vol. Rice, James, illus. 2003. (Night Before Christmas Ser.). (ENG.). 32p. (J). (gr. k-3). 16.99 (978-1-58980-152-3(0)) Pelican Publishing Co., Inc.

Davis, Donald. Don't Kill Santa! Christmas Stories. 2006. (ENG., Illus.). 128p. (J). (gr. 3-7). 14.95 (978-0-87483-746-9(4)) August Hse. Pubs., Inc.

Davis, Lowrey. Papa's Storybook. 2008. 116p. 19.99 (978-1-60791-100-5(0)); pap. 11.99 (978-1-60791-099-2(3)) Salem Author Services.

DeCarmelo, Marie. A Little Christmas Story. 2008. 40p. pap. 18.95 (978-0-557-02844-3(2)) Lulu Pr., Inc.

Dede, Vivian Hughes. Elizabeth's Christmas Story. Morris, Susan, illus. 2004. 16p. (J). 1.99 (978-0-7586-0478-1(5)) Concordia Publishing Hse.

deGroat, Diane. Jingle Bells, Homework Smells. deGroat, Diane, illus. 2003. (ENG., Illus.). 32p. (J). (gr. -1-3). pap. 6.99 (978-0-688-17545-0(7)) HarperCollins Pubs.

—Jingle Bells, Homework Smells. deGroat, Diane, illus. 2008. (Illus.). (J). (gr. -1-3). pap. 16.95 incl. audio (978-1-4301-0419-3(8)) Live Oak Media.

DeLand, M. Maitland. Baby Santa's Worldwide Christmas Adventure. Wilson, Phil, illus. 2010. 32p. (J). 14.95 (978-1-60832-062-2(6)) Greenleaf Book Group.

DeLand, M. Maitland. Baby Santa & the Lost Letters. 2011. (Illus.). 36p. (J). 14.95 (978-1-60832-194-0(0)) Greenleaf Book Group.

Dellinger, Hampton. Thanks for Nothing: How Willie & Abe Saved Thanksgiving. 2008. 24p. 12.99 (978-0-615-24971-1(X)) Dellinger, Hampton.

delMazo, Deborah. No Cookies for Christmas: The Story of Grandma's Missing Package. Horsfall, Jacqueline, ed. Balvanz, Gwynessa, illus. 2010. 32p. (J). pap. 9.95 (978-0-615-32691-7(9)) Zoombird Bks.

Delrusso, Diana. Pages, the Book-Maker Elf. Schwab, Jordan, illus. 2008. 68p. pap. 23.49 (978-1-4343-9844-4(7)) AuthorHouse.

Demas, Corinne. Two Christmas Mice. Roth, Stephanie, illus. 2005. (ENG.). 32p. (J). (gr. -1-3). 16.95 (978-0-8234-1785-8(9)) Holiday Hse., Inc.

Dempster, Al. Walt Disney's Santa's Toy Shop. 2015. (Illus.). (J). **(978-0-7364-3402-7(X))** Mouse Works.

Denis, Erik & LeBlanc, Natalie. The Bubble. 2005. 16p. 10.10 (978-1-4116-6424-1(8)) Lulu Pr., Inc.

DePalma, Johnny & Crabapple, Molly. Once upon a Christmas Tree - A Holiday Fairy Tale. 2007. 88p. pap. 10.50 (978-0-615-15448-0(4)) Umbrelly Bks.

dePaola, Tomie. Four Friends at Christmas. dePaola, Tomie, illus. 2009. (ENG., Illus.). 32p. (J). (gr. -1-1). 12.99 (978-1-4169-9175-5(1), Aladdin) Simon & Schuster Children's Publishing.

—Joy to the World: Christmas Stories & Songs. dePaola, Tomie, illus. 2010. (ENG., Illus.). 112p. (J). (gr. -1-2). 24.99 (978-0-399-25536-6(2), G.P. Putnam's Sons Books for Young Readers) Penguin Young Readers Group.

—Joy to the World: Tomie's Christmas Stories. dePaola, Tomie, illus. 2013. (ENG., Illus.). 112p. (J). (gr. -1-2). 12.99 (978-0-14-750952-9(1), Puffin Books) Penguin Young Readers Group.

—My First Christmas. dePaola, Tomie, illus. 2008. (ENG., Illus.). 14p. (J). (gr. -1-k). bds. 6.99 (978-0-448-44860-2(2), Grosset & Dunlap) Penguin Young Readers Group.

dePaola, Tomie. Strega Nona Does It Again. 2017. lib. bdg. 19.65 **(978-0-606-39784-1(1))** Turtleback Bks.

Depken, Kristen L. Merry Christmas, Woody. 2013. lib. bdg. 13.55 (978-0-606-32213-3(2), Turtleback) Turtleback Bks.

—Merry Christmas, Woody (Disney/Pixar Toy Story) RH Disney Staff, illus. 2013. (Pictureback Ser.). (ENG.). 16p. (J). (gr. -1-2). 3.99 (978-0-7364-3070-8(9), RH/Disney) Random Hse. Children's Bks.

—Rudolph the Red-Nosed Reindeer. Karl, Linda, illus. 2014. (My Readers Ser.). (ENG.). 32p. (J). (gr. k-2). 15.99 (978-1-250-05044-1(8), 9781250050441) Square Fish.

DePrisco, Dorothea. Randall Reindeer's Naughty & Nice Report. Reagan, Susan, illus. 2011. (ENG.). (J). (gr. -1-3). 24.95 (978-1-61524-365-5(8), Intervisual/Piggy Toes) Bendon, Inc.

Desjardins, India. Marguerite's Christmas. Blanchet, Pascal, illus. 2015. (ENG.). 72p. (J). (gr. 2). 19.95 (978-1-59270-178-0(7)) Enchanted Lion Bks., LLC.

DeStefano, Anthony. Little Star. Elliott, Mark, illus. 2013. (ENG.). 36p. (J). 14.99 (978-0-7369-5859-2(2)) Harvest Hse. Pubs.

deVet, L. J. Teddy's Christmas Wish. Zabarylo-Duma, Ewa, illus. 2013. (ENG.). 48p. (J). (978-0-9873686-0-7(5)); pap. (978-0-9873686-1-4(3)) Print-Rite Publishers.

Dewdney, Anna. Llama Llama Holiday Drama. 2010. (Llama Llama Ser.). (ENG.). 40p. (J). (gr. -1-k). 17.99 (978-0-670-01161-2(4), Viking Books for Young Readers) Penguin Young Readers Group.

—Llama Llama Jingle Bells. Dewdney, Anna, illus. 2014. (Llama Llama Ser.). (ENG., Illus.). 14p. (J). (— 1). bds. 5.99 (978-0-451-46980-9(1), Viking Books for Young Readers) Penguin Young Readers Group.

DiCamillo, Kate. Great Joy. Ibatoulline, Bagram, illus. (ENG.). 32p. (J). (gr. -1-3). 2010. 8.99 (978-0-7636-4996-8(1)) 2007. 16.99 (978-0-7636-2920-5(0)) Candlewick Pr.

Dickens, Charles. A Christmas Carol. 2008. (Illus.). 116p. (Orig.). pap. 7.99 (978-1-60450-545-0(1), Serenity Pubs.) Arc Manor.

—A Christmas Carol. 2005. 92p. (Orig.). (gr. 4-6). per. 6.95 (978-1-933652-47-4(0)) Bed Bks.

—A Christmas Carol. 2003. (ENG.). 128p. (Orig.). (C). pap. 16.95 (978-0-7593-9886-3(0), Cengage Learning) CENGAGE Learning.

—A Christmas Carol. Lynch, P. J., illus. 2006. (ENG.). 160p. (Orig.). (J). (gr. 5-6). 19.99 (978-0-7636-3120-8(5)) Candlewick Pr.

—A Christmas Carol. Bryant, Clive, ed. Collins, Mike & Offredi, James, illus. 2012. (ENG.). 160p. (Orig.). (gr. 6). lib. bdg. 24.95 (978-1-907127-40-3(2)) Classical Comics GBR. Dist: Publishers Group West (PGW).

—A Christmas Carol. Howell, Keith, tr. Roach, David & Offredi, James, illus. 2008. (ENG.). 144p. (Orig.). (gr. 4-18). pap. 16.95 (978-1-906332-51-8(7)); pap. 16.95 (978-1-906332-52-5(5)) Classical Comics GBR. (Classical Comics, Ltd.). Dist: Publishers Group West (PGW).

—A Christmas Carol. 2008. 160p. (Orig.). (gr. 5-6). pap. 11.95 (978-1-4341-0214-0(9)) Editorium, The.

—A Christmas Carol. 2006. (Illus.). 61p. (Orig.). (J). lib. bdg. 30.77 (978-1-4242-1016-9(X)) Fitzgerald Bks.

—A Christmas Carol. 2009. 84p. (Orig.). (gr. -1-18). pap. 19.99 (978-1-4432-6003-9(7)) General Bks. LLC.

—A Christmas Carol. Helquist, Brett, illus. 2009. (ENG.). 40p. (Orig.). (J). (gr. k). 17.99 (978-0-06-165099-4(4)) HarperCollins Pubs.

—A Christmas Carol. 2008. (Puffin Classics Ser.). (ENG., Illus.). 160p. (Orig.). (J). (gr. 5-7). 5.99 (978-0-14-132452-4(X), Puffin Books) Penguin Young Readers Group.

—A Christmas Carol. Donnelly, Karen, illus. 2013. (Charles Dickens Ser.). (ENG.). 64p. (Orig.). pap. 6.95 (978-1-906230-02-9(1)) Real Reads Ltd. GBR. Dist: Casemate Pubs. & Bk. Distributors, LLC.

—A Christmas Carol. 2004. (Aladdin Classics Ser.). (ENG.). 128p. (Orig.). (J). pap. 5.99 (978-0-689-87180-1(5), Simon & Schuster/Paula Wiseman Bks.) Simon & Schuster/Paula Wiseman Bks.

—A Christmas Carol. Andrews, Gary, illus. 2008. (Fast Track Classics Ser.). 46p. (Orig.). (J). (gr. 4-7). pap. 10.00 (978-1-4190-5087-9(7)) Steck-Vaughn.

—A Christmas Carol. McKowen, Scott, illus. 2009. (Sterling Unabridged Classics Ser.). (ENG.). 96p. (Orig.). (J). (gr. 5). 9.95 (978-1-4027-6690-9(4)) Sterling Publishing Co., Inc.

—Christmas Carol. 2004. (Fast Track Classics Ser.). (Illus.). 48p. (J). pap. (978-0-237-52686-3(7)) Evans Brothers, Ltd.

—A Christmas Carol. 2009. (Foundation Classics Ser.). 56p. (J). (gr. 5-9). lib. bdg. 27.95 (978-1-60754-850-8(X)) Windmill Bks.

—A Christmas Carol. Sanchez Almara, Dono & Almara, Dono Sanchez, illus. 2015. (Graphic Revolve: Common Core Editions Ser.). (ENG.). 72p. (gr. 2-3). lib. bdg. 27.99 (978-1-4965-0370-1(8)) Stone Arch Bks.

—A Christmas Carol. Blake, Quentin, illus. unabr. ed. 2004. (Chrysalis Childrens Classics Ser.). 190p. (Orig.). (YA). pap. (978-1-84365-063-8(0), Pavilion Children's Books) Pavilion Bks.

—A Christmas Carol, 1 vol. 2010. (Illustrated Classics Ser.). (ENG., Illus.). 64p. (Orig.). (YA). (gr. 9-12). pap. 9.95 (978-1-56254-890-2(5)) Saddleback Educational Publishing, Inc.

—A Christmas Carol: Being a Ghost Story of Christmas. 2013. (Cambridge Library Collection - Fiction & Poetry Ser.). (ENG., Illus.). 186p. pap. 28.99 *(978-1-108-05714-1(4))* Cambridge Univ. Pr.

—A Christmas Carol: Prestwick House Literary Touchstone Edition. 2005. 86p. (YA). per. 3.99 *(978-1-58049-579-0(6),* PWH5796) Prestwick Hse., Inc.

—A Christmas Carol - Spotlight Edition. 2004. 102p. (YA). per. 5.95 *(978-1-58049-551-6(6),* PWH5516) Prestwick Hse., Inc.

—A Christmas Carol & the Remembrance of Mugby. 2012. (Classics Illustrated Deluxe Graphic Nove Ser.). (ENG., Illus.). 96p. (J). (gr. 2-8). pap. 11.99 *(978-1-59707-345-5(8),* 9781597073455) Papercutz.

—A Christmas Carol the Graphic Novel - Original Text: British Edition. Collins, Mike et al, illus. 2008. 160p. (Orig.). pap. *(978-1-906332-17-4(7))* Classical Comics.

—The Cricket on the Hearth. 2004. reprint ed. pap. 15.95 *(978-1-4191-5807-0(4));* pap. 1.99 *(978-1-4192-5807-7(9))* Kessinger Publishing, LLC.

—The Cricket on the Hearth. l.t. ed. 2005. 128p. pap. 17.95 *(978-1-59688-048-1(1),* 1-59688-048-1) Large Print Bk. Co., The.

Dickens, Charles & Wright, Brett. Scrooge #worstgiftever. 2016. (OMG Classics Ser.). (ENG., Illus.). 112p. (YA). (gr. 9). 9.99 *(978-0-399-55064-5(X),* Random Hse. Bks. for Young Readers) Random Hse. Children's Bks.

Dickens, Charles, et al. Christmas Books & Stories. 2004. (YA). cd-rom, audio compact disk 25.00 *(978-0-917466-15-1(2))* Samizdat Express.

Dickinson, Asa Don & Skinner, Ada M. The Children's Book of Christmas Stories. 2004. reprint ed. pap. 24.95 *(978-1-4191-5657-1(8));* pap. 1.99 *(978-1-4192-5657-8(2))* Kessinger Publishing, LLC.

Diesen, Deborah. The Not Very Merry Pout-Pout Fish. Hanna, Dan, illus. (Pout-Pout Fish Adventure Ser.). (ENG.). (J). 2017. 34p. bds. 7.99 *(978-0-374-30459-1(9),* 9780374304591) 2015. 32p. (gr. -1-1). 16.99 *(978-0-374-35549-4(5),* 9780374355494) Farrar, Straus & Giroux. (Farrar, Straus & Giroux (BYR)).

Dineen, Kaite. What Santa Wants You to Know: A Story of Santa's Love for Jesus, 1 vol. 2010. 34p. pap. 24.95 *(978-1-4489-7071-1(7))* PublishAmerica, Inc.

Disney Book Group. Disney 5-Minute Christmas Stories. Disney Storybook Art Team, illus. 2016. (5-Minute Stories Ser.). (ENG.). 192p. (J). (gr. 1-3). 12.99 *(978-1-4847-2741-6(X))* Disney Pr.

—Frozen Olaf's Night Before Christmas Book & CD. Disney Storybook Art Team, illus. 2015. (ENG.). 32p. (J). (gr. 1-3). 12.99 *(978-1-4847-2468-2(2))* Disney Pr.

Disney Book Group & Rogers, Tom. Elena of Avalor Feliz Navidad: A Royal Christmas. Disney Storybook Art Team, illus. 2016. (ENG.). 48p. (J). (gr. 1-3). 12.99 *(978-1-4847-4792-6(5))* Disney Pr.

Disney Book Group Staff. Mickey Saves Santa. Disney Storybook Artists Staff, illus. 2009. (ENG.). 24p. (J). (gr. -1-k). pap. 5.99 *(978-1-4231-1846-6(4))* Disney Pr.

Disney Book Group Staff & Higginson, Sheila Sweeny. Doc Mcstuffins a Very Mcstuffins Christmas. Disney Storybook Artists Staff & Disney Storybook Art Team, illus. 2014. (ENG.). 24p. (J). (gr. -1-k). pap. 5.99 *(978-1-4847-0698-5(6))* Disney Pr.

Disney Book Group Staff, et al. Disney Christmas Storybook Collection. Disney Storybook Artists Staff, illus. 2014. (Storybook Collection). (ENG.). 304p. (J). (gr. -1-k). 16.99 *(978-1-4231-8450-8(5))* Disney Pr.

Disney Princess Holiday: Cinderella So This Is Christmas/Beauty & the Beast One Magical Christmas/Ariel's Christmas under the Sea. unabr. ed. 2005. (Disney's Read along Collection Ser.). (J). pap. *(978-0-7634-1146-6(9))* Walt Disney Records.

DiTaranto, Cynthia A. Krismas Karol the Nigerian Dwarf Goat. 2010. 24p. 14.95 *(978-1-4269-3016-4(X))* Trafford Publishing.

Dittmer, Cherie. Angel Angel. 2004. (Illus.). 32p. (J). 7.99 *(978-0-7586-0062-2(3))* Concordia Publishing Hse.

Dittrick, A. L., as told by. Once upon A Christmas: The 4th Wiseman. 2007. (Illus.). (J). 3.95 net. *(978-0-9767578-0-1(X),* Ink Well Publishing) Ink Well.

Dixon, Bob. Holiday Bunny. 2009. 28p. pap. 13.99 *(978-1-4490-0436-1(9))* AuthorHouse.

Dodd, Melissa. Santa Sheds, 1 vol. 2009. 17p. pap. 24.95 *(978-1-60749-208-5(3))* America Star Bks.

Dodson, Bert. Helping Santa: My First Christmas Adventure with Grandma. Dodson, Bert, illus. 2011. (ENG., Illus.). 32p. (J). (gr. 1-3). 17.95 *(978-1-59373-093-2(4))* Bunker Hill Publishing, Inc.

Doherty, Glen. Eddie's Christmas Surprise. 2012. 28p. pap. 12.99 *(978-1-4797-0976-2(X))* Xlibris Corp.

Doles, Sean Patrick. Saving Mr. Bingle: A New Orleans Christmas Fairy Tale. num. ed. 2004. 176p. per. 9.95 *(978-0-9758996-0-1(0))* New Orleans Stories.

Donaldson, Julia. Christmas with Princess Mirror-Belle. Monks, Lydia, illus. 2016. (Princess Mirror-Belle Ser.). (ENG.). 112p. (J). (gr. k-6). 14.99 *(978-1-5098-1426-8(4))* Pan Macmillan GBR. Dist: Independent Pubs. Group.

—Stick Man. Scheffler, Axel, illus. (ENG.). 32p. (J). (gr. -1-3). 2016. 12.99 *(978-0-545-94789-3(8))* 2009. 16.99 *(978-0-545-15761-2(7))* Scholastic, Inc. (Levine, Arthur A. Bks.).

Donovan, Dan. A Christmas Tail! 2008. 28p. pap. 14.50 *(978-1-4389-1220-2(X))* AuthorHouse.

Donovan, Jane Monroe. Small, Medium & Large. Donovan, Jane Monroe, illus. 2010. (ENG., Illus.). 32p. (J). (gr. 1-4). 15.95 *(978-1-58536-447-3(9),* 202172) Sleeping Bear Pr.

Dorman, Brandon. Santa's Stowaway. Dorman, Brandon, illus. 2009. (ENG., Illus.). 40p. (J). (gr. -1-3). 16.99 *(978-0-06-135188-4(1),* Greenwillow Bks.) HarperCollins Pubs.

Doman, Dave. Tree Talkers: A Christmas Story, 1 vol. Swope, Brenda, illus. 2009. 32p. pap. 24.95 *(978-1-61546-180-6(9))* America Star Bks.

Dorner, Nancy L. Crackerjack the Christmas Cat. Alphenaar, Pamela L., illus. 2008. 40p. pap. 16.95 *(978-0-9818488-0-8(X))* Ajoyin Publishing, Inc.

Dougherty, Brandi. The Littlest Elf. Richards, Kirsten, illus. 2012. (ENG.). 24p. (J). (gr. -1-k). pap. 4.99 *(978-0-545-43654-0(0))* Scholastic, Inc.

—The Littlest Elf. Richards, Kristen, illus. 2012. (J). pap. *(978-0-545-48978-2(4),* WestBow Pr.) Scholastic, Inc.

Douglas, Ryke. Tock a Tick. 2007. 32p. per. 11.95 *(978-1-59800-756-5(4))* Outskirts Pr., Inc.

Dove, S. R. Gabriel the First Christmas Dragon, 1 vol. 2009. 39p. pap. 24.95 *(978-1-60836-855-6(6))* America Star Bks.

Dragovich, Joe. The Empty Hook. 2013. (ENG.). 36p. pap. 13.95 *(978-1-4497-7819-4(4),* WestBow Pr.) Author Solutions, Inc.

Draper, Melissa J. Holly the Christmas Collie. Kravanek, J. Elise, illus. 2004. 63p. (J). *(978-0-9741081-3-1(8))* Acres Publishing.

Dreyer, Nicole E. Joseph's Christmas Story. Ebert, Len, illus. 2004. (ENG.). 16p. (J). 1.99 *(978-0-570-07577-6(7))* Concordia Publishing Hse.

D'shindia, Albert. The Fable Musical. 2012. 56p. (gr. -1). pap. 10.95 *(978-1-4567-9978-6(9))* AuthorHouse.

Dubin, Lawrence. Santa's Big Red Hat. 2012. (ENG.). (J). pap. 20.00 *(978-1-4675-3866-4(3))* Independent Pub.

Duggan, Janet. The Christmas Story As Told by Assellus the Christmas Donkey. Robertson, Catherine, illus. 2009. (ENG.). 44p. *(978-0-9563389-1-4(7))* Janet Duggan.

Dukes, LeRoy L. Christmas on Chill Street. 2005. (J). 6.99 *(978-0-9664506-2-0(0))* Dukes World, Inc.

Duncan, Brenda. Reese - the Dog Who Almost Ruined Christmas. 2012. 24p. pap. 17.99 *(978-1-4772-6105-7(2))* AuthorHouse.

Duncan Gurley, Ann. Esbe's Halo. 2009. 108p. (J). pap. 15.95 *(978-1-4327-3453-4(9))* Outskirts Pr., Inc.

Dunham, Terri Hoover. The Legend of Papa Noel: A Cajun Christmas Story. Knorr, Laura, illus. 2006. (Legends Ser.). (ENG.). 32p. (J). (gr. -1-3). 17.95 *(978-1-58536-256-1(5))* Sleeping Bear Pr.

Dunrea, Olivier. Merry Christmas, Ollie! (Gossie & Friends Ser.). (ENG., Illus.). (J). (gr. k — 1). 2011. 30p. bds. 6.99 *(978-0-547-37016-3(4))* 2008. 32p. 12.95 *(978-0-618-53242-1(0))* Houghton Mifflin Harcourt Publishing Co.

—Merry Christmas, Ollie (Reader) 2015. (Gossie & Friends Ser.). (ENG., Illus.). 32p. (J). (gr. -1 — 1). pap. 3.99 *(978-0-544-55394-1(2),* HMH Books For Young Readers) Houghton Mifflin Harcourt Publishing Co.

Dunsany, Taylor. The Little Witch Who Lost Her Broom & Other Stories. 2008. 48p. pap. 8.95 *(978-0-595-52506-5(7))* iUniverse, Inc.

Durrant, George D. Sam's Christmas Wish. Burr, Dan, illus. 2014. (ENG.). 32p. (J). (gr. 3). 17.99 *(978-1-60907-606-1(0),* Shadow Mountain) Shadow Mountain Publishing.

Duval, Kathy. The Three Bears' Christmas. Meisel, Paul, illus. (ENG.). 32p. (J). (gr. -1-3). 2006. 6.95 *(978-0-8234-2039-1(6))* 2005. 16.95 *(978-0-8234-1871-8(5))* Holiday Hse., Inc.

—The Three Bears' Christmas. Meisel, Paul, illus. 2007. (J). *(978-0-545-05421-8(4))* Scholastic, Inc.

Duvall, John. The Great Spruce. Gibbon, Rebecca, illus. 2016. (ENG.). 40p. (J). (gr. k-3). 17.99 *(978-0-399-16084-4(1),* G.P. Putnam's Sons Books for Young Readers) Penguin Young Readers Group.

Dyan, Penelope. Bunny Love! a Book about Home & Bunnies. Dyan, Penelope, illus. 2013. (Illus.). 34p. pap. 11.95 *(978-1-61477-084-8(0))* Bellissima Publishing, LLC.

—Easter Eggs & Bunny Wishes. 2011. (Illus.). 34p. pap. 11.95 *(978-1-935630-61-6(X))* Bellissima Publishing, LLC.

—Why Angels Sing! Dyan, Penelope, illus. 2012. (Illus.). 34p. pap. 11.95 *(978-1-61477-065-7(4))* Bellissima Publishing, LLC.

Easterling, Anne S. Ozzie the Great Christmas Crocodile. 2006. (Illus.). 12p. (J). 3.95 *(978-0-9768890-4-5(8))* ASE Media.

Eaton, Kay A. Gleason, the Christmas Giraffe. 2009. 28p. pap. 12.50 *(978-1-4389-3010-7(0))* AuthorHouse.

Ebanks, Timali. A Caymanian Heritage Series: Christmas Time. 2013. 24p. pap. 12.50 *(978-1-4575-1726-6(4))* Dog Ear Publishing, LLC.

Ebbeler, Jeffrey, illus. Jingle Bells. 2009. (ENG.). 20p. (J). (gr. -1-k). bds. 6.99 *(978-0-8249-1827-9(4),* Ideal Pubns.) Worthy Publishing.

—Jingle Bells - Musical. 2009. (ENG.). 20p. (J). (gr. -1-k). bds. 12.99 *(978-0-8249-1829-3(0),* Ideal Pubns.) Worthy Publishing.

Ebie, Mora. Little Mouse's Hawaiian Christmas Present. Braffet, Holly, illus. 2011. 28p. (J). *(978-1-56647-956-1(8))* Mutual Publishing LLC.

Ebiringa, Chudy. The, Adventures of Ella at Bulukutu Stream. 2011. (ENG.). 50p. pap. 11.95 *(978-1-4327-6655-9(4))* Outskirts Pr., Inc.

Edwards, Nicholas. The Adventures of Santa Paws. 2010. (Santa Paws Ser.). (ENG.). 336p. (J). (gr. 3-7). pap. 7.99 *(978-0-545-22551-9(5),* Scholastic Paperbacks) Scholastic, Inc.

Eismann, Sheila F. & Putz, Ali F. The Christmas Tin. Richardson, Cathie, illus. 2013. 40p. pap. 9.95 *(978-0-9897133-8-2(5))* Desert Sage Pr.

Ellen, Chantal. The Reason for the Season. Pierre-Louis, Phillip, illus. 2007. 32p. (J). (gr. k-2). 15.95 *(978-0-9786786-1-6(3))* Lions Den Publishing, LLC.

Elliott, Ann. GypsyBridge Friends: The Gift. 2003. 46p. pap. 12.95 *(978-0-9721825-1-5(9))* Open Vision Entertainment Corp.

Ellis, Gwen. The First Christmas, 1 vol. Pichon, Liz, illus. 2007. 10p. (J). bds. 15.99 *(978-0-8254-5538-4(3))* Kregel Pubns.

Emmett, Jonathan. The Santa Trap, 1 vol. Bernatene, Poly, illus. 2012. (ENG.). 32p. (J). 15.95 *(978-1-56145-670-3(5))* Peachtree Pubs.

Encarnacion, Elizabeth. Rudolph, the Red-Nosed Reindeer. 2007. (Miniature Editions Ser.). (ENG., Illus.). 128p. (gr. 1-17). 5.95 *(978-0-7624-3098-7(2))* Running Pr. Bk. Pubs.

Encyclopaedia Britannica, Inc. Staff, compiled by. I Wish Daddy Didn't Drink So Much. 2008. 49.95 *(978-1-59339-667-1(8))* Encyclopaedia Britannica, Inc.

Enge-Grandbois, Kathryn L. Suzy Q: Book 2. 2012. 32p. pap. 24.95 *(978-1-4626-6970-7(0))* America Star Bks.

Engelbreit, Mary. Mary Engelbreit's A Merry Little Christmas: Celebrate from A to Z. Engelbreit, Mary, illus. 2006. (ENG., Illus.). 40p. (J). (gr. -1-3). lib. bdg. 17.89 *(978-0-06-074159-4(7))* HarperCollins Pubs.

—Mary Engelbreit's a Merry Little Christmas: Celebrate from A to Z. Engelbreit, Mary, illus. 2010. (ENG., Illus.). 40p. (J). (gr. -1-3). pap. 6.99 *(978-0-06-074160-0(0))* HarperCollins Pubs.

—Mary Engelbreit's Nutcracker. Engelbreit, Mary, illus. 2011. (ENG., Illus.). 40p. (J). (gr. -1-3). 17.99 *(978-0-06-088579-3(3))* HarperCollins Pubs.

—Queen of Christmas. Engelbreit, Mary, illus. 2003. (Ann Estelle Stories Ser.). (Illus.). (J). 32p. 16.99 *(978-0-06-058608-9(7));* 127.92 *(978-0-06-056903-7(4));* 159.90 *(978-0-06-056902-0(6))* HarperCollins Pubs.

Erickson, John R. The Wounded Buzzard on Christmas Eve. Holmes, Gerald L., illus. 2011. (Hank the Cowdog Ser.: No. 13). (ENG.). 112p. (J). (gr. 3-6). pap. 5.99 *(978-1-59188-113-1(7))* Maverick Bks., Inc.

Erickson, Patricia. The Little Christmas Tree. 2012. 24p. (-18). pap. 17.99 *(978-1-4772-8610-4(1))* AuthorHouse.

Eriksen, Valanee. Christmas Bells & Hero's Tails. 2015. (Illus.). vi, 90p. (J). pap. 7.99 *(978-1-4621-1737-6(6))* Cedar Fort, Inc./CFI Distribution.

Erwin, Kay. A Sheepdog's Christmas. 2008. 56p. pap. 10.99 *(978-1-60647-698-7(X))* Salem Author Services.

Etheridge, Judy. Olivia's Wish. 2009. 32p. pap. 21.99 *(978-1-4415-3915-1(8))* Xlibris Corp.

Etherington Dilks, Barbara. The Snowman. 2015. (ENG.). 50p. (J). (gr. 2-3). mass mkt. 14.95 *(978-1-78612-050-2(X),* 81054dbd-4c58-4cbd-98dc-c4631d79a99c) Austin, Stan AUS. Dist: Bookmasters Distribution.

Eubank, Patricia Reeder. Countdown to Christmas. 2003. (ENG., Illus.). 14p. (J). (gr. -1-k). bds. 9.95 *(978-0-8249-6505-1(1),* Ideal Pubns.) Worthy Publishing.

Evans, Clay Bonnyman. The Winter Witch. Bender, Robert, illus. 2005. (ENG.). 32p. (J). (gr. -1-3). 16.95 *(978-0-8234-1615-8(1))* Holiday Hse., Inc.

Evans, Richard. The Christmas Candle. Collins, Jacob, illus. (ENG.). 32p. (J). (gr. -1-3). 2007. 9.99 *(978-1-4169-5047-9(8))* 2006. 8.99 *(978-1-4169-2682-5(8))* Simon & Schuster Bks. For Young Readers. (Simon & Schuster Bks. For Young Readers).

—The Light of Christmas. Craig, Daniel, illus. 2016. (ENG.). 32p. (J). (gr. -1-3). 9.99 *(978-1-4814-6612-7(7),* Aladdin) Simon & Schuster Children's Publishing.

Evert, Lori. The Christmas Wish. Breiehagen, Per, illus. Breiehagen, Per, photos by. 2013. (ENG.). 48p. (J). (gr. -1-2). 17.99 *(978-0-449-81681-3(8),* Random Hse. Bks. for Young Readers) Random Hse. Children's Bks.

—The Christmas Wish. Breiehagen, Per, illus. Breiehagen, Per, photos by. 2013. (J). *(978-0-449-81942-5(6))* Random Hse., Inc.

—The Reindeer Wish. Breiehagen, Per, illus. Breiehagen, Per, photos by. 2015. (ENG.). 48p. (J). (gr. -1-2). 20.99 *(978-0-375-97335-2(4),* Random Hse. Bks. for Young Readers) Random Hse. Children's Bks.

Ewing, Juliana Horatia. The Brownies & Other Tales. 2007. 140p. per. *(978-1-4065-2523-6(5))* Dodo Pr.

—A Great Emergency & Other Tales. 2007. 188p. per. *(978-1-4065-2525-0(1))* Dodo Pr.

Fairbairn, Lee-Anne. Oh, Deer! Christmas Magic: If You Believe Dreams Do Really Come True. 2012. 20p. pap. 14.99 *(978-1-4525-6225-4(3))* Balboa Pr.

—Osiepna! Hono e Krismas. 2013. 20p. pap. 14.99 *(978-1-4525-8785-1(X),* Balboa Pr.) Author Solutions, Inc.

Falconer, Ian. Olivia Helps with Christmas. Falconer, Ian, illus. (Classic Board Bks.). (ENG., Illus.). (J). (gr. -1-2). 2013. 40p. bds. 7.99 *(978-1-4424-9446-6(8))* 2007. 58p. 19.99 *(978-1-4169-0786-2(6))* Simon & Schuster Children's Publishing. (Atheneum Bks. for Young Readers).

Falki, Pamela Marie. The Perfect Christmas Tree: Petrie & Toby's Holiday Adventure. 2009. 24p. pap. 11.49 *(978-1-4343-9983-0(4))* AuthorHouse.

Falzon, Adrienne. What Is an Angel? Salzberg, Helen, illus. 2012. 32p. 18.99 *(978-0-9855562-2-8(6))* Blue Note Pubns.

Fambro, Sonja Grimsley. Santa Spent the Night with Me! 2011. 52p. pap. 25.06 *(978-1-4634-4626-0(8))* AuthorHouse.

—When Santa Goes to Church. 2011. 84p. pap. 32.26 *(978-1-4634-5983-3(1))* AuthorHouse.

Famularo, Joe. Chiara's Bite of the Big Apple: A Happy Book. 2013. 28p. pap. 16.09 *(978-1-4669-5274-4(1))* Trafford Publishing.

Fant, Donna. Scotty's Dream: Book & CD. Axford, Elizabeth C., ed. McKeown, David, illus. 2004. (ENG.). 16p. (J). audio compact disk 14.99 *(978-1-931844-17-8(8),* PP1034) Piano Pr.

Farr, Dan. Mr. Finnegan's Giving Chest. 2005. (Illus.). 32p. (J). (gr. -1-3). 19.95 incl. audio compact disk *(978-1-59038-555-5(1),* Shadow Mountain) Shadow Mountain Publishing.

Faulkner, Keith. Charlie Chimp's Christmas: A Pop-up Extravaganza of Festive Friends. Lambert, Jonathan, illus. 2006. 12p. (J). (gr. -1-3). reprint ed. 10.00 *(978-1-4223-5446-9(6))* DIANE Publishing Co.

Favorite Little Golden Books for Christmas, 5 vols. 2012. (ENG., Illus.). 24p. (J). (gr. k-k). 24.95 *(978-0-307-97745-8(5),* Golden Bks.) Random Hse. Children's Bks.

Fearne, Peter. My Week with Father Christmas. 2006. 176p. per. *(978-1-84667-021-3(7))* Derwent Pr., The.

Fedatova, Marina, illus. The 12 Elves: A New Christmas Tradition. 2010. (ENG.). 18p. (J). (gr. -1-k). bds. 12.99 *(978-1-4424-1684-0(X),* Little Simon) Little Simon.

Federici, Diane Marie. The Christmas Stocking. 2006. (J). pap. 8.00 *(978-0-8059-6874-3(1))* Dorrance Publishing Co., Inc.

Felden, Georgia. When Jesus Hired Santa. 2006. (J). pap. *(978-0-9790444-8-9(0))* Dynasty Publishing, Inc.

Feldman, Thea. Rudolph the Red-Nosed Reindeer - The Classic Story. Madrid, Erwin, illus. 50th ed. 2014. (Rudolph the Red-Nosed Reindeer Ser.). (ENG.). 40p. (J). (gr. -1-3). 12.99 *(978-1-250-04760-1(9),* 9781250047601) Square Fish.

Feldman, Thea & Auerbach, Annie. The Snow Family: A Winter's Tale. Alderson, Lisa, illus. 2005. 12p. (J). 13.00 *(978-0-7567-9460-6(9))* DIANE Publishing Co.

Feliciano, Jose. Feliz Navidad: Two Stories Celebrating Christmas. Diaz, David, illus. 2005. 23p. (J). reprint ed. 16.00 *(978-0-7567-8587-1(1))* DIANE Publishing Co.

Ferguson, Sarah & Duchess of York Staff. Little Red's Christmas Story. Williams, Sam, illus. 2011. (ENG.). 40p. (J). (gr. -1-2). pap. 19.99 *(978-1-4424-3076-1(1),* Simon & Schuster/Paula Wiseman Bks.) Simon & Schuster/Paula Wiseman Bks.

Fernandez, Rafael. Diego's Family Christmas. McGee, Warner, illus. 2008. (Go, Diego, Go! Ser.). (ENG.). 16p. (J). (gr. -1-k). bds. 5.99 *(978-1-4169-5836-9(3),* Simon Spotlight/Nickelodeon) Simon Spotlight/Nickelodeon.

Ferrante, Joanne. Where Do the Christmas Trees Go? 2003. (Illus.). 32p. (J). 15.95 *(978-0-9721949-0-7(8))* Window Seat Publishing.

Field, Ellen. Merry Ham-Ham Christmas. Haefele, Steve, illus. 2003. (Hamtaro Ser.). (ENG.). 32p. (J). pap. 3.99 *(978-0-439-54249-4(9),* Scholastic Paperbacks) Scholastic, Inc.

Field, Eugene. Profitable Tales. 2007. 308p. pap. 29.95 *(978-1-4344-9217-3(6));* per. 19.95 *(978-1-4344-9123-7(4))* Wildside Pr., LLC.

Figueredo, D. H. The Road to Santiago. Torrecilla, Pablo, illus. 2003. (ENG.). 32p. (J). 16.95 *(978-1-58430-059-5(0))* Lee & Low Bks., Inc.

Figueredo, Dan & Torrecilla, Pablo. The Road to Santiago. 2016. (ENG., Illus.). 32p. (J). (gr. 1-4). 9.95 ***(978-1-62014-317-9(8))*** Lee & Low Bks., Inc.

Finley, Martha. Christmas with Grandma Elsie. 2006. 28.95 *(978-1-4218-2988-3(6));* pap. 13.95 *(978-1-4218-3088-9(4))* 1st World Publishing, Inc.

—Christmas with Grandma Elsie. l.t. ed. 2007. (ENG.). 216p. pap. 22.99 *(978-1-4346-2529-8(X))* Creative Media Partners, LLC.

Finn, Rebecca. Rudy Learns to Fly. 6. 2012. (Sparkly Christmas Ser.). (ENG., Illus.). 12p. (J). (gr. -1-k). bds. 5.99 *(978-0-230-75386-0(8))* Macmillan Pubs., Ltd. GBR. Dist: Independent Pubs. Group.

Fiore, Keith M. Leni the Pug: The Comet Christmas Caper. Sacui, Alexandru, illus. 2006. 95p. per. 29.50 *(978-0-9785773-0-8(2))* Brownstone Monkey Productions, Inc.

Fischer, Jean & Thomas Nelson Publishing Staff. A Star for Me, 1 vol. Steele-Morgan, Alexandra, illus. 2014. (ENG.). 20p. (J). bds. 14.99 *(978-0-529-11212-5(4))* Nelson, Thomas Inc.

Fiset, Pierre & Ferraro, Damiano. A Gopher's Christmas Adventure. 2012. 70p. pap. *(978-0-9877632-2-8(9))* Flower Pr.

Fisher, Kimball. Finding Baby Jesus. 2015. 12p. (J). pap. 3.99 *(978-1-4621-1698-0(1))* Cedar Fort, Inc./CFI Distribution.

—Finding the Baby Jesus. 2012. 36p. pap. 5.99 *(978-0-9884132-1-4(3))* TFG.

Fisher, Phyllis Mae Richardson. Twiglet the Little Christmas Tree. Fisher, Phyllis Mae Richardson & Fisher, Douglas W., illus. 2003. (J). 30.00 *(978-0-9745615-1-6(7),* Twiglet The Little Christmas Tree); 186p. 12.00 *(978-0-9745615-4-7(1))* PJs Corner.

Fitzgerald, Linda, creator. Stellar: The Teeniest, Tiniest Star in the WHOLE Universe! 2003. (Illus.). 86p. (J). per. 19.95 *(978-0-9745745-0-9(3),* 102049562) Turning Point LLC.

Fitzhugh, Louise. Harriet the Spy. 50th anniv. ed. 2014. (ENG.). 336p. (J). (gr. 3-7). 17.99 *(978-0-385-37610-5(3),* Delacorte Bks. for Young Readers) Random Hse. Children's Bks.

Fitzsimmons, Jim. The Prince, the Fairy & the Fouly. 2014. (ENG., Illus.). 204p. pap. *(978-1-78306-233-1(9))* Troubador Publishing Ltd.

Flathers, Sean. 'Twas a Shepherd's First Christmas. 2010. 26p. pap. 12.99 *(978-0-88144-230-4(5),* Thorncrown Publishing) Yorkshire Publishing Group.

Fletcher, Corina, et al. The Little Christmas Tree. 2016. (ENG., Illus.). 16p. (J). (gr. -1-k). 19.99 *(978-1-4052-7566-8(9))* Egmont Bks., Ltd. GBR. Dist: Independent Pubs. Group.

Flinn, Lias. Unwrapping the Christmas Creche. 18.00 *(978-0-687-05441-1(9))* Abingdon Pr.

Flinn, Lisa & Younger, Barbara. The Christmas Garland. Corvino, Lucy, tr. Corvino, Lucy, illus. 2003. 32p. (J). 14.95 *(978-0-8249-5460-4(2),* Ideal Pubns.) Worthy Publishing.

Flor Ada, Alma. Celebrate Christmas & Three Kings Day with Pablo & Carlitos. Torres, Walter, illus. 2006. (Cuentos para Celebrar / Stories to Celebrate Ser.). 30p. (gr. k-6). per. 11.95 *(978-1-59820-136-9(0))* Santillana USA Publishing Co., Inc.

Flora, James, creator. Kangaroo for Christmas. 2011. (ENG., Illus.). 40p. (J). (gr. -1-3). 16.95 *(978-1-59270-113-1(2))* Enchanted Lion Bks., LLC.

Fogelin, Adrian. My Brother's Hero, 1 vol. 2005. (ENG.). 224p. (J). (gr. 3-7). reprint ed. pap. 7.95 *(978-1-56145-352-8(8))* Peachtree Pubs.

Fogle, Robin. The Shepherd Boy's Christmas. 2005. (J). pap. 1.79 *(978-1-59317-105-6(6))* Warner Pr., Inc.

Foley, Alyssa Christine. A Secret at Half Past Noon: A Christmas Story. 2008. 28p. pap. 13.99 *(978-1-4389-2013-9(X))* AuthorHouse.

Follow the Star 5 Book Set. 2004. 10p. (J). bds. 7.49 *(978-0-570-07189-1(5))* Concordia Publishing Hse.

Ford, Bernette. Ballet Kitty: Christmas Recital. Williams, Sam, illus. 2012. (ENG.). 32p. (J). (gr. -1-1). 16.95 *(978-1-907152-12-2(1))* Boxer Bks., Ltd. GBR. Dist: Sterling Publishing Co., Inc.

Ford, RoShawn T. Marty & the Magical Christmas Tree. 2012. 24p. pap. 17.99 *(978-1-4772-3719-9(4))* AuthorHouse.

Forster, David. Dreamer in the Snows. 2017. (ENG.). 312p. pap. 15.95 ***(978-1-78629-823-2(6),*** 44efd4ae-c88b-4fbf-af8b-a77e619889dd) Austin, Stan AUS. Dist: Bookmasters Distribution.

Forward, Toby. The Christmas Mouse. Brown, Ruth, illus. 2007. (ENG.). 40p. (J). (gr. k-2). pap. 13.95 *(978-1-84270-583-4(0))* Andersen Pr. GBR. Dist: Independent Pubs. Group.

Foster, Jesse, et al. The Night Before Christmas in Africa, 1 vol. Christodoulou, Jean, illus. 2010. (Night Before Christmas Ser.). (ENG.). 32p. (J). (gr. k-3). 16.99 *(978-1-58980-847-8(9))* Pelican Publishing Co., Inc.

Fox, Adrienne. Starstruck. 2012. 126p. 27.45 *(978-1-4772-3558-4(2));* pap. 15.18 *(978-1-4772-3556-0(6))* AuthorHouse.

Franklin, Kathleen. Uncle Holly saves Christmas. 2010. (Illus.). 32p. 14.89 *(978-1-4520-9689-6(9))* AuthorHouse.

Franks, Pam. The Magic Gingerbread House. 2015. (ENG.). 32p. (J). 19.95 *(978-1-931721-10-3(6),* 9781931721103) Bright Sky Pr.

C
D

Frazee, Marla. Santa Claus the World's Number One Toy Expert. 2010. (ENG., Illus.). 32p. (J). (gr. -1-3). pap. 7.99 (978-0-547-48074-9(1)) Houghton Mifflin Harcourt Publishing Co.

Frazier, Kelly. The Red Sock Christmas. Matthes, Justice, illus. 2008. 25p. pap. 24.95 (978-1-60610-704-1(6)) America Star Bks.

Frederick, Heather Vogel. Home for the Holidays. 2011. (Mother-Daughter Book Club Ser.). (ENG.). 352p. (J). (gr. 4-7). 18.99 (978-1-4424-0685-8(2), Simon & Schuster Bks. For Young Readers) Simon & Schuster Bks. For Young Readers.

—A Little Women Christmas. Ibatoulline, Bagram, illus. 2014. (ENG.). 32p. (J). (gr. -1-3). 17.99 (978-1-4424-1359-7(X), Simon & Schuster Bks. For Young Readers) Simon & Schuster Bks. For Young Readers.

Freeberg, Jane. The Scallop Christmas. Sheckels, Astrid, illus. 2011. (ENG.). 36p. (J). 16.95 (978-1-934031-25-4(9), 9781934031254) Islandport Pr., Inc.

Freedman, Claire. Aliens Love Panta Claus. Cort, Ben, illus. 2011. (Underpants Bks.). (ENG.). 32p. (J). (gr. -1-2). 16.99 (978-1-4424-2830-0(9), Simon & Schuster/Paula Wiseman Bks.) Simon & Schuster/Paula Wiseman Bks.

—A Magical Christmas. Yerrill, Gail, illus. (J). 2016. (ENG.). 22p. (gr. -1-k). bds. 6.99 (978-1-58925-236-3(5)) 2008. 24p. (gr. 4-7). 12.95 (978-1-58925-828-0(2)) Tiger Tales.

Freedman, Claire, et al. My Little Box of Christmas Stories: One Winter's Night/Hurry, Santa!/a Magical Christmas/the Gift of Christmas/the Special Christmas Tree/the Christmas Bear. Mendez, Simon & Warnes, Tim, illus. 2013. (ENG.). (J). (gr. -1-1). pap. 8.95 (978-1-58925-443-5(0)) Tiger Tales.

Freeman, Don. Christmas Is Here, Corduroy! 2007. (Corduroy Ser.). (ENG., Illus.). 16p. (J). (gr. -1-k). 5.99 (978-0-448-44650-9(2), Grosset & Dunlap) Penguin Young Readers Group.

Freeman, Emily. God Bless Your Way: A Christmas Journey. Burr, Dan, illus. 2007. 32p. (J). (gr. -1-3). 19.95 incl. audio compact disk (978-1-59038-806-8(2)) Deseret Bk. Co.

Freeman, Martha. Who Is Stealing the 12 Days of Christmas? 2008. (ENG., Illus.). 200p. (J). (gr. 3-7). pap. 7.95 (978-0-8234-2167-1(8)) Holiday Hse., Inc.

Freeman, Trudy. Shaggy Nick. 2011. 28p. pap. 15.99 (978-1-4653-4763-3(1)) Xlibris Corp.

French, Jackie. Christmas Wombat. Whatley, Bruce, illus. 2012. (ENG.). 32p. (J). (gr. -1-3). 16.99 (978-0-547-86872-1(3)) Houghton Mifflin Harcourt Publishing Co.

—Josephine Wants to Dance. Whatley, Bruce, illus. 2008. 32p. (J). pap. (978-0-207-20080-9(7)) HarperCollins Pubs. Australia.

Friedman, Laurie. Merry Christmas, Mary Christmas! Durst, Kathryn, illus. 2017. (ENG.). 32p. (J). (gr. -1-3). lib. bdg. 17.99 **(978-1-4677-9261-5(6)**, Carolrhoda Bks.) Lerner Publishing Group.

Froeb, Lori. Fisher-Price Little People Christmastime Is Here! 2015. (Fisher Price Lift the Flap Ser.). (ENG., Illus.). 10p. (J). (gr. -1-k). bds. 9.99 (978-0-7944-3534-9(3)) Reader's Digest Assn., Inc., The.

Frrich, Lewandowski & Riccards, Michael. It's Christmas Again! Delisle, Kathryn H., illus. 2007. 32p. (J). 14.95 (978-1-929039-44-9(1)) Ambassador Bks., Inc.

Fry, Michael & Jackson, Bradley. The Naughty List. Fry, Michael, illus. 2015. (ENG., Illus.). 240p. (J). (gr. 3-7). 12.99 (978-0-06-235475-4(2)) HarperCollins Pubs.

Fuggle, Debbie. The Two Little Fir Trees. 2012. 28p. pap. 32.70 (978-1-4691-3253-2(2)) Xlibris Corp.

Furlong, Reynolds Cynthia. S Is for Star: A Christmas Alphabet. Carroll, Pam, illus. 2004. (ENG.). 40p. (J). (gr. k-6). pap. 6.95 (978-1-58536-247-9(6)) Sleeping Bear Pr.

Fyfe, Connie. Grandma's Christmas Candy. 2011. 24p. pap. 12.79 (978-1-4567-5437-2(8)) AuthorHouse.

Gale Editor, ed. A Christmas Carol: The Graphic Novel. 2011. (Classic Graphic Novel Collection Ser.). 160p. (YA). (gr. 7-12). lib. bdg. 34.80 (978-1-4205-0630-3(7)) Cengage Gale.

Gallo, Tina. OLIVIA & the Christmas Party. Rose, Drew, illus. 2011. (Olivia TV Tie-In Ser.). (ENG.). 32p. (J). (gr. -1-1). 4.99 (978-1-4424-3070-9(2), Simon Scribbles) Simon Scribbles.

Gamble, Adam. Good Night North Pole. Jasper, Mark, illus. 2012. (Good Night Our World Ser.). (ENG.). 20p. (J). (gr. k — 1). bds. 9.95 (978-1-60219-071-9(2), 1350772) Good Night Bks.

Gandolfi, Claudine. The Night Before Christmas dot.com. Barbas, Kerren, illus. 2005. (Charming Petites Ser.). 80p. 4.95 (978-0-88088-844-8(X)) Peter Pauper Pr. Inc.

—The Night Before Dog-Mas. Anagost, Karen, illus. 2007. (Petite Plush Kit Ser.). 64p. (J). (gr. -1-3). 9.95 (978-1-59359-883-9(1)) Peter Pauper Pr. Inc.

Ganzer, Diane. Patrick the Wayward Setter: A Christmas Miracle. 2005. 60p. pap. 16.95 (978-1-4137-8351-3(1)) PublishAmerica, Inc.

Garcia, Gloria. Navidad. (SPA.). 8p. 9.95 (978-84-272-7278-1(2)) Molino, Editorial ESP. Dist: Distribooks, Inc.

Garcia, Jeffrey. Santa Claus & the Molokai Mules. 2009. 32p. 17.95 (978-0-9840942-0-2(2)) Garcia, Jeffrey.

Garis, Howard Roger. Johnnie & Billie Bushytail. 2004. reprint ed. pap. 15.95 (978-1-4191-2786-1(1)); pap. 1.99 (978-1-4192-2786-8(6)) Kessinger Publishing, LLC.

Garland, Michael. Oh, What a Christmas! Garland, Michael, illus. 2011. (ENG., Illus.). 40p. (J). (gr. -1-3). 16.99 (978-0-545-24210-3(X), Scholastic Pr.) Scholastic, Inc.

Garner, Ellen. Santa's Elves & the Tickets. Street, James, illus. 2012. 56p. pap. 12.99 (978-0-615-55920-9(4)) EG Bks.

Garrow, Rhonda. Michaela & the Christmas Village. 2011. 24p. pap. 11.32 (978-1-4634-8751-5(7)) AuthorHouse.

Garza, Xavier. Charro Claus & the Tejas Kid. 2008. (SPA & ENG., Illus.). 40p. (J). (gr. k-6). 17.95 (978-1-933693-24-8(X)) Cinco Puntos Pr.

Gates, Josephine Scribner. The Turkey Doll. Flass, E. C., illus. 2007. 62p. (J). lib. bdg. 59.00 (978-1-60304-016-7(1)) Dollworks.

Gausselin, Richard J. How the Grandmas & Grandpas Saved Christmas. 2012. 24p. pap. 17.99 (978-1-4772-4771-6(8)) AuthorHouse.

George, Kallie. The Lost Gift: A Christmas Story. Graegin, Stephanie, illus. 2016. (ENG.). 40p. (J). (gr. -1-3). 17.99 (978-0-553-52481-9(X), Schwartz & Wade Bks.) Random Hse. Children's Bks.

Gerber, Carole. The Twelve Days of Christmas in Ohio. Ebbeler, Jeffrey, illus. 2014. (Twelve Days of Christmas in America Ser.). (ENG.). 40p. (J). (gr. k). 12.95 (978-1-4549-0890-6(4)) Sterling Publishing Co., Inc.

Gerencher, Jane. Santa's Sugar. Patch, Michael, illus. 2012. 51p. 15.50 (978-0-9852501-3-3(5)) Inkwell Books LLC.

Gerlach-Babb nee Maines, Mary & Gerlach, Susan. Best Christmas Gift. 2007. (ENG.). 52p. per. 16.95 (978-1-4241-6389-2(7)) America Star Bks.

Geronimo Stilton Staff. The Christmas Toy Factory. 2006. (Geronimo Stilton Ser.: 27). (ENG., Illus.). 128p. (J). (gr. 2-5). pap. 7.99 (978-0-439-84118-4(6), Scholastic Paperbacks) Scholastic, Inc.

Gerver, Jane E. Christmas Shapes. Davis, Nancy & Davis, Kathryn Lynn, illus. 2010. (ENG.). 14p. (J). (gr. -1 — 1). bds. 6.99 (978-1-4169-9759-7(8), Little Simon) Little Simon.

Gevry, C. C. A Christmas Kindness. Mabey, Coline, illus. 2012. 24p. pap. 11.99 (978-0-9852661-4-1(7)) 4RV Publishing, LLC.

Gibbs, D. Renee. The Special Little Christmas Tree. 2003. (Illus.). (J). bds. 14.95 (978-0-9741406-0-5(0)) Cranberry Quill Publishing Co.

Gibson, Sherri L. In the Mind of a Child: Children's Stories. 2013. 36p. pap. 24.95 (978-1-62709-750-5(3)) America Star Bks.

Gifford, Peggy. Moxy Maxwell Does Not Love Writing Thank-You Notes. Fisher, Valorie, illus. 2009. (Moxy Maxwell Ser.). (ENG.). 192p. (J). (gr. 2-5). 6.99 (978-0-375-84343-3(4), Yearling) Random Hse. Children's Bks.

Gillam, David. Gingertown. Gilliam, David, illus. 2012. 216p. (J). 29.99 (978-1-60131-122-1(2)) Big Tent Bks.

Gilley, Jane. Christmas on Troglodyte Hill - Book Three of the Troglodyte Trilogy. 2008. 16p. pap. (978-1-906210-71-7(3)) Grosvenor Hse. Publishing Ltd.

Gillingham, Sara. Cozy Christmas: A Touch-and-Feel Book. 2016. (Sago Mini Ser.). (ENG., Illus.). 14p. (J). (gr. -1 — 1). bds. 6.99 (978-1-4998-0324-2(9)) Little Bee Books Inc.

Gillmor, Don. The Christmas Orange. 2004. (Illus.). (J). (gr. k-3). spiral bd. (978-0-616-03035-6(5)) Canadian National Institute for the Blind/Institut National Canadien pour les Aveugles.

Gingrich, Callista. Christmas in America. Arciero, Susan, illus. 2015. (Ellis the Elephant Ser.). (ENG.). 40p. (J). (gr. -1-3). 16.99 (978-1-62157-345-6(1), Regnery Kids) Regnery Publishing, Inc., An Eagle Publishing Co.

Ginolfi, Art. The Tiny Snowflake. 2005. 32p. (J). pap. 3.99 (978-1-4003-0684-8(1)) Nelson, Thomas Inc.

Glaser, Byron & Higashi, Sandra. Zolocolor! Christmas Doodling. Glaser, Byron & Higashi, Sandra, illus. 2012. (ENG., Illus.). 96p. (J). pap. 7.99 (978-1-4424-4592-5(0), Little Simon) Little Simon.

Glaser, P. H. Chrystallia & the Source of Light. 2011. (Illus.). 196p. (J). 18.99 (978-1-60832-232-9(7)) Greenleaf Book Group.

Godden, Rumer. The Story of Holly & Ivy. Cooney, Barbara, illus. 2006. (ENG.). 32p. (J). (gr. k-3). 17.99 (978-0-670-06219-5(7), Viking Books for Young Readers) Penguin Young Readers Group.

Godley, Marie. The Special Christmas Bear. 2007. (Illus.). 52p. per. (978-1-84748-005-7(5)) Athena Pr.

Goertzen, Angelina. Tinsel the Christmas Tree. 2009. 32p. pap. 12.49 (978-1-4389-8569-5(X)) AuthorHouse.

Gold, Maya & Fitzhugh, Louise. Harriet the Spy, Double Agent. 2007. (Harriet the Spy Adventures Ser.). (ENG.). 160p. (J). (gr. 3-7). 6.99 (978-0-440-41691-3(4), Yearling) Random Hse. Children's Bks.

Golden Books. Christmas Magic! (Frosty the Snowman) Golden Books, illus. 2016. (Color & Paint Plus Stickers Ser.). (ENG., Illus.). 128p. (J). (gr. -1-2). pap. 9.99 (978-0-399-55224-3(3), Golden Bks.) Random Hse. Children's Bks.

—Happy Holi-Doodles! Moroney, Christopher, illus. 2012. (Doodle Book Ser.). (ENG.). 128p. (J). (gr. -1-2). pap. 5.99 (978-0-307-93198-6(6), Golden Bks.) Random Hse. Children's Bks.

—It's Time for Christmas! (Bubble Guppies) Golden Books, illus. 2014. (Big Coloring Book Ser.). (ENG., Illus.). 48p. (J). (gr. -1-2). pap. 6.99 (978-0-385-38409-4(2), Golden Bks.) Random Hse. Children's Bks.

—One Sparkly Christmas (Shimmer & Shine) Golden Books, illus. 2016. (Hologramatic Sticker Book Ser.). (ENG., Illus.). 64p. (J). (gr. -1-2). pap. 4.99 (978-0-399-55298-4(7), Golden Bks.) Random Hse. Children's Bks.

—The Pups Save Christmas! (Paw Patrol) Moore, Harry, illus. 2015. (Big Golden Book Ser.). (ENG.). 48p. (J). (gr. -1-2). 9.99 (978-0-553-52391-1(0), Golden Bks.) Random Hse. Children's Bks.

—A Very Puppy Christmas! (PAW Patrol) MJ Illustrations, illus. 2016. (Color Plus Cardstock & Stickers Ser.). (ENG.). 32p. (J). (gr. -1-2). pap. 5.99 (978-0-399-55356-1(8), Golden Bks.) Random Hse. Children's Bks.

Golden Books Staff. Christmas Is Coming! (Dora the Explorer) McGee, Warner, illus. 2011. (Glitter Sticker Book Ser.). (ENG.). 64p. (J). (gr. -1-2). pap. 4.99 (978-0-375-87393-5(7), Golden Bks.) Random Hse. Children's Bks.

—A Very Krabby Christmas (SpongeBob SquarePants) Aikins, Dave, illus. 2011. (Glitter Sticker Book Ser.). (ENG.). 64p. (J). (gr. -1-2). pap. 4.99 (978-0-375-87392-8(9), Golden Bks.) Random Hse. Children's Bks.

Golden Books Staff, et al. Christmas Favorites. Catusanu, Mircea & Wilkin, Eloise, illus. 2009. (Little Golden Book Favorites Ser.). (ENG.). 80p. (J). (gr. -1-2). 6.99 (978-0-375-85778-2(8), Golden Bks.) Random Hse. Children's Bks.

Goldman, Dara. Boris & Stella & the Perfect Gift. 2013. (ENG.). (J). (978-1-58536-859-4(8)) Sleeping Bear Pr.

Goldrush, Jds. The Christmas Caf. 2013. 20p. (J). pap. 24.95 (978-1-63004-357-5(5)) America Star Bks.

Goldsack, Gaby, et al. The Little Fir Tree. 2003. (Traditional Christmas Stories Ser.). 32p. (J). 4.98 (978-0-7525-8846-9(X)) Parragon, Inc.

Goldstone, Bruce & Poortvliet, Rien. A Gnome's Christmas. 2004. (ENG., Illus.). 48p. (gr. 8-17). 14.95 (978-0-8109-5017-7(0)) Abrams, Inc.

Gomi, Taro. Presents Through the Window. 2016. (ENG., Illus.). 36p. (J). (gr. -1-k). 15.99 (978-1-4521-5138-0(5)) Chronicle Bks. LLC.

Goodings, Christina & Hudson, Annabel. My Look & Point First Christmas Stick-a-Story Book. 2014. (ENG., Illus.). 16p. (J). (gr. -1-k). 6.99 (978-0-7459-6396-9(X)) Lion Hudson PLC GBR. Dist: Independent Pubs. Group.

Goodrich, Carter & Moore, Clement C. A Creature Was Stirring: One Boy's Night Before Christmas. Goodrich, Carter, illus. 2006. (ENG., Illus.). 40p. (J). (gr. -1-3). 17.99 (978-0-689-86399-8(3), Simon & Schuster Bks. For Young Readers) Simon & Schuster Bks. For Young Readers.

Gordon, Leslie M. The Homeless Christmas Tree. Bailey, Court, illus. 2005. 48p. (J). 19.95 (978-1-933285-09-2(5)) Brown Books Publishing Group.

Gordon, Peggy T. Santa's Secret. 2009. 24p. pap. 15.99 (978-1-4415-5330-0(4)) Xlibris Corp.

Gorgas, Paula Blais. The Perfect Purple Present. 2007. (Illus.). (J). 20p. per. 11.99 (978-0-9797574-4-0(4)); 24p. 24.99 (978-0-9794660-4-5(0)); 24p. per. 12.99 (978-0-9794660-5-2(9)) Dragonfly Publishing, Inc.

Goudge, Elizabeth. I Saw Three Ships. Tomes, Margot, illus. 2008. (ENG.). 64p. (J). 15.95 (978-1-56792-369-8(0)) Godine, David R. Pub.

Gould, M&R. The Bleeks: The Bleek Family's First Christmas, 1 vol. Hurst, Debbie, illus. 2010. 30p. pap. 24.95 (978-1-4489-2770-8(6)) PublishAmerica, Inc.

Govan, Nina & Olive and Moss Staff. Michael the Monkey. 2014. (Olive & Moss Ser.). (ENG., Illus.). 10p. (J). (— 1). bds. 8.99 (978-1-4052-6001-5(7)) Egmont Bks., Ltd. GBR. Dist: Independent Pubs. Group.

Gownley, Jim. Amelia & the Other Side of Yuletide: #4, 1 vol. Gownley, Jim, illus. 2011. (Amelia Rules! Ser.). (ENG., Illus.). 36p. 24.21 (978-1-59961-790-9(0)) Spotlight.

Gownley, Jimmy. A Very Ninja Christmas. Gownley, Jimmy, illus. 2009. (Amelia Rules! Ser.). (ENG., Illus.). 80p. (J). (gr. 2-7). pap. 7.99 (978-1-4169-8959-2(5), Atheneum Bks. for Young Readers) Simon & Schuster Children's Publishing.

Grace, Ann Marie. The Secret Gift. 2013. 18p. pap. 12.99 (978-1-4808-0411-1(8)) Archway Publishing.

Graire, Virginie, illus. Snowman. 2016. (ENG.). 12p. (J). (gr. -1 — 1). bds. 6.99 (978-1-4998-0344-0(3)) Little Bee Books Inc.

Grampa Ralph. Santa's New Boots, 1 vol. 2010. 48p. pap. 16.95 (978-1-4489-5981-5(0)) America Star Bks.

Grandpa. The Beginning of Meet the Müsh-Mice: (a Visit to the North Pole) 2012. 34p. 29.95 (978-1-4626-9377-1(6)) America Star Bks.

Grandpa Casey. Meet the Müsh-Mice. Brennan, Lisa, illus. 2012. 28p. 24.95 (978-1-4626-9380-1(6)) America Star Bks.

Grant, Carolyn E. Christmas in Maggie's Neighborhood. 2009. 24p. pap. 12.99 (978-1-4490-0633-4(7)) AuthorHouse.

Grant, Cindy M. Itty-Bitty Jesus Is Born Christmas Storybook. 2005. (J). pap. 1.29 (978-1-59317-117-9(X)) Warner Pr., Inc.

Gray, Kes. Nuddy Ned's Christmas. Parsons, Garry, illus. 2016. (ENG.). 32p. (J). 20.99 (978-1-4088-6598-9(X), 9781408865989, Bloomsbury USA Childrens) Bloomsbury Publishing USA.

Green, John, et al. Let It Snow: Three Holiday Romances. (ENG.). 368p. (YA). (gr. 7). 2014. mass mkt. 7.99 (978-0-14-751501-8(7)) 2008. pap. 10.99 (978-0-14-241214-5(7)) Penguin Young Readers Group. (Speak).

Green, Rod. Santa Claus: The Magical World of Father Christmas. 2014. (ENG., Illus.). 32p. (J). (gr. 1). 12.95 (978-1-78312-076-5(2)) Carlton Bks., Ltd. GBR. Dist: Sterling Publishing Co., Inc.

Green, Sylvia. The Soft-Hearted Sheepdog. Kavanagh, Peter, illus. 2003. 144p. (J). (978-0-439-62569-2(6)) Scholastic, Inc.

Greenberg, David E. The Ugly Brown Pear. 2010. 40p. pap. 12.96 (978-0-557-28055-1(9)) Lulu Pr., Inc.

Greenberg, Nicki. The Naughtiest Reindeer. Greenberg, Nicki, illus. 2014. (ENG., Illus.). 32p. (J). (gr. -1-k). 14.99 (978-1-74331-304-6(7)) Allen & Unwin AUS. Dist: Independent Pubs. Group.

Greene, Rhonda Gowler. Santa's Stuck. Cole, Henry, illus. 2006. (ENG.). 32p. (J). (gr. -1-3). pap. 5.99 (978-0-14-240686-1(4), Puffin Books) Penguin Young Readers Group.

Greene, Stephanie. Christmas at Stony Creek. Sheban, Chris, illus. 2007. 96p. (gr. -1-3). lib. bdg. 15.89 (978-0-06-121487-5(6)) HarperCollins Pubs.

—Princess Posey & the Christmas Magic. 2013. (Princess Posey, First Grader Ser.: 7). (ENG.). 96p. (J). (gr. k-3). pap. 4.99 (978-0-14-242734-7(9), Puffin Books) Penguin Young Readers Group.

—Princess Posey & the Christmas Magic. Sisson, Stéphanie Roth, illus. 2013. (Princess Posey, First Grader Ser.: 7). (ENG.). 96p. (J). (gr. k-3). 13.99 (978-0-399-16363-0(8), G.P. Putnam's Sons Books for Young Readers) Penguin Young Readers Group.

Gregory, Larry. A Christmas Surprise. Woolmer, Nancy, illus. 2004. 24p. pap. 24.95 (978-1-4137-3014-2(0)) PublishAmerica, Inc.

Grein, Josh. Petunia Bobbin & the Baby Robin: A Christmas Adventure. 2012. 48p. (-18). 28.95 (978-1-4582-0614-5(9)); pap. 20.95 (978-1-4582-0615-2(7)) Author Solutions, Inc. (Abbott Pr.).

Greive, Bradley Trevor. Every Day Is Christmas. 2007. (ENG., Illus.). 120p. 9.99 (978-0-7407-6860-6(3)) Andrews McMeel Publishing.

Griffin, Donna. The Twelve Days of Christmas in Indiana. Cummings, Troy, illus. 2014. (Twelve Days of Christmas in America Ser.). (ENG.). 40p. (J). (gr. k). 12.95 (978-1-4549-0888-3(2)) Sterling Publishing Co., Inc.

Griffin Mims, Nancy. The Christmas Geese. 2013. 42p. 16.95 (978-1-940224-05-3(5)) Taylor and Seale Publishing, LLC.

Griffiths, Allen & Godinez, Mary. Rusty Finds a Home: A Christmas Miracle. Ulrich, Kelly, illus. 2012. 32p. pap. (978-1-4602-0937-0(0)) FriesenPress.

Grim, Katie. Gingerbread Land. Johnson, Jake, illus. 2007. (ENG.). 24p. (J). (gr. 1-18). 19.95 (978-1-58117-635-3(X), Intervisual/Piggy Toes) Bendon, Inc.

Grimmer, Constance Marie. Santa's Christmas Dogs: A Legend Begins... 2009. 28p. pap. 15.49 (978-1-4490-5920-0(1)) AuthorHouse.

Grindley, Sally. Home for Christmas. Littlewood, Karin, illus. 2004. (ENG.). 32p. (J). (gr. k-17). 15.95 (978-1-84507-071-7(2), Frances Lincoln) Quarto Publishing Group UK GBR. Dist: Hachette Bk. Group.

Grogan, John. Marley's Christmas Pageant. Cowdrey, Richard, illus. 2013. (Marley Ser.). (ENG.). 16p. (J). (gr. -1-3). pap. 6.99 (978-0-06-185382-1(8), HarperFestival) HarperCollins Pubs.

—A Very Marley Christmas. Cowdrey, Richard, illus. (Marley Ser.). (ENG.). 40p. (J). (gr. -1-3). 2014. 9.99 (978-0-06-211367-2(4)) 2008. 17.99 (978-0-06-137292-6(7)) HarperCollins Pubs.

—A Very Marley Christmas. Cowdrey, Richard, illus. (ENG.). 32p. pap. (978-0-00-728723-9(2), HarperCollins Children's Bks.) HarperCollins Pubs. Ltd.

Grosset & Dunlap. Berry Merry Holiday Treasury. 2014. (Strawberry Shortcake Ser.). (ENG.). 160p. (J). (gr. -1-k). 9.99 (978-0-448-48360-3(2), Grosset & Dunlap) Penguin Young Readers Group.

Gruber Jr., Fernan M. Santa's Reindeer Hay. 2012. 24p. pap. 17.99 (978-1-4685-9501-7(6)) AuthorHouse.

Guerrera, Jeannette D. The Christmas Witch. 2012. 24p. pap. 17.99 (978-1-4685-6226-2(6)) AuthorHouse.

Guiffre, William. The First Gift of Christmas. Baron, Cheri Ann, illus. 2008. 32p. (J). (gr. -1-3). pap. 9.95 (978-1-931650-33-5(0)) Bks. for Children Publishing.

Guiffre, William A. The First Gift of Christmas. Baron, Cheri Ann, illus. 2003. 36p. (J). (gr. -1-3). lib. bdg. 17.95 (978-1-931650-21-2(7)) Bks. for Children Publishing.

Gutman, Anne. Cadeau de Noel. (FRE.). pap. 17.95 (978-2-01-224134-3(4)) Hachette Groupe Livre FRA. Dist: Distribooks, Inc.

—Gaspard & Lisa's Christmas Surprise. Hallensleben, Georg, illus. 2012. (ENG.). 32p. (J). (gr. k-3). pap. 6.99 (978-0-449-81013-2(5), Dragonfly Bks.) Random Hse. Children's Bks.

—Gaspard & Lisa's Christmas Surprise. Hallensleben, Georg, illus. 2012. lib. bdg. 17.20 (978-0-606-26782-3(4), Turtleback) Turtleback Bks.

Gutman, Dan. The Christmas Genie. Santat, Dan, illus. (ENG.). (J). (gr. 3-7). 2010. 176p. pap. 6.99 (978-1-4169-9002-4(X)) 2009. 160p. 16.99 (978-1-4169-9001-7(1)) Simon & Schuster Bks. For Young Readers. (Simon & Schuster Bks. For Young Readers).

Guttiere, Benedicte. When Christmas Comes. 2011. (Funny Faces Ser.). (Illus.). 14p. bds. (978-1-84089-710-4(4)) Zero to Ten, Ltd.

—When Christmas Comes - Welsh Edition. Guttiere, Benedicte, illus. 2011. (Funny Faces Ser.). (Illus.). 14p. bds. (978-1-84089-711-1(2)) Zero to Ten, Ltd.

Gwilym, Mari & Thomas, Dylan. Am Ddolig! 2005. (WEL., Illus.). 48p. pap. (978-0-86243-530-1(7)) Y Lolfa.

H M Bricker & Bricker, Howard Michael. The Christmas Santa Had No Beard. Dall, John, illus. 2011.Tr. of Navidad Que Santa Claus No Tovo Barba. (ENG & SPA.). 34p. (J). 15.45 (978-0-615-42163-6(6)) H M Bricker.

Hague, Michael & Hague, Kathleen. Michael Hague's Treasury of Christmas Carols. 2011. (ENG., Illus.). 48p. (J). 9.95 (978-1-4027-7812-4(0)) Sterling Publishing Co., Inc.

Haig, Matt. A Boy Called Christmas. Mould, Chris, illus. 2016. (ENG.). 240p. (J). (gr. 3-7). 16.99 (978-0-399-55265-6(0), Knopf Bks. for Young Readers) Random Hse. Children's Bks.

Haile, Carol J. Christmas Cows. Haile, Carol J., illus. 2012. (ENG., Illus.). 40p. (J). 19.95 (978-0-9711236-5-6(9)) Firenze Pr.

Hale, Bruce. Clark the Shark Loves Christmas. Francis, Guy, illus. 2016. (Clark the Shark Ser.). 32p. (J). (gr. -1-3). 17.99 (978-0-06-237452-3(4)) HarperCollins Pubs.

Hall, Annalisa. Sheppard's Last Lamb. Worthen, Alex, illus. 2016. (ENG.). 32p. (J). (gr. -1-3). 14.99 (978-1-4621-1853-3(4), Bonneville Bks.) Cedar Fort, Inc./CFI Distribution.

—Tak & Lolly: Santa Clause at Church. 2009. 51p. pap. 6.99 (978-0-557-04923-3(7)) Lulu Pr., Inc.

Hall, Donald. Lucy's Christmas. McCurdy, Michael, illus. 2007. (ENG.). 32p. (J). (gr. 1). pap. 10.95 (978-1-56792-342-1(9)) Godine, David R. Pub.

Hall, Noelle. Emily & the Captain. D'Souza, Mel, illus. 2012. (ENG.). 32p. pap. (978-1-894377-15-7(X)) Breakwater Bks., Ltd.

Hall, Rohan. The Little Boy. 2005. (Illus.). 34p. (J). spiral bd. 14.95 (978-0-9729187-7-0(9)) Foundation For Cosmetic Surgery, The.

Hallinan, P. K. Christmas at Grandma's House. 2006. (ENG., Illus.). 32p. (J). (gr. -1-3). 8.95 (978-0-8249-5535-9(8), 1262731, Ideal Pubns.) Worthy Publishing.

—That's What a Friend Is! 2003. (ENG.). 24p. (J). bds. 6.95 (978-0-8249-5468-0(8), Ideal Pubns.) Worthy Publishing.

—Today Is Christmas! Hallinan, P. K., illus. 2008. (ENG., Illus.). 26p. (J). (gr. -1-k). bds. 6.99 (978-0-8249-1804-0(5), Ideal Pubns.) Worthy Publishing.

Hamilton, Annie. The Unforgettable Night. 2013. (Illus.). 70p. pap. (978-1-78148-617-7(4)) Grosvenor Hse. Publishing Ltd.

Hamley, Dennis. Yule Logs. 2005. 96p. per. (978-1-904529-17-0(8), Back to Front) Solidus.

Hammon, Darrel L. Christmas Beneath the Lake: From the Adventures of Bob the Bullfrog. 2012. (ENG.). (J). (-18). 35p. pap. 17.95 (978-1-4787-1910-6(9)); 25p. pap. 23.95 (978-1-4327-7916-0(8)) Outskirts Pr., Inc.

Hampton, Randall. A Christmas Kiss. l.t. ed. 2005. (Illus.). 48p. (J). per. 16.95 (978-1-59879-048-1(X)) Lifevest Publishing, Inc.

Hand, Cynthia. The Afterlife of Holly Chase. 2017. 400p. (YA). (gr. 8). 17.99 **(978-0-06-231850-3(0)**, HarperTeen) HarperCollins Pubs.

Hanlin, Beverly Austin. Little Lamb: A Christmas Story. 2006. (J). pap. 8.00 (978-0-8059-7128-6(9)) Dorrance Publishing Co., Inc.

Hanna, Margaret Leis. Canneh, the Reluctant Christmas Camel. Weltner, Dave, illus. l.t. ed. 2003. 26p. (J). 7.95 (978-0-9706654-7-8(4)) Sprite Pr.

Hannigan, Kate. Winter Wonders. Hughes, Brooke Boynton, illus. 2016. (Cupcake Cousins Ser.: Bk. 3). (ENG.). 240p. (J). (gr. 3-7). 16.99 (978-1-4847-1663-2(9)) Hyperion Bks. for Children.

Hanrion, Patricia. The Jingle Bell Bum. 2012. (J). pap. 2.99 (978-1-4621-1106-0(8)) Cedar Fort, Inc./CFI Distribution.

Hansen, Eric. Ian, Ceo, North Pole. 2008. 108p. pap. 9.95 *(978-1-60693-554-5(2),* Eloquent Bks.) Strategic Book Publishing & Rights Agency (SBPRA).

Hanson, Bonnie Compton. The Impossible Christmas Present. 2004. (Ponytail Girls Ser.). (Illus.). 208p. (J). pap. 7.99 *(978-1-58411-030-9(9),* Legacy Pr.) Rainbow Pubs. & Legacy Pr.

Hapka, Cathy, pseud. Picture Me Christmas Princess. Hill, Heather C. & Roush, April, illus. 2003. (Picture Me Holiday Ser.). 10p. (J). (gr. -1-18). bds. 6.99 *(978-1-57151-571-1(2))* Playhouse Publishing.

Harden, Pamela. Abc's from the Whippety Wood: The Magic in Nature. 2013. (Illus.). 32p. pap. 9.95 *(978-0-9897216-0-8(4))* TheWhippetyWood.

Hardie, Jill. The Sparkle Box: The Story of a Very Special Christmas Gift. Komacki, Christine, illus. 2012. 32p. (J). 19.99 *(978-0-8249-5647-9(8),* Ideal Pubns.) Worthy Publishing.

Hardin, Becky. Shug E Bear. 2008. 24p. pap. 19.99 *(978-1-4389-3247-7(2))* AuthorHouse.

Hardin, Holly. Aurora of the Northern Lights. 2009. 31p. (J). pap. 18.95 *(978-1-4327-2439-9(8))* Outskirts Pr., Inc.

Hargreaves, Roger. Mr. Christmas Sticker Activity Book. Hargreaves, Adam, illus. 2010. (Mr. Men & Little Miss Ser.). (ENG.). 24p. (J). (gr. -1-2). act. bk. ed. 4.99 *(978-0-8431-2670-9(1),* Price Stern Sloan) Penguin Young Readers Group.

Harper, Stephan J. One Christmas Story. Steuerwald, Joy, illus. 2003. 32p. (J). lib. bdg. 16.95 *(978-0-9741800-0-7(9))* Inspire Press, Inc.

Harris, Annmarie. The Nutcracker. Jay, Alison, illus. 2010. (ENG.). 40p. (J). (gr. -1-k). 16.99 *(978-0-8037-3285-8(6),* Dial Bks) Penguin Young Readers Group.

Harris, Danielle. The Second Chance Sant. 2012. 28p. pap. 24.95 *(978-1-4626-6778-9(3))* America Star Bks.

Harris, Jim. Dinosaur's Night Before Christmas, 1 vol. Harris, Jim, illus. 2010. (Night Before Christmas Ser.). (ENG., Illus.). 40p. (J). (gr. k-3). 16.99 *(978-1-58980-850-8(9))* Pelican Publishing Co., Inc.

Harrison, Michael. Cop's Night Before Christmas, 1 vol. Miles, David, illus. 2010. (Night Before Christmas Ser.). (ENG.). 32p. (J). (gr. k-3). 16.99 *(978-1-58980-800-3(2))* Pelican Publishing Co., Inc.

Harrod-Eagles, Cynthia. It's Holiday Time! Baccala, Gladys, illus. 2012. (ENG.). 18p. (J). bds. *(978-1-58925-640-8(9))* Tiger Tales.

Harry, Rebecca. Snow Bunny's Christmas Wish. Harry, Rebecca, illus. 2013. (ENG., Illus.). 32p. (J). (gr. -1-3). 16.99 *(978-0-545-54103-9(4),* Orchard Bks.) Scholastic, Inc.

Hartman, Bob. The Lion Storyteller Christmas Book. Nagy, Krisztina Kallai, illus. 2013. (Storyteller Tales Ser.). (ENG.). 128p. (J). (gr. k-2). pap. 14.99 *(978-0-7459-6379-2(X))* Lion Hudson PLC GBR. Dist: Independent Pubs. Group.

Hartwell, David G., ed. Christmas Magic. 2016. (ENG.). 496p. (Orig.). pap. 18.99 *(978-0-7653-1580-9(7),* 9780765315809, Tor Bks.) Doherty, Tom Assocs., LLC.

Hartwright, Gianna. The Befana Drama. 2013. 352p. pap. *(978-0-9575697-6-8(9))* Gianna Della Luna Publishing.

Harvey, A. W. Llewellyn. Christmas Stories: For the Young & Young at Heart. 2012. 114p. (gr. -1). pap. 12.06 *(978-1-4669-5800-5(6))* Trafford Publishing.

Hassett, Ann. The Finest Christmas Tree. Hassett, John, illus. 2010. (ENG.). 32p. (J). (gr. -1-3). pap. 6.99 *(978-0-547-40623-7(1))* Houghton Mifflin Harcourt Publishing Co.

Hatch, Justina. Charlie the Caterpillar, 1 vol. 2010. 44p. pap. 24.95 *(978-1-4489-9256-0(7))* PublishAmerica, Inc.

Hatfield, Kara. The Real Story of Sant. 2011. 30p. pap. 16.95 *(978-1-4626-1022-8(6))* America Star Bks.

Hawley, Jim. Homer & Friends. 2012. 50p. pap. *(978-1-77097-709-9(0))* FriesenPress.

Hawthorne, Reita Rea. Finding Christmas. 2013. 24p. pap. 12.45 *(978-1-4908-1160-4(5),* WestBow Pr.) Author Solutions, Inc.

Hayes, J. B. Freddy the Frog's First Christmas. 2012. 44p. pap. 21.99 *(978-1-4772-2870-8(5))* AuthorHouse.

Hayes, Karel. The Christmas Visitors. 2013. (ENG., Illus.). 32p. (J). (gr. -1-3). 16.95 *(978-1-60893-248-1(6))* Down East Bks.

Haynes, Anne S. Little Tree Makes a New Year's Resolution. 2013. 28p. pap. 24.95 *(978-1-4241-0479-6(3))* America Star Bks.

Hays, Helen Ashe. The Adventures of Prince Lazybones: And Other Stories. 2007. 152p. pap. 19.99 *(978-1-4264-8474-2(7));* 168p. pap. 21.99 *(978-1-4264-8532-9(8))* Creative Media Partners, LLC.

Hays, Patricia Quinn. First Dog. 2012. (ENG.). (J). 14.95 *(978-1-59982-273-0(3));* pap. *(978-1-59982-274-7(1))* St. Mary's Pr. of MN.

Head, Jean. Andrew's Christmas Dream. 2012. 28p. pap. 5.00 *(978-1-937260-19-4(4))* Sleepytown Pr.

Healey, Richard (Dick). Holly the Christmas Dove. 2005. 36p. (J). 13.28 *(978-1-4116-5496-9(X))* Lulu Pr., Inc.

Hearn, Sam. Christmas at Last! Dann, Penny, illus. 2015. (ENG.). 16p. (J). (gr. -1-k). bds. 10.99 *(978-0-545-79455-8(2),* Cartwheel Bks.) Scholastic, Inc.

Heckler, Naomi & Kyelberg, Hope. The Adventures of Little Caesar ... Little Caesar's Christmas Adventure. 2008. 32p. pap. 14.98 *(978-0-557-00878-0(6))* Lulu Pr., Inc.

Hegarty, Patricia. Five Busy Elves. Woolf, Julia, illus. 2014. (ENG.). 22p. (J). (gr. -1-k). bds. 8.99 *(978-1-58925-561-6(5))* Tiger Tales.

Heible, Beverly. A Christmas Party on River Row. 2012. 98p. 22.95 *(978-1-62709-018-6(5));* pap. 17.95 *(978-1-4626-9575-1(2))* America Star Bks.

Heidecker, Samie. Who's Looking at Whom? Christmas, 1 vol. 2010. 38p. 24.95 *(978-1-4489-4855-0(X))* PublishAmerica, Inc.

Heierbacher, Michael. Yo Ho Ho Merry Christmas. 2010. (Illus.). 28p. (J). pap. 15.95 *(978-1-4327-6484-5(5))* Outskirts Pr., Inc.

Heisler, H. T. A. The Innkeeper's Daughter: A Christmas Story & Music Score. 2013. 40p. pap. *(978-0-9917756-2-0(7))* Daisy Harriette Tina Anne Heisler.

Helmer, Marilyn. One Splendid Tree. Eastman, Dianne, illus. 2007. (ENG.). 32p. (J). (gr. -1-3). 6.95 *(978-1-55453-166-0(7))* Kids Can Pr., Ltd. CAN. Dist: Hachette Bk. Group.

Helmintoller, Matt & Baiz, Mark. One December Night. 2013. 30p. pap. 16.95 *(978-1-4908-1576-3(7),* WestBow Pr.) Author Solutions, Inc.

Hendershot, Eric. A Horse for Christmas. 2012. pap. 8.99 *(978-1-4621-1078-0(9))* Cedar Fort, Inc./CFI Distribution.

Henderson, Richard. One Christmas Night. Shackelford, David, illus. 2008. 32p. (J). 15.95 *(978-0-615-17629-1(1))* St. Clair Publishing.

Hendry, Diana. The Very Snowy Christmas. Chapman, Jane, illus. (J). 2013. (ENG.). 16p. (gr. -1). bds. 8.95 *(978-1-58925-617-0(4))* 2007. 32p. pap. 6.95 *(978-1-58925-406-0(6))* 2005. 32p. (gr. -1-2). 15.95 *(978-1-58925-051-2(6))* Tiger Tales.

Hennessey, David G. A Cricket's Christmas: the Bethlehem Story. 2009. 151p. pap. 15.30 *(978-0-557-04685-0(8))* Lulu Pr., Inc.

Henry, Juliann. The Little Shepherd Girl: A Christmas Story. Madsen, Jim, illus. 2007. 32p. (J). (gr. -1-3). 14.99 *(978-0-7814-4513-9(2))* Cook, David C.

Henry, O. The Gift of the Magi. Zwerger, Lisbeth, illus. 2006. (ENG.). 32p. (J). (gr. 1-4). 17.99 *(978-1-4169-3586-5(X),* Simon & Schuster Bks. For Young Readers) Simon & Schuster Bks. For Young Readers.

—The Gift of the Magi: A Story about Giving. Jaekel, Susan M., illus. 2006. (J). *(978-1-59939-084-0(1),* Reader's Digest Young Families, Inc.) Studio Fun International.

Herman, Gail. Christmas Wishes. Marderosian, Mark, illus. 2004. (J). *(978-0-439-66763-0(1))* Scholastic, Inc.

Herman, R. A. The Littlest Christmas Tree. Rogers, Jacqueline, illus. 2007. (ENG.). 32p. (J). (gr. -1-3). pap. 3.99 *(978-0-439-54007-0(0))* Scholastic, Inc.

Hernandez, Anna Marie Eloise. O Holy Night. 2012. 26p. pap. 16.99 *(978-1-4497-4616-2(0),* WestBow Pr.) Author Solutions, Inc.

Herzing, Nancy. The Night the Angels Came. 2012. 46p. pap. 19.99 *(978-1-62419-373-6(0))* Salem Author Services.

Heyer, Carol. The First Christmas. Heyer, Carol, illus. 2007. (ENG., Illus.). 32p. (J). (gr. k-3). 8.99 *(978-0-8249-5566-3(8),* Ideal Pubns.) Worthy Publishing.

—Humphrey's First Christmas. Heyer, Carol, illus. 2008. (ENG., Illus.). 32p. (J). (gr. -1-3). 14.99 *(978-0-8249-5559-5(5),* Ideal Pubns.) Worthy Publishing.

Higginson, Sheila Sweeny. Jingle Bell Doc. Disney Book Group Staff et al, illus. 2013. (ENG.). 12p. (J). (gr. -1-k). bds. 6.99 *(978-1-4231-8386-0(X))* Disney Pr.

—A Very McStuffins Christmas. 2014. (Doc Mcstuffins 8X8 Ser.). (J). lib. bdg. 16.00 *(978-0-606-35908-5(7))* Turtleback Bks.

Hill, Eric. First Christmas. Hill, Eric, illus. 2000. (Spot Ser.). (ENG., Illus.). 20p. (J). (gr. -1-k). 7.99 *(978-0-14-240202-3(8),* Warne) Penguin Young Readers Group.

—Spot's Christmas Plush Doll. Hill, Eric, illus. 2005. (Illus.). (J). 11.00 *(978-0-399-24472-8(7),* Putnam Juvenile) Penguin Publishing Group.

Hill, Kathi Harper. The Christmas Closet & Other Works. 2012. (ENG.). 48p. 16.99 *(978-1-936815-58-6(3))* Yawn's Bks. & More, Inc.

Hillenbrand, Will. Asleep in the Stable. 2004. (ENG., Illus.). 32p. (J). (gr. k-3). tchr. ed. 16.95 *(978-0-8234-1824-4(3))* Holiday Hse., Inc.

—Cock-a-Doodle Christmas!, 0 vols. 2010. (ENG.). 32p. (J). (gr. -1-2). pap. 6.99 *(978-0-7614-5718-3(6),* 9780761457183, Amazon Children's Publishing) Amazon Publishing.

Hillert, Margaret. Feliz Navidad, Querido Dragón. Pullan, Jack, illus. 2017. (BeginningtoRead Ser.).Tr. of Merry Christmas, Dear Dragon. (ENG & SPA.). 32p. (J). (-2). 22.60 ***(978-1-59953-838-9(5))*** Norwood Hse. Pr.

Hillert, Margaret. Merry Christmas, Dear Dragon. Pullan, Jack, illus. 2016. (BeginningtoRead Ser.). (ENG.). 32p. (J). (-2). lib. bdg. 22.60 *(978-1-59953-775-7(3));* (gr. -1-2). pap. 11.94 *(978-1-60357-888-2(9))* Norwood Hse. Pr.

Hills, Tad. It's Time for Christmas! Hills, Tad, illus. (Duck & Goose Ser.). (ENG., Illus.). 22p. (J). 2011. (gr. -1 — 1). bds. 10.99 *(978-0-375-87112-2(8))* 2010. (gr. k — 1). bds. 7.99 *(978-0-375-86484-1(9))* Random Hse. Children's Bks. (Schwartz & Wade Bks.).

Hindmarsh, Ted C. The Elf & the Magic Windows: A Christmas Fairy Tale. 2008. pap. 2.99 *(978-1-59955-179-1(9))* Cedar Fort, Inc./CFI Distribution.

Hiscox, Don. The Sled. 2011. 32p. pap. 21.99 *(978-1-4568-1971-2(2))* Xlibris Corp.

Hobbie, Holly. I'll Be Home for Christmas. 2008. (Toot & Puddle Ser.: 5). (ENG.). 32p. (gr. -1-3). pap. 6.99 *(978-0-316-03383-1(9))* Little, Brown Bks. for Young Readers.

—Toot & Puddle: Let It Snow. 2016. (Toot & Puddle Ser.: 11). (ENG.). 32p. (J). (gr. -1-3). 6.99 *(978-0-316-35224-6(1))* Little, Brown Bks. for Young Readers.

Hobeika, Noelia, tr. The Pied Piper of Hamelin. Baas, Thomas, illus. 2016. (ENG.). 48p. (J). (gr. -1-3). 19.95 *(978-3-89955-767-1(0))* Die Gestalten Verlag DEU. Dist: Penguin Random Hse. LLC.

Hodges, Meredith. Jasper: A Christmas Caper. Shields, Bonnie, illus. 2004. 85p. (J). 24.95 *(978-1-928624-20-2(0))* Lucky 3 Ranch, Inc.

Hodgson, Julie. The Magic of Christmas. 2007. 26p. 18.95 *(978-1-84799-350-2(8))* Lulu Pr., Inc.

Hoepfner, John P. The Tale of Magic Pixie Dust. 2011. 34p. pap. 16.95 *(978-1-4560-6811-0(3))* PublishAmerica, Inc.

Hoff, Syd. Danny & the Dinosaur: a Very Dino Christmas. Hoff, Syd & Cutting, David, illus. 2017. 24p. (J). (gr. -1-3). pap. 6.99 ***(978-0-06-241046-7(6),*** HarperFestival) HarperCollins Pubs.

Hoffer, Rod. The Strange Christmas Dream. 2012. 64p. pap. 24.99 *(978-1-4772-5949-8(X))* AuthorHouse.

Hoffmann, E. T. A. The Nutcracker. Neugroschel, Joachim, tr. from GER. 2014. (Penguin Christmas Classics Ser.: 4). (ENG., Illus.). 128p. (gr. 12). 16.00 *(978-0-14-312250-0(9),* Penguin Classics) Penguin Publishing Group.

—The Nutcracker. Hess, Christina, illus. 2016. (Classic Edition Ser.: 10). (ENG.). 64p. (J). 19.95 *(978-1-60433-630-6(7),* Applesauce Pr.) Cider Mill Pr. Bk. Pubs., LLC.

—The Nutcracker & the Mouse King. Scheiner, A. & Wenckebach, L. W. R., illus. 2013. Orig. Title: Nutcracker & the King of the Mice. 88p. pap. *(978-1-909115-77-4(0))* Planet, The.

Hoffmann, E. T. A. & Ventura, Paola Fratalocchi. The Nutcracker. 2010. (ENG., Illus.). 32p. (J). 14.99 *(978-0-7944-2044-4(3))* Reader's Digest Assn., Inc., The.

Holder, Jennifer. God Made You Special. Nobens, C. A., illus. 2015. (Happy Day Ser.). (ENG.). 16p. (J). pap. 2.49 *(978-1-4964-1110-5(2),* Happy Day) Tyndale Hse. Pubs.

Holder, Mig, et al. Papa Panov's Special Day. Downing, Julie, illus. 3rd ed. 2014. (ENG.). 32p. (gr. k-2). pap. 8.99 *(978-0-7459-4564-4(3))* Lion Hudson PLC GBR. Dist: Independent Pubs. Group.

Holdren, Mark W. Spirit Wolf. 2004. (Illus.). 158p. reprint ed. pap. 13.95 *(978-0-9760648-0-0(4))* Powell Hill Pr.

Holland, Trish & Ford, Christine. The Soldiers' Night Before Christmas. Manders, John, illus. 2006. (Big Little Golden Book Ser.). (ENG.). 32p. (J). (gr. -1-2). 10.99 *(978-0-375-83795-1(7),* Golden Bks.) Random Hse. Children's Bks.

Hollins, Jack. Charlie's Christmas Adventure. 2006. 16.95 *(978-0-9788725-0-2(9))* Alli Kat Publishing.

Holm, H. R. Forever Santa. 2009. 14p. (J). pap. 2.99 *(978-1-59955-345-0(7))* Cedar Fort, Inc./CFI Distribution.

Holm, Jennifer L. Little Babymouse & the Christmas Cupcakes. Holm, Matthew, illus. 2016. (ENG.). 40p. (J). (gr. -1-2). 17.99 *(978-1-101-93743-3(2),* Random Hse. Bks. for Young Readers) Random Hse. Children's Bks.

Holm, Jennifer L. & Holm, Matthew. A Very Babymouse Christmas. Holm, Jennifer L. & Holm, Matthew, illus. 2011. (Babymouse Ser.: 15). (ENG., Illus.). 96p. (J). (gr. 2-5). 12.99 *(978-0-375-96779-5(6));* pap. 6.99 *(978-0-375-86779-8(1))* Random Hse. Children's Bks. (Random Hse. Bks. for Young Readers).

Holm, M. S. The Arborist. Sayles, Susana, illus. 2007. (ENG.). 104p. (J). 16.95 *(978-0-9796199-1-5(2));* pap. 11.95 *(978-0-9796199-3-9(9))* Great West Publishing. (Sentry Bks.).

Holt, Gretta Scott. The Reindeer Who Was Afraid to Fly. 2008. 24p. pap. 11.49 *(978-1-4389-1709-2(0))* AuthorHouse.

Holt, Kimberly Willis. Piper Reed, Rodeo Star. Davenier, Christine, illus. 2011. (Piper Reed Ser.: 5). (ENG.). 160p. (J). (gr. 3-6). 15.99 *(978-0-8050-9007-9(X),* 9780805090079, Holt, Henry & Co. Bks. For Young Readers) Holt, Henry & Co.

—Piper Reed, Rodeo Star. Davenier, Christine, illus. 2012. (Piper Reed Ser.: 5). (ENG.). 176p. (J). (gr. 3-6). pap. 6.99 *(978-1-250-00409-3(8),* 9781250004093) Square Fish.

Holthaus, Abbey. The Treasures of Christmas. Downs, Braden, illus. 2008. 126p. pap. 19.95 *(978-1-60672-152-0(6))* America Star Bks.

Holub, Joan. The Knights Before Christmas. Magoon, Scott, illus. 2015. (ENG.). 32p. (J). (gr. k-3). 16.99 *(978-0-8050-9932-4(8),* 9780805099324, Holt, Henry & Co. Bks. For Young Readers) Holt, Henry & Co.

Honolulu Theatre for Youth Staff. Christmas Talk Story. 2003. 88p. (J). 14.95 incl. audio compact disk *(978-1-57306-172-8(7))* Bess Pr., Inc.

Hood, Jack B., illus. The Legend of Holly Boy. rev. ed. 38p. (J). (gr. -1-12). pap. 3.95 *(978-0-9640474-2-6(X))* Latino, Frank Publishing Co.

Hooke, R. Schuyler. Thomas' Night Before Christmas. Courtney, Richard, illus. 2013. (Little Golden Book Ser.). (ENG.). 24p. (J). (gr. -1-k). 4.99 *(978-0-449-81663-9(X),* Golden Bks.) Random Hse. Children's Bks.

Hoover, Helen. Great Wolf & the Good Woodsman. Bowen, Betsy, illus. 2005. (Fesler-Lampert Minnesota Heritage Ser.). 40p. (J). (gr. -1-7). 14.95 *(978-0-8166-4445-2(4))* Univ. of Minnesota Pr.

Hope, Laura Lee. Bunny Brown & His Sister Sue at Christmas Tree Cove. 2007. 176p. 27.95 *(978-1-4218-3887-8(7),* 1st World Library - Literary Society) 1st World Publishing, Inc.

—Bunny Brown & His Sister Sue at Christmas Tree Cove. 2007. (ENG.). 138p. pap. 18.99 *(978-1-4346-3592-1(9));* 152p. pap. 21.99 *(978-1-4346-3593-8(7))* Creative Media Partners, LLC.

Hopkins, Charles. Santa's Frost Covered Sleigh Lay Broken in the Snow. 2007. pap. 17.00 *(978-0-8059-8935-9(8))* Dorrance Publishing Co., Inc.

Hopkins, Suzette. Little Wolf's Christmas. Taylor, Jill, illus. 2004. (Little Wolf & Friends Ser.). 19p. (J). 12.95 *(978-1-932133-72-1(0))* Writers' Collective, The.

Horácek, Petr. Suzy Goose & the Christmas Star. Horácek, Petr, illus. 2009. (ENG., Illus.). 32p. (J). (gr. -1-2). 15.99 *(978-0-7636-4487-1(0))* Candlewick Pr.

—Suzy Goose & the Christmas Star: Midi Edition. Horácek, Petr, illus. 2010. (ENG., Illus.). 32p. (J). (gr. -1-2). 7.99 *(978-0-7636-5000-1(5))* Candlewick Pr.

Horman, Marnie. Carrie's Silver Christmas Tree. 2007. 32p. per. 12.95 *(978-1-4327-1615-8(8))* Outskirts Pr., Inc.

Horse, Harry. Little Rabbit's Christmas. Horse, Harry, illus. 2007. (Illus.). 32p. (J). (gr. k-3). 15.95 *(978-1-56145-419-8(2))* Peachtree Pubs.

Horsfall, S. J. Jodie & Lilly & the Joy of Christmas. 2010. 19p. 12.95 *(978-1-4452-4148-7(X))* Lulu Pr., Inc.

Horton, Jim. The Foot Log Incident. 2008. 30p. pap. 24.95 *(978-1-60610-706-5(2))* America Star Bks.

Houghton Mifflin and Company Publishing Staff & Rey, H. A. The Family Christmas Treasury with CD & Downloadable Audio. 2013. (ENG., Illus.). 288p. (J). (gr. -1-3). 18.99 *(978-0-544-09249-5(X))* Houghton Mifflin Harcourt Publishing Co.

Houts, Michelle. Winterfrost. (ENG.). 272p. (J). (gr. 3-7). 2016. pap. 7.99 *(978-0-7636-9101-1(1))* 2014. (Illus.). 16.99 *(978-0-7636-6565-4(7))* Candlewick Pr.

Howard, Elizabeth Fitzgerald. Chita's Christmas Tree. 2007. (ENG.). 32p. (J). (gr. -1-3). 13.99 *(978-1-4169-6156-7(9),* Simon & Schuster/Paula Wiseman Bks.) Simon & Schuster/Paula Wiseman Bks.

Howarth, Jill, illus. Jingle Bells. 2015. (ENG.). 8p. (J). (gr. -1-17). bds. 10.95 *(978-0-7624-5842-4(9),* Running Pr. Kids) Running Pr. Bk. Pubs.

Howe, James. The Fright Before Christmas. Mack, Jeff, illus. (Bunnicula & Friends Ser.: 5). (ENG.). 48p. (J). (gr. 1-3). 2007. pap. 3.99 *(978-0-689-86941-9(X))* 2006. 16.99 *(978-0-689-86939-6(8))* Simon Spotlight. (Simon Spotlight).

Howell, Alice O. Lara's First Christmas. Mailer, Maggie, illus. 2004. (ENG.). 96p. (J). pap. 9.95 *(978-0-88010-553-8(4),* Bell Pond Bks.) SteinerBooks, Inc.

Howells, William Dean. Christmas Every Day. (J). lib. bdg. 16.95 *(978-0-8488-1866-1(0))* Amereon Ltd.

—Christmas Every Day & Other Stories. 2008. 68p. pap. 9.99 *(978-1-59547-634-0(2))* NuVision Pubns., LLC.

Howie, Vickie. Knock, Knock! Who's There at Christmas? MacLean, Moira, illus. 2004. 20p. (J). bds. 9.49 *(978-0-7586-0649-5(4))* Concordia Publishing Hse.

Hubery, Julia. When Grandma Saved Christmas. Pedler, Caroline, illus. 2014. (ENG.). 32p. (J). (gr. -1-3). 16.99 *(978-1-58925-164-9(4))* Tiger Tales.

Huck, Jeremy. Charlie, the Christmas Caterpillar, & Marvin Mouse. 2013. 16p. pap. 24.95 *(978-1-62709-632-4(9))* America Star Bks.

Huddy, Delia. The Christmas Eve Tree. Sutton, Emily, illus. 2016. (ENG.). 40p. (J). (gr. k-3). 16.99 *(978-0-7636-7917-0(8))* Candlewick Pr.

Hudson, Mary C. Crossing the Chasm: The Sled. 2006. 3p. (J). pap. 10.00 *(978-0-9722937-2-3(8))* Hudson, Mary C.

Hughes, John H. B. Jiminy Tish - the Animal's Christmas. 2009. 61p. pap. 39.95 *(978-1-4092-9279-1(7))* Lulu Pr., Inc.

Hughes, Julie. The Fantastic Christmas. Sharpley, Kate, illus. 2013. 34p. pap. *(978-0-9868344-9-3(1))* Yodoki Inc.

Hughes, Shirley. Alfie's Christmas. 2013. (Alfie Ser.). (ENG., Illus.). 32p. (J). (gr. k-2). 22.99 *(978-0-370-33230-7(X))* Transworld Publishers Ltd. GBR. Dist: Independent Pubs. Group.

—The Christmas Eve Ghost. Hughes, Shirley, illus. 2010. (ENG., Illus.). 32p. (J). (gr. -1-3). 15.99 *(978-0-7636-4472-7(2))* Candlewick Pr.

—Lucy & Tom's Christmas. Date not set. 32p. (J). pap. *(978-0-05-004509-1(1))* Addison-Wesley Longman, Inc.

Hulse, Kris. A Cowhand Christmas. Hulse, Kris, illus. 2006. (Illus.). 32p. (J). lib. bdg. 21.95 *(978-0-9761128-6-0(8))* KB Bks. & More.

Hulst, W. G. van de & Hulst, Willem G. van de, illus. The Search for Christmas. 2014. (J). *(978-1-928136-12-5(5))* Inheritance Pubns.

Humphreys, Stephen. Harold Saves Christmas: A Harold & Charlie adventure Story. 2011. (Illus.). 28p. pap. 12.49 *(978-1-4520-9994-1(4))* AuthorHouse.

Hunt, Zoe. Azarels Christmas Wish. 2007. (J). per. 10.95 *(978-1-934345-20-7(2))* SouthWest Pubns.

Hunt, Zoe Paton. Azrael's Magical Moment. 2008. 24p. pap. 18.95 *(978-1-60693-070-0(2),* Strategic Bk. Publishing) Strategic Book Publishing & Rights Agency (SBPRA).

Hunter, Sara Hoagland. The Lighthouse Santa. Miner, Julia, illus. 2011. 36p. (J). (gr. -1-3). 17.95 *(978-1-61168-006-5(9))* Univ. Pr. of New England.

Hunter, Todd H. Elf Night: A Christmas Story. Gavrilovskiy, Olga, illus. 2006. 52p. (J). (gr. -1-7). 16.95 *(978-0-9788085-0-1(9))* Tetoca Pr.

Huser, Glen & Rose, Martin. Jeremy's Christmas Wish. 2005. (Illus.). viii, 40p. (J). 5.95 *(978-0-9686899-2-9(2))* Hodgepog Bks. CAN. Dist: Fitzhenry & Whiteside, Ltd.

Huws, Emily & Gomer, Gwasg. CAE Berllan. 2005. (WEL.). 28p. 5.99 *(978-1-85902-998-5(1))* Gomer Pr. GBR. Dist: Gomer Pr.

Hyde, Margaret. Mo Smells Christmas: A Scentsational Journey. Giacomini, Amanda, illus. 4th ed. 2010. (Mo's Nose Ser.). (ENG.). 24p. (J). (gr. k-k). 17.95 *(978-0-9816255-6-0(8))* Mo's Nose, LLC.

Hysen, Sylvia. A Very Dairy Christmas. 2005. 290p. 24.95 *(978-0-9763365-6-3(1))* 1st Impression Publishing.

Ikaris, Despoina. The Little Red Jacket: A True Almost Christmas Almost Mystery Almost Ghost Story for Children And Certain Grown-Ups. 2008. 48p. pap. 10.99 *(978-1-60647-898-1(2))* Salem Author Services.

Inches, Alison. Santa Claus Is Green! How to Have an Eco-Friendly Christmas. Kirwan, Wednesday, illus. 2009. (Little Green Bks.). (ENG.). 24p. (J). (gr. -1-1). pap. 5.99 *(978-1-4169-7223-5(4),* Little Simon) Little Simon.

Inkpen, Mick. Kipper: Kipper's Christmas Eve. 2016. (Kipper Ser.). (ENG., Illus.). 26p. (J). (gr. -1-k). bds. 8.99 *(978-1-4449-3029-0(X))* Hachette Children's Group GBR. Dist: Hachette Bk. Group.

—Tickly Christmas. 2016. (Wibbly Pig Ser.). (ENG., Illus.). 32p. (J). (gr. -1-k). pap. 8.99 *(978-1-4449-2410-7(9))* Hachette Children's Group GBR. Dist: Hachette Bk. Group.

Inman, Robert. The Christmas Bus. Baskin, Lyle, illus. 2006. 77p. 19.95 *(978-0-9760963-6-8(6))* Novello Festival Pr.

Ioan, Elwyn. Ici'r Dôl A'r Cathod Nadolig. 2005. (WEL., Illus.). 36p. pap. *(978-0-86243-361-1(4))* Y Lolfa.

Iosue, Marilyn. Santa's Busy Day. 2007. pap. 17.00 *(978-0-8059-8761-4(4))* Dorrance Publishing Co., Inc.

Issim, Beth. The Empty Christmas Sack. 2009. (Illus.). 54p. pap. *(978-1-84748-683-7(5))* Athena Pr.

It's Time for Christmas. 2003. (J). per. *(978-1-57657-919-0(0));* per. *(978-1-57657-807-0(0))* Paradise Pr., Inc.

Ivey, Lisa. The Christmas Tree That Didn't Get Picked. 2007. 64p. per. 19.95 *(978-1-4241-8276-3(X))* America Star Bks.

Jackson, Ciandress. Chloe the Jumbo Jet the Best Cancelled Christmas Ever. 2013. 28p. pap. 9.99 *(978-1-61286-200-2(4))* Avid Readers Publishing Group.

Jackson, Kate. Santa's Special Helper: A Spot-the-Difference Christmas Adventure! 2016. (ENG.). 18p. (J). bds. 7.99 *(978-1-4926-4175-9(8),* 9781492641759, Sourcebooks Jabberwocky) Sourcebooks, Inc.

Jackson, Kathryn. The Animals' Merry Christmas. Scarry, Richard, illus. 2005. (ENG.). 72p. (J). (gr. -1-2). 15.99 *(978-0-375-83341-0(2),* Golden Bks.) Random Hse. Children's Bks.

—Richard Scarry's the Animals' Merry Christmas. Scarry, Richard, illus. 2016. (Little Golden Book Ser.). (ENG.). 24p. (J). (-k). 4.99 *(978-1-101-93842-3(0),* Golden Bks.) Random Hse. Children's Bks.

Jalonen, Nicole. Baby's Magical Night. 2011. 28p. pap. 15.99 *(978-1-4628-5419-6(2))* Xlibris Corp.

James, Brian. Yo-Ho-Ho! Zivoin, Jennifer, illus. 2008. (Pirate School Ser.: 7). (ENG.). 64p. (J). (gr. 1-3). pap. 3.99 *(978-0-448-44887-9(4),* Grosset & Dunlap) Penguin Young Readers Group.

James, Emma J. A Surprise for Santa. James, Emma J., illus. (Illus.). 32p. (Orig.). (J). (gr. -1-3). pap. *(978-1-885935-02-1(1))* Appalachian Log Publishing Co., The.

James, Eric. Santa's Sleigh Is on Its Way to Alabama. Dunn, Robert, illus. 2015. (ENG.). 32p. (J). (-2). 12.99

C D

(978-1-4926-2763-0(1), Sourcebooks Jabberwocky) Sourcebooks, Inc.

—Santa's Sleigh Is on Its Way to California. Dunn, Robert, illus. 2015. (ENG.). 32p. (J). (-2). 12.99 (978-1-4926-2747-0(X), Sourcebooks Jabberwocky) Sourcebooks, Inc.

—Santa's Sleigh Is on Its Way to Colorado. Dunn, Robert, illus. 2015. (ENG.). 32p. (J). (-2). 12.99 (978-1-4926-2756-2(9), Sourcebooks Jabberwocky) Sourcebooks, Inc.

—Santa's Sleigh Is on Its Way to Florida. Dunn, Robert, illus. 2015. (ENG.). 32p. (J). (-2). 12.99 (978-1-4926-2743-2(7), Sourcebooks Jabberwocky) Sourcebooks, Inc.

—Santa's Sleigh Is on Its Way to Georgia. Dunn, Robert, illus. 2015. (ENG.). 32p. (J). (-2). 12.99 (978-1-4926-2744-9(5), Sourcebooks Jabberwocky) Sourcebooks, Inc.

—Santa's Sleigh Is on Its Way to Illinois. Dunn, Robert, illus. 2015. (ENG.). 32p. (J). (-2). 12.99 (978-1-4926-2746-3(1), Sourcebooks Jabberwocky) Sourcebooks, Inc.

—Santa's Sleigh Is on Its Way to Indiana. Dunn, Robert, illus. 2015. (ENG.). 32p. (J). (-2). 12.99 (978-1-4926-2753-1(4), Sourcebooks Jabberwocky) Sourcebooks, Inc.

—Santa's Sleigh Is on Its Way to Iowa. Dunn, Robert, illus. 2015. (ENG.). 32p. (J). (-2). 12.99 (978-1-4926-2749-4(6), Sourcebooks Jabberwocky) Sourcebooks, Inc.

—Santa's Sleigh Is on Its Way to Kentucky. Dunn, Robert, illus. 2015. (ENG.). 32p. (J). (-2). 12.99 (978-1-4926-2761-6(5), Sourcebooks Jabberwocky) Sourcebooks, Inc.

—Santa's Sleigh Is on Its Way to Louisiana. Dunn, Robert, illus. 2015. (ENG.). 32p. (J). (-2). 12.99 (978-1-4926-2762-3(3), Sourcebooks Jabberwocky) Sourcebooks, Inc.

—Santa's Sleigh Is on Its Way to Michigan. Dunn, Robert, illus. 2015. (ENG.). 32p. (J). (-2). 12.99 (978-1-4926-2741-8(0), Sourcebooks Jabberwocky) Sourcebooks, Inc.

—Santa's Sleigh Is on Its Way to Missouri. Dunn, Robert, illus. 2015. (ENG.). 32p. (J). (-2). 12.99 (978-1-4926-2759-3(3), Sourcebooks Jabberwocky) Sourcebooks, Inc.

—Santa's Sleigh Is on Its Way to My House. Dunn, Robert, illus. 2015. (ENG.). 32p. (J). (-2). 12.99 (978-1-4926-2740-1(2), Sourcebooks Jabberwocky) Sourcebooks, Inc.

—Santa's Sleigh Is on Its Way to New Jersey. Dunn, Robert, illus. 2015. (ENG.). 32p. (J). (-2). 12.99 (978-1-4926-2758-6(5), Sourcebooks Jabberwocky) Sourcebooks, Inc.

—Santa's Sleigh Is on Its Way to New York. Dunn, Robert, illus. 2015. (ENG.). 32p. (J). (-2). 12.99 (978-1-4926-2751-7(8), Sourcebooks Jabberwocky) Sourcebooks, Inc.

—Santa's Sleigh Is on Its Way to North Carolina. Dunn, Robert, illus. 2015. (ENG.). 32p. (J). (-2). 12.99 (978-1-4926-2750-0(X), Sourcebooks Jabberwocky) Sourcebooks, Inc.

—Santa's Sleigh Is on Its Way to Ohio. Dunn, Robert, illus. 2015. (ENG.). 32p. (J). (-2). 12.99 (978-1-4926-2742-5(9), Sourcebooks Jabberwocky) Sourcebooks, Inc.

—Santa's Sleigh Is on Its Way to Pennsylvania. Dunn, Robert, illus. 2015. (ENG.). 32p. (J). (-2). 12.99 (978-1-4926-2745-6(3), Sourcebooks Jabberwocky) Sourcebooks, Inc.

—Santa's Sleigh Is on Its Way to South Carolina. Dunn, Robert, illus. 2015. (ENG.). 32p. (J). (-2). 12.99 (978-1-4926-2757-9(7), Sourcebooks Jabberwocky) Sourcebooks, Inc.

—Santa's Sleigh Is on Its Way to Tennessee. Dunn, Robert, illus. 2015. (ENG.). 32p. (J). (-2). 12.99 (978-1-4926-2752-4(6), Sourcebooks Jabberwocky) Sourcebooks, Inc.

—Santa's Sleigh Is on Its Way to Texas. Dunn, Robert, illus. 2015. (ENG.). 32p. (J). (-2). 12.99 (978-1-4926-2739-5(9), Sourcebooks Jabberwocky) Sourcebooks, Inc.

—Santa's Sleigh Is on Its Way to Virginia. Dunn, Robert, illus. 2015. (ENG.). 32p. (J). (-2). 12.99 (978-1-4926-2754-8(2), Sourcebooks Jabberwocky) Sourcebooks, Inc.

—Santa's Sleigh Is on Its Way to Washington. Dunn, Robert, illus. 2015. (ENG.). 32p. (J). (-2). 12.99 (978-1-4926-2760-9(7), Sourcebooks Jabberwocky) Sourcebooks, Inc.

—Santa's Sleigh Is on Its Way to Wisconsin. Dunn, Robert, illus. 2015. (ENG.). 32p. (J). (-2). 12.99 (978-1-4926-2755-5(0), Sourcebooks Jabberwocky) Sourcebooks, Inc.

—Santa's Sleigh Is on Its Way to Alaska: A Christmas Adventure. Dunn, Robert, illus. 2016. (ENG.). 32p. (J). (-2). 12.99 (978-1-4926-4314-2(9), 9781492643142, Sourcebooks Jabberwocky) Sourcebooks, Inc.

—Santa's Sleigh Is on Its Way to Albuquerque: A Christmas Adventure. Dunn, Robert, illus. 2016. (ENG.). 32p. (J). (-2). 12.99 (978-1-4926-4315-9(7), 9781492643159, Sourcebooks Jabberwocky) Sourcebooks, Inc.

—Santa's Sleigh Is on Its Way to Arizona: A Christmas Adventure. Dunn, Robert, illus. 2016. (ENG.). 32p. (J). (-2). 12.99 (978-1-4926-4316-6(5), 9781492643166, Sourcebooks Jabberwocky) Sourcebooks, Inc.

—Santa's Sleigh Is on Its Way to Arkansas: A Christmas Adventure. Dunn, Robert, illus. 2016. (ENG.). 32p. (J). (-2). 12.99 (978-1-4926-4317-3(3), 9781492643173, Sourcebooks Jabberwocky) Sourcebooks, Inc.

—Santa's Sleigh Is on Its Way to Boise: A Christmas Adventure. Dunn, Robert, illus. 2016. (ENG.). 32p. (J). (-2). 12.99 (978-1-4926-4318-0(1), 9781492643180, Sourcebooks Jabberwocky) Sourcebooks, Inc.

—Santa's Sleigh Is on Its Way to Boston: A Christmas Adventure. Dunn, Robert, illus. 2016. (ENG.). 32p. (J). (-2). 12.99 (978-1-4926-4319-7(X), 9781492643197, Sourcebooks Jabberwocky) Sourcebooks, Inc.

—Santa's Sleigh Is on Its Way to Calgary: A Christmas Adventure. Dunn, Robert, illus. 2016. (ENG.). 32p. (J). (-2). 12.99 (978-1-4926-4320-3(3), 9781492643203, Sourcebooks Jabberwocky) Sourcebooks, Inc.

—Santa's Sleigh Is on Its Way to Canada: A Christmas Adventure. Dunn, Robert, illus. 2016. (ENG.). 32p. (J). (-2). 12.99 (978-1-4926-4321-0(1), 9781492643210, Sourcebooks Jabberwocky) Sourcebooks, Inc.

—Santa's Sleigh Is on Its Way to Charleston: A Christmas Adventure. Dunn, Robert, illus. 2016. (ENG.). 32p. (J). (-2). 12.99 (978-1-4926-4322-7(X), 9781492643227, Sourcebooks Jabberwocky) Sourcebooks, Inc.

—Santa's Sleigh Is on Its Way to Chicago: A Christmas Adventure. Dunn, Robert, illus. 2016. (ENG.). 32p. (J). (-2). 12.99 (978-1-4926-4323-4(8), 9781492643234, Sourcebooks Jabberwocky) Sourcebooks, Inc.

—Santa's Sleigh Is on Its Way to Cincinnati: A Christmas Adventure. Dunn, Robert, illus. 2016. (ENG.). 32p. (J). (-2). 12.99 (978-1-4926-4324-1(6), 9781492643241, Sourcebooks Jabberwocky) Sourcebooks, Inc.

—Santa's Sleigh Is on Its Way to Connecticut: A Christmas Adventure. Dunn, Robert, illus. 2016. (ENG.). 32p. (J). (-2). 12.99 (978-1-4926-4325-8(4), 9781492643258, Sourcebooks Jabberwocky) Sourcebooks, Inc.

—Santa's Sleigh Is on Its Way to Delaware: A Christmas Adventure. Dunn, Robert, illus. 2016. (ENG.). 32p. (J). (-2). 12.99 (978-1-4926-4326-5(2), 9781492643265, Sourcebooks Jabberwocky) Sourcebooks, Inc.

—Santa's Sleigh Is on Its Way to Edmonton: A Christmas Adventure. Dunn, Robert, illus. 2016. (ENG.). 32p. (J). (-2). 12.99 (978-1-4926-4327-2(0), 9781492643272, Sourcebooks Jabberwocky) Sourcebooks, Inc.

—Santa's Sleigh Is on Its Way to Hawaii: A Christmas Adventure. Dunn, Robert, illus. 2016. (ENG.). 32p. (J). (-2). 12.99 (978-1-4926-4328-9(9), 9781492643289, Sourcebooks Jabberwocky) Sourcebooks, Inc.

—Santa's Sleigh Is on Its Way to Idaho: A Christmas Adventure. Dunn, Robert, illus. 2016. (ENG.). 32p. (J). (-2). 12.99 (978-1-4926-4329-6(7), 9781492643296, Sourcebooks Jabberwocky) Sourcebooks, Inc.

—Santa's Sleigh Is on Its Way to Kansas: A Christmas Adventure. Dunn, Robert, illus. 2016. (ENG.). 32p. (J). (-2). 12.99 (978-1-4926-4330-2(0), 9781492643302, Sourcebooks Jabberwocky) Sourcebooks, Inc.

—Santa's Sleigh Is on Its Way to Kansas City: A Christmas Adventure. Dunn, Robert, illus. 2016. (ENG.). 32p. (J). (-2). 12.99 (978-1-4926-4331-9(9), 9781492643319, Sourcebooks Jabberwocky) Sourcebooks, Inc.

—Santa's Sleigh Is on Its Way to Las Vegas: A Christmas Adventure. Dunn, Robert, illus. 2016. (ENG.). 32p. (J). (-2). 12.99 (978-1-4926-4332-6(7), 9781492643326, Sourcebooks Jabberwocky) Sourcebooks, Inc.

—Santa's Sleigh Is on Its Way to Maine: A Christmas Adventure. Dunn, Robert, illus. 2016. (ENG.). 32p. (J). (-2). 12.99 (978-1-4926-4334-0(3), 9781492643340, Sourcebooks Jabberwocky) Sourcebooks, Inc.

—Santa's Sleigh Is on Its Way to Maryland: A Christmas Adventure. Dunn, Robert, illus. 2016. (ENG.). 32p. (J). (-2). 12.99 (978-1-4926-4335-7(1), 9781492643357, Sourcebooks Jabberwocky) Sourcebooks, Inc.

—Santa's Sleigh Is on Its Way to Mississippi: A Christmas Adventure. Dunn, Robert, illus. 2016. (ENG.). 32p. (J). (-2). 12.99 (978-1-4926-4337-1(8), 9781492643371, Sourcebooks Jabberwocky) Sourcebooks, Inc.

—Santa's Sleigh Is on Its Way to Montana: A Christmas Adventure. Dunn, Robert, illus. 2016. (ENG.). 32p. (J). (-2). 12.99 (978-1-4926-4338-8(6), 9781492643388, Sourcebooks Jabberwocky) Sourcebooks, Inc.

—Santa's Sleigh Is on Its Way to Nebraska: A Christmas Adventure. Dunn, Robert, illus. 2016. (ENG.). 32p. (J). (-2). 12.99 (978-1-4926-4339-5(4), 9781492643395, Sourcebooks Jabberwocky) Sourcebooks, Inc.

—Santa's Sleigh Is on Its Way to Nevada: A Christmas Adventure. Dunn, Robert, illus. 2016. (ENG.). 32p. (J). (-2). 12.99 (978-1-4926-4340-1(8), 9781492643401, Sourcebooks Jabberwocky) Sourcebooks, Inc.

—Santa's Sleigh Is on Its Way to New England: A Christmas Adventure. Dunn, Robert, illus. 2016. (ENG.). 32p. (J). (-2). 12.99 (978-1-4926-4341-8(6), 9781492643418, Sourcebooks Jabberwocky) Sourcebooks, Inc.

—Santa's Sleigh Is on Its Way to New Hampshire: A Christmas Adventure. Dunn, Robert, illus. 2016. (ENG.). 32p. (J). (-2). 12.99 (978-1-4926-4342-5(4), 9781492643425, Sourcebooks Jabberwocky) Sourcebooks, Inc.

—Santa's Sleigh Is on Its Way to New Mexico: A Christmas Adventure. Dunn, Robert, illus. 2016. (ENG.). 32p. (J). (-2). 12.99 (978-1-4926-4343-2(2), 9781492643432, Sourcebooks Jabberwocky) Sourcebooks, Inc.

—Santa's Sleigh Is on Its Way to New York City: A Christmas Adventure. Dunn, Robert, illus. 2016. (ENG.). 32p. (J). (-2). 12.99 (978-1-4926-4344-9(0), 9781492643449, Sourcebooks Jabberwocky) Sourcebooks, Inc.

—Santa's Sleigh Is on It's Way to Newfoundland: A Christmas Adventure. Dunn, Robert, illus. 2016. (ENG.). 32p. (J). (-2). 12.99 (978-1-4926-4505-4(2), 9781492645054, Sourcebooks Jabberwocky) Sourcebooks, Inc.

—Santa's Sleigh Is on Its Way to North Dakota: A Christmas Adventure. Dunn, Robert, illus. 2016. (ENG.). 32p. (J). (-2). 12.99 (978-1-4926-4345-6(9), 9781492643456, Sourcebooks Jabberwocky) Sourcebooks, Inc.

—Santa's Sleigh Is on It's Way to Nova Scotia: A Christmas Adventure. Dunn, Robert, illus. 2016. (ENG.). 32p. (J). (-2). 12.99 (978-1-4926-4508-5(7), 9781492645085, Sourcebooks Jabberwocky) Sourcebooks, Inc.

—Santa's Sleigh Is on Its Way to Oklahoma: A Christmas Adventure. Dunn, Robert, illus. 2016. (ENG.). 32p. (J). (-2). 12.99 (978-1-4926-4346-3(7), 9781492643463, Sourcebooks Jabberwocky) Sourcebooks, Inc.

—Santa's Sleigh Is on Its Way to Omaha: A Christmas Adventure. Dunn, Robert, illus. 2016. (ENG.). 32p. (J). (-2). 12.99 (978-1-4926-4347-0(5), 9781492643470, Sourcebooks Jabberwocky) Sourcebooks, Inc.

—Santa's Sleigh Is on Its Way to Oregon: A Christmas Adventure. Dunn, Robert, illus. 2016. (ENG.). 32p. (J). (-2). 12.99 (978-1-4926-4348-7(3), 9781492643487, Sourcebooks Jabberwocky) Sourcebooks, Inc.

—Santa's Sleigh Is on Its Way to Philadelphia: A Christmas Adventure. Dunn, Robert, illus. 2016. (ENG.). 32p. (J). (-2). 12.99 (978-1-4926-4350-0(5), 9781492643500, Sourcebooks Jabberwocky) Sourcebooks, Inc.

—Santa's Sleigh Is on Its Way to Pittsburgh: A Christmas Adventure. Dunn, Robert, illus. 2016. (ENG.). 32p. (J). (-2). 12.99 (978-1-4926-4351-7(3), 9781492643517, Sourcebooks Jabberwocky) Sourcebooks, Inc.

—Santa's Sleigh Is on Its Way to Portland: A Christmas Adventure. Dunn, Robert, illus. 2016. (ENG.). 32p. (J). (-2). 12.99 (978-1-4926-4352-4(1), 9781492643524, Sourcebooks Jabberwocky) Sourcebooks, Inc.

—Santa's Sleigh Is on Its Way to Rhode Island: A Christmas Adventure. Dunn, Robert, illus. 2016. (ENG.). 32p. (J). (-2). 12.99 (978-1-4926-4353-1(X), 9781492643531, Sourcebooks Jabberwocky) Sourcebooks, Inc.

—Santa's Sleigh Is on Its Way to San Francisco: A Christmas Adventure. Dunn, Robert, illus. 2016. (ENG.). 32p. (J). (-2). 12.99 (978-1-4926-4354-8(8), 9781492643548, Sourcebooks Jabberwocky) Sourcebooks, Inc.

—Santa's Sleigh Is on Its Way to South Dakota: A Christmas Adventure. Dunn, Robert, illus. 2016. (ENG.). 32p. (J). (-2). 12.99 (978-1-4926-4355-5(6), 9781492643555, Sourcebooks Jabberwocky) Sourcebooks, Inc.

—Santa's Sleigh Is on Its Way to St. Louis: A Christmas Adventure. Dunn, Robert, illus. 2016. (ENG.). 32p. (J). (-2). 12.99 (978-1-4926-4356-2(4), 9781492643562, Sourcebooks Jabberwocky) Sourcebooks, Inc.

—Santa's Sleigh Is on Its Way to Tampa Bay: A Christmas Adventure. Dunn, Robert, illus. 2016. (ENG.). 32p. (J). (-2). 12.99 (978-1-4926-4357-9(2), 9781492643579, Sourcebooks Jabberwocky) Sourcebooks, Inc.

—Santa's Sleigh Is on Its Way to Tulsa: A Christmas Adventure. Dunn, Robert, illus. 2016. (ENG.). 32p. (J). (-2). 12.99 (978-1-4926-4359-3(9), 9781492643593, Sourcebooks Jabberwocky) Sourcebooks, Inc.

—Santa's Sleigh Is on Its Way to Utah: A Christmas Adventure. Dunn, Robert, illus. 2016. (ENG.). 32p. (J). (-2). 12.99 (978-1-4926-4360-9(2), 9781492643609, Sourcebooks Jabberwocky) Sourcebooks, Inc.

—Santa's Sleigh Is on Its Way to Vermont: A Christmas Adventure. Dunn, Robert, illus. 2016. (ENG.). 32p. (J). (-2). 12.99 (978-1-4926-4362-3(9), 9781492643623, Sourcebooks Jabberwocky) Sourcebooks, Inc.

—Santa's Sleigh Is on Its Way to Washington, D. C. A Christmas Adventure. Dunn, Robert, illus. 2016. (ENG.). 32p. (J). (-2). 12.99 (978-1-4926-4363-0(7), 9781492643630, Sourcebooks Jabberwocky) Sourcebooks, Inc.

—Santa's Sleigh Is on Its Way to West Virginia: A Christmas Adventure. Dunn, Robert, illus. 2016. (ENG.). 32p. (J). (-2). 12.99 (978-1-4926-4364-7(5), 9781492643647, Sourcebooks Jabberwocky) Sourcebooks, Inc.

—Santa's Sleigh Is on Its Way to Wyoming: A Christmas Adventure. Dunn, Robert, illus. 2016. (ENG.). 32p. (J). (-2). 12.99 (978-1-4926-4365-4(3), 9781492643654, Sourcebooks Jabberwocky) Sourcebooks, Inc.

James G. Normand. Santa's Secret Trick. 2009. (Illus.). 52p. pap. 20.49 (978-1-4389-5788-3(2)) AuthorHouse.

James, Hollis. Santa's Christmas Genies (Shimmer & Shine) Laviosa, Mattia Francesco, illus. 2016. (Big Golden Book Ser.). (ENG.). 32p. (J). (gr. -1-2). 9.99 (978-0-399-55121-5(2), Golden Bks.) Random Hse. Children's Bks.

James, Rosalind. Bertie Rides Again. 2012. (Illus.). 126p. 29.99 (978-1-4771-2272-3(9)) Xlibris Corp.

Jameson, Louise. Christmas in Gabba Land. Style Guide Staff, illus. 2009. (Yo Gabba Gabba! Ser.). (ENG.). 12p. (J). (gr. -1-k). bds. 7.99 (978-1-4169-9167-0(0), Simon Spotlight) Simon Spotlight.

Jamieson, Tom. Sproutzilla vs. Christmas. Byrne, Mike, illus. 2016. (ENG.). 32p. (J). (gr. -1-1). pap. 10.99 **(978-1-5098-2278-2(X))** Pan Macmillan GBR. Dist: Independent Pubs. Group.

Jane, Pamela. Little Elfie One. Manning, Jane, illus. 2015. (ENG.). 32p. (J). (gr. -1-3). 17.99 (978-0-06-220673-2(7)) HarperCollins Pubs.

Janovitz, Marilyn. We Love Christmas! 2007. (ENG., Illus.). 32p. (J). (gr. -1-3). 9.95 (978-0-7358-2089-0(9)) North-South Bks., Inc.

Jarvis, Cathy. Red Beard Santa's Biker Buddy. 2013. 36p. pap. 15.49 (978-1-4669-9587-1(4)) Trafford Publishing.

Jatkowska, Ag. Santa Sticker Fun. Jatkowska, Ag, illus. 2016. (ENG., Illus.). 56p. (J). (gr. -1-3). pap. 9.99 **(978-1-5098-2786-2(2))** Pan Macmillan GBR. Dist: Independent Pubs. Group.

Jatkowska, Ag, illus. The Christmas Treasure Hunt. 2014. (ENG.). 10p. (J). (gr. -1-k). 15.99 (978-0-230-76863-5(6)) Pan Macmillan GBR. Dist: Independent Pubs. Group.

Jeanfield. Twinkle, a Christmas Story. 2009. 36p. pap. 13.95 (978-1-60693-745-7(6), Eloquent Bks.) Strategic Book Publishing & Rights Agency (SBPRA).

Jeffers, Susan. Jingle Bells. Jeffers, Susan, illus. 2017. (Illus.). 40p. (J). (gr. -1-3). 17.99 **(978-0-06-236020-5(5))** HarperCollins Pubs.

—The Nutcracker. Jeffers, Susan, illus. 2007. (Illus.). 40p. (J). (gr. -1-3). 17.89 (978-0-06-074387-1(5)); (ENG., 17.99 (978-0-06-074386-4(7)) HarperCollins Pubs.

—The Twelve Days of Christmas. Jeffers, Susan, illus. 2013. (ENG., Illus.). 40p. (J). (gr. -1-3). 17.99 (978-0-06-206615-2(3)) HarperCollins Pubs.

Jeffers, Susan, illus. The Twelve Days of Christmas. 2013. (J). (978-0-06-206616-9(1)) Harper & Row Ltd.

Jeffs, Stephanie. Llygoden y Nadolig. Wyn, Delyth, tr. from ENG. Thorne, Jenny, illus. 2005. (WEL.). 28p. (978-1-85994-497-4(3)) Cyhoeddiadau'r Gair.

Jenkins, Peter. When Father Christmas Resigned. Jenkins, Sandra, illus. 2012. 36p. pap. (978-1-908775-94-8(7)) Legend Pr.

Jennings, Sharon. Jingle Bats. Malloy, Kalle, illus. 72p. pap. (978-1-897039-22-9(0)) High Interest Publishing (HIP).

Jensen, Kimberly. Always the Elf. Harmon, Glenn, illus. 2007. 38p. (J). (gr. -1-3). 15.99 (978-1-59955-086-2(5)) Cedar Fort, Inc./CFI Distribution.

Jewett, Sarah Orne. Betty Leicester's Christmas. 2004. reprint ed. pap. 15.95 (978-1-4191-0979-9(0)); pap. 1.99 (978-1-4192-0979-6(5)) Kessinger Publishing, LLC.

Jitchotvisut, Donna M. Mittens for Christmas. 2009. 376p. 31.95 (978-1-4401-0372-8(0)); pap. 21.95 (978-1-4401-0370-4(4)) iUniverse, Inc.

Johansen, Tesia. The Christmas Secret. Johnson, Gary & Johansen, Tesia, illus. 2011. 28p. pap. 24.95 (978-1-4626-3242-8(4)) America Star Bks.

John Taylor, Jeannie St. Penguin's Special Christmas Tree. l.t. ed. 2012. 36p. (J). pap. (978-1-4596-3452-7(7)) ReadHowYouWant.com, Ltd.

Johnson, Crockett. Harold at the North Pole. Johnson, Crockett, illus. 2015. (ENG., Illus.). 48p. (J). (gr. -1-3). 16.99 (978-0-06-242861-5(6)) HarperCollins Pubs.

Johnson, Florence. The Christmas ABC. Wilkin, Eloise, illus. 2013. (Little Golden Book Ser.). (ENG.). 24p. (J). (-k). 4.99 (978-0-307-97891-2(5), Golden Bks.) Random Hse. Children's Bks.

Johnson, Gerald J. J. Misty's Christmas Present, 1 vol. Miltenberger, Jeri & Miltenberger, Dave, illus. 2010. 32p. 24.95 (978-1-4512-1330-0(1)) PublishAmerica, Inc.

—The Mouse Family Christmas, 1 vol. Bousum, Julie, illus. 2009. 26p. pap. 24.95 (978-1-61546-536-1(7)) America Star Bks.

Johnson, Shane L., illus. OLIVIA & the Christmas Present. 2011. (Olivia TV Tie-In Ser.). (ENG.). 24p. (J). (gr. -1-2). 9.99 (978-1-4424-3624-4(7), Simon Spotlight) Simon Spotlight.

Johnston, Joe. Snag & Me - Christmas Miracle in Blanchard Forks. Johnston, Joe, illus. 2004. (Illus.). (YA). per. 10.00 (978-1-932496-15-4(7)) Penman Publishing, Inc.

Jones, Carl. Rudy the Rangifer & Why Her Nose Turned Orange. 2007. 64p. pap. 14.99 (978-0-9748266-3-9(4)) Grampa Jones's Publishing Co.

Jones, Debra. Christmas & the Little Dolls. Bullock Jr., Michael A., illus. 2011. 24p. pap. 24.95 (978-1-4560-6679-6(X)) America Star Bks.

Jones, Ernest, illus. The Great Mix Up. 2005. (ENG.). 42p. (J). 17.99 (978-0-9772282-0-1(7)) B. T. Brooks.

Jones, Sandy. Anya's Gift: A Tale of Two Christmases, 1 vol. Yourell, Pam, illus. 2009. 48p. pap. 24.95 (978-1-61546-129-5(9)) America Star Bks.

Jordan, L. W. Santa Heads South: Casey's Christmas Surprise. Lasson, Matt, illus. 2008. 40p. per. 24.95 (978-1-60441-374-8(3)) America Star Bks.

Jorgenson, Norman. In Flanders Fields. Harrison-Lever, Brian, illus. 2010. (ENG.). 32p. (J). (gr. -1-3). pap. 9.95 (978-1-894965-83-5(3)) Simply Read Bks. CAN. Dist: Ingram Publisher Services.

Joseph, Costa & Christopher, Romero. Puffs In: Christmas in Puffville. Rachel, Drapkin, illus. 2013. 46p. pap. 15.95 (978-1-62882-016-4(0)) Keith Pubns., LLC.

Joslin, Mary. The Fourth Wise Man. Johnson, Richard, illus. 2007. 28p. (J). (gr. -1-2). 14.99 (978-0-7814-4545-0(0)) Cook, David C.

Joslin, Mary & Ray, Jane. The Lion Classic Christmas Stories. 2014. (ENG., Illus.). 96p. (J). (gr. 2-7). 16.99 (978-0-7459-6299-3(8)) Lion Hudson PLC GBR. Dist: Independent Pubs. Group.

Jumbo Christmas Coloring & Activity Book. (Illus.). 300p. (J). mass mkt. (978-0-87449-054-1(5)) Unisystems, Inc.

"Just Right" Authors and Artists, "Just Right". Merry Christmas Stories. 2014. (ENG., Illus.). 128p. (J). (gr. k-3). pap. 9.99 (978-0-486-49492-0(6)) Dover Pubns., Inc.

Justice, Joseph. Lawyer's Week Before Christmas, 1 vol. Alikhan, Salima, illus. 2010. (Night Before Christmas Ser.). (ENG.). 32p. (J). (gr. 4-8). 16.99 (978-1-58980-739-6(1)) Pelican Publishing Co., Inc.

Kalz, Jill. No Snow for Christmas, 1 vol. Erkocak, Sahin, illus. 2013. (Pfeffernut County Ser.). (ENG.). 32p. (gr. 3-4). 8.99 (978-1-4795-2158-6(2), Fiction Picture Bks.) Picture Window Bks.

Kann, Victoria. Merry Pinkmas! Kann, Victoria, illus. 2013. (Pinkalicious Ser.). (ENG., Illus.). 24p. (J). (gr. -1-3). pap. 6.99 (978-0-06-218912-7(3), HarperFestival) HarperCollins Pubs.

Karpinski, David. Sarah's Christmas Presence. 2006. 58p. pap. 8.95 (978-0-7414-3411-1(3)) Infinity Publishing.

Kaserman, James & Kaserman, Sarah Jane. How the Pirates Saved Christmas. 2005. (Illus.). 64p. (J). per. 5.99 (978-0-9674081-2-5(1), (239)939-4845) Pirate Publishing International.

Kästner, Erich. The Flying Classroom. Bell, Anthea, tr. from GER. 2015. (ENG., Illus.). 176p. (YA). (gr. 5-12). pap. 13.95 (978-1-78269-056-6(5), Pushkin Children's Bks.) Steerforth Pr.

Katris Gonis, Theofania. An Icon for Christmas: Sophia's Gift: an Icon Christmas Story to Color. Deshamais, Margo, illus. 2005. (ENG.). 24p. (J). (gr. k-3). pap. 5.95 (978-1-880971-94-9(1)) Light & Life Publishing Co.

Katz, Alan. Where Did They Hide My Presents? Silly Dilly Christmas Songs. Catrow, David, illus. 2008. (ENG.). 32p. (J). (gr. -1-3). 6.99 (978-1-4169-6830-6(X), McElderry, Margaret K. Bks.) McElderry, Margaret K. Bks.

Katz, Karen. Counting Christmas. Katz, Karen, illus. 2007. (Classic Board Bks.). (ENG., Illus.). 32p. (J). (gr. -1-1). bds. 7.99 (978-1-4169-3624-4(6), Little Simon) Little Simon.

—Counting Christmas. Katz, Karen, illus. 2003. (ENG., Illus.). 32p. (J). (gr. -1-1). 16.99 (978-0-689-84925-1(7), McElderry, Margaret K. Bks.) McElderry, Margaret K. Bks.

—Where Is Baby's Christmas Present? Katz, Karen, illus. 2009. (ENG., Illus.). 14p. (J). (gr. -1 — 1). bds. 7.99 (978-1-4169-7145-0(9), Little Simon) Little Simon.

Keane, Michael. The Night Santa Got Lost: How NORAD Saved Christmas. Garland, Michael, illus. (ENG.). 28p. (J). (gr. -1). 2012. 14.95 (978-1-59698-810-1(X), Little Patriot Pr.) 2015. 16.99 (978-1-62157-398-2(2), Regnery Kids) Regnery Publishing, Inc., An Eagle Publishing Co.

Kelly, L. Meme's Christmas Stories. 2005. pap. 16.95 (978-1-4241-0026-2(7)) America Star Bks.

Kelso, Mary Jean. One Family's Christmas. Snider, K. C., illus. 24p. 2012. 19.95 (978-1-61633-308-9(1)) 2008. pap. 10.95 (978-1-935137-05-4(0)) Guardian Angel Publishing, Inc.

Kennedy, Bryan. Charlie's Favorite Christmas. 2012. 26p. pap. 5.95 (978-0-9885358-0-0(7)) Bryan-Kennedy Entertainment, LLC.

Kerr, Judith. Mog's Christmas. unabr. ed. 2005. (ENG., Illus.). 32p. (J). pap. 14.00 incl. audio compact disk *(978-0-00-719366-0(1))* HarperCollins Pubs.

Kibblesmith, Daniel & Quach, A. P. Santa's Husband. 2017. 32p. 16.99 ***(978-0-06-274874-4(2)***, Collins Design) HarperCollins Pubs.

Kidd, Paul T. Father Christmas Adventures: Unexpected Tales of Christmas Magic. 2012. (ENG.). 92p. pap. *(978-1-901864-12-0(X))* Cheshire Henbury.

Kilgore, Lee. The Riddle of the Rustled Reindeer: A Christmas Mystery. 2009. 50p. pap. 16.95 *(978-1-61546-863-8(3))* America Star Bks.

Killen, Nicola. The Little Reindeer. Killen, Nicola, illus. 2017. (ENG., Illus.). 32p. (J). (gr. -1-3). 15.99 *(978-1-4814-8686-6(1)*, Simon & Schuster/Paula Wiseman Bks.) Simon & Schuster/Paula Wiseman Bks.

Kilpatrick, Leanne. One Night on Earth: The Story of Christmas. 2013. 28p. pap. *(978-0-906672-82-2(1))* Oleander Pr., The.

Kim, Cecil. Little Moon's Christmas: Imagination - Objects. Cowley, Joy, ed. Horácek, Petr, illus. 2015. (Step up - Creative Thinking Ser.). (ENG.). 32p. (gr. -1-2). 7.99 *(978-1-925246-63-6(9))*; 26.65 *(978-1-925246-11-7(6))*; 26.65 *(978-1-925246-37-7(X))* ChoiceMaker Pty. Ltd., The AUS. (Big and SMALL). Dist: Lerner Publishing Group.

—Little Moon's Christmas: Imagination - Objects. Cowley, Joy, ed. Horácek, Petr, illus. 2015. (Step up - Creative Thinking Ser.). (ENG.). 32p. (gr. -1-2). 26.65 *(978-1-925186-39-0(3))* Lerner Publishing Group.

Kimmel, Elizabeth Cody. My Penguin Osbert. Lewis, H. B., illus. (ENG.). 40p. (J). (gr. -1-3). 2011. pap. 6.99 *(978-0-7636-5730-7(1))* 2008. 7.99 *(978-0-7636-3692-0(4))* 2004. 16.99 *(978-0-7636-1699-1(0))* Candlewick Pr.

King, Emily. Clopper & the Night Travelers. Olson, Ed, illus. 2007. 32p. (J). (gr. -1-3). 10.99 *(978-0-8254-3066-4(6))* Kregel Pubns.

—Clopper the Christmas Donkey, 1 vol. Olson, Ed, illus. 2003. 32p. (J). 12.99 *(978-0-8254-3069-5(0))* Kregel Pubns.

Kinney, Jeff. The Third Wheel. 2012. (ENG.). (J). (gr. 3-7). pap. 8.49 *(978-1-4197-0729-2(9))* Abrams, Inc.

Kirby, Susan E. A No-Fuss Christmas. 2010. (J). *(978-1-60682-059-9(1))* BJU Pr.

Kirk, David. Nova's Christmas Creation. 2006. (Nova the Robot Ser.). 32p. (J). 12.99 *(978-0-448-43994-5(8))* Penguin Publishing Group.

Kirk, Janice. The Christmas Redwood. Kirk, Janice, illus. 2007. (Illus.). 56p. per. 18.95 *(978-1-60290-147-6(3))* OakTara Publishing Group LLC.

Kirkle, Diane Luise. Rachel Serves a Stew. Batson, Susann, illus. 2009. 28p. pap. 10.95 *(978-1-935137-59-7(X))* Guardian Angel Publishing, Inc.

Kladstrup, Kristin. The Gingerbread Pirates. Tavares, Matt, illus. (ENG.). 32p. (J). (gr. -1-3). 2009. 16.99 *(978-0-7636-3223-6(6))* 2012. 9.99 *(978-0-7636-6233-2(X))* Candlewick Pr.

Kleinberg, Naomi. Elmo's Christmas Snowman (Sesame Street) Brannon, Tom, illus. 2013. (ENG.). 12p. (J). (— 1). bds. 6.99 *(978-0-449-81257-0(X)*, Random Hse. Bks. for Young Readers) Random Hse. Children's Bks.

—Elmo's Countdown to Christmas (Sesame Street) Brannon, Tom, illus. 2016. (Lift-The-Flap Ser.). (ENG.). 12p. (J). (-k). bds. 6.99 *(978-0-399-55213-7(8)*, Random Hse. Bks. for Young Readers) Random Hse. Children's Bks.

—Have Yourself a Furry Little Christmas. Womble, Louis, illus. 2007. (ENG.). 12p. (J). (gr. k — 1). bds. 4.99 *(978-0-375-84133-0(4)*, Random Hse. Bks. for Young Readers) Random Hse. Children's Bks.

Klimo, Kate. Dragon Keepers #6: the Dragon at the North Pole. Shroades, John, illus. (Dragon Keepers Ser.). (ENG.). 176p. (J). (gr. 3-7). 2014. 6.99 *(978-0-375-87117-7(9)*, Yearling) 2013. 15.99 *(978-0-375-87066-8(0)*, Random Hse. Bks. for Young Readers) Random Hse. Children's Bks.

Klise, Kate. Shall I Knit You a Hat? A Christmas Yarn. Klise, M. Sarah, illus. 2007. (ENG.). 32p. (J). (gr. -1-2). per. 8.99 *(978-0-312-37139-5(X)*, 9780312371395) Square Fish.

Knapman, Timothy. A Very Pirate Christmas. Ayto, Russell, illus. 2015. (ENG.). 32p. (J). (gr. -1-k). pap. 11.99 *(978-1-4052-6504-1(3))* Egmont Bks., Ltd. GBR. Dist: Independent Pubs. Group.

Knecht, Eileen. Christine's Christmas Crib. 2009. 40p. pap. 18.49 *(978-1-4389-2265-2(5))* AuthorHouse.

Kneen, Maggie. The Christmas Surprise. Kneen, Maggie, illus. 2006. (Illus.). 18p. (J). (gr. k-4). reprint ed. 16.00 *(978-0-7567-9837-6(X))* DIANE Publishing Co.

—The First Christmas: An Angel Came to Nazareth. 2010. (ENG., Illus.). 24p. (J). (gr. -1-1). 9.99 *(978-0-8118-7662-9(4))* Chronicle Bks. LLC.

Knight, Hilary. The Night Before Christmas. 2004. (J). 15.89 *(978-0-06-000995-3(0))*; 14.99 *(978-0-06-000994-6(2))* HarperCollins Pubs.

Knights, Harry B. Angel's Star. 2006. (J). lib. bdg. 20.00 *(978-0-9632248-8-0(3))* Synergetic Pubns., Inc.

—Luigi & the Lost Wish, 1 vol. Calico World Entertainment Staff, illus. 2003. (Nicholas Stories Ser.: 4). (ENG.). 56p. (J). (gr. k-3). 16.95 *(978-1-58980-162-2(8))* Pelican Publishing Co., Inc.

—The Maiden Voyage of Kris Kringle, 1 vol. Calico World Entertainment Staff, illus. 2003. (Nicholas Stories Ser.: 3). (ENG.). 56p. (J). (gr. k-3). 16.95 *(978-1-58980-161-5(X))* Pelican Publishing Co., Inc.

Knott, Joan. Merry Christmas, Marushka! Fronliche Weihnachten, Marie! Knott, Marie, ed. 2006. (J). 7.95 *(978-0-9779895-1-5(8))* Knott, Joan.

Knowlen, Maralee Burdick. Ian's Christmas Tree. 2012. 48p. pap. 24.95 *(978-1-4626-8932-3(9))* America Star Bks.

Koch, Theresa F. The Gift of Laughter. 2007. 16p. per. 24.95 *(978-1-4241-8343-2(X))* America Star Bks.

Konecny, Linda. Dave's First Christmas. 2011. 26p. pap. 9.99 *(978-1-61379-817-1(2))* Salem Author Services.

Koontz, Dean. Robot Santa: The Further Adventures of Santa's Twin. Parks, Phil, illus. 2004. (Santa's Twin Ser.: Bk. 2). 72p. (J). 20.89 *(978-0-06-050944-6(9))* HarperCollins Pubs.

—Santa's Twin. Parks, Phil, illus. 2004. (Santa's Twin Ser.: Bk. 1). (ENG.). 64p. pap. 12.95 *(978-0-06-057223-5(X)*, William Morrow Paperbacks) HarperCollins Pubs.

Korman, Justine. The Poky Little Puppy's First Christmas. Korman, Justine, illus. 2014. (Little Golden Board Book Ser.). (ENG., Illus.). 26p. (J). (-k). bds. 7.99 *(978-0-385-38473-5(4)*, Golden Bks.) Random Hse. Children's Bks.

Kowalik, Susie. Lumen: The Star That Shone for the Visit of the Composer-Conductor. 2013. 24p. pap. 10.99 *(978-1-4624-0539-8(8)*, Inspiring Voices) Author Solutions, Inc.

Krackow, Eric T. Have an Abominably Good Day, 1 vol. 2010. (ENG., Illus.). 64p. (J). 16.99 *(978-0-7643-3496-2(4)*, 9780764334962) Schiffer Publishing, Ltd.

Krackow, Eric T. & Krackow, Krackow. Bill the Snowman, 1 vol. 2009. (ENG., Illus.). 64p. (J). 16.99 *(978-0-7643-3219-7(8)*, 9780764332197) Schiffer Publishing, Ltd.

Krenina, Katya, illus. The Spider's Gift: A Ukrainian Christmas Story. 2005. (ENG.). 32p. (J). (gr. -1-3). 16.95 *(978-0-8234-1743-8(3))* Holiday Hse., Inc.

Krensky, Stephen. How Santa Lost His Job. Schindler, S. D., illus. 2004. (ENG.). 32p. (J). (gr. -1-3). 7.99 *(978-0-689-87147-4(3)*, Simon & Schuster Bks. For Young Readers) Simon & Schuster Bks. For Young Readers.

—The Last Christmas Tree. Campion, Pascal, illus. 2014. (ENG.). 32p. (J). (gr. -1-k). 16.99 *(978-0-8037-3757-0(2)*, Dial Bks) Penguin Young Readers Group.

Kroll, Steven. The Biggest Christmas Tree Ever. Bassett, Jeni, illus. 2009. (ENG.). 32p. (J). (gr. -1-3). pap. 4.99 *(978-0-545-12119-4(1)*, Cartwheel Bks.) Scholastic, Inc.

—Pooch on the Loose: A Christmas Adventure, 0 vols. Garland, Michael, illus. 2013. (ENG.). 40p. (J). (gr. -1-3). pap. 9.99 *(978-0-7614-5443-4(8)*, 9780761454434, Two Lions) Amazon Publishing.

Kroll, Steven & Droll. Pooch on the Loose: A Christmas Adventure, 1 vol. Garland, Michael, illus. 2005. (ENG.). 32p. (J). (gr. -1-3). 14.95 *(978-0-7614-5239-3(7))* Marshall Cavendish Corp.

Krueger, Diane. Blessly's Carrotnog Christmas Book & Coloring Book. Krueger, Diane & Westenbroek, Ken, illus. 2004. 14.99 *(978-0-9763695-1-6(6))* Hope Harvest Publishing.

Krulik, Nancy. Holly's Jolly Christmas. John and Wendy Staff, illus. 2009. (Katie Kazoo, Switcheroo Ser.: No. 8). (ENG.). 160p. (J). (gr. 2-4). pap. 4.99 *(978-0-448-45218-0(9)*, Grosset & Dunlap) Penguin Young Readers Group.

—The Twelve Burps of Christmas. Blecha, Aaron, illus. 2012. (George Brown, Class Clown Ser.: No. 1). (ENG.). 192p. (J). (gr. 2-4). pap. 5.99 *(978-0-448-45680-5(X)*, Grosset & Dunlap) Penguin Young Readers Group.

—The Twelve Burps of Christmas. 2012. (George Brown, Class Clown Ser.: No. 1). lib. bdg. 16.00 *(978-0-606-26652-9(6)*, Turtleback) Turtleback Bks.

Kuc, Jessica. Mawby the Christmas Pony. 2011. 36p. pap. 15.14 *(978-1-4634-2521-0(X))* AuthorHouse.

Kuhn, Douglas Wolcik. Animals' Christmas Gift. Cimino, Nicole C., ed. 2011. 24p. pap. 24.95 *(978-1-4560-5244-7(6))* America Star Bks.

Kulka, Joe. Christmas Coal Man. Kulka, Joe, illus. 2015. (ENG., Illus.). 32p. (J). (gr. k-3). lib. bdg. 17.99 *(978-1-4677-1607-9(3)*, Carolrhoda Bks.) Lerner Publishing Group.

—The Christmas Coal Man. Kulka, Joe, illus. 2015. (ENG., Illus.). 32p. (J). (gr. k-3). 17.99 *(978-1-4677-8808-3(2)*, Carolrhoda Bks.) Lerner Publishing Group.

Kurtz, John. Claus Kids Christmas Coloring Book. 2011. (Dover Holiday Coloring Book Ser.). (ENG.). 32p. (J). (gr. k-5). pap. 3.99 *(978-0-486-48292-7(8))* Dover Pubns., Inc.

—Claus Kids Super Sticker Book: A Year-Round Christmas Celebration. 2011. (Dover Sticker Bks.). (ENG., Illus.). 6p. (J). (gr. k-5). 7.99 *(978-0-486-48295-8(2))* Dover Pubns., Inc.

Kurtz, Pauline. Das Deutsche Haus. 2013. 36p. pap. 13.95 *(978-1-4908-0732-4(2)*, WestBow Pr.) Author Solutions, Inc.

Kvasnosky, Laura McGee. Zelda & Ivy One Christmas. Kvasnosky, Laura McGee, illus. 2013. (Candlewick Sparks Ser.). (ENG., Illus.). 40p. (J). (gr. k-4). pap. 3.99 *(978-0-7636-6865-5(6))* Candlewick Pr.

Kyriakou, Marie. Mike the Little Bean: Christmas with Mike. 2012. (Illus.). 32p. pap. 22.88 *(978-1-4772-4646-7(0))* AuthorHouse.

L & M Trustam. Turn Left for Christmas. 2011. (Illus.). 28p. pap. 12.19 *(978-1-4567-7084-6(5))* AuthorHouse.

La Porte, Mary Ellen. The Almost Christmas Story. 2011. 44p. pap. 18.99 *(978-1-4520-9946-0(4))* AuthorHouse.

Ladybird Christmas Time. 2016. (ENG., Illus.). 72p. (J). (gr. 2-4). 16.99 *(978-0-241-26302-0(6))* Penguin Bks., Ltd. GBR. Dist: Independent Pubs. Group.

Lagerlöf, Selma. The Holy Night. Wikland, Ilon, illus. 2004. 40p. (J). 17.00 *(978-0-86315-467-6(0))* Floris Bks. GBR. Dist: SteinerBooks, Inc.

LaMaster, Melissa. Appaloosa Tales with a Christmas Spirit. 2006. 48p. pap. 16.95 *(978-1-4241-3153-2(7))* PublishAmerica, Inc.

Lamerton, Todd. A Tale from Flurryville: The Berg's Big Surprise. 2003. 28p. 7.61 *(978-0-7575-0655-0(0))* Kendall Hunt Publishing Co.

Lamson, Deborah Ann. The Nativity Lighting. 2008. (Illus.). 36p. pap. 15.95 *(978-1-4343-9521-4(9))* AuthorHouse.

Landon, Angela. The Innkeeper's Wife: A Christmas Story. 2012. 48p. pap. 19.99 *(978-1-4772-9248-8(9))* AuthorHouse.

Lane, Queen, illus. & creator. It's Christmas Time (Babytown Storybook) Lane, Queen, creator. 2005. (BABYTOWN Ser.: Bk. 4). 36p. (J). spiral bd. 15.00 *(978-0-9772738-1-2(4))* Quebla.

Lange, Willem. Favor Johnson: A Christmas Story. Dodson, Bert, illus. 2009. (ENG.). 32p. (J). (gr. 1-3). 16.95 *(978-1-59373-082-6(9))* Bunker Hill Publishing, Inc.

Langen, Annette. Felix's Christmas Around the World. Droop, Constanza, illus. 2003. (ENG.). 40p. (J). 14.99 *(978-1-59384-036-5(5))* Parklane Publishing.

Lankford, Mary D. Christmas USA. Dugan, Karen, illus. 2006. 48p. (J). (gr. 3-7). 16.99 *(978-0-688-15012-9(8)*, Collins) HarperCollins Pubs.

Lansley, Oliver. Holly & Ivan's Christmas Adventure. 2012. (ENG., Illus.). 96p. (J). (gr. k-5). pap. 16.95 *(978-1-84943-136-1(1))* Oberon Bks., Ltd. GBR. Dist: Consortium Bk. Sales & Distribution.

Larson, Michael J. Nature's Christmas Story. 2010. 28p. pap. 10.95 *(978-1-4497-0569-5(3)*, WestBow Pr.) Author Solutions, Inc.

L.A.S., Alex. Magnificent Sir Johnny & Santa Claus. 2011. 36p. pap. 24.95 *(978-1-4626-3401-9(X))* America Star Bks.

Laughing Elephant Staff, creator. Cats' Christmas ABC. 2012. (Christmas Ser.). (Illus.). 54p. pap. 4.95 *(978-1-59583-393-8(5)*, 9781595833938) Laughing Elephant.

Laura Lee Hope. Bunny Brown & His Sister Sue at Christmas Tree Cove. 2007. 176p. per. 12.95 *(978-1-4218-3987-5(3)*, 1st World Library - Literary Society) 1st World Publishing, Inc.

Lavonne, Victoria. Twas the Night at the Capitol: A Narrative Featuring the First African American Family. 2012. 28p. pap. 24.95 *(978-1-4626-9799-1(2))* America Star Bks.

Lawless, Mary Ann. The Proud Christmas Tree. McCool, Arlene, illus. 2006. (J). 12.95 *(978-0-9772795-0-0(2))* Tuesday's Child.

Lawrence, Gregory. A Christmas Surprise, 1 vol. 2010. 24p. 24.95 *(978-1-4512-1457-4(X))* PublishAmerica, Inc.

Lê, Christine & Lê, Michel, illus. The Hawai'i Snowman. 2008. (J). 14.95 *(978-1-56647-879-3(0))* Mutual Publishing LLC.

Leake, Trish. The Christmas Dream. 2012. 24p. pap. 12.95 *(978-0-9882034-7-1(2))* Barringer Publishing.

Ledray, Michael. Fifi Loves You! 2010. 40p. pap. 21.00 *(978-0-557-27099-6(5))* Lulu Pr., Inc.

Lee, Quinlan B. A Christmas Tree for Me: A New Holiday Tradition for Your Family. Basaluzzo, Constanza, illus. 2013. (ENG.). 32p. (J). (gr. -1-2). 14.99 *(978-0-7944-3018-4(X))* Reader's Digest Assn., Inc., The.

Lee, Stan. Stan Lee's Superhero Christmas. Jessell, Tim, illus. 2nd ed. 2016. (ENG.). (J). (gr. k-2). 27.95 ***(978-1-59687-526-5(7)***, ipicturebooks) ibooks, Inc.

Lee, Stan. Superhero Christmas. Jessell, Tim, illus. 2004. 32p. (J). (gr. -1-2). 16.89 *(978-0-06-056560-2(8))* HarperCollins Pubs.

Leeds, Robert X. Christmas Tails. Stetz, Ken, illus. rev. ed. 2005. 55p. (J). 16.95 *(978-0-9674025-7-4(3))* EPIC Publishing Co.

Leighton, Maxinne Rhea. An Ellis Island Christmas. Nolan, Dennis, illus. 2005. (ENG.). 32p. (J). (gr. k-3). pap. 6.99 *(978-0-14-240506-2(X)*, Puffin Books) Penguin Young Readers Group.

Leighton, Noreen. Mr Tilly & the Christmas Lights. Wilson, Lorna, illus. 2013. 38p. pap. *(978-0-9573315-7-0(6))* Tatterdemalion Blue.

Lenton, Steven. Five Christmas Penguins. 2016. (ENG., Illus.). 12p. (J). (gr. -1). bds. 9.99 *(978-1-62686-822-9(0)*, Silver Dolphin Bks.) Readerlink Distribution Services, LLC.

Lepage, Michaele. A Year at Santa's Workshop. 2009. 32p. pap. 14.55 *(978-1-4343-7989-4(2))* AuthorHouse.

LePage, Michaele L. & Lovass-Nagy, Nicole. A Year at the North Pole. 2009. 31p. 16.95 *(978-0-557-06430-4(9))* Lulu Pr., Inc.

Lespérance, Colette. Baby's First Christmas. 2009. 16p. pap. 12.99 *(978-1-4490-2169-6(7))* AuthorHouse.

Letter to Santa. 2003. (Traditional Christmas Stories Ser.). 32p. (J). 4.98 *(978-0-7525-8845-2(1))* Parragon, Inc.

Lewandowski, James E. The Christmas Box: An Eerie Tale of the Perfect Gift. 2009. (ENG.). 132p. pap. 10.95 *(978-0-9821084-3-7(5))* Prairie Hills Publishing.

Lewis, Anne G. A Perfect Tree for Christmas. Stahlberg, Carina, illus. 2013. (ENG.). (J). pap. 7.99 *(978-1-935666-55-4(X))* Nodin Pr.

Lewis, Anne Margaret. The Runaway Santa. Zenz, Aaron, illus. 2015. (ENG.). 40p. (J). (gr. -1-k). 15.99 *(978-1-63450-589-5(1)*, Sky Pony Pr.) Skyhorse Publishing Co., Inc.

Lewis, Beverly & Querin, Pamela. Annika's Secret Wish. 2006. (Illus.). 32p. (J). (gr. k-4). reprint ed. 15.00 *(978-0-7567-9876-5(0))* DIANE Publishing Co.

Lewis, J. Patrick, et al. First Dog's White House Christmas. Bowers, Tim, illus. 2010. (ENG.). 32p. (J). (gr. 1-4). 15.95 *(978-1-58536-503-6(3)*, 202197) Sleeping Bear Pr.

Lewis, Regina N. The Smallest Toy Store, A Christmas Story. Moore, Phyllis M., illus. 2004. 44p. (J). per. 12.95 *(978-0-9672585-8-4(8))* CyPress Pubns.

Lichtwardt, Rita, illus. Barbie - A Perfect Christmas. 2011. (Book & Jewelry Ser.). (ENG.). 24p. (J). (gr. -1-1). 10.99 *(978-0-7944-2319-3(1)*, Reader's Digest Children's Bks.) Studio Fun International.

Light, Steve. The Christmas Giant. Light, Steve, illus. 2010. (ENG., Illus.). 32p. (J). (gr. -1-2). 15.99 *(978-0-7636-4692-9(X))* Candlewick Pr.

Lincoln, Dallas Ford. The Sawmill Sant. 2011. 36p. pap. 16.95 *(978-1-4626-4335-6(3))* America Star Bks.

Lindman. Flicka, Ricka, Dicka & Their New Skates: Updated Edition with Paperdolls. Lindman, illus. 2011. (Flicka, Ricka, Dicka Ser.). (ENG., Illus.). 32p. (J). (gr. k-3). 9.99 *(978-0-8075-2496-1(4))* Whitman, Albert & Co.

Lindman, Maj. Flicka, Ricka, Dicka & Their New Skates. Lindman, Maj, illus. 2011. (ENG., Illus.). 32p. (J). (gr. k-3). 9.99 *(978-0-8075-2491-6(3))* Whitman, Albert & Co.

Lionheart, Amelia. The Dolphin Heptad. 2009. 200p. (gr. 4-6). pap. 14.95 *(978-1-4401-8028-6(8))* iUniverse, Inc.

Lisa Catanzarite. What the World Is Like to Bea Moore: Dear Santa. 2009. 60p. pap. 16.43 *(978-1-4269-2115-5(2))* Trafford Publishing.

Little Bee Books Staff. Our Christmas Tree: A Touch-and-Feel Book. 2015. (ENG., Illus.). 12p. (J). (gr. -1-1). 6.99 *(978-1-4998-0145-3(9))* Little Bee Books Inc.

Little Fish Christmas Merchandiser. (J). 128.16 *(978-0-8307-2909-8(7)*, Gospel Light) Gospel Light Pubns.

Little Miss Muffet: 6 Small Books. (gr. k-2). 23.00 *(978-0-7635-8503-7(3))* Rigby Education.

Little, Paul D. The Christmas Chips. 2009. 44p. pap. 15.50 *(978-1-60860-578-1(7)*, Eloquent Bks.) Strategic Book Publishing & Rights Agency (SBPRA).

The Littlest Christmas Tree. 2005. 45.00 *(978-0-916773-85-4(X))* Book Peddlers.

Litton, Jonathan. Planet Pop-Up: Bear's Merry Christmas. Anderson, Nicola, illus. 2015. (Planet Pop-Up Ser.). (ENG.). 12p. (J). (gr. -1). 12.95 *(978-1-62686-486-3(1)*, Silver Dolphin Bks.) Readerlink Distribution Services, LLC.

—Surprise: A Book of Christmas Shapes. Galloway, Fhiona, illus. 2014. (ENG.). 16p. (J). (gr. -1-k). bds. 7.99 *(978-1-58925-567-8(4))* Tiger Tales.

Litwin, Eric. Pete the Cat Saves Christmas. Dean, James, illus. (Pete the Cat Ser.). 40p. (J). (gr. -1-3). 2014. (ENG.). 17.99 *(978-0-06-211062-6(4))* 2012. lib. bdg. 18.89 *(978-0-06-211063-3(2))* HarperCollins Pubs.

Lizana, Robert V. Two Weeks Before Christmas. 2012. 24p. pap. 17.99 *(978-1-4772-7164-3(3))* AuthorHouse.

Locurto, Ian N. The Christmas Penny. 2010. 20p. 11.99 *(978-1-4490-7100-4(7))* AuthorHouse.

Lombardi, Elizabeth L. Jonathan's Journey. 2012. (ENG.). (J). *(978-1-62148-014-3(3))* SteinerBooks, Inc.

Lomumo, Inez Regina. Love at Christmas I, II, & III. 2006. 9.00 *(978-0-8059-8822-2(X))* Dorrance Publishing Co., Inc.

Londa And Pop-Pop. On Christmas Day. Harrell, Symear, illus. 2011. 16p. pap. 24.95 *(978-1-4560-7078-6(9))* America Star Bks.

Long, Loren. The Drummer Boy. Long, Loren, illus. 2008. (ENG., Illus.). 40p. (J). (gr. -1-k). 18.99 *(978-0-399-25174-0(X)*, Philomel Bks.) Penguin Young Readers Group.

—Drummer Boy. Long, Loren, illus. 2012. (ENG., Illus.). 40p. (J). (gr. -1-k). mass mkt. 7.99 *(978-0-14-242341-7(6)*, Puffin Books) Penguin Young Readers Group.

—An Otis Christmas. Long, Loren, illus. 2013. (Otis Ser.: Bk. 4). (ENG., Illus.). 40p. (J). (gr. -1-2). 17.99 *(978-0-399-16395-1(6)*, Philomel Bks.) Penguin Publishing Group.

—An Otis Christmas. Long, Loren, illus. 2016. (Otis Ser.). (ENG., Illus.). 38p. (J). (gr. -1-2). bds. 8.99 *(978-0-399-54811-6(4)*, Philomel Bks.) Penguin Young Readers Group.

Long, Mary Evelyn Curton. The First Christmas Gift. 2012. 16p. (-18). pap. 15.99 *(978-1-4772-8836-8(8))* AuthorHouse.

Long, Melinda. The Twelve Days of Christmas in South Carolina. Mai-Wyss, Tatjana, illus. 2010. (Twelve Days of Christmas in America Ser.). (ENG.). 40p. (J). (gr. k). 12.95 *(978-1-4027-6672-5(6))* Sterling Publishing Co., Inc.

Longacre, Tracy Ardella. A Very Merry Ferret Christmas. 2008. 76p. pap. 19.95 *(978-1-60703-836-8(6))* America Star Bks.

Lord, Grant. Tales of Rex Riley Aged 10 & a Bit, It's A Dog's Life. 2009. 141p. pap. 12.95 *(978-1-4092-4782-1(1))* Lulu Pr., Inc.

Love, Maryann Cusimano. You Are My Miracle. Ichikawa, Satomi, illus. (ENG.). (J). (gr. -1 — 1). 2012. 28p. bds. 6.99 *(978-0-399-25791-9(8))* 2005. 32p. 16.99 *(978-0-399-24037-9(3))* Penguin Young Readers Group. (Philomel Bks.).

Lowell, Susan. A Very Hairy Christmas. Harris, Jim, illus. 2012. (J). *(978-1-933855-80-6(0))* Rio Nuevo Pubs.

Loyd, Mark. Big Ben: A Little Known Story. Loyd, Mark, illus. 2005. (Illus.). (J). *(978-0-9773317-1-0(7))* Too Fun Publshing.

Lucado, Max. Itsy Bitsy Christmas: You're Never Too Little for His Love, 1 vol. 2016. (ENG., Illus.). 26p. (J). bds. 8.99 *(978-0-7180-8887-3(5))* Nelson, Thomas Inc.

Lunn, Janet. One Hundred Shining Candles. Grater, Lindsay, illus. 2008. (ENG.). 32p. (J). (gr. k-3). 17.95 *(978-0-88776-889-7(X)*, Tundra Bks.) Tundra Bks. CAN. Dist: Penguin Random Hse. LLC.

Luton, Mildred. Christmas Time in the Mountains. Peattie, Gary, illus. 2003. 44p. (Orig.). (gr. 1-6). pap. 6.95 *(978-0-87516-434-2(X))* DeVorss & Co.

Lutz, Nancie Anne. Patsy & Freckles Make Christmas Cookies. Lutz, Nancie Anne, illus. 2005. (Illus.). 25p. (J). *(978-0-9760064-1-1(3))* Dollworks.

Luzio-Poitras, Linda Di. Kitchi's Christmas Wish. 2009. 32p. pap. 12.99 *(978-1-4490-2121-4(2))* AuthorHouse.

Lynch, Diane M., ed. Celebrate the Season! Twelve Short Stories for Advent & Christmas. 2010. (J). (gr. 3-6). pap. 7.95 *(978-0-8198-1585-9(3))* Pauline Bks. & Media.

Maccarone, Grace. The Nutcracker. Chauffrey, Célia, illus. 2016. (ENG.). 40p. (J). (gr. -1-3). 17.99 *(978-1-4998-0281-8(1))* Little Bee Books Inc.

MacDonald, Betty Bard. Nancy & Plum. GrandPré, Mary, illus. 2011. (ENG.). 240p. (J). (gr. 3-7). 7.99 *(978-0-375-85986-1(1)*, Yearling) Random Hse. Children's Bks.

MacGregor, Doug. The Incredible Tongue Twister That Swallowed My Sister: Another Santa Story by Doug MacGregor. MacGregor, Doug, illus. ltd. ed. 2006. (Illus.). 40p. (J). per. *(978-0-9654843-5-0(1))* MacGregor, Doug.

MacGuire, Maxine. Maddie & the Naughty Elf: Santa Learns a Lesson, 1 vol. 2010. 36p. 24.95 *(978-1-4489-8250-9(2))* PublishAmerica, Inc.

Mackall, Dandi Daley. The Legend of St. Nicholas: A Story of Christmas Giving, 1 vol. Cowdrey, Richard, illus. 2014. (ENG.). 32p. (J). 16.99 *(978-0-310-73115-3(1))* Zonderkidz.

—The Legend of the Christmas Cookie, 1 vol. Cowdrey, Richard, illus. 2015. (ENG.). 32p. (J). 16.99 *(978-0-310-74767-3(8))* Zonderkidz.

—Natalie Really Very Much Wants to Be a Star, 1 vol. Blakeslee, Lys, illus. 2009. (That's Nat! Ser.). (ENG.). 96p. (J). (gr. 1-4). pap. 4.99 *(978-0-310-71567-2(9))* Zonderkidz.

—One Small Donkey for Little Ones, 1 vol. 2016. (ENG., Illus.). 20p. (J). bds. 8.99 *(978-0-7180-8247-5(8))* Nelson, Thomas Inc.

Mackall, Dandi Daley & Kingsbury, Karen. The Gift of the Christmas Cookie: Sharing the True Meaning of Jesus' Birth, 1 vol. Chabrian, Deborah L., illus. 2008. (ENG.). 32p. (J). (gr. -1-2). 16.99 *(978-0-310-71328-9(5))* Zonderkidz.

MacKey, Garry. Joey: The Christmas Kangaroo. 2012. 24p. pap. 9.95 *(978-1-4575-1592-7(X))* Dog Ear Publishing, LLC.

MacLachlan, Patricia. The True Gift. Floca, Brian, illus. 2013. (ENG.). 112p. (J). (gr. 2-6). pap. 6.99 *(978-1-4424-8858-8(1)*, Atheneum Bks. for Young Readers) Simon & Schuster Children's Publishing.

—The True Gift: A Christmas Story. Floca, Brian, illus. 2009. (ENG.). 96p. (J). (gr. 2-6). 14.99 *(978-1-4169-9081-9(X)*, Atheneum Bks. for Young Readers) Simon & Schuster Children's Publishing.

MacLennan, David. Santa's Stormy Christmas Eve. Parkinson, Cheryl, tr. Parkinson, Cheryl, illus. 2004. 32p. 7.95 *(978-0-9731960-0-9(9))* Full Satchel Pr. CAN. Dist: Wilson & Assocs.

C D

Macor, Jim. Frazier Fir, A Christmas Fable. Macor, Jim, illus. 2007. (Illus.). 32p. (J). 17.95 *(978-0-9785551-3-9(9))* Zuber Publishing.

Mad Libs Staff. Mr. Men Little Miss Christmas Mad Libs. 2014. (Mr. Men & Little Miss Ser.). (ENG.). 48p. (J). (gr. -1-2). 4.99 *(978-0-8431-8240-8(7),* Mad Libs) Penguin Young Readers Group.

Madaras, Diana. Kitty Humbug's Christmas Tail. Madaras, Diana & Nielsen, Ric, illus. 2009. 24p. 17.99 *(978-1-892344-56-4(4))* Palomino Publishing.

Maddock, Lisa. The Bridezilla Who Stole Christmas: A Teddy & Pip Story. 2009. 108p. pap. 9.95 *(978-1-60844-258-4(6))* Dog Ear Publishing, LLC.

Mader, C. Roger, illus. Stowaway in a Sleigh. 2016. (ENG.). 32p. (J). (gr. -1-3). 17.99 *(978-0-544-48174-9(7),* HMH Books For Young Readers) Houghton Mifflin Harcourt Publishing Co.

Maggie's Christmas Wish. l.t. ed. 2004. (Illus.). 69p. (J). per. 15.00 *(978-0-9764406-0-4(1))* James, JoAnn.

The Magic of Christmas: A Treasury of Holiday Stories. 2008. (Illus.). 117p. (J). *(978-1-4351-1073-1(0))* Barnes & Noble, Inc.

Magnusson, Sally. Horace & the Christmas Mystery. Stone, Norman, illus. 2015. (ENG.). 48p. (J). (gr. k). 14.99 ***(978-1-84502-791-9(4))*** Black and White Publishing Ltd. GBR. Dist: Independent Pubs. Group.

Magsamen, Sandra. Merry Christmas, Little One! 2010. (Padded Cloth Covers with Lift-The-Flaps Ser.). (ENG., Illus.). 10p. (J). (gr. -1-17). bds. 7.99 *(978-0-316-07003-4(3))* Little, Brown Bks. for Young Readers.

Maguire, Gregory. Matchless: An Illumination of Hans Christian Andersen's Classic the Little Match Girl. 2010. (ENG., Illus.). 112p. pap. 12.99 *(978-0-06-200482-6(4),* Harper Paperbacks) HarperCollins Pubs.

Maher, Liam. The Plumber & the Wishing Well. May, Gin, illus. 2012. 24p. (gr. k-3). 19.95 *(978-1-61633-269-3(7));* pap. 10.95 *(978-1-61633-268-6(9))* Guardian Angel Publishing, Inc.

Maiden, Cecil. The Molliwumps. Price, Christine, illus. 2004. 160p. 12.95 *(978-0-9714612-9-1(5))* Green Mansion Pr. LLC.

Major, Kevin. The House of Wooden Santas, 1 vol. Pratt, Ned, photos by. gif. ed. 2004. (ENG., Illus.). 96p. (J). 34.95 *(978-0-88995-249-2(3))* Red Deer Pr. CAN. Dist: Fitzhenry & Whiteside, Ltd.

Make Believe Ideas. Katie the Candy Cane Fairy Storybook. 2013. (ENG.). 32p. (J). 15.99 *(978-1-78235-526-7(X))* Make Believe Ideas GBR. Dist: Nelson, Thomas Inc.

Mallonee, Dennis & Wilson, Shawn V. The Adventures of Chrissie Claus: Volume 1, Vol. 1. 2009. 116p. (Orig.). pap. 21.50 *(978-0-929729-01-5(3))* Heroic Publishing, Inc.

Malone, Beni & White, Marian Frances. The Sights Before Christmas, 1 vol. Erdelji, Darka, illus. 2007. (ENG.). 32p. (J). (gr. -1-2). per. 8.95 *(978-1-894294-94-2(7),* Tuckamore Bks) Creative Bk. Publishing CAN. Dist: Orca Bk. Pubs. USA.

Man-Kong, Mary. Barbie in a Christmas Carol. Random House Editors, illus. 2010. (Pictureback(R) Ser.). (ENG.). 24p. (J). (gr. -1-2). pap. 3.99 *(978-0-375-86482-7(2),* Random Hse. Bks. for Young Readers) Random Hse. Children's Bks.

—Christmas Parade! (Frosty the Snowman) Golden Books, illus. 2015. (Big Coloring Book Ser.). (ENG.). 48p. (J). (gr. -1-2). pap. 6.99 *(978-0-553-52273-0(6),* Golden Bks.) Random Hse. Children's Bks.

—Holiday Style (Barbie) 2014. (Big Coloring Book Ser.). (ENG.). 48p. (J). (gr. -1-2). pap. 6.99 *(978-0-385-38339-4(8),* Golden Bks.) Random Hse. Children's Bks.

Man-Kong, Mary & Tillworth, Mary. A Perfect Christmas (Barbie) Golden Books Staff, illus. 2011. (Pictureback(R) Ser.). (ENG.). 16p. (J). (gr. -1-2). pap. 3.99 *(978-0-375-87363-8(5),* Random Hse. Bks. for Young Readers) Random Hse. Children's Bks.

A Manatee Christmas. 2007. (Illus.). 32p. (J). lib. bdg. 15.99 *(978-0-9771059-7-7(0))* Thomas Expressions, LLC.

Mancil, Arlene. The Angel Explains Christmas Blessings. McKinnon, Joy, illus. 2008. 16p. pap. 24.95 *(978-1-60813-297-3(8))* America Star Bks.

Maner, Dee. Artie: The First Artificial Christmas Tree. 2016. (ENG.). 32p. (J). 19.95 *(978-1-942945-28-4(0),* 9781942945284) Bright Sky Pr.

Manzano, Sonia. Miracle on 133rd Street. Priceman, Marjorie, illus. 2015. (ENG.). 48p. (J). (gr. -1-3). 17.99 *(978-0-689-87887-9(7))* Simon & Schuster Children's Publishing.

Marchi, Mary V. The Web in the Halo: A Tale of a Spider Who Learns about Christmas. 2012. 32p. pap. 19.99 *(978-1-4685-6624-6(5))* AuthorHouse.

Marcos, Teri. Bethlehem's Gift. 2013. 24p. pap. 12.45 *(978-1-4908-0901-4(5),* WestBow Pr.) Author Solutions, Inc.

Marie, Barbara. Snowy & Felix Find Christmas. 2009. 24p. pap. 11.49 *(978-1-4389-7392-0(6))* AuthorHouse.

Marr, Andrew. Born in the Darkest Time of Year: Stories for the Season of the Christ Child. 2004. 180p. (J). pap. 13.95 *(978-0-595-32633-4(1))* iUniverse, Inc.

Marsh, Carole. The Legend of the Candy Cane. 2003. 12p. (J). (gr. k-4). pap. 2.95 *(978-0-635-02124-3(2))* Gallopade International.

—The Story of the Christmas Tree. 2003. 12p. (J). (gr. k-4). pap. 2.95 *(978-0-635-02150-2(1))* Gallopade International.

—The White House Christmas Mystery. (Real Kids, Real Places Ser.). (J). 2009. 146p. 18.99 *(978-0-635-06996-2(2),* Marsh, Carole Mysteries) 2003. 160p. (gr. 2-8). 14.95 *(978-0-635-01666-9(4))* 2003. 160p. (gr. 2-8). pap. 5.95 *(978-0-635-01664-5(8))* Gallopade International.

Marshall, Geraldine Ann. Spider's Gift: A Christmas Story. Sorge, Rebecca, illus. 2016. 40p. (J). pap. 14.95 *(978-0-8198-9058-0(8))* Pauline Bks. & Media.

Marshall, Jane Garrett. The Christmas Tree That Cried. Tomasek, Dean, illus. 2013. 106p. pap. 24.99 *(978-0-9896247-0-1(6))* WRB Pub.

Marshall, Kate. Mokes, Mines & Mayhem. 2008. 120p. pap. 10.95 *(978-1-60693-357-2(4),* Eloquent Bks.) Strategic Book Publishing & Rights Agency (SBPRA).

Marsoli, Lisa Ann. Rudolph the Red-Nosed Reindeer Pop-Up Book. Finch, Keith Andrew, illus. 2014. (ENG.). 12p. (J). (gr. -1). 19.95 *(978-1-62686-197-8(8),* Silver Dolphin Bks.) Readerlink Distribution Services, LLC.

Martin, Ann M. 'Tis the Season. 2007. (Main Street Ser.). (Illus.). 195p. (J). (gr. 4-7). 14.65 *(978-0-7569-8327-7(4))* Perfection Learning Corp.

Martin, Ann M. & Godwin, Laura. The Doll People's Christmas. Helquist, Brett, illus. 2016. (ENG.). 48p. (J). (gr. -1-k). 17.99 *(978-1-4847-2339-5(2))* Hyperion Bks. for Children.

Martin, David. Christmas Tree. Sweet, Melissa, illus. 2015. (ENG.). 26p. (J). (gr. -1-2). 5.99 *(978-0-7636-7968-2(2))* Candlewick Pr.

Martin, David Lozell. Christmas Tree. Sweet, Melissa, illus. 2009. (ENG.). 26p. (J). (— 1). bds. 5.99 *(978-0-7636-3030-0(6))* Candlewick Pr.

Martin, Maria G. The Christmas Crown. Stratman, Kay, illus. 2010. 20p. pap. 10.95 *(978-1-60911-442-8(6),* Eloquent Bks.) Strategic Book Publishing & Rights Agency (SBPRA).

Martini, T. J. Christmas Lost & Found. Kiejna, Magdalenea, illus. 2017. (J). per. 15.99 *(978-0-9705018-7-5(0))* Wings, Inc.

Marvel Book Group Staff & Macri, Thomas. Happy Holidays! from the Avengers. Lim, Ron, illus. 2016. (ENG.). 24p. (J). (gr. 1-3). pap. 5.99 *(978-1-4847-8200-2(3),* Marvel Pr.) Disney Publishing Worldwide.

Mason, Tom & Danko, Dan. A Christmas Surprise. Shannon, David et al, illus. 2011. (Jon Scieszka's Trucktown Ser.). (ENG.). 12p. (J). (gr. -1-k). 7.99 *(978-1-4169-4193-4(2),* Simon & Schuster Bks. For Young Readers) Simon & Schuster Bks. For Young Readers.

Masse, Stephen V. The Taste of Snow. 2011. (ENG., Illus.). 216p. (J). 20.00 *(978-0-9799638-1-0(8))* Good Harbor Pr.

Masterson, Madeline Ann. Wonka's Christmas Story. 2015. (ENG.). 36p. (J). (gr. 2-3). mass mkt. 11.95 *(978-1-78612-086-1(0),* 470e8853-74bf-4cb8-9970-ad8b75618e44) Austin, Stan AUS. Dist: Bookmasters Distribution.

Matheron, Annaliese. Ninja Nan & Her Merry Men. 2013. 180p. pap. *(978-1-909411-22-7(1))* Mauve Square Publishing.

Matsuura, Richard & Matsuura, Ruth. Hawaiian Christmas Story. Chao, Linus, illus. (J). 8.95 *(978-1-887916-01-1(6))* Orchid Isle Publishing Co.

Matteson, George & Ursone, Adele. The Christmas Tugboat: How the Rockefeller Center Christmas Tree Came to New York City. Ransome, James E., illus. 2015. (ENG.). 48p. (J). (gr. -1-3). 6.99 *(978-0-544-55548-8(1),* HMH Books For Young Readers) Houghton Mifflin Harcourt Publishing Co.

Matthews, John and Caitlin. StoryWorld: Christmas Tales: Create-A-Story Kit. 2011. (Storyworld Ser.). (ENG., Illus.). (J). (gr. 4-7). 9.99 *(978-0-7636-5573-0(2),* Templar) Candlewick Pr.

—StoryWorld: Tales from the Haunted House: Create-A-Story Kit. 2011. (Storyworld Ser.). (ENG., Illus.). (J). (gr. 4-7). 9.99 *(978-0-7636-5568-6(6),* Templar) Candlewick Pr.

Mauthe, Deb. The Bishop's Christmas Tree. 2011. 24p. pap. 12.74 *(978-1-4634-3572-1(X))* AuthorHouse.

May, Robert L. Rudolph Shines Again. Caparo, Antonio Javier, illus. 2015. (ENG.). 40p. (J). (gr. -1-1). 17.99 *(978-1-4424-7498-7(X),* Little Simon) Little Simon.

Mayer, Mercer. Merry Christmas, Little Critter! Mayer, Mercer, illus. 2004. (Little Critter Ser.). (ENG., Illus.). 16p. (J). (gr. -1-1). pap. 6.99 *(978-0-06-053972-6(0),* HarperFestival) HarperCollins Pubs.

Mayhew, James. Katie's London Christmas. 2016. (Katie Ser.). (ENG., Illus.). 32p. (J). (gr. -1-k). pap. 10.99 *(978-1-4083-2642-8(6),* Orchard Bks.) Hachette Children's Group GBR. Dist: Hachette Bk. Group.

McAdam, Claudia Cangilla. The Christmas Tree Cried: The Story of the White House Christmas Tree. Crum, Anna-Maria, illus. 2004. 32p. (J). 16.95 *(978-0-9748995-5-8(0),* 1236093) Two Sons Pr., Inc.

McAnulty, Stacy. Dear Santasaurus. Kaminsky, Jef, illus. 2013. (ENG.). 32p. (J). (gr. k-3). 15.95 *(978-1-59078-876-9(1))* Boyds Mills Pr.

McCann, Thomas P. "Tom". The Tree Nobody Wanted: A Christmas Story. 2007. 14.95 *(978-0-9797407-0-1(3))* Exeter Pr.

McCardell, Ken. BibleRhymes' Christmas Story, bk. 3. Chirco, Antonella, illus. ed. 2008. (BibleRhymes Ser.: 3). 28p. (J). 17.95 *(978-0-9790605-2-6(4),* BibleRhymes) BibleRhymes Publishing, L.L.C.

McCarthy, Rebecca. Save This Christmas! May, Jason J., illus. 2012. (Lego City Ser.). (ENG.). 24p. (J). (gr. -1-3). pap. 3.99 *(978-0-545-45727-9(0))* Scholastic, Inc.

Mccarthy, Rebecca L. Save This Christmas! 2012. (LEGO City 8X8 Ser.). lib. bdg. 13.55 *(978-0-606-26767-0(0),* Turtleback) Turtleback Bks.

McCaughrean, Geraldine & Hoffmann, E. T. A. The Nutcracker: A Magic Theater Book. Swamer, Kristina, illus. 2012. (ENG.). 24p. (J). (gr. 1-17). 19.99 *(978-1-4521-0669-4(X))* Handprint Bks.

McClatchy, Lisa & Knight, Hilary. Eloise Decorates for Christmas. Lyon, Tammie Speer & Lyon, Tammie, illus. 2007. (Eloise Ser.). (ENG.). 32p. (J). (gr. -1-1). pap. 3.99 *(978-1-4169-4978-7(X),* Simon Spotlight) Simon Spotlight.

McClure, Beverly Stowe. Tumbleweed Christmas. McKenna, Bridgett, illus. 2011. 24p. pap. 13.99 *(978-0-9832740-4-9(5))* 4RV Publishing, LLC.

McCormack, Chris. The Fight Before Christmas. Lunn, Naomi, illus. 2013. 44p. (J). pap. *(978-0-9572875-4-9(2))* Batmack Ltd.

McCourt, Lisa. Merry Christmas, Stinky Face. Moore, Cyd, illus. (ENG.). 32p. (J). (— 1). 2016. 3.99 *(978-1-338-02919-2(3))* 2008. bds. 6.99 *(978-0-439-73123-2(2))* Scholastic, Inc. (Cartwheel Bks.).

McCray, Ed. Jill Chill & the Baron of Glacier Mountain: Wonder Tales from the Book of Ed. Brewer, Tammy & Harms, Cathy, eds. McCray, Ed, illus. 2003. (Illus.). 150p. (J). mass mkt. 14.95 *(978-1-929515-26-4(X),* Solovisions) Comic Library International.

McCue, Lisa. The Animals' Advent. 2010. (ENG., Illus.). 14p. (J). (gr. k — 1). 5.99 *(978-0-375-85815-4(6),* Random Hse. Bks. for Young Readers) Random Hse. Children's Bks.

McCullough, L. E. Silent Night: A Christmas Story. Maxwell, Cassandre, illus. 2006. 24p. (J). 7.95 *(978-0-88271-009-9(5))* Regina Pr., Malhame & Co.

—We Three Kings: A Christmas Story. Maxwell, Cassandre, illus. 2006. 24p. (J). 7.95 *(978-0-88271-010-5(9))* Regina Pr., Malhame & Co.

McCutcheon, John. Christmas in the Trenches, 1 vol. Sorensen, Henri, illus. 2006. (ENG.). 32p. (J). (gr. 1-5). 18.95 *(978-1-56145-374-0(9))* Peachtree Pubs.

McDade Jr, Bert M. Why Santa Claus Comes at Christmas. Swope, Brenda, illus. 2011. 32p. pap. 24.95 *(978-1-4560-0921-2(4))* America Star Bks.

McDonald, Megan. Happy New Year, Julie, Bk. 3. McAliley, Susan & Hunt, Robert, illus. 2007. (American Girl Ser.). (ENG.). 88p. (J). (gr. 3-7). 12.95 *(978-1-59369-292-6(7))* American Girl Publishing, Inc.

McGougan, Kathy. Buddy's Christmas Joy. 2011. 20p. pap. 12.95 *(978-1-4634-3763-3(3))* AuthorHouse.

McGrath, Barbara Barbieri & Togel, Peggy. The M & M's(r) Brand Christmas Gift Book. 2004. (Illus.). 12p. (J). (gr. -1-3). bds. 6.95 *(978-1-57091-421-8(4))* Charlesbridge Publishing, Inc.

McGrath, Milo & McGrath, Chris. South Pole Santa. 2007. 68p. pap. 12.50 *(978-1-84799-221-5(8))* Lulu Pr., Inc.

McGrory, Anik, illus. The Christmas Fox. 2016. (ENG.). 32p. (J). (gr. -1-2). 16.99 *(978-1-101-93500-2(6),* Knopf Bks. for Young Readers) Random Hse. Children's Bks.

McGuirk, Leslie. Ho, Ho, Ho, Tucker! McGuirk, Leslie, illus. 2010. (Candlewick Storybook Animations Ser.). (ENG., Illus.). 32p. (J). (-k). 8.99 *(978-0-7636-5043-8(9))* Candlewick Pr.

McHugh, Rosetta. Poodiky Oglethorpe's First Christmas, 1 vol. 2010. 30p. 24.95 *(978-1-4512-0119-2(2))* PublishAmerica, Inc.

McIntosh, Maria J. Evenings at Donaldson Manor: Or- the Christmas Guest. 2007. (ENG.). 222p. per. 20.99 *(978-1-4346-4259-2(3));* 252p. per. 23.99 *(978-1-4346-4260-8(7))* Creative Media Partners, LLC.

McIntyre, Sharyn. Christmas Tea with the Angels. 2007. 112p. 24.95 *(978-1-4327-1457-4(0))* Outskirts Pr., Inc.

McKay, Hilary. Forever Rose. (ENG.). 304p. (J). 2009. (gr. 4-9). pap. 6.99 *(978-1-4169-5487-3(2))* 2008. (Illus.). (gr. 5-9). 17.99 *(978-1-4169-5486-6(4))* McElderry, Margaret K. Bks. (McElderry, Margaret K. Bks.).

McKee, David, illus. Elmer's Christmas. 2011. (Andersen Press Picture Books Ser.). (J). 16.95 *(978-0-7613-8088-7(4))* Andersen Pr. GBR. Dist: Lerner Publishing Group.

McKissack, Patricia C. The All-I'll-Ever-Want Christmas Doll. Pinkney, Jerry, illus. 2007. (J). *(978-0-375-83615-2(2),* Schwartz & Wade Bks.) Random Hse. Children's Bks.

—The All-I'll-Ever-Want Christmas Doll. Pinkney, Jerry, illus. 2007. (ENG.). 40p. (J). (gr. -1-3). 17.99 *(978-0-375-83759-3(0),* Schwartz & Wade Bks.) Random Hse. Children's Bks.

McLean, Michael & McLean, Scott. Fairy Tale Christmas. 2014. (ENG., Illus.). 176p. (J). (gr. 3-9). 15.99 *(978-1-60907-930-7(2),* Shadow Mountain) Shadow Mountain Publishing.

McMorrow, T. E. & Hoffmann, E. T. A. Nutcracker in Harlem. Ransome, James, illus. 2017. 32p. (J). (gr. -1-3). 17.99 *(978-0-06-117598-5(6))* HarperCollins Pubs.

McNamara, Margaret. The Fairy Bell Sisters - Christmas Fairy Magic. 2014. (Fairy Bell Sisters Ser.: 6). (ENG.). 144p. (J). (gr. 1-5). pap. 4.99 *(978-0-06-226723-8(X))* HarperCollins Pubs.

—Secret Santa. Gordon, Mike, illus. 2012. (Robin Hill School Ser.). (ENG.). 32p. (J). (gr. -1-1). 15.99 *(978-1-4424-3649-7(2));* pap. 3.99 *(978-1-4424-3648-0(4))* Simon Spotlight. (Simon Spotlight).

McPherson, Heather L. A. Sonja's Wish. Cartwright, Christina, illus. 2012. 26p. (J). pap. 11.95 *(978-1-61863-394-1(5))* Bookstand Publishing.

Meachen Rau, Dana. Holiday Time. 2004. (Compass Point Early Reader Ser.). (J). 18.60 *(978-0-7565-0571-4(2))* Compass Point Bks.

Meadows, Daisy. Holly the Christmas Fairy. Ripper, Georgie, illus. 2007. (Rainbow Magic Ser.). (ENG.). 176p. (Orig.). (J). (gr. -1-3). pap. 6.99 *(978-0-439-92880-9(X),* Scholastic Paperbacks) Scholastic, Inc.

—Natalie the Christmas Stocking Fairy. 2014. (Rainbow Magic — Special Edition Ser.). lib. bdg. 17.20 *(978-0-606-36055-5(7))* Turtleback Bks.

—Paige the Christmas Play Fairy. 2010. (Rainbow Magic Ser.). (ENG.). 192p. (J). (gr. 2-5). pap. 6.99 *(978-0-545-22177-1(3),* Scholastic Paperbacks) Scholastic, Inc.

—Rainbow Magic Special Edition: Cheryl the Christmas Tree Fairy. 2012. (Rainbow Magic Special Edition Ser.). (ENG.). 176p. (J). (gr. 2-5). pap. 6.99 *(978-0-545-45571-8(5),* Scholastic Paperbacks) Scholastic, Inc.

—Rainbow Magic Special Edition: Natalie the Christmas Stocking Fairy. 2014. (Rainbow Magic Special Edition Ser.). (ENG.). 176p. (J). (gr. 2-5). pap. 6.99 *(978-0-545-60540-3(7),* Scholastic Paperbacks) Scholastic, Inc.

—Stella the Star Fairy. Ripper, Georgie, illus. 2008. (Rainbow Magic Ser.). (ENG.). 192p. (J). (gr. -1-3). pap. 6.99 *(978-0-545-06776-8(6),* Scholastic Paperbacks) Scholastic, Inc.

Mears, Richard Chase. Saint Nick & the Space Nicks. Westerfield, William Stephen, illus. l.t. ed. 2004. 32p. (J). 16.95 *(978-0-9754056-0-4(8))* Tuxedo Blue, LLC.

Melinda, Shoals, illus. The Spritelees: A Christmas Tale about Kindness. 2006. 32p. (J). 16.00 *(978-0-9773460-0-4(5))* Spritelee Enterprises.

Menard, Michele R. Cardinal Christmas. 2013. 36p. pap. 11.95 *(978-0-9891734-5-2(3))* Four Menards, The.

Mendonsa, Mark. A Sermon for a Sleigh. 2004. (J). pap. 15.95 *(978-1-59433-020-9(4))* Publication Consultants.

Menear, Linda. The Little Groundhog Discovers the True Meaning of Christmas. 2011. 24p. pap. 24.95 *(978-1-4626-3288-6(2))* America Star Bks.

Merry Christmas USA. 2007. (J). bds. 21.95 *(978-0-9745191-3-5(8))* Lynn Tyner Mitchum & James Rogers.

Mervis (Pantoja), Judith. Yuyi & la Ram: Yuyi y la Rama. 2012. 24p. pap. 17.99 *(978-1-4685-7600-9(3))* AuthorHouse.

Metivier, Gary. Cody & Grandpa's Christmas Tradition, 1 vol. Van Wagoner, Traci, illus. 2016. (ENG.). 32p. (J). (gr. k-3). 16.99 *(978-1-4556-2170-5(6))* Pelican Publishing Co., Inc.

Meyer, Brigit. The Christmas Surprise. Mussenbrock, Anne, illus. 2004. 10p. (J). bds. 5.99 *(978-1-59384-061-7(6))* Parklane Publishing.

—Merry Christmas, Little Bear. Mussenbrock, Anne, illus. 2004. 10p. (J). bds. 5.99 *(978-1-59384-062-4(4))* Parklane Publishing.

Miceli, Robert L. The Adventures of Twilight. 2008. 80p. pap. 22.50 *(978-1-60693-241-4(1),* Strategic Bk. Publishing) Strategic Book Publishing & Rights Agency (SBPRA).

Michael, Alexander. Until Wishes Are Fulfilled. 2007. (ENG.). 154p. per. 13.50 *(978-1-84426-408-7(4))* Upfront Publishing Ltd. GBR. Dist: Printondemand-worldwide.com.

Middleton, Nancy. The Zookeeper's Christmas Eve. 2009. 36p. pap. 16.50 *(978-1-60693-302-2(7),* Eloquent Bks.) Strategic Book Publishing & Rights Agency (SBPRA).

Milbourne, Anna. Very First Christmas. 2006. 24p. (J). 9.99 *(978-0-7945-1474-7(X),* Usborne) EDC Publishing.

Miller, Bernice Joyce. Nicholas' Christmas Eve Journey! 2009. 24p. pap. 11.49 *(978-1-4389-8279-3(8))* AuthorHouse.

Miller, Jennifer. Christmas Tails. Knight, Vanessa, illus. 2009. 56p. pap. 17.26 *(978-1-4251-8987-7(3))* Trafford Publishing.

Miller-Johnston, Renee. Double Trouble for Courtney Logan Kennedy, 1 vol. 2009. 88p. pap. 19.95 *(978-1-60836-384-1(8))* America Star Bks.

Miller-Stehr, Felicia. Are You Chanukah or Christmas? 2008. 32p. pap. 17.99 *(978-1-4343-9517-7(0))* AuthorHouse.

Mills, Patricia Anne. Stevie's First Christmas. 2009. 28p. pap. 12.49 *(978-1-4490-3452-8(7))* AuthorHouse.

Mirabile, Michele. Choir of Angels. 2013. (Illus.). 25p. pap. 4.99 *(978-1-4621-1361-3(3),* Horizon Pubs.) Cedar Fort, Inc./CFI Distribution.

Mitchell, Gloria. The Mouse That Went to Find Christmas. Johnson, Jerome A., illus. (J). pap. *(978-0-9706186-0-3(3))* Fourth Generation Pubs.

Mitter, Matt. Elmo's Christmas Hugs. Brannon, Tom, illus. 2012. (Hugs Book Ser.). (ENG.). 12p. (J). (gr. -1-k). bds. 10.99 *(978-0-7944-2703-0(0),* Reader's Digest Children's Bks.) Studio Fun International.

—Fisher-Price Little People: Santa's Helpers. 2016. (ENG.). 12p. (J). (gr. -1-k). bds. 5.99 *(978-0-7944-3799-2(0))* Studio Fun International.

Mlawer, Teresa, tr. from ENG. Olivia Se Prepara para la Navidad. Falconer, Ian, illus. 2008.Tr. of Olivia Helps with Christmas. (SPA.). 58p. (J). (gr. k-1). 16.99 *(978-1-933032-42-9(1))* Lectorum Pubns., Inc.

Mobley, Cyn. A Very Airey Christmas. 2004. pap. 16.00 *(978-0-9724136-0-2(X))* Greyhound Bks.

Mock, Chara. The Cajun Nutcracker, 1 vol. Cassels, Jean, illus. 2011. (ENG.). 32p. (J). (gr. k-3). 16.99 *(978-1-58980-978-9(5))* Pelican Publishing Co., Inc.

Moeri, Louise. Star Mother's Youngest Child. Hyman, Trina Schart, illus. 30th ed. 2005. (ENG.). 48p. (J). (gr. -1-3). 8.95 *(978-0-618-61509-4(1))* Houghton Mifflin Harcourt Publishing Co.

Mogensen, Jan. Go to Sleep, Little Bear. 2005. (ENG., Illus.). 32p. (J). (gr. -1-3). *(978-0-86315-490-4(5))* Floris Bks.

Molyneux, Caroline. A 1940 Christmas. 2012. 16p. pap. 15.99 *(978-1-4772-2899-9(3))* AuthorHouse.

Monroe, Colleen. A Wish to Be a Christmas Tree. Monroe, Michael Glenn, illus. 2005. (Holiday Ser.). (ENG.). 20p. (J). (gr. -1-1). bds. 8.99 *(978-1-58536-269-1(7),* 202284) Sleeping Bear Pr.

Monroe Donovan, Jane. Winter's Gift. Monroe Donovan, Jane, illus. 2004. (Holiday Ser.). (ENG., Illus.). 32p. (J). 16.95 *(978-1-58536-231-8(X))* Sleeping Bear Pr.

Montgomery Gibson, Jane. My Christmas Friend. Montgomery Gibson, Jane, illus. 2005. (Illus.). (YA). bds. 8.99 *(978-1-4183-0066-1(7))* Christ Inspired, Inc.

Moore, Clement C. C'Etait la Veille de Noel. Santore, Charles, illus. 2012. (FRE.). 48p. (J). 18.95 *(978-1-60433-300-8(6),* Applesauce Pr.) Cider Mill Pr. Bk. Pubs., LLC.

—Grumpy Santa. Spiridellis, Gregg & Spiridellis, Evan, illus. 2003. (ENG.). (J). *(978-0-439-53039-2(3),* Orchard Bks.) Scholastic, Inc.

—Magie de Noel. pap. 16.95 *(978-2-07-054886-6(4))* Gallimard, Editions FRA. Dist: Distribooks, Inc.

—My First Night Before Christmas. Newsom, Tom, illus. 2008. (ENG.). 12p. (J). 9.95 *(978-1-58117-808-1(5),* Intervisual/Piggy Toes) Bendon, Inc.

—The Night Before Christmas. Newsom, Tom, illus. 2007. (ENG.). 18p. (J). (gr. -1-3). 19.95 *(978-1-4037-2947-7(6),* Intervisual/Piggy Toes) Bendon, Inc.

—The Night Before Christmas. 2010. 32p. pap. 7.99 *(978-0-8249-5623-3(0),* Ideal Pubns.) Worthy Publishing.

—The Night Before Christmas. Watson, Richard Jesse, illus. 2006. (ENG.). 40p. (J). (gr. -1-3). 16.99 *(978-0-06-075741-0(8))* HarperCollins Pubs.

—The Night Before Christmas. 2005. (Classic Illustrated Ser.: CLAS). (ENG., Illus.). 44p. (J). (gr. -1-17). 7.95 *(978-0-8118-5028-5(5))* Chronicle Bks. LLC.

—The Night Before Christmas, Set. gif. ed. 2012. (ENG.). 48p. (J). 29.95 *(978-1-60433-296-4(4),* Applesauce Pr.) Cider Mill Pr. Bk. Pubs., LLC.

—The Night Before Christmas: A Bedtime Shadow Book. 2006. (Illus.). 8p. (J). 12.99 *(978-1-59359-942-3(0))* Peter Pauper Pr. Inc.

—The Night Before Christmas: A Christmas Treasury. (Illus.). 12p. (J). 4.95 *(978-1-58989-101-2(5))* Thurman Hse., LLC.

—La Nochebuena, 1. Alvarez, Lourdes, tr. Eldredge, Larry, illus. 2005.Tr. of Twas the Night Before Christmas. (SPA.). 28p. (J). bds. 12.95 *(978-1-58173-257-3(0))* Sweetwater Pr.

Moore, Clement C., ed. & illus. The Night Before Christmas. Moore, Clement C., illus. Price, Margaret Evans, illus. 2004. (Shape Bks.). (ENG.). 16p. (J). (gr. -1-3). pap. 9.95 *(978-1-59583-009-8(X),* 9781595830098, Green Tiger Pr.) Laughing Elephant.

Moore, Clement C. & Denslow, W. w. Denslow's Night Before Christmas. 2014. (ENG., Illus.). 72p. (J). (gr. k-3). pap. 9.99 *(978-0-486-78333-8(2))* Dover Pubns., Inc.

Morgan, Ruth. Happy Christmas Sglod. Carpenter, Suzanne, illus. 2003. (WEL & ENG.). 32p. pap. 12.95 *(978-1-84323-261-2(8))* Beekman Bks., Inc.

Morning, Carey. The Shepherd Girl of Bethlehem: A Nativity Story. Marks, Alan, illus. 2016. (ENG.). 32p. (J). (gr. -1-k). pap. 8.99 *(978-0-7459-6232-0(7))* Lion Hudson PLC GBR. Dist: Independent Pubs. Group.

Morpurgo, Michael. The Best Christmas Present in the World. Foreman, Michael, illus. 2004. (ENG.). 48p. (J). (gr. k-4). 9.99 *(978-1-4052-1518-3(6))* Egmont Bks., Ltd. GBR. Dist: Independent Pubs. Group.

—Christmas Stories. Allsopp, Sophie et al, illus. 2016. (ENG.). 240p. (J). (gr. k-3). pap. 23.99 *(978-1-4052-6911-7(1))* Egmont Bks., Ltd. GBR. Dist: Independent Pubs. Group.

—Michael Morpurgo Christmas Stories. 2014. (ENG., Illus.). 192p. (J). (gr. -1-2). pap. 15.99 *(978-1-4052-6895-0(6))* Egmont Bks., Ltd. GBR. Dist: Independent Pubs. Group.

—Mimi & the Mountain Dragon. Stephens, Helen, illus. 2015. (ENG.). 48p. (J). (gr. 2-4). 9.99 *(978-1-4052-6934-6(0))* Egmont Bks., Ltd. GBR. Dist: Independent Pubs. Group.

Morris, David. My Twins First Christmas. 2008. (Illus.). 24p. (J). pap. 14.95 *(978-0-9799885-0-9(0))* New Year Publishing.

Morris, Tony, illus. Papa Panov's Special Day. 2017. (ENG.). 32p. (J). (gr. k-2). 7.99 ***(978-0-7459-6562-8(8))*** Lion Hudson PLC GBR. Dist: Independent Pubs. Group.

Morse, Rose. The Everlasting Evergreen. 2009. 32p. pap. 18.01 *(978-0-557-21209-5(X))* Lulu Pr., Inc.

Morse, William A. Bip & the Bulb. 2009. 64p. pap. 23.49 *(978-1-4490-2498-7(X))* AuthorHouse.

Mortimer, Anne. Christmas Mouse. Mortimer, Anne, illus. 2013. (ENG., Illus.). 24p. (J). (gr. -1-3). 12.99 *(978-0-06-208928-1(5),* Tegen, Katherine Bks) HarperCollins Pubs.

Moulton, Mark K. The Visit. Winget, Susan, illus. 2003. 56p. (J). 14.95 *(978-0-8249-5475-8(0),* Ideal Pubns.) Worthy Publishing.

Moulton, Mark Kimball. A Cricket's Carol. Blowers, Lisa, illus. 2004. 32p. (J). 14.95 *(978-0-8249-5488-8(2),* Ideal Pubns.) Worthy Publishing.

—Reindeer Christmas. Good, Karen Hillard, illus. 2008. (ENG.). 40p. (J). (gr. -1-3). 15.99 *(978-1-4169-6108-6(9),* Simon & Schuster/Paula Wiseman Bks.) Simon & Schuster/Paula Wiseman Bks.

Mucha Aydlott, Julie A. My Favorite Time of Year. Mucha-Sullivan, Kalie A. & Mucha-Sullivan, Emily V., illus. I.t. ed. 2004. 22p. (J). 5.95 *(978-0-9746093-2-4(3))* San Diego Business Accounting Solutions a Non CPA Firm.

Muecke, Anne & Moore, Clement C. The Dinosaurs' Night Before Christmas. Hale, Nathan, illus. 2008. (ENG.). 36p. (J). (gr. -1-3). 18.99 *(978-0-8118-6322-3(0))* Chronicle Bks. LLC.

Muldrow, Diane. Frosty the Snowman. Golden Books, illus. 2013. (Big Golden Board Book Ser.). (ENG.). 22p. (J). (-k). bds. 10.99 *(978-0-385-37870-3(X),* Golden Bks.) Random Hse. Children's Bks.

Mullarkey, Lisa. The Purr-Fect-O Present: Book 10, 1 vol. Harris, Phyllis, illus. 2012. (Katharine the Almost Great Ser.). (ENG.). 80p. (J). (gr. 1-4). 27.07 *(978-1-61641-831-1(1))* Magic Wagon.

Murnaugh, Lene. Touch of Christmas. Skrbic, Melissa, illus. I.t. ed. 2003. 28p. per. 9.95 *(978-1-932344-19-6(5))* Thornton Publishing, Inc.

Mumford, Carole. Christmas Vacation in Colorado: A Magnificent Six Adventure, 1 vol. 2009. 75p. pap. 19.95 *(978-1-60749-231-3(8))* America Star Bks.

Mun-Ensor, Michelle. The Faithful Christmas. 2011. 28p. pap. 24.95 *(978-1-4560-7077-9(0))* America Star Bks.

Muncaster, Harriet. The Biggest Smallest Christmas Present. Muncaster, Harriet, illus. 2016. (ENG., Illus.). 32p. (J). (-k). 16.99 *(978-0-399-16432-3(4),* G.P. Putnam's Sons Books for Young Readers) Penguin Young Readers Group.

Mundt, A. S. The Letter. 2011. 36p. pap. 14.49 *(978-1-4634-3936-1(9))* AuthorHouse.

Murail, Marie-aude & Murail, Elvire. Santa's Last Present. Blake, Quentin, illus. 2004. (ENG.). 32p. (J). (gr. 3-7). 12.95 *(978-1-56145-319-1(6))* Peachtree Pubs.

Murguia, Bethanie Deeney. The Best Parts of Christmas. Murguia, Bethanie Deeney, illus. 2015. (ENG., Illus.). 32p. (J). (gr. -1-2). 14.99 *(978-0-7636-7556-1(3))* Candlewick Pr.

Murphy, Mary. Christmas Is the Best Bit. 2004. (Illus.). 28p. (Orig.). (J). pap. 6.95 *(978-0-7497-4252-2(6))* Egmont Bks., Ltd. GBR. Dist: Trafalgar Square Publishing.

Murphy, Michael E. Candy Cane Christmas. 2006. 16p. (J). *(978-1-59975-434-5(7))* Independent Pub.

Murphy, Susan White. D. J. 's Special Tree. 2012. 50p. (-18). pap. 8.95 *(978-1-4759-5983-3(4))* iUniverse, Inc.

Murphy, T. M. Saving Santa's Seals. Taylor, Adam, illus. 2009. (LeapKids Ser.). (ENG.). 170p. (J). (gr. 1-5). pap. 10.95 *(978-0-9815148-8-8(X))* Leapfrog Pr.

Murray, Kiel. Mater Saves Christmas. 2009. (ENG.). 48p. (J). (gr. -1-2). 12.99 *(978-1-4231-1695-0(X))* Disney Pr.

Murray, Laura & McPike, Elizabeth. The Gingerbread Man Loose at Christmas. Lowery, Mike, illus. 2015. (ENG.). 32p. (J). (gr. k-k). 16.99 *(978-0-399-16866-6(4),* G.P. Putnam's Sons Books for Young Readers) Penguin Young Readers Group.

Murray, Scott. Granny's Christmas Blunder. 2012. 28p. pap. 18.00 *(978-1-4772-0990-5(5))* AuthorHouse.

My Crazy Christmas Catastrophe Cat. 2003. (Illus.). 22p. (J). 9.95 *(978-0-9744751-1-0(4))* Timothy Lane Pr.

My First Book of Christmas Stories. 2003. (J). 8.99 *(978-1-59384-014-3(4))* Parklane Publishing.

My Little Christmas Library. 2008. (Pocket Libraries Ser.). 5p. bds. *(978-1-4075-3193-9(X))* Parragon, Inc.

My Treasury of Christmas Stories. Date not set. 192p. (J). 12.98 *(978-1-4054-1295-7(X))* Parragon, Inc.

Myers, Janice Limb. Carolee Sings in the Christmas Choir: A Christmas Story for Children of All Ages. Velica, Teodora, illus. 2013. 48p. pap. 13.77 *(978-0-9897175-1-9(8))* LJM Publishing.

Myers, Tim J. The Christmas Stick: A Children's Story. Yilmaz, Necdet, illus. 2014. (ENG.). 32p. (J). pap. 13.99 *(978-1-61261-571-4(6))* Paraclete Pr., Inc.

Naliboff, Jane. The Only One Club. Hopkins, Jeff, illus. 2013. (ENG.). 32p. (J). (gr. k-2). 6.95 *(978-1-936261-30-7(8))* Flashlight Pr.

Nancy St. Paul-Martin. Go to the Nurse: Peanut Puffs & Snicker-Doodles. 2009. 28p. pap. 15.49 *(978-1-4389-7653-2(4))* AuthorHouse.

Natale, Noel. The Adventures of Nicholas: The Boy Who Grew up to Become Santa Claus. 2004. (Illus.). 127p. (YA). per. 17.99 *(978-0-9753349-0-4(5))* Open Bk. Publishing Co.

Navillus, Nell. God's Christmas Gift. McCallum, Jodie, illus. 2006. (J). *(978-1-58173-595-6(2))* Sweetwater Pr.

—Happy Birthday, Jesus. McCallum, Jodie, illus. 2007. (J). *(978-1-60261-264-8(1))* Cliff Road Bks.

Naylor, Phyllis Reynolds. A Shiloh Christmas. 2015. (Shiloh Quartet Ser.). (ENG., Illus.). 256p. (J). (gr. 3-7). 17.99 *(978-1-4814-4151-3(5))* Simon & Schuster Children's Publishing.

Nazoa, Aquiles. Retablillo de Navidad. Oliver, Maria Fernanda, illus.Tr. of Christmas Nativity. (SPA.). (J). (gr. 3-5). 10.95 *(978-980-257-067-6(2))* Ekare, Ediciones VEN. Dist: Lectorum Pubns., Inc.

Neely, Kirk H. Santa Almost Got Caught: Stories for Thanksgiving, Christmas, & the New Year. Cash, Emory, illus. 2011. 152p. pap. 14.99 *(978-1-4575-0477-8(4))* Dog Ear Publishing, LLC.

Neff, Fred. The Memory Tree. Montmeat, Jack, illus. 2008. 36p. pap. 14.99 *(978-1-59858-854-5(0))* Dog Ear Publishing, LLC.

Neill, Patricia S. Christmas Is a Gift from God. 2008. (Illus.). 24p. (J). 7.00 *(978-0-8059-7845-2(3))* Dorrance Publishing Co., Inc.

Nelson, S. D. Coyote Christmas: A Lakota Story. 2007. (ENG., Illus.). 40p. (J). (gr. 1-4). 18.95 *(978-0-8109-9367-9(8),* Abrams Bks. for Young Readers) Abrams, Inc.

Nesbø, Jo. Silent (but Deadly) Night. Lowery, Mike, illus. 2017. (J). pap. ***(978-1-5344-1000-8(7),*** Simon & Schuster/Paula Wiseman Bks.) Simon & Schuster/Paula Wiseman Bks.

Neusner, Dena, et al. Danny Dozer's Perfect Christmas Tree. 2007. (ENG., Illus.). 12p. (J). (gr. -1-3). pap. 9.95 *(978-0-7624-3141-0(5))* Running Pr. Bk. Pubs.

New Mexico Night Before Christmas. 2006. (YA). per. 19.99 *(978-0-9710675-5-4(4))* 2020 Vision Pr.

New York City Ballet, New York. George Balanchine's the Nutcracker. Docampo, Valeria, illus. 2016. (ENG.). 40p. (J). (gr. -1-3). 17.99 *(978-1-4814-5829-0(9),* Little Simon) Little Simon.

Newberry, Gabriel S. Elli & Gabe's Big Christmas Adventure. 2012. 20p. pap. 13.77 *(978-1-4669-6941-4(5))* Trafford Publishing.

Newton, Lesley. Ralphie's Christmas Story, 1 vol. 2010. 16p. pap. 24.95 *(978-1-4489-2674-9(2))* PublishAmerica, Inc.

Nez, John Abbott. The Twelve Days of Christmas in Washington. Nez, John Abbott, illus. 2011. (Twelve Days of Christmas in America Ser.). (ENG., Illus.). 40p. (J). (gr. k-3). 12.95 *(978-1-4027-7068-5(5))* Sterling Publishing Co., Inc.

Nickelodeon. PAW Patrol: the Night Before Christmas. 2016. (ENG.). 10p. (J). (gr. -1-k). bds. 8.99 *(978-0-7944-3800-5(8),* Reader's Digest Children's Bks.) Studio Fun International.

Night & Day Studios. Peekaboo Presents. Lunn, Corey, illus. 2015. (Peekaboo Ser.). (ENG.). 20p. (J). (— 1). bds. 7.99 *(978-0-7636-7567-7(9),* Candlewick Entertainment) Candlewick Pr.

Nikola-lisa, W. & Nikola-lisa, W. Hallelujah! A Christmas Celebration. Saint James, Synthia, illus. 2009. (ENG.). 36p. (J). (gr. -1-3). 10.99 *(978-1-4424-0224-9(5),* Atheneum Bks. for Young Readers) Simon & Schuster Children's Publishing.

Nivens, Karen. Benjamin P. Blizzard: Welcome to Christmastown. Grisham, Jason, illus. 2007. 48p. (J). per. *(978-0-9798154-1-6(X))* Living Waters Publishing Co.

Noble, Trinka Hakes. Apple Tree Christmas. Noble, Trinka Hakes, illus. 2005. (Holiday Ser.). (ENG., Illus.). 32p. (J). (gr. -1-3). 16.95 *(978-1-58536-270-7(0))* Sleeping Bear Pr.

Noël, Alyson. Five Days of Famous. 2016. (ENG.). 304p. (J). (gr. 5). 16.99 *(978-0-553-53796-3(2),* Delacorte Bks. for Young Readers) Random Hse. Children's Bks.

Norman, Travis D. Christmas Island. Baker, David, illus. 2011. 28p. pap. 24.95 *(978-1-4560-9800-1(4))* America Star Bks.

Norris, Jeannine Q. Tonight You Are My Baby: Mary's Christmas Gift. Ladwig, Tim, illus. 2010. (HarperBlessings Ser.). (ENG.). 30p. (J). (gr. -1-k). bds. 7.99 *(978-0-06-147999-1(3),* HarperFestival) HarperCollins Pubs.

Norris, Leslie. Albert, Lucille & the Two Williams. 2007. (Illus.). 40p. (J). per. 20.00 *(978-0-9766261-3-8(6))* Clandestine Pr., The.

Nosy Crow Staff. Bizzy Bear: Christmas Helper. Davies, Benji, illus. 2016. (Bizzy Bear Ser.). (ENG.). 8p. (J). (— 1). bds. 6.99 *(978-0-7636-8004-6(4),* Nosy Crow) Candlewick Pr.

—Can You Say It, Too? Jingle! Jingle! Braun, Sebastien, illus. 2015. (Can You Say It, Too? Ser.). (ENG.). 10p. (J). (— 1). bds. 8.99 *(978-0-7636-8002-2(8),* Nosy Crow) Candlewick Pr.

Numeroff, Laura Joffe. If You Take a Mouse to the Movies. 2004. (Illus.). (J). (gr. k-3). spiral bd. *(978-0-616-11129-1(0));* spiral bd. *(978-0-616-11128-4(2))* Canadian National Institute for the Blind/Institut National Canadien pour les Aveugles.

—If You Take a Mouse to the Movies. Bond, Felicia, illus. 2009. (If You Give... Ser.). (ENG.). 72p. (J). (gr. -1-3). 18.99 *(978-0-06-176280-2(6))* HarperCollins Pubs.

—Merry Christmas, Mouse! Bond, Felicia, illus. 2007. (If You Give... Ser.). (ENG.). 24p. (J). (gr. -1 — 1). bds. 6.99 *(978-0-06-134499-2(0))* HarperCollins Pubs.

The Nutcracker. 2003. (Illus.). 32p. (J). 4.98 *(978-1-4054-0982-7(7))* Parragon, Inc.

Nyaradi, J. A. Catching Santa. 2006. 140p. pap. 11.95 *(978-0-7414-3462-3(8))* Infinity Publishing.

O., Lila. Lulabelle's Jewels: The Christmas Wish of Mrs. Claus. 2008. 20p. pap. 12.49 *(978-1-4389-3189-0(1))* AuthorHouse.

O, Lila & O., Lila. Lula Belle's Jewels: The Christmas Wish of Mrs. Claus. 2011. 28p. pap. 17.50 *(978-1-4634-3326-0(3))* AuthorHouse.

Obed, Ellen Bryan. Who Would Like a Christmas Tree? A Tree for All Seasons. Hunter, Anne, illus. 2009. (ENG.). 32p. (J). (gr. -1-3). 16.00 *(978-0-547-04625-9(1))* Houghton Mifflin Harcourt Publishing Co.

O'Brien, Mandie. Molly's Christmas Gift. 2010. 50p. pap. 9.99 *(978-1-60911-840-2(5),* Eloquent Bks.) Strategic Book Publishing & Rights Agency (SBPRA).

Ochoa, Mary Lou. Andy's Arctic Party. 2009. 20p. pap. 9.14 *(978-1-4269-0943-6(8))* Trafford Publishing.

O'Connor, Jane. Splendiferous Christmas. Glasser, Robin Preiss, illus. (Fancy Nancy Ser.). 32p. (J). (gr. -1-2). 2011. (ENG.). 17.99 *(978-0-06-123590-0(3))* 2009. lib. bdg. 18.89 *(978-0-06-123591-7(1))* HarperCollins Pubs.

O'Donnell, Kevin & Gon, Zang Sung. Stone Age Santa. Kim, Boo Young et al, illus. 2007. (ENG.). 184p. (J). (gr. 4-7). per. 11.95 *(978-1-58818-153-4(7))* Hill Street Pr., LLC.

O'Leary-Coggins, Annette. The Rescueteers' Christmas Mission: Book 2. 2010. 168p. 22.95 *(978-1-4502-3085-8(7));* pap. 12.95 *(978-1-4502-3087-2(3))* iUniverse, Inc.

Olek, Lisa B. Yoshka's Journey to Christmas. Gruenfelder, Robin, illus. 2012. 70p. (J). 21.95 *(978-1-60131-125-2(7),* Castlebridge Bks.) Big Tent Bks.

Olsen, Bevan. The Innkeeper's Christmas. 2010. (Illus.). 12p. (J). pap. 2.99 *(978-1-59955-433-4(X))* Cedar Fort, Inc./CFI Distribution.

Olson, Cynthia. Cherise's Christmas Wish. 2005. 145p. pap. 24.95 *(978-1-4137-5664-7(6))* America Star Bks.

O'Meara, Sandra F. Charli's First Christmas. 2010. 28p. pap. 28.03 *(978-1-4500-7325-7(5))* Xlibris Corp.

Ondrias, Rachel. Kolby, the Skating Bear: A Kalamazoo Christmas. Scarborough, Casey, illus. 2007. (ENG.). 32p. (J). 16.95 *(978-1-933660-29-5(5),* Tadpole Pr. 4 Kids) Smooth Sailing Pr., LLC.

O'Neal-Thorpe, Rochelle. The Doll at the Christmas Bazaar: Christmas Miracles. Penn, Karen V., illus. 2010. 32p. (J). pap. 9.95 *(978-0-9823906-2-7(9))* Wiggles Pr.

The Ooshes the Night Before Christmas. 2004. (J). mass mkt. *(978-1-932233-03-2(2))* Aurora Libris Corp.

Oppenheim, Joanne F. El Milagro de la Primera Flora de Nochebuena: Un Cuento Mexicano Sobre la Navidad. Negrin, Fabian, illus. 2003. (SPA & ENG.). 32p. (J). 16.99 *(978-1-84148-308-5(7))* Barefoot Bks., Inc.

—The Miracle of the First Poinsettia. Negrin, Fabian, illus. 2003. (ENG.). 32p. (J). 16.99 *(978-1-84148-245-3(5))* Barefoot Bks., Inc.

—Miracle of the First Poinsettia. Negrin, Fabian, illus. 32p. 8.99 *(978-1-84148-364-1(8))* Barefoot Bks., Inc.

Organ, Betty. Peter's Christmas Eve Adventure, 1 vol. Martin, Shawn, illus. 2010. (ENG.). 32p. (J). (gr. k-1). 10.95 *(978-1-897174-68-5(3),* Tuckamore Bks) Creative Bk. Publishing CAN. Dist: Orca Bk. Pubs. USA.

O'Ryan, Ray. A Green Christmas! Jack, Colin, illus. 2013. (Galaxy Zack Ser.: 6). (ENG.). 128p. (J). (gr. k-2). 16.99 *(978-1-4424-8225-8(7));* pap. 4.99 *(978-1-4424-8224-1(9));* pap. 4.99 *(978-1-4424-8224-1(9))* Little Simon. (Little Simon).

—A Green Christmas! 2013. (Galaxy Zack Ser.: 6). lib. bdg. 14.75 *(978-0-606-35185-0(X))* Turtleback Bks.

Osborne, Mary Pope. Christmas in Camelot. 2009. (Magic Tree House Merlin Missions Ser.: 1). lib. bdg. 16.00 *(978-0-606-06386-9(2),* Turtleback) Turtleback Bks.

—A Ghost Tale for Christmas Time. 2012. (Magic Tree House Merlin Missions Ser.: 16). lib. bdg. 16.00 *(978-0-606-26808-0(1),* Turtleback) Turtleback Bks.

—Navidad en Camelot. 2015. (Casa De árbol Ser.: 29). (SPA., Illus.). 144p. (J). (gr. 2-4). pap. 5.99 *(978-1-63245-532-1(3))* Lectorum Pubns., Inc.

Osborne, Rick. Legend of the Christmas Stocking: An Inspirational Story of a Wish Come True, 1 vol. Griffin, Jim, illus. 2004. (ENG.). 32p. (J). 17.99 *(978-0-310-70898-8(2))* Zonderkidz.

Ottersley, Martha T. Guess Who Loves Christmas! Hall, Susan, illus. 2014. (Guess Who Ser.). (ENG.). 10p. (J). (gr. -1-k). 10.99 *(978-0-7944-3210-2(7))* Reader's Digest Assn., Inc., The.

Oubre, Glenn. The Twelve Days of a Berry Christmas. 2012. (ENG.). pap. 14.00 *(978-1-4675-3296-9(7))* Independent Pub.

Oud, Pauline. Christmas with Lily & Milo. 2012. (Clavis Toddler: Language Development Ser.). (ENG.). 30p. (J). (gr. k — 1). 12.95 *(978-1-60537-128-3(9))* Cobblestone Publishing Co.

Our Shinning Christmas Tree. 2003. (J). per. *(978-1-57657-911-4(5))* Paradise Pr., Inc.

Outram, Evelyn. Sav & Josh O Lucky's Christmas Adventure & Magic Street. 2010. 56p. pap. 17.95 *(978-1-60911-876-1(6),* Eloquent Bks.) Strategic Book Publishing & Rights Agency (SBPRA).

Pace, Terri L. The Christmas Dream, 1 vol. 2009. 116p. pap. 19.95 *(978-1-60813-532-5(2))* America Star Bks.

Pachek, Mary C. Isabella & the Merry Mouse House: A Christmas Story Coloring Book. Noad, Jordan, illus. 2009. 34p. pap. 14.49 *(978-1-4389-8467-4(7))* AuthorHouse.

Padilla, Gerane & Sky. Penelope Potts & the Christmas Pup. 2009. 32p. pap. 16.49 *(978-1-4490-4781-8(5))* AuthorHouse.

Page, J. & Rainier, S. T. Ben & Elvis: The Miracle of a Stormy Christmas. Moyer, J., illus. 2012. 28p. pap. 8.99 *(978-0-9829669-4-5(6))* Elv Enterprises.

Page, Nick & Page, Claire. Finger Puppet Books Christmas Story. 2009. (Finger Puppet Bks.). (Illus.). 12p. (gr. -1-k). bds. 12.99 *(978-1-84610-573-9(0))* Make Believe Ideas GBR. Dist: Nelson, Thomas Inc.

Page, Thomas Nelson. Santa Claus's Partner. 2006. 64p. pap. *(978-1-84702-187-8(5))* Echo Library.

Palacios, Laura. Ten Hardworking Elves. 2009. 40p. pap. 17.95 *(978-0-557-22319-0(9))* Lulu Pr., Inc.

Paladin, Frank. Hole in My Stocking. Amber, Holly & Lin, Melanie, illus. 2005. 24p. (J). per. 16.95 *(978-0-9763635-4-5(2))* Beyond the Stars Pubns.

Pallotta, Jerry. Dinosaur Christmas. McWilliam, Howard, illus. (J). (gr. k-2). 2013. (ENG.). 32p. 12.99 *(978-0-545-43360-0(6))* 2011. *(978-0-545-24963-8(5))* Scholastic, Inc.

—Santa Pups. Terry, Will, illus. 2016. (ENG.). 32p. (J). (gr. -1-k). 6.99 *(978-0-545-48479-4(0))* Scholastic, Inc.

Pankiw, Dr Mary & Pankiw, Mary. Misilla Mouse. 2011. 32p. pap. *(978-1-4269-5476-4(X))* Trafford Publishing (UK) Ltd.

Paradis, Anne. Caillou: the Little Christmas Artist. Sévigny, Eric, illus. 2013. (Coloring & Activity Book Ser.). (ENG.). 64p. (J). (gr. -1-1). 8.99 *(978-2-89718-065-2(X))* Caillouet, Gerry.

Parker, Amy. Tiny Blessings: for a Merry Christmas (large Trim) Walsh, Sarah, illus. 2016. (ENG.). 10p. (J). (gr. -1-17). bds. 9.95 ***(978-0-7624-6209-4(4),*** Running Pr.) Running Pr. Bk. Pubs.

Parker, Emma Rae. Papa's Book of Mormon Christmas. 2015. (Illus.). (J). 14.99 *(978-1-4621-1741-3(4))* Cedar Fort, Inc./CFI Distribution.

Parker, Laurie. It Really Said Christmas. Parker, Laurie, illus. 2005. (Illus.). (J). pap. 17.95 *(978-0-9772096-0-6(1))* Wild Hare Publishing.

—It Really Said Christmas. Parker, Laurie, illus. 2003. (Illus.). (J). *(978-0-9729615-0-9(X))* Parker, Laurie.

Parker, Robert H. The Little Crooked Christmas Tree. Long, DeWayne Lee, illus. 2012. 32p. (J). pap. 15.00 *(978-0-9837382-9-9(7),* Catch the Spirit of Appalachia) Ammons Communications, Ltd.

Parry, Linda & Parry, Alan. Christmastime with Mr Bear. 2006. 12p. (J). bds. 11.99 *(978-0-7847-1469-0(X),* 04389) Standard Publishing.

Partridge, Helen L. Blinky: The Bear Who Wouldn't Hibernate. 2008. 32p. per. 24.95 *(978-1-4241-9261-8(7))* America Star Bks.

Pasquali, Elena. Santa's Midnight Sleighride. Vagnozzi, Barbara, illus. 2013. (Finger-Trail Animal Tales Ser.). (ENG.). 10p. (J). (gr. -1-k). bds. 9.99 *(978-0-7459-6242-9(4))* Lion Hudson PLC GBR. Dist: Independent Pubs. Group.

Paterson, Katherine. A Stubborn Sweetness & Other Stories for the Christmas Season. 2013. (ENG.). 200p. 16.00 *(978-0-664-23915-2(3))* Westminster John Knox Pr.

Patricelli, Leslie. Fa la La. Patricelli, Leslie, illus. 2012. (Leslie Patricelli Board Bks.). (ENG., Illus.). 26p. (J). (gr. k — 1). bds. 6.99 *(978-0-7636-3247-2(3))* Candlewick Pr.

Patterson, James. SantaKid. Garland, Michael, illus. 2004. (ENG.). 48p. (J). (gr. -1-1). 17.99 *(978-0-316-00061-1(2),* Jimmy Patterson) Little Brown & Co.

Paul, Ellis. The Night the Lights Went Out on Christmas. Brundage, Scott, illus. 2015. (ENG.). 32p. (J). (gr. -1-3). 16.99 *(978-0-8075-4543-0(0))* Whitman, Albert & Co.

Pauline Wall & Shelley Smith. What the Owl Saw: (a Christmas Story) 2012. 20p. pap. 15.19 *(978-1-4669-2813-8(1))* Trafford Publishing.

Paulson, Michael W. The Baker Street Bunch No. 1: A Double Mystery Book. I.t. ed. 2004. (Illus.). 154p. (J). per. *(978-0-9754241-0-0(6))* MiMar Publishing.

Payne-Sylvester, Linda. Here Comes Christmas & the Teddy Bears Get Ready. 2012. (ENG.). pap. 12.95 *(978-1-4675-5249-3(6))* Independent Pub.

Pearson, Carol Lynn. A Christmas Thief. 2008. 80p. 12.99 *(978-1-59955-184-5(5))* Cedar Fort, Inc./CFI Distribution.

—A Christmas Thief: A Novel. 2003. 67p. 14.95 *(978-0-8294-1764-7(8))* Loyola Pr.

—The Modern Magi. 2009. 80p. pap. 7.99 *(978-1-59955-354-2(6))* Cedar Fort, Inc./CFI Distribution.

Pearson, Judith Frank. Chester the Christmas Church Mouse. 2013. 18p. pap. 9.95 *(978-1-61493-176-8(3))* Peppertree Pr., The.

Pease, Elaine. Tallie's Christmas Lights Surprise!, 1 vol. Crum, Anna-Maria, illus. 2012. (ENG.). 32p. (J). (gr. k-3). 16.99 *(978-1-4556-1586-5(2))* Pelican Publishing Co., Inc.

Peaslee Levine, Martha. The Twelve Days of Christmas in Pennsylvania. Dougherty, Rachel, illus. 2014. (Twelve Days of Christmas in America Ser.). (ENG.). 40p. (J). (gr. k). 12.95 *(978-1-4549-0889-0(0))* Sterling Publishing Co., Inc.

Peet, Amanda & Troyer, Andrea. Dear Santa, Love, Rachel Rosenstein. Davenier, Christine, illus. 2015. (ENG.). 40p. (J). (gr. -1-2). 20.99 *(978-0-553-51062-1(2));* 17.99 *(978-0-553-51061-4(4))* Random Hse. Children's Bks. (Doubleday Bks. for Young Readers).

Pelham, David. Here Comes Santa: A Mini Holiday Pop-Up. Pelham, David, illus. 2008. (ENG., Illus.). 18p. (J). 11.99 *(978-1-4169-5440-8(6),* Little Simon) Little Simon.

Pennington, Norma C. & Schuller, Sheldon V. The Unopened Gift, 1 vol. 2010. 18p. 24.95 *(978-1-4489-7670-6(7))* PublishAmerica, Inc.

Perez, Vivian. Stolen Stories for My Nieces. 2007. (ENG.). 68p. per. 19.95 *(978-1-4241-6679-4(9))* America Star Bks.

Perla, Victoria. When Santa Turned Green. 2007. (Illus.). 44p. (J). *(978-0-9799454-0-3(2))* Brinsights, LLC.

Perrigo, Brad. Tuffy Mcnasty: The Rogue Elf Who Terrorized Christmas! 2012. 48p. pap. 21.88 *(978-1-4669-6147-0(3))* Trafford Publishing.

Perry, Rex, illus. 'Twas the Night Before Christmas. 2004. 24p. (J). lib. bdg. 8.00 *(978-1-4242-0641-4(3))* Fitzgerald Bks.

Peschke, Marci. Daisy Has the Holiday Blues, 1 vol., Bk. 5. Pilz, MH, illus. 2011. (Growing up Daisy Ser.). (ENG.). 80p. (gr. 3-8). 27.07 *(978-1-61641-118-3(X),* Calico Chapter Bks) Magic Wagon.

Peyo. The Smurfs Christmas. 2013. (Smurfs Graphic Novels Ser.). (ENG., Illus.). 56p. (J). (gr. 2-5). 10.99 *(978-1-59707-452-0(7),* 9781597074520); pap. 5.99 *(978-1-59707-451-3(9),* 9781597074513) Papercutz.

Phillips, Dixie. Baby Jesus Is Missing. Snider, K. C., illus. 2009. 16p. pap. 9.95 *(978-1-61633-000-2(7))* Guardian Angel Publishing, Inc.

Phillips, Dixie & Sharon, et al. Camiles Journey Master Playbook with Musical Scores. 2012. 44p. pap. 29.95 *(978-1-61633-196-2(8))* Guardian Angel Publishing, Inc.

Phillips, Jean. The Meaning of Christmas: A Children's Story in Picture & Verse. 2005. (ENG., Illus.). 24p. pap. 7.95 *(978-0-929292-67-0(7),* 800-747-0738) Hannibal Bks.

Pick, Alice. Jamey's Promise, 1 vol. 2009. 61p. pap. 19.95 *(978-1-61582-547-9(9))* America Star Bks.

Pienkowski, Jan. The First Noel: A Christmas Carousel. Pienkowski, Jan et al, illus. 2004. (ENG.). 1p. (J). (gr. k-12). 14.99 *(978-0-7636-2190-2(0))* Candlewick Pr.

Pierpont, James Lord. Jingle Bells. Siewert, Pauline, illus. 2015. (ENG.). 14p. (J). (— 1). 12.99 *(978-0-7636-8197-5(0))* Candlewick Pr.

—Jingle Bells. Samuel, Janet, illus. 2014. 24p. (J). bds. 6.99 *(978-0-8249-1941-2(6),* Ideal Pubns.) Worthy Publishing.

—Jingle Bells: A Magical Cut-Paper Edition. Puttapipat, Niroot, illus. 2015. (ENG.). 12p. (J). (gr. -1-3). 19.99 *(978-0-7636-7821-0(X))* Candlewick Pr.

Pingk, Rubin. Samurai Santa: A Very Ninja Christmas. Pingk, Rubin, illus. 2015. (ENG., Illus.). 40p. (J). (gr. -1-3). 17.99 *(978-1-4814-3057-9(2),* Simon & Schuster Bks. For Young Readers) Simon & Schuster Bks. For Young Readers.

Pingry, Patricia A. Dear Santa... Rasmussen, Wendy, illus. 2005. (ENG.). 24p. (J). (gr. -1-k). bds. 6.95 *(978-0-8249-6618-8(X),* Ideal Pubns.) Worthy Publishing.

—On Christmas Morning. Barretta, Gene, illus. 2007. (ENG.). 26p. (J). (gr. -1-3). bds. 6.99 *(978-0-8249-6713-0(5),* Ideal Pubns.) Worthy Publishing.

Pink, A. J. The Fox at Christmas. 2009. (Illus.). 52p. pap. *(978-1-84748-586-1(3))* Athena Pr.

Pinson, Joseph. Big Wooley's Christmas. 2011. 32p. pap. 12.99 *(978-1-4634-1202-9(9))* AuthorHouse.

Pitchford, Dean. Nickel Bay Nick. 2014. (ENG.). 272p. (J). (gr. 3-7). pap. 7.99 *(978-0-14-751227-7(1),* Puffin Books) Penguin Young Readers Group.

Pittar, Gill. Milly, Molly & the Secret Scarves. 2004. 28p. *(978-1-86972-027-8(X))* Milly Molly Bks.

C
D

—Milly, Molly & the Secret Scarves (book w/dolls) 2006. 28p. pap. *(978-1-877337-42-0(0))* Milly Molly Bks.

Plehal, Christopher J. Yes, Virginia: There Is a Santa Claus. Bernardin, James, illus. 2010. (ENG.). 32p. (J). (gr. -1-2). 16.99 *(978-0-06-200173-3(6))* HarperCollins Pubs.

Plemmons, Fred Maurice. What Day Is It, Ralphie? 2008. 24p. pap. 12.99 *(978-1-4389-2705-3(3))* AuthorHouse.

Plume, Ilse. The Twelve Days of Christmas. 2005. (ENG., Illus.). 32p. (J). (gr. 1). 17.95 *(978-1-56792-300-1(3))* Godine, David R. Pub.

Pohl, Dora & Kremer, Kevin. Maggie's Christmas Miracle. Ely, Dave, illus. 2010. 78p. (J). pap. 4.99 *(978-0-9824611-2-9(7))* Snow In Sarasota Publishing.

Polacco, Patricia. Christmas Tapestry. 2008. (ENG.). 48p. (J). (gr. 1-4). pap. 7.99 *(978-0-14-241165-0(5),* Puffin Books) Penguin Young Readers Group.

—Gifts of the Heart. Polacco, Patricia, illus. 2013. (ENG., Illus.). 40p. (J). (gr. k-3). 17.99 *(978-0-399-16094-3(9),* G.P. Putnam's Sons Books for Young Readers) Penguin Young Readers Group.

—An Orange for Frankie. Polacco, Patricia, illus. 2004. (ENG., Illus.). 48p. (J). (gr. 1-4). 17.99 *(978-0-399-24302-8(X),* Philomel Bks.) Penguin Young Readers Group.

Politi, Leo. Pedro: The Angel of Olvera Street. 2009. (ENG., Illus.). 32p. 14.95 *(978-0-89236-990-4(6))* Oxford Univ. Pr., Inc.

Pollard, Tara. Season's Christmas Quest: The Dog's Story. 2012. 138p. (gr. 1-1). 21.95 *(978-1-4759-4008-4(4));* pap. 11.95 *(978-1-4759-4009-1(2))* iUniverse, Inc.

Pollock, Beth. Harley's Gift, 1 vol. 2007. (Lorimer Streetlights Ser.). (ENG.). 128p. (J). (gr. 2-5). 7.95 *(978-1-55028-992-3(6),* 9781550289923) Lorimer, James & Co., Ltd., Pubs. CAN. Dist: Casemate Pubs. & Bk. Distributors, LLC.

Poltamees, Welleran & Laughing Elephant Staff, compiled by. The Laughing Elephant's Book of Christmas. 2013. (ENG., Illus.). 96p. 12.95 *(978-1-59583-626-7(8))* Laughing Elephant.

Pongetti, Freda, illus. & adapted by. Why the Chimes Rang. Pongetti, Freda, adapted by. 2007. 18p. (J). 21.00 net. *(978-0-9796625-0-8(8))* GDG Publishing.

Ponko, Cindy. Cartwheel Katie's Christmas. 2007. (Illus.). 16p. (J). 15.50 *(978-0-9768230-7-0(1))* Some Kids I Know, LLC.

Ponko, Cindy A. Gary's Forever Christmas Tree. 2006. (Illus.). (J). *(978-0-9768230-2-5(0))* Some Kids I Know.

Porteous, Barbara. Little Cloud's Christmas Adventure. 2011. (Illus.). 32p. pap. 15.66 *(978-1-4520-0176-0(6))* AuthorHouse.

Posner-Sanchez, Andrea. The Christmas Party. Random House Disney Staff, illus. 2014. (Step into Reading Ser.). (ENG.). 24p. (J). (gr. -1-1). 4.99 *(978-0-7364-3279-5(5),* RH/Disney) Random Hse. Children's Bks.

—Cinderella's Fairy Merry Christmas. Marrucchi, Elisa, illus. 2009. (Pictureback(R) Ser.). (ENG.). 24p. (J). (gr. -1-2). pap. 3.99 *(978-0-7364-2622-0(1),* RH/Disney) Random Hse. Children's Bks.

Potter, Beatrix. The Tailor of Gloucester, 1 vol. Jorgensen, David, illus. 2007. (Rabbit Ears: A Classic Tale Ser.). (ENG.). 40p. (gr. -1-3). 25.65 *(978-1-59961-312-3(3))* Spotlight.

Powell-Tuck, Maudie. A Very Merry Christmas. Guile, Gill, illus. 2014. (ENG.). 22p. (J). (gr. -1-k). bds. 8.99 *(978-1-58925-560-9(7))* Tiger Tales.

Poydar, Nancy. Brave Santa. 2004. (ENG., Illus.). 32p. (J). (gr. k-3). tchr. ed. 16.95 *(978-0-8234-1821-3(9))* Holiday Hse., Inc.

Prati, Elisa. Mio Libro di Natale. pap. 24.95 *(978-88-09-02754-1(X))* Giunti Gruppo Editoriale ITA. Dist: Distribooks, Inc.

Preston, Sarah. The, Adventures of Abby. 2011. (ENG.). 30p. (J). pap. 14.95 *(978-1-4327-7566-7(9))* Outskirts Pr., Inc.

Priddy, Roger. Christmas. (Mini Tab Ser.). (ENG.). (J). 2016. 16p. bds. 5.99 *(978-0-312-52051-9(4),* 9780312520519) 2015. 12p. (gr. -1 — 1). bds. 4.99 *(978-0-312-51895-0(1),* 9780312518950) St. Martin's Pr. (Priddy Bks.).

—Little Friends: Home for Christmas. 2016. (Little Friends Ser.). (ENG.). 12p. (J). bds. 8.99 *(978-0-312-52144-8(8),* 9780312521448, Priddy Bks.) St. Martin's Pr.

—Santa Claus. 2012. (Funny Faces Ser.). (ENG., Illus.). 10p. (J). (gr. -1-1). bds. 8.99 *(978-0-312-51558-4(8),* 9780312515584, Priddy Bks.) St. Martin's Pr.

—Santa Express. 2013. (Shaped Board Bks.). (ENG., Illus.). 6p. (J). (gr. -1-k). bds. 6.99 *(978-0-312-51619-2(3),* 9780312516192, Priddy Bks.) St. Martin's Pr.

—Shiny Shapes: My Christmas Star. 2016. (Shiny Shapes Ser.). (ENG.). 10p. (J). bds. 7.99 *(978-0-312-52052-6(2),* 9780312520526, Priddy Bks.) St. Martin's Pr.

Pride, Wallace. The Mighty Christmas Oak. 2008. 19p. pap. 24.95 *(978-1-60672-752-2(4))* PublishAmerica, Inc.

Primavera, Elise. Auntie Claus: Home for the Holidays. Primavera, Elise, illus. 2009. (ENG., Illus.). 40p. (J). (gr. -1-3). 17.99 *(978-1-4169-5485-9(6),* Simon & Schuster/Paula Wiseman Bks.) Simon & Schuster/Paula Wiseman Bks.

—Auntie Claus & the Key to Christmas. 2011. (ENG., Illus.). 40p. (J). (gr. -1-3). pap. 7.99 *(978-0-547-57679-4(X))* Houghton Mifflin Harcourt Publishing Co.

—Auntie Claus Gift Edition. Primavera, Elise, illus. 2015. (ENG., Illus.). 40p. (J). (gr. -1-3). 17.99 *(978-0-544-53872-6(2),* HMH Books For Young Readers) Houghton Mifflin Harcourt Publishing Co.

Pritchard, Mark A. Billy Christmas. 2012. (ENG.). 350p. (YA). (gr. 7). pap. 16.95 *(978-0-9826251-8-7(9))* Santa Fe Writers Project.

Provencio, Marta. The Christmas Dragon. 2013. 24p. pap. 12.99 *(978-1-4808-0379-4(0))* Archway Publishing.

Publications International Ltd. Staff, creator. Christmas Stories. 2007. (Pop-up Treasury Ser.). (Illus.). (J). (gr. -1-3). 12.98 *(978-1-4127-8837-3(4))* Publications International, Ltd.

Publications International Ltd. Staff, ed. Christmas Small Saddle Stitch, Pack. 2010. 16p. (J). pap. 5.98 *(978-1-4127-9916-4(3))* Publications International, Ltd.

—First Look & Find Little Elf. 2013. 18p. (J). bds. *(978-1-4508-7093-1(7),* 1450870937) Phoenix International Publications, Inc.

—Mickey Mouse Clubhouse: Sing-along Christmas Songs: Holiday Play-a-Song Book. 2010. 10p. (J). bds. 12.98 *(978-1-4127-7862-6(X))* Publications International, Ltd.

—Night Before Christmas Giant Look & Find. 2010. 24p. (J). 15.98 *(978-1-4508-0408-0(X))* Publications International, Ltd.

—Record a Story: 'Twas the Night Before Christmas. 2010. 20p. (J). (gr. k-3). bds. 19.99 *(978-1-4508-0201-7(X),* 145080201X) Phoenix International Publications, Inc.

—Rudolph the Red-Nosed Reindeer (Book & Plush) 2011. 8p. (J). bds. 11.98 *(978-1-4508-2170-4(7))* Publications International, Ltd.

—Sesame Street: Merry Christmas, Elmo! 2010. 8p. (J). bds. 5.98 *(978-1-60553-980-5(5))* Phoenix International Publications, Inc.

—Sesame Street: Merry Christmas, Elmo! (Book & Plush) 2011. 8p. (J). bds. 11.98 *(978-1-4508-2169-8(3))* Publications International, Ltd.

Purnell, Ann. Christmas Tree Farm. Weber, Jill, illus. 2006. (ENG.). 32p. (J). (gr. -1-3). 16.95 *(978-0-8234-1886-2(3))* Holiday Hse., Inc.

Quintanilla, Billie. The Greatest Mousemas Ever! Barnum, Tabatha, illus. 2012. 36p. 24.95 *(978-1-4626-9725-0(9));* pap. 24.95 *(978-1-4626-5236-5(0))* America Star Bks.

R., Charlie. The Christmas Mama Santa Delivered the Toys. 2012. 36p. 19.95 *(978-1-4626-6824-3(0))* PublishAmerica, Inc.

Rabe, Tish. The Cat in the Hat Knows a Lot about Christmas! (Dr. Seuss/Cat in the Hat) Mathieu, Joe, illus. 2013. (Big Golden Book Ser.). (ENG.). 48p. (J). (gr. -1-1). 9.99 *(978-0-449-81495-6(5),* Golden Bks.) Random Hse. Children's Bks.

—Cooking with the Grinch (Dr. Seuss) Brannon, Tom, illus. 2017. (Step into Reading Ser.). (ENG.). 32p. (J). (gr. -1-1). pap. 4.99 ***(978-1-5247-1462-8(3))***; lib. bdg. 12.99 ***(978-1-5247-1463-5(1))*** Random Hse. Children's Bks. (Random Hse. Bks. for Young Readers).

—Home for Christmas. Brannon, Tom, illus. 2012. (Step into Reading Ser.). (ENG.). 48p. (J). (gr. k-3). pap. 3.99 *(978-0-307-97625-3(4),* Random Hse. Bks. for Young Readers) Random Hse. Children's Bks.

—A Reindeer's First Christmas / New Friends for Christmas. 2012. (Cat in the Hat Knows a Lot about That Ser.). lib. bdg. 14.75 *(978-0-606-26787-8(5),* Turtleback) Turtleback Bks.

Rader, Laura. The Twelve Days of Christmas in California. Rader, Laura, illus. 2009. (Twelve Days of Christmas in America Ser.). (ENG., Illus.). 40p. (J). (gr. k-3). 12.95 *(978-1-4027-6247-5(X))* Sterling Publishing Co., Inc.

—When Santa Lost His Ho! Ho! Ho! Rader, Laura, illus. 2008. (ENG., Illus.). 40p. (J). (gr. -1-3). 14.99 *(978-0-06-114139-3(9))* HarperCollins Pubs.

Radzinski, Kandy. What Cats Want for Christmas. Radzinski, Kandy, illus. rev. ed. 2007. (ENG., Illus.). 32p. (J). (gr. k-6). 16.95 *(978-1-58536-340-7(5))* Sleeping Bear Pr.

—What Dogs Want for Christmas. Radzinski, Kandy, illus. 2008. (ENG., Illus.). 32p. (J). (gr. k-6). 16.95 *(978-1-58536-363-6(4))* Sleeping Bear Pr.

Rae, Jaci. Collista's Search for the True Meaning of Christmas. 2007. (Illus.). 59p. per. 14.95 *(978-0-9746229-1-0(5))* North Shore Records, Inc.

Rainey, Barbara. What God Wants for Christmas. Walker, John, illus. 2011. (J). (gr. 4-7). pap. 29.99 incl. audio compact disk *(978-1-60200-428-3(5))* FamilyLife.

Raley, Hugh W. Erin the Excellent Elf. 2013. 20p. pap. 12.95 *(978-1-4908-0533-7(8),* WestBow Pr.) Author Solutions, Inc.

Ralph, Grampa. How Santa Knows. 2007. 56p. pap. 16.95 *(978-1-4241-2284-4(8))* America Star Bks.

Rand, Ted & Moore, Clement C. The Night Before Christmas. 2012. (ENG., Illus.). 32p. (J). (gr. -1-3). 19.95 *(978-0-7358-4099-7(7))* North-South Bks., Inc.

Randall, Marilyn. Elmer the Christmas Elf. 2009. 32p. 18.95 *(978-0-557-15333-6(6))* Lulu Pr., Inc.

Random House. Frosty's First Christmas (Frosty the Snowman) Cucca, Vincenzo & Hao, Katrina Mae, illus. 2016. (Nifty Lift-And-Look Ser.). (ENG.). 12p. (J). (-k). bds. 6.99 *(978-0-399-55012-6(7),* RH/Disney) Random Hse. Children's Bks.

—Holiday Helpers! (PAW Patrol) Random House, illus. 2016. (Pictureback(R) Ser.). (ENG., Illus.). 24p. (J). (gr. -1-2). pap. 5.99 *(978-0-399-55874-0(8),* Random Hse. Bks. for Young Readers) Random Hse. Children's Bks.

—It's a SpongeBob Christmas! (SpongeBob SquarePants) Random House, illus. 2013. (Pictureback(R) Ser.). (ENG., Illus.). 24p. (J). (gr. -1-2). 3.99 *(978-0-385-37856-7(4),* Random Hse. Bks. for Young Readers) Random Hse. Children's Bks.

—Plankton's Christmas Surprise! (SpongeBob SquarePants) Martinez, Heather, illus. 2013. (Pictureback(R) Ser.). (ENG.). 16p. (J). (gr. -1-2). 4.99 *(978-0-449-81851-0(9),* Random Hse. Bks. for Young Readers) Random Hse. Children's Bks.

—Santa's Little Helpers (Team Umizoomi) Ostrom, Bob, illus. 2013. (Pictureback(R) Ser.). (ENG.). 16p. (J). (gr. -1-2). 4.99 *(978-0-449-81881-7(0),* Random Hse. Bks. for Young Readers) Random Hse. Children's Bks.

Random House Editors. Don't Be a Jerk, It's Christmas! Random House Editors, illus. 2013. (Big Golden Book Ser.). (ENG., Illus.). 40p. (J). (gr. -1-2). 12.99 *(978-0-449-81766-7(0),* Random Hse. Bks. for Young Readers) Random Hse. Children's Bks.

Rangel, Graciela. Anthony's Christmas Journey. 2006. (ENG.). 80p. pap. 9.95 *(978-1-59526-650-7(X),* Llumina Christian Bks.) Aeon Publishing Inc.

Ransom, Candice. The Twelve Days of Christmas in Washington, D. C. Hollander, Sarah, illus. 2010. (Twelve Days of Christmas in America Ser.). (ENG.). 40p. (J). (gr. k). 12.95 *(978-1-4027-6394-6(8))* Sterling Publishing Co., Inc.

Rasmussen, Liz, illus. Too Fat to Fly. 2007. 32p. (J). 16.95 *(978-0-9793517-0-9(7))* Silver Bells Publishing Hse.

Rath, Tom H. Donkey Oatie's Christmas Pageant. Townshend, Katie, illus. 2013. 24p. pap. *(978-0-9918033-6-1(1))* Wood Islands Prints.

Raum, Elizabeth. The Christmas Star. Johnson, Meredith, illus. (ENG.). (J). (gr. -1-k). 2008. 32p. per. 3.99 *(978-0-8249-5567-0(6))* 2005. 28p. bds. 7.95 *(978-0-8249-6620-1(1))* Worthy Publishing. (Ideal Pubns.).

Ravera, Giuseppe. Gingerbread Man House. Pagnoni, Roberta & Rigo, Laura, illus. 2015. (ENG.). 8p. (J). (gr. -1-k). bds. 6.99 *(978-0-7641-6784-3(7))* Barron's Educational Series, Inc.

—Snowflake. 2014. (ENG., Illus.). 10p. (J). (gr. -1 — 1). bds. 6.99 *(978-0-7641-6719-5(7))* Barron's Educational Series, Inc.

Rawlinson, Julia. Fletcher & the Snowflake Christmas. Beeke, Tiphanie, illus. 2010. (ENG.). 32p. (J). (gr. -1-2). 16.99 *(978-0-06-199033-5(7),* Greenwillow Bks.) HarperCollins Pubs.

Ray, Lynn. The Angel's Christmas. 2013. (ENG., Illus.). 32p. (J). (gr. -1-3). 16.95 *(978-1-927018-39-2(0))* Simply Read Bks. CAN. Dist: Ingram Publisher Services.

Ray, Mary Lyn. Christmas Farm. Root, Barry, illus. 2008. (ENG.). 40p. (J). (gr. -1-3). 17.99 *(978-0-15-216290-0(9))* Houghton Mifflin Harcourt Publishing Co.

Read, Miss. The Christmas Mouse. Goodall, John S., illus. (J). lib. bdg. 14.95 *(978-0-8488-1452-6(5))* Amereon Ltd.

Reagan, Jean. How to Catch Santa. Wildish, Lee, illus. 2015. (ENG.). 32p. (J). (gr. -1-3). 17.99 *(978-0-553-49839-4(8));* lib. bdg. 20.99 *(978-0-553-49840-0(1))* Random Hse. Children's Bks. (Knopf Bks. for Young Readers).

Reasoner, Charles. Winter Friends, 1 vol. Reasoner, Charles & Jones, Anna, illus. 2013. (Charles Reasoner Holiday Bks.). (ENG.). 10p. (J). (gr. -1 — 1). bds. 4.99 *(978-1-4048-8156-3(5))* Picture Window Bks.

Reavis, Vicky 'A' Blevins. The Night Before Christmas. 2013. 72p. pap. 17.95 *(978-1-4241-2838-9(2))* America Star Bks.

Rebmann, Charles. Christmas Stories from the Jersey Cape. 2003. 94p. pap. 9.95 *(978-0-595-29692-7(0))* iUniverse, Inc.

The Recipe for Christmas Snow. 2003. (Illus.). 36p. per. 12.90 *(978-0-9743840-3-0(8))* Creek Sound Bks.

Rees, Douglas. Jeannette Claus Saves Christmas. Latyk, Olivier, illus. 2010. (ENG.). 40p. (J). (gr. k-3). 16.99 *(978-1-4169-2686-3(0),* McElderry, Margaret K. Bks.) McElderry, Margaret K. Bks.

Reese, Michael. Christmas Party on the Farm. 2004. (J). per. 14.95 *(978-0-9746213-0-2(7))* Sabre Publishing Hse., Inc.

Regan, Patricia, illus. Musical Christmas Tree. 2017. (ENG.). 16p. (J). (gr. -1-1). bds. 10.99 ***(978-0-7641-6899-4(1))*** Barron's Educational Series, Inc.

Regnew, Tera. Christopher Cricket's Christmas. 2011. 16p. pap. *(978-1-4269-9687-0(X))* Trafford Publishing (UK) Ltd.

Reid, Pamela Carrington. Little One. Tolman, Tom, illus. 2010. (J). *(978-1-59811-574-1(X))* Covenant Communications.

Reindeer. 2003. (Shaped Board Books Ser.). 14p. (J). (gr. -1-k). bds. 9.95 *(978-0-7525-8850-6(8))* Parragon, Inc.

Reinheimer, Melinda. A Christmas Tea. 2004. (J). per. 7.95 *(978-1-59196-756-9(2))* Instant Pub.

Reiss, Mike. How Murray Saved Christmas. Catrow, David, illus. 2004. (ENG.). 32p. (J). (gr. -1-2). 6.99 *(978-0-14-250145-0(X),* Puffin Books) Penguin Young Readers Group.

—Merry Un-Christmas. Catrow, David, illus. 2006. 32p. (J). (gr. -1-2). lib. bdg. 16.89 *(978-0-06-059127-4(7))* HarperCollins Pubs.

Remkiewicz, Frank, illus. The Twelve Days of Christmas in Florida. (Twelve Days of Christmas in America Ser.). (ENG.). (J). (— 1). 2017. 22p. bds. 7.95 ***(978-1-4549-2283-4(4))*** 2008. 40p. 12.95 *(978-1-4027-3817-3(X))* Sterling Publishing Co., Inc.

Repicci, Albert. The Littlest Angel: A Christmas Story. 2012. 36p. pap. 21.99 *(978-1-4691-9547-6(X))* Xlibris Corp.

Rey, H. A. Christmas Countdown. 2009. (Curious George Ser.). (ENG., Illus.). 14p. (J). (gr. k — 1). bds. 7.99 *(978-0-547-23863-0(0))* Houghton Mifflin Harcourt Publishing Co.

—Curious about Christmas. 2011. (Curious Baby Curious George Ser.). (ENG., Illus.). 12p. (J). (gr. k — 1). bds. 8.99 *(978-0-547-58841-4(0))* Houghton Mifflin Harcourt Publishing Co.

—Feliz Navidad, Jorge el Curioso. Young, Mary O'Keefe, illus. 2012. (Curious George Ser.).Tr. of Merry Christmas, Curious George. (ENG & SPA.). 32p. (J). (gr. -1-3). 10.99 *(978-0-547-74503-9(6))* Houghton Mifflin Harcourt Publishing Co.

Rey, H. A., et al. Merry Christmas, Curious George. Young, Mary O'Keefe, illus. 2012. (Curious George Ser.). (ENG.). 32p. (J). (gr. -1-3). 9.99 *(978-0-547-76054-4(X))* Houghton Mifflin Harcourt Publishing Co.

Reynolds, Carl. The Turkey Mountain Gang's.... Christmas Adventure! 2010. 44p. pap. 18.49 *(978-1-4520-6514-4(4))* AuthorHouse.

Reynolds, Peter H. The Smallest Gift of Christmas. Reynolds, Peter H., illus. 2013. (ENG., Illus.). 40p. (J). (gr. -1-2). 14.00 *(978-0-7636-6103-8(1))* Candlewick Pr.

Reynolds, Peter H., illus. Star Bright: A Christmas Story. 2014. (ENG.). 40p. (J). (gr. -1-3). 17.99 *(978-1-4169-5858-1(4),* Atheneum Bks. for Young Readers) Simon & Schuster Children's Publishing.

Rhodes, Tiffany. What I Learned This Christmas. 2013. (Illus.). 42p. pap. 15.99 *(978-0-9899099-1-4(3))* Bee Creative, LLC.

Ricci, Christine. Dora's Starry Christmas. Studios, A&J, illus. 2005. 24p. (J). lib. bdg. 9.00 *(978-1-4242-0980-4(3))* Fitzgerald Bks.

—Navidad Estelar de Dora. Ziegler, Argentina Palacios, tr. A and J Studios Staff, illus. 2005. (Dora the Explorer Ser.). (SPA.). 24p. (J). pap. 3.99 *(978-1-4169-1183-8(9),* Libros Para Ninos) Libros Para Ninos.

Richardson, Faith. Angel Walker. 2003. Orig. Title: The Sea, the Song & the Trumpetfish. (Illus.). 172p. (J). 19.95 *(978-0-9744989-2-8(0));* pap. 12.95 *(978-0-9744989-3-5(9))* Fox Song Bks.

Richardson, Kiowa. The Christmas Kangaroo: Written & Illustrated by Kiowa Richardson. 2012. 16p. pap. 7.95 *(978-1-4497-4329-1(3),* WestBow Pr.) Author Solutions, Inc.

Richardson, Linda. The Gift. 2003. (J). 6.95 *(978-1-59094-021-1(0),* Jawbreakers for Kids) Jawbone Publishing Corp.

Richmond, Marianne. You Are My Merry. (ENG., 32p. (J). (-2). 2017. Illus.). pap. 4.99 ***(978-1-4926-6064-4(7))*** 2015. 16.99 *(978-1-4926-2894-1(8))* Sourcebooks, Inc. (Sourcebooks Jabberwocky).

Rickett, Sally. Minky the Shoebox Monkey - a Little Monkey with a Long Way to Go. 2010. 54p. pap. 17.95 *(978-1-60860-625-2(2),* Strategic Bk. Publishing) Strategic Book Publishing & Rights Agency (SBPRA).

Ricks, Kimber Orson. Discovering Santa: A Christmas Story. 2005. 7.99 *(978-1-55517-862-8(6))* Cedar Fort, Inc./CFI Distribution.

Rigo, L., illus. Little Reindeer. 2014. (Mini People Shape Bks.). (ENG.). 10p. (J). (gr. -1-2). bds. 4.99 *(978-0-7641-6736-2(7))* Barron's Educational Series, Inc.

Riley, Penelope A. Christmas Away! A Duckie Dan Adventure Book. 2012. 48p. pap. 21.99 *(978-1-4772-7554-2(1))* AuthorHouse.

Rimes, Rebecca. Hippie Hippopotamus. 2011. 24p. (gr. 10-12). pap. 12.74 *(978-1-4634-0855-8(2))* AuthorHouse.

Rissik, Maureen. Christmas Box: A Holiday Gift to Unlock & Treasure. 2007. (Illus.). 24p. 9.95 *(978-0-7624-3039-0(7),* Running Pr. Bk. Pubs.) Running Pr. Bk. Pubs.

Ritchie, Joseph R. Where's Santa? Halverson, Lydia, illus. 2006. (ENG.). 14p. (J). (gr. -1-k). bds. 7.95 *(978-0-8249-6673-7(2),* Ideal Pubns.) Worthy Publishing.

Rivers-Moore, Debbie. Five Christmas Reindeer. Everitt-Stewart, Andrew, illus. 2015. (ENG.). 10p. (J). (gr. -1 — 1). bds. 8.99 *(978-1-4998-0169-9(6))* Little Bee Books Inc.

Rivers, Phoebe. Spirits of the Season. 2012. (Saranormal Ser.: 4). (ENG.). 160p. (J). (gr. 3-7). 15.99 *(978-1-4424-5379-1(6));* pap. 6.99 *(978-1-4424-5223-7(4))* Simon Spotlight. (Simon Spotlight).

Rives, J. G. Where Are My Christmas Presents? Young, Dot, illus. 2007. 44p. (J). 17.95 *(978-0-9790014-0-6(4))* Sterli Publishing.

Rix, Jamie. Tough Turkey. 2003. (ENG., Illus.). 240p. pap. *(978-0-440-86479-0(8),* Yearling) Random Hse. Children's Bks.

Robbins, Dennis L. A Soldier's Christmas. 2011. 44p. pap. 21.99 *(978-1-4653-4097-9(1))* Xlibris Corp.

Robertson, Charmaine. My Christmas List. 2016. (Rosen REAL Readers: Social Studies Nonfiction / Fiction: Family, Community, & the World Ser.). 12p. (gr. 1-k). pap. 6.33 *(978-1-5081-2550-1(3),* Rosen Classroom) Rosen Publishing Group, Inc., The.

Robertson, Si & Nelson, Ashley Howard. Uncle Si, the Christmas Elf: Work Hard, Nap Hard. Gilpin, Stephen, illus. 2014. (ENG.). 48p. (J). (gr. -1-3). 29.99 *(978-1-4814-1821-8(1),* Simon & Schuster Bks. For Young Readers) Simon & Schuster Bks. For Young Readers.

Robinson, Barbara. The Best Christmas Pageant Ever. Cornell, Laura, illus. 2011. (ENG.). 40p. (J). (gr. -1-3). 16.99 *(978-0-06-089074-2(6))* HarperCollins Pubs.

—The Best Christmas Pageant Ever. 2005. (ENG., Illus.). 128p. (J). (gr. 3-7). pap. 5.99 *(978-0-06-440275-0(4))* HarperCollins Pubs.

—The Best Christmas Pageant Ever. 2009. 8.32 *(978-0-7848-1246-4(2),* Everbind) Marco Bk. Co.

—The Best Christmas Pageant Ever. 2005. (Illus.). 108p. (gr. 3-7). 16.00 *(978-0-7569-6531-0(4))* Perfection Learning Corp.

—The Best Christmas Pageant Ever. 2005. (J). 16.00 *(978-0-88103-998-6(5),* Turtleback) Turtleback Bks.

Robinson, George. Elmer the Elf & the Magical Jingle Bells, 1 vol. Foster, Janet, illus. 2008. (ENG.). 33p. 24.95 *(978-1-60610-606-8(6))* America Star Bks.

Robinson, Michelle. Goodnight Santa: The Perfect Bedtime Book. East, Nick, illus. 2015. (Goodnight Ser.). (ENG.). 32p. (gr. -1 — 1). pap. 7.99 *(978-1-4380-0660-4(8))* Barron's Educational Series, Inc.

Rocha, Toni. Magic in the Air. 2013. 166p. pap. 19.99 *(978-1-4797-8467-7(2))* Xlibris Corp.

Roche, Lynne. The Happiest Christmas. 2005. (Illus.). 32p. (J). *(978-1-932485-27-1(9))* Reverie Publishing Co.

Rockas, Leo. Mice Make War. 2007. 53p. 16.95 *(978-1-4241-5708-2(0))* America Star Bks.

Rodrigues, Naomi. Molly Mouse & the Christmas Mystery. 2013. 24p. pap. 15.99 *(978-1-4797-6511-9(2))* Xlibris Corp.

Rogala, Judy. The Dog Days of Christmas. Stroede, Paul, illus. 2012. 32p. (J). 12.95 *(978-1-59598-219-3(1),* Goblin Fern Pr.) HenschelHAUS Publishing.

Rogers, Kenny & Junkerman, Kelly. Kenny Rogers Presents the Toy Shoppe. 2004. (Illus.). 30p. (J). (gr. 4-8). reprint ed. 16.00 *(978-0-7567-7758-6(5))* DIANE Publishing Co.

Romance, Trisha. A Star for Christmas. 2007. (ENG., Illus.). 40p. (J). (gr. k-12). 22.95 *(978-0-88776-836-1(9),* Tundra Bks.) Tundra Bks. CAN. Dist: Penguin Random Hse. LLC.

Rooks, Elizabeth. Where Does Santa Go on Vacation after Christmas? 2012. 24p. pap. 17.99 *(978-1-4772-6535-2(X))* AuthorHouse.

—Where Does Santa Work after Christmas? 2012. 24p. pap. 17.99 *(978-1-4772-9210-5(1))* AuthorHouse.

Rookstool, Yakiri. A Christmas Star. 2009. 80p. pap. 9.95 *(978-1-60693-855-3(X),* Eloquent Bks.) Strategic Book Publishing & Rights Agency (SBPRA).

Rose, Laura Lopez. Chester the Christmas Cookie Jar. 2008. 24p. per. 24.95 *(978-1-60441-228-4(3))* PublishAmerica, Inc.

Rose, M. E. Kangaroo Christmas. Keenan, Brona, illus. 2007. (ENG.). 140p. (YA). 10.95 *(978-1-896209-89-0(0))* Bayeux Arts, Inc. CAN. Dist: Chicago Distribution Ctr.

Rose, Nancy. Merry Christmas, Squirrels! 2015. (ENG., Illus.). 32p. (J). (gr. -1-3). 17.00 *(978-0-316-30257-9(0))* Little, Brown Bks. for Young Readers.

Rosenthal, Amy Krouse. Christmas Cookies: Bite-Size Holiday Lessons. Dyer, Jane, illus. 2008. 40p. (J). (gr. k-5). lib. bdg. 13.89 *(978-0-06-058025-4(9));* (ENG.). 12.99 *(978-0-06-058024-7(0))* HarperCollins Pubs.

Ross, Darien. The Carr House Cats at Christmas. 2012. 36p. pap. 18.41 *(978-1-4669-4794-8(2))* Trafford Publishing.

Ross, Tony, illus. The Nights Before Christmas: 24 Classic Christmas Stories to Read Aloud. 2017. (ENG.). 240p. (J). (gr. 4-6). 25.95 ***(978-1-84939-580-9(2))*** Andersen Pr. GBR. Dist: Independent Pubs. Group.

Rouss, Sylvia. Littlest Tree. Binus, Ari, illus. 2005. 32p. (J). pap. 9.95 *(978-1-932687-26-2(2),* Devora Publishing) Simcha Media Group.

Rowland, Teresa. Blusher's First Christmas. 2012. 64p. (-18). pap. 20.95 *(978-1-4525-0718-7(X))* Balboa Pr.

Rox, John. I Want a Hippopotamus for Christmas. Whatley, Bruce, illus. 2005. 32p. (J). (gr. -1-3). 17.99 *(978-0-06-052942-0(3))* HarperCollins Pubs.

Roy, Alene Adele. The Legend of Dragonfly Pond: Coloring Book. 2008. 56p. pap. 11.99 *(978-1-4343-4628-5(5))* AuthorHouse.

Roy, Kasi. Elizabeth Dreams: And the Christmas House Clock. 2011. 96p. pap. 12.10 *(978-1-4520-1864-5(2))* AuthorHouse.

Roy, Ronald. Calendar Mysteries #12: December Dog. Gurney, John Steven, illus. 2014. (Calendar Mysteries Ser.:

12). (ENG.). 80p. (J). (gr. 1-4). 4.99 *(978-0-385-37168-1(3)*, Random Hse. Bks. for Young Readers) Random Hse. Children's Bks.
—December Dog. 2014. (Calendar Mysteries Ser.: 12). lib. bdg. 14.75 *(978-0-606-36019-7(0))* Turtleback Bks.
Royther, Chris. Zippy's Christmas Tree. 2011. 36p. pap. 24.95 *(978-1-4560-9864-3(0))* America Star Bks.
Rozanski, Lillian. House of Shod. 2012. 20p. pap. 13.80 *(978-1-4669-7254-4(8))* Trafford Publishing.
Rubel, David. The Carpenter's Gift: A Christmas Tale about the Rockefeller Center Tree. LaMarche, Jim, illus. 2011. (ENG.). 48p. (J). (gr. k-4). 17.99 *(978-0-375-86922-8(0)*, Random Hse. Bks. for Young Readers) Random Hse. Children's Bks.
Rucker, David. The Valley of the Christmas Trees: A Legend. Laster, Brenda, illus. 2007. 41p. (J). (gr. -1-3). 14.95 *(978-1-931643-94-8(6))* Seven Locks Pr.
Rudnicki, Richard, illus. A Christmas Dollhouse, 1 vol. 2012. (ENG.). 32p. (J). (gr. -1-3). 18.95 *(978-1-55109-868-5(7))* Nimbus Publishing, Ltd. CAN. Dist: Orca Bk. Pubs. USA.
Rudolph. 2012. (Illus.). (J). *(978-1-4351-4386-9(8))* Barnes & Noble, Inc.
Rudolph the Red-Nosed Reindeer. 2004. 4p. (J). 3.95 *(978-0-634-09040-0(2))* Leonard, Hal Corp.
Rudolph the Red-Nosed Reindeer. 2014. (ENG., Illus.). 40p. (J). (gr. -1-1). 17.99 *(978-1-4424-7495-6(5)*, Little Simon) Little Simon.
Ruelle, Karen Gray. The Crunchy, Munchy Christmas Tree. Ruelle, Karen Gray, illus. 2003. (Holiday House Readers Ser.). (ENG., Illus.). 32p. (J). (gr. k-3). tchr. ed. 14.95 *(978-0-8234-1787-2(5))* Holiday Hse., Inc.
—Crunchy, Munchy Christmas Tree. 2003. (ENG., Illus.). 32p. (J). (gr. k-3). pap. 4.95 *(978-0-8234-1799-5(9))* Holiday Hse., Inc.
Ruff, Zeata P. The Gumdrop Tree. Ruff, Zeata P. & Ruff, Jim, illus. 2013. 34p. 16.95 *(978-1-937449-25-4(4))* YAV.
Running Press Staff, ed. A Treasury of Christmas Classics: Includes the Night Before Christmas, the Twelve Days of Christmas, & the Nutcracker. 2014. (ENG., Illus.). 128p. (J). (gr. 3-17). 14.95 *(978-0-7624-5495-2(4)*, Running Pr. Kids) Running Pr. Bk. Pubs.
Running Press Staff & Parker, Amy. Tiny Blessings: for a Merry Christmas. Walsh, Sarah, illus. 2016. (ENG.). 10p. (J). (gr. -1-17). bds. 7.95 *(978-0-7624-6095-3(4)*, Running Pr. Kids) Running Pr. Bk. Pubs.
Running Press Staff & Sesame Workshop Staff. Sesame Street: a Very Elmo Christmas. 2016. (ENG., Illus.). 52p. (J). (gr. -1-17). 12.95 *(978-0-7624-6140-0(3)*, Running Pr. Kids) Running Pr. Bk. Pubs.
Russo, Frank M. The Sleigh. Cittadino, Kyle & Cittadino, Kristen, illus. 2012. 24p. pap. 24.95 *(978-1-4626-7662-0(6))* America Star Bks.
Russo, Mallory Kate. The Hotel Christmas. 2012. 24p. pap. 24.95 *(978-1-4626-8060-3(7))* America Star Bks.
Rusu, Meredith. A Merry Shopkins Christmas. 2016. (Shopkins Ser.). (ENG.). 24p. (J). (gr. -1-3). pap. 4.99 *(978-1-338-03800-2(1))* Scholastic, Inc.
Ryan, Cheryl, et al. My Christmas Treasury. Bassett, Jeni et al, illus. 2012. (ENG.). 96p. (J). (gr. -1-3). 8.99 *(978-0-545-43647-2(8))* Scholastic, Inc.
Ryan, Mary C., illus. & text. Twitcher Mcgee & the Wonderful Tree. Ryan, Mary C., text. 2008. 12p. (J). 4.95 *(978-0-9678115-3-6(8))* Dragonseed Pr.
Rylant, Cynthia. Henry & Mudge & a Very Merry Christmas. Stevenson, Suçie, illus. 2005. (Henry & Mudge Ser.). 40p. (gr. -1-3). 14.00 *(978-0-7569-5816-9(4))* Perfection Learning Corp.
—Henry & Mudge & a Very Merry Christmas. Stevenson, Suçie, illus. (Henry & Mudge Ser.: 25). (ENG.). 40p. (J). (gr. k-2). 2005. pap. 3.99 *(978-0-689-83448-6(9))* 2004. 16.99 *(978-0-689-81168-5(3))* Simon Spotlight. (Simon Spotlight).
Sabuda, Robert. The Christmas Story. 2016. (ENG.). 12p. (J). (gr. k-3). 35.00 *(978-0-7636-8326-9(4))* Candlewick Pr.
—The 12 Days of Christmas. Sabuda, Robert, illus. 10th anniv. ed. 2006. (ENG., Illus.). 14p. (J). (gr. -1-3). 34.99 *(978-1-4169-2792-1(1)*, Little Simon) Little Simon.
Sachs, Harley L. A Troll for Christmas & Other Stories. 2009. (ENG., Illus.). 240p. (J). pap. 14.99 *(978-1-934841-80-8(3)*, Zumaya Thresholds) Zumaya Pubns. LLC.
Sacre, Antonio. La Noche Buena: A Christmas Story. Dominguez, Angela, illus. 2010. (ENG.). 32p. (J). (gr. k-2). 17.95 *(978-0-8109-8967-2(0)*, Abrams Bks. for Young Readers) Abrams, Inc.
Sammy & the White Christmas. 2004. (J). per. 15.99 *(978-0-9753533-9-4(X))* Golden Eagle Publishing Hse., Inc.
Sander, Sonia & Bridwell, Norman. Clifford Helps Santa. Cuddy, Robbin, illus. 2006. (Clifford the Big Red Dog Ser.). (J). pap. *(978-0-439-90456-8(0))* Scholastic, Inc.
Sanders, Rob. Cowboy Christmas. Manders, John, illus. 2012. (ENG.). 32p. (J). (gr. k-k). 10.99 *(978-0-375-86985-3(9)*, Golden Bks.) Random Hse. Children's Bks.
Sanrio. Merry Christmas, Hello Kitty! 2014. (ENG., Illus.). 24p. (J). (gr. k-2). 6.95 *(978-1-4197-1376-7(0)*, Abrams Bks. for Young Readers) Abrams, Inc.
Sansone, V. K. The Carpenter & His Wife. 2009. 32p. pap. 14.98 *(978-0-557-19204-5(8))* Lulu Pr., Inc.
—Katie Bear & Friends (Book One) 2009. 36p. pap. 16.97 *(978-0-557-09358-8(9))* Lulu Pr., Inc.
Santa the Chimney Sweep/the Candy Cane That Found a Home: Wee Voices Collection. 2005. (Illus.). 37p. per. 6.95 *(978-0-9764444-9-7(6))* E. J. Publishing.
Santa's Christmas Cookies. 2003. (J). per. *(978-1-57657-708-0(2))* Paradise Pr., Inc.
Santa's Twinkly Christmas Eve. 2008. (Light up Book Ser.). 8p. *(978-1-4075-3500-5(5))* Parragon, Inc.
Santa's Workshop. 2004. (J). per. *(978-1-57657-450-8(4))* Paradise Pr., Inc.
Santiago, Esmeralda. Una Muneca para el Dia de Reyes. Torres-Vidal, Nina, tr. from ENG. Sanchez, Enrique O., illus. 2005.Tr. of Doll for Navidades. (SPA & ENG.). 32p. (J). (gr. -1-3). per. 5.99 *(978-0-439-75510-8(7))* Scholastic, Inc.
Santomero, Angela C. Merry Christmas, Daniel Tiger! Fruchter, Jason, illus. 2015. (Daniel Tiger's Neighborhood Ser.). (ENG.). 14p. (J). (gr. -1-2). bds. 6.99 *(978-1-4814-4660-0(6)*, Simon Spotlight) Simon Spotlight.
Santore, Charles. Cuento de Nochebuena: Una Visita de San Nicolas. 2012. (ENG & SPA.). 48p. (J). 18.95 *(978-1-60433-299-5(9)*, Applesauce Pr.) Cider Mill Pr. Bk. Pubs., LLC.
Santoro, Scott. Candy Cane Lane. Santoro, Scott, illus. 2016. (ENG., Illus.). 48p. (J). (gr. -1-3). 17.99 *(978-1-4814-5661-6(X)*, Simon & Schuster Bks. For Young Readers) Simon & Schuster Bks. For Young Readers.
Sapp, Karen, illus. Ellie's Christmas. 2013. (J). *(978-1-4351-4835-2(5))* Barnes & Noble, Inc.
Sargent, Dave & Sargent, Pat. Sweetpea: (Purple Corn Welsh) Be Happy, 30 vols., Vol. 58. Lenoir, Jane, illus. 2003. (Saddle up Ser.: Vol. 58). 42p. (J). pap. 10.95 *(978-1-56763-816-5(3))*; lib. bdg. 23.60 *(978-1-56763-815-8(5))* Ozark Publishing.
Sam, Amélie & Trouillot, Virgile. Happy Holidays. 2009. (Groove High Ser.). (Illus.). 112p. (YA). (gr. 5-8). 31.95 *(978-1-60754-526-2(8))*; pap. 15.25 *(978-1-60754-527-9(6))* Windmill Bks.
Sattler, Jennifer. A Chick 'n' Pug Christmas. 2014. (ENG., Illus.). 32p. (J). (gr. -1-1). 16.99 *(978-1-59990-602-7(3)*, 9781599906027, Bloomsbury USA Childrens) Bloomsbury Publishing USA.
Sattler, Jennifer Gordon, illus. A Chick 'n' Pug Christmas. 2014. (J). *(978-1-61963-463-3(5))* Bloomsbury Pr.
Sauer, Tammi. The Twelve Days of Christmas in Oklahoma. Hutto, Victoria, illus. 2012. (Twelve Days of Christmas in America Ser.). (ENG.). 40p. (J). (gr. k-3). 12.95 *(978-1-4027-9224-3(7))* Sterling Publishing Co., Inc.
Sawyer, Ruth. This Way to Christmas. 2004. reprint ed. pap. 22.95 *(978-1-4179-3854-4(4))* Kessinger Publishing, LLC.
Say, Allen. Tree of Cranes. Say, Allen, illus. 2009. (ENG., Illus.). 32p. (J). (gr. -1-3). pap. 7.99 *(978-0-547-24830-1(X))* Houghton Mifflin Harcourt Publishing Co.
Scali, Jacob, et al. Sprucy: The Tallest Christmas Tree. Carrier, Jason, illus. 2011. (ENG.). 32p. (J). (gr. k-4). 14.99 *(978-1-4634-2468-8(X)*, 9781463424688) AuthorHouse.
Scarry, Patricia M. The Sweet Smell of Christmas. Miller, J. P., illus. 2003. (Scented Storybook Ser.). (ENG.). 36p. (J). (gr. -1-2). 9.99 *(978-0-375-82643-6(2)*, Golden Bks.) Random Hse. Children's Bks.
Scarry, Richard. Christmas Mice. Scarry, Richard, illus. 2014. (Little Golden Book Ser.). (ENG., Illus.). 24p. (J). (-k). 4.99 *(978-0-385-38421-6(1)*, Golden Bks.) Random Hse. Children's Bks.
—The Night Before the Night Before Christmas! Scarry, Richard, illus. 2014. (ENG., Illus.). 48p. (J). (gr. -1-2). 14.99 *(978-0-385-38804-7(7)*, Golden Bks.) Random Hse. Children's Bks.
—Richard Scarry's Best Christmas Book Ever! 2010. (ENG., Illus.). 44p. (J). (gr. -1-2). 12.95 *(978-1-4027-7218-4(1))* Sterling Publishing Co., Inc.
—Richard Scarry's Christmas Tales, 4 vols. 2011. (My Mini Book Collection). (ENG., Illus.). 48p. (J). (gr. -1 — 1). 6.95 *(978-1-4027-8567-2(4))* Sterling Publishing Co., Inc.
Schaefer, Jack. Stubby Pringle's Christmas. Bjorklund, Lorence, illus. 2017. (ENG.). 48p. pap. 16.95 ***(978-0-8263-5865-3(9))*** Univ. of New Mexico Pr.
Scheidies, Carolyn R. WHERE IS CAT? She's Obviously Been Here! 2007. 50p. pap. 14.88 *(978-0-615-16673-5(3))* C R Pubns.
Schermbrucker, Reviva. An African Christmas Cloth. 2007. (ENG.). 36p. 27.95 *(978-1-77009-081-1(9))* Jacana Media ZAF. Dist: Independent Pubs. Group.
Schertle, Alice. Little Blue Truck's Christmas. McElmurry, Jill, illus. 2014. (Little Blue Truck Ser.). (ENG.). 24p. (J). (— 1). 14.99 *(978-0-544-32041-3(7)*, HMH Books For Young Readers) Houghton Mifflin Harcourt Publishing Co.
Schick-Jacobowitz, Jeannie, et al. A Bit of Applause for Mrs. Claus. 2012. (ENG.). 32p. (J). (-3). 15.99 *(978-1-4022-7085-7(2)*, Sourcebooks Jabberwocky) Sourcebooks, Inc.
Schlafer, Linda. A Gift for the Christ Child: A Christmas Folktale. Wilson, Anne, illus. 2004. 26p. (gr. -1-3). 15.95 *(978-0-8294-1606-0(4))* Loyola Pr.
Schliewen, Richard. Paulina's Teddy Bear Journey. Visaya, Artemio, illus. 2012. 104p. pap. 19.95 *(978-1-4626-9597-3(3))* America Star Bks.
Schmoll, Edie. Holly, the Christmas Tree Fairy. 2012. 24p. pap. 15.99 *(978-1-4797-2087-3(9))* Xlibris Corp.
Schneider, Antonie. Advent Storybook: 24 Stories to Share Before Christmas. Miller, Marisa, tr. from GER. Dusikova, Maja, illus. 2005. (ENG.). 64p. (J). (gr. -1-3). 17.95 *(978-0-7358-1963-4(7))* North-South Bks., Inc.
Schneider, Richard H. The Christmas Pea Coat. Bond, Higgins, illus. 2004. 32p. (J). 14.95 *(978-0-8249-5474-1(2)*, Ideal Pubns.) Worthy Publishing.
Scholastic, Inc. Staff. Merry Christmas, Lego City! 2012. (Lego City Ser.). (ENG.). 16p. (J). (gr. -1-k). pap. 6.99 *(978-0-545-42396-0(1))* Scholastic, Inc.
Scholastic, Inc. Staff, contrib. by. Peppa's Christmas Wish. 2013. (Peppa Pig Ser.). (ENG.). 24p. (J). (gr. -1-k). 4.99 *(978-0-545-56511-0(1))* Scholastic, Inc.
Schonewill, Lisa. Tell Me Mama, Is Santa Claus Real? 2005. (J). pap. 9.00 *(978-0-8059-6373-1(1))* Dorrance Publishing Co., Inc.
Schram, Scott. The Last Noel: A Christmas Musical for Children. 2007. (ENG.). pap. 64.95 *(978-0-7390-4487-2(7))* Alfred Publishing Co., Inc.
Schrewe, Suzanne. Hello Little Snowflake: A Christmas Miracle. 2010. 24p. pap. 12.48 *(978-1-4497-0799-6(8)*, WestBow Pr.) Author Solutions, Inc.
Schulman, Janet. 10 Trim-the-Tree'ers. Davick, Linda, illus. 2011. (ENG.). 32p. (J). (gr. -1 — 1). bds. 6.99 *(978-0-375-87302-7(3)*, Knopf Bks. for Young Readers) Random Hse. Children's Bks.
Schultz, Heidi. The Twelve Dreams of Christmas. 2012. pap. 11.95 *(978-0-7414-7532-9(4))* Infinity Publishing.
Schulz, Charles. A Charlie Brown Christmas, 1 vol. 2013. (Peanuts Picture Bks.). (ENG., Illus.). 48p. (J). (gr. -1-4). lib. bdg. 24.21 *(978-1-61479-029-7(9))* ABDO Publishing Co.
—A Charlie Brown Christmas. Running Press Staff, ed. 2010. (ENG., Illus.). 10p. (J). (gr. -1-3). 22.95 *(978-0-7624-4004-7(X))* Running Pr. Bk. Pubs.
—A Charlie Brown Christmas: The Making of a Tradition. 2013. (ENG.). 192p. 19.99 *(978-0-06-227214-0(4))* HarperCollins Pubs.
—Christmas Is Together-Time. Schulz, Charles, illus. 2006. (Peanuts(r) Ser.). (ENG., Illus.). 72p. 6.95 *(978-1-933662-37-4(9))* Cider Mill Pr. Bk. Pubs., LLC.
Schulz, Charles M. Be Joyful: Peanuts Wisdom to Carry You Through. 2014. (ENG., Illus.). 72p. (J). (gr. k-17). 7.95 *(978-0-7624-4719-0(2)*, Running Pr. Kids) Running Pr. Bk. Pubs.
—A Charlie Brown Christmas. deluxe ed. 2003. (Miniature Editions Ser.). (ENG., Illus.). 128p. (gr. 1-17). 5.95 *(978-0-7624-1601-1(7))* Running Pr. Bk. Pubs.
—A Charlie Brown Christmas Kit: A Book & Tree. 2007. (Miniature Editions Ser.). (ENG., Illus.). 128p. (gr. 1-17). pap. 9.95 *(978-0-7624-3145-8(8))* Running Pr. Bk. Pubs.
Schwarzkopf, Tom. Trouble Twins Save Christmas, 1 vol. 2007. (ENG.). 96p. (J). (gr. 3-7). pap. 10.95 *(978-1-55109-619-3(6))* Nimbus Publishing, Ltd. CAN. Dist: Orca Bk. Pubs. USA.
Schweitzer, C. V. The Making of an Angel. 2012. 48p. (-18). pap. 31.99 *(978-1-4797-3502-0(7))* Xlibris Corp.
Scillian, Devin. Memoirs of an Elf. Bowers, Tim, illus. 2014. (ENG.). 32p. (J). (gr. 1-4). 16.99 *(978-1-58536-910-2(1)*, 203676) Sleeping Bear Pr.
Scott, Christina. All in A Night's Work. 2006. (J). lib. bdg. 19.95 *(978-1-933732-19-0(9))* Big Ransom Studio.
—The Chimney. 2006. (J). lib. bdg. 19.95 *(978-1-933732-18-3(0))* Big Ransom Studio.
—The North Pole. 2006. (J). lib. bdg. 19.95 *(978-1-933732-17-6(2))* Big Ransom Studio.
Scott, D. P. The Christmas Elf. Hayward, Roy, illus. 2013. 86p. pap. *(978-0-9880635-2-5(2))* Scott, Daren.
Scott, Elizabeth M. Adventures with Mama Scottie & the Kids. Jackson, Kay Whytock, illus. 2008. 60p. pap. 8.95 *(978-0-595-51760-2(9))* iUniverse, Inc.
Scott, Eric. Santa & the Cyberspace Plot. 2013. 114p. pap. 7.99 *(978-1-78333-397-4(9))* Acorn Bks.
Scotton, Rob. Christmas Countdown. Scotton, Rob, illus. 2015. (Splat the Cat Ser.). (ENG., Illus.). 12p. (J). (gr. -1 — 1). bds. 6.99 *(978-0-06-197865-4(5)*, HarperFestival) HarperCollins Pubs.
—Merry Christmas, Splat. Scotton, Rob, illus. (Splat the Cat Ser.). (ENG., Illus.). 40p. (J). (gr. -1-2). 2013. 9.99 *(978-0-06-212450-0(1))* 2009. 16.99 *(978-0-06-083160-8(X))* HarperCollins Pubs.
—Russell's Christmas Magic. Scotton, Rob, illus. 2007. (Illus.). 32p. (J). (gr. -1-2). lib. bdg. 17.89 *(978-0-06-059855-6(7))* HarperCollins Pubs.
Scripture Teachers: Solomon & Friends Learn about the Christmas Story. 2003. pap. *(978-0-9712894-4-4(1))* Lighthouse Christian Products Co.
Seaberg, Richard Leonard. Elmoson the Christmas Goat. 2009. 20p. pap. 15.95 *(978-1-4490-2321-8(5))* AuthorHouse.
Sears, Gale. The Missing Christmas Treasure. Johnson, Meredith, illus. 2012. (J). *(978-1-60861-283-3(X))* Covenant Communications, Inc.
Sedgwick, Patricia Louise. Santa's Key. deluxe ed. 2004. (Illus.). 12.95 incl. audio compact disk *(978-0-9688190-1-2(X))* F. D. & D. Corp. CAN. Dist: Hushion Hse. Publishing, Ltd.
Sedrak, Asham. The Santa Claus Fox. 2011. 28p. pap. 13.59 *(978-1-4670-2484-6(8))* AuthorHouse.
See, Marcia A. The Candy Cane Rain. 2006. (Illus.). 53p. (J). (gr. -1-7). per. 12.95 *(978-1-60002-218-0(9)*, 4315) Mountain Valley Publishing, LLC.
Seglie, Susan & Schiefelbein, Janis. Sissy's Christmas Program. Zagorski, Astrid, tr. Papish, Adam, illus. 2003. (ENG & SPA.). (J). 4.95 *(978-0-9747243-1-7(9))* Seglie, Susan M.
Sehlin, Gunhild. Mary's Little Donkey: And the Flight to Egypt, 1 vol. Latham, Hugh & Maclean, Donald, trs. from SWE. Verheijen, Jan, illus. 2nd rev. ed. 2004. (ENG.). 160p. (J). (gr. 3-6). pap. 12.00 *(978-0-86315-064-7(0))* Floris Bks. GBR. Dist: SteinerBooks, Inc.
Seigerman, Michelle. A Christmastime Book of Rhymes. 2005. 35p. pap. 13.08 *(978-1-4116-4960-6(5))* Lulu Pr., Inc.
Sellaro, Brendan. Space Santa Holiday Hero. 2012. (ENG., Illus.). 32p. (J). 16.95 *(978-0-938467-60-1(3))* Headline Bks., Inc.
Senior, Suzy. Tales from Christmas Wood. Newman, James, illus. 2016. (ENG.). 32p. (J). (gr. k-4). 16.99 *(978-0-7459-7666-2(2))* Lion Hudson PLC GBR. Dist: Independent Pubs. Group.
Senior, Suzy. Tales from Christmas Wood Activity Book. Newman Gray, James, illus. 2017. (ENG.). 24p. (J). (gr. k-4). 7.99 ***(978-0-7459-7694-5(8))*** Lion Hudson PLC GBR. Dist: Independent Pubs. Group.
Sesko, Frank & Sesko, Mary Ann. Santa & Sam's Big Secret. 2007. 48p. per. 14.95 *(978-1-4327-0769-9(8))* Outskirts Pr., Inc.
Seus. Wie der Grinch Weihnachen. pap. 14.95 *(978-3-492-23722-2(3))* Piper Verlag GmbH DEU. Dist: Distribooks, Inc.
Seuss, Dr. Comment le Grinch a Vvolé Noël! 2013. (FRE & ENG., Illus.). 64p. (J). (gr. -1-3). 12.95 *(978-1-61243-244-1(1))* Ulysses Pr.
—The Grinch's Great Big Flap Book. 2014. (Great Big Board Book Ser.). (ENG.). 12p. (J). (-k). bds. 12.99 *(978-0-385-38494-0(7)*, Random Hse. Bks. for Young Readers) Random Hse. Children's Bks.
—How the Grinch Stole Christmas! Seuss, Dr., illus. 50th ed. 2007. (ENG., Illus.). 64p. pap. *(978-0-00-725860-4(7)*, HarperCollins) HarperCollins Pubs. Ltd.
—How the Grinch Stole Christmas! Jonaitis, Alice, ed. Seuss, Dr., illus. deluxe ed. 2014. (Classic Seuss Ser.). (ENG., Illus.). 64p. (J). (gr. k-4). 25.99 *(978-0-679-89153-6(6)*, Random Hse. Bks. for Young Readers) Random Hse. Children's Bks.
—How the Grinch Stole Christmas! Book & Grinch. 2015. (Classic Seuss Ser.). (ENG.). 64p. (J). (gr. k-4). 26.99 *(978-0-553-52445-1(3)*, Random Hse. Bks. for Young Readers) Random Hse. Children's Bks.
Sevonna. Simon, the Christmas Tree Fle. 2012. 32p. pap. 21.99 *(978-1-4771-3105-3(1))* Xlibris Corp.
Shannon, David. It's Christmas, David! Shannon, David, illus. 2010. (ENG., Illus.). 32p. (J). (gr. -1-3). 17.99 *(978-0-545-14311-0(X)*, Blue Sky Pr., The) Scholastic, Inc.
Sharkey, Niamh. Santasaurus. Sharkey, Niamh, illus. (ENG., Illus.). 32p. (J). (gr. -1-2). 2008. pap. 3.99 *(978-0-7636-3890-0(0))* 2005. 15.99 *(978-0-7636-2671-6(6))* Candlewick Pr.
Shaw, Stephanie. A Cookie for Santa. Robert, Bruno, illus. 2014. (ENG.). 32p. (J). (gr. 1-4). 15.99 *(978-1-58536-883-9(0)*, 203675) Sleeping Bear Pr.
Shea, Bob. Dinosaur vs. Santa. Shea, Bob, illus. 2014. (Dinosaur vs. Book Ser.). (ENG., Illus.). 30p. (J). (gr. -1-k). bds. 7.99 *(978-1-4231-6824-9(0))* Hyperion Bks. for Children.
Shearon, Lillian Nicholson. The Little Mixer. 2005. reprint ed. pap. 15.95 *(978-1-4179-1802-7(0))* Kessinger Publishing, LLC.
Shein, Erik Daniel. The Forgotton Ornament. Reker, Martin, ed. Safar, Lina, illus. 2010. 32p. (J). pap. 16.95 *(978-0-9765358-2-9(3))* Ark Watch Holdings LLC.
Shein, Erik Daniel & Reker, Martin. The Forgotten Ornament. Safar, Lina, illus. 2010. (J). pap. 11.95 *(978-0-578-05938-9(X))* Ark Watch Holdings LLC.
Shelton, Rick. Hoggle's Christmas. Gates, Donald, illus. 2007. 80p. (J). pap. 11.95 *(978-1-60306-026-4(X))* NewSouth, Inc.
Shepherd, Anita. The Santa Genie. 2012. 50p. pap. 7.95 *(978-0-9882368-0-6(X))* New Eden Publishing.
Shepherd, Jodie. Merry Christmas, Rarity! Fletcher, Lyn, illus. 2006. (My Little Pony Ser.). 32p. (J). (gr. -1-1). pap., act. bk. ed. 3.99 *(978-0-06-079472-9(0)*, HarperFestival) HarperCollins Pubs.
Sherratt, Tana. Santa's Magic Dust. 2012. 28p. pap. 24.95 *(978-1-4626-8037-5(2))* America Star Bks.
Shoshan, Beth. Mess Monsters at Christmas. 2009. 24p. (J). pap. 6.99 *(978-1-60010-560-9(2)*, Worthwhile Bks.) Idea & Design Works, LLC.
Silvano, Wendi J. Turkey Claus, 0 vols. Harper, Lee, illus. 2012. (ENG.). 40p. (J). (gr. -1-3). 16.99 *(978-0-7614-6239-2(2)*, 9780761462392, Two Lions) Amazon Publishing.
Simmons, Lynn. Bo & the Christmas Bandit, 1 vol. Lyne, Alison, illus. 2009. (Bo Ser.). (ENG.). 128p. (J). (gr. 3-6). pap. 8.95 *(978-1-58980-723-5(5))* Pelican Publishing Co., Inc.
Simon, Francesca. Horrid Henry's Christmas. Ross, Tony, illus. 2009. (Horrid Henry Ser.: 0). (ENG.). 112p. (J). (gr. 2-5). pap. 5.99 *(978-1-4022-1782-1(X)*, Sourcebooks Jabberwocky) Sourcebooks, Inc.
Simon, Mary Manz. My March to the Manger (die-Cut) A Celebration of Jesus' Birth. Scudamore, Angelika, illus. 2016. (ENG.). 14p. (J). (gr. -1 — 1). bds. 12.99 *(978-1-4336-4525-9(4)*, B&H Kids) B&H Publishing Group.
Simons, Joseph. Under a Living Sky, 1 vol. 2005. (Orca Young Readers Ser.). (ENG., Illus.). 112p. (J). (gr. 3-6). per. 5.95 *(978-1-55143-355-4(9))* Orca Bk. Pubs. USA.
Sing to Baby Jesus. 2013. (Illus.). 32p. (J). 14.99 *(978-1-62108-071-8(4))* Covenant Communications, Inc.
Singer, Marilyn. Tallulah's Nutcracker. Boiger, Alexandra, illus. 2013. (ENG.). 48p. (J). (gr. -1-3). 16.99 *(978-0-547-84557-9(X))* Houghton Mifflin Harcourt Publishing Co.
Skead, Robert. Elves Can't Tackle. 2004. (J). pap. 7.99 *(978-1-929478-64-4(X))* Cross Training Publishing.
Skrentny, Jan. The Christmas Moose. 2008. 36p. pap. 18.95 *(978-1-4389-2807-4(6))* AuthorHouse.
Smale, Denise L. Santa I Moved! 2012. 20p. pap. 24.95 *(978-1-4626-9241-5(9))* America Star Bks.
Small, Lily. Hailey the Hedgehog. 2016. (Fairy Animals of Misty Wood Ser.). (ENG., Illus.). 144p. (J). pap. 5.99 *(978-1-62779-735-1(1)*, 9781627797351, Holt, Henry & Co. Bks. For Young Readers) Holt, Henry & Co.
Smallman, Steve. Santa Is Coming to Alabama. Dunn, Robert, illus. 2013. (ENG.). 32p. (J). (-3). 9.99 *(978-1-4022-8821-0(2)*, Sourcebooks Jabberwocky) Sourcebooks, Inc.
—Santa Is Coming to Alaska. Dunn, Robert, illus. 2013. (ENG.). 32p. (J). (-3). 9.99 *(978-1-4022-9517-1(0)*, Sourcebooks Jabberwocky) Sourcebooks, Inc.
—Santa Is Coming to Albuquerque. Dunn, Robert, illus. 2013. (ENG.). 32p. (J). (-3). 9.99 *(978-1-4022-9042-8(X)*, Sourcebooks Jabberwocky) Sourcebooks, Inc.
—Santa Is Coming to Arizona. Dunn, Robert, illus. 2012. (ENG.). 32p. (J). (-3). 9.99 *(978-1-4022-7545-6(5)*, Sourcebooks Jabberwocky) Sourcebooks, Inc.
—Santa Is Coming to Arkansas. Dunn, Robert, illus. 2013. (ENG.). 32p. (J). (-3). 9.99 *(978-1-4022-9066-4(7)*, Sourcebooks Jabberwocky) Sourcebooks, Inc.
—Santa Is Coming to Asheville. Dunn, Robert, illus. 2013. (ENG.). 32p. (J). (-3). 9.99 *(978-1-4022-9030-5(6)*, Sourcebooks Jabberwocky) Sourcebooks, Inc.
—Santa Is Coming to Atlanta. Dunn, Robert, illus. 2015. (ENG.). 32p. (J). (-3). 9.99 *(978-1-4926-2640-4(6)*, Sourcebooks Jabberwocky) Sourcebooks, Inc.
—Santa Is Coming to Austin. Dunn, Robert, illus. 2013. (ENG.). 32p. (J). (-3). 9.99 *(978-1-4022-8973-6(1)*, Sourcebooks Jabberwocky) Sourcebooks, Inc.
—Santa Is Coming to Baltimore. Dunn, Robert, illus. 2015. (ENG.). 32p. (J). (-3). 9.99 *(978-1-4926-2652-7(X)*, Sourcebooks Jabberwocky) Sourcebooks, Inc.
—Santa Is Coming to Bellingham. Dunn, Robert, illus. 2013. (ENG.). 32p. (J). (-3). 9.99 *(978-1-4022-9130-2(2)*, Sourcebooks Jabberwocky) Sourcebooks, Inc.
—Santa Is Coming to Bentonville. Dunn, Robert, illus. 2013. (ENG.). 32p. (J). (-3). 9.99 *(978-1-4022-9109-8(4)*, Sourcebooks Jabberwocky) Sourcebooks, Inc.
—Santa Is Coming to Birmingham. Dunn, Robert, illus. 2013. (ENG.). 32p. (J). (-3). 9.99 *(978-1-4022-9106-7(X)*, Sourcebooks Jabberwocky) Sourcebooks, Inc.
—Santa Is Coming to Boise. Dunn, Robert, illus. 2013. (ENG.). 32p. (J). (-3). 9.99 *(978-1-4022-9118-0(3)*, Sourcebooks Jabberwocky) Sourcebooks, Inc.
—Santa Is Coming to Boston. Dunn, Robert, illus. 2012. (ENG.). 32p. (J). (-3). 9.99 *(978-1-4022-7506-7(4)*, Sourcebooks Jabberwocky) Sourcebooks, Inc.
—Santa Is Coming to Boulder. Dunn, Robert, illus. 2015. (ENG.). 32p. (J). (-3). 9.99 *(978-1-4926-2659-6(7)*, Sourcebooks Jabberwocky) Sourcebooks, Inc.
—Santa Is Coming to Bozeman. Dunn, Robert, illus. 2013. (ENG.). 32p. (J). (-3). 9.99 *(978-1-4022-9045-9(4)*, Sourcebooks Jabberwocky) Sourcebooks, Inc.

C
D

—Santa Is Coming to Brooklyn. Dunn, Robert, illus. 2013. (ENG.). 32p. (J). (-3). 9.99 (978-1-4022-9003-9(9), Sourcebooks Jabberwocky) Sourcebooks, Inc.
—Santa Is Coming to Buffalo. Dunn, Robert, illus. 2013. (ENG.). 32p. (J). (-3). 9.99 (978-1-4022-8858-6(1), Sourcebooks Jabberwocky) Sourcebooks, Inc.
—Santa Is Coming to Cajun Country. Dunn, Robert, illus. 2015. (ENG.). 32p. (J). (-3). 9.99 (978-1-4926-2665-7(1), Sourcebooks Jabberwocky) Sourcebooks, Inc.
—Santa Is Coming to Calgary. Dunn, Robert, illus. 2013. (ENG.). 32p. (J). (-3). 11.99 (978-1-4022-8988-0(X), Sourcebooks Jabberwocky) Sourcebooks, Inc.
—Santa Is Coming to California. Dunn, Robert, illus. 2012. (ENG.). 32p. (J). (-3). 9.99 (978-1-4022-7515-9(3), Sourcebooks Jabberwocky) Sourcebooks, Inc.
—Santa Is Coming to Canada. Dunn, Robert, illus. 2013. (ENG.). 32p. (J). (-3). 11.99 (978-1-4022-8839-5(5), Sourcebooks Jabberwocky) Sourcebooks, Inc.
—Santa Is Coming to Cape Cod. Dunn, Robert, illus. 2013. (ENG.). 32p. (J). (-3). 9.99 (978-1-4022-9078-7(0), Sourcebooks Jabberwocky) Sourcebooks, Inc.
—Santa Is Coming to Charleston. Dunn, Robert, illus. 2013. (ENG.). 32p. (J). (-3). 9.99 (978-1-4022-8985-9(5), Sourcebooks Jabberwocky) Sourcebooks, Inc.
—Santa Is Coming to Chattanooga. Dunn, Robert, illus. 2015. (ENG.). 32p. (J). (-3). 9.99 (978-1-4926-2651-0(1), Sourcebooks Jabberwocky) Sourcebooks, Inc.
—Santa Is Coming to Chicago. Dunn, Robert, illus. 2012. (ENG.). 32p. (J). (-3). 9.99 (978-1-4022-7509-8(9), Sourcebooks Jabberwocky) Sourcebooks, Inc.
—Santa Is Coming to Cincinnati. Dunn, Robert, illus. 2013. (ENG.). 32p. (J). (-3). 9.99 (978-1-4022-8997-2(9), Sourcebooks Jabberwocky) Sourcebooks, Inc.
—Santa Is Coming to Colorado. Dunn, Robert, illus. 2013. (ENG.). 32p. (J). (-3). 9.99 (978-1-4022-8815-9(8), Sourcebooks Jabberwocky) Sourcebooks, Inc.
—Santa Is Coming to Columbus. Dunn, Robert, illus. 2013. (ENG.). 32p. (J). (-3). 9.99 (978-1-4022-9036-7(5), Sourcebooks Jabberwocky) Sourcebooks, Inc.
—Santa Is Coming to Delaware. Dunn, Robert, illus. 2013. (ENG.). 32p. (J). (-3). 9.99 (978-1-4022-9508-9(1), Sourcebooks Jabberwocky) Sourcebooks, Inc.
—Santa Is Coming to Denver. Dunn, Robert, illus. 2015. (ENG.). 32p. (J). (-3). 9.99 (978-1-4926-2644-2(9), Sourcebooks Jabberwocky) Sourcebooks, Inc.
—Santa Is Coming to des Moines. Dunn, Robert, illus. 2015. (ENG.). 32p. (J). (-3). 9.99 (978-1-4926-2646-6(5), Sourcebooks Jabberwocky) Sourcebooks, Inc.
—Santa Is Coming to Duluth. Dunn, Robert, illus. 2013. (ENG.). 32p. (J). (-3). 9.99 (978-1-4022-9027-5(6), Sourcebooks Jabberwocky) Sourcebooks, Inc.
—Santa Is Coming to Durango. Dunn, Robert, illus. 2013. (ENG.). 32p. (J). (-3). 9.99 (978-1-4022-9133-3(7), Sourcebooks Jabberwocky) Sourcebooks, Inc.
—Santa Is Coming to Edmonton. Dunn, Robert, illus. 2013. (ENG.). 32p. (J). (-3). 11.99 (978-1-4022-8991-0(X), Sourcebooks Jabberwocky) Sourcebooks, Inc.
—Santa Is Coming to Florida. Dunn, Robert, illus. 2012. (ENG.). 32p. (J). (-3). 9.99 (978-1-4022-7527-2(7), Sourcebooks Jabberwocky) Sourcebooks, Inc.
—Santa Is Coming to Georgia. Dunn, Robert, illus. 2013. (ENG.). 32p. (J). (-3). 9.99 (978-1-4022-8794-7(1), Sourcebooks Jabberwocky) Sourcebooks, Inc.
—Santa Is Coming to Grand Rapids. Dunn, Robert, illus. 2015. (ENG.). 32p. (J). (-3). 9.99 (978-1-4926-2657-2(0), Sourcebooks Jabberwocky) Sourcebooks, Inc.
—Santa Is Coming to Green Bay. Dunn, Robert, illus. 2013. (ENG.). 32p. (J). (-3). 9.99 (978-1-4022-9112-8(4), Sourcebooks Jabberwocky) Sourcebooks, Inc.
—Santa Is Coming to Hawaii. Dunn, Robert, illus. 2013. (ENG.). 32p. (J). (-3). 9.99 (978-1-4022-9009-1(8), Sourcebooks Jabberwocky) Sourcebooks, Inc.
—Santa Is Coming to Hollywood. Dunn, Robert, illus. 2015. (ENG.). 32p. (J). (-3). 9.99 (978-1-4926-2664-0(3), Sourcebooks Jabberwocky) Sourcebooks, Inc.
—Santa Is Coming to Honolulu. Dunn, Robert, illus. 2015. (ENG.). 32p. (J). (-3). 9.99 (978-1-4926-2653-4(8), Sourcebooks Jabberwocky) Sourcebooks, Inc.
—Santa Is Coming to Houston. Dunn, Robert, illus. 2015. (ENG.). 32p. (J). (-3). 9.99 (978-1-4926-2631-2(7), Sourcebooks Jabberwocky) Sourcebooks, Inc.
—Santa Is Coming to Idaho. Dunn, Robert, illus. 2013. (ENG.). 32p. (J). (-3). 9.99 (978-1-4022-9511-9(1), Sourcebooks Jabberwocky) Sourcebooks, Inc.
—Santa Is Coming to Illinois. Dunn, Robert, illus. 2013. (ENG.). 32p. (J). (-3). 9.99 (978-1-4022-9103-6(5), Sourcebooks Jabberwocky) Sourcebooks, Inc.
—Santa Is Coming to Indiana. Dunn, Robert, illus. 2013. (ENG.). 32p. (J). (-3). 9.99 (978-1-4022-8803-6(4), Sourcebooks Jabberwocky) Sourcebooks, Inc.
—Santa Is Coming to Indianapolis. Dunn, Robert, illus. 2015. (ENG.). 32p. (J). (-3). 9.99 (978-1-4926-2636-7(8), Sourcebooks Jabberwocky) Sourcebooks, Inc.
—Santa Is Coming to Iowa. Dunn, Robert, illus. 2013. (ENG.). 32p. (J). (-3). 9.99 (978-1-4022-8818-0(2), Sourcebooks Jabberwocky) Sourcebooks, Inc.
—Santa Is Coming to Jacksonville. Dunn, Robert, illus. 2015. (ENG.). 32p. (J). (-3). 9.99 (978-1-4926-2635-0(X), Sourcebooks Jabberwocky) Sourcebooks, Inc.
—Santa Is Coming to Kansas. Dunn, Robert, illus. 2013. (ENG.). 32p. (J). (-3). 9.99 (978-1-4022-9121-0(3), Sourcebooks Jabberwocky) Sourcebooks, Inc.
—Santa Is Coming to Kansas City. Dunn, Robert, illus. 2013. (ENG.). 32p. (J). (-3). 9.99 (978-1-4022-8855-5(7), Sourcebooks Jabberwocky) Sourcebooks, Inc.
—Santa Is Coming to Kentucky. Dunn, Robert, illus. 2013. (ENG.). 32p. (J). (-3). 9.99 (978-1-4022-8824-1(7), Sourcebooks Jabberwocky) Sourcebooks, Inc.
—Santa Is Coming to Las Vegas. Dunn, Robert, illus. 2013. (ENG.). 32p. (J). (-3). 9.99 (978-1-4022-8836-4(0), Sourcebooks Jabberwocky) Sourcebooks, Inc.
—Santa Is Coming to Los Angeles. Dunn, Robert, illus. 2013. (ENG.). 32p. (J). (-3). 9.99 (978-1-4022-8830-2(1), Sourcebooks Jabberwocky) Sourcebooks, Inc.
—Santa Is Coming to Louisiana. Dunn, Robert, illus. 2012. (ENG.). 32p. (J). (-3). 9.99 (978-1-4022-7536-4(6), Sourcebooks Jabberwocky) Sourcebooks, Inc.
—Santa Is Coming to Louisville. Dunn, Robert, illus. 2015. (ENG.). 32p. (J). (-3). 9.99 (978-1-4926-2639-8(2), Sourcebooks Jabberwocky) Sourcebooks, Inc.
—Santa Is Coming to Lubbock. Dunn, Robert, illus. 2013. (ENG.). 32p. (J). (-3). 9.99 (978-1-4022-9136-4(1), Sourcebooks Jabberwocky) Sourcebooks, Inc.
—Santa Is Coming to Maine. Dunn, Robert, illus. 2013. (ENG.). 32p. (J). (-3). 9.99 (978-1-4022-9069-5(1), Sourcebooks Jabberwocky) Sourcebooks, Inc.
—Santa Is Coming to Manchester. Dunn, Robert, illus. 2013. (ENG.). 32p. (J). (-3). 9.99 (978-1-4022-9115-9(9), Sourcebooks Jabberwocky) Sourcebooks, Inc.
—Santa Is Coming to Maryland. Dunn, Robert, illus. 2013. (ENG.). 32p. (J). (-3). 9.99 (978-1-4022-8812-8(3), Sourcebooks Jabberwocky) Sourcebooks, Inc.
—Santa Is Coming to Memphis. Dunn, Robert, illus. 2015. (ENG.). 32p. (J). (-3). 9.99 (978-1-4926-2643-5(0), Sourcebooks Jabberwocky) Sourcebooks, Inc.
—Santa Is Coming to Miami. Dunn, Robert, illus. 2013. (ENG.). 32p. (J). (-3). 9.99 (978-1-4022-9051-0(9), Sourcebooks Jabberwocky) Sourcebooks, Inc.
—Santa Is Coming to Michigan. Dunn, Robert, illus. 2012. (ENG.). 32p. (J). (-3). 9.99 (978-1-4022-7539-5(0), Sourcebooks Jabberwocky) Sourcebooks, Inc.
—Santa Is Coming to Minnesota. Dunn, Robert, illus. 2012. (ENG.). 32p. (J). (-3). 9.99 (978-1-4022-7530-2(7), Sourcebooks Jabberwocky) Sourcebooks, Inc.
—Santa Is Coming to Mississippi. Dunn, Robert, illus. 2013. (ENG.). 32p. (J). (-3). 9.99 (978-1-4022-9015-2(2), Sourcebooks Jabberwocky) Sourcebooks, Inc.
—Santa Is Coming to Missoula. Dunn, Robert, illus. 2015. (ENG.). 32p. (J). (-3). 9.99 (978-1-4926-2656-5(2), Sourcebooks Jabberwocky) Sourcebooks, Inc.
—Santa Is Coming to Missouri. Dunn, Robert, illus. 2013. (ENG.). 32p. (J). (-3). 9.99 (978-1-4022-8809-8(3), Sourcebooks Jabberwocky) Sourcebooks, Inc.
—Santa Is Coming to Montana. Dunn, Robert, illus. 2013. (ENG.). 32p. (J). (-3). 9.99 (978-1-4022-9018-3(7), Sourcebooks Jabberwocky) Sourcebooks, Inc.
—Santa Is Coming to My House. Dunn, Robert, illus. 2012. (ENG.). 32p. (J). (-3). 9.99 (978-1-4022-7775-7(X), Sourcebooks Jabberwocky) Sourcebooks, Inc.
—Santa Is Coming to Naperville. Dunn, Robert, illus. 2013. (ENG.). 32p. (J). (-3). 9.99 (978-1-4022-9063-3(2), Sourcebooks Jabberwocky) Sourcebooks, Inc.
—Santa Is Coming to Naples. Dunn, Robert, illus. 2013. (ENG.). 32p. (J). (-3). 9.99 (978-1-4022-9048-0(9), Sourcebooks Jabberwocky) Sourcebooks, Inc.
—Santa Is Coming to Nebraska. Dunn, Robert, illus. 2013. (ENG.). 32p. (J). (-3). 9.99 (978-1-4022-9072-5(1), Sourcebooks Jabberwocky) Sourcebooks, Inc.
—Santa Is Coming to Nevada. Dunn, Robert, illus. 2013. (ENG.). 32p. (J). (-3). 9.99 (978-1-4022-9523-2(5), Sourcebooks Jabberwocky) Sourcebooks, Inc.
—Santa Is Coming to New England. Dunn, Robert, illus. 2012. (ENG.). 32p. (J). (-3). 9.99 (978-1-4022-7551-7(X), Sourcebooks Jabberwocky) Sourcebooks, Inc.
—Santa Is Coming to New Jersey. Dunn, Robert, illus. 2013. (ENG.). 32p. (J). (-3). 9.99 (978-1-4022-8797-8(6), Sourcebooks Jabberwocky) Sourcebooks, Inc.
—Santa Is Coming to New Mexico. Dunn, Robert, illus. 2013. (ENG.). 32p. (J). (-3). 9.99 (978-1-4022-9520-1(0), Sourcebooks Jabberwocky) Sourcebooks, Inc.
—Santa Is Coming to New York. Dunn, Robert, illus. 2012. (ENG.). 32p. (J). (-3). 9.99 (978-1-4022-7503-6(X), Sourcebooks Jabberwocky) Sourcebooks, Inc.
—Santa Is Coming to New York City. Dunn, Robert, illus. 2015. (ENG.). 32p. (J). (-3). 9.99 (978-1-4926-2662-6(7), Sourcebooks Jabberwocky) Sourcebooks, Inc.
—Santa Is Coming to Niagara Falls. Dunn, Robert, illus. 2015. (ENG.). 32p. (J). (-3). 9.99 (978-1-4926-2655-8(4), Sourcebooks Jabberwocky) Sourcebooks, Inc.
—Santa Is Coming to North Dakota. Dunn, Robert, illus. 2013. (ENG.). 32p. (J). (-3). 9.99 (978-1-4022-9514-0(6), Sourcebooks Jabberwocky) Sourcebooks, Inc.
—Santa Is Coming to Northern Virginia. Dunn, Robert, illus. 2015. (ENG.). 32p. (J). (-3). 9.99 (978-1-4926-2663-3(5), Sourcebooks Jabberwocky) Sourcebooks, Inc.
—Santa Is Coming to Notre Dame. Dunn, Robert, illus. 2013. (ENG.). 32p. (J). (-3). 9.99 (978-1-4022-9024-4(1), Sourcebooks Jabberwocky) Sourcebooks, Inc.
—Santa Is Coming to Ohio. Dunn, Robert, illus. 2012. (ENG.). 32p. (J). (-3). 9.99 (978-1-4022-7554-8(4), Sourcebooks Jabberwocky) Sourcebooks, Inc.
—Santa Is Coming to Oklahoma. Dunn, Robert, illus. 2013. (ENG.). 32p. (J). (-3). 9.99 (978-1-4022-9012-1(8), Sourcebooks Jabberwocky) Sourcebooks, Inc.
—Santa Is Coming to Oklahoma City. Dunn, Robert, illus. 2015. (ENG.). 32p. (J). (-3). 9.99 (978-1-4926-2637-4(6), Sourcebooks Jabberwocky) Sourcebooks, Inc.
—Santa Is Coming to Omaha. Dunn, Robert, illus. 2013. (ENG.). 32p. (J). (-3). 9.99 (978-1-4022-9006-0(3), Sourcebooks Jabberwocky) Sourcebooks, Inc.
—Santa Is Coming to Oregon. Dunn, Robert, illus. 2013. (ENG.). 32p. (J). (-3). 9.99 (978-1-4022-9075-6(6), Sourcebooks Jabberwocky) Sourcebooks, Inc.
—Santa Is Coming to Orlando. Dunn, Robert, illus. 2015. (ENG.). 32p. (J). (-3). 9.99 (978-1-4926-2633-6(3), Sourcebooks Jabberwocky) Sourcebooks, Inc.
—Santa Is Coming to Ottawa. Dunn, Robert, illus. 2013. (ENG.). 32p. (J). (-3). 11.99 (978-1-4022-8994-1(4), Sourcebooks Jabberwocky) Sourcebooks, Inc.
—Santa Is Coming to Philadelphia. Dunn, Robert, illus. 2012. (ENG.). 32p. (J). (-3). 9.99 (978-1-4022-7518-0(8), Sourcebooks Jabberwocky) Sourcebooks, Inc.
—Santa Is Coming to Pittsburgh. Dunn, Robert, illus. 2013. (ENG.). 32p. (J). (-3). 9.99 (978-1-4022-8982-8(0), Sourcebooks Jabberwocky) Sourcebooks, Inc.
—Santa Is Coming to Portland. Dunn, Robert, illus. 2012. (ENG.). 32p. (J). (-3). 9.99 (978-1-4022-7772-6(5), Sourcebooks Jabberwocky) Sourcebooks, Inc.
—Santa Is Coming to Providence. Dunn, Robert, illus. 2015. (ENG.). 32p. (J). (-3). 9.99 (978-1-4926-2660-2(0), Sourcebooks Jabberwocky) Sourcebooks, Inc.
—Santa Is Coming to Raleigh-Durham. Dunn, Robert, illus. 2015. (ENG.). 32p. (J). (-3). 9.99 (978-1-4926-2642-8(2), Sourcebooks Jabberwocky) Sourcebooks, Inc.
—Santa Is Coming to Rapid City. Dunn, Robert, illus. 2015. (ENG.). 32p. (J). (-3). 9.99 (978-1-4926-2658-9(9), Sourcebooks Jabberwocky) Sourcebooks, Inc.
—Santa Is Coming to Salt Lake City. Dunn, Robert, illus. 2015. (ENG.). 32p. (J). (-3). 9.99 (978-1-4926-2645-9(7), Sourcebooks Jabberwocky) Sourcebooks, Inc.
—Santa Is Coming to San Antonio. Dunn, Robert, illus. 2015. (ENG.). 32p. (J). (-3). 9.99 (978-1-4926-2632-9(5), Sourcebooks Jabberwocky) Sourcebooks, Inc.
—Santa Is Coming to San Francisco. Dunn, Robert, illus. 2012. (ENG.). 32p. (J). (-3). 9.99 (978-1-4022-7548-7(X), Sourcebooks Jabberwocky) Sourcebooks, Inc.
—Santa Is Coming to San Jose. Dunn, Robert, illus. 2015. (ENG.). 32p. (J). (-3). 9.99 (978-1-4926-2641-1(4), Sourcebooks Jabberwocky) Sourcebooks, Inc.
—Santa Is Coming to Santa Cruz. Dunn, Robert, illus. 2013. (ENG.). 32p. (J). (-3). 9.99 (978-1-4022-9057-2(8), Sourcebooks Jabberwocky) Sourcebooks, Inc.
—Santa Is Coming to Santa Fe. Dunn, Robert, illus. 2013. (ENG.). 32p. (J). (-3). 9.99 (978-1-4022-9124-1(8), Sourcebooks Jabberwocky) Sourcebooks, Inc.
—Santa Is Coming to Savannah. Dunn, Robert, illus. 2013. (ENG.). 32p. (J). (-3). 9.99 (978-1-4022-8979-8(0), Sourcebooks Jabberwocky) Sourcebooks, Inc.
—Santa Is Coming to Seattle. Dunn, Robert, illus. 2015. (ENG.). 32p. (J). (-3). 9.99 (978-1-4926-2649-7(X), Sourcebooks Jabberwocky) Sourcebooks, Inc.
—Santa Is Coming to Sioux Falls. Dunn, Robert, illus. 2015. (ENG.). 32p. (J). (-3). 9.99 (978-1-4926-2650-3(3), Sourcebooks Jabberwocky) Sourcebooks, Inc.
—Santa Is Coming to South Dakota. Dunn, Robert, illus. 2013. (ENG.). 32p. (J). (-3). 9.99 (978-1-4022-9021-3(7), Sourcebooks Jabberwocky) Sourcebooks, Inc.
—Santa Is Coming to St. Louis. Dunn, Robert, illus. 2013. (ENG.). 32p. (J). (-3). 9.99 (978-1-4022-9000-8(4), Sourcebooks Jabberwocky) Sourcebooks, Inc.
—Santa Is Coming to Tampa Bay & St. Petersburg. Dunn, Robert, illus. 2013. (ENG.). 32p. (J). (-3). 9.99 (978-1-4022-9054-1(3), Sourcebooks Jabberwocky) Sourcebooks, Inc.
—Santa Is Coming to Tennessee. Dunn, Robert, illus. 2013. (ENG.). 32p. (J). (-3). 9.99 (978-1-4022-8806-7(9), Sourcebooks Jabberwocky) Sourcebooks, Inc.
—Santa Is Coming to Texas. Dunn, Robert, illus. 2012. (ENG.). 32p. (J). (-3). 9.99 (978-1-4022-7512-8(9), Sourcebooks Jabberwocky) Sourcebooks, Inc.
—Santa Is Coming to the Carolinas. Dunn, Robert, illus. 2012. (ENG.). 32p. (J). (-3). 9.99 (978-1-4022-7586-9(2), Sourcebooks Jabberwocky) Sourcebooks, Inc.
—Santa Is Coming to the Great Smoky Mountains. Dunn, Robert, illus. 2013. (ENG.). 32p. (J). (-3). 9.99 (978-1-4022-9033-6(0), Sourcebooks Jabberwocky) Sourcebooks, Inc.
—Santa Is Coming to the Quad Cities. Dunn, Robert, illus. 2013. (ENG.). 32p. (J). (-3). 9.99 (978-1-4022-9060-2(6), Sourcebooks Jabberwocky) Sourcebooks, Inc.
—Santa Is Coming to the Rockies. Dunn, Robert, illus. 2012. (ENG.). 32p. (J). (-3). 9.99 (978-1-4022-7593-7(5), Sourcebooks Jabberwocky) Sourcebooks, Inc.
—Santa Is Coming to the Twin Cities. Dunn, Robert, illus. 2015. (ENG.). 32p. (J). (-3). 9.99 (978-1-4926-2647-3(3), Sourcebooks Jabberwocky) Sourcebooks, Inc.
—Santa Is Coming to the Valley of the Sun. Dunn, Robert, illus. 2015. (ENG.). 32p. (J). (-3). 9.99 (978-1-4926-2666-4(X), Sourcebooks Jabberwocky) Sourcebooks, Inc.
—Santa Is Coming to Toledo. Dunn, Robert, illus. 2015. (ENG.). 32p. (J). (-3). 9.99 (978-1-4926-2654-1(6), Sourcebooks Jabberwocky) Sourcebooks, Inc.
—Santa Is Coming to Toronto. Dunn, Robert, illus. 2012. (ENG.). 32p. (J). (-3). 9.99 (978-1-4022-7521-0(8), Sourcebooks Jabberwocky) Sourcebooks, Inc.
—Santa Is Coming to Tucson. Dunn, Robert, illus. 2013. (ENG.). 32p. (J). (-3). 9.99 (978-1-4022-8976-7(6), Sourcebooks Jabberwocky) Sourcebooks, Inc.
—Santa Is Coming to Tulsa. Dunn, Robert, illus. 2013. (ENG.). 32p. (J). (-3). 9.99 (978-1-4022-9039-8(X), Sourcebooks Jabberwocky) Sourcebooks, Inc.
—Santa Is Coming to Utah. Dunn, Robert, illus. 2013. (ENG.). 32p. (J). (-3). 9.99 (978-1-4022-8827-2(1), Sourcebooks Jabberwocky) Sourcebooks, Inc.
—Santa Is Coming to Vancouver. Dunn, Robert, illus. 2012. (ENG.). 32p. (J). (-3). 9.99 (978-1-4022-7542-5(0), Sourcebooks Jabberwocky) Sourcebooks, Inc.
—Santa Is Coming to Vermont. Dunn, Robert, illus. 2013. (ENG.). 32p. (J). (-3). 9.99 (978-1-4022-9127-2(2), Sourcebooks Jabberwocky) Sourcebooks, Inc.
—Santa Is Coming to Virginia. Dunn, Robert, illus. 2013. (ENG.). 32p. (J). (-3). 9.99 (978-1-4022-8800-5(X), Sourcebooks Jabberwocky) Sourcebooks, Inc.
—Santa Is Coming to Washington. Dunn, Robert, illus. 2012. (ENG.). 32p. (J). (-3). 9.99 (978-1-4022-7524-1(2), Sourcebooks Jabberwocky) Sourcebooks, Inc.
—Santa Is Coming to Washington DC. Dunn, Robert, illus. 2013. (ENG.). 32p. (J). (-3). 9.99 (978-1-4022-8833-3(6), Sourcebooks Jabberwocky) Sourcebooks, Inc.
—Santa Is Coming to West Virginia. Dunn, Robert, illus. 2013. (ENG.). 32p. (J). (-3). 9.99 (978-1-4022-9100-5(0), Sourcebooks Jabberwocky) Sourcebooks, Inc.
—Santa Is Coming to Wichita. Dunn, Robert, illus. 2015. (ENG.). 32p. (J). (-3). 9.99 (978-1-4926-2638-1(4), Sourcebooks Jabberwocky) Sourcebooks, Inc.
—Santa Is Coming to Wisconsin. Dunn, Robert, illus. 2012. (ENG.). 32p. (J). (-3). 9.99 (978-1-4022-7533-3(1), Sourcebooks Jabberwocky) Sourcebooks, Inc.
Smallman, Steve, et al. My First Santa's Coming to Michigan. Dunn, Robert, illus. 2015. (ENG.). 18p. (J). bds. 9.99 (978-1-4926-2873-6(5), Sourcebooks Jabberwocky) Sourcebooks, Inc.
—My First Santa's Coming to Minnesota. Dunn, Robert, illus. 2015. (ENG.). 18p. (J). bds. 9.99 (978-1-4926-2879-8(4), Sourcebooks Jabberwocky) Sourcebooks, Inc.
—My First Santa's Coming to New Jersey. Dunn, Robert, illus. 2015. (ENG.). 18p. (J). bds. 9.99 (978-1-4926-2882-8(4), Sourcebooks Jabberwocky) Sourcebooks, Inc.
—My First Santa's Coming to Ohio. Dunn, Robert, illus. 2015. (ENG.). 18p. (J). bds. 9.99 (978-1-4926-2876-7(X), Sourcebooks Jabberwocky) Sourcebooks, Inc.
—My First Santa's Coming to My House. Dunn, Robert, illus. 2015. (ENG.). 18p. (J). bds. 9.99 (978-1-4926-2885-9(9), Sourcebooks Jabberwocky) Sourcebooks, Inc.
Smart Kidz, creator. Jingle Bells. 2013. (ENG., Illus.). 12p. (gr. -1). bds. 12.99 (978-1-939658-03-6(9), Smart Kids) Penton Overseas, Inc.
Smart Kidz Media, creator. O Christmas Tree! 2013. (ENG., Illus.). 12p. (J). bds. 12.99 (978-1-939658-05-0(5), Smart Kids) Penton Overseas, Inc.
—Silent Night. 2013. (ENG., Illus.). 12p. (J). bds. 12.99 (978-1-939658-01-2(2), Smart Kids) Penton Overseas, Inc.
—Up on the Housetop! 2013. (ENG., Illus.). 12p. (J). bds. 12.99 (978-1-939658-04-3(7), Smart Kids) Penton Overseas, Inc.
Smath, Jerry, et al. Merry Christmas: A Storybook Collection. 2007. (Merry Christmas Ser.). (ENG., Illus.). 96p. (J). (gr. -1-k). 8.99 (978-0-545-01341-3(0), Cartwheel Bks.) Scholastic, Inc.
Smith, Brendan Powell. The Christmas Story: The Brick Bible for Kids. 2012. (ENG., Illus.). 32p. (J). (gr. -1-k). 12.95 (978-1-62087-173-7(4), 620173, Sky Pony Pr.) Skyhorse Publishing Co., Inc.
Smith, Cliff. New Magical Holiday Stories. 2005. pap. 31.99 (978-1-4134-7971-3(5)) Xlibris Corp.
Smith, Elva S. Christmas in Legend & Story. 2009. (Illus.). 240p. pap. 10.95 (978-1-59915-387-2(4)) Yesterday's Classics.
Smith, Elva S. & Hazeltine, Alice I. Christmas in Legend & Story: A Book for Boys & Girls. 2007. pap. 19.99 (978-1-4346-2190-0(1)); (ENG.). 200p. pap. 21.99 (978-1-4346-2250-1(9)) Creative Media Partners, LLC.
Smith, Eveline Maria. A Christmas to Remember. 2008. 88p. 26.95 (978-1-4357-4699-2(6)); pap. 12.95 (978-1-4357-4698-5(8)) Lulu Pr., Inc.
Smith, Joel D. Santa's Secret Deal: Who Else Signed It, & Where You Can Find Proof of the Deal in Your Room Right Now. 2012. 30p. pap. 14.25 (978-1-4575-1458-6(3)) Dog Ear Publishing, LLC.
Smith, John A. A Special Christmas for Oscar, 1 vol. 2010. 32p. 24.95 (978-1-4512-0999-0(1)) 2004. 31p. pap. 24.95 (978-1-4137-2892-7(8)) PublishAmerica, Inc.
Smith, Karen Cecil. An Old Salem Christmas, 1840. Phipps, Bebe, illus. 2008. (J). 14.95 (978-1-933251-46-2(8)) Parkway Pubs., Inc.
Smith, Kim, illus. Home Alone: The Classic Christmas Storybook. 2015. (Pop Classics Ser.). (ENG.). 40p. (J). (gr. -1-3). 18.95 (978-1-59474-858-5(6)) Quirk Bks.
Smith, Miss Diane Pearl. Princess S Magickal Christmas. 2012. 28p. pap. (978-0-9878503-0-0(X)) Rainbowchild.
Smith, Nancy. The Christmas Duck. 2012. (ENG.). (J). pap. (978-1-4675-1988-5(X)) Independent Pub.
Smith, Nikki Shannon. The Little Christmas Elf. Mitchell, Susan, illus. 2011. (Little Golden Book Ser.). (ENG.). 24p. (J). (gr. -1-k). 4.99 (978-0-375-87348-5(1), Golden Bks.) Random Hse. Children's Bks.
Snedeker, Erin. The Littlest Elf: Marvin Mcgee & the Candle of Fate. Drotleff, David J., illus. 2010. 44p. pap. 15.50 (978-1-60911-194-6(X), Eloquent Bks.) Strategic Book Publishing & Rights Agency (SBPRA).
Snell, Gordon. Twas the Day after Christmas. Delonas, Sean, illus. Date not set. 32p. (J). (gr. -1-3). 5.99 (978-0-06-443675-5(6)) HarperCollins Pubs.
—Twelve Days of Christmas. Date not set. (Illus.). 32p. (J). (gr. -1-3). 5.99 (978-0-06-443674-8(8)) HarperCollins Pubs.
Snicket, Lemony, pseud. The Latke Who Couldn't Stop Screaming: A Christmas Story. Scott, Daniel, ed. Brown, Lisa, illus. 2007. (ENG.). 48p. (gr. 2-7). 12.00 (978-1-932416-87-9(0)) McSweeney's Publishing.
—The Lump of Coal. Helquist, Brett, illus. 2008. 40p. (J). (gr. -1). lib. bdg. 14.89 (978-0-06-157425-2(2)); (ENG.). 12.99 (978-0-06-157428-3(7)) HarperCollins Pubs.
Snively, Carolyn. Zippo's First Christmas. 2012. 19.95 (978-0-7414-7383-7(6)); pap. 11.95 (978-0-7414-7382-0(8)) Infinity Publishing.
Snow, Alan. How Santa Really Works. Snow, Alan, illus. 2007. (ENG., Illus.). 48p. (J). (gr. -1-3). 7.99 (978-1-4169-5000-4(1), Atheneum Bks. for Young Readers) Simon & Schuster Children's Publishing.
Snow, Susie. The Old Cookie Jar. Motz, Mike, illus. 2012. 34p. pap. 19.99 (978-1-61996-595-9(X)) Salem Author Services.
Snow X-mas. 2004. (J). per. (978-1-57657-384-6(2)) Paradise Pr., Inc.
Snowman. 2003. (Shaped Board Books Ser.). 14p. (J). (gr. -1-k). bds. 9.95 (978-0-7525-8852-0(4)) Parragon, Inc.
Snyder, Casey. Miss Fit the Dog Saves Christmas. 2013. 20p. pap. 24.95 (978-1-62709-358-3(3)) America Star Bks.
Sobel, Gerrie. Jacob & His Magical Flying Bears. Torres, Dottie, illus. 2009. 32p. pap. 12.95 (978-1-936051-16-8(8)) Peppertree Pr., The.
Solheim, James. Santa's Secrets Revealed: All Your Questions Answered about Santa's Super Sleigh, His Flying Reindeer, & Other Wonders. Gott, Barry, illus. 2004. (Carolrhoda Picture Books Ser.). 40p. (J). (gr. k-3). 15.95 (978-1-57505-600-5(3)) Lerner Publishing Group.
Solomon, Martha. Christmas in Da Hood. 2012. 28p. pap. 12.50 (978-0-9883126-3-0(8)) iScribe Pubns. LLC.
Sonja Johannesen & Alice Johannesen. Ola & Jens' Christmas Adventure. 2011. 32p. pap. 21.99 (978-1-4628-6498-0(8)) Xlibris Corp.
Soper, Stuart A. Milky Saves Christmas. 2011. (Illus.). 290p. pap. 16.00 (978-1-60976-193-6(6), Strategic Bk. Publishing) Strategic Book Publishing & Rights Agency (SBPRA).
Soprano, Sophie, illus. Laughing All the Way. 2008. (J). (978-1-59811-642-7(8)) Covenant Communications.
Sorenson, Margo. Ambrose & the Princess. Szegedi, Katalin, illus. 2005. (ENG.). 32p. (J). (gr. -1-3). 16.95 (978-0-8146-3043-3(X)) Liturgical Pr.
Sortland, Bjorn. The Dream Factory Starring Anna & Henry. Christianson, Emily V. & Hedin, Robert, trs. from NOR. Elling, Lars, illus. 2003. (Picture Bks.). 40p. (J). (gr. -1-3). 15.95 (978-0-87614-009-3(6), Carolrhoda Bks.) Lerner Publishing Group.
Sovago-Royal, Sandra. Magimus. 2009. 33p. (J). pap. 19.95 (978-1-4327-4375-8(9)) Outskirts Pr., Inc.

Sowards, Ben. Asleep on the Hay: A Dust Bowl Christmas. Sowards, Ben, illus. 2015. (Illus.). (J). 17.99 *(978-1-62972-067-8(4)*, Ensign Peak) Deseret Bk. Co.

Sowards, Ben, illus. Christmas Oranges. 2004. 32p. 17.95 *(978-1-59156-098-2(5))* Covenant Communications, Inc.

Spain, Susan Rosson. The Twelve Days of Christmas in Georgia. Dulemba, Elizabeth O., illus. 2010. (Twelve Days of Christmas in America Ser.). (ENG.). 40p. (J). (gr. k). 12.95 *(978-1-4027-7008-1(1))* Sterling Publishing Co., Inc.

Spangler, Paula Jeanne. Abigail's Christmas: Christmas Mom Reveals A Newborn. 2010. 48p. pap. 20.49 *(978-1-4490-8104-1(5))* AuthorHouse.

—Abigail's Christmas ~ Christmas Mom Reveals A Newborn. 2004. 17p. (J). pap. 14.08 *(978-1-4116-1045-3(8))* Lulu Pr., Inc.

Sparks, Favre. The Ugly Brown Cup. 2013. 12p. pap. 9.00 *(978-1-62516-468-1(8)*, Strategic Bk. Publishing) Strategic Book Publishing & Rights Agency (SBPRA).

Speare, Jean. A Candle for Christmas, 1 vol. Blades, Ann, illus. (ENG.). 32p. (J). pap. 4.95 *(978-0-88899-149-2(5))* Groundwood Bks. CAN. Dist: Publishers Group West (PGW).

Special X-mas Tree. 2004. (J). per. *(978-1-57657-386-0(9))* Paradise Pr., Inc.

Spencer, Debbie. Monty & His Amazing Adventures at Christmas. 2015. (ENG.). 25p. (J). (gr. 2-3). mass mkt. 13.95 *(978-1-78554-708-9(9)*, c404417d-e519-44a9-b243-445d307c70e4) Austin, Stan AUS. Dist: Bookmasters Distribution.

Spencer, John Nicholas. Sleigh Ride with Santa. Spencer, Kay Kincannon, illus. 2012. (ENG.). 26p. (J). pap. 14.95 *(978-1-61296-140-8(1))* Black Rose Writing.

Sperring, Mark. How Many Sleeps 'til Christmas? Braun, Sebastein, illus. 2014. (ENG.). 32p. (J). (gr. -1-3). 16.99 *(978-1-58925-160-1(1))* Tiger Tales.

Spiewak, Chet. An Ornament's Tale. 2006. (Illus.). 32p. (J). spiral bd. 16.95 *(978-0-9785827-0-8(5))* CWS Studios, Inc.

Spinelli, Eileen. Together at Christmas. Lee, Bin, illus. 2012. (ENG.). 24p. (J). (gr. -1-3). 15.99 *(978-0-8075-8010-3(4))* Whitman, Albert & Co.

—When Christmas Came. Parmenter, Wayne, illus. 2006. (ENG.). 32p. (J). (gr. k-3). bds. 16.95 *(978-0-8249-5507-6(2)*, Ideal Pubns.) Worthy Publishing.

Spinner, Stephanie. The Nutcracker. Malone, Peter, illus. 2008. (ENG.). 40p. (J). (gr. -1-2). 17.99 *(978-0-375-84464-5(3)*, Knopf Bks. for Young Readers) Random Hse. Children's Bks.

Spirin, Gennady. The Twelve Days of Christmas. Spirin, Gennady, illus. ltd. ed. 2009. (Illus.). 32p. (J). (gr. -1-3). 16.99 *(978-0-7614-5607-0(4))* Marshall Cavendish Corp.

Spitz, Mary Y. Mint's Christmas Message. Pierce, Joanne Y., illus. 2003. 32p. 14.95 *(978-0-9724570-0-2(3))* Mother Moose Pr.

Spohn, Bruce. Christmas Hope. 2011. 114p. pap. 19.95 *(978-1-4560-7541-5(1))* America Star Bks.

Spoon, Cynthia. The Ice Angel. Harr, Lynn, illus. 2006. 24p. (J). (gr. -1-3). per. 8.50 *(978-1-60002-280-7(4)*, 4233) Mountain Valley Publishing, LLC.

Springer, David. Patch Quilt Santa. 2005. 16p. 11.95 *(978-1-4116-3761-0(5))* Lulu Pr., Inc.

Stahel, Merry Kesner. Jennifer's Christmas Gift. 2005. 48p. pap. 8.93 *(978-1-4116-4029-0(2))* Lulu Pr., Inc.

Stahl, Deborah Joan. The Man Called Christmas. 2004. (Illus.). 32p. (YA). per. *(978-0-9755174-0-6(6))* Stahl Pubns.

Stanton, Melissa. My Pen Pal, Santa. Bell, Jennifer A., illus. 2013. (ENG.). 32p. (J). (gr. -1-2). 9.99 *(978-0-375-86992-1(1)*, Random Hse. Bks. for Young Readers) Random Hse. Children's Bks.

Starr, Barbara May. A Home for Finn: The Tail of an Alaska Rescue Dog, 1 vol. 2009. 23p. pap. 24.95 *(978-1-60749-679-3(8))* America Star Bks.

Stead, Judy. The Twelve Days of Christmas in North Carolina. Stead, Judy, illus. 2009. (Twelve Days of Christmas in America Ser.). (ENG., Illus.). 40p. (J). (gr. k). 12.95 *(978-1-4027-4467-9(6))* Sterling Publishing Co., Inc.

Stead, Judy, illus. The Twelve Days of Christmas in North Carolina. 2017. (Twelve Days of Christmas in America Ser.). (ENG.). 22p. (J). (— 1). bds. 7.95 ***(978-1-4549-2285-8(0))*** Sterling Publishing Co., Inc.

Steele, Margaret. Wuz Da Nite Befo: A Pidgin Christmas Story in Hawaii. Chang, Roy, illus. 2005. 24p. 10.95 *(978-1-56647-750-5(6))* Mutual Publishing LLC.

Steers, Billy. Tractor Mac Countdown to Christmas. 2016. (Tractor Mac Ser.). (ENG., Illus.). 16p. (J). bds. 6.99 *(978-0-374-30120-0(4)*, 9780374301200, Farrar, Straus & Giroux (BYR)) Farrar, Straus & Giroux.

—Tractor Mac Saves Christmas. 2015. (Tractor Mac Ser.). (ENG., Illus.). 32p. (J). (gr. -1-2). 8.99 *(978-0-374-30112-5(3)*, 9780374301125, Farrar, Straus & Giroux (BYR)) Farrar, Straus & Giroux.

Stein, Garth. Enzo & the Christmas Tree Hunt! Alley, R. W., illus. 2015. (ENG.). 40p. (J). (gr. -1-3). 17.99 *(978-0-06-229532-3(2))* HarperCollins Pubs.

Steinkraus, Kyla. Case of the Christmas Concert Catastrophe. 2015. (ENG.). 64p. (gr. 3-6). 29.95 *(978-1-63430-379-8(2))* Rourke Educational Media.

Stephens, Ann Marie. Christmas for Bly & Ray. Bolan, Michael P., illus. 2003. 45p. (J). per. 11.95 *(978-0-9729285-0-2(2)*, 0-9729285-0-2) Kinkachoo Pr., The.

Stepp, Shirley. Santa Lost His Cell Phone. 2012. 24p. 24.95 *(978-1-4626-5479-6(7))* America Star Bks.

Stevens-Egerton, Drema. Three Wishes for Christmas: A Stevens Children Adventure. 2007. 35p. pap. 24.95 *(978-1-60441-780-7(3))* America Star Bks.

Stevens, K. T. Christmas Stories for Children & the Young at Heart! 2012. 40p. pap. 24.95 *(978-1-4626-9166-1(8))* America Star Bks.

Stevenson, James. Night after Christmas. 2003. (ENG.). 32p. (J). pap. 2.95 *(978-0-590-41600-9(6))* Scholastic, Inc.

Stewart, Jennifer J. The Twelve Days of Christmas in Arizona. Avril, Lynne, illus. 2010. (Twelve Days of Christmas in America Ser.). (ENG.). 40p. (J). (gr. k). 12.95 *(978-1-4027-7036-4(7))* Sterling Publishing Co., Inc.

Stewart, Judy. 'Twas the Two Weeks of Christmas Break. 2008. pap. 17.00 *(978-0-8059-8657-0(X))* Dorrance Publishing Co., Inc.

Stilton, Geronimo. Christmas Catastrophe. 2007. (Geronimo Stilton Ser.). (Illus.). 93p. (J). (gr. 2-5). 14.65 *(978-0-7569-8804-3(7))* Perfection Learning Corp.

—Christmas Catastrophe. 2007. (Geronimo Stilton Special Edition Ser.). (ENG., Illus.). 128p. (J). (gr. 2-5). pap. 8.99 *(978-0-545-00902-7(2)*, Scholastic Paperbacks) Scholastic, Inc.

—A Christmas Tale. 2005. (Geronimo Stilton Special Edition Ser.). (ENG., Illus.). 64p. (J). (gr. 2-5). 7.99 *(978-0-439-79131-1(6)*, Scholastic Paperbacks) Scholastic, Inc.

—Merry Christmas, Geronimo! Wolf, Matt, illus. 2004. (Geronimo Stilton Ser.: No. 12). 113p. (J). lib. bdg. 10.00 *(978-1-4242-0281-2(7))* Fitzgerald Bks.

—Merry Christmas, Geronimo! Wolf, Matt, illus. 2004. (Geronimo Stilton Ser.: 12). (ENG.). 128p. (J). (gr. 2-5). pap. 7.99 *(978-0-439-55974-4(X)*, Scholastic Paperbacks) Scholastic, Inc.

—A Very Merry Christmas. 2008. (Geronimo Stilton Ser.: 35). (ENG.). 128p. (J). (gr. 2-5). pap. 7.99 *(978-0-545-02135-7(9)*, Scholastic Paperbacks) Scholastic, Inc.

Stine, R. L. Young Scrooge: A Very Scary Christmas Story. 2016. (ENG.). 192p. (J). 16.99 *(978-1-250-07015-9(5)*, 9781250070159) Feiwel & Friends.

—Young Scrooge: A Very Scary Christmas Story. 2017. (J). lib. bdg. 18.40 ***(978-0-606-40587-4(9))*** Turtleback Bks.

Stine, R. L. The 12 Screams of Christmas. 2014. (Goosebumps Most Wanted Special Edition Ser.: 2). (ENG.). 192p. (J). (gr. 3-7). pap. 7.99 *(978-0-545-62777-1(X)*, Scholastic Paperbacks) Scholastic, Inc.

—The 12 Screams of Christmas. 2014. (Goosebumps Most Wanted Ser.). lib. bdg. 18.40 *(978-0-606-36066-1(2))* Turtleback Bks.

Stimkorb, Patricia. A Place for the King: Christmas from the Angels Point of View. Bock, Suzanne, illus. 2004. 48p. (J). 15.99 *(978-0-9758709-6-9(3)*, 12420) Journey Stone Creations, LLC.

Stoeke, Janet Morgan. Minerva Louise on Christmas Eve. Stoeke, Janet Morgan, illus. 2009. (ENG., Illus.). 32p. (J). (gr. -1-k). pap. 6.99 *(978-0-14-241449-1(2)*, Puffin Books) Penguin Young Readers Group.

Stone Arch Books. Christmas & New Year's Eve, 1 vol. Nguyen, Dustin, illus. 2014. (Batman: Li'l Gotham Ser.). (ENG.). 32p. (gr. 2-3). 22.60 *(978-1-4342-9217-9(7))* Stone Arch Bks.

Stone, Julia. Little Bear's Sparkly Christmas. Muss, Angela, illus. 2014. (ENG.). 6p. (J). (gr. -1-k). 8.99 *(978-0-7459-6262-7(9))* Lion Hudson PLC GBR. Dist: Independent Pubs. Group.

The Story of Christmas. 2014. (Boardbooks - Board Book Ser.). (ENG.). 10p. (J). (gr. -1-k). bds. 6.99 *(978-0-7944-3198-3(4)*, Reader's Digest Children's Bks.) Studio Fun International.

Stowe, Harriet Beecher. The First Christmas of New England & O. 2006. 108p. per. 9.95 *(978-1-59818-758-8(9))* Aegypan.

Streblow, Mary. A Martian for Christmas. 2007. (ENG.). 32p. per. 23.95 *(978-1-4303-0794-5(3))* Lulu Pr., Inc.

Streeter, Lord Ronald. Grumpy Brother Christmas. 2008. 28p. pap. 16.50 *(978-1-60693-566-8(6)*, Strategic Bk. Publishing) Strategic Book Publishing & Rights Agency (SBPRA).

Strutz, Amuel U. Santa's New Reindeer Team. 2009. (Illus.). 60p. pap. 24.99 *(978-1-4389-6455-3(2))* AuthorHouse.

Stuart, Ruth McEnery. A Christmas Guest. 2004. reprint ed. pap. 15.95 *(978-1-4191-0046-8(7))*; pap. 1.99 *(978-1-4192-0046-5(1))* Kessinger Publishing, LLC.

Suderman, Colleen C. Norgee & the Christmas Tree: A Norgee Story. 2013. 28p. pap. 24.95 *(978-1-4560-0981-6(8))* America Star Bks.

Sullivan, E. J. How Santa Got His Elves. Eldredge, Ernie, illus. 2006. (J). (gr. -1-3). 9.95 *(978-1-58173-308-2(9))* Sweetwater Pr.

Susan A. McCoy. The Christmas That Saved Pie Town. 2009. 56p. pap. 23.99 *(978-1-4389-4027-4(0))* AuthorHouse.

Swad, Libby White. A Christmas Tree. 2011. 32p. pap. *(978-1-77067-342-7(3))* FriesenPress.

Swanson, Maggie, illus. & retold by. The Kitten's Christmas Lullaby. Swanson, Maggie, retold by. 2007. (J). (gr. -1-3). 8.95 *(978-0-88271-064-8(8))* Regina Pr., Malhame & Co.

Swickle, Dvora. The Legend of Santa Owl. 2012. 64p. pap. *(978-1-897512-65-4(1))* Saga Bks.

Swigut, Bernadetta. First Star: Vigilja- First Star. 2006. (J). 16.99 *(978-0-9790026-0-1(5))* Steinschneider, Bernadetta.

Sykes, Julie. Bless You, Santa! Warnes, Tim, illus. 2004. 32p. (J). tchr. ed. 15.95 *(978-1-58925-041-3(9))* Tiger Tales.

—Shhh! Warnes, Tim, illus. 2006. (Storytime Board Bks.). 18p. (J). (gr. -1-1). bds. 6.95 *(978-1-58925-796-2(0))* Tiger Tales.

Sylvester, Merrill. Ho-Ho Where Did All My Reindeer Go? The Chicken Leg Detective Service. 2011. 72p. pap. 19.95 *(978-1-4626-0794-5(2))* America Star Bks.

Sypolt, Carl W. Fibber Lygood at Christmas, Easter, & St. Patrick's Day. 2006. 108p. (J). pap. 10.95 *(978-0-7414-2982-7(9))* Infinity Publishing.

The Talking Christmas Tree. 2003. (J). per. *(978-1-57657-925-1(5))* Paradise Pr., Inc.

Tangvald, Christine Harder. The Best Thing about Christmas. Nobens, C. A., illus. 2014. (Faith That Sticks Bks.). (ENG.). 27p. (J). pap. 3.99 *(978-1-4964-0087-1(9))* Tyndale Hse. Pubs.

Tanigawa, Nagaru. The Disappearance of Haruhi Suzumiya. 2010. (Haruhi Suzumiya Ser.: 4). (ENG., Illus.). 192p. (YA). (gr. 10-17). pap. 18.00 *(978-0-316-03889-8(X))* Little, Brown Bks. for Young Readers.

Tapler, Judy. Santa Horse. Kohler, Michelle, illus. 2008. 36p. pap. 16.99 *(978-1-4389-2290-4(6))* AuthorHouse.

Tapley-Milton, Katherine. The Adventures of Sir Lancelot the Cat. 2013. 16p. pap. 7.99 *(978-1-4497-8838-4(6)*, WestBow Pr.) Author Solutions, Inc.

Taplin, Sam. My First Christmas Keyboard Book. 2015. (My First Keyboard Bks.). (ENG.). 20p. (J). 18.99 *(978-0-7945-3580-3(1)*, Usborne) EDC Publishing.

Tarkington, Booth. Beasley's Christmas Party. 2005. 76p. pap. 10.95 *(978-1-4218-0407-1(7)*, 1st World Library - Literary Society) 1st World Publishing, Inc.

—Beasley's Christmas Party. Clements, Ruth Sypherd, illus. 2004. reprint ed. pap. 15.95 *(978-1-4179-0186-9(1))* Kessinger Publishing, LLC.

—Beasley's Christmas Party. 2004. reprint ed. pap. 1.99 *(978-1-4192-0925-3(6))* Kessinger Publishing, LLC.

Tavares, Matt, illus. 'Twas the Night Before Christmas. 2006. (ENG.). 32p. (J). (gr. k-12). 8.99 *(978-0-7636-3118-5(3))* Candlewick Pr.

Taylor, C. Brian. Atop the Tree Top: A Christmas Story. Butler, Sharon, illus. 2003. (J). 15.95 *(978-0-9747054-0-8(3))* Rilly Silly Bk. Co., The.

Taylor, Lillian Webb. Santa's Musical Elves. 2009. 28p. pap. 12.25 *(978-1-60860-146-2(3)*, Strategic Bk. Publishing) Strategic Book Publishing & Rights Agency (SBPRA).

Taylor, Pat Eytcheson. Scamper Tangles with Christmas. 2012. 56p. pap. 15.00 *(978-0-9845630-4-3(0))* Catch-A-Winner Publishing.

Tazewell, Charles. The Littlest Angel. lthr. 29.95 *(978-0-8249-5333-1(9)*, Ideal Pubns.) Worthy Publishing.

—The Littlest Angel. Micich, Paul, illus. (ENG.). 32p. (J). (gr. -1-3). 2008. 8.99 *(978-0-8249-5575-5(7))* 2007. pap. 3.99 *(978-0-8249-5549-6(8))* Worthy Publishing. (Ideal Pubns.).

—The Littlest Angel. Porfirio, Guy, illus. 2004. 32p. (J). 16.95 *(978-0-8249-5473-4(4)*, Ideal Pubns.) Worthy Publishing.

Teitelbaum, Michael. Garfield & the Santa Spy. Fentz, Mike, illus. 2004. 92p. (J). *(978-0-439-70543-1(6))* Scholastic, Inc.

TerKeurst, Lysa. The Sweetest Story Ever Told: A New Christmas Tradition for Families. Sparks, Michal, illus. 2003. 32p. 9.99 *(978-0-8024-7094-2(7))* Moody Pubs.

Testa, Maggie. OLIVIA Counts down to Christmas. Johnson, Shane L., illus. 2012. (Olivia TV Tie-In Ser.). (ENG.). 16p. (J). (gr. -1-1). pap. 6.99 *(978-1-4424-5747-8(3)*, Simon Spotlight) Simon Spotlight.

Tewkesbury, Alexa. The Camel Who Found Christmas. 2007. (ENG., Illus.). 32p. (J). *(978-1-85345-427-1(3))* Crusade for World Revival.

—The Perfect Christmas Present. 2008. (ENG.). 32p. (J). *(978-1-85345-476-9(1))* Crusade for World Revival.

Thaler, Mike. The Christmas Party from the Black Lagoon. Lee, Jared, illus. 2006. 64p. (J). pap. *(978-0-439-87160-0(3))* Scholastic, Inc.

—The Secret Santa from the Black Lagoon. Lee, Jared D., illus. 2014. 64p. (J). *(978-0-545-78519-8(7))* Scholastic, Inc.

—The Three Wise Guys, 1 vol. Lee, Jared, illus. 2010. (Tales from the Back Pew Ser.). (ENG.). 32p. (J). (gr. 1-4). pap. 3.99 *(978-0-310-71593-1(8))* Zonderkidz.

Thanos, Jerald. A Princess Christmas. 2009. 32p. pap. 14.49 *(978-1-4389-6752-3(7))* AuthorHouse.

Thayer, Jane. The Puppy Who Wanted a Boy. McCue, Lisa, illus. 2005. (ENG.). 32p. (J). (gr. -1-3). pap. 6.99 *(978-0-06-052698-6(X))* HarperCollins Pubs.

The Bee Guru, Gregg McMahan. Christmas Honey. 2012. (Illus.). 20p. pap. 11.60 *(978-1-4669-5471-7(X))* Trafford Publishing.

Theer, Justine M. The Backwards Town, 1 vol. 2010. 82p. pap. 19.95 *(978-1-4489-5361-5(8))* America Star Bks.

Thomas Nelson. Twas the Night Before Christmas. 2016. (ENG.). 32p. (J). (gr. -1-7). pap. *(978-1-78598-443-3(8))* Make Believe Ideas.

Thomas, Patricia. Mouse's Christmas Cookie, 0 vols. Nez, Jon, illus. 2013. (ENG.). 24p. (J). (gr. -1-2). 14.99 *(978-1-4778-4704-6(9)*, 9781477847046, Amazon Children's Publishing) Amazon Publishing.

Thompson, David. The Nine Clues of Christmas, 1 vol. 2009. 172p. pap. 24.95 *(978-1-60813-410-6(5))* America Star Bks.

Thompson, Emily Weisner & Hussey, Mandy. But What If There's No Chimney? Lampe, Kate, illus. 2016. (ENG.). 24p. 12.00 *(978-0-253-02392-6(0))* Indiana Univ. Pr.

Thompson, Emma. The Christmas Tale of Peter Rabbit. Taylor, Eleanor, illus. 2013. (Peter Rabbit Ser.). (ENG.). 72p. (J). (gr. -1-2). 20.00 *(978-0-7232-7694-4(3)*, Warne) Penguin Young Readers Group.

Thompson, Kimberly. Toulouse Tangled up in Lights. Easey, Chris, illus. 2011. 64p. (J). 19.95 *(978-0-9818976-1-5(4))* Little Pigeon Bks.

Thompson, Lauren. A Christmas Gift for Mama. Burke, Jim, illus. 2003. (J). pap. 16.95 *(978-0-590-30726-0(6))* Scholastic, Inc.

—The Christmas Magic. Muth, Jon J., illus. 2009. (ENG.). 40p. (J). (gr. -1-3). 16.99 *(978-0-439-77497-0(7)*, Scholastic Pr.) Scholastic, Inc.

—Mouse's First Christmas. Erdogan, Buket, illus. 2003. (ENG.). 32p. (J). (gr. -1-3). 7.99 *(978-0-689-86348-6(9)*, Simon & Schuster Bks. For Young Readers) Simon & Schuster Bks. For Young Readers.

—Mouse's First Christmas. Erdogan, Buket, illus. 2003. (gr. -1-1). lib. bdg. 18.40 *(978-0-613-91039-2(7)*, Turtleback) Turtleback Bks.

—One Starry Night. Bean, Jonathan, illus. (ENG.). 32p. (J). 2011. (gr. -1-3). lib. bdg. 17.99 *(978-0-689-82851-5(9))* 2003. 6.99 *(978-0-689-84215-3(5))* McElderry, Margaret K. Bks. (McElderry, Margaret K. Bks.).

Thoms, Susan Collins. The Twelve Days of Christmas in Michigan. Pilutti, Deb, illus. (Twelve Days of Christmas in America Ser.). (ENG.). (J). (— 1). 2017. 22p. bds. 7.95 ***(978-1-4549-2284-1(2))*** 2010. 40p. 12.95 *(978-1-4027-6351-9(4))* Sterling Publishing Co., Inc.

Thorup, Bryce. Doctor Matthews' Family Christmas. Muller, Ruth, illus. 2005. (J). 18.95 *(978-0-9765964-1-7(5))* Round Tower Pr.

Tiger Tales, ed. & compiled by. My Favorite Christmas Stories. Tiger Tales, compiled by. 2015. (ENG.). 128p. (J). (gr. -1-3). 12.99 *(978-1-68010-200-0(1))* Tiger Tales.

Tiger Tales Staff. Five Minute Christmas Stories. 2014. (ENG.). 292p. (J). (gr. -1-3). 14.99 *(978-1-58925-525-8(9))* Tiger Tales.

Tillman, Nancy. The Spirit of Christmas. Tillman, Nancy, illus. 2009. (ENG., Illus.). 32p. (J). (gr. -1-3). 17.99 *(978-0-312-54965-7(2)*, 9780312549657) Feiwel & Friends.

Tillworth, Mary. Dora's Christmas Star (Dora the Explorer) Miller, Victoria, illus. 2013. (Pictureback(R) Ser.). (ENG.). 16p. (J). (gr. -1-2). 4.99 *(978-0-449-81780-3(6)*, Random Hse. Bks. for Young Readers) Random Hse. Children's Bks.

—Happy Holidays, Bubble Guppies! (Bubble Guppies) Jackson, Mike, illus. 2013. (Pictureback(R) Ser.). (ENG.). 16p. (J). (gr. -1-2). 4.99 *(978-0-449-81779-7(2)*, Random Hse. Bks. for Young Readers) Random Hse. Children's Bks.

Timmo. The Magic Christmas Fairy. 2008. 32p. pap. 17.95 *(978-1-4092-3707-5(9))* Lulu Pr., Inc.

Tingwald, July Ann. Orrie's Christmas. Powell, James, illus. 2007. 42p. 9.00 *(978-0-9706728-5-8(3))* New Millenium Pr., The.

Todd, Michelle, illus. Santa's Workshop. 2017. (ENG.). 12p. (J). (gr. -1-1). 12.99 ***(978-1-4380-5007-2(0))*** Barron's Educational Series, Inc.

Tolan, Stephanie S. Bartholomew's Blessing. Moore, Margie, illus. 2004. 32p. (J). (gr. -1-3). lib. bdg. 16.89 *(978-0-06-001198-7(X))* HarperCollins Pubs.

Tolkien, J. R. R. Letters from Father Christmas. Tolkien, Baillie, ed. 2004. (ENG., Illus.). 128p. pap. 23.99 *(978-0-618-51265-2(9))* Houghton Mifflin Harcourt Publishing Co.

Tolley, Diane Stringam. Kris Kringle's Magic. 2012. 169p. (J). 14.99 *(978-1-4621-1105-3(X))* Cedar Fort, Inc./CFI Distribution.

Toner, Gerald R. Lipstick Like Lindsay's & Other Christmas Stories, 1 vol. Haynes, Joyce, illus. 2005. (ENG.). 112p. per. 14.95 *(978-1-58980-357-2(4))* Pelican Publishing Co., Inc.

Top Ten Clues You're Clueless. 2014. (ENG.). 304p. (YA). (gr. 8). pap. 9.99 *(978-0-06-227242-3(X))* HarperCollins Pubs.

Torgrimsen, Reidun. Timmy's Christmas, a Very Special Pig from Sugar Valley & His Best Friend. 2012. 30p. 24.95 *(978-1-62709-149-7(1))* America Star Bks.

Torres, Christopher S. Salma & the Christmas Star. Hildebrandt, Lowell, illus. 2010. 24p. 12.99 *(978-1-4490-8981-8(X))* AuthorHouse.

Toska, Mary Lou. The Shepherd Boy. 2013. 32p. pap. 24.95 *(978-1-62709-475-7(X))* America Star Bks.

Treasury of Christmas Tales. bds. 15.98 *(978-0-7853-0820-1(2))* Publications International, Ltd.

Tripp, Valerie. Kit's Surprise. Rane, Walter & McAliley, Susan, illus. 2004. (American Girls Collection: Bk. 3). (ENG.). 71p. (gr. 2-18). 12.95 *(978-1-58485-021-2(3))* American Girl Publishing, Inc.

Trivette, Donna K. One Special Christmas. 2012. 44p. pap. 24.95 *(978-1-4626-9363-4(6))* America Star Bks.

Trodd, Mark. Hippo in the Stable. 2012. 36p. pap. 32.70 *(978-1-4797-1561-9(1))* Xlibris Corp.

Tucker, David J. Stickman World Larry & George have a Merry Christmas. 2005. 23p. (J). 11.68 *(978-1-4116-5615-4(6))* Lulu Pr., Inc.

Tullis, Jamie. Rudolph, I Think You Need Glasses! 2012. 24p. pap. 15.99 *(978-1-4797-1624-1(3))* Xlibris Corp.

Tully, Justin. Lost from the Christmas Mansion. 2008. 141p. pap. 16.95 *(978-1-4092-5106-4(3))* Lulu Pr., Inc.

Turman, Evelyn. J. B. 's Christmas Presents. Turman, Adam, illus. l.t. ed. 2004. 28p. (J). 15.95 *(978-0-9753042-0-4(8))* Turman, E.

Turner, Christina. Hello Santa! Turner, Christina, illus. 2007. (Illus.). 16p. (J). (gr. -1). bds. 7.95 *(978-0-9790347-0-1(1))* Mackenzie Smiles, LLC.

Tutor, Margaret. A Make-Do Christmas, 1 vol. 2009. 74p. pap. 19.95 *(978-1-4489-0849-3(3))* America Star Bks.

The Twelve Rabbids of Christmas. 2014. (Rabbids Invasion Ser.). (ENG., Illus.). 24p. (J). (gr. -1-3). pap. 4.99 *(978-1-4814-2032-7(1)*, Simon Spotlight) Simon Spotlight.

Twin Sisters(r), et al. The First Christmas Sing-A-Story Book. 2016. (ENG.). 16p. (J). bds. 9.99 *(978-1-63409-900-4(1))* Barbour Publishing, Inc.

Twinkle Toes. 2011. (ENG., Illus.). 36p. (J). 15.95 *(978-1-935268-57-4(0))* Halo Publishing International.

Tyler, William H. The Little Wolf Cubs' Christmas Gift. 2011. 48p. pap. *(978-1-4269-7443-4(4))* Trafford Publishing (UK) Ltd.

Ulmer, Louise. The Bible That Wouldn't Burn: How the Tyndale English Version of the Bible Came About. 2nd l.t. ed. 2003. (Illus.). 32p. 4.95 *(978-0-941367-01-1(0))* Peach Blossom Pubns.

Uncle Markie. Piglette & Bobo Christmas in Palm Springs. 2003. (YA). ring bd. 9.95 *(978-1-933129-10-5(7))* Studio 403.

Underwood, Deborah. The Christmas Quiet Book. Liwska, Renata, illus. (ENG.). 32p. (J). (gr. -1-3). 2017. pap. 7.99 ***(978-1-328-74056-4(0)***, HMH Books For Young Readers) 2012. 12.99 *(978-0-547-55863-9(5))* Houghton Mifflin Harcourt Publishing Co.

Ungerer, Tomi. Christmas Eve at the Mellops' 2011. (ENG., Illus.). 32p. (gr. -1-2). 12.95 *(978-0-7148-6250-7(9))* Phaidon Pr., Inc.

Unrau, Adela. That Was a Nice Surprise, 1 vol. Friesen, Anni, illus. 2010. 16p. 24.95 *(978-1-4489-5744-6(3))* PublishAmerica, Inc.

Unser, Virginia. The Night Before Cat-Mas. Anagost, Karen, illus. 2007. (Petite Plush Kit Ser.). 64p. (J). (gr. -1-3). 9.95 *(978-1-59359-882-2(3))* Peter Pauper Pr. Inc.

Urmy, Deanne, ed. Merry Christmas: Best - Loved Stories & Carols. Green, Donna, illus. 2004. 90p. (J). (gr. 4-8). reprint ed. 20.00 *(978-0-7567-7580-3(9))* DIANE Publishing Co.

Vainio, Pirkko. Little Bunny Finds Christmas. Vainio, Pirkko, illus. 2008. (ENG., Illus.). 32p. (J). (gr. -1-3). 16.95 *(978-0-7358-2221-4(2))* North-South Bks., Inc.

Vaitonis, Steven. Edison the Christmas Elf & the Imperfect Perfect Toy. Blue, Melissa, illus. 2014. 32p. (J). (gr. -1-1). pap. 12.95 *(978-1-939930-33-0(2)*, Belle Isle Bks.) Brandylane Pubs., Inc.

Valentine, Peggy. Katie's Christmas. 2010. 28p. pap. 13.59 *(978-1-4520-5230-4(1))* AuthorHouse.

Van Allsburg, Chris. The Polar Express. 30th anniv. ed. 2015. (ENG., Illus.). 32p. (J). (gr. -1-3). 19.99 *(978-0-544-58014-5(1)*, HMH Books For Young Readers) Houghton Mifflin Harcourt Publishing Co.

—The Polar Express: Sam's Edition. annot. ed. 2006. (J). (gr. k-3). 35.00 *(978-0-618-83659-8(4))* Houghton Mifflin Harcourt Trade & Reference Pubs.

—The Polar Express Big Book. 2014. (ENG., Illus.). 32p. (J). (gr. -1-3). 29.99 *(978-0-544-45798-0(6)*, HMH Books For Young Readers) Houghton Mifflin Harcourt Publishing Co.

Van Dyke, Henry. The Other Wise Man. 2004. pap. 11.95 incl. audio compact disk *(978-1-932226-34-8(6))* Wizard Academy Pr.

—The Sad Shepherd: A Christmas Story, & the Unruly Sprite. 2007. 48p. per. *(978-1-4065-4725-2(5))* Dodo Pr.

—The Story of the Other Wise Man. 2007. 52p. per. *(978-1-4065-4728-3(X))* Dodo Pr.

van Genechten, Guido. Ricky's Christmas Tree. 2011. (Ricky Ser.). (ENG., Illus.). 32p. (J). (gr. -1-k). 16.95 *(978-1-60537-106-1(8))* Cobblestone Publishing Co.

C
D

Van King, L. The Dwarf in the Drawer: A Mischievous Parody. Gonzales, Chuck, illus. 2013. (ENG.). 32p. (J). 19.99 *(978-1-250-04143-2(0)*, 9781250041432) Square Fish.
Van Liew Cassels, Rosemary. Santa's Dilemm. 2008. 48p. pap. 24.50 *(978-1-4389-0881-6(4))* AuthorHouse.
Van Scott, Miriam. Candy Canes in Bethlehem. Van Wagoner, Traci, illus. 2012. (J). 7.95 *(978-0-8198-1606-1(X))* Pauline Bks. & Media.
Van Steenwyk, Elizabeth. Prairie Christmas. Himler, Ronald, illus. 2006. 32p. (J). (gr. k). 17.00 *(978-0-8028-5280-9(7)*, Eerdmans Bks For Young Readers) Eerdmans, William B. Publishing Co.
Van Syckle, A. & Schwartz, Josh. The OC: 'twas the Night Before Chrismukkah. 2005. 206p. (YA). *(978-1-4156-3915-3(9))* Scholastic, Inc.
Vandepeer, Helen. Gifts. 2008. 76p. pap. 35.80 *(978-0-557-03191-7(5))* Lulu Pr., Inc.
VanDerwest, Steven M. Reuben's First Christmas Crow. 2012. 40p. pap. 13.95 *(978-1-4497-5164-7(4)*, WestBow Pr.) Author Solutions, Inc.
Varicak, Rebecca. The Journey of a Toys for Tots Toy! 2012. 24p. pap. 15.99 *(978-1-4772-8601-2(2))* AuthorHouse.
Vaswani, Navina. A Wonderful Christmas. 2004. (YA). per. *(978-0-9754818-5-1(1))* Creative Bk. Pubs.
Vasylenko, Veronica. Deck the Halls. Tiger Tales Staff, ed. 2011. (ENG., Illus.). 20p. bds. 8.95 *(978-1-58925-868-6(1))* Tiger Tales.
—Jingle Bells. Tiger Tales Staff, ed. 2011. (ENG., Illus.). 20p. bds. 8.95 *(978-1-58925-869-3(X))* Tiger Tales.
Velasquez, Eric. Grandma's Gift. Velasquez, Eric, illus. 2013. (ENG., Illus.). 32p. (J). (gr. k-1). pap. 9.99 *(978-0-8027-3536-2(3)*, 9780802735362, Bloomsbury USA Childrens) Bloomsbury Publishing USA.
Ventline, D. Min. Tale So True of My Christmas Tree: Everything Belongs in Our World. 2008. 16p. pap. 10.99 *(978-1-4389-1094-9(0))* AuthorHouse.
Verney, Jeff. The Christmas Book of Hope. 2006. (Illus.). 36p. 14.95 *(978-0-9771250-0-5(9))* JRV Publishing.
Vernick, Shirley Reva. The Black Butterfly. 2014. (ENG.). 226p. (J). 19.95 *(978-1-935955-79-5(9))* Cinco Puntos Pr.
Verrett, Michael. Cozmo the Elf. 2010. 86p. pap. 32.00 *(978-0-557-25717-1(4))* Lulu Pr., Inc.
—Galid's Christmas Wish. 2010. 44p. pap. 22.90 *(978-0-557-29109-0(7))* Lulu Pr., Inc.
Victoria, Marie Alexandra. A Christmas Tale. 2013. 40p. pap. *(978-3-944704-09-8(6))* Nothnagle, Alan. Edition Graugans.
Villa, Leesan. The Angel on Top of the Tree. 2011. 68p. pap. 31.99 *(978-1-4628-7837-6(7))* Xlibris Corp.
Villarreal, Tanya E. Izzie's First Christmas, 1 vol. Villarreal, Tanya E., illus. 2009. (Illus.). 28p. pap. 24.95 *(978-1-61546-093-9(4))* America Star Bks.
Vischer, Frans. A Very Fuddles Christmas. Vischer, Frans, illus. 2013. (ENG., Illus.). 32p. (J). (gr. -1-2). 15.99 *(978-1-4169-9156-4(5)*, Aladdin) Simon & Schuster Children's Publishing.
Vlahakis, Andrea. Christmas Eve Blizzard, 1 vol. Schongut, Emanuel, illus. 2005. (ENG.). 32p. (J). (gr. k-4). 15.95 *(978-0-9764943-3-1(7))* Arbordale Publishing.
Von Dornheim, Curt H. The Little Baron's Christmas Angel. Date not set. (Illus.). 64p. 12.95 *(978-0-89404-222-5(X))* Aztex Corp.
Voutila, Ritva, illus. The Nutcracker. 2016. (ENG.). 32p. (J). (gr. k-3). 18.99 *(978-1-74297-778-2(2))* Little Hare Bks. AUS. Dist: Independent Pubs. Group.
Waddell, Martin. Room for a Little One: A Christmas Tale. Cockcroft, Jason, illus. 2008. (ENG.). 26p. (J). (gr. -1-2). bds. 7.99 *(978-1-4169-6177-2(1)*, Little Simon) Little Simon.
—Room for a Little One: A Christmas Tale. Cockcroft, Jason, illus. (ENG.). 32p. (J). (gr. -1-3). 2006. 11.99 *(978-1-4169-2518-7(X))* 2004. 18.99 *(978-0-689-86841-2(3))* McElderry, Margaret K. Bks. (McElderry, Margaret K. Bks.).
Walburg, Lori. The Legend of the Candy Cane: The Inspirational Story of Our Favorite Christmas Candy, 1 vol. Bernardin, James & Cowdrey, Richard, illus. ed. 2012. (ENG.). 32p. (J). 15.99 *(978-0-310-73012-5(0))* Zonderkidz.
Walker, Anna. I Love Christmas. Walker, Anna, illus. 2009. (ENG., Illus.). 32p. (J). (gr. -1-1). 9.99 *(978-1-4169-8317-0(1)*, Simon & Schuster Bks. For Young Readers) Simon & Schuster Bks. For Young Readers.
Walker, John, illus. The Story of Christmas: The Birth of Jesus. 2008. (ENG.). 24p. (J). (gr. 2). 19.95 *(978-1-58117-793-0(3)*, Intervisual/Piggy Toes) Bendon, Inc.
Walker-Renner, Christa. Santa's Magic. 2009. 20p. pap. 11.00 *(978-1-4389-8206-9(2))* AuthorHouse.
Walker, Susan Eileen. I Know the Quigglebush Heroes. 2008. 53p. pap. 16.95 *(978-1-60672-587-0(4))* America Star Bks.
Wallace, Adam. How to Catch an Elf. Elkerton, Andy, illus. 2016. (ENG.). 32p. (J). (-3). 10.99 *(978-1-4926-4631-0(8)*, 9781492646310, Sourcebooks Jabberwocky) Sourcebooks, Inc.
Wallace, Adam. Only YOU Can Save Christmas! A Help-The-Elf Adventure. Bruner, Garth, illus. 2017. (ENG.). 40p. (J). (gr. 1-5). 16.99 ***(978-1-4926-4136-0(7)***, Sourcebooks Jabberwocky) Sourcebooks, Inc.
Wallace, Bill. The Dog Who Thought He Was Santa. 2007. (ENG., Illus.). 224p. (J). (gr. 4-7). 17.95 *(978-0-8234-2114-5(7))* Holiday Hse., Inc.
—The Dog Who Thought He Was Santa. 2008. (ENG.). 192p. (J). (gr. 3-7). pap. 5.99 *(978-1-4169-4816-2(3)*, Aladdin) Simon & Schuster Children's Publishing.
Wallace, Carol. The Santa Secret. Björkman, Steve, illus. 2007. (Holiday House Readers: Level 2 Ser.). (ENG.). 40p. (J). (gr. -1-3). 15.95 *(978-0-8234-2022-3(1))*; pap. 4.95 *(978-0-8234-2126-8(0))* Holiday Hse., Inc.
Wallace, Nancy K. The Christmas Cats, 1 vol. Housley, Cathren, illus. 2011. (ENG.). 32p. (J). (gr. k-3). 16.99 *(978-1-58980-979-6(3))* Pelican Publishing Co., Inc.
—The Haunted Sleepover, 1 vol. Chronister, Amanda, illus. 2013. (Abby & the Book Bunch Ser.). (ENG.). 80p. (J). (gr. 2-5). 27.07 *(978-1-61641-913-4(X))* Magic Wagon.
Wallace, R. Mike. Saunter. 2009. 36p. pap. 10.75 *(978-1-60693-994-9(7)*, Strategic Bk. Publishing) Strategic Book Publishing & Rights Agency (SBPRA).
Walls, Sarah. Christmas Kitten: Special Delivery. 2010. 20p. 10.49 *(978-1-4490-9750-9(2))* AuthorHouse.
Walter, C. Lyn. The Five Dollar Christmas Tree. 2009. 24p. pap. 16.99 *(978-1-4490-3467-2(5))* AuthorHouse.
Walters, Catherine. The Special Christmas Tree. Taylor-Kielty, Simon, illus. 2012. (J). *(978-1-4351-4315-9(9))* Barnes & Noble, Inc.
Walton, Rick. Bunny Christmas: A Family Celebration. Miglio, Paige, illus. 2004. 32p. (J). (ENG.). 15.99 *(978-0-06-008415-8(4))*; lib. bdg. 16.89 *(978-0-06-008416-5(2))* HarperCollins Pubs.
Walz, C. E. Mary's Treasure Box. Merz, Bruno, illus. 2015. (ENG.). 32p. (J). (gr. -1-3). 12.99 *(978-1-4336-8394-7(6)*, B&H Kids) B&H Publishing Group.
Wampol, Pam & Woodard, Heather. Oscar's Dreamzz: The Story of Santa's First Elf. 2013. 40p. pap. *(978-1-4602-0414-6(X))* FriesenPress.
Wan, Joyce. You Are My Merry Little Christmas. Wan, Joyce, illus. 2016. (ENG., Illus.). 14p. (J). (— 1). 6.99 *(978-0-545-88093-0(9)*, Cartwheel Bks.) Scholastic, Inc.
Wang, Jack, et al. E.T.A. Hoffman's the Nutcracker. 2016. (ENG., Illus.). 24p. (J). (gr. -1 — 1). bds. 9.95 *(978-1-4521-5248-6(9))* Chronicle Bks. LLC.
Wangerin, Walter, Jr. Probity Jones & the Fear Not Angel. Ladwig, Tim, illus. 2005. 32p. (J). (gr. 1-4). 16.95 *(978-1-55725-457-3(5))* Paraclete Pr., Inc.
Ward, Candace, ed. Children's Christmas Stories & Poems. 2011. (Dover Children's Thrift Classics Ser.). (ENG., Illus.). 96p. (J). (gr. 3-8). pap. 4.00 *(978-0-486-28656-3(8))* Dover Pubns., Inc.
Warne. Merry Christmas, Peter! 2014. (Peter Rabbit Animation Ser.). (ENG.). 32p. (J). (gr. -1-k). 9.99 *(978-0-14-135173-5(X)*, Warne) Penguin Young Readers Group.
Warner, Marty, et al. The Little Girl in the Yellow Dress. 2005. 26p. 14.99 *(978-1-4116-3148-9(X))* Lulu Pr., Inc.
Warner, Sally. Ellray Jakes Rocks the Holidays! 2014. (EllRay Jakes Ser.: 7). lib. bdg. 16.00 *(978-0-606-36188-0(X))* Turtleback Bks.
—Rocks the Holidays! Biggs, Brian, illus. 2014. (EllRay Jakes Ser.: 7). (ENG.). 160p. (J). (gr. 1-3). 14.99 *(978-0-451-46909-0(7)*, Viking Books for Young Readers) Penguin Young Readers Group.
Warren, G. A. Starr Light & the Christmas Story. Ciesinska, Izabela, illus. 2009. 32p. (J). 14.95 *(978-1-935268-09-3(0))* Halo Publishing International.
Warwick, Ellen. The Twelve Days of Christmas in Canada. Smith, Kim, illus. 2016. (Twelve Days of Christmas in America Ser.). (ENG.). 22p. (J). (— 1). bds. 9.50 *(978-1-4549-2056-4(4))* Sterling Publishing Co., Inc.
Washington, LaVonne & Washington, LaShawn. How the Grinch Hare Became a Christian. 2005. 37p. 11.95 *(978-1-4116-2322-4(3))* Lulu Pr., Inc.
Watt, Fiona. Christmas Eve. Wells, Rachel, illus. 2007. (Luxury Touchy-Feely Board Bks). 10p. (J). (gr. -1-k). bds. 11.99 *(978-0-7945-1478-5(2)*, Usborne) EDC Publishing.
—Christmas Mice. 2004. (Big Touchy Feely Board Bks.). (Illus.). 10p. (J). 11.95 *(978-0-7945-0482-3(5)*, Usborne) EDC Publishing.
—Little Children's Christmas Music Book. 2012. (Little Children's Music Book Ser.). 24p. (J). bds. 18.99 *(978-0-7945-3328-1(0)*, Usborne) EDC Publishing.
—The Nativity. Wells, Rachel, illus. 2005. (Usborne Touchy-Feely Board Bks.). 10p. (J). (gr. -1-k). bds. 15.95 *(978-0-7945-1172-2(4)*, Usborne) EDC Publishing.
—Santa Claus. 2004. (Sparkly Touchy-Feely Board Bks.). 10p. (J). 15.95 *(978-0-7945-0830-2(8)*, Usborne) EDC Publishing.
—Sparkly Christmas Angel. Kightley, Rosalinda, illus. 2007. (Luxury Touchy-Feely Board Bks). 10p. (J). (gr. -1-k). bds. 15.99 *(978-0-7945-1477-8(4)*, Usborne) EDC Publishing.
Watt, Mélanie. Scaredy Squirrel Prepares for Christmas. Watt, Mélanie, illus. 2012. (ENG., Illus.). 80p. (J). (gr. -1-3). 17.95 *(978-1-55453-469-2(0))* Kids Can Pr., Ltd. CAN. Dist: Hachette Bk. Group.
Wax, Wendy. Animal Family Christmas. 2007. (ENG.). 20p. (J). 14.95 *(978-1-58117-625-4(2)*, Intervisual/Piggy Toes) Bendon, Inc.
Webster, Christy. Elmo's Merry Christmas/Oscar's Grouchy Christmas (Sesame Street) 2016. (Pictureback(R) Ser.). (ENG., Illus.). 24p. (J). (-k). 4.99 *(978-1-101-93923-9(0)*, Random Hse. Bks. for Young Readers) Random Hse. Children's Bks.
—A Perfect Christmas. Random House Staff, illus. 2011. (Step into Reading Ser.). (ENG.). 32p. (J). (gr. -1-1). pap. 3.99 *(978-0-375-86932-7(8)*, Random Hse. Bks. for Young Readers) Random Hse. Children's Bks.
Webster, Clare L., retold by. The Elf, 1 vol. 2009. 27p. pap. 24.95 *(978-1-60836-775-7(4))* America Star Bks.
Webster, Michelle B. The Christmas of Miracles. 2004. 136p. per. 12.95 *(978-0-9753117-0-7(0))* Four Sonkist Angels.
Weinand, Margaret & Johnson, Thomas M. Tommy's Treasured Christmas Tree. 2012. 24p. pap. 15.99 *(978-1-4797-2325-6(8))* Xlibris Corp.
Weinberg, Jennifer Liberts. Christmas Toys. 2012. (Step into Reading Level 2 Ser.). lib. bdg. 13.55 *(978-0-606-26796-0(4)*, Turtleback) Turtleback Bks.
Weinberger, David J. Answers to a Christmas Question. 2012. (ENG.). (J). pap. *(978-1-4675-2381-3(X))* Independent Pub.
—Answers to a Christmas Question Coloring Book. 2012. (ENG.). (J). pap. *(978-1-4675-2380-6(1))* Independent Pub.
Weiskal, N. J. C Is for the Christ Child. 2009. 32p. pap. 8.00 *(978-1-935125-55-6(9))* Robertson Publishing.
Welborn, Amy. Bambinelli Sunday: A Christmas Blessing. Engelhart, Ann, illus. 2013. (ENG.). 32p. (J). (gr. k-2). 15.99 *(978-1-61636-649-0(4))* Franciscan Media.
Weldon, George. It Could Only Happen at Christmas. 2008. 80p. pap. 10.49 *(978-1-4389-3737-3(7))* AuthorHouse.
Wells, Rosemary. Max's Christmas. 2013. (Max & Ruby Ser.). (ENG.). 32p. (J). (gr. -1-k). 8.99 *(978-0-14-750947-5(5)*, Puffin Books) Penguin Young Readers Group.
—Max's Christmas. 2013. (Max Ruby Ser.). lib. bdg. 18.40 *(978-0-606-32139-6(X)*, Turtleback) Turtleback Bks.
—McDuff's New Friend with Plush Box Set. 2003. (Illus.). 28p. (J). 14.99 *(978-0-7868-1866-2(2)*, Disney Editions) Disney Pr.
Wenger, Brahm. Dewey's Magical Sleigh, from the Dewey Doo-it Series. 2005. (ENG., Illus.). 32p. (J). (gr. -1-2). 15.95 incl. lp *(978-0-9745143-6-9(5))* RandallFraser Publishing.
Weninger, Brigitte. 24 Stories for Advent. Tharlet, Eve, illus. 2015. (ENG.). 120p. (J). 19.95 *(978-0-7358-4229-8(9))* North-South Bks., Inc.
Werkema, Mark A. The Flight Before Christmas. 2004. (YA). pap. 13.95 *(978-1-58961-306-5(6))* PageFree Publishing, Inc.
Werner, James R. Dave's Christmas Surprise & a Puppy Named Oxley. 2008. 28p. pap. 14.95 *(978-1-4327-3298-1(6))* Outskirts Pr., Inc.
Westerman, Rob. The Legend of Kalikimaka: Alohalani, Kalikimaka Auntie. Tahleh, Eleykaa, illus. 2003. 32p. (J). 12.95 *(978-0-9761992-0-5(3))* Gold Boy Music & Pubn.
Westerman, Robert. Alohalani Kalikimaka Auntie: Sheet Music & Lyrics. Westerman, Robert, . 2006. (Illus.). 12p. (J). 6.95 *(978-0-9761992-1-2(1))* Gold Boy Music & Pubn.
Weston Woods Staff, creator. Fletcher & the Snowflake Christmas. 2011. 29.95 *(978-0-545-42619-0(7))* Weston Woods Studios, Inc.
—Morris's Disappearing. 2011. 18.95 *(978-0-439-72855-3(X))* Weston Woods Studios, Inc.
—Morris's Disappearing Bag. 2011. 38.75 *(978-0-439-72858-4(4))* Weston Woods Studios, Inc.
—Too Many Tamales. 2011. 38.75 *(978-0-439-84580-9(7))*; 18.95 *(978-0-439-87361-1(4))* Weston Woods Studios, Inc.
Whalen, Diane. Tales of the Christmas Store. 2011. 92p. pap. 9.99 *(978-1-4567-1783-4(9))* AuthorHouse.
Wheeler, Jordan & Jackson, Dennis. Christmas at Wapos Bay, 1 vol. 2005. (From Many Peoples Ser.). (ENG.). 152p. (J). (gr. 4-7). per. 7.95 *(978-1-55050-324-1(3))* Coteau Bks. CAN. Dist: Orca Bk. Pubs. USA.
Wheeler, Lisa. The Christmas Boot. Pinkney, Jerry, illus. 2016. (ENG.). 32p. (J). (gr. -1-3). 17.99 *(978-0-8037-4134-8(0)*, Dial Bks) Penguin Young Readers Group.
—Uncles & Antlers. Floca, Brian, illus. 2014. (ENG.). 40p. (J). (gr. -1-3). 17.99 *(978-1-4814-3018-0(1)*, Atheneum Bks. for Young Readers) Simon & Schuster Children's Publishing.
Wheiler, Robert. Snowflake a Christmas Gift. 2010. 39p. pap. 11.50 *(978-0-557-47524-7(4))* Lulu Pr., Inc.
Where Is Baby's Christmas Present? A Lift-The-Flap Book/Lap Edition. 2014. (ENG., Illus.). 14p. (J). (gr. -1 — 1). bds. 12.99 *(978-1-4424-0363-5(2)*, Little Simon) Little Simon.
White, Pam. Buddy's First White Christmas. 2008. 16p. pap. 9.95 *(978-1-4389-3154-8(9))* AuthorHouse.
White, Prentice L. Christmas at Mimi's. 2012. 24p. (-18). pap. 14.00 *(978-1-4772-4856-0(0))* AuthorHouse.
White, S.D. Sing along with the Santa Claus That Never Saw a Child. 2008. 20p. pap. 12.89 *(978-1-4389-0305-7(7))* AuthorHouse.
Whitehouse, Anna. The Last Sant. 2012. 118p. pap. *(978-1-78176-289-9(9))* FeedARead.com.
Whitlock, Matt. Punk's Christmas Carol: A Punk 'n Patch Book. Whitlock, Matt, illus. 2006. (Illus.). 32p. (J). (gr. -1-3). 16.95 *(978-0-9769057-1-4(X))* Little Hero.
Whybrow, Ian. Miss Wire's Christmas Surprise. Chichester Clark, Emma, illus. 2007. 45p. (J). (gr. -1-3). pap. 3.95 *(978-0-7534-6136-5(6)*, Kingfisher) Roaring Brook Pr.
Wick, Walter. Christmas Board Book (Can You See What I See?) 2015. (Can You See What I See? Ser.). (ENG.). 24p. (J). (gr. -1-k). bds. 6.99 *(978-0-545-83183-3(0)*, Cartwheel Bks.) Scholastic, Inc.
Wiggin, Kate Douglas. The Birds' Christmas Carol. 2006. 80p. pap. 9.45 *(978-1-59462-392-9(9)*, 428, Book Jungle) Standard Pubns., Inc.
—The Bird's Christmas Carol. 2008. 88p. (gr. 4-7). pap. 8.95 *(978-1-60664-191-0(3))* Aegypan.
—The Bird's Christmas Carol. 2011. 88p. (gr. 4-7). 20.95 *(978-1-4638-9984-4(X))* Rodgers, Alan Bks.
—The Birds' Christmas Carol. (J). reprint ed. lib. bdg. 48.00 *(978-0-7426-1056-9(X))* Classic Bks.
—The Birds' Christmas Carol. 2004. reprint ed. pap. 1.99 *(978-1-4179-9945-3(4))*; pap. 15.95 *(978-1-4179-9995-8(0))* Kessinger Publishing, LLC.
—The Old Peabody Pew. 60p. 2011. 16.95 *(978-1-4638-9983-7(1))* 2009. pap. 7.95 *(978-1-60664-315-0(0))* Rodgers, Alan Bks.
Wild, Anne. Christmas Carousel: The Story of the Nativity in Five Scenes to Cut Out & Make. (Illus.). (J). pap. 10.00 *(978-0-906212-64-6(2))* Tarquin Pubns. GBR. Dist: Parkwest Pubns., Inc.
Wilde, Irma & dePaola, Tomie. The Christmas Puppy. Wilde, Irma, illus. 2015. (G&d Vintage Ser.). (ENG., Illus.). 24p. (J). (-k). bds. 9.99 *(978-0-448-48765-6(9)*, Grosset & Dunlap) Penguin Young Readers Group.
Wilder, Laura Ingalls. A Little House Christmas Treasury: Festive Holiday Stories. Williams, Garth, illus. 2005. (Little House Ser.). (ENG.). 144p. (J). (gr. 3-7). 14.99 *(978-0-06-076918-5(1))* HarperCollins Pubs.
Wilhite, Cindy. Santa He Sees You When. 2009. 28p. 18.65 *(978-0-557-12852-5(8))* Lulu Pr., Inc.
Wilkes, Irene. Elvie Saves Christmas. Montgomery, Jason, illus. 2010. 48p. (J). pap. 21.95 *(978-1-59299-537-0(3))* Inkwater Pr.
Wilkin, Esther. Baby's Christmas. Wilkin, Eloise, illus. 2017. (Little Golden Book Ser.). (ENG.). 24p. (J). (-k). 4.99 ***(978-1-5247-2051-3(8)***, Golden Bks.) Random Hse. Children's Bks.
Wilkin, Esther. Baby's Christmas. Wilkin, Eloise, illus. 2012. (Golden Baby Ser.). (ENG.). 26p. (J). (gr. k — 1). bds. 6.99 *(978-0-375-87058-3(X)*, Golden Bks.) Random Hse. Children's Bks.
Wilkinson, Thomas M. Willie-off-the-Pickleboat. 2009. 71p. pap. 12.99 *(978-0-557-06181-5(4))* Lulu Pr., Inc.
Willey, Margaret. A Clever Beatrice Christmas. Solomon, Heather M., illus. 2006. (ENG.). 40p. (J). (gr. -1-2). 19.99 *(978-0-689-87017-0(5)*, Atheneum Bks. for Young Readers) Simon & Schuster Children's Publishing.
Williams, Hap. Henry the Elf. Graves, Michelle, illus. 2012. 28p. pap. 24.95 *(978-1-4626-8999-6(X))* America Star Bks.
Williams, Lisa E. The Christmas Hippo. 2012. (Illus.). 28p. pap. 16.95 *(978-1-4497-2474-0(4)*, WestBow Pr.) Author Solutions, Inc.
Williams, Mark. Hooty & Pig: The Missing Christmas Pudding. Garrett, Keith, illus. 2013. 24p. pap. *(978-1-78132-133-1(7))* SilverWood Bks.
Williams, Sam. Santa's Toys. Gill, Tim, illus. 2003. 14p. bds. *(978-1-85602-274-3(9)*, Pavilion Children's Books) Pavilion Bks.
Williams, Thomas. The Christmas Chair. l.t. ed. 2004. (Illus.). 27p. (J). audio compact disk 22.95 *(978-0-9763633-0-9(5))* Williams, Thomas.
Williamson, Barbara. Wishbone. 2007. (Illus.). 24p. (J). per. 12.95 *(978-1-60002-197-8(2)*, 4216) Mountain Valley Publishing, LLC.
Williamson, K. E. Kayla & the Christmas Monkey. 2010. 28p. pap. 15.49 *(978-1-4520-9749-7(6))* AuthorHouse.
Wilson, Budge & Roscoe, Terry. The Imperfect Perfect Christmas. 2004. (ENG., Illus.). 48p. (J). pap. *(978-1-895900-66-8(2))* Pottersfield Pr.
Wilson, Janet. LSU Night Before Christmas. Verrett, Michael, illus. 2013. (ENG.). (J). 14.95 *(978-1-62086-484-5(3))* Mascot Bks., Inc.
Wilson, Karma. Bear Stays up for Christmas. Chapman, Jane, illus. 2011. (Bear Bks.). (ENG.). 34p. (J). (gr. -1 — 1). bds. 7.99 *(978-1-4424-2790-7(6)*, Little Simon) Little Simon.
—Bear Stays up for Christmas. Chapman, Jane, illus. (Bear Bks.). (ENG.). 40p. (J). (gr. -1-3). 2008. 9.99 *(978-1-4169-5896-3(7))* 2004. 17.99 *(978-0-689-85278-7(9))* McElderry, Margaret K. Bks. (McElderry, Margaret K. Bks.).
—Mortimer's Christmas Manger. Chapman, Jane, illus. 2007. (ENG.). 40p. (J). (gr. -1-3). 9.99 *(978-1-4169-5049-3(4)*, McElderry, Margaret K. Bks.) McElderry, Margaret K. Bks.
Wilson, Matthew. Scrooge & Santa GN. 2011. (Illus.). 100p. pap. 14.95 *(978-1-897548-98-1(2))* Arcana Studio, Inc.
Witt, Janice. Harold Discovers Santa's Secret: A Very Long Dog with a Very Big Heart. Reznicek, Curtis, illus. 2013. 40p. pap. 11.99 *(978-1-63022-442-4(1))* Speedy Publishing LLC.
Woebkenberg, Valerie & Ingels, Diane. The Story the Little Christmas Tree Told. 2012. pap. 11.95 *(978-0-7414-8095-8(6))* Infinity Publishing.
Wolf, Carol A. Foggy Dog Discovers Christmas. 2012. 40p. pap. 16.46 *(978-1-4669-6253-8(4))* Trafford Publishing.
Wolf, Jackie. My Sparkle Present. 2003. (Sparkle Shape Bks.). (Illus.). 10p. (J). (gr. -1-18). bds. 6.99 *(978-1-57151-715-9(4))* Playhouse Publishing.
Wolfe, Frances. The Little Toy Shop. Wolfe, Frances, illus. 2008. (ENG., Illus.). 32p. (J). (gr. -1-2). 19.95 *(978-0-88776-865-1(2)*, Tundra Bks.) Tundra Bks. CAN. Dist: Penguin Random Hse. LLC.
Wolfe, Greg. Shmelf the Hanukkah Elf. McWilliam, Howard, illus. 2016. (ENG.). 32p. (J). 16.99 *(978-1-61963-521-0(6)*, 9781619635210, Bloomsbury USA Childrens) Bloomsbury Publishing USA.
Wolper, Joanna. The Man Who Could Be Santa. 2008. (Illus.). 78p. (J). pap. *(978-0-88092-765-9(8))*; lib. bdg. *(978-0-88092-764-2(X))* Royal Fireworks Publishing Co.
Wondra, Ashley E. Kelsey's Coat. 2008. 28p. pap. 15.99 *(978-1-4363-2987-3(6))* Xlibris Corp.
Wood, A. J. The Christmas Hat. Kneen, Maggie, illus. 2004. (ENG.). 24p. (J). *(978-1-55168-267-9(2))* Fenn, H. B. & Co., Ltd.
Wood, Amanda & Kneen, Maggie. Christmas in the Mouse House. Kneen, Maggie, illus. 2011. (ENG., Illus.). 16p. (J). (gr. -1-2). 14.99 *(978-0-7636-5287-6(3)*, Templar) Candlewick Pr.
Wood, David. The Little House on Buchanan Street. 2007. 24p. per. 12.95 *(978-1-934246-64-1(6))* Peppertree Pr., The.
Wood, Francis Eusene. The Christmas Letter. Wood, Christine & Marken, Jon, eds. McDermott, Robert, illus. Wood, Christine, photos by. 2007. pap. 9.95 *(978-0-9746372-6-6(2))* Tip-Of-The-Moon Publishing Co.
Wood, Maryrose. The Mysterious Howling. Klassen, Jon, illus. (Incorrigible Children of Ashton Place Ser.: 1). (ENG.). (J). (gr. 3-7). 2015. 288p. pap. 6.99 *(978-0-06-236693-1(9))*Bk. I. 2010. 272p. 16.99 *(978-0-06-179105-5(9))* HarperCollins Pubs.
Woodrum, Margaret. The Christmas Tree Fort. Woodrum, Larry, illus. 2010. 32p. pap. 13.00 *(978-1-60911-329-2(2)*, Eloquent Bks.) Strategic Book Publishing & Rights Agency (SBPRA).
Woods, Cindy Smith. The Happy, Happy Christmas Book. 2011. 58p. pap. 16.95 *(978-1-4626-4064-5(8))* America Star Bks.
Woolf, Julia, illus. Gingerbread Joy. 2008. (ENG.). 10p. (J). bds. 4.95 *(978-1-58117-814-2(X)*, Intervisual/Piggy Toes) Bendon, Inc.
—Snowman Surprise. 2008. (ENG.). 10p. (J). bds. 4.95 *(978-1-58117-812-8(3)*, Intervisual/Piggy Toes) Bendon, Inc.
—Special Star. 2008. (ENG.). 10p. (J). bds. 4.95 *(978-1-58117-815-9(8)*, Intervisual/Piggy Toes) Bendon, Inc.
Woollatt, Margaret. The Twelve Days of Christmas in New Jersey. Rossi, Richard, illus. 2008. (Twelve Days of Christmas in America Ser.). (ENG.). 40p. (J). (gr. k). 12.95 *(978-1-4027-3816-6(1))* Sterling Publishing Co., Inc.
Worre, John Arthur. The Gospel According to Scrooge: A Dickens of A Tale. 2010. 120p. 25.49 *(978-1-4520-7794-9(0))*; pap. 15.99 *(978-1-4520-7793-2(2))* AuthorHouse.
Worstine, Waneta Cotner. Grandma's Yam. 2012. 38p. pap. 16.95 *(978-1-4497-6661-0(7)*, WestBow Pr.) Author Solutions, Inc.
Worthington, Jennifer & Shoals, Melinda, illus. The Gift That Saved Christmas. 2008. 40p. (J). 17.00 *(978-0-9773460-1-1(3))* Spritelee Enterprises.
Wright, Jason F. Penny's Christmas Jar Party. Sowards, Ben, illus. 2009. 32p. (J). 17.95 *(978-1-60641-167-4(5)*, Shadow Mountain) Shadow Mountain Publishing.
Wright, Sally Ann. Christmas Baby. 2008. 14p. (J). 12.99 *(978-1-4003-1301-3(5))* Nelson, Thomas Inc.
Wurst, Thomas Scott. Pearl's Christmas Present. Wurst, Thomas Scott, illus. 2006. (Illus.). 40p. (J). 20.00 *(978-0-9772441-1-9(3))* Pearl & Dotty.
X-mas Morning. 2004. (J). per. *(978-1-57657-387-7(7))* Paradise Pr., Inc.
X-mas Trees are Special. 2004. (J). per. *(978-1-57657-452-2(0))* Paradise Pr., Inc.
Yardley, Liz. The Firefly Legacy - Book Vi. Yardley, Liz, illus. 2013. (Illus.). 336p. pap. *(978-0-9872013-1-7(X))* BlueFlower Bks.
Yates, Philip. A Pirate's Twelve Days of Christmas. Serra, Sebastià, illus. 2012. (ENG.). 32p. (J). (gr. -1-1). 14.95 *(978-1-4027-9225-0(5))* Sterling Publishing Co., Inc.
Yaun, Ellen R. A Christmas Problem for Samuel James. Murphy, Betsy, illus. 59p. (J). (gr. 2-5). pap. 5.95 *(978-0-9673970-1-6(4))* Blue Chip Publishing.
Yelchin, Eugene & Kuryla, Mary. Heart of a Snowman. Yelchin, Eugene & Kuryla, Mary, illus. 2009. (ENG., Illus.). 40p. (J). (gr. -1-3). 16.99 *(978-0-06-125926-5(8))* HarperCollins Pubs.

Yolen, Jane. How Do Dinosaurs Say Merry Christmas? Teague, Mark, illus. 2012. (How Do Dinosaurs... ? Ser.). (ENG.). 40p. (J). (gr. -1-k). 16.99 *(978-0-545-41678-8(7),* Blue Sky Pr., The) Scholastic, Inc.
—Under the Star: A Christmas Counting Story. van Kampen, Vlasta, illus. 2009. (ENG.). 24p. (J). (gr. -1-k). *(978-1-55470-201-5(1))* Me to We.
Yoon, Salina. Penguin's Christmas Wish. 2016. (Penguin Ser.). (ENG.). 40p. (J). 14.99 *(978-1-68119-155-3(5),* 9781681191553, Bloomsbury USA Childrens) Bloomsbury Publishing USA.
Yoon, Salina, illus. My Shimmery Christmas Book. 2005. 10p. (J). bds. 8.95 *(978-1-58117-045-0(9),* Intervisual/Piggy Toes) Bendon, Inc.
Young, Francis Kerr. The Paperweight. Steele, Andrew & Clement, Devyn, illus. 2008. 39p. pap. 24.95 *(978-1-60610-034-9(3))* America Star Bks.
Young, H. M. (Hal). The huskies & the christmas Fawn. 2007. 56p. pap. 9.95 *(978-1-4357-0070-3(8))* Lulu Pr., Inc.
Young, Jeanna & Johnson, Jacqueline Kinney. A Royal Christmas to Remember, 1 vol. Aranda, Omar, illus. 2016. (Princess Parables Ser.). (ENG.). 32p. (J). 14.99 *(978-0-310-74802-1(X))* Zonderkidz.
Young, Marlene Lauster. Before Summer's End. 2012. 36p. (-18). pap. 20.99 *(978-1-4772-6810-0(3))* AuthorHouse.
Young, Ned. Zoomer's Out-of-This-World Christmas. Young, Ned, illus. 2013. (ENG., Illus.). 32p. (J). (gr. -1-3). 17.99 *(978-0-06-199959-8(8))* HarperCollins Pubs.
Ytreeide, Arnold. Tabitha's Travels: A Family Story for Advent. 2004. 170p. pap. 12.99 *(978-0-8307-3501-3(1),* Regal Bks.) Gospel Light Pubns.
Zabrosky, Joseph & Jacobs, Nathaniel. The Christmas Tree, 4 vols., 4bks. l.t. ed. 2005. (Illus.). 32p. (J). per. *(978-0-9768831-3-5(9))* Elohim Bks.
Zamora, Nancy. Back in the Band. 2007. 94p. pap. 19.95 *(978-1-60441-818-7(4))* America Star Bks.
Zepeda, Monique. Las Pinatas. Graullera, Fabiola, illus.Tr. of Pinatas. (SPA.). 26p. (J). (gr. 3-5). pap. 6.95 *(978-968-19-0612-2(8))* Santillana USA Publishing Co., Inc.
Ziefert, Harriet. The Best Smelling Christmas Book Ever: 9 Scents to Scratch & Sniff! Rader, Laura, illus. 2004. 18p. (J). (gr. k-4). reprint ed. 13.00 *(978-0-7567-7600-8(7))* DIANE Publishing Co.
Ziegesar, Cecily von. Adored. 2009. (It Girl Ser.: 8). (ENG.). 240p. (YA). (gr. 10-17). pap. 9.99 *(978-0-316-02509-6(7),* Tingley, Megan Bks.) Little, Brown Bks. for Young Readers.
Ziegler, Jennifer. Revenge of the Angels. 2015. (ENG.). 256p. (J). (gr. 3-7). 16.99 *(978-0-545-83899-3(1),* Scholastic Pr.) Scholastic, Inc.
Zobel-Nolan, Allia. Peek & Find Christmas Story. Cox, Steve, illus. 2004. 14p. (J). bds. 7.49 *(978-0-7586-0718-8(0))* Concordia Publishing Hse.
Zomerdyke, Joy. Polar & Grizzly Find Christmas. 2013. 24p. pap. 17.99 *(978-1-4817-1155-5(5))* AuthorHouse.
Zondervan Staff & Poth, Karen. Yuletide Ice Cube Fair, 1 vol. 2014. (Big Idea Books / VeggieTales Ser.). (ENG.). 24p. (J). pap. 3.99 *(978-0-310-74623-2(X))* Zonderkidz.
Zondervan Staff & Walburg, Lori. The Legend of the Candy Cane, 1 vol. Cowdrey, Richard, illus. 2014. (ENG.). 30p. (J). bds. 9.99 *(978-0-310-74672-0(8))* Zonderkidz.
Zondervan Staff & Zonderkidz Editors. The Shepherds Watch, 1 vol. 2012. (Flip Book Ser.). (ENG.). 96p. (J). pap. 3.99 *(978-0-310-72688-3(3))* Zonderkidz.
Zoomer's Out-Of-This-World Christmas. 2013. (Illus.). (J). *(978-0-06-199960-4(1))* Harper & Row Ltd.
Zuber, Diane C. The Broken Doll. Firtl, Mary Meehan, illus. 2006. (ENG.). 32p. (J). (gr. -1-3). incl. audio compact disk *(978-0-9785551-1-5(2))* Zuber Publishing.
Zullo, Allan. Christmas Miracle Pets: Animals Who Saved the Day. 2012. 119p. (J). *(978-0-545-38573-2(3))* Scholastic, Inc.

CHRISTMAS—POETRY

see also Carols

Angelou, Maya. Amazing Peace: A Christmas Poem, 1 vol. Johnson, Steve & Fancher, Lou, illus. 2008. (ENG.). 40p. (J). (gr. k-12). 18.99 *(978-0-375-84150-7(4),* Schwartz & Wade Bks.) Random Hse. Children's Bks.
Black, Baxter A. Rudolph's Night Off. Patterson, Bill, illus. 2011. (ENG.). 32p. (J). (gr. -1-3). 19.95 *(978-0-939343-54-6(1))* Coyote Cowboy Co.
Brallier, Christine, illus. The Night Before Christmas. 2013. (ENG.). 32p. (J). 16.99 *(978-0-9789688-2-3(4))* Brownian Bee Pr.
Brown, Tricia. Alaskan Night Before Christmas, 1 vol. Stacy, Alan, illus. 2008. (Night Before Christmas Ser.). (ENG.). 32p. (gr. 1-3). 16.99 *(978-1-58980-554-5(2))* Pelican Publishing Co., Inc.
Browning, Tom & Moore, Clement C. The Night Before Christmas. 2014. (ENG., Illus.). 40p. (J). (gr. k). pap. 6.95 *(978-1-4549-1355-9(X))* Sterling Publishing Co., Inc.
Byrd, Bill Scott. The Story of Rap & Tap. Ayzenberg, Nina, illus. 2006. 9.95 *(978-0-9776805-0-4(9))* Byrd, Fay T.
Carney, Larry, adapted by. The Gingerbread Man's Christmas. deluxe ed. 2009. (ENG., Illus.). 24p. (J). 6.95 *(978-1-60072-109-0(5))* PC Treasures, Inc.
—The Little Mermaid's Christmas. deluxe ed. 2009. (ENG., Illus.). 24p. (J). 6.95 *(978-1-60072-110-6(9))* PC Treasures, Inc.
—The Three Little Pig's Christmas. 2009. (ENG., Illus.). 24p. (J). 6.95 *(978-1-60072-123-6(0))* PC Treasures, Inc.
Dabija, Violeta, illus. The Twelve Days of Christmas. 2013. (ENG.). 24p. (J). 18.99 *(978-0-7945-3330-4(2),* Usborne) EDC Publishing.
Davis, David. Librarian's Night Before Christmas, 1 vol. Harris, Jim, illus. 2007. (Night Before Christmas Ser.). (ENG.). 32p. (J). (gr. k-3). 16.99 *(978-1-58980-336-7(1))* Pelican Publishing Co., Inc.
—The Southern Twelve Days of Christmas, 1 vol. Camling, Candace, illus. 2013. (ENG.). 32p. (J). (gr. k-3). 16.99 *(978-1-4556-1773-9(3))* Pelican Publishing Co., Inc.
Dickman, Jean M. Santa in Space. l.t. ed. 2003. (Illus.). 32p. (J). per. 9.95 *(978-0-9743718-0-1(7))* Tintagel Publications.
Dinola, Jack. Two Squirrels & a Mouse: A Christmas Story. 2013. 36p. pap. 16.95 *(978-1-4582-1236-8(X),* Abbott Pr.) Author Solutions, Inc.
Dover, et al. A Christmas Treasury. Price, Margaret Evans et al, illus. 2014. (ENG.). 96p. (J). (gr. 1-5). pap. 12.99 *(978-0-486-78184-6(4))* Dover Pubns., Inc.
Downing, Julie. The Night Before Christmas. Downing, Julie, illus. 2013. (ENG., Illus.). 32p. (J). (gr. -1-3). 16.99 *(978-1-4814-2151-5(4),* Simon & Schuster Bks. For Young Readers) Simon & Schuster Bks. For Young Readers.
Duvoisin, Roger & Moore, Clement C. The Night Before Christmas. 2014. (ENG., Illus.). 40p. (J). (gr. k-12). 16.99 *(978-0-385-75459-0(0),* Knopf Bks. for Young Readers) Random Hse. Children's Bks.
Dyan, Penelope. Christmas Is — -A Time to Remember, to Smile & to Share. Dyan, Penelope, illus. 2009. (Illus.). 44p. pap. 11.95 *(978-1-935118-46-6(3))* Bellissima Publishing, LLC.
Field, Eugene. Christmas Tales & Christmas Verse. Storer, Florence, illus. 2007. 100p. per. *(978-1-4065-2387-4(9))* Dodo Pr.
—Christmas Tales & Christmas Verse. 2006. 148p. per. 16.99 *(978-1-4255-1074-9(4))* Michigan Publishing.
Hollins, Paula. Christmas Makes Words! A Selection of Words That Can Be Made from the Letters in the Word Christmas, with Humorous Poems & Colorful Illustr. 2013. (Illus.). 36p. pap. 10.95 *(978-0-9897278-9-1(0))* PHD Ink.
Hopkins, Lee Bennett. Christmas Presents: Holiday Poetry. Hall, Melanie W., illus. 2004. (I Can Read Bks.). 32p. (J). (gr. k-3). 15.99 *(978-0-06-008054-9(X));* lib. bdg. 16.89 *(978-0-06-008055-6(8))* HarperCollins Pubs.
Johnston, Tony. Noel. Chee, Cheng-Khee, illus. 2005. (ENG.). 32p. (J). (gr. k-3). lib. bdg. 16.95 *(978-1-57505-752-1(2),* Carolrhoda Bks.) Lerner Publishing Group.
Johnstone, Michael. Christmas Hugs. 2003. (Forever Friends Ser.). (Illus.). 64p. pap. 3.95 *(978-1-84357-027-1(0))* Contender Entertainment Group GBR. Dist: Independent Pubs. Group.
Kirk, Daniel & Moore, Clement C. 'Twas the Night Before Christmas. 2015. (ENG., Illus.). 32p. (J). (gr. -1-3). 16.95 *(978-1-4197-1233-3(0),* Abrams Bks. for Young Readers) Abrams, Inc.
Layne, Steven. The Principal's Night Before Christmas, 1 vol. Rice, James, illus. 2004. (Night Before Christmas Ser.). (ENG.). 32p. (J). (gr. k-3). 16.99 *(978-1-58980-252-0(7))* Pelican Publishing Co., Inc.
Lewis, J. Patrick. Under the Kissletoe: Christmastime Poems. Shepperson, Rob, illus. 2007. (ENG.). 32p. (J). (gr. 2-4). 16.95 *(978-1-59078-438-9(3),* Wordsong) Boyds Mills Pr.
Lewis, Maud. Christmas with the Rural Mail BB, 1 vol. 2011. (ENG., Illus.). 24p. (J). (gr. -1-2). bds. 12.95 *(978-1-55109-790-9(7))* Nimbus Publishing, Ltd. CAN. Dist: Orca Bk. Pubs. USA.
Macy, Carolyn. Hawaiian Night Before Christmas, 1 vol. Macy, Carolyn, illus. 2008. (Night Before Christmas Ser.). (ENG., Illus.). 32p. (gr. 1-3). 16.99 *(978-1-58980-598-9(4))* Pelican Publishing Co., Inc.
McWilliams, Amanda & Moore, Clement C. Ozark Night Before Christmas, 1 vol. Rice, James, illus. 2004. (Night Before Christmas Ser.). (ENG.). 32p. (J). (gr. k-3). 16.99 *(978-1-58980-056-4(7))* Pelican Publishing Co., Inc.
Medina, Tony. Just Us. 2004. (Illus.). 48p. (J). (gr. 4-18). pap. 6.95 *(978-0-940975-75-0(0),* Sankofa Bks.) Just Us Bks., Inc.
Moore, Clement C. Cuento de Nochebuena. Santore, Charles, illus. 2013. (ENG.). 24p. (J). bds. 9.95 *(978-1-60433-451-7(7),* Applesauce Pr.) Cider Mill Pr. Bk. Pubs., LLC.
—Era la Víspera de Navidad. 2012.Tr. of Twas the Night Before Christmas. (SPA., Illus.). 32p. (J). 16.95 *(978-0-9879023-5-1(0))* Grafton and Scratch Pubs. CAN. Dist: Bookmasters Distribution.
—The Night Before Christmas. Fujikawa, Gyo, illus. 2007. (ENG.). 32p. (J). (gr. -1-2). 9.95 *(978-1-4027-5065-6(X))* Sterling Publishing Co., Inc.
—The Night Before Christmas. 2006. (J). per. 9.95 *(978-1-4276-0967-0(5))* Aardvark Global Publishing.
—The Night Before Christmas. 2012. (ENG.). 32p. 11.50 *(978-1-84135-796-6(0))* Award Pubns. Ltd. GBR. Dist: Parkwest Pubns., Inc.
—The Night Before Christmas. Fisher, Henry, illus. 2013. 26p. (J). *(978-1-4351-4927-4(0))* Barnes & Noble, Inc.
—The Night Before Christmas. Barrett, Angela, illus. 2012. 30p. (J). *(978-1-4351-4416-3(3))* Barnes & Noble, Inc.
—The Night Before Christmas. Adolphe, Joseph, illus. 2013. (J). 19.95 *(978-1-59530-953-2(5))* Hallmark Card, Inc.
—The Night Before Christmas. Kesler, Matt, illus. 2012. 16p. (J). 29.95 *(978-1-59530-407-0(X))* Hallmark Card, Inc.
—The Night Before Christmas. Engelbreit, Mary, illus. 2011. (ENG.). 40p. (J). (gr. -1-3). 9.99 *(978-0-06-208944-1(7))* HarperCollins Pubs.
—The Night Before Christmas. Watson, Richard Jesse, illus. 2008. (ENG.). 40p. (J). (gr. -1-3). pap. 6.99 *(978-0-06-075744-1(2))* HarperCollins Pubs.
—The Night Before Christmas. Whatley, Bruce, illus. 2004. (ENG.). 32p. (J). (gr. -1 — 1). bds. 6.99 *(978-0-06-073917-1(7),* HarperFestival) HarperCollins Pubs.
—The Night Before Christmas. 2014. (ENG., Illus.). 32p. (J). (gr. -1-k). 10.99 *(978-1-4449-0243-3(1))* Hodder & Stoughton GBR. Dist: Hachette Bk. Group.
—The Night Before Christmas. dePaola, Tomie, illus. 2010. (ENG.). 24p. (J). (gr. -1). bds. 8.95 *(978-0-8234-2284-5(4))* Holiday Hse., Inc.
—The Night Before Christmas. 2008. *(978-1-58865-498-4(2))* Kidsbooks, LLC.
—The Night Before Christmas. Caparo, Antonio Javier, illus. 2017. (ENG.). 40p. (J). (gr. -1-2). 17.99 ***(978-1-5344-0085-6(0),*** Little Simon) Little Simon.
—The Night Before Christmas. 2009. (Illus.). 23p. pap. *(978-0-462-09940-8(7))* Marshall Cavendish.
—The Night Before Christmas. Zwerger, Lisbeth, illus. 2014. (Minedition Minibooks Ser.). (ENG.). 32p. (J). (gr. -1-k). 9.99 *(978-988-8240-88-3(9))* Neugebauer, Michael (Publishing) Limited HKG. Dist: Independent Pubs. Group.
—The Night Before Christmas. Rand, Ted, illus. 2014. (ENG.). 32p. (J). 17.95 *(978-0-7358-4106-2(3))* North-South Bks., Inc.
—The Night Before Christmas. Newsom, Tom, illus. 2012. (J). *(978-1-4508-5375-0(7))* Publications International, Ltd.
—The Night Before Christmas. 2015. (Big Golden Board Book Ser.). (ENG., Illus.). 24p. (J). (-k). bds. 10.99 *(978-0-553-52226-6(4),* Golden Bks.) Random Hse. Children's Bks.
—The Night Before Christmas. Malvern, Corinne, illus. (Little Golden Board Book Ser.). (ENG.). (J). 2014. 26p. (-k). bds. 7.99 *(978-0-385-38474-2(2))* 2011. 24p. (gr. -1-k). 4.99 *(978-0-375-86359-2(1))* Random Hse. Children's Bks. (Golden Bks.).
—The Night Before Christmas. 2007. (ENG., Illus.). 26p. (gr. -1-17). bds. 5.95 *(978-0-7624-3014-7(1))* Running Pr. Bk. Pubs.
—The Night Before Christmas. Ercolini, David, illus. 2015. (ENG.). 32p. (J). (gr. -1-k). 16.99 *(978-0-545-39112-2(1),* Orchard Bks.) Scholastic, Inc.
—The Night Before Christmas. 2012. 28p. (gr. -1-2). 14.95 *(978-1-61382-397-2(5))* Simon & Brown.
—The Night Before Christmas. Bell, Bill, illus. 2011. (ENG.). 32p. (J). (gr. k-2). 6.95 *(978-1-61608-470-7(7),* 608470, Sky Pony Pr.) Skyhorse Publishing Co., Inc.
—The Night Before Christmas, 1 vol. Cone, William, illus. 2005. (Rabbit Ears: A Classic Tale Ser.). (ENG.). 32p. (J). (gr. 2-7). 25.65 *(978-1-59197-751-3(7))* Spotlight.
—The Night Before Christmas. Eldredge, Larry, illus. 2006. (Night Before Christmas Ser.). 32p. (J). 9.95 *(978-1-58173-306-8(2));* 26p. bds. 9.95 *(978-1-58173-300-6(3))* Sweetwater Pr.
—The Night Before Christmas. Nowakowski, Marcin, illus. 2016. (ENG.). 32p. (J). (gr. -1-1). pap. 9.99 *(978-1-78445-346-6(3))* Top That! Publishing PLC GBR. Dist: Independent Pubs. Group.
—The Night Before Christmas. Rackham, Arthur, illus. 2012. 32p. pap. 5.99 *(978-1-61720-437-1(4))* Wilder Pubns., Corp.
—The Night Before Christmas. Samuel, Janet, illus. 2012. (ENG.). 24p. (J). bds. 6.99 *(978-0-8249-1884-2(3),* Ideal Pubns.) Worthy Publishing.
—The Night Before Christmas. 2010. (Illus.). 32p. (J). 9.99 *(978-0-8249-5627-1(3),* Ideal Pubns.) Worthy Publishing.
—The Night Before Christmas. Mills, Donald, illus. 2008. 30p. (J). (gr. -1-k). pap. 3.95 *(978-0-8249-5514-4(5),* Ideal Pubns.) Worthy Publishing.
—The Night Before Christmas. Price, Margaret Evans, illus. 2009. (Dover Children's Classics Ser.). (ENG.). 16p. (J). (gr. k-5). pap. 6.99 *(978-0-486-47369-7(4))* Dover Pubns., Inc.
—The Night Before Christmas. Puybaret, Eric, illus. 2010. (Book & CD Ser.). (ENG.). 26p. (J). (gr. k-4). 19.95 *(978-1-936140-06-0(3))* Charlesbridge Publishing, Inc.
—The Night Before Christmas. Gurney, John Steven, illus. 2006. (ENG.). (J). (gr. -1-3). 9.99 *(978-0-439-89557-6(X))* Scholastic, Inc.
—The Night Before Christmas. 2013. (ENG., Illus.). 40p. (J). (gr. -1-3). 18.00 *(978-0-316-07018-8(1))* Little, Brown Bks. for Young Readers.
—The Night Before Christmas. Reid, Barbara, illus. 2014. (ENG.). 32p. (J). (gr. -1-3). 16.99 *(978-0-8075-5625-2(4))* Whitman, Albert & Co.
—The Night Before Christmas. Set. Santore, Charles, illus. gif. ed. 2013. (ENG.). 48p. (J). 14.95 *(978-1-60433-437-1(1),* Applesauce Pr.) Cider Mill Pr. Bk. Pubs., LLC.
—The Night Before Christmas. Reid, Barbara, illus. adapted ed. 2016. (ENG.). 36p. pap. 6.95 ***(978-1-945546-47-1(6))*** Frederic Thomas USA, Inc.
—The Night Before Christmas. Tudor, Tasha, illus. 10th anniv. ed. 2009. 32p. pap. 6.99 *(978-0-316-18947-7(2))* Hachette Bk. Group.
—The Night Before Christmas. Engelbreit, Mary, illus. rev. ed. (ENG.). 40p. (J). (gr. -1-3). 2006. 17.99 *(978-0-06-008160-7(0))*Set. 2007. 25.00 *(978-0-06-136495-2(9),* HarperFestival) HarperCollins Pubs.
—The Night Before Christmas. Birmingham, Christian, illus. 10th anniv. ed. 2005. (ENG.). 48p. (J). (gr. -1-3). 9.95 *(978-0-7624-2416-0(8))* Running Pr. Bk. Pubs.
—The Night Before Christmas: A Brick Story. Brack, Amanda, illus. 2015. (ENG.). 32p. (J). (gr. -1). 12.99 *(978-1-63450-179-8(9),* Sky Pony Pr.) Skyhorse Publishing Co., Inc.
—The Night Before Christmas: A Magical Cut-Paper Edition. Puttapipat, Niroot, illus. 2007. (ENG.). 24p. (J). (gr. -1-3). 19.99 *(978-0-7636-3469-8(7))* Candlewick Pr.
—The Night Before Christmas: A Visit from St. Nicholas. 2008. 48p. 18.99 *(978-1-60641-066-0(0))* Deseret Bk. Co.
—The Night Before Christmas: Or, a Visit from St. Nicholas. Santore, Charles, illus. 2011. 41p. (J). *(978-1-60464-033-5(2))* Appleseed Pr. Bk. Pub. LLC.
—The Night Before Christmas: Peek Inside the 3D Windows. Alderson, Lisa, illus. 2013. (ENG.). 12p. (J). (gr. -1-3). 16.99 *(978-1-84322-923-0(4),* Armadillo) Anness Publishing GBR. Dist: National Bk. Network.
—The Night Before Christmas: The Classic Heirloom Edition. Santore, Charles, illus. 2016. (ENG.). 48p. (J). 24.95 *(978-1-60433-677-1(3),* Applesauce Pr.) Cider Mill Pr. Bk. Pubs., LLC.
—The Night Before Christmas / by Clement C Moore; Illustrated by Arthur Rackham. 2011. 34p. pap. 11.99 *(978-1-4181-9416-1(6))* Michigan Publishing.
—The Night Before Christmas Mini Edition. Santore, Charles, illus. 2011. (Little Seedling Edition Ser.: 1). (ENG.). 44p. (J). 6.95 *(978-1-60433-244-5(1),* Applesauce Pr.) Cider Mill Pr. Bk. Pubs., LLC.
—'Twas the Night Before Christmas. Whelan, Kat, illus. 2010. (ENG.). 24p. (J). (gr. -1-2). 12.95 *(978-1-58925-858-7(4))* Tiger Tales.
—Twas the Night Before Christmas. 2013. (ENG., Illus.). 32p. (J). pap. 7.95 *(978-0-9879023-1-3(8))* Grafton and Scratch Pubs. CAN. Dist: Bookmasters Distribution.
—Twas the Night Before Christmas: Santa Claus for the Benefit of Children of the 21st Century. 2012. (ENG., Illus.). 32p. (J). 15.95 *(978-0-9879023-0-6(X),* 9780987902306) Grafton and Scratch Pubs. CAN. Dist: Bookmasters Distribution.
—A Visit from St. Nicholas. Nast, Thomas, illus. 2006. (ENG.). 24p. (gr. -1-1). pap. 24.95 *(978-1-55709-592-3(2))* Applewood Bks.
Moore, Clement C., ed. & illus. The Night Before Christmas. Moore, Clement C., illus. Winget, Susan, illus. 2004. 32p. 18.00 *(978-0-7412-1939-8(5))* Lang Graphics, Ltd.
—The Night Before Christmas. Moore, Clement C., illus. Gorsline, Douglas, illus. 32p. (J). Random Hse. Children's Bks.
—The Night Before Christmas. Moore, Clement C., illus. Porfirio, Guy, illus. 2004. 20p. (J). 9.95 *(978-0-8249-6553-2(1),* Ideal Pubns.) Worthy Publishing.
Moore, Clement C. & Curto Family, The. The Night Before Christmas. Creative Illustrations Studio & Good Times At Home LLC, illus. 2012. (J). pap. 9.99 *(978-0-9840338-5-0(8))* Good Times at Home LLC.
Moore, Clement C. & Linz, Peter. The Night Before Christmas. Gurney, John Steven, illus. 2006. (ENG.). 32p. (J). (gr. -1-3). 18.95 *(978-0-439-89843-0(9))* Scholastic, Inc.
Moore, Clement C., et al. C'était la Veille de Noel. 2012.Tr. of Twas the Night Before Christmas. (FRE.). 32p. (J). 16.95 *(978-0-9879023-6-8(9))* Grafton and Scratch Pubs. CAN. Dist: Bookmasters Distribution.
Morgan, Gaby. Christmas Poems. Scheffler, Axel, illus. unabr. ed. 2014. (ENG.). 176p. (J). pap. 9.99 *(978-1-4472-5463-8(5))* Pan Macmillan GBR. Dist: Independent Pubs. Group.
Moses, Grandma, illus. The Night Before Christmas. 2007. (ENG.). 32p. (J). (gr. k-4). 17.95 *(978-0-7893-1568-7(8))* Universe Publishing.
The Night Before Christmas. 2003. (Traditional Christmas Stories Ser.). 32p. (J). 4.98 *(978-0-7525-8847-6(8))* Parragon, Inc.
Peet, Inez M. Celebrating Christmas: A Collection of Poems for Children. 2011. (ENG.). 70p. pap. 24.95 *(978-1-4327-6438-8(1))* Outskirts Pr., Inc.
Phillips, Betty Lou & Herndon, Roblyn. The Night Before Christmas in New York, 1 vol. Dickert, Sheryl, illus. 2013. (ENG.). 32p. 9.99 *(978-1-4236-3440-9(3))* Gibbs Smith, Publisher.
—The Night Before Christmas in Texas, 1 vol. Dickert, Sheryl, illus. 2013. (ENG.). 32p. 9.99 *(978-1-4236-3509-3(4))* Gibbs Smith, Publisher.
Piper, Sophie. The Lion Book of Christmas Poems. 2015. (ENG., Illus.). 64p. (J). (gr. 2-6). 8.99 *(978-0-7459-6510-9(5))* Lion Hudson PLC GBR. Dist: Independent Pubs. Group.
Prelutsky, Jack. It's Christmas! Hafner, Marylin, illus. 2012. (I Can Read Level 3 Ser.). (ENG.). 48p. (J). (gr. k-3). pap. 3.99 *(978-0-06-053708-1(6),* Greenwillow Bks.) HarperCollins Pubs.
—It's Christmas! 2012. (I Can Read! Level 3 Ser.). (J). lib. bdg. 13.55 *(978-0-606-26862-2(6),* Turtleback) Turtleback Bks.
Robinson, Gary. Native American Twelve Days of Christmas. Hummingbird, Jesse T., illus. 2011. (ENG.). 32p. (J). 19.95 *(978-1-57416-105-2(9))* Clear Light Pubs.
Santore, Charles, illus. The Night Before Christmas. 2011. (Classic Edition Ser.). (ENG.). 44p. (J). (gr. -1). 19.95 *(978-1-60433-237-7(9),* Applesauce Pr.) Cider Mill Pr. Bk. Pubs., LLC.
Sesame Workshop. 'Twas the Night Before Christmas on Sesame Street! 2014. (Sesame Street Scribbles Cookie Monster Ser.: 0). (ENG., Illus.). 32p. (J). (-3). 10.99 *(978-1-4022-9740-3(8),* Sourcebooks Jabberwocky) Sourcebooks, Inc.
Spirin, Gennady, illus. The Night Before Christmas, 0 vols. ltd. ed. 2006. (ENG.). 32p. (J). (gr. -1-3). 16.99 *(978-0-7614-5298-0(2),* 9780761452980, Amazon Children's Publishing) Amazon Publishing.
Stephens, Courtney. My Christmas Child. 2012. 40p. pap. 13.95 *(978-1-4497-3755-9(2),* WestBow Pr.) Author Solutions, Inc.
Stiegemeyer, Julie. Baby in a Manger. Wong, Nicole, illus. 2004. 32p. (J). (gr. k-4). 9.99 *(978-0-7586-0726-3(1))* Concordia Publishing Hse.
Townsend, Una Belle. Racecar Driver's Night Before Christmas, 1 vol. Anderson, Rick, illus. 2008. (Night Before Christmas Ser.). (ENG.). 32p. (gr. 1-3). 16.99 *(978-1-58980-565-1(8))* Pelican Publishing Co., Inc.
Ward, Candace, ed. Children's Christmas Stories & Poems. 2011. (Dover Children's Thrift Classics Ser.). (ENG., Illus.). 96p. (J). (gr. 3-8). pap. 4.00 *(978-0-486-28656-3(8))* Dover Pubns., Inc.
Wick, Walter. Can You See What I See? Night Before Christmas. Wick, Walter, photos by. 2005. (Can You See What I See? Ser.). (ENG., Illus.). 40p. (J). (gr. -1-3). 13.99 *(978-0-439-76927-3(2),* Cartwheel Bks.) Scholastic, Inc.
Yates, Philip. A Pirate's Night Before Christmas. Serra, Sebastiá, illus. (ENG.). 32p. (J). (gr. -1-1). 2014. pap. 6.95 *(978-1-4549-1357-3(6))* 2008. 14.95 *(978-1-4027-4257-6(6))* Sterling Publishing Co., Inc.

CHRISTMAS CARDS

see Greeting Cards

CHRISTMAS CAROLS

see Carols

CHRISTMAS COOKING

Coll-Seck, Jayden. My Russian Grandmother Cooks Special Food for Christmas, 01 vols., 1. 2016. (Rosen REAL Readers: Social Studies Nonfiction / Fiction: Family, Community, & the World Ser.). (ENG.). 12p. (J). pap. 6.33 *(978-1-5081-1815-2(9),* Rosen Classroom) Rosen Publishing Group, Inc., The.
Disney Book Group Staff. A Merry Christmas Cookbook. Disney Storybook Artists Staff, illus. 2014. (ENG.). 64p. (J). (gr. 1-3). 10.99 *(978-1-4231-6322-0(2))* Disney Pr.
Dog 'n' Bone Books Staff & CICO Kidz Staff, compiled by. My First Christmas Craft Book: 35 Fun Festive Projects for Children Aged 7+ 2016. (ENG., Illus.). 128p. (J). (gr. 7-11). pap. 14.95 *(978-1-78249-381-5(6),* 1782493816, CICO Books) Ryland Peters & Small GBR. Dist: WIPRO.
Gilpin, R. & Atkinson, C. Christmas Cooking. 2004. (Activity Bks.). (ENG.). 1p. (J). pap. 6.95 *(978-0-7945-0056-6(0),* Usborne) EDC Publishing.
Gilpin, Rebecca & Atkinson, Catherine. Yummy Little Cookbook. Taylor, Non et al, illus. rev. ed. 2007. (Children's Cooking Ser.). (ENG.). 96p. (J). (gr. -1-3). 7.99 *(978-0-7945-1655-0(6),* Usborne) EDC Publishing.
Johnson, Kristin & Cummins, Mimi. Christmas Cookies Are for Giving: Recipes, Stories & Tips for Making Heartwarming Gifts. 2003. (Illus.). 208p. 16.95 *(978-0-9723473-9-6(9))* Tyr Publishing.
Lynette, Rachel. Let's Throw a Christmas Party! 2011. (J). 49.50 *(978-1-4488-2732-9(9));* pap. 8.25 *(978-1-4488-2731-2(0));* lib. bdg. 22.60 *(978-1-4488-2571-4(7))* Rosen Publishing Group, Inc., The. (PowerKids Pr.).

C D

Marsh, Carole. Christmas: Activities, Crafts, Recipes & More! 2003. 32p. (J). (gr. 1-7). pap. 6.95 *(978-0-635-02172-4(2))* Gallopade International.

—Christmas Recipes from the Past. 2003. 12p. (J). (gr. k-4). pap. 2.95 *(978-0-635-02153-3(6))* Gallopade International.

Owen, Ruth. Christmas Sweets & Treats. 2012. (Holiday Cooking for Kids! Ser.). (ENG., Illus.). 32p. (J). (gr. 3-6). 26.50 *(978-1-4488-8081-2(5))*; pap. 11.75 *(978-1-4488-8128-4(5))* Windmill Bks.

Pratt, Leonie & Atkinson, Catherine. Christmas Fairy Cooking. Sage, Molly, illus. Allman, Howard, photos by. 2006. (Usborne Activities Ser.). (ENG.). 32p. (J). (gr. -1-3). pap. 8.99 *(978-0-7945-1118-0(X),* Usborne) EDC Publishing.

Price, Roger & Stern, Leonard. Holly, Jolly Mad Libs. 2009. (Mad Libs Ser.). (ENG.). 224p. (J). (gr. 3-7). 6.99 *(978-0-8431-8950-6(9),* Mad Libs) Penguin Young Readers Group.

Schuette, Sarah L. A Christmas Cookbook: Simple Recipes for Kids, 1 vol. 2011. (First Cookbooks Ser.). (ENG.). 24p. (gr. 1-2). lib. bdg. 25.32 *(978-1-4296-5999-4(8),* First Facts) Capstone Press of Coughlan Cos.

Usborne Books, creator. The Usborne Big Book of Christmas Things to Make & Do. 2013. (ENG., Illus.). 128p. pap. 14.99 *(978-0-7945-2950-5(X),* Usborne) EDC Publishing.

CHRISTMAS DECORATIONS

Aston, Al. A Message for Mary. Hutchinson, Joy, illus. 2005. 16p. 2.00 *(978-1-84427-176-4(5))* Scripture Union GBR. Dist: Send The Light Distribution LLC.

—The Shepherds' Surprise. Hutchinson, Joy, illus. 2005. 16p. pap., pap. 2.00 *(978-1-84427-178-8(1))* Scripture Union GBR. Dist: Send The Light Distribution LLC.

Bicknell, Joanna. Dress Up: The Christmas Story. 2005. (Illus.). 12p. (J). (gr. -1-3). per., bds. *(978-1-905051-93-9(X))* Make Believe Ideas.

Boase, Petra. Christmas Crafts for Kids: 50 Step-By-Step Decorations & Gift Ideas for Festive Fun. 2013. (ENG., Illus.). 96p. (J). (gr. k-5). 13.99 *(978-1-84322-945-2(5),* Armadillo) Anness Publishing GBR. Dist: National Bk. Network.

Cannon, Nick & Carey, Mariah. Roc & Roe's Twelve Days of Christmas. Ford, A. G., illus. 2014. (ENG.). 32p. (J). (gr. -1-k). 17.99 *(978-0-545-51950-2(0),* Orchard Bks.) Scholastic, Inc.

d'Allancé, Mireille. Dejame Decorar El Arbol De Navidad. (SPA.). 36p. *(978-84-95150-36-3(0))* Corimbo, Editorial S.L.

Dog 'n' Bone Books Staff & CICO Kidz Staff, compiled by. My First Christmas Craft Book: 35 Fun Festive Projects for Children Aged 7+ 2016. (ENG., Illus.). 128p. (J). (gr. 7-11). pap. 14.95 *(978-1-78249-381-5(6),* 1782493816, CICO Books) Ryland Peters & Small GBR. Dist: WIPRO.

Edgar, Val. How to Be Brilliant at Christmas Time. 2004. (Illus.). 48p. pap. 30.00 *(978-1-897675-63-2(1))* Brilliant Pubns. GBR. Dist: Parkwest Pubns., Inc.

Gibson, R. & Watt, F. Things to Make & Do for Christmas. 2004. (Illus.). 32p. (J). pap., act. bk. ed. 6.95 *(978-0-7945-0338-3(1))* EDC Publishing.

Gilpin, Rebecca. Christmas fairy things to make & Do. Fearn, Katrina, illus. 2004. 34p. (J). pap. 6.95 *(978-0-7945-0835-7(9),* Usborne) EDC Publishing.

Glow in the Dark Advent Sticker Book. (Illus.). 16p. (J). (gr. -1-5). 6.99 *(978-0-8254-7233-6(4))* Kregel Pubns.

Goodings, Christina. Christmas - Fun Things to Make & Do. 2017. (ENG.). 104p. (J). (gr. k-2). spiral bd. 9.99 ***(978-0-7459-7616-7(6))*** Lion Hudson PLC GBR. Dist: Independent Pubs. Group.

Goodings, Christina. Whizzy Bizzy Christmas Fun Book. 2004. (ENG., Illus.). 32p. (J). (gr. k-4). pap. 5.50 *(978-0-7459-4888-1(X))* Lion Hudson PLC GBR. Dist: Independent Pubs. Group.

Green, Jonathan, et al. Christmas Unwrapped: A Kid's Winter Wonderland of Holiday Trivia. 2011. (ENG., Illus.). 64p. (J). (gr. 1-5). 12.95 *(978-1-61608-469-1(3),* 608469, Sky Pony Pr.) Skyhorse Publishing Co., Inc.

Harpine, Elaine C. Christment Tree Pattern: 21 Christian Ornaments on the Meaning of Christmas. 2004. (Illus.). 86p. pap. 12.95 *(978-1-56608-102-3(5))* Meriwether Publishing, Ltd.

Imperato, Teresa. Ten Christmas Lights: Count the Lights from One to Ten! Parry, Jo, illus. 2005. (ENG.). 20p. (J). 10.95 *(978-1-58117-321-5(0),* Intervisual/Piggy Toes) Bendon, Inc.

Kalman, Bobbie. A Visual Dictionary of Christmas Long Ago. 2010. (Crabtree Visual Dictionaries Ser.). (ENG.). 32p. (J). (gr. 1-7). pap. *(978-0-7787-3526-7(5))* Crabtree Publishing Co.

Kaye, Teri, ed. Christmas Crafts on a Budget: Over 100 Project Ideas. 2005. 19.99 *(978-0-9759636-2-1(1))* Gizmo Enterprises, Inc.

Lim, Annalees. Christmas Crafts, 01 vols., 1. 2016. (10-Minute Crafts Ser.). (ENG., Illus.). 24p. (J). pap. 10.60 *(978-1-5081-9077-6(1),* Windmill Bks.) Rosen Publishing Group, Inc., The.

Llimós, Anna. Earth-Friendly Christmas Crafts in 5 Easy Steps. 2013. (Earth-Friendly Crafts in 5 Easy Steps Ser.). 32p. (J). (gr. 3-4). pap. 7.95 *(978-1-4644-0307-1(4),* Enslow Elementary) Enslow Pubs., Inc.

Llimós Plomer, Anna. Earth-Friendly Christmas Crafts in 5 Easy Steps. 2013. (Earth-Friendly Crafts in 5 Easy Steps Ser.). (Illus.). 32p. (J). lib. bdg. 23.94 *(978-0-7660-4188-2(3))* Enslow Pubs., Inc.

Lynette, Rachel. Let's Throw a Christmas Party! 2011. (J). 49.50 *(978-1-4488-2732-9(9))*; pap. 8.25 *(978-1-4488-2731-2(0))*; lib. bdg. 22.60 *(978-1-4488-2571-4(7))* Rosen Publishing Group, Inc., The. (PowerKids Pr.).

Marsh, Carole. Christmas: Activities, Crafts, Recipes & More! 2003. 32p. (J). (gr. 1-7). pap. 6.95 *(978-0-635-02172-4(2))* Gallopade International.

McGee, Randel. Celebrate Christmas with Paper Crafts. 2015. (Celebrate Holidays with Paper Crafts Ser.). 48p. (J). (gr. 3-4). 25.27 *(978-0-7660-6355-6(0))* Enslow Pubs., Inc.

—Paper Crafts for Christmas. (Paper Craft Fun for Holidays Ser.). (Illus.). 48p. (J). (gr. 3-4). 2012. pap. 8.95 *(978-1-4644-0321-7(X))* 2009. lib. bdg. 25.27 *(978-0-7660-2952-1(2))* Enslow Pubs., Inc. (Enslow Elementary).

Miller, Mirella S. Christmas Crafts. Gallagher-Cole, Mernie, illus. 2016. (Holiday Crafts Ser.). (ENG.). 24p. (J). (gr. k-3). 28.50 *(978-1-5038-0816-4(5),* 210652) Child's World, Inc., The.

Minor, Florence F. & Minor, Wendell. Christmas Tree! Minor, Wendell, illus. 2005. (ENG., Illus.). 40p. (J). (gr. -1-3). 16.99 *(978-0-06-056034-8(7),* Tegen, Katherine Bks) HarperCollins Pubs.

Munro, Roxie. Christmastime in New York City. 2014. (ENG., Illus.). 32p. (J). (gr. -1-3). 14.95 *(978-0-7893-2740-6(6))* Rizzoli International Pubns., Inc.

Noble, Marty. Fun with Christmas Ornaments Stencils. 2006. (Dover Stencils Ser.). (ENG., Illus.). 6p. (J). (gr. -1-5). pap. 1.50 *(978-0-486-44893-0(2))* Dover Pubns., Inc.

Owen, Cheryl. Gifts for Kids to Make. 2005. (ENG., Illus.). 128p. (gr. -1-17). pap. 14.95 *(978-0-600-61502-6(2),* Hamlyn) Octopus Publishing Group GBR. Dist: Hachette Bk. Group.

Owen, Ruth. Christmas & Hanukkah Origami. 2012. (Holiday Origami Ser.). (ENG., Illus.). 32p. (J). (gr. 3-6). 26.50 *(978-1-4488-7860-4(8))*; pap. 11.75 *(978-1-4488-7919-9(1))* Rosen Publishing Group, Inc., The. (PowerKids Pr.).

Owen, Ruth. Handmade Christmas Crafts. 2016. (Handmade Holiday Crafts Ser.). 00032p. (J). pap. 10.50 ***(978-1-4824-6081-0(5))*** Stevens, Gareth Publishing LLLP.

Patchett, Fiona. Rabbits. rev. ed. 2004. (First Pets Ser.). 32p. (J). 12.99 *(978-1-58086-588-3(7))* EDC Publishing.

Peter, Val J., creator. Gifts for a Joyous Christmas: From the Kids at Boys Town. 2004. 164p. pap. 5.95 *(978-1-889322-39-1(3),* 19-015) Boys Town Pr.

Pomaska, Anna. Shiny Christmas Balls Ornaments. 2006. (Dover Little Activity Books Stickers Ser.). (ENG., Illus.). 2p. (J). (gr. -1-5). 1.50 *(978-0-486-44943-2(2))* Dover Pubns., Inc.

Press, Judy. Big Fun Christmas Crafts & Activities: Over 200 Quick & Easy Activities for Holiday Fun! Cole, Sarah, illus. 2006. (ENG.). 128p. (J). (gr. -1-3). 16.95 *(978-0-8249-6787-1(9))*; pap. 12.95 *(978-0-8249-6786-4(0))* Worthy Publishing. (Ideal Pubns.).

Rigg, Annie & Woram, Catherine. Fun Christmas Crafts to Make & Bake: Over 60 Festive Projects to Make with Your Kids. 2012. (ENG., Illus.). 160p. *(978-1-84975-273-2(7))* Ryland Peters & Small.

Robinson, Fay. Christmas Crafts. 2004. (Fun Holiday Crafts Kids Can Do! Ser.). (Illus.). 32p. (J). lib. bdg. 23.94 *(978-0-7660-2257-7(9))* Enslow Pubs., Inc.

Sneesby, Frederick. A Believer's Christmas. 2008. 92p. pap. 15.25 *(978-1-4389-0031-5(7))* AuthorHouse.

Sturgill, Ruthy. Christmas Tree Advent Calendar: A Country Quilted & Appliquéd Project. 2006. 96p. pap. 24.95 *(978-1-59800-539-4(1))* Outskirts Pr., Inc.

Torres, J. Christmas Eve. Harpster, Steve, illus. 2006. (Scribble & Sing Ser.). (ENG.). 80p. (J). 4.99 *(978-1-4169-2731-0(X),* Simon Scribbles) Simon Scribbles.

Twin Sisters(r), et al. Easy-To-Make Christmas Crafts for Kids. 2016. (I'm Learning the Bible Activity Book Ser.). (ENG.). 32p. (J). pap. 4.99 *(978-1-63409-803-8(X))* Barbour Publishing, Inc.

Watt, Fiona. Christmas Art Ideas. 2004. (Art Ideas Ser.). 64p. (J). pap. 14.95 *(978-0-7945-0833-3(2),* Usborne) EDC Publishing.

—Christmas decorations & Cards. 2005. 34p. (J). pap. 8.95 *(978-0-7945-0795-4(6),* Usborne) EDC Publishing.

—Christmas Decorations to Cut, Fold & Stick. 2012. (Christmas Decorations Ser.). 200p. (J). pap. 9.99 *(978-0-7945-3327-4(2),* Usborne) EDC Publishing.

—50 Christmas Things to Make & Do. 2006. (Activity Cards Ser.). (Illus.). 50p. (J). 9.99 *(978-0-7945-1217-0(8),* Usborne) EDC Publishing.

Watt, Fiona & Gilpin, Rebecca. The Usborne Big Book of Christmas Things to Make & Do. Fearn, Katrina, illus. 2005. 99p. (J). *(978-0-439-81506-2(1))* Scholastic, Inc.

Who's Coming to Stay?, 1 vol. 2014. 12p. (J). bds. 5.99 *(978-0-8254-4206-3(0))* Kregel Pubns.

Woram, Catherine. Christmas Crafting with Kids. Wreford, Polly, photos by. 2011. (ENG., Illus.). 128p. pap. *(978-1-84975-141-4(2))* Ryland Peters & Small.

—Christmas Crafting with Kids: 35 Projects for the Festive Season. 2008. (ENG., Illus.). 128p. (J). *(978-1-84597-700-9(9))* Ryland Peters & Small.

25 Crafts for Christmas. 2015. (ENG., Illus.). 32p. (J). (gr. -1-2). pap. 9.99 *(978-0-7459-6387-7(0))* Lion Hudson PLC GBR. Dist: Independent Pubs. Group.

CHRISTMAS ENTERTAINMENTS

see also Christmas Plays

Angel's Christmas Party Activity Fun. 2003. (Christmas Activity Bks.). (Illus.). 128p. (J). 3.98 *(978-0-7525-6499-9(4))* Parragon, Inc.

Dowling, Iris. Christmas Program Ideas. 2004. 96p. per. 7.95 *(978-0-9749836-1-5(6))* Faithful Life Pubs.

Gordon, Lynn. 52 Christmas Activities. Johnson, Karen, illus. 2004. (52 Ser.: 52SE). (ENG.). 52p. (J). (gr. k-4). 6.95 *(978-0-8118-4123-8(5))* Chronicle Bks. LLC.

Hill, Grace Livingston. The Best Birthday: A Christmas Entertainment for Children. (J). (gr. 5-6). 15.95 *(978-0-89190-404-5(2))* Amereon Ltd.

Johnson, Kristin & Cummins, Mimi. Christmas Cookies Are for Giving: Recipes, Stories & Tips for Making Heartwarming Gifts. 2003. (Illus.). 208p. 16.95 *(978-0-9723473-9-6(9))* Tyr Publishing.

Marsh, Carole. Christmas: Activities, Crafts, Recipes & More! 2003. 32p. (J). (gr. 1-7). pap. 6.95 *(978-0-635-02172-4(2))* Gallopade International.

Milbourne, Anna. Christmas Activities. Cartwright, Stephen, illus. 2004. (Activity Books). 32p. (J). pap. 6.95 *(978-0-7945-0564-6(3),* Usborne) EDC Publishing.

Rollins, Jack & Nelson, Steve. Frosty the Snowman. Halverson, Lydia, illus. 2005. 18p. (J). (gr. -1-k). bds. 9.95 *(978-0-8249-6595-2(7),* Ideal Pubns.) Worthy Publishing.

Snowman's Winter Coloring Fun. Date not set. (Christmas Activity Bks.). (Illus.). 128p. (J). pap. 3.98 *(978-0-7525-6670-2(9))* Parragon, Inc.

CHRISTMAS MUSIC

Andreasen, Dan, illus. The Twelve Days of Christmas. 2012. (ENG.). 32p. (J). (gr. k-2). 14.99 *(978-1-58536-834-1(2),* 202344) Sleeping Bear Pr.

Andrews, Pam. A Christmas Carol: A Christmas Musical for Children about Giving. 2003. (ENG., Illus.). 120p. pap. 7.99 *(978-0-8341-7372-9(7),* MC-538) Lillenas Publishing Co.

—Joyland: A Children's Christmas Musical Teaching the Blessing of Giving. 2006. (ENG., Illus.). 136p. pap. 7.99 *(978-0-8341-7482-5(0),* MC-561) Lillenas Publishing Co.

—A Shepherd's Story: An Easy-to-Sing Christmas Musical for Children. 2003. (ENG., Illus.). 32p. pap. 5.99 *(978-0-8341-7366-8(2),* MC-542) Lillenas Publishing Co.

Andrews, Pam & Andrews, Pam. Cross Country: A Children's Musical That Reminds Us to Race to the Cross. 2003. (ENG., Illus.). 112p. pap. 7.99 *(978-0-8341-7235-7(6),* MB-911) Lillenas Publishing Co.

Bergerac. A First Book of Christmas Songs for the Beginning Pianist: With Downloadable MP3s. 2014. (ENG.). 48p. (gr. -1). pap. 6.95 *(978-0-486-78007-8(4))* Dover Pubns., Inc.

Berlin, Irving. White Christmas. Hague, Michael, illus. 2010. (ENG.). 32p. (J). 16.99 *(978-0-06-029123-5(0))* HarperCollins Pubs.

Bible Visuals International Staff, compiled by. Christmas Collection. 2004. (Illus.). (J). cd-rom *(978-1-933206-39-4(X),* 8001) Bible Visuals International, Inc.

Bonnet, Rosalinde. Very First Christmas Carols. 2011. (Very First Words Board Book Ser.). 12p. (J). ring bd. 6.99 *(978-0-7945-3117-1(2),* Usborne) EDC Publishing.

Boys Choir of Harlem Staff. O Holy Night: Christmas with the Boys Choir of Harlem. Ringgold, Faith, illus. 2004. 40p. (J). 19.89 *(978-0-06-051819-6(7))* HarperCollins Pubs.

Cannon, Nick & Carey, Mariah. Roc & Roe's Twelve Days of Christmas. Ford, A. G., illus. 2014. (ENG.). 32p. (J). (gr. -1-k). 17.99 *(978-0-545-51950-2(0),* Orchard Bks.) Scholastic, Inc.

Canwell, Peter & Evry, Philip. Christmas Dove & the Woodcutter. 2007. (ENG.). pap. 10.25 *(978-0-86175-328-4(3))* Alfred Publishing Co., Inc.

The Christmas Carol Book. (Illus.). 10p. (J). bds. *(978-2-89393-929-2(5))* Phidal Publishing, Inc./Editions Phidal, Inc.

Clydesdale, David T., contrib. by. Angel Alert! The Night That Heaven Came Down. 2007. (Illus.). 125p. pap. 6.95 *(978-5-557-71504-1(5),* Word Music) Word Entertainment.

—The Little Drummer Boy: Behind the Music. 2007. (Illus.). 127p. pap. 6.95 *(978-5-557-71490-7(1),* Word Music) Word Entertainment.

Combs, Katie. The Present Is the Future: A Kids' Christmas Musical about the Gift of Hope. 2010. (ENG.). 80p. pap. 7.99 *(978-0-8341-7783-3(8),* 9780834177833) Lillenas Publishing Co.

Davis, Katherine K., et al. The Little Drummer Boy: Sheet. 2012. (Signature Ser.). (ENG.). 4p. pap. 3.50 *(978-0-7390-9154-8(9))*; pap. 3.50 *(978-0-7390-9152-4(2))*; pap. 3.50 *(978-0-7390-9153-1(0))* Alfred Publishing Co., Inc.

Dealey, Erin. Deck the Walls: A Wacky Christmas Carol. Ward, Nick, illus. 2013. (ENG.). 32p. (J). (gr. 1-3). 14.99 *(978-1-58536-857-0(1),* 202892) Sleeping Bear Pr.

Feldstein, Sandy & Clark, Larry. Christmas Suprise. 2005. (YA). pap. 40.00 *(978-1-932895-97-1(3))* PlayinTime Productions, Inc.

—Christmas Suprise - Conductor Score. 2005. (J). pap. 6.00 *(978-1-932895-98-8(1))* PlayinTime Productions, Inc.

—Christmas Toyland. 2004. (YA). pap. 50.00 *(978-1-932895-08-7(6))* PlayinTime Productions, Inc.

—Christmas Toyland - conductor's Score. 2004. (YA). pap. 8.00 *(978-1-932895-09-4(4))* PlayinTime Productions, Inc.

Golden Books Staff. The Twelve Days of Christmas: A Christmas Carol. Beckett, Sheilah, illus. 2015. (Little Golden Book Ser.). (ENG.). 24p. (J). (gr. k-k). 4.99 *(978-0-307-00149-8(0),* Golden Bks.) Random Hse. Children's Bks.

Hal Leonard Corp. Staff, creator. Violin Classics - Advanced Level. 2009. (ENG.). 112p. pap. 16.95 *(978-1-4234-2852-7(8),* 1423428528, G Schirmer, Inc.) Leonard, Hal Corp.

Hussey, Christopher. Abracadabra Christmas Showstoppers Clarinet, 1 vol. 2015. (Abracadabra Ser.). (ENG.). 32p. (J). (gr. k-4). pap. 22.95 ***(978-1-4729-2053-9(8))*** HarperCollins Pubs. Ltd. GBR. Dist: Independent Pubs. Group.

—Abracadabra Christmas Showstoppers Trumpet, 1 vol. 2015. (Abracadabra Ser.). (ENG.). 32p. (J). pap. 22.95 ***(978-1-4729-2052-2(X))*** HarperCollins Pubs. Ltd. GBR. Dist: Independent Pubs. Group.

Julian, Alison, illus. The 12 Days of Christmas. 2005. (J). *(978-1-74157-281-0(9))* Hinkler Bks. Pty, Ltd.

Kragen, Emma. The Twelve Dogs of Christmas. 2004. 16p. 14.99 *(978-1-4003-9404-3(X))* Nelson, Thomas Inc.

Long, Laurel. The Twelve Days of Christmas. Long, Laurel, illus. 2014. (ENG., Illus.). 32p. (J). (gr. -1-2). pap. 8.99 *(978-0-14-751286-4(7),* Puffin Books) Penguin Young Readers Group.

—The Twelve Days of Christmas. 2011. (ENG.). 32p. (J). (gr. -1-2). 16.99 *(978-0-8037-3357-2(7),* Dial Bks) Penguin Young Readers Group.

Manson, Christopher, illus. Good King Wenceslas. 2004. 25p. (J). (gr. k-4). reprint ed. 15.00 *(978-0-7567-8226-9(0))* DIANE Publishing Co.

Moore, Bette Dale. My Best-est Friend: A Simple Christmas Music Program for Preschoolers. 2010. (ENG., Illus.). 64p. pap. 19.99 *(978-0-8341-7785-7(4),* 9780834177857) Lillenas Publishing Co.

Moore, Clement C. A Christmas Carol. (Illus.). 12p. (J). 4.95 *(978-1-58989-103-6(1))* Thurman Hse., LLC.

National Gallery of Art Staff. Hark! The Herald Angels Sing: The National Gallery, London. (Illus.). 48p. (J). (gr. k-18). *(978-0-7112-0814-8(X))* ReiseArt Buchhandlung GmbH.

Neale, John M. Good King Wenceslas. Ladwig, Tim, illus. 2005. (ENG.). 32p. (J). (gr. k-17). 17.00 *(978-0-8028-5209-0(2),* Eerdmans Bks For Young Readers) Eerdmans, William B. Publishing Co.

Newsom, Tom, illus. The First Noel. 2006. 14p. (J). (gr. k-4). reprint ed. 8.00 *(978-1-4223-5413-1(X))* DIANE Publishing Co.

Pingry, Patricia A. & Urbano, Aide. One Baby Jesus/Un Nino Dios. Edelson, Wendy, illus. 2003. (ENG & SPA.). 30p. (J). pap. 3.95 *(978-0-8249-5472-7(6),* Ideal Pubns.) Worthy Publishing.

Pinksterboer, Hugo. Pocket-Info Gesang: (German Text) 2004. (ENG.). 164p. pap. 13.95 *(978-3-7957-5536-2(0),* 3795755360) Schott Music Corp.

Pizzoli, Greg. The Twelve Days of Christmas. Pizzoli, Greg, illus. 2017. (ENG., Illus.). 56p. (J). (gr. -1-k). 16.99 ***(978-1-4847-5031-5(4))*** Hyperion Bks. for Children.

Rauenhorst, Linda. Fröhliche Weihnachten: Learning Songs & Traditions in German. Collier, Roberta, illus. 2007. (Teach Me Ser.). (GER & ENG.). 32p. (J). (gr. -1-3). 19.95 *(978-1-59972-063-0(9))* Teach Me Tapes, Inc.

Ray, Jane. The Twelve Days of Christmas. 2011. (ENG., Illus.). 32p. (J). (gr. -1-2). 16.99 *(978-0-7636-5735-2(2))* Candlewick Pr.

Ringgold, Faith, illus. O Holy Night: Christmas with the Boys Choir of Harlem. 2006. 30p. (J). (gr. 4-8). 19.00 *(978-1-4223-5512-1(8))* DIANE Publishing Co.

Robertson, Barny & Robertson, Carter, told to. The Christmas Puzzle: An Easy-to-Sing, Easy-to-Stage Kids' Christmas Musical about How We're All Part of God's Picture. 2010. (ENG.). 48p. pap. 5.99 *(978-0-8341-7784-0(6),* 9780834177840) Lillenas Publishing Co.

Rossi, Sophia. Buon Natale: Learning Songs & Traditions in Italian. Kelleher, Kathie, illus. 2007. (Teach Me Ser.). (ITA & SPA.). 32p. (J). (gr. -1-3). 19.95 *(978-1-59972-067-8(1))* Teach Me Tapes, Inc.

Schiller, David. Christmas Sing-Along Car-I-Oke. Robinson, Tim, illus. 2005. (ENG.). 64p. (J). (gr. -1-8). bds. 15.95 *(978-0-7611-3984-3(2),* 13984) Workman Publishing Co., Inc.

Schram, Scott. The Last Noel, Director's Score: A Christmas Musical for Children. 2007. (ENG., Illus.). 36p. pap. 24.95 *(978-0-7390-4482-7(6))* Alfred Publishing Co., Inc.

Snell, Gordon. Twelve Days: A Christmas Countdown. O'Malley, Kevin, illus. 2005. 30p. (J). (gr. -1-2). reprint ed. 16.00 *(978-0-7567-9403-3(X))* DIANE Publishing Co.

St. James, Rebecca. Friendly Beasts: An Old English Christmas Carol, 1 vol. Vojtech, Anna, illus. 2012. (ENG.). 32p. (J). 16.99 *(978-0-310-72012-6(5))* Zonderkidz.

Tiger Tales, ed. Jingle Bells: A Collection of Songs & Carols. Kolvanovic, Dubravka, illus. 2014. (ENG.). 22p. (J). (gr. -1-k). bds. 8.99 *(978-1-58925-568-5(2))* Tiger Tales.

Torme, Mel. The Christmas Song: Chestnuts Roasting on an Open Fire. Barrette, Doris, illus. 2007. 32p. (J). (gr. -1-2). lib. bdg. 17.89 *(978-0-06-072226-5(6))* HarperCollins Pubs.

Tormé, Mel. The Christmas Song: Chestnuts Roasting on an Open Fire. Barrette, Doris, illus. 2007. (J). lib. bdg. 6.99 *(978-0-06-072227-2(4))* HarperCollins Pubs.

Traditional. O Little Town of Bethlehem. Beauvois, Nathalie, illus. 2014. 16p. (J). bds. 12.99 *(978-0-8249-1933-7(5),* Ideal Pubns.) Worthy Publishing.

Twin Sisters(r) Staff. Christmas Songs 4 Kids 3. 2009. 12.99 *(978-1-57583-971-4(7))* Twin Sisters IP, LLC.

—The Christmas Story. 2009. 9.99 *(978-1-59922-408-4(9))* Twin Sisters IP, LLC.

—Santa Songs & More Boxed Set- 2 books. 2009. 12.99 *(978-1-59922-152-6(7))* Twin Sisters IP, LLC.

—The Twelve Days of Christmas. 2009. 16p. 4.99 *(978-1-59922-415-2(1))* Twin Sisters IP, LLC.

—Up on the Housetop. 2009. 16p. 4.99 *(978-1-59922-414-5(3))* Twin Sisters IP, LLC.

—The 12 Days of Christmas. 2009. 9.99 *(978-1-59922-407-7(0))* Twin Sisters IP, LLC.

Tyrrell, Frances, illus. The Huron Carol. 2004. 32p. 16.00 *(978-0-8028-5263-2(7))* Eerdmans, William B. Publishing Co.

Vasylenko, Veronica, illus. Jingle Bells. 2007. (Padded Board Bks.). 18p. (J). (gr. -1-k). bds. 7.95 *(978-1-58925-821-1(5))* Tiger Tales.

Wallace, Ian. The Huron Carol, 1 vol. 2013. (ENG., Illus.). 32p. (J). (gr. -1). 14.95 *(978-1-55498-394-0(0))* Groundwood Bks. CAN. Dist: Publishers Group West (PGW).

Watt, Fiona. Baby's First Christmas. 2009. (Baby Board Books with CD Ser.). 10p. (J). (gr. -1). bds. 14.99 *(978-0-7945-1902-5(4),* Usborne) EDC Publishing.

Weston Woods Staff, creator. The Little Drummer Boy. 2011. 38.75 *(978-0-439-93227-1(0))*; 18.95 *(978-0-439-93213-4(0))* Weston Woods Studios, Inc.

Wheeler, Jody. The First Noel. 2010. (Illus.). 24p. (J). (gr. -1-3). 14.99 *(978-0-8249-5621-9(4),* Ideal Pubns.) Worthy Publishing.

Wood, Don. Joyeux Noel, Ours Affamé! 2004. (FRE., Illus.). (J). (gr. -1-18). spiral bd. *(978-0-616-14601-9(9))* Canadian National Institute for the Blind/Institut National Canadien pour les Aveugles.

CHRISTMAS PLAYS

Baker, Steve & Golden, Mark. The Kings of Christmas. 2004. (Illus.). 24p. 15.99 *(978-0-9752895-2-5(7))* Shepherd's Workshop, LLC, The.

Carver, Patty & Carusone, Leo P. The Elves & the Shoemaker: A Musical Holiday Fable. 2013. 47p. ***(978-0-87602-396-9(0))*** Family Plays.

Doonan, Gladys & Sorensen, Rebekah M. Crown Him King! A Christmas Program. 2005. (Illus.). 29p. *(978-1-59402-299-9(2))* Regular Baptist Pr.

Goulding, Dorothy J. Three Christmas Plays. 20p. (J). (gr. 3-6). reprint ed. *(978-0-88020-103-2(7))* Dramatic Publishing Co.

Hezlep, William. How Come Christmas? 2003. (Theater for Young Audiences Ser.). 18p. (J). pap. 5.00 *(978-0-88734-424-4(0))* Players Pr., Inc.

Howie, Vicki. Story Plays for Christmas: Three Plays Complete with Stories & Interactive Activities. Doggett, Sue, ed. 2005. (ENG.). 84p. pap. *(978-1-84101-400-5(1))* Bible Reading Fellowship.

Lee, Nate. Pushing the Boundaries: And Five Other Dramas for Tweens. 2004. (Illus.). 48p. (J). (gr. -1-7). 6.00 *(978-0-687-06587-5(9))* Abingdon Pr.

McCaslin, Nellie. Christmas Fiesta. 2003. 55p. (Orig.). (J). (gr. k-6). pap. 5.00 *(978-0-88734-400-8(3))* Players Pr., Inc.

—The Christmas Lamb. 2003. (Players Press Nellie McCaslin Ser.). 55p. (Orig.). (J). (gr. k-5). pap. 5.00 *(978-0-88734-479-4(8))* Players Pr., Inc.

—A Miracle in the Christmas City: Playscript. 2003. (Players Press Nellie McCaslin Ser.). 16p. (YA). (gr. k-12). pap. 5.00 *(978-0-88734-437-4(2))* Players Pr., Inc.

Meacham, Liz. Three Wise Women: A Christmas Story / A Christmas Play. l.t. ed. 2006. (Illus.). 54p. per. 10.99 *(978-1-59879-222-5(9))* Lifevest Publishing, Inc.

Preston, Elizabeth. The Very Best Christmas Plays for Kids. 2007. 290p. (J). (gr. 3-8). 24.95 *(978-0-8238-0312-5(0))* Kalmbach Publishing Co., Bks. Div.

Smiley, Kendra. One Rehearsal Christmas Plays: The Easiest Christmas Plays Ever. 2004. (Bible Funstuff Ser.). (ENG.).

96p. (gr. 4-18). pap. 19.99 *(978-0-7814-4120-9(X),* 078144120X) Cook, David C.

CHRISTOLOGY

see Jesus Christ

CHRONOLOGY

see Calendars; Time

CHRONOLOGY, HISTORICAL

see also Calendars

also subdivision History—Chronology under names of countries, e.g. United States—History—Chronology

Chandler, Fiona. Encyclopedia of World History. rev. ed. 2011. (World History Ser.). 416p. (J). ring bd. 39.99 *(978-0-7945-2688-7(8),* Usborne) EDC Publishing.

History Makers. 2003. 320p. 5.98 *(978-1-4054-0325-2(X))* Parragon, Inc.

Jackson, Ellen B. Turn of the Century: Eleven Centuries of Children & Change. Ellis, Jan Davey, illus. 2003. (ENG.). 32p. (J). (gr. k-3). pap. 8.95 *(978-0-88106-370-7(3))* Charlesbridge Publishing, Inc.

Moskal, Greg. The History of Space Exploration: Sequencing Events Chronologically on a Timeline. 2009. (PowerMath Ser.). (ENG., Illus.). 24p. (gr. 3-4). pap. 8.25 *(978-0-8239-8850-1(3),* PowerKids Pr.) Rosen Publishing Group, Inc., The.

CHURCH

see also Christianity

Bagley, Val Chadwick & Beckstrand, Tamara, trs. My Little Book about Prayer. Bagley, Val Chadwick, illus. 2004. (Illus.). (J). bds. 10.95 *(978-1-59156-096-8(9))* Covenant Communications, Inc.

Berndt, Clarence & Rathmann, Rodney L. A Bible History: In the Words of Holy Scripture: With Illustrations, Maps, & Notes. 2003. (Illus.). 480p. stu. ed. 19.75 *(978-0-7586-0288-6(X))* Concordia Publishing Hse.

Boling, Ruth L. Come Worship with Me: A Journey Through the Church Year. Carrier, Tracey Dahle, illus. 2010. (J). 13.00 *(978-0-664-23717-2(7))* Westminster John Knox Pr.

Drion, Donna. Stop & Look at God's World. 2008. (Stop & Look Ser.). 32p. (J). (gr. -1-3). *(978-1-84625-133-7(8))* DayOne Pubns.

—Stop & Look at Yourself. 2008. (Stop & Look Ser.). (Illus.). 32p. (J). (gr. -1-3). *(978-1-84625-132-0(X))* DayOne Pubns.

Elkins, Stephen. Tell Me about Church. 2014. (Train 'Em Up Ser.). (ENG.). 24p. (J). pap. 4.99 *(978-1-4143-9681-1(3))* Tyndale Hse. Pubs.

Falkenhain, John Mark. I Don't Want to Go to Church: Turning the Struggle into a Celebration. Alley, R. W., illus. 2009. (J). pap. 7.95 *(978-0-87029-423-5(7))* Abbey Pr.

Fawcett, Cheryl & Newman, Robert C. Kids' Questions about Church & the Future. Mazellan, Ron, illus. 2003. 79p. pap. *(978-1-59402-084-1(1))* Regular Baptist Pr.

Fewins, Clive & Open Churches Trust Staff. Be a Church Detective: A Young Person's Guide to Old Churches. Davies, Taffy, illus. 2005. (ENG.). 48p. (J). pap. 12.99 *(978-1-85311-628-5(9),* Canterbury Pr. Norwich) Hymns Ancient & Modern Ltd GBR. Dist: Westminster John Knox Pr.

Frevert, Patricia. Sunday & Every Day: My Little Book of Unitarian Universalism. 2010. (J). pap. 5.00 *(978-1-55896-555-3(6),* Skinner Hse. Bks.) Unitarian Universalist Assn.

George, Enzo. Westminster Abbey. 2017. (Crypts, Tombs, & Secret Rooms Ser.). 48p. (gr. 4-5). pap. 84.30 ***(978-1-5382-0646-1(3))*** Stevens, Gareth Publishing LLLP.

Hall, Annalisa. The Holy Ghost Is Like a Blanket. Egbert, Corey, illus. 2013. (ENG.). 32p. (J). (gr. 3-7). 14.99 *(978-1-4621-1229-6(3))* Cedar Fort, Inc./CFI Distribution.

MacKenzie, Carine. My 1st Book about the Church. 2010. (My First Bks.). (ENG., Illus.). 64p. (J). pap. 3.99 *(978-1-84550-570-7(0),* 9781845505707) Christian Focus Pubns. GBR. Dist: Bookmasters Distribution.

Stiegemeyer, Julie & Mitter, Kathy. Things I Do in Church. 2003. (Illus.). 20p. (J). bds. 5.49 *(978-0-7586-0126-1(3))* Concordia Publishing Hse.

Stohs, Anita. Here Is the Church. Mitter, Kathy, illus. 2009. 32p. (J). (gr. -1). 8.99 *(978-0-7586-1633-3(3))* Concordia Publishing Hse.

Todd, Richard E. Church: A Bible Study Wordbook for Kids. 2009. (Children's Wordbooks Ser.). (ENG., Illus.). 32p. (gr. 4-7). pap. 5.99 *(978-1-60066-196-9(3))* WingSpread Publishers.

Tyndale, prod. My Church. 2014. (Happy Day Ser.). (ENG.). 32p. (J). pap. 2.99 *(978-1-4143-9488-6(8))* Tyndale Hse. Pubs.

Whitehurst, Susan. The Pilgrims Before the Mayflower. 2009. (Library of the Pilgrims Ser.). 24p. (gr. 3-4). 42.50 *(978-1-60853-915-4(6),* PowerKids Pr.) Rosen Publishing Group, Inc., The.

Wright, Briana. What Is a Temple? Burnette, Emily, illus. 2016. (ENG.). (J). 14.99 *(978-1-4621-1748-2(1))* Cedar Fort, Inc./CFI Distribution.

CHURCH AND STATE

see also Freedom of Religion

Espejo, Roman. Civil Liberties. 2009. (Opposing Viewpoints Ser.). (ENG., Illus.). 240p. (YA). (gr. 10-12). pap. 29.45 *(978-0-7377-4355-5(7),* LML02109-245310);No. 9. pap. 42.95 *(978-0-7377-4356-2(5),* LML02109-245369) Cengage Gale. (Greenhaven Pr., Inc.).

Harrison, Geoffrey C. & Scott, Thomas F. Church & State. Stewart, Mark & Kennedy, Mike, eds. 2014. (Great Debates Ser.). (ENG.). 48p. (J). (gr. 5-8). lib. bdg. 29.27 *(978-1-59953-589-0(0))* Norwood Hse. Pr.

MacDonald, Joan Vos. Religion & Free Speech Today: A Pro/con Debate. 2008. (Issues in Focus Today Ser.). (Illus.). 112p. (J). (gr. k-6). lib. bdg. 33.27 *(978-0-7660-2915-6(8))* Enslow Pubs., Inc.

Marzilli, Alan. Religion in Public Schools. 2003. (Point/Counterpoint Ser.). (Illus.). 112p. (C). (gr. 9-13). 35.00 *(978-0-7910-7484-8(6),* Chelsea Hse.) Facts On File, Inc.

Merino, Noel. Civil Liberties. 2013. (Opposing Viewpoints Ser.). (ENG., Illus.). 224p. (gr. 10-12). pap. 33.80 *(978-0-7377-6305-8(1),* Greenhaven Pr., Inc.) Cengage Gale.

Merino, Noël. Civil Liberties. 2013. (Opposing Viewpoints Ser.). (ENG., Illus.). 224p. (gr. 10-12). lib. bdg. 48.80 *(978-0-7377-6304-1(3),* Greenhaven Pr., Inc.) Cengage Gale.

Mountjoy, Shane. Engel V. Vitale: School Prayer & the Establishment Clause. 2006. (Great Supreme Court Decisions Ser.). (Illus.). 128p. (YA). (gr. 5-9). lib. bdg. 32.95 *(978-0-7910-9241-5(0))* Facts On File, Inc.

New, David W. Religious Freedom in America for Beginners. 2004. (Illus.). 63p. (YA). 4.95 *(978-0-9721333-3-3(X))* Pocket Pubn., A.

Porterfield, Jason. The Separation of Church & State: Interpreting the Constitution. 2014. (Understanding the United States Constitution Ser.). (Illus.). 112p. (YA). (gr. 7-12). 35.60 *(978-1-4777-7508-0(0))* Rosen Publishing Group, Inc., The.

Uilmann, Carol & Zott, Lynn M. Religious Liberty. 2014. (Opposing Viewpoints Ser.). (ENG., Illus.). 224p. (gr. 7-12). pap. 33.80 *(978-0-7377-6665-3(4));* lib. bdg. 48.80 *(978-0-7377-6664-6(6))* Cengage Gale. (Greenhaven Pr., Inc.).

CHURCH ARCHITECTURE

see also Cathedrals; Church Buildings; Temples

Kuhlman, Thomas, et al. The Beauty of Thy House: The History, Art & Architecture of Saint Cecilia Cathedral Omaha. 2005. (Illus.). lib. bdg. 39.95 *(978-0-9745410-7-5(9));* per. 14.95 *(978-0-9745410-6-8(0))* Omaha Bks.

Michelangelo. Sistine Chapel Coloring Book. 2004. (Dover Art Coloring Book Ser.). (ENG., Illus.). 32p. (J). (gr. 3-8). spiral bd. 4.95 *(978-0-486-43334-9(X))* Dover Pubns., Inc.

CHURCH BELLS

see Bells

CHURCH BIOGRAPHY

see Christian Biography

CHURCH BUILDINGS

see also Cathedrals; Church Architecture

Dill, Pamela Wescovich. Katrina's Rainbow: The Miracle of the Storm Crosses. 2006. (Illus.). 42p. (J). 17.99 *(978-1-59879-302-4(0))* Lifevest Publishing, Inc.

Goldsworthy, Kaite. St. Paul's Cathedral. 2014. (J). *(978-1-4896-1154-3(1))* Weigl Pubs., Inc.

Macaulay, David. Mosque. 2008. (ENG., Illus.). 96p. (YA). (gr. 4-7). pap. 9.95 *(978-0-547-01547-7(X))* Houghton Mifflin Harcourt Publishing Co.

Nanji, Shenaaz. Vatican City. 2014. (J). *(978-1-4896-1158-1(4))* Weigl Pubs., Inc.

Rasmussen, Jason. The House of the Lord: A Pop-Up Book. 2011. 32p. (J). 29.99 *(978-1-60641-939-7(0))* Deseret Bk. Co.

Synder, Bernadette. 131 Fun-Damental Facts for Catholic Kids: Liturgy, Litanies, Rituals, Rosaries, Symbols, Sacraments & Sacred Scripture. Sharp, Chris, illus. 2006. (Liguori's Fun Facts Ser.). 144p. (J). (gr. 3-7). per. 12.99 *(978-0-7648-1502-7(4))* Liguori Pubns.

Wilson, Cristi. Just Because. Wilson, Cristi, illus. l.t. ed. 2006. (Illus.). 24p. (J). (gr. -1-3). per. 10.99 *(978-1-59879-251-5(2))* Lifevest Publishing, Inc.

CHURCH BUILDINGS—FICTION

Acevedo, Ari. Juan Bobo Sends the Pig to Mass. Wrenn, Tom, illus. 2008. (Story Cove Ser.). (SPA & ENG.). 24p. (J). (gr. -1-3). pap. 4.95 *(978-0-87483-883-1(5))* August Hse. Pubs., Inc.

Peabody, Beth Leone. Chocolate Pie Therapy. 2008. 40p. pap. 18.49 *(978-1-4343-9684-6(3))* AuthorHouse.

Rubright, Lynn. Mama's Window. Smith, Duane, illus. 2005. 89p. (J). 16.95 *(978-1-57480-160-6(0))* Lee & Low Bks., Inc.

Saddleback Educational Publishing, ed. Shelter, 1 vol. 2013. (Heights Ser.). (ENG.). 52p. (gr. 5-8). 7.95 *(978-1-62250-046-8(6))* Saddleback Educational Publishing, Inc.

CHURCH DENOMINATIONS

see Sects

CHURCH FESTIVALS

see Fasts and Feasts

CHURCH HISTORY

see also Church and State; Jews; Missions; Monasticism and Religious Orders; Popes; Protestantism; Reformation; Sects

also names of countries, states, etc. with the subdivision Church History (e.g. United States—Church History; etc.)

Anderson, Dale. Churches & Religion in the Middle Ages. 2005. (World Almanac Library of the Middle Ages). (Illus.). 48p. (gr. 5-12). lib. bdg. 31.00 *(978-0-8368-5892-1(1),* Gareth Stevens Secondary Library) Stevens, Gareth Publishing LLLP.

—Monks & Monasteries in the Middle Ages. 2005. (World Almanac Library of the Middle Ages). 48p. (gr. 5-12). pap. 14.05 *(978-0-8368-5906-5(5));* (Illus.). lib. bdg. 31.00 *(978-0-8368-5897-6(2))* Stevens, Gareth Publishing LLLP. (Gareth Stevens Secondary Library).

Appleton, E. R. & Cadman, S. Parkes. An Outline of Religion. 2005. pap. 50.95 *(978-1-4179-8460-2(0))* Kessinger Publishing, LLC.

Bartolotta, Kenneth L. The Inquisition: The Quest for Absolute Religious Power. 2017. (World History Ser.). 104p. (YA). (gr. 7-7). lib. bdg. 39.90 ***(978-1-5345-6049-9(1),*** Lucent Pr.) Greenhaven Publishing LLC.

Bible Visuals International Staff, compiled by. The Church Vol. 15: New Testament. 2006. (Illus.). (J). pap. *(978-1-932381-45-0(7),* 1015) Bible Visuals International, Inc.

Boekestein, William. The Quest for Comfort: The Story of the Heidelberg Catechism. Hughes, Evan, illus. 2011. 32p. (J). pap. 10.00 *(978-1-60178-152-9(0))* Reformation Heritage Bks.

DeKock, Paul & Yount, David. The Next Step. 2004. (Illus.). (YA). (gr. 8-12). 40.00 *(978-1-57336-406-5(1),* I7130) Interaction Pubs., Inc.

Eastwood, Kay. Places of Worship in the Middle Ages. 2003. (Medieval World Ser.). (ENG., Illus.). 32p. (J). (gr. 5). pap. *(978-0-7787-1379-1(2));* lib. bdg. *(978-0-7787-1347-0(4))* Crabtree Publishing Co.

Flatt, Lizann. Religion in the Renaissance. 2009. (ENG., Illus.). 32p. (J). (gr. 5-7). *(978-0-7787-4597-6(X));* (gr. 6-9). pap. *(978-0-7787-4617-1(8))* Crabtree Publishing Co.

Gilmour, Richard. Bible History. 2009. 120.00 *(978-1-60724-278-9(8))* Gorgias Pr., LLC.

Heroes of the Faith. (Illus.). 176-208p. (J). (gr. 5). 179.50 *(978-0-7910-4916-7(7),* Chelsea Hse.) Facts On File, Inc.

Higgins, Richard Stockton. The Trace of the True Cross. 2008. 56p. pap. 7.95 *(978-1-4327-1489-5(9))* Outskirts Pr., Inc.

Hodges, George. Saints & Heroes to the End of the Middle Ages (Yesterday's Classics) 2006. (Illus.). 188p. (J). per. 9.95 *(978-1-59915-093-2(X))* Yesterday's Classics.

Kingdom Leaders Solving Church Problems. (YA). *(978-0-7673-9456-7(9))* LifeWay Christian Resources.

Kuipers, Ken. A. D. A Study of Church History. (Crossroads Ser.). 143p. (gr. 6-8). stu. ed. 9.50 *(978-0-930265-44-1(0),* 120010) Faith Alive Christian Resources.

Morgan, Julian. Constantine: Ruler of Christian Rome. 2009. (Ancient Leaders Ser.). 112p. (gr. 5-8). 66.50 *(978-1-61511-422-1(X),* Rosen Reference) Rosen Publishing Group, Inc., The.

Nardo, Don. The Birth of Christianity. 2011. (World Religions & Beliefs Ser.). 112p. (gr. 7-12). 28.95 *(978-1-59935-145-2(5))* Reynolds, Morgan Inc.

Nichols, Stephen J. & Bustard, Ned. The Church History ABCs: Augustine & 25 Other Heroes of the Faith. 2010. 32p. (J). 16.99 *(978-1-4335-1472-2(9))* Crossway.

Notgrass, Ray. Exploring World History. 2014. (Illus.). *(978-1-60999-061-9(7))* Notgrass Co.

Phillips, Shannon & Garland, Nick. Celebrating a Century: The Birth & Growth of First Baptist Church Broken Arrow. Schilling, Sarah Phillips, ed. 2005. per. 24.95 *(978-0-9764103-3-1(8))* Daylight Pubs.

Ross, Melanie H. & Guymon-King. Primary Partners. 2004. cd-rom 11.95 *(978-1-57734-691-3(2))* Covenant Communications, Inc.

Rostrom, Laura Lee. My Church History Storybook. 2003. (Illus.). 288p. (J). 19.95 *(978-1-55517-698-3(4),* 76984) Cedar Fort, Inc./CFI Distribution.

Schomp, Virginia. The Church. 2010. (Life in Victorian England Ser.). 80p. (gr. 6). 34.21 *(978-1-60870-031-8(3))* Marshall Cavendish GBR. Dist: Marshall Cavendish Corp.

Tracy, Kathleen. The Life & Times of Constantine. 2005. (Biography from Ancient Civilizations Ser.). (Illus.). 48p. (J). (gr. 4-8). lib. bdg. 29.95 *(978-1-58415-343-6(1))* Mitchell Lane Pubs., Inc.

Van Der Veer, Andrew. Bible Lessons for Juniors, Book 4: The Early Church. 2007. 88p. (J). 6.00 *(978-1-60178-015-7(X))* Reformation Heritage Bks.

Welch, Laura & Hodge, Bodie, eds. Big Book of History: A 15' Fold-Out Time-line from Creation to Modern Computers. 2011. (J). lib. bdg. 21.99 *(978-0-89051-623-2(5))* Master Bks.

Withrow, Brandon & Withrow, Mindy. Monks & Mystics: Chronicles of the Medieval Church, Vol. 2. 2005. (History Lives Ser.). (ENG., Illus.). 224p. (J). (gr. 3-7). per. 9.99 *(978-1-84550-083-2(0),* 9781845500832) Christian Focus Pubns. GBR. Dist: Bookmasters Distribution.

—Peril & Peace: Chronicles of the Ancient Church, Vol. 1. 2014. (History Lives Ser.). (ENG., Illus.). 240p. (J). (gr. 3-7). per. 9.99 *(978-1-84550-082-5(2),* 9781845500825) Christian Focus Pubns. GBR. Dist: Bookmasters Distribution.

Yonge, Charlotte M. The Chosen People: A Compendium of Sacred & Church History for School-Children. 2007. (ENG.). 202p. pap. 20.99 *(978-1-4264-2274-4(1));* 214p. pap. 22.99 *(978-1-4264-2309-3(8))* Creative Media Partners, LLC.

—The Chosen People A Compendium of Sacred & Church History for School Children. 2004. reprint ed. pap. 1.99 *(978-1-4192-5664-6(5));* pap. 22.95 *(978-1-4191-5664-9(0))* Kessinger Publishing, LLC.

CHURCH HISTORY—FICTION

Lee, Kathy. Rome in Flames. 2005. 144p. pap. *(978-1-84427-089-7(0))* Scripture Union.

Leslie, Emma. From Bondage to Freedom: A Tale of the Times of Mohammed. Symmons, Sheeres, illus. 2007. 308p. 24.95 *(978-1-934671-10-8(X))* Salem Ridge Press LLC.

—Out of the Mouth of the Lion: Or, the Church in the Catacombs. Felter and Gunston & Butterworth and Heath, illus. 2007. 296p. 24.95 *(978-1-934671-04-7(5));* per. 14.95 *(978-1-934671-05-4(3))* Salem Ridge Press LLC.

—Sowing Beside All Waters: A Tale of the World in the Church. Morgin, W. J. & W., E., illus. 2007. 300p. 24.95 *(978-1-934671-06-1(1));* per. 14.95 *(978-1-934671-07-8(X))* Salem Ridge Press LLC.

Millsap, Ella. A Portrait of a Church in Stone: The Keeper of the Honeybees. 2013. 62p. (J). pap. 12.00 *(978-0-9891960-3-1(8))* Professional Publishing Hse. LLC.

Polland, Madeleine. City of the Golden House. 2006. (J). per. 14.95 *(978-0-9766386-4-3(9))* Hillside Education.

Pope, Amy. Big Church. Meier, Paul, illus. 2004. (J). bds. 9.99 *(978-1-4183-0008-1(X))* Christ Inspired, Inc.

Spinelli, Eileen. When Christmas Came. Parmenter, Wayne, illus. 2006. (ENG.). 32p. (J). (gr. k-3). bds. 16.95 *(978-0-8249-5507-6(2),* Ideal Pubns.) Worthy Publishing.

CHURCH HISTORY—REFORMATION

see Reformation

CHURCH MUSIC

see also Carols; Hymns

Advance Cal-Tech Inc. Staff. Let's Praise & Play: Children's Christian Mini-Piano Book. Kung, Edward, ed. McKig, Susan, illus. 36p. (J). (gr. -1-6). *(978-0-943759-00-5(5))* Advance Cal Tech, Inc.

Andrews, Pam. The First Action Heroes: A Musical for Children about the Power of God. 2005. (ENG., Illus.). 120p. pap. 7.99 *(978-0-8341-7471-9(5),* MB-949) Lillenas Publishing Co.

—Journey of Praise: An Easy-to-Sing, Easy-to-Stage Musical for Children. 2005. (ENG., Illus.). 40p. pap. 5.99 *(978-0-8341-7457-3(X),* MB-955) Lillenas Publishing Co.

—We Can Praise! An Easy-to-Sing, Easy-to-Stage Mini-Musical for Children. 2007. (ENG.). 64p. pap. 5.99 *(978-0-8341-7594-5(0),* 0834175940) Lillenas Publishing Co.

Andrews, Pam, et al. The Easter Tree: An Easy-to-Sing, Easy-to-Stage Children's Easter Musical. 2006. (ENG.). 64p. pap. 5.99 *(978-0-8341-7538-9(X),* 083417538X) Lillenas Publishing Co.

Barden, Christine H., et al. Music for Little Mozarts — Little Mozarts Go to Church, Bk 1-2: 10 Favorite Hymns, Spirituals & Sunday School Songs. 2008. (Music for Little Mozarts Ser.: Bk 1-2). (ENG.). 24p. (J). pap. 6.00 *(978-0-7390-5689-9(1))* Alfred Publishing Co., Inc.

—Music for Little Mozarts — Little Mozarts Go to Church, Bk 3-4: 10 Favorite Hymns, Spirituals & Sunday School Songs. 2008. (Music for Little Mozarts Ser.: Bk 3-4). (ENG.). 24p. (J). pap. 6.00 *(978-0-7390-5690-5(5))* Alfred Publishing Co., Inc.

Belpulsi, Peter A. & Belpulsi, Nathalie B. As the Saying Goes, Vol. 2. 2005. (Illus.). 145p. (gr. 1-7). *(978-1-882614-21-9(6))* Globe Pubs.

Bible Visuals International Staff, compiled by. A Christian's Belief. 2005. (Illus.). (J). pap. *(978-1-932381-17-7(1),* 6120) Bible Visuals International, Inc.

—Hark! the Herald Angels Sing. 2006. (Illus.). (J). pap. *(978-1-932381-95-5(3),* 6200) Bible Visuals International, Inc.

Clydesdale, David T., contrib. by. King of the Jungle: The God of Creation Is Lord of My Heart. 2007. (Illus.). 116p. pap. 6.95 *(978-5-557-71505-8(3),* Word Music) Word Entertainment.

—The Little Drummer Boy: Behind the Music. 2007. (Illus.). 127p. pap. 6.95 *(978-5-557-71490-7(1),* Word Music) Word Entertainment.

Cunningham, Edie. Trust & Obey: A Visualized Gospel Song. Anthoine, Leila et al, illus. 2005. 20p. (J). pap. *(978-1-932381-20-7(1),* 6480) Bible Visuals International, Inc.

Discovering Music: Bible Story: David, the Music Maker. (Scripture Bites Ser.). (Illus.). (J). 7.99 *(978-0-7847-9008-3(6),* 00705) Standard Publishing.

Forsythe, Gary & Kee, Ed, creators. Crazy Praise, Volume 4: Unison. 2008. 81p. (J). (gr. -1-3). pap. 7.99 *(978-5-557-38267-0(4))* Brentwood-Benson Music Publishing.

Just a Closer Walk. 7.50 *(978-0-8054-5921-0(9))* B&H Publishing Group.

Kishimoto, Yuko, illus. God Will Take Care of You. 2007. (ENG.). 16p. (J). pap. *(978-1-932381-18-4(X),* 6160) Bible Visuals International, Inc.

Miffleton, Jack. Sing a Song of Joy. (J). (gr. k-6). pap. 15.00 *(978-0-937690-87-1(2),* 6111) World Library Pubns.

Mississippi Staff. Best of Mississippi Childrens. 2004. pap. *(978-5-550-05701-8(8))* Nairi.

Music-Children's. 3.50 *(978-0-8054-5876-3(X))* B&H Publishing Group.

Neal, Sharon, ed. Who Is He in Yonder Stall? Jarrett, Sandra, illus. 2008. (ENG.). 24p. (J). pap. *(978-1-932381-21-4(X),* 6500) Bible Visuals International, Inc.

Oden, Annette. Born to Worship: A Contemporary Kids Musical for Every Season: Unison/2-Part Book. 2008. 64p. pap. 8.95 *(978-5-557-38656-2(4))* Point of Grace Entertainment Group.

Playaway, creator. Scripture Memory Songs. 2008. (Playaway Adult Nonfiction Ser.). (J). (gr. -1-3). 59.99 *(978-1-59922-325-4(2))* Findaway World, LLC.

Ross, Mary H. Primary Partners Singing Fun. Guymon-King, Jennette, illus. 2004. *(978-1-59156-793-6(9))* Covenant Communications.

Thomas Nelson Publishing Staff. Dance Praise Expansion Pack Vol 2: Hip-Hop/Rap. 2008. cd-rom 24.95 *(978-0-9754280-3-0(9))* Nelson, Thomas Inc.

Tornquist, Carol. Music in Me - A Piano Method for Young Christian Students: Lesson (Reading Music) Level 5. 2007. (ENG.). 48p. pap. 8.95 *(978-1-4234-1884-9(0),* 1423418840) Leonard, Hal Corp.

Turck, Mary C. Freedom Song: Young Voices & the Struggle for Civil Rights. 2008. (ENG., Illus.). 160p. (J). (gr. 4). pap. 18.95 *(978-1-55652-773-9(X))* Chicago Review Pr., Inc.

Woog, Adam. The History of Gospel Music. 2005. (Music Library). (ENG., Illus.). 112p. (J). (gr. 4-7). lib. bdg. 34.45 *(978-1-59018-735-7(0),* Lucent Bks.) Cengage Gale.

CHURCH OF CHRIST OF LATTER-DAY SAINTS

see Mormons and Mormonism

CHURCH OF CHRIST, SCIENTIST

see Christian Science

CHURCH SETTLEMENTS

see Social Settlements

CHURCHILL, WINSTON, 1874-1965

Barber, Nicola. Churchill & the Battle of Britain: Days of Decision, 1 vol. 2013. (Days of Decision Ser.). (ENG.). 64p. (gr. 7-8). 35.99 *(978-1-4329-7634-7(6));* pap. 10.95 *(978-1-4329-7641-5(9))* Heinemann-Raintree.

Conklin, Wendy. Winston Churchill, 1 vol. 2007. (Primary Source Readers Ser.). (ENG.). 32p. (J). (gr. 4-4). pap. 8.99 *(978-0-7439-0669-2(1))* Shell Educational Publishing.

Daynes, Katie. Winston Churchill. Tomlins, Karen, illus. 2006. (Usborne Famous Lives Gift Bks.). 64p. (J). (gr. 2-5). 8.99 *(978-0-7945-1258-3(5),* Usborne) EDC Publishing.

Hamilton, Janice. Winston Churchill. 2006. (and E Biography Ser.). (Illus.). 112p. (J). (gr. 3-7). lib. bdg. 27.93 *(978-0-8225-3419-8(3),* Twenty-First Century Bks.) Lerner Publishing Group.

Kesselring, Mari. How to Analyze the Works of Winston Churchill, 1 vol. 2013. (Essential Critiques Set 4 Ser.). (ENG.). 112p. (J). (gr. 6-12). lib. bdg. 35.64 *(978-1-61783-649-7(4),* Essential Library) ABDO Publishing Co.

Labrecque, Ellen & dePaola, Tomie. Who Was Winston Churchill? Hoare, Jerry & Harrison, Nancy, illus. 2015. (Who Was? Ser.). (ENG.). 112p. (J). (gr. 3-7). 5.99 *(978-0-448-48300-9(9),* Grosset & Dunlap) Penguin Young Readers Group.

Ridley, Sarah. Winston Churchill: ...And World War II. 2013. (History Makers Ser.). (Illus.). 24p. (J). (gr. 2-4). lib. bdg. 25.65 *(978-1-59771-393-1(7))* Sea-To-Sea Pubns.

Roxburgh, Ellis. Adolf Hitler vs. Winston Churchill: Foes of World War II. 2015. (History's Greatest Rivals Ser.). (ENG.). 48p. (J). (gr. 6-8). lib. bdg. 31.95 *(978-1-4824-2205-4(0))* Stevens, Gareth Publishing LLLP.

Selbert, Kathryn. War Dogs. Selbert, Kathryn, illus. 2016. (ENG., Illus.). 48p. (J). (gr. 2-5). pap. 7.95 *(978-1-58089-415-9(1))* Charlesbridge Publishing, Inc.

Trussell-Cullen, Alan. Winston Churchill. 2009. pap. 13.25 *(978-1-60559-072-1(X))* Hameray Publishing Group, Inc.

Vander Hook, Sue. Winston Churchill: British Prime Minister & Statesman, 1 vol. 2009. (Essential Lives Set 3 Ser.). (ENG.,

Illus.). 112p. (J). (gr. 6-12). lib. bdg. 35.64 *(978-1-60453-523-5(7))* ABDO Publishing Co.

Wood, Douglas. Franklin & Winston: A Christmas That Changed the World. Moser, Barry, illus. 2011. (ENG.). 40p. (J). (gr. 1-4). 16.99 *(978-0-7636-3383-7(6))* Candlewick Pr.

CHURCHYARDS

see Cemeteries

CICERO, MARCUS TULLIUS

Forsyth, Fiona. Cicero: Defender of the Republic. (Ancient Leaders Ser.). 112p. (gr. 5-8). 2009. 66.50 *(978-1-61511-420-7(3))* 2003. (Illus.). (YA). lib. bdg. 34.60 *(978-0-8239-3590-1(6))* Rosen Publishing Group, Inc., The. (Rosen Reference).

Hess, Debra. On Trial in Rome: Cicero Versus Caesr. 2007. (Read on! Special Edition: Level AA Ser.). (Illus.). 23p. pap. 18.51 *(978-1-4190-3517-3(7))* Steck-Vaughn.

Leoni, Cristiana. In Caesar's Rome with Cicero. Cappon, Manuela, illus. 2008. (Come See My City Ser.). 48p. (gr. 4-8). lib. bdg. 28.50 *(978-0-7614-4328-5(2)*, Benchmark Bks.) Marshall Cavendish Corp.

Lowery, Zoe & Forsyth, Fiona. Cicero. 2016. (Leaders of the Ancient World Ser.). 00112p. (J). (gr. 6-6). 37.10 *(978-1-5081-7258-1(7))* Rosen Publishing Group, Inc., The.

Tracy, Kathleen. The Life & Times of Cicero. 2006. (Biography from Ancient Civilizations Ser.). (Illus.). 48p. (J). (gr. 4-8). lib. bdg. 29.95 *(978-1-58415-510-2(8))* Mitchell Lane Pubs., Inc.

CINCINNATI BENGALS (FOOTBALL TEAM)

Angst, Frank. Chad Johnson. 2009. (Superstars of Pro Football Ser.). (Illus.). 64p. (YA). (gr. 5-18). lib. bdg. 22.95 *(978-1-4222-0556-3(8))* Mason Crest.

Burgess, Zack. Meet the Cincinnati Bengals. 2016. (Big Picture Sports Ser.). (ENG., Illus.). 24p. (J). (gr. k-3). lib. bdg. 22.60 *(978-1-59953-724-5(9))* Norwood Hse. Pr.

Frederick, Sara. The History of the Cincinnati Bengals. 2004. (NFL Today Ser.). (Illus.). 32p. (YA). (gr. 5-9). 18.95 *(978-1-58341-292-3(1))* Creative Co., The.

Gilbert, Sara. NFL Today: Cincinnati Bengals. 2013. (NFL Today Ser.). (ENG., Illus.). 48p. (J). (gr. 4-7). pap. 12.00 *(978-0-89812-851-2(X)*, Creative Paperbacks) Creative Co., The.

—The Story of the Cincinnati Bengals. 48p. 2013. (Illus.). (J). 35.65 *(978-1-60818-298-5(3)*, Creative Education) 2009. (YA). (gr. 5-9). 22.95 *(978-1-58341-751-5(6))* Creative Co., The.

Gitlin, Martin. Cincinnati Bengals, 1 vol. 2010. (Inside the NFL Ser.). (ENG.). 48p. (YA). (gr. 3-6). lib. bdg. 32.79 *(978-1-61714-007-5(4))* ABDO Publishing Co.

Glave, Tom. Cincinnati Bengals. 2015. (Insider's Guide to Pro Football Ser.). (ENG.). 32p. (J). (gr. k-3). 28.50 *(978-1-63143-992-6(8)*, 208827) Child's World, Inc., The.

Morey, Allan. The Cincinnati Bengals Story. 2016. (NFL Teams Ser.). (ENG., Illus.). 32p. (J). (gr. 3-7). lib. bdg. 26.95 *(978-1-62617-361-3(3)*, Torque Bks.) Bellwether Media.

Stewart, Mark. The Cincinnati Bengals. rev. ed. 2012. (Team Spirit Ser.). (ENG.). 48p. (J). (gr. 3-6). lib. bdg. 29.27 *(978-1-59953-518-0(1))* Norwood Hse. Pr.

Wyner, Zach. Cincinnati Bengals. 2014. (Inside the NFL Ser.). (ENG., Illus.). 32p. (J). (gr. 4-7). lib. bdg. 28.55 *(978-1-4896-0806-2(0)*, AV2 by Weigl) Weigl Pubs., Inc.

CINCINNATI REDS (BASEBALL TEAM)

Connery-Boyd, Peg. Cincinnati Reds Activity Book. 2016. (Hawk's Nest Activity Bks.: 0). (ENG.). 64p. (J). (gr. k-3). pap. 8.99 *(978-1-4926-3563-5(4))* Sourcebooks, Inc.

Gilbert, Sara. Cincinnati Reds. 2013. (Illus.). 24p. (J). 25.65 *(978-1-60818-263-3(0)*, Creative Education) Creative Co., The.

—World Series Champs: Cincinnati Reds. 2013. (World Series Champions Ser.). (ENG.). 24p. (J). (gr. 1-3). pap. 7.99 *(978-0-89812-814-7(5)*, Creative Paperbacks) Creative Co., The.

Gitlin, Martin. Cincinnati Reds, 1 vol. 2011. (Inside MLB Ser.). (ENG., Illus.). 48p. (YA). (gr. 3-6). lib. bdg. 32.79 *(978-1-61714-040-2(6))* ABDO Publishing Co.

Gitlin, Marty. Cincinnati Reds, 1 vol. 2014. (Inside MLB Ser.). (ENG., Illus.). 48p. (J). (gr. 3-6). lib. bdg. 32.79 *(978-1-62403-466-4(7)*, SportsZone) ABDO Publishing Co.

Goodman, Michael E. The Story of the Cincinnati Reds. 2011. (J). 35.65 *(978-1-60818-037-0(9)*, Creative Education) Creative Co., The.

Stewart, Mark. The Cincinnati Reds. 2012. (Team Spirit Ser.). 48p. (J). (gr. 3-6). lib. bdg. 29.27 *(978-1-59953-478-7(9))* Norwood Hse. Pr.

CINEMA

see Motion Pictures

CINEMATOGRAPHY

Apodaca, Blanca. All in a Day's Work: Animator, 1 vol. 2nd rev. ed. 2013. (TIME for KIDS(r) Nonfiction Readers Ser.). (ENG.). 64p. (J). (gr. 5-5). pap. 10.99 *(978-1-4333-4907-2(8))*; (Illus.). pap. 31.96 *(978-1-4333-7430-2(7))* Teacher Created Materials, Inc.

Bancroft, Tom & Hunter, Nick. Animator: The Coolest Jobs on the Planet, 1 vol. 2014. (Coolest Jobs on the Planet Ser.). (ENG., Illus.). 48p. (gr. 6-6). 32.65 *(978-1-4109-6640-7(2))*; pap. 8.99 *(978-1-4109-6646-9(1))* Heinemann-Raintree.

Bellmont, Laura & Brink, Emily. Animation Lab for Kids: Fun Art Projects for Making Stop-Motion Movies. 2016. (Lab Ser.). (ENG.). 144p. pap. 24.99 *(978-1-63159-118-1(5)*, Quarry Bks.) Quarto Publishing Group USA.

Bradley, Timothy J. FX! Computer-Generated Imagery. 2017. (TIME for KIDS(r) Nonfiction Readers Ser.). (Illus.). 64p. (J). (gr. 7-7). pap. 10.99 *(978-1-4938-3614-7(5))* Teacher Created Materials, Inc.

Buckley, Annie. Making Movies. 2006. (Reading Rocks! Ser.). (ENG., Illus.). 32p. (J). (gr. 2-5). 28.50 *(978-1-59296-746-9(9)*, 200731) Child's World, Inc., The.

—Movies. 2008. (21st Century Skills Innovation Library: Innovation in Entertainment Ser.). (ENG.). 32p. (gr. 4-8). lib. bdg. 28.50 *(978-1-60279-222-7(4)*, 200153) Cherry Lake Publishing.

Careers in Focus: Animation. 2010. (Careers in Focus Ser.). (Illus.). 208p. (J). (gr. 6-12). 32.95 *(978-0-8160-8015-1(1)*, Ferguson Publishing Co.) Facts On File, Inc.

Conley, Robyn. Motion Pictures. 2006. (Inventions That Shaped the World Ser.). (Illus.). 80p. (gr. 5-8). 19.95 *(978-0-7569-6859-5(3))* Perfection Learning Corp.

Connolly, Sean. Movies & Video. 2010. 34.25 *(978-1-59920-346-1(4))* Black Rabbit Bks.

De Angelis, Gina. Motion Pictures: Making Cinema Magic. 2003. (Innovators Ser.: Vol. 11). (Illus.). 144p. (gr. 5-18). lib. bdg. 21.95 *(978-1-881508-78-6(1))* Oliver Pr., Inc.

Disney Book Group Staff, et al. Layout & Background. 2011. (ENG., Illus.). 282p. (gr. -1-17). 50.00 *(978-1-4231-3866-2(X)*, Disney Editions) Disney Pr.

Fingeroth, Danny. Backstage at an Animated Series. 2003. (High Interest Bks.). (ENG., Illus.). 48p. (YA). (gr. 7-12). pap. 6.95 *(978-0-516-24385-6(3)*, Children's Pr.) Scholastic Library Publishing.

Garza, Sarah. Action! Making Movies, 1 vol. 2nd rev. ed. 2013. (Nonfiction Readers Ser.). (ENG., Illus.). 64p. (J). (gr. 5-5). pap. 31.96 *(978-1-4333-7448-7(X))* Teacher Created Materials, Inc.

Gilbert, Sara. Built for Success: the Story of Pixar. 2015. (Built for Success Ser.). (ENG.). 48p. (J). (gr. 5-8). pap. 12.00 *(978-0-89812-983-0(4)*, Creative Paperbacks) Creative Co., The.

Green, Julie. Super Smart Information Strategies: Shooting Video to Make Learning Fun. 2010. (Explorer Library: Information Explorer Ser.). (ENG.). 32p. (gr. 4-8). lib. bdg. 28.50 *(978-1-60279-955-4(5)*, 200635) Cherry Lake Publishing.

Gregory, Josh. Animation. 2014. (ENG., Illus.). 64p. (J). 30.00 *(978-0-531-20613-3(0))* Scholastic Library Publishing.

Horn, Geoffrey M. Movie Stunts & Special Effects. 2006. (Making Movies Ser.). (Illus.). 32p. (gr. 5-8). lib. bdg. 26.00 *(978-0-8368-6840-1(4))* Stevens, Gareth Publishing LLLP.

Labrecque, Ellen. Multimedia Artist & Animator. 2016. (21st Century Skills Library: Cool Vocational Careers Ser.). (ENG.). 32p. (J). (gr. 4-7). 29.93 *(978-1-63471-064-0(9)*, 208335) Cherry Lake Publishing.

Larson, Jeff. FX! Lighting & Sound (Grade 7) 2017. (TIME for KIDS(r) Nonfiction Readers Ser.). (Illus.). 64p. (gr. 7-7). pap. 10.99 ***(978-1-4938-3612-3(9))*** Teacher Created Materials, Inc.

Lenburg, Jeff. William Hanna & Joseph Barbera. 2011. (Legends of Animation Ser.). (Illus.). 168p. (gr. 6-12). 34.95 *(978-1-60413-837-5(8)*, Chelsea Hse.) Facts On File, Inc.

Lenburg, Jeff & Kurtz, Bob. Career Opportunities in Animation. 2011. (Career Opportunities Ser.). 320p. (C). (gr. 9). pap. 18.95 *(978-0-8160-8183-7(2)*, Checkmark Bks.); 2nd rev. ed. 49.50 *(978-0-8160-8182-0(4)*, Ferguson Publishing Co.) Facts On File, Inc.

Levete, Sarah. Maker Projects for Kids Who Love Animation. 2016. (Be a Maker! Ser.). (ENG., Illus.). 32p. (J). (gr. 5-8). *(978-0-7787-2244-1(9))* Crabtree Publishing Co.

Masura, Shauna. Record It! Shooting & Editing Digital Video. 2012. (Explorer Junior Library: Information Explorer Junior Ser.). (ENG.). 24p. (gr. 1-4). 28.50 *(978-1-61080-484-4(8)*, 202094); pap. 12.79 *(978-1-61080-658-9(1)*, 202268) Cherry Lake Publishing.

Mooney, Carla. Stephen Hillenburg SpongeBob SquarePants: SpongeBob SquarePants. 2015. (Illus.). 80p. (YA). lib. bdg. *(978-1-60152-866-7(3))* ReferencePoint Pr., Inc.

Mullins, Matt. Special Effects Technician. 2011. (21st Century Skills Library: Cool Arts Careers Ser.). (ENG.). 32p. (gr. 4-8). lib. bdg. 28.50 *(978-1-61080-134-8(2)*, 201146) Cherry Lake Publishing.

Omoth, Tyler. Busting Boredom with Technology. 2017. (Boredom Busters Ser.). (ENG., Illus.). 32p. (gr. 3-4). lib. bdg. 27.99 *(978-1-5157-4705-5(0))* Capstone Press of Coughlan Cos.

Owen, Ruth. Creating Visual Effects for Movies As a CGI Artist. 2016. (Get to Work with Science & Technology Ser.). (ENG.). 32p. (J). (gr. 2-7). 19.95 *(978-1-910549-89-6(4))* Bearport Publishing Co., Inc.

Parker, Steve. Robots in Fiction & Films. 2010. (Robot World Ser.). 32p. (J). 28.50 *(978-1-60753-073-2(2))* Amicus Publishing.

Parker, Steve & Pipe, Jim. Robots in Fiction & Films. 2011. (On the Edge Ser.). 32p. (YA). (gr. 3-6). lib. bdg. 28.50 *(978-1-59920-515-1(7))* Black Rabbit Bks.

Reid, Emily. Space Claymation. 2016. (Claymation Sensation Ser.). 32p. (gr. 3-3). pap. 11.75 *(978-1-4994-8100-6(4)*, Windmill Bks.) Rosen Publishing Group, Inc., The.

Segall, Miriam. Career Building Through Digital Moviemaking. (Digital Career Building Ser.). 64p. 2009. (gr. 6-6). 58.50 *(978-1-61512-164-9(1))* 2007. (Illus.). (YA). (gr. 7-12). lib. bdg. 29.25 *(978-1-4042-1945-8(5))* Rosen Publishing Group, Inc., The.

Snyder, Gail. Seth Mcfarlane Family Guy: Family Guy. 2015. (Illus.). 80p. (YA). lib. bdg. *(978-1-60152-864-3(7))* ReferencePoint Pr., Inc.

Spence, Kelly. Get into Claymation. 2017. (Get-Into-It Guides). (ENG.). 32p. (J). (gr. 3-6). ***(978-0-7787-3400-0(5))***; (Illus.). pap. ***(978-0-7787-3404-8(8))*** Crabtree Publishing Co.

Tieck, Sarah. Walt Disney, 1 vol. 2010. (First Biographies Set 6 Ser.). (ENG., Illus.). 32p. (J). (gr. 1-4). 27.07 *(978-1-60453-984-4(4))* ABDO Publishing Co.

Wessling, Katherine. Backstage at a Movie Set. 2003. (High Interest Bks.). (ENG., Illus.). 48p. (J). (gr. 7-12). pap. 6.95 *(978-0-516-24387-0(X)*, Children's Pr.) Scholastic Library Publishing.

Woog, Adam. Trey Parker, Matt Stone, & South Park: South Park. 2015. (ENG., Illus.). 80p. (YA). lib. bdg. *(978-1-60152-868-1(X))* ReferencePoint Pr., Inc.

CINEMATOGRAPHY—SPECIAL EFFECTS

Cohn, Jessica. Animator. 2009. (Cool Careers: Cutting Edge Ser.). 32p. (gr. 5-8). (ENG.). pap. 10.50 *(978-1-4339-2152-0(9))*; lib. bdg. 26.00 *(978-1-4339-1953-4(2))* Stevens, Gareth Publishing LLLP.

Hammelef, Danielle S. Awesome Special Effects. 2015. (Awesome Special Effects Ser.). (ENG.). 32p. (gr. 1-2). lib. bdg. 106.60 *(978-1-4914-2552-7(0)*, Blazers) Capstone Press of Coughlan Cos.

—Explosive Scenes: Fireballs, Furious Storms, & More Live Special Effects. 2015. (Awesome Special Effects Ser.). (ENG.). 32p. (gr. 1-2). lib. bdg. 26.65 *(978-1-4914-2003-4(0))* Capstone Press of Coughlan Cos.

—Eye-Popping CGI: Computer-Generated Special Effects. 2015. (Awesome Special Effects Ser.). (ENG.). 32p. (gr. 1-2). lib. bdg. 26.65 *(978-1-4914-2001-0(4))* Capstone Press of Coughlan Cos.

Miller, Ron. Special Effects: An Introduction to Movie Magic. Miller, Ron, illus. 2006. (ENG., Illus.). 128p. (gr. 7-12). 26.60 *(978-0-7613-2918-3(8))* Lerner Publishing Group.

Ridley, Frances J. Special Effects. 2009. (ENG., Illus.). 32p. (J). (gr. 6-8). lib. bdg. *(978-0-7787-3824-4(8))* Crabtree Publishing Co.

CIPHERS

see also Cryptography; Writing

Anderson, Rane. Cryptography. 2017. (J). pap. 9.97 ***(978-1-4938-3624-6(2))*** Teacher Created Materials, Inc.

Blake, Spencer. Spyology. Steer, Dugald A., ed. Blake, Spencer et al, illus. 2008. (Ologies Ser.: 7). (ENG.). 32p. (J). (gr. 3-7). 25.99 *(978-0-7636-4048-4(4))* Candlewick Pr.

Brian, Sarah Jane. Brainiac's Secret Agent: Fun Activities for Spies of All Ages. 2005. (Activity Journal Ser.). 128p. act. bk. ed. 12.99 *(978-0-88088-446-4(0))* Peter Pauper Pr. Inc.

Burrows, Terry. Codes, Ciphers, & Cartography: Math Goes to War. 2017. (STEM on the Battlefield Ser.). (ENG., Illus.). 48p. (J). (gr. 4-6). 31.99 ***(978-1-5124-3927-4(4)***, Lerner Pubns.) Lerner Publishing Group.

Byers, Ann. Uncracked Codes & Cyphers. 2016. (Cryptography: Code Making & Code Breaking Ser.). 00064p. (J). (gr. 8-8). 34.45 *(978-1-5081-7310-6(9))* Rosen Publishing Group, Inc., The.

Capstone Press. Making & Breaking Codes, 1 vol. 2010. (Making & Breaking Codes Ser.). (ENG.). 32p. lib. bdg. 79.95 *(978-1-4296-5943-7(2)*, Edge Bks.) Capstone Press of Coughlan Cos.

Cleary, Brian P. I'm & Won't, They're & Don't: What's a Contraction? Gable, Brian, illus. (Words Are CATegorical (r) Ser.). (ENG.). 32p. (gr. 2-5). 2012. pap. 6.95 *(978-0-7613-8504-2(5)*, Millbrook Pr.) 2010. (J). lib. bdg. 16.95 *(978-0-8225-9155-9(3))* Lerner Publishing Group.

Colson, Mary. Destroy after Reading: The World of Secret Codes. 2010. (Culture in Action Ser.). (ENG.). 32p. (gr. 3-6). 30.65 *(978-1-4109-3927-2(8)*, NA-r) Heinemann-Raintree.

Freedman, Jeri. Famous Cryptographers. 2016. (Cryptography: Code Making & Code Breaking Ser.). 00064p. (J). (gr. 8-8). 34.45 *(978-1-5081-7312-0(5))* Rosen Publishing Group, Inc., The.

Gregory, Jillian. Breaking Secret Codes, 1 vol. 2010. (Making & Breaking Codes Ser.). (ENG.). 32p. (gr. 3-4). lib. bdg. 27.99 *(978-1-4296-4568-3(7)*, Edge Bks.) Capstone Press of Coughlan Cos.

—Making Secret Codes, 1 vol. 2010. (Making & Breaking Codes Ser.). (ENG.). 32p. (gr. 3-4). lib. bdg. 27.99 *(978-1-4296-4567-6(9)*, Edge Bks.) Capstone Press of Coughlan Cos.

Groves. Knots & Knocks, Bk. 16. Date not set. (Illus.). 32p. (J). pap. 129.15 *(978-0-582-18059-8(7))* Addison-Wesley Longman, Ltd. GBR. Dist: Trans-Atlantic Pubns., Inc.

Hall, Kirsten. Top Secret. Simard, Remy, illus. 2003. 64p. (J). *(978-0-439-50133-0(4))* Scholastic, Inc.

La Bella, Laura. Ciphers, Codes, Algorithms, & Keys. 2016. (Cryptography: Code Making & Code Breaking Ser.). 00064p. (J). (gr. 8-8). 34.45 *(978-1-5081-7306-9(0))* Rosen Publishing Group, Inc., The.

Levy, Janey. Breaking the Code with Cryptography: Analyzing Patterns. (Math for the Real World Ser.). (Illus.). 32p. 2009. (ENG.). (gr. 6-7). pap. 10.00 *(978-1-4042-6089-4(7))* 2007. (YA). (gr. 5-9). lib. bdg. 25.25 *(978-1-4042-3368-3(7))* Rosen Publishing Group, Inc., The.

Making & Breaking Codes, 1 vol. 2010. (Making & Breaking Codes Ser.). (ENG.). 32p. (gr. 3-4). lib. bdg. 83.97 *(978-1-4296-4570-6(9)*, Edge Bks.) Capstone Press of Coughlan Cos.

McFadzean, Lesley. Creating & Cracking Codes. 2013. (Discovery Education: Discoveries & Inventions Ser.). 32p. (J). (gr. 3-6). pap. 10.00 *(978-1-4777-1500-0(2))*; pap. 60.00 *(978-1-4777-1501-7(0))*; lib. bdg. 25.25 *(978-1-4777-1329-7(8))* Rosen Publishing Group, Inc., The. (PowerKids Pr.).

Menotti, Andrea. How to Tackle Puzzles, Unravel Riddles, Crack Codes, & Other Ways to Bend Your Brain. 2004. (Illus.). 80p. (J). *(978-0-439-57905-6(8))* Scholastic, Inc.

Meyer, Susan. The History of Cryptography. 2016. (Cryptography: Code Making & Code Breaking Ser.). 00064p. (J). (gr. 8-8). 34.45 *(978-1-5081-7304-5(4))* Rosen Publishing Group, Inc., The.

Mitchell, Susan K. Spy Codes & Ciphers. 2011. (Secret World of Spies Ser.). (Illus.). 48p. (J). (gr. 2-5). lib. bdg. 25.27 *(978-0-7660-3709-0(6))*; (gr. 4-18). pap. 8.95 *(978-1-59845-353-9(X))* Enslow Pubs., Inc.

O'Hare, J. Dragonball Z: Book of Heroes (and Villains) 2005. (Illus.). 48p. *(978-0-439-80172-0(9))* Scholastic, Inc.

Over 50 Secret Codes. 2017. (Activity Puzzle Bks.). (ENG.). (J). pap. 5.99 ***(978-0-7945-3967-2(X)***, Usborne) EDC Publishing.

Peirce, Lincoln. Big Nate Boredom Buster: Super Scribbles, Cool Comix, & Lots of Laughs. Peirce, Lincoln, illus. 2011. (Big Nate Activity Book Ser.: 1). (ENG., Illus.). 224p. (J). (gr. 3-7). 10.99 *(978-0-06-206094-5(5))* HarperCollins Pubs.

Schwartz, Heather E. Code-Breaker & Mathematician Alan Turing. 2017. (J). ***(978-1-5124-9980-3(3))*** Lerner Publishing Group.

CIPHERS—FICTION

see Code and Cipher Stories

CIRCULATION OF THE BLOOD

see Blood—Circulation

CIRCUMNAVIGATION

see Voyages around the World

CIRCUS

see also Animals—Training

Al Circo, Al Circo! 2003. 63.50 *(978-0-8136-8085-9(9))*; suppl. ed. 8.95 *(978-0-8136-8082-8(4))* Modern Curriculum Pr.

Alcott, Louisa May. Under the Lilacs. l.t. ed. 2005. 444p. pap. *(978-1-84637-059-5(0))* Echo Library.

Anorak Press Staff & Olmedillas, Cathy, compiled by. Anorak: The Happy Mag For Kids. 2012. (ENG., Illus.). 64p. (J). pap. 9.99 *(978-1-4236-3317-4(2)*, Anorak Pr.) Gibbs Smith, Publisher.

Bontinck, Helga. At the Circus. 2006. (Simple Steps to Drawing Ser.). (Illus.). 24p. (gr. k-3). lib. bdg. 23.00 *(978-0-8368-6312-3(7)*, Gareth Stevens Learning Library) Stevens, Gareth Publishing LLLP.

Centore, Michael. Entertainment Industry, Vol. 10. 2016. (Stem in Current Events Ser.). (Illus.). 64p. (J). (gr. 7). 23.95 *(978-1-4222-3590-4(4))* Mason Crest.

Chambers, Mary & Meinking, Mary. Who Walks the Tight Rope? Working at a Circus. 2010. (Wild Work Ser.). (ENG.). 32p. (gr. 1-2). 29.99 *(978-1-4109-3852-7(2)*, Read Me!) Heinemann-Raintree.

The Circus: Individual Title Six-Packs. (Literatura 2000 Ser.). (gr. -1-1). 28.00 *(978-0-7635-0027-6(5))* Rigby Education.

Circus: Level A. 8p. 24.95 *(978-0-7802-9105-8(0))* Wright Group/McGraw-Hill.

Color All About: The Circus: A Giant Coloring Book about Going to the Circus. 2004. (Illus.). (J). (SPA & ENG.). *(978-0-9763307-9-0(2))*; *(978-0-9763307-1-4(7))* Food Marketing Consultants, Inc.

Delafosse, Claude & Krawczyk, Sabine. Let's Look at the Circus. Krawczyk, Sabine, illus. 2012. (ENG., Illus.). 38p. (J). (gr. k-3). pap. 11.99 *(978-1-85103-367-6(X))* Moonlight Publishing, Ltd. GBR. Dist: Independent Pubs. Group.

Dover Staff. Circus Surprise: Silly Sticker Story. 2004. (Dover Little Activity Bks.). (ENG.). 4p. (J). (gr. 3-5). pap. 1.50 *(978-0-486-43951-8(8))* Dover Pubns., Inc.

Elya, Susan Middleton. Say Hola to Spanish at the Circus. Lopez, Loretta, illus. 2013. (ENG.). 32p. (J). (gr. -1-5). pap. 8.95 *(978-1-58430-042-7(6))* Lee & Low Bks., Inc.

Encyclopaedia Britannica, Inc. Staff, compiled by. Discover English with Ben & Bella: Series 3: in the Circus. 2010. 180.00 *(978-1-61535-350-7(X))* Encyclopaedia Britannica, Inc.

Fleming, Candace. The Great & Only Barnum: The Tremendous, Stupendous Life of Showman P. T. Barnum. Fenwick, Ray, illus. 2009. (ENG.). 160p. (J). (gr. 3-7). 19.99 *(978-0-375-84197-2(0)*, Schwartz & Wade Bks.) Random Hse. Children's Bks.

Giulieri, Anne. Circus Tricks, 1 vol. Meldrum, Ned, photos by. 2012. (Engage Literacy Green Ser.). (ENG., Illus.). 32p. (gr. k-2). pap. 5.99 *(978-1-4296-9006-5(2)*, Engage Literacy) Capstone Press of Coughlan Cos.

Gordon, Carol. Super Smart Information Strategies: Make the Grade. 2010. (Explorer Library: Information Explorer Ser.). (ENG.). 32p. (gr. 4-8). pap. 14.21 *(978-1-61080-259-8(4)*, 200907); lib. bdg. 28.50 *(978-1-60279-642-3(4)*, 200345) Cherry Lake Publishing.

Granfield, Linda. Circus. (Illus.). (J). 19.95 *(978-0-88899-292-5(0))* Groundwood Bks. CAN. Dist: Publishers Group West (PGW).

Greenwall, Jessica. First Sticker Book Circus. 2013. (First Sticker Bks). 16p. (J). pap. 6.99 *(978-0-7945-3342-7(6)*, Usborne) EDC Publishing.

Hunter, Nick. Silly Circus Tricks, 1 vol. 2013. (Try This at Home! Ser.). (ENG., Illus.). 32p. (gr. 1-2). pap. 8.29 *(978-1-4109-5010-9(7))*; lib. bdg. 29.99 *(978-1-4109-5003-1(4))* Heinemann-Raintree. (Read Me!).

Klepeis, Alicia Z. Hot Coal Walking, Hooping, & Other Mystifying Circus Science. 2017. (Circus Science Ser.). (ENG.). 32p. (gr. 3-4). lib. bdg. 27.99 ***(978-1-5157-7281-1(0)***, Edge Bks.) Capstone Press of Coughlan Cos.

Levinson, Cynthia. Watch Out for Flying Kids!, 1 vol. 2015. (ENG., Illus.). 216p. (J). (gr. 5-9). 22.95 *(978-1-56145-821-9(X))* Peachtree Pubs.

Levy, Barbara Soloff. How to Draw Circus Pictures. 2007. (Dover How to Draw Ser.). (ENG., Illus.). 32p. (J). (gr. -1-5). pap. 2.95 *(978-0-486-45647-8(1))* Dover Pubns., Inc.

Lobel, Anita. Animal Antics: A to Z. Lobel, Anita, illus. 2005. (Illus.). 32p. (J). lib. bdg. 16.89 *(978-0-06-051815-8(4))* HarperCollins Pubs.

Lusted, Marcia Amidon. Contortion, German Wheels, & Other Mind-Bending Circus Science. 2017. (Circus Science Ser.). (ENG.). 32p. (gr. 3-4). lib. bdg. 27.99 ***(978-1-5157-7282-8(9)***, Edge Bks.) Capstone Press of Coughlan Cos.

—Trapeze, Perch Poles, & Other High-Flying Circus Science. 2017. (Circus Science Ser.). (ENG.). 32p. (gr. 3-4). lib. bdg. 27.99 ***(978-1-5157-7284-2(5)***, Edge Bks.) Capstone Press of Coughlan Cos.

Mara, Wil. Fire-Breathing, Sword-Swallowing, & Other Death-Defying Circus Science. 2017. (Circus Science Ser.). (ENG.). 32p. (gr. 3-4). lib. bdg. 27.99 ***(978-1-5157-7283-5(7)***, Edge Bks.) Capstone Press of Coughlan Cos.

Nobleman, Marc Tyler. Contortionists & Cannons: An Acrobatic Look at the Circus. 2010. (Culture in Action Ser.). (ENG.). 32p. (gr. 3-6). 30.65 *(978-1-4109-3919-7(7)*, NA-r) Heinemann-Raintree.

Nunn, Daniel. Eddie & Ellie's Opposites at the Circus, 1 vol. 2013. (Eddie & Ellie's Opposites Ser.). (ENG.). 24p. (gr. -1-k). 22.65 *(978-1-4109-5341-4(6))*; pap. 7.95 *(978-1-4109-5346-9(7))* Heinemann-Raintree. (NA-r).

Paulding, Barbara. Circus Scratch & Sketch: An Art Activity Book. Zschock, Martha, illus. 2009. (Scratch & Sketch Ser.). 64p. (J). (gr. -1). spiral bd. 14.99 *(978-1-59359-832-7(7))* Peter Pauper Pr. Inc.

Regan, Lisa. Circus Performer. 2012. (Stage School Ser.). (ENG., Illus.). 32p. (J). (gr. 3-6). 25.25 *(978-1-4488-8093-5(9))*; pap. 10.00 *(978-1-4488-8152-9(8))* Windmill Bks.

Royston, Angela. Diary of a Circus Performer, 1 vol. 2013. (Diary of A... Ser.). (ENG.). 32p. (gr. 1-3). 27.32 *(978-1-4329-7580-7(3))*; pap. 8.95 *(978-1-4329-7587-6(0))* Heinemann-Raintree. (Heinemann First Library).

Sévigny, Eric, illus. Caillou, Circus Fun - Beginner Reader. 2016. (Read with Caillou Ser.). (ENG.). 32p. (J). (gr. -1-k). 3.99 *(978-2-89718-343-1(8))* Caillouet, Gerry.

Stills, Caroline. Mice Mischief: Math Facts in Action. Rossell, Judith, illus. 2014. (ENG.). 24p. (J). (gr. -1-1). 16.95 *(978-0-8234-2947-9(4))* Holiday Hse., Inc.

Turnbull, Stephanie. A Circus Star. 2016. (How to Be... Ser.). 24p. (gr. 2-6). 28.50 *(978-1-62588-367-4(6)*, Smart Apple Media) Black Rabbit Bks.

Urrea, Lourdes. El Circo. rev. ed. 2006. (Ediciones Castillo Castillo Del Terror Ser.).Tr. of Circus. (SPA & ENG.). 132p. (J). (gr. 6-9). pap. 6.95 *(978-970-20-0330-4(X))* Castillo, Ediciones, S. A. de C. V. MEX. Dist: Macmillan.

van Genechten, Guido. Circus 123. 2013. (ENG.). 32p. (J). (gr. -1-k). 13.95 *(978-1-60537-162-7(9))* Cobblestone Publishing Co.

Yoyo Books Staff. At the Circus: Learning Words Series. 2004. 12p. bds. *(978-90-5843-606-1(3))* YoYo Bks.

3D Circus Puzzle Book. 12p. (J). *(978-2-89393-867-7(1))* Phidal Publishing, Inc./Editions Phidal, Inc.

CIRCUS—FICTION

Adler, David A. Young Cam Jansen & the Circus Mystery. Natti, Susanna, illus. 2013. (Young Cam Jansen Ser.: 17). (ENG.). 32p. (J). (gr. 1-3). pap. 3.99 *(978-0-448-46614-9(7)*, Penguin Young Readers) Penguin Young Readers Group.

Alborozo. The Acrobat. 2013. (Child's Play Library). (ENG., Illus.). 32p. (J). *(978-1-84643-634-5(6))* Child's Play International Ltd.

Alexander, Heather. Be a Star! Le Feyer, Diane, illus. 2015. (Amazing Stardust Friends Ser.: 2). (ENG.). 96p. (J). (gr. 1-3). pap. 4.99 *(978-0-545-75754-6(1))* Scholastic, Inc.

—Step into the Spotlight! Le Feyer, Diane, illus. 2015. (Amazing Stardust Friends Ser.: 1). (ENG.). 96p. (J). (gr. 1-3). pap. 4.99 *(978-0-545-75752-2(5))* Scholastic, Inc.

Alger, Horatio. Young Acrobat. 2007. 19.95 *(978-1-4344-8845-9(4))*; pap. 9.95 *(978-1-4344-8844-2(6))* Wildside Pr., LLC.

Almond, David. The Boy Who Swam with Piranhas. Jeffers, Oliver, illus. 2015. (ENG.). 256p. (J). (gr. 4-7). pap. 7.99 *(978-0-7636-7680-3(2))* Candlewick Pr.

Awdry, W. Animals Everywhere! Courtney, Richard, illus. 2011. (Step into Reading Ser.). (ENG.). 32p. (J). (gr. -1-1). pap. 3.99 *(978-0-375-86812-2(7)*, Random Hse. Bks. for Young Readers) Random Hse. Children's Bks.

Barker, Mary Ann. A Circus Day Adventure for Emma & Jake. 2012. 28p. pap. 18.65 *(978-1-4771-2849-7(2))* Xlibris Corp.

Barnum, P. T. Dick Broadhead: A Story of Perilous Adve. 2006. pap. 30.95 *(978-1-4286-1959-3(3))* Kessinger Publishing, LLC.

Barnum, Vance. Joe Strong, the Boy Fire-Eater. 2006. pap. *(978-1-4065-0922-9(1))* Dodo Pr.

—Joe Strong the Boy Fire-Eater. 2007. 180p. 25.96 *(978-1-4218-3912-7(1)*, 1st World Library - Literary Society) 1st World Publishing, Inc.

Barton, Byron. My Bike. Barton, Byron, illus. 2015. (ENG., Illus.). 40p. (J). (gr. -1-3). 16.99 *(978-0-06-233699-6(1)*, Collins Design) HarperCollins Pubs.

—My Bike Board Book. Barton, Byron, illus. 2016. (Illus.). 40p. (J). (gr. -1-3). bds. 7.99 *(978-0-06-233701-6(7)*, Greenwillow Bks.) HarperCollins Pubs.

—My Bike Lap Book. Barton, Byron, illus. 2016. (Illus.). 40p. (J). (gr. -1-3). pap. 12.99 *(978-0-06-233702-3(5)*, Greenwillow Bks.) HarperCollins Pubs.

Beasley, Cassie. Circus Mirandus. 2016. (SPA.). 25.99 *(978-84-246-5686-7(5))* La Galera, S.A. Editorial ESP. Dist: Lectorum Pubns., Inc.

—Circus Mirandus. (ENG., Illus.). 304p. (J). (gr. 4-7). 2016. pap. 8.99 *(978-0-14-751554-4(8)*, Puffin Books) 2015. 17.99 *(978-0-525-42843-5(7)*, Dial Bks) Penguin Young Readers Group.

—Circus Mirandus. 2016. (ENG.). 304p. (J). (gr. 3-7). 19.65 *(978-0-606-39311-9(0))* Turtleback Bks.

Bentley, Sue. Circus Surprise #7. Swan, Angela, illus. 2014. (Magic Ponies Ser.: 7). (ENG.). 128p. (J). (gr. 1-3). 4.99 *(978-0-448-46734-4(8)*, Grosset & Dunlap) Penguin Young Readers Group.

—A Circus Wish #6, 6 vols. Farley, Andrew & Swan, Angela, illus. 2009. (Magic Kitten Ser.: 6). (ENG.). 128p. (J). (gr. 1-3). pap. 5.99 *(978-0-448-45062-9(3)*, Grosset & Dunlap) Penguin Young Readers Group.

Berkeley, Jon. The Palace of Laughter. Dorman, Brandon, illus. (Wednesday Tales Ser.: No. 1). (J). (gr. 3-7). 2007. (ENG.). 464p. pap. 8.99 *(978-0-06-075509-6(1))* 2006. 427p. 16.99 *(978-0-06-075507-2(5)*, Julie Andrews Collection) HarperCollins Pubs.

—The Tiger's Egg. Dorman, Brandon, illus. (Wednesday Tales Ser.: No. 2). (J). 2009. (ENG.). 432p. pap. 7.99 *(978-0-06-075512-6(1)*, Harper Trophy) 2007. 416p. (gr. 3-7). 16.99 *(978-0-06-075510-2(5)*, Julie Andrews Collection) HarperCollins Pubs.

Blackmon, Rodney Allan. A Kitten Named Buddy, Buddy's Circus. 2013. 20p. pap. 24.95 *(978-1-62709-674-4(4))* America Star Bks.

Bloncourt, Nelson & Botero, Fernando. Botero: Paintings & Works on Paper. Polyansky, Nikita, illus. 2013. (ENG.). 252p. 125.00 *(978-0-9881745-1-1(0))* Glitterati, Inc.

Bloomfield, Kevin. Mr. Biggs at the Circus. 2012. (ENG.). 32p. 16.95 *(978-1-936299-99-7(2)*, Raven Tree Pr.,Csi) Continental Sales, Inc.

—Mr. Biggs at the Circus / el Sr. Grande en el Circo. 2012. (ENG.). 32p. 16.95 *(978-1-936299-98-0(4)*, Raven Tree Pr.,Csi) Continental Sales, Inc.

Blythe, Enid. Three Boys & a Circus. (Illus.). 144p. (J). (gr. k-6). pap. 5.95 *(978-0-09-987870-4(4))* Random Hse. GBR. Dist: Trafalgar Square Publishing.

Blyton, Enid. Enid Blyton Circus Stories. (Illus.). (J). 11.95 *(978-0-09-914131-0(0))* Random Hse. GBR. Dist: Trafalgar Square Publishing.

Bond, Michael. Paddington at the Circus. Alley, R. W., illus. 2016. (Paddington Ser.). 32p. (J). (gr. -1-3). 17.99 *(978-0-06-231843-5(8))* HarperCollins Pubs.

Bowman, Patty. The Amazing Hamweenie Escapes! Bowman, Patty, illus. 2015. (Amazing Hamweenie Ser.: 2). (ENG., Illus.). 32p. (J). (gr. k-3). 16.99 *(978-0-399-25689-9(X)*, Philomel Bks.) Penguin Young Readers Group.

Bowser, Kimberly M. The Circus Dogs. 2012. 20p. pap. 24.95 *(978-1-4626-6524-2(1))* America Star Bks.

Bridwell, Norman. Clifford at the Circus. 2011. (Be Big! Work Together Ser.). (ENG., Illus.). (gr. -1-3). 14.00 *(978-0-60686-965-9(5))* Perfection Learning Corp.

—Clifford at the Circus. (Clifford, the Big Red Dog Ser.). (Illus.). (J). (gr. k-2). 6.95 *(978-0-590-68639-6(9))* Scholastic, Inc.

—Clifford at the Circus. Bridwell, Norman, illus. 2010. (Clifford 8x8 Ser.). (ENG., Illus.). 32p. (J). (gr. -1-3). pap. 3.99 *(978-0-545-21584-8(6)*, Cartwheel Bks.) Scholastic, Inc.

Bridwell, Norman & Scholastic, Inc. Staff. Clifford's Bedtime Story Box. Bridwell, Norman, illus. 2013. (ENG., Illus.). (J). (gr. -1-k). pap. 10.99 *(978-0-545-61521-1(6))* Scholastic, Inc.

Brooks, Chelsey. Yokeville Yokinton. 2008. 42p. pap. 24.95 *(978-1-60703-823-8(4))* America Star Bks.

Brooks, Walter R. Freddy & the Baseball Team from Mars. Wiese, Kurt, illus. 2011. (ENG.). 256p. 10.99 *(978-1-59020-696-6(7)*, 902696) Overlook Pr., The.

—Freddy the Pied Piper. Wiese, Kurt, illus. 2014. (ENG.). 272p. (gr. 4-13). pap. 10.99 *(978-1-4683-0915-7(3)*, 460915) Overlook Pr., The.

—Freddy the Pilot. Wiese, Kurt, tr. 2012. (ENG., Illus.). 256p. (gr. 4-13). pap. 10.99 *(978-1-59020-867-0(6)*, 902867) Overlook Pr., The.

Brown, Elizabeth R. The Wineberry Diner. 2011. 44p. pap. 24.95 *(978-1-4560-7936-9(0))* America Star Bks.

Bullock, Kathleen. The Clown-Around Kids. Bullock, Kathleen, illus. 2012. (ENG., Illus.). (J). pap. 10.95 *(978-1-61633-223-5(9))* Guardian Angel Publishing, Inc.

Candlewick Press. Peppa Pig & the Backyard Circus. 2017. (Peppa Pig Ser.). (ENG.). 32p. (J). (gr. -1-2). 12.99 *(978-0-7636-9437-1(1)*, Candlewick Entertainment) Candlewick Pr.

Carlson, Melody. The Day the Circus Came to Town. Butterfield, Ned, illus. 2004. 31p. (gr. -1-3). 14.99 *(978-1-58134-158-4(X))* Crossway.

Carr, Fran. Wilbur Runs Away. 2004. (Illus.). 80p. pap. *(978-1-84401-304-3(9))* Athena Pr.

Carretero, Mónica. FLEA CIRCUS. 2011. (Mini-Animalist Ser.). (ENG., Illus.). 32p. (J). (gr. k-2). *(978-84-938240-0-6(3))* D P & G Military Pubs.

Chadwick, Jennie. The Peach Tree Kids: Circus Fleas. 2012. 96p. pap. 9.99 *(978-1-61897-455-6(6)*, Strategic Bk. Publishing) Strategic Book Publishing & Rights Agency (SBPRA).

Chaud, Benjamin. The Bear's Surprise. 2015. (ENG., Illus.). 32p. (J). (gr. -1-k). 17.99 *(978-1-4521-4028-5(6))* Chronicle Bks. LLC.

Christie, Jacky. Roger's Big Adventure. 2005. (J). pap. 8.00 *(978-0-8059-6889-7(X))* Dorrance Publishing Co., Inc.

Circus Animals. (Puzzle Shapes Ser.). 10p. (J). bds. *(978-2-89393-787-8(X))* Phidal Publishing, Inc./Editions Phidal, Inc.

Circus Fever. 2008. (Illus.). 32p. (J). 14.95 *(978-0-9796380-0-8(3))* Three Wishes Publishing Co.

The Circus Mystery, 6 vols., Vol. 2. (Woodland Mysteriestm Ser.). 133p. (gr. 3-7). 42.50 *(978-0-7802-7942-1(5))* Wright Group/McGraw-Hill.

Coerr, Eleanor. Circus Day in Japan: Bilingual English & Japanese Text. Matsunari, Yumi, tr. 2010. (ENG & JPN., Illus.). 48p. (J). (gr. -1-3). 15.95 *(978-4-8053-1059-5(6))* Tuttle Publishing.

Coerr, Eleanor & Matsunari, Yumi. Circus Day in Japan: Bilingual English & Japanese Text. 2016. (ENG & JPN., Illus.). 48p. (J). (gr. -1-3). 9.95 *(978-0-8048-4743-8(6))* Tuttle Publishing.

Cooper, Page. Amigo, Circus Horse. Pitz, Henry, illus. 2011. 240p. 46.95 *(978-1-258-06394-8(8))* Literary Licensing, LLC.

Corder, Zizou. Lionboy. 2004. (ENG., Illus.). 304p. (J). (gr. 3-7). reprint ed. pap. 8.99 *(978-0-14-240226-9(5)*, Puffin Books) Penguin Young Readers Group.

Costain, Meredith. Stella, Circus Star. McGowan, Shane, illus. 2015. (Legends in Their Own Lunchbox Ser.). (ENG.). 56p. (gr. 2-3). pap. 7.99 *(978-1-4966-0255-8(2)*, Legends in Their Own Lunchbox) Capstone Classroom.

Coulson-Staak, Louise. Clarisse the Cow: A Circus Adventure. 2012. 28p. pap. 12.50 *(978-1-61897-735-9(0)*, Strategic Bk. Publishing) Strategic Book Publishing & Rights Agency (SBPRA).

Coulton, Mia. Circus Fish. Coulton, Mia, photos by. 2008. (ENG., Illus.). pap. 5.35 *(978-1-933624-29-7(9))* Maryruth Bks., Inc.

Cowley, Joy. Smarty Pants at the Circus. 2009. pap. 8.25 *(978-1-60559-243-5(9))* Hameray Publishing Group, Inc.

—Smarty Pants at the Circus Big Book. 2010. 48.25 *(978-1-60559-249-7(8))* Hameray Publishing Group, Inc.

Crow, Marilee. Cartwheel Annie. Snider, K. C., illus. 2009. 24p. pap. 10.95 *(978-1-935137-71-9(9))* Guardian Angel Publishing, Inc.

Cunningham, Ann. The Adventures of Bossie & the Circus. 2009. 20p. pap. 11.99 *(978-1-4389-3947-6(7))* AuthorHouse.

Dale, Elizabeth. Circus Fun! Gausden, Vicki, illus. (Reading Ladder Ser.). (ENG.). 48p. (J). (gr. k-2). 2016. 7.99 *(978-1-4052-8232-1(0))* 2014. pap. 7.99 *(978-1-4052-7069-4(1))* Egmont Bks., Ltd. GBR. Dist: Independent Pubs. Group.

Damjan, Mischa. The Clown Said No. 2004. (Illus.). (J). (gr. k-3). spiral bd. *(978-0-616-14569-2(1))* Canadian National Institute for the Blind/Institut National Canadien pour les Aveugles.

Daniel, Beverly. The Adventures of Madilyn Millicent Middleton-Mew. Daniel, Cindy, ed. Daniel, Beverly, illus. 2013. (Illus.). 64p. pap. 8.95 *(978-0-9789429-6-0(5))* Batelier Publishing.

Darlington, Edgar. The Circus Boys on the Mississippi. 2007. 116p. per. *(978-1-4068-4235-7(4))* Echo Library.

Darlington, Edgar B. The Circus Boys on the Flying Rings. 2005. 220p. pap. 12.95 *(978-1-4218-1122-2(7)*, 1st World Library - Literary Society) 1st World Publishing, Inc.

Darlington, Edgar B. P. The Circus Boys Across Continent or Making the Start in the Sawdust Life. 2004. reprint ed. pap. 22.95 *(978-1-4191-5679-3(9))*; pap. 1.99 *(978-1-4192-5679-0(3))* Kessinger Publishing, LLC.

—The Circus Boys Across the Continent. 2005. 27.95 *(978-1-4218-1020-1(4))*; 212p. pap. 12.95 *(978-1-4218-1120-8(0))* 1st World Publishing, Inc. (1st World Library - Literary Society).

—The Circus Boys Across the Continent. 2007. 116p. per. *(978-1-4068-4236-4(2))* Echo Library.

—The Circus Boys in Dixie Land. 2005. 27.95 *(978-1-4218-1021-8(2))*; 220p. pap. 12.95 *(978-1-4218-1121-5(9))* 1st World Publishing, Inc. (1st World Library - Literary Society).

—The Circus Boys in Dixie Land or Winning the Plaudits of the Sunny South. 2004. reprint ed. pap. 22.95 *(978-1-4191-5680-9(2))*; pap. 1.99 *(978-1-4192-5680-6(7))* Kessinger Publishing, LLC.

—The Circus Boys on the Mississippi. 2005. 27.95 *(978-1-4218-1023-2(9))*; 220p. pap. 12.95 *(978-1-4218-1123-9(5))* 1st World Publishing, Inc. (1st World Library - Literary Society).

—The Circus Boys on the Mississippi or Afloat with the Big Show on the Big River. 2004. reprint ed. pap. 1.99 *(978-1-4192-5681-3(5))*; pap. 22.95 *(978-1-4191-5681-6(0))* Kessinger Publishing, LLC.

—The Circus Boys on the Plains or the Young Advance Agents Ahead of the Show. 2004. reprint ed. pap. 1.99 *(978-1-4192-5682-0(3))*; pap. 22.95 *(978-1-4191-5682-3(9))* Kessinger Publishing, LLC.

Das, Christina. Oomph-Pa-Pa at the Circus. l.t. ed. 2005. (Illus.). 32p. (J). 15.95 *(978-0-9763082-2-5(3)*, A JuneOne Production) JuneOne Publishing Hub.

Denslow, W. w. Denslow's One Ring Circus. 2013. (ENG., Illus.). 84p. pap. 24.95 *(978-1-4290-9804-5(X))* New-York Historical Society.

Destiny, A. & Kahler, A. R. Love Is in the Air. 2015. 221p. (YA). *(978-1-4814-2377-9(0)*, Simon Pulse) Simon Pulse.

Devine, Ginger. Hooray for the Circus: A Story of Sam the Lamb. 2008. 36p. pap. 16.99 *(978-1-4389-1826-6(7))* AuthorHouse.

Disney Staff. Dumbo. (FRE.). 96p. (J). (gr. k-5). pap. 9.95 *(978-0-7859-8849-6(1))* French & European Pubns., Inc.

Dixon, Franklin W. One False Step. 2005. (Hardy Boys II Ser.: No. 189). 150p. (J). lib. bdg. 15.00 *(978-1-59054-846-2(9))* Fitzgerald Bks.

Dolan, Penny. Joey the Juggler, 1 vol. Robert, Bruno, illus. 2013. (Start Reading Ser.). (ENG.). 24p. (gr. k-1). pap. 7.95 *(978-1-4765-4109-9(4))* Capstone Press of Coughlan Cos.

—Lola Fanola, 1 vol. Robert, Bruno, illus. 2013. (Start Reading Ser.). (ENG.). 24p. (gr. k-1). pap. 7.95 *(978-1-4765-4113-6(2))* Capstone Press of Coughlan Cos.

—Princess Rani, 1 vol. Robert, Bruno, illus. 2013. (Start Reading Ser.). (ENG.). 24p. (gr. k-1). pap. 7.95 *(978-1-4765-4131-0(0))* Capstone Press of Coughlan Cos.

Doolin, Jimmy. The Day the Circus Came to My Backyard. l.t. ed. 2003. 39p. lib. bdg. *(978-0-9710432-4-4(8))* Children's Literacy Pubns.

Downs, Mike. You See a Circus, I See... McGrory, Anik, illus. 2006. (ENG.). 32p. (J). (gr. -1-3). pap. 7.95 *(978-1-58089-155-4(1))* Charlesbridge Publishing, Inc.

D'shindia, Albert. The Fable Musical. 2012. 56p. (gr. -1). pap. 10.95 *(978-1-4567-9978-6(9))* AuthorHouse.

Dubrule, Jackie. Little John, God, & the Circus. Swope, Brenda, illus. 2011. 32p. pap. 24.95 *(978-1-4560-0978-6(8))* America Star Bks.

Edwards, Wallace. The Painted Circus: P. T. Vermin Presents a Mesmerizing Menagerie of Trickery & Illusion Guaranteed to Beguile & Bamboozle the Beholder. Edwards, Wallace, illus. 2007. (ENG., Illus.). 32p. (J). (gr. 1-4). 17.95 *(978-1-55337-720-7(6))* Kids Can Pr., Ltd. CAN. Dist: Hachette Bk. Group.

EEBOO Staff, creator. Circus Animals' Adventures Write Me a Story - #WSADV. 2008. (J). pap. *(978-1-59461-282-4(X))* eeBoo Corp.

Elga Learns to Juggle. 2006. (J). 6.99 *(978-0-9770918-0-5(5))* Forelle Graphics.

Elwell, Telva & Kelley, Barbara. Ellasense Misses the Train. Elwell, Telva, illus. 2004. (Illus.). 48p. (J). per. 12.95 *(978-0-9754591-0-2(4))* Cubby Hole Tales.

Falconer, Ian. Olivia Saves the Circus. 2004. (Olivia Ser.). (J). (gr. k-2). spiral bd. *(978-0-616-11111-6(8))*; spiral bd. *(978-0-616-11110-9(X))* Canadian National Institute for the Blind/Institut National Canadien pour les Aveugles.

—Olivia Saves the Circus. Falconer, Ian, illus. 2010. (Classic Board Bks.). (ENG., Illus.). 36p. (J). (gr. -1-2). bds. 7.99 *(978-1-4424-1287-3(9)*, Atheneum Bks. for Young Readers) Simon & Schuster Children's Publishing.

Faris, Stephanie. Piper Morgan Joins the Circus. 2016. (Piper Morgan Ser.: 1). (ENG., Illus.). 112p. (J). (gr. 1-4). pap. 5.99 *(978-1-4814-5708-8(X)*, Aladdin) Simon & Schuster Children's Publishing.

The Farmer & the Clown. 2014. (ENG., Illus.). 32p. (J). (gr. -1-3). 17.99 *(978-1-4424-9744-3(0)*, Beach Lane Bks.) Beach Lane Bks.

Farrell, Darren. Doug-Dennis & the Flyaway Fib. 2010. (ENG.). 40p. (J). (gr. k-3). 16.99 *(978-0-8037-3437-1(9)*, Dial Bks) Penguin Young Readers Group.

Fleischman, Paul. Sidewalk Circus. Hawkes, Kevin, illus. 2007. (ENG.). 32p. (J). (gr. k-4). 7.99 *(978-0-7636-2795-9(X))* Candlewick Pr.

—Sidewalk Circus. Hawkes, Kevin, illus. 2007. (gr. k-4). 18.00 *(978-0-7569-8182-2(4))* Perfection Learning Corp.

Fleming, Candace. Emma's Circus. Davenier, Christine, illus. 2017. (ENG.). 40p. (J). 17.99 *(978-0-374-39907-8(7)*, 9780374399078, Farrar, Straus & Giroux (BYR)) Farrar, Straus & Giroux.

Ford, Ron. Cindy's Backyard Circus. 2006. (Neighborhood Readers Ser.). (ENG.). 16p. (gr. 1-3). pap. 6.50 *(978-1-4042-7136-4(8)*, Rosen Classroom) Rosen Publishing Group, Inc., The.

—El circo de Cindy (Cindy's Backyard Circus) 2006. (Lecturas del barrio (Neighborhood Readers) Ser.). (SPA.). 16p. (gr. 1-3). pap. 6.50 *(978-1-4042-7138-8(4)*, Rosen Classroom) Rosen Publishing Group, Inc., The.

Garant, Andre J. The Circus Kids. 2008. 140p. pap. 11.99 *(978-1-4389-2833-3(5))* AuthorHouse.

Garcia-Webb, Peter. Aeron. 2008. 32p. E-Book 15.99 *(978-0-9924756-9-7(4)*, Philomel) Penguin Publishing Group.

A Garden Circus. 2003. (J). 9.99 *(978-0-9740847-5-6(1))* GiGi Bks.

Garis, Howard R. Umboo, the Elephant. 2008. 108p. pap. 9.95 *(978-1-60664-156-9(5))* Aegypan.

Garis, Howard Roger. Tom Cardiff's Circus. King, W. B., illus. 2005. reprint ed. pap. 28.95 *(978-1-4179-3393-8(3))* Kessinger Publishing, LLC.

—Umboo, the Elephant. 2005. 26.95 *(978-1-4218-0956-4(7))*; 132p. pap. 10.95 *(978-1-59540-656-9(5))* 1st World Publishing, Inc. (1st World Library - Literary Society).

Garis, Lilian C. Let's Play Circus. 2005. pap. 24.95 *(978-1-4179-9394-9(4))* Kessinger Publishing, LLC.

Gay, Marie-Louise & Homel, David. The Traveling Circus, 1 vol. 2015. (ENG., Illus.). 144p. (J). (gr. 1-5). 15.95 *(978-1-55498-420-6(3))* Groundwood Bks. CAN. Dist: Publishers Group West (PGW).

George, Kallie. The Melancholic Mermaid. Halpin, Abigail, illus. 2011. (ENG.). 64p. (J). (gr. k-4). 16.95 *(978-1-897476-53-6(1))* Simply Read Bks. CAN. Dist: Ingram Publisher Services.

Gibeau, Claire Janvier. The Circus in Grandpa's Day. 2009. 16p. pap. 8.49 *(978-1-4490-3382-8(2))* AuthorHouse.

Gilkey, Gail. Freckles & the Circus. 2004. (J). per. 9.95 *(978-0-9662983-3-8(0))* Windy Hill Pr.

Glass, Calliope. Disney Tails Dumbo & Mama. Disney Storybook Art Team, illus. 2016. (Disney Tails Ser.). (ENG.). 10p. (J). (gr. -1 — 1). bds. 6.99 *(978-1-4847-2955-7(2))* Disney Pr.

Glaze, Dave. The Light-Fingered Gang, 1 vol. 2005. (1912: the Mackenzie Davis Files Ser.). (ENG.). 168p. (J). (gr. 3-7). per. 7.95 *(978-1-55050-326-5(X))* Coteau Bks. CAN. Dist: Orca Bk. Pubs. USA.

Glennon, Michelle. Duncan the Circus Dinosaur. Glennon, Michelle, illus. 2008. (Illus.). 21p. (J). 16.95 *(978-0-9796625-5-3(9))* GDG Publishing.

Godley, Christina. Lion at the Gateway. 2010. 36p. pap. 16.99 *(978-1-4520-4508-5(9))* AuthorHouse.

Gordon, Lynn, et al. Circus Fantastico. 2010. (ENG., Illus.). 38p. (J). (gr. k-3). 16.99 *(978-0-7407-9199-4(0))* Andrews McMeel Publishing.

Grant, Myrna. Ivan & the Moscow Circus. 2006. (Flamingo Fiction 9-13s Ser.). (ENG., Illus.). 160p. (J). (gr. 4-7). per. 6.99 *(978-1-84550-135-8(7)*, 4a6719e2-1a18-4f7c-9b8f-fed8a960777e) Christian Focus Pubns. GBR. Dist: Bookmasters Distribution.

Graves, Keith. Second Banana. 2015. (ENG., Illus.). 32p. (J). (gr. 2-5). 17.99 *(978-1-59643-883-5(5)*, 9781596438835) Roaring Brook Pr.

Gravett, Emily. Wolf Won't Bite! Gravett, Emily, illus. 2012. (ENG., Illus.). 32p. (J). (gr. -1-1). 16.99 *(978-1-4424-2763-1(9)*, Simon & Schuster Bks. For Young Readers) Simon & Schuster Bks. For Young Readers.

Gray, Clio. Peder & the Skincatcher. 2013. 188p. (J). pap. *(978-1-78299-157-1(3))* FeedARead.com.

Guettier, Bénédicte. At the Circus. 2011. (Funny Faces Ser.). (Illus.). 14p. bds. *(978-1-84089-678-7(7))* Zero to Ten, Ltd.

Guettier, Nancy. Circus in the Sky. 2013. (ENG.). 36p. (gr. 1-5). pap. 9.95 *(978-1-61448-672-5(7))*; 19.00 *(978-1-61448-644-2(1))* Morgan James Publishing.

Guttier, Benedicte. At the Circus - Welsh Edition. 2011. (Funny Faces Ser.). (WEL., Illus.). 14p. bds. *(978-1-84089-686-2(8))* Zero to Ten, Ltd.

Hapka, Catherine, pseud. Horse Diaries #12: Luna. Sanderson, Ruth, illus. 2015. (Horse Diaries). (ENG.). 160p. (J). (gr. 3-7). lib. bdg. 12.99 *(978-0-553-53371-2(1)*, Random Hse. Bks. for Young Readers) Random Hse. Children's Bks.

—Luna. 2015. (Horse Diaries: 12). lib. bdg. 18.40 *(978-0-606-37711-9(5))* Turtleback Bks.

Happy Books. A Day at the Circus. 2012. (Day at ... Bks.). (ENG., Illus.). 8p. (J). bds. 7.99 *(978-0-7641-6531-3(3))* Barron's Educational Series, Inc.

Harkness, Peter T. Andy the Acrobat or Out with the Greatest Show on Earth. 2007. 120p. per. *(978-1-4068-3830-5(6))* Echo Library.

Harmening, Gail. How Did Clancey Get His Color?, 1 vol. 2009. 45p. pap. 24.95 *(978-1-60836-440-4(2))* America Star Bks.

Harrison, Hannah E. Extraordinary Jane. 2014. (ENG.). 40p. (J). (gr. -1-k). 16.99 *(978-0-8037-3914-7(1)*, Dial Bks) Penguin Young Readers Group.

Haydon, David J. The Spuds - the Circus Comes to Town. 2012. 20p. pap. *(978-1-78222-051-0(8))* Paragon Publishing, Rothersthorpe.

Hensley, Sarah M. Caillov Visits the Circus. Storch, Ellen N., illus. l.t. ed. 2005. (HRL Board Book Ser.). (J). (gr. -1-k). pap. 10.95 *(978-1-57332-309-3(8)*, HighReach Learning, Incorporated) Carson-Dellosa Publishing, LLC.

Hill, Clare. Granddad's Circus & Other Stories. 2004. 41p. pap. 19.95 *(978-1-4137-3647-2(5))* PublishAmerica, Inc.

Hillert, Margaret. Circus Fun. Masheris, Bob, illus. 2016. (BeginningtoRead Ser.). (ENG.). 32p. (J). (gr. -1-2). pap. 11.94 *(978-1-60357-937-7(0))*; (gr. k-2). 22.60 *(978-1-59953-796-2(6))* Norwood Hse. Pr.

—It's Circus Time, Dear Dragon. Pullan, Jack, illus. 2016. (BeginningtoRead Ser.). (ENG.). 32p. (J). (-2). lib. bdg. 22.60 *(978-1-59953-772-6(9))*; (gr. 1-2). pap. 11.94 *(978-1-60357-885-1(4))* Norwood Hse. Pr.

Hillert, Margaret. Vamos Al Circo, Querido Dragón. Pullan, Jack, illus. 2017. (BeginningtoRead Ser.).Tr. of It's Circus Time, Dear Dragon. (ENG & SPA.). 32p. (J). (-2). 22.60 ***(978-1-59953-835-8(0))*** Norwood Hse. Pr.

Hirota, Denise. The Circus Poster. 2011. 58p. pap. 9.99 *(978-1-60911-292-9(X)*, Eloquent Bks.) Strategic Book Publishing & Rights Agency (SBPRA).

Hope, Laura Lee. Bunny Brown & His Sister Sue Playing C. 2006. 26.95 *(978-1-4218-2977-7(0))*; pap. 11.95 *(978-1-4218-3077-3(9))* 1st World Publishing, Inc.

Houck, Colleen. Tiger's Curse, Bk. 1. 2012. (Tiger's Curse Ser.: Bk. 1). (ENG.). 456p. (J). (gr. 7). pap. 9.95 *(978-1-4549-0249-2(3))* Sterling Publishing Co., Inc.

—Tiger's Curse. 2012. (Tiger's Curse Ser.: Bk. 1). lib. bdg. 20.80 *(978-0-606-23822-9(0)*, Turtleback) Turtleback Bks.

Howard, J. J. That Time I Joined the Circus. 2013. (ENG.). 272p. (J). (gr. 7). 17.99 *(978-0-545-43381-5(9))* Scholastic, Inc.

Hubbard, L. Ron. If I Were You: Literature Guide for Teachers & Librarians, Based on Common Core ELA Standards for Classrooms 6-9, Kit. 2014. (gr. 6-10). 22.95 *(978-1-61986-295-1(6))* Galaxy Pr., LLC.

Hubbard, L. Ron, contrib. by. If I Were You: Literature Guide for Teachers & Librarians, Based on Common Core ELA Standards for Classrooms 6-9. 2013. (Stories from the Golden Age Ser.). (ENG.). 35p. (gr. 6-9). pap., tchr. ed. 14.95 *(978-1-61986-201-2(8))* Galaxy Pr., LLC.

Hunt, Bonnie. The Missing Chimp: A Grayson Twins Adventures, 1 vol. 2009. 100p. pap. 19.95 *(978-1-60813-481-6(4))* America Star Bks.

Hyland, Betty. Tressa & the Lost Circus of Ireland. 2004. 85p. (YA). pap. 10.95 *(978-0-7414-2268-2(9))* Infinity Publishing.

Ingram, Doreen. My Sanctuary: A Place I Call Home - Keepers of the Wild. Josh Green, illus. 2013. 54p. pap. 17.50 *(978-1-62516-273-1(1)*, Strategic Bk. Publishing) Strategic Book Publishing & Rights Agency (SBPRA).

James, Rosalind. Bertie Rides Again. 2012. (Illus.). 126p. 29.99 *(978-1-4771-2272-3(9))* Xlibris Corp.

Jan Baer: And the Mystery of the Silent Circus. 2005. (J). per. 10.00 *(978-1-930052-29-1(4))* Cherokee Bks.

Jeffery, John. Freddie & the Garden Circus. 2015. (ENG.). 47p. (J). (gr. 2-3). mass mkt. 14.95 *(978-1-78455-729-4(3)*, ffaea993-f2af-431a-bb31-29d73a42d220) Austin, Stan AUS. Dist: Bookmasters Distribution.

Johnson, Lois Walfrid. The Runaway Clown. 2009. (Orig.). (J). 8.99 (978-0-88062-282-0(2)) Mott Media.

Keene, Carolyn. Big Top Flop. Francis, Peter, illus. 2016. (Nancy Drew Clue Book Ser.: 4). (ENG.). 96p. (J). (gr. 1-4). pap. 5.99 (978-1-4814-3752-3(6), Aladdin) Simon & Schuster Children's Publishing.

Kelly, Lynne. Chained, 1 vol. 2012. (ENG.). 256p. (J). (gr. 5-9). 17.99 (978-0-374-31237-4(0), 9780374312374, Farrar, Straus & Giroux (BYR)) Farrar, Straus & Giroux.

Kenah, Katharine. The Best Teacher in Second Grade. Carter, Abby, illus. 2006. (I Can Read Bks.). 48p. (J). (gr. -1-3). lib. bdg. 17.89 (978-0-06-053565-0(2)) HarperCollins Pubs.

Kidd, Ron. Magical Circus Train. Boyd, Patti, illus. 16p. (J). (gr. -1-18). 19.95 (978-0-9627001-5-6(0)) Futech Educational Products, Inc.

Klein, Adria F. Circus Train, 1 vol. Cameron, Craig, illus. 2013. (Train Time Ser.). (ENG.). 32p. (gr. -1-1). pap. 5.95 (978-1-4342-4883-1(6)); lib. bdg. 22.65 (978-1-4342-4188-7(2)) Stone Arch Bks.

Klise, Kate. The Circus Goes to Sea. Klise, M. Sarah, illus. (Three-Ring Rascals Ser.). (ENG.). 160p. (J). 2015. (gr. 2-5). pap. 5.95 (978-1-61620-481-5(8)) 2014. 15.95 (978-1-61620-365-8(X), 73365) Algonquin Bks. of Chapel Hill.

—Little Rabbit & the Meanest Mother on Earth. Klise, M. Sarah, illus. (ENG.). 32p. (J). (gr. -1-3). 2015. 6.99 (978-0-544-45611-2(4), HMH Books For Young Readers) 2010. 17.99 (978-0-15-206201-9(7)) Houghton Mifflin Harcourt Publishing Co.

—Pop Goes the Circus! Klise, M. Sarah, illus. 2015. (Three-Ring Rascals Ser.: 4). (ENG.). 144p. (J). (gr. 2-5). pap. 5.95 (978-1-61620-547-8(4)); 15.95 (978-1-61620-464-8(8)) Algonquin Bks. of Chapel Hill.

—Secrets of the Circus. Klise, M. Sarah, illus. 2016. (Three-Ring Rascals Ser.: 5). (ENG.). 128p. (J). (gr. 2-5). pap. 5.95 (978-1-61620-640-6(3)); 15.95 (978-1-61620-566-9(0)) Algonquin Bks. of Chapel Hill.

Klise, Kate & Klise, M. Sarah. The Greatest Star on Earth. Klise, M. Sarah, illus. 2014. (Three-Ring Rascals Ser.: 2). (ENG., Illus.). 144p. (J). (gr. 2-5). 15.95 (978-1-61620-245-3(9), 73245) Algonquin Bks. of Chapel Hill.

—The Show Must Go On! 2013. (Three-Ring Rascals Ser.: 1). (ENG., Illus.). 160p. (J). (gr. 2-5). 15.95 (978-1-61620-244-6(0), 73244) Algonquin Bks. of Chapel Hill.

Krosoczka, Jarrett J. Ollie the Purple Elephant. 2011. (ENG.). 40p. (J). (gr. -1-2). 16.99 (978-0-375-86654-8(X), Knopf Bks. for Young Readers) Random Hse. Children's Bks.

Lamb, Jowana. Makhi & the Run Away Elephant. 2012. 28p. pap. 15.99 (978-1-4771-3820-5(X)) Xlibris Corp.

Landry, Leo. Eat Your Peas, Ivy Louise! 2005. (J). (gr. -1-k). 12.00 (978-0-618-58112-2(X)) Houghton Mifflin Harcourt Trade & Reference Pubs.

Lee, Quinlan B. The Circus Comes to Town. 2005. (Illus.). (J). (978-0-439-77931-9(6)) Scholastic, Inc.

Lee, Rex. Rann Braden Circus Showman A Circus Adve. 2006. (Illus.). pap. 27.95 (978-1-4286-5861-5(0)) Kessinger Publishing, LLC.

Lester, Alison. The Circus Horse. Harvey, Roland, illus. 2009. (ENG.). 64p. (J). (gr. k-3). pap. 4.99 (978-0-8118-6656-9(4)) Chronicle Bks. LLC.

Levez, Olivia. The Circus. 2017. (ENG.). 288p. (gr. 7). pap. 11.99 (978-1-78607-094-4(4)) Oneworld Pubns. GBR. Dist: Publishers Group West (PGW).

Liberto, Lorenzo, et al. Practice Makes Perfect / la Práctica Hace al Maestro. Torres, Irving, illus. 2004. (ENG & SPA.). 32p. (J). lib. bdg. 20.00 (978-0-9743668-2-1(X)) Harvest Sun Pr., LLC.

Little Engine-Circus Friends. 2005. (J). (978-1-4194-0005-6(3)) Paradise Pr., Inc.

Lockwood, Vicki. The Magnificent Lizzie Brown & the Devil's Hound, 1 vol. 2014. (Magnificent Lizzie Brown Ser.). (ENG., Illus.). 200p. (gr. 5-9). lib. bdg. 26.65 (978-1-4342-7941-5(3)) Stone Arch Bks.

—The Magnificent Lizzie Brown & the Fairy Child. Hans, Stephanie, illus. 2015. (Magnificent Lizzie Brown Ser.). (ENG.). 200p. (gr. 5-9). 10.95 (978-1-62370-210-6(0)) Stone Arch Bks.

—The Magnificent Lizzie Brown & the Ghost Ship. Hans, Stephanie, illus. 2015. (Magnificent Lizzie Brown Ser.). (ENG.). 200p. (gr. 5-9). lib. bdg. 26.65 (978-1-4342-9806-5(X)) Stone Arch Bks.

—The Magnificent Lizzie Brown & the Mysterious Phantom, 1 vol. 2014. (Magnificent Lizzie Brown Ser.). (ENG., Illus.). 200p. (gr. 5-9). 10.95 (978-1-62370-069-0(8)); lib. bdg. 26.65 (978-1-4342-7940-8(5)) Stone Arch Bks.

—The Magnificent Lizzie Brown & the Mysterious Phantom, 1 vol. Hans, Stephanie, illus. 2014. (ENG.). 200p. (J). pap. (978-1-4342-7942-2(1)) Stone Arch Bks.

Loffredo, Edward. The Adventures of the First Buffarillo. 2013. 28p. pap. 13.95 (978-1-4808-0195-0(X)) Archway Publishing.

Lofting, Hugh. The Story of Doctor Dolittle: The Circus Crocodile. Kanzler, John, illus. 2008. (Easy Reader Classics Ser.). (ENG.). 32p. (gr. 3-7). lib. bdg. 24.21 (978-1-59961-339-0(5)) Spotlight.

MacDonald, Suse. Circus Opposites: An Interactive Extravaganza! MacDonald, Suse, illus. 2010. (ENG., Illus.). 20p. (J). (gr. -1-2). 11.99 (978-1-4169-7154-2(8), Little Simon) Little Simon.

Mack, Tracy & Citrin, Michael. The Fall of the Amazing Zalindas. 2006. (Illus.). 259p. (J). (978-1-4287-0951-5(7), Orchard Bks.) Scholastic, Inc.

—Fall of the Amazing Zalindas. 2009. (Sherlock Holmes & the Baker St. Irregulars Ser.: 1). (ENG.). 272p. (J). (gr. 3-7). 6.99 (978-0-545-06939-7(4), Scholastic Paperbacks) Scholastic, Inc.

Mahy, Margaret. Maddigan's Fantasia. 2012. (ENG.). 512p. (J). (gr. 5-9). pap. 22.99 (978-1-4424-6053-9(9), McElderry, Margaret K. Bks.) McElderry, Margaret K. Bks.

Marinaro, Stacy. Carter Meets Ella the Elephant. 2008. 20p. pap. 10.95 (978-0-615-20883-1(5)) Marinaro, Stacy.

Martín Anguita, Carmen & Carmen, Martín Anguita. Una Tarde en el Circo. Cortazar, Alicia Canas, illus. 2008. (SPA.). 32p. (J). 10.99 (978-84-241-5459-2(2)) Everest Editora ESP. Dist: Lectorum Pubns., Inc.

Mary, Nanette. Ashby, the Happy Little Elephant. 2007. (Illus.). 40p. (J). per. 12.95 (978-0-9787112-7-6(0), 01002) New World Publishing.

Mary-Todd, Jonathan. The Giant. 2014. (Bareknuckle Ser.). 104p. (YA). (gr. 6-12). lib. bdg. 27.93 (978-1-4677-1457-0(7), Darby Creek) Lerner Publishing Group.

Mattaino, J. F. Cotton Candy Circus & Other Performances. 2006. 22.00 (978-0-8059-8804-8(1)) Dorrance Publishing Co., Inc.

Mayer, Mercer. Good for Me & You. Mayer, Mercer, illus. 2004. (Little Critter Ser.). (ENG., Illus.). 24p. (J). (gr. -1-2). pap. 3.99 (978-0-06-053948-1(8), HarperFestival) HarperCollins Pubs.

Mayhew, James. Bubble & Squeak. Vulliamy, Clara, illus. 2013. (J). (978-1-4351-4770-6(7)) Barnes & Noble, Inc.

Mayo, Margaret. Polly of the Circus. 2004. reprint ed. pap. 1.99 (978-1-4192-4251-9(2)); pap. 15.95 (978-1-4191-4251-2(8)) Kessinger Publishing, LLC.

McCaffery, William, illus. The Flea Circus. 2013. (J). (978-0-307-97997-1(0)); lib. bdg. (978-0-375-97132-7(7)) Random Hse. Children's Bks.

McCaughrean, Geraldine. The Kite Rider. 2003. (Illus.). 320p. (YA). (gr. 8-18). pap. 8.99 (978-0-06-441091-5(9), HarperTeen) HarperCollins Pubs.

McCully, Emily Arnold. Mirette on the High Wire. 2004. (J). (gr. k-3). spiral bd. (978-0-616-01716-6(2)); spiral bd. (978-0-616-01717-3(0)) Canadian National Institute for the Blind/Institut National Canadien pour les Aveugles.

McKee, David. Big-Top Benn. 2011. (ENG., Illus.). 48p. (J). (gr. -1-3). 14.50 (978-1-85437-961-0(5)) Tate Publishing, Ltd. GBR. Dist: Abrams, Inc.

Medina Rosas, Juana. ABC Pasta. 2017. (ENG., Illus.). 40p. (J). (— 1). 17.99 (978-1-101-99978-3(0), Viking Books for Young Readers) Penguin Young Readers Group.

Miller, Lindsey Michael. The Circus. Griswold, Phillip, illus. 2005. 32p. (J). (gr. -1-3). 13.95 (978-0-9709104-8-6(7)) Hickory Tales Publishing.

Mills, Joyce C. & Crowley, Richard J. Sammy the Elephant & Mr. Camel: A Story to Help Children Overcome Bedwetting. Pillo, Cary, illus. 2nd ed. 2005. 32p. (J). 14.95 (978-1-59147-247-6(4)); pap. 9.95 (978-1-59147-248-3(2)) American Psychological Assn. (Magination Pr.).

Mitchell, Lebbeus. The Circus Comes to Town. 2008. 128p. 21.99 (978-0-554-35343-2(1)) 2008. 128p. 24.99 (978-0-554-26040-2(9)) 2007. (ENG.). 116p. pap. 18.99 (978-1-4346-0376-0(8)) 2007. 126p. pap. 19.99 (978-1-4346-0388-3(1)) Creative Media Partners, LLC.

—The Circus Comes to Town. 2008. (Illus.). 132p. pap. (978-1-4099-1485-3(2)) Dodo Pr.

—The Circus Comes to Town. 2010. (Illus.). 74p. pap. 14.14 (978-1-153-69785-9(8)) General Bks. LLC.

—The Circus Comes to Town. 2010. 120p. pap. (978-1-4076-1796-1(6)) HardPr.

Moore, Natascha. The Circus der Zirkus. 2012. 28p. pap. 19.99 (978-1-4772-0706-2(6)) AuthorHouse.

Morgan, Allen. Matthew & the Midnight Hospital. 2004. (Illus.). (J). (gr. k-3). spiral bd. (978-0-616-01529-2(1)) Canadian National Institute for the Blind/Institut National Canadien pour les Aveugles.

Moulton, Mark. Mr Sparrows Merry Fairy Circus. Good, Karen, illus. 2004. 24p. 18.00 (978-0-7412-1940-4(9)) Lang Graphics, Ltd.

Mr Brown: KinderReaders Individual Title Six-Packs. (Kinderstarters Ser.). 8p. (gr. -1-1). 21.00 (978-0-7635-8653-9(6)) Rigby Education.

Muller, Rachel. Ten Thumb Sam, 1 vol. 2007. (Orca Young Readers Ser.). (ENG., Illus.). 128p. (J). (gr. 3-6). per. 5.95 (978-1-55143-699-9(X)) Orca Bk. Pubs. USA.

Murray, Carol. Hurry Up! Garbot, Dave, illus. 2003. (Rookie Readers Ser.). (ENG.). 32p. (J). 19.50 (978-0-516-22585-2(5), Children's Pr.) Scholastic Library Publishing.

Murray, Guillermo. Te Dije Que No Miraras. rev. ed. 2005. (Ediciones Castillo Castillo Del Terror Ser.). (SPA & ENG.). 100p. (J). (gr. -1-7). pap. 6.95 (978-970-20-0308-3(3)) Castillo, Ediciones, S. A. de C. V. MEX. Dist: Macmillan.

Natl Children's Book & Literacy Alliance. The Exquisite Corpse Adventure. 2011. (ENG., Illus.). 288p. (J). (gr. 4-7). pap. 7.99 (978-0-7636-5773-4(5)) Candlewick Pr.

Naughton, Patrick. Colonel Tiger on the Raft. 2010. 76p. pap. 12.95 (978-1-4452-6095-2(6)) Lulu Pr., Inc.

Nelson, Charlie. The Circus Life. l.t. ed. 2003. (Illus.). 22p. (J). per. 7.95 (978-1-932338-25-6(X)) Lifevest Publishing, Inc.

Nickel, Scott. Jimmy Sniffles Dognapped! 2007. (J). (gr. 3-5). 31.92 incl. cd-rom (978-1-4342-0372-4(7)); 21.52 incl. audio compact disk (978-1-4342-0379-3(4)) Stone Arch Bks.

Nunes, Lygia Bojunga. La Cuerda Floja. (SPA.). 136p. (YA). (gr. 5-8). (978-84-204-3122-2(2), AF1749) Ediciones Alfaguara ESP. Dist: Lectorum Pubns., Inc.

Ogden, Charles. High Wire. Carton, Rick, illus. 2006. (Edgar & Ellen Ser.: 5). (ENG.). 208p. (J). (gr. 3-7). 24.99 (978-1-4169-1500-3(1), Simon & Schuster/Paula Wiseman Bks.) Simon & Schuster/Paula Wiseman Bks.

O'Neal, Jayce. Crazy Circus World. 2009. (Illus.). 40p. (978-1-55452-372-6(9)) Essence Publishing.

Oppel, Kenneth. The Boundless. Tierney, Jim, illus. 2014. (ENG.). 336p. (J). (gr. 3-7). 17.99 (978-1-4424-7288-4(X), Simon & Schuster Bks. For Young Readers) Simon & Schuster Bks. For Young Readers.

Orloff, Karen Kaufman. Nightlight Detective: Big Top Circus Mystery. Smith, Jamie, illus. 2013. 42p. spiral bd. 12.99 (978-1-4413-1227-3(7)) Peter Pauper Pr. Inc.

Orth, Jack. Happy Days: Book 1. Sunshine, Mary Lou, illus. 2013. 50p. (J). pap. 9.95 (978-1-61863-545-7(X)) Bookstand Publishing.

—Happy Days: Book 2. Sunshine, Mary Lou, illus. 2013. 50p. (J). pap. 9.95 (978-1-61863-546-4(8)) Bookstand Publishing.

—Happy Days: Book 3. Sunshine, Mary Lou, illus. 2013. 50p. (J). pap. 9.95 (978-1-61863-547-1(6)) Bookstand Publishing.

Ostow, Micol. Louise Trapeze Can SO Save the Day. Barrager, Brigette, illus. 2016. (Louise Trapeze Ser.). (ENG.). 112p. (J). (gr. 1-4). 5.99 (978-0-553-49750-2(2)); 14.99 (978-0-553-49747-2(2)) Random Hse. Children's Bks. (Random Hse. Bks. for Young Readers).

—Louise Trapeze Did NOT Lose the Juggling Chickens. Barrager, Brigette, illus. 2016. (Louise Trapeze Ser.). (ENG.). 112p. (J). (gr. 1-4). lib. bdg. 17.99 (978-0-553-49744-1(8), Random Hse. Bks. for Young Readers) Random Hse. Children's Bks.

—Louise Trapeze Is Totally 100% Fearless. Barrager, Brigette, illus. 2015. (Louise Trapeze Ser.: 1). (ENG.). 112p. (J). (gr. 1-4). 14.99 (978-0-553-49739-7(1), Random Hse. Bks. for Young Readers) Random Hse. Children's Bks.

—Louise Trapeze Will NOT Lose a Tooth. Barrager, Brigette, illus. 2017. (Louise Trapeze Ser.). (ENG.). 112p. (J). (gr. 1-4). 14.99 (978-0-553-49751-9(0), Random Hse. Bks. for Young Readers) Random Hse. Children's Bks.

Otis, James. Toby Tyler: Or Ten Weeks with a Circus. 2013. 178p. pap. 15.00 (978-0-9831857-8-9(6)) MPR Publishing.

—Toby Tyler, or Ten Weeks with a Circus. 2007. 100p. (gr. 4-7). per. (978-1-4068-4370-5(9)) Echo Library.

Paquette, Jessica E. Sophie the Clown in Crinkle Town. 2013. 258p. (gr. 4-6). 26.95 (978-1-4759-7322-8(5)); pap. 16.95 (978-1-4759-7321-1(7)) iUniverse, Inc.

Parker, Emma. At the Circus. 2010. (Illus.). 20p. pap. (978-1-877561-52-8(5)) First Edition Ltd.

Parsley, Elise. If You Ever Want to Bring a Circus to the Library, Don't! 2017. (Magnolia Says DON'T! Ser.). (ENG., Illus.). 40p. (J). (gr. -1-3). 17.99 (978-0-316-37661-7(2)) Little Brown & Co.

Patterson, Teri Jo. Corky & Lizzie Go to the Circus. 2012. 108p. pap. 19.95 (978-1-4626-9192-0(7)) America Star Bks.

Peck, George W. Peck's Bad Boy at the Circus. 2007. (ENG.). 200p. pap. 21.99 (978-1-4264-4090-8(1)); 178p. pap. 19.99 (978-1-4264-4031-1(6)) Creative Media Partners, LLC.

—Peck's Bad Boy at the Circus. 2004. reprint ed. pap. 1.99 (978-1-4192-4055-3(2)) Kessinger Publishing, LLC.

Peoples, Alan, illus. James the Circus Boy. 2013. 80p. pap. 11.99 (978-1-62839-474-0(9)) Salem Author Services.

Pernice, Clare. Circus Girl. 2014. (ENG., Illus.). 40p. (J). (gr. -1-3). 16.95 (978-1-927018-36-1(6), 9781927018361) Simply Read Bks. CAN. Dist: Ingram Publisher Services.

Petrowski, Carol. The Clown Who Wears Many Hats. 2011. 24p. pap. 15.99 (978-1-4653-3700-9(8)) Xlibris Corp.

Price, Reynolds. A Perfect Friend. 2013. (ENG.). (J). pap. 4.99 (978-0-689-83148-5(X), Simon & Schuster/Paula Wiseman Bks.) Simon & Schuster/Paula Wiseman Bks.

Pruitt, Kat. Si Si the Circus Cat. Griftner, Rebecca, illus. 2011. (ENG.). 24p. (J). pap. 12.95 (978-0-9844037-2-1(8)) Pruggus Publishing.

Puerto, Carlos & Puerto, Carlos. Las Alas de la Pantera. (Barco de Vapor). (SPA.). 128p. (YA). (gr. 5-8). (978-84-348-4667-8(5)) SM Ediciones.

Punter, Russell. Cow Takes a Bow. Blunt, Fred, illus. 2014. (Usborne Phonics Readers Ser.). (ENG.). (J). pap. 6.99 (978-0-7945-3368-7(X), Usborne) EDC Publishing.

Resnick, Jacqueline. The Daring Escape of the Misfit Menagerie. 2013. (Misfit Menagerie Ser.: 1). (ENG.). 320p. (J). (gr. 3-7). pap. 7.99 (978-1-59514-589-5(3), Razorbill) Penguin Young Readers Group.

Rey, H. A. & Rey, Margret. Circus Act. 2008. (Curious George Ser.). (ENG., Illus.). 16p. (J). (gr. -1-3). 5.99 (978-0-618-99909-5(4)) Houghton Mifflin Harcourt Publishing Co.

Rice, James, illus. Gaston Joins the Circus, 1 vol. 2015. (ENG.). 32p. (J). (gr. k-3). pap. 9.95 (978-1-4556-2092-0(0)) Pelican Publishing Co., Inc.

—Gaston(r) Joins the Circus, 1 vol. 2015. (ENG.). 32p. (J). (gr. k-3). 16.99 (978-1-4556-2129-3(3)) Pelican Publishing Co., Inc.

Rider, Cynthia. Circus. Aguilar, Sandra, illus. 2013. (Start Reading Ser.). (ENG.). 24p. (gr. k-1). pap. 7.95 (978-1-4765-4091-7(8)) Capstone Press of Coughlan Cos.

Ross, Barbara & Beatty, Nicholas. The Goops Circus: A Whimsical Telling of Do-Good Tales. Camille, Diana, illus. 2010. (Goops Ser.). 58p. (J). 19.95 incl. audio compact disk (978-0-9712368-4-4(4)) Goops Unlimited.

Rothstein, Arminio & Brixler, Andreas. TOBY & TOBIAS: Die Abenteuer aus dem ZiRKUS HABAKUK. 2010. 134p. pap. 14.90 (978-3-8391-0292-3(8)) Bks. on Demand.

Roy, Ron. August Acrobat. Gurney, John Steven, illus. 2012. (Calendar Mysteries Ser.: 8). (ENG.). 80p. (J). (gr. 1-4). 4.99 (978-0-375-86886-3(0)); lib. bdg. 12.99 (978-0-375-96886-0(5)) Random Hse. Children's Bks. (Random Hse. Bks. for Young Readers).

—August Acrobat. 2012. (Calendar Mysteries Ser.: 8). lib. bdg. 14.75 (978-0-606-26403-7(5), Turtleback) Turtleback Bks.

Russell Brown, Eleanor. A C Robat Goes to Circus School. 2009. 32p. pap. 14.49 (978-1-4389-3939-1(6)) AuthorHouse.

Sally the Great: Individual Title Six-Packs. (gr. k-1). 23.00 (978-0-7635-9026-0(6)) Rigby Education.

Sander, Sonia. Big-Top Scooby-Doo! Movie Reader. 2012. (Scooby Doo Reader Ser.). lib. bdg. 13.55 (978-0-606-26542-3(2), Turtleback) Turtleback Bks.

Santillo, LuAnn. At the Circus, 6 vols. Santillo, LuAnn, ed. 2003. (Half-Pint Kids Readers Ser.). (Illus.). 42p. (J). (gr. -1-1). pap. 6.95 (978-1-59256-112-4(8)) Half-Pint Kids, Inc.

—The Best Show. Santillo, LuAnn, ed. 2003. (Half-Pint Kids Readers Ser.). (Illus.). 7p. (J). (gr. -1-1). pap. 1.00 (978-1-59256-117-9(9)) Half-Pint Kids, Inc.

—The Big Top. Santillo, LuAnn, ed. 2003. (Half-Pint Kids Readers Ser.). (Illus.). 7p. (J). (gr. -1-1). pap. 1.00 (978-1-59256-113-1(6)) Half-Pint Kids, Inc.

—Good Food. Santillo, LuAnn, ed. 2003. (Half-Pint Kids Readers Ser.). (Illus.). 7p. (J). (gr. -1-1). pap. 1.00 (978-1-59256-118-6(7)) Half-Pint Kids, Inc.

—The Lion Tamer. Santillo, LuAnn, ed. 2003. (Half-Pint Kids Readers Ser.). (Illus.). 7p. (J). (gr. -1-1). pap. 1.00 (978-1-59256-115-5(2)) Half-Pint Kids, Inc.

—The Tight Rope. Santillo, LuAnn, ed. 2003. (Half-Pint Kids Readers Ser.). (Illus.). 7p. (J). (gr. -1-1). pap. 1.00 (978-1-59256-114-8(4)) Half-Pint Kids, Inc.

Scalzo, Linda V. Carazona's Coloring Book. l.t. ed. 2004. (Illus.). 8p. (J). 2.99 (978-0-9753724-3-2(2)) Carazona Creations LLC.

—El circo llega al Pueblo: Version de Lectura Temprana. Torres, Marcela H., tr. Spalinski, Amanda, illus. l.t. ed. 2005. (SPA.). 24p. per. 9.99 (978-0-9753724-2-5(4)) Carazona Creations LLC.

—The Circus Is coming to Town: Early Reader Version. Spalinski, Amanda, illus. l.t. ed. 2005. 24p. (J). per. 9.99 (978-0-9753724-1-8(6)) Carazona Creations LLC.

—The Circus Is Coming to Town: Full-Length Version. l.t. ed. 2004. (Illus.). 32p. (J). 9.99 (978-0-9753724-0-1(8)) Carazona Creations LLC.

Schachner, Judy. Skippyjon Jones Cirque de Ole. 2012. (Skippyjon Jones Ser.). (ENG.). 32p. (J). (gr. -1-k). 17.99 (978-0-8037-3782-2(3), Dial Bks) Penguin Young Readers Group.

Schrecengost, Maity. High above the Hippodrome. 2007. (J). (gr. 3-6). pap. 13.95 (978-0-9771079-7-1(3), Chapin Hse. Bks.) Florida Historical Society.

Scott, Elaine. Secrets of the Cirque Medrano. 2008. (ENG., Illus.). 216p. (J). (gr. 5-9). 15.95 (978-1-57091-712-7(4)) Charlesbridge Publishing, Inc.

—The Spanish Web: An Encounter with Picasso. 2004. (Art Encounters Ser.). (J). 15.95 (978-0-8230-0410-2(4)); pap. 6.99 (978-0-8230-0413-3(9)) Watson-Guptill Pubns., Inc.

Sedgwick, Julian. The Black Dragon. Moffett, Patricia, illus. 2016. (Mysterium Ser.: 1). (ENG.). 352p. (gr. 4-8). 18.99 (978-1-4677-7567-0(3)); 38.65 (978-1-4677-9555-5(0)) Lerner Publishing Group. (Carolrhoda Bks.).

—The Palace of Memory. Moffett, Patricia, illus. 2017. (Mysterium Ser.: 2). (ENG.). 352p. (J). (gr. 4-8). 18.99 (978-1-4677-7568-7(1), Carolrhoda Bks.) Lerner Publishing Group.

Segal, Andrew. Clarissa the Clown. Scott, Peter & JessT, Grant, illus. 2007. 32p. per. (978-1-905823-20-8(7)) Panoma Pr. Ltd.

Seidon, Bonnie Bale. The Adventures of Trevor & the Tiger. 2012. 104p. 21.79 (978-1-4669-4389-6(0)); pap. 11.79 (978-1-4669-4391-9(2)) Trafford Publishing.

Shan Shan, Kathryn. Everyday Circus. Wilson, Lynda Farrington, illus. 2013. 48p. pap. 10.97 (978-1-939896-01-8(0)) Levity Pr.

Shepple, Sue Ann. Christopher & Grammy Join the Circus. 2011. 28p. pap. 15.99 (978-1-4628-6245-0(4)) Xlibris Corp.

Shire, Poppy. Sparkle the Circus Pony. Berg, Ron, illus. 2007. (Magic Pony Carousel Ser.: 1). (ENG.). 96p. (J). (gr. 2-5). pap. 3.99 (978-0-06-083779-2(9)) HarperCollins Pubs.

Sileo, Frank J. Don't Put Yourself down in Circus Town: A Story about Self-Confidence. Cornelison, Sue, illus. 2014. (J). pap. (978-1-4338-1914-8(7), Magination Pr.) American Psychological Assn.

The Silly Circus. 2007. (Illus.). 29p. (J). pap. 14.95 (978-0-615-18357-2(3)) Carolyn & Kristina's Bookshelf.

Silverstein, Shel. Lafcadio, el Leon Que Disparo al Cazador. Rioja, Alberto Jimenez, tr. from ENG. 2011.Tr. of Lafcadio, the Lion Who Shot Back. (SPA., Illus.). 112p. (J). (gr. 2-3). pap. 16.99 (978-1-933032-74-0(X)) Lectorum Pubns., Inc.

Silvestri, Linda. Clementina & the Hooey-Phooey Circus Troupe. 2007. (ESP., Illus.). (YA). 12.95 (978-0-9710696-8-8(9)) Jorlan Publishing, Inc.

Slobodkina, Esphyr. Circus Caps for Sale. Slobodkina, Esphyr, illus. 2004. (Illus.). 40p. (J). (gr. -1-2). reprint ed. 17.00 (978-0-7567-8345-7(3)) DIANE Publishing Co.

Slobodkina, Esphyr & Slobodkina. Circus Caps for Sale. Slobodkina, Esphyr, illus. 2004. (ENG., Illus.). 48p. (J). (gr. -1-3). reprint ed. pap. 7.99 (978-0-06-443793-6(0)) HarperCollins Pubs.

Smith, Alex T. Claude at the Circus, 1 vol. Smith, Alex T., illus. (Claude Ser.). (ENG., Illus.). 96p. (J). (gr. 2-4). 2017. pap. 7.95 (978-1-56145-980-3(1)) 2013. 12.95 (978-1-56145-702-1(7)) Peachtree Pubs.

Soderberg, Erin. The Quirks in Circus Quirkus. 2014. (Quirks Ser.). (ENG., Illus.). (YA). (gr. 3-6). 256p. pap. 7.99 (978-1-61963-663-7(8), 9781619636637); 240p. 13.99 (978-1-59990-790-1(9), 9781599907901) Bloomsbury Publishing USA. (Bloomsbury USA Childrens).

Starkey, R. Hawk. Mysterious Magical Circus Family Kids: The Chocolate Cake Turkey Lip Crumb Trail Mystery Adventure. 2008. 192p. pap. 13.95 (978-1-4327-3096-3(7)) Outskirts Pr., Inc.

Stine, R. L. A Nightmare on Clown Street. 2015. (Goosebumps: Most Wanted Ser.: 7). (ENG.). 160p. (J). (gr. 3-7). pap. 6.99 (978-0-545-62774-0(5), Scholastic Paperbacks) Scholastic, Inc.

Studio Mouse, ed. Jojo's Circus Get up & Move! Flat Learn & Carry 4 Board Books & CD. rev. ed. 2007. (ENG.). 12.99 (978-1-59069-548-7(8)) Studio Mouse LLC.

Sturgis, Brenda Reeves. 10 Turkeys in the Road, 0 vols. Slonim, David, illus. 2011. (ENG.). 32p. (J). (gr. -1-1). 16.99 (978-0-7614-5847-0(6), 9780761458470, Amazon Children's Publishing) Amazon Publishing.

Teele, Elinor. The Mechanical Mind of John Coggin. 2016. (Illus.). 352p. (J). (gr. 3-7). 16.99 (978-0-06-234510-3(9), Waldon Pond Pr.) HarperCollins Pubs.

ten Cate, Marijke. Who Has the Biggest Bottom. 2013. (ENG., Illus.). 32p. (J). (gr. -1). 17.95 (978-1-935954-25-5(3), 9781935954255) Lemniscaat USA.

Thurmond, Joey. Nojoe Makes New Friends. 2009. 16p. pap. 10.99 (978-1-4490-4156-4(6)) AuthorHouse.

Tibo, Gilles. Simon et le Petit Cirque. 2004.Tr. of Simon at the Circus. (FRE.). (J). (gr. -1-2). spiral bd. (978-0-616-01846-0(0)) Canadian National Institute for the Blind/Institut National Canadien pour les Aveugles.

—Le Voyage du Funambule. 2004. (Mon Roman Ser.). (FRE., Illus.). 64p. (J). (gr. 2). pap. (978-2-89021-701-0(9)) Diffusion du livre Mirabel (DLM).

Toft, Di. The Twilight Circus. 2011. (Wolven Ser.: 2). (ENG.). 384p. (J). (gr. 3-7). 17.99 (978-0-545-29492-8(4), Chicken Hse., The) Scholastic, Inc.

Touma, Patricia. Happy Times, the Adventures of Ish & Mish Vol. 1: Ish & Mish Go to the Circus. 2005. per. 7.00 (978-1-58396-873-4(3)) Blue Unicorn Edition, LLC.

Tripp, Jenny. Pete & Fremont. Manders, John, illus. 2008. (ENG.). 192p. (J). (gr. 3-7). pap. 12.95 (978-0-15-206238-5(6)) Houghton Mifflin Harcourt Publishing Co.

Valdes, Leslie. At the Carnival. Roper, Robert, illus. 2005. (Dora the Explorer Ser.). (ENG.). 24p. (J). pap. 3.99 (978-0-689-85841-3(8), Simon Spotlight/Nickelodeon) Simon Spotlight/Nickelodeon.

Van Dusen, Chris. The Circus Ship. Van Dusen, Chris, illus. (ENG., Illus.). 40p. (J). (gr. -1-3). 2015. 6.99 (978-0-7636-5592-1(9)) 2009. 16.99 (978-0-7636-3090-4(X)) Candlewick Pr.

Vance Barnum. Joe Strong the Boy Fire-Eater. 2007. 180p. per. 11.95 *(978-1-4218-4012-3(X)*, 1st World Library - Literary Society) 1st World Publishing, Inc.

Villeneuve, Anne. The Red Scarf. 2010. (ENG., Illus.). 40p. (J). (gr. k-3). 17.95 *(978-0-88776-989-4(6)*, Tundra Bks.) Tundra Bks. CAN. Dist: Penguin Random Hse. LLC.

Walder, Lysa. Katie the Paramedic. 2009. (Illus.). 28p. pap. 12.49 *(978-1-4389-7134-6(6))* AuthorHouse.

Wallace, Morgan the Magnificent. (J). 16.95 *(978-0-88899-056-3(1)*, Libros Tigrillo) Groundwood Bks. CAN. Dist: Publishers Group West (PGW).

Wallace, Ian. Morgan the Magnificent. (J). 5.95 *(978-0-88899-166-9(5)*, Libros Tigrillo) Groundwood Bks. CAN. Dist: Publishers Group West (PGW).

Walters, Eric. Tiger by the Tail. 2009. (ENG.). 176p. (J). (gr. 6). pap. *(978-1-55488-175-8(7))* Beach Holme Pubs., Ltd.

Wegman, William. 3... 2... 1... Circus! 2014. (ENG., Illus.). 24p. (J). (— 1). bds. 6.99 *(978-0-8037-3934-5(6)*, Dial Bks) Penguin Young Readers Group.

Weidensee, Ralph. The Cry'N Lion. 2010. 28p. pap. 21.99 *(978-1-4415-7923-2(0))* Xlibris Corp.

Weinberg, Jennifer Liberts. Fly, Dumbo, Fly! Kurtz, John & Lo Raso, Carlo, illus. 2012. (Step into Reading Ser.). (ENG.). 32p. (J). (gr. -1-1). pap. 3.99 *(978-0-7364-2044-0(4)*, RH/Disney) Random Hse. Children's Bks.

Weston Woods Staff, creator. Caps for Sale. 2011. 38.75 *(978-0-439-72925-3(4))*; 18.95 *(978-0-439-72924-6(6))* Weston Woods Studios, Inc.

Wheeler, J. D. Gummery & Lubber. 2008. 56p. pap. 16.95 *(978-1-60563-432-6(8))* America Star Bks.

Wilson, Audrey. Dante Goes to the Circus. 2009. 28p. pap. 13.99 *(978-1-4389-6779-0(9))* AuthorHouse.

Wundram, Bill. Finnius: The Tale of a Lost Little Elephant. Tucker, Eric, illus. 2003. (J). *(978-1-59152-011-5(8)*, Sweetgrass Bks.) Farcountry Pr.

Yeoman, John & Blake, Quentin. The Fabulous Foskett Family Circus. 2015. (ENG., Illus.). 32p. (J). (gr. -1-k). pap. 9.99 *(978-1-78344-035-1(X))* Andersen Pr. GBR. Dist: Independent Pubs. Group.

Yep, Laurence. When the Circus Came to Town. Wang, Suling, illus. 2004. 112p. (J). (gr. 3-5). 13.65 *(978-0-7569-2969-5(5))* Perfection Learning Corp.

Yolen, Jane & Stemple, Adam. The Last Changeling. 2014. (Seelie Wars Ser.). (ENG.). 304p. (J). (gr. 3-7). 16.99 *(978-0-670-01435-4(4)*, Viking Books for Young Readers) Penguin Young Readers Group.

Zimmer, Tracie Vaughn & Vaughn Zimmer, Tracie. The Floating Circus. 2008. (ENG.). 208p. (YA). (gr. 3-7). 16.99 *(978-1-59990-185-5(4)*, 9781599901855, Bloomsbury USA Childrens) Bloomsbury Publishing USA.

CIRCUS—PICTORIAL WORKS

Hruby, Patrick. ABC Is for Circus. 2013. (ENG., Illus.). 56p. (J). 16.95 *(978-1-62326-006-4(X))* AMMO Bks., LLC.

—ABC Is for Circus: Hardcover Popular Edition. 2017. (ENG., Illus.). 56p. 9.95 *(978-1-62326-107-8(4))* AMMO Bks., LLC.

Tullet, Hervé. The Finger Circus Game. Oceano Editorial Staff, ed. 2013. (ENG., Illus.). 14p. 12.95 *(978-0-7148-6531-7(1))* Phaidon Pr., Inc.

CIRCUS—POETRY

Janeczko, Paul B. Worlds Afire. 2007. (ENG., Illus.). 112p. (YA). (gr. 7-18). per. 7.99 *(978-0-7636-3400-1(X))* Candlewick Pr.

CITIES AND TOWNS

Here are entered works on cities and towns. For works on large cities and their surrounding areas use Metropolitan Areas. General works on the government of cities are entered under Municipal Government. General works on local government other than that of cities are entered under Local Government.

see also Markets; Sociology, Urban; Streets

also headings beginning with the word Municipal; and names of individual cities and towns

Alaina, Maria. Shapes in the City, 1 vol. (Wonder Readers Next Steps: Math Ser.). (ENG.). (gr. -1-1). 2013. 20p. lib. bdg. 22.65 *(978-1-4765-0035-5(5))* 2011. 16p. pap. 35.94 *(978-1-4296-8147-6(0))* 2011. 32p. pap. 5.99 *(978-1-4296-7811-7(9))* Capstone Press of Coughlan Cos. (Wonder Readers).

Anderson, Mercedes Padrino. Cities & Towns in the Middle Ages. 2005. (World Almanac Library of the Middle Ages). (Illus.). 48p. (gr. 5-12). pap. 14.05 *(978-0-8368-5902-7(2)*, Gareth Stevens Secondary Library) Stevens, Gareth Publishing LLLP.

Anderson, Mercedes Padrino & Padrino, Mercedes. Cities & Towns in the Middle Ages. 2005. (World Almanac Library of the Middle Ages). (Illus.). 48p. (gr. 5-12). lib. bdg. 31.00 *(978-0-8368-5893-8(X)*, Gareth Stevens Secondary Library) Stevens, Gareth Publishing LLLP.

Austen, Mary. We Live in a Small Town, 01 vols., 1. 2016. (American Communities Ser.). (ENG.). 24p. (J). 23.60 *(978-1-5081-4195-2(9))*; pap. 8.25 *(978-1-5081-4193-8(2))* Rosen Publishing Group, Inc., The. (PowerKids Pr.).

Barber, Nicola. City Homes. 2007. (Homes Around the World Ser.). (ENG., Illus.). 32p. (J). (gr. 3-7). pap. *(978-0-7787-3554-0(0))* Crabtree Publishing Co.

Benjamin, Tina. Where I Live. 2015. (Inside My World Ser.). (ENG.). 24p. (J). (gr. k-k). 22.60 *(978-1-4824-1813-2(4))* Stevens, Gareth Publishing LLLP.

Benjamin, Tina & Bockman, Charlotte. Donde Yo Vivo: Where I Live. 2015. (SPA & ENG.). 24p. *(978-1-4824-2366-2(9))* Stevens, Gareth Publishing LLLP.

Blanche, David. A Day in My Town. 2012. (InfoMax Readers Ser.). (ENG., Illus.). 16 pp.p. (J). (gr. k-1). pap. 7.00 *(978-1-4488-8977-8(4)*, Rosen Classroom) Rosen Publishing Group, Inc., The.

Bodden, Valerie. A City. (My First Look At Ser.). 24p. (J). 2011. (ENG.). (gr. 1-17). pap. 7.99 *(978-1-926722-29-0(9)*, Creative Paperbacks) 2007. (Illus.). (gr. -1-3). lib. bdg. 24.25 *(978-1-58341-512-2(2)*, Creative Education) Creative Co., The.

—A Farming Town. 2007. (My First Look at: Communities Ser.). (Illus.). 24p. (J). (gr. -1-3). lib. bdg. 24.25 *(978-1-58341-513-9(0)*, Creative Education) Creative Co., The.

—My First Look at - A Town. 2007. (My First Look at: Communities Ser.). (Illus.). 24p. (J). (gr. -1-3). lib. bdg. 24.25 *(978-1-58341-515-3(7)*, Creative Education) Creative Co., The.

—A Suburb. (My First Look At Ser.). 24p. (J). 2011. (ENG.). (gr. 1-17). pap. 7.99 *(978-1-926722-31-3(0)*, Creative Paperbacks) 2007. (Illus.). (gr. -1-3). lib. bdg. 24.25 *(978-1-58341-514-6(9)*, Creative Education) Creative Co., The.

—A Town. 2011. (My First Look At Ser.). (ENG.). 24p. (J). (gr. 1-17). pap. 7.99 *(978-1-926722-32-0(9)*, Creative Paperbacks) Creative Co., The.

Boudreau, Hélène, et al. Life in a Residential City. 2010. (Learn about Urban Life Ser.). (ENG., Illus.). 32p. (J). (gr. 3-6). pap. *(978-0-7787-7403-7(1))*; lib. bdg. *(978-0-7787-7393-1(0))* Crabtree Publishing Co.

Bradley, Timothy J. Wild Cities, 1 vol. 2nd rev. ed. 2013. (Nonfiction Readers Ser.). (ENG., Illus.). 48p. (J). (gr. 4-4). pap. 29.96 *(978-1-4807-1099-3(7))* Shell Educational Publishing.

Bruce, Julia. Conquest! Can You Build a Roman City? Dennis, Peter, illus. 2009. (Step into History Ser.). 32p. (J). (gr. 2-5). lib. bdg. 23.94 *(978-0-7660-3478-5(X))* Enslow Pubs., Inc.

Bullard, Lisa. This Is My Town. Becker, Paula J., illus. 2016. (Cloverleaf Books (tm) — Where I Live Ser.). (ENG.). 24p. (J). (gr. k-2). 25.32 *(978-1-4677-9522-7(4)*, Millbrook Pr.) Lerner Publishing Group.

Chambers, Catherine. Stickmen's Guide to Cities in Layers. Dean, Venitia & De Quay, John Paul, illus. 2016. (Stickmen's Guides to This Incredible Earth Ser.). (ENG.). 32p. (J). (gr. 3-6). 26.65 *(978-1-5124-0620-7(1))* Lerner Publishing Group.

City. 2007. (Busy Books Small Ser.). 5p. *(978-1-4054-9496-0(4))* Parragon, Inc.

City Senses: Big Book: Level F. 16p. 31.50 *(978-0-322-00374-3(1))* Wright Group/McGraw-Hill.

Clark Sawyer, J. Patterns in the City. 2015. (J). lib. bdg. *(978-1-62724-336-0(4))* Bearport Publishing Co., Inc.

Claybourne, Anna. 1001Things to Spot in the Town. 2009. (1001 Things to Spot Ser.). 32p. (J). 9.99 *(978-0-7945-2514-9(8)*, Usborne) EDC Publishing.

Cornell, Kari. Life in the City. 2016. (Illus.). 24p. (J). *(978-0-87659-714-9(2))* Gryphon Hse., Inc.

Dawson, Emily C. The City. 2010. (My Community Ser.). 24p. (J). 25.65 *(978-1-60753-022-0(8))* Amicus Publishing.

Doherty, Gillian. 1001 Cosa Que Buscar En Pueblos y Ciudades. 2004. (SPA., Illus.). 32p. (J). (gr. -1-18). lib. bdg. 14.95 *(978-1-58086-351-3(5)*, EU31233) EDC Publishing.

Doherty, Gillian & Claybourne, Anna. Los Pueblos Del Mundo - Internet Linked. 2004. (Titles in Spanish Ser.). (SPA.). 96p. (J). pap. 14.95 *(978-0-7460-5068-2(2)*, Usborne) EDC Publishing.

Dyer, Hadley. Watch This Space: Designing, Defending & Sharing Public Spaces. Ngui, Marc, illus. 2010. (ENG.). 80p. (J). (gr. 5-9). 18.95 *(978-1-55453-293-3(0))* Kids Can Pr., Ltd. CAN. Dist: Hachette Bk. Group.

Emberley, Rebecca. My City/ Mi Ciudad. 2005. (ENG., Illus.). 10p. (J). (gr. -1 — 1). bds. 6.99 *(978-0-316-00051-2(5))* Little, Brown Bks. for Young Readers.

Espejo, Roman. Urban America. 2011. (Opposing Viewpoints Ser.). 240p. (J). lib. bdg. 42.95 *(978-0-7377-5249-6(1)*, Greenhaven Pr., Inc.) Cengage Gale.

Faulkner, Nicholas. A Visual History of Houses & Cities Around the World. 2016. (Visual History of the World Ser.). 00096p. (J). (gr. 8-8). 37.10 *(978-1-4994-6572-3(6))* Rosen Publishing Group, Inc., The.

Felix, Rebecca. Patterns in the City. 2015. (21st Century Basic Skills Library: Patterns All Around Ser.). (ENG.). 24p. (J). (gr. k-3). pap. 12.79 *(978-1-63188-938-7(9)*, 206013) Cherry Lake Publishing.

Figorito, C. In the City: Learning the Soft C Sound. 2009. (PowerPhonics Ser.). 24p. (gr. 1-1). 39.90 *(978-1-60851-452-6(8)*, PowerKids Pr.) Rosen Publishing Group, Inc., The.

Flatt, Lizann. Life in a Suburban City. 2010. (Learn about Urban Life Ser.). (ENG., Illus.). 32p. (J). (gr. 3-6). lib. bdg. *(978-0-7787-7394-8(9))*; (gr. 4-9). pap. *(978-0-7787-7404-4(X))* Crabtree Publishing Co.

—Life in an Industrial City. 2010. (Learn about Urban Life Ser.). (ENG., Illus.). 32p. (J). (gr. 4-9). pap. *(978-0-7787-7402-0(3))*; lib. bdg. *(978-0-7787-7392-4(2))* Crabtree Publishing Co.

Flores, Mina. The Growth of the American City: Immigrants & Migrants Travel for Work, 01 vols., 1. 2016. (Spotlight on Immigration & Migration Ser.). (ENG., Illus.). 24p. (J). pap. 10.00 *(978-1-5081-4076-4(6)*, PowerKids Pr.) Rosen Publishing Group, Inc., The.

Franceschelli, Christopher. Cityblock. Peskimo, illus. 2016. (Alphablock Ser.). (ENG.). 96p. (J). (gr. -1-k). bds. 16.95 *(978-1-4197-2189-2(5)*, Abrams Appleseed) Abrams, Inc.

Fretland VanVoorst, Jenny. Las Formas en la Ciudad. 2015.Tr. of Shapes in the City. (SPA., Illus.). 24p. (J). lib. bdg. *(978-1-62031-246-9(8)*, Bullfrog Bks.) Jump! Inc.

—Shapes in the City. 2015. (Illus.). 24p. (J). lib. bdg. *(978-1-62031-200-1(X)*, Bullfrog Bks.) Jump! Inc.

Gale Editors & Merino, Noël. Urban Sprawl. 2014. (Current Controversies Ser.). (ENG., Illus.). 224p. (gr. 7-12). pap. 32.00 *(978-0-7377-6248-8(9)*, Greenhaven Pr., Inc.) Cengage Gale.

Geatches, Hazel. Cities, Level 2. 2012. (ENG., Illus.). 40p. pap. 9.38 *(978-0-19-464682-6(3))* Oxford Univ. Pr., Inc.

George, Enzo. Russia's City of the Dead. 2017. (Crypts, Tombs, & Secret Rooms Ser.). 48p. (gr. 4-5). pap. 84.30 ***(978-1-5382-0644-7(7))*** Stevens, Gareth Publishing LLLP.

Gibson, Brylee. Megacities. 2007. (Connectors Ser.). (gr. 2-5). pap. *(978-1-877453-07-6(2))* Global Education Systems Ltd.

Gifford, Clive. 100 Facts Around Town. Kearney, Brendan, illus. 2015. (ENG.). 14p. (J). (gr. -1-1). 12.99 *(978-1-4052-7171-4(X))* Egmont Bks., Ltd. GBR. Dist: Independent Pubs. Group.

Gordon, Sharon. At Home in the City. 2005. (Bookworms Ser.). (SPA., Illus.). 32p. (J). (gr. 3-7). lib. bdg. *(978-0-7614-1960-0(8)*, Benchmark Bks.) Marshall Cavendish Corp.

—At Home in the City/Mi Casa en la Ciudad. 2006. (Bookworms Ser.). (ENG & SPA., Illus.). 32p. (gr. k-2). lib. bdg. 15.95 *(978-0-7614-2452-9(0))* Marshall Cavendish Corp.

—Mi Casa en la Ciudad. 2006. (Bookworms Ser.). (SPA., Illus.). 32p. (gr. k-2). lib. bdg. 15.95 *(978-0-7614-2372-0(9))* Marshall Cavendish Corp.

Guin, Valerie. In the City. 2005. (One World (Smart Apple Media) Ser.). (Illus.). 30p. (J). (gr. 3-6). lib. bdg. 27.10 *(978-1-58340-696-0(4))* Black Rabbit Bks.

Hamilton, Robert. Encyclopedia of Amazing Places: Discover Famous Wonders of the World. 2012. (Illus.). 224p. (J). *(978-1-4351-4347-0(7))* Barnes & Noble, Inc.

Harcourt School Publishers Staff. Where We Live, Unit 2. 3rd ed. 2003. (Harcourt Brace Social Studies). pap. 76.00 *(978-0-15-341067-3(1))* Harcourt Schl. Pubs.

Harrison, Nicholas. A Day in a City. 2009. (Time Goes By Ser.). (ENG.). (gr. k-3). pap. 39.62 *(978-0-7613-4711-8(9))* Lerner Publishing Group.

Heywood, Rosie. The Great City Search. 2004. (Great Searches Ser.). 32p. (J). lib. bdg. 16.95 *(978-1-58086-626-2(3)*, Usborne) EDC Publishing.

Hinds, Kathryn. The City. (Life in the Medieval Muslim World Ser.). (gr. 6-18). 2008. 96p. lib. bdg. 34.21 *(978-0-7614-3089-6(X))* 2006. (Illus.). 80p. lib. bdg. 34.21 *(978-0-7614-2184-9(X))* 2004. (Illus.). 80p. 34.21 *(978-0-7614-1655-5(2))* Marshall Cavendish Corp. (Benchmark Bks.).

Holland, Gini. I Live in a Town. 2004. (Weekly Reader Early Learning Library). (Illus.). 24p. (gr. k-3). pap. 8.15 *(978-0-8368-4090-2(9))*; lib. bdg. 22.00 *(978-0-8368-4083-4(6))* Stevens, Gareth Publishing LLLP. (Weekly Reader Leveled Readers).

—I Live in a Town/Vivo en un Pueblo. Coffey, Colleen & Carrillo, Consuelo, trs. 2004. (Weekly Reader Early Learning Library). (SPA & ENG., Illus.). 24p. (gr. k-3). pap. 8.15 *(978-0-8368-4138-1(7))*; lib. bdg. 22.00 *(978-0-8368-4131-2(X))* Stevens, Gareth Publishing LLLP. (Weekly Reader Leveled Readers).

—I Live in the City. 2004. (Where I Live Ser.). (Illus.). 24p. (gr. k-3). lib. bdg. 22.00 *(978-0-8368-4078-0(X)*, Weekly Reader Leveled Readers) Stevens, Gareth Publishing LLLP.

—I Live in the City/Vivo en la Ciudad. Coffey, Colleen & Carrillo, Consuelo, trs. 2004. (Weekly Reader Early Learning Library). (SPA & ENG., Illus.). 24p. (gr. k-3). lib. bdg. 22.00 *(978-0-8368-4126-8(3)*, Weekly Reader Leveled Readers) Stevens, Gareth Publishing LLLP.

—Where I Live, 6 bks. Incl. I Live in a Town. lib. bdg. 22.00 *(978-0-8368-4083-4(6))*; I Live in the City. lib. bdg. 22.00 *(978-0-8368-4078-0(X))*; I Live in the Country. lib. bdg. 22.00 *(978-0-8368-4079-7(8))*; I Live in the Desert. lib. bdg. 22.00 *(978-0-8368-4080-3(1))*; I Live in the Mountains. lib. bdg. 22.00 *(978-0-8368-4081-0(X))*; (gr. k-3)., Weekly Reader Leveled Readers (Where I Live Ser.). (Illus.). 24p. 2004. 119.58 o.p. *(978-0-8368-4077-3(1)*, Weekly Reader) Stevens, Gareth Publishing LLLP.

Hurtig, Jennifer. Capitals. 2008. (U. S. Sites & Symbols Ser.). (Illus.). 48p. (J). (gr. 3-5). lib. bdg. 29.05 *(978-1-59036-896-1(7))*; (gr. 4-6). pap. 10.95 *(978-1-59036-897-8(5))* Weigl Pubs., Inc.

Hyde, Natalie. Population Patterns: What Factors Determine the Location & Growth of Human Settlements? 2010. (Investigating Human Migration & Settlement Ser.). (ENG., Illus.). 48p. (J). (gr. 5-8). *(978-0-7787-5182-3(1))*; pap. *(978-0-7787-5197-7(X))* Crabtree Publishing Co.

In the City. (Early Intervention Levels Ser.). 23.10 *(978-0-7362-0019-6(3))* CENGAGE Learning.

In the City: Individual Title, 6 Packs. (gr. -1-2). 23.00 *(978-0-7635-8809-0(1))* Rigby Education.

James, Trisha. I Know Places Around Town. 2017. (What I Know Ser.). 24p. (gr. k-k). pap. 8.15 ***(978-1-4824-6305-7(9))*** Stevens, Gareth Publishing LLLP.

Jones, Tammy. My Town. 2009. (Sight Word Readers Set A Ser.). (J). *(978-1-60719-147-6(4))* Newmark Learning LLC.

Kenney, Sean. Cool City. Kenney, Sean, illus. 2011. (ENG., Illus.). 32p. (J). (gr. -1-3). 12.99 *(978-0-8050-8762-8(1)*, 9780805087628, Holt, Henry & Co. Bks. For Young Readers) Holt, Henry & Co.

Kirst, Sean. The Soul of Central New York: Syracuse Stories by Sean Kirst. 2016. (ENG., Illus.). 400p. pap. 29.95 *(978-0-8156-1083-0(1)*, 4188) Syracuse Univ. Pr.

Koh, Frederick. The 10 Most Fascinating Cities. 2008. (J). 14.99 *(978-1-55448-499-7(5))* Scholastic Library Publishing.

Labrecque, Ellen. Living in a City. 2015. (Places We Live Ser.). (ENG.). 32p. (gr. 1-3). 27.32 *(978-1-4846-0805-0(4)*, Heinemann First Library) Heinemann-Raintree.

Laval, Thierry. Look & Find Your World. 2016. (Look & Find Ser.). (ENG.). 14p. (J). 18.99 *(978-0-531-22239-3(X)*, Children's Pr.) Scholastic Library Publishing.

Li, Maggie. Where Can I Go? Amazing Cities: Amazing World City Maps & Facts. Li, Maggie, illus. 2016. (ENG., Illus.). 64p. (J). (gr. -1-2). 18.99 *(978-1-84365-274-8(9)*, Pavilion) Pavilion Bks. GBR. Dist: Independent Pubs. Group.

Linde, Barbara M. Urban Sprawl, Vol. 1. 2014. (Habitat Havoc Ser.). 32p. (J). (gr. 3-4). (ENG.). pap. 10.50 *(978-1-4339-9868-3(8))*; 26.60 *(978-1-4339-9866-9(1))* Stevens, Gareth Publishing LLLP.

Litchfield, Jo. Town. 2004. (Look & Say Board Books Ser.). (Illus.). 10p. (J). 7.95 *(978-0-7945-0701-5(8)*, Usborne) EDC Publishing.

Loggins, Trace. Farm Life, City Life. 2013. (Rosen Readers Ser.). (ENG.). 24p. (J). (gr. 2-3). pap. 8.25 *(978-1-4777-2248-0(3))*; pap. 49.50 *(978-1-4777-2249-7(1))* Rosen Publishing Group, Inc., The. (Rosen Classroom).

Lonely Planet Publications Staff. Lonely Planet Let's Explore... Cities, 1 vol. 2017. (Lonely Planet Kids Ser.). (ENG., Illus.). (J). pap. 9.99 *(978-1-78657-230-1(3)*, 5380) Lonely Planet Pubns.

—World Search - Busy Places, 1 vol. 2014. (Lonely Planet Kids Ser.). (ENG.). 16p. (J). 14.99 *(978-1-74321-918-8(0)*, 4636) Lonely Planet Pubns.

Lonely Planet Publications Staff & Feroze, Jen. How Cities Work, 1 vol. 2016. (Lonely Planet Kids Ser.). (ENG., Illus.). 24p. (J). 18.99 *(978-1-78657-022-2(X)*, 5192) Lonely Planet Pubns.

Macdonald, Fiona. Inca Town. Mark, Bergin, illus. 2017. (Time Traveler's Guide Ser.). 48p. (gr. 3-7). 37.10 ***(978-1-911242-01-7(6))*** Book Hse. GBR. Dist: Black Rabbit Bks.

MacDonald, Margaret. Big Cities. 2011. (Learn-Abouts Ser.). (Illus.). 16p. (J). pap. 7.95 *(978-1-59920-614-1(5))* Black Rabbit Bks.

Mackley, Daniel. The City in the Roman Empire. 2016. (Life in the Roman Empire Ser.). 80p. (J). 35.64 *(978-1-5026-2259-4(9))* Cavendish Square Publishing.

Malam, John. Greek Town. Antram, David, illus. 2017. (Time Traveler's Guide Ser.). 48p. (gr. 3-7). 37.10 ***(978-1-911242-00-0(8))*** Book Hse. GBR. Dist: Black Rabbit Bks.

Manhof, Errol. My Community. 2009. (Real Life Readers Ser.). 8p. (gr. k-1). pap. 5.15 *(978-1-4042-7991-9(1)*, Rosen Classroom) Rosen Publishing Group, Inc., The.

Mara, Wil. What Should I Do? Near a Busy Street. 2011. (Community Connections: What Should I Do? Ser.). (ENG., Illus.). 24p. (J). (gr. 2-5). lib. bdg. 25.64 *(978-1-61080-051-8(6)*, 1330910) Cherry Lake Publishing.

Markovics, Joyce L. City Colors: From Taxis to Skyscrapers. 2015. (Illus.). 24p. (J). lib. bdg. *(978-1-62724-322-3(4))* Bearport Publishing Co., Inc.

—Los Colores de la Ciudad: De Los Taxis a Los Rascacielos. 2014. (Los Colores Cuentan una Historia Ser.). (SPA.). 24p. (J). (gr. -1-3). lib. bdg. 23.93 *(978-1-62724-464-0(6))* Bearport Publishing Co., Inc.

Marsico, Katie. Good Manners in Public, 1 vol. Haslam, John, illus. 2009. (Good Manners Matter! Ser.). (ENG.). 32p. (J). (gr. -1-2). 28.50 *(978-1-60270-610-1(7))* Magic Wagon.

—What's It Like to Live Here? City. 2014. (Community Connections: What's It Like to Live Here? Ser.). (ENG., Illus.). 24p. (J). (gr. 2-5). 25.64 *(978-1-62431-564-0(X)*, 203244) Cherry Lake Publishing.

—What's It Like to Live Here? Suburb. 2014. (Community Connections: What's It Like to Live Here? Ser.). (ENG., Illus.). 24p. (J). (gr. 2-5). pap. 12.79 *(978-1-62431-584-8(4)*, 203261) Cherry Lake Publishing.

Martell, Hazel Mary. Roman Town. Mark, Bergin, illus. 2017. (Time Traveler's Guide Ser.). 48p. (gr. 3-7). 37.10 ***(978-1-911242-02-4(4))*** Book Hse. GBR. Dist: Black Rabbit Bks.

Matthews, Colin. I Know People Around Town. 2017. (What I Know Ser.). 24p. (J). (gr. k-k). pap. 8.15 ***(978-1-4824-6301-9(6))*** Stevens, Gareth Publishing LLLP.

McAllan, Kate. Urban Habitats. 2013. (Discovery Education: Habitats Ser.). 32p. (J). (gr. 3-6). 25.25 *(978-1-4777-1327-3(1))*; pap. 10.00 *(978-1-4777-1489-8(8))* Rosen Publishing Group, Inc., The. (PowerKids Pr.).

McDowell, Pamela. Small Town. 2016. (Illus.). 24p. (J). pap. *(978-1-4896-3614-0(5))* Weigl Pubs., Inc.

Michele, Tracey. Getting Around the City. 2011. (Learn-Abouts Ser.). (Illus.). 16p. (J). pap. 7.95 *(978-1-59920-622-6(6))* Black Rabbit Bks.

Milbourne, Anna. 1001 Things to Spot in the Town. 2004. (1001 Things to Spot Ser.). (SPA & ENG., Illus.). 32p. (J). (gr. -1-18). 1p. pap. 6.99 *(978-0-7460-2953-4(5))*; 32p. lib. bdg. 14.99 *(978-1-58086-332-2(9))* EDC Publishing.

Milich, Zoran. City 123. 2005. (ENG., Illus.). 32p. (J). (gr. -1-k). 16.95 *(978-1-55337-540-1(8))* Kids Can Pr., Ltd. CAN. Dist: Hachette Bk. Group.

Millard, Anne. A Street Through Time. Noon, Steve, illus. 2012. (ENG.). 48p. (J). (gr. 5-12). 17.99 *(978-0-7566-9792-1(1)*, DK Children) Dorling Kindersley Publishing, Inc.

Miller, Jake. Who's Who in a Neighborhood. (Communities at Work Ser.). 24p. (gr. 2-2). 2009. 42.50 *(978-1-61511-897-7(7))* 2005. (Illus.). (J). lib. bdg. 22.60 *(978-1-4042-2785-9(7))* 2005. (ENG., Illus.). pap. 8.25 *(978-1-4042-5024-6(7))* Rosen Publishing Group, Inc., The. (PowerKids Pr.).

—Who's Who in an Urban Community. (Communities at Work Ser.). 24p. (gr. 2-2). 2009. 42.50 *(978-1-61511-901-1(9))* 2005. (Illus.). (J). lib. bdg. 22.60 *(978-1-4042-2790-3(3))* Rosen Publishing Group, Inc., The. (PowerKids Pr.).

Mills, Nathan & Jamison, Linc. Getting Around Our City. 2012. (Rosen Readers Ser.). (ENG., Illus.). 16p. (J). (gr. k-1). pap. 7.00 *(978-1-4488-8722-4(4)*, Rosen Classroom) Rosen Publishing Group, Inc., The.

Morgan, Sally. Changing Planet: What Is the Environmental Impact of Human Migration & Settlement? 2010. (Investigating Human Migration & Settlement Ser.). (ENG., Illus.). 48p. (J). (gr. 5-8). *(978-0-7787-5179-3(1))*; pap. *(978-0-7787-5194-6(5))* Crabtree Publishing Co.

My Cousin Jake: Individual Title Six-Packs. (gr. -1-2). 27.00 *(978-0-7635-9463-3(6))* Rigby Education.

Obadina, Tunde. Population & Overcrowding. Ojakorotu, Victor & Rotberg, Robert I., eds. 2013. (Africa: Progress & Problems Ser.: 13). (Illus.). 112p. (J). (gr. 7-18). 24.95 *(978-1-4222-2945-3(9))* Mason Crest.

Owings, Lisa. Craco: The Medieval Ghost Town. 2017. (Abandoned Places Ser.). (ENG., Illus.). 24p. (J). (gr. 3-7). lib. bdg. 25.95 ***(978-1-62617-695-9(7)***, Torque Bks.) Bellwether Media.

Padrino, Mercedes. Feudalism & Village Life in the Middle Ages. 2005. (World Almanac Library of the Middle Ages). (Illus.). 48p. (gr. 5-12). lib. bdg. 31.00 *(978-0-8368-5894-5(8)*, Gareth Stevens Secondary Library) Stevens, Gareth Publishing LLLP.

Park, Louise. Ancient Cities. 2013. (Discovery Education: Ancient Civilizations Ser.). (ENG., Illus.). 32p. (J). (gr. 3-6). pap. 10.00 *(978-1-4777-0097-6(8))*; lib. bdg. 25.25 *(978-1-4777-0056-3(0))* Rosen Publishing Group, Inc., The.

Pearson, Claudia. This Way, Watson! A Map & Directions Primer, 1 vol. 2017. (ENG.). 32p. (J). 12.99 ***(978-1-4236-4765-2(3))*** Gibbs Smith, Publisher.

Porter, Esther. Peeking under the City. Lozano, Andres, illus. 2016. (What's Beneath Ser.). (ENG.). 32p. (gr. -1-3). lib. bdg. 27.32 *(978-1-4795-8665-3(X))* Picture Window Bks.

Price, Sean Stewart. The Kids' Guide to Lost Cities, 1 vol. 2011. (Kids' Guides). (ENG.). 32p. (gr. 3-4). 27.99 *(978-1-4296-6009-9(0)*, Edge Bks.) Capstone Press of Coughlan Cos.

Priddy, Roger. Around the Town. 2015. (Treasure Hunt Ser.). (ENG., Illus.). 10p. (J). (gr. -1 — 1). bds. 8.99 *(978-0-312-51797-7(1)*, 9780312517977, Priddy Bks.) St. Martin's Pr.

—Playtown. 2014. (Playtown Ser.). (ENG.). 16p. (J). (gr. -1-k). bds. 12.99 *(978-0-312-51737-3(8)*, 9780312517373, Priddy Bks.) St. Martin's Pr.

C D

Publishers, Chelsea House, creator. Global Cities Set, 12-Volumes. 2007. (Global Cities Ser.). (gr. 5-8). 360.00 (978-0-7910-9680-2(7), Chelsea Hse.) Facts On File, Inc.

Raby, Charlotte. City Tours. 2017. (ENG., Illus.). 48p. (J). pap. 8.99 **(978-0-00-820882-0(4))** HarperCollins Pubs. Ltd. GBR. Dist: Independent Pubs. Group.

Randall, Jory. My Day in the City. 2009. (Kid's Life! Ser.). 24p. (J). (ENG.). pap. 8.25 (978-1-4358-2469-0(5)); (Illus.). lib. bdg. 22.60 (978-1-4042-8075-5(8)) Rosen Publishing Group, Inc., The. (PowerKids Pr.).

Rau, Dana Meachen & National Geographic Learning Staff. In the City. 2010. (Rise & Shine Ser.). (ENG.). (C). pap. 18.95 (978-0-7614-3306-4(6)) National Geographic School Publishing, Inc.

Raum, Elizabeth. Birth & Death of a City. 2007. (Illus.). 32p. (J). (978-1-4062-0505-3(2)) Steck-Vaughn.

Riggs, Sandy. Safe Streets. 2006. (Reader's Clubhouse Level 2 Reader Ser.). (ENG., Illus.). 24p. (J). (gr. 1-4). pap. 3.99 (978-0-7641-3300-8(4)) Barron's Educational Series, Inc.

Rogers, Amy B. We Live in a City, 01 vols., 1. 2016. (American Communities Ser.). (ENG., Illus.). 24p. (J). pap. 8.25 (978-1-5081-4189-1(4), PowerKids Pr.) Rosen Publishing Group, Inc., The.

Romanek, Trudee. Life in a Commercial City. 2010. (Learn about Urban Life Ser.). (ENG., Illus.). 32p. (J). (gr. 4-9). pap. (978-0-7787-7401-3(5)); lib. bdg. (978-0-7787-7391-7(4)) Crabtree Publishing Co.

Rossi, Renzo. In Nineteenth Century London with Dickens. Baldanzi, Alessandro, illus. 2008. (Come See My City Ser.). 48p. (gr. 4-8). lib. bdg. 28.50 (978-0-7614-4333-9(9), Benchmark Bks.) Marshall Cavendish Corp.

Rotner, Shelley. Senses in the City. Rotner, Shelley, photos by. 2008. (Shelley Rotner's Early Childhood Library Ser.). (ENG., Illus.). 32p. (gr. -1-2). lib. bdg. 23.93 (978-0-8225-7502-3(7)) Lerner Publishing Group.

Rowe, Brooke. What City Should You Live In? 2016. (Best Quiz Ever Ser.). (ENG., Illus.). 32p. (J). (gr. 4-8). 29.93 (978-1-63471-105-0(X), 208531, 45th Parallel Press) Cherry Lake Publishing.

Rowell, Rebecca. The 12 Most Amazing American Cities. 2014. (ENG., Illus.). 32p. (J). (978-1-63235-007-7(6)) Pr. Room Editions LLC.

Ryan, Pam Muñoz. Our California. López, Rafael, illus. 2008. (ENG.). 48p. (J). (gr. 1-4). 18.95 (978-1-58089-116-5(0)); per. 9.95 (978-1-58089-117-2(9)) Charlesbridge Publishing, Inc.

La Salvaguardia de las Ciudades. (Colección Biblioteca Juvenil de Ecología). (SPA., Illus.). (YA). (gr. 5-8). (978-958-04-3262-3(7), NR7196) Norma S.A. COL. Dist: Lectorum Pubns., Inc.

Samuels, Charlie. Forgotten Cities. 2012. (ENG.). 32p. (J). pap. (978-0-7787-8012-0(0)) Crabtree Publishing Co.

Schaefer, Lola M. How Did This City Grow? 2011. (Early Connections Ser.). (J). (978-1-61672-636-2(9)) Benchmark Education Co.

Schomp, Virginia. The City. 2010. (Life in Victorian England Ser.). (Illus.). 80p. (gr. 6). 34.21 (978-1-60870-029-5(1)) Marshall Cavendish Corp.

Segal, Robin. ABC in Tulsa. 2009. (All 'Bout Cities Ser.). (ENG.). 32p. (J). (gr. -1-k). (978-1-935139-03-4(7)) Murray Hill Bks., LLC.

Sharp, Jean. Contando Por la Ciudad. Walter, Lorin, illus. 2007. (Matemáticas en Nuestro Mundo (Math in Our World) Ser.). (SPA.). 24p. (gr. 1-2). lib. bdg. 22.00 (978-0-8368-8486-9(8), Weekly Reader Leveled Readers) Stevens, Gareth Publishing LLLP.

—Counting in the City. Walter, Lorin, illus. 2007. (Math in Our World Ser.). 24p. (gr. 1-2). pap. 8.15 (978-0-8368-8477-7(9)); lib. bdg. 22.00 (978-0-8368-8468-5(X)) Stevens, Gareth Publishing LLLP. (Weekly Reader Leveled Readers).

Siemens, Jared. City. 2015. (Illus.). 24p. (J). pap. (978-1-4896-3598-3(X)) Weigl Pubs., Inc.

Silate, Jennifer. Your Mayor: Local Government in Action. 2009. (Primary Source Library of American Citizenship Ser.). 32p. (gr. 5-5). 47.90 (978-1-61511-237-1(5), Rosen Reference) Rosen Publishing Group, Inc., The.

Snedden, Robert. The Growth of Cities. 2004. (Earth's Changing Landscape Ser.). (J). lib. bdg. 28.50 (978-1-58340-474-4(0)) Black Rabbit Bks.

Steedman, Scott. Egyptian Town. Antram, David, illus. 2017. (Time Traveler's Guide Ser.). 48p. (gr. 3-7). 37.10 **(978-1-910706-99-2(X))** Book Hse. GBR. Dist: Black Rabbit Bks.

Stefoff, Rebecca. Cities & Towns. 2007. (ENG., Illus.). 96p. (C). (gr. 6-18). lib. bdg. 140.00 (978-0-7656-8109-6(9), Y181735) Routledge.

—The Medieval World. 2004. (World Historical Atlases Ser.). (Illus.). 48p. (gr. 5). 26.95 (978-0-7614-1642-5(0), Benchmark Bks.) Marshall Cavendish Corp.

Sterling, Kristin. Living in Urban Communities. 2008. (First Step Nonfiction - Communities Ser.). (Illus.). 23p. (J). lib. bdg. 18.60 (978-0-8225-8597-8(9), Lerner Pubns.); pap. 34.95 (978-0-8225-9480-2(3)) Lerner Publishing Group.

Stuckey, Rachel. Your Guide to Medieval Society. 2017. (Destination: Middle Ages Ser.). (ENG., Illus.). 32p. (J). **(978-0-7787-2991-4(5))**; pap. **(978-0-7787-2997-6(4))** Crabtree Publishing Co.

Summers, Portia. My Urban Community. 2016. (Zoom in on Communities Ser.). 24p. (J). (gr. 2-2). pap. 9.35 (978-0-7660-7829-1(9)) Enslow Pubs., Inc.

Tardif, Benoît, illus. Metropolis. 2016. (ENG.). 72p. (J). (gr. -1-3). 17.95 (978-1-77138-721-7(1)) Kids Can Pr., Ltd. CAN. Dist: Hachette Bk. Group.

Thomas, R. Kayeen. Light: Stories of Urban Resurrection. 2004. 90p. per. 12.00 (978-0-9759582-0-9(8)) MarWel Enterprises, Inc.

Tidey, John & Tidey, Jackie. People & Cities. 2008. (China Ser.). 32p. (gr. 4-18). lib. bdg. 18.56 (978-0-7614-3158-9(6), Benchmark Bks.) Marshall Cavendish Corp.

Urban Habitats. 2013. (Discovery Education: Habitats Ser.). 32p. (J). (gr. 3-6). pap. 60.00 (978-1-4777-1490-4(1), PowerKids Pr.) Rosen Publishing Group, Inc., The.

Ventura, Piero. Book of Cities. 2009. (ENG., Illus.). 64p. (J). (gr. k-12). 18.95 (978-0-7893-1821-3(0)) Universe Publishing.

Verderosa, Laura. In Our Town. 2010. (Sight Word Readers Ser.). (J). 3.49 (978-1-60719-609-9(3)) Newmark Learning LLC.

Walker, Rob. Mapping Towns & Cities. 2010. (Mapping Our World Ser.). 32p. (gr. 4). 28.50 (978-1-60870-120-9(4)) Marshall Cavendish Corp.

Watson, Danielle. The City in Medieval Europe. 2016. (Life in Medieval Europe Ser.). (Illus.). 80p. (J). (gr. 6-6). 35.64 (978-1-5026-1880-1(X)) Cavendish Square Publishing.

Weil, Ann. The World's Most Amazing Lost Cities, 1 vol. 2011. (Landmark Top Tens Ser.). (ENG.). 32p. (gr. 3-5). pap. 8.29 (978-1-4109-4250-0(3)); 30.65 (978-1-4109-4239-5(2)) Heinemann-Raintree. (Raintree Perspectives).

Wirkner, Linda. Learning about Urban Growth in America with Graphic Organizers. 2009. (Graphic Organizers in Social Studies). 24p. (gr. 3-4). 42.50 (978-1-61513-087-0(X), PowerKids Pr.) Rosen Publishing Group, Inc., The.

CITIES AND TOWNS—FICTION

Achebe, Chinua. Chike & the River. Rodriguez, Edel, illus. 2011. (ENG.). 96p. (YA). pap. 12.00 (978-0-307-47386-8(4), Penguin Books) Penguin Publishing Group.

Allstun, Gina. Related. 2007. 63p. pap. 8.50 (978-1-4303-1229-1(7)) Lulu Pr., Inc.

Alonso, Fernando. Celiana y la Ciudad Sumergida. (Superbks./Superlibros).Tr. of Celiana & the Enchanted City. (J). (gr. k-1). pap. 6.95 (978-0-88272-495-9(9)) Santillana USA Publishing Co., Inc.

Anderson, Sara. Noisy City Day (2015 Board Book) Anderson, Sara, illus. 2015. (ENG., Illus.). 12p. (J). (gr. -1-1). bds. 10.95 (978-1-943459-00-1(2)) Sara Anderson Children's Bks.

—Noisy City Night (2015 Board Book) Anderson, Sara, illus. 2015. (ENG., Illus.). 12p. (J). (gr. -1-1). bds. 10.95 (978-1-943459-01-8(0)) Sara Anderson Children's Bks.

ARISE Foundation Staff & Benson, Susan. 31 of Taneka's Urban Life Tales (Instructor's Manual) 2011. (Illus.). 100p. (J). pap., tchr. ed. 19.95 (978-1-58614-099-1(X)) Arise Foundation.

Arrenhius, Ingela. Welcome to Curiosity! The Lift-the-Flap Tour of a Very Small Town. 2017. (ENG., Illus.). 22p. (J). (gr. -1 — 1). 16.99 **(978-1-4521-6157-0(7))** Chronicle Bks. LLC.

Baker, Jeannie. Home. Baker, Jeannie, illus. 2004. (ENG., Illus.). 32p. (J). (gr. k-5). 16.99 (978-0-06-623935-4(4), Greenwillow Bks.) HarperCollins Pubs.

Base, Graeme. Uno's Garden. 2006. (ENG., Illus.). 44p. (J). (gr. -1-3). 19.95 (978-0-8109-5473-1(7)) Abrams, Inc.

Bauer, Marion Dane. Little Dog, Lost. Bell, Jennifer A., illus. (ENG.). 208p. (J). (gr. 3-7). 2013. pap. 6.99 (978-1-4424-3424-0(4)) 2012. 16.99 (978-1-4424-3423-3(6)) Simon & Schuster Children's Publishing. (Atheneum Bks. for Young Readers).

Bee, William. Migloo's Day. Bee, William, illus. 2015. (ENG., Illus.). (J). (gr. -1-2). 14.99 (978-0-7636-7374-1(9)) Candlewick Pr.

Berry, Eileen M. Looking for Home. Manning, Maurie J., illus. 2006. 75p. (J). (gr. -1-3). per. (978-1-59166-493-2(4)) BJU Pr.

Biggs, Brian. Tinyville Town Gets to Work! 2016. (Tinyville Town Ser.). (ENG., Illus.). 32p. (J). (gr. -1-k). 16.95 (978-1-4197-2133-5(X), Abrams Appleseed) Abrams, Inc.

Blackstone, Stella. Bear about Town (Oso en las Ciudad) Harter, Debbie, illus. 2010. (ENG, SPA & FRE.). 24p. (J). (gr. -1-1). pap. 6.99 (978-1-84686-377-6(5)) Barefoot Bks., Inc.

—Oso en la Ciudad. Sarfatti, Esther, tr. Harter, Debbie, illus. 2003. (Bear Ser.). (SPA.). 24p. (J). pap. 6.99 (978-1-84148-776-2(7)) Barefoot Bks., Inc.

Blakemore, Megan Frazer. The Spy Catchers of Maple Hill. 2014. (ENG.). 320p. (YA). (gr. 3-6). 16.99 (978-1-61963-348-3(5), 9781619633483, Bloomsbury USA Childrens) Bloomsbury Publishing USA.

Blance, Ellen & Cook, Tony. Monster Comes to the City. Date not set. (Illus.). 16p. pap. 129.15 (978-0-582-18588-3(2)) Addison-Wesley Longman, Ltd. GBR. Dist: Trans-Atlantic Pubns., Inc.

—Monster Goes Around Town. Date not set. (Illus.). 38p. pap. 129.15 (978-0-582-19309-3(5)) Addison-Wesley Longman, Ltd. GBR. Dist: Trans-Atlantic Pubns., Inc.

Bloomfield, Kevin. Mr. Biggs in the City. Bloomfield, Kevin, illus. 2011. (ENG & SPA., Illus.). 32p. (gr. -1-3). lib. bdg. 16.95 (978-1-936299-26-3(7), Raven Tree Pr.,Csi) Continental Sales, Inc.

Brooks, Felicity. Noisy Town. 2008. (Usborne Busy Sounds Ser.). (Illus.). 10p. (J). (gr. -1-3). bds. 15.99 (978-0-7945-2041-0(3), Usborne) EDC Publishing.

Brown, Peter. The Curious Garden. 2009. (ENG., Illus.). 40p. (J). (gr. -1-3). 18.99 (978-0-316-01547-9(4)) Little Brown & Co.

—The Curious Garden. 2010. (J). 37.75 (978-1-4407-7744-8(6)); 39.75 (978-1-4407-7742-4(X)); 39.75 (978-1-4407-7738-7(1)); 194.75 (978-1-4407-7739-4(X)); 1.25 (978-1-4407-7745-5(4)); 37.75 (978-1-4407-7740-0(3)) Recorded Bks., Inc.

—Mr. Tiger Goes Wild. 2013. (ENG.). 48p. (J). 126.00 (978-0-316-25551-6(3)); (Illus.). (gr. -1-1). 18.00 (978-0-316-20063-9(8)) Little, Brown Bks. for Young Readers.

Brown, Tameka Fryer. Around Our Way on Neighbors' Day. Riley-Webb, Charlotte, illus. 2010. (ENG.). 32p. (J). (gr. k-2). 16.95 (978-0-8109-8971-9(9), Abrams Bks. for Young Readers) Abrams, Inc.

Burleigh, Robert. Clang! Clang! Beep! Beep! Listen to the City. Giacobbe, Beppe, illus. 2009. (ENG.). 32p. (J). (gr. -1-2). 17.99 (978-1-4169-4052-4(9), Simon & Schuster/Paula Wiseman Bks.) Simon & Schuster/Paula Wiseman Bks.

—Zoom! Zoom! Sounds of Things That Go in the City. Carpenter, Tad, illus. 2014. (ENG.). 32p. (J). (gr. -1-3). 17.99 (978-1-4424-8315-6(6), Simon & Schuster Bks. For Young Readers) Simon & Schuster Bks. For Young Readers.

Burton, Virginia Lee. The Little House. Burton, Virginia Lee, illus. 2009. (ENG., Illus.). 42p. (J). (gr. -1 — 1). bds. 7.99 (978-0-547-13104-7(6)) Houghton Mifflin Harcourt Publishing Co.

—The Little House, 1 vol. (Read along Book & CD Ser.). (ENG., Illus.). 44p. (J). (gr. -1-3). 2007. audio compact disk 10.99 (978-0-618-91651-1(2)) 70th anniv. ed. 2012. lib. bdg. 17.99 (978-0-547-79044-2(9)) Houghton Mifflin Harcourt Publishing Co.

C D Stampley Enterprises, creator. Billy & Baxter on City Streets, 4 vols. 2005. (Illus.). 24p. (J). (gr. -1 — 1). 8.95 (978-1-58087-101-3(1)) Stampley, C. D. Enterprises, Inc.

Campoy, F. Isabel & Howell, Theresa. Maybe Something Beautiful: How Art Transformed a Neighborhood. López, Rafael, illus. 2016. (ENG.). 40p. (J). (gr. -1-3). 16.99 (978-0-544-35769-3(8), HMH Books For Young Readers) Houghton Mifflin Harcourt Publishing Co.

Champion, Dionne N., et al. The Spirit of the Baobab Tree. Champion, Dionne N. & Champion, Daryl, illus. 2008. 37p. (J). 31.99 (978-1-4363-7842-0(7)) Xlibris Corp.

The Citiscapes Series, Big bk. (J). pap. 23.00 (978-1-56843-024-9(8)) EMG Networks.

City. (Busy Books Large Ser.). 5p. (978-1-4054-9500-4(6)) Parragon, Inc.

Cochran, Matthew. The Yagoos Go to Town. 2008. 32p. pap. 23.95 (978-1-4357-2377-1(5)) Lulu Pr., Inc.

Cole, Henry. Spot, the Cat. Cole, Henry, illus. 2016. (ENG., Illus.). 32p. (J). (gr. -1-3). 17.99 (978-1-4814-4225-1(2), Little Simon) Little Simon.

Colman, Michelle Sinclair. Urban Babies Wear Black. Dion, Nathalie, illus. 2005. (Urban Babies Wear Black Book Ser.). (ENG.). 20p. (J). (gr. k — 1). bds. 6.99 (978-1-58246-158-8(9), Tricycle Pr.) Random Hse. Children's Bks.

Cousins, Lucy. Maisy Goes to the City. Cousins, Lucy, illus. 2014. (Maisy Ser.). (ENG., Illus.). 32p. (J). (gr. -1-2). 6.99 (978-0-7636-6834-1(6)) Candlewick Pr.

—Maisy Goes to the City. 2014. (Maisy First Experiences Ser.). lib. bdg. 17.20 (978-0-606-35157-7(4)) Turtleback Bks.

Cowley, Joy. Mrs. WishyWashy & the Big Wash. 2009. pap. 8.25 (978-1-60559-235-0(8)) Hameray Publishing Group, Inc.

—Mrs. WishyWashy & the Big Wash Big Book. 2010. 48.25 (978-1-60559-247-3(1)) Hameray Publishing Group, Inc.

Curato, Mike. Little Elliot, Big City. Curato, Mike, illus. 2014. (Little Elliot Ser.). (ENG., Illus.). 40p. (J). (gr. -1-3). 16.99 (978-0-8050-9825-9(9), 9780805098259, Holt, Henry & Co. Bks. For Young Readers) Holt, Henry & Co.

Dairman, Tara. The Great Hibernation. 2017. (ENG.). 272p. (J). (gr. 3-7). lib. bdg. 19.99 **(978-1-5247-1786-5(X)**, Lamb, Wendy Bks.) Random Hse. Children's Bks.

De la Peña, Matt. Last Stop on Market Street. Robinson, Christian, illus. 2015. (ENG.). 32p. (J). 16.99 (978-0-399-25774-2(8), G.P. Putnam's Sons Books for Young Readers) Penguin Publishing Group.

Dean, Myers Walter. Fast Sam, Cool Clyde, & Stuff. 2014. (ENG.). 192p. (J). (gr. 12-12). 11.24 (978-1-63245-241-2(3)) Lectorum Pubns., Inc.

Doyle, Brian. Easy Avenue, 1 vol. 2nd ed. 2004. (ENG.). 122p. (YA). pap. 6.95 (978-0-88899-605-3(5)) Groundwood Bks. CAN. Dist: Publishers Group West (PGW).

East, Jacqueline, illus. The Town Mouse & the Country Mouse. 2007. (First Reading Level 4 Ser.). 48p. (J). (gr. -1-3). 8.99 (978-0-7945-1613-0(0), Usborne) EDC Publishing.

Egan, Tim. Dodsworth in Paris. Egan, Tim, illus. 2010. (Dodsworth Book Ser.). (ENG., Illus.). 48p. (J). (gr. 1-4). pap. 3.99 (978-0-547-33192-8(4)) Houghton Mifflin Harcourt Publishing Co.

—Metropolitan Cow. 2004. (J). (gr. k-3). spiral bd. (978-0-616-07231-8(7)) Canadian National Institute for the Blind/Institut National Canadien pour les Aveugles.

Engram, Teta. Baxter & the Sidewalk Alligator. Holland, Lisa Tomms, illus. 2009. 32p. pap. 12.99 (978-1-4389-9367-6(6)) AuthorHouse.

Fleischman, Paul. Sidewalk Circus. Hawkes, Kevin, illus. 2007. (ENG.). 32p. (J). (gr. k-4). 7.99 (978-0-7636-2795-9(X)) Candlewick Pr.

—Sidewalk Circus. Hawkes, Kevin, illus. 2007. (gr. k-4). 18.00 (978-0-7569-8182-2(4)) Perfection Learning Corp.

Fox, Paula. Maurice's Room. Fetz, Ingrid, illus. 2010. (ENG.). 64p. (J). (gr. 2-5). pap. 6.99 (978-1-4424-1678-9(5), Simon & Schuster/Paula Wiseman Bks.) Simon & Schuster/Paula Wiseman Bks.

Galante, Cecilia. Willowood. 2010. (ENG.). 272p. (J). (gr. 4-8). 16.99 (978-1-4169-8022-3(9), Simon & Schuster/Paula Wiseman Bks.) Simon & Schuster/Paula Wiseman Bks.

Gamble, Adam & Jasper, Mark. Good Night Twin Cities. Palmer, Ruth, illus. 2015. (Good Night Our World Ser.). (ENG.). 20p. (J). (— 1). bds. 9.95 (978-1-60219-232-4(4)) Good Night Bks.

Godwin, Laura. One Moon, Two Cats. Tanaka, Yoko, illus. 2011. (ENG.). 32p. (J). (gr. -1-1). 16.99 (978-1-4424-1202-6(X), Atheneum Bks. for Young Readers) Simon & Schuster Children's Publishing.

Golden Books. Welcome to the City! (Dora & Friends) Sciarrone, Claudio, illus. 2014. (Color Plus Chunky Crayons Ser.). (ENG.). 48p. (J). (gr. -1-2). pap. 3.99 (978-0-385-38412-4(2), Golden Bks.) Random Hse. Children's Bks.

Gordon, Amy. Twenty Gold Falcons. 2010. (ENG.). 240p. (J). (gr. 3-7). 16.95 (978-0-8234-2252-4(6)) Holiday Hse., Inc.

Grant, Karima. Sofie & the City. Montecalvo, Janet, illus. 2006. (ENG.). 32p. (J). (gr. 1-3). 15.95 (978-1-59078-273-6(9)) Boyds Mills Pr.

Griesmer, Russell. My Hometown. Wong, Priscilla, illus. 2015. (ENG.). 40p. (gr. 1-4). 15.95 (978-1-62370-174-1(0)) Capstone Young Readers of Coughlan Cos.

Guest, Elissa Haden. Iris & Walter. 2012. (Iris & Walter — Green Light Reader Ser.). lib. bdg. 13.55 (978-0-606-24229-5(5), Turtleback) Turtleback Bks.

Gulledge, Laura Lee. Page by Paige. 2011. (ENG., Illus.). 192p. (YA). (gr. 7-17). 18.95 (978-0-8109-9721-9(5)); pap. 9.95 (978-0-8109-9722-6(3)) Abrams, Inc. (Amulet Bks.).

Hamilton, Libby & Haworth, Katie. Through the Town. Shuttlewood, Craig, illus. 2015. (ENG.). 10p. (J). (gr. -1 — 1). bds. 6.99 (978-1-4998-0076-0(2)) Little Bee Books Inc.

Handprint Staff. Traffic Town. 2007. (J). 8.95 (978-1-59354-186-6(4)) Handprint Bks.

Harris, Nicholas. A Day in a City. (Time Goes By Ser.). 24p. (gr. k-3). 2009. (ENG.). pap. 6.95 (978-1-58013-797-3(0), First Avenue Editions) 2008. (Illus.). (J). lib. bdg. 22.60 (978-1-58013-552-8(8)) Lerner Publishing Group.

Harrison, Lisi. The Clique. 2004. (Clique Ser.: 1). (ENG.). 224p. (YA). (gr. 7-17). pap. 9.99 (978-0-316-70129-7(7), Poppy) Little, Brown Bks. for Young Readers.

—Invasion of the Boy Snatchers. 2005. (Clique Ser.: 4). (ENG.). 256p. (YA). (gr. 7-17). per. 9.99 (978-0-316-70134-1(3), Poppy) Little, Brown Bks. for Young Readers.

Hays, Ethel, illus. The Town Mouse & the Country Mouse. 2007. (Shape Bks.). (ENG.). 14p. (J). (gr. -1-3). pap. 9.95 (978-1-59583-192-7(4), 9781595831927, Green Tiger Pr.) Laughing Elephant.

Hicks, Faith Erin. The Nameless City. 2016. (Nameless City Ser.: 1). (ENG., Illus.). 240p. (J). pap. 14.99 (978-1-62672-156-2(4), 9781626721562, First Second Bks.) Roaring Brook Pr.

High, Linda Oatman. Tenth Avenue Cowboy. Farnsworth, Bill, illus. 2008. 32p. (J). (gr. 4-7). 17.00 (978-0-8028-5330-1(7), Eerdmans Bks For Young Readers) Eerdmans, William B. Publishing Co.

Hillert, Margaret. City Fun. Lewis, K. E., illus. 2016. (BeginningtoRead Ser.). (ENG.). 32p. (J). (gr. -1-2). pap. 11.94 (978-1-60357-975-9(3)); 21st ed. (gr. k-2). 22.60 (978-1-59953-813-6(X)) Norwood Hse. Pr.

—Come Play with Me. Chow, Derrick, illus. 2016. (BeginningtoRead Ser.). (ENG.). 32p. (J). (gr. -1-2). pap. 11.94 (978-1-60357-976-6(1)) Norwood Hse. Pr.

Hinton, S. E. Rumble Fish. 2006. 21.50 (978-0-8446-7283-0(1)) Smith, Peter Pub., Inc.

Hinton, Susan E. & E Hinton, Susan. La Ley de la Calle. 2015. (ENG & SPA., Illus.). 128p. (YA). pap. 13.95 (978-607-01-2325-2(5), Alfaguara) Santillana USA Publishing Co., Inc.

Hipscher, Jerome. White Slavery. 2004. 78p. (YA). pap. 8.95 (978-0-595-31441-6(4)) iUniverse, Inc.

Hitchcock, Fleur. Shrunk! 2016. (Shrunk! Adventure Ser.: 1). (ENG., Illus.). 256p. (J). (gr. 3-7). pap. 9.99 (978-1-84812-480-6(5)) Bonnier Publishing GBR. Dist: Independent Pubs. Group.

Holt, Kimberly Willis. When Zachary Beaver Came to Town. unabr. ed. 2004. 227p. (J). (gr. 5-9). pap. 36.00 incl. audio (978-0-8072-8394-3(0), Listening Library) Random Hse. Audio Publishing Group.

Howell, Lauren. If I Was the Mayor. Dawson, Sheldon, illus. 2005. 32p. (J). per. (978-0-9735798-1-9(1)) Three Bears Publishing.

Hrachovec, Anna. Adventures in Mochimochi Land: Tall Tales from a Tiny, Knitted World. 2015. (ENG., Illus.). 144p. pap. 19.99 (978-0-385-34459-3(7), Potter Craft) Potter/TenSpeed/Harmony.

Hudgins, Mary Jane. The Town of Nowhere, 1 vol. Hudgins, Tim, illus. 2009. 17p. pap. 24.95 (978-1-60672-544-3(0)) America Star Bks.

Hunter, Erin. The Empty City. (Survivors Ser.: 1). (J). (gr. 3-7). 2013. (ENG.). 304p. pap. 7.99 (978-0-06-210258-4(3)) 2012. (ENG.). 288p. 16.99 (978-0-06-210256-0(7)) 2012. 288p. lib. bdg. 17.89 (978-0-06-210257-7(5)) HarperCollins Pubs.

—The Empty City. 2013. (Survivors Ser.: 1). (J). lib. bdg. 18.40 (978-0-606-31803-7(8), Turtleback) Turtleback Bks.

Hurst, Elise. Imagine a City. 2016. (ENG., Illus.). 32p. (J). (gr. -1-2). 16.99 (978-1-101-93457-9(3), Doubleday Bks. for Young Readers) Random Hse. Children's Bks.

Hurwitz, Gregg. The Rains. 2016. (Rains Brothers Ser.). (ENG.). 352p. (YA). 17.99 (978-0-7653-8267-2(9), 9780765382672, Tor Teen) Doherty, Tom Assocs., LLC.

Isadora, Rachel. Say Hello! Isadora, Rachel, illus. 2010. (ENG., Illus.). 32p. (J). (gr. -1-k). 16.99 (978-0-399-25230-3(4), G.P. Putnam's Sons Books for Young Readers) Penguin Young Readers Group.

Jakubowski, Michele. Mick's Buried Treasure. Pinelli, Amerigo, illus. 2016. (Sleuths of Somerville Ser.). (ENG.). 144p. (gr. 4-6). lib. bdg. 25.99 (978-1-4965-3178-0(7)) Stone Arch Bks.

—Secrets in Somerville. Pinelli, Amerigo, illus. 2016. (Sleuths of Somerville Ser.). (ENG.). 144p. (gr. 4-6). lib. bdg. 25.99 (978-1-4965-3175-9(2)) Stone Arch Bks.

Jamieson, Victoria. Bea Rocks the Flock. 2009. (J). (gr. -1-3). 17.89 (978-1-59990-357-6(1)) Bloomsbury Publishing USA.

Jenkins, Amanda. City Kids, Country Kids. 2006. (J). pap. (978-1-4108-6184-9(8)) Benchmark Education Co.

Jennings, Patrick. Bat & Rat. Cordell, Matthew, illus. 2012. (ENG.). 40p. (J). (gr. k-2). 16.95 (978-1-4197-0160-3(6), Abrams Bks. for Young Readers) Abrams, Inc.

Jones, Judith. You're from Where Grandma? 2011. 24p. pap. 12.99 (978-1-4568-8150-4(7)) Xlibris Corp.

Jones, Traci L. Standing Against the Wind. 2010. (ENG.). 208p. (YA). (gr. 7-9). pap. 11.99 (978-0-312-62293-0(7), 9780312622930) Square Fish.

The Journey. 2003. 170p. (YA). per. 10.95 (978-0-9713292-8-7(1)) Aim Higher Bks.

Joyce, Rita. Johnny Peppertoes. 2005. (J). per. 9.95 (978-1-59094-092-1(X)) Jawbone Publishing Corp.

Kauflin, Chris. Smiletown's Big Snow Day. 2006. (J). per. 14.95 (978-0-9785132-0-7(7), Smiletown Bks.) Smile-a-Lot, LLP.

Kessler, Leonard P. Mr. Pine's Purple House. Kessler, Leonard P., illus. 40th anniv. ed. 2005. (Illus.). 64p. (J). 16.00 (978-1-930900-32-5(5)) Purple Hse. Pr.

Kibbe, Pat. Mrs. Kiddy & the Moonbooms. 2010. 112p. pap. 9.95 (978-1-4401-9968-4(X)) iUniverse, Inc.

Kiernan, Patrick. Good Morning, City. Campion, Pascal, illus. 2016. (ENG.). 32p. (J). 16.99 (978-0-374-30346-4(0), 9780374303464, Farrar, Straus & Giroux (BYR)) Farrar, Straus & Giroux.

Knowles, Jo. Read Between the Lines. 2015. (ENG.). 336p. (YA). (gr. 9). 16.99 (978-0-7636-6387-2(5)) Candlewick Pr.

Kurtz, Jane. Anna Was Here. 2013. (ENG.). 288p. (J). (gr. 3-7). 16.99 (978-0-06-056493-3(8), Greenwillow Bks.) HarperCollins Pubs.

—Lanie's Real Adventures. Papp, Robert, illus. 2010. (American Girl Today Ser.). (ENG.). 112p. (YA). (gr. 3-18). 12.95 (978-1-59369-685-6(X)) American Girl Publishing, Inc.

—Lemon Sand. 2011. (J). lib. bdg. 17.89 (978-0-06-056494-0(6), Greenwillow Bks.) HarperCollins Pubs.

Lamba, Marie & Lamba, Baldev. Green, Green: A Community Gardening Story. Sanchez, Sonia, illus. 2017. (ENG.). 32p. (J). 17.99 (978-0-374-32797-2(1), 9780374327972, Farrar, Straus & Giroux (BYR)) Farrar, Straus & Giroux.

Lee, Cecelia In. The Alphabets. 2010. 292p. 25.99 (978-1-4520-3626-7(8)); pap. 15.59 (978-1-4520-3625-0(X)) AuthorHouse.

Lindsay, Bruce. The Hometown Weekly: Good News for a Change: Humorous Tales from Parley Grove. 2008. 111p. pap. (978-1-59811-600-7(2)) Covenant Communications.

The check digit for ISBN-10 appears in parentheses after the full ISBN-13

Lobel, Arnold. On Market Street. 2006. (J). (gr. -1-2). 17.20 *(978-0-8085-3705-2(9)*, Turtleback) Turtleback Bks.

Martin, Amy. Symphony City. 2011. (ENG., Illus.). 48p. (J). (gr. -1-4). 17.95 *(978-1-936365-39-5(1))* McSweeney's Publishing.

Mayer, Mercer. This Is My Town. Mayer, Mercer, illus. 2008. (My First I Can Read Ser.). (ENG., Illus.). 32p. (J). (gr. -1-3). pap. 3.99 *(978-0-06-083549-1(4))* HarperCollins Pubs.

McCully, Emily Arnold. Little Ducks Go. McCully, Emily Arnold, illus. 2015. (I Like to Read(r) Ser.). (ENG., Illus.). 24p. (J). (gr. -1-2). 6.99 *(978-0-8234-3300-1(5))* Holiday Hse., Inc.

McKenzie, Lyn. Betsy, Girl Scout of Woodward Center 1935. 2007. 244p. (YA). pap. 17.95 net. *(978-0-9722839-0-8(0))* Just Write Bks.

Meister, Cari. Snorp: The City Monster. Messner, Dennis, illus. 2009. (Monster Friends Ser.). (ENG.). 32p. (gr. 2-3). 22.65 *(978-1-4342-1632-8(2))* Stone Arch Bks.

—Snorp el Monstruo de la Ciudad/Snorp the City Monster, 1 vol. Heck, Claudia M., tr. from ENG. Messner, Dennis, illus. 2012. (Los Amigos Monstruos/Monster Friends Ser.). (MUL & SPA.). 32p. (gr. 2-3). lib. bdg. 22.65 *(978-1-4342-3783-5(4)*, Bilingual Stone Arch Readers) Stone Arch Bks.

Melvin, Treva. Mr. Samuel's Penny. 2014. (Elizabeth Parrot Landers Mysteries Ser.: 1). (ENG.). 264p. (YA). pap. 10.95 *(978-1-929345-04-5(6))* Poisoned Pen Pr.

Michels, Dia L. Look What I See! Where Can I Be? In the Neighborhood. Bowles, Michael J. N., illus. 2005. (Look What I See! Where Can I Be? Ser.: Vol. 1). (ENG.). 32p. (J). (gr. -1-12). 9.95 *(978-1-930775-00-8(8))* Platypus Media, L.L.C.

Montgomery, R. A. Fire! 2015. (ENG.). 80p. (Orig.). (J). pap. 7.99 *(978-1-937133-49-8(4))* Chooseco LLC.

Morrison, David. The Mind Map Level 3 Lower-Intermediate. 2009. (ENG.). 80p. pap. 12.75 *(978-84-8323-537-9(4))* Cambridge Univ. Pr.

Murray, Diana. City Shapes. Collier, Bryan, illus. 2016. (ENG.). 40p. (J). (gr. -1-3). 17.99 *(978-0-316-37092-9(4))* Little Brown & Co.

Nœ–ez, Marisa. CHOCOLATE. 2007. (ENG., Illus.). 36p. (J). 17.95 *(978-84-96788-83-1(0))* OQO, Editora ESP. Dist: Baker & Taylor Bks.

Nelson, Mary Beth & Linn, Laurent, illus. Elmo's Big Word Book/el Libro Grande de Palabras de Elmo. Barrett, John E., photos by. 2006. (Elmo's Big Word Book/el Libro Grande de Palabras de Elmo Ser.). (SPA, ENG, MUL & ANG.). 12p. (J). (gr. -1 — 1). bds. 8.95 *(978-0-87358-906-2(8))* Cooper Square Publishing Llc.

Neri, G. Chess Rumble. Watson, Jesse Joshua, illus. 2007. (ENG.). 64p. (J). (gr. 3-7). 18.95 *(978-1-58430-279-7(8))* Lee & Low Bks., Inc.

Ochsner, Gina. The Hidden Letters of Velta B. 2017. (ENG.). 320p. pap. 14.99 *(978-0-544-70304-9(9))* Houghton Mifflin Harcourt Publishing Co.

Palatini, Margie. Hogg, Hogg, & Hog. Palatini, Margie, illus. 2011. (ENG., Illus.). 32p. (J). (gr. -1-3). 15.99 *(978-1-4424-0322-2(5)*, Simon & Schuster Bks. For Young Readers) Simon & Schuster Bks. For Young Readers.

Paltenghi, Madalena. Remus Goes to Town. Anderson, C. W., illus. 2011. 32p. 35.95 *(978-1-258-10024-7(X))* Literary Licensing, LLC.

Pearson, Debora. Big City Song. Reed, Lynn Rowe, illus. 2006. (ENG.). 32p. (J). (gr. -1-3). 16.95 *(978-0-8234-1988-3(6))* Holiday Hse., Inc.

Pearson, Luke, illus. Hilda & the Bird Parade. 2013. (Hildafolk Ser.). (ENG.). 44p. (J). (gr. k). 24.00 *(978-1-909263-06-2(0))* Flying Eye Bks. GBR. Dist: Consortium Bk. Sales & Distribution.

Perry, Gina. Small. 2017. (ENG.). 40p. (J). (gr. -1-3). 17.99 ***(978-1-4998-0401-0(6))*** Little Bee Books Inc.

Peschke, Marci. Green Queen, 1 vol. Mourning, Tuesday, illus. 2014. (Kylie Jean Ser.). (ENG.). 112p. (gr. 2-3). 22.65 *(978-1-4795-2351-1(8)*, Kylie Jean) Picture Window Bks.

Pinkwater, Daniel M. Beautiful Yetta's Hanukkah Kitten. Pinkwater, Jill, illus. 2014. (ENG.). 32p. (J). (gr. -1-2). 17.99 *(978-0-312-62134-6(5)*, 9780312621346) Feiwel & Friends.

Pitchford, Dean. Nickel Bay Nick. 2014. (ENG.). 272p. (J). (gr. 3-7). pap. 7.99 *(978-0-14-751227-7(1)*, Puffin Books) Penguin Young Readers Group.

Priddy, Roger. Toddler Town - City. 2014. (Toddler Town Ser.). (ENG.). 10p. (J). (gr. -1 — 1). bds. 7.99 *(978-0-312-51673-4(8)*, 9780312516734, Priddy Bks.) St. Martin's Pr.

Raschka, Chris. New York Is English, Chattanooga Is Creek. Raschka, Chris, illus. 2005. (ENG., Illus.). 40p. (J). (gr. -1-2). 17.99 *(978-0-689-84600-7(2)*, Atheneum/Richard Jackson Bks.) Simon & Schuster Children's Publishing.

Reasoner, Charles. A Day Around Town. 2009. (Inside Outside Board Bks.). (Illus.). (J). bds. 10.99 *(978-1-934650-53-0(6))* Just For Kids Pr., LLC.

Reidy, Jean. All Through My Town. Timmers, Leo, illus. 2015. (ENG.). 26p. (J). (gr. -1-k). bds. 7.99 *(978-1-61963-562-3(3)*, 9781619635623, Bloomsbury USA Childrens) Bloomsbury Publishing USA.

Richmond, Lori. Pax & Blue. Richmond, Lori, illus. 2017. (ENG., Illus.). 32p. (J). (gr. -1-3). 17.99 *(978-1-4814-5132-1(4)*, Simon & Schuster/Paula Wiseman Bks.) Simon & Schuster/Paula Wiseman Bks.

Robeson, K. S. Chloe & Bia Bk. 2: Tales from Wind Creek. 2003. 96p. per. 8.95 *(978-0-9723530-1-4(1))* Falcor Bks.

Ross, Cathy. Tater Town. 2007. (Illus.). 20p. (J). spiral bd. 16.00 *(978-0-9797832-0-3(8))* Ross, Cathy.

Rubin, Susan Goldman. Jacob Lawrence in the City. 2009. (ENG., Illus.). 24p. (J). (gr. -1 — 1). bds. 7.99 *(978-0-8118-6582-1(7))* Chronicle Bks. LLC.

Russell, Natalie. Brown Rabbit in the City. 2010. (ENG.). 40p. (J). (gr. -1-k). 16.99 *(978-0-670-01234-3(3)*, Viking Books for Young Readers) Penguin Young Readers Group.

Russo, David Anson. The Great Treasure Hunt. Russo, David Anson, illus. 2011. (ENG., Illus.). 28p. (J). (gr. k-3). pap. 14.99 *(978-1-4424-4342-6(1)*, Simon & Schuster Bks. For Young Readers) Simon & Schuster Bks. For Young Readers.

Sander, Sonia. Help Is on the Way! 2009. (Lego City Ser.). (ENG.). 32p. (J). (gr. -1-k). pap. 3.99 *(978-0-545-15068-2(X))* Scholastic, Inc.

Sarcone-Roach, Julia. The Bear Ate Your Sandwich. 2015. (ENG., Illus.). 40p. (J). (gr. -1-2). 16.99 *(978-0-375-85860-4(1))*; lib. bdg. 19.99 *(978-0-375-95860-1(6))* Random Hse. Children's Bks. (Knopf Bks. for Young Readers).

Sarfati, Sonia. La Ville Engloutie. 2003. (Roman Jeunesse Ser.). (FRE.). 96p. (YA). (gr. 4-7). pap. *(978-2-89021-179-7(7))* Diffusion du livre Mirabel (DLM).

Scarry, Richard. Richard Scarry's Busytown on the Go! 2015. (ENG., Illus.). 18p. (J). (gr. -1-k). bds. 7.99 *(978-0-7641-6776-8(6))* Barron's Educational Series, Inc.

—Richard Scarry's Good Morning, Busytown! 2015. (ENG., Illus.). 18p. (J). (gr. -1-k). bds. 7.99 *(978-0-7641-6777-5(4))* Barron's Educational Series, Inc.

—Richard Scarry's Postman Pig & His Busy Neighbors. Scarry, Richard, illus. 2015. (Pictureback(R) Ser.). (ENG., Illus.). 32p. (J). (gr. -1-2). pap. 4.99 *(978-0-385-38419-3(X)*, Random Hse. Bks. for Young Readers) Random Hse. Children's Bks.

Scattergood, Augusta. Glory Be. (ENG.). 208p. (J). (gr. 3-7). 2014. pap. 6.99 *(978-0-545-33181-4(1))* 2012. 16.99 *(978-0-545-33180-7(3))* Scholastic, Inc. (Scholastic Pr.).

Scher, Paula. The Brownstone. 2016. (ENG., Illus.). 32p. (J). (gr. -1-3). 17.95 *(978-1-61689-428-3(8))* Princeton Architectural Pr.

Schertle, Alice. Little Blue Truck Leads the Way. McElmurry, Jill, illus. (Little Blue Truck Ser.). (ENG.). (J). 2016. 38p. (— 1). bds. 12.99 *(978-0-544-70899-0(7)*, HMH Books For Young Readers) 2012. 40p. (gr. -1-3). 26.99 *(978-0-547-85060-3(3))* 2015. 38p. (— 1). bds. 7.99 *(978-0-544-56805-1(2)*, HMH Books For Young Readers) Houghton Mifflin Harcourt Publishing Co.

Schneider, Peter. Der Mauerspringer. (GER.). pap. 18.95 *(978-3-499-13532-3(9))* Rowohlt Taschenbuch Verlag GmbH DEU. Dist: Distribooks, Inc.

Schotz, Leo D. Rooftop. 2005. (Illus.). 32p. (J). 15.95 *(978-0-9741319-7-9(0))* 4N Publishing LLC.

Schraff, Anne. Urban Underground Sample Set. Saddleback Educational Publishing Staff, ed. 2011. (Urban Underground Ser.). (YA). 89.50 *(978-1-61651-256-9(3))* Saddleback Educational Publishing, Inc.

Schwartz, Joanne. Town Is by the Sea, 1 vol. Smith, Sydney, illus. 2017. (ENG.). 52p. (J). (gr. k-4). 19.95 *(978-1-55498-871-6(3))* Groundwood Bks. CAN. Dist: Publishers Group West (PGW).

Seredy, Kate. Philomena. Seredy, Kate, illus. 2008. (Illus.). 93p. (J). pap. 11.95 *(978-1-932350-19-7(5))* Bethlehem Bks.

Shulevitz, Uri. One Monday Morning. Shulevitz, Uri, illus. 2003. (ENG., Illus.). 48p. (J). (gr. -1-1). reprint ed. pap. 8.99 *(978-0-374-45648-1(8)*, 9780374456481) Square Fish.

—One Monday Morning. 2003. (J). (gr. -1-2). lib. bdg. 18.40 *(978-0-613-71877-6(1)*, Turtleback) Turtleback Bks.

Shusterman, Neal. Red Rider's Hood. 2006. (Dark Fusion Ser.: 3). (ENG.). 192p. (YA). (gr. 7-18). 6.99 *(978-0-14-240678-6(3)*, Speak) Penguin Young Readers Group.

Sidman, Joyce. Before Morning. Krommes, Beth, illus. 2016. (ENG.). 48p. (J). (gr. -1-3). 17.99 *(978-0-547-97917-5(7)*, HMH Books For Young Readers) Houghton Mifflin Harcourt Publishing Co.

Silverman, Erica. Wake up, City! Fournier, Laure, illus. 2016. (ENG.). 32p. (J). (gr. -1-3). 16.99 *(978-1-4998-0173-6(4))* Little Bee Books Inc.

Silverstein, Shel. Lafcadio, el Leon Que Disparo al Cazador. Rioja, Alberto Jimenez, tr. from ENG. 2011.Tr. of Lafcadio, the Lion Who Shot Back. (SPA., Illus.). 112p. (J). (gr. 2-3). pap. 16.99 *(978-1-933032-74-0(X))* Lectorum Pubns., Inc.

Singer, Marilyn. City Lullaby. Cneut, Carll, illus. 2007. (ENG.). 32p. (J). (gr. -1-3). 16.99 *(978-0-618-60703-7(X))* Houghton Mifflin Harcourt Publishing Co.

Sís, Peter. Madlenka. Sís, Peter, illus. 2010. (ENG., Illus.). 48p. (J). (gr. -1-3). pap. 8.99 *(978-0-312-65912-7(1)*, 9780312659127) Square Fish.

Smiletown's Little Coloring Book. 2006. (J). 3.99 *(978-0-9785132-1-4(5)*, Smiletown Bks.) Smile-a-Lot, LLP.

Smiletown's Upside Down. 2007. (J). per. 14.95 *(978-0-9785132-3-8(1))* Smile-a-Lot, LLP.

Smith, Alex T. Claude in the City, 1 vol. Smith, Alex T., illus. 2015. (Claude Ser.). (ENG., Illus.). 96p. (J). (gr. 2-4). pap. 7.95 *(978-1-56145-843-1(0))* Peachtree Pubs.

Smith, Charles R., Jr. Chameleon. 2010. (ENG., Illus.). 384p. (YA). (gr. 7). pap. 7.99 *(978-0-7636-4660-8(1))* Candlewick Pr.

Snicket, Lemony, pseud. File Under - 13 Suspicious Incidents. Seth, illus. 2014. (ENG.). 272p. (J). (gr. 3-17). 12.00 *(978-0-316-28403-5(3))* Little, Brown Bks. for Young Readers.

Soderberg, Erin. Monkey See, Monkey Zoo. Francis, Guy, illus. 2010. (ENG.). 160p. (YA). (gr. 2-4). pap. 5.99 *(978-1-59990-558-7(2)*, 9781599905587, Bloomsbury USA Childrens) Bloomsbury Publishing USA.

Sommer, Carl. Light Your Candle. James, Kennon, illus. 2014. (J). pap. *(978-1-57537-957-9(0))* Advance Publishing, Inc.

—Light Your Candle(Enciende Tu Vela) James, Kennon, illus. 2009. (Another Sommer-Time Story Bilingual Ser.). (SPA & ENG.). 48p. (J). lib. bdg. 16.95 *(978-1-57537-157-3(X))* Advance Publishing, Inc.

—Mayor for a Day. Westbrook, Dick, illus. 2014. (J). pap. *(978-1-57537-959-3(7))* Advance Publishing, Inc.

—Mayor for a Day: Alcalde Por un Dia. Westbrook, Dick, illus. 2009. (Another Sommer-Time Story Bilingual Ser.). (SPA & ENG.). 48p. (J). lib. bdg. 16.95 *(978-1-57537-159-7(6))* Advance Publishing, Inc.

Stamey, Marsha. The Man in the Clouds, 1 vol. Jones, Seth, illus. 2009. 21p. pap. 24.95 *(978-1-60836-730-6(4))* PublishAmerica, Inc.

Stevens, Courtney. Dress Codes for Small Towns. 2017. 352p. (YA). (gr. 9). 17.99 ***(978-0-06-239851-2(2)***, HarperTeen) HarperCollins Pubs.

Stewart, Sarah. The Journey. Smalls, David, illus. pap. 18.95 incl. audio compact disk *(978-1-59112-344-6(5))*; pap. incl. audio *(978-0-87499-924-2(3))*; pap. 16.95 incl. audio *(978-0-87499-922-8(7))*; pap. incl. audio compact disk *(978-1-59112-556-3(1))* Live Oak Media.

—The Journey. Small, David, illus. 2006. (ENG.). 40p. (J). (gr. k-4). reprint ed. pap. 8.99 *(978-0-374-40010-1(5)*, 9780374400101) Square Fish.

Suen, Anastasia. In the Big City. Myer, Ed, illus. 2012. (ENG.). 24p. (gr. k-1). pap. 8.95 *(978-1-61810-302-4(4))* Rourke Educational Media.

Tafolla, Carmen. What Can You Do with a Paleta? Morales, Magaly, illus. (ENG.). 32p. (J). (gr. -1-2). 2014. 7.99 *(978-0-385-75537-5(6)*, Dragonfly Bks.) 2009. 14.99 *(978-1-58246-221-9(6)*, Tricycle Pr.) Random Hse. Children's Bks.

—What Can You Do with a Paleta? (¿Que Puede Hacer con una Paleta?) Morales, Magaly, illus. 2009. (SPA & ENG.). 32p. (J). (gr. -1-2). 14.99 *(978-1-58246-289-9(5)*, Tricycle Pr.) Random Hse. Children's Bks.

Teckentrup, Britta, illus. Busy Bunny Days: In the Town, on the Farm & at the Port. 2014. (ENG.). 56p. (J). (gr. -1-3). 17.99 *(978-1-4521-1700-3(4))* Chronicle Bks. LLC.

Terry, Chris L. Zero Fade. Knabb, Jacob & Vance, Leonard, eds. 2013. (ENG., Illus.). 294p. (gr. 6). pap. 12.00 *(978-0-9884804-3-8(3)*, 1362831) Curbside Splendor Publishing.

Tonatiuh, Duncan. Dear Primo: A Letter to My Cousin. 2010. (ENG., Illus.). 32p. (J). (gr. k-2). 16.95 *(978-0-8109-3872-4(3)*, Abrams Bks. for Young Readers) Abrams, Inc.

Townsend, Wendy. Lizard Love. 2013. 198p. 18.95 *(978-1-60898-151-9(7))* namelos llc.

—The Sundown Rule. 2011. (J). (gr. 5-9). 18.95 *(978-1-60898-099-4(5))* namelos llc.

Tracy, Blaise. The Inside Out & Upside Town. 2008. 24p. pap. 17.95 *(978-1-4327-2484-9(3))* Outskirts Pr., Inc.

Tub Tales: The City. 2003. (Illus.). 10p. (J). 6.00 *(978-0-9713507-1-7(X)*, 842) Panline U.S.A., Inc.

Viau, Nancy. City Street Beat. 2015. (Illus.). 32p. (J). *(978-1-4896-3855-7(5))* Weigl Pubs., Inc.

Vigilante, Danette. The Trouble with Half a Moon. 2015. (ENG.). 208p. (J). (gr. 5). 7.99 *(978-0-14-751550-6(5)*, Puffin Books) Penguin Young Readers Group.

Vivian, Siobhan. The Last Boy & Girl in the World. 2016. (ENG., Illus.). 432p. (YA). (gr. 9). 17.99 *(978-1-4814-5229-8(0)*, Simon & Schuster Bks. For Young Readers) Simon & Schuster Bks. For Young Readers.

Wallace-Brodeur, Ruth. Home by Five. 2010. (ENG.). 32p. (J). (gr. -1-3). 9.99 *(978-1-4424-1438-9(3)*, McElderry, Margaret K. Bks.) McElderry, Margaret K. Bks.

Wasserman, Robin. The Waking Dark. 2013. (ENG.). 464p. (YA). (gr. 9). 17.99 *(978-0-375-86877-1(1)*, Knopf Bks. for Young Readers) Random Hse. Children's Bks.

Webb, Steve. City Kitty Cat. Le Huche, Magali, illus. 2015. (ENG.). 32p. (J). (gr. -1-3). 17.99 *(978-1-4814-4331-9(3)*, Simon & Schuster Bks. For Young Readers) Simon & Schuster Bks. For Young Readers.

Weston Woods Staff, creator. Goggles! 2011. 29.95 *(978-0-439-85317-0(6))* Weston Woods Studios, Inc.

—The Little House. 2011. 38.75 *(978-0-439-72748-8(0))*; 18.95 *(978-0-439-72746-4(4))* Weston Woods Studios, Inc.

Wiggin, Kate Douglas. Rebecca of Sunnybrook Farm. 2003. (Dover Children's Evergreen Classics Ser.). (ENG.). 240p. (J). (gr. 3-8). pap. 4.50 *(978-0-486-42845-1(1))* Dover Pubns., Inc.

—Rebecca of Sunnybrook Farm. 2005. pap. 30.95 *(978-1-4179-1457-9(2))* Kessinger Publishing, LLC.

—Rebecca of Sunnybrook Farm. 2003. (Aladdin Classics Ser.). (ENG.). 368p. (J). pap. 7.99 *(978-0-689-86001-0(3)*, Aladdin) Simon & Schuster Children's Publishing.

—Rebecca of Sunnybrook Farm. Akib, Jamel, illus. 2007. (Classic Starts(tm) Ser.). (ENG.). 160p. (J). (gr. 2-4). 6.95 *(978-1-4027-3693-3(2))* Sterling Publishing Co., Inc.

—Rebecca of Sunnybrook Farm. 2004. reprint ed. pap. 19.95 *(978-1-4179-9996-5(9))*; pap. 1.99 *(978-1-4179-9946-0(2))* Kessinger Publishing, LLC.

Willis Hudson, Cheryl. From Where I Stand. 2008. (Illus.). 32p. (gr. -1-3). 6.95 *(978-1-60349-002-3(7)*, Marimba Bks.) Hudson Publishing Group, The.

Winter, Jonah. Steel Town. Widener, Terry, illus. 2008. (ENG.). 40p. (J). (gr. -1-3). 19.99 *(978-1-4169-4081-4(2)*, Atheneum Bks. for Young Readers) Simon & Schuster Children's Publishing.

Yaccarino, Dan. Doug Unplugged. (ENG.). 40p. (J). (gr. k-4). 2016. 7.99 *(978-0-375-85921-2(7)*, Dragonfly Bks.) 2013. (Illus.). 16.99 *(978-0-375-86643-2(4)*, Knopf Bks. for Young Readers) Random Hse. Children's Bks.

Yee, Wong Herbert. Did You See Chip? Ovresat, Laura, illus. 2004. (Green Light Readers Level 2 Ser.). (ENG.). 24p. (J). (gr. -1-3). pap. 3.95 *(978-0-15-205096-2(5))* Houghton Mifflin Harcourt Publishing Co.

Young, Judy. Digger y Daisy Van a la Ciudad (Digger & Daisy Go to the City) Sullivan, Dana, illus. 2016. (I AM a READER: Digger & Daisy Ser.). (SPA & ENG.). 32p. (J). (gr. k-2). 9.99 *(978-1-62753-954-8(9)*, 204177) Sleeping Bear Pr.

Young, Judy & Sullivan, Dana. Digger & Daisy Go to the City. 2015. (I AM a READER!: Digger & Daisy Ser.). (ENG., Illus.). 32p. (J). (gr. k-2). pap. 4.99 *(978-1-58536-848-8(2)*, 203821) Sleeping Bear Pr.

CITIES AND TOWNS—HISTORY

Broutin, Christian. The Town. Broutin, Christian, illus. 2012. (ENG., Illus.). 36p. (J). (gr. -1-k). spiral bd. 12.99 *(978-1-85103-395-9(5))* Moonlight Publishing, Ltd. GBR. Dist: Independent Pubs. Group.

Flatt, Lizann. Cities & Statecraft in the Renaissance. 2009. (Renaissance World Ser.). (ENG.). 32p. (J). (gr. 6-9). pap. *(978-0-7787-4615-7(1))*; (Illus.). (gr. 5-7). *(978-0-7787-4595-2(3))* Crabtree Publishing Co.

Hinds, Kathryn. The City. 2007. (Life in Elizabethan England Ser.). 80p. (J). (gr. 4-7). lib. bdg. 32.79 *(978-0-7614-2544-1(6)*, Benchmark Bks.) Marshall Cavendish Corp.

Lusted, Marcia Amidon. America's Colonization & Settlement. 2011. (Explorer Library: Language Arts Explorer Ser.). (ENG.). 32p. (gr. 4-8). pap. 14.21 *(978-1-61080-282-6(9)*, 201205); lib. bdg. 28.50 *(978-1-61080-194-2(6)*, 201164) Cherry Lake Publishing.

Markovics, Joyce L. Ghostly Towns. 2017. (Tiptoe into Scary Places Ser.). (ENG., Illus.). 24p. (J). (gr. k-3). 18.95 *(978-1-68402-051-5(4))* Bearport Publishing Co., Inc.

Steele, Philip & Dorling Kindersley Publishing Staff. A City Through Time. Noon, Steve, illus. 2013. (ENG.). 48p. (J). (gr. 2-5). 17.99 *(978-1-4654-0249-3(7)*, DK Children) Dorling Kindersley Publishing, Inc.

Sundance/Newbridge LLC Staff. Why Cities Grow. 2004. (Reading PowerWorks Ser.). (gr. 1-3). 37.50 *(978-0-7608-9281-7(4))*; pap. 6.10 *(978-0-7608-9282-4(2))* Sundance/Newbridge Educational Publishing.

CITIES AND TOWNS—PICTORIAL WORKS

Jakobsen, Kathy. My New York. Jakobsen, Kathy, illus. anniv. rev. ed. 2005. (Illus.). 54p. (J). (gr. k-4). 19.00 *(978-0-7567-8588-8(X))* DIANE Publishing Co.

—My New York. Jakobsen, Kathy, illus. anniv. ed. 2003. (ENG., Illus.). 48p. (J). (gr. -1-3). 20.00 *(978-0-316-92711-6(2))* Little, Brown Bks. for Young Readers.

CITIES AND TOWNS—PLANNING

see City Planning

CITIES AND TOWNS—POETRY

Brooks, Gwendolyn. Bronzeville Boys & Girls. Ringgold, Faith, illus. 2015. (ENG.). 48p. (J). (gr. -1-3). pap. 6.99 *(978-0-06-443772-1(8)*, Amistad) HarperCollins Pubs.

Moore, Lilian. Mural on Second Avenue & Other City Poems. Karas, Roma, illus. 2005. (ENG.). 32p. (J). (gr. k-4). 16.99 *(978-0-7636-1987-9(6))* Candlewick Pr.

CITIES AND TOWNS, RUINED, EXTINCT, ETC.

see Extinct Cities

CITIES AND TOWNS—UNITED STATES

Aveni, Anthony. Buried Beneath Us: Discovering the Ancient Cities of the Americas. Roy, Katherine, illus. 2013. (ENG.). 96p. (J). (gr. 4-8). 18.99 *(978-1-59643-567-4(4)*, 9781596435674) Roaring Brook Pr.

Basher, Simon, et al. States & Capitals: United We Stand! 2014. (Basher History Ser.). (ENG., Illus.). 128p. (J). (gr. 5-9). 14.99 *(978-0-7534-7138-8(8)*, 9780753471388, Kingfisher) Roaring Brook Pr.

Beckett, Leslie. We Live in a State Capital, 01 vols., 1. 2016. (American Communities Ser.). (ENG., Illus.). 24p. (J). pap. 8.25 *(978-1-5081-4196-9(7)*, PowerKids Pr.) Rosen Publishing Group, Inc., The.

Brown, Rachel K. Daily Life in a Southern Colonial Town: St. Augustine. 2003. (J). *(978-1-58417-014-3(X))*; pap. *(978-1-58417-077-8(8))* Lake Street Pubs.

Cleveland, Will & Alvarez, Mark. Yo, Sacramento! (And All Those Other State Capitals You Don't Know) - Memorize Them All (Forever) in 20 Minutes-Without Trying! Nation, Tate, illus. 2011. (ENG.). 128p. (J). (gr. 3-7). pap. 7.95 *(978-1-935212-38-6(9)*, Prospecta Pr.) Easton Studio Pr., LLC.

Colligan, L. H. The City. 2014. (J). pap. *(978-1-62712-883-4(2))*; 80p. (YA). (gr. 6-8). lib. bdg. 35.64 *(978-1-62712-882-7(4))* Cavendish Square Publishing.

Liberman, Sherri. A Historical Atlas of the Industrial Age & the Growth of America's Cities. (United States: Historical Atlases of the Growth of a New Nation Ser.). 64p. 2009. (gr. 5-5). 61.20 *(978-1-60854-254-3(8))* 2005. (Illus.). (J). (gr. 7-12). lib. bdg. 31.95 *(978-1-4042-0205-4(6))* Rosen Publishing Group, Inc., The.

Murdico, Suzanne J. Possibilities & Problems in America's New Urban Centers: The Rise of Cities. (America's Industrial Society in the 19th Century Ser.). 32p. 2009. (gr. 4-4). 47.90 *(978-1-61511-338-5(X))* 2004. (Illus.). (gr. 5-8). pap. 10.00 *(978-0-8239-4277-0(5))* Rosen Publishing Group, Inc., The.

Ryan, Pam Muñoz. Nuestra California. López, Rafael, illus. 2008.Tr. of Our California. (SPA & ENG.). 48p. (J). (gr. 1-4). 17.95 *(978-1-58089-226-1(4))* Charlesbridge Publishing, Inc.

Segal, Robin. ABC in Miami: And the Beaches. 2008. (All 'Bout Cities Ser.). (ENG & SPA.). 32p. (J). (gr. -1-k). *(978-0-9719697-2-8(8))* Murray Hill Bks., LLC.

—ABC in San Francisco. 2008. (All 'Bout Cities Ser.). (ENG.). 32p. (J). (gr. -1-k). *(978-0-9719697-9-7(5))* Murray Hill Bks., LLC.

—ABC in the City. 2008. (All 'Bout Cities Ser.). (ENG.). 32p. (J). (gr. -1-k). *(978-0-9719697-3-5(6))* Murray Hill Bks., LLC.

Staeger, Rob. The Boom Towns. 2004. (History of the Old West Ser.). (Illus.). 64p. (YA). (gr. 5-18). lib. bdg. 19.95 *(978-1-59084-068-9(2))* Mason Crest.

Williams, Jack S. Townspeople & Ranchers of the California Mission Frontier. 2009. (People of the California Missions Ser.). 64p. (gr. 4-4). 58.50 *(978-1-60851-161-7(8)*, PowerKids Pr.) Rosen Publishing Group, Inc., The.

Wirkner, Linda. Learning about Urban Growth in America with Graphic Organizers. 2005. (Graphic Organizers in Social Studies). (Illus.). 24p. (J). (gr. 3-5). lib. bdg. 22.60 *(978-1-4042-2809-2(8)*, PowerKids Pr.) Rosen Publishing Group, Inc., The.

CITIES AND TOWNS IN ART

Carroll, Colleen. How Artists See Work/Play/Families/America Set 2, 4 vols., Set. 2008. (How Artists See Ser.). (ENG., Illus.). 192p. (J). (gr. k-7). 45.00 *(978-0-7892-0965-8(9))* Abbeville Pr., Inc.

CITIZENSHIP

see also Patriotism; Suffrage

Anderson, Nancy. I Am a Citizen of the United States. 2016. (Rosen REAL Readers: Social Studies Nonfiction / Fiction: Family, Community, & the World Ser.). 12p. (gr. 1-k). pap. 6.33 *(978-1-5081-2323-1(3)*, Rosen Classroom) Rosen Publishing Group, Inc., The.

Barraclough, Sue. Honestidad, 1 vol. 2010. (Explorar el Civismo Ser.). (SPA.). 32p. (gr. 1-3). 27.32 *(978-1-4329-4458-2(4))*; pap. 8.29 *(978-1-4329-4466-7(5))* Heinemann-Raintree.

—Sharing. 2016. (Exploring Citizenship Ser.). (ENG.). 32p. pap. 8.29 *(978-1-4846-4003-6(9)*, Heinemann First Library) Heinemann-Raintree.

Benchmark Education Company, LLC Staff, compiled by. Eve Bunting's World of Stories & Citizenship. 2005. spiral bd. 225.00 *(978-1-4108-5807-8(3))* Benchmark Education Co.

—Government & Citizenship. 2005. (English Explorers Ser.). (J). spiral bd. 265.00 *(978-1-4108-5767-5(0))* Benchmark Education Co.

—Government & Citizenship: Theme Set. 2006. (J). 121.00 *(978-1-4108-7096-4(0))* Benchmark Education Co.

—GOVT & Citizenship. 2006. spiral bd. 330.00 *(978-1-4108-7007-0(3))* Benchmark Education Co.

—Social Studies Theme: GOVT & Citizenship. 2005. spiral bd. 115.00 *(978-1-4108-5331-8(4))* Benchmark Education Co.

Boothroyd, Jennifer. What Is Citizenship? 2015. (ENG., Illus.). 24p. (gr. k-2). pap. 6.99 *(978-1-4677-8623-2(3)*, Lerner Pubns.) Lerner Publishing Group.

Brown, Liz. Civics. 2007. (Social Studies Essential Skills Ser.). (Illus.). 24p. (J). (gr. 4-7). lib. bdg. 24.45 *(978-1-59036-765-0(0))*; per. 8.95 *(978-1-59036-766-7(9))* Weigl Pubs., Inc.

Byers, Ann. Immigration: Interpreting the Constitution. 2014. (Understanding the United States Constitution Ser.). 112p. (YA). (gr. 7-12). 35.60 *(978-1-4777-7512-7(9))* Rosen Publishing Group, Inc., The.

Cherry Lake Publishing Staff, compiled by. Citizens & their Governments. 2010. 32p. lib. bdg. 199.50 *(978-1-60279-108-4(2)*, 200001) Cherry Lake Publishing.

Citizenship & Character: Understanding America's Civic Values. 2003. 180p. (YA). per. 49.95 incl. cd-rom *(978-1-932785-00-5(0))* Bill of Rights Institute, The.

Clay, Kathryn. The Pledge of Allegiance: Introducing Primary Sources. 2016. (Introducing Primary Sources Ser.). (ENG., Illus.). 32p. (gr. 1-2). lib. bdg. 27.99 *(978-1-4914-8227-8(3))* Capstone Press of Coughlan Cos.

Coan, Sharon. Being a Good Citizen (Foundations) 2015. (TIME for KIDS(r) Nonfiction Readers Ser.). (ENG., Illus.). 12p. (gr. k-k). 4.99 *(978-1-4938-2066-5(4))* Teacher Created Materials, Inc.

Coll-Seck, Jayden. I'm a Good Citizen, 01 vols., 1. 2016. (Rosen REAL Readers: Social Studies Nonfiction / Fiction: Family, Community, & the World Ser.). (ENG.). 12p. (J). pap. 6.33 *(978-1-5081-1761-2(6)*, Rosen Classroom) Rosen Publishing Group, Inc., The.

Conklin, Wendy. Power, People, & Change. 2016. (Primary Source Readers Ser.). (Illus.). 32p. (gr. 2-2). 8.99 *(978-1-4938-2548-6(8))* Teacher Created Materials, Inc.

Donovan, Sandy. Does My Voice Count? A Book about Citizenship. 2014. (Show Your Character Ser.). (ENG., Illus.). 32p. (gr. 1-3). lib. bdg. 26.60 *(978-1-4677-1366-5(X)*, Lerner Pubns.) Lerner Publishing Group.

Explore Citizenship, 3 vols., Set. Incl. Constitution Day. Griffin, Maeve. 22.60 *(978-1-4358-2978-7(6))*; Elections: Choosing Our Leaders. Bamaton, Paul. 22.60 *(978-1-4358-2979-4(4))*; Why We Need Laws. Wilberforce, Bertram. lib. bdg. 22.60 *(978-1-4358-2977-0(8))*; 24p. (J). (gr. 3-5). 2009. Set lib. bdg. 63.75 *(978-1-4358-3020-2(2)*, PowerKids Pr.) Rosen Publishing Group, Inc., The.

Falk, Laine. We Are Citizens. 2009. (Scholastic News Nonfiction Readers Ser.). (ENG.). 24p. (J). (gr. 1-2). pap. 6.95 *(978-0-531-21448-0(6)*, Children's Pr.); lib. bdg. 22.00 *(978-0-531-21349-0(8))* Scholastic Library Publishing.

Fiehn, Terry & Fiehn, Julia. This Is Citizenship. 2nd ed. 2008. (Illus.). 96p. pap., stu. ed. 39.50 *(978-0-340-94712-8(8))* Hodder Education Group GBR. Dist: Trans-Atlantic Pubns., Inc.

Fisher, Douglas & McGraw-Hill Staff. Civics Today: Citizenship, Economics, & You - Active Reading Note-Taking Guide. 2nd ed. 2004. (Civics Today: Citzshp Econ You Ser.). (ENG., Illus.). 454p. (gr. 6-10). stu. ed. 12.80 *(978-0-07-865611-8(7)*, 0078656117) McGraw-Hill Education.

Fowler, Leona. Our Class Rules: Digital Citizenship. 2017. (Computer Science for the Real World Ser.). 12p. (gr. 6-7). pap. 7.05 ***(978-1-5383-5164-2(1)***, Rosen Classroom) Rosen Publishing Group, Inc., The.

Gagne, Tammy. Your Guide to Becoming a United States Citizen. 2013. (My Guide to U.S. Citizenship Ser.). (ENG.). (J). (gr. 4-6). lib. bdg. 29.95 *(978-1-61228-449-1(3))* Mitchell Lane Pubs., Inc.

Glassman, Bruce. Citizenship. 2009. (Character Counts! Ser.). 48p. (gr. 4-5). 53.00 *(978-1-61511-835-9(7))* Rosen Publishing Group, Inc., The.

Glassman, Bruce S. Citizenship. 2008. (Illus.). 48p. (J). pap. 9.95 *(978-1-60108-503-0(6)*, Bearing Bks.); (YA). (gr. 3-6). lib. bdg. 29.25 *(978-1-60108-502-3(8))* Red Cygnet Pr.

Hanson, Anders. Do Something for Others: The Kids' Book of Citizenship, 1 vol. 2014. (What We Stand For Ser.). (ENG.). 24p. (gr. 5-10). lib. bdg. 25.65 *(978-1-62403-292-9(3)*, Super SandCastle) ABDO Publishing Co.

Harcourt School Publishers Staff. Good Citizen, No. 2. 2nd ed. 2003. (Illus.). (gr. 1). pap. 139.70 *(978-0-15-337557-6(4))* Harcourt Schl. Pubs.

Harper, Leslie. Cómo Mantenerse Informado. 2014. (Sé un líder de la Comunidad (Be a Community Leader) Ser.). (SPA.). 32p. (J). (gr. 4-6). pap. 60.00 *(978-1-4777-6923-2(4)*, PowerKids Pr.) Rosen Publishing Group, Inc., The.

—Cómo Mantenerse Informados. 2014. (Sé un líder de la Comunidad (Be a Community Leader) Ser.). (SPA.). 32p. (J). (gr. 4-6). lib. bdg. 26.25 *(978-1-4777-6921-8(8)*, PowerKids Pr.) Rosen Publishing Group, Inc., The.

—How to Stay Informed. 2014. (Be a Community Leader Ser.). 32p. (J). (gr. 4-6). lib. bdg. 26.25 *(978-1-4777-6701-6(0)*, PowerKids Pr.) Rosen Publishing Group, Inc., The.

—What Are Rights & Responsibilities? 2012. (Civics Q & A Ser.). (ENG., Illus.). 24p. (J). (gr. 3-6). 22.60 *(978-1-4488-7437-8(8))*; pap. 8.25 *(978-1-4488-7510-8(2))* Rosen Publishing Group, Inc., The. (PowerKids Pr.).

—What Is Citizenship? 2012. (Civics Q & A Ser.). (ENG., Illus.). 24p. (J). (gr. 3-6). pap. 8.25 *(978-1-4488-7508-5(0))*; lib. bdg. 22.60 *(978-1-4488-7435-4(1))* Rosen Publishing Group, Inc., The. (PowerKids Pr.).

Hay, Jeff. Amendment XIV: Citizenship for All. 2008. (Constitutional Amendments Ser.). (ENG., Illus.). 112-144p. (YA). (gr. 9-12). lib. bdg. 37.90 *(978-0-7377-4124-7(4)*, LML02109-243013) Cengage Gale.

Higgins, Melissa. I Am a Good Citizen, 1 vol. 2014. (I Don't Bully Ser.). (ENG.). 24p. (gr. k-1). lib. bdg. 21.99 *(978-1-4765-4071-9(3)*, Pebble Bks.) Capstone Press of Coughlan Cos.

Hoffman, Mary Ann. I Am a Good Citizen. 2011. (Kids of Character Ser.). (Illus.). 24p. (J). (gr. 1-3). pap. 8.15 *(978-1-4339-4851-0(6))*; lib. bdg. 22.60 *(978-1-4339-4850-3(8))* Stevens, Gareth Publishing LLLP.

—I Am a Good Citizen / Soy un buen Ciudadano. 2011. (Kids of Character / Chicos con carácter Ser.). (ENG & SPA., Illus.). 24p. (J). (gr. -1-2). 22.60 *(978-1-4339-4854-1(0))* Stevens, Gareth Publishing LLLP.

Hotchkins, Dewayne. We Are Citizens of the World. 2016. (Rosen REAL Readers: Social Studies Nonfiction / Fiction: Family, Community, & the World Ser.). 12p. (gr. 1-k). pap. 6.33 *(978-1-5081-2332-3(2)*, Rosen Classroom) Rosen Publishing Group, Inc., The.

Howell, Sara. El Camino a la Ciudadania. 2014. (Mosaico Americano: la Inmigración Hoy en día (the American Mosaic: Immigration Today) Ser.). (SPA., Illus.). 24p. (J). (gr. 3-6). pap. 8.25 *(978-1-4777-6825-9(4)*, PowerKids Pr.) Rosen Publishing Group, Inc., The.

—Los Derechos de Los Inmigrantes, Los Derechos de Los Ciudadanos. 2014. (Mosaico Americano: la Inmigración Hoy en día (the American Mosaic: Immigration Today) Ser.). (SPA., Illus.). 24p. (J). (gr. 3-6). lib. bdg. 23.60 *(978-1-4777-6819-8(X)*, PowerKids Pr.) Rosen Publishing Group, Inc., The.

—Los Refugiados. 2014. (Mosaico Americano: la Inmigración Hoy en día (the American Mosaic: Immigration Today) Ser.). (SPA & ENG., Illus.). 24p. (J). (gr. 3-6). pap. 8.25 *(978-1-4777-6817-4(3)*, PowerKids Pr.) Rosen Publishing Group, Inc., The.

—The Path to Citizenship. 2014. (American Mosaic: Immigration Today Ser.). 24p. (J). (gr. 3-6). 23.60 *(978-1-4777-6736-8(3))*; pap. 49.50 *(978-1-4777-6648-4(0))* Rosen Publishing Group, Inc., The. (PowerKids Pr.).

—Refugees. 2014. (American Mosaic: Immigration Today Ser.). (Illus.). 24p. (J). (gr. 3-6). pap. 49.50 *(978-1-4777-6649-1(9)*, PowerKids Pr.) Rosen Publishing Group, Inc., The.

Hudak, Heather C. Roles & Responsibilities of Canadian Citizens: Government of Canada. 2010. (Illus.). 32p. pap. *(978-1-55388-684-6(4))* Weigl Educational Pubs. Ltd.

Hudak, Heather C., ed. Roles & Responsibilities of Canadian Citizens: Government of Canada. 2010. (Illus.). 32p. *(978-1-55388-680-8(1))* Weigl Educational Pubs. Ltd.

James, Emily. How to Be a Good Citizen: A Question & Answer Book about Citizenship. 2017. (Character Matters Ser.). (ENG.). 32p. (gr. 1-2). lib. bdg. 27.32 ***(978-1-5157-7195-1(4)***, Aplus Bks.) Capstone Press of Coughlan Cos.

Jianmei, Wang. America: My Hom, Your Country. 2009. pap. 29.00 *(978-1-61584-424-1(4))* Independent Pub.

Kawa, Dominic. Sasha Is a Good Citizen. 2013. (InfoMax Readers Ser.). (ENG.). 24p. (J). (gr. 2-3). pap. 8.25 *(978-1-4777-2366-1(8))*; pap. 49.50 *(978-1-4777-2367-8(6))* Rosen Publishing Group, Inc., The. (Rosen Classroom).

Keller, Ellen. Kids Are Citizens. 2007. (Reading Expeditions Ser.). (ENG., Illus.). 32p. (J). pap. 17.95 *(978-0-7922-8683-7(9))* CENGAGE Learning.

Kenney, Karen. Civic Responsibilities. 2014. (ENG.). 24p. (gr. 3-5). 28.50 *(978-1-62717-685-9(3))* Rourke Educational Media.

Kishel, Ann-Marie. Citizenship. 2006. (First Step Nonfiction Ser.). (Illus.). 23p. (J). (gr. 3-7). lib. bdg. 18.60 *(978-0-8225-6398-3(3)*, Lerner Pubns.) Lerner Publishing Group.

Lansford, Tom. Citizenship & Immigration, Vol. 8. Lansford, Tom, ed. 2016. (Foundations of Democracy Ser.). (Illus.). 64p. (J). (gr. 7). 23.95 *(978-1-4222-3626-0(9))* Mason Crest.

Leavitt, Amie Jane. United States Laws of Citizenship. 2013. (My Guide to U.S. Citizenship Ser.). (ENG.). (J). (gr. 4-6). lib. bdg. 29.95 *(978-1-61228-448-4(5))* Mitchell Lane Pubs., Inc.

Loria, Laura. What Is Citizenship? 2015. (Let's Find Out! Government Ser.). (ENG., Illus.). 32p. (J). (gr. 2-3). 23.45 *(978-1-62275-976-7(1)*, Britannica Educational Publishing) Rosen Publishing Group, Inc., The.

Manolis, Kay & Todd, Anne. John F. Kennedy: A Life of Citizenship. 2007. (People of Character Ser.). (ENG., Illus.). 24p. (J). (gr. 2-5). lib. bdg. 25.95 *(978-1-60014-087-7(4))* Bellwether Media.

Marshall, Shelley. Molly the Great Respects the Flag: A Book about Being a Good Citizen. Mahan, Ben, illus. 2010. (Character Education with Super Ben & Molly the Great Ser.). 24p. (J). 22.60 *(978-0-7660-3519-5(0))*; pap. 7.95 *(978-0-7660-3744-1(4))* Enslow Pubs., Inc. (Enslow Elementary).

Mason, Helen. Be an Active Citizen at Your School. 2016. (Citizenship in Action Ser.). (ENG.). 24p. (J). (gr. 1-4). *(978-0-7787-2600-5(2))*; pap. *(978-0-7787-2606-7(1))* Crabtree Publishing Co.

Matthas, Seth. Our Family Rules: Digital Citizenship. 2017. (Computer Science for the Real World Ser.). 8p. (gr. 5-6). pap. 6.20 ***(978-1-5383-5083-6(1)***, Rosen Classroom) Rosen Publishing Group, Inc., The.

Maury, Rob. Citizenship: Rights & Responsibilities. (Major American Immigration Ser.). (YA). 2010. (Illus.). 64p. (gr. 9-12). lib. bdg. 22.95 *(978-1-4222-0618-8(1))* 2007. pap. 9.95 *(978-1-4222-0685-0(8))* Mason Crest.

McNamara, Andrew. Being a Good Citizen. 2009. (Real Life Readers Ser.). 16p. (gr. 2-3). pap. 7.05 *(978-1-4358-0071-7(0)*, Rosen Classroom) Rosen Publishing Group, Inc., The.

O'Connor, Barbara. Citizenship. 2004. (Illus.). pap. 7.95 *(978-0-8225-4743-3(0))* Lerner Publishing Group.

Parker, Vic. Exploring Citizenship, 7 vols., Set. Incl. Acting Responsibly. (ENG.). 32p. (gr. 1-3). 2009. 26.65 *(978-1-4329-3315-9(9)*, Heinemann First Library); (Exploring Citizenship Ser.). (ENG.). 32p. 2009. Set lib. bdg. 109.28 o.p. *(978-1-4329-3318-0(3)*, Heinemann First Library) Heinemann-Raintree.

Pegis, Jessica. What Is Citizenship? 2016. (Citizenship in Action Ser.). (ENG.). 24p. (J). (gr. 1-4). *(978-0-7787-2596-1(0))* Crabtree Publishing Co.

Phillips, Miriam. President for the Day! Digital Citizenship. 2017. (Computer Science for the Real World Ser.). 12p. (gr. 6-7). pap. 7.05 ***(978-1-5383-5162-8(5)***, Rosen Classroom) Rosen Publishing Group, Inc., The.

Raatma, Lucia. Citizenship. 2013. (21st Century Junior Library: Character Education Ser.). (ENG., Illus.). 24p. (J). (gr. 1-4). 25.64 *(978-1-62431-154-3(7)*, 202936); pap. 12.79 *(978-1-62431-286-1(1)*, 202938) Cherry Lake Publishing.

—Citizenship. 2012. (Cornerstones of Freedom, Third Ser.). (ENG., Illus.). 64p. (J). pap. 8.95 *(978-0-531-28164-2(7))*; (gr. 4-6). lib. bdg. 30.00 *(978-0-531-23064-0(3))* Scholastic Library Publishing. (Children's Pr.).

Remy, Richard C., et al. Civics Today: Citizenship, Economics, & You. 3rd ed. 2006. (Illus.). 710p. (J). 90.64 *(978-0-07-874574-4(8)*, 9780078745744) Glencoe/McGraw-Hill.

—Civics Today: Citizenship, Economics, & You. 2nd ed. 2004. (Civics Today: Citzshp Econ You Ser.). (ENG., Illus.). 710p. (gr. 7-10). lib. bdg., stu. ed. 115.68 *(978-0-07-860970-1(4)*, 0078609704) McGraw-Hill Higher Education.

Reynolds, Shaye. I Am an American Citizen. 2013. (Rosen Readers Ser.). (ENG.). 24p. (J). (gr. 2-3). pap. 49.50 *(978-1-4777-2377-7(3))*; pap. 8.25 *(978-1-4777-2376-0(5))* Rosen Publishing Group, Inc., The. (Rosen Classroom).

Rothstein, Evelyn. Clara Becomes a Citizen. Uhlig, Elizabeth, illus. 2009. (ENG.). (J). pap. 12.95 *(978-0-9786745-7-1(X))* Marble Hse. Editions.

Scholastic Library Publishing. A True Book—Civics. 2012. (J). 116.00 *(978-0-531-26000-5(3)*, Children's Pr.) Scholastic Library Publishing.

Scholastic News Nonfiction Readers: We the Kids (Citizenship), 5 vols., Set. Incl. Let's Be Friends. Miller, Amanda. lib. bdg. 22.00 *(978-0-531-21344-5(7))*; Let's Vote on It! Behrens, Janice. lib. bdg. 22.00 *(978-0-531-21346-9(3))*; We Are Alike, We Are Different. Behrens, Janice. lib. bdg. 22.00 *(978-0-531-21347-6(1))*; We Are Citizens. Falk, Laine. lib. bdg. 22.00 *(978-0-531-21349-0(8))*; We Help Out at School. Miller, Amanda. lib. bdg. 22.00 *(978-0-531-21345-2(5)*, Children's Pr.); 24p. (J). (gr. 1-2). 2009. Set lib. bdg. 110.00 *(978-0-531-21036-9(7)*, Children's Pr.) Scholastic Library Publishing.

Skog, Jason. Citizenship, 1 vol. Brown, Kelly, illus. 2008. (Cartoon Nation Ser.). (ENG.). 32p. (gr. 3-4). 30.65 *(978-1-4296-1331-6(9)*, Graphic Library) Capstone Press of Coughlan Cos.

Small, Mary. Being a Good Citizen: A Book about Citizenship, 1 vol. Previn, Stacey, illus. 2005. (Way to Be! Ser.). (ENG.). 24p. (gr. k-2). lib. bdg. 26.65 *(978-1-4048-1050-1(1))* Picture Window Bks.

Springdale Elementary 5/6 Class, The Students Of Valerie Dockendorff's. What If ?, 1 vol. 2012. (ENG.). 24p. (J). (gr. -1-3). pap. 9.95 *(978-1-894838-65-8(3))* Nimbus Publishing, Ltd. CAN. Dist: Orca Bk. Pubs. USA.

Steinagle, Jason. Citizenship: What It Means to Be from Texas. 2014. (Spotlight on Texas Ser.). (ENG., Illus.). 32p. (J). (gr. 3-4). 26.25 *(978-1-4777-4546-5(7)*, Rosen Classroom) Rosen Publishing Group, Inc., The.

Stout, Carol A. Proud to Be an American, 1. 2004. (Illus.). 168p. pap. 6.95 *(978-1-886161-08-5(9))* Millennium Marketing & Publishing.

Sundance/Newbridge LLC Staff. Being a Good Citizen. 2004. (Reading PowerWorks Ser.). (gr. 1-3). 37.50 *(978-0-7608-8940-4(6))*; pap. 6.10 *(978-0-7608-8941-1(4))* Sundance/Newbridge Educational Publishing.

Wells, Naomi. What Does Citizenship Mean? Digital Citizenship. 2017. (Computer Science for the Real World Ser.). 16p. (gr. 7-8). pap. 7.95 ***(978-1-5383-5241-0(9)***, Rosen Classroom) Rosen Publishing Group, Inc., The.

Wyatt, Valerie. How to Build Your Own Country. Fredericks, Karen & Rix, Fred, illus. 2009. (CitizenKid Ser.). (ENG.). 40p. (J). (gr. 3-7). 17.95 *(978-1-55453-310-7(4))* Kids Can Pr., Ltd. CAN. Dist: Hachette Bk. Group.

CITRUS FRUITS—FICTION

Polacco, Patricia. An Orange for Frankie. Polacco, Patricia, illus. 2004. (ENG., Illus.). 48p. (J). (gr. 1-4). 17.99 *(978-0-399-24302-8(X)*, Philomel Bks.) Penguin Young Readers Group.

CITY GOVERNMENT

see Municipal Government

CITY LIFE

see Cities and Towns

CITY PLANNING

see also Housing; Urban Renewal

Delafosse, Claude, et al. Let's Look at Life below the City. 2012. (ENG., Illus.). 38p. (J). (gr. k-3). pap. 11.99 *(978-1-85103-313-3(0))* Moonlight Publishing, Ltd. GBR. Dist: Independent Pubs. Group.

Drummond, Allan. Pedal Power. 2017. (ENG., Illus.). 40p. (J). 17.99 *(978-0-374-30527-7(7)*, 9780374305277, Farrar, Straus & Giroux (BYR)) Farrar, Straus & Giroux.

Houghton, Gillian. Careers in Urban Planning. 2005. (Career Resource Library). (Illus.). 192p. (YA). (gr. 7-12). lib. bdg. 34.60 *(978-0-8239-3658-8(9))* Rosen Publishing Group, Inc., The.

Kopp, Megan. Maker Projects for Kids Who Love Designing Communities. 2017. 32p. (J). ***(978-0-7787-2879-5(X))*** Crabtree Publishing Co.

Lankford, Ronnie D. Green Cities. 2011. (At Issue Ser.). (ENG.). 128p. (gr. 12-12). pap. 27.80 *(978-0-7377-5152-9(5))*; lib. bdg. 39.40 *(978-0-7377-5151-2(7))* Cengage Gale. (Greenhaven Pr., Inc.).

Lomberg, Michelle. Avoiding Gridlock. Schwartzenberger, Tina, ed. 2004. (Understanding Global Issues). (Illus.). 56p. (J). (gr. 10-12). lib. bdg. 28.50 *(978-1-58340-357-0(4))* Weigl Pubs., Inc.

Lyles, Brian & Lyles, Jason. The LEGO Neighborhood Book: Build Your Own Town! 2014. (ENG., Illus.). 204p. (J). (gr. 5). 19.95 *(978-1-59327-571-6(4))* No Starch Pr., Inc.

Macaulay, David. City: A Story of Roman Planning & Construction. 2012. 21.00 *(978-1-61383-577-7(9))* Perfection Learning Corp.

Mason, Helen. Urban Planner. 2014. (Creative Careers Ser.). 48p. (J). (gr. 4-8). pap. 84.30 *(978-1-4824-0933-8(X))* Stevens, Gareth Publishing LLLP.

Romanek, Trudee. Life in a Commercial City. 2010. (Learn about Urban Life Ser.). (ENG., Illus.). 32p. (J). (gr. 4-9). pap. *(978-0-7787-7401-3(5))*; lib. bdg. *(978-0-7787-7391-7(4))* Crabtree Publishing Co.

Snedden, Robert. The Growth of Cities. 2004. (Earth's Changing Landscape Ser.). (J). lib. bdg. 28.50 *(978-1-58340-474-4(0))* Black Rabbit Bks.

Yomtov, Nel. Urban Planner. 2015. (21st Century Skills Library: Cool STEAM Careers Ser.). (ENG., Illus.). 32p. (J). (gr. 4-7). 29.93 *(978-1-63362-009-4(3)*, 205948) Cherry Lake Publishing.

CITY PLANNING—HISTORY

Lang, Glenna & Wunsch, Marjory. Genius of Common Sense: Jane Jacobs & the Story of the Death & Life of Great American Cities. 2012. pap. 15.95 *(978-1-56792-456-5(5))* Godine, David R. Pub.

Lang, Glenna W. & Wunsch, Marjory. Genius of Common Sense: Jane Jacobs & the Story of the Death & Life of Great American Cities. 2009. (ENG., Illus.). 128p. (YA). (gr. 5-18). 17.95 *(978-1-56792-384-1(4))* Godine, David R. Pub.

CIVICS

see Citizenship; Political Science; United States—Politics and Government

CIVIL DISOBEDIENCE

see Government, Resistance to; Passive Resistance

CIVIL DISORDERS

see Riots

CIVIL ENGINEERING

see also Bridges; Canals; Dams; Excavation; Harbors; Hydraulic Engineering; Irrigation; Masonry; Mechanical Engineering; Military Engineering; Mining Engineering; Public Works; Railroad Engineering; Reclamation of Land; Rivers; Roads; Streets; Subways; Surveying; Tunnels; Water-Supply

Borchelt, Kelly L. The Longest Tunnel. 2004. (Extreme Places Ser.). (ENG., Illus.). 48p. (J). 27.50 *(978-0-7377-1882-9(X)*, Greenhaven Pr., Inc.) Cengage Gale.

Carmichael, L. E. Amazing Feats of Civil Engineering, 1 vol. 2014. (Great Achievements in Engineering Ser.). (ENG.). 112p. (J). (gr. 6-12). lib. bdg. 35.64 *(978-1-62403-427-5(6)*, Essential Library) ABDO Publishing Co.

Crabtree Staff & Solway, Andrew. Civil Engineering & the Science of Structures. 2012. (ENG., Illus.). 32p. (J). pap. *(978-0-7787-7501-0(1))* Crabtree Publishing Co.

Ebner, Aviva. Engineering Science Experiments. 2011. (Experiments for Future Scientists Ser.). (Illus.). 164p. (J). (gr. 5-8). 35.00 *(978-1-60413-852-8(1))* Facts On File, Inc.

Enz, Tammy. Build Your Own Car, Rocket, & Other Things That Go, 1 vol. (Build It Yourself Ser.). (ENG., 32p. (gr. 3-4). 2011. Illus.). pap. 8.29 *(978-1-4296-6260-4(3))* 2010. lib. bdg. 27.99 *(978-1-4296-5437-1(6))* Capstone Press of Coughlan Cos. (Edge Bks.).

Gibson, Brylee. Wonders of the World Megastructures. 2007. (Connectors Ser.). (gr. 2-5). pap. *(978-1-877453-20-5(X))* Global Education Systems Ltd.

Glatzer, Jenna. The Story Behind the Name. 2015. (Story Behind the Name Ser.). (ENG.). 32p. (gr. 2-3). 114.60 *(978-1-4795-8008-8(2))* Picture Window Bks.

Glenn, John. Civil Engineers!, Vol. 10. 2015. (Scientists in Action Ser.). (Illus.). 48p. (J). (gr. 5). lib. bdg. 20.95 *(978-1-4222-3421-1(5))* Mason Crest.

Greathouse, Lisa. Big Digs: Construction Site, 1 vol. 2nd rev. ed. 2014. (TIME for KIDS(r) Nonfiction Readers Ser.). (ENG., Illus.). 32p. (J). (gr. 3-3). pap. 25.96 *(978-1-4807-1077-1(6))* Shell Educational Publishing.

—Big Digs - Construction Site, 1 vol. 2nd rev. ed. 2011. (Nonfiction Readers Ser.). (ENG.). 32p. (J). (gr. 3-3). pap. 8.99 *(978-1-4333-3662-1(6))* Teacher Created Materials, Inc.

Gregory, Helen. Changing the Land, 1 vol. 2011. (Wonder Readers Early Level Ser.). (ENG.). (gr. -1-1). 32p. pap. 5.99 *(978-1-4296-7800-1(3))*; 16p. pap. 35.94 *(978-1-4296-8076-9(8))* Capstone Press of Coughlan Cos. (Wonder Readers).

Hayes, Amy. Building Bridges & Roads: Civil Engineers, 01 vols., 1. 2016. (Engineers Rule Ser.). (ENG., Illus.). 32p. (J). pap. 11.75 *(978-1-5081-4532-5(6)*, PowerKids Pr.) Rosen Publishing Group, Inc., The.

Jango-Cohen, Judith. Dump Trucks on the Move. 2011. (Lightning Bolt Books Vroom-Vroom Ser.). (ENG.). 32p. (gr. k-2). lib. bdg. 26.60 *(978-0-7613-3917-5(5))* Lerner Publishing Group.

Kissock, Heather, ed. Eiffel Tower. 2011. (J). (gr. 4-6). pap. 12.95 *(978-1-61690-770-9(3)*, AV2 by Weigl); (Illus.). 24p. (gr. 2-5). 27.13 *(978-1-61690-766-2(5))* Weigl Pubs., Inc.

Klobuchar, Lisa. How Did They Do That? 2005. (Real Deal Ser.). (Illus.). 32p. (J). pap. *(978-0-7608-9633-4(X))* Sundance/Newbridge Educational Publishing.

Macaulay, David. City: A Story of Roman Planning & Construction. 2012. 21.00 *(978-1-61383-577-7(9))* Perfection Learning Corp.

Marciniak, Kristin. Astounding Structures. 2018. (ENG.). 32p. (gr. 3-6). 31.35 ***(978-1-63235-418-1(7)***, 12-Story Library) Pr. Room Editions LLC.

Masters, Nancy Robinson. Heavy Equipment Operator. 2010. (21st Century Skills Library: Cool Careers Ser.). (ENG.). 32p. (gr. 4-8). lib. bdg. 28.50 *(978-1-60279-941-7(5)*, 200627) Cherry Lake Publishing.

Mattern, Joanne. Built to Last. 2011. (ENG., Illus.). 48p. (gr. 4-6). pap. 10.95 *(978-1-61741-989-8(3))* Rourke Educational Media.

Meister, Cari. Totally Amazing Facts about Stuff We've Built. 2017. (Mind Benders Ser.). (ENG.). 112p. (gr. 1-3). lib. bdg. 23.32 *(978-1-5157-4753-6(0))* Capstone Press of Coughlan Cos.

Miller, Ron. Seven Wonders of Engineering. 2010. (Seven Wonders Ser.). (Illus.). 80p. (J). (gr. 5-9). lib. bdg. 33.26 *(978-0-7613-4237-3(0))* Twenty First Century Bks.

Oxlade, Chris. Constructions for Towering Intellects. (Illus.). 128p. (J). pap. 8.99 *(978-0-340-68994-3(3))* Hodder & Stoughton GBR. Dist: Trafalgar Square Publishing.

Rooney, Thomas L. Tobey Boland & the Blackstone Canal. Donovan, Patte, illus. 2005. 30p. (J). *(978-1-929039-30-2(1))* Ambassador Bks., Inc.

Samuels, Charlie. The Rise of Industry (1700-1800) 2010. (Science Highlights: A Gareth Stevens Timeline Ser.). (ENG.). 48p. (J). (gr. 6-8). pap. 14.05 *(978-1-4339-4146-7(5))*; lib. bdg. 31.95 *(978-1-4339-4145-0(7))* Stevens, Gareth Publishing LLLP. (Gareth Stevens Secondary Library).

Silivanch, Annalise. Rebuilding America's Infrastructure. 2010. (In the News Ser.). (ENG.). 64p. (YA). pap. 12.95 *(978-1-4488-1676-7(9))*; (gr. 7-12). lib. bdg. 31.95 *(978-1-4358-9444-0(8))* Rosen Publishing Group, Inc., The.

Sjonger, Rebecca. Geotechnical Engineering & Earth's Materials & Processes. 2015. (ENG., Illus.). 32p. (J). *(978-0-7787-7506-5(2))* Crabtree Publishing Co.

Solway, Andrew. Civil Engineering & the Science of Structures. 2012. (ENG.). 32p. (J). *(978-0-7787-7496-9(1))* Crabtree Publishing Co.

Squire, Ann O. Extreme Bridges. 2014. (ENG.). 48p. (J). lib. bdg. 29.00 *(978-0-531-20745-1(5))* Scholastic Library Publishing.

Stefoff, Rebecca. Building Bridges. 2015. (Great Engineering Ser.). (ENG.). 32p. (J). (gr. 3-4). pap. 10.58 *(978-1-5026-0597-9(X))* Cavendish Square Publishing.
—Building Dams. 2015. (Great Engineering Ser.). (ENG.). 32p. (J). (gr. 3-4). pap. 10.58 *(978-1-5026-0594-8(5))* Cavendish Square Publishing.
—Building Roads. 2015. (Great Engineering Ser.). (ENG.). 32p. (J). (gr. 3-4). pap. 10.58 *(978-1-5026-0603-7(8))* Cavendish Square Publishing.
—Building Tunnels. 2015. (Great Engineering Ser.). (ENG.). 32p. (J). (gr. 3-4). pap. 10.58 *(978-1-5026-0600-6(3))* Cavendish Square Publishing.
Way, Steve & Bailey, Gerry. Structures. 2009. (Simply Science Ser.). (Illus.). 32p. (YA). (gr. 3-6). lib. bdg. 26.00 *(978-1-4339-0036-5(X))* Stevens, Gareth Publishing LLLP.
Woods, Mary B. & Woods, Michael. Ancient Construction: From Tents to Towers. 2005. (Ancient Technology Ser.). (Illus.). 96p. (gr. 6-12). 25.26 *(978-0-8225-2998-9(X))* Lerner Publishing Group.
Woods, Michael & Woods, Mary B. Ancient Transportation Technology: From Oars to Elephants. 2011. (Technology in Ancient Cultures Ser.). (ENG., Illus.). 96p. (J). (gr. 6-12). lib. bdg. 31.93 *(978-0-7613-6524-2(9))* Lerner Publishing Group.

CIVIL ENGINEERING—FICTION

Hancock, H. Irving. The Young Engineers in Arizona, or Laying Tracks on the Man-Killer Quicksand. 2004. reprint ed. pap. 1.99 *(978-1-4192-8913-2(6))* Kessinger Publishing, LLC.

CIVIL GOVERNMENT

see Political Science; United States—Politics and Government

CIVIL LIBERTY

see Liberty

CIVIL RIGHTS

see also Assembly, Right of; Freedom of Religion; Freedom of Speech; Freedom of the Press; Liberty
also subdivision Civil rights under classes of persons and names of ethnic groups

Altobello, Albert & Wadhams, Doyle. The 10 Most Important Civil Rights Decisions. 2008. 14.99 *(978-1-55448-528-4(2))* Scholastic Library Publishing.
Archer, Jules. Treason in America: Disloyalty Versus Dissent. 2016. (Jules Archer History for Young Readers Ser.). (ENG.). 208p. (J). (gr. 6). 16.99 *(978-1-63450-628-1(6),* Sky Pony Pr.) Skyhorse Publishing Co., Inc.
Atkins, Laura & Yogi, Stan. Fred Korematsu Speaks Up. 2017. (Illus.). 103p. (J). *(978-1-59714-368-4(5))* Heyday.
Bednar, Chuck. Rosa Parks. 2010. (Transcending Race in America Ser.). (Illus.). 64p. (YA). (gr. 5-18). lib. bdg. 22.95 *(978-1-4222-1615-6(2))* Mason Crest.
Bill of Rights Institute, text. Celebrate the Constitution. 2007. 20p. (YA). 4.95 *(978-1-932785-30-2(2))* Bill of Rights Institute, The.
Braun, Eric. Taking Action for Civil & Political Rights. 2016. (Who's Changing the World? Ser.). (ENG., Illus.). 48p. (J). (gr. 4-6). 33.32 *(978-1-4677-9394-0(9));* 50.65 *(978-1-4677-9665-1(4),* Lerner Pubns.) Lerner Publishing Group.
Cahill, Bryon. Freedom of Speech & Expression. 2013. (Four Freedoms Ser.). (ENG., Illus.). 32p. (J). (gr. 3-6). lib. bdg. 19.95 net. *(978-1-937529-91-8(6))* Red Chair Pr.
Civic Participation: Working for Civil Rights. 2016. (Civic Participation: Working for Civil Rights Ser.). 00032p. (J). (gr. 5-5). 157.50 *(978-1-4994-2630-4(5),* PowerKids Pr.) Rosen Publishing Group, Inc., The.
Civil Rights Struggles Around the World, 4 vols., Set. Incl. Equal Rights Is Our Minimum Demand: The Women's Rights Movement in Iran 2005. Childress, Diana. (Illus.). 160p. 38.60 *(978-0-7613-5770-4(X));* Gay Power! The Stonewall Riots & the Gay Rights Movement 1969. Kuhn, Betsy. 144p. 38.60 *(978-0-7613-5768-1(8));* Today the World Is Watching You: The Little Rock Nine & the Fight for School Integration 1957. Magoon, Kekla. (Illus.). 160p. 38.60 *(978-0-7613-5767-4(X));* You Are Now on Indian Land: The American Indian Occupation of Alcatraz Island, California, 1969. Goldstein, Margaret J. 160p. lib. bdg. 38.60 *(978-0-7613-5769-8(6));* (gr. 9-12). 2011. Set lib. bdg. 154.40 *(978-0-7613-7474-9(4),* Twenty-First Century Bks.) Lerner Publishing Group.
Coil, Suzanne M. The Civil Rights Movement. (Liberty & Justice For All Ser.). (Illus.). 64p. (J). (gr. 5-8). lib. bdg. 15.98 *(978-0-8050-2987-1(7),* Twenty-First Century Bks.) Lerner Publishing Group.
Collins, Terry. Liberty, 1 vol. Bascle, Brian, illus. 2009. (Cartoon Nation Ser.). (ENG.). 32p. (gr. 3-4). lib. bdg. 30.65 *(978-1-4296-2340-7(3),* Graphic Library) Capstone Press of Coughlan Cos.
Ditchfield, Christin. Knowing Your Civil Rights. 2004. (True Bks.). (ENG., Illus.). 48p. (J). (gr. 3-5). pap. 6.95 *(978-0-516-27910-7(6),* Children's Pr.) Scholastic Library Publishing.
Duckworth, Katie. Education. 2004. (Children's Rights Ser.). (J). lib. bdg. 27.10 *(978-1-58340-419-5(8))* Black Rabbit Bks.
Engdahl, Sylvia. Welfare. 2010. (Issues on Trial Ser.). (ENG.). 240p. 42.15 *(978-0-7377-5110-9(X),* Greenhaven Pr., Inc.) Cengage Gale.
Esherick, Joan. Guaranteed Rights: The Legislation that Protects Youth with Special Needs. 2004. (Youth with Special Needs Ser.). (Illus.). 128p. (YA). lib. bdg. 24.95 *(978-1-59084-742-8(3))* Mason Crest.
Fredericks, Carrie. Amendment XIV: Due Process. 2009. (Constitutional Amendments Ser.). (ENG., Illus.). 160p. (gr. 10-12). lib. bdg. 43.20 *(978-0-7377-4125-4(2),* LML02109-243014) Cengage Gale.
Freedman, Russell. In Defense of Liberty: The Story of America's Bill of Rights. 2003. (ENG., Illus.). 208p. (J). (gr. 4-6). tchr. ed. 24.95 *(978-0-8234-1585-4(6))* Holiday Hse., Inc.
Fridell, Ron. Cruzan V. Missouri & the Right to Die Debate: Debating Supreme Court Decisions. 2005. (Debating Supreme Court Decisions Ser.). (Illus.). 128p. (J). (gr. 8-18). lib. bdg. 27.94 *(978-0-7660-2356-7(7))* Enslow Pubs., Inc.
Friedman, Lauri S. The Patriot Act. 2008. (Introducing Issues with Opposing Viewpoints Ser.). (ENG., Illus.). 144p. (YA). (gr. 7-10). 36.95 *(978-0-7377-4172-8(4),* Greenhaven Pr., Inc.) Cengage Gale.
Harper, Leslie. What Are Rights & Responsibilities? 2012. (Civics Q & A Ser.). (ENG., Illus.). 24p. (J). (gr. 3-6). 22.60 *(978-1-4488-7437-8(8));* pap. 8.25 *(978-1-4488-7510-8(2))* Rosen Publishing Group, Inc., The. (PowerKids Pr.).
Harrison, Geoffrey C. & Scott, Thomas F. The Fight for Freedom. Stewart, Mark & Kennedy, Mike, eds. 2014. (Great Debates Ser.). (ENG.). 48p. (J). (gr. 5-8). lib. bdg. 29.27 *(978-1-59953-588-3(2))* Norwood Hse. Pr.
Harrison, Jean. Home. 2004. (Children's Rights Ser.). (J). lib. bdg. 27.10 *(978-1-58340-418-8(X))* Black Rabbit Bks.
Haskins, James. Freedom Rides: Journey for Justice. 2005. (Illus.). 88p. (J). (gr. 4-17). per. 10.95 *(978-0-940975-94-1(7),* Sankofa Bks.) Just Us Bks., Inc.
Haugen, David M. Disabilities. Greenhaven Press Editors & Gale Editors, eds. 2014. (Teen Rights & Freedoms Ser.). (ENG., Illus.). 176p. (gr. 10-12). lib. bdg. 42.00 *(978-0-7377-6995-1(5),* Greenhaven Pr., Inc.) Cengage Gale.
Henneberg, Susan, ed. LGBT Rights. 2017. (Current Controversies Ser.). 224p. (YA). (gr. 10-12). pap. 32.00 ***(978-1-5345-0035-8(9))***; lib. bdg. 46.40 ***(978-1-5345-0019-8(7))*** Greenhaven Publishing LLC. (Greenhaven Publishing).
Individual Rights & Civic Responsibility, 8 bks. Incl. Right to Bear Arms. Sommers, Michael A. lib. bdg. 34.60 *(978-0-8239-3232-0(X));* Right to Privacy. Garrett, Brandon. lib. bdg. 34.60 *(978-0-8239-3236-8(2));* Right to Vote. Isler, Claudia. lib. bdg. 34.60 *(978-0-8239-3235-1(4));* Women's Rights. Ching, Jacqueline & Ching, Juliet. lib. bdg. 34.60 *(978-0-8239-3233-7(8));* 64p. (YA). (gr. 7-12). 2001. (Illus.). Set lib. bdg. 212.00 *(978-0-8239-9203-4(9))* Rosen Publishing Group, Inc., The.
Johnson, Terry. Legal Rights, 6 vols. 2005. (American Rights Ser.). (Illus.). 144p. (gr. 5-8). 35.00 *(978-0-8160-5665-1(X))* Facts On File, Inc.
Kawa, Katie. Bill of Rights. 2016. (Documents of American Democracy Ser.). (Illus.). 32p. (J). (gr. 5-5). pap. 10.00 *(978-1-4994-2073-9(0),* PowerKids Pr.) Rosen Publishing Group, Inc., The.
Keller, Susanna. The Bill of Rights. 2016. (Let's Find Out! Primary Sources Ser.). 00032p. (J). (gr. 2-3). lib. bdg. 24.45 *(978-1-5081-0399-8(2))* Rosen Publishing Group, Inc., The.
Leavitt, Amie Jane. The Bill of Rights in Translation: What It Really Means. 2016. (Kids' Translations Ser.). (ENG.). 32p. (gr. 3-4). pap. 8.10 *(978-1-5157-4218-0(0),* Fact Finders) Capstone Press of Coughlan Cos.
The LGBTQ+ Guide to Beating Bullying. 2017. (LGBTQ+ Guide to Beating Bullying Ser.). 64p. (gr. 12-11). pap. 64.75 ***(978-1-4994-6645-4(5),*** Rosen Young Adult) Rosen Publishing Group, Inc., The.
Lüsted, Marcia Amidon. Lyndon B. Johnson & the Civil Rights ACT. 2017. (J). ***(978-1-5383-8048-2(X))*** Rosen Publishing Group, Inc., The.
Manion, Jennifer. Safia AMA Jan. 2011. (J). lib. bdg. *(978-0-8225-9038-5(7))* Twenty First Century Bks.
Mara, Wil. Rights & Values. 2016. (21st Century Skills Library: a Citizen's Guide Ser.). (ENG., Illus.). 32p. (J). (gr. 4-7). 29.93 *(978-1-63471-071-8(1),* 208363) Cherry Lake Publishing.
Marsh, Carole. I'm Reading about Civil Rights. 2016. (I'm Reading About Ser.). (ENG., Illus.). (J). lib. bdg. 24.99 ***(978-0-635-12223-0(5))***; pap. 7.99 ***(978-0-635-12224-7(3))*** Gallopade International.
Mason, Jennifer. The Right to Petition. 2016. (Our Basic Freedoms Ser.). 00048p. (J). pap. 14.05 ***(978-1-4824-6115-2(3))*** Stevens, Gareth Publishing LLLP.
Merino, Noel. Civil Liberties. 2012. (Global Viewpoints Ser.). (ENG., Illus.). 224p. (gr. 10-12). pap. 31.70 *(978-0-7377-6437-6(6),* Greenhaven Pr., Inc.) Cengage Gale.
Merino, No'l, ed. Civil Liberties. 2012. (Global Viewpoints Ser.). (ENG., Illus.). 224p. (J). (gr. 10-12). lib. bdg. 40.45 *(978-0-7377-6261-7(6),* Greenhaven Pr., Inc.) Cengage Gale.
Miller, Debra A. Civil Liberties. 2009. (Hot Topics Ser.). (ENG., Illus.). 128p. (gr. 7-10). 39.40 *(978-1-4205-0080-6(5),* Lucent Bks.) Cengage Gale.
—The Patriot Act. 2007. (Hot Topics Ser.). (ENG., Illus.). 112p. (YA). (gr. 7-12). lib. bdg. 33.95 *(978-1-59018-981-8(7),* LML02109-229790) Cengage Gale.
Murray, Julie. Martin Luther King, Jr. Day, 1 vol. 2005. (Buddy Book Ser.). (ENG., Illus.). 24p. (gr. k-4). 25.65 *(978-1-59197-589-2(1),* Buddy Bks.) ABDO Publishing Co.
Nelson, Kadir. Heart & Soul: The Story of America & African Americans. 2013. (J). lib. bdg. 19.65 *(978-0-606-35050-1(0),* Turtleback) Turtleback Bks.
Our Basic Freedoms. 2016. (Our Basic Freedoms Ser.). 00048p. (J). lib. bdg. 191.70 ***(978-1-4824-6076-6(9))*** Stevens, Gareth Publishing LLLP.
Pauly, Robert J. Speech, Media, & Protest, Vol. 8. Lansford, Tom, ed. 2016. (Foundations of Democracy Ser.). 64p. (J). (gr. 7). 23.95 *(978-1-4222-3633-8(1))* Mason Crest.
Pezzi, Bryan. Craig Kielburger: Ma Vie. Karvonen, Tanjah, tr. from ENG. 2011. (FRE., Illus.). 24p. (YA). (gr. 2-4). *(978-1-77071-428-1(6))* Weigl Educational Pubs. Ltd.
Rees, Peter. Liberty: Blessing or Burden? 2007. (Shockwave: the Human Experience Ser.). (ENG., Illus.). 36p. (J). (gr. 3-5). 25.00 *(978-0-531-17760-0(2),* Children's Pr.) Scholastic Library Publishing.
Rivera, Sheila. Bill of Rights, 1 vol. 2004. (American Moments Ser.). (ENG.). 48p. (gr. 4-8). 27.07 *(978-1-59197-279-2(5),* Abdo & Daughters) ABDO Publishing Co.
Rondeau, Amanda. Freedom. 2003. (United We Stand Ser.). (ENG., Illus.). 24p. (J). (gr. k-3). lib. bdg. 24.21 *(978-1-57765-878-8(7),* SandCastle) ABDO Publishing Co.
Rossi, Anna Maria. The Struggle for Equality. 2007. (Rise & Shine Ser.). (ENG., Illus.). 40p. (J). pap. 19.95 *(978-0-7922-4559-9(8))* CENGAGE Learning.
Shamir, Ruby. What's the Big Deal about Freedom. Faulkner, Matt, illus. 2017. (What's the Big Deal About Ser.). (ENG.). 32p. (J). (gr. -1-3). 17.99 *(978-0-399-54728-7(2),* Philomel Bks.) Penguin Young Readers Group.
Shull, Jodie A. Words of Promise: A Story about James Weldon Johnson. Stetz, Ken, illus. 2005. (Creative Minds Biographies Ser.). (ENG.). 64p. (gr. 4-8). lib. bdg. 22.60 *(978-1-57505-755-2(7),* Carolrhoda Bks.) Lerner Publishing Group.
Sikora, Frank & Batcheler, Michelle. Frank M. Johnson, Jr: Courageous Judge. 2009. (Illus.). 104p. *(978-1-59421-045-7(4))* Seacoast Publishing, Inc.
Spangenburg, Ray & Moser, Kit. Civil Liberties. 2005. (Open for Debate Ser.). (Illus.). 128p. (YA). (gr. 7-12). lib. bdg. 42.79 *(978-0-7614-1886-3(5))* Marshall Cavendish Corp.
Stearman, Kaye. Freedom of Information. 2017. (Ethical Debates Ser.). (ENG., Illus.). 48p. (J). (gr. 6-11). pap. 12.99 ***(978-0-7502-9746-2(8),*** Wayland) Hachette Children's Group GBR. Dist: Hachette Bk. Group.
Stefoff, Rebecca. Security V. Privacy. 2007. (Open for Debate Ser.). (Illus.). 128p. (gr. 7-7). lib. bdg. 42.79 *(978-0-7614-2578-6(0),* Benchmark Bks.) Marshall Cavendish Corp.
Telgen, Diane. Brown V. Board of Education. 2005. (Defining Moments Ser.). (Illus.). 256p. (gr. 7-12). 55.00 *(978-0-7808-0775-4(8))* Omnigraphics, Inc.
Venter, Sahm. Human Rights Day March 21. 2008. (Exploring Our National Days Ser.). (ENG.). 70p. 20.95 *(978-1-77009-321-8(4))* Jacana Media ZAF. Dist: Independent Pubs. Group.
Warner, Jody Nyasha. Viola Desmond Won't Be Budged, 1 vol. Rudnicki, Richard & Junaid, Bushra, illus. 2010. (ENG.). 32p. (J). (gr. k-4). 18.95 *(978-0-88899-779-1(5))* Groundwood Bks. CAN. Dist: Publishers Group West (PGW).
Winters, Robert. Freedom of Assembly & Petition. 2006. (Bill of Rights Ser.). (ENG., Illus.). 135p. (J). (gr. 3-7). lib. bdg. 37.90 *(978-0-7377-3544-4(9),* Greenhaven Pr., Inc.) Cengage Gale.
Wittmann, Kelly. The Right to Bear Arms. 2016. (Our Basic Freedoms Ser.). 00048p. (J). pap. 14.05 ***(978-1-4824-6112-1(9))*** Stevens, Gareth Publishing LLLP.
World Book, Inc Staff, contrib. by. Aboriginal Rights Movement. 2011. (Illus.). 64p. (J). *(978-0-7166-1499-9(5))* World Bk., Inc.

CIVIL RIGHTS—UNITED STATES

Adler, David A. Dr. Martin Luther King, Jr: A Historical Perspective. Bootman, Colin, illus. 2003. (ENG.). 48p. (J). (gr. k-3). pap. 7.99 *(978-0-8234-1803-9(0))* Holiday Hse., Inc.
Alarcon, Roben. The Constitution & the Bill of Rights, 1 vol. 2004. (Primary Source Readers Ser.). (ENG.). 24p. (J). (gr. 5-5). pap. 8.99 *(978-0-7439-8783-7(7))* Shell Educational Publishing.
American Rights Set. 2005. (American Rights Ser.). 160p. (gr. 5-8). 175.00 *(978-0-8160-6488-5(1))* Facts On File, Inc.
Anderson, Dale. The FBI & Civil Rights. 2009. (FBI Story Ser.). 64p. (J). (gr. 4-7). lib. bdg. 22.95 *(978-1-4222-0569-3(X))* Mason Crest.
—The Seneca Falls Women's Rights Convention. 2004. (Landmark Events in American History Ser.). (Illus.). 48p. (J). (gr. 5-12). lib. bdg. 31.00 *(978-0-8368-5389-6(X),* Gareth Stevens Secondary Library) Stevens, Gareth Publishing LLLP.
Baxter, Roberta. The Bill of Rights, 1 vol. 2012. (Documenting U. S. History Ser.). (ENG.). 48p. (gr. 3-6). pap. 9.95 *(978-1-4329-6760-4(6),* NA-h) Heinemann-Raintree.
Brezina, Corona. Fifth Amendment: Double Jeopardy, Self-Incrimination, & Due Process of Law. 2011. (Amendments to the United States Constitution: the Bill of Rights Ser.). (ENG., Illus.). 64p. (J). pap. 12.95 *(978-1-4488-2306-2(4),* Rosen Reference) Rosen Publishing Group, Inc., The.
—The Fifth Amendment: Double Jeopardy, Self-Incrimination, & Due Process of Law. 2011. (Amendments to the United States Constitution: the Bill of Rights Ser.). (Illus.). 64p. (YA). (gr. 5-9). lib. bdg. 31.95 *(978-1-4488-1260-8(7))* Rosen Publishing Group, Inc., The.
Brinkman, Patricia. The Bill of Rights. 2006. (J). pap. *(978-1-4108-6452-9(9))* Benchmark Education Co.
Carson, Mary Kay. What Was Your Dream, Dr. King? And Other Questions About... Martin Luther King, Jr. Madsen, Jim, illus. 2013. (Good Question! Ser.). (ENG.). 32p. (J). (gr. 2). pap. 5.95 *(978-1-4027-9045-4(7))* Sterling Publishing Co., Inc.
Ching, Jacqueline. Women's Rights. 2009. (Individual Rights & Civic Responsibility Ser.). 128p. (gr. 7-12). 63.90 *(978-1-61513-518-9(9))* Rosen Publishing Group, Inc., The.
Crewe, Sabrina & Ingram, Scott. The 1963 Civil Rights March. 2005. (Events That Shaped America Ser.). (Illus.). 32p. (gr. 3-6). lib. bdg. 26.00 *(978-0-8368-3411-6(9),* Gareth Stevens Learning Library) Stevens, Gareth Publishing LLLP.
Dils, Tracey E. 12 Questions about the Bill of Rights. 2017. (Examining Primary Sources Ser.). (ENG., Illus.). 32p. (J). (gr. 3-6). 21.95 *(978-1-63235-282-8(6))* Pr. Room Editions LLC.
Ditchfield, Christin. Knowing Your Civil Rights. 2004. (True Bks.). (ENG., Illus.). 48p. (J). (gr. 3-5). pap. 6.95 *(978-0-516-27910-7(6),* Children's Pr.) Scholastic Library Publishing.
Donnelly, Karen. The Bill of Rights. 2009. (Primary Source Library of American Citizenship Ser.). 32p. (gr. 5-5). 47.90 *(978-1-61511-221-0(9),* Rosen Reference) Rosen Publishing Group, Inc., The.
—Cruzan V. Missouri: The Right to Die. 2009. (Supreme Court Cases Through Primary Sources Ser.). 64p. (gr. 5-8). 58.50 *(978-1-60853-246-9(1))* Rosen Publishing Group, Inc., The.
Espejo, Roman. Civil Liberties. 2009. (Opposing Viewpoints Ser.). (ENG., Illus.). 240p. (YA). (gr. 10-12). pap. 29.45 *(978-0-7377-4355-5(7),* LML02109-245370);No. 9. pap. 42.95 *(978-0-7377-4356-2(5),* LML02109-245369) Cengage Gale. (Greenhaven Pr., Inc.).
Ferris, Jeri Chase. Demanding Justice: A Story about Mary Ann Shadd Cary. Smith, Kimanne, illus. 2003. (Creative Minds Biographies Ser.). (ENG.). 64p. (gr. 4-8). 22.60 *(978-1-57505-177-2(X));* pap. 8.95 *(978-0-87614-928-7(X),* Carolrhoda Bks.) Lerner Publishing Group.
Fradin, Dennis Brindell. The Bill of Rights. 2008. (Turning Points in U. S. History Ser.). 48p. (gr. 3-18). lib. bdg. 31.36 *(978-0-7614-3009-4(1),* Benchmark Bks.) Marshall Cavendish Corp.
Freedman, Jeri. America Debates Civil Liberties & Terrorism. 2009. (America Debates Ser.). 64p. (gr. 5-6). 58.50 *(978-1-61511-331-6(2),* Rosen Reference) Rosen Publishing Group, Inc., The.
—America Debates Privacy Versus Security. 2007. (America Debates Ser.). (Illus.). 64p. (YA). (gr. 5-9). lib. bdg. 31.95 *(978-1-4042-1929-8(3))* Rosen Publishing Group, Inc., The.
Freedom of Speech DBA. 2003. spiral bd. 16.95 *(978-1-56004-150-4(1))* Social Studies Schl. Service.
Freedom of the Press DBA. 2003. spiral bd. 16.95 *(978-1-56004-149-8(8))* Social Studies Schl. Service.
Furgang, Kathy. Ninth Amendment: Rights Retained by the People. 2011. (Amendments to the United States Constitution: the Bill of Rights Ser.). (ENG., Illus.). 64p. (J). pap. 12.95 *(978-1-4488-2310-9(2),* Rosen Reference) Rosen Publishing Group, Inc., The.
—The Ninth Amendment: Rights Retained by the People. 2011. (Amendments to the United States Constitution: the Bill of Rights Ser.). (Illus.). 64p. (YA). (gr. 5-9). lib. bdg. 31.95 *(978-1-4488-1264-6(X))* Rosen Publishing Group, Inc., The.
Gillam, Scott. Civil Liberties, 1 vol. 2007. (Essential Viewpoints Set 1 Ser.). (ENG., Illus.). 112p. (J). (gr. 6-12). lib. bdg. 35.64 *(978-1-59928-858-1(3))* ABDO Publishing Co.
Gold, Susan Dudley. Freedom of Information ACT. 2011. (Landmark Legislation 2 Ser.). 128p. (gr. 7). 39.93 *(978-1-60870-485-9(8))* Marshall Cavendish GBR. Dist: Marshall Cavendish Corp.
Goldstein, Margaret J. You Are Now on Indian Land: The American Indian Occupation of Alcatraz Island, California, 1969. 2011. (Civil Rights Struggles around the World Ser.). (ENG.). 160p. (gr. 9-12). lib. bdg. 38.60 *(978-0-7613-5769-8(6))* Lerner Publishing Group.
Gorman, Jacqueline Laks. Cuáles Son Tus Derechos Básicos? 2008. (Conoce tu gobierno (Know Your Government) Ser.). (SPA., Illus.). 24p. (gr. 1-4). lib. bdg. 22.00 *(978-0-8368-8850-8(2),* Weekly Reader Leveled Readers) Stevens, Gareth Publishing LLLP.
—What Are Your Basic Rights? 2008. (Know Your Government Ser.). 24p. (gr. 1-4). pap. 8.15 *(978-0-8368-8845-4(6));* (Illus.). lib. bdg. 22.00 *(978-0-8368-8840-9(5))* Stevens, Gareth Publishing LLLP. (Weekly Reader Leveled Readers).
Gorman, Jacqueline Laks, et al. Cuáles Son Tus Derechos Básicos? 2008. (Conoce tu gobierno (Know Your Government) Ser.). (SPA.). 24p. (gr. 1-4). pap. 8.15 *(978-0-8368-8855-3(3),* Weekly Reader Leveled Readers) Stevens, Gareth Publishing LLLP.
Hanson, Anders. Land of the Free: The Kids' Book of Freedom, 1 vol. 2014. (What We Stand For Ser.). (ENG.). 24p. (gr. 5-10). lib. bdg. 25.65 *(978-1-62403-295-0(8),* Super SandCastle) ABDO Publishing Co.
Hayes, Amy. Disability Rights Movement. 2016. (Civic Participation: Working for Civil Rights Ser.). 00032p. (J). (gr. 5-5). pap. 10.00 *(978-1-4994-2679-3(8),* PowerKids Pr.) Rosen Publishing Group, Inc., The.
Hernandez, Daniel. They Call Me a Hero: A Memoir of My Youth. 2013. (ENG., Illus.). 240p. (YA). (gr. 7). 17.99 *(978-1-4424-6228-1(0),* Simon & Schuster Bks. For Young Readers) Simon & Schuster Bks. For Young Readers.
Hunter, Miranda. Story of Latino Civil Rights: Fighting for Justice. 2007. (Hispanic Heritage Ser.). (Illus.). 112p. (YA). lib. bdg. 22.95 *(978-1-59084-934-7(5))* Mason Crest.
Isaacs, Sally & Bedeksy, Baron. Understanding the Bill of Rights. 2008. (Documenting Early America Ser.). (ENG.). 32p. (J). (gr. 3-6). pap. *(978-0-7787-4379-8(9))* Crabtree Publishing Co.
Jones, Molly. First Amendment: Freedom of Speech, the Press, & Religion. 2011. (Amendments to the United States Constitution: the Bill of Rights Ser.). (ENG., Illus.). 64p. (YA). pap. 12.95 *(978-1-4488-2302-4(1),* Rosen Reference) Rosen Publishing Group, Inc., The.
—The First Amendment: Freedom of Speech, the Press, & Religion. 2011. (Amendments to the United States Constitution: the Bill of Rights Ser.). (Illus.). 64p. (YA). (gr. 5-9). lib. bdg. 31.95 *(978-1-4488-1252-3(6))* Rosen Publishing Group, Inc., The.
Jones, Phillip & Marzilli, Alan. Freedom of Information. 2nd rev. ed. 2012. (Point/Counterpoint Ser.). (Illus.). 128p. (C). (gr. 9). 35.00 *(978-1-60413-906-8(4),* Chelsea Hse.) Facts On File, Inc.
King, Martin Luther, Jr. I Have a Dream, 1 vol. Nelson, Kadir, illus. 2012. (ENG.). 40p. (J). (gr. k-12). 18.99 *(978-0-375-85887-1(3),* Schwartz & Wade Bks.) Random Hse. Children's Bks.
Kootz, Russell & Seidman, David. Understanding Civil Rights. 2011. (Personal Freedom & Civic Duty Ser.). (Illus.). 184p. (J). lib. bdg. 35.95 *(978-1-4488-4666-5(8))* Rosen Publishing Group, Inc., The.
Kowalski, Kathiann M. A Pro/con Look at Homeland Security: Safety vs. Liberty After 9/11. 2008. (Issues in Focus Today Ser.). (Illus.). 112p. (J). (gr. 3-7). lib. bdg. 33.27 *(978-0-7660-2914-9(X))* Enslow Pubs., Inc.
Landau, Elaine. The Civil Rights Movement in America. 2003. (Cornerstones of Freedom Ser.). (ENG., Illus.). 48p. (YA). (gr. 4-7). 26.00 *(978-0-516-24219-4(9))* Scholastic Library Publishing.
Leavitt, Amie Jane. The Bill of Rights. 2011. (My Guide to the Constitution Ser.). (Illus.). 48p. (J). (gr. 3-6). lib. bdg. 29.95 *(978-1-58415-947-6(2))* Mitchell Lane Pubs., Inc.
—The Bill of Rights in Translation: What It Really Means. 2017. (Kids' Translations Ser.). (ENG.). 32p. (gr. 3-4). lib. bdg. 27.32 ***(978-1-5157-9138-6(6),*** Fact Finders) Capstone Press of Coughlan Cos.
Leavitt, Amie Jane. The Bill of Rights in Translation [Scholastic]: What It Really Means. 2010. (Kids' Translations Ser.). 32p. pap. 0.50 *(978-1-4296-5951-2(3),* Fact Finders) Capstone Press of Coughlan Cos.
Lüsted, Marcia Amidon. Lyndon B. Johnson & the Civil Rights ACT. 2017. (J). pap. ***(978-1-5081-7746-3(5))*** Rosen Publishing Group, Inc., The.
Lusted, Marcia Amidon & Thain, Gerald J. Tinker v. Des Moines: The Right to Protest in Schools, 1 vol. 2012. (Landmark Supreme Court Cases Ser.). (ENG., Illus.). 160p. (J). (gr. 6-12). 37.07 *(978-1-61783-477-6(7))* ABDO Publishing Co.
MacBain-Stephens, Jennifer. Women's Suffrage: Giving the Right to Vote to All Americans. 2009. (Progressive Movement 1900-1920: Efforts to Reform America's New Industrial Society Ser.). 32p. (gr. 3-4). 47.90 *(978-1-60854-175-1(4))* Rosen Publishing Group, Inc., The.

Magoon, Kekla. Media Censorship, 1 vol. 2009. (Essential Viewpoints Set 4 Ser.). (ENG., Illus.). 112p. (J). (gr. 6-12). lib. bdg. 35.64 *(978-1-60453-533-4(4))* ABDO Publishing Co.

Mara, Wil. Thurgood Marshall: Champion for Civil Rights. 2004. (Great Life Stories Ser.). (ENG., Illus.). 125p. (J). 30.50 *(978-0-531-12058-3(9),* Watts, Franklin) Scholastic Library Publishing.

Marcovitz, Harold. Privacy Rights & the Patriot Act, 1 vol. 2008. (Essential Viewpoints Set 2 Ser.). (ENG., Illus.). 112p. (J). (gr. 6-12). lib. bdg. 35.64 *(978-1-60453-059-9(6))* ABDO Publishing Co.

McCormick, Anita Louise. Rosa Parks & the Montgomery Bus Boycott. 2017. (J). ***(978-1-5383-8061-1(7))***; pap. ***(978-1-5383-8062-8(5))*** Rosen Publishing Group, Inc., The.

Merino, Noel. Civil Liberties. 2013. (Opposing Viewpoints Ser.). (ENG., Illus.). 224p. (gr. 10-12). pap. 33.80 *(978-0-7377-6305-8(1),* Greenhaven Pr., Inc.) Cengage Gale.

Merino, Noël. Civil Liberties. 2013. (Opposing Viewpoints Ser.). (ENG., Illus.). 224p. (gr. 10-12). lib. bdg. 48.80 *(978-0-7377-6304-1(3),* Greenhaven Pr., Inc.) Cengage Gale.

Meyer, Susan. Affirmative Action. 2017. (J). pap. ***(978-1-5383-8011-6(0))*** Rosen Publishing Group, Inc., The.

Mirman, Heather Moehn. Issues in Drug Abuse. 2003. (Contemporary Issues Ser.). (ENG., Illus.). 112p. (YA). (gr. 7-10). 30.85 *(978-1-59018-035-8(6),* Lucent Bks.) Cengage Gale.

Mitchell, Don. The Freedom Summer Murders. 2014. (ENG.). 256p. (J). (gr. 9). 18.99 *(978-0-545-47725-3(5),* Scholastic Pr.) Scholastic, Inc.

Monk, Linda R. The Words We Live By: Your Annotated Guide to the Constitution. annot. rev. ed. 2004. (ENG., Illus.). 304p. (gr. -1-17). pap. 18.99 *(978-0-7868-8620-3(X))* Hyperion Pr.

Personal Freedom & Civic Duty: Set 2. 2013. (Personal Freedom & Civic Duty Ser.). 112p. (YA). (gr. 7-12). 207.60 *(978-1-4488-9472-7(7))* Rosen Publishing Group, Inc., The.

Personal Freedom & Civic Duty: Sets 1 - 2. 2013. (Personal Freedom & Civic Duty Ser.). 112p. (YA). (gr. 7-12). 484.40 *(978-1-4777-0614-5(3))* Rosen Publishing Group, Inc., The.

Schwartz, Heather E. The Civil Rights Act of 1964: A Primary Source Exploration of the Landmark Legislation. 2014. (We Shall Overcome Ser.). (ENG.). 32p. (gr. 3-4). lib. bdg. 27.32 *(978-1-4914-0224-5(5))* Capstone Press of Coughlan Cos.

Smith, Rich. The Bill of Rights: Defining Our Freedoms, 1 vol. 2007. (Bill of Rights Ser.). (ENG.). 32p. (gr. 4-8). 27.07 *(978-1-59928-913-7(X),* Abdo & Daughters) ABDO Publishing Co.

Stanton, Terence M. The Bill of Rights: What It Means to You. 2009. (Real Life Readers Ser.). 32p. (gr. 4-5). pap. 10.00 *(978-1-4358-0169-1(5),* Rosen Classroom); 32p. (gr. 4-4). 47.90 *(978-1-61511-370-5(3),* PowerKids Pr.); (J). lib. bdg. 25.25 *(978-1-4358-2992-3(1),* PowerKids Pr.) Rosen Publishing Group, Inc., The.

Stearman, Kaye. Freedom of Information. 2011. (Ethical Debates Ser.). (ENG., Illus.). 48p. (YA). (gr. 5-8). pap. 11.75 *(978-1-4488-7008-0(9))*; lib. bdg. 29.25 *(978-1-4488-6019-7(9))* Rosen Publishing Group, Inc., The. (Rosen Reference).

Taylor-Butler, Christine. The Bill of Rights. 2007. (True Book(tm), a — American History Ser.). (ENG., Illus.). 48p. (J). (gr. 3-5). lib. bdg. 31.00 *(978-0-531-12627-1(7),* Children's Pr.) Scholastic Library Publishing.

—The Bill of Rights: American History. 2008. (True Bks.). (ENG., Illus.). 48p. (J). (gr. 3-5). pap. 6.95 *(978-0-531-14777-1(0),* Children's Pr.) Scholastic Library Publishing.

Thomas, William David. ¿Cuáles Son Los Derechos Básicos de Los Ciudadanos? 2008. (Mi gobierno de Estados Unidos (My American Government) Ser.). (SPA.). 32p. (gr. 3-7). pap. 10.50 *(978-0-8368-8876-8(6),* Gareth Stevens Learning Library) Stevens, Gareth Publishing LLLP.

—¿Cuáles son los derechos básicos de los ciudadanos? 2008. (Mi gobierno de Estados Unidos (My American Government) Ser.). (SPA., Illus.). 32p. (gr. 3-7). lib. bdg. 26.00 *(978-0-8368-8871-3(5),* Gareth Stevens Learning Library) Stevens, Gareth Publishing LLLP.

—What Are Citizens' Basic Rights? 2008. (My American Government Ser.). 32p. (gr. 3-7). pap. 10.50 *(978-0-8368-8866-9(9),* Gareth Stevens Learning Library) Stevens, Gareth Publishing LLLP.

—What Are Citizens' Basic Rights? 2008. (My American Government Ser.). (Illus.). 32p. (gr. 3-7). lib. bdg. 26.00 *(978-0-8368-8861-4(8),* Gareth Stevens Learning Library) Stevens, Gareth Publishing LLLP.

Vaughn, Wally G. & Davis, Mattie Campbell, eds. The Selma Campaign, 1963-1965: The Decisive Battle of the Civil Rights Movement. 2006. (ENG., Illus.). 244p. pap. 19.95 *(978-0-912469-44-7(7))* Majority Pr., The.

Watson, Stephanie. Gay Rights Movement, 1 vol. 2013. (Essential Library of Social Change Ser.). (ENG.). 112p. (J). (gr. 6-12). lib. bdg. 35.64 *(978-1-61783-887-3(X),* Essential Library) ABDO Publishing Co.

Wolfe, James & Stair, Nancy L. Understanding the Bill of Rights. 2015. (Primary Sources of American Political Documents Ser.). (ENG., Illus.). 112p. (J). (gr. 7-7). 37.27 *(978-0-7660-6882-7(X))* Enslow Pubs., Inc.

Wright, Susan. The Civil Rights Act Of 1964: Landmark Anti-Discrimination Legislation. 2009. (Library of American Laws & Legal Principles Ser.). 48p. (gr. 5-8). 53.00 *(978-1-60853-463-0(4),* Rosen Reference) Rosen Publishing Group, Inc., The.

—The Civil Rights Act Of 1964: Landmark Antidiscrimination Legislation. 2005. (Library of American Laws & Legal Principles Ser.). (Illus.). 48p. (YA). (gr. 7-12). lib. bdg. 29.25 *(978-1-4042-0455-3(5))* Rosen Publishing Group, Inc., The.

Yero, Judith Lloyd & National Geographic Learning Staff. The Bill of Rights. 2007. (Reading Expeditions Ser.). (ENG., Illus.). 32p. (J). pap. 17.95 *(978-0-7922-4552-0(0))* CENGAGE Learning.

CIVIL RIGHTS DEMONSTRATIONS

see also African Americans—Civil Rights

Aretha, David. Sit-Ins & Freedom Rides. 2009. (Civil Rights Movement Ser.). 128p. (J). (gr. 4-7). 28.95 *(978-1-59935-098-1(X))* Reynolds, Morgan Inc.

—The Story of the Civil Rights March on Washington for Jobs & Freedom in Photographs. 2014. (Story of the Civil Rights Movement in Photographs Ser.). 48p. (J). lib. bdg. 25.27 *(978-0-7660-4238-4(3))* Enslow Pubs., Inc.

Bausum, Ann & National Geographic Kids Staff. The March Against Fear: The Last Great Walk of the Civil Rights Movement & the Emergence of Black Power. 2017. (ENG., Illus.). 144p. (J). (gr. 7-9). 18.99 *(978-1-4263-2665-3(3),* National Geographic Children's Bks.) National Geographic Society.

Crewe, Sabrina & Ingram, Scott. The 1963 Civil Rights March. 2005. (Events That Shaped America Ser.). (Illus.). 32p. (gr. 3-6). lib. bdg. 26.00 *(978-0-8368-3411-6(9),* Gareth Stevens Learning Library) Stevens, Gareth Publishing LLLP.

Krull, Kathleen. What Was the March on Washington? Tomkinson, Tim, illus. 2013. (What Was? Ser.). (ENG.). 112p. (J). (gr. 3-7). pap. 5.99 *(978-0-448-46287-5(7),* Grosset & Dunlap) Penguin Young Readers Group.

—What Was the March on Washington? 2013. (What Was... ? Ser.). lib. bdg. 16.00 *(978-0-606-29974-9(2),* Turtleback) Turtleback Bks.

Kurtz, Jane. Martin's Dream. Bates, Amy June, illus. 2008. (Ready-To-Reads Ser.). (ENG.). 32p. (J). (gr. -1-1). pap. 3.99 *(978-1-4169-2774-7(3),* Simon Spotlight) Simon Spotlight.

Maloof, Torrey. You Are There! March on Washington, August 28, 1963. 2nd ed. 2017. (TIME for KIDS(r) Nonfiction Readers Ser.). 32p. (gr. 8-8). 8.99 ***(978-1-4938-3929-2(2))*** Teacher Created Materials, Inc.

—You Are There! March on Washington, August 28 1963. 2017. (Time for Kids Nonfiction Readers Ser.). lib. bdg. 19.65 ***(978-0-606-40288-0(8))*** Turtleback Bks.

Miller, Jake. Sit-Ins & Freedom Rides: The Power of Nonviolent Resistance. 2004. (Library of the Civil Rights Movement Ser.). (Illus.). 24p. (J). lib. bdg. 22.60 *(978-0-8239-6253-2(9),* PowerKids Pr.) Rosen Publishing Group, Inc., The.

—The 1963 March on Washington: Speeches & Songs for Civil Rights. (Library of the Civil Rights Movement Ser.). 24p. 2009. (gr. 3-3). 42.50 *(978-1-60853-893-5(1))* 2004. (Illus.). (J). lib. bdg. 22.60 *(978-0-8239-6255-6(5))* Rosen Publishing Group, Inc., The. (PowerKids Pr.).

Schwartz, Heather E. The March on Washington: A Primary Source Exploration of the Pivotal Protest, 1 vol. 2014. (We Shall Overcome Ser.). (ENG.). 32p. (gr. 3-4). lib. bdg. 27.32 *(978-1-4914-0223-8(7))* Capstone Press of Coughlan Cos.

Swain, Gwenyth. Riding to Washington. Geister, David, illus. 2007. (Tales of Young Americans Ser.). (ENG.). 32p. (YA). (gr. 6-12). 17.95 *(978-1-58536-324-7(3))* Sleeping Bear Pr.

Tisdale, Rachel. The March on Washington, 1 vol., 1. 2014. (We Shall Overcome Ser.). (ENG.). 32p. (J). (gr. 3-6). 26.25 *(978-1-4777-6069-7(5),* PowerKids Pr.) Rosen Publishing Group, Inc., The.

Weston Woods Staff, creator. March on! the Day My Brother Martin Changed the World. 2011. 18.95 *(978-0-545-31398-8(8))*; 38.75 *(978-0-545-31399-5(6))* Weston Woods Studios, Inc.

CIVIL RIGHTS MOVEMENTS

Adamson, Heather. The Civil Rights Movement: An Interactive History Adventure. 2016. (You Choose: History Ser.). (ENG.). 112p. (gr. 3-4). pap. 6.95 *(978-1-5157-4263-0(6),* You Choose Bks.) Capstone Press of Coughlan Cos.

—The Civil Rights Movement [Scholastic]: An Interactive History Adventure. (You Choose: History Ser.). 112p. 2010. pap. 0.86 *(978-1-4296-5179-0(2))* 2009. (gr. 3-4). pap. 0.86 *(978-1-4296-4047-3(2))* Capstone Press of Coughlan Cos. (You Choose Bks.).

Adler, David A. Heroes for Civil Rights. Farnsworth, Bill, illus. 2007. (ENG.). 32p. (J). (gr. -1-3). 17.95 *(978-0-8234-2008-7(6))* Holiday Hse., Inc.

Archer, Jules. They Had a Dream: The Struggles of Four of the Most Influential Leaders of the Civil Rights Movement, from Frederick Douglass to Marcus Garvey to Martin Luther King Jr. & Malcolm X. 2016. (Jules Archer History for Young Readers Ser.). (ENG., Illus.). 272p. (J). (gr. 6). 16.99 *(978-1-63450-194-1(2),* Sky Pony Pr.) Skyhorse Publishing Co., Inc.

Aretha, David. Black Power. 2011. (Civil Rights Movement Ser.). (Illus.). 128p. (gr. 7-12). 28.95 *(978-1-59935-164-3(1))* Reynolds, Morgan Inc.

—Freedom Summer. 2007. (Civil Rights Movement Ser.). (Illus.). 128p. (J). (gr. 3-7). lib. bdg. 27.95 *(978-1-59935-059-2(9))* Reynolds, Morgan Inc.

—The Murder of Emmett Till. 2007. (Civil Rights Movement Ser.). (Illus.). 160p. (J). (gr. 3-7). lib. bdg. 27.95 *(978-1-59935-057-8(2))* Reynolds, Morgan Inc.

—Selma & the Voting Rights Act. 2007. (Civil Rights Movement Ser.). (Illus.). 128p. (J). (gr. 3-7). lib. bdg. 27.95 *(978-1-59935-056-1(4))* Reynolds, Morgan Inc.

—Sit-Ins & Freedom Rides. 2009. (Civil Rights Movement Ser.). 128p. (J). (gr. 4-7). 28.95 *(978-1-59935-098-1(X))* Reynolds, Morgan Inc.

Asselin, Kristine Carlson. Martin Luther King Jr: Civil Rights Leader, 1 vol. 2013. (Essential Lives Set 8 Ser.). (ENG.). 112p. (J). (gr. 6-12). lib. bdg. 35.64 *(978-1-61783-891-0(8),* Essential Library) ABDO Publishing Co.

Banting, Erinn. The Civil Rights Movement. 2008. (African American History Ser.). (Illus.). 48p. (YA). (gr. 5-8). lib. bdg. 29.05 *(978-1-59036-882-4(7))*; pap. 10.95 *(978-1-59036-883-1(5))* Weigl Pubs., Inc.

—Civil Rights Movement. 2013. (J). *(978-1-62127-190-1(0))*; pap. *(978-1-62127-196-3(X))* Weigl Pubs., Inc.

Bausum, Ann. Freedom Riders: John Lewis & Jim Zwerg on the Front Lines of the Civil Rights Movement. 2005. (ENG., Illus.). 80p. (gr. 5-18). 18.95 *(978-0-7922-4173-7(8))*; lib. bdg. 28.90 *(978-0-7922-4174-4(6))* National Geographic Society. (National Geographic Children's Bks.).

Belinda, Rochelle. Witnesses to Freedom: Young People Who Fought for Civil Rights. 2014. (ENG.). 116p. (J). 12.24 *(978-1-63245-230-6(8))* Lectorum Pubns., Inc.

Benson, Kathleen & Haskins, Jim. John Lewis in the Lead: A Story of the Civil Rights Movement, 1 vol. Andrews, Benny, illus. 2006. (ENG.). 40p. (gr. 2-7). 17.95 *(978-1-58430-250-6(X))* Lee & Low Bks., Inc.

bjornlund, lydia. The Civil Rights Movement. 2012. (Illus.). 96p. (J). lib. bdg. *(978-1-60152-478-2(1))* ReferencePoint Pr., Inc.

Bjornlund, Lydia. Rosa Parks & the Montgomery Bus Boycott. 2007. (Lucent Library of Black History Ser.). (ENG., Illus.). 128p. (gr. 8-12). lib. bdg. 39.40 *(978-1-4205-0010-3(4),* Lucent Bks.) Cengage Gale.

Boehme, Gerry. John Lewis & Desegregation. 2016. (Primary Sources of the Civil Rights Movement Ser.). (Illus.). 64p. (J). (gr. 6-6). 34.21 *(978-1-5026-1868-9(0))* Cavendish Square Publishing.

Boerst, William J. Marching in Birmingham. 2007. (Civil Rights Movement Ser.). (Illus.). 112p. (J). (gr. 3-7). lib. bdg. 27.95 *(978-1-59935-055-4(6))* Reynolds, Morgan Inc.

Brimner, Larry Dane. Black & White: The Confrontation Between Reverend Fred L. Shuttlesworth & Eugene Bull Connor. 2011. (ENG., Illus.). 112p. (J). (gr. 6). 17.95 *(978-1-59078-766-3(8),* Calkins Creek) Boyds Mills Pr.

Bringle, Jennifer. The Civil Rights Act Of 1964. 2014. (Celebration of the Civil Rights Movement Ser.). (Illus.). 80p. (J). (gr. 7-12). 34.25 *(978-1-4777-7739-8(3))* Rosen Publishing Group, Inc., The.

Byers, Ann. African-American History from Emancipation to Today: Rising above the Ashes of Slavery. 2004. (Slavery in American History Ser.). (Illus.). 128p. (J). lib. bdg. 27.94 *(978-0-7660-2153-2(X))* Enslow Pubs., Inc.

Capek, Michael. Civil Rights Movement, 1 vol. 2013. (Essential Library of Social Change Ser.). (ENG.). 112p. (J). (gr. 6-12). lib. bdg. 35.64 *(978-1-61783-885-9(3),* Essential Library) ABDO Publishing Co.

A Celebration of the Civil Rights Movement. 2014. (Celebration of the Civil Rights Movement Ser.). 80p. (YA). (gr. 7-12). 205.50 *(978-1-4777-7751-0(2))* Rosen Publishing Group, Inc., The.

Civil Rights Leaders, bks. 13, vol. 13. Incl. A. Philip Randolph & the African American Labor Movement. Miller, Calvin Craig. (Illus.). 160p. (YA). (gr. 6-12). 2005. 26.95 *(978-1-931798-50-1(8))*; Eternal Vigilance: The Story of Ida B. Wells-Barnett. Hinman, Bonnie. 128p. (gr. 6-10). 2011. lib. bdg. 28.95 *(978-1-59935-111-7(0))*; Freedom Cannot Rest: Ella Baker & the Civil Rights Movement. Bohannon, Lisa Frederiksen. (Illus.). 176p. (YA). (gr. 6-12). 2005. lib. bdg. 26.95 *(978-1-931798-71-6(0))*; Liberator: The Story of William Lloyd Garrison. Esty, Amos. 144p. 2011. 28.95 *(978-1-59935-137-7(4))*; No Compromise: The Story of Harvey Milk. Aretha, David. 100p. (YA). (gr. 5-9). 2009. lib. bdg. 28.95 *(978-1-59935-129-2(3))*; No Easy Answers: Bayard Rustin & the Civil Rights Movement. (Illus.). 160p. (J). (gr. 6-12). 2005. 26.95 *(978-1-931798-43-3(5))*; Roy Wilkins: Leader of the NAACP. Miller, Calvin Craig. (Illus.). 176p. (YA). (gr. 6-12). 2005. 26.95 *(978-1-931798-49-5(4))*; Stranger in My Own House: The Story of W. E. B. du Bois. Hinman, Bonnie. (Illus.). 176p. (gr. 6-12). 2005. 28.95 *(978-1-931798-45-7(1))*; Unbound & Unbroken: The Story of Frederick Douglass. Esty, Amos. 144p. (gr. 8-10). 2011. 28.95 *(978-1-59935-136-0(6))*; 2008. Set lib. bdg. 376.35 *(978-1-931798-99-0(0))* Reynolds, Morgan Inc.

The Civil Rights Movement Set, vols. 13, vol. 13. Incl. Black Power. Aretha, David. (Illus.). 128p. (gr. 7-12). 2011. 28.95 *(978-1-59935-164-3(1))*; Freedom Summer. Aretha, David. (Illus.). 128p. (J). (gr. 3-7). 2007. lib. bdg. 27.95 *(978-1-59935-059-2(9))*; Marching in Birmingham. Boerst, William J. (Illus.). 112p. (J). (gr. 3-7). 2007. lib. bdg. 27.95 *(978-1-59935-055-4(6))*; Murder of Emmett Till. Aretha, David. (Illus.). 160p. (J). (gr. 3-7). 2007. lib. bdg. 27.95 *(978-1-59935-057-8(2))*; Selma & the Voting Rights Act. Aretha, David. (Illus.). 128p. (J). (gr. 3-7). 2007. lib. bdg. 27.95 *(978-1-59935-056-1(4))*; Sit-Ins & Freedom Rides. Aretha, David. 128p. (J). (gr. 4-7). 2009. 28.95 *(978-1-59935-098-1(X))*; Trial of the Scottsboro Boys. Aretha, David. (Illus.). 128p. (J). (gr. 4-7). 2007. lib. bdg. 27.95 *(978-1-59935-058-5(0))*; 2007. Set lib. bdg. 376.35 *(978-1-59935-073-8(4))* Reynolds, Morgan Inc.

Conklin, Wendy. Civil Rights Movement, 1 vol. 2007. (Primary Source Readers Ser.). (ENG.). 32p. (J). (gr. 5-5). pap. 8.99 *(978-0-7439-0670-8(5))* Shell Educational Publishing.

Crayton, Lisa A. Freedom Riders. 2017. (J). ***(978-1-5383-8027-7(7))***; pap. ***(978-1-5383-8026-0(9))*** Rosen Publishing Group, Inc., The.

Crompton, Sam. Georgia & the Modern Civil Rights Movement. 2017. (Spotlight on Georgia Ser.). 32p. (gr. 9-10). pap. 11.75 ***(978-1-5081-5976-6(9)***, PowerKids Pr.) Rosen Publishing Group, Inc., The.

Cruz, Barbara C. The Fight for Latino Civil Rights. 2015. (Our Shared History Ser.). (ENG., Illus.). 128p. (J). (gr. 7-7). lib. bdg. 37.27 *(978-0-7660-7006-6(9))* Enslow Pubs., Inc.

Cruz, Bàrbara C. Triumphs & Struggles for Latino Civil Rights. 2008. (From Many Cultures, One History Ser.). (Illus.). 128p. (J). (gr. 5-18). lib. bdg. 33.27 *(978-0-7660-2804-3(6))* Enslow Pubs., Inc.

Deal, Heidi. Perspectives on the Civil Rights Movement. 2018. (ENG.). 32p. (gr. 3-6). ***(978-1-63235-398-6(9)***, 12-Story Library) Pr. Room Editions LLC.

Ditchfield, Christin. Knowing Your Civil Rights. 2004. (True Bks.). (ENG., Illus.). 48p. (J). (gr. 3-5). pap. 6.95 *(978-0-516-27910-7(6),* Children's Pr.) Scholastic Library Publishing.

Ellis, Carol. African American Activists. 2012. (J). pap. *(978-1-4222-2384-0(1))* Mason Crest.

—African American Activists. Hill, Marc Lamont, ed. 2012. (Major Black Contributions from Emancipation to Civil Rights Ser.). 64p. (J). (gr. 5). 22.95 *(978-1-4222-2371-0(X))* Mason Crest.

Fandel, Jennifer. Martin Luther King, Jr. 2005. (Genius Ser.). (Illus.). 48p. (J). (gr. 5-9). lib. bdg. 21.95 *(978-1-58341-329-6(4),* Creative Education) Creative Co., The.

—Martin Luther King, Jr: Great Civil Rights Leader, 1 vol. Bascle, Brian, illus. 2006. (Graphic Biographies Ser.). (ENG.). 32p. (gr. 3-4). 30.65 *(978-0-7368-6498-5(9),* Graphic Library) Capstone Press of Coughlan Cos.

Feinstein, Stephen. Inspiring African-American Civil Rights Leaders. 2012. (African-American Collective Biographies Ser.). (Illus.). 112p. (J). (gr. 5-18). 33.27 *(978-1-59845-136-8(7))* Enslow Pubs., Inc.

—Read about Martin Luther King, Jr. 2004. (I Like Biographies! Ser.). (Illus.). 24p. (J). lib. bdg. 24.95 *(978-0-7660-2300-0(1))* Enslow Pubs., Inc.

Finlayson, Reggie. We Shall Overcome: The History of the American Civil Rights Movement. 2005. (People's History Ser.). (Illus.). 96p. (gr. 6-12). lib. bdg. 26.60 *(978-0-8225-0647-8(5))* Lerner Publishing Group.

Fradin, Dennis Brindell. The Montgomery Bus Boycott. 2009. (Turning Points in U. S. History Ser.). 48p. (gr. 3-18). 31.36 *(978-0-7614-4258-5(8))* Marshall Cavendish Corp.

Freedman, Russell. Because They Marched: The People's Campaign for Voting Rights That Changed America. 2014. (ENG., Illus.). 96p. (J). (gr. 5-12). 20.00 *(978-0-8234-2921-9(0))* Holiday Hse., Inc.

—Freedom Walkers: The Story of the Montgomery Bus Boycott. 2009. (ENG., Illus.). 112p. (J). (gr. 3-7). pap. 14.95 *(978-0-8234-2195-4(3))* Holiday Hse., Inc.

Frey, Wendy. Citizen Heroes. 2007. (Illus.). 68p. (J). *(978-1-4105-0887-4(0))*; *(978-1-4105-0888-1(9))* Johnston, Don Inc.

Ganeri, Anita. I Have a Dream: Martin Luther King, Jr. & the Fight for Equal Rights. 2013. (Turning Points in History Ser.). (Illus.). 48p. (gr. 5-12). 37.10 *(978-1-59920-972-2(1))* Black Rabbit Bks.

Gelfand, Dale Evva. Coretta Scott King: Civil Rights Activist. 2nd rev. ed. 2006. (Black Americans of Achievement Legacy Edition Ser.). (Illus.). 137p. (YA). (gr. 7-12). lib. bdg. 35.00 *(978-0-7910-9522-5(3))* Facts On File, Inc.

George, Enzo. The Civil Rights Movement. 2015. (Primary Sources in U. S. History Ser.). (ENG., Illus.). 48p. (J). (gr. 4-4). 31.36 *(978-1-5026-0496-5(5))* Cavendish Square Publishing.

Gitlin, Martin. The Montgomery Bus Boycott: A History Perspectives Book. 2013. (Perspectives Library). (ENG., Illus.). 32p. (J). (gr. 4-8). 28.50 *(978-1-62431-418-6(X),* 202792); pap. 14.21 *(978-1-62431-494-0(5),* 202794) Cherry Lake Publishing.

Green, Richard L., et al, eds. A Salute to Black Civil Rights Leaders. Dobson, S. Gaston, illus. (Empak "Black History" Publication). (J). pap. 1.00 *(978-0-9616156-3-5(X))* Empak Publishing Co.

Haldy, Emma E. Martin Luther King, Jr. Bane, Jeff, illus. 2016. (My Early Library: My Itty-Bitty Bio Ser.). (ENG.). 24p. (J). (gr. k-1). 28.50 *(978-1-63470-477-9(0),* 207639) Cherry Lake Publishing.

Hally, Ashleigh. Coretta Scott King. 2012. (Illus.). 24p. (J). *(978-1-935884-78-1(6))*; pap. *(978-1-935884-84-2(0))* State Standards Publishing, LLC.

Hardy, P. Stephen & Hardy, Sheila. Extraordinary People of the Civil Rights Movement. 2006. (Extraordinary People Ser.). (ENG., Illus.). 288p. (J). (gr. 6-18). lib. bdg. 40.00 *(978-0-516-25461-6(8),* Children's Pr.) Scholastic Library Publishing.

Hasday, Judy L. Women in the Civil Rights Movement. 2012. (J). pap. *(978-1-4222-2366-6(3))* Institute of Physics Publishing.

—Women in the Civil Rights Movement. 2012. 64p. (J). (gr. 5). 22.95 *(978-1-4222-2356-7(6))* Mason Crest.

Haskins, James. Freedom Rides: Journey for Justice. 2005. (Illus.). 88p. (J). (gr. 4-17). per. 10.95 *(978-0-940975-94-1(7),* Sankofa Bks.) Just Us Bks., Inc.

Haskins, Jim. Delivering Justice: W. W. Law & the Fight for Civil Rights. Andrews, Benny, illus. 2008. (ENG.). 32p. (J). (gr. k-3). pap. 7.99 *(978-0-7636-3880-1(3))* Candlewick Pr.

Haskins, Jim, et al. John Lewis in the Lead: A Story of the Civil Rights Movement, 1 vol. 2006. (ENG., Illus.). 40p. (J). pap. 11.95 *(978-1-60060-849-0(3))* Lee & Low Bks., Inc.

Hazen, Walter. Reform Movement. 2005. (Illus.). 112p. pap. 12.95 *(978-1-59647-085-9(2))* Good Year Bks.

Hermann, Spring. The Struggle for Equality: Women & Minorities in America. 2006. (American Saga Ser.). (Illus.). 128p. (J). (gr. 5-9). lib. bdg. 33.27 *(978-0-7660-2573-8(X))* Enslow Pubs., Inc.

Herr, Melody. Sitting for Equal Service: Lunch Counter Sit-Ins, United States, 1960s. 2010. (Civil Rights Struggles around the World Ser.). (ENG.). 160p. (gr. 9-12). lib. bdg. 38.60 *(978-0-8225-8970-9(2))* Lerner Publishing Group.

Higgins, Nadia. The Split History of the Civil Rights Movement: A Perspectives Flip Book, 1 vol. 2014. (Perspectives Flip Bks.). (ENG.). 64p. (gr. 5-6). lib. bdg. 33.99 *(978-0-7565-4736-3(9),* CPB Grades 4-8) Compass Point Bks.

Hinton, Kerry. The Black Power Movement & Civil Unrest. 2017. (J). pap. ***(978-1-5383-8016-1(1))*** Rosen Publishing Group, Inc., The.

—Sit-Ins & Nonviolent Protest. 2017. (J). pap. ***(978-1-5383-8064-2(1)***, Rosen Young Adult) Rosen Publishing Group, Inc., The.

Honders, Christine. Mexican American Rights Movement. 2016. (Civic Participation: Working for Civil Rights Ser.). 00032p. (J). (gr. 5-5). pap. 10.00 *(978-1-4994-2684-7(4),* PowerKids Pr.) Rosen Publishing Group, Inc., The.

Hooks, Gwendolyn. If You Were a Kid During the Civil Rights Movement. 2017. (If You Were a Kid Ser.). (ENG., Illus.). 32p. (J). lib. bdg. 26.00 *(978-0-531-22384-0(1),* Children's Pr.) Scholastic Library Publishing.

Houtman, Jacqueline, et al. Bayard Rustin: The Invisible Activist. 2014. (J). pap. *(978-1-937768-58-4(9))* QuakerPress.

Howard, Melanie A. Civil Rights Marches, 1 vol. 2004. (American Moments Ser.). (ENG.). 48p. (gr. 4-8). 27.07 *(978-1-59197-282-2(5),* Abdo & Daughters) ABDO Publishing Co.

Hunter-Gault, Charlayne. To the Mountaintop: My Journey Through the Civil Rights Movement. 2014. (New York Times Ser.). (ENG., Illus.). 224p. (YA). (gr. 7). pap. 12.99 *(978-1-250-04062-6(0),* 9781250040626) Square Fish.

Jeffrey, Gary. Malcolm X & the Fight for African American Unity. 2012. (Graphic History of the Civil Rights Movement Ser.). (Illus.). 24p. (J). (gr. 3-8). pap. 8.15 *(978-1-4339-7488-5(6))*; lib. bdg. 23.95 *(978-1-4339-7487-8(8))* Stevens, Gareth Publishing LLLP.

—Martin Luther King Jr. & the March on Washington. 2012. (Graphic History of the Civil Rights Movement Ser.). (Illus.). 24p. (J). (gr. 3-8). pap. 8.15 *(978-1-4339-7492-2(4))*; lib. bdg. 23.95 *(978-1-4339-7491-5(6))* Stevens, Gareth Publishing LLLP.

—Rosa Parks & the Montgomery Bus Boycott. 2012. (Graphic History of the Civil Rights Movement Ser.). (Illus.). 24p. (J). (gr. 3-8). pap. 8.15 *(978-1-4339-7500-4(9))*; lib. bdg. 23.95 *(978-1-4339-7499-1(1))* Stevens, Gareth Publishing LLLP.

Jones, Joyce Adams. Remembering the Marches in Selma, Alabama. 2006. 8.00 *(978-0-8059-7237-5(4))* Dorrance Publishing Co., Inc.

Kallen, Stuart A. Women of the Civil Rights Movement. 2005. (Women in History Ser.). (ENG., Illus.). 112p. (YA). (gr. 7-10). lib. bdg. 32.45 *(978-1-59018-569-8(2),* Lucent Bks.) Cengage Gale.

Kanefield, Teri. The Girl from the Tar Paper School: Barbara Rose Johns & the Advent of the Civil Rights Movement. 2014. (ENG., Illus.). 56p. (J). (gr. 3-7). 19.95 *(978-1-4197-0796-4(5),* Abrams Bks. for Young Readers) Abrams, Inc.

Kimmel, Allison Crotzer. The Montgomery Bus Boycott. 2015. (We Shall Overcome Ser.). (ENG.). 32p. (gr. 3-4). lib. bdg. 27.32 *(978-1-4914-2043-0(X))* Capstone Press of Coughlan Cos.

King, Martin Luther, Jr. I Have a Dream. 2007. (Illus.). 40p. (J). (gr. -1-3). 14.65 *(978-0-7569-8119-8(0))* Perfection Learning Corp.

—I Have a Dream, 1 vol. Nelson, Kadir, illus. 2012. (ENG.). 40p. (J). (gr. k-12). 18.99 *(978-0-375-85887-1(3),* Schwartz & Wade Bks.) Random Hse. Children's Bks.

Kittinger, Jo S. Rosa's Bus: The Ride to Civil Rights. Walker, Steven, illus. (ENG.). 40p. (J). 2017. (gr. 1-4). pap. 7.95 *(978-1-62979-848-6(7),* Calkins Creek) 2010. (gr. 2-4). 17.95 *(978-1-59078-722-9(6))* Boyds Mills Pr.

Koestler-Grack, Rachel A. School in the Civil Rights Movement. 2016. (It's Back to School ... Way Back! Ser.). (ENG., Illus.). 32p. (gr. 3-4). lib. bdg. 27.32 *(978-1-5157-2099-7(3),* Fact Finders) Capstone Press of Coughlan Cos.

Koosman, Melissa. The Fall of Apartheid in South Africa. 2009. (Monumental Milestones Ser.). 48p. (YA). (gr. 4-7). lib. bdg. 29.95 *(978-1-58415-736-6(4))* Mitchell Lane Pubs., Inc.

Krull, Kathleen & Freeman, Laura. Coretta Scott King: I Kept on Marching. 2015. (Women Who Broke the Rules Ser.). (ENG., Illus.). 48p. (J). (gr. 1-4). pap. 6.99 *(978-0-8027-3827-1(3),* 9780802738271, Bloomsbury USA Childrens) Bloomsbury Publishing USA.

Krumm, Brian. The Little Rock Nine: A Primary Source Exploration of the Battle for School Integration, 1 vol. 2014. (We Shall Overcome Ser.). (ENG.). 32p. (gr. 3-4). lib. bdg. 27.32 *(978-1-4914-0225-2(3))* Capstone Press of Coughlan Cos.

Kuhn, Betsy. The Force Born of Truth: Mohandas Gandhi & the Salt March, India, 1930. 2010. (Civil Rights Struggles around the World Ser.). (ENG., Illus.). 160p. (gr. 9-12). lib. bdg. 38.60 *(978-0-8225-8968-6(0))* Lerner Publishing Group.

Landau, Elaine. The Civil Rights Movement in America. 2003. (Cornerstones of Freedom Ser.). (ENG., Illus.). 48p. (YA). (gr. 4-7). 26.00 *(978-0-516-24219-4(9))* Scholastic Library Publishing.

Levinson, Cynthia. We've Got a Job: The 1963 Birmingham Children's March, 1 vol. 2015. (ENG.). 180p. (gr. 5-9). pap. 13.95 *(978-1-56145-844-8(9))* Peachtree Pubs.

—The Youngest Marcher: The Story of a Young Civil Rights Activist. Brantley-Newton, Vanessa, illus. 2017. (ENG.). 40p. (J). (gr. k-5). 17.99 *(978-1-4814-0070-1(3))* Simon & Schuster, Inc.

Levinson, Cynthia Y. We've Got a Job: The 1963 Birmingham Children's March, 1 vol. 2012. (ENG.). 192p. (J). 19.95 *(978-1-56145-627-7(6))* Peachtree Pubs.

Levy, Debbie. We Shall Overcome: The Story of a Song. Brantley-Newton, Vanessa, illus. 2013. (ENG.). 32p. (J). (gr. 1-3). 16.99 *(978-1-4231-1954-8(1))* Hyperion Bks. for Children.

Linney, Susan. Martin Luther King, Jr: With a Discussion of Responsibility. 2004. (Values in Action Ser.). (J). *(978-1-59203-069-9(6))* Learning Challenge, Inc.

Loughran, P. J., illus. Turning 15 on the Road to Freedom: My Story of the Selma Voting Rights March. 2015. (ENG.). 128p. (YA). (gr. 7). 19.99 *(978-0-8037-4123-2(5),* Dial Bks) Penguin Young Readers Group.

Mahoney, Emily Jankowski. American Civil Rights Movement. 2016. (Civic Participation: Working for Civil Rights Ser.). 00032p. (J). (gr. 5-5). pap. 10.00 *(978-1-4994-2791-2(3),* PowerKids Pr.) Rosen Publishing Group, Inc., The.

Main, Mary & Thomason, Cathy. African-Americans in Law & Politics. 2012. (J). pap. *(978-1-4222-2391-8(4))* Mason Crest.

—African-Americans in Law & Politics. Hill, Marc Lamont, ed. 2012. (Major Black Contributions from Emancipation to Civil Rights Ser.). 64p. (J). (gr. 5). 22.95 *(978-1-4222-2378-9(7))* Mason Crest.

Malaspina, Ann. Nelson Mandela: Fighting to Dismantle Apartheid. 2017. (Rebels with a Cause Ser.). 128p. (YA). (gr. 8-8). lib. bdg. 37.27 ***(978-0-7660-8517-6(1))*** Enslow Pubs., Inc.

Maloof, Torrey. Martin Luther King Jr: Destined to Lead. 2016. (Primary Source Readers Ser.). (Illus.). 32p. (gr. 2-2). 8.99 *(978-1-4938-2559-2(3))* Teacher Created Materials, Inc.

Marsico, Katie. The Montgomery Bus Boycott: Milestone of the Civil Rights Movement. 2011. (Perspectives on 3 Ser.). (Illus.). 112p. (J). (gr. 7). 39.93 *(978-1-60870-447-7(5))* Marshall Cavendish Corp.

Martin, Oscar, Jr., creator. Civil Rights Leaders. l.t. ed. 2004. (Illus.). 25p. (J). E-Book 19.95 incl. cd-rom *(978-0-9748416-9-4(2))* Build Your Story.

Mattern, Joanne. Coretta Scott King: Civil Rights Activist. (Women Who Shaped History Ser.). 24p. 2009. (gr. 2-3). 42.50 *(978-1-60854-816-3(3))* 2003. (Illus.). (J). lib. bdg. 19.95 *(978-0-8239-6504-5(X))* Rosen Publishing Group, Inc., The. (PowerKids Pr.).

Mayer, Robert H. When the Children Marched: The Birmingham Civil Rights Movement. 2008. (Prime (Middle/Senior) Ser.). (Illus.). 176p. (J). (gr. 3-7). lib. bdg. 35.94 *(978-0-7660-2930-9(1))* Enslow Pubs., Inc.

McNeese, Tim. The Civil Rights Movement: Striving for Justice. 2007. (Reform Movements in American History Ser.). (Illus.). 156p. (YA). (gr. 7-12). lib. bdg. 32.50 *(978-0-7910-9504-1(5))* Facts On File, Inc.

McPherson, Stephanie Sammartino. Biography Coretta Scott King. 2007. (Biography Ser.). (Illus.). 112p. (YA). (gr. 7-12). lib. bdg. 29.27 *(978-0-8225-7156-8(0))* Twenty First Century Bks.

McWhorter, Diane. A Dream of Freedom: The Civil Rights Movement from 1954 to 1968. 2004. (ENG., Illus.). 160p. (J). (gr. 3-7). pap. 22.99 *(978-0-439-57678-9(4),* Scholastic Nonfiction) Scholastic, Inc.

Michelson, Richard. As Good As Anybody. Colón, Raúl, illus. 2013. (ENG.). 40p. (J). (gr. 1-4). 7.99 *(978-0-385-75387-6(X),* Dragonfly Bks.) Random Hse. Children's Bks.

Miller, Calvin Craig. A. Philip Randolph & the African American Labor Movement. 2005. (Civil Rights Leaders Ser.). (Illus.). 160p. (YA). (gr. 6-12). 26.95 *(978-1-931798-50-1(8))* Reynolds, Morgan Inc.

Miller, Jake. The March from Selma to Montgomery: African Americans Demand the Vote. (Library of the Civil Rights Movement Ser.). 24p. 2009. (gr. 3-3). 42.50 *(978-1-60853-894-2(X))* 2004. (Illus.). (J). lib. bdg. 22.60 *(978-0-8239-6254-9(7))* Rosen Publishing Group, Inc., The. (PowerKids Pr.).

—Sit-Ins & Freedom Rides: The Power of Nonviolent Resistance. (Library of the Civil Rights Movement Ser.). 24p. 2009. (gr. 3-3). 42.50 *(978-1-60853-892-8(3))* 2004. (Illus.). (J). lib. bdg. 22.60 *(978-0-8239-6253-2(9))* Rosen Publishing Group, Inc., The. (PowerKids Pr.).

Mis, Melody S. Meet Coretta Scott King. (Civil Rights Leaders Ser.). 24p. (gr. 2-3). 2009. 42.50 *(978-1-61511-851-9(9),* PowerKids Pr.) 2008. (Illus.). (YA). lib. bdg. 22.60 *(978-1-4042-4211-1(2))* Rosen Publishing Group, Inc., The.

—Meet Martin Luther King Jr. 2009. (Civil Rights Leaders Ser.). 24p. (gr. 2-3). 42.50 *(978-1-61511-854-0(3),* PowerKids Pr.) Rosen Publishing Group, Inc., The.

—Meet Martin Luther King Jr. 2008. (Civil Rights Leaders Ser.). (Illus.). 24p. (YA). (gr. 2-5). lib. bdg. 22.60 *(978-1-4042-4209-8(0))* Rosen Publishing Group, Inc., The.

Mortensen, Lori. Voices of the Civil Rights Movement. 2015. (We Shall Overcome Ser.). (ENG.). 32p. (gr. 3-4). lib. bdg. 27.32 *(978-1-4914-2044-7(8))* Capstone Press of Coughlan Cos.

Mortensen, Lori & Kimmel, Allison Crotzer. We Shall Overcome. 2015. (We Shall Overcome Ser.). (ENG.). 32p. (gr. 3-4). pap. 15.90 *(978-1-4914-2475-9(3),* Fact Finders) Capstone Press of Coughlan Cos.

Nagelhout, Ryan. Martin Luther King Jr. 2015. (Heroes of Black History Ser.). (ENG.). 32p. (J). (gr. 3-4). 26.60 *(978-1-4824-2906-0(3))* Stevens, Gareth Publishing LLLP.

Nathan, Amy. Round & Round Together: Taking a Merry-Go-Round Ride into the Civil Rights Movement. 2011. (Nautilus Ser.). (ENG., Illus.). 200p. (gr. 4-10). pap. 14.95 *(978-1-58988-071-9(4))* Dry, Paul Bks., Inc.

Nelson, Kadir. Heart & Soul: The Story of America & African Americans. Nelson, Kadir, illus. 2013. (ENG., Illus.). 112p. (J). (gr. 1-5). pap. 8.99 *(978-0-06-173079-5(3))* HarperCollins Pubs.

Nelson, Maria. Coretta Scott King. 2011. (Civil Rights Crusaders Ser.). 24p. (gr. 2-5). (J). pap. 8.15 *(978-1-4339-5680-5(2),* Gareth Stevens Learning Library); (YA). lib. bdg. 22.60 *(978-1-4339-5678-2(0))* Stevens, Gareth Publishing LLLP.

No Easy Answers: Bayard Rustin & the Civil Rights Movement. 2005. (Civil Rights Leaders Ser.). (Illus.). 160p. (J). (gr. 6-12). 26.95 *(978-1-931798-43-3(5))* Reynolds, Morgan Inc.

Ollhoff, Jim. The Civil Rights Movement, 1 vol. 2011. (African American History Ser.). (ENG., Illus.). 32p. (YA). (gr. 5-9). 27.07 *(978-1-61714-709-8(5))* ABDO Publishing Co.

—Courage & Growth, 1 vol. 2011. (African American History Ser.). (ENG., Illus.). 32p. (YA). (gr. 5-9). lib. bdg. 27.07 *(978-1-61714-711-1(7))* ABDO Publishing Co.

Osborne, Linda Barrett. Miles to Go for Freedom: Segregation & Civil Rights in the Jim Crow Years. 2012. (ENG., Illus.). 128p. (J). (gr. 3-7). 25.99 *(978-1-4197-0020-0(0),* Abrams Bks. for Young Readers) Abrams, Inc.

Partridge, Elizabeth. Marching for Freedom: Walk Together, Children, & Don't You Grow Weary. 2009. (ENG.). 80p. (J). (gr. 5-18). 19.99 *(978-0-670-01189-6(4),* Viking Books for Young Readers) Penguin Young Readers Group.

Perry, M. LaVora. A History of the Civil Rights Movement. 2012. (J). pap. *(978-1-4222-2395-6(7))* Mason Crest.

—A History of the Civil Rights Movement. Hill, Marc Lamont, ed. 2012. (Major Black Contributions from Emancipation to Civil Rights Ser.). 64p. (J). (gr. 5). 22.95 *(978-1-4222-2382-6(5))* Mason Crest.

Petruccio, Steven James. History of the Civil Rights Movement Coloring Book. 2011. (Dover History Coloring Book Ser.). (ENG., Illus.). 32p. (gr. 3-5). pap. 3.99 *(978-0-486-47846-3(7))* Dover Pubns., Inc.

Pinkney, Andrea Davis. Sit-In: How Four Friends Stood up by Sitting Down. 2010. (ENG., Illus.). 40p. (J). (gr. 1-17). 18.99 *(978-0-316-07016-4(5))* Little, Brown Bks. for Young Readers.

Primary Sources of the Abolitionist Movement. 2015. (Primary Sources of the Abolitionist Movement Ser.). (ENG.). 64p. (J). (gr. 6-6). 273.68 *(978-1-5026-0368-5(3))* Cavendish Square Publishing.

Primary Sources of the Civil Rights Movement. 2016. (Primary Sources of the Civil Rights Movement Ser.). 64p. (gr. 6-6). lib. bdg. 239.47 *(978-1-5026-1826-9(5))* Cavendish Square Publishing.

Randolph, Joanne. African American Politicians & Civil Rights Activists. 2017. (J). ***(978-0-7660-9252-5(6))*** Enslow Pubs., Inc.

Rappaport, Doreen. Nobody Gonna Turn Me 'Round: Stories & Songs of the Civil Rights Movement. Evans, Shane W., illus. 2006. (ENG.). 64p. (J). (gr. 4-7). 19.99 *(978-0-7636-1927-5(2))* Candlewick Pr.

—Nobody Gonna Turn Me 'Round: Stories & Songs of the Civil Rights Movement. Evans, Shane W., illus. 2008. (ENG.). 64p. (J). (gr. 4-7). pap. 9.99 *(978-0-7636-3892-4(7))* Candlewick Pr.

Regis, Frankye. A Voice from the Civil Rights Era, 1 vol. 2004. (Voices of Twentieth-Century Conflict Ser.). (Illus.). 184p. (C). 43.00 *(978-0-313-32998-2(2),* GR2998, Greenwood) ABC-CLIO, LLC.

Rice, Dona Herwick & Isecke, Harriet. Civil Rights: Freedom Riders, 1 vol. 2009. (Building Fluency Through Reader's Theater Ser.). (ENG., Illus.). 32p. (J). (gr. 3-5). pap. 7.99 *(978-1-4333-0554-2(2))* Teacher Created Materials, Inc.

Rissman, Rebecca. The Black Power Movement, 1 vol. 2014. (African-American History Ser.). (ENG.). 48p. (gr. 8-12). 32.79 *(978-1-62403-144-1(7))* ABDO Publishing Co.

Robert Sheldon Stradford. Dj's First Parade. 2009. 44p. pap. 19.99 *(978-1-4389-5864-4(1))* AuthorHouse.

Roome, Hugh. Martin Luther King Jr. 2017. (Rookie Biographies Ser.). (ENG.). 32p. (J). pap. 5.95 ***(978-0-531-23861-5(X),*** Children's Pr.) Scholastic Library Publishing.

Rubin, Susan Goldman. Freedom Summer: The 1964 Struggle for Civil Rights in Mississippi. (ENG.). 144p. (J). 2016. 14.95 *(978-0-8234-3557-9(1))* 2014. (Illus.). (gr. 5). 18.95 *(978-0-8234-2920-2(2))* Holiday Hse., Inc.

Ruffin, Frances E. Martin Luther King & the March on Washington. 2014. (Penguin Young Readers, L3 Ser.). (ENG.). 48p. (J). (gr. 1-2). 8.24 *(978-1-63245-254-2(5))* Lectorum Pubns., Inc.

Sapet, Kerrily. John Lewis. 2009. (Political Profiles Ser.). 100p. (YA). (gr. 5-9). 28.95 *(978-1-59935-130-8(7))* Reynolds, Morgan Inc.

Schuetz, Rachael Law. The Long Road to Change: An American Story of Civil Rights & Barack Obama's Journey to the White House. 2009. 36p. (J). 16.00 *(978-0-615-27983-1(X))* NRS Enterprises.

Schuldt, Lori Meek. Martin Luther King, Jr: With Profiles of Mohandas K. Gandhi & Nelson Mandela. 2006. (Biographical Connections Ser.). (Illus.). 112p. (J). *(978-0-7166-1822-5(2))* World Bk., Inc.

Schuman, Michael A. & Schraff, Anne E. Martin Luther King Jr: Fighting for Civil Rights. 2017. (Rebels with a Cause Ser.). 128p. (gr. 8-8). lib. bdg. 37.27 ***(978-0-7660-8511-4(2))*** Enslow Pubs., Inc.

Schwartz, Heather E. Freedom Riders: A Primary Source Exploration of the Struggle for Racial Justice. 2014. (We Shall Overcome Ser.). (ENG.). 32p. (gr. 3-4). lib. bdg. 27.32 *(978-1-4914-0222-1(9))* Capstone Press of Coughlan Cos.

Schwartz, Heather E. Locked up for Freedom: Civil Rights Protesters at the Leesburg Stockade. 2017. (ENG., Illus.). 64p. (J). (gr. 5-8). lib. bdg. 33.32 ***(978-1-4677-8597-6(0),*** Millbrook Pr.) Lerner Publishing Group.

Schwartz, Heather E., et al. We Shall Overcome, 1 vol. 2014. (We Shall Overcome Ser.). (ENG.). 32p. (gr. 3-4). 109.28 *(978-1-4914-0226-9(1),* Fact Finders) Capstone Press of Coughlan Cos.

Sepahban, Lois. 12 Incredible Facts about the Montgomery Bus Boycott. 2015. (Turning Points in US History Ser.). (ENG., Illus.). 32p. (J). (gr. 3-5). *(978-1-63235-132-6(3),* 12-Story Library) Pr. Room Editions LLC.

Shange, Ntozake. Coretta Scott. Nelson, Kadir, illus. (ENG.). 32p. (J). (gr. -1-4). 2011. pap. 6.99 *(978-0-06-125366-9(9))* 2009. 17.99 *(978-0-06-125364-5(2))* HarperCollins Pubs. (Tegen, Katherine Bks).

Sharp, Anne Wallace. Women Civil Rights Leaders. 2012. (Lucent Library of Black History Ser.). (ENG., Illus.). 128p. (J). (gr. 7-10). 39.40 *(978-1-4205-0880-2(6),* Lucent Bks.) Cengage Gale.

Shelton, Paula Young. Child of the Civil Rights Movement. Colón, Raúl, illus. 2013. (ENG.). 48p. (J). (gr. -1-3). 7.99 *(978-0-385-37606-8(5),* Dragonfly Bks.) Random Hse. Children's Bks.

Spence, Kelly. Martin Luther King Jr. & Peaceful Protest. 2016. (Primary Sources of the Civil Rights Movement Ser.). (Illus.). 64p. (J). (gr. 6-6). 34.21 *(978-1-5026-1864-1(8))* Cavendish Square Publishing.

Spilsbury, Richard. Who Marched for Civil Rights?, 1 vol. HL Studios Staff, illus. 2014. (Primary Source Detectives Ser.). (ENG.). 64p. (gr. 7-8). lib. bdg. 35.99 *(978-1-4329-9604-8(5))* Heinemann-Raintree.

Staley, Erin. Martin Luther King Jr. & the Speech That Inspired the World. 2014. (Celebration of the Civil Rights Movement Ser.). 80p. (YA). (gr. 7-12). 34.25 *(978-1-4777-7745-9(8))* Rosen Publishing Group, Inc., The.

Stanley, George E. Coretta Scott King: First Lady of Civil Rights. Madsen, Jim & Henderson, Meryl, illus. 2008. (Childhood of Famous Americans Ser.). (ENG.). 224p. (J). (gr. 3-7). pap. 7.99 *(978-1-4169-6800-9(8),* Simon & Schuster/Paula Wiseman Bks.) Simon & Schuster/Paula Wiseman Bks.

Stanmyre, Jackie F. Coretta Scott King & the Center for Nonviolent Social Change. 2016. (Primary Sources of the Civil Rights Movement Ser.). (Illus.). 64p. (J). (gr. 6-6). 34.21 *(978-1-5026-1876-4(1))* Cavendish Square Publishing.

Staton, Hilarie N. Civil Rights. 2015. (ENG.). 48p. (J). *(978-0-7787-1549-8(3))* Crabtree Publishing Co.

Supples, Kevin, et al. The Civil Rights Movement. 2006. (Nonfiction Reading & Writing Workshops Ser.). (ENG., Illus.). 40p. (J). pap. 19.95 *(978-0-7922-8628-8(6))* CENGAGE Learning.

Tisdale, Rachel. The Freedom Riders, 1 vol., 1. 2014. (We Shall Overcome Ser.). (ENG.). 32p. (J). (gr. 3-6). 26.25 *(978-1-4777-6061-1(X),* PowerKids Pr.) Rosen Publishing Group, Inc., The.

—The Montgomery Bus Boycott, 1 vol., 1. 2014. (We Shall Overcome Ser.). (ENG., Illus.). 32p. (J). (gr. 3-6). 26.25 *(978-1-4777-6053-6(9),* PowerKids Pr.) Rosen Publishing Group, Inc., The.

—The Woolworth's Sit-In, 1 vol., 1. 2014. (We Shall Overcome Ser.). (ENG.). 32p. (J). (gr. 3-6). 26.25 *(978-1-4777-6065-9(2),* PowerKids Pr.) Rosen Publishing Group, Inc., The.

Tonatiuh, Duncan. Separate Is Never Equal: Sylvia Mendez & Her Family's Fight for Desegregation. 2014. (ENG., Illus.). 40p. (J). (gr. 1-4). 18.95 *(978-1-4197-1054-4(0),* Abrams Bks. for Young Readers) Abrams, Inc.

Toth, Henrietta. The Murder of Emmett Till. 2017. pap. ***(978-1-5383-8054-3(4))*** Rosen Publishing Group, Inc., The.

Tougas, Shelley. Birmingham 1963: How a Photograph Rallied Civil Rights Support, 1 vol. 2011. (Captured History Ser.). (ENG.). 64p. (gr. 5-7). pap. 9.10 *(978-0-7565-4446-1(7));* lib. bdg. 34.65 *(978-0-7565-4398-3(3))* Compass Point Bks. (CPB Grades 4-8).

Turck, Mary C. Freedom Song: Young Voices & the Struggle for Civil Rights. 2008. (ENG., Illus.). 160p. (J). (gr. 4). pap. 18.95 *(978-1-55652-773-9(X))* Chicago Review Pr., Inc.

Uschan, Michael V. The Civil Rights Movement. 2010. (American History Ser.). (ENG.). 128p. 34.80 *(978-1-4205-0261-9(1),* Lucent Bks.) Cengage Gale.

—James Foreman & SNCC. Greenhaven Press Staff, ed. 2013. (Lucent Library of Black History Ser.). (ENG., Illus.). 128p. (J). (gr. 7-10). lib. bdg. 39.40 *(978-1-4205-0920-5(9),* Lucent Bks.) Cengage Gale.

—Reconstruction. 2007. (Lucent Library of Black History Ser.). (ENG., Illus.). 128p. (gr. 3-7). lib. bdg. 39.40 *(978-1-4205-0009-7(0),* Lucent Bks.) Cengage Gale.

Vietze, Andrew. The Life & Death of Martin Luther King Jr. 2017. (J). ***(978-1-5383-8038-3(2));*** pap. ***(978-1-5383-8039-0(0))*** Rosen Publishing Group, Inc., The.

Waxman, Laura Hamilton. Coretta Scott King. 2008. pap. 52.95 *(978-0-8225-9387-4(4));* (ENG., Illus.). 48p. (gr. 3-6). lib. bdg. 27.93 *(978-0-8225-7168-1(4),* Lerner Pubns.) Lerner Publishing Group.

Weakland, Mark. When Martin Luther King Jr. Wore Roller Skates. Ballesteros, Patrick, illus. 2016. (Leaders Doing Headstands Ser.). (ENG.). 32p. (gr. 2-3). pap. 7.95 *(978-1-5158-0137-5(3))* Picture Window Bks.

Weatherford, Carole Boston. The Beatitudes: From Slavery to Civil Rights. Ladwig, Tim, illus. 2009. (ENG.). 36p. (J). (gr. 3-7). 17.00 *(978-0-8028-5352-3(8),* Eerdmans Bks For Young Readers) Eerdmans, William B. Publishing Co.

—Voice of Freedom: Fannie Lou Hamer, Spirit of the Civil Rights Movement. Holmes, Ekua, illus. 2015. (ENG.). 56p. (J). (gr. 4-7). 17.99 *(978-0-7636-6531-9(2))* Candlewick Pr.

Weil, Ann. Medgar Evers, 1 vol. 2012. (American Biographies Ser.). (ENG.). 48p. (gr. 4-6). pap. 9.95 *(978-1-4329-6465-8(8),* NA-h) Heinemann-Raintree.

—Medgar Evers, 1 vol. Oxford Bible Staff, illus. 2012. (American Biographies Ser.). (ENG.). 48p. (gr. 4-6). lib. bdg. 32.65 *(978-1-4329-6454-2(2),* NA-h) Heinemann-Raintree.

Welch, Catherine A. Children of the Civil Rights Era. 2005. (Picture the American Past Ser.). (Illus.). 48p. (J). (gr. 2-5). lib. bdg. 22.60 *(978-1-57505-481-0(7))* Lerner Publishing Group.

Winter, Max. Civil Rights Movement, 1 vol. 2014. (African-American History Ser.). (ENG.). 48p. (gr. 8-12). lib. bdg. 32.79 *(978-1-62403-145-8(5))* ABDO Publishing Co.

Woog, Adam. The Fight Renewed: The Civil Rights Movement. 2005. (Lucent Library of Black History). (ENG., Illus.). 112p. (YA). (gr. 7-10). lib. bdg. 33.45 *(978-1-59018-701-2(6),* Lucent Bks.) Cengage Gale.

World Book, Inc Staff, contrib. by. Aboriginal Rights Movement. 2011. (Illus.). 64p. (J). *(978-0-7166-1499-9(5))* World Bk., Inc.

—African American Civil Rights Movement. 2010. (J). *(978-0-7166-1500-2(2))* World Bk., Inc.

Zeiger, Jennifer. The Civil Rights Movement. 2011. (Cornerstones of Freedom, Third Ser.). (Illus.). 64p. (J). (ENG.). pap. 8.95 *(978-0-531-26554-3(4));* (ABK., lib. bdg. 30.00 *(978-0-531-25029-7(6))* Scholastic Library Publishing. (Children's Pr.).

CIVIL RIGHTS MOVEMENTS—FICTION

Armistead, John. The Return of Gabriel. Gregory, Fran, illus. 2004. 218p. (gr. 3-8). 17.45 *(978-0-7569-3460-6(5))* Perfection Learning Corp.

Birtha, Becky. Grandmama's Pride. Bootman, Colin, illus. 2005. (ENG.). 32p. (J). (gr. 2-3). 16.99 *(978-0-8075-3028-3(X))* Whitman, Albert & Co.

Brandeis, Gayle. My Life with the Lincolns. 2010. (ENG.). 256p. (J). (gr. 5-9). 34.99 *(978-0-8050-9013-0(4),* 9780805090130, Holt, Henry & Co. Bks. For Young Readers) Holt, Henry & Co.

Burg, Shana. A Thousand Never Evers. 2009. (ENG.). 320p. (J). (gr. 3-7). 7.99 *(978-0-440-42209-9(4),* Yearling) Random Hse. Children's Bks.

Dowell, Frances O'Roark. Ten Miles Past Normal. (ENG., 224p. (YA). (gr. 7). 2012. Illus.). pap. 9.99 *(978-1-4169-9586-9(2))* 2011. 16.99 *(978-1-4169-9585-2(4))* Simon & Schuster Children's Publishing. (Atheneum Bks. for Young Readers).

Johnson, Angela. A Sweet Smell of Roses. Velasquez, Eric, illus. (ENG.). 32p. (J). 2007. (gr. k-3). 7.99 *(978-1-4169-5361-6(2))* 2005. (gr. -1-3). 17.99 *(978-0-689-83252-9(4))* Simon & Schuster Bks. For Young Readers. (Simon & Schuster Bks. For Young Readers).

Magoon, Kekla. Fire in the Streets. 2013. (ENG., Illus.). 352p. (J). (gr. 5-9). pap. 7.99 *(978-1-4424-2231-5(9),* Aladdin) Simon & Schuster Children's Publishing.

—The Rock & the River. (ENG.). 304p. (J). (gr. 5-9). 2010. pap. 7.99 *(978-1-4169-7803-9(8))* 2009. 17.99 *(978-1-4169-7582-3(9))* Simon & Schuster Children's Publishing. (Aladdin).

Magoon, Kekla & Keene, Carolyn. Strangers on a Train. 2013. (Nancy Drew Diaries: 2). (ENG.). 208p. (J). (gr. 3-7). pap. 6.99 *(978-1-4169-9073-4(9),* Aladdin) Simon & Schuster Children's Publishing.

Mazellan, Ron, illus. We Will Walk. 2005. 16p. (J). pap. *(978-0-7367-2919-2(4))* Zaner-Bloser, Inc.

McKissack, Fredrick L. This Generation of Americans. 2004. 150p. (J). lib. bdg. 16.92 *(978-1-4242-0769-5(X))* Fitzgerald Bks.

McKissack, Patricia C. Abby Takes a Stand. James, Gordon C., illus. 2007. 104p. (J). *(978-0-439-02797-7(7))* Scholastic, Inc.

Medearis, Angela Shelf. Singing for Dr. King. Hu, Ying-Hwa & Van Wright, Cornelius, illus. 2004. 32p. (J). lib. bdg. 15.00 *(978-1-4242-0237-9(X))* Fitzgerald Bks.

Nolan, Han. A Summer of Kings. 2006. 334p. (J). *(978-1-4156-7340-9(3))* Harcourt Trade Pubs.

Pinkney, Andrea Davis. Boycott Blues: How Rosa Parks Inspired a Nation. Pinkney, Brian, illus. 2008. (ENG.). 40p. (J). (gr. k-3). 16.99 *(978-0-06-082118-0(3),* Greenwillow Bks.) HarperCollins Pubs.

Raven, Margot Theis. Let Them Play. Ellison, Chris, illus. 2005. (ENG.). 32p. (J). (gr. 1-4). 17.99 *(978-1-58536-260-8(3),* 202075) Sleeping Bear Pr.

Reynolds, Aaron. Back of the Bus. Cooper, Floyd, illus. (ENG.). 32p. (J). (gr. 1-3). 2013. 8.99 *(978-0-14-751058-7(9),* Puffin Books) 2010. 16.99 *(978-0-399-25091-0(3),* Philomel Bks.) Penguin Young Readers Group.

Scholastic, Inc. Staff & Medearis, Angela Shelf. Singing for Dr. King. Van Wright, Cornelius & Hu, Ying-Hwa, illus. 2004. (Just for You Ser.). (ENG.). 32p. (gr. k-3). pap. 3.99 *(978-0-439-56855-5(2),* Teaching Resources) Scholastic, Inc.

Stroud, Bettye. Belle, the Last Mule at Gee's Bend: A Civil Rights Story. Holyfield, John, illus. 2016. (ENG.). (J). (gr. k-3). 7.99 *(978-0-7636-8769-4(3))* Candlewick Pr.

Stroud, Bettye & Ramsey, Calvin Alexander. Belle, the Last Mule at Gee's Bend: A Civil Rights Story. Holyfield, John,

C D

illus. 2011. (ENG.). 32p. (J). (gr. k-3). 16.99 *(978-0-7636-4058-3(1))* Candlewick Pr.

Tuck, Pamela M. As Fast As Words Could Fly, 1 vol. Velasquez, Eric, illus. 2013. (ENG.). 40p. (J). 18.95 *(978-1-60060-348-8(3))* Lee & Low Bks., Inc.

Vaught, Susan. Things Too Huge to Fix by Saying Sorry. 2016. (ENG., Illus.). 352p. (J). (gr. 5-9). 16.99 *(978-1-4814-2279-6(0)*, Simon & Schuster Bks. For Young Readers) Simon & Schuster Bks. For Young Readers.

—Things Too Huge to Fix by Saying Sorry. 2017. (ENG.). 368p. (J). (gr. 5-9). pap. 7.99 ***(978-1-4814-2280-2(4)***, Simon & Schuster/Paula Wiseman Bks.) Simon & Schuster/Paula Wiseman Bks.

Williams-Garcia, Rita. One Crazy Summer. 2009. (KOR.). 272p. (J). pap. *(978-89-7199-494-8(0))* Dolbegae Publishing Co.

—One Crazy Summer. (J). (gr. 4-7). 2011. (ENG.). 240p. pap. 7.99 *(978-0-06-076090-8(7))* 2010. (ENG.). 224p. 16.99 *(978-0-06-076088-5(5))* 2010. 224p. lib. bdg. 16.89 *(978-0-06-076089-2(3))* HarperCollins Pubs. (Amistad).

—One Crazy Summer. (J). 2011. 1.25 *(978-1-4498-2201-9(0))* 2010. 69.75 *(978-1-4498-2197-5(9))* 2010. 67.75 *(978-1-4498-2199-9(5))* Recorded Bks., Inc.

—One Crazy Summer. 2011. (J). lib. bdg. 17.20 *(978-0-606-23555-6(8)*, Turtleback) Turtleback Bks.

CIVIL RIGHTS WORKERS

Adler, David A. Heroes for Civil Rights. Farnsworth, Bill, illus. 2007. (ENG.). 32p. (J). (gr. -1-3). 17.95 *(978-0-8234-2008-7(6))* Holiday Hse., Inc.

—A Picture Book of Rosa Parks. Casilla, Robert, illus. 2015. 32p. pap. 8.00 *(978-1-61003-405-0(8))* Center for the Collaborative Classroom.

Alexander, Florence. Dare to Be. . . Martin Luther King Jr. Whitmore, Yvette, illus. 2003. (ENG & SPA.). 17p. (J). 3.99 *(978-0-915960-65-1(6))* Ebon Research Systems Publishing, LLC.

Aretha, David. Freedom Summer. 2007. (Civil Rights Movement Ser.). (Illus.). 128p. (J). (gr. 3-7). lib. bdg. 27.95 *(978-1-59935-059-2(9))* Reynolds, Morgan Inc.

—Sit-Ins & Freedom Rides. 2009. (Civil Rights Movement Ser.). 128p. (J). (gr. 4-7). 28.95 *(978-1-59935-098-1(X))* Reynolds, Morgan Inc.

Ashby, Ruth. Rosa Parks: Freedom Rider. 2008. (Sterling Biographies(r) Ser.). (ENG., Illus.). 128p. (J). (gr. 5). pap. 5.95 *(978-1-4027-4865-3(5))* Sterling Publishing Co., Inc.

Asim, Jabari. Preaching to the Chickens: The Story of Young John Lewis. Lewis, E. B., illus. 2016. (ENG.). 32p. (J). (gr. k-3). 17.99 *(978-0-399-16856-7(7)*, Nancy Paulsen Books) Penguin Young Readers Group.

Bader, Bonnie. Who Was Martin Luther King, Jr. ? Wolf, Elizabeth & Harrison, Nancy, illus. 2007. (Who Was? Ser.). (ENG.). 112p. (J). (gr. 3-7). pap. 5.99 *(978-0-448-44723-0(1)*, Grosset & Dunlap) Penguin Young Readers Group.

—Who Was Martin Luther King, Jr. ? Wolf, Elizabeth, illus. 2008. (Who Was... ? Ser.). 105p. (J). (gr. 2-5). 12.65 *(978-0-7569-8935-4(3))* Perfection Learning Corp.

Bailey, Gerry & Foster, Karen. Martin Luther King Jr.'s Microphone. Radford, Karen & Noyes, Leighton, illus. 2008. (Stories of Great People Ser.). (ENG.). 40p. (J). (gr. 3-8). pap. *(978-0-7787-3711-7(X))*; lib. bdg. *(978-0-7787-3689-9(X))* Crabtree Publishing Co.

Banting, Erinn. Rosa Parks. 2005. (Great African American Women for Kids Ser.). (Illus.). 24p. (J). (gr. 2-3). lib. bdg. 26.00 *(978-1-59036-336-2(1))*; (gr. 3-7). per. 8.95 *(978-1-59036-342-3(6))* Weigl Pubs., Inc.

Bausum, Ann & National Geographic Kids Staff. The March Against Fear: The Last Great Walk of the Civil Rights Movement & the Emergence of Black Power. 2017. (ENG., Illus.). 144p. (J). (gr. 7-9). 18.99 *(978-1-4263-2665-3(3)*, National Geographic Children's Bks.) National Geographic Society.

Belinda, Rochelle. Witnesses to Freedom: Young People Who Fought for Civil Rights. 2014. (ENG.). 116p. (J). 12.24 *(978-1-63245-230-6(8))* Lectorum Pubns., Inc.

Benson, Kathleen & Haskins, Jim. John Lewis in the Lead: A Story of the Civil Rights Movement, 1 vol. Andrews, Benny, illus. 2006. (ENG.). 40p. (gr. 2-7). 17.95 *(978-1-58430-250-6(X))* Lee & Low Bks., Inc.

Boehme, Gerry. John Lewis & Desegregation. 2016. (Primary Sources of the Civil Rights Movement Ser.). (Illus.). 64p. (J). (gr. 6-6). 34.21 *(978-1-5026-1868-9(0))* Cavendish Square Publishing.

Bolden, Tonya. M. L. K. The Journey of a King. Adelman, Bob, ed. 2007. (ENG., Illus.). 128p. (J). (gr. 5-9). 27.95 *(978-0-8109-5476-2(1)*, Abrams Bks. for Young Readers) Abrams, Inc.

Brandt, Keith & Mattern, Joanne. Rosa Parks: Freedom Rider. Griffith, Gershom, illus. 2006. 54p. (J). pap. *(978-0-439-66045-7(9))* Scholastic, Inc.

Brimner, Larry Dane. We Are One: The Story of Bayard Rustin. 2007. (ENG., Illus.). 48p. (J). (gr. 4-6). 18.95 *(978-1-59078-498-3(7))* Boyds Mills Pr.

Bull, Angela. The Story of Martin Luther King, Level 4. 2009. (DK Readers Ser.). (ENG.). 48p. (J). (gr. 3-7). 3.99 *(978-0-7566-5615-7(X)*, DK Children) Dorling Kindersley Publishing, Inc.

Carson, Mary Kay. What Was Your Dream, Dr. King? And Other Questions About... Martin Luther King, Jr. Madsen, Jim, illus. 2013. (Good Question! Ser.). (ENG.). 32p. (J). (gr. 2). pap. 5.95 *(978-1-4027-9045-4(7))* Sterling Publishing Co., Inc.

Civil Rights Leaders, bks. 13, vol. 13. Incl. A. Philip Randolph & the African American Labor Movement. Miller, Calvin Craig. (Illus.). 160p. (YA). (gr. 6-12). 2005. 26.95 *(978-1-931798-50-1(8))*; Eternal Vigilance: The Story of Ida B. Wells-Barnett. Hinman, Bonnie. 128p. (gr. 6-10). 2011. lib. bdg. 28.95 *(978-1-59935-111-7(0))*; Freedom Cannot Rest: Ella Baker & the Civil Rights Movement. Bohannon, Lisa Frederiksen. (Illus.). 176p. (YA). (gr. 6-12). 2005. lib. bdg. 26.95 *(978-1-931798-71-6(0))*; Liberator: The Story of William Lloyd Garrison. Esty, Amos. 144p. 2011. 28.95 *(978-1-59935-137-7(4))*; No Compromise: The Story of Harvey Milk. Aretha, David. 100p. (YA). (gr. 5-9). 2009. lib. bdg. 28.95 *(978-1-59935-129-2(3))*; No Easy Answers: Bayard Rustin & the Civil Rights Movement. (Illus.). 160p. (J). (gr. 6-12). 2005. 26.95 *(978-1-931798-43-3(5))*; Roy Wilkins: Leader of the NAACP. Miller, Calvin Craig. (Illus.). 176p. (YA). (gr. 6-12). 2005. 26.95 *(978-1-931798-49-5(4))*; Stranger in My Own House: The Story of W. E. B. du Bois. Hinman, Bonnie. (Illus.). 176p. (gr. 6-12). 2005. 28.95 *(978-1-931798-45-7(1))*; Unbound & Unbroken: The Story of Frederick Douglass. Esty, Amos. 144p. (gr. 8-10). 2011. 28.95 *(978-1-59935-136-0(6))*; 2008. Set lib. bdg. 376.35 *(978-1-931798-99-0(0))* Reynolds, Morgan Inc.

Connors, Kathleen. The Life of Rosa Parks, Vol. 1. 2014. (Famous Lives Ser.). (ENG.). 24p. (J). (gr. 1-2). 22.60 *(978-1-4824-0419-7(2))* Stevens, Gareth Publishing LLLP.

Crayton, Lisa A. Freedom Riders. 2017. (J). ***(978-1-5383-8027-7(7))***; pap. ***(978-1-5383-8026-0(9))*** Rosen Publishing Group, Inc., The.

Crompton, Samuel Willard. Desmond Tutu: Fighting Apartheid. 2007. (Modern Peacemakers Ser.). (Illus.). 112p. (YA). (gr. 9-12). lib. bdg. 30.00 *(978-0-7910-9221-7(6))* Facts On File, Inc.

Daly, Ruth. Rosa Parks. 2014. (J). *(978-1-4896-2452-9(X))* Weigl Pubs., Inc.

Deal, Heidi. Perspectives on the Civil Rights Movement. 2018. (ENG.). 32p. (gr. 3-6). ***(978-1-63235-398-6(9)***, 12-Story Library) Pr. Room Editions LLC.

Denenberg, Barry. Nelson Mandela: No Easy Walk to Freedom. 2014. (ENG.). 240p. (J). (gr. 3-7). pap. 7.99 *(978-0-545-66911-5(1))* Scholastic, Inc.

DeRubertis, Barbara. Let's Celebrate Martin Luther King, Jr. Day. Griffith, Gershom, illus. 2013. (Holidays & Heroes Ser.). 32p. (gr. 1-3). pap. 7.95 *(978-1-57565-638-0(8))* Kane Press, Inc.

Deutsch, Stacia & Cohon, Rhody. Hot Pursuit: Murder in Mississippi. Orback, Craig, illus. 2010. (ENG.). 40p. (J). (gr. 3-5). pap. 7.95 *(978-0-7613-3956-4(6))*; lib. bdg. 17.95 *(978-0-7613-3955-7(8))* Lerner Publishing Group. (Kar-Ben Publishing).

D'Orio, Wayne. Al Sharpton. 2nd rev. ed. 2011. (Black Americans of Achievement Legacy Edition Ser.). 128p. (gr. 6-12). 35.00 *(978-1-60413-834-4(3))* Facts On File, Inc.

Dray, Philip. Yours for Justice, Ida B. Wells: The Daring Life of a Crusading Journalist, 1 vol. Alcorn, Stephen, illus. 2008. (ENG.). 48p. (J). (gr. 5-9). 18.95 *(978-1-56145-417-4(6))* Peachtree Pubs.

Dubowski, Cathy East. Rosa Parks: Don't Give In! 2005. (Defining Moments Ser.). (Illus.). 32p. (J). (gr. 2-5). lib. bdg. 25.27 *(978-1-59716-078-0(4))* Bearport Publishing Co., Inc.

Dunn, Joeming W. Martin Luther King, Jr, 1 vol. Allen, Chris, illus. 2008. (Bio-Graphics Ser.). (ENG.). 32p. 28.50 *(978-1-60270-175-5(X)*, Graphic Planet- Nonfiction) ABDO Publishing Co.

Edison, Erin. Rosa Parks, 1 vol. 2013. (Great Women in History Ser.). (ENG.). 24p. (gr. k-1). pap. 6.29 *(978-1-62065-863-5(1))*; pap. 35.70 *(978-1-62065-864-2(X))*; (Illus.). lib. bdg. 21.99 *(978-1-62065-071-4(1))* Capstone Press of Coughlan Cos. (Pebble Bks.).

Edwards, Pamela Duncan. The Bus Ride That Changed History: The Story of Rosa Parks. Shanahan, Danny, illus. 2009. (ENG.). 32p. (J). (gr. -1-3). pap. 6.99 *(978-0-547-07674-4(6))* Houghton Mifflin Harcourt Publishing Co.

Fandel, Jennifer. Martin Luther King, Jr. 2005. (Genius Ser.). (Illus.). 48p. (J). (gr. 5-9). lib. bdg. 21.95 *(978-1-58341-329-6(4)*, Creative Education) Creative Co., The.

—Martin Luther King, Jr: Great Civil Rights Leader, 1 vol. Bascle, Brian, illus. 2006. (Graphic Biographies Ser.). (ENG.). 32p. (gr. 3-4). 30.65 *(978-0-7368-6498-5(9)*, Graphic Library) Capstone Press of Coughlan Cos.

Feinstein, Stephen. Inspiring African-American Civil Rights Leaders. 2012. (African-American Collective Biographies Ser.). (Illus.). 112p. (J). (gr. 5-18). 33.27 *(978-1-59845-136-8(7))* Enslow Pubs., Inc.

Ferris, Jeri Chase. Demanding Justice: A Story about Mary Ann Shadd Cary. Smith, Kimanne, illus. 2003. (Creative Minds Biographies Ser.). (ENG.). 64p. (gr. 4-8). 22.60 *(978-1-57505-177-2(X))*; pap. 8.95 *(978-0-87614-928-7(X)*, Carolrhoda Bks.) Lerner Publishing Group.

Fine, Edith Hope. Rosa Parks: Meet a Civil Rights Hero. 2004. (Meeting Famous People Ser.). (Illus.). 32p. (J). lib. bdg. 23.94 *(978-0-7660-2099-3(1))* Enslow Pubs., Inc.

Finlayson, Reggie. Nelson Mandela. pap. 9.95 *(978-0-8225-5743-2(6))*; 2005. (ENG., Illus.). 112p. (gr. 5-12). lib. bdg. 27.93 *(978-0-8225-2644-5(1)*, Lerner Pubns.) Lerner Publishing Group.

Fleming, Alice. Martin Luther King, Jr. A Dream of Hope. 2008. (Sterling Biographies(r) Ser.). (ENG., Illus.). 128p. (J). (gr. 5). pap. 5.95 *(978-1-4027-4439-6(0))* Sterling Publishing Co., Inc.

Flowers, Arthur. I See the Promised Land: A Life of Martin Luther King, Jr., 1 vol. Chitrakar, Manu, illus. rev. ed. 2013. (ENG.). 156p. (J). (gr. 6). 16.95 *(978-1-55498-328-5(2))* Groundwood Bks. CAN. Dist: Publishers Group West (PGW).

Foy, Debbie. Civil-Rights Activists. 2012. (Black History Makers Ser.). (ENG.). 24p. (J). (gr. 3-8). pap. 8.25 *(978-1-4488-7054-7(2))*; lib. bdg. 22.60 *(978-1-4488-6638-0(3))* Rosen Publishing Group, Inc., The. (PowerKids Pr.).

Freedman, Russell. Freedom Walkers: The Story of the Montgomery Bus Boycott. (ENG., Illus.). 112p. (J). 2009. (gr. 3-7). pap. 14.95 *(978-0-8234-2195-4(3))* 2006. (gr. 5-10). 18.95 *(978-0-8234-2031-5(0))* Holiday Hse., Inc.

Frey, Wendy. Citizen Heroes. 2007. (Illus.). 68p. (J). *(978-1-4105-0887-4(0))*; *(978-1-4105-0888-1(9))* Johnston, Don Inc.

Ganeri, Anita. I Have a Dream: Martin Luther King, Jr. & the Fight for Equal Rights. 2013. (Turning Points in History Ser.). (Illus.). 48p. (gr. 5-12). 37.10 *(978-1-59920-972-2(1))* Black Rabbit Bks.

Gelfand, Dale Evva. Coretta Scott King: Civil Rights Activist. 2nd rev. ed. 2006. (Black Americans of Achievement Legacy Edition Ser.). (Illus.). 137p. (YA). (gr. 7-12). lib. bdg. 35.00 *(978-0-7910-9522-5(3))* Facts On File, Inc.

Giovanni, Nikki. Rosa. Collier, Bryan, illus. 2007. (ENG.). 40p. (J). (gr. -1-3). per. 8.99 *(978-0-312-37602-4(2)*, 9780312376024) Square Fish.

—Rosa. Collier, Bryan, illus. 2011. (J). (gr. 2-5). 29.95 *(978-0-545-04261-1(5))* Weston Woods Studios, Inc.

Gosman, Gillian. Martin Luther King, Jr. 2011. (Life Stories Ser.). (Illus.). 24p. (J). pap. 8.25 *(978-1-4488-2755-8(8)*, PowerKids Pr.); (gr. 1-4). lib. bdg. 22.60 *(978-1-4488-2583-7(0)*, PowerKids Pr.); (ENG & SPA., (gr. 1-4). lib. bdg. 22.60 *(978-1-4488-3217-0(9))* Rosen Publishing Group, Inc., The.

—Rosa Parks. 2011. (Life Stories Ser.). (Illus.). 24p. (J). pap. 8.25 *(978-1-4488-2757-2(4)*, PowerKids Pr.); (ENG & SPA., (gr. 1-4). lib. bdg. 22.60 *(978-1-4488-3218-7(7))*; (gr. 1-4). lib. bdg. 22.60 *(978-1-4488-2584-4(9)*, PowerKids Pr.) Rosen Publishing Group, Inc., The.

Gotsch, Patrice. Martin Luther King, Jr. Changing Lives. Arreola, Gil, illus. 2006. 19p. pap. 6.30 *(978-1-55501-779-8(7))* Ballard & Tighe Pubs.

Green, Richard L., et al, eds. A Salute to Black Civil Rights Leaders. Dobson, S. Gaston, illus. (Empak "Black History" Publication). (J). pap. 1.00 *(978-0-9616156-3-5(X))* Empak Publishing Co.

Haldy, Emma E. Martin Luther King, Jr. Bane, Jeff, illus. 2016. (My Early Library: My Itty-Bitty Bio Ser.). (ENG.). 24p. (J). (gr. k-1). 28.50 *(978-1-63470-477-9(0)*, 207639) Cherry Lake Publishing.

—Rosa Parks. Bane, Jeff, illus. 2016. (My Early Library: My Itty-Bitty Bio Ser.). (ENG.). 24p. (J). (gr. k-1). 28.50 *(978-1-63470-481-6(9)*, 207655) Cherry Lake Publishing.

Hall, M. C. Martin Luther King, Jr. Civil Rights Leader, 1 vol. Soud, illus. 2008. (Beginner Biographies Ser.). (ENG.). 32p. (gr. -1-3). 28.50 *(978-1-60270-251-6(9)*, Looking Glass Library- Nonfiction) Magic Wagon.

Hally, Ashleigh. Coretta Scott King. 2012. (Illus.). 24p. (J). *(978-1-935884-78-1(6))*; pap. *(978-1-935884-84-2(0))* State Standards Publishing, LLC.

Hardy, P. Stephen & Hardy, Sheila. Extraordinary People of the Civil Rights Movement. 2006. (Extraordinary People Ser.). (ENG., Illus.). 288p. (J). (gr. 6-18). lib. bdg. 40.00 *(978-0-516-25461-6(8)*, Children's Pr.) Scholastic Library Publishing.

Hasday, Judy L. Women in the Civil Rights Movement. 2012. (J). pap. *(978-1-4222-2366-6(3))* Institute of Physics Publishing.

—Women in the Civil Rights Movement. 2012. 64p. (J). (gr. 5). 22.95 *(978-1-4222-2356-7(6))* Mason Crest.

Haskins, Jim, et al. John Lewis in the Lead: A Story of the Civil Rights Movement, 1 vol. 2006. (ENG., Illus.). 40p. (J). pap. 11.95 *(978-1-60060-849-0(3))* Lee & Low Bks., Inc.

Helfand, Lewis & Teitelbaum, Michael. Martin Luther King. Banerjee, Sankha, illus. 2013. (Campfire Graphic Novels Ser.). (ENG.). 88p. (YA). (gr. 5). pap. 11.99 *(978-93-80028-69-9(5)*, Campfire) Steerforth Pr.

Henneberg, Susan. James Baldwin, 1 vol. 2015. (ENG.). 112p. (YA). 35.60 *(978-1-4777-7897-5(7)*, Rosen Young Adult) Rosen Publishing Group, Inc., The.

Herweck, Dona. Martin Luther King Jr., 1 vol. 2nd rev. ed. 2011. (TIME for KIDS(r) Nonfiction Readers Ser.). (ENG.). 28p. (J). (gr. 2-2). pap. 6.99 *(978-1-4333-3641-6(3))* Teacher Created Materials, Inc.

Hinman, Bonnie. Eternal Vigilance: The Story of Ida B. Wells-Barnett. 2011. (Civil Rights Leaders Ser.). 128p. (gr. 6-10). lib. bdg. 28.95 *(978-1-59935-111-7(0))* Reynolds, Morgan Inc.

Hinton, KaaVonia. Martin Luther King, Jr. 2008. (What's So Great About... ? Ser.). (Illus.). 32p. (YA). (gr. 2-4). lib. bdg. 25.70 *(978-1-58415-724-3(0))* Mitchell Lane Pubs., Inc.

Hoe, Susan C. Rosa Parks. 2009. (Sharing the American Dream Ser.). 64p. (YA). (gr. 7-12). 22.95 *(978-1-4222-0597-6(5))* Mason Crest.

Hoose, Phillip. Claudette Colvin: Twice Toward Justice. 2010. (ENG., Illus.). 160p. (YA). (gr. 8-12). pap. 9.99 *(978-0-312-66105-2(3)*, 9780312661052) Square Fish.

House, Catherine. Voices Against Injustice: Ten Christians Who Spoke Out for Justice. 2007. (ENG.). 192p. (J). per. 7.99 *(978-1-84550-280-5(9)*, b2aa8a18-ff3a-4b6a-b14a-f5fd55dbd02e) Christian Focus Pubns. GBR. Dist: Bookmasters Distribution.

Houtman, Jacqueline, et al. Bayard Rustin: The Invisible Activist. 2014. (J). pap. *(978-1-937768-58-4(9))* QuakerPress.

Hull, Mary. Rosa Parks: Civil Rights Leader. 2nd rev. ed. 2006. (Black Americans of Achievement Ser.). (Illus.). 122p. (YA). (gr. 7-12). lib. bdg. 35.00 *(978-0-7910-9523-2(1))* Facts On File, Inc.

Hull, Mary & Gelfand, Dale Evva. Rosa Parks. 2nd rev. ed. 2008. (Black Americans of Achievement: Legacy Edition Ser.). 128p. (gr. 6-12). pap. 11.95 *(978-1-60413-325-7(2)*, Checkmark Bks.) Facts On File, Inc.

Hurt, Avery Elizabeth. Rosa Parks: Civil Rights Activist. 2017. (J). ***(978-1-5383-8105-2(2))*** Rosen Publishing Group, Inc., The.

Jazynka, Kitson. National Geographic Readers: Rosa Parks. 2015. (Readers Bios Ser.). (ENG., Illus.). 32p. (J). (gr. k-3). pap. 3.99 *(978-1-4263-2141-2(4)*, National Geographic Children's Bks.) National Geographic Society.

Jeffrey, Gary. Martin Luther King Jr. The Life of a Civil Rights Leader. 2009. (Graphic Nonfiction Biographies Ser.). (ENG.). 48p. (YA). (gr. 4-5). 58.50 *(978-1-61513-021-4(7)*, Rosen Reference) Rosen Publishing Group, Inc., The.

—Martin Luther King Jr. The Life of a Civil Rights Leader. Forsey, Chris, illus. 2007. (Graphic Nonfiction Biographies Ser.). (ENG.). 48p. (YA). (gr. 4-7). lib. bdg. 31.95 *(978-1-4042-0858-2(5))* Rosen Publishing Group, Inc., The.

—Martin Luther King Jr. The Life of a Civil Rights Leader. Forsey, Christopher, illus. 2007. (Graphic Biographies Ser.). (ENG.). 48p. (gr. 5-8). pap. 14.05 *(978-1-4042-0921-3(2))* Rosen Publishing Group, Inc., The.

—Medgar Evers & the NAACP. 2012. (Graphic History of the Civil Rights Movement Ser.). 24p. (J). (gr. 3-8). pap. 8.15 *(978-1-4339-7496-0(7))*; lib. bdg. 23.95 *(978-1-4339-7495-3(9))* Stevens, Gareth Publishing LLLP.

Jones, Rob Lloyd. Martin Luther King, Jr. 2006. (Illus.). 62p. (J). pap. *(978-0-439-02299-6(1))* Scholastic, Inc.

Juarez, Christine. Hector P. Garcia. 2016. (Great Hispanic & Latino Americans Ser.). (ENG.). 24p. (gr. k-1). lib. bdg. 21.99 *(978-1-5157-1891-8(3)*, Pebble Bks.) Capstone Press of Coughlan Cos.

Kaiser, Lisbeth. Maya Angelou. Salaberria, Leire, illus. 2016. (Little People, Big Dreams Ser.). (ENG.). 32p. (J). (gr. k-3). 14.99 *(978-1-84780-889-9(1)*, Frances Lincoln Children's Bks.) Quarto Publishing Group UK GBR. Dist: Hachette Bk. Group.

Kanefield, Teri. The Girl from the Tar Paper School: Barbara Rose Johns & the Advent of the Civil Rights Movement. 2014. (ENG., Illus.). 56p. (J). (gr. 3-7). 19.95 *(978-1-4197-0796-4(5)*, Abrams Bks. for Young Readers) Abrams, Inc.

Kishel, Ann-Marie. Rosa Parks: A Life of Courage. 2006. (Pull Ahead Books-Biographies Ser.). (ENG., Illus.). 32p. (gr. k-3). lib. bdg. 22.60 *(978-0-8225-3478-5(9)*, Lerner Pubns.) Lerner Publishing Group.

—Rosa Parks: Una Vida de Valentia. Translations.com Staff, tr. 2006. (Libros para Avanzar-Biografías (Pull Ahead Books-Biographies) Ser.). (ENG & SPA., Illus.). 32p. (gr. k-3). lib. bdg. 22.60 *(978-0-8225-6239-9(1))* Lerner Publishing Group.

Kortemeier, Todd. Unsung Heroes of Social Justice. 2017. (Unsung Heroes Ser.). (ENG., Illus.). 32p. (J). (gr. 3-6). 21.95 *(978-1-63235-310-8(5))* Pr. Room Editions LLC.

Krull, Kathleen & Freeman, Laura. Coretta Scott King: I Kept on Marching. 2015. (Women Who Broke the Rules Ser.). (ENG., Illus.). 48p. (J). (gr. 1-4). pap. 6.99 *(978-0-8027-3827-1(3)*, 9780802738271, Bloomsbury USA Childrens) Bloomsbury Publishing USA.

Krumm, Brian. The Little Rock Nine: A Primary Source Exploration of the Battle for School Integration, 1 vol. 2014. (We Shall Overcome Ser.). (ENG.). 32p. (gr. 3-4). lib. bdg. 27.32 *(978-1-4914-0225-2(3))* Capstone Press of Coughlan Cos.

Kurtz, Jane. Martin's Dream. Bates, Amy June, illus. 2008. (Ready-To-Reads Ser.). (ENG.). 32p. (J). (gr. -1-1). pap. 3.99 *(978-1-4169-2774-7(3)*, Simon Spotlight) Simon Spotlight.

Labrecque, Ellen. Who Was Maya Angelou? Putra, Dede, illus. 2016. 105p. (J). ***(978-1-4844-6937-8(2)***, Grosset & Dunlap) Penguin Publishing Group.

Levinson, Cynthia. The Youngest Marcher: The Story of a Young Civil Rights Activist. Brantley-Newton, Vanessa, illus. 2017. (ENG.). 40p. (J). (gr. k-5). 17.99 *(978-1-4814-0070-1(3))* Simon & Schuster, Inc.

Linde, Barbara M. Jesse Jackson. 2011. (Civil Rights Crusaders Ser.). 24p. (gr. 2-5). (J). pap. 8.15 *(978-1-4339-5684-3(5)*, Gareth Stevens Learning Library); (YA). lib. bdg. 22.60 *(978-1-4339-5682-9(9))* Stevens, Gareth Publishing LLLP.

—Malcolm X. 2011. (Civil Rights Crusaders Ser.). 24p. (J). (gr. 2-5). pap. 8.15 *(978-1-4339-5688-1(8)*, Gareth Stevens Learning Library); lib. bdg. 22.60 *(978-1-4339-5686-7(1))* Stevens, Gareth Publishing LLLP.

—Martin Luther King Jr. 2011. (Civil Rights Crusaders Ser.). (Illus.). 24p. (gr. 2-5). (J). pap. 8.15 *(978-1-4339-5692-8(6)*, Gareth Stevens Learning Library); (YA). lib. bdg. 22.60 *(978-1-4339-5690-4(X))* Stevens, Gareth Publishing LLLP.

—Rosa Parks. 2011. (Civil Rights Crusaders Ser.). (Illus.). 24p. (gr. 2-5). (J). pap. 8.15 *(978-1-4339-5696-6(9)*, Gareth Stevens Learning Library); (YA). lib. bdg. 22.60 *(978-1-4339-5694-2(2))* Stevens, Gareth Publishing LLLP.

MacMillan, Dianne M. Martin Luther King, Jr. Day. rev. ed. 2008. (Best Holiday Bks.). (Illus.). 48p. (J). (gr. 3-7). lib. bdg. 25.27 *(978-0-7660-3043-5(1))* Enslow Pubs., Inc.

Maloof, Torrey. Martin Luther King Jr. Destined to Lead. 2016. (Primary Source Readers Ser.). (Illus.). 32p. (gr. 2-2). 8.99 *(978-1-4938-2559-2(3))* Teacher Created Materials, Inc.

Manolis, Kay & Leslie, Tonya. Rosa Parks: A Life of Courage. 2007. (People of Character Ser.). (ENG., Illus.). 24p. (J). (gr. 2-5). lib. bdg. 25.95 *(978-1-60014-088-4(2))* Bellwether Media.

Mara, Wil. Martin Luther King Jr. 2013. (Rookie Biographies(r) Ser.). (ENG.). 32p. (J). pap. 5.95 *(978-0-531-24704-4(X))*; lib. bdg. 23.00 *(978-0-531-24738-9(4))* Scholastic Library Publishing.

—Rosa Parks. (Rookie Biographies Ser.). (ENG., Illus.). 32p. (J). (gr. 1-2). 2004. pap. 4.95 *(978-0-516-27916-9(5))* 2007. pap. 4.95 *(978-0-531-12592-2(0))* Scholastic Library Publishing. (Children's Pr.).

—Rosa Parks: Mother of the Civil Rights Movement. 2014. (Rookie Biographies(tm) Ser.). (ENG.). 32p. (J). lib. bdg. 25.00 *(978-0-531-20561-7(4))*; pap. 5.95 *(978-0-531-21204-2(1))* Scholastic Library Publishing.

Mattern, Joanne. Coretta Scott King: Civil Rights Activist. (Women Who Shaped History Ser.). 24p. 2009. (gr. 2-3). 42.50 *(978-1-60854-816-3(3))* 2003. (Illus.). (J). lib. bdg. 19.95 *(978-0-8239-6504-5(X))* Rosen Publishing Group, Inc., The. (PowerKids Pr.).

McDonough, Yona Zeldis. Who Was Rosa Parks? Harrison, Nancy & Marchesi, Stephen, illus. 2010. (Who Was? Ser.). (ENG.). 112p. (J). (gr. 3-7). pap. 5.99 *(978-0-448-45442-9(4)*, Grosset & Dunlap) Penguin Young Readers Group.

McKissack, Patricia C. & McKissack, Fredrick L. Ida B. Wells-Barnett: Fighter for Justice. 2013. (Famous African Americans Ser.). 24p. (J). (gr. k-3). pap. 7.95 *(978-1-4644-0198-5(5)*, Enslow Elementary); (Illus.). 22.60 *(978-0-7660-4108-0(5))* Enslow Pubs., Inc.

McPherson, Stephanie Sammartino. Biography Coretta Scott King. 2007. (Biography Ser.). (Illus.). 112p. (YA). (gr. 7-12). lib. bdg. 29.27 *(978-0-8225-7156-8(0))* Twenty First Century Bks.

Medearis, Angela Shelf. Coretta Scott King: Dare to Dream. Rich, Anna, illus. 2014. (Women of Our Time Ser.). (ENG.). 96p. (J). (gr. 3-7). 7.99 *(978-0-14-751363-2(4)*, Puffin Books) Penguin Young Readers Group.

Meltzer, Brad. I Am Martin Luther King, Jr. Eliopoulos, Christopher, illus. 2016. (Ordinary People Change the World Ser.). (ENG.). 40p. (J). (gr. k-3). 14.99 *(978-0-525-42852-7(6)*, Dial Bks) Penguin Young Readers Group.

—I Am Rosa Parks. Eliopoulos, Christopher, illus. 2014. (Ordinary People Change World Ser.). (ENG.). 40p. (J). (gr. -1-k). 14.99 *(978-0-8037-4085-3(9)*, Dial Bks) Penguin Publishing Group.

Michelson, Richard. As Good As Anybody. Colón, Raúl, illus. 2013. (ENG.). 40p. (J). (gr. 1-4). 7.99 *(978-0-385-75387-6(X)*, Dragonfly Bks.) Random Hse. Children's Bks.

Miller, Calvin Craig. A. Philip Randolph & the African American Labor Movement. 2005. (Civil Rights Leaders Ser.). (Illus.). 160p. (YA). (gr. 6-12). 26.95 *(978-1-931798-50-1(8))* Reynolds, Morgan Inc.

Miller, Connie Colwell. Rosa Parks & the Montgomery Bus Boycott, 1 vol. Kalal, Dan, illus. 2006. (Graphic History Ser.). (ENG.). 32p. (gr. 3-4). 30.65 *(978-0-7368-6495-4(4),* Graphic Library) Capstone Press of Coughlan Cos.

—Rosa Parks & the Montgomery Bus Boycott, 1 vol. Kalal, Dan, illus. 2006. (Graphic History Ser.). (ENG.). 32p. (gr. 3-4). per. 8.10 *(978-0-7368-9658-0(9),* Graphic Library) Capstone Press of Coughlan Cos.

Mis, Melody S. Civil Rights Leaders, 6 vols., Set. Incl. Meet Al Sharpton. lib. bdg. 22.60 *(978-1-4042-4213-5(9));* Meet Coretta Scott King. lib. bdg. 22.60 *(978-1-4042-4211-1(2));* Meet Jesse Jackson. lib. bdg. 22.60 *(978-1-4042-4212-8(0));* Meet Malcolm X. lib. bdg. 22.60 *(978-1-4042-4214-2(7));* Meet Martin Luther King Jr. lib. bdg. 22.60 *(978-1-4042-4209-8(0));* Meet Rosa Parks. lib. bdg. 22.60 *(978-1-4042-4210-4(4));* (Illus.). 24p. (YA). (gr. 2-5). 2008. 2009. Set lib. bdg. 127.50 *(978-1-4042-4240-1(6))* Rosen Publishing Group, Inc., The.

—Meet Al Sharpton. (Civil Rights Leaders Ser.). 24p. (gr. 2-3). 2009. 42.50 *(978-1-61511-850-2(0),* PowerKids Pr.) 2008. (Illus.). (YA). lib. bdg. 22.60 *(978-1-4042-4213-5(9))* Rosen Publishing Group, Inc., The.

—Meet Coretta Scott King. (Civil Rights Leaders Ser.). 24p. (gr. 2-3). 2009. 42.50 *(978-1-61511-851-9(9),* PowerKids Pr.) 2008. (Illus.). (YA). lib. bdg. 22.60 *(978-1-4042-4211-1(2))* Rosen Publishing Group, Inc., The.

—Meet Jesse Jackson. (Civil Rights Leaders Ser.). 24p. (gr. 2-3). 2009. 42.50 *(978-1-61511-852-6(7),* PowerKids Pr.) 2008. (Illus.). (YA). lib. bdg. 22.60 *(978-1-4042-4212-8(0))* Rosen Publishing Group, Inc., The.

—Meet Martin Luther King Jr. 2009. (Civil Rights Leaders Ser.). 24p. (gr. 2-3). 42.50 *(978-1-61511-854-0(3),* PowerKids Pr.) Rosen Publishing Group, Inc., The.

—Meet Martin Luther King Jr. 2008. (Civil Rights Leaders Ser.). (Illus.). 24p. (YA). (gr. 2-5). lib. bdg. 22.60 *(978-1-4042-4209-8(0))* Rosen Publishing Group, Inc., The.

—Meet Rosa Parks. (Civil Rights Leaders Ser.). 24p. (gr. 2-3). 2009. 42.50 *(978-1-61511-855-7(1),* PowerKids Pr.) 2008. (Illus.). (YA). lib. bdg. 22.60 *(978-1-4042-4210-4(4))* Rosen Publishing Group, Inc., The.

Mitchell, Don. The Freedom Summer Murders. 2014. (ENG.). 256p. (J). (gr. 9). 18.99 *(978-0-545-47725-3(5),* Scholastic Pr.) Scholastic, Inc.

Moore, Johnny Ray. The Story of Martin Luther King Jr. Wummer, Amy, illus. 2016. (J). *(978-0-8249-1974-0(2),* Ideal Pubns.) Worthy Publishing.

Morretta, Alison. Ida B. Wells-Barnett & the Crusade Against Lynching. 2016. (Primary Sources of the Civil Rights Movement Ser.). (Illus.). 64p. (J). (gr. 6-6). 34.21 *(978-1-5026-1874-0(5))* Cavendish Square Publishing.

—Rosa Parks & Civil Disobedience. 2016. (Primary Sources of the Civil Rights Movement Ser.). (Illus.). 64p. (J). (gr. 6-6). 34.21 *(978-1-5026-1870-2(2))* Cavendish Square Publishing.

Morris, Roz. Rosa Parks: Mother of the Civil Rights Movement. 2003. (Alabama Roots Biography Ser.). (Illus.). 109p. (J). *(978-1-878561-57-2(X))* Seacoast Publishing, Inc.

Myers, Walter Dean. Ida B. Wells: Let the Truth Be Told. Christensen, Bonnie, illus. (ENG.). 40p. (J). (gr. -1-3). 2015. pap. 6.99 *(978-0-06-054468-3(5))* 2008. 16.99 *(978-0-06-027705-5(X))* HarperCollins Pubs. (Amistad).

—I've Seen the Promised Land: The Life of Dr. Martin Luther King, Jr. Jenkins, Leonard, illus. 2012. (ENG.). 40p. (J). (gr. -1-3). pap. 6.99 *(978-0-06-225002-5(7),* Amistad) HarperCollins Pubs.

Nagelhout, Ryan. Martin Luther King Jr. 2015. (Heroes of Black History Ser.). (ENG.). 32p. (J). (gr. 3-4). 26.60 *(978-1-4824-2906-0(3))* Stevens, Gareth Publishing LLLP.

Nelson, Maria. Coretta Scott King. 2011. (Civil Rights Crusaders Ser.). 24p. (gr. 2-5). (J). pap. 8.15 *(978-1-4339-5680-5(2),* Gareth Stevens Learning Library); (YA). lib. bdg. 22.60 *(978-1-4339-5678-2(0))* Stevens, Gareth Publishing LLLP.

Nichols, Kaitlyn. Martin Luther King. 2009. pap. 13.25 *(978-1-60559-065-3(7))* Hameray Publishing Group, Inc.

Norwich, Grace. Martin Luther King, Jr. Alba, Elisabeth, illus. 2012. (I Am Ser.: 4). (ENG.). 128p. (J). (gr. 2-5). pap. 5.99 *(978-0-545-44780-5(1),* Scholastic Paperbacks) Scholastic, Inc.

Patrick, Denise Lewis. A Lesson for Martin Luther King, Jr. Pate, Rodney S., illus. 2003. (Ready-To-read COFA Ser.). (ENG.). 32p. (J). (gr. k-2). pap. 3.99 *(978-0-689-85397-5(1),* Simon Spotlight) Simon Spotlight.

Pingry, Patricia A. Meet Rosa Parks. Walker, Steven, illus. 2008. (ENG.). 32p. (J). (gr. k-3). per. 7.99 *(978-0-8249-5578-6(1),* Ideal Pubns.) Worthy Publishing.

—The Story of Coretta Scott King. Walker, Steven, illus. 2007. (ENG.). 26p. (J). (gr. 3-7). bds. 7.69 *(978-0-8249-6717-8(8),* Ideal Pubns.) Worthy Publishing.

—The Story of Rosa Parks. Walker, Steven, illus. (J). 2016. *(978-0-8249-1967-0(4))* 2008. (ENG.). 24p. (gr. 3-7). bds. 7.69 *(978-0-8249-6687-4(2))* Worthy Publishing. (Ideal Pubns.).

Ponto, Joanna & Gnojewski, Carol. Martin Luther King Jr. Day. 2016. (Story of Our Holidays Ser.). (Illus.). 32p. (J). pap. 10.52 *(978-0-7660-8340-0(3))* Enslow Pubs., Inc.

Ridley, Sarah. Martin Luther King: ...And the Fight for Equality. 2013. (History Makers Ser.). (Illus.). 24p. (J). (gr. 2-4). 25.65 *(978-1-59771-389-4(9))* Sea-To-Sea Pubns.

Rinaldo, Denise. Rosa Parks: With a Discussion of Courage. 2003. (Values in Action Ser.). (J). *(978-1-59203-061-3(0))* Learning Challenge, Inc.

Ringgold, Faith. If a Bus Could Talk: The Story of Rosa Parks. Ringgold, Faith, illus. 2003. (ENG., Illus.). 32p. (J). (gr. k-4). pap. 7.99 *(978-0-689-85676-1(8),* Aladdin) Simon & Schuster Children's Publishing.

Rivera, Sheila. Martin Luther King Jr. Una Vida de Determinación. Translations.com Staff, tr. 2006. (Libros para Avanzar-Biografías (Pull Ahead Books-Biographies) Ser.). (ENG & SPA., Illus.). 32p. (gr. k-3). lib. bdg. 22.60 *(978-0-8225-6237-5(5))* Lerner Publishing Group.

Roop, Peter & Roop, Connie. Let's Dream, Martin Luther King, Jr.! 2004. (Scholastic Chapter Book Biography Ser.). (Illus.). 59p. (J). pap. *(978-0-439-55443-5(8))* Scholastic, Inc.

Rose, Or N. Abraham Joshua Heschel: Man of Spirit, Man of Action. 2003. (ENG., Illus.). 80p. pap. 9.95 *(978-0-8276-0758-3(X))* Jewish Pubn. Society.

Rowh, Mark. The Life of W. E. B. du Bois: Civil Rights Champion. 2015. (Legendary African Americans Ser.). 96p. (J). (gr. 6-12). pap. 10.95 *(978-0-7660-6281-8(3))* Enslow Pubs., Inc.

Rubin, Susan Goldman. Freedom Summer: The 1964 Struggle for Civil Rights in Mississippi. (ENG.). 144p. (J). 2016. 14.95 *(978-0-8234-3557-9(1))* 2014. (Illus.). (gr. 5). 18.95 *(978-0-8234-2920-2(2))* Holiday Hse., Inc.

Ruiz, Rachel. When Rosa Parks Went Fishing. Fedele, Chiara, illus. 2017. (Leaders Doing Headstands Ser.). (ENG.). 32p. (gr. 2-3). lib. bdg. 27.99 ***(978-1-5158-1574-7(9))*** Picture Window Bks.

Rustad, Martha E. H. & Leslie, Tonya. Martin Luther King, Jr: A Life of Fairness. 2007. (People of Character Ser.). (ENG., Illus.). 24p. (J). (gr. 2-5). lib. bdg. 25.95 *(978-1-60014-090-7(4))* Bellwether Media.

Saddleback Educational Publishing Staff, ed. Martin Luther King Jr., 1 vol. unabr. ed. 2008. (Graphic Biographies Ser.). (ENG., Illus.). 25p. (YA). (gr. 9-12). pap. 7.95 *(978-1-59905-227-4(X))* Saddleback Educational Publishing, Inc.

Sapet, Kerrily. John Lewis. 2009. (Political Profiles Ser.). 100p. (YA). (gr. 5-9). 28.95 *(978-1-59935-130-8(7))* Reynolds, Morgan Inc.

Schraff, Anne E. Ida B. Wells-Barnett: Strike a Blow Against Glaring Evil. 2008. (African-American Biography Library). (Illus.). 128p. (J). (gr. 6-18). lib. bdg. 33.27 *(978-0-7660-2704-6(X))* Enslow Pubs., Inc.

—Rosa Parks: Tired of Giving In. 2005. (African-American Biography Library). (Illus.). 128p. (J). (gr. 6-12). lib. bdg. 33.27 *(978-0-7660-2463-2(6))* Enslow Pubs., Inc.

Schuldt, Lori Meek. Martin Luther King, Jr: With Profiles of Mohandas K. Gandhi & Nelson Mandela. 2006. (Biographical Connections Ser.). (Illus.). 112p. (J). *(978-0-7166-1822-5(2))* World Bk., Inc.

Schuman, Michael A. The Life of Martin Luther King, Jr: Leader for Civil Rights. 2014. (Legendary African Americans Ser.). (Illus.). 96p. (J). (gr. 6-12). 27.94 *(978-0-7660-6147-7(7))* Enslow Pubs., Inc.

Schuman, Michael A. & Schraff, Anne E. Martin Luther King Jr: Fighting for Civil Rights. 2017. (Rebels with a Cause Ser.). 128p. (gr. 8-8). lib. bdg. 37.27 ***(978-0-7660-8511-4(2))*** Enslow Pubs., Inc.

Shange, Ntozake. Coretta Scott. Nelson, Kadir, illus. (ENG.). 32p. (J). (gr. -1-4). 2011. pap. 6.99 *(978-0-06-125366-9(9))* 2009. 17.99 *(978-0-06-125364-5(2))* HarperCollins Pubs. (Tegen, Katherine Bks).

Shea, Therese. Rosa Parks, 1 vol. 2015. (ENG., Illus.). 32p. (J). 23.45 *(978-1-62275-697-1(5),* Britannica Educational Publishing) Rosen Publishing Group, Inc., The.

Shone, Rob. Rosa Parks: The Life of a Civil Rights Heroine. Spender, Nick, illus. 2007. (Graphic Nonfiction Biographies Ser.). (ENG.). 48p. (J). (gr. 4-7). lib. bdg. 31.95 *(978-1-4042-0864-3(X))* Rosen Publishing Group, Inc., The.

—Rosa Parks: The Life of a Civil Rights Heroine. Spender, Nik, illus. 2007. (Graphic Biographies Ser.). (ENG.). 48p. (gr. 5-8). pap. 14.05 *(978-1-4042-0927-5(1))* Rosen Publishing Group, Inc., The.

Spilsbury, Richard. Who Marched for Civil Rights?, 1 vol. HL Studios Staff, illus. 2014. (Primary Source Detectives Ser.). (ENG.). 64p. (gr. 7-8). lib. bdg. 35.99 *(978-1-4329-9604-8(5))* Heinemann-Raintree.

Staley, Erin. Martin Luther King Jr. & the Speech That Inspired the World. 2014. (Celebration of the Civil Rights Movement Ser.). 80p. (YA). (gr. 7-12). 34.25 *(978-1-4777-7745-9(8))* Rosen Publishing Group, Inc., The.

Stamper, G. C. Nelson Mandela. 2005. (Illus.). 32p. (J). pap. *(978-0-7367-2922-2(4))* Zaner-Bloser, Inc.

Stille, Darlene R. Eleanor Roosevelt: First Lady & Civil Rights Activist, 1 vol. Sprunger, Reed, illus. 2013. (Beginner Biographies Set 2 Ser.). (ENG.). 32p. (J). (gr. -1-4). 28.50 *(978-1-61641-941-7(5))* Magic Wagon.

Stotts, Stuart. Father Groppi: Marching for Civil Rights. 2013. (Badger Biographies Ser.). (ENG., Illus.). 160p. (J). pap. 12.95 *(978-0-87020-575-0(7))* Wisconsin Historical Society.

Summer, L. S. Rosa Parks. 2009. (Journey to Freedom Ser.). (ENG., Illus.). 32p. (J). (gr. 4-7). 29.93 *(978-1-60253-133-8(1),* 200399) Child's World, Inc., The.

Taylor-Butler, Christine. Rosa Parks. 2015. (ENG., Illus.). 48p. (J). pap. 6.95 *(978-0-531-21209-7(2),* Orchard Bks.) Scholastic Library Publishing.

Tieck, Sarah. Rosa Parks, 1 vol. 2006. (Buddy Book Ser.). (ENG., Illus.). 32p. (gr. -1-3). 27.07 *(978-1-59679-788-8(6),* Buddy Bks.) ABDO Publishing Co.

Time for Kids Editors. Rosa Parks: Civil Rights Pioneer. 2006. (Time for Kids Ser.). (ENG., Illus.). 48p. (J). (gr. 2-4). pap. 3.99 *(978-0-06-057624-0(3),* Collins) HarperCollins Pubs.

—Rosa Parks: Civil Rights Pioneer. 2007. (Time for Kids Biographies Ser.). (Illus.). 44p. (gr. 2-4). 14.00 *(978-0-7569-8110-5(7))* Perfection Learning Corp.

Tisdale, Rachel. The Freedom Riders, 1 vol., 1. 2014. (We Shall Overcome Ser.). (ENG.). 32p. (J). (gr. 3-6). 26.25 *(978-1-4777-6061-1(X),* PowerKids Pr.) Rosen Publishing Group, Inc., The.

Uschan, Michael V. James Foreman & SNCC. Greenhaven Press Staff, ed. 2013. (Lucent Library of Black History Ser.). (ENG., Illus.). 128p. (J). (gr. 7-10). lib. bdg. 39.40 *(978-1-4205-0920-5(9),* Lucent Bks.) Cengage Gale.

Vietze, Andrew. The Life & Death of Malcolm X. 2017. (J). pap. ***(978-1-5383-8031-4(5),*** Rosen Young Adult) Rosen Publishing Group, Inc., The.

—The Life & Death of Martin Luther King Jr. 2017. (J). ***(978-1-5383-8038-3(2));*** pap. ***(978-1-5383-8039-0(0))*** Rosen Publishing Group, Inc., The.

Wallace, Rich. Blood Brother: Jonathan Daniels & His Sacrifice for Civil Rights. 2016. (ENG., Illus.). 352p. (J). (gr. 4). 18.95 *(978-1-62979-094-7(X),* Calkins Creek) Boyds Mills Pr.

Ward, Jill. Martin Luther King, Jr: Georgia, My State Biographies. l.t. ed. 2008. (ENG., Illus.). 24p. (J). (gr. k-2). 22.60 *(978-1-935077-01-5(5));* pap. 22.60 *(978-1-935077-08-4(2))* State Standards Publishing, LLC.

Warren, Nagueyalti. Grandfather of Black Studies: W.E.B. du Bois. 2011. (J). *(978-1-59221-821-9(0));* (ENG., Illus.). 258p. pap. *(978-1-59221-822-6(9))* Africa World Pr.

Watkins, Angela Farris. My Uncle Martin's Big Heart. Velasquez, Eric, illus. 2010. (ENG.). 32p. (J). (gr. k-2). 19.95 *(978-0-8109-8975-7(1),* Abrams Bks. for Young Readers) Abrams, Inc.

Waxman, Laura Hamilton. Coretta Scott King. 2008. pap. 52.95 *(978-0-8225-9387-4(4));* (ENG., Illus.). 48p. (gr. 3-6). lib. bdg. 27.93 *(978-0-8225-7168-1(4),* Lerner Pubns.) Lerner Publishing Group.

Weakland, Mark. When Martin Luther King Jr. Wore Roller Skates. Ballesteros, Patrick, illus. 2017. 31p. (J). *(978-1-5158-0141-2(1))* 2016. (ENG.). 32p. (gr. 2-3). lib. bdg. 27.99 *(978-1-4795-9685-0(X))* Picture Window Bks.

Weidt, Maryann N. Rosa Parks. (History Maker Bios Ser.). (Illus.). (J). 2004. 48p. pap. 8.95 *(978-0-8225-4805-8(4))* 2003. 47p. 26.60 *(978-0-8225-4673-3(6))* Lerner Publishing Group. (Lerner Pubns.).

Weston Woods Staff, creator. Martin's Big Words. 2011. 18.95 *(978-0-545-15251-8(8));* 38.75 *(978-0-545-15256-3(9))* Weston Woods Studios, Inc.

—Rosa. 2011. 18.95 *(978-0-545-14962-4(2));* 38.75 *(978-0-545-14963-1(0))* Weston Woods Studios, Inc.

Wheeler, Jill C. Rosa Parks, Set II. 2003. (Breaking Barriers Ser.). 64p. (gr. 3-8). 27.07 *(978-1-57765-640-1(7),* Abdo & Daughters) ABDO Publishing Co.

Wittrock, Jeni. W. E. B. du Bois. 2014. (Great African-Americans Ser.). (ENG., Illus.). 24p. (gr. k-1). lib. bdg. 21.99 *(978-1-4914-0505-5(8),* Pebble Bks.) Capstone Press of Coughlan Cos.

Woll, Kris. Nelson Mandela: South African President & Civil Rights Activist, 1 vol. 2014. (Newsmakers Ser.). (ENG., Illus.). 48p. (J). (gr. 3-6). lib. bdg. 32.79 *(978-1-62403-643-9(0))* ABDO Publishing Co.

Zullo, Allan. 10 True Tales: Young Civil Rights Heroes. 2014. (10 True Tales Ser.). (ENG.). 192p. (J). (gr. 3-7). pap. 5.99 *(978-0-545-76974-7(4))* Scholastic, Inc.

CIVIL SERVICE

Here are entered general works on the history and development of public service. Works on public personnel administration, including the duties of civil service employees, their salaries, pensions, etc., are entered under the name of the country, state or city with the subdivision Officials and Employees.

see also names of countries, cities, etc. with the subdivision Officials and Employees, e.g. United States—Officials and Employees

Dawson, Emily C. Town Leaders. 2010. (My Community Ser.). 24p. (J). 25.65 *(978-1-60753-025-1(2))* Amicus Publishing.

Ginyard, John. What Is the Job of a Corrections Officer? 2006. (YA). per. 6.95 *(978-1-59094-113-3(6))* Jawbone Publishing Corp.

Hernandez, Daniel. They Call Me a Hero: A Memoir of My Youth. 2013. (ENG., Illus.). 240p. (YA). (gr. 7). 17.99 *(978-1-4424-6228-1(0),* Simon & Schuster Bks. For Young Readers) Simon & Schuster Bks. For Young Readers.

Kishel, Ann-Marie. Government Services. 2007. (First Step Nonfiction - Government Ser.). (ENG., Illus.). 24p. (gr. k-2). lib. bdg. 23.93 *(978-0-8225-6397-6(5),* Lerner Pubns.) Lerner Publishing Group.

Marsico, Katie. Working at a Bank. 2008. (21st Century Junior Library: Careers Ser.). (ENG.). 24p. (gr. 2-5). lib. bdg. 25.64 *(978-1-60279-270-8(4),* 200175) Cherry Lake Publishing.

Monroe Peterson, Judy. Who Are Community Workers? 2017. (Let's Find Out! Communities Ser.). 32p. (J). (gr. 6-8). 24.45 ***(978-1-68048-739-8(6));*** pap. 12.90 ***(978-1-68048-737-4(X))*** Rosen Publishing Group, Inc., The. (Britannica Educational Publishing).

Randolph, Joanne. Dennis Tito: First Space Tourist. 2009. (Reading Room Collection 2 Ser.). 24p. (gr. 3-4). 42.50 *(978-1-60851-962-0(7),* PowerKids Pr.) Rosen Publishing Group, Inc., The.

Ruffin, David C. The Duties & Responsibilities of the Secretary of Health & Human Services. 2009. (Your Government in Action Ser.). 32p. (gr. 3-3). 43.90 *(978-1-60854-917-7(8),* PowerKids Pr.) Rosen Publishing Group, Inc., The.

Sullivan, Laura L. Sir Henry Morgan. 2015. (J). lib. bdg. *(978-1-62713-308-1(9))* Cavendish Square Publishing.

Zamosky, Lisa. Government Leaders Then & Now, 1 vol. 2006. (Primary Source Readers Ser.). (ENG.). 32p. (J). (gr. 2-2). pap. 8.99 *(978-0-7439-9386-9(1))* Shell Educational Publishing.

CIVIL WAR, GREAT BRITAIN, 1642-1649

see Great Britain—History—Puritan Revolution, 1642-1660

CIVIL WAR, U. S., 1861-1865

see United States—History—Civil War, 1861-1865

CIVILIZATION

see also Anthropology; Archaeology; Art; Bronze Age; Culture; Education; Ethics; Ethnology; Industries; Inventions; Learning and Scholarship; Manners and Customs; Religions; Science and Civilization; Social Problems; Technology and Civilization

also names of countries, states, etc. with the subdivision Civilization, e.g. United States—Civilization

Ahmad, Iftikhar. World Cultures: A Global Mosaic, 8 vols, l.t. ed. 2004. 2467p. (YA). (gr. 6-9). 1236.00 *(978-0-13-036895-9(4),* A-L00012-00) Prentice Hall Pr.

Ancient Cultures & Civilizations. 2016. (Ancient Cultures & Civilizations Ser.). 32p. (gr. 5-5). 157.50 *(978-1-4994-2247-4(4));* pap. 60.00 *(978-1-5081-5247-7(0))* Rosen Publishing Group, Inc., The. (PowerKids Pr.).

Anglo-Saxons. 2016. (Ladybird Histories Ser.). (ENG., Illus.). 64p. (J). (gr. 2-4). pap. 9.99 *(978-0-7232-9442-9(9))* Penguin Bks., Ltd. GBR. Dist: Independent Pubs. Group.

Barter, James. The Ancient Persians. 2005. (Lost Civilizations Ser.). (Illus.). 112p. (J). (gr. 4-7). lib. bdg. 29.95 *(978-1-59018-621-3(4),* Lucent Bks.) Cengage Gale.

Benchmark Education Company, LLC Staff, compiled by. One World, Many Cultures: Theme Set. 2006. (J). 240.00 *(978-1-4108-7066-7(9))* Benchmark Education Co.

—World Cultures: Theme Set. 2006. (J). 215.00 *(978-1-4108-7129-9(0))* Benchmark Education Co.

Bingham, Jane. Vikings. 2017. (Explore! Ser.). (ENG., Illus.). 32p. (J). (gr. 4-6). pap. 12.99 ***(978-0-7502-9737-0(9),*** Wayland) Hachette Children's Group GBR. Dist: Hachette Bk. Group.

Burncrot, Curt & Dunlap, Shiree. Testing Targets: For Streams of Civilization. Zyp, Nicole, ed. 2004. 19p. (YA). (gr. 9-12). pap. 5.00 *(978-1-888786-43-9(4))* Basic Skills Assessment & Educational Services.

—Testing Targets: For Streams of Civilization, Vol. 2. Zyp, Nikki & Robinson, Heidi, eds. 2004. 20p. (YA). (gr. 9-12). pap. 5.00 *(978-1-888786-45-3(0))* Basic Skills Assessment & Educational Services.

Butterfield, Moira. Anglo-Saxons. 2017. (Britain in the Past Ser.). (ENG., Illus.). 32p. (J). (gr. 4-6). pap. 12.99 ***(978-1-4451-4062-9(4),*** Franklin Watts) Hachette Children's Group GBR. Dist: Hachette Bk. Group.

—Art & Culture. 2017. (Discover the Anglo-Saxons Ser.). (ENG., Illus.). 32p. (J). (gr. 4-6). pap. 11.99 *(978-1-4451-3343-0(1),* Franklin Watts) Hachette Children's Group GBR. Dist: Hachette Bk. Group.

—Everyday Life. 2016. (ENG., Illus.). 32p. (J). (gr. 2-4). 17.99 *(978-1-4451-4815-1(3),* Franklin Watts) Hachette Children's Group GBR. Dist: Hachette Bk. Group.

—Warriors & Weapons. 2016. (ENG., Illus.). 32p. (J). (gr. 2-4). 17.99 *(978-1-4451-4816-8(1),* Franklin Watts) Hachette Children's Group GBR. Dist: Hachette Bk. Group.

Ceceri, Kathy. World Myths & Legends: 25 Projects You Can Build Yourself. Braley, Shawn, illus. 2010. (Build It Yourself Ser.). (ENG.). 128p. (J). (gr. 3-7). pap. 15.95 *(978-1-934670-43-9(X))* Octavio Publishing.

Challen, Paul. Hail! Hail! Ancient Chinese. 2010. (ENG.). 32p. (J). *(978-0-7787-6621-6(7));* pap. *(978-0-7787-6628-5(4))* Crabtree Publishing Co.

Chambers, Catherine. African Culture, 1 vol. 2012. (Global Cultures Ser.). (ENG.). 48p. (gr. 4-6). pap. 9.95 *(978-1-4329-6785-7(1));* 32.65 *(978-1-4329-6776-5(2))* Heinemann-Raintree. (NA-h).

Chelsea House Publishing Staff. Journey into Civilization Set. (Illus.). (J). (gr. 3-7). pap. 79.50 *(978-0-7910-3773-7(8),* Chelsea Hse.) Facts On File, Inc.

Christopher, Nick. What Makes a Civilization? 2013. (Rosen Readers Ser.). (ENG.). 24p. (J). (gr. 3-4). pap. 8.25 *(978-1-4777-2557-3(1));* pap. 49.50 *(978-1-4777-2558-0(X))* Rosen Publishing Group, Inc., The. (Rosen Classroom).

Clements, J. M. Vikings. 2012. (Illus.). 205p. (J). *(978-1-4351-4591-7(7))* Metro Bks.

Cline, Eric H. & Rubalcaba, Jill. Digging for Troy: From Homer to Hisarlik. Brannen, Sarah S., illus. 2011. (ENG.). 80p. (J). (gr. 4-7). 17.95 *(978-1-58089-326-8(0));* pap. 9.95 *(978-1-58089-327-5(9))* Charlesbridge Publishing, Inc.

Corrick, James A. The Rough, Stormy Age of Vikings: The Disgusting Details about Viking Life, 1 vol. 2010. (Disgusting History Ser.). (ENG.). 32p. (gr. 3-4). lib. bdg. 27.32 *(978-1-4296-5405-0(8),* Fact Finders) Capstone Press of Coughlan Cos.

Covert, Kim, et al. Great Civilizations. 2011. (Great Civilizations Ser.). (ENG.). 32p. (gr. 3-4). pap. 24.30 *(978-1-4296-7241-2(2),* Fact Finders) Capstone Press of Coughlan Cos.

Cultural Atlas for Young People, 8 vols., Set. 3rd ed. Incl. Africa. 3rd rev. ed. Murray, Jocelyn. 35.00 *(978-0-8160-6826-5(7));* Ancient China. Allan, Tony. 35.00 *(978-0-8160-6827-2(5));* Ancient Egypt. 3rd rev. ed. Harris, Geraldine. 35.00 *(978-0-8160-6823-4(2));* Ancient Greece. 3rd rev. ed. Powell, Anton. 35.00 *(978-0-8160-6821-0(6));* Ancient Maya & Aztec Civilization. 3rd rev. ed. Mitchell, Peter. 35.00 *(978-0-8160-6820-3(8));* Ancient Mesopotamia. 3rd rev. ed. Hunter, Erica C. D. 35.00 *(978-0-8160-6824-1(0));* Ancient Rome. 3rd rev. ed. Corbishley, Mike. 35.00 *(978-0-8160-6822-7(4));* Middle Ages. 3rd rev. ed. Corbishley, Mike. 35.00 *(978-0-8160-6825-8(9));* (YA). (gr. 5-9). 2007. (Cultural Atlas for Young People Ser.). (Illus.). 96p. 2007. 280.00 *(978-0-8160-7218-7(3),* Chelsea Hse.) Facts On File, Inc.

Cultures of the World - Group 17, 6 vols. Incl. Bangladesh. Whyte, Mariam. (gr. 5-12). 1999. lib. bdg. 37.07 *(978-0-7614-0869-7(X));* Czech Republic. Sioras, Efstathia. (gr. 5-12). 1999. lib. bdg. 37.07 *(978-0-7614-0870-3(3));* Democratic Republic of the Congo. Heale, Jay. (gr. 5-12). 1999. lib. bdg. 37.07 *(978-0-7614-0874-1(6));* Kuwait. O'Shea, Maria. (gr. 5-12). 1999. lib. bdg. 37.07 *(978-0-7614-0871-0(1));* Senegal. Berg, Elizabeth. (gr. 5-12). 1999. lib. bdg. 37.07 *(978-0-7614-0872-7(X));* Uruguay. Jermyn, Leslie. (J). (gr. k-17). 1998. lib. bdg. 37.07 *(978-0-7614-0873-4(8));* 128p. (Illus.). 222.43 *(978-0-7614-0868-0(1),* Benchmark Bks.) Marshall Cavendish Corp.

Cultures of the World - Group 19, 6 vols. Incl. Cote d'Ivoire. Sheehan, Patricia. lib. bdg. 37.07 *(978-0-7614-0980-9(7));* Uganda. Barlas, Robert. lib. bdg. 37.07 *(978-0-7614-0981-6(5));* 128p. (gr. 5-12). 2000. (Illus.). 222.43 *(978-0-7614-0975-5(0),* Benchmark Bks.) Marshall Cavendish Corp.

Cultures of the World - Group 20, 6 vols. Incl. Fiji. NgCheong-Lum, Roseline. lib. bdg. 37.07 *(978-0-7614-0996-0(3));* Guyana. Jermyn, Leslie. lib. bdg. 37.07 *(978-0-7614-0994-6(7));* 128p. (gr. 5-12). 2000. (Illus.). 222.43 *(978-0-7614-0991-5(2),* Benchmark Bks.) Marshall Cavendish Corp.

Deady, Kathleen W. & Dubois, Muriel L. Ancient China: Beyond the Great Wall. 2011. (Great Civilizations Ser.). (ENG.). 32p. (gr. 3-4). pap. 47.70 *(978-1-4296-7234-4(X),* Fact Finders) Capstone Press of Coughlan Cos.

Dillard, Sheri. Viking Warriors. 2015. (Ancient Warriors Ser.). (ENG.). 32p. (J). (gr. 2-5). 28.50 *(978-1-63143-761-8(5),* 208593) Child's World, Inc., The.

Doeden, Matt. The Chinese: Life in China's Golden Age. Hiti, Sam, illus. 2009. (Life in Ancient Civilizations Ser.). (ENG.). 48p. (gr. 3-6). lib. bdg. 29.27 *(978-0-8225-8681-4(9),* Millbrook Pr.) Lerner Publishing Group.

Dorling Kindersley Publishing Staff. Children Just Like Me. 2016. (ENG., Illus.). 80p. (J). (gr. 2-5). 19.99 *(978-1-4654-5392-1(X),* DK Children) Dorling Kindersley Publishing, Inc.

Dowling, Lucy. Why Why Why... Were Vikings So Fierce? 2010. (Why Why Why Ser.). 32p. (YA). (gr. 1-3). lib. bdg. 18.95 *(978-1-4222-1591-3(1))* Mason Crest.

Dubois, Muriel L., et al. Great Civilizations. 2011. (Great Civilizations Ser.). (ENG.). 32p. (gr. 3-4). pap. 190.80 *(978-1-4296-7242-9(0));* lib. bdg. 81.96 *(978-1-4296-6833-0(4))* Capstone Press of Coughlan Cos. (Fact Finders).

C D

Exploring World Cultures. 2015. (Exploring World Cultures Ser.). (ENG.). 32p. (J). (gr. 3-4). 171.00 *(978-1-5026-0376-0(4))* Cavendish Square Publishing.
Farndon, John. A History of Civilization Illustrated History Encyclopedia: The Great Landmarks in the Development of Mankind. 2006. (Illus.). 256p. (gr. 7-10). reprint ed. pap. 22.00 *(978-1-4223-5514-5(4))* DIANE Publishing Co.
The First Humans & Early Civilizations. 2016. (First Humans & Early Civilizations Ser.). 64p. (gr. 6-6). 172.25 *(978-1-4777-8552-2(3))*; pap. 64.75 *(978-1-4994-6423-8(1))* Rosen Publishing Group, Inc., The. (Rosen Young Adult).
Flatt, Lizann. Early Islamic Empires. 2013. (Life in the Early Islamic World Ser.). (ENG., Illus.). 48p. (J). pap. *(978-0-7787-2178-9(7))* Crabtree Publishing Co.
Gagne, Tammy. The Celts of the British Isles. 2012. (Explore Ancient Worlds Ser.). (Illus.). 48p. (J). (gr. 3-6). lib. bdg. 29.95 *(978-1-61228-283-1(0))* Mitchell Lane Pubs., Inc.
Grant, Neil. Everyday Life of the Vikings. 2005. (Uncovering History Ser.). (Illus.). 46p. (J). (gr. 6-9). lib. bdg. 29.95 *(978-1-58340-706-5(5))* Black Rabbit Bks.
Gray, Nigel. A Country Far Away. Philippe, Dupasquier, illus. 2012. 32p. pap. *(978-0-9808760-2-4(8))* Vivid Publishing.
Green, Jen. Ancient Celts: Archaeology Unlocks the Secrets of the Celts' Past. 2008. (National Geographic Investigates Ser.). (ENG., Illus.). 64p. (J). (gr. 5). lib. bdg. 27.90 *(978-1-4263-0226-8(6))*, National Geographic Children's Bks.) National Geographic Society.
Green, Jen & National Geographic Kids Staff. Ancient Celts: Archaeology Unlocks the Secrets of the Celts' Past. 2008. (National Geographic Investigates Ser.). (ENG., Illus.). 64p. (J). (gr. 5). 17.95 *(978-1-4263-0225-1(8))*, National Geographic Children's Bks.) National Geographic Society.
Hale, Vincent, ed. Mesopotamian Gods & Goddesses, 1 vol., 1. 2014. (Gods & Goddesses of Mythology Ser.). (ENG.). 112p. (YA). (gr. 7-12). 32.90 *(978-1-62275-161-7(2))* Rosen Publishing Group, Inc., The.
Harrell, Nancy. Ninos de el Mundo/ Children of the World. 2008. 60p. pap. 23.99 *(978-1-4389-4202-5(8))* AuthorHouse.
Hawes, Alison. What the Romans Did for the World. 2010. (Crabtree Connections Ser.). (ENG.). 24p. (J). (gr. 3-6). *(978-0-7787-9943-6(3))*; pap. *(978-0-7787-9965-8(4))* Crabtree Publishing Co.
Haywood, John. Home, Family & Everyday Life Through the Ages: Compare the Food, Homes & Daily Lives of Ancient People from All the Major Civilizations. 2008. (ENG., Illus.). 64p. (J). (gr. 4-7). pap. 12.99 *(978-1-84476-602-4(0))* Anness Publishing GBR. Dist: National Bk. Network.
Helgren. People, Places & Change: The Western World. 5th ed. 2005. (Holt People, Places, & Change: an Introduction to World Studies). (ENG., Illus.). 600p. (gr. 8-8). pap. 84.05 *(978-0-03-037643-6(2))* Houghton Mifflin Harcourt Publishing Co.
History Channel, History & Steinberg, Don. Ancient Aliens. 2015. (ENG., Illus.). 112p. (J). (gr. 3-7). 19.99 *(978-1-62672-064-0(9))*, 9781626720640) Roaring Brook Pr.
—The Young Investigator's Guide to Ancient Aliens. 2015. (ENG., Illus.). 112p. (J). (gr. 3-7). pap. 14.99 *(978-1-62672-063-3(0))*, 9781626720633) Roaring Brook Pr.
Housel, Debra J. World Cultures Through Time, 1 vol. rev. ed. 2007. (Leveled Texts). (ENG., Illus.). 144p. (gr. 4-12). 39.99 *(978-1-4258-0083-3(1))* Shell Educational Publishing.
Hunter, Nick. Ancient Treasures, 1 vol. 2013. (Treasure Hunters Ser.). (ENG., Illus.). 48p. (gr. 5-8). pap. 9.25 *(978-1-4109-4957-8(5))*; lib. bdg. 29.99 *(978-1-4109-4950-9(8))* Heinemann-Raintree.
Husain, Shahrukh. The Vikings. 2005. (Stories from Ancient Civilizations Ser.). (Illus.). 32p. (J). (gr. 4-18). lib. bdg. 27.10 *(978-1-58340-621-2(2))*, 1236428) Black Rabbit Bks.
Hynson, Colin. How People Lived in Viking Times. 2008. (How People Lived Ser.). (Illus.). 30p. (J). lib. bdg. 26.50 *(978-1-4042-4434-4(4))*, PowerKids Pr.) Rosen Publishing Group, Inc., The.
James Baldwin. Fifty Famous Stories Retold. 2009. (Illus.). 132p. pap. 5.95 *(978-1-60386-206-6(4))*, Merchant Bks.) Rough Draft Printing.
Jupo, Frank. Time to Spare: The Story of Man's Leisure Hours. 2011. 66p. 36.95 *(978-1-258-07710-5(8))* Literary Licensing, LLC.
Kalman, Bobbie. We Are the Earth. 2009. (Our Multicultural World Ser.). (ENG., Illus.). 32p. (J). (gr. 1-4). pap. *(978-0-7787-4649-2(6))* Crabtree Publishing Co.
Krieg, Katherine. What We Get from Greek Mythology. 2015. (21st Century Skills Library: Mythology & Culture Ser.). (ENG., Illus.). 32p. (J). (gr. 3-6). 29.93 *(978-1-63188-913-4(3))*, 205976) Cherry Lake Publishing.
—What We Get from Norse Mythology. 2015. (21st Century Skills Library: Mythology & Culture Ser.). (ENG., Illus.). 32p. (J). (gr. 3-6). 29.93 *(978-1-63188-914-1(1))*, 205980) Cherry Lake Publishing.
Lasseter, Rollin, ed. History: All Ye Lands. (Illus.). 360p. (J). (gr. 6). 55.00 *(978-0-89870-944-5(X))* Ignatius Pr.
MacLeod, Elizabeth, et al. A History of Just about Everything: 180 Events, People & Inventions That Changed the World. Leng, Qin, illus. 2013. (ENG.). 124p. (J). (gr. 3-7). 21.95 *(978-1-55453-775-4(4))* Kids Can Pr., Ltd. CAN. Dist: Hachette Bk. Group.
Marsico, Katie. What We Get from Celtic Mythology. 2015. (21st Century Skills Library: Mythology & Culture Ser.). (ENG.). 32p. (J). (gr. 3-6). 29.93 *(978-1-63188-910-3(9))*, 205964) Cherry Lake Publishing.
Miles, John C. Everyday Life, Art & Culture. 2016. (Discover the Vikings Ser.). (ENG., Illus.). 32p. (J). (gr. 2-4). 17.99 *(978-1-4451-4887-8(0))*, Franklin Watts) Hachette Children's Group GBR. Dist: Hachette Bk. Group.
Millard, Anne & Millard, Anne. Misterios de las Civilizaciones Perdidas. (Coleccion Misterios De). (SPA., Illus.). 48p. (YA). (gr. 5-8). 19.95 *(978-84-348-5638-7(7))*, SM5948) SM Ediciones ESP. Dist: AIMS International Bks., Inc., Lectorum Pubns., Inc.
Mincks, Margaret. What We Get from Roman Mythology. 2015. (21st Century Skills Library: Mythology & Culture Ser.). (ENG., Illus.). 32p. (J). (gr. 3-6). pap. 14.21 *(978-1-63188-931-8(1))*, 205985) Cherry Lake Publishing.
National Geographic Editors. 1001 Inventions & Awesome Facts from Muslim Civilization. 2012. (ENG., Illus.). 96p. (J). (gr. 3-7). 14.95 *(978-1-4263-1258-8(X))*, National Geographic Children's Bks.) National Geographic Society.
O'Donnell, Kerri. The Ancient Civilizations of Greece & Rome: Solving Algebraic Equations. (PowerMath Ser.). 32p. (gr. 5-6). 2009. (ENG.). pap. 10.00 *(978-1-4042-5123-6(5))*, PowerKids Pr.) 2005. (Illus.). (YA). lib. bdg. 25.25 *(978-1-4042-2930-3(2))* Rosen Publishing Group, Inc., The.
—The Ancient Civilizations of Greece & Rome: Solving Algebraic Equations Big Book. 2005. (Math for the REAL World Ser.). (J). pap. 39.95 *(978-1-4042-5292-9(4))*, Rosen Classroom) Rosen Publishing Group, Inc., The.
—The Ancient Civilizations of Greece & Rome: Solving Algebraic Equations (Big Book) 2005. (Math for the REAL World Ser.). 32p. 47.50 *(978-1-4042-5222-6(3))*, Rosen Classroom) Rosen Publishing Group, Inc., The.
Owings, Lisa. What We Get from Egyptian Mythology. 2015. (21st Century Skills Library: Mythology & Culture Ser.). (ENG., Illus.). 32p. (J). (gr. 3-6). pap. 14.21 *(978-1-63188-928-8(1))*, 205973) Cherry Lake Publishing.
Phipps, Liza & Thompson, Avril. Vikings. 2017. (History Showtime Ser.). (ENG., Illus.). 32p. (J). (gr. 2-4). pap. 11.99 *(978-1-4451-1487-3(9))*, Franklin Watts) Hachette Children's Group GBR. Dist: Hachette Bk. Group.
Powell, Jillian. The Vikings. 2010. (Gruesome Truth about Ser.). (ENG.). 32p. (J). (gr. 4-6). lib. bdg. 22.60 *(978-1-61533-221-2(9))* Windmill Bks.
Reid, Struan. Hands-on History Projects: Art & Craft. 2008. (ENG., Illus.). 64p. (J). (gr. 4-7). pap. 7.99 *(978-1-84476-618-5(7))* Anness Publishing GBR. Dist: National Bk. Network.
Richards, Jon. Art, Culture, & Sports. 2016. (Mapographica Ser.). (ENG., Illus.). 32p. (J). (gr. 3-6). *(978-0-7787-2655-5(X))* Crabtree Publishing Co.
Richardson, Hazel. Life of the Ancient Celts. 2005. (Peoples of the Ancient World Ser.). (ENG., Illus.). 32p. (J). (gr. -1-7). pap. *(978-0-7787-2075-1(6))*; lib. bdg. *(978-0-7787-2045-4(4))* Crabtree Publishing Co.
—Life of the Ancient Vikings. 2005. (Peoples of the Ancient World Ser.). (ENG., Illus.). 32p. (J). (gr. -1-9). pap. *(978-0-7787-2074-4(8))*; lib. bdg. *(978-0-7787-2044-7(6))* Crabtree Publishing Co.
Romero, Libby. Discover People. 2006. (J). pap. *(978-1-4108-6485-7(5))* Benchmark Education Co.
Rossi, Ann. Two Cultures Meet - Native American & European. 2006. (Language, Literacy, & Vocabulary - Reading Expeditions Ser.). (ENG., Illus.). 40p. (J). pap. 19.95 *(978-0-7922-8679-0(0))* CENGAGE Learning.
Rustad, Martha E. H. & Hiti, Samuel. The Babylonians: Life in Ancient Babylon. 2009. (Life in Ancient Civilizations Ser.). (Illus.). 48p. (J). (gr. 3-6). lib. bdg. 29.27 *(978-0-8225-8682-1(7))*, Millbrook Pr.) Lerner Publishing Group.
Samuels, Charlie. Timeline of the Muslim World. 2010. (History Highlights: A Gareth Stevens Timeline Ser.). (Illus.). 48p. (gr. 6-8). (J). pap. 14.05 *(978-1-4339-3490-2(6))*; (YA). lib. bdg. 31.95 *(978-1-4339-3489-6(2))* Stevens, Gareth Publishing LLLP. (Gareth Stevens Secondary Library).
Schomp, Virginia. The Ancient Mesopotamians. 2008. (Myths of the World Ser.). 96p. (gr. 6-18). lib. bdg. 34.21 *(978-0-7614-3095-7(4))*, Benchmark Bks.) Marshall Cavendish Corp.
Smith, Daniel. World Cultures Explained, 1 vol. 2015. (ENG.). 136p. (J). 38.25 *(978-1-4777-8130-2(7))*, Rosen Young Adult) Rosen Publishing Group, Inc., The.
Steele, Philip. The Chinese Empire. 2009. (Passport to the Past Ser.). (Illus.). 64p. (YA). (gr. 5-8). lib. bdg. 31.95 *(978-1-4358-5174-0(9))* Rosen Publishing Group, Inc., The.
Thompson, Ben. The Vikings. (Guts & Glory Ser.: 2). (ENG., Illus.). 320p. (J). (gr. 3-7). 2016. pap. 6.99 *(978-0-316-32057-3(9))* 2015. 17.00 *(978-0-316-32056-6(0))* Little, Brown Bks. for Young Readers.
Ticktock Media, Ltd. Staff. Civilizations: The History of the Ancient World. 2009. (ENG.). 128p. (J). (gr. 4-7). pap. 12.95 *(978-1-84696-831-0(3))*, TickTock Books) Octopus Publishing Group GBR. Dist: Independent Pubs. Group.
Toth, Henrietta. Viking Explorers. 2016. (Spotlight on Explorers & Colonization Ser.). 48p. (J). (gr. 6-6). pap. 11.75 *(978-1-4777-8832-5(8))* Rosen Publishing Group, Inc., The.
The Vikings. 2014. (Ladybird Histories Ser.). (ENG., Illus.). 64p. (J). (gr. 2-4). 13.99 ***(978-0-7232-8841-1(0))*** Penguin Bks., Ltd. GBR. Dist: Independent Pubs. Group.
Wayland Publishers & Bingham, Jane. Vikings. 2017. (Explore! Ser.). (ENG., Illus.). 32p. (J). (gr. 4-6). 17.99 *(978-0-7502-9548-2(1))*, Wayland) Hachette Children's Group GBR. Dist: Hachette Bk. Group.
Wildwood, Gretchen. Ancient Mesopotamian Civilization. Cantucci, Alessandro & Morandi, Andrea, illus. 2009. (Ancient Civilizations & Their Myths & Legends Ser.). (YA). (gr. 5-9). lib. bdg. 29.25 *(978-1-4042-8037-3(5))* Rosen Publishing Group, Inc., The.
Williams, Brian. How We Live. 2010. (What About... Ser.). (Illus.). 40p. (J). (gr. 6-8). lib. bdg. 19.95 *(978-1-4222-1560-9(1))* Mason Crest.
—What about How We Live. 2008. 40p. pap. *(978-1-84810-069-5(8))* Miles Kelly Publishing, Ltd.
Zenescope Entertainment Staff, et al. Mankind Vol. 1: The Story of All of Us. 2012. (ENG., Illus.). 120p. (J). pap. 14.99 *(978-1-937068-68-4(4))*, 9781937068684) Zenescope Entertainment.
—Mankind Vol. 2: The Story of All of Us. 2012. (ENG., Illus.). 120p. (J). pap. 14.99 *(978-1-937068-69-1(2))*, 9781937068691) Zenescope Entertainment.
Zimmerman, Larry J. Exploring the Life, Myth, & Art of Native Americans. 2009. (Civilizations of the World Ser.). (YA). (gr. 7-12). lib. bdg. 42.60 *(978-1-4358-5614-1(7))* Rosen Publishing Group, Inc., The.

CIVILIZATION, AMERICAN

see America—Civilization; United States—Civilization

CIVILIZATION, ANCIENT

see also Prehistoric Peoples

Abdo. Ancient Civilizations, 1 vol. 2014. (Ancient Civilizations Ser.: 8). (ENG.). 112p. (J). (gr. 6-12). lib. bdg. 285.12 *(978-1-62403-534-0(5))*, Essential Library) ABDO Publishing Co.
Ancient Civilizations. 2005. (Ancient Civilizations Ser.). (Illus.). 32p. (gr. 4-6). 224.00 *(978-0-7910-9089-3(2))*, Chelsea Clubhouse) Facts On File, Inc.
Ancient Civilizations: Egypt, Greece, & Rome. 2004. (Primary Source Big Bookstm Ser.). 24p. (gr. 4-8). 43.95 *(978-0-8239-4590-0(1))* Rosen Publishing Group, Inc., The.
Ancient Civilizations Classroom Library. (gr. 2-5). lib. bdg. 22.95 *(978-0-7368-4552-6(6))* Red Brick Learning.
Ancient Civilizations Complete Unit. 2004. (Early Civilizations Ser.). (ENG., Illus.). 48p. (gr. 3-4). pap. 190.80 *(978-0-7368-4551-9(8))* Capstone Press of Coughlan Cos.
Anderson, Zachary. Ancient Civilizations of Western Asia & the Mediterranean: From the Hittites to the Phoenicians. 2015. (Exploring the Ancient & Medieval Worlds Ser.). (ENG., Illus.). 160p. (J). (gr. 8-8). 45.64 *(978-1-5026-0568-9(6))* Cavendish Square Publishing.
—The Origins of Civilization: From Early Humans to the Babylonians. 2015. (Exploring the Ancient & Medieval Worlds Ser.). (ENG., Illus.). 160p. (J). (gr. 8-8). 45.64 *(978-1-5026-0566-5(X))* Cavendish Square Publishing.
Antram, David, illus. You Wouldn't Want To... Ancient Civilization, 4 bks., Set. Incl. Assyrian Soldier! An Ancient Army You'd Rather Not Join. Matthews, Rupert. (gr. 2-5). 29.00 *(978-0-531-18727-2(6))*; Be a Sumerian Slave! A Life of Hard Labor You'd Rather Avoid. Morley, Jacqueline. (gr. 4-7). 29.00 *(978-0-531-18728-9(4))*, Watts, Franklin); Tutankhamen! A Mummy Who Really Got Meddled With. Stewart, David. (gr. 2-5). 29.00 *(978-0-531-18725-8(X))*; You Wouldn't Want to Be Cleopatra! An Egyptian Ruler You'D Rather Not Be. Pipe, Jim. (gr. 2-5). 29.00 *(978-0-531-18726-5(8))*, Watts, Franklin); (Illus.). 32p. (J). 2007. 114.00 o.p. *(978-0-531-17738-9(6))*, Watts, Franklin) Scholastic Library Publishing.
AZ Books Staff. Ancient Asia. Kazimirova, Karina & Snezhana, Ivinskaya, eds. 2012. (Mysteries of History Ser.). (ENG.). 18p. (J). (gr. 1-3). bds. 17.95 *(978-1-61889-091-7(3))* AZ Bks. LLC.
—Ancient Egypt. Ulasevich, Olga, ed. 2012. (Mysteries of History Ser.). (ENG.). 18p. (J). (gr. 1-3). bds. 17.95 *(978-1-61889-092-4(1))* AZ Bks. LLC.
—Ancient Rome. Naumovets, Elena & Svistunova, Natalia, eds. 2012. (Mysteries of History Ser.). (ENG.). 18p. (J). (gr. 1-3). bds. 17.95 *(978-1-61889-090-0(5))* AZ Bks. LLC.
Bahn, Paul. Ancient Civilizations Explained, 1 vol., 1. 2014. (Guide for Curious Minds Ser.). (ENG.). 136p. (YA). (gr. 7-12). 38.25 *(978-1-4777-2975-5(5))* Rosen Publishing Group, Inc., The.
Barber, Nicola. Lost Cities, 1 vol. 2013. (Treasure Hunters Ser.). (ENG., Illus.). 48p. (gr. 5-8). pap. 9.25 *(978-1-4109-4959-2(1))*; lib. bdg. 29.99 *(978-1-4109-4952-3(4))* Heinemann-Raintree.
—Tomb Explorers, 1 vol. 2013. (Treasure Hunters Ser.). (ENG.). 48p. (gr. 5-8). pap. 9.25 *(978-1-4109-4962-2(1))*; lib. bdg. 29.99 *(978-1-4109-4955-4(9))* Heinemann-Raintree.
The Beginning of Civilization in Sumer: The Advent of Written Communication. (YA). (gr. 6-9). spiral bd., tchr.'s planning gde. ed. 11.50 *(978-0-382-40978-3(7))* Cobblestone Publishing Co.
Bell, Michael & Quie, Sarah. Ancient Egyptian Civilization. D'Ottavi, Francesca, illus. 2009. (Ancient Civilizations & Their Myths & Legends Ser.). 48p. (YA). (gr. 5-9). lib. bdg. 29.25 *(978-1-4042-8034-2(0))* Rosen Publishing Group, Inc., The.
Benchmark Education Company, LLC Staff, compiled by. Ancient Civilization. 2005. (English Explorers Ser.). (J). spiral bd. 265.00 *(978-1-4108-5772-9(7))* Benchmark Education Co.
—Ancient Civilizations. 2006. spiral bd. 330.00 *(978-1-4108-7012-4(X))* Benchmark Education Co.
—Ancient Civilizations: Theme Set. 2006. (J). 183.00 *(978-1-4108-7140-4(1))* Benchmark Education Co.
—Early River Civilizations. 2006. spiral bd. 330.00 *(978-1-4108-7011-7(1))* 2005. (J). spiral bd. 265.00 *(978-1-4108-5773-6(5))* Benchmark Education Co.
—Early River Civilizations: Theme Set. 2006. (J). 183.00 *(978-1-4108-7139-8(8))* Benchmark Education Co.
—Social Studies Theme: Ancient Civilizations. 2005. spiral bd. 115.00 *(978-1-4108-5327-1(6))* Benchmark Education Co.
—Social Studies Theme: Early River Civilizations. 2005. spiral bd. 115.00 *(978-1-4108-5325-7(X))* Benchmark Education Co.
Biography from Ancient Civilizations, 6 Bks, Set. (Illus.). (gr. 4-8). lib. bdg. *(978-1-58415-320-7(2))* Mitchell Lane Pubs., Inc.
Biography from Ancient Civilizations: Legends, Folklore, & Stories of Ancient Worlds, 28 vols., Set. Incl. Life & Times of Aristotle. Whiting, Jim. (Illus.). 48p. (gr. 3-7). 2006. lib. bdg. 29.95 *(978-1-58415-508-9(6))*; Life & Times of Cicero. Tracy, Kathleen. (Illus.). 48p. (gr. 4-8). 2006. lib. bdg. 29.95 *(978-1-58415-510-2(8))*; Life & Times of Herodotus. Whiting, Jim. (Illus.). 48p. (gr. 3-7). 2006. lib. bdg. 29.95 *(978-1-58415-509-6(4))*; Life & Times of Hippocrates. Whiting, Jim. (Illus.). 48p. (gr. 3-7). 2006. lib. bdg. 29.95 *(978-1-58415-512-6(4))*, 1259600); Life & Times of King Arthur: The Evolution of the Legend. Harkins, Susan & Harkins, William H. (Illus.). 48p. (gr. 3-7). 2006. lib. bdg. 29.95 *(978-1-58415-513-3(2))*; Life & Times of Nostradamus. Roberts, Russell. (Illus.). 48p. (gr. 4-8). 2007. lib. bdg. 29.95 *(978-1-58415-544-7(2))*; Life & Times of Plato. Whiting, Jim. (Illus.). 48p. (gr. 3-7). 2006. lib. bdg. 29.95 *(978-1-58415-507-2(8))*, 1259591); Life & Times of Pythagoras. Harkins, Susan Sales & Harkins, William H. (Illus.). 48p. (gr. 4-8). 2007. lib. bdg. 29.95 *(978-1-58415-545-4(0))*; Set. (gr. 4-8). 2005. lib. bdg. *(978-1-58415-407-5(1))*; (J). (Biography from Ancient Civilizations Ser.). 2007. Set lib. bdg. 838.60 *(978-1-58415-546-1(9))* Mitchell Lane Pubs., Inc.
Bow, James. Hidden Worlds. 2013. (ENG., Illus.). 32p. (J). *(978-0-7787-1124-7(2))*; pap. *(978-0-7787-1128-5(5))* Crabtree Publishing Co.
Brooks, Philip. Ancient Civilizations: How People Lived Around the World & Through the Ages. 2016. (ENG., Illus.). 64p. (J). (gr. -1-12). 12.99 *(978-1-86147-695-1(7))*, Armadillo) Anness Publishing GBR. Dist: National Bk. Network.
—The Story of Ancient Civilizations. 2010. (Journey Through History Ser.). (ENG.). 64p. (YA). lib. bdg. 31.95 *(978-1-4488-0624-9(0))*, Rosen Reference) Rosen Publishing Group, Inc., The.
Brooks, Phillip. Exploring History: Ancient Civilizations. 2008. (ENG., Illus.). 64p. (J). (gr. 4-7). pap. 12.99 *(978-1-84476-493-8(1))* Anness Publishing GBR. Dist: National Bk. Network.
Burrell, Carol M. Scavella. Did Greek Soldiers Really Hide Inside the Trojan Horse? And Other Questions about the Ancient World. 2010. (Is That a Fact? Ser.). (ENG.). 40p. (gr. 4-6). lib. bdg. 26.60 *(978-0-7613-4912-9(X))* Lerner Publishing Group.
Clarke, Penny. The Story of Mummies. 2013. (Illus.). 63p. (J). *(978-1-4351-5032-4(5))* Barnes & Noble, Inc.
Coletti, Sharon. Everything You Need to Teach Ancient Civilizations. 2005. (YA). ring bd. 149.95 *(978-1-933558-10-3(5))* InspirEd Educators.
Collins. Collins Fascinating Facts - Amazing Places. rev. ed. 2016. (Collins Fascinating Facts Ser.). (ENG.). 72p. (J). (gr. 1-3). pap. 10.99 *(978-0-00-816919-0(5))* HarperCollins Pubs. Ltd. GBR. Dist: Independent Pubs. Group.
Collinson, Clare. The Ancient & Classical World 500 BC to AD 600. 2010. (CC: Atlas of World History Ser.). 112p. (gr. 6-12). 42.80 *(978-1-933834-66-5(8))* Brown Bear Bks.
—The First Civilizations to 500 BC. 2010. (CC: Atlas of World History Ser.). 112p. (gr. 6-12). 42.80 *(978-1-933834-65-8(X))* Brown Bear Bks.
Cottrell, George. Ancient Greece. 2017. (Unlocking Ancient Civilizations Ser.). (J). (gr. 4-5). 32p. pap. 10.50 ***(978-1-5345-2029-5(5))***; pap. 63.00 ***(978-1-5345-2030-1(9))***; 32p. lib. bdg. 27.25 ***(978-1-5345-2031-8(7))*** Greenhaven Publishing LLC. (KidHaven Publishing).
Croy, Anita. Exploring the Past. 2010. (Invisible Worlds Ser.). 48p. (gr. 4). 28.50 *(978-0-7614-4194-6(8))* Marshall Cavendish GBR. Dist: Marshall Cavendish Corp.
Culp, Jennifer. Ancient Chinese Technology. 2016. (Spotlight on the Rise & Fall of Ancient Civilizations Ser.). 48p. (J). (gr. 6-6). pap. 11.75 *(978-1-4777-8897-4(2))* Rosen Publishing Group, Inc., The.
Discovering Ancient Civilizations. 2016. (Discovering Ancient Civilizations Ser.). 32p. (gr. 3-3). pap. 63.00 *(978-1-4824-5319-5(3))*; lib. bdg. 159.60 *(978-1-4824-4973-0(0))* Stevens, Gareth Publishing LLLP.
Discovery Education. 2013. (Discovery Education Ser.). 32p. (J). (gr. 3-6). 1035.25 *(978-1-4777-1555-0(X))*; pap. 2460.00 *(978-1-4777-2737-9(X))*; pap. 410.00 *(978-1-4777-2736-2(1))* Rosen Publishing Group, Inc., The. (PowerKids Pr.).
Dixon, Darla, illus. What Really Happened in Ancient Times: A Collection of Historical Biographies, 4. 2007. (What Really Happened Ser.). 240p. per. 15.95 *(978-1-932786-21-7(X))* Knowledge Quest.
Doeden, Matt. Tools & Treasures of the Ancient Maya. 2014. (Searchlight Books: What Can We Learn from Early Civilizations? Ser.). (ENG., Illus.). 40p. (gr. 3-5). lib. bdg. 27.93 *(978-1-4677-1431-0(3))*, Lerner Pubns.) Lerner Publishing Group.
Dorling Kindersley Publishing Staff & Fullman, Joseph. Ancient Civilizations. 2013. (DK Eyewitness Bks.). (ENG.). 72p. (J). (gr. 3-7). 16.99 *(978-1-4654-0887-7(8))*, DK Children) Dorling Kindersley Publishing, Inc.
Ellermeyer, Deborah & Rowell, Judy. Ancient Civilizations Reader's Theater Vol. 2246: Develop Reading Fluency & Text Comprehension Skills. Hults, Alaska, ed. Hillam, Corbin & Vangsgard, Amy, illus. 2004. 96p. (J). pap. 12.99 *(978-1-59198-041-4(0))*, 2246) Creative Teaching Pr., Inc.
Evan-Moor. History Pockets: Ancient Civilizations, Grades 1-3. 2003. (ENG., Illus.). 96p. (J). (gr. 1-3). pap., suppl. ed. 14.99 *(978-1-55799-900-9(7))*, EMC 3701) Evan-Moor Educational Pubs.
Foley, E., et al. Cultures of the World: Group 10, 6 vols. 2nd rev. ed. 2005. (Cultures of the World 10 Ser.). (Illus.). 144p. (gr. 6-18). lib. bdg. 256.74 *(978-0-7614-2023-1(1))*, Benchmark Bks.) Marshall Cavendish Corp.
Ganeri, Anita. Ancient Egypt: The Complete Homework Solution. 2010. (Study Buddies Ser.). (ENG.). 32p. (J). (gr. 4-7). pap. 6.95 *(978-1-84898-183-6(X))*, TickTock Books) Octopus Publishing Group GBR. Dist: Independent Pubs. Group.
Ganeri, Anita & West, David. The Curse of King Tut's Tomb & Other Ancient Discoveries. 2011. (Incredible True Adventures Ser.). (ENG.). 48p. (YA). (gr. 5-8). pap. 11.75 *(978-1-4488-6661-8(8))*; lib. bdg. 29.25 *(978-1-4488-6657-1(X))* Rosen Publishing Group, Inc., The.
Gray, Susan H. Scholastic News Nonfiction Readers: Prehistoric World, 6 bks., Set. Incl. Dinosaur Armor. 22.00 *(978-0-531-17481-4(6))*; Dinosaur Dig! 22.00 *(978-0-531-17482-1(4))*; Dinosaur Eggs. 22.00 *(978-0-531-17483-8(2))*; Dinosaur Teeth. 22.00 *(978-0-531-17484-5(0))*; Dinosaur Tracks. 22.00 *(978-0-531-17485-2(9))*; (Illus.). 24p. (J). (gr. 1-2). 2007. 114.00 o.p. *(978-0-531-12605-9(6))*, Children's Pr.) Scholastic Library Publishing.
Halstead, Rachel & Reid, Struan. Everyday Life in the Ancient World: Learn about Houses, Homes & What the Romans, Celts, Egyptians & Other Peoples of the Past Used to Eat. 2009. (ENG., Illus.). 64p. (J). (gr. 4-7). pap. 7.99 *(978-1-84476-711-3(6))* Anness Publishing GBR. Dist: National Bk. Network.
Harcourt School Publishers Staff. Horizons with Ancient Civilizations. 4th ed. 2004. (gr. 3). 53.20 *(978-0-15-344221-6(2))* Harcourt Schl. Pubs.
—Horizons with Ancient Civilizations, Grade 3. 4th ed. 2004. Vol. 1. tchr. ed. 104.40 *(978-0-15-344222-3(0))* Vol. 2. tchr. ed. 104.40 *(978-0-15-344223-0(9))* Harcourt Schl. Pubs.
HarrisNic. EMPIRE: RISE AND FALL LOW INTERMEDIATE BOOK WITH ONLINE ACCESS. 2014. (ENG., Illus.). 24p. (J). pap. 9.50 *(978-1-107-62844-1(X))* Cambridge Univ. Pr.
Harrison, Paul. Uncovering Mummies & Other Mysteries of the Ancient World. 2010. (Extreme! Ser.). (ENG.). 32p. (gr. 3-4). pap. 47.70 *(978-1-4296-5117-2(2))*, Fact Finders) Capstone Press of Coughlan Cos.
Hattstein, Markus. Prehistory, First Empires, & the Ancient World: From the Stone Age to 900 CE. 2012. (Witness to History: A Visual Chronicle of the World Ser.). (ENG., Illus.). 200p. (J). (gr. 7-12). 46.50 *(978-1-4488-7222-0(7))* Rosen Publishing Group, Inc., The.
Haywood, John. Through the Ages: Gods, Beliefs & Ceremonies. 2008. (ENG., Illus.). 64p. (J). (gr. 4-7). pap. 12.99 *(978-1-84476-601-7(2))* Anness Publishing GBR. Dist: National Bk. Network.

Haywood, John, ed. The Illustrated History Encyclopedia Everyday Life in the Ancient World: How People Lived & Worked Through the Ages. 2015. (ENG., Illus.). 256p. pap. 13.99 *(978-1-86147-457-5(1),* Armadillo) Anness Publishing GBR. Dist: National Bk. Network.

Hibbert, Adam. World Wonders. 2010. (Unpredictable Nature Ser.). 48p. (J). (gr. 3-18). lib. bdg. 19.95 *(978-1-4222-2008-5(7))* Mason Crest.

Hile, Lori, et al. Daily Life In... 2015. (Daily Life in Ancient Civilizations Ser.). (ENG.). 48p. (gr. 3-6). pap. 44.95 *(978-1-4846-2584-2(6),* Heinemann InfoSearch) Heinemann-Raintree.

Holm, Kirsten C. Everyday Life in the Maya Civilization. 2012. (Jr. Graphic Ancient Civilizations Ser.). (ENG.). 24p. (J). (gr. 3-6). pap. 10.60 *(978-1-4488-6393-8(7));* lib. bdg. 25.25 *(978-1-4488-6217-7(5))* Rosen Publishing Group, Inc., The.

Howell, Izzi & Martin, Claudia. The Indus Valley. 2017. (Explore! Ser.). (ENG., Illus.). 32p. (J). (gr. 4-6). 16.99 ***(978-1-5263-0086-7(9),*** Wayland) Hachette Children's Group GBR. Dist: Hachette Bk. Group.

Hunter, Nick, et al. Hero Journals. 2013. (Hero Journals). (ENG.). 48p. (gr. 4-6). 199.92 *(978-1-4109-5362-9(9));* pap. 53.94 *(978-1-4109-5369-8(6))* Heinemann-Raintree. (NA-r).

Hurdman, Charlotte, et al. Living History: What Life Was Like in Ancient Times. 2011. (ENG., Illus.). 512p. (J). (gr. -1-12). 17.99 *(978-1-84322-937-7(4))* Anness Publishing GBR. Dist: National Bk. Network.

Hyde, Natalie. History Mysteries Revealed. 2010. (ENG., Illus.). 32p. (J). pap. *(978-0-7787-7429-7(5));* (gr. 4-7). lib. bdg. *(978-0-7787-7414-3(7))* Crabtree Publishing Co.

Hynson, Colin. Ancient Rome: The Complete Homework Solution. 2010. (Study Buddies Ser.). (ENG.). 32p. (J). (gr. 4-7). pap. 6.95 *(978-1-84898-182-9(1),* TickTock Books) Octopus Publishing Group GBR. Dist: Independent Pubs. Group.

Kemp, Ellwood W. Streams of History: Ancient Rome (Yesterday's Classics) 2008. 104p. per. 7.95 *(978-1-59915-256-1(8))* Yesterday's Classics.

Life in Ancient Civilizations, 6 vols., Set. Incl. Aztecs: Life in Tenochtitlan. Doeden, Matt. Hiti, Samuel, illus. lib. bdg. 29.27 *(978-0-8225-8684-5(3),* Millbrook Pr.); Babylonians: Life in Ancient Babylon. Rustad, Martha E. H. & Hiti, Samuel. (J). lib. bdg. 29.27 *(978-0-8225-8682-1(7),* Millbrook Pr.); Chinese: Life in China's Golden Age. Doeden, Matt. Hiti, Sam, illus. lib. bdg. 29.27 *(978-0-8225-8681-4(9),* Millbrook Pr.); Greeks: Life in Ancient Greece. Levine, Michelle. Hiti, Samuel, illus. lib. bdg. 29.27 *(978-0-8225-8680-7(0),* Lerner Pubns.); Romans: Life in Ancient Rome. Sonnebom, Liz. Hiti, Samuel, illus. lib. bdg. 29.27 *(978-0-8225-8679-1(7),* Millbrook Pr.); 48p. (gr. 3-6). 2009. Set lib. bdg. 175.62 *(978-0-8225-8678-4(9),* Millbrook Pr.) Lerner Publishing Group.

Macdonald, Fiona, et al. The Incredible Ancient History Book Box: Includes Fascinating Facts, 120 Step-by-Step Projects & over 3000 Amazing Pictures, 8 vols. 2012. (ENG., Illus.). 64p. (J). (gr. 3-7). pap. 20.00 *(978-1-84322-800-4(9))* Anness Publishing GBR. Dist: National Bk. Network.

Maloy, Jackie. The Ancient Maya. (True Book(tm), a — Ancient Civilizations Ser.). (ENG.). 48p. (J). 2009. (gr. 2-5). 31.00 *(978-0-531-25229-1(9))* 2010. (Illus.). (gr. 3-5). pap. 6.95 *(978-0-531-24110-3(6))* Scholastic Library Publishing.

Marks, Anthony & Tingay, Graham. Romans - Internet Linked. 2005. (Illustrated World History Ser.). 96p. (J). pap. 12.95 *(978-0-7945-0429-8(9),* Usborne) EDC Publishing.

Marsh, Carole. Ancient Civilizations - Common Core Lessons & Activities. 2015. (Common Core Ser.). (ENG.). (J). pap. 4.99 *(978-0-635-11986-5(2))* Gallopade International.

Matthews, Rupert & Van Pelt, Todd. Ancient Chinese Civilization. D'Ottavi, Francesca, illus. 2009. (Ancient Civilizations & Their Myths & Legends Ser.). 48p. (J). (gr. 5-9). lib. bdg. 29.25 *(978-1-4042-8035-9(9))* Rosen Publishing Group, Inc., The.

Merrill, Yvonne Y. Ancient People: Art Activities about Mesopotamia, Egypt, & Islam. Simpson, Mary, illus. 2003. (Hands-on Ser.). (ENG.). 88p. (J). (gr. 4-7). pap. 20.00 *(978-0-9643177-8-9(8))* KK.

Morris, Neil. Ancient World. 2003. (Knowledge Masters Ser.). (Illus.). 32p. (YA). pap. incl. cd-rom *(978-1-903954-49-2(5),* Pavilion Children's Books) Pavilion Bks.

—The Atlas of Ancient Civilizations. De Luca, Daniela, illus. 2008. (ENG.). 28p. (J). (gr. -1-3). 17.95 *(978-88-900466-0-5(0))* McRae Bks. Srl ITA. Dist: Independent Pubs. Group.

—Lost Cities. 2009. (Amazing History Ser.). (Illus.). 32p. (J). (gr. 4-7). pap. 7.95 *(978-1-59920-209-9(3))* Black Rabbit Bks.

Nardo, Don. Daily Life in Ancient Civilizations. 2015. (Daily Life in Ancient Civilizations Ser.). (ENG.). 48p. (gr. 3-6). lib. bdg. 133.28 *(978-1-4846-0832-6(1),* Heinemann InfoSearch) Heinemann-Raintree.

—Early River Civilizations. 2011. (World History Ser.). (Illus.). 112p. (J). 28.95 *(978-1-59935-140-7(4))* Reynolds, Morgan Inc.

Nelson, Jo. Historium. Wilkinson, Richard, illus. 2015. (Welcome to the Museum Ser.). (ENG.). 112p. (J). (gr. 3-7). 35.00 *(978-0-7636-7984-2(4),* Big Picture Press) Candlewick Pr.

Niver, Heather Moore. Archaeology: Excavating Our Past. 2014. (Study of Science Ser.). 160p. (YA). (gr. 7-12). 35.25 *(978-1-62275-403-8(4))* Rosen Publishing Group, Inc., The.

O'Donnell, Kerri. The Ancient Civilizations of Greece & Rome: Solving Algebraic Equations. 2009. (PowerMath: Proficiency Plus Ser.). 32p. (gr. 4-5). 47.90 *(978-1-60851-417-5(X),* PowerKids Pr.) Rosen Publishing Group, Inc., The.

Park, Louise. Ancient Cities. 2013. (Discovery Education: Ancient Civilizations Ser.). (ENG., Illus.). 32p. (J). (gr. 3-6). pap. 10.00 *(978-1-4777-0097-6(8));* lib. bdg. 25.25 *(978-1-4777-0056-3(0))* Rosen Publishing Group, Inc., The.

Passport to the Past, 8 vols., Set. Incl. Ancient Egypt. Steele, Philip. 64p. (J). (gr. 4-7). lib. bdg. 31.95 *(978-1-4358-5173-3(0));* Ancient Greece. Tames, Richard. 61p. (J). (gr. 4-7). lib. bdg. 31.95 *(978-1-4358-5175-7(7));* Ancient India. Ali, Daud. 64p. (YA). (gr. 4-7). lib. bdg. 31.95 *(978-1-4358-5169-6(2));* Aztec & Maya Worlds. MacDonald, Fiona. 64p. (J). (gr. 4-7). lib. bdg. 31.95 *(978-1-4358-5170-2(6));* Chinese Empire. Steele, Philip. 64p. (YA). (gr. 5-8). lib. bdg. 31.95 *(978-1-4358-5174-0(9));* Mesopotamia. Oakes, Lorna. 64p. (J). (gr. 4-7). lib. bdg. 31.95 *(978-1-4358-5172-6(2));* Roman Empire. Steele, Philip. 64p. (J). (gr. 4-7). lib. bdg. 31.95 *(978-1-4358-5176-4(5));* World of North American Indians. Stotter, Mike. 64p. (YA). (gr. 4-7). lib. bdg. 31.95 *(978-1-4358-5171-9(4));* (Illus.). 2009. Set lib. bdg. 234.00 *(978-1-4358-5215-0(X))* Rosen Publishing Group, Inc., The.

People from the Past: Level Q, 6 vols., Vol. 3. (Explorers Ser.). 32p. (gr. 3-6). 44.95 *(978-0-7699-0623-2(0))* Shortland Pubns. (U. S. A.) Inc.

Pistone, Nicholas. Art & Culture of Ancient Rome. 2010. (Ancient Art & Cultures Ser.). 40p. (YA). (gr. 5-8). lib. bdg., E-Book 53.00 *(978-1-61532-965-6(X))* Rosen Publishing Group, Inc., The.

Pistone, Nicholas, et al. Art & Culture of Ancient Rome. 2010. (Ancient Art & Cultures Ser.). (Illus.). 40p. (J). pap. 11.75 *(978-1-61532-885-7(8));* (YA). (gr. 5-8). lib. bdg. 26.50 *(978-1-4358-3591-7(3))* Rosen Publishing Group, Inc., The.

Price, Sean Stewart. The Kids' Guide to Lost Cities, 1 vol. 2011. (Kids' Guides). (ENG.). 32p. (gr. 3-4). 27.99 *(978-1-4296-6009-9(0),* Edge Bks.) Capstone Press of Coughlan Cos.

Pye, Michael & Dalley, Kirsten, eds. Ancient Secret Societies & Lost Knowledge, 01 vols., 1. 2016. (Ancient Secrets & Alien Gods Ser.). (ENG.). 224p. (YA). 38.25 *(978-1-5081-7100-3(9),* Rosen Young Adult) Rosen Publishing Group, Inc., The.

Rector, Rebecca Kraft. The Early River Valley Civilizations. 2016. (First Humans & Early Civilizations Ser.). 64p. (J). (gr. 6-6). pap. 12.95 *(978-1-4994-6326-2(X))* Rosen Publishing Group, Inc., The.

Rinaldo, Denise. Cities of the Dead: Finding Lost Civilizations. 2008. (24/7: Science Behind the Scenes Ser.). (ENG., Illus.). 64p. (J). (gr. 9-12). 29.00 *(978-0-531-12079-8(1));* pap. 7.95 *(978-0-531-18739-5(X))* Scholastic Library Publishing. (Watts, Franklin).

Rosen Publishing Staff. Exploring Ancient Civilizations, 1 vol. 2015. (Exploring Ancient Civilizations Ser.). (ENG.). 48p. (YA). 155.10 *(978-1-62275-814-2(5),* Britannica Educational Publishing) Rosen Publishing Group, Inc., The.

Samuels, Charlie. Forgotten Cities. 2012. (ENG.). 32p. (J). pap. *(978-0-7787-8012-0(0))* Crabtree Publishing Co.

—Timeline of the Classical World. 2010. (History Highlights: A Gareth Stevens Timeline Ser.). (Illus.). 48p. (gr. 6-8). (J). pap. 14.05 *(978-1-4339-3481-0(7));* (YA). lib. bdg. 31.95 *(978-1-4339-3480-3(9))* Stevens, Gareth Publishing LLLP. (Gareth Stevens Secondary Library).

Scurman, Ike & Malam, John. Ancient Roman Civilization. D'Ottavi, Francesca, illus. 2009. (Ancient Civilizations & Their Myths & Legends Ser.). 48p. (YA). (gr. 5-9). lib. bdg. 29.25 *(978-1-4042-8038-0(3))* Rosen Publishing Group, Inc., The.

Shone, Rob. Ancient Treasures. Spender, Nick, illus. 2008. (Graphic Nonfiction Ser.). (ENG.). 48p. (gr. 3-8). pap. 14.05 *(978-1-4042-9593-3(3));* (YA). (gr. 5-9). lib. bdg. 31.95 *(978-1-4042-1089-9(X))* Rosen Publishing Group, Inc., The.

Shukin, Barbara. Ancient History Portfolio: A History of First Civilizations Through the Classical Age. 2004. (Illus.). (J). ring bd. 29.95 *(978-0-9762918-0-0(0))* Homeschool Journey.

Smith, Miranda & Steele, Philip. Ancient Worlds: A Thrilling Adventure Through the Ancient Worlds. 2016. (Navigators Ser.). (ENG., Illus.). 80p. (J). 15.99 *(978-0-7534-7239-2(2),* 9780753472392, Kingfisher) Roaring Brook Pr.

Somervill, Barbara A. Ancient Maya. 2012. (Ancient World Ser.). (ENG.). 112p. (J). pap. 9.95 *(978-0-531-25981-8(1));* (gr. 6-9). lib. bdg. 34.00 *(978-0-531-25181-2(0))* Scholastic Library Publishing.

Spielvogel, Jackson J., et al. World History Journey Across Time: The Early Ages, Course 1. 2004. (MS Wh Jat Early Age V-1 (ga) Ser.). (ENG., Illus.). 568p. (gr. 6-9). stu. ed. 87.56 *(978-0-07-860309-9(9),* 0078603099) McGraw-Hill Higher Education.

Spotlight on Ancient Civilizations. 2013. (Spotlight on Ancient Civilizations Ser.). 24p. (J). (gr. 3-4). (ENG.). 424.80 *(978-1-4777-1154-5(6));* pap. 891.00 *(978-1-4777-2692-1(6));* pap. 148.50 *(978-1-4777-2691-4(8))* Rosen Publishing Group, Inc., The. (PowerKids Pr.).

Spotlight on the Rise & Fall of Ancient Civilizations. 2016. (Spotlight on the Rise & Fall of Ancient Civilizations Ser.). 48p. (gr. 6-6). 571.50 *(978-1-4777-8959-9(6),* Rosen Young Adult) Rosen Publishing Group, Inc., The.

Spotlight on the Rise & Fall of Ancient Civilizations: China. 2016. (Spotlight on the Rise & Fall of Ancient Civilizations Ser.). 48p. (gr. 6-6). 190.50 *(978-1-4777-8957-5(X));* pap. 70.50 *(978-1-4994-6415-3(0))* Rosen Publishing Group, Inc., The. (Rosen Young Adult).

Spotlight on the Rise & Fall of Ancient Civilizations: India. 2016. (Spotlight on the Rise & Fall of Ancient Civilizations Ser.). 48p. (gr. 6-6). 190.50 *(978-1-4777-8956-8(1));* pap. 70.50 *(978-1-4994-6417-7(7))* Rosen Publishing Group, Inc., The. (Rosen Young Adult).

Stern, Steven L. Wretched Ruins. 2010. (Scary Places Ser.). (Illus.). 32p. (YA). (gr. 4-7). lib. bdg. 25.27 *(978-1-936087-55-6(3))* Bearport Publishing Co., Inc.

Technology in the Ancient World. 2013. (Technology in the Ancient World Ser.). 48p. (J). (gr. 4-6). 191.70 *(978-1-4339-9686-3(3));* pap. 505.80 *(978-1-4339-9766-2(5));* pap. 84.30 *(978-1-4339-9765-5(7))* Stevens, Gareth Publishing LLLP.

Tectum, compiled by. Our Amazing World: Discover cultural sites 1, from the Unesco World Heritage, 1 vol. 2011. (ENG.). 32p. 14.95 *(978-90-79761-06-7(0))* Tectum B.V.B.A. BEL. Dist: Innovative Logistics.

Tectum Publishers Staff, compiled by. Our Amazing World: Discover cultural sites 2, from the Unesco World Heritage, 1 vol. 2011. (ENG.). 32p. 14.95 *(978-90-79761-07-4(9))* Tectum B.V.B.A. BEL. Dist: Innovative Logistics.

Van Vleet, Carmella. Seven Wonders of the World: Discover Amazing Monuments to Civilization with 20 Projects. Rizvi, Farah, illus. 2011. (Build It Yourself Ser.). (ENG.). 128p. (J). (gr. 3-7). 21.95 *(978-1-934670-82-8(0));* pap. 15.95 *(978-1-936313-73-0(1))* Open City Bks.

VanVoorst, Jennifer Fretland. The Ancient Maya, 1 vol. 2012. (Exploring the Ancient World Ser.). (ENG., Illus.). 48p. (gr. 5-6). 29.32 *(978-0-7565-4564-2(1))* Compass Point Bks.

—The Ancient Maya, 1 vol. 2012. (Exploring the Ancient World Ser.). (ENG., Illus.). 48p. (gr. 5-6). pap. 9.10 *(978-0-7565-4584-0(6))* Compass Point Bks.

von Däniken, Erich. Alien Contact in Ancient Greece, 01 vols., 1. 2016. (Ancient Secrets & Alien Gods Ser.). (ENG.). 224p. (YA). 38.25 *(978-1-5081-7103-4(3),* Rosen Young Adult) Rosen Publishing Group, Inc., The.

—Aliens of the Ancient World, 01 vols., 1. 2016. (Ancient Secrets & Alien Gods Ser.). (ENG.). 224p. (YA). 38.25 *(978-1-5081-7101-0(7),* Rosen Young Adult) Rosen Publishing Group, Inc., The.

von Daniken, Erich. The Mysterious Master Builders of the Stone Age, 01 vols., 1. 2016. (Ancient Secrets & Alien Gods Ser.). (ENG.). 224p. (YA). 38.25 *(978-1-5081-7102-7(5),* Rosen Young Adult) Rosen Publishing Group, Inc., The.

Waldron, Melanie. Geography Matters in Ancient Civilizations. 2015. (Geography Matters in Ancient Civilizations Ser.). (ENG.). 48p. (gr. 3-6). lib. bdg. 133.28 *(978-1-4846-0966-8(2),* Heinemann InfoSearch) Heinemann-Raintree.

Walker, Kathryn. Mysteries of the Ancients. 2009. (Unsolved! Ser.). (ENG., Illus.). 32p. (J). (gr. 3-5). pap. *(978-0-7787-4160-2(5));* (gr. 4-6). lib. bdg. *(978-0-7787-4147-3(8))* Crabtree Publishing Co.

Weil, Ann. The World's Most Amazing Lost Cities, 1 vol. 2011. (Landmark Top Tens Ser.). (ENG.). 32p. (gr. 3-5). pap. 8.29 *(978-1-4109-4250-0(3));* 30.65 *(978-1-4109-4239-5(2))* Heinemann-Raintree. (Raintree Perspectives).

Wood, Alix. Mummification. Wood, Alix, illus. 2013. (Illus.). 32p. (J). (gr. 4-6). 26.60 *(978-1-4339-9588-0(3));* pap. 10.50 *(978-1-4339-9589-7(1));* pap. 63.00 *(978-1-4339-9590-3(5))* Stevens, Gareth Publishing LLLP.

World Book, Inc Staff, contrib. by. The Secrets of Ancient Tombs. 2014. (J). *(978-0-7166-2661-9(6))* World Bk., Inc.

Writing in the Ancient World. (Illus.). (J). (gr. 3-6). 103.50 *(978-0-8239-7291-3(7),* Reading Power) Rosen Publishing Group, Inc., The.

York, M. J. 12 Ancient Mysteries. 2017. (Scary & Spooky Ser.). (ENG., Illus.). 32p. (J). (gr. 3-6). 21.95 *(978-1-63235-291-0(5))* Pr. Room Editions LLC.

Zumbusch, Amelie von. Ancient Roman Geography. 2013. (Spotlight on Ancient Civilizations: Rome Ser.). (ENG., Illus.). 24p. (J). (gr. 3-4). pap. 10.00 *(978-1-4777-0891-0(X),* PowerKids Pr.) Rosen Publishing Group, Inc., The.

Zumbusch, Amelie Von & Von Zumbusch, Amelie. Ancient Roman Geography. 2013. (Spotlight on Ancient Civilizations: Rome Ser.). (ENG., Illus.). 24p. (J). (gr. 3-4). 23.60 *(978-1-4777-0779-1(4),* PowerKids Pr.) Rosen Publishing Group, Inc., The.

CIVILIZATION, ARAB

Hinds, Kathryn. Life in the Medieval Muslim World, 4 bks., Set. Incl. City. lib. bdg. 34.21 *(978-0-7614-3089-6(X));* Countryside. (J). lib. bdg. 34.21 *(978-0-7614-3091-9(1));* Faith. (Illus.). lib. bdg. 34.21 *(978-0-7614-3092-6(X));* Palace. lib. bdg. 34.21 *(978-0-7614-3088-9(1));* 96p. (gr. 6-18). (Life in the Medieval Muslim World Ser.). 2008. Set lib. bdg. 136.84 *(978-0-7614-3086-5(5),* Benchmark Bks.) Marshall Cavendish Corp.

Hussain, Saima S. The Arab World Thought of It: Inventions, Innovations, & Amazing Facts. 2013. (We Thought of It Ser.). (ENG., Illus.). 48p. (J). (gr. 5-7). pap. 11.95 *(978-1-55451-476-2(2),* 9781554514762); 2nd ed. 19.95 *(978-1-55451-477-9(0),* 9781554514779) Annick Pr., Ltd. CAN. Dist: Publishers Group West (PGW).

CIVILIZATION—FICTION

Coombs, Rachel. A Year in a Castle. 2009. (Time Goes By Ser.). (ENG.). 24p. (gr. k-3). pap. 6.95 *(978-1-58013-796-6(2),* First Avenue Editions) Lerner Publishing Group.

Crew, Gary. The Viewer. Tan, Shaun, illus. 2003. (ENG.). 32p. (J). (gr. 1-6). 16.95 *(978-1-894965-02-6(7))* Simply Read Bks. CAN. Dist: Ingram Publisher Services.

Cronin, Bernie. One Step Ahead: An Adventure in Jordan. 2010. (ENG.). 52p. pap. *(978-1-84748-791-9(2))* Athena Pr.

Dehoratius. Follow Your Fates Exile of Aeneas. 2010. (Illus.). x, 113p. (J). pap. 12.00 *(978-0-86516-709-4(5))* Bolchazy-Carducci Pubs.

Driscoll, Laura. My Brother, the Knight. Smath, Jerry, illus. 2004. (Social Studies Connects). 32p. (J). (gr. 1-3). pap. 5.95 *(978-1-57565-140-8(8))* Kane Press, Inc.

Fleischman, Paul. Weslandia. braille ed. 2004. (Illus.). (J). (gr. k-3). spiral bd. *(978-0-616-01641-1(7))* Canadian National Institute for the Blind/Institut National Canadien pour les Aveugles.

—Weslandia. Hawkes, Kevin, illus. 2006. (gr. -1-3). 17.00 *(978-0-7569-6566-2(7))* Perfection Learning Corp.

Gilligan, Shannon. Struggle down Under. Burphon, S. et al, illus. 2007. (Choose Your Own Adventure Ser.: No. 21). 123p. (J). (gr. 4-7). pap. 6.99 *(978-1-933390-21-5(2))* Chooseco LLC.

Iturralde, Edna. Caminantes del Sol. Gonzalez, Santiago et al, illus. 2003. (SPA.). 163p. (J). (gr. 5-8). pap. 14.95 *(978-9978-07-431-2(7))* Santillana USA Publishing Co., Inc.

MacDonald, Beverley. Written in Blood: A Brief History of Civilisation (With All the Gory Bits Left In) Weldon, Andrew, illus. 2004. (ENG.). 216p. (J). (gr. 8-8). pap. 11.95 *(978-1-86508-792-4(0))* Allen & Unwin AUS. Dist: Independent Pubs. Group.

Mallory, Alex. Wild. 2014. (ENG.). 448p. (YA). (gr. 8). 17.99 *(978-0-06-221874-2(3),* HarperTeen) HarperCollins Pubs.

Mary-Todd, Jonathan. Pig City. 2012. (After the Dust Settled Ser.). (ENG.). 112p. (YA). (gr. 6-12). pap. 7.95 *(978-0-8225-8746-0(7),* Darby Creek); lib. bdg. 27.93 *(978-0-7613-8328-4(X))* Lerner Publishing Group.

McClure, C. R. The Legend of Papa Balloon, 1 vol. Kemen, Steven, illus. 2013. (ENG.). 40p. (J). 16.99 *(978-0-7643-4410-7(2),* 9780764344107) Schiffer Publishing, Ltd.

McCormack, Caren McNelly. The Fiesta Dress: A Quinceanera Tale, 0 vols. Aviles, Martha, illus. 2012. (ENG.). 42p. (J). (gr. k-4). pap. 7.99 *(978-0-7614-6236-1(8),* 9780761462361, Amazon Children's Publishing) Amazon Publishing.

Newton, R. H. Oceannis. 2010. pap. 16.95 *(978-0-7414-5911-4(6))* Infinity Publishing.

Page, Cecelia Frances. Adventures on Ancient Continents. 2007. 172p. per. 13.95 *(978-0-595-46358-9(4))* iUniverse, Inc.

Reformation & Enlightenment. 2004. (Stories in History Ser.). (gr. 6-12). *(978-0-618-14223-1(1),* 2-00243) Holt McDougal.

Tomkins, D. Michael. The World Below. 2006. (YA). 39.95 *(978-0-9774451-2-7(7))* DSA Publishing & Design, Inc.

CIVILIZATION, GREEK

see Greece—Civilization

CIVILIZATION—HISTORY

Bailey, Linda. Adventures in Ancient China. Slavin, Bill, illus. 2008. (Good Times Travel Agency Ser.). (ENG.). 48p. (J). (gr. 4-6). 8.95 *(978-1-55337-454-1(1))* Kids Can Pr., Ltd. CAN. Dist: Hachette Bk. Group.

Buy Sets 1, 2, And 3. 2005. (Primary Sources of World Culturestm Ser.). (Illus.). 128p. (gr. 4-8). lib. bdg. *(978-1-4042-2970-9(1))* Rosen Publishing Group, Inc., The.

Civilizations of the World, Set. 2016. (Civilizations of the World Ser.). (ENG.). 144p. (J). (gr. 8-8). lib. bdg. 270.60 *(978-1-4994-6378-1(2))* Rosen Publishing Group, Inc., The.

Corrick, James A., et al. Disgusting History: The Smelliest, Dirtiest Eras of the Past 10,000 Years. 2014. (Disgusting History Ser.). (ENG.). 240p. pap. 12.95 *(978-1-4765-7745-6(5),* Fact Finders) Capstone Press of Coughlan Cos.

Cultures of the World, Group 8. 2005. 222.43 *(978-0-7614-1844-3(X))* Marshall Cavendish Corp.

Dickmann, Nancy & Spilsbury, Louise. History Hunters. 2016. (History Hunters Ser.). (ENG.). 32p. (gr. 3-4). lib. bdg. 167.94 *(978-1-5157-2571-8(5),* Edge Bks.) Capstone Press of Coughlan Cos.

DuMont, Brianna. Fantastic Fugitives: Criminals, Cutthroats, & Slaves Who Changed History (While on the Run!) Straker, Bethany, illus. 2016. (Changed History Ser.). (ENG.). 192p. (J). (gr. 3-7). 16.99 *(978-1-63220-412-7(6),* Sky Pony Pr.) Skyhorse Publishing Co., Inc.

Faulkner, Nicholas. A Visual History of the Great Civilizations. 2016. (Visual History of the World Ser.). 00096p. (J). (gr. 8-8). 37.10 *(978-1-4994-6574-7(2))* Rosen Publishing Group, Inc., The.

Harris, Nicolas. El Libro de Saber: Civilizaciones y Conocimiento. (Coleccion Enciclopedia Ilustrada del Conocimiento).Tr. of Book of Knowledge about Civilizations. (SPA., Illus.). 64p. (J). (gr. 3-5). 7.96 *(978-84-7630-750-2(0))* Editorial Libsa, S.A. ESP. Dist: Lectorum Pubns., Inc.

Heigren. People, Places & Change: The Eastern Hemisphere. 5th ed. 2005. (Holt People, Places, & Change: an Introduction to World Studies). (ENG., Illus.). 576p. (gr. 8-8). 84.05 *(978-0-03-037573-6(8))* Houghton Mifflin Harcourt Publishing Co.

MacDonald, Fiona. History of Culture. 2004. (Culture Encyclopedia Ser.). (Illus.). 40p. (YA). (gr. 5-18). lib. bdg. 19.95 *(978-1-59084-477-9(7))* Mason Crest.

Martell, Hazel Mary, et al. The Big Book of Civilizations. 2008. (ENG.). 184p. (J). (gr. 4-18). 22.95 *(978-88-89272-96-1(1))* McRae Bks. Srl ITA. Dist: Independent Pubs. Group.

McGraw-Hill Education. Human Heritage: A World History. 3rd ed. 2005. (Merrill Human Heritage Ser.). (ENG.). (gr. 6-9). cd-rom 142.12 *(978-0-07-873136-5(4),* 0078731364) McGraw-Hill Higher Education.

McGraw-Hill Staff. Human Heritage, Spanish Reading Essentials & Study Guide, Student Edition. 2005. pap. 18.00 *(978-0-07-869627-5(5))* Glencoe/McGraw-Hill.

Moore, Christopher. From Then to Now: A Short History of the World. Krystoforski, Andrej, illus. 2011. (ENG.). 192p. (J). (gr. 5-18). 25.95 *(978-0-88776-540-7(8),* Tundra Bks.) Tundra Bks. CAN. Dist: Penguin Random Hse. LLC.

Primary Sources of World Cultures Set 3. 2005. (Illus.). 128p. (gr. 4-8). lib. bdg. 207.60 *(978-1-4042-2969-3(8))* Rosen Publishing Group, Inc., The.

Stanton, Mary & Hyma, Albert. Streams of Civilization Vol. 1: Earliest Times to the Discovery of the New World. 2007. (Illus.). 410p. (YA). (gr. 7-12). pap. 19.95 *(978-1-930367-43-2(0),* CLP79555) Christian Liberty Pr.

Stevens, Stefan. Understanding Civilizations. 2013. (InfoMax Readers Ser.). (ENG.). 24p. (J). (gr. 3-4). pap. 49.50 *(978-1-4777-2620-4(9));* pap. 8.25 *(978-1-4777-2619-8(5))* Rosen Publishing Group, Inc., The. (Rosen Classroom).

Why'd They Do That? Strange Customs of the Past. 2013. (Why'd They Do That? Strange Customs of the Past Ser.). 32p. (J). (gr. 4-6). 159.60 *(978-1-4339-9684-9(7));* pap. 378.00 *(978-1-4339-9812-6(2));* pap. 63.00 *(978-1-4339-9811-9(4))* Stevens, Gareth Publishing LLLP.

Wood, A. J. & Jolley, Mike. The Spot the Mistake: Lands of Long Ago. Castle, Frances, illus. 2017. (Spot the Mistake Ser.). (ENG.). 48p. (J). (gr. 2-5). 19.99 *(978-1-84780-964-3(2),* Wide Eyed Editions) Quarto Publishing Group UK GBR. Dist: Hachette Bk. Group.

World Book, Inc Staff, contrib. by. Explore & Learn — People in Place & Time. 2008. (J). *(978-0-7166-3020-3(6))* World Bk., Inc.

CIVILIZATION, MEDIEVAL

see also Art, Medieval; Chivalry; Feudalism; Middle Ages; Monasticism and Religious Orders

Allan, Tony, et al. Exploring the Life, Myth, & Art of the Medieval World. 2016. (Civilizations of the World Ser.). (ENG.). 144p. (J). (gr. 8-8). lib. bdg. 45.10 *(978-1-4994-6395-8(2))* Rosen Publishing Group, Inc., The.

Allen, Kathy. The Horrible, Miserable Middle Ages: The Disgusting Details about Life During Medieval. 2011. (Disgusting History Ser.). (ENG.). 32p. (gr. 3-4). pap. 47.70 *(978-1-4296-6479-0(7),* Fact Finders) Capstone Press of Coughlan Cos.

—The Horrible, Miserable Middle Ages: The Disgusting Details about Life During Medieval Times. (Disgusting History Ser.). (ENG.). 32p. (gr. 3-4). 2011. pap. 8.10 *(978-1-4296-6350-2(2))* 2010. lib. bdg. 27.32 *(978-1-4296-3958-3(X))* Capstone Press of Coughlan Cos. (Fact Finders).

Anderson, Mercedes Padrino. Cities & Towns in the Middle Ages. 2005. (World Almanac Library of the Middle Ages). (Illus.). 48p. (gr. 5-12). pap. 14.05 *(978-0-8368-5902-7(2),* Gareth Stevens Secondary Library) Stevens, Gareth Publishing LLLP.

Anderson, Mercedes Padrino & Padrino, Mercedes. Cities & Towns in the Middle Ages. 2005. (World Almanac Library of the Middle Ages). (Illus.). 48p. (gr. 5-12). lib. bdg. 31.00 *(978-0-8368-5893-8(X),* Gareth Stevens Secondary Library) Stevens, Gareth Publishing LLLP.

Anderson, Zachary. The Fall of Rome & the Rise of Constantinople. 2015. (Exploring the Ancient & Medieval Worlds Ser.). (ENG., Illus.). 160p. (J). (gr. 8-8). lib. bdg. 45.64 *(978-1-5026-0574-0(0))* Cavendish Square Publishing.

Arnold, Tedd. Castles. 2017. (Fly Guy Presents Ser.). lib. bdg. 13.55 ***(978-0-606-39716-2(7))*** Turtleback Bks.

Bailey Publishing Staff & Elgin, Kathy. The Medieval World. 2009. (Costume Source Bks). (Illus.). 32p. (gr. 6-12). 35.00 *(978-1-60413-378-3(3),* Chelsea Hse.) Facts On File, Inc.

Barter, James. A Medieval Knight. 2005. (Working Life Ser.). (ENG., Illus.). 112p. (YA). (gr. 7-10). lib. bdg. 29.95 *(978-1-59018-580-3(3),* Lucent Bks.) Cengage Gale.

Bauer, Susan Wise. The Middle Ages Vol. 2: From the Fall of Rome to the Rise of the Renaissance. 2003. (Story of the World: Vol. 2). (ENG., Illus.). 1p. 21.95 *(978-0-9714129-8-9(7));* 336p. (J). pap. 16.95 *(978-0-9714129-3-4(6),* SOTW2) Well-Trained Mind Pr.

Baum, Margaux & Hopkins, Andrea. The Lives of Women in the Middle Ages. 2016. (J). *(978-1-4994-6467-2(3))* Rosen Publishing Group, Inc., The.

Benduhn, Tea. La Edad Media. 2007. (vida en el pasado (Life Long Ago) Ser.). (SPA., Illus.). 24p. (gr. 1-4). pap. 8.15 *(978-0-8368-8040-3(4));* lib. bdg. 22.00 *(978-0-8368-8035-9(8))* Stevens, Gareth Publishing LLLP. (Weekly Reader Leveled Readers).

—The Middle Ages. 2007. (Life Long Ago Ser.). (Illus.). 24p. (gr. 1-4). pap. 8.15 *(978-0-8368-7789-2(6));* lib. bdg. 22.00 *(978-0-8368-7784-7(5))* Stevens, Gareth Publishing LLLP. (Weekly Reader Leveled Readers).

Bhote, Themina. Charlemagne: Life & Times of an Early Medieval Emperor. 2004. (Leaders of the Middle Ages Ser.). (Illus.). 112p. (YA). (gr. 5-9). lib. bdg. 34.60 *(978-1-4042-0161-3(0))* Rosen Publishing Group, Inc., The.

—Charlemagne: The Life & Times of an Early Medieval Emperor. 2009. (Leaders of the Middle Ages Ser.). 112p. (gr. 5-8). 66.50 *(978-1-61513-896-8(X),* Rosen Reference) Rosen Publishing Group, Inc., The.

Bingham, Jane. Medieval world - internet Linked. Firenze, Inklink, illus. rev. ed. 2004. 96p. (J). pap. 14.95 *(978-0-7945-0815-9(4),* Usborne) EDC Publishing.

Bodden, Valerie. Castles. 2007. (Built to Last Ser.). (Illus.). 24p. (J). (gr. 3-7). lib. bdg. 24.25 *(978-1-58341-561-0(0),* Creative Education) Creative Co., The.

Bower & Bower, Bert. History Alive! The Medieval World & Beyond. 2011. (Illus.). xiv, 505p. (J). *(978-1-58371-916-9(4))* Teachers' Curriculum Institute.

Boyer, Crispin. National Geographic Kids Everything Castles: Capture These Facts, Photos, & Fun to Be King of the Castle! 2011. (National Geographic Kids Everything Ser.). (ENG., Illus.). 64p. (J). (gr. 3-7). 25.90 *(978-1-4263-0804-8(3));* pap. 12.95 *(978-1-4263-0803-1(5))* National Geographic Society. (National Geographic Children's Bks.).

Butterfield, Moira. Knight. 2009. (Medieval Lives Ser.). (J). 32.80 *(978-1-59920-168-9(2))* Black Rabbit Bks.

Chambers, Catherine. Why Why Why... Did Knights Wear Heavy Armor? 2010. (Why Why Why Ser.). (Illus.). 32p. (J). (gr. 1-3). lib. bdg. 18.95 *(978-1-4222-1575-3(X))* Mason Crest.

Claybourne, Anna. Knight Survival Guide. 2011. (ENG.). 24p. (J). pap. *(978-0-7787-7877-6(0));* (gr. 3-6). *(978-0-7787-7855-4(X))* Crabtree Publishing Co.

Clements, Gillian. Medieval Castle. 2009. (Building History Ser.). (Illus.). 32p. (J). (gr. 3-5). 27.10 *(978-1-59771-145-6(4))* Sea-To-Sea Pubns.

Coggins, Jack. The Illustrated Book of Knights. 2006. (Dover Children's Classics Ser.). (ENG., Illus.). 112p. (J). (gr. 3-8). per. 14.95 *(978-0-486-45134-3(8))* Dover Pubns., Inc.

Coombs, Rachel. A Year in a Castle. (Time Goes By Ser.). (gr. k-3). 2009. (ENG.). pap. 39.62 *(978-0-7613-4715-6(1))* 2008. (Illus.). 24p. (J). lib. bdg. 22.60 *(978-1-58013-550-4(1))* Lerner Publishing Group.

Dargie, Richard. Knights & Castles. 2008. (Age of Castles Ser.). (Illus.). 48p. (J). (gr. 4-8). lib. bdg. 29.25 *(978-1-4042-4295-1(3),* PowerKids Pr.) Rosen Publishing Group, Inc., The.

Delaware, Steven S. Art & Culture of the Medieval World. 2010. (Ancient Art & Cultures Ser.). 40p. (YA). (gr. 5-8). lib. bdg., E-Book 53.00 *(978-1-61532-966-3(8))* Rosen Publishing Group, Inc., The.

Delaware, Steven S., et al. Art & Culture of the Medieval World. 2010. (Ancient Art & Cultures Ser.). (Illus.). 40p. (J). pap. 11.75 *(978-1-61532-887-1(4));* (YA). (gr. 5-8). lib. bdg. 26.50 *(978-1-4358-3592-4(1))* Rosen Publishing Group, Inc., The. (Rosen Reference).

Dixon, Darla, illus. What Really Happened During the Middle Ages: A Collection of Historical Biographies, 4. 2007. (What Really Happened Ser.). 222p. per. 15.95 *(978-1-932786-22-4(8))* Knowledge Quest.

Dorling Kindersley Publishing Staff. Castles & Knights. 2014. (Eye Wonder Ser.). (ENG.). 56p. (J). (gr. k-4). 10.99 *(978-1-4654-1562-2(9),* DK Children) Dorling Kindersley Publishing, Inc.

Dorling Kindersley Publishing Staff & Langley, Andrew. Medieval Life. 2011. (DK Eyewitness Bks.). (ENG.). 72p. (J). (gr. 3-7). 16.99 *(978-0-7566-7316-1(X),* DK Children) Dorling Kindersley Publishing, Inc.

Dwyer, Helen. The Middle Ages, 600 to 1492. 2010. (CC: Atlas of World History Ser.). 112p. (gr. 6-12). 42.80 *(978-1-933834-67-2(6))* Brown Bear Bks.

Eastwood, Kay. Life in a Castle. 2004. (Medieval World Ser.). (ENG., Illus.). 32p. (J). (gr. 5). pap. *(978-0-7787-1375-3(X))* Crabtree Publishing Co.

—The Life of a Knight. 2003. (Medieval World Ser.). (ENG., Illus.). 32p. (J). (gr. 5). pap. *(978-0-7787-1374-6(1))* Crabtree Publishing Co.

—Medieval Society. 2003. (Medieval World Ser.). (ENG., Illus.). 32p. (J). (gr. 5). pap. *(978-0-7787-1377-7(6))* Crabtree Publishing Co.

—Women & Girls in the Middle Ages. 2003. (Medieval World Ser.). (ENG., Illus.). 32p. (J). (gr. 5). pap. *(978-0-7787-1378-4(4))* Crabtree Publishing Co.

Elliott, Lynne. Clothing in the Middle Ages. 2004. (Medieval World Ser.). (ENG., Illus.). 32p. (J). pap. *(978-0-7787-1383-8(0))* Crabtree Publishing Co.

Firth, Rachel. Knights & Armor. Gaudenzi, Giacinto & Montgomery, Lee, illus. 2006. 95p. (J). (gr. 4-7). 17.99 *(978-0-7945-1279-8(8),* Usborne) EDC Publishing.

Foran, Racquel. Knights, 1 vol. 2013. (Great Warriors Ser.). (ENG.). 48p. (J). (gr. 3-6). lib. bdg. 32.79 *(978-1-61783-724-1(5));* (Illus.). pap. 15.64 *(978-1-61783-774-6(1),* Core Library) ABDO Publishing Co.

Galloway, Priscilla. Archers, Alchemists, & 98 Other Medieval Jobs You Might Have Loved or Loathed. Newbigging, Martha, illus. 5th ed. 2003. (Jobs in History Ser.). (ENG.). 96p. (J). (gr. 4-7). pap. 16.95 *(978-1-55037-810-8(4),* 9781550378108) Annick Pr., Ltd. CAN. Dist: Publishers Group West (PGW).

Gelfand, Dale Evva. Charlemagne. 2003. (Ancient World Leaders Ser.). (Illus.). 112p. (gr. 6-12). 30.00 *(978-0-7910-7224-0(X),* Chelsea Hse.) Facts On File, Inc.

Gigliotti, Jim. Knight Life. 2008. (Reading Rocks! Ser.). (ENG., Illus.). 32p. (J). (gr. 2-5). 28.50 *(978-1-60253-100-0(5),* 200761) Child's World, Inc., The.

Gitlin, Marty. The Totally Gross History of Medieval Europe, 01 vols., 1. 2016. (Totally Gross History Ser.). (ENG.). 48p. (J). pap. 11.75 *(978-1-4994-3764-5(1),* Rosen Central) Rosen Publishing Group, Inc., The.

Gravett, Christopher. Knight. 2015. (DK Eyewitness Bks.). (ENG., Illus.). 72p. (J). (gr. 3-7). 19.99 *(978-1-4654-3574-3(3),* DK Children) Dorling Kindersley Publishing, Inc.

—Real Knights: Over 20 True Stories of Chivalrous Deeds. James, John, illus. 2005. (ENG.). 48p. (J). (gr. 3-9). 15.95 *(978-1-59270-034-9(9))* Enchanted Lion Bks., LLC.

Gregory, Josh. If You Were a Kid in a Medieval Castle. 2017. (If You Were a Kid Ser.). (ENG.). 32p. (J). lib. bdg. 26.00 *(978-0-531-22385-7(X),* Children's Pr.) Scholastic Library Publishing.

Gunderson, Jessica. Gothic Art: Movements in Art. 2015. (Illus.). 80p. (J). *(978-1-60818-532-0(X),* Creative Education) Creative Co., The.

Guy, John. Medieval Life. 2004. (Illus.). 32p. (J). (gr. 4-7). pap. 6.95 *(978-1-86007-002-0(7),* TickTock Books) Octopus Publishing Group GBR. Dist: Independent Pubs. Group.

Hamilton, John. Knights & Heroes, 1 vol. 2006. (Fantasy & Folklore Ser.). (ENG., Illus.). 32p. (gr. 5-8). 27.07 *(978-1-59679-336-1(8),* Abdo & Daughters) ABDO Publishing Co.

Hanawalt, Barbara. The European World, 400-1450. 2006. (Illus.). 189p. 32.95 *(978-0-19-522267-8(9))* Oxford Univ. Pr., Inc.

Hanawalt, Barbara A. The European World, 400-1450. 2005. (Medieval & Early Modern World Ser.). (ENG., Illus.). 192p. (YA). 36.95 *(978-0-19-517844-9(0))* Oxford Univ. Pr., Inc.

Hanel, Rachael. Life as a Knight: An Interactive History Adventure. 2010. (You Choose: Warriors Ser.). (ENG.). 112p. (gr. 3-4). pap. 41.70 *(978-1-4296-5098-4(2),* You Choose Bks.) Capstone Press of Coughlan Cos.

Hanel, Rachael. Knights. 2007. (Fearsome Fighters Ser.). (Illus.). 48p. (J). (gr. 3-6). lib. bdg. 31.35 *(978-1-58341-536-8(X))* Creative Co., The.

Hardyman, Robyn. Horrible Jobs in Medieval Times, Vol. 1. 2014. (History's Most Horrible Jobs Ser.). 48p. (J). (gr. 5-6). (ENG.). 31.95 *(978-1-4824-0337-4(4));* pap. 14.05 *(978-1-4824-0339-8(0))* Stevens, Gareth Publishing LLLP.

Hattstein, Markus & Udelhoven, Hermann-Josef. The Middle Ages & the Early Modern Period: From the 5th Century to the 18th Century. 2012. (Witness to History: A Visual Chronicle of the World Ser.). (ENG., Illus.). 200p. (J). (gr. 7-12). 46.50 *(978-1-4488-7223-7(5))* Rosen Publishing Group, Inc., The.

Helstrom, Kraig. Knights. 2011. (History's Greatest Warriors Ser.). (ENG., Illus.). 24p. (J). (gr. 3-7). lib. bdg. 25.95 *(978-1-60014-629-9(5),* Torque Bks.) Bellwether Media.

Hinds, Kathryn. Everyday Life in Medieval Europe. 2008. (Everyday Life in... Ser.). 288p. (gr. 6-18). lib. bdg. 42.79 *(978-0-7614-3927-1(7),* Benchmark Bks.) Marshall Cavendish Corp.

—Life in the Medieval Muslim World, 4 bks., Set. Incl. City. lib. bdg. 34.21 *(978-0-7614-3089-6(X));* Countryside. (J). lib. bdg. 34.21 *(978-0-7614-3091-9(1));* Faith. (Illus.). lib. bdg. 34.21 *(978-0-7614-3092-6(X));* Palace. lib. bdg. 34.21 *(978-0-7614-3088-9(1));* 96p. (gr. 6-18). (Life in the Medieval Muslim World Ser.). 2008. Set lib. bdg. 136.84 *(978-0-7614-3086-5(5),* Benchmark Bks.) Marshall Cavendish Corp.

Hopkins, Andrea. Damsels Not in Distress: The Lives of Medieval Women. 2004. (Library of the Middle Ages Ser.). (Illus.). 64p. (YA). (gr. 5-9). lib. bdg. 31.95 *(978-0-8239-3992-3(8))* Rosen Publishing Group, Inc., The.

—Damsels Not in Distress: The True Story of Women in Medieval Times. 2009. (Library of the Middle Ages Ser.). 64p. (gr. 5-8). 58.50 *(978-1-60853-898-0(2),* Rosen Reference) Rosen Publishing Group, Inc., The.

Hull, Robert. Peasant. 2009. (Illus.). 45p. (J). 32.80 *(978-1-59920-172-6(0))* Black Rabbit Bks.

—Stonemason. 2009. (J). 32.80 *(978-1-59920-173-3(9))* Black Rabbit Bks.

Hunt, Norman Bancroft. Living in the Middle Ages. 2008. (Living in the Ancient World Ser.). (Illus.). 96p. (YA). (gr. 7-12). 35.00 *(978-0-8160-6341-3(9))* Facts On File, Inc.

Jeffrey, Gary. Crusades. 2014. (ENG., Illus.). 48p. (J). *(978-0-7787-0397-6(5))* Crabtree Publishing Co.

Jones, Molly. Medieval Knights. 2015. (Ancient Warriors Ser.). (ENG.). 32p. (J). (gr. 2-5). 28.50 *(978-1-63143-755-7(0),* 208587) Child's World, Inc., The.

Kallen, Stuart A. Life During the Crusades. 2014. (Living History Ser). (ENG., Illus.). 80p. (J). lib. bdg. *(978-1-60152-720-2(9))* ReferencePoint Pr., Inc.

Kenney, Karen Latchana. Harsh or Heroic? The Middle Ages. 2007. (Shockwave: History & Politics Ser.). (ENG., Illus.). 36p. (J). (gr. 3-5). 25.00 *(978-0-531-17754-9(8),* Children's Pr.) Scholastic Library Publishing.

Kerns, Ann. Did Castles Have Bathrooms? And Other Questions about the Middle Ages. 2010. (Is That a Fact? Ser.). (ENG.). 40p. (gr. 4-6). lib. bdg. 26.60 *(978-0-7613-4915-0(4))* Lerner Publishing Group.

Knights & Warriors. 2009. (FACT ATLAS Ser.). 72p. (J). pap. 13.99 *(978-0-8437-0859-2(X))* Hammond World Atlas Corp.

Lee, Adrienne. Knights, 1 vol. Martin, Cynthia, illus. 2013. (Legendary Warriors Ser.). (ENG.). 32p. (gr. 1-2). 26.65 *(978-1-4765-3115-1(3),* Blazers) Capstone Press of Coughlan Cos.

Lee, Brian, illus. A Castle. 2005. (What's Inside? Ser.). (J). *(978-0-7607-6568-5(5))* backpackbook.

Levy, Janey. 20 Fun Facts about Women of the Middle Ages. 2015. (Fun Fact File: Women in History Ser.). (ENG., Illus.). 32p. (J). (gr. 2-3). pap. 10.50 *(978-1-4824-2824-7(5))* Stevens, Gareth Publishing LLLP.

Life in Medieval Europe. 2016. (Life in Medieval Europe Ser.). 80p. (gr. 6-6). lib. bdg. 142.56 *(978-1-5026-1822-1(2))* Cavendish Square Publishing.

Llimós, Anna. Medieval Castle Adventure Crafts. 2010. (Fun Adventure Crafts Ser.). (Illus.). 32p. (J). pap. 7.95 *(978-0-7660-3735-9(5),* Enslow Elementary) Enslow Pubs., Inc.

Macdonald, Fiona. Do You Want to Be a Medieval Knight? 2015. (Do You Want to Be... Ser.). (Illus.). 32p. (gr. 3-6). 28.50 *(978-1-909645-35-6(4))* Book Hse. GBR. Dist: Black Rabbit Bks.

MacDonald, Fiona. Knights & Castles. 2009. (History Explorers Ser.). (ENG.). 24p. (J). (gr. k-2). pap. 5.95 *(978-1-84696-215-8(3),* TickTock Books) Octopus Publishing Group GBR. Dist: Independent Pubs. Group.

—Knights, Castles, & Warfare in the Middle Ages. 2005. (World Almanac Library of the Middle Ages). (Illus.). 48p. (gr. 5-12). lib. bdg. 31.00 *(978-0-8368-5895-2(6),* Gareth Stevens Secondary Library) Stevens, Gareth Publishing LLLP.

Macdonald, Fiona. The Medieval Chronicles: Vikings, Knights, & Castles. Antram, David, illus. 2013. 92p. (J). *(978-1-4351-5067-6(8))* Barnes & Noble, Inc.

—You Wouldn't Want to Be a Medieval Knight! Armor You'd Rather Not Wear. Antram, David, illus. 2013. (ENG.). (J). 40p. pap. 9.95 *(978-0-531-23851-6(2));* 32p. 29.00 *(978-0-531-27100-1(5))* Scholastic Library Publishing. (Watts, Franklin).

MacDonald, Fiona & Macdonald, Fiona. You Wouldn't Want to Be in a Medieval Dungeon! Prisoners You'd Rather Not Meet. Antram, David, illus. 2003. (You Wouldn't Want to Ser.). (ENG.). 32p. (J). 29.00 *(978-0-531-12312-6(X),* Watts, Franklin) Scholastic Library Publishing.

Mason, Paul. Want to Be a Knight? 2011. (ENG.). 24p. (J). pap. *(978-0-7787-7867-7(3));* (gr. 3-6). *(978-0-7787-7845-5(2))* Crabtree Publishing Co.

Matthews, Rupert. Battle at the Castle. 2014. (DK Readers Ser.). (ENG., Illus.). 32p. (J). (gr. 1-3). 14.99 *(978-1-4654-2004-6(5),* DK Children) Dorling Kindersley Publishing, Inc.

Matthews, Rupert & Dorling Kindersley Publishing Staff. Battle at the Castle. 2014. (DK Readers Ser.). (ENG., Illus.). 32p. (J). (gr. 1-3). pap. 3.99 *(978-1-4654-2005-3(3),* DK Children) Dorling Kindersley Publishing, Inc.

Miles, Liz. Meet the Medievals. 2014. (Encounters with the Past Ser.). 32p. (J). (gr. 3-6). 26.60 *(978-1-4824-0889-8(9))* Stevens, Gareth Publishing LLLP.

Murrell, Deborah Jane. Knights & Armor. 2008. (Medieval Warfare Ser.). 32p. (gr. 5-8). (J). lib. bdg. 26.00 *(978-0-8368-9210-9(0),* Gareth Stevens Secondary Library); pap. 10.50 *(978-0-8368-9337-3(9))* Stevens, Gareth Publishing LLLP.

Murrell, Deborah Jane & Dennis, Peter. Knight. 2012. (Illus.). 32p. (gr. 3-5). pap. 8.95 *(978-1-926853-54-3(7))* Saunders Bk. Co. CAN. Dist: RiverStream Publishing.

Nagle, Jeanne, ed. Feudalism, Monarchies, & Nobility. 2014. (Political & Economic Systems Ser.). 312p. (J). (gr. 9-12). 45.00 *(978-1-62275-347-5(X))* Rosen Publishing Group, Inc., The.

Nardo, Don. Medeival Europe: Medieval Europe. 2011. (World History Ser.). (gr. 7-12). 28.95 *(978-1-59935-172-8(2))* Reynolds, Morgan Inc.

Nikola-lisa, W. Till Year's Good End. Manson, Christopher, illus. 2009. (ENG.). 36p. (J). (gr. 1-4). 12.99 *(978-1-4424-0225-6(3),* Atheneum Bks. for Young Readers) Simon & Schuster Children's Publishing.

O'Brian, Pliny. Feudalism in Medieval Europe. 2015. (Exploring the Ancient & Medieval Worlds Ser.). (ENG., Illus.). 160p. (J). (gr. 8-8). lib. bdg. 45.64 *(978-1-5026-0681-5(X))* Cavendish Square Publishing.

Padrino, Mercedes. Feudalism & Village Life in the Middle Ages. 2005. (World Almanac Library of the Middle Ages). (Illus.). 48p. (gr. 5-12). lib. bdg. 31.00 *(978-0-8368-5894-5(8),* Gareth Stevens Secondary Library) Stevens, Gareth Publishing LLLP.

Park, Louise. Life in the Middle Ages. 2013. (Discovery Education: Ancient Civilizations Ser.). (ENG., Illus.). 32p. (J). (gr. 3-6). pap. 10.00 *(978-1-4777-0095-2(1));* lib. bdg. 25.25 *(978-1-4777-0055-6(2))* Rosen Publishing Group, Inc., The. (PowerKids Pr.).

Park, Louise & Love, Timothy. The Medieval Knights. 2009. (Ancient & Medieval People Ser.). 32p. (gr. 5). 28.50 *(978-0-7614-4444-2(0))* Marshall Cavendish GBR. Dist: Marshall Cavendish Corp.

Platt, Richard & Biesty, Stephen. Castle. (Illus.). 32p. (J). pap. 21.95 *(978-0-590-24346-9(2))* Scholastic, Inc.

Powell, Jillian & Buckingham, Matt. The Middle Ages. 2010. (Gruesome Truth about Ser.). (ENG.). 32p. (J). (gr. 4-6). lib. bdg. 22.60 *(978-1-61533-219-9(7))* Windmill Bks.

Pratt, Laura. Medieval Times. 2013. (Illus.). 32p. (J). *(978-1-62127-338-7(5))* Weigl Pubs., Inc.

Reid, Struan. Castle Life. 2008. (Age of Castles Ser.). (Illus.). 48p. (J). (gr. 4-8). lib. bdg. 29.25 *(978-1-4042-4292-0(9),* PowerKids Pr.) Rosen Publishing Group, Inc., The.

Riggs, Kate. Knights. 2011. (Great Warriors Ser.). 24p. (J). (ENG.). (gr. 1-3). pap. 9.99 *(978-0-89812-572-6(3),* Creative Paperbacks); (Illus.). (gr. k-2). 16.95 *(978-1-60818-001-1(8),* Creative Education) Creative Co., The.

Ross, Stewart. Medieval Europe, 1 vol. 2010. (Research It! Ser.). (ENG., Illus.). 56p. (gr. 6-9). lib. bdg. 34.65 *(978-1-4329-3498-9(8),* NA-h) Heinemann-Raintree.

Schlesinger, Arthur M., Jr., intro. Ancient World Leaders. (Illus.). (gr. 6-12). lib. bdg. *(978-0-7910-8056-6(0),* Chelsea Hse.) Facts On File, Inc.

Sepahban, Lois. Mongol Warriors. 2015. (Ancient Warriors Ser.). (ENG.). 32p. (J). (gr. 2-5). 28.50 *(978-1-63143-756-4(9),* 208588) Child's World, Inc., The.

Shapiro, Stephen. It's a Feudal, Feudal World: A Different Medieval History. Kinnaird, Ross, illus. 2013. (ENG.). 48p. (J). (gr. 4-8). lib. bdg. 24.95 *(978-1-55451-553-0(X),* 9781554515530); 2nd ed. pap. 14.95 *(978-1-55451-552-3(1),* 9781554515523) Annick Pr., Ltd. CAN. Dist: Publishers Group West (PGW).

Snedden, Robert. The Medieval World. 2009. (Technology in Times Past Ser.). (Illus.). 46p. (J). (gr. 4-7). pap. *(978-1-897563-65-6(5))* Saunders Bk. Co.

Stefoff, Rebecca. The Medieval World. 2004. (World Historical Atlases Ser.). (Illus.). 48p. (gr. 5). 26.95 *(978-0-7614-1642-5(0),* Benchmark Bks.) Marshall Cavendish Corp.

Stiefel, Chana. Sweaty Suits of Armor: Could You Survive Being a Knight? Kelley, Gerald, illus. 2011. (Ye Yucky Middle Ages Ser.). 48p. (J). (gr. 5-18). pap. 8.95 *(978-1-59845-376-8(9));* (gr. 7-12). lib. bdg. 25.27 *(978-0-7660-3784-7(3))* Enslow Pubs., Inc.

—Ye Castle Stinketh: Could You Survive Living in a Castle? Kelley, Gerald, illus. 2011. (Ye Yucky Middle Ages Ser.). 48p. (J). (gr. 5-18). pap. 8.95 *(978-1-59845-374-4(2));* (gr. 7-12). lib. bdg. 25.27 *(978-0-7660-3786-1(X))* Enslow Pubs., Inc.

Storey, Rita. Knights & Castles. 2013. (Have Fun with Arts & Crafts Ser.). 32p. (gr. 4-7). 31.35 *(978-1-59920-899-2(7))* Black Rabbit Bks.

Stuckey, Rachel. Your Guide to Medieval Society. 2017. (Destination: Middle Ages Ser.). (ENG., Illus.). 32p. (J). ***(978-0-7787-2991-4(5));*** pap. ***(978-0-7787-2997-6(4))*** Crabtree Publishing Co.

Taylor, Barbara. The Amazing History of Castles & Knights. 2016. (ENG., Illus.). 64p. (J). (gr. -1-12). 12.99 *(978-1-86147-717-0(1),* Armadillo) Anness Publishing GBR. Dist: National Bk. Network.

—The Amazing World Of: Castles. 2008. (ENG., Illus.). 64p. (J). (gr. 4-7). pap. 12.99 *(978-1-84476-599-7(7))* Anness Publishing GBR. Dist: National Bk. Network.

Trembinski, Donna. Medieval Myths, Legends, & Songs. 2005. (Medieval World Ser.). (ENG., Illus.). 32p. (J). (gr. 5-9). lib. bdg. *(978-0-7787-1359-3(8))* Crabtree Publishing Co.

Turnbull, Stephanie. Castles: Information for Young Readers - Level 1. King, Colin, illus. 2007. (Usborne Beginners Ser.). 32p. (J). 4.99 *(978-0-7945-1335-1(2),* Usborne) EDC Publishing.

Vonne, Mira. Gross Facts about the Middle Ages. 2017. (Gross History Ser.). (ENG., Illus.). 32p. (gr. 1-2). lib. bdg. 26.65 *(978-1-5157-4153-4(2))* Capstone Press of Coughlan Cos.

Watson, Danielle. The Castle in Medieval Europe. 2016. (Life in Medieval Europe Ser.). (Illus.). 80p. (J). (gr. 6-6). 35.64 *(978-1-5026-1878-8(8))* Cavendish Square Publishing.

—The Countryside in Medieval Europe. 2016. (Life in Medieval Europe Ser.). (Illus.). 80p. (J). (gr. 6-6). 35.64 *(978-1-5026-1882-5(6))* Cavendish Square Publishing.

West, David. Lots of Things You Want to Know about Knights: ... & Some You Don't! 2015. (Lots of Things You Want to Know About Ser.). (Illus.). 24p. (J). 28.50 *(978-1-62588-091-8(X))* Black Rabbit Bks.

Whiting, Jim. The Life & Times of Charlemagne. 2005. (Biography from Ancient Civilizations Ser.). (Illus.). 48p. (J). (gr. 4-8). lib. bdg. 29.95 *(978-1-58415-346-7(6))* Mitchell Lane Pubs., Inc.

Wilkinson, Carole. How to Live in the Dark Ages. 2007. 96p. (J). pap. *(978-1-4207-0725-0(6))* Sundance/Newbridge Educational Publishing.

Wilson, Phil, illus. Medieval Castle: A Three Dimensional. 2004. (ENG.). (J). 22.00 *(978-1-58117-365-9(2),* Intervisual/Piggy Toes) Bendon, Inc.

Woog, Adam. The Early Middle Ages. 2011. (Understanding World History Ser.). (ENG., Illus.). 96p. (YA). (gr. 7-12). lib. bdg. 27.95 *(978-1-60152-151-4(0))* ReferencePoint Pr., Inc.

—A Medieval Knight. 2003. (Daily Life Ser.). (ENG., Illus.). 48p. (J). (gr. 4-6). pap. 27.00 *(978-0-7377-0992-6(8),* Kidhaven) Cengage Gale.

World Book, Inc Staff, contrib. by. The Age of Knights & Castles. 2011. (J). *(978-0-7166-1787-7(0))* World Bk., Inc.

Wroble, Lisa A. Kids in the Middle Ages. (Kids Throughout History Ser.). 24p. 2009. (gr. 3-3). 42.50 *(978-1-61513-895-1(1))* 2004. (J). 22.60 *(978-1-4042-2666-1(4))* Rosen Publishing Group, Inc., The. (PowerKids Pr.).

Zannos, Susan. The Life & Times of Marco Polo. 2004. (Biography from Ancient Civilizations Ser.). (Illus.). 48p. (J). (gr. 4-8). lib. bdg. 29.95 *(978-1-58415-264-4(8))* Mitchell Lane Pubs., Inc.

CIVILIZATION, MODERN

see also History, Modern; Renaissance

Bailey, Viola & Wise, Ella. Victorian Times. Date not set. (Focus on History Ser.). (Illus.). 64p. (J). pap. 129.15 *(978-0-582-18240-0(9))* Addison-Wesley Longman, Ltd. GBR. Dist: Trans-Atlantic Pubns., Inc.

Baker, Patricia. Fashions of a Decade: The 1940s. 2nd rev. ed. 2006. (Fashions of a Decade Ser.). (Illus.). 64p. (gr. 6-12). 35.00 *(978-0-8160-6720-6(1))* Facts On File, Inc.

—Fashions of a Decade: The 1950s. 2nd rev. ed. 2006. (Fashions of a Decade Ser.). (Illus.). 64p. (gr. 6-12). 35.00 *(978-0-8160-6721-3(X))* Facts On File, Inc.

Bauer, Susan Wise & Weiss, Jim. Early Modern Times Vol. 3: From Elizabeth the First to the Forty-Niners. 2nd unabr. ed. 2008. (Story of the World Ser.: 0). (ENG.). 1p. cd-rom 49.95 *(978-1-933339-17-7(9),* 333917) Well-Trained Mind Pr.

Bennett, Doraine. Greece & Our American Heritage. 2009. (J). *(978-1-935077-71-8(6));* pap. *(978-1-935077-72-5(4))* State Standards Publishing, LLC.

Catel, Patrick. What Did the Ancient Chinese Do for Me?, 1 vol. 2010. (Linking the Past & Present Ser.). (ENG.). 32p. (gr. 3-6). pap. 8.29 *(978-1-4329-3754-6(5),* Heinemann InfoSearch) Heinemann-Raintree.

—What Did the Ancient Egyptians Do for Me?, 1 vol. 2010. (Linking the Past & Present Ser.). (ENG., Illus.). 32p. (gr. 3-6). 33.32 *(978-1-4329-3742-3(1));* pap. 8.29 *(978-1-4329-3749-2(9))* Heinemann-Raintree. (Heinemann InfoSearch).

—What Did the Ancient Greeks Do for Me?, 1 vol. 2010. (Linking the Past & Present Ser.). (ENG.). 32p. (gr. 3-6). pap. 8.29 *(978-1-4329-3753-9(7),* Heinemann InfoSearch) Heinemann-Raintree.

—What Did the Ancient Romans Do for Me?, 1 vol. 2010. (Linking the Past & Present Ser.). (ENG., Illus.). 32p. (gr. 3-6). 33.32 *(978-1-4329-3743-0(X));* pap. 8.29

(978-1-4329-3750-8(2)) Heinemann-Raintree. (Heinemann InfoSearch).

Collins. Collins Fascinating Facts - Amazing Places. rev. ed. 2016. (Collins Fascinating Facts Ser.). (ENG.). 72p. (J). (gr. 1-3). pap. 10.99 (978-0-00-816919-0(5)) HarperCollins Pubs. Ltd. GBR. Dist: Independent Pubs. Group.

Connikie, Yvonne. Fashions of a Decade: The 1960s. 2nd rev. ed. 2006. (Fashions of a Decade Ser.). (Illus.). 64p. (gr. 6-12). 35.00 (978-0-8160-6722-0(8)) Facts On File, Inc.

Costantino, Maria. Fashions of a Decade: The 1930s. 2nd rev. ed. 2006. (Fashions of a Decade Ser.). (Illus.). 64p. (gr. 6-12). 35.00 (978-0-8160-6719-0(8)) Facts On File, Inc.

Cultures of the World - Group 14. 2nd rev. ed. Incl. Algeria. Kagda, Falaq & Latif, Zawiah Abdul. lib. bdg. 42.79 (978-0-7614-2085-9(1), Benchmark Bks.); Armenia. Dhilawala, Sakina. (Illus.). lib. bdg. 42.79 (978-0-7614-2029-3(0)); Lithuania. Kagda, Sakina & Latif, Zawiah Abdul. lib. bdg. 42.79 (978-0-7614-2087-3(8), Benchmark Bks.); Luxembourg. Sheehan, Patricia & Dhilawala, Sakina. lib. bdg. 42.79 (978-0-7614-2088-0(6), Benchmark Bks.); Tahiti. NgCheong-Lum, Roseline. lib. bdg. 42.79 (978-0-7614-2089-7(4), Benchmark Bks.); Ukraine. Bassis, Volodymyr & Dhilawala, Sakina. lib. bdg. 42.79 (978-0-7614-2090-3(8), Benchmark Bks.); 144p. (gr. 6). (Cultures of the World 14 Ser.). 2007. Set lib. bdg. 256.74 (978-0-7614-2084-2(3), Benchmark Bks.) Marshall Cavendish Corp.

Dubois, Muriel L. Ancient Rome: A Mighty Empire. 2011. (Great Civilizations Ser.). (ENG.). 32p. (gr. 3-4). pap. 47.70 (978-1-4296-7240-5(4)); lib. bdg. 27.32 (978-1-4296-6832-3(6)) Capstone Press of Coughlan Cos. (Fact Finders).

F, Professor Charles, ed. Modern World Cultures, 10 Vols., Set. 2006. (Modern World Cultures Ser.). 100p. (gr. 6-12). 270.00 (978-0-7910-9323-8(9), Chelsea Hse.) Facts On File, Inc.

Facts on File, Inc. Staff, ed. Fashions of a Decade, 8 Vols., Set. 2006. (Fashions of a Decade Ser.). (Illus.). 64p. (gr. 6-12). 280.00 (978-0-8160-7059-6(8)) Facts On File, Inc.

Harvey, Miles. Look What Came from Africa. 2003. (Look What Came from... Ser.). (ENG., Illus.). 32p. (J). (gr. 2-4). pap. 6.95 (978-0-531-16626-0(0)) Scholastic Library Publishing.

Herald, Jacqueline. Fashions of a Decade: The 1920s. 2nd rev. ed. 2006. (Fashions of a Decade Ser.). (Illus.). 64p. (gr. 6-12). 35.00 (978-0-8160-6718-3(X)) Facts On File, Inc.

—Fashions of a Decade: The 1970s. 2nd rev. ed. 2006. (Fashions of a Decade Ser.). (Illus.). 64p. (gr. 6-12). 35.00 (978-0-8160-6723-7(6)) Facts On File, Inc.

Hibbert, Adam. World Wonders. 2010. (Unpredictable Nature Ser.). 48p. (J). (gr. 3-18). lib. bdg. 19.95 (978-1-4222-2008-5(7)) Mason Crest.

Hills, Ken. 1940s. (Take Ten Years Ser.). (Illus.). 47p. (J). pap. (978-0-237-51681-9(0)) Evans Brothers, Ltd.

Hoyle, Geoffrey. 2011: Living in the Future. Anderson, Alasdair, illus. 2010. (ENG.). 64p. 15.95 (978-1-59583-430-0(3), 9781595834300, Darling & Co.) Laughing Elephant.

Hughes, Shirley. A Brush with the Past, 1900-1950: The Years That Changed Our Lives. 2005. (ENG., Illus.). 112p. (gr. 5-18). 45.00 (978-0-370-32839-3(6)) Random Hse. GBR. Dist: Independent Pubs. Group.

Kerrigan, Juliet. Ancient Greeks & Why They Matter to Us, Bd. 16. 2017. (ENG., Illus.). 56p. (J). pap. 8.99 **(978-0-00-820892-9(1))** HarperCollins Pubs. Ltd. GBR. Dist: Independent Pubs. Group.

Levy, Patricia. From Punk Rock to Perestroika: The Mid 1970s to the Mid 1980s. 2005. (Modern Eras Uncovered Ser.). (Illus.). 56p. (J). pap. (978-1-4109-1798-0(3)) Steck-Vaughn.

—From Speakeasies to Stalinism: The 1920s to the Mid-1930s. 2005. (Modern Eras Uncovered Ser.). (Illus.). 56p. (J). pap. (978-1-4109-1794-2(0)) Steck-Vaughn.

—Modern Eras Uncovered: From Beatlemania to Watergate. 2005. (Modern Eras Uncovered Ser.). (Illus.). 56p. (J). (978-1-84443-965-2(8)); (978-1-84443-955-3(0)) Steck-Vaughn.

—Modern Eras Uncovered: From Compact Discs to the Gulf War. 2005. (Modern Eras Uncovered Ser.). (Illus.). 56p. (J). (978-1-84443-967-6(4)); (978-1-84443-957-7(7)) Steck-Vaughn.

—Modern Eras Uncovered: From Punk Rock to Perestroika. 2005. (Modern Eras Uncovered Ser.). (Illus.). 56p. (J). (978-1-84443-966-9(6)); (978-1-84443-956-0(9)) Steck-Vaughn.

—Modern Eras Uncovered: From the World Wide Web to September 11. 2005. (Modern Eras Uncovered Ser.). (Illus.). 56p. (J). (978-1-84443-968-3(2)) Steck-Vaughn.

Levy, Patricia & Sheehan, Sean. From Compact Discs to the Gulf War: The Mid 1980s to the Early 1990s. 2005. (Modern Eras Uncovered Ser.). (Illus.). 56p. (J). pap. (978-1-4109-1799-7(1)) Steck-Vaughn.

—From the World Wide Web to September 11: The Early 1990s to 2001. 2005. (Modern Eras Uncovered Ser.). (Illus.). 56p. (J). pap. (978-1-4109-1800-0(9)) Steck-Vaughn.

—Modern Eras Uncovered: From the World Wide Web to September 11. 2005. (Modern Eras Uncovered Ser.). (Illus.). 56p. (J). (978-1-84443-958-4(5)) Steck-Vaughn.

McEvoy, Anne. Fashions of a Decade: The 1990s. 2nd rev. ed. 2006. (Fashions of a Decade Ser.). (Illus.). 64p. (gr. 6-12). 35.00 (978-0-8160-6725-1(2)) Facts On File, Inc.

One World or Many? 2010. (Global Connections Ser.). (Illus.). 120p. (gr. 5-8). 35.00 (978-1-60413-284-7(1), Chelsea Hse.) Facts On File, Inc.

Perritano, John. Education, Poverty, & Inequality. 2017. (Illus.). 64p. (J). (978-1-4222-3634-5(X)) Mason Crest.

—The Making of the Modern World: 1945 to the Present: Culture & Customs in a Connected World, Vol. 9. 2016. (Making of the Modern World: 1945 to the Present Ser.: Vol. 9). (ENG., Illus.). 64p. (J). (gr. 7-12). 23.95 (978-1-4222-3635-2(8)) Mason Crest.

—Science & Technology, Vol. 9. van Dijk, Ruud, ed. 2016. (Making of the Modern World: 1945 to the Present Ser.). (Illus.). 64p. (J). (gr. 7). 23.95 (978-1-4222-3641-3(2)) Mason Crest.

Raum, Elizabeth. What Did the Aztecs Do for Me?, 1 vol. 2010. (Linking the Past & Present Ser.). (ENG.). 32p. (gr. 3-6). 33.32 (978-1-4329-3744-7(8)); pap. 8.29 (978-1-4329-3751-5(0)) Heinemann-Raintree. (Heinemann InfoSearch).

—What Did the Vikings Do for Me?, 1 vol. 2010. (Linking the Past & Present Ser.). (ENG., Illus.). 32p. (gr. 3-6). 33.32 (978-1-4329-3745-4(6)); pap. 8.29 (978-1-4329-3752-2(9)) Heinemann-Raintree. (Heinemann InfoSearch).

Robson, David. The Decade of The 2000s. 2011. (Understanding World History Ser.). (ENG., Illus.). 96p. (YA). (gr. 7-12). lib. bdg. 27.95 (978-1-60152-187-3(1)) ReferencePoint Pr., Inc.

Rowe, Brooke. What Decade Do You Belong In? 2016. (Illus.). 32p. (J). (978-1-63470-508-0(4)) Cherry Lake Publishing.

Rustad, Martha E. H. Great Leaders & Thinkers of Ancient Greece, 1 vol. 2014. (Ancient Greece Ser.). (ENG.). 24p. (gr. 1-2). 25.32 (978-1-4914-0275-7(X)) Capstone Press of Coughlan Cos.

Sharman, Margaret. Take Ten Years 1900s. (Illus.). 46p. (J). (978-0-237-51257-6(2)) Evans Brothers, Ltd.

Sheehan, Sean. From Beatlemania to Watergate: The Early 1960s to the Mid 1970s. 2005. (Modern Eras Uncovered Ser.). (Illus.). 56p. (J). pap. (978-1-4109-1797-3(5)) Steck-Vaughn.

—From Jessie Owens to Hiroshima: The Mid 1930s to 1945. 2005. (Modern Eras Uncovered Ser.). (Illus.). 56p. (J). pap. (978-1-4109-1795-9(9)) Steck-Vaughn.

—From Television to the Berlin Wall: The Mid-1940s to the Early 1960s. 2005. (Modern Eras Uncovered Ser.). (Illus.). 56p. (J). pap. (978-1-4109-1796-6(7)) Steck-Vaughn.

—From the Wright Brothers to the Treaty of Versailles: The 1900s to 1918. 2005. (Modern Eras Uncovered Ser.). (Illus.). 56p. (J). pap. (978-1-4109-1793-5(2)) Steck-Vaughn.

—Modern Eras Uncovered: From Jesse Owens to Hiroshima. 2005. (Modern Eras Uncovered Ser.). (Illus.). 56p. (J). (978-1-84443-962-1(3)); (978-1-84443-952-2(6)) Steck-Vaughn.

—Modern Eras Uncovered: From Speakeasies to Stalinism. 2005. (Modern Eras Uncovered Ser.). (Illus.). 56p. (J). (978-1-84443-961-4(5)) Steck-Vaughn.

—Modern Eras Uncovered: From Television to the Berlin Wall. 2005. (Modern Eras Uncovered Ser.). (Illus.). 56p. (J). (978-1-84443-963-8(1)) Steck-Vaughn.

—Modern Eras Uncovered: From the Wright Brothers to the Treaty of Versailles. 2005. (Modern Eras Uncovered Ser.). (Illus.). 56p. (J). (978-1-84443-960-7(7)); (978-1-84443-950-8(X)) Steck-Vaughn.

Sheehan, Sean & Levy, Pat. Modern Eras Uncovered: From Speakeasies to Stalinism. 2005. (Modern Eras Uncovered Ser.). (Illus.). 56p. (J). (978-1-84443-951-5(8)) Steck-Vaughn.

—Modern Eras Uncovered: From Television to the Berlin Wall. 2005. (Modern Eras Uncovered Ser.). (Illus.). 56p. (J). pap. (978-1-84443-953-9(4)) Steck-Vaughn.

Sherman, Patrice. The Enlightenment: A Revolution in Reason, 1 vol. 2012. (Primary Source Readers Ser.). (ENG.). 32p. (J). (gr. 5-5). pap. 8.99 (978-1-4333-5013-9(0)) Teacher Created Materials, Inc.

Van Vleet, Carmella. Seven Wonders of the World: Discover Amazing Monuments to Civilization with 20 Projects. Rizvi, Farah, illus. 2011. (Build It Yourself Ser.). (ENG.). 128p. (J). (gr. 3-7). 21.95 (978-1-934670-82-8(0)); pap. 15.95 (978-1-936313-73-0(1)) Open City Bks.

World Book People & Places 2004 Edition, 6 vols. rev. ed. 2004. (Illus.). 1,632p. (gr. 4-18). pap. 299.00 (978-0-7166-3754-7(5)) World Bk., Inc.

CIVILIZATION AND SCIENCE

see Science and Civilization

CIVILIZATION AND TECHNOLOGY

see Technology and Civilization

CLAIRVOYANCE

see also Divination; Extrasensory Perception; Fortune-Telling; Hypnotism; Thought Transference

Green, Carl R. & Sanford, William R. Sensing the Unknown. Kelley, Gerald, illus. 2011. (Investigating the Unknown Ser.). 48p. (J). (gr. 5-18). pap. 8.95 (978-1-59845-303-4(3)); 25.27 (978-0-7660-3823-3(8)) Enslow Pubs., Inc.

CLARK, GEORGE ROGERS, 1752-1818

Roberts, Russell. The Life & Times of George Rogers Clark. 2006. (Profiles in American History Ser.). (Illus.). 48p. (J). (gr. 3-7). lib. bdg. 29.95 (978-1-58415-448-8(9)) Mitchell Lane Pubs., Inc.

Stokes, Betty Southard. Postcards from George, 1763-1781: George Rogers Clark Writes Home to Virginia from the Kentucky Wilderness. Cable, Annette, illus. 2010. (J). (978-1-935497-12-7(X)) Butler Bk. Publishing.

CLARK, WILLIAM, 1770-1838

Adler, David A. A Picture Book of Lewis & Clark. Himler, Ronald, illus. 2003. (ENG.). 32p. (J). (gr. k-3). tchr. ed. 17.95 (978-0-8234-1735-3(2)) Holiday Hse., Inc.

Bodden, Valerie. Through the American West. (Great Expeditions Ser.). (Illus.). 48p. (J). 2012. (ENG.). (gr. 4-7). pap. 12.00 (978-0-89812-663-1(0), Creative Paperbacks) 2011. 35.65 (978-1-60818-065-3(4), Creative Education) Creative Co., The.

Crompton, Samuel Willard. Lewis & Clark. 2009. (Great Explorers Ser.). (Illus.). 120p. (J). (gr. 6-12). 30.00 (978-1-60413-418-6(6), Chelsea Hse.) Facts On File, Inc.

Ditchfield, Christin. The Lewis & Clark Expedition. 2006. (True Bks.). (ENG., Illus.). 48p. (J). (gr. 3-7). pap. 6.95 (978-0-516-25222-3(4), Children's Pr.) Scholastic Library Publishing.

Espinosa, Rod. Lewis & Clark, 1 vol. Espinosa, Rod, illus. 2007. (Bio-Graphics Ser.). (ENG., Illus.). 32p. (gr. 3-6). 28.50 (978-1-60270-069-7(9), Graphic Planet- Nonfiction) ABDO Publishing Co.

Fox, Suzanne G. Meriwether Lewis & William Clark: The Corp of Discovery & the Exploration of the American Frontier. 2009. (Library of American Lives & Times Ser.). 112p. (gr. 5-5). 69.20 (978-1-60853-493-7(6)) Rosen Publishing Group, Inc., The.

Fruge, William. Lewis & Clark: A Journey West. 2009. (Real Life Readers Ser.). 24p. (gr. 3-4). pap. 8.25 (978-1-4358-0040-3(0), Rosen Classroom) Rosen Publishing Group, Inc., The.

Ganeri, Anita. On Expedition with Lewis & Clark. 2010. (ENG.). 32p. (J). (gr. 3-5). (978-0-7787-9896-5(8)); (Crabtree Connections Ser.: No. 2). pap. (978-0-7787-9917-7(4)) Crabtree Publishing Co.

Gondosch, Linda. Where Did Sacagawea Join the Corps of Discovery? And Other Questions about the Lewis & Clark Expedition. 2011. (Six Questions of American History Ser.). (ENG.). 48p. (gr. 4-6). pap. 9.95 (978-0-7613-7131-1(1)); pap. 56.72 (978-0-7613-7644-6(5)); lib. bdg. 30.60 (978-0-7613-5226-6(0)) Lerner Publishing Group.

Hillstrom, Laurie Collier. The Lewis & Clark Expedition. 2015. (Defining Moments Ser.). (Illus.). 240p. (J). lib. bdg. 60.00 (978-0-7808-1417-2(7)) Omnigraphics, Inc.

Jeffrey, Gary. The Explorations of Lewis & Clark. Riley, Terry, illus. 2012. (Graphic History of the American West Ser.). (ENG.). 24p. (J). (gr. 3-8). pap. 8.15 (978-1-4339-6737-5(5), Gareth Stevens Learning Library); (gr. 4-7). lib. bdg. 23.95 (978-1-4339-6735-1(9)) Stevens, Gareth Publishing LLLP.

Keller, Susanna. The True Story of Lewis & Clark. 2013. (What Really Happened? Ser.). (ENG., Illus.). 24p. (J). (gr. 3-6). pap. 8.25 (978-1-4488-9846-6(3)); lib. bdg. 22.60 (978-1-4488-9694-3(0)) Rosen Publishing Group, Inc., The. (PowerKids Pr.).

Levy, Janey. Lewis & Clark in Their Own Words, Vol. 1. 2014. (Eyewitness to History Ser.). 32p. (J). (gr. 4-5). (ENG.). pap. 10.50 (978-1-4339-9930-7(7)); 26.60 (978-1-4339-9929-1(3)) Stevens, Gareth Publishing LLLP.

Lynette, Rachel. Meriwether Lewis & William Clark. 2013. (Pioneer Spirit: the Westward Expansion Ser.). 24p. (J). (gr. 3-6). 22.60 (978-1-4777-0783-8(2)); pap. 49.50 (978-1-4777-0900-9(2)); (ENG., Illus.). pap. 8.25 (978-1-4777-0899-6(5)) Rosen Publishing Group, Inc., The. (PowerKids Pr.).

Marsh, Carole. Meriwether Lewis & William Clark: Explorers of the Uncharted West: Explorers of the Uncharted West. 2003. 12p. (gr. k-4). 2.95 (978-0-635-02133-5(1)) Gallopade International.

Micklos, John, Jr. Discovering the West: The Expedition of Lewis & Clark, 1 vol. 2014. (Adventures on the American Frontier Ser.). (ENG.). 32p. (gr. 3-4). 27.32 (978-1-4914-0185-9(0), Fact Finders) Capstone Press of Coughlan Cos.

Molzahn, Arlene Bourgeois. Lewis & Clark: American Explorers. 2003. (Explorers! Ser.). (Illus.). 48p. (J). (gr. 1-4). lib. bdg. 25.27 (978-0-7660-2067-2(3)) Enslow Pubs., Inc.

Morley, Jacqueline. You Wouldn't Want to Explore with Lewis & Clark! An Epic Journey You'd Rather Not Make. Bergin, Mark, illus. 2013. (You Wouldn't Want to... Ser.). (ENG.). 32p. (J). 29.00 (978-0-531-25942-9(0)); pap. 9.95 (978-0-531-23039-8(2)) Scholastic Library Publishing. (Watts, Franklin).

—You Wouldn't Want to Explore with Lewis & Clark! An Epic Journey You'd Rather Not Make. 2013. (You Wouldn't Want To... Ser.). lib. bdg. 20.80 (978-0-606-31633-0(7), Turtleback) Turtleback Bks.

Mulhall, Jill K. Lewis & Clark. 2017. (Primary Source Readers Ser.). (Illus.). 32p. (J). (gr. 4-5). pap. 8.99 (978-1-4938-3886-8(5)) Teacher Created Materials, Inc.

Orr, Tamra. The Lewis & Clark Expedition: A Primary Source History of the Journey of the Corps of Discovery. (Primary Sources in American History Ser.). 64p. (gr. 5-8). 2009. 58.50 (978-1-60851-498-4(6)) 2004. (Illus.). lib. bdg. 31.95 (978-0-8239-4005-9(5), Rosen Reference) Rosen Publishing Group, Inc., The.

Perritano, John. The Lewis & Clark Expedition. 2010. (True Book Ser.). (ENG.). 48p. (J). (gr. 3-5). pap. 6.95 (978-0-531-21245-5(9), Children's Pr.) Scholastic Library Publishing.

Petrie, Kristin. Lewis & Clark, 1 vol. 2007. (Explorers Set 2 Ser.). (ENG., Illus.). 32p. (gr. 4-7). 27.07 (978-1-59679-743-7(6), Checkerboard Library) ABDO Publishing Co.

Ransom, Candice. Lewis & Clark. 2003. (History Maker Bios Ser.). (Illus.). 48p. (J). (gr. 2-4). 26.60 (978-0-8225-0394-1(8), Lerner Pubns.) Lerner Publishing Group.

Robinson, Kate. Lewis & Clark: Exploring the American West. 2010. (Great Explorers of the World Ser.). (Illus.). 112p. (J). (gr. 7-12). 33.27 (978-1-59845-124-5(3)) Enslow Pubs., Inc.

Rodger, Ellen. Lewis & Clark: Opening the American West. 2005. (In the Footsteps of Explorers Ser.). (ENG., Illus.). 32p. (J). (gr. -1-9). pap. (978-0-7787-2446-9(8)); lib. bdg. (978-0-7787-2410-0(7)) Crabtree Publishing Co.

Sapp, Richard. Lewis & Clark on Their Journey to the Pacific. 2006. (In the Footsteps of American Heroes Ser.). (Illus.). 64p. (gr. 5-12). lib. bdg. 34.00 (978-0-8368-6429-8(8), Gareth Stevens Secondary Library) Stevens, Gareth Publishing LLLP.

Schanzer, Rosalyn. How We Crossed the West: The Adventures of Lewis & Clark. 2012. (ENG.). 48p. (J). (gr. 3-7). lib. bdg. 27.00 (978-1-4263-1328-8(4), National Geographic Children's Bks.) National Geographic Society.

Smalley, Carol Parenzan. Lewis & Clark. 2008. (What's So Great About...? Ser.). (Illus.). 32p. (YA). (gr. 2-4). lib. bdg. 25.70 (978-1-58415-725-0(9)) Mitchell Lane Pubs., Inc.

Smith, Jeff. William Clark: Explorer & Diplomat. 2016. (ENG., Illus.). 48p. (J). pap. 27.00 (978-1-61248-178-4(7)) Truman State Univ. Pr.

St. George, Judith. What Was the Lewis & Clark Expedition? Foley, Tim, illus. 2014. (What Was? Ser.). (ENG.). 112p. (J). (gr. 3-7). pap. 5.99 (978-0-448-47901-9(X), Penguin Workshop) Penguin Young Readers Group.

—What Was the Lewis & Clark Expedition? 2014. (What Was...? Ser.). lib. bdg. 16.00 (978-0-606-36185-9(5)) Turtleback Bks.

Stille, Darlene R. The Journals of Lewis & Clark, 1 vol. 2012. (Documenting U. S. History Ser.). (ENG.). 48p. (gr. 3-6). pap. 9.95 (978-1-4329-6763-5(0)); lib. bdg. 32.65 (978-1-4329-6754-3(1)) Heinemann-Raintree. (NA-h).

Stuckey, Rachel. Explore with Lewis & Clark. 2014. (ENG., Illus.). 32p. (J). (978-0-7787-1247-3(8)); pap. (978-0-7787-1259-6(1)) Crabtree Publishing Co.

Swanson, Jennifer. Lewis & Clark. 2016. (Spotlight on Explorers & Colonization Ser.). 00048p. (J). (gr. 6-6). pap. 11.75 (978-1-5081-7237-6(4)) Rosen Publishing Group, Inc., The.

CLASS CONFLICT

see Social Conflict

CLASS DISTINCTION

see Social Classes

CLASS STRUGGLE

see Social Conflict

CLASSES (MATHEMATICS)

see Set Theory

CLASSICAL ANTIQUITIES

see also Archaeology; Art, Greek; Art, Roman; Mythology, Classical

also names of countries, cities, etc. with the subdivision Antiquities, e.g. Greece—Antiquities

Fuhr, Ute & Sautai, Raoul. Let's Look for Lost Treasure. 2012. (ENG., Illus.). 38p. (J). (gr. k-3). pap. 11.99 (978-1-85103-291-4(6)) Moonlight Publishing, Ltd. GBR. Dist: Independent Pubs. Group.

Marsico, Katie. The Oldest & the Newest. 2015. (True Book(tm) — Extreme Places Ser.). (ENG., Illus.). 48p. (J). pap. 6.95 (978-0-531-21785-6(X), Children's Pr.) Scholastic Library Publishing.

CLASSICAL ART

see Art, Greek; Art, Roman

CLASSICAL BIOGRAPHY

see Greece—Biography; Rome—Biography

CLASSICAL LANGUAGES

see Latin Language

CLASSICAL MYTHOLOGY

see Mythology, Classical

CLAY, CASSIUS, 1942-2016

see Ali, Muhammad, 1942-2016

CLAY, HENRY, 1777-1852

Heinrichs, Ann & Burgan, Michael. Henry Clay: The Great Compromiser. 2004. (Our People Ser.). (ENG., Illus.). 32p. (J). (gr. 3-6). 29.93 (978-1-59296-174-0(6), 200639) Child's World, Inc., The.

Tibbitts, Alison Davis. Henry Clay: From War Hawk to the Great Compromiser. 2003. (Historical American Biographies Ser.). (Illus.). 128p. (J). lib. bdg. 27.94 (978-0-7660-1980-5(2)) Enslow Pubs., Inc.

CLAY

see also Modeling

Frankish, Lorraine. 30 Fun Ways to Learn with Clay & Squishy Stuff. 2011. (30 Fun Ways to Learn Ser.). (ENG.). 80p. (gr. -1-k). pap. 12.95 (978-0-87659-371-4(6), Gryphon House Inc) Gryphon Hse., Inc.

Fun with Clay. 2013. (Fun With Ser.). (ENG., Illus.). 40p. (J). (gr. 3-7). (978-1-77132-068-9(0)) SpiceBox Products Ltd.

Haab, Sherri. Clay So Cute! 21 Polymer Clay Projects for Cool Charms, Itty-Bitty Animals, & Tiny Treasures. 2009. (ENG.). 112p. pap. 14.95 (978-0-8230-9899-6(0), Potter Craft) Potter/TenSpeed/Harmony.

Hammonds, Heather. Modellieren MIT Knete. 2005. (GER., Illus.). 64p. (J). (978-3-937495-94-1(0)) Mud Puddle, Inc.

How-To Library (Set), 26 vols. 2014. (How-To Library). (ENG.). 32p. (J). (gr. 3-6). pap. 369.46 (978-1-63137-796-9(5), 205348) Cherry Lake Publishing.

Jennings, Terry. Clay. 2006. (Illus.). 32p. (YA). (gr. 1-18). lib. bdg. 27.10 (978-1-932333-02-2(9)) Chrysalis Education.

Llimos Plomer, Anna & Parramon's Editorial Team Staff. Clay. 2003. (Let's Create! Ser.). (Illus.). 32p. (gr. 1-4). lib. bdg. 26.00 (978-0-8368-3746-9(0), Gareth Stevens Learning Library) Stevens, Gareth Publishing LLLP.

Petelinsek, Kathleen. Making Clay Bead Crafts. Petelinsek, Kathleen, illus. 2014. (How-To Library). (ENG., Illus.). 32p. (J). (gr. 3-6). 28.50 (978-1-63137-777-8(9), 205351) Cherry Lake Publishing.

—Modeling Clay Creations. Petelinsek, Kathleen, illus. 2014. (How-To Library). (ENG., Illus.). 32p. (J). (gr. 3-6). 28.50 (978-1-63137-783-9(3), 205375) Cherry Lake Publishing.

Quan, Adalucia. The Magic of Clay. 2003. (Illus.). 29p. (J). 18.95 (978-0-9742956-0-2(4)) Cholita Prints & Pub. Co.

Smith, Thomasina. Crafty Fun with Clay! 25 Brilliant Ideas, from Pretty Pots to Scary Monsters. 2015. (ENG., Illus.). 64p. (J). (gr. 3-7). 9.99 (978-1-86147-417-9(2), Armadillo) Anness Publishing GBR. Dist: National Bk. Network.

Stephens, Cassie. Clay Lab for Kids: 52 Projects to Make, Model, & Mold with Air-Dry, Polymer, & Homemade Clay. 2017. (Lab Ser.). (ENG., Illus.). 144p. (J). (gr. -1-5). pap. 24.99 (978-1-63159-270-6(X), Quarry Bks.) Quarto Publishing Group USA.

Storey, Rita. Clay. 2007. (How We Use Materials/Watts Ser.). (Illus.). 30p. (J). (gr. 4-7). lib. bdg. 28.50 (978-1-59920-000-2(7)) Black Rabbit Bks.

Taus-Bolstad, Stacy. From Clay to Bricks. Richter, Cheryl R., photos by. 2003. (Start to Finish Ser.). (ENG., Illus.). 24p. (gr. k-3). lib. bdg. 19.93 (978-0-8225-4663-4(9)) Lerner Publishing Group.

CLAY MODELING

see Modeling

CLEANING

see also House Cleaning; Soap

Baker, Sue. Wash Day! Stockham, Jess, illus. 2006. (Blanket Babies Ser.). (ENG.). 12p. (J). (gr. -1-k). bds. (978-1-904550-89-1(4)) Child's Play International Ltd.

Dayton, Connor. Street Sweepers. 2012. (Illus.). 24p. (J). 49.50 (978-1-4488-5073-0(8)); pap. 8.25 (978-1-4488-5072-3(X)); lib. bdg. 22.60 (978-1-4488-4961-1(6)) Rosen Publishing Group, Inc., The. (PowerKids Pr.).

Fortuna, Lois. Let's Clean Up! 2016. (We Can Do It! Ser.). (ENG.). 24p. (J). (gr. k-k). pap. 8.15 (978-1-4824-3813-0(5)) Stevens, Gareth Publishing LLLP.

Kishel, Ann-Marie. Custodian. 2007. (First Step Nonfiction Ser.). (J). pap. 3.95 (978-0-8225-6845-2(4)) Lerner Publishing Group.

Mitchell, Melanie. Killing Germs. 2006. (Pull Ahead Books: Health Ser.). (ENG., Illus.). 32p. (gr. k-3). pap. 7.95 (978-0-8225-2772-5(3)) Lerner Publishing Group.

Rissman, Rebecca. Cleaning Up: Comparing Past & Present, 1 vol. 2014. (Comparing Past & Present Ser.). (ENG.). 24p. (gr. -1-1). lib. bdg. 22.65 (978-1-4329-8989-7(8), Acorn) Heinemann-Raintree.

Verdick, Elizabeth. Clean-Up Time. Heinlen, Marieka, illus. 2008. (Toddler Tools Ser.). (ENG.). 24p. (J). (gr. k — 1). bds. 7.95 (978-1-57542-298-5(0)) Free Spirit Publishing, Inc.

CLEANLINESS

see Health

CLEARING OF LAND
see Reclamation of Land

CLEMENS, SAMUEL LANGHORNE, 1835-1910
see Twain, Mark, 1835-1910

CLEMENTE, ROBERTO, 1934-1972

Anderson, Sheila. Roberto Clemente. 2008. pap. 40.95 *(978-0-8225-9476-5(5))* Lerner Publishing Group.
—Roberto Clemente: A Life of Generosity. 2008. (Pull Ahead Bks.). (Illus.). 32p. (J). (gr. -1-3). lib. bdg. 22.60 *(978-0-8225-8586-2(3)*, Lerner Pubns.) Lerner Publishing Group.
Anderson, Sheila & National Geographic Learning Staff. Roberto Clemente: A Life of Generosity. 2010. (ENG.). 32p. (C). (gr. k-3). pap. 12.95 *(978-0-8225-8619-7(3))* National Geographic School Publishing, Inc.
Benjamin, Lisa. Baseball Dreams: The Story of Roberto Clemente. (Voices Reading Ser.). (Illus.). 32p. (J). *(978-0-7367-2912-3(7))* Zaner-Bloser, Inc.
Boehme, Gerry. Roberto Clemente: The Pride of Puerto Rico. 2016. (Game-Changing Athletes Ser.). (ENG., Illus.). 112p. (J). (gr. 9-9). lib. bdg. 42.79 *(978-1-5026-1058-4(2))* Cavendish Square Publishing.
Buckley, James, Jr. Who Was Roberto Clemente? Hammond, Ted & Harrison, Nancy, illus. 2014. (Who Was? Ser.). (ENG.). 112p. (J). (gr. 3-7). 5.99 *(978-0-448-47961-3(3)*, Grosset & Dunlap) Penguin Young Readers Group.
Buckley, James. Who Was Roberto Clemente? 2014. (Who Was... ? Ser.). lib. bdg. 16.00 *(978-0-606-36170-5(7))* Turtleback Bks.
Fischer, David. Roberto Clemente. 2004. (Trailblazers of the Modern World Ser.). (Illus.). 48p. (gr. 5-12). pap. 14.05 *(978-0-8368-5264-6(8))*; lib. bdg. 31.00 *(978-0-8368-5495-4(0))* Stevens, Gareth Publishing LLLP. (Gareth Stevens Secondary Library).
Ford, Carin T. Roberto Clemente: Baseball Legend. 2005. (Latino Biography Library). (Illus.). 128p. (J). (gr. 6-12). lib. bdg. 33.27 *(978-0-7660-2485-4(7))* Enslow Pubs., Inc.
Franchino, Vicky. Roberto Clemente. 2007. (21st Century Skills Library: Life Skills Biographies Ser.). (ENG.). 48p. (gr. 4-8). lib. bdg. 31.36 *(978-1-60279-073-5(6)*, 200047) Cherry Lake Publishing.
Gigliotti, Jim. I Am #8: Roberto Clemente. 2013. (I Am Ser.: 8). (ENG.). 128p. (J). (gr. 2-5). pap. 5.99 *(978-0-545-53381-2(3)*, Scholastic Paperbacks) Scholastic, Inc.
Guzmán, Lila & Guzmán, Rick. Roberto Clemente: Baseball Hero. 2006. (Famous Latinos Ser.). (Illus.). 32p. (J). (gr. 3-7). lib. bdg. 23.94 *(978-0-7660-2640-7(X)*, Enslow Elementary) Enslow Pubs., Inc.
—Roberto Clemente: Heroe del Beisbol. 2007. (Latinos Famosos Ser.). (SPA., Illus.). 32p. (J). (gr. 3-7). lib. bdg. 23.94 *(978-0-7660-2675-9(2)*, Enslow Elementary) Enslow Pubs., Inc.
Lace, William W. Roberto Clemente, Baseball Hall of Famer. 2006. (Twentieth Century's Most Influential Hispanics Ser.). (ENG., Illus.). 104p. (YA). (gr. 7-12). lib. bdg. 34.80 *(978-1-59018-969-6(8))* Cengage Gale.
Marquez, Heron. Roberto Clemente: Baseball's Humanitarian Hero. 2005. (Trailblazer Biography Ser.). (Illus.). 112p. (J). (gr. 3-7). lib. bdg. 30.60 *(978-1-57505-767-5(0))* Lerner Publishing Group.
Marsh, Carole. Roberto Clemente: Baseball Hero & Humanitarian: Baseball Hero & Humanitarian. 2003. 12p. (gr. k-4). 2.95 *(978-0-635-02140-3(4))* Gallopade International.
Perdomo, Willie. Clemente! Collier, Bryan, illus. 2010. (ENG.). 32p. (J). (gr. 1-5). 17.99 *(978-0-8050-8224-1(7)*, 9780805082241, Holt, Henry & Co. Bks. For Young Readers) Holt, Henry & Co.
Rice, Dona. Roberto Clemente, 1 vol. 2nd rev. ed. 2014. (TIME for KIDS(r) Nonfiction Readers Ser.). (ENG., Illus.). 32p. (J). (gr. 3-3). pap. 25.96 *(978-1-4807-1092-4(X))* Shell Educational Publishing.
—Roberto Clemente, 1 vol. 2nd rev. ed. 2012. (Nonfiction Readers Ser.). (ENG.). 32p. (J). (gr. 3-3). pap. 8.99 *(978-1-4333-3683-6(9))* Teacher Created Materials, Inc.
Roberto Clemente, Atleta y Heroe. 2003. 94.95 *(978-0-8136-9218-0(0))*; pap. 48.95 *(978-0-8136-9206-7(7))* Modern Curriculum Pr.
Roberts, Jerry. Roberto Clemente: Baseball Player. 2005. (Ferguson Career Biographies Ser.). (Illus.). 128p. (gr. 6-12). 25.00 *(978-0-8160-6072-6(X)*, Ferguson Publishing Co.) Facts On File, Inc.
Rodriguez Gonzalez, Tania. Roberto Clemente. 2012. (Superstars of Baseball ENGLISH Ser.). 32p. (J). (gr. 4). 19.95 *(978-1-4222-2697-1(2))*; (SPA., Illus.). 19.95 *(978-1-4222-2644-5(1))* Mason Crest.
Thornley, Stew. Roberto Clemente. 2006. (Sports Heroes & Legends Ser.). (ENG., Illus.). 120p. (gr. 5-12). lib. bdg. 30.60 *(978-0-8225-5962-7(5))* Lerner Publishing Group.
Winter, Jonah. Roberto Clemente: Pride of the Pittsburgh Pirates. Colón, Raúl, illus. (ENG.). 40p. (J). (gr. -1-3). 2008. 7.99 *(978-1-4169-5082-0(6))* 2005. 17.99 *(978-0-689-85643-3(1))* Simon & Schuster Children's Publishing. (Atheneum Bks. for Young Readers).

CLEOPATRA, QUEEN OF EGYPT, -30 B.C.

Adams, Michelle Medlock. The Life & Times of Cleopatra. 2005. (Biography from Ancient Civilizations Ser.). (Illus.). 48p. (J). (gr. 4-8). lib. bdg. 29.95 *(978-1-58415-335-1(0))* Mitchell Lane Pubs., Inc.
Albee, Sarah. Julius Caesar, Cleopatra. 2011. (Readers' & Writers' Genre Workshop Ser.). (YA). pap. *(978-1-4509-3023-9(9))* Benchmark Education Co.
Bailey, Gerry & Foster, Karen. Cleopatra's Coin. Radford, Karen & Noyes, Leighton, illus. 2008. (Stories of Great People Ser.). (ENG.). 40p. (J). (gr. 3-8). pap. *(978-0-7787-3707-0(1))*; lib. bdg. *(978-0-7787-3685-1(7))* Crabtree Publishing Co.
Blackaby, Susan. Cleopatra: Egypt's Last & Greatest Queen. 2009. (Sterling Biographies(r) Ser.). (ENG., Illus.). 128p. (J). (gr. 5-18). pap. 5.95 *(978-1-4027-5710-5(7))* Sterling Publishing Co., Inc.
Caravantes, Peggy. Cleopatra: Powerful Leader or Ruthless Pharaoh? 2015. (Perspectives on History Ser.). (ENG.). 32p. (gr. 3-4). lib. bdg. 27.32 *(978-1-4914-2042-3(1))* Capstone Press of Coughlan Cos.
Connors, Kathleen. The Life of Cleopatra, Vol. 1. 2014. (Famous Lives Ser.). (ENG.). 24p. (J). (gr. 1-2). 22.60 *(978-1-4824-0384-8(6))* Stevens, Gareth Publishing LLLP.
Daynes, Katie. Cleopatra. 2005. (Famous Lives Gift Books Ser.). 64p. (J). 8.95 *(978-0-7945-0868-5(5)*, Usborne) EDC Publishing.
Jeffrey, Gary. Cleopatra: The Life of an Egyptian Queen. 2009. (Graphic Nonfiction Biographies Ser.). (Illus.). 48p. (YA). (gr. 4-5). 58.50 *(978-1-61513-015-3(2)*, Rosen Reference) Rosen Publishing Group, Inc., The.
Jeffrey, Gary & Ganeri, Anita. Cleopatra: The Life of an Egyptian Queen. 2005. (Graphic Nonfiction Biographies Ser.). (Illus.). 48p. (YA). (gr. 4-7). lib. bdg. 31.95 *(978-1-4042-0242-9(0))* Rosen Publishing Group, Inc., The.
Kramer, Barbara. National Geographic Readers: Cleopatra. 2015. (Readers Bios Ser.). (ENG., Illus.). 48p. (J). (gr. 1-4). pap. 3.99 *(978-1-4263-2137-5(6)*, National Geographic Children's Bks.) National Geographic Society.
Lowery, Zoe & Morgan, Julian. Cleopatra. 2016. (Leaders of the Ancient World Ser.). 00112p. (J). (gr. 6-6). 37.10 *(978-1-5081-7254-3(4))* Rosen Publishing Group, Inc., The.
Miller, Ron & Browning, Sommer. Cleopatra. 2008. (Ancient World Leaders Ser.). (Illus.). 104p. (gr. 6-12). lib. bdg. 30.00 *(978-0-7910-9582-9(7)*, Chelsea Hse.) Facts On File, Inc.
Nardo, Don. Cleopatra. 2016. (ENG.). 80p. (J). 38.60 *(978-1-60152-948-0(1))* ReferencePoint Pr., Inc.
—Cleopatra: Egypt's Last Pharoah. 2005. (Lucent Library of Historical Eras). (ENG., Illus.). 112p. (YA). (gr. 7-10). lib. bdg. 33.45 *(978-1-59018-660-2(5)*, Lucent Bks.) Cengage Gale.
Norwich, Grace. Cleopatra. 2014. (I Am Ser.: 10). (ENG., Illus.). 128p. (J). (gr. 2-5). pap. 5.99 *(978-0-545-58753-2(0)*, Scholastic Paperbacks) Scholastic, Inc.
Pack, Mary Fisk. Cleopatra: "Serpent of the Nile" Malone, Peter, illus. 2011. (Thinking Girl's Treasury of Dastardly Dames Ser.). (ENG.). 32p. (J). (gr. 3-8). 18.95 *(978-0-9834256-0-1(4))* Goosebottom Bks. LLC.
Pipe, Jim. You Wouldn't Want to Be Cleopatra! An Egyptian Ruler You'd Rather Not Be. Antram, David, illus. 2007. (You Wouldn't Want to... Ser.). (ENG.). 32p. (J). (gr. 2-5). pap. 9.95 *(978-0-531-18923-8(6)*, Watts, Franklin) Scholastic Library Publishing.
—You Wouldn't Want to Be Cleopatra! An Egyptian Ruler You'D Rather Not Be. Antram, David, illus. 2007. (You Wouldn't Want to... Ser.). (ENG.). 32p. (J). (gr. 2-5). 29.00 *(978-0-531-18726-5(8)*, Watts, Franklin) Scholastic Library Publishing.
—You Wouldn't Want to Be Cleopatra! (Revised Edition) 2017. (You Wouldn't Want to... Ancient Civilizations Ser.). (ENG., Illus.). 32p. (J). lib. bdg. 29.00 *(978-0-531-23834-9(2)*, Watts, Franklin) Scholastic Library Publishing.
Ross, Stewart. Clever Cleo. Shields, Sue, illus. 32p. pap. 9.99 *(978-0-7502-2853-4(9))* Hodder & Stoughton GBR. Dist: Trafalgar Square Publishing.
Roxburgh, Ellis. Cleopatra vs. the Roman Empire: Power, Conquest, & Tragedy. 2016. (History's Greatest Rivals Ser.). (ENG., Illus.). 48p. (J). (gr. 6-8). pap. 14.05 *(978-1-4824-4223-6(X))* Stevens, Gareth Publishing LLLP.
Shakespeare, William. Antony & Cleopatra. Heims, Neil & Bloom, Harold, eds. 2008. (Bloom's Shakespeare Through the Ages Ser.). 290p. (YA). (gr. 9-12). 50.00 *(978-0-7910-9630-7(0))* Facts On File, Inc.
Shecter, Vicky Alvear. Cleopatra Rules! The Amazing Life of the Original Teen Queen. 2013. (ENG., Illus.). 176p. (J). (gr. 6-9). pap. 9.95 *(978-1-62091-032-0(2))* Boyds Mills Pr.
Streissguth, Tom. Queen Cleopatra. 2007. (Illus.). 112p. (J). pap. 9.95 *(978-0-8225-7061-5(0))* Lerner Publishing Group.
Uhl, Xina M. Cleopatra: Queen of Egypt. 2017. (Women Who Changed History Ser.). 48p. (gr. 10-12). 26.85 ***(978-1-68048-639-1(X)***, Britannica Educational Publishing) Rosen Publishing Group, Inc., The.
Worth, Richard. Cleopatra: Queen of Ancient Egypt. 2006. (Rulers of the Ancient World Ser.). (Illus.). 160p. (YA). (gr. 6-12). lib. bdg. 29.27 *(978-0-7660-2559-2(4))* Enslow Pubs., Inc.

CLEOPATRA, QUEEN OF EGYPT, -30 B.C.—FICTION

Cleopatra the Ambitious: What Made Them Famous? 2006. 156p. (J). per. 15.00 *(978-1-931195-97-3(8))* KiwE Publishing, Ltd.
Effie Mae Shearin. Cleopatra: Glory to Her Race. 2006. 85p. 20.00 *(978-1-4257-0545-9(6))*; pap. 10.00 *(978-1-4257-0544-2(8))* Xlibris Corp.
Ewert, Marcus. Mummy Cat. Brown, Lisa, illus. 2015. (ENG.). 48p. (J). (gr. 1-4). 16.99 *(978-0-544-34082-4(5)*, Clarion Bks.) Houghton Mifflin Harcourt Trade & Reference Pubs.
Kraljic, Helena. Cleopatra. 2017. (SPA.). 32p. (J). (gr. 1-4). 16.95 ***(978-84-9145-008-5(4)***, Picarona Editorial) Ediciones Obelisco ESP. Dist: Spanish Pubs., LLC.
Lopez, David Mark. Walk Like an Egyptian. 2006. (J). (gr. 3-7). *(978-0-9744097-0-2(7))* Lopez, David.
Maihack, Mike. Secret of the Time Tablets (Cleopatra in Space #3) 2016. (Cleopatra in Space Ser.: 3). (ENG.). 192p. (J). (gr. 3-7). pap. 12.99 *(978-0-545-83867-2(3)*, Graphix) Scholastic, Inc.
—Target Practice. 2014. (Cleopatra in Space Ser.: 1). (ENG.). 176p. (J). (gr. 3-7). 22.99 *(978-0-545-52842-9(9)*, Graphix) Scholastic, Inc.
Meyer, Carolyn. Cleopatra Confesses. (ENG.). 304p. (YA). (gr. 7). 2012. pap. 11.99 *(978-1-4169-8728-4(2))* 2011. 16.99 *(978-1-4169-8727-7(4))* Simon & Schuster/Paula Wiseman Bks. (Simon & Schuster/Paula Wiseman Bks.).
Premonville, Marie de & Volpari, Daniela. Cleopatra: Queen of the Nile. 2012. (Big Picture Book Ser.). (ENG., Illus.). 48p. (J). (gr. 2). 14.95 *(978-2-7338-2096-4(6))* Auzou, Philippe Editions FRA. Dist: Consortium Bk. Sales & Distribution.
Shecter, Vicky Alvear. Cleopatra's Moon. (ENG.). 368p. (J). (gr. 9). 2013. pap. 9.99 *(978-0-545-22131-3(5))* 2011. 18.99 *(978-0-545-22130-6(7))* Scholastic, Inc. (Levine, Arthur A. Bks.).
Surget, Alain & Yeardley, Glynne. Caesar, Who's He? Parme, Fabrice, illus. 2014. 95p. (J). *(978-1-4351-5328-8(6))* Barnes & Noble, Inc.
—Cleopatra Must Be Saved! Parme, Fabrice, illus. 2014. 95p. (J). *(978-1-4351-5329-5(4))* Barnes & Noble, Inc.
—Danger at the Circus! Parme, Fabrice, illus. 2014. 95p. (J). *(978-1-4351-5334-9(0))* Barnes & Noble, Inc.
—Prisoners in the Pyramid. Parme, Fabrice, illus. 2014. 94p. (J). *(978-1-4351-5326-4(X))* Barnes & Noble, Inc.
Twist, Clint. Cleopatra: Queen of Egypt. Andrew, Ian, illus. 2012. (Historical Notebooks Ser.). (ENG.). 30p. (J). (gr. 3-7). 19.99 *(978-0-7636-6095-6(7)*, Templar) Candlewick Pr.
White, Dorine. The Emerald Ring (Cleopatra's Legacy) 2013. 183p. (YA). pap. 13.99 *(978-1-4621-1133-6(5)*, Horizon Pubs.) Cedar Fort, Inc./CFI Distribution.

CLERGY
see also Monasticism and Religious Orders

Aykroyd, Clarissa. Savage Satire: The Story of Jonathan Swift. 2006. (World Writers Ser.). (Illus.). 160p. (J). (gr. 3-7). lib. bdg. 27.95 *(978-1-59935-027-1(0))* Reynolds, Morgan Inc.
Bader, Bonnie. Who Was Martin Luther King, Jr.? Wolf, Elizabeth & Harrison, Nancy, illus. 2007. (Who Was? Ser.). (ENG.). 112p. (J). (gr. 3-7). pap. 5.99 *(978-0-448-44723-0(1)*, Grosset & Dunlap) Penguin Young Readers Group.
Benge, Janet & Benge, Geoff. Christian Heroes - Then & Now - John Wesley: The World, His Parish. 2007. (Christian Heroes Ser.). (ENG.). 192p. (YA). (gr. 3-7). pap. 9.99 *(978-1-57658-382-1(1))* YWAM Publishing.
—Francis Asbury: Circuit Rider. 2013. (Christian Heroes: Then & Now Ser.). (ENG.). 189p. (YA). (gr. 3-7). pap. 9.99 *(978-1-57658-737-9(1))* YWAM Publishing.
Bozzuti-Jones, Mark Francisco. The Miter Fits Just Fine: A Story about the Rt. Rev. Barbara Clementine Harris, Suffragan Bishop, Diocese of Massachusetts. 2003. (ENG.). 86p. pap. 10.95 *(978-1-56101-220-6(3))* Cowley Pubns.
Brown, Terrell. Reverend Run (Run-D. M. C.) 2008. (Hip-Hop Ser.). (Illus.). 64p. (YA). (gr. 7-12). lib. bdg. 22.95 *(978-1-4222-0127-5(9))* Mason Crest.
Carr, Simonetta. Athanasius. Abraxas, Matt, illus. 2011. 64p. (J). 18.00 *(978-1-60178-151-2(2))* Reformation Heritage Bks.
DeDomenico, Elizabeth Marie. Saint John Vianney: A Priest for All People. Hatke, Ben, illus. 2008. (Encounter the Saints Ser.). 122p. (J). (gr. 4-7). pap. 7.95 *(978-0-8198-7115-2(X))* Pauline Bks. & Media.
D'Orio, Wayne. Al Sharpton. 2nd rev. ed. 2011. (Black Americans of Achievement Legacy Edition Ser.). 128p. (gr. 6-12). 35.00 *(978-1-60413-834-4(3))* Facts On File, Inc.
Fandel, Jennifer. Martin Luther King, Jr. 2005. (Genius Ser.). (Illus.). 48p. (J). (gr. 5-9). lib. bdg. 21.95 *(978-1-58341-329-6(4)*, Creative Education) Creative Co., The.
Feinstein, Stephen. Read about Martin Luther King, Jr. 2004. (I Like Biographies! Ser.). (Illus.). 24p. (J). lib. bdg. 24.95 *(978-0-7660-2300-0(1))* Enslow Pubs., Inc.
Ficocelli, Elizabeth. Where Do Deacons Come From? Wirrenga, Shannon, illus. 2011. 20p. (J). pap. 7.99 *(978-1-936453-03-0(7))* Bezalel Bks.
—Where Do Priests Come From? Wirrenga, Shannon, illus. 2010. (J). pap. 7.99 *(978-0-9844864-0-3(2))* Bezalel Bks.
Gosman, Gillian. Martin Luther King, Jr. 2011. (Life Stories Ser.). (Illus.). 24p. (J). pap. 8.25 *(978-1-4488-2755-8(8)*, PowerKids Pr.); (gr. 1-4). lib. bdg. 22.60 *(978-1-4488-2583-7(0)*, PowerKids Pr.); (ENG & SPA., (gr. 1-4). lib. bdg. 22.60 *(978-1-4488-3217-0(9))* Rosen Publishing Group, Inc., The.
Granfield, Linda. Out of Slavery: The Journey to Amazing Grace. Wilson, Janet, illus. 2009. (ENG.). 40p. (J). (gr. k-12). 15.95 *(978-0-88776-915-3(2)*, Tundra Bks.) Tundra Bks. CAN. Dist: Penguin Random Hse. LLC.
House, Catherine. Voices Against Injustice: Ten Christians Who Spoke Out for Justice. 2007. (ENG.). 192p. (J). per. 7.99 *(978-1-84550-280-5(9)*, b2aa8a18-ff3a-4b6a-b14a-f5fd55dbd02e) Christian Focus Pubns. GBR. Dist: Bookmasters Distribution.
Intosh, Kenneth Mc & McIntosh, Kenneth. Clergy. Riggs, Ernestine G. & Gholar, Cheryl, eds. 2013. (Careers with Character Ser.: 18). 96p. (J). (gr. 7-18). 22.95 *(978-1-4222-2753-4(7))* Mason Crest.
Jones, Rob Lloyd. Martin Luther King, Jr. 2006. (Illus.). 62p. (J). pap. *(978-0-439-02299-6(1))* Scholastic, Inc.
Linney, Susan. Martin Luther King, Jr: With a Discussion of Responsibility. 2004. (Values In Action Ser.). (J). *(978-1-59203-069-9(6))* Learning Challenge, Inc.
Mallin, Jay. Al Sharpton: Community Activist. 2007. (Great Life Stories Ser.). (Illus.). 111p. (J). *(978-0-531-13672-0(8)*, Franklin Watts) Hachette Children's Group.
Martin. Dietrich Bonhoeffer. 2011. (Champion of Freedom Ser.). (gr. 7-12). 28.95 *(978-1-59935-169-8(2))* Reynolds, Morgan Inc.
McCormick, Patricia. The Plot to Kill Hitler: Dietrich Bonhoeffer: Pastor, Spy, Unlikely Hero. 2016. (Illus.). 192p. (J). (gr. 3). 18.99 *(978-0-06-241108-2(X))* HarperCollins Pubs.
Miller, Reagan & Boyle, Sarah B. What Is a Theocracy? 2012. (Forms of Government Ser.). (ENG.). 48p. (J). (gr. 5-9). lib. bdg. *(978-0-7787-5319-3(0))* Crabtree Publishing Co.
Mis, Melody S. Meet Al Sharpton. (Civil Rights Leaders Ser.). 24p. (gr. 2-3). 2009. 42.50 *(978-1-61511-850-2(0)*, PowerKids Pr.) 2008. (Illus.). (YA). lib. bdg. 22.60 *(978-1-4042-4213-5(9))* Rosen Publishing Group, Inc., The.
Nichols, Kaitlyn. Martin Luther King. 2009. pap. 13.25 *(978-1-60559-065-3(7))* Hameray Publishing Group, Inc.
Sims, Rudine. Bishop Daniel A. Payne: Great Black Leader. 2009. (Illus.). 70p. (J). (gr. 3-7). pap. 12.95 *(978-1-933491-15-8(9))* Just Us Bks., Inc.
Stotts, Stuart. Father Groppi: Marching for Civil Rights. 2013. (Badger Biographies Ser.). (ENG., Illus.). 160p. (J). pap. 12.95 *(978-0-87020-575-0(7))* Wisconsin Historical Society.
Tucker, Margaret E. Biography of Richard Bullard: From Shoe Cobbler in England to Minister for Jesus Christ in America. 2003. pap. 6.75 *(978-0-9672363-3-9(9))* Heritage Publishing.
Watkins, Angela Farris. My Uncle Martin's Big Heart. Velasquez, Eric, illus. 2010. (ENG.). 32p. (J). (gr. k-2). 19.95 *(978-0-8109-8975-7(1)*, Abrams Bks. for Young Readers) Abrams, Inc.
Weston Woods Staff, creator. Martin's Big Words. 2011. 38.75 *(978-0-545-15256-3(9))*; 18.95 *(978-0-545-15251-8(8))* Weston Woods Studios, Inc.
Windle, Jeanette & Clements, Jan. Yandicu: Ein Medizinmann Wird Evangelist. Date not set.Tr. of Yandicu - From Witch Doctor to Evangelist. (GER., Illus.). (J). (gr. 2-7). pap. *(978-0-9617490-5-7(9))* Gospel Missionary Union.
Winget, Mary. Martin Luther King, Jr. 2004. (History Maker Bios Ser.). (Illus.). 48p. (J). pap. 8.95 *(978-0-8225-4804-1(6)*, Lerner Pubns.) Lerner Publishing Group.

CLERGY—FICTION

A. L. O. E. The Triumph over Midian. 2006. 344p. per. 23.99 *(978-1-4255-3466-0(X))* Michigan Publishing.
Beeton, Abigail. A Pastor's Predicament. 2011. 42p. pap. 16.95 *(978-1-4560-6605-5(6))* America Star Bks.
Burney, Claudia Mair. Exorsistah, No. 1. 2008. (ENG.). 272p. (YA). pap. 9.95 *(978-1-4165-6133-0(1)*, Gallery Bks.) Gallery Bks.
Easton, Kelly. Walking on Air. 2010. (ENG.). 240p. (YA). (gr. 7). pap. 11.99 *(978-1-4424-1437-2(5)*, McElderry, Margaret K. Bks.) McElderry, Margaret K. Bks.
Friedland, Joyce, ed. Lizzie Bright & the Buckminster Boy: Novel-Ties Study Guide. 2007. 36p. pap. 16.95 *(978-0-7675-3558-8(8))* Learning Links Inc.
Fyne, Olga M. Be Satisfied with Who You Are. Mathis, Leslie, illus. 2013. 24p. pap. 9.99 *(978-1-61286-142-5(3))* Avid Readers Publishing Group.
Hawthorne, Nathaniel. Scarlet Letter. 2014. (Differentiated Timeless Classics Ser.). (ENG.). 80p. (YA). (gr. 9-12). 12.95 *(978-1-62250-716-0(9))* Saddleback Educational Publishing, Inc.
—The Scarlet Letter - Spotlight Edition. Grudzina, Douglas, ed. 2004. (Illus.). 150p. (YA). per. 5.95 *(978-1-58049-550-9(8)*, PWH5508) Prestwick Hse., Inc.
Jolley, Alana L. If You Give a Padre a Peppertree. 2008. 24p. pap. 15.99 *(978-1-4257-9308-1(8))* Xlibris Corp.
Keeling, Annie E. Andrew Golding A Tale of the Great Plague. 2004. reprint ed. pap. 1.99 *(978-1-4192-0694-8(X))*; pap. 15.95 *(978-1-4191-0694-1(5))* Kessinger Publishing, LLC.
Kiely, Brendan. The Gospel of Winter. 2014. (ENG., Illus.). 304p. (YA). (gr. 9). 19.99 *(978-1-4424-8489-4(6)*, McElderry, Margaret K. Bks.) McElderry, Margaret K. Bks.
Lasky, Kathryn. Lucy. 2012. (Daughters of the Sea Ser.: 3). (ENG.). 320p. (J). (gr. 7). 17.99 *(978-0-439-78312-5(7)*, Scholastic Pr.) Scholastic, Inc.
Leslie, Emma. The Captives: Or, Escape from the Druid Council. 2007. 200p. 22.95 *(978-1-934671-02-3(9))*; per. 12.95 *(978-1-934671-03-0(7))* Salem Ridge Press LLC.
Manning, Dennis & Crisalli, Joseph. The Emeritus Peabody Mysteries. 2008. 212p. pap. 13.98 *(978-1-4303-2186-6(5))* Lulu Pr., Inc.
McGinty, Alice B. Rabbi Benjamin's Buttons. Reinhardt, Jennifer Black, illus. (ENG.). 32p. (J). (gr. -1-3). 2017. pap. 7.99 *(978-1-58089-433-3(X))* 2014. lib. bdg. 17.95 *(978-1-58089-432-6(1))* Charlesbridge Publishing, Inc.
Muschla, Gary Robert. The Sword & the Cross. 2009. (YA). pap. *(978-0-88092-472-6(1))* Royal Fireworks Publishing Co.
Naylor, Phyllis Reynolds. A Shiloh Christmas. 2015. (Shiloh Quartet Ser.). (ENG., Illus.). 256p. (J). (gr. 3-7). 17.99 *(978-1-4814-4151-3(5))* Simon & Schuster Children's Publishing.
Schmidt, Gary D. Lizzie Bright & the Buckminster Boy. 2013. (ENG.). 224p. (J). (gr. 5-7). pap. 7.99 *(978-0-544-02279-9(3))* Houghton Mifflin Harcourt Publishing Co.
Seaman, John E. The Captain's Secret: A Lost Boy's Odyssey in Old New York. 2008. 220p. pap. 15.95 *(978-0-595-51753-4(6))* iUniverse, Inc.
Shan, Darren, pseud. Bec. 2008. (ENG.). 256p. (YA). (gr. 10-17). pap. 10.00 *(978-0-316-01390-1(0))* Little, Brown Bks. for Young Readers.
Spinelli, Eileen. When Christmas Came. Parmenter, Wayne, illus. 2006. (ENG.). 32p. (J). (gr. k-3). bds. 16.95 *(978-0-8249-5507-6(2)*, Ideal Pubns.) Worthy Publishing.
Voigt, Cynthia. Come a Stranger. 2012. (Tillerman Cycle Ser.: 5). (ENG., Illus.). 256p. (YA). (gr. 7). 18.99 *(978-1-4424-5063-9(0))*; pap. 7.99 *(978-1-4424-2882-9(1))* Simon & Schuster Children's Publishing. (Atheneum Bks. for Young Readers).
Whelan, Gloria. A Time to Keep Silent. 2004. 144p. (J). pap. 8.00 *(978-0-8028-5255-7(6))* Eerdmans, William B. Publishing Co.

CLERGY—POLITICAL ACTIVITY

Colbert, David. Martin Luther King Jr. 2008. (10 Days Ser.). (ENG.). 160p. (J). (gr. 3-8). pap. 7.99 *(978-1-4169-6805-4(9)*, Aladdin) Simon & Schuster Children's Publishing.
Jakoubek, Robert E. Martin Luther King, Jr. Civil Rights Leader. 2004. (Black Americans of Achievement Ser.). (Illus.). 112p. (gr. 6-12). 35.00 *(978-0-7910-8161-7(3)*, Chelsea Hse.) Facts On File, Inc.

CLERGY—VOCATIONAL GUIDANCE

McIntosh, Kenneth. Clergy. 2004. (Careers with Character Ser.). (Illus.). 96p. (YA). (gr. 7-18). lib. bdg. 22.95 *(978-1-59084-311-6(8))* Mason Crest.

CLERICAL WORK—TRAINING
see Business Education

CLERKS (SALESMENSHIP)
see Sales Personnel

CLEVELAND, GROVER, 1837-1908

Kelley, K. C. Grover Cleveland: The 22nd & 24th President. 2016. (First Look at America's Presidents Ser.). (ENG., Illus.). 24p. (J). (gr. -1-3). 17.95 *(978-1-944102-67-8(1))* Bearport Publishing Co., Inc.
Markel, Rita J. Grover Cleveland. 2006. (Presidential Leaders Ser.). (Illus.). 112p. (J). (gr. 3-7). lib. bdg. 29.27 *(978-0-8225-1494-7(X)*, Lerner Pubns.) Lerner Publishing Group.
Otfinoski, Steven. Grover Cleveland. 2010. (Presidents & Their Times 4 Ser.). 96p. (gr. 6). 34.21 *(978-0-7614-4811-2(X))* Marshall Cavendish GBR. Dist: Marshall Cavendish Corp.
Rissman, Rebecca. Grover Cleveland. 2017. (Premier Presidents Ser.). (ENG.). 24p. (J). (gr. 1-4). lib. bdg. 27.07 *(978-1-5038-1646-6(X)*, 211489) Child's World, Inc., The.
Rumsch, BreAnn. Grover Cleveland, 1 vol. (ENG., Illus.). 40p. 2016. (J). *(978-1-68078-088-8(3))* 2009. (YA). (gr. 3-6). 27.07 *(978-1-60453-446-7(X))* ABDO Publishing Co.
Tecco, Betsy Dru. How to Draw the Life & Times of Grover Cleveland. (Kid's Guide to Drawing the Presidents of the United States of America Ser.). 2009. 32p. (gr. 4-4). 50.50 *(978-1-61511-142-8(5)*, PowerKids Pr.) 2006. (YA). (gr. 2-5). 26.50 *(978-1-4042-2999-0(X))* Rosen Publishing Group, Inc., The.
Venezia, Mike. Grover Cleveland: Twenty-Second & Twenty-Fourth President, 1885-1889, 1893-1897. Venezia, Mike, illus. 2006. (Getting to Know the U. S. Presidents Ser.).

(ENG., Illus.). 32p. (J). (gr. 3-7). pap. 7.95 *(978-0-516-25402-9(2))*; lib. bdg. 28.00 *(978-0-516-22627-9(4))* Scholastic Library Publishing. (Children's Pr.).

Young, Jeff C. Grover Cleveland: A MyReportLinks. Com Book. 2003. (Presidents Ser.). (Illus.). 48p. (J). lib. bdg. 25.26 *(978-0-7660-5128-7(5)*, MyReportLinks.com Bks.) Enslow Pubs., Inc.

CLEVELAND (OHIO)

Pfingsten, Ralph. From Rockport to West Park. 2004. 45.00 net. *(978-0-9759618-0-3(2))* Marshall, John High Schl. Alumni Assn.

CLEVELAND (OHIO)—FICTION

Ashkenas, Bruce. Sick Street. 2011. 102p. pap. 9.95 *(978-1-257-04901-1(1))* Lulu Pr., Inc.

Garsee, Jeannine. Before, after, & Somebody in Between. 2008. (ENG., Illus.). 368p. (YA). (gr. 9-12). pap. 8.99 *(978-1-59990-292-0(3)*, 9781599902920, Bloomsbury USA Childrens) Bloomsbury Publishing USA.

Jacobs, Lily. The Littlest Bunny in Cleveland. Dunn, Robert, illus. 2016. (ENG.). 32p. (J). (-7). 9.99 *(978-1-4926-3353-2(4)*, 9781492633532, Sourcebooks Jabberwocky) Sourcebooks, Inc.

Johnson, Angela. Bird. 2006. (ENG.). 144p. (YA). (gr. 7-18). reprint ed. 6.99 *(978-0-14-240544-4(2)*, Puffin Books) Penguin Young Readers Group.

Perry, M. LaVora. Taneesha Never Disparaging. Cooper, Floyd, illus. 2008. (ENG.). 216p. (J). (gr. 2-7). pap. 8.95 *(978-0-86171-550-3(0))* Wisdom Pubns.

Smallman, Steve. Santa Is Coming to Cleveland. Dunn, Robert, illus. 2014. (ENG.). 32p. (J). (-3). 9.99 *(978-1-4926-0703-8(7)*, Sourcebooks Jabberwocky) Sourcebooks, Inc.

Thompson Ii, Roger E. A Sister's Love: A Novel. 2007. 80p. per. 8.95 *(978-0-595-44549-3(7))* iUniverse, Inc.

CLEVELAND BROWNS (FOOTBALL TEAM)

Burgess, Zack. Meet the Cleveland Browns. 2016. (Big Picture Sports Ser.). (ENG., Illus.). 24p. (J). (gr. k-3). lib. bdg. 22.60 *(978-1-59953-726-9(5))* Norwood Hse. Pr.

Gilbert, Sara. The History of the Cleveland Browns. 2004. (NFL Today Ser.). (Illus.). 32p. (YA). (gr. 5-9). 18.95 *(978-1-58341-293-0(X))* Creative Co., The.

—NFL Today: Cleveland Browns. 2013. (NFL Today Ser.). (ENG., Illus.). 48p. (J). (gr. 4-7). pap. 12.00 *(978-0-89812-852-9(8)*, Creative Paperbacks) Creative Co., The.

—The Story of the Cleveland Browns. 2013. (J). 35.65 *(978-1-60818-299-2(1)*, Creative Education) 2009. 48p. (YA). (gr. 5-9). 22.95 *(978-1-58341-752-2(4))* Creative Co., The.

Gitlin, Martin. Cleveland Browns, 1 vol. 2010. (Inside the NFL Ser.). (ENG.). 48p. (YA). (gr. 3-6). lib. bdg. 32.79 *(978-1-61714-008-2(2))* ABDO Publishing Co.

Glave, Tom. Cleveland Browns. 2015. (Insider's Guide to Pro Football Ser.). (ENG.). 32p. (J). (gr. k-3). 28.50 *(978-1-63143-993-3(6)*, 208828) Child's World, Inc., The.

Morey, Allan. The Cleveland Browns Story. 2016. (NFL Teams Ser.). (ENG., Illus.). 32p. (J). (gr. 3-7). lib. bdg. 26.95 *(978-1-62617-362-0(1)*, Torque Bks.) Bellwether Media.

Wyner, Zach. Cleveland Browns. 2014. (Inside the NFL Ser.). (ENG., Illus.). 32p. (J). (gr. 4-7). lib. bdg. 28.55 *(978-1-4896-0810-9(9)*, AV2 by Weigl) Weigl Pubs., Inc.

CLEVELAND INDIANS (BASEBALL TEAM)

Connery-Boyd, Peg. Cleveland Indians. 2016. (Hawk's Nest Activity Bks.: 0). (ENG.). 64p. (J). (gr. k-3). pap., act. bk. ed. 8.99 *(978-1-4926-3562-8(6))* Sourcebooks, Inc.

Feller, Bob. Hello, Slider! 2007. (J). 14.95 *(978-1-932888-88-1(8))* Mascot Bks., Inc.

Gitlin, Martin. Cleveland Indians, 1 vol. 2011. (Inside MLB Ser.). (ENG., Illus.). 48p. (YA). (gr. 3-6). lib. bdg. 32.79 *(978-1-61714-041-9(4))* ABDO Publishing Co.

Gitlin, Marty. Cleveland Indians, 1 vol. 2014. (Inside MLB Ser.). (ENG., Illus.). 48p. (J). (gr. 3-6). lib. bdg. 32.79 *(978-1-62403-467-1(5)*, SportsZone) ABDO Publishing Co.

LeBoutillier, Nate. The Story of the Cleveland Indians. 2011. (J). 35.65 *(978-1-60818-038-7(7)*, Creative Education) Creative Co., The.

Pueschner, Gordon. The Story of the Cleveland Indians. 2007. (Baseball, the Great American Game Ser.). (Illus.). 48p. (YA). (gr. 4-7). lib. bdg. 32.80 *(978-1-58341-485-9(1))* Creative Co., The.

Stewart, Mark. The Cleveland Indians. 2012. (Team Spirit Ser.). 48p. (J). (gr. 3-6). lib. bdg. 29.27 *(978-1-59953-479-4(7))* Norwood Hse. Pr.

CLIFF DWELLERS AND CLIFF DWELLINGS

see also Mounds and Mound Builders

Anderson, Dale. The Anasazi Culture at Mesa Verde. 2003. (Landmark Events in American History Ser.). (Illus.). 48p. (gr. 5-12). lib. bdg. 31.00 *(978-0-8368-5371-1(7)*, Gareth Stevens Secondary Library) Stevens, Gareth Publishing LLLP.

Blake, Kevin & Yates, Martha. Cliff Dwellings: Empty Windows. 2015. (Abandoned: Towns Without People Ser.). (ENG.). 32p. (J). (gr. 2-7). lib. bdg. 26.60 *(978-1-62724-522-7(7))* Bearport Publishing Co., Inc.

Collins, Terry, et al. The Mesa Verde Cliff Dwellers: An Isabel Soto Archaeology Adventure, 1 vol. 2010. (Graphic Expeditions Ser.). (ENG.). 32p. (gr. 3-4). pap. 8.10 *(978-1-4296-4861-5(9))*; pap. 47.70 *(978-1-4296-5144-8(X))* Capstone Press of Coughlan Cos. (Graphic Library).

—The Mesa Verde Cliff Dwellers: An Isabel Soto Archaeology Adventure, 1 vol. Anderson, Bill, illus. 2010. (Graphic Expeditions Ser.). (ENG.). 32p. (gr. 3-4). lib. bdg. 30.65 *(978-1-4296-3971-2(7)*, Graphic Library) Capstone Press of Coughlan Cos.

Fay, Gail. Secrets of Mesa Verde: Cliff Dwellings of the Pueblo, 1 vol. 2014. (Archaeological Mysteries Ser.). (ENG.). 32p. (gr. 3-4). lib. bdg. 27.99 *(978-1-4765-9918-2(1))* Capstone Press of Coughlan Cos.

CLIFFORD, THE BIG RED DOG (FICTITIOUS CHARACTER)—FICTION

Aboff, Marcie. Santa's Big Red Helper. Haefele, Steve, illus. 2005. (Clifford Ser.). (ENG.). 80p. (J). (gr. k — 1). 2.99 *(978-0-439-79150-2(2))* Scholastic, Inc.

Bridwell, Norman. Clifford & the Halloween Parade. Bridwell, Norman, illus. 2004. (Scholastic Reader, Level 1 Ser.). (ENG., Illus.). 32p. (J). (gr. -1-3). 3.99 *(978-0-439-09834-2(3))* Scholastic, Inc.

—Clifford at the Circus. (Clifford, the Big Red Dog Ser.). (Illus.). (J). (gr. k-2). 6.95 *(978-0-590-68639-6(9))* Scholastic, Inc.

—Clifford Collection. Bridwell, Norman, illus. 2012. (ENG., Illus.). 192p. (J). (gr. -1-k). 12.99 *(978-0-545-45013-3(6))* Scholastic, Inc.

—Clifford Goes to Dog School. 2010. (Clifford 8x8 Ser.). (gr. -1-2). lib. bdg. 13.55 *(978-0-613-45580-0(0)*, Turtleback) Turtleback Bks.

—Clifford Goes to Kindergarten. 2015. (Clifford Ser.). (ENG., Illus.). 32p. (J). (gr. -1-k). pap. 3.99 *(978-0-545-82335-7(8))* Scholastic, Inc.

—Clifford Sees America. 2012. (Scholastic Reader Level 1 Ser.). (ENG.). 32p. (J). (gr. -1-3). pap. 3.99 *(978-0-545-23144-2(2)*, Cartwheel Bks.) Scholastic, Inc.

—Clifford Sees America. 2012. (Clifford: Scholastic Readers Level 1 Ser.). lib. bdg. 13.55 *(978-0-606-23908-0(1)*, Turtleback) Turtleback Bks.

—Clifford Takes a Trip. Bridwell, Norman, illus. 2011. (Clifford Ser.). (ENG., Illus.). 32p. (J). (gr. -1-k). pap. 3.99 *(978-0-545-21591-6(9)*, Cartwheel Bks.) Scholastic, Inc.

—Clifford the Big Red Dog. 2006. (Clifford Ser.). (ENG.). (J). (gr. -1-3). 18.95 *(978-0-439-87593-6(5))* Scholastic, Inc.

—Clifford the Big Red Dog. 2010. (Clifford 8x8 Ser.). lib. bdg. 13.55 *(978-0-88103-203-1(4)*, Turtleback) Turtleback Bks.

—Clifford the Small Red Puppy. 2007. (Clifford Ser.). (ENG.). (J). (gr. -1-3). 18.95 *(978-0-439-02313-9(0))* Scholastic, Inc.

—Clifford Va al Doctor. Bridwell, Norman, illus. 2011. (Scholastic Reader Level 1 Ser.).Tr. of Clifford Goes to the Doctor. (SPA., Illus.). 32p. (J). (gr. -1-3). pap. 3.99 *(978-0-545-34118-9(3)*, Scholastic en Espanol) Scholastic, Inc.

—Clifford Visits the Zoo. Bridwell, Norman, illus. 2014. (ENG., Illus.). 40p. (J). (— 1). 12.99 *(978-0-545-66896-5(4))* Scholastic, Inc.

—Clifford y la Hora de Dormir. 2003. (Clifford Ser.).Tr. of Clifford's Bedtime. (SPA & ENG., Illus.). 7p. (J). (— 1). 4.99 *(978-0-439-54568-6(4)*, Scholastic en Espanol) Scholastic, Inc.

—Clifford y la Hora del Bano. 2003. (Clifford Ser.).Tr. of Clifford's Bathtime. (SPA & ENG., Illus.). 16p. (J). (— 1). bds. 4.99 *(978-0-439-54567-9(6)*, Scholastic en Espanol) Scholastic, Inc.

—Clifford y los Sondios de los Animales. 2003. (Clifford Ser.).Tr. of Clifford's Animal Sounds. (SPA & ENG.). 7p. (J). (— 1). bds. 4.99 *(978-0-439-55109-0(9)*, Scholastic en Espanol) Scholastic, Inc.

—Clifford's Bedtime Story. Bridwell, Norman, illus. 2013. (Clifford Ser.). (ENG., Illus.). 20p. (J). (gr. -1-k). bds. 8.99 *(978-0-545-49577-6(6))* Scholastic, Inc.

—Clifford's Birthday Party. Bridwell, Norman, illus. 50th anniv. ed. 2013. (Clifford Ser.). (ENG., Illus.). 32p. (J). (gr. -1-3). pap. 4.99 *(978-0-545-47956-1(8))* Scholastic, Inc.

—Clifford's Christmas. Bridwell, Norman, illus. 2011. (Clifford 8x8 Ser.). (ENG., Illus.). 32p. (J). (gr. -1-k). pap. 3.99 *(978-0-545-21596-1(X)*, Cartwheel Bks.) Scholastic, Inc.

—Clifford's Christmas Treasury. 2005. (Illus.). 96p. (gr. -1-3). pap. 10.99 *(978-0-439-79137-3(5))* Scholastic, Inc.

—Clifford's Day with Dad. Bridwell, Norman, illus. 2011. (Clifford 8x8 Ser.). (ENG., Illus.). 32p. (J). (gr. -1-k). pap. 3.99 *(978-0-545-21593-0(5)*, Cartwheel Bks.) Scholastic, Inc.

—Clifford's Field Day. 2012. (Scholastic Reader Level 1 Ser.). (ENG.). 32p. (J). (gr. -1-3). pap. 3.99 *(978-0-545-22325-6(3)*, Cartwheel Bks.) Scholastic, Inc.

—Clifford's Field Day. 2012. (Clifford: Scholastic Readers Level 1 Ser.). lib. bdg. 13.55 *(978-0-606-23907-3(3)*, Turtleback) Turtleback Bks.

—Clifford's First Christmas. (Clifford, the Big Red Dog Ser.). (FRE., Illus.). (J). (gr. k-2). pap. 5.99 *(978-0-590-24374-2(8))* Scholastic, Inc.

—Clifford's First Halloween. Bridwell, Norman, illus. 2010. (Clifford Ser.). (ENG., Illus.). 20p. (J). (gr. k — 1). bds. 6.99 *(978-0-545-21774-3(1)*, Cartwheel Bks.) Scholastic, Inc.

—Clifford's Halloween. Bridwell, Norman, illus. 2011. (Clifford 8x8 Ser.). (ENG., Illus.). 32p. (J). (gr. -1-k). pap. 3.99 *(978-0-545-21595-4(1)*, Cartwheel Bks.) Scholastic, Inc.

—Clifford's Happy Easter. Bridwell, Norman, illus. 2011. (Clifford 8x8 Ser.). (ENG., Illus.). 32p. (J). (gr. -1-k). pap. 3.99 *(978-0-545-21587-9(0)*, Cartwheel Bks.) Scholastic, Inc.

—Clifford's Manners. 2010. (Clifford 8x8 Ser.). (ENG., Illus.). 32p. (J). (gr. -1-3). pap. 3.99 *(978-0-545-21586-2(2)*, Cartwheel Bks.) Scholastic, Inc.

—Clifford's Puppy Days. 2010. (Clifford 8x8 Ser.). (ENG., Illus.). 32p. (J). (gr. -1-3). pap. 3.99 *(978-0-545-21583-1(8)*, Cartwheel Bks.) Scholastic, Inc.

—Clifford's School Story Box. Bridwell, Norman, illus. 2015. (ENG., Illus.). (J). (gr. -1-k). 10.99 *(978-0-545-83737-8(5))* Scholastic, Inc.

—Clifford's Sports Day. (Clifford, the Big Red Dog Ser.). (Illus.). 32p. (J). (gr. k-2). pap. 5.99 *(978-0-590-16002-5(8))* Scholastic, Inc.

—Clifford's Tricks. (Clifford, the Big Red Dog Ser.). (FRE., Illus.). (J). (gr. k-2). pap. 5.99 *(978-0-590-73954-2(9))* Scholastic, Inc.

—La Coleccion. Bridwell, Norman, illus. 2012. (Clifford Ser.). (SPA., Illus.). 192p. (J). (gr. -1-k). 12.99 *(978-0-545-45692-0(4)*, Scholastic en Espanol) Scholastic, Inc.

Bridwell, Norman & Scholastic, Inc. Staff. The Big Red Dog. 2010. (Clifford Ser.). (ENG.). (J). (gr. -1-3). pap. 12.99 incl. audio compact disk *(978-0-545-25415-1(9))* Scholastic, Inc.

—Clifford the Big Red Dog. Bridwell, Norman, illus. unabr. ed. 2006. (Clifford Ser.). (ENG., Illus.). (J). (gr. -1-3). 9.99 *(978-0-439-87587-5(0))* Scholastic, Inc.

—Clifford's Bedtime Story Box. Bridwell, Norman, illus. 2013. (ENG., Illus.). (J). (gr. -1-k). pap. 10.99 *(978-0-545-61521-1(6))* Scholastic, Inc.

Brooke, Samantha. Apple-Picking Day! Durk, Jim, illus. 2007. (Clifford's Puppy Days Ser.). (J). *(978-0-545-02841-7(8))* Scholastic, Inc.

Davis, Guy. Spring Garden Sticker Storybook. 2005. (Clifford's Puppy Days Ser.). *(978-0-439-69046-1(3))* Scholastic, Inc.

Denega, Danielle & Bridwell, Norman. Pumpkin Patch Puppy. 2006. (Illus.). 26p. (J). pap. *(978-0-439-87764-0(4))* Scholastic, Inc.

Fisch, Sarah. The Smallest Snowman. Durk, Jim, illus. 2006. (J). *(978-0-439-81616-8(5))* Scholastic, Inc.

McVeigh, Mark, et al. Clifford for President. LaPadula, Tom, illus. 2004. (Clifford's Big Red Reader Ser.). (ENG.). 32p. (J). (gr. -1-3). pap. 3.99 *(978-0-439-69391-2(8))* Scholastic, Inc.

CLIMATE

Here are entered works on climate as it relates to man and to plant and animal life, including the effects of changes of climate. Works limited to the climate of a particular region are entered under the name of the place with the subdivision Climate. Works on the state of the atmosphere at a given time and place with respect to heat and cold, wetness or dryness, calm or storm, are entered under Weather. Scientific works on the atmosphere, especially weather factors, are entered under Meteorology.

see also Meteorology; Rain and Rainfall; Seasons; Weather

Aitken, Stephen. Ecosystems at Risk. 2013. 64p. (J). (gr. 5-8). 31.36 *(978-1-60870-463-7(7))*; pap. 15.28 *(978-1-62712-043-2(2))* Cavendish Square Publishing.

—Fever at the Poles, 1 vol. 2011. (Climate Change Ser.). (ENG., Illus.). 32p. (J). (gr. k-3). 28.50 *(978-1-61641-671-3(8))* Magic Wagon.

—Fever in the Oceans, 1 vol. 2011. (Climate Change Ser.). (ENG., Illus.). 32p. (J). (gr. k-3). 28.50 *(978-1-61641-672-0(6))* Magic Wagon.

—Ocean Life. 2013. (Climate Crisis Ser.). (Illus.). 64p. (J). (gr. 5-8). 31.36 *(978-1-60870-460-6(2))* Cavendish Square Publishing.

—People. 2013. (Illus.). 64p. (J). (gr. 5-8). 31.36 *(978-1-60870-461-3(0))* Cavendish Square Publishing.

—Plants & Insects. 2013. 64p. (J). (gr. 5-8). 31.36 *(978-1-60870-462-0(9))*; pap. 15.28 *(978-1-62712-042-5(4))* Cavendish Square Publishing.

Aitken, Stephen, illus. People in Trouble. 2011. (J). *(978-1-61641-675-1(0))* Magic Wagon.

Allaby, Michael. Atmosphere: A Scientific History of Air, Weather, & Climate. Garratt, Richard, illus. 2009. (Discovering the Earth Ser.). 242p. (C). (gr. 9-18). 39.95 *(978-0-8160-6098-6(3))* Facts On File, Inc.

Anderson, Michael. Investigating Earth's Weather. 2011. (J). lib. bdg. 31.70 *(978-1-61530-499-8(1))* Rosen Publishing Group, Inc., The.

Arnold, Caroline. A Warmer World. Hogan, Jamie, illus. 2012. (ENG.). 32p. (J). (gr. 2-5). pap. 7.95 *(978-1-58089-267-4(1))* Charlesbridge Publishing, Inc.

Baker, Stuart. In Temperate Zones. 2009. (Climate Change Ser.). 32p. (gr. 4). 28.50 *(978-0-7614-4441-1(6))* Marshall Cavendish Corp.

Basher, Simon. Basher Science: Climate Change. 2015. (Basher Science Ser.). (ENG., Illus.). 128p. (J). (gr. 5). pap. 8.99 *(978-0-7534-7175-3(2)*, 9780753471753, Kingfisher) Roaring Brook Pr.

Bassett, John. Experiments with Weather & Climate. 2010. (Cool Science Ser.). 32p. (J). (gr. 5-6). lib. bdg. 28.00 *(978-1-4339-3447-6(7))*; (Illus.). pap. 10.50 *(978-1-4339-3448-3(5))* Stevens, Gareth Publishing LLLP. (Gareth Stevens Learning Library).

Benchmark Education Company. Weather & Climate (Teacher Guide) 2005. *(978-1-4108-4635-8(0))* Benchmark Education Co.

Benchmark Education Company, LLC Staff, compiled by. Weather & Seasons. 2006. (J). 265.00 *(978-1-4108-7031-5(6))* Benchmark Education Co.

Benoit, Peter. Climate Change. 2011. (True Bk Ser.). 48p. (J). (ENG.). pap. 6.95 *(978-0-531-28106-2(X))*; (gr. 3-5). 29.00 *(978-0-531-20557-0(6))* Scholastic Library Publishing. (Children's Pr.).

Besel, Jennifer M. The Hottest Places on Earth. 2010. (Extreme Planet Ser.). (ENG.). 24p. (gr. 1-2). lib. bdg. 25.32 *(978-1-4296-3964-4(4)*, First Facts) Capstone Press of Coughlan Cos.

Bethune, Helen. Why Do Glaciers Grind? 2010. (Solving Science Mysteries Ser.). (Illus.). 24p. (YA). (gr. 3-6). lib. bdg. 22.60 *(978-1-4488-0391-0(8))* Rosen Publishing Group, Inc., The.

The Big Picture - Climate. 2010. (Big Picture: Climate Ser.). (ENG.). 24p. (gr. 1-2). pap. 166.80 *(978-1-4296-5827-0(4)*, First Facts) Capstone Press of Coughlan Cos.

Biomes Atlases, Set. 2nd ed. Incl. Arctic Tundra & Polar Deserts. Woodford, Chris. 34.65 *(978-1-4329-4172-7(0))*; Deserts & Semideserts. Allaby, Michael. 34.65 *(978-1-4329-4175-8(5))*; Mountains & Highlands. Harris, Tim. 34.65 *(978-1-4329-4174-1(7))*; Shrublands. Burnie, David. 34.65 *(978-1-4329-4178-9(X))*; Taiga. Day, Trevor. 34.65 *(978-1-4329-4179-6(8))*; Temperate Forests. Woodward, John. (Illus.). 34.65 *(978-1-4329-4180-2(1))*; Temperate Grasslands. Hoare, Ben. 34.65 *(978-1-4329-4181-9(X))*; Tropical Forests. Jackson, Tom. 34.65 *(978-1-4329-4177-2(1))*; Tropical Grasslands. Morgan, Ben. 34.65 *(978-1-4329-4182-6(8))*; Wetlands. Beatty, Richard. 34.65 *(978-1-4329-4183-3(6))*; (gr. 6-9). (Biomes Atlases Ser.). (ENG.). 64p. 2010. Set lib. bdg. 346.50 *(978-1-4329-4184-0(4))* Heinemann-Raintree.

Birch, Robin. Climate Change. 2009. (Weather & Climate Ser.). 32p. (gr. 3). 28.50 *(978-0-7614-4473-2(4))* Marshall Cavendish Corp.

—Earth's Climate. 2009. (Weather & Climate Ser.). 32p. (gr. 3). 28.50 *(978-0-7614-4471-8(8))* Marshall Cavendish Corp.

—Extreme Weather. 2009. (Weather & Climate Ser.). 32p. (gr. 3). 28.50 *(978-0-7614-4468-8(8))* Marshall Cavendish Corp.

Bishop, Amanda. Climate Change. 2008. (Saving Our World Ser.). 32p. (gr. 4-18). lib. bdg. 28.50 *(978-0-7614-3219-7(1)*, Benchmark Bks.) Marshall Cavendish Corp.

Boothroyd, Jennifer. What Is Climate? 2014. (First Step Nonfiction - Let's Watch the Weather Ser.). 24p. (gr. k-2). (Illus.). pap. 6.95 *(978-1-4677-4498-0(0))*; (ENG.). lib. bdg. 23.93 *(978-1-4677-3918-4(9)*, Lerner Pubns.) Lerner Publishing Group.

Bow, James. Earth's Secrets. 2010. (Invisible Worlds Ser.). 48p. (gr. 4). 28.50 *(978-0-7614-4196-0(4))* Marshall Cavendish GBR. Dist: Marshall Cavendish Corp.

Brannon, Cecelia H. A Look at Erosion & Weathering. 2016. (Rock Cycle Ser.). (ENG.). 32p. (J). (gr. 3-4). pap. 10.52 *(978-0-7660-7278-7(9))* Enslow Pubs., Inc.

Brasch, Nicolas & Rigby Education Staff. A Moving World. 2004. (Rigby PM Plus Extension Ser.). (ENG., Illus.). 32p. (gr. 4-5). pap. 9.05 *(978-0-7578-9260-8(4))* Rigby Education.

Bredeson, Carmen. Deadly Storm Alert! The Dangerous el Niño & la Niña. 2012. (Disasters — People in Peril Ser.). (Illus.). 48p. (J). (gr. 5-18). 25.27 *(978-0-7660-4014-4(3))* Enslow Pubs., Inc.

Burgan, Michael. Climate Change & the Polar Regions. 2017. (Exploring the Polar Regions Today Ser.: Vol. 8). (ENG.). (YA). (gr. 7-12). 23.95 ***(978-1-4222-3868-4(7))*** Mason Crest.

Canavan, Roger. You Wouldn't Want to Live Without Extreme Weather! Bergin, Mark, illus. 2015. (You Wouldn't Want to Live Without... Ser.). (ENG.). (J). 40p. pap. 9.95 *(978-0-531-21408-4(7))*; 32p. lib. bdg. 29.00 *(978-0-531-21365-0(X))* Scholastic Library Publishing. (Watts, Franklin).

—You Wouldn't Want to Live Without Extreme Weather! 2015. (You Wouldn't Want to Live Without Ser.). lib. bdg. 20.80 *(978-0-606-36711-0(X))* Turtleback Bks.

Capstone Press. Climate, 1 vol. 2010. (Big Picture Ser.). (ENG.). 32p. lib. bdg. 95.96 *(978-1-4296-5927-7(0)*, First Facts) Capstone Press of Coughlan Cos.

Cardenas, Ernesto & Saavedra, Patricia. El estado del Tiempo. I.t. ed. 2006. (SPA., Illus.). 16p. pap. 4.95 *(978-1-933668-22-2(9))* Milo Educational Bks. & Resources.

Cardenas, Ernesto A. The Four Seasons of the Year. 2009. pap. 4.95 *(978-1-60698-092-7(0))* Milo Educational Bks. & Resources.

Changing Climates. 2010. (Global Connections Ser.). (Illus.). 120p. (gr. 5-8). 35.00 *(978-1-60413-291-5(4)*, Chelsea Hse.) Facts On File, Inc.

Changing Habitats. 2015. (Illus.). 44p. (J). *(978-0-7166-2708-1(6))* World Bk., Inc.

Christie, Peter. 50 Climate Questions: A Blizzard of Blistering Facts. Kinnaird, Ross, illus. 2012. (50 Questions Ser.). (ENG.). 120p. (J). (gr. 3-8). 22.95 *(978-1-55451-375-8(8)*, 9781554513758); pap. 14.95 *(978-1-55451-374-1(X)*, 9781554513741) Annick Pr., Ltd. CAN. Dist: Publishers Group West (PGW).

Corporate Contributor Staff & O'Brien, Cynthia. Climate Maps. 2012. (ENG.). 32p. (J). pap. *(978-0-7787-4496-2(5))*; lib. bdg. *(978-0-7787-4491-7(4))* Crabtree Publishing Co.

Cunningham, Anne C. & Green, Kenneth. Climate Change: A Threat to All Life on Earth. 2016. (End of Life As We Know It Ser.). (ENG., Illus.). 128p. (J). (gr. 7-8). lib. bdg. 37.27 *(978-0-7660-7284-8(3))* Enslow Pubs., Inc.

Davies, Nicola & Lovelock, James. Gaia Warriors. 2011. (ENG., Illus.). 192p. (J). (gr. 5-9). pap. 14.99 *(978-0-7636-4808-4(6))* Candlewick Pr.

Daynes, Katie. See Inside Weather & Climate IR. 2015. (See Inside Board Bks.). (ENG.). 16p. (J). (gr. k-5). 14.99 *(978-0-7945-2161-5(4)*, Usborne) EDC Publishing.

Desonie, Dana. Climate. 2007. (Our Fragile Planet Ser.). (Illus.). 199p. (YA). (gr. 7-12). lib. bdg. 35.00 *(978-0-8160-6214-0(5))* Facts On File, Inc.

Dorion, Christiane. How the Weather Works: A Hands-On Guide to Our Changing Climate. Young, Beverley, illus. 2011. (Explore the Earth Ser.). (ENG.). 20p. (J). (gr. 2-5). 19.99 *(978-0-7636-5262-3(8)*, Templar) Candlewick Pr.

Eagen, Rachel. Flood & Monsoon Alert! 3rd rev. ed. 2011. (ENG., Illus.). 32p. (J). pap. *(978-0-7787-1624-2(4))* Crabtree Publishing Co.

Encyclopaedia Britannica, Inc. Staff, compiled by. Britannica Illustrated Science Library: Climate, 16 vols. 2008. (Illus.). (J). 29.95 *(978-1-59339-386-1(5))* Encyclopaedia Britannica, Inc.

—Learn & Explore: Earth's Changing Environment. 2010. (gr. 7-12). 24.95 *(978-1-61535-339-2(9))* Encyclopaedia Britannica, Inc.

Espejo, Roman. Adaptation & Climate Change. 2012. (At Issue Ser.). (ENG.). 128p. (gr. 10-12). pap. 27.80 *(978-0-7377-6142-9(3))*; lib. bdg. 39.40 *(978-0-7377-6141-2(5))* Cengage Gale. (Greenhaven Pr., Inc.).

Flannery, Tim. We Are the Weather Makers: The History of Climate Change. 2010. (ENG., Illus.). 320p. (YA). (gr. 9). pap. 12.99 *(978-0-7636-4656-1(3))* Candlewick Pr.

Forces of Nature. 2009. (Illus.). 47p. (J). *(978-0-7166-9822-7(6))* World Bk., Inc.

Ganeri, Anita. El Sol. 2004. (tiempo de aqui (Weather Around You- Spanish) Ser.). (SPA.). 24p. (gr. 1-4). lib. bdg. 22.00 *(978-0-8368-4365-1(7)*, Weekly Reader Leveled Readers) Stevens, Gareth Publishing LLLP.

—Wild Weather, 1 vol. 2012. (Extreme Nature Ser.). (ENG.). 32p. (gr. 1-3). pap. 8.29 *(978-1-4109-4704-8(1))*; lib. bdg. 29.99 *(978-1-4109-4699-7(1))* Heinemann-Raintree. (Read Me!).

George, Charles & George, Linda. Climate Change Research. 2010. (Inside Science Ser.). (YA). (gr. 7-12). 26.95 *(978-1-60152-128-6(6))* ReferencePoint Pr., Inc.

Gosman, Gillian. What Do You Know about Weather & Climate? 2013. (20 Questions: Earth Science Ser.). (ENG., Illus.). 24p. (J). (gr. 3-6). pap. 8.25 *(978-1-4488-9860-2(9)*, PowerKids Pr.) Rosen Publishing Group, Inc., The.

Greek, Joe. Weather & Climate. 2017. (J). ***(978-1-5383-0032-9(X))*** Rosen Publishing Group, Inc., The.

Green, Jen. Changing Climates. 2006. (Illus.). 32p. (YA). (gr. 4-18). lib. bdg. 27.10 *(978-1-59389-118-3(0))* Chrysalis Education.

Gregory, Cam. Why Are Polar Bears in Danger? 2014. (Little Books of Answers: Level e Ser.). (Illus.). 16p. (gr. k-2). pap. 7.95 *(978-1-927136-44-7(X))* Three Crows Media NZL. Dist: RiverStream Publishing.

Gregory, Josh. Climate Scientist. 2013. (21st Century Skills Library: Cool STEM Careers Ser.). (ENG.). 32p. (J). (gr. 4-8). 28.50 *(978-1-62431-002-7(8)*, 202459); pap. 14.21 *(978-1-62431-026-3(5)*, 202461) Cherry Lake Publishing.

Gunderson, Jessica. Global Warming. 2010. (Earth Issues Ser.). 48p. (YA). (gr. 5-18). 23.95 *(978-1-58341-982-3(9)*, Creative Education) Creative Co., The.

Hall, Julie. A Hot Planet Needs Cool Kids: Understanding Climate Change & What You can do About it. 2007. 88p. (J). pap. 15.99 *(978-0-615-15585-2(5))* Green Goat Bks.

Hirschmann, Kris & Herndon, Ryan, compiled by. Guinness World Records, up Close. 2007. (Illus.). 47p. *(978-0-439-89828-7(5))* Scholastic, Inc.

Hollar, Sherman. Pioneers in the World of Weather & Climatology. 2012. (Inventors & Innovators Ser.). (ENG.,

CD

Illus.). 112p. (YA). (gr. 7-12). 65.80 *(978-1-61530-787-6(7))*; 32.90 *(978-1-61530-702-9(8))* Rosen Publishing Group, Inc., The.

Holt, Rinehart and Winston Staff. Environmental Science Chptr. 13: Atmosphere & Climate. 4th ed. Date not set. pap. 11.20 *(978-0-03-068073-1(5))* Holt McDougal.

—Holt Science & Technology Chapter 16: Earth Science: Understanding the Weather. 5th ed. 2004. (Illus.). pap. 12.86 *(978-0-03-030323-4(0))* Holt McDougal.

—Holt Science & Technology Chapter 17: Earth Science: Climate. 5th ed. 2004. (Illus.). pap. 12.86 *(978-0-03-030326-5(5))* Holt McDougal.

Houghton Gosman, Gillian. What Do You Know about Weather & Climate? 2013. (20 Questions: Earth Science Ser.). 24p. (J). (gr. 3-6). 22.60 *(978-1-4488-9701-8(7)*, PowerKids Pr.) Rosen Publishing Group, Inc., The.

Howell, Laura. Introduction to Weather & Climate Change. 2004. (Geography Ser.). (ENG., Illus.). 96p. (J). pap. 14.95 *(978-0-7945-0629-2(1))* EDC Publishing.

—Introduction to Weather & Climate Change. Furnival, Keith, illus. 2004. (Geography Ser.). 96p. (J). (gr. 5). lib. bdg. 22.95 *(978-1-58086-613-2(1)*, Usborne) EDC Publishing.

Hunter, Nick. Science vs. Climate Change. 2013. (Science Fights Back Ser.). (Illus.). 48p. (gr. 4-6). 31.95 *(978-1-4339-8678-9(7))*; pap. 14.05 *(978-1-4339-8679-6(5))* Stevens, Gareth Publishing LLLP. (Gareth Stevens Learning Library).

Hunter, Rebecca. Climate Change. 2012. (Eco Alert! Ser.). (Illus.). 32p. (gr. 4-6). lib. bdg. 28.50 *(978-1-59771-295-8(7))* Sea-To-Sea Pubns.

Joanne, O'Sullivan. Bizarre Weather: Howling winds, pouring rain, blazing heat, freezing cold, huge hurricanes, violent earthquakes, tsunami's, tornadoes & more of nature's Fury. 2013. (ENG., Illus.). 160p. (J). pap. 7.95 *(978-1-936140-72-5(1)*, Imagine Publishing) Charlesbridge Publishing, Inc.

Johnson, Rebecca L. Investigating Climate Change: Scientists' Search for Answers in a Warming World. 2008. (Discovery! Ser.). (ENG., Illus.). 112p. (gr. 6-12). lib. bdg. 31.93 *(978-0-8225-6792-9(X))* Lerner Publishing Group.

Juettner, Bonnie. Climate Change. 2011. (J). *(978-1-60217-030-8(4))* Erickson Pr.

Kallio, Jamie. 12 Things to Know about Climate Change. 2015. (ENG., Illus.). 32p. (J). *(978-1-63235-028-2(9))* Pr. Room Editions LLC.

Kalman, Bobbie. What Is Climate? 2012. (ENG.). 32p. (J). *(978-0-7787-2773-6(4))*; pap. *(978-0-7787-2778-1(5))* Crabtree Publishing Co.

Kudlinski, Kathleen V. Boy, Were We Wrong about the Weather! Serra, Sebastià, illus. 2015. (ENG.). 32p. (J). (gr. -1-3). 16.99 *(978-0-8037-3793-8(9)*, Dial Bks) Penguin Young Readers Group.

Kummer, Patricia K. Africa. 2013. (J). *(978-0-7614-8088-4(9))* Marshall Cavendish Corp.

—Asia. 2014. (J). *(978-0-7614-8090-7(0))* Marshall Cavendish Corp.

—The Changing Climate of Asia. 2014. 48p. pap. 12.93 *(978-1-62712-443-0(8))* Cavendish Square Publishing.

—The Changing Climate of North America. 2014. 48p. pap. 12.93 *(978-1-62712-452-2(7))* Cavendish Square Publishing.

Kusky, Timothy. Climate Change: Shifting Glaciers, Deserts, & Climate Belts. 2008. (Hazardous Earth Ser.). (Illus.). 156p. (gr. 6-12). 39.50 *(978-0-8160-6466-3(0))* Facts On File, Inc.

Lanz, Helen. Having the Energy. 2012. (Go Green Ser.). (Illus.). 32p. (J). (gr. 3-6). lib. bdg. 28.50 *(978-1-59771-301-6(5))* Sea-To-Sea Pubns.

Lawrence, Ellen. What Is Climate? 2012. (Weather Wise Ser.). 24p. (J). (gr. -1-3). lib. bdg. 23.93 *(978-1-61772-401-5(7))* Bearport Publishing Co., Inc.

Linde, Barbara. Climates of the World: Identifying & Comparing Mean, Median, & Mode. 2009. (PowerMath: Proficiency Plus Ser.). 32p. (gr. 4-5). 47.90 *(978-1-60851-407-6(2)*, PowerKids Pr.) Rosen Publishing Group, Inc., The.

Linde, Barbara M. Climates of the World: Identifying & Comparing Mean, Median, & Mode. (PowerMath Ser.). 32p. 2009. (ENG., Illus.). (gr. 5-6). pap. 10.00 *(978-1-4042-5125-0(1)*, PowerKids Pr.) 2005. (Illus.). (YA). (gr. 5-9). lib. bdg. 25.25 *(978-1-4042-2932-7(9))* 2005. 47.50 *(978-1-4042-5219-6(3)*, Rosen Classroom) Rosen Publishing Group, Inc., The.

—Deforestation & Desertification: Text Pairs. 2008. (Bridges/Navigators Ser.). (J). (gr. 6). 94.00 *(978-1-4108-8432-9(5))* Benchmark Education Co.

—Weather & Climate. 2005. (J). pap. *(978-1-4108-4587-0(7))* Benchmark Education Co.

Macdonald, Margaret. When Does This Tree Grow Best? 2014. (Little Books of Answers: Level a Ser.). (Illus.). 16p. (gr. k-2). pap. 7.95 *(978-1-927136-04-1(0))* Three Crows Media NZL. Dist: RiverStream Publishing.

Magic Wagon Staff & ABDO Publishing Company Staff. Climate Change, 1 vol. 2011. (Climate Change Ser.). (ENG., Illus.). 32p. 114.00 *(978-1-61641-669-0(6)*, Looking Glass Library) Magic Wagon.

Mahaney, Ian F. Climate Maps. (Map It! Ser.). 24p. 2009. (gr. 3-4). 42.50 *(978-1-61514-354-2(8)*, PowerKids Pr.) 2006. (Illus.). (YA). (gr. 2-5). lib. bdg. 22.60 *(978-1-4042-3058-3(0))* Rosen Publishing Group, Inc., The.

Maloof, Torrey. Climate, 1 vol. 2015. (Science Readers: Content & Literacy Ser.). (ENG., Illus.). 32p. (gr. 3-3). pap. 8.99 *(978-1-4807-4649-7(5))* Teacher Created Materials, Inc.

McCutcheon, Chuck. What Are Global Warming & Climate Change? Answers for Young Readers. 2010. (World's of Wonder Ser.). (ENG., Illus.). 114p. (J). (gr. 4-18). 34.95 *(978-0-8263-4745-9(2))* Univ. of New Mexico Pr.

Mooney, Carla. Climate & Weather. 2012. (ENG.). 48p. (gr. 4-6). pap. 10.95 *(978-1-61810-258-4(3))* Rourke Educational Media.

Nakaya, Andrea C. What Are the Consequences of Climate Change? 2016. (ENG.). 80p. (J). (gr. 5-12). lib. bdg. *(978-1-68282-078-0(5))* ReferencePoint Pr., Inc.

Nardo, Don. Climate Change. 2009. (Extreme Threats Ser.). 112p. (J). lib. bdg. 28.95 *(978-1-59935-119-3(6))* Reynolds, Morgan Inc.

Natural Cycles & Climate Change. 2015. (Illus.). 48p. (J). *(978-0-7166-2711-1(6))* World Bk., Inc.

Natural Resources Defense Council Staff, et al. Simple Steps Toward a Healthier Earth. Carpenter, Tad, illus. 2010. (ENG.). 80p. (J). (gr. 3-17). pap., act. bk. ed. 12.99 *(978-0-8118-7141-9(X))* Chronicle Bks. LLC.

Nemeth, Jason D. The Atmosphere. 2012. (Our Changing Earth Ser.). (ENG., Illus.). 24p. (J). (gr. 3-6). pap. 8.25 *(978-1-4488-6298-6(1)*, PowerKids Pr.); lib. bdg. 22.60 *(978-1-4488-6170-5(5))* Rosen Publishing Group, Inc., The.

—Climate Change. 2012. (Our Changing Earth Ser.). (ENG.). 24p. (J). (gr. 3-6). pap. 8.25 *(978-1-4488-6290-0(6)*, PowerKids Pr.); lib. bdg. 22.60 *(978-1-4488-6166-8(7))* Rosen Publishing Group, Inc., The.

O'Connell, Bailey. Earth's Rainiest Places. 2015. (Earth's Most Extreme Places Ser.). (ENG.). 24p. (J). (gr. 2-3). pap. 8.15 *(978-1-4824-1910-8(6))* Stevens, Gareth Publishing LLLP.

Orme, Helen. Climate Change. 2008. (Earth in Danger Ser.). (Illus.). 32p. (YA). (gr. 3-6). lib. bdg. 25.27 *(978-1-59716-723-9(1)*, 1284355) Bearport Publishing Co., Inc.

Oxlade, Chris. Climate Change. 2010. (J). 34.25 *(978-1-59920-319-5(7))* Black Rabbit Bks.

Peterson, Cris. Harvest Year. Upitis, Alvis, photos by. 2009. (ENG., Illus.). 32p. (J). pap. 10.95 *(978-1-59078-783-0(8))* Boyds Mills Pr.

Pinna, Lorenzo. El Clima. (SPA.). 326p. (YA). (gr. 5-8). *(978-84-7131-928-9(4))* Editex, Editorial S.A. ESP. Dist: Lectorum Pubns., Inc.

Rajczak, Kristen. The Climate Zones. 2014. (Map Basics Ser.). (Illus.). 24p. (J). (gr. 2-5). 22.60 *(978-1-4824-0800-3(7))* Stevens, Gareth Publishing LLLP.

Reilly, Kathleen M. Explore Weather & Climate! With 25 Great Projects. Stone, Bryan, illus. 2012. (Explore Your World Ser.). (ENG.). 96p. (J). (gr. k-4). pap. 12.95 *(978-1-936313-84-6(7))* Open City Bks.

Ride, Sally & O'Shaughnessy, Tam. Mission Planet Earth: Our World & Its Climate - And How Humans Are Changing Them. 2009. (ENG., Illus.). 80p. (YA). (gr. 4-9). 19.95 *(978-1-59643-310-6(8)*, 9781596433106) Roaring Brook Pr.

Ripley's Believe It Or Not! Staff, et al. Extreme Earth: Fun, Facts, & Earth-Shattering Stories... 2010. (Twist Ser.: 7). (ENG., Illus.). 48p. (J). 12.95 *(978-1-893951-78-5(2))* Ripley Entertainment, Inc.

Rowell, Rebecca. Weather & Climate Through Infographics. Dean, Venitia, illus. 2013. (Super Science Infographics Ser.). (ENG.). 32p. (gr. 3-5). pap. 8.95 *(978-1-4677-1595-9(6))*; lib. bdg. 26.60 *(978-1-4677-1292-7(2)*, Lerner Pubns.) Lerner Publishing Group.

Rustad, Martha E. H. The Driest Places on Earth. 2010. (Extreme Planet Ser.). (ENG.). 24p. (gr. 1-2). lib. bdg. 25.32 *(978-1-4296-3962-0(8)*, First Facts) Capstone Press of Coughlan Cos.

—The Wettest Places on Earth, 1 vol. 2010. (Extreme Planet Ser.). (ENG.). 24p. (gr. 1-2). lib. bdg. 25.32 *(978-1-4296-3966-8(0)*, First Facts) Capstone Press of Coughlan Cos.

Senker, Cath. Focus on Climate Zones. 2017. (Focus on Climate Zones Ser.). (ENG.). 48p. (gr. 4-6). 133.28 *(978-1-4846-3801-9(8)*, Heinemann InfoSearch) Heinemann-Raintree.

—Temperate Climates. 2017. (Focus on Climate Zones Ser.). (ENG., Illus.). 48p. (gr. 4-6). pap. 4.95 *(978-1-4846-3786-9(0))*; lib. bdg. 33.32 *(978-1-4846-3782-1(8))* Heinemann-Raintree. (Heinemann InfoSearch).

Shuckburgh, Emily & Chambers, Catherine. Polar Scientist: The Coolest Jobs on the Planet, 1 vol. HL Studios Staff, illus. 2014. (Coolest Jobs on the Planet Ser.). (ENG.). 48p. (gr. 6-6). pap. 8.99 *(978-1-4109-6648-3(8))* Heinemann-Raintree.

Simpson, Kathleen. Extreme Weather: Science Tackles Global Warming & Climate Change. 2008. (National Geographic Investigates Ser.). (ENG., Illus.). 64p. (J). (gr. 5). lib. bdg. 27.90 *(978-1-4263-0281-7(9)*, National Geographic Children's Bks.) National Geographic Society.

Simpson, Kathleen & National Geographic Kids Staff. Extreme Weather: Science Tackles Global Warming & Climate Change. 2008. (National Geographic Investigates Science Ser.). (ENG., Illus.). 64p. (J). (gr. 5). 17.95 *(978-1-4263-0359-3(9)*, National Geographic Children's Bks.) National Geographic Society.

Singer, Marilyn. On the Same Day in March. 2014. 17.00 *(978-1-63419-675-8(9))* Perfection Learning Corp.

Soll, Karen. Coldest Places on the Planet. 2016. (Extreme Earth Ser.). (ENG., Illus.). 24p. (gr. k-1). lib. bdg. 26.65 *(978-1-4914-8340-4(7)*, Pebble Plus) Capstone Press of Coughlan Cos.

Solway, Andrew. Climate Change. 2010. (World at Risk Ser.). (YA). (gr. 5-9). 34.25 *(978-1-59920-376-8(6))* Black Rabbit Bks.

Spalding, Frank. Catastrophic Climate Change & Global Warming. 2010. (Doomsday Scenarios: Separating Fact from Fiction Ser.). 64p. (YA). (gr. 5-8). E-Book 58.50 *(978-1-4488-1204-2(6))* Rosen Publishing Group, Inc., The.

Spilsbury, Louise. What Is Weather?, 1 vol., 1. 2014. (Let's Find Out! Ser.). (ENG.). 32p. (gr. 3-6). 23.45 *(978-1-62275-276-8(7))* Rosen Publishing Group, Inc., The.

Squire, Ann O. Extreme Weather. 2014. (True Book(tm), a — Extreme Science Ser.). (ENG.). 48p. (J). lib. bdg. 31.00 *(978-0-531-20743-7(9))* Scholastic Library Publishing.

Stein, Paul. Droughts of the Future. 2009. (Library of Future Weather & Climate Ser.). 64p. (gr. 5-5). 58.50 *(978-1-60853-644-3(0))* Rosen Publishing Group, Inc., The.

—Storms of the Future. 2009. (Library of Future Weather & Climate Ser.). 64p. (gr. 5-5). 58.50 *(978-1-60853-651-1(3))* Rosen Publishing Group, Inc., The.

Storad, Conrad J. Studying Weather & Climates. 2011. (ENG., Illus.). 24p. (gr. 2-3). pap. 8.95 *(978-1-61741-951-5(6))* Rourke Educational Media.

Thompson, Clifford. Climatologists!, Vol. 10. 2015. (Scientists in Action Ser.). (Illus.). 48p. (J). (gr. 5). 20.95 *(978-1-4222-3422-8(3))* Mason Crest.

Townsend, John. Is Our Weather Getting Worse? 2010. (Crabtree Connections Ser.). (ENG.). 24p. (J). (gr. 3-6). *(978-0-7787-9957-3(3))*; pap. *(978-0-7787-9979-5(4))* Crabtree Publishing Co.

Twist, Clint. Extreme Earth. 2010. (Ripley Twists Ser.). (Illus.). 48p. (J). (gr. 3-18). lib. bdg. 19.95 *(978-1-4222-1829-7(5)*, 1318258) Mason Crest.

Twist, Clint, et al. Extreme Earth. 2009. (Ripley Twists Ser.). (Illus.). 48p. (J). (gr. 3-18). pap. 8.95 *(978-1-4222-2067-2(2)*, 1318258) Mason Crest.

Viegas, Jennifer, ed. Critical Perspectives on Planet Earth. 2006. (Scientific American Critical Anthologies on Environment & Climate Ser.). (Illus.). 278p. (J). (gr. 3-7). 37.95 *(978-1-4042-0687-8(6))* Rosen Publishing Group, Inc., The.

What Do You Know about Weather & Climate? 2013. (20 Questions: Earth Science Ser.). 24p. (J). (gr. 3-6). pap. 49.50 *(978-1-4488-9861-9(7)*, PowerKids Pr.) Rosen Publishing Group, Inc., The.

Whitfield, David. Rainbows. 2012. (Sky Science Ser.). (ENG., Illus.). 24p. (J). (gr. 3-7). lib. bdg. 27.13 *(978-1-61913-099-9(8)*, 1346030, AV2 by Weigl) Weigl Pubs., Inc.

World Book, Inc. Staff. Food, Water, & Climate Change. 2016. (Illus.). 48p. (J). *(978-0-7166-2705-0(1))* World Bk., Inc.

CLIMATOLOGY

see Climate

CLINTON, BILL, 1946-

Bailer, Darice. William Clinton. 2016. (Premier Presidents Ser.). (ENG.). 24p. (J). (gr. 1-4). 27.07 *(978-1-5038-0880-5(7)*, 210730) Child's World, Inc., The.

Benson, Michael. Bill Clinton. 2003. (Presidential Leaders Ser.). (ENG., Illus.). 112p. (gr. 6-12). 29.27 *(978-0-8225-0819-9(2))* Lerner Publishing Group.

Dunn, Joeming & Dunn, Ben. Bill Clinton: 42nd U. S. President, 1 vol. 2011. (Presidents of the United States Bio-Graphics Ser.). (ENG., Illus.). 32p. (YA). (gr. 3-6). 28.50 *(978-1-61641-645-4(9))* Magic Wagon.

Gregory, Josh. Bill Clinton. 2014. (ENG.). 64p. (J). pap. 8.95 *(978-0-531-25825-5(4))*; lib. bdg. 30.00 *(978-0-531-21329-2(3))* Scholastic Library Publishing.

Gross, M. J. How to Draw the Life & Times of William Jefferson Clinton. 2009. (Kid's Guide to Drawing the Presidents of the United States of America Ser.). 32p. (gr. 4-4). 50.50 *(978-1-61511-166-4(2)*, PowerKids Pr.) Rosen Publishing Group, Inc., The.

Gross, Miriam J. How to Draw the Life & Times of William Jefferson Clinton. 2007. (Kid's Guide to Drawing the Presidents of the United States of America Ser.). (Illus.). 32p. (YA). (gr. 2-5). 26.50 *(978-1-4042-3018-7(1))* Rosen Publishing Group, Inc., The.

Hansen, Grace. Bill Clinton, 1 vol. 2014. (United States President Biographies Ser.). (ENG.). 24p. (J). (gr. 4-8). lib. bdg. 28.50 *(978-1-62970-087-8(8))* ABDO Publishing Co.

—Bill Clinton. 2015. (Biografías de Los Presidentes de Los Estados Unidos Ser.). (SPA., Illus.). 24p. (gr. k-1). pap. 7.95 *(978-1-4966-0405-7(9))* Capstone Classroom.

Lee, Sally. William Jefferson Clinton, 1 vol. (Presidential Biographies Ser.). (ENG.). 24p. (gr. k-1). 2014. pap. 6.29 *(978-1-4765-9627-3(1)*, Pebble Bks.) 2012. (Illus.). lib. bdg. 26.65 *(978-1-4296-8585-6(9)*, Pebble Plus) Capstone Press of Coughlan Cos.

Mapua, Jeff. Bill & Hillary Clinton. 2014. (Making a Difference: Leaders Who Are Changing the World Ser.). 48p. (YA). (gr. 5-8). 25.85 *(978-1-62275-425-0(5))*; pap. 84.30 *(978-1-62275-428-1(X))*; pap. 14.05 *(978-1-62275-427-4(1))* Rosen Publishing Group, Inc., The.

Marcovitz, Hal. Bill Clinton. 2004. (Childhoods of the Presidents Ser.). (Illus.). 48p. (J). (gr. 4-18). lib. bdg. 17.95 *(978-1-59084-273-7(1))* Mason Crest.

Mattern, Joanne. Hillary Rodham Clinton, 1 vol. 2008. (First Ladies Set 1 Ser.). (ENG., Illus.). 32p. (YA). (gr. 1-4). 27.07 *(978-1-59928-792-8(7))* ABDO Publishing Co.

McCollum, Sean. Bill Clinton. 2005. (Encyc of Presidents, 2ND Ser.). (ENG., Illus.). 112p. (YA). (gr. 5-9). 34.00 *(978-0-516-22980-5(X))* Scholastic Library Publishing.

McPherson, Stephanie Sammartino. Bill Clinton. 2009. pap. 52.95 *(978-0-7613-4960-0(X))* 2008. (ENG.). 48p. (gr. 3-6). 27.93 *(978-0-8225-7986-1(3)*, Lerner Pubns.) Lerner Publishing Group.

O'Shei, Tim. Bill Clinton: A MyReportLinks. Com Book. 2003. (Presidents Ser.). (Illus.). 48p. (J). lib. bdg. 25.26 *(978-0-7660-5149-2(8)*, MyReportLinks.com Bks.) Enslow Pubs., Inc.

Rumsch, BreAnn. Bill Clinton, 1 vol. 2009. (United States Presidents Ser.). (ENG., Illus.). 40p. (YA). (gr. 3-6). 27.07 *(978-1-60453-447-4(8))* ABDO Publishing Co.

Schuman, Michael A. Bill Clinton. rev. ed. 2003. (United States Presidents Ser.). (Illus.). 128p. (J). (gr. 5-12). lib. bdg. 27.94 *(978-0-7660-2032-0(0))* Enslow Pubs., Inc.

Venezia, Mike. Bill Clinton: Forty-Second President, 1993-2001. Venezia, Mike, illus. 2007. (Getting to Know the U. S. Presidents Ser.). (ENG., Illus.). 32p. (J). (gr. 3-4). 28.00 *(978-0-516-22646-0(0)*, Children's Pr.) Scholastic Library Publishing.

CLINTON, DEWITT, 1769-1828

Kleinmartin, Hex. The Erie Canal. 2016. (Expanding America Ser.). (ENG., Illus.). 96p. (J). (gr. 8-8). lib. bdg. 42.79 *(978-1-5026-0966-3(5))* Cavendish Square Publishing.

CLINTON, HILLARY RODHAM, 1947-

Abrams, Dennis. Hillary Rodham Clinton: Politician. 2009. (Women of Achievement Ser.). (Illus.). 144p. (gr. 6-12). 35.00 *(978-1-60413-077-5(6)*, Chelsea Hse.) Facts On File, Inc.

Blashfield, Jean F. Hillary Clinton. 2010. (Leading Women Ser.). 96p. (YA). (gr. 7-12). 39.93 *(978-0-7614-4954-6(X))* Marshall Cavendish Corp.

Blohm, Craig E. Hillary Clinton. 2016. (ENG.). 80p. (J). 38.60 *(978-1-60152-950-3(3))* ReferencePoint Pr., Inc.

Blumenthal, Karen. Hillary Rodham Clinton: A Woman Living History. 2016. (ENG., Illus.). 448p. (J). 18.99 *(978-1-250-06014-3(1)*, 9781250060143) Feiwel & Friends.

Bodden, Valerie. Hillary Clinton: Historic Leader, 1 vol. 2009. (Essential Lives Set 4 Ser.). (ENG., Illus.). 112p. (J). (gr. 6-12). lib. bdg. 35.64 *(978-1-60453-699-7(3))* ABDO Publishing Co.

Burgan, Michael. Hillary Clinton, 1 vol. 2014. (Extraordinary Women Ser.). (ENG.). 48p. (gr. 6-6). lib. bdg. 32.65 *(978-1-4109-5941-6(4))* Heinemann-Raintree.

Burlingame, Jeff. Hillary Clinton: A Life in Politics. 2008. (People to Know Today Ser.). (Illus.). 112p. (J). (gr. 3-7). lib. bdg. 33.27 *(978-0-7660-2892-0(5))* Enslow Pubs., Inc.

Carosella, Melissa. Hillary Clinton: Shattering the Glass Ceiling. 2016. (Primary Source Readers Focus On Ser.). (Illus.). 32p. (gr. 4-4). pap. 8.99 ***(978-1-4258-3289-6(X))*** Teacher Created Materials, Inc.

Carosella, Melissa. Hillary Rodham Clinton: First Lady, Senator, & Secretary of State, 1 vol. 2011. (Primary Source Readers Ser.). (ENG.). 32p. (J). (gr. 4-4). pap. 8.99 *(978-1-4333-1508-4(4))* Teacher Created Materials, Inc.

Corey, Shana. Hillary Clinton: the Life of a Leader. Gustavson, Adam, illus. 2016. (Step into Reading Ser.). (ENG.). 48p. (J). (gr. k-3). 3.99 *(978-1-101-93235-3(X)*, Random Hse. Bks. for Young Readers) Random Hse. Children's Bks.

Cunningham, Anne C. & Burlingame, Jeff. Hillary Clinton: Former First Lady & Secretary of State. 2017. (Influential Lives Ser.). 128p. (gr. 7-8). lib. bdg. 37.27 ***(978-0-7660-8501-5(5))*** Enslow Pubs., Inc.

Doak, Robin S. Hillary Clinton. 2013. (True Book™—Biographies Ser.). (ENG., Illus.). 48p. (J). pap. 6.95 *(978-0-531-23877-6(6))*; lib. bdg. 29.00 *(978-0-531-21906-5(2))* Scholastic Library Publishing.

Egan, Jill. Hillary Rodham Clinton. 2009. (People We Should Know Ser.). (ENG., Illus.). 48p. (J). (gr. 3-5). pap. 10.50 *(978-1-4339-2193-3(6))*; lib. bdg. 31.00 *(978-1-4339-2188-9(X))* Stevens, Gareth Publishing LLLP. (Gareth Stevens Learning Library).

Epstein, Dwayne. Hillary Clinton. (People in the News Ser.). (Illus.). (J). 2010. 128p. 33.95 *(978-1-4205-0268-8(9))* 2006. (ENG., 112p. (gr. 3-7). lib. bdg. 32.45 *(978-1-4205-0031-8(7))* Cengage Gale. (Lucent Bks.).

Fitzgerald, Stephanie. Hillary Clinton. rev. ed. 2017. (Rookie Biographies(tm) Ser.). (ENG., Illus.). 32p. (J). lib. bdg. 25.00 ***(978-0-531-22931-6(9))*** Scholastic Library Publishing.

—Rookie Biographies: Hillary Clinton (Revised Edition) 2017. (Rookie Biographies Ser.). (ENG., Illus.). 32p. (J). pap. 5.95 ***(978-0-531-23406-8(1))*** Scholastic Library Publishing.

Freedman, Jeri. Hillary Rodham Clinton: Profile of a Leading Democrat. (Career Profiles Ser.). 112p. 2009. (gr. 9-10). 63.90 *(978-1-61511-794-9(6))* 2007. (YA). (gr. 7-12). lib. bdg. 34.60 *(978-1-4042-1910-6(2))* Rosen Publishing Group, Inc., The.

Guernsey, JoAnn B. Hillary Rodham Clinton. 2005. (Biography Ser.). (Illus.). 112p. (J). (gr. 6-18). pap. 7.95 *(978-0-8225-9613-4(X))* Lerner Publishing Group.

Guernsey, Joann Bren. Hillary Rodham Clinton. 2005. (Biography Ser.). (Illus.). 112p. (J). (gr. 3-7). lib. bdg. 29.27 *(978-0-8225-2372-7(8)*, Lerner Pubns.) Lerner Publishing Group.

—Hillary Rodham Clinton: Secretary of State. 2009. (USA TODAY Lifeline Biographies Ser.). (ENG.). 112p. (gr. 6-12). lib. bdg. 34.60 *(978-0-7613-5122-1(1))* Lerner Publishing Group.

Harness, Cheryl. Hillary Clinton: American Woman of the World. 2016. (Real-Life Story Ser.). (ENG., Illus.). 192p. (J). (gr. 3-7). 17.99 *(978-1-4814-6057-6(9)*, Aladdin) Simon & Schuster Children's Publishing.

Kawa, Katie. Hillary Clinton. 2016. (Superwomen Role Models Ser.). 32p. (J). (gr. 4-3). 26.25 *(978-1-5081-4806-7(6)*, PowerKids Pr.) Rosen Publishing Group, Inc., The.

Krull, Kathleen. Hillary Rodham Clinton: Dreams Taking Flight. Bates, Amy June, illus. 2015. (ENG.). 48p. (J). (gr. k-5). 17.99 *(978-1-4814-5113-0(8)*, Simon & Schuster Bks. For Young Readers) Simon & Schuster Bks. For Young Readers.

Lee, Sally. Hillary Clinton, 1 vol. 2010. (First Ladies Ser.). (ENG.). 24p. (gr. k-1). lib. bdg. 26.65 *(978-1-4296-5327-5(2)*, Pebble Plus) Capstone Press of Coughlan Cos.

Levinson, Cynthia. Hillary Rodham Clinton: Do All the Good You Can. 2016. (Illus.). 352p. (J). (gr. 3-7). pap. 6.99 *(978-0-06-238729-5(4))* HarperCollins Pubs.

Mapua, Jeff. Bill & Hillary Clinton. 2014. (Making a Difference: Leaders Who Are Changing the World Ser.). 48p. (YA). (gr. 5-8). 25.85 *(978-1-62275-425-0(5))*; pap. 84.30 *(978-1-62275-428-1(X))*; pap. 14.05 *(978-1-62275-427-4(1))* Rosen Publishing Group, Inc., The.

—Hillary Clinton, 1 vol. 2015. (ENG., Illus.). 32p. (J). 23.45 *(978-1-62275-689-6(4)*, Britannica Educational Publishing) Rosen Publishing Group, Inc., The.

Markel, Michelle. Hillary Rodham Clinton: Some Girls Are Born to Lead. Pham, LeUyen, illus. 2016. 40p. (J). (gr. -1-3). 17.99 *(978-0-06-238122-4(9))* HarperCollins Pubs.

Mattern, Joanne. Hillary Rodham Clinton, 1 vol. 2008. (First Ladies Set 1 Ser.). (ENG., Illus.). 32p. (YA). (gr. 1-4). 27.07 *(978-1-59928-792-8(7))* ABDO Publishing Co.

Riddolls, Tom & Wearing, Judy. Hillary Clinton. 2009. (Remarkable People Ser.). (Illus.). 24p. (J). (gr. 4-6). pap. 8.95 *(978-1-60596-621-2(5))*; lib. bdg. 24.45 *(978-1-60596-620-5(7))* Weigl Pubs., Inc.

Ruiz, Rachel. When Hillary Rodham Clinton Played Ice Hockey. Doneva, Steliyana, illus. 2017. (Leaders Doing Headstands Ser.). (ENG.). 32p. (gr. 2-3). lib. bdg. 27.99 ***(978-1-5158-1573-0(0))*** Picture Window Bks.

Ryan, Bernard. Hillary Rodham Clinton: First Lady & Senator. 2004. (Ferguson Career Biographies Ser.). (Illus.). 160p. (gr. 6-12). 25.00 *(978-0-8160-5544-9(0)*, Ferguson Publishing Co.) Facts On File, Inc.

Shepherd, Jodie. Hillary Clinton. 2015. (Rookie Biographies(r) Ser.). (ENG., Illus.). 32p. (J). lib. bdg. 23.00 *(978-0-531-20592-1(4))* Scholastic Library Publishing.

Sherman, Jill. Donald Trump: Outspoken Personality & President. 2017. (Gateway Biographies Ser.). (ENG., Illus.). 48p. (J). (gr. 4-8). lib. bdg. 26.65 *(978-1-5124-2596-3(6))* Lerner Publishing Group.

Summers, Portia. Hillary Clinton: Politician & Activist. 2017. (Junior Biographies Ser.). 24p. (J). (gr. 3-4). lib. bdg. 22.60 ***(978-0-7660-8670-8(4))*** Enslow Pubs., Inc.

Tieck, Sarah. Hillary Rodham Clinton, 1 vol. 2010. (First Biographies Set 6 Ser.). (ENG.). 32p. (J). (gr. 1-4). 27.07 *(978-1-60453-983-7(6))* ABDO Publishing Co.

Tracy, Kathleen. The Historic Fight for the 2008 Democratic Presidential Nomination: The Clinton View. 2009. (Monumental Milestones Ser.). (Illus.). 48p. (YA). (gr. 4-7). lib. bdg. 29.95 *(978-1-58415-731-1(3))* Mitchell Lane Pubs., Inc.

Wells, Catherine. Hillary Clinton. 2007. (Political Profiles Ser.). (Illus.). 112p. (YA). (gr. 5-9). lib. bdg. 27.95 *(978-1-59935-047-9(5))* Reynolds, Morgan Inc.

Wheeler, Jill C. Hillary Rodham Clinton. 2003. (Breaking Barriers Ser.). 64p. (gr. 3-8). 27.07 *(978-1-57765-741-5(1),* Abdo & Daughters) ABDO Publishing Co.

Winter, Jonah. Hillary. Colón, Raúl, illus. 2016. (ENG.). 40p. (J). (gr. -1-3). lib. bdg. 20.99 *(978-0-553-53389-7(4),* Schwartz & Wade Bks.) Random Hse. Children's Bks.

Winter, Jonah & Colón, Raúl. Hillary. 2016. (ENG., Illus.). 40p. (J). (gr. -1-3). 17.99 *(978-0-553-53388-0(6),* Schwartz & Wade Bks.) Random Hse. Children's Bks.

CLIPPER SHIPS

Fern, Tracey E. Dare the Wind: The Record-Breaking Voyage of Eleanor Prentiss & the Flying Cloud. McCully, Emily Arnold, illus. 2014. (ENG.). 540p. (J). (gr. k-3). 17.99 *(978-0-374-31699-0(6),* 9780374316990, Farrar, Straus & Giroux (BYR)) Farrar, Straus & Giroux.

Sanford, Candace. Captain Nathaniel Brown Palmer. Scala, Susan, illus. 2007. 96p. (YA). pap. 14.95 *(978-0-9773725-9-1(6))* Flat Hammock Pr.

CLIPPER SHIPS—FICTION

McKenzie, Lyn. Lavinia's Shoes. 2007. (J). pap. 12.95 *(978-0-9788628-5-5(6))* Just Write Bks.

CLOCKS AND WATCHES

see also Sundials

Adler, David. Time Zones. Miller, Edward, illus. 2011. (ENG.). 32p. (J). pap. 7.95 *(978-0-8234-2385-9(9))* Holiday Hse., Inc.

Adler, David A. Time Zones. Miller, Edward, III, illus. 2010. (ENG.). 32p. (J). (gr. 1-5). 17.95 *(978-0-8234-2201-2(1))* Holiday Hse., Inc.

Alaina, Maria. Measuring Time, 1 vol. (Wonder Readers Next Steps: Math Ser.). (ENG.). (gr. -1-1). 2013. 20p. 22.65 *(978-1-4765-2369-9(X))* 2011. 16p. pap. 35.94 *(978-1-4296-8129-2(2))* Capstone Press of Coughlan Cos. (Wonder Readers).

Baxter, Nicola. Learn to Tell Time: With Magnets to Use Again & Again! Elliott, Rebecca, illus. 2013. (ENG.). 16p. (J). (gr. -1-12). bds. 17.99 *(978-1-84322-638-3(3),* Armadillo) Anness Publishing GBR. Dist: National Bk. Network.

Benchmark Education Company, LLC Staff, compiled by. Measuring Time: Theme Set. 2006. (J). 274.00 *(978-1-4108-7074-2(X))* Benchmark Education Co.

Dapice, Carmine. Lets Rhyme with Time. 2013. 38p. pap. 13.95 *(978-1-4497-8822-3(X),* WestBow Pr.) Author Solutions, Inc.

Faulkner, Keith & Tyger, Rory. Time's Up! Faulkner, Keith & Tyger, Rory, illus. Lambert, Jonathan, illus. 2003. (J). *(978-0-439-56155-6(8))* Scholastic, Inc.

French, Cathy. You Can Make a Timer. 2011. (Early Connections Ser.). (J). *(978-1-61672-243-2(6))* Benchmark Education Co.

Ganeri, Anita. From Candle to Quartz Clock. (Illus.). 30p. (J). *(978-0-237-51534-8(2))* Evans Brothers, Ltd.

Gardner, Robert. How Quick Is Quick? Science Projects with Time. 2015. (Hot Science Experiments Ser.). 48p. (J). (gr. 3-4). 25.27 *(978-0-7660-6610-6(X));* pap. 8.95 *(978-0-7660-6611-3(8),* Enslow Elementary) Enslow Pubs., Inc.

—It's about Time! Science Projects: How Long Does It Take? 2003. (Sensational Science Experiments Ser.). (Illus.). 48p. (J). (gr. 1-4). lib. bdg. 25.27 *(978-0-7660-2012-2(6))* Enslow Pubs., Inc.

Heos, Bridget. Telling Time. Longhi, Katya, illus. 2015. (Math World Ser.). 24p. (J). lib. bdg. 27.10 *(978-1-60753-461-7(4))* Amicus Publishing.

Herbst, Kailee. Lots of Clocks: Learning about Tools That Measure Time. 2009. (Math for the Real World: Early Emergent Ser.). (ENG., Illus.). 8p. (gr. k-1). pap. 5.15 *(978-0-8239-8858-7(9))* Rosen Publishing Group, Inc., The.

Hickman, Debbie. The Exasperated Clock. Taylor, Adam, illus. 2013. 40p. pap. *(978-1-4602-1811-2(6))* FriesenPress.

Holden, Arianne. It's Fun to Learn about Time: A Busy Picture Book Full of Fabulous Facts & Things to Do! 2016. (ENG., Illus.). 32p. (J). (gr. -1-12). pap. 9.99 *(978-1-86147-729-3(5))* Anness Publishing, Inc.

Hutmacher, Kimberly M. Hours. 2012. (It's about Time Ser.). (ENG.). 24p. (gr. k-1). pap. 35.70 *(978-1-4296-9351-6(7));* (Illus.). pap. 6.29 *(978-1-4296-9350-9(9))* Capstone Press of Coughlan Cos. (Pebble Bks.).

—Hours, 1 vol. 2012. (It's about Time Ser.). (ENG., Illus.). 24p. (gr. k-1). lib. bdg. 21.99 *(978-1-4296-8577-1(8),* Pebble Bks.) Capstone Press of Coughlan Cos.

—It's about Time. 2012. (It's about Time Ser.). (ENG.). 24p. (gr. k-1). pap. 17.85 *(978-1-4296-9356-1(8));* pap. 107.10 *(978-1-4296-9357-8(6));* lib. bdg. 65.97 *(978-1-4296-9165-9(4))* Capstone Press of Coughlan Cos. (Pebble Bks.).

—Minutes. 2012. (It's about Time Ser.). (ENG.). 24p. (gr. k-1). pap. 35.70 *(978-1-4296-9353-0(3));* (Illus.). pap. 6.29 *(978-1-4296-9352-3(5));* (Illus.). lib. bdg. 21.99 *(978-1-4296-8576-4(X))* Capstone Press of Coughlan Cos. (Pebble Bks.).

—Seconds, 1 vol. 2012. (It's about Time Ser.). (ENG.). 24p. (gr. k-1). pap. 6.29 *(978-1-4296-9354-7(1));* pap. 35.70 *(978-1-4296-9355-4(X))* Capstone Press of Coughlan Cos. (Pebble Bks.).

—Seconds, 1 vol. 2012. (It's about Time Ser.). (ENG.). 24p. (gr. k-1). lib. bdg. 21.99 *(978-1-4296-8575-7(1),* Pebble Bks.) Capstone Press of Coughlan Cos.

Jackson, Lora Z. Around the Clock: A Story about Telling Time. Martin, Miles J., illus. 2011. 58p. 36.95 *(978-1-258-06483-9(9))* Literary Licensing, LLC.

Keller, Shana. Ticktock Banneker's Clock. Gardner, David C., illus. 2016. (ENG.). 32p. (J). (gr. 1-4). 16.99 *(978-1-58536-956-0(X),* 204114) Sleeping Bear Pr.

Klutz Editors. Design Your Own Charm Watch. 2005. (ENG., Illus.). 26p. (YA). 21.95 *(978-1-57054-212-1(0))* Klutz.

Koscielniak, Bruce. About Time: A First Look at Time & Clocks. 2004. (ENG., Illus.). 32p. (J). (gr. 2-5). tchr. ed. 17.99 *(978-0-618-39668-9(3))* Houghton Mifflin Harcourt Publishing Co.

Levy, Janey. Keeping Time Through the Ages: The History of Tools Used to Measure Time. (PowerMath Ser.). 32p. 2009. (ENG., Illus.). (gr. 4-5). pap. 10.00 *(978-0-8239-8917-1(8))* 2009. (gr. 4-5). 47.90 *(978-1-60851-396-3(3))* 2004. (Illus.). (J). lib. bdg. 25.25 *(978-0-8239-8993-5(3))* Rosen Publishing Group, Inc., The. (PowerKids Pr.).

Macdonald, Fiona. You Wouldn't Want to Live Without Clocks & Calendars! Antram, David, illus. 2015. (You Wouldn't Want to Live Without... Ser.). (ENG.). 32p. (J). lib. bdg. 29.00 *(978-0-531-21928-7(3),* Watts, Franklin) Scholastic Library Publishing.

Mara, Wil. The Clock. 2006. (Inventions That Shaped the World Ser.). (ENG., Illus.). 80p. (J). (gr. 5-8). per. 9.95 *(978-0-531-16743-4(7),* Watts, Franklin) Scholastic Library Publishing.

McConnell, William. What Makes Clocks Tick? 2009. (Real Life Readers Ser.). 24p. (gr. 3-5). pap. 8.25 *(978-1-4358-0230-8(6),* Rosen Classroom) Rosen Publishing Group, Inc., The.

McEwan, Rebecca. Telling Time Through the Ages & Comó medir el tiempo desde la antigüedad hasta nuestros Días: 6 English, 6 Spanish Adaptations. 2011. (ENG & SPA.). (J). 89.00 net. *(978-1-4108-5673-9(9))* Benchmark Education Co.

Metz, Lorijo. Using Clocks & Stopwatches. 2013. (Science Tools Ser.). (ENG., Illus.). 24p. (J). (gr. 3-6). 22.60 *(978-1-4488-9689-9(4));* pap. 8.25 *(978-1-4488-9836-7(6))* Rosen Publishing Group, Inc., The. (PowerKids Pr.).

Michele, Tracey. Clocks. 2011. (Learn-Abouts Ser.). (Illus.). 16p. (J). pap. 7.95 *(978-1-59920-639-4(0))* Black Rabbit Bks.

Miller, Ray, et al. Beat the Clock Sports. Thorp, Cameron, illus. 2007. 48p. (J). *(978-0-439-02189-0(8))* Scholastic, Inc.

Moldovo, Eustacia & Murphy, Patricia J. Learning to Tell Time with Puppies & Kittens. 2017. (J). pap. ***(978-0-7660-9075-0(2))*** Enslow Pubs., Inc.

Nagelhout, Ryan. The Problem with Early Clocks. 2015. (Bloopers of Invention Ser.). (ENG., Illus.). 24p. (J). (gr. 2-3). 22.60 *(978-1-4824-2770-7(2))* Stevens, Gareth Publishing LLLP.

Peters, Scott. Clock Watch. 2011. (Early Connections Ser.). (J). *(978-1-61672-319-4(X))* Benchmark Education Co.

—Today. 2011. (Early Connections Ser.). (J). *(978-1-61672-338-5(6))* Benchmark Education Co.

Randolph, Joanne. All about an Hour. (It's about Time Ser.). 24p. 2009. (gr. 1-1). 42.50 *(978-1-61513-631-5(2),* PowerKids Pr.) 2007. (Illus.). (J). (gr. k-2). lib. bdg. 22.60 *(978-1-4042-3766-7(6))* Rosen Publishing Group, Inc., The.

—All about an Hour/Las Horas. 2009. (It's about Time/Los libros del tiempo Ser.). (SPA.). 24p. (gr. 1-1). 42.50 *(978-1-61513-627-8(4),* Editorial Buenas Letras) Rosen Publishing Group, Inc., The.

—All about an Hour/Las Horas. Brusca, Maria Cristina, tr. from ENG. 2007. (It's about Time / Los Libros Del Tiempo Ser.). (ENG & SPA., Illus.). 24p. (J). (gr. k-2). lib. bdg. 22.60 *(978-1-4042-7626-0(2))* Rosen Publishing Group, Inc., The.

Reinke, Beth Bence. Measuring Time with a Clock. Petelinsek, Kathleen, illus. 2014. (Explorer Junior Library: Math Explorer Junior Ser.). (ENG.). 24p. (J). (gr. 1-4). 28.50 *(978-1-62431-650-0(6),* 203112) Cherry Lake Publishing.

Scheunemann, Pam. Time to Learn about Measuring Time, 1 vol. 2008. (Time Ser.). (ENG., Illus.). 24p. (J). (gr. k-3). lib. bdg. 24.21 *(978-1-60453-016-2(2))* ABDO Publishing Co.

Spilsbury, Richard & Spilsbury, Louise. The Clock, 1 vol. 2011. (Tales of Invention Ser.). (ENG.). 32p. (gr. 3-5). pap. 8.95 *(978-1-4329-4886-3(5));* 30.65 *(978-1-4329-4877-1(6))* Heinemann-Raintree. (NA-h).

Steffora, Tracey. Horas, Minutos y Segundos. 2011. (Medir el Tiempo Ser.). (SPA.). 24p. (gr. -1-1). 22.65 *(978-1-4329-5630-1(2));* pap. 6.29 *(978-1-4329-5637-0(X))* Heinemann-Raintree. (Bellota).

—Hours, Minutes, & Seconds, 1 vol. 2011. (Measuring Time Ser.). (ENG.). 24p. (gr. -1-1). 22.65 *(978-1-4329-4900-6(4),* Acorn) Heinemann-Raintree.

—Relojes y Calendarios. 2011. (Medir el Tiempo Ser.). (SPA.). 24p. (gr. -1-1). pap. 6.29 *(978-1-4329-5635-6(3),* Bellota) Heinemann-Raintree.

Thomas, Mary Ann. Our Train Trip: Learning to Add Times by the Half Hour. 2009. (Math for the REAL World Ser.). 12p. (gr. 1-2). pap. 5.90 *(978-0-8239-8849-5(X),* Rosen Classroom) Rosen Publishing Group, Inc., The.

Woodford, Chris. Time. 2012. (Measure up Math Ser.). (Illus.). 32p. (J). (gr. 4-6). 26.60 *(978-1-4339-7453-3(3));* pap. 10.50 *(978-1-4339-7454-0(1))* Stevens, Gareth Publishing LLLP. (Gareth Stevens Learning Library).

Yo-Kai Watch. Seek & Find. 2016. (ENG., Illus.). 24p. (J). (gr. 1-4). 8.99 *(978-0-316-39621-9(4))* Little, Brown Bks. for Young Readers.

CLOCKS AND WATCHES—FICTION

Adams, Clint. My Watch Doesn't Tell Time. 2006. (YA). per. *(978-0-9768375-4-1(4))* Credo Italia.

Adams, Gary. The Little Clock Who Had No Hands. 2010. 36p. pap. 15.99 *(978-1-4490-6106-7(0))* AuthorHouse.

Archambault, John. Boom Chicka Rock. Chitwood, Suzanne Tanner & Chitwood, Suzanne, illus. 2004. (ENG.). 32p. (J). (gr. -1-k). 16.99 *(978-0-399-23587-0(6),* Philomel Bks.) Penguin Young Readers Group.

Baker, Keith. Hickory Dickory Dock. 2007. (ENG., Illus.). 32p. (J). (gr. -1-3). 17.99 *(978-0-15-205818-0(4))* Houghton Mifflin Harcourt Publishing Co.

Barnett, Mac, et al. The Clock Without a Face. Teplin, Scott & Rex, Adam, illus. 2010. (ENG.). 30p. (gr. 2-18). bds. 19.95 *(978-1-934781-71-5(1))* McSweeney's Publishing.

Berg, Jean Horton. Pierre, the Young Watchmaker. D'Adamo, Anthony, illus. 2011. 190p. 42.95 *(978-1-258-08171-3(7))* Literary Licensing, LLC.

Berg, Jean Horton & dePaola, Tomie. The Noisy Clock Shop. Seiden, Art, illus. 2015. (G&d Vintage Ser.). (ENG.). 32p. (J). (gr. -1-k). bds. 7.99 *(978-0-448-48216-3(9),* Grosset & Dunlap) Penguin Young Readers Group.

Brooks, Brian. Oopsy Daisy's Bad Day. Brooks, Brian, illus. 2007. (Illus.). (J). 62p. (J). reprint ed. 13.00 *(978-1-4223-9004-7(7))* DIANE Publishing Co.

Coates, Kimberly & Coates, Ashley. If I Only Knew How to Tell Time. 2013. 32p. pap. 19.99 *(978-1-4772-9963-0(7))* AuthorHouse.

Collier, James Lincoln. The Clock. 2003. (Great Inventions Ser.). (Illus.). 128p. (gr. 8-18). lib. bdg. 29.95 *(978-0-7614-1538-1(6),* Benchmark Bks.) Marshall Cavendish Corp.

Cunliffe, John. Postman Pat Mends a Clock. (Illus.). 20p. (J). pap. 11.99 *(978-0-340-73718-7(2))* Hodder & Stoughton GBR. Dist: Trafalgar Square Publishing.

Danziger, Paula. It's Justin Time, Amber Brown. Ross, Tony, illus. (Amber Brown Ser.). 9.95 *(978-1-59112-294-4(5))* Live Oak Media.

—Justo a Tiempo, Ambar Dorado. Ross, Tony, illus. 2007. (Amber Brown Ser.). (SPA.). 48p. (gr. k-3). per. 8.95 *(978-1-59820-595-4(1),* Alfaguara) Santillana USA Publishing Co., Inc.

d'Lacey, Chris. Gauge. 2010. (Dragons of Wayward Crescent Ser.: No. 2). (ENG.). 112p. (J). (gr. 2-5). 9.99 *(978-0-545-16831-1(7),* Orchard Bks.) Scholastic, Inc.

Dodd, Emma, illus. Tick Tock Dog: A Tell the Time Book - with a Special Movable Clock! 2016. (ENG.). 12p. (J). (gr. -1-12). bds. 14.99 *(978-1-86147-718-7(X),* Armadillo) Anness Publishing GBR. Dist: National Bk. Network.

Douglas, Ryke. Tock a Tick. 2007. 32p. per. 11.95 *(978-1-59800-756-5(4))* Outskirts Pr., Inc.

Escott, Jamison. The Clockmaker of Mullen. Escott, Esther, illus. 2004. 24p. (J). pap. 8.95 *(978-1-57733-127-8(3),* Papillon Publishing) Blue Dolphin Publishing, Inc.

Funk, Rachel. Christabelle in the Museum of Time. 2007. 217p. pap. 14.95 *(978-1-4303-2572-7(0))* Lulu Pr., Inc.

Gilmore, Rachna. Grandpa's Clock, 1 vol. Meissner, Amy, illus. 2006. (ENG.). 32p. (J). (gr. -1-3). 17.95 *(978-1-55143-333-2(8))* Orca Bk. Pubs. USA.

Grant, Gavin J. & Link, Kelly, eds. Steampunk! an Anthology of Fantastically Rich & Strange Stories. 2013. (ENG.). 432p. (YA). (gr. 9). pap. 16.99 *(978-0-7636-5797-0(2))* Candlewick Pr.

Harris, Trudy. The Clock Struck One: A Time-Telling Tale. Hartman, Carrie, illus. 2009. (Math Is Fun! Ser.). (ENG.). 32p. (gr. k-2). 19.99 *(978-0-8225-9067-5(0),* Millbrook Pr.) Lerner Publishing Group.

Howard, Kate. The Misadventures of Jibanyan, Bk. 1. 2016. (Yo-Kai Watch Ser.: 1). (ENG.). 64p. (J). (gr. 2-5). pap. 4.99 *(978-1-338-05462-0(7))* Scholastic, Inc.

Hunt, Mabel Leigh. The Peddler's Clock. Jones, Elizabeth Orton, illus. 2011. 30p. 35.95 *(978-1-258-09998-5(5))* Literary Licensing, LLC.

James, Lincoln. Sal Sleeps In. 2006. (Neighborhood Readers Ser.). (ENG.). 8p. (gr. -1-3). pap. 5.15 *(978-1-4042-5780-1(2),* Rosen Classroom) Rosen Publishing Group, Inc., The.

Jaskiewicz, A. E. Hickory & the Big Clock. 2006. (ENG.). 56p. per. 16.95 *(978-1-4241-6024-2(3))* America Star Bks.

Keene, Carolyn. Stop the Clock. 2005. (Nancy Drew Ser.: 12). 160p. (J). lib. bdg. 15.00 *(978-1-59054-815-8(9))* Fitzgerald Bks.

Kids Can Press Staff, ed. Franklin & the Stopwatch. 2007. (Kids Can Read Ser.). (ENG., Illus.). 32p. (J). (gr. 1-2). 14.95 *(978-1-55337-890-7(3))* Kids Can Pr., Ltd. CAN. Dist: Hachette Bk. Group.

Konishi, Noriyuki. Yo-kai Watch, Vol. 1. 2015. (ENG., Illus.). 192p. (J). pap. 9.99 *(978-1-4215-8251-1(1))* Viz Media.

—Yo-kai Watch, Vol. 2. 2015. (ENG., Illus.). 192p. (J). pap. 9.99 *(978-1-4215-8252-8(X))* Viz Media.

Lach, Hope Carlin. Mr. Contrareloj. 2011. (SPA.). 20p. 13.99 *(978-1-4567-2624-9(2))* AuthorHouse.

—Mr. Counter Clockwise. 2010. 20p. (J). pap. 13.99 *(978-1-4520-4805-5(3))* AuthorHouse.

MacCaughrean, Geraldine, et al. El Reloj de Mi Abuela. Lambert, Stephen, illus. 2003. (SPA.). 32p. (J). (gr. k-2). 14.99 *(978-84-241-8643-2(5))* Everest Editora ESP. Dist: Lectorum Pubns., Inc.

McClintock, Norah. Watch Me, 1 vol. 2008. (Orca Currents Ser.). (ENG.). (J). (gr. 5-9). 112p. 16.95 *(978-1-55469-040-4(4));* 128p. pap. 9.95 *(978-1-55469-039-8(0))* Orca Bk. Pubs. USA.

Metzger, Steve. Dancing Clock. Nez, John Abbott, illus. 2011. (ENG.). 32p. 12.95 *(978-1-58925-100-7(8));* (J). pap. 7.95 *(978-1-58925-429-9(5))* Tiger Tales.

Mirarchi, Anthony J. The King's Challenge. 2007. (Cristo's Chronicles Ser.). (ENG., Illus.). 224p. (YA). (gr. 4-7). pap. *(978-1-933255-32-3(3))* DNA Pr.

Molesworth. The Cuckoo Clock. 2007. (ENG.). 122p. pap. 18.99 *(978-1-4346-4245-5(3))* Creative Media Partners, LLC.

—The Cuckoo Clock. 2007. 172p. per. 12.99 *(978-1-59986-835-6(0))* Filiquarian Publishing, LLC.

—The Cuckoo Clock. l.t. ed. 2007. 132p. pap. 19.99 *(978-1-4346-4246-2(1))* Creative Media Partners, LLC.

Molesworth & Molesworth, Mary Louisa S. The Cuckoo Clock. 2008. 112p. 23.95 *(978-1-60664-856-8(X));* pap. 9.95 *(978-1-60664-103-3(4))* Aegypan.

Molesworth, Mary Louisa. The Cuckoo Clock. 2004. reprint ed. pap. 19.95 *(978-1-4191-5839-1(2));* pap. 1.99 *(978-1-4192-5839-8(7))* Kessinger Publishing, LLC.

Pilegard, Virginia Walton. The Warlord's Alarm, 1 vol. Debon, Nicolas, illus. 2006. (Warlord's Ser.). (ENG.). 32p. (J). (gr. k-3). 16.99 *(978-1-58980-378-7(7))* Pelican Publishing Co., Inc.

Priddy, Roger & Crimi-Trent, Ellen. My School Day. 2013. (Schoolies Ser.). (ENG., Illus.). 32p. (J). (gr. -1-1). 14.99 *(978-0-312-51607-9(X),* 9780312516079, Priddy Bks.) St. Martin's Pr.

Publications International Ltd. Staff, ed. Exploring Time with Dora Clock. 2004. 10p. (J). bds. 16.98 *(978-1-4127-3050-1(3),* 7228800) Publications International, Ltd.

Pullman, Philip. El Reloj Mecanico. Netzel, Carmen, tr. 2005. (Escritura desatada Ser.). (SPA.). 112p. (J). 15.95 *(978-84-406-8065-5(1))* Ediciones B ESP. Dist: Independent Pubs. Group.

Pyle, Howard. Pepper & Salt & the Wonder Clock, Set. Pyle, Howard, illus. 2006. (Foundations Ser.). (Illus.). 385p. (J). 45.00 *(978-1-933859-14-9(8))* ISI Bks.

Rusu, Meredith. Yo-Kai Watch. Scholastic, illus. 2016. (Yo-Kai Watch Ser.). (ENG.). 32p. (J). (gr. -1-3). pap. 3.99 *(978-1-338-05444-6(9))* Scholastic, Inc.

Scholastic, Inc. Staff. Tickety Toc: Let's Tell Time! 2014. (Tickety Toc Ser.). (ENG.). 16p. (J). (gr. -1-k). 8.99 *(978-0-545-66252-9(4))* Scholastic, Inc.

Silver Dolphin en Español Editors. Llegs la hora del baile: Time for the Ball, Spanish-Language Edition. 2005. (SPA., Illus.). 22p. (J). *(978-970-718-287-5(3),* Silver Dolphin en Español) Advanced Marketing, S. de R. L. de C. V.

Smith, C. Michelle. Skeeter Sneeter Doodlebop. Foreman, A., illus. 2009. 24p. pap. 15.63 *(978-1-934840-54-2(8))* Nimble Bks. LLC.

Stead, Philip C. A Home for Bird. Stead, Philip C., illus. 2012. (ENG., Illus.). 32p. (J). (gr. -1-3). 17.99 *(978-1-59643-711-1(1),* 9781596437111) Roaring Brook Pr.

Stewart, Trenton Lee. The Secret Keepers. Sudyka, Diana, illus. 2017. (ENG.). 512p. (J). (gr. 3-7). pap. 8.99 ***(978-0-316-38954-9(4))*** Little, Brown Bks. for Young Readers.

—The Secret Keepers. 2016. (ENG., Illus.). 512p. (J). (gr. 3-7). 18.99 *(978-0-316-38955-6(2))* Little, Brown Bks. for Young Readers.

—The Secret Keepers. 2017. (J). lib. bdg. 19.65 ***(978-0-606-40551-5(8))*** Turtleback Bks.

Stimson, James. Thirteen O'Clock. Stimson, James, illus. 2005. (ENG., Illus.). 40p. (J). (gr. -1-2). 15.95 *(978-0-8118-4839-8(6))* Chronicle Bks. LLC.

Stine, R. L. The Big Blueberry Barf-Off! Park, Trip, illus. 2005. (Rotten School Ser.: No. 1). 128p. (J). (ENG.). 6.99 *(978-0-06-078586-4(1));* lib. bdg. 14.89 *(978-0-06-078587-1(X))* HarperCollins Pubs.

—The Big Blueberry Barf-Off!, 1 vol. Park, Trip, illus. 2011. (Rotten School Ser.: No. 1). (ENG.). 128p. (gr. 2-5). 24.21 *(978-1-59961-825-8(7))* Spotlight.

—The Big Blueberry Barf-Off! Park, Trip, illus. 2008. (Rotten School Ser.: 1). (ENG.). 128p. (J). (gr. 3-7). pap. 5.99 *(978-0-06-078588-8(8))* HarperCollins Pubs.

Thompson, Kate. I Can Tell the Time. Green, Barry, illus. 2014. (I Can Bks.). (ENG.). 12p. (J). (gr. -1). 7.99 *(978-1-78244-825-9(X))* Top That! Publishing PLC GBR. Dist: Independent Pubs. Group.

Tulien, Sean, et al. Clock King's Time Bomb, 1 vol. Schoening, Dan, illus. 2011. (Flash Ser.). (ENG.). 56p. (gr. 2-3). pap. 4.95 *(978-1-4342-3412-4(6));* lib. bdg. 26.65 *(978-1-4342-2626-6(3))* Stone Arch Bks. (DC Super Heroes).

Turley, Sandy. The Clock & the Mouse: A Teaching Rhyme about Time. Peterson, Sara & Lindstrom, Brita, illus. 2006. 32p. (J). lib. bdg. 26.95 *(978-0-9778548-0-6(9))* Helps4Teachers.

CLOG DANCING

see Folk Dancing

CLOISTERS (RELIGIOUS COMMUNITIES)

see Monasteries

CLONING

Barber, Nicola. Cloning & Genetic Engineering. 2012. (Both Sides of the Story Ser.). (ENG., Illus.). 48p. (J). (gr. 5-8). lib. bdg. 29.25 *(978-1-4488-7187-2(5),* Rosen Reference) Rosen Publishing Group, Inc., The.

Fritz, Sandy. Genomics & Cloning. 2003. (Hot Science Ser.). (J). lib. bdg. 28.50 *(978-1-58340-365-5(5))* Black Rabbit Bks.

Goodnough, David. The Debate over Human Cloning. 2003. (Hot Pro/Con Issues Ser.). (Illus.). 64p. (YA). (gr. 6-12). lib. bdg. 27.93 *(978-0-7660-1818-1(0))* Enslow Pubs., Inc.

Haugen, David M. The Ethics of Cloning. 2009. (At Issue Ser.). (ENG., Illus.). 128p. (gr. 10-12). pap. 24.45 *(978-0-7377-4311-1(5),* Greenhaven Pr., Inc.) Cengage Gale.

Henneberg, Susan. Cloning. 2015. (Red Rhino Nonfiction Ser.). (J). lib. bdg. 20.80 *(978-0-606-37199-5(0))* Turtleback Bks.

Jones, Phill. Reproduction & Cloning. 2nd rev. ed. 2012. (Science Foundations Ser.). 136p. (gr. 6-12). 35.00 *(978-1-61753-025-8(5),* Chelsea Hse.) Facts On File, Inc.

Kafka, Tina. Cloning. 2007. (Hot Topics Ser.). (ENG., Illus.). 111p. (YA). (gr. 7-12). lib. bdg. 33.95 *(978-1-59018-979-5(5))* Cengage Gale.

Langwith, Jacqueline. Cloning. 2012. (Opposing Viewpoints Ser.). (ENG., Illus.). 224p. (gr. 10-12). lib. bdg. 48.80 *(978-0-7377-5713-2(2))* Cengage Gale.

Langwith, Jacqueline, ed. Cloning. 2012. (Opposing Viewpoints Ser.). (ENG., Illus.). 240p. (J). (gr. 10-12). pap. 29.45 *(978-0-7377-5714-9(0),* Greenhaven Pr., Inc.) Cengage Gale.

Levine, Aaron D. Cloning. 2009. (World Issues Today Ser.). (J). lib. bdg. 37.95 *(978-1-4358-5168-9(4))* Rosen Publishing Group, Inc., The.

Nardo, Don. Cloning. (Lucent Library of Science & Technology). (Illus.). 2005. (ENG.). 112p. (YA). (gr. 7-10). lib. bdg. 30.85 *(978-1-59018-773-9(3),* Lucent Bks.) 2003. 48p. (J). 24.95 *(978-1-56711-782-0(1),* Blackbirch Pr., Inc.) Cengage Gale.

Panno, Joseph. Animal Cloning: The Science of Nuclear Transfer. 2nd rev. ed. 2010. (New Biology Ser.). 248p. (gr. 6-12). 40.00 *(978-0-8160-6847-0(X))* Facts On File, Inc.

Rogers, Kara. Cloning. 2015. (Biotechnology Revolution Ser.). (ENG., Illus.). 128p. (J). (gr. 10-10). 38.75 *(978-1-62275-576-9(6),* Britannica Educational Publishing) Rosen Publishing Group, Inc., The.

Roleff, Tamara L. Cloning. 2008. (Compact Research Ser.). (Illus.). 112p. (YA). (gr. 7-12). lib. bdg. 25.95 *(978-1-60152-049-4(2))* ReferencePoint Pr., Inc.

Thomas, Isabel. Should Scientists Pursue Cloning?, 1 vol. 2012. (Sci-Hi: Science Issues Ser.). (ENG.). 48p. (gr. 4-4). lib. bdg. 33.32 *(978-1-4109-4463-4(8),* Sci-Hi) Heinemann-Raintree.

Wimmer, Teresa. Cloning: Dolly the Sheep. 2008. (What in the World? Ser.). (Illus.). 48p. 22.95 *(978-1-58341-652-5(8),* Creative Education) Creative Co., The.

Woodward, John. The Ethics of Human Cloning. 2004. (Opposing Viewpoints Ser.). (ENG.). 91p. (gr. 10-12). pap. 22.50 *(978-0-7377-2187-4(1),* Greenhaven Pr., Inc.) Cengage Gale.

CLONING—FICTION

Anaya, Rudolfo. ChupaCabra & the Roswell UFO. 2008. (ENG.). 144p. (YA). (gr. 9-18). 9.95 *(978-0-8263-4469-4(0))* Univ. of New Mexico Pr.

Breslin, Theresa. Mutant. 2012. (Stoke Books Titles Ser.). 64p. (J). (gr. 5-8). pap. 45.32 *(978-0-7613-9220-0(3));* lib. bdg. 22.60 *(978-1-78112-027-9(7))* Stoke Bks.

Castle, M. E. Cloneward Bound. 2013. (Clone Chronicles Ser.: No. 2). (ENG.). 272p. (J). (gr. 3-7). pap. 6.99

C
D

(978-1-60684-473-1(3), Darby Creek) Lerner Publishing Group.

—Game of Clones. (Clone Chronicles Ser.: No. 3). (ENG.). 256p. (J). (gr. 3-7). 2014. 15.99 (978-1-60684-234-8(X))No. 3. 2015. pap. 6.99 (978-1-60684-538-7(1)) Lerner Publishing Group. (Darby Creek).

—Popular Clone. 2012. (Clone Chronicles: No. 1). (ENG.). 320p. (J). (gr. 3-7). pap. 6.99 (978-1-60684-414-4(8)); 15.99 (978-1-60684-232-4(3)) Lerner Publishing Group. (Darby Creek).

Cave, Patrick. The Selected. 2010. (ENG.). 416p. (YA). (gr. 9-18). 17.99 (978-1-4169-1573-7(7), Atheneum Bks. for Young Readers) Simon & Schuster Children's Publishing.

—Sharp North. 2009. (ENG.). 528p. (YA). (gr. 9). pap. 8.99 (978-1-4169-1223-1(1), Atheneum Bks. for Young Readers) Simon & Schuster Children's Publishing.

Cohn, Rachel. Beta. 2013. (Beta Novel Ser.). (ENG., Illus.). 336p. (YA). (gr. 9-17). pap. 9.99 (978-1-4231-5734-2(6)) Hyperion Pr.

—Emergent. 2014. (Beta Novel Ser.). (ENG.). 288p. (YA). (gr. 9-17). 17.99 (978-1-4231-5720-5(6)) Hyperion Bks. for Children.

Crashland. 2014. (Twinmaker Ser.: 2). (ENG.). 480p. (YA). (gr. 8). 17.99 (978-0-06-220324-3(X)) HarperCollins Pubs.

Disney Book Group Staff. Pining Away. 2014. (Gravity Falls Ser.: 1). (J). lib. bdg. 14.75 (978-0-606-35287-1(2)) Turtleback Bks.

Farmer, Nancy. The House of the Scorpion. 2004. (ENG., Illus.). 400p. (YA). (gr. 7). reprint ed. pap. 11.99 (978-0-689-85223-7(1), Atheneum Bks. for Young Readers) Simon & Schuster Children's Publishing.

—The House of the Scorpion. 2004. 380p. (gr. 6). lib. bdg. 22.10 (978-1-4176-1900-9(7), Turtleback) Turtleback Bks.

—The Lord of Opium. 2013. (ENG., Illus.). 432p. (YA). (gr. 7). 17.99 (978-1-4424-8254-8(0)) Simon & Schuster Children's Publishing.

Farnell, Chris. Mark II. 2006. (ENG., Illus.). 144p. (gr. 8-10). per. 14.95 (978-0-9547913-9-1(8), Tindal Street Pr.) Profile Bks. Ltd. GBR. Dist: Independent Pubs. Group.

Gaither, Stefanie. Into the Abyss. 2016. (ENG., Illus.). 352p. (YA). (gr. 7). 18.99 (978-1-4814-4995-3(8), Simon & Schuster Bks. For Young Readers) Simon & Schuster Bks. For Young Readers.

Girard, Geoffrey. Project Cain. 2013. (ENG., Illus.). 368p. (YA). (gr. 9). 17.99 (978-1-4424-7696-7(6), Simon & Schuster Bks. For Young Readers) Simon & Schuster Bks. For Young Readers.

Haddix, Margaret Peterson. Double Identity. 2007. 218p. (gr. 5-9). 17.00 (978-0-7569-8190-7(5)) Perfection Learning Corp.

—Double Identity. (ENG.). (J). (gr. 5-9). 2007. 192p. pap. 7.99 (978-0-689-87379-9(4)) 2005. 224p. 16.99 (978-0-689-87374-4(3)) Simon & Schuster Bks. For Young Readers. (Simon & Schuster Bks. For Young Readers).

—Double Identity. rev. l.t. ed. 2007. (Literacy Bridge Young Adult Ser.). 299p. (J). (gr. 5-9). 22.95 (978-0-7862-9702-3(6)) Thorndike Pr.

Hopper, Ada. A Case of the Clones. Ricks, Sam, illus. 2016. (DATA Set Ser.: 5). (ENG.). 128p. (J). (gr. k-4). pap. 5.99 (978-1-4814-7113-8(9), Little Simon) Little Simon.

Horowitz, Anthony. Point Blanc. 2004. (Alex Rider Ser.: Bk. 2). (SPA.). 264p. pap. 7.95 (978-84-414-1410-5(6)) Editorial Edaf, S.L. ESP. Dist: Spanish Pubs., LLC.

—Point Blank. 2006. (Alex Rider Ser.). (ENG.). 320p. (J). (gr. 5-18). 8.99 (978-0-14-240612-0(0), Puffin Books) Penguin Young Readers Group.

Incomprehensible, Vordak T. & Seegert, Scott. Double Trouble. Martin, John, illus. 2012. (Vordak the Incomprehensible Ser.: No. 3). (ENG.). 192p. (J). (gr. 5). 13.99 (978-1-60684-372-7(9), Darby Creek) Lerner Publishing Group.

Kerner, Charlotte. Blueprint. Crawford, Elizabeth D., tr. from GER. 2003. (Young Adult Fiction Ser.). 192p. (YA). (gr. 9-12). 16.95 (978-0-8225-0080-3(9), Carolrhoda Bks.) Lerner Publishing Group.

Koosis, Lisa A. Resurrecting Sunshine. 2016. (ENG.). 320p. (YA). (gr. 8-12). 16.99 (978-0-8075-6943-6(7)) Whitman, Albert & Co.

Korman, Gordon. Criminal Destiny. 2016. (Masterminds Ser.: 2). 320p. (J). (gr. 3-7). 16.99 (978-0-06-230002-7(4)) HarperCollins Pubs.

—Criminal Destiny. 2017. (Masterminds Ser.: 2). (J). lib. bdg. 18.40 **(978-0-606-39612-7(8))** Turtleback Bks.

Korman, Gordon. Masterminds. (Masterminds Ser.: 2). (J). (gr. 3-7). 2017. 336p. 7.99 (978-0-06-230003-4(2)) 2016. 352p. pap. 7.99 (978-0-06-229999-4(9)) 2015. 336p. 16.99 (978-0-06-229996-3(4)) HarperCollins Pubs.

—Masterminds. 2016. (Masterminds Ser.: 1). (J). lib. bdg. 18.40 (978-0-606-38138-3(4)) Turtleback Bks.

Krokos, Dan. False Future. 2014. (False Memory Novel Ser.). (ENG., Illus.). 320p. (YA). (gr. 9-17). 17.99 (978-1-4231-4987-3(4)) Hyperion Bks. for Children.

—False Sight. 2014. (False Memory Novel Ser.). (ENG., Illus.). 352p. (YA). (gr. 7-12). pap. 8.99 (978-1-4231-4986-6(6)) Hyperion Bks. for Children.

The Lord of Opium. 2014. (ENG., Illus.). 448p. (YA). (gr. 7). pap. 12.99 (978-1-4424-8255-5(9), Atheneum Bks. for Young Readers) Simon & Schuster Children's Publishing.

Lucas, Luke. Falls the Shadow. 2014. (ENG., Illus.). 352p. (YA). (gr. 7). 18.99 (978-1-4424-9753-5(X), Simon & Schuster Bks. For Young Readers) Simon & Schuster Bks. For Young Readers.

Mandanna, Sangu. The Lost Girl. 2012. (ENG.). 432p. (YA). (gr. 8). 17.99 (978-0-06-208231-2(0)) HarperCollins Pubs.

Nancy, Farmer. The House of the Scorpion. 2014. (ENG.). 400p. (YA). (gr. 3-6). 14.24 (978-1-63245-268-9(5)) Lectorum Pubns., Inc.

The New Olympians. 2014. (Pegasus Ser.: 3). (ENG., Illus.). 448p. (J). (gr. 3-7). pap. 8.99 (978-1-4424-4416-4(9), Simon & Schuster/Paula Wiseman Bks.) Simon & Schuster/Paula Wiseman Bks.

O'Hara, Mo. Jurassic Carp. Jagucki, Marek, illus. 2017. (My Big Fat Zombie Goldfish Ser.: 6). (ENG.). 224p. (J). pap. 6.99 **(978-1-250-10260-7(X)**, 9781250102607) Square Fish.

O'Hearn, Kate. The New Olympians. 2014. (Pegasus Ser.: 3). (ENG., Illus.). 432p. (J). (gr. 3-7). 17.99 (978-1-4424-4415-7(0), Simon & Schuster/Paula Wiseman Bks.) Simon & Schuster/Paula Wiseman Bks.

Patrick, Cat. The Originals. (ENG.). (YA). (gr. 7-17). 2014. 320p. pap. 10.00 (978-0-316-21945-7(2)) 2013. 304p. 18.00 (978-0-316-21943-3(6)) Little, Brown Bks. for Young Readers.

Project Cain. 2014. (ENG., Illus.). 384p. (YA). (gr. 9). pap. 11.99 (978-1-4424-7698-1(2), Simon & Schuster Bks. For Young Readers) Simon & Schuster Bks. For Young Readers.

Reynolds, Peter H. So Few of Me. Reynolds, Peter H., illus. 2006. (ENG., Illus.). 32p. (J). (gr. k-12). 15.00 (978-0-7636-2623-5(6)) Candlewick Pr.

Scroggs, Kirk. Snoop Troop: Attack of the Ninja Potato Clones. 2015. (Snoop Troop Ser.: 2). (ENG., Illus.). 192p. (J). (gr. 1-4). 13.99 (978-0-316-24277-6(2)) Little, Brown Bks. for Young Readers.

Skurzynski, Gloria. Afterwar. 2011. (ENG., Illus.). 528p. (YA). (gr. 7). pap. 9.99 (978-1-4424-1681-9(5), Atheneum Bks. for Young Readers) Simon & Schuster Children's Publishing.

—The Clones Bk. 2. 2007. (ENG.). 192p. (YA). (gr. 7). pap. 10.95 (978-1-4169-5560-3(7), Simon Pulse) Simon Pulse.

Stevens, Garrett. Who Cloned the President? Friedland, Joyce & Kessler, Rikki, eds. 2007. (Novel-Ties Ser.). (Illus.). 30p. pap. 16.95 (978-0-7675-1543-6(9)) Learning Links Inc.

Sutton, Laurie S. Night of a Thousand Doomsdays, 1 vol. Vecchio, Luciano, illus. 2013. (Man of Steel Ser.). (ENG.). 88p. (gr. 2-3). 26.65 (978-1-4342-4487-1(3)) Stone Arch Bks.

—Night of a Thousand Doomsdays. Vecchio, Luciano, illus. 2013. (Man of Steel Ser.). (ENG.). 88p. (gr. 2-3). pap. 5.95 (978-1-4342-4827-5(5)) Stone Arch Bks.

Traver., N. K. & Traver, N. K. Duplicity. 2015. (ENG.). 256p. (YA). (gr. 9-12). 18.99 (978-1-250-05914-7(3), 9781250059147, Dunne, Thomas Bks.) St. Martin's Pr.

Van Dolzer, Krista. The Sound of Life & Everything. 2015. (ENG.). 272p. (J). (gr. 5). 16.99 (978-0-399-16775-1(7), G.P. Putnam's Sons Books for Young Readers) Penguin Young Readers Group.

Werlin, Nancy. Double Helix. 2005. (ENG.). 256p. (YA). (gr. 7-6). pap. 7.99 (978-0-14-240327-3(X), Puffin Books) Penguin Young Readers Group.

Williams, Sean. Hollowgirl: A Twinmaker Novel. 2015. (Twinmaker Ser.: 3). (ENG.). 512p. (YA). (gr. 8). 17.99 (978-0-06-220327-4(4)) HarperCollins Pubs.

CLOTHIERS

see Clothing Trade

CLOTHING AND DRESS

Here are entered works dealing with clothing from a practical standpoint including the art of dress. Descriptive and historical works on the costume of particular countries or periods are entered under Costume.

see also Buttons; Costume; Costume Design; Dressmaking; Fashion; Hats; Shoes

Adamson, Heather. Clothes in Many Cultures. 2016. (Life Around the World Ser.). (ENG.). 24p. (gr. k-1). pap. 7.29 (978-1-5157-4237-1(7), Pebble Plus) Capstone Press of Coughlan Cos.

Ajmera, Maya, et al. What We Wear: Dressing up Around the World. 2012. (ENG., Illus.). 32p. (J). (gr. -1-3). pap. 7.95 (978-1-58089-417-3(8)) Charlesbridge Publishing, Inc.

Albee, Sarah. Why'd They Wear That? From Hair Shirts to Hoop Skirts, Platform Shoes to Tattoos, a Fashion History of of the World. 2015. (ENG., Illus.). 192p. (J). (gr. 5-7). 19.99 (978-1-4263-1919-8(3), National Geographic Children's Bks.) National Geographic Society.

Appel, Dee. Let's Play Dress Up. Francour, Kathleen, photos by. Date not set. (Tiny Times Board Book Ser.). (Illus.). 10p. (J). bds. 5.99 (978-0-7369-0563-3(4)) Harvest Hse. Pubs.

Arrowsmith, Vicky. Sticker Dolly Dressing Costumes & Parties. 2012. (Sticker Dolly Dressing Ser.). 24p. (J). pap. 8.99 (978-0-7945-3134-8(2), Usborne) EDC Publishing.

Atlantic, Leonard. We Play Dress-Up! 2017. (Ways to Play Ser.). 24p. (gr. k-k). pap. 8.15 **(978-1-4824-6345-3(8))** Stevens, Gareth Publishing LLLP.

Baggott, Stella & Arrowsmith, Vicker. Popstars & Movie Stars CV. 2011. (Sticker Dolly Dressing Ser.). 24p. (J). pap. 14.99 (978-0-7945-2887-4(2), Usborne) EDC Publishing.

Bailey Publishing Staff. A History of Fashion & Costume Set. 2005. (History of Fashion & Costume Ser.). 512p. (gr. 6-12). 280.00 (978-0-8160-5943-0(8)) Facts On File, Inc.

Bailey Publishing Staff & Elgin, Kathy. Elizabethan England. 2009. (Costume Source Bks). (Illus.). 64p. (gr. 6-12). 35.00 (978-1-60413-379-0(1), Chelsea Hse.) Facts On File, Inc.

Bailey Publishing Staff & McEvoy, Anne. The 20s & 30s. 2009. (Costume Source Bks). (Illus.). 32p. (gr. 6-12). 35.00 (978-1-60413-383-7(X), Chelsea Hse.) Facts On File, Inc.

Bailey Publishing Staff & Steer, Deirdre Clancy. The 1980s & 1990s. 2009. (Costume Source Bks). (Illus.). 32p. (gr. 6-12). 35.00 (978-1-60413-386-8(4), Chelsea Hse.) Facts On File, Inc.

Bailey Publishing Staff, et al. Colonial America. 2009. (Costume Source Bks). (Illus.). 32p. (gr. 6-12). 35.00 (978-1-60413-380-6(5), Chelsea Hse.) Facts On File, Inc.

Baker, Patricia. Fashions of a Decade: The 1940s. 2nd rev. ed. 2006. (Fashions of a Decade Ser.). (Illus.). 64p. (gr. 6-12). 35.00 (978-0-8160-6720-6(1)) Facts On File, Inc.

—Fashions of a Decade: The 1950s. 2nd rev. ed. 2006. (Fashions of a Decade Ser.). (Illus.). 64p. (gr. 6-12). 35.00 (978-0-8160-6721-3(X)) Facts On File, Inc.

Ball, Jacqueline A. Clothing Creations: From T-Shirts to Flip-Flops. 2006. (Which Came First? Ser.). (Illus.). 32p. (J). (gr. 3-6). lib. bdg. 25.27 (978-1-59716-128-2(4)) Bearport Publishing Co., Inc.

Barbie Tiara. 2004. (Marketing Support Ser.). (J). (978-1-57584-455-8(9), Reader's Digest Children's Bks.) Studio Fun International.

Baum, Margaux & Scott, Margaret. Fashion & Clothing. 2016. (Life in the Middle Ages Ser.). 00064p. (J). (gr. 5-5). 34.45 (978-1-4994-6468-9(1)) Rosen Publishing Group, Inc., The.

Beckett-Bowman, Lucy. Sticker Dolly Dressing Bridesmaids. 2009. (Sticker Dolly Dressing Ser.). 24p. (J). pap. 8.99 (978-0-7945-2519-4(9), Usborne) EDC Publishing.

—Sticker Dolly Dressing on Vacation. 2009. (Sticker Dolly Dressing Ser.). 24p. (J). pap. 8.99 (978-0-7945-2369-5(2), Usborne) EDC Publishing.

—Sticker Dolly Dressing Popstars. 2009. (Sticker Dolly Dressing Ser.). 26p. (J). pap. 8.99 (978-0-7945-2360-2(9), Usborne) EDC Publishing.

Behnke, Alison. The Little Black Dress & Zoot Suits: Depression & Wartime Fashions from the 1930s to the 1950s. 2011. (Dressing a Nation: the History of U. S. Fashion Ser.). (ENG., Illus.). 64p. (gr. 5-12). lib. bdg. 31.93 (978-0-7613-5892-3(7), Twenty-First Century Bks.) Lerner Publishing Group.

Behrens, Janice. This Is the Way We Dress. 2009. (Scholastic News Nonfiction Readers Ser.). (ENG.). 24p. (J). (gr. 1-2). lib. bdg. 22.00 (978-0-531-21338-4(2)) Scholastic Library Publishing.

Berendes, Mary. Clothes/la Ropa. Petelinsek, Kathleen, illus. 2008. (WordBooks/Libros de Palabras Ser.). (SPA & ENG.). 24p. (J). (gr. k-3). 25.64 (978-1-59296-989-0(5), 201089) Child's World, Inc., The.

Berry, Joy. Getting Dressed. 2009. (ENG.). 40p. (J). (gr. k — 1). bds. 7.95 (978-1-60577-009-3(4)) Berry, Joy Enterprises.

—I Love Getting Dressed. Regan, Dana, illus. 2010. (Teach Me About Ser.). (ENG.). 20p. (J). (gr. k — 1). bds. 5.99 (978-1-60577-014-7(0)) Berry, Joy Enterprises.

Bily, Cynthia A. Dress Codes in Schools. Gale, ed. 2014. (Issues That Concern You Ser.). (ENG., Illus.). 144p. (gr. 7-10). lib. bdg. 42.00 (978-0-7377-6930-2(0), Greenhaven Pr., Inc.) Cengage Gale.

Bingham, Jane. Japan. 2008. (Costume Around the World Ser.). (Illus.). 32p. (gr. 4-6). 28.00 (978-0-7910-9770-0(6), Chelsea Clubhouse) Facts On File, Inc.

—Mexico. 2008. (Costume Around the World Ser.). (Illus.). 32p. (gr. 4-6). 28.00 (978-0-7910-9771-7(4), Chelsea Clubhouse) Facts On File, Inc.

Bix, Jasper. Dressing for the Cold. 2016. (Winter Fun Ser.). (ENG.). 24p. (J). (gr. k-k). pap. 8.15 (978-1-4824-3751-5(1)) Stevens, Gareth Publishing LLLP.

Blake, Susannah. Crafts for Styling Your Wardrobe. 2013. (Eco Chic Ser.). 32p. (J). lib. bdg. 23.94 (978-0-7660-4316-9(9)); (gr. 4-12). pap. 7.95 (978-1-4644-0577-8(8)) Enslow Pubs., Inc.

Blaxland, Wendy. Helmets. 2009. (How Are They Made? Ser.). (Illus.). 32p. (gr. 4-6). lib. bdg. 18.56 (978-0-7614-4755-9(5)) Marshall Cavendish Corp.

—T-Shirts. 2008. (How Are They Made? Ser.). (Illus.). 32p. (J). (gr. 4-18). lib. bdg. 18.56 (978-0-7614-3812-0(2), Benchmark Bks.) Marshall Cavendish Corp.

Boase, Petra. Terrific T-Shirt Fun: 25 Tremendous T-Shirt Designs & Creations to Try! 2013. (ENG., Illus.). 64p. (J). (gr. 2-6). 9.99 (978-1-84322-748-9(7), Armadillo) Anness Publishing GBR. Dist: National Bk. Network.

Bolte, Mari. All-American Girl Style: Fun Fashions You Can Sketch, 1 vol. Otero, Sole, illus. 2013. (Drawing Fun Fashions Ser.). (ENG.). 32p. (gr. 3-4). lib. bdg. 27.99 (978-1-62065-039-4(8), Snap Bks.) Capstone Press of Coughlan Cos.

—Fab Fashions You Can Make & Share, 1 vol. Franco, Paula, illus. 2014. (Sleepover Girls Crafts Ser.). (ENG.). 32p. (gr. 3-4). lib. bdg. 27.99 (978-1-4914-1735-5(8), Snap Bks.) Capstone Press of Coughlan Cos.

—Girly Girl Style: Fun Fashions You Can Sketch, 1 vol. Hagel, Brooke, illus. 2013. (Drawing Fun Fashions Ser.). (ENG.). 32p. (gr. 3-4). lib. bdg. 27.99 (978-1-62065-035-6(5), Snap Bks.) Capstone Press of Coughlan Cos.

—Harajuku Style: Fun Fashions You Can Sketch, 1 vol. Hagel, Brooke, illus. 2013. (Drawing Fun Fashions Ser.). (ENG.). 32p. (gr. 3-4). lib. bdg. 27.99 (978-1-62065-034-9(7), Snap Bks.) Capstone Press of Coughlan Cos.

Bone, Emily. Sticker Dolly Dressing Around the World. 2011. (Sticker Dolly Dressing Ser.). 24p. (J). pap. 8.99 (978-0-7945-2968-0(2), Usborne) EDC Publishing.

—Sticker Dolly Dressing Dream Jobs. 2012. (Sticker Dolly Dressing Ser.). 24p. (J). pap. 8.99 (978-0-7945-3253-6(5), Usborne) EDC Publishing.

Bonnice, Sherry. Folk Fashion. 2004. (North American Folklore Ser.). (Illus.). 112p. (YA). (gr. 7-18). lib. bdg. 22.95 (978-1-59084-338-3(X)) Mason Crest.

Boothroyd, Jennifer. Clothes. 2006. (First Step Nonfiction Ser.). (Illus.). 8p. (J). pap. 3.95 (978-0-8225-5732-6(0), Lerner Pubns.) Lerner Publishing Group.

Bowman, Lucy. Sticker Dolly Dressing Fashion Long Ago. Baggott, Stella, illus. 2010. (Sticker Dolly Dressing Ser.). 24p. (J). pap. 8.99 (978-0-7945-2547-7(4), Usborne) EDC Publishing.

Brides. Date not set. (Dressing My Dolly Ser.). (Illus.). 16p. (J). 2.98 (978-1-4054-0474-7(4)) Parragon, Inc.

Brocklehurst, Ruth. Clothes & Fashion Sticker Book IR. Lardot, Christopher, illus. 2013. (Clothes & Fashion Sticker Book Ser.). 31p. (J). pap. 9.99 (978-0-7945-3235-2(7), Usborne) EDC Publishing.

Brooks, Felicity. Getting Dressed. Widdowson, Kay, illus. 2010. (Sticker Bks). 16p. (J). pap. 6.99 (978-0-7945-2668-9(3), Usborne) EDC Publishing.

Bullard, Lisa. My Clothes, Your Clothes. 2015. (Cloverleaf Books (tm) — Alike & Different Ser.). (ENG., Illus.). 24p. (J). (gr. k-2). lib. bdg. 23.99 (978-1-4677-4902-2(8)) Lerner Publishing Group.

—My Clothes, Your Clothes. Kurilla, Renee, illus. 2015. (Cloverleaf Books (tm) — Alike & Different Ser.). (ENG.). 24p. (gr. k-2). pap. 6.99 (978-1-4677-6030-0(7), Millbrook Pr.) Lerner Publishing Group.

Butterfield, Moira. Clothes Around the World. 2016. (Children Like Us Ser.). (ENG., Illus.). 32p. (J). (gr. 3-3). pap. 10.58 (978-1-5026-0834-5(0), 1399882) Cavendish Square Publishing.

Butterworth, Chris. Where Did My Clothes Come From? Gaggiotti, Lucia, illus. 2015. (ENG.). 32p. (J). (gr. k-3). 12.99 (978-0-7636-7750-3(7)) Candlewick Pr.

Butterworth, Christine. Where Did My Clothes Come From? Gaggiotti, Lucia, illus. 2017. (Exploring the Everyday Ser.). (ENG.). 32p. (J). (gr. k-3). 5.99 **(978-0-7636-9518-7(1))** Candlewick Pr.

Cain, Marie Mowery. Dress for the Weather. 2013. (Big Books, Blue Ser.). (ENG & SPA., Illus.). 16p. pap. 33.00 (978-1-59246-010-6(0)) Big Books, by George!

Carluccio, Maria. D Is for Dress Up: The ABCs of What We Wear. 2016. (ENG., Illus.). 36p. (J). (gr. -1-k). 15.99 (978-1-4521-4025-4(1)) Chronicle Bks. LLC.

Carnegy, Vicky. Fashions of a Decade: The 1980s. 2nd rev. ed. 2006. (Fashions of a Decade Ser.). (Illus.). 64p. (gr. 6-12). 35.00 (978-0-8160-6724-4(4)) Facts On File, Inc.

Carole, Bonnie. School Uniforms, Yes or No. 2015. (ENG.). 24p. (gr. k-3). 28.50 (978-1-63430-348-4(2)) Rourke Educational Media.

Chorba, April & Johnson, Anne Akers. Fashion Forms. 2012. (ENG.). 68p. (J). (gr. 3). 24.99 (978-0-545-44935-9(9)) Klutz.

Claybourne, Anna. Accessories for All. 2013. (Illus.). 32p. (J). lib. bdg. 27.10 (978-1-59920-694-3(3)) Black Rabbit Bks.

Clothes: KinderFacts Individual Title Six-Packs. (Kinderstarters Ser.). 8p. (gr. -1-1). 21.00 (978-0-7635-8743-7(5)) Rigby Education.

Clothes-Ropa Bilingual Board Book. 2008. (ENG & SPA.). (J). pap. 5.99 (978-0-9727886-9-4(7)) Osmosis, LLC.

Cobb, Vicki. Sneakers. 2006. (Where's the Science Here? Ser.). (Illus.). 48p. (J). (gr. 3-5). 23.93 (978-0-7613-2772-1(X), Millbrook Pr.) Lerner Publishing Group.

Collins, Elaine Banks. I Like Dressing Up. Floyd, John, Jr., illus. 2005. (J). bds. 5.95 (978-0-9752860-5-0(6)) OurRainbow Pr., LLC.

Connikie, Yvonne. Fashions of a Decade: The 1960s. 2nd rev. ed. 2006. (Fashions of a Decade Ser.). (Illus.). 64p. (gr. 6-12). 35.00 (978-0-8160-6722-0(8)) Facts On File, Inc.

Conrad, Lauren. Lauren Conrad Style. 2012. (ENG.). 240p. (YA). (gr. 8). pap. 12.99 (978-0-06-198969-8(X)) HarperCollins Pubs.

Costantino, Maria. Fashions of a Decade: The 1930s. 2nd rev. ed. 2006. (Fashions of a Decade Ser.). (Illus.). 64p. (gr. 6-12). 35.00 (978-0-8160-6719-0(8)) Facts On File, Inc.

Cullis, Megan. Sticker Dressing Heroes. 2012. (Sticker Dressing Ser.). 24p. (J). pap. 8.99 (978-0-7945-3267-3(5), Usborne) EDC Publishing.

Daynes, Katie. Fabulous Story of Fashion. Mistry, Nilesh, illus. 2006. (Young Reading Series 2 Gift Bks.). 64p. (J). (gr. 2-5). 8.99 (978-0-7945-1263-7(1), Usborne) EDC Publishing.

—The Revealing Story of Underwear. Mistry, Nilesh, illus. 2006. (Young Reading Series 2 Gift Bks.). 64p. (J). (gr. 2-5). 8.99 (978-0-7945-1352-8(2), Usborne) EDC Publishing.

D'Cruz, Anna-Marie. Make Your Own Purses & Bags. 2009. (Do It Yourself Projects! Ser.). (ENG.). 24p. (J). (gr. 3-5). pap. 9.40 (978-1-4358-2929-9(8), PowerKids Pr.) Rosen Publishing Group, Inc., The.

deCarufel, Laura. Learn to Speak Fashion: A Guide to Creating, Showcasing, & Promoting Your Style. Kulak, Jeff & Owlkids Books Inc. Staff, illus. 2012. (Learn to Speak Ser.). (ENG.). 96p. (J). (gr. 4-8). pap. 14.95 (978-1-926973-42-5(9), Owlkids) Owlkids Bks. Inc. CAN. Dist: Publishers Group West (PGW).

Diva Girls. Date not set. (Dressing My Dolly Ser.). (Illus.). 16p. (J). 2.98 (978-1-4054-0475-4(2)) Parragon, Inc.

Dorling Kindersley Publishing Staff. Fashion. 2014. (ENG.). 96p. (J). (gr. 2-4). pap. 12.99 (978-1-4654-1653-7(6), DK Children) Dorling Kindersley Publishing, Inc.

—The Fashion Book. 2014. (ENG.). 160p. (YA). (gr. 8-12). 15.99 (978-1-4654-2284-2(6), DK Children) Dorling Kindersley Publishing, Inc.

Doudna, Kelly. Clothing Around the World, 1 vol. 2004. (Around the World Ser.). (ENG., Illus.). 24p. (J). (gr. k-3). lib. bdg. 24.21 (978-1-59197-565-6(4), SandCastle) ABDO Publishing Co.

—Look Your Best!, 1 vol. 2007. (Character Concepts Ser.). (ENG., Illus.). 24p. (J). (gr. k-3). lib. bdg. 24.21 (978-1-59928-737-9(4), SandCastle) ABDO Publishing Co.

Draper, Allison Stark. Clothing, Costumes & Uniforms Throughout American History, 6 bks. Incl. What People Wore During the American Revolution. lib. bdg. 22.60 (978-0-8239-5666-1(0), PKCLRE); What People Wore During the Civil War. lib. bdg. 22.60 (978-0-8239-5669-2(5), PKCLCI); What People Wore in Early America. lib. bdg. 22.60 (978-0-8239-5664-7(4), PKCLEA); What People Wore on Southern Plantations. lib. bdg. 22.60 (978-0-8239-5668-5(7), PKCLPL); 24p. (J). (gr. 3). 2001. (Illus.). Set lib. bdg. 117.00 (978-0-8239-7060-5(4), PKCLAM, PowerKids Pr.) Rosen Publishing Group, Inc., The.

—What People Wore During the American Revolution. 2009. (Clothing, Costumes, & Uniforms Throughout American History Ser.). 24p. (gr. 3-3). 42.50 (978-1-61511-875-5(6), PowerKids Pr.) Rosen Publishing Group, Inc., The.

—What People Wore During the Civil War. 2009. (Clothing, Costumes, & Uniforms Throughout American History Ser.). 24p. (gr. 3-3). 42.50 (978-1-61511-876-2(4), PowerKids Pr.) Rosen Publishing Group, Inc., The.

—What People Wore in Early America. 2009. (Clothing, Costumes, & Uniforms Throughout American History Ser.). 24p. (gr. 3-3). 42.50 (978-1-61511-881-6(0), PowerKids Pr.) Rosen Publishing Group, Inc., The.

—What People Wore on Southern Plantations. 2009. (Clothing, Costumes, & Uniforms Throughout American History Ser.). 24p. (gr. 3-3). 42.50 (978-1-61511-882-3(9), PowerKids Pr.) Rosen Publishing Group, Inc., The.

Dressing with Pride: Six-Pack. (Greetings Ser.: Vol. 2). (gr. 3-5). 31.00 (978-0-7635-1764-9(X)) Rigby Education.

Drews, Judith. Lucas: Magnetic Dress-up Doll. 2014. (ENG., Illus.). 1p. (J). (gr. -1-2). 14.95 (978-3-89955-721-3(2)) Die Gestalten Verlag DEU. Dist: Penguin Random Hse. LLC.

Dunn, Mary R. I Want to Be a Fashion Designer. 2009. (Dream Jobs Ser.). 24p. (gr. 2-3). 42.50 (978-1-61512-206-6(0), PowerKids Pr.) Rosen Publishing Group, Inc., The.

Dybvik, Tina. Cute Clothes for the Crafty Fashionista, 1 vol. 2011. (Fashion Craft Studio Ser.). (ENG.). 32p. (gr. 3-4). lib. bdg. 27.99 (978-1-4296-6553-7(X), Snap Bks.) Capstone Press of Coughlan Cos.

Eck, Kristin. Hide-and-Seek Clothes. 2004. (Hide-And-Seek Books). (Illus.). (J). lib. bdg. 21.25 (978-1-4042-2705-7(9), PowerKids Pr.) Rosen Publishing Group, Inc., The.

—Hide & Seek Clothes. 2009. (Tough Toddler Bks). 16p. (gr. k-k). 42.50 (978-1-60854-569-8(5), PowerKids Pr.) Rosen Publishing Group, Inc., The.

Elgin, Kathy. France. 2008. (Costume Around the World Ser.). (Illus.). 32p. (gr. 4-6). 28.00 (978-0-7910-9766-3(8), Chelsea Clubhouse) Facts On File, Inc.

—India. 2008. (Costume Around the World Ser.). (Illus.). 32p. (gr. 4-6). 28.00 (978-0-7910-9768-7(4), Chelsea Clubhouse) Facts On File, Inc.

—Italy. 2008. (Costume Around the World Ser.). (Illus.). 32p. (gr. 4-6). 28.00 (978-0-7910-9769-4(2), Chelsea Clubhouse) Facts On File, Inc.

—Spain. 2008. (Costume Around the World Ser.). (Illus.). 32p. (gr. 4-6). 28.00 (978-0-7910-9772-4(2), Chelsea Clubhouse) Facts On File, Inc.

Elliott, Lynne. Clothing in the Middle Ages. 2004. (Medieval World Ser.). (ENG., Illus.). 32p. (J). pap. (978-0-7787-1383-8(0)) Crabtree Publishing Co.

Facts on File, Inc. Staff, ed. Fashions of a Decade, 8 Vols., Set. 2006. (Fashions of a Decade Ser.). (Illus.). 64p. (gr. 6-12). 280.00 (978-0-8160-7059-6(8)) Facts On File, Inc.

Fashion Designer. 2008. (Cool Creations Style Folder Ser.). 32p. pap. (978-1-4075-1651-6(5)) Parragon, Inc.

Felix, Rebecca. Mini Wearables. 2017. (Mini Makers Ser.). (ENG.). 32p. (J). (gr. 2-5). 12.99 **(978-1-5124-3843-7(X)**, Lerner Pubns.); 39.99 **(978-1-5124-3842-0(1)**, Lerner Pubns.); 39.99 **(978-1-5124-2813-1(2)**, Lerner Pubns.); (Illus.). 26.65 (978-1-5124-2635-9(0)) Lerner Publishing Group.

Fields, Stella. Accessory Projects for a Lazy Crafternoon. 2016. (Lazy Crafternoon Ser.). (ENG.). 32p. (gr. 3-4). lib. bdg. 27.99 (978-1-5157-1436-1(5), Snap Bks.) Capstone Press of Coughlan Cos.

Focus on Fashion! 2004. (Bratz Ser.). (J). 1.49 (978-0-7666-1225-9(2), 99215) Modern Publishing.

Fontichiaro, Kristin. Hacking Fashion. 2016. (21st Century Skills Innovation Library: Makers As Innovators Ser.). (ENG., Illus.). 32p. (J). (gr. 4-8). lib. bdg. 29.93 (978-1-63471-416-7(4), 208443) Cherry Lake Publishing.

—Hacking Fashion: Fleece. 2015. (21st Century Skills Innovation Library: Makers As Innovators Ser.). (ENG., Illus.). 32p. (J). (gr. 4-8). pap. 14.21 (978-1-63362-404-7(8), 206925) Cherry Lake Publishing.

—Hacking Fashion: T- Shirts. 2015. (21st Century Skills Innovation Library: Makers As Innovators Ser.). (ENG.). 32p. (J). (gr. 4-8). 29.93 (978-1-63188-871-7(4), 206064) Cherry Lake Publishing.

Foster, Dara. Now You See It! Pupstyle Red Carpet Pups. Foster, Dara, photos by. 2013. (ENG., Illus.). 64p. (J). (gr. 2-5). pap. 5.99 (978-0-545-53245-7(0)) Math Solutions.

Foy, Debbie. Pants, Vest, Getting Dressed! 2017. (All by Myself Ser.). (ENG., Illus.). 20p. (J). (gr. -1-k). pap. 6.99 (978-0-7502-9620-5(8), Wayland) Hachette Children's Group GBR. Dist: Hachette Bk. Group.

Freistadt, Margo. Kate Spade. 2011. (Profiles in Fashion Ser.). (Illus.). 112p. 28.95 (978-1-59935-154-4(4)) Reynolds, Morgan Inc.

Galford, Ellen. Festivals. 2004. (Twentieth-Century Developments in Fashion & Costume Ser.). (Illus.). 64p. (YA). (gr. 7-18). lib. bdg. 19.95 (978-1-59084-423-6(8)) Mason Crest.

—Religious Costumes. 2004. (Twentieth-Century Developments in Fashion & Costume Ser.). (Illus.). 64p. (YA). (gr. 7-18). lib. bdg. 19.95 (978-1-59084-429-8(7)) Mason Crest.

Gardner, Jane P. Fashion Science, Vol. 11. Lewin, Russ, ed. 2015. (Science 24/7 Ser.). (Illus.). 48p. (J). (gr. 5). 20.95 (978-1-4222-3409-9(6)) Mason Crest.

Giulieri, Anne. The Lost Sock, 1 vol. Bailey, Martin, illus. 2012. (Engage Literacy Red Ser.). (ENG.). 32p. (gr. k-2). pap. 5.99 (978-1-4296-8940-3(4), Engage Literacy) Capstone Press of Coughlan Cos.

Gogerly, Liz. United States. 2008. (Costume Around the World Ser.). (Illus.). 32p. (gr. 4-6). 28.00 (978-0-7910-9774-8(9), Chelsea Clubhouse) Facts On File, Inc.

Greathead, Helen. Clothes & Shoes. 2006. (Design & Make Ser.). (Illus.). 32p. (J). (gr. 4-7). lib. bdg. 28.50 (978-1-58340-956-5(4)) Black Rabbit Bks.

Greene, Jacqueline Dembar. The Triangle Shirtwaist Factory Fire. 2007. (Code Red Ser.). (Illus.). 32p. (YA). (gr. 2-5). lib. bdg. 25.27 (978-1-59716-359-0(7)) Bearport Publishing Co., Inc.

Gunzi, Christiane. Clothes. 2003. (My Very First Look At Ser.). (SPA & ENG., Illus.). 24p. (J). (gr. -1-k). 9.95 (978-1-58728-672-8(6)); pap. 5.95 (978-1-58728-686-5(6)) Cooper Square Publishing Llc.

Harcourt School Publishers Staff. Going Outside to Play. 3rd ed. 2003. (Trophies English Language Learners Ser.). (Illus.). (J). pap. 3.20 (978-0-15-327569-2(3)) Harcourt Schl. Pubs.

Harper, Kathryn. Dressing for the Weather Green Band. Sims, Sean, illus. 2016. (Cambridge Reading Adventures Ser.). (ENG.). 16p. pap. 6.56 (978-1-316-50324-9(0)) Cambridge Univ. Pr.

Harris, Carol & Brown, Mike. Accessories. 2004. (Twentieth-Century Developments in Fashion & Costume Ser.). (Illus.). 64p. (YA). (gr. 7-18). lib. bdg. 19.95 (978-1-59084-419-9(X)) Mason Crest.

—Children's Costumes. 2004. (Twentieth-Century Developments in Fashion & Costume Ser.). (Illus.). 64p. (YA). (gr. 7-18). lib. bdg. 19.95 (978-1-59084-420-5(3)) Mason Crest.

—Men's Costumes. 2004. (Twentieth-Century Developments in Fashion & Costume Ser.). (Illus.). 64p. (YA). (gr. 7-18). lib. bdg. 19.95 (978-1-59084-422-9(X)) Mason Crest.

Harrison, Paul. Ancient Roman Clothes. 2010. (Ancient Communities: Roman Life Ser.). 32p. (J). (ENG.). pap. 10.60 (978-1-61532-308-1(2)); (Illus.). (gr. 3-6). lib. bdg. 26.50 (978-1-61532-304-3(X)) Rosen Publishing Group, Inc., The. (PowerKids Pr.).

Havelin, Kate. Hoopskirts, Union Blues, & Confederate Grays: Civil War Fashions from 1861 to 1865. 2011. (Dressing a Nation: the History of U. S. Fashion Ser.). (ENG., Illus.). 64p. (gr. 5-12). lib. bdg. 31.93 (978-0-7613-5889-3(7), Twenty-First Century Bks.) Lerner Publishing Group.

Hayes, Amy. Turning Wool into Sweaters. 2015. (Step-By-Step Transformations Ser.). (ENG., Illus.). 24p. (J). (gr. 1-1). 24.21 (978-1-5026-0455-2(8)) Cavendish Square Publishing.

Herald, Jacqueline. Fashions of a Decade: The 1920s. 2nd rev. ed. 2006. (Fashions of a Decade Ser.). (Illus.). 64p. (gr. 6-12). 35.00 (978-0-8160-6718-3(X)) Facts On File, Inc.

—Fashions of a Decade: The 1970s. 2nd rev. ed. 2006. (Fashions of a Decade Ser.). (Illus.). 64p. (gr. 6-12). 35.00 (978-0-8160-6723-7(6)) Facts On File, Inc.

Hewitt, Sally. Happy Dresser. Cameron, Craig, illus. 2003. 14p. (J). pap. 10.95 (978-1-57145-733-2(X), Silver Dolphin Bks.) Readerlink Distribution Services, LLC.

Holland, Trish. Wash & Dry. Kumar, Vinay, illus. 2010. 24p. (J). (978-1-60617-119-6(4)) Teaching Strategies, LLC.

—Who's Got the Button? 2010. (J). (978-1-60617-118-9(6)) Teaching Strategies, LLC.

Horne, Jane & Page, Claire. Magnetics Fashion Show. 2007. (Magnetics Ser.). (Illus.). 14p. (J). (gr. -1-k). (978-1-84610-471-8(8)) Make Believe Ideas.

Hughes, Susan. No Girls Allowed: Tales of Daring Women Dressed as Men for Love, Freedom & Adventure. Dawson, Willow, illus. 2008. (ENG.). 80p. (J). (gr. 4-7). 16.95 (978-1-55453-177-6(2)); pap. 8.95 (978-1-55453-178-3(0)) Kids Can Pr., Ltd. CAN. Dist: Hachette Bk. Group.

Hurley, Jo. Looking Good! How to Get Stylin' with Your Friends. Morley, Taia, illus. 2007. 64p. (J). (978-0-439-02013-8(1)) Scholastic, Inc.

Hyun, Kim. Getting Dressed: A Book about Dressing, with Tabs for Older Babies. 2016. (Chat About Ser.). (ENG., Illus.). 22p. (J). bds. 9.99 **(978-1-5098-0457-3(9))** Pan Macmillan GBR. Dist: Independent Pubs. Group.

Ibrahim, Yasmin. I Can Wear Hijab Anywhere! Zulkifli, Azhari, illus. 2010. (ENG.). 15p. (J). (gr. -1-k). bds. 9.95 (978-0-86037-319-3(3)) Kube Publishing Ltd. GBR. Dist: Consortium Bk. Sales & Distribution.

Ikids. Fashion Girls Around the World. 2010. (ENG., Illus.). 10p. (J). (gr. -1-1). 19.99 (978-1-58476-960-6(2)) Innovative Kids.

Johnson, Anne Akers, ed. Bead Loom Bracelets. 2008. (ENG., Illus.). 60p. (J). (gr. 7). 24.95 (978-1-59174-504-4(7)) Klutz.

Jupo, Frank. Nothing to Wear but Clothes. 2012. 50p. 35.95 (978-1-258-23157-6(3)) Literary Licensing, LLC.

Kachidurian, Debbie, et al. Accessorize Yourself! 77 Projects to Personalize Your Look. 2016. (Craft It Yourself Ser.). (ENG., Illus.). 144p. (gr. 3-4). pap. 14.95 (978-1-62370-645-6(9)) Capstone Young Readers of Coughlan Cos.

Kalman, Bobbie. The Clothes I Wear. 2010. (My World Ser.). (ENG., Illus.). 16p. (J). (gr. k-2). (978-0-7787-9424-0(5)); pap. (978-0-7787-9468-4(7)) Crabtree Publishing Co.

—I Move Like This. 2010. (My World Ser.). (ENG., Illus.). 16p. (J). (gr. k-2). (978-0-7787-9429-5(6)); pap. (978-0-7787-9473-8(3)) Crabtree Publishing Co.

Kaner, Etta. Have You Ever Seen a Duck in a Raincoat? Szuc, Jeff, illus. 2009. (Have You Ever Seen Ser.). (ENG.). 32p. (J). (gr. -1-2). 14.95 (978-1-55453-246-9(9)) Kids Can Pr., Ltd. CAN. Dist: Hachette Bk. Group.

Kawa, Katie. Claire's Clothing Drive: Represent & Solve Problems Involving Subtraction. 2014. (Rosen Common Core Math Readers Ser.). 24p. (J). (gr. 2-3). (ENG.). pap. 49.50 (978-1-4777-4634-9(X)); (Illus.). 23.60 (978-1-4777-6399-5(6)) Rosen Publishing Group, Inc., The. (Rosen Classroom).

Kimmel, Allison Crotzer. Prepped & Punked: Bringing 1980s & 1990s Flair to Your Wardrobe, 1 vol. 2014. (Fashion Forward Ser.). (ENG.). 64p. (gr. 4-5). lib. bdg. 34.65 (978-1-4765-4000-9(4)) Capstone Press of Coughlan Cos.

Koontz, Robin. El Traje Nuevo Del Rey. 2012. (SPA & ENG.). 24p. (gr. 2-3). pap. 8.95 (978-1-61810-547-9(7)) Rourke Educational Media.

Krohn, Katherine E. Calico Dresses & Buffalo Robes: American West Fashions from the 1840s to the 1890s. 2011. (Dressing a Nation: the History of U. S. Fashion Ser.). (ENG., Illus.). 64p. (gr. 5-12). lib. bdg. 31.93 (978-0-7613-5890-9(0), Twenty-First Century Bks.) Lerner Publishing Group.

Krulik, Nancy. Prom! The Complete Guide to a Truly Spectacular Night. Johnson, Kim, illus. 2003. 96p. (YA). 8.00 (978-0-7567-9038-7(7)) DIANE Publishing Co.

Kuskowski, Alex. Cool Refashion. 2015. (Cool Refashion Ser.: Vol. 6). (ENG.). 32p. (J). lib. bdg. 171.00 (978-1-62403-699-6(6)) ABDO Publishing Co.

—Cool Refashioned Jeans: Fun & Easy Fashion Projects, 1 vol. 2016. (ENG.). 32p. (J). (978-1-62403-701-6(1)) ABDO Publishing Co.

—Cool Refashioned Scarves & Ties: Fun & Easy Fashion Projects, 1 vol. 2016. (ENG.). 32p. (J). (978-1-62403-703-0(8)) ABDO Publishing Co.

—Cool Refashioned Sweaters: Fun & Easy Fashion Projects, 1 vol. 2016. (ENG.). 32p. (J). (978-1-62403-704-7(6)) ABDO Publishing Co.

—Cool Refashioned T-Shirts: Fun & Easy Fashion Projects, 1 vol. 2016. (ENG.). 32p. (J). (978-1-62403-705-4(4)) ABDO Publishing Co.

Kyi, Tanya Lloyd. 50 Underwear Questions: A Bare-All History. Kinnaird, Ross, illus. 2011. (50 Questions Ser.). (ENG.). 120p. (J). (gr. 3-18). 21.95 (978-1-55451-353-6(7), 9781554513536); pap. 12.95 (978-1-55451-352-9(9), 9781554513529) Annick Pr., Ltd. CAN. Dist: Publishers Group West (PGW).

Langston-George, Rebecca. All Dolled Up: Bringing 1920s & 1930s Flair to Your Wardrobe, 1 vol. 2014. (Fashion Forward Ser.). (ENG.). 64p. (gr. 4-5). lib. bdg. 34.65 (978-1-4765-3997-3(9)) Capstone Press of Coughlan Cos.

Laughlin, Kara L., et al. Accessorize Yourself! 2016. (Accessorize Yourself! Ser.). (ENG.). 48p. (gr. 4-5). lib. bdg. 138.60 (978-1-4914-8696-2(1)) Capstone Press of Coughlan Cos.

—Fashion Craft Studio. 2011. (Fashion Craft Studio Ser.). (ENG.). 32p. (gr. 3-4). lib. bdg. 139.95 (978-1-4296-6555-1(6), Snap Bks.) Capstone Press of Coughlan Cos.

Lavis, Rose Brenda. Christopher's New Suit. 2010. 24p. pap. 11.49 (978-1-4490-3606-5(6)) AuthorHouse.

Lawrence, Ellen. The Clothes We Wear. 2015. (My World Your World Ser.). (ENG.). 24p. (J). (gr. -1-3). lib. bdg. 23.93 (978-1-910549-14-8(2)) Bearport Publishing Co., Inc.

Learn to Tie Shoelaces. 2003. (Illus.). (J). bds. 4.98 (978-1-4054-1146-2(5)) Parragon, Inc.

Lewis, Clare. Clothes Around the World, 1 vol. 2014. (Around the World Ser.). (ENG., Illus.). 24p. (gr. -1-1). 22.65 (978-1-4846-0374-1(5), Acorn) Heinemann-Raintree.

Liddle, Charlotte. Pimp Your Pumps: 35 Easy Ways to Transform Your Shoes. 2014. (ENG., Illus.). 128p. (J). (gr. 7-11). pap. 14.95 (978-1-78249-106-4(6), CICO Books) Ryland Peters & Small GBR. Dist: WIPRO.

Loewen, Nancy & Skelley, Paula. Clothing of the World. 2015. (Go Go Global Ser.). (ENG., Illus.). 32p. (gr. 1-2). pap. 7.95 (978-1-4914-3928-9(9)) Capstone Press of Coughlan Cos.

Look at Me! KinderWords Individual Title, 6 Packs. (Kinderstarters Ser.). 8p. (gr. -1-1). 21.00 (978-0-7635-8704-8(4)) Rigby Education.

Lundsten, Apryl. The Girls' Life Guide to Being a Style Superstar! Parett, Lisa, illus. 2004. 124p. (J). (978-0-439-44984-7(7)) Scholastic, Inc.

MacDonald, Margaret. What Do New Clothes Cost? 2011. (Learn-Abouts Ser.). (Illus.). 16p. (J). pap. 7.95 (978-1-59920-615-8(3)) Black Rabbit Bks.

Maggio, Viqui. Baby Tease. 2008. (ENG.). 16p. bds. 10.00 (978-1-933572-08-6(6)) Centro Bks., LLC.

Malam, John. Journey of a T-Shirt, 1 vol. 2012. (Journey of A... Ser.). (ENG.). 32p. (gr. 1-3). pap. 8.29 (978-1-4329-6611-9(1), Heinemann First Library) Heinemann-Raintree.

Marzollo, Jean. Pierre the Penguin. Regan, Laura, illus. 2010. (ENG.). 32p. (J). (gr. -1-2). 15.95 (978-1-58536-485-5(1)) Sleeping Bear Pr.

Mason, Paul. How Big Is Your Clothing Footprint? 2009. (Environmental Footprints Ser.). 32p. (gr. 4). 28.50 (978-0-7614-4410-7(6)) Marshall Cavendish Corp.

Masters, Nancy Robinson. Jeans. 2007. (21st Century Skills Library: Global Products Ser.). (ENG., Illus.). 32p. (gr. 4-8). lib. bdg. 28.50 (978-1-60279-029-2(9), 200025) Cherry Lake Publishing.

Maurer, Tracy Nelson. Fabulous Fashion Crafts. 2009. (Illus.). 32p. (J). pap. 8.95 (978-1-60694-503-2(3)) Rourke Educational Media.

McCarthy, Meghan. Earmuffs for Everyone! How Chester Greenwood Became Known As the Inventor of Earmuffs. McCarthy, Meghan, illus. 2015. (ENG., Illus.). 48p. (J). (gr. -1-3). 17.99 (978-1-4814-0637-6(X), Simon & Schuster/Paula Wiseman Bks.) Simon & Schuster/Paula Wiseman Bks.

McCullough, Missy, illus. Fashion Stylist - Autumn/Winter Collection. 2015. (ENG.). 52p. (J). (gr. 1-7). pap. 12.95 (978-1-78067-599-2(2)) King, Laurence Publishing GBR. Dist: Hachette Bk. Group.

McDonald, Fiona. Everyday Clothes Through History. 2006. (Why Do We Wear? Ser.). (Illus.). 32p. (gr. 2-6). lib. bdg. 26.00 (978-0-8368-6853-1(6), Gareth Stevens Learning Library) Stevens, Gareth Publishing LLLP.

—Shoes & Boots Through History. 2006. (Why Do We Wear? Ser.). (Illus.). 32p. (gr. 2-6). lib. bdg. 26.00 (978-0-8368-6857-9(9), Gareth Stevens Learning Library) Stevens, Gareth Publishing LLLP.

—Uniforms Through History. 2006. (Why Do We Wear? Ser.). (Illus.). 32p. (gr. 2-6). lib. bdg. 26.00 (978-0-8368-6858-6(7), Gareth Stevens Learning Library) Stevens, Gareth Publishing LLLP.

McEvoy, Anne. Fashions of a Decade: The 1990s. 2nd rev. ed. 2006. (Fashions of a Decade Ser.). (Illus.). 64p. (gr. 6-12). 35.00 (978-0-8160-6725-1(2)) Facts On File, Inc.

McPhail, David. I Get Dressed. 2015. (ENG., Illus.). 12p. (J). (gr. -1 — 1). bds. 5.99 (978-1-62672-147-0(5), 9781626721470) Roaring Brook Pr.

Meachen Rau, Dana. Clothing in American History. 2006. (How People Lived in America Ser.). (Illus.). 24p. (gr. 1-4). pap. 8.15 (978-0-8368-7212-5(6), Weekly Reader Leveled Readers) Stevens, Gareth Publishing LLLP.

—La Ropa en la Historia de América. 2006. (Como era la vida en America (How People Lived in America) Ser.). (SPA., Illus.). 24p. (gr. 1-4). pap. 8.15 (978-0-8368-7440-2(4), Weekly Reader Leveled Readers) Stevens, Gareth Publishing LLLP.

—La Ropa en la Historia de America. 2006. (Como era la vida en America (How People Lived in America) Ser.). (SPA., Illus.). 24p. (gr. 1-4). lib. bdg. 22.00 (978-0-8368-7433-4(1), Weekly Reader Leveled Readers) Stevens, Gareth Publishing LLLP.

Meachen Rau, Dana & Meachen Rau, Dana. Clothing in American History. 2006. (How People Lived in America Ser.). (Illus.). 24p. (gr. 1-4). lib. bdg. 22.00 (978-0-8368-7205-7(3), Weekly Reader Leveled Readers) Stevens, Gareth Publishing LLLP.

Meinking, Mary. Stylish Shoes for the Crafty Fashionista, 1 vol. 2011. (Fashion Craft Studio Ser.). (ENG.). 32p. (gr. 3-4). lib. bdg. 27.99 (978-1-4296-6554-4(8), Snap Bks.) Capstone Press of Coughlan Cos.

Mercer, Abbie. Happy Halloween. 2009. (Holiday Fun Ser.). 24p. (gr. 2-3). 42.50 (978-1-61513-375-8(5), PowerKids Pr.) Rosen Publishing Group, Inc., The.

Miles, Liz. Clothes: From Fur to Fair Trade. 2010. (Timeline History Ser.). (ENG., Illus.). 32p. (gr. 3-5). 29.99 (978-1-4329-3803-1(7), NA-h) Heinemann-Raintree.

Milet Publishing Staff. Clothes. 2014. (My First Bilingual Book Ser.). (Illus.). 20p. (J). (— 1). (ENG & KOR.). bds. 7.99 (978-1-84059-865-0(4)); (SPA & ENG., bds. 7.99 (978-1-84059-870-4(0)) Milet Publishing.

—Clothes - My First Bilingual Book. 2014. (My First Bilingual Book Ser.). (Illus.). 20p. (J). (— 1). (ENG & ITA.). bds. 7.99 (978-1-84059-864-3(6)); (ENG & CHI., bds. 7.99 (978-1-84059-860-5(3)); (POR & ENG., bds. 7.99 (978-1-84059-867-4(0)); (ENG & VIE., bds. 7.99 (978-1-84059-873-5(5)) Milet Publishing.

—My First Bilingual Book - Clothes. 2014. (My First Bilingual Book Ser.). (Illus.). 20p. (J). (— 1). (ENG & RUS.). bds. 7.99 (978-1-84059-868-1(9)); (ENG & TUR., bds. 7.99 (978-1-84059-871-1(9)); (ENG & URD., bds. 7.99 (978-1-84059-872-8(7)); (ENG & ARA., bds. 7.99 (978-1-84059-858-2(1)); (ENG, POL & POR., bds. 7.99 (978-1-84059-866-7(2)); (ENG & BEN., bds. 7.99 (978-1-84059-859-9(X)); (ENG & PER., bds. 7.99 (978-1-84059-861-2(1)); (ENG & GER., bds. 7.99 (978-1-84059-863-6(8)); (ENG & SOM., bds. 7.99 (978-1-84059-869-8(7)); (FRE & ENG., bds. 7.99 (978-1-84059-862-9(X)) Milet Publishing.

Miller, Shauna, creator. Penny Chic: How to Be Stylish on a Real Girl's Budget. 2014. (ENG., Illus.). 192p. (J). (gr. 7-17). 16.99 (978-0-316-23656-0(X), Poppy) Little, Brown Bks. for Young Readers.

Mitchell, Alycen. The Performing Arts. 2004. (Twentieth-Century Developments in Fashion & Costume Ser.). (Illus.). 64p. (YA). (gr. 7-18). lib. bdg. 19.95 (978-1-59084-426-7(2)) Mason Crest.

Moore, Elizabeth. Clothes Around the World. 2011. (Wonder Readers Emergent Level Ser.). (ENG.). (gr. -1-1). 16p. pap. 35.94 (978-1-4296-8077-6(6)); 32p. pap. 5.99 (978-1-4296-7862-9(3)) Capstone Press of Coughlan Cos. (Wonder Readers).

Morley, Jacqueline. Fashion: The History of Clothes. 2014. (Illus.). 32p. (J). (978-1-4351-5629-6(3)) Barnes & Noble, Inc.

Morris, Ting. Arts & Crafts of Ancient Greece. Young, Emma, illus. 2006. (Arts & Crafts of Ser.). 32p. (J). lib. bdg. 28.50 (978-1-58340-912-1(2), 1262692) Black Rabbit Bks.

Muehlenhardt, Amy Bailey. Drawing & Learning about Fashion: Using Shapes & Lines, 1 vol. Muehlenhardt, Amy Bailey, illus. 2005. (Sketch It! Ser.). (ENG., Illus.). 24p. (gr. k-4). lib. bdg. 26.65 (978-1-4048-1191-1(5), 1243855) Picture Window Bks.

Murphy, Charles. Clothing Around the World. 2016. (Adventures in Culture Ser.). 00024p. (J). pap. 8.15 **(978-1-4824-5579-3(X))** Stevens, Gareth Publishing LLLP.

Murray, Julie. Sheep to Sweater, 1 vol. 2006. (Beginning to End Set 1 - 8 Titles Ser.). (ENG., Illus.). 24p. (gr. k-4). 25.65 (978-1-59679-914-1(5), Buddy Bks.) ABDO Publishing Co.

Murray, Laura K. Lululemon Athletica. 2015. (Illus.). 48p. (J). (978-1-60818-558-0(3), Creative Education) Creative Co., The.

National Geographic Learning. What Should I Wear? 2009. (Inside the USA Ser.). (ENG., Illus.). 16p. (C). pap. 13.95 (978-0-7362-7063-2(9)) CENGAGE Learning.

Nelson, Robin. Clothing. 2004. (First Step Nonfiction - Basic Human Needs Ser.). (ENG., Illus.). 8p. (gr. -1-1). pap. 4.95 (978-0-8225-3927-8(6), Lerner Pubns.) Lerner Publishing Group.

—From Cotton to T-Shirt. 2013. (Start to Finish, Second Series: Everyday Products Ser.). (ENG., Illus.). 24p. (gr. k-3). lib. bdg. 23.93 (978-0-7613-6561-7(3), Lerner Pubns.) Lerner Publishing Group.

Nunn, Daniel. Old Clothes, 1 vol. 2011. (From Trash to Treasures Ser.). (ENG.). 24p. (gr. k-2). 23.32 (978-1-4329-5149-8(1), Heinemann Read & Learn) Heinemann-Raintree.

O'Brien, Joan. Fashion Accessories Stickers. 2003. (Dover Little Activity Bks.). (ENG., Illus.). 4p. 1.50 (978-0-486-43071-3(5)) Dover Pubns., Inc.

Okawa, Junko & Uonca Staff. Carefree Clothes for Girls: 20 Patterns for Outdoor Frocks, Playdate Dresses, & More. 2009. (Make Good: Crafts + Life Ser.). (ENG., Illus.). 96p. pap. 21.95 (978-1-59030-717-5(8), Roost Books) Shambhala Pubns., Inc.

Olson, Nathan. Levi Strauss & Blue Jeans, 1 vol. Hoover, Dave et al, illus. 2006. (Inventions & Discovery Ser.). (ENG.). 32p. (gr. 3-4). 30.65 (978-0-7368-6484-8(9), Graphic Library) Capstone Press of Coughlan Cos.

—Levi Strauss & Blue Jeans. Barnett, Charles, III et al, illus. 2006. (Inventions & Discovery Ser.). (ENG.). 32p. (gr. 3-4). pap. 8.10 (978-0-7368-9646-7(5), Graphic Library) Capstone Press of Coughlan Cos.

Party Clothes. 2004. (Jasper the Cat Set 1 Ser.). (J). 7.33 (978-1-58453-279-8(3)) Pioneer Valley Bks.

Patteson, Nelda. Adina de Zavala: "Angel of the Alamo" Her Life Story Presented Through the Clothes She Wore. Patteson, Nelda, illus. 2003. (Women of Texas Ser.: Vol. 3). Orig. Title: Angel of the Alamo. (Illus.). 32p. (J). (gr. 4-8). pap. 14.95 (978-0-9629001-2-9(5)) Smiley Co.

Peacock, John. The Story of Costume. 2006. (ENG., Illus.). 48p. 19.95 (978-0-500-51309-5(0), 551309) Thames & Hudson.

Perham, Molly. Customize Your Clothes: Over 50 Simple, Fun Ideas to Transform Your Wardrobe & Accessories. Perham, Molly, ed. 2009. (ENG., Illus.). 64p. (J). (gr. 4-7). 12.99 (978-0-7548-1745-1(8)) Anness Publishing GBR. Dist: National Bk. Network.

Petelinsek, Kathleen. Making Sock Puppets. Petelinsek, Kathleen, illus. 2014. (How-To Library). (ENG., Illus.). 32p. (J). (gr. 3-6). 28.50 (978-1-63137-782-2(5), 205371) Cherry Lake Publishing.

Peterson, Megan Cooley & Rustad, Martha E. H. Kid Style: Cool Clothes for You!, 1 vol. 2014. (Make It Mine Ser.). (ENG.). 24p. (gr. k-1). lib. bdg. 26.65 (978-1-4765-3971-3(5), Pebble Plus) Capstone Press of Coughlan Cos.

Phillips, Jennifer. Adorable Accessories: Paper Creations to Wear, 1 vol. 2013. (Paper Creations Ser.). (ENG.). 32p. (gr. 3-4). lib. bdg. 27.99 (978-1-62065-043-1(6), Snap Bks.) Capstone Press of Coughlan Cos.

Pratt, Leonie. Sticker Dolly Dressing Ballerinas. Baggott, Stella & Leyhane, Vici, illus. 2007. (Usborne Activities Ser.). 24p. (J). (gr. -1-3). pap. 8.99 (978-0-7945-1392-4(1), Usborne) EDC Publishing.

—Sticker Dolly Dressing Fairies. Baggott, Stella & Leyhane, Vici, illus. 2007. (Usborne Activities Ser.). 24p. (J). (gr. -1-3). pap. 8.99 (978-0-7945-1391-7(3), Usborne) EDC Publishing.

Publishers, Chelsea House, creator. Costume & Fashion Source Books, 8-Volumes. 2009. (Costume & Fashion Source Bks). (gr. 6-12). 280.00 (978-1-60413-646-3(4), Chelsea Hse.) Facts On File, Inc.

Rau, Dana Meachen. Athletic Shoes. 2007. (21st Century Skills Library: Global Products Ser.). (ENG., Illus.). 32p. (gr. 4-8). lib. bdg. 28.50 (978-1-60279-027-8(2), 200020) Cherry Lake Publishing.

Raum, Elizabeth. The Scoop on Clothes, Homes, & Daily Life in Colonial America. (Life in the American Colonies Ser.). (ENG.). 32p. (gr. 3-4). 2017. pap. 8.10 **(978-1-5157-9746-3(5))** 2011. 27.32 (978-1-4296-6138-6(0)) 2011. pap. 47.70 (978-1-4296-7214-6(5)) Capstone Press of Coughlan Cos. (Fact Finders).

Rayner, Amanda. What We Wear. 2005. (One World (Smart Apple Media) Ser.). (Illus.). 30p. (J). (gr. 3-6). lib. bdg. 27.10 (978-1-58340-694-6(8)) Black Rabbit Bks.

Ready to Wear. (Totally Girls Ser.). 16p. (J). (978-2-7643-0187-6(1)) Phidal Publishing, Inc./Editions Phidal, Inc.

Reid, Struan & Halstead, Rachel. Clothes: Discover How People Dressed Around the World With 30 Great Step-by-Step Projects. 2008. (ENG.). 64p. (J). (gr. 4-7). pap. 7.99 (978-1-84476-523-2(7)) Anness Publishing GBR. Dist: National Bk. Network.

Richards, Jon. Clothes. 2005. (How Things Have Changed Ser.). (Illus.). 32p. (J). (gr. 3-7). lib. bdg. 27.10 *(978-1-59389-195-4(4))* Chrysalis Education.

Ridley, Sarah. A Cotton T-Shirt. 2006. (How It's Made Ser.). (Illus.). 32p. (gr. 1-4). lib. bdg. 26.00 *(978-0-8368-6294-2(5),* Gareth Stevens Learning Library) Stevens, Gareth Publishing LLLP.

Rissman, Rebecca. Clothes, 1 vol. 2013. (Picture This! Ser.). (ENG.). 24p. (gr. -1-k). pap. 9.95 *(978-1-4109-5258-5(4),* NA-r) Heinemann-Raintree.

Rissman, Rebecca. Fashion Hacks: Your Fashion Failures Solved! 2017. (Beauty Hacks Ser.). (ENG.). 48p. (gr. 4-5). lib. bdg. 31.32 ***(978-1-5157-6827-2(9))*** Capstone Press of Coughlan Cos.

Rooney, Anne. China. 2008. (Costume Around the World Ser.). (Illus.). 32p. (gr. 4-6). 28.00 *(978-0-7910-9765-6(X),* Chelsea Clubhouse) Facts On File, Inc.

—The Eighteenth Century. Woolf, Alex, ed. 2005. (History of Fashion & Costume Ser.). (Illus.). 64p. (gr. 6-12). 35.00 *(978-0-8160-5948-5(9))* Facts On File, Inc.

—The 50s & 60s. 2009. (Costume Source Bks). (Illus.). 32p. (gr. 6-12). 35.00 *(978-1-60413-385-1(6),* Chelsea Hse.) Facts On File, Inc.

Rosa-Mendoza, Gladys. My Clothes/Mi Ropa. Abello, Patricia & Weber, Amy, eds. Collier, Mary, illus. 2005. (#1 Bilingual Board Book Ser.). (SPA & ENG.). 20p. (J). (gr. -1). bds. 6.95 *(978-1-931398-15-2(1))* Me+Mi Publishing.

Ross, Kathy. Jazzy Jewelry, Pretty Purses, & More! Bosch, Nicole in den, illus. 2009. (Girl Crafts Ser.). (ENG.). 48p. (gr. 2-5). pap. 7.95 *(978-1-58013-883-3(7),* Millbrook Pr.) Lerner Publishing Group.

Sachse, Dina, illus. My Clothes: 12 Lift-N-Learn Flashcards about Clothes, 26 vols. 2013. (Early Start Singles Ser.). (ENG.). 12p. (J). *(978-1-77132-101-3(6))* SpiceBox Products Ltd.

Safran, Sheri. Let's Dress! Fuller, Rachel, illus. 2011. (ENG.). 20p. (J). (gr. -1-2). 18.99 *(978-1-85707-725-4(3))* Tango Bks. GBR. Dist: Independent Pubs. Group.

Salzmann, Mary Elizabeth. Money for Clothes, 1 vol. 2010. (Your Piggy Bank: A Guide to Spending & Saving for Kids! Ser.). (ENG.). 24p. (J). (gr. k-3). 27.07 *(978-1-61641-027-8(2))* Magic Wagon.

Schumacher, Bev. Dress Up. 2007. 20p. (J). lib. bdg. 9.95 *(978-0-9768706-4-7(9))* Learning Props.

—Dress Up (Chinese/English) 2012. 20p. (J). pap. 8.95 *(978-1-935292-47-0(1))* Learning Props.

Scott, Margaret. Medieval Clothing & Costumes: Displaying Wealth & Class in Medieval Times. 2009. (Library of the Middle Ages Ser.). 64p. (gr. 5-8). 58.50 *(978-1-60853-900-0(8),* Rosen Reference) Rosen Publishing Group, Inc., The.

Senker, Cath. Germany. 2008. (Costume Around the World Ser.). (Illus.). 32p. (gr. 4-6). 28.00 *(978-0-7910-9767-0(6),* Chelsea Clubhouse) Facts On File, Inc.

—Saudi Arabia. 2008. (Costume Around the World Ser.). (Illus.). 32p. (gr. 4-6). 28.00 *(978-0-7910-9773-1(0),* Chelsea Clubhouse) Facts On File, Inc.

Sills, Leslie. From Rags to Riches: A History of Girls' Clothing in America. (ENG., Illus.). 48p. (J). 2007. (gr. 5-18). pap. 6.95 *(978-0-8234-2048-3(5))* 2005. 17.95 *(978-0-8234-1708-7(5))* Holiday Hse., Inc.

Sipi, Claire. One Direction Dress-Up Sticker Book. 2012. (ENG., Illus.). 28p. 6.95 *(978-1-60710-713-2(9),* Silver Dolphin Bks.) Readerlink Distribution Services, LLC.

Skinner, Tina. Fashionable Clothing from the Sears Catalogs, Mid-1940s. 2003. (ENG., Illus.). 160p. (gr. 10-13). pap. 29.95 *(978-0-7643-1858-0(6),* 9780764318580) Schiffer Publishing, Ltd.

Slee, Natasha. Design Line: History of Women's Fashion. Mander, Sanna, illus. 2015. (ENG.). 16p. (J). (gr. 5). 17.99 *(978-0-7636-7962-0(3),* Big Picture Press) Candlewick Pr.

Smith, Alastair. Clothes & Fashion Then & Now. 2004. (Usborne Flip Flaps Ser.). (SPA & ENG., Illus.). 1p. (J). (gr. 2-18). pap. 7.95 *(978-0-7460-3098-1(3))* EDC Publishing.

Smith, Paula. Clothing in Different Places. 2015. (Learning about Our Global Community Ser.). (ENG.). 24p. (J). *(978-0-7787-2010-2(1))* Crabtree Publishing Co.

Sohn, Emily & Klobuchar, Lisa. Fabric: It's Got You Covered! 2011. (IScience Readers Ser.). 24p. (J). (gr. k-2). lib. bdg. 21.27 *(978-1-59953-406-0(1))* Norwood Hse. Pr.

Song, Sok. Everyday Origami: A Foldable Fashion Guide. Song, Sok, illus. 2016. (Fashion Origami Ser.). (ENG., Illus.). 48p. (gr. 4-5). lib. bdg. 31.99 *(978-1-5157-1630-3(9))* Capstone Press of Coughlan Cos.

—Origami Accessories: A Foldable Fashion Guide. Song, Sok, illus. 2016. (Fashion Origami Ser.). (ENG., Illus.). 48p. (gr. 4-5). lib. bdg. 31.99 *(978-1-5157-1623-5(6))* Capstone Press of Coughlan Cos.

—Origami Outfits: A Foldable Fashion Guide. Song, Sok, illus. 2016. (Fashion Origami Ser.). (ENG., Illus.). 48p. (gr. 4-5). lib. bdg. 31.99 *(978-1-5157-1631-0(7))* Capstone Press of Coughlan Cos.

Sonnebom, Liz. Far Out Fashion: Bringing 1960s & 1970s Flair to Your Wardrobe, 1 vol. 2014. (Fashion Forward Ser.). (ENG., Illus.). 64p. (gr. 4-5). lib. bdg. 34.65 *(978-1-4765-3999-7(5))* Capstone Press of Coughlan Cos.

Stamper, Judith Bauer. Who Wears What? 2010. (J). *(978-1-60617-120-2(8))* Teaching Strategies, LLC.

Staniford, Linda. Clothes. 2015. (Wants vs Needs Ser.). (ENG., Illus.). 24p. (gr. k-2). 23.32 *(978-1-4846-0944-6(1),* Heinemann Read & Learn) Heinemann-Raintree.

Stardoll. Sticker Catwalk Dress Up. 2013. (Stardoll Ser.). (ENG.). 24p. (J). (gr. 2-4). pap. 6.99 *(978-0-85751-176-8(9))* Transworld Publishers Ltd. GBR. Dist: Independent Pubs. Group.

—Sticker Holiday Dress Up. 2013. (Stardoll Ser.). (ENG.). 24p. (J). (gr. 2-4). pap. 6.99 *(978-0-85751-177-5(7))* Transworld Publishers Ltd. GBR. Dist: Independent Pubs. Group.

Steele, Philip. The Nineteenth Century. 2005. (History of Fashion & Costume Ser.). (Illus.). 64p. (gr. 6-12). 35.00 *(978-0-8160-5950-8(0))* Facts On File, Inc.

Sterling Children's, Sterling. Clothes/la Ropa. 2016. (Say & Play Ser.). (ENG., Illus.). 28p. (J). (— 1). bds. 4.95 *(978-1-4549-1997-1(3))* Sterling Publishing Co., Inc.

Sterling Publishing Co., Inc. Clothes. 2016. (Say & Play Ser.). (ENG., Illus.). 28p. (J). (— 1). bds. 4.95 *(978-1-4549-1971-1(X))* Sterling Publishing Co., Inc.

Streissguth, Tom. Fashion & Dress Codes. 2011. (Life—a How-To Guide Ser.). (Illus.). 128p. (J). (gr. 6-18). pap. 10.95 *(978-1-59845-313-3(0))* Enslow Pubs., Inc.

—Fashion & Dress Codes: A How-to Guide. 2011. (Life—a How-To Guide Ser.). (Illus.). 128p. (J). lib. bdg. 33.27 *(978-0-7660-3444-0(5))* Enslow Pubs., Inc.

Swain, Gwenyth. Get Dressed! 2011. (Small World Ser.). (Illus.). 24p. bds. *(978-1-84089-675-6(2))* Zero to Ten, Ltd.

Swain, Ruth Freeman. Underwear: What We Wear under There. O'Brien, John A., illus. 2008. (ENG.). 32p. (J). (gr. 1-5). 16.95 *(978-0-8234-1920-3(7))* Holiday Hse., Inc.

Tanaka, Rin. Motorcycle Jackets: Ultimate Biker's Fashions, 1 vol. 2003. (ENG., Illus.). 304p. (gr. 10-13). 69.95 *(978-0-7643-1849-8(7),* 9780764318498) Schiffer Publishing, Ltd.

Taschek, Karen. The Civil War. 2009. (Costume Source Bks). (Illus.). 32p. (gr. 6-12). 35.00 *(978-1-60413-381-3(3),* Chelsea Hse.) Facts On File, Inc.

Tejidos. (One Hundred One Things to Do Ser.). (SPA.). (J). (gr. 3-5). pap. 4.76 *(978-950-724-207-6(4))* Lumen ARG. Dist: Lectorum Pubns., Inc.

Then & Now, 6 Pack. (Discovery World Ser.). 16p. (gr. 1-2). 28.00 *(978-0-7635-8463-4(0))* Rigby Education.

Tierney, Tom. Late Victorian & Edwardian Fashions. 2005. (Dover Fashion Coloring Book Ser.). (ENG., Illus.). 32p. (gr. 3-5). 4.99 *(978-0-486-44458-1(9))* Dover Pubns., Inc.

Top That!, creator. Dressing-up Fun: Learn to Lace. 2006. (Illus.). 16p. (J). (gr. -1-3). *(978-1-84666-013-9(0))* Top That! Publishing PLC.

Torres, Laura. Rock Your Wardrobe. 2012. (Illus.). 32p. (gr. 3-5). pap. 8.95 *(978-1-926853-89-5(X))* Saunders Bk. Co. CAN. Dist: RiverStream Publishing.

The Trend-Setters: Paper Doll Cut-Out Book. 2006. (J). pap. 8.95 *(978-0-9787319-2-2(1))* Kolluri, Alina M.

Turnbull, Stephanie. Accessories: Style Secrets for Girls. 2014. (Girl Talk Ser.). (ENG., Illus.). 32p. (J). (gr. 4-8). pap. 9.95 *(978-1-77092-200-6(8))* Saunders Bk. Co. CAN. Dist: RiverStream Publishing.

—Wardrobe Makeovers. 2016. (Sleepover Secrets Ser.). 24p. (gr. 2-6). 28.50 *(978-1-62588-381-0(1),* Smart Apple Media) Black Rabbit Bks.

Tuxworth, Nicola. Clothes. 2014. (ENG., Illus.). 20p. (J). (gr. -1 — 1). bds. 6.99 *(978-1-84322-861-5(0),* Armadillo) Anness Publishing GBR. Dist: National Bk. Network.

Tyler, Jenny. Baby's Very First Getting Dressed. 2009. (Baby's Very First Board Bks). 10p. (J). (gr. -1). bds. 6.99 *(978-0-7945-2609-2(8),* Usborne) EDC Publishing.

Verderosa, Laura. Dad Likes New Clothes. 2010. (Sight Word Readers Ser.). (J). 3.49 *(978-1-60719-605-1(0))* Newmark Learning LLC.

Vize, Dania. My Dress up Book. 2005. (Illus.). 12p. (J). (gr. -1-3). per., bds. *(978-1-905051-36-6(0))* Make Believe Ideas.

Walker, Kate. Clothing. 2010. (Recycling Ser.). 32p. (gr. 1). 28.50 *(978-1-60870-128-5(X))* Marshall Cavendish GBR. Dist: Marshall Cavendish Corp.

Walton, Ruth. Let's Get Dressed: Find Out about Clothes & Fabric. 2013. (Let's Find Out Ser.). (Illus.). 32p. (J). (gr. k-5). 28.50 *(978-1-59771-383-2(X))* Sea-To-Sea Pubns.

Watson, Stephanie. Streetwear Fashion. Kubley, Ashley Newsome, illus. 2014. (What's Your Style? Ser.). (ENG.). 48p. (gr. 5-8). lib. bdg. 30.60 *(978-1-4677-1471-6(2),* Lerner Pubns.) Lerner Publishing Group.

Watt, Fiona. Sticker Dolly Dressing Back to School. 2012. (Sticker Dolly Dressing Ser.). 34p. (J). pap. 8.99 *(978-0-7945-3303-8(5),* Usborne) EDC Publishing.

—Sticker Dolly Dressing Ballerinas & Dolls (Combined Volume) 2008. (Sticker Dolly Dressing Ser.). (Illus.). 48p. (J). pap. 14.99 *(978-0-7945-2382-4(X),* Usborne) EDC Publishing.

—Sticker Dolly Dressing Dancers. Baggott, Stella, illus. 2011. (Sticker Dolly Dressing Ser.). 24p. (J). pap. 8.99 *(978-0-7945-2931-4(3),* Usborne) EDC Publishing.

—Sticker Dolly Dressing Dolls. Leyhane, Vici & Baggott, Stella, illus. 2006. (Usborne Activities Ser.). 23p. (J). pap. 8.99 *(978-0-7945-1389-4(1),* Usborne) EDC Publishing.

—Sticker Dolly Dressing Fashion Activity Book. 2017. (Sticker Dolly Dressing Fashion Designer Ser.). (ENG.). 96p. (J). pap. 14.99 ***(978-0-7945-3988-7(2),*** Usborne) EDC Publishing.

—Sticker Dolly Dressing Princesses. Leyhane, Vici & Baggott, Stella, illus. 2007. (Sticker Dolly Dressing Ser.). 32p. (J). pap. 8.99 *(978-0-7945-1390-0(5),* Usborne) EDC Publishing.

—Sticker Dolly Dressing Princesses & Fairies (Combined Volume) 2008. (Sticker Dolly Dressing Ser.). (Illus.). 48p. (J). pap. 14.99 *(978-0-7945-2418-0(4),* Usborne) EDC Publishing.

—Sticker Dolly Dressing Shopping Girls. 2012. (Sticker Dolly Dressing Ser.). 24p. (J). pap. 8.99 *(978-0-7945-3254-3(3),* Usborne) EDC Publishing.

—Sticker Dolly Dressing Sportsgirls. 2011. (Sticker Dolly Dressing Ser.). 24p. (J). pap. 8.99 *(978-0-7945-3003-7(6),* Usborne) EDC Publishing.

—Sticker Dolly Dressing Travel. 2012. (Sticker Dolly Dressing Ser.). 34p. (J). pap. 8.99 *(978-0-7945-3313-7(2),* Usborne) EDC Publishing.

—Sticker Dolly Dressing Weddings. Baggott, Stella, illus. 2011. (Usborne Activities Ser.). 24p. (J). 8.99 *(978-0-7945-3105-8(9),* Usborne) EDC Publishing.

—Tie-a-Bow Book. 2008. (Tie-a-Bow Book Ser.). 10p. (J). bds. 9.99 *(978-0-7945-1528-7(2),* Usborne) EDC Publishing.

Watt, Fiona, des. Sticker Dolly Dressing Princess Kit. 2011. (Activity Kit Ser.). 24p. (J). pap. 15.99 *(978-1-60130-278-6(9),* Usborne) EDC Publishing.

Weaver, Janice. From Head to Toe: Bound Feet, Bathing Suits, & Other Bizarre & Beautiful Things. Blake, Francis, illus. 2003. (ENG.). 80p. (J). (gr. 5-9). pap. 16.95 *(978-0-88776-654-1(4),* Tundra Bks.) Tundra Bks. CAN. Dist: Penguin Random Hse. LLC.

Weekly Reader Editorial Staff. Things I Wear. 2006. (Things in My World Ser.). (Illus.). 16p. (gr. -1-2). lib. bdg. 19.00 *(978-0-8368-6812-8(9),* Weekly Reader Leveled Readers) Stevens, Gareth Publishing LLLP.

—Things I Wear (Las cosas que me Pongo) 2006. (Things in My World/ Las cosas de mi mundo Ser.). (ENG & SPA., Illus.). 16p. (gr. -1-2). lib. bdg. 19.00 *(978-0-8368-7224-8(X),* Weekly Reader Leveled Readers) Stevens, Gareth Publishing LLLP.

Weekly Reader Editorial Staff, contrib. by. Things I Wear. 2006. (Things in My World/ Las cosas de mi mundo Ser.). (ENG & SPA., Illus.). 16p. (gr. -1-2). pap. 5.30 *(978-0-8368-7231-6(2),* Weekly Reader Leveled Readers) Stevens, Gareth Publishing LLLP.

Weston Woods Staff, creator. Charlie Needs a Cloak. 2004. 38.75 *(978-1-55592-383-9(6));* 18.95 *(978-1-55592-382-2(8))* Weston Woods Studios, Inc.

What I Like to Wear, 6 Pack. (gr. -1-2). 23.00 *(978-0-7635-9016-1(9))* Rigby Education.

Whittaker, Helen. Clothing. 2011. (Living Green Ser.). 32p. (gr. 3). 28.50 *(978-1-60870-572-6(2))* Marshall Cavendish Corp.

Williamson, Froser, illus. My Clothes: Individual Title Six-Packs. (Sails Literacy Ser.). 16p. (gr. k-18). 27.00 *(978-0-7635-4392-1(6))* Rigby Education.

Wood, Alix. Hair & Makeup Design. 2017. (Design It! Ser.). 32p. (gr. 3-4). pap. 63.00 ***(978-1-5382-0783-3(4))*** Stevens, Gareth Publishing LLLP.

Wood, Anita. Fashion Doodles, 1 vol. Kalis, Jennifer, illus. 2014. (ENG.). 240p. (J). pap. 16.99 *(978-1-4236-3607-6(4))* Gibbs Smith, Publisher.

CLOTHING AND DRESS—FICTION

A Caribbean Experience Con Amor. There's a Coqui in My Shoe! 2007. (Illus.). 66p. (J). 21.99 *(978-0-9797641-0-3(6))* Chi Chi Rodriguez Bks.

Abdel-Fattah, Randa. Does My Head Look Big in This? 2007. 360p. (YA). 25.66 *(978-1-4287-4610-7(2),* Follettbound) Follett School Solutions.

—Does My Head Look Big in This? 2008. (ENG.). 368p. (J). (gr. 7). pap. 9.99 *(978-0-439-92233-3(X),* Scholastic Paperbacks) Scholastic, Inc.

Adams, Colleen. Playing in the Snow. (Neighborhood Readers Ser.). (ENG.). 8p. 2007. 29.95 *(978-1-4042-7059-6(0))* 2006. (gr. -1-3). pap. 5.15 *(978-1-4042-5657-6(1))* Rosen Publishing Group, Inc., The. (Rosen Classroom).

Adler, David A. Young Cam Jansen & the Molly Shoe Mystery, No. 14. Natti, Susanna, illus. 2009. (Young Cam Jansen Ser.: 14). (ENG.). 32p. (J). (gr. 1-3). mass mkt. 3.99 *(978-0-14-241402-6(6),* Penguin Young Readers) Penguin Young Readers Group.

Afyouni, Hassan. Lucky Shirt: The Lucky Series. 2010. 32p. pap. 12.99 *(978-1-4490-1703-3(7))* AuthorHouse.

Alford, Douglas J. Cozy Clozy. 2006. (J). 25.00 *(978-1-933589-95-4(7))* Scripture Mastery Resources!

Alger, Horatio. Making His Way. 2005. 28.95 *(978-1-4218-1456-8(0));* 260p. pap. 13.95 *(978-1-4218-1556-5(7))* 1st World Publishing, Inc. (1st World Library - Literary Society).

Alien Nine: Ultimate Collection, Vol. 3. 2003. (Illus.). 224p. pap. 15.95 *(978-1-58664-893-0(4),* CMX 64203G, CPM Manga) Central Park Media Corp.

Alkhayyat, Mithaa. My Own Special Way. Sharafeddini, Fatima, tr. Fidawi, Maya, illus. 2012. (ENG.). 64p. (J). (gr. -1-k). pap. 7.99 *(978-1-4440-0320-8(8),* Orion Children's Bks.) Hachette Children's Group GBR. Dist: Hachette Bk. Group.

Andersen, Hans Christian. The Emperor's New Clothes. 2005. (SPA.). 12p. (J). pap. *(978-958-30-1782-7(5))* Panamericana Editorial.

—El Traje Nuevo del Emperador.Tr. of Emperor's New Clothes. (SPA., Illus.). 48p. (J). (gr. 3-5). *(978-84-241-5527-8(0),* EV0621) Everest Editora ESP. Dist: Lectorum Pubns., Inc.

—El Traje Nuevo del Emperador.Tr. of Emperor's New Clothes. (SPA.). 64p. (J). 9.50 *(978-84-207-3349-4(0))* Grupo Anaya, S.A. ESP. Dist: AIMS International Bks., Inc.

—We Both Read-The Emperor's New Clothes. 2014. (Illus.). 44p. (J). 9.95 *(978-1-60115-269-5(8))* Treasure Bay, Inc.

Andersen, Hans Christian & Fowler, Gloria. The Red Shoes. Yung Yoo, Sun, illus. 2008. (ENG.). 32p. (J). (gr. -1-3). 16.95 *(978-1-934429-06-8(6))* AMMO Bks., LLC.

Andersen, Hans Christian & Starbright Foundation Staff. The Emperor's New Clothes. Burton, Virginia Lee, illus. 2004. (ENG.). 48p. (J). (gr. -1-3). pap. 6.95 *(978-0-618-34420-8(9))* Houghton Mifflin Harcourt Publishing Co.

Anthony, Irie. Pants & Shoes & Reading the News. 2009. 20p. pap. 12.00 *(978-1-4490-3249-4(4))* AuthorHouse.

Applegate, Katherine. Don't Swap Your Sweater for a Dog. Biggs, Brian, illus. 2008. (Roscoe Riley Rules Ser.: 3). (ENG.). 96p. (J). (gr. 1-5). 15.99 *(978-0-06-114886-6(5));* pap. 4.99 *(978-0-06-114885-9(7))* HarperCollins Pubs.

Arciniegas, Triunfo. La Verdadera Historia del Gato con Botas. (SPA.). (J). 8.95 *(978-958-04-7348-0(X))* Norma S.A. COL. Dist: Distribuidora Norma, Inc.

Ashburn, Boni. I Had a Favorite Dress. Denos, Julia, illus. 2011. (ENG.). 32p. (J). (gr. k-2). 16.95 *(978-1-4197-0016-3(2),* Abrams Bks. for Young Readers) Abrams, Inc.

Avery, Kristin. La Colcha de Retazos, Level 3. Flor Ada, Alma, tr. McPhail, David, illus. 2003. (Dejame Leer Ser.). (SPA.). 16p. (J). (gr. -1-3). 6.50 *(978-0-673-36303-9(1),* Good Year Bks.) Celebration Pr.

Aylesworth, Jim. My Grandfather's Coat. McClintock, Barbara, illus. 2014. (ENG.). 32p. (J). (gr. -1-3). 17.99 *(978-0-439-92545-7(2),* Scholastic Pr.) Scholastic, Inc.

AZ Books Staff. Fashion Ideas. Batan, Natalia, ed. 2012. (Fashion Ideas Ser.). (ENG.). 60p. (J). bds. 15.95 *(978-1-61889-075-7(1))* AZ Bks. LLC.

Babiak, Alexandra Brittany. The Runaway Jacket, 1 vol. 2009. 40p. pap. 24.95 *(978-1-60749-332-7(2))* America Star Bks.

Barnett, Mac. Extra Yarn. Klassen, Jon, illus. 2012. (ENG.). 40p. (J). (gr. -1-3). 17.99 *(978-0-06-195338-5(5))* HarperCollins Pubs.

Bartels, Korin. A Secret in My Shoes. l.t. ed. 2005. (Illus.). 20p. (J). per. 10.00 *(978-1-59879-031-3(5))* Lifevest Publishing, Inc.

Batt, Tanya Robyn. The Fabrics of Fairytale: Stories Spun from Far & Wide. Griffin, Rachel, illus. 2007. (ENG.). 80p. (J). (gr. -1-3). pap. 16.99 *(978-1-84686-089-8(X))* Barefoot Bks., Inc.

Baum, L. Frank. The Woggle-Bug Book. 2008. 52p. pap. 7.95 *(978-1-60664-008-1(9))* Aegypan.

Beaton, Clare, illus. Daisy Gets Dressed. 2005. 24p. (J). 15.99 *(978-1-84148-794-6(5))* Barefoot Bks., Inc.

Beaumont, Karen. Hats off to You! Pham, LeUyen, illus. 2017. (ENG.). 40p. (J). (gr. -1-3). 16.99 *(978-0-545-47423-8(X),* Scholastic Pr.) Scholastic, Inc.

Beck, Glenn, et al. The Christmas Sweater. Dorman, Brandon, illus. 2009. (ENG.). 40p. (J). (gr. -1-2). 17.99 *(978-1-4169-9543-2(9),* Aladdin) Simon & Schuster Children's Publishing.

Beinstein, Phoebe. ¡A nadar, Boots! (Swim, Boots, Swim!) Roper, Robert, illus. 2009. (Dora la Exploradora Ser.). (SPA.). 24p. (J). pap. 3.99 *(978-1-4169-7939-5(5),* Libros Para Ninos) Libros Para Ninos.

—Swim, Boots, Swim! Roper, Robert, illus. 2009. (Dora the Explorer Ser.: 29). (ENG.). 24p. (J). (gr. -1-2). pap. 3.99 *(978-1-4169-7195-5(5),* Simon Spotlight/Nickelodeon) Simon Spotlight/Nickelodeon.

Bellamy, Doug. My Blankee. 2013. 28p. pap. 12.79 *(978-1-4120-6923-6(8))* Trafford Publishing.

Benton, Jim. My Pants Are Haunted! Benton, Jim, illus. 2004. (Dear Dumb Diary Ser.: 2). (ENG., Illus.). 144p. (J). (gr. 2-5). mass mkt. 6.99 *(978-0-439-62905-8(5),* Scholastic Paperbacks) Scholastic, Inc.

Berkshire, Mary Ann. The Black Glove. 2011. 42p. pap. 16.95 *(978-1-4560-6841-7(5))* America Star Bks.

Bester, Maryanne. The Long Trousers. Bester, Shayle, illus. 2009. (Cool Nguni Ser.). (ENG.). 32p. (J). (gr. 2-4). pap. 12.00 *(978-1-77009-499-4(7))* Jacana Media ZAF. Dist: Independent Pubs. Group.

Biedrzycki, David. Me & My Dragon: Scared of Halloween. Biedrzycki, David, illus. 2013. (ENG., Illus.). 32p. (J). (gr. -1-3). pap. 7.95 *(978-1-58089-659-7(6))* Charlesbridge Publishing, Inc.

Black, Michael Ian. Naked! Ohi, Debbie Ridpath, illus. 2014. (ENG.). 40p. (J). (gr. -1-3). 17.99 *(978-1-4424-6738-5(X),* Simon & Schuster Bks. For Young Readers) Simon & Schuster Bks. For Young Readers.

Blackburn, Sheila M. Stewie Scraps & the Giant Joggers. 2008. 76p. pap. *(978-1-903853-86-3(9))* Brilliant Pubns.

Blankenship, LeeAnn. Mr. Tuggle's Troubles. Dugan, Karen, illus. 2005. (ENG.). 32p. (J). (gr. k-3). 15.95 *(978-1-59078-196-8(1))* Boyds Mills Pr.

Blessing, Charlotte. New Old Shoes. Phillips, Gary R., illus. 2009. (ENG.). 32p. (J). (gr. k-3). 16.95 *(978-0-9792035-6-5(2))* Pleasant St. Pr.

Bobs neue Stiefel. pap. 12.95 *(978-3-89748-674-4(1))* Dino Entertainment AG DEU. Dist: Distribooks, Inc.

Boelts, Maribeth. Those Shoes. Jones, Noah Z., illus. 2009. (ENG.). 40p. (J). (gr. k-3). pap. 6.99 *(978-0-7636-4284-6(3))* Candlewick Pr.

Boswall, Nigel. Jerry's Trousers. Melling, David, illus. 2003. (ENG.). 26p. (J). pap. 4.99 *(978-0-333-68359-0(5))* Macmillan Pubs., Ltd. GBR. Dist: Trafalgar Square Publishing.

Bowman, Lucy. Sticker Dolly Dressing on Vacation (Revised Cover) 2015. (Sticker Dolly Dressing Ser.). (ENG.). 24+p. (J). (gr. k-5). pap. 8.99 *(978-0-7945-3555-1(0),* Usborne) EDC Publishing.

Boynton, Sandra. Azul el Sombrero, Verde el Sombrero. Boynton, Sandra, illus. 2003.Tr. of Blue Hat, Green Hat. (SPA., Illus.). 14p. (J). (gr. -1 — 1). bds. 5.99 *(978-0-689-86304-2(7),* Libros Para Ninos) Libros Para Ninos.

Brashares, Ann. Forever in Blue: The Fourth Summer of the Sisterhood. 2008. (Sisterhood of the Traveling Pants Ser.: Bk. 4). (ENG.). 416p. (YA). (gr. 7-12). pap. 9.99 *(978-0-385-73401-1(8),* Ember) Random Hse. Children's Bks.

—Girls in Pants. 2006. (Sisterhood of the Traveling Pants Ser.: Bk. 3). (ENG.). 384p. (YA). (gr. 7-12). reprint ed. per. 9.99 *(978-0-553-37593-0(8),* Ember) Random Hse. Children's Bks.

—The Sisterhood of the Traveling Pants. 2003. (Sisterhood of the Traveling Pants Ser.: Bk. 1). (ENG.). 336p. (YA). (gr. 7-18). pap. 9.99 *(978-0-385-73058-7(6),* Ember) Random Hse. Children's Bks.

—The Sisterhood of the Traveling Pants Set: The Sisterhood of the Traveling Pants - The Second Summer of the Sisterhood - Girls in Pants, 3 vols. 2006. (Sisterhood of the Traveling Pants Ser.: Vols. 1-3). (ENG.). (YA). pap., pap., pap. 26.85 *(978-0-385-73424-0(7),* Ember) Random Hse. Children's Bks.

Braun, Sebastian, illus. I'm a Clown! 2012. (Look at Me Ser.). (ENG.). 12p. (J). bds. *(978-1-84643-472-3(6))* Child's Play International Ltd.

—I'm a Monster! 2012. (Look at Me Ser.). (ENG.). 12p. (J). bds. *(978-1-84643-470-9(X))* Child's Play International Ltd.

—I'm a Robot! 2012. (Look at Me Ser.). (ENG.). 12p. (J). bds. *(978-1-84643-469-3(6))* Child's Play International Ltd.

—I'm an Alien! 2012. (Look at Me Ser.). (ENG.). 12p. (J). bds. *(978-1-84643-471-6(8))* Child's Play International Ltd.

Brett, Jan. El Sombrero. (Buenas Noches Ser.).Tr. of Hat. (SPA.). (J). *(978-958-04-4169-4(3))* Norma S.A.

Brimner, Larry Dane. The Cool Coats. Tripp, Christine, illus. 2003. (Rookie Choices Ser.). 31p. (J). (gr. 1-2). 13.60 *(978-0-7569-3259-6(9))* Perfection Learning Corp.

—The Cool Coats. Tripp, Christine, illus. 2003. (Rookie Choices Ser.). (ENG.). 32p. (gr. 1-2). pap. 5.95 *(978-0-516-27834-6(7));* (J). 20.50 *(978-0-516-22545-6(6))* Scholastic Library Publishing. (Children's Pr.).

Brundage, Frances. The Cats' Pajamas. Brundage, Frances, illus. 2006. (Shape Bks.). (ENG., Illus.). 16p. (J). (gr. -1-3). 9.95 *(978-1-59583-054-8(5),* 9781595830548) Laughing Elephant.

Burks, James. Beep & Bah. Burks, James, illus. 2012. (Carolrhoda Picture Bks.). (ENG., Illus.). 32p. (J). (gr. k-3). lib. bdg. 16.95 *(978-0-7613-6567-9(2))* Lerner Publishing Group.

Bursting at the Seams. 2014. (Sew Zoey Ser.: 10). (ENG., Illus.). 176p. (J). (gr. 3-7). pap. 6.99 *(978-1-4814-1964-2(1),* Simon Spotlight) Simon Spotlight.

Byars, Betsy. Dead Letter. 2006. (Herculeah Jones Mystery Ser.). (ENG.). 160p. (J). (gr. 3-7). 5.99 *(978-0-14-240564-2(7),* Puffin Books) Penguin Young Readers Group.

Campbell, K. G. Lester's Dreadful Sweaters. Campbell, K. G., illus. 2012. (ENG., Illus.). 32p. (J). (gr. -1-3). 16.95 *(978-1-55453-770-9(3))* Kids Can Pr., Ltd. CAN. Dist: Hachette Bk. Group.

Capotosto, Anthony. No Shoes Required. 2005. 49p. pap. 8.00 *(978-1-4116-2523-5(4))* Lulu Pr., Inc.

Capucilli, Alyssa Satin. Katy Duck Meets the Babysitter. Cole, Henry, illus. 2012. (Katy Duck Ser.). (ENG.). 24p. (J). (gr.

-1-1). 15.99 *(978-1-4424-5242-8(0))*; pap. 3.99 *(978-1-4424-5241-1(2))* Simon Spotlight. (Simon Spotlight).

—Katy Duck's Happy Halloween. Cole, Henry, illus. 2014. (Katy Duck Ser.). (ENG.). 24p. (J). (gr. -1-1). pap. 3.99 *(978-1-4424-9806-8(4)*, Simon Spotlight) Simon Spotlight.

Carmen & Thane Johnson. Dogs Don't Wear Underwear. Bianca & Annie West, illus. 2009. 20p. pap. 12.99 *(978-1-4389-4128-8(5))* AuthorHouse.

Cate, Marijke Ten. Where Is My Sock? Cate, Marijke Ten, illus. 2010. (ENG., Illus.). 24p. (J). (gr. -1-1). 16.95 *(978-1-59078-808-0(7)*, Lemniscaat) Boyds Mills Pr.

Caudle, Ruth. Yvette, Annette & Renette. 2007. (Illus.). 32p. (J). 16.99 *(978-0-9793039-0-6(7))* Haiti World.

Chapman, Jared. Fruits in Suits. 2017. (ENG., Illus.). 40p. (J). (gr. -1-k). 14.95 *(978-1-4197-2298-1(0)*, Abrams Appleseed) Abrams, Inc.

—Vegetables in Underwear. 2015. (ENG., Illus.). 40p. (J). (gr. -1-k). 14.95 *(978-1-4197-1464-1(3))* Abrams, Inc.

Cheshire, Marc. Eloise Dresses Up: 50 Reusable Stickers! Hahner, Chris, illus. 2005. (Eloise Ser.). (ENG.). 12p. (J). (gr. -1-1). pap. 6.99 *(978-0-689-87455-0(3)*, Little Simon) Little Simon.

Children's Press, contrib. by. The Three Little Kittens Get Dressed. 2009. (Rookie Preschool-NEW Ser.). (ENG.). 24p. (J). pap. 6.95 *(978-0-531-24579-8(9)*, Children's Pr.) Scholastic Library Publishing.

Chodos-Irvine, Margaret. Ella Sarah Gets Dressed. 2003. (ENG., Illus.). 40p. (J). (gr. -1-3). 17.99 *(978-0-15-216413-3(8))* Houghton Mifflin Harcourt Publishing Co.

Christiansen, Candace. The Mitten Tree. Greenstein, Elaine, illus. (ENG.). 32p. 2009. (J). (gr. -1-1). pap. 10.95 *(978-1-55591-733-3(X))* 2008. pap. 7.95 *(978-1-55591-698-5(8))* Fulcrum Publishing.

Church, Caroline Jayne. Here Comes Halloween! Church, Caroline Jayne, illus. 2009. (ENG., Illus.). 8p. (J). (gr. k — 1). bds. 7.99 *(978-0-545-11815-6(8)*, Cartwheel Bks.) Scholastic, Inc.

—Let's Get Dressed! Church, Caroline Jayne, illus. 2012. (ENG., Illus.). 10p. (J). (gr. -1 — 1). bds. 7.99 *(978-0-545-43637-3(0))* Scholastic, Inc.

Chwast, Seymour. Get Dressed! 2012. (ENG., Illus.). 18p. (J). (gr. -1 — 1). 14.95 *(978-1-4197-0107-8(X)*, Abrams Appleseed) Abrams, Inc.

Ciccone, Madonna L. & Madonna. A Perfect Pair. Fulvimari, Jeffrey, illus. 2008. (English Roses Ser.: 8). (ENG.). 128p. (J). (gr. 3-7). 9.99 *(978-0-14-241125-4(6)*, Puffin Books) Penguin Young Readers Group.

Clarke, Jane. I'm Not Wearing That! Mostyn, David, illus. 2005. (ENG.). 24p. (J). lib. bdg. 23.65 *(978-1-59646-716-3(9))* Dingles & Co.

Classic Goosebumps & Stine, R. L. The Haunted Mask. 2008. (Classic Goosebumps Ser.: 4). (ENG.). 144p. (J). (gr. 3-7). 6.99 *(978-0-545-03521-7(X)*, Scholastic Paperbacks) Scholastic, Inc.

Cleary, Beverly. Socks. Tiegreen, Alan & Dockray, Tracy, illus. 2015. (Avon Camelot Bks.). (ENG.). 160p. (J). (gr. 3-7). pap. 6.99 *(978-0-380-70926-7(0))* HarperCollins Pubs.

Cocca-Leffler, Maryann. Mr. Tanen's Ties. Cocca-Leffler, Maryann, illus. 2004. (ENG., Illus.). 32p. (J). (gr. k-2). pap. 6.95 *(978-0-8075-5302-2(6))* Whitman, Albert & Co.

Cohen, Miriam. Layla's Head Scarf, 1 vol. Himler, Ronald, illus. 2009. (ENG.). 32p. (J). (gr. -1-3). 15.95 *(978-1-59572-177-8(0))*; pap. 5.95 *(978-1-59572-178-5(9))* Star Bright Bks., Inc.

Connelly, Peggy. My Quirky, Oddball, Eccentric, Unpredictable Grandma. 2006. (ENG.). 112p. per. 19.95 *(978-1-4241-4486-0(8))* PublishAmerica, Inc.

Cooper, Ilene. Lucy's Tricks & Treats. Merrell, David, illus. 2012. (Lucy Ser.). (ENG.). 112p. (J). (gr. 1-4). 4.99 *(978-0-375-86997-6(2)*, Random Hse. Bks. for Young Readers) Random Hse. Children's Bks.

Cortes, Mary. Where on Earth Did My Sock Go? 2006. (J). per. 15.95 *(978-0-9787788-3-5(9))* LUMEN-US Pubns.

Cousins, Lucy. Maisy's Clothes/La Ropa de Maisy. Cousins, Lucy, illus. 2009. (Maisy Ser.). (SPA & ENG., Illus.). 16p. (J). (gr. -1-2). bds. 5.99 *(978-0-7636-4518-2(4))* Candlewick Pr.

Coven, Wanda. Heidi Heckelbeck in Disguise. 2012. (Heidi Heckelbeck Ser.: 4). lib. bdg. 16.00 *(978-0-606-26329-0(2)*, Turtleback) Turtleback Bks.

Cowley, Joy. Smarty No Pants. 2009. pap. 8.25 *(978-1-60559-239-8(0))* Hameray Publishing Group, Inc.

Croissant-Madden, Gayle. My Wild, Wild Hair! Croissant-Madden, Gayle, illus. 2006. (Illus.). (J). 10.00 *(978-0-9786478-0-3(7))* airjam.com.

Crow, Marilee. Does Heaven Get Mail? Snider, K. C., illus. 2008. 24p. pap. 10.95 *(978-1-935137-12-2(3))* Guardian Angel Publishing, Inc.

Cunnane, Kelly. Deep in the Sahara. Hadadi, Hoda, illus. 2013. (ENG.). 40p. (J). (gr. -1-3). 17.99 *(978-0-375-87034-7(2)*, Schwartz & Wade Bks.) Random Hse. Children's Bks.

Currey, Anna. Truffle Goes to Town. Currey, Anna, illus. 2003. (Illus.). 32p. (YA). *(978-1-85602-429-7(6)*, Pavilion Children's Books) Pavilion Bks.

Cuyler, Margery. Princess Bess Gets Dressed. Maione, Heather Harms & Maione, Heather, illus. 2009. (ENG.). 32p. (J). (gr. -1-3). 15.99 *(978-1-4169-3833-0(8)*, Simon & Schuster Bks. For Young Readers) Simon & Schuster Bks. For Young Readers.

Czajak, Paul. Monster Needs a Costume. Grieb, Wendy, illus. (Monster & Me Ser.). (ENG.). 32p. (J). (-k). 2014. 6.99 *(978-1-938063-38-1(4))* 2013. 16.95 *(978-1-938063-09-1(0))* Mighty Media Pr. (Mighty Media Kids).

Dale, Jay. Dress-Up Day, 1 vol. Heyworth, Heather, illus. 2012. (Engage Literacy Green Ser.). (ENG.). 32p. (gr. k-2). pap. 5.99 *(978-1-4296-9003-4(8)*, Engage Literacy) Capstone Press of Coughlan Cos.

—Letter to Sam, 1 vol. Zamazing, Cherie, illus. 2012. (Engage Literacy Green Ser.). (ENG.). 32p. (gr. k-2). pap. 5.99 *(978-1-4296-9033-1(X)*, Engage Literacy) Capstone Press of Coughlan Cos.

—Shopping for Socks, 1 vol. Jackson, Katy, illus. 2012. (Engage Literacy Red Ser.). (ENG.). 32p. (gr. k-2). pap. 5.99 *(978-1-4296-8942-7(0)*, Engage Literacy) Capstone Press of Coughlan Cos.

David And Stephanie Williams. The Pajamazon Amazon vs the Goofers Twofers. 2013. 98p. pap. 5.99 *(978-0-9910562-0-0(5))* One Million Words, LLC.

Davies, Dalene. Sock Monster's Invade Earth: Hold on to Your Socks! 2006. 74p. pap. 12.26 *(978-1-4116-8227-6(0))* Lulu Pr., Inc.

Davies, Jacqueline. Panda Pants. Hanson, Sydney, illus. 2016. (ENG.). 32p. (J). (gr. -1-2). 17.99 *(978-0-553-53576-1(5)*, Knopf Bks. for Young Readers) Random Hse. Children's Bks.

Davis, Jacky. Do You Like These Boots? Soman, David, illus. 2014. (Ladybug Girl Ser.). (ENG.). 32p. (J). (gr. k-1). pap. 3.99 *(978-0-448-46503-6(5)*, Penguin Young Readers) Penguin Young Readers Group.

—Do You Like These Boots? 2014. (Penguin Young Readers Level 1 Ser.). lib. bdg. 13.55 *(978-0-606-34507-1(8)*, Turtleback) Turtleback Bks.

Davis, Jacky & Soman, David. Ladybug Girl Dresses Up! Soman, David, illus. 2010. (Ladybug Girl Ser.). (ENG., Illus.). 14p. (J). (gr. -1 — 1). bds. 5.99 *(978-0-448-45373-6(8)*, Grosset & Dunlap) Penguin Young Readers Group.

Dean, James. Too Cool for School. 2014. (Pete the Cat I Can Read Ser.). (J). lib. bdg. 13.55 *(978-0-606-35062-4(4)*, Turtleback) Turtleback Bks.

deGroat, Diane. Trick or Treat, Smell My Feet, 4 bks., Set. 2008. (J). (gr. -1-2). pap. 37.95 incl. audio *(978-1-4301-0426-1(0))*; pap. 39.95 incl. audio compact disk *(978-1-4301-0428-5(7))* Live Oak Media.

Depken, Kristen L. Dream Closet. 2013. (Barbie Step into Reading Level 3 Ser.). lib. bdg. 13.55 *(978-0-606-32194-5(2)*, Turtleback) Turtleback Bks.

Dewdney, Anna. Llama Llama Trick or Treat. Dewdney, Anna, illus. 2014. (Llama Llama Ser.). (ENG., Illus.). 14p. (J). (— 1). bds. 5.99 *(978-0-451-46978-6(X)*, Viking Books for Young Readers) Penguin Publishing Group.

Di Franco, Armand L. The Gloves. 2013. 24p. pap. 24.95 *(978-1-62709-989-9(1))* America Star Bks.

Dipucchio, Kelly. Dress-Up Mess-Up. Ross, Heather, illus. 2013. (Crafty Chloe Ser.). (ENG.). 40p. (J). (gr. -1-3). 16.99 *(978-1-4424-2124-0(X))* Simon & Schuster Children's Publishing.

Disney Book Group Staff & Higginson, Sheila Sweeny. Minnie: Minnie's Costume Contest. Disney Storybook Artists Staff, illus. 2014. (ENG.). 12p. (J). (gr. -1-k). bds. 7.99 *(978-1-4231-9427-9(6))* Disney Pr.

Disney Book Group Staff & Kelman, Marcy. Minnie's Purse. Disney Storybook Artists Staff, illus. 2014. (ENG.). 20p. (J). (gr. -1-k). 9.99 *(978-1-4231-8492-8(0))* Disney Pr.

—Sofia the First Sofia's Purse. Disney Storybook Artists Staff, illus. 2014. (ENG.). 20p. (J). (gr. -1-k). 9.99 *(978-1-4231-8493-5(9))* Disney Pr.

Disney Minnie, Disney. Disney Minnie - My Colorful Closet. 2014. (ENG.). 10p. (J). (gr. -1-1). 12.99 *(978-0-7944-3141-9(0))* Reader's Digest Assn., Inc., The.

Dlugolecki, Michele. Mr. Mish Mosh & His Wash. 2007. 17.00 *(978-0-8059-8878-9(5))* Dorrance Publishing Co., Inc.

Donaldson, Julia. Hippo Has a Hat. Sharratt, Nick, illus. 2007. (ENG.). 24p. (J). (gr. k-k). pap. 8.99 *(978-1-4050-2192-0(6))* Macmillan Pubs., Ltd. GBR. Dist: Independent Pubs. Group.

Donnanna. Jamie & the Cheesy Foot Monster. 2010. (Illus.). 44p. pap. 16.99 *(978-1-4490-9785-1(5))* AuthorHouse.

Doodler, Todd H. Veggies with Wedgies. Doodler, Todd H., illus. 2014. (ENG., Illus.). 32p. (J). (gr. -1-k). 14.99 *(978-1-4424-9340-7(2)*, Little Simon) Little Simon.

Dressing Up: Individual Title Six-Packs. (Chiquilibros Ser.). (gr. k-1). 23.00 *(978-0-7635-0421-2(1))*; 28.00 *(978-0-7635-0028-3(3))* Rigby Education.

Du Bois, Crystal L. Where Are My Socks? 2012. 28p. pap. 16.09 *(978-1-4669-0586-3(7))* Trafford Publishing.

Duder, Tessa. Carpet of Dreams. Wilson, Mark, illus. 2008. 32p. pap. *(978-0-207-19991-2(4))* HarperCollins Pubs. Australia.

Duke, Shirley Smith. No Bows!, 1 vol. Mattheson, Jenny, illus. 2006. (ENG.). 32p. (J). (gr. k-1). 15.95 *(978-1-56145-356-6(0))* Peachtree Pubs.

Dunrea, Olivier. Gossie. 2007. (Gossie & Friends Ser.). (ENG., Illus.). 32p. (J). (gr. -1 — 1). bds. 6.99 *(978-0-618-74791-7(5))* Houghton Mifflin Harcourt Publishing Co.

—Gossie & Gertie. 2006. (Illus.). 32p. pap. *(978-1-4063-0119-9(1))* Walker Bks., Ltd.

—Ollie the Stomper. 2007. (Gossie & Friends Ser.). (ENG., Illus.). 32p. (J). (gr. -1-k). bds. 6.95 *(978-0-618-75504-2(7))* Houghton Mifflin Harcourt Publishing Co.

Dyan, Penelope. Arianna's Shoes. Dyan, Penelope, illus. 2008. (Illus.). 44p. pap. 11.95 *(978-1-935118-33-6(1))* Bellissima Publishing, LLC.

—Little Miss Chris & the Incredible Red Shoes. Dyan, Penelope, illus. 2009. (Illus.). 44p. pap. 11.95 *(978-1-935118-49-7(8))* Bellissima Publishing, LLC.

—Tammy's Left Shoe — -As Opposed to Her Right. Dyan, Penelope, illus. 2008. (Illus.). 44p. pap. 11.95 *(978-1-935118-41-1(2))* Bellissima Publishing, LLC.

Edgson, Alison, illus. The Emperor's New Clothes. 2007. (Flip-Up Fairy Tales Ser.). (ENG.). 24p. (J). (gr. -1-2). audio compact disk *(978-1-84643-093-0(3))* Child's Play International Ltd.

Eggleton, Jill. Clown's Pants. Smith, Craig, illus. 2003. (Rigby Sails Early Ser.). (ENG.). 16p. (gr. 1-2). pap. 6.95 *(978-0-7578-8723-9(6))* Houghton Mifflin Harcourt Publishing Co.

Eilers, Roxanne. The Chocolate Brown Coat, 1 vol. 2010. 44p. pap. 24.95 *(978-1-4489-8540-1(4))* PublishAmerica, Inc.

Ellis, Dianne. Rusty Rumble & His Smelly Socks. 2012. 36p. pap. 32.70 *(978-1-4691-9914-6(9))* Xlibris Corp.

—Rusty Rumble's Day at the Beach. 2012. 40p. pap. 32.70 *(978-1-4797-0360-9(5))* Xlibris Corp.

Emerson, Carl. Monster Boy & the Halloween Parade, 1 vol. Levin, Lon, illus. 2010. (Monster Boy Set 2 Ser.). (ENG.). 32p. (J). (gr. k-3). 28.50 *(978-1-60270-777-1(4))* ABDO Publishing Co.

Ewert, Marcus. 10,000 Dresses. Ray, Rex, illus. 2008. (ENG.). 32p. (J). (gr. k-4). 14.95 *(978-1-58322-850-0(0)*, Triangle Square) Seven Stories Pr.

Faber, Toni Tuso. The Poodle Tales: Book Nine. Rudd, Benton, illus. 2013. 24p. 16.99 *(978-0-9897168-2-6(1))* Mindstir Media.

Faircloth, M. L. Seana's New Accessory. Margolis, Al, illus. 2012. 26p. 19.95 *(978-1-61863-407-8(0))* Bookstand Publishing.

Faye. Jazzy Shoes. l.t. ed. 2006. (ENG., Illus.). 28p. per. 9.95 *(978-1-4327-0176-5(2))* Outskirts Pr., Inc.

Feeney, Tatyana. Little Owl's Orange Scarf. 2013. (ENG.). 32p. (J). (— 1). 16.99 *(978-0-449-81411-6(4)*, Knopf Bks. for Young Readers) Random Hse. Children's Bks.

Feldman, Thea. Princess Party. 2006. 3p. 5.99 *(978-1-932915-33-4(8))* Sandvik Publishing.

Fiesta Girls: A Paper Doll Cut-Out Book. 2006. (J). pap. 8.95 *(978-0-9787319-0-8(5))* Kolluri, Alina M.

Fine, Anne. Billy y el Vestido Rosa. Dupasquier, Philippe, illus. 2003.Tr. of Bill's New Frock. (SPA.). 100p. (J). (gr. 3-5). pap. 8.95 *(978-958-24-0175-7(3))* Santillana USA Publishing Co., Inc.

Flam, Chanie. Shoe, Shoe. (Goldie Gold Board Book Ser.: Vol. 4). (Illus.). (J). (gr. -1-1). bds. 4.95 *(978-1-58330-028-2(7))* Feldheim Pubs.

Fleming, Denise. Maggie & Michael Get Dressed. Fleming, Denise, illus. 2016. (ENG., Illus.). 40p. (J). 17.99 *(978-0-8050-8794-9(X)*, 9780805087949, Holt, Henry & Co. Bks. For Young Readers) Holt, Henry & Co.

Fliess, Sue. A Dress for Me!, 0 vols. Laughead, Mike, illus. 2012. (ENG.). 24p. (J). (gr. k-3). 12.99 *(978-0-7614-6148-7(5)*, 9780761461487, Amazon Children's Publishing) Amazon Publishing.

Florian, Douglas. I Love My Hat, 0 vols. Keiser, Paige, illus. 2014. (ENG.). 24p. (J). (gr. -1-2). 16.99 *(978-1-4778-4780-0(4)*, 9781477847800, Amazon Children's Publishing) Amazon Publishing.

Ford, Bernette. No More Blanket for Lambkin! Williams, Sam, illus. 2010. (Ducky & Piggy Ser.). (ENG.). 26p. (J). (gr. k — 1). bds. 6.95 *(978-1-906250-47-8(2))* Boxer Bks., Ltd. GBR. Dist: Sterling Publishing Co., Inc.

Frank, Hannah. The Ballet Shoes. 2008. 44p. pap. 18.49 *(978-1-4389-1025-3(8))* AuthorHouse.

Freedman, Claire. Aliens in Underpants Save the World. Cort, Ben, illus. 2012. (Underpants Bks.). (ENG.). 32p. (J). (gr. -1-2). 17.99 *(978-1-4424-2768-6(X)*, Simon & Schuster/Paula Wiseman Bks.) Simon & Schuster/Paula Wiseman Bks.

French, Vivian. Polly's Pink Pajamas. Heap, Sue, illus. 2010. (ENG.). 32p. (J). (gr. -1-2). 14.99 *(978-0-7636-4807-7(8))* Candlewick Pr.

Friden, Chris. Pajamatime with P.J. Zapater Oliva, Carlos & Glazier, Garth, illus. 2008. (J). *(978-0-9758785-9-0(X))*; *(978-0-9801849-5-2(9))* Haydenburri Lane.

Fridman, Sashi. The Last Pair of Shoes. Seva, illus. 2006. 32p. (J). 13.95 *(978-0-8266-0031-8(X))* Merkos L'Inyonei Chinuch.

Friedman, Becky. No Red Sweater for Daniel. Fruchter, Jason, illus. 2016. (Daniel Tiger's Neighborhood 8X8 Ser.). (ENG.). 24p. (gr. -1-k). 13.55 *(978-0-606-39246-4(7))* Turtleback Bks.

—What Is Daniel Wearing? Fruchter, Jason, illus. 2015. (Daniel Tiger's Neighborhood Ser.). (ENG.). 14p. (J). (gr. -1 — 1). 8.99 *(978-1-4814-2899-6(3)*, Simon Spotlight) Simon Spotlight.

Friedman, Laurie. A Style All Her Own. Watts, Sharon, illus. 2005. 32p. (J). (gr. -1-3). lib. bdg. 15.95 *(978-1-57505-599-2(6))* Lerner Publishing Group.

Fruchter, Jason, illus. You're Still You! 2016. (Daniel Tiger's Neighborhood Ser.). (ENG.). 12p. (J). (gr. -1-k). bds. 5.99 *(978-1-4814-6743-8(3)*, Simon Spotlight) Simon Spotlight.

Fuller, Bob, illus. The Costume Trunk. 2011. (J). *(978-1-936169-01-6(0))* Paddywhack Lane LLC.

Garis, Howard Roger. The Curlytops at Uncle Franks Ranch. 2005. 192p. pap. 11.95 *(978-1-4218-1566-4(4)*, 1st World Library - Literary Society) 1st World Publishing, Inc.

Garza, Carmen Lomas. Vejigante-Masquerader. (J). (gr. 2-4). *(978-0-590-45777-4(2)*, SO7640) Scholastic, Inc.

Gassman, Julie A. Crabby Pants, 1 vol. Watson, Richard, illus. 2010. (Little Boost Ser.). (ENG.). 32p. (gr. k-3). lib. bdg. 23.99 *(978-1-4048-6165-7(3)*, Little Boost) Picture Window Bks.

Gayle, Christine. Dottie the Sock: How I Found My Pair! 2009. 32p. pap. 12.99 *(978-1-4389-8041-6(8))* AuthorHouse.

Geis, Patricia. Let's Get Dressed! Folch, Sergio, illus. 2009. (Good Habits with Coco & Tula Ser.). 16p. (J). (gr. -1-k). bds. 11.40 *(978-1-60754-409-8(1))* Windmill Bks.

Gerstenblit, Rivke. Baruch & His Disappearing Yarmulke. Judowitz, Chani, illus. 2014. 32p. (J). *(978-1-4226-1530-0(8))* Mesorah Pubns., Ltd.

Gibbs, Gail L. What about Those Pants? 2012. 24p. pap. 15.99 *(978-1-4691-7338-2(7))* Xlibris Corp.

Gibson, Beatrice. The Legend of the Sandals. 2008. 28p. pap. 15.99 *(978-1-4363-9169-6(5))* Xlibris Corp.

Gill, Vince. The Emperor's New Clothes: A Country Storybook. Newsom, Carol, illus. 2006. 30p. (J). (gr. 4-8). reprint ed. 17.00 *(978-1-4223-5729-3(5))* DIANE Publishing Co.

Gilson, Jamie. Bug in a Rug. deGroat, Diane, illus. 2003. (ENG.). 80p. (J). pap. 7.95 *(978-0-618-31670-0(1))* Houghton Mifflin Harcourt Publishing Co.

Glass, Eleri. The Red Shoes. Spires, Ashley, illus. 2008. (ENG.). 36p. (J). (gr. -1-3). 16.95 *(978-1-894965-78-1(7))* Simply Read Bks. CAN. Dist: Ingram Publisher Services.

Godin, Thelma Lynne. How to Dress a Dragon. Barclay, Eric, illus. 2016. (ENG.). 40p. (J). (gr. -1-k). 16.99 *(978-0-545-67846-9(3)*, Scholastic Pr.) Scholastic, Inc.

Goethals, Angela. The Sisterhood of the Traveling Pants. 2004. (Sisterhood of the Traveling Pants Ser.: Bk. 1). 320p. (YA). (gr. 7-18). pap. 40.00 incl. audio *(978-0-8072-2286-7(0)*, Listening Library) Random Hse. Audio Publishing Group.

Goldberg, Whoopi. Toeshoe Trouble. Roos, Maryn, illus. 2009. (ENG.). 160p. (J). (gr. 1-17). pap. 4.99 *(978-0-7868-5261-1(5)*, Jump at the Sun) Hyperion Bks. for Children.

Gomi, Taro. What Do You Wear? 2017. (ENG., Illus.). 20p. (J). bds. 6.99 *(978-1-4521-5028-4(1))* Chronicle Bks. LLC.

Goodrich, Carter. Zorro Gets an Outfit. Goodrich, Carter, illus. 2012. (ENG., Illus.). 48p. (J). (gr. -1-3). 15.99 *(978-1-4424-3535-3(6)*, Simon & Schuster Bks. For Young Readers) Simon & Schuster Bks. For Young Readers.

Gordon, Mike, illus. The Emperor's New Clothes. 2006. 24p. (J). (gr. -1-3). 9.99 *(978-0-7945-1350-4(6)*, Usborne) EDC Publishing.

Goulis, Julie. The Topsy-Turvy Towel. Ferguson, John H., illus. 2006. 32p. (J). (gr. -1-2). 14.95 *(978-0-9754621-2-6(1))* Bubblegum Bks.

Graf, Mike & Morden, Richard. Dirt on My Shoe. 2008. (Rigby Focus Forward: Level L Ser.). (Illus.). 24p. (J). (gr. 4-7). pap. *(978-1-4190-3805-1(2)*, Rigby) Pearson Education Australia.

Greene, Carol. Buttons. 2007. 94p. (gr. 2-2). 24.99 *(978-1-4257-7420-2(2))*; per. 15.99 *(978-1-4257-7419-6(9))* Xlibris Corp.

Hall, Francois, illus. The Emperor's New Clothes. 2007. (First Fairy Tales Ser.). 32p. (J). (gr. -1-3). lib. bdg. 28.50 *(978-1-59771-071-8(7)*, 1262700) Sea-To-Sea Pubns.

Hall, John. What If I Pulled This Thread. Gilpin, Stephen, illus. 2006. 48p. 12.99 *(978-1-59379-067-7(8))* White Stone Bks.

Harley, Bill. Dirty Joe the Pirate: A True Story. Davis, Jack E., illus. 2008. (ENG.). 32p. (J). (gr. k-3). 17.99 *(978-0-06-623780-0(7))* HarperCollins Pubs.

Harrison, Lisi. Best Friends for Never. 2004. (Clique Ser.: 2). (ENG.). 208p. (YA). (gr. 7-17). pap. 9.99 *(978-0-316-70131-0(9)*, Poppy) Little, Brown Bks. for Young Readers.

Harry How Books. Just Luke. l.t. ed. 2006. (ENG., Illus.). 28p. per. 9.95 *(978-1-4327-0178-9(9))* Outskirts Pr., Inc.

Hart, Caryl. Don't Put Your Pants on Your Head, Fred! Hodgkinson, Leigh, illus. 2012. (ENG.). 32p. (J). (gr. -1-k). pap. 9.99 *(978-1-4083-0917-9(3))* Hodder & Stoughton GBR. Dist: Hachette Bk. Group.

Harvey, Damian. Mr. Fox's Socks. Rescek, Sanja, illus. 2004. (ENG.). 16p. (J). lib. bdg. 23.65 *(978-1-59646-678-4(2))* Dingles & Co.

Haselhurst, Maureen. The Emperor's New Uniform. Kennedy, Kelly, illus. 2015. (ENG.). 32p. (J). *(978-0-7787-1933-5(2))* Crabtree Publishing Co.

Hasta Manana Zapatos: See You Tomorrow Shoes. 2006. (J). *(978-0-9743359-2-6(4))* Murdock Publishing Co.

Hayes, Joe. The Lovesick Skunk. Castro L., Antonio, illus. (ENG.). 32p. (J). 2016. 7.95 *(978-1-941026-04-5(4))* 2010. 16.95 *(978-1-933693-81-1(9))* Cinco Puntos Pr.

Healey, Vittoria. Dave & V. 2017. (ENG.). 130p. pap. 11.95 ***(978-1-78629-009-0(X)***, ec9a5ae7-407e-4080-a583-db914a29dfe6) Austin, Stan AUS. Dist: Bookmasters Distribution.

Heape, David. R. That's What Friends Do. l.t. ed. 2006. (ENG., Illus.). 28p. per. 9.95 *(978-1-4327-0177-2(0))* Outskirts Pr., Inc.

Hefner, Elizabeth. The Great Laundry Rebellion. 2008. 38p. pap. 14.95 *(978-0-557-00886-5(7))* Lulu Pr., Inc.

Higginson, Sheila Sweeny & Disney Book Group Staff. Chilly Catches a Cold. Disney Storybook Art Team, illus. 2013. (ENG.). 24p. (J). (gr. -1-k). pap. 3.99 *(978-1-4231-7509-4(3))* Disney Pr.

Higi, Laf. Sock Thing. 2009. 16p. pap. 12.99 *(978-1-4490-0402-6(4))* AuthorHouse.

Hill, Amye Rose. The Amazing Mr. Buddy. 10th ed. 2005. (Illus.). (J). 6.99 *(978-0-9769234-0-4(8))* Zany Angel Projects LLC.

Himler, Ronald. Dancing Boy, 1 vol. Himler, Ronald, illus. 2005. (ENG., Illus.). 32p. (J). (gr. -1-k). 15.95 *(978-1-59572-020-7(0))* Star Bright Bks., Inc.

Hinman, Bobbie. The Sock Fairy. Bridgeman, Kristi, illus. 2008. (ENG.). 32p. (J). (gr. -1-1). 16.95 *(978-0-9786791-1-8(3))* Best Fairy Bks.

Hoberman, Mary Ann. I Like Old Clothes. Barton, Patrice, illus. 2012. (ENG.). 32p. (J). (gr. k-3). 16.99 *(978-0-375-86951-8(4)*, Knopf Bks. for Young Readers) Random Hse. Children's Bks.

Hoffman, Sarah & Hoffman, Ian. Jacob's New Dress. Case, Chris, illus. 2014. (ENG.). 32p. (J). (gr. -1-3). 16.99 *(978-0-8075-6373-1(0))* Whitman, Albert & Co.

Hore, Rosie. Sticker Dolly Dressing Wartime Fashion IR. 2015. (Historical Sticker Dolly Dressing Ser.). (ENG.). 24+ 10p. (J). (gr. k-5). pap. 9.99 *(978-0-7945-3474-5(0)*, Usborne) EDC Publishing.

Houdek, Andi. J P S Halloween Parade. Collier, Kevin, illus. 2012. 20p. pap. 9.95 *(978-1-61633-263-1(8))* Guardian Angel Publishing, Inc.

Howard, Jennifer. Lucy & the Land of Lost Socks. 2009. 56p. pap. 10.49 *(978-1-4389-5362-5(3))* AuthorHouse.

Howard, Kate. The Duck Vinci Code & Other Tales. 2013. (ENG.). 112p. (J). (gr. 2-5). pap. 4.99 *(978-0-545-49291-1(2))* Scholastic, Inc.

Hubble, Meagan R. Where Your Underwear Goes. 2011. 28p. pap. 13.95 *(978-1-4567-3463-3(6))* AuthorHouse.

Hudson, Cheryl Willis. Clothes I Love to Wear. 2008. (Illus.). 24p. (J). (gr. -1-3). 3.99 *(978-1-60349-004-7(3)*, Marimba Bks.) Hudson Publishing Group, The.

Hughes, Shirley. Alfie's Feet. Hughes, Shirley, illus. 2009. (Alfie Ser.). (ENG., Illus.). 32p. (J). (gr. -1-k). pap. 9.99 *(978-1-86230-784-1(9)*, Red Fox) Random House Children's Books GBR. Dist: Independent Pubs. Group.

Huser, Glen. Stitches, 1 vol. 2004. (ENG.). 200p. (J). (gr. 4-7). pap. 9.95 *(978-0-88899-578-0(4))* Groundwood Bks. CAN. Dist: Publishers Group West (PGW).

Hutton, John. Blanket: Baby Unplugged. Kang, Andrea, illus. 2011. (Baby Unplugged Ser.). (ENG.). 14p. (J). (— 1). bds. 7.99 *(978-1-936669-00-4(5))* Blue Manatee Press.

I Love to Dress Up. 2003. (J). per. *(978-1-57657-960-2(3))* Paradise Pr., Inc.

Ikids Staff. Just Like My Mommy. Baruzzi, Agnese, illus. 2009. (ENG.). 20p. (J). (gr. 1-17). 19.99 *(978-1-58476-664-3(6))* Innovative Kids.

Inglee, K. B. Farmer's Daughter, Miller's Son. 2003. 62p. (J). pap. 9.95 *(978-0-7414-1667-4(0))* Infinity Publishing.

Jakary, Lin. I Lost My Sock. Olson, Ryan, illus. 2008. 40p. (J). (gr. -1-3). 16.99 *(978-1-934867-01-3(2))* Wocto Publishing.

Jakobs, D. My Little Pony: Tricks & Treats. 2014. (ENG., Illus.). 24p. (J). (gr. -1-3). pap. 5.99 *(978-0-316-24795-5(2))* Little, Brown Bks. for Young Readers.

Jeanne, Diana. Nathalie's Socks. Rose, Nathalie, illus. 2004. 51p. (J). mass mkt. 7.95 *(978-0-9727583-9-0(9))* Taylor-Dth Publishing.

Jeffers, Oliver. The New Sweater. Jeffers, Oliver, illus. 2012. (Hueys Ser.: 1). (ENG., Illus.). 32p. (J). (gr. -1-2). 17.99 *(978-0-399-25767-4(5)*, Philomel Bks.) Penguin Young Readers Group.

Jeffs, Dixie. The Little Pink Dress. 2012. 24p. 24.95 *(978-1-4626-5853-4(9))* America Star Bks.

Jenkins, Amanda. Hodja's Fine Coat: A Tale from Turkey. 2006. (J). pap. *(978-1-4108-6174-0(0))* Benchmark Education Co.

Jocelyn, Marthe. Hannah & the Seven Dresses. 2006. (Illus.). 23p. (J). (gr. k-4). reprint ed. 15.00 *(978-1-4223-5552-7(7))* DIANE Publishing Co.

—Hannah & the Seven Dresses. 2005. (ENG.). 32p. (J). (gr. -1-k). pap. 7.95 *(978-0-88776-749-4(4),* Tundra Bks.) Tundra Bks. CAN. Dist: Penguin Random Hse. LLC.

—Ready for Autumn. 2008. (ENG., Illus.). 16p. (J). (gr. k-k). bds. 7.95 *(978-0-88776-861-3(X),* Tundra Bks.) Tundra Bks. CAN. Dist: Penguin Random Hse. LLC.

—Ready for Spring. 2008. (ENG., Illus.). 16p. (J). (gr. k-k). bds. 7.95 *(978-0-88776-849-1(0),* Tundra Bks.) Tundra Bks. CAN. Dist: Penguin Random Hse. LLC.

—Ready for Summer. 2008. (ENG., Illus.). 16p. (J). (gr. -1-k). bds. 7.95 *(978-0-88776-860-6(1),* Tundra Bks.) Tundra Bks. CAN. Dist: Penguin Random Hse. LLC.

—Ready for Winter. 2008. (ENG., Illus.). 16p. (J). (gr. -1-k). bds. 7.95 *(978-0-88776-848-4(2),* Tundra Bks.) Tundra Bks. CAN. Dist: Penguin Random Hse. LLC.

Johnson, Joanna. Phoebe's Sweater. Johnson, Eric, illus. 2010. (ENG.). 38p. (J). 18.95 *(978-0-578-04697-6(0))* Slate Falls Pr., LLC.

Johnston, Tony. Levi Strauss Gets a Bright Idea: A Fairly Fabricated Story of a Pair of Pants. Innerst, Stacy, illus. 2011. (ENG.). 32p. (J). (gr. -1-3). 16.99 *(978-0-15-206145-6(2))* Houghton Mifflin Harcourt Publishing Co.

Jones, Christianne C. Dani el Dinosaurio, 1 vol. Lozano, Clara, tr. from ENG. Epstein, Len, illus. 2006. (Read-It! Readers en Español: Story Collection). (SPA.). 24p. (gr. -1-3). lib. bdg. 21.32 *(978-1-4048-2706-6(4),* Easy Readers) Picture Window Bks.

Jones, Dennis. The Life of Socks. 2004. 27p. pap. 24.95 *(978-1-4137-2774-6(3))* PublishAmerica, Inc.

Kane, Gillian. The Witch Who Liked to Wear Pink. Povey, Andrea, illus. 2013. 24p. pap. 11.50 *(978-1-62516-315-8(0),* Strategic Bk. Publishing) Strategic Book Publishing & Rights Agency (SBPRA).

Karp, Ken, illus. Will You Wear a Blue Hat? 2009. (Rookie Toddler: Sing along Toddler Ser.). (ENG.). 12p. (J). (gr. -1). bds. 6.95 *(978-0-531-24549-1(7))* Scholastic Library Publishing.

Kathleen, Jo Ann. NATALIA, O' MIA, WHITE LACES & SHOES. l.t. ed. 2006. (ENG., Illus.). 28p. per. 9.95 *(978-1-4327-0314-1(5))* Outskirts Pr., Inc.

Katschke, Judy. Ready, Set, Boo! Elsom, Clare, illus. 2014. 32p. (J). pap. *(978-0-545-75843-7(2))* Scholastic, Inc.

Keene, Carolyn. Double Take. Pamintuan, Macky, illus. 2009. (Nancy Drew & the Clue Crew Ser.: 21). (ENG.). 112p. (J). (gr. 1-4). pap. 5.99 *(978-1-4169-7812-1(7),* Aladdin) Simon & Schuster Children's Publishing.

Kellogg, Steven. The Missing Mitten Mystery. Kellogg, Steven, illus. 2004. (Picture Puffins Ser.). (Illus.). (gr. -1-3). 17.00 *(978-0-7569-2581-9(9))* Perfection Learning Corp.

Khoo, Rowena. Where Is My Sock? 2012. 76p. pap. 42.05 *(978-1-4771-5459-5(0))* Xlibris Corp.

Kimmel, Eric A. Joha Makes a Wish: A Middle Eastern Tale, 0 vols. Rayyan, Omar, illus. 2013. (ENG.). 40p. (J). (gr. k-3). pap. 7.99 *(978-1-4778-1687-5(9),* 9781477816875, Amazon Children's Publishing) Amazon Publishing.

King, Tom. Coyote's New Suit. Wales, Johnny, illus. 2009. (ENG.). 40p. (J). (gr. k-3). pap. *(978-1-55470-239-8(9))* Me to We.

Klein, Abby. Halloween Parade. McKinley, John, illus. 2009. (Ready, Freddy! Reader List: No. 3). 32p. (J). *(978-0-545-14174-1(5))* Scholastic, Inc.

Klinting, Lars. Beaver the Tailor: A How-to Picture Book. Klinting, Lars, illus. 2004. Orig. Title: Castor Syr.. (Illus.). 32p. (J). (gr. k-3). reprint ed. 17.00 *(978-0-7567-7213-0(3))* DIANE Publishing Co.

Kondrchek, Jamie & Rasemas, Joe. What Should I Wear Today? (Que Ropa Me Pondre Hoy?) Vega, Eida de la, tr. Rasemas, Joe, illus. 2009. (Day in the Life Ser.). (ENG & SPA., Illus.). 32p. (J). (gr. -1-1). 25.70 *(978-1-58415-839-4(5))* Mitchell Lane Pubs., Inc.

Koontz, Robin Michal. Lizzie Little, the Sky Is Falling! Koontz, Robin Michal, illus. 2011. (ENG., Illus.). 24p. (gr. 2-3). pap. 8.95 *(978-1-61236-029-4(7))* Rourke Educational Media.

Kraegel, Kenneth. Green Pants. Kraegel, Kenneth, illus. 2017. (ENG., Illus.). 40p. (J). (gr. -1-2). 15.99 *(978-0-7636-8840-0(1))* Candlewick Pr.

Kragh, Abby. Thomas, Berkley, & the Missing Socks. 2012. (ENG.). (J). pap. 12.99 *(978-1-4675-4433-7(7))* Independent Pub.

Kramer, Alan. The Completely Cool Clothing Company. 2006. (J). pap. *(978-1-4108-6180-1(5))* Benchmark Education Co.

Krauss, Trisha. Charlotte's Very Own Dress. 2016. (ENG., Illus.). 40p. (J). (gr. -1-2). 16.99 *(978-0-553-52095-8(4),* Random Hse. Bks. for Young Readers) Random Hse. Children's Bks.

Kushner, Elisabeth. The Purim Superhero. Byrne, Mike, illus. 2013. (Purim Ser.). (ENG.). 32p. (J). (gr. -1-3). lib. bdg. 17.95 *(978-0-7613-9061-9(8),* Kar-Ben Publishing) Lerner Publishing Group.

Lainez, René Colato. My Shoes & I. Broeck, Fabricio Vanden, illus. 2010. (ENG.). 32p. (J). (gr. 2-4). 16.95 *(978-1-59078-385-6(9))* Boyds Mills Pr.

Lamaro, Glenda. Max Goes to Kindy. Ratyna, Linda, illus. 2009. 36p. pap. 16.44 *(978-1-4251-8830-6(3))* Trafford Publishing.

Lambert, Nat. Magnetic Dressing up Fairies. 2014. (ENG.). 10p. (J). (gr. -1-k). 9.99 *(978-1-78244-798-6(9))* Top That! Publishing PLC GBR. Dist: Independent Pubs. Group.

—Magnetic Dressing up Princesses. 2014. (ENG.). 10p. (J). (gr. -1-k). 9.99 *(978-1-78244-799-3(7))* Top That! Publishing PLC GBR. Dist: Independent Pubs. Group.

Leonard, Marcia. Pantalones Nuevos, No! Handelman, Dorothy, photos by. 2005.Tr. of No New Pants! (Illus.). 32p. (J). (ENG & SPA.). (gr. -1-1). pap. 4.99 *(978-0-8225-3297-2(2));* (SPA., (gr. 1-1). per. 5.95 *(978-0-8225-3296-5(4),* Ediciones Lerner) Lerner Publishing Group.

Lester, Helen. The Sheep in Wolf's Clothing. Munsinger, Lynn, illus. 2014. (Laugh-Along Lessons Ser.). (ENG.). 32p. (J). (gr. -1-3). 8.99 *(978-0-544-23300-3(X),* HMH Books For Young Readers) Houghton Mifflin Harcourt Publishing Co.

Levy, Janey. What Would I Wear? 2006. (Neighborhood Readers Ser.). (ENG.). 12p. (gr. -1-3). pap. 5.90 *(978-1-4042-6682-7(8),* Rosen Classroom) Rosen Publishing Group, Inc., The.

Levy, Michael. The Inspiring Story of Little Goody Two Shoes. 2007. 139p. (YA). per. 12.95 *(978-0-9668069-9-1(9))* Point of Life, Inc.

Lipp, Frederick. Fatima. Lindmark, Margaret, illus. 2006. 32p. (J). pap. *(978-1-59336-302-4(8))* Mondo Publishing.

Little, Awen. Sid y Bwystfil Bwyta Sanau. 2009. (WEL., Illus.). 32p. pap. 14.49 *(978-1-4389-2711-4(8))* AuthorHouse.

Lodge, Jo. Flip Flap, Mr Croc: A Mix & Match Book. 2014. (ENG., Illus.). 14p. (J). (gr. -1-k). 8.99 *(978-1-4449-0992-0(4))* Hodder & Stoughton GBR. Dist: Hachette Bk. Group.

Lombardi, Kristine A. Lovey Bunny. 2015. (Lovey Bunny Ser.). (ENG., Illus.). 32p. (J). (gr. -1-2). 14.95 *(978-1-4197-1485-6(6),* Abrams Bks. for Young Readers) Abrams, Inc.

London, Jonathan. Froggy Gets Dressed, 1 vol. Remkiewicz, Frank, illus. 2007. (Froggy Ser.). (ENG.). 15p. (J). (gr. -1-k). 9.99 *(978-0-14-240870-4(0),* Puffin Books) Penguin Young Readers Group.

Long, Ethan. Chamelia. 2011. (ENG., Illus.). 40p. (J). (gr. -1-3). 16.99 *(978-0-316-08612-7(6))* Little, Brown Bks. for Young Readers.

Lord, Cynthia. Hot Rod Hamster & the Haunted Halloween Party. Anderson, Derek & Paprocki, Greg, illus. 2015. (Scholastic Reader, Level 2 Ser.). (ENG.). 32p. (J). (gr. k-2). pap. 3.99 *(978-0-545-81528-4(2),* Scholastic Pr.) Scholastic, Inc.

—Hot Rod Hamster & the Haunted Halloween Party! Anderson, Derek, illus. 2015. (ENG.). 32p. (J). (gr. -1-3). 16.99 *(978-0-545-81529-1(0),* Scholastic Pr.) Scholastic, Inc.

Lougher, Jenny. Ted & His New Trousers. 2008. 24p. pap. *(978-1-905553-31-0(5))* BookPublishingWorld.

Lovett, Darrell. Hi, I'm Alex. l.t. ed. 2006. (ENG., Illus.). 28p. per. 9.95 *(978-1-4327-0195-6(9))* Outskirts Pr., Inc.

—My Dog Tony. l.t. ed. 2006. (ENG., Illus.). 28p. per. 9.95 *(978-1-4327-0187-1(8))* Outskirts Pr., Inc.

Low, Chen-Chen-Chen. Lizzie May & the Shoelaces. 2009. 44p. pap. 29.99 *(978-1-4092-5739-4(8))* Lulu Pr., Inc.

Lueck, Andrew M. Chicabee. 2006. (Illus.). 32p. (gr. -1-3). 16.95 *(978-0-9774547-0-9(3))* Lueck Studios.

Magsamen, Sandra. Boo, Boo, I Love You! 2015. (ENG., Illus.). 10p. (J). (gr. -1 — 1). bds. 7.99 *(978-0-316-25514-1(9))* Little, Brown Bks. for Young Readers.

Mama Doo. Trevor's Adventure in Button Land, 1 vol. 2008. (ENG.). 47p. pap. 24.95 *(978-1-60672-349-4(9))* America Star Bks.

Manion, Denaé. Sock Stealing Thieves! 2011. 16p. (gr. 1-2). pap. 12.50 *(978-1-4567-5733-5(4))* AuthorHouse.

Marguerita, Ann. Fannie Annie & Her Little White Shoes. 2008. (Illus.). 68p. per. *(978-1-84748-259-4(7))* Athena Pr.

Martin, Justin McCory. The Mystery of the Missing Socks. Kennedy, Kelly, illus. 2004. (Grammar Tales Ser.). (ENG.). 16p. (J). (gr. 3-7). pap. 3.25 *(978-0-439-45823-8(4))* Scholastic, Inc.

Martine, Victoria. The 100 Dollar Sock. 2011. 24p. (gr. -1). pap. 11.32 *(978-1-4567-6677-1(5))* AuthorHouse.

Mason, Christopher. Little Bunny Comfy Pants. 2011. 20p. pap. 24.95 *(978-1-4626-0900-0(7))* America Star Bks.

Matthews, Elli. The Everyday Easter Dress. Matthews, John, illus. 2011. 24p. pap. 24.95 *(978-1-4560-9411-9(4))* America Star Bks.

McArthur, Nancy. The Mystery of the Plant That Ate Dirty Socks. 2004. 162p. pap. 11.95 *(978-0-595-33693-7(0),* Backinprint.com) iUniverse, Inc.

McBride, Maurice & Wallace, Jessica K. Oliver Vance Pull up Your Pants! Jackson, Anthony B., illus. 2011. 32p. (J). 13.95 *(978-1-935802-06-8(2))* Father & Son Publishing.

McCoid, Uldine. Little Girls Play Dress Up. 2011. 28p. (gr. -1). pap. 12.03 *(978-1-4567-6841-6(7))* AuthorHouse.

McCord, Joseph Lennon. Where Do Socks Go? Eller, Sydney, illus. 2012. 32p. pap. 24.95 *(978-1-4626-6624-9(8))* America Star Bks.

McCrimmon, Linda. Can You Please tie My Shoes? 2007. (J). 10.95 *(978-0-9796978-2-1(4))* G Publishing LLC.

Mckee, David. Elmer & Super El. McKee, David, illus. 2012. (Andersen Press Picture Bks). (ENG.). 32p. (J). (gr. -1-3). 16.95 *(978-0-7613-8989-7(X))* Lerner Publishing Group.

McKenna, Kerin Elaine. I Like Shoes. 2006. 17.00 *(978-0-8059-9020-1(8))* Dorrance Publishing Co., Inc.

McKissack, Patricia C. & McKissack, Fredrick L. El Closet de Bessey, la Desordenada. Regan, Dana, illus. 2003. (Rookie Reader Español Ser.).Tr. of Messy Bessey's Closet. (SPA.). 32p. (J). (gr. k-2). pap. 4.95 *(978-0-516-27796-7(0),* Children's Pr.) Scholastic Library Publishing.

McLoughlin, Coleen. Passion for Fashion. 2008. (Coleen Style Queen Ser.: 1). (ENG.). 160p. (J). pap. 7.99 *(978-0-00-727739-1(3),* HarperCollins Children's Bks.) HarperCollins Pubs. Ltd. GBR. Dist: HarperCollins Pubs.

McMahon, Kara. Dress up Dora! Aikins, Dave, illus. 2009. (Dora the Explorer Ser.). (ENG.). 12p. (J). 8.99 *(978-1-4169-6067-6(8),* Simon Spotlight/Nickelodeon) Simon Spotlight/Nickelodeon.

McNally, Amber. Henry & the World of the Missing Socks. 2008. 60p. pap. 16.95 *(978-1-60563-288-9(0))* America Star Bks.

McNamara, Margaret. The Fairy Bell Sisters No. 3: Golden at the Fancy-Dress Party. Denos, Julia, illus. 2013. (Fairy Bell Sisters Ser.: 3). (ENG.). 144p. (J). (gr. 1-5). pap. 4.99 *(978-0-06-222807-9(2))* HarperCollins Pubs.

—The Fairy Bell Sisters #3: Golden at the Fancy-Dress Party. Denos, Julia, illus. 2013. (Fairy Bell Sisters Ser.: 3). (ENG.). 144p. (J). (gr. 1-5). 15.99 *(978-0-06-222808-6(0))* HarperCollins Pubs.

—One Hundred Days (Plus One) Gordon, Mike, illus. 2003. (Ready-to-Read Robin Hill School Ser.). 32p. (J). (gr. -1-3). 11.65 *(978-0-7569-1805-7(7))* Perfection Learning Corp.

McQuinn, Anna. Wanda's Washing Machine. McCafferty, Jan, illus. 2005. 20p. (J). (gr. -1-2). 12.95 *(978-1-58925-768-9(5))* Tiger Tales.

Meadows, Daisy. Cassidy the Costume Fairy. 2012. (Rainbow Magic — the Princess Fairies Ser.: 2). lib. bdg. 14.75 *(978-0-606-26170-8(2),* Turtleback) Turtleback Bks.

—Flora the Dress-Up Fairy. 2010. (Rainbow Magic Ser.). (ENG., Illus.). 192p. (J). (gr. 2-5). 6.99 *(978-0-545-22176-4(5),* Scholastic Paperbacks) Scholastic, Inc.

Meredith, Susan Markowitz. Frances the Fairy Dressmaker. 2011. (Early Connections Ser.). (J). *(978-1-61672-663-8(6))* Benchmark Education Co.

Mincher, Scott. The Blanket. 2009. 48p. pap. 15.99 *(978-1-4415-6632-4(5))* Xlibris Corp.

Mitchell, Dawn. A Bird in a Bathing Suit. 2010. 24p. (J). pap. 12.95 *(978-1-4327-5404-4(1))* Outskirts Pr., Inc.

The Mitten. (Blue-Ribbon Listen-and-Read Ser.). (Orig.). (J). (gr. -1-2). pap. 5.95 incl. audio *(978-0-590-63092-4(X))* Scholastic, Inc.

Mom Dresses Up. 2003. (Mom & Dad Ser.). (J). 7.33 *(978-1-58453-254-5(8))* Pioneer Valley Bks.

Morgan-McCray, Sheila. Untied Shoes. 2008. 28p. pap. 9.95 *(978-1-4327-1093-4(1))* Outskirts Pr., Inc.

Morningforest, Chris & Raymond, Rebecca. Princess Underdrawers & the Dragon. 2006. 37p. (J). pap. 15.58 *(978-1-4116-8837-7(6))* Lulu Pr., Inc.

Moses, Brian. Animal Pants! Boretzki, Anja, illus. 2012. (ENG.). 24p. (J). (gr. -1-k). pap. 8.99 *(978-0-230-73614-6(9))* Macmillan Pubs., Ltd. GBR. Dist: Independent Pubs. Group.

Moses, Jennifer Anne. Tales from My Closet. 2014. (ENG.). 304p. (J). (gr. 7-9). 17.99 *(978-0-545-51608-2(0),* Scholastic Pr.) Scholastic, Inc.

Moss, Marissa. The Vampire Dare! Moss, Marissa, illus. 2011. (Daphne's Diary of Daily Disasters Ser.). (ENG., Illus.). 80p. (J). (gr. 2-5). pap. 5.99 *(978-1-4424-1737-3(4));* lib. bdg. 9.99 *(978-1-4424-2677-1(2))* Simon & Schuster/Paula Wiseman Bks. (Simon & Schuster/Paula Wiseman Bks.).

Moss, Miriam. Bare Bear. McQuillan, Mary, illus. 2005. (ENG.). 32p. (J). 16.95 *(978-0-8234-1934-0(7))* Holiday Hse., Inc.

Mulford, Carolyn. The Feedsack Dress. 2007. (YA). per. 7.95 *(978-0-9713497-4-2(6))* Cave Hollow Pr.

Munro, Maisie. Shoes. Hale, Jenny, illus. 2009. (ENG., Illus.). 9p. (J). (gr. k — 1). bds. 5.95 *(978-1-921272-30-1(9))* Little Hare Bks. AUS. Dist: Independent Pubs. Group.

—Slippers. Hale, Jenny, illus. 2009. (ENG.). 9p. (J). (gr. k — 1). bds. 5.95 *(978-1-921272-31-8(7))* Little Hare Bks. AUS. Dist: Independent Pubs. Group.

Munsch, Robert. Kiss Me, I'm Perfect! Martchenko, Michael, illus. 2008. (J). (gr. -1-3). 11.65 *(978-0-7569-9007-7(6))* Perfection Learning Corp.

—Smelly Socks. 2005. 15.00 *(978-0-7569-5139-9(9))* Perfection Learning Corp.

Murguia, Bethanie Deeney. Zoe Gets Ready. 2012. (ENG.). 40p. (J). (gr. -1-k). 17.99 *(978-0-545-34215-5(5),* Levine, Arthur A. Bks.) Scholastic, Inc.

Murphy, Peg. I Can Do Anything. l.t. ed. 2006. (ENG., Illus.). 28p. per. 9.95 *(978-1-4327-0175-8(4))* Outskirts Pr., Inc.

My Holiday Dress. 2003. (J). per. *(978-1-57657-929-9(8))* Paradise Pr., Inc.

Nagy, Jennifer. Goats in Coats. Broughton, Ilona & Szijgyarto, Cynthia, illus. 2009. 20p. pap. 12.99 *(978-1-4389-6586-4(9))* AuthorHouse.

Nasser, Sarah. Busy Ben Gets Dressed. 2012. 24p. pap. 28.03 *(978-1-4771-5456-4(6))* Xlibris Corp.

Nees, Susan. Picture Day. 2013. (Missy's Super Duper Royal Deluxe Ser.: 1). (ENG., Illus.). 80p. (J). (gr. k-2). 15.99 *(978-0-545-49609-4(8));* pap. 4.99 *(978-0-545-43851-3(9))* Scholastic, Inc.

—Picture Day. 2013. (Missy's Super Duper Royal Deluxe Ser.: 1). lib. bdg. 14.75 *(978-0-606-31979-9(4),* Turtleback) Turtleback Bks.

Nolan, Allia Zobel. God's Winter Wonderland. Mitchell, Melanie, illus. 2006. 10p. (J). bds. 8.99 *(978-0-8254-5526-1(X))* Kregel Pubns.

Noland, Charles. The Adventures of Drew & Ellie: The Daring Rescue. Moyer, Tom, illus. 2nd ed. 2006. 92p. (J). per. 7.95 *(978-0-9789297-2-5(1))* TMD Enterprises.

O'Connor, Jane. Apples Galore! 2013. (Fancy Nancy - I Can Read! Ser.). (J). lib. bdg. 13.55 *(978-0-606-32150-1(0),* Turtleback) Turtleback Bks.

—Fancy Day in Room 1-A. 2012. (Fancy Nancy - I Can Read! Ser.). (J). lib. bdg. 13.55 *(978-0-606-26259-0(8),* Turtleback) Turtleback Bks.

—Fancy Nancy: Pajama Day. Drainville, Beth et al, illus. 2009. (I Can Read Level 1 Ser.). (ENG.). 32p. (J). (gr. -1-3). 16.99 *(978-0-06-170371-3(0))* HarperCollins Pubs.

—Fancy Nancy: Too Many Tutus. Glasser, Robin Preiss, illus. 2012. (I Can Read Level 1 Ser.). (ENG.). 32p. (J). (gr. -1-3). 16.99 *(978-0-06-208308-1(2))* HarperCollins Pubs.

—Fancy Nancy & the Posh Puppy. Glasser, Robin Preiss, illus. 2007. (Fancy Nancy Ser.). 32p. (J). (gr. -1-2). (ENG.). 17.99 *(978-0-06-054213-9(6));* lib. bdg. 18.89 *(978-0-06-054215-3(2))* HarperCollins Pubs.

—Fancy Nancy Loves! Loves!! Loves!!! Glasser, Robin Preiss & Bracken, Carolyn, illus. 2007. (Fancy Nancy Ser.). (ENG.). 12p. (J). (gr. -1-2). pap. 6.99 *(978-0-06-123599-3(7),* HarperFestival) HarperCollins Pubs.

—Nancy la Elegante, 1 vol. Valenzuela, Liliana, tr. from ENG. Glasser, Robin Preiss, illus. 2008. (Fancy Nancy Ser.). (SPA.). 32p. (J). (gr. -1-2). 17.99 *(978-0-06-143528-7(7))* HarperCollins Pubs.

—Pajama Day. Drainville, Beth et al, illus. 2009. (I Can Read Level 1 Ser.). (ENG.). 32p. (J). (gr. -1-3). pap. 3.99 *(978-0-06-170370-6(2))* HarperCollins Pubs.

—Too Many Tutus. Glasser, Robin Preiss, illus. 2012. (I Can Read Level 1 Ser.). (ENG.). 32p. (J). (gr. -1-3). pap. 3.99 *(978-0-06-208307-4(4))* HarperCollins Pubs.

—Too Many Tutus. 2012. (Fancy Nancy - I Can Read! Ser.). (J). lib. bdg. 13.55 *(978-0-606-27124-0(4),* Turtleback) Turtleback Bks.

O'donnell, Tamara J. Grand Mommy's Dress up Box. 2006. (J). *(978-0-9790337-1-1(3))* Crosam Pr.

Olsen, Sylvia. Yetsa's Sweater, 1 vol. Larson, Joan, illus. 2007. (ENG.). 40p. (J). (gr. -1-5). 19.95 *(978-1-55039-155-8(0))* Sono Nis Pr. CAN. Dist: Orca Bk. Pubs. USA.

Oud, Pauline. Getting Dressed with Lily & Milo. Oud, Pauline, illus. 2010. (Lily & Milo Ser.). (ENG., Illus.). 30p. (J). (gr. k — 1). 12.95 *(978-1-60537-060-6(6))* Cobblestone Publishing Co.

—Going to the Beach with Lily & Milo. Oud, Pauline, illus. 2011. (Lily & Milo Ser.). (ENG., Illus.). 28p. (J). (gr. k — 1). 12.95 *(978-1-60537-094-1(0))* Cobblestone Publishing Co.

Ouida. Bebee. 2007. 120p. per. *(978-1-4068-4372-9(5))* Echo Library.

Owens, Robert. Indian Ways. 2008. 76p. pap. 14.54 *(978-1-4357-3702-0(4))* Lulu Pr., Inc.

Parker, Emma. Groat & the Coat. 2010. (Illus.). pap. *(978-1-877547-99-7(9))* First Edition Ltd.

—What Will JoJo Be? 2010. (Illus.). pap. *(978-1-877561-06-1(1))* First Edition Ltd.

Payne, Jackson. The Stork & the Birthday Stocking. Williams, Jean, illus. 2009. 24p. pap. 12.00 *(978-1-4389-8146-8(5))* AuthorHouse.

Peck, J. L. Mr Crabby Pants & the Zoo. 2012. 24p. pap. 17.99 *(978-1-4685-7953-6(3))* AuthorHouse.

Peña-Solis, Marcia. Minna Vu & Her Super Special One of a Kind Fabulous Sparkly New Shoes. 2009. 40p. pap. 21.99 *(978-1-4363-8578-7(4))* Xlibris Corp.

Pennypacker, Sara. Stuart Goes to School. Matje, Martin, illus. 2005. (ENG.). 64p. (J). (gr. -1-3). reprint ed. per. 5.99 *(978-0-439-30183-1(1),* Scholastic Paperbacks) Scholastic, Inc.

Peters, Judy. The Little Blue Curtain. 2008. pap. 9.00 *(978-0-8059-8790-4(8))* Dorrance Publishing Co., Inc.

Pin, Isabel. Bumblebee Blues. James, J. Alison, tr. from GER. 2003. (Illus.). 32p. (J). (gr. k-3). 15.95 *(978-0-7358-1813-2(4));* lib. bdg. 16.50 *(978-0-7358-1814-9(2))* North-South Bks., Inc. (Michael Neugebauer Bks.).

Pitchford, Dean. Captain Nobody. 2010. (ENG.). 208p. (J). (gr. 3-7). 6.99 *(978-0-14-241667-9(3),* Puffin Books) Penguin Young Readers Group.

Pliszka, Jodi. Bella & Gizmo's Adventures: Bella Gets A New Sweater. 2005. (Illus.). 24p. (J). per. 18.95 *(978-1-933449-04-3(7))* Nightengale Pr.

—Bella & Gizmo's Adventures — Bella Gets A New Sweater. 2005. 32p. (J). per. 18.95 *(978-1-933449-26-5(8))* Nightengale Pr.

Plourde, Lynn. Bella's Fall Coat. Gal, Susan, illus. 2016. (ENG.). 40p. (J). (gr. -1-k). 17.99 *(978-1-4847-2697-6(9))* Disney Pr.

Pochocki, Ethel. Rosebud & Red Flannel. 2014. (ENG., Illus.). 32p. (J). (gr. k-4). 16.95 *(978-1-60893-306-8(7))* Down East Bks.

Polak, Monique. The Leggings Revolt, 1 vol. 2016. (Orca Currents Ser.). (ENG.). 144p. (J). (gr. 5-9). pap. 9.95 *(978-1-4598-1189-8(5))* Orca Bk. Pubs. USA.

—Leggings Revolt. 2016. (Orca Currents Ser.). lib. bdg. 20.80 *(978-0-606-38696-8(3))* Turtleback Bks.

Pomranz, Craig. Made by Raffi. Chamberlain, Margaret, illus. 2016. (ENG.). 40p. (J). (gr. 1-4). pap. 9.99 *(978-1-84780-596-6(5),* Frances Lincoln) Quarto Publishing Group UK GBR. Dist: Hachette Bk. Group.

Prelutsky, Jack. The Frogs Wore Red Suspenders. Mathers, Petra, illus. 2005. (ENG.). 64p. (J). (gr. k-5). reprint ed. pap. 6.99 *(978-0-06-073776-4(X),* Greenwillow Bks.) HarperCollins Pubs.

Pressler, Mirjam. Let Sleeping Dogs Lie. Macki, Erik J., tr. from GER. 2007. (ENG.). 208p. (J). (gr. 9-12). 16.95 *(978-1-932425-84-0(5),* Front Street) Boyds Mills Pr.

Price, W. Morris. A Gnu with a Shoe. 2009. 20p. pap. 10.49 *(978-1-4389-4388-6(1))* AuthorHouse.

Probasco, Teri. Blue Jean Gum. 35p. (J). (gr. -1-4). pap. 5.90 *(978-0-932970-95-4(8))* Printit Pr.

Prochovnic, Dawn Babb. One Trick for One Treat: Sign Language for Numbers, 1 vol. Bauer, Stephanie, illus. 2012. (ENG.). 32p. 28.50 *(978-1-61641-838-0(9),* Looking Glass Library) Magic Wagon.

—Wear a Silly Hat: Sign Language for Clothing, 1 vol. Bauer, Stephanie, illus. 2009. (Story Time with Signs & Rhymes Ser.). (ENG.). 32p. (gr. -1-3). 28.50 *(978-1-60270-674-3(3),* Looking Glass Library) ABDO Publishing Co.

Punnett, Dick. Help Dress Priscilla: A Talk-along Book. Dunnington, Tom, illus. 2nd ed. 2005. (Talk-Along Bks.). 32p. (J). pap. 6.99 *(978-0-9657211-3-4(2))* Tomoka Pr.

Raden, Tammy. Priscilla Play. 2010. 28p. 12.49 *(978-1-4520-0808-0(6))* AuthorHouse.

Rainforth, Hannah. Barnaby Bennett, 1 vol. Teo, Ali, illus. 2008. (ENG.). 32p. (J). (gr. -1-3). pap. 5.95 *(978-1-59572-156-3(8))* Star Bright Bks., Inc.

—Barnaby Bennett. Teo, Ali, illus. 2007. 32p. (J). (gr. -1-3). pap. 10.00 *(978-1-86969-232-2(2))* Univ. of Hawaii Pr.

Reidy, Jean. Too Purpley! Leloup, Geneviève, illus. (Too! Bks.). (ENG.). (J). (gr. -1 — 1). 2011. 26p. bds. 7.99 *(978-1-59990-679-9(1),* 9781599906799) 2010. 32p. 11.99 *(978-1-59990-307-1(5),* 9781599903071) Bloomsbury Publishing USA. (Bloomsbury USA Childrens).

Reiner, Angela. You Can't Dance in Those Pants. 2008. 28p. pap. 18.65 *(978-1-4363-6798-1(0))* Xlibris Corp.

Rey, H. A., et al. Curious George Cleans Up. 2007. (Curious George Ser.). (ENG., Illus.). 24p. (J). (gr. -1-3). 3.99 *(978-0-618-73759-8(6))* Houghton Mifflin Harcourt Publishing Co.

Reynolds, Aaron. Creepy Pair of Underwear! Brown, Peter, illus. 2017. (ENG.). 48p. (J). (gr. -1-3). 17.99 *(978-1-4424-0298-0(9),* Simon & Schuster Bks. For Young Readers) Simon & Schuster Bks. For Young Readers.

Richards, Kirsten, illus. My Little Beauty Shop: A Girly Girl Book. 2009. (ENG.). 12p. (J). bds. 6.95 *(978-1-58117-857-9(3),* Intervisual/Piggy Toes) Bendon, Inc.

Rifkin, Sherri & Bennett, Olivia. The Allegra Biscotti Collection. 2010. (ENG., Illus.). 256p. (J). (gr. 6-8). pap. 11.99 *(978-1-4022-4391-2(X),* Sourcebooks Jabberwocky) Sourcebooks, Inc.

Rim, Sujean. Birdie's Big-Girl Dress. 2011. (Birdie Ser.). (ENG., Illus.). 40p. (J). (gr. -1-3). 16.99 *(978-0-316-13287-9(X))* Little Brown & Co.

Rim, Sujean, illus. Birdie's Big-Girl Shoes. 2009. (Birdie Ser.). (ENG.). 40p. (J). (gr. -1-3). 17.99 *(978-0-316-04470-7(9))* Little, Brown Bks. for Young Readers.

Rippin, Sally. The Robot Blues. Spartels, Stephanie, illus. 2014. (ENG.). 48p. (J). pap. 4.99 *(978-1-61067-124-8(4))* Kane Miller.

Rizzi, Kathleen. What's in My Dresser?, 1 vol. Riggs, Jenna, illus. 2013. (ENG.). 32p. (J). bds. 7.99 *(978-1-59572-165-5(7))* Star Bright Bks., Inc.

Robert, Na'ima Bint. The Swirling Hijaab. Mistry, Nilesh, illus. 2004. 24p. (J). *(978-1-85269-910-9(8));* (SER & ENG.). pap. *(978-1-85269-180-6(8));* (POR & ENG.). pap.

(978-1-85269-179-0(4)); (ITA & ENG.). pap. *(978-1-85269-167-7(0))*; (GER & ENG.). pap. *(978-1-85269-165-3(4))*; (PER & ENG.). pap. *(978-1-85269-163-9(8))*; (BEN & ENG.). pap. *(978-1-85269-160-8(3))*; (URD & ENG.). pap. *(978-1-85269-143-1(3))*; (ARA & ENG.). pap. *(978-1-85269-119-6(0))*; (PAN & ENG.). pap. *(978-1-85269-178-3(6))*; (CZE & ENG.). pap. *(978-1-85269-629-0(X))*; (SOM & ENG.). pap. *(978-1-85269-181-3(6))*; (SPA & ENG.). pap. *(978-1-85269-182-0(4))*; (TAM & ENG.). pap. *(978-1-85269-188-2(3))*; (TUR & ENG.). pap. *(978-1-85269-189-9(1))* Mantra Lingua.

Ross, Tony. Centipede's One Hundred Shoes. Ross, Tony, illus. rev. ed. 2003. (ENG., Illus.). 32p. (J). (gr. -1-3). 18.99 *(978-0-8050-7298-3(5)*, 9780805072983, Holt, Henry & Co. Bks. For Young Readers) Holt, Henry & Co.

Rudnick, Paul. Gorgeous. 2013. (ENG.). 336p. (J). (gr. 9). 18.99 *(978-0-545-46426-0(9)*, Scholastic Pr.) Scholastic, Inc.

Rylant, Cynthia. Henry & Mudge & Mrs. Hopper's House. Bracken, Carolyn, illus. 2004. (Ready-to-Read Ser.). 40p. (gr. k-2). 14.00 *(978-0-7569-2200-9(3))* Perfection Learning Corp.

Sanford, Barry. The Shoes. 2007. 84p. per. 19.95 *(978-1-4241-8700-3(1))* America Star Bks.

Santa's Suit. 2006. (Little Elf Set 1 Ser.). (J). 7.33 *(978-1-932570-71-7(3))* Pioneer Valley Bks.

Sava, Scott Christian. Magic Carpet. 2010. (Illus.). 110p. (J). pap. 11.99 *(978-1-60010-563-0(7))* Idea & Design Works, LLC.

Schertle, Alice. The Skeleton in the Closet. Jobling, Curtis, illus. 2003. (ENG.). 32p. (J). (gr. 1-18). 15.99 *(978-0-688-17738-6(7))* HarperCollins Pubs.

Schmauss, Judy Kentor. Parade Day. Chewning, Randy, illus. 2006. (Reader's Clubhouse Level 2 Reader Ser.). (ENG.). 24p. (J). (gr. 1-4). pap. 3.99 *(978-0-7641-3293-3(8))* Barron's Educational Series, Inc.

Schmid, Susan Maupin. Ghost of a Chance. Marlin, Lissy, illus. 2017. (100 Dresses Ser.: 2). (ENG.). 320p. (J). (gr. 3-7). 16.99 *(978-0-553-53373-6(8)*, Random Hse. Bks. for Young Readers) Random Hse. Children's Bks.

—If the Magic Fits. (100 Dresses Ser.: 1). (ENG.). (J). (gr. 3-7). 2017. 320p. 7.99 ***(978-0-553-53369-9(X)***, Yearling) 2016. (Illus.). 304p. 16.99 *(978-0-553-53366-8(5)*, Random Hse. Bks. for Young Readers) Random Hse. Children's Bks.

Scholastic, Inc. Staff & Giovanni, Nikki. The Girls in the Circle. Johnson, Cathy Ann, illus. 2004. (Just for You Ser.). (ENG.). 32p. pap. 3.99 *(978-0-439-56861-6(7)*, Teaching Resources) Scholastic, Inc.

Scholastic Library Publishing. The Three Little Kittens Get Dressed. 2009. (Rookie Preschool Ser.). 24p. (J). (gr. -1). lib. bdg. 23.00 *(978-0-531-24404-3(0)*, Children's Pr.) Scholastic Library Publishing.

Schwartz, Amy. Polka Dots for Poppy. 2016. (ENG., Illus.). 32p. (J). 16.95 *(978-0-8234-3431-2(1))* Holiday Hse., Inc.

Scotton, Rob. Scaredy-Cat, Splat! Scotton, Rob, illus. (Splat the Cat Ser.). (Illus.). 40p. (J). (gr. -1-3). 2015. (ENG.). 9.99 *(978-0-06-236897-3(4))* 2010. (ENG., 16.99 *(978-0-06-117760-6(1))* 2010. lib. bdg. 17.89 *(978-0-06-117761-3(X))* HarperCollins Pubs.

Shaw, Gina. Oh My! Ginny Fry! Barton, Patrice, illus. 2010. 48p. (J). *(978-0-545-24384-1(X))* Scholastic, Inc.

Shaw-Lott, Karen. The Binky Fairy. Marquez, Erick, illus. 2009. 12p. pap. 11.00 *(978-1-60844-271-3(3))* Dog Ear Publishing, LLC.

Shoebridge-Bloom, Melanie. Eleanor. 2009. 21p. 14.95 *(978-0-557-01597-9(9))* Lulu Pr., Inc.

Shuff, Lana Tanaka. Kira Helps A Friend. l.t. ed. 2007. (ENG., Illus.). 28p. (J). per. 9.95 *(978-1-4327-0810-8(4))* Outskirts Pr., Inc.

Siclari, Theresa. The Case of the Missing Hairpin, 1 vol. 2009. 25p. pap. 24.95 *(978-1-60813-865-4(8))* America Star Bks.

Siegal, Ida. Party Drama! (Emma Is on the Air #2) 2015. (Emma Is on the Air Ser.: 2). (ENG.). 128p. (J). (gr. 2-5). pap. 4.99 *(978-0-545-68695-2(4)*, Scholastic Paperbacks) Scholastic, Inc.

Silvano, Wendi. Turkey Trouble, 0 vols. 2009. (ENG., Illus.). 32p. (J). (gr. -1-2). 15.99 *(978-0-7614-5529-5(9)*, 9780761455295, Two Lions) Amazon Publishing.

Smith, Adam. Other People's Shoes. 2008. 36p. pap. 18.50 *(978-1-60693-383-1(3)*, Eloquent Bks.) Strategic Book Publishing & Rights Agency (SBPRA).

Smith, Clete Barrett. Magic Delivery. Dziekan, Michal, illus. 2014. (ENG.). 288p. (J). (gr. 3-7). 16.99 *(978-1-4231-6597-2(7))* Hyperion Bks. for Children.

Smith, Diana M. Every Sock Needs a Mate. 2009. 36p. pap. 17.49 *(978-1-4389-2636-0(7))* AuthorHouse.

Smith, Jeff. Little Mouse Gets Ready. 2009. (ENG., Illus.). 32p. (J). (gr. -1-3). 12.95 *(978-1-935179-01-6(2))* TOON Books / RAW Junior, LLC.

—Little Mouse Gets Ready. 2013. (Toon Books Level 1 Ser.). lib. bdg. 14.75 *(978-0-606-31593-7(4)*, Turtleback) Turtleback Bks.

—Little Mouse Gets Ready, Level 1. 2013. (ENG., Illus.). 32p. (J). (gr. -1-3). pap. 6.99 *(978-1-935179-24-5(1))* TOON Books / RAW Junior, LLC.

Smith, Lauren E. Ashley Enright & the Darnell Diamonds, 1 vol. 2009. 90p. pap. 19.95 *(978-1-60836-332-2(5))* America Star Bks.

Soffe, Caroline Dawn. Bluebell Wood. 2011. 166p. pap. 24.95 *(978-1-4560-5235-5(7))* America Star Bks.

Solomon, Michelle & Pereira, Lavinia. Too Big! Faust, Laurie A., illus. 2009. 24p. pap. 10.96 *(978-1-4251-8949-5(0))* Trafford Publishing.

Soman, David & Davis, Jacky. Doodle All Day with Ladybug Girl. Soman, David, illus. 2014. (Ladybug Girl Ser.). (ENG., Illus.). 32p. (J). (gr. -1-k). 6.99 *(978-0-448-47859-3(5)*, Grosset & Dunlap) Penguin Young Readers Group.

—Who Can Play? 2013. (Penguin Young Readers Level 1 Ser.). lib. bdg. 13.55 *(978-0-606-32148-8(9)*, Turtleback) Turtleback Bks.

Sparklington, Madame & Gurney, Stella. Princess: A Glittering Guide for Young Ladies. Allsop, Sophie et al, illus. 2006. (Genuine & Moste Authentic Guide Ser.: 2). (ENG.). 26p. (J). (gr. 1-4). 15.99 *(978-0-7636-3430-8(1))* Candlewick Pr.

Stephens, Jane. Katie's Too-Big Coat. 2014. (ENG., Illus.). 32p. (J). (gr. -1-3). 16.99 *(978-1-4814-2532-2(3)*, Simon & Schuster Bks. For Young Readers) Simon & Schuster Bks. For Young Readers.

Stevenson-Ringo, Angela. Keith's Shoes. 2009. 28p. pap. 9.95 *(978-1-4327-2344-6(8))* Outskirts Pr., Inc.

—Where Are My Shoes? 2009. 28p. pap. 9.95 *(978-1-4327-2343-9(X))* Outskirts Pr., Inc.

Sticker Dolly Dressing Around the World (Revised) 2017. (Sticker Dolly Dressing Ser.). (ENG.). (J). pap. 9.99 ***(978-0-7945-3980-1(7)***, Usborne) EDC Publishing.

Sticker Dolly Dressing on Vacation (Revised) 2017. (Sticker Dolly Dressing Ser.). (ENG.). (J). pap. 9.99 ***(978-0-7945-3791-3(X)***, Usborne) EDC Publishing.

Stine, Megan, et al. War of the Wardrobes. 2003. (ENG., Illus.). 112p. *(978-0-00-714468-6(7)*, HarperCollins Children's Bks.) HarperCollins Pubs. Ltd.

Stine, R. L. The Scream of the Haunted Mask. 2008. (Goosebumps HorrorLand Ser.: No. 4). (Illus.). 139p. (J). (gr. 4-7). 13.65 *(978-0-7569-8818-0(7))* Perfection Learning Corp.

Stinson, Kathy. One More Clue, 1 vol. 2005. (Lorimer Streetlights Ser.). (ENG.). 104p. (J). (gr. 2-5). 7.95 *(978-1-55028-888-9(1)*, 9781550288889) Lorimer, James & Co., Ltd., Pubs. CAN. Dist: Casemate Pubs. & Bk. Distributors, LLC.

—Red Is Best. Lewis, Robin Baird, illus. 2006. (ENG.). 32p. (J). (gr. -1-1). 7th ed. 19.95 *(978-1-55451-052-8(X)*, 9781554510528) 9th anniv. ed. pap. 6.95 *(978-1-55451-051-1(1)*, 9781554510511) Annick Pr., Ltd. CAN. Dist: Publishers Group West (PGW).

Stripling, Ashley. No clothes for Ashley. 2004. 27p. pap. 24.95 *(978-1-4137-1826-3(4))* PublishAmerica, Inc.

Strohm, Stephanie Kate. Confederates Don't Wear Couture: A Tale of Heartache, Haunting, & Hoop Skirts. 2013. (ENG.). 240p. (YA). (gr. 7). pap. 13.99 *(978-0-547-97258-9(X))* Houghton Mifflin Harcourt Publishing Co.

Su, Lucy. Play Dressing Up. Su, Lucy, illus. 2003. (Kitten & Baby Kitten Ser.). (Illus.). 24p. (J). bds. *(978-1-85602-463-1(6)*, Pavilion Children's Books) Pavilion Bks.

Taback, Simms. Joseph Had a Little Overcoat. Taback, Simms, illus. (Illus.). pap. incl. audio compact disk *(978-1-59112-608-9(8))* Live Oak Media.

Tafolla, Carmen. What Can You Do with a Rebozo? ?Qué Puedes Hacer con un Rebozo? Córdova, Amy & Cordova, Amy, illus. 2009. (SPA & ENG.). 32p. (J). (gr. -1-2). pap. 7.99 *(978-1-58246-271-4(2)*, Tricycle Pr.) Random Hse. Children's Bks.

—What Can You Do with a Rebozo? (¿Qué Puedes Hacer Con un Rebozo?) Córdova, Amy & Córdova, Amy, illus. 2009. (SPA & ENG.). 30p. (J). (gr. -1-2). 14.99 *(978-1-58246-270-7(4)*, Tricycle Pr.) Random Hse. Children's Bks.

The Tale of Jackie Berry. 2005. (J). per. 12.95 *(978-0-9677047-5-3(8))* Marble Hse. Editions.

Taylor, Chloe. Lights, Camera, Fashion! Zhang, Nancy, illus. 2013. (Sew Zoey Ser.: 3). (ENG.). 176p. (J). (gr. 3-7). 15.99 *(978-1-4424-8980-6(4))*; pap. 5.99 *(978-1-4424-8979-0(0))* Simon Spotlight. (Simon Spotlight).

Teddy Tender-Heart: Paper Doll Cut-Out Book. 2006. (J). pap. 5.95 *(978-0-9787319-6-0(4))* Kolluri, Alina M.

Terrell, Andrea M. The Adventures of Sammy the Squirrel: Buying Shoes. Mitchell, Anthony W., illus. 2008. (ENG.). 28p. pap. 13.99 *(978-1-4343-5608-6(6))* AuthorHouse.

Thayer, Kristi. The Life of Pajamas. 2008. 20p. pap. 11.00 *(978-1-60693-221-6(7)*, Eloquent Bks.) Strategic Book Publishing & Rights Agency (SBPRA).

Thompson, Carol. Dressing Up. Thompson, Carol, illus. 2017. (Amazing Me! Ser.: 4). (ENG., Illus.). 12p. (J). (gr. k-k). bds. ***(978-1-84643-960-5(4))*** Child's Play International Ltd.

Tomizawa, Hitoshi. Alien Nine 2, Vol. 2. Pannone, Frank, ed. Jackson, Laura & Kobayashi, Yoko, trs. from JPN. Tomizawa, Hitoshi, illus. 2003. (Illus.). 224p. (gr. 11-18). pap. 15.95 *(978-1-58664-892-3(6)*, CMX 64202G, CPM Manga) Central Park Media Corp.

Tomos, Angharad. Y Llipryn Llwyd. 2005. (WEL., Illus.). 48p. pap. *(978-0-86243-095-5(X))* Y Lolfa.

Too Many Clothes: Individual Title Six-Packs. (Literatura 2000 Ser.). (gr. k-1). 28.00 *(978-0-7635-0068-9(2))* Rigby Education.

Torres, Veronica Hilda. My Mommy's Sweater. Rottinger, Amy, illus. 2013. 24p. pap. 12.95 *(978-1-61244-203-7(X))* Halo Publishing International.

Trottier, Maxine. The Long White Scarf. Craig, David, illus. 2005. (ENG.). 32p. (J). *(978-1-55005-147-6(4))* Fitzhenry & Whiteside, Ltd.

Tunkin, David & National Geographic Learning Staff. New Clothes. 2007. (Windows on Literacy Ser.). (ENG., Illus.). 12p. (J). pap. 10.95 *(978-0-7922-8947-0(1))* CENGAGE Learning.

Twinkle Toes. 2011. (ENG., Illus.). 36p. (J). 15.95 *(978-1-935268-57-4(0))* Halo Publishing International.

Valente, Shannon. The Puddle That Ate My Boot! 2009. 16p. pap. 10.79 *(978-1-4389-5325-0(9))* AuthorHouse.

Van Durme, Leen. Mo & Mac: Socks On! Van Durme, Leen, illus. 2013. (ENG., Illus.). 16p. (J). (— 1). 9.95 *(978-1-60537-176-4(9))* Cobblestone Publishing Co.

Van Fleet, Mara & Wade, Sarah. The Very Mixed-Up Princess. 2009. (Mix & Match Ser.). (ENG., Illus.). 14p. (J). (gr. -1-3). bds. 8.99 *(978-0-7944-1775-8(2))* Reader's Digest Assn., Inc., The.

Van Kersen, Elizabeth. Who's Riley. 2005. (Illus.). 50p. (J). per. 8.99 *(978-1-932338-90-4(X))* Lifevest Publishing, Inc.

Van Slyke, Rebecca. Where Do Pants Go? Robertson, Chris, illus. 2016. (ENG.). 40p. (J). (gr. -1). 9.95 *(978-1-4549-1592-8(7))* Sterling Publishing Co., Inc.

Vantrease, Norma. Ants in My Pants. Cox, Steve, illus. 2004. (Rookie Readers Ser.). 31p. (J). 12.60 *(978-0-7569-4280-9(2))* Perfection Learning Corp.

Vest, Bonnie A. Tuxedo, Oreo, & Socks. 2009. 20p. pap. 10.49 *(978-1-4389-5065-5(9))* AuthorHouse.

Vestiti Nuovi dell Imperatore. pap. 14.95 *(978-88-04-45657-5(4))* Mondadori ITA. Dist: Distribooks, Inc.

Vize, Dania. My Princess Dress up Storybook. 2005. (Illus.). 12p. (J). (gr. -1-3). bds. *(978-1-905051-84-7(0))* Make Believe Ideas.

Wade, Barrie. The Emperor's New Clothes. O'kif, A., illus. 2017. (Must Know Stories: Level 2 Ser.). (ENG.). 32p. (J). (gr. 1-3). pap. 4.99 ***(978-1-4451-4659-1(2)***, Franklin Watts) Hachette Children's Group GBR. Dist: Hachette Bk. Group.

Wake, Shelley. Wrinkly Socks Make Me Giggle. Tufts, N. Jo, illus. 2005. (ENG.). 16p. (gr. k-2). pap. 7.95 *(978-1-57874-086-4(X)*, Kaeden Bks.) Kaeden Corp.

Walker, Anna. Hurry up, Alfie! 2016. (ENG., Illus.). 24p. (J). (gr. -1-3). 14.99 *(978-0-544-58654-3(9))* Houghton Mifflin Harcourt Publishing Co.

Walker, Melzina. Little Melvin's Blue Coat. 2007. (Illus.). 32p. (J). pap. 8.00 *(978-0-8059-7389-1(3))* Dorrance Publishing Co., Inc.

Wang, Margaret. The Right Shoes for Me! Kightly, Rosalinda, illus. 2006. (ENG.). 12p. (J). (gr. -1-k). bds. 9.95 *(978-1-58117-494-6(2)*, Intervisual/Piggy Toes) Bendon, Inc.

Waterton, Betty. A Bumblebee Sweater, 1 vol. LaFave, Kim, illus. 2007. (ENG.). 32p. (J). (gr. -1-3). *(978-1-55455-028-9(9))* Fitzhenry & Whiteside, Ltd.

Watkins, Rowboat. Pete with No Pants. 2017. (ENG., Illus.). 40p. (J). 16.99 *(978-1-4521-4401-6(X))* Chronicle Bks. LLC.

Watson, J. D. My Socks Don't Match. 2004. 41p. pap. 24.95 *(978-1-4137-1935-2(X))* PublishAmerica, Inc.

Watt, Fiona, des. Sticker Dolly Dressing Princess Kit. 2011. (Acitivity Kit Ser.). 24p. (J). pap. 15.99 *(978-1-60130-278-6(9)*, Usborne) EDC Publishing.

Webb, Sarah. Bridesmaid Blitz. 2012. (Ask Amy Green Ser.: 3). (ENG., Illus.). 320p. (YA). (gr. 7). pap. 6.99 *(978-0-7636-5157-2(5))* Candlewick Pr.

Weissman, Elissa Brent. Standing for Socks. Sonkin, Jessica, illus. (ENG.). 224p. (J). (gr. 3-7). 2010. pap. 6.99 *(978-1-4169-9777-1(6))* 2009. 15.99 *(978-1-4169-4801-8(5))* Simon & Schuster Children's Publishing. (Atheneum Bks. for Young Readers).

Wells, Rosemary. Max's New Suit. 2003. (Max & Ruby Ser.). (ENG.). 12p. (J). (gr. 1 — 1). bds. 6.99 *(978-0-670-88718-7(8)*, Viking Books for Young Readers) Penguin Young Readers Group.

West, Tracey. The Clothing Capers. Harrington, Rich, illus. 2007. 96p. (J). pap. *(978-0-439-91452-9(3))* Scholastic, Inc.

Weston, Robert Paul. Prince Puggly of Spud & the Kingdom of Spiff. 2013. (ENG., Illus.). 224p. (J). (gr. 3-7). 15.99 *(978-1-59514-567-3(2)*, Razorbill) Penguin Young Readers Group.

Weston Woods Staff, creator. Owen. 2011. (SPA.). 18.95 *(978-0-439-02177-7(4))*; 38.75 *(978-0-439-02178-4(2))*; 29.95 *(978-0-439-02310-8(6))* Weston Woods Studios, Inc.

White, Mark. The Wolf in Sheep's Clothing: A Retelling of Aesop's Fable, 1 vol. Pérez, Sara Rojo, illus. 2013. (My First Classic Story Ser.). (ENG.). 24p. (gr. k-3). pap. 7.10 *(978-1-4795-1857-9(3)*, My First Classic Story) Picture Window Bks.

White, Mark & Aesop Enterprise Inc. Staff. The Wolf in Sheep's Clothing: A Retelling of Aesop's Fable, 1 vol. Pérez, Sara Rojo, illus. 2011. (My First Classic Story Ser.). (ENG.). 24p. (gr. k-3). lib. bdg. 22.65 *(978-1-4048-6509-9(8)*, My First Classic Story) Picture Window Bks.

Willems, Mo. Naked Mole Rat Gets Dressed. Willems, Mo, illus. 2009. (ENG., Illus.). 40p. (J). (gr. -1 — 1). 16.99 *(978-1-4231-1437-6(X))* Hyperion Pr.

Willems, Mo, et al, narrated by. Naked Mole Rat Gets Dressed. 2011. (J). (gr. -1-2). 29.95 *(978-0-545-29678-6(1))* Weston Woods Studios, Inc.

Williamson, Greg. Why Do I Have to Wear Glasses? Popko, Wendy, illus. 2005. (J). 12.99 *(978-0-9666076-5-9(1))* Peerless Publishing, L.L.C.

—Why Do I Have to Wear Glasses? Popkp, Wendy, illus. 2005. (J). pap. 7.99 *(978-0-9666076-3-5(5))* Peerless Publishing, L.L.C.

Wojtowycz, David, illus. What Will You Wear, Claude? 2004. 10p. (J). (gr. -1-3). reprint ed. 8.00 *(978-0-7567-8259-7(7))* DIANE Publishing Co.

Wood, Maryrose. How I Found the Perfect Dress. 2008. (ENG.). 240p. (YA). (gr. 9-18). 11.00 *(978-0-425-21939-3(9)*, Berkley) Penguin Publishing Group.

Written By Dana Wright; Illustrated By S. Crazy Pants. 2011. 20p. pap. 24.95 *(978-1-4626-3469-9(9))* America Star Bks.

Yazzie, Seraphine G. Beauty Beside Me: Stories of My Grandmother's Skirts. Ruffenach, Jessie Eve, ed. Whitethorne, Baje, Sr., illus. 2011. (NAV & ENG.). 32p. (J). (gr. -1-3). 17.95 *(978-1-893354-77-7(6))* Salina Bookshelf Inc.

Yee, Wong Herbert. A Brand-New Day with Mouse & Mole. (Mouse & Mole Story Ser.). (ENG., Illus.). 48p. (J). (gr. 1-4). 2012. pap. 3.99 *(978-0-547-72209-2(5))* 2008. 15.00 *(978-0-618-96676-9(5))* Houghton Mifflin Harcourt Publishing Co.

—A Brand-New Day with Mouse & Mole. 2012. (Green Light Readers — Level 3 Ser.). lib. bdg. 13.55 *(978-0-606-24437-4(9)*, Turtleback) Turtleback Bks.

Yoon, Salina. Penguin Gets Dressed! Yoon, Salina, illus. 2010. (Illus.). 10p. bds. 7.95 *(978-1-60747-750-1(5)*, Pickwick Pr.) Phoenix Bks., Inc.

Yost, Beth. The Mysterious Sock Caper. 2007. 20p. per. 10.95 *(978-1-4327-1242-6(X))* Outskirts Pr., Inc.

Young, Annemarie. Let's Go Out, 1 vol. Redshaw, Louise, illus. 2013. (Start Reading Ser.). (ENG.). 24p. (gr. k-1). pap. 7.95 *(978-1-4765-3193-9(5))*; pap. 41.94 *(978-1-4765-3223-3(0))* Capstone Press of Coughlan Cos.

Yum, Hyewon. The Twins' Blanket. Yum, Hyewon, illus. 2011. (ENG., Illus.). 40p. (J). (gr. -1-1). 17.99 *(978-0-374-37972-8(6)*, 9780374379728, Farrar, Straus & Giroux (BYR)) Farrar, Straus & Giroux.

Zabel, Vivian. I Like Pink. Nielson, Ginger, illus. 2013. 28p. pap. 12.99 *(978-0-9889617-1-5(7))* 4RV Publishing, LLC.

Zemke, Deborah. Green Boots, Blue Hair, Polka-Dot Underwear. Zemke, Deborah, illus. 2007. (I'm Going to Read(r) Ser.). (ENG., Illus.). 28p. (J). (gr. k-1). pap. 3.95 *(978-1-4027-4245-3(2))* Sterling Publishing Co., Inc.

Zitkus, K S. Krissi Swan: Cover-up Girl. 2007. 120p. per. 10.95 *(978-0-595-42674-4(3))* iUniverse, Inc.

CLOTHING TRADE

Brill, Marlene Targ. Annie Shapiro & the Clothing Workers' Strike. 2010. pap. 56.72 *(978-0-7613-6924-0(4))* Lerner Publishing Group.

Broyles, Janell. The Triangle Shirtwaist Factory Fire Of 1911. 2009. (Tragic Fires Throughout History Ser.). 48p. (gr. 5-8). 53.00 *(978-1-60854-584-1(9)*, Rosen Reference) Rosen Publishing Group, Inc., The.

Downs, Alison. For People Who Are into Fashion. 2016. (Cool Careers Without College Ser.). 00104p. (J). (gr. 7-7). 38.45 *(978-1-5081-7278-9(1))* Rosen Publishing Group, Inc., The.

Espejo, Roman. Fashion Industry. 2010. (Opposing Viewpoints Ser.). (Illus.). 240p. (J). 42.95 *(978-0-7377-4512-2(6))*; pap. 29.45 *(978-0-7377-4513-9(4))* Cengage Gale.

Fashion. 2007. (What Can I Do Now? Ser.). (Illus.). 168p. (YA). (gr. 7-12). 32.95 *(978-0-8160-6029-0(0))* Facts On File, Inc.

Giacabello, John. Careers in the Fashion Industry. 2009. (Career Resource Library). 192p. (gr. 7-12). 63.90 *(978-1-60853-405-0(7))* Rosen Publishing Group, Inc., The.

Greathead, Helen. My T-Shirt & Other Clothing. 2016. (Well Made, Fair Trade Ser.). (ENG., Illus.). 32p. (J). (gr. 5-8). *(978-0-7787-2716-3(5))* Crabtree Publishing Co.

Greathouse, Lisa. Backstage Pass: Fashion, 1 vol. 2nd rev. ed. 2014. (TIME for KIDS(r) Nonfiction Readers Ser.). (ENG., Illus.). 32p. (J). (gr. 3-3). pap. 25.96 *(978-1-4807-1076-4(8))* Shell Educational Publishing.

Hobbs, Mike. Fashion. 2013. (Young Entrepreneurs' Club Ser.). 48p. (gr. 5-11). lib. bdg. 37.10 *(978-1-59920-922-7(5))* Black Rabbit Bks.

Markel, Michelle. Brave Girl: Clara & the Shirtwaist Makers' Strike of 1909. Sweet, Melissa, illus. 2013. (ENG.). 32p. (J). (gr. -1-3). 17.99 *(978-0-06-180442-7(8))* HarperCollins Pubs.

McAlpine, Margaret. Working in the Fashion Industry. 2005. (My Future Career Ser.). (Illus.). 64p. (gr. 3-7). lib. bdg. 27.00 *(978-0-8368-4774-1(1)*, Gareth Stevens Learning Library) Stevens, Gareth Publishing LLLP.

McPherson, Stephanie Sammartino. Levi Strauss. 2007. (History Maker Bios Ser.). (Illus.). 48p. (J). (gr. 3-7). lib. bdg. 26.60 *(978-0-8225-6581-9(1)*, Lerner Pubns.) Lerner Publishing Group.

Miller, Mirella S. Working in Fashion. 2018. (ENG.). 32p. (gr. 3-6). ***(978-1-63235-445-7(4)***, 12-Story Library) Pr. Room Editions LLC.

Senker, Cath. Topshop. 2017. (Big Business Ser.). (ENG., Illus.). 32p. (J). (gr. 4-6). pap. 11.99 *(978-0-7502-8944-3(9)*, Wayland) Hachette Children's Group GBR. Dist: Hachette Bk. Group.

Spilsbury, Louise. The True Cost of Fashion. 2014. (ENG., Illus.). 48p. (J). *(978-0-7787-0483-6(1))*; pap. *(978-0-7787-0487-4(4))* Crabtree Publishing Co.

Teen Vogue Staff. The Teen Vogue Handbook: An Insider's Guide to Careers in Fashion. 2009. (ENG., Illus.). 304p. (YA). (gr. 7-18). pap. 24.95 *(978-1-59514-261-0(4)*, Razorbill) Penguin Young Readers Group.

Thomas, Isabel. Being a Fashion Stylist. 2012. (On the Radar: Awesome Jobs Ser.). (ENG., Illus.). 32p. (gr. 4-8). lib. bdg. 26.60 *(978-0-7613-7778-8(6)*, Lerner Pubns.) Lerner Publishing Group.

Vescia, Monique. Fashion. 2010. (Career Launcher Ser.). (C). (gr. 9). 182p. 34.95 *(978-0-8160-7965-0(X)*, Ferguson Publishing Co.); 192p. pap. 14.95 *(978-0-8160-7987-2(0)*, Checkmark Bks.) Facts On File, Inc.

Walker, Kate. Clothing. 2010. (Recycling Ser.). 32p. (gr. 1). 28.50 *(978-1-60870-128-5(X))* Marshall Cavendish GBR. Dist: Marshall Cavendish Corp.

Walton, Ruth. Let's Get Dressed: Find Out about Clothes & Fabric. 2013. (Let's Find Out Ser.). (Illus.). 32p. (J). (gr. k-5). 28.50 *(978-1-59771-383-2(X))* Sea-To-Sea Pubns.

Wilson, Rosie. Fashion Industry. 2010. (Closer Look: Global Industries Ser.). (ENG.). 48p. (YA). lib. bdg. 29.25 *(978-1-4358-9631-4(9)*, Rosen Reference) Rosen Publishing Group, Inc., The.

CLOTHING TRADE—FICTION

Cleary, Beverly. Socks. Tiegreen, Alan & Dockray, Tracy, illus. 2015. (Avon Camelot Bks.). (ENG.). 160p. (J). (gr. 3-7). pap. 6.99 *(978-0-380-70926-7(0))* HarperCollins Pubs.

Hansen, Jeff. Alibriana Visits the Branch Office. 2009. 36p. pap. 16.99 *(978-1-4389-4534-7(5))* AuthorHouse.

CLOUD, ALEX (FICTITIOUS CHARACTER)—FICTION

Lichtenheld, Tom. Cloudette. Lichtenheld, Tom, illus. 2011. (ENG., Illus.). 40p. (J). (gr. -1-2). 17.99 *(978-0-8050-8776-5(1)*, 9780805087765, Holt, Henry & Co. Bks. For Young Readers) Holt, Henry & Co.

CLOUD SEEDING

see Weather Control

CLOUDS

Bauer, Marion Dane. Clouds. Wallace, John, illus. 2004. (Weather Ready-To-Reads Ser.). (ENG.). 32p. (J). (gr. -1-1). pap. 3.99 *(978-0-689-85441-5(2)*, Simon Spotlight) Simon Spotlight.

Bodden, Valerie. Clouds. 2012. (J). 25.65 *(978-1-60818-146-9(4)*, Creative Education) Creative Co., The.

—Our Wonderful Weather: Clouds. 2014. (Our Wonderful Weather Ser.). (ENG., Illus.). 24p. (J). (gr. 1-3). pap. 9.99 *(978-0-89812-721-8(1)*, Creative Paperbacks) Creative Co., The.

Braidich, Shelby. Learning about Clouds. 2006. (Rosen Real Readers Big Bookstm Ser.). (ENG.). 8p. (gr. k-1). 29.95 *(978-1-4042-6208-9(3))* Rosen Publishing Group, Inc., The.

Capstone Press. Strange but True. 2010. (Strange but True Ser.). (ENG.). 32p. lib. bdg. 101.28 *(978-1-4296-5909-3(2)*, Blazers) Capstone Press of Coughlan Cos.

Clouds: Individual Title Six-Packs. (Literatura 2000 Ser.). (gr. 2-3). 33.00 *(978-0-7635-0222-5(7))* Rigby Education.

Cox Cannons, Helen. Clouds, 1 vol. 2014. (Weather Wise Ser.). (ENG., Illus.). 24p. (gr. -1-1). 22.65 *(978-1-4846-0544-8(6)*, Acorn) Heinemann-Raintree.

Del Moral, Susana. El Mundo A Mi Alrededor: El Cielo. Zaidi, Nadeem, illus. 2005. (Baby Einstein: Libros de Carton Ser.). (SPA.). 12p. (J). (gr. -1). bds. *(978-970-718-312-4(8)*, Silver Dolphin en Español) Advanced Marketing, S. de R. L. de C. V.

Delano, Marfe Ferguson. Explore My World Clouds. 2015. (Explore My World Ser.). (ENG.). 32p. (J). (gr. -1-2). pap. 4.99 *(978-1-4263-1879-5(0)*, National Geographic Children's Bks.) National Geographic Society.

dePaola, Tomie. The Cloud Book. 2010. (CHI., Illus.). 31p. (J). *(978-986-241-116-2(3))* Asian Culture Co., Ltd.

Doudna, Kelly. It Is Cloudy, 1 vol. 2003. (Weather Ser.). (ENG., Illus.). 24p. (J). (gr. k-3). lib. bdg. 24.21 *(978-1-57765-773-6(X)*, SandCastle) ABDO Publishing Co.

Doudna, Kelly & Craig, Diane. Cloud or Fog?, 1 vol. 2016. (This or That? Weather Ser.). (ENG., Illus.). 24p. (J). (gr. k-4). 25.65 *(978-1-62403-953-9(7))* ABDO Publishing Co.

Edison, Erin. Clouds, 1 vol. 2011. (Weather Basics Ser.). (ENG.). 24p. (gr. k-1). pap. 7.29 *(978-1-4296-7077-7(0))*; pap. 41.70 *(978-1-4296-7083-8(5))*; lib. bdg. 26.65 *(978-1-4296-6057-0(0))* Capstone Press of Coughlan Cos. (Pebble Plus).

Edison, Erin & Saunders-Smith, Gail. Nubes. Strictly Spanish LLC. Staff, tr. from ENG. 2013. (Lo Básico Sobre el Tiempo/Weather Basics Ser.).Tr. of Clouds. (SPA, ENG & MUL.). 24p. (gr. k-1). lib. bdg. 26.65 *(978-1-62065-162-9(9))* Capstone Press of Coughlan Cos.

Fleisher, Paul. Vapor, Rain, & Snow: The Science of Clouds & Precipitation. 2010. (Weatherwise Ser.). (ENG.). 48p. (gr. 4-8). lib. bdg. 29.27 *(978-0-8225-7534-4(5))* Lerner Publishing Group.

Hall, Katharine. Nubes: Un Libro de Comparación y Contraste, 1 vol. 2015. (SPA.). 32p. (J). (gr. k-3). pap. 9.95 *(978-1-62855-465-6(7))* Arbordale Publishing.

Hansen, Grace. Clouds, 1 vol. 2016. (ENG., Illus.). 24p. (J). *(978-1-62970-931-4(X))* ABDO Publishing Co.

—Las Nubes. 2016. (Clima Ser.). (SPA.). 24p. (J). (gr. 1-6). pap. 7.95 *(978-1-4966-0692-1(2))* Capstone Classroom.

Harper, Scott. Clouds! 2013. (InfoMax Readers Ser.). (ENG.). 24p. (J). (gr. 2-3). pap. 49.50 *(978-1-4777-2285-5(8))*; pap. 8.25 *(978-1-4777-2284-8(X))* Rosen Publishing Group, Inc., The. (Rosen Classroom).

Herriges, Ann. Clouds. 2006. (Weather Ser.). (ENG., Illus.). 24p. (J). (gr. k-3). lib. bdg. 25.95 *(978-1-60014-024-2(6))* Bellwether Media.

Higgins, Nadia. What Kind of Clouds? Infante, Sara, illus. 2017. (Water All Around Us Ser.). (ENG.). 24p. (gr. 1-3). 33.99 ***(978-1-68410-061-3(5))*** Cantata Learning.

Hirschmann, Kris. It's Cloudy!, 1 vol. 2008. (What's It Like Out? Ser.). (ENG.). 32p. (gr. k-6). 27.07 *(978-1-59928-943-4(1))*, Checkerboard Library) ABDO Publishing Co.

Jensen, Belinda. Weather Clues in the Sky: Clouds. Kurilla, Renee, illus. 2016. (Bel the Weather Girl Ser.). (ENG.). 24p. (J). (gr. -1-3). 25.32 *(978-1-4677-7963-0(6))*, Millbrook Pr.) Lerner Publishing Group.

Korb, Rena. Crazy about Clouds, 1 vol. Reibeling, Brandon, illus. 2007. (Science Rocks Ser.). (ENG.). 32p. (gr. -1-4). 28.50 *(978-1-60270-037-6(0))*, Looking Glass Library-Nonfiction) Magic Wagon.

Las Nubes: Individual Title Six-Packs. (Literatura 2000 Ser.). (SPA.). (gr. 2-3). 33.00 *(978-0-7635-1267-5(2))* Rigby Education.

Lawrence, Ellen. What Are Clouds? 2012. (Weather Wise Ser.). 24p. (J). (gr. -1-3). lib. bdg. 23.93 *(978-1-61772-404-6(1))* Bearport Publishing Co., Inc.

Lowery, Lawrence. Clouds, Rain, Clouds Again. 2013. (I Wonder Why Ser.). (ENG., Illus.). 36p. (J). (gr. k-3). pap. 11.95 *(978-1-938946-12-7(X))* National Science Teachers Assn.

Manners, Jane. Clouds. 2004. (ENG., Illus.). 16p. (J). (gr. 1-1). pap. 10.92 *(978-0-7652-5153-4(1))*, Celebration Pr.) Pearson Schl.

Maunsell, Simonne. Fluffy Clouds. 2013. 20p. pap. 10.95 *(978-1-4525-7180-5(5))*, Balboa Pr.) Author Solutions, Inc.

McAuliffe, Bill. Clouds. 2017. (J). ***(978-1-60818-823-9(X))***, Creative Education) 2010. 47p. (YA). (gr. 4-7). lib. bdg. 23.95 *(978-1-58341-926-7(8))* Creative Co., The.

Meister, Cari. Kit & Mateo Journey into the Clouds: Learning about Clouds, 1 vol. Record, Adam, illus. 2013. (Take It Outside Ser.). (ENG.). 24p. (gr. k-2). pap. 8.95 *(978-1-4795-1936-1(7))*; lib. bdg. 27.32 *(978-1-4048-8315-4(0))* Picture Window Bks.

Montgomery, Mary Sue. A Cloud Is a Cloud Is a What? You've got to be Kidding, 1 vol. 2010. 34p. 24.95 *(978-1-4489-4360-9(4))* PublishAmerica, Inc.

Morgan, Emily. Next Time You See a Cloud. 2017. (Next Time You See Ser.). (ENG., Illus.). 32p. (J). (gr. 2-4). pap. 12.95 *(978-1-938946-36-3(7))* National Science Teachers Assn.

Nelson, Robin. Cloudy. (First Step Nonfiction - Kinds of Weather Ser.). (ENG., Illus.). 8p. (gr. -1-1). 2015. 11.99 *(978-1-5124-1036-5(5))* 2005. pap. 4.95 *(978-0-8225-5368-7(6))*, Lerner Pubns.) Lerner Publishing Group.

Nelson, Robin & National Geographic Learning Staff. A Cloudy Day. 2010. (Rise & Shine Ser.). (ENG., Illus.). 24p. (C). (gr. k-2). pap. 10.95 *(978-0-8225-1961-4(5))* National Geographic School Publishing, Inc.

Orr, Tamra. I Spy in the Sky the Clouds. 2011. (Randy's Corner Ser.). (Illus.). 32p. (J). (gr. k-3). lib. bdg. 25.70 *(978-1-58415-974-2(X))* Mitchell Lane Pubs., Inc.

Peppas, Lynn. How Do Clouds Form? 2012. (ENG.). 24p. (J). pap. *(978-0-7787-4480-1(9))* Crabtree Publishing Co.

—What Are Cirrus Clouds? 2012. (ENG.). 24p. (J). *(978-0-7787-4473-3(6))*; pap. *(978-0-7787-4478-8(7))* Crabtree Publishing Co.

—What Are Cumulus Clouds? 2012. (ENG.). 24p. (J). pap. *(978-0-7787-4479-5(5))* Crabtree Publishing Co.

—What Are Stratus Clouds? 2012. (ENG.). 24p. (J). *(978-0-7787-4476-4(0))*; pap. *(978-0-7787-4481-8(7))* Crabtree Publishing Co.

Pope, Kristen. What Is the Difference Between Clouds & Fog? 2016. (Everyday Earth Science Ser.). (ENG.). 24p. (J). (gr. k-3). 27.07 *(978-1-5038-0794-5(0))*, 210629) Child's World, Inc., The.

Rockwell, Anne F. Clouds. Date not set. 40p. (J). (gr. -1-1). lib. bdg. 16.89 *(978-0-06-029102-0(8))* HarperCollins Pubs.

—Clouds. Lessac, Frané, illus. 2008. (Let's-Read-And-Find-Out Science 1 Ser.). (ENG.). 40p. (J). (gr. -1-1). pap. 5.99 *(978-0-06-445220-5(4))* HarperCollins Pubs.

Sabin, Patricia T. If I Could Fly I Would Play among the Clouds. 2012. 40p. pap. 20.99 *(978-1-4772-7936-6(9))* AuthorHouse.

Scholastic, Inc. Staff, contrib. by. Shapes in the Sky. 2016. (Rookie Toddlers Ser.). (ENG.). 12p. (J). bds. 6.95 *(978-0-531-22457-1(0))*, Children's Pr.) Scholastic Library Publishing.

Schuetz, Kristin. Cloud Cover. 2015. (Understanding Weather Ser.). (ENG., Illus.). 24p. (J). (gr. k-3). lib. bdg. 25.95 *(978-1-62617-250-0(1))*, Blastoff! Readers) Bellwether Media.

Sherman, Josepha. Shapes in the Sky: A Book about Clouds. Wesley, Omarr, illus. 2003. (Amazing Science: Weather Ser.). (ENG.). 24p. (gr. -1-3). 26.65 *(978-1-4048-0097-7(2))*; per. 8.95 *(978-1-4048-0341-1(6))* Picture Window Bks.

Shifler, Ann. The Lone, Lone Cloud. Birky, Rachael, illus. 2012. 28p. pap. 16.00 *(978-1-58158-133-1(5))* McDougal Publishing Co.

Sterling, Kristin. It's Cloudy Today. 2009. (Lightning Bolt Books — What's the Weather Like? Ser.). (ENG., Illus.). 32p. (gr. k-2). 26.60 *(978-0-7613-4256-4(7))*, Lerner Pubns.); pap. 7.95 *(978-0-7613-5019-4(5))* Lerner Publishing Group.

Strange but True, 1 vol. 2010. (Strange but True Ser.). (ENG.). 32p. (gr. 1-2). lib. bdg. 106.60 *(978-1-4296-4554-6(7))*, Blazers) Capstone Press of Coughlan Cos.

Tanner, S. Clouds: Learning the CL Sound. 2009. (PowerPhonics Ser.). 24p. (gr. 1-1). 39.90 *(978-1-60851-439-7(0))*, PowerKids Pr.) Rosen Publishing Group, Inc., The.

Trueit, Trudi Strain. Cloudy Days. 2009. (Benchmark Rebus: Weather Watch Ser.). 24p. (gr. k-1). 15.95 *(978-0-7614-4011-6(9))* Marshall Cavendish Corp.

Webster, Christine. Clouds. (Sky Science Ser.). (Illus.). 24p. (J). 2012. (ENG.). (gr. 4-7). lib. bdg. 27.13 *(978-1-61913-539-0(6))*, AV2 by Weigl) 2006. (gr. 3-7). lib. bdg. 24.45 *(978-1-59036-411-6(2))* 2006. pap. 8.95 *(978-1-59036-417-8(1))* Weigl Pubs., Inc.

—Clouds with Code. 2012. (Sky Science Ser.). (ENG., Illus.). 24p. (J). (gr. 4-7). pap. 12.95 *(978-1-61913-541-3(8))*, AV2 by Weigl) Weigl Pubs., Inc.

Wilshire, Florence A. Messages from the Skies. 2005. 82p. pap. 7.42 *(978-1-4116-4316-1(X))* Lulu Pr., Inc.

The Years of Tears & His Glory, 1. 2003. (Illus.). 240p. per. 10.00 *(978-0-9740882-0-4(X))*, YoT1) C & H Pubns.

CLOWNS

Chwast, Seymour. Bobo's Smile. Chwast, Seymour, illus. 2012. (ENG., Illus.). 32p. (J). (gr. 1-3). 14.99 *(978-1-56846-221-9(2))*, Creative Editions) Creative Co., The.

The Clown: Individual Title Six-Packs. (Chiquilibros Ser.). (gr. k-1). 23.00 *(978-0-7635-0409-0(2))* Rigby Education.

Gordon, Nick. Rodeo Clown. 2013. (Dangerous Jobs Ser.). (ENG., Illus.). 24p. (J). (gr. 3-7). lib. bdg. 25.95 *(978-1-60014-896-5(4))*, Torque Bks.) Bellwether Media.

Kupperberg, Paul. Rodeo Clowns. 2009. (World of Rodeo Ser.). 48p. (gr. 6-6). 53.00 *(978-1-60854-308-3(0))*, Rosen Reference) Rosen Publishing Group, Inc., The.

McManus, Donald. Emmett Kelly: The Greatest Clown on Earth. 2014. (ENG., Illus.). 48p. (J). lib. bdg. 24.00 *(978-1-61248-120-3(5))* Truman State Univ. Pr.

Stolzenberg, Mark. Be a Clown. 2003. (Illus.). 160p. (YA). (gr. 4-12). pap. 10.95 *(978-0-8069-5804-0(9))* Sterling Publishing Co., Inc.

Wilkerson, J. L. Sad-Face Clown: Emmett Kelly. 2004. (Great Heartlanders Ser.). (Illus.). 118p. (J). per. 9.95 *(978-0-9664470-9-5(3))*, AB7093) Acorn Bks.

CLOWNS—FICTION

Adler, David A. Bones & the Clown Mix-Up Mystery, No. 8. Newman, Barbara Johansen, illus. 2011. (Bones Ser.: 8). (ENG.). 32p. (J). (gr. 1-3). 3.99 *(978-0-14-241825-3(0))*, Penguin Young Readers) Penguin Young Readers Group.

August, Elaine. It Only Snows in Brooklyn. 2012. 30p. 24.95 *(978-1-4626-9438-9(1))*; 32p. pap. 24.95 *(978-1-4626-7588-3(3))* America Star Bks.

Belczyk, David. Sometimes Form, Sometimes Vessel. Heming, Kathy, ed. 2009. (Mimi's Kids Ser.: vol. 4). (ENG., Illus.). 120p. pap. 14.95 *(978-0-9712383-8-1(3))* Culturatti Ink.

Brown, Eleanor Russell. Break A Leg They Yelled to the Clown. 2010. 32p. 14.49 *(978-1-4520-7366-8(X))* AuthorHouse.

Bullock, Kathleen. The Clown-Around Kids. Bullock, Kathleen, illus. 2012. (ENG., Illus.). (J). pap. 10.95 *(978-1-61633-223-5(9))* Guardian Angel Publishing, Inc.

Cassidy, Anne. Toby's Trousers. Lewis, Jan, illus. 2005. (Reading Corner Ser.). 24p. (J). (gr. k-3). lib. bdg. 22.80 *(978-1-59771-009-1(1))* Sea-To-Sea Pubns.

Circus Fever. 2008. (Illus.). 32p. (J). 14.95 *(978-0-9796380-0-8(3))* Three Wishes Publishing Co.

Clowns. Date not set. 9.95 *(978-0-89868-287-8(8))* ARO Publishing Co.

Condon, Bill. Riley Clowns Around. Hopgood, Andrew, illus. 2015. (Legends in Their Own Lunchbox Ser.). (ENG.). 48p. (gr. 1-2). pap. 7.99 *(978-1-4966-0240-4(4))*, Legends in Their Own Lunchbox) Capstone Classroom.

Cowley, Joy. Smarty Pants at the Circus Big Book. 2010. 48.25 *(978-1-60559-249-7(8))* Hameray Publishing Group, Inc.

Damschroder, Scott. The Crazy Carnival Clown We Call Croc. 2006. (Illus.). 40p. (J). lib. bdg. 19.95 *(978-0-9754728-1-1(X))* Big Ransom Studio.

Darke, J. A. The Grin in the Dark. Evergreen, Nelson, illus. 2015. (Spine Shivers Ser.). (ENG.). 128p. (gr. 3-4). lib. bdg. 26.65 *(978-1-4965-0217-9(5))* Stone Arch Bks.

Divine, Miss Jill. Miles Smiles. 2008. 88p. pap. 15.95 *(978-1-4092-5052-4(0))* Lulu Pr., Inc.

Eggleton, Jill. Clown's Pants. Smith, Craig, illus. 2003. (Rigby Sails Early Ser.). (ENG.). 16p. (gr. 1-2). pap. 6.95 *(978-0-7578-8723-9(6))* Houghton Mifflin Harcourt Publishing Co.

—Clown's Party. Smith, Craig, illus. 2003. (Rigby Sails Early Ser.). (ENG.). 16p. (gr. 1-2). pap. 6.95 *(978-0-7578-8669-0(8))* Houghton Mifflin Harcourt Publishing Co.

Elga Learns to Juggle. 2006. (J). 6.99 *(978-0-9770918-0-5(5))* Forelle Graphics.

Fancher, Joseph. Sydney's Travels Through Dreamland Part. 2006. 48p. pap. 16.95 *(978-1-4241-3690-2(3))* PublishAmerica, Inc.

The Farmer & the Clown. 2014. (ENG., Illus.). 32p. (J). (gr. -1-3). 17.99 *(978-1-4424-9744-3(0))*, Beach Lane Bks.) Beach Lane Bks.

Friend, Gaythel Boggs & Miller, Dalton. Foundation of a Clown, 1 vol. 2010. 58p. pap. 19.95 *(978-1-4489-8253-0(7))* America Star Bks.

Giamanco, Candice (Bucky). The Sweet Circus. 2012. 36p. pap. 24.95 *(978-1-4626-8537-0(4))* America Star Bks.

Harmening, Gail. How Did Clancey Get His Color?, 1 vol. 2009. 45p. pap. 24.95 *(978-1-60836-440-4(2))* America Star Bks.

Hodes, Loren. Who Would Have Guessed? It's All for the Best! Hodes, Loren, illus. 2006. (Illus.). 32p. (J). (gr. -1-3). 13.95 *(978-1-932443-48-6(7))* Judaica Pr., Inc., The.

Holden, Pam. The Surprise Visitor, 6 pack. Holt, Richard, illus. 2009. (Red Rocket Readers Ser.). (ENG.). 16p. (gr. 2-2). pap. *(978-1-877363-85-6(5))* Flying Start Bks.

Huston, Donna. The Woe down Clown. 2006. (J). spiral bd. 19.95 *(978-0-9771192-1-9(1))* Shayne Publishing.

I Am Jumping, 6 Packs. (Sails Literacy Ser.). 16p. (gr. k-18). 27.00 *(978-0-7635-4404-1(3))* Rigby Education.

I Can Laugh, 6 Packs. (Sails Literacy Ser.). 16p. (gr. k-18). 27.00 *(978-0-7635-4397-6(7))* Rigby Education.

I Like Hats: Individual Title, 6 Packs. (Sails Literacy Ser.). 16p. (gr. k-18). 27.00 *(978-0-7635-4401-0(9))* Rigby Education.

Klein, Adria F. Circus Train & the Clowns, 1 vol. Cameron, Craig, illus. 2013. (Train Time Ser.). (ENG.). 32p. (gr. -1-1). pap. 5.95 *(978-1-4342-6195-3(6))*; pap. 29.70 *(978-1-4342-6303-2(7))*; lib. bdg. 22.65 *(978-1-4342-4782-7(1))* Stone Arch Bks.

Kline, Trish & Donev, Mary. Don't Frown, Clown! KA Reader 9. 2007. (Illus.). 32p. (J). per. 20.00 *(978-1-934307-02-1(5))* Ghost Hunter Productions.

Lee, Vanessa Rose. Funny Jimmy. 2011. 28p. pap. 21.00 *(978-1-4567-2347-7(2))* AuthorHouse.

Lubar, David. Dunk. 2004. (ENG.). 272p. (YA). (gr. 7-18). reprint ed. pap. 7.99 *(978-0-618-43909-6(9))* Houghton Mifflin Harcourt Publishing Co.

MacDonald, Steven. Just Clowning Around: Two Stories. McPhail, David, illus. 2003. (Green Light Readers — Level 1 Ser.). 20p. (gr. -1-3). lib. bdg. 13.50 *(978-0-613-66362-5(4))*, Turtleback) Turtleback Bks.

Moncure, Jane Belk. A Color Clown Comes to Town: A Book about Recognizing Colors. Girouard, Patrick, illus. 2013. (Magic Castle Readers Ser.). (ENG.). 32p. (J). (gr. -1-2). 25.64 *(978-1-62323-565-9(0))*, 206299) Child's World, Inc., The.

Montgomery Gibson, Jane. Sit down, Clown! Montgomery Gibson, Jane, illus. 2005. (Illus.). (J). bds. 8.99 *(978-1-4183-0040-1(3))* Christ Inspired, Inc.

Paquette, Jessica E. Sophie the Clown in Crinkle Town. 2013. 258p. (gr. 4-6). 26.95 *(978-1-4759-7322-8(5))*; pap. 16.95 *(978-1-4759-7321-1(7))* iUniverse, Inc.

Parker, Meeta. Cookie the Clown. 2007. 56p. per. 16.95 *(978-1-4241-7917-6(3))* America Star Bks.

Petrowski, Carol. The Clown Who Wears Many Hats. 2011. 24p. pap. 15.99 *(978-1-4653-3700-9(8))* Xlibris Corp.

The Printing Machine: Individual Title Six-Packs. (Literatura 2000 Ser.). (gr. 1-2). 28.00 *(978-0-7635-0105-1(0))* Rigby Education.

Ray, Crystol T. Grumpy the Clown. 2011. 24p. pap. 24.95 *(978-1-4560-6627-7(7))* America Star Bks.

Richards, J. Danielle Jennson, Life Lessons of a Little Clown. 2006. 72p. per. 8.95 *(978-1-59824-187-7(7))* E-BookTime LLC.

Rostoker-Gruber, Karen. Maddie the Mitzvah Clown. 2016. (J). *(978-1-68115-523-4(0))* Behrman Hse., Inc.

Russell Brown, Eleanor. A C Robat Goes to Circus School. 2009. 32p. pap. 14.49 *(978-1-4389-3939-1(6))* AuthorHouse.

Santillo, LuAnn. Funny Clowns. Santillo, LuAnn, ed. 2003. (Half-Pint Kids Readers Ser.). (Illus.). 7p. (J). (gr. -1-1). pap. 1.00 *(978-1-59256-116-2(0))* Half-Pint Kids, Inc.

Sara & the Crying Clown. 2006. (J). *(978-1-933343-15-0(X))* Stabenfeldt Inc.

Scalzo, Linda V. Carazona's Coloring Book. l.t. ed. 2004. (Illus.). 8p. (J). 2.99 *(978-0-9753724-3-2(2))* Carazona Creations LLC.

—The Circus Is Coming to Town: Full-Length Version. l.t. ed. 2004. (Illus.). 32p. (J). 9.99 *(978-0-9753724-0-1(8))* Carazona Creations LLC.

Segal, Andrew. Clarissa the Clown. Scott, Peter & JessT, Grant, illus. 2007. 32p. per. *(978-1-905823-20-8(7))* Panoma Pr. Ltd.

Shan, Darren, pseud. Zom-B, Bk. 10. 2015. (Zom-B Ser.: 10). (ENG., Illus.). 208p. (YA). (gr. 7-17). 15.99 *(978-0-316-21422-3(1))* Little, Brown Bks. for Young Readers.

Shipton, Paul. Clown School. Blake, Beccy, illus. 2005. (ENG.). 24p. (J). lib. bdg. 23.65 *(978-1-59646-752-1(5))* Dingles & Co.

The Silly Circus. 2007. (Illus.). 29p. (J). pap. 14.95 *(978-0-615-18357-2(3))* Carolyn & Kristina's Bookshelf.

Stewart, Paul & Riddell, Chris. Far-Flung Adventures: Corby Flood. 2012. (Far-Flung Adventures Ser.). (ENG.). 256p. (J). (gr. 3-7). 7.99 *(978-0-385-75097-4(8))*, Yearling) Random Hse. Children's Bks.

Stine, R. L. A Nightmare on Clown Street. 2015. (Goosebumps: Most Wanted Ser.: 7). (ENG.). 160p. (J). (gr. 3-7). pap. 6.99 *(978-0-545-62774-0(5))*, Scholastic Paperbacks) Scholastic, Inc.

Los tres Bobos: Individual Title, 6 Packs. (Literatura 2000 Ser.). (SPA.). (gr. 2-3). 33.00 *(978-0-7635-1274-3(5))* Rigby Education.

Turner, Mary. Colored Balloons & Clowns. 2012. 28p. pap. 21.99 *(978-1-4771-0004-2(0))* Xlibris Corp.

Ward, Matthew. The Fantastic Family Whipple. 2014. (Fantastic Family Whipple Ser.: 1). (ENG.). 400p. (J). (gr. 3-7). pap. 8.99 *(978-1-59514-690-8(3))*, Razorbill) Penguin Young Readers Group.

Weston Woods Staff, creator. Clown of God. 2011. 38.75 *(978-0-545-14915-0(0))* Weston Woods Studios, Inc.

—The Clown of God. 2011. 18.95 *(978-0-545-08632-5(9))*; 29.95 *(978-0-545-08638-7(8))* Weston Woods Studios, Inc.

CLUBS

Blackmon, Clarissa. Join the Club! Foundations for Multiplication. 2014. (Rosen Common Core Math Readers Ser.). 24p. (J). (gr. 2-3). (ENG.). pap. 49.50 *(978-1-4777-4643-1(9))*; (Illus.). 23.60 *(978-1-4777-6425-1(9))* Rosen Publishing Group, Inc., The. (Rosen Classroom).

Gold, Susan Dudley. Roberts v. Jaycees: Women's Rights. 2008. (Supreme Court Milestones Ser.). 128p. (gr. 7-18). lib. bdg. 42.79 *(978-0-7614-2952-4(2))*, Benchmark Bks.) Marshall Cavendish Corp.

The Robotics Club: Teaming up to Build Robots. 2011. (Robotics Ser.). (Illus.). 32p. (YA). pap. 11.75 *(978-1-4488-2251-5(3))* Rosen Publishing Group, Inc., The.

Rowe, Brooke. What Club Should You Try? 2015. (Illus.). 32p. (J). *(978-1-63470-033-7(3))* Cherry Lake Publishing.

Shea, Therese. The Robotics Club: Teaming up to Build Robots. 2011. (Robotics Ser.). (Illus.). 48p. (YA). (gr. 5-9). lib. bdg. 29.25 *(978-1-4488-1237-0(2))* Rosen Publishing Group, Inc., The.

Winter, Jonah. Paul Revere & the Bell Ringers. Dodson, Bert, illus. 2003. (Ready-To-read COFA Ser.). (ENG.). 32p. (J). (gr. k-2). pap. 3.99 *(978-0-689-85635-8(0))*, Simon Spotlight) Simon Spotlight.

CLUBS—FICTION

Angleberger, Tom. The Rat with the Human Face. 2015. (Qwikpick Papers). (ENG., Illus.). 160p. (J). (gr. 3-7). 12.95 *(978-1-4197-1489-4(9))*, Amulet Bks.) Abrams, Inc.

Archer, Nick & McDonald, Megan. Rule of Three. 2010. (Sisters Club Ser.: 2). (ENG., Illus.). 240p. (J). (gr. 3-7). pap. 5.99 *(978-0-7636-4830-5(2))* Candlewick Pr.

—Rule of Three. Consolazio, Pamela A., illus. 2009. (Sisters Club Ser.: 2). (ENG.). 240p. (J). (gr. 3-7). 15.99 *(978-0-7636-4153-5(7))* Candlewick Pr.

Arensen, Shel. The Poison Arrow Tree. 2003. (Rugendo Rhino Ser.). (Illus.). 128p. (J). pap. 5.99 *(978-0-8254-2041-2(5))* Kregel Pubns.

Badger, Meredith. Fairy School Dropout Undercover. 2011. (Fairy School Ser.: 2). (ENG., Illus.). 160p. (J). (gr. 2-4). pap. 14.99 *(978-0-312-61951-0(0))*, 9780312619510) Square Fish.

Baker, Kim. Pickle: The (Formerly) Anonymous Prank Club of Fountain Point Middle School. Probert, Tim, illus. 2014. (ENG.). 256p. (J). (gr. 3-7). pap. 7.99 *(978-1-250-04427-3(8))*, 9781250044273) Square Fish.

Baker, Kimberly. Pickle: The (Formerly) Anonymous Prank Club of Fountain Point Middle School. Probert, Tim, illus. 2012. (ENG.). 240p. (J). (gr. 3-7). 16.99 *(978-1-59643-765-4(0))*, 9781596437654) Roaring Brook Pr.

Barkley, Callie. All about Ellie. Riti, Marsha, illus. 2013. (Critter Club Ser.: 2). (ENG.). 128p. (J). (gr. k-2). 15.99 *(978-1-4424-5789-8(9))*; pap. 5.99 *(978-1-4424-5788-1(0))* Little Simon. (Little Simon).

—All about Ellie. 2013. (Critter Club Ser.: 2). lib. bdg. 16.00 *(978-0-606-27024-3(8))*, Turtleback) Turtleback Bks.

—Amy Is a Little Bit Chicken. Bishop, Tracy, illus. 2015. (Critter Club Ser.: 13). (ENG.). 128p. (J). (gr. k-4). pap. 5.99 *(978-1-4814-5174-1(X))*, Little Simon) Little Simon.

—Amy Meets Her Stepsister. Riti, Marsha, illus. 2013. (Critter Club Ser.: 5). (ENG.). 128p. (J). (gr. k-2). 15.99 *(978-1-4424-8216-6(8))*; pap. 5.99 *(978-1-4424-8215-9(X))* Little Simon. (Little Simon).

—Amy Meets Her Stepsister. 2013. (Critter Club Ser.: 5). lib. bdg. 16.00 *(978-0-606-32320-8(1))*, Turtleback) Turtleback Bks.

—Amy on Park Patrol. Bishop, Tracy, illus. 2017. (Critter Club Ser.: 17). (ENG.). 128p. (J). (gr. k-3). pap. 5.99 ***(978-1-4814-9432-8(5))***, Little Simon) Little Simon.

—The Critter Club: Amy & the Missing Puppy; All about Ellie; Liz Learns a Lesson. Riti, Marsha, illus. 2014. (Critter Club Ser.). (ENG.). 368p. (J). (gr. k-4). pap. 8.99 *(978-1-4814-2770-8(9))*, Little Simon) Little Simon.

—Ellie the Flower Girl. Bishop, Tracy, illus. 2016. (Critter Club Ser.: 14). (ENG.). 128p. (J). (gr. k-4). pap. 5.99 *(978-1-4814-6718-6(2))*, Little Simon) Little Simon.

—Liz at Marigold Lake. Riti, Marsha, illus. 2014. (Critter Club Ser.: 7). (ENG.). 128p. (J). (gr. k-4). pap. 5.99 *(978-1-4424-9525-8(1))*, Little Simon) Little Simon.

—Liz at Marigold Lake. 2014. (Critter Club Ser.: 7). lib. bdg. 16.00 *(978-0-606-35445-5(X))* Turtleback Bks.

—Liz Learns a Lesson. Riti, Marsha, illus. 2013. (Critter Club Ser.: 3). (ENG.). 128p. (J). (gr. -1-2). 16.99 *(978-1-4424-6770-5(3))*; pap. 5.99 *(978-1-4424-6768-2(1))* Little Simon. (Little Simon).

—Liz Learns a Lesson. 2013. (Critter Club Ser.: 3). lib. bdg. 16.00 *(978-0-606-32032-0(6))*, Turtleback) Turtleback Bks.

—Liz's Night at the Museum. Bishop, Tracy, illus. 2016. (Critter Club Ser.: 15). (ENG.). 128p. (J). (gr. k-4). pap. 5.99 *(978-1-4814-7164-0(3))*, Little Simon) Little Simon.

—Marion Takes a Break. Riti, Marsha, illus. 2013. (Critter Club Ser.: 4). (ENG.). 128p. (J). (gr. k-2). 16.99 *(978-1-4424-6773-6(8))*; pap. 5.99 *(978-1-4424-6772-9(X))* Little Simon. (Little Simon).

—Marion Takes a Break. 2013. (Critter Club Ser.: 4). lib. bdg. 16.00 *(978-0-606-32045-0(8))*, Turtleback) Turtleback Bks.

—Marion Takes Charge. Riti, Marsha, illus. 2015. (Critter Club Ser.: 12). (ENG.). 128p. (J). (gr. k-4). pap. 5.99 *(978-1-4814-2408-0(4))*, Little Simon) Little Simon.

Barshaw, Ruth McNally. The Ellie McDoodle Diaries: Most Valuable Player. Barshaw, Ruth McNally, illus. 2013. (Ellie Mcdoodle Diaries). (ENG., Illus.). 192p. (YA). (gr. 3-6). 12.99 *(978-1-61963-176-2(8))*, 9781619631762, Bloomsbury USA Childrens) Bloomsbury Publishing USA.

Bateman, Teresa. The Bully Blockers Club. Urbanovic, Jackie, illus. 2004. (ENG.). 32p. (J). (gr. 1-3). 6.99 *(978-0-8075-0919-7(1))* Whitman, Albert & Co.

Bauer, Marion Dane. The Double-Digit Club. 2004. (ENG.). 126p. (J). (gr. 4-6). tchr. ed. 16.95 *(978-0-8234-1805-3(7))* Holiday Hse., Inc.

Berk, Sheryl & Berk, Carrie. Baby Cakes. 2014. (Cupcake Club Ser.: 5). (ENG.). 160p. (J). (gr. 3-6). pap. 6.99 *(978-1-4022-8330-7(X))*, Sourcebooks Jabberwocky) Sourcebooks, Inc.

—Bakers on Board. 2016. (Cupcake Club Ser.: 9). (ENG.). 128p. (J). (gr. 3-7). pap. 7.99 *(978-1-4926-2085-3(8))*, 9781492620853, Sourcebooks Jabberwocky) Sourcebooks, Inc.

—Cupcake Club Box Set: Books 1-3. 2013. (Cupcake Club Ser.: 0). (ENG.). (J). (gr. 3-6). 19.99 *(978-1-4022-9139-5(6))*, Sourcebooks Jabberwocky) Sourcebooks, Inc.

—Icing on the Cake. 2013. (Cupcake Club Ser.: 4). (ENG.). 160p. (J). (gr. 3-6). pap. 6.99 *(978-1-4022-8327-7(X))*, Sourcebooks Jabberwocky) Sourcebooks, Inc.

—Royal Icing: The Cupcake Club. 2014. (Cupcake Club Ser.: 6). (ENG.). 144p. (J). (gr. 3-7). pap. 6.99 *(978-1-4022-8333-8(4))*, Sourcebooks Jabberwocky) Sourcebooks, Inc.

—Sugar & Spice: The Cupcake Club. 2015. (Cupcake Club Ser.: 7). (ENG.). 160p. (J). (gr. 3-7). pap. 6.99 *(978-1-4022-8336-9(9))*, Sourcebooks Jabberwocky) Sourcebooks, Inc.

—Sweet Victory. 2015. (Cupcake Club Ser.: 8). (ENG.). 128p. (J). (gr. 3-7). pap. 6.99 (978-1-4926-2082-2(3), Sourcebooks Jabberwocky) Sourcebooks, Inc.

Borden, Louise. The John Hancock Club. Gustavson, Adam, illus. 2007. (ENG.). 48p. (J). (gr. 2-5). 17.99 (978-1-4169-1813-4(2), McElderry, Margaret K. Bks.) McElderry, Margaret K. Bks.

Bourgeois, Paulette. Franklin's Secret Club. 2004. (Illus.). (J). (gr. k-3). spiral bd. (978-0-616-01593-3(3)); spiral bd. (978-0-616-01594-0(1)) Canadian National Institute for the Blind/Institut National Canadien pour les Aveugles.

Brezenoff, Steve. I Dare You! Hilliker, Phillip, illus. 2008. (Vortex Bks.). (ENG.). 112p. (gr. 2-3). 26.65 (978-1-4342-0798-2(6), Vortex Bks.) Stone Arch Bks.

Brinley, Bertrand R. The Big Chunk of Ice: The Last Known Adventure of the Mad Scientists' Club. Geer, Charles, illus. 2005. (Mad Scientist Club Ser.). 275p. (J). (gr. 3-7). 18.95 (978-1-930900-29-5(5)) Purple Hse. Pr.

—The Big Kerplop! The Original Adventure of the Mad Scientist's Club. Geer, Charles, illus. 2003. 238p. (J). 17.95 (978-1-930900-22-6(8)) Purple Hse. Pr.

—The Mad Scientists' Club. Geer, Charles, illus. 50th ed. 2011. (J). 18.95 (978-1-930900-53-0(8)) Purple Hse. Pr.

Brody, Jessica. The Karma Club. 2011. (ENG.). 288p. (YA). (gr. 7-12). pap. 10.99 (978-0-312-67473-1(2), 9780312674731) Square Fish.

Bryant, Bonnie. Horse Play. 2007. (Saddle Club(R) Ser.: No. 7). (ENG.). 144p. (J). (gr. 3-7). 5.99 (978-0-553-15754-3(X), Yearling) Random Hse. Children's Bks.

Bui-Quang, Phuong-Mai. Tea Club. 2006. (YA). per. 10.95 (978-1-59971-581-0(3)) Aardvark Global Publishing.

Carlson, Melody. Raising Faith, 1 vol. 2016. (Faithgirlz / Girls of Harbor View Ser.). (ENG.). 272p. (J). pap. 9.99 (978-0-310-75375-9(9)) Zonderkidz.

Chebatte, Helen. Bro. 2016. (ENG.). 240p. (YA). (gr. 7). pap. 14.99 **(978-1-76012-550-9(4))** Hardie Grant Egmont Pty, Ltd. AUS. Dist: Independent Pubs. Group.

Cleary, Beverly. Henry & the Clubhouse. Darling, Louis et al, illus. 2014. (Henry Huggins Ser.: 5). (ENG.). 224p. (J). (gr. 3-7). 16.99 (978-0-688-21381-7(2)) HarperCollins Pubs.

Clements, Andrew. The Losers Club. 2017. (ENG.). 240p. (J). (gr. 3-7). 16.99 **(978-0-399-55755-2(5)**, Random Hse. Bks. for Young Readers) Random Hse. Children's Bks.

Cosson, M. J. The Mystery of the Old Car. 2005. (Cover-to-Cover Kooties Club Mysteries Ser.). (Illus.). 56p. (J). (gr. k-3). lib. bdg. 14.95 (978-0-7569-4606-7(9)) Perfection Learning Corp.

The Critter Club Collection: A Purrfect Four-Book Boxed Set: Amy & the Missing Puppy; All about Ellie; Liz Learns a Lesson; Marion Takes a Break. 2014. (Critter Club Ser.). (ENG., Illus.). 512p. (J). (gr. k-4). pap. 23.99 (978-1-4814-0664-2(7), Little Simon) Little Simon.

Crutcher, Chris. Period 8. 2013. 288p. (YA). (gr. 9). (ENG.). 17.99 (978-0-06-191480-5(0)); lib. bdg. 18.89 (978-0-06-191481-2(9)) HarperCollins Pubs. (Greenwillow Bks.).

Danko, Dan & Mason, Tom. The Brotherhood of Rotten Babysitters. Gott, Barry, illus. 5th ed. 2005. (ENG.). 144p. (J). (gr. 3-7). pap. 15.99 (978-0-316-15895-4(X)) Little, Brown Bks. for Young Readers.

Dave & Matt. Yuck's Fart Club. Baines, Nigel, illus. 2013. (Yuck Ser.). (ENG.). 112p. (J). (gr. 2-5). pap. 6.99 (978-1-4424-8152-7(8), Simon & Schuster/Paula Wiseman Bks.) Simon & Schuster/Paula Wiseman Bks.

Davis, Eleanor. Secret Science Alliance. 2010. (J). (978-1-59990-143-5(9)) Bloomsbury Publishing USA.

—The Secret Science Alliance. Davis, Eleanor, illus. 2009. (ENG., Illus.). 160p. (YA). (gr. 3-6). pap. 16.99 (978-1-59990-396-5(2), 9781599903965, Bloomsbury USA Childrens) Bloomsbury Publishing USA.

—The Secret Science Alliance & the Copycat Crook. Davis, Eleanor, illus. 2009. (ENG., Illus.). 160p. (J). (gr. 3-6). 18.99 (978-1-59990-142-8(0), 9781599901428, Bloomsbury USA Childrens) Bloomsbury Publishing USA.

De la Cruz, Melissa. Popularity Takeover. 2015. (Ashley Project Ser.: 4). (ENG., Illus.). 272p. (J). (gr. 4-8). 17.99 (978-1-4814-0974-2(3), Aladdin) Simon & Schuster Children's Publishing.

Decker-Ahmed, Stasia. The Weirder the Better. 2011. (ENG.). 175p. (J). (gr. 4-6). pap. 8.99 (978-0-930773-97-7(7)) Black Heron Pr.

DeLaCroix, Alice. How to Survive a Totally Boring Summer. Fisher, Cynthia, illus. 2007. (ENG.). 96p. (J). (gr. 1-4). 16.95 (978-0-8234-2024-7(8)) Holiday Hse., Inc.

Deriso, Christine Hurley. The Right-Under Club: Second Stage. 2010. (J). (978-0-385-73621-3(5)); lib. bdg. (978-0-385-90593-0(9)) Random House Publishing Group. (Delacorte Pr).

deRubertis, Barbara. Corky Cub's Crazy Caps. Alley, R. W., illus. 2010. (Animal Antics A to Z Ser.). 32p. (J). lib. bdg. 22.60 (978-1-57565-306-8(0)); (ENG.). (gr. -1-3). pap. 7.95 (978-1-57565-302-0(8)) Kane Press, Inc.

deRubertis, Barbara & DeRubertis, Barbara. Corky Cub's Crazy Caps. Alley, R. W., illus. 2012. (Animal Antics A to Z Ser.). 32p. (J). (gr. 2 — 1). cd-rom 7.95 (978-1-57565-396-9(6)) Kane Press, Inc.

Dinan, Kurt. Don't Get Caught. 2016. (ENG.). 336p. (YA). (gr. 8-12). pap. 10.99 (978-1-4926-3014-2(4), 9781492630142) Sourcebooks, Inc.

Draper, Sharon M. The Battle of Jericho. (Jericho Trilogy Ser.: 1). (ENG., Illus.). (YA). (gr. 7). 2017. 320p. pap. 9.99 **(978-1-4814-9029-0(X)**, Atheneum/Caitlyn Dlouhy Books) 2003. 304p. 19.99 (978-0-689-84232-0(5), Atheneum Bks. for Young Readers) Simon & Schuster Children's Publishing.

—The Battle of Jericho. 2005. (Jericho Trilogy Ser.). (ENG., Illus.). 352p. (YA). (gr. 7). mass mkt. 7.99 (978-0-689-84233-7(3), Simon Pulse) Simon Pulse.

—The Buried Bones Mystery. Watson, Jesse Joshua, illus. 2011. (Clubhouse Mysteries Ser.: 1). (ENG.). 112p. (J). (gr. 3-7). pap. 5.99 (978-1-4424-2709-9(4), Aladdin) Simon & Schuster Children's Publishing.

—The Buried Bones Mystery. Watson, Jesse Joshua, illus. 2011. (Clubhouse Mysteries Ser.: 1). (ENG.). 112p. (J). (gr. 3-7). lib. bdg. 15.99 (978-1-4424-2710-5(8), Simon & Schuster/Paula Wiseman Bks.) Simon & Schuster/Paula Wiseman Bks.

Durand, Hallie. Just Desserts. Davenier, Christine, illus. (ENG.). (J). (gr. 2-5). 2011. 224p. pap. 5.99 (978-1-4169-6388-2(X)) 2010. 208p. 15.99 (978-1-4169-6387-5(1)) Simon & Schuster Children's Publishing. (Atheneum Bks. for Young Readers).

Elliott, David. The Cool Crazy Crickets Club. Meisel, Paul, illus. 2010. (ENG.). 48p. (J). (gr. 1-4). 5.99 (978-0-7636-4659-2(8)) Candlewick Pr.

—The Cool Crazy Crickets to the Rescue. Meisel, Paul, illus. 2010. (ENG.). 48p. (J). (gr. 1-4). 5.99 (978-0-7636-4658-5(X)) Candlewick Pr.

English, Karen. Nikki & Deja. Freeman, Laura, illus. 2009. (ENG.). 80p. (J). (gr. -1-3). pap. 5.99 (978-0-547-13362-1(6)) Houghton Mifflin Harcourt Publishing Co.

Eulberg, Elizabeth. The Lonely Hearts Club. (ENG.). 304p. (J). 2011. (gr. 3-7). pap. 8.99 (978-0-545-14032-4(3)) 2010. (gr. 9-12). 17.99 (978-0-545-14031-7(5)) Scholastic, Inc.

Feldman, Thea. ASPCA Pet Rescue Club - Too Big to Run. 2015. (ENG.). 128p. (J). (gr. 1-3). lib. bdg. 16.99 (978-0-7944-3513-4(0), Reader's Digest Children's Bks.) Studio Fun International.

Frederick, Heather Vogel. Mother-Daughter Book Camp. 2016. (Mother-Daughter Book Club Ser.). (ENG., Illus.). 336p. (J). (gr. 5-9). 16.99 (978-1-4424-7183-2(2), Simon & Schuster Bks. For Young Readers) Simon & Schuster Bks. For Young Readers.

—The Mother-Daughter Book Club. (Mother-Daughter Book Club Ser.). (ENG.). (J). 2008. 288p. (gr. 4-7). pap. 7.99 (978-1-4169-7079-8(7)) 2007. (Illus.). 256p. (gr. 5-7). 17.99 (978-0-689-86412-4(4)) Simon & Schuster Bks. For Young Readers. (Simon & Schuster Bks. For Young Readers).

—Pies & Prejudice. (Mother-Daughter Book Club Ser.). (ENG.). (J). (gr. 4-7). 2011. 400p. pap. 8.99 (978-1-4424-2019-9(7)) 2010. 384p. 15.99 (978-1-4169-7431-4(8)) Simon & Schuster Bks. For Young Readers. (Simon & Schuster Bks. For Young Readers).

—Wish You Were Eyre. 2013. (Mother-Daughter Book Club Ser.). (ENG.). 480p. (J). (gr. 4-9). pap. 7.99 (978-1-4424-3065-5(6), Simon & Schuster Bks. For Young Readers) Simon & Schuster Bks. For Young Readers.

Freeman, Martha. Campfire Cookies. 2016. (Secret Cookie Club Ser.). (ENG., Illus.). 288p. (J). (gr. 3-7). 16.99 (978-1-4814-4821-5(8), Simon & Schuster/Paula Wiseman Bks.) Simon & Schuster/Paula Wiseman Bks.

—P. S. Send More Cookies. 2017. (Secret Cookie Club Ser.). (ENG., Illus.). 336p. (J). (gr. 3-7). 16.99 **(978-1-4814-4824-6(2)**, Simon & Schuster/Paula Wiseman Bks.) Simon & Schuster/Paula Wiseman Bks.

Freeman, Martha. The Secret Cookie Club. 2015. (Secret Cookie Club Ser.). (ENG., Illus.). 304p. (J). (gr. 3-7). 16.99 (978-1-4814-1046-5(6), Simon & Schuster Bks. For Young Readers) Simon & Schuster Bks. For Young Readers.

Gabriel, Nat. Bubble Trouble. Nez, John, illus. 2004. 32p. (J). lib. bdg. 20.00 (978-1-4242-1085-5(2)) Fitzgerald Bks.

—Bubble Trouble. Nez, John, tr. Nez, John, illus. 2004. (Science Solves It! Ser.). 32p. (J). pap. 5.95 (978-1-57565-133-0(5)) Kane Press, Inc.

—Bubble Trouble. Nez, John, illus. 2004. (Science Solves It Ser.). 32p. (gr. -1-3). 15.00 (978-0-7569-4286-1(1)) Perfection Learning Corp.

Gallagher, Diana G. Whatever! The Complicated Life of Claudia Cristina Cortez, 1 vol. Garvey, Brann, illus. 2007. (Claudia Cristina Cortez Ser.). (ENG.). 88p. (gr. 2-3). pap. 6.10 (978-1-59889-880-4(9)); lib. bdg. 26.65 (978-1-59889-839-2(6)) Stone Arch Bks. (Claudia Cristina Cortez).

Galvin, Laura Gates. Mickey Mouse Clubhouse Fun with Numbers & Shapes. 2008. (ENG.). 20p. (J). (gr. -1-3). 9.99 (978-1-59069-655-2(7)) Studio Mouse LLC.

Garant, Andre J. Jake's Tree House. 2010. 128p. pap. 10.99 (978-1-4490-8369-4(2)) AuthorHouse.

Gene, Barbara. Lamar Montgomery & the Freaky Faces Club. 2006. (J). per. 14.95 (978-1-889743-50-9(X)) Robbie Dean Pr.

Gownley, Jimmy. Amelia's Life During Wartime, 1 vol. 2013. (Amelia Rules! Set 2 Ser.). (ENG.). 36p. (J). (gr. 3-6). 24.21 (978-1-61479-073-0(6)) Spotlight.

Grovet, Heather. Super Star Problems. 2008. (J). pap. 5.97 (978-0-8163-2255-8(4)) Pacific Pr. Publishing Assn.

Gutman, Dan. The Get Rich Quick Club. (ENG.). 128p. (J). 2006. (gr. 3-7). pap. 5.99 (978-0-06-053442-4(7)) 2004. 15.99 (978-0-06-053440-0(0)) HarperCollins Pubs.

Hambrick, Sharon. Tommy's Clubhouse. Manning, Maurie J., tr. Manning, Maurie J., illus. 2003. (Fig Street Kids Ser.). 78p. (J). (gr. 1-2). pap. 7.49 (978-1-57924-993-9(0)) BJU Pr.

—Tommy's Race. Manning, Maurie J., illus. 2004. (Fig Street Kids Ser.). 95p. (J). (gr. 1-2). 7.49 (978-1-59166-286-0(9)) BJU Pr.

—Tommy's Rocket. Manning, Maurie J., illus. 2003. (Fig Street Kids Ser.). 83p. (J). (gr. 1-2). 7.49 (978-1-59166-186-3(2)) BJU Pr.

Hamilton, Elizabeth L. Christopher Cat's Character Club. 2003. (Character Critters Ser.: No. 1). (Illus.). 32p. (J). (gr. -1-3). per. 5.95 (978-0-9713749-2-8(9), Character-in-Action) Quiet Impact, Inc.

Hammel, Sara. The Underdogs. 2016. (ENG.). 320p. (J). 16.99 (978-0-374-30161-3(1), 9780374301613, Farrar, Straus & Giroux (BYR)) Farrar, Straus & Giroux.

—The Underdogs. 2017. (J). lib. bdg. 18.40 **(978-0-606-39936-4(4))** Turtleback Bks.

Hancock, H. Irving. The High School Boys' Canoe Club. rev. ed. 2006. 220p. 27.95 (978-1-4218-1753-8(5)); pap. 12.95 (978-1-4218-1853-5(1)) 1st World Publishing, Inc. (1st World Library - Literary Society).

—The High School Boys' Canoe Club. 2007. 184p. per. (978-1-4065-1983-9(9)) Dodo Pr.

Hapka, Catherine, pseud. ASPCA Pet Rescue Club: the Lonely Pony. 2015. (Pet Rescue Club Ser.: 3). (ENG., Illus.). 128p. (J). (gr. 1-3). lib. bdg. 16.99 (978-0-7944-3454-0(1)) Reader's Digest Assn., Inc., The.

—A New Home for Truman. Regan, Dana, illus. 2015. (Pet Rescue Club Ser.: 1). (ENG.). 128p. (J). (gr. 1-3). lib. bdg. 16.99 (978-0-7944-3351-2(0)) Reader's Digest Assn., Inc., The.

—A New Home for Truman. Regan, Dana, illus. 2015. (Pet Rescue Club Ser.: 1). (ENG.). 128p. (J). (gr. 1-3). pap. 5.99 (978-0-7944-3312-3(X)) Studio Fun International.

—No Time for Hallie. Regan, Dana, illus. 2015. (Pet Rescue Club Ser.: 2). (ENG.). 128p. (J). (gr. 1-3). lib. bdg. 16.99 (978-0-7944-3352-9(9)) Reader's Digest Assn., Inc., The.

—No Time for Hallie. Regan, Dana, illus. 2015. (Pet Rescue Club Ser.: 2). (ENG.). 128p. (J). (gr. 1-3). pap. 5.99 (978-0-7944-3313-0(8)) Studio Fun International.

—Too Big to Run. 2015. (Pet Rescue Club Ser.: 4). (ENG.). 128p. (J). (gr. 1-3). pap. 5.99 (978-0-7944-3453-3(3), Reader's Digest Children's Bks.) Studio Fun International.

Hapka, Cathy, pseud. ASPCA Pet Rescue Club Collection, Bks. 1-3. Regan, Dana, illus. 2016. (Pet Rescue Club Ser.: 5). (ENG.). 384p. (J). (gr. 1-3). pap. 8.99 (978-0-7944-3572-1(6), Reader's Digest Children's Bks.) Studio Fun International.

Hartinger, Brent. Geography Club. (ENG.). 240p. 2003. (J). 17.99 (978-0-06-001221-2(8)) 2004. (YA). (gr. 9). reprint ed. pap. 9.99 (978-0-06-001223-6(4), HarperTeen) HarperCollins Pubs.

Heller, Alyson. Touchdown! Björkman, Steve, illus. 2010. (After-School Sports Club Ser.). (ENG.). 32p. (J). (gr. -1-1). pap. 3.99 (978-1-4169-9413-8(0), Simon Spotlight) Simon Spotlight.

Herrera, Robin. Hope Is a Ferris Wheel. 2014. (ENG., Illus.). 272p. (YA). (gr. 3-7). 16.95 (978-1-4197-1039-1(7), Amulet Bks.) Abrams, Inc.

Holt, Kimberly Willis. Piper Reed, Campfire Girl. Davenier, Christine, illus. 2010. (Piper Reed Ser.: 4). (ENG.). 160p. (J). (gr. 3-6). 15.99 (978-0-8050-9006-2(1), 9780805090062, Holt, Henry & Co. Bks. For Young Readers) Holt, Henry & Co.

—Piper Reed, Campfire Girl. Davenier, Christine, illus. 2011. (Piper Reed Ser.: 4). (ENG.). 176p. (J). (gr. 3-6). pap. 6.99 (978-0-312-67482-3(1), 9780312674823) Square Fish.

Hooks, Gwendolyn. The Best Trick: A Pet Club Story, 1 vol. Byrne, Mike, illus. 2010. (Pet Club Ser.). (ENG.). 32p. (gr. 1-2). 22.65 (978-1-4342-2052-3(4)); pap. 6.25 (978-1-4342-2794-2(4)) Stone Arch Bks.

—The Cat Food Mystery: A Pet Club Story, 1 vol. Byrne, Mike, illus. 2011. (Pet Club Ser.). (ENG.). 32p. (gr. 1-2). pap. 6.25 (978-1-4342-3051-5(1)); lib. bdg. 22.65 (978-1-4342-2511-5(9)) Stone Arch Bks.

—Find the Cat! A Pet Club Story. Byrne, Mike, illus. 2010. (Pet Club Ser.). (ENG.). 32p. (gr. 1-2). pap. 6.25 (978-1-4342-2795-9(2)) Stone Arch Bks.

—The Lucky Charm: A Pet Club Story, 1 vol. Byrne, Mike, illus. 2011. (Pet Club Ser.). (ENG.). 32p. (gr. 1-2). pap. 6.25 (978-1-4342-3052-2(X)) Stone Arch Bks.

—The Noisy Night: A Pet Club Story, 1 vol. Byrne, Mike, illus. 2010. (Pet Club Ser.). (ENG.). 32p. (gr. 1-2). 22.65 (978-1-4342-2049-3(4)); pap. 6.25 (978-1-4342-2793-5(6)) Stone Arch Bks.

—The Pet Wash: A Pet Club Story, 1 vol. Byrne, Mike, illus. 2011. (Pet Club Ser.). (ENG.). 32p. (gr. 1-2). pap. 6.25 (978-1-4342-3054-6(6)); lib. bdg. 22.65 (978-1-4342-2514-6(3)) Stone Arch Bks.

—Pets at the Party: A Pet Club Story, 1 vol. Byrne, Mike, illus. 2010. (Pet Club Ser.). (ENG & ABK.). 32p. (gr. 1-2). 22.65 (978-1-4342-2054-7(0)); pap. 6.25 (978-1-4342-2796-6(0)) Stone Arch Bks.

Hopper, Ada. A Case of the Clones. Ricks, Sam, illus. 2016. (DATA Set Ser.: 5). (ENG.). 128p. (J). (gr. k-4). pap. 5.99 (978-1-4814-7113-8(9), Little Simon) Little Simon.

—Don't Disturb the Dinosaurs. Ricks, Sam, illus. 2016. (DATA Set Ser.: 2). (ENG.). 128p. (J). (gr. k-4). pap. 5.99 (978-1-4814-5731-6(4), Little Simon) Little Simon.

—Invasion of the Insects. Ricks, Sam, illus. 2017. (DATA Set Ser.: 6). (ENG.). 128p. (J). (gr. -1-4). 16.99 (978-1-4814-7117-6(1), Little Simon) Little Simon.

—March of the Mini Beasts. Ricks, Sam, illus. 2016. (DATA Set Ser.: bk.1). (ENG.). 128p. (J). (gr. k-4). pap. 5.99 (978-1-4814-5728-6(4), Little Simon) Little Simon.

—Robots Rule the School. Ricks, Sam, illus. 2016. (DATA Set Ser.: bk.4). (ENG.). 128p. (J). (gr. k-4). pap. 5.99 (978-1-4814-6312-6(8), Little Simon) Little Simon.

—The Sky Is Falling. Ricks, Sam, illus. 2016. (DATA Set Ser.: bk.3). (ENG.). 128p. (J). (gr. k-4). pap. 5.99 (978-1-4814-6309-6(8), Little Simon) Little Simon.

Howe, James. Horace & Morris, but Mostly Dolores. Waldrod, Amy, illus. 2003. pap. 39.95 incl. audio compact disk (978-1-59112-538-9(3)); pap. 37.95 incl. audio (978-1-59112-243-2(0)) Live Oak Media.

—Horace & Morris but Mostly Dolores. Walrod, Amy, illus. 2003. 30p. (J). (gr. -1-3). 15.65 (978-0-7569-2936-7(9)) Perfection Learning Corp.

In the Clubhouse. 2003. (J). per. (978-1-57657-872-8(0)) Paradise Pr., Inc.

Jaimet, Kate. Dunces Rock, 1 vol. 2014. (ENG.). 224p. (J). (gr. 4-7). pap. 9.95 (978-1-4598-0585-9(2)) Orca Bk. Pubs. USA.

Jennings, Sharon. Jingle Bats. Malloy, Kalle, illus. 72p. pap. (978-1-897039-22-9(0)) High Interest Publishing (HIP).

Johnson-Crouse, Donna C. The Whispering Kids Club: The Ruby Ring. 2005. 90p. (J). pap. 12.00 (978-1-886098-17-6(4)) Gye Nyame Hse.

Jung, Mike. Geeks, Girls, & Secret Identities. Maihack, Mike, illus. 2012. (J). (ENG.). 320p. (gr. 3-7). 16.99 (978-0-545-33548-5(5)); pap. (978-0-545-33549-2(3)) Scholastic, Inc. (Levine, Arthur A. Bks.).

Kaye, Marilyn. Teammates. 2014. (ENG., Illus.). 80p. (J). (gr. 3-7). pap. 13.99 (978-1-4814-2887-3(X), Simon & Schuster/Paula Wiseman Bks.) Simon & Schuster/Paula Wiseman Bks.

Keene, Carolyn. Double Take. Pamintuan, Macky, illus. 2009. (Nancy Drew & the Clue Crew Ser.: 21). (ENG.). 112p. (J). (gr. 1-4). pap. 5.99 (978-1-4169-7812-1(7), Aladdin) Simon & Schuster Children's Publishing.

—Earth Day Escapade. Pamintuan, Macky, illus. 2009. (Nancy Drew & the Clue Crew Ser.: 18). (ENG.). 96p. (J). (gr. 1-4). pap. 5.99 (978-1-4169-7218-1(8), Aladdin) Simon & Schuster Children's Publishing.

—Treasure Trouble. Pamintuan, Macky, illus. 2009. (Nancy Drew & the Clue Crew Ser.: 20). (ENG.). 112p. (J). (gr. 1-4). pap. 4.99 (978-1-4169-7809-1(7), Aladdin) Simon & Schuster Children's Publishing.

—Unicorn Uproar. Pamintuan, Macky, illus. 2009. (Nancy Drew & the Clue Crew Ser.: 22). (ENG.). 96p. (J). (gr. 1-4). pap. 4.99 (978-1-4169-7810-7(0), Aladdin) Simon & Schuster Children's Publishing.

Keeney, Stephen S. Spencer the Adventurer & the Castle of Bran. 2009. (ENG.). 256p. (J). pap. 14.99 (978-1-934135-31-0(3), Zumaya Thresholds) Zumaya Pubns. LLC.

Kehret, Peg. Desert Danger. 2008. (Frightmares Ser.). (ENG.). 128p. (J). (gr. 3-7). pap. 7.99 (978-1-4169-9111-3(5), Simon & Schuster/Paula Wiseman Bks.) Simon & Schuster/Paula Wiseman Bks.

—Race to Disaster. 2008. (ENG.). 128p. (J). (gr. 3-7). pap. 7.99 (978-1-4169-9108-3(5), Simon & Schuster/Paula Wiseman Bks.) Simon & Schuster/Paula Wiseman Bks.

—Screaming Eagles. 2008. (ENG.). 128p. (J). (gr. 3-7). pap. 7.99 (978-1-4169-9106-9(9), Simon & Schuster/Paula Wiseman Bks.) Simon & Schuster/Paula Wiseman Bks.

Kelly, David A. The Football Fumble. Brundage, Scott, illus. 2016. (Most Valuable Players Ser.: 3). (ENG.). 128p. (J). (gr. 1-4). 4.99 (978-0-553-51325-7(7), Random Hse. Bks. for Young Readers) Random Hse. Children's Bks.

—The Gold Medal Mess. Brundage, Scott, illus. 2016. (Most Valuable Players Ser.: 1). (ENG.). 128p. (J). (gr. 1-4). 4.99 (978-0-553-51319-6(2), Random Hse. Bks. for Young Readers) Random Hse. Children's Bks.

—The Soccer Surprise. Brundage, Scott, illus. 2016. (Most Valuable Players Ser.: 2). (ENG.). 128p. (J). (gr. 1-4). 4.99 (978-0-553-51322-6(2), Random Hse. Bks. for Young Readers) Random Hse. Children's Bks.

Kerrin, Jessica Scott. Martin Bridge: Onwards & Upwards! Kelly, Joseph, illus. 2009. (Martin Bridge Ser.). (ENG.). 112p. (J). (gr. 2-5). 6.95 (978-1-55453-161-5(6)) Kids Can Pr., Ltd. CAN. Dist: Hachette Bk. Group.

Kraft, Erik P. Lenny & Mel after-School Confidential. Kraft, Erik P., illus. 2012. (Lenny & Mel Ser.). (ENG., Illus.). 64p. (J). (gr. 2-5). pap. 6.99 (978-1-4424-6314-1(7), Simon & Schuster/Paula Wiseman Bks.) Simon & Schuster/Paula Wiseman Bks.

Leedy, Loreen. The Monster Money Book. Leedy, Loreen, illus. 2005. (ENG., Illus.). 32p. (J). (gr. k-3). pap. 6.95 (978-0-8234-1558-8(9)) Holiday Hse., Inc.

Lewis, Beverly. Girls Only! 2008. (Girls Only (Go!) Ser.: Vols. 5-8). (ENG.). (J). (gr. 4-7). 510p. pap. 20.00 (978-0-7642-0462-3(9)); Vols. 1-4. 512p. pap. 16.00 (978-0-7642-0461-6(0)) Bethany Hse. Pubs.

Lockhart, E. The Disreputable History of Frankie Landau-Banks. 2009. (ENG.). 352p. (J). (gr. 5-9). pap. 9.99 (978-0-7868-3819-6(1)) Hyperion Pr.

—The Disreputable History of Frankie Landau-Banks. l.t. ed. 2009. (ENG.). 502p. (YA). 23.95 (978-1-4104-1439-7(6)) Thorndike Pr.

Long, Ethan. Fright Club. 2015. (ENG., Illus.). 32p. (J). (gr. -1-2). 16.99 (978-1-61963-337-7(X), 9781619633377, Bloomsbury USA Childrens) Bloomsbury Publishing USA.

Luper, Eric. Seth Baumgartner's Love Manifesto. 2010. (ENG.). 304p. (YA). (gr. 8-18). 16.99 (978-0-06-182753-2(3)) HarperCollins Pubs.

Lytton, Deborah. Ruby Starr. 2017. (Ruby Starr Ser.: 1). (ENG.). 272p. (J). (gr. 3-7). pap. 7.99 **(978-1-4926-4577-1(X)**, Sourcebooks Jabberwocky) Sourcebooks, Inc.

MacDonald, Maryann. No Room for Francie. Richards, Virginia Helen, illus. 2010. 64p. (J). (gr. 1-3). pap. 6.95 (978-0-8198-5168-0(X)) Pauline Bks. & Media.

Manushkin, Fran. Best Club. Lyon, Tammie, illus. 2016. (Katie Woo Ser.). (ENG.). 32p. (gr. k-2). lib. bdg. 21.32 (978-1-4795-9639-3(6)) Picture Window Bks.

—Pedro's Mystery Club. Lyon, Tammie, illus. 2016. (Pedro Ser.). (ENG.). 32p. (gr. k-2). lib. bdg. 21.32 (978-1-5158-0084-2(9)) Pedro Pubns. GBR. Dist: Capstone Pub.

Maple, Daphne. Top Dog. Metayer, Annabelle, illus. 2016. (Roxbury Park Dog Club Ser.: 3). 224p. (J). (gr. 3-7). pap. 6.99 (978-0-06-232771-0(2)) HarperCollins Pubs.

Martin, Ann M. Dawn on the Coast. (Baby-Sitters Club Ser.: No. 23). 10p. (J). (gr. 3-7). pap. 3.95 (978-0-590-42007-5(0)) Scholastic, Inc.

—Dawn y los Mensajes Aterradores. Peraire del Molino, Conchita, tr. (Club de Las Canguro Ser.: Vol. 2).Tr. of Beware, Dawn! (SPA.). 134p. (J). 9.95 (978-84-272-2602-9(0)) Molino, Editorial ESP. Dist: AIMS International Bks., Inc.

—Kristy's Great Idea. 2010. (Baby-Sitters Club Ser.: 1). (ENG.). 176p. (J). (gr. 3-7). 6.99 (978-0-545-17475-6(9), Scholastic Paperbacks) Scholastic, Inc.

—Kristy's Great Idea. Telgemeier, Raina, illus. rev. ed. 2015. (Baby-Sitters Club Graphix Ser.: 1). (ENG.). 192p. (J). (gr. 3-7). 24.99 (978-0-545-81386-0(7), Graphix) Scholastic, Inc.

Martin, Ann M. & Telgemeier, Raina. Baby-Sitters Club Graphix, Bks. 1-4, Set. Telgemeier, Raina, illus. 2016. (Baby-Sitters Club Graphix Ser.). (ENG., Illus.). 192p. (J). (gr. 3-7). pap. 43.96 (978-1-338-11898-8(6)) Scholastic, Inc.

McDonald, Megan. Cloudy with a Chance of Boys. (Sisters Club Ser.: 3). (ENG., Illus.). 272p. (J). (gr. 3-7). 2012. pap. 5.99 (978-0-7636-5577-8(5)) 2011. 15.99 (978-0-7636-4615-8(6)) Candlewick Pr.

—The Sisters Club. 2008. (Sisters Club Ser.: 1). (ENG., Illus.). 208p. (J). (gr. 3-7). pap. 5.99 (978-0-7636-3251-9(1)) Candlewick Pr.

—The Sisters Club. 2008. (Sisters Club Ser.: 1). lib. bdg. 16.00 (978-1-4178-1785-6(2), Turtleback) Turtleback Bks.

McIntosh, Kenneth. Close-Up: Forensic Photography. 2009. (J). pap. 24.95 (978-1-4222-1455-8(9)) Mason Crest.

—Close-Up: Forensic Photography, 5 vols. Sanborn, Casey, illus. 2007. (Crime Scene Club Ser.: Bk. 5). 144p. (YA). (gr. 9-12). lib. bdg. 24.95 (978-1-4222-0251-7(8)) Mason Crest.

McMahon, P. J. Case of the Psychic Hamster. Manders, John, illus. 2005. 153p. (J). lib. bdg. 15.38 (978-1-4242-0404-5(6)) Fitzgerald Bks.

—Case of the Singing Sea Dragons. Manders, John, illus. 2005. 153p. (J). lib. bdg. 15.38 (978-1-4242-0406-9(2)) Fitzgerald Bks.

—Case of the Smiling Shark. Manders, John, illus. 2004. 116p. (J). lib. bdg. 15.38 (978-1-4242-0402-1(X)) Fitzgerald Bks.

Metz, Melinda. S. M. A. R. T. S. & the Invisible Robot. McKenzie, Heath, illus. 2015. (S. M. A. R. T. S. Ser.). (ENG.). 128p. (gr. 3-6). 22.65 (978-1-4965-0463-0(1)) S.M.A.R.T.S. Learning System.

—S. M. A. R. T. S. & the Missing UFO. McKenzie, Heath, illus. 2015. (S. M. A. R. T. S. Ser.). (ENG.). 128p. (gr. 3-6). lib. bdg.

C
D

22.65 *(978-1-4965-0466-1(6))* S.M.A.R.T.S. Learning System.

—S. M. A. R. T. S. & the Poison Plates. McKenzie, Heath, illus. 2015. (S. M. A. R. T. S. Ser.). (ENG.). 128p. (gr. 3-6). 22.65 *(978-1-4965-0464-7(X))* S.M.A.R.T.S. Learning System.

Meyerhoff, Jenny. Green Thumbs-Up! Chatelain, Éva, illus. 2015. (Friendship Garden Ser.: 1). (ENG.). 176p. (J). (gr. 2-5). pap. 5.99 *(978-1-4814-3904-6(9),* Aladdin) Simon & Schuster Children's Publishing.

—Pumpkin Spice. Chatelain, Éva, illus. 2015. (Friendship Garden Ser.: 2). (ENG.). 144p. (J). (gr. 2-5). pap. 5.99 *(978-1-4814-3909-1(X),* Aladdin) Simon & Schuster Children's Publishing.

—Pumpkin Spice. 2015. (Friendship Garden Ser.: 2). lib. bdg. 16.00 *(978-0-606-37833-8(2))* Turtleback Bks.

Mills, Charles. The Bandit of Benson Park. 2003. (Honors Club Story Ser.: Vol. 1). 127p. (J). *(978-0-8163-1977-0(4))* Pacific Pr. Pubns.

—The Great Sleepy-Time Stew Rescue. 2004. (Honors Club Story Ser.: Vol. 4). (Illus.). 127p. (J). 7.99 *(978-0-8163-2009-7(8))* Pacific Pr. Publishing Assn.

—The Secret of Scarlett Cove. 2004. (Honors Club Story Ser.: Bk. 3). 127p. (J). 7.99 *(978-0-8163-1999-2(5))* Pacific Pr. Publishing Assn.

Moore, Stephanie Perry & Moody Publishing Staff. Believing in Hope. 2009. (Yasmin Peace Ser.: 2). (ENG.). 176p. (gr. 7-10). pap. 7.99 *(978-0-8024-8603-5(7),* Lift Every Voice) Moody Pubs.

Morgan, Matthew, et al. Yuck's Fart Club. Baines, Nigel, illus. 2013. (Yuck Ser.). (ENG.). 112p. (J). (gr. 2-5). 15.99 *(978-1-4424-8153-4(6),* Simon & Schuster/Paula Wiseman Bks.) Simon & Schuster/Paula Wiseman Bks.

Naylor, Phyllis Reynolds. All but Alice. 2011. (Alice Ser.: 4). (ENG.). 192p. (J). (gr. 5-9). pap. 6.99 *(978-1-4424-2756-3(6),* Atheneum Bks. for Young Readers) Simon & Schuster Children's Publishing.

Neal, Terry L. The Find It Club & the Prankster. 2008. 151p. pap. 24.95 *(978-1-60610-959-5(6))* America Star Bks.

Nelson, Wendy Watson. The Not Even Once Club: My Promise to Heavenly Father. Dorman, Brandon, illus. 2013. 18.99 *(978-1-60907-337-4(1))* Deseret Bk. Co.

O'Connor, Jane. Explorer Extraordinaire! Glasser, Robin Preiss, illus. 2009. (Fancy Nancy Ser.). (ENG.). 32p. (J). (gr. -1-2). 12.99 *(978-0-06-168486-9(4))* HarperCollins Pubs.

Parish, Herman. Amelia Bedelia Chapter Book #6: Amelia Bedelia Cleans Up (POB) Avril, Lynne, illus. 2015. (Amelia Bedelia Ser.). (ENG.). 160p. (J). (gr. 1-5). 9.99 *(978-0-06-233403-9(4),* Greenwillow Bks.) HarperCollins Pubs.

—Amelia Bedelia Cleans Up. Avril, Lynne, illus. 2015. (Amelia Bedelia Ser.). (ENG.). 160p. (J). (gr. 1-5). pap. 4.99 *(978-0-06-233400-8(X),* Greenwillow Bks.) HarperCollins Pubs.

—Amelia Bedelia Joins the Club. Avril, Lynne, illus. 2014. (I Can Read Level 1 Ser.). (ENG.). 32p. (J). (gr. -1-3). 16.99 *(978-0-06-222131-5(0));* pap. 3.99 *(978-0-06-222130-8(2))* HarperCollins Pubs. (Greenwillow Bks.).

Patterson, Valerie O. Operation Oleander. 2013. (ENG.). 192p. (J). (gr. 5-7). 16.99 *(978-0-547-24437-2(1))* Houghton Mifflin Harcourt Publishing Co.

Preble, Laura. The Queen Geek Social Club. 2006. (ENG.). 336p. (YA). (gr. 7-18). 15.00 *(978-0-425-21164-9(9),* Berkley) Penguin Publishing Group.

Publications International Ltd. Staff, ed. Mickey Mouse Clubhouse. 2010. 128p. (J). pap. 12.98 *(978-1-60553-129-8(4),* PIL Kids) Publications International, Ltd.

—Mickey Mouse Clubhouse: Ask a Silly Question. 2010. (J). bds. 5.98 *(978-1-60553-037-6(9))* Phoenix International Publications, Inc.

Reynolds, Aaron. Carnivores. Newman, Jeff & Santat, Dan, illus. 2013. (ENG.). 40p. (J). (gr. -1-3). 16.99 *(978-0-8118-6690-3(4))* Chronicle Bks. LLC.

Riehecky, Janet. The Red Door Detective Club Mysteries, 4 bks., Set. Halverson, Lydia, illus. (J). (gr. 3-6). lib. bdg. 51.80 *(978-1-56674-900-8(X))* Forest Hse. Publishing Co., Inc.

Rippin, Sally. Spooky House. Fukuoka, Aki, illus. (J). 2015. (ENG.). 96p. pap. 4.99 *(978-1-61067-311-2(5))* 2014. 89p. *(978-1-61067-332-7(8))* Kane Miller.

Rosenberg, Aaron. Flood: Race Against Time. 2016. (S. T. E. M. Squad Ser.). (ENG.). 224p. (J). (gr. 3-10). pap. 7.99 *(978-1-4380-0805-9(8))* Barron's Educational Series, Inc.

Rylant, Cynthia. Annie & Snowball & the Book Bugs Club. Stevenson, Suçie, illus. (Annie & Snowball Ser.: 9). (ENG.). 40p. (J). (gr. k-2). 2012. pap. 3.99 *(978-1-4169-7201-3(3))* 2011. 16.99 *(978-1-4169-7199-3(8))* Simon Spotlight. (Simon Spotlight).

—Annie & Snowball & the Book Bugs Club. 2012. (Annie & Snowball Ready-To-Read Ser.). lib. bdg. 13.55 *(978-0-606-23692-8(9),* Turtleback) Turtleback Bks.

—Annie & Snowball & the Teacup Club. Stevenson, Suçie, illus. (Annie & Snowball Ser.: 3). (ENG.). 40p. (J). (gr. k-2). 2009. pap. 3.99 *(978-1-4169-1461-7(7))* 2008. 16.99 *(978-1-4169-0940-8(0))* Simon Spotlight. (Simon Spotlight).

Schreiber, Ellen. Cryptic Cravings. 2012. (Vampire Kisses Ser.: 8). (ENG.). 240p. (YA). (gr. 8). pap. 9.99 *(978-0-06-168947-5(5),* Tegen, Katherine Bks) HarperCollins Pubs.

Shannon Simmons. The Community Club: #1 Aubrey & the Fight for Life. 2009. 112p. pap. 10.95 *(978-1-4401-7616-6(7))* iUniverse, Inc.

Sharmat, Marjorie Weinman & Sharmat, Mitchell. The Green Toenails Gang. Brunkus, Denise, illus. 2nd ed. 2005. (Olivia Sharp: Agent for Secrets Ser.). (ENG.). 80p. (J). (gr. 3-7). per. 5.99 *(978-0-440-42063-7(6),* Yearling) Random Hse. Children's Bks.

Sheinmel, Courtney. The Kindness Club. 2016. (Kindness Club Ser.). (ENG.). 224p. (J). 15.99 *(978-1-68119-091-4(5),* 9781681190914, Bloomsbury USA Childrens) Bloomsbury Publishing USA.

Shusterman, Neal. The Shadow Club Rising. 2003. (ENG.). 208p. (YA). (gr. 7-7). 6.99 *(978-0-14-250089-7(5),* Speak) Penguin Young Readers Group.

Simon, Coco. Alexis: The Icing on the Cupcake. 2014. (Cupcake Diaries: 20). lib. bdg. 17.20 *(978-0-606-35786-9(6))* Turtleback Bks.

—Alexis Cool as a Cupcake. 2012. (Cupcake Diaries: 8). (ENG., Illus.). 160p. (J). (gr. 3-7). pap. 6.99 *(978-1-4424-5080-6(0),* Simon Spotlight) Simon Spotlight.

—Alexis the Icing on the Cupcake. 2014. (Cupcake Diaries: 20). (ENG., Illus.). 160p. (J). (gr. 3-7). pap. 6.99 *(978-1-4814-0468-6(7),* Simon Spotlight) Simon Spotlight.

—Emma: Lights! Camera! Cupcakes! 2014. (Cupcake Diaries: 19). lib. bdg. 17.20 *(978-0-606-35437-0(9))* Turtleback Bks.

—Emma on Thin Icing. 2013. (Cupcake Diaries: 3). (ENG., Illus.). 160p. (J). (gr. 3-7). 15.99 *(978-1-4424-7492-5(0),* Simon Spotlight) Simon Spotlight.

—Emma on Thin Icing. 2011. (Cupcake Diaries: 3). lib. bdg. 17.20 *(978-0-606-23734-5(8),* Turtleback) Turtleback Bks.

—Emma, Smile & Say Cupcake! 2012. (Cupcake Diaries: 11). (ENG.). 160p. (J). (gr. 3-7). pap. 6.99 *(978-1-4424-5398-2(2),* Simon Spotlight) Simon Spotlight.

—Katie & the Cupcake Cure; Mia in the Mix; Emma on Thin Icing, 3 in 1 bks. 2015. (Cupcake Diaries). (ENG., Illus.). 480p. (J). (gr. 3-7). pap. 8.99 *(978-1-4814-5756-9(X),* Simon Spotlight) Simon Spotlight.

—Katie & the Cupcake War. 2012. (Cupcake Diaries: 9). (ENG.). 160p. (J). (gr. 3-7). pap. 6.99 *(978-1-4424-5373-9(7),* Simon Spotlight) Simon Spotlight.

—Mia: Fashion Plates & Cupcakes. 2014. (Cupcake Diaries: 18). lib. bdg. 16.00 *(978-0-606-35436-3(0))* Turtleback Bks.

—Mia Fashion Plates & Cupcakes. 2014. (Cupcake Diaries: 18). (ENG., Illus.). 160p. (J). (gr. 3-7). pap. 5.99 *(978-1-4424-9790-0(4),* Simon Spotlight) Simon Spotlight.

Singleton, Linda Joy. The Curious Cat Spy Club. 2015. (Curious Cat Spy Club Ser.: 1). (ENG.). 256p. (J). (gr. 3-7). 14.99 *(978-0-8075-1376-7(8))* Whitman, Albert & Co.

—Kelsey the Spy. 2016. (Curious Cat Spy Club Ser.: 3). (ENG.). 288p. (J). (gr. 3-7). 14.99 *(978-0-8075-1380-4(6))* Whitman, Albert & Co.

—The Mystery of the Zorse's Mask. 2016. (Curious Cat Spy Club Ser.: 2). (ENG.). 272p. (J). (gr. 3-7). pap. 9.99 *(978-0-8075-1383-5(0))* Whitman, Albert & Co.

Standish, Burt L. Frank Merriwell's Club. Rudman, Jack, ed. 2003. (Frank Merriwell Ser.). 29.95 *(978-0-8373-9368-1(X));* pap. 9.95 *(978-0-8373-9068-0(0))* Merriwell, Frank Inc.

Steps To Literacy Staff, compiled by. The Freaky Joe Club: Gen027. 2005. (ENG., Illus.). (J). pap. *(978-1-60015-069-2(1))* Steps To Literacy, LLC.

Stevenson, Sarah Jamila. The Latte Rebellion. 2011. (ENG., Illus.). 336p. (YA). (gr. 9-18). pap. 9.95 *(978-0-7387-2278-8(2),* Flux) North Star Editions.

Stout, Shawn K. Miss Matched. Martini, Angela, illus. 2013. (Not-So-Ordinary Girl Ser.: 2). (ENG.). 176p. (J). (gr. 1-5). pap. 5.99 *(978-1-4424-7404-8(1),* Aladdin) Simon & Schuster Children's Publishing.

—Miss Matched. Martini, Angela, illus. 2013. (Not-So-Ordinary Girl Ser.: 2). (ENG.). 160p. (J). (gr. 1-5). 15.99 *(978-1-4424-7405-5(X),* Simon & Schuster/Paula Wiseman Bks.) Simon & Schuster/Paula Wiseman Bks.

Studio Mouse Staff. Mickey Mouse Clubhouse Count Along. rev. ed. 2007. (ENG.). 36p. 12.99 *(978-1-59069-613-2(1))* Studio Mouse LLC.

Tamaki, Mariko. Saving Montgomery Sole. 2016. (ENG.). 240p. (YA). 17.99 *(978-1-62672-271-2(4),* 9781626722712) Roaring Brook Pr.

—Saving Montgomery Sole. 2017. (ENG.). 240p. (YA). pap. 9.99 *(978-1-250-10440-3(8),* 9781250104403) Square Fish.

—Saving Montgomery Sole. 2017. (YA). lib. bdg. 20.85 ***(978-0-606-39584-7(9))*** Turtleback Bks.

Tanigawa, Nagaru. The Boredom of Haruhi Suzumiya. 2010. (Haruhi Suzumiya Ser.: 3). (ENG., Illus.). 224p. (YA). (gr. 10-17). 24.00 *(978-0-316-03886-7(5));* pap. 18.00 *(978-0-316-03887-4(3))* Little, Brown Bks. for Young Readers.

—The Disappearance of Haruhi Suzumiya. 2010. (Haruhi Suzumiya Ser.: 4). (ENG., Illus.). 192p. (YA). (gr. 10-17). pap. 18.00 *(978-0-316-03889-8(X))* Little, Brown Bks. for Young Readers.

—The Dissociation of Haruhi Suzumiya. 2013. (Haruhi Suzumiya Ser.: 9). (ENG., Illus.). 192p. (YA). (gr. 10-17). pap. 8.99 *(978-0-316-03894-2(6))* Little, Brown Bks. for Young Readers.

—The Intrigues of Haruhi Suzumiya. 2012. (Haruhi Suzumiya Ser.: 7). (ENG.). 288p. (YA). (gr. 10-17). 15.99 *(978-0-316-03895-9(4))* Little, Brown Bks. for Young Readers.

—The Rampage of Haruhi Suzumiya. 2011. (Haruhi Suzumiya Ser.: 4). (ENG.). 240p. (YA). (gr. 10-17). pap. 18.00 *(978-0-316-03884-3(9))* Little, Brown Bks. for Young Readers.

—The Sigh of Haruhi Suzumiya. 2009. (Haruhi Suzumiya Ser.: Bk. 1). (Illus.). 208p. (YA). (gr. 10-18). 14.99 *(978-0-316-03881-2(4))* Hachette Bk. Group.

—The Sigh of Haruhi Suzumiya, Bk. 1. 2009. (Haruhi Suzumiya Ser.: 2). (ENG., Illus.). 208p. (YA). (gr. 10-17). pap. 18.00 *(978-0-316-03879-9(2))* Little, Brown Bks. for Young Readers.

—The Surprise of Haruhi Suzumiya. 2013. (Haruhi Suzumiya Ser.: 10). (ENG., Illus.). 368p. (YA). (gr. 10-17). 24.00 *(978-0-316-03898-0(9));* pap. 10.99 *(978-0-316-03897-3(0))* Little, Brown Bks. for Young Readers.

—The Wavering of Haruhi Suzumiya. 2011. (Haruhi Suzumiya Ser.: 6). (ENG & JPN.). 208p. (YA). (gr. 10-17). pap. 18.00 *(978-0-316-03892-8(X))* Little, Brown Bks. for Young Readers.

Viz Media. Fairy Dreams. 2013. (Winx Club Ser.: 5). lib. bdg. 17.20 *(978-0-606-26987-2(8),* Turtleback) Turtleback Bks.

VIZ Media, . & Straffi, Iginio. WINX Club, Vol. 7. 2013. (ENG.). 96p. (J). pap. 6.99 *(978-1-4215-4204-1(8))* Viz Media.

VIZ Media Staff & Straffi, Iginio. WINX Club, Vol. 5. 2013. (ENG.). 96p. (J). pap. 6.99 *(978-1-4215-4163-1(7))* Viz Media.

VIZ Media Staff & Straffi, Iginio. WINX Club, Vol. 6. 2013. (ENG.). 96p. (J). pap. 6.99 *(978-1-4215-4203-4(X))* Viz Media.

Young, Kristi. The Secret Club - the Powder Puff Club Book 1. 2007. (ENG.). 140p. (J). per. 12.95 *(978-1-59594-070-4(7),* Wingspan Pr.) WingSpan Publishing.

Zevin, Gabrielle. In the Age of Love & Chocolate. 2014. (Birthright Ser.: 3). (ENG.). 320p. (YA). (gr. 7). pap. 10.99 *(978-1-250-05071-7(5),* 9781250050717) Square Fish.

COACHING (ATHLETICS)

Ferguson. Coaches & Fitness Professionals. 2nd rev. ed. 2008. (Careers in Focus Ser.). 188p. (gr. 6-12). 32.95 *(978-0-8160-7284-2(1),* Ferguson Publishing Co.) Facts On File, Inc.

Hunsaker, Jennifer. Athletic Trainers. 2017. (Careers in Healthcare Ser.: Vol. 13). (ENG.). (YA). (gr. 7-12). 23.95 ***(978-1-4222-3795-3(8))*** Mason Crest.

Nagle, Jeanne M. Careers in Coaching. 2005. (Careers). (Illus.). 192p. (YA). (gr. 7-12). lib. bdg. 31.95 *(978-0-8239-2966-5(3),* CACOAC) Rosen Publishing Group, Inc., The.

—Choosing a Career as a Coach. 2005. (World of Work Ser.). (Illus.). 64p. (YA). (gr. 7-12). lib. bdg. 31.95 *(978-0-8239-3285-6(0))* Rosen Publishing Group, Inc., The.

Pettiford, Rebecca. Coaches. 2015. (J). lib. bdg. 25.65 *(978-1-62031-155-4(0),* Bullfrog Bks.) Jump! Inc.

COAL MINES AND MINING

see also Mining Engineering

Andrekson, Judy. Gunner: Hurricane Horse. Parkins, David, illus. 2010. (True Horse Stories Ser.). (ENG.). 104p. (J). (gr. 4-7). pap. 7.99 *(978-0-88776-905-4(5),* Tundra Bks.) Tundra Bks. CAN. Dist: Penguin Random Hse. LLC.

Bailey, Diane. Coal Power. 2014. (J). *(978-1-60818-408-8(0),* Creative Education) Creative Co., The.

—Harnessing Energy: Coal Power. 2015. (Harnessing Energy Ser.). (ENG.). 48p. (J). (gr. 5-8). pap. 12.00 *(978-0-89812-994-6(X),* Creative Paperbacks) Creative Co., The.

Belton, Blair. How Coal Is Formed. 2016. (From the Earth: How Resources Are Made Ser.). (Illus.). 32p. (J). (gr. 4-3). pap. 10.50 *(978-1-4824-4703-3(7))* Stevens, Gareth Publishing LLLP.

Bethea, Nikole Brooks. Oil & Coal. 2013. (Explorer Library: Language Arts Explorer Ser.). (ENG.). 32p. (gr. 4-8). 28.50 *(978-1-61080-897-2(5),* 202567); pap. 14.21 *(978-1-61080-922-1(X),* 202569) Cherry Lake Publishing.

Burgan, Michael. Breaker Boys: How a Photograph Helped End Child Labor, 1 vol. 2011. (Captured History Ser.). (ENG.). 64p. (gr. 5-7). pap. 9.10 *(978-0-7565-4510-9(2),* CPB Grades 4-8) Compass Point Bks.

Goodman, James A. Two Weeks Under: The Sheppton Mine Disaster Miracle. 2004. (Illus.). 144p. per. 12.95 *(978-0-9709630-4-8(1))* Coal Hole Productions.

Gordon, Nick. Coal Miner. 2013. (Dangerous Jobs Ser.). (ENG., Illus.). 24p. (J). (gr. 3-7). lib. bdg. 25.95 *(978-1-60014-893-4(X),* Torque Bks.) Bellwether Media.

Green, Robert. Coal. 2009. (21st Century Skills Library: Power Up! Ser.). (ENG.). 32p. (gr. 4-8). lib. bdg. 28.50 *(978-1-60279-508-2(8),* 200323) Cherry Lake Publishing.

Hemenway, Scott. Anthracite Collieries & Railroads of the Western Middle Field. 2008. *(978-1-931014-08-3(6))* Garrigues Hse. Pubs.

Malam, John. You Wouldn't Want to Be a 19th-Century Coal Miner in England! A Dangerous Job You'd Rather Not Have. Antram, David, illus. 2006. (You Wouldn't Want to Ser.). (ENG.). 32p. (J). (gr. 2-5). 29.00 *(978-0-531-14971-3(4))* Scholastic Library Publishing.

Owings, Lisa. Battleship Island: The Deserted Island. 2017. (Abandoned Places Ser.). (ENG., Illus.). 24p. (J). (gr. 3-7). lib. bdg. 25.95 ***(978-1-62617-693-5(0),*** Torque Bks.) Bellwether Media.

Parker, Steve. Coal, Vol. 12. 2015. (North American Natural Resources Ser.). 64p. (J). (gr. 7). 23.95 *(978-1-4222-3379-5(0))* Mason Crest.

—Coal. 2004. (Science Files Ser.). (Illus.). 32p. (gr. 2-6). lib. bdg. 26.00 *(978-0-8368-4029-2(1),* Gareth Stevens Learning Library) Stevens, Gareth Publishing LLLP.

Parks, Peggy J. Coal Power. 2010. (Compact Research Ser.). 96p. (YA). (gr. 7-12). 26.95 *(978-1-60152-107-1(3))* ReferencePoint Pr., Inc.

Pipe, Jim. Coal. 2011. (J). 28.50 *(978-1-59604-213-1(3))* Black Rabbit Bks.

Ruby, Lois. Strike! Mother Jones & the Colorado Coal Field War. 2012. (Illus.). 224p. (J). pap. 8.95 *(978-0-86541-141-8(7))* Filter Pr., LLC.

COAL MINES AND MINING—FICTION

Almond, David. Kit's Wilderness. unabr. ed. 2004. 240p. (J). (gr. 7-18). pap. 36.00 incl. audio *(978-0-8072-8216-8(2),* Listening Library) Random Hse. Audio Publishing Group.

Anderson, T. Neill. Horrors of History: Massacre of the Miners. 2015. (ENG., Illus.). 144p. (YA). (gr. 7). lib. bdg. 16.95 *(978-1-58089-520-0(4))* Charlesbridge Publishing, Inc.

Benyo, Richard. The South Street Gang vs. the Coalcracker Cyclops. 2010. (ENG.). 151p. pap. 8.00 *(978-1-58966-208-7(3))* Univ. of Scranton Pr.

Brown, Elizabeth Ferguson & Boyds Mills Press Staff. Coal Country Christmas. Stevenson, Harvey, illus. 2003. (ENG.). 32p. (J). (gr. 1-7). 15.95 *(978-1-59078-020-6(5))* Boyds Mills Pr.

Carter, Anne Laurel. Out of the Deeps, 1 vol. Debon, Nicolas, illus. 2008. (ENG.). 32p. (J). (gr. -1-3). 19.95 *(978-1-55143-559-6(4))* Orca Bk. Pubs. USA.

Ellis, Deborah. No Ordinary Day, 1 vol. (ENG.). (J). (gr. 3-7). 2014. 160p. pap. 9.95 *(978-1-55498-108-3(5))* 2011. 144p. 16.95 *(978-1-55498-134-2(4))* Groundwood Bks. CAN. Dist: Publishers Group West (PGW).

Green, Connie Jordan. Emmy. 2nd ed. 2007. (J). pap. 15.00 *(978-1-60454-000-0(1))* Iris Publishing Group, Inc., The.

Haas, Jessie. Chase. 2007. 256p. (J). (gr. 5-9). lib. bdg. 17.89 *(978-0-06-112851-6(1))* HarperCollins Pubs.

Hart, Alison. Finder, Coal Mine Dog, 1 vol. Montgomery, Michael G., illus. 2015. (Dog Chronicles Ser.). (ENG.). 185p. (J). (gr. 2-5). 12.95 *(978-1-56145-860-8(0))* Peachtree Pubs.

Hendry, Frances. Atlantis. l.t. ed. 2007. 228p. per. *(978-1-905665-20-4(2))* Pollinger In Print.

Kehret, Peg. The Ghost's Grave. 2007. 224p. pap. 5.99 *(978-0-14-280819-1(9),* Puffin) Penguin Publishing Group.

Knight, Mary. Saving Wonder. 2016. (ENG.). 288p. (J). (gr. 3-7). 16.99 *(978-0-545-82893-2(7),* Scholastic Pr.) Scholastic, Inc.

Kulka, Joe. Christmas Coal Man. Kulka, Joe, illus. 2015. (ENG., Illus.). 32p. (J). (gr. k-3). lib. bdg. 17.99 *(978-1-4677-1607-9(3),* Carolrhoda Bks.) Lerner Publishing Group.

Laskas, Gretchen Moran. The Miner's Daughter. 2007. (ENG.). 256p. (YA). (gr. 7-12). 17.99 *(978-1-4169-1262-0(2),* Simon & Schuster Bks. For Young Readers) Simon & Schuster Bks. For Young Readers.

Mobley, Jeannie. Katerina's Wish. 2012. (ENG., Illus.). 256p. (J). (gr. 3-7). 15.99 *(978-1-4424-3343-4(4),* McElderry, Margaret K. Bks.) McElderry, Margaret K. Bks.

Norton, Andre. Ralestone Luck. 2006. pap. *(978-1-4068-3557-1(9))* Echo Library.

Rosenberg, Madelyn. Canary in the Coal Mine. 2013. (ENG., Illus.). 192p. (J). (gr. 2-7). 16.95 *(978-0-8234-2600-3(9))* Holiday Hse., Inc.

Sherman, V. T. The Call of the Beaver Patrol: Or A Break in the Glacier. 2007. (ENG.). 238p. pap. 20.99 *(978-1-4346-3570-9(8))* Creative Media Partners, LLC.

—The Call of the Beaver Patrol: Or a Break in the Glacier. l.t. ed. 2007. (ENG.). 270p. pap. 23.99 *(978-1-4346-3571-6(6))* Creative Media Partners, LLC.

Smucker, Anna. No Star Nights. Johnson, Steve & Fancher, Lou, illus. 2012. 40p. (J). pap. 8.95 *(978-1-891852-82-4(5))* Quarrier Pr.

Sullivan, Paul. Breaker at Dawn. 2010. (J). pap. *(978-0-88092-705-5(4))* Royal Fireworks Publishing Co.

Swindells, Robert. Blackout. 2011. (ENG.). 224p. (J). (gr. 3-6). pap. 9.99 *(978-0-552-56154-9(1))* Transworld Publishers Ltd. GBR. Dist: Independent Pubs. Group.

Wallace, Bill. The Dog Who Thought He Was Santa. 2007. (ENG., Illus.). 224p. (J). (gr. 4-7). 17.95 *(978-0-8234-2114-5(7))* Holiday Hse., Inc.

—The Dog Who Thought He Was Santa. 2008. (ENG.). 192p. (J). (gr. 3-7). pap. 5.99 *(978-1-4169-4816-2(3),* Aladdin) Simon & Schuster Children's Publishing.

Wilson, John. Red Goodwin. 2006. (ENG., Illus.). 170p. (J). per. *(978-1-55380-034-7(6))* Ronsdale Pr.

Witschen, Kay. Johnny Coalboy. Luckemeyer, Norma, illus. 2003. (J). per. 5.95 *(978-0-9741352-0-5(8))* Dwitt Publishing.

Woodson, Marion. Charlotte's Vow. 2006. (ENG.). 144p. (J). (gr. 4). pap., tchr. ed. 8.95 *(978-0-88878-413-1(9))* Dundurn CAN. Dist: Ingram Publisher Services.

Yep, Laurence. The Traitor. 2004. (Golden Mountain Chronicles). 310p. (J). (gr. 5). 14.65 *(978-0-7569-3457-6(5))* Perfection Learning Corp.

COAL OIL

see Petroleum

COASTAL SIGNALS

see Signals and Signaling

COAT COLOR OF ANIMALS

see Animals—Color

COATS OF ARMS

see Heraldry

COBB, TY, 1886-1961

Abrams, Dennis. Ty Cobb. 2007. (Baseball Superstars Ser.). (Illus.). 130p. (YA). (gr. 7-12). lib. bdg. 30.00 *(978-0-7910-9439-6(1))* Facts On File, Inc.

COCHISE, APACHE CHIEF, 1805?-1874

Dean, Arlan. With All My Might: Cochise & the Indian Wars. (Great Moments in American History Ser.). 32p. (gr. 3-3). 2009. 47.90 *(978-1-61513-137-2(X))* 2004. (Illus.). (J). lib. bdg. 22.50 *(978-0-8239-4338-8(0),* Rosen Reference) Rosen Publishing Group, Inc., The.

Phillips, Larissa. Cochise: Apache Chief. (Primary Sources of Famous People in American History Ser.). 32p. 2009. (gr. 2-3). 47.90 *(978-1-60851-660-5(1))* 2004. (ENG., Illus.). (gr. 4-8). pap. 10.00 *(978-0-8239-4177-3(9),* Rosen Classroom) Rosen Publishing Group, Inc., The.

—Cochise: Apache Chief / Cochise: Jefe Apache. 2009. (Famous People in American History/Grandes personajes en la historia de los Estados Unidos Ser.). (ENG & SPA.). 32p. (gr. 2-3). 47.90 *(978-1-61512-540-1(X),* Editorial Buenas Letras) Rosen Publishing Group, Inc., The.

—Cochise: Jefe Apache. de la Vega, Eida, tr. from ENG. 2004. (Grandes Personajes en la Historia de Los Estados Unidos Ser.). (ENG & SPA., Illus.). 32p. (gr. 3-6). pap. 10.00 *(978-0-8239-4223-7(6))* Rosen Publishing Group, Inc., The.

—Cochise: Jefe apache (Cochise: Apache Chief) 2009. (Grandes personajes en la historia de los Estados Unidos (Famous People in American History) Ser.). (SPA.). 32p. (gr. 2-3). 47.90 *(978-1-61512-792-4(5),* Editorial Buenas Letras) Rosen Publishing Group, Inc., The.

COCHISE, APACHE CHIEF, 1805?-1874—FICTION

La Farge, Oliver. Cochise of Arizona. 2014. 222p. pap. 24.95 *(978-0-86534-675-8(5))* Sunstone Pr.

COCHRANE, ELIZABETH, 1867-1922

see Bly, Nellie, 1867-1922

COCKROACHES

Amstutz, Lisa J. Cockroaches, 1 vol. 2013. (Creepy Crawlers Ser.). (ENG., Illus.). 24p. (gr. k-1). lib. bdg. 26.65 *(978-1-4765-2063-6(1),* Pebble Plus) Capstone Press of Coughlan Cos.

Bodden, Valerie. Cockroaches. 2013. (Illus.). 24p. (J). 25.65 *(978-1-60818-232-9(0),* Creative Education) Creative Co., The.

—Creepy Creatures: Cockroaches. 2013. (Creepy Creatures Ser.). (ENG., Illus.). 24p. (J). (gr. 1-3). pap. 7.99 *(978-0-89812-795-9(5),* Creative Paperbacks) Creative Co., The.

Carr, Aaron. Cockroaches. 2014. (J). *(978-1-4896-1038-6(3))* Weigl Pubs., Inc.

Field, Jon Eben. Scurrying Cockroaches. 2010. (Creepy Crawlies Ser.). (ENG.). 32p. (J). (gr. 3-6). *(978-0-7787-2502-2(2));* pap. *(978-0-7787-2509-1(X))* Crabtree Publishing Co.

Goldish, Meish. Hungry Cockroaches. 2008. (No Backbone! Ser.). (Illus.). 24p. (J). (gr. k-3). lib. bdg. 21.28 *(978-1-59716-588-4(3))* Bearport Publishing Co., Inc.

Green, Emily K. Cockroaches. 2006. (World of Insects Ser.). (ENG., Illus.). 24p. (J). (gr. k-3). lib. bdg. 25.95 *(978-1-60014-010-5(6))* Bellwether Media.

Helget, Nicole. Cochroaches. 2007. (Bugbooks Ser.). (Illus.). 24p. (J). (gr. -1-3). lib. bdg. 24.25 *(978-1-58341-540-5(8),* Creative Education) Creative Co., The.

Herriott, Charlotte. Rat vs. Cockroach. 2015. (Bizarre Beast Battles Ser.). (ENG.). 24p. (J). (gr. 2-3). pap. 8.15 *(978-1-4824-2788-2(5))* Stevens, Gareth Publishing LLLP.

Kravetz, Jonathan. Cockroaches. (Gross Bugs Ser.). 24p. 2009. (gr. 3-4). 42.50 *(978-1-61513-227-0(9))* 2006. (Illus.).

(J). 22.60 *(978-1-4042-3043-9(2))* Rosen Publishing Group, Inc., The. (PowerKids Pr.).

Nelson, Robin. Crawling Cockroaches. 2016. (First Step Nonfiction — Backyard Critters Ser.). (ENG., Illus.). 24p. (J). (gr. k-2). 23.99 *(978-1-5124-0881-2(6))* Lerner Publishing Group.

Petrie, Kristin. Cockroaches, 1 vol. 2009. (Bugs! Ser.). (ENG.). 32p. (gr. 3-6). 27.07 *(978-1-60453-066-7(9),* Checkerboard Library) ABDO Publishing Co.

—Madagascar Hissing Cockroaches, 1 vol. 2012. (Unique Pets Ser.). (ENG.). 24p. (J). (gr. 3-6). lib. bdg. 25.65 *(978-1-61783-441-7(6),* Checkerboard Library) ABDO Publishing Co.

Roza, Greg. Repulsive Roaches. 2011. (World of Bugs Ser.). (Illus.). 24p. (gr. k-2). 69.20 *(978-1-4339-6144-1(X));* (J). (gr. -1-2). lib. bdg. 22.60 *(978-1-4339-4607-3(6))* Stevens, Gareth Publishing LLLP.

Schuetz, Kari. Hissing Cockroaches. 2015. (Creepy Crawlies Ser.). (ENG., Illus.). 24p. (J). (gr. k-3). lib. bdg. 25.95 *(978-1-62617-223-4(4),* Blastoff! Readers) Bellwether Media.

Schuh, Mari. Cockroaches. 2015. (J). lib. bdg. 25.65 *(978-1-62031-161-5(5),* Bullfrog Bks.) Jump! Inc.

Silverstein, Alvin, et al. Hissing Cockroaches: Cool Pets! Kelley, Gerald, illus. 2011. (Far-Out & Unusual Pets Ser.). 48p. (J). (gr. 2-5). lib. bdg. 25.27 *(978-0-7660-3685-7(5))* Enslow Pubs., Inc.

COCKROACHES—FICTION

Blake-Brekke, Carri. Billy Bully Bug: Learns a Lesson in Hawaii. Melton, Jodi, illus. 2003. (Mrs. B's Story Time... With a Twist! Ser.). 20p. (J). pap. 11.95 incl. audio compact disk *(978-0-9720549-2-8(8))* Mom's Pride Enterprises.

Cannon, Janell. Crickwing. 2005. (ENG., Illus.). 48p. (J). (gr. -1-3). reprint ed. pap. 7.99 *(978-0-15-205061-0(2))* Houghton Mifflin Harcourt Publishing Co.

—Crickwing. 2005. (Illus.). (gr. 1-4). 17.00 *(978-0-7569-5051-4(1))* Perfection Learning Corp.

Conly, Jane Leslie. Impetuous R., Secret Agent. Leick, Bonnie, illus. 2008. (ENG.). 240p. (gr. 3-7). 16.99 *(978-1-4231-0418-6(8))* Hyperion Pr.

Cuenca, Hector. La Cucarachita Martina. 2008. (SPA., Illus.). 32p. (J). (gr. -1-3). 14.99 *(978-1-933032-36-8(7))* Lectorum Pubns., Inc.

de Las Casas, Dianne. Madame Poulet & Monsieur Roach, 1 vol. Gentry, Marita, illus. 2009. (ENG.). 32p. (J). (gr. k-3). 16.99 *(978-1-58980-686-3(7))* Pelican Publishing Co., Inc.

Deedy, Carmen Agra. Martina the Beautiful Cockroach, 1 vol. Austin, Michael, illus. 2014. (ENG.). 32p. (J). (gr. -1-3). pap. 8.95 *(978-1-56145-787-8(6))* Peachtree Pubs.

—Martina the Beautiful Cockroach. 2014. lib. bdg. 19.60 *(978-0-606-35654-1(1))* Turtleback Bks.

—Martina the Beautiful Cockroach: A Cuban Folktale, 1 vol. Austin, Michael, illus. 2007. (ENG.). 32p. (J). (gr. k-3). 16.95 *(978-1-56145-399-3(4))* Peachtree Pubs.

—Martina una Cucarachita Muy Linda: Un Cuento Cubano, 1 vol. Austin, Michael, illus. 2010. (SPA.). 32p. (J). pap. 8.95 *(978-1-56145-532-4(6))* Peachtree Pubs.

—Martina una Cucarachita Muy Linda: Un Cuento Cubano. De la Torre, Cristina, tr. Austin, Michael, illus. 2007. (SPA.). 32p. (J). (gr. -1-3). 17.95 *(978-1-56145-425-9(7))* Peachtree Pubs.

Doodler, Todd H. Revenge of the Roach! 2016. (Super Fly Ser.). (ENG., Illus.). 128p. (J). pap. 6.99 *(978-1-61963-381-0(7),* 9781619633810, Bloomsbury USA Childrens) Bloomsbury Publishing USA.

Driscoll, Laura & Random House Disney Staff. Smash Trash! Cortes, Mario et al, illus. 2008. (Step into Reading Ser.). (ENG.). 32p. (J). (gr. k-3). pap. 3.99 *(978-0-7364-2515-5(2),* RH/Disney) Random Hse. Children's Bks.

Freeman, Martha. The Case of the Bug on the Run. 2014. (First Kids Mystery Ser.: 6). (ENG.). 144p. (J). (gr. 2-7). pap. 6.99 *(978-0-8234-3188-5(6))* Holiday Hse., Inc.

—The Case of the Bug on the Run: First Kids Mystery #6. 2013. (First Kids Mystery Ser.: 6). (ENG.). 144p. (J). (gr. 2-7). 16.95 *(978-0-8234-2872-4(9))* Holiday Hse., Inc.

Gil, Carmen. Story of a Cockroach. 2012. (Mini-Animalist Ser.). (ENG., Illus.). 32p. (J). (gr. -1-2). *(978-84-15241-22-5(4))* D P & G Military Pubs.

Harlen, Jonathan. The Cockroach War. rev. ed. 2005. (ENG., Illus.). 204p. (Orig.). (J). (gr. 3-7). pap. 7.95 *(978-1-74114-490-1(6))* Allen & Unwin AUS. Dist: Independent Pubs. Group.

Matheson, Jason. Buzzbomb: Adventures in the Forbidden Zone. Hope, Bill, illus. 2013. 80p. (J). pap. *(978-1-925011-26-5(7))* Australian Self Publishing Group/ Inspiring Pubs.

Mccants, Bruce C. Legend of the White Cockroach. 2012. 120p. 20.95 *(978-1-4759-4791-5(7));* pap. 10.95 *(978-1-4759-4792-2(5))* iUniverse, Inc.

Pochocki, Ethel. The Blessing of the Beasts. Moser, Barry, illus. 2014. (ENG.). 40p. (J). pap. 15.99 *(978-1-61261-582-0(1))* Paraclete Pr., Inc.

Pochocki, Ethel & Helms, Hal M. The Blessing of the Beasts. Moser, Barry, illus. 2007. (ENG.). 40p. (gr. -1-3). 18.95 *(978-1-55725-502-0(4))* Paraclete Pr., Inc.

Speck, Katie. Maybelle Goes to School. Tagyos, Paul Rátz de, illus. 2015. (Maybelle Ser.). (ENG.). 64p. (J). (gr. 2-5). 16.99 *(978-0-8050-9158-8(0),* 9780805091588, Holt, Henry & Co. Bks. For Young Readers) Holt, Henry & Co.

Speck, Katie & De Tagyos, Paul Rátz. Maybelle & the Haunted Cupcake. 2012. (Maybelle Ser.). (ENG., Illus.). 64p. (J). (gr. 2-5). 16.99 *(978-0-8050-9468-8(7),* 9780805094688, Holt, Henry & Co. Bks. For Young Readers) Holt, Henry & Co.

Tandy, Clive. Quarry Grove. 2008. 60p. per. 11.59 *(978-1-4251-4974-1(X))* Trafford Publishing.

Thomas, Susan. Beyond the Mist: Sequel to Mist on the Window. 2012. 352p. pap. 24.34 *(978-1-4772-4627-6(4))* AuthorHouse.

Wenz, Graham D. The Day a Cockroach Crawled under My Door: This Book Won't Be a Bore! 2012. 44p. pap. 21.99 *(978-1-4797-0761-4(9))* Xlibris Corp.

COCOA

see also Chocolate

Frydenborg, Kay. Chocolate: Sweet Science & Dark Secrets of the World's Favorite Treat. 2015. (ENG., Illus.). 256p. (YA). (gr. 7). 18.99 *(978-0-544-17566-2(2),* HMH Books For Young Readers) Houghton Mifflin Harcourt Publishing Co.

Grout, Phil. Harvest of Hope. 2003. (Illus.). 96p. per. 13.95 *(978-0-9708816-2-5(2))* Publishers@TreeHouse, The.

Murray, Julie. Cocoa Bean to Chocolate, 1 vol. 2006. (Beginning to End Ser.). (ENG.). 24p. (gr. k-4). 25.65 *(978-1-59679-835-9(1),* Buddy Bks.) ABDO Publishing Co.

Rajczak, Kristen. Creative Cocoa Recipes. 2014. (Ingredients for a Healthy Life Ser.). (Illus.). 24p. (J). (gr. 2-5). 22.60 *(978-1-4824-0559-0(8))* Stevens, Gareth Publishing LLLP.

COCOONS

see Butterflies; Caterpillars; Moths; Silkworms

CODE AND CIPHER STORIES

Alfonsi, Alice. The Code Red Cases. Harrington, Rich, illus. 2006. 96p. (J). *(978-0-439-91447-5(7))* Scholastic, Inc.

Baldacci, David. Day of Doom, Bk. 6. 2013. (39 Clues: Cahills vs. Vespers Ser.: Bk. 6). (ENG., Illus.). 272p. (J). (gr. 3-7). 12.99 *(978-0-545-32416-8(5))* Scholastic, Inc.

Base, Graeme, et al. Dinosaurs in Your Backyard: The Coolest, Scariest Creatures Ever Found in the USA! 2009. (ENG., Illus.). 32p. (J). (gr. 1-4). 16.95 *(978-0-8109-7099-1(6),* Abrams Bks. for Young Readers) Abrams, Inc.

Beck, W. H. Malcolm under the Stars. Lies, Brian, illus. (ENG.). 272p. (J). (gr. 2-5). 2016. pap. 7.99 *(978-0-544-81312-0(X))* 2015. 16.99 *(978-0-544-39267-0(1))* Houghton Mifflin Harcourt Publishing Co. (HMH Books For Young Readers).

Child, Lauren. Ruby Redfort Feel the Fear. Child, Lauren, illus. 2016. (Ruby Redfort Ser.). (ENG., Illus.). 528p. (J). (gr. 5-9). 16.99 *(978-0-7636-5470-2(1))* Candlewick Pr.

—Take Your Last Breath. Child, Lauren, illus. 2014. (Ruby Redfort Ser.: 2). (ENG., Illus.). 432p. (J). (gr. 5-9). pap. 7.99 *(978-0-7636-6932-4(6))* Candlewick Pr.

Clark, Henry. The Book That Proves Time Travel Happens. 2015. (ENG., Illus.). 416p. (J). (gr. 3-7). 17.00 *(978-0-316-40617-8(1))* Little Brown & Co.

Doyle, Bill. Trapped! The 2031 Journal of Otis Fitzmorgan. 6th ed. 2006. (ENG., Illus.). 144p. (J). (gr. 3-7). per. 16.99 *(978-0-316-05754-7(1))* Little, Brown Bks. for Young Readers.

Doyle, Bill H. Betrayed! The 1977 Journal of Zeke Moorie. 4th ed. 2006. (ENG., Illus.). 144p. (J). (gr. 3-7). per. 16.99 *(978-0-316-05741-7(X))* Little, Brown Bks. for Young Readers.

Ellis, Julie & Stewart, Christen. Lizzie's Hidden Message. 2008. (Rigby Focus Forward: Level N Ser.). (Illus.). 24p. (J). (gr. 4-7). pap. *(978-1-4190-3839-6(7),* Rigby) Pearson Education Australia.

Ford, John C. & Wells, Rosemary. The Cipher. 2015. (ENG.). 320p. (YA). (gr. 7). bds. 17.99 *(978-0-670-01542-9(3),* Viking Books for Young Readers) Penguin Young Readers Group.

Gutman, Dan. From Texas with Love. 2014. (Genius Files Ser.: 4). (ENG.). 304p. (J). (gr. 3-7). pap. 6.99 *(978-0-06-182775-4(4))* HarperCollins Pubs.

—From Texas with Love. 2014. (Genius Files Ser.: 4). (J). lib. bdg. 17.20 *(978-0-606-36462-1(5))* Turtleback Bks.

Hicks, Clifford B. Alvin's Secret Code. Sokol, Bill, illus. 2015. (J). pap. 9.99 *(978-1-930900-85-1(6))* Purple Hse. Pr.

Hirsch, Jeff. Breakaway. 2014. (39 Clues Ser.: Bk. 2). (ENG., Illus.). 192p. (J). (gr. 3-7). 12.99 *(978-0-545-52142-0(4))* Scholastic, Inc.

Korman, Gordon. The Emperor's Code. 2010. (39 Clues Ser.: 8). (ENG., Illus.). 192p. (J). (gr. 3-7). 12.99 *(978-0-545-06048-6(6))* Scholastic, Inc.

—The Medusa Plot. 2011. (39 Clues: Cahills vs. Vespers Ser.: 1). (ENG., Illus.). 224p. (J). (gr. 3-7). 12.99 *(978-0-545-32409-0(2),* Scholastic Pr.); 12.99 *(978-0-545-29839-1(3))* Scholastic, Inc.

Lerangis, Peter. The Viper's Nest. 2010. (39 Clues Ser.: Bk. 7). (J). 49.99 *(978-1-61637-711-3(9))* Findaway World, LLC.

—The Viper's Nest. 2010. (39 Clues Ser.: 7). (ENG., Illus.). 192p. (J). (gr. 3-7). 12.99 *(978-0-545-06047-9(8))* Scholastic, Inc.

London, C. Alexander & Scholastic, Inc. Staff. Mission Hindenburg. 2015. (39 Clues: Doublecross Ser.: 2). (ENG., Illus.). 192p. (J). (gr. 3-7). 12.99 *(978-0-545-76743-9(1))* Scholastic, Inc.

Mone, Gregory. Fish. 2010. (J). *(978-0-545-11631-2(7),* Scholastic Pr.) Scholastic, Inc.

Park, Linda Sue. Storm Warning. 2010. (39 Clues Ser.: 9). (ENG.). 192p. (J). (gr. 3-7). 12.99 *(978-0-545-09067-4(9));* (Illus.). 12.99 *(978-0-545-06049-3(4))* Scholastic, Inc.

Peers, Bobbie. William Wenton & the Impossible Puzzle. 2017. (William Wenton Ser.: 1). (ENG., Illus.). 272p. (J). (gr. 3-7). 16.99 ***(978-1-4814-7825-0(7),*** Aladdin) Simon & Schuster Children's Publishing.

Peterson Haddix, Margaret. EL DESAFÍO FINAL: THE 39 CLUES 10. 2013. (SPA.). 304p. (J). pap. 14.99 *(978-84-08-10876-4(X))* Noguer y Caralt Editores, S. A. ESP. Dist: Lectorum Pubns., Inc.

Richards, Justin. The Chaos Code. 2007. (ENG.). 400p. (YA). (gr. 7-12). 17.95 *(978-1-59990-124-4(2),* 9781599901244, Bloomsbury USA Childrens) Bloomsbury Publishing USA.

Riley, Clifford. Operation Trinity. 2012. (39 Clues: the Cahill Files Ser.). (ENG.). 144p. (J). (gr. 3-7). 9.99 *(978-0-545-43143-9(3))* Scholastic, Inc.

Ringwald, Whitaker. The Secret Cipher. 2016. (Secret Box Ser.: 2). 272p. (J). (gr. 3-7). pap. 6.99 *(978-0-06-221618-2(X),* Tegen, Katherine Bks) HarperCollins Pubs.

—The Secret Cipher: A Secret Box Book. 2015. (Secret Box Ser.: 2). (ENG.). 256p. (J). (gr. 3-7). 16.99 *(978-0-06-221617-5(1),* Tegen, Katherine Bks) HarperCollins Pubs.

Sparkes, Ali. Chameleon Chaos. Collins, Ross, illus. 2014. (S. W. I. T. C. H. Ser.: 10). (ENG.). 112p. (J). (gr. 2-5). lib. bdg. 27.93 *(978-1-4677-2113-4(1),* Darby Creek) Lerner Publishing Group.

—Gecko Gladiator. Collins, Ross, illus. 2014. (S. W. I. T. C. H. Ser.: 12). (ENG.). 104p. (J). (gr. 2-5). lib. bdg. 27.93 *(978-1-4677-2115-8(8),* Darby Creek) Lerner Publishing Group.

—Lizard Loopy. Collins, Ross, illus. 2014. (S. W. I. T. C. H. Ser.: 9). (ENG.). 104p. (J). (gr. 2-5). lib. bdg. 27.93 *(978-1-4677-2112-7(3),* Darby Creek) Lerner Publishing Group.

—Turtle Terror. Collins, Ross, illus. 2014. (S. W. I. T. C. H. Ser.: 11). (ENG.). 104p. (J). (gr. 2-5). lib. bdg. 27.93 *(978-1-4677-2114-1(X),* Darby Creek) Lerner Publishing Group.

Standiford, Natalie. Countdown, Bk. 3. 2014. (39 Clues: Unstoppable Ser.: 3). (ENG., Illus.). 192p. (J). (gr. 3-7). 12.99 *(978-0-545-52145-1(9))* Scholastic, Inc.

Stilton, Geronimo. The Mona Mousa Code. Wolf, Matt, illus. 2005. (Geronimo Stilton Ser.: No. 15). 113p. (J). lib. bdg. 10.00 *(978-1-4242-0284-3(1))* Fitzgerald Bks.

Stokes, Jonathan W. Addison Cooke & the Treasure of the Incas. 2016. (Addison Cooke Ser.). (ENG., Illus.). 336p. (J). (gr. 3-7). 16.99 *(978-0-399-17377-6(3),* Philomel Bks.) Penguin Young Readers Group.

Stone, Phoebe. The Romeo & Juliet Code. 2012. (ENG.). 320p. (J). (gr. 3-7). pap. 7.99 *(978-0-545-21827-6(6),* Levine, Arthur A. Bks.) Scholastic, Inc.

Walters, Eric & Spreekmeester, Kevin. Death by Exposure. 2nd ed. 2006. (ENG., Illus.). 88p. (J). (gr. 4-8). pap. 9.99 *(978-1-55002-632-0(1),* Dundurn Pr.) Dundurn CAN. Dist: Ingram Publisher Services.

Warner, Penny. The Code Busters Club, Case #2: the Haunted Lighthouse. 2013. (Code Busters Club Ser.). (ENG.). 208p. (J). (gr. 4-7). pap. 6.99 *(978-1-60684-455-7(5),* Darby Creek) Lerner Publishing Group.

—The Code Busters Club, Case #3: the Mystery of the Pirate's Treasure. 2014. (ENG.). 192p. (J). (gr. 3-7). pap. 6.99 *(978-1-60684-517-2(9),* Darby Creek) Lerner Publishing Group.

—The Code Busters Club, Case #4: the Mummy's Curse. 2014. (ENG., Illus.). 224p. (J). (gr. 3-7). 16.99 *(978-1-60684-459-5(8),* Darby Creek) Lerner Publishing Group.

—The Hunt for the Missing Spy. 2016. (Code Busters Club Ser.: 5). (ENG.). 168p. (J). (gr. 3-6). 16.99 *(978-1-5124-0304-6(0))* Lerner Publishing Group.

—Mystery of the Pirate's Treasure. 2013. (Code Busters Club Ser.). (ENG.). 192p. (J). (gr. 4-7). 16.99 *(978-1-60684-457-1(1),* Darby Creek) Lerner Publishing Group.

—The Secret of the Puzzle Box. 2016. (Code Busters Club Ser.: 6). (ENG.). 192p. (J). (gr. 3-6). 16.99 *(978-1-5124-0307-7(5));* 33.32 *(978-1-5124-0900-0(6))* Lerner Publishing Group. (Darby Creek).

—The Secret of the Skeleton Key. (Code Busters Club Ser.). (ENG.). 224p. (J). (gr. 4-7). 2012. pap. 6.99 *(978-1-60684-390-1(7))* 2011. (Illus.). 15.99 *(978-1-60684-162-4(9))* Lerner Publishing Group. (Darby Creek).

Wells, Marcia. Doom at Grant's Tomb. Calo, Marcos, illus. 2017. (Eddie Red Undercover Ser.: 3). (ENG.). 208p. (J). (gr. 5-7). pap. 6.99 *(978-0-544-93733-8(3),* HMH Books For Young Readers) Houghton Mifflin Harcourt Publishing Co.

West, Tracey. The Secret Cipher Cases. Harrington, Rich, illus. 2006. 96p. (J). *(978-0-439-91448-2(5))* Scholastic, Inc.

CODE NAMES

see Ciphers

CODY, WILLIAM FREDERICK, 1846-1917

see Buffalo Bill, 1846-1917

COFFEE

Cervone, Barbara, ed. In Our Village: Boto, Ethiopia Through the Eyes of Its Youth. 2012. (Illus.). 90p. pap. 12.95 *(978-0-9815595-6-8(5))* Next Generation Pr.

Gilbert, Sara. Built for Success: The\Story of Starbucks. 2008. (Built for Success Ser.). (Illus.). 46p. (YA). (gr. 5-9). 22.95 *(978-1-58341-609-9(9))* Creative Co., The.

—The Story of Starbucks. 2011. (Built for Success Ser.). (ENG.). 48p. (J). (gr. 4-7). pap. 12.00 *(978-0-89812-737-9(8),* Creative Paperbacks) Creative Co., The.

Greenhaven Press Editors. Caffeine. 2016. (At Issue Ser.). (ENG.). 128p. (J). (gr. 10-12). 39.40 *(978-0-7377-7380-4(4),* Greenhaven Pr., Inc.) Cengage Gale.

Morganelli, Adrianna. The Biography of Coffee. 2006. (How Did That Get Here? Ser.). (ENG., Illus.). 32p. (J). (gr. 4-7). pap. *(978-0-7787-2524-4(3),* 1259496); lib. bdg. *(978-0-7787-2488-9(3),* 1259496) Crabtree Publishing Co.

Sanders, Susan & Sandbeck, Fletcher. Coffee Roasting at Home: The Magic Bean. l.t. ed. 2003. (Magic Bean Coffee Books: Vol. 1). (Illus.). viii, 145p. pap. 17.95 *(978-0-9709730-0-9(4),* MB001) Cumuli.

Snyder, R. Bradley & Engelsgjerd, Marc. What Every Child Needs to Know about Coffee. 2014. (ENG.). 22p. (-k). 8.95 *(978-1-940705-02-6(9))* Need To Know Publishing.

Sobol, Richard. Growing Peace: A Story of Farming, Music, & Religious Harmony, 1 vol. 2016. (ENG., Illus.). 40p. (J). 18.95 *(978-1-60060-450-8(1))* Lee & Low Bks., Inc.

Walker, Ida. Natural & Everyday Drugs: A False Sense of Security. 2012. (J). pap. *(978-1-4222-2456-4(2))* Mason Crest.

—Natural & Everyday Drugs: A False Sense of Security. Henningfield, Jack E., ed. 2012. (Illicit & Misused Drugs Ser.). 128p. (J). (gr. 7). 24.95 *(978-1-4222-2437-3(6))* Mason Crest.

COFFEE—FICTION

Mohamed, Sultan, tr. & illus. The Story of Coffee. Mohamed, Sultan, illus. 2003. (ENG & AMH.). 24p. (J). (gr. 4-5). 15.99 *(978-0-9605670-9-6(7))* Ananse Pr.

Springer, Kristina. The Espressologist. 2011. (ENG.). 208p. (YA). (gr. 7-12). pap. 15.99 *(978-0-312-65923-3(7))* Square Fish.

Steffen, Tim. Mom's Cup of Coffee: The (Incr)Edible Adventures of Allie Quirk. 2012. (Illus.). 65p. (J). pap. *(978-0-9779518-5-7(5))* Cardinal Pr.

COGNITION

see Knowledge, Theory of

COHAN, GEORGE M. (GEORGE MICHAEL), 1878-1942

Schwaeber, Barbie. Grand Old Flag. Nussbaum, Ben, ed. Pamintuan, Macky & Wang, Qi, illus. 2006. (Smithsonian American Favorites Ser.). (ENG.). 32p. (J). (gr. -1-3). 9.85 *(978-1-59249-650-1(4))* Soundprints.

Schwaeber, Barbie H. Grand Old Flag. Nussbaum, Ben, ed. Wang, Qi, illus. 2006. (Smithsonian American Favorites Ser.). (ENG.). 32p. (J). (gr. 3-7). 14.95 *(978-1-59249-649-5(0))* Soundprints.

COIN COLLECTING

see Coins

COINS

see also Numismatics

Anderson, Jill. Money Math with Sebastian Pig & Friends at the Farmer's Market. Amy Huntington, illus. 2013. (Math Fun with Sebastian Pig & Friends! Ser.). 32p. (J). (gr. k-3). pap. 7.95 *(978-0-7660-5983-2(9),* Enslow Elementary) Enslow Pubs., Inc.

—Money Math with Sebastian Pig & Friends at the Farmer's Market. Huntington, Amy, illus. 2009. (Math Fun with Sebastian Pig & Friends! Ser.). 32p. (J). (gr. k-3). lib. bdg. 23.94 *(978-0-7660-3364-1(3))* Enslow Pubs., Inc.

Brennan-Nelson, Denise. Penny: The Forgotten Coin. Monroe, Michael Glenn, illus. 2003. (ENG.). 32p. (J). (gr. k-6). 15.95 *(978-1-58536-128-1(3))* Sleeping Bear Pr.

Bullard, Lisa. This Is My State. Conger, Holli, illus. 2016. (Cloverleaf Books (tm) — Where I Live Ser.). (ENG.). 24p. (J). (gr. k-2). 25.32 *(978-1-4677-9523-4(2))* Lerner Publishing Group.

Cleary, Brian. A Dollar, a Penny, How Much & How Many? Gable, Brian, illus. 2014. (Math Is CATegorical (r) Ser.). (ENG.). 32p. (gr. k-3). pap. 6.95 *(978-1-4677-2629-0(X),* Millbrook Pr.) Lerner Publishing Group.

Cleary, Brian P. A Dollar, a Penny, How Much & How Many? Gable, Brian, illus. 2012. (Math Is CATegorical (r) Ser.). (ENG.). 32p. (gr. k-3). lib. bdg. 16.95 *(978-0-8225-7882-6(4),* Millbrook Pr.) Lerner Publishing Group.

Coins & Money. 2015. (Coins & Money Ser.). (ENG.). 24p. (J). (gr. 1-1). pap., pap., pap. 297.00 *(978-1-4994-1276-5(2),* PowerKids Pr.) Rosen Publishing Group, Inc., The.

Crewe, Sabrina. Canadian Coins. 2015. (Canadian Symbols Ser.). (ENG.). 24p. (gr. k-1). lib. bdg. 26.65 *(978-1-4914-7093-0(3),* Pebble Plus) Capstone Press of Coughlan Cos.

Fitzgerald, Lee. Quarters! 2015. (Coins & Money Ser.). (ENG.). 24p. (J). (gr. 1-1). 23.60 *(978-1-4994-0503-3(0),* PowerKids Pr.) Rosen Publishing Group, Inc., The.

Hallberg, Garth Risk. The Penny: A Little History of Luck. 2008. (Memoire Ser.). (ENG.). 79p. 25.00 *(978-2-7594-0304-2(1))* Assouline FRA. Dist: Two Rivers Distribution.

Heos, Bridget. Counting Change. Longhi, Katya, illus. 2015. (Math World Ser.). 24p. (J). lib. bdg. 27.10 *(978-1-60753-462-4(2))* Amicus Publishing.

Hill, Mary. Pennies. 2005. (Welcome Bks.). (ENG., Illus.). 24p. (J). (gr. -1-2). pap. 4.95 *(978-0-516-25172-1(4),* Children's Pr.) Scholastic Library Publishing.

Jones, Tammy. Look at the Coins. 2009. (Sight Word Readers Set A Ser.). (J). 3.49 net. *(978-1-60719-155-1(5))* Newmark Learning LLC.

—We Can Use Coins. 2006. (Early Explorers Ser.). (J). pap. *(978-1-4108-6042-2(6))* Benchmark Education Co.

Kompelien, Tracy. I Know about Money, It Is So Funny!, 1 vol. 2007. (Math Made Fun Ser.). (ENG., Illus.). 24p. (J). (gr. k-3). lib. bdg. 24.21 *(978-1-59928-527-6(4),* SandCastle) ABDO Publishing Co.

Meachen Rau, Dana. Coins. 2010. (Money & Banks Ser.). (Illus.). 24p. (gr. 2-5). pap. 8.15 *(978-1-4339-3378-3(0))* Stevens, Gareth Publishing LLLP.

—Las Monedas (Coins) 2010. (Dinero y los Bancos (Money & Banks) Ser.). (SPA., Illus.). 24p. (gr. 2-5). pap. 8.15 *(978-1-4339-3712-5(3))* Stevens, Gareth Publishing LLLP.

Michaels, Chris. Our Tag Sale. 2010. (Sight Word Readers Ser.). (J). 3.49 *(978-1-60719-627-3(1))* Newmark Learning LLC.

Money - Set 1: Coins That Add Up. 2005. (J). spiral bd. 19.90 *(978-0-9770248-4-1(9))* Sidedoor Publishing LLC.

Morgan, Elizabeth. Nickels! 2015. (Coins & Money Ser.). (ENG., Illus.). 24p. (J). (gr. 1-1). 23.60 *(978-1-4994-0501-9(4),* PowerKids Pr.) Rosen Publishing Group, Inc., The.

Otfinoski, Steve. Coin Collecting for Kids. Graham, Jack, illus. 2007. (ENG.). 12p. (J). (gr. 2-7). spiral bd. 17.99 *(978-1-58476-624-7(7),* IKIDS) Innovative Kids.

Rau, Dana Meachen. Coins. 2010. (Money & Banks Ser.). (Illus.). 24p. (J). (gr. 2-5). lib. bdg. 22.00 *(978-1-4339-3377-6(2))* Stevens, Gareth Publishing LLLP.

Reid, Margarette S. Lots & Lots of Coins. Kelley, True, illus. 2011. (ENG.). 32p. (J). (gr. 1-3). 16.99 *(978-0-525-47879-9(5),* Dutton Books for Young Readers) Penguin Young Readers Group.

Rowe, Brooke. Shining a Penny. Bane, Jeff, illus. 2016. (My Early Library: My Science Fun Ser.). (ENG.). 24p. (J). (gr. k-1). 28.50 *(978-1-63471-030-5(4),* 208200) Cherry Lake Publishing.

Stuart, Carrie. Kinds of Coins: Learning the Values of Pennies, Nickels, Dimes & Quarters. 2009. (Math for the REAL World Ser.). 12p. (gr. 1-2). pap. 5.90 *(978-0-8239-8862-4(7),* Rosen Classroom) Rosen Publishing Group, Inc., The.

Whitman Publishing, ed. Adventure Across the States: Collecting State Quarters & Other Coins. 2006. (Official Whitman Guidebook Ser.). (Illus.). 92p. per. 4.99 *(978-0-7948-2050-3(6))* Whitman Publishing LLC.

Williams, Rozanne Lanczak. Learning about Coins. Jarrett, Michael, photos by. 2004. (I Can Do Math Ser.). (Illus.). 24p. (gr. k-3). lib. bdg. 22.00 *(978-0-8368-4110-7(7),* Gareth Stevens Learning Library) Stevens, Gareth Publishing LLLP.

Yearling, Tricia & Summers, Portia. One Dollar: How Many Pennies? 2016. (Value of Money Ser.). (Illus.). 24p. (J). (gr. 2-1). pap. 9.35 *(978-0-7660-7685-3(7))* Enslow Pubs., Inc.

COINS—FICTION

Afyouni. Ed.D., Hassan. Lucky Penny: The Lucky Series. 2012. 32p. pap. 19.95 *(978-1-4520-2328-1(X))* AuthorHouse.

Beck, W. H. Malcolm under the Stars. Lies, Brian, illus. (ENG.). 272p. (J). (gr. 2-5). 2016. pap. 7.99 *(978-0-544-81312-0(X))* 2015. 16.99 *(978-0-544-39267-0(1))* Houghton Mifflin Harcourt Publishing Co. (HMH Books For Young Readers).

Borden, Louise. Kindergarten Luck. Godbout, Geneviève, illus. 2015. (ENG.). 32p. (J). (gr. -1-k). 16.99 *(978-1-4521-1394-4(7))* Chronicle Bks. LLC.

Burack, Emilie Christie. The Runaway's Gold. 2015. (ENG., Illus.). 320p. (YA). (gr. 3-9). 16.95 *(978-1-4197-1369-9(8),* Amulet Bks.) Abrams, Inc.

Cartwheel: A Sequel to Double Eagle. 2013. (ENG.). 252p. (YA). 17.00 *(978-0-9844460-3-2(6))* Bucking Horse Bks.

Collard, Sneed B., III. Double Eagle. 1 vol. 2011. (ENG.). 256p. pap. 7.95 *(978-1-56145-599-7(7),* Peachtree Junior) Peachtree Pubs.

C

D

Cotler, Steve. Cheesie Mack Is Not a Genius or Anything. McCauley, Adam, illus. 2011. (Cheesie Mack Ser.). (ENG.). 240p. (J). (gr. 3-7). 15.99 (978-0-375-86437-7(7), Random Hse. Bks. for Young Readers) Random Hse. Children's Bks.
Dahl, Michael. The Crushing Coin. Vecchio, Luciano, illus. 2016. (Batman Tales of the Batcave Ser.). (ENG.). 40p. (gr. 1-3). lib. bdg. 24.65 (978-1-4965-4014-0(X), DC Super Heroes) Stone Arch Bks.
Freeman, Martha. The Case of the Piggy Bank Thief: First Kids Mystery #4. 2013. (First Kids Mystery Ser.: 4). (ENG.). 144p. (J). (gr. 1-5). pap. 6.99 (978-0-8234-2916-5(4)) Holiday Hse., Inc.
Gordon, Amy. Twenty Gold Falcons. (ENG.). 240p. (J). (gr. 3-7). 2012. pap. 8.99 (978-0-8234-2656-0(4)) 2010. 16.95 (978-0-8234-2252-4(6)) Holiday Hse., Inc.
Juarbe, Cynthia. Callie the Caterpillar Collects Coins. 2011. 24p. pap. 13.50 (978-1-4520-5641-8(2)) AuthorHouse.
Klise, Kate. Till Death Do Us Bark. 2012. (43 Old Cemetery Road Ser.: 3). lib. bdg. 17.20 (978-0-606-26543-0(0), Turtleback) Turtleback Bks.
Klise, Kate & Klise, M. Sarah. Till Death Do Us Bark. Klise, Kate & Klise, M. Sarah, illus. 2011. (43 Old Cemetery Road Ser.: 3). (ENG., Illus.). 144p. (J). (gr. 2-5). 16.99 (978-0-547-40036-5(5)) Houghton Mifflin Harcourt Publishing Co.
Lubar, David. Dinosaur Disaster. Loveridge, Matt, illus. 2013. (Looniverse Ser.: 3). (ENG.). 96p. (J). (gr. 1-3). 15.99 (978-0-545-49605-6(5)); pap. 4.99 (978-0-545-49606-3(3)) Scholastic, Inc.
—Dinosaur Disaster. 2013. (Looniverse Ser.: 3). lib. bdg. 14.75 (978-0-606-32367-3(8), Turtleback) Turtleback Bks.
—Meltdown Madness. Loveridge, Matt, illus. 2013. (Looniverse Ser.: 2). (ENG.). 96p. (J). (gr. 1-3). 15.99 (978-0-545-49603-2(9)); pap. 4.99 (978-0-545-49604-9(7)) Scholastic, Inc.
—Meltdown Madness. 2013. (Looniverse Ser.: 2). lib. bdg. 14.75 (978-0-606-31983-6(2), Turtleback) Turtleback Bks.
—Stranger Things. Loveridge, Matt, illus. 2013. (Looniverse Ser.: 1). (ENG.). 96p. (J). (gr. 1-3). pap. 4.99 (978-0-545-49602-5(0)) Scholastic, Inc.
—Stranger Things. 2013. (Looniverse Ser.: 1). lib. bdg. 14.75 (978-0-606-31982-9(4), Turtleback) Turtleback Bks.
May, Eleanor. Albert Helps Out: Counting Money. Melmon, Deborah, illus. 2017. (Mouse Math (r) Ser.). (ENG.). 32p. (gr. -1-1). 7.95 (978-1-57565-860-5(7)) Kane Press, Inc.
—Albert Helps Out: Counting Money. Melmon, Deborah, illus. 2017. (Mouse Math (r) Ser.). (ENG.). 32p. (gr. -1-1). lib. bdg. 22.65 (978-1-57565-857-5(7)); 34.65 **(978-1-57565-863-6(1))** Kane Press, Inc.
Melvin, Treva. Mr. Samuel's Penny. 2014. (Elizabeth Parrot Landers Mysteries Ser.: 1). (ENG.). 264p. (YA). pap. 10.95 (978-1-929345-04-5(6)) Poisoned Pen Pr.
Nam, Jeong-hee & Cowley, Joy. Lion, King & Coin. Sforza, Lucia, illus. 2017. (J). 10.00 **(978-0-8028-5475-9(3)**, Eerdmans Bks For Young Readers) Eerdmans, William B. Publishing Co.
Nathan, Sarah. Jasmine: The Missing Coin, 1 vol. Studio IBOIX, illus. 2012. (Disney Princesses Set 2 Ser.). (ENG.). 96p. (J). (gr. 2-6). lib. bdg. 24.21 (978-1-59961-182-2(1)) Spotlight.
Rose, Simon. Les Loonies: Les Emblèmes Canadiens. McMann, Julie, tr. from ENG. 2011. (FRE.). 24p. (YA). (gr. 2-4). (978-1-77071-409-0(X)) Weigl Educational Pubs. Ltd.
Sainsbury, Adam. The Coin. 2005. 84p. (YA). pap. 9.96 (978-1-4116-5358-0(0)) Lulu Pr., Inc.
Stine, R. L. Heads, You Lose. 2010. (Goosebumps Horrorland Ser.: 15). (ENG.). 160p. (J). (gr. 3-7). 6.99 (978-0-545-16196-1(7), Scholastic Paperbacks) Scholastic, Inc.
Sutton, Laurie S. Two-Face Face-Off. Vecchio, Luciano, illus. 2016. (Batman & Robin Adventures Ser.). (ENG.). 88p. (gr. 2-3). lib. bdg. 26.65 (978-1-4965-2535-2(3), DC Super Heroes) Stone Arch Bks.
Trivas, Tracy. The Wish Stealers. 2011. (ENG.). 288p. (J). (gr. 3-7). pap. 7.99 (978-1-4169-8726-0(6), Aladdin) Simon & Schuster Children's Publishing.
Vermazen, Eve. Dogtales: Sebastian & the Destiny Stone. 2012. 36p. pap. 32.70 (978-1-4797-4032-1(2)) Xlibris Corp.
Warrington, Dean Grey. Perfiction. 2007. 188p. per. 13.95 (978-0-595-43758-0(3)) iUniverse, Inc.
Williams, Suzanne. The Lucky Penny? Carter, Abby, illus. 2004. 56p. (J). lib. bdg. 15.00 (978-1-4242-0909-5(9)) Fitzgerald Bks.
Yasuda, Anita. The Mystery Coins, 1 vol. Harpster, Steve, illus. 2013. (Dino Detectives Ser.). (ENG.). 32p. (gr. 1-2). lib. bdg. 22.65 (978-1-4342-5972-1(2)) Stone Arch Bks.
—Mystery Coins. Harpster, Steve, illus. 2013. (Dino Detectives Ser.). (ENG.). 32p. (gr. 1-2). pap. 5.95 (978-1-4342-6201-1(4)) Stone Arch Bks.
Yasuda, Anita & Harpster, Steve. The Mystery Coins. 2013. (Dino Detectives Ser.). (ENG.). 32p. (gr. 1-2). pap. 29.70 (978-1-4342-6228-8(6)) Stone Arch Bks.

COLD

Amstutz, Lisa J. Discover Cryobiology. 2016. (Searchlight Books (tm) — What's Cool about Science? Ser.). (ENG., Illus.). 40p. (J). (gr. 3-5). 30.65 (978-1-5124-0807-2(7)) Lerner Publishing Group.
Berger, Melvin & Berger, Gilda. Cold Weather. 2010. (Illus.). 16p. (J). (978-0-545-16084-1(7)) Scholastic, Inc.
Canavan, Thomas. Cool Experiments with Heat & Cold. Linley, Adam, illus. 2017. (Mind-Blowing Science Experiments Ser.). 32p. (gr. 4-5). pap. 63.00 **(978-1-5382-0729-1(X))** Stevens, Gareth Publishing LLLP.
Corcorane, Ann. Hot & Cold. 2011. (Wonder Readers Emergent Level Ser.). (ENG.). (gr. -1-1). 16p. pap. 35.94 (978-1-4296-8095-0(4)); 32p. pap. 5.99 (978-1-4296-7865-0(8)) Capstone Press of Coughlan Cos. (Wonder Readers).
Faulk, Michelle. The Case of the Sneezy Popcorn: Annie Biotica Solves Respiratory System Disease Crimes. 2013. (Body System Disease Investigations Ser.). 48p. (J). (gr. 5-12). lib. bdg. 25.27 (978-0-7660-3946-9(3)) Enslow Pubs., Inc.
Gardner, Robert. How Hot Is Hot? Science Projects with Temperature. 2015. (Hot Science Experiments Ser.). 48p. (J). (gr. 3-4). 25.27 (978-0-7660-6605-2(3)); pap. 8.95 (978-0-7660-6606-9(1), Enslow Elementary) Enslow Pubs., Inc.
—Really Hot Science Projects with Temperature: How Hot Is It? How Cold Is It? 2003. (Sensational Science Experiments Ser.). (Illus.). 48p. (J). lib. bdg. 25.27 (978-0-7660-2015-3(0)) Enslow Pubs., Inc.
Guillain, Charlotte. Caliente o Frío, 1 vol. 2010. (Las Propiedades de Los Materiales Ser.). (SPA.). 24p. (gr. -1-1). 22.65 (978-1-4329-4239-7(5)); pap. 6.29 (978-1-4329-4247-2(6)) Heinemann-Raintree. (Bellota).
HarrisNic. HOW COOL IS COLD! LOW INTERMEDIATE BOOK WITH ONLINE ACCESS. 2014. (ENG.). 24p. (J). pap. 9.50 (978-1-107-65803-5(9)) Cambridge Univ. Pr.
Hawkins, Jay. Hot Stuff: The Science of Heat & Cold. 2013. (Big Bang Science Experiments Ser.). (ENG., Illus.). 32p. (gr. 3-6). 26.50 (978-1-4777-0321-2(7)); pap. 11.75 (978-1-4777-0363-2(2)) Windmill Bks.
Hughes, Susan. Is It Hot or Cold? 2012. (ENG., Illus.). 24p. (J). (978-0-7787-2049-2(7)); pap. (978-0-7787-2056-0(X)) Crabtree Publishing Co.
Hughes, Tom. Hot & Cold. 2016. (All about Opposites Ser.). (Illus.). 24p. (J). pap. 9.35 (978-0-7660-8110-9(9)) Enslow Pubs., Inc.
Jeffries, Joyce. Hot & Cold. 2013. (Dinosaur School Ser.). (Illus.). 24p. (gr. -1-1). 22.60 (978-1-4339-8091-6(0)); pap. 8.15 (978-1-4339-8092-3(4)) Stevens, Gareth Publishing LLLP.
Jennings, Terry. Hot & Cold. 2009. (Science Alive Ser.). (Illus.). 32p. (J). (gr. -1-2). pap. (978-1-897563-55-7(8)) Saunders Bk. Co.
Keiser, Cody. Is It Hot or Is It Cold? Describe & Compare Measurable Attributes. 2013. (InfoMax Math Readers Ser.). (ENG., Illus.). 16p. (J). (gr. k-1). pap. 7.00 (978-1-4777-2012-7(X), Rosen Classroom) Rosen Publishing Group, Inc., The.
Lindeen, Mary. Hot & Cold. 2017. (BeginningtoRead Ser.). (ENG.). 32p. (J). (-2). 22.60 **(978-1-59953-883-9(0))**; pap. 11.94 **(978-1-68404-102-2(3))** Norwood Hse. Pr.
Lipschultz, Wes. Is It Hot or Cold? Learning to Use a Thermometer. 2009. (Math for the REAL World Ser.). 12p. (gr. 1-2). pap. 5.90 (978-0-8239-8848-8(1), Rosen Classroom) Rosen Publishing Group, Inc., The.
Marshall Cavendish Benchmark, prod. Hot/Cold. 2nd rev. ed. 2011. (Bookworms 2nd Edition: Opposites Ser.). 16p. (gr. k-1). 21.36 (978-1-60870-409-5(2)) Marshall Cavendish Corp.
Oxlade, Chris. Enfriar, 1 vol. 2010. (Materiales Cambiantes Ser.).Tr. of Cooling. (SPA.). 32p. (gr. 1-3). 27.32 (978-1-4329-4430-8(4)); pap. 8.95 (978-1-4329-4435-3(5)) Heinemann-Raintree.
Rooke, Thom. A Germ's Journey, 1 vol. Trimmer, Tony, illus. (Follow It! Ser.). (ENG.). 24p. (gr. 1-3). 2011. pap. 7.49 (978-1-4048-6710-9(4)) 2010. lib. bdg. 26.65 (978-1-4048-6268-5(4)) Picture Window Bks.
Rustad, Martha E. H. Today Is a Cold Day. 2017. (What Is the Weather Today? Ser.). (ENG., Illus.). 24p. (gr. k-2). pap. 6.29 (978-1-4966-0947-2(6), Pebble Bks.) Capstone Press of Coughlan Cos.
Sheehan, Thomas F. Para Calentarse, para Refrescarse (Keeping Warm, Keeping Cool) Sarfatti, Esther, tr. 2005. (Ciencia Citadina Ser.). (ENG & SPA., Illus.). 24p. (J). (gr. 3-7). lib. bdg. 21.36 (978-1-59515-666-2(6)) Rourke Educational Media.
Smith, Sian. Hot & Cold, 1 vol. 2014. (Opposites Ser.). (ENG.). 24p. (gr. -1-1). pap. 5.99 (978-1-4846-0334-5(6), Acorn) Heinemann-Raintree.
Solway, Andrew. Secrets of Heat & Cold. 2010. (Science Secrets Ser.). 32p. (gr. 4). 28.50 (978-1-60870-138-4(7)) Marshall Cavendish GBR. Dist: Marshall Cavendish Corp.
Stille, Darlene R. & Picture Window Books Staff. La Temperatura: Caliente y Frio. Robledo, Sol, tr. from ENG. Boyd, Sheree, illus. 2007. (Ciencia Asombrosa Ser.). (SPA.). 24p. (gr. k-4). 26.65 (978-1-4048-3234-3(3)) Picture Window Bks.
World Book, Inc Staff, contrib. by. Icy Worlds. 2011. (J). (978-0-7166-1788-4(9)) World Bk., Inc.

COLD WAR

Here are entered works on the post World War II rivalry between western capitalist nations led by the United States and eastern communist nations led by the Soviet Union.

Baker, Lawrence W. Cold War Reference Library Cumulative Index. 2003. (Cold War Reference Library). (ENG.). 85p. (J). 5.00 (978-0-7876-7667-4(5), UXL) Cengage Gale.
—Immigration & Migration Reference. 2004. (US Immigration & Migration Reference Library). (ENG.). (J). 5.00 (978-0-7876-7734-3(5), UXL) Cengage Gale.
Bearce, Stephanie. Top Secret Files - The Cold War: Spies, Secrets, Special Missions, & Hidden Facts about the CIA, KGB, & MI6. rev. ed. 2015. (Top Secret Files of History Ser.: 0). (ENG., Illus.). 125p. (J). (gr. 4-7). pap. 8.95 (978-1-61821-419-5(5)) Prufrock Pr.
Beyer, Mark. Nuclear Weapons & the Cold War. (Library of Weapons of Mass Destruction Ser.). 64p. 2009. (gr. 5-5). 58.50 (978-1-60853-953-6(9)) 2005. (Illus.). (J). lib. bdg. 31.95 (978-1-4042-0290-0(0)) Rosen Publishing Group, Inc., The.
Bodden, Valerie. The Cold War. 2007. (Days of Change Ser.). (Illus.). 48p. (YA). (gr. 4-7). lib. bdg. 31.35 (978-1-58341-546-7(7)) Creative Co., The.
Bodden, Valerie & Riggs, Kate. The End of the Cold War. 2017. (Turning Points Ser.). (ENG., Illus.). 48p. (J). (gr. 7-12). pap. 12.00 (978-1-62832-344-3(2), Creative Paperbacks) Creative Co., The.
Bougie, Matt. Strategic Inventions of the Cold War. 2016. (Tech in the Trenches Ser.). (ENG., Illus.). 112p. (J). (gr. 9-9). 42.79 (978-1-5026-1022-5(1)) Cavendish Square Publishing.
Brownell, Richard. The Cold War. 2008. (American History Ser.). (ENG., Illus.). 96-128p. (gr. 7-10). 34.80 (978-1-4205-0032-5(5), Lucent Bks.) Cengage Gale.
Byers, Ann. The Legacy of the Cold War. 2017. (J). **(978-1-5026-2865-7(1))** Cavendish Square Publishing.
Clare, John D. Cold War & After. 2nd rev. ed. 2005. (Illus.). 64p. pap. 26.50 (978-0-340-81480-2(2), Hodder Education) Hodder Education Group GBR. Dist: Trans-Atlantic Pubns., Inc.
The Cold War & Postwar America 1946-1963. 2010. (Discovering U. S. History Ser.). (Illus.). 136p. (gr. 5-8). 35.00 (978-1-60413-360-8(0), Chelsea Hse.) Facts On File, Inc.
Conklin, Wendy. The Cold War, 1 vol. 2007. (Primary Source Readers Ser.). (ENG.). 32p. (J). (gr. 5-5). pap. 8.99 (978-0-7439-0672-2(1)) Shell Educational Publishing.
—Cold War Leaders, 1 vol. 2007. (Primary Source Readers Ser.). (ENG.). 32p. (J). (gr. 4-4). pap. 8.99 (978-0-7439-0673-9(X)) Shell Educational Publishing.
Corona, Laurel. War Within a War: Vietnam & the Cold War. 2004. (Lucent Library of Historical Eras). (ENG., Illus.). 112p. (J). 33.45 (978-1-59018-389-2(4), Lucent Bks.) Cengage Gale.
Crawford, Steve. Cold War. 2010. (FAYFT: Modern Military History Ser.). 64p. (gr. 4-10). 39.95 (978-1-933834-52-8(8)) Brown Bear Bks.
Day, Meredith, ed. The Cold War. 2016. (Political & Diplomatic History of the Modern World Ser.). 224p. (J). (gr. 10-10). 46.00 (978-1-68048-358-1(7)) Rosen Publishing Group, Inc., The.
DeMarco, Neil & Aylett, J. F. Cold War & After. 2nd rev. ed. 2005. (Illus.). 64p. pap. 32.50 (978-0-340-81479-6(9)) Hodder Education Group GBR. Dist: Trans-Atlantic Pubns., Inc.
Doeden, Matt. The Berlin Wall: An Interactive Modern History Adventure, 1 vol. 2014. (You Choose: Modern History Ser.). (ENG.). 112p. (gr. 3-4). 31.99 (978-1-4914-0354-9(3), You Choose Bks.) Capstone Press of Coughlan Cos.
Duling, Kaitlyn. Nuclear Proliferation, the Military-Industrial Complex, & the Arms Race. 2017. (J). **(978-1-5026-2730-8(2))** Cavendish Square Publishing.
Dunn, Joeming. The Fall of the Berlin Wall, 1 vol. 2008. (Graphic History Ser.). (ENG., Illus.). 32p. 28.50 (978-1-60270-182-3(2), Graphic Planet- Nonfiction) ABDO Publishing Co.
George, Enzo. The Cold War. 2015. (Primary Sources in U. S. History Ser.). (ENG., Illus.). 48p. (J). (gr. 4-4). 31.36 (978-1-5026-0498-9(1)) Cavendish Square Publishing.
Goodman, Michael E. Cold War Spies. 2015. (Illus.). 48p. (J). (978-1-60818-599-3(0), Creative Education) Creative Co., The.
—Cold War Spies: Wartime Spies. 2016. (Wartime Spies Ser.). (ENG.). 48p. (J). (gr. 5-9). pap. 12.00 (978-1-62832-204-0(7), Creative Paperbacks) Creative Co., The.
Gottfried, Ted. The Cold War. Reim, Melanie, illus. 2003. (Rise & Fall of the Soviet Union Ser.). (ENG.). 160p. (gr. 7-12). lib. bdg. 29.20 (978-0-7613-2560-4(3), Twenty-First Century Bks.) Lerner Publishing Group.
Hanes, Sharon M., et al. Cold War: Almanac, 2 vols. 2003. (U-X-L Cold War Reference Library). (Illus.). (J). (978-0-7876-9087-8(2)); 200p. 55.00 (978-0-7876-7662-9(4)); (ENG., 376p. lib. bdg. 191.00 (978-0-7876-9089-2(9)) Cengage Gale. (UXL).
—Cold War: Biographies, 2 vols. 2003. (U-X-L Cold War Reference Library). (Illus.). (J). xxxv, 473p. (978-0-7876-7665-0(9)); (ENG., 474p. 191.00 (978-0-7876-7663-6(2)); xxxv, 473p. (978-0-7876-7664-3(0)) Cengage Gale. (UXL).
—Cold War - Primary Sources. 2003. (Cold War Reference Library). (ENG., Illus.). 400p. (J). 106.00 (978-0-7876-7666-7(7), UXL) Cengage Gale.
—Cold War Reference Library: Includes Cumulative Index, 5.0. Incl. Cold War: Almanac. 200p. 55.00 (978-0-7876-7662-9(4)); Cold War: Biographies. 474p. 191.00 (978-0-7876-7663-6(2)); Cold War - Primary Sources. 400p. 106.00 (978-0-7876-7666-7(7)); (J). (Cold War Reference Library). (ENG., Illus.). 800p. 2003. Set lib. bdg. 458.00 (978-0-7876-7609-4(8), UXL) Cengage Gale.
Harrison, Paul. The Cold War. 2005. (How Did It Happen? Ser.). (ENG., Illus.). 48p. (YA). (gr. 7-10). lib. bdg. 32.10 (978-1-59018-603-9(6), Lucent Bks.) Cengage Gale.
—Why Did the Cold War Happen? 2010. (Moments in History Ser.). 48p. (ENG.). (J). (gr. 6-8). pap. 14.05 (978-1-4339-4167-2(8), Gareth Stevens Secondary Library); (Illus.). (YA). (gr. 5-9). lib. bdg. 31.95 (978-1-4339-4166-5(X)) Stevens, Gareth Publishing LLLP.
Herwick Rice, Dona & Isecke, Harriet. Cold War: Communism on Trial, 1 vol. 2009. (Building Fluency Through Reader's Theater Ser.). (ENG.). 32p. (J). (gr. 3-5). pap. 7.99 (978-1-4333-0555-9(0)) Teacher Created Materials, Inc.
Hyde, Natalie. The Cold War & the Cuban Missile Crisis. 2016. (ENG., Illus.). 48p. (J). (978-0-7787-2570-1(7)) Crabtree Publishing Co.
Johnson, Jordan. Sputnik & the Space Race. 2017. (J). **(978-1-5026-2732-2(9))** Cavendish Square Publishing.
Kallen, Stuart A. Primary Sources. 2003. (American War Library). (ENG., Illus.). 112p. (J). 30.85 (978-1-59018-243-7(X), Lucent Bks.) Cengage Gale.
Keeley, Jennifer. Containing the Communists: America's Foreign Entanglements. 2003. (American War Library). (ENG., Illus.). 112p. (J). 30.85 (978-1-59018-225-3(1), Lucent Bks.) Cengage Gale.
Langston-George, Rebecca. Deep-Cover Spies & Double-Crossers of the Cold War. 2017. (Spies! Ser.). (ENG., Illus.). 64p. (gr. 5-6). lib. bdg. 33.99 (978-0-7565-5497-2(7), CPB Grades 4-8) Compass Point Bks.
Levering, Ralph B. The Cold War, 1945-1991. Eisenstadt, Abraham S. & Franklin, John Hope, eds. 2003. (American History Ser.). (Illus.). 200p. (J). (gr. 11-12). pap. 13.95 (978-0-88295-912-2(3)) Davidson, Harlan Inc.
Mason, Paul. Did Anything Good Come Out of the Cold War?, 01 vols., 1. 2016. (Innovation Through Adversity Ser.). (ENG.). 48p. (J). 30.25 (978-1-5081-7066-2(5), Rosen Young Adult) Rosen Publishing Group, Inc., The.
Maus, Derek C., ed. Living under the Threat of Nuclear War. 2005. (Living Through the Cold War Ser.). (ENG., Illus.). 143p. (YA). (gr. 10-12). lib. bdg. 37.90 (978-0-7377-2130-0(8), Greenhaven Pr., Inc.) Cengage Gale.
Morgan, Kayla. The Cold War, 1 vol. 2010. (Essential Events Set 5 Ser.). (ENG., Illus.). 112p. (J). (gr. 6-12). lib. bdg. 35.64 (978-1-61613-681-9(2)) ABDO Publishing Co.
Piddock, Charles. The Cold War. 2016. (Illus.). 48p. (J). (978-1-5105-1282-5(9)) SmartBook Media, Inc.
Richardson, Erik. NATO, the Warsaw Pact, & the Iron Curtain. 2017. (J). **(978-1-5026-2727-8(2))** Cavendish Square Publishing.
Riggs, Kate. The End of the Cold War. 2016. (Illus.). 48p. (J). (978-1-60818-748-5(9), Creative Education) Creative Co., The.
Roxburgh, Ellis. John F. Kennedy vs. Nikita Khrushchev. 2015. (History's Greatest Rivals Ser.). (ENG., Illus.). 48p. (J). (gr. 6-8). lib. bdg. 31.95 (978-1-4824-2221-4(2)) Stevens, Gareth Publishing LLLP.
Sasley, Brent. The Cold War in the Middle East, 1950-1991. 2009. (Making of the Middle East Ser.). (Illus.). 80p. (YA). (gr. 7-18). lib. bdg. 22.95 (978-1-4222-0173-2(2)) Mason Crest.
Sheehan, Sean. The Cold War. 2003. (Questioning History Ser.). (Illus.). 64p. (J). (gr. 5). lib. bdg. 28.50 (978-1-58340-266-5(7)) Black Rabbit Bks.
Sherman, Josepha. The Cold War. 2004. (Chronicle of America's Wars Ser.). (Illus.). 96p. (J). (gr. 5-12). 27.93 (978-0-8225-0150-3(3)) Lerner Publishing Group.
Small, Cathleen. The Collapse of Communism & the Break up of the Soviet Union. 2017. (J). **(978-1-5026-2728-5(0))** Cavendish Square Publishing.
Stanley, George Edward. America & the Cold War (1949-1969) 2005. (Primary Source History of the United States Ser.). (Illus.). 48p. (gr. 5-12). lib. bdg. 31.00 (978-0-8368-5830-3(1), Gareth Stevens Secondary Library) Stevens, Gareth Publishing LLLP.
Tracy, Kathleen. The Fall of the Berlin Wall. 2005. (Monumental Milestones Ser.). (Illus.). 48p. (YA). (gr. 4-7). lib. bdg. 29.95 (978-1-58415-405-1(5)) Mitchell Lane Pubs., Inc.
Ziff, John. The Cold War, Vol. 11. Musteen, Jason R., ed. 2015. (Major U. S. Historical Wars Ser.). (Illus.). 64p. (J). (gr. 7). lib. bdg. 23.95 (978-1-4222-3355-9(3)) Mason Crest.

COLLAGE

Chapman, Gillian & Robson, Pam. Making Art with Wood. 2007. (Everyday Art Ser.). (Illus.). 32p. (YA). (gr. 4-7). lib. bdg. 26.50 (978-1-4042-3726-1(7)) Rosen Publishing Group, Inc., The.
Collage. (Jump Ser.). (Illus.). 36p. (J). (gr. 2-6). pap. (978-1-882210-34-3(4)) Action Publishing, Inc.
Hanson, Anders. Cool Collage: The Art of Creativity for Kids, 1 vol. 2009. (Cool Art Ser.). (ENG.). 32p. (gr. 3-6). 28.50 (978-1-60453-146-6(0), Checkerboard Library) ABDO Publishing Co.
Henry, Sally. Collage. 2009. (Make Your Own Art Ser.). (Illus.). 32p. (ENG.). (gr. 2-6). pap. 11.75 (978-1-4358-2642-7(6)); (J). (gr. 3-6). lib. bdg. 26.50 (978-1-4358-2509-3(8)) Rosen Publishing Group, Inc., The. (PowerKids Pr.).
Hodge, Anthony. Collage. 2006. (SPA.). 32p. (978-958-30-1835-0(X)) Panamericana Editorial.
Johnson, Susan & Johnson, Wil. Making Collages. 2003. (Illus.). 32p. (J). pap. 6.00 (978-1-59034-183-4(X)) Mondo Publishing.
Luxbacher, Irene. 123 I Can Collage! Luxbacher, Irene, illus. 2009. (Starting Art Ser.). (ENG., Illus.). 24p. (J). (gr. -1-2). 14.95 (978-1-55453-313-8(9)); pap. 6.95 (978-1-55453-314-5(7)) Kids Can Pr., Ltd. CAN. Dist: Hachette Bk. Group.
Medina, Sarah. Having Fun with Collage. 2007. (Fun Art Projects Ser.). (Illus.). 24p. (J). (gr. 4-7). lib. bdg. 25.25 (978-1-4042-3721-6(6), PowerKids Pr.) Rosen Publishing Group, Inc., The.
QEB Let's Start! Art National Book Stores Edition: Collage. 2006. (J). per. (978-1-59566-301-6(0)) QEB Publishing Inc.
Rubin, Susan Goldman. Matisse Dance for Joy. 2008. (ENG., Illus.). 26p. (J). (gr. -1 — 1). bds. 6.99 (978-0-8118-6288-2(7)) Chronicle Bks. LLC.
Sabini, Oscar. Paper Zoo. 2015. (ENG., Illus.). 20p. (J). (gr. -1-3). 19.95 (978-1-61689-439-3(3)) Princeton Architectural Pr.
Thomas, Isabel. Collages, 1 vol. 2011. (Start with Art Ser.). (ENG.). 24p. (gr. k-2). 23.32 (978-1-4329-5020-0(7), Heinemann Read & Learn) Heinemann-Raintree.

COLLECTING

see Collectors and Collecting

COLLECTIONS OF LITERATURE

see Short Stories

also names of literatures and literary forms with the subdivision Collections, e.g. English Literature—Collections; Poetry—Collections

COLLECTIVE SETTLEMENTS

Hunter, David. Teen Life among the Amish & Other Alternative Communities: Choosing a Lifestyle. 2009. (Youth in Rural North America Ser.). 96p. (J). (gr. 7-18). lib. bdg. 22.95 (978-1-4222-0017-9(5)) Mason Crest.

COLLECTIVE SETTLEMENTS—FICTION

Berry, Kit. Solstice at Stonewylde. 2011. (ENG.). 400p. (gr. 13-17). 10.99 (978-0-575-09887-9(2), Gollancz) Orion Publishing Group, Ltd. GBR. Dist: Hachette Bk. Group.
Finneyfrock, Karen. Starbird Murphy & the World Outside. 2014. (ENG.). 384p. (YA). (gr. 7). 17.99 (978-0-670-01276-3(9), Viking Books for Young Readers) Penguin Young Readers Group.
Hurwitz, Laura. Disappear Home. 2015. (ENG.). 256p. (J). (gr. 8-12). 16.99 (978-0-8075-2468-8(9)) Whitman, Albert & Co.
Ostow, Micol. Family. 2011. (ENG.). 384p. (J). (gr. 9). 17.99 (978-1-60684-155-6(6), Carolrhoda Lab™) Lerner Publishing Group.
Reed, Amy. Over You. 2013. (ENG., Illus.). 320p. (YA). (gr. 9). 16.99 (978-1-4424-5696-9(5), Simon Pulse) Simon Pulse.

COLLECTIVISM

see Communism; Socialism

COLLECTORS AND COLLECTING

see also names of natural specimens with the subdivision Collection and Preservation, e.g. Zoological Specimens—Collection and Preservation

Allen, Tom & Allen, Susan. American Oil Cans Identification & Price Guide. Allen, Tom & Allen, Susan, eds. 2003. (Illus.). 128p. (YA). per. 24.95 (978-0-9728607-0-3(3)) Dean's Bks., Inc.
Eng, Loman & Eng, Petula. Collecting American Belleek, 1 vol. 2003. (ENG., Illus.). 160p. 39.95 (978-0-7643-1860-3(8), 9780764318603) Schiffer Publishing, Ltd.
Eury, Michael. Captain Action: The Original Super-Hero Action Figure. 2003. (ENG., Illus.). 160p. pap. 15.95

(978-1-893905-17-7(9), 9781893905177) TwoMorrows Publishing.

Forest, Christopher. The Kids' Guide to Collecting Stuff, 1 vol. 2010. (Kids' Guides). (ENG.). 32p. (gr. 3-4). lib. bdg. 27.99 *(978-1-4296-5442-5(2)*, Edge Bks.) Capstone Press of Coughlan Cos.

Grice, Gordon. Cabinet of Curiosities: A Kid's Guide to Collecting & Understanding the Wonders of the Natural World. 2015. (ENG., Illus.). 200p. (J). (gr. 3-12). 24.95 *(978-0-7611-6927-7(X))* Workman Publishing Co., Inc.

Kravitz, Robert J. A Collector's Guide to Fractional Currency: The Pocket Change of the Union Soldier. collector's ed. 2003. (Illus.). 262p. pap. 29.95 *(978-0-918501-46-2(6)*, RK-2003, Archives Pr.) Media Assocs.

McMullan, Tigre. Collectible Girlie Glasses, 1 vol. 2003. (ENG., Illus.). 128p. pap. 24.95 *(978-0-7643-1862-7(4)*, 9780764318627) Schiffer Publishing, Ltd.

Miller, Martin. Antiques Source Book: The Definitive Guide to Retail Prices for Antiques & Collectables. (Illus.). 613p. pap. *(978-0-681-35573-6(5))* Carlton Bks., Ltd.

Mitchell, James O. Her Black Sparkles! (Illus.). pap. 7.50 *(978-0-9646017-1-0(0))* Thirty-Three Hundred Pr.

O'Neill, David & Sullivan, Janet O'Neill. Collecting Rose O'Neill's Kewpies, 1 vol. 2003. (ENG., Illus.). 160p. (gr. 10-13). pap. 29.95 *(978-0-7643-1855-9(1)*, 9780764318559) Schiffer Publishing, Ltd.

Pratt, Michael E. Mid-Century Modern Dinnerware: Ak-Sar-Ben to Paden City Pottery - A Pictorial Guide. 2003. (ENG., Illus.). 224p. (gr. 10-13). 39.95 *(978-0-7643-1736-1(9)*, 9780764317361) Schiffer Publishing, Ltd.

Rendall, Richard & Abrams, Elise. Hand-Painted Porcelain Plates: Nineteenth Century to the Present, 1 vol. 2003. (ENG., Illus.). 240p. (gr. 10-13). 59.99 *(978-0-7643-1692-0(3)*, 9780764316920) Schiffer Publishing, Ltd.

Turnbull, Stephanie. Cool Stuff to Collect. 2014. (Cool Stuff Ser.). 32p. (gr. 2-5). 31.35 *(978-1-62588-187-6(8))* Black Rabbit Bks.

Walk, John. Fenton Special Orders: 1980-Present: QVC; Mary Walrath; Martha Stewart; Cracker Barrel; JC Penney; National Fenton Glass Society; & Fenton Art Glass Club of America, 1 vol. 2003. (ENG., Illus.). 239p. 29.95 *(978-0-7643-1813-9(6)*, 9780764318139) Schiffer Publishing, Ltd.

COLLECTORS AND COLLECTING—FICTION

Beeny, Emily. Hector the Collector. Graegin, Stephanie, illus. 2017. (ENG.). 40p. (J). 17.99 *(978-1-62672-296-5(X)*, 9781626722965) Roaring Brook Pr.

Bessesen, Brooke. Zachary Z. Packrat & His Amazing Collections. Campbell, Jenney, illus. 2008. 40p. pap. 19.95 *(978-1-932082-83-8(2))* Arizona Highways.

Best, Cari. When We Go Walking, 0 vols. Brooker, Kyrsten, illus. 2013. (ENG.). 32p. (J). (gr. -1-3). 17.99 *(978-1-4778-1648-6(8)*, 9781477816486, Amazon Children's Publishing) Amazon Publishing.

Boniface, William. The Hero Revealed. Gilpin, Stephen, illus. 2008. (Extraordinary Adventures of Ordinary Boy Ser.: 1). (ENG.). 320p. (J). (gr. 3-7). pap. 6.99 *(978-0-06-077466-0(5))* HarperCollins Pubs.

Broach, Elise. James to the Rescue. Murphy, Kelly, illus. 2015. (Masterpiece Adventures Ser.: 2). (ENG.). 112p. (J). (gr. 1-4). 15.99 *(978-1-62779-316-2(X)*, 9781627793162, Holt, Henry & Co. Bks. For Young Readers) Holt, Henry & Co.

Bunting, Eve. Anna's Table. Morley, Taia, illus. 2003. (ENG.). 32p. (J). (gr. 3-6). 16.95 *(978-1-55971-841-7(2))* Cooper Square Publishing Llc.

Chaconas, Dori. Best Friends No. 1. McCue, Lisa, illus. 2010. (Cork & Fuzz Ser.: 1). (ENG.). 32p. (J). (gr. 1-3). mass mkt. 3.99 *(978-0-14-241593-1(6)*, Penguin Young Readers) Penguin Young Readers Group.

—The Collectors, 4 vols. McCue, Lisa, illus. 2010. (Cork & Fuzz Ser.: 4). (ENG.). 32p. (J). (gr. 1-3). mass mkt. 3.99 *(978-0-14-241714-0(9)*, Penguin Young Readers) Penguin Young Readers Group.

—Cork & Fuzz - The Collectors. McCue, Lisa, illus. 2008. (Cork & Fuzz Ser.: 4). (ENG.). 32p. (J). (gr. k-3). 13.99 *(978-0-670-06286-7(3)*, Viking Books for Young Readers) Penguin Young Readers Group.

Cooper & the Enchanted Metal Detector. 2013. (ENG.). 250p. (J). pap. 9.95 *(978-1-60898-150-2(9))* namelos llc.

Dahlin, Adam A. Junk Collector School. Sandin, Joan, tr. from SWE. Akerman, Emma, illus. 2007. 32p. (J). (gr. -1-3). 16.00 *(978-91-29-66736-3(4))* R & S Bks. SWE. Dist: Macmillan.

deRubertis, Barbara. Una Coleccion para Kate (A Collection for Kate) Fiammenghi, Gioia, illus. 2007. (Math Matters Ser.). (SPA.). 29p. (J). (gr. -1-3). pap. 5.95 *(978-1-57565-240-5(4))* Kane Press, Inc.

Donaldson, Julia. The Giants & the Joneses. Swearingen, Greg, illus. 2008. (ENG.). 224p. (J). (gr. 3-5). pap. 14.99 *(978-0-312-37961-2(7)*, 9780312379612) Square Fish.

Doudna, Kelly. Pack Rat. Chawla, Neena, illus. 2006. (Fact & Fiction Ser.). 24p. (J). pap. 48.42 *(978-1-59679-956-1(0))* ABDO Publishing Co.

—La Rata Coleccionista, 1 vol. Chawla, Neena, illus. 2007. (Cuentos de Animales Ser.).Tr. of Pack Rat. (SPA & ENG.). 24p. (J). (gr. k-3). lib. bdg. 24.21 *(978-1-59928-671-6(8)*, SandCastle) ABDO Publishing Co.

Dussling, Jennifer. Whatcha Got? Wummer, Amy, illus. 2004. (Social Studies Connects). 32p. (J). (gr. 1-3). pap. 5.95 *(978-1-57565-143-9(2))* Kane Press, Inc.

Fleischman, Paul. The Matchbox Diary. Ibatoulline, Bagram, illus. 2013. (ENG.). 40p. (J). (gr. 1-4). 16.99 *(978-0-7636-4601-1(6))* Candlewick Pr.

—The Matchbox Diary. Ibatoulline, Bagram, illus. 2016. (ENG.). 40p. (J). (gr. 1-4). 18.40 *(978-0-606-39097-2(9))* Turtleback Bks.

Griffin, Molly Beth. Rhoda's Rock Hunt. Bell, Jennifer A., illus. 2014. (ENG.). 32p. (J). (gr. -1-2). 16.95 *(978-0-87351-950-2(7))* Minnesota Historical Society Pr.

Hillert, Margaret. I Like Things. (J). 4.95 *(978-0-87895-683-8(2))* Modern Curriculum Pr.

—I Like Things. Hopkins, Jeff, illus. 2016. (BeginningtoRead Ser.). (ENG.). 32p. (J). (gr. 1-2). 22.60 *(978-1-59953-817-4(2))* Norwood Hse. Pr.

Hills, Frederic F. & Hills, Tad. Rocket's 100th Day of School. 2014. (Rocket Ser.). (ENG.). 32p. (J). (gr. 1-4). pap. 3.99 *(978-0-385-39097-2(1)*, Random Hse. Bks. for Young Readers) Random Hse. Children's Bks.

Jocelyn, Marthe. Hannah's Collections. 2004. (ENG., Illus.). 32p. (J). (gr. -1-k). reprint ed. pap. 7.95 *(978-0-88776-690-9(0)*, Tundra Bks.) Tundra Bks. CAN. Dist: Penguin Random Hse. LLC.

Kehew, George & Kehew, Roger. Brett the Collector. 2011. 36p. pap. 24.95 *(978-1-4626-1254-3(7))* America Star Bks.

Kleven, Elisa. The Puddle Pail. Kleven, Elisa, illus. 2007. (ENG., Illus.). 32p. (J). (gr. -1-2). pap. 6.99 *(978-1-58246-206-6(2)*, Tricycle Pr.) Random Hse. Children's Bks.

Lakritz, Deborah. Joey & the Giant Box. Byrne, Mike, illus. 2015. (J). (ENG.). 32p. (J). (gr. -1-2). lib. bdg. 17.95 *(978-1-4677-1953-7(6))*; 6.99 *(978-1-4677-6205-2(9))* Lerner Publishing Group. (Kar-Ben Publishing).

Levin, Betty. The Unmaking of Duncan Veerick. 2007. (ENG.). 212p. (J). (gr. 9-12). 16.95 *(978-1-932425-96-3(9)*, Front Street) Boyds Mills Pr.

Mass, Wendy. 13 Gifts. 2013. (ENG.). 352p. (J). (gr. 3-7). pap. 6.99 *(978-0-545-31004-8(0))* Scholastic, Inc.

—13 Gifts. 2013. (Willow Falls Ser.: 3). lib. bdg. 17.20 *(978-0-606-31957-7(3)*, Turtleback) Turtleback Bks.

Meachen Rau, Dana. Stickers, Shells, & Snowglobes. 2004. (Compass Point Early Reader Ser.). (J). 18.60 *(978-0-7565-0574-5(7))* Compass Point Bks.

Osterweil, Adam. Cooper & the Enchanted Metal Detector. 2013. (ENG.). 250p. (J). 18.95 *(978-1-60898-149-6(5))* namelos llc.

Shearer, Alex. Canned. 2008. (J). *(978-0-439-90310-3(6)*, Scholastic Pr.) Scholastic, Inc.

Wimmer, Sonja. The Word Collector. 2012. (ENG., Illus.). 32p. (J). (gr. k-2). *(978-84-15241-34-8(8))* D P & G Military Pubs.

COLLECTS

see Prayers

COLLEGE AND SCHOOL JOURNALISM

Manual for Scholastic Newspaper Publishing. 2006. 32.95 net. *(978-1-56004-259-4(1))* Social Studies Schl. Service.

COLLEGE ATHLETICS

see Athletics

COLLEGE CHOICE

Greenfeld, Barbara & Weinstein, Robert A. The Kids' College Almanac Fourth Edition: A First Look at College. 4th ed. 2010. (ENG., Illus.). 352p. pap. 16.95 *(978-1-59357-736-0(2)*, JIST Works) JIST Publishing.

Lee, Danielle. JumpStart Your Future: A Guide for the College-Bound Christian. 2006. (Illus.). iii, 123p. (YA). per. 12.99 *(978-0-9769298-9-5(9))* Olive Pr., The.

Piehl, Norah, ed. Choosing a College. 2012. (Issues That Concern You Ser.). (ENG., Illus.). 144p. (gr. 7-10). lib. bdg. 42.00 *(978-0-7377-5691-3(8))* Cengage Gale.

Read, Marya, creator & contrib. by. An Educated Choice Journal. Read, Marya, contrib. by. 2003. 133p. (YA). *(978-1-929931-11-8(5))* Intrepid Films, LLC.

Rugg, Frederick E. Thirty Questions & Answers on the Colleges. (YA). 9th rev. ed. 2003. 20p. pap. 9.95 *(978-1-883062-52-1(7))* 10th rev. ed. 2004. 20p. pap. 9.95 *(978-1-883062-56-9(X))* 11th rev. ed. 2005. 21p. pap. 9.95 *(978-1-883062-61-3(6))* Rugg's Recommendations.

Zmich, Elizabeth & Adler, Penny. Check Yourself into College: A Quick & Easy Guide for High School Students. 2003. (Illus.). 120p. (YA). pap. 29.99 *(978-1-878234-03-2(X)*, IBT-100) NETWORK Inc., The.

COLLEGE ENTRANCE REQUIREMENTS

see Universities and Colleges—Entrance Requirements

COLLEGE JOURNALISM

see College and School Journalism

COLLEGE PERIODICALS

see College and School Journalism

COLLEGE STUDENTS

Easley, Michael F. Look Out, College, Here I Come! 2007. (J). *(978-0-8106-2037-7(5))*; pap. *(978-0-8106-2038-4(3))* National Education Assn.

Greenfeld, Barbara & Weinstein, Robert A. The Kids' College Almanac Fourth Edition: A First Look at College. 4th ed. 2010. (ENG., Illus.). 352p. pap. 16.95 *(978-1-59357-736-0(2)*, JIST Works) JIST Publishing.

Jones, Molly. 21st-Century Education & Careers: Options & Strategies. 2011. (Young Man's Guide to Contemporary Issues Ser.). (ENG.). 104p. (YA). (gr. 9-12). lib. bdg. 34.60 *(978-1-4488-5526-1(8))* Rosen Publishing Group, Inc., The.

Wilson, CeCe. Andre's Father Goes to School. 2015. (Rosen REAL Readers: STEM & STEAM Collection). (ENG.). 8p. pap. 5.46 *(978-1-4994-9695-6(8)*, Rosen Classroom) Rosen Publishing Group, Inc., The.

COLLEGE TEACHERS

see Educators; Teachers

COLLEGES

see Universities and Colleges

COLLIE

Albert, Terry. Collie Animal Planet: Dogs 101. 2016. (Animal PlanetTM: Dogs 101 Ser.). (ENG., Illus.). 144p. (J). (gr. 3-7). 15.95 *(978-0-7938-3739-7(1))* TFH Pubns., Inc.

Bozzo, Linda. I Like Collies! 2012. (Discover Dogs with the American Canine Association Ser.). (Illus.). 24p. (J). (gr. k-3). pap. 7.95 *(978-1-4644-0121-3(7)*, Enslow Elementary) Enslow Pubs., Inc.

Collard, Sneed B., III. Shep: Our Most Loyal Dog. Yardley, Joanna, illus. 2006. (ENG.). 32p. (J). (gr. k-6). 16.95 *(978-1-58536-259-2(X))* Sleeping Bear Pr.

Finne, Stephanie. Collies, 1 vol. 2014. (Dogs Set 12 Ser.). (ENG.). 24p. (J). (gr. 3-6). 25.65 *(978-1-62403-673-6(2))* ABDO Publishing Co.

Fitzpatrick, Anne. Collies. 2003. (Dog Breeds Ser.). 24p. (J). lib. bdg. 21.35 *(978-1-58340-315-0(9))* Black Rabbit Bks.

Green, Sara. Collies. 2010. (Dog Breeds Ser.). (ENG., Illus.). 24p. (J). (gr. 2-5). lib. bdg. 25.95 *(978-1-60014-299-4(0))* Bellwether Media.

Scuh, Mari. Collies. 2017. (Awesome Dogs Ser.). (ENG.). 24p. (J). (gr. k-3). 25.95 ***(978-1-62617-612-6(4)***, Blastoff! Readers) Bellwether Media.

COLLIES

see Collie

COLOMBIA

Barghoorn, Linda. A Refugee's Journey from Colombia. 2017. 32p. (J). ***(978-0-7787-3672-1(5))*** Crabtree Publishing Co.

Blackford, Cheryl. Colombia. 2011. (Country Explorers Ser.). (ENG., Illus.). 48p. (gr. 2-4). lib. bdg. 29.27 *(978-0-7613-6417-7(X))* Lerner Publishing Group.

Croy, Anita & National Geographic Kids Staff. Countries of the World - Colombia. 2008. (Countries of the World Ser.). (ENG., Illus.). 64p. (J). (gr. 5). lib. bdg. 27.90 *(978-1-4263-0257-2(6)*, National Geographic Children's Bks.) National Geographic Society.

Downing, David. Colombia. 2009. (Global Hotspots Ser.). 32p. (gr. 5-18). lib. bdg. 18.56 *(978-0-7614-4759-7(8))* Marshall Cavendish Corp.

Gelletly, LeeAnne. Colombia. (South America Today Ser.). 64p. 2009. (Illus.). (J). (gr. 4-7). 21.95 *(978-1-4222-0635-5(1))* 2007. (YA). (gr. 7-18). pap. 9.95 *(978-1-4222-0702-4(1))* Mason Crest.

—Colombia, Vol. 13. Henderson, James D., ed. 2015. (Discovering South America: History, Politics, & Culture Ser.). (Illus.). 64p. (J). (gr. 7). lib. bdg. 22.95 *(978-1-4222-3298-9(0))* Mason Crest.

Hand, Carol. Colombia, 1 vol. 2013. (Countries of the World Set 2 Ser.). (ENG.). 144p. (J). (gr. 6-12). lib. bdg. 37.07 *(978-1-61783-628-2(1)*, Essential Library) ABDO Publishing Co.

Markovics, Joyce. Colombia. 2016. (Countries We Come From Ser.: 4). (ENG., Illus.). 32p. (J). (gr. -1-3). lib. bdg. 19.95 *(978-1-943553-34-1(3))* Bearport Publishing Co., Inc.

Murcia, Rebecca Thatcher. Meet Our New Student from Colombia. 2008. (Meet Our New Student Ser.). (Illus.). 48p. (J). (gr. 1-5). lib. bdg. 29.95 *(978-1-58415-650-5(3))* Mitchell Lane Pubs., Inc.

Murray, Julie. Colombia, 1 vol. 2016. (Explore the Countries Set 3 Ser.). (ENG., Illus.). 40p. (J). (gr. 2-5). 29.93 *(978-1-68078-066-6(2))* ABDO Publishing Co.

National Geographic Learning, National Geographic Learning. Out of War. 2006. (Reader's Workshop Ser.). (ENG.). 104p. (C). pap. 19.95 *(978-0-7362-3139-8(0))* National Geographic School Publishing, Inc.

Sheen, Barbara, ed. Foods of Colombia. 2012. (Taste of Culture Ser.). (ENG., Illus.). 64p. (J). (gr. 3-6). lib. bdg. 30.45 *(978-0-7377-5948-8(8)*, Kidhaven) Cengage Gale.

Simmons, Walter. Colombia. 2012. (Exploring Countries Ser.). (ENG., Illus.). 32p. (J). (gr. 3-7). lib. bdg. 26.95 *(978-1-60014-727-2(5)*, Blastoff! Readers) Bellwether Media.

Thatcher Murcia, Rebecca. We Visit Colombia. 2010. (Your Land & My Land Ser.). (Illus.). 64p. (J). (gr. 3-6). lib. bdg. 33.95 *(978-1-58415-885-1(9))* Mitchell Lane Pubs., Inc.

Wiseman, Blaine. Colombia. 2016. (J). ***(978-1-5105-1899-5(1))*** SmartBook Media, Inc.

—Colombia. 2016. (Illus.). 32p. (J). *(978-1-4896-4609-5(4))* Weigl Pubs., Inc.

Yomtov, Nel. Colombia. 2014. (Enchantment of the World Ser.: 2). (ENG.). 144p. (J). lib. bdg. 40.00 *(978-0-531-22013-9(3))* Scholastic Library Publishing.

COLOMBIA—FICTION

Balletta, Janet. The Legend of the Colombian Mermaid. Mejía, Estella, illus. 2013. 36p. (J). pap. 14.95 *(978-0-9856762-9-2(9))* WRB Pub.

Bowen, Carl & Fuentes, Benny. Eagle Down, 1 vol. Tortosa, Wilson, illus. 2013. (Shadow Squadron Ser.). (ENG.). 112p. (gr. 4-8). lib. bdg. 26.65 *(978-1-4342-4606-6(X))* Stone Arch Bks.

Durango, Julia. The Walls of Cartagena. Pohrt, Tom, illus. 2008. (ENG.). 160p. (J). (gr. 3-7). 15.99 *(978-1-4169-4102-6(9)*, Simon & Schuster Bks. For Young Readers) Simon & Schuster Bks. For Young Readers.

Gómez Cerda, Alfredo. Barro de Medellín/ Mud of Medellin. Lopez, Xan, illus. 2010. (SPA.). 146p. (YA). (gr. 5-8). *(978-84-263-6849-2(2))* Vives, Luis Editorial (Edelvives).

Medina, Juana. Juana & Lucas. Medina, Juana, illus. 2016. (ENG., Illus.). 96p. (J). (gr. k-3). 14.99 *(978-0-7636-7208-9(4))* Candlewick Pr.

Morrison, David. The Mind Map Level 3 Lower-Intermediate. 2009. (ENG.). 80p. pap. 12.75 *(978-84-8323-537-9(4))* Cambridge Univ. Pr.

Mulder, Michelle. Yeny & the Children for Peace, 1 vol. 2008. (Kids' Power Book Ser.). (ENG., Illus.). 104p. (J). (gr. 3-8). pap. 14.95 *(978-1-897187-45-6(9))* Second Story Pr. CAN. Dist: Orca Bk. Pubs. USA.

Whitney, Barbara I. Barbara's Quest to Find a Messenger: Journeys I & II. 2009. 40p. pap. 19.49 *(978-1-4415-0159-2(2))* Xlibris Corp.

Withers, Pam. First Descent. (ENG., Illus.). (YA). (gr. 7). 2014. 266p. pap. 9.99 *(978-1-77049-412-1(X))* 2011. 268p. 17.95 *(978-1-77049-257-8(7))* Tundra Bks. CAN. (Tundra Bks.). Dist: Penguin Random Hse. LLC.

COLON, CRISTOBAL, 1451-1506

see Columbus, Christopher, 1451-1506

COLONIAL HISTORY (UNITED STATES)

see United States—History—Colonial Period, ca. 1600-1775

COLONIAL LIFE AND CUSTOMS (UNITED STATES)

see United States—History—Colonial Period, ca. 1600-1775; United States—Social Life and Customs—Colonial Period, ca. 1600-1775

COLOR

see also Dyes and Dyeing

Abril, Paco & Francisco, Abril Berán. Colores que se Aman. Decis, Anne, illus. 2004.Tr. of Colors that Love Each Other. (SPA.). 32p. (J). (gr. 2-3). 14.99 *(978-84-241-7989-2(7))* Everest Editora ESP. Dist: Lectorum Pubns., Inc.

Ackland, Nick. Colors. Bradley, Jennie, illus. 2016. (Baby Sparkler Ser.). (ENG.). 10p. (J). (gr. -1 — 1). bds. 5.99 *(978-0-7641-6855-0(X))* Barron's Educational Series, Inc.

—Colors. 2015. (Bright Beginnings Ser.). (ENG.). 20p. (J). (gr. -1 — 1). bds. 6.99 *(978-0-7641-6742-3(1))* Barron's Educational Series, Inc.

Adams, Herschelle. Color Bind. 2011. 49p. (J). pap. 19.95 *(978-1-4327-6336-7(9))*; pap. 21.95 *(978-1-4327-6977-2(4))* Outskirts Pr., Inc.

Adamson, Heather. Blue in Nature. 2013. (ENG., Illus.). 24p. (J). lib. bdg. 25.65 *(978-1-62031-040-3(6))* Jump! Inc.

Aigner-Clark, Julie. Baby Einstein Colores: Libro con Ventanas. Zaidi, Nadeem, illus. 2007. (Baby Einstein Ser.). 5p. (J). (gr. -1). *(978-970-718-469-5(8)*, Silver Dolphin en Español) Advanced Marketing, S. de R. L. de C. V.

—El Mundo de Color de Van Gogh. 2004. (Baby Einstein Ser.). (SPA., Illus.). 12p. (J). bds. *(978-970-718-158-8(3)*, Silver Dolphin en Español) Advanced Marketing, S. de R. L. de C. V.

—Una Ventana Al Color. Zaidi, Nadeem, illus. 2007. (Baby Einstein Ser.). 10p. (J). (gr. -1-k). *(978-970-718-454-1(X)*, Silver Dolphin en Español) Advanced Marketing, S. de R. L. de C. V.

Alda, Arlene. Except the Color Grey. 2011. (ENG., Illus.). 24p. (J). (gr. k-k). 16.95 *(978-1-77049-284-4(4)*, Tundra Bks.) Tundra Bks. CAN. Dist: Penguin Random Hse. LLC.

Alexander, Emmett. Colores / Sort It by Color. de la Vega, Eida, tr. from ENG. 2015. (Vamos a Agrupar Por... / Sort It Out! Ser.). (ENG & SPA., Illus.). 24p. (J). (gr. k-1). lib. bdg. 22.60 *(978-1-4824-3215-2(3))* Stevens, Gareth Publishing LLLP.

—Sort It by Color. 2015. (Sort It Out! Ser.). (ENG., Illus.). 24p. (J). (gr. k-1). pap. 8.15 *(978-1-4824-2565-9(3))* Stevens, Gareth Publishing LLLP.

Alvarez, Lourdes M. Colores. 2004. (Mi primer libro Ser.). (SPA., Illus.). 9p. (J). bds. 3.95 *(978-1-933050-01-0(2))* Sweetwater Pr.

—My First Book Colors. Brooks, David, illus. 2005. (My First Book Ser.). 9p. (J). (gr. -1-1). bds. 3.95 *(978-1-933050-07-2(1))* Sweetwater Pr.

Annette Roeder. Edgar Degas: Coloring Book. 2011. (ENG.). 32p. (J). (gr. 1-4). pap. 8.95 *(978-3-7913-7064-4(2))* Prestel Verlag GmbH & Co KG. DEU. Dist: Penguin Random Hse. LLC.

Arps, Melissa. Colors. 2006. (Illus.). (J). *(978-0-7364-2381-6(8))* Random Hse., Inc.

ArsEdition, illus. Winter Magic: Beautiful Holiday Patterns to Color. 2015. (Color Magic Ser.). (ENG.). 80p. pap. 12.99 *(978-1-4380-0733-5(7))* Barron's Educational Series, Inc.

Austin, Richard. Pocket Piggies Colors! The Teacup Pigs of Pennywell Farm. Austin, Richard, photos by. 2014. (ENG., Illus.). 22p. (J). bds. 5.95 *(978-0-7611-7980-1(1)*, 17980) Workman Publishing Co., Inc.

Award, Anna. My First Colours. 2012. (ENG., Illus.). 10p. (J). bds. 6.50 *(978-1-84135-557-3(7))*; bds. 9.95 *(978-1-84135-558-0(5))* Award Pubns. Ltd. GBR. Dist: Parkwest Pubns., Inc.

AZ Books Staff. Colors. Slusar, Julia, ed. 2012. (Pull It Out Ser.). (ENG.). 10p. (J). (gr. -1 — 1). 7.95 *(978-1-61889-193-8(6))* AZ Bks. LLC.

—Colors & Shapes. Petrovskaya, Olga, ed. 2012. (Matching Game Ser.). (ENG.). 18p. (J). (gr. -1-k). spiral bd. 4.95 *(978-1-61889-201-0(0))* AZ Bks. LLC.

Azadi, Azita. Thank You Sun. 2009. 32p. pap. 16.50 *(978-1-4269-2197-1(7))* Trafford Publishing.

Baby's First Colors Book. 2004. 10p. (J). bds. 4.99 *(978-1-85854-920-0(5))* Brimax Books Ltd. GBR. Dist: Byeway Bks.

Baggott, Stella, illus. Baby's Very First Colors Book. 2009. (Baby Board Bks). 10p. (J). bds. 6.99 *(978-0-7945-2467-8(2)*, Usborne) EDC Publishing.

Bambi727 & Bambi727. Having Fun with Colors' & Numbers' I wrote this book in hopes our younger children would enjoy & have fun learning their colors' & Numbers' 2009. 32p. pap. 14.49 *(978-1-4389-6226-9(6))* AuthorHouse.

Barnes, Brynne. Colors of Me. Nelson, Annika M., illus. 2011. (ENG.). 28p. 15.95 *(978-1-58536-541-8(6))* Sleeping Bear Pr.

Barradas, Michele. Rainbow of Shapes: Learn shapes & Colors. 2008. 20p. pap. 15.95 *(978-1-4389-0177-0(1))* AuthorHouse.

Barton, Chris. The Day-Glo Brothers: The True Story of Bob & Joe Switzer's Bright Ideas & Brand-New Colors. Persiani, Tony, illus. 2009. (ENG.). 44p. (J). (gr. 2-5). 19.95 *(978-1-57091-673-1(X))* Charlesbridge Publishing, Inc.

Base, Graeme. The Water Hole: Coloring Book. 2004. (ENG., Illus.). 32p. (J). (gr. -1-4). pap. 9.95 *(978-0-8109-8735-7(X))* Abrams, Inc.

Bass, Jennifer Vogel. Edible Colors. Bass, Jennifer Vogel, photos by. (ENG., Illus.). (J). 2016. 30p. bds. 7.99 *(978-1-62672-284-2(6)*, 9781626722842) 2014. 32p. (gr. -1-k). 12.99 *(978-1-62672-002-2(9)*, 9781626720022) Roaring Brook Pr.

Begin Smart Books Staff, contrib. by. What Colour Is Your Apple? 2010. (Illus.). 14p. (J). bds. *(978-1-60906-006-0(7))* Begin Smart LLC.

Benduhn, Tea. What Is Color? 2009. (Get Art Smart Ser.). (ENG., Illus.). 24p. (J). (gr. k-3). pap. *(978-0-7787-5137-3(6))*; lib. bdg. *(978-0-7787-5123-6(6))* Crabtree Publishing Co.

Beveridge, Dorothy. Birding in Belize with Colours. Beveridge, Jim, photos by. 2013. (Illus.). 32p. pap. *(978-976-8142-55-9(3))* Producciones de la Hamaca.

Bicknell, J. Buby Baby Colors_Padded. 2010. 12p. pap. *(978-1-84879-164-0(X))* Make Believe Ideas.

Bicknell, Joanna. My First BK of Animals. 2010. 16p. (J). bds. 8.99 *(978-1-84879-361-3(8))* Make Believe Ideas GBR. Dist: Nelson, Thomas Inc.

Blyton, Enid, et al. My First Colours & Shapes. 2013. (ENG., Illus.). 20p. (J). bds. 11.50 *(978-1-84135-760-7(X))* Award Pubns. Ltd. GBR. Dist: Parkwest Pubns., Inc.

Bolchazy, Marie Carducci. Quo Colore Est?/What Color Is It? 2003. (I Am Reading Latin Ser.). (ENG & LAT., Illus.). 64p. (J). (gr. k-3). 10.00 *(978-0-86516-539-7(4))* Bolchazy-Carducci Pubs.

Bond, G. T. GT Bond's Absolutely Stupendous Book of Colors. 2007. 60p. pap. 24.95 *(978-0-615-14642-3(2))* S & S Pr.

Boos, Andre, illus. Hi! Read, Stick & Learn about Animals. Little Bears are Brown. 2004. 20p. (J). pap. 6.99 *(978-1-59496-003-1(8))* Teora USA LLC.

Boothroyd, Jennifer. Light Makes Colors. 2014. (First Step Nonfiction - Light & Sound Ser.). (Illus.). 24p. (J). (gr. k-2). pap. 6.95 *(978-1-4677-4502-4(2))*; (ENG., lib. bdg. 23.93 *(978-1-4677-3914-6(6)*, Lerner Pubns.) Lerner Publishing Group.

Borene, Mark R. Welcome to the Ground. 2009. (Illus.). 20p. pap. 10.49 *(978-1-4389-8268-7(2))* AuthorHouse.

—Welcome to the School. 2009. 20p. pap. 10.49 *(978-1-4389-7752-2(2))* AuthorHouse.

Bourgoing, Pascale & Valat, Pierre-Marie. Colours. Peyrols, Sylvaine, illus. 2006. (ENG.). 40p. (J). (gr. k-3). pap. 11.99

C
D

(978-1-85103-088-0(3)) Moonlight Publishing, Ltd. GBR. Dist: Independent Pubs. Group.

Box, Su & Brown, Jo. My Rainbow Book of Bedtime Prayers. Brown, Jo & Brown, Joan, illus. 2009. (ENG.). 14p. (J). (gr. k-k). bds. 9.99 (978-0-7459-6165-1(7)) Lion Hudson PLC GBR. Dist: Independent Pubs. Group.

—My Rainbow Book of Everyday Prayers. Brown, Jo, illus. 2009. (ENG., Illus.). 16p. (J). (gr. k-k). bds. 9.99 (978-0-7459-6166-8(5)) Lion Hudson PLC GBR. Dist: Independent Pubs. Group.

Boyd, Nicole. Let's Brush Our Teeth. 2008. (Rosen Real Readers: Upper Emergent Ser.). (ENG., Illus.). 12p. (gr. 1-2). pap. 5.90 (978-0-8239-8133-5(9)) Rosen Publishing Group, Inc., The.

Boye, B. D. The Look Book. Boye, B. D., illus. l.t. ed. 2004. (Illus.). 20p. (J). per. 4.99 (978-0-9768078-1-0(5), 100001) Innerchild Publishing, Inc.

Bradshaw, Georgine & Wrighton, Charlene. Set of Color Mini-Books (29 Titles) Clark, Irene, illus. 2005. (J). 39.95 (978-1-886441-42-2(1), CMB4356) Zoo-phonics, Inc.

Brainy Baby Quad Book. 2005. (Brainy Baby Ser.). 40p. (J). bds. 10.39 (978-1-59394-240-3(0)) Bendon, Inc.

Brame, Kimberly. My Abc & Color Bible Book. 2009. 16p. pap. 12.24 (978-1-4389-4174-5(9)) AuthorHouse.

Brocket, Jane. Ruby, Violet, Lime: Looking for Color. Brocket, Jane, photos by. 2011. (Jane Brocket's Clever Concepts Ser.). (ENG., Illus.). 32p. (gr. -1-2). lib. bdg. 26.60 (978-0-7613-4612-8(0)) Lerner Publishing Group.

Brooks, Felicity. Big Book of Colors. 2015. (Big Book of Colors Ser.). (ENG.). 26p. (J). 15.99 (978-0-7945-2840-9(6), Usborne) EDC Publishing.

—Lift-out Colors Book. 2008. (Shapes & Colors Jigsaw Bks). 12p. (J). bds. 12.99 (978-0-7945-2136-3(3), Usborne) EDC Publishing.

—Very First Colors Board Book. 2010. (Very First Words Board Bks). 10p. (J). bds. 6.99 (978-0-7945-2763-1(9), Usborne) EDC Publishing.

Brown, Lisa, illus. Baby Fix My Car. 2006. (ENG.). 12p. bds. 6.95 (978-1-932416-56-5(0)) McSweeney's Publishing.

Brown, Margery W. Book of Colors: Meet the Color Family. Blair, Culverson & Simpson, Howard, illus. 2nd ed. 2004. (Afro-Bets Ser.). 24p. (J). (gr. -1-1). pap. 3.95 (978-0-940975-57-6(2), Sankofa Bks.) Just Us Bks., Inc.

Brown, Robert L. Daddy Grows Colors, 1 vol. 2009. 28p. pap. 24.95 (978-1-60836-124-3(1)) America Star Bks.

Bruna, Dick. My Vest Is White. 2012. (ENG., Illus.). 28p. 7.95 (978-1-84976-075-1(6)) Tate Publishing, Ltd. GBR. Dist: Abrams, Inc.

Bullard, Lisa. Brown Food Fun [Ars Scribendi (Netherlands)]. 2010. (Eat Your Colors Ser.). 32p. lib. bdg. 2.50 (978-1-4296-5231-5(4), Aplus Bks.) Capstone Press of Coughlan Cos.

—Green Food Fun [Ars Scribendi (Netherlands)]. 2010. (Eat Your Colors Ser.). 32p. lib. bdg. 2.50 (978-1-4296-5232-2(2), Aplus Bks.) Capstone Press of Coughlan Cos.

—Orange Food Fun [Ars Scribendi (Netherlands)]. 2010. (Eat Your Colors Ser.). 32p. lib. bdg. 2.50 (978-1-4296-5233-9(0), Aplus Bks.) Capstone Press of Coughlan Cos.

—Red Food Fun, 1 vol. 2006. (Eat Your Colors Ser.). (ENG., Illus.). 32p. (gr. 1-2). 27.32 (978-0-7368-5383-5(9), Aplus Bks.) Capstone Press of Coughlan Cos.

—Red Food Fun [Ars Scribendi (Netherlands)]. 2010. (Eat Your Colors Ser.). 32p. lib. bdg. 2.50 (978-1-4296-5234-6(9), Aplus Bks.) Capstone Press of Coughlan Cos.

Burke, Zoe. Charley Harper's Book of Colors. Harper, Charley, illus. 2015. (ENG.). 24p. (J). bds. 10.95 (978-0-7649-7261-4(8), POMEGRANATE KIDS) Pomegranate Communications, Inc.

Burlew, Rich, creator. The Order of the Stick Coloring Book. 2012. (Illus.). 32p. (YA). pap. 4.99 (978-0-9854139-0-3(5)) Giant in the Playground.

Byers, Helen. Colors of France. Byers, Helen, illus. 2005. (Colors of the World Ser.). (Illus.). 24p. (gr. 3-6). 5.95 (978-1-57505-565-7(1)) Lerner Publishing Group.

Byeway Books, creator. Colors. 2011. (My First Picture Fun Bks.). (ENG., Illus.). 24p. (gr. -1-k). bds. 5.99 (978-1-60176-021-0(3)) Byeway Bks.

Cain, Marie Mowery. A Splash of Colors. 2013. (Big Books, Blue Ser.). (ENG & SPA., Illus.). 16p. pap. 33.00 (978-1-59246-015-1(1)) Big Books, by George!

—Water Colors. 2013. (Big Books, Red Ser.). (ENG & SPA., Illus.). 16p. pap. 33.00 (978-1-59246-228-5(6)) Big Books, by George!

Canetti, Yanitzia. Colores escolares/School Colors: A World of Color. 2010. (ENG & SPA.). 24p. (J). pap. 6.99 (978-1-59835-272-6(5), BrickHouse Education) Cambridge BrickHouse, Inc.

—Colorful Shapes/Figuras de Colores: A World of Color. 2010. (SPA & ENG.). 24p. (J). pap. 6.99 (978-1-59835-278-8(4), BrickHouse Education) Cambridge BrickHouse, Inc.

—Colorful Sights Paisajes de Colores: A World of Color. 2010. (SPA & ENG.). 24p. (J). pap. 6.99 (978-1-59835-280-1(6), BrickHouse Education) Cambridge BrickHouse, Inc.

—Colors on Colors/Colores Sobre Colores: A World of Color. 2010. (SPA & ENG.). 24p. (J). pap. 6.99 (978-1-59835-276-4(8), BrickHouse Education) Cambridge BrickHouse, Inc.

—Musical Colors/Colores Musicales: A World of Color. 2010. 24p. (J). pap. 6.99 (978-1-59835-267-2(9), BrickHouse Education) Cambridge BrickHouse, Inc.

—Party Colors/Colores Festivos: A World of Color. 2010. (ENG & SPA.). 24p. (J). pap. 6.99 (978-1-59835-274-0(1), BrickHouse Education) Cambridge BrickHouse, Inc.

—Sporty Colors/Colores Deportivos: A World of Color. 2010. (ENG & SPA.). 24p. (J). pap. 6.99 (978-1-59835-268-9(7), BrickHouse Education) Cambridge BrickHouse, Inc.

—Tasty Colors/Colores de Sabores: A World of Color. 2010. (SPA & ENG.). 24p. (J). pap. 6.99 (978-1-59835-270-2(9), BrickHouse Education) Cambridge BrickHouse, Inc.

Cantillo, Oscar. Blue Around Me. 2015. (J). lib. bdg. (978-1-62713-346-3(1)) Cavendish Square Publishing.

—Green Around Me. 2015. (Color in My World Ser.). (ENG., Illus.). 24p. (J). (gr. 3-3). pap. 8.22 (978-1-5026-0276-3(8)) Cavendish Square Publishing.

—Purple Around Me. 2015. (Color in My World Ser.). (ENG., Illus.). 24p. (J). (gr. 3-3). pap. 8.22 (978-1-5026-0072-1(2)) Cavendish Square Publishing.

Carle, Eric. Colors (Colores) 2008. (World of Eric Carle Ser.). (SPA & ENG., Illus.). 12p. (J). (gr. -1 — 1). bds. 8.99 (978-0-448-44883-1(1), Grosset & Dunlap) Penguin Young Readers Group.

—My Very First Book of Colors. Carle, Eric, illus. 2005. (ENG., Illus.). 20p. (J). (gr. -1 — 1). bds. 5.99 (978-0-399-24386-8(0), Philomel Bks.) Penguin Young Readers Group.

—What's Your Favorite Color? 2017. (ENG., Illus.). 40p. (J). 17.99 (978-0-8050-9614-9(0), 9780805096149, Holt, Henry & Co. Bks. For Young Readers) Holt, Henry & Co.

Carolan, Dr. Where Are My Slippers? A Book of Colors. Carolan, Joanna F., illus. 2005. 32p. (J). pap. 16.95 (978-0-9715333-6-3(9)) Banana Patch Pr.

Carole, Bonnie. Black & White in Winter. 2015. (SPA.). 24p. (gr. -1-1). pap. 8.95 (978-1-63430-081-0(5)) Rourke Educational Media.

—Blue & Yellow in Summer. 2015. (ENG.). 24p. (gr. -1-1). pap. 8.95 (978-1-63430-079-7(3)) Rourke Educational Media.

Carpenter, Tad. I Say, You Say Colors! 2014. (ENG., Illus.). 18p. (J). (gr. -1 — 1). bds. 6.99 (978-0-316-20072-1(7)) Little, Brown Bks. for Young Readers.

Carr, Aaron. Diseños de Las Plantas. 2012. (SPA.). (J). (978-1-61913-207-8(9)) Weigl Pubs., Inc.

—Explorando Los Colores. 2012. (SPA & ENG.). (J). (978-1-61913-206-1(0)) Weigl Pubs., Inc.

—Exploring Colors. 2011. (J). (978-1-61690-591-0(3)); lib. bdg. 27.13 (978-1-61690-947-5(1)) Weigl Pubs., Inc.

Carson-Dellosa Publishing Staff. Colors & Shapes. 2006. (ENG., Illus.). 54p. (gr. -1-1). 2.99 (978-0-7696-4689-3(1), Brighter Child) Carson-Dellosa Publishing, LLC.

—Colors, Grades PK - K. 2010. (Home Workbooks Ser.). (ENG.). 64p. (gr. -1-k). pap. 4.49 (978-1-60418-765-6(4)) Carson-Dellosa Publishing, LLC.

Carter, David A. White Noise: A Pop-Up Book for Children of All Ages. Carter, David A., illus. 2009. (ENG., Illus.). 20p. (J). (gr. -1-3). 27.99 (978-1-4169-4094-4(4), Little Simon) Little Simon.

—Yellow Square: A Pop-Up Book for Children of All Ages. Carter, David A., illus. 2008. (ENG., Illus.). 20p. (J). (gr. -1-3). 19.99 (978-1-4169-4093-7(6), Little Simon) Little Simon.

Cartwright, Shannon. Alaska 1 2 3: Colors & Numbers. 2005. (Illus.). (J). (978-0-9772297-0-3(X)) Taku Graphics.

Casteel, Seth. Underwater Doggies Colors. 2014. (ENG., Illus.). 18p. (J). (gr. -1 — 1). bds. 6.99 (978-0-316-37365-4(6)) Little, Brown Bks. for Young Readers.

Chandler, Shannon & Accord Publishing Staff. Colors. 2011. (ENG., Illus.). 10p. (J). bds. 10.99 (978-1-4494-0831-2(1)) Andrews McMeel Publishing.

Chaplain, Dawn. One Red Apple. 2008. 23p. pap. 24.95 (978-1-60703-020-1(9)) America Star Bks.

Charles, Faustin. The Selfish Crocodile Book of Colours. Terry, Michael, illus. 2013. (Selfish Crocodile Ser.). (ENG.). 14p. (J). bds. 10.99 (978-1-4088-1449-9(8), 9781408814499, Bloomsbury USA Childrens) Bloomsbury Publishing USA.

Charly, Harry T. Learning Colors Is Fun. 2009. 20p. pap. 10.49 (978-1-4389-3998-8(1)) AuthorHouse.

Children's Press, contrib. by. Red, Blue, & Yellow Too! 2009. (Rookie Preschool Ser.). (ENG.). 24p. (J). (gr. -1). lib. bdg. 23.00 (978-0-531-24403-6(2), Children's Pr.) Scholastic Library Publishing.

Children's Press (New York, N.Y.) Staff, contrib. by. Can You Find Colors? 2010. (J). (978-85-312-5231-0(8)) Children's Pr., Ltd.

Childrens Press Staff & Scholastic, Inc. Staff, contrib. by. Can You Find Colors? 2010. (Rookie Toddler: First Concepts Ser.). (ENG., Illus.). 12p. (J). bds. 6.95 (978-0-531-25231-4(0), Children's Pr.) Scholastic Library Publishing.

Chopra, Hayma. Mixing Colors at School. 2017. (Wonderful World of Colors Ser.). 24p. (gr. 4-6). pap. 8.25 **(978-1-5383-2171-3(8)**, PowerKids Pr.) Rosen Publishing Group, Inc., The.

Christian, Cheryl. What's in My Garden? A Book of Colors. Ericsson, Annie Beth, illus. 2009. 16p. (J). (gr. -1). bds. 6.25 (978-1-59572-166-2(5)) Star Bright Bks., Inc.

Clark Sawyer, J. Animal Colors: What They Mean. 2014. (Little Bits: Colors Tell a Story Ser.). (ENG.). 24p. (J). (gr. -1-3). lib. bdg. 23.93 (978-1-62724-321-6(6)) Bearport Publishing Co., Inc.

—Holiday Colors: Our Favorite Days. 2015. (Illus.). 24p. (J). lib. bdg. (978-1-62724-325-4(9)) Bearport Publishing Co., Inc.

—Los Colores de la Selva Tropical: Hermosos y Brillantes. 2014. (Los Colores Cuentan una Historia Ser.). (SPA.). 24p. (J). (gr. -1-3). lib. bdg. 23.93 (978-1-62724-468-8(9)) Bearport Publishing Co., Inc.

—Los Colores de Las Celebraciones: Nuestros Días Favoritos. 2014. (Los Colores Cuentan una Historia Ser.). (SPA.). 24p. (J). (gr. -1-3). lib. bdg. 23.93 (978-1-62724-467-1(0)) Bearport Publishing Co., Inc.

—Los Colores de Los Animales: Qué Significan. 2014. (Los Colores Cuentan una Historia Ser.). (SPA., Illus.). 24p. (J). (gr. -1-3). lib. bdg. 23.93 (978-1-62724-463-3(8)) Bearport Publishing Co., Inc.

—Rain Forest Colors: Bright & Beautiful. 2014. (Little Bits: Colors Tell a Story Ser.). (ENG.). 24p. (J). (gr. -1-3). lib. bdg. 23.93 (978-1-62724-326-1(7)) Bearport Publishing Co., Inc.

Clearwater, Gary. Colors at the Races. 2017. (Wonderful World of Colors Ser.). 24p. (gr. 4-6). pap. 8.25 **(978-1-5081-6167-7(4)**, PowerKids Pr.) Rosen Publishing Group, Inc., The.

Cleland, Jo. I Can Make Colors. 2006. (Science about Me Ser.). (Illus.). 8p. (J). (gr. 3-7). pap. 5.95 (978-1-59515-925-0(8)) Rourke Educational Media.

Clement, Debbie. Red, White, & Blue. 2010. 19.95 (978-0-578-06631-8(9)) Rainbows Within Reach.

Coan, Sharon. Light Makes a Rainbow, 1 vol. (Science Readers: Content & Literacy Ser.). (ENG., Illus.). 24p. (gr. 1-1). 2015. (J). 22.96 (978-1-4938-1153-3(3)) 2014. pap. 8.99 (978-1-4807-4566-7(9)) Teacher Created Materials, Inc.

Coirault, Christine. Colors. 2008. (Gymboree Play & Music Ser.). (ENG., Illus.). 24p. (J). (gr. -1). bds. (978-1-55470-039-4(6)) Me to We.

Coirault, Christine, illus. My First Book of Learning. 2009. (J). (978-1-74089-930-7(X)) Fog City Pr.

Cole, Ian. Colors. 2008. 17p. pap. 24.95 (978-1-60610-273-2(7)) America Star Bks.

Collins Easy Learning Staff & HarperCollins UK Staff. Shapes, Colours & Patterns, Bk. 1. 2008. (Collins Easy Learning Age 3-5 Ser.). (ENG.). 88p. (J). pap. 4.99 (978-0-00-730092-1(1)) HarperCollins Pubs. Ltd. GBR. Dist: Independent Pubs. Group.

Color by Numbers Sparkly Sticker Book. Date not set. (Illus.). 16p. (J). 3.98 (978-1-4054-0991-9(6)) Parragon, Inc.

Color in My World. 2015. (Color in My World Ser.). (ENG.). 24p. (J). (gr. 3-3). 145.26 (978-1-5026-0285-5(7)); 49.32 (978-1-5026-0328-9(4)) Cavendish Square Publishing.

Color Set 1: Shades of Coolor. 2005. (J). spiral bd. 23.40 (978-0-9770248-8-9(1)) Sidedoor Publishing LLC.

Colores. (Coleccion Mi Primer Libro). (SPA., Illus.). (J). 13.95 (978-84-207-3778-2(X), ANY875) Grupo Anaya, S.A. ESP. Dist: Continental Bk. Co., Inc.

Colores. (Coleccion Libritos Acordeon). (SPA., Illus.). 10p. (J). pap. 5.50 (978-950-11-0792-0(2), SGM922) Sigmar ARG. Dist: Continental Bk. Co., Inc.

Los Colores (Colors) (SPA.). (J). 6.95 (978-968-419-049-8(2)) Grijalbo, Editorial MEX. Dist: AIMS International Bks., Inc.

Colores en el zoologico: Colors at the Zoo. 2005. (Take-Home Bks.). (SPA.). (YA). (gr. -1-3). 15.75 (978-0-8215-1208-1(0)) Sadlier, William H. Inc.

Colores en el zoologico/Colors at the Zoo. 2005. (Libros en Espanol Para Ninos Ser.). (SPA.). (YA). (gr. -1-1). 11.97 (978-0-8215-0998-2(5)) Sadlier, William H. Inc.

Colorful Days. 2014. (DK Readers Ser.). (ENG.). 32p. (J). (gr. -1-1). pap. 3.99 (978-1-4654-1674-2(9), DK Children) Dorling Kindersley Publishing, Inc.

Colors! (Amazing Animals Ser.). 32p. (J). (gr. 1). pap. (978-1-882210-77-0(8)) Action Publishing, Inc.

Colors! 2003. (J). per. (978-1-57657-914-5(X)); per. (978-1-57657-916-9(6)) Paradise Pr., Inc.

Colors! Date not set. (Illus.). 16p. (J). 2.98 (978-0-7525-9453-8(2)) Parragon, Inc.

Colors! (Rainbow Ryhmes Ser.). 12p. (J). bds. (978-2-7643-0174-6(X)) Phidal Publishing, Inc./Editions Phidal, Inc.

Colors All Around. (Colors All Around Ser.). (ENG.). 32p. (gr. 1-2). 2011. pap. 238.50 (978-1-4296-6178-2(X)) 2010. lib. bdg. 109.28 (978-1-4296-5260-5(8)) Capstone Press of Coughlan Cos. (Aplus Bks.).

Colors All Around: KinderConcepts Individual Title Six-Packs. (Kinderstarters Ser.). 8p. (gr. -1-1). 21.00 (978-0-7635-8722-2(2)) Rigby Education.

Colors & Shapes. rev. ed. 2007. (ENG., Illus.). 28p. (J). (gr. -1-1). 16.99 (978-1-59069-505-0(4), 1C1000) Studio Mouse LLC.

Conceptis Puzzles. Dots! Super Connect-the-Dots Puzzles. 2008. (ENG., Illus.). 96p. (J). (gr. 2). spiral bd. 12.95 (978-1-4027-5521-7(X), Puzzlewright) Sterling Publishing Co., Inc.

Connelly, Neil O. Colors. Thornburgh, Rebecca, illus. 10p. (J). (gr. -1). bds. 3.95 (978-1-58989-003-9(5)) Thurman Hse., LLC.

Corporate Contibutor Staff & West, David. Dinosaur Colors. 2012. (ENG.). 24p. (J). (978-0-7787-7454-9(6)); pap. (978-0-7787-7459-4(7)) Crabtree Publishing Co.

Corrigan, Kathleen. My First Colours, 1 vol. 2015. (Maple Leaf Learners Ser.). (ENG.). 20p. bds. 7.99 (978-1-62370-222-9(4)) Capstone Young Readers of Coughlan Cos.

Coss, Lauren. Let's Sort by Color. 2014. (21st Century Basic Skills Library: Sorting Ser.). (ENG., Illus.). 24p. (J). (gr. k-3). 22.79 (978-1-63137-634-4(9), 205319) Cherry Lake Publishing.

Cottin, Menena. The Black Book of Colors. Amado, Elisa, tr. from SPA. Faria, Rosana & Faria, Rosana, illus. 2008. (ENG.). 24p. (J). (gr. k-5). 17.95 (978-0-88899-873-6(2)) Groundwood Bks. CAN. Dist: Publishers Group West (PGW).

Cox, Tracey M. Shaping up the Year. Bell, Samantha, illus. 2009. 24p. pap. 10.95 (978-1-935137-73-3(5)) Guardian Angel Publishing, Inc.

Cummings, Priscilla. Chesapeake Rainbow, 1 vol. Aiken, David, illus. 2009. (ENG.). 30p. 11.95 (978-0-87033-556-3(1), 9780870335563, Cornell Maritime Pr./Tidewater Pubs.) Schiffer Publishing, Ltd.

Dahl, Michael. Brown, 1 vol. 2005. (Colors Bks.). (ENG., Illus.). 32p. (gr. 1-2). 27.32 (978-0-7368-3669-2(1), Aplus Bks.) Capstone Press of Coughlan Cos.

—Brown: Seeing Brown All Around Us. 2005. (Colors Bks.). (ENG., Illus.). 32p. (gr. 1-2). per. 8.10 (978-0-7368-6071-1(6), Aplus Bks.) Capstone Press of Coughlan Cos.

Dalmatian Press Staff. Pop & Shine Colors. 2008. (ENG.). 12p. (J). bds. 10.95 (978-1-58117-673-5(2), Intervisual/Piggy Toes) Bendon, Inc.

Davies, Ann & Ne, Harriet. Teddy Is Yellow. (Illus.). 10p. (J). 9.95 (978-1-85479-258-7(X)) O'Mara, Michael Bks., Ltd. GBR. Dist: Trans-Atlantic Pubns., Inc.

de Klerk, Roger, illus. Foxy Learns Colors. 2009. (Foxy Learns Ser.). 16p. (J). pap. 4.95 (978-1-59496-181-6(6)) Teora USA LLC.

—Foxy Learns Shapes. 2009. (Foxy Learns Ser.). 16p. (J). pap. 4.95 (978-1-59496-179-3(4)) Teora USA LLC.

—Foxy Learns to Add. 2009. (Foxy Learns Ser.). 16p. (J). pap. 4.95 (978-1-59496-178-6(6)) Teora USA LLC.

Deeds, Christopher. Light & Color: What We See. 2013. (InfoMax Readers Ser.). (ENG.). 24p. (J). (gr. 3-4). pap. 49.50 (978-1-4777-2638-9(1)); (Illus.). pap. 8.25 (978-1-4777-2637-2(3)) Rosen Publishing Group, Inc., The. (Rosen Classroom).

Del Moral, S., tr. Colores. 2006. (Disney Learning (Silver Dolphin en Espanol) Ser.). (Illus.). 22p. (J). (gr. -1). (978-970-718-430-5(2), Silver Dolphin en Español) Advanced Marketing, S. de R. L. de C. V.

Delessert, Etienne, creator. Full Color. 2014. (ENG., Illus.). 32p. (J). (gr. -1-k). 15.99 (978-1-56846-266-0(2), Creative Editions) Creative Co., The.

Deneux, Xavier. Colours. 2013. (ENG.). 20p. (J). (gr. -1 — 1). bds. 14.99 (978-1-4521-1726-3(8)) Chronicle Bks. LLC.

DePrisco, Dorothea. Apple. Taxali, Gary, illus. 2005. (Plush Learning Books Ser.). 10p. (J). bds. 6.95 (978-1-58117-191-4(9), Intervisual/Piggy Toes) Bendon, Inc.

—Lemon. Taxali, Gary, illus. 2005. (Plush Learning Books Ser.). 10p. (J). bds. 6.95 (978-1-58117-194-5(3), Intervisual/Piggy Toes) Bendon, Inc.

DeSimone, Corkey Hay. The Planet Hue. DeSimone, Corkey Hay, illus. 2003. (Illus.). (J). 14.95 (978-0-9747921-0-1(1)) Gentle Giraffe Pr.

Diaz, James & Diaz, Francesca. Making Colors: A Pop-Up Book. 2014. (ENG.). 10p. (J). (gr. k). 19.95 (978-1-85707-853-4(5)) Tango Bks. GBR. Dist: Independent Pubs. Group.

Dicmas, Courtney. Colours. Dicmas, Courtney, illus. 2017. (Wild! Concepts Ser.: 4). (ENG., Illus.). 14p. (J). bds. **(978-1-84643-995-7(7))** Child's Play International Ltd.

Dingles, Molly. Black as a Bat. Velez, Walter, illus. 2005. (Community of Color Ser.). 32p. (J). pap. 10.95 (978-1-59646-334-9(1)); per. 10.95 (978-1-59646-335-6(X)) Dingles & Co.

—Black as a Bat/Negro como un Murcielago. Velez, Walter, illus. (Community of Color Ser.). 32p. (J). 2005. (ENG & SPA.). pap. 10.95 (978-1-59646-100-0(4)) 2005. (ENG & SPA.). per. 10.95 (978-1-59646-106-2(3)) 2003. (SPA.). lib. bdg. 21.65 (978-1-891997-33-4(5)) Dingles & Co.

—Blue as a Blueberry. Velez, Walter, illus. 2005. (Community of Color Ser.). 32p. (J). (ACE.). pap. 10.95 (978-1-59646-328-8(7)); per. 10.95 (978-1-59646-329-5(5)) Dingles & Co.

—Blue as a Blueberry/Azul como un Arandano. Velez, Walter, illus. 2005. (Community of Color Ser.). (ENG & SPA.). 32p. (J). pap. 10.95 (978-1-59646-097-3(0)); per. 10.95 (978-1-59646-103-1(9)) Dingles & Co.

—Blue as a Blueberry/Bleu comme un Bleuet. Velez, Walter, illus. 2004. (Community of Color Ser.).Tr. of Bleu comme un Bleuet. (ENG & FRE.). 32p. (J). lib. bdg. 21.65 (978-1-891997-72-3(6)) Dingles & Co.

—Brown as an Acorn. Velez, Walter, illus. (Community of Color Ser.). 32p. (J). 2005. per. 10.95 (978-1-59646-347-9(3)) 2004. pap. 10.95 (978-1-59646-346-2(5)) Dingles & Co.

—Brown as an Acorn/Marrón como una Bellota. Velez, Walter, illus. (Community of Color Ser.).Tr. of Marrón como una Bellota. (ENG & SPA.). 32p. (J). 2005. per. 10.95 (978-1-59646-109-3(8)) 2004. lib. bdg. 21.65 (978-1-891997-37-2(8)) Dingles & Co.

—Gray as a Dolphin. Velez, Walter, illus. (Community of Color Ser.). 32p. (J). 2005. per. 10.95 (978-1-59646-343-1(0)) 2004. pap. 10.95 (978-1-59646-342-4(2)) Dingles & Co.

—Gray as a Dolphin/Gris como un Delfin. Velez, Walter, illus. 2004. (Community of Color Ser.).Tr. of Gris como un Delfin. (ENG & SPA.). 32p. (J). pap. 10.95 (978-1-59646-092-8(X)); lib. bdg. 21.65 (978-1-891997-58-7(0)) Dingles & Co.

—Gray as a Dolphin/Gris como un Delfin. Velez, Walter, illus. 2005. (Community of Color Ser.). (ENG & SPA.). 32p. (J). per. 10.95 (978-1-59646-110-9(1)) Dingles & Co.

—Green as a Frog. Velez, Walter, illus. 2005. (Community of Color Ser.). 32p. (J). pap. 10.95 (978-1-59646-330-1(9)); per. 10.95 (978-1-59646-331-8(7)) Dingles & Co.

—Green as a Frog/Verde como una Rana. Velez, Walter, illus. 2005. (Community of Color Ser.). (ENG & SPA.). 32p. (J). pap. 10.95 (978-1-59646-098-0(9)); per. 10.95 (978-1-59646-104-8(7)) Dingles & Co.

—Green as a Frog/Vert comme une Grenouille. Velez, Walter, illus. 2004. (Community of Color Ser.).Tr. of Vert comme une Grenouille. (ENG & FRE.). 32p. (J). lib. bdg. 21.65 (978-1-891997-71-6(8)) Dingles & Co.

—Orange as a Pumpkin. Velez, Walter, illus. 2005. (Community of Color Ser.). 32p. (J). pap. 10.95 (978-1-59646-332-5(5)); per. 10.95 (978-1-59646-333-2(3)) Dingles & Co.

—Orange as a Pumpkin/Anaranjado como una Calabaza. Velez, Walter, illus. (Community of Color Ser.).Tr. of Anaranjado como una Calabaza. 32p. (J). 2005. (ENG & SPA.). pap. 10.95 (978-1-59646-099-7(7)) 2005. (ENG & SPA.). per. 10.95 (978-1-59646-105-5(5)) 2003. lib. bdg. 21.65 (978-1-891997-31-0(9)) Dingles & Co.

—Orange as a Pumpkin/Orange comme une Citrouille. Velez, Walter, illus. 2004. (Community of Color Ser.).Tr. of Orange comme une Citrouille. (ENG & FRE.). 32p. (J). lib. bdg. 21.65 (978-1-891997-69-3(6)) Dingles & Co.

—Pink as a Piglet. Velez, Walter, illus. (Community of Color Ser.). 32p. (J). 2005. pap. 10.95 (978-1-59646-336-3(8)) 2005. per. 10.95 (978-1-59646-337-0(6)) 2004. lib. bdg. 21.65 (978-1-891997-25-9(4)) Dingles & Co.

—Pink as a Piglet/Rosa como un Cerdito. Velez, Walter, illus. (Community of Color Ser.).Tr. of Rosa como un Cerdito. 32p. (J). 2005. (ENG & SPA.). pap. 10.95 (978-1-59646-348-6(1)) 2005. (ENG & SPA.). per. 10.95 (978-1-59646-349-3(X)) 2004. (SPA & ENG.). lib. bdg. 21.65 (978-1-891997-34-1(3)) Dingles & Co.

—Purple as a Plum. Velez, Walter, illus. (Community of Color Ser.). 32p. (J). 2005. pap. 10.95 (978-1-59646-338-7(4)) 2005. per. 10.95 (978-1-59646-339-4(2)) 2004. lib. bdg. 21.65 (978-1-891997-24-2(6)) Dingles & Co.

—Purple as a Plum/Morado como una Ciruela. Velez, Walter, illus. (Community of Color Ser.). 32p. (J). 2005. (ENG & SPA.). pap. 10.95 (978-1-59646-350-9(3)) 2005. (ENG & SPA.). per. 10.95 (978-1-59646-351-6(1)) 2004. lib. bdg. 21.65 (978-1-891997-32-7(7)) Dingles & Co.

—Purple as a Plum/Violet comme une Prune. Velez, Walter, illus. 2004. (Community of Color Ser.).Tr. of Violet comme une Prune. (ENG & FRE.). 32p. (J). lib. bdg. 21.65 (978-1-891997-68-6(8)) Dingles & Co.

—Red as a Fire Truck. Velez, Walter, illus. 2005. (Community of Color Ser.). 32p. (J). pap. 10.95 (978-1-59646-324-0(4)); per. 10.95 (978-1-59646-325-7(2)) Dingles & Co.

—Red as a Fire Truck/Rojo como un camion de Bomberos. Velez, Walter, illus. 2005. (Community of Color Ser.).Tr. of Rojo Como un Camion de Bomberos. (ENG & SPA.). 32p. (J). pap. 10.95 (978-1-59646-095-9(4)); per. 10.95 (978-1-59646-101-7(2)) Dingles & Co.

—Red as a Firetruck/Rouge comme un camion de Pompiers. Velez, Walter, illus. 2004. (Community of Color Ser.).Tr. of Rouge comme un camion de Pompiers. (ENG & FRE.). 32p. (J). lib. bdg. 21.65 (978-1-891997-73-0(4)) Dingles & Co.

—Turquoise as a Parakeet. Velez, Walter, illus. 2005. (Community of Color Ser.). (J). 32p. pap. 10.95 (978-1-59646-344-8(9)); 2005p. per. 10.95 (978-1-59646-345-5(7)) Dingles & Co.

—Turquoise as a Parakeet/Turquesa como un Periquito. Velez, Walter, illus. (Community of Color Ser.).Tr. of Turquesa como un Periquito. (ENG & SPA.). 32p. (J). 2005. per. 10.95 *(978-1-59646-107-9(1))* 2004. pap. 10.95 *(978-1-59646-094-2(6))* 2004. lib. bdg. 21.65 *(978-1-891997-60-0(2))* Dingles & Co.
—White as a Seashell. Velez, Walter, illus. 2005. (Community of Color Ser.). 32p. (J). pap. 10.95 *(978-1-59646-340-0(6))*; per. 10.95 *(978-1-59646-341-7(4))* Dingles & Co.
—White as a Seashell/Blanco como una concha Marina. Velez, Walter, illus. (Community of Color Ser.).Tr. of Blanco como una concha Marina. (ENG & SPA.). (J). 2005. 2005p. per. 10.95 *(978-1-59646-108-6(X))* 2004. 32p. pap. 10.95 *(978-1-59646-091-1(1))* 2004. 32p. lib. bdg. 21.65 *(978-1-891997-38-9(6))* Dingles & Co.
—Yellow as a Lemon. Velez, Walter, illus. 2005. (Community of Color Ser.). 32p. (J). pap. 10.95 *(978-1-59646-326-4(0))*; per. 10.95 *(978-1-59646-327-1(9))* Dingles & Co.
—Yellow as a Lemon/Amarillo como un Limon. Velez, Walter, illus. 2005. (Community of Color Ser.). (ENG & SPA.). 32p. (J). pap. 10.95 *(978-1-59646-096-6(2))*; per. 10.95 *(978-1-59646-102-4(0))* Dingles & Co.
—Yellow as a Lemon/Jaune comme un Citron. Velez, Walter, illus. 2004. (Community of Color Ser.).Tr. of Jaune comme un Citron. (ENG & FRE.). 32p. (J). lib. bdg. 21.65 *(978-1-891997-70-9(X))* Dingles & Co.
Disney Book Group. Disney Baby My First Colors. Disney Storybook Art Team, illus. 2016. (ENG.). 10p. (J). (gr. -1 — 1). bds. 6.99 *(978-1-4847-2943-4(9))* Disney Pr.
Disney Publishing Staff. Rainbow Colors, 15 vols. 2003. (It's Fun to Learn Ser.). (Illus.). 32p. (J). (gr. -1-3). 3.99 *(978-1-57973-135-9(X))* Advance Pubs. LLC.
Disney Staff, contrib. by. Write, Slide & Learn Disney Mickey Mouse Clubhouse: Colors & Shapes. 2011. (Disney Write, Slide & Learn Ser.). 12p. (J). 9.99 *(978-1-74183-850-3(9))* Hinkler Bks. Pty. Ltd. AUS. Dist: Ideals Pubns.
Dorling Kindersley Publishing Staff. Baby - Colors! 2010. (ENG.). 16p. (J). (gr. -1 — 1). bds. 6.99 *(978-0-7566-5567-9(6)*, DK Children) Dorling Kindersley Publishing, Inc.
—Color Illusions. 2014. (ENG.). 32p. (J). (gr. 2-5). 19.99 *(978-1-4654-2285-9(4)*, DK Children) Dorling Kindersley Publishing, Inc.
—Colorful World. 2006. (Fun Flaps Ser.). (ENG., Illus.). 20p. (J). (gr. -1-k). bds. 4.99 *(978-0-7566-2007-3(4)*, DK Children) Dorling Kindersley Publishing, Inc.
—Colors. (Baby Touch & Feel Ser.). (ENG., (J). 2016. Illus.). 14p. (— 1). bds. 5.99 *(978-1-4654-5470-6(5))* 2014. 16p. (gr. -1 — 1). bds. 7.99 *(978-1-4654-1992-7(6))* 2009. (Illus.). 12p. (gr. -1-k). bds. 6.99 *(978-0-7566-5227-2(8))* Dorling Kindersley Publishing, Inc. (DK Children).
—Doodlepedia. 2012. (ENG.). 112p. (J). (gr. 1-4). 12.99 *(978-0-7566-9011-3(0)*, DK Children) Dorling Kindersley Publishing, Inc.
—Flaptastic: Colors. 2016. (ENG., Illus.). 12p. (J). (— 1). bds. 9.99 *(978-1-4654-5619-9(8)*, DK Children) Dorling Kindersley Publishing, Inc.
—My First Colors. 2015. (My First Bks.). (ENG., Illus.). 36p. (J). (gr. -1 — 1). bds. 5.99 *(978-1-4654-2898-1(4)*, 1383273, DK Children) Dorling Kindersley Publishing, Inc.
—My First Colors: Let's Learn Them All! 2010. (Tab Board Bks.). (ENG.). 28p. (J). (gr. -1 — 1). bds. 9.99 *(978-0-7566-7141-9(8)*, DK Children) Dorling Kindersley Publishing, Inc.
—Pop-Up Peekaboo! - Colors. 2013. (ENG.). 12p. (J). (gr. -1 — 1). bds. 9.99 *(978-1-4654-0156-4(3)*, DK Children) Dorling Kindersley Publishing, Inc.
—Pull the Tab: Colors. 2015. (ENG., Illus.). 10p. (J). (— 1). bds. 6.99 *(978-1-4654-3856-0(4)*, DK Children) Dorling Kindersley Publishing, Inc.
—Rainbow Colors Peekaboo! 2008. (ENG.). 12p. (J). (gr. -1-k). bds. 6.99 *(978-0-7566-3760-6(0)*, DK Children) Dorling Kindersley Publishing, Inc.
—Sophie la Girafe: Sophie Peekaboo Colors. 2017. (ENG.). 14p. (J). (— 1). bds. 6.99 *(978-1-4654-5624-3(4)*, DK Children) Dorling Kindersley Publishing, Inc.
—Squeaky Baby Bath: Colors: Colors. 2014. (ENG.). 14p. (J). (gr. -1 — 1). 6.99 *(978-1-4654-2462-4(8)*, DK Children) Dorling Kindersley Publishing, Inc.
Draze, Dianne. Attribute Block - Thinking Activities - Sequences. 2005. (ENG.). 32p. pap. 9.95 *(978-1-59363-053-9(0))* Prufrock Pr.
Dunne, Abbie. Light. 2016. (Physical Science Ser.). (ENG., Illus.). 24p. (gr. k-1). lib. bdg. 26.65 *(978-1-5157-0937-4(X)*, Pebble Plus) Capstone Press of Coughlan Cos.
Durber, Matt, illus. First Colors. Allman, Howard & MMStudios, photos by. 2006. (Usborne Look & Say Ser.). 18p. (J). (gr. -1-k). bds. 14.99 *(978-0-7945-1348-1(4)*, Usborne) EDC Publishing.
Eck, Kristin. Colors in My House. (Board Bks.). (gr. k-1). 2009. 16p. 23.90 *(978-1-61511-639-3(7))* 2004. (Illus.). (J). lib. bdg. 8.95 *(978-1-4042-2698-2(2))* Rosen Publishing Group, Inc., The. (PowerKids Pr.).
Ellis, Belinda. Baby See-A-Shape Colors. 2005. (Baby See a Shape Ser.). (Illus.). 12p. (gr. -1 — 1). per., bds. *(978-1-84610-021-5(6))* Make Believe Ideas.
Endle, Kate. What Is Green? A Colors Book by Kate Endle. 2010. (ENG., Illus.). 18p. (J). (gr. k-k). bds. 9.99 *(978-1-57061-648-8(5)*, Little Bigfoot) Sasquatch Bks.
Enslow, Brian. Fall Colors. 2011. (All about Colors of the Seasons Ser.). (Illus.). 24p. (J). (gr. -1-18). pap. 7.95 *(978-1-59845-264-8(9)*, Enslow Elementary) Enslow Pubs., Inc.
—Spring Colors. 2011. (All about Colors of the Seasons Ser.). (Illus.). 24p. (J). (gr. -1-18). pap. 7.95 *(978-1-59845-265-5(7)*, Enslow Elementary) Enslow Pubs., Inc.
—Summer Colors. 2011. (All about Colors of the Seasons Ser.). (Illus.). 24p. (J). (gr. -1-18). pap. 7.95 *(978-1-59845-266-2(5)*, Enslow Elementary) Enslow Pubs., Inc.
—Winter Colors. 2011. (All about Colors of the Seasons Ser.). (Illus.). 24p. (J). (gr. -1-18). pap. 7.95 *(978-1-59845-268-6(1)*, Enslow Elementary) Enslow Pubs., Inc.
Ericsson, Annie Beth & Christian, Cheryl. ¿Que hay en mi Jardin? (Spanish/English) Un libro de colores/A Book of Colors. del Risco, Eida, tr. 2009. (ENG & SPA., Illus.). 16p. (J). bds. 6.25 *(978-1-59572-181-5(9))* Star Bright Bks., Inc.
Estellon, Pascale. The Color-Play Coloring Book. 2012. (ENG.). 24p. (J). (gr. -1-3). 16.99 *(978-1-4521-0545-1(6))* Chronicle Bks. LLC.
Evanson, Ashley. New York: A Book of Colors. Evanson, Ashley, illus. 2015. (Hello, World Ser.). (ENG., Illus.). 14p. (J). (— 1). bds. 6.99 *(978-0-448-48913-1(9)*, Grosset & Dunlap) Penguin Young Readers Group.
Fairies Coloring Book: Charming Pictures of the Sprites from Folklore. 2013. (Chartwell Coloring Bks.). (ENG.). 128p. pap. 7.99 *(978-0-7858-3040-5(5)*, 0785830405, Chartwell) Book Sales, Inc.
Felder, Monica. Juggling Colors. 2013. (Illus.). 28p. pap. 11.95 *(978-1-61863-472-6(0))* Bookstand Publishing.
Feldman, Thea. ASPCA Mix & Match Pets: A Colors & Counting Book. 2015. (Mix & Match Ser.: 1). (ENG.). 12p. (J). (gr. -1-k). 8.99 *(978-0-7944-3299-7(9)*, Reader's Digest Children's Bks.) Studio Fun International.
Felix, Rebecca. Patterns at the Zoo. 2015. (21st Century Basic Skills Library: Patterns All Around Ser.). (ENG., Illus.). 24p. (J). (gr. k-3). pap. 12.79 *(978-1-63188-935-6(4)*, 206001) Cherry Lake Publishing.
Filipek, Nina. Colors. O'Toole, Jeanette, illus. 2009. (Bright Basics Ser.). 12p. (J). (gr. -1-k). bds. 11.40 *(978-1-60754-687-0(6))* Windmill Bks.
Fiol, Maria A., tr. Eating the Rainbow (Spanish/English), 1 vol. 2010. (Libro de Comidas de Colores/Colorful Food Bks.). (ENG., Illus.). 16p. (J). bds. 6.95 *(978-1-59572-203-4(3))* Star Bright Bks., Inc.
—Que Sabroso Arco Iris!, 1 vol. 2010. (Libro de Comidas de Colores Ser.).Tr. of Eating the Rainbow. (SPA., Illus.). 32p. (J). bds. 6.95 *(978-1-59572-225-6(4))* Star Bright Bks., Inc.
Fisher, Valorie. Everything I Need to Know Before I'm Five. Fisher, Valorie, illus. 2011. (ENG., Illus.). 40p. (J). (gr. k-k). 17.99 *(978-0-375-86865-8(8)*, Schwartz & Wade Bks.) Random Hse. Children's Bks.
Flash Kids Editors, ed. Colors & Shapes: Grade Pre-K-K (Flash Skills) 2010. (Flash Skills Ser.). (ENG.). 64p. (J). pap. 3.95 *(978-1-4114-3470-7(6)*, Spark Publishing Group) Sterling Publishing Co., Inc.
Flores, Cory, illus. Bugs on Parade: A Counting Book. 2006. 8p. (J). *(978-1-58970-400-8(2))* Lakeshore Learning Materials.
Flowerpot Press, creator. Animals Coloring Book. 2013. (Sockheadz Ser.). (ENG., Illus.). 72p. (J). (gr. -1-3). 4.99 *(978-1-77093-546-4(0))* Flowerpot Pr.
—Dinosaurs Coloring Book. 2013. (Sockheadz Ser.). (ENG., Illus.). 72p. (J). (gr. -1-3). 4.99 *(978-1-77093-544-0(4))* Flowerpot Pr.
—Ghosts & Goblins Coloring Book. 2013. (ENG., Illus.). 72p. (J). (gr. -1-3). 4.99 *(978-1-77093-317-0(4))* Flowerpot Pr.
—Monsters Coloring Book. 2013. (Sockheadz Ser.). (ENG., Illus.). 72p. (J). (gr. -1-3). 4.99 *(978-1-77093-545-7(2))* Flowerpot Pr.
—Princesses Coloring Book. 2013. (Sockheadz Ser.). (ENG., Illus.). 72p. (J). (gr. -1-3). 4.99 *(978-1-77093-543-3(6))* Flowerpot Pr.
Forte, Imogene. Ready to Learn Shapes & Colors. 2003. (Illus.). 64p. per. 7.95 *(978-0-86530-593-9(5))* Incentive Pubns., Inc.
Foster, Jane. Jane Foster's Black & White. 2016. (ENG., Illus.). 26p. (J). (gr. -1 — 1). bds. 8.99 *(978-1-4998-0255-9(2))* Little Bee Books Inc.
—Jane Foster's Colors. 2016. (ENG., Illus.). 26p. (J). (gr. -1 — 1). bds. 7.99 *(978-1-4998-0256-6(0))* Little Bee Books Inc.
Freeman, Lisa Show. The Colors of God. 2010. 28p. 16.95 *(978-1-4269-3063-8(1))* Trafford Publishing.
Furgang, Kathy. A Rainbow Party. 2011. (Early Connections Ser.). (J). *(978-1-61672-569-3(9))* Benchmark Education Co.
G., Ashley. Critter Colors. G., Ashley, illus. 2015. (ENG., Illus.). 28p. (J). (gr. -1-k). bds. 7.99 *(978-1-4814-4218-3(X)*, Little Simon) Little Simon.
Ganeri, Anita. Colorful Creatures. 2016. (Illus.). 79p. (J). ***(978-1-4351-6383-6(4))*** Barnes & Noble, Inc.
Gardner, Robert & Conklin, Joshua. A Kid's Book of Experiments with Color. 2016. (Surprising Science Experiments Ser.). (ENG.). 48p. (J). (gr. 4-4). pap. 11.70 *(978-0-7660-7199-5(5))*; (Illus.). lib. bdg. 27.93 *(978-0-7660-7201-5(0))* Enslow Pubs., Inc.
Gates, Valerie. The Other Colors: An ABC Book. Cutting, Ann, photos by. 2013. (ENG., Illus.). 56p. (J). (gr. -1-k). 14.95 *(978-1-62087-537-7(3)*, 620537, Sky Pony Pr.) Skyhorse Publishing Co., Inc.
George, Chris. Colors. 2017. (Early Concepts Ser.). 24p. (gr. 4-6). 23.60 ***(978-1-5081-6209-4(3)***, PowerKids Pr.) Rosen Publishing Group, Inc., The.
George, Patrick. Magic Colors. 2013. (ENG., Illus.). 28p. (J). (gr. -1-1). 14.95 *(978-1-907967-54-2(0))* Boxer Bks., Ltd. GBR. Dist: Sterling Publishing Co., Inc.
Ghigna, Charles. Wonders of the Color Wheel. Jatkowska, Ag, illus. 2013. (My Little School House Ser.). (ENG.). 24p. (gr. -1-2). 21.99 *(978-1-4048-8307-9(X))* Picture Window Bks.
—The Wonders of the Color Wheel. Jatkowska, Ag, illus. 2014. 24p. (J). pap. *(978-1-4795-1927-9(8))* Picture Window Bks.
Gibbs, Edward. I Spy on the Farm. Gibbs, Edward, illus. 2016. (ENG., Illus.). 22p. (J). (gr. -1-k). bds. 7.99 *(978-0-7636-8530-0(5)*, Templar) Candlewick Pr.
Giles, Angela & Picthall, Chez. Colours & Shapes. Calver, Paul, illus. 2015. (ENG.). 6p. (J). 9.99 *(978-1-909763-42-5(X))* Award Pubns. Ltd. GBR. Dist: Parkwest Pubns., Inc.
Girard, Alexander. Alexander Girard Color. 2011. (ENG., Illus.). 58p. (J). bds. 14.95 *(978-1-934429-77-8(5))* AMMO Bks., LLC.
Girard, Alexander, illus. Alexander Girard Coloring Book. 2014. (ENG.). 30p. pap. 9.95 *(978-1-934429-86-0(4))* AMMO Bks., LLC.
Glaser, Rebecca. Red in Nature. 2013. (ENG.). 24p. (J). lib. bdg. 25.65 *(978-1-62031-036-6(8))* Jump! Inc.
Glick, Dvorah. Red Is My Rimon: A Jewish Child's Book of Colors. Ackerman, Dena, illus. 2012. 32p. (J). 12.95 *(978-1-929628-71-1(4))* Hachai Publishing.
Gonyea, Mark. A Book about Color: A Clear & Simple Guide for Young Artists. Gonyea, Mark, illus. 2010. (ENG., Illus.). 96p. (YA). (gr. 4-9). 19.99 *(978-0-8050-9055-0(X)*, 9780805090550, Holt, Henry & Co. Bks. For Young Readers) Holt, Henry & Co.
Gordon, Sharon. El Amarillo. 2007. (Colores Ser.). (SPA.). 24p. (gr. k-1). lib. bdg. 15.95 *(978-0-7614-2863-3(1)*, Benchmark Bks.) Marshall Cavendish Corp.
—El Anaranjado. 2007. (Colores Ser.). (SPA.). 24p. (gr. k-1). lib. bdg. 15.95 *(978-0-7614-2860-2(7)*, Benchmark Bks.) Marshall Cavendish Corp.
—El Azul. 2007. (Colores Ser.). (SPA.). 24p. (gr. k-1). lib. bdg. 15.95 *(978-0-7614-2858-9(5)*, Benchmark Bks.) Marshall Cavendish Corp.
—Blue/El Azul. 2007. (Colors/Los Colores Ser.). (SPA & ENG.). 24p. (gr. k-1). lib. bdg. 15.95 *(978-0-7614-2873-2(9)*, Benchmark Bks.) Marshall Cavendish Corp.
—Green. 2004. (SPA & ENG., Illus.). 23p. (J). 21.36 *(978-0-7614-1773-6(7)*, Benchmark Bks.) Marshall Cavendish Corp.
—Green/El Verde. 2007. (Colors/Los Colores Ser.). (SPA & ENG.). 24p. (gr. k-1). lib. bdg. 15.95 *(978-0-7614-2874-9(7)*, Benchmark Bks.) Marshall Cavendish Corp.
—El Morado. 2007. (Colores Ser.). (SPA.). 24p. (gr. k-1). lib. bdg. 15.95 *(978-0-7614-2861-9(5)*, Benchmark Bks.) Marshall Cavendish Corp.
—Orange/El Anaranjado. 2007. (Colors/Los Colores Ser.). (ENG & SPA.). 24p. (gr. k-1). lib. bdg. 15.95 *(978-0-7614-2875-6(5)*, Benchmark Bks.) Marshall Cavendish Corp.
—Purple/El Morado. 2007. (Colors/Los Colores Ser.). (SPA & ENG.). 24p. (gr. k-1). lib. bdg. 15.95 *(978-0-7614-2876-3(3)*, Benchmark Bks.) Marshall Cavendish Corp.
—Red/El Rojo. 2007. (Colors/Los Colores Ser.). (SPA & ENG.). 24p. (gr. k-1). lib. bdg. 15.95 *(978-0-7614-2878-7(X)*, Benchmark Bks.) Marshall Cavendish Corp.
—El Rojo. 2007. (Colores Ser.). (SPA.). 24p. (gr. k-1). lib. bdg. 15.95 *(978-0-7614-2862-6(3)*, Benchmark Bks.) Marshall Cavendish Corp.
—El Verde. 2007. (Colores Ser.). (SPA.). 24p. (gr. k-1). lib. bdg. 15.95 *(978-0-7614-2859-6(3)*, Benchmark Bks.) Marshall Cavendish Corp.
—Yellow. 2004. (SPA & ENG., Illus.). 23p. (J). 21.36 *(978-0-7614-1772-9(9)*, Benchmark Bks.) Marshall Cavendish Corp.
—Yellow/El Amarillo. 2007. (Colors/Los Colores Ser.). (SPA & ENG.). 24p. (gr. k-1). lib. bdg. 15.95 *(978-0-7614-2879-4(8)*, Benchmark Bks.) Marshall Cavendish Corp.
Goslin, Angela. True Colours. 2011. (Illus.). 72p. pap. 30.85 *(978-1-4567-8672-4(5))* AuthorHouse.
Greathouse, Lisa. Farm Animals: Classifying & Sorting. rev. ed. 2011. (Mathematics Readers Ser.). (ENG.). 32p. (J). (gr. k-k). pap. 8.99 *(978-1-4333-3442-9(9))* Teacher Created Materials, Inc.
—Wild Animals, Level K. rev. ed. 2011. (Mathematics Readers Ser.). (ENG.). 32p. (J). (gr. k-k). pap. 8.99 *(978-1-4333-3443-6(7))* Teacher Created Materials, Inc.
Grossman, Laurie. Colors of Israel. Byers, Helen, illus. (Colors of the World Ser.). 24p. 2005. (gr. 3-6). lib. bdg. 19.93 *(978-1-57505-382-0(9))* 2003. (J). (gr. 1-4). pap. 5.95 *(978-1-57505-523-7(6))* Lerner Publishing Group.
Guidone, Lisa M. What Happens at a Crayon Factory? 2008. (Where People Work Ser.). 24p. (gr. -1-3). (J). lib. bdg. 22.00 *(978-0-8368-9273-4(9))*; pap. 8.15 *(978-0-8368-9372-4(7))* Stevens, Gareth Publishing LLLP. (Weekly Reader Leveled Readers).
Gulliver, Amanda, illus. Colors. 2011. (Baby Rattle Bks.). 12p. (J). (gr. -1-k). 5.99 *(978-0-7641-6391-3(4))* Barron's Educational Series, Inc.
Gunzi, Christane. Colours. 2nd rev. ed. 2015. (ENG., Illus.). 34p. (J). 7.99 *(978-1-906572-20-4(8))* Award Pubns. Ltd. GBR. Dist: Parkwest Pubns., Inc.
Gunzi, Christiane. Los Colores. 2004. (My Very First Look At Ser.).Tr. of Colors. (SPA & ENG., Illus.). 32p. (J). (gr. -1-k). pap. 5.95 *(978-1-58728-411-3(1))* Cooper Square Publishing Llc.
—Colours. 2015. (ENG., Illus.). 6p. (J). 7.99 *(978-1-907604-95-9(2))* Award Pubns. Ltd. GBR. Dist: Parkwest Pubns., Inc.
Gürth, Per-Henrik. Canada in Colours. Gürth, Per-Henrik, illus. 2011. (ENG., Illus.). 24p. (J). (gr. -1 — 1). bds. 8.95 *(978-1-55453-757-0(6))* Kids Can Pr., Ltd. CAN. Dist: Hachette Bk. Group.
—Canada in Colours. Gürth, Per-Henrik, illus. 2013. (ENG., Illus.). 24p. (J). (gr. -1 — 1). pap. 7.95 *(978-1-55453-760-0(6))* Kids Can Pr., Ltd. CAN. Dist: Hachette Bk. Group.
Hale, Natalie. So Many Colors. 2003. (J). spiral bd. 9.95 *(978-0-9702698-5-0(4))* Special Reads for Special Needs.
Hale, Rachael. Baby Colors. 2009. (ENG., Illus.). 20p. (J). (gr. -1 — 1). bds. 6.99 *(978-0-316-04452-3(0))* Little Brown & Co.
Harmon, Minnie P. Golden's Shapes & Colors. 2011. 36p. pap. 21.99 *(978-1-4628-6253-5(5))* Xlibris Corp.
Hellier, Catherine. Baby's World of Colors. Ferri, Francesca, illus. 2010. (Baby's Bks.). (ENG.). 6p. (J). (gr. -1-k). 12.99 *(978-0-7641-4539-1(8))* Barron's Educational Series, Inc.
Helman, Andrea. Southwest Colors. Jecan, Gavriel, photos by. 2011. (Illus.). 24p. (J). 12.95 *(978-1-933855-64-6(9))* Rio Nuevo Pubs.
Herold, Vickey. Light & Color. 2006. (J). pap. *(978-1-4108-6488-8(X))* Benchmark Education Co.
Hicks, Barbara Jean. I Like Colors. Prap, Lila, illus. 2006. 24p. (J). (gr. -1-3). 9.95 *(978-1-58925-057-4(5))* Tiger Tales.
Hill, Emma. My First Book of Colors: A Pull-Out Toddler Book. 2014. (My First Book Ser.). (ENG., Illus.). 12p. (J). (gr. -1 — 1). bds. 6.99 *(978-1-77085-314-0(6)*, 9781770853140) Firefly Bks., Ltd.
Hills, Tad. Duck & Goose Colors. Hills, Tad, illus. 2015. (Duck & Goose Ser.). (ENG., Illus.). 22p. (J). (— 1). bds. 7.99 *(978-0-553-50806-2(7)*, Schwartz & Wade Bks.) Random Hse. Children's Bks.
Hnatov, Catherine. Yum, Yum (Spanish/English), 1 vol. 2011. (ENG., Illus.). 32p. (J). bds. 5.95 *(978-1-59572-276-8(9))* Star Bright Bks., Inc.
Hogan, Martina, illus. Rainbow Zoo. 2016. (Early Birds Ser.). (ENG.). 12p. (J). (gr. -1 — 1). bds. 6.99 *(978-1-4998-0209-2(9))* Little Bee Books Inc.
Holden, Arianne. It's Fun to Learn about Colors: A Busy Picture Book Full of Fabulous Facts & Things to Do! 2016. (ENG., Illus.). 32p. 9.99 *(978-1-86147-710-1(4)*, Armadillo) Anness Publishing GBR. Dist: National Bk. Network.
Holden, Pam. I Like to Paint, 8, Set. 2009. (Red Rocket Readers Ser.). (ENG., Illus.). 16p. (gr. -1-1). pap. *(978-1-877435-97-3(X))* Flying Start Bks.
Horácek, Petr. Las Fresas Son Rojas. Horácek, Petr, illus. 2014. (ENG & SPA., Illus.). 16p. (J). (-k). bds. 5.99 *(978-0-7636-7393-2(5))* Candlewick Pr.
Horne, Jane. Baby First Concepts: Colors. 2007. (Busy Baby Ser.). (Illus.). 12p. (gr. -1-k). per., bds. *(978-1-84610-469-5(6))* Make Believe Ideas.
—Busy Baby Sparklies 4 Volume Boxed Set: Baby's First Box of Books. 2007. (Illus.). 12p. (gr. -1-k). bds., bds. *(978-1-84610-565-4(X))* Make Believe Ideas.
—Sparklies Colors. 2008. (Illus.). 12p. (gr. -1-k). bds. *(978-1-84610-608-8(7))* Make Believe Ideas.
Horstschäfer, Felicitas. Flowers: Make Your Own Mobile Inspired by Emil Nolde. 2014. (ENG., Illus.). 16p. (J). (gr. 1-4). pap. 9.95 *(978-3-7913-7188-7(6))* Prestel Verlag GmbH & Co KG. DEU. Dist: Penguin Random Hse. LLC.
Houblon, Marie. A World of Colors: Seeing Colors in a New Way. 2009. (ENG., Illus.). 48p. (J). (gr. -1-2). 25.90 *(978-1-4263-0559-7(1))*; 16.95 *(978-1-4263-0556-6(7))* National Geographic Society. (National Geographic Children's Bks.).
Hudson, Amanda. This Is My Ball. 2008. (Our Toys Ser.). (Illus.). 16p. (gr. -1-2). (J). lib. bdg. 19.00 *(978-0-8368-9252-9(6))*; pap. 5.30 *(978-0-8368-9351-9(4))* Stevens, Gareth Publishing LLLP. (Weekly Reader Leveled Readers).
Hudson, Amanda & Nations, Susan. This Is My Ball/Ésta es mi Pelota. 2008. (Our Toys/Nuestros Juguetes Ser.). (SPA.). 16p. (gr. -1-2). pap. 5.30 *(978-0-8368-9355-7(7)*, Weekly Reader Leveled Readers) Stevens, Gareth Publishing LLLP.
—This Is My Ball/Ésta Es Mi Pelota. 2008. (Our Toys/Nuestros Juguetes Ser.). (SPA & ENG., Illus.). 16p. (J). (gr. -1-2). lib. bdg. 19.00 *(978-0-8368-9256-7(9)*, Weekly Reader Leveled Readers) Stevens, Gareth Publishing LLLP.
Hvass & Hannibal. Technicolor Treasure Hunt: Learn to Count with Nature. 2016. (ENG.). 14p. (J). (gr. -1-k). bds. 12.99 *(978-1-84780-780-9(1)*, Wide Eyed Editions) Quarto Publishing Group UK GBR. Dist: Hachette Bk. Group.
Hvass, Nan Na & Hannibal, Sofie, illus. Technicolour Treasure Hunt: Learn to Count with Nature. 2016. (ENG.). 14p. (J). bds. 12.99 *(978-1-84780-744-1(5)*, Wide Eyed Editions) Quarto Publishing Group UK GBR. Dist: Littlehampton Bk Services, Ltd.
I Like Red: Individual Title, 6 Packs. (Sails Literacy Ser.). 16p. (gr. k-18). 27.00 *(978-0-7635-4402-7(7))* Rigby Education.
Icibaci, Neusa, tr. Eating the Rainbow (Portuguese/English), 1 vol. 2010. (Um Colorido Livro de Alimentos/Colorful Food Bks.). (ENG., Illus.). 20p. (J). 6.95 *(978-1-59572-204-1(1))* Star Bright Bks., Inc.
Imperato, Teresa. Colors All Around: A Turn & Pop Book. Petrone, Valeria, illus. 2005. (Turn & Pop Book Ser.). 10p. (J). bds. 5.95 *(978-1-58117-277-5(X)*, Intervisual/Piggy Toes) Bendon, Inc.
In Full Color. 2004. per. *(978-1-932948-08-0(2))* Student Pr. Initiative.
Innovative Kids Staff, creator. Soft Shapes - Colors. 2010. (ENG.). 8p. (J). (gr. -1 — 1). 10.99 *(978-1-58476-963-7(7))* Innovative Kids.
Ivancic, Linda. What Is the Color Spectrum? 2016. (Unseen Science Ser.). (ENG., Illus.). 32p. (J). (gr. 3-3). pap. 10.58 *(978-1-5026-0920-5(7))* Cavendish Square Publishing.
Jackson, Tom. Experiments with Light & Color. 2010. (Cool Science Ser.). (Illus.). 32p. (J). (gr. 5-6). pap. 10.50 *(978-1-4339-3454-4(X))*; lib. bdg. 28.00 *(978-1-4339-3453-7(1)*, 1309304) Stevens, Gareth Publishing LLLP. (Gareth Stevens Learning Library).
Jaramillo, Gloria. Busy Kids' Colors, Shapes & Sizes. Poirier, Nadine, illus. 2008. (Busy Kids Ser.). 36p. (J). (gr. -1-k). bds. 12.99 *(978-2-7641-1677-7(2))* Gardner Pubns.
Jenkins, Steve. The Animal Book: A Collection of the Fastest, Fiercest, Toughest, Cleverest, Shyest - And Most Surprising - Animals on Earth. Jenkins, Steve, illus. 2013. (ENG., Illus.). 208p. (J). (gr. 1-4). 24.99 *(978-0-547-55799-1(X))* Houghton Mifflin Harcourt Publishing Co.
Jennings, Terry. Light & Dark. 2009. (Science Alive Ser.). (Illus.). 32p. (J). (gr. 4-7). pap. *(978-1-897563-56-4(6))* Saunders Bk. Co.
Jensen, Karl, et al. Flowers for Grandma. 2007. (Windows on Literacy Ser.). (ENG., Illus.). 12p. (J). pap. 10.95 *(978-0-7922-8457-4(7))* CENGAGE Learning.
Jocelyn, Marthe. One Some Many. Slaughter, Tom, illus. (ENG.). (J). (gr. k-k). 2006. 16p. bds. 7.95 *(978-0-88776-789-0(3))* 2004. 32p. 11.95 *(978-0-88776-675-6(7))* Tundra Bks. CAN. (Tundra Bks.). Dist: Penguin Random Hse. LLC.
Jones, Christianne C. Camping in Green, 1 vol. Ouren, Todd, illus. 2007. (Know Your Colors Ser.). (ENG.). 24p. (gr. -1-1). lib. bdg. 26.65 *(978-1-4048-3107-0(X)*, 1265677) Picture Window Bks.
Jordan, Christopher. Hockey Colors. 2011. (My First NHL Book Ser.). (ENG.). 30p. (J). (gr. k-k). bds. 6.95 *(978-1-77049-349-0(2)*, Fenn-Tundra) Tundra Bks. CAN. Dist: Penguin Random Hse. LLC.
—Hockey Colours. 2010. (My First NHL Bks.). (ENG., Illus.). 30p. (J). (gr. -1). bds. *(978-1-55168-368-3(7))* Me to We.
—Hockey Colours. 2011. (ENG., Illus.). 30p. (J). (-k). bds. 8.99 *(978-1-77049-322-3(0))* Tundra Bks. CAN. Dist: Random Hse., Inc.
—NASCAR Colors. 2012. (My First NASCAR Racing Ser.). (ENG., Illus.). 26p. (J). (gr. k-k). bds. 7.95 *(978-1-77049-430-5(8)*, Fenn-Tundra) Tundra Bks. CAN. Dist: Penguin Random Hse. LLC.
Kalman, Bobbie. ¿De Qué Color Es? 2008.Tr. of What Color Is It? (SPA.). 24p. (J). pap. *(978-0-7787-8735-8(4))* Crabtree Publishing Co.
—I Eat a Rainbow: Me Como un Arco Iris. 2010. (SPA, ENG & MUL.). 16p. (J). pap. *(978-0-7787-8263-6(8))*; lib. bdg. *(978-0-7787-8270-4(0))* Crabtree Publishing Co.
—Me Como un Arco Iris. 2010. (SPA.). 16p. (J). pap. *(978-0-7787-8578-1(5))*; lib. bdg. *(978-0-7787-8552-1(1))* Crabtree Publishing Co.
—What Color Is It? 2007. (Looking at Nature Ser.). (ENG., Illus.). 24p. (J). (gr. -1-2). pap. *(978-0-7787-3338-6(6))*; lib. bdg. *(978-0-7787-3318-8(1))* Crabtree Publishing Co.

Kalz, Jill. Colors. Banks, Timothy, illus. 2013. (Wizard of Oz Ser.). (ENG.). 24p. (gr. 1-2). 27.99 (978-1-4765-3764-1(X)) Capstone Press of Coughlan Cos.

Kassinger, Ruth. Dyes: From Sea Snails to Synthetics. 2003. (Material World Ser.). (Illus.). 80p. (gr. 6-8). lib. bdg. 25.90 (978-0-7613-2112-5(8), Twenty-First Century Bks.) Lerner Publishing Group.

Katz, Karen. Baby's Colors. Katz, Karen, illus. 2010. (ENG., Illus.). 14p. (J). (gr. -1 — 1). bds. 6.99 (978-1-4169-9821-1(7), Little Simon) Little Simon.

Keating, Jess. Pink Is for Blobfish. 2016. (World of Weird Animals Ser.). (ENG., Illus.). 48p. (J). (gr. k-3). 16.99 (978-0-553-51227-4(7), Knopf Bks. for Young Readers) Random Hse. Children's Bks.

Keiser, Melissa. My Airplane Book-Colors. 2005. (Board Book Ser.). (ENG., Illus.). 12p. (J). (gr. -1-12). bds. 6.95 (978-1-59373-042-0(X)) Bunker Hill Publishing, Inc.

Kenison, Misti, illus. France - The Tiny Traveler: A Book of Colors. 2015. (ENG.). 24p. (J). (— 1). bds. 5.95 (978-1-62914-609-6(9), Sky Pony Pr.) Skyhorse Publishing Co., Inc.

Kenney, Karen Latchana. The Science of Color: Investigating Light. 1 vol. 2016. (Science in Action Ser.). (ENG., Illus.). 32p. (J). (gr. 3-6). 27.07 (978-1-62403-960-7(X)) ABDO Publishing Co.

Khan, Hena. Golden Domes & Silver Lanterns: A Muslim Book of Colors. Amini, Mehrdokht, illus. 2015. (ENG.). 32p. (J). (gr. -1-k). 7.99 (978-1-4521-4121-3(5)) Chronicle Bks. LLC.

Kiely, Orla. Colors. Kiely, Orla, illus. 2012. (ENG., Illus.). 20p. (J). (gr. -1 — 1). bds. 12.99 (978-0-8050-9491-6(1), 9780805094916, Holt, Henry & Co. Bks. For Young Readers) Holt, Henry & Co.

Kim, illus. Colors All Around. 2008. (SPA & ENG.). 28p. (J). pap. 8.95 (978-1-60448-009-2(2)) Lectura Bks.

Kissinger, Katie. All the Colors We Are/Todos Los Colores de Nuestra Piel: The Story of How We Get Our Skin Color/la Historia de Por Que Tenemos Diferentes Colores de Piel. 2014. (ENG., Illus.). 32p. (J). (gr. -1-5). 16.95 (978-1-60554-079-5(X)) Redleaf Pr.

Kitamura, Satoshi. Colours. Kitamura, Satoshi, illus. 2007. (Collins Big Cat Ser.). (ENG., Illus.). 48p. (J). (gr. -1-1). pap. 5.99 (978-0-00-718663-1(0)) HarperCollins Pubs. Ltd. GBR. Dist: Independent Pubs. Group.

Koski, Mary B. Color, Color, Where Are You, Color? Mason, Janeen, illus. 2004. (ENG.). (J). 28p. bds. 7.95 (978-1-930650-34-3(5)); 32p. (gr. 1-3). 14.95 (978-1-930650-35-0(3)) mTrellis Publishing, Inc.

La Jars, David. One, Two, Red & Blue. rev. ed. 2004. (Talk Together Ser.). (Illus.). 24p. (J). (gr. -1-k). pap. 5.95 (978-1-58728-019-1(1), Two-Can Publishing) T&N Children's Publishing.

Lamb, Stacey. Colors Sticker Coloring Book. 2011. (First Sticker Coloring Book Ser.). 32p. (J). pap. 5.99 (978-0-7945-2965-9(8), Usborne) EDC Publishing.

Lauber, Patricia. What You Never Knew about Beds, Bedrooms, & Pajamas. Manders, John, illus. 2008. (ENG.). 40p. (J). (gr. 1-4). 6.99 (978-1-4169-6738-5(9), Simon & Schuster Bks. For Young Readers) Simon & Schuster Bks. For Young Readers.

Law, Felicia. Colors. Knight, Paula, illus. 2015. (Patchwork Ser.). (ENG.). 24p. (J). (gr. k-3). pap. 11.94 (978-1-60357-799-1(8)) Norwood Hse. Pr.

Lawrence, Ellen. Color. 2013. (Science Slam: FUN-Damental Experiments Ser.). 24p. (J). (gr. -1-3). lib. bdg. 23.93 (978-1-61772-738-2(5)) Bearport Publishing Co., Inc.

Layne, Carmela C. I See Many Colors Around My House: Los Colores que Veo Por Mi Casa. Layne, Carmela C., ed. Arevalo, Jose Daniel, illus. l.t. ed. 2005. (SPA.). 24p. (J). (gr. -1-3). pap. 6.95 (978-0-9769538-0-7(3)) Pannycake Pubn.

Layton, Neil. Go Wild with Colors. 2004. (Illus.). 12p. (J). bds. 9.95 (978-1-84458-044-6(X), Pavilion Children's Books) Pavilion Bks.

Lazoo Publishing Staff. Colors! 2010. (ENG., Illus.). 10p. (J). bds. 6.99 (978-1-934734-56-8(X)) Seven Footer Pr.

Learning Colors. 2010. (Colors Bks.). 32p. lib. bdg. 155.94 (978-1-4296-5195-0(4), Aplus Bks.) Capstone Press of Coughlan Cos.

Learning Company Books Staff, ed. Reader Rabbit Fun with Colors. 2004. (Illus.). 32p. (J). pap. (978-0-7630-7738-9(0)) Magma.

Lewis, Jan. Look & Learn with Little Dino: Colour Fun. Lewis, Jan, illus. 2014. (ENG., Illus.). 24p. (J). (gr. -1-2). bds. 6.99 (978-1-86147-380-6(X), Armadillo) Anness Publishing GBR. Dist: National Bk. Network.

Lewis, Jan, illus. Ask Me about Colours: Lift the Flaps & Find the Answers! 2016. (ENG.). 14p. (J). (gr. -1-12). 10.99 (978-1-86147-775-0(9), Armadillo) Anness Publishing GBR. Dist: National Bk. Network.

—My First Colours. 2014. (ENG.). 24p. (J). (gr. -1-k). bds. 6.99 (978-1-86147-374-5(5), Armadillo) Anness Publishing GBR. Dist: National Bk. Network.

El Libro de Contar de los Chocolates M & M's Brand. 2004. 32p. (J). pap. 6.95 (978-1-57091-370-9(6)) Charlesbridge Publishing, Inc.

Lift & See Colors. (Baby Goldstars Lift Out Eva Ser.). 5p. (978-1-4054-9313-0(5)) Parragon, Inc.

Lilly, Melinda. Color. Thompson, Scott M., illus. 2003. 24p. (J). 22.79 (978-1-58952-646-4(5)) Rourke Educational Media.

Linda, Winder. Glitter: My First Book of Shapes Numbers Colors & the Alphabet Gods Way. 2003. (978-1-892354-65-3(3)) Educational Publishing Concepts, Inc.

Lindeen, Mary. Color & Shape. 2017. (BeginningtoRead Ser.). (ENG.). 32p. (J). (-2). 22.60 (978-1-59953-882-2(2)); pap. 11.94 (978-1-68404-101-5(5)) Norwood Hse. Pr.

Lionni, Leo. Colors, Numbers, Letters. 2010. (ENG., Illus.). 40p. (J). (gr. k — 1). bds. 10.99 (978-0-375-85474-3(6), Knopf Bks. for Young Readers) Random Hse. Children's Bks.

Little, Richard. We Love Purple! 2016. (Our Favorite Colors Ser.). (ENG., Illus.). 24p. (J). (gr. k-k). pap. 8.15 (978-1-4824-3735-5(X)) Stevens, Gareth Publishing LLLP.

—We Love Red! 2016. (Our Favorite Colors Ser.). (ENG., Illus.). 24p. (J). (gr. k-k). pap. 8.15 (978-1-4824-3739-3(2)) Stevens, Gareth Publishing LLLP.

—We Love Yellow! 2016. (Our Favorite Colors Ser.). (ENG., Illus.). 24p. (J). (gr. k-k). pap. 8.15 (978-1-4824-3743-0(0)) Stevens, Gareth Publishing LLLP.

Littlefield, Holly. Colors of India. Porter, Janice Lee, illus. 2003. (Colors of the World Ser.). 24p. (J). (gr. 1-4). 5.95 (978-1-57505-368-4(3)) Lerner Publishing Group.

Litton, Jonathan. Touch & Feel Colors. Galloway, Fhiona, illus. 2017. (My Little World Ser.). (ENG.). 10p. (J). (gr. -1-k). bds. 8.99 (978-1-68010-510-0(8)) Tiger Tales.

Lluch, Alex A. I Like to Learn Colors: Curious Penguin. 2011. (ENG.). 32p. (J). (gr. -1-k). bds. 4.95 (978-1-934386-02-6(2)) WS Publishing.

—Let's Leap Ahead Colors & Shapes. 2012. (ENG.). 80p. (J). (gr. -1). spiral bd. 9.95 (978-1-936061-66-2(X)) WS Publishing.

Lovejoy, Sharon. The Little Green Island with a Little Red House: A Book of Colors & Critters. 2015. (ENG., Illus.). 32p. (J). (gr. -1-2). 10.95 (978-1-60893-464-5(0)) Down East Bks.

Lowery, Lawrence F. Light & Color: I Wonder Why. Wood, Muriel, illus. 2014. (I Wonder Why Ser.). (ENG.). 36p. (J). (gr. k-3). pap. 11.95 (978-1-938946-51-6(0)) National Science Teachers Assn.

Luckiesh, Matthew. The Language of Color. (Illus.). xii, 28p. (gr. 2). reprint ed. lib. bdg. (978-0-7222-3055-8(9)) Library Reprints, Inc.

Ludgate, Kevin. Pilgrim Village: A Thanksgiving Diorama, 1 vol. 2010. (ENG., Illus.). 32p. (J). pap. 9.99 (978-0-7643-3563-1(4), 9780764335631) Schiffer Publishing, Ltd.

Mack, Steve. Coloring. Flash Kids Editors, ed. 2012. (Flash Kids Preschool Activity Bks.). (ENG., Illus.). 80p. (J). pap. 5.95 (978-1-4114-5806-2(0), Spark Publishing Group) Sterling Publishing Co., Inc.

Mackall, Dandi Daley. Easter Colors Sticker Book. Fyffe, Brian, illus. 2004. 10p. (J). (gr. -1-18). bds. 4.99 (978-1-57151-723-4(5)) Playhouse Publishing.

MacRobert, Tristan. Colors at the Garage Sale. 2017. (Wonderful World of Colors Ser.). 24p. (gr. 4-6). pap. 8.25 (978-1-5383-2167-6(X), PowerKids Pr.) Rosen Publishing Group, Inc., The.

Make Believe Ideas Staff. Baby Fun Colors. 2005. (Illus.). 10p. (gr. -1 — 1). per. (978-1-905051-17-5(4)) Make Believe Ideas.

Makeeff, Cyndi Sue. Inky Winky Spider Colors by the Bay. Riley, Kevin, illus. 2006. 32p. (J). pap. 7.99 (978-0-9778310-2-9(7)) New Vision Entertainment, LLC.

Manolis, Kay. Color. 2008. (First Science Ser.). (ENG., Illus.). 24p. (J). (gr. 2-5). lib. bdg. 25.95 (978-1-60014-227-7(3)) Bellwether Media.

—Color. 2011. (Blastoff! Readers Ser.). (ENG.). 24p. (J). pap. 5.95 (978-0-531-28450-6(6), Children's Pr.) Scholastic Library Publishing.

Mara, Wil. Why Is the Sky Blue? 2006. (Tell Me Why, Tell Me How Ser.). (Illus.). 32p. (J). (gr. 3-7). lib. bdg. 28.50 (978-0-7614-2108-5(4), Benchmark Bks.) Marshall Cavendish Corp.

Mark R. Borene, R. Borene & Mark R Borene. Welcome to the Farm: Book 2 of Welcome to the World. 2009. (Illus.). 20p. pap. 10.49 (978-1-4389-6549-9(4)) AuthorHouse.

—Welcome to the Sky. 2009. (Illus.). 20p. pap. 10.49 (978-1-4389-7088-2(9)) AuthorHouse.

Markovics, Joyce L. City Colors: From Taxis to Skyscrapers. 2015. (Illus.). 24p. (J). lib. bdg. (978-1-62724-322-3(4)) Bearport Publishing Co., Inc.

—Farm Colors: From Purple Plums to Pink Pigs. 2014. (Little Bits: Colors Tell a Story Ser.). (ENG.). 24p. (J). (gr. -1-3). lib. bdg. 23.93 (978-1-62724-323-0(2)) Bearport Publishing Co., Inc.

—Food Colors: From Blueberries to Beets. 2014. (Little Bits: Colors Tell a Story Ser.). (ENG.). 24p. (J). (gr. -1-3). lib. bdg. 23.93 (978-1-62724-324-7(0)) Bearport Publishing Co., Inc.

—Los Colores de la Ciudad: De Los Taxis a Los Rascacielos. 2014. (Los Colores Cuentan una Historia Ser.). (SPA.). 24p. (J). (gr. -1-3). lib. bdg. 23.93 (978-1-62724-464-0(6)) Bearport Publishing Co., Inc.

—Los Colores de la Granja: De Las Ciruelas Moradas a Los Cerdos Rosados. 2014. (Los Colores Cuentan una Historia Ser.). (SPA.). 24p. (J). (gr. -1-3). lib. bdg. 23.93 (978-1-62724-465-7(4)) Bearport Publishing Co., Inc.

—Los Colores de Las Estaciones: Cómo Cambian. 2014. (Los Colores Cuentan una Historia Ser.). (SPA.). 24p. (J). (gr. -1-3). lib. bdg. 23.93 (978-1-62724-469-5(7)) Bearport Publishing Co., Inc.

—Los Colores de Los Alimentos: De Los Arándanos a la Remolacha. 2014. (Los Colores Cuentan una Historia Ser.). (SPA., Illus.). 24p. (J). (gr. -1-3). lib. bdg. 23.93 (978-1-62724-466-4(2)) Bearport Publishing Co., Inc.

—The Seasons' Colors: How They Change. 2015. (Illus.). 24p. (J). lib. bdg. (978-1-62724-327-8(5)) Bearport Publishing Co., Inc.

Matisse, Henri & Phaidon Editors. Blue & Other Colours: With Henri Matisse. 2016. (ENG., Illus.). 30p. bds. 9.95 (978-0-7148-7132-5(X)) Phaidon Pr., Inc.

Maynard, Christopher & White, Terry. Why Are Zebras Black & White? Questions Children Ask about Colour. (Why Bks.). (Illus.). 24p. (J). pap. 10.99 (978-0-590-24946-1(0)) Scholastic, Inc.

McBratney, Sam. Colors Everywhere. Jeram, Anita, illus. 2007. (Guess How Much I Love You Ser.). (ENG.). 24p. (J). (-k). bds. 7.99 (978-0-7636-3545-9(6)) Candlewick Pr.

McGrath, Barbara Barbieri. Christmas Colors & Counting. Tagel, Peggy, illus. 2016. (First Celebrations Ser.). (ENG.). 12p. (J). (— 1). bds. 6.95 (978-1-58089-531-6(X)) Charlesbridge Publishing, Inc.

—The M & M's(r) Brand Color Pattern Book. Glass, Roger, illus. 2004. 32p. (J). (gr. -1-3). 16.95 (978-1-57091-416-4(8)); pap. 6.95 (978-1-57091-417-1(6)) Charlesbridge Publishing, Inc.

—The M & M's(r) Brand Counting Book. Glass, Roger, illus. rev. ed. 2004. 32p. (J). 16.95 (978-1-57091-367-9(6)); pap. 6.95 (978-1-57091-368-6(4)) Charlesbridge Publishing, Inc.

—Mas Matematicas con los Chocolates de M & M's Brand. Mlawer, Teresa, tr. Glass, Roger, illus. 2004. (SPA.). 32p. (J). pap. 6.95 (978-1-57091-481-2(8), CH30498) Charlesbridge Publishing, Inc.

—Teddy Bear Patterns. Nihoff, Tim, illus. 2013. (McGrath Math Ser.). (ENG.). 32p. (J). (gr. -1-3). pap. 7.95 (978-1-58089-423-4(2)); lib. bdg. 16.95 (978-1-58089-422-7(4)) Charlesbridge Publishing, Inc.

—Teddy Bear, Teddy Bear, School Day Math. Nihoff, Tim, illus. 2012. (McGrath Math Ser.). (ENG.). 32p. (J). (gr. -1-3). 16.95 (978-1-58089-420-3(8)); pap. 7.95 (978-1-58089-421-0(6)) Charlesbridge Publishing, Inc.

McKay, Sindy. Too Many Cats: Demasiados Gatos. 2010. (SPA., Illus.). 41p. (J). (978-1-60115-039-4(3)) Treasure Bay, Inc.

—We Both Read Bilingual Edition-Too Many Cats/Demasiados Gatos. Johnson, Meredith, illus. 2011. (ENG & SPA.). 44p. (J). pap. 4.99 (978-1-60115-040-0(7)) Treasure Bay, Inc.

Melnikov, Julian. Our Colorful World. 2017. (Wonderful World of Colors Ser.). 24p. (gr. 4-6). pap. 8.25 (978-1-5383-2163-8(7), PowerKids Pr.) Rosen Publishing Group, Inc., The.

Metropolitan Museum of Art Staff, contrib. by. Color Magic Sticker Play Book. 2008. (ENG., Illus.). 16p. (J). (gr. k-2). spiral bd. 25.95 (978-0-8109-7126-4(7), Abrams Bks. for Young Readers) Abrams, Inc.

Metsola, Aino-Maija. Colors. 2016. (Learning Garden Ser.). (ENG.). 16p. (J). (gr. -1-k). bds. 9.99 (978-1-84780-705-2(4), Wide Eyed Editions) Quarto Publishing Group UK GBR. Dist: Hachette Bk. Group.

—Colours: With Lift-Flap Surprises on Every Page. 2015. (Learning Garden Ser.). (ENG., Illus.). 14p. (J). bds. 9.99 (978-1-84780-609-3(0), Wide Eyed Editions) Quarto Publishing Group UK GBR. Dist: Littlehampton Bk Services, Ltd.

Micco, Trudy. I See Blue. 2010. (All about Colors Ser.). (Illus.). 24p. (J). 22.60 (978-0-7660-3788-5(6)); pap. 7.95 (978-1-59845-163-4(4)) Enslow Pubs., Inc. (Enslow Elementary).

—I See Green. 2010. (All about Colors Ser.). (Illus.). 24p. (J). 22.60 (978-0-7660-3789-2(4)); pap. 7.95 (978-1-59845-164-1(2)) Enslow Pubs., Inc. (Enslow Elementary).

—I See Orange. 2010. (All about Colors Ser.). (Illus.). 24p. (J). 22.60 (978-0-7660-3791-5(6)); pap. 7.95 (978-1-59845-166-5(9)) Enslow Pubs., Inc. (Enslow Elementary).

—I See Purple. 2010. (All about Colors Ser.). (Illus.). 24p. (J). 22.60 (978-0-7660-3792-2(4)); pap. 7.95 (978-1-59845-167-2(7)) Enslow Pubs., Inc. (Enslow Elementary).

—I See Red. 2010. (All about Colors Ser.). (Illus.). 24p. (J). 22.60 (978-0-7660-3787-8(8)); pap. 7.95 (978-1-59845-162-7(6)) Enslow Pubs., Inc. (Enslow Elementary).

—I See Yellow. 2010. (All about Colors Ser.). (Illus.). 24p. (J). 22.60 (978-0-7660-3790-8(8)); pap. 7.95 (978-1-59845-165-8(0)) Enslow Pubs., Inc. (Enslow Elementary).

Michele, Tracey. Make a Color. 2011. (Learn-Abouts Ser.). (Illus.). 16p. (J). pap. 7.95 (978-1-59920-596-0(3)) Black Rabbit Bks.

Miesen, Christina & Novick, Mary. Colours & Shapes: With Flip the Flap Pages. 2013. (Mini Marvels Ser.). (ENG., Illus.). 10p. (J). (gr. -1-k). 9.99 (978-1-921049-62-0(6)) Little Hare Bks. AUS. Dist: Independent Pubs. Group.

Milet Publishing Staff. Colors. (My First Bilingual Book Ser.). 24p. (J). (gr. k — 1). 2011. (ENG.). bds. 7.99 (978-1-84059-606-9(6)) 2011. (ENG.). bds. 8.99 (978-1-84059-597-0(3)) 2010. (SPA & ENG., Illus.). bds. 7.99 (978-1-84059-539-0(6)) Milet Publishing.

—Colors - My First Bilingual Book. 2011. (My First Bilingual Book Ser.). (ENG.). 24p. (J). (gr. k — 1). bds. 7.99 (978-1-84059-601-4(5)); bds. 7.99 (978-1-84059-599-4(X)) Milet Publishing.

—Colours. 2010. (My First Bilingual Book Ser.). (Illus.). 24p. (J). (gr. k — 1). (ENG & CHI.). bds. 7.99 (978-1-84059-561-1(2)); (ENG & JPN., bds. 7.99 (978-1-84059-563-5(9)); (KOR & ENG., bds. 7.99 (978-1-84059-564-2(7)); (VIE & ENG., bds. 7.99 (978-1-84059-569-7(8)) Milet Publishing.

—Colours - My First Bilingual Book. 2010. (My First Bilingual Book Ser.). (Illus.). 24p. (J). (gr. k — 1). (ENG & POL.). bds. 8.99 (978-1-84059-538-3(8)); (URD & ENG., bds. 7.99 (978-1-84059-568-0(X)); (SOM & ENG., bds. 7.99 (978-1-84059-567-3(1)); (RUS & ENG., bds. 7.99 (978-1-84059-566-6(3)); (POR & ENG., bds. 7.99 (978-1-84059-565-9(5)); (PER & ENG., bds. 7.99 (978-1-84059-562-8(0)); (ARA & ENG., bds. 7.99 (978-1-84059-560-4(4)); (ENG & ITA., bds. 8.99 (978-1-84059-537-6(X)); (ENG & GER., bds. 8.99 (978-1-84059-536-9(1)) Milet Publishing.

—My First Bilingual Book - Colors. 2011. (My First Bilingual Book Ser.). (ENG.). 24p. (J). (gr. k — 1). bds. 7.99 (978-1-84059-603-8(1)); bds. 7.99 (978-1-84059-602-1(3)); bds. 7.99 (978-1-84059-598-7(1)); bds. 7.99 (978-1-84059-604-5(X)); bds. 7.99 (978-1-84059-600-7(7)) Milet Publishing.

—My First Bilingual Book - Colors (English-Urdu) 2011. (My First Bilingual Book Ser.). (ENG.). 24p. (J). (gr. k — 1). bds. 7.99 (978-1-84059-605-2(8)) Milet Publishing.

—My First Bilingual Book - Colours. 2010. (My First Bilingual Book Ser.). (Illus.). 24p. (J). (gr. k — 1). (FRE & ENG.). bds. 8.99 (978-1-84059-535-2(3)); (ENG & TUR., bds. 7.99 (978-1-84059-540-6(X)) Milet Publishing.

Milich, Zoran. City Colors. (ENG., Illus.). 24p. (J). (gr. -1-k). 2006. 6.95 (978-1-55337-981-2(0)) 2004. 14.95 (978-1-55337-542-5(4)) Kids Can Pr., Ltd. CAN. Dist: Hachette Bk. Group.

Miller, Margaret. I Love Colors. Miller, Margaret, photos by. 2009. (Look Baby! Bks.). (ENG., Illus.). 14p. (J). (gr. -1 — 1). bds. 4.99 (978-1-4169-7888-6(7), Little Simon) Little Simon.

Mills, Nathan & Star, Pat. Describe It: Size, Shape, & Color. 2012. (Rosen Readers Ser.). (ENG., Illus.). 16p. (J). (gr. k-1). pap. 7.00 (978-1-4488-8755-2(0), Rosen Classroom) Rosen Publishing Group, Inc., The.

Minnerly, Denise Bennett. Painting the Town. 2009. (ENG.). 32p. (J). 15.95 (978-1-56290-616-0(X)) Crystal Productions.

Mitchell, Melanie S. Black. 2004. (First Step Nonfiction - Colors Ser.). (ENG., Illus.). 8p. (gr. -1-1). pap. 4.95 (978-0-8225-3891-2(1), Lerner Pubns.) Lerner Publishing Group.

—Blue. 2004. (First Step Nonfiction - Colors Ser.). (ENG., Illus.). 8p. (gr. -1-1). pap. 4.95 (978-0-8225-3892-9(X), Lerner Pubns.) Lerner Publishing Group.

—Brown. 2004. (First Step Nonfiction - Colors Ser.). (ENG., Illus.). 8p. (gr. -1-1). pap. 4.95 (978-0-8225-3893-6(8), Lerner Pubns.) Lerner Publishing Group.

—Green. 2004. (First Step Nonfiction - Colors Ser.). (ENG., Illus.). 8p. (gr. -1-1). pap. 4.95 (978-0-8225-3894-3(6), Lerner Pubns.) Lerner Publishing Group.

—Orange. 2004. (First Step Nonfiction - Colors Ser.). (ENG., Illus.). 8p. (gr. -1-1). pap. 4.95 (978-0-8225-3895-0(4), Lerner Pubns.) Lerner Publishing Group.

—Purple. 2004. (First Step Nonfiction - Colors Ser.). (ENG., Illus.). 8p. (gr. -1-1). pap. 4.95 (978-0-8225-3896-7(2), Lerner Pubns.) Lerner Publishing Group.

—Red. 2004. (First Step Nonfiction - Colors Ser.). (ENG., Illus.). 8p. (gr. -1-1). pap. 4.95 (978-0-8225-3897-4(0), Lerner Pubns.) Lerner Publishing Group.

—Yellow. 2004. (First Step Nonfiction - Colors Ser.). (ENG., Illus.). 8p. (gr. -1-1). pap. 4.95 (978-0-8225-3898-1(9), Lerner Pubns.) Lerner Publishing Group.

Moore, Cassandra. Shape/Color Master. 2007. (Illus.). 75p. (J). spiral bd. 12.95 (978-1-886297-30-2(4)) Omega Publishing Hse.

Moore-Chambers, Robin. Dark Skin, Light Skin, Straight or Nappy... It's All Good! An Educational Coloring Book about the Beauty & Diversity of African-American Features. 2011. 47p. pap. 12.95 (978-1-4327-3545-6(4)) Outskirts Pr., Inc.

Mullen, Amy. Colors of New England. 2017. (Naturally Local Ser.). (ENG., Illus.). 20p. (J). (gr. -1-k). bds. 8.95 (978-1-938093-99-9(2)) Duo Pr. LLC.

Murray, Julie. Color, 1 vol. 2006. (First Science - 12 Titles Ser.). (ENG., Illus.). 24p. (gr. k-4). 25.65 (978-1-59679-821-2(1), Buddy Bks.) ABDO Publishing Co.

My Big Box of Colors, Shapes, & Numbers: Contains Twenty Beautifully Illustrated Board Books. (Illus.). (J). bds. (978-1-904613-80-0(2)) O'Mara, Michael Bks., Ltd.

Nancy Giorgio-Kupiec. Nanje's Imagination or Is It ? 2009. 20p. pap. 10.49 (978-1-4389-7068-4(4)) AuthorHouse.

National Geographic Kids Staff. Colors! 2012. (ENG., Illus.). 24p. (J). (gr. k-k). bds. 6.99 (978-1-4263-0929-8(5), National Geographic Children's Bks.) National Geographic Society.

Naughton, Diane. True Colors Intermediate Book with Online Access, 1 vol. 2014. (ENG., Illus.). 28p. (J). pap. 9.50 (978-1-107-66068-7(8)) Cambridge Univ. Pr.

Nguyen, An Mai. Let's Learn Colors in Vietnamese. 2006. (VIE & ENG., Illus.). (J). bds. 6.95 (978-0-9776482-1-4(4)) Viet Baby, LLC.

Nixon, Mallory. The Color Cats. 2009. 28p. pap. 12.99 (978-1-4389-9798-8(1)) AuthorHouse.

Nobens, Cheryl, illus. Colores - Colors. 2006. (ENG & SPA.). (J). bds. 5.99 (978-1-934113-03-5(4)) Little Cubans, LLC.

Norma Staff, ed. Colores. 2005. 14p. (978-958-04-8068-6(0)) Norma S.A.

Novoa, Teresa, illus. Azul. (Cocorolos Ser.). (SPA.). 12p. (J). (gr. -1-k). bds. 7.95 (978-84-294-6923-3(0)) Santillana USA Publishing Co., Inc.

Nunn, Daniel. Brown, 1 vol. 2012. (Colors All Around Us Ser.). (ENG.). 24p. (gr. -1-k). lib. bdg. 25.99 (978-1-4329-5752-0(X)) Heinemann-Raintree.

—The Colors. 2013. (True or False? Ser.). (ENG.). 24p. (gr. -1-1). pap. 6.29 (978-1-4109-5072-7(7), NA-r) Heinemann-Raintree.

—Colors, 1 vol. 2013. (True or False? Ser.). (ENG.). 20p. (gr. -1-1). bds. 7.99 (978-1-4109-5085-7(9), NA-r) Heinemann-Raintree.

—The Colors - True or False? 2013. (True or False? Ser.). (ENG.). 24p. (gr. -1-1). lib. bdg. 22.65 (978-1-4109-5066-6(2), NA-r) Heinemann-Raintree.

—Colors in English, 1 vol. 2012. (World Languages - Colors Ser.). (ENG.). 24p. (gr. 1-3). pap. 6.29 (978-1-4329-6663-8(4)); lib. bdg. 21.99 (978-1-4329-6656-0(1)) Heinemann-Raintree. (Acorn).

—Colors in French: Les Couleurs, 1 vol. 2012. (World Languages - Colors Ser.). (ENG, FRE & MUL.). 24p. (gr. 1-3). pap. 6.29 (978-1-4329-6658-4(8)); lib. bdg. 22.65 (978-1-4329-6651-5(0)) Heinemann-Raintree. (Acorn).

—Colors in German: Die Farben, 1 vol. 2012. (World Languages - Colors Ser.). (ENG, GER & MUL.). 24p. (gr. 1-3). pap. 6.29 (978-1-4329-6660-7(X)); lib. bdg. 22.65 (978-1-4329-6653-9(7)) Heinemann-Raintree. (Acorn).

—Colors in Italian: I Colori, 1 vol. 2012. (World Languages - Colors Ser.). (ENG, ITA & MUL.). 24p. (gr. 1-3). pap. 6.29 (978-1-4329-6662-1(6)); lib. bdg. 22.65 (978-1-4329-6655-3(3)) Heinemann-Raintree. (Acorn).

—Colors in Polish: Kolory, 1 vol. 2012. (World Languages - Colors Ser.). (ENG, POL & MUL.). 24p. (gr. 1-3). pap. 6.29 (978-1-4329-6661-4(8)); lib. bdg. 22.65 (978-1-4329-6654-6(5)) Heinemann-Raintree. (Acorn).

—Colors in Spanish: Los Colores, 1 vol. 2012. (World Languages - Colors Ser.). (ENG, SPA & MUL.). 24p. (gr. 1-3). pap. 6.29 (978-1-4329-6659-1(6), Acorn) Heinemann-Raintree.

—Red, 1 vol. 2012. (Colors All Around Us Ser.). (ENG., Illus.). 24p. (gr. -1-k). lib. bdg. 25.99 (978-1-4329-5747-6(3)) Heinemann-Raintree.

—White, 1 vol. 2012. (Colors All Around Us Ser.). (ENG., Illus.). 24p. (gr. -1-k). lib. bdg. 25.99 (978-1-4329-5751-3(1)) Heinemann-Raintree.

—Yellow, 1 vol. 2012. (Colors All Around Us Ser.). (ENG., Illus.). 24p. (gr. -1-k). lib. bdg. 25.99 (978-1-4329-5748-3(1)) Heinemann-Raintree.

Nunn, Daniel & Rissman, Rebecca. Pink, 1 vol. 2012. (Colors All Around Us Ser.). (ENG., Illus.). 24p. (gr. -1-k). lib. bdg. 25.99 (978-1-4329-5750-6(3)) Heinemann-Raintree.

O'Connell, Emma. We Love Blue! 2016. (Our Favorite Colors Ser.). (ENG., Illus.). 24p. (J). (gr. k-k). pap. 8.15 (978-1-4824-3723-2(6)) Stevens, Gareth Publishing LLLP.

—We Love Green! 2016. (Our Favorite Colors Ser.). (ENG., Illus.). 24p. (J). (gr. k-k). pap. 8.15 (978-1-4824-3727-0(9)) Stevens, Gareth Publishing LLLP.

—We Love Orange! 2016. (Our Favorite Colors Ser.). (ENG., Illus.). 24p. (J). (gr. k-k). pap. 8.15 (978-1-4824-3731-7(7)) Stevens, Gareth Publishing LLLP.

Omary, Rachel, illus. Shapes & Colors in Dari. 2004. 5p. (J). spiral bd. 14.95 (978-0-9740535-7-8(0)) Knight Publishing.

—Shapes & Colors in Farsi. l.t. ed. 2004. 5p. (J). spiral bd. 14.95 *(978-0-9740535-6-1(2))* Knight Publishing.
—Shapes & Colors in Pashto. l.t. ed. 2004. 5p. (J). spiral bd. 14.95 *(978-0-9740535-8-5(9))* Knight Publishing.
Omoto, Garrett, illus. Na Waihooluu. 2006.Tr. of Colors. (HAW & ENG.). 16p. (J). 8.95 *(978-1-933835-00-6(1))* Partners in Development Foundation.
Orero, Maria Jesus. Nico y los Colores. 2006. (Nico Collection). (SPA & ESP., Illus.). 12p. (gr. -1-2). per., bds. 6.99 *(978-84-272-6153-2(5))* Molino, Editorial ESP. Dist: Santillana USA Publishing Co., Inc.
Osburn, Mary Rose. I Know Colors. 2016. (What I Know Ser.). 00024p. (J). pap. 8.15 *(978-1-4824-5445-1(9))* Stevens, Gareth Publishing LLLP.
Pacovská, Kveta. The Sun Is Yellow. 2012. (ENG., Illus.). 32p. (J). 24.95 *(978-1-84976-064-5(0))* Tate Publishing, Ltd. GBR. Dist: Abrams, Inc.
Page, Liza & Innovative Kids Staff. Colors - E-Z Page Turners. Larrañaga, Ana Martín, illus. 2008. (ENG.). 12p. (J). (gr. -1 — 1). bds. 5.99 *(978-1-58476-655-1(7))* Innovative Kids.
Pallotta, Jerry. Butterfly Colors & Counting. Bersani, Shennen, illus. 2013. (ENG.). 10p. (J). (— 1). bds. 5.95 *(978-1-57091-899-5(6))* Charlesbridge Publishing, Inc.
Pantone. Pantone: Color Cards: 18 Oversized Flash Cards. Gibbs, Andrew, illus. 2013. (Pantone Ser.). (ENG.). 19p. (J). (gr. -1 — 1). 15.95 *(978-1-4197-0626-4(8)*, Abrams Appleseed) Abrams, Inc.
—Pantone: Color Puzzles: 6 Color-Matching Puzzles. Carpenter, Tad, illus. 2013. (Pantone Ser.). (ENG.). 12p. (J). (gr. -1-k). 16.95 *(978-1-4197-0939-5(9)*, Abrams Appleseed) Abrams, Inc.
Pantone, Inc Staff, contrib. by. Pantone - Box of Colour: 6 Mini Board Books!, 6 vols. 2012. (ENG., Illus.). 60p. (J). (gr. -1 — 1). 12.95 *(978-1-4197-0515-1(6))* Abrams, Inc.
Parker, Andy. Mekanimals: Clockwork Safari, Spanish-Language Edition. 2005. (Mekanimals Ser.). (SPA., Illus.). 8p. (J). bds. *(978-970-718-322-3(5)*, Silver Dolphin en Español) Advanced Marketing, S. de R. L. de C. V.
—Mekanimals: Robotic Reef, Spanish-Language Edition. 2005. (Mekanimals Ser.). (SPA., Illus.). 8p. (J). bds. *(978-970-718-321-6(7)*, Silver Dolphin en Español) Advanced Marketing, S. de R. L. de C. V.
Parker, Ant, illus. Amazing Machines First Concepts: Colors. 2015. (ENG.). 12p. (J). (gr. -1-1). bds. 5.99 *(978-0-7534-7233-0(3)*, 9780753472330, Kingfisher) Roaring Brook Pr.
Payne, Yadira V. !Viva los Colores! Payne, Yadira V., ed. 2004. (MUL., Illus.). (J). pap. 12.50 *(978-0-9747350-0-9(0))* Payne, Yadira V. Publishing.
Penton Overseas, Inc. Staff. Colors, Shapes & Sizes. abr. ed. 2003. (J). (gr. -1-3). 12.99 incl. audio, cd-rom *(978-1-894677-24-0(2))* Kidzup Productions.
Peros, Tracey E. Colors Make the World a Brighter Place. 2011. 28p. pap. 12.99 *(978-1-4634-1461-0(7))* AuthorHouse.
Phaidon Editors & Matisse, Henri. Blue & Other Colors. 2016. (ENG., Illus.). 30p. (gr. -1 — 1). bds. 9.95 *(978-0-7148-7142-4(7))* Phaidon Pr., Inc.
Phidal Publishing Staff, ed. Colors. (Turn & Learn Ser.). 12p. (J). *(978-2-7643-0077-0(8))* Phidal Publishing, Inc./Editions Phidal, Inc.
Phillips, A. Color My Soul. 2009. 50p. pap. 15.99 *(978-1-4415-5830-5(6))* Xlibris Corp.
Phillips, Dee. Colors. 2009. (Christmas Lift the Flap Ser.). (ENG.). 10p. (J). (gr. -1-k). bds. 5.95 *(978-1-84696-966-9(2)*, TickTock Books) Octopus Publishing Group GBR. Dist: Independent Pubs. Group.
—First Addition. 2009. (Christmas Lift the Flap Ser.). (ENG.). 10p. (J). (gr. -1-k). bds. 5.95 *(978-1-84696-967-6(0)*, TickTock Books) Octopus Publishing Group GBR. Dist: Independent Pubs. Group.
—First Words. 2009. (Christmas Lift the Flap Ser.). (ENG.). 10p. (J). (gr. -1-k). bds. 5.95 *(978-1-84696-968-3(9)*, TickTock Books) Octopus Publishing Group GBR. Dist: Independent Pubs. Group.
—Numbers. 2009. (Christmas Lift the Flap Ser.). (ENG.). 10p. (J). (gr. -1-k). bds. 5.95 *(978-1-84696-969-0(7)*, TickTock Books) Octopus Publishing Group GBR. Dist: Independent Pubs. Group.
Picou, Lin. Pink Toys, Yes or No. 2015. (ENG.). 24p. (gr. k-3). 28.50 *(978-1-63430-346-0(6))* Rourke Educational Media.
Picthall, Chez, creator. Flip Flap Colours: A Turn-the-Flap Book! 2014. (ENG., Illus.). 36p. pap. 10.00 *(978-1-906572-79-2(8))* Award Pubns. Ltd. GBR. Dist: Parkwest Pubns., Inc.
Pimot, Dr Karen Hutchins & Pimot, Karen Hutchins. The Colors of Myself. Klanot, Sameon Clay, illus. 2010. 20p. pap. 12.95 *(978-1-936051-96-0(6))* Peppertree Pr., The.
Poitier, Anton, illus. Colors: Match the Words & Colors. 2014. (Twisters Ser.). (ENG.). 10p. (J). (gr. -1 — 1). bds. 7.99 *(978-0-7641-6687-7(5))* Barron's Educational Series, Inc.
Polinsky, Paige V. Super Simple Experiments with Light & Color: Fun & Innovative Science Projects. 2016. (ENG., Illus.). 32p. (J). *(978-1-68078-171-7(5))* ABDO Publishing Co.
Powell, Debbie. Make It Grow. 2016. (ENG., Illus.). 16p. (J). (gr. -1-2). 14.99 *(978-1-84780-789-2(5)*, Frances Lincoln Children's Bks.) Quarto Publishing Group UK GBR. Dist: Hachette Bk. Group.
Powell, Jennifer. The Colors of Mackinac Island. Powell, Jennifer, photos by. 2015. (ENG., Illus.). 30p. (J). (gr. 1-2). 10.95 *(978-1-933272-49-8(X))* Thunder Bay Pr.
Priddy Books Staff. First Concepts: Colors. 2003. (Illus.). bds. 8.95 *(978-0-312-49233-5(2)*, Priddy Bks.) St. Martin's Pr.
Priddy Books Staff & Priddy, Roger. Colors. rev. ed. 2004. (Bright Baby Ser.). (ENG., Illus.). 26p. (J). (gr. -1 — 1). bds. 4.99 *(978-0-312-49247-2(2)*, 9780312492472, Priddy Bks.) St. Martin's Pr.
Priddy, Roger. Baby's First Colors. 2016. (Baby's First Ser.). (ENG., Illus.). 8p. (J). bds. 7.99 *(978-0-312-51949-0(4)*, 9780312519490, Priddy Bks.) St. Martin's Pr.
—Big Board Books Colors, ABC, Numbers. 2008. (First 100 Ser.). (ENG.). 14p. (J). (gr. -1 — 1). bds. 8.95 *(978-0-312-50219-5(2)*, 9780312502195, Priddy Bks.) St. Martin's Pr.
—Busy Babies Colors. 2010. 8p. (J). bds. 4.99 *(978-0-312-50853-1(0)*, Priddy Bks.) St. Martin's Pr.
—Colores. 2005. (Happy Baby Ser.).Tr. of Colors. (SPA & ENG., Illus.). 28p. (J). (gr. -1 — 1). bds. 5.95 *(978-0-312-49234-2(0)*, 9780312492342, Priddy Bks.) St. Martin's Pr.
—Colors. (Little Friends Ser.). (ENG.). (J). 2016. 12p. bds. 14.99 *(978-0-312-52005-2(0)*, 9780312520052) 2015. (Illus.). 14p. (gr. -1 — 1). bds. 9.99 *(978-0-312-51793-9(9)*, 9780312517939) 2013. (Illus.). 10p. (gr. -1 — 1). bds. 7.99 *(978-0-312-51606-2(1)*, 9780312516062) 2013. (Illus.). 10p. (gr. -1 — 1). bds. 4.99 *(978-0-312-51514-0(6)*, 9780312515140) 2008. 14p. (gr. -1 — 1). bds. 4.95 *(978-0-312-50425-0(X)*, 9780312504250) St. Martin's Pr. (Priddy Bks.).
—Colors/Colores. 2007. (Bright Baby Ser.). (ENG & SPA., Illus.). 12p. (J). (gr. -1 — 1). bds. 4.95 *(978-0-312-50297-3(4)*, 9780312502973, Priddy Bks.) St. Martin's Pr.
—Counting Colors. 2007. (ENG., Illus.). 20p. (J). (gr. -1-1). 8.95 *(978-0-312-50137-2(4)*, 9780312501372, Priddy Bks.) St. Martin's Pr.
—Hello Baby, Set. 2013. (Hello Baby Ser.). (ENG.). (J). (gr. -1 — 1). 19.99 *(978-0-312-51641-3(X)*, 9780312516413, Priddy Bks.) St. Martin's Pr.
—Kitty's Color Activity Book. Crimi-Trent, Ellen, illus. 2014. (Schoolies Ser.). (ENG.). 76p. (J). (gr. -1-1). pap. 6.99 *(978-0-312-51675-8(4)*, 9780312516758, Priddy Bks.) St. Martin's Pr.
—Let's Say Our Colors. 2009. (Simple First Words Ser.). (ENG.). 12p. (J). (gr. -1 — 1). bds. 14.95 *(978-0-312-50643-8(0)*, 9780312506438, Priddy Bks.) St. Martin's Pr.
—Little Alphaprints: Colors. 2015. (Alphaprints Ser.). (ENG., Illus.). 10p. (J). (gr. -1 — 1). bds. 5.99 *(978-0-312-51829-5(3)*, 9780312518295, Priddy Bks.) St. Martin's Pr.
—Numbers Colors Shapes. 2011. (First 100 Ser.). (ENG., Illus.). 26p. (J). (gr. -1 — 1). bds. 5.99 *(978-0-312-51081-7(0)*, 9780312510817, Priddy Bks.) St. Martin's Pr.
—Picture Fit Board Books: a Traffic Jam of Trucks: A Colors Book. 2017. (Picture Fit Ser.). (ENG., Illus.). 14p. (J). bds. 8.99 *(978-0-312-52160-8(X)*, 9780312521608, Priddy Bks.) St. Martin's Pr.
—Picture Fit Board Books: a Traffic Jam of Trucks (Large) A Colors Book. 2017. (Picture Fit Ser.). (ENG., Illus.). 14p. (J). bds. 12.99 *(978-0-312-52172-1(3)*, 9780312521721, Priddy Bks.) St. Martin's Pr.
—Play & Learn: Colors. 2014. (Play & Learn Ser.). (ENG.). 10p. (J). (gr. -1-k). bds. 12.99 *(978-0-312-51751-9(3)*, 9780312517519, Priddy Bks.) St. Martin's Pr.
—Pull the Tab: Colors. 2016. (Pull the Tab Ser.). (ENG.). 10p. (J). bds. 8.99 *(978-0-312-52069-4(7)*, 9780312520694, Priddy Bks.) St. Martin's Pr.
—Sneak-a-Peek Colors. 2015. (Sneak-A-Peek Ser.). (ENG., Illus.). 12p. (J). (gr. -1 — 1). bds. 7.99 *(978-0-312-51799-1(8)*, 9780312517991, Priddy Bks.) St. Martin's Pr.
—Sticker Early Learning: Colors. 2016. (ENG., Illus.). 24p. (J). pap. 4.99 *(978-0-312-52016-8(6)*, 9780312520168, Priddy Bks.) St. Martin's Pr.
Pristash, Nicole. Blue. 2010. (My Colorful World Ser.). (ENG., Illus.). 16p. (J). bds. 11.95 *(978-1-4358-9314-6(X)*, 1307085, PowerKids Pr.) Rosen Publishing Group, Inc., The.
—Green. 2010. (My Colorful World Ser.). (ENG., Illus.). 16p. (J). bds. 11.95 *(978-1-4358-9317-7(4)*, 1307086, PowerKids Pr.) Rosen Publishing Group, Inc., The.
—Orange. 2010. (My Colorful World Ser.). (ENG., Illus.). 16p. (J). bds. 11.95 *(978-1-4358-9316-0(6)*, 1307087, PowerKids Pr.) Rosen Publishing Group, Inc., The.
—Purple. 2010. (My Colorful World Ser.). (ENG., Illus.). 16p. (J). bds. 11.95 *(978-1-4358-9318-4(2)*, PowerKids Pr.) Rosen Publishing Group, Inc., The.
—Red. 2010. (My Colorful World Ser.). (ENG., Illus.). 16p. (J). bds. 11.95 *(978-1-4358-9313-9(1)*, 1307089, PowerKids Pr.) Rosen Publishing Group, Inc., The.
—Yellow. 2010. (My Colorful World Ser.). (ENG., Illus.). 16p. (J). bds. 11.95 *(978-1-4358-9315-3(8)*, 1307090, PowerKids Pr.) Rosen Publishing Group, Inc., The.
Professor Q's Chinese-English Language Books: Yán Sè - Colors. 2006. (J). *(978-0-9743359-5-7(9))* Murdock Publishing Co.
Prosper, Tanzia. He Chose a Coat for Me! 2011. 44p. 17.95 *(978-1-4497-1316-4(5)*, WestBow Pr.) Author Solutions, Inc.
Publications International Ltd. Staff, ed. Fun to Color. 2010. 96p. (J). 5.98 *(978-1-60553-645-3(8))* Phoenix International Publications, Inc.
Ranchetti, Sebastiano. Animals in Color (Animales en Color) 2008. (Learn with Animals;Aprende con los animales Ser.). (SPA & ENG.). 24p. (gr. -1-2). pap. 8.15 *(978-0-8368-9042-6(6)*, Weekly Reader Leveled Readers) Stevens, Gareth Publishing LLLP.
—Animals in Color/Animales en Color. 2008. (Learn with Animals/Aprende con los Animales Ser.). (SPA & ENG., Illus.). 24p. (gr. -1-2). lib. bdg. 22.00 *(978-0-8368-9037-2(X)*, Weekly Reader Leveled Readers) Stevens, Gareth Publishing LLLP.
Ranchetti, Sebastiano & Nations, Susan. Animals in Color. 2008. (Learn with Animals Ser.). 24p. (gr. -1-2). pap. 8.15 *(978-0-8368-8826-3(X))*; lib. bdg. 22.00 *(978-0-8368-8821-8(9))* Stevens, Gareth Publishing LLLP. (Weekly Reader Leveled Readers).
Random House. Team Colors (Paw Patrol) Random House, illus. 2015. (Board Book Ser.). (ENG., Illus.). 24p. (J). (— 1). bds. 6.99 *(978-0-553-49771-7(5)*, Random Hse. Bks. for Young Readers) Random Hse. Children's Bks.
Random House Staff. Colors Everywhere! (Bubble Guppies) Random House Staff, illus. 2013. (Board Book Ser.). (ENG., Illus.). 24p. (J). (-k). bds. 4.99 *(978-0-449-81782-7(2)*, Random Hse. Bks. for Young Readers) Random Hse. Children's Bks.
Ranson, Erin. Magnetic Color Safari. Parry, Jo, illus. 2007. 10p. (J). (gr. -1 — 3). *(978-1-84666-361-1(X)*, Tide Mill Pr.) Top That! Publishing PLC.
Rao, Lisa. I Love to Color. Yoe! Studio Staff, illus. 2009. (Yo Gabba Gabba! Ser.). (ENG.). 32p. (J). (gr. -1-1). 3.99 *(978-1-4169-6871-9(7)*, Simon Scribbles) Simon Scribbles.
Raven, Paul. A Story of Colours. 2011. 20p. pap. *(978-1-4269-7220-1(2))* Trafford Publishing (UK) Ltd.
Raz, Rachel. The Colors of Israel. Raz, Rachel, photos by. 2015. (ENG., Illus.). 24p. (J). (gr. -1-2). 7.99 *(978-1-4677-5540-5(0))*; lib. bdg. 17.99 *(978-1-4677-5539-9(7))* Lerner Publishing Group. (Kar-Ben Publishing).
Rea, Thelma. I Wonder Why the Sky Is Blue. 2009. (Reading Room Collection 2 Ser.). 24p. (gr. 3-4). 42.50 *(978-1-60851-973-6(2)*, PowerKids Pr.) Rosen Publishing Group, Inc., The.
Reader's Digest Editors & Zobel-Nolan, Allia. See the Sea! A Book about Colors. Terry, Michael, illus. 2004. (Googly Eyes Ser.). (ENG.). 10p. (J). (-1). bds. 7.99 *(978-0-7944-0291-4(7)*, Reader's Digest Children's Bks.) Studio Fun International.
Reasoner, Charles. Colors in the Garden. Pitt, Sarah, illus. 2009. (3D Board Bks.). 12p. (J). (gr. -1-k). bds. 9.99 *(978-1-934650-40-0(4))* Just For Kids Pr., LLC.
Rebman, Nick. Who Is Wearing Blue? A Book about Colors. 2016. (Concept Fun Ser.). (ENG.). 16p. (J). (gr. -1-2). 25.64 *(978-1-5038-0770-9(3)*, 210618) Child's World, Inc., The.
Reich, Kass. This Little Hamster, 1 vol. 2013. (ENG., Illus.). 24p. (J). (gr. -1-k). bds. 9.95 *(978-1-4598-0410-4(4))* Orca Bk. Pubs. USA.
Reinke, Beth Bence. Why Do Leaves Change Color? 2016. (Everyday Earth Science Ser.). (ENG.). 24p. (J). (gr. k-3). 27.07 *(978-1-5038-0797-6(5)*, 210633) Child's World, Inc., The.
Ren&apos, et al. Investigating Why Leaves Change Their Color. 2009. (Science Detectives Ser.). (Illus.). 24p. (J). (gr. 2-5). lib. bdg. 22.60 *(978-1-4042-4485-6(9))* Rosen Publishing Group, Inc., The.
Repchuk, Caroline. Fairy Colors. O'Neill, Rachael, illus. 2007. (ENG.). 5p. (J). (gr. k — 1). bds. 5.99 *(978-0-439-88704-5(6)*, Cartwheel Bks.) Scholastic, Inc.
Rice, Dona Herweck. Colores, 1 vol. 2nd rev. ed. 2011. (Nonfiction Readers Ser.). (SPA.). 12p. (J). (gr. 1-1). pap. 4.99 *(978-1-4333-4405-3(X))* Teacher Created Materials, Inc.
—Colors, 1 vol. 2nd rev. ed. 2014. (TIME for KIDS(r) Nonfiction Readers Ser.). (ENG., Illus.). 12p. (J). (gr. 1-1). pap. 15.96 *(978-1-4807-1005-4(9))* Shell Educational Publishing.
—Colors, 1 vol. 2nd rev. ed. 2011. (Nonfiction Readers Ser.). (ENG.). 12p. (J). (gr. 1-1). pap. 4.99 *(978-1-4333-3566-2(2))* Teacher Created Materials, Inc.
Rigol, Francesc, illus. Dan & Din Learn Colors. 2009. (Learning with Dan & Din Ser.). 12p. (J). (gr. -1-k). bds. 11.40 *(978-1-60754-401-2(6))* Windmill Bks.
Riley, Peter. Light & Seeing. 2007. (Essential Science/Watts Ser.). (Illus.). 32p. (J). (gr. 4-7). lib. bdg. 28.50 *(978-1-59920-028-6(7))* Black Rabbit Bks.
Rinaldo, Luana, illus. Matching Puzzle Cards - Colors. 2012. (ENG.). 36p. (J). (gr. k-12). 9.99 *(978-1-60905-220-1(X))* Blue Apple Bks.
Rissman, Rebecca. Blue, 1 vol. 2012. (Colors All Around Us Ser.). (ENG.). 24p. (gr. -1-k). lib. bdg. 25.99 *(978-1-4329-5745-2(7))* Heinemann-Raintree.
—Orange, 1 vol. 2012. (Colors All Around Us Ser.). (ENG., Illus.). 24p. (gr. -1-k). lib. bdg. 25.99 *(978-1-4329-5749-0(X))* Heinemann-Raintree.
Rivera, Sheila. What Color Is It? 2005. (First Step Nonfiction - Properties of Matter Ser.). (ENG.). 8p. (gr. -1-1). pap. 4.95 *(978-0-8225-5409-7(7)*, Lerner Pubns.) Lerner Publishing Group.
Roeder, Annette. Leonardo Da Vinci: Coloring Book. 2011. (ENG.). 32p. (J). (gr. 1-4). pap. 8.95 *(978-3-7913-7065-1(0))* Prestel Verlag GmbH & Co KG. DEU. Dist: Penguin Random Hse. LLC.
—Vincent Van Gogh. Prestel, ed. 2009. (ENG.). 32p. (J). (gr. 1-4). pap. 8.95 *(978-3-7913-4331-0(9))* Prestel Verlag GmbH & Co KG. DEU. Dist: Penguin Random Hse. LLC.
Romaine, Claire. Matemáticas con Mascotas / Math with Pets. de la Vega, Eida, tr. 2016. (¡Matemáticas en Todas Partes! / Math Is Everywhere! Ser.). (ENG & SPA.). 24p. (gr. k-k). lib. bdg. 22.60 *(978-1-4824-5216-7(2))* Stevens, Gareth Publishing LLLP.
Ronay, Laura. Kids Like Me... Learn Colors. Kishimoto, Jon Wayne, illus. 2008. (ENG.). 16p. (J). (gr. -1-1). 11.95 *(978-1-60613-001-8(3))* Woodbine Hse.
Rosa-Mendoza, Gladys. Colors & Shapes. Cifuentes, Carolina, ed. Noiset, Michele, illus. 2004. (English-Spanish Foundations Ser.).Tr. of Los Colores y las Figuras. (ENG & SPA.). 20p. (J). bds. 6.95 *(978-0-9679748-3-5(6))* Me+Mi Publishing.
Ross, Kathy. Kathy Ross Crafts Colors. Barger, Jan, illus. 2003. (Crafts from Kathy Ross Ser.). 48p. (J). lib. bdg. 23.93 *(978-0-7613-2651-9(0)*, Millbrook Pr.) Lerner Publishing Group.
Rossetti, Christina. What Is Pink? Carr, Holly, illus. 2003. 24p. pap. *(978-1-894915-13-7(5))* Rubicon Publishing, Inc.
Ruble, Eugene. Learning the Basics of Color. Ruble, Eugene, illus. 2010. (Illus.). 16p. pap. 9.95 *(978-1-61633-063-7(5))* Guardian Angel Publishing, Inc.
Rupp, Kristina. Colors in the Jungle. 2016. (1-3Y Ecosystems Ser.). (ENG., Illus.). 16p. (J). pap. 5.99 *(978-1-63437-463-7(0))* American Reading Co.
Rustad, Martha E. H. Green Foods. 2016. (Colorful Foods Ser.). (ENG.). 24p. (gr. k-1). lib. bdg. 21.99 *(978-1-5157-2372-1(0)*, Pebble Bks.) Capstone Press of Coughlan Cos.
—Orange Foods. 2016. (Colorful Foods Ser.). (ENG.). 24p. (gr. k-1). lib. bdg. 21.99 *(978-1-5157-2370-7(4)*, Pebble Bks.) Capstone Press of Coughlan Cos.
—Red Foods. 2016. (Colorful Foods Ser.). (ENG.). 24p. (gr. k-1). lib. bdg. 21.99 *(978-1-5157-2373-8(9)*, Pebble Bks.) Capstone Press of Coughlan Cos.
—Yellow Foods. 2016. (Colorful Foods Ser.). (ENG.). 24p. (gr. k-1). lib. bdg. 21.99 *(978-1-5157-2371-4(2)*, Pebble Bks.) Capstone Press of Coughlan Cos.
Salas, Laura Purdie. Colors of Fall. (Colors All Around Ser.). (ENG.). 32p. (gr. 1-2). 2011. pap. 47.70 *(978-1-4296-6152-2(6))* 2010. lib. bdg. 27.32 *(978-1-4296-5256-8(X))* Capstone Press of Coughlan Cos. (Aplus Bks.).
—Colors of Insects. 2011. (Colors All Around Ser.). (ENG.). 32p. (gr. 1-2). pap. 47.70 *(978-1-4296-6154-6(2)*, Aplus Bks.) Capstone Press of Coughlan Cos.
—Colors of Sports, 1 vol. 2011. (Colors All Around Ser.). (ENG.). 32p. (gr. 1-2). pap. 8.10 *(978-1-4296-6149-2(6))*; pap. 47.70 *(978-1-4296-6150-8(X))* Capstone Press of Coughlan Cos. (Aplus Bks.).
—Colors of the Ocean. 2011. (Colors All Around Ser.). (ENG.). 32p. (gr. 1-2). pap. 47.70 *(978-1-4296-6156-0(9)*, Aplus Bks.) Capstone Press of Coughlan Cos.
—Colors of Weather. (Colors All Around Ser.). (ENG.). 32p. (gr. 1-2). 2011. pap. 47.70 *(978-1-4296-6158-4(5))* 2010. lib. bdg. 27.32 *(978-1-4296-5258-2(6))* Capstone Press of Coughlan Cos. (Aplus Bks.).
SAMi. Let's Learn Colors & Shapes. 2012. (Illus.). (J). *(978-1-60905-243-0(9))* Handprint Bks.
Samuel, Y. D. Learning with Strawberry & Friends: C o l o u r S. 2009. (Illus.). 16p. pap. 8.49 *(978-1-4389-3538-6(2))* AuthorHouse.
San Antonio Museum of Art Staff & Budnick, Madeleine. Colores Everywhere! Colors in English & Spanish. 2013. (ArteKids Ser.). (ENG & SPA., Illus.). 16p. (J). (gr. k-k). bds. 7.95 *(978-1-59534-139-6(0))* Trinity Univ. Pr.
Sanchez, Richard. Colores (Colors) (SPA.). (J). 4.95 *(978-84-243-2191-8(X))* Publicaciones Fher, S.A. ESP. Dist: AIMS International Bks., Inc.
Sanderson, Geoff. What Color Is It? 2009. (Real Life Readers Ser.). 8p. (gr. k-1). pap. 5.15 *(978-1-4042-7971-1(7)*, Rosen Classroom) Rosen Publishing Group, Inc., The.
Sandviks HOP, Inc. Staff, contrib. by. My Colors Wipe-off Board Book with DVD. DVD 10.99 *(978-1-60143-896-6(6))* HOP, LLC.
Santillana & Dorling Kindersley Publishing Staff. Colores. (Ensename Ser.). (SPA., Illus.). 16p. (J). (gr. -1-k). bds. 6.95 *(978-1-58986-325-5(9))* Santillana USA Publishing Co., Inc.
Sarfatti, Esther. Colors: Blue. 2007. (Concepts (Discovery Library) Ser.). (Illus.). 24p. (J). (gr. -1-k). lib. bdg. *(978-1-60044-517-0(9))* Rourke Educational Media.
—Colors: Green. 2007. (Concepts (Discovery Library) Ser.). (Illus.). 24p. (J). (gr. -1-k). lib. bdg. *(978-1-60044-518-7(7))* Rourke Educational Media.
Sargent, Daina. Colors & the Number 1, 11 vols. Lenoir, Jane, illus. (Learn to Read Ser.: 11). 24p. (J). 2005. pap. 10.95 *(978-1-59381-031-3(8))* 2004. lib. bdg. 20.95 *(978-1-59381-030-6(X))* Ozark Publishing.
—Colors & the Number 10, 11 vols. Lenoir, Jane, illus. l.t. ed. 2004. (Learn to Read Ser.). 24p. (J). lib. bdg. 20.95 *(978-1-59381-048-1(2))* Ozark Publishing.
—Colors & the Number 10/Los Colores y el Número 10, 11 vols. Lenoir, Jane, illus. 2005. (Learn to Read Ser.: 11). (ENG & SPA.). 24p. (J). pap. 10.95 *(978-1-59381-147-1(0))*; lib. bdg. 20.95 *(978-1-59381-146-4(2))* Ozark Publishing.
—Colors & the Number 2, 11 vols. Lenoir, Jane, illus. 2004. (Learn to Read Ser.: 11). 24p. (J). pap. 10.95 *(978-1-59381-033-7(4))*; lib. bdg. 20.95 *(978-1-59381-032-0(6))* Ozark Publishing.
—Colors & the Number 4, 11 vols. Lenoir, Jane, illus. 2005. (Learn to Read Ser.). 24p. (J). pap. 10.95 *(978-1-59381-037-5(7))* Ozark Publishing.
—Colors & the Number 6, 11 vols. Lenoir, Jane, illus. l.t. ed. 2004. (Learn to Read Ser.). 24p. (J). lib. bdg. 20.95 *(978-1-59381-040-5(7))* Ozark Publishing.
—Colors & the Number 7, 11 vols. Lenoir, Jane, illus. l.t. ed. 2004. (Learn to Read Ser.). 24p. (J). lib. bdg. 20.95 *(978-1-59381-042-9(3))* Ozark Publishing.
—Colors & the Number 8, 11 vols. Lenoir, Jane, illus. l.t. ed. 2004. (Learn to Read Ser.). 24p. (J). lib. bdg. 20.95 *(978-1-59381-044-3(X))* Ozark Publishing.
—Colors & the Number 9, 11 vols. Lenoir, Jane, illus. l.t. ed. 2004. (Learn to Read Ser.). 24p. (J). lib. bdg. 20.95 *(978-1-59381-046-7(6))* Ozark Publishing.
—Introduction to Colors & Numbers, 11 vols. Lenoir, Jane, illus. l.t. ed. 2004. (Learn to Read Ser.: 11). 24p. (J). lib. bdg. 20.95 *(978-1-59381-050-4(4))* Ozark Publishing.
—Introduction to Colors & Numbers/Introduccion a los Colores Numeros, 11 vols. Lenoir, Jane, illus. l.t. ed. 2005. (Learn to Read Ser.: 11). (SPA & ENG.). 24p. (J). pap. 10.95 *(978-1-59381-149-5(7))* Ozark Publishing.
Saunders, Helen B., creator. Sweet Faces Coloring Book. 2004. (J). 5.95 *(978-0-9763143-1-8(2))* Happy Heart Kids Publishing.
Saviola, Ava. Dinosaur Colors. 2012. (Dinosaur School Ser.). (Illus.). 24p. (J). (gr. -1-1). pap. 8.15 *(978-1-4339-7140-2(2))*; lib. bdg. 22.60 *(978-1-4339-7139-6(9))* Stevens, Gareth Publishing LLLP.
Sawalski, Katreena. Let's Paint Our Cars. 2017. (Wonderful World of Colors Ser.). 24p. (gr. 4-6). pap. 8.25 **(978-1-5383-2098-3(3)**, PowerKids Pr.) Rosen Publishing Group, Inc., The.
Scarry, Richard. My School Backpack: With 4 Books! 2012. (Illus.). (J). *(978-1-4380-8502-9(8))* Barron's Educational Series, Inc.
Scholastic, Inc. Staff. Carry & Learn Colors. Ward, Sarah G., illus. 2015. (ENG.). 10p. (J). (gr. -1 — 1). bds. 7.99 *(978-0-545-78385-9(2)*, Cartwheel Bks.) Scholastic, Inc.
Scholastic, Inc. Staff, contrib. by. Color with Clifford the Big Red Dog. 2015. (With Clifford the Big Red Dog Ser.). (ENG.). 48p. (gr. -1-1). pap. 4.99 *(978-0-545-81960-2(1)*, Teaching Resources) Scholastic, Inc.
—My Favorite Color Is... 2016. (Rookie Toddlers Ser.). (ENG., Illus.). 12p. (J). bds. 6.95 *(978-0-531-22456-4(2)*, Children's Pr.) Scholastic Library Publishing.
—Red Apple, Green Pear: A Book of Colors. 2013. (ENG.). 12p. (J). bds. 6.95 *(978-0-531-27258-9(3))* Scholastic Library Publishing.
—Red Truck, Yellow Bus: A Book of Colors. 2012. (Rookie Toddler Ser.). (ENG., Illus.). 12p. (J). bds. 6.95 *(978-0-531-20852-6(4)*, Children's Pr.) Scholastic Library Publishing.
—What Is Blue? 2015. (Rookie Toddler(tm) Ser.). (ENG., Illus.). 12p. (J). bds. 6.95 *(978-0-531-21267-7(X)*, Children's Pr.) Scholastic Library Publishing.
—What Is Pink? 2015. (Rookie Toddler(tm) Ser.). (ENG., Illus.). 12p. (J). bds. 6.95 *(978-0-531-21266-0(1)*, Children's Pr.) Scholastic Library Publishing.

C
D

—What Is Red? 2016. (Rookie Toddler(tm) Ser.). (ENG., Illus.). 12p. (J). bds. 6.95 (978-0-531-22622-3(0), Children's Pr.) Scholastic Library Publishing.

—What Is Yellow? 2016. (Rookie Toddler(tm) Ser.). (ENG.). 12p. (J). bds. 6.95 (978-0-531-22623-0(9), Children's Pr.) Scholastic Library Publishing.

Scholastic, Inc. Staff, ed. Close-Up Colors. (Changing Picture Bks.). (Illus.). (J). pap. 9.99 (978-0-590-24642-2(9)) Scholastic, Inc.

Scholastic Teaching Resources Staff. Preschool Basic Skills: Colors, Shapes & More. 2012. (Preschool Basic Skills Ser.). (ENG.). 48p. pap. 6.99 (978-0-545-42969-6(2)) Teacher's Friend Pubns., Inc.

School Zone Publishing Company Staff. Colors & Shapes. 2005. (ENG.). 64p. (J). (gr. -1-k). pap., wbk. ed. 3.99 (978-1-58947-357-7(4)) School Zone Publishing Co.

School Zone Staff. Bilingual Colors, Shapes & More. 2004. (ENG.). (J). 2.99 (978-1-58947-988-3(2)) School Zone Publishing Co.

Schuette, Sarah L. Colors & Patterns! A Spot-It, Learn-It Challenge, 1 vol. 2014. (Spot It, Learn It! Ser.). (ENG.). 32p. (gr. 1-2). lib. bdg. 27.32 (978-1-4765-4011-5(X), Aplus Bks.) Capstone Press of Coughlan Cos.

—Morado: Mira el Morado Que Te Rodea. 2007. (Colores/Colors Ser.).Tr. of Purple - Seeing Purple All Around Us. (MUL & SPA., Illus.). 32p. (gr. 1-2). 27.32 (978-1-4296-0009-5(8), A+ Bilingue/Bilingual) Capstone Press of Coughlan Cos.

Schuh, Mari C. Crayola Summer Colors. 2017. (Crayola (r) Seasons Ser.). (ENG.). 24p. (J). (gr. -1-3). 26.65 **(978-1-5124-3290-9(3))** Lerner Publishing Group.

Schumacher, Bev. What Color Is It? 2004. (ENG., Illus.). 20p. (J). lib. bdg. 9.95 (978-0-9741549-7-8(0)) Learning Props.

—What Color Is It? / de Que Color Es? 2004. (SPA & CHI., Illus.). 20p. (J). lib. bdg. 9.95 (978-0-9741549-0-9(3)) Learning Props.

—What Color Is It? (Chinese/English) 2012. 20p. (J). pap. 8.95 (978-1-935292-50-0(1)) Learning Props.

Schwartz, Betty Ann. What Makes a Rainbow? Turner, Dona, illus. 2006. (Magic Ribbon Books). (ENG.). 14p. (J). 4.95 (978-1-58117-220-1(6), Intervisual/Piggy Toes) Bendon, Inc.

Scott, Colin. Speedy Kids Coloring Book. 2013. (ENG.). 50p. 12.55 (978-1-63022-416-5(2), Speedy Kids (Children's Fiction)) Speedy Publishing LLC.

Scott, MaryJo. Corduroy's Colors. McCue, Lisa, illus. 2016. (Corduroy Ser.). (ENG.). 14p. (J). (— 1). bds. 5.99 (978-0-451-47247-2(0), Viking Books for Young Readers) Penguin Young Readers Group.

Script, Roseanne D'Erasmo. I AM a Rainbow. 2011. 24p. pap. 12.99 (978-1-4567-4358-1(9)) AuthorHouse.

Seeger, Laura Vaccaro. Lemons Are Not Red. Seeger, Laura Vaccaro, illus. 2006. (ENG., Illus.). 32p. (J). (gr. -1-k). pap. 8.99 (978-1-59643-195-9(4), 9781596431959) Square Fish.

Shapes anc colors shaped layer Book. 2006. (J). bds. 4.99 (978-1-934004-08-1(1)) Byeway Bks.

Shulman, Mark. There's No Blue on a Bagel. Miline, Bill, photos by. 2006. (Illus.). 12p. (J). (gr. k-4). reprint ed. 6.00 (978-1-4223-5711-8(2)) DIANE Publishing Co.

Silver Dolphin en Español Editors. Disney Tesoro de libros de Calcomanias: Disney Sticker Book Treasury, Spanish-Language Edition. 2007. (Illus.). 48p. (J). (978-970-718-447-3(7), Silver Dolphin en Español) Advanced Marketing, S. de R. L. de C. V.

Simon, Seymour. Seymour Simon's Silly Riddles & Jokes Coloring Book. Kendrick, D., illus. 2013. (Dover Coloring Bks.). (ENG.). 48p. (J). (gr. 2-5). pap. 4.99 (978-0-486-48045-9(3)) Dover Pubns., Inc.

Simson, Dana. Colors. 2003. (Dana Simson Chunky Books Ser.). 10p. (J). bds. 2.95 (978-1-74047-261-6(6)) Book Co. Publishing Pty, Ltd., The AUS. Dist: Penton Overseas, Inc.

Slaughter, Tom. One, Two, Three. 2003. (ENG., Illus.). 24p. (J). (gr. k-k). 12.95 (978-0-88776-664-0(1), Tundra Bks.) Tundra Bks. CAN. Dist: Penguin Random Hse. LLC.

Sper, Emily. Follow the Yarn: A Book of Colors. Sper, Emily, illus. 2016. (ENG., Illus.). 24p. (J). (gr. -1 — 1). bds. 7.99 (978-0-9754902-8-0(1), 9780975490280) Jump Pr.

Spurr, Elizabeth. The Farm Life. Björkman, Steve, illus. 2005. (ENG.). 32p. (J). (gr. k-3). tchr. ed. 16.95 (978-0-8234-1777-3(8)) Holiday Hse., Inc.

Star Bright Books, creator. Eating the Rainbow (Vietnamese/English), 1 vol. 2010. (Sach Ve Thuc Pham Day Mau Sac/Eating the Rainbow Ser.). (VIE & ENG., Illus.). 20p. (J). 6.95 (978-1-59572-219-5(X)) Star Bright Bks., Inc.

Steck-Vaughn Staff. Head for Home: Colors & Shapes. 2004. (Illus.). pap. (978-0-7398-8554-3(5)) Steck-Vaughn.

Stella, Heather. Get Ready for Pre-K: Numbers, Shapes & Colors - 249 Fun Exercises for Mastering Basic Skills. 2013. (Get Ready for School Ser.). (ENG.). 128p. (J). (gr. -1-17). pap. 7.95 (978-1-57912-936-1(6), 81936, Black Dog & Leventhal Pubs. Inc.) Hachette Bks.

Sterling Children's, Sterling. Web Colors. 2016. (Code Babies Ser.). (ENG., Illus.). 12p. (J). (gr. -1). bds. 9.95 (978-1-4549-2158-5(7)) Sterling Publishing Co., Inc.

Sterling, Kristin. Black Everywhere. 2010. (Lightning Bolt Books — Colors Everywhere Ser.). (ENG., Illus.). 32p. (gr. k-2). pap. 7.95 (978-0-7613-5660-8(6)); lib. bdg. 26.60 (978-0-7613-4591-6(4), Lerner Pubns.) Lerner Publishing Group.

—Blue Everywhere. 2010. (Lightning Bolt Books — Colors Everywhere Ser.). (ENG., Illus.). 32p. (gr. k-2). pap. 7.95 (978-0-7613-5657-8(6)); lib. bdg. 26.60 (978-0-7613-4588-6(4), Lerner Pubns.) Lerner Publishing Group.

—Brown Everywhere. 2010. pap. 45.32 (978-0-7613-6987-5(2)); (ENG., Illus.). 32p. pap. 7.95 (978-0-7613-6046-9(8)); (ENG., Illus.). 32p. lib. bdg. 26.60 (978-0-7613-5438-3(7), Lerner Pubns.) Lerner Publishing Group.

—Gray Everywhere. 2010. pap. 45.32 (978-0-7613-6988-2(0)); (ENG., Illus.). 32p. pap. 7.95 (978-0-7613-6047-6(6)); (ENG., Illus.). 32p. lib. bdg. 26.60 (978-0-7613-5439-0(5), Lerner Pubns.) Lerner Publishing Group.

—Green Everywhere. 2010. pap. 45.32 (978-0-7613-6985-1(6)); (ENG., Illus.). 32p. pap. 7.95 (978-0-7613-6044-5(1)); (ENG., Illus.). 32p. lib. bdg. 26.60 (978-0-7613-5436-9(0), Lerner Pubns.) Lerner Publishing Group.

—Lightning Bolt Books: Colors Everywhere, 12 vols., Set. Incl. Black Everywhere. lib. bdg. 26.60 (978-0-7613-4591-6(4)); Blue Everywhere. lib. bdg. 26.60 (978-0-7613-4588-6(4)); Brown Everywhere. lib. bdg. 26.60 (978-0-7613-5438-3(7)); Gray Everywhere. lib. bdg. 26.60 (978-0-7613-5439-0(5)); Green Everywhere. lib. bdg. 26.60 (978-0-7613-5436-9(0)); Orange Everywhere. lib. bdg. 26.60 (978-0-7613-5435-2(2)); Pink Everywhere. lib. bdg. 26.60 (978-0-7613-5440-6(9)); Purple Everywhere. lib. bdg. 26.60 (978-0-7613-5437-6(9)); Red Everywhere. lib. bdg. 26.60 (978-0-7613-4590-9(6)); Silver & Gold Everywhere. lib. bdg. 26.60 (978-0-7613-4593-0(0)); White Everywhere. lib. bdg. 26.60 (978-0-7613-4592-3(2)); Yellow Everywhere. lib. bdg. 26.60 (978-0-7613-4589-3(2)); (Illus.). 32p. (gr. k-2). 2010. 2009. Set lib. bdg. 303.12 (978-0-7613-4587-9(6), Lerner Pubns.) Lerner Publishing Group.

—Orange Everywhere. 2010. pap. 45.32 (978-0-7613-6984-4(8)); (ENG., Illus.). 32p. pap. 7.95 (978-0-7613-6043-8(3)); (ENG., Illus.). 32p. lib. bdg. 26.60 (978-0-7613-5435-2(2), Lerner Pubns.) Lerner Publishing Group.

—Pink Everywhere. 2010. pap. 45.32 (978-0-7613-6989-9(9)); (ENG., Illus.). 32p. pap. 7.95 (978-0-7613-6048-3(4)); (ENG., Illus.). 32p. lib. bdg. 26.60 (978-0-7613-5440-6(9), Lerner Pubns.) Lerner Publishing Group.

—Purple Everywhere. 2010. pap. 45.32 (978-0-7613-6986-8(4)); (ENG., Illus.). 32p. pap. 7.95 (978-0-7613-6045-2(X)); (ENG., Illus.). 32p. lib. bdg. 26.60 (978-0-7613-5437-6(9), Lerner Pubns.) Lerner Publishing Group.

—Red Everywhere. 2010. (Lightning Bolt Books — Colors Everywhere Ser.). (ENG., Illus.). 32p. (gr. k-2). pap. 7.95 (978-0-7613-5659-2(2)); lib. bdg. 26.60 (978-0-7613-4590-9(6), Lerner Pubns.) Lerner Publishing Group.

—Silver & Gold Everywhere. 2010. (Lightning Bolt Books — Colors Everywhere Ser.). (ENG., Illus.). 32p. (gr. k-2). pap. 7.95 (978-0-7613-5662-2(2)); lib. bdg. 26.60 (978-0-7613-4593-0(0), Lerner Pubns.) Lerner Publishing Group.

—White Everywhere. 2010. (Lightning Bolt Books — Colors Everywhere Ser.). (ENG., Illus.). 32p. (gr. k-2). pap. 7.95 (978-0-7613-5661-5(4)); lib. bdg. 26.60 (978-0-7613-4592-3(2), Lerner Pubns.) Lerner Publishing Group.

—Yellow Everywhere. 2010. (Lightning Bolt Books — Colors Everywhere Ser.). (ENG., Illus.). 32p. (gr. k-2). pap. 7.95 (978-0-7613-5658-5(4)); lib. bdg. 26.60 (978-0-7613-4589-3(2), Lerner Pubns.) Lerner Publishing Group.

Sterling Publishing Co., Inc. Colors. 2012. (Say & Play Ser.). (ENG., Illus.). 28p. (J). (gr. k — 1). bds. 4.95 (978-1-4027-9892-4(X)) Sterling Publishing Co., Inc.

—Colors/Colores. 2013. (Say & Play Ser.). (ENG & SPA., Illus.). 28p. (J). (— 1). bds. 4.95 (978-1-4549-1038-1(0)) Sterling Publishing Co., Inc.

Stevens, Madeline. Orange Around Me. 2015. (Color in My World Ser.). (ENG., Illus.). 24p. (J). (gr. 3-3). pap. 8.22 (978-1-5026-0069-1(2)) Cavendish Square Publishing.

—Red Around Me. 2015. (J). lib. bdg. (978-1-62713-348-7(8)) Cavendish Square Publishing.

Stewart, Melissa. Why Are Animals Blue? 2009. (Rainbow of Animals Ser.). (Illus.). 32p. (J). (gr. k-3). lib. bdg. 23.94 (978-0-7660-3251-4(5)) Enslow Pubs., Inc.

—Why Are Animals Green? 2009. (Rainbow of Animals Ser.). (Illus.). 32p. (J). (gr. k-3). lib. bdg. 23.94 (978-0-7660-3252-1(3)) Enslow Pubs., Inc.

—Why Are Animals Orange? 2009. (Rainbow of Animals Ser.). (Illus.). 32p. (J). (gr. k-3). lib. bdg. 23.94 (978-0-7660-3250-7(7)) Enslow Pubs., Inc.

—Why Are Animals Purple? 2009. (Rainbow of Animals Ser.). (Illus.). 32p. (J). (gr. k-3). lib. bdg. 23.94 (978-0-7660-3254-5(X)) Enslow Pubs., Inc.

—Why Are Animals Red? 2009. (Rainbow of Animals Ser.). (Illus.). 32p. (J). (gr. k-3). lib. bdg. 23.94 (978-0-7660-3249-1(3)) Enslow Pubs., Inc.

—Why Are Animals Yellow? 2009. (Rainbow of Animals Ser.). (Illus.). 32p. (J). (gr. k-3). lib. bdg. 23.94 (978-0-7660-3253-8(1)) Enslow Pubs., Inc.

—Why Do We See Rainbows? 2008. (Tell Me Why, Tell Me How Ser.). (Illus.). 32p. (gr. 3-18). lib. bdg. 29.93 (978-0-7614-2919-7(0), Benchmark Bks.) Marshall Cavendish Corp.

Stockland, Patricia M. Black, 1 vol. Woolf, Julia, illus. 2008. (Colors Ser.). (ENG.). 24p. (gr. -1-2). 27.07 (978-1-60270-255-4(1), 1285037, Looking Glass Library-Nonfiction) Magic Wagon.

—Blue, 1 vol. Woolf, Julia, illus. 2008. (Colors Ser.). (ENG.). 24p. (gr. -1-2). 27.07 (978-1-60270-256-1(X), 1285038, Looking Glass Library- Nonfiction) Magic Wagon.

—Brown, 1 vol. Woolf, Julia, illus. 2011. (Colors Set 2 Ser.). (ENG.). 24p. (gr. -1-2). 27.07 (978-1-61641-135-0(X), Looking Glass Library- Nonfiction) Magic Wagon.

—Colors, 6 vols., Set 2. Woolf, Julia, illus. Incl. Brown. 27.07 (978-1-61641-135-0(X)); Gray. 27.07 (978-1-61641-136-7(8)); Orange. 27.07 (978-1-61641-137-4(6)); Pink. 27.07 (978-1-61641-138-1(4)); Purple. 27.07 (978-1-61641-139-8(2)); Tan. 27.07 (978-1-61641-140-4(6)); (gr. -1-2). (Colors Set 2 Ser.). (Illus.). 24p. 2011. 162.42 (978-1-61641-134-3(1), Looking Glass Library- Nonfiction) Magic Wagon.

—Gray, 1 vol. Woolf, Julia, illus. 2011. (Colors Set 2 Ser.). (ENG.). 24p. (gr. -1-2). 27.07 (978-1-61641-136-7(8), Looking Glass Library- Nonfiction) Magic Wagon.

—Green, 1 vol. Woolf, Julia, illus. 2008. (Colors Ser.). (ENG.). 24p. (gr. -1-2). 27.07 (978-1-60270-257-8(8), 1285039, Looking Glass Library- Nonfiction) Magic Wagon.

—Orange, 1 vol. Woolf, Julia, illus. 2011. (Colors Set 2 Ser.). (ENG.). 24p. (gr. -1-2). 27.07 (978-1-61641-137-4(6), Looking Glass Library- Nonfiction) Magic Wagon.

—Pink, 1 vol. Woolf, Julia, illus. 2011. (Colors Set 2 Ser.). (ENG.). 24p. (gr. -1-2). 27.07 (978-1-61641-138-1(4), Looking Glass Library- Nonfiction) Magic Wagon.

—Purple, 1 vol. Woolf, Julia, illus. 2011. (Colors Set 2 Ser.). (ENG.). 24p. (gr. -1-2). 27.07 (978-1-61641-139-8(2), Looking Glass Library- Nonfiction) Magic Wagon.

—Red, 1 vol. Woolf, Julia, illus. 2008. (Colors Ser.). (ENG.). 24p. (gr. -1-2). 27.07 (978-1-60270-258-5(6), 1285040, Looking Glass Library- Nonfiction) Magic Wagon.

—Tan, 1 vol. Woolf, Julia, illus. 2011. (Colors Set 2 Ser.). (ENG.). 24p. (gr. -1-2). 27.07 (978-1-61641-140-4(6), Looking Glass Library- Nonfiction) Magic Wagon.

—White, 1 vol. Woolf, Julia, illus. 2008. (Colors Ser.). (ENG.). 24p. (gr. -1-2). 27.07 (978-1-60270-259-2(4), 1285041, Looking Glass Library- Nonfiction) Magic Wagon.

—Yellow, 1 vol. Woolf, Julia, illus. 2008. (Colors Ser.). (ENG.). 24p. (gr. -1-2). 27.07 (978-1-60270-260-8(8), 1285042, Looking Glass Library- Nonfiction) Magic Wagon.

Strelitski, Mies & de Hartog, Arnold. Woobie Paints: A Discovery of Color. 2005. (ENG., Illus.). 32p. (J). (gr. -1-3). 16.95 (978-1-59249-472-9(2), 1F001) Soundprints.

Studio Mouse. Princess Colors & Shapes Pack. 2003. (ENG., Illus.). 36p. (J). (gr. -1-3). 12.99 (978-1-59069-366-7(3), 1A501) Studio Mouse LLC.

Suttle, Darlene. On that Mountain So Hilly! 2011. 28p. (gr. -1). pap. 16.95 (978-1-4497-1529-8(X), WestBow Pr.) Author Solutions, Inc.

Tauber, Sabine. Hieronymus Bosch: Coloring Book. 2014. (ENG., Illus.). 32p. (J). (gr. 1-4). pap. 8.95 (978-3-7913-7176-4(2)) Prestel Verlag GmbH & Co KG. DEU. Dist: Penguin Random Hse. LLC.

Teacher's Friend Publications Staff, creator. Color & Shape Puzzles. 2006. (Scholastic Hands-on Learning Ser.). (ENG., Illus.). 12.99 (978-0-439-82388-3(9), Teaching Resources) Scholastic, Inc.

Thornborough, Kathy. Colors & Shapes. Petelinsek, Kathleen, illus. 2014. (Talking Hands Ser.). (ENG.). 24p. (J). (gr. k-3). 25.64 (978-1-62687-315-5(1), 207155) Child's World, Inc., The.

Thurmond, Cindy. What If There Were No Colors? 2004. (Illus.). 44p. (J). 16.95 (978-0-9760685-0-1(8)) Overview Publishing.

Ticktock Media, Ltd. Staff. Favorite Foods: Colors & Shapes. 2008. (Tab Bks.). (ENG.). 10p. (J). (gr. -1-k). bds. 4.95 (978-1-84696-821-1(6), TickTock Books) Octopus Publishing Group GBR. Dist: Independent Pubs. Group.

Tiger Tales Staff, creator. First Colors. 2013. (My First Lift & Learn Ser.). (ENG., Illus.). 10p. (gr. -1). bds. 7.99 (978-1-58925-633-0(6)) Tiger Tales.

Tildes, Phyllis Limbacher. Baby's First Book of Birds & Colors. Tildes, Phyllis Limbacher, illus. 2017. (ENG., Illus.). 18p. (J). (— 1). bds. 7.99 (978-1-58089-742-6(8)) Charlesbridge Publishing, Inc.

Timmy Turtle Learns Colors. (Board Bks.). (Illus.). 6p. (J). (gr. -1-k). 4.99 (978-0-7847-1120-0(8), 03528, Bean Sprouts) Standard Publishing.

Tocci, Salvatore. Experiments with Colors. 2003. (True Bks.). (ENG., Illus.). 48p. (J). 25.00 (978-0-516-22785-6(8), Children's Pr.) Scholastic Library Publishing.

Top That Publishing Staff, ed. Colors. 2004. (Magnetic Play & Learn Ser.). (Illus.). 12p. (J). (978-1-84510-047-6(6)) Top That! Publishing PLC.

Trace & Color (Pre-K) 2003. (J). (978-1-58232-043-4(8)) ECS Learning Systems, Inc.

Trapp, Kyrima. Que? Como? Por Que?: Los Colores. 2007. (Illus.). 16p. (J). (gr. -1). (978-970-718-491-6(4), Silver Dolphin en Español) Advanced Marketing, S. de R. L. de C. V.

Trazos, Ritmo Y Color: Francisco Icaza. 2005. (Coleccion Los Grandes Para Los Mas Pequenos Ser.). (SPA.). (J). pap. 8.95 (978-968-7381-50-3(7)) Tecolote, Ediciones, S.A. de C.V. MEX. Dist: Iaconi, Maruccia Bk. Imports.

Tullet, Hervé. The Game of Red, Yellow & Blue. 2012. (Tullet Game Ser.). (ENG., Illus.). 14p. (gr. -1-1). 9.95 (978-0-7148-6481-5(1)) Phaidon Pr., Inc.

Tuxworth, Nicola. Colors. 2005. (Learn-A-Word Picture Bks.). (ENG., Illus.). 12p. (J). (gr. -1-k). bds. 6.99 (978-0-7548-1418-4(1)) Anness Publishing GBR. Dist: National Bk. Network.

—Colours. 2014. (ENG., Illus.). 20p. (J). (gr. -1-12). bds. 6.99 (978-1-84322-749-6(5), Armadillo) Anness Publishing GBR. Dist: National Bk. Network.

Twine, Alice. My Favorite Book of Colors. 2008. (Board Bks.). (Illus.). 14p. (J). (gr. -1-k). bds. 11.95 (978-1-4042-4254-8(6)) Rosen Publishing Group, Inc., The.

Upgrade kit dsm-3 Color&light. (J). 2004. (978-1-59242-527-3(5)) 2003. (978-1-59242-410-8(4)) Delta Education, LLC.

Urban, Chieu Anh. Hooray for Spring! Urban, Chieu Anh, illus. 2016. (Color Wonder Ser.). (ENG., Illus.). 14p. (J). (gr. -1 — 1). bds. 7.99 (978-1-4814-8720-7(5), Little Simon) Little Simon.

Usilton, Terry. Color Guard Competition. 2004. (Let's Go Team Ser.). (Illus.). 64p. (YA). (gr. 5-18). lib. bdg. 19.95 (978-1-59084-537-0(4)) Mason Crest.

Utarid, Anjana. Count Me In. 2008. 24p. pap. 12.95 (978-1-60264-281-2(8)) Virtualbookworm.com Publishing, Inc.

Valat, Pierre-Marie, et al. El Color. (SPA., Illus.). 40p. (J). (978-84-348-3471-2(5), CO9914) SM Ediciones.

Vance, Cynthia. Red, Yellow, Blue & You. Whitman, Candace, illus. 2008. (My First Colors Ser.). (ENG.). 30p. (J). (gr. -1 — 1). 8.95 (978-0-7892-0969-6(1)) Abbeville Pr., Inc.

Vendittelli, Marie. Colors. 2016. (Picture This Ser.). (ENG., Illus.). 32p. (J). (gr. -1-3). bds. 7.99 (978-0-544-51264-1(2), HMH Books For Young Readers) Houghton Mifflin Harcourt Publishing Co.

Votry, Kim & Waller, Curt. A Book of Colors. 2003. (Illus.). 16p. (J). pap. 7.95 (978-1-56368-147-9(1)) Gallaudet Univ. Pr.

Walden, Libby. Touch & Feel First Words. Galloway, Fhiona, illus. 2017. (My Little World Ser.). (ENG.). 10p. (J). (gr. -1-k). bds. 8.99 **(978-1-68010-521-6(3))** Tiger Tales.

Wallace, B. My Books of Colors Slipcase. 2007. (Illus.). 12p. (gr. -1-k). pap., per. (978-1-84610-561-6(7)) Make Believe Ideas.

Walter Foster Creative Team. Marvel's Avengers Colors: Learn Colors with Reusable Chalkboard Pages! 2017. (ENG., Illus.). 14p. (J). (gr. -1-1). bds. 12.95 **(978-1-63322-255-7(1)**, Walter Foster Jr) Quarto Publishing Group USA.

Walter Foster Creative Team Staff, et al. The Big Book of Color: An Adventurous Journey into the Magical & Marvelous World of Color! 2015. (Big Book Ser.). (ENG.). 128p. (J). (gr. k-3). pap. 14.95 (978-1-60058-435-0(7)) Quarto Publishing Group USA.

Walter, Nancy. Bumpsie's Colorful Garden. 2005. 8p. (J). bds. 5.99 (978-0-9770957-1-1(1)) Turtle Time Bks.

Washington, Joi. The Pink Book. 2011. (Color My World Ser.). 20p. pap. 39.62 (978-1-61541-447-5(9)) American Reading Co.

—The Pink Book. Washington, Joi, illus. 2010. (1-3Y Color My World Ser.). (ENG., Illus.). 20p. (J). (gr. k-2). pap. 5.99 (978-1-61541-161-0(5)) American Reading Co.

Watt, Mélanie. Colors. Watt, Mélanie, illus. 2005. (Learning with Animals Ser.). (ENG., Illus.). 24p. (J). (gr. -1 — 1). bds. 5.95 (978-1-55337-830-3(X)) Kids Can Pr., Ltd. CAN. Dist: Hachette Bk. Group.

—Leon the Chameleon. Watt, Mélanie, illus. 2003. (ENG., Illus.). 32p. (J). (gr. -1-k). pap. 7.95 (978-1-55337-527-2(0)) Kids Can Pr., Ltd. CAN. Dist: Hachette Bk. Group.

—Leon the Chameleon. 2003. (J). (gr. k-3). lib. bdg. 18.40 (978-0-613-62429-9(7), Turtleback) Turtleback Bks.

Way, Steve & Bailey, Gerry. Light & Color. 2008. (Simply Science Ser.). (Illus.). 32p. (YA). (gr. 3-6). lib. bdg. 26.00 (978-0-8368-9229-1(1)) Stevens, Gareth Publishing LLLP.

Weakland, Mark. Football Colors, 1 vol. 2013. (SI Kids Rookie Bks.). (ENG.). (gr. 1-2). 20p. bds. 7.95 (978-1-4296-9966-2(3)); 32p. lib. bdg. 27.32 (978-1-4296-9959-4(0)) Capstone Press of Coughlan Cos.

Weill, Cynthia & Cinco Puntos Press Staff. Colores de la Vida: Mexican Folk Art Colors in English & Spanish. 2011. (First Concepts in Mexican Folk Art Ser.). (SPA & ENG., Illus.). 32p. (J). (gr. -1-k). 14.95 (978-1-933693-82-8(7)) Cinco Puntos Pr.

What Color Am I? (Peek A Boo Pockets Ser.). (Illus.). 12p. (J). bds. (978-2-89393-975-9(9)) Phidal Publishing, Inc./Editions Phidal, Inc.

Wildsmith, Brian. Animal Colors, 1 vol. 2009. (BEN & ENG., Illus.). 16p. (J). bds. 4.99 (978-1-59572-135-8(5)) Star Bright Bks., Inc.

—Animal Colors, 1 vol. wintranslation.com, tr. 2009. (ARA & ENG., Illus.). 16p. (J). bds. 4.99 (978-1-59572-168-6(1)) Star Bright Bks., Inc.

—Brian Wildsmith's Animal Colors, 1 vol. 2007. (ENG., Illus.). 16p. (J). (gr. -1). bds. 4.99 (978-1-59572-118-1(5)) Star Bright Bks., Inc.

—Brian Wildsmith's Animal Colors, 1 vol. Wildsmith, Brian, illus. (Illus.). 16p. (J). 2004. (NAV.). 4.99 (978-1-932065-34-3(2), 718-784-9112) 2003. (TAG., 4.99 (978-1-932065-30-5(X), 1-718-784-9112) 2003. (KOR., 4.99 (978-1-932065-28-2(8), 1-718-784-9112) Star Bright Bks., Inc.

—Brian Wildsmith's Animal Colors (Simplified Mandarin) Wildsmith, Brian, illus. 2004. (CHI., Illus.). 16p. (J). bds. 4.95 (978-1-932065-52-7(0), 7187849112) Star Bright Bks., Inc.

—Brian Wildsmith's Animal Colors (Traditional Cantonese) Wildsmith, Brian, illus. 2004. (CHI., Illus.). 16p. (J). bds. 4.99 (978-1-932065-53-4(9)) Star Bright Bks., Inc.

Wildsmith, Brian, illus. Brian Wildsmith's Animal Colors. 16p. (J). 2004. (VIE.). bds. 4.95 (978-1-932065-51-0(2)) 2003. (POR.). bds. 4.95 (978-1-932065-27-5(X), 1-718-784-9112) Star Bright Bks., Inc.

William H. Sadlier Staff. Colors at the Zoo. 2005. (Emergent Library: Vol. 2). (gr. -1-1). 24.00 net. (978-0-8215-8939-7(3)) Sadlier, William H. Inc.

Wilson, Anne, illus. My First Box of Books: 1 2 3 Colours Animals, 3 vols. 2016. (ENG.). 72p. (J). (gr. -1-2). bds. 9.99 (978-1-86147-416-2(4), Armadillo) Anness Publishing GBR. Dist: National Bk. Network.

wintranslation.com, tr. Eating the Rainbow (French/English), 1 vol. 2010. (Livre D'Aliments Colores/Colorful Food Bks.). (ENG & FRE., Illus.). 20p. (J). 6.95 (978-1-59572-218-8(1)) Star Bright Bks., Inc.

Wonderful World of Colors. 2017. (Wonderful World of Colors Ser.). 24p. (gr. 4-6). 141.60 **(978-1-5081-6197-4(6))**; pap. 49.50 **(978-1-5081-6199-8(2))** Rosen Publishing Group, Inc., The. (PowerKids Pr.).

Wood, Jakki. Moo Moo, Brown Cow. 2004. (Illus.). (J). (gr. -1-18). spiral bd., bds. (978-0-616-14613-2(2)) Canadian National Institute for the Blind/Institut National Canadien pour les Aveugles.

Wyatt, Katherine. The Science of Light & Color. 2013. (Rosen Readers Ser.). (ENG.). 24p. (J). (gr. 3-4). pap. 8.25 (978-1-4777-2575-7(X)); pap. 49.50 (978-1-4777-2576-4(8)) Rosen Publishing Group, Inc., The. (Rosen Classroom).

Yates, Gene. The Chameleon Colors Book. 2004. (Illus.). (J). (978-1-58865-182-2(7)) Kidsbooks, LLC.

Yates, Irene. Colour. 2004. (Activities for 3-5 Year Olds Ser.). (Illus.). 32p. pap. 11.00 (978-1-897675-26-7(7)) Brilliant Pubns. GBR. Dist: Parkwest Pubns., Inc.

Yellow. 2004. (Illus.). 10p. (J). 3.99 (978-1-85997-884-9(3)) Byeway Bks.

Yoon, Salina, creator. Bug Buddies: A Sparkling Little Colors Book. 2005. (ENG., Illus.). 12p. (J). bds. 5.95 (978-1-58117-166-2(8), Intervisual/Piggy Toes) Bendon, Inc.

Yorke, Jane & Dorling Kindersley Publishing Staff. Colors & Shapes Touch & Feel Picture Cards. Thomson, Maria & Hester, Elizabeth, eds. 2005. (My 1st T&F Picture Cards Ser.). (ENG., Illus.). 16p. (J). (gr. -1 — 1). 9.99 (978-0-7566-1516-1(X), DK Children) Dorling Kindersley Publishing, Inc.

Your Baby Can Learn! Colors, Vol. 1. 2007. (J). 7.95 (978-1-931026-12-3(2)) Infant Learning Co., The.

Zemlicka, Shannon. Colors of China. Porter, Janice Lee, illus. 2005. (Colors of the World Ser.). 24p. (gr. 3-6). lib. bdg. 19.93 (978-1-57505-478-0(7)) Lerner Publishing Group.

—Colors of Russia. Reeves, Jeni, illus. (Colors of the World Ser.). 24p. (J). 2005. (gr. 3-6). lib. bdg. 19.93 (978-1-57505-513-8(9)) 2003. (gr. 1-4). pap. 5.95 (978-1-57505-564-0(3)) Lerner Publishing Group.

Zoller, Arthur David. Fish Colors. 2004. 14p. (J). (gr. -1-k). bds. 6.95 (978-0-88106-073-7(9)) Charlesbridge Publishing, Inc.

Zuckerman, Andrew, photos by. Creature Colors. 2014. (ENG., Illus.). 20p. (J). (gr. -1 — 1). bds. 7.99 (978-1-4521-1668-6(7)) Chronicle Bks. LLC.

Zuckerman, Rory. Colorful Sleepy Sheep. Roos, Maryn, illus. 2004. (J). bds. 12.95 *(978-0-9749305-1-0(2))* Castle Pacific Publishing.

—Colorful Sleepy Sheep. Roos, Maryn, illus. 2007. (Sleepy Sheep Ser.). (J). (gr. -1). bds. 7.95 incl. audio compact disk *(978-0-9796393-2-6(8))* Little Lion Pr.

COLOR—FICTION

Albee, Sarah. Kidoozle Kids & the Great Color Chase! 2004. (Illus.). 12p. bds. 9.95 *(978-1-932915-03-7(6))* Sandvik Publishing.

Allaway, Al. Laughing Flowers & Blooming Animals. 2009. 32p. pap. 17.95 *(978-0-557-04195-4(3))* Lulu Pr., Inc.

Anderson, Airlie. Cat's Colors. Anderson, Airlie, illus. 2016. (Child's Play Library). (ENG., Illus.). 32p. (J). (gr. k-2). *(978-1-84643-761-8(X))* Child's Play International Ltd.

—Cat's Colours. Anderson, Airlie, illus. 2016. (Child's Play Library). (ENG., Illus.). 32p. (J). pap. *(978-1-84643-760-1(1))* Child's Play International Ltd.

Andrew, Carol B. The Colorful Secret: An Interactive Book to Learn about Colors. 2005. (Illus.). (J). *(978-1-933577-01-2(0))* Learning Wood, LLC.

Andrews McMeel Publishing, LLC Staff. Colors. Stone, Kate, illus. 2015. (ENG.). 12p. (J). bds. 10.99 *(978-1-4494-5587-3(5))* Andrews McMeel Publishing.

Anholt, Laurence. Matisse: the King of Color. 2007. (Anholt's Artists Books for Children Ser.). (ENG., Illus.). 32p. (J). (gr. 1-3). 16.99 *(978-0-7641-6047-9(8))* Barron's Educational Series, Inc.

Arnold, Tedd. Vincent Paints His House. (ENG.). 32p. (J). (gr. -1-3). 2016. 6.99 *(978-0-8234-3686-6(1))* 2015. (Illus.). 16.95 *(978-0-8234-3210-3(6))* Holiday Hse., Inc.

Aryal, Aimee. Hello Big Red! Craig, Megan, illus. 2004. 24p. (J). 19.95 *(978-1-932888-24-9(1))* Mascot Bks., Inc.

Aspinall, Sarah. Penguins Love Colors. Aspinall, Sarah, illus. 2016. (ENG., Illus.). 40p. (J). (gr. -1-k). 17.99 *(978-0-545-87654-4(0),* Blue Sky Pr., The) Scholastic, Inc.

August, Rachel. Adventures of Libby Nickel: Why Are There Colors? 2011. 33p. (J). pap. 19.95 *(978-1-4327-7078-5(0))* Outskirts Pr., Inc.

Austin, Mike. Monsters Love Colors. Austin, Mike, illus. 2013. (ENG., Illus.). 40p. (J). (gr. -1-3). 15.99 *(978-0-06-212594-1(X))* HarperCollins Pubs.

Averous, Helene. Jaune. Dumont, Madeleine, illus. 2013. 38p. pap. *(978-981-07-5312-2(8))* MHC Asia Group.

—Rouge. Coevoet, Sylvie, illus. 2013. 38p. pap. *(978-967-10358-2-5(5))* MHC Asia Group.

—Yellow. Dumont, Madeleine, illus. 2013. 38p. pap. *(978-981-07-5311-5(X))* MHC Asia Group.

AZ Books, creator. What Color? 2012. (Smarty Ser.). (ENG., Illus.). 10p. (J). (gr. -1 — 1). 9.95 *(978-1-61889-249-2(5))* AZ Bks. LLC.

AZ Books Staff. Colores - Colorful Animals: Colorful Animals. Gorbachenok, Ekaterina, ed. 2012. (Spanish for Kids Ser.). (ENG & SPA.). 10p. (J). (gr. -1-k). bds. 11.95 *(978-1-61889-136-5(7))* AZ Bks. LLC.

Baby Bear Sees Blue. 2014. (Baby Bear Ser.). (ENG., Illus.). 42p. (J). (gr. -1 — 1). bds. 7.99 *(978-1-4814-1503-3(4),* Little Simon) Little Simon.

Badescu, Ramona. Pomelo Explores Color. Chaud, Benjamin, illus. 2012. (Pomelo the Garden Elephant Ser.). (ENG.). 120p. (J). (gr. -1). 15.95 *(978-1-59270-126-1(4))* Enchanted Lion Bks., LLC.

Baker, Alan. Brown Rabbit's Busy Day. 2017. (Little Rabbit Bks.). (ENG.). 24p. (J). 12.99 *(978-0-7534-7337-5(2),* 9780753473375, Kingfisher) Roaring Brook Pr.

Baker, Keith. Big Fat Hen Big Book. Baker, Keith, illus. 2010. (ENG., Illus.). 32p. (J). (gr. -1-3). 26.99 *(978-0-547-32859-1(1))* Houghton Mifflin Harcourt Publishing Co.

—Little Green Peas: A Big Book of Colors. Baker, Keith, illus. 2014. (Peas Ser.). (ENG., Illus.). 40p. (J). (gr. -1-3). 17.99 *(978-1-4424-7660-8(5),* Beach Lane Bks.) Beach Lane Bks.

Baker, Ryan. How I Would Paint the World? 2006. (ENG.). 48p. per. 15.95 *(978-1-59800-969-9(9))* Outskirts Pr., Inc.

Banner, Angela. Ant & Bee & the Rainbow. 2014. (Ant & Bee Ser.). (ENG., Illus.). 96p. (J). (gr. -1-k). 7.99 *(978-1-4052-6674-1(0))* Egmont Bks., Ltd. GBR. Dist: Independent Pubs. Group.

Bee, William. Stanley's Colors, 1 vol. Bee, William, illus. 2016. (Stanley Ser.). (ENG., Illus.). 20p. (J). (gr. -1-k). bds. 6.95 *(978-1-56145-948-3(8),* Freestone) Peachtree Pubs.

Beinstein, Phoebe. Dora Explora los Colores. Hall, Susan & Hall, Susan, illus. 2007. (Dora la Exploradora Ser.).Tr. of Dora Explores Colors. (SPA & ENG.). 14p. (J). (gr. -1). bds. 4.99 *(978-1-4169-4726-4(4),* Libros Para Ninos) Libros Para Ninos.

Berenstain, Jan & Berenstain, Mike. God Made the Colors, 1 vol. 2013. (I Can Read! / Berenstain Bears / Living Lights Ser.). (ENG.). 32p. (J). pap. 3.99 *(978-0-310-72507-7(0))* Zonderkidz.

Berkove, Lawrence I. How Butterflies Got Colored Wings. Barshishat, Malka Michaela, illus. 2017. (J). pap. ***(978-1-5011-4872-9(9))*** Meadowbrook Pr.

Berry, Ron. The Easter Bunny's Colorful Day! 2008. (Slide-N-Color Bks.). (Illus.). 10p. (J). (gr. -1). bds. 6.99 *(978-0-8249-6698-0(8),* Ideal Pubns.) Worthy Publishing.

Bird, Benjamin. Scooby-Doo's Color Mystery. 2015. (Scooby-Doo! Little Mysteries Ser.). (ENG., Illus.). 20p. (gr. -1 — 1). bds. 7.99 *(978-1-62370-176-5(7))* Capstone Press of Coughlan Cos.

—Superman Colors, 1 vol. Beavers, Ethen, illus. 2014. (DC Board Bks.). (ENG.). 20p. (gr. -1 — 1). bds. 5.99 *(978-1-4795-5890-2(7))* Picture Window Bks.

Birkett, Georgie. Red, Blue, Peekaboo! Birkett, Georgie, illus. 2015. (Felty Flaps Ser.). (ENG., Illus.). 10p. (J). (— 1). bds. 9.99 *(978-1-4472-6099-8(6))* Pan Macmillan GBR. Dist: Independent Pubs. Group.

Blackstone, Stella. Cleo's Color Book. Mockford, Caroline, illus. 2006. 0032p. (J). 15.99 *(978-1-905236-30-5(1))* Barefoot Bks., Inc.

Blackstone, Stella & Harter, Debbie. Can You See the Red Balloon? 2004. (Illus.). 32p. (J). pap. 6.99 *(978-1-84148-788-5(0))* Barefoot Bks., Inc.

Blevins, Wiley. Colors All Around. Kreloff, Elliott, illus. 2016. (Basic Concepts Ser.). (ENG.). 24p. (J). (gr. -1-1). lib. bdg. 14.99 *(978-1-63440-080-0(1))* Red Chair Pr.

Bolam, Emily, illus. Colors. 2009. 10p. (J). (gr. -1-k). 5.95 *(978-1-58925-845-7(2))* Tiger Tales.

Boldt, Mike. Colors Versus Shapes. Boldt, Mike, illus. 2014. (ENG., Illus.). 40p. (J). (gr. -1-3). 16.99 *(978-0-06-210303-1(2))* HarperCollins Pubs.

Bonilla, Rocio, illus. What Colour Is a Kiss? 2016. (ENG.). 32p. (J). (-k). lib. bdg. 16.95 *(978-1-58089-739-6(8))* Charlesbridge Publishing, Inc.

Bronn, Charles Heil. The Sun, the Moon, & the Gardener's Son. Kami, Y. Z., illus. 2006. 30p. (J). (gr. 4-12). reprint ed. 16.00 *(978-1-4223-5222-9(6))* DIANE Publishing Co.

Bryant, Megan E. Colorasaurus. Powell, Luciana Navarro, illus. 2012. (ENG.). 20p. (J). (gr. -1 — 1). bds. 9.99 *(978-1-4521-0814-8(5))* Chronicle Bks. LLC.

Buffomante, Maya. How Pandas Became Black & White. 2012. 24p. pap. *(978-1-4602-0613-3(4))* FriesenPress.

Burton, Lamonica. Good Mothers Come in All Colors. 2012. 20p. pap. 19.95 *(978-1-4772-2044-3(5))* AuthorHouse.

Bushman, Janet. A Shiny Red Apple. 2010. 16p. 8.95 *(978-1-4389-7861-1(8))* AuthorHouse.

Buxton, Jane. In My Garden. Teo, Ali, illus. 2010. (ENG.). 8p. (gr. k-1). pap. 7.95 *(978-1-61181-033-2(7),* Kaeden Bks.) Kaeden Corp.

Cabrera, Jane. Cat's Colors. 2015. 32p. pap. 8.00 *(978-1-61003-526-2(7))* Center for the Collaborative Classroom.

Caicco, Joseph. Adventures of the Rainbow Guardians: When the Color Came Down. 2013. 40p. pap. *(978-1-4602-1451-0(X))* FriesenPress.

Calder, C. J. Busy Truck, 1 vol. Rooney, Ronnie & Peterson, Shauna, illus. 2012. (Truck Buddies Ser.). (ENG.). 16p. (gr. -1-k). bds. 7.95 *(978-1-4342-4388-1(5))* Stone Arch Bks.

—Fast Truck. Rooney, Ronnie & Peterson, Shauna, illus. 2012. (Truck Buddies Ser.). (ENG.). 16p. (gr. -1-k). bds. 7.95 *(978-1-4342-4389-8(3))* Stone Arch Bks.

—Muddy Truck, 1 vol. Rooney, Ronnie & Peterson, Shauna, illus. 2012. (Truck Buddies Ser.). (ENG.). 16p. (gr. -1-k). bds. 7.95 *(978-1-4342-4390-4(7))* Stone Arch Bks.

Calvert, Ellen Hasenecz. Nine Goldfish in David's Pond. Fleming, Diana Trucks, illus. 2013. 36p. pap. 14.99 *(978-1-936745-18-0(6))* Nuevo Bks.

Campbell, Corbin. The Little Blue Man. 2011. 32p. pap. 13.99 *(978-1-257-37707-7(8))* Lulu Pr., Inc.

Campbell, Rod. Colour Bugs. 2003. (ENG., Illus.). 10p. (J). bds. 4.95 *(978-0-333-73338-7(X))* Macmillan Pubs., Ltd. GBR. Dist: Trafalgar Square Publishing.

Carle, Eric. The Artist Who Painted a Blue Horse. Carle, Eric, illus. (ENG., Illus.). (J). (gr. -1 — 1). 2013. 22p. bds. 7.99 *(978-0-399-16402-6(2))* 2011. 32p. 17.99 *(978-0-399-25713-1(6))* Penguin Young Readers Group. (Philomel Bks.).

—My First Busy Book. Carle, Eric, illus. 2015. (World of Eric Carle Ser.). (ENG., Illus.). 12p. (J). bds. 14.99 *(978-1-4814-5791-0(8),* Little Simon) Little Simon.

Carle, Eric & Chronicle Books Staff. Stage & Play: Brown Bear, Brown Bear, What Do You See? 2015. (ENG., Illus.). 8p. (J). (gr. -1-1). 16.99 *(978-1-4521-4320-0(X))* Chronicle Bks. LLC.

Carothers, Nina. Pink Ink's Purpose. Nilsen, Richard J., ed. Padovano, Chris, illus. 2013. 36p. pap. 12.97 *(978-1-937376-26-0(5))* All Star Pr.

—The Wonderful World of Color Olors. Nilsen, Richard J., ed. Padovano, Chris, illus. 2013. 36p. pap. 12.97 *(978-1-937376-28-4(1))* All Star Pr.

Carter, David A. Colors: A Bugs Pop-Up Concept Book. Carter, David A., illus. 2010. (David Carter's Bugs Ser.). (ENG., Illus.). 16p. (J). (gr. -1-1). 8.99 *(978-1-4424-0830-2(8),* Little Simon) Little Simon.

—Opposites: A Bugs Pop-Up Concept Book. Carter, David A., illus. 2010. (David Carter's Bugs Ser.). (ENG., Illus.). 16p. (J). (gr. -1-1). 7.99 *(978-1-4424-0829-6(4),* Little Simon) Little Simon.

Catalanotto, Peter. Kitten Red, Yellow, Blue. Catalanotto, Peter, illus. 2005. (ENG., Illus.). 32p. (J). (gr. -1-k). 18.99 *(978-0-689-86562-6(7),* Atheneum/Richard Jackson Bks.) Simon & Schuster Children's Publishing.

Chapman, Joan. The Lonely Crayon. 2006. (Neighborhood Readers Ser.). (ENG.). 16p. (gr. 1-3). pap. 6.50 *(978-1-4042-7212-5(7),* Rosen Classroom) Rosen Publishing Group, Inc., The.

Chen, Julia. On the Way Home. Stewart, Fion, illus. 2009. (J). *(978-0-7877550-6-5(5))* Heryin Publishing Corp.

Chernesky, Felicia Sanzari. Sugar White Snow & Evergreens: A Winter Wonderland of Color. Swan, Susan, illus. 2014. (ENG.). 32p. (J). (gr. -1-3). 16.99 *(978-0-8075-7234-4(9))* Whitman, Albert & Co.

Collier, Talina L. Jacob & the Orange. 2012. 20p. pap. 24.95 *(978-1-4626-8046-7(1))* America Star Bks.

—Jacob & the Turtle Race. 2012. 28p. pap. 24.95 *(978-1-4626-8045-0(3))* America Star Bks.

Color Board Books 800595, 4. 2005. (J). bds. *(978-1-59794-034-4(8))* Environments, Inc.

Coloring Fun: Coloring/Activity Book (English) 2006. (Illus.). (J). 2.99 *(978-1-933934-20-4(4))* Mighty Kids Media.

Coloring Fun: Coloring/Activity Book (Spanish) 2006. (Illus.). (J). 2.99 *(978-1-933934-21-1(2))* Mighty Kids Media.

Coloring Fun: English/Spanish. 2006. (Illus.). (J). 2.99 *(978-1-933934-24-2(7))* Mighty Kids Media.

Colors All Day. (J). 26.20 *(978-0-8136-8399-7(8));* (gr. -1-3). 59.50 *(978-0-8136-7918-1(4))* Modern Curriculum Pr.

Coulton, Mia. Danny Likes Red. Coulton, Mia, photos by. 2003. (ENG., Illus.). pap. 5.35 *(978-0-9720295-2-0(4))* Maryruth Bks., Inc.

Cousineau-Peiffer, Trisha. Have You Ever Heard of a Rainbow Farm. Everett-Hawkes, Bonnie, illus. 2006. 32p. (J). 12.95 *(978-0-9792084-1-6(6))* Dream Ridge Pr.

—Have You Ever Heard of a Rainbow Farm: The Missing Color Kittens. Everett-Hawkes, Bonnie, illus. 2007. 48p. (J). per. 15.95 *(978-0-9792084-2-3(4))* Dream Ridge Pr.

Cousins, Lucy. Maisy's First Colors: A Maisy Concept Book. Cousins, Lucy, illus. 2013. (Maisy Ser.). (ENG., Illus.). 14p. (J). (-k). bds. 6.99 *(978-0-7636-6804-4(4))* Candlewick Pr.

Cox, Katie, des. Little Hands Colors. 2009. (Little Hands (Make Believe Ideas) Ser.). (ENG., Illus.). 24p. (gr. -1-k). 6.99 *(978-1-84610-959-1(0))* Make Believe Ideas GBR. Dist: Nelson, Thomas Inc.

Crews, Donald. Ten Black Dots Board Book. Crews, Donald, illus. 2010. (ENG., Illus.). 32p. (J). (gr. -1-3). bds. 7.99 *(978-0-06-185779-9(3),* Greenwillow Bks.) HarperCollins Pubs.

Cronin, B. B. The Lost House. 2016. (ENG., Illus.). 40p. (J). (gr. -1-2). 18.99 *(978-1-101-99921-9(7),* Viking Books for Young Readers) Penguin Young Readers Group.

Cyr, Joe. Magical Trees & Crayons: Great Stories. 2006. (Illus.). pap. 9.95 *(978-0-9778525-6-7(3))* Peppertree Pr., The.

Dalmatian Press Staff. Maggie's Colorful Garden. 2008. (ENG.). 5p. bds. 4.95 *(978-1-58117-727-5(5),* Intervisual/Piggy Toes) Bendon, Inc.

Dargento, Beverly. Spot the Dot. 2008. 16p. pap. 9.49 *(978-1-4389-2287-4(6))* AuthorHouse.

Davis, Anne Shirley. No Red Suit for Santa? 2008. 16p. pap. 8.49 *(978-1-4389-2418-2(6))* AuthorHouse.

Davis, Jacky. Do You Like These Boots? Soman, David, illus. 2014. (Ladybug Girl Ser.). (ENG.). 32p. (J). (gr. k-1). pap. 3.99 *(978-0-448-46503-6(5),* Penguin Young Readers) Penguin Young Readers Group.

—Do You Like These Boots? 2014. (Penguin Young Readers Level 1 Ser.). lib. bdg. 13.55 *(978-0-606-34507-1(8),* Turtleback) Turtleback Bks.

Daywalt, Drew. The Day the Crayons Came Home. Jeffers, Oliver, illus. 2015. (ENG.). 48p. (J). (gr. k-3). 18.99 *(978-0-399-17275-5(0),* Philomel Bks.) Penguin Publishing Group.

—The Day the Crayons Quit. 2014. (CHI.). 32p. (J). *(978-7-5448-3406-3(9))* Jieli Publishing Hse.

—The Day the Crayons Quit, 2 vols. Jeffers, Oliver, illus. (ENG.). (J). (gr. -1-2). 2016. 88p. 40.00 *(978-0-399-54892-5(0))* 2013. 40p. 17.99 *(978-0-399-25537-3(0))* Penguin Young Readers Group. (Philomel Bks.).

de Brunhoff, Laurent. Babar's Book of Color. rev. ed. 2012. (ENG., Illus.). 40p. (J). (gr. k-2). 16.95 *(978-1-4197-0339-3(0),* Abrams Bks. for Young Readers) Abrams, Inc.

Deak, Gloria. The Kissing Skunks. Nathan, Cheryl, illus. 2006. 40p. (J). (gr. -1). 16.95 *(978-1-932065-46-6(6))* Star Bright Bks., Inc.

Dean, James, illus. I Love My White Shoes. 2010. (Pete the Cat Ser.). (J). lib. bdg. *(978-0-06-107623-7(6))* HarperCollins Pubs.

Denos, Julia. Swatch: the Girl Who Loved Color. Denos, Julia, illus. 2016. (Illus.). 40p. (J). (gr. -1-3). 17.99 *(978-0-06-236638-2(6))* HarperCollins Pubs.

Desmazieres, Sandra. Emma & Her Friends: A Book about Colors. 2006. (Picture Bks.). (Illus.). 28p. (gr. k-3). lib. bdg. 24.00 *(978-0-8368-6997-2(4),* Gareth Stevens Learning Library) Stevens, Gareth Publishing LLLP.

—Emma y Sus Amigos: Un Libro Sobre los Colores. 2006. (Picture Bks.). (SPA., Illus.). 28p. (gr. k-3). lib. bdg. 24.00 *(978-0-8368-6998-9(2),* Gareth Stevens Learning Library) Stevens, Gareth Publishing LLLP.

Desrochers, Diane O. The Little Tree That Would Be Great. Boucher, Julie, illus. 2009. 36p. pap. 14.95 *(978-0-9819727-7-0(2))* Fiction Publishing, Inc.

DeVogt, Rindia M. Tommy Hare & the Color Purple, 1 vol. Trogdon, Kathryn, illus. 2009. (ENG.). 22p. pap. 24.95 *(978-1-61582-827-2(3))* America Star Bks.

Dhar, Lisa Jane. Aisha Goes in Search of Colour. Zulkifi, Azhari, illus. 2009. (ENG.). 32p. (J). (gr. k-2). 6.95 *(978-0-86037-472-5(6))* Kube Publishing Ltd. GBR. Dist: Consortium Bk. Sales & Distribution.

Disney, Pixar Cars, ed. Red Light, Green Light: Action Opposites. 2009. (ENG.). 20p. 9.99 *(978-1-59069-780-1(4))* Studio Mouse LLC.

Dobbins, Jan. Driving My Tractor. Sim, David, illus. 2009. (ENG.). 32p. (J). (gr. -1-3). 16.99 incl. audio compact disk *(978-1-84686-356-5(9))* Barefoot Bks., Inc.

Doerrfeld, Cori. Penny Loves Pink. 2011. (ENG., Illus.). 40p. (J). (gr. -1-3). 15.99 *(978-0-316-05458-4(5))* Little, Brown Bks. for Young Readers.

Dompierre, Judith. Jennie's Search for Colors & Numbers. 2012. 38p. 29.95 *(978-1-4626-9277-4(X));* 40p. pap. 24.95 *(978-1-4626-6487-0(3))* America Star Bks.

Dompierre, Judith E. Jennie's Search for Colors & Numbers. 2012. 40p. pap. 24.95 *(978-1-4626-9331-3(8))* America Star Bks.

Donahue, Laurie. Mr. Blue a Job for You. Bryan, Hintz, illus. 2010. 32p. (J). 15.95 *(978-0-9799116-2-0(1))* LifeSong Pubs.

Dorling Kindersley Publishing Staff. Baby - Tractor! 2012. (ENG.). 16p. (J). (gr. -1 — 1). bds. 6.99 *(978-0-7566-8998-8(8),* DK Children) Dorling Kindersley Publishing, Inc.

—Colors & Shapes. 2009. (Baby Touch & Feel Ser.). (ENG.). 14p. (J). (gr. -1 — 1). bds. 5.99 *(978-0-7566-4300-3(7),* DK Children) Dorling Kindersley Publishing, Inc.

Dudar, Judy. I Spy a Bunny, 1 vol. Rudnicki, Richard, illus. 2009. (ENG.). 32p. (J). (gr. -1-2). 17.95 *(978-1-55109-700-8(1))* Nimbus Publishing, Ltd. CAN. Dist: Orca Bk. Pubs. USA.

Dude, Rosanna Eubank. Natalia's Favorite Color. Eubank, Patricia Reeder, illus. 2008. (ENG.). 32p. (J). (gr. -1-3). 12.99 *(978-0-8249-5523-6(4),* Ideal Pubns.) Worthy Publishing.

Duvoisin, Roger. The House of Four Seasons. 2017. (ENG., Illus.). 40p. (J). (gr. -1-1). 16.95 *(978-1-68137-098-9(0),* NYR Children's Collection) New York Review of Bks., Inc., The.

Ebia, Iris. Get up & Go! 2011. 32p. pap. 12.95 *(978-1-4634-4827-1(9))* AuthorHouse.

Edwards, Amelia. Carousel Colors, 1 vol. rev. ed. 2013. (Fiction Readers Ser.). (ENG., Illus.). 12p. (J). (gr. 1-1). pap. 4.99 *(978-1-4333-5447-2(0));* pap. 12.96 *(978-1-4807-1126-6(8))* Shell Educational Publishing.

Ehlert, Lois. Planting a Rainbow. Ehlert, Lois, illus. 2003. (ENG., Illus.). 32p. (J). (gr. k — 1). bds. 7.99 *(978-0-15-204633-0(X))* Houghton Mifflin Harcourt Publishing Co.

—Planting a Rainbow: Lap-Sized Board Book. 2008. (ENG., Illus.). 32p. (J). (gr. -1 — 1). bds. 11.99 *(978-0-15-206304-7(8))* Houghton Mifflin Harcourt Publishing Co.

Eliot, Hannah. If Everything Were Blue. Lalalimola, illus. 2015. (ENG.). 16p. (J). (gr. -1-k). bds. 8.99 *(978-1-4814-3539-0(6),* Little Simon) Little Simon.

Elzina, Philda. Purple Is the Magic Colour. 2008. 36p. pap. 12.95 *(978-1-4327-1805-3(3))* Outskirts Pr., Inc.

Emanuel, Effie Ann. Charles Chameleon. 2007. 32p. per. 24.95 *(978-1-4241-8621-1(8))* America Star Bks.

Emma Treehouse Ltd. My Toys. Davis, Caroline, illus. 2007. (Easy Flaps Ser.). 10p. (J). (gr. -1). bds. 6.95 *(978-1-58925-825-9(8))* Tiger Tales.

Esperanza, Charles George, illus. Red, Yellow, Blue, & a Dash of White, Too! 2015. (ENG.). 40p. (J). (gr. -1-k). 16.99 *(978-1-62914-624-9(2),* Sky Pony Pr.) Skyhorse Publishing Co., Inc.

Evans, Cordelia. Colors Are the Best! 2016. (Yo Gabba Gabba! Ser.). (ENG., Illus.). 24p. (J). (gr. -1-1). pap. 3.99 *(978-1-4814-5658-6(X),* Simon Spotlight) Simon Spotlight.

Fabbella, Teresa. Forever Friends. Giaquinta, Maria, illus. 2010. 26p. pap. 9.95 *(978-1-60911-366-7(7),* Eloquent Bks.) Strategic Book Publishing & Rights Agency (SBPRA).

Feiffer, Kate. Double Pink. Ingman, Bruce, illus. (ENG.). 32p. (J). (gr. -1-1). 2013. 7.99 *(978-1-4424-6033-1(4))* 2005. 17.99 *(978-0-689-87190-0(2))* Simon & Schuster/Paula Wiseman Bks. (Simon & Schuster/Paula Wiseman Bks.).

Félix, Lucie. Apples & Robins. 2016. (ENG., Illus.). 56p. (J). (gr. k-3). 16.99 *(978-1-4521-3264-8(X))* Chronicle Bks. LLC.

Felix, Monique. The Colors. Felix, Monique, illus. 2013. (ENG., Illus.). 32p. (J). (gr. -1-k). 12.99 *(978-1-56846-234-9(4),* Creative Editions) Creative Co., The.

Ficocelli, Elizabeth. Kid Tea, 0 vols. Dibley, Glin, illus. 2013. (ENG.). 36p. (J). (gr. -1-k). pap. 9.99 *(978-1-4778-4738-1(3),* 9781477847381, Amazon Children's Publishing) Amazon Publishing.

—Kid Tea. Dibley, Glin, illus. 2009. 32p. (J). (gr. -1). bds. 7.99 *(978-0-7614-5533-2(7))* Marshall Cavendish Corp.

Fischer, Kelly. The Most Beautiful Color of All. Duckworth, Michelle, illus. 2011. (ENG.). 36p. (J). 19.50 *(978-1-58385-281-1(6))* ktf-writers-studio.

Fishman, Linda Charles. The Little Girl Who Loves Colors: Book Four of Grandma's Girls. 2012. 24p. pap. 17.99 *(978-1-4772-9277-8(2))* AuthorHouse.

Fleming, Denise. Lunch. 2014. 32p. pap. 8.00 *(978-1-61003-225-4(X))* Center for the Collaborative Classroom.

—Maggie & Michael Get Dressed. Fleming, Denise, illus. 2016. (ENG., Illus.). 40p. (J). 17.99 *(978-0-8050-8794-9(X),* 9780805087949, Holt, Henry & Co. Bks. For Young Readers) Holt, Henry & Co.

Flying Frog Pub, creator. Color Fun with Elmo & Friends. 2011. (ENG., Illus.). 14p. (J). (gr. -1-k). bds. 3.99 *(978-1-60745-031-3(3))* Flying Frog Publishing.

Foley, Greg. Purple Little Bird. Foley, Greg, illus. 2011. (ENG., Illus.). 32p. (J). (gr. -1-2). 14.99 *(978-0-06-200828-2(5))* HarperCollins Pubs.

Fontes, Justine. Black Meets White. Waring, Geoff, illus. 2005. (ENG.). 24p. (J). (— 1). 12.99 *(978-0-7636-1933-6(7))* Candlewick Pr.

Furgang, Kathy. A Rainbow Party & una fiesta de Colores: 6 English, 6 Spanish Adaptations. 2011. (ENG & SPA.). (J). 75.00 net. *(978-1-4108-5645-6(3))* Benchmark Education Co.

Futterer, Kurt. Emile. Gray, Bronwen et al, trs. from GER. Futterer, Ralf, illus. 2004. (ENG.). 32p. (J). *(978-1-931561-95-2(8))* MacAdam/Cage Publishing, Inc.

Galvin, Laura. Pooh & Friends Colors & Shapes. 2008. (ENG.). 24p. (J). (gr. -1). 4.99 *(978-1-59069-736-8(7))* Studio Mouse LLC.

Galvin, Laura Gates. Musical Fun: Colors & Patterns. Williams, Tracee, ed. 2011. (Carry a Tune Ser.). (ENG., Illus.). 22p. (J). (gr. -1-1). pap. 4.99 incl. audio compact disk *(978-1-60727-305-9(5))* Studio Mouse LLC.

Garcia, Marc Khayam, illus. Color Me & My Pals: The Adventures of Billy Butterfly' Coloring Book. 2003. (J). 3.95 *(978-0-9747628-3-8(0))* BKB Group, Inc., The.

Gerstein, Mordicai. The Night World. 2015. (ENG., Illus.). 40p. (J). (gr. -1-3). 18.00 *(978-0-316-18822-7(0))* Little Brown & Co.

Gilbert, Frances. I Love Pink! Unten, Eren, illus. 2017. (Step into Reading Ser.). (ENG.). 32p. (J). (gr. -1-1). 3.99 *(978-1-101-93737-2(8),* Random Hse. Bks. for Young Readers) Random Hse. Children's Bks.

—I Love Pink. Unten, Eren, illus. 2017. (Step into Reading Ser.). (ENG.). 32p. (J). (gr. -1-1). lib. bdg. 12.99 *(978-1-101-93738-9(6),* Random Hse. Bks. for Young Readers) Random Hse. Children's Bks.

Gildea, Shir. Loving All the Colors. Gildea, Shir, illus. 2009. (Illus.). 24p. pap. 10.95 *(978-1-4269-0713-5(3))* Trafford Publishing.

Gomi, Taro. Hide & Seek. 2013. (ENG., Illus.). 22p. (J). (gr. -1 — 1). bds. 6.99 *(978-1-4521-0840-7(4))* Chronicle Bks. LLC.

Gonzalez, Maya Christina. My Colors, My World. Gonzalez, Maya Christina, illus. 2013.Tr. of Mis Colores, Mi Mundo. (ENG & SPA., Illus.). 32p. (J). pap. 9.95 *(978-0-89239-278-0(9),* Children's Book Press) Lee & Low Bks., Inc.

—My Colors, My World. 2007.Tr. of Mis Colores, Mi Mundo. (ENG & SPA., Illus.). 24p. (J). (gr. -1-3). 16.95 *(978-0-89239-221-6(5))* Lee & Low Bks., Inc.

Gottlieb, Suzanne. What Is Red? Bobri, Vladimir, illus. 2016. (ENG.). 24p. (J). 20.00 *(978-1-85124-458-4(1))* Bodleian Library GBR. Dist: Chicago Distribution Ctr.

Grandfeather Press. Roly Poly Napoleon Discovers Colors. 2011. (ENG., Illus.). 36p. (J). pap. 6.99 *(978-0-9832355-0-7(3))* Grandfeather Pr.

Gravett, Emily. Blue Chameleon. Gravett, Emily, illus. 2011. (ENG., Illus.). 32p. (J). (gr. -1-1). 16.99 *(978-1-4424-1958-2(X),* Simon & Schuster Bks. For Young Readers) Simon & Schuster Bks. For Young Readers.

Green, Judy. The Little Blue Octopus. 2009. 28p. pap. 21.99 *(978-1-4415-3393-7(1))* Xlibris Corp.

Gregory, Byron. Little Gray & the Wockelbog Woods. 2008. 32p. pap. 24.95 *(978-1-60610-835-2(2))* America Star Bks.

Grey, Chelsea Gillian. Princess Colors. 2004. (Early Learning Ser.). (Illus.). 36p. (J). (gr. -1-3). 12.99 incl. audio compact disk *(978-1-59069-370-4(1),* 1A102) Studio Mouse LLC.

Guettier, Nancy. Roy G. Biv Is Mad at Me Because I Love Pink! Vera, Andrew, illus. 2013. (ENG.). 36p. (gr. -1-2). pap. 9.95 *(978-1-61448-671-8(9),* 9781614486718) Morgan James Publishing.

—Roy G. Biv Is Mad at Me Because I Love Pink! 2013. (ENG., Illus.). 36p. (gr. -1-2). 19.95 (978-1-61448-642-8(5)) Morgan James Publishing.

Guy, Ginger Foglesong. Bravo! Moreno, Rene King, illus. 2010. (SPA & ENG.). 32p. (J). (gr. -1-k). 16.99 (978-0-06-173180-8(3), Greenwillow Bks.) HarperCollins Pubs.

Guy, Ginger Foglesong & Guy, Ginger F. Siesta. Moreno, Rene King, illus. 2005. (ENG & SPA.). 32p. (J). (gr. -1-k). 17.99 (978-0-06-056061-4(4), Greenwillow Bks.) HarperCollins Pubs.

Hall, Michael. It's an Orange Aardvark! Hall, Michael, illus. 2014. (ENG., Illus.). 40p. (J). (gr. -1-3). 17.99 (978-0-06-225206-7(2), Greenwillow Bks.) HarperCollins Pubs.

—Red: A Crayon's Story. Hall, Michael, illus. 2015. (ENG., Illus.). 40p. (J). (gr. -1-3). 17.99 (978-0-06-225207-4(0), Greenwillow Bks.) HarperCollins Pubs.

Halligan, Jim & Newman, John. Seeing Red. 2003. 176p. pap. 6.95 (978-0-86327-903-4(1)) Wolfhound Pr. IRL. Dist: Interlink Publishing Group, Inc.

Hancock, Dennis & Hancock, Shawn. What If There Are No Colors. Hancock, Uyen, illus. 2012. 36p. 24.95 (978-1-4626-7203-5(5)) America Star Bks.

Hanton, Sophie. Colors by the Sea. 2009. (Mag-NUT-Tics! Ser.). (Illus.). (J). bds. 9.99 (978-1-934650-73-8(0)) Just For Kids Pr., LLC.

Hardy, Sarah Frances. Paint Me! Hardy, Sarah Frances, illus. 2014. (ENG., Illus.). 32p. (J). (-k). 14.95 (978-1-62873-813-1(8), Sky Pony Pr.) Skyhorse Publishing Co., Inc.

Harmening, Gail. How Did Clancey Get His Color?, 1 vol. 2009. 45p. pap. 24.95 (978-1-60836-440-4(2)) America Star Bks.

Harris, Patricia. The Car of Many Colors. 2017. (Colorful Cars Ser.). 24p. (gr. 4-6). pap. 8.25 **(978-1-5383-2087-7(8)**, PowerKids Pr.) Rosen Publishing Group, Inc., The.

Harris, Sally M. Color Me Happy. Paplinksie, Cecilia, illus. 2009. 24p. pap. 10.95 (978-1-935137-75-7(1)) Guardian Angel Publishing, Inc.

Harrison, Casey. I'm an Ostrich. 2012. 24p. pap. 9.99 (978-0-9853650-4-2(8)) Mindstir Media.

Harshman, Marc & Ryan, Cheryl. Red Are the Apples. Zahares, Wade, illus. 2007. (ENG.). 32p. (J). (gr. -1-3). pap. 6.99 (978-0-15-206065-7(0)) Houghton Mifflin Harcourt Publishing Co.

Haynes, Martha Sue. The Ladies of Color. 2011. (Illus.). 16p. (gr. 1-2). pap. 9.49 (978-1-4520-9877-7(8)) AuthorHouse.

Hazekamp, Michelle R. The Rainbow in My Pocket. Buehrle, Jacquelyn, illus. 2011. 28p. pap. 24.95 (978-1-4560-0927-4(3)) America Star Bks.

Hicer, Nancy. Rosa's Painting. 2015. (Rosen REAL Readers: STEM & STEAM Collection). (ENG.). 8p. pap. 5.46 (978-1-4994-9608-6(7), Rosen Classroom) Rosen Publishing Group, Inc., The.

Hicks, Barbara Jean. I Like Black & White. Prap, Lila, illus. 2006. 24p. (J). (gr. -1-3). 9.95 (978-1-58925-056-7(7)) Tiger Tales.

Hillert, Margaret. Dear Dragon's Colors 1 ,2, 3. Schimmell, David, illus. 2010. (BeginningtoRead Ser.). 32p. (J). (gr. k-2). lib. bdg. 22.60 (978-1-59953-376-6(6)) Norwood Hse. Pr.

—I Like Things. (J). 4.95 (978-0-87895-683-8(2)) Modern Curriculum Pr.

—I Like Things. Hopkins, Jeff, illus. 2016. (BeginningtoRead Ser.). (ENG.). 32p. (J). (gr. 1-2). 22.60 (978-1-59953-817-4(2)) Norwood Hse. Pr.

—It's St. Patrick's Day, Dear Dragon. Schimmell, David, illus. 2008. (BeginningtoRead Ser.). 32p. (J). (gr. k-2). lib. bdg. 22.60 (978-1-59953-161-8(5)) Norwood Hse. Pr.

—It's St. Patrick's Day, Dear Dragon. del Risco, Eida, tr. Schimmell, David, illus. 2008. (BeginningtoRead Ser.). 32p. (J). (-2). pap. 11.94 (978-1-60357-086-2(1)) Norwood Hse. Pr.

—¿Qué Tengo en el Bolsillo, Querido Dragón? Fernandez, Queta, tr. from ENG. Schimmell, David, illus. 2014. (BeginningtoRead Ser.).Tr. of What's in My Pocket, Dear Dragon? (ENG & SPA.). 32p. (J). (-2). lib. bdg. 22.60 (978-1-59953-611-8(0)) Norwood Hse. Pr.

—Querido Dragón, Los Colores y 1, 2, 3 /Dear Dragon's Colors 1, 2, 3. del Risco, Eida, tr. Schimmell, David, illus. 2011. (BeginningtoRead Ser.). 32p. (J). (-2). pap. 11.94 (978-1-60357-554-6(5)) Norwood Hse. Pr.

—Querido Dragón, los Colores y 1, 2, 3 /Dear Dragon's Colors 1, 2, 3. del Risco, Eida, tr. from ENG. Schimmell, David, illus. 2011. (BeginningtoRead Ser.). 32p. (J). (gr. k-2). lib. bdg. 22.60 (978-1-59953-470-1(3)) Norwood Hse. Pr.

—What's in My Pocket, Dear Dragon? Schimmell, David, illus. 2014. (BeginningtoRead Ser.). (ENG.). 32p. (J). (-2). pap. 11.94 (978-1-60357-415-0(8)); lib. bdg. 22.60 (978-1-59953-579-1(3)) Norwood Hse. Pr.

Hnatov, Catherine. Yum, Yum, 1 vol. 2011. (ENG., Illus.). 32p. (J). (gr. -1). bds. 5.95 (978-1-59572-275-1(0)) Star Bright Bks., Inc.

Holub, Joan & Williams, Suzanne. Iris the Colorful. 2014. (Goddess Girls Ser.: 14). (ENG., Illus.). 272p. (J). (gr. 3-7). pap. 7.99 (978-1-4424-8823-6(9), Aladdin) Simon & Schuster Children's Publishing.

—Iris the Colorful. 2014. (Goddess Girls Ser.: 14). lib. bdg. 18.40 (978-0-606-35792-0(0)) Turtleback Bks.

Hooks, Bell. Skin Again. Raschka, Chris, illus. 2017. (ENG.). 40p. (J). (gr. -1-k). 12.99 **(978-1-4847-9923-9(2)**, Jump at the Sun) Hyperion Bks. for Children.

Hopgood, Tim. Wow! Said the Owl. Hopgood, Tim, illus. 2009. (ENG., Illus.). 32p. (J). (gr. -1-k). 16.99 (978-0-374-38518-7(1), 9780374385187, Farrar, Straus & Giroux (BYR)) Farrar, Straus & Giroux.

Hopkins, Jane. Diving for Colors in Hawaii: A Color Identification Book for Keiki. Bosgra, Johann, illus. 2003. (ENG.). 18p. (J). (gr. -1-1). bds. 7.95 (978-0-9729905-1-6(8)) Beachhouse Publishing, LLC.

Horacek, Judy. Yellow Is My Color Star. Horacek, Judy, illus. 2014. (ENG., Illus.). 32p. (J). (gr. -1-3). 16.99 (978-1-4424-9299-8(6), Beach Lane Bks.) Beach Lane Bks.

Howard-Parham, Pam. Caillou Finds Colors. Gillen, Lisa P., illus. l.t. ed. 2005. (HRL Board Book Ser.). (J). (gr. -1-k). bds. 10.95 (978-1-57332-313-0(6), HighReach Learning, Incorporated) Carson-Dellosa Publishing, LLC.

Hufnal, Amy. The Language of Color. 2012. 28p. pap. 15.99 (978-1-4691-5933-1(3)) Xlibris Corp.

Humu the Little Fish Who Wished Away His Colors. 2003. (J). 10.99 (978-0-89610-548-5(2)) Island Heritage Publishing.

Husar, Stephane. Cat & Mouse Learn the Colors! Mehee, Loic, illus. 2015. (Av2 Fiction Readalong 2016 Ser.). (ENG.). (J). lib. bdg. 34.28 (978-1-4896-3813-7(X), AV2 by Weigl) Weigl Pubs., Inc.

Hyde, Margaret. Mo Smells Blue: A Scentsational Journey. Giacomini, Amanda, illus. 3rd ed. 2010. (Mo's Nose Ser.). (ENG.). 24p. (J). (gr. k-k). 17.95 (978-0-9816255-4-6(1)) Mo's Nose, LLC.

—Mo Smells Green: A Scentsational Journey. Giacomini, Amanda, illus. 2009. (Mo's Nose Ser.). (ENG.). 16p. (J). (gr. k-k). 17.95 (978-0-9816255-2-2(5)) Mo's Nose, LLC.

I Love Birds. 2004. (Illus.). 26p. (J). lib. bdg. 12.95 (978-0-9748165-0-0(7)) Jaylil Publishing Co.

Jackson, Ellen B. The Seven Seas. Slavin, Bill & Melo, Esperanca, illus. 2010. (ENG.). 36p. (J). (gr. -1-3). 16.00 (978-0-8028-5341-7(2), Eerdmans Bks For Young Readers) Eerdmans, William B. Publishing Co.

Jakubowski, Kristan E. Paint the Town. 2008. 24p. pap. 11.85 (978-1-4343-6912-3(9)) AuthorHouse.

James, Carol. The Lady Who Loved Hats, 1 vol. 2009. 44p. pap. 24.95 (978-1-60813-777-0(5)) America Star Bks.

Johnson, Karrissa. What Would We Do Without the Color Blue? 2012. 20p. pap. 14.99 (978-1-4678-7027-6(7)) AuthorHouse.

Jones, Damon S. My Colorful Day. 2011. 28p. pap. 13.99 (978-1-4634-2959-1(2)) AuthorHouse.

Joyce, William. The Numberlys. Joyce, William & Ellis, Christina, illus. 2014. (ENG.). 56p. (J). (gr. -1-2). 17.99 (978-1-4424-7343-0(6), Atheneum Bks. for Young Readers) Simon & Schuster Children's Publishing.

Kahn, Colleen Alyssa. The Peadoaks, 1 vol. 2010. 36p. 24.95 (978-1-4489-4774-4(X)) America Star Bks.

Kane, Kim. Esther's Rainbow. Acton, Sara, illus. 2015. (ENG.). 32p. (J). (gr. -1-k). 16.99 (978-1-925266-28-3(1)) Allen & Unwin AUS. Dist: Independent Pubs. Group.

Kann, Victoria. Love, Pinkalicious. Kann, Victoria, illus. 2009. (Pinkalicious Ser.). (ENG., Illus.). 12p. (J). (gr. -1-2). pap. 6.99 (978-0-06-192731-7(7), HarperFestival) HarperCollins Pubs.

—The Perfectly Pink Collection. Kann, Victoria, illus. 2010. (Pinkalicious Ser.). (ENG., Illus.). 100p. (J). (gr. k-3). 15.99 (978-0-06-199048-9(5), HarperFestival) HarperCollins Pubs.

—Pink-a-Rama. Kann, Victoria, illus. 2012. (I Can Read Level 1 Ser.). (ENG., Illus.). 96p. (J). (gr. k-3). pap. 16.99 (978-0-06-198966-7(5)) HarperCollins Pubs.

—Pinkalicious. Kann, Victoria, illus. 2013. (Pinkalicious Ser.). (ENG., Illus.). 192p. (J). (gr. -1-3). 11.99 (978-0-06-218800-7(3)) HarperCollins Pubs.

—Pinkalicious: Crazy Hair Day. Kann, Victoria, illus. 2014. (Pinkalicious Ser.). (ENG., Illus.). 24p. (J). (gr. -1-3). pap. 3.99 (978-0-06-218768-0(6), HarperFestival) HarperCollins Pubs.

—Pinkalicious: Pink Around the Rink. Kann, Victoria, illus. 2010. (I Can Read Level 1 Ser.). (ENG., Illus.). 32p. (J). (gr. -1-3). 16.99 (978-0-06-192880-2(1)); pap. 3.99 (978-0-06-192879-6(8)) HarperCollins Pubs.

—Pinkalicious: School Rules! Kann, Victoria, illus. 2010. (I Can Read Level 1 Ser.). (ENG., Illus.). 32p. (J). (gr. -1-3). 16.99 (978-0-06-192886-4(0)) HarperCollins Pubs.

—Pinkalicious - Soccer Star. Kann, Victoria, illus. 2012. (I Can Read Level 1 Ser.). (ENG., Illus.). 32p. (J). (gr. -1-3). pap. 3.99 (978-0-06-198964-3(9)) HarperCollins Pubs.

—Pinkalicious - The Pinkamazing Storybook Collection. 2013. (Pinkalicious Ser.). (J). lib. bdg. 23.30 (978-0-606-31783-2(X), Turtleback) Turtleback Bks.

—Pinkalicious & the New Teacher. Kann, Victoria, illus. 2014. (Pinkalicious Ser.). (ENG., Illus.). 24p. (J). (gr. -1-3). pap. 6.99 (978-0-06-218913-4(1), HarperFestival) HarperCollins Pubs.

—Pinkalicious & the Pink Drink. Kann, Victoria, illus. 2010. (Pinkalicious Ser.). (ENG., Illus.). 24p. (J). (gr. -1-3). pap. 3.99 (978-0-06-192732-4(5), HarperFestival) HarperCollins Pubs.

—Pinkalicious & the Pink Drink. 2010. (Pinkalicious Ser.). (J). lib. bdg. 13.55 (978-0-606-14868-9(X), Turtleback) Turtleback Bks.

—Pinkalicious & the Pink Hat Parade. Kann, Victoria, illus. 2012. (Pinkalicious Ser.). (ENG., Illus.). 24p. (J). (gr. -1-2). pap. 6.99 (978-0-06-198960-5(6), HarperFestival) HarperCollins Pubs.

—Pinkalicious & the Pink Pumpkin. Kann, Victoria, illus. 2011. (Pinkalicious Ser.). (ENG., Illus.). 16p. (J). (gr. -1-2). pap. 6.99 (978-0-06-198961-2(4), HarperFestival) HarperCollins Pubs.

—The Pinkalicious Take-Along Storybook Set. Kann, Victoria, illus. 2015. (Pinkalicious Ser.). (ENG., Illus.). 120p. (J). (gr. -1-3). pap. 11.99 (978-0-06-241080-1(6), HarperFestival) HarperCollins Pubs.

—The Pinkatastic. Kann, Victoria, illus. 2011. (Pinkalicious Ser.). (ENG., Illus.). 100p. (J). (gr. -1-2). pap. 12.99 (978-0-06-192889-5(5), HarperFestival) HarperCollins Pubs.

—The Pinkerrific Playdate. Kann, Victoria, illus. 2011. (I Can Read Level 1 Ser.). (ENG., Illus.). 32p. (J). (gr. -1-3). 16.99 (978-0-06-192884-0(4)); pap. 3.99 (978-0-06-192883-3(6)) HarperCollins Pubs.

—The Princess of Pink Slumber Party. Kann, Victoria, illus. 2012. (I Can Read Level 1 Ser.). (ENG., Illus.). 32p. (J). (gr. -1-3). 16.99 (978-0-06-198963-6(0)); pap. 3.99 (978-0-06-198962-9(2)) HarperCollins Pubs.

—Purpledoodles. Kann, Victoria, illus. 2012. (Pinkalicious Ser.). (ENG., Illus.). 128p. (J). (gr. -1-7). pap. 12.99 (978-0-06-208586-3(7), HarperFestival) HarperCollins Pubs.

—The Royal Tea Party. Kann, Victoria, illus. 2014. (I Can Read Level 1 Ser.). (ENG., Illus.). 32p. (J). (gr. -1-3). pap. 3.99 (978-0-06-218791-8(0)) HarperCollins Pubs.

—School Rules! Kann, Victoria, illus. 2010. (I Can Read Level 1 Ser.). (ENG., Illus.). 32p. (J). (gr. -1-3). pap. 3.99 (978-0-06-192885-7(2)) HarperCollins Pubs.

—Tickled Pink. Kann, Victoria, illus. 2010. (Pinkalicious Ser.). (ENG., Illus.). 24p. (J). (gr. -1-3). pap. 3.99 (978-0-06-192877-2(1), HarperFestival) HarperCollins Pubs.

—Tickled Pink. Kann, Victoria, illus. 2010. (Pinkalicious Ser.). (Illus.). (J). lib. bdg. 13.55 (978-0-606-14869-6(8), Turtleback) Turtleback Bks.

Kann, Victoria & Kann, Elizabeth. Pinkalicious. Kann, Victoria, illus. (Pinkalicious Ser.). (Illus.). 40p. (J). 2016. (ENG.). (gr. -1-3). 17.99 (978-0-06-077639-8(0)) 2011. (SPA.). (gr. k-3). 17.99 (978-0-06-179959-4(9)) 2006. (gr. -1-3). lib. bdg. 17.89 (978-0-06-077640-4(4)) HarperCollins Pubs.

—Purplicious. Kann, Victoria, illus. 2007. (Illus.). 40p. (J). (gr. k-3). (ENG.). 17.99 (978-0-06-124405-6(8)); lib. bdg. 17.89 (978-0-06-124406-3(6)) HarperCollins Pubs.

Kasper, Beth. Billy's Secret. 2013. 36p. pap. 16.95 (978-1-4808-0344-2(8)) Archway Publishing.

Kelly, Martin. Color Train, Color Train! Luiz, Fernando, illus. 2009. 20p. bds. 12.99 (978-0-8249-1437-0(6), Ideal Pubns.) Worthy Publishing.

—Skeleton Stretch. 2011. (Stretchies Glow-in-the-Dark Bk Ser.). 16p. (J). 8.99 (978-0-8249-1522-3(4)) SmartInk Bks., LLC.

Khan, Hena. Golden Domes & Silver Lanterns: A Muslim Book of Colors. Amini, Mehrdokht, illus. 2012. (ENG.). 32p. (J). (gr. -1-2). 17.99 (978-0-8118-7905-7(4)) Chronicle Bks. LLC.

Kidd, Ron. Bookee Presents Colors, Shapes & Sounds. Nord, Mary, illus. (Talking Book Adventures Ser.). 12p. (J). (gr. -1-18). 16.95 (978-0-9627001-1-8(8)) Futech Educational Products, Inc.

King-Chai, Sharon. Lucy Ladybug. 2016. (ENG., Illus.). 32p. (J). (gr. -1-2). 16.99 (978-0-553-51005-8(3), Random Hse. Bks. for Young Readers) Random Hse. Children's Bks.

Klausmeier, Jesse. Open This Little Book. Lee, Suzy, illus. 2013. (ENG.). 40p. (J). (gr. -1-3). 16.99 (978-0-8118-6783-2(8)) Chronicle Bks. LLC.

Klein, Adria F. Circus Train, 1 vol. Cameron, Craig, illus. 2013. (Train Time Ser.). (ENG.). 32p. (gr. -1-1). pap. 5.95 (978-1-4342-4883-1(6)); lib. bdg. 22.65 (978-1-4342-4188-7(2)) Stone Arch Bks.

—Circus Train & the Clowns, 1 vol. Cameron, Craig, illus. 2013. (Train Time Ser.). (ENG.). 32p. (gr. -1-1). pap. 5.95 (978-1-4342-6195-3(6)); pap. 29.70 (978-1-4342-6303-2(7)); lib. bdg. 22.65 (978-1-4342-4782-7(1)) Stone Arch Bks.

—The Full Freight Train, 1 vol. Cameron, Craig, illus. 2013. (Train Time Ser.). (ENG.). 32p. (gr. -1-1). pap. 5.95 (978-1-4342-6197-7(2)); pap. 29.70 (978-1-4342-6301-8(0)); lib. bdg. 22.65 (978-1-4342-4784-1(8)) Stone Arch Bks.

—Train Time. 2013. (Train Time Ser.). (ENG.). 32p. (gr. -1-1). pap. 23.80 (978-1-4342-4902-9(6)) Stone Arch Bks.

Kleinberg, Naomi. Elmo's Colors (Sesame Street) 2016. (Pictureback(R) Ser.). (ENG., Illus.). 24p. (J). (gr. -1-2). 4.99 (978-1-101-93200-1(7), Random Hse. Bks. for Young Readers) Random Hse. Children's Bks.

Kolanovic, Dubravka. Wipe-Clean Colours. Kolanovic, Dubravka, illus. 2009. (Honey Hill Ser.). (ENG., Illus.). 12p. (J). (gr. -1-k). bds. 9.99 (978-0-230-70915-7(X)) Macmillan Pubs., Ltd. GBR. Dist: Independent Pubs. Group.

Kono, Erin Eitter. Every Color. 2016. (ENG., Illus.). 32p. (J). (gr. -1-3). 16.99 (978-0-8037-4132-4(4), Dial Bks) Penguin Young Readers Group.

Krajenbrink Hulin, Yvonne. My Magic Box of Shapes. 2013. 28p. pap. 11.99 (978-0-9794133-7-7(0)) TV Acres Bks.

Kravetz, Nathan. A Horse of Another Color. 2011. 68p. (gr. 4-6). pap. 10.95 (978-1-4620-0591-8(8)) iUniverse, Inc.

Kumin, Maxine. What Color Is Caesar? Friend, Alison, illus. 2010. (ENG.). 56p. (J). (gr. -1-k). 16.99 (978-0-7636-3432-2(8)) Candlewick Pr.

Labuda, Scott A. The Color of People. Franfou Studio, illus. 2011. (ENG.). 34p. (J). (gr. -1-3). 15.95 (978-1-935268-94-9(5)) Halo Publishing International.

Lallemand, Orianne. The Wolf Who Wanted to Change His Color. Thuillier, Eléonore, illus. 2012. (My Little Picture Book Ser.). (ENG.). 32p. (J). (gr. -1-2). pap. 6.95 (978-2-7338-1945-6(3)) Auzou, Philippe Editions FRA. Dist: Consortium Bk. Sales & Distribution.

Lavender, Todd. Farmer Fred & His Hen So Red. Lavender, Todd, illus. 2012. (Illus.). 48p. pap. 9.99 (978-0-9850410-0-7(5)) Akmaeon Publishing, LLC.

Law, Felicia. Colors. Knight, Paula, illus. 2015. (Patchwork Ser.). (ENG.). 24p. (J). (gr. k-3). lib. bdg. 22.60 (978-1-59953-709-2(5)) Norwood Hse. Pr.

Lehrhaupt, Adam. I Don't Draw, I Color! Sala, Felicita, illus. 2017. (ENG.). 32p. (J). (gr. -1-3). 17.99 (978-1-4814-6275-4(X), Simon & Schuster/Paula Wiseman Bks.) Simon & Schuster/Paula Wiseman Bks.

Leopold, Nikia Speliakos Clark. Adam's Crayons. Nemett, Barry & Nemett, Laini, illus. 2011. (J). (978-0-9817519-1-7(1)) Galileo Pr.

Lewis, Bisa, as told by. How Flowers Get Their Colors. 2005. (J). (978-0-9745469-9-5(2)) Ashley & Taylor Publishing, Co.

Lewis, Janaka Bowman. Brown All Over. 2012. 20p. (-18). pap. 17.99 (978-1-4772-9129-0(6)) AuthorHouse.

Lewis, T. Caroline's Beautiful Pictures. 2012. 16p. pap. 15.99 (978-1-4772-6195-8(8)) AuthorHouse.

Linton, Chandra S. Colors, Colors, Colors, A World Filled with Colors, Who Made Them? 2011. 20p. (gr. 2-4). pap. 15.49 (978-1-4567-6355-8(5)) AuthorHouse.

Lionni, Leo. A Color of His Own. Lionni, Leo, illus. 2006. (ENG., Illus.). 40p. (J). (gr. -1-k). reprint ed. 12.95 (978-0-375-83697-8(7), Knopf Bks. for Young Readers) Random Hse. Children's Bks.

—A Color of His Own: (Spanish-English Bilingual Edition) Lionni, Leo, illus. 2016. (ENG & SPA., Illus.). 32p. (J). (gr. -1-k). bds. 7.99 (978-0-553-53873-1(X), Knopf Bks. for Young Readers) Random Hse. Children's Bks.

—Little Blue & Little Yellow. (ENG.). (J). (gr. -1-2). 2011. 42p. bds. 7.99 (978-0-375-87290-7(6)) 2009. 48p. 16.99 (978-0-375-86013-4(3)) Random Hse. Children's Bks. (Knopf Bks. for Young Readers).

—Su Propio Color. Mlawer, Teresa, tr. from ENG. 2007. (SPA., Illus.). 32p. (J). (gr. k-2). 12.99 (978-1-933032-14-6(6)) Lectorum Pubns., Inc.

Little Bear, Shena. How the lone wolf got her Name. 2008. 80p. pap. 9.95 (978-0-578-00171-5(3)) Stone Castle Publishing.

Little Bee Books Staff & Brook-Piper, Holly. Fun with Colors. Max and Sid Staff, illus. 2015. (Tiny Touch Ser.). (ENG.). 12p. (J). (gr. -1 — 1). bds. 4.99 (978-1-4998-0001-2(0)) Little Bee Books Inc.

Little Dragon Catches Colors. 2008. (Little Dragon Tab Board Book Ser.). 6p. bds. (978-1-4075-2666-9(9)) Parragon, Inc.

Litton, Jonathan. Red Car, Blue Car. Verrall, Lisa, illus. 2015. (My Little World Ser.). (ENG.). 12p. (J). (gr. -1-2). bds. 8.99 (978-1-68010-506-3(X)) Tiger Tales.

Litwin, Eric. I Love My White Shoes. Dean, James, illus. 2010. (Pete the Cat Ser.). 40p. (J). (gr. -1-3). (ENG.). 17.99 (978-0-06-190622-0(0)); lib. bdg. 17.89 (978-0-06-190623-7(9)) HarperCollins Pubs.

Litwin, Eric & Dean, James. I Love My White Shoes. 2010. (Pete the Cat Ser.). pap. (978-0-545-41966-6(2)) Scholastic, Inc.

Lloyd, Ashley. Red, 1 vol. Matkovich, Gregory, illus. 2009. 19p. pap. 24.95 (978-1-61546-913-0(3)) PublishAmerica, Inc.

Lluch, Alex. Do I Look Good in Color? Defenbaugh, David, illus. 2006. (ENG.). 30p. (J). (gr. -1-1). bds. 7.95 (978-1-887169-57-8(1)) WS Publishing.

Lobel, Arnold. The Arnold Lobel Treasury. 2014. (ENG., Illus.). 160p. (J). (gr. 1-4). pap. 14.99 (978-0-486-78078-8(3)) Dover Pubns., Inc.

Lodge, Jo. Little Roar's Red Boots. 2013. (ENG., Illus.). 20p. (J). (gr. -1-k). 8.99 (978-1-4449-0482-6(5)) Hodder & Stoughton GBR. Dist: Hachette Bk. Group.

Logan, J. Gavin. Plum Bunny. 2008. 52p. pap. 16.95 (978-1-60563-654-2(1)) America Star Bks.

Lopata-Kurzweil, Ruti. A Story of Colors: And Much More! 2012. 36p. pap. 15.50 (978-1-4669-1946-4(9)) Trafford Publishing.

Lumley, Jemima. The Journey Home from Grandpa's. Fatus, Sophie, illus. 2006. (ENG.). 24p. (J). pap. 6.99 (978-1-84686-029-4(6)); (gr. -1-k). 9.99 (978-1-84686-026-3(1)); (gr. -1-3). 16.99 (978-1-905236-37-4(9)) Barefoot Bks., Inc.

Lumley, Jemima & Penner, Fred. The Journey Home from Grandpa's. Fatus, Sophie, illus. 2011. (ENG.). 24p. (J). (gr. -1-2). 9.99 (978-1-84686-658-6(8)) Barefoot Bks., Inc.

Lunablau, Jani. Little Snowflake. 2006. (ENG., Illus.). 32p. (J). (gr. -1-k). (978-1-59692-139-9(0)) MacAdam/Cage Publishing, Inc.

Lund, Laurel. When Glory Got Her Glow Back: A Glowworm's Tail. 2012. 32p. (-18). pap. 16.99 (978-1-4525-6011-3(0)) Balboa Pr.

Luning, Barbara. The Quilted Zoo. 2008. 28p. pap. 15.99 (978-1-4363-1778-8(9)) Xlibris Corp.

Lynch, Jay. Otto's Orange Day. Cammuso, Frank, illus. 2013. (ENG.). 40p. (J). (gr. -1-3). pap. 4.99 (978-1-935179-27-6(6)) TOON Books / RAW Junior, LLC.

—Otto's Orange Day. Mouly, Francoise, ed. Cammuso, Frank, illus. 2008. (ENG.). 40p. (J). (gr. -1-3). 12.95 (978-0-9799238-2-1(4)) TOON Books / RAW Junior, LLC.

Lynch, Jay & Cammuso, Frank. Otto's Orange Day, 1 vol. 2013. (Toon Bks). (ENG.). 36p. (J). (gr. 2-3). lib. bdg. 27.07 (978-1-61479-154-6(6)) Spotlight.

—Otto's Orange Day. 2013. (Toon Books Level 3 Ser.). lib. bdg. 14.75 (978-0-606-32103-7(9), Turtleback) Turtleback Bks.

MacKoul, Eva. The Pig Who Didn't Want to Be Pink. 2013. 24p. pap. 12.45 (978-1-4908-0071-4(9), WestBow Pr.) Author Solutions, Inc.

Maddox, Jake. Striker Assist, 1 vol. Tiffany, Sean, illus. 2012. (Jake Maddox Sports Stories Ser.). (ENG.). 72p. (gr. 2-3). pap. 5.95 (978-1-4342-4208-2(0)) Stone Arch Bks.

Mancil, Arlene. The Garden Fairy. 2008. 32p. pap. 24.95 (978-1-60441-735-7(8)) PublishAmerica, Inc.

Mara, Nichole. All Aboard! Let's Ride a Train. Kolb, Andrew, illus. 2017. (ENG.). 10p. (J). (gr. -1 — 1). bds. 9.95 **(978-1-4197-2567-8(X)**, Abrams Appleseed) Abrams, Inc.

Marino Walters, Jennifer. Amazing Autumn. Nez, John, illus. 2016. (Seasons Ser.). (ENG.). 24p. (J). (gr. -1-1). lib. bdg. 25.32 (978-1-63440-045-9(3)) Red Chair Pr.

—Surprising Spring. Nez, John, illus. 2016. (Seasons Ser.). (ENG.). 24p. (J). (gr. -1-1). lib. bdg. 25.32 (978-1-63440-047-3(X)) Red Chair Pr.

Martin, Bill, Jr. Brown Bear, Brown Bear, What Do You See? Carle, Eric, illus. (Brown Bear & Friends Ser.). (J). 2012. (ENG.). 28p. (gr. -1-k). bds. 12.99 (978-0-8050-9577-7(2), 9780805095777) 2010. (ENG.). 40p. (gr. -1-2). 8.99 (978-0-8050-9244-8(7), 9780805092448) 2007. 32p. pap. 7.95 (978-0-8050-8797-0(4)) 3rd anniv. ed. 2008. (ENG.). 32p. (gr. -1-k). pap. 27.95 (978-0-8050-8718-5(4), 9780805087185) 50th anniv. ed. 2016. (ENG.). 28p. bds. 9.99 (978-1-62779-722-1(X), 9781627797221) Holt, Henry & Co. (Holt, Henry & Co. Bks. For Young Readers).

—Brown Bear, Brown Bear, What Do You See? / Oso Pardo, Oso Pardo, ¿qué Ves Ahí? (Bilingual Board Book - Spanish Edition) Carle, Eric, illus. 2017. (ENG.). 28p. (J). bds. 9.99 **(978-1-250-15232-9(1)**, 9781250152329, Holt, Henry & Co. Bks. For Young Readers) Holt, Henry & Co.

Martin, Bill, Jr. Brown Bear, Brown Bear, What Do You See? 50th Anniversary Edition with Audio CD. Carle, Eric, illus. 2016. (Brown Bear & Friends Ser.). (ENG.). 32p. (J). 19.99 (978-1-62779-721-4(1), 9781627797214, Holt, Henry & Co. Bks. For Young Readers) Holt, Henry & Co.

Marvel Press Book Group. Mighty Colors. 2016. (ENG.). 20p. (J). (gr. -1 — 1). bds. 7.99 (978-1-4847-3270-0(7), Marvel Pr.) Disney Publishing Worldwide.

Matsi, Maria. A Week in the Life of the Chromasomas. 2009. (Illus.). 156p. pap. (978-1-84748-619-6(3)) Athena Pr.

Matthias, Catherine & Sharp, Gene. Demasiados Globos. Sharp, Gene, illus. 2011. (Rookie Ready to Learn Español Ser.). (SPA., Illus.). 40p. (J). pap. 5.95 (978-0-531-26792-9(X)); lib. bdg. 23.00 (978-0-531-26124-8(7)) Scholastic Library Publishing. (Children's Pr.).

McBratney, Sam. Guess How Much I Love You: Colors. Jeram, Anita, illus. 2013. (Guess How Much I Love You Ser.). (ENG.). 14p. (J). (—1). bds. 4.99 (978-0-7636-6476-3(6)) Candlewick Pr.

McClymer, Kelly. Must Love Black. 2008. (ENG.). 192p. (YA). (gr. 7-18). pap. 8.99 (978-1-4169-4903-9(8), Simon Pulse) Simon Pulse.

McCoy, Angie. Starchild's Adventures on Earth. McCoy, Derrick, illus. 2011. 24p. pap. 24.95 (978-1-4560-5053-5(2)) America Star Bks.

McCue, Lisa. Quiet Bunny's Many Colors. 2011. (ENG., Illus.). 32p. (J). (gr. -1-1). 14.95 (978-1-4027-7209-2(2)) Sterling Publishing Co., Inc.

McCumbers, Jaime. Don't Step on the Flowers! 2008. 12p. per. 24.95 (978-1-4241-9092-8(4)) America Star Bks.

McDonald, Megan. Judy Moody's Best Mood Ever Coloring & Activity Book. Reynolds, Peter H., illus. 2011. (Judy Moody Ser.). (ENG.). 32p. (J). (gr. -1-2). pap. 3.99 (978-0-7636-5707-9(7)) Candlewick Pr.

McDunn, Linda L. The Color of Me. Knutson, Barbara, illus. 2004. (ENG.). 32p. 16.95 (978-0-8146-2952-9(0)) Liturgical Pr.

McElroy, Jean. Baby's Colorful World. 2011. (ENG.). 14p. (J). (gr. -1 — 1). 4.99 (978-1-4424-1197-5(X), Little Simon) Little Simon.

McGrath, Barbara Barbieri. Halloween Colors. Tagel, Peggy, illus. 2016. (First Celebrations Ser.). (ENG.). 12p. (J). (— 1). bds. 6.95 (978-1-58089-533-0(6)) Charlesbridge Publishing, Inc.

—Teddy Bear Counting. Nihoff, Tim, illus. 2010. (McGrath Math Ser.). (ENG.). 32p. (J). (gr. -1-2). 16.95 (978-1-58089-215-5(9)); pap. 7.95 (978-1-58089-216-2(7)) Charlesbridge Publishing, Inc.

McGrath, Barbara Barbieri & Tagel, Peggy. Parade Colors. 2017. (First Celebrations Ser.). (ENG., Illus.). 12p. (J). (— 1). bds. 6.99 (978-1-58089-536-1(0)) Charlesbridge Publishing, Inc.

McKay, Sindy. We Both Read-Too Many Cats. Johnson, Meredith, illus. 2003. (We Both Read Ser.). 44p. (J). (gr. k-18). 7.99 (978-1-891327-49-0(6)); pap. 4.99 (978-1-891327-50-6(X)) Treasure Bay, Inc.

McKee, David. Elmer's Colours. Mo'Allim, Nur M., tr. 2004. (Elmer Ser.). (ENG & SOM., Illus.). 14p. (J). (gr. -1). bds. 8.95 (978-1-84059-397-6(0)) Milet Publishing.

—Elmer's Colours. Al-Hamdi, Ahmed, tr. 2004. (Elmer Ser.). (ARA & ENG., Illus.). 14p. (J). (gr. -1). bds. 8.95 (978-1-84059-395-2(4)) Milet Publishing.

—Elmer's Colours. Umicini, Roberta, tr. 2004. (Elmer Ser.). (ENG & ITA., Illus.). 14p. (J). (gr. -1). bds. 8.95 (978-1-84059-396-9(2)) Milet Publishing.

—Elmer's Colours (English-Polish) 2010. (Elmer Ser.). (POL & ENG., Illus.). 16p. (J). (gr. k — 1). bds. 8.95 (978-1-84059-531-4(0)) Milet Publishing.

McLoughlin, Nancy. Color Me Orange. 2011. 36p. pap. 13.95 (978-1-4497-2293-7(8), WestBow Pr.) Author Solutions, Inc.

McTrustry, Chris. Red Goes Green, 1 vol. rev. ed. 2013. (Fiction Readers Ser.). (ENG., Illus.). 32p. (J). (gr. 3-3). pap. 8.99 (978-1-4333-5641-4(4)) Shell Educational Publishing.

Meadows, Daisy. The Rainbow Fairies. 2010. (Scholastic Reader Level 2 Ser.). (ENG.). 32p. (J). (gr. 1-3). pap. 3.99 (978-0-545-22291-4(5), Cartwheel Bks.) Scholastic, Inc.

—Ruby the Red Fairy. Ripper, Georgie, illus. 2005. (Rainbow Magic Ser.: 1). (ENG.). 80p. (Orig.). (J). (gr. -1-3). pap. 4.99 (978-0-439-73861-3(X)) Scholastic, Inc.

Meet the Colors Board Book. 2007. (Preschool Prep Ser.). (J). bds. 7.99 (978-0-9770215-5-0(6)) Preschool Prep Co.

Meet the Colors Lift the Flap Book. 2007. (Preschool Prep Ser.). (J). bds. 9.99 (978-0-9770215-4-3(8)) Preschool Prep Co.

Melling, David. Colour with Splosh! 2017. (Splosh Ser.). (ENG., Illus.). 32p. (J). (gr. -1-k). pap. 7.99 **(978-1-4449-3181-5(4))** Hachette Children's Group GBR. Dist: Hachette Bk. Group.

Messenger, Lois. Fairy Magic & the Healing Rainbow Colours. 2013. 36p. pap. 15.95 (978-1-4525-7663-3(7), Balboa Pr.) Author Solutions, Inc.

Michalak, Jamie. Fairy Tea Party. Watanabe, Kaori, illus. 2008. 24p. (J). (gr. -1-3). bds. 7.95 (978-1-58925-840-2(1)) Tiger Tales.

Michalczewski, Raime. Monsters of a Different Color: Being Different Is Beautiful. 2011. 36p. pap. 18.99 (978-1-4567-2769-7(9)) AuthorHouse.

Milne, A. A. Winnie the Pooh's Colors. Shepard, Ernest H., illus. 2009. (Winnie-The-Pooh Ser.). (ENG.). 20p. (J). (gr. -1 — 1). bds. 6.99 (978-0-525-42083-5(5), Dutton Books for Young Readers) Penguin Young Readers Group.

Mockford, Caroline & Blackstone, Stella. Cleo's Color Book. Mockford, Caroline, illus. 2007. (Cleo Ser.). (ENG., Illus.). 24p. (J). (gr. -1-k). bds. 6.99 (978-1-84686-060-7(1)) Barefoot Bks., Inc.

Moncure, Jane Belk. A Color Clown Comes to Town: A Book about Recognizing Colors. Girouard, Patrick, illus. 2013. (Magic Castle Readers Ser.). (ENG.). 32p. (J). (gr. -1-2). 25.64 (978-1-62323-565-9(0), 206299) Child's World, Inc., The.

Moore, Ann C. The Colors Join Hands for A Surprise. 2010. 24p. pap. 12.79 (978-1-4520-7572-3(7)) AuthorHouse.

Moore, Debbie. Penelope, the Peculiar Purple Porpoise. 2011. 48p. pap. 24.95 (978-1-4560-6577-5(7)) America Star Bks.

Moriarty, Jaclyn. A Corner of White. 2013. (Colors of Madeleine Ser.: 1). (ENG.). 384p. (J). (gr. 7). 18.99 (978-0-545-39736-0(7), Levine, Arthur A. Bks.) Scholastic, Inc.

—The Cracks in the Kingdom. 2014. (Colors of Madeleine Ser.: 2). (ENG.). 480p. (J). (gr. 7). 18.99 (978-0-545-39738-4(3), Levine, Arthur A. Bks.) Scholastic, Inc.

—A Tangle of Gold. 2016. (Colors of Madeleine Ser.: 3). (ENG.). 480p. (YA). (gr. 7). 18.99 (978-0-545-39740-7(5), Levine, Arthur A. Bks.) Scholastic, Inc.

My First Gators Book. 2004. (J). bds. 8.95 (978-0-9754317-0-2(6)) JEM Bks., Inc.

My First Hurricanes Book. 2004. (J). bds. 8.95 (978-0-9754317-2-6(2)) JEM Bks., Inc.

Myers, Stacy Erin. Lil Bug. 2012. 56p. pap. 11.99 (978-1-929845-56-9(1)) DeFranco Entertainment.

Nagy, Jennifer. Goats in Coats. Broughton, Ilona & Szijgyarto, Cynthia, illus. 2009. 20p. pap. 12.99 (978-1-4389-6586-4(9)) AuthorHouse.

Nettrour, Nelani. The Dragon Lands Bk. 1: The Ripple. Nettrour, Heather, illus. 2003. 100p. pap. 11.95 (978-1-929381-46-3(8), Third Millennium Publishing) Sci Fi-Arizona, Inc.

Newman, Patrice Tomasetti. Beautiful Colors. 2013. 24p. pap. 24.95 (978-1-63000-660-0(2)) America Star Bks.

Nikola-lisa, W. & Nikola-lisa, W. Hallelujah! A Christmas Celebration. Saint James, Synthia, illus. 2009. (ENG.). 36p. (J). (gr. -1-3). 10.99 (978-1-4424-0224-9(5), Atheneum Bks. for Young Readers) Simon & Schuster Children's Publishing.

Norman, Kim. I Know a Wee Piggy. Cole, Henry, illus. 2012. (ENG.). 32p. (J). (gr. -1-k). 16.99 (978-0-8037-3735-8(1), Dial Bks) Penguin Young Readers Group.

O. Shelley Dunn. Brown Like You. 2009. 24p. pap. 14.99 (978-1-4389-5089-1(6)) AuthorHouse.

Oe, Patricia Daly. Blue Mouse, Yellow Mouse. Oe, Patricia Daly, illus. 2007. (R. I. C. Story Chest Ser.). (Illus.). 20p. (J). (gr. -1-k). 11.95 incl. audio compact disk (978-1-74126-439-5(1)) R.I.C. Pubns. AUS. Dist: SCB Distributors.

Ohrt, Kate. The Rainbow Book. 2011. (ENG.). 18p. (J). (gr. -1-1). pap. 9.99 (978-1-4494-0171-9(6)) Andrews McMeel Publishing.

O'Leary, John. Goldilocks: A Pop-Up Book. O'Leary, John, illus. 2015. (ENG., Illus.). 16p. (J). (gr. -1-k). 19.99 (978-1-85707-888-6(8)) Tango Bks. GBR. Dist: Independent Pubs. Group.

Oliver, Veronica A. The Rainbow Colors: Learning Primary & Secondary Colors. 2011. 20p. 11.59 (978-1-4269-4805-3(0)) Trafford Publishing.

Otoshi, Kathryn. One. pap. (978-0-9723946-5-9(6)); 2008. (ENG., Illus.). 32p. (J). (gr. -1). 17.95 (978-0-9723946-4-2(8)) KO Kids Bks.

Pan, Hui-Mei. What's in Grandma's Grocery Bag?, 1 vol. 2004. (ENG., Illus.). 32p. (J). bds. 6.25 (978-1-887734-97-4(X)) Star Bright Bks., Inc.

—What's in Grandma's Grocery Bag? (Spanish/English), 1 vol. del Risco, Eida, tr. 2004. (ENG & SPA., Illus.). 32p. (J). bds. 5.95 (978-1-932065-12-1(1)) Star Bright Bks., Inc.

Pantone. Pantone: Colors. Dardik, Helen, illus. 2012. (Pantone Ser.). (ENG.). 20p. (J). (gr. -1-k). bds. 9.95 (978-1-4197-0180-1(0), Abrams Appleseed) Abrams, Inc.

Paschkis, Julie. P. Zonka Lays an Egg, 1 vol. Paschkis, Julie, illus. 2015. (ENG., Illus.). 32p. (J). (gr. 1-3). 16.95 (978-1-56145-819-6(8)) Peachtree Pubs.

Paterson, Brian. The Picnic: Board Book. 2006. (ENG., Illus.). 16p. (J). (gr. -1). bds. 6.99 (978-0-00-717421-8(7), HarperCollins Children's Bks.) HarperCollins Pubs. Ltd. GBR. Dist: Trafalgar Square Publishing.

Patricelli, Leslie. Hop! Hop! Patricelli, Leslie, illus. 2015. (Leslie Patricelli Board Bks.). (ENG., Illus.). 26p. (J). (— 1). bds. 6.99 (978-0-7636-6319-3(0)) Candlewick Pr.

Patterson, Christine. Conversation in the Crayon Box. 2004. 12p. (J). per. 9.33 (978-1-4116-0672-2(8)) Lulu Pr., Inc.

Patterson, Christine D. Conversation in the Crayon Box. 2008. 24p. per. 12.95 (978-1-4327-1469-7(4)) Outskirts Pr., Inc.

Paul Frank Industries & Gillingham, Sara. I Love Color: A Paul Frank Book. 2011. (ENG.). 10p. (J). (gr. -1 — 1). bds. 8.99 (978-1-4521-0222-1(8)) Chronicle Bks. LLC.

Peek, Merle & Giblin, James Cross. Mary Wore Her Red Dress & Henry Wore His Green Sneakers, 1 vol. 2006. (Read along Book & CD Ser.). (ENG., Illus.). 32p. (J). (gr. k — 1). audio compact disk 10.99 (978-0-618-75249-2(8)) Houghton Mifflin Harcourt Publishing Co.

Penn, Audrey. A Color Game for Chester Raccoon. Gibson, Barbara Leonard, illus. 2012. (Kissing Hand Ser.). (ENG.). 14p. (J). (gr. -1-k). bds. 7.95 (978-1-933718-58-3(7)) Tanglewood Pr.

Petersen, Pat. Make the World Pink, I Think. Danilewicz, Jamie, illus. 2012. 26p. 24.95 (978-1-4626-3028-8(6)) America Star Bks.

Pfister, Marcus. Rainbow Fish Colors. 2013. (Rainbow Fish Ser.). (ENG., Illus.). 12p. (J). (gr. 1-1). bds. 7.95 (978-0-7358-4147-5(0)) North-South Bks., Inc.

Phillips, Matthew. Ingo Flamingo, 1 vol. 2009. 19p. pap. 24.95 (978-1-60836-340-7(6)) America Star Bks.

Piggy Toes Press, creator. Color Party! 2007. (ENG., Illus.). 12p. (gr. -1-k). bds. 7.99 (978-1-58117-585-1(X), Intervisual/Piggy Toes) Bendon, Inc.

Pimot, Karen Hutchins. Rainbows Are the Best. Allen, Sandra Hutchins, illus. 2009. 24p. pap. 12.95 (978-1-936051-01-4(X)) Peppertree Pr., The.

Plummer, David & Archambault, John. I Paint a Rainbow. Hollander, Sarah, illus. 2007. (J). (978-1-58669-228-5(3)); (978-1-58669-227-8(5)) Childcraft Education Corp.

Portis, Antoinette. A Penguin Story. Portis, Antoinette, illus. 2008. (ENG., Illus.). 40p. (J). (gr. -1-3). 17.99 (978-0-06-145688-6(8)) HarperCollins Pubs.

Power Of The Pencil. Round. 2013. 64p. pap. 24.99 (978-1-4817-0913-2(5)) AuthorHouse.

Priddy, Roger. Best Friends: We Are Better Together. 2016. (Best Friends Ser.). (ENG., Illus.). 20p. (J). bds. 9.99 (978-0-312-51964-3(8), 9780312519643, Priddy Bks.) St. Martin's Pr.

—Color Attack! 2015. (ENG.). 96p. (J). (gr. k-2). pap. 9.99 (978-0-312-51845-5(5), 9780312518455, Priddy Bks.) St. Martin's Pr.

Prochovnic, Dawn Babb. See the Colors: Sign Language for Colors, 1 vol. Bauer, Stephanie, illus. 2009. (Story Time with Signs & Rhymes Ser.). (ENG.). 32p. (gr. -1-3). 28.50 (978-1-60270-671-2(9), Looking Glass Library) ABDO Publishing Co.

Propaganda, Amanda. People Flavors. 2006. (Illus.). (J). 6.00 (978-1-60149-000-1(3)) Punkin Pr.

Publications International Ltd. Staff, ed. Dora the Explorer: Island Adventure (Talking Look & Find) 2010. 16p. (J). bds. 12.98 (978-1-60553-471-8(4)) Publications International, Ltd.

—Where in the World. 2010. 18p. (J). bds. 12.98 (978-1-4127-4464-5(4), PIL Kids) Publications International, Ltd.

Pugliano-Martin, Carol. Little Lion. 2011. (Early Connections Ser.). (J). (978-1-61672-585-3(0)) Benchmark Education Co.

Punnett, Dick. Name Lizzy's Colors: A Talk-along Book. Punnett, Yvonne, ed. 2nd ed. 2005. (Talk-Along Bks.). (Illus.). 32p. (J). pap. 6.99 (978-0-9657211-6-5(7)) Tomoka Pr.

Pym, Tasha & Pichon, Liz. Colour Bears. 2006. (Collins Big Cat Ser.). (ENG., Illus.). 56p. (J). (gr. -1-k). pap. 5.99 (978-0-00-718652-5(5)) HarperCollins Pubs. Ltd. GBR. Dist: Independent Pubs. Group.

Pynn, Susan. Jelly Bean Row, 1 vol. Pratt, Liz, illus. 2011. (ENG.). 32p. (J). (gr. k-5). pap. 9.95 (978-1-897174-80-7(2), Tuckamore Bks) Creative Bk. Publishing CAN. Dist: Orca Bk. Pubs. USA.

Rainbow of Colors. 2003. (J). per. (978-1-57657-952-7(2)) Paradise Pr., Inc.

Rainbow Town: Individual Title Six-Packs. (Sails Literacy Ser.). 16p. (gr. k-18). 27.00 (978-0-7635-4441-6(8)) Rigby Education.

The Rainbow Week. 2013. (Illus.). 26p. 16.99 (978-0-9896660-0-8(X)) Sojourner Stories.

Rainforth, Hannah. Barnaby Bennett. Teo, Ali, illus. 2007. 32p. (J). (gr. -1-3). pap. 10.00 (978-1-86969-232-2(2)) Univ. of Hawaii Pr.

Rand, Ann. What Can I Be? King, Ingrid Fiksdahl, illus. 2016. (ENG.). 32p. (J). (gr. -1-1). 17.95 (978-1-61689-472-6(5)) Princeton Architectural Pr.

Random House. Racing Colors! (Blaze & the Monster Machines) Random House, illus. 2016. (ENG., Illus.). 24p. (J). (gr. -1 — 1). bds. 6.99 (978-0-553-53892-2(6), Random Hse. Bks. for Young Readers) Random Hse. Children's Bks.

—Show Your Colors! (Teenage Mutant Ninja Turtles) Spaziante, Patrick, illus. 2015. (Board Book Ser.). (ENG.). 24p. (J). (— 1). bds. 4.99 (978-0-553-49776-2(6), Random Hse. Bks. for Young Readers) Random Hse. Children's Bks.

Rappa, Desiree & Brian, illus. Big Red. 2003. (J). 4.95 (978-0-9722027-0-1(6)) Covered Bridge Bks.

Rathmell, Donna & Rathmell, Doreen. Octavia & Her Purple Ink Cloud, 1 vol. McLennan, Connie, illus. 2006. (ENG.). 32p. (J). (gr. -1-2). 15.95 (978-0-9764943-5-5(3)) Arbordale Publishing.

Reasoner, Charles. Color Crunch! 2009. (Bite Bks.). (Illus.). (J). bds. 7.99 (978-1-934650-15-8(3)) Just For Kids Pr., LLC.

Red & Green Choices by Green Irene: Cindy T's Circle Time. 2003. (J). 16.00 (978-0-9742280-2-0(8)) Green Irene.

Reed, Jennifer Bond. Doodle Girl. Foster, Jack, illus. 2012. 20p. pap. 9.95 (978-1-61633-341-6(3)) Guardian Angel Publishing, Inc.

Reiner, Angela. You Can't Dance in Those Pants. 2008. 28p. pap. 18.65 (978-1-4363-6798-1(0)) Xlibris Corp.

Rey, H. A. Curious George Colors Eggs. 2012. (Curious George Ser.). (ENG., Illus.). 24p. (J). (gr. -1-3). pap. 3.99 (978-0-547-31585-0(6)) Houghton Mifflin Harcourt Publishing Co.

—Curious George Colors Eggs (CGTV Reader) 2012. (Curious George Ser.). (ENG., Illus.). 24p. (J). (gr. -1-3). 12.99 (978-0-547-55904-9(6)) Houghton Mifflin Harcourt Publishing Co.

Riggs, Kate. Colors of Nature. Domeniconi, Paolo, illus. 2017. (ENG.). 14p. (J). (gr. -1 — 1). bds. 8.99 (978-1-56846-299-8(9), Creative Education) Creative Co., The.

Rinker, Sherri Duskey. Steam Train, Dream Train Colors. Lichtenheld, Tom, illus. 2016. (ENG.). 20p. (J). (gr. -1 — 1). bds. 7.99 (978-1-4521-4915-8(1)) Chronicle Bks. LLC.

Robinson, Jennifer. Isabella's Shoes. 2009. 20p. pap. 10.95 (978-1-60860-553-8(1), Strategic Bk. Publishing) Strategic Book Publishing & Rights Agency (SBPRA).

Rochester, Mary Frances. The Turquoise Monkey. 2010. 48p. pap. 17.99 (978-1-4490-7260-5(7)) AuthorHouse.

Rockhill, Dennis. Meadow Dance. 2007. (Wonderlands Ser.).Tr. of Danza de la Pradera. (ENG., Illus.). 32p. (J). (gr. -1-3). 16.95 (978-0-9741992-5-2(7), Raven Tree Pr.,Csi) Continental Sales, Inc.

Rodriguez, Paul. What Color Are You? Rodriguez, Paul, illus. 2003. (Illus.). 32p. (J). lib. bdg. 15.99 (978-0-9744770-2-2(8)) Rodro.

Rogers, Alan. En Forme de Bateau. 2003. (Little Giants Ser.). (FRE., Illus.). 16p. (J). (gr. -1-k). 5.95 (978-1-58728-177-8(5), Two-Can Publishing) T&N Children's Publishing.

—Ours Vert. 2003. (Little Giants Ser.). (SPA., Illus.). 16p. (J). (gr. -1-k). 5.95 (978-1-58728-180-8(5), Two-Can Publishing) T&N Children's Publishing.

Rotner, Shelley & Kelly, Sheila M. Shades of People. 2010. (ENG., Illus.). 32p. (J). (gr. -1-k). pap. 7.99 (978-0-8234-2305-7(0)) Holiday Hse., Inc.

—Shades of People. Rotner, Shelley, photos by. 2009. (ENG., Illus.). 32p. (J). (gr. -1-k). 17.95 (978-0-8234-2191-6(0)) Holiday Hse., Inc.

Rowles, Louis. Ida Claire Decorates with Flair. Brownlee, Sunny, illus. 2004. 24p. (J). pap. (978-0-9708748-1-8(2)) Rowles, Louis.

Rubinger, Ami. I Dream of an Elephant. Rubinger, Ami, illus. 2010. (ENG., Illus.). 28p. (J). (gr. k-k). 13.95 (978-0-7892-1058-6(4), Abbeville Kids) Abbeville Pr., Inc.

Ruffenach, Jessie, ed. Baby Learns about Colors. Thomas, Peter, tr. from NAV. Blacksheep, Beverly, illus. 2004. (ENG & NAV.). 16p. (J). (gr. -1-12). 7.95 (978-1-893354-48-7(2)) Salina Bookshelf Inc.

Rusch, Elizabeth. A Day with No Crayons. Cameron, Chad, illus. 2007. (ENG.). 32p. (J). (gr. -1-3). 15.95 (978-0-87358-910-9(6)) Cooper Square Publishing Llc.

Saltzberg, Barney. Redbird: Colors, Colors, Everywhere! 2015. (ENG., Illus.). 22p. (J). bds. 5.95 (978-0-7611-8185-9(7)) Workman Publishing Co., Inc.

Salzano, Tammi. One Rainy Day. Wood, Hannah, illus. 2011. (ENG.). 24p. (J). (gr. -1-k). bds. 8.95 (978-1-58925-860-0(6)) Tiger Tales.

SAMi. Flip-a-Face: Colors. (J). bds. 8.95 (978-1-59354-137-8(6)) Blue Apple Bks.

Sandall, Ellie. Daisy Plays Hide-and-Seek. Sandall, Ellie, illus. 2012. (ENG., Illus.). 32p. (J). (gr. -1-k). pap. 8.99 (978-1-4052-5457-1(2)) Egmont Bks., Ltd. GBR. Dist: Independent Pubs. Group.

Sanders, Roy E. Land of Pink. Patzelt, Kasie, illus. 2007. (Not So Far Ago Ser.). 37p. (J). (gr. -1-3). 19.99 (978-1-59879-327-7(6)) Lifevest Publishing, Inc.

Sargent, Daina. Colors & the Number 10, 11 vols. Lenoir, Jane, illus. 2004. (Learn to Read Ser.: 11). 24p. (J). pap. 10.95 (978-1-59381-049-8(0)); per. 9.95 (978-1-59381-527-1(1)) Ozark Publishing.

—Colors & the Number 1/Los Colores y el Número 1, 11 vols. Lenoir, Jane, illus. 2004. (Learn to Read Ser.: 11). (SPA & ENG.). 24p. (J). pap. 10.95 (978-1-59381-129-7(2)) Ozark Publishing.

—Colors & the Number 2, 11 vols. Lenoir, Jane, illus. 2004. (Learn to Read Ser.: 11). 24p. (J). per. 10.95 (978-1-59381-529-5(8)) Ozark Publishing.

—Colors & the Number 2/Los Colores y el Número 2, 11 vols. Lenoir, Jane, illus. 2004. (Learn to Read Ser.: 11).Tr. of Los colores y el Nùmero 2. (SPA & ENG.). 24p. (J). pap. 10.95 (978-1-59381-131-0(4)); lib. bdg. 20.95 (978-1-59381-130-3(6)) Ozark Publishing.

—Colors & the Number 3, 11 vols. Lenoir, Jane, illus. 2004. (Learn to Read Ser.: 11). 24p. (J). pap. 10.95 (978-1-59381-530-1(1)); pap. 10.95 (978-1-59381-035-1(0)) Ozark Publishing.

—Colors & the Number 3/Los Colores y el Número 3, 11 vols. Lenoir, Jane, illus. 2004. (Learn to Read Ser.: 11).Tr. of Los colores y el el Nùmero 3. (SPA & ENG.). 24p. (J). pap. 10.95 (978-1-59381-133-4(0)); lib. bdg. 20.95 (978-1-59381-132-7(2)) Ozark Publishing.

—Colors & the Number 4, 11 vols. Lenoir, Jane, illus. 2004. (Learn to Read Ser.: 11). 24p. (J). per. 10.95 (978-1-59381-531-8(X)) Ozark Publishing.

—Colors & the Number 4/Los colores y el Número 4, 11 vols. Lenoir, Jane, illus. 2004. (Learn to Read Ser.: 11).Tr. of Los colores y el Número 4. (SPA & ENG.). 24p. (J). pap. 10.95 (978-1-59381-135-8(7)); lib. bdg. 20.95 (978-1-59381-134-1(9)) Ozark Publishing.

—Colors & the Number 5, 11 vols. Lenoir, Jane, illus. 2004. (Learn to Read Ser.: 11). 24p. (J). pap. 10.95 (978-1-59381-039-9(3)); per. 10.95 (978-1-59381-532-5(8)) Ozark Publishing.

—Colors & the Number 5/Los colores y el Número 5, 11 vols. Lenoir, Jane, illus. 2004. (Learn to Read Ser.: 11).Tr. of Los colores y el Número 5. (SPA & ENG.). 24p. (J). pap. 10.95 (978-1-59381-137-2(3)); lib. bdg. 20.95 (978-1-59381-136-5(5)) Ozark Publishing.

—Colors & the Number 6, 11 vols. Lenoir, Jane, illus. 2004. (Learn to Read Ser.: 11). 24p. (J). pap. 10.95 (978-1-59381-041-2(5)); per. 10.95 (978-1-59381-533-2(6)) Ozark Publishing.

—Colors & the Number 7, 11 vols. Lenoir, Jane, illus. 2004. (Learn to Read Ser.: 11). 24p. (J). pap. 10.95 (978-1-59381-043-6(1)); per. 10.95 (978-1-59381-534-9(4)) Ozark Publishing.

—Colors & the Number 7/Los Colores y el Número 7, 11 vols. Lenoir, Jane, illus. 2004. (Learn to Read Ser.: 11).Tr. of Los colores y el Número 7. (SPA & ENG.). 24p. (J). pap. 10.95 (978-1-59381-141-9(1)); lib. bdg. 20.95 (978-1-59381-140-2(3)) Ozark Publishing.

—Colors & the Number 8, 11 vols. Lenoir, Jane, illus. 2004. (Learn to Read Ser.: 11). 24p. (J). pap. 10.95 (978-1-59381-045-0(8)) Ozark Publishing.

—Colors & the Number 8/Los Colores y el Número 8, 11 vols. Lenoir, Jane, illus. 2004. (Learn to Read Ser.: 11).Tr. of Los colores y el Número 8. (SPA & ENG.). 24p. (J). pap. 10.95 (978-1-59381-143-3(8)); lib. bdg. 20.95 (978-1-59381-142-6(X)) Ozark Publishing.

—Colors & the Number 9, 11 vols. Lenoir, Jane, illus. 2004. (Learn to Read Ser.: 11). 24p. (J). pap. 10.95 (978-1-59381-047-4(4)) Ozark Publishing.

—Colors & the Number 9/Los Colores y el Número 9, 11 vols. Lenoir, Jane, illus. 2004. (Learn to Read Ser.: 11).Tr. of Los colores y el Número 9. (SPA & ENG.). 24p. (J). pap. 10.95 (978-1-59381-145-7(4)); lib. bdg. 20.95 (978-1-59381-144-0(6)) Ozark Publishing.

—Introduction to Colors & Niumbers, 11 vols. Lenoir, Jane, illus. 2005. (Learn to Read Ser.: 11). 24p. (J). pap. 10.95 (978-1-59381-051-1(2)) Ozark Publishing.

—Introduction to Colors & Numbers, 11 vols. Lenoir, Jane, illus. 2005. (Learn to Read Ser.: 11). 24p. (J). per. 10.95 (978-1-59381-528-8(X)) Ozark Publishing.

—Introduction to Colors & Numbers (BL) Introduccion a los colores y a los Numeros, 11 vols. Lenoir, Jane, illus. 2004. (Learn to Read Ser.: 11). (SPA & ENG.). 24p. (J). lib. bdg. 20.95 (978-1-59381-148-8(9)) Ozark Publishing.

Saunders, Katie & Little Bee Books Staff. Color Fun! An Abacus Book. Saunders, Katie, illus. 2015. (Baby Steps Ser.). (ENG., Illus.). 14p. (J). (gr. -1 — 1). bds. 7.99 (978-1-4998-0006-7(1)) Little Bee Books Inc.

Scanlon, Jack. Rainbow Zoo. 2006. (Neighborhood Readers Ser.). (ENG., Illus.). 8p. (gr. -1-3). pap. 5.15 (978-1-4042-6686-5(0), Rosen Classroom) Rosen Publishing Group, Inc., The.

Scarry, Richard. Richard Scarry's All the Colors of Busytown. 2013. (Richard Scarry's Concept Bks.). (ENG.). 18p. (J). (gr. -1 — 1). bds. 7.99 (978-0-7641-6601-3(8)) Barron's Educational Series, Inc.

Schachner, Judy. Color Crazy. Schachner, Judy, illus. 2007. (Skippyjon Jones Ser.). (ENG., Illus.). 12p. (J). (gr. -1 — 1). bds. 6.99 (978-0-525-47782-2(9), Dutton Books for Young Readers) Penguin Young Readers Group.

Scholastic. Peppa's First Colors (Peppa Pig) Eone, illus. 2017. (Peppa Pig Ser.). (ENG.). 10p. (J). (gr. -1-k). bds. 7.99 **(978-1-338-18257-6(9))** Scholastic, Inc.

Scholastic, Inc. Staff. My First Book of Colors. 2016. (Scholastic Early Learners Ser.). (ENG.). 14p. (J). (gr. -1 — 1). bds. 6.99 (978-0-545-90341-7(6)) Scholastic, Inc.

Scholastic, Inc. Staff, contrib. by. Red Pepper, Yellow Squash: A Book of Colors. 2014. (Rookie Toddler(r) Ser.). (ENG.). 12p. (J). bds. 6.95 (978-0-531-20917-2(2)) Scholastic Library Publishing.

Schwartz, Betty & Seresin, Lynn. You're It, Little Red Fish! A Back-And-Forth Color Book. Powell, Luciana Navarro, illus. 2015. (J). (978-1-62370-235-9(6)) Capstone Young Readers of Coughlan Cos.

Scott, Eric. The Day the Rainbow Ended. 2013. 90p. pap. 7.99 (978-1-78333-419-3(3)) Acorn Bks.

Seeger, Laura Vaccaro. Green. 2014. (KOR.). 36p. (J). (978-89-7938-085-9(2)) Dasan Publishing Hse.

—Green. Seeger, Laura Vaccaro, illus. 2012. (ENG., Illus.). 36p. (J). (gr. -1-1). 16.99 (978-1-59643-397-7(3), 9781596433977) Roaring Brook Pr.

Sergeyeva, Marina. Nikki & Nick Are Great Friends to Pick. Sergeyeva, Marina, illus. 2012. (Illus.). 34p. 19.95 (978-0-9834735-4-1(4)) Leo Publishing.

Seuss, Dr. One Fish, Two Fish, Red Fish, Blue Fish Book & CD, 1 vol. 2005. (Book & CD Ser.). (ENG., Illus.). 64p. (J). (gr. -1-2). 9.95 (978-0-375-83497-4(4), Random Hse. Bks. for Young Readers) Random Hse. Children's Bks.

Shannon, George. White Is for Blueberry. Dronzek, Laura, illus. 2005. 40p. (J). (gr. -1). lib. bdg. 17.89 (978-0-06-029276-8(8)) HarperCollins Pubs.

Shannon, George & Shannon. White Is for Blueberry. Dronzek, Laura, illus. 2005. (ENG.). 40p. (J). (gr. -1-3). 17.99 (978-0-06-029275-1(X), Greenwillow Bks.) HarperCollins Pubs.

Sharpe, Jeannie w. Once There Was an Orange Truck. 2005. 37p. (J). 15.95 *(978-0-9763117-0-6(4))* Sharpe, Jeannie W.

Shaw, M. Beatryce. Mr. Browne & the Rose Show: A Child's Perception of "Different" Date not set. 40p. (J). (gr. k-4). pap. 7.95 *(978-1-929234-02-8(3))* Schooner Pubns.

Shea, Therese. Sam's New Shoes. 2006. (Neighborhood Readers Ser.). (ENG.). 8p. (gr. -1-3). pap. 5.15 *(978-1-4042-5651-4(2),* Rosen Classroom) Rosen Publishing Group, Inc., The.

Shepard, C. Lori & the Sky of Colors. 2008. 28p. pap. 24.95 *(978-1-4241-9094-2(0))* America Star Bks.

Shukla, Subir. The Boy Who Loved Colour. Sabnani, Nina, illus. 2004. (ENG & HIN.). (J). *(978-81-8146-042-4(1))* Tulika Pubs.

Shulman, Mark. Foxy Fox. Chambers, Sally, illus. 2004. 8p. (J). bds. 6.95 *(978-1-58925-738-2(3))* Tiger Tales.

Silva, Angel R. Morenit. 2012. 28p. pap. 15.99 *(978-1-4691-7288-0(7))* Xlibris Corp.

Sim, David. Jump Freddy, Jump! Sim, David, illus. 2007. (ENG., Illus.). 12p. (J). (gr. -1-k). 12.99 *(978-1-85707-659-2(1))* Tango Bks. GBR. Dist: Independent Pubs. Group.

Simone, Val Edward. Proton Gator & Friends Coloring Book. McGill, Joshua, illus. 2011. 32p. (J). pap. 5.99 *(978-1-935296-27-0(2))* Morningside Publishing, LLC.

Skotnicki, Jill. Ham & Beans: Have You Seen the Color Green? 2010. 28p. pap. 12.49 *(978-1-4520-6452-9(0))* AuthorHouse.

Smith, Danna. Pirate Nap: A Book of Colors. Petrone, Valeria, illus. 2011. (ENG.). 40p. (J). lib. bdg. 14.99 *(978-0-547-57531-5(9))* Houghton Mifflin Harcourt Publishing Co.

Smythe, Theresa. Chester's Colorful Easter Eggs. Smythe, Theresa, illus. 2013. (ENG., Illus.). 24p. (J). (gr. -1-k). 12.99 *(978-0-8050-9326-1(5),* 9780805093261, Holt, Henry & Co. Bks. For Young Readers) Holt, Henry & Co.

Soundar, Chitra. Chasing the Pot of Gold. Amrein, Paul, illus. 2006. 32p. (J). E-Book 5.00 incl. cd-rom *(978-1-933090-36-8(7))* Guardian Angel Publishing, Inc.

Spencer, Alison Hill. Bird Color. 1 vol. 2013. (Adventure Boardbook Ser.). (ENG.). 22p. (J). (gr. -1-k). bds. 6.95 *(978-1-59193-428-8(1))* Adventure Pubns.

Srinivasan, Divya. Little Owl's Colors. Srinivasan, Divya, illus. 2015. (ENG., Illus.). 18p. (J). (— 1). 5.99 *(978-0-451-47456-8(2),* Viking Books for Young Readers) Penguin Young Readers Group.

Stevens, Rita. Glumpkins. 2004. 28p. pap. 10.99 *(978-1-4116-1281-5(7))* Lulu Pr., Inc.

Stinson, Kathy. Red Is Best. Lewis, Robin Baird, illus. 6th ed. 2011. (ENG.). 26p. (J). (gr. -1 — 1). bds. 7.99 *(978-1-55451-364-2(2),* 9781554513642) Annick Pr., Ltd. CAN. Dist: Publishers Group West (PGW).

Stone, Connie. A Tractor Green Day. Barnes, Garry, illus. 2008. 36p. pap. 24.95 *(978-1-60474-948-9(2))* PublishAmerica, Inc.

Strasser, Stephanie. Blue Bananas. 2010. 28p. pap. 12.49 *(978-1-4490-5327-7(0))* AuthorHouse.

Street, Sesame. Elmo's Guessing Game about Colors/Elmo y Su Juego de Adivinar Los Colores. 2006. (Elmo's Guessing Game about Colors / Elmo y Su Juego de Adivinar Los Colores Ser.). (SPA, ENG & MUL., Illus.). 10p. (J). (gr. -1 — 1). bds. 5.95 *(978-0-87358-905-5(X))* Cooper Square Publishing Llc.

Strom, Maria Diaz. Joe Arco Iris y Yo. Strom, Maria Diaz, illus. 2008.Tr. of Rainbow Joe & Me. (SPA., Illus.). 32p. (J). (gr. -1-3). pap. 9.95 *(978-1-60060-278-8(9))* Lee & Low Bks., Inc.

Studio Mouse Staff. Musical Fun: Colors & Patterns. rev. ed. 2008. (ENG., Illus.). 24p. (J). 4.99 *(978-1-59069-605-7(0))* Studio Mouse LLC.

—Sesame Street Colors & Shapes. 2008. (ENG.). 36p. (J). (gr. -1). 12.99 *(978-1-59069-741-2(3))* Studio Mouse LLC.

Sullivan, Tom. Blue vs. Yellow. Sullivan, Tom, illus. 2017. (Illus.). 48p. (J). (gr. -1-3). 17.99 ***(978-0-06-245295-5(9))*** HarperCollins Pubs.

Sweeney, Monica. How the Crayons Saved the Rainbow. Parker-Thomas, Feronia, illus. 2016. (ENG.). 32p. (J). (gr. -1-k). 16.99 *(978-1-5107-0583-8(X),* Sky Pony Pr.) Skyhorse Publishing Co., Inc.

Tafuri, Nancy. Blue Goose. Tafuri, Nancy, illus. 2010. (Classic Board Bks.). (ENG., Illus.). 34p. (J). (gr. -1 — 1). bds. 7.99 *(978-1-4169-2835-5(9),* Little Simon) Little Simon.

—Blue Goose. Tafuri, Nancy, illus. 2008. (ENG., Illus.). 32p. (J). (gr. -1-3). 17.99 *(978-1-4169-2834-8(0),* Simon & Schuster Bks. For Young Readers) Simon & Schuster Bks. For Young Readers.

Tashiro, Chisato. Chameleon's Colors. Martens, Marianne, tr. from JPN. 2007. (Michael Neugebauer Books Ser.). (ENG., Illus.). 32p. (J). (gr. -1-3). pap. 7.95 *(978-0-7358-2111-8(9))* North-South Bks., Inc.

Tate, Bernice & Tate, Andrew. Zanzy's Purple Cheese & Orange Peas. 2010. 20p. 14.95 *(978-1-4490-9174-3(1))* AuthorHouse.

Telchin, Eric. The Black & White Factory. Funck, Diego, illus. 2016. (ENG.). 40p. (J). (gr. -1-k). 17.99 *(978-1-4998-0277-1(3))* Little Bee Books Inc.

Texier, Ophélie & Baumann, Anne-Sophie. Colors. 2009. (Little Discoveries: Ser.). (ENG., Illus.). 6p. (J). (gr. -1-k). bds. 8.95 *(978-0-7892-0982-5(9),* Abbeville Kids) Abbeville Pr., Inc.

Thaler, Mike. St. Patrick's Day from the Black Lagoon. Lee, Jared, illus. 2011. 61p. (J). *(978-0-545-27328-2(5))* Scholastic, Inc.

Thomas & Friends, Thomas &. Thomas & Friends: Thomas Speeds Along. 2015. (Lift-The-Flap Ser.: 1). (ENG.). 10p. (J). (gr. -1-k). 11.99 *(978-0-7944-3480-9(0),* Reader's Digest Children's Bks.) Studio Fun International.

Thong, Roseanne Greenfield. Green Is a Chile Pepper. 2016. (J). lib. bdg. 18.40 *(978-0-606-39431-4(1))* Turtleback Bks.

—Green Is a Chile Pepper: A Book of Colors. 2014. (Multicultural Shapes & Colors Ser.). (Illus.). 40p. (J). lib. bdg. 28.50 *(978-1-60753-707-6(9))* Amicus Publishing.

—Green Is a Chile Pepper: A Book of Colors. Parra, John, illus. 2014. (ENG & SPA.). 40p. (J). (gr. -1-k). 16.99 *(978-1-4521-0203-0(1))* Chronicle Bks. LLC.

—Red Is a Dragon. Lin, Grace, illus. 2014. 40p. pap. 7.00 *(978-1-61003-333-6(7))* Center for the Collaborative Classroom.

—Red Is a Dragon: A Book of Colors. 2014. (Multicultural Shapes & Colors Ser.). (Illus.). 40p. (J). lib. bdg. 28.50 *(978-1-60753-565-2(3))* Amicus Publishing.

—Red Is a Dragon: A Book of Colors. Lin, Grace, illus. 2008. (ENG.). 40p. (J). (gr. -1-17). pap. 7.99 *(978-0-8118-6481-7(2))* Chronicle Bks. LLC.

Thorpe, Kiki. Dónde Está Boots? - Cuento para Levantar la Tapita. Savitsky, Steven, illus. 2005. (Dora the Explorer Ser.).Tr. of Where Is Boots? - A Lift-the-Flap Story. (SPA.). 16p. (J). pap. 5.99 *(978-1-4169-0621-6(5),* Libros Para Ninos) Libros Para Ninos.

Tierney, Melissa. Elly's True Colors. 2009. 32p. pap. 14.99 *(978-1-4389-3901-8(9))* AuthorHouse.

Tillis, Dionne. Willameana Whitney White & the Magical Butterfly. 2012. 24p. pap. 17.99 *(978-1-4685-7286-5(5))* AuthorHouse.

Top That Publishing Staff, ed. Millie the Millipede: Collects Colors as She Munches Her Way Through the Pages. Elliott, Rebecca, illus. 2007. (Story Book Ser.). 20p. (J). (gr. -1). bds. *(978-1-84666-274-4(5),* Tide Mill Pr.) Top That! Publishing PLC.

Top That! Color Safari (large Version) Parry, Jo, illus. 2007. 10p. (J). (gr. -1). *(978-1-84666-554-7(X),* Tide Mill Pr.) Top That! Publishing PLC.

Treml, Renee. Colour for Curlews. Treml, Renee, illus. 2013. (ENG., Illus.). 32p. (J). (gr. -1). 17.99 *(978-1-74275-921-0(1))* Random Hse. Australia AUS. Dist: Independent Pubs. Group.

Tullet, Hervé. ¡Mezclalo Bien! 2017.Tr. of Couleurs. (ENG & SPA., Illus.). 64p. (J). 15.99 *(978-1-4521-5933-1(5))* Chronicle Bks. LLC.

—Let's Play! 2016. (ENG., Illus.). 68p. (J). (gr. -1-k). 15.99 *(978-1-4521-5477-0(5))* Chronicle Bks. LLC.

—Mix It Up! 2014.Tr. of Couleurs. (ENG., Illus.). 56p. (J). (gr. -1-k). 15.99 *(978-1-4521-3735-3(8))* Chronicle Bks. LLC.

Tullet, Hervé & Perez, Peter L. Presiona Aqui. Perez, Peter L., illus. 2012. (SPA & ENG., Illus.). 56p. (J). (gr. -1-3). 15.99 *(978-1-4521-1287-9(8))* Chronicle Bks. LLC.

Turner, Taquila Lanina. New Friends. 2011. 32p. pap. 21.99 *(978-1-4568-5670-0(7))* Xlibris Corp.

Tusa, Tricia. Follow Me. 2011. (ENG., Illus.). 40p. (J). (gr. -1-3). 16.99 *(978-0-547-27201-6(4))* Houghton Mifflin Harcourt Publishing Co.

Tyson, Delilah Cottingham. Color Us Rainbow. 2012. 24p. pap. 15.99 *(978-1-4797-5711-4(X))* Xlibris Corp.

Ungerer, Tomi. Rufus. 2015. (ENG.). 32p. (gr. -1-2). 16.95 *(978-0-7148-7049-6(8))* Phaidon Pr., Inc.

—Rufus: The Bat Who Loved Colours. 2015. (ENG., Illus.). 32p. 16.95 *(978-0-7148-6972-8(4))* Phaidon Pr., Inc.

Van Fleet, Mara. Little Color Fairies. Van Fleet, Mara, illus. 2012. (ENG., Illus.). 16p. (J). (gr. -1-1). 14.99 *(978-1-4424-3434-9(1),* Simon & Schuster/Paula Wiseman Bks.) Simon & Schuster/Paula Wiseman Bks.

Van Fleet, Matthew. Color Dog. Stanton, Brian, illus. Stanton, Brian, photos by. 2015. (ENG.). 22p. (J). (gr. -1-k). 19.99 *(978-1-4814-4986-1(9),* Simon & Schuster Bks. For Young Readers) Simon & Schuster Bks. For Young Readers.

—Monday the Bullfrog. Van Fleet, Matthew, illus. 2010. (ENG., Illus.). 20p. (J). (gr. -1). 24.99 *(978-1-4424-0958-3(4),* Simon & Schuster/Paula Wiseman Bks.) Simon & Schuster/Paula Wiseman Bks.

Van Fleet, Matthew. Tails. 2017. (ENG., Illus.). 20p. (J). (— 1). 14.99 ***(978-1-328-88685-9(9),*** HMH Books For Young Readers) Houghton Mifflin Harcourt Publishing Co.

van Genechten, Guido. Porque Te Quiero Tanto. 2003. (SPA., Illus.). 28p. (J). (gr. k-3). 15.95 *(978-970-29-0912-5(0))* Santillana USA Publishing Co., Inc.

Van Pelt, Jason. The Color Wheel. 2013. 28p. pap. 24.95 *(978-1-4626-9697-0(X))* America Star Bks.

Venditti, Stacey Marie. Stashi the Rainbow Star: Her Journey Home. Provenzano, Jeannine, illus. 2008. 52p. pap. 24.95 *(978-1-60474-786-7(2))* America Star Bks.

Vetsch, Rita Kaye. The Many Colors of Friendship. 2009. 40p. pap. 16.50 *(978-1-60693-756-3(1),* Eloquent Bks.) Strategic Book Publishing & Rights Agency (SBPRA).

Vilarrubias, Pia. KIKO SALE DEL LIBRO. (SPA.). 36p. 11.95 *(978-84-207-1252-9(3))* Grupo Anaya, S.A. ESP. Dist: Distribooks, Inc.

Vision, Mutiya & Vision, David. The Land of Expression. Alcantara, Ignacio, illus. 2009. (ENG.). 48p. 15.00 *(978-0-9816254-0-9(1))* Von Curtis Publishing.

Walsh, Ellen Stoll. Mouse Paint: Lap-Sized Board Book. 2006. (ENG., Illus.). 15p. (J). (gr. k — 1). bds. 11.99 *(978-0-15-205533-2(9))* Houghton Mifflin Harcourt Publishing Co.

—Mouse Paint - Pintura de Ratón. 2010. (ENG & SPA., Illus.). 30p. (J). (gr. k — 1). bds. 4.99 *(978-0-547-33332-8(3))* Houghton Mifflin Harcourt Publishing Co.

Walters, Jennifer Marino. Amazing Autumn. Nez, John, illus. 2016. (Seasons Ser.). (ENG.). 24p. (J). (gr. -1-1). pap. 6.99 *(978-1-63440-120-3(4))* Red Chair Pr.

Warner, Carl. A World of Food: Discover Magical Lands Made of Things You Can Eat! 2012. (ENG., Illus.). 32p. (J). (gr. k-2). 18.95 *(978-1-4197-0162-7(2),* Abrams Bks. for Young Readers) Abrams, Inc.

Warren, Donna E. Colors of the Rainbow. 2011. 26p. pap. 12.00 *(978-1-61204-318-0(6),* Eloquent Bks.) Strategic Book Publishing & Rights Agency (SBPRA).

Watsuki, Nobuhiro. Busou Renkin Vol. 2: Fade to Black. (Illus.). 203p. (YA). pap. *(978-4-08-873567-0(0))* Shuei-Sha.

Watt, Fiona. Hide-and-Seek Dragons. Fiorin, Fabiano, illus. 2007. (Touchy-Feely Flap Bks). 10p. (J). (gr. -1-k). bds. 16.99 *(978-0-7945-1590-4(8),* Usborne) EDC Publishing.

Weeks, Sarah. Counting Ovejas. Diaz, David, illus. 2006. (ENG & SPA.). 40p. (J). (gr. -1-2). 18.99 *(978-0-689-86750-7(6),* Atheneum Bks. for Young Readers) Simon & Schuster Children's Publishing.

—Who's under That Hat? A Lift-the-Flap Pop-up Adventure. Carter, David A., illus. 2006. 14p. (J). (gr. -1-2). 14.00 *(978-1-4223-5440-7(7))* DIANE Publishing Co.

Wellington, Monica. Colors for Zena. 2013. (ENG., Illus.). 32p. (J). (gr. -1-k). 16.99 *(978-0-8037-3743-3(2),* Dial Bks) Penguin Young Readers Group.

Weston Woods Staff, creator. Mr. Rabbit & the Lovely Present. 2011. 18.95 *(978-0-439-72859-1(2));* 38.75 *(978-0-439-72860-7(6))* Weston Woods Studios, Inc.

—Mr Rabbit & the Lovely Present. 2011. 29.95 *(978-0-439-73502-5(5))* Weston Woods Studios, Inc.

—Planting a Rainbow. 2011. 18.95 *(978-0-439-80643-5(7));* 38.75 *(978-0-439-80645-9(3));* 29.95 *(978-0-439-80436-3(1))* Weston Woods Studios, Inc.

Widdowson, Kay, illus. Please, Mr. Crocodile. 2006. (Lift-the-Flap Books (Child's Play) Ser.). (ENG.). 24p. (J). (gr. -1-1). *(978-1-84643-025-1(9))* Child's Play International Ltd.

Wilcox, Michael. Colors Around Us. Barber, Julia, illus. 2004. 32p. (J). per. 19.95 *(978-1-931780-32-2(3))* School of Color Publishing.

—What Is Color. 2004. (Illus.). 32p. (J). per. 19.95 *(978-1-931780-31-5(5))* School of Color Publishing.

Wildsmith, Brian. Animal Colors. Wildsmith, Brian, illus. 2004. (PER., Illus.). 16p. (J). bds. 4.99 *(978-1-932065-42-8(3))* Star Bright Bks., Inc.

Williams, S. L. Polka-Dot Maddy's Birthday Fun: Colors of the Rainbow. 2008. 36p. pap. 24.95 *(978-1-60672-908-3(X))* America Star Bks.

Williams, Sue. I Went Walking. Vivas, Julie, illus. 2014. 32p. pap. 27.00 *(978-1-61003-230-8(6))* Center for the Collaborative Classroom.

—I Went Walking. Vivas, Julie, illus. 2004. (J). (gr. -1-2). audio compact disk 28.95 *(978-1-59112-720-8(3))* 2003. pap. 39.95 incl. audio compact disk *(978-1-59112-721-5(1))* Live Oak Media.

Williamson, Rose. Look at Me! Look at Me! Marts, Doreen, illus. 2014. (ENG.). 32p. (J). (gr. -1-k). 16.95 *(978-1-62914-617-1(X),* Sky Pony Pr.) Skyhorse Publishing Co., Inc.

Wilson, Karma. Bear Sees Colors. Chapman, Jane, illus. 2014. (Bear Bks.). (ENG.). 32p. (J). (gr. -1-2). 16.99 *(978-1-4424-6536-7(0),* McElderry, Margaret K. Bks.) McElderry, Margaret K. Bks.

Windsor, Herbert C. The Colour Monster. 2009. (Illus.). 32p. pap. 12.99 *(978-1-4490-1056-0(3))* AuthorHouse.

Wolff, Ashley. Baby Bear Sees Blue. Wolff, Ashley, illus. 2012. (Baby Bear Ser.). (ENG., Illus.). 40p. (J). (gr. -1-1). 17.99 *(978-1-4424-1306-1(9),* Beach Lane Bks.) Beach Lane Bks.

Written By Dana Wright; Illustrated By S. Crazy Pants. 2011. 20p. pap. 24.95 *(978-1-4626-3469-9(9))* America Star Bks.

Yang, Belle. Summertime Rainbow: A Mandarin Chinese-English Bilingual Book of Colors. Yang, Belle, illus. 2012. (ENG & CHI., Illus.). 22p. (J). (gr. k — 1). bds. 6.99 *(978-0-7636-5280-7(6))* Candlewick Pr.

Yates, Gene, illus. The Chameleon Colors Book. 2006. (J). *(978-1-58865-361-1(7))* Kidsbooks, LLC.

Ying, Jonathan. Not Quite Black & White. Ying, Victoria, illus. 2016. 32p. (J). (gr. -1-3). 14.99 *(978-0-06-238066-1(4))* HarperCollins Pubs.

Yolen, Jane. ¿Cómo Aprenden los Colores los Dinosaurios? Teague, Mark, illus. 2006. (How Do Dinosaurs... Ser.).Tr. of How Do Dinosaurs Learn Their Colors? (SPA.). 12p. (J). (gr. -1-k). bds. 6.99 *(978-0-439-87192-1(1),* Scholastic en Espanol) Scholastic, Inc.

—How Do Dinosaurs Learn Their Colors? Teague, Mark, illus. 2006. (How Do Dinosaurs... Ser.). (ENG.). 12p. (J). (gr. -1-k). bds. 6.99 *(978-0-439-85653-9(1),* Blue Sky Pr., The) Scholastic, Inc.

Yoon, Salina. Kaleidoscope. 2012. (ENG.). 18p. (J). (gr. -1-17). bds. 12.99 *(978-0-316-18641-4(4))* Little, Brown Bks. for Young Readers.

Yost-Filgate, Susan. Jesse's Book of Colors. Filgate, Leonard, illus. 2009. (ENG.). 22p. (J). (gr. -1-12). bds. 7.95 *(978-1-934960-43-1(8),* Raven Tree Pr.,Csi) Continental Sales, Inc.

Young, Jessica. My Blue Is Happy. Chien, Catia, illus. 2013. (ENG.). 32p. (J). (gr. -1-3). 15.99 *(978-0-7636-5125-1(7))* Candlewick Pr.

Yoyo. Toddler's First Puzzle Fun — Blue. 2005. 96p. pap. *(978-90-5843-615-3(2))* YoYo Bks.

—Toddler's First Puzzle Fun — Green. 2005. 96p. pap. *(978-90-5843-614-6(4))* YoYo Bks.

—Toddler's First Puzzle Fun — Red. 2005. 96p. pap. *(978-90-5843-613-9(6))* YoYo Bks.

—Toddler's First Puzzle Fun — Yellow. 2005. 96p. pap. *(978-90-5843-616-0(0))* YoYo Bks.

Zabel, Vivian. I Like Pink. Nielson, Ginger, illus. 2013. 28p. pap. 12.99 *(978-0-9889617-1-5(7))* 4RV Publishing, LLC.

Zipf, Sean. What Color Is Spring? Antkowski, Marygrace, illus. 2008. 36p. pap. 24.95 *(978-1-60703-005-8(5))* America Star Bks.

Zuravicky, Orli. A Color for Sketch: A Book about Colors. Castellano, Giuseppe, illus. 2011. (Mister Doodle Ser.). (ENG.). 34p. (J). (gr. -1-k). bds. 7.99 *(978-1-4424-3154-6(7),* Little Simon) Little Simon.

COLOR—POETRY

Casher, Debby Lightman. Color Doodles. 2010. 16p. 11.99 *(978-1-4520-7493-1(3))* AuthorHouse.

Novoa, Teresa, illus. Rojo. (Cocorolos Ser.). (SPA.). 12p. (J). (gr. -1-k). bds. 7.95 *(978-84-294-6921-9(4))* Santillana USA Publishing Co., Inc.

Radmanovic, Rada. Color Me Trendy. Radmanovic, Ljubica, illus. 2010. 68p. pap. 14.99 *(978-1-4520-5795-8(8))* AuthorHouse.

Sidman, Joyce. Red Sings from Treetops: A Year in Colors. Zagarenski, Pamela, illus. 2009. (ENG.). 32p. (J). (gr. -1-3). 17.99 *(978-0-547-01494-4(5))* Houghton Mifflin Harcourt Publishing Co.

—Red Sings from Treetops: A Year in Colors. 2010. (J). 38.75 *(978-1-4498-2608-6(3));* 36.75 *(978-1-4498-2606-2(7));* 36.75 *(978-1-4498-2610-9(5));* 184.75 *(978-1-4498-2605-5(9))* Recorded Bks., Inc.

Tugeau, Jeremy, illus. Seeing Colors with Mother Goose. 1 vol. 2011. (Mother Goose Nursery Rhymes Ser.). (ENG.). 32p. (gr. -1-2). 28.50 *(978-1-61641-146-6(5),* Looking Glass Library) ABDO Publishing Co.

COLOR ETCHINGS

see Prints

COLOR OF ANIMALS

see Animals—Color

COLOR OF MAN

see Human Skin Color

COLORADO

Altman, Linda Jacobs & Fitzgerald, Stephanie. Colorado. 2014. (It's My State! (r) Ser.). (Illus.). 80p. (J). (gr. 4-8). lib. bdg. 34.21 *(978-1-62712-482-9(9))* Cavendish Square Publishing.

Barker, Jane Valentine. Trappers & Traders. Downing, Sybil, ed. (Colorado Heritage Ser.). (Illus.). 36p. (J). (gr. k-6). reprint ed. pap. 6.95 *(978-1-878611-03-1(8))* Silver Rim Pr.

Barker, Jane Valentine & Downing, Sybil. Mountain Treasures. (Colorado Heritage Ser.). (Illus.). 44p. (J). (gr. k-6). reprint ed. pap. 7.95 *(978-1-878611-01-7(1))* Silver Rim Pr.

Bledsoe, Sara. Colorado. 2012. (J). lib. bdg. 25.26 *(978-0-7613-4524-4(8),* Lerner Pubns.) Lerner Publishing Group.

Boys & Girls Club of Downtown Toronto Staff. C Is for Colorado. 2012. (See My State Ser.). (ENG., Illus.). 32p. (J). (gr. -1-3). 14.99 *(978-0-88240-776-0(7),* West Winds Pr.) Graphic Arts Ctr. Publishing Co.

Deady, Kathleen W. Colorado. 2006. (Portraits of the States Ser.). (Illus.). 32p. (gr. 2-6). pap. 10.50 *(978-0-8368-4681-2(8));* lib. bdg. 26.00 *(978-0-8368-4662-1(1))* Stevens, Gareth Publishing LLLP. (Gareth Stevens Learning Library).

Elish, Dan & Ayer, Eleanor. Colorado. 2nd rev. ed. 2005. (Celebrate the States Ser.). (Illus.). 144p. (gr. 6-7). lib. bdg. 42.79 *(978-0-7614-2019-4(3),* Benchmark Bks.) Marshall Cavendish Corp.

Feinstein, Stephen. Colorado: A MyReportLinks.com Book. 2003. (States Ser.). (Illus.). 48p. (J). (gr. 4-10). lib. bdg. 25.26 *(978-0-7660-5029-7(7),* MyReportLinks.com Bks.) Enslow Pubs., Inc.

Finn, Denny Von. Stanley Hotel. 2013. (Scariest Places on Earth Ser.). (ENG., Illus.). 24p. (J). (gr. 3-7). lib. bdg. 25.95 *(978-1-60014-950-4(2),* Torque Bks.) Bellwether Media.

Frisch, Nate. Rocky Mountains National Park: Preserving America. 2016. (Preserving America Ser.). (ENG.). 48p. (J). (gr. 5-9). pap. 12.00 *(978-1-62832-182-1(2),* Creative Paperbacks) Creative Co., The.

Gish, Steven, et al. Ethiopia. 2nd rev. ed. 2006. (Cultures of the World Ser.). (Illus.). 144p. (gr. 6-7). lib. bdg. 42.79 *(978-0-7614-2025-5(8),* Benchmark Bks.) Marshall Cavendish Corp.

Justesen, Kim Williams. Hey Ranger! Kids Ask Questions about Rocky Mountain National Park. Newhouse, Judy, illus. 2005. (Hey Ranger! Ser.). (ENG.). 48p. (J). (gr. -1-12). pap. 9.95 *(978-0-7627-3848-9(0),* Falcon Guides) Globe Pequot Pr., The.

Kirchner, Jason. Colorado. 2016. (States Ser.). (ENG., Illus.). 32p. (gr. 3-4). lib. bdg. 27.32 *(978-1-5157-0392-1(4))* Next Page Pr., The.

Lowery, Linda & Porter, Janice Lee. Tia Clara Brown. 2005. (Yo Solo (On My Own) Ser.).Tr. of Aunt Clara Brown. (SPA., Illus.). 48p. (J). (gr. 2-5). 23.93 *(978-0-8225-3128-9(3),* Ediciones Lerner) Lerner Publishing Group.

Marsh, Carole. Colorado Current Events Projects: 30 Cool, Activities, Crafts, Experiments & More for Kids to Do to Learn about Your State! 2003. (Colorado Experience Ser.). 32p. (gr. k-8). pap. 5.95 *(978-0-635-02025-3(4),* Marsh, Carole Bks.) Gallopade International.

—The Colorado Experience Pocket Guide. 2004. (Colorado Experience! Ser.). (Illus.). 96p. (J). (gr. 3-8). pap. 6.95 *(978-0-7933-9602-3(6))* Gallopade International.

—Colorado Geography Projects: 30 Cool, Activities, Crafts, Experiments & More for Kids to Do to Learn about Your State! 2003. (Colorado Experience Ser.). 32p. (gr. k-5). pap. 5.95 *(978-0-635-01825-0(X),* Marsh, Carole Bks.) Gallopade International.

—Colorado Government Projects: 30 Cool, Activities, Crafts, Experiments & More for Kids to Do to Learn about Your State! 2003. (Colorado Experience Ser.). 32p. (gr. k-5). pap. 5.95 *(978-0-635-01925-7(6),* Marsh, Carole Bks.) Gallopade International.

—Colorado Jeopardy! Answers & Questions about Our State! 2004. (Colorado Experience! Ser.). (Illus.). 32p. (J). (gr. 3-8). pap. 7.95 *(978-0-7933-9604-7(2))* Gallopade International.

—Colorado "Jography" A Fun Run Thru Our State! 2004. (Colorado Experience! Ser.). 32p. (J). (gr. 3-8). pap. 7.95 *(978-0-7933-9605-4(0))* Gallopade International.

—Colorado People Projects: 30 Cool, Activities, Crafts, Experiments & More for Kids to Do to Learn about Your State! 2003. (Colorado Experience Ser.). 32p. (gr. k-5). pap. 5.95 *(978-0-635-01975-2(2),* Marsh, Carole Bks.) Gallopade International.

—Colorado Symbols & Facts Projects: 30 Cool, Activities, Crafts, Experiments & More for Kids to Do to Learn about Your State! 2003. (Colorado Experience Ser.). 32p. (gr. k-5). pap. 5.95 *(978-0-635-01874-8(8),* Marsh, Carole Bks.) Gallopade International.

—Colorado's Big Activity Book. 2004. (Colorado Experience! Ser.). (Illus.). 96p. (J). (gr. 2-6). pap. 9.95 *(978-0-7933-9606-1(9))* Gallopade International.

—The Cool Colorado Coloring Book. 2004. (Colorado Experience! Ser.). (Illus.). 32p. (J). (gr. k-2). pap. 3.95 *(978-0-7933-9607-8(7))* Gallopade International.

—My First Book about Colorado. 2004. (Colorado Experience! Ser.). (Illus.). 32p. (J). (gr. k-4). pap. 7.95 *(978-0-7933-9603-0(4))* Gallopade International.

Maynard, Charles W. Zebulon Pike: Soldier-Explorer of the American Southwest. 2009. (Famous Explorers of the American West Ser.). 24p. (gr. 3-4). 42.50 *(978-1-61512-506-7(X),* PowerKids Pr.) Rosen Publishing Group, Inc., The.

Murray, Julie. Colorado. 1 vol. 2006. (Buddy Book Ser.). (ENG., Illus.). 32p. (gr. k-4). 27.07 *(978-1-59197-665-3(0),* Buddy Bks.) ABDO Publishing Co.

Obregon, Jose Maria. Colorado. 2005. (Bilingual Library of the United States of America Ser.: Set 1). (ENG & SPA., Illus.). 32p. (J). (gr. 3-6). lib. bdg. 25.25 *(978-1-4042-3070-5(X))* Rosen Publishing Group, Inc., The.

Obregón, José María. Colorado. 2009. (Bilingual Library of the United States of America Ser.). (ENG & SPA.). 32p. (gr. 2-2). 47.90 *(978-1-60853-346-6(8),* Editorial Buenas Letras) Rosen Publishing Group, Inc., The.

Olhoff, Jim. Colorado. 1 vol. 2009. (United States Ser.). (ENG., Illus.). 48p. (YA). (gr. 2-5). 27.07 *(978-1-60453-641-6(1))* ABDO Publishing Co.

O'Neill, Elizabeth. Alfred Visits Colorado. 2007. (Illus.). 24p. (J). pap. 12.00 *(978-0-9790240-4-7(8))* Global Business Information Strategies, Inc.

Payne, Christine N. Kid Places in Colorado Springs. 2003. (J). spiral bd. 8.95 *(978-0-9740643-0-7(0))* Payne, Christine.
Perry, Phyllis J. Colorado Fun: Activities for on the Road & at Home. Tarr, Lisa M., illus. 2007. 80p. (J). (gr. 1-7). pap. 12.95 *(978-1-55566-402-2(4),* Johnson Bks.) Bower Hse.
Peterson, Sheryl. Colorado. 2008. (This Land Called America Ser.). 32p. (YA). (gr. 3-6). 22.95 *(978-1-58341-621-0(5))* Creative Co., The.
Quasha, Jennifer. How to Draw Colorado's Sights & Symbols. 2009. (Kid's Guide to Drawing America Ser.). 32p. (gr. k-k). 50.50 *(978-1-61511-050-6(X),* PowerKids Pr.) Rosen Publishing Group, Inc., The.
Somervill, Barbara A. Colorado. 2014. (America the Beautiful Ser.: 3). (ENG.). 144p. (J). lib. bdg. 40.00 *(978-0-531-24878-2(X))* Scholastic Library Publishing.
Spotlight on Colorado. 2015. (Spotlight on Colorado Ser.). (ENG.). 32p. (J). (gr. 4-5). pap., pap., pap. 900.00 *(978-1-4994-1605-3(9),* PowerKids Pr.) Rosen Publishing Group, Inc., The.
Trumbull, Jamie. Barney Ford: Pioneer Businessman. 2010. (ENG & SPA., Illus.). 50p. (J). pap. 8.95 *(978-0-86541-115-9(8))* Filter Pr., LLC.
Walker, Cynthia. Colorado. Hamilton, Harriet, tr. 2006. (Rookie Espanol: Geografia: Estados (Geography: States) Ser.). (SPA., Illus.). 32p. (J). (gr. k-2). per. 5.95 *(978-0-516-25045-8(0),* Children's Pr.) Scholastic Library Publishing.
Walsh, Steve. Enos Mills: Rocky Mountain Conservationist. 2011. (ENG & SPA., Illus.). 64p. (J). pap. 8.95 *(978-0-86541-122-7(0))* Filter Pr., LLC.
Wyner, Zach. Denver Nuggets. 2014. (On the Hardwood Ser.). (gr. 3-8). pap. 8.95 *(978-1-61570-905-2(3))* Scobre Pr. Corp.
Zeiger, Jennifer. Colorado. 2017. (True Book — My United States Ser.). (ENG.). 48p. (J). pap. 7.95 ***(978-0-531-23283-5(2))***; lib. bdg. 31.00 ***(978-0-531-25253-6(1))*** Scholastic Library Publishing. (Children's Pr.).

COLORADO—FICTION

Alger, Horatio. Do & Dare: Or, A Brave Boy's Fight for Fortune. 2006. 182p. pap. 19.99 *(978-1-4264-0880-9(3))*; 170p. pap. 21.99 *(978-1-4264-0861-8(7))* Creative Media Partners, LLC.
—Do & Dare: Or, A Brave Boy's Fight for Fortune. 2006. pap. *(978-1-4065-0701-0(6))* Dodo Pr.
Anderson, Renae. Upon the Heads of the Children. 2009. 236p. 25.75 *(978-1-60860-483-8(7),* Strategic Bk. Publishing) Strategic Book Publishing & Rights Agency (SBPRA).
Anderson, T. Neill. Horrors of History: Massacre of the Miners. 2015. (ENG., Illus.). 144p. (YA). (gr. 7). lib. bdg. 16.95 *(978-1-58089-520-0(4))* Charlesbridge Publishing, Inc.
Archer, Jennifer. The Shadow Girl. 2013. (ENG.). 336p. (YA). (gr. 8). pap. 9.99 *(978-0-06-183460-8(2),* HarperTeen) HarperCollins Pubs.
Ashman, Linda. The Twelve Days of Christmas in Colorado. 2011. (Twelve Days of Christmas in America Ser.). (ENG., Illus.). 40p. (J). (gr. k-3). 12.95 *(978-1-4027-7463-8(X))* Sterling Publishing Co., Inc.
Atkinson, Elizabeth. Lisa's Totally Unforgettable Winter. 2006. (ENG.). 56p. per. 16.95 *(978-1-4241-6249-9(1))* America Star Bks.
Avi. The Good Dog. 2003. (ENG.). 256p. (J). (gr. 3-7). mass mkt. 7.99 *(978-0-689-83825-5(5),* Atheneum Bks. for Young Readers) Simon & Schuster Children's Publishing.
—Prairie School. Farnsworth, Bill, illus. 2003. (I Can Read Level 4 Ser.). (ENG.). 48p. (J). (gr. 3-4). pap. 3.99 *(978-0-06-051318-4(7))* HarperCollins Pubs.
—Prairie School. Farnsworth, Bill, illus. 2003. (I Can Read Bks.). 47p. (gr. 3-7). 14.00 *(978-0-7569-1452-3(4))* Perfection Learning Corp.
—The Secret School. 2003. (ENG., Illus.). 176p. (J). (gr. 2-5). pap. 7.99 *(978-0-15-204699-6(2),* 53582853) Houghton Mifflin Harcourt Publishing Co.
—The Secret School. 2003. 157p. (J). (gr. 3-7). 13.60 *(978-0-7569-1625-1(9))* Perfection Learning Corp.
Aviation Publications Staff & National Geographic Learning Staff. Hard Gold: The Colorado Gold Rush of 1859. 2010. (Rise & Shine Ser.). (ENG.). 240p. (C). (gr. 3-7). pap. 10.95 *(978-1-4231-0520-6(6))* National Geographic School Publishing, Inc.
Barbour, Ralph Henry. The Lilac Girl. 2006. (Illus.). pap. *(978-1-4065-0778-2(4))* Dodo Pr.
Barker, Jane Valentine. Building Up. pap. 7.95 *(978-1-878611-07-9(0))* Silver Rim Pr.
Barker, Jane Valentine & Downing, Sybil. Colorado Heritage Series, 10 vols., Set. (Illus.). (J). (gr. -1-8). reprint ed. pap. 9.50 *(978-1-878611-00-0(3))* Silver Rim Pr.
Barone, Michelle. Out of the Ordinary. (Adventures in History Ser.). 120p. 2004. (Illus.). (J). pap. *(978-1-932663-08-2(8))* 2nd ed. 2005. (ENG.). (YA). pap. 9.95 *(978-1-932663-10-5(X))* History Compass, LLC.
Bezek, Lyn. Daisy: The Cripple Creek Donkey. 2004. (J). pap. 7.95 *(978-1-932738-09-4(6))* Western Reflections Publishing Co.
—Ribbon the Border Collie: From Herder to Healer. 2008. (J). pap. 11.95 *(978-1-932738-51-3(7))* Western Reflections Publishing Co.
Biggs, Suzanne K. Charlie Christmas. 2012. 124p. (gr. 4-6). 20.95 *(978-1-4759-4157-9(9))*; pap. 10.95 *(978-1-4759-4155-5(2))* iUniverse, Inc.
Bjornson, Nancy. Mustangs, Fires & Snakes. 2007. (J). *(978-1-930596-84-9(7))* Amherst Pr.
Blake, Christine & Lopez, Jill. Signs, Signs, Everywhere Signs. 2008. 32p. pap. 15.95 *(978-1-4327-2523-5(8))* Outskirts Pr., Inc.
Blanchet, Deborah A. The Hat. 2009. 122p. 29.99 *(978-1-4415-4624-1(3))*; pap. 19.99 *(978-1-4415-4623-4(5))* Xlibris Corp.
Blizzard: Colorado 1886. 2014. (Survivors Ser.). (ENG., Illus.). 160p. (J). (gr. 3-7). pap. 6.99 *(978-1-4814-0969-8(7),* Aladdin) Simon & Schuster Children's Publishing.
Bollback, Anthony G. Rescue at Cripple Creek. 2012. 178p. pap. 8.99 *(978-0-9849359-3-2(2))* Finding the Cause, LLC.
Bouse, Susan & Gamble, Adam. Good Night Denver. Veno, Joe, illus. 2007. (Good Night Our World Ser.). (ENG.). 20p. (J). (gr. k — 1). bds. 9.95 *(978-1-60219-006-1(2))* Good Night Bks.
Bowen, Carl. Hot Spot. Lee, Marc, illus. 2016. (Firestormers Ser.). (ENG.). 112p. (gr. 4-8). lib. bdg. 26.65 *(978-1-4965-3307-4(0))* Stone Arch Bks.
Brown, Lenoard. The Adventure of Paul & Page in Colorado: (Idennital Twins) l.t. ed. 2011. (ENG.). 32p. pap. 12.50 *(978-1-4635-6139-0(3))* CreateSpace Independent Publishing Platform.
Bryant, Annie. Freestyle with Avery. 2009. (Beacon Street Girls Ser.). (ENG.). 240p. (J). (gr. 4-8). pap. 8.99 *(978-1-4169-6435-3(5),* Aladdin) Simon & Schuster Children's Publishing.
Burnham, Niki. Goddess Games. 2008. (ENG.). 256p. (YA). (gr. 9-12). pap. 8.99 *(978-1-4169-2772-3(7),* Simon Pulse) Simon Pulse.
Callies, Debi. Frog Mill. 2008. 20p. pap. 24.95 *(978-1-60703-091-1(8))* America Star Bks.
Colorado, Papa. Nui & Kiwi's Fantastic Adventures. 2011. 70p. pap. 19.95 *(978-1-4626-2806-3(0))* PublishAmerica, Inc.
Covey, Ken. The Adventures of a Little Boy Named Kenny. 2008. 68p. pap. 10.95 *(978-1-4327-3110-6(6))* Outskirts Pr., Inc.
Dahlstrom, S. J. The Elk Hunt: The Adventure Begins. 2013. (Adventures of Wilder Good Ser.). (ENG., Illus.). 110p. (J). (gr. 3). pap. 8.95 *(978-1-58988-087-0(0))* Dry, Paul Bks., Inc.
Danneberg, Julie. Family Reminders. Shelley, John, illus. 2009. (ENG.). 112p. (J). (gr. 3-7). 14.95 *(978-1-58089-320-6(1))* Charlesbridge Publishing, Inc.
Davies, Jocelyn. A Beautiful Dark. (ENG.). (YA). (gr. 8). 2012. 416p. pap. 9.99 *(978-0-06-199066-3(3))* 2011. 400p. 17.99 *(978-0-06-199065-6(5))* HarperCollins Pubs. (HarperTeen).
—A Fractured Light. 2013. (ENG.). 368p. (YA). (gr. 8). pap. 9.99 *(978-0-06-199068-7(X),* HarperTeen) HarperCollins Pubs.
—A Radiant Sky. 2014. (ENG.). 384p. (YA). (gr. 8). pap. 9.99 *(978-0-06-199070-0(1),* HarperTeen) HarperCollins Pubs.
de Gramont, Nina. Meet Me at the River. (ENG., Illus.). 384p. (YA). (gr. 9). 2014. pap. 11.99 *(978-1-4169-8016-2(4),* Atheneum Bks. for Young Readers) 2013. 17.99 *(978-1-4169-8014-8(8))* Simon & Schuster Children's Publishing.
Diller, Janelle. Mystery of the Ballerina Ghost. Turner, Adam, illus. 2013. 104p. (J). pap. 5.99 *(978-1-936376-00-1(8))* WorldTrek Publishing.
Downing, Sybil & Barker, Jane Valentine. Happy Harvest. (Colorado Heritage Ser.). (Illus.). 43p. (J). reprint ed. pap. 7.95 *(978-1-878611-02-4(X))* Silver Rim Pr.
—Mesas to Mountains. (Colorado Heritage Ser.). (Illus.). 47p. (J). (gr. -1-8). reprint ed. pap. 7.95 *(978-1-878611-04-8(6))* Silver Rim Pr.
Du Jardin, Rosamond. Marcy Catches Up. 2003. (YA). pap. 12.95 *(978-1-930009-75-2(5),* 800-691-7779) Image Cascade Publishing.
Duble, Kathleen Benner. Phantoms in the Snow. 2011. (ENG.). 240p. (J). (gr. 7-7). 17.99 *(978-0-545-19770-0(8),* Scholastic Pr.) Scholastic, Inc.
Edwards, Jean E. Adventure Tales: For Kids Who Want to Become Better Readers. 2012. 102p. 24.99 *(978-1-4771-4118-2(9))* Xlibris Corp.
Edwards, Lori. Fire Fawn. 2013. 58p. pap. 8.99 *(978-1-4525-7703-6(X),* Balboa Pr.) Author Solutions, Inc.
Ernst, Kathleen. Whistler in the Dark. 2009. (Mysteries Through Time Ser.). 144 - 176p. (YA). (gr. 4-8). 31.95 *(978-1-60754-429-6(6))*; pap. 15.25 *(978-1-60754-432-6(6))* Windmill Bks.
French, Jennifer. Fidgets. 2007. 132p. pap. 9.95 *(978-1-59663-531-9(2),* Castle Keep Pr.) Rock, James A. & Co. Pubs.
Funk, Rachel. Christabelle in the Museum of Time. 2007. 217p. pap. 14.95 *(978-1-4303-2572-7(0))* Lulu Pr., Inc.
Gamble, Adam & Mackey, Bill. Good Night Colorado. Rosen, Anne, illus. 2012. (Good Night Our World Ser.). (ENG.). 20p. (J). (gr. k — 1). bds. 9.95 *(978-1-60219-055-9(0))* Good Night Bks.
Gerwitz, Felice & Gerwitz, Christina. Dinosaur Quest at Diamond Peak, 3, Vol. 2. 2nd rev. ed. 2007. (Truth Seeker's Mystery Ser.). 208p. (YA). per. 8.99 *(978-1-931941-11-2(4))* Media Angels, Inc.
Gill, J. Duddy. The Secret of Ferrell Savage. Chaghatzbanian, Sonia, illus. (ENG.). 176p. (J). (gr. 3-7). 2015. pap. 7.99 *(978-1-4424-6018-8(0))* 2014. 15.99 *(978-1-4424-6017-1(2))* Simon & Schuster Children's Publishing. (Atheneum Bks. for Young Readers).
Griffin, Lydia. Prunes & Rupe. Hunt, Judith, illus. 2007. 32p. (J). 16.00 *(978-0-86541-086-2(0))* Filter Pr., LLC.
Gulliksen, Anne. The Smartest Dog on the Planet. 2012. 32p. pap. 14.98 *(978-1-4575-0973-5(3))* Dog Ear Publishing, LLC.
Halls, Kelly Milner. Blazing Courage. Parks, Phil, illus. 2015. (ENG.). 96p. (J). (gr. 4-8). lib. bdg. 25.32 *(978-1-4677-7219-8(4))*; (Animal Rescues Ser.: 1). 6.99 *(978-1-4677-8990-5(9))* Lerner Publishing Group. (Darby Creek).
Hamilton, Sable. Free Spirit. 2015. (Stardust Stables Ser.). (ENG.). 160p. (gr. 3-6). lib. bdg. 22.65 *(978-1-4342-9792-1(6))* Stone Arch Bks.
—A Star Is Born. 2015. (Stardust Stables Ser.). (ENG.). 160p. (gr. 3-6). lib. bdg. 22.65 *(978-1-4342-9790-7(X))* Stone Arch Bks.
—Stardust Stables. 2015. (Stardust Stables Ser.). (ENG.). 160p. (gr. 3-6). lib. bdg. 67.95 *(978-1-4965-0112-7(8),* Stardust Stables) Stone Arch Bks.
—Wildfire. 2015. (Stardust Stables Ser.). (ENG.). 160p. (gr. 3-6). lib. bdg. 22.65 *(978-1-4342-9791-4(8))* Stone Arch Bks.
Hancock, H. Irving. The Young Engineers in Colorado. rev. ed. 2006. 212p. 27.95 *(978-1-4218-1744-6(6))*; pap. 12.95 *(978-1-4218-1844-3(2))* 1st World Publishing, Inc. (1st World Library - Literary Society).
—The Young Engineers in Colorado. 2007. 180p. per. *(978-1-4065-1993-8(6))* Dodo Pr.
Henty, George Alfred. In the Heart of the Rockies. l.t. ed. 2006. 322p. pap. 24.99 *(978-1-4264-3253-8(4))* Creative Media Partners, LLC.
—In the Heart of the Rockies. 2004. reprint ed. pap. 27.95 *(978-1-4191-2600-0(8))*; pap. 1.99 *(978-1-4192-2600-7(2))* Kessinger Publishing, LLC.
Hill, Carolyn Swan. A Summer to Remember. 2013. 256p. (YA). (gr. 10-12). pap. 17.99 *(978-1-4624-0543-5(6),* Inspiring Voices) Author Solutions, Inc.
Hoban, Russell. A Birthday for Frances. Hoban, Lillian, illus. 2012. (I Can Read Level 2 Ser.). (ENG.). 48p. (J). (gr. k-3). pap. 3.99 *(978-0-06-083797-6(7))* HarperCollins Pubs.
Howell, Troy. The Dragon of Cripple Creek. 2011. (ENG., Illus.). 400p. (J). (gr. 3-7). 16.95 *(978-0-8109-9713-4(4),* Amulet Bks.) Abrams, Inc.
Jacobs, Lily. The Littlest Bunny in Colorado: An Easter Adventure. 2015. (ENG.). 32p. (J). (-3). 9.99 *(978-1-4926-1057-1(7),* Sourcebooks Jabberwocky) Sourcebooks, Inc.
James, Eric. A Halloween Scare in Colorado. Le Ray, Marina, illus. 2014. (ENG.). 32p. (J). (-5). 9.99 *(978-1-4926-0582-9(4),* 9781492605829, Sourcebooks Jabberwocky) Sourcebooks, Inc.
—Santa's Sleigh Is on Its Way to Colorado. Dunn, Robert, illus. 2015. (ENG.). 32p. (J). (-2). 12.99 *(978-1-4926-2756-2(9),* Sourcebooks Jabberwocky) Sourcebooks, Inc.
Jenkins, Jerry B. & Fabry, Chris. Dead End. 2006. (Red Rock Mysteries Ser.: 15). (ENG.). 248p. (YA). (gr. 3-7). per. 6.99 *(978-1-4143-0154-9(5),* Tyndale Kids) Tyndale Hse. Pubs.
—Double Fault. 2005. (Red Rock Mysteries Ser.: 7). (ENG.). 272p. (YA). pap. 6.99 *(978-1-4143-0146-4(4),* Tyndale Kids) Tyndale Hse. Pubs.
—Hollywood Holdup. 2006. (Red Rock Mysteries Ser.: 12). (ENG.). 224p. (YA). (gr. 8-12). per. 6.99 *(978-1-4143-0151-8(0),* Tyndale Kids) Tyndale Hse. Pubs.
—Instant Menace. 2006. (Red Rock Mysteries Ser.: 9). (ENG.). 256p. (YA). (gr. 3-7). per. 6.99 *(978-1-4143-0148-8(0),* Tyndale Kids) Tyndale Hse. Pubs.
—Phantom Writer. 2005. (Red Rock Mysteries Ser.: 6). (ENG.). 256p. (YA). pap. 5.99 *(978-1-4143-0145-7(6),* Tyndale Kids) Tyndale Hse. Pubs.
—Wind Chill. 2006. (Red Rock Mysteries Ser.: 14). (ENG.). 240p. (YA). (gr. 3-7). per. 6.99 *(978-1-4143-0153-2(7),* Tyndale Kids) Tyndale Hse. Pubs.
Kahler, Janet C. 1918 Covered Wagon Adventure. 2006. (Illus.). 94p. per. 10.95 *(978-1-57258-444-0(0),* 945-6305) TEACH Services, Inc.
Kelsey, Stacy. Meet the Pro's with Sproket the Moto Dog, 1 vol. 2010. 38p. 24.95 *(978-1-4489-4785-0(5))* PublishAmerica, Inc.
Lacy, Sandy Allbee. Pepe & Lupita & the Great Yawn Jar. Schrom, Garren, illus. 2013. 36p. pap. 10.95 *(978-1-60494-923-0(6))* Wheatmark, Inc.
Laybourne, Emmy. Monument 14. 2012. (Monument 14 Ser.: 1). (ENG.). 304p. (YA). (gr. 8-13). 17.99 *(978-0-312-56903-7(3),* 9780312569037) Feiwel & Friends.
Luxa, Sue. A Cabin in Cripple Creek. 2004. (Illus.). 99p. (J). pap. 8.95 *(978-1-932738-04-9(5),* 1234249) Western Reflections Publishing Co.
—Denver Days. 2004. (Illus.). 82p. (J). pap. 8.95 *(978-1-890437-98-5(0),* 1234247) Western Reflections Publishing Co.
—One Golden Summer. 2004. (Illus.). 80p. (J). pap. 8.95 *(978-1-890437-99-2(9),* 1234248) Western Reflections Publishing Co.
Mac Iver, Kathi. Ghosts of the Mining District. 2003. (Illus.). 60p. 9.95 *(978-0-9651272-1-9(4))* Columbine Pr.
MacLean, Kerry Lee, creator. Pigs Ski over Colorado: The Top Ten Reasons Winter Is the Piggies Favorite Season. 2005. (J). per. 15.95 *(978-0-9652998-7-9(2))* On the Spot! Bks.
Maddox, Jake. Snowboard Hero. 2015. (Jake Maddox JV Ser.). (ENG.). 96p. (gr. 3-4). lib. bdg. 25.99 *(978-1-4342-9636-8(9))* Stone Arch Bks.
—Touchdown Triumph. Aburto, Jesus, illus. 2015. (Jake Maddox Sports Stories Ser.). (ENG.). 72p. (gr. 2-3). lib. bdg. 25.32 *(978-1-4965-0492-0(5))* Stone Arch Bks.
Marsh, Carole. The Mystery in the Rocky Mountains. 2009. (Real Kids, Real Places Ser.). (Illus.). 145p. (J). lib. bdg. 18.99 *(978-0-635-07000-5(6),* Marsh, Carole Mysteries) Gallopade International.
Martin, Rebecca. The Treasure Hunt. 2015. (Amish Frontier Ser.). (ENG., Illus.). 160p. (J). (gr. 2-7). pap. 8.99 *(978-0-7369-6369-5(3))* Harvest Hse. Pubs.
McKinty, Adrian. Deviant. 2011. (ENG.). 368p. (YA). (gr. 9-17). 16.95 *(978-0-8109-8420-2(2),* Amulet Bks.) Abrams, Inc.
McMahan, Gregg. Christmas Honey. 2012. (ENG.). pap. 10.00 *(978-1-4675-5319-3(0))* Independent Pub.
Merrill, Karen Grill. Oh, What a State I'm In: The USA in Rhyme & Riddle, 1 vol. Grill, Gerald, illus. 2010. 48p. pap. 24.95 *(978-1-4489-7979-0(X))* PublishAmerica, Inc.
Mills, Claudia. How Oliver Olson Changed the World. Maione, Heather Harms, illus. 2009. (ENG.). 112p. (J). (gr. 2-5). 15.95 *(978-0-374-33487-1(0),* 9780374334871, Farrar, Straus & Giroux (BYR)) Farrar, Straus & Giroux.
—How Oliver Olson Changed the World. Maione, Heather, illus. 2011. (ENG.). 128p. (J). (gr. 2-5). pap. 6.99 *(978-0-312-67282-9(9),* 9780312672829) Square Fish.
Mills, Tricia. Heartbreak River. 2009. (YA). *(978-1-59514-220-7(7),* Razorbill) Penguin Publishing Group.
Mobley, Jeannie. Katerina's Wish. (ENG., Illus.). (J). (gr. 3-7). 2014. 272p. pap. 8.99 *(978-1-4424-3344-1(2))* 2012. 256p. 15.99 *(978-1-4424-3343-4(4))* McElderry, Margaret K. Bks. (McElderry, Margaret K. Bks.).
Morrow, Dj. Two Bears Short. 2013. 28p. pap. 24.95 *(978-1-62709-822-9(4))* America Star Bks.
Mostoller, Marcia. Emma's Dilemm. 2011. 42p. pap. 16.95 *(978-1-4560-9859-9(4))* America Star Bks.
Mumford, Carole. Christmas Vacation in Colorado: A Magnificent Six Adventure, 1 vol. 2009. 75p. pap. 19.95 *(978-1-60749-231-3(8))* America Star Bks.
Myers, Edward. Climb or Die. 2nd ed. 2016. 154p. (J). pap. *(978-1-932727-12-8(4))* Montemayor Pr.
—Solos en la Montaña. 2016. (SPA.). 157p. (J). pap. *(978-1-932727-18-0(3))* Montemayor Pr.
Myers, Tim J. The Thunder Egg. Coleman, Winfield, illus. 2015. (ENG.). 28p. (J). (gr. k-4). 15.95 *(978-1-937786-39-7(0),* Wisdom Tales) World Wisdom, Inc.
Nesbit, Troy. Sand Dune Pony, Vol. 2013. (Wilderness Mystery Ser.). (ENG., Illus.). 248p. (J). (gr. 3-7). pap. 12.95 *(978-1-58979-811-3(2))* Taylor Trade Publishing.
Nuzum, K. A. The Leanin' Dog. (ENG.). 256p. (J). (gr. 3-7). 2010. pap. 6.99 *(978-0-06-113936-9(X))* 2008. 15.99 *(978-0-06-113934-5(3))* HarperCollins Pubs.
Oceanak, Karla. Dumbstruck. Spanjer, Kendra, illus. 2011. (Aldo Zelnick Comic Novel Ser.: 4). (ENG.). 160p. (J). (gr. 3-7). 12.95 *(978-1-934649-16-9(3))* Bailiwick Pr.
Oldfield, Jenny. Crazy Horse. 2009. (Horses of Half Moon Ranch Ser.: 3). (ENG.). 160p. (J). (gr. 4-7). pap. 9.99 *(978-1-4022-1702-9(1),* Sourcebooks Jabberwocky) Sourcebooks, Inc.
Olson, Lute. Hello, Wilbur! De Angel, M., illus. 2007. 24p. (J). lib. bdg. 14.95 *(978-1-932888-40-9(3))* Mascot Bks., Inc.
Osorio, Rick. The Great Adventure of Sally Rock & el Lobo. 2007. (ENG.). 96p. per. 19.95 *(978-1-4241-5869-0(9))* America Star Bks.
Parkhurst, Johanna. Here's to You, Zeb Pike. 2016. (ENG., Illus.). (J). 24.99 ***(978-1-63533-027-4(0),*** Harmony Ink Pr.) Dreamspinner Pr.
Parkhurst, Johanna. Here's to You, Zeb Pike [Library Edition]. 2014. 180p. pap. 14.99 *(978-1-62798-526-0(3),* Harmony Ink Pr.) Dreamspinner Pr.
Perkins, T. J. The Secret in Phantom Forest: A Kim & Kelly Mystery. 2004. (Illus.). 130p. (YA). 10.99 *(978-0-9777538-1-9(6))* GumShoe Press.
Peters, Julie Anne. Lies My Girlfriend Told Me. 2017. (ENG.). 256p. (YA). (gr. 10-17). pap. 9.99 ***(978-0-316-23495-5(8))*** Little, Brown Bks. for Young Readers.
Peters, Julie Anne. She Loves You, She Loves You Not... 2011. (ENG.). 288p. (YA). (gr. 10-17). 17.99 *(978-0-316-07874-0(3))* Little, Brown Bks. for Young Readers.
Ralph, Donna J. Critter Chronicles: Stories of Critters in a Colorado Wildlife Rehabilitator's Life. 2007. 200p. per. 16.95 *(978-0-595-47858-3(1))* iUniverse, Inc.
Raschke, Erik. The Book of Samuel: A Novel. 2009. (ENG.). 256p. (YA). (gr. 4-7). pap. 18.99 *(978-0-312-37969-8(2),* 9780312379698, St. Martin's Griffin) St. Martin's Pr.
Roaring Fork Conservancy (Basalt, Colo.) Staff, contrib. by. Dee Dee the Fryingpan River Dipper. 2017. (J). ***(978-1-883551-90-2(0),*** Maple Corners Press) Attic Studio Publishing Hse.
Sage, David. Adzul, the Heirs of the Medallion Book 1. 2013. 168p. pap. 7.99 *(978-0-9894210-0-3(7))* Sage, David.
Sappenfield, Heather. The View from Who I Was. 2015. (ENG.). 336p. (YA). pap. 11.99 *(978-0-7387-4174-1(4),* Flux) North Star Editions.
Sargent, Dave & Sargent, Pat. The Colorado Blizzard: Be Determined, 10 vols., Vol. 8. Lenoir, Jane, illus. l.t. ed. 2004. (Colorado Cowboys Ser.: 8). 32p. (J). (gr. 3-8). lib. bdg. 23.60 *(978-1-59381-026-9(1))* Ozark Publishing.
Scott, Joanna I. Stanley the Moose: Book One of the Woodsie Tails Series. 2009. (Illus.). 40p. (J). 19.95 net. *(978-0-9795678-1-0(5))* Cherakota Publishing.
Seaman, John E. On the Road with Ruben Doyle. 2010. 170p. 29.99 *(978-1-4500-3196-7(X))*; pap. 19.99 *(978-1-4500-3195-0(1))* Xlibris Corp.
Searching for Silverheels. 2014. (ENG., Illus.). 304p. (J). (gr. 5-9). 16.99 *(978-1-4814-0029-9(0),* McElderry, Margaret K. Bks.) McElderry, Margaret K. Bks.
Shaw, Tucker. The Girls. 2010. (ENG.). 224p. (YA). (gr. 7-11). pap. 7.95 *(978-0-8109-8991-7(3),* Amulet Bks.) Abrams, Inc.
Shaw, Tucker & Luce, Clare Boothe. The Girls. 2009. (ENG.). 208p. (YA). (gr. 7-11). 17.95 *(978-0-8109-8348-9(6),* Amulet Bks.) Abrams, Inc.
Sherman, M. Zachary. Fall Line, Vol. 3. Majado, Caio & Emery, Thomas, illus. 2011. (Tony Hawk's 900 Revolution Ser.). (ENG.). 128p. (gr. 3-4). pap. 7.19 *(978-1-4342-3453-7(3))*; lib. bdg. 26.65 *(978-1-4342-3204-5(2))* Stone Arch Bks. (Tony Hawk's 900 Revolution).
Shusterman, Neal. The Accelerati Trilogy Book Three Hawking's Hallway. 2017. (Accelerati Trilogy Ser.). (ENG.). 368p. (J). (gr. 5-9). pap. 8.99 *(978-1-4231-5521-8(1))* Hyperion Bks. for Children.
—Edison's Alley. 2016. (Accelerati Trilogy Ser.: Bk. 2). (ENG.). 256p. (J). (gr. 5-9). pap. 7.99 *(978-1-4231-5517-1(3))* Hyperion Bks. for Children.
Shusterman, Neal & Elfman, Eric. Edison's Alley. 2015. (Accelerati Trilogy Ser.: Bk. 2). (ENG.). 256p. (J). (gr. 5-9). 16.99 *(978-1-4231-4806-7(1))* Hyperion Bks. for Children.
—Tesla's Attic. 2014. (Accelerati Trilogy Ser.: Bk. 1). (ENG.). 256p. (J). (gr. 3-7). 16.99 *(978-1-4231-4803-6(7))* Hyperion Bks. for Children.
Silvano, Wendi. Love Is All Around Colorado. Czernichowska, Joanna, illus. 2016. (ENG.). 32p. (J). (-6). 12.99 *(978-1-4926-2914-6(6),* Sourcebooks Jabberwocky) Sourcebooks, Inc.
Smallman, Steve. Santa Is Coming to Boulder. Dunn, Robert, illus. 2015. (ENG.). 32p. (J). (-3). 9.99 *(978-1-4926-2659-6(7),* Sourcebooks Jabberwocky) Sourcebooks, Inc.
—Santa Is Coming to Colorado. Dunn, Robert, illus. 2013. (ENG.). 32p. (J). (-3). 9.99 *(978-1-4022-8815-9(8),* Sourcebooks Jabberwocky) Sourcebooks, Inc.
—Santa Is Coming to the Rockies. Dunn, Robert, illus. 2012. (ENG.). 32p. (J). (-3). 9.99 *(978-1-4022-7593-7(5),* Sourcebooks Jabberwocky) Sourcebooks, Inc.
Stone, Judith. Billie the Buffalo Goes to Town. 2008. 20p. pap. 12.95 *(978-1-4389-2877-7(7))* AuthorHouse.
Sully, Katherine. Night-Night Colorado. Kolanovic, Dubravka & Poole, Helen, illus. 2016. (ENG.). 20p. (J). (-1). bds. 9.99 *(978-1-4926-3938-1(9),* 9781492639381, Sourcebooks Jabberwocky) Sourcebooks, Inc.
Summers, Gillian. The Goblin's Curse: The Scions of Shadow Trilogy, Book 3. 2012. (Faire Folk Saga Ser.: 6). (ENG.). 312p. (YA). pap. 9.95 *(978-0-7387-1572-8(7),* Flux) North Star Editions.
Taylor, Kim. Cissy Funk. Date not set. 224p. (YA). (gr. 5-18). mass mkt. 4.99 *(978-0-06-440880-6(9))* HarperCollins Pubs.
The Bee Guru, Gregg McMahan. Christmas Honey. 2012. (Illus.). 20p. pap. 11.60 *(978-1-4669-5471-7(X))* Trafford Publishing.
Whitmore, Hugh. The Three Madelines. Wilson, Raylene Jenee & Gibbons, Deanna, illus. 2012. 124p. pap. 15.95 *(978-0-9848314-4-9(4))* Sincerity Publishing.
Wise, Keith. Isabella's Playmate. 2011. 278p. pap. 27.95 *(978-1-4560-7320-6(6))* America Star Bks.

C
D

Wonderley, Stanley. A Boy & His Horse. 2012. 19.95 *(978-0-7414-7806-1(4))*; pap. 11.95 *(978-0-7414-7805-4(6))* Infinity Publishing.

Zarr, Sara. How to Save a Life. 2012. (ENG.). 368p. (YA). (gr. 7-17). pap. 10.99 *(978-0-316-03605-4(6))* Little, Brown Bks. for Young Readers.

COLORADO—HISTORY

Alderman, Tyrone. Mining & Ranching in Early Colorado: Boom & Bust, & Back Again, 01 vols., 1. 2016. (Spotlight on Colorado Ser.). (ENG.). 48p. (J). (gr. 4-5). pap. 11.75 *(978-1-4994-1489-9(7)*, PowerKids Pr.) Rosen Publishing Group, Inc., The.

Altman, Linda Jacobs & Fitzgerald, Stephanie. Colorado. 2nd rev. ed. 2010. (It's My State! Ser.). 80p. (gr. 3-18). lib. bdg. 31.36 *(978-1-60870-046-2(1))* Marshall Cavendish Corp.

Bankoff, Samuel. Famous Coloradans, 01 vols., 1. 2016. (Spotlight on Colorado Ser.). (ENG.). 48p. (J). (gr. 4-5). pap. 11.75 *(978-1-4994-1530-8(3)*, PowerKids Pr.) Rosen Publishing Group, Inc., The.

Barker, Jane Valentine & Downing, Sybil. Adventures in the West. (Colorado Heritage Ser.). (Illus.). 40p. (J). reprint ed. pap. 7.95 *(978-1-878611-05-5(4))* Silver Rim Pr.

Beckwith, Cheryl. William Bent: Frontiersman. 2011. (ENG & SPA., Illus.). 60p. (J). pap. 8.95 *(978-0-86541-117-3(4))* Filter Pr., LLC.

Benchmark Education Company. The Mesa Verde Communities (Teacher Guide) 2005. *(978-1-4108-4679-2(2))* Benchmark Education Co.

Blegen, Daniel. Bob Sakata: American Farmer. 2009. (Now You Know Bio Ser.: 13). (Illus.). 102p. (J). pap. 8.95 *(978-0-86541-093-0(3))* Filter Pr., LLC.

Brennan-Nelson, Denise. Little Colorado. Urban, Helle, illus. 2011. (My Little State Ser.). (ENG.). 22p. (J). 9.95 *(978-1-58536-530-2(0))* Sleeping Bear Pr.

Cieply, Angela. The Economy of Colorado, 01 vols., 1. 2016. (Spotlight on Colorado Ser.). (ENG.). 48p. (J). (gr. 4-5). pap. 11.75 *(978-1-4994-1506-3(0)*, PowerKids Pr.) Rosen Publishing Group, Inc., The.

Dolphin, Colleen. Rocky's Outdoor Adventure: A Story about Colorado, 1 vol. Doucet, Bob, illus. 2011. (Fact & Fable: State Stories Set 3 Ser.). (ENG.). 24p. (J). (gr. -1-2). lib. bdg. 25.65 *(978-1-61714-684-8(6))* ABDO Publishing Co.

Downey, Matthew T. & Pettit, Jenny. Discover Colorado: Its People, Places, & Times. 2015. (Illus.). vii, 337p. (J). *(978-1-60732-357-0(5))* Univ. Pr. of Colorado.

Downs, Pamela. Colorado Today: Influences from Many Cultures, 01 vols., 1. 2016. (Spotlight on Colorado Ser.). (ENG.). 48p. (J). (gr. 4-5). pap. 11.75 *(978-1-4994-1519-3(2)*, PowerKids Pr.) Rosen Publishing Group, Inc., The.

Durrie, Karen. Colorado: Colorful Colorado. 2012. (J). *(978-1-61913-331-0(8))*; pap. *(978-1-61913-332-7(6))* Weigl Pubs., Inc.

Fackler, David. Governing the Centennial State, 01 vols., 1. 2016. (Spotlight on Colorado Ser.). (ENG.). 48p. (J). (gr. 4-5). pap. 11.75 *(978-1-4994-1513-1(3)*, PowerKids Pr.) Rosen Publishing Group, Inc., The.

Flood, Nancy Bo. Sand to Stone: And Back Again. Kuyper, Tony, photos by. 2009. (ENG., Illus.). 32p. (J). (gr. -1-k). pap. 9.95 *(978-1-55591-657-2(0))* Fulcrum Publishing.

Glaser, Jason. Colorado: The Centennial State. 2010. (Our Amazing States Ser.). 24p. (J). (ENG.). pap. 8.25 *(978-1-4358-9776-2(5))*; (Illus.). (gr. 2-3). lib. bdg. 22.60 *(978-1-4358-9344-3(1))* Rosen Publishing Group, Inc., The. (PowerKids Pr.).

Halls, Kelly Milner. The Story of the Hoover Dam: A History Perspectives Book. 2014. (Perspectives Library). (ENG., Illus.). 32p. (J). (gr. 4-8). 28.50 *(978-1-62431-668-5(9)*, 203236) Cherry Lake Publishing.

Hamilton, John. Rocky Mountain National Park. 2008. (National Parks Set II Ser.). 32p. (gr. 4-9). 27.07 *(978-1-60453-094-0(4)*, Abdo & Daughters) ABDO Publishing Co.

Harvey, Dan. Rocky Mountain: Colorado, Utah, Wyoming, Vol. 19. 2015. (Let's Explore the States Ser.). (Illus.). 64p. (J). (gr. 5). 23.95 *(978-1-4222-3332-0(4))* Mason Crest.

Hasday, Judy L. Forty-Nine Minutes of Madness: The Columbine High School Shooting. 2012. (Disasters — People in Peril Ser.). (Illus.). 48p. (J). (gr. 5-18). 25.27 *(978-0-7660-4013-7(5))* Enslow Pubs., Inc.

Heos, Bridget. Colorado: Past & Present. 2010. (United States: Past & Present Ser.). (ENG.). 48p. (YA). pap. 11.75 *(978-1-4358-9530-0(4))*; lib. bdg. 29.25 *(978-1-4358-9477-8(4))* Rosen Publishing Group, Inc., The. (Rosen Reference).

Jerome, Kate B. Lucky to Live in Colorado. 2017. (Arcadia Kids Ser.). (ENG., Illus.). 32p. (J). 16.99 ***(978-0-7385-2781-9(5))*** Arcadia Publishing.

Keils, Deanne. The Mesa Verde Communities. 2005. (J). pap. *(978-1-4108-4631-0(8))* Benchmark Education Co.

Kids: Descubre el rio Colorado. 2003. (SPA.). (J). *(978-1-888631-42-5(2))* Project WET Foundation.

Krudwig, Vickie L. We Are the Noochew - A Brief History of the Ute People & their Colorado Connection. 2004. (Illus.). 76p. (J). spiral bd. *(978-0-9700127-1-5(3))* Sweet Success Pr.

Laney, Mark. The Land & Resources of Colorado, 01 vols., 1. 2016. (Spotlight on Colorado Ser.). (ENG.). 48p. (J). (gr. 4-5). pap. 11.75 *(978-1-4994-1438-7(2)*, PowerKids Pr.) Rosen Publishing Group, Inc., The.

Lassieur, Allison. Stanley Hotel: A Chilling Interactive Adventure. 2017. (You Choose: Haunted Places Ser.). (ENG., Illus.). 112p. (gr. 3-4). lib. bdg. 31.99 *(978-1-5157-3650-9(4)*, You Choose Bks.) Capstone Press of Coughlan Cos.

Laughlin, Rosemary. The Ludlow Massacre Of 1913-14. 2006. (American Workers Ser.). (Illus.). 144p. (J). (gr. 6-12). lib. bdg. 26.95 *(978-1-931798-86-0(9))* Reynolds, Morgan Inc.

Lohr, Ruth. The First Coloradans: Native Americans in Colorado, 01 vols., 1. 2016. (Spotlight on Colorado Ser.). (ENG.). 48p. (J). (gr. 4-5). pap. 11.75 *(978-1-4994-1444-8(7)*, PowerKids Pr.) Rosen Publishing Group, Inc., The.

Lowery, Linda. Aunt Clara Brown: Official Pioneer. Porter, Janice Lee, illus. 2006. (On My Own Biographies Ser.). 48p. 16.95 *(978-0-7569-6699-7(X))* Perfection Learning Corp.

Marsh, Carole. Colorado History Projects: 30 Cool, Activities, Crafts, Experiments & More for Kids to Do to Learn about Your State! 2003. (Colorado Experience Ser.). 32p. (gr. k-5). pap. 5.95 *(978-0-635-01775-8(X)*, Marsh, Carole Bks.) Gallopade International.

—Exploring Colorado Through Project-Based Learning. 2016. (Colorado Experience Ser.). (ENG.). (J). pap. 9.99 *(978-0-635-12330-5(4))* Gallopade International.

Marsico, Katie. The Colorado River. 2013. (Explorer Library: Social Studies Explorer Ser.). (ENG.). 32p. (J). (gr. 4-8). 28.50 *(978-1-62431-014-0(1)*, 202507); pap. 14.21 *(978-1-62431-038-6(9)*, 202509) Cherry Lake Publishing.

—The Rio Grande. 2013. (Explorer Library: Social Studies Explorer Ser.). (ENG.). 32p. (J). (gr. 4-8). 28.50 *(978-1-62431-012-6(5)*, 202499); pap. 14.21 *(978-1-62431-036-2(2)*, 202501) Cherry Lake Publishing.

McLuskey, Krista. Colorado. 2011. (Guide to American States Ser.). (Illus.). 48p. (J). (gr. 3-6). 29.99 *(978-1-61690-778-5(9))*; *(978-1-61690-453-1(4))* Weigl Pubs., Inc.

—Colorado: The Centennial State. 2016. (J). ***(978-1-5105-2085-1(6))***; *(978-1-5105-0662-6(4))* SmartBook Media, Inc.

—Colorado: The Centennial State. 2016. (J). *(978-1-4896-4830-3(5))* Weigl Pubs., Inc.

Meinking, Mary. What's Great about Colorado? 2014. (Our Great States Ser.). (ENG., 32p. (gr. 2-5). Illus.). pap. 7.95 *(978-1-4677-4536-9(7))*; lib. bdg. 26.60 *(978-1-4677-3350-2(4)*, Lerner Pubns.) Lerner Publishing Group.

Miller, Amy. Colorado. 2008. (ENG.). 80p. (J). pap. 7.95 *(978-0-531-20802-1(8)*, Children's Pr.) Scholastic Library Publishing.

Morgenstern, Gretchen L. The Privilege of Colorado Citizenship: Rights & Responsibilities, 01 vols., 1. 2016. (Spotlight on Colorado Ser.). (ENG.). 48p. (J). (gr. 4-5). pap. 11.75 *(978-1-4994-1525-4(7)*, PowerKids Pr.) Rosen Publishing Group, Inc., The.

Noel, Thomas J. & Smith, Duane A. Colorado: The Highest State. 2nd ed. 2011. (ENG., Illus.). 400p. (gr. 4-4). 34.95 *(978-1-60732-144-6(0))* Univ. Pr. of Colorado.

Perry, Phyllis J. A Kid's Look at Colorado. 2005. (ENG., Illus.). 216p. (J). (gr. 3-7). pap. 15.95 *(978-1-55591-856-9(5))* Fulcrum Publishing.

Perry, Phyllis Jean. Bold Women in Colorado History. 2012. (J). pap. *(978-0-87842-584-6(5))* Mountain Pr. Publishing Co., Inc.

Robles, David Alan. The Natural History of Colorado, 01 vols., 1. 2016. (Spotlight on Colorado Ser.). (ENG.). 48p. (J). (gr. 4-5). pap. 11.75 *(978-1-4994-1536-0(2)*, PowerKids Pr.) Rosen Publishing Group, Inc., The.

Roundtree, Abigail. Pathway to Statehood: The Territory of Colorado Joins the Union, 01 vols., 1. 2016. (Spotlight on Colorado Ser.). (ENG.). 48p. (J). (gr. 4-5). pap. 11.75 *(978-1-4994-1467-7(6)*, PowerKids Pr.) Rosen Publishing Group, Inc., The.

Schmidt, Elton. Colorado's Changing Cities: Then & Now, 01 vols., 1. 2016. (Spotlight on Colorado Ser.). (ENG.). 48p. (J). (gr. 4-5). pap. 11.75 *(978-1-4994-1497-4(8)*, PowerKids Pr.) Rosen Publishing Group, Inc., The.

Shea, Therese. Colorado's Trailblazers: Pioneers in Science, Technology, & Engineering, 01 vols., 1. 2016. (Spotlight on Colorado Ser.). (ENG.). 48p. (J). pap. 11.75 *(978-1-4994-1875-0(2)*, PowerKids Pr.) Rosen Publishing Group, Inc., The.

Skelton, Renee. A Kid's Guide to Exploring Black Canyon of the Gunnison National Park. 2003. (Illus.). 12p. (J). pap. 4.95 *(978-1-58369-035-2(2))* Western National Parks Assn.

Tieck, Sarah. Colorado, 1 vol. 2012. (Explore the United States Ser.). (ENG., Illus.). 32p. (J). (gr. 2-5). 28.50 *(978-1-61783-344-1(4))* ABDO Publishing Co.

Vescia, Peter. The Pikes Peak Gold Rush, 01 vols., 1. 2016. (Spotlight on Colorado Ser.). (ENG.). 48p. (J). (gr. 4-5). pap. 11.75 *(978-1-4994-1456-1(0)*, PowerKids Pr.) Rosen Publishing Group, Inc., The.

Virden, William & Borg, Mary. My Colorado Teacher Guide. 2010. 43p. pap. 3.95 *(978-1-59363-656-2(3))* Prufrock Pr.

Walker, Cynthia. Colorado. 2005. (Rookie Español Geografía Ser.). (ENG & SPA., Illus.). 32p. (J). (gr. k-2). lib. bdg. 19.50 *(978-0-516-25244-5(5)*, Children's Pr.) Scholastic Library Publishing.

Zirkelbach, Grace. Charles Boettcher: Colorado Business Leader. 2011. (ENG & SPA., Illus.). 48p. (J). pap. 8.95 *(978-0-86541-118-0(2))* Filter Pr., LLC.

COLORADO RIVER AND VALLEY

Barter, James E. The Colorado. 2003. (Rivers of the World Ser.). (Illus.). 112p. (J). 28.70 *(978-1-59018-059-4(3)*, Lucent Bks.) Cengage Gale.

Bryan, Dale-Marie. The Colorado River. 2006. (Rookie Read-About Geography Ser.). (ENG., Illus.). 32p. (J). (gr. 1-2). pap. 5.95 *(978-0-516-21447-4(0)*, Children's Pr.) Scholastic Library Publishing.

Marsico, Katie. The Colorado River. 2013. (Explorer Library: Social Studies Explorer Ser.). (ENG.). 32p. (J). (gr. 4-8). 28.50 *(978-1-62431-014-0(1)*, 202507); pap. 14.21 *(978-1-62431-038-6(9)*, 202509) Cherry Lake Publishing.

McNeese, Tim. The Colorado River. 2004. (Rivers in American Life & Times Ser.). (Illus.). 120p. (C). (gr. 9-13). 32.50 *(978-0-7910-7726-9(8)*, Chelsea Hse.) Facts On File, Inc.

Souza, Dorothy M. John Wesley Powell. 2004. (Watts Library). (ENG., Illus.). 64p. (J). (gr. 5-7). pap. 8.95 *(978-0-531-16653-6(8)*, Watts, Franklin) Scholastic Library Publishing.

COLORADO ROCKIES (BASEBALL TEAM)

Connery-Boyd, Peg. Colorado Rockies. 2016. (Hawk's Nest Activity Bks.: 0). (ENG.). 64p. (J). (gr. k-3). pap., act. bk. ed. 8.99 *(978-1-4926-3377-8(1))* Sourcebooks, Inc.

Goodman, Michael E. The Story of the Colorado Rockies. 2011. (J). 35.65 *(978-1-60818-039-4(5)*, Creative Education) Creative Co., The.

Howell, Brian. Colorado Rockies, 1 vol. (Inside MLB Ser.). (ENG., 48p. (gr. 3-6). 2011. Illus.). (YA). lib. bdg. 32.79 *(978-1-61714-042-6(2))* 2014. lib. bdg. 32.79 *(978-1-62403-468-8(3)*, SportsZone) ABDO Publishing Co.

Omoth, Tyler. The Story of the Colorado Rockies. 2007. (Baseball, the Great American Game Ser.). (Illus.). 48p. (YA). (gr. 4-7). lib. bdg. 32.80 *(978-1-58341-486-6(X))* Creative Co., The.

Stewart, Mark. The Colorado Rockies. 2012. (Team Spirit Ser.). 48p. (J). (gr. 3-6). lib. bdg. 29.27 *(978-1-59953-480-0(0))* Norwood Hse. Pr.

COLORED PEOPLE (UNITED STATES)

see African Americans

COLORING BOOKS

Abato, Andrew. Alphabet Mandalas - Beautiful Letter-Based Mandalas for Colouring in, Learning & Meditation. 2010. 56p. pap. 14.90 *(978-3-8391-4871-6(5))* Bks. on Demand.

—Car Mandalas - Beautiful Mandalas Featuring Cars for Colouring In. 2010. 52p. pap. 15.50 *(978-3-8391-3390-3(4))* Bks. on Demand.

—Celtic Mandalas - Beautiful Mandalas & Patterns for Colouring in, Relaxation & Meditation. 2010. 52p. pap. 15.50 *(978-3-8391-3799-4(3))* Bks. on Demand.

—Christmas Mandalas - Beautiful Christmas Mandalas for Colouring In. 2010. 52p. pap. 15.50 *(978-3-8391-4000-0(5))* Bks. on Demand.

—Decorative Mandalas - Beautiful Mandalas & Patterns for Colouring in, Relaxation & Meditation. 2010. 52p. pap. 15.50 *(978-3-8391-4019-2(6))* Bks. on Demand.

—Fantasy Mandalas - Beautiful Mandalas & Ornamentation for Colouring in, Relaxation & Meditation. 2010. 54p. pap. 15.50 *(978-3-8391-4075-8(7))* Bks. on Demand.

—Farmyard Mandalas - Beautiful Mandalas with a Farmyard Theme for Colouring In. 2010. 52p. pap. 15.50 *(978-3-8391-4427-5(2))* Bks. on Demand.

—Horse Mandalas - Beautiful Horse Mandalas for Colouring in & Meditation. 2010. 52p. pap. 15.50 *(978-3-8391-4417-6(5))* Bks. on Demand.

—Love Mandalas - Beautiful Love Mandalas for Colouring in, Dreaming, Relaxation & Meditation. 2010. 52p. pap. 15.50 *(978-3-8391-4472-5(8))* Bks. on Demand.

ABC coloring Book. 2006. (YA). per. 2.99 *(978-1-59872-431-8(2))* Instant Pub.

ABC Coloring Book. 2004. 3.00 *(978-1-880960-11-0(7))* Scripture Memory Fellowship International.

ABCs of the Bible Coloring Book. (Illus.). 16p. (J). pap. 1.50 *(978-0-87162-873-2(2)*, E6036) Warner Pr., Inc.

Abraham, Chuck. Intricate Eggs: 45 Easter Designs to Color. 2008. (ENG., Illus.). 96p. (J). (gr. -1-17). pap. 6.95 *(978-0-7624-3178-6(4))* Running Pr. Bk. Pubs.

Abrahamson, Bobbie. Sunflower: A Pony's Story. 2012. 36p. pap. *(978-1-105-60309-9(1))* Lulu.com.

Abstract Adventure II: A Kaleidoscopia Coloring Book. 2006. (Illus.). 25p. (J). (gr. k-16). 8.95 *(978-0-929636-66-5(X))* Syren Bk. Co.

Adam, Sarah E., illus. Abby in Vermont Coloring & Activity Book. 2008. 32p. (J). 4.95 *(978-0-9793790-1-7(6))* Howard Printing, Inc.

Adam, Winky. Around the World Coloring Book. 2005. (Dover History Coloring Book Ser.). (ENG.). 32p. (J). (gr. 3-6). pap. 3.99 *(978-0-486-43983-9(6))* Dover Pubns., Inc.

—Color by Number. 2006. (Dover Coloring Bks.). (ENG., Illus.). 32p. (J). (gr. -1-2). pap. 4.99 *(978-0-486-45343-9(X))* Dover Pubns., Inc.

Adams, William J. Goin' to the Zoo Coloring Book: Vamos Al Zoologico. Stiglich, Tom, illus. 2007. (ENG & SPA.). (J). pap. 3.95 *(978-0-9772757-3-1(6))* Mandy & Andy Bks., Inc.

Adatto, Miryam. Creative Haven Dreamscapes Coloring Book. 2013. (Adult Coloring Ser.). (ENG.). 64p. (gr. 3). pap. 5.99 *(978-0-486-49422-7(5))* Dover Pubns., Inc.

Adly, Muhammad S. Learn & Color (For Children) 24p. *(978-1-894264-45-7(2))* Al-Attique Pubs., Inc.

The Advantage Max-4 HD Waterfowl Coloring & Activity Book. 2003. (J). pap. *(978-0-9745863-0-4(7))* Cypress Knees Publishing.

Agredo, Mary & Agredo, Javier. Creative Haven Hamsa Designs Coloring Book. 2014. (Adult Coloring Ser.). (ENG., Illus.). 64p. (gr. 6). pap. 5.99 *(978-0-486-49454-8(3))* Dover Pubns., Inc.

—Creative Haven Nature Fractals Coloring Book. 2014. (Adult Coloring Ser.). (ENG., Illus.). 64p. (gr. 6). pap. 5.99 *(978-0-486-49498-2(5))* Dover Pubns., Inc.

Al-Kinani, Maarja. Islamic. 2010. 74p. pap. 69.50 *(978-1-4461-6416-7(0))* Lulu Pr., Inc.

Alcott, Louisa May & Steadman, Barbara. Little Women Coloring Book. 2013. (Dover Classic Stories Coloring Book Ser.). (ENG., Illus.). 48p. (J). (gr. -1-8). pap. 4.99 *(978-0-486-29943-3(0))* Dover Pubns., Inc.

Alden, Peter C. Mammals. Reid, Fiona, illus. 2nd ed. 2013. (Peterson Field Guide Color-In Bks.). (ENG.). 10p. (J). 8.95 *(978-0-544-03254-5(3))* Houghton Mifflin Harcourt Publishing Co.

Alden, Peter C. & Peterson, Roger Tory. Birds. Peterson, Roger Tory, ed. Sill, John, illus. 2nd ed. 2013. (Peterson Field Guide Color-In Bks.). (ENG.). 64p. (J). 8.95 *(978-0-544-02692-6(6))* Houghton Mifflin Harcourt Publishing Co.

Aliens & Space. Date not set. (Illus.). 64p. (J). 2.98 *(978-1-4054-0446-4(9))* Parragon, Inc.

Allen, Katy C. Dingo & Willy's Donuts. DePaolo, Daniel, illus. 2012. 74p. pap. 6.99 *(978-0-9857160-3-5(7))*; pap. 6.99 *(978-0-9857160-1-1(0))* Baysmore Bks.

Altmann, Scott. Mermaids — Sirens of the Sea. 2009. (Dover Coloring Bks.). (ENG., Illus.). 32p. (J). (gr. 1-5). pap. 3.99 *(978-0-486-46990-4(5))* Dover Pubns., Inc.

Amery, Heather. First Hundred Words Coloring Book. 2009. (First Hundred Words Ser.). 32p. (J). (gr. k). pap. 5.99 *(978-0-7945-2485-2(0)*, Usborne) EDC Publishing.

—What's Happening on the Farm? Cartwright, Stephen, illus. rev. ed. 2006. (What's Happening? Ser.). 32p. (J). (gr. -1-3). 5.99 *(978-0-7945-1288-0(7)*, Usborne) EDC Publishing.

Amoss, Berthe. Draw Yourself into a Starlit Journey. 2003. 32p. (J). spiral bd. 12.95 *(978-1-59325-004-1(5))* Word Among Us Pr.

—Draw Yourself into the Ark with Noah & His Family. 2003. 32p. (J). spiral bd. 12.95 *(978-1-59325-003-4(7))* Word Among Us Pr.

Andriamanga, Faratiana, illus. Amazing Animals. 2016. (Coloring Studio Ser.: 2). (ENG.). 48p. (J). (gr. 1-17). pap. 8.99 *(978-0-316-39288-4(X))* Little, Brown Bks. for Young Readers.

Angell, Ian O. Creative Haven Geometric Allover Patterns Coloring Book. 2013. (Adult Coloring Ser.). (ENG., Illus.). 64p. (gr. 6). pap. 5.99 *(978-0-486-78164-8(X))* Dover Pubns., Inc.

Anglin, Dawnice. God's Creation Bible Coloring Book: Bible Coloring Book. 2007. (Illus.). 24p. (J). per. 6.99 *(978-0-9801320-0-7(2))* Basic Black Publishing.

Animal Faces. 16p. (J). 1.89 *(978-0-7847-1020-3(1))* Standard Publishing.

Animals of the Bible. (Illus.). 16p. (J). pap. 1.50 *(978-0-87162-874-9(0)*, E6035) Warner Pr., Inc.

Arcturus Publishing. My Drawing, Doodling & Coloring Book. 2015. (ENG.). 256p. (J). 16.95 *(978-1-78404-796-2(1)*, 9781784047962) Arcturus Publishing GBR. Dist: Bookmasters Distribution.

Arcturus Publishing Staff. Lots to Spot: Dinosaurs. 2017. (ENG., Illus.). 48p. (J). (gr. k-5). 9.99 ***(978-1-78428-475-6(0)***, 9781784284756) Arcturus Publishing GBR. Dist: Bookmasters Distribution.

—Lots to Spot: Farm. 2017. (ENG., Illus.). 48p. (J). (gr. k-5). 9.99 ***(978-1-78428-476-3(9)***, 9781784284763) Arcturus Publishing GBR. Dist: Bookmasters Distribution.

Arena Verlag. Kids' Mandalas. 2004. (ENG., Illus.). 64p. (J). pap. 4.95 *(978-1-4027-1720-8(2))* Sterling Publishing Co., Inc.

Armstrong, Gregory D. Count with Buddy Coloring Book. 2013. 24p. pap. 12.99 *(978-0-9895026-5-8(1))* Armstrong, Greg.

ArsEdition, illus. Blossom Magic: Beautiful Floral Patterns to Color. 2015. (Color Magic Ser.). (ENG.). 80p. pap. 12.99 *(978-1-4380-0731-1(0))* Barron's Educational Series, Inc.

An Artist's Coloring Book. 2004. (J). 5.95 *(978-0-9749672-0-2(3))* JINKS Studio Art & Publishing.

Ashar, Linda C. Kerry Bog Pony Sketch & Coloring Book 2004. (Illus.). (J). 4.00 *(978-0-9749728-0-0(0))* Thornapple Farms, LLC.

Aston, Paul, tr. Claude Monet. Kutschbach, Doris, illus. 2006. (ENG.). 32p. (J). (gr. 1-4). 8.95 *(978-3-7913-3713-5(0))* Prestel Verlag GmbH & Co KG. DEU. Dist: Penguin Random Hse. LLC.

—Coloring Book: Wassily Kandinsky. Kutschbach, Doris, illus. 2006. (ENG.). 32p. (J). (gr. 1-4). 8.95 *(978-3-7913-3712-8(2))* Prestel Verlag GmbH & Co KG. DEU. Dist: Penguin Random Hse. LLC.

At the Barbershop, 6 vols. (Multicultural Programs Ser.). 16p. (gr. 1-3). 24.95 *(978-0-7802-9209-3(X))* Wright Group/McGraw-Hill.

Attanasio, Fabiana. Snow White Coloring Book. 2016. (ENG., Illus.). 80p. (J). (gr. k). pap. 9.95 *(978-1-4549-2092-2(0))* Sterling Publishing Co., Inc.

Attansia, Fabiana, illus. Alice in Wonderland Coloring Book. 2016. (ENG.). 80p. (J). (gr. k). pap. 9.95 *(978-1-4549-2089-2(0))* Sterling Publishing Co., Inc.

—Peter Pan Coloring Book. 2016. (ENG.). 80p. (J). (gr. k). pap. 9.95 *(978-1-4549-2090-8(4))* Sterling Publishing Co., Inc.

Atwood, Karen. Halloween Coloring Book. 2011. (ENG.). 26p. pap. 5.38 *(978-1-4679-1124-5(0))* CreateSpace Independent Publishing Platform.

Aunt Judy. Chickens on the go! coloring Book. 2008. (Illus.). 32p. (J). pap. 2.50 *(978-0-9780693-5-3(8))* McEwen, Judith A.

AWARD & Award, Anna. Dot to Dot Count & Colour Fun. 2015. (ENG.). 16p. (J). pap. 3.99 *(978-1-78270-122-4(2))*; pap. 3.99 *(978-1-78270-124-8(9))*; pap. 3.99 *(978-1-78270-125-5(7))*; pap. 3.99 *(978-1-78270-123-1(0))* Award Pubns. Ltd. GBR. Dist: Parkwest Pubns., Inc.

Award, Anna. My First Colouring Book. 2012. (ENG.). 16p. (J). pap. 3.25 *(978-1-84135-014-1(1))*; (Illus.). pap. 3.25 *(978-1-84135-016-5(8))*; (Illus.). pap. 3.25 *(978-1-84135-013-4(3))* Award Pubns. Ltd. GBR. Dist: Parkwest Pubns., Inc.

—My First Colouring Fun - 123: Copy the Colors to Complete the Picture. 2012. (ENG.). 16p. (J). pap. 3.25 *(978-1-84135-891-8(6))* Award Pubns. Ltd. GBR. Dist: Parkwest Pubns., Inc.

—My First Colouring Fun - Abc: Copy the Colors to Complete the Pictures. 2012. (ENG.). 16p. (J). pap. 3.25 *(978-1-84135-890-1(8))* Award Pubns. Ltd. GBR. Dist: Parkwest Pubns., Inc.

Award Publications Limited, creator. My First Bumper Copy Colouring Book. 2013. (ENG., Illus.). 64p. (J). (gr. -1-3). pap. 8.50 *(978-1-84135-999-1(8))* Award Pubns. Ltd. GBR. Dist: Parkwest Pubns., Inc.

Award Publications Staff. Octopus. 2012. (ENG., Illus.). 16p. (J). 3.25 *(978-1-84135-819-2(3))* Award Pubns. Ltd. GBR. Dist: Parkwest Pubns., Inc.

Award Staff & Award, Anna. Sticker Fun & Colouring. 2015. (ENG.). 48p. (J). pap. 7.99 *(978-1-78270-012-8(9))* Award Pubns. Ltd. GBR. Dist: Parkwest Pubns., Inc.

Awdry, W. Bust My Buffers! (Thomas & Friends) 2014. (Color Plus 1,000 Stickers Ser.). (ENG.). 64p. (J). (gr. -1-2). pap. 9.99 *(978-0-385-38537-4(4)*, Golden Bks.) Random Hse. Children's Bks.

—Rail Blazers! (Thomas & Friends) Durk, Jim, illus. 2011. (Paint Box Book Ser.). (ENG.). 48p. (J). (gr. -1-2). pap. 3.99 *(978-0-375-87390-4(2)*, Golden Bks.) Random Hse. Children's Bks.

Awdry, Wilbert V. The Secret of the Mine. Durk, Jim, illus. 2013. (Glow-In-the-Dark Sticker Book Ser.). (ENG.). 48p. (J). (gr. -1-2). pap. 3.99 *(978-0-449-81711-7(3)*, Golden Bks.) Random Hse. Children's Bks.

—Thomas' Giant Puzzle Book (Thomas & Friends) Durk, Jim, illus. 2012. (Giant Coloring Book Ser.). (ENG.). 40p. (J). (gr. -1-2). pap. 9.99 *(978-0-307-97690-1(4)*, Golden Bks.) Random Hse. Children's Bks.

Awesome Activity. 2004. 80p. (J). act. bk. ed. 4.99 *(978-1-85997-688-3(3))* Byeway Bks.

Awesome Coloring. 2004. 80p. (J). act. bk. ed. 4.99 *(978-1-85997-689-0(1))* Byeway Bks.

AZ Books. Bright Colors. 2013. (Matching Pictures Ser.). (ENG.). 20p. (J). (gr. -1-k). bds. 5.95 *(978-1-61889-310-9(6))* AZ Bks. LLC.

AZ Books, creator. My Favorite Pet. 2013. (Velvet Fantasy Ser.). (ENG., Illus.). 16p. (J). (gr. k-3). pap. 4.95 *(978-1-61889-293-5(2))* AZ Bks. LLC.

—Stylish Gifts. 2013. (Velvet Fantasy Ser.). (ENG., Illus.). 16p. (J). (gr. 1-3). pap. 4.95 *(978-1-61889-296-6(7))* AZ Bks. LLC.

AZ Books Staff. Stylish Girls. 2013. (Velvet Fantasy Ser.). (ENG., Illus.). 16p. (J). (gr. 1-3). pap. 4.95 *(978-1-61889-292-8(4))* AZ Bks. LLC.

Baggott, Stella, illus. Advent Calendar to Color. 2011. (Coloring Bks.). (J). ring bd. 7.99 *(978-0-7945-3136-2(9)*, Usborne) EDC Publishing.

—Lots of Things to Find & Color in Fairyland. 2015. (Lots of Things to Find & Color Ser.). (ENG.). 96p. (J). (gr. k-5). pap. 12.99 *(978-0-7945-3329-8(9)*, Usborne) EDC Publishing.

Bain, Michelle. The Adventures of Thumbs up Johnnie Reading Heart to Heart Thumbs up Johnnie, Little Digit & the Special Delivery: Reading Heart to Heart, Coloring & Activity Book. 2006. (J). pap. 7.95 *(978-0-9761421-5-7(5))*; (Illus.). pap. 7.95 *(978-0-9795832-5-4(X))* Pixie Stuff LLC.

Bak, Jenny. Color & Poster Book. Middleton, Gayle & Edwards, Ken, illus. 2006. (My Little Pony Ser.). 32p. (J). (gr. -1-1). 3.99 *(978-0-06-079470-5(4)*, HarperFestival) HarperCollins Pubs.

Baker, Kelly A. & Baker, Robin J. Spark - Fancy Fish Coloring Book. 2015. (ENG., Illus.). 64p. (J). (gr. 1-4). pap. 5.99 *(978-0-486-80220-6(5))* Dover Pubns., Inc.

Baker, Michael. Thinker Doodles A1: Think, Draw, & Color. 2010. (Thinker Doodles Ser.). 45p. (gr. k-1). pap. 8.99 *(978-0-89455-870-2(6))* Critical Thinking Co., The.

—Thinker Doodles Beginning: Think, Draw, & Color. 2010. (Thinker Doodles Ser.). 48p. (gr. -1 — 1). pap. 8.99 *(978-0-89455-869-6(2))* Critical Thinking Co., The.

Baker, Robin J. & Baker, Kelly A. Creative Haven Garden Party Stained Glass Coloring Book. 2014. (Adult Coloring Ser.). (ENG., Illus.). 32p. (gr. 3). pap. 7.99 *(978-0-486-79827-1(5))* Dover Pubns., Inc.

—3-D Coloring Book — Fish Frenzy! 2012. (Dover 3-D Coloring Book Ser.). (ENG., Illus.). 32p. (J). (gr. 2-6). pap. 5.99 *(978-0-486-49011-3(4))* Dover Pubns., Inc.

Baker, Robin J. & McElwain, Kelly A. Garden Party! Flower Designs to Color. 2011. (Dover Nature Coloring Book Ser.). (ENG.). 32p. (gr. 3-5). pap. 3.99 *(978-0-486-48035-0(6))* Dover Pubns., Inc.

—3-D Coloring Book — Flower Power! 2nd ed. 2012. (Dover 3-D Coloring Book Ser.). (ENG., Illus.). 32p. (J). (gr. 2-6). pap. 5.99 *(978-0-486-49012-0(2))* Dover Pubns., Inc.

Baker, Robin J., et al. Awesome Animal Designs. 2012. (Adult Coloring Ser.). (ENG., Illus.). 64p. (gr. 3). pap. 5.99 *(978-0-486-49135-6(8))* Dover Pubns., Inc.

—Crazy Paisley. 2012. (Adult Coloring Ser.). (ENG., Illus.). 64p. (gr. 3). pap. 5.99 *(978-0-486-49086-1(6))* Dover Pubns., Inc.

Baldeon, David, text. Color Your Own Marvel Tsum Tsum. 2017. (ENG., Illus.). 120p. (J). (gr. -1-17). pap. 9.99 ***(978-1-302-90714-3(X))*** Marvel Worldwide, Inc.

Ballerinas. Date not set. (Dot to Dot Ser.). 64p. (J). 2.98 *(978-1-4054-0449-5(3))* Parragon, Inc.

Balloon Books Staff. I Can Draw. 2003. (ENG., Illus.). 18p. (J). pap., wbk. ed. 3.95 *(978-1-4027-0494-9(1)*, Balloon Bks.) Sterling Publishing Co., Inc.

—Kindergarten Color & Learn. 2003. (ENG., Illus.). 64p. (J). pap. 4.95 *(978-1-4027-0498-7(4)*, Balloon Bks.) Sterling Publishing Co., Inc.

Baran, Robert J. The Bonsai Coloring Book. Steele, Paul, illus. 2005. 5.95 net. *(978-0-9659913-5-3(0))* Pyramid Dancer Pubns.

Barard, Brooke. Believe in Yourself: Coloring Book. 2013. 4.99 *(978-0-9898437-2-0(6))* One in Me, The.

Barbaresi, Nina. Animal Word Puzzles Coloring Book. 81st ed. 2013. (Dover Coloring Bks.). (ENG., Illus.). 48p. (J). (gr. 1-4). pap. 3.99 *(978-0-486-26848-4(9))* Dover Pubns., Inc.

—Firefighters Coloring Book. 2003. (Dover Coloring Bks.). (ENG., Illus.). 32p. (J). (gr. -1-2). pap. 3.99 *(978-0-486-42646-4(7))* Dover Pubns., Inc.

Barbaresi, Nina & Beylon, Cathy. Horses & Ponies: Coloring & Sticker Fun. 2006. (Dover Coloring Bks.). (ENG., Illus.). 32p. (J). (gr. 3-8). pap. 4.99 *(978-0-486-45220-3(4))* Dover Pubns., Inc.

Barker, Cicely Mary. Flower Fairies Alphabet Coloring Book. 2010. (Flower Fairies Ser.). (ENG.). 24p. (J). (gr. -1-2). 4.99 *(978-0-7232-6496-5(1)*, Warne) Penguin Young Readers Group.

Barlow, Dave. Tome of Knowledge; Volcanoes. 2005. (ENG., Illus.). 20p. (YA). per. 4.95 *(978-0-9725230-9-7(X))* Wandering Sage Pubns., LLC.

Barlowe, Dot. America the Beautiful to Paint or Color. 2006. (Dover Art Coloring Book Ser.). (ENG., Illus.). 48p. (gr. 3-8). per. 5.99 *(978-0-486-44811-4(8))* Dover Pubns., Inc.

—The Birdwatcher's Coloring Book. 2012. (Dover Nature Coloring Book Ser.). (ENG.). 32p. (gr. 3-5). pap. 3.99 *(978-0-486-48794-6(6))* Dover Pubns., Inc.

—Creative Haven Country Scenes Coloring Book. 2014. (Adult Coloring Ser.). (ENG.). 64p. (gr. 3). pap. 5.99 *(978-0-486-49455-5(1))* Dover Pubns., Inc.

—Forest Animals. 2011. (Dover Nature Coloring Book Ser.). (ENG.). 32p. (J). (gr. 1-5). pap. 5.99 *(978-0-486-47894-4(7))* Dover Pubns., Inc.

—Nautical Scenes to Paint or Color. 2007. (Dover Art Coloring Book Ser.). (ENG., Illus.). 48p. (gr. 3-8). 5.99 *(978-0-486-45693-5(5))* Dover Pubns., Inc.

—Rocky Mountains Plants & Animals. 2004. (Dover Nature Coloring Book Ser.). (ENG., Illus.). 32p. (gr. 3-8). pap. 3.99 *(978-0-486-43045-4(6))* Dover Pubns., Inc.

—A Walk in the Woods. 2003. (Dover Nature Coloring Book Ser.). (ENG., Illus.). 32p. (gr. 6-8). pap. 3.99 *(978-0-486-42644-0(0))* Dover Pubns., Inc.

Barney Color & Activity Prepack. 2003. (J). 179.40 *(978-0-439-47364-4(0))* Scholastic, Inc.

Bartfeld, Martha & Hutchinson, Alberta. Infinite Coloring Mandala Designs. 2009. (Dover Design Coloring Bks.). (ENG., Illus.). 96p. (gr. 3-5). pap. 9.99 incl. cd-rom *(978-0-486-46949-2(2))* Dover Pubns., Inc.

Basford, Johanna. Enchanted Forest. 2015. (J). lib. bdg. 28.10 *(978-0-606-37118-6(4))* Turtleback Bks.

—Secret Garden: An Inky Treasure Hunt & Coloring Book. 2013. (J). lib. bdg. 28.10 *(978-0-606-37119-3(2))* Turtleback Bks.

Battaglioli, Peter. What to Doodle? Crazy Faces. 2013. (Dover Doodle Bks.). (ENG.). 48p. (J). (gr. 2-5). pap. 4.99 *(978-0-486-49100-4(5))* Dover Pubns., Inc.

Bauer, Susan Wise. The Middle Ages. 2003. (Story of the World: Vol. 2). (ENG., Illus.). 200p. (J). act. bk. ed. 29.95 *(978-0-9714129-4-1(4)*, AB2) Well-Trained Mind Pr.

Bechtold, Phyllis. Seymour Bluffs Activities Coloring Book. 2006. 32p. spiral bd. 5.95 *(978-0-9728538-3-5(9))* Arnica Publishing.

Beck, Ernie. Skinni Mini & Friends in the Valley of Hope. Beck, Blaze, illus. 2012. 74p. pap. 13.99 *(978-0-9858398-5-7(6))* Mindstir Media.

Beck, Lauren. All about Me Children's Coloring Journal. Anderson, Lexie, illus. 2015. (J). pap. 4.99 *(978-1-4621-1707-9(4)*, Horizon Pubs.) Cedar Fort, Inc./CFI Distribution.

Bell, A. L. Jr. Comics Coloring (Fun Time) 2005. 20p. 7.00 *(978-1-4116-3758-0(5))* Lulu Pr., Inc.

Bell-Myers, Darcy. The Animal Babies ABC Book of Ballet. 2013. (Dover Coloring Bks.). (ENG.). 32p. (J). (gr. -1-3). pap. 3.99 *(978-0-486-49814-0(X))* Dover Pubns., Inc.

—The Animal Babies ABC Book of Princesses. 2013. (ENG.). 32p. (J). (gr. -1-3). pap. 3.99 *(978-0-486-49811-9(5))* Dover Pubns., Inc.

Bell, N. Wayne. Childrens' Economics: A Book on Money & Finance. I.t. ed. 2004. (Illus.). 32p. (J). per. *(978-0-9729753-5-3(7))* Really Big Coloring Bks., Inc.

—The Really Big Book of Zoo Animals. I.t. ed. 2004. (Illus.). 32p. (J). per. *(978-0-9729753-6-0(5))* Really Big Coloring Bks., Inc.

Belovitch, Jeanne & Bonnevie, Bonnie. New York City Firsts: A Coloring Book for Families about New York History & America's. Belovitch, Jeanne, ed. 2004. 19p. (J). (gr. -1-6). pap. 3.00 *(978-0-9722969-1-5(3))* CMB Publishing Co.

BELTEI, Nadia. Emily's BOOKS: Coloring & Activity book, age Level: 2-3 (B&W) 2010. 39p. pap. 7.47 *(978-0-557-32886-4(1))* Lulu Pr., Inc.

Berenstain, Jan & Berenstain, Stan. The Berenstain Bears Giant Coloring & Activity Book. 2013. (ENG.). 272p. (J). (gr. -1-2). pap. 7.99 *(978-0-486-49341-1(5))* Dover Pubns., Inc.

Berenstain, Jan, et al. The Berenstain Bears — a Bear Country Alphabet Coloring Book. 2014. (ENG.). 48p. (J). (gr. -1). pap. 4.99 *(978-0-486-49470-8(5))* Dover Pubns., Inc.

—The Berenstain Bears' Count on Numbers Coloring Book. 2014. (ENG.). 48p. (J). (gr. -1). pap. 4.99 *(978-0-486-49469-2(1))* Dover Pubns., Inc.

Berenstain, Stan, et al. The Berenstain Bears' Sleepover, Vol. 3. Berenstain, Stan et al, illus. 2008. (I Can Read Level 1 Ser.). (ENG.). 32p. (J). (gr. k-3). pap., act. bk. ed. 3.99 *(978-0-06-057415-4(1))* HarperCollins Pubs.

Bernath, Stefen. Common Weeds. 2013. (Dover Nature Coloring Book Ser.). (ENG., Illus.). 48p. (J). (gr. 3-8). pap. 4.99 *(978-0-486-23308-6(1))* Dover Pubns., Inc.

Berrios, Frank & RH Disney Staff. Shapes, Colors, Counting & More! (Disney/Pixar Cars) RH Disney Staff, illus. 2013. (Friendship Box Ser.). (ENG., Illus.). 48p. (J). (gr. -1-2). bds. 10.99 *(978-0-7364-3105-7(5)*, RH/Disney) Random Hse. Children's Bks.

The Best Thing about Easter Coloring Book. 2006. 16p. (J). pap. 1.99 *(978-0-7847-1351-8(0)*, 22128) Standard Publishing.

Betanzos, Sue, illus. My New Backyard Garden. 2006.Tr. of Mi Nuevo Jardin del Traspatio. (SPA & ENG.). (J). *(978-0-9792253-0-7(2))* Tucson Botanical Gardens.

Beylon, Cathy. All Aboard! Trains Activity & Coloring Book. 2006. (Dover Children's Activity Bks.). (ENG., Illus.). 32p. (J). (gr. -1-2). pap., act. bk. ed. 3.99 *(978-0-486-45174-9(7))* Dover Pubns., Inc.

—Animal Opposites. 2008. (Dover Coloring Bks.). (ENG., Illus.). 32p. (J). (gr. -1-2). pap. 3.99 *(978-0-486-46197-7(1))* Dover Pubns., Inc.

—At the Aquarium/en el Acuario: Bilingual Coloring Book. Gongora, Oscar, tr. 2011. (Dover Children's Bilingual Coloring Book Ser.). (ENG & SPA., Illus.). 32p. (J). (gr. k-6). pap. 3.99 *(978-0-486-47813-5(0))* Dover Pubns., Inc.

—At the Zoo/en el Zoologico: Bilingual Coloring Book. Gongora, Oscar, tr. 2011. (Dover Children's Bilingual Coloring Book Ser.). (ENG & SPA., Illus.). 32p. (J). (gr. k-6). pap. 3.99 *(978-0-486-47814-2(9))* Dover Pubns., Inc.

—BOOST Mother Goose Coloring Book. 2013. (BOOST Educational Ser.). (ENG.). 32p. (J). (gr. 1-2). pap. 4.99 *(978-0-486-49414-2(4))* Dover Pubns., Inc.

—Christmas Family Fun Coloring Book. 2006. (Dover Holiday Coloring Book Ser.). (ENG., Illus.). 32p. (J). (gr. 1-5). 3.99 *(978-0-486-44749-0(9))* Dover Pubns., Inc.

—Going Camping. 2004. (Dover Coloring Bks.). (ENG.). 32p. (J). (gr. -1-2). pap. 3.99 *(978-0-486-43984-6(4))* Dover Pubns., Inc.

—Halloween Stained Glass Coloring Book. 2007. (Holiday Stained Glass Coloring Book Ser.). (ENG., Illus.). 32p. (J). (gr. -1-2). 6.99 *(978-0-486-45677-5(3))* Dover Pubns., Inc.

—Happy Halloween Stained Glass Jr. Coloring Book. 2012. (Dover Stained Glass Coloring Book Ser.). (ENG.). 32p. (J). (gr. -1-5). pap. 3.99 *(978-0-486-49872-0(7))* Dover Pubns., Inc.

—Hearts Stained Glass Coloring Book. 2004. (Dover Stained Glass Coloring Book Ser.). (ENG., Illus.). 8p. (J). (gr. k-3). pap. 1.99 *(978-0-486-43844-3(9))* Dover Pubns., Inc.

—I Love Ballet/Me Encanta el Ballet: Bilingual Coloring Book. Gongora, Oscar, tr. 2011. (Dover Children's Bilingual Coloring Book Ser.). (ENG & SPA., Illus.). 32p. (J). (gr. k-5). pap. 3.99 *(978-0-486-47815-9(7))* Dover Pubns., Inc.

—I Love Pets Coloring Book. 2014. (ENG.). 64p. (J). (gr. -1-3). pap. 3.99 *(978-0-486-77964-5(5))* Dover Pubns., Inc.

—I Love Tropical Fish. 2008. (Dover Nature Coloring Book Ser.). (ENG., Illus.). 32p. (J). (gr. -1-2). 3.99 *(978-0-486-46221-9(8))* Dover Pubns., Inc.

—Let's Color Together — Horses & Ponies. 2014. (ENG., Illus.). 64p. (J). (gr. -1-3). pap. 3.99 *(978-0-486-77974-4(2))* Dover Pubns., Inc.

—Merry-Go-Round Stained Glass Coloring Book. 2003. (Dover Stained Glass Coloring Book Ser.). (ENG., Illus.). 8p. (J). (gr. -1-5). pap. 1.50 *(978-0-486-43000-3(6))* Dover Pubns., Inc.

—Mother Goose Coloring Book. 2004. (Dover Classic Stories Coloring Book Ser.). (ENG., Illus.). 32p. (J). (gr. -1-2). pap. 3.99 *(978-0-486-43696-8(9))* Dover Pubns., Inc.

—My Plane Trip. 2005. (Dover Coloring Bks.). (ENG., Illus.). 32p. (J). (gr. -1-2). pap. 3.99 *(978-0-486-43982-2(8))* Dover Pubns., Inc.

—Nature ABC Coloring Book. 2005. (Dover Coloring Bks.). (ENG., Illus.). 32p. (J). (gr. -1-3). 3.99 *(978-0-486-44448-2(1))* Dover Pubns., Inc.

—Noah's Ark. 2003. (Dover Classic Stories Coloring Book Ser.). (ENG., Illus.). 32p. (J). (gr. -1-2). pap. 3.99 *(978-0-486-42373-9(5))* Dover Pubns., Inc.

—Old Macdonald's Farm. 2003. (Dover Coloring Bks.). (ENG., Illus.). 32p. (J). (gr. -1-2). pap. 3.99 *(978-0-486-43034-8(0))* Dover Pubns., Inc.

—Safety First Coloring Book. 2006. (Dover Coloring Bks.). (ENG., Illus.). 32p. (J). (gr. -1-2). pap. 3.99 *(978-0-486-45164-0(X))* Dover Pubns., Inc.

—Teddy Bear Family Stained Glass Coloring Book. 2003. (Dover Stained Glass Coloring Book Ser.). (ENG., Illus.). 16p. (J). (gr. -1-5). pap. 1.50 *(978-0-486-42617-4(3))* Dover Pubns., Inc.

Beylon, Cathy & Barbaresi, Nina. I Love Butterflies. 2007. (Dover Nature Coloring Book Ser.). (ENG., Illus.). 32p. (J). (gr. -1-2). pap. 4.99 *(978-0-486-45659-1(5))* Dover Pubns., Inc.

Bible Heroes. 2006. 16p. (J). pap. 1.99 *(978-0-7847-1354-9(5)*, 22123) Standard Publishing.

Bickico Enterprises Staff, concept. BabyKids: The Color Book. 2003. 16p. (J). pap. 2.95 *(978-0-9746508-2-1(X))* Bickico Enterprises, Inc.

Big Little Coloring Book. 2004. 192p. (J). act. bk. ed. 4.99 *(978-1-85997-234-2(9))* Byeway Bks.

Biggs, Brian. Blue Bus, Red Balloon: A Book of Colors. Biggs, Brian, illus. 2013. (ENG., Illus.). 24p. (J). (gr. -1 — 1). bds. 7.99 *(978-0-06-195814-4(X))* HarperCollins Pubs.

Bing & Bong's Colouring Book. 2003. (Bing & Bong's Tiny Planets Ser.). (Illus.). 24p. *(978-1-84222-876-0(5))* Carlton Bks., Ltd.

Bishop, Jennie. Jonah & the Big Fish Coloring Book. 2007. (Illus.). 16p. (J). pap. 1.89 *(978-1-59317-206-0(0))* Warner Pr., Inc.

—The Squire & the Scroll Coloring Book. 2005. (J). pap. 1.79 *(978-1-59317-085-1(8))* Warner Pr., Inc.

Blackbird Publishing Staff. Mr. HookWorm Coloring Book. 2007. (Illus.). 32p. (J). per. 1.50 *(978-0-9789798-7-4(7))* Blackbird's World Publishing Co.

Blackmon, Rosalind. Inventions Created by African Americans: An Educational Coloring Book. 2012. 60p. 24.99 *(978-1-4415-6339-2(3))*; pap. 15.99 *(978-1-4415-6338-5(5))* Xlibris Corp.

Blaisdell, Bob & Green, John. Adventures of Hercules Coloring Book. 2014. (Dover Classic Stories Coloring Book Ser.). (ENG., Illus.). 32p. (J). (gr. 4-7). pap. 3.99 *(978-0-486-29766-8(7))* Dover Pubns., Inc.

Blake, William. William Blake Stained Glass Colouring Book. 2005. (Dover Pictorial Archive Ser.). (ENG., Illus.). 16p. (gr. 3-5). pap. 5.95 *(978-0-486-44667-7(0))* Dover Pubns., Inc.

Blazin' Hot: Coloring/Activity Book (English) 2005. (Illus.). (J). 2.99 *(978-0-9770455-0-1(1))* Mighty Kids Media.

Blazin' Hot: Coloring/Activity Book (English) Incl. Stickers. 2007. (J). 2.99 *(978-1-933934-51-8(4))* Mighty Kids Media.

Blendy Pens Activity Book. 2006. (J). spiral bd., act. bk. ed. *(978-0-9770652-0-2(0))* Color Loco, LLC.

Bloomfield. Wild Utah Coloring Book. (J). pap. 2.95 *(978-0-915749-12-6(2))* Earthwalk Pr.

Bohn, Kendall. Abstract Adventure. 2009. (Kaleidoscopia Coloring Book Ser.). (Illus.). (J). 8.95 *(978-0-929636-98-6(8))* Itasca Bks.

—Abstract Adventure V. 2009. 56p. pap. 8.95 *(978-0-929636-01-6(5))* Syren Bk. Co.

Bohn, Kendall, illus. The Original Abstract Adventure. 2009. 54p. pap. 8.95 *(978-0-929636-99-3(6))* Syren Bk. Co.

Bonforte, Lisa. Farm Animals Coloring Book. 2012. (Dover Little Activity Bks.). (ENG., Illus.). 64p. (J). (gr. k-3). pap. 1.99 *(978-0-486-29781-1(0))* Dover Pubns., Inc.

Boosel, Brian D. The Saint Vincent Coloring Book Gabler, Michael, illus. 2005. 36p. (J). 9.99 *(978-0-9708216-7-6(0))* St. Vincent Archabbey Pubns.

Boughton, Samantha. Day at the Zoo Adventure Coloring Book. 2014. (ENG., Illus.). 48p. (J). (gr. k). pap. 4.99 *(978-0-486-49154-7(4))* Dover Pubns., Inc.

—Dino Island Adventure Coloring Book. 2014. (ENG., Illus.). 48p. (J). (gr. k). pap. 4.99 *(978-0-486-49155-4(2))* Dover Pubns., Inc.

—Under the Sea Adventure Coloring Book. 2013. (ENG., Illus.). 48p. (J). (gr. k-5). pap. 4.99 *(978-0-486-49166-0(8))* Dover Pubns., Inc.

Bowers, A., et al. Mushrooms of the World with Pictures to Color. 2013. (Dover Nature Coloring Book Ser.). (ENG., Illus.). 48p. (J). (gr. 3-12). pap. 4.99 *(978-0-486-24643-7(4))* Dover Pubns., Inc.

Bowman, Lucy. Drawing, Doodling & Coloring Book Girls. 2012. (Activity Cards Ser.). 128p. (J). pap. 13.99 *(978-0-7945-3297-0(7)*, Usborne) EDC Publishing.

—Spooky Doodles. 2012. (Doodles Cards Ser.). 50p. (J). 9.99 *(978-0-7945-2902-4(X)*, Usborne) EDC Publishing.

Bowsher, Alice, illus. Lift-The-Flap & Color Jungle. 2017. (Lift-the-flap & Color Ser.). (ENG.). 10p. (J). (gr. -1-k). pap. 8.99 ***(978-1-84780-931-5(6)***, Frances Lincoln Children's Bks.) Quarto Publishing Group UK GBR. Dist: Hachette Bk. Group.

—Lift-The-Flap & Color Ocean. 2017. (Lift-The-flap & Color Ser.). (ENG.). 10p. (J). (gr. -1-k). pap. 8.99 ***(978-1-84780-932-2(4)***, Frances Lincoln Children's Bks.) Quarto Publishing Group UK GBR. Dist: Hachette Bk. Group.

Boyer, Melody. Great American Pony Ride. Johnson, Dolores Uselman, illus. 32p. (J). 2.00 *(978-0-9704876-3-6(0))* First Mom's Club, The.

Brabham, Barbara. Donkey Tales — Color with Paco! [English/Spanish Versions]. 2006. (J). 2.95 *(978-1-882185-86-3(2))* Cornerstone Publishing, Inc.

Bradley, Barbara. Hawaiian Kids Cook & Color Book. pap. 5.95 *(978-0-930492-43-4(9))* Hawaiian Service, Inc.

Brett, Anna. Ballerina Theater: Color & Create Your Own Beautiful 3D Scenes. 2017. (3D Colorscapes Ser.). (ENG.). 48p. (J). (gr. 3-7). bds. 10.99 *(978-0-7641-6882-6(7))* Barron's Educational Series, Inc.

British Broadcasting Corporation Children's Books Staff. T Is for Tardis. Howling, Adam, illus. 2017. (ENG.). 60p. (J). 9.99 ***(978-1-4059-2998-1(7)***, 9781405929981) Penguin Bks., Ltd. GBR. Dist: Diamond Comic Distributors, Inc.

Britto, Romero. Color Play! An Interactive Pop Art Book. Britto, Romero, illus. 2011. (ENG., Illus.). 12p. (J). (gr. -1-k). 10.99 *(978-1-4169-9622-4(2)*, Little Simon) Little Simon.

Broberg, Penelope Northrop. Sleuthy Gumshoe: The Remarkable Detective. 2011. 32p. (gr. -1). pap. 14.39 *(978-1-4567-6404-3(7))* AuthorHouse.

Brocklehurst, Ruth. Vintage Fashion Coloring Book IR. 2015. (Patterns to Color Ser.). (ENG.). 32p. (J). (gr. k-5). pap. 5.99 *(978-0-7945-3490-5(2)*, Usborne) EDC Publishing.

Brodsky, Irene. Queen Esther's New Coloring Book. Steyert, Bill, illus. 2011. 39p. pap. 17.95 *(978-1-4327-6771-6(2))* Outskirts Pr., Inc.

Brown, Barbara J. The Many Different Ways to Worship: Is apart of everyday Life. 2009. 48p. pap. 11.99 *(978-1-4490-3275-3(3))* AuthorHouse.

Buckingham, Faye. The Calm Coloring Book for Creative Kids. 2016. (ENG.). 96p. (J). pap. 9.95 *(978-1-78599-091-5(8)*, f30044e7-0cb9-4f77-b14a-f44baa13183d) Arcturus Publishing GBR. Dist: Bookmasters Distribution.

Bugs Bunny & Friends. 2008. (Super Big Coloring Book Ser.). 224p. pap. *(978-1-4075-3407-7(6))* Parragon, Inc.

Bulleman, Curtis David. Let's Color Together — Cool Cars. 2014. (ENG., Illus.). 64p. (J). (gr. -1-3). pap. 3.99 *(978-0-486-77971-3(8))* Dover Pubns., Inc.

Bulleman, Curtis David & Coloring Books Staff. Car Crazy! 2011. (Dover 3-D Coloring Book Ser.). (ENG., Illus.). 32p. (J). (gr. 2-6). 5.99 *(978-0-486-48418-1(1))* Dover Pubns., Inc.

Bumpers, Katrina. Alphabet Fun, Book 2: Coloring & Activity Book. 2008. (Illus.). 64p. (gr. -1-3). pap. 10.95 *(978-0-9797208-1-9(8))* K's Kids Publishing.

Bumpers, Katrina B. Alphabet Fun, Book 1: Coloring & Activity Book. Lopez, Eddie, ed. Bourrouet, Jonathan, illus. 2008. 64p. pap. 10.95 *(978-0-9797208-0-2(X))* K's Kids Publishing.

Bunnell, Jacinta. Sometimes the Spoon Runs Away with Another Spoon Coloring Book. Kusinitz, Nat, illus. 2010. (Reach & Teach Ser.). (ENG.). 32p. pap. 10.00 *(978-1-60486-329-1(3))* PM Pr.

Burke, Fatti & Burke, John. Irelandopedia Activity Book: With Colouring Pages, a Huge Pull-Out Map of Ireland & Lots of Things to See & Do. 2016. (ENG., Illus.). 32p. (J). pap. 16.00 *(978-0-7171-7149-1(3))* M.H. Gill & Co. U. C. IRL. Dist: Dufour Editions, Inc.

Burke, John & Burke, Fatti. Historopedia Activity Book: With Colouring Pages, a Huge Pull-Out Timeline Poster & Lots of Things to See & Do. 2017. (ENG.). 32p. (J). pap. 17.00 ***(978-0-7171-7573-4(1))*** M.H. Gill & Co. U. C. IRL. Dist: Dufour Editions, Inc.

Burnett, Frances Hodgson. A Little Princess Coloring Book. Kliros, Thea, illus. abr. ed. 2013. (Dover Coloring Bks.). (ENG.). 48p. (J). (gr. 1-5). pap. 4.99 *(978-0-486-40561-2(3))* Dover Pubns., Inc.

—The Secret Garden Coloring Book. Kliros, Thea, illus. 2014. (ENG.). 48p. (J). (gr. 4-7). pap. 4.99 *(978-0-486-27680-9(5))* Dover Pubns., Inc.

Burns, T. D. BOOST Rocks & Minerals Coloring Book. 2013. (BOOST Educational Ser.). (ENG.). 48p. (J). (gr. 3-5). pap. 5.99 *(978-0-486-49437-1(3))* Dover Pubns., Inc.

Burton, Manja. Foldables - Princesses, Ponies, Mermaids & More: Never-Ending Fun to Color, Fold & Flip. 2016. (ENG.). 32p. (J). (gr. 1-4). pap. 3.99 *(978-0-486-80451-4(8))* Dover Pubns., Inc.

—Foldables - Trucks, Dinosaurs, Monsters & More: Never-Ending Fun to Color, Fold & Flip. 2016. (ENG.). 32p. (J). (gr. 1-4). pap. 3.99 *(978-0-486-80452-1(6))* Dover Pubns., Inc.

Buster Books, et al. Colour Away Your Worries. Bigwood, John, illus. 2017. (ENG.). 112p. (J). (gr. 1-6). 13.99 ***(978-1-78055-309-2(9))*** O'Mara, Michael Bks., Ltd. GBR. Dist: Independent Pubs. Group.

Buster Books Staff & Kronheimer, Ann. The Ice Princess. 2015. (ENG.). 32p. (J). (gr. 1-4). pap. 6.99 ***(978-1-78055-363-4(3))*** O'Mara, Michael Bks., Ltd. GBR. Dist: Independent Pubs. Group.

Buzz. (Disney Fun Shaped Coloring Ser.). 64p. pap. *(978-1-4054-9381-9(X))* Parragon, Inc.

Cache, Dee. ABC's of Boating Terms, 1 vol. 2012. (ENG., Illus.). 32p. (J). pap. 6.99 *(978-0-7643-3982-0(6)*, 9780764339820) Schiffer Publishing, Ltd.

Caillou: Colors & Shapes. 2003. 32p. pap., wbk. ed. 14.95 incl. cd-rom *(978-1-57791-029-9(X))* Brighter Minds Children's Publishing.

Camping Caper: Coloring/Activity Book (English) incl. Stickers. 2007. (Illus.). (J). 2.99 *(978-1-933934-65-5(4))* Mighty Kids Media.

Candlewick Press Staff. Winter at Hogwarts, Set. 2016. (ENG.). 48p. (J). (gr. 3-7). 15.99 *(978-0-7636-9589-7(0))* Candlewick Pr.

Carbone, Courtney. Power-Packed! (DC Super Friends) Golden Books, illus. 2014. (Deluxe Stickerific Ser.). (ENG.). 64p. (J). (gr. -1-2). pap. 5.99 *(978-0-385-38720-0(2)*, Golden Bks.) Random Hse. Children's Bks.

Care Bears Coloring Books. 2004. (J). act. bk. ed. 1.29 *(978-0-7666-0921-1(9)*, 99390) Modern Publishing.

Carle, Eric. My Own Very Busy Spider Coloring Book. Carle, Eric, illus. 2004. (ENG., Illus.). 32p. (J). (gr. -1-k). 5.99 *(978-0-399-24309-7(7)*, Philomel Bks.) Penguin Young Readers Group.

—My Own Very Hungry Caterpillar. Carle, Eric, illus. 2003. (ENG., Illus.). 32p. (J). (gr. -1-k). 5.99 *(978-0-399-24207-6(4)*, Philomel Bks.) Penguin Young Readers Group.

—My Own Very Lonely Firefly Coloring Book. Carle, Eric, illus. 2006. (ENG., Illus.). 32p. (J). (gr. -1-k). 5.99 *(978-0-399-24646-3(0)*, Philomel Bks.) Penguin Young Readers Group.

—My Own Very Quiet Cricket Coloring Book. Carle, Eric, illus. 2005. (ENG., Illus.). 32p. (J). (gr. -1-k). 5.99 *(978-0-399-24475-9(1)*, Philomel Bks.) Penguin Young Readers Group.

—The World of Eric Carle Big Coloring Book (the World of Eric Carle) Carle, Eric, illus. 2011. (Big Coloring Book Ser.). (ENG., Illus.). 48p. (J). (gr. -1-2). pap. 6.99 *(978-0-375-87351-5(1)*, Golden Bks.) Random Hse. Children's Bks.

Carlsbad Caverns & Guadalupe Mountains Color Book. 2003. (YA). pap. *(978-0-916907-08-2(2))* Carlsbad Caverns Guadalupe Mountains Assn.

Carlson, Jr. Autism Coloring Book. Carlson, Kevin, illus. 2009. 50p. pap. 9.95 *(978-1-60264-383-3(0))* Virtualbookworm.com Publishing, Inc.

C
D

Carlton Publishing Group. My Mandalas. 2016. (Cool & Calm Coloring for Kids Ser.). (ENG.). 48p. (J). (gr. 2-6). pap. 6.99 (978-1-4380-0884-4(8)) Barron's Educational Series, Inc.

Carlton Publishing Group, illus. Magical Designs & Color-By-Numbers. 2016. (Cool & Calm Coloring for Kids Ser.). (ENG.). 48p. (J). (gr. 2-6). pap. 6.99 (978-1-4380-0927-8(5)) Barron's Educational Series, Inc.

Carney, Larry. Jeff Gordon. PC Treasures Staff, ed. Houghton, Chris & Morrison, Jeff, illus. 2009. (Nascar Drivers Coloring/Sticker Book Ser.). (ENG.). 96p. (J). pap. 6.95 (978-1-60072-162-5(1)) PC Treasures, Inc.

—Tony Stewart. PC Treasures Staff, ed. Morrison, Jeff, illus. 2009. (Nascar Drivers Coloring/Sticker Book Ser.). (ENG.). 96p. (J). pap. 6.95 (978-1-60072-166-3(4)) PC Treasures, Inc.

Caro, Joe. Santa's Christmas Train Coloring Book. Shih, Lin, illus. 2005. 32p. pap. (978-0-9628078-5-5(0)) Cowboy Collector Pubns.

Carole Marsh. Chicago Coloring & Activity Book. 2004. (City Bks.). 24p. (gr. k-5). pap. 3.95 (978-0-635-02227-1(3)) Gallopade International.

—Dallas Coloring & Activity Book. 2004. (City Bks.). 24p. (gr. k-5). pap. 3.95 (978-0-635-02231-8(1)) Gallopade International.

—Los Angeles Coloring & Activity Book. 2004. (City Bks.). 24p. (gr. k-5). pap. 3.95 (978-0-635-02229-5(X)) Gallopade International.

—New England Coloring. 2004. (City Bks.). 24p. (gr. k-5). pap., act. bk. ed. 3.95 (978-0-635-02233-2(8)) Gallopade International.

—New York City Coloring & Activity Book. 2004. (City Bks.). 24p. (gr. k-5). pap. 3.95 (978-0-635-02226-4(5)) Gallopade International.

—San Francisco Coloring & Activity Book. 2004. (City Bks.). 24p. (J). (gr. k-5). pap., act. bk. ed. 3.95 (978-0-635-02228-8(1)) Gallopade International.

—Washington Dc Coloring & Activity Book. 2004. (City Bks.). 24p. (gr. k-5). pap. 3.95 (978-0-635-02232-5(X)) Gallopade International.

Carpenter, Chad. Tundra Alaska Coloring Book. (J). pap. 3.00 (978-1-878100-32-0(7)) Todd Communications.

Carroll, Lewis, pseud. Alice in Wonderland Giant Poster & Coloring Book. Tenniel, John, illus. 2012. (ENG.). 48p. (gr. -1-17). pap. 12.95 (978-1-4197-0089-7(8), Abrams Image) Abrams, Inc.

Carson-Dellosa Publishing Staff. Dot-to-Dot Bible Pictures: Make Personal Connections to God's Word! 2004. (Fun Faith-Builders Ser.). (ENG.). 32p. (gr. -1-k). pap. 4.99 (978-0-88724-219-9(7), CD-2040) Carson-Dellosa Publishing, LLC.

Carson-Dellosa Publishing Staff, compiled by. Dot-to-Dot Bible Pictures, Grades 1-3: Make Personal Connections to God's Word! 2004. (Fun Faith-Builders Ser.). (ENG.). 32p. (gr. 1-3). pap. 4.99 (978-0-88724-220-5(0), CD-2041) Carson-Dellosa Publishing, LLC.

Cartwright, Steven, illus. Farmyard Tales Sticker Coloring Book. 2011. (Coloring Bks). 20p. (J). pap. 5.99 (978-0-7945-2959-8(3), Usborne) EDC Publishing.

Cash, Marie Romero. Santos: A Coloring Book of New Mexican Saints. 2008. 80p. (J). pap. 10.95 (978-0-86534-701-4(8)) Sunstone Pr.

Cass, Kiera. The Selection Coloring Book. Flor, Martina, illus. 2016. 96p. (J). (gr. 8). pap. 15.99 (978-0-06-264114-4(X), HarperTeen) HarperCollins Pubs.

Cassettari, James. Monster Trucks Coloring Book. 2015. (ENG.). 32p. (J). (gr. k). pap. 3.99 (978-0-486-79794-6(5)) Dover Pubns., Inc.

Catwalk Model: Clothes, Shoes & Accessories to Draw & Color. 2012. (ENG.). 144p. (J). spiral bd. 10.95 (978-1-84837-916-9(1)) Arcturus Publishing GBR. Dist: Bookmasters Distribution.

Celebrate Jesus! Coloring/Activity Book. 2006. (Illus.). 32p. (J). (gr. -1-2). pap., act. bk. ed. 2.89 (978-0-7847-1125-5(9), 22090) Standard Publishing.

Charge of the Goddess. 2007. (Illus.). 20p. (J). 10.00 (978-0-9795206-4-8(9)) Unseen Gallery.

Children of the Bible: Dot-to-Dot Coloring Book. (Illus.). 16p. (J). pap. 1.50 (978-0-87162-979-1(8), E4652) Warner Pr., Inc.

Chouette Publishing Staff. Caillou - The Little Artist. Sevigny, Eric, illus. 2011. (Coloring & Activity Book Ser.). (ENG.). 96p. (J). (gr. -1-1). 7.95 (978-2-89450-809-1(3)) Caillouet, Gerry.

Christensen, Catherine, told to. Blessing the Nephite Children. 2016. (ENG.). (J). bds. 10.99 (978-1-4621-1875-5(5)) Cedar Fort, Inc./CFI Distribution.

Christmas Coloring Fun Christmas Carols. 2004. (J). per. 6.95 (978-1-885920-47-8(4)) Pyramid Publishing, Inc.

Christmas Coloring Fun Santa Relaxing. 2004. (J). per. 6.95 (978-1-885920-48-5(2)) Pyramid Publishing, Inc.

Christmas Coloring Fun Santa's New Sled. 2004. (J). per. 6.95 (978-1-885920-88-1(1)) Pyramid Publishing, Inc.

Christmas Coloring Fun Snowman. 2004. (J). per. 6.95 (978-1-885920-90-4(3)) Pyramid Publishing, Inc.

Christmas Fun Coloring Book. 2006. 16p. (J). pap. 1.99 (978-0-7847-1745-5(1), 04371) Standard Publishing.

Chu, Carol & Chang, Lulu. The Fashion Coloring Book. 2012. (ENG., Illus.). 128p. (YA). (gr. 7). pap. 14.99 (978-0-547-55395-5(1)) Houghton Mifflin Harcourt Publishing Co.

Cibos, Lindsay. Little Pony Coloring Book. 2015. (ENG.). 48p. (J). pap. 6.99 (978-1-4403-4387-2(X), Impact) F&W Media, Inc.

Cicierega, Emmy. Gravity Falls Don't Color This Book! A Cursed Coloring Book. Ramirez, Stephanie, illus. 2017. (ENG.). 64p. pap. 12.99 **(978-1-368-00899-0(2))** Disney Pr.

Ciminera, Siobhan & Testa, Maggie. Dancey Dance. Yoe! Studio Staff, illus. 2009. (Yo Gabba Gabba! Ser.). (ENG.). 32p. (J). (gr. -1-1). 4.99 (978-1-4169-7100-9(9), Simon Scribbles) Simon Scribbles.

Clark, Christian. Mr. Clark's Awesome Designs Coloring Book. 2006. (ENG.). 60p. per. 11.95 (978-1-59800-883-8(8)) Outskirts Pr., Inc.

Clark, Isabel. Sticker & Colour- in Playbook: On the Farm. Tulip, Jenny, illus. 2016. (ENG.). 16p. (J). (gr. -1-12). pap. 4.99 (978-1-86147-748-4(1)) Anness Publishing, Inc.

Clarke, Isabel. Sticker & Color-In Playbook: With over 50 Reusable Stickers: Teddy Bear Sizes. Tulip, Jenny, illus. 2016. (ENG.). 16p. (J). (gr. -1-12). pap. 4.99 (978-1-86147-736-1(8), Armadillo) Anness Publishing GBR. Dist: National Bk. Network.

Cloyne, Rachel. The Alice in Wonderland Colouring Book. Cloyne, Rachel, illus. 2015. (ENG., Illus.). 32p. (J). (gr. 1-4). pap. 6.99 **(978-1-78055-353-5(6))** O'Mara, Michael Bks., Ltd. GBR. Dist: Independent Pubs. Group.

—The Fairy Tale Colouring Book. Cloyne, Rachel, illus. 2014. (ENG., Illus.). 32p. (J). (gr. 1-4). pap. 8.99 **(978-1-78055-252-1(1))** O'Mara, Michael Bks., Ltd. GBR. Dist: Independent Pubs. Group.

Coches. (Coleccion Mundo Maravilloso).Tr. of Drawing Cars. (SPA.). (J). (gr. 3-5). (978-84-348-4429-2(X)) SM Ediciones.

Cole, Heidi & Vogl, Nancy. Am I a Color Too? Purnell, Gerald, illus. 2005. 32p. (J). (gr. -1-3). 15.95 (978-0-9740190-5-5(4)) Illumination Arts Publishing Co., Inc.

Cole, Hugh M. Postman Pat. 2012. (Illus.). xxv, 720p. **(978-0-7948-3770-9(0))** Whitman Publishing LLC.

Collins, Erica. Aloha Activity Book. Collins, Erica, illus. 2009. (Illus.). 24p. pap. 4.98 (978-1-933735-59-7(7)) Pacifica Island Art, Inc.

Color All About: A Giant Coloring Book about Dinosaurs: Dinosaurs. 2004. (SPA & ENG., Illus.). 36p. (J). (978-1-59949-001-4(3)) Food Marketing Consultants, Inc.

Color All About: A Giant Coloring Book about Fun Things to do at School: Back to School. 2004. (Illus.). 36p. (J). (978-1-59949-005-2(6)) Food Marketing Consultants, Inc.

Color All About: A Giant Coloring Book about Loving Our Pets: Pets. 2004. (Illus.). 36p. (J). (978-1-59949-002-1(1)) Food Marketing Consultants, Inc.

Color All About: A Giant Coloring Book about Summer Vacation: Summer Vacation. 2004. (Illus.). 36p. (J). (978-1-59949-006-9(4)) Food Marketing Consultants, Inc.

Color All About: A Giant Coloring Book about the Alphabet: the Alphabet. 2004. (SPA & ENG., Illus.). 36p. (J). (978-1-59949-000-7(5)) Food Marketing Consultants, Inc.

Color All About: A Giant Coloring Book about the County Fair: the County Fair. 2004. (SPA & ENG., Illus.). 36p. (J). (978-1-59949-004-5(8)) Food Marketing Consultants, Inc.

Color All About: A Giant Coloring Book about Work & Play on the Farm: the Farm. 2004. (SPA & ENG., Illus.). 36p. (J). (978-1-59949-003-8(X)) Food Marketing Consultants, Inc.

Color All About: America: A Giant Coloring Book about the Birth of a Nation. 2004. (Illus.). (J). (978-0-9763307-3-8(3)) Food Marketing Consultants, Inc.

Color All About: Christmas: A Giant Coloring Book about Christmas. 2004. (SPA & ENG., Illus.). (J). (978-0-9763307-7-6(6)) Food Marketing Consultants, Inc.

Color All About: Christmas: A Giant Coloring Book for Christmas. 2004. (Illus.). (J). (978-0-9763307-0-7(9)) Food Marketing Consultants, Inc.

Color All About: Santa: A Giant Coloring Book about What Santa Does When It's Not Christmas. 2004. (Illus.). (J). (978-0-9763307-4-5(1)); (SPA & ENG.). (978-0-9763307-8-3(4)) Food Marketing Consultants, Inc.

Color All About: The Circus: A Giant Coloring Book about Going to the Circus. 2004. (Illus.). (J). (SPA & ENG.). (978-0-9763307-9-0(2)); (978-0-9763307-1-4(7)) Food Marketing Consultants, Inc.

Color All About: The County Fair: A Giant Coloring Book about Having Fun When the Fair Comes to Town. 2004. (Illus.). (J). (978-0-9763307-6-9(8)) Food Marketing Consultants, Inc.

Color All About: The Farm: A Giant Coloring Book about Having Fun on a Farm. 2004. (Illus.). (J). (978-0-9763307-5-2(X)) Food Marketing Consultants, Inc.

Color All About: The Zoo: A Coloring Book about Going to the Zoo. 2004. (Illus.). (J). (978-0-9763307-2-1(5)) Food Marketing Consultants, Inc.

Color Me Monet. 2004. (J). (978-0-9765917-1-9(5)) EDUKIT, L.L.C.

Color My Mouse - Calendar Mice. 2004. (J). pap. (978-0-9764719-1-2(4)) MiceWorks.

Color My Mouse - Summer Mice. 2005. (J). pap. (978-0-9764719-2-9(2)) MiceWorks.

Color Splitz. 2006. (J). spiral bd. 12.99 (978-0-9770652-1-9(9)) Color Loco, LLC.

Colorado Coloring Book. 2003. (J). (978-0-9726022-0-4(8)) Mountain States Specialties.

Coloring Book Assortment. 2003. (J). per. (978-1-932435-22-1(0)) Cardinal Brands, Inc.

Coloring Book Lets Celebrate G. 2006. 16p. (J). pap. 1.99 (978-0-7847-1526-0(2), 22140) Standard Publishing.

Coloring Book Let's Remember Jesus. 2006. 16p. (J). pap. 1.99 (978-0-7847-1525-3(4), 22139) Standard Publishing.

Coloring Book Story of David. 2004. pap. (978-1-931471-12-1(6)) United Bible Societies, African Regional Ctr.

Coloring Book/Intermediate/Bible Fun Old Testament. 2006. (J). 14.99 (978-1-59317-146-9(3)) Warner Pr., Inc.

Coloring Fun: Coloring/Activity Book (English) 2006. (Illus.). (J). 2.99 (978-1-933934-20-4(4)) Mighty Kids Media.

Coloring Fun: Coloring/Activity Book (Spanish) 2006. (Illus.). (J). 2.99 (978-1-933934-21-1(2)) Mighty Kids Media.

Coloring Fun: English/Spanish. 2006. (Illus.). (J). 2.99 (978-1-933934-24-2(7)) Mighty Kids Media.

Coloring Fun Book. 2004. 80p. (J). act. bk. ed. 4.99 (978-1-85997-387-5(6)) Byeway Bks.

Coloring Fun of the U. S. States Images & Facts. 2003. (Illus.). 40p. (J). 3.95 (978-0-9729026-3-2(5)) Midwest Cylinder Management, Inc.

Colors, 6 Bks, Set. 2004. (J). 128.14 (978-0-7614-1769-9(9)) Marshall Cavendish Corp.

Come Aboard Noah's Ark Coloring Book. abr. ed. (J). pap. 1.99 (978-0-8423-3535-5(8)) Tyndale Hse. Pubs.

Conant, Susan Sens. Lewis & Clark's Journey of Discovery: A Guide for Young Explorers. Lynn, Rick, illus. 2004. 48p. (J). pap. (978-0-9725584-1-9(1)) Little Blue Pr.

Concordia Publishing House. The Story of Christmas Coloring & Activity Book. 2015. (ENG.). 96p. (J). pap. 3.99 (978-0-7586-5223-2(2)) Concordia Publishing Hse.

—The Story of Jesus Coloring & Activity Book. 2015. (ENG.). 96p. (J). pap. 3.99 (978-0-7586-5222-5(4)) Concordia Publishing Hse.

Conley, Nia. Ray's School Daze. l.t. ed. 2003. (Illus.). 30p. (J). (978-0-9743781-2-1(7)) Urban Edge Publishing Co.

Conroy, Jim & Alexander, Basia. Messages from Trees Set 1: A Coloring Book for the Young & Young-At-Heart. 2013. (ENG., Illus.). 32p. (J). pap. 8.00 (978-0-9834114-5-1(X)) Plant Kingdom Communications.

Cookie Jar Entertainment Inc Staff. Doodlebops Count to Ten. 2007. 32p. mass mkt. 4.99 (978-1-60095-356-9(5), Doodlebops) Cookie Jar.

Cookie Jar Publishing Staff. Don't Pull the Rope: Kids' Favorite Rock Band! 2006. (Illus.). 32p. 2.99 (978-1-933799-00-1(5)) Midpoint Trade Bks., Inc.

Cookie Jar Publishing Staff, creator. Doodlebops: Friends & Favorites. 2007. (Doodlebops Ser.). (Illus.). 96p. (J). (gr. -1-3). 2.99 (978-1-60095-256-2(9)) Midpoint Trade Bks., Inc.

—Doodlebops: Let's Get on the Bus! 2007. (Doodlebops Ser.). (Illus.). 96p. (J). (gr. -1-3). 2.99 (978-1-60095-255-5(0)) Midpoint Trade Bks., Inc.

Cool by the Pool: Coloring / Activity Book incl Snipe. 2007. (Illus.). (J). 2.99 (978-0-9770455-8-7(7)) Mighty Kids Media.

Cool by the Pool: Coloring/Activity Book. 2005. (Illus.). (J). 2.99 (978-0-9770455-2-5(8)) Mighty Kids Media.

Cool Things Press. 75 Cool Things to Color. 2008. 80p. pap. 12.95 (978-0-615-20795-7(2)) Cool Things Pr.

—75 Cool Things to Cut Out. 2008. 152p. pap. 15.95 (978-0-615-20796-4(0)) Cool Things Pr.

Cooper, Heather, et al. Jacob Has Cancer: His Friends Want to Help. McMillion, Lindsey, illus. 2012. (ENG.). 16p. (J). (gr. k-2). pap. 3.50 (978-1-60443-012-7(5)) American Cancer Society, Inc.

Cooper, Jenny, illus. Forest Life to Color. 2013. (Nature Coloring Bks). 32p. (J). pap. 5.99 (978-0-7945-3305-2(1), Usborne) EDC Publishing.

—Rainforest to Color. 2013. (Nature Coloring Bks). 32p. (J). pap. 5.99 (978-0-7945-3306-9(X), Usborne) EDC Publishing.

Copeland, Peter F. Blackbeard & Other Notorious Pirates. 2005. (Dover History Coloring Book Ser.). (ENG., Illus.). 32p. (J). (gr. 3-8). 3.99 (978-0-486-44003-3(6)) Dover Pubns., Inc.

—Columbus Discovers America Coloring Book. 2014. (ENG., Illus.). 48p. (J). (gr. 3-8). pap. 4.99 (978-0-486-25542-2(5)) Dover Pubns., Inc.

—Daniel Boone Coloring Book. 2006. (Dover History Coloring Book Ser.). (ENG., Illus.). 32p. (J). (gr. 3-5). 3.99 (978-0-486-44738-4(3)) Dover Pubns., Inc.

—George Washington Coloring Book. 2003. (Dover History Coloring Book Ser.). (ENG., Illus.). 48p. (J). (gr. 3-8). pap. 4.99 (978-0-486-42647-1(5)) Dover Pubns., Inc.

—Scenes of Olde New York Coloring Book. 2009. (Dover History Coloring Book Ser.). (ENG.). 48p. (gr. 3-8). pap. 4.99 (978-0-486-47494-6(1)) Dover Pubns., Inc.

Copeland, Peter F., et al. Big Book of the Old West to Color. 2008. (Dover History Coloring Book Ser.). (ENG., Illus.). 144p. (gr. 3-8). 8.95 (978-0-486-46679-8(5)) Dover Pubns., Inc.

Corley, Nikolett. Zendoodle Coloring: Birds & Butterflies: Delicate Beauties to Color & Display. 2017. (ENG., Illus.). 128p. pap. 13.99 (978-1-250-12823-2(4), 9781250128232, St. Martin's Griffin) St. Martin's Pr.

Count & Color (Pre-K) 2003. (J). (978-1-58232-042-7(X)) ECS Learning Systems, Inc.

Courtauld, Sarah & Dickens, Rosie. Art Coloring Book with Stickers. 2012. (Art Coloring Book with Stickers Ser.). 32p. (J). pap. 8.99 (978-0-7945-2976-5(3), Usborne) EDC Publishing.

Couzens, Dominic & Nurney, David. Color Yourself Smart: Dinosaurs. 2013. (Color Yourself Smart Ser.). (ENG., Illus.). 128p. 19.95 (978-1-60710-573-2(X), Thunder Bay Pr.) Readerlink Distribution Services, LLC.

Covington, Jean. Nanny Planted Love: Color Book. 2006. (J). per. 6.99 (978-1-933732-13-8(X)) Big Ransom Studio.

COX, Margaret. The Soul-pearl. 2010. 169p. pap. 11.50 (978-1-4457-5679-0(X)) Lulu Pr., Inc.

Craig, Carol. Floral Fairies Coloring Book. 2015. (ENG.). 32p. (J). (gr. 3-8). pap. 3.99 (978-0-486-78327-7(8)) Dover Pubns., Inc.

Craig, Gary. I Can Be Anything Creative Activity Book. Craig, Gary, illus. 2006. (Illus.). 41p. (J). pap. 5.99 (978-0-9786813-2-6(0)) Elora Pr.

Creepy Crawlies. Date not set. (Dot to Dot Ser.). (Illus.). 64p. (J). 2.98 (978-1-4054-0447-1(7)) Parragon, Inc.

Criscuolo, Jill. I Want To... Coloring Book. 2013. 48p. (gr. -1). pap. 9.89 (978-1-4669-7625-2(X)); 40p. (gr. 4-6). pap. 16.46 (978-1-4669-7629-0(2)) Trafford Publishing.

Crispiels, Giada, illus. Wildlife of New York Coloring Book: A Five-Borough Coloring Book. 2016. (ENG.). 60p. 14.95 (978-0-7892-1255-9(2)) Abbeville Pr., Inc.

Crop Circle Coloring Book. 2005. (J). (978-0-9719583-6-4(X)) Onstott, Scott.

Crossling, Nick. Alhambra Stained Glass Coloring Book. 2008. (Dover Design Stained Glass Coloring Book Ser.). (ENG., Illus.). 32p. (gr. 3-8). per. 7.99 (978-0-486-46531-9(4)) Dover Pubns., Inc.

Crossling, Nick & Coloring Books Staff. Arabic Floral Patterns Coloring Book. 2012. (Dover Design Coloring Bks.). (ENG., Illus.). 32p. (J). (gr. 3-5). pap. 3.99 (978-0-486-47847-0(5)) Dover Pubns., Inc.

Crossling, Nick & Creative Haven. Creative Haven Alhambra Designs. 2013. (Adult Coloring Ser.). (ENG., Illus.). 64p. (gr. 3). pap. 5.99 (978-0-486-49316-9(4)) Dover Pubns., Inc.

Crow, Nosy. The Coloring Book of Cards & Envelopes: Christmas. Jones, Rebecca, illus. 2016. (ENG.). 74p. (J). (gr. k-12). pap. 10.99 (978-0-7636-9242-1(5), Nosy Crow) Candlewick Pr.

Crownover, Amy & Crownover, Dean. My Perfect Man Coloring & Activity Book. 2006. (Illus.). 32p. 12.95 (978-0-9785425-0-4(9)) Retro Recess.

Cullis, Megan. Birds to Color. Cooper, Jenny, illus. 2012. (Coloring Bks). 32p. (J). pap. 5.99 (978-0-7945-3285-7(3), Usborne) EDC Publishing.

—Butterflies Coloring Book. Cooper, Jenny, illus. 2012. (Coloring Bks). 32p. (J). pap. 5.99 (978-0-7945-3113-3(X), Usborne) EDC Publishing.

Curry, Don, ed. DC Heroes Ultimate Color & Activity Set. 2005. (J). pap. 9.99 (978-0-696-22892-6(0)) Meredith Bks.

Dahlen, Noelle. Christmas Cheer! Stained Glass Coloring Book. 2010. (Holiday Stained Glass Coloring Book Ser.). (ENG., Illus.). 32p. (gr. 2-5). pap. 7.99 (978-0-486-47936-1(6)) Dover Pubns., Inc.

—Owls Coloring Book. 2014. (Dover Coloring Bks.). (ENG.). 32p. (J). (gr. k). pap. 3.99 (978-0-486-78033-7(3)) Dover Pubns., Inc.

—Spark - Cool Cats Coloring Book. 2015. (Dover Coloring Bks.). (ENG., Illus.). 64p. (J). (gr. 1-4). pap. 5.99 (978-0-486-80058-5(X)) Dover Pubns., Inc.

—Spark - Horses Coloring Book. 2016. (ENG., Illus.). 64p. (J). (gr. 1-4). pap. 5.99 (978-0-486-80212-1(4)) Dover Pubns., Inc.

—Spark - Owls Coloring Book. 2015. (Dover Coloring Bks.). (ENG., Illus.). 64p. (J). (gr. 1-4). pap. 5.99 (978-0-486-80211-4(6)) Dover Pubns., Inc.

Dalmatian Press Staff. A Lesson In... Thankfulness: Book to Color with Stickers. 2003. (Big Idea's Veggie Tales Ser.). (ENG., Illus.). 32p. (J). pap. 2.99 (978-1-4037-0293-7(4), Spirit Pr.) Bendon, Inc.

—Paint Box Book to Color. 2003. (Big Idea's Veggie Tales Ser.). (ENG., Illus.). 32p. (J). pap. 3.99 (978-1-4037-0338-5(8), Spirit Pr.) Bendon, Inc.

—You Are Special! Coloring Activity Book with Stickers. 2003. (ENG., Illus.). 64p. (J). pap. 1.89 (978-1-4037-0814-4(2), Spirit Pr.) Bendon, Inc.

—Zany Fun! Coloring Activity Book with Stickers. (ENG.). 64p. (J). pap. 1.89 (978-1-4037-0813-7(4), Spirit Pr.) Bendon, Inc.

Danger Alert: Coloring/Activity Book. 2006. (Illus.). (J). 2.99 (978-1-933934-05-1(0)) Mighty Kids Media.

Danger Alert: Coloring/Activity Book (English) Incl. Stickers. 2007. (J). 2.99 (978-1-933934-54-9(9)) Mighty Kids Media.

Daniel. (Divertidas Historias Biblicas para Ninos Ser.). (SPA.). (J). 3.49 (978-0-7899-0599-4(X), 496646) Editorial Unilit.

Daniel. (Illus.). 16p. (J). (gr. -1-3). pap. 1.69 (978-0-7847-0712-8(X), 22032, Bean Sprouts) Standard Publishing.

Daste, Larry. Alphabet Search: Activity & Coloring Book. 2007. (Dover Children's Activity Bks.). (ENG., Illus.). 48p. (J). (gr. k-3). 4.99 (978-0-486-46196-0(3)) Dover Pubns., Inc.

Daumain, Thibaut. Minecraft Dot-To-Dot: Awesome Scenes & Incredible Challenges to Complete & Color. 2017. (ENG.). 64p. (J). (gr. 3-7). pap. 9.99 **(978-1-4380-1076-2(1))** Barron's Educational Series, Inc.

David, Hop & Coloring Books Staff. Surreal Visions Coloring Book. 2012. (Dover Coloring Bks.). (ENG., Illus.). 32p. (J). (gr. 3-5). pap. 3.99 (978-0-486-48837-0(3)) Dover Pubns., Inc.

David, Juliet. Bible Stories Painting Book, 1 vol., Bk. 3. Abbott, Simon, illus. 2014. (ENG.). 24p. (J). 7.99 (978-1-85985-995-7(X), Candle Bks.) Lion Hudson PLC GBR. Dist: Kregel Pubns.

—My Little Promise Bible Colouring Book, 1 vol. Barnard, Lucy, illus. 2016. 48p. (J). pap. 6.99 (978-1-78128-307-3(9), Candle Bks.) Lion Hudson PLC GBR. Dist: Kregel Pubns.

Davidson, Annie. Colour Together: Nature. 2016. (ENG., Illus.). 64p. (J). (gr. k-2). pap. 16.99 **(978-1-78344-517-2(3))** Andersen Pr. GBR. Dist: Independent Pubs. Group.

Davidson, Mike, et al, illus. Draw What? A Doodling, Drawing, & Coloring Book. 2014. (ENG.). (J). (gr. -1-3). (978-1-74352-285-1(1)) Hinkler Bks. Pty, Ltd.

Davies, Hannah. The Big Fabulous Colouring Book. 2017. (ENG.). 48p. (J). (gr. 3). pap. 14.99 **(978-1-78055-452-5(4))** O'Mara, Michael Bks., Ltd. GBR. Dist: Independent Pubs. Group.

Davies, Hannah & Gunnell, Beth, illus. Pretty Patterns: Beautiful Patterns to Color! 2013. (ENG.). 96p. (J). (gr. -1-2). 7.99 (978-1-4424-5181-0(5), Little Simon) Little Simon.

Davies, Hannah & Ryan, Nellie, illus. Pretty Costumes: Beautiful Costumes to Color! 2013. (ENG.). 96p. (J). (gr. -1-2). 7.99 (978-1-4424-5180-3(7), Little Simon) Little Simon.

Davis, Bertha. Jay's Friend Kitty Brew Jumbo Coloring & Activity Book. Bowman, Todd A., illus. 2013. 26p. pap. 9.99 (978-0-9899472-1-3(1)) Kids At Heart Publishing, LLC.

Davis, Jenny. The U. S. Lawyer-Presidents Coloring & Activity Book. 2008. (ENG.). 32p. (J). (gr. -1-3). pap. 5.95 (978-1-59031-976-5(1)) American Bar Assn.

Davis, Jenny B. The U. S. Supreme Court Coloring Book. 3rd ed. 2014. (ENG., Illus.). 32p. (J). (gr. 1-12). pap. 5.95 (978-1-62722-399-7(1)) American Bar Assn.

Davis, Regina & Spencer, Carolyn Royer. Señor Smarty Pantaloons & the Mystery of the Missing Teachers. 2011. 32p. (gr. 1-2). pap. 17.59 (978-1-4567-4557-8(3)) AuthorHouse.

DC Comics Staff. Batman Jumbo Color & Activity Book. Meredith Books Staff et al, eds. 2005. 400p. (J). pap. 5.99 (978-0-696-22722-6(3)) Meredith Bks.

de Moulor, Claire, illus. Extraordinary Machines. 2016. (Coloring Studio Ser.: 3). (ENG.). 32p. (J). (gr. 1-17). pap. 7.99 (978-0-316-39289-1(8)) Little, Brown Bks. for Young Readers.

De Sturtz, Mari. God Gave Me. 2004. (ENG & SPA.). 32p. 1.99 (978-0-7586-0293-0(6)) Concordia Publishing Hse.

—God Is. 2004. (ENG & SPA.). 32p. 1.99 (978-0-7586-0292-3(8)) Concordia Publishing Hse.

Deal, Darlene. Play with Your Food & Learn How to Eat Right: Nutritional Book about Fruits & Vegetables. 2004. (ENG & SPA., Illus.). 22p. (J). (gr. 1-4). pap. 9.95 (978-0-9747299-0-9(6)) Deal, Darlene.

Debacque, Pascal. Create Your Own Mandalas — Fantasy. 2013. (ENG.). 32p. (J). (gr. -1-12). 6.99 (978-0-486-49373-2(3)) Dover Pubns., Inc.

Demand, Carlo. Airplanes of World War I Coloring Book. 2013. (Dover History Coloring Book Ser.). (ENG., Illus.). 48p. (J). (gr. 3-12). pap. 4.99 (978-0-486-23807-4(5)) Dover Pubns., Inc.

—Classic Racing Cars of the World Coloring Book. 2013. (Dover Coloring Bks.). (ENG., Illus.). 48p. (J). (gr. 3-8). pap. 4.99 (978-0-486-24294-1(3)) Dover Pubns., Inc.

Dennison, Mysha. Reverie: A Coloring Retreat. 2016. (ENG.). (J). pap. 12.99 (978-1-4621-1839-7(9)) Cedar Fort, Inc./CFI Distribution.

Desplechin, Mar. Verte. pap. 19.95 (978-2-211-04178-2(7)) Archimede Editions FRA. Dist: Distribooks, Inc.

Diaz, Wendy Umm Uthman. Nuestros Oficios. 2012. (ENG.). (J). pap. 12.99 (978-1-4675-3282-2(7)) Independent Pub.

Dickason, Chris. The Clever Kids' Colouring Book: Genius. Dickason, Chris, illus. 2015. (ENG., Illus.). 32p. (J). (gr. 1). pap. 6.99 **(978-1-78055-318-4(8))** O'Mara, Michael Bks., Ltd. GBR. Dist: Independent Pubs. Group.

—The Diggers & Trucks Colouring Book. Dickason, Chris, illus. 2017. (ENG., Illus.). 64p. (J). (gr. k-2). pap. 6.99 **(978-1-78055-250-7(5))** O'Mara, Michael Bks., Ltd. GBR. Dist: Independent Pubs. Group.

Dickason, Chris & Buster Books Staff. The Planes, Trains & Cars Colouring Book. Dickason, Chris, illus. 2017. (ENG., Illus.). 64p. (J). (gr. k-2). pap. 6.99 **(978-1-78055-251-4(3))** O'Mara, Michael Bks., Ltd. GBR. Dist: Independent Pubs. Group.

Dickens, Rosie. My Very First Art Coloring Book with Stickers. 2012. (Art Ser.). 24p. (J). pap. 5.99 *(978-0-7945-3273-4(X)*, Usborne) EDC Publishing.

Diddle Doodle - Blue. 2004. (Diddle Doodle Coloring Pads Ser.). 24p. (J). act. bk. ed. 3.99 *(978-1-904586-30-2(9))* Byeway Bks.

Diddle Doodle - Red. 2004. (Diddle Doodle Coloring Pads Ser.). 24p. (J). act. bk. ed. 3.99 *(978-1-904586-29-6(5))* Byeway Bks.

Dieterichs, Shelley. Let's Color Together — Fabulous Fairies. 2014. (ENG., Illus.). 64p. (J). (gr. -1-3). pap. 3.99 *(978-0-486-77972-0(6))* Dover Pubns., Inc.

Dieterichs, Shelley, et al. Fabulous Fairies Coloring Book. 2011. (Dover Coloring Bks.). (ENG.). 32p. (J). (gr. -1-3). pap. 3.99 *(978-0-486-48267-5(7))* Dover Pubns., Inc.

Dinosaur Coloring Book. (Illus.). (J). Bk. 1. pap. 1.99 *(978-1-59340-008-8(X))*Bk. 2. pap. 1.99 *(978-1-59340-009-5(8))* Grandreams Bks., Inc.

Disney Book Group. Disney Princess Storybook Collection: Tales to Finish. Disney Storybook Art Team, illus. 2017. (Storybook Collection: Tales to Finish Ser.). (ENG.). 128p. (J). (gr. 1-3). 10.99 *(978-1-4847-8957-5(1))* Disney Pr.

—Disney*Pixar Storybook Collection: Tales to Finish. Disney Storybook Art Team, illus. 2017. (Disney*Pixar Storybook Collection: Tales to Finish Ser.). (ENG.). 128p. (J). (gr. 1-3). 10.99 *(978-1-4847-9942-0(9))* Disney Pr.

Disney Book Group. Elena of Avalor un Dia para Recordar (Spanish Edition) Disney Storybook Art Team, illus. 2017. (ENG.). 24p. (J). (gr. 1-3). pap. 5.99 **(978-1-368-00110-6(6))** Disney Pr.

Disney Book Group & Rogers, Tom. Elena of Avalor a Day to Remember. Disney Storybook Art Team, illus. 2017. (ENG.). 24p. (J). (gr. 1-3). pap. 5.99 **(978-1-4847-4791-9(7))** Disney Pr.

Dobson, Shirley. God Answers Prayer: Coloring Book. 2004. 16p. 1.49 *(978-0-8307-2750-6(7)*, Gospel Light) Gospel Light Pubns.

—God Cares for Me Coloring Book: A Read-To-Me Bible Story Coloring Book about Paul's Journey. 2003. (Coloring Bks.). (ENG.). 14p. (J). (gr. -1-3). 1.99 *(978-0-8307-3270-8(5))* Gospel Light Pubns.

—God Helps Me Share: Coloring Book about Abigail & David. 2004. (Illus.). 12p. pap. 1.49 *(978-0-8307-2894-7(5)*, Gospel Light) Gospel Light Pubns.

—God Made the World Coloring Book. 2004. (Illus.). 16p. 1.49 *(978-0-8307-2487-1(7)*, Gospel Light) Gospel Light Pubns.

—God Made the World Coloring Book: 100-Unit Counter Merchandiser. 2004. 16p. 99.00 *(978-0-8307-2488-8(5)*, Gospel Light) Gospel Light Pubns.

—God's Little Helper Coloring Book. 2004. (Illus.). 16p. pap. 1.49 *(978-0-8307-2188-7(6)*, Gospel Light) Gospel Light Pubns.

—Jesus Takes Care of Me Coloring Book: A Read-to-Me Bible Story Coloring Book about Jesus' Feeding 5,000 People. 2004. 1.49 *(978-0-8307-3540-2(2)*, Gospel Light) Gospel Light Pubns.

Dobson, Shirley, contrib. by. God Gives Me Joy Coloring Book. 2004. 16p. 1.49 *(978-0-8307-3054-4(0)*, Gospel Light) Gospel Light Pubns.

Dodd, Emma. Dog's Colorful Day: A Messy Story about Colors & Counting. 2003. (gr. k-3). 16.00 *(978-0-613-57720-5(5)*, Turtleback) Turtleback Bks.

Doell, Glenn, illus. & concept. Creative Coloring Books: The What If. . . series. Doell, Glenn, concept. 2003. (What If. . . ser.). 41p. (J). spiral bd. 8.95 *(978-0-9742438-0-1(9))* Curtis Elliott Designs, Ltd.

Donahue, Peter. All Aboard! Trains Stained Glass Coloring Book. 2011. (Dover Stained Glass Coloring Book Ser.). (ENG., Illus.). 32p. (J). (gr. -1-2). pap. 6.99 *(978-0-486-47896-8(3))* Dover Pubns., Inc.

—Build a Poster Coloring Book — ABC & 123. 2010. (Dover Build a Poster Coloring Book Ser.). (ENG., Illus.). 48p. (J). (gr. 3-5). pap. 4.99 *(978-0-486-47946-0(3))* Dover Pubns., Inc.

—Cars & Trucks Stained Glass Coloring Book. 2010. (Dover Stained Glass Coloring Book Ser.). (ENG., Illus.). 32p. (J). (gr. -1-5). pap. 6.99 *(978-0-486-47706-0(1))* Dover Pubns., Inc.

—Classic Arabian Nights Stained Glass Coloring Book. 2011. (Dover Stained Glass Coloring Book Ser.). (ENG., Illus.). 32p. (J). (gr. 3-5). pap. 6.99 *(978-0-486-47609-4(X))* Dover Pubns., Inc.

—Farm & Zoo. 2010. (Dover Build a Poster Coloring Book Ser.). (ENG., Illus.). 48p. (J). (gr. 3-5). pap. 4.99 *(978-0-486-47947-7(1))* Dover Pubns., Inc.

—Robot Mazes. 2008. (Dover Children's Activity Bks.). (ENG., Illus.). 48p. (J). (gr. k-5). pap. 4.99 *(978-0-486-46825-9(9))* Dover Pubns., Inc.

—Things That Fly Stained Glass Coloring Book. 2012. (Dover Stained Glass Coloring Book Ser.). (ENG., Illus.). 32p. (J). (gr. k-5). pap. 6.99 *(978-0-486-49866-9(2))* Dover Pubns., Inc.

—Things That Go Coloring Book: Cars, Trucks, Planes, Trains & More! 2015. (ENG.). 32p. (J). (gr. -1-2). pap. 3.99 *(978-0-486-79814-1(3))* Dover Pubns., Inc.

Donahue, Peter & Coloring Books Staff. Mix & Match ROBOTS. 2012. (Dover Mix & Match Coloring Book Ser.). (ENG.). 48p. (J). (gr. 2-5). pap. 4.99 *(978-0-486-48847-9(0))* Dover Pubns., Inc.

—Robot Buddies Stained Glass Coloring Book. 2012. (Dover Stained Glass Coloring Book Ser.). (ENG., Illus.). 32p. (J). (gr. k-5). pap. 6.99 *(978-0-486-48673-4(7))* Dover Pubns., Inc.

Donahue, Peter & Wright, Blanche Fisher. The Real Mother Goose Stained Glass Coloring Book. 2010. (Dover Stained Glass Coloring Book Ser.). (ENG., Illus.). 32p. (J). (gr. 1-5). pap. 6.99 *(978-0-486-47341-3(4))* Dover Pubns., Inc.

Donahue, Peter, et al. Mix & Match FANTASY CREATURES. 2012. (Dover Mix & Match Coloring Book Ser.). (ENG., Illus.). 48p. (J). (gr. 2-5). pap. 4.99 *(978-0-486-48848-6(9))* Dover Pubns., Inc.

Dorling Kindersley Publishing Staff, ed. Doodlepedia - Wow. 2012. (ENG.). 96p. (J). (gr. 2-5). pap. 12.99 *(978-0-7566-9800-3(6)*, DK Children) Dorling Kindersley Publishing, Inc.

Douglas, Bettye. Safari Oklahoma Presents: The Magic of Christmas Around the World. Douglas, Bettye, ed. Douglas, Punchye, illus. (Multicultural). 16p. (J). (gr. k-6). 5.00 *(978-0-9703183-4-3(0))* Douglas, Bettye Forum, Inc., The.

Douglas, Punchye. Safari Oklahoma Presents: Thanksgiving History Coloring Book. (Illus.). 16p. (J). (gr. k-6). 5.00 *(978-0-9703183-3-6(2))* Douglas, Bettye Forum, Inc., The.

Douglas, Punchye, illus. Safari Oklahoma Presents Operation Safe 2000: Halloween Coloring Book. (Safari Oklahoma Presents). 16p. (J). (gr. k-6). 5.00 *(978-0-9703183-2-9(4))* Douglas, Bettye Forum, Inc., The.

Dover. Geometric Stained Glass Coloring Book: Deluxe Edition with 48 Stained Glass Sheets. 2010. (Dover Design Stained Glass Coloring Book Ser.). (ENG., Illus.). 96p. (J). (gr. 2-5). pap. 14.99 *(978-0-486-47549-3(2))* Dover Pubns., Inc.

Dover Publications Inc. Staff, ed. Boxed/Decorate for Halloween Fun Kit. 2008. (Dover Fun Kits Ser.). (ENG.). 12p. (J). (gr. 1). pap. 16.95 *(978-0-486-46792-4(9))* Dover Pubns., Inc.

—Boxed/Samurai Kit. 2008. (ENG.). 12p. (gr. 1). pap. 19.99 *(978-0-486-46691-0(4))* Dover Pubns., Inc.

—Revolutionary War, Kit. 2009. (ENG.). 4p. (J). (gr. 5). 19.99 *(978-0-486-47356-7(2))* Dover Pubns., Inc.

Dover Staff & Noble, Marty. Art Masterpieces to Color: 60 Great Paintings from Botticelli to Picasso. 2004. (Dover Art Coloring Book Ser.). (ENG., Illus.). 128p. (gr. 3-8). pap. 8.95 *(978-0-486-43381-3(1))* Dover Pubns., Inc.

Down on the Farm Coloring Book. 2004. (J). mass mkt. *(978-0-9745863-9-7(0))* Cypress Knees Publishing.

Doyle, Arthur Conan. Sherlock Holmes: The Hound of the Baskervilles. abr. ed. 2009. (Dover Classic Stories Coloring Book Ser.). (ENG., Illus.). 48p. (J). (gr. 3-8). pap. 4.99 *(978-0-486-47416-8(X))* Dover Pubns., Inc.

Doyle, Richard & Noble, Marty. Fairyland Stained Glass Coloring Book. 2003. (Dover Stained Glass Coloring Book Ser.). (ENG., Illus.). 16p. (gr. 3-8). pap. 7.99 *(978-0-486-43049-2(9))* Dover Pubns., Inc.

Dragons: Coloring Book. 2007. (Illus.). 20p. (J). 10.00 *(978-0-9795206-5-5(7))* Unseen Gallery.

Drake, Ernest. Dragonology Coloring Book. 2016. (Ologies Ser.). (ENG.). 64p. (J). (gr. 3-7). pap. 14.99 *(978-0-7636-9530-9(0))* Candlewick Pr.

Dreamworks Animation Publishing, LLC. Olivia's Big Day Coloring Book. Kurtz, John, illus. 2015. (Dover Paper Dolls Ser.). (ENG.). 64p. (J). (gr. 2-5). pap. 6.99 *(978-0-486-80279-4(5))* Dover Pubns., Inc.

Dubinski, Lisa. A Gift to Give & Coloring Book. 2010. 32p. pap. 17.99 *(978-0-557-60224-7(6))* Lulu Pr., Inc.

Duhgam, P. Island Hopping with Anancy. 24p. *(978-976-8184-11-5(6))* LMH Publishing, Ltd.

Dukes, Dorothy. The Coloring Book. 2009. 89p. pap. 10.96 *(978-0-557-03529-8(5))* Lulu Pr., Inc.

Duling, Jean Saunders. Marco Island A-Z: A Coloring Book for You. Duling, Jean Saunders, ed. 2003. (Illus.). 36p. (J). (gr. -1-6). pap. 5.95 *(978-0-9743445-0-8(8))* Duling Designs.

Dupeyron, Sarah, illus. The ABC's of Vermont Coloring Book. 2007. 32p. (J). 4.95 *(978-0-9793790-0-0(8))* Howard Printing, Inc.

Dupont, Monsieur, illus. Imaginary Cities. 2016. (Coloring Studio Ser.: 4). (ENG.). 48p. (J). (gr. 1-17). pap. 8.99 *(978-0-316-39291-4(X))* Little, Brown Bks. for Young Readers.

Dutton, Michael. Amazing Carbon Footprint Facts. 2010. (Dover Nature Coloring Book Ser.). (ENG., Illus.). 32p. (J). (gr. 2-5). pap. 3.99 *(978-0-486-47552-3(2))* Dover Pubns., Inc.

—Exploring Ecosystems! An Environmentally Friendly Coloring Book. 2009. (Dover Nature Coloring Book Ser.). (ENG., Illus.). 32p. (J). (gr. k-2). pap. 3.99 *(978-0-486-46988-1(3))* Dover Pubns., Inc.

—The Water Cycle Coloring Book. 2012. (Dover Nature Coloring Book Ser.). (ENG.). 32p. (J). (gr. 2-5). pap. 3.99 *(978-0-486-47988-0(9))* Dover Pubns., Inc.

Dutton, Michael & Coloring Books Staff. Habitats Coloring Book. 2012. (Dover Nature Coloring Book Ser.). (ENG., Illus.). 32p. (J). (gr. 2-5). pap. 3.99 *(978-0-486-48709-0(1))* Dover Pubns., Inc.

Dutton, Michael & Roytman, Arkady. 3-D Coloring Book — Vampires & Zombies. 2011. (Dover 3-D Coloring Book Ser.). (ENG., Illus.). 32p. (J). (gr. 2-6). pap. 5.99 *(978-0-486-48415-0(7))* Dover Pubns., Inc.

Dwyer, Kerry, illus. Rhett's Colorful Campus Tour- Boston University A-Z. 2004. (J). 9.99 *(978-1-933069-03-6(1))* Odd Duck Ink, Inc.

Easter. (Illus.). (gr. 1-4). 3.00 *(978-0-570-05524-2(5)*, 54-1034) Concordia Publishing Hse.

Eckel, Jessie. The Boys' Coloring Book. 2013. (ENG.). 128p. (J). (gr. -1-2). pap. 8.95 *(978-1-4549-0716-9(9))* Sterling Publishing Co., Inc.

—The Girls' Coloring Book. 2013. (ENG.). 128p. (J). (gr. -1-2). pap. 8.95 *(978-1-4549-0717-6(7))* Sterling Publishing Co., Inc.

Eddy, Randon T., illus. DILLO the Coloring Book. 2006. 53p. (J). pap. 6.95 *(978-0-9769332-1-2(7))* Jungle Hse. Pubns.

Educational Adventures, creator. Cool by the Pool: Coloring/Activity Book (Spanish) w/ Snipe. 2007. (Illus.). (J). per. 2.99 *(978-1-933934-73-0(5))* Mighty Kids Media.

—Danger Alert: Coloring/Activity Book (Spanish) w/ Snipe. 2006. (Illus.). (J). 2.99 *(978-1-933934-06-8(9))* Mighty Kids Media.

—Free Wheelin' Coloring/Activity Book (English) w/ Snipe. 2007. (J). 2.99 *(978-1-933934-52-5(2))* Mighty Kids Media.

—Poison Patrol: Coloring/Activity Book (Spanish) w/ Snipe. 2006. (Illus.). (J). 2.99 *(978-1-933934-02-0(6))* Mighty Kids Media.

—Street Smarts: Coloring/Activity Book (Spanish) w/ Snipe. 2006. (Illus.). (J). 2.99 *(978-1-933934-19-8(0))* Mighty Kids Media.

Egmont Books. Christmas Doodle & Colouring Book. 2014. (ENG., Illus.). 128p. (J). (gr. -1). pap. 16.99 *(978-1-4052-7351-0(8))* Egmont Bks., Ltd. GBR. Dist: Independent Pubs. Group.

Elder, Jeremy. Animal Kaleidoscope Designs Coloring Book. 2017. (Dover Coloring Bks.). (ENG., Illus.). 32p. (J). (gr. 3-6). pap. 3.99 *(978-0-486-80883-3(1))* Dover Pubns., Inc.

—ComicQuest ZOMBIES UNLEASHED. 2013. (Dover Children's Activity Bks.). (ENG.). 48p. (J). (gr. 3-8). pap. 4.99 *(978-0-486-49943-7(X))* Dover Pubns., Inc.

—Creative Haven Steampunk Devices Coloring Book. 2014. (Adult Coloring Ser.). (ENG., Illus.). 64p. (J). (gr. 3). pap. 5.99 *(978-0-486-49443-2(8))* Dover Pubns., Inc.

—Graffiti Art Coloring Book. 2016. (Dover Coloring Bks.). (ENG.). 32p. (YA). pap. 3.99 *(978-0-486-80457-6(7))* Dover Pubns., Inc.

—Hot Rod Tattoos Stained Glass Coloring Book. 2013. (Dover Stained Glass Coloring Book Ser.). (ENG., Illus.). 32p. (J). (gr. 3-8). pap. 6.99 *(978-0-486-48829-5(2))* Dover Pubns., Inc.

—Japanese Tattoo Art Stained Glass Coloring Book. 2010. (Dover Design Stained Glass Coloring Book Ser.). (ENG., Illus.). 32p. (J). (gr. 1-5). pap. 7.99 *(978-0-486-47533-2(6))* Dover Pubns., Inc.

—Monsters Destroyed My City! Stained Glass Coloring Book. 2011. (Dover Stained Glass Coloring Book Ser.). (ENG., Illus.). 32p. (J). (gr. 2-5). pap. 6.99 *(978-0-486-47910-1(2))* Dover Pubns., Inc.

—Neon Lights Stained Glass Coloring Book. 2014. (Dover Stained Glass Coloring Book Ser.). (ENG., Illus.). 32p. (J). (gr. 3). pap. 6.99 *(978-0-486-48598-0(6))* Dover Pubns., Inc.

—Sci-Fi Stained Glass Coloring Book. 2009. (Dover Stained Glass Coloring Book Ser.). (ENG., Illus.). 32p. (J). (gr. -1-5). pap. 6.99 *(978-0-486-47151-8(9))* Dover Pubns., Inc.

—Space Agent. 2010. (Dover Children's Activity Bks.). (ENG., Illus.). 48p. (J). (gr. 2-5). pap. 4.99 *(978-0-486-47828-9(9))* Dover Pubns., Inc.

Elder, Jeremy & Coloring Books for Grownups Staff. In the Wild Stained Glass Coloring Book. 2013. (Dover Stained Glass Coloring Book Ser.). (ENG., Illus.). 32p. (J). (gr. 3-8). pap. 7.99 *(978-0-486-49942-0(1))* Dover Pubns., Inc.

Eliot, Hannah. Sweet Treats. Ingham, Julie, illus. 2014. (Dream Doodle Draw! Ser.). (ENG.). 96p. (J). (gr. -1-2). pap. 7.99 *(978-1-4814-0452-5(0)*, Little Simon) Little Simon.

Elliott, Mel. Color Me Swoon: The Beefcake Activity Book for Good Color-Inners As Well As Beginners. 2013. (ENG.). 128p. (gr. 12). pap. 14.00 *(978-0-399-16547-4(9)*, TarcherPerigee) Penguin Publishing Group.

Ellison, Renee. Character Traits Coloring Book pages PDF Files. 2003. (J). cd-rom 8.00 *(978-0-9749455-5-2(2))* Cross-Over.

Endangered Mammals - Africa: An Educational Coloring Book. (J). (gr. 3-18). pap. 1.99 *(978-0-86545-213-8(X))* Spizzirri Pr., Inc.

Endangered Mammals - Asia & China: An Educational Coloring Book. (J). (gr. 3-18). pap. 1.99 *(978-0-86545-214-5(8))* Spizzirri Pr., Inc.

Endangered Mammals - South America: An Educational Coloring Book. (J). pap. 1.99 *(978-0-86545-215-2(6))* Spizzirri Pr., Inc.

Engelbreit, Mary. Color Me Too. Engelbreit, Mary, illus. 2016. (Illus.). 96p. (J). (gr. -1-3). pap. 15.99 *(978-0-06-256258-6(4))* HarperCollins Pubs.

—Mary Engelbreit's Color ME Christmas. Engelbreit, Mary, illus. 2016. (Illus.). 96p. (J). (gr. -1-3). pap. 15.99 *(978-0-06-256260-9(6))* HarperCollins Pubs.

—Mary Engelbreit's Color ME Christmas Book of Postcards. Engelbreit, Mary, illus. 2017. (Illus.). 20p. (J). (gr. -1). pap. 9.99 **(978-0-06-266327-6(5))** HarperCollins Pubs.

Engelbreit, Mary. Mary Engelbreit's Color ME Coloring Book. Engelbreit, Mary, illus. 2015. (Illus.). 96p. (J). (gr. -1-3). pap. 15.99 *(978-0-06-244561-2(8))* HarperCollins Pubs.

Erte. Erte Fashions Coloring Book. Noble, Marty, ed. 2003. (Dover Fashion Coloring Book Ser.). (ENG., Illus.). 32p. (gr. 6-8). pap. 4.99 *(978-0-486-43041-6(3))* Dover Pubns., Inc.

Ertekin, Betul. This World I Love Coloring & Activity Book. 2011. (ENG.). 48p. pap. 3.95 *(978-1-59784-234-1(6))* Tughra Bks.

Evans, Brad. Bishop Museum Color & Activity Book. 2004. (Illus.). 24p. (J). pap. 4.95 *(978-1-58178-034-5(6))* Bishop Museum Pr.

Extreme Sports Coloring Book. 2004. (J). mass mkt. 5.99 *(978-0-9763757-0-8(2))* Cypress Knees Publishing.

Eyre, Jane. Creatures of the New Jersey Pine Barrens Coloring Book, 1 vol. Eyre, Jane, illus. 2004. (Illus.). 36p. spiral bd. 6.00 *(978-0-9762483-0-9(1))* Fun Fitness Publishing.

Falini, Nancy Patin. Gluten-Free Friends: An Activity Book for Kids. 2003. (Illus.). 64p. (J). 18.95 *(978-1-889374-09-3(1))* Savory Palate, Inc.

Fay, Claire. Color, Snap, App! My First Animated Coloring Book. Fay, Claire, illus. 2017. (ENG., Illus.). 32p. (J). (gr. k-4). pap. 9.99 **(978-0-7636-9347-3(2))** Candlewick Pr.

Fearn, Katrina, illus. & des. First Dot-To-Dot Dinosaurs. Fearn, Katrina, des. 2013. (First Dot-To-Dot Ser.). 16p. (J). pap. 5.99 *(978-0-7945-3341-0(8)*, Usborne) EDC Publishing.

Feelings Garden Coloring & Activity Book. 2005. (J). *(978-0-9768827-2-5(8))* Prevention Through Puppetry, Inc.

Felix the Cat/el Gato Felix: The Professor's Mix-Up/El Lio Del Profesor. 2005. (J). 64p. pap. *(978-0-9762071-5-3(X))*; 32p. pap. *(978-0-9762071-8-4(4))*; 64p. pap. 3.99 *(978-0-9762071-2-2(5))* Big City Publishing.

Felix the Cat/el Gato Felix: World of Fun. 2005. 32p. (J). pap. *(978-0-9762071-6-0(8))* Big City Publishing.

Ferguson, Suzanie P. Ferris, Color & Activity Book: Libro de Colorear & Actividad. Date not set. (ENG & SPA., Illus.). 28p. (Orig.). (J). (gr. k-6). pap. *(978-0-9658745-1-9(6))* Ferguson, Suzanie Pamela.

Filmer, Mary, et al. Farmer Frank: Educational Fire Safety, Poetry & Story Colouring Book. 2010. 50p. pap. 9.99 *(978-1-60911-721-4(2)*, Eloquent Bks.) Strategic Book Publishing & Rights Agency (SBPRA).

Fisher, Phyllis Mae Richardson. Twiglet's Coloring Book. 2004. (J). 14.00 *(978-0-9745615-2-3(5))* PJs Corner.

Fisher, Phyllis Mae Richardson, illus. Rueben & Rachel's Paper Doll Coloring Book. Fisher, Phyllis Mae Richardson, . 2003. (J). 8.00 *(978-0-9745615-0-9(9))* PJs Corner.

Flags over Corydon Coloring Book. 2005. (J). 4.95 *(978-0-9769829-1-3(9))* Dorcas Pubns., LLC.

Flanagan, Anne. Family Saints Col/Act Bk. 24p. pap. 1.25 *(978-0-8198-2678-7(2)*, 332-097) Pauline Bks. & Media.

—Miracles of Jesus Act/Col Bk. 24p. pap. 1.25 *(978-0-8198-4836-9(0)*, 332-225) Pauline Bks. & Media.

Flier, Marcel. Colour Your Day: A Spiritual Colouring Book, 1 vol. 2015. (ENG., Illus.). 32p. 7.99 *(978-0-85721-696-0(1)*, Monarch Bks.) Lion Hudson PLC GBR. Dist: Kregel Pubns.

—Colour Your Life: A Spiritual Colouring Book, 1 vol. 2015. (ENG., Illus.). 32p. 7.99 *(978-0-85721-695-3(3)*, Monarch Bks.) Lion Hudson PLC GBR. Dist: Kregel Pubns.

—Colour Your World: A Spiritual Colouring Book, 1 vol. 2016. (ENG., Illus.). 32p. 7.99 *(978-0-85721-726-4(7)*, Monarch Bks.) Lion Hudson PLC GBR. Dist: Kregel Pubns.

Flip along Fun. (Illus.). 22p. (J). (gr. -1-k). spiral bd. *(978-1-56021-374-1(4)*, #221) W.J. Fantasy, Inc.

Flowerpot Press, creator. Trick-Or-Treat Coloring Book. 2013. (ENG., Illus.). 72p. (J). pap. 4.99 *(978-1-77093-319-4(0))* Flowerpot Pr.

—Wacky Witch Coloring Book. 2013. (ENG., Illus.). 72p. (J). (gr. -1-3). 4.99 *(978-1-77093-316-3(6))* Flowerpot Pr.

Fluckiger, Kory. Mylands. 2010. pap. 9.95 *(978-0-615-15654-5(1))* Fluckiger, Kory.

Fogle, Robin. Baby Moses Coloring Book. 2007. (Illus.). 16p. (J). pap. 1.89 *(978-1-59317-189-6(7))* Warner Pr., Inc.

—Daniel & the Lions' Den Coloring Book. 2007. (Illus.). 16p. (J). pap. 1.89 *(978-1-59317-191-9(9))* Warner Pr., Inc.

—David & Golaith Coloring Book. 2007. (Illus.). 16p. (J). pap. 1.89 *(978-1-59317-205-3(2))* Warner Pr., Inc.

—The Easter Story Coloring Book. 2007. (Illus.). 16p. (J). pap. 1.89 *(978-1-59317-190-2(0))* Warner Pr., Inc.

—My Favorite Bible Stories Color-by-number. 2007. (Illus.). 16p. (J). pap. 1.89 *(978-1-59317-208-4(7))* Warner Pr., Inc.

Foldvary-Anderson, Carol. Heart to Heart Stained Glass Coloring Book. 2012. (Dover Stained Glass Coloring Book Ser.). (ENG., Illus.). 32p. (gr. 3-5). pap. 6.99 *(978-0-486-48648-2(6))* Dover Pubns., Inc.

—Hearts & Roses Stained Glass Coloring Book. 2009. (Dover Design Stained Glass Coloring Book Ser.). (ENG., Illus.). 32p. (gr. 3-8). pap. 6.99 *(978-0-486-47023-8(7))* Dover Pubns., Inc.

—Words of Love Stained Glass Coloring Book. 2011. (Dover Design Stained Glass Coloring Book Ser.). (ENG., Illus.). 32p. (gr. 3-8). pap. 6.99 *(978-0-486-47707-7(X))* Dover Pubns., Inc.

—3-D Coloring Book — Hearts. 2012. (Dover 3-D Coloring Book Ser.). (ENG., Illus.). 32p. (J). (gr. 2-6). pap. 5.99 *(978-0-486-49013-7(0))* Dover Pubns., Inc.

Formas y Colores. (Coleccion Picaros Peluchines). (SPA.). (J). 5.50 *(978-950-11-0400-4(1)*, SGM400) Sigmar ARG. Dist: Continental Bk. Co., Inc.

Fowler, Eleri. Easter to Color. Fowler, Eleri, illus. 2017. (Illus.). 96p. (J). (gr. -1). pap. 15.99 *(978-0-06-256996-7(1))* HarperCollins Pubs.

—My Mother, My Heart. Fowler, Eleri, illus. 2016. (Illus.). 96p. (J). (gr. -1). pap. 15.99 *(978-0-06-247938-9(5))* HarperCollins Pubs.

—Words of Love to Color. Fowler, Eleri, illus. 2016. (Illus.). 96p. (J). (gr. -1). pap. 15.99 *(978-0-06-256608-9(3))* HarperCollins Pubs.

Frances, Dee. Pink Milk Sea Coloring Book. Patrick, Scot, illus. Date not set. 32p. (J). pap. 3.00 *(978-1-885519-26-9(5))* DDDD Pubns.

—The Pink Milk Sea Coloring Book. Date not set. (J). 3.00 *(978-1-885519-58-0(3))* DDDD Pubns.

Francis. More Saints of the Eucharist. 2006. (J). 2.50 *(978-0-9778570-1-2(8))* MOS, Inc.

Frantz, Jennifer. Color & Iron-Ons Book. Middleton, Gayle, illus. 2005. (My Little Pony Ser.). 32p. (J). (gr. -1-1). 3.99 *(978-0-06-074441-0(3)*, HarperFestival) HarperCollins Pubs.

Fredrikson, Magnus. Skateboarding Coloring Book. 2011. (ENG., Illus.). 64p. mass mkt. 9.95 *(978-91-85639-45-8(1))* Dokument forlag, Fotograf Malcolm Jacobsson SWE. Dist: SCB Distributors.

Free Wheelin' Coloring/Activity Book (English) 2005. (Illus.). (J). 2.99 *(978-0-9770455-7-0(9))* Mighty Kids Media.

Freeborn, Andrew J., illus. Colorways: For Days. abr. ed. 2005. 32p. pap. *(978-0-9769575-0-8(7))* N8TIVE.

French, Felicity. Colour & Frame? Patterns. 2016. (ENG.). 64p. pap. 12.95 *(978-1-78243-585-3(9))* O'Mara, Michael Bks., Ltd. GBR. Dist: Independent Pubs. Group.

—Colour & Frame - Nature. 2016. (ENG.). 64p. pap. 12.95 *(978-1-78243-584-6(0))* O'Mara, Michael Bks., Ltd. GBR. Dist: Independent Pubs. Group.

French, Matt. The Uncolored Book for You to Color, 1 vol. 2012. (ENG., Illus.). 80p. (J). pap. 12.99 *(978-0-7643-4087-1(5)*, 9780764340871) Schiffer Publishing, Ltd.

Frey, Daniel J., illus. Jacy's Coloring & Activity Book. 2006. 32p. (J). 3.00 *(978-0-9755314-2-6(5))* Majestic Publishing, LLC.

Frey, Lisa A. The Story of Monet & Renoir. Frey, Lisa A. & Darroch, Jane, eds. Darroch, Jane & Riley, Scott, illus. 2004. (Color & Learn Book Ser.). 32p. (gr. k-4). pap. 12.99 *(978-0-9707110-1-4(8))* Starshell Pr., Ltd.

Fried, Miriam. My Jelly Bean Book. 2005. (Illus.). (J). *(978-1-57400-049-8(7))* Data Trace Publishing, Co.

Frog. 2004. (Peek-A-Boo Coloring Pads Ser.). 48p. (J). act. bk. ed. 3.99 *(978-1-85997-394-3(9))* Byeway Bks.

Fulcher, Roz. Color & Learn Easy Italian Phrases for Kids. 2015. (Dover Little Activity Bks.). (ENG.). 64p. (J). (gr. k-3). pap. 1.99 *(978-0-486-80359-3(7))* Dover Pubns., Inc.

—Color & Learn Easy Spanish Phrases for Kids. 2015. (Dover Little Activity Bks.). (ENG.). 64p. (J). (gr. k-3). pap. 1.99 *(978-0-486-79759-5(7))* Dover Pubns., Inc.

Funko. The World of Pop! 2012. (ENG.). (J). pap. *(978-1-4675-3615-8(6))* Independent Pub.

Gache, Stephen Vance. The Real Mother Goose Coloring Book. Wright, Blanche Fisher, illus. 2009. (Dover Classic Stories Coloring Book Ser.). (ENG.). 32p. (J). (gr. k-5). pap. 3.99 *(978-0-486-46991-1(3))* Dover Pubns., Inc.

Gaiman, NEil. Neil Gaiman Coloring Book. Thompson, Jill, illus. 2017. 96p. (J). (gr. 3-7). pap. 15.99 *(978-0-06-265297-3(4)*, HarperFestival) HarperCollins Pubs.

C D

Gallo, Tina. Brava OLIVIA. Rose, Drew, illus. 2009. (Olivia TV Tie-In Ser.). (ENG.). 32p. (J). (gr. -1-1). 4.99 *(978-1-4169-8521-1(2),* Simon Scribbles) Simon Scribbles.

Galvin, Laura Gates. Chirp's Colors. 2006. (Peep & the Big Wide World Ser.). (ENG., Illus.). 24p. (J). (gr. -1-2). 15.99 *(978-1-59249-518-4(4),* 1C300) Soundprints.

Garaway, Margaret K. Old Hogan Coloring Book. (J). pap. 2.50 *(978-0-9638851-1-1(1))* Old Hogan Publishing Co.

Garlington, William R. The Great Divide: Coloring & Activity Book. 2004. (Illus.). (J). 5.95 *(978-0-9708395-4-1(5))* Legacy Publishing Services, Inc.

Gaskin, Terri. Me & My Brother: Coloring Book. 2011. 24p. pap. 11.32 *(978-1-4567-6031-1(9))* AuthorHouse.

Gaspas, Diane & Creative Haven Staff. Creative Haven Chinese Designs Coloring Book. 2013. (Adult Coloring Ser.). (ENG., Illus.). 64p. (gr. 3). pap. 5.99 *(978-0-486-49313-8(X))* Dover Pubns., Inc.

Gaspas, Dianne. Southwest Indian Designs Coloring Book. 2003. (Dover Design Coloring Bks.). (ENG., Illus.). 32p. (gr. 3-8). pap. 3.99 *(978-0-486-43042-3(1))* Dover Pubns., Inc.

Gaudet, Mary Kate. Peppa Pig: Coloring & Activity Book & Crayons. 2007. (Peppa Pig Ser.). 32p. (J). pap. 4.99 *(978-0-06-117374-5(6),* Harper Entertainment) HarperCollins Pubs.

Gaugler, Gil. Samantha's Coloring Box, 1 vol. 2009. 26p. pap. 24.95 *(978-1-61546-210-0(4))* America Star Bks.

Gawron, Gay, illus. The New Hampshire Coloring Book. 2008. 40p. (YA). pap. 8.95 *(978-0-9801672-0-7(5))* Hobblebush Bks.

Gee, Allison. Animal Dreams: Coloring Book. 2009. 52p. pap. 14.99 *(978-1-4389-9014-9(6))* AuthorHouse.

Gerovasiliou, Oreanthy. Yuri the Lion: Three Stories. 2010. (Illus.). 48p. pap. 13.00 *(978-1-60888-069-0(9))* Nimble Bks. LLC.

Giannotta, Andres Bernardo. Manga Stained Glass Coloring Book. 2011. (Dover Stained Glass Coloring Book Ser.). (ENG., Illus.). 32p. (J). (gr. 3-5). pap. 6.99 *(978-0-486-47809-8(2))* Dover Pubns., Inc.

GIANTmicrobes(r). GIANTmicrobes — Cells Coloring Book. Cutting, David, illus. 2014. (ENG.). 32p. (J). (gr. k-5). pap. 3.99 *(978-0-486-78017-7(1))* Dover Pubns., Inc.

—GIANTmicrobes — Germs & Microbes Coloring Book. Cutting, David, illus. 2014. (ENG.). 32p. (J). (gr. k-5). pap. 3.99 *(978-0-486-78018-4(X))* Dover Pubns., Inc.

Giddy Up Staff. Backyardigans Color Blast. 2009. (J). 72p. 5.99 *(978-1-59524-216-7(3));* 24p. 7.99 *(978-1-59524-187-0(6))* Giddy Up, LLC.

—Transformers Color N Carry II. 2009. (J). act. bk. ed. 6.99 *(978-1-59524-269-3(4))* Giddy Up, LLC.

Giddy Up Staff, contrib. by. Barbie Color Blast Mini. 2009. 4.99 *(978-1-59524-118-4(3))* Giddy Up, LLC.

—Barbie Water Wow Book. 2009. 6.99 *(978-1-59524-274-7(0))* Giddy Up, LLC.

—Camp Rock Surprize Ink Book. 2009. (J). 6.99 *(978-1-59524-448-2(4))* Giddy Up, LLC.

—Diego Color Blast. 2009. (J). 7.99 *(978-1-59524-271-6(6))* Giddy Up, LLC.

—Diego Surprize Ink Book. 2009. (J). 6.99 *(978-1-59524-214-3(7))* Giddy Up, LLC.

—Dora Color Blast Mini. 2009. 4.99 *(978-1-59524-119-1(1))* Giddy Up, LLC.

—Dora Rub N Color Mini. 2009. 4.99 *(978-1-59524-319-5(4))* Giddy Up, LLC.

—My Little Pony Color N Carry II. 2009. 108p. 5.99 *(978-1-932125-93-1(0))* Giddy Up, LLC.

—Rub N Color Large Kit. 2009. (J). 14.99 *(978-0-9788778-0-4(2))* Giddy Up, LLC.

—Rub N Color Small Kit. 2009. (J). 6.99 *(978-0-9788778-3-5(7))* Giddy Up, LLC.

—Spiderman Color Blast Mini. 2009. 4.99 *(978-1-59524-488-8(3))* Giddy Up, LLC.

—Spiderman Surprize Ink Book. 2009. (J). 6.99 *(978-1-59524-036-1(5))* Giddy Up, LLC.

—Spiderman Surprize Ink Book2. 2009. 6.99 *(978-1-59524-100-9(0))* Giddy Up, LLC.

—Spiderman Water Wow Book. 2009. 6.99 *(978-1-59524-273-0(2))* Giddy Up, LLC.

—Sponge Bob Rub N Color Mini. 2009. 4.99 *(978-1-59524-443-7(3))* Giddy Up, LLC.

—SpongeBob Surprize Ink Book 4. 2009. 6.99 *(978-1-59524-205-1(8))* Giddy Up, LLC.

—Thomas Tank Rub N Color Mini Book. 2009. 4.99 *(978-1-59524-321-8(6))* Giddy Up, LLC.

—Thomas Tank Surprize Ink Book. 2009. 6.99 *(978-1-59524-288-4(0))* Giddy Up, LLC.

—Thomas Tank Water Wow Book. 2009. 6.99 *(978-1-59524-290-7(2))* Giddy Up, LLC.

—Tigger & Pooh Surprize Ink Book. 2009. (J). 6.99 *(978-1-59524-289-1(9))* Giddy Up, LLC.

—Transformers Animated Water Wow Book. 2009. 6.99 *(978-1-59524-434-5(4))* Giddy Up, LLC.

Gill, Shelley. If I Were a Whale. Brooks, Erik, illus. 2017. (ENG.). 20p. (J). (— 1). bds. 9.99 *(978-1-63217-104-7(X),* Little Bigfoot) Sasquatch Bks.

Ginyard, John. What Is the Job of a Corrections Officer? 2006. (YA). per. 6.95 *(978-1-59094-113-3(6))* Jawbone Publishing Corp.

Giovanni, Nikki. Rosa Storytime Set, 1 vol. Collier, Bryan, illus. unabr. ed. 2014. (ENG.). 40p. (J). (gr. -1-3). 12.99 *(978-1-4272-4397-3(2),* 9781427243973) Macmillan Audio.

Gittins, Sheri. The Christmas Journey. 2005. (J). pap. 1.79 *(978-1-59317-106-3(4))* Warner Pr., Inc.

Giulieri, Anne. Here Is a Robot, 1 vol. Kreinberg, Sylvia, photos by. 2012. (Engage Literacy Magenta Ser.). (ENG., Illus.). 32p. (gr. k-2). pap. 5.99 *(978-1-4296-8848-2(3),* Engage Literacy) Capstone Press of Coughlan Cos.

Gladly's Bible Lands Coloring Book. 2003. (J). spiral bd. *(978-0-9706684-7-9(3))* Cortright Fellowship Pr.

Glaser, Byron & Higashi, Sandra. Zolocolor! Doodling Between Black & White. Glaser, Byron & Higashi, Sandra, illus. 2011. (ENG., Illus.). 96p. (J). 7.99 *(978-1-4424-2261-2(0),* Little Simon) Little Simon.

—Zolocolor! Christmas Doodling. Glaser, Byron & Higashi, Sandra, illus. 2012. (ENG., Illus.). 96p. (J). pap. 7.99 *(978-1-4424-4592-5(0),* Little Simon) Little Simon.

Godfrey, Jan. Mira! (SPA., Illus.). 24p. (J). 2.95 *(978-958-607-886-3(8))* Sociedad de San Pablo ESP. Dist: St Pauls/Alba Hse. Pubs.

God's World of Animals. 2006. 16p. (J). pap. 1.99 *(978-0-7847-1019-7(8),* 22120) Standard Publishing.

Golden Books. Championship Colors! (Blaze & the Monster Machines) Golden Books, illus. 2017. (Jumbo Coloring Book Ser.). (ENG., Illus.). 224p. (J). (gr. -1-2). pap. 6.99 ***(978-1-5247-6558-3(9),*** Golden Bks.) Random Hse. Children's Bks.

—Dream Big! (Shimmer & Shine) Golden Books, illus. 2016. (Big Coloring Book Ser.). (ENG., Illus.). 48p. (J). (gr. -1-2). pap. 6.99 *(978-1-101-93673-3(8),* Golden Bks.) Random Hse. Children's Bks.

—Extreme Team! (SpongeBob SquarePants) Golden Books, illus. 2013. (Deluxe Coloring Book Ser.). (ENG., Illus.). 96p. (J). (gr. k-3). pap. 3.99 *(978-0-307-98227-8(0),* Golden Bks.) Random Hse. Children's Bks.

—From Army Ants to Zebrafish: Animals That Hop, Fly & Swish! (Dr. Seuss/Cat in the Hat) Ruiz, Aristides, illus. 2013. (Deluxe Stickerific Ser.). (ENG.). 64p. (J). (gr. -1-2). pap. 5.99 *(978-0-449-81432-1(7),* Golden Bks.) Random Hse. Children's Bks.

—Fry Cook Freak-Out! (SpongeBob SquarePants) Petrossi, Fabrizio, illus. 2014. (Color Plus Chunky Crayons Ser.). (ENG.). 48p. (J). (gr. -1-2). pap. 3.99 *(978-0-385-37430-9(5),* Golden Bks.) Random Hse. Children's Bks.

—Giant Adventures. Golden Books, illus. 2015. (Big Coloring Book Ser.). (ENG., Illus.). 48p. (J). (gr. -1-2). pap. 6.99 *(978-0-553-52292-1(2),* Golden Bks.) Random Hse. Children's Bks.

—Hooray for Dora! (Dora the Explorer) Golden Books, illus. 2012. (Super Jumbo Coloring Book Ser.). (ENG., Illus.). 416p. (J). (gr. -1-2). pap. 10.99 *(978-0-307-93093-4(9),* Golden Bks.) Random Hse. Children's Bks.

—It's Time for Christmas! (Bubble Guppies) Golden Books, illus. 2014. (Big Coloring Book Ser.). (ENG., Illus.). 48p. (J). (gr. -1-2). pap. 6.99 *(978-0-385-38409-4(2),* Golden Bks.) Random Hse. Children's Bks.

—Join the Team! (Team Umizoomi) Golden Books, illus. 2012. (Big Coloring Book Ser.). (ENG., Illus.). 48p. (J). (gr. -1-2). pap. 6.99 *(978-0-307-93138-2(2),* Golden Bks.) Random Hse. Children's Bks.

—Jumbo Coloring Adventures! (Nickelodeon) Golden Books, illus. 2015. (Super Jumbo Coloring Book Ser.). (ENG., Illus.). 416p. (J). (gr. -1-2). pap. 10.99 *(978-0-553-52087-3(3),* Golden Bks.) Random Hse. Children's Bks.

—Just Yelp for Help! (PAW Patrol) Golden Books, illus. 2015. (Giant Coloring Book Ser.). (ENG., Illus.). 40p. (J). (gr. -1-2). pap. 9.99 *(978-0-553-53386-6(X),* Golden Bks.) Random Hse. Children's Bks.

—Let's Get Epic! (Teenage Mutant Ninja Turtles) Golden Books, illus. 2014. (Big Coloring Book Ser.). (ENG., Illus.). 48p. (J). (gr. -1-2). pap. 6.99 *(978-0-385-37849-9(1),* Golden Bks.) Random Hse. Children's Bks.

—Let's Make a Splash! (Bubble Guppies) Golden Books, illus. 2014. (Jumbo Coloring Book Ser.). (ENG., Illus.). 224p. (J). (gr. -1-2). pap. 5.99 *(978-0-385-37437-8(2),* Golden Bks.) Random Hse. Children's Bks.

—No Job Is Too Big! (Paw Patrol) Golden Books, illus. 2015. (Big Coloring Book Ser.). (ENG., Illus.). 48p. (J). (gr. -1-2). pap. 6.99 *(978-0-553-52276-1(0),* Golden Bks.) Random Hse. Children's Bks.

—On the Farm (Bubble Guppies) Jackson, Mike, illus. 2012. (Super Color with Stickers Ser.). (ENG.). 96p. (J). (gr. -1-2). pap. 3.99 *(978-0-307-93096-5(3),* Golden Bks.) Random Hse. Children's Bks.

—PAW Patrol Awesome Sticker Collection (PAW Patrol) Golden Books, illus. 2017. (4 Color Plus 1,000 Stickers Ser.). (ENG., Illus.). 64p. (J). (gr. -1-2). pap. 12.99 ***(978-1-5247-1682-0(0),*** Golden Bks.) Random Hse. Children's Bks.

—Peeps Full-Color Activity Book (Peeps) Golden Books, illus. 2017. (Full-Color Activity Book with Stickers Ser.). (ENG., Illus.). 48p. (J). (gr. -1-2). pap. 5.99 *(978-1-5247-1909-8(9),* Golden Bks.) Random Hse. Children's Bks.

—Plank-Ton's Big Plan! Golden Books, illus. movie tie-in ed. 2015. (Big Coloring Book Ser.). (ENG., Illus.). 48p. (J). (gr. -1-2). pap. 6.99 *(978-0-553-50827-7(X),* Golden Bks.) Random Hse. Children's Bks.

—Puptacular Rescues! (Paw Patrol) Golden Books, illus. 2016. (Jumbo Coloring Book Ser.). (ENG., Illus.). 224p. (J). (gr. -1-2). pap. 5.99 *(978-0-553-53905-9(1),* Golden Bks.) Random Hse. Children's Bks.

—Race Against Time (Mr. Peabody & Sherman) Fransisco, Tina, illus. 2014. (Super Color with Stickers Ser.). (ENG.). 96p. (J). (gr. -1-2). pap. 3.99 *(978-0-385-37151-3(9),* Golden Bks.) Random Hse. Children's Bks.

—Ruff-Ruff Rescues! (Paw Patrol) Golden Books, illus. 2015. (Color & Paint Plus Stickers Ser.). (ENG., Illus.). 128p. (J). (gr. -1-2). pap. 9.99 *(978-0-553-52080-4(6),* Golden Bks.) Random Hse. Children's Bks.

—Sewer Squad! Chabot, Jacob, illus. 2013. (Deluxe Stickerific Ser.). (ENG.). 64p. (J). (gr. -1-2). pap. 5.99 *(978-0-307-98226-1(2),* Golden Bks.) Random Hse. Children's Bks.

—Shimmer & Shine. Golden Books, illus. 2016. (Hologramatic Sticker Book Ser.). (ENG., Illus.). 64p. (J). (gr. -1-2). pap. 4.99 *(978-0-399-55791-0(1),* Golden Bks.) Random Hse. Children's Bks.

—Silly Costume Contest (Team Umizoomi) Fruchter, Jason, illus. 2014. (Glow-In-the-Dark Sticker Book Ser.). (ENG.). 48p. (J). (gr. -1-2). pap. 3.99 *(978-0-385-38413-1(0),* Golden Bks.) Random Hse. Children's Bks.

—Sticker Swim-Sation! (Bubble Guppies) Golden Books, illus. 2014. (Color Plus 1,000 Stickers Ser.). (ENG., Illus.). 64p. (J). (gr. -1-2). pap. 9.99 *(978-0-385-37510-8(7),* Golden Bks.) Random Hse. Children's Bks.

—Thomas & Friends 6-Movie Coloring Collection. Durk, Jim, illus. 2016. (Jumbo Coloring Book Ser.). (ENG.). 224p. (J). (gr. -1-2). pap. 5.99 *(978-1-101-94019-8(0),* Golden Bks.) Random Hse. Children's Bks.

—Tons of Fun with Thomas (Thomas & Friends) 2016. (ENG.). 80p. (J). (gr. -1-2). pap. 6.99 *(978-1-101-93724-2(6),* Golden Bks.) Random Hse. Children's Bks.

—Trainloads of Color (Thomas & Friends) 2014. (Color & Paint Plus Stickers Ser.). (ENG.). 128p. (J). (gr. -1-2). pap. 9.99 *(978-0-385-37513-9(1),* Golden Bks.) Random Hse. Children's Bks.

—Welcome to Wonderland! (Dora the Explorer) Miller, Victoria, illus. 2014. (Color Plus Chunky Crayons Ser.). (ENG.). 48p. (J). (gr. -1-2). pap. 3.99 *(978-0-449-81760-5(1),* Golden Bks.) Random Hse. Children's Bks.

Golden Books & Berrios, Frank. Mutants Rule! (Teenage Mutant Ninja Turtles) Golden Books, illus. 2013. (Color & Paint Plus Stickers Ser.). (ENG., Illus.). 128p. (J). (gr. -1-2). pap. 9.99 *(978-0-449-81952-4(3),* Golden Bks.) Random Hse. Children's Bks.

Golden Books Staff. A Big Easter Adventure (Peter Cottontail) 2012. (Big Coloring Book Ser.). (ENG.). 48p. (J). (gr. -1-2). pap. 6.99 *(978-0-375-86557-2(8),* Golden Bks.) Random Hse. Children's Bks.

—Catch a Wave! Golden Books Staff, illus. 2009. (Color Plus Chunky Crayons Ser.). (ENG., Illus.). 48p. (J). (gr. -1-2). pap. 3.99 *(978-0-375-85107-0(0),* Golden Bks.) Random Hse. Children's Bks.

—Christmas Is Coming! (Dora the Explorer) McGee, Warner, illus. 2011. (Glitter Sticker Book Ser.). (ENG.). 64p. (J). (gr. -1-2). pap. 4.99 *(978-0-375-87393-5(7),* Golden Bks.) Random Hse. Children's Bks.

—Danger from the Deep. 2009. (Deluxe Coloring Book Ser.). (ENG., Illus.). 96p. (J). (gr. -1-2). pap. 3.99 *(978-0-375-85328-9(6),* Golden Bks.) Random Hse. Children's Bks.

—Dora the Explorer Fun Kit!, Kit. Golden Books Staff, illus. 2010. (Fun Kit Ser.). (ENG., Illus.). 64p. (J). (gr. -1-2). 9.99 *(978-0-375-86527-5(6),* Golden Bks.) Random Hse. Children's Bks.

—Easter Deliveries. Golden Books Staff, illus. 2010. (Color Plus Chunky Crayons Ser.). (ENG., Illus.). 48p. (J). (gr. -1-2). pap. 3.99 *(978-0-375-85747-8(8),* Golden Bks.) Random Hse. Children's Bks.

—Friends from Sodor. Hit Entertainment Staff, illus. 2008. (Deluxe Paint Box Book Ser.). (ENG.). 128p. (J). (gr. -1-2). pap. 7.99 *(978-0-375-84292-4(6),* Golden Bks.) Random Hse. Children's Bks.

—The Great Crayon Race. 2012. (Color Plus Chunky Crayons Ser.). (ENG.). 48p. (J). (gr. -1-2). pap. 3.99 *(978-0-307-93027-9(0),* Golden Bks.) Random Hse. Children's Bks.

—Here Comes Bubble Bunny! (Bubble Guppies) MJ Illustrations Staff, illus. 2014. (Hologramatic Sticker Book Ser.). (ENG.). 48p. (J). (gr. -1-2). pap. 3.99 *(978-0-385-37497-2(6),* Golden Bks.) Random Hse. Children's Bks.

—Jumbo Coloring Party. Golden Books Staff, illus. 2010. (Jumbo Coloring Book Ser.). (ENG., Illus.). 224p. (J). (gr. -1-2). pap. 5.99 *(978-0-375-86352-3(4),* Golden Bks.) Random Hse. Children's Bks.

—Kite Riders! (Team Umizoomi) Fruchter, Jason, illus. 2012. (Color Plus Chunky Crayons Ser.). (ENG.). 48p. (J). (gr. -1-2). pap. 3.99 *(978-0-375-86119-2(X),* Golden Bks.) Random Hse. Children's Bks.

—The Lorax Deluxe Doodle Book. Gerardi, Jan, illus. 2013. (Super Coloring Book Ser.). (ENG.). 256p. (J). (gr. -1-2). pap. 9.99 *(978-0-449-81061-3(5),* Golden Bks.) Random Hse. Children's Bks.

—The Lorax Doodle Book. Gerardi, Jan, illus. 2012. (Doodle Book Ser.). (ENG.). 128p. (J). (gr. -1-2). pap. 5.99 *(978-0-307-92982-2(5),* Golden Bks.) Random Hse. Children's Bks.

—Private Eyes (SpongeBob SquarePants) 2012. (3-D Coloring Book Ser.). (ENG.). 32p. (J). (gr. -1-2). pap. 4.99 *(978-0-307-92994-5(9),* Golden Bks.) Random Hse. Children's Bks.

—Puppy Hugs & Kisses! Golden Books Staff & Lovett, Nate, illus. 2016. (Hologramatic Sticker Book Ser.). (ENG.). 64p. (J). (gr. -1-2). pap. 4.99 *(978-0-399-55878-8(0),* Golden Bks.) Random Hse. Children's Bks.

—Puppy Power! (Paw Patrol) Golden Books Staff & Lovett, Nate, illus. 2014. (Color Plus Chunky Crayons Ser.). (ENG.). 48p. (J). (gr. -1-2). pap. 3.99 *(978-0-385-38445-2(9),* Golden Bks.) Random Hse. Children's Bks.

—Rescue Team! Durk, Jim, illus. 2010. (Big Coloring Book Ser.). (ENG.). 48p. (J). (gr. -1-2). pap. 6.99 *(978-0-375-86160-4(2),* Golden Bks.) Random Hse. Children's Bks.

—Santa's Big Big Book to Color. 2006. (Jumbo Coloring Book Ser.). (ENG., Illus.). 80p. (J). (gr. -1-2). 4.99 *(978-0-375-83651-0(9),* Golden Bks.) Random Hse. Children's Bks.

—SpongeBob's Best Days! Golden Books Staff, illus. 2010. (Jumbo Coloring Book Ser.). (ENG., Illus.). 224p. (J). (gr. -1-2). pap. 5.99 *(978-0-375-86351-6(6),* Golden Bks.) Random Hse. Children's Bks.

—Travel with Thomas. Santanach, Tino, illus. 2007. (Deluxe Coloring Book Ser.). (ENG.). 96p. (J). (gr. -1-2). pap. 3.99 *(978-0-375-83953-5(4),* Golden Bks.) Random Hse. Children's Bks.

—A Tree for Me! Gerardi, Jan, illus. 2012. (Stickerific Ser.). (ENG.). 48p. (J). (gr. k — 1). pap. 3.99 *(978-0-307-92981-5(7),* Golden Bks.) Random Hse. Children's Bks.

Golden Twomey, Emily, illus. Amazing Copycat Coloring Book: Cool Pictures to Copy & Complete. 2015. (ENG.). 48p. (J). (gr. 1-4). pap. 6.99 *(978-1-4380-0635-2(7))* Barron's Educational Series, Inc.

—Creative Copycat Coloring Book: Cool Pictures to Copy & Complete. 2016. (Copycat Coloring Bks.). (ENG.). 48p. (J). (gr. 1-5). pap. 6.99 *(978-1-4380-0840-0(6))* Barron's Educational Series, Inc.

Golding, Elizabeth. Challenging Coloring: Millions of Animals: Over 90 Awesome Coloring Pages. Mallet, Lisa et al, illus. 2017. (Challenging... Bks.). (ENG.). 96p. (J). (gr. 3-7). pap. 7.99 *(978-1-4380-0978-0(X))* Barron's Educational Series, Inc.

—My First Mazes: Over 50 Fantastic Puzzles. 2017. (My First Activity Bks.). (ENG.). 64p. (J). (gr. -1-2). pap. 5.99 *(978-1-4380-1003-8(6))* Barron's Educational Series, Inc.

Goodhart, Pippa & Sharratt, Nick. You Choose! (ENG., Illus.). 32p. (J). 19.99 *(978-0-385-60176-4(X),* Doubleday Children's) Random House Children's Books GBR. Dist: Trafalgar Square Publishing.

Goodridge, Teresa. Pretty Princess Coloring Book. 2016. (Dover Coloring Bks.). (ENG.). 32p. (J). (gr. -1-2). pap. 3.99 *(978-0-486-80446-0(1))* Dover Pubns., Inc.

Gordon, Bob. Lift & Learn Colors. Snaith, Andy, photos by. 2006. (Illus.). 24p. (gr. -1 — 1). per., bds. *(978-1-84610-028-4(3))* Make Believe Ideas.

Gospel Light Publications Staff, creator. The Best Gift: Forgiveness: A Read-to-Me Bible Story Coloring Book about Jesus & the Paralyzed Man. 2007. (Illus.). 12p. (J). (gr. -1-3). 1.49 *(978-0-8307-4428-2(2),* Gospel Light) Gospel Light Pubns.

Got, Yves. Sam's Pop-up Schoolhouse. Got, Yves, illus. 2004. (Illus.). 6p. (J). (gr. k-4). reprint ed. 17.00 *(978-0-7567-8065-4(9))* DIANE Publishing Co.

Gottesman, Eric. Color Your Own Patriotic Posters. 2003. (Dover Art Coloring Book Ser.). (ENG., Illus.). 32p. (J). (gr. 3-8). 3.99 *(978-0-486-42650-1(5))* Dover Pubns., Inc.

—I Love America Stained Glass Coloring Book. 2003. (Dover Stained Glass Coloring Book Ser.). (ENG., Illus.). 32p. (J). (gr. 3-8). pap. 7.99 *(978-0-486-43050-8(2))* Dover Pubns., Inc.

—Wizards & Dragons Stained Glass Coloring Book. 2003. (Dover Stained Glass Coloring Book Ser.). (ENG., Illus.). 32p. (J). (gr. 3-5). pap. 7.99 *(978-0-486-42770-6(6))* Dover Pubns., Inc.

Gottesman, Eric & Coloring Books for Adults. Classic Tattoo Designs Coloring Book. 2006. (Dover Design Coloring Bks.). (ENG., Illus.). 32p. (gr. 8). pap. 3.99 *(978-0-486-44759-9(6))* Dover Pubns., Inc.

Grack, David. Birds of the Northwoods. 2007. (Color & Learn Ser.). (ENG., Illus.). 64p. (J). (gr. 3-4). per., act. bk. ed. 7.95 *(978-1-59193-166-9(5))* Adventure Pubns.

Graham, Patti. And That Is Why We Teach: A Celebration of Teachers. Wellman, Megan D., illus. 2008. (ENG.). 32p. (J). (gr. 4-7). 17.95 *(978-1-933916-23-1(0))* Nelson Publishing & Marketing.

Grama, Getta. Swirling Designs. 2013. (ENG., Illus.). 40p. pap. 6.95 *(978-1-60705-775-8(1))* C & T Publishing.

Gran Libro de Oro. 2003. (SPA., Illus.). 9.95 *(978-84-7971-268-6(6))* Servilibro Ediciones, S.A. ESP. Dist: Giron Bks.

Grange, James. The 1990s Coloring Book: All That & a Box of Crayons (Psych! Crayons Not Included.) 2013. (ENG., Illus.). 64p. pap. 10.00 *(978-1-61243-224-3(7))* Ulysses Pr.

Grau, Maritta, ed. The ABCs of Frederick Maryland: A Historic Coloring Book. Grau, Ryon, illus. 2007. 32p. 8.95 *(978-0-9772559-0-0(5))* Grau, Ryon.

Gray, Susan. Colorful Ohio! A Bird's Eye View with Worthington Cardinal, 7 bks. Gray, Susan & Messer, Celia, illus. 2003. 28p. (J). 4.95 *(978-0-9742862-5-9(7))* Two's Company.

Green, John. Arabian Nights Coloring Book. 2004. (Dover Classic Stories Coloring Book Ser.). (ENG., Illus.). 32p. (J). (gr. 3-8). pap. 3.95 *(978-0-486-43635-7(7))* Dover Pubns., Inc.

—Beowulf. 2007. (Dover Classic Stories Coloring Book Ser.). (ENG., Illus.). 32p. (J). (gr. 3-8). 3.99 *(978-0-486-45655-3(2))* Dover Pubns., Inc.

—Cathedrals of the World Coloring Book. 2013. (Dover Coloring Bks.). (ENG., Illus.). 48p. (gr. 3-12). pap. 4.99 *(978-0-486-28339-5(9))* Dover Pubns., Inc.

—Creative Haven Wildflowers Stained Glass Coloring Book. 2014. (Adult Coloring Ser.). (ENG., Illus.). 32p. (gr. 6). pap. 7.99 *(978-0-486-79601-7(9))* Dover Pubns., Inc.

—Dogs to Paint or Color. 2008. (Dover Art Coloring Book Ser.). (ENG., Illus.). 48p. (gr. 3-5). pap. 5.99 *(978-0-486-46541-8(1))* Dover Pubns., Inc.

—Fairy World Stained Glass Coloring Book. 2004. (Dover Stained Glass Coloring Book Ser.). (ENG., Illus.). 8p. (J). (gr. 1-4). pap. 1.99 *(978-0-486-43846-7(5))* Dover Pubns., Inc.

—Favorite Horses. 2005. (Dover Nature Coloring Book Ser.). (ENG., Illus.). 32p. (J). (gr. 3-8). 3.99 *(978-0-486-44010-1(9))* Dover Pubns., Inc.

—Great Racehorses. 2006. (Dover Nature Coloring Book Ser.). (ENG., Illus.). 32p. (J). (gr. 3-5). pap. 3.99 *(978-0-486-45162-6(3))* Dover Pubns., Inc.

—Great Scenes from Horror Stories. 2012. (Dover Classic Stories Coloring Book Ser.). (ENG.). 32p. (gr. 3-5). pap. 3.99 *(978-0-486-48840-0(3))* Dover Pubns., Inc.

—Heavenly Snowflakes Stained Glass Coloring Book. 2006. (Dover Stained Glass Coloring Book Ser.). (ENG., Illus.). 8p. (J). (gr. k-3). 1.99 *(978-0-486-44923-4(8))* Dover Pubns., Inc.

—Horse Anatomy. 2006. (Dover Nature Coloring Book Ser.). (ENG., Illus.). 32p. (gr. 6-8). 3.99 *(978-0-486-44813-8(4))* Dover Pubns., Inc.

—Horses of the Old West. 2007. (Dover Nature Coloring Book Ser.). (ENG., Illus.). 32p. (gr. 3-8). 3.99 *(978-0-486-45675-1(7))* Dover Pubns., Inc.

—Horses Stained Glass Coloring Book. 2004. (Dover Nature Stained Glass Coloring Book Ser.). (ENG., Illus.). 32p. (J). (gr. 3-8). pap. 6.99 *(978-0-486-43341-7(2))* Dover Pubns., Inc.

—Indian Life in Pre-Columbian North America Coloring Book. 2013. (Dover History Coloring Book Ser.). (ENG., Illus.). 48p. (gr. 3-12). pap. 4.99 *(978-0-486-28047-9(0))* Dover Pubns., Inc.

—The Language of Flowers Coloring Book, 2 vols. 2004. (Dover Nature Coloring Book Ser.). (ENG., Illus.). 32p. (gr. 6-8). pap. 3.99 *(978-0-486-43035-5(9))* Dover Pubns., Inc.

—Monkeys & Apes Coloring Book. 2013. (Dover Nature Coloring Book Ser.). (ENG., Illus.). 48p. (J). (gr. 3-12). pap. 4.99 *(978-0-486-25798-3(3))* Dover Pubns., Inc.

—Musical Instruments Stained Glass Coloring Book. 2006. (Dover Stained Glass Coloring Book Ser.). (ENG., Illus.). 8p. (J). (gr. -1-5). pap. 1.50 *(978-0-486-44936-4(X))* Dover Pubns., Inc.

—Old Testament Scenes Stained Glass Coloring Book. 2009. (Dover Stained Glass Coloring Book Ser.). (ENG., Illus.). 32p. (gr. 3-5). pap. 6.99 *(978-0-486-46763-4(5))* Dover Pubns., Inc.

—Pirate Queens: Notorious Women of the Sea. 2014. (Dover Coloring Bks.). (ENG.). 32p. (gr. 3). pap. 3.99 *(978-0-486-78334-5(0))* Dover Pubns., Inc.

—Pirates Stained Glass Coloring Book. 2004. (Dover Stained Glass Coloring Book Ser.). (ENG., Illus.). 32p. (J). (gr. 3-8). pap. 6.99 *(978-0-486-43731-6(0))* Dover Pubns., Inc.

—Popes Coloring Book. 2015. (ENG.). 32p. (gr. 3). pap. 3.99 (978-0-486-79236-1(6)) Dover Pubns., Inc.
—Samurai Stained Glass Coloring Book. 2008. (Dover Stained Glass Coloring Book Ser.). (ENG., Illus.). 32p. (gr. 3-8). 6.99 (978-0-486-46558-6(6)) Dover Pubns., Inc.
—Samurai Warriors. 2008. (Dover History Coloring Book Ser.). (ENG., Illus.). 32p. (gr. 3-8). 3.95 (978-0-486-46559-3(4)) Dover Pubns., Inc.
—Sparta! Warriors of the Ancient World. 2013. (Dover History Coloring Book Ser.). (ENG.). 32p. (gr. 3-12). pap. 3.99 (978-0-486-49813-3(1)) Dover Pubns., Inc.
—The War of the Worlds. 2005. (Dover Classic Stories Coloring Book Ser.). (ENG., Illus.). 32p. (gr. 3-8). 3.95 (978-0-486-44455-0(4)) Dover Pubns., Inc.
—Wildflowers GemGlow Stained Glass Coloring Book. 2009. (Dover Nature Stained Glass Coloring Book Ser.). (ENG., Illus.). 32p. (J). (gr. 1-5). pap. 7.99 (978-0-486-47148-8(9)) Dover Pubns., Inc.
—Women of the Bible. 2006. (Dover Classic Stories Coloring Book Ser.). (ENG., Illus.). 32p. (J). (gr. 3-8). 3.99 (978-0-486-45193-0(3)) Dover Pubns., Inc.
—Wonderful World of Horses Coloring Book. 2005. (Dover Nature Coloring Book Ser.). (ENG., Illus.). 32p. (J). (gr. 3-5). 3.99 (978-0-486-44465-9(1)) Dover Pubns., Inc.
—World of Cats to Paint or Color. 2007. (Dover Art Coloring Book Ser.). (ENG., Illus.). 48p. (gr. 3-8). 5.99 (978-0-486-46233-2(1)) Dover Pubns., Inc.
Green, John & Appelbaum, Stanley. Life in Old Japan Coloring Book. 2008. (Dover History Coloring Book Ser.). (ENG.). 48p. (J). (gr. 1-5). pap. 4.99 (978-0-486-46883-9(6)) Dover Pubns., Inc.
Green, John & Coloring Books Staff. Amazing Angels Stained Glass Coloring Book. 2011. (Dover Stained Glass Coloring Book Ser.). (ENG., Illus.). 32p. (gr. 3-8). pap. 7.99 (978-0-486-48047-3(X)) Dover Pubns., Inc.
—Glorious Angels Coloring Book. 2013. (Dover Coloring Bks.). (ENG.). 32p. (gr. 3-5). pap. 3.99 (978-0-486-48046-6(1)) Dover Pubns., Inc.
Green, John, et al. Merry Christmas! Stained Glass Coloring Book. 2008. (Holiday Stained Glass Coloring Book Ser.). (ENG., Illus.). 96p. (gr. 1-5). pap. 12.99 (978-0-486-46944-7(1)) Dover Pubns., Inc.
Green, Yuko. Let's Learn about JAPAN: Activity & Coloring Book. 2013. (Dover Children's Activity Bks.). (ENG.). 48p. (J). (gr. 1-5). pap. 4.99 (978-0-486-48993-3(0)) Dover Pubns., Inc.
—Let's Learn about MEXICO: Activity & Coloring Book. 2013. (Dover Children's Activity Bks.). (ENG.). 48p. (J). (gr. 1-5). pap. 4.99 (978-0-486-48994-0(9)) Dover Pubns., Inc.
—Naia & Kohola. 2010. 20p. pap. 6.95 (978-1-59700-803-7(6)) Island Heritage Publishing.
—The Nativity Activity & Coloring Book. 2013. (Dover Holiday Coloring Book Ser.). (ENG.). 48p. (J). (gr. k-4). pap. 4.99 (978-0-486-49717-4(8)) Dover Pubns., Inc.
Greenaway, Kate. Mother Goose Coloring Book. Perkins, Nancy, illus. 2013. (Dover Coloring Bks.). (ENG.). 48p. (J). (gr. -1-8). pap. 4.99 (978-0-486-22883-9(5)) Dover Pubns., Inc.
Greenwell, Jessica. Animal Coloring Book with Stickers. 2009. (Sticker Coloring Bks). 16p. (J). pap. 5.99 (978-0-7945-2506-4(7), Usborne) EDC Publishing.
—Fairies Sticker Coloring Book. 2012. (First Sticker Coloring Bks). 16p. (J). pap. 5.99 (978-0-7945-3129-4(6), Usborne) EDC Publishing.
—Farm Coloring Sticker Book. 2009. (Sticker Coloring Bks). 16p. (J). pap. 5.99 (978-0-7945-2512-5(1), Usborne) EDC Publishing.
—My First Coloring Book. 2011. (First Sticker Coloring Book Ser.). 46p. (J). pap. 10.99 (978-0-7945-2964-2(X), Usborne) EDC Publishing.
Greenwood, Rebecca J. Scripture Princesses Coloring Book. 2016. (ENG.). (J). pap. 4.99 (978-1-4621-1832-8(1)) Cedar Fort, Inc./CFI Distribution.
Gregory, Charles Matthew. Mika's Musik Coloring Book. 2006. (ENG.). (J). 24.00 (978-0-9766442-4-8(X)) Gregory, Charles Matthew.
Gregory, Jeannette. Once upon A Time. 2004. (J). 6.99 (978-0-9754779-8-4(6)) Chosen Word Publishing.
Grey, Rochelle, text. My RiverPlace on the Schuylkill Coloring Book. 2006. (Illus.). 12p. (J). (978-0-9785538-0-7(2)) RiverPlace Development Corp.
Griffiths, Andy & Griffiths, Jill. The Treehouse Fun Book. Denton, Terry, illus. 2016. (Treehouse Bks.). (ENG.). 192p. (J). 12.99 (978-1-250-11775-5(5), 9781250117755) Feiwel & Friends.
Grumpy Cat, Grumpy. Grumpy Cat Coloring Book. 2014. (ENG.). 64p. (J). (gr. 6-12). pap. 5.99 (978-0-486-79163-0(7)) Dover Pubns., Inc.
Guesné, Maude, illus. Once upon a Time. 2016. (Coloring Studio Ser.: 1). (ENG.). 32p. (J). (gr. 1-17). pap. 7.99 (978-0-316-39292-1(8)) Little, Brown Bks. for Young Readers.
Gul, Hasibe, et al. My Wonderful Body. 2011. (ENG.). 16p. (J). (gr. -1 — 1). pap. 3.95 (978-1-59784-241-9(9)) Tughra Bks.
—Nutritious Vegetables. 2011. (ENG.). 16p. (J). (gr. -1 — 1). pap. 3.95 (978-1-59784-239-6(7)) Tughra Bks.
Gunnell, Beth, et al. Girls' Gorgeous World: Doodling & Colouring. Jackson, Katy et al, illus. 2015. (ENG.). 128p. (J). (gr. 2). pap. 12.99 (978-1-78055-151-7(7)) O'Mara, Michael Bks., Ltd. GBR. Dist: Independent Pubs. Group.
Gunzl, Christiane & Gunzl, Christiane. Colours. 2014. (ENG., Illus.). 20p. 8.95 (978-1-907604-24-9(3)) Award Pubns. Ltd. GBR. Dist: Parkwest Pubns., Inc.
Guzman, Maria Del C. Sheep of Many Colors: Coloring Book. Lovell, Edith, illus. 2013. 26p. pap. 5.99 (978-0-9855639-4-3(X)) Guzman, Maria del C.
Hachette Book Group. Beautiful Winter. 2016. (Coloring Space Ser.: 8). (ENG.). 64p. (J). (gr. 1-17). 9.99 (978-0-316-35957-3(2)) Little, Brown Bks. for Young Readers.
—Connect the Dots. 2016. (Coloring Space Ser.: 6). (ENG.). 32p. (J). (gr. 1-17). 7.99 (978-0-316-35959-7(9)) Little, Brown Bks. for Young Readers.
Haley, Amanda. Un Mundo de Peques. 2004. (SPA., Illus.). 34p. (J). 17.99 (978-84-95620-97-2(9)) Brosquil Edicions, S.L. ESP. Dist: Lectorum Pubns., Inc.
Hall, Susan T. Happy Halloween Coloring Book. 2013. (Dover Holiday Coloring Book Ser.). (ENG., Illus.). 32p. (J). (gr. -1-8). pap. 3.99 (978-0-486-49218-6(4)) Dover Pubns., Inc.
Hallmark, Darla, illus. More Dragons: Coloring Book by Darla Hallmark. 2007. 20p. (YA). 10.00 (978-0-9795206-8-6(1)) Unseen Gallery.
Halpin, D. I Learn about Jesus Col/Act Bk. 32p. pap. 1.25 (978-0-8198-3686-1(9), 332-139) Pauline Bks. & Media.
—My Guardian Angel Col/Act Bk. 24p. pap. 1.25 (978-0-8198-4825-3(5), 332-216) Pauline Bks. & Media.
Halpin, D. Thomas. The Beatitudes Coloring & Activity Book. Richards, Virginia Helen, illus. 2006. (J). 1.95 (978-0-8198-2359-5(7)) Pauline Bks. & Media.
—Holy Eucharist. Richards, Virginia Helen, illus. 2005. 32p. (J). (gr. 4-7). 1.95 (978-0-8198-3387-7(8), 332-425) Pauline Bks. & Media.
Halpin, D. Thomas & Richards, Virginia Helen. Saint Paul. Halpin, D. Thomas & Richards, Virginia Helen, illus. 2008. (COMIColor Saints Ser.: 1). (Illus.). (J). 2.95 (978-0-8198-7109-1(5)) Pauline Bks. & Media.
Ham, Ken & Ham, Mally. D Is for Dinosaur Coloring Book. 2016. (Illus.). 32p. (J). pap. 4.99 **(978-1-68344-015-4(3))** Master Bks.
—N Is for Noah Coloring Book. 2016. (Illus.). 32p. (J). pap. 4.99 **(978-1-68344-016-1(1))** Master Bks.
Handford, Martin. Where's Waldo? the Coloring Collection. Handford, Martin, illus. 2017. (Where's Waldo? Ser.). (ENG., Illus.). 80p. (J). (gr. k-12). pap. 12.99 (978-0-7636-9577-4(7)) Candlewick Pr.
Hansen, Doug, illus. The Sierra Adventure Coloring Book: Featuring Yosemite National Park. 2013. (ENG.). 24p. (J). (gr. -1-2). pap. 4.95 (978-1-930238-39-8(8)) Yosemite Assn.
Happy Thanksgiving Coloring Book. 2006. 16p. (J). pap. 1.99 (978-0-7847-1744-8(3), 04370) Standard Publishing.
Hargreaves, Roger. Little Miss Princess & the Very Special Wedding. 2011. (Mr. Men & Little Miss Ser.). (ENG., Illus.). 24p. (J). (gr. -1-3). (978-1-4052-5996-5(5)) Egmont Bks., Ltd.
—Mr. Christmas Sticker Activity Book. Hargreaves, Adam, illus. 2010. (Mr. Men & Little Miss Ser.). (ENG.). 24p. (J). (gr. -1-2). act. bk. ed. 4.99 (978-0-8431-2670-9(1), Price Stern Sloan) Penguin Young Readers Group.
Harper, Betty. Color My World Vol. 1: Early Elvis (Coloring Book) Harper, Betty, illus. 2004. (Illus.). 32p. (J). 4.95 (978-0-932117-42-7(2)) Osborne Enterprises Publishing.
Harper, Marrisa and Normita. ABC Book. 2005. 58p. 8.19 (978-1-4116-2660-7(5)) Lulu Pr., Inc.
Harper, Valentina. Creative Coloring Animals: Art Activity Pages to Relax & Enjoy! 2014. (ENG., Illus.). 72p. pap. 9.99 (978-1-57421-971-5(5), Design Originals) Fox Chapel Publishing Co., Inc.
Harrell, Antoinette. Nurturing My Family Tree: Genealogy for Children. 2010. 52p. pap. 28.99 (978-1-4490-6541-6(4)) AuthorHouse.
Harris, Patricia. Ben's Color Book. 2017. (Teddy's Colorful World Ser.). 24p. (gr. 4-6). 23.60 **(978-1-5081-6168-4(2)**, PowerKids Pr.) Rosen Publishing Group, Inc., The.
Harston, David, illus. Michigan Coloring Book. 2005. 24p. (J). pap. (978-1-893624-32-0(3)) Penrod/Hiawatha Co.
Harvest House Publishers. The Jesus Bible for Kids Coloring Book. International Publishing Services Pty Ltd, illus. 2017. (ENG.). 160p. (J). 9.99 (978-0-7369-6999-4(3)) Harvest Hse. Pubs.
Hashanah, Rosh & Kippur, Yom. Rosh Hashanah & Yom Kippur Coloring Book. 2.99 (978-1-58330-168-5(2)) Feldheim Pubs.
Hasibe, Gul & Balci. Delicious Fruits. 2011. (ENG.). 16p. (J). (gr. -1 — 1). pap. 3.95 (978-1-59784-240-2(0)) Tughra Bks.
Hawaiian Kids Coloring Book. No. 1. pap. 4.95 (978-0-930492-41-0(2))No. 2. pap. 4.95 (978-0-930492-42-7(0)) Hawaiian Service, Inc.
Hawkes, Spencer, illus. Beagles in My Bed Coloring Book. 2005. 50p. (J). 5.95 (978-0-9774563-1-4(5)) Ladd, David Pr.
Hay DeSimone, Corkey. Air & Space Activity & Coloring Book: An Early Introduction to the History of Flight. Hay DeSimone, Corkey, illus. 2006. (Illus.). (J). 7.95 (978-0-9747921-4-9(4)) Gentle Giraffe Pr.
—Dinosaur Explore Activity & Coloring Book: Dinosaurs designed for their littlest Fans. Hay DeSimone, Corkey, illus. 2006. (Illus.). (J). 4.95 (978-0-9777394-0-0(6)) Gentle Giraffe Pr.
—Mammal Animal Coloring & Activity Book: What Is a mammal? You are a mammal Too! 2005. (Illus.). (J). pap. 4.95 (978-0-9747921-2-5(8)) Gentle Giraffe Pr.
—Panda Promise Activity & Coloring Book. Hay DeSimone, Corkey, illus. 2006. (Illus.). (J). 4.95 (978-0-9747921-9-4(5)) Gentle Giraffe Pr.
Hay, Sam. Beauty & the Beast. Jackson, Katy, illus. 2017. (3D Colouring & Activity Ser.). (ENG.). 24p. (J). (gr. 1-4). pap. 11.99 **(978-1-4052-8160-7(X))** Egmont Bks., Ltd. GBR. Dist: Independent Pubs. Group.
—The Nutcracker. Dudziuk, Kasia, illus. 2017. (3D Colouring & Activity Ser.). (ENG.). 24p. (J). (gr. 1-4). pap. 11.99 **(978-1-4052-7912-3(5))** Egmont Bks., Ltd. GBR. Dist: Independent Pubs. Group.
Hays, Susan. Nature Friends Creativity Book. 2003. (Illus.). 52p. (J). 11.95 (978-0-9729192-0-3(1)) Art & Soul Expressions.
Hecht, Kristina. 1, 2, 3, My Daddy & Me. 2007. 16p. per. 24.95 (978-1-4241-8940-3(3)) America Star Bks.
Hecker, Vera. Mystic World Coloring Book. Hecker, Vera, illus. 2007. (Illus.). (YA). per. (978-0-9799729-1-1(4)) Banta, Sandra.
Heighton, Mary Beth & Laskey, Andrew. What I Do When You're Not Home. 1 vol. 2009. 38p. pap. 24.95 (978-1-60813-167-9(X)) America Star Bks.
Hein, Connie L. Toliver in Time: For a Fourth of July Celebration. Theobald, Denise, illus. 2003. 40p. (J). lib. bdg. 19.95 (978-0-9740855-8-6(8)); per. 12.95 (978-0-9740855-9-3(6)) Still Water Publishing.
Hell-Höflinger, Philippa. My First Coloring Dictionary from a to Z. 2012. 56p. pap. (978-3-8482-0712-1(5)) Books on Demand GmbH.
Heller, Elaine. Half 'n Half Animals A1: Think, Draw, & Color. 2010. (Half 'n Half Animals Ser.). 48p. (gr. k-1). pap. 8.99 (978-0-89455-867-2(6)) Critical Thinking Co., The.
Heller, Ruth. Sea Life. Heller, Ruth, illus. 2009. (Designs for Coloring Ser.). (ENG., Illus.). 64p. (J). (gr. 1-3). 6.99 (978-0-448-45204-3(9), Grosset & Dunlap) Penguin Young Readers Group.
—Spring Has Sprung. 2009. (Designs for Coloring Ser.). (ENG.). 384p. (J). (gr. 1-4). 10.99 (978-0-448-45099-5(2), Grosset & Dunlap) Penguin Young Readers Group.
Heller, Ruth, illus. Wildflowers. 2011. (Designs for Coloring Ser.). (ENG.). 64p. (J). (gr. 1-4). 6.99 (978-0-448-45462-7(9), Grosset & Dunlap) Penguin Young Readers Group.
Hellman, Charles S. Luckysports Abc's Coloring Book. Tiritilli, Robert A., illus. 2013. 50p. pap. 5.40 (978-0-935938-46-3(X)) LuckySports.
Hendler, Muncie. Infinite Designs Coloring Book. 2006. (Dover Design Coloring Bks.). (ENG., Illus.). 32p. (J). (gr. 3-8). 3.99 (978-0-486-44892-3(4)) Dover Pubns., Inc.
Herrero, M. N. Mi Libro de Seguridad Infantil. (SPA.). 95p. (J). pap. 7.95 (978-968-416-831-2(4), FN8314) Fernandez USA Publishing.
Hicks, Angie, illus. Colour by Numbers. 2012. (ENG.). 16p. (J). 3.25 (978-1-84135-860-4(6)) Award Pubns. Ltd. GBR. Dist: Parkwest Pubns., Inc.
—Mermaid. 2012. (ENG.). 16p. (J). 3.25 (978-1-84135-859-8(2)) Award Pubns. Ltd. GBR. Dist: Parkwest Pubns., Inc.
—Shark. 2012. (ENG.). 16p. (J). 3.25 (978-1-84135-858-1(4)) Award Pubns. Ltd. GBR. Dist: Parkwest Pubns., Inc.
Highlights, creator. The Jumbo Book of Things to Find & Color. 2017. (Highlights(tm) Jumbo Books & Pads Ser.). (ENG.). 256p. (J). (gr. -1-k). pap. 12.99 (978-1-62979-779-3(0), Highlights) Boyds Mills Pr.
The Hiking & Camping Coloring Book. 2004. (J). mass mkt. (978-0-9745863-8-0(2)) Cypress Knees Publishing.
Hill, Eric. Spot Aprende los Colores. (SPA.). pap. 4.95 (978-950-07-1965-0(7)) Editorial Sudamericana S.A. ARG. Dist: Distribooks, Inc.
Hillary: The Coloring Book. 2014. (ENG., Illus.). 64p. pap. 10.00 (978-1-61243-369-1(3)) Ulysses Pr.
Hillert, Margaret. Dear Dragon's Colors 1, 2, 3. Schimmell, David, illus. 2010. (BeginningtoRead Ser.). 32p. (J). (-2). pap. 11.94 (978-1-60357-100-5(0)) Norwood Hse. Pr.
Hilltree, Angela. ABC Coloring Book: Creation Science & Geology. 2004. (Illus.). 26p. (J). 6.50 (978-1-931941-10-5(6)) Media Angels, Inc.
Hirsch, Ancilla. Holy Mass Col & Act Bk. 32p. pap. 1.25 (978-0-8198-3380-8(0), 332-118) Pauline Bks. & Media.
La Historias de Jeremias Coloring Book. (SPA.). 32p. pap. 1.95 (978-1-931471-94-7(0)) United Bible Societies Association Inc.
Hoerner, L. Fanciful Fairies & Dazzling Dragons Coloring Book. 2013. (ENG.). 32p. (gr. 3-6). pap. 3.99 (978-0-486-49979-6(0)) Dover Pubns., Inc.
Holokai, Ben W., Jr. Myths & Legends of Hawai'i Coloring Book. 2004. (Illus.). 32p. 5.95 (978-1-57306-212-1(X)) Bess Pr., Inc.
Holt, William T. Brand New Shoes Coloring & Activity Book. 2013. (Illus.). 66p. pap. 5.75 (978-0-9895062-1-2(5)) SeartStudio Publishing.
Hood, Karen Jean Matsko. Adventure Travel Activity & Coloring Book. Whispering Pine Press International, ed. Hatakeyama, Hiroshi, tr. Hatakeyama, Hiroshi, illus. 2014. (Hood Activity & Coloring Book Ser.). (ENG & JPN.). 160p. (J). spiral bd. 19.95 (978-1-59649-334-6(8)); per. 19.95 (978-1-59210-590-8(4)) Whispering Pine Pr. International, Inc.
—Adventure Travel Activity & Coloring Book: Activity & Coloring Book Series. 2006. (Educational Activity & Coloring Book Ser.). (Illus.). (J). 17.95 (978-1-930948-58-7(1)) Whispering Pine Pr. International, Inc.
—Adventures of My Dentist & the Tooth Fairy: Activity & Coloring Book, bk. 2. Whispering Pine Press International, Inc. Staff, ed. Artistic Book and Web Design, illus. 2013. (ENG & JPN.). 174p. (J). pap. 19.95 (978-1-59649-535-7(9)) Whispering Pine Pr. International, Inc.
—Adventures of My Dentist & Tooth Fairy Activity & Coloring Book: Activity & Coloring Book. Whispering Pine Press International, Inc. Staff, ed. Keyama, Hiroshi Hata, tr. Keyama, Hiroshi Hata, illus. 2010. (ENG.). 160p. (J). pap. 9.95 (978-1-930948-76-1(X)) Whispering Pine Pr. International, Inc.
—Gaited Horse Activity & Coloring Book. Whispering Pine Press International, ed. Artistic Design Service Staff, illus. 2014. (Hood Activity & Coloring Book Ser.). 160p. (J). bk. 4. spiral bd. 21.95 (978-1-59649-628-6(2)) Vol. 4. (ENG.). per. 19.95 (978-1-59210-591-5(2)) Whispering Pine Pr. International, Inc.
—Gaited Horse Activity & Coloring Book-English/German/Spanish Edition. Whispering Pine Press International, Inc. Staff, ed. Artistic Book and Web Design, illus. 2010. (ENG, GER & SPA.). 160p. (J). per. 19.95 (978-1-59649-522-7(7)) Whispering Pine Pr. International, Inc.
—Girls Can Do Activity & Coloring Book. Whispering Pine Press International, Inc. Staff, ed. Artistic Book and Web Design, illus. 2010. (ENG & JPN.). 160p. (J). per. 13.95 (978-1-59210-593-9(9)) Whispering Pine Pr. International, Inc.
—Girls Can Do Activity & Coloring Book, Vol. 5. Whispering Pine Press International, ed. 2014. (Educational Activity & Coloring Book Ser.). (ENG., Illus.). 170p. (J). spiral bd. 21.95 (978-1-930948-54-9(9)) Whispering Pine Pr. International, Inc.
—Girls Can Do Journal: A Daily Journal, bk. 5. Whispering Pine Press International, ed. Artistic Design Services, illus. 2014. (Educational Activity & Coloring Book Ser.). 164p. (J). spiral bd. 15.95 (978-1-59649-361-2(5)) Whispering Pine Pr. International, Inc.
—Icelandic Horse Activity & Coloring Book, Vol. 6. Whispering Pine Press International, ed. Artistic Design Service Staff, illus. 2nd ed. 2014. (Educational Activity & Coloring Book Ser.). (ENG, ICE & GER.). 160p. (J). spiral bd. 21.95 (978-1-59649-364-3(X)) Whispering Pine Pr. International, Inc.
—Icelandic Horse Activity & Coloring Book: Activity & Coloring Book, Vol. 6. Whispering Pine Press International, ed. Artistic Design Service Staff, illus. 2014. (Hood Activity & Coloring Book Ser.). (ENG, GER & ICE.). 160p. (J). per. 19.95 (978-1-59210-595-3(5)) Whispering Pine Pr. International, Inc.
—Kids' Kindness Activity & Coloring Book, Vol. 9. Whispering Pine Press International, ed. Artistic Design Service Staff, illus. 2015. (Hood Activity & Coloring Book Ser.). 170p. (J). spiral bd. 21.95 (978-1-59808-753-6(3)); per. 19.95 (978-1-59808-752-9(5)) Whispering Pine Pr. International, Inc.
—My Dentist & the Tooth Fairy: Activity & Coloring Book, bk. 10. Whispering Pine Press International, Inc. Staff, ed. 2013. (Hood Activity & Coloring Book Ser.). (ENG., Illus.). 160p. (J). pap. 19.95 (978-1-59210-596-0(3)) Whispering Pine Pr. International, Inc.
—Washington State: Activity & Coloring Book. 2014. (J). spiral bd. 19.95 (978-1-59649-434-3(4)); 19.95 (978-1-930948-56-3(5)) Whispering Pine Pr. International, Inc.
HOP, LLC. Hooked on Learning Coloring. 2006. 64p. 3.79 (978-1-933863-92-4(7)) HOP, LLC.
Houghton Mifflin Harcourt Publishing Company Staff. Draw It! Color It! Creatures. Gravett, Emily et al, illus. 2016. (ENG.). 120p. (J). 11.99 (978-0-544-77979-2(7), HMH Books For Young Readers) Houghton Mifflin Harcourt Publishing Co.
Hoyle, Leighanna. Dinosaur Circus: A Cretaceous Coloring Book. 2016. (ENG., Illus.). 44p. (J). (gr. k-2). pap. 5.99 (978-1-57826-637-1(8), Hatherleigh Pr.) Hatherleigh Co., Ltd., The.
—Mysterious Creatures: A Cryptid Coloring Book & Field Reference Guide. 2016. (ENG., Illus.). 44p. (J). (gr. k-2). pap. 5.99 (978-1-57826-638-8(6), Hatherleigh Pr.) Hatherleigh Co., Ltd., The.
Hruby, Patrick. Natural Wonders: A Patrick Hruby Coloring Book. 2011. (ENG.). 32p. pap. 9.95 (978-1-934429-71-6(6)) AMMO Bks., LLC.
Huberts, Al. Hockey Canada's Learn All about Hockey: Color & Activity. Bailey, Frank, illus. 2012. (Rule 1, Sports Color & Activity Bks.). (ENG.). 176p. (J). (gr. -1-3). pap. 9.99 (978-1-77049-436-7(7), Fenn-Tundra) Tundra Bks. CAN. Dist: Penguin Random Hse. LLC.
—Learn All about Soccer: Color & Activity. Bailey, Frank, illus. 2013. (Rule 1, Sports Color & Activity Bks.). (ENG.). 176p. (J). (gr. -1-3). pap. 9.99 (978-1-77049-506-7(1), Fenn-Tundra) Tundra Bks. CAN. Dist: Penguin Random Hse. LLC.
Hughes, Bill. Texas History Coloring Book & Punch Out Playset. 2004. (Illus.). 16p. (J). 4.95 (978-0-9746784-0-5(6)) Great Big Comics, Big Tex Films.
Hughes, Sarah Anne. Reptiles & Amphibians. Peterson, Roger Tory, ed. Hughes, Sarah Anne, illus. 2nd ed. 2013. (Peterson Field Guide Color-In Bks.). (ENG., Illus.). 64p. (J). 8.95 (978-0-544-02695-7(0)) Houghton Mifflin Harcourt Publishing Co.
Hummingbird, Sandy & Hummingbird, Jesse T. Cherokee Clothing Activity Book. 2006. (Illus.). 31p. (J). (gr. -1-3). pap., act. bk. ed. 4.95 (978-1-57067-180-7(X), Native Voices) Book Publishing Co.
Hunter, Hannah Klaus. Be Happy & Color! Mindful Activities & Coloring Pages for Kids. 2016. (ENG.). 96p. (J). (gr. k-6). pap. 12.95 (978-1-63322-101-7(6), Walter Foster Jr) Quarto Publishing Group USA.
Hunter, Llyn. Sea Life GemGlow Stained Glass Coloring Book. 2009. (Dover Nature Stained Glass Coloring Book Ser.). (ENG., Illus.). 32p. (J). (gr. -1-5). pap. 7.99 (978-0-486-47149-5(7)) Dover Pubns., Inc.
Hutchinson, Alberta. Mystical Mandala Coloring Book. 2007. (Dover Design Coloring Bks.). (ENG., Illus.). 32p. (J). (gr. 3-8). 3.99 (978-0-486-45694-2(3)) Dover Pubns., Inc.
Hutchinson, Alberta & Creative Haven Staff. Lotus Designs. 2012. (Adult Coloring Ser.). (ENG., Illus.). 64p. (gr. 3). pap. 5.99 (978-0-486-49089-2(0)) Dover Pubns., Inc.
—Square Mandalas. 2012. (Adult Coloring Ser.). (ENG., Illus.). 64p. (J). (gr. 3). pap. 5.99 (978-0-486-49094-6(7)) Dover Pubns., Inc.
I Am Coloring Book. 2004. 3.00 (978-1-880960-27-1(3)) Scripture Memory Fellowship International.
I Love You Daddy Color. 2006. 96p. pap. 2.99 (978-0-7666-2226-5(6)) Modern Publishing.
I Love You Grandma Color. 2006. 96p. pap. 2.99 (978-0-7666-2228-9(2)) Modern Publishing.
I Love You Grandpa Color. 2006. 96p. pap. 2.99 (978-0-7666-2227-2(4)) Modern Publishing.
I Love You Mommy Color. 2006. 96p. pap. 2.99 (978-0-7666-2225-8(8)) Modern Publishing.
Ilya & Hillyer. Colour Me Bad: Stress Out, Colour in, Deface, Obliterate. 2016. (ENG.). 96p. pap. 10.99 (978-1-4721-3720-3(5), Constable) Little, Brown Book Group Ltd. GBR. Dist: Hachette Bk. Group.
Inglis, Karen. Ferdinand Fox's Big Sleep Colouring Book. Kundalic, Damir, illus. 2013. 32p. pap. (978-0-9569323-4-1(7)) Well Said Pr.
Ingram, Zoe. America the Beautiful to Color: A Road Trip to Color By. Ingram, Zoe, illus. 2017. (Illus.). 96p. (J). (gr. -1). pap. 15.99 (978-0-06-256990-5(2)) HarperCollins Pubs.
—Wise Words to Color - Inspiration to Live & Color By. Ingram, Zoe, illus. 2016. (Illus.). 96p. (J). (gr. -1). pap. 15.99 (978-0-06-248192-4(4)) HarperCollins Pubs.
Intermediate/Bible Fun New Testament: Coloring Book. 2006. (J). 14.99 (978-1-59317-147-6(1)) Warner Pr., Inc.
Ioan, Elwyn & Gruffudd, Lefi. Llyfr Lliwio Guto Nyth Brân. 2005. (WEL., Illus.). 16p. pap. (978-0-86243-707-7(5)) Y Lolfa.
Izzo, Donna. Frilly Lilly. 2011. 28p. pap. 15.99 (978-1-4628-7708-9(7)) Xlibris Corp.
Jackson, Antonia. The Lion Bible Verses Colouring Book. French, Felicity, illus. 2017. (ENG.). 32p. (J). (gr. 2-4). pap. 7.99 (978-0-7459-7689-1(1)) Lion Hudson PLC GBR. Dist: Independent Pubs. Group.
—The Lion Psalms Colouring Book. French, Felicity, illus. 2016. (ENG.). 32p. (J). (gr. 2-4). pap. 7.99 (978-0-7459-7618-1(2)) Lion Hudson PLC GBR. Dist: Independent Pubs. Group.
Jackson, Katy, illus. Pretty Fashions: Beautiful Fashions to Color! 2014. (ENG.). 96p. (J). (gr. -1-2). 7.99 (978-1-4424-8386-6(5), Little Simon) Little Simon.
James, Setria. Doodles: Alphabet Coloring Fun. 2010. 32p. (gr. -1 — 1). 14.49 (978-1-4520-9085-6(8)) AuthorHouse.
Jarzabek, Ela & Wood, Hannah. The Baby Animals: Colouring Book. Jarzabek, Ela & Wood, Hannah, illus. 2017. (ENG., Illus.). 64p. (J). (gr. -1-3). pap. 6.99 (978-1-78055-306-1(4))

O'Mara, Michael Bks., Ltd. GBR. Dist: Independent Pubs. Group.

Jay, Aye. Punk Rock Fun Time Activity Book. 2009. (ENG., Illus.). 48p. pap. *(978-1-55022-872-4(2))* Filmer Ltd.

Jefferson, E. Louis. The Little Caterpillar-A Story of Kindness-Companion Coloring Book. 2012. 52p. pap. 8.00 *(978-1-105-92194-0(8))* Lulu Pr., Inc.

—The Little Tadpole-A Story of Friendship: Companion Coloring Book. 2012. 48p. pap. 7.00 *(978-1-105-61123-0(X))* Lulu.com GBR. Dist: Lulu Pr., Inc.

Jensen, Valerie K. Romeo & Juliet: The Coloring Book. 2011. 80p. pap. 11.99 *(978-1-4567-5051-0(8))* AuthorHouse.

Jesus & His Disciples: Coloring Book. (Illus.). 16p. (J). pap. 1.50 *(978-0-87162-856-5(2)*, E6040) Warner Pr., Inc.

Jesus Is Alive! Coloring Book. 2006. 16p. (J). pap. 1.99 *(978-0-7847-1353-2(7)*, 22122) Standard Publishing.

Jesus Is Born. 2004. *(978-0-8294-9909-4(1))* Loyola Pr.

Jesus Miracles. 2004. (gr. 3-4). pap. 6.95 *(978-0-382-30784-3(4))* Cobblestone Publishing Co.

Johnson, Brian. Creative Haven Abstract Designs Coloring Book. 2014. (Adult Coloring Ser.). (ENG.). 64p. (gr. 3). pap. 5.99 *(978-0-486-77956-0(4))* Dover Pubns., Inc.

Johnstone, Michael. Sticker & Color-In Playbook: Teddy Bear Colours. Tulip, Jenny, illus. 2016. (ENG.). 16p. (J). (gr. -1-12). pap. 4.99 *(978-1-86147-749-1(X)*, Armadillo) Anness Publishing GBR. Dist: National Bk. Network.

—Sticker & Color-In Playbook: Teddy Bear Shapes. Tulip, Jenny, illus. 2016. (ENG.). 16p. (J). (gr. -1-12). pap. 4.99 *(978-1-86147-734-7(1)*, Armadillo) Anness Publishing GBR. Dist: National Bk. Network.

Jones, B. J. Let's Color Korea - Everyday Life in Traditional. 2005. (ENG., Illus.). 26p. (J). (gr. k-3). pap. 12.50 *(978-0-930878-98-6(1))* Hollym International Corp.

Jones, Kirk. Lisa the Ministering Mole: Meet the Mole. Jones, Kirk, illus. 2004. (Illus.). 24p. (J). bds. 5.00 net. *(978-0-9759688-0-2(7))* Jones, Kirk.

Joseph: A Bible Story to Color. (Illus.). 16p. (J). pap. 1.50 *(978-0-87162-812-1(0)*, E6026) Warner Pr., Inc.

Joseph: Very Easy Coloring Fun. (Coloring Bks.). (Illus.). 16p. (J). (gr. -1-k). pap. 1.69 *(978-0-7847-0711-1(1)*, 22031, Bean Sprouts) Standard Publishing.

Joseph & the Colorful Coat: A Little Story in Color. (Illus.). 16p. (J). pap. 1.50 *(978-0-87162-733-9(7)*, E4313) Warner Pr., Inc.

Jumbo Christmas Coloring & Activity Book. (Illus.). 300p. (J). mass mkt. *(978-0-87449-054-1(5))* Unisystems, Inc.

Jumbo Coloring. Date not set. (Illus.). 256p. (J). 5.98 *(978-1-4054-0699-4(2))* Parragon, Inc.

Kachmann, Rudy. Kid Scripts: Just What the Doctor Ordered. Lynch, Dan, illus. 2005. (ENG.). 48p. (J). spiral bd. 12.95 *(978-1-893270-38-1(6))* Evangel Author Services.

Kann, Victoria. Pinkalicious 123: A Counting Book. Kann, Victoria, illus. 2016. (Pinkalicious Ser.). (Illus.). 32p. (J). (gr. -1 — 1). bds. 7.99 *(978-0-06-243757-0(7)*, HarperFestival) HarperCollins Pubs.

Katz, David. DC Super Heroes Colors, Shapes & More! 2012. (DC Super Heroes Ser.). (ENG.). 20p. (J). (gr. -1 — 1). bds. 9.99 *(978-1-935703-73-0(0))* Downtown Bookworks.

Kauffman, Judy. The Lord God Made Them All. 2003. (Illus.). 40p. 1.90 *(978-0-7399-2347-4(1)*, 2927) Rod & Staff Pubs., Inc.

Kaylor, J. Garcia. Animal Magic Coloring Pages. 2012. (ENG.). pap. 11.99 *(978-1-4675-2458-2(1))* Independent Pub.

Kershner, Gerry. Lancaster Landmarks Coloring Book. Kershner, Gerry, illus. 2006. (Illus.). 25p. (J). 4.50 *(978-1-60126-010-9(5))* Masthof Pr.

Kesinger, Brian. Coloring with Your Octopus: A Coloring Book for Domesticated Cephalopods. 2014. (ENG., Illus.). 48p. pap. 12.00 *(978-1-61404-010-1(9))* Baby Tattoo Bks.

King Features Syndicate Division. Betty Boop Coloring Book. 2015. (ENG.). 64p. (J). (gr. 3-6). pap. 6.99 *(978-0-486-80170-4(5))* Dover Pubns., Inc.

KING, R. O. N. S. The emerald Fire. 2010. 166p. pap. 11.50 *(978-1-4461-3748-2(1))* Lulu Pr., Inc.

—The Soul-pearl. 2010. 169p. pap. 11.50 *(978-1-4457-5542-7(4))* Lulu Pr., Inc.

King, Sally, illus. Desert Blooms. 2007. 39p. pap. 7.95 *(978-1-55566-405-3(9)*, Johnson Bks.) Bower Hse.

Kipling, Rudyard. The Jungle Book: a Coloring Book. 2016. (ENG., Illus.). 96p. (J). (gr. k). pap. 12.99 *(978-1-62686-702-4(X)*, Silver Dolphin Bks.) Readerlink Distribution Services, LLC.

Klimit, Gustav. Coloring Book Gustav Klimt. 2007. (ENG., Illus.). 32p. (J). (gr. 1-4). 8.95 *(978-3-7913-3790-6(4))* Prestel Verlag GmbH & Co KG. DEU. Dist: Penguin Random Hse. LLC.

Kline, C. A. & Lauder, M. F. Halloween Night. 2012. 24p. pap. 17.99 *(978-1-4772-7417-0(0))* AuthorHouse.

Klug, Kirsten. Healthy Smiles! 2011. (Illus.). 12p. (J). pap. 6.50 *(978-0-9798173-6-6(6))* Bamboo River Pr.

Klutz Editors, contrib. by. Shrinky Dinks Refill, Pack. (ENG.). 8p. 8.95 *(978-1-57054-585-6(5))* Klutz.

Koenigsberg, Phyllis & Winkler, Ziporah, creators. Color My Alef Bet. 2004. (J). 2.99 *(978-965-90462-5-6(1))* Mazo Pubs.

Koski, Mary B. Color, Color, Where Are You, Color? Mason, Janeen, illus. 2004. (ENG.). (J). 28p. bds. 7.95 *(978-1-930650-34-3(5))*; 32p. (gr. 1-3). 14.95 *(978-1-930650-35-0(3))* mTrellis Publishing, Inc.

Krause, Maria. Hokusai Coloring Book. 2015. (ENG.). 32p. (J). (gr. 1-4). pap. 8.95 *(978-3-7913-7215-0(7))* Prestel Verlag GmbH & Co KG. DEU. Dist: Penguin Random Hse. LLC.

Kronheimer, Ann. The Fairy Colouring Book. Kronheimer, Ann, illus. 2014. (ENG., Illus.). 64p. (J). (gr. 1). pap. 8.99 ***(978-1-78055-343-6(9))*** O'Mara, Michael Bks., Ltd. GBR. Dist: Independent Pubs. Group.

—The Peter Pan Colouring Book. 2017. (ENG.). 32p. (J). (gr. 1-4). pap. 6.99 ***(978-1-78055-435-8(4))*** O'Mara, Michael Bks., Ltd. GBR. Dist: Independent Pubs. Group.

—The Wonderful Wizard of Oz Colouring Book. 2017. (ENG.). 32p. (J). (gr. 1-4). pap. 8.99 ***(978-1-78055-436-5(2))*** O'Mara, Michael Bks., Ltd. GBR. Dist: Independent Pubs. Group.

Kronheimer, Ann, illus. Pretty Princesses: Beautiful Princesses to Color! 2014. (ENG.). 96p. (J). (gr. -1-2). 7.99 *(978-1-4424-8385-9(7)*, Little Simon) Little Simon.

Kryttre, Krystine. The Coloring Book. 2015. (ENG., Illus.). 100p. (J). pap. 5.95 *(978-0-86719-524-8(X))* Last Gasp of San Francisco.

Kumon, creator. Let's Color! 2005. (Kumon Workbooks Ser.). (Illus.). 40p. (J). (gr. -1). per., wbk. ed. 5.95 *(978-1-933241-11-1(X))* Kumon Publishing North America, Inc.

Kumon Publishing, creator. More Let's Color! 2006. (Kumon First Steps Workbooks Ser.). (Illus.). 40p. (gr. -1). per. 5.95 *(978-1-933241-32-6(2))* Kumon U.S.A., Inc.

—My Book of Coloring: Ages 2-3-4. 2006. (Kumon Workbooks Ser.). (ENG., Illus.). 80p. (J). (gr. -1-k). per. 7.95 *(978-1-933241-28-9(4))* Kumon Publishing North America, Inc.

—My Book of Coloring at the Zoo: Ages 3, 4, 5. 2007. (Kumon Workbooks Ser.). (Illus.). 80p. per. 7.95 *(978-1-933241-39-5(X))* Kumon Publishing North America, Inc.

Kurtz, John. Claus Kids Christmas Coloring Book. 2011. (Dover Holiday Coloring Book Ser.). (ENG.). 32p. (J). (gr. k-5). pap. 3.99 *(978-0-486-48292-7(8))* Dover Pubns., Inc.

—FLIP OUTS — Bird Bash: Color Your Own Cartoon! 2015. (ENG., Illus.). 64p. (J). (gr. k-3). pap. 1.99 *(978-0-486-79485-3(7))* Dover Pubns., Inc.

—Silly Snowmen Coloring Book. 2015. (ENG.). 32p. (J). (gr. -1-2). pap. 3.99 *(978-0-486-79743-4(0))* Dover Pubns., Inc.

—Spot-The-Differences Grumpy Cat Coloring Book. 2017. (Dover Little Activity Bks.). (ENG.). 64p. (gr. k-3). pap. 1.99 ***(978-0-486-81959-4(0))*** Dover Pubns., Inc.

Kurtz, John. Unicorn Fun Coloring Book. 2014. (ENG., Illus.). 32p. (J). (gr. k-5). pap. 3.99 *(978-0-486-78196-9(8))* Dover Pubns., Inc.

Kurtz, John & Kurtz, Sandrina. The Big & Little Farm Coloring Book: Featuring Romy the Cow. 2015. (ENG.). 32p. (J). (gr. -1-2). pap. 3.99 *(978-0-486-78341-3(3))* Dover Pubns., Inc.

—Chef Lorenzo's Foods Around the World Coloring Book. 2015. (ENG.). 32p. (J). (gr. k). pap. 3.99 *(978-0-486-79000-8(2))* Dover Pubns., Inc.

La Beree, Brian, illus. Herbert the Tadpole in the Big Change: Color-Me Version. 2007. 48p. (J). 6.95 *(978-0-9800736-0-7(X))* Sophrose Entertainment Inc.

Laberis, Stephanie & Coloring Books Staff. Mix & Match ZOO ANIMALS. 2012. (Dover Mix & Match Coloring Book Ser.). (ENG.). 48p. (J). (gr. 2-5). pap. 4.99 *(978-0-486-48849-3(7))* Dover Pubns., Inc.

LaFontaine, Bruce. The Adventures of Ulysses. 2014. (Dover Classic Stories Coloring Book Ser.). (ENG., Illus.). 32p. (J). (gr. 4-6). pap. 3.99 *(978-0-486-43328-8(5))* Dover Pubns., Inc.

—All about the Weather. 2004. (Dover Nature Coloring Book Ser.). (ENG., Illus.). 48p. (J). (gr. 3-8). pap. 4.99 *(978-0-486-43036-2(7))* Dover Pubns., Inc.

—BOOST the Story of the Wright Brothers Coloring Book. 2013. (BOOST Educational Ser.). (ENG.). 32p. (J). (gr. 3-5). pap. 4.99 *(978-0-486-49440-1(3))* Dover Pubns., Inc.

—Classic Cars Coloring Book. 2007. (Dover History Coloring Book Ser.). (ENG., Illus.). 112p. (gr. 3-8). 9.95 *(978-0-486-46067-3(3))* Dover Pubns., Inc.

—Construction Trucks Stained Glass Coloring Book. 2004. (Dover Stained Glass Coloring Book Ser.). (ENG., Illus.). 8p. (J). pap. 1.50 *(978-0-486-44106-1(7))* Dover Pubns., Inc.

—Famous Trains. 2005. (Dover History Coloring Book Ser.). (ENG., Illus.). 32p. (J). (gr. 3-8). 3.99 *(978-0-486-44009-5(5))* Dover Pubns., Inc.

—International Space Station. 2003. (Dover History Coloring Book Ser.). (ENG., Illus.). 32p. (J). (gr. 6-8). pap. 3.95 *(978-0-486-42379-1(4))* Dover Pubns., Inc.

—Luxury Cars Coloring Book. 2005. (Dover History Coloring Book Ser.). (ENG., Illus.). 32p. (gr. 3-5). per. 3.99 *(978-0-486-44436-9(8))* Dover Pubns., Inc.

—Railroad Engines from Around the World Coloring Book. 2003. (Dover History Coloring Book Ser.). (ENG., Illus.). 48p. (J). (gr. 3-8). pap. 4.99 *(978-0-486-42378-4(6))* Dover Pubns., Inc.

—Tanks & Armored Vehicles. 2013. (Dover History Coloring Book Ser.). (ENG., Illus.). 48p. (J). (gr. 3-8). pap. 4.99 *(978-0-486-41317-4(9))* Dover Pubns., Inc.

—Warriors Through the Ages. 2013. (Dover History Coloring Book Ser.). (ENG., Illus.). 48p. (J). (gr. 3-12). pap. 4.99 *(978-0-486-42071-4(X))* Dover Pubns., Inc.

Lamb, Stacey. ABC Coloring Book with Stickers. 2010. (Sticker Coloring Bks). 16p. (J). pap. 5.99 *(978-0-7945-2786-0(8)*, Usborne) EDC Publishing.

Larousse Color ABC y 123 (Amarillo), Vol. 1. 2003. (SPA., Illus.). 6p. (J). 2.98 *(978-970-22-0163-2(2))* Larousse, Ediciones, S. A. de C. V. MEX. Dist: Giron Bks.

Larsen, Jill. There's a Moose on the Loose Coloring Book. 2004. (J). pap. 4.99 *(978-0-9755200-0-0(8))* Kids, Critters & Country Publishing.

Larson, Angela. Norman PhartEphant: The coloring Book. 2009. pap. *(978-1-61623-787-5(2))* Independent Pub.

The Laughing Lavender Field. 2005. (J). 5.00 *(978-0-9765731-0-4(5))* DTJ, LLC.

Lawson, Jim. Jim Lawson's Dinosaurs Coloring Book. 2016. (ENG.). 32p. (J). (gr. 2-5). pap. 3.99 *(978-0-486-80503-0(4))* Dover Pubns., Inc.

Lazoo Publishing Staff. Holes! A Coloring Book. Oku, Makiko, tr. 2009. (King of Play Ser.). (ENG., Illus.). 64p. (J). (gr. -1). pap. 7.95 *(978-1-934734-12-4(8))* Seven Footer Pr.

—Imagine That! A Coloring Book for Growing Young Minds. Miyakoshi, Junko, tr. 2009. (King of Play Ser.). (ENG.). 200p. (gr. -1). pap. 14.95 *(978-1-934734-05-6(5))* Seven Footer Pr.

Lazoo Publishing Staff & ZOO, La. Let's Color! A Coloring Book Like No Other. Miyakoshi, Junko, tr. 2009. (King of Play Ser.). (ENG.). 128p. (gr. -1). pap. 12.95 *(978-1-934734-02-5(0))* Seven Footer Pr.

Leonard, Barry, ed. NASCAR Jumbo Coloring & Activity Book, 2 vols. 2004. (Illus.). 150p. (J). (gr. k-4). reprint ed. pap. 12.00 *(978-0-7567-7715-9(1))* DIANE Publishing Co.

Leonhard, Herb, illus. The Faerie Garden Coloring Book. 2004. 24p. (J). 3.50 *(978-0-9763555-0-2(7))* Prancing Pony, The.

Levin, Freddie. ABC Stained Glass Coloring Book. 2010. (Dover Stained Glass Coloring Book Ser.). (ENG., Illus.). 32p. (J). (gr. -1-2). pap. 6.99 *(978-0-486-47334-5(1))* Dover Pubns., Inc.

—Chanukah Coloring Book. 2011. (Dover Holiday Coloring Book Ser.). (ENG., Illus.). 32p. (J). (gr. -1-2). pap. 3.99 *(978-0-486-48286-6(3))* Dover Pubns., Inc.

—Goodnight Stained Glass Coloring Book. 2009. (Dover Stained Glass Coloring Book Ser.). (ENG., Illus.). 32p. (J). (gr. -1-2). pap. 6.99 *(978-0-486-47293-5(0))* Dover Pubns., Inc.

Levivier, Juliette. Prayers Around the Crib. Gravier, Anne, illus. 2012. (ENG.). 46p. (J). (gr. -1-3). 9.99 *(978-1-58617-773-7(7))* Ignatius Pr.

Levy, Barbara Soloff. Dinosaurs Dot-to-Dot. 2006. (Dover Children's Activity Bks.). (ENG., Illus.). 32p. (J). (gr. -1-2). pap. 3.99 *(978-0-486-45320-0(0))* Dover Pubns., Inc.

Lewis, Rachel. Cook's Coloring Book: Simple Recipes for Beginners, 1 vol. Lewis, Rachel, illus. 2015. (ENG., Illus.). 144p. pap. 12.99 *(978-1-4236-3845-2(X))* Gibbs Smith, Publisher.

Library Of Congress, creator. The Wizard of Oz Coloring Book. 2011. (Illus.). (J). (gr. -1-3). pap. 7.95 *(978-0-7649-5990-5(5))* Pomegranate Communications, Inc.

Lidner, D. B. The A,B, C's of Firefighting & Fire Safety. 2009. pap. 3.95 *(978-1-61584-189-9(X))* Independent Pub.

Lincoln, Jerri. The Little Unicorn Who Could Coloring Book. 2012. 34p. pap. 7.77 *(978-1-938322-00-6(2))* Ralston Store Publishing.

Linn, Susie. Coloring: Early Learning Through Art. 2017. (Arty Mouse Creativity Bks.). (ENG.). 48p. (J). (gr. -1-k). pap. 6.99 *(978-1-78445-625-2(X))* Top That! Publishing PLC GBR. Dist: Independent Pubs. Group.

Lipniewska, Dominika, illus. 100 Coloring Book. 2015. (ENG.). 20p. (gr. -1-2). pap. 12.95 *(978-1-84976-381-3(X))* Tate Publishing, Ltd. GBR. Dist: Abrams, Inc.

, Liverpool Football Club, Liverpool Football Club. The Official Liverpool FC Sticker Colouring Book. 2014. (ENG.). 24p. (J). (gr. -1-3). pap. 8.99 *(978-1-78097-326-5(8))* Carlton Bks., Ltd. GBR. Dist: Independent Pubs. Group.

Lluch, Alex. Do I Look Good in Color? Defenbaugh, David, illus. 2006. (ENG.). 32p. (J). (gr. -1-k). 14.95 *(978-1-887169-63-9(6))* WS Publishing.

Lockman, Vic. Catechism for Young Children Coloring Book. Lockman, Vic, illus. 2003. (Illus.). 24p. (J). (gr. -1-3). *(978-0-936175-41-6(9))* Lockman, Vic.

Lockwood, Mark W. Learn About... Texas Birds. Ivy, Elena T., illus. 2007. (ENG.). 52p. (J). (gr. 1-7). pap. 10.95 *(978-0-292-71685-8(0))* Univ. of Texas Pr.

Lodge, Jo. Colour & Stick, Mr Croc. 2013. (ENG.). 24p. (J). (gr. -1-k). pap. 5.99 *(978-1-4449-1308-8(5))* Hodder & Stoughton GBR. Dist: Hachette Bk. Group.

Longhi, Phoebe. The Steampunk Coloring & Activity Book: Containing Illustrations, Recipes, Formulas & Other Activities to Entertain & Entice Creativity for the Prevention of Ennui & General Malaise among the Youth of Today & Their Progenitors. 2012. (ENG., Illus.). 64p. pap. 11.95 *(978-1-933149-63-9(9))* Manic D Pr.

The Looney Tunes Gang. 2008. (Super Big Coloring Book Ser.). 224p. pap. *(978-1-4075-3408-4(4))* Parragon, Inc.

Lopes, Marilyn/Jansen. Amaryllis of Hawaii Big Coloring Book: Drawings of Hawaii to Color. 2007. (ENG & HAW., Illus.). (YA). pap. 5.00 *(978-0-9761070-5-7(8))* Jansen, Marilyn.

—Amaryllis of Hawaii Pocket Coloring Book: Drawings of Hawaii to Color. 2007. (ENG & HAW., Illus.). (J). pap. 3.00 *(978-0-9761070-7-1(4))* Jansen, Marilyn.

Lots of Things to Find & Color for Christmas. 2011. (Activity Bks). 96p. (J). pap. 12.99 *(978-0-7945-3174-4(1)*, Usborne) EDC Publishing.

Lucas Film Book Group. Star Wars Color by Number. 2017. (ENG.). 128p. (YA). (gr. 7-12). pap. 14.99 ***(978-1-368-00568-5(3)***, Disney Lucasfilm Press) Disney Publishing Worldwide.

Luetkemeyer, Jenny. Jesus, I Trust in You! The Story of Saint Faustina, Missionary of Divine Mercy. Kiszkurno, Irene & Chacon, Cesar, trs. Clifford, Caroline, illus. 2004. (SPA & POL.). 32p. (J). (gr. k-5). 5.00 *(978-0-9747571-2-4(8))* Catholic World Mission.

Lumsden, Colin, illus. Apostles. 2003. (Bible Colour & Learn Ser.). 32p. pap. 2.50 *(978-1-903087-51-0(1))* DayOne Pubns. GBR. Dist: Send The Light Distribution LLC.

—Hebrews Men of Faith. 2003. (Bible Colour & Learn Ser.). 32p. pap. 2.50 *(978-1-903087-52-7(X))* DayOne Pubns. GBR. Dist: Send The Light Distribution LLC.

—John the Baptist. 2003. (Bible Colour & Learn Ser.). 32p. pap. 2.50 *(978-1-903087-44-2(9))* DayOne Pubns. GBR. Dist: Send The Light Distribution LLC.

—Miracles of Jesus. 2003. (Bible Colour & Learn Ser.). 32p. pap. 2.50 *(978-1-903087-48-0(1))* DayOne Pubns. GBR. Dist: Send The Light Distribution LLC.

—Parables of Jesus. 2003. (Bible Colour & Learn Ser.). 32p. pap. 2.50 *(978-1-903087-47-3(3))* DayOne Pubns. GBR. Dist: Send The Light Distribution LLC.

—People in the Life of Jesus. 2003. (Bible Colour & Learn Ser.). 32p. pap. 2.50 *(978-1-903087-49-7(X))* DayOne Pubns. GBR. Dist: Send The Light Distribution LLC.

—People in the Life of Paul. 2003. (Bible Colour & Learn Ser.). 32p. pap. 2.50 *(978-1-903087-50-3(3))* DayOne Pubns. GBR. Dist: Send The Light Distribution LLC.

—Story of Mary. 2003. (Bible Colour & Learn Ser.). 32p. pap. 2.50 *(978-1-903087-43-5(0))* DayOne Pubns. GBR. Dist: Send The Light Distribution LLC.

—Story of Paul. 2003. (Bible Colour & Learn Ser.). 32p. pap. 2.50 *(978-1-903087-46-6(5))* DayOne Pubns. GBR. Dist: Send The Light Distribution LLC.

—Story of Peter. 2003. (Bible Colour & Learn Ser.). 32p. pap. 2.50 *(978-1-903087-45-9(7))* DayOne Pubns. GBR. Dist: Send The Light Distribution LLC.

Lynn, Richard & Nova Blue. Historic Savannah, GA Coloring Book. Claughton, Dena, ed. Hale, Jason, illus. 2003. 32p. *(978-0-9725584-0-2(3))* Nova Blue, Inc.

Maas, Sarah J. A Court of Thorns & Roses. 2017. (ENG.). 96p. (YA). pap. 15.99 *(978-1-68119-576-6(3)*, 9781681195766, Bloomsbury USA Childrens) Bloomsbury Publishing USA.

Mac a'Bháird, Natasha & Nolan, Alan. My Ireland. 2016. (ENG., Illus.). 24p. (J). pap., act. bk. ed. 12.00 *(978-1-84717-834-3(0))* O'Brien Pr., Ltd., The IRL. Dist: Dufour Editions, Inc.

MacKenzie, Carine. Bible Heroes - Noah. 2013. (Bible Art Ser.). (ENG.). 16p. (J). pap., act. bk. ed. 1.99 *(978-1-85792-823-5(7)*, 68bc0ad9-0c11-4662-b243-81a7a41e4b52) Christian Focus Pubns. GBR. Dist: Bookmasters Distribution.

—Bible Heroes Elijah. 2005. (Bible Art Ser.). (ENG.). 16p. (J). act. bk. ed. 1.99 *(978-1-84550-089-4(X)*, 7336c626-8c11-4b07-8c54-3f395d9c105e) Christian Focus Pubns. GBR. Dist: Bookmasters Distribution.

—Bible Heroes Gideon. 2005. (Bible Art Ser.). (ENG.). 16p. (J). act. bk. ed. 1.99 *(978-1-84550-090-0(3)*, c413bdb8-6ed2-450e-92b3-3dfe97e1313e) Christian Focus Pubns. GBR. Dist: Bookmasters Distribution.

—Bible Heroes Joseph. 2005. (Bible Art Ser.). (ENG.). 16p. (J). act. bk. ed. 1.99 *(978-1-84550-091-7(1)*, 75cca856-6fd6-454b-a66f-ffec2e980d5d) Christian Focus Pubns. GBR. Dist: Bookmasters Distribution.

—Bible Heroes Paul. 2003. (Bible Art Ser.). (ENG.). 16p. (J). pap., act. bk. ed. 1.99 *(978-1-85792-824-2(5)*, 12d15b76-219d-4db7-8c1c-00d98ebbf2d3, Christian Focus) Christian Focus Pubns. GBR. Dist: Bookmasters Distribution.

—Bible Heroes Peter. 2003. (Bible Art Ser.). (ENG.). 16p. (J). pap., act. bk. ed. 1.99 *(978-1-85792-826-6(1)*, dbea3229-6423-4a2f-ae08-1b09081b7a52, Christian Focus) Christian Focus Pubns. GBR. Dist: Bookmasters Distribution.

—Colour the Bible: Romans-2Thessalonians. 2008. (Bible Art Ser.). (ENG.). 16p. (J). pap., act. bk. ed. 1.99 *(978-1-85792-765-8(6)*, b708e0eb-808e-45e7-a211-9c686cb6fb8a) Christian Focus Pubns. GBR. Dist: Bookmasters Distribution.

—Colour the Bible Bk. 3: Hosea-Malachi. 2008. (Bible Art Ser.). (ENG.). 16p. (J). pap., act. bk. ed. 1.99 *(978-1-85792-763-4(X)*, 70a53dae-b5fa-4bde-9de2-74ed9816d955) Christian Focus Pubns. GBR. Dist: Bookmasters Distribution.

—God Knows Everything. 2010. (Bible Art Ser.). (ENG.). 16p. (J). pap., act. bk. ed. 1.99 *(978-1-85792-636-1(6)*, 85aaec2f-54d4-4638-b373-5432ebbedcfe) Christian Focus Pubns. GBR. Dist: Bookmasters Distribution.

—Mary - Bible Heroes. 2013. (Bible Art Ser.). (ENG.). 16p. (J). pap., act. bk. ed. 1.99 *(978-1-85792-828-0(8)*, 4b90cc51-2f0f-48b9-b374-403691fd0ae7) Christian Focus Pubns. GBR. Dist: Bookmasters Distribution.

—The Special Birthday. Taylor, Roger, illus. 2010. (Bible Art Ser.). (ENG.). 16p. (J). pap., act. bk. ed. 1.99 *(978-1-85792-307-0(3)*, 5f23bf65-609d-44d1-a663-6837ba53cdc3) Christian Focus Pubns. GBR. Dist: Bookmasters Distribution.

MacKenzie, Catherine. What God Says: Creation. 2006. (Bible Art Ser.). (ENG.). 16p. (J). pap. 1.99 *(978-1-84550-219-5(1)*, 9781845502195) Christian Focus Pubns. GBR. Dist: Bookmasters Distribution.

—What God Says: Holiness. 2006. (Bible Art Ser.). (ENG.). 16p. (J). pap. 1.99 *(978-1-84550-214-0(0)*, b02e9199-6885-4e88-a17e-a6a1c0336f7f) Christian Focus Pubns. GBR. Dist: Bookmasters Distribution.

—What God Says: Redemption. 2006. (Bible Art Ser.). (ENG.). 16p. (J). pap. 1.99 *(978-1-84550-217-1(5)*, 8569bbc5-8685-4fb0-bdac-f94bc832dd0b) Christian Focus Pubns. GBR. Dist: Bookmasters Distribution.

—What God Says: Repenting. 2006. (Bible Art Ser.). (ENG.). 16p. (J). pap. 1.99 *(978-1-84550-216-4(7)*, a801aa9a-3026-4eb2-ba54-9b04f6b60757) Christian Focus Pubns. GBR. Dist: Bookmasters Distribution.

—What God Says: Resurrection. 2006. (Bible Art Ser.). (ENG.). 16p. (J). pap. 1.99 *(978-1-84550-218-8(3)*, e8deff6e-314a-430c-82a4-8f17c4d053fc) Christian Focus Pubns. GBR. Dist: Bookmasters Distribution.

—What God Says: Salvation. 2006. (Bible Art Ser.). (ENG.). 16p. (J). pap. 1.99 *(978-1-84550-215-7(9)*, e667eba6-d3ae-4232-b172-352a5debcd69) Christian Focus Pubns. GBR. Dist: Bookmasters Distribution.

Maclaine, James. Drawing, Doodling & Coloring Blue Book. 2015. (Doodle Bks.). (ENG.). 128p. (J). (gr. k-5). pap. 13.99 *(978-0-7945-3443-1(0)*, Usborne) EDC Publishing.

—Drawing, Doodling & Coloring Book Boys. 2012. (Activity Cards Ser.). 128p. (J). pap. 13.99 *(978-0-7945-3296-3(9)*, Usborne) EDC Publishing.

MacNeill, Scott. How Things Work Vehicles - Motorcycle. 2013. (ENG.). 48p. (J). (gr. 3-8). pap. 4.99 *(978-0-486-49221-6(4))* Dover Pubns., Inc.

Macrae, Tammy Vallieres & Lucente-Rizzo, Susan. Jeffrey Finds His Way. 2012. 72p. pap. 8.99 *(978-1-4525-4724-4(6))* Balboa Pr.

Maderna, Victoria. Look & Find Letters to Color. 2013. (Dover Coloring Bks.). (ENG., Illus.). 32p. (J). (gr. -1-2). pap. 3.99 *(978-0-486-48702-1(4))* Dover Pubns., Inc.

—Look & Find Numbers to Color. 2014. (ENG.). 48p. (J). (gr. k-5). pap. 4.99 *(978-0-486-49464-7(0))* Dover Pubns., Inc.

—Look & Find Opposites to Color. 2014. (ENG.). 48p. (J). (gr. k-5). pap. 4.99 *(978-0-486-49463-0(2))* Dover Pubns., Inc.

—Look & Find Shapes to Color. 2011. (Dover Children's Activity Bks.). (ENG.). 48p. (J). (gr. -1-2). pap. 4.99 *(978-0-486-47991-0(9))* Dover Pubns., Inc.

—Playful Pictures — Animals. 2013. (ENG., Illus.). 32p. (J). (gr. -1-8). pap. 3.99 *(978-0-486-49268-1(0))* Dover Pubns., Inc.

Magruder, Trula & David, Chris. Art Starts: Every Page Illustrated by You! 2006. (ENG., Illus.). 80p. (J). (gr. 4-7). spiral bd. 9.95 *(978-1-59369-152-3(1)*, American Girl) American Girl Publishing, Inc.

Mahoney, Jean. Swan Lake Ballet Theatre. Seddon, Viola Anne, illus. 2009. (ENG.). 16p. (J). (gr. 1-4). 24.99 *(978-0-7636-4396-6(3))* Candlewick Pr.

Mai, Lily. Bertie Boom's Trip to the Moon. 2010. (Illus.). 20p. 12.49 *(978-1-4520-1379-4(9))* AuthorHouse.

Majewski, Anthony M. T. & Maximus. Color with Max! Activity & Coloring Book. Majewski, Julie, illus. 2010. 16p. (J). pap., act. bk. ed. 4.99 *(978-0-615-38985-1(6))* Emarketing Of Michigan, LLC.

Maland, Nick, illus. Colour in the Queen: Celebrate the Queen's Life with 15 Frameable Prints. 2016. (ENG.). 32p. (J). (gr. -1-2). pap. 9.99 *(978-1-84780-884-4(0)*, Frances Lincoln Children's Bks.) Quarto Publishing Group UK GBR. Dist: Hachette Bk. Group.

Maldonado, Luis, illus. Friends Having Fun. Maldonado, Luis, . 2007. 48p. (J). 3.95 *(978-0-9790699-1-8(2))* Empty Harbor Productions, LLC.

Mallet, Lisa, et al, illus. Challenging Coloring: A Book Full of Creative Coloring. 2016. (Challenging... Bks.). (ENG.). 96p. (J). (gr. 3-7). pap. 7.99 *(978-1-4380-0780-9(9))* Barron's Educational Series, Inc.

Man-Kong, Mary. Barbie Loves Horses (Barbie) Duarte, Pamela, illus. 2013. (Color Plus Stencil Ser.). (ENG.). 64p. (J). (gr. -1-2). pap. 5.99 *(978-0-449-81612-7(5)*, Golden Bks.) Random Hse. Children's Bks.

—Easter Stencil Fun! (Peter Cottontail) Karl, Linda, illus. 2014. (Color Plus Stencil Ser.). (ENG.). 64p. (J). (gr. -1-2). pap. 5.99 *(978-0-385-37442-2(9)*, Golden Bks.) Random Hse. Children's Bks.

—A Fin-Tastic Journey! Golden Books Staff, illus. 2012. (Color Plus Chunky Crayons Ser.). (ENG.). 48p. (J). (gr. k-k). pap. 3.99 *(978-0-307-92978-5(7)*, Golden Bks.) Random Hse. Children's Bks.

—Friends, Fashion, & Fun! (Barbie) Golden Books Staff & Das Group Staff, illus. 2012. (Jumbo Coloring Book Ser.). (ENG.). 224p. (J). (gr. -1-2). pap. 5.99 *(978-0-375-87358-4(9)*, Golden Bks.) Random Hse. Children's Bks.

—Get Your Glam On! (Barbie) 2015. (Super Jumbo Coloring Book Ser.). (ENG.). 416p. (J). (gr. -1-2). pap. 10.99 *(978-0-553-52165-8(9)*, Golden Bks.) Random Hse. Children's Bks.

—Happy, Jolly Fun! (Frosty the Snowman) Golden Books, illus. 2014. (Color Plus Chunky Crayons Ser.). (ENG.). 48p. (J). (gr. -1-2). pap. 3.99 *(978-0-385-38723-1(7)*, Golden Bks.) Random Hse. Children's Bks.

—Holiday Style (Barbie) 2014. (Big Coloring Book Ser.). (ENG.). 48p. (J). (gr. -1-2). pap. 6.99 *(978-0-385-38339-4(8)*, Golden Bks.) Random Hse. Children's Bks.

—I Can Be a Rock Star. Golden Books Staff, illus. 2010. (Pictureback(R) Ser.). (ENG.). 16p. (J). (gr. -1-2). pap. 3.99 *(978-0-375-86545-9(4)*, Golden Bks.) Random Hse. Children's Bks.

—Mermaid Style. 2014. (Color Plus Chunky Crayons Ser.). (ENG., Illus.). 48p. (J). (gr. -1-2). pap. 3.99 *(978-0-385-37306-7(6)*, Golden Bks.) Random Hse. Children's Bks.

—Sensational Style. Golden Books Staff, illus. 2010. (Big Coloring Book Ser.). (ENG.). 48p. (J). (gr. -1-2). pap. 6.99 *(978-0-375-86490-2(3)*, Golden Bks.) Random Hse. Children's Bks.

—Sparkling Style. Golden Books Staff, illus. 2010. (Deluxe Coloring Book Ser.). (ENG.). 96p. (J). (gr. -1-2). pap. 3.99 *(978-0-375-86031-7(2)*, Golden Bks.) Random Hse. Children's Bks.

Man-Kong, Mary, et al. Glimmer, Shimmer, & Shine! Golden Books Staff, illus. 2010. (Hologramatic Sticker Book Ser.). (ENG.). 48p. (J). (gr. -1-2). pap. 3.99 *(978-0-375-86032-4(0)*, Golden Bks.) Random Hse. Children's Bks.

Mankita, Jay. Elar. 2013. (Illus.). 38p. (J). pap. 9.95 *(978-1-935734-49-9(0))* Kitanie Bks.

Marabout & Abrams Noterie Staff. Butterflies. 2015. (ENG., Illus.). 144p. pap. 9.95 *(978-1-4197-1980-6(7)*, Abrams Noterie) Abrams, Inc.

Marinaro, Stacy. The Cat who rules the Star Mice. 2009. 32p. pap. 15.95 *(978-0-557-08180-6(7))* Lulu Pr., Inc.

Marsh, Carole. America's National Parks Coloring & Activity Book. 2016. (Non-State Ser.). (ENG., Illus.). (J). pap. 5.99 *(978-0-635-12460-9(2))* Gallopade International.

—Barack Obama Presidential Coloring Book! 2008. (Here & Now Ser.). (J). 5.99 *(978-0-635-07050-0(2))* Gallopade International.

—The Cool Arkansas Coloring Book. 2004. (Carole Marsh Arkansas Bks.). (Illus.). 32p. (J). (gr. k-2). pap. 3.95 *(978-0-7933-9850-8(9))* Gallopade International.

—The Cool Colorado Coloring Book. 2004. (Colorado Experience! Ser.). (Illus.). 32p. (J). (gr. k-2). pap. 3.95 *(978-0-7933-9607-8(7))* Gallopade International.

—The Cool Connecticut Coloring Book. 2004. (Connecticut Experience! Ser.). (Illus.). 32p. (J). (gr. k-2). pap. 3.95 *(978-0-7933-9583-5(6))* Gallopade International.

—The Cool Kansas Coloring Book. 2004. (Carole Marsh Kansas Bks.). (Illus.). 32p. (J). (gr. k-2). pap. 3.95 *(978-0-7933-9856-0(8))* Gallopade International.

—Donald Trump: Presidential Coloring & Activity Book. 2017. (Here & Now Ser.). (ENG., Illus.). (J). (gr. 3-7). 5.99 ***(978-0-635-12561-3(7))*** Gallopade International.

—Farm Days A-Z Coloring Book. Ford, Yvonne, illus. 2009. 28p. (J). 5.99 *(978-0-635-07421-8(4))* Gallopade International.

—Heroes & Helpers Coloring Book. 2004. 24p. (J). (gr. k-2). pap. 3.95 *(978-0-635-01093-3(3))* Gallopade International.

—Hispanic Heritage Coloring Book. 2003. 24p. (gr. k-2). pap. 3.95 *(978-0-635-02117-5(X))* Gallopade International.

—Indiana Coloring Book! 2004. (Illus.). 32p. (J). (gr. k-2). pap. 3.95 *(978-0-7933-9854-6(1))* Gallopade International.

—The Kentucky Coloring Book. 2004. (Kentucky Experience! Ser.). (Illus.). 32p. (J). (gr. k-2). pap. 3.95 *(978-0-7933-9471-5(6))* Gallopade International.

—The Louisiana Coloring Book. 2004. (Louisiana Experience! Ser.). (Illus.). 32p. (J). (gr. k-2). pap. 3.95 *(978-0-7933-9551-4(8))* Gallopade International.

—Louisiana Jography. 2004. (Louisiana Experience! Ser.). (Illus.). 32p. (J). (gr. 3-8). pap. 7.95 *(978-0-7933-9549-1(6))* Gallopade International.

—The Magnificent Michigan Coloring Book. 2004. (Michigan Experience! Ser.). (Illus.). 32p. (J). (gr. k-2). pap. 3.95 *(978-0-7933-9567-5(4))* Gallopade International.

—The Magnificent Missouri Coloring Book. 2004. (Missouri Experience! Ser.). (Illus.). 32p. (J). (gr. k-2). pap. 3.95 *(978-0-7933-9575-0(5))* Gallopade International.

—The Marvelous Maryland Coloring Book! 2004. (Maryland Experience! Ser.). (Illus.). 32p. (J). (gr. k-2). pap. 3.95 *(978-0-7933-9615-3(8))* Gallopade International.

—Mississippi "Jography" A Fun Run Thru Our State! 2004. (Mississippi Experience! Ser.). (Illus.). 32p. (J). (gr. 3-8). pap. 7.95 *(978-0-7933-9557-6(7))* Gallopade International.

—Native American Coloring Book. Corsey, Jenny, ed. 2004. (Native American Heri Ser.). (Illus.). 24p. (J). (gr. k-2). 3.95 *(978-0-635-02398-8(9))* Gallopade International.

—The Nifty New Jersey Coloring Book. 2004. (New Jersey Experience! Ser.). (Illus.). 32p. (J). (gr. k-2). pap. 3.95 *(978-0-7933-9473-9(2))* Gallopade International.

—The Nifty New York Coloring Book. 2004. (New York Experience! Ser.). 32p. (Orig.). (J). (gr. k-2). pap. 3.95 *(978-0-635-00164-1(0))* Gallopade International.

—The Nifty North Carolina Coloring Book. 2004. (North Carolina Experience! Ser.). (Illus.). 32p. (J). (gr. k-2). pap. 3.95 *(978-0-7933-9472-2(4))* Gallopade International.

—The Out-of-This-World Oklahoma Coloring Book! 2004. (Oklahoma Experience! Ser.). (Illus.). 32p. (J). (gr. k-2). 3.95 *(978-0-7933-9599-6(2))* Gallopade International.

—Peachtree City Coloring Book! 2005. 24p. (gr. k-2). pap. 4.95 *(978-0-635-06196-6(1))* Gallopade International.

—The Proud Pennsylvania Coloring Book. 2004. (Pennsylvania Experience! Ser.). (Illus.). 32p. (J). (gr. k-2). pap. 3.95 *(978-0-7933-9591-0(7))* Gallopade International.

—The Terrific Tennessee Coloring Book! 2004. (Carole Marsh Tennessee Bks.). (Illus.). 32p. (J). (gr. k-2). 3.95 *(978-0-7933-9870-6(3))* Gallopade International.

—The Wonderful Wisconsin Coloring Book. 2004. (Wisconsin Experience! Ser.). (Illus.). 32p. (J). (gr. k-2). pap. 3.95 *(978-0-7933-9543-9(7))* Gallopade International.

Marshall, Natalie, illus. Colors in the Ocean. 2017. (Touch & Learn Bks.). (ENG.). 12p. (J). (gr. -1 — 1). bds. 5.99 ***(978-1-4380-5001-0(1))*** Barron's Educational Series, Inc.

Martin, Courtney Autumn, et al, illus. Life in Color: A Coloring Book of Teenage Confusion, Creativity, & Discovery. 2016. (ENG.). 96p. (gr. 9-11). pap. 12.95 *(978-1-63079-059-2(1))* Switch Pr.

Marvel Comics. Color Your Own Marvel Masters. 2017. (ENG., Illus.). 120p. (J). (gr. -1-17). pap. 9.99 ***(978-1-302-90273-5(3))*** Marvel Worldwide, Inc.

—Color Your Own Spider-Man. 2017. (ENG., Illus.). 120p. (J). (gr. -1-17). pap. 9.99 ***(978-1-302-90370-1(5))*** Marvel Worldwide, Inc.

—Color Your Own Thor. 2017. (ENG., Illus.). 120p. (J). (gr. -1-17). 9.99 ***(978-1-302-90378-7(0))*** Marvel Worldwide, Inc.

Masters, Neil. Aircrafts Coloring Book. 2013. (ENG.). 42p. 12.92 *(978-1-62884-652-2(6)*, Baby Professor (Education Kids)) Speedy Publishing LLC.

—Butterflies Coloring Book. 2013. (ENG.). 34p. 12.07 *(978-1-62884-656-0(9)*, Baby Professor (Education Kids)) Speedy Publishing LLC.

—Trucks Coloring Book. 2013. (ENG.). 32p. 12.48 *(978-1-62884-654-6(2)*, Baby Professor (Education Kids)) Speedy Publishing LLC.

—Wild Animals Coloring Book. 2013. (ENG.). 42p. 12.92 *(978-1-62884-653-9(4)*, Baby Professor (Education Kids)) Speedy Publishing LLC.

—Working Vehicles Coloring Book. 2013. (ENG.). 32p. 11.98 *(978-1-62884-655-3(0)*, Baby Professor (Education Kids)) Speedy Publishing LLC.

Matsunaga, Judd, illus. King's Kids Coloring Book. Fleming, Jesse, photos by. Date not set. (SPA.). 32p. (J). *(978-0-9703880-4-9(7))* King's Kids Trading Cards, Inc.

Matsunaga, Judd & Fleming, Jesse, illus. King's Kids Coloring Book. Date not set. 32p. (J). *(978-0-9703880-3-2(9))* King's Kids Trading Cards, Inc.

Mattox, Brenda Sneathen. Favorite Ballets Coloring Book. 2004. (Dover Fashion Coloring Book Ser.). (ENG., Illus.). 32p. (J). (gr. 3-8). pap. 3.99 *(978-0-486-43646-3(2))* Dover Pubns., Inc.

—Nutcracker Ballet Coloring Book. 2005. (Dover Holiday Coloring Book Ser.). (ENG., Illus.). 32p. (J). (gr. 3-8). 3.99 *(978-0-486-44022-4(2))* Dover Pubns., Inc.

—Wedding Traditions from Around the World Coloring Book. 2007. (Dover Fashion Coloring Book Ser.). (ENG., Illus.). 32p. (gr. 3-5). 3.99 *(978-0-486-46232-5(3))* Dover Pubns., Inc.

May, Darcy. Fairies to Paint or Color. 2008. (Dover Art Coloring Book Ser.). (ENG., Illus.). 48p. (gr. 3-5). pap. 5.99 *(978-0-486-46544-9(6))* Dover Pubns., Inc.

—Garden Fairies GemGlow Stained Glass Coloring Book. 2009. (Dover Stained Glass Coloring Book Ser.). (ENG., Illus.). 32p. (J). (gr. 1-5). pap. 7.99 *(978-0-486-47146-4(2))* Dover Pubns., Inc.

May, Stephan. Leo the Entrepreneurial Hippo. 2008. (Illus.). 56p. pap. 10.95 *(978-1-4401-0480-0(8))* iUniverse, Inc.

Mazurkiewicz, Jessica. Abstractions. 2009. (Dover Design Coloring Bks.). (ENG., Illus.). 32p. (gr. 3-6). pap. 3.99 *(978-0-486-46836-5(4))* Dover Pubns., Inc.

—Alphascapes. 2013. (Dover Design Coloring Bks.). (ENG.). 32p. (J). (gr. 1-5). pap. 3.99 *(978-0-486-49010-6(6))* Dover Pubns., Inc.

—Animals Mosaics Coloring Book. 2014. (Adult Coloring Ser.). (ENG., Illus.). 64p. (gr. 3). pap. 5.99 *(978-0-486-78177-8(1))* Dover Pubns., Inc.

—COLORTWIST — Blue Coloring Book. 2013. (Dover Coloring Bks.). (ENG.). 64p. (J). (gr. -1-8). pap. 5.99 *(978-0-486-49971-0(5))* Dover Pubns., Inc.

—COLORTWIST — Green Coloring Book. 2013. (Dover Coloring Bks.). (ENG.). 64p. (J). (gr. -1-8). pap. 5.99 *(978-0-486-49945-1(6))* Dover Pubns., Inc.

—COLORTWIST — Pink Coloring Book. 2013. (Dover Coloring Bks.). (ENG.). 64p. (J). (gr. -1-8). pap. 5.99 *(978-0-486-49946-8(4))* Dover Pubns., Inc.

—COLORTWIST — Purple Coloring Book. 2013. (Dover Coloring Bks.). (ENG.). 64p. (J). (gr. -1-8). pap. 5.99 *(978-0-486-49947-5(2))* Dover Pubns., Inc.

—Coral Reef Stained Glass Coloring Book. 2008. (Dover Nature Stained Glass Coloring Book Ser.). (ENG., Illus.). 32p. (gr. 1-5). pap. 7.99 *(978-0-486-46789-4(9))* Dover Pubns., Inc.

—Creative Haven Beautiful Butterfly Designs Coloring Book. 2013. (Adult Coloring Ser.). (ENG.). 64p. (gr. 3). pap. 5.99 *(978-0-486-49456-2(X))* Dover Pubns., Inc.

—Creative Haven Magnificent Mosaics Stained Glass Coloring Book. 2014. (Adult Coloring Ser.). (ENG., Illus.). 32p. (gr. 3). pap. 7.99 *(978-0-486-79829-5(1))* Dover Pubns., Inc.

—Creative Haven Simply Abstract Stained Glass Coloring Book. 2014. (Adult Coloring Ser.). (ENG., Illus.). 32p. (gr. 3). pap. 7.99 *(978-0-486-79831-8(3))* Dover Pubns., Inc.

—Creatures of the Night Stained Glass Coloring Book. 2010. (Dover Nature Stained Glass Coloring Book Ser.). (ENG., Illus.). 32p. (J). (gr. 2-5). pap. 7.99 *(978-0-486-47688-9(X))* Dover Pubns., Inc.

—Forever Inspired Coloring Book - Unicorns & Mystical Creatures. 2016. (ENG., Illus.). 96p. (J). (gr. 3-7). pap. 7.99 *(978-1-944686-22-2(3)*, Racehorse Publishing) Skyhorse Publishing Co., Inc.

—Forever Inspired Coloring Book: Fairyworld. 2016. (ENG., Illus.). 96p. (J). (gr. 3-7). pap. 7.99 *(978-1-944686-23-9(1)*, Racehorse Publishing) Skyhorse Publishing Co., Inc.

—HalloweenScapes. 2011. (Dover Holiday Coloring Book Ser.). (ENG.). 32p. (J). (gr. 2-5). pap. 3.99 *(978-0-486-48179-1(4))* Dover Pubns., Inc.

—Haunted House Activity Book. 2010. (Dover Little Activity Bks.). (ENG., Illus.). 64p. (J). (gr. k-3). pap. 1.50 *(978-0-486-47522-6(0))* Dover Pubns., Inc.

—Magnificent Mosaics. 2009. (Dover Design Coloring Bks.). (ENG., Illus.). 32p. (J). (gr. 1-5). pap. 3.99 *(978-0-486-46989-8(1))* Dover Pubns., Inc.

—Santa's Busy Workshop Stained Glass Jr. Coloring Book. 2012. (Dover Stained Glass Coloring Book Ser.). (ENG.). 32p. (J). (gr. -1-5). pap. 3.99 *(978-0-486-49870-6(0))* Dover Pubns., Inc.

—Santa's Workshop Stained Glass Coloring Book. 2008. (Holiday Stained Glass Coloring Book Ser.). (ENG., Illus.). 32p. (J). (gr. 3-5). pap. 6.99 *(978-0-486-46937-9(9))* Dover Pubns., Inc.

—Seashell Patterns Coloring Book. 2011. (Dover Nature Coloring Book Ser.). (ENG.). 32p. (J). (gr. 3-5). pap. 3.99 *(978-0-486-47559-2(X))* Dover Pubns., Inc.

—SPARK - Mandalas Coloring Book. 2015. (ENG., Illus.). 64p. (J). (gr. 1-4). pap. 5.99 *(978-0-486-80214-5(0))* Dover Pubns., Inc.

—Spark - Mosaics Coloring Book. 2016. (ENG., Illus.). 64p. (J). (gr. k-3). pap. 5.99 *(978-0-486-80213-8(2))* Dover Pubns., Inc.

—Wonder Wings Butterfly Coloring Book. 2015. (ENG., Illus.). 32p. (J). (gr. -1-5). pap. 3.99 *(978-0-486-78937-8(3))* Dover Pubns., Inc.

—3-D Coloring Book — Abstractions. 2014. (Dover 3-D Coloring Book Ser.). (ENG., Illus.). 32p. (J). (gr. 3-5). pap. 5.99 *(978-0-486-48416-7(5))* Dover Pubns., Inc.

—3-D Coloring Book — Butterflies. 2011. (Dover 3-D Coloring Book Ser.). (ENG., Illus.). 32p. (J). (gr. 3-5). pap. 5.99 *(978-0-486-48161-6(1))* Dover Pubns., Inc.

—3-D Coloring Book — Crazy Christmas. 2011. (Dover 3-D Coloring Book Ser.). (ENG., Illus.). 32p. (J). (gr. 2-6). pap. 5.99 *(978-0-486-48409-9(2))* Dover Pubns., Inc.

—3-D Coloring Book — Happy Halloween. 2011. (Dover 3-D Coloring Book Ser.). (ENG., Illus.). 32p. (J). (gr. 2-6). pap. 5.99 *(978-0-486-48411-2(4))* Dover Pubns., Inc.

—3-D Coloring Book — Mosaic Madness. 2011. (Dover 3-D Coloring Book Ser.). (ENG., Illus.). 32p. (J). (gr. 3-5). pap. 5.99 *(978-0-486-48104-3(2))* Dover Pubns., Inc.

Mazurkiewicz, Jessica & Coloring Books Staff. Creatures of the Deep Stained Glass Coloring Book. 2012. (Dover Stained Glass Coloring Book Ser.). (ENG., Illus.). 32p. (J). (gr. 3-5). pap. 6.99 *(978-0-486-48523-2(4))* Dover Pubns., Inc.

—Organic Designs Coloring Book. 2011. (Dover Coloring Bks.). (ENG., Illus.). 32p. (J). (gr. 2-5). pap. 3.99 *(978-0-486-47987-3(0))* Dover Pubns., Inc.

Mazurkiewicz, Jessica & Dahlen, Noelle. 3-D Coloring Book — Here Comes Santa Claus! 2011. (Dover 3-D Coloring Book Ser.). (ENG., Illus.). 32p. (J). (gr. 2-6). pap. 5.99 *(978-0-486-48413-6(0))* Dover Pubns., Inc.

Mazurkiewicz, Jessica & Noble, Marty. 3-D Coloring Book - Christmas Designs. 2013. (Dover 3-D Coloring Book Ser.). (ENG.). 128p. (J). (gr. 3-12). pap. 9.99 *(978-0-486-49343-5(1))* Dover Pubns., Inc.

Mazurkiewicz, Jessica, et al. Floral Designs. 2012. (Adult Coloring Ser.). (ENG., Illus.). 32p. (gr. 1). pap. 5.99 *(978-0-486-47245-4(0))* Dover Pubns., Inc.

—Skyscapes. 2012. (Adult Coloring Ser.). (ENG.). 32p. (J). (gr. 3). pap. 5.99 *(978-0-486-48834-9(9))* Dover Pubns., Inc.

McBratney, Sam. Guess How Much I Love You Coloring Book. Jeram, Anita, illus. 2017. (Guess How Much I Love You Ser.). (ENG.). 96p. (J). (gr. k-12). pap. 7.99 *(978-0-7636-9467-8(3))* Candlewick Pr.

McCabe, Dennis, illus. Haunted Halloween: Color & Create with Spooky Stickers. 2004. 10p. (J). (gr. -1-18). bds. 4.99 *(978-1-57151-730-2(8))* Playhouse Publishing.

McCabe, Gusty. The Most Important Critter in the Whole Wide World: Why the Coyote Howls at Night. 2013. 40p. pap. 19.57 *(978-1-4669-8759-3(6))* Trafford Publishing.

McCalment, Ray & McCalment, Diana. Route 66 Fun Coloring Book. 2006. (J). *(978-0-9793902-0-3(6))* Designs For Progress, Inc.

McDevitt, Bradley. Oddly Adorable Coloring Book 1. Leon, Richard, ed. 2007. (Illus.). 16p. (J). 4.95 *(978-0-9797080-2-2(8))* Dark Skull Studios.

McDonald, Jake. The Dinosaur Colouring Book. McDonald, Jake, illus. 2017. (ENG., Illus.). 64p. (J). (gr. k-3). 6.99 ***(978-1-78055-351-1(X))*** O'Mara, Michael Bks., Ltd. GBR. Dist: Independent Pubs. Group.

McDONALD, Steve, illus. Fantastic Cities: A Coloring Book of Amazing Places Real & Imagined. 2015. (ENG.). 80p. pap. 14.95 *(978-1-4521-4957-8(7))* Chronicle Bks. LLC.

McElroy, Bonnie & Mandala Publishing Staff. Jagannath Coloring Book. McElroy, Bonnie, illus. l.t. ed. 2007. (ENG., Illus.). 32p. (J). 6.95 *(978-0-945475-29-3(2)*, 1203) Mandala Publishing.

—Nimai Coloring Book. 2004. (ENG.). 43p. (J). (gr. k). *(978-1-932771-59-6(X))* Mattei Medien GmbH.

McElroy, Bonnie, et al. Damodara Coloring Book. 2004. (ENG.). 32p. (J). (gr. k). *(978-1-932771-60-2(3))* Mattei Medien GmbH.

—Jagannatha Coloring Book. 2004. (ENG.). 33p. (J). (gr. k). *(978-1-932771-62-6(X))* Mattei Medien GmbH.

McGraw, Mike. Doodle Land. 2010. 28p. pap. 13.99 *(978-1-4520-1290-2(3))* AuthorHouse.

McHale, Conor. Ancient Ireland Colouring Book: From Newgrange to the Vikings. McHale, Conor, illus. 2014. (ENG., Illus.). 32p. (J). pap. 12.00 *(978-1-84717-629-5(1))* O'Brien Pr., Ltd., The IRL. Dist: Dufour Editions, Inc.

McIntyre, Sasha & Ghione, Yvette. Franklin's Easter: A Sticker Activity Book. 2004. (ENG., Illus.). 16p. (J). 6.95 *(978-1-55337-521-0(1))* Kids Can Pr., Ltd. CAN. Dist: Hachette Bk. Group.

McKendry, Sam. Curious Kitties: A Color Book. Mitchell, Melanie, illus. 2007. (ENG.). 14p. (J). (gr. -1-3). bds. 5.95 *(978-1-58117-554-7(X)*, Intervisual/Piggy Toes) Bendon, Inc.

McVey, Randall, et al. Mesmerizing Mandalas. 2012. (Adult Coloring Ser.). (ENG., Illus.). 64p. (gr. 3). pap. 5.99 *(978-0-486-49961-1(8))* Dover Pubns., Inc.

Mead, Brian. Creatures of the Deep Coloring Book. 2003. 32p. (J). (gr. -1-3). pap. 3.99 *(978-0-9717509-3-7(9))* Mead, Brian Publishing.

—Monsters of the Ice Age Coloring Book. 2003. 32p. (J). (gr. -1-3). pap. 3.99 *(978-0-9717509-2-0(0))* Mead, Brian Publishing.

Mead, David. Noah's Babies Colors & Caring. Byers, Brian, illus. 2005. 22p. (J). bds. 6.95 *(978-0-9746440-7-3(2))* Virtue Bks.

Mead, Pumima. Bibia Tells Her Story! 2010. 24p. 14.50 *(978-1-4490-4753-5(X))* AuthorHouse.

Medsker, Lynne. Zendala Coloring Book. 2015. (Dover Design Coloring Bks.). (ENG., Illus.). 32p. (gr. 4-7). pap. 3.99 *(978-0-486-80251-0(5))* Dover Pubns., Inc.

Meislin, Barbara. No One Can Ever Steal Your Rainbow. Webber, Helen, illus. 2005. 28p. 19.75 incl. audio compact disk *(978-0-9714506-0-8(9))* Purple Lady Productions.

Meithrin, Mudiad Ysgolion. Llyfr Lliwio Dydd a Nos. 2005. (WEL & ENG., Illus.). 26p. pap. *(978-1-870222-48-8(2))* Mudiad Ysgolion Meithrin.

Menges, Jeff A. House of Horror Stained Glass Coloring Book. 2009. (Dover Stained Glass Coloring Book Ser.). (ENG., Illus.). 32p. (gr. 6-8). pap. 6.99 *(978-0-486-47452-6(6))* Dover Pubns., Inc.

Mercer, Erin. How Do You Count To 10? 2011. 16p. pap. 9.95 *(978-1-4634-3296-6(8))* AuthorHouse.

Mercer, Henry C., et al. Color Me Pennsylvania: Our Heritage. 2007. (Illus.). 22p. (J). pap. 12.00 *(978-1-4223-1491-3(X))* DIANE Publishing Co.

Meredith Books Staff, ed. Fantastic Four Classic Color & Activity Book with Poster. 2005. 400p. pap. 6.99 *(978-0-696-22511-6(5))* Meredith Bks.

—Spider-Man Color & Activity Book with Poster. 2005. 400p. pap. 6.99 *(978-0-696-22401-0(1))* Meredith Bks.

Meredith, Samantha & Wyk, Hanri van, illus. Weddings Sticker Color Book. 2011. (First Sticker Coloring Bks). 20p. (J). pap. 5.99 *(978-0-7945-3108-9(3)*, Usborne) EDC Publishing.

Meredith, Susan. Flowers to Color. Cooper, Jenny, illus. 2013. (Nature Coloring Bks). 32p. (J). pap. 5.99 *(978-0-7945-3058-7(3)*, Usborne) EDC Publishing.

—Undersea Life to Color. Cooper, Jenny, illus. 2014. (ENG.). (J). pap. 5.99 *(978-0-7945-2854-6(6)*, Usborne) EDC Publishing.

Meredith, Susan & Cullis, Megan. Nature to Color. Cooper, Jenny, illus. 2013. (ENG.). 96p. (J). 9.99 *(978-0-7945-1913-1(X)*, Usborne) EDC Publishing.

Messenger, Norman. IMAGINA. (Coleccion Mundo Maravilloso). (SPA.). 20p. (J). (gr. 3-5). *(978-84-348-4430-8(3))* SM Ediciones.

Messersmith, Heather. Seasons. 2005. pap. 23.50 *(978-1-4208-6698-8(2))* AuthorHouse.

Meza, Martin. Martin Meza's Color Me in Coloring Book. 2007. (ENG., Illus.). 72p. per. 9.70 *(978-1-4116-9168-1(7))* Lulu Pr., Inc.

Michael O'Mara Books. Cool Coloring for Kids: Express Yourself Through Color. 2016. (ENG., Illus.). 128p. (J). (gr. 3). pap. 12.95 *(978-1-4549-2053-3(X))* Sterling Publishing Co., Inc.

Michelangelo. Sistine Chapel Coloring Book. 2004. (Dover Art Coloring Book Ser.). (ENG., Illus.). 32p. (J). (gr. 3-8). spiral bd. 4.95 *(978-0-486-43334-9(X))* Dover Pubns., Inc.

Miller, Eileen Rudisill. Happy Easter Stained Glass Coloring Book. 2010. (Holiday Stained Glass Coloring Book Ser.). (ENG., Illus.). 32p. (J). (gr. -1-8). pap. 6.99 *(978-0-486-47296-6(5))* Dover Pubns., Inc.

—Mermaids Stained Glass Coloring Book. 2008. (Dover Stained Glass Coloring Book Ser.). (ENG., Illus.). 32p. (J). (gr. 3-8). 6.99 *(978-0-486-46555-5(1))* Dover Pubns., Inc.

—Princess Coloring Book. 2012. (Dover Coloring Bks.). (ENG.). 32p. (J). (gr. -1-3). pap. 3.99 *(978-0-486-49917-8(0))* Dover Pubns., Inc.

—Princess Leonora Stained Glass Coloring Book. 2007. (Dover Stained Glass Coloring Book Ser.). (ENG., Illus.). 16p. (J). (gr. 3-8). 5.95 *(978-0-486-45957-8(8))* Dover Pubns., Inc.

—Princess Stained Glass Jr. Coloring Book. 2012. (Dover Stained Glass Coloring Book Ser.). (ENG.). 32p. (J). (gr. -1-5). pap. 3.99 *(978-0-486-49871-3(9))* Dover Pubns., Inc.

—True Love Stained Glass Coloring Book. 2011. (Dover Stained Glass Coloring Book Ser.). (ENG., Illus.). 32p. (gr. 3-8). pap. 6.99 *(978-0-486-47835-7(1))* Dover Pubns., Inc.

Miller, Mona. Call of the Wild! Golden Books Staff & Fruchter, Jason, illus. 2011. (Color Plus Chunky Crayons Ser.). (ENG.). 48p. (J). (gr. -1-2). pap. 3.99 *(978-0-375-86158-1(0)*, Golden Bks.) Random Hse. Children's Bks.

—Hey, Buddy! Fruchter, Jason, illus. 2010. (Super Coloring Book Ser.). (ENG.). 96p. (J). (gr. -1-2). pap. 3.99 *(978-0-375-86155-0(6)*, Golden Bks.) Random Hse. Children's Bks.

—A Very Busy Coloring Book. Golden Books, illus. 2013. (Jumbo Coloring Book Ser.). (ENG.). 224p. (J). (gr. -1-2). pap. 5.99 *(978-0-449-81609-7(5)*, Golden Bks.) Random Hse. Children's Bks.

Millhoff, Brian L. The Micronesian Coloring Book. 2nd l.t. ed. 2006. (Illus.). 68p. (J). per. 6.50 net. *(978-0-9790111-0-8(8))* M-m-mauleg Publishing.

Mills, Cindy, illus. Cass Railroad Fun Book. 2007. 32p. (J). pap. 2.95 *(978-0-929915-74-6(7))* Headline Bks., Inc.

Miner, Julie Dobson. EEK! Monsters Coloring Book. 2017. (Dover Coloring Bks.). (ENG., Illus.). 32p. (J). (gr. -1-2). pap. 3.99 *(978-0-486-81441-4(6))* Dover Pubns., Inc.

Mischel, Jenny Ann. Animal Alphabet. Bell-Myers, Darcy, illus. 2006. (J). bds. *(978-0-9769239-0-9(4))* Perfect 4 Preschool.

Mitchell, George. My handwriting & colouring Book. 2009. 64p. pap. 13.95 *(978-1-4452-3485-4(8))* Lulu Pr., Inc.

Mitchell, Lori, illus. & compiled by. Marfan Syndrome A-Z. Mitchell, Lori, compiled by. 2007. 36p. (J). pap. *(978-0-918335-14-2(0))* National Marfan Foundation, The.

Mitzo Thompson, Kim, et al. Coloring Journal for Girls. 2017. (ENG.). 64p. (J). spiral bd. 9.99 ***(978-1-68322-195-1(8))*** Barbour Publishing, Inc.

Modern Painters Staff & Quarto Generic Staff. Colour It! Various Artists, illus. 2004. (ENG.). 36p. (J). (gr. -1-17). pap. 7.95 *(978-1-84507-275-9(8)*, Frances Lincoln) Quarto Publishing Group UK GBR. Dist: Hachette Bk. Group.

Modern Publishing, creator. Friends, Silliness & Fun! 2011. (Lalaloopsy Ser.). (ENG., Illus.). (J). (gr. -1-3). 2.99 *(978-0-7666-4082-5(5))* Modern Publishing.

C
D

—Once upon a Zoo! 2011. (Fisher-Price Luv U Zoo Ser.). (ENG., Illus.). (J). (gr. -1-3). 2.99 *(978-0-7666-3830-3(8))* Modern Publishing.

—Sew Much Fun! 2011. (Lalaloopsy Ser.). (ENG., Illus.). (J). (gr. -1-3). 2.99 *(978-0-7666-4083-2(3))* Modern Publishing.

—Traintastic Crew! 2011. (Chuggington Ser.). (ENG., Illus.). (J). (gr. -1-3). 2.99 *(978-0-7666-3982-9(7))* Modern Publishing.

—Wheels to the Rails! 2011. (Chuggington Ser.). (ENG., Illus.). (J). (gr. -1-3). 2.99 *(978-0-7666-3981-2(9))* Modern Publishing.

Modern Publishing Staff. Fisher-Price Laugh, Smile & Learn. 2009. 96p. (J). (gr. -1). pap. 2.99 *(978-0-7666-3488-6(4))* Modern Publishing.

—Fisher-Price Spike the Ultra Dinosaur. 2009. (Giant Coloring & Activity Bks.). 96p. (J). (gr. -1). pap. 2.99 *(978-0-7666-3491-6(4))* Modern Publishing.

—Zhu Zhu Pets Giant Coloring & Activity Book: Furry Friends! 2010. 96p. (J). pap. 2.99 *(978-0-7666-3764-1(6))* Modern Publishing.

—Zhu Zhu Pets Giant Coloring & Activity Book: Happy Hamsters! 2010. 96p. (J). pap. 2.99 *(978-0-7666-3765-8(4))* Modern Publishing.

Modern Publishing Staff, ed. Here Comes Tonka. 2005. pap. 2.99 *(978-0-7666-1875-6(7))* Modern Publishing.

—Make Way for Tonka. 2005. 32p. pap. 2.99 *(978-0-7666-1874-9(9))* Modern Publishing.

Monet, Claude & Noble, Marty. Colorier Vos Propres Tableaux de Monet. 2013. (Dover Children's Bilingual Coloring Book Ser.). (FRE & ENG.). 64p. (gr. 3-12). pap. 5.99 *(978-0-486-49328-2(8))* Dover Pubns., Inc.

Montes, Graciela. Federico Dice No. (SPA.). 16p. pap. 9.95 *(978-950-07-1158-6(3))* Editorial Sudamericana S.A. ARG. Dist: Distribooks, Inc.

—Federico Se Hizo Pis. (SPA.). pap. 9.95 *(978-950-07-0851-7(5))* Editorial Sudamericana S.A. ARG. Dist: Distribooks, Inc.

Montgomery, Kelly. SPARK Wildlife Designs Coloring Book. 2016. (Dover Coloring Bks.). (ENG., Illus.). 64p. (J). (gr. 1-4). pap. 5.99 *(978-0-486-81092-8(5))* Dover Pubns., Inc.

Montgomery, Kelly & Creative Haven Staff. Sea Life Designs Coloring Book. 2012. (Adult Coloring Ser.). (ENG., Illus.). 64p. (gr. 3). pap. 5.99 *(978-0-486-49088-5(2))* Dover Pubns., Inc.

Moorash, Marc. The Romanti-Goth A to Z Coloring Book. 2006. (Illus.). 32p. 7.99 *(978-0-9778989-0-9(3))* Seraphemera Bks.

More Unicorns. 2007. (Illus.). 20p. (J). 10.00 *(978-0-9795206-6-2(5))* Unseen Gallery.

Morrison, Denis. Gumball. 2010. 32p. pap. 7.19 *(978-0-557-33389-9(X))* Lulu Pr., Inc.

Mossy Moose Alaska: Coloring & Activity Book. (J). pap. 5.00 *(978-0-9677477-2-9(4))* "Grandma's Hope Notes".

Mostofizadeh, Hoomaz. MMA Coloring Book: Mixed Martial Arts Coloring Book. 2012. (ENG.). 52p. pap. 5.99 *(978-1-937981-60-0(6))* Mikazuki Publishing Hse.

Msmh. Learning to Count, Alphabets a-J & Colours. 2013. 16p. pap. 12.68 *(978-1-4669-7416-6(8))* Trafford Publishing.

Mucklow, Lacy. Color Me Fearless: Nearly 100 Coloring Templates to Boost Strength & Courage. Porter, Angela, illus. 2016. (Zen Coloring Book Ser.). (ENG.). 208p. pap. 16.99 *(978-1-63106-195-0(X)*, Race Point Publishing) Quarto Publishing Group USA.

Mucklow, Lacy & Porter, Angela. Color Me to Sleep: Nearly 100 Coloring Templates to Promote Relaxation & Restful Sleep. 2016. (Zen Coloring Book Ser.). (ENG., Illus.). 208p. pap. 16.99 *(978-1-63106-237-7(9)*, Race Point Publishing) Quarto Publishing Group USA.

Mukherjee, Aiswarya & S., Bijan, illus. My Family! ABCs with Keesha. 2011. (J). pap. 2.99 *(978-0-9767273-9-2(0))* Dodi Pr.

Music. ABCs & Much More Activity & Coloring Book. 2008. (Illus.). 177p. (J). pap. 14.95 *(978-0-9818635-1-1(5))* Music, Movement & Magination Bks.

My Activity Time Coloring Pad. 2003. 80p. (J). 3.98 *(978-1-4054-1968-0(7))* Parragon, Inc.

My Bumper Fun Coloring. Date not set. (My Bumper Activity Ser.). (Illus.). 128p. (J). 3.98 *(978-0-7525-8295-5(X))* Parragon, Inc.

My First Book of Trucks. 2004. (Illus.). 18p. (J). bds. 5.99 *(978-1-85854-431-1(9))* Brimax Books Ltd. GBR. Dist: Byeway Bks.

My First Coloring Book. 2004. 72p. (J). act. bk. ed. 3.99 *(978-1-85997-692-0(1))* Byeway Bks.

My First Coloring Book of Spansih Words. 1000th ed. 2003. (ENG & SPA., Illus.). 34p. (J). 5.95 *(978-0-9722999-0-9(4))* Three Sisters Pr.

My Playtime Coloring Pad. 2003. 80p. (J). 3.98 *(978-1-4054-1967-3(9))* Parragon, Inc.

My Pocket Coloring Rainbow. 2003. (Illus.). 192p. (J). 1.49 *(978-1-4054-0882-0(0))* Parragon, Inc.

My Pocket Coloring Snail. 2003. (Illus.). 192p. (J). 1.49 *(978-1-4054-0883-7(9))* Parragon, Inc.

My Pocket Dot to Dot Boat. 2003. (Illus.). 192p. (J). 1.49 *(978-1-4054-0884-4(7))* Parragon, Inc.

My Pocket Dot to Dot Rocket. Date not set. (Illus.). 192p. (J). 1.49 *(978-1-4054-0885-1(5))* Parragon, Inc.

Narayan, Jasmine. Color with Me, Grandma! Color, Create, & Connect with Your Grandchild. Davies, Hannah, illus. 2017. (Side-By-Side Book Ser.). (ENG.). 128p. (J). (gr. -1-2). pap. 12.99 *(978-1-63106-306-0(5)*, Race Point Publishing) Quarto Publishing Group USA.

Natural History Museum. Sticker Art Ocean. Craig & Karl, illus. 2017. (Sticker Art Ser.). (ENG.). 24p. (J). (gr. -1-k). pap. 7.99 ***(978-1-78603-005-4(5)**, Frances Lincoln Children's Bks.)* Quarto Publishing Group UK GBR. Dist: Hachette Bk. Group.

Nelson, Andy. The Carl Larsson Coloring Book. 2nd ed. 2004. (Illus.). 96p. (Orig.). (J). (gr. 1-6). pap. 8.95 *(978-0-929636-25-2(2))* Syren Bk. Co.

—The Renaissance Painters Coloring Book: Donatello, Raphael, Leonardo & Michelangelo. 2nd ed. 2004. (Illus.). 96p. (J). (gr. 1-6). pap. 8.95 *(978-0-929636-27-6(9))* Syren Bk. Co.

Nelson, Cyndi. Rocky Mountain Mushrooms: Edible & Poisonous. 2nd rev. ed. 2007. (Illus.). 43p. pap. 7.95 *(978-1-55566-404-6(0)*, Johnson Bks.) Bower Hse.

Nemmers, Lee. Scratch & Sketch Trace-Along Robots: An Art Activity Book for Artistic Inventors of All Ages. Wheeler, David Cole, illus. 2015. (ENG.). 64p. (J). 14.99 *(978-1-4413-1812-1(7)*, 9781441318121) Peter Pauper Pr. Inc.

Neusner, Dena Wallenstein. Colors of Spring. McKee, Darren, illus. 2003. (Barney Ser.). (ENG.). 32p. (J). pap., act. bk. ed. 3.99 *(978-1-58668-305-4(5))* Scholastic, Inc.

Nevis, Lance. Silly Stew. Laible MBA, Steve William, ed. Piper, Tom, illus. 2012. 50p. pap. 10.99 *(978-0-9850142-9-2(6))* Kodel Group, LLC, The.

New Frontiers Group. There's Nobody Like You! The World of Howie & Friends. 2006. (Illus.). (J). 2.99 *(978-1-58597-370-5(X))* Leathers Publishing.

Newman-D'Amico, Fran. All about America: Facts & Fun. 2008. (Dover Little Activity Bks.). (ENG., Illus.). 64p. (J). (gr. 1-4). pap. 1.99 *(978-0-486-46573-9(X))* Dover Pubns., Inc.

—BOOST Favorite Fairy Tales Coloring Book. 2013. (BOOST Educational Ser.). (ENG.). 32p. (J). (gr. -1-k). pap. 4.99 *(978-0-486-49403-6(9))* Dover Pubns., Inc.

—Bugs Activity & Coloring Book. 2007. (Dover Children's Activity Bks.). (ENG., Illus.). 32p. (J). (gr. 1-3). pap. 3.99 *(978-0-486-46199-1(8))* Dover Pubns., Inc.

—Halloween Fun. 2005. (Dover Holiday Coloring Book Ser.). (ENG., Illus.). 32p. (J). (gr. k-3). 3.99 *(978-0-486-44699-8(9))* Dover Pubns., Inc.

Nichols, Catherine. Color Yourself Smart: Masterpieces of Art. Bright, Joe, illus. 2013. (Color Yourself Smart Ser.). (ENG.). 128p. 19.95 *(978-1-60710-572-5(1)*, Thunder Bay Pr.) Readerlink Distribution Services, LLC.

Nilsson, Oscar. Lowrider Coloring Book. 2011. (ENG., Illus.). 64p. pap. 9.95 *(978-91-85639-41-0(9))* Dokument forlag, Fotograf Malcolm Jacobsson SWE. Dist: SCB Distributors.

Nip It in the Bud. 2003. (Humble Heart Ser.). (J). spiral bd. *(978-0-9746148-3-0(1))* Common Courtesy.

Noble, Marty. Angels. 2008. (Dover Coloring Bks.). (ENG.). 32p. (gr. 3-5). pap. 3.99 *(978-0-486-46775-7(9))* Dover Pubns., Inc.

—Artful Eggs from Around the World Stained Glass Coloring Book. 2011. (Dover Design Stained Glass Coloring Book Ser.). (ENG., Illus.). 32p. (gr. 3-8). pap. 7.99 *(978-0-486-48025-1(9))* Dover Pubns., Inc.

—Chinese Kites Stained Glass Coloring Book. 2008. (Dover Design Stained Glass Coloring Book Ser.). (ENG., Illus.). 32p. (gr. 3-8). pap. 6.99 *(978-0-486-46942-3(5))* Dover Pubns., Inc.

—Christmas. 2011. (Build Window Stained Glass Coloring Book Ser.). (ENG., Illus.). 32p. (J). (gr. 3-5). pap. 6.99 *(978-0-486-48394-8(0))* Dover Pubns., Inc.

—Color Your Own Classic Movie Posters. 2006. (Dover Art Coloring Book Ser.). (ENG., Illus.). 32p. (gr. 6-8). pap. 4.99 *(978-0-486-44812-1(6))* Dover Pubns., Inc.

—Color Your Own Great Fairy Tale Illustrations. 2008. (Dover Art Coloring Book Ser.). (ENG., Illus.). 32p. (gr. 3-5). pap. 4.99 *(978-0-486-46788-7(0))* Dover Pubns., Inc.

—Color Your Own Great Flower Paintings. 2004. (Dover Art Coloring Book Ser.). (ENG., Illus.). 32p. (gr. 3-8). pap., spiral bd. 4.99 *(978-0-486-43335-6(8))* Dover Pubns., Inc.

—Color Your Own Poster Masterpieces. 2008. (Dover Art Coloring Book Ser.). (ENG.). 32p. (gr. 3-8). pap. 4.99 *(978-0-486-45680-5(3))* Dover Pubns., Inc.

—Creative Haven Incredible Insect Designs Coloring Book. 2014. (Adult Coloring Ser.). (ENG., Illus.). 64p. (gr. 3). pap. 5.99 *(978-0-486-49499-9(3))* Dover Pubns., Inc.

—Creative Haven Mandalas Stained Glass Coloring Book. 2014. (Adult Coloring Ser.). (ENG., Illus.). 32p. (gr. 6). pap. 7.99 *(978-0-486-79602-4(7))* Dover Pubns., Inc.

—Creative Haven Mexican Folk Art Coloring Book. 2014. (Adult Coloring Ser.). (ENG.). 64p. (gr. 3). pap. 5.99 *(978-0-486-49451-7(9))* Dover Pubns., Inc.

—Creative Haven Paisley Designs Stained Glass Coloring Book. 2014. (Adult Coloring Ser.). (ENG., Illus.). 32p. (gr. 3). pap. 7.99 *(978-0-486-79830-1(5))* Dover Pubns., Inc.

—Creative Haven Tibetan Designs Coloring Book. 2013. (Adult Coloring Ser.). (ENG.). 64p. (gr. 3). pap. 5.99 *(978-0-486-49449-4(7))* Dover Pubns., Inc.

—Creative Haven Wild Horses Stained Glass Coloring Book. 2014. (Adult Coloring Ser.). (ENG., Illus.). 32p. (gr. 3). pap. 7.99 *(978-0-486-79828-8(3))* Dover Pubns., Inc.

—Decorative Tile Designs. 2006. (Dover Design Coloring Bks.). (ENG., Illus.). 32p. (gr. 3-8). 3.99 *(978-0-486-45195-4(X))* Dover Pubns., Inc.

—Dover Masterworks: Color Your Own American Folk Art Paintings. 2014. (Adult Coloring Ser.). (ENG.). 64p. (gr. 3). pap. 5.99 *(978-0-486-77939-3(4))* Dover Pubns., Inc.

—Fairy Babies Stained Glass Coloring Book. 2006. (Dover Stained Glass Coloring Book Ser.). (ENG., Illus.). 8p. (J). (gr. -1-5). 1.50 *(978-0-486-44916-6(5))* Dover Pubns., Inc.

—Fairy Princesses Stained Glass Coloring Book. 2003. (Dover Stained Glass Coloring Book Ser.). (ENG., Illus.). 8p. (J). (gr. 1-4). pap. 1.99 *(978-0-486-43001-0(4))* Dover Pubns., Inc.

—Famous Fairy Tales Coloring Book. 2013. (Dover Coloring Bks.). (ENG.). 32p. (gr. -1-8). pap. 3.99 *(978-0-486-49707-5(0))* Dover Pubns., Inc.

—Floral Mandalas Stained Glass Coloring Book. 2011. (Dover Design Stained Glass Coloring Book Ser.). (ENG., Illus.). 32p. (gr. 3-5). pap. 7.99 *(978-0-486-48312-2(6))* Dover Pubns., Inc.

—Garden Flowers Stained Glass Coloring Book. 2003. (Dover Stained Glass Coloring Book Ser.). (ENG., Illus.). 8p. (J). (gr. 1-4). pap. 1.99 *(978-0-486-42618-1(1))* Dover Pubns., Inc.

—Goddesses Coloring Book. 2012. (Dover Coloring Bks.). (ENG.). 32p. (gr. 6-8). pap. 3.99 *(978-0-486-48028-2(3))* Dover Pubns., Inc.

—Heart Mandalas Coloring Book. 2013. (ENG.). 32p. (gr. 3-12). pap. 3.99 *(978-0-486-49219-3(2))* Dover Pubns., Inc.

—Impressionist Art. 2009. (Dover Stained Glass Coloring Book Ser.). (ENG., Illus.). 32p. (gr. 6-8). pap. 6.99 *(978-0-486-46538-8(1))* Dover Pubns., Inc.

—Japanese Designs Stained Glass Coloring Book. 2006. (Dover Design Stained Glass Coloring Book Ser.). (ENG., Illus.). 16p. (gr. 6-8). 6.99 *(978-0-486-45175-6(5))* Dover Pubns., Inc.

—Little Dancers. 2005. (Dover Stained Glass Coloring Book Ser.). (ENG., Illus.). 8p. (J). (gr. -1-5). 1.50 *(978-0-486-44494-9(5))* Dover Pubns., Inc.

—Mandalas GemGlow Stained Glass Coloring Book. 2010. (Dover Design Stained Glass Coloring Book Ser.). (ENG., Illus.). 32p. (J). (gr. 1-5). pap. 7.99 *(978-0-486-47478-6(X))* Dover Pubns., Inc.

—Medieval Tapestries Coloring Book. 2004. (Dover Fashion Coloring Book Ser.). (ENG., Illus.). 32p. (gr. 6-8). pap. 3.99 *(978-0-486-43686-9(1))* Dover Pubns., Inc.

—Mexican Designs Stained Glass Coloring Book. 2012. (Dover Stained Glass Coloring Book Ser.). (ENG., Illus.). 32p. (gr. 3-5). pap. 6.99 *(978-0-486-49008-3(4))* Dover Pubns., Inc.

—Nativity Stained Glass Coloring Book. 2004. (Holiday Stained Glass Coloring Book Ser.). (ENG., Illus.). 32p. (J). (gr. -1-5). pap. 7.99 *(978-0-486-43527-5(X))* Dover Pubns., Inc.

—Paisley Designs Coloring Book. 2008. (Dover Design Coloring Bks.). (ENG., Illus.). 32p. (gr. 3-8). 3.99 *(978-0-486-45642-3(0))* Dover Pubns., Inc.

—Vampires Coloring Book. 2010. (Dover Coloring Bks.). (ENG., Illus.). 32p. (gr. 6-8). pap. 3.99 *(978-0-486-47848-7(3))* Dover Pubns., Inc.

—Wild Cards Stained Glass Coloring Book. 2010. (Dover Stained Glass Coloring Book Ser.). (ENG., Illus.). 32p. (gr. 3-8). pap. 6.99 *(978-0-486-47451-9(8))* Dover Pubns., Inc.

—3-D Coloring Book — Horses. 2014. (Dover 3-D Coloring Book Ser.). (ENG., Illus.). 32p. (J). (gr. 2). pap. 5.99 *(978-0-486-49474-6(8))* Dover Pubns., Inc.

—3-D Coloring Book — Mystic Mandalas. 2011. (Dover 3-D Coloring Book Ser.). (ENG., Illus.). 32p. (J). (gr. 3-5). pap. 5.99 *(978-0-486-48102-9(6))* Dover Pubns., Inc.

—3-D Coloring Book — Paisley Designs. 2014. (Dover 3-D Coloring Book Ser.). (ENG., Illus.). 32p. (J). (gr. 6-8). pap. 5.99 *(978-0-486-48427-3(0))* Dover Pubns., Inc.

Noble, Marty & Coloring Books for Adults. Ancient Mexican Designs. 2004. (Dover Design Coloring Bks.). (ENG., Illus.). 32p. (J). (gr. 6-8). pap. 3.99 *(978-0-486-43633-3(0))* Dover Pubns., Inc.

Noble, Marty & Coloring Books Staff. Day of the Dead (Dia de los Muertos) 2011. (Dover Stained Glass Coloring Book Ser.). (ENG., Illus.). 32p. (gr. 3-8). pap. 6.99 *(978-0-486-48033-6(X))* Dover Pubns., Inc.

Noble, Marty & Creative Haven. Creative Haven African Designs Coloring Book. 2013. (Adult Coloring Ser.). (ENG., Illus.). 64p. (gr. 3). pap. 5.99 *(978-0-486-49309-1(1))* Dover Pubns., Inc.

Noble, Marty & Creative Haven Staff. Creative Haven Day of the Dead Coloring Book. 2013. (Adult Coloring Ser.). (ENG., Illus.). 64p. (gr. 3). pap. 5.99 *(978-0-486-49213-1(3))* Dover Pubns., Inc.

—Steampunk Designs. 2013. (Adult Coloring Ser.). (ENG., Illus.). 64p. (gr. 3). pap. 5.99 *(978-0-486-49919-2(7))* Dover Pubns., Inc.

Noble, Marty & Da Vinci, Leonardo. Leonardo Da Vinci Stained Glass. 2006. (Dover Stained Glass Coloring Book Ser.). (ENG., Illus.). 32p. (gr. 3-8). 6.99 *(978-0-486-45059-9(7))* Dover Pubns., Inc.

Noble, Marty & Dover, A. T. Impressionist Art Masterpieces to Color: 60 Great Paintings from Renoir to Gauguin. 2007. (Dover Art Coloring Book Ser.). (ENG., Illus.). 128p. (gr. 6-8). per. 9.95 *(978-0-486-45135-0(6))* Dover Pubns., Inc.

Noble, Marty, et al. Mosaic Masterpieces. 2012. (Adult Coloring Ser.). (ENG., Illus.). 64p. (gr. 3). pap. 5.99 *(978-0-486-49748-8(8))* Dover Pubns., Inc.

Noe, Ida, et al. Zendoodle Color-By-Number: Sea Life: Underwater Worlds to Color & Display. 2017. (ENG., Illus.). 128p. pap. 13.99 ***(978-1-250-14074-6(9)**, 9781250140746*, St. Martin's Griffin) St. Martin's Pr.

Nosy Crow Staff. The Coloring Book of Cards & Envelopes: a Year of Celebrations. Jones, Rebecca, illus. 2017. (ENG.). 74p. (J). (gr. k-12). pap. 15.99 *(978-0-7636-9529-3(7)*, Nosy Crow) Candlewick Pr.

—The Coloring Book of Cards & Envelopes: Flowers & Butterflies. Jones, Rebecca, illus. 2016. (ENG.). 74p. (J). (gr. k-12). pap. 10.99 *(978-0-7636-9244-5(1)*, Nosy Crow) Candlewick Pr.

—The Coloring Book of Cards & Envelopes: Nature. Jones, Rebecca, illus. 2016. (ENG.). 74p. (J). (gr. k-12). pap. 10.99 *(978-0-7636-9245-2(X)*, Nosy Crow) Candlewick Pr.

—The Coloring Book of Cards & Envelopes: Summertime. Jones, Rebecca, illus. 2017. (ENG.). 74p. (J). (gr. k-12). pap. 10.99 *(978-0-7636-9340-4(5)*, Nosy Crow) Candlewick Pr.

Notarfrancesco, Lisa Christiano & Padovano, Chris. Catherine the Caterpillar & Friends Coloring Book: A Children's Guide to Autism. 2014. (ENG.). 72p. pap. 1.95 *(978-1-63443-539-0(7))* Primedia eLaunch LLC.

O'Brien, Joan. Christmas Around the World Coloring Book. 2003. (Dover Holiday Coloring Book Ser.). (ENG., Illus.). 32p. (J). (gr. -1-5). pap. 3.99 *(978-0-486-42651-8(3))* Dover Pubns., Inc.

O'Connor, Jane. Express Yourself! A Doodle & Draw Book. Glasser, Robin Preiss, illus. 2011. (Fancy Nancy Ser.). (ENG.). 64p. (J). (gr. -1-3). pap. 6.99 *(978-0-06-188281-4(X)*, HarperFestival) HarperCollins Pubs.

—Fashionista. Glasser, Robin Preiss, illus. 2011. (Fancy Nancy Ser.). (ENG.). 32p. (J). (gr. -1-3). pap., act. bk. ed. 4.99 *(978-0-06-188266-1(6)*, HarperFestival) HarperCollins Pubs.

Oliveri, Lisa L. The Last Pacifier. Fisher, Marianne, illus. 2013. 36p. pap. 24.95 *(978-1-62709-860-1(7))* America Star Bks.

Olson, Marie. Tlingit Coloring Book. 24p. (J). pap. 6.00 *(978-1-57833-051-5(3))* Todd Communications.

Olszewski, Raymond VanCe. Chucky the Car: A Children's Story & Coloring Book. 2010. (Illus.). 20p. 12.95 *(978-1-4490-6821-9(9))* AuthorHouse.

One Hundred Color & Activity Book: Tom & Jerry. 56p. (J). (gr. -1-3). pap. *(978-1-57041-000-0(3))* Rose Art Industries, Inc.

One Starry Night Coloring & Activity. 2005. mass mkt. 2.25 *(978-1-59317-006-6(8))* Warner Pr., Inc.

O'Neil, Patrick. Washington Farm-Toons Coloring & Activity Book. Pastars, Chris, illus. 2nd ed. 2003. (J). *(978-0-9742610-0-3(9))* Applied Database Technology, Inc.

Orange. 2004. (Illus.). 10p. (J). 3.99 *(978-1-85997-885-6(1))* Byeway Bks.

O'Toole, Patrick & Coloring Books Staff. Alphabetimals Coloring Book. 2012. (Dover Coloring Bks.). (ENG.). 32p. (J). (gr. -1-2). pap. 3.99 *(978-0-486-48700-7(8))* Dover Pubns., Inc.

The Outdoor Youth Adventures Bass Fishing Coloring Book. 2003. (J). pap. *(978-0-9745863-4-2(X))* Cypress Knees Publishing.

The Outdoor Youth Adventures Freshwater Fishing Coloring & Activity Book. 2004. (J). pap. *(978-0-9745863-7-3(4))* Cypress Knees Publishing.

The Outdoor Youth Adventures Saltwater Fishing Activity & Coloring Book. 2003. (J). pap. *(978-0-9745863-2-8(3))* Cypress Knees Publishing.

The Outdoor Youth Adventures Trout Fishing Activity & Coloring Book. 2003. (J). pap. *(978-0-9745863-5-9(8))* Cypress Knees Publishing.

The Outdoor Youth Adventures Young Hunter's Coloring Book. 2004. (J). pap. *(978-0-9745863-6-6(6))* Cypress Knees Publishing.

Oye! (SPA.). (J). 2.95 *(978-958-607-884-9(1))* Sociedad de San Pablo ESP. Dist: St Pauls/Alba Hse. Pubs.

Ozten the NonDogmatic Artist, Ozten. Understanding Terror: A Fun-Filled Coloring & Activity Book. 2004. 5.00 *(978-0-9752966-0-8(4))* Ozten.

Pacileo, Cindy, creator. The Virtues Activity & Coloring Book, Ages 5-7. 2005. (J). 4.50 *(978-0-9741930-0-7(3))* Changing-Times.net.

—The Virtues Activity & Coloring Book, Ages 8-10. 2005. (J). 4.50 *(978-0-9741930-1-4(1))* Changing-Times.net.

Paddock, Susan Star. I Want to Be a Christian: The Story of Blessed Kateri Tekakwitha. Jaurequi, Leticia & Gomez, Elisa, trs. Matheny, Jean Sherlock, illus. 2004. (J). *(978-0-9747571-8-6(7))* Catholic World Mission.

Page, Terry. The Fathers of the Friendly Forest Coloring Book. Page, Terry, illus. (Illus.). 32p. (J). (gr. -1-5). pap. 3.00 *(978-1-887864-39-8(3))* Boo Bks., Inc.

—The Saddest Centaur Coloring Book. Page, Terry, illus. (Illus.). 32p. (J). (gr. -1-5). pap. 3.00 *(978-1-887864-37-4(7))* Boo Bks., Inc.

Pain, Catherine. Alphabet for Colouring In. 2008. 112p. pap. 16.95 *(978-1-4092-1024-5(3))* Lulu Pr., Inc.

Panian, Angie & Panian, Tyler. Creature Clash! Mix & Match Coloring Book. 2014. (ENG., Illus.). 64p. (J). (gr. 1-4). pap. 12.99 *(978-1-4521-1267-1(3))* Chronicle Bks. LLC.

Paolini, Christopher. The Official Eragon Coloring Book. Ciruelo, illus. 2017. (Inheritance Cycle Ser.). (ENG.). 96p. (J). (gr. 7-12). pap. 15.99 ***(978-1-5247-1874-9(2)**,* Knopf Bks. for Young Readers) Random Hse. Children's Bks.

Paprocki, Beth. Storyland: the Marvelous Mcrittersons — Road Trip to Grandma's: A Story Coloring Book. Paprocki, Greg, illus. 2015. (ENG.). 32p. (J). (gr. k-5). pap. 3.99 *(978-0-486-79383-2(4))* Dover Pubns., Inc.

Paradis, Anne. Caillou: the Little Christmas Artist. Sévigny, Eric, illus. 2013. (Coloring & Activity Book Ser.). (ENG.). 64p. (J). (gr. -1-1). 8.99 *(978-2-89718-065-2(X))* Caillouet, Gerry.

Parks, Carmen. Farmers Market/Día de Mercado. Flor Ada, Alma & Campoy, F. Isabel, trs. from ENG. Martinez, Edward, illus. 2010. (Green Light Readers Level 2 Ser.). (SPA & ENG.). 28p. (J). (gr. -1-3). pap. 3.99 *(978-0-547-36900-6(X))* Houghton Mifflin Harcourt Publishing Co.

Parr, Todd. Todd Parr Create Your Own Planet. 2010. (ENG.). 240p. (J). (gr. -1-4). 14.99 *(978-0-8118-7146-4(0))* Chronicle Bks. LLC.

Parr, Todd & Chronicle Books Staff. Save the Blue. 2009. (ENG.). 160p. (J). (gr. -1-3). 9.99 *(978-0-8118-7153-2(3))* Chronicle Bks. LLC.

Parrish, Fayrene. Pancho Saves the Day: Shipmates Learning Adventures Venture. Parrish, Fayrene, illus. 2010. (Illus.). 42p. (J). 15.95 *(978-0-9826717-8-8(4))* Parrish, Fayrene.

Patterson, Maurice. Children's Computer Learning Cartoon Coloring Book. 2003. spiral bd. 10.95 *(978-1-932257-21-2(7))* Network CPU Learning Technologies.

Pauba, Judy. A Tale of Two Dogs. 2006. (Illus.). 32p. (J). per. 5.95 *(978-0-9747994-1-4(6))* Julenda Enterprises.

PC Treasures Staff, ed. Barney's Giant Coloring & Activity Book. 2009. (ENG., Illus.). 384p. (J). pap. 3.99 *(978-1-60072-220-2(2))* PC Treasures, Inc.

—Dale Earnhardt Jr. 2009. (Nascar Drivers Coloring Book Ser.). (ENG., Illus.). 96p. (J). 2.99 *(978-1-60072-150-2(8))*; 6.95 *(978-1-60072-163-2(X))* PC Treasures, Inc.

—Jeff Gordon. 2009. (Nascar Drivers Coloring Book Ser.). (ENG., Illus.). 96p. (J). 2.99 *(978-1-60072-151-9(6))* PC Treasures, Inc.

—Jimmie Johnson. 2009. (Nascar Drivers Coloring Book Ser.). (ENG., Illus.). 96p. (J). pap. 2.99 *(978-1-60072-152-6(4))*; Vol. 48. 6.95 *(978-1-60072-161-8(3))* PC Treasures, Inc.

—Kyle Busch. 2010. (Nascar Drivers Coloring/Sticker Book Ser.). (ENG., Illus.). 96p. (J). 6.95 *(978-1-60072-165-6(6))* PC Treasures, Inc.

—Tony Stewart. 2009. (Nascar Drivers Coloring Book Ser.). (ENG., Illus.). 96p. (J). pap. 2.99 *(978-1-60072-160-1(5))* PC Treasures, Inc.

Pearl, Michael & Bulanadi, Danny. Good & Evil Pt. 2: Abraham, Pt. 2. 2007. (ENG., Illus.). 12p. (J). pap. 2.99 *(978-0-9786372-5-5(9))* No Greater Joy Ministries, Inc.

Pearlstein, Don. Make Your Own Laptop: Color & Build Your Own Computer! Stillerman, Robbie, illus. 2011. (Dover Children's Activity Bks.). (ENG.). 24p. (J). (gr. k-3). pap. 9.99 *(978-0-486-48532-4(3))* Dover Pubns., Inc.

Peel, Yana. Color for Baby. 2014. (ENG.). (J). (gr. k — 1). bds. 21.99 *(978-0-7636-7124-2(X)*, Big Picture Press) Candlewick Pr.

Penix, Sherry. San Diego Activity & Coloring Book for All Ages. Berman, Linda, illus. Date not set. (J). pap. *(978-0-9670612-0-7(2))*; pap. *(978-0-9670612-1-4(0))* Sher-A-Craft.

Penrod. Indiana Coloring Book. 2005. pap. *(978-1-893624-40-5(4))* Penrod/Hiawatha Co.

—Ohio Coloring Book. 2005. pap. *(978-1-893624-41-2(2))* Penrod/Hiawatha Co.

Perlow, Janet, illus. Show Dog Coloring Book. 2007. 40p. (J). pap. 4.95 *(978-0-9795049-1-4(0))* Kidz Entertainment, Inc.

Peter Pauper Press, Inc., creator. Rosie & Crayon. 2017. (ENG.). 34p. (J). 16.99 ***(978-1-4413-2287-6(6))*** Peter Pauper Pr. Inc.

Petruccio, Steven. At the Construction Site (en el Sitio de Construccion) Gongora, Oscar, tr. 2011. (Dover Children's Bilingual Coloring Book Ser.). (ENG & SPA., Illus.). 32p. (J). (gr. k-6). pap. 3.99 *(978-0-486-46368-1(0))* Dover Pubns., Inc.

Petruccio, Steven James. American Heroes Coloring Book. 2013. (ENG.). 48p. (J). (gr. 3-6). pap. 4.99 *(978-0-486-49895-9(6))* Dover Pubns., Inc.

—American Legends & Tall Tales. 2011. (Dover Classic Stories Coloring Book Ser.). (ENG., Illus.). 32p. (J). (gr. 3-6). pap. 3.99 *(978-0-486-47786-2(X))* Dover Pubns., Inc.

—BOOST Trucks Coloring Book. 2013. (BOOST Educational Ser.). (ENG.). 32p. (J). (gr. 1-2). pap. 4.99 *(978-0-486-49411-1(X))* Dover Pubns., Inc.

—History of the Civil Rights Movement Coloring Book. 2011. (Dover History Coloring Book Ser.). (ENG., Illus.). 32p. (gr. 3-5). pap. 3.99 *(978-0-486-47846-3(7))* Dover Pubns., Inc.

—The History of the White House Coloring Book. 2010. (Dover History Coloring Book Ser.). (ENG.). 32p. (gr. 3-5). pap. 3.99 *(978-0-486-47556-1(5))* Dover Pubns., Inc.

—Let's Build a House! Coloring Book. 2017. (Dover Coloring Bks.). (ENG.). 32p. (J). (gr. 1-4). pap. 3.99 *(978-0-486-81213-7(8))* Dover Pubns., Inc.

—Rodeo Coloring Book. 2004. (Dover History Coloring Book Ser.). (ENG., Illus.). 32p. (J). (gr. -1-2). pap. 3.99 *(978-0-486-43330-1(7))* Dover Pubns., Inc.

Petruccio, Steven James & Coloring Books Staff. Roadside Attractions Coloring Book: Weird & Wacky Landmarks from Across the USA! 2012. (Dover Coloring Bks.). (ENG., Illus.). 32p. (gr. 3-5). pap. 3.99 *(978-0-486-48695-6(8))* Dover Pubns., Inc.

Pfeil, Susan. Professor Kiwi, Explorer of the Seven Seas: The Eye of Easter Island. 2005. (J). per. 6.95 *(978-1-59094-062-4(8))* Jawbone Publishing Corp.

Pfister, Marcus. Rainbow Fish Deep Sea Adventure Sticker & Coloring Storybook. 2010. (Rainbow Fish Ser.). (ENG.). 24p. (gr. -1-2). 5.95 *(978-0-7358-2318-1(9))* North-South Bks., Inc.

Phillips, Dee & Ticktock Media, Ltd. Staff. What Do Cats Do? 2009. (What Do Animals Do? Ser.). (ENG.). 5p. (J). (gr. k — 1). bds. 4.95 *(978-1-84696-958-4(1)*, TickTock Books) Octopus Publishing Group GBR. Dist: Independent Pubs. Group.

—What Do Kangaroos Do? 2009. (What Do Animals Do? Ser.). (ENG.). 5p. (J). (gr. k — 1). bds. 4.95 *(978-1-84696-959-1(X)*, TickTock Books) Octopus Publishing Group GBR. Dist: Independent Pubs. Group.

—What Do Monkeys Do? 2009. (What Do Animals Do? Ser.). (ENG.). 5p. (J). (gr. k — 1). bds. 4.95 *(978-1-84696-960-7(3)*, TickTock Books) Octopus Publishing Group GBR. Dist: Independent Pubs. Group.

—What Do Rabbits Do? 2009. (What Do Animals Do? Ser.). (ENG.). 5p. (J). (gr. k — 1). bds. 4.95 *(978-1-84696-961-4(1)*, TickTock Books) Octopus Publishing Group GBR. Dist: Independent Pubs. Group.

Phillips, Jillian & Kurtz, John. Our Five Senses Coloring Book. 2014. (ENG.). 160p. (J). (gr. -1-3). pap. 5.99 *(978-0-486-77966-9(1))* Dover Pubns., Inc.

A Picture & A Promise: Coloring Book. 2003. (J). spiral bd. *(978-0-9706684-6-2(5))* Cortright Fellowship Pr.

Pierce, Terry. Coral Reefs A to Z Coloring Book. Kofsky, Kristen, illus. 2003. 32p. 4.95 *(978-1-57306-122-3(0))* Bess Pr., Inc.

—Surfing A to Z Coloring Book. Kofsky, Kristen, illus. 2004. 24p. pap. 4.95 *(978-1-57306-178-0(6))* Bess Pr., Inc.

—Volcanoes A to Z Coloring Book. Villalobos, Ethel M., illus. 2003. 24p. pap. 4.95 *(978-1-57306-123-0(9))* Bess Pr., Inc.

Pierce, Terry & Kofsky, Kristen. Dangerous Sea Creatures A to Z Coloring Book. 2004. (Illus.). 24p. pap. 4.95 *(978-1-57306-177-3(8))* Bess Pr., Inc.

Pingry, Patricia A. America the Beautiful: A Patriotic Coloring Book. 2005. (ENG.). 46p. (J). pap. 4.35 *(978-0-8249-5504-5(8)*, Ideal Pubns.) Worthy Publishing.

Platten, Carl. Once upon a Dragon: A Colouring Book. 2012. 48p. 24.99 *(978-1-4691-9369-4(8))*; pap. 15.99 *(978-1-4691-9368-7(X))* Xlibris Corp.

Poison Patrol: Coloring/Activity Book (English) 2005. (Illus.). (J). 2.99 *(978-1-933934-01-3(8))* Mighty Kids Media.

Poison Patrol: Coloring/Activity (English) Incl. Posters, Stickers. 2007. (J). 2.99 *(978-1-933934-53-2(0))* Mighty Kids Media.

Pomaska, Anna. BOOST Dinosaurs Coloring Book. 2013. (BOOST Educational Ser.). (ENG.). 32p. (J). (gr. 1-2). pap. 4.99 *(978-0-486-49415-9(2))* Dover Pubns., Inc.

—Mandalas Coloring Book. 2014. (ENG.). 64p. (J). (gr. -1-3). pap. 3.99 *(978-0-486-77959-1(9))* Dover Pubns., Inc.

—My First Geometric Designs Coloring Book. 2010. (Dover Coloring Bks.). (ENG., Illus.). 32p. (J). (gr. -1-2). pap. 3.99 *(978-0-486-47557-8(3))* Dover Pubns., Inc.

—My First Mandalas - Animals. 2010. (Dover Coloring Bks.). (ENG., Illus.). 32p. (J). (gr. -1-2). pap. 3.99 *(978-0-486-47558-5(1))* Dover Pubns., Inc.

—My First Mandalas Coloring Book. 2008. (Dover Coloring Bks.). (ENG., Illus.). 32p. (J). (gr. -1-2). 3.99 *(978-0-486-46556-2(X))* Dover Pubns., Inc.

—Same & Different. 2007. (Dover Coloring Bks.). (ENG., Illus.). 32p. (J). (gr. k-3). pap. 3.99 *(978-0-486-46107-6(6))* Dover Pubns., Inc.

—3-D Coloring Book — My First Animal Mandalas. 2011. (Dover 3-D Coloring Book Ser.). (ENG., Illus.). 32p. (J). (gr. -1-2). pap. 5.99 *(978-0-486-48103-6(4))* Dover Pubns., Inc.

—3-D Coloring Book — My First Geometric Designs. 2011. (Dover 3-D Coloring Book Ser.). (ENG., Illus.). 32p. (J). (gr. -1-2). pap. 5.99 *(978-0-486-48110-4(7))* Dover Pubns., Inc.

Pomaska, Anna & Coloring Books Staff. My First Mandalas - Nature. 2012. (Dover Coloring Bks.). (ENG., Illus.). 32p. (J). (gr. -1-3). pap. 3.99 *(978-0-486-48708-3(3))* Dover Pubns., Inc.

Pope, Miller. ABC-Pirate-Coloring Book. 2012. (ENG.). (J). pap. 5.99 *(978-1-4507-8603-4(0))* Independent Pub.

Porter, Angela. Forever Inspired: Angela Porter's Tropical Rainforest Hidden Pictures. 2017. (ENG., Illus.). 96p. (J). (gr. 3-7). pap. 7.99 *(978-1-944686-54-3(1)*, Racehorse Publishing) Skyhorse Publishing Co., Inc.

Potter, Beatrix. Peter Rabbit Rainbow Shapes & Colors. Potter, Beatrix, illus. 2006. (Peter Rabbit Seedlings Ser.). (ENG., Illus.). 10p. (J). (gr. k-18). bds. 5.99 *(978-0-7232-5722-6(1)*, Puffin) Penguin Publishing Group.

Power Block Kids/Cabritos Del Bloque De Energia. 2005. 64p. (J). pap. *(978-0-9762071-4-6(1)*, 371-008) Big City Publishing.

Prechtel, Jeff. Mountain Men — the History of Fur Trapping Coloring Book. 2015. (Dover History Coloring Book Ser.). (ENG.). 30p. (J). (gr. 3-6). pap. 3.99 *(978-0-486-79968-1(9))* Dover Pubns., Inc.

Prestel. Botticelli: Coloring Book, 1 vol. 2016. (ENG.). 32p. (J). (gr. 1-4). pap. 8.95 *(978-3-7913-7227-3(0))* Prestel Verlag GmbH & Co KG. DEU. Dist: Penguin Random Hse. LLC.

Prestel, creator. Salvador Dali. 2007. (ENG., Illus.). 32p. (J). (gr. 1-4). 8.95 *(978-3-7913-3888-0(9))* Prestel Verlag GmbH & Co KG. DEU. Dist: Penguin Random Hse. LLC.

Prestel, ed. Coloring Book: Great Artists. 2012. (ENG.). 32p. (J). (gr. 1-4). pap. 8.95 *(978-3-7913-7089-7(8))* Prestel Verlag GmbH & Co KG. DEU. Dist: Penguin Random Hse. LLC.

—Coloring Book: Turner. 2012. (ENG.). 32p. (J). (gr. 1-4). pap. 8.95 *(978-3-7913-7090-3(1))* Prestel Verlag GmbH & Co KG. DEU. Dist: Penguin Random Hse. LLC.

Prestel Publishing. Colouring Book Antoni Gaudi. 2014. (ENG.). 32p. (J). (gr. 1-4). pap. 8.95 *(978-3-7913-7203-7(3))* Prestel Verlag GmbH & Co KG. DEU. Dist: Penguin Random Hse. LLC.

—Roy Lichtenstein: Coloring Book. 2013. (ENG., Illus.). 32p. (J). (gr. 1-4). pap. 8.95 *(978-3-7913-7146-7(0))* Prestel Verlag GmbH & Co KG. DEU. Dist: Penguin Random Hse. LLC.

Prestel Publishing, creator. Edward Hopper Coloring Book. 2007. (ENG., Illus.). 32p. (J). (gr. 1-4). 8.95 *(978-3-7913-3809-5(9))* Prestel Verlag GmbH & Co KG. DEU. Dist: Penguin Random Hse. LLC.

Prestofillipo, Mary Nazarene, tr. The Story of Creation. Flamini, Lorella, illus. 2005. Orig. Title: Piccola storia della Creazione. (ITA.). 36p. (J). pap. 12.95 *(978-0-8198-7093-3(5))* Pauline Bks. & Media.

Priddy, Roger. Dinosaur. 2012. (ENG., Illus.). 36p. (J). (gr. -1-1). pap., act. bk. ed. 4.99 *(978-0-312-51329-0(1)*, 9780312513290, Priddy Bks.) St. Martin's Pr.

Princess Adjepong. My First Shapes & Numbers Colouring Book. 2013. 52p. pap. 27.45 *(978-1-4817-9519-7(8))* AuthorHouse.

Prothero, Tiffany. Let's Go Green! An Earth-Friendly Coloring Book. 2009. (Dover Nature Coloring Book Ser.). (ENG., Illus.). 32p. (J). (gr. -1-2). pap. 3.99 *(978-0-486-46817-4(8))* Dover Pubns., Inc.

Pruett, Mary, illus. Color the Western Birds. 2010. (Pruett Ser.). (ENG.). 32p. (J). pap. 4.99 *(978-0-87108-957-1(2))* Pruett Publishing Co.

Publications International Ltd. Staff, ed. My Colors Book. 2011. 32p. (J). bds. 5.98 *(978-1-4508-1022-7(5))* Publications International, Ltd.

Publishers, Hancock House Publishers. Raptors - Birds of Prey Coloring Book. 2005. (Illus.). 24p. (J). pap. 4.95 *(978-0-88839-600-6(7))* Hancock Hse. Pubs.

—Wildlife Coloring Book. 2004. (Illus.). 24p. (J). pap. 4.95 *(978-0-88839-599-3(X))* Hancock Hse. Pubs.

Publishing, Autumn. I Want to Color BIG Pictures. 2009. 80p. pap. 12.99 *(978-1-60095-389-7(1))* Carson-Dellosa Publishing, LLC.

Publishing, Racehorse & Grahame, Kenneth. Classics to Color: the Wind in the Willows. 2016. (ENG., Illus.). 80p. (J). (gr. 1-6). pap. 8.99 *(978-1-63158-114-4(7)*, Racehorse Publishing) Skyhorse Publishing Co., Inc.

Pyle, Robert Michael & Peterson, Roger Tory. Butterflies. Peterson, Roger Tory, ed. Hughes, Sarah Anne, illus. 2nd ed. 2013. (Peterson Field Guide Color-In Bks.). (ENG.). 64p. (J). 8.95 *(978-0-544-03339-9(6))* Houghton Mifflin Harcourt Publishing Co.

R, J. Ff: The Weedy Sea Dragon Coloring Book (Standard Version) 2013. 38p. (J). pap. 9.95 *(978-1-935734-53-6(9))* Kitanie Bks.

Rabe, Tish. Wings & Paws & Fins & Claws. Ruiz, Aristides, illus. 2010. (Deluxe Coloring Book Ser.). (ENG.). 96p. (J). (gr. -1-2). pap. 3.99 *(978-0-375-85928-1(4)*, Golden Bks.) Random Hse. Children's Bks.

Radtke, Becky. At the State Fair Coloring Book. 2004. (Dover Coloring Bks.). (ENG., Illus.). 32p. (J). (gr. -1-2). pap. 2.95 *(978-0-486-43339-4(0))* Dover Pubns., Inc.

Radtke, Becky J. Christmas Color by Number. 2015. (Dover Children's Activity Bks.). (ENG.). 32p. (J). (gr. -1-2). pap. 3.99 *(978-0-486-80051-6(2))* Dover Pubns., Inc.

—Halloween Color by Number. 2017. (Dover Children's Activity Bks.). (ENG.). 32p. (J). (gr. -1-2). pap. 3.99 *(978-0-486-81216-8(2))* Dover Pubns., Inc.

Rainbow Publishers Staff. Coloring Plus Activities: Jesus Our Lord & Savior. 2004. (Illus.). 64p. (J). (gr. -1-3). pap. 9.95 *(978-0-937282-17-5(0)*, RB37162) Rainbow Pubs. & Legacy Pr.

—Coloring Plus Activities: Living the Christian Life. 2004. (Illus.). 64p. (J). (gr. -1-3). pap. 9.95 *(978-0-937282-18-2(9)*, RB37166) Rainbow Pubs. & Legacy Pr.

Rakos, Lynnda. Let's Color Together — Princesses, Mermaids & Fairies. 2014. (ENG., Illus.). 64p. (J). (gr. -1-3). pap. 3.99 *(978-0-486-77976-8(9))* Dover Pubns., Inc.

—Let's Color Together — Robots. 2014. (ENG., Illus.). 64p. (J). (gr. -1-3). pap. 3.99 *(978-0-486-77977-5(7))* Dover Pubns., Inc.

Rakos, Lynnda, et al. Princesses, Mermaids & Fairies Coloring Book. 2012. (Dover Coloring Bks.). (ENG.). 32p. (J). (gr. -1-2). pap. 3.99 *(978-0-486-48664-2(8))* Dover Pubns., Inc.

Random House. Dreamworks. Random House, illus. 2017. (Adult Coloring Book Ser.). (ENG., Illus.). 96p. (J). (gr. k-12). pap. 14.99 ***(978-1-5247-6879-9(0)***, Random Hse. Bks. for Young Readers) Random Hse. Children's Bks.

Random House. Holiday Helpers! (PAW Patrol) Random House, illus. 2016. (Pictureback(R) Ser.). (ENG., Illus.). 24p. (J). (gr. -1-2). pap. 5.99 *(978-0-399-55874-0(8)*, Random Hse. Bks. for Young Readers) Random Hse. Children's Bks.

Random House Disney Staff. A Christmas Carol: a Coloring Classic. Aleksic, Vladimir & Ware, Kate, illus. 2016. (ENG.). 80p. (gr. k-12). pap. 15.99 *(978-1-5247-1319-5(8)*, Doubleday Bks. for Young Readers) Random Hse. Children's Bks.

Rao, Lisa. Surf's Up. Merkel, Joe F. & Sazaklis, John, illus. 2007. (Surf's Up Ser.). 32p. (J). (gr. -1-2). 4.99 *(978-0-06-115335-8(4)*, Harper Entertainment) HarperCollins Pubs.

Rea, Monique F. Toulouse the Moose Coloring Book. 2007. (J). *(978-0-9788926-3-0(1))* Trails of Discovery.

Read & Color Book Series. Date not set. (Illus.). (J). (gr. -1-5). pap. *(978-0-86545-223-7(7))* Spizzirri Pr., Inc.

The Really Big Butterfly Coloring Book ' A Teaching & Learning Tool. 2004. Orig. Title: Same. (J). per. 7.95 *(978-0-9729753-2-2(2))* Really Big Coloring Bks., Inc.

The Realtree Deer Hunting Activity & Coloring Book. 2003. (J). pap. *(978-0-9745863-1-1(5))* Cypress Knees Publishing.

The Realtree Hunting Coloring Book. 2003. (J). pap. *(978-0-9745863-3-5(1))* Cypress Knees Publishing.

Rechlin, Ted. ComicQuest TIME TRAVEL TROUBLE. 2013. (Dover Children's Activity Bks.). (ENG.). 48p. (J). (gr. 3-8). pap. 4.99 *(978-0-486-49949-9(9))* Dover Pubns., Inc.

—Superheroes Stained Glass Coloring Book. 2012. (Dover Stained Glass Coloring Book Ser.). (ENG., Illus.). 32p. (J). (gr. 2-5). pap. 6.99 *(978-0-486-49036-6(X))* Dover Pubns., Inc.

Rechlin, Ted & Coloring Books Staff. Build a Poster Coloring Book — Robots & Wreckage. 2012. (Dover Build a Poster Coloring Book Ser.). (ENG.). 48p. (J). (gr. 3-5). pap. 4.99 *(978-0-486-48646-8(X))* Dover Pubns., Inc.

Reidy, Hannah. Crazy Creature Colors. Mackie, Clare, illus. 2003. (Crazy Creatures Ser.). 26p. (J). pap. *(978-1-84089-221-5(8))* Zero to Ten, Ltd.

Rentfro, Jeanne. Cowboy Country Coloring Book. 2007. (Illus.). (J). per. 5.00 *(978-0-9761128-9-1(2))* KB Bks. & More.

Rey, H. A. Plumber's Helper. Meyer, Emily, ed. 2010. (Curious George Ser.). (ENG., Illus.). 24p. (J). (gr. -1-3). pap. 4.99 *(978-0-547-23589-9(5))* Houghton Mifflin Harcourt Publishing Co.

Rey, H. A. & Rey, Margret. Curious George Super Sticker Coloring Book. 2008. (Curious George Ser.). (ENG., Illus.). 64p. (J). (gr. -1-3). 12.99 *(978-0-618-99877-7(2))* Houghton Mifflin Harcourt Publishing Co.

RH Disney. Taken by Storm/How to Be a Great Racer. RH Disney, illus. 2017. (Pictureback(R) Ser.). (ENG., Illus.). 48p. (J). (gr. -1-2). pap. 5.99 ***(978-0-7364-3727-1(4)***, RH/Disney) Random Hse. Children's Bks.

RH Disney Staff. Monster Hide-and-Seek. RH Disney Staff, illus. 2013. (Glow-In-the-Dark Board Book Ser.). (ENG., Illus.). 12p. (J). (-k). bds. 6.99 *(978-0-7364-3032-6(6)*, Golden/Disney) Random Hse. Children's Bks.

Rhodes, Karen. God's Word Then & Now Activity Book. 2007. (Illus.). 16p. (J). pap. 1.89 *(978-1-59317-207-7(9))* Warner Pr., Inc.

Ricci, Christine & Golden Books Staff. Bug Hunt. Savitsky, Steve et al, illus. 2008. (Color Plus Chunky Crayons Ser.). (ENG.). 48p. (J). (gr. -1-2). pap. 3.99 *(978-0-375-84298-6(5)*, Golden Bks.) Random Hse. Children's Bks.

Rich, J. Milton. Heavenly Fathers Plan of Salvation Coloring Book. Knaupp, Andrew & Koford, Adam, illus. 2003. 108p. (J). per. 7.95 *(978-0-9726670-2-9(4))* Rich Publishing.

Richards, V. H. First Christmas Color Act Bk. 24p. pap. 1.25 *(978-0-8198-2677-0(4)*, 332-096) Pauline Bks. & Media.

Riders in the Sky: Cartoon Cowboy Coloring Book. 2004. (J). *(978-0-9746784-1-2(4))* Great Big Comics, Big Tex Films.

Riordan, Rick. Percy Jackson & the Olympians the Percy Jackson Coloring Book. Robinson, Keith, illus. 2017. (Percy Jackson & the Olympians Ser.). (ENG.). 96p. (J). (gr. 3-7). pap. 15.99 ***(978-1-4847-8779-3(X))*** Hyperion Bks. for Children.

Rivera, Mirabelle. What Is your favorite Color? 2008. 20p. pap. 24.95 *(978-1-4241-8454-5(1))* America Star Bks.

Rivera, Nicole. The Sweet Smell of Freedom (Max's Mini Coloring Book) 2011. (ENG.). 36p. pap. 7.99 *(978-1-4610-7649-0(8))* CreateSpace Independent Publishing Platform.

Rivers-Moore, Debbie. Colin Car: Bath Books That Float. Moulding, Lynne, illus. 2012. (Water Wheels Ser.). (ENG.). 8p. (J). 5.99 *(978-1-4380-7221-0(X))* Barron's Educational Series, Inc.

Robert, Cerny. My Kingdom Pal Adventure Color Activity Book. 2004. (Illus.). 32p. (J). *(978-0-9748251-1-3(5)*, 10000) Zoe Life Publishing.

Roberts, Shelly. Sissy & the Old Crow (Coloring Book) 2006. (Illus.). 36p. (J). per. 6.50 *(978-0-9789798-3-6(4)*, 978-0-9789798-3-6) Blackbird's World Publishing Co.

Robinson, Alise. Shining Stars: A Colors Book. Reich, Carin, illus. 2005. (Space Craze Ser.). 16p. (J). (gr. -1-k). per., bds. 6.95 *(978-1-58117-392-5(X)*, Intervisual/Piggy Toes) Bendon, Inc.

Robinson, Beth. The Safe Family Coloring Book. 2013. (Illus.). 20p. (J). mass mkt. 3.99 *(978-0-9799092-4-5(4))* Robinson, Beth.

Roeder, Annette. The Art Coloring Book. 2012. (ENG.). 128p. (J). (gr. 1-4). pap. 12.95 *(978-3-7913-7108-5(8))* Prestel Verlag GmbH & Co KG. DEU. Dist: Penguin Random Hse. LLC.

Rogers, Kirsteen. Christmas Coloring Book. 2009. (Coloring Bks). 34p. (J). pap. 5.99 *(978-0-7945-2438-8(9)*, Usborne) EDC Publishing.

—Christmas Patterns Coloring Book. 2011. (Coloring Bks). 32p. (J). pap. 5.99 *(978-0-7945-3184-3(9)*, Usborne) EDC Publishing.

—Spooky Coloring Book. 2012. (Coloring Bks). 32p. (J). pap. 5.99 *(978-0-7945-2546-0(6)*, Usborne) EDC Publishing.

Rogers, Kirsteen & Everall, Nayera. Patterns Coloring Book. 2011. (Coloring Books Ser.). 26p. (J). pap. 5.99 *(978-0-7945-2967-3(4)*, Usborne) EDC Publishing.

Romano, Elaine. The Magic Potato - la Papa Magica: Story & coloring book in English & Spanish, 1. Nielsen, Emily, tr. Winchel, Heidi, illus. 2nd ed. 2004. (SPA.). 20p. (J). 3.00 *(978-0-9728225-3-4(4))* Mill Park Publishing.

Rose, Drew, illus. God's Heroes. 2005. (Bible Activity Bks.). 94p. (J). (gr. -1-3). 2.99 *(978-0-7814-4313-5(X)*, 078144313X) Cook, David C.

—God's Son, Jesus. 2005. (Bible Activity Bks.). 94p. (J). (gr. -1-3). 2.99 *(978-0-7814-4314-2(8)*, 0781443148) Cook, David C.

—God's World. 2005. (Bible Activity Bks.). 94p. (J). (gr. -1-3). 2.99 *(978-0-7814-4312-8(1)*, 0781443121) Cook, David C.

Roytman, Arkady. The Adventures of King Arthur Coloring Book. 2013. (ENG., Illus.). 32p. (J). (gr. 3-12). pap. 3.99 *(978-0-486-49829-4(8))* Dover Pubns., Inc.

—Build-a-Window Halloween Stained Glass Coloring Book. 2011. (Build Window Stained Glass Coloring Book Ser.). (ENG., Illus.). 32p. (J). (gr. 3-5). pap. 6.99 *(978-0-486-48391-7(6))* Dover Pubns., Inc.

—Fairy Princess. 2010. (Dover Build a Poster Coloring Book Ser.). (ENG., Illus.). 48p. (J). (gr. 3-5). pap. 4.99 *(978-0-486-47943-9(9))* Dover Pubns., Inc.

—Fantasy Warriors Stained Glass Coloring Book. 2010. (Dover Stained Glass Coloring Book Ser.). (ENG., Illus.). 32p. (J). (gr. 3-5). pap. 6.99 *(978-0-486-47372-7(4))* Dover Pubns., Inc.

—GOAL! the Hockey Coloring Book. 2013. (Dover Coloring Bks.). (ENG.). 32p. (J). (gr. 2-5). pap. 3.99 *(978-0-486-49889-8(1))* Dover Pubns., Inc.

—Greek & Roman Gods Stained Glass Coloring Book. 2009. (Dover Stained Glass Coloring Book Ser.). (ENG., Illus.). 32p. (J). (gr. 2-5). pap. 6.99 *(978-0-486-46995-9(6))* Dover Pubns., Inc.

—Knights & Dragons. 2010. (Dover Build a Poster Coloring Book Ser.). (ENG., Illus.). 48p. (J). (gr. 3-5). pap. 4.99 *(978-0-486-47942-2(0))* Dover Pubns., Inc.

—Maneki Neko Lucky Cat Coloring Book. 2015. (Dover Clip Art Design Tools Ser.). (ENG., Illus.). 32p. (J). (gr. 2-5). pap. 3.99 *(978-0-486-79930-8(1))* Dover Pubns., Inc.

—Martial Arts Coloring Book. 2013. (Dover Coloring Bks.). (ENG., Illus.). 32p. (J). (gr. 3-5). pap. 3.99 *(978-0-486-49023-6(8))* Dover Pubns., Inc.

—Pixelations Coloring Book. 2015. (ENG., Illus.). 32p. (J). (gr. 3-8). pap. 3.99 *(978-0-486-79200-2(5))* Dover Pubns., Inc.

—The Soccer Coloring Book. 2016. (Dover Coloring Bks.). (ENG.). 32p. (J). (gr. 2-5). pap. 3.99 *(978-0-486-80481-1(X))* Dover Pubns., Inc.

—Treasures of King Tut's Tomb Stained Glass Coloring Book. 2009. (Dover Stained Glass Coloring Book Ser.). (ENG., Illus.). 32p. (J). (gr. -1-5). pap. 6.99 *(978-0-486-46996-6(4))* Dover Pubns., Inc.

—Vampire Nights. 2010. (Dover Stained Glass Coloring Book Ser.). (ENG., Illus.). 32p. (J). (gr. 3-5). pap. 6.99 *(978-0-486-47638-4(3))* Dover Pubns., Inc.

—World of Dragons Coloring Book. 2014. (Dover Coloring Bks.). (ENG., Illus.). 32p. (J). (gr. 3-7). pap. 3.99 *(978-0-486-49445-6(4))* Dover Pubns., Inc.

Roytman, Arkady, illus. Extreme Sports. 2008. (Dover Coloring Bks.). (ENG.). 32p. (J). (gr. k-5). pap. 3.99 *(978-0-486-46688-0(4))* Dover Pubns., Inc.

Roytman, Arkady & Coloring Books Staff. Outer Space. 2011. (Build Window Stained Glass Coloring Book Ser.). (ENG., Illus.). 32p. (J). (gr. 3-5). pap. 6.99 *(978-0-486-48392-4(4))* Dover Pubns., Inc.

Roytman, Arkady, et al. Build a Poster Coloring Book — Atlantis. 2012. (Dover Build a Poster Coloring Book Ser.). (ENG., Illus.). 48p. (J). (gr. 3-5). pap. 4.99 *(978-0-486-48644-4(3))* Dover Pubns., Inc.

—Build a Poster Coloring Book — Space. 2012. (Dover Build a Poster Coloring Book Ser.). (ENG., Illus.). 48p. (J). (gr. 3-5). pap. 4.99 *(978-0-486-48645-1(1))* Dover Pubns., Inc.

RSPB Garden Nature Colouring Book. 2013. (ENG., Illus.). 48p. pap. 7.95 *(978-1-4081-9250-4(0)*, 9781408192504, A&C Black Childrens & Educational) Bloomsbury Publishing Plc GBR. Dist: Macmillan.

RSPB Wild Nature Colouring Book. 2013. (ENG., Illus.). 48p. pap. 7.95 *(978-1-4081-9249-8(7)*, 9781408192498, A&C Black Childrens & Educational) Bloomsbury Publishing Plc GBR. Dist: Macmillan.

Rudolph's Sleigh Ride Coloring Fun. Date not set. (Christmas Activity Bks.). (Illus.). 128p. (J). pap. 3.98 *(978-0-7525-6671-9(7))* Parragon, Inc.

Rugg, Michael. Bigfoot Discovery Book. 2005. (Illus.). 32p. (J). pap., act. bk. ed. 5.95 *(978-0-88839-592-4(2))* Hancock Hse. Pubs.

Rugg, Michael & Kieffer, Steve. Dinosaur Coloring Book. 2005. (Illus.). 24p. (J). pap. 4.95 *(978-0-88839-593-1(0))* Hancock Hse. Pubs.

Running Press Staff. Posters to Color: Space. 2016. (ENG., Illus.). 24p. (J). (gr. -1-17). pap. 9.95 *(978-0-7624-5997-1(2)*, Running Pr. Kids) Running Pr. Bk. Pubs.

Saborea & Huele!Tr. of Taste & Small! (SPA.). (J). 2.95 *(978-958-607-887-0(6))* Sociedad de San Pablo ESP. Dist: St Pauls/Alba Hse. Pubs.

Salem, Iosi. A Mitzva for Zelda Coloring Book. 2008. 48p. (J). pap. 6.95 *(978-1-934440-38-4(8)*, Pitspopany Pr.) Simcha Media Group.

Salem, Iosi, illus. The Mr. Mentch Coloring Book. 2008. (J). (gr. -1-3). 6.95 *(978-1-934440-37-7(X)*, Pitspopany Pr.) Simcha Media Group.

The Saltwater Game Fish Coloring Book. 2005. (J). mass mkt. *(978-0-9763757-1-5(0))* Cypress Knees Publishing.

Sam & Sarge. 2004. (J). 5.00 *(978-0-9767215-1-2(1))* Family Guidance & Outreach Ctr. of Lubbock.

Sanchez, John Joseph P. Illuminating the Legacy: A Coloring & Activity Book of the CNMI's History. Ogo, Luis S., illus. 2006. 106p. (J). (gr. 4-5). pap. *(978-1-878453-89-1(0))* Univ. of Guam, Micronesian Area Research Ctr.

Sanders, Jane. Nighttime Slumber, 1 vol. 2017. (ENG., Illus.). 22p. (J). bds. 9.99 *(978-1-4236-4714-0(9))* Gibbs Smith, Publisher.

Sands, Emily. Egyptology Coloring Book. 2017. (Ologies Ser.). (ENG.). 64p. (J). (gr. 5). pap. 14.99 *(978-0-7636-9531-6(9))* Candlewick Pr.

Santore, Charles, illus. The Wizard of Oz Coloring Book. 2017. (ENG.). 96p. (J). pap. 10.99 ***(978-1-60433-706-8(0)***, Applesauce Pr.) Cider Mill Pr. Bk. Pubs., LLC.

Sargent, Daina. Colors & the Number 6/Los Colores y el Número 6, 11 vols. Lenoir, Jane, illus. 2005. (Learn to Read Ser.: 11). (ENG & SPA.). 24p. (J). pap. 10.95 *(978-1-59381-139-6(X))* Ozark Publishing.

Sargent, Daina & Lenoir, Jane. Colors & the Number 6/Los colores y el Número 6, 11 vols. 2005. (Learn to Read Ser.).Tr. of Los colores y el Número 6. (ENG & SPA., Illus.). 24p. (J). lib. bdg. 20.95 *(978-1-59381-138-9(1))* Ozark Publishing.

Sato, Koichi. Infinite Coloring Dazzling Designs. 2009. (Dover Design Coloring Bks.). (ENG., Illus.). 96p. (gr. 3-5). pap. 8.99 incl. cd-rom *(978-0-486-46950-8(6))* Dover Pubns., Inc.

Sawyers, William. What Am I? Bugs. 2005. 65p. (J). pap. 16.01 *(978-1-4116-3402-2(0))* Lulu Pr., Inc.

Say It with a Puffin: 50 Colour-In Postcards. 2016. (ENG.). 50p. (J). (gr. 2-4). 14.99 ***(978-0-14-136860-3(8))*** Penguin Bks., Ltd. GBR. Dist: Independent Pubs. Group.

Sazaklis, John. Design & Draw. 2012. (Dark Knight Rises Ser.). (ENG.). 64p. (J). (gr. -1-3). pap., act. bk. ed. 6.99 *(978-0-06-213226-0(1)*, HarperFestival) HarperCollins Pubs.

Scalzo, Linda V. Carazona's Coloring Book. l.t. ed. 2004. (Illus.). 8p. (J). 2.99 *(978-0-9753724-3-2(2))* Carazona Creations LLC.

Schmidt, Carol. Butterfly Alphabet Coloring Book. 2007. (Dover Coloring Bks.). (ENG., Illus.). 32p. (J). (gr. -1-5). 3.99 *(978-0-486-45843-4(1))* Dover Pubns., Inc.

—Butterfly Fairies Stained Glass Coloring Book. 2011. (Dover Stained Glass Coloring Book Ser.). (ENG., Illus.). 32p. (gr. 3-8). pap. 7.99 *(978-0-486-48034-3(8))* Dover Pubns., Inc.

—Creative Haven Kaleidoscope Designs Stained Glass Coloring Book. 2014. (Adult Coloring Ser.). (ENG., Illus.). 32p. (gr. 6). pap. 7.99 *(978-0-486-79605-5(1))* Dover Pubns., Inc.

—Creative Haven Patchwork Quilt Designs Coloring Book. 2014. (Adult Coloring Ser.). (ENG., Illus.). 64p. (gr. 3). pap. 5.99 *(978-0-486-78031-3(7))* Dover Pubns., Inc.

—Witches Stained Glass Coloring Book. 2010. (Dover Stained Glass Coloring Book Ser.). (ENG., Illus.). 96p. (gr. 3-8). pap. 6.99 *(978-0-486-47654-4(5))* Dover Pubns., Inc.

Schmidt, Carol & Coloring Books Staff. Japanese Stencil Designs Stained Glass Coloring Book. 2012. (Dover Stained Glass Coloring Book Ser.). (ENG.). 32p. (gr. 3-5). pap. 6.99 *(978-0-486-48504-1(8))* Dover Pubns., Inc.

Schmidt, Nathan, illus. Zoey & the Zones: Coloring Book, 2. 2003. 0.99 *(978-0-9718120-7-9(1))* HealthSprings, LLC.

Schmitz, Mark. Manga Boys Coloring Book. 2013. (Dover Coloring Bks.). (ENG., Illus.). 48p. (J). (gr. -1-8). pap. 4.99 *(978-0-486-49710-5(0))* Dover Pubns., Inc.

Scholastic. Harry Potter Magical Places & Characters Postcard Coloring Book. 2016. (ENG.). 40p. (J). (gr. 3). pap. 9.99 *(978-1-338-13294-6(6))* Scholastic, Inc.

—Harry Potter Magical Places & Characters Poster Coloring Book. 2016. (Harry Potter Ser.). (ENG.). 40p. (J). (gr. 3). pap. 24.99 *(978-1-338-13292-2(X))* Scholastic, Inc.

—The World of the Hunger Games: The Official Coloring Book. 2016. (ENG.). 96p. (J). (gr. 7). pap. 15.99 *(978-1-338-09619-4(2))* Scholastic, Inc.

Scholastic & Marsham, Liz. Fantastic Beasts & Where to Find Them: Coloring & Creativity Book. 2016. (ENG.). 80p. (J). (gr. 3-7). pap. 8.99 *(978-1-338-11680-9(0))* Scholastic, Inc.

Scholastic, Inc. Staff. Coloring Cute. 2016. (ENG.). 72p. (J). (gr. 2-5). 16.99 *(978-1-338-10398-4(9))* Klutz.

—Harry Potter - The Coloring Book. 2015. (ENG.). 96p. (J). (gr. 3-5). pap. 15.99 *(978-1-338-02999-4(1))* Scholastic, Inc.

—Harry Potter Postcard Coloring Book. 2016. (ENG.). 40p. (J). (gr. 3). pap. 9.99 *(978-1-338-04575-8(X))* Scholastic, Inc.

Scholastic, Inc. Staff, contrib. by. Colors in the Cold. 2016. (Rookie Toddler(tm) Ser.). (ENG.). 12p. (J). bds. 6.95 *(978-0-531-22699-5(9)*, Children's Pr.) Scholastic Library Publishing.

Scholastic Inc, Staff, contrib. by. Harry Potter Magical Artifacts Poster Coloring Book. 2017. (Harry Potter Ser.: 3). (ENG.). 40p. (J). (gr. 3). pap. 24.99 ***(978-1-338-13293-9(8))*** Scholastic, Inc.

Scholastic, Inc. Staff, contrib. by. Harry Potter: Magical Creatures Postcard Coloring Book. 2016. (Harry Potter Ser.). (ENG.). 40p. (J). (gr. 3). pap. 9.99 *(978-1-338-05459-0(7))* Scholastic, Inc.

—Harry Potter Poster Coloring Book. 2016. (Harry Potter Ser.). (ENG.). 40p. (J). (gr. 3). pap. 24.99 *(978-1-338-05460-6(0))* Scholastic, Inc.

Scholastic, Inc. Staff & Klutz Editors. Coloring Crush. 2015. (ENG.). 78p. (J). (gr. 3-7). 16.99 *(978-0-545-93097-0(9))* Klutz.

Scholastic Magazines, inc Staff, contrib. by. Harry Potter - Magical Creatures Coloring Book. 2016. (Harry Potter Ser.: Bk. 2). (ENG.). 96p. (J). (gr. 3). pap. 15.99 *(978-1-338-03000-6(0))* Scholastic, Inc.

—Harry Potter: Magical Artifacts Coloring Book. 2016. (ENG.). 96p. (J). (gr. 3-7). pap. 15.99 *(978-1-338-03002-0(7))* Scholastic, Inc.

—Harry Potter Magical Places & Characters Coloring Book. 2016. (ENG.). 96p. (J). (gr. 3). pap. 15.99 *(978-1-338-03001-3(9))* Scholastic, Inc.

Scholastic Teaching Resources Staff. Harry Potter Coloring Book: Celebratory Edition: The Best of Harry Potter Coloring. 2016. (ENG.). 96p. (J). (gr. 3). pap. 15.99 *(978-1-338-16660-6(3))* Scholastic, Inc.

School Zone Staff. My First Dot-To-Dots. 2009. (J). pap. 1.50 net. *(978-1-60159-246-0(9))* School Zone Publishing Co.

—My First Hidden Pictures. 2009. (J). pap. 2.99 *(978-1-60159-251-4(5))* School Zone Publishing Co.

—My First Mazes. 2009. (J). pap. 2.99 *(978-1-60159-247-7(7))* School Zone Publishing Co.

Schwartz, Suzanne & Schwartz, Robert. The Christmas Palm Tree: A Storybook to Color. Schwartz, Suzanne & Schwartz, Robert, illus. l.t. ed. 2005. (Illus.). 22p. (J). spiral bd. 3.99 *(978-0-9764152-3-7(2))* Seascay Productions.

—My Friend Hibby Picture & Coloring Book Set, 2 vols. 2005. (Illus.). 46p. (J). spiral bd. 8.00 *(978-0-9764152-2-0(4))* Seascay Productions.

Schwartz, Suzanne & Schwartz, Robert, illus. Hibby's Coloring Book. 2005. 24p. (J). spiral bd. 3.95 *(978-0-9764152-1-3(6))* Seascay Productions.

Scott, Colin. Speedy Kids Coloring Book. 2013. (ENG.). 50p. 12.55 *(978-1-63022-416-5(2)*, Speedy Kids (Children's Fiction)) Speedy Publishing LLC.

Seal, Daisy, selected by. Cute Animals: Color by Numbers. 2016. (Hobbies & Craft Ser.). (ENG., Illus.). 128p. pap. 15.99 *(978-1-78664-043-7(0)*, 9781786640437) Flame Tree Publishing GBR. Dist: Bookmasters Distribution.

—Exotic Birds: Color by Numbers. 2016. (Hobbies & Craft Ser.). (ENG., Illus.). 128p. pap. 15.99 *(978-1-78664-042-0(2)*, 9781786640420) Flame Tree Publishing GBR. Dist: Bookmasters Distribution.

The Seasons of Mount Rushmore Coloring Book. 2006. (J). *(978-0-9752617-7-4(0))* Mount Rushmore Bookstores.

Serrano, Shea. Bun B's Rapper Coloring & Activity Book. 2013. (ENG.). 48p. pap., act. bk. ed. 12.95 *(978-1-4197-1041-4(9)*, Abrams Image) Abrams, Inc.

Sesame's: A Giant Coloring Book about Fun Things to do at School. 2006. (J). 6.99 *(978-1-59949-495-1(7))* Food Marketing Consultants, Inc.

Sesame's: A Giant Coloring Book about Fun Things to do over the Summer. 2006. (J). 6.99 *(978-1-59949-496-8(5))* Food Marketing Consultants, Inc.

Sesame's: A Giant Coloring Book that Introduces Kids to the Alphabet: the ABCs of Sesame Street. 2006. (J). 6.99 *(978-1-59949-498-2(1))* Food Marketing Consultants, Inc.

Sesame's: A Giant Coloring Book that Teaches about Opposites. 2006. (J). 6.99 *(978-1-59949-497-5(3))* Food Marketing Consultants, Inc.

Sesame's: A Giant Coloring Book that teaches Healthy Eating Habits. 2006. (J). 6.99 *(978-1-59949-499-9(X))* Food Marketing Consultants, Inc.

Seuss. I Can Draw It Myself, by Me, Myself. 2017. (ENG.). 64p. (J). (gr. -1-2). 16.99 ***(978-1-101-93960-4(5)***, Random Hse. Bks. for Young Readers) Random Hse. Children's Bks.

Seuss, Dr. I Can Draw It Myself, by Me, Myself. 2011. (Classic Seuss Ser.). (ENG., Illus.). 36p. (J). (gr. -1-2). pap. 4.99 *(978-0-375-86600-5(0)*, Golden Bks.) Random Hse. Children's Bks.

Sexton, Brenda. Have a Silly Easter! 2017. (Mad Libs Junior Ser.). (ENG., Illus.). 32p. (J). (gr. -1-k). 7.99 *(978-0-8431-3125-3(X)*, Mad Libs) Penguin Young Readers Group.

Sforza, Daniella, ed. Savannah Blue's Activity Book/Libro de Actividades de Savannah Azul. Spagnoli, Maria Eugenia, tr. Rakusin, Sudie, illus. 2005.Tr. of Libro de Actividades de Savannah Azul. (SPA & ENG.). 48p. (J). 10.95 *(978-0-9664805-4-2(6))* Winged Willow Pr.

Shaffer, Christy. Fairies Around the World. 2009. (Dover Coloring Bks.). (ENG.). 32p. (gr. 3-8). pap. 3.99 *(978-0-486-47289-8(2))* Dover Pubns., Inc.

—Magical Unicorns Stained Glass Coloring Book. 2004. (Dover Stained Glass Coloring Book Ser.). (ENG., Illus.). 32p. (gr. 3-8). pap. 6.99 *(978-0-486-43705-7(1))* Dover Pubns., Inc.

Shaw, Henry. Creative Haven Geometric Genius Stained Glass Coloring Book. 2014. (Adult Coloring Ser.). (ENG.). 32p. (gr. 3). pap. 7.99 *(978-0-486-79832-5(1))* Dover Pubns., Inc.

Shaw-Russell, Susan. Cool Cupcakes Coloring Book. 2016. (ENG., Illus.). 32p. (J). (gr. k-3). pap. 3.99 *(978-0-486-78229-4(8))* Dover Pubns., Inc.

—A Day with the Dinosaurs Sticker Activity Book. 2011. (Dover Little Activity Books Stickers Ser.). (ENG., Illus.). 4p. (J). (gr. k-3). 1.99 *(978-0-486-47236-2(1))* Dover Pubns., Inc.

—Spark - Amazing Animals Coloring Book. 2016. (ENG.). 64p. (J). (gr. 1-5). pap. 5.99 *(978-0-486-80715-7(0))* Dover Pubns., Inc.

Shealy, Dennis & Miryam. Favorites: I'm a Truck/The Happy Man & His Dump Truck/I'm a Monster Truck. Staake, Bob et al, illus. 2011. (Little Golden Book Favorites Ser.). (ENG.). 80p. (J). (gr. -1-2). 7.99 *(978-0-375-86549-7(7)*, Golden Bks.) Random Hse. Children's Bks.

Sheely, Tiffany, illus. Captain William Clark's Great Montana Adventure. 2003. 32p. (J). mass mkt. 3.95 *(978-0-9711667-0-7(6))* Outlook Publishing, Inc.

Shepherd Mountain Press Staff. What Can You See on the Coast? A Shepherd Mountain Press Coloring Book. 2003. (Illus.). 36p. (J). pap. 4.50 *(978-0-9749282-0-3(8))* Shepherd Mountain Pr.

Sherman, Janice. Colorful Critters Color Match Coloring Book. 2007. (ENG., Illus.). 10p. (J). pap. 1.99 *(978-0-9797139-3-4(5))* Jan's Bks.

Shirley Dobson Bible Story Coloring Book Sampler Merchandiser. 129.00 *(978-0-8307-2753-7(1)*, Gospel Light) Gospel Light Pubns.

Shirley Dobson Bible Story Coloring Book Sampler Merchandiser: 55 Unit Mini-Merch. 70.95 *(978-0-8307-3024-7(9)*, Gospel Light) Gospel Light Pubns.

Shoup, Andrew J. Andy & Elmer's Apple Dumpling Adventure. 2nd ed. 2007. (J). 16.95 *(978-0-9720436-3-2(2))* TokoBooks, LLC.

—Andy & Elmer's Apple Dumpling Adventure Coloring & Activity Book. Shoup, Andrew J., illus. 2007. (Illus.). 36p. (J). 3.95 *(978-0-9720436-2-5(4))* TokoBooks, LLC.

Shumate, A. M. The True-Color Book. 2003. (Illus.). 120p. pap. 44.95 *(978-1-894921-14-5(3))* Briston Hse. CAN. Dist: Independent Pubs. Group.

Sibbett, Ed, Jr., et al. Japanese Prints. 2012. (Adult Coloring Ser.). (ENG., Illus.). 64p. (gr. 3). pap. 5.99 *(978-0-486-49136-3(6))* Dover Pubns., Inc.

—3-D Coloring Book — Merry Christmas. 2011. (Dover 3-D Coloring Book Ser.). (ENG., Illus.). 32p. (J). (gr. 2-6). pap. 5.99 *(978-0-486-48414-3(9))* Dover Pubns., Inc.

Sibbett, Ed JR. & Sibbett, Jr., Ed, Ed. Birds GemGlow Stained Glass Coloring Book. 2010. (Dover Nature Stained Glass Coloring Book Ser.). (ENG., Illus.). 32p. (J). (gr. -1-5). pap. 7.99 *(978-0-486-47476-2(3))* Dover Pubns., Inc.

Sibbett, Jr., Ed, Ed. Butterfly GemGlow Stained Glass Coloring Book. 2009. (Dover Nature Stained Glass Coloring Book Ser.). (ENG., Illus.). 32p. (J). (gr. 1-5). pap. 7.99 *(978-0-486-47147-1(0))* Dover Pubns., Inc.

Sileo, Cinzia. Robots. 2016. (Coloring Space Ser.: 5). (ENG.). 32p. (J). (gr. 1-17). 7.99 *(978-0-316-35973-3(4))* Little, Brown Bks. for Young Readers.

Silver Dolphin. Beauty & the Beast: a Coloring Book. 2017. (Classic Coloring Book Ser.). (ENG., Illus.). 96p. (J). (gr. k). pap. 15.99 *(978-1-62686-885-4(9)*, Silver Dolphin Bks.) Readerlink Distribution Services, LLC.

Silver Dolphin & Andersen, Hans Christian. Little Mermaid: a Coloring Book. Dulac, Edmund, illus. 2017. (Classic Coloring Book Ser.). (ENG.). 96p. (J). (gr. k). pap. 15.99 *(978-1-62686-886-1(7)*, Silver Dolphin Bks.) Readerlink Distribution Services, LLC.

Sim, David. Matt's Hat: A Find the Hat Color Book, 2 bks. Sim, David, illus. 2003. (Illus.). 10p. (J). 7.95 *(978-1-58117-197-6(8)*, Intervisual/Piggy Toes) Bendon, Inc.

Simard, Remy, illus. Busy Day Coloring Storybook. 2003. (Rainbow Fish & Friends Ser.). 24p. (J). mass mkt. 2.99 *(978-1-59014-132-8(6))* Night Sky Bks.

—Favorite Places Coloring Storybook. 2003. (Rainbow Fish & Friends Ser.). 24p. (J). mass mkt. 2.99 *(978-1-59014-133-5(4))* Night Sky Bks.

Simon and Schuster UK Staff. Colour in 5 SOS! 2014. (ENG.). 32p. (J). 5.99 *(978-1-4711-2469-3(X)*, Simon & Schuster Children's) Simon & Schuster, Ltd. GBR. Dist: Simon & Schuster, Inc.

—Colour in One Direction! 2014. (ENG.). 32p. (J). pap. 5.99 *(978-1-4711-1867-8(3)*, Simon & Schuster Children's) Simon & Schuster, Ltd. GBR. Dist: Simon & Schuster, Inc.

—Ultimate Boy Band Pack! 2014. (ENG.). 48p. (J). 8.99 *(978-1-4711-2473-0(8)*, Simon & Schuster Children's) Simon & Schuster, Ltd. GBR. Dist: Simon & Schuster, Inc.

Simon-Kerr, Julia. Princess Party Paint Book. Edwards, Ken, illus. 2005. (My Little Pony Ser.). 32p. (J). 3.99 *(978-0-06-074699-5(8)*, HarperFestival) HarperCollins Pubs.

Simon, Seymour. Seymour Simon's Silly Riddles & Jokes Coloring Book. Kendrick, D., illus. 2013. (Dover Coloring Bks.). (ENG.). 48p. (J). (gr. 2-5). pap. 4.99 *(978-0-486-48045-9(3))* Dover Pubns., Inc.

Simone, Val Edward. Proton Gator & Friends Coloring Book. McGill, Joshua, illus. 2011. 32p. (J). pap. 5.99 *(978-1-935296-27-0(2))* Morningside Publishing, LLC.

Siuda, Erik. Creative Haven Floral Tattoo Designs Coloring Book. 2014. (Adult Coloring Ser.). (ENG., Illus.). 64p. (gr. 6). pap. 5.99 *(978-0-486-49629-0(5))* Dover Pubns., Inc.

—Creative Haven Polynesian Designs Coloring Book. 2014. (Adult Coloring Ser.). (ENG., Illus.). 64p. (gr. 6). pap. 5.99 *(978-0-486-78965-1(9))* Dover Pubns., Inc.

—Dolphin Dream Designs Coloring Book. 2015. (ENG., Illus.). 32p. (J). (gr. 3). pap. 3.99 *(978-0-486-78966-8(7))* Dover Pubns., Inc.

Siuda, Erik & Creative Haven. Creative Haven Modern Tattoo Designs Coloring Book. 2013. (Adult Coloring Ser.). (ENG., Illus.). 64p. (gr. 6). pap. 5.99 *(978-0-486-49326-8(1))* Dover Pubns., Inc.

Skiles, Janet. Color & Count. 2015. (Dover Coloring Bks.). (ENG.). 32p. (J). (gr. -1-2). pap. 3.99 *(978-0-486-79405-1(9))* Dover Pubns., Inc.

Skiles, Janet & Coloring Books Staff. How to Care for Your Cat: A Color & Learn Guide for Kids. 2011. (Dover Children's Activity Bks.). (ENG., Illus.). 32p. (J). (gr. -1-3). pap. 3.99 *(978-0-486-48148-7(4))* Dover Pubns., Inc.

—How to Care for Your Dog: A Color & Learn Guide for Kids. 2011. (Dover Children's Activity Bks.). (ENG., Illus.). 32p. (J). (gr. -1-2). pap. 3.99 *(978-0-486-48149-4(2))* Dover Pubns., Inc.

Skinner. Forbidden Activities for Neglected Children. 2014. (ENG., Illus.). 36p. pap. 9.95 *(978-0-86719-798-3(6))* Last Gasp of San Francisco.

Smart Kids Publishing Staff, creator. Down on the Farm Bath Book. 2007. (Rub a Dub Fun in the Tub Ser.). (ENG., Illus.). 12p. (gr. -1-k). 8.99 *(978-0-8249-6721-5(6)*, Ideal Pubns.) Worthy Publishing.

—My Princess Bath Book. 2008. (ENG., Illus.). 12p. (gr. -1-k). 8.99 *(978-0-8249-6720-8(8)*, Ideal Pubns.) Worthy Publishing.

Smith, A. G. Beautiful Butterflies Stained Glass Coloring Book. 2003. (Dover Nature Stained Glass Coloring Book Ser.). (ENG., Illus.). 32p. (J). (gr. 3-5). pap. 7.99 *(978-0-486-43061-4(8))* Dover Pubns., Inc.

—BOOST Story of the Vikings Coloring Book. 2013. (BOOST Educational Ser.). (ENG.). 48p. (J). (gr. 3-5). pap. 5.99 *(978-0-486-49439-5(X))* Dover Pubns., Inc.

—Creative Haven Geometric Star Designs Coloring Book. 2013. (Adult Coloring Ser.). (ENG.). 64p. (gr. 3). pap. 5.99 *(978-0-486-77936-2(X))* Dover Pubns., Inc.

—Creative Haven Tiffany Designs Stained Glass Coloring Book. 2014. (Adult Coloring Ser.). (ENG., Illus.). 32p. (gr. 6). pap. 7.99 *(978-0-486-79603-1(5))* Dover Pubns., Inc.

—Easy Kaleidoscope Stained Glass Coloring Book. 2005. (Dover Stained Glass Coloring Book Ser.). (ENG., Illus.). 8p. (J). (gr. k-3). pap. 1.99 *(978-0-486-44182-5(2))* Dover Pubns., Inc.

—FRENCH EDITION of Gargoyles & Medieval Monsters Coloring Book. 2013. (Dover Children's Bilingual Coloring Book Ser.). (FRE & ENG.). 48p. (J). (gr. 3-12). pap. 4.99 *(978-0-486-49327-5(X))* Dover Pubns., Inc.

—Little Mandalas Stained Glass Coloring Book. 2006. (Dover Stained Glass Coloring Book Ser.). (ENG., Illus.). 8p. (J). (gr. k-3). 1.99 *(978-0-486-44937-1(8))* Dover Pubns., Inc.

—Masks of the World Coloring Book. 2003. (Dover History Coloring Book Ser.). (ENG., Illus.). 32p. (J). (gr. 3-8). pap. 3.99 *(978-0-486-43039-3(1))* Dover Pubns., Inc.

—Snowflake Designs Stained Glass Coloring Book. 2007. (Dover Design Stained Glass Coloring Book Ser.). (ENG., Illus.). 32p. (J). (gr. 3-8). 6.99 *(978-0-486-45769-7(9))* Dover Pubns., Inc.

—Starbursts Stained Glass Coloring Book. 2005. (Dover Stained Glass Coloring Book Ser.). (ENG., Illus.). 8p. (J). (gr. k-3). pap. 1.99 *(978-0-486-44460-4(0))* Dover Pubns., Inc.

—Visual Illusions Stained Glass Coloring Book. 2008. (Dover Design Stained Glass Coloring Book Ser.). (ENG., Illus.). 32p. (gr. 3-8). pap. 6.99 *(978-0-486-46563-0(2))* Dover Pubns., Inc.

—Wonders of the World Coloring Book. 2003. (Dover History Coloring Book Ser.). (ENG., Illus.). 32p. (gr. 3-8). pap. 3.99 *(978-0-486-43044-7(8))* Dover Pubns., Inc.

Smith, A. G. & Mason, Randy. History of American Automobile Coloring Book. 2014. (ENG., Illus.). 48p. (J). (gr. 6). pap. 4.99 *(978-0-486-26315-1(0))* Dover Pubns., Inc.

Smith, Dororthy. Noah's Ark Coloring Book. 2007. (Illus.). 16p. (J). pap. 1.89 *(978-1-59317-188-9(9))* Warner Pr., Inc.

Smith Novelty Company Staff. Monterey & Carmel Coloring Book. 2006. (J). pap. 5.99 *(978-1-932387-23-0(4))* Smith Novelty Co., Inc.

Smokey's Coloring Book. (J). (SPA.). 29.50 *(978-1-56230-212-2(4))*; 29.50 *(978-1-56230-055-5(5))* Syndistar, Inc.

Snider, Brandon T. Spider-Man Doodles. Montalvo-Lagos, Tomás, illus. 2017. (Doodle Book Ser.). (ENG.). 128p. (J). (gr. 1-3). pap. 12.99 ***(978-1-4847-8771-7(4)***, Marvel Pr.) Disney Publishing Worldwide.

Snow, Philip. Birds of the Bible. Snow, Philip, illus. 2005. (Bible Discover & Colour Ser.). (Illus.). 32p. (J). (gr. -1-7). 4.00 *(978-1-903087-89-3(9))* DayOne Pubns. GBR. Dist: Send The Light Distribution LLC.

—Places of the Bible. Snow, Philip, illus. 2005. (Bible Discover & Colour Ser.). (Illus.). 32p. (J). (gr. -1-7). 4.00 *(978-1-903087-90-9(2))* DayOne Pubns. GBR. Dist: Send The Light Distribution LLC.

—Plants of the Bible. Snow, Philip, illus. 2005. (Bible Discover & Colour Ser.). (Illus.). 32p. (J). (gr. -1-7). 4.00 *(978-1-903087-91-6(0))* DayOne Pubns. GBR. Dist: Send The Light Distribution LLC.

Snowman's Winter Coloring Fun. Date not set. (Christmas Activity Bks.). (Illus.). 128p. (J). pap. 3.98 *(978-0-7525-6670-2(9))* Parragon, Inc.

Snozek, Lee Anne & Coloring Books for Adults. Simply Circular Designs Coloring Book. 2005. (Dover Design Coloring Bks.). (ENG., Illus.). 32p. (gr. 3-5). 3.99 *(978-0-486-44461-1(9))* Dover Pubns., Inc.

Soffer, Ruth. Animal Illustrations to Paint or Color. 2007. (Dover Art Coloring Book Ser.). (ENG., Illus.). 48p. (J). (gr. 3-8). 5.99 *(978-0-486-45696-6(X))* Dover Pubns., Inc.

—Baby Animals Coloring Book. 2004. (Dover Coloring Bks.). (ENG., Illus.). 32p. (J). (gr. -1-2). pap. 3.99 *(978-0-486-43331-8(5))* Dover Pubns., Inc.

—Birds Alphabet Coloring Book. 2005. (Dover Nature Coloring Book Ser.). (ENG., Illus.). 32p. (J). (gr. -1-5). 3.99 *(978-0-486-44035-4(4))* Dover Pubns., Inc.

—Birds in Flight Coloring Book. 2013. (ENG.). 32p. (gr. 3-12). pap. 3.99 *(978-0-486-49735-8(6))* Dover Pubns., Inc.

—BOOST Arctic & Antarctic Life Coloring Book. 2013. (BOOST Educational Ser.). (ENG.). 48p. (J). (gr. 3-5). pap. 5.99 *(978-0-486-49430-2(6))* Dover Pubns., Inc.

—BOOST North American Desert Life Coloring Book. 2013. (BOOST Educational Ser.). (ENG.). 48p. (J). (gr. 3-5). pap. 5.99 *(978-0-486-49436-4(5))* Dover Pubns., Inc.

—Butterflies & Flowers to Paint or Color. 2005. (Dover Art Coloring Book Ser.). (ENG., Illus.). 48p. (gr. 3-8). per. 5.99 *(978-0-486-44496-3(1))* Dover Pubns., Inc.

—The Cat Lovers. 2007. (Dover Nature Coloring Book Ser.). (ENG., Illus.). 32p. (gr. 3-5). 3.99 *(978-0-486-46200-4(5))* Dover Pubns., Inc.

—Cats Stained Glass Coloring Book. 2009. (Dover Nature Stained Glass Coloring Book Ser.). (ENG., Illus.). 32p. (gr. -1-8). pap. 7.99 *(978-0-486-46994-2(8))* Dover Pubns., Inc.

—Creative Haven in Full Bloom Coloring Book. 2014. (Adult Coloring Ser.). (ENG.). 64p. (gr. 3). pap. 5.99 *(978-0-486-49453-1(5))* Dover Pubns., Inc.

—Dogs Stained Glass Coloring Book. 2010. (Dover Nature Stained Glass Coloring Book Ser.). (ENG., Illus.). 32p. (J). (gr. 2-5). pap. 6.99 *(978-0-486-47802-9(5))* Dover Pubns., Inc.

—Favorite Birds Stained Glass Coloring Book. 2004. (Dover Nature Stained Glass Coloring Book Ser.). (ENG., Illus.). 32p. (gr. 3-8). pap. 7.99 *(978-0-486-43690-6(X))* Dover Pubns., Inc.

—The Flower Garden Coloring Book. 2005. (Dover Nature Coloring Book Ser.). (ENG., Illus.). 32p. (gr. 3-8). 3.99 *(978-0-486-44497-0(X))* Dover Pubns., Inc.

—Garden Flowers Alphabet. 2004. (Dover Design Coloring Bks.). (ENG., Illus.). 32p. (J). (gr. -1-5). pap. 3.99 *(978-0-486-43595-4(4))* Dover Pubns., Inc.

—Great Barrier Reef Coloring Book. 2007. (Dover Nature Coloring Book Ser.). (ENG., Illus.). 32p. (gr. 3-8). 3.99 *(978-0-486-45689-8(7))* Dover Pubns., Inc.

—Nature Alphabets Coloring Book. 2006. (Dover Nature Coloring Book Ser.). (ENG., Illus.). 96p. (J). (gr. -1-5). 7.95 *(978-0-486-45921-9(7))* Dover Pubns., Inc.

—Sea Life Alphabet Coloring Book. 2003. (Dover Nature Coloring Book Ser.). (ENG., Illus.). 32p. (J). (gr. -1-2). pap. 3.99 *(978-0-486-42653-2(X))* Dover Pubns., Inc.

—Swampland Plants & Animals Coloring Book. 2011. (Dover Nature Coloring Book Ser.). (ENG., Illus.). 48p. (J). (gr. 3-5). pap. 4.99 *(978-0-486-29625-8(3))* Dover Pubns., Inc.

Soffer, Ruth, et al. Big Book of Sea Life to Color. 2008. (Dover Nature Coloring Book Ser.). (ENG., Illus.). 144p. (J). (gr. 3-5). 8.95 *(978-0-486-46681-1(7))* Dover Pubns., Inc.

Sorensen, "Miss Nancy". Alexa's Rainbow. 2008. 16p. pap. 8.49 *(978-1-4343-9342-5(9))* AuthorHouse.

Sotnik, Katherine, illus. Choir of Angels Coloring Book. 2012. (Holy Imitation Ser.). (ENG.). 72p. (J). (gr. -1-3). 4.95 *(978-1-58617-588-7(2))* Ignatius Pr.

Sovak, Jan. Alaskan Wildlife Coloring Book. 2006. (Dover Nature Coloring Book Ser.). (ENG., Illus.). 32p. (J). (gr. 1-5). pap. 3.99 *(978-0-486-45221-0(2))* Dover Pubns., Inc.

—Build a Giant Poster Coloring Book — Under the Sea. 2013. (Dover Build a Poster Coloring Book Ser.). (ENG., Illus.). 48p. (J). (gr. 2-6). pap. 4.99 *(978-0-486-49139-4(0))* Dover Pubns., Inc.

—Deadly Creatures Coloring Book. 2011. (Dover Nature Coloring Book Ser.). (ENG., Illus.). 32p. (J). (gr. 3-8). pap. 3.99 *(978-0-486-47655-1(3))* Dover Pubns., Inc.

—Deadly Insects & Arachnids. 2013. (Dover Nature Coloring Book Ser.). (ENG.). 32p. (J). (gr. 3-5). pap. 3.99 *(978-0-486-49054-0(8))* Dover Pubns., Inc.

—Dinosaurs! Coloring Book. 2009. (Dover Nature Coloring Book Ser.). (ENG., Illus.). 32p. (J). (gr. 1-5). pap. 3.99 *(978-0-486-46987-4(5))* Dover Pubns., Inc.

—Dinosaurs of the Cretaceous Era. 2009. (Dover Nature Coloring Book Ser.). (ENG., Illus.). 32p. (J). (gr. 2-5). pap. 3.99 *(978-0-486-47264-5(7))* Dover Pubns., Inc.

—Dinosaurs of the Triassic Era. 2010. (Dover Nature Coloring Book Ser.). (ENG., Illus.). 32p. (J). (gr. 2-5). pap. 3.99 *(978-0-486-47265-2(5))* Dover Pubns., Inc.

—Dinosaurs Stained Glass Coloring Book. 2005. (Dover Nature Stained Glass Coloring Book Ser.). (ENG., Illus.). 16p. (J). (gr. 1-5). pap. 7.99 *(978-0-486-44668-4(9))* Dover Pubns., Inc.

—Endangered Animals. 2009. (Dover Nature Coloring Book Ser.). (ENG., Illus.). 32p. (J). (gr. 1-5). pap. 3.99 *(978-0-486-46793-1(7))* Dover Pubns., Inc.

—Fairy World. 2011. (Build Window Stained Glass Coloring Book Ser.). (ENG., Illus.). 32p. (J). (gr. 3-5). pap. 6.99 *(978-0-486-48393-1(2))* Dover Pubns., Inc.

—Giants & Ogres Coloring Book. 2004. (Dover Coloring Bks.). (ENG., Illus.). 32p. (J). (gr. 3-8). pap. 3.95 *(978-0-486-43680-7(2))* Dover Pubns., Inc.

—Let's Explore! Sea Animals. 2011. (Dover Nature Coloring Book Ser.). (ENG.). 32p. (J). (gr. 1-5). pap. 5.99 *(978-0-486-47895-1(5))* Dover Pubns., Inc.

—Lizards. 2006. (Dover Nature Coloring Book Ser.). (ENG., Illus.). 32p. (J). (gr. 1-5). 3.99 *(978-0-486-44820-6(7))* Dover Pubns., Inc.

—Lost in the Amazon: Hidden Pictures. 2011. (Dover Children's Activity Bks.). (ENG., Illus.). 48p. (J). (gr. 3-6). pap. 4.99 *(978-0-486-48230-9(8))* Dover Pubns., Inc.

—Manatees Coloring Book. 2010. (Dover Nature Coloring Book Ser.). (ENG., Illus.). 32p. (J). (gr. 2-5). pap. 3.99 *(978-0-486-47390-1(2))* Dover Pubns., Inc.

—Prehistoric Man Coloring Book. 2005. (Dover History Coloring Book Ser.). (ENG., Illus.). 32p. (J). (gr. 3-5). 3.99 *(978-0-486-44432-1(5))* Dover Pubns., Inc.

—Rain Forest Wildlife. 2008. (Dover Nature Stained Glass Coloring Book Ser.). (ENG., Illus.). 32p. (J). (gr. 3-8). pap. 6.99 *(978-0-486-41554-3(6))* Dover Pubns., Inc.

—3-D Coloring Book — Dangerous Animals. 2012. (Dover 3-D Coloring Book Ser.). (ENG., Illus.). 32p. (J). (gr. 2-6). pap. 5.99 *(978-0-486-48419-8(X))* Dover Pubns., Inc.

—3-D Coloring Book — Dinosaurs. 2011. (Dover 3-D Coloring Book Ser.). (ENG., Illus.). 32p. (J). (gr. 3-5). pap. 5.99 *(978-0-486-48162-3(X))* Dover Pubns., Inc.

Sovak, Jan & Coloring Books Staff. Build a Poster Coloring Book — Dinosaurs. 2012. (Dover Build a Poster Coloring Book Ser.). (ENG.). 48p. (J). (gr. 3-5). pap. 4.99 *(978-0-486-48647-5(8))* Dover Pubns., Inc.

Sowash, Rick. Heroes of Ohio Coloring Book. 2003. (J). 5.95 *(978-0-9762412-6-3(9))* Sowash, Rick Publishing Co.

Sparrow, Shanti. Colors. 2016. (ENG., Illus.). 22p. (J). (— 1). bds. 6.95 *(978-1-4549-2082-3(3))* Sterling Publishing Co., Inc.

Spear, Kevin. David & the Giant. 2005. (Illus.). (J). pap. 1.79 *(978-1-59317-087-5(4))* Warner Pr., Inc.

Spearman, David. What Will I Grow up to Be?, 1 vol. Spearman, Davidx & Spearman, Terry, illus. 2009. 34p. pap. 24.95 *(978-1-60749-728-8(X))* America Star Bks.

Spenceley, Angela. Virgin Islands Coloring Book. 2006. (Illus.). 24p. (J). 2.00 net. *(978-0-9778913-9-9(9))* Coconut Pr., LLC.

Spenceley, Angela, compiled by. Pirate Coloring & Sticker Book: Your Complete Guide to Famous Pirates. l.t. ed. 2006. (Illus.). 24p. (J). pap. 8.95 *(978-0-9702168-6-1(6))* Coconut Pr., LLC.

Spider-Man Coloring. 2003. (J). per. *(978-1-57657-904-6(2))* Paradise Pr., Inc.

Spiderman Coloring. 2003. (J). per. *(978-1-57657-905-3(0))* Paradise Pr., Inc.

Spirit Press, creator. The Lord Told Noah. 2006. (ENG., Illus.). 48p. (J). (gr. -1-3). 2.99 *(978-1-4037-2003-0(7),* Spirit Pr.) Bendon, Inc.

Spizzirri, Linda, ed. Counting & Coloring Dinosaurs. (Illus.). 32p. (J). (gr. 1-8). pap. 4.98 incl. audio *(978-0-86545-044-8(7))* Spizzirri Pr., Inc.

—Northeast Indians. (Illus.). 32p. (J). (gr. 1-8). pap. 4.98 incl. audio *(978-0-86545-040-0(4))* Spizzirri Pr., Inc.

—Northwest Indians. (Illus.). 32p. (J). (gr. 1-8). pap. 4.98 incl. audio *(978-0-86545-047-9(1))* Spizzirri Pr., Inc.

Standard Publishing Staff. God Loves Me Coloring Pages: For Toddlers & 2s. Bausman, Mary, illus. 2016. (ENG.). 192p. (J). 16.99 *(978-0-7847-1796-7(6),* 02446) Standard Publishing.

—Thru-the-Bible Coloring Pages, (Ages 3-6) Skiles, Janet, illus. 2016. (ENG.). 240p. (J). (gr. -1-3). 16.99 *(978-0-7847-1783-7(4),* 02272) Standard Publishing.

—Thru-the-Bible Coloring Pages, Ages 6-8. Skiles, Janet, illus. 2016. (ENG.). 240p. (J). (gr. -1-3). 16.99 *(978-0-7847-1785-1(0),* 02274) Standard Publishing.

Stanley, Stephen. The Haunted Maze. 2013. (ENG., Illus.). 32p. (J). (gr. 3-8). pap. 5.99 *(978-0-486-49134-9(X))* Dover Pubns., Inc.

Stark, Freddy. Gray's Anatomy: A Fact-Filled Coloring Book. 2011. (ENG.). 128p. (J). (gr. -1-17). pap. 12.95 *(978-0-7624-4073-3(2))* Running Pr. Bk. Pubs.

StarKidz: I Am Who I Am. l.t. ed. 2003. (Illus.). 28p. (J). 16.95 *(978-0-9743964-1-5(9))* World of Angels, A.

Steere, Marcia. Tales from My Coloring Book. 2012. (ENG.). (J). pap. *(978-1-4675-2531-2(6))* Independent Pub.

Steffek, Tracey H. Coloring Fun with Words: Learn to Spell & Remember Difficult Words Through Coloring. 2012. 56p. pap. 12.95 *(978-1-4772-0633-1(7))* AuthorHouse.

Stegenga, Wil. Sacred Yantra Coloring Book. 2009. (Dover Design Coloring Bks.). (ENG., Illus.). 32p. (gr. 3-5). pap. 3.99 *(978-0-486-47081-8(4))* Dover Pubns., Inc.

Stegenga, Wil & Coloring Books for Adults. Geometric Whirlwind Coloring Book. 2010. (Dover Design Coloring Bks.). (ENG., Illus.). 32p. (J). (gr. 3-5). pap. 3.99 *(978-0-486-47391-8(0))* Dover Pubns., Inc.

—Heart Designs. 2008. (Dover Design Coloring Bks.). (ENG., Illus.). 32p. (gr. 3-8). 3.99 *(978-0-486-46537-1(3))* Dover Pubns., Inc.

Stegenga, Wil & Coloring Books Staff. Geometric Motifs. 2012. (Dover Design Coloring Bks.). (ENG., Illus.). 32p. (J). (gr. 3-5). pap. 3.99 *(978-0-486-48998-8(1))* Dover Pubns., Inc.

Stein, Erin K. Peppa Pig: Paint Book. 2007. (Peppa Pig Ser.). 32p. (J). pap. 4.99 *(978-0-06-117376-9(2),* Harper Entertainment) HarperCollins Pubs.

Sterling Children's, Sterling. Color Your Own Doll's House. 2016. (ENG., Illus.). 32p. (J). (gr. 2). pap. 7.95 *(978-1-4549-2222-3(2))* Sterling Publishing Co., Inc.

—Coloring Book of Visual Tricks & Optical Illusions: Color the Patterns to Reveal Eye-Popping Effects! 2017. (ENG., Illus.). 96p. (J). (gr. 3). pap. 9.95 ***(978-1-4549-2565-1(5))*** Sterling Publishing Co., Inc.

Sterling Children's, Sterling. Make a Yellow Dot the Sun. 2017. (ENG., Illus.). 96p. (J). (gr. k-6). pap. 12.95 *(978-1-4549-2288-9(5))* Sterling Publishing Co., Inc.

Sterling Publishing Co., Inc. Begin Smart(tm) Play Colors/Colores Juego. 2016. (Begin Smart(tm) Ser.). (ENG & SPA., Illus.). 16p. (J). (— 1). bds. 8.95 *(978-1-4549-1757-1(1))* Sterling Publishing Co., Inc.

Stevenson, Patricia. The Z Family Coloring Book. 2012. 60p. (gr. -1). pap. 8.99 *(978-1-4582-0242-0(9),* Abbott Pr.) Author Solutions, Inc.

Stewart, Pat. Hans Christian Andersen Fairy Tales Stained Glass Coloring Book. 2004. (Dover Stained Glass Coloring Book Ser.). (ENG., Illus.). 16p. (J). (gr. -1-5). pap. 5.95 *(978-0-486-43770-5(1))* Dover Pubns., Inc.

—Little Circus Stained Glass Coloring Book. 2004. (Dover Stained Glass Coloring Book Ser.). (ENG., Illus.). 8p. (J). (gr. -1-5). pap. 1.50 *(978-0-486-43303-5(X))* Dover Pubns., Inc.

—Wedding Stained Glass Coloring Book. 2003. (Dover Stained Glass Coloring Book Ser.). (ENG., Illus.). 8p. (J). (gr. -1-5). pap. 1.50 *(978-0-486-43003-4(0))* Dover Pubns., Inc.

Stoinich, Elisabetta, illus. Good Night Stories for Rebel Girls: Coloring Book. 2016. (ENG.). pap. 9.00 ***(978-0-9978958-0-3(2))*** Timbuktu Labs, Inc.

Stoker, Bram. Dracula. 2009. (Dover Classic Stories Coloring Book Ser.). (ENG., Illus.). 48p. (J). (gr. 3-8). pap. 4.99 *(978-0-486-47414-4(3))* Dover Pubns., Inc.

Stoll, Scott & Stoll, Kristen. God's Garden Friends. 2012. (ENG.). pap. *(978-1-4675-2486-5(7))* Independent Pub.

Strangway, Melissa. Finding Hope. 2012. 82p. pap. 11.65 *(978-1-61933-676-6(6))* FastPrncl, Inc.

Street Smarts: Coloring/Activity Book (English) Incl. Stickers. 2006. (Illus.). (J). 2.99 *(978-1-933934-18-1(2))* Mighty Kids Media.

Stuart, Natalie. Monster Alphabet. 2013. (ENG.). 54p. 13.00 *(978-1-62884-649-2(6),* Baby Professor (Education Kids)) Speedy Publishing LLC.

Sturtz, Maria. Coloring Book in the Bible. 2004. 32p. (J). 1.79 *(978-0-7586-0106-3(9))* Concordia Publishing Hse.

—Coloring Book Living for Jesus. 2004. 32p. (J). 1.79 *(978-0-7586-0107-0(7))* Concordia Publishing Hse.

—God Gave Me. 2004. 32p. (J). 1.79 *(978-0-7586-0105-6(0))* Concordia Publishing Hse.

—God Gave Me Spanish. 2004. (SPA.). 32p. 1.99 *(978-0-7586-0059-2(3))* Concordia Publishing Hse.

—God Is. 2004. 32p. (J). 1.79 *(978-0-7586-0104-9(2))* Concordia Publishing Hse.

—God Is Spanish. 2004. (SPA.). 32p. 1.99 *(978-0-7586-0058-5(5))* Concordia Publishing Hse.

—Spanish Coloring in the Bible. 2004. (SPA.). 32p. 1.99 *(978-0-7586-0060-8(7))* Concordia Publishing Hse.

—Spanish Coloring Living for Je. 2004. (SPA.). 32p. 1.99 *(978-0-7586-0061-5(5))* Concordia Publishing Hse.

Summers, Sue L. Eye Spy Program: Early Youth Education Program. (J). (gr. k-3). pap. 15.00 *(978-0-9676616-1-2(7))* Media Alert!

—Programa Espio Con los Ojos: Programa de Educacion para Jovenes. (SPA.). (J). (gr. k-3). pap. 15.00 *(978-0-9676616-2-9(5))* Media Alert!

Sun, Ming-Ju. Creative Haven Japanese Kimono Designs Coloring Book. 2013. (Adult Coloring Ser.). (ENG., Illus.). 64p. (gr. 3). pap. 5.99 *(978-0-486-49344-2(X))* Dover Pubns., Inc.

—Godey's Fashions. 2005. (Dover Fashion Coloring Book Ser.). (ENG., Illus.). 32p. (gr. 6-8). 3.99 *(978-0-486-43998-3(4))* Dover Pubns., Inc.

—Old-Time Children's Fashions Coloring Book. 2005. (Dover Fashion Coloring Book Ser.). (ENG., Illus.). 32p. (gr. 3-5). 3.95 *(978-0-486-44484-0(8))* Dover Pubns., Inc.

Sun, Ming-Ju & Creative Haven Staff. Creative Haven Art Nouveau Fashions Coloring Book. 2013. (Adult Coloring Ser.). (ENG., Illus.). 64p. (gr. 3). pap. 5.99 *(978-0-486-49211-7(7))* Dover Pubns., Inc.

—Flower Fashion Fantasies. 2012. (Adult Coloring Ser.). (ENG., Illus.). 64p. (gr. 3). pap. 5.99 *(978-0-486-49863-8(8))* Dover Pubns., Inc.

Super Coloring Pad. Date not set. (Illus.). 384p. (J). 7.98 *(978-0-7525-9574-0(1))* Parragon, Inc.

Swanson, Maggie. Awesome Animals Coloring Book. 2016. (Dover Coloring Bks.). (ENG.). 32p. (J). (gr. k-2). pap. 3.99 *(978-0-486-80496-5(8))* Dover Pubns., Inc.

—Best-Loved Aesop's Fables Coloring Book. 2015. (ENG.). 48p. (J). (gr. k-4). pap. 4.99 *(978-0-486-79747-2(3))* Dover Pubns., Inc.

—Floral Fantasies Stained Glass Coloring Book. 2013. (Dover Stained Glass Coloring Book Ser.). (ENG., Illus.). 32p. (gr. 3-8). pap. 7.99 *(978-0-486-49807-2(7))* Dover Pubns., Inc.

—Let's Color Together — Sun, Moon & Stars. 2014. (ENG., Illus.). 64p. (J). (gr. -1-3). pap. 3.99 *(978-0-486-77970-6(X))* Dover Pubns., Inc.

—My Backyard Color by Number. 2017. (ENG.). 32p. (J). (gr. -1-2). pap. 3.99 *(978-0-486-81461-2(0))* Dover Pubns., Inc.

—My Storybook Paper Dolls. 2013. (Dover Paper Dolls Ser.). (ENG., Illus.). 32p. (J). (gr. 1). pap. 9.99 *(978-0-486-48989-6(2))* Dover Pubns., Inc.

—Spark - Flower Fun Coloring Book. 2016. (ENG., Illus.). 64p. (J). (gr. k-3). pap. 5.99 *(978-0-486-80215-2(9))* Dover Pubns., Inc.

—Spark - Sun, Moon & Stars Coloring Book. 2015. (Dover Coloring Bks.). (ENG., Illus.). 64p. (J). (gr. 1-4). pap. 5.99 *(978-0-486-80216-9(7))* Dover Pubns., Inc.

—SPARK Sea Life Designs Coloring Book. 2016. (Dover Coloring Bks.). (ENG.). 64p. (J). (gr. 1-4). pap. 5.99 *(978-0-486-81025-6(9))* Dover Pubns., Inc.

—Sun, Moon & Stars Designs to Color. 2013. (ENG., Illus.). 32p. (gr. 3-8). pap. 3.99 *(978-0-486-49227-8(3))* Dover Pubns., Inc.

—Zany Zoo Stained Glass Jr. Coloring Book. 2012. (Dover Stained Glass Coloring Book Ser.). (ENG.). 32p. (J). (gr. -1-5). pap. 3.99 *(978-0-486-49869-0(7))* Dover Pubns., Inc.

Sykes, Andy. The Hexjibber Colouring & Activity Book. 2007. 84p. pap. 14.95 *(978-1-4303-2817-9(7))* Lulu Pr., Inc.

Tagel, Peggy, illus. Color My World Blue. 2005. (J). *(978-1-58987-101-4(4))* Kindermusik International.

Tallarico, Tony. Find & Color Activity Book. 2007. (Dover Children's Activity Bks.). (ENG., Illus.). 48p. (J). (gr. 3-5). 4.99 *(978-0-486-45679-9(X))* Dover Pubns., Inc.

Tanana, Mary. Christmas to Color. Tanana, Mary, illus. 2015. (Illus.). 96p. (J). (gr. -1). pap. 15.99 *(978-0-06-244379-3(8))* HarperCollins Pubs.

Taplin, Sam. Pirates First Coloring Book. 2012. (First Sticker Coloring Bks). 16p. (J). pap. 6.99 *(978-0-7945-3260-4(8),* Usborne) EDC Publishing.

Tarbox, Charlene. Creative Haven Beautiful Flower Arrangements Coloring Book. 2013. (Adult Coloring Ser.). (ENG., Illus.). 64p. (gr. 3). pap. 5.99 *(978-0-486-49345-9(8))* Dover Pubns., Inc.

—Floral Beauty Coloring Book. 2006. (Dover Nature Coloring Book Ser.). (ENG., Illus.). 96p. (J). (gr. 3-8). 7.95 *(978-0-486-45922-6(5))* Dover Pubns., Inc.

Tate, Suzanne. Color with the Wright Brothers: See How They Made History. Melvin, James, illus. 2003. (Suzanne Tate's History Ser.). 32p. (J). pap. 2.95 *(978-1-878405-41-8(1))* Nags Head Art, Inc.

Taylor, Jo. Sneaker Designs Coloring Book. 2017. (Dover Coloring Bks.). (ENG.). 32p. (J). (gr. 1-4). pap. 3.99 *(978-0-486-80935-9(8))* Dover Pubns., Inc.

Tebo, Mary Elizabeth. Feast Days & Holy Days: Dias Festivos de la Iglesia. Richards, Virginia Helen, illus. 2007. 32p. (J). lab manual ed. 1.95 *(978-0-8198-2682-4(0))* Pauline Bks. & Media.

Teis, Kyra. Look!, 1 vol. 2005. (ENG., Illus.). 16p. (J). (gr. -1). bds. 6.95 *(978-1-59572-022-1(7))* Star Bright Bks., Inc.

Temko, Florence. Cut & Color Things That Go. 2006. (Dover Children's Activity Bks.). (ENG., Illus.). 32p. (J). (gr. -1-5). 3.95 *(978-0-486-45294-4(8))* Dover Pubns., Inc.

Templar Books. Monsters & Heroes of the Realms: a Dungeons & Dragons Coloring Book. 2016. (Ologies Ser.). (ENG.). 96p. (J). (gr. 5). pap. 14.99 *(978-0-7636-9424-1(X))* Candlewick Pr.

Tenenbaum, Frances & Peterson, Roger Tory. Wildflowers. Peterson, Roger Tory, ed. Savage, Virginia, illus. 2013. (Peterson Field Guide Color-In Bks.). (ENG.). 64p. (J). 8.95 *(978-0-544-02697-1(7))* Houghton Mifflin Harcourt Publishing Co.

Tennyson, Patrick & Bickford, Nicole. Tarantula Tracks: Rosie's Wild Adventure. l.t. ed. 2004. (Illus.). 32p. (J). 2.95 *(978-0-9729000-1-0(2))* Butterfly Pavilion.

Thank You, God, for Christmas Coloring Book. 2006. 16p. (J). pap. 1.99 *(978-0-7847-1261-0(1),* 22119) Standard Publishing.

The Broons. The Broons Colouring Book. 2016. (ENG., Illus.). 64p. (J). pap. 11.99 ***(978-1-910230-36-7(7))*** Black and White Publishing Ltd. GBR. Dist: Independent Pubs. Group.

Thenen, Peter Von & Creative Haven Staff. Creative Haven Prismatic Designs Coloring Book. 2013. (Adult Coloring Ser.). (ENG., Illus.). 64p. (gr. 3). pap. 5.99 *(978-0-486-49312-1(1))* Dover Pubns., Inc.

Things I See in God's World. (Illus.). 16p. (J). pap. 1.50 *(978-0-87162-957-9(7),* E4997) Warner Pr., Inc.

Thiruvalluvar. Tirukkural Manthiram Coloring Book with Meditation. 2006. (ENG, FRE & ZUL., Illus.). (J). 5.00 incl. audio *(978-0-9676212-3-4(2))* International Tamil Language Foundation.

Thivierge, Claude. BOOST the World of Turtles Coloring Book. 2013. (BOOST Educational Ser.). (ENG.). 32p. (J). (gr. 3-5). pap. 4.99 *(978-0-486-49442-5(X))* Dover Pubns., Inc.

—The World of Turtles. 2009. (Dover Nature Coloring Book Ser.). (ENG., Illus.). 32p. (J). (gr. 1-5). pap. 3.99 *(978-0-486-46854-9(2))* Dover Pubns., Inc.

Thomas, Keith A. Cross-Lengua Coloring Book for Kids. Thomas, Keith A., illus. l.t. ed. 2004. (ENG & SPA., Illus.). 22p. (J). (gr. 3-18). pap. *(978-0-9617451-2-7(6))* KALEXT Productions, LLC.

Thomas, Louis, illus. A Walk on the Wild Side: Filled with Facts & over 60 Creatures. 2016. (ENG.). 80p. (J). (gr. k-3). 19.99 *(978-1-84780-914-8(6),* Frances Lincoln Children's Bks.) Quarto Publishing Group UK GBR. Dist: Hachette Bk. Group.

Thomas Nelson. A Hole Lot of Fun. 2016. (ENG., Illus.). 64p. (J). (gr. k-4). pap. *(978-1-78598-150-0(1))* Make Believe Ideas.

—My Perfect Pug Doodle Pet. 2015. (ENG.). 98p. (J). (gr. -1-7). pap. *(978-1-78393-961-9(3))* Make Believe Ideas.

—My Utterly Fluttery Coloring Book. 2015. (ENG.). 98p. (J). (gr. -1-2). pap. *(978-1-78393-555-0(3))* Make Believe Ideas.

Thompson, Lauren. Little Quack Loves Colors. Anderson, Derek, illus. 2009. (Super Chubbies Ser.). (ENG.). 26p. (J). (gr. -1 — 1). bds. 5.99 *(978-1-4169-6094-2(5),* Little Simon) Little Simon.

Thong, Roseanne Greenfield. Green Is a Chile Pepper: A Book of Colors. Parra, John, illus. 2016. (ENG.). 40p. (J). (gr. -1-k). 7.99 *(978-1-4521-5645-3(X))* Chronicle Bks. LLC.

Tierney, Tom. Fashions from India. 2013. (Dover Fashion Coloring Book Ser.). (ENG., Illus.). 48p. (J). (gr. 3-12). pap. 4.99 *(978-0-486-43040-9(5))* Dover Pubns., Inc.

—Fashions of the Old South Coloring Book. 2004. (Dover Fashion Coloring Book Ser.). (ENG., Illus.). 32p. (J). (gr. 3-8). pap. 3.99 *(978-0-486-43876-4(7))* Dover Pubns., Inc.

—Fashions of the Roaring Twenties Coloring Book. 2013. (Dover Coloring Bks.). (ENG., Illus.). 32p. (gr. 3-12). pap. 3.99 *(978-0-486-49950-5(2))* Dover Pubns., Inc.

—Mexican Folk Dance Paper Dolls. 2013. (Dover Paper Dolls Ser.). (ENG.). 32p. (gr. 3-8). pap. 9.99 *(978-0-486-48831-8(4))* Dover Pubns., Inc.

Tigger. (Disney Fun Shaped Coloring Ser.). 64p. pap. *(978-1-4054-9264-5(3))* Parragon, Inc.

Toca! (J). 2.95 *(978-958-607-885-6(X))* Sociedad de San Pablo COL. Dist: St Pauls/Alba Hse. Pubs.

Touched by Him: Bible Story Coloring Book. 2006. (ENG, CHI & RUS.). (J). 1.99 *(978-0-9777446-0-2(4))* Childrens Bible Society.

Toufexis, George. Great Explorers Activity Book. 2012. (Dover Children's Activity Bks.). (ENG.). 48p. (J). (gr. 2-6). pap. 4.99 *(978-0-486-48367-2(3))* Dover Pubns., Inc.

—History's Mysteries! Animals: Activity Book. 2012. (Dover Children's Activity Bks.). (ENG.). 48p. (J). (gr. 3-8). pap. 4.99 *(978-0-486-48699-4(0))* Dover Pubns., Inc.

—History's Mysteries! Dinosaurs: Activity Book. 2012. (Dover Children's Activity Bks.). (ENG.). 48p. (J). (gr. 3-8). pap. 4.99 *(978-0-486-48698-7(2))* Dover Pubns., Inc.

—MONSTER MASH-Up — Aliens Meet Their Match. 2012. (Dover Coloring Bks.). (ENG.). 48p. (J). (gr. 3-8). pap. 4.99 *(978-0-486-48949-0(3))* Dover Pubns., Inc.

—MONSTER MASH-Up — Dinosaurs Face Destruction. 2012. (Dover Coloring Bks.). (ENG.). 48p. (J). (gr. 3-8). pap. 4.99 *(978-0-486-48950-6(7))* Dover Pubns., Inc.

—Nelson Mandela Coloring Book. 2014. (ENG.). 32p. (J). (gr. 3-8). pap. 3.99 *(978-0-486-78813-5(X))* Dover Pubns., Inc.

—River Monsters of the World. 2014. (ENG., Illus.). 32p. (J). (gr. 3-8). pap. 3.99 *(978-0-486-49627-5(9))* Dover Pubns., Inc.

—The Unbelievable Cryptozoology Coloring Book. 2014. (ENG.). 32p. (J). (gr. 3-8). pap. 3.99 *(978-0-486-78053-5(8))* Dover Pubns., Inc.

—World Atlas Activity & Coloring Book. 2014. (ENG.). 64p. (J). (gr. 3-5). pap. 5.99 *(978-0-486-78121-1(6))* Dover Pubns., Inc.

Toufexis, George & Coloring Books Staff. Sharks! Coloring Book. 2013. (Dover Nature Coloring Book Ser.). (ENG.). 32p. (J). (gr. 2-5). pap. 3.99 *(978-0-486-49028-1(9))* Dover Pubns., Inc.

Toufexis, George, et al. Sharks. 2011. (Dover 3-D Coloring Book Ser.). (ENG., Illus.). 32p. (J). (gr. 2-6). 5.99 *(978-0-486-48426-6(2))* Dover Pubns., Inc.

Toutz-Hager, Tanya. Goddesses of Legend & Myth: A Coloring Book Celebrating the Heroines of Ancient Europe. Stockton, Greta & Philbrick, Katie, illus. Date not set. 40p. (YA). (gr. 4-12). pap. 8.95 *(978-0-9672107-0-4(4))* MoonStar Pr.

Tracey, Andrée. Buddies NOT Bullies Rule! 2016. (Dover Coloring Bks.). (ENG.). 32p. (J). (gr. k-3). pap. 3.99 *(978-0-486-80148-3(9))* Dover Pubns., Inc.

—Marvelous Me! a Personalized Coloring Book. 2016. (Dover Coloring Bks.). (ENG.). 32p. (J). (gr. -1-3). pap. 4.99 *(978-0-486-80758-4(4))* Dover Pubns., Inc.

Traeger, Heather. Rabbiting on Nowingi - A Coloring Book: A Bush Kid Loving the Red Soil, Australian Bush Animals & Starry Nights! 2011. 48p. (gr. 1-2). pap. 9.89 *(978-1-4269-9510-1(5))* Trafford Publishing.

Trafford, Adrienne. Cat & Dog See the World Coloring Book. 2014. (ENG., Illus.). 32p. (J). (gr. -1-5). pap. 3.99 *(978-0-486-49468-5(3))* Dover Pubns., Inc.

—The Journey Coloring Book, 1 vol. 2011. (ENG., Illus.). 48p. pap. 9.99 *(978-0-7643-3784-0(X),* 9780764337840, Schiffer Publishing Ltd) Schiffer Publishing, Ltd.

—SPARK Cat & Dog Around the World Coloring Book. 2017. (Dover Coloring Bks.). (ENG.). 64p. (J). (gr. 1-4). pap. 5.99 *(978-0-486-81433-9(5))* Dover Pubns., Inc.

—Tarot Designs Coloring Book. 2014. (ENG., Illus.). 32p. (J). (gr. 6-8). pap. 3.99 *(978-0-486-49460-9(8))* Dover Pubns., Inc.

Traini, Agostino. Christmas Find & Color. 2009. (Dover Children's Activity Bks.). (ENG., Illus.). 48p. (J). (gr. -1-2). pap. 4.99 *(978-0-486-47112-9(8))* Dover Pubns., Inc.

—Springtime Find & Color. 2009. (Dover Children's Activity Bks.). (ENG., Illus.). 46p. (J). (gr. 1-5). pap. 4.99 *(978-0-486-47336-9(8))* Dover Pubns., Inc.

Triplett, Annette. From the Farm to You Coloring Book. Vale, Joe, ed. Murphy, Dennis, illus. 2012. 28p. (J). *(978-0-933842-34-2(1))* Univ. of Missouri, Extension.

Tudosa-Fundureanu, Lucia. Coloring Book Happy Vegetables. Chabvepi-Tudosa, Patricia, tr. Lazar, Ligia, illus. 2012. 50p. pap. 11.95 *(978-1-936629-17-6(8))* Reflection Publishing.

Tulip, Jenny, illus. Sticker & Color-In Playbook: The Teddy Bear Dance. 2016. (ENG.). 16p. (J). (gr. -1-12). pap. 4.99 *(978-1-86147-751-4(1),* Armadillo) Anness Publishing GBR. Dist: National Bk. Network.

—Sticker & Colour-In Playbook: With over 60 Reusable Stickers - Teddy Bear ABC. 2016. (ENG.). 16p. (J). (gr. -1-12). pap. 4.99 *(978-1-86147-745-3(7),* Armadillo) Anness Publishing GBR. Dist: National Bk. Network.

Tullet, Hervé. Doodle Cook. Barbour, Susan, tr. from FRE. 2011. (ENG., Illus.). 48p. pap. 14.95 *(978-0-7148-6070-1(0))* Phaidon Pr., Inc.

Turnbull, S. Trains. 2004. (Discovery Program Ser.). (SPA., Illus.). 48p. (J). (gr. 3-18). lib. bdg. 16.95 *(978-1-58086-410-7(4))* EDC Publishing.

Turner, Gary. Guitar Method for Young Beginners, Book 1. Stewart, James, illus. 2006. (Young Beginner Giant Coloring Bks.). 36p. pap. incl. audio compact disk *(978-1-86469-096-5(8))* LearnToPlayMusic.com Pty Ltd.

—Keyboard Method for Young Beginners, Book 1. Stewart, James, illus. 2006. (Young Beginner Giant Coloring Bks.). 48p. pap. incl. audio compact disk *(978-1-86469-097-2(6))* LearnToPlayMusic.com Pty Ltd.

—Piano Method for Young Beginners, Book 1. Stewart, James, illus. 2006. (Young Beginner Giant Coloring Bks.). 44p. pap. incl. audio compact disk *(978-1-86469-098-9(4))* LearnToPlayMusic.com Pty Ltd.

—Recorder Method for Young Beginners, Book 1. Stewart, James, illus. 2006. (Young Beginner Giant Coloring Bks.). 36p. pap. *(978-1-86469-099-6(2))* LearnToPlayMusic.com Pty Ltd.

Turton, Karalynn Teresa. The Passion for Children: Bilingual (English & Spanish) Guide to the Passion of Christ, 1 bk. Ruiz, Jeanette, tr. Burnett, Anne, illus. 2005. (J). 3.00 *(978-0-9765180-0-6(7))* Catholic World Mission.

Twin Sisters(r), et al. The Story of Christmas: Coloring & Activity Book. 2016. (ENG.). 32p. (J). pap. 4.99 *(978-1-63409-801-4(3))* Barbour Publishing, Inc.

Tyndale, prod. Big Bible Fun Color & Learn, Vol. 1. 2014. (Happy Day Ser.). (ENG.). 96p. (J). pap. 2.49 *(978-1-4143-9500-5(0))* Tyndale Hse. Pubs.

—The Gigantic Coloring Book of Bible Stories. 2014. (ENG.). 384p. (J). pap. 5.99 *(978-1-4143-9498-5(5))* Tyndale Hse. Pubs.

—The Gigantic Coloring Book of God's World. 2014. (ENG.). 320p. (J). pap. 5.99 *(978-1-4143-9499-2(3))* Tyndale Hse. Pubs.

Urban, Erin & Romano, Alexis, eds. Sailors' Snug Harbor Coloring Book. 2005. (Illus.). (J). spiral bd. *(978-0-9623017-1-1(X))* Noble Maritime Collection, The.

Valle, Anita. Best Princess Coloring Book. 2012. 50p. pap. 10.50 *(978-1-105-54804-8(X))* Lulu Pr., Inc.

Vamos a Divertirnos, 4 bks., Set. (SPA & ENG.). 120p. (J). pap. 9.95 *(978-970-607-688-5(3),* LA6883) Larousse, Ediciones, S. A. de C. V. MEX. Dist: Continental Bk. Co., Inc.

van Gogh, Vincent & Noble, Marty. Van Gogh Stained Glass Coloring Book. 2007. (Dover Stained Glass Coloring Book Ser.). (ENG., Illus.). 32p. (gr. 6-8). 6.99 *(978-0-486-45671-3(4))* Dover Pubns., Inc.

Van Leeuwed, Wendy. Agents of God Activity Book. 2007. (Illus.). 16p. (J). pap. 1.89 *(978-1-59317-193-3(5))* Warner Pr., Inc.

Van Leeuwen, Wendy. Miracle Man Activity Book. 2007. (Illus.). 16p. (J). pap. 1.89 *(978-1-59317-209-1(5))* Warner Pr., Inc.

—The Ten Commandments Activity Book. 2007. (Illus.). 16p. (J). pap. 1.89 *(978-1-59317-210-7(9))* Warner Pr., Inc.

Veggie Tales Cast. Veggietales Lots of Fun Color. rev. ed. 2004. (ENG., Illus.). 400p. (J). pap. 5.99 *(978-1-4037-0538-9(0),* Spirit Pr.) Bendon, Inc.

Verlag, Arena. Kids' Magical Mandalas. 2004. (ENG., Illus.). 64p. (J). pap. 4.95 *(978-1-4027-1721-5(0))* Sterling Publishing Co., Inc.

Vic Visits Ground Zero. 2004. (J). *(978-0-9761102-0-0(2))* Adams, Evelyn.

Voce, Karma. Forever Inspired Coloring Book: Paris Fashions. 2016. (ENG., Illus.). 96p. (J). (gr. 3-7). pap. 7.99

(978-1-944686-60-4(6), Racehorse Publishing) Skyhorse Publishing Co., Inc.

Volke, Gordon. Big World Activity Sticker Book, Vol. 2. 2004. (Illus.). 16p. 7.25 *(978-1-84161-130-3(1))* Ravette Publishing, Ltd. GBR. Dist: Parkwest Pubns., Inc.

Walke, Ted, illus. & compiled by. Boating Safety Sidekicks Color a Fish: Freshwater Fish Coloring Book. Walke, Ted, compiled by. 2008. 28p. (J). *(978-0-9718864-4-5(X))* Within Reach, Inc.

Walker, Gary C. Confederate Coloring & Learning Book. Breaux, Joe Ann, illus. 2004. 41p. (J). (gr. 1-7). pap. 4.95 *(978-0-9617898-5-5(9))* A & W Enterprises.

Walker, Sylvia. The Art Museum: A Sticker Story Coloring Book. 2011. (Dover Coloring Bks.). (ENG.). 32p. (J). (gr. 1-5). pap. 5.99 *(978-0-486-48039-8(9))* Dover Pubns., Inc.

—At the Wedding. 2009. (Dover Coloring Bks.). (ENG., Illus.). 32p. (J). (gr. -1-3). pap. 3.99 *(978-0-486-46778-8(3))* Dover Pubns., Inc.

—Halloween ABC Coloring Book. 2011. (Dover Holiday Coloring Book Ser.). (ENG.). 32p. (J). (gr. -1-3). pap. 3.99 *(978-0-486-48175-3(1))* Dover Pubns., Inc.

—Happy New Year Around the World. 2012. (Dover Holiday Coloring Book Ser.). (ENG., Illus.). 32p. (J). (gr. -1-3). pap. 3.99 *(978-0-486-48988-9(4))* Dover Pubns., Inc.

—Let's Color Together — My Sleepover. 2014. (ENG., Illus.). 64p. (J). (gr. -1-3). pap. 3.99 *(978-0-486-77973-7(4))* Dover Pubns., Inc.

—My Sleepover Coloring Book. 2010. (Dover Coloring Bks.). (ENG., Illus.). 32p. (J). (gr. -1-4). pap. 3.99 *(978-0-486-47656-8(1))* Dover Pubns., Inc.

—Our New Baby Coloring Book. 2014. (Dover Coloring Bks.). (ENG.). 32p. (J). (gr. -1-2). pap. 3.99 *(978-0-486-49462-3(4))* Dover Pubns., Inc.

—Storyland: We're Moving! A Story Coloring Book. 2015. (Dover Coloring Bks.). (ENG., Illus.). 32p. (J). (gr. k-5). pap. 3.99 *(978-0-486-79412-9(1))* Dover Pubns., Inc.

Walker, Sylvia & Coloring Books Staff. Easter Egg Hunt Coloring Book. 2012. (Dover Holiday Coloring Book Ser.). (ENG., Illus.). 32p. (J). (gr. -1-3). pap. 3.99 *(978-0-486-48521-8(8))* Dover Pubns., Inc.

Wallace, Melissa. It's Great to Be a Baton Rouge Kid: An a-Z Coloring Book, 1 vol. 2017. (ENG., Illus.). 32p. pap. 4.95 ***(978-1-4556-2373-0(3))*** Pelican Publishing Co., Inc.

Wallace, Melissa. It's Great to Be a NOLA Kid: An a-Z Coloring Book, 1 vol. 2015. (ENG., Illus.). 32p. (J). pap. 4.95 *(978-1-4556-2052-4(1))* Pelican Publishing Co., Inc.

Walter Foster Creative Team. Animals: 30+ Fun & Relaxing Color-by-Number Projects to Engage & Entertain. 2016. (Color by Number Ser.). (ENG.). 112p. pap. 17.95 *(978-1-63322-099-7(0)*, Walter Foster) Quarto Publishing Group USA.

—Sticker Pictures - Animals. 2017. (Sticker & Color-By-Number Ser.). (ENG., Illus.). 48p. (J). (gr. k-3). pap. 9.95 *(978-1-63322-279-3(9)*, Walter Foster Jr) Quarto Publishing Group USA.

—Sticker Pictures - Pets: Stick, Color & Create One Sticker at a Time! 2017. (Sticker & Color-By-Number Ser.). (ENG., Illus.). 48p. (J). (gr. k-3). pap. 9.95 *(978-1-63322-278-6(0)*, Walter Foster Jr) Quarto Publishing Group USA.

Walters, Kathy. Circles into Another World, the Amazing World of Coloring: Prelude. 2012. 50p. pap. 8.99 *(978-1-4525-5454-9(4))* Balboa Pr.

Warner Press, creator. The Best Christmas Gift Ever: Coloring & Activity Book. 2008. (J). (gr. -1-3). pap. 11.34 *(978-1-59317-324-1(5))* Warner Pr., Inc.

—Bible Sports Heroes: Great Lessons You Can Learn from God's Favorite Athletes Activity Book. 2008. (J). (gr. -1-3). pap. 11.34 *(978-1-59317-325-8(3))* Warner Pr., Inc.

—Learning the Lord's Prayer: Coloring & Activity Book. 2008. (J). (gr. -1-3). pap. 11.34 *(978-1-59317-323-4(7))* Warner Pr., Inc.

—My Favorite Bible Stories Coloring Book. 2009. (Illus.). (gr. -1-2). 4.50 *(978-1-59317-352-4(0))* Warner Pr., Inc.

—The Ten Commandments Coloring Book. 2009. (Illus.). 16p. (J). (gr. -1-2). pap. 11.34 *(978-1-59317-340-1(7))* Warner Pr., Inc.

—Zacchaeus Climbs a Tree Coloring Book. 2009. (ENG., Illus.). 16p. (J). (gr. -1-k). pap. 11.34 *(978-1-59317-337-1(7))* Warner Pr., Inc.

Warner Press Kids, creator. The Jelly Bean Prayer Coloring & Activity Book. 2009. (Illus.). (J). (gr. -1-2). 11.34 *(978-1-59317-348-7(2))* Warner Pr., Inc.

—The Jelly Bean Witness. 2009. 16p. (J). (gr. 1-5). pap. 11.34 *(978-1-59317-350-0(4))* Warner Pr., Inc.

—Jesus Is Born: Coloring Book. 2008. 16p. (J). (gr. -1-3). pap. 11.34 *(978-1-59317-322-7(9))* Warner Pr., Inc.

Warner Press Staff. Jesus in My Heart Coloring Books Intermediate. 2005. 2.69 *(978-0-87162-939-5(9))* Warner Pr., Inc.

—Jesus Loves Me Coloring Book Pre-K. 2005. (J). pap. 2.69 *(978-1-59317-017-2(3))* Warner Pr., Inc.

Watt, Fiona. Christmas Magic Painting Book. 2015. (Magic Painting Bks.). (ENG.). 32p. (J). (gr. k-5). pap. 9.99 *(978-0-7945-3577-3(1)*, Usborne) EDC Publishing.

—Drawing, Doodling & Coloring Fashion. Miller, Antonia, illus. 2013. (Activity Bks). 128p. (J). pap. 13.99 *(978-0-7945-3336-6(1)*, Usborne) EDC Publishing.

—Lots of Things to Find & Color. 2011. 96p. pap. 12.99 *(978-0-7945-2963-5(1)*, Usborne) EDC Publishing.

—The Usborne Book of Drawing, Doodling & Coloring Book. Harrison, Erica & Lovell, Katie, illus. 2010. 126p. (J). pap. 13.99 *(978-0-7945-2788-4(4))* EDC Publishing.

—The Usborne Color by Numbers Book. Harrison, Erica, illus. 2014. (ENG.). (J). pap. 5.99 *(978-0-7945-3251-2(9)*, Usborne) EDC Publishing.

Waycott, Flora. Winter Wonderland to Color. Waycott, Flora, illus. 2016. (Illus.). 96p. (J). (gr. -1). pap. 15.99 *(978-0-06-256997-4(X))* HarperCollins Pubs.

Webber, John, et al, illus. The Childhood of Jesus / la niñez de Jesús. 2007. Tr. of niñez de Jesús. (ENG & SPA.). 24p. (J). pap. 3.50 *(978-0-9801121-5-3(X))* Holy Heroes LLC.

Weber, Amy & Creative Haven Staff. Creative Haven Curious Creatures Coloring Book. 2013. (Adult Coloring Ser.). (ENG., Illus.). 64p. (gr. 3). pap. 5.99 *(978-0-486-49269-8(9))* Dover Pubns., Inc.

Weinberger, David J. Answers to a Christmas Question Coloring Book. 2012. (ENG.). (J). pap. *(978-1-4675-2380-6(1))* Independent Pub.

Wekelo, Kerry Alison. Audrey's Coloring & Activity Book: Let's Do Yoga. 2012. 48p. (gr. -1). pap. 12.95 *(978-1-4772-4366-4(6))* AuthorHouse.

Wellington, Monica. Color & Cook BREAKFAST. 2010. (Dover Coloring Bks.). (ENG., Illus.). 32p. (J). (gr. -1-3). pap. 4.99 *(978-0-486-47763-3(0))* Dover Pubns., Inc.

—Color & Cook CUPCAKES. 2009. (Dover Coloring Bks.). (ENG., Illus.). 32p. (J). (gr. -1-3). pap. 4.99 *(978-0-486-47113-6(6))* Dover Pubns., Inc.

—Color & Cook HEALTHY SNACKS. 2010. (Dover Coloring Bks.). (ENG., Illus.). 32p. (J). (gr. -1-3). pap. 4.99 *(978-0-486-47449-6(6))* Dover Pubns., Inc.

—Color & Cook PIZZA. 2009. (Dover Coloring Bks.). (ENG., Illus.). 32p. (J). (gr. -1-3). pap. 4.99 *(978-0-486-47114-3(4))* Dover Pubns., Inc.

—Color & Cook Story Coloring Book. 2014. (ENG.). 160p. (J). (gr. -1-5). pap. 5.99 *(978-0-486-77967-6(X))* Dover Pubns., Inc.

—Color & Cook TEA PARTY! 2013. (ENG.). 32p. (J). (gr. -1-3). pap. 4.99 *(978-0-486-49270-4(2))* Dover Pubns., Inc.

—Color & Garden FLOWERS. 2011. (Dover Coloring Bks.). (ENG., Illus.). 32p. (J). (gr. -1-3). pap. 4.99 *(978-0-486-47860-9(2))* Dover Pubns., Inc.

—Color & Garden VEGETABLES. 2011. (Dover Children's Activity Bks.). (ENG., Illus.). 32p. (J). (gr. -1-3). pap. 4.99 *(978-0-486-47959-0(5))* Dover Pubns., Inc.

Wells, Rachel. Farm. 2011. (That's Not My.... Coloring Books Ser.). 32p. (J). pap. 4.99 *(978-0-7945-3011-2(7)*, Usborne) EDC Publishing.

—That's Not My Christmas Coloring Book. 2011. (That's Not My... Coloring Book Ser.). 32p. (J). pap. 4.99 *(978-0-7945-3155-3(5)*, Usborne) EDC Publishing.

Welsh Books Staff. Llyfr Lliwio Sali Mali. 2nd ed. 2005. (WEL., Illus.). 24p. pap. *(978-1-902416-88-5(0))* Cymdeithas Lyfrau Ceredigion.

Werden's class. Nunamiut ABC: A Child's View of Life in an Alaska Village. Written & Illustrated by the 4th & 5th Graders of Anaktuvuk Pass, Alaska. Werden's class, illus. 2003. (Illus.). 28p. (J). 3.95 *(978-0-930931-54-4(8))* Alaska Geographic Assn.

West, Grace. Australian Colouring Book. 2016. (ENG.). 112p. 11.95 *(978-0-670-07933-9(2))* Penguin Books Australia AUS. Dist: Independent Pubs. Group.

Whatmore, Candace. Monsters Coloring Book. 2012. (Coloring Bks). 32p. (J). pap. 5.99 *(978-0-7945-3195-9(4)*, Usborne) EDC Publishing.

Whatmore, Candice. 25 Postcards to Color. 2013. (Greeting Cards Ser.). 25p. (J). 7.99 *(978-0-7945-3293-2(4)*, Usborne) EDC Publishing.

Whelon, Chuck. Dinoscenes. 2009. (Dover Coloring Bks.). (ENG., Illus.). 32p. (J). (gr. -1-5). pap. 3.99 *(978-0-486-47263-8(9))* Dover Pubns., Inc.

—Word Play: Write Your Own Crazy Comics, No. 1. 2011. (Dover Children's Activity Bks.). (ENG., Illus.). 64p. (J). (gr. 3-5). pap. 5.99 *(978-0-486-48165-4(4))* Dover Pubns., Inc.

—Word Play! - Write Your Own Crazy Comics, No. 2. 2011. (Dover Children's Activity Bks.). (ENG., Illus.). 64p. (J). (gr. 3-5). pap. 5.99 *(978-0-486-48166-1(2))* Dover Pubns., Inc.

White, Elga Haymon. A Children's Adventure Duo: Thad the Sailor & Little Miss Lavendar. Freudiger, Victoria, ed. Bjornsen, Holly, illus. 2007. 130p. (J). per. 13.95 *(978-0-9785728-2-2(3))* Digi-Tall Media.

Who Lives in the Coral Reef. 2004. (J). 6.95 *(978-0-931548-12-3(8))* Island Heritage Publishing.

A Whole World to Colour In. 2017. (Asterix Ser.). (ENG.). 112p. (J). (gr. 4-6). 19.99 *(978-1-5101-0238-5(8)*, Orion Children's Bks.) Hachette Children's Group GBR. Dist: Hachette Bk. Group.

Why I Believe in Jesus: A Finish-the-Picture Coloring Book. (Illus.). 16p. (J). pap. 1.50 *(978-0-87162-814-5(7)*, E6027) Warner Pr., Inc.

The Wiggles Coloring & Activity Books. 2004. (J). act. bk. ed. 0.99 *(978-0-7666-1048-4(9)*, 99530); act. bk. ed. 0.99 *(978-0-7666-1047-7(0)*, 99530); act. bk. ed. 0.99 *(978-0-7666-1049-1(7)*, 99530) Modern Publishing.

The Wiggles Giant Coloring & Activity Books. 2004. (J). act. bk. ed. 1.99 *(978-0-7666-1050-7(0)*, 49220); act. bk. ed. 1.99 *(978-0-7666-1051-4(9)*, 49220) Modern Publishing.

Wik, John. Visual Chaos Stained Glass Coloring Book. 2011. (Dover Design Stained Glass Coloring Book Ser.). (ENG., Illus.). 32p. (J). (gr. 3-5). pap. 6.99 *(978-0-486-47562-2(X))* Dover Pubns., Inc.

Wik, John & Coloring Books for Adults. Deco Tech: Geometric Coloring Book. 2010. (Dover Design Coloring Bks.). (ENG., Illus.). 32p. (J). (gr. 1-5). pap. 3.99 *(978-0-486-47546-2(8))* Dover Pubns., Inc.

Wik, John & Creative Haven Staff. Creative Haven Tessellation Patterns Coloring Book. 2013. (Adult Coloring Ser.). (ENG., Illus.). 64p. (J). (gr. 3). pap. 5.99 *(978-0-486-49165-3(X))* Dover Pubns., Inc.

Wilde, Cindy, illus. Beautiful Copycat Coloring Book: Pretty Pictures to Copy & Complete. 2015. (ENG.). 48p. (J). (gr. 1-4). pap. 6.99 *(978-1-4380-0636-9(5))* Barron's Educational Series, Inc.

Wilde, Cindy, et al, illus. Color with Me. 2016. (ENG.). 96p. (J). (gr. 1-6). spiral bd. 12.95 *(978-1-4549-1930-8(2))* Sterling Publishing Co., Inc.

—Color with Mom. 2016. (ENG.). 96p. (J). (gr. 1-6). spiral bd. 12.95 *(978-1-4549-1931-5(0))* Sterling Publishing Co., Inc.

Wilde, Cindy & French, Felicity, illus. Beautiful Coloring. 2016. (ENG.). 128p. (J). (gr. 2-6). pap. 12.95 *(978-1-4549-1885-1(3))* Sterling Publishing Co., Inc.

Wilson, Ray. Kelsey's Lessons on Africa Vol 2. 2013. 42p. pap. 12.00 *(978-0-9857741-1-0(8))* Village Publishing.

Wilson, Todd. Southwest Desert Animal Coloring Book. (J). pap. 2.00 *(978-0-918080-86-8(X))* Rio Nuevo Pubs.

Winslow, Jeremy. Hours of Coloring Fun with Shapes & Patterns. 2011. 182p. 30.99 *(978-1-4568-8227-3(9))*; pap. 20.99 *(978-1-4568-8226-6(0))* Xlibris Corp.

Witcher, John. 123 & Me. 2009. 28p. pap. 13.99 *(978-1-4389-6896-4(5))* AuthorHouse.

Witty One Funny Family Fotos Coloring Book. 2003. (J). *(978-1-932435-17-7(4))* Cardinal Brands, Inc.

Witty One Restickable Coloring Book - Animal Morphs. 2003. (Illus.). (J). per. *(978-1-932435-05-4(0))* Cardinal Brands, Inc.

Witty One Restickable Coloring Book - Invisible. 2003. per. *(978-1-932435-15-3(8))* Cardinal Brands, Inc.

Witty One Restickable Coloring Book - Noah's Ark. 2003. per. *(978-1-932435-06-1(9))* Cardinal Brands, Inc.

Witty One Restickable Coloring Book - under the Sea. 2003. per. *(978-1-932435-10-8(7))*; per. *(978-1-932435-00-9(X))* Cardinal Brands, Inc.

Witty One Restickable Sticker Search Coloring Book. 2003. (J). spiral bd. *(978-1-932435-08-5(5))* Cardinal Brands, Inc.

Wonderland Unicorns: Coloring book by Darla Hallmark. 2007. (Illus.). 20p. (YA). 10.00 *(978-0-9795206-1-7(4))* Unseen Gallery.

Wood, David. The Little House on Buchanan Street. 2007. 24p. per. 12.95 *(978-1-934246-64-1(6))* Peppertree Pr., The.

Wooding, Sharon. Mark Twain in Nevada, a History Coloring Book for Children. l.t. ed. 2003. (Illus.). 25p. (J). pap. 5.95 *(978-0-9727757-0-0(6))*; (SPA.). pap. 5.95 *(978-0-9727757-1-7(4))* Susy & Livy Pubns.

Workman Publishing, Workman. Paint by Sticker Kids: Create 10 Pictures One Sticker at a Time. 2016. (Paint by Sticker Ser.). (ENG., Illus.). 34p. (J). (gr. k-5). 9.95 *(978-0-7611-8941-1(6))* Workman Publishing Co., Inc.

The World of Eric Carle My Color Wheel Activity Kit. 2007. (J). 16.99 *(978-0-9794445-2-4(7))* Loew-Cornell, Inc.

The World of Eric Carle My Warm & Cool Color Activity Kit. 2007. (J). 16.99 *(978-0-9794445-5-5(1))* Loew-Cornell, Inc.

Wright, Shannon. Dinosaurs & Monsters Coloring Book. 2013. (ENG.). 38p. 13.00 *(978-1-62884-683-6(6)*, Baby Professor (Education Kids)) Speedy Publishing LLC.

—Wild Wild Animals Coloring Book. 2013. (ENG.). 30p. 8.89 *(978-1-62884-680-5(1)*, Baby Professor (Education Kids)) Speedy Publishing LLC.

Wummel, Jeanette. Zendoodle Coloring: Playful Puppies: Furry Friends to Color & Display. 2017. (ENG., Illus.). 128p. pap. 13.99 *(978-1-250-14158-3(3)*, 9781250141583, St. Martin's Griffin) St. Martin's Pr.

Wyland: Ocean Life. 2010. (Illus.). 24p. (J). pap. 6.95 *(978-1-884840-91-3(4))* Wyland Worldwide, LLC.

Wynne, Patricia J. Creative Haven NatureScapes Coloring Book. 2014. (Adult Coloring Ser.). (ENG.). 64p. (gr. 3). pap. 5.99 *(978-0-486-49450-0(0))* Dover Pubns., Inc.

—Creative Haven SeaScapes Coloring Book. 2013. (Adult Coloring Ser.). (ENG.). 64p. (gr. 3). pap. 5.99 *(978-0-486-49423-4(3))* Dover Pubns., Inc.

—King Tut Coloring Book. 2005. (Dover History Coloring Book Ser.). (ENG., Illus.). 32p. (J). (gr. 3-5). 3.99 *(978-0-486-44444-4(9))* Dover Pubns., Inc.

Wynne, Patricia J. & MacPhee, Ross. Race to the South Pole Coloring Book. 2010. (Dover History Coloring Book Ser.). (ENG.). 32p. (gr. 3-8). pap. 3.99 *(978-0-486-47668-1(5))* Dover Pubns., Inc.

Wynne, Patricia J. & Silver, Donald M. BOOST My First Human Body Coloring Book. 2013. (BOOST Educational Ser.). (ENG.). 32p. (J). (gr. 1-2). pap. 4.99 *(978-0-486-49410-4(1))* Dover Pubns., Inc.

Yacoubou, Jeanne. I Am a Rainbow Child Coloring-Story Book. Stebakova, Elena, illus. 2005. 16p. (J). *(978-0-9788737-4-5(2))* Alaafia Kids Co.

—Wanna Play? Coloring-Story Book. Stebakova, Elena, illus. 2005. 16p. (J). *(978-0-9788737-5-2(0))* Alaafia Kids Co.

—What's My Heritage? Coloring-Story Book. Stebakova, Elena, illus. 2006. 24p. (J). *(978-0-9788737-2-1(6))* Alaafia Kids Co.

Yoon, Salina, creator. Country Pals: A Sparkling Little Colors Book. 2005. (Sparkling Little Colors Book Ser.). (ENG., Illus.). 12p. (J). bds. 5.95 *(978-1-58117-167-9(6)*, Intervisual/Piggy Toes) Bendon, Inc.

—Little Friends: A Sparkling Little Colors Book, 4 vols. 2005. (ENG., Illus.). 12p. (J). bds. 5.95 *(978-1-58117-168-6(4)*, Intervisual/Piggy Toes) Bendon, Inc.

Yoon, Sarah. To the Moon: The World's Tallest Coloring Book. 2016. (ENG.). 14p. (J). (gr. -1-3). pap. 14.95 *(978-1-78067-757-6(X))* King, Laurence Publishing GBR. Dist: Hachette Bk. Group.

—To the Ocean Deep: The Longest Colouring Book in the World. 2016. (ENG.). 14p. (J). (gr. -1-3). pap. 14.95 *(978-1-78067-770-5(7))* King, Laurence Publishing GBR. Dist: Hachette Bk. Group.

Zaboly, Gary. Barack Obama Coloring Book. 2009. (Dover History Coloring Book Ser.). (ENG., Illus.). 32p. (J). (gr. 3-6). pap. 3.99 *(978-0-486-47320-8(1))* Dover Pubns., Inc.

—Frederick Douglass Coloring Book. 2014. (ENG.). 32p. (gr. 4). pap. 3.99 *(978-0-486-49215-5(X))* Dover Pubns., Inc.

—Story of World War I. 2013. (Dover History Coloring Book Ser.). (ENG.). 48p. (gr. 3-12). pap. 4.99 *(978-0-486-49791-4(7))* Dover Pubns., Inc.

Zambarano, Richard, illus. Wilbur & Wilma's Colorful Campus Tour - University of Arizona A-Z. 2004. (J). 9.99 *(978-1-933069-02-9(3))* Odd Duck Ink, Inc.

Zarrika's Horse Show Coloring & Activity Book. 2006. (J). *(978-0-9758663-3-7(8))* Zarrika, Ltd.

Zimmerman, Beverly. Bridal Planner. 2013. (ENG.). 49p. pap. 29.99 *(978-1-932676-80-8(5))* Vision Pubs., LLC.

Zimmerman, Erik. Booga-Boo - Coloring Book. 2005. (Illus.). 32p. (J). per. 7.99 *(978-1-59879-009-2(9))* Lifevest Publishing, Inc.

Zinjiba-Nyakutya, Peshie. From Adam to Noah in Coloring Pages: Genesis 1 To 9. Chitombo, Patience, illus. 2012. 64p. pap. 12.50 *(978-1-61897-769-4(5)*, Strategic Bk. Publishing) Strategic Book Publishing & Rights Agency (SBPRA).

Zondervan. The Beginner's Bible Coloring Book, 1 vol. 2017. (Beginner's Bible Ser.). (ENG.). 64p. (J). pap. 4.99 *(978-0-310-75955-3(2))* Zonderkidz.

—Faithgirlz Promises for You Coloring Devotional: 60 Days Discovering God's Hope & Love, 1 vol. 2017. (Faithgirlz Ser.). (ENG.). 128p. (J). 12.99 *(978-0-310-76119-8(0))* Zonderkidz.

Zondervan Staff. Beginners Bible Super Duper Mighty Jumbo Coloring Book, 1 vol. 2012. (Beginner's Bible Ser.). (ENG.). 384p. (J). pap. 6.99 *(978-0-310-72498-8(8))* Zonderkidz.

—Believe - Coloring Book: Think, Act, & Be Like Jesus, 1 vol. Pamintuan, Macky, illus. 2015. (ENG.). 64p. (J). pap. 4.99 *(978-0-310-75222-6(1))* Zonderkidz.

Zourelias, Diana. All Around New York City Mini Coloring Book. 2015. (Dover Little Activity Bks.). (ENG.). 64p. (J). (gr. k-3). pap. 1.99 *(978-0-486-79752-6(X))* Dover Pubns., Inc.

—A Barrel of Monkeys & Other Animal Groups. 2015. (Dover Coloring Bks.). (ENG.). 32p. (J). (gr. 1-5). pap. 3.99 *(978-0-486-78465-6(7))* Dover Pubns., Inc.

—Build a Giant Poster Coloring Book — United States Map. 2013. (Dover Build a Poster Coloring Book Ser.). (ENG., Illus.). 48p. (J). (gr. 3-5). pap. 4.99 *(978-0-486-49152-3(8))* Dover Pubns., Inc.

—First Ladies Fascinating Facts. 2012. (Dover History Coloring Book Ser.). (ENG.). 48p. (J). (gr. 3-5). pap. 4.99 *(978-0-486-49832-4(8))* Dover Pubns., Inc.

—Fun Facts about Everyday Inventions. 2013. (Dover Coloring Bks.). (ENG.). 32p. (J). (gr. 3-8). pap. 3.99 *(978-0-486-49778-5(X))* Dover Pubns., Inc.

—Monster Bugs. 2010. (Dover Nature Coloring Book Ser.). (ENG.). 32p. (J). (gr. 1-5). pap. 3.99 *(978-0-486-47673-5(1))* Dover Pubns., Inc.

—Monster Reptiles: A Close-Up Coloring Book. 2012. (Dover Nature Coloring Book Ser.). (ENG.). 32p. (J). (gr. 1-5). pap. 3.99 *(978-0-486-48252-1(9))* Dover Pubns., Inc.

—Presidential Pets Coloring Book. 2009. (Dover History Coloring Book Ser.). (ENG., Illus.). 32p. (J). (gr. 3-8). pap. 3.99 *(978-0-486-47450-2(X))* Dover Pubns., Inc.

—SPARK Silly Sea Life Find It! Color It! 2016. (Dover Coloring Bks.). (ENG.). 64p. (J). (gr. 1-4). pap. 5.99 *(978-0-486-81095-9(X))* Dover Pubns., Inc.

—SPARK U. S. A. Fun Find It! Color It! 2017. (Dover Coloring Bks.). (ENG.). 64p. (J). (gr. 1-4). pap. 5.99 ***(978-0-486-81893-1(4))*** Dover Pubns., Inc.

Zourelias, Diana. Weird & Wacky Jobs. 2015. (Dover Coloring Bks.). (ENG.). 48p. (J). (gr. k). pap. 4.99 *(978-0-486-78011-5(2))* Dover Pubns., Inc.

Zourelias, Diana & Coloring Books Staff. Monster Sea Creatures. 2012. (Dover Nature Coloring Book Ser.). (ENG., Illus.). 32p. (J). (gr. 1-5). pap. 3.99 *(978-0-486-48505-8(6))* Dover Pubns., Inc.

Zourelias, Diana, et al. Mix & Match PRINCESSES. 2012. (Dover Mix & Match Coloring Book Ser.). (ENG.). 48p. (J). (gr. 2-5). pap. 4.99 *(978-0-486-48846-2(2))* Dover Pubns., Inc.

Zschock, Heather. Wild Safari: An Art Activity Book for Imaginative Artists of All Ages. Barbas, Kerren, illus. 2005. (Activity Journal Ser.). 64p. (J). (gr. -1-7). 12.99 *(978-1-59359-971-3(4))* Peter Pauper Pr. Inc.

2006-2007 Tongue River Elementary 3rd Graders, text. Sheridan County History ABC Coloring & Activity Book - 2007. 2006-2007 Tongue River Elementary 3rd Graders, . 2007. (Illus.). 32p. (J). 3.95 *(978-0-9792871-1-4(1))* Sherian County Historical Society Pr.

COLORS

see Color

COLT, SAMUEL, 1814-1892

Wyckoff, Edwin Brit. The Man Behind the Gun: Samuel Colt & His Revolver. 2010. (Genius at Work! Great Inventor Biographies Ser.). (Illus.). 32p. (J). 23.94 *(978-0-7660-3446-4(1))* Enslow Pubs., Inc.

COLUMBIA RIVER AND VALLEY

Jackson, Tom. The Columbia River. 2003. (Rivers of North America Ser.). (Illus.). 32p. (gr. 2-6). lib. bdg. 26.00 *(978-0-8368-3754-4(1)*, Gareth Stevens Learning Library) Stevens, Gareth Publishing LLLP.

Lashnits, Tom. Columbia River. 2004. (Rivers in American Life & Times Ser.). (Illus.). 120p. (C). (gr. 9-13). 32.50 *(978-0-7910-7728-3(4)*, Chelsea Hse.) Facts On File, Inc.

COLUMBUS, CHRISTOPHER, 1451-1506

Abnett, Dan. Christopher Columbus & the Voyage of 1492. Q2A Staff, illus. 2007. (Jr. Graphic Biographies Ser.). (ENG.). 24p. (gr. 3-8). pap. 10.60 *(978-1-4042-2143-7(3)*, PowerKids Pr.) Rosen Publishing Group, Inc., The.

—Christopher Columbus & the Voyage Of 1492. (Jr. Graphic Biographies Ser.). (ENG.). 24p. (J). (gr. 2-3). 2009. 47.90 *(978-1-61513-810-4(2)*, PowerKids Pr.) 2007. (Illus.). lib. bdg. 25.25 *(978-1-4042-3390-4(3))* Rosen Publishing Group, Inc., The.

—Cristóbal Colón y el Viaje de 1942. 2009. (Historietas Juveniles: Biografías (Jr. Graphic Biographies) Ser.). (SPA & ENG., Illus.). 24p. (J). (gr. 2-5). 25.25 *(978-1-4358-8559-2(7))*; (gr. 3-8). pap. 10.60 *(978-1-4358-3312-8(0))* Rosen Publishing Group, Inc., The.

Allen, Kathy & Krueger, Jennifer. When Did Columbus Arrive in the Americas? And Other Questions about Columbus's Voyages. 2012. (Six Questions of American History Ser.). (ENG.). 48p. (gr. 4-6). pap. 56.72 *(978-0-7613-9240-8(8))*; pap. 9.95 *(978-0-7613-7127-4(3))*; lib. bdg. 30.60 *(978-0-7613-5327-0(5))* Lerner Publishing Group.

Aller, Susan Bivin. Christopher Columbus. 2003. (History Maker Bios Ser.). (Illus.). 48p. (J). (gr. 3-5). lib. bdg. 26.60 *(978-0-8225-0398-9(0))* Lerner Publishing Group.

Aloian, Molly. Columbus Day. 2010. (ENG., Illus.). 32p. (J). *(978-0-7787-4760-4(3))*; pap. *(978-0-7787-4778-9(6))* Crabtree Publishing Co.

Bach, Nancy. Cristoforo Colombo e la Pasta Al Pomodoro - Christopher Columbus & the Pasta with Tomato Sauce: A Bilingual Picture Book (Italian-English Text) Latti, Leo, illus. 2013. 30p. pap. *(978-1-938712-06-7(4))* Roxby Media Ltd.

Bader, Bonnie. Who Was Christopher Columbus? Harrison, Nancy, illus. 2013. (Who Was? Ser.). (ENG.). 112p. (J). (gr. 3-7). pap. 5.99 *(978-0-448-46333-9(4)*, Grosset & Dunlap) Penguin Young Readers Group.

—Who Was Christopher Columbus? 2013. (Who Was... ? Ser.). lib. bdg. 16.00 *(978-0-606-31684-2(1)*, Turtleback) Turtleback Bks.

Bailey, Gerry & Foster, Karen. Columbus's Chart. Radford, Karen & Noyes, Leighton, illus. 2008. (Stories of Great People Ser.). (ENG.). 40p. (J). (gr. 3-8). pap. *(978-0-7787-3708-7(X))*; lib. bdg. *(978-0-7787-3686-8(5))* Crabtree Publishing Co.

Benge, Janet & Benge, Geoff. Heroes of History - Christopher Columbus: Across the Ocean Sea. 2005. (Heroes of History Ser.). (ENG.). 191p. (YA). (gr. 5). pap. 9.99 *(978-1-932096-23-1(X))* Emerald Bks.

Berne, Emma Carlson. Did Christopher Columbus Really Discover America? And Other Question about the New World. 2015. (Good Question! Ser.). (ENG., Illus.). 32p. (J).

The check digit for ISBN-10 appears in parentheses after the full ISBN-13

(gr. 2). pap. 5.95 *(978-1-4549-1259-0(6))* Sterling Publishing Co., Inc.

—Did Christopher Columbus Really Discover America? And Other Questions about the New World. 2015. (Good Question! Ser.). (ENG., Illus.). 40p. (J). (gr. 2). 12.95 *(978-1-4549-1258-3(8))* Sterling Publishing Co., Inc.

Bodden, Valerie. Columbus Reaches the New World. 2009. (Days of Change Ser.). (Illus.). 48p. (YA). (gr. 4-7). 22.95 *(978-1-58341-732-4(X))* Creative Co., The.

Burgan, Michael. Christopher Columbus: Opening the Americas to European Exploration. 2004. (Proud Heritage: the Hispanic Library). (ENG., Illus.). 40p. (J). (gr. 3-6). 29.93 *(978-1-59296-142-9(8)*, 200002) Child's World, Inc., The.

Collier, James Lincoln. Christopher Columbus: To the New World. 2006. (Great Explorations Ser.). (Illus.). 80p. (J). (gr. 3-7). lib. bdg. 32.79 *(978-0-7614-2221-1(8)*, Benchmark Bks.) Marshall Cavendish Corp.

Conklin, Wendy. Christopher Columbus, 1 vol. 2004. (Primary Source Readers Ser.). (SPA & ENG.). 24p. (J). (gr. 4-4). pap. 8.99 *(978-0-7439-8741-7(1))* Shell Educational Publishing.

Connelly, Jack. Christopher Columbus: Discovering the Americas. 2015. (Incredible Explorers Ser.). (ENG., Illus.). 64p. (J). (gr. 7-7). 34.21 *(978-1-5026-0171-1(0))* Cavendish Square Publishing.

Craats, Rennay. Columbus Day. (American Celebrations Ser.). (Illus.). 24p. (J). 2010. (gr. 3-5). pap. 11.95 *(978-1-60596-933-6(8))* 2010. (gr. 3-5). lib. bdg. 25.70 *(978-1-60596-775-2(0))* 2004. lib. bdg. 24.45 *(978-1-59036-106-1(7))* 2004. (gr. 1-3). per. 8.95 *(978-1-59036-164-1(4))* Weigl Pubs., Inc.

Dash, Meredith. Día de la Raza. 2015. (Días Festivos Ser.). (SPA & ENG., Illus.). 24p. (gr. k-1). pap. 7.95 *(978-1-4966-0417-0(2))* Capstone Classroom.

Dayton, Connor. Columbus Day. 2012. (American Holidays Ser.). (ENG., Illus.). 24p. (J). (gr. k-3). pap. 8.25 *(978-1-4488-6248-1(5)*, PowerKids Pr.) Rosen Publishing Group, Inc., The.

—Columbus Day: Día de la Raza. Alamán, Eduardo, tr. from ENG. 2012. (American Holidays / Celebraciones en los Estados Unidos Ser.). (SPA & ENG., Illus.). 24p. (J). (gr. k-3). lib. bdg. 22.60 *(978-1-4488-6711-0(8)*, PowerKids Pr.) Rosen Publishing Group, Inc., The.

Demi. Columbus, 0 vols. Demi, illus. 2012. (ENG., Illus.). 64p. (J). (gr. 3-7). 19.99 *(978-0-7614-6167-8(1)*, 9780761461678, Amazon Children's Publishing) Amazon Publishing.

DeRubertis, Barbara. Let's Celebrate Columbus Day. Sperling, Thomas, illus. 2014. (Holidays & Heroes Ser.). 32p. (J). (gr. 1-3). pap. 7.95 *(978-1-57565-634-2(5))* Kane Press, Inc.

Donohue, Moira Rose. Christopher Columbus. 2013. (Illus.). 24p. (J). *(978-1-938813-04-7(9))*; pap. *(978-1-938813-08-5(1))* State Standards Publishing, LLC.

Feinstein, Stephen. Columbus: Opening up the New World. 2009. (Great Explorers of the World Ser.). (Illus.). 112p. (J). (gr. 7-12). lib. bdg. 33.27 *(978-1-59845-101-6(4))* Enslow Pubs., Inc.

Guillain, Charlotte. Great Explorers. 2015. (Collins Big Cat Ser.). (ENG.). 24p. (J). (gr. 2-2). pap. 7.95 *(978-0-00-759119-0(5))* HarperCollins Pubs. Ltd. GBR. Dist: Independent Pubs. Group.

Gunderson, Jessica. Christopher Columbus: New World Explorer or Fortune Hunter?, 1 vol. 2013. (Perspectives on History Ser.). (ENG.). 32p. (gr. 3-4). 27.32 *(978-1-4765-0242-7(0))*; pap. 7.95 *(978-1-4765-3406-0(3))* Capstone Press of Coughlan Cos. (Fact Finders).

Healy, Nick. Christopher Columbus. 2003. (Explorers of the Unknown Ser.). (J). *(978-1-58417-034-1(4))*; pap. *(978-1-58417-097-6(2))* Lake Street Pubs.

Herr, Melody. Exploring the New World: An Interactive History Adventure. 2016. (You Choose: History Ser.). (ENG.). 112p. (gr. 3-4). pap. 6.95 *(978-1-5157-4258-6(X)*, You Choose Bks.) Capstone Press of Coughlan Cos.

Hoogenboom, Lynn. Christopher Columbus. 2009. (Primary Source Library of Famous Explorers Ser.). 24p. (gr. 4-4). 42.50 *(978-1-60854-119-5(3)*, PowerKids Pr.) Rosen Publishing Group, Inc., The.

—Christopher Columbus: A Primary Source Biography. 2006. (Primary Source Library of Famous Explorers Ser.). (Illus.). 24p. (YA). (gr. 2-5). lib. bdg. 22.60 *(978-1-4042-3036-1(X))* Rosen Publishing Group, Inc., The.

Hunter, Nick. Christopher Columbus & Neil Armstrong. 2015. (Comparing People from the Past Ser.). (ENG., Illus.). 32p. (gr. 3-3). pap. 6.49 *(978-1-4846-0920-0(4)*, Heinemann First Library) Heinemann-Raintree.

Kallen, Stuart A. A Journey with Christopher Columbus. 2017. (Primary Source Explorers Ser.). (ENG.). 40p. (J). (gr. 3-5). lib. bdg. 30.65 *(978-1-5124-0772-3(0))* Lerner Publishing Group.

Keller, Susanna. The True Story of Christopher Columbus. 2013. (What Really Happened? Ser.). (ENG., Illus.). 24p. (J). (gr. 3-6). pap. 8.25 *(978-1-4488-9842-8(0))*; lib. bdg. 22.60 *(978-1-4488-9692-9(4))* Rosen Publishing Group, Inc., The. (PowerKids Pr.).

Kneib, Martha. Christopher Columbus: Master Italian Navigator in the Court of Spain. 2009. (Library of Explorers & Exploration Ser.). 112p. (gr. 5-8). 66.50 *(978-1-60853-601-6(7)*, Rosen Reference) Rosen Publishing Group, Inc., The.

Kudlinski, Kathleen. Christopher Columbus: Young Explorer. 2005. 199p. (J). lib. bdg. 18.46 *(978-1-4242-1727-4(X))* Fitzgerald Bks.

—Christopher Columbus: Young Explorer. 2005. (Childhood of World Figures Ser.). (ENG.). 208p. (J). (gr. 3-7). pap. 10.99 *(978-0-689-87648-6(3)*, Simon & Schuster/Paula Wiseman Bks.) Simon & Schuster/Paula Wiseman Bks.

Landau, Elaine. Celebrating Columbus Day. 2012. (Celebrating Holidays Ser.). 48p. (J). (gr. 3-4). (Illus.). pap. 8.95 *(978-1-59845-400-0(5))*; 25.27 *(978-0-7660-4033-5(X))* Enslow Pubs., Inc. (Enslow Elementary).

—Discovering a New World: Would You Sail with Columbus? 2014. (What Would You Do? Ser.). (Illus.). 48p. (J). (gr. 3-4). lib. bdg. 25.27 *(978-0-7660-4222-3(7)*, Enslow Elementary) Enslow Pubs., Inc.

Leavitt, Amie Jane. Christopher Columbus. 2007. (What's So Great About...? Ser.). (Illus.). 32p. (J). (gr. 2-4). lib. bdg. 25.70 *(978-1-58415-578-2(7))* Mitchell Lane Pubs., Inc.

Macdonald, Fiona. You Wouldn't Want to Sail with Christopher Columbus! (Revised Edition) 2014. (You Wouldn't Want to... Ser.). (ENG.). 32p. (J). lib. bdg. 29.00 *(978-0-531-21177-9(0)*, Watts, Franklin) Scholastic Library Publishing.

Malam, John. Columbus Reaches the Americas. 2003. (Dates with History Ser.). 45p. (J). lib. bdg. 28.50 *(978-1-58340-411-9(2))* Black Rabbit Bks.

Mann, Charles. 1493 for Young People: From Columbus's Voyage to Globalization. 2016. (For Young People Ser.). (ENG., Illus.). 416p. (J). (gr. 7). pap. 18.95 *(978-1-60980-663-7(8)*, Triangle Square) Seven Stories Pr.

Mattern, Joanne. Celebrate Columbus Day. 2006. (Celebrate Holidays Ser.). (Illus.). 104p. (J). (gr. 5-6). lib. bdg. 33.27 *(978-0-7660-2580-6(2))* Enslow Pubs., Inc.

McCormick, Lisa Wade. Christopher Columbus. 2005. (Scholastic News Nonfiction Readers Ser.). (ENG., Illus.). 24p. (J). (gr. 1-2). lib. bdg. 22.00 *(978-0-516-24938-4(X))* Scholastic Library Publishing.

McNeese, Tim. Christopher Columbus & the Discovery of the Americas, Explorers of New Lands. Goetzmann, William H., ed. 2005. (Explorers of New Lands Ser.). (Illus.). 100p. (gr. 5-8). lib. bdg. 30.00 *(978-0-7910-8613-1(5))* Facts On File, Inc.

Molzahn, Arlene Bourgeois. Christopher Columbus: Famous Explorer. 2003. (Explorers! Ser.). (Illus.). 48p. (J). (gr. 1-4). lib. bdg. 25.27 *(978-0-7660-2066-5(5))* Enslow Pubs., Inc.

Morganelli, Adrianna. Christopher Columbus: Sailing to a New World. 2005. (In the Footsteps of Explorers Ser.). (ENG., Illus.). 32p. (J). (gr. -1-9). pap. *(978-0-7787-2445-2(X))*; lib. bdg. *(978-0-7787-2409-4(3))* Crabtree Publishing Co.

Murray, Julie. Columbus Day, 1 vol. 2005. (Holidays Ser.). (ENG.). 24p. (gr. k-4). 25.65 *(978-1-59197-587-8(5)*, Buddy Bks.) ABDO Publishing Co.

Nelson, Robin. Columbus Day. 2009. (First Step Nonfiction - American Holidays Ser.). (J). (gr. k-2). 19.93 *(978-0-7613-4928-0(6))* Lerner Publishing Group.

O'Brien, Cynthia. Explore with Christopher Columbus. 2014. (ENG., Illus.). 32p. (J). *(978-0-7787-1245-9(1))*; pap. *(978-0-7787-1257-2(5))* Crabtree Publishing Co.

Ollhoff, Jim. Christopher Columbus. 2013. (Great Explorers Ser.). 32p. (J). (gr. 5-9). lib. bdg. 27.07 *(978-1-61783-964-1(7)*, Abdo & Daughters) ABDO Publishing Co.

Otfinoski, Steven. The Voyages of Christopher Columbus: Set Of 6. 2011. (Navigators Ser.). (J). pap. 48.00 net. *(978-1-4108-5105-5(2))* Benchmark Education Co.

—The Voyages of Christopher Columbus: Text Pairs. 2008. (Bridges/Navigators Ser.). (J). (gr. 5). 89.00 *(978-1-4108-8425-1(2))* Benchmark Education Co.

Petrie, Kristin. Christopher Columbus, 1 vol. 2004. (Explorers Set 1 Ser.). (ENG., Illus.). 32p. (gr. k-6). 27.07 *(978-1-59197-595-3(6)*, Checkerboard Library) ABDO Publishing Co.

Ponto, Joanna. Columbus Day. 2016. (Story of Our Holidays Ser.). (Illus.). 32p. (J). (gr. 3-3). pap. 10.52 *(978-0-7660-7654-9(7))* Enslow Pubs., Inc.

Randall, Jesseca. Christopher Columbus: Navigated by God - A Historical Children's Novel about One of the Most Important Figures of the Age of Exploration. 2009. 124p. pap. 11.99 *(978-1-60791-926-1(5))* Salem Author Services.

Reis, Ronald A. Christopher Columbus & the Age of Exploration for Kids: With 21 Activities. 2013. (For Kids Ser.). (ENG., Illus.). 160p. (J). (gr. 4). pap. 16.95 *(978-1-61374-674-5(1))* Chicago Review Pr., Inc.

Saguchi, Kensaku. Biographical Comics: Christopher Columbus: The Merchant Adventurer. Miyazoe, Ikuo, illus. 2012. (Biographical Comic Ser.). (ENG.). 152p. (J). (gr. 3-6). 18.99 *(978-1-4215-4973-6(5))*; pap. 9.99 *(978-1-4215-4974-3(3))* Shogakukan JPN. Dist: Simon & Schuster, Inc.

Sís, Peter. Follow the Dream: The Story of Christopher Columbus. Sís, Peter, illus. 2003. (ENG., Illus.). 40p. (J). (gr. -1-2). 15.95 *(978-0-679-80628-8(0)*, Knopf Bks. for Young Readers) Random Hse. Children's Bks.

Wade, Mary Dodson. Christopher Columbus. (Rookie Biographies(r) Ser.). (ENG., Illus.). 32p. (J). 2014. lib. bdg. *(978-0-531-20559-4(2))* 2014. pap. 5.95 *(978-0-531-21202-8(5))* 2003. (gr. 1-2). pap. 4.95 *(978-0-516-27769-1(3)*, Children's Pr.) Scholastic Library Publishing.

—Christopher Columbus: Famous Explorer, 1 vol. Whigham, Rod & Barnett, Charles, III, illus. 2007. (Graphic Biographies Ser.). (ENG.). 32p. (gr. 3-4). per. 8.10 *(978-0-7368-7905-7(6)*, 1264941, Graphic Library) Capstone Press of Coughlan Cos.

Wade, Mary Dodson & Capstone Press Staff. Christopher Columbus: Famous Explorer, 1 vol. Whigham, Rod & Barnett, Charles, III, illus. 2007. (Graphic Biographies Ser.). (ENG.). 32p. (gr. 3-4). 30.65 *(978-0-7368-6853-2(4)*, 1264941, Graphic Library) Capstone Press of Coughlan Cos.

West, David. Christopher Columbus: The Life of a Master Navigator & Explorer. 2009. (Graphic Nonfiction Biographies Ser.). (ENG.). 48p. (YA). (gr. 4-5). 58.50 *(978-1-61513-014-6(4)*, Rosen Reference) Rosen Publishing Group, Inc., The.

West, David & Gaff, Jackie. Christopher Columbus: The Life of a Master Navigator & Explorer. 2005. (Graphic Nonfiction Biographies Ser.). (ENG., Illus.). 48p. (J). (gr. 4-7). lib. bdg. 31.95 *(978-1-4042-0243-6(9))* Rosen Publishing Group, Inc., The.

COLUMBUS, CHRISTOPHER, 1451-1506—FICTION

Hi-stories Presents Christopher Cowlumbus. 2004. (Illus.). 58p. (J). *(978-0-9763233-0-3(3))* Little Germ That Could...Creations, Inc., The.

Histories presents Christopher Cowlumbus. 2006. (J). bds. 14.99 *(978-0-9763233-3-4(8))* Little Germ That Could...Creations, Inc., The.

King, Thomas. A Coyote Columbus Story, 1 vol. Monkman, William Kent, illus. 2007. (ENG.). 32p. (J). (gr. -1-k). pap. 8.95 *(978-0-88899-830-9(9))* Groundwood Bks. CAN. Dist: Publishers Group West (PGW).

Losada, Basilio. Cristobal Colon. (SPA., Illus.). 160p. (YA). 11.95 *(978-84-7281-053-2(4)*, AF1053) Auriga, Ediciones S.A. ESP. Dist: Continental Bk. Co., Inc.

Whittier, Mary Ann. Tales from 1492. (YA). (gr. 7-18). lib. bdg. 19.99 *(978-0-89824-981-1(3))* Royal Fireworks Publishing Co.

COLUMBUS DAY

Aloian, Molly. Columbus Day. 2010. (ENG., Illus.). 32p. (J). *(978-0-7787-4760-4(3))*; pap. *(978-0-7787-4778-9(6))* Crabtree Publishing Co.

Craats, Rennay. Columbus Day. (American Celebrations Ser.). (Illus.). 24p. (J). 2010. (gr. 3-5). pap. 11.95 *(978-1-60596-933-6(8))* 2010. (gr. 3-5). lib. bdg. 25.70 *(978-1-60596-775-2(0))* 2004. lib. bdg. 24.45 *(978-1-59036-106-1(7))* 2004. (gr. 1-3). per. 8.95 *(978-1-59036-164-1(4))* Weigl Pubs., Inc.

Dash, Meredith. Columbus Day, 1 vol. 2014. (National Holidays Ser.). (ENG., Illus.). 24p. (J). (gr. 4-8). lib. bdg. 28.50 *(978-1-62970-043-4(6))* ABDO Publishing Co.

—Día de la Raza. 2015. (Días Festivos Ser.). (SPA & ENG., Illus.). 24p. (gr. k-1). pap. 7.95 *(978-1-4966-0417-0(2))* Capstone Classroom.

Dayton, Connor. Columbus Day. 2012. (American Holidays Ser.). (ENG., Illus.). 24p. (J). (gr. k-3). pap. 8.25 *(978-1-4488-6248-1(5))*; lib. bdg. 22.60 *(978-1-4488-6145-3(4))* Rosen Publishing Group, Inc., The. (PowerKids Pr.).

—Columbus Day: Día de la Raza. Alamán, Eduardo, tr. from ENG. 2012. (American Holidays / Celebraciones en los Estados Unidos Ser.). (SPA & ENG., Illus.). 24p. (J). (gr. k-3). lib. bdg. 22.60 *(978-1-4488-6711-0(8)*, PowerKids Pr.) Rosen Publishing Group, Inc., The.

DeRubertis, Barbara. Let's Celebrate Columbus Day. Sperling, Thomas, illus. 2014. (Holidays & Heroes Ser.). 32p. (J). (gr. 1-3). pap. 7.95 *(978-1-57565-634-2(5))* Kane Press, Inc.

Landau, Elaine. Celebrating Columbus Day. 2012. (Celebrating Holidays Ser.). 48p. (J). (gr. 3-4). (Illus.). pap. 8.95 *(978-1-59845-400-0(5))*; 25.27 *(978-0-7660-4033-5(X))* Enslow Pubs., Inc. (Enslow Elementary).

Mattern, Joanne. Celebrate Columbus Day. 2006. (Celebrate Holidays Ser.). (Illus.). 104p. (J). (gr. 5-6). lib. bdg. 33.27 *(978-0-7660-2580-6(2))* Enslow Pubs., Inc.

Murray, Julie. Columbus Day, 1 vol. 2005. (Holidays Ser.). (ENG.). 24p. (gr. k-4). 25.65 *(978-1-59197-587-8(5)*, Buddy Bks.) ABDO Publishing Co.

Nelson, Robin. Columbus Day. 2009. (First Step Nonfiction - American Holidays Ser.). (J). (gr. k-2). 19.93 *(978-0-7613-4928-0(6))* Lerner Publishing Group.

Ponto, Joanna. Columbus Day. 2016. (Story of Our Holidays Ser.). (Illus.). 32p. (J). (gr. 3-3). pap. 10.52 *(978-0-7660-7654-9(7))* Enslow Pubs., Inc.

COLUMBUS DAY—FICTION

Park, Barbara. Shipwrecked, No. 23. Brunkus, Denise, illus. 2005. (Junie B. Jones Ser.: No. 6). (ENG.). 96p. (J). (gr. 1-4). mass mkt. 4.99 *(978-0-375-82805-8(2)*, Random Hse. Bks. for Young Readers) Random Hse. Children's Bks.

COLUMNISTS

see Journalists

COMEDY

Doyle, Alfreda C. Alfreda's Reader's Theatre: Comedy Club. Date not set. (Illus.). (J). spiral bd. 8.95 *(978-1-56820-362-1(4))* Story Time Stories That Rhyme.

Guillain, Charlotte. Writing & Staging Funny Plays. 2016. (Writing & Staging Plays Ser.). (ENG., Illus.). 48p. (gr. 4-6). lib. bdg. 33.32 *(978-1-4846-2769-3(5)*, Heinemann InfoSearch) Heinemann-Raintree.

Jasheway, Leigh Anne. 101 Comedy Games for Children & Grown-Ups. 2014. (SmartFun Activity Bks.). (ENG., Illus.). 168p. (gr. 1). pap. 14.95 *(978-0-89793-700-9(7)*, Hunter Hse.) Turner Publishing Co.

Ramsay, Jana & Ramsay, Nicole. Comedy. 2014. (Urban Entrepreneurs Ser.). (gr. 3-8). 27.99 *(978-1-61570-885-7(5))* Scobre Pr. Corp.

Ramsay, Nicole. Comedy. 2014. (Urban Entrepreneurs Ser.). (gr. 3-8). pap. 8.99 *(978-1-61570-871-0(5))* Scobre Pr. Corp.

COMETS

Anthony, David. Exploring Comets & Asteroids. 2017. (J). ***(978-1-5345-2248-0(4)**, KidHaven Publishing)* Greenhaven Publishing LLC.

Asimov, Isaac & Hantula, Richard. Comets & Meteors. 2005. (Isaac Asimov's 21st Century Library of the Universe). (Illus.). 32p. (gr. 2-6). lib. bdg. 26.00 *(978-0-8368-3966-1(8)*, Gareth Stevens Learning Library) Stevens, Gareth Publishing LLLP.

Atkinson, Stuart. Comets, Asteroids, & Meteors, 1 vol. 2012. (Astronaut Travel Guides). (ENG.). 48p. (gr. 3-6). pap. 9.95 *(978-1-4109-4576-1(6))*; lib. bdg. 32.65 *(978-1-4109-4567-9(7))* Heinemann-Raintree. (NA-r).

Carson, Mary Kay. Far-Out Guide to Asteroids & Comets. 2010. (Far-Out Guide to the Solar System Ser.). (Illus.). 48p. (J). pap. 8.95 *(978-1-59845-191-7(X)*, Enslow Elementary) Enslow Pubs., Inc.

Carson, Mary Kay & Library Association Staff. Far-Out Guide to Asteroids & Comets. 2010. (Far-Out Guide to the Solar System Ser.). 48p. (J). (gr. 2-5). 25.27 *(978-0-7660-3188-3(8))* Enslow Pubs., Inc.

Chiger, Arielle & Houk Maley, Adrienne. 20 Fun Facts about Asteroids & Comets. 2014. (Fun Fact File: Space! Ser.). 32p. (J). (gr. 2-5). 25.25 *(978-1-4824-0791-4(4))*; pap. 10.50 *(978-1-4824-0792-1(2))* Stevens, Gareth Publishing LLLP.

Chrismer, Melanie. Comets. 2008. (Scholastic News Nonfiction Readers Ser.). (ENG., Illus.). 24p. (J). (gr. 1-2). pap. 6.95 *(978-0-531-14759-7(2))* Scholastic Library Publishing.

Cole, Michael D. Comets & Asteroids: Ice & Rocks in Space. 2003. (Countdown to Space Ser.). (Illus.). 48p. (J). (gr. 4-10). lib. bdg. 23.93 *(978-0-7660-1954-6(3))* Enslow Pubs., Inc.

Comets. 2015. (J). *(978-1-60818-481-1(1)*, Creative Education) Creative Co., The.

Dickmann, Nancy. Exploring Comets, Asteroids, & Other Objects in Space. 2015. (Spectacular Space Science Ser.). (ENG., Illus.). 48p. (J). (gr. 5-6). 30.25 *(978-1-4994-3637-2(8)*, Rosen Central) Rosen Publishing Group, Inc., The.

Gifford, Clive. The Solar System, Meteors, & Comets. 2015. (Watch This Space! Ser.). (ENG., Illus.). 32p. (J). (gr. 3-7). lib. bdg. *(978-0-7787-2023-2(3))* Crabtree Publishing Co.

Glaser, Chaya & Sawyer, J. Clark. Icy Comets: Sometimes Have Tails. 2015. (Out of This World Ser.). (ENG.). 24p. (J). (gr. -1-3). lib. bdg. 23.93 *(978-1-62724-572-2(3))* Bearport Publishing Co., Inc.

Graham, Ian. Asteroids & Comets. 2015. (Space Ser.). (Illus.). 24p. (gr. 3-6). lib. bdg. 28.50 *(978-1-62588-207-3(6))* Black Rabbit Bks.

Howard, Fran. Asteroids, Comets, & Meteoroids, 1 vol. 2008. (Universe Ser.). (ENG.). 32p. (gr. k-4). 27.07 *(978-1-59928-925-0(3)*, Buddy Bks.) ABDO Publishing Co.

Hunter, Nick. Comets, 1 vol. 2013. (Night Sky: & Other Amazing Sights in Space Ser.). (ENG.). 32p. (gr. 1-3). 27.32 *(978-1-4329-7514-2(5))*; pap. 8.95 *(978-1-4329-7519-7(6))* Heinemann-Raintree. (Heinemann First Library).

Kortenkamp, Steve. Asteroids, Comets, & Meteoroids, 1 vol. 2011. (Solar System & Beyond Ser.). (ENG.). 32p. (gr. 3-4). pap. 8.10 *(978-1-4296-7223-8(4))*; pap. 47.70 *(978-1-4296-7224-5(2))* Capstone Press of Coughlan Cos. (Fact Finders).

Lawrence, Ellen. Comets, Meteors, & Asteroids: Voyagers of the Solar System. 2013. (Zoom into Space Ser.). 24p. (J). (gr. -1-3). lib. bdg. 23.93 *(978-1-909673-22-9(6))* Ruby Tuesday Books Limited GBR. Dist: Bearport Publishing Co., Inc.

Mason Crest. Comets & Meteors, Vol. 7. 2016. (Solar System Ser.: Vol. 7). (ENG., Illus.). 48p. (J). (gr. 5-8). 20.95 *(978-1-4222-3548-5(3))* Mason Crest.

Miller, Ron. Asteroids, Comets, & Meteors. 2006. (Worlds Beyond Ser.). (Illus.). 80p. (J). (gr. 5-9). 27.93 *(978-0-7613-2363-1(5)*, Twenty-First Century Bks.) Lerner Publishing Group.

—Seven Wonders of Asteroids, Comets, & Meteors. 2011. (Seven Wonders Ser.). (ENG.). 80p. (gr. 5-8). lib. bdg. 33.26 *(978-0-7613-5451-2(4))* Lerner Publishing Group. (Extreme Threats

Nardo, Don. Asteroids & Comets. 2009. (Extreme Threats Ser.). 112p. (YA). lib. bdg. 28.95 *(978-1-59935-121-6(8))* Reynolds, Morgan Inc.

Nicolson, Cynthia. Discover Space Rocks. Slavin, Bill, illus. 2006. 32p. (J). lib. bdg. 15.38 *(978-1-4242-1195-1(6))* Fitzgerald Bks.

Nicolson, Cynthia Pratt & Nicolson, Cynthia. Discover Space Rocks. Slavin, Bill, illus. 2006. (Kids Can Read Ser.). (ENG.). 32p. (J). (gr. 1-3). 3.95 *(978-1-55337-901-0(2))* Kids Can Pr., Ltd. CAN. Dist: Hachette Bk. Group.

Orme, David. Comets. 2007. (Trailblazers Ser.). (ENG., Illus.). 36p. pap. *(978-1-84167-424-7(9))* Ransom Publishing Ltd.

—Comets. 2009. (Fact to Fiction Ser.). (Illus.). 36p. (J). 16.95 *(978-0-7569-9277-4(X))*; pap. 6.95 *(978-0-7891-7899-2(0))* Perfection Learning Corp.

Orme, Helen & Orme, David. Let's Explore Comets & Asteroids. 2007. (Space Launch! Ser.). (Illus.). 24p. (gr. 1-4). pap. 8.15 *(978-0-8368-8132-5(X))*; lib. bdg. 23.00 *(978-0-8368-7947-6(3))* Stevens, Gareth Publishing LLLP. (Gareth Stevens Learning Library).

Parker, Steve. Space Objects: Comets, Asteroids & Meteors. 2007. (Earth & Space Ser.). (Illus.). 48p. (YA). (gr. 5-9). lib. bdg. 29.25 *(978-1-4042-3738-4(0))* Rosen Publishing Group, Inc., The.

Pobst, Sandy. Life of a Comet: Set Of 6. 2011. (Navigators Ser.). (J). pap. 50.00 net. *(978-1-4108-6242-6(9))* Benchmark Education Co.

—Life of a Comet: Text Pairs. 2008. (Bridges/Navigators Ser.). (J). (gr. 6). 94.00 *(978-1-4108-8443-5(0))* Benchmark Education Co.

Rajczak, Kristen. Comets. 2012. (Nature's Light Show Ser.). (Illus.). 24p. (J). (gr. 2-5). pap. 8.15 *(978-1-4339-7020-7(1))*; lib. bdg. 22.60 *(978-1-4339-7019-1(8))* Stevens, Gareth Publishing LLLP.

Reilly, Carmel. Comets, Asteroids, & Meteoroids. 2011. (Sky Watching Ser.). 32p. (gr. 2-4). 28.50 *(978-1-60870-579-5(X))* Marshall Cavendish GBR. Dist: Marshall Cavendish Corp.

Riggs, Kate. Across the Universe: Comets. 2015. (Across the Universe Ser.). (ENG.). 24p. (J). (gr. 1-3). pap. 9.99 *(978-1-62832-081-7(8)*, Creative Paperbacks) Creative Co., The.

Romero, Libby. Comets. 2006. (J). pap. *(978-1-4108-6505-2(3))* Benchmark Education Co.

—Discover Comets. 2006. (J). pap. *(978-1-4108-6508-3(8))* Benchmark Education Co.

Roza, Greg. Comets & Asteroids: Space Rocks. 2010. (Our Solar System Ser.). 24p. (J). (gr. k-3). (ENG.). pap. 8.15 *(978-1-4339-3816-0(2))*; (Illus.). lib. bdg. 22.60 *(978-1-4339-3815-3(4))* Stevens, Gareth Publishing LLLP.

Sawyer, J. Clark. Los Cometas Helados: A Veces Tienen Colas. 2015. (Fuera de Este Mundo Ser.). (SPA., Illus.). 24p. (J). (gr. -1-3). lib. bdg. 23.93 *(978-1-62724-589-0(8))* Bearport Publishing Co., Inc.

Sherman, Josepha. Asteroids, Meteors, & Comets. 2009. (Space!). 64p. (gr. 5-18). lib. bdg. 32.79 *(978-0-7614-4252-3(9))* Marshall Cavendish Corp.

Silverman, Buffy. Exploring Dangers in Space: Asteroids, Space Junk, & More. 2011. (Searchlight Books Whats Amazing about Space Ser.). (ENG., Illus.). (gr. 3-5). pap. 51.01 *(978-0-7613-8414-4(6))*; 40p. pap. 8.95 *(978-0-7613-7882-2(0))*; 40p. lib. bdg. 27.93 *(978-0-7613-5446-8(8))* Lerner Publishing Group.

Sparrow, Giles. Destination Asteroids, Comets, & Meteors. 2009. (Destination Solar System Ser.). (Illus.). 32p. (J). 25.25 *(978-1-4358-3449-1(6))*; pap. 10.00 *(978-1-4358-3469-9(0))* Rosen Publishing Group, Inc., The. (PowerKids Pr.).

Stiefel, Chana. Comets & Meteors: Shooting Through Space. 2014. (ENG.). 24p. (gr. k-3). 28.50 *(978-1-62717-732-0(9))* Rourke Educational Media.

The Sun. 2017. (Illus.). 40p. (J). ***(978-1-4222-3547-8(5))*** Mason Crest.

Vogt, Gregory. Meteors & Comets. 2010. (Early Bird Astronomy Ser.). (ENG.). 48p. (gr. 2-5). lib. bdg. 26.60 *(978-0-7613-3876-5(4))* Lerner Publishing Group.

Waldeck, Aaron. Space Rocks: A Look at Asteroids & Comets. 2003. (Rosen Real Readers Big Bookstm Ser.). (ENG.). 24p. (gr. 3-4). 43.95 *(978-0-8239-8729-0(9))* Rosen Publishing Group, Inc., The.

—Space Rocks: A Look at Asteroids & Comets. 2009. (Reading Room Collection 2 Ser.). 24p. (gr. 3-4). 42.50 *(978-1-60851-990-3(2)*, PowerKids Pr.) Rosen Publishing Group, Inc., The.

Way, Jennifer. Exploring Comets. (Objects in the Sky Ser.). 24p. (gr. 3-3). 2009. 42.50 *(978-1-60851-137-2(5))* 2007. (Illus.). (J). lib. bdg. 22.60 *(978-1-4042-3469-7(1))* Rosen Publishing Group, Inc., The. (PowerKids Pr.).

Weakland, Mark. The Lonely Existence of Asteroids & Comets, 1 vol. Lazzati, Laura & Aón, Carlos, illus. 2012. (Adventures in Science Ser.). (ENG.). 32p. (gr. 3-4). pap.

C
D

8.10 *(978-1-4296-7987-9(5)*, Graphic Library) Capstone Press of Coughlan Cos.

—The Lonely Existence of Asteroids & Comets. Aón, Carlos & Lazzati, Laura, illus. 2012. (Adventures in Science Ser.). (ENG.). 32p. (gr. 3-4). pap. 47.70 *(978-1-4296-8465-1(8))*; lib. bdg. 30.65 *(978-1-4296-7546-8(2))* Capstone Press of Coughlan Cos. (Graphic Library).

Wilkins, Mary-Jane. Asteroids, Comets, & Meteors. 2017. (Fast Track: Our Solar System Ser.). 24p. (gr. k-3). 28.50 ***(978-1-78121-368-1(2))*** Brown Bear Bks.

Windsor. Sail Main4 Comets Nf. 2003. (Rigby Sails Ser.). (ENG.). 32p. (gr. 4-4). pap. 9.50 *(978-0-7578-8507-5(1))* Rigby Education.

World Book, Inc Staff, contrib. by. Neptune, Comets, & Dwarf Planets. 2010. (J). *(978-0-7166-9538-7(3))* World Bk., Inc.

COMIC BOOKS, STRIPS, ETC.

see also Cartoons and Comics

Abdo, Kenny. Comic Relief, 1 vol. Doucet, Bob, illus. 2013. (Haven't Got a Clue! Ser.). (ENG.). 80p. (J). (gr. 3-6). lib. bdg. 27.07 *(978-1-61641-951-6(2)*, Calico Chapter Bks) Magic Wagon.

Abnett, Dan. A Pier Too Far. Hansen, Jimmy, illus. 2005. (Wallace & Gromit Ser.). (ENG.). 48p. 12.95 *(978-1-84023-953-9(0)*, Titan Bks.) Titan Bks. Ltd. GBR. Dist: Penguin Random Hse. LLC.

Adachi, Mitsuru. Cross Game, Vol. 4. Adachi, Mitsuru, illus. 2011. (ENG., Illus.). 376p. pap. 14.99 *(978-1-4215-3768-9(0))* Viz Media.

Allegri, Natasha. Fionna & Cake Mathematical. Allegri, Natasha, illus. 2014. (Adventure Time Ser.: 1). (ENG., Illus.). 192p. (J). (gr. 4). 39.99 *(978-1-60886-391-4(3))* Boom! Studios.

Allegri, Natasha, illus. Adventure Time - Fionna & Cake. Allegri, Natasha, . 2013. (ENG.). 176p. (J). (gr. 4). pap. 19.99 *(978-1-60886-338-9(7))* Boom! Studios.

Allen, John. Anime & Manga. 2014. (Discovering Art). (ENG., Illus.). 80p. (J). lib. bdg. *(978-1-60152-696-0(2))* ReferencePoint Pr., Inc.

Amara, Philip. So, You Want to Be a Comic Book Artist? The Ultimate Guide on How to Break into Comics! 2012. (Be What You Want Ser.). (ENG., Illus.). 176p. (J). (gr. 3-7). 17.99 *(978-1-58270-358-9(2))*; pap. 9.99 *(978-1-58270-357-2(4))* Aladdin/Beyond Words.

American Graphic. (American Graphic Ser.). (ENG.). 32p. (gr. 3-4). 2011. pap. 286.20 *(978-1-4296-6439-4(8))* 2010. pap. 40.50 *(978-1-4296-6271-0(9))* Capstone Press of Coughlan Cos. (Graphic Library).

Anderson, Jeff, et al. The Lion Comic Book Hero Bible. 2015. (ENG., Illus.). 192p. 19.95 *(978-0-7459-5617-6(3))* Lion Hudson PLC GBR. Dist: Independent Pubs. Group.

Anderson, M. T. Yvain: The Knight of the Lion. Offermann, Andrea, illus. 2017. (ENG.). 144p. (J). (gr. 7). 19.99 *(978-0-7636-5939-4(8))* Candlewick Pr.

Antram, David. Drawing Manga Monsters. 2015. (Art Class: the Art of Drawing Manga Ser.). (ENG., Illus.). 32p. (gr. 2-6). 31.35 *(978-1-62588-352-0(8))* Black Rabbit Bks.

—Drawing Manga Villians. 2015. (Art Class: the Art of Drawing Manga Ser.). (ENG., Illus.). 32p. (gr. 2-6). 31.35 *(978-1-62588-354-4(4))* Black Rabbit Bks.

—How to Draw Manga Warriors. 2010. (How to Draw Ser.). (Illus.). 32p. (YA). (gr. 6-18). pap. 11.75 *(978-1-4488-1609-5(2))*; lib. bdg. 26.50 *(978-1-4488-1581-4(9))* Rosen Publishing Group, Inc., The. (PowerKids Pr.).

Anzai, Nobuyuki & Caselman, Lance. Flame of Recca. Anzai, Nobuyuki, illus. 2006. (Flame of Recca Ser.). (ENG., Illus.). 208p. pap. 9.99 *(978-1-4215-0250-2(X))*; Vol. 17. pap. 9.99 *(978-1-4215-0381-3(6))* Viz Media.

Aoki, Takao. Beyblade. Aoki, Takao, illus. 2006. (Beyblade Ser.). (ENG., Illus.). 208p. Vol. 9. pap. 7.99 *(978-1-4215-0249-6(6))* Vol. 10. pap. 7.99 *(978-1-4215-0380-6(8))* Viz Media.

Arakawa, Hiromu. Fullmetal Alchemist, Vol. 26. Arakawa, Hiromu, illus. 2011. (ENG., Illus.). 193p. pap. 9.99 *(978-1-4215-3962-1(4))* Viz Media.

Arni, Samhita & Valmiki. Sita's Ramayana, 1 vol. Chitrakar, Moyna, illus. 2011. (ENG.). 152p. (J). (gr. 4). 24.95 *(978-1-55498-145-8(X))* Groundwood Bks. CAN. Dist: Publishers Group West (PGW).

Ashihara, Hinako. Sos. Ashihara, Hinako, illus. 2005. (Sos Ser.). (ENG., Illus.). 192p. (YA). pap. 9.99 *(978-1-59116-735-8(3))* Viz Media.

Autry, Gene. Gene Autry Comics V1, No 58, December 1951: The Mysterious Arrows. 2011. 40p. pap. 35.95 *(978-1-258-01939-6(6))* Literary Licensing, LLC.

—Gene Autry Comics, V1, No 73, March 1953: The Double Game. 2011. 48p. pap. 35.95 *(978-1-258-01938-9(8))* Literary Licensing, LLC.

Avery, Ben & Rogers, Bud. Berlin Breakout, 1 vol. Gaudiamo, Adi Darda, illus. 2008. (Z Graphic Novels / TimeFlyz Ser.). (ENG.). 160p. (J). (gr. 4-7). pap. 6.99 *(978-0-310-71363-0(3))* Zondervan.

Avery, Ben G. Pyramid Peril, 1 vol. Gaudiamo, Adi Darda, illus. 2007. (Z Graphic Novels / TimeFlyz Ser.). (ENG.). 160p. (J). (gr. 3-7). pap. 6.99 *(978-0-310-71361-6(7))* Zondervan.

—Turtle Trouble, 1 vol. Gaudiamo, Adi Darda, illus. 2007. (Z Graphic Novels / TimeFlyz Ser.). (ENG.). 160p. (J). (gr. 3-7). pap. 6.99 *(978-0-310-71362-3(5))* Zondervan.

Baltazar, Art & Aureliani, Franco, creators. Patrick the Wolf Boy Vols. 3 & 4: Giant Size Collection. 2004. (J). pap. 15.00 *(978-0-9749941-1-6(1))* Blind Wolf Studios.

Baumann, Susan K. Black Civil War Soldiers: The 54th Massachusetts Regiment. 2013. (Jr. Graphic African American History Ser.). (ENG., Illus.). 24p. (J). (gr. 3-6). pap. 10.60 *(978-1-4777-1457-7(X))*; lib. bdg. 25.25 *(978-1-4777-1316-7(6))* Rosen Publishing Group, Inc., The. (PowerKids Pr.).

—Harriet Tubman. 2013. (Jr. Graphic African American History Ser.). 24p. (J). (gr. 3-6). 25.25 *(978-1-4777-1312-9(3))*; pap. 10.60 *(978-1-4777-1449-2(9))* Rosen Publishing Group, Inc., The. (PowerKids Pr.).

Beacham, Travis, et al. Tales from Year Zero. 2013. (Pacific Rim Ser.). (ENG., Illus.). 128p. (gr. 8-17). 24.99 *(978-0-7851-5394-8(2))* Legendary Comics.

Beck, William F. Bible Stories in Pictures. Rogers, Ruth W. et al, illus. 2nd ed. 2003.Tr. of Bible Stories in Pictures. (ALB, SPA & SWE.). 376p. pap. 10.65 *(978-1-931891-08-0(7))* Multi-Language Pubns.

Beechen, Adam. Divide & Conquer, 1 vol. Barberi, Carlo & Wong, Walden, illus. 2013. (Justice League Unlimited Ser.). (ENG.). 32p. (gr. 2-3). lib. bdg. 22.60 *(978-1-4342-4713-1(9))* Stone Arch Bks.

Bell, Cece. El Deafo. Lasky, David, illus. 2014. (ENG.). 248p. (J). (gr. 3-7). 21.95 *(978-1-4197-1020-9(6))*; pap. 10.95 *(978-1-4197-1217-3(9))* Abrams, Inc. (Amulet Bks.).

—El Deafo. 2014. (J). lib. bdg. 22.05 *(978-0-606-36148-4(0))* Turtleback Bks.

Belmonte, David. Creating Horror Comics. 2015. (Illus.). 32p. (J). *(978-1-4777-5924-0(7)*, PowerKids Pr.) Rosen Publishing Group, Inc., The.

Benintendi, Stephen F. PowerMark Seeker Series Issue 1: Quest for Truth. 2003. (SPA.). (J). 0.25 *(978-0-9729135-1-5(3))* PowerMark Productions.

—PowerMark Seeker Series Issue 2: Let there Be... Light. 2003. (J). 1.75 *(978-0-9729135-2-2(1))* PowerMark Productions.

—PowerMark Seeker Series Issue 3: Sabotage. 2003. (ENG & SPA.). (J). 1.75 *(978-0-9729135-3-9(X))* PowerMark Productions.

Benintendi, Steve. PowerMark Issue 6 5-PK. 2003. 32p. (J). pap. 14.75 *(978-0-9725121-0-7(1))* PowerMark Productions.

Beranek, Adam, et al. Silent Forest, 1. Burke, Chris et al, illus. 2004. 136p. per. 11.95 *(978-0-9752582-0-0(6))* Silent Devil Productions.

Bergen, Lara. Tutu Twins. Pastel, Elyse & Pastel, Elyse, illus. 2008. (ENG.). 24p. (J). (gr. k-17). per. 3.99 *(978-1-58476-615-5(8))* Innovative Kids.

Bergin, Mark. How to Draw Comic Book Heroes. 2010. (How to Draw Ser.). (Illus.). 32p. (YA). (gr. 6-18). pap. 11.75 *(978-1-4488-1604-0(1))*; lib. bdg. 26.50 *(978-1-4488-1579-1(7))* Rosen Publishing Group, Inc., The. (PowerKids Pr.).

Berne, Emma. What Are Graphic Novels? 2014. (Name That Text Type! Ser.). (Illus.). 32p. (gr. 2-4). pap. 7.95 *(978-1-4677-4517-8(0))* Lerner Publishing Group.

Berne, Emma Carlson. What Are Graphic Novels? 2014. (Illus.). 32p. (gr. 2-4). lib. bdg. 26.60 *(978-1-4677-3666-4(X)*, Lerner Pubns.) Lerner Publishing Group.

Berry, Stéphane, prod. Spies in Disguise, Vol. 1. 2004. (Teen Ser.). (Illus.). pap. 14.99 *(978-1-59532-286-9(8)*, Tokyopop Kids) TOKYOPOP, Inc.

Bertozzi, Nick. Shackleton: Antarctic Odyssey. Bertozzi, Nick, illus. 2014. (ENG., Illus.). 128p. (YA). (gr. 7-12). pap. 16.99 *(978-1-59643-451-6(1)*, First Second Bks.) Roaring Brook Pr.

Biskup, Agnieszka. Amazing Story of Space Travel. Pop Art Properties Staff, illus. 2013. (STEM Adventures Ser.). (ENG.). 32p. (gr. 3-4). 30.65 *(978-1-4765-0124-6(6)*, Graphic Library) Capstone Press of Coughlan Cos.

—D-Day: June 6 1944, 1 vol. 2014. (24-Hour History Ser.). (ENG.). 48p. (gr. 3-5). pap. 8.95 *(978-1-4329-9301-6(1)*, NA-h) Heinemann-Raintree.

—Super Cool Forces & Motion Activities with Max Axiom. Baez, Marcelo, illus. 2015. (Max Axiom Science & Engineering Activities Ser.). (ENG.). 32p. (gr. 3-4). lib. bdg. 30.65 *(978-1-4914-2079-9(0)*, Graphic Library) Capstone Press of Coughlan Cos.

Biskup, Agnieszka & Collins, Terry. American Graphic. Pope, Richie, illus. 2012. (American Graphic Ser.). (ENG.). 32p. (gr. 3-4). pap. 572.40 *(978-1-4296-9339-4(8))*; pap. 15.90 *(978-1-4296-9494-0(7))*; pap. 89.10 *(978-1-4296-9338-7(X))* Capstone Press of Coughlan Cos. (Graphic Library).

Biskup, Agnieszka, et al. Graphic Science & Engineering in Action. Baez, Marcelo, illus. 2013. (Graphic Science & Engineering in Action Ser.). (ENG.). 32p. (gr. 3-4). lib. bdg. 122.60 *(978-1-4296-9938-9(8)*, Graphic Library) Capstone Press of Coughlan Cos.

Black Civil War Soldiers: The 54th Massachusetts Regiment. 2013. (Jr. Graphic African American History Ser.). 24p. (J). (gr. 3-6). pap. 63.60 *(978-1-4777-1458-4(8)*, PowerKids Pr.) Rosen Publishing Group, Inc., The.

Blackman, Haden. Darth Vader & the Lost Command: Vol 1, 1 vol. 2012. (Star Wars: Darth Vader & the Lost Command Ser.). (ENG., Illus.). 24p. (J). 24.21 *(978-1-59961-980-4(6)*, Graphic Novels) Spotlight.

—Darth Vader & the Lost Command: Vol 2, 1 vol. Leonardi, Rick, illus. 2012. (Star Wars: Darth Vader & the Lost Command Ser.). (ENG.). 24p. (J). 24.21 *(978-1-59961-981-1(4)*, Graphic Novels) Spotlight.

—Darth Vader & the Lost Command: Vol 3, 1 vol. Leonardi, Rick, illus. 2012. (Star Wars: Darth Vader & the Lost Command Ser.). (ENG.). 24p. (J). 24.21 *(978-1-59961-982-8(2)*, Graphic Novels) Spotlight.

—Darth Vader & the Lost Command: Vol 4, 1 vol. Leonardi, Rick, illus. 2012. (Star Wars: Darth Vader & the Lost Command Ser.). (ENG.). 24p. (J). 24.21 *(978-1-59961-983-5(0)*, Graphic Novels) Spotlight.

—Darth Vader & the Lost Command: Vol 5, 1 vol. Leonardi, Rick, illus. 2012. (Star Wars: Darth Vader & the Lost Command Ser.). (ENG.). 24p. (J). 24.21 *(978-1-59961-984-2(9)*, Graphic Novels) Spotlight.

Bolte, Mari. Encountering Ghosts: Eyewitness Accounts, 1 vol. Kako, Franco, illus. 2014. (Eyewitness to the Unexplained Ser.). (ENG.). 32p. (gr. 3-4). 30.65 *(978-1-4914-0245-0(8)*, Graphic Library) Capstone Press of Coughlan Cos.

—Flight to Freedom! Nickolas Flux & the Underground Railroad, 1 vol. Foster, Brad W. & Simmons, Mark, illus. 2014. (Nickolas Flux History Chronicles Ser.). (ENG.). 32p. (gr. 3-4). lib. bdg. 30.65 *(978-1-4914-0254-2(7)*, Graphic Library) Capstone Press of Coughlan Cos.

—Sleepover Girls Crafts: Amazing Recipes You Can Make & Share, 1 vol. Franco, Paula, illus. 2014. (Sleepover Girls Crafts Ser.). (ENG.). 64p. (gr. 3-4). pap. 9.95 *(978-1-62370-197-0(X))* Capstone Press of Coughlan Cos.

Bowers, Rick. Superman Versus the Ku Klux Klan: The True Story of How the Iconic Superhero Battled the Men of Hate. 2012. (Illus.). 160p. pap. *(978-0-545-43745-5(8))* Scholastic, Inc.

Bowman, Chris. The Hindenburg Disaster. 2014. (Disaster Stories Ser.). (ENG., Illus.). 24p. (J). (gr. 3-8). 29.95 *(978-1-62617-153-4(X)*, Black Sheep) Bellwether Media.

Britt, Fanny. Jane, the Fox & Me, 1 vol. Ouriou, Susan & Morelli, Christelle, trs. from FRE. Arsenault, Isabelle, illus. 2013. (ENG.). 104p. (J). (gr. 5). 19.95 *(978-1-55498-360-5(6))* Groundwood Bks. CAN. Dist: Publishers Group West (PGW).

Brontë, Emily. Wuthering Heights. Bryant, Clive, ed. Burns, John M., illus. 2011. (ENG.). 160p. lib. bdg. 24.95 *(978-1-907127-80-9(1))* Classical Comics GBR. Dist: Publishers Group West (PGW).

Brown, Jeffrey. Jedi Academy. Brown, Jeffrey, illus. 2013. (Star Wars Jedi Academy Ser.: Bk. 1). (Illus.). 160p. (J). (ENG.). (gr. 3-7). 12.99 *(978-0-545-50517-8(8))*; pap. *(978-0-545-60999-9(2))* Scholastic, Inc.

—The Phantom Bully. 2015. (Star Wars: Jedi Academy Ser.: 3). (ENG., Illus.). 176p. (J). (gr. 3-7). 12.99 *(978-0-545-62126-7(7))* Scholastic, Inc.

—Return of the Padawan. Brown, Jeffrey, illus. 2014. (Star Wars Jedi Academy Ser.: Bk. 2). (ENG., Illus.). 176p. (J). (gr. 3-7). 12.99 *(978-0-545-62125-0(9))* Scholastic, Inc.

Burgan, Michael. Benedict Arnold: American Hero & Traitor, 1 vol. Beatty, Terry, illus. 2007. (Graphic Biographies Ser.). (ENG.). 32p. (gr. 3-4). per. 8.10 *(978-0-7368-7906-4(4)*, Graphic Library) Capstone Press of Coughlan Cos.

Burnham, Erik. Ghostbusters. Schoening, Dan, illus. 2016. (ENG.). 24p. (J). *(978-1-61479-485-1(5))* Spotlight.

Burroughs, Edgar Rice. The Land That Time Forgot: Graphic Novel. Jones, K. L., illus. 2011. (Campfire Graphic Novels Ser.). (ENG.). 72p. (YA). (gr. 5-12). pap. 9.99 *(978-93-80028-38-5(5)*, Campfire) Steerforth Pr.

Byrne, Eugene. Darwin: A Graphic Biography. Gurr, Simon, illus. 2013. (ENG.). 100p. (J). (gr. 7). pap. 9.95 *(978-1-58834-352-9(9)*, Smithsonian Bks.) Smithsonian Institution Scholarly Pr.

Cabiya, Pedro, creator. Anima Sola: Hambre. 2003. (SPA.). 40p. (YA). pap. 8.95 *(978-0-9745825-0-4(6))* Zemi Comics.

Camagajevac, Seb. Creating Fantasy Comics. 2015. (J). *(978-1-4777-5904-2(2))* Rosen Publishing Group, Inc., The.

Cameron, Don, et al. The World's Finest Comics. rev. ed. 2004. (Batman Ser.: Vol. 2). (ENG., Illus.). 228p. (YA). 49.95 *(978-1-4012-0163-0(6))* DC Comics.

Camper, Cathy. Low Riders in Space. Raúl, III, illus. 2014. (ENG & SPA.). 112p. (J). (gr. 3-7). pap. 9.99 *(978-1-4521-2869-6(3))*;Bk. 1. 22.99 *(978-1-4521-2155-0(9))* Chronicle Bks. LLC.

Campos, Leo. Creating Manga Comics, 1 vol. 2015. (ENG., Illus.). 32p. (J). lib. bdg. 27.50 *(978-1-4777-5926-4(3)*, PowerKids Pr.) Rosen Publishing Group, Inc., The.

Cardarelli, Alyn. Captain Virtue & the Champions of Justice. 2012. 38p. pap. 19.99 *(978-1-4685-0955-7(1))* AuthorHouse.

Careers in Focus: Comic Books & Graphic Novels. 4th rev. ed. 2011. (Careers in Focus Ser.). 220p. (gr. 6-12). 32.95 *(978-0-8160-8038-0(0)*, Ferguson Publishing Co.) Facts On File, Inc.

Carre, Lilli. Tippy & the Night Parade. Carre, Lilli, illus. 2014. (ENG., Illus.). 32p. (J). (gr. -1-3). 12.95 *(978-1-935179-57-3(8))* TOON Books / RAW Junior, LLC.

Carroll, Lewis, pseud. Alice. 2004. (ENG., Illus.). 112p. (J). pap. 8.95 *(978-0-9716338-3-4(5)*, 9780971633834) About Comics.

Castellucci, Cecil. Odd Duck. Varon, Sara, illus. 2013. (ENG.). 96p. (J). (gr. 1-5). 15.99 *(978-1-59643-557-5(7)*, 9781596435575, First Second Bks.) Roaring Brook Pr.

Cauvin, Raoul. Dad's Got Class. 2009. (Cedric Ser.: 2). (ENG., Illus.). 48p. (J). (gr. 4-7). pap. 11.95 *(978-1-84918-003-0(2))* CineBook GBR. Dist: National Bk. Network.

—What Got into Him?, Vol. Laudec, illus. 2011. (Cedric Ser.: 3). (ENG.). 48p. (J). (gr. 3-17). pap. 11.95 *(978-1-84918-081-8(4))* CineBook GBR. Dist: National Bk. Network.

Chambers, Ailin. Manga. 2014. (Ready, Set, Draw! Ser.). 32p. (J). (gr. 2-5). 26.60 *(978-1-4824-0918-5(6))* Stevens, Gareth Publishing LLLP.

Chan, Mari. Super Fun Kids. 2003. 4.99 *(978-1-56971-922-0(5))* Dark Horse Comics.

Chandler, Matt, retold by. The Trojan War: A Graphic Retelling. 2015. (Ancient Myths Ser.). (ENG.). 32p. (gr. 3-4). lib. bdg. 30.65 *(978-1-4914-2074-4(X)*, Graphic Library) Capstone Press of Coughlan Cos.

Chantler, Scott. The Sign of the Black Rock. Chantler, Scott, illus. 2011. (Three Thieves Ser.: 2). (ENG., Illus.). 112p. (J). (gr. 4-7). pap. 7.95 *(978-1-55453-417-3(8))* Kids Can Pr., Ltd. CAN. Dist: Hachette Bk. Group.

Chiacchiera, Moreno. Creating Funny Comics. 2015. (Illus.). 32p. *(978-1-4777-5912-7(3))* Rosen Publishing Group, Inc., The.

Clamp Staff. Cardcaptor Sakura, Vol. 4. Clamp Staff, illus. rev. ed. 2005. (Illus.). 200p. (J). pap. 9.99 *(978-1-59182-881-5(3)*, Tokyopop Kids) TOKYOPOP, Inc.

Claremont, Chris & Lopresti, Aaron. Excalibur: Forging the Sword. 2004. (X-Men Ser.). (Illus.). 96p. 9.99 *(978-0-7851-1527-4(7))* Marvel Worldwide, Inc.

Collins, Terry. The Assassination of John F. Kennedy: November 22 1963, 1 vol. 2014. (24-Hour History Ser.). (ENG.). 48p. (gr. 3-5). pap. 8.95 *(978-1-4329-9300-9(3)*, NA-h) Heinemann-Raintree.

—The Assassination of Martin Luther King, Jr: April 4 1968, 1 vol. 2014. (24-Hour History Ser.). (ENG.). 48p. (gr. 3-5). pap. 8.95 *(978-1-4329-9302-3(X)*, NA-h) Heinemann-Raintree.

—Escape from Pompeii: An Isabel Soto Archaeology Adventure. 2010. (Graphic Expeditions Ser.). (ENG., Illus.). 32p. (gr. 3-4). pap. 47.70 *(978-1-4296-5714-3(6)*, Graphic Library) Capstone Press of Coughlan Cos.

—Stake a Claim! Nickolas Flux & the California Gold Rush, 1 vol. Ginevra, Dante, illus. 2014. (Nickolas Flux History Chronicles Ser.). (ENG.). 32p. (gr. 3-4). lib. bdg. 30.65 *(978-1-4765-3944-7(8)*, Graphic Library) Capstone Press of Coughlan Cos.

Collins, Terry, et al. American Graphic. Hayden, Seitu & Kinsella, Pat, illus. 2012. (American Graphic Ser.). (ENG.). 32p. (gr. 3-4). lib. bdg. 61.30 *(978-1-4296-9162-8(X)*, Graphic Library) Capstone Press of Coughlan Cos.

The Comic Adventures of Felix the Cat. 2004. (Illus.). 128p. (YA). per. 12.95 *(978-0-615-12660-9(X))* Felix Comics, Inc.

Comic Book Facts. 2003. (Illus.). pap. 5.60 *(978-0-7398-7514-8(0))* Steck-Vaughn.

Conway, Gerry, et al. Super-Villain Team-Up. 2004. (Marvel Heroes Ser.). (Illus.). 552p. (YA). pap. 16.99 *(978-0-7851-1545-8(5))* Marvel Worldwide, Inc.

Cook, Trevor & Miles, Lisa. Drawing Manga. 2011. (Drawing Is Fun Ser.). (Illus.). 32p. (J). (gr. 1-3). pap. 10.50 *(978-1-4339-5067-4(7)*, Gareth Stevens Learning Library); lib. bdg. 26.60 *(978-1-4339-5024-7(3))* Stevens, Gareth Publishing LLLP.

Corsetto, Danielle. Adventure Time: Pixel Princesses. 2013. lib. bdg. 23.30 *(978-0-606-35464-6(6))* Turtleback Bks.

—Adventure Time - Seeing Red. 2014. lib. bdg. 23.30 *(978-0-606-35465-3(4))* Turtleback Bks.

—Pixel Princesses, Vol. 2. Sterling, Zack, illus. 2013. (Adventure Time Ser.: 2). (ENG.). 160p. (J). (gr. 3). pap. 11.99 *(978-1-60886-329-7(8))* Boom! Studios.

Craddock, Erik. Ninja Slice. Craddock, Erik, illus. 2010. (Stone Rabbit Ser.: No. 5). (ENG., Illus.). 96p. (J). (gr. 3-7). pap. 6.99 *(978-0-375-86723-1(6)*, Random Hse. Bks. for Young Readers) Random Hse. Children's Bks.

Craver, Marcella Marino. Shield Up! Pinelli, Amerigo, illus. 2014. 64p. (J). pap. *(978-1-4338-1651-2(2)*, Magination Pr.) American Psychological Assn.

Creative Team at Walter Foster Publishing Staff. Spongebob Squarepants - The Bikini Bottom Collection. 2012. (Licensed Learn to Draw Ser.). (ENG., Illus.). 64p. (J). (gr. 1-3). pap. 9.95 *(978-1-60058-297-4(4)*, 1600582974) Quarto Publishing Group USA.

Dalrymple, Farel. The Wrenchies. Dalrymple, Farel, illus. 2014. (ENG., Illus.). 304p. (YA). (gr. 9). pap. 19.99 *(978-1-59643-421-9(X)*, 9781596434219, First Second Bks.) Roaring Brook Pr.

David, Peter. Out of the Shadows. Thomas, LeSean, illus. 2007. (Teenage Mutant Ninja Turtles Ser.). (ENG.). 96p. pap. 12.95 *(978-1-84576-146-2(4)*, Titan Bks.) Titan Bks. Ltd. GBR. Dist: Penguin Random Hse. LLC.

Davis, Adam. Guardians of the Galaxy. 2014. (ENG., Illus.). 24p. (J). (gr. -1-3). pap. 3.99 *(978-0-316-29319-8(9))* Little, Brown Bks. for Young Readers.

—Guardians of the Galaxy: Rocket & Groot Fight Back. 2014. (ENG., Illus.). 24p. (J). (gr. -1-3). pap. 4.99 *(978-0-316-29323-5(7))* Little, Brown Bks. for Young Readers.

Dawson, Willow. Lila & Ecco's Do-It-Yourself Comics Club. Dawson, Willow, illus. 2010. (ENG., Illus.). 112p. (J). (gr. 3-7). 7.95 *(978-1-55453-439-5(9))*; 16.95 *(978-1-55453-438-8(0))* Kids Can Pr., Ltd. CAN. Dist: Hachette Bk. Group.

DC Comics Staff, et al. Death of Superman. Kahan, Bob, ed. rev. ed. 2011. (Superman Ser.). (ENG., Illus.). 168p. (YA). pap. 12.99 *(978-1-56389-097-0(6))* DC Comics.

Denton, Shannon, et al. Komikwerks Presents Nuts & Bolts 2004. (Illus.). 144p. (YA). per. 9.95 *(978-0-9742803-2-5(1))* Komikwerks, LLC.

—Zapt!, Vol. 1. 2006. (Zapt! Ser.). (Illus.). 96p. pap. 5.99 *(978-1-59816-588-3(7))* TOKYOPOP, Inc.

Deshpande, Sanjay. In Defense of the Realm: Graphic Novel. Sharma, Lalit Kumar, illus. 2011. (Campfire Graphic Novels Ser.). (ENG.). 104p. (YA). (gr. 3-7). pap. 12.99 *(978-93-80028-64-4(4)*, Campfire) Steerforth Pr.

Dickens, Charles. A Christmas Carol the Graphic Novel - Original Text: British Edition. Collins, Mike et al, illus. 2008. 160p. (Orig.). pap. *(978-1-906332-17-4(7))* Classical Comics.

Disney Staff, creator. Bambi. 2005. (Illus.). 96p. pap. 14.99 *(978-1-59532-715-4(0)*, Tokyopop Kids) TOKYOPOP, Inc.

Disney Staff, prod. Sparring & Charring. 2004. (Lilo & Stitch: Vol. 2). (Illus.). 96p. pap. 14.99 *(978-1-59532-068-1(7)*, Tokyopop Kids) TOKYOPOP, Inc.

Dobbyn, Nigel. Creating Science Fiction Comics. 2015. (Illus.). 32p. (J). *(978-1-4777-5932-5(8)*, PowerKids Pr.) Rosen Publishing Group, Inc., The.

Doctorow, Cory. In Real Life. Wang, Jen, illus. 2014. (ENG.). 192p. (YA). (gr. 7). pap. 17.99 *(978-1-59643-658-9(1)*, 9781596436589, First Second Bks.) Roaring Brook Pr.

Doering Tourville, Amanda. A Visit to the Police Station. Thompson, Jeffrey, illus. 2011. (First Graphics: My Community Ser.). (ENG.). 24p. (gr. 1-2). pap. 35.70 *(978-1-4296-6402-8(9))* Capstone Press of Coughlan Cos.

Dorling Kindersley Publishing Staff. LEGO(r) DC Comics Super Heroes the Awesome Guide. 2017. (ENG.). 96p. (J). (gr. 2). 16.99 ***(978-1-4654-6078-3(0))***; lib. bdg. 16.99 ***(978-1-4654-6315-9(1))*** Dorling Kindersley Publishing, Inc. (DK Children).

Dorling Kindersley Publishing Staff. Marvel the Avengers. 2015. (ENG.). 96p. (J). (gr. 2-5). pap. 12.99 *(978-1-4654-3249-0(3)*, DK Children) Dorling Kindersley Publishing, Inc.

Dorsey, Angela. Horse Angel Comic: Rough Diamond. 2007. (YA). pap. *(978-1-933343-66-2(4))* Stabenfeldt Inc.

—Horse Angel Comic - the Desert King. 2008. (J). pap. *(978-1-933343-82-2(6))* Stabenfeldt Inc.

Doyle, Arthur Conan. Sherlock Holmes & a Scandal in Bohemia. Rohrbach, Sophie, illus. 2010. (On the Case with Holmes & Watson Ser.: 1). (ENG.). 48p. (J). (gr. 4-6). lib. bdg. 27.93 *(978-0-7613-6185-5(5))* Lerner Publishing Group.

—Sherlock Holmes & the Adventure at the Abbey Grange. Rohrbach, Sophie, illus. 2010. (On the Case with Holmes & Watson Ser.: 2). (ENG.). 48p. (J). (gr. 4-6). lib. bdg. 27.93 *(978-0-7613-6189-3(8))* Lerner Publishing Group.

—Sherlock Holmes & the Adventure of Black Peter. Rohrbach, Sophie & Morrow, J. T., illus. 2012. (On the Case with Holmes & Watson Ser.). 48p. (J). (gr. 4-6). pap. 39.62 *(978-0-7613-9274-3(2))*; (ENG.). pap. 6.95 *(978-0-7613-7100-7(1))* Lerner Publishing Group. (Graphic Universe™).

—Sherlock Holmes & the Adventure of the Blue Gem. Rohrbach, Sophie, illus. 2010. (On the Case with Holmes & Watson Ser.: 3). (ENG.). 48p. (J). (gr. 4-6). lib. bdg. 27.93 *(978-0-7613-6190-9(1))* Lerner Publishing Group.

—Sherlock Holmes & the Adventure of the Cardboard Box. Rohrbach, Sophie & Morrow, J. T., illus. 2012. (On the Case with Holmes & Watson Ser.). 48p. (J). (gr. 4-6). pap. 39.62 *(978-0-7613-9275-0(0))*; (ENG.). pap. 6.95 *(978-0-7613-7098-7(6))* Lerner Publishing Group. (Graphic Universe™).

—Sherlock Holmes & the Adventure of the Dancing Men. Rohrbach, Sophie, illus. 2010. (On the Case with Holmes & Watson Ser.: 4). (ENG.). 48p. (J). (gr. 4-6). lib. bdg. 27.93 *(978-0-7613-6188-6(X))* Lerner Publishing Group.

—Sherlock Holmes & the Adventure of the Sussex Vampire. Rohrbach, Sophie, illus. 2010. (On the Case with Holmes &

Watson Ser.: 6). (ENG.). 48p. (J). (gr. 4-6). lib. bdg. 27.93 *(978-0-7613-6187-9(1))* Lerner Publishing Group.
—Sherlock Holmes & the Adventure of the Three Garridebs. Rohrbach, Sophie & Morrow, J. T., illus. 2012. (On the Case with Holmes & Watson Ser.). 48p. (J). (gr. 4-6). pap. 39.62 *(978-0-7613-9276-7(9))*; (ENG.). pap. 6.95 *(978-0-7613-7099-4(4))* Lerner Publishing Group. (Graphic Universe™).
—Sherlock Holmes & the Boscombe Valley Mystery. Rohrbach, Sophie & Morrow, J. T., illus. 2011. (On the Case with Holmes & Watson Ser.: 10). (ENG.). 48p. (J). (gr. 4-6). 27.93 *(978-0-7613-7089-5(7))*; pap. 6.95 *(978-0-7613-7097-0(8))* Lerner Publishing Group. (Graphic Universe™).
—Sherlock Holmes & the Gloria Scott. Rohrbach, Sophie & Morrow, J. T., illus. 2012. (On the Case with Holmes & Watson Ser.: 14). (ENG.). 48p. (J). (gr. 4-6). lib. bdg. 27.93 *(978-0-7613-7093-2(5))* Lerner Publishing Group.
—Sherlock Holmes & the Gloria Scott. Rohrbach, Sophie & Morrow, J. T., illus. 2012. (On the Case with Holmes & Watson Ser.). 48p. (J). (gr. 4-6). pap. 39.62 *(978-0-7613-9277-4(7))*; (ENG.). pap. 6.95 *(978-0-7613-7101-4(X))* Lerner Publishing Group. (Graphic Universe™).
DreamWorks Animation Staff. Shrek 2. 2004. (Illus.). pap. 14.99 *(978-1-59182-912-6(7)*, Tokyopop Kids) TOKYOPOP, Inc.
Dufaux, Jean. Rapaces. Marini, Enrico, illus. 2004. (SPA.). Vol. 1. 56p. pap. 17.95 *(978-1-59497-003-0(3))* Vol. 2. 56p. pap. 17.95 *(978-1-59497-004-7(1))* Vol. 3. 64p. pap. 17.95 *(978-1-59497-005-4(X))* Public Square Bks.
Dumas, Alexandre. The Man in the Iron Mask. 2003. (Saddleback Classics Ser.). (Illus.). 48p. (J). per. 17.95 *(978-1-56254-528-4(0)*, SP5280); 79p. (YA). (gr. 8-12). per. 6.95 *(978-1-56254-527-7(2)*, SP5272) Saddleback Educational Publishing, Inc.
—The Three Musketeers. Tayal, Amit, illus. 2011. (Campfire Graphic Novels Ser.). (ENG.). 104p. (YA). (gr. 3-7). pap. 12.99 *(978-93-80028-57-6(1)*, Campfire) Steerforth Pr.
Dunn, Ben. How to Draw Manga. 2004. (Illus.). 344p. (YA). pap. 3.25 *(978-1-59412-063-3(3))* Mud Puddle, Inc.
Dunn, Joeming. Barack Obama: 44th U. S. President, 1 vol. Espinosa, Rod, illus. 2011. (Presidents of the United States Bio-Graphics Ser.). (ENG.). 32p. (YA). (gr. 3-6). 28.50 *(978-1-61641-648-5(3))* Magic Wagon.
Dunn, Joeming & Espinosa, Rod. John Adams: 2nd U. S. President, 1 vol. 2011. (Presidents of the United States Bio-Graphics Ser.). (ENG., Illus.). 32p. (YA). (gr. 3-6). 28.50 *(978-1-61641-644-7(0))* Magic Wagon.
Elder, Jeremy. Space Agent. 2010. (Dover Children's Activity Bks.). (ENG., Illus.). 48p. (J). (gr. 2-5). pap. 4.99 *(978-0-486-47828-9(9))* Dover Pubns., Inc.
Eliot, Jan. You Can't Say Boobs on Sunday No. 2: The Second Collection of the Syndicated Cartoon Stone Soup. 2004. (Illus.). 192p. pap. 13.95 *(978-0-9674102-0-3(7))* Four Panel Pr.
Elliott, Craig. Racer Buddies-Opening Day at Daytona. William, Harper, illus. 2004. 40p. (J). per. 12.95 *(978-0-9746445-0-9(1)*, 1234022) Powerband, LLC.
Ennis, Garth. A Rage in Arkham. 2009. (ENG., Illus.). 144p. (YA). pap. 14.99 *(978-1-56389-314-8(2))* DC Comics.
—Until the End of the World. 2nd rev. ed. 2011. (Preacher Ser.). (ENG., Illus.). 264p. (YA). pap. 17.99 *(978-1-56389-312-4(6))* DC Comics.
Enz, Tammy. Amazing Story of Cell Phone Technology. Pop Art Properties Staff, illus. 2013. (STEM Adventures Ser.). (ENG.). 32p. (gr. 3-4). 30.65 *(978-1-4765-0137-6(8)*, Graphic Library) Capstone Press of Coughlan Cos.
—Engineering a Totally Rad Skateboard with Max Axiom, Super Scientist, 1 vol. Pop Art Studios, illus. 2013. (Graphic Science & Engineering in Action Ser.). (ENG.). 32p. (gr. 3-4). pap. 8.10 *(978-1-62065-703-4(1)*, Graphic Library) Capstone Press of Coughlan Cos.
—Engineering a Totally Rad Skateboard with Max Axiom, Super Scientist, 1 vol. Pop Art Studios Staff, illus. 2013. (Graphic Science & Engineering in Action Ser.). (ENG.). 32p. (gr. 3-4). lib. bdg. 30.65 *(978-1-4296-9935-8(3)*, Graphic Library) Capstone Press of Coughlan Cos.
—Terrific Tale of Television Technology. Pop Art Properties Staff, illus. 2013. (STEM Adventures Ser.). (ENG.). 32p. (gr. 3-4). 30.65 *(978-1-4765-0138-3(6)*, Graphic Library); pap. 8.95 *(978-1-4765-3458-9(6))* Capstone Press of Coughlan Cos.
Enz, Tammy, et al. Graphic Science & Engineering in Action. Baez, Marcelo, illus. 2013. (Graphic Science & Engineering in Action Ser.). (ENG.). 32p. (gr. 3-4). pap. 31.80 *(978-1-62065-707-2(4))*; pap. 190.80 *(978-1-62065-708-9(2))* Capstone Press of Coughlan Cos. (Graphic Library).
Eppard, Jon. Manga. 2012. (ENG., Illus.). 24p. (J). pap. *(978-1-60014-857-6(3))*; (gr. 3-8). lib. bdg. 25.95 *(978-1-60014-812-5(3)*, Express Bks.) Bellwether Media.
EZ Comics, ed. James A. Baker, III: The Authorised Comic Book Biography. 2009. (ENG., Illus.). 44p. (YA). *(978-0-9795887-3-0(1))* EZ Comics.
Fearing, Mark & Rummel, Tim. Earthling! 2012. (ENG., Illus.). 248p. (J). (gr. 3-7). 22.99 *(978-0-8118-7106-8(1))* Chronicle Bks. LLC.
—Earthling. 2012. (ENG., Illus.). 248p. (J). (gr. 3-7). pap. 12.99 *(978-1-4521-0906-0(0))* Chronicle Bks. LLC.
Fedyszyn, Kirra. Molly Brown. 2014. (Jr. Graphic American Legends Ser.). (Illus.). 24p. (J). (gr. 3-6). pap. 10.60 *(978-1-4777-7201-0(4)*, PowerKids Pr.) Rosen Publishing Group, Inc., The.
Ferri, Jean-Yves. Asterix & the Missing Scroll. Conrad, Didier, illus. 2015. (ENG.). 48p. (J). (gr. 4-6). 17.99 *(978-1-5101-0045-9(8)*, Asterix) Hachette Children's Group GBR. Dist: Hachette Bk. Group.
Filippi, Denis Pierre, et al. Muse. 2013. (Muse Ser.). (ENG., Illus.). 104p. 34.95 *(978-1-59465-038-3(1)*, 9781594650383) Humanoids, Inc.
Fisch, Sholly. Just My Luck, 1 vol. Brizuela, Dario, illus. 2013. (DC Super Friends Ser.). (ENG.). 32p. (gr. 1-2). lib. bdg. 22.60 *(978-1-4342-4702-5(3))* Stone Arch Bks.
—Nothing to Fear, 1 vol. McKenny, Stewart & Moy, Phil, illus. 2013. (DC Super Friends Ser.). (ENG.). 32p. (gr. 1-2). lib. bdg. 22.60 *(978-1-4342-4703-2(1))* Stone Arch Bks.
Flowers, Arthur. I See the Promised Land: A Life of Martin Luther King, Jr., 1 vol. Chitrakar, Manu, illus. rev. ed. 2013. (ENG.). 156p. (J). (gr. 6). 16.95 *(978-1-55498-328-5(2))* Groundwood Bks. CAN. Dist: Publishers Group West (PGW).
Fontes, Ron & Fontes, Justine, creators. Ron & Justine Fontes Present Tales of the Terminal Diner. 2004. (Illus.). 96p. (YA). per. 9.95 *(978-0-9754615-0-1(8)*, 001) Critter Publishing.
Forget, Tom. Art Spiegelman. 2009. (Library of Graphic Novelists Ser.). 112p. (gr. 7-12). 63.90 *(978-1-60853-652-8(1))* Rosen Publishing Group, Inc., The.
Freeman, Aaron & Rosenzweig, Sharon. The Comic Torah: Reimagining the Good Book. 2010. (Illus.). 128p. (J). 36.00 *(978-1-934730-53-9(X))* Yehuda, Ben Pr.
—The Comic Torah: Reimagining the Very Good Book. Rosenzweig, Sharon, illus. 2010. (ENG., Illus.). 128p. (J). pap. 19.95 *(978-1-934730-54-6(8))* Yehuda, Ben Pr.
Fridolfs, Derek. Secret Hero Society- Study Hall of Justice. Nguyen, Dustin, illus. 2016. 176p. (J). pap. ***(978-1-76027-653-9(7))*** Scholastic, Inc.
Friends of Lulu Presents: Broad Appeal. 2003. (YA). per. 9.95 *(978-0-9740960-1-8(6))* Friends of Lulu.
Furman, Simon. Revenge of the Fallen, 1 vol. Davis-Hunt, Jon, illus. 2010. (Transformers: Revenge of the Fallen Movie Adaptation Ser.). (ENG.). 24p. (J). (gr. 3-6). Vol. 1. 24.21 *(978-1-59961-726-8(9))* Vol. 2. 24.21 *(978-1-59961-727-5(7))* Spotlight.
—Revenge of the Fallen, 1 vol., Vol. 3. Milne, Alex, illus. 2010. (Transformers: Revenge of the Fallen Movie Adaptation Ser.). (ENG.). 24p. (J). (gr. 3-6). 24.21 *(978-1-59961-728-2(5))* Spotlight.
—Revenge of the Fallen, 1 vol., Vol. 4. Davis-Hunt, Jon, illus. 2010. (Transformers: Revenge of the Fallen Movie Adaptation Ser.). (ENG.). 24p. (J). (gr. 3-6). 24.21 *(978-1-59961-729-9(3))* Spotlight.
Gaiman, NEil. Hansel & Gretel. Mattotti, Lorenzo, illus. 2014. (ENG.). (J). (gr. 2-7). 56p. 16.95 *(978-1-935179-62-7(4))*; 60p. 29.95 *(978-1-935179-65-8(9))* TOON Books / RAW Junior, LLC.
Gaiman, NEil & Russell, P. Craig. The Graveyard Book Graphic Novel. Russell, P. Craig, illus. 2014. (ENG., Illus.). (J). (gr. 3-7). Vol. 1. 192p. 19.99 *(978-0-06-219481-7(X))* Vol. 2. 176p. 19.99 *(978-0-06-219483-1(6))* HarperCollins Pubs.
Gale Editor, ed. Romeo & Juliet: The Graphic Novel. 2011. (Classic Graphic Novel Collection Ser.). (Illus.). 160p. (J). (gr. 7-12). lib. bdg. 34.80 *(978-1-4205-0631-0(5))* Cengage Gale.
Gallagher, Michael. X-Men, Magneto's Master Plan. Severin, Marie, illus. 24p. (YA). (gr. k-18). 12.95 *(978-0-9627001-6-3(9))* Futech Educational Products, Inc.
Ganeri, Anita. United States of America. Isik, Semur, illus. 2015. (Country Guides, with Benjamin Blog & His Inquisitive Dog Ser.). (ENG.). 32p. (gr. 1-3). 29.99 *(978-1-4109-6851-7(0)*, Read Me!) Heinemann-Raintree.
Garcia, Tracy J. Thomas Edison. 2013. (Jr. Graphic American Inventors Ser.). (ENG., Illus.). 24p. (J). (gr. 3-6). pap. 10.60 *(978-1-4777-0137-9(0))*; lib. bdg. 25.25 *(978-1-4777-0076-1(5))* Rosen Publishing Group, Inc., The. (PowerKids Pr.).
Giannotta, Andres Bernardo & Drawing Staff. How to Draw Manga. 2010. (Dover How to Draw Ser.). (ENG., Illus.). 64p. (J). (gr. 3-5). pap. 5.99 *(978-0-486-47662-9(6))* Dover Pubns., Inc.
Gianopoulos, Andrea & Barnett, Charles, III. Isaac Newton & the Laws of Motion, 1 vol. Miller, Phil, illus. 2007. (Inventions & Discovery Ser.). (ENG.). 32p. (gr. 3-4). pap. 8.10 *(978-0-7368-7899-9(8)*, 1264949, Graphic Library) Capstone Press of Coughlan Cos.
Gilchrist, Ellen. Adventures of TinTin. 2009. Vol. 6. pap. 18.99 *(978-0-316-18990-3(1))* Vol. 7. pap. 18.99 *(978-0-316-18992-7(8))* Little, Brown Bks. for Young Readers.
Gill, Joel Christian. Strange Fruit Vol. 1: Uncelebrated Narratives from Black History. 2014. (ENG., Illus.). 176p. (YA). (gr. 7). pap. 23.95 *(978-1-938486-29-6(3))* Fulcrum Publishing.
Gomdori Co. Staff & Han, Hyun-dong. Survive! Inside the Human Body, Vol. 1: The Digestive System. 2013. (ENG., Illus.). 184p. (gr. 2). pap. 17.95 *(978-1-59327-471-9(8))* No Starch Pr., Inc.
—Survive! Inside the Human Body, Vol. 2: The Circulatory System. 2013. (ENG., Illus.). 180p. (gr. 2). pap. 17.95 *(978-1-59327-472-6(6))* No Starch Pr., Inc.
—Survive! Inside the Human Body, Vol. 3: The Nervous System. 2013. (ENG., Illus.). 184p. (gr. 2). pap. 17.95 *(978-1-59327-473-3(4))* No Starch Pr., Inc.
Goodwin, Vincent. The Adventure of the Blue Carbuncle, 1 vol. Dunn, Ben, illus. 2012. (Graphic Novel Adventures of Sherlock Holmes Set 2 Ser.). (ENG.). 48p. (J). (gr. 3-8). lib. bdg. 29.93 *(978-1-61641-891-5(5)*, Graphic Planet) Magic Wagon.
—The Adventure of the Copper Beeches, 1 vol. Dunn, Ben, illus. 2012. (Graphic Novel Adventures of Sherlock Holmes Set 2 Ser.). (ENG.). 48p. (J). (gr. 3-8). lib. bdg. 29.93 *(978-1-61641-892-2(3)*, Graphic Planet) Magic Wagon.
—The Adventure of the Engineer's Thumb, 1 vol. Dunn, Ben, illus. 2012. (Graphic Novel Adventures of Sherlock Holmes Set 2 Ser.). (ENG.). 48p. (J). (gr. 3-8). lib. bdg. 29.93 *(978-1-61641-893-9(1)*, Graphic Planet) Magic Wagon.
—The Adventure of the Solitary Cyclist, 1 vol. Dunn, Ben, illus. 2012. (Graphic Novel Adventures of Sherlock Holmes Set 2 Ser.). (ENG.). 48p. (J). (gr. 3-8). lib. bdg. 29.93 *(978-1-61641-894-6(X)*, Graphic Planet) Magic Wagon.
—The Adventure of the Three Students, 1 vol. Dunn, Ben, illus. 2012. (Graphic Novel Adventures of Sherlock Holmes Set 2 Ser.). (ENG.). 48p. (J). (gr. 3-8). lib. bdg. 29.93 *(978-1-61641-895-3(8)*, Graphic Planet) Magic Wagon.
—The Adventure of Wisteria Lodge, 1 vol. Dunn, Ben, illus. 2012. (Graphic Novel Adventures of Sherlock Holmes Set 2 Ser.). (ENG.). 48p. (J). (gr. 3-8). lib. bdg. 29.93 *(978-1-61641-896-0(6)*, Graphic Planet) Magic Wagon.
Goscinny, René. Asterix & Cleopatra. Uderzo, Albert, illus. 2004. (ENG.). 48p. 17.99 *(978-0-7528-6606-2(0)*, Orion) Orion Publishing Group, Ltd. GBR. Dist: Hachette Bk. Group.
—Asterix & the Banquet. Uderzo, Albert, illus. 2004. (ENG.). 48p. 17.99 *(978-0-7528-6608-6(7)*, Orion) Orion Publishing Group, Ltd. GBR. Dist: Hachette Bk. Group.
—Asterix & the Cauldron. Uderzo, Albert, illus. 2004. (ENG.). 48p. 17.99 *(978-0-7528-6628-4(1)*, Orion) Orion Publishing Group, Ltd. GBR. Dist: Hachette Bk. Group.
—Asterix & the Class Act. Uderzo, Albert, illus. 2004. (ENG.). 56p. pap. 12.99 *(978-0-7528-6640-6(0)*, Orion) Orion Publishing Group, Ltd. GBR. Dist: Hachette Bk. Group.
—Asterix & the Golden Sickle. Uderzo, Albert, illus. 2004. (ENG.). 48p. 17.99 *(978-0-7528-6612-3(5)*, Orion) Orion Publishing Group, Ltd. GBR. Dist: Hachette Bk. Group.
—Asterix & the Normans. (Illus.). (J). pap. 9.95 *(978-0-02-497290-3(8))* International Language Centre.
—Asterix aux Jeux Olympiques. (FRE.). (J). pap. 21.95 *(978-2-01-210144-9(5))* Hachette Groupe Livre FRA. Dist: Distribooks, Inc.
—Asterix et Cleopatre. (FRE.). (J). pap. 21.95 *(978-2-01-210138-8(0))*; (Illus.). 21.95 *(978-2-01-210111-1(9))* Hachette Groupe Livre FRA. Dist: Distribooks, Inc.
—Asterix et les Normaands. (FRE.). (J). pap. 21.95 *(978-2-01-210141-8(0))* Hachette Groupe Livre FRA. Dist: Distribooks, Inc.
—Asterix in Britain. Uderzo, Albert, illus. 2004. (ENG.). 48p. 17.99 *(978-0-7528-6618-5(4)*, Orion) Orion Publishing Group, Ltd. GBR. Dist: Hachette Bk. Group.
—Asterix in Spain. Uderzo, Albert, illus. 2004. (ENG.). 48p. 17.99 *(978-0-7528-6630-7(3)*, Orion) Orion Publishing Group, Ltd. GBR. Dist: Hachette Bk. Group.
—Asterix in Switzerland. Uderzo, Albert, illus. 2004. (ENG.). 48p. 17.99 *(978-0-7528-6634-5(6)*, Orion) Orion Publishing Group, Ltd. GBR. Dist: Hachette Bk. Group.
—Asterix Omnibus 11: Asterix & the Actress; Asterix & the Class Act; Asterix & the Falling Sky. Uderzo, Albert, illus. 2011. (ENG.). 168p. (J). (gr. 4-6). pap. 22.99 *(978-1-4440-0426-7(3)*, Orion) Orion Publishing Group, Ltd. GBR. Dist: Hachette Bk. Group.
—Asterix Omnibus 3: Asterix & the Big Fight; Asterix in Britain; Asterix & the Normans. Uderzo, Albert, illus. 2011. (ENG.). 156p. (J). (gr. 4-6). 29.99 *(978-1-4440-0427-4(1)*, Orion) Orion Publishing Group, Ltd. GBR. Dist: Hachette Bk. Group.
—Asterix the Legionary. Uderzo, Albert, illus. 2004. (ENG.). 48p. 17.99 *(978-0-7528-6620-8(6)*, Orion) Orion Publishing Group, Ltd. GBR. Dist: Hachette Bk. Group.
—The Daltons Always on the Run. Morris, illus. 2012. (Lucky Luke Ser.: 34). (ENG.). 48p. (J). (gr. 3-12). pap. 11.95 *(978-1-84918-119-8(5))* CineBook GBR. Dist: National Bk. Network.
—The Gaul. Uderzo, Albert, illus. 2004. (ENG.). 48p. 17.99 *(978-0-7528-6604-8(4)*, Orion) Orion Publishing Group, Ltd. GBR. Dist: Hachette Bk. Group.
Goscinny, René & Morris Publishing Company Staff. The Grand Duke. 2011. (Lucky Luke Ser.: 29). (ENG., Illus.). 48p. (gr. 3-17). pap. 11.95 *(978-1-84918-083-2(0))* CineBook GBR. Dist: National Bk. Network.
—The Singing Wire. 2012. (Lucky Luke Ser.: 35). (ENG., Illus.). 48p. (J). (gr. 3-9). pap. 11.95 *(978-1-84918-123-5(3))* CineBook GBR. Dist: National Bk. Network.
Goscinny, René & Uderzo, Albert. Asterix & Caesar's Gift. 2004. (ENG., Illus.). 48p. 17.99 *(978-0-7528-6645-1(1)*, Orion) Orion Publishing Group, Ltd. GBR. Dist: Hachette Bk. Group.
—Asterix & Cleopatra. Uderzo, Albert, illus. 2004. (ENG., Illus.). 48p. pap. 12.99 *(978-0-7528-6607-9(9)*, Orion) Orion Publishing Group, Ltd. GBR. Dist: Hachette Bk. Group.
—Asterix & the Big Fight. 2004. (ENG., Illus.). 48p. 17.99 *(978-0-7528-6616-1(8)*, Orion) Orion Publishing Group, Ltd. GBR. Dist: Hachette Bk. Group.
—Asterix & the Big Fight. Uderzo, Albert, illus. 2004. (ENG., Illus.). 48p. pap. 12.99 *(978-0-7528-6617-8(6)*, Orion) Orion Publishing Group, Ltd. GBR. Dist: Hachette Bk. Group.
—Asterix & the Class Act. Bell, Anthea & Hockridge, Derek, trs. from FRE. Uderzo, Albert, illus. 2003. (ENG., Illus.). 56p. 17.99 *(978-0-7528-6068-8(2)*, Orion) Orion Publishing Group, Ltd. GBR. Dist: Hachette Bk. Group.
—Asterix & the Great Crossing. 2004. (ENG., Illus.). 48p. 17.99 *(978-0-7528-6647-5(8)*, Orion) Orion Publishing Group, Ltd. GBR. Dist: Hachette Bk. Group.
—Asterix & the Laurel Wreath. Uderzo, Albert, illus. 2004. (ENG., Illus.). 48p. 17.99 *(978-0-7528-6636-9(2)*, Orion) Orion Publishing Group, Ltd. GBR. Dist: Hachette Bk. Group.
—Asterix & the Normans. Uderzo, Albert, illus. 2004. (ENG., Illus.). 48p. 17.99 *(978-0-7528-6622-2(2)*, Orion) Orion Publishing Group, Ltd. GBR. Dist: Hachette Bk. Group.
—Asterix & the Soothsayer. Uderzo, Albert, illus. 2004. (ENG., Illus.). 48p. 17.99 *(978-0-7528-6641-3(9)*, Orion) Orion Publishing Group, Ltd. GBR. Dist: Hachette Bk. Group.
—Asterix at the Olympic Games. Uderzo, Albert, illus. 2004. (ENG., Illus.). 48p. 17.99 *(978-0-7528-6626-0(5)*, Orion) Orion Publishing Group, Ltd. GBR. Dist: Hachette Bk. Group.
—Asterix in Britain. Uderzo, Albert, illus. 2004. (ENG., Illus.). 48p. pap. 12.99 *(978-0-7528-6619-2(2)*, Orion) Orion Publishing Group, Ltd. GBR. Dist: Hachette Bk. Group.
—Asterix in Spain. Uderzo, Albert, illus. 2004. (ENG., Illus.). 48p. pap. 12.99 *(978-0-7528-6631-4(1)*, Orion) Orion Publishing Group, Ltd. GBR. Dist: Hachette Bk. Group.
—Asterix the Gladiator. Uderzo, Albert, illus. 2004. (ENG., Illus.). 48p. 17.99 *(978-0-7528-6610-9(9)*, Orion) Orion Publishing Group, Ltd. GBR. Dist: Hachette Bk. Group.
—Asterix the Legionary. Uderzo, Albert, illus. 2004. (ENG., Illus.). 48p. pap. 12.99 *(978-0-7528-6621-5(4)*, Orion) Orion Publishing Group, Ltd. GBR. Dist: Hachette Bk. Group.
—Los Laureles del Cesar. (SPA.). 48p. 9.95 *(978-84-7510-031-9(7))* Grijalbo-Dargaud, S.A. Editores ESP. Dist: Distribooks, Inc.
Goscinny, René & Uderzo, M. Asterix el Galo. (SPA., Illus.). (J). (gr. 7-10). 24.95 *(978-0-8288-4933-3(1))* French & European Pubns., Inc.
—Streit um Asterix. (GER., Illus.). (J). 24.95 *(978-0-8288-4906-7(4))* French & European Pubns., Inc.
Gownley, Jimmy. Her Permanent Record. Gownley, Jimmy, illus. 2012. (Amelia Rules! Ser.). (ENG., Illus.). 160p. (J). (gr. 2-7). 19.99 *(978-1-4169-8615-7(4))*; pap. 11.99 *(978-1-4169-8614-0(6))* Simon & Schuster Children's Publishing. (Atheneum Bks. for Young Readers).
—What Makes You Happy. Gownley, Jimmy, illus. 2009. (Amelia Rules! Ser.). (ENG., Illus.). 176p. (J). (gr. 2-7). pap. 12.99 *(978-1-4169-8605-8(7)*, Atheneum Bks. for Young Readers) Simon & Schuster Children's Publishing.
—The Whole World's Crazy. Gownley, Jimmy, illus. 2009. (Amelia Rules! Ser.). (ENG., Illus.). 176p. (J). (gr. 2-7). pap. 12.99 *(978-1-4169-8604-1(9)*, Atheneum Bks. for Young Readers) Simon & Schuster Children's Publishing.
Gran, Meredith. Marceline & the Scream Queens. Gran, Meredith, illus. 2013. (Adventure Time Ser.). (ENG., Illus.). 128p. (J). (gr. 4). pap. 19.99 *(978-1-60886-313-6(1))* Boom! Studios.
Gray, Peter. Animals. 2006. (Drawing Manga Ser.). (Illus.). 32p. (YA). (gr. 3-6). lib. bdg. 26.50 *(978-1-4042-3329-4(6))* Rosen Publishing Group, Inc., The.
—Female Action Figures. 2009. (Drawing Manga Ser.). 32p. (gr. 4-4). 50.50 *(978-1-61512-197-7(8))* Rosen Publishing Group, Inc., The.
—Heroes & Villains. (Drawing Manga Ser.). 32p. 2009. (gr. 4-4). 50.50 *(978-1-61512-198-4(6))* 2006. (Illus.). (YA). (gr. 3-6). lib. bdg. 26.50 *(978-1-4042-3330-0(X))* Rosen Publishing Group, Inc., The.
—Male Action Figures. 2009. (Drawing Manga Ser.). 32p. (gr. 4-4). 50.50 *(978-1-61512-199-1(4))* Rosen Publishing Group, Inc., The.
—Monsters. 2006. (Drawing Manga Ser.). (Illus.). 32p. (YA). (gr. 3-6). lib. bdg. 26.50 *(978-1-4042-3331-7(8))* Rosen Publishing Group, Inc., The.
—Robots. 2009. (Drawing Manga Ser.). 32p. (gr. 4-4). 50.50 *(978-1-61512-201-1(X))* Rosen Publishing Group, Inc., The.
Gray, Peter C. Female Action Figures. 2006. (Drawing Manga Ser.). (Illus.). 32p. (J). (gr. 3-6). lib. bdg. 26.50 *(978-1-4042-3327-0(X))* Rosen Publishing Group, Inc., The.
—Male Action Figures. 2006. (Drawing Manga Ser.). (Illus.). 32p. (YA). (gr. 3-6). lib. bdg. 26.50 *(978-1-4042-3328-7(8))* Rosen Publishing Group, Inc., The.
—Robots. 2006. (Drawing Manga Ser.). (Illus.). 32p. (YA). (gr. 3-6). lib. bdg. 26.50 *(978-1-4042-3332-4(6))* Rosen Publishing Group, Inc., The.
Green Egg Media. Power Bible 2: Moses, Leader of the Israelites. 2011. (ENG., Illus.). (J). pap. 14.99 *(978-1-937212-01-8(7))* Green Egg Media, Inc.
—Power Bible 5: The Kingdom Becomes Divided. 2011. (ENG., Illus.). (J). pap. 14.99 *(978-1-937212-04-9(1))* Green Egg Media, Inc.
—Power Bible 6: Destruction & a Promise. 2011. (ENG., Illus.). (J). pap. 14.99 *(978-1-937212-05-6(X))* Green Egg Media, Inc.
Guinea Pig, Pet Shop Private Eye, 3 vols., Set. 2010. (J). (gr. 2-5). lib. bdg. 55.86 *(978-0-7613-4597-8(3)*, Graphic Universe™) Lerner Publishing Group.
Guojing. The Only Child. 2015. (ENG., Illus.). 112p. (J). (gr. k-4). 22.99 *(978-0-553-49705-2(7)*, Schwartz & Wade Bks.) Random Hse. Children's Bks.
Hajikete BB. 2005. (J). pap. 9.99 *(978-1-59182-598-2(9))*; Vol. 2. pap. 9.99 *(978-1-59182-599-9(7))*; Vol. 3. pap. 9.99 *(978-1-59182-600-2(4))*; Vol. 4. pap. 9.99 *(978-1-59182-601-9(2))*; Vol. 5. pap. 9.99 *(978-1-59182-602-6(0))* TOKYOPOP, Inc.
Hale, Nathan. Big Bad Ironclad! 2012. (Nathan Hale's Hazardous Tales Ser.). (ENG., Illus.). 128p. (J). (gr. 3-7). 12.95 *(978-1-4197-0395-9(1)*, Amulet Bks.) Abrams, Inc.
—Donner Dinner Party. 2013. (Nathan Hale's Hazardous Tales Ser.). (ENG., Illus.). 128p. (J). (gr. 3-7). 12.99 *(978-1-4197-0856-5(2)*, Amulet Bks.) Abrams, Inc.
—One Dead Spy. 2012. (Nathan Hale's Hazardous Tales Ser.). (ENG., Illus.). 128p. (J). (gr. 3-7). 12.95 *(978-1-4197-0396-6(X)*, Amulet Bks.) Abrams, Inc.
—One Trick Pony. 2017. (ENG., Illus.). 128p. (J). (gr. 3-7). 14.95 *(978-1-4197-2128-1(3)*, Amulet Bks.) Abrams, Inc.
—Treaties, Trenches, Mud, & Blood. 2014. (Nathan Hale's Hazardous Tales Ser.). (ENG., Illus.). 128p. (J). (gr. 3-7). 12.95 *(978-1-4197-0808-4(2)*, Amulet Bks.) Abrams, Inc.
—Treaties, Trenches, Mud, & Blood. 2017. (Nathan Hale's Hazardous Tales Ser.). (J). lib. bdg. 24.45 ***(978-0-606-40707-6(3))*** Turtleback Bks.
Hale, Nathan. The Underground Abductor. 2015. (Nathan Hale's Hazardous Tales Ser.). (ENG., Illus.). 128p. (J). (gr. 3-9). 12.95 *(978-1-4197-1536-5(4)*, Amulet Bks.) Abrams, Inc.
—The Underground Abductor. 2017. (Nathan Hale's Hazardous Tales Ser.). (J). lib. bdg. 24.45 ***(978-0-606-40708-3(1))*** Turtleback Bks.
Hale, Shannon & Hale, Dean. Rapunzel's Revenge. Hale, Nathan, illus. 2008. (ENG.). 144p. (YA). (gr. 5-8). pap. 16.99 *(978-1-59990-288-3(5)*, 9781599902883, Bloomsbury USA Childrens) Bloomsbury Publishing USA.
Hanna, Kevin & Fagan, Dave. Creature Academy GN. 2011. (Illus.). 80p. (YA). pap. 14.95 *(978-1-897548-53-0(2))* Arcana Studio, Inc.
Harbo, Christopher L. Frankenstein's Monster & Scientific Methods, 1 vol. Aón, Carlos, illus. 2013. (Monster Science Ser.). (ENG.). 32p. (gr. 3-4). pap. 8.10 *(978-1-62065-816-1(X)*, Graphic Library) Capstone Press of Coughlan Cos.
—Frankenstein's Monster & Scientific Methods. An, Carlos, illus. 2013. (Monster Science Ser.). (ENG.). 32p. (gr. 3-4). pap. 47.70 *(978-1-62065-817-8(8)*, Graphic Library) Capstone Press of Coughlan Cos.
—Frankenstein's Monster & Scientific Methods, 1 vol. Aón, Carlos, illus. 2013. (Monster Science Ser.). (ENG.). 32p. (gr. 3-4). lib. bdg. 30.65 *(978-1-4296-9931-0(0)*, Graphic Library) Capstone Press of Coughlan Cos.
Harris, Joe. Narda. 2005. (J). *(978-0-9772259-0-3(9))* Character Arts.
Harris, Tony, illus. The Invincible Iron Man(r): Disassembled. 2007. (ENG.). 144p. (YA). (gr. 8-17). pap. 14.99 *(978-0-7851-1653-0(2))* Marvel Worldwide, Inc.
Hart, Chris. Manga Mania Romance: Drawing Shojo Girls & Bishie Boys. 2008. (Manga Mania(tm) Ser.). (ENG., Illus.). 144p. (gr. 5-18). pap. 19.95 *(978-1-933027-43-2(6)*, Hart, Chris Bks.) Sixth&Spring Bks.
Hart, Christopher. Draw Manga Villans! 2004. (XTreme Art Ser.). (ENG., Illus.). 64p. (J). (gr. 2-4). pap. 7.95 *(978-0-8230-0370-9(1)*, Watson-Guptill) Potter/TenSpeed/Harmony.

C
D

—Kids Draw Manga. 2004. (Kids Draw Ser.). (ENG., Illus.). 64p. (J). (gr. 2-4). pap. 11.95 (978-0-8230-2623-4(X), Watson-Guptill) Potter/TenSpeed/Harmony.
—Xtreme Art: Ultimate Book of Trace-and-Draw Manga. 2009. (ENG., Illus.). 192p. (J). pap. 21.95 (978-0-8230-9806-4(0), Watson-Guptill) Potter/TenSpeed/Harmony.
—Young Artists Draw Manga. 2011. (ENG.). 144p. (J). (gr. 3-7). pap. 14.99 (978-0-8230-2657-9(4), Watson-Guptill) Potter/TenSpeed/Harmony.
Hartland, Jessie. Bon Appétit! The Delicious Life of Julia Child. Hartland, Jessie, illus. 2012. (ENG., Illus.). 48p. (J). (gr. k-12). 17.99 (978-0-375-86944-0(1)); 20.99 (978-0-375-96944-7(6)) Random Hse. Children's Bks. (Schwartz & Wade Bks.).
—Steve Jobs: Insanely Great. 2015. (ENG., Illus.). 240p. (YA). (gr. 7). 22.95 (978-0-307-98295-7(5), Schwartz & Wade Bks.) Random Hse. Children's Bks.
Harukaze, Santa. Pokemon Pocket Comics, Vols. 1 & 2 2016. (Pokemon Ser.: 1). (ENG., Illus.). 576p. (J). pap. 16.99 (978-1-4215-8964-0(8)) Viz Media.
—Pokémon XY Pocket Comics. 2016. (Pokemon Ser.: 3). (ENG., Illus.). 240p. (J). pap. 10.99 (978-1-4215-8693-9(2)) Viz Media.
Hatke, Ben. Legends of Zita the Spacegirl. Hatke, Ben, illus. 2012. (Zita the Spacegirl Ser.: 2). (ENG., Illus.). 224p. (J). (gr. 3-7). 19.99 (978-1-59643-806-4(1), 9781596438064); pap. 12.99 (978-1-59643-447-9(3), 9781596434479) Roaring Brook Pr. (First Second Bks.).
—Legends of Zita the Spacegirl. 2012. (Zita the Spacegirl Ser.: 2). (J). lib. bdg. 24.50 (978-0-606-26708-3(5), Turtleback) Turtleback Bks.
—Zita the Spacegirl. Hatke, Ben, illus. 2011. (Zita the Spacegirl Ser.: 1). (ENG., Illus.). 192p. (J). (gr. 3-7). 19.99 (978-1-59643-695-4(6), 9781596436954); pap. 12.99 (978-1-59643-446-2(5), 9781596434462) Roaring Brook Pr. (First Second Bks.).
—Zita the Spacegirl. 2011. (Zita the Spacegirl Ser.: 1). (J). lib. bdg. 24.50 (978-0-606-21623-4(5), Turtleback) Turtleback Bks.
Hayes, Geoffrey. Benny & Penny in the Toy Breaker. Mouly, Francoise, ed. Hayes, Geoffrey, illus. 2010. (Benny & Penny Ser.). (ENG., Illus.). 32p. (J). (gr. -1-3). 12.95 (978-1-935179-07-8(1)) TOON Books / RAW Junior, LLC.
Helfand, Lewis. Abraham Lincoln: From the Log Cabin to the White House - Campfire Heroes Line. Jones, K. L. & Manikandan, illus. 2013. (Campfire Graphic Novels Ser.). (ENG.). 108p. (YA). (gr. 5-12). pap. 12.99 (978-93-80741-21-5(9), Campfire) Steerforth Pr.
—Photo Booth. Nagar, Sachin, illus. 2011. (Campfire Graphic Novels Ser.). (ENG.). 80p. (YA). (gr. 3-7). pap. 9.99 (978-93-80028-65-1(2), Campfire) Steerforth Pr.
—400 BC: The Story of the Ten Thousand. Singh, Lalit Kumar, illus. 2011. (Campfire Graphic Novels Ser.). (ENG.). 72p. (YA). (gr. 5-12). pap. 9.99 (978-93-80028-61-3(X), Campfire) Steerforth Pr.
Helfand, Lewis & Teitelbaum, Michael. Martin Luther King. Banerjee, Sankha, illus. 2013. (Campfire Graphic Novels Ser.). (ENG.). 88p. (YA). (gr. 5). pap. 11.99 (978-93-80028-69-9(5), Campfire) Steerforth Pr.
Hellman, Charles & Tiritilli, Robert. Beisbol Humor. 2008. (Illus.). 32p. (J). (gr. -1-3). pap. 4.95 (978-0-935938-43-2(5)) Williams, Michael.
Henderson, Sam. Scene but Not Heard. 2013. (ENG., Illus.). 128p. (J). (gr. 2-5). 14.95 (978-1-60309-089-6(4), 9781603090896) Top Shelf Productions.
Henson, Jim & Juhl, Jerry. Tale of Sand. Christy, Stephen & Robinson, Chris, eds. Perez, Ramon, illus. 2011. (ENG.). 120p. (YA). (gr. 2). 29.95 (978-1-936393-09-1(3)) Boom Entertainment, Inc.
Hergé. The Adventures of Tintin, 8. collector's gif. ed. Set. 2008. (ENG.). (gr. 3-17). 165.00 (978-0-316-00668-2(8)) Vol. 1. 2009. 192p. 18.99 (978-0-316-18979-8(0)) Vol. 2. 2009. 192p. 18.99 (978-0-316-18983-5(9)) Vol. 3. 2009. 192p. 18.99 (978-0-316-18986-6(3)) Vol. 4. 2009. 192p. 18.99 (978-0-316-18987-3(1)) Little, Brown Bks. for Young Readers.
—America. 2004. (Adventures of Tintin Ser.). Orig. Title: Tintin en Amerique. (Illus.). 124p. 24.95 (978-0-86719-904-8(0)) Last Gasp of San Francisco.
—Tintin in America. 2011. (Adventures of Tintin: Young Readers Edition Ser.). Orig. Title: Tintin en Amerique. (ENG., Illus.). 96p. (J). (gr. 3-17). pap. 9.99 (978-0-316-13380-7(9)) Little, Brown Bks. for Young Readers.
Hester, Beth Landis & Dorling Kindersley Publishing Staff. Secret World of the Ninja. 2015. (ENG., Illus.). 96p. (J). (gr. 2-5). 16.99 (978-1-4654-2078-7(9), DK Children) Dorling Kindersley Publishing, Inc.
Hickey, Brenda, et al, illus. My Little Pony: Art Is Magic! Art Is Magic! 2015. (My Little Pony Ser.). (ENG.). 148p. pap. 19.99 (978-1-63140-467-2(9), 9781631404672) Idea & Design Works, LLC.
Hijioka, Makoto. Pokemon: Giratina & the Sky Warrior!, Vol. 4. Hijioka, Makoto, illus. 2009. (ENG., Illus.). 192p. (J). pap. 9.99 (978-1-4215-2701-7(4)) Viz Media.
Himekawa, Akira. The Legend of Zelda, Vol. 6. Himekawa, Akira, illus. 2009. (ENG., Illus.). 200p. (J). pap. 9.99 (978-1-4215-2332-3(9)) Viz Media.
Hinds, Gareth. The Merchant of Venice. Hinds, Gareth, illus. 2008. (ENG., Illus.). 80p. (YA). (gr. 7-12). pap. 12.99 (978-0-7636-3025-6(X)) Candlewick Pr.
—The Odyssey. Hinds, Gareth, illus. 2010. (ENG., Illus.). 256p. (YA). (gr. 7-18). 24.99 (978-0-7636-4266-2(5)); pap. 14.99 (978-0-7636-4268-6(1)) Candlewick Pr.
—Romeo & Juliet. Hinds, Gareth, illus. 2013. (ENG., Illus.). 144p. (YA). (gr. 7). 21.99 (978-0-7636-5948-6(7)); pap. 12.99 (978-0-7636-6807-5(9)) Candlewick Pr.
—Romeo & Juliet (Graphic Adaptation) 2013. lib. bdg. 24.50 (978-0-606-32098-6(9), Turtleback) Turtleback Bks.
Hinds, Gareth & Shakespeare, William. The Merchant of Venice. Hinds, Gareth, illus. 2008. (ENG., Illus.). 80p. (YA). (gr. 7-12). 21.99 (978-0-7636-3024-9(1)) Candlewick Pr.
Historia Gráficas Set [Steps to Literacy]. 2010. (Historia Gráficas Ser.). pap. 79.50 (978-1-4296-5248-3(9), Graphic Library en espanol) Capstone Press of Coughlan Cos.
Hiwatari, Saki. Please Save My Earth, Vol. 12. Hiwatari, Saki, illus. 2005. (Please Save My Earth Ser.: 12). (ENG., Illus.). 184p. pap. 9.99 (978-1-59116-987-1(9)) Viz Media.
Hoena, B. A. Theseus & the Minotaur: A Graphic Retelling. 2015. (Ancient Myths Ser.). (ENG., Illus.). 32p. (gr. 3-4). lib. bdg. 30.65 (978-1-4914-2075-1(8), Graphic Library) Capstone Press of Coughlan Cos.
Hoena, Blake, retold by. The Voyages of Odysseus: A Graphic Retelling. 2015. (Ancient Myths Ser.). (ENG., Illus.). 32p. (gr. 3-4). lib. bdg. 30.65 (978-1-4914-2076-8(6), Graphic Library) Capstone Press of Coughlan Cos.
Hoena, Blake A. The Puzzling Pluto Plot: Eek & Ack, 1 vol. Harpster, Steve, illus. 2008. (Graphic Sparks Ser.). (ENG.). 40p. (gr. 1-3). pap. 5.95 (978-1-4342-0502-5(9), Graphic Sparks) Stone Arch Bks.
Holkins, Jerry. Attack of the Bacon Robots!, Vol. 1. Krahulik, Mike, illus. 2006. (Penny Arcade Ser.). (ENG.). 168p. pap. 12.95 (978-1-59307-444-9(1)) Dark Horse Comics.
Holm, Jennifer L. Sunny Side Up. Holm, Matthew, illus. 2015. (ENG.). 224p. (J). (gr. 3-7). 23.99 (978-0-545-74165-1(3)); pap. 12.99 (978-0-545-74166-8(1)) Scholastic, Inc. (Graphix).
Horowitz, Anthony. Stormbreaker. Damerum, Kanako et al, illus. 2006. (Alex Rider Ser.). (ENG.). 144p. (J). (gr. 5-18). pap. 14.99 (978-0-399-24633-3(9), Philomel Bks.) Penguin Young Readers Group.
Hosler, Jay. Last of the Sandwalkers. 2015. (ENG., Illus.). 320p. (YA). (gr. 5). pap. 17.99 (978-1-62672-024-4(X), 9781626720244, First Second Bks.) Roaring Brook Pr.
Hunter, Erin. After the Flood. Barry, James L. & Hunt, John, illus. 2012. (Warriors Manga Ser.: 3). (ENG.). 112p. (J). (gr. 3-7). pap. 7.99 (978-0-06-200838-1(2)) HarperCollins Pubs.
—Return to the Clans. Hudson, Don, illus. 2009. (Warriors Manga Ser.: 3). (ENG.). 112p. (J). (gr. 3-7). pap. 6.99 (978-0-06-154794-2(8)) HarperCollins Pubs.
—Warriors Manga - Graystripe's Adventure, 3 vols., Set. Barry, James, illus. 2009. (Warriors Manga Ser.). 336p. (J). (gr. 3-7). pap. 16.99 (978-0-06-178228-2(9)) HarperCollins Pubs.
Ihara, Shigekatsu. Pokémon Vol. 8: Diamond & Pearl Adventure! Ihara, Shigekatsu, illus. 2010. (ENG., Illus.). 192p. (J). pap. 9.99 (978-1-4215-3671-2(4)) Viz Media.
Inada, Koji & Sanjo, Riku. Beet the Vandel Buster, Vol. 3. Inada, Koji, illus. 2005. (Beet the Vandel Buster Ser.: 3). (ENG., Illus.). 216p. pap. 7.99 (978-1-59116-693-1(4)) Viz Media.
—Beet the Vandel Buster, Vol. 9. Sanjo, Riku, illus. 2006. (ENG., Illus.). 208p. pap. 7.99 (978-1-4215-0270-0(4)) Viz Media.
Inagaki, Riichiro. Eyeshield 21, Vol. 7. Murata, Yusuke, illus. 2006. (Eyeshield 21 Ser.: 7). (ENG.). 208p. pap. 9.99 (978-1-4215-0405-6(7)) Viz Media.
—Eyeshield 21, Vol. 4. Murata, Yusuke, illus. 2005. (ENG.). 200p. pap. 9.99 (978-1-4215-0074-4(4)) Viz Media.
—Eyeshield 21, Vol. 6. Murata, Yusuke, illus. 2006. (ENG.). 208p. pap. 9.99 (978-1-4215-0274-8(7)) Viz Media.
Izumi, Kaneyoshi. Seiho Boys' High School!, Vol. 3. Izumi, Kaneyoshi, illus. 2010. (ENG., Illus.). 200p. pap. 9.99 (978-1-4215-3733-7(8)) Viz Media.
Jacques, Brian. Redwall. Blevins, Bret, illus. 2007. (Redwall Ser.). (ENG.). 148p. (J). (gr. 5-18). 12.99 (978-0-399-24481-0(6), Philomel Bks.) Penguin Young Readers Group.
Jamieson, Victoria. All's Faire in Middle School, 9 vols. 2017. (ENG.). (J). pap. 116.91 **(978-0-525-48668-8(2))**; (Illus.). 248p. (gr. 4-7). 20.99 **(978-0-525-42998-2(0))**; (Illus.). 248p. (gr. 4-7). pap. 12.99 **(978-0-525-42999-9(9))** Penguin Young Readers Group. (Dial Bks).
—All's Faire in Middle School. 2017. lib. bdg. 24.50 **(978-0-606-40484-6(8))** Turtleback Bks.
Jamieson, Victoria. Roller Girl. 2015. (ENG., Illus.). 240p. (J). (gr. 4-7). 20.99 (978-0-525-42967-8(0)); pap. 12.99 (978-0-8037-4016-7(6)) Penguin Young Readers Group. (Dial Bks).
—Roller Girl. 2015. (J). lib. bdg. 24.50 (978-0-606-37112-4(5)) Turtleback Bks.
Jeffery, Gary & Petty, Kate. Abraham Lincoln: The Life of America's Sixteenth President. Lacey, Mike, illus. 2005. (Graphic Biographies Ser.). (ENG.). 48p. (gr. 5-8). pap. 14.05 (978-1-4042-5164-9(2)) Rosen Publishing Group, Inc., The.
Jeffrey, Gary. Autopsies: Pathologists at Work. 2009. (Graphic Forensic Science Ser.). (ENG.). 48p. (YA). (gr. 5-5). 58.50 (978-1-61512-941-6(3), Rosen Reference) Rosen Publishing Group, Inc., The.
—Crusades. 2014. (ENG., Illus.). 48p. (J). (978-0-7787-0397-6(5)) Crabtree Publishing Co.
Jensen Shaffer, Jody. Vampires & Light, 1 vol. Gervasio, illus. 2013. (Monster Science Ser.). (ENG.). 32p. (gr. 3-4). pap. 8.10 (978-1-62065-820-8(8), Graphic Library) Capstone Press of Coughlan Cos.
Johns, Geoff, et al. Teen Titans, Vol. 1. rev. ed. 2004. (Teen Titans Go! Ser.: Vol. 1). (ENG., Illus.). 192p. pap. 16.99 (978-1-4012-0308-5(6)) DC Comics.
Jolley, Dan & Hunter, Erin. The Rise of Scourge. Kurkoski, Bettina, illus. 2008. (Warriors Manga Ser.: 4). 82p. (J). (gr. 3-7). lib. bdg. 17.20 (978-1-4178-3120-3(0), Turtleback) Turtleback Bks.
Jones, Richard & Santillan, Jorge. Manga Animals. 2012. (Learn to Draw Manga Ser.). (ENG., Illus.). 32p. (J). (gr. 4-6). pap. 11.75 (978-1-4488-7943-4(4)); lib. bdg. 26.50 (978-1-4488-7872-7(1)) Rosen Publishing Group, Inc., The. (PowerKids Pr.).
—Manga Dinosaurs. 2012. (Learn to Draw Manga Ser.). (ENG., Illus.). 32p. (J). (gr. 4-6). pap. 11.75 (978-1-4488-7944-1(2)); lib. bdg. 26.50 (978-1-4488-7873-4(X)) Rosen Publishing Group, Inc., The. (PowerKids Pr.).
—Manga Dragons. 2012. (Learn to Draw Manga Ser.). (ENG., Illus.). 32p. (J). (gr. 4-6). pap. 11.75 (978-1-4488-7945-8(0)); lib. bdg. 26.50 (978-1-4488-7874-1(8)) Rosen Publishing Group, Inc., The. (PowerKids Pr.).
—Manga Martial Arts Figures. 2012. (Learn to Draw Manga Ser.). (ENG., Illus.). 32p. (J). (gr. 4-6). pap. 11.75 (978-1-4488-7946-5(9)); lib. bdg. 26.50 (978-1-4488-7875-8(6)) Rosen Publishing Group, Inc., The. (PowerKids Pr.).
—Manga Superheroes. 2012. (Learn to Draw Manga Ser.). (ENG., Illus.). 32p. (J). (gr. 4-6). pap. 11.75 (978-1-4488-7948-9(5)); lib. bdg. 26.50 (978-1-4488-7877-2(2)) Rosen Publishing Group, Inc., The. (PowerKids Pr.).
Jr. Graphic Ghost Stories. 2014. (Jr. Graphic Ghost Stories Ser.). 24p. (J). (gr. 3-6). 157.50 (978-1-4777-7092-4(5), PowerKids Pr.) Rosen Publishing Group, Inc., The.
Jurevicius, Nathan. The Adventures of Scarygirl. 2013. (ENG., Illus.). 156p. (J). (gr. 4-7). pap. 13.99 (978-1-74237-293-8(7)) Allen & Unwin AUS. Dist: Independent Pubs. Group.
Kabaya, Kosuke. Android Angels. 2014. (ENG., Illus.). 158p. (YA). pap. 14.95 (978-1-939012-10-4(4), 9781939012104) Gen Manga Entertainment, Inc.
Kadono, Eiko & Miyazaki, Hayao. Kiki's Delivery Service, Vol. 2. 2006. (Kiki's Delivery Service Film Comics Ser.: 2). (ENG., Illus.). 208p. (gr. 1). pap. 9.99 (978-1-59116-749-5(3)) Viz Media.
Kanietzko, Bryan. Avatar Vol. 2: The Last Airbender. 2006. (Illus.). 96p. (J). pap. 7.99 (978-1-59532-892-2(0), Tokyopop Kids) TOKYOPOP, Inc.
Kanietzko, Bryan & DiMartino, Michael Dante. Avatar: The Last Airbender. 2006. (Avatar Ser.: Vol. 3). (Illus.). 96p. pap. 7.99 (978-1-59816-757-3(X), Tokyopop Kids) TOKYOPOP, Inc.
Kanzaka, Hajime & Yoshinaka, Shoko. Super-Explosive Demon Story: Return, 7 vols., Vol. 4. 2004. (Slayers Ser.). (Illus.). 192p. 9.99 (978-1-58664-914-2(0), CMX 64604G, CPM Manga) Central Park Media Corp.
Kibuishi, Kazu. Escape from Lucien. 2014. (Amulet Ser.: Bk. 6). (ENG., Illus.). 224p. (J). (gr. 3-7). pap. 12.99 (978-0-545-43315-0(0), Graphix) Scholastic, Inc.
—Escape from Lucien. 2014. (Amulet Ser.: 6). lib. bdg. 24.50 (978-0-606-36039-5(5)) Turtleback Bks.
—Firelight. 2016. (Amulet Ser.: 7). (ENG., Illus.). 208p. (J). (gr. 3-7). 24.99 (978-0-545-83966-2(1)); pap. 12.99 (978-0-545-43316-7(9)) Scholastic, Inc. (Graphix).
—Firelight. 2016. (Amulet Ser.: 7). (ENG., Illus.). 224p. (J). (gr. 3-7). lib. bdg. 24.50 (978-0-606-38070-6(1)) Turtleback Bks.
—Prince of the Elves. 2012. (Amulet Ser.: 5). (ENG., Illus.). 208p. (J). (gr. 3-7). pap. 12.99 (978-0-545-20889-5(0), Graphix) Scholastic, Inc.
—Prince of the Elves. 2012. (Amulet Ser.: 5). lib. bdg. 24.50 (978-0-606-26499-0(X), Turtleback) Turtleback Bks.
Kill Me, Kiss Me, Vol. 5. 2005. (YA). pap. 9.99 (978-1-59182-597-5(0)) TOKYOPOP, Inc.
Kim, Chuck & Alvarez, Richard. Best of Looney Tunes, Vol. 1. Koth, Brett, illus. 2016. (ENG.). 144p. (J). (gr. 4-7). pap. 12.99 (978-1-4012-6359-1(3)) DC Comics.
Kincade, Chris. Encountering Aliens: Eyewitness Accounts, 1 vol. Mallea, Cristian, illus. 2014. (Eyewitness to the Unexplained Ser.). (ENG.). 32p. (gr. 3-4). 30.65 (978-1-4914-0244-3(X), Graphic Library) Capstone Press of Coughlan Cos.
Kishimoto, Masashi. Naruto, Vol. 52. Kishimoto, Masashi, illus. 2011. (ENG., Illus.). 192p. pap. 9.99 (978-1-4215-3957-7(8)) Viz Media.
Knight, Christo. The Adventures of Charlz from Marz: Book I Going Home. 2009. (Illus.). 54p. (J). 14.95 (978-0-9763250-0-0(4)) DreamerLand.
Knudtsen, Ken. My Monkey's Name Is Jennifer. 2003. (ENG., Illus.). 152p. (gr. 11-18). pap. 15.95 (978-0-943151-71-7(6), 9780943151717) Slave Labor Bks.
Kobayashi, Tatsuyoshi, illus. Thomas Edison: Genius of the Electric Age. 2011. (Biographical Comic Ser.). (ENG.). 152p. (J). (gr. 2-6). 18.99 (978-1-4215-4236-2(6)) Shogakukan JPN. Dist: Simon & Schuster, Inc.
Kochalka, James. The Best Little Ghost in the World! 2008. (Johnny Boo Ser.: 1). (ENG., Illus.). 40p. (J). (gr. 2-5). 9.95 (978-1-60309-013-1(4), 9781603090131) Top Shelf Productions.
Kolpin, Molly, et al. First Graphics: Body Systems. Jones, Chris B., illus. 2012. (First Graphics: Body Systems Ser.). (ENG.). 24p. (gr. 1-2). pap. 178.50 (978-1-4296-9333-2(9)); pap. 25.16 (978-1-4296-9332-5(0)); lib. bdg. 71.97 (978-1-4296-9158-1(1)) Capstone Press of Coughlan Cos.
Konishi, Noriyuki. Yo-kai Watch, Vol. 6. 2016. (Yo-Kai Watch Ser.: 6). (ENG., Illus.). 192p. (J). pap. 9.99 (978-1-4215-9217-6(7)) Viz Media.
Koontz, Robin. Hide & Seek Moon: The Moon Phases, 1 vol. Davidson, Chris, illus. 2011. (First Graphics: Nature Cycles Ser.). (ENG.). 24p. (gr. 1-2). pap. 6.29 (978-1-4296-6229-1(8)) Capstone Press of Coughlan Cos.
—Water Goes Round: The Water Cycle. Davidson, Chris, illus. 2011. (First Graphics: Nature Cycles Ser.). (ENG.). 24p. (gr. 1-2). pap. 35.70 (978-1-4296-6400-4(2)) Capstone Press of Coughlan Cos.
Korb, Rena. Science Rocks! CD + Book Set. Reibeling, Brandon, illus. 2008. (Science Rocks! (CD+Book) Ser.). (J). (gr. 3). lib. bdg. 324.84 (978-1-60270-210-3(1)) ABDO Publishing Co.
Korte, Steve. DC Super-Pets Character Encyclopedia, 1 vol. Baltazar, Art, illus. 2013. (DC Super-Pets Ser.). (ENG.). 128p. (gr. 1-3). pap. 7.95 (978-1-4048-8297-3(9), DC Super-Pets) Picture Window Bks.
Krefta, Ben. Step by Step Manga. 2013. (ENG., Illus.). 64p. (J). pap. 7.95 (978-1-84858-863-9(1)) Arcturus Publishing GBR. Dist: Bookmasters Distribution.
Kreuger, Jim & Averdonz, N. R. My Double-Edged Life, 1 vol. Padilla, Ariel, illus. 2007. (Z Graphic Novels / Tomo Ser.). (ENG.). 160p. (J). (gr. 3-7). pap. 6.99 (978-0-310-71301-2(3)) Zondervan.
Krosoczka, Jarrett J. Lunch Lady & the Summer Camp Shakedown. 2010. (Lunch Lady Ser.). (ENG.). 96p. (J). (gr. 3-7). pap. 6.99 (978-0-375-86095-9(9)); lib. bdg. 12.99 (978-0-375-96095-6(3)) Random Hse. Children's Bks. (Knopf Bks. for Young Readers).
Krpata, Mitch. The Lost Expedition. Merritt, Kory, illus. 2016. (Poptropica Ser.). (ENG.). 112p. (J). (gr. 1-4). 9.95 (978-1-4197-2129-8(1), Amulet Bks.) Abrams, Inc.
Kudo, Maki. The Pokémon Cookbook: Easy & Fun Recipes. 2016. (Pokemon Ser.: 1). (ENG., Illus.). 80p. 14.99 (978-1-4215-8989-3(3)) Viz Media.
Kumar, Naresh, illus. The Dusk Society. 2011. (Campfire Graphic Novels Ser.). (ENG.). 88p. (YA). (gr. 3-7). pap. 11.99 (978-93-80028-63-7(6), Campfire) Steerforth Pr.
Kunkel, Mike & Heuser, Randy. The Land of Sokmunster. 2004. (ENG., Illus.). 60p. 14.95 (978-0-9721259-2-5(2), 9780972125925) Astonish Comics.
Kurumada, Masami. Knights of the Zodiac (Saint Seiya), Vol. 11. Kurumada, Masami, illus. 2005. (ENG., Illus.). 184p. pap. 7.95 (978-1-59116-993-2(3)) Viz Media.
—Knights of the Zodiac (Saint Seiya), Vol. 6. Kurumada, Masami, illus. 2004. (ENG., Illus.). 200p. pap. 7.95 (978-1-59116-525-5(3)) Viz Media.
—Knights of the Zodiac, Vol. 5. Kurumada, Masami, illus. 2004. (ENG., Illus.). 200p. pap. 7.95 (978-1-59116-470-8(2)) Viz Media.
Kusaka, Hidenori. Pokemon Adventures. 2015. (Pokemon Adventures Ser.: 27). lib. bdg. 20.85 (978-0-606-37244-2(X)) Turtleback Bks.
—Pokémon Adventures Vol. 1: Black & White. Yamamoto, Satoshi, illus. 2013. (ENG.). 104p. (J). pap. 9.99 (978-1-4215-5898-1(X)) Viz Media.
—Pokémon Adventures Vol. 1: Diamond & Pearl/Platinum. 2011. (ENG., Illus.). 208p. (J). pap. 9.99 (978-1-4215-3816-7(4)) Viz Media.
—Pokémon Adventures Vol. 2: Diamond & Pearl/Platinum. 2011. (ENG., Illus.). 208p. (J). pap. 9.99 (978-1-4215-3817-4(2)) Viz Media.
—Pokémon Adventures Vol. 3: Diamond & Pearl/Platinum. Satoshi, Yamamoto, illus. 2011. (ENG.). 200p. (J). pap. 9.99 (978-1-4215-3818-1(0)) Viz Media.
—Pokémon Adventures Vol. 5: Diamond & Pearl/Platinum. Yamamoto, Satoshi, illus. 2012. (ENG.). 208p. (J). pap. 9.99 (978-1-4215-3913-3(6)) Viz Media.
—Pokémon Adventures Vol. 9: Black & White. Yamamoto, Satoshi, illus. 2015. (ENG.). 208p. (J). pap. 9.99 (978-1-4215-7961-0(8)) Viz Media.
—Pokémon Adventures Vol. 9: Diamond & Pearl/Platinum. Yamamoto, Satoshi, illus. 2013. (Pokemon Ser.: 9). (ENG.). 192p. (J). pap. 9.99 (978-1-4215-5405-1(4)) Viz Media.
—Pokémon Adventures Vol. 11: Diamond & Pearl/Platinum. Yamamoto, Satoshi, illus. 2014. (ENG.). 192p. (J). pap. 9.99 (978-1-4215-6179-0(4)) Viz Media.
—Pokémon Adventures - Diamond & Pearl/Platinum. Yamamoto, Satoshi, illus. (ENG.). (J). Vol. 6. 2012. 208p. pap. 9.99 (978-1-4215-3914-0(4)) Vol. 7. 2013. 192p. pap. 9.99 (978-1-4215-4247-8(1)) Viz Media.
—Pokémon Adventures: Black & White, Vol. 2. Yamamoto, Satoshi, illus. 2013. (ENG.). 192p. (J). pap. 9.99 (978-1-4215-5899-8(8)) Viz Media.
—Pokémon Adventures: Black & White, Vol. 6. Yamamoto, Satoshi, illus. 2015. (ENG.). 224p. (J). pap. 9.99 (978-1-4215-7181-2(1)) Viz Media.
—Pokémon Adventures: Black & White, Vol. 7. Yamamoto, Satoshi, illus. 2015. (ENG.). 208p. (J). pap. 9.99 (978-1-4215-7836-1(0)) Viz Media.
—Pokémon Adventures: Diamond & Pearl/Platinum, Vol. 4. 2012. (ENG., Illus.). 216p. (J). pap. 9.99 (978-1-4215-3912-6(8)) Viz Media.
—Pokémon Adventures: Diamond & Pearl/Platinum, Vol. 8. Yamamoto, Satoshi, illus. 2013. (ENG.). 192p. (J). pap. 9.99 (978-1-4215-5404-4(6)) Viz Media.
—Pokémon Adventures Diamond & Pearl / Platinum Box Set, Set, Vols. 1-11. Yamamoto, Satoshi, illus. 2014. (ENG.). 2304p. (J). pap. 89.99 (978-1-4215-7777-7(1)) Viz Media.
—Pokémon Adventures Fire Red & Leaf Green / Emerald Box Set, Vol. 1. Yamamoto, Satoshi, illus. 2015. (ENG.). 1576p. (J). pap. 54.99 (978-1-4215-8278-8(3)) Viz Media.
—Pokémon Adventures Gold & Silver Box Set (set includes Vol. 8-14) 2012. (ENG.). 1552p. (J). pap. 54.99 (978-1-4215-5007-7(5)) Viz Media.
—Pokémon Adventures: Heart Gold Soul Silver, Vol. 1. 2013. (ENG., Illus.). 208p. (J). pap. 9.99 (978-1-4215-5900-1(5)) Viz Media.
—Pokémon Adventures: Heart Gold Soul Silver, Vol. 2. 2013. (ENG., Illus.). 272p. (J). pap. 9.99 (978-1-4215-5901-8(3)) Viz Media.
—Pokémon Adventures Red & Blue Box Set (set includes Vol. 1-7) 2012. (ENG., Illus.). 1504p. (J). pap. 54.99 (978-1-4215-5006-0(7)) Viz Media.
—Pokémon Adventures Ruby & Sapphire Box Set, Set, Vols. 15-22. Yamamoto, Satoshi, illus. 2014. (ENG.). 1576p. (J). pap. 59.99 (978-1-4215-7776-0(3)) Viz Media.
—Pokémon Adventures, Vol. 1 (2nd Edition) Kusaka, Hidenori, illus. 2nd ed. 2009. (ENG., Illus.). 200p. (J). pap. 9.99 (978-1-4215-3054-3(6)) Viz Media.
—Pokémon Adventures, Vol. 10. Kusaka, Hidenori, illus. 2010. (ENG., Illus.). 200p. (J). pap. 9.99 (978-1-4215-3063-5(5)) Viz Media.
—Pokémon Adventures, Vol. 11. Mato, illus. 2011. (ENG.). 208p. (J). pap. 9.99 (978-1-4215-3545-6(9)) Viz Media.
—Pokémon Adventures, Vol. 12. Mato, illus. 2011. (ENG.). 208p. (J). pap. 9.99 (978-1-4215-3546-3(7)) Viz Media.
—Pokémon Adventures, Vol. 13. 2011. (ENG., Illus.). 208p. (J). pap. 9.99 (978-1-4215-3547-0(5)) Viz Media.
—Pokémon Adventures, Vol. 14. 2011. (ENG., Illus.). 208p. (J). pap. 9.99 (978-1-4215-3548-7(3)) Viz Media.
—Pokémon Adventures, Vol. 15. Mato, illus. 2013. (ENG.). 144p. (J). pap. 9.99 (978-1-4215-3549-4(1)) Viz Media.
—Pokémon Adventures, Vol. 16. Mato, illus. 2013. (ENG.). 208p. (J). pap. 9.99 (978-1-4215-3550-0(5)) Viz Media.
—Pokémon Adventures, Vol. 17. Mato, illus. 2013. (ENG.). 208p. (J). pap. 9.99 (978-1-4215-3551-7(3)) Viz Media.
—Pokémon Adventures, Vol. 18. Mato, illus. 2013. (ENG.). 192p. (J). pap. 9.99 (978-1-4215-3552-4(1)) Viz Media.
—Pokémon Adventures, Vol. 19. Mato, illus. 2013. (ENG.). 192p. (J). pap. 9.99 (978-1-4215-3553-1(X)) Viz Media.
—Pokémon Adventures, Vol. 2 (2nd Edition) Kusaka, Hidenori, illus. 2nd ed. 2009. (ENG., Illus.). 200p. (J). pap. 9.99 (978-1-4215-3055-0(4)) Viz Media.
—Pokémon Adventures, Vol. 20. Mato, illus. 2014. (ENG.). 208p. (J). pap. 9.99 (978-1-4215-3554-8(8)) Viz Media.
—Pokémon Adventures, Vol. 22. Yamamoto, Satoshi, illus. 2014. (ENG.). 184p. (J). pap. 9.99 (978-1-4215-3556-2(4)) Viz Media.
—Pokémon Adventures, Vol. 26. Mato, illus. 2015. (ENG.). 144p. (J). pap. 9.99 (978-1-4215-3560-9(2)) Viz Media.
—Pokémon Adventures, Vol. 27. Mato, illus. 2015. (ENG.). 208p. (J). pap. 9.99 (978-1-4215-3561-6(0)) Viz Media.
—Pokémon Adventures, Vol. 28. Mato, illus. 2015. (ENG.). 208p. (J). pap. 9.99 (978-1-4215-3562-3(9)) Viz Media.

—Pokémon Adventures, Vol. 29. Yamamoto, Satoshi, illus. 2015. (ENG.). 224p. (J). pap. 9.99 (978-1-4215-3563-0(7)) Viz Media.
—Pokémon Adventures, Vol. 3 (2nd Edition) Kusaka, Hidenori, illus. 2nd ed. 2009. (ENG., Illus.). 240p. (J). pap. 9.99 (978-1-4215-3056-7(2)) Viz Media.
—Pokémon Adventures, Vol. 4 (2nd Edition) Kusaka, Hidenori, illus. 2nd ed. 2009. (ENG., Illus.). 216p. (J). pap. 9.99 (978-1-4215-3057-4(0)) Viz Media.
—Pokémon Adventures, Vol. 5 (2nd Edition) Kusaka, Hidenori, illus. 2nd ed. 2010. (ENG., Illus.). 208p. (J). pap. 9.99 (978-1-4215-3058-1(9)) Viz Media.
—Pokémon Adventures, Vol. 6 (2nd Edition) Kusaka, Hidenori, illus. 2nd ed. 2010. (ENG., Illus.). 208p. (J). pap. 9.99 (978-1-4215-3059-8(7)) Viz Media.
—Pokémon Adventures, Vol. 7 (2nd Edition) Kusaka, Hidenori, illus. 2nd ed. 2010. (ENG., Illus.). 200p. (J). pap. 9.99 (978-1-4215-3060-4(0)) Viz Media.
—Pokémon Adventures, Vol. 8. Kusaka, Hidenori, illus. 2010. (ENG., Illus.). 200p. (J). pap. 9.99 (978-1-4215-3061-1(9)) Viz Media.
—Pokémon Adventures, Vol. 9. Kusaka, Hidenori, illus. 2010. (ENG., Illus.). 224p. (J). pap. 9.99 (978-1-4215-3062-8(7)) Viz Media.
—Pokémon Black & White, Vol. 10. Yamamoto, Satoshi, illus. 2013. (ENG.). 96p. (J). pap. 4.99 (978-1-4215-5894-3(7)) Viz Media.
—Pokémon Black & White, Vol. 11. Yamamoto, Satoshi, illus. 2013. (ENG.). 96p. (J). pap. 4.99 (978-1-4215-5895-0(5)) Viz Media.
—Pokémon Black & White, Vol. 4. 2011. (ENG.). 80p. (J). pap. 4.99 (978-1-4215-4114-3(9)) Viz Media.
—Pokémon Black & White, Vol. 5. Yamamoto, Satoshi, illus. 2012. (ENG.). 96p. (J). pap. 4.99 (978-1-4215-4280-5(3)) Viz Media.
—Pokémon Black & White, Vol. 7. Yamamoto, Satoshi, illus. 2012. (ENG.). 96p. (J). pap. 4.99 (978-1-4215-4282-9(X)) Viz Media.
—Pokémon Black & White, Vol. 8. Yamamoto, Satoshi, illus. 2012. (ENG.). 96p. (J). pap. 4.99 (978-1-4215-4283-6(8)) Viz Media.
—Pokémon Black & White, Vol. 9. Yamamoto, Satoshi, illus. 2013. (ENG.). 96p. (J). pap. 4.99 (978-1-4215-5893-6(9)) Viz Media.
Labaff, Stephanie. Draw Cartoon People in 4 Easy Steps: Then Write a Story. LaBaff, Tom, illus. 2012. (Drawing in 4 Easy Steps Ser.). 48p. (J). (gr. 3-18). pap. 8.95 (978-1-4644-0016-2(4), Enslow Elementary) Enslow Pubs., Inc.
LaBaff, Stephanie. Draw Superheroes in 4 Easy Steps: Then Write a Story. LaBaff, Tom, illus. 2012. (Drawing in 4 Easy Steps Ser.). 48p. (J). (gr. 3-18). pap. 8.95 (978-1-4644-0015-5(6), Enslow Elementary) Enslow Pubs., Inc.
Labatt, Mary. Lake Monster Mix-Up. Rioux, Jo-Anne, illus. 2009. (Sam & Friends Mystery Ser.). (ENG.). 96p. (J). (gr. 2-5). 7.95 (978-1-55337-302-5(2)); 16.95 (978-1-55337-822-8(9)) Kids Can Pr., Ltd. CAN. Dist: Hachette Bk. Group.
Lakin, Patricia. The Colorful Story of Comics. McClurkan, Rob, illus. 2016. (History of Fun Stuff Ser.). (ENG.). 48p. (J). (gr. 1-3). pap. 3.99 (978-1-4814-7144-2(9), Simon Spotlight) Simon Spotlight.
Lamb, Braden. Adventure Time. Paroline, Shelli, illus. 2014. (Adventure Time Ser.: 3). (ENG.). 128p. (J). (gr. 4). 34.99 (978-1-60886-347-1(6)) Boom! Studios.
Lambil, Willy & Raoul, Cauvin. The Blues in Black & White. 2004. (Blue Tunics Ser.: Vol. 1). (Illus.). (J). 12.45 (978-0-9752688-0-3(5)) Reney Editions, Inc.
Langridge, Roger. The Muppet Show Comic Book - Muppet Mash. Langridge, Roger, illus. 2011. (Muppet Show Ser.). (Illus.). 128p. pap. 9.99 (978-1-60886-611-3(4)) Boom! Studios.
Larson, Hope. Compass South. Mock, Rebecca, illus. 2016. (Four Points Ser.: 1). (ENG.). 224p. (J). 17.99 (978-0-374-30043-2(7), 9780374300432, Farrar, Straus & Giroux (BYR)) Farrar, Straus & Giroux.
Lee, Frank. Creating the Cover for Your Graphic Novel. 2012. (How to Draw Your Own Graphic Novel Ser.). (ENG.). 32p. (J). (gr. 4-6). pap. 12.30 (978-1-4488-6457-7(7)); lib. bdg. 26.50 (978-1-4488-6436-2(4)) Rosen Publishing Group, Inc., The. (PowerKids Pr.).
—Drawing Action in Your Graphic Novel. 2012. (How to Draw Your Own Graphic Novel Ser.). (ENG.). 32p. (J). (gr. 4-6). pap. 12.30 (978-1-4488-6451-5(8)); lib. bdg. 26.50 (978-1-4488-6477-5(1)) Rosen Publishing Group, Inc., The. (PowerKids Pr.).
—Penciling, Inking, & Coloring Your Graphic Novel. 2012. (How to Draw Your Own Graphic Novel Ser.). (ENG.). 32p. (J). (gr. 4-6). pap. 12.30 (978-1-4488-6455-3(0)); lib. bdg. 26.50 (978-1-4488-6435-5(6)) Rosen Publishing Group, Inc., The. (PowerKids Pr.).
Lee, Sally. Healthy Snacks, Healthy You! [Scholastic]. Swift, Gary, illus. 2013. (First Graphics: Myplate & Healthy Eating Ser.). (ENG.). (gr. 1-2). pap. 0.50 (978-1-4765-3129-8(3)) Capstone Press of Coughlan Cos.
Lee, Stan. Stan Lee's How to Draw Superheroes. 2013. lib. bdg. 39.15 (978-0-606-31949-2(2), Turtleback) Turtleback Bks.
Lemke, Amy J. Dinosaurs for Breakfast, 1 vol. Bradley, Jessica, illus. 2013. (Comics Land Ser.). (ENG.). 32p. (gr. k-2). lib. bdg. 25.32 (978-1-4342-4029-3(0)) Stone Arch Bks.
Lemke, Donald B. Chameleon Cage Match! Eliopoulos, Chris, illus. 2013. (Lucha Lizards Ser.). (ENG.). 48p. (gr. 1-3). pap. 5.95 (978-1-4342-3874-0(1)); lib. bdg. 23.99 (978-1-4342-3285-4(9)) Stone Arch Bks.
Lemke, Donald B., et al. Lecciones Sobre la Seguridad en el Trabajo Científico. Smith, Tod G., illus. 2013. (Ciencia Gráfica Ser.). (SPA.). 32p. (gr. 3-4). lib. bdg. 30.65 (978-1-62065-183-4(1)) Capstone Press of Coughlan Cos.
Lepp, Royden. Secrets of the Cell, Vol. 2. Lepp, Royden, illus. 2017. (Rust Ser.: 2). (ENG., Illus.). 144p. (J). (gr. 5). pap. 14.99 (978-1-60886-895-7(8), Archaia Entertainment) Boom! Studios.
Liniers, Ricardo. The Big Wet Balloon. Liniers, Ricardo, illus. 2013. (ENG., Illus.). 32p. (J). (gr. -1-3). 12.95 (978-1-935179-32-0(2)) TOON Books / RAW Junior, LLC.
Liu, Na. Little White Duck: A Childhood in China. 2012. (Single Titles Ser.). (ENG., Illus.). 108p. (gr. 4-7). (J). lib. bdg. 29.27 (978-0-7613-6587-7(7)); pap. 9.95 (978-0-7613-8115-0(5)) Lerner Publishing Group. (Graphic Universe™).
Ma, Wing Shing. A Tale of No Name, Vol. 1. 2005. (Storm Riders Ser.). (Illus.). 300p. (YA). pap. 7.95 (978-1-58899-375-5(2)) ComicsOne Corp./Dr. Masters.
MacPherson, Dwight L. Lil' Hellions. O'Reilly, Sean Patrick, ed. 2011. (Illus.). 82p. (YA). pap., pap. 14.95 (978-1-926914-37-4(6)) Arcana Studio, Inc.
Makura, Sho. Panda Man to the Rescue! Kato, Haruhi, illus. 2010. (ENG.). 96p. (J). pap. 7.99 (978-1-4215-3520-3(3)) Viz Media.
Mallonee, Dennis & Wilson, Shawn V. The Adventures of Chrissie Claus: Volume 1, Vol. 1. 2009. 116p. (Orig.). pap. 21.50 (978-0-929729-01-5(3)) Heroic Publishing, Inc.
Mancusi, Mari. Gamer Girl. 2010. (ENG.). 256p. (YA). (gr. 7-18). 7.99 (978-0-14-241509-2(X), Speak) Penguin Young Readers Group.
Marazano, Richard. The Sons of Ares, 2 vols. Ponzio, Jean-Michel, illus. 2009. (Chimpanzee Complex Ser.: 1). (ENG.). 56p. pap. 13.95 (978-1-84918-002-3(4)) CineBook GBR. Dist: National Bk. Network.
Mariolle, Mathieu. Even for A Dreamer Like Me. 3rd rev. ed. 2010. pap. 56.72 (978-0-7613-6960-8(0)) Lerner Publishing Group.
Martin Ann, M. Claudia & Mean Janine. Telgemeier, Raina, illus. 2016. (Baby-Sitters Club Graphix Ser.: 4). (ENG.). 176p. (J). (gr. 3-7). 24.99 (978-0-545-88623-9(6), Graphix) Scholastic, Inc.
Martin, Ann M. Claudia & Mean Janine. Telgemeier, Raina, illus. rev. ed. 2016. (Baby-Sitters Club Graphix Ser.: 4). (ENG.). 176p. (J). (gr. 3-7). pap. 10.99 (978-0-545-88622-2(8), Graphix) Scholastic, Inc.
Martin, Ann M. & Telgemeier, Raina. Baby-Sitters Club Graphix, Bks. 1-4, Set. Telgemeier, Raina, illus. 2016. (Baby-Sitters Club Graphix Ser.). (ENG., Illus.). 192p. (J). (gr. 3-7). pap. 43.96 (978-1-338-11898-8(6)) Scholastic, Inc.
Marvel Books Staff & Wyatt, Chris. Guardians of the Galaxy. 2014. (ENG.). 144p. (J). (gr. 3-7). pap. 6.99 (978-0-316-29324-2(5)) Little, Brown Bks. for Young Readers.
Mayhall, Robin. The Quest for Dragon Mountain. Martinez, Alitha E., illus. 2010. (Twisted Journeys (r) Ser.: 16). (ENG.). 112p. (J). (gr. 4-7). lib. bdg. 27.93 (978-0-8225-9261-7(4)) Lerner Publishing Group.
McBride, Earvin, Jr. The Bowdery Rodeo Cowboys of Texas. McBride, Earvin, Jr., illus. 2nd unabr. ed. 2003. (Earvin MacBride's Amazing Sci-Fi & Adventure Heroes Ser.). (Illus.). 329p. (J). (gr. 7-12). pap. 4.95 (978-1-892511-07-2(X)) MacBride, E. J. Pubn., Inc.
—Earvin MacBride's Amazing Sci-Fi & Adventure Heroes, 7 vols. McBride, Earvin, Jr., illus. 2nd unabr. ed. 2003. (Illus.). (J). (gr. 7-12). pap. 25.95 (978-1-892511-05-8(3)) MacBride, E. J. Pubn., Inc.
—The Eerie Adventures of Detective Omar Mendez. McBride, Earvin, Jr., illus. 2nd unabr. ed. 2003. (Earvin MacBride's Amazing Sci-Fi & Adventure Heroes Ser.). (Illus.). 329p. (J). (gr. 7-12). pap. 5.95 (978-1-892511-08-9(8)) MacBride, E. J. Pubn., Inc.
—Space - M. D. 3001. McBride, Earvin, Jr., illus. 2nd unabr. ed. 2003. (Earvin MacBride's Amazing Sci-Fi & Adventure Heroes Ser.). (Illus.). 329p. (J). (gr. 7-12). pap. 4.95 (978-1-892511-09-6(6)) MacBride, E. J. Pubn., Inc.
McDonnell, Patrick. The Mutts Diaries. 2014. (Mutts Kids Ser.: 1). (ENG., Illus.). 224p. (J). pap. 9.99 (978-1-4494-5870-6(X)) Andrews McMeel Publishing.
McLachlan, Brian & Owlkids Books Inc. Staff. Draw Out the Story: Ten Secrets to Creating Your Own Comics. 2013. (ENG., Illus.). 144p. (J). (gr. 2-7). pap. 11.95 (978-1-77147-003-2(8)); (gr. 3-7). 18.95 (978-1-926973-83-8(6)) Owlkids Bks. Inc. CAN. (Owlkids). Dist: Publishers Group West (PGW).
Megami Deluxe Volume 3. 2008. (Illus.). 100p. (YA). pap. 19.95 (978-1-56970-780-7(4)) Digital Manga Publishing.
Midthun, Joseph & Hiti, Samuel. Addition. 2013. (Illus.). 32p. (J). (978-0-7166-1431-9(6)) World Bk., Inc.
—Division. 2013. (Illus.). 32p. pap. (978-0-7166-1474-6(X)) World Bk., Inc.
Midthun, Joseph & Samuel, Hiti. Multiplication. 2013. (Illus.). 32p. (J). pap. (978-0-7166-1476-0(6)) World Bk., Inc.
Mignola, Mike. Batman/Hellboy/Starman (En Español) Riera, Ernest, tr. from ENG. 2004. (SPA., Illus.). 64p. (YA). pap. 12.95 (978-1-59497-025-2(4)) Public Square Bks.
Miller, Frank. Alcohol, Chicas y Balas. 2006. (Sin City Ser.).Tr. of Frank Miller's Sin City: Booze, Broads, & Bullets. (SPA., Illus.). 151p. (YA). (gr. 11). per. 15.00 (978-1-59497-021-4(1)) Public Square Bks.
—Sin City: Valores Familiares 2005.Tr. of Sin City: Family Values. (SPA., Illus.). 128p. pap. 15.00 (978-1-59497-017-7(3)) Public Square Bks.
Mishkin, Dan. The Warren Commission Report: A Graphic Investigation into the Kennedy Assassination. Colón, Ernie & Drozd, Jerzy, illus. 2014. (ENG.). 160p. pap. 17.95 (978-1-4197-1231-9(4), Abrams ComicArts) Abrams, Inc.
Miyasaka, Kaho. Kare First Love, 10 vols. Miyasaka, Kaho, illus. 2004. (Kare First Love Ser.: 2). (ENG., Illus.). 200p. pap. 9.95 (978-1-59116-395-4(1)) Viz Media.
—Kare First Love, 10 vols. Watanabe, Akira, tr. from JPN. Miyasaka, Kaho, illus. 2004. (Kare First Love Ser.: 1). (ENG., Illus.). 200p. pap. 9.95 (978-1-59116-394-7(3)) Viz Media.
Miyazaki, Hayao. Kiki's Delivery Service Film Comic, Vol. 1. 2006. (Kiki's Delivery Service Film Comics Ser.: 1). (ENG., Illus.). 144p. pap. 9.99 (978-1-59116-724-2(8)) Viz Media.
—My Neighbor Totoro, Vol. 1. Miyazaki, Hayao, illus. 2004. (ENG., Illus.). 152p. pap. 9.99 (978-1-59116-647-4(0)) Viz Media.
—My Neighbor Totoro, Vol. 2, 4 vols. Miyazaki, Hayao, illus. 2004. (ENG., Illus.). 152p. pap. 9.99 (978-1-59116-684-9(5)) Viz Media.
—My Neighbor Totoro, Vol. 3. Miyazaki, Hayao, illus. 2004. (ENG., Illus.). 152p. pap. 9.99 (978-1-59116-699-3(3)) Viz Media.
—My Neighbor Totoro, Vol. 4. Miyazaki, Hayao, illus. 2005. (ENG., Illus.). 152p. pap. 9.99 (978-1-59116-700-6(0)) Viz Media.
—Nausicaä of the Valley of the Wind. Miyazaki, Hayao, illus. 2nd ed. 2004. (ENG., Illus.). Vol. 6. 168p. pap. 12.99 (978-1-59116-354-1(4)) Vol. 7. 232p. pap. 12.99 (978-1-59116-355-8(2)) Viz Media.
Moore, Alan, et al. Promethea, Bk. 2. 2nd rev. ed. 2003. (ENG., Illus.). 176p. pap. 17.99 (978-1-56389-957-7(4), Wildstorm) DC Comics.
Morimoto, Sango. Taro & the Magic Pencil. Morimoto, Sango, illus. 2010. (ENG., Illus.). 104p. (J). pap. 7.99 (978-1-4215-3524-1(6)) Viz Media.
Morse, Scott. Magic Pickle. Morse, Scott, illus. 2008. (Magic Pickle Ser.). (ENG., Illus.). 112p. (J). (gr. 2-5). pap. 9.99 (978-0-439-87995-8(7), Graphix) Scholastic, Inc.
Moss, Marissa. The Vampire Dare! Moss, Marissa, illus. 2011. (Daphne's Diary of Daily Disasters Ser.). (ENG., Illus.). 80p. (J). (gr. 2-5). lib. bdg. 9.99 (978-1-4424-2677-1(2), Simon & Schuster/Paula Wiseman Bks.) Simon & Schuster/Paula Wiseman Bks.
Mowry, Chris. Revenge of the Fallen: Alliance, 1 vol. Milne, Alex, illus. 2010. (Transformers: Revenge of the Fallen Movie Prequel Ser.). (ENG.). 24p. (J). (gr. 3-6). Vol. 1. 24.21 (978-1-59961-717-6(X)) Vol. 2. 24.21 (978-1-59961-718-3(8)) Vol. 3. 24.21 (978-1-59961-719-0(6)) Vol. 4. 24.21 (978-1-59961-720-6(X)) Spotlight.
Naifeh, Ted. Courtney Crumrin & the Prince of Nowhere. Nozemack, Joe & Beaton, Jill, eds. 2008. (Illus.). 54p. (J). pap. 5.95 (978-1-932664-86-7(6)) Oni Pr., Inc.
—Courtney Crumrin Volume 1: The Night Things Special Edition. 2012. (ENG., Illus.). 144p. (YA). 19.99 (978-1-934964-77-4(8), 9781934964774) Oni Pr., Inc.
—The League of Ordinary Gentleman. 2011. (Courtney Crumrin Tales Ser.). (Illus.). 56p. (J). (gr. 2). pap. 5.99 (978-1-934964-68-2(9)) Oni Pr., Inc.
Najman, Alexander. The Assassin GN. O'Reilly, Sean Patrick, ed. 2014. (Illus.). 50p. (YA). pap. 14.95 (978-1-897548-09-7(5)) Arcana Studio, Inc.
Napoli, Donna Jo. Fish Girl. 2017. (ENG.). (J). (gr. 5-7). lib. bdg. 30.60 **(978-0-606-39824-4(4))** Turtleback Bks.
Napoli, Donna Jo & Wiesner, David. Fish Girl. Wiesner, David, illus. 2017. (ENG., Illus.). 192p. (J). (gr. 5-7). 25.00 (978-0-544-81512-4(2)); pap. 17.99 (978-0-547-48393-1(7)) Houghton Mifflin Harcourt Trade & Reference Pubs. (Clarion Bks.).
Nelson, O. T. The Girl Who Owned a City: Graphic Novel. Delk, Chrissy, illus. 2012. (Single Titles Ser.). (ENG.). 128p. (YA). (gr. 5-12). lib. bdg. 29.27 (978-0-7613-4903-7(0), Graphic Universe™) Lerner Publishing Group.
Nickel, Scott. Blast to the Past, 1 vol. Harpster, Steve, illus. 2006. (Time Blasters Ser.). (ENG.). 40p. (gr. 1-3). 23.99 (978-1-59889-033-4(6), Graphic Sparks) Stone Arch Bks.
—Blastoff to the Secret Side of the Moon!, 1 vol. Bradley, Jessica, illus. 2013. (Comics Land Ser.). (ENG.). 32p. (gr. k-2). 7.95 (978-1-4342-4273-0(0)); lib. bdg. 25.32 (978-1-4342-4031-6(2)) Stone Arch Bks.
Nishida, Masaki. Drawing Manga Animals. 2009. (How to Draw Manga Ser.). 24p. (gr. 3-3). 47.90 (978-1-61513-437-3(9), PowerKids Pr.) Rosen Publishing Group, Inc., The.
—Drawing Manga Dinosaurs. (How to Draw Manga Ser.). 24p. 2009. (gr. 3-3). 47.90 (978-1-61513-438-0(7), PowerKids Pr.) 2007. (Illus.). (J). (gr. -1-3). lib. bdg. 25.25 (978-1-4042-3845-9(X)) Rosen Publishing Group, Inc., The.
—Drawing Manga Insects. (How to Draw Manga Ser.). 24p. (gr. 3-3). 2009. 47.90 (978-1-61513-439-7(5), PowerKids Pr.) 2007. (Illus.). (J). lib. bdg. 25.25 (978-1-4042-3847-3(6)) Rosen Publishing Group, Inc., The.
—Drawing Manga Martial Arts Figures. (How to Draw Manga Ser.). 24p. (gr. 3-3). 2009. 47.90 (978-1-61513-440-3(9), PowerKids Pr.) 2007. (Illus.). (J). lib. bdg. 25.25 (978-1-4042-3850-3(6)) Rosen Publishing Group, Inc., The.
—Drawing Manga Vehicles. (How to Draw Manga Ser.). 24p. 2009. (gr. 3-3). 47.90 (978-1-61513-442-7(5), PowerKids Pr.) 2007. (Illus.). (J). (gr. 5-8). lib. bdg. 25.25 (978-1-4042-3848-0(4)) Rosen Publishing Group, Inc., The.
Nobleman, Marc Tyler & Besel, Jennifer M. The Captivating, Creative, Unusual History of Comic Books, 1 vol. 2010. (Unusual Histories Ser.). (ENG.). 48p. (gr. 3-4). lib. bdg. 31.99 (978-1-4296-4790-8(6)) Capstone Press of Coughlan Cos.
North, Ryan. Adventure Time, Vol. 2. Paroline, Shelli & Lamb, Braden, illus. 2013. (Adventure Time Ser.: 1). (ENG.). 128p. (J). (gr. 4). 34.99 (978-1-60886-321-1(2)) Boom! Studios.
—Adventure Time Vol. 2. Paroline, Shelli & Lamb, Braden, illus. 2013. (Adventure Time Ser.). (ENG.). 112p. (J). (gr. 4). pap. 14.99 (978-1-60886-323-5(9)) Boom! Studios.
—Adventure Time Vol. 3. Paroline, Shelli & Lamb, Braden, illus. 2013. (Adventure Time Ser.). (ENG.). 112p. (J). (gr. 4). pap. 14.99 (978-1-60886-317-4(4)) Boom! Studios.
North, Ryan & Lamb, Branden. Adventure Time, Vol. 1. Paroline, Shelli, illus. 2012. (Adventure Time Ser.). (ENG.). 128p. (J). (gr. 4). pap. 14.99 (978-1-60886-280-1(1)) Boom! Studios.
O'Brien, Anne Sibley. The Legend of Hong Kil Dong: The Robin Hood of Korea. O'Brien, Anne Sibley, illus. 2008. (ENG., Illus.). 48p. (J). (gr. 4-7). per. 8.95 (978-1-58089-303-9(1)) Charlesbridge Publishing, Inc.
Oceanak, Karla. Finicky. Spanjer, Kendra, illus. 2012. (Aldo Zelnick Comic Novel Ser.: 6). (ENG.). 160p. (J). (gr. 3-7). 12.95 (978-1-934649-24-4(4)) Bailiwick Pr.
O'Connor, George. Aphrodite: Goddess of Love. O'Connor, George, illus. 2013. (Olympians Ser.: 6). (ENG., Illus.). 80p. (J). (gr. 4-9). 18.99 (978-1-59643-947-4(5), 9781596439474); pap. 10.99 (978-1-59643-739-5(1), 9781596437395) Roaring Brook Pr. (First Second Bks.).
—Ares. O'Connor, George, illus. 2015. (Olympians Ser.: 7). (ENG., Illus.). 80p. (J). (gr. 4-9). pap. 10.99 (978-1-62672-013-8(4), 9781626720138, First Second Bks.) Roaring Brook Pr.
—Hades: Lord of the Dead. O'Connor, George, illus. 2012. (Olympians Ser.: 4). (ENG., Illus.). 80p. (J). (gr. 4-9). 17.99 (978-1-59643-761-6(8), 9781596437616); pap. 9.99 (978-1-59643-434-9(1), 9781596434349) Roaring Brook Pr. (First Second Bks.).
—Poseidon: Earth Shaker. O'Connor, George, illus. 2013. (Olympians Ser.: 5). (ENG., Illus.). 80p. (J). (gr. 4-9). 18.99 (978-1-59643-828-6(2), 9781596438286); pap. 9.99 (978-1-59643-738-8(3), 9781596437388) Roaring Brook Pr. (First Second Bks.).
O'Donnell, Liam. Max Finder Mystery, Vol. 2. Cho, Michael & Owlkids Books Inc. Staff, illus. 2007. (Max Finder Mystery Collected Casebook Ser.: 2). (ENG.). 96p. (J). (gr. 3-6). 9.95 (978-2-89579-121-8(X)) Owlkids Bks. Inc. CAN. Dist: Publishers Group West (PGW).
—Max Finder Mystery Collected Casebook, Vol. 1. Cho, Michael & Owlkids Books Inc. Staff, illus. 2006. (Max Finder Mystery Collected Casebook Ser.: 1). (ENG.). 96p. (J). (gr. 3-6). pap. 9.95 (978-2-89579-116-4(3), Owlkids) Owlkids Bks. Inc. CAN. Dist: Publishers Group West (PGW).
—Max Finder Mystery Collected Casebook Vol. 3, Vol. 3. Cho, Michael & Owlkids Books Inc. Staff, illus. 2007. (Max Finder Mystery Collected Casebook Ser.: 3). (ENG.). 96p. (J). (gr. 3-6). pap. 9.95 (978-2-89579-149-2(X), Owlkids) Owlkids Bks. Inc. CAN. Dist: Publishers Group West (PGW).
—Soccer Sabotage: A Graphic Guide Adventure, 1 vol. Deas, Mike, illus. 2009. (Graphic Guides). (ENG.). 64p. (J). (gr. 3-7). pap. 9.95 (978-1-55143-884-9(4)) Orca Bk. Pubs. USA.
O'Donnell, Liam & Barnett III, Charles. The Shocking World of Electricity with Max Axiom, Super Scientist, 1 vol. Dominguez, Richard, illus. 2007. (Graphic Science Ser.). (ENG.). 32p. (gr. 3-4). pap. 8.10 (978-0-7368-7888-3(2), 1264936, Graphic Library) Capstone Press of Coughlan Cos.
O'Malley, Tom. Top Trumps Marvel Heroes. 2008. (Illus.). 192p. pap. (978-1-84425-477-4(1)) Haynes Manuals, Inc.
Ord, Mandy. Sensitive Creatures. Ord, Mandy, illus. 2012. (ENG., Illus.). 296p. (YA). (gr. 9). pap. 19.95 (978-1-74237-216-7(3)) Allen & Unwin AUS. Dist: Independent Pubs. Group.
Orr, Tamra. Manga Artists. 2008. (Extreme Careers Ser.). (Illus.). 64p. (YA). (gr. 5-9). lib. bdg. 31.95 (978-1-4042-1854-3(8)) Rosen Publishing Group, Inc., The.
Orr, Tamra B. Manga Artists. 2009. (Extreme Careers Ser.). 64p. (gr. 5-5). 58.50 (978-1-61512-400-8(4), Rosen Reference) Rosen Publishing Group, Inc., The.
Ottaviani, Jim. T-Minus: The Race to the Moon. Cannon, Kevin & Cannon, Zander, illus. 2009. (ENG.). 128p. (J). (gr. 3-7). 21.99 (978-1-4169-8682-9(0), Simon & Schuster/Paula Wiseman Bks.) Simon & Schuster/Paula Wiseman Bks.
Panev, Aleksandar. Queen Nzinga. Steffibauer, Thomas, illus. 2007. 48p. (J). lib. bdg. 23.08 (978-1-4242-1641-3(9)) Fitzgerald Bks.
Patrick, Jean L. S. The Baseball Adventure of Jackie Mitchell, Girl Pitcher vs. Babe Ruth. Hammond, Ted & Carbajal, Richard, illus. 2011. (History's Kid Heroes Ser.). (ENG.). 32p. (gr. 3-5). pap. 8.95 (978-0-7613-7072-7(2), Graphic Universe™) Lerner Publishing Group.
Peanuts 2. Date not set. (J). pap. 108.00 (978-0-590-39640-0(4)) Scholastic, Inc.
Peirce, Lincoln. Big Nate: Game On! Peirce, Lincoln, illus. 2013. (Big Nate Ser.: 6). (ENG., Illus.). 224p. (J). pap. 9.99 (978-1-4494-2777-1(4)) Andrews McMeel Publishing.
Peters, Stephanie. The Adventures of Tintin: The Chapter Book. 2011. (J). lib. bdg. 14.75 (978-0-606-23444-3(6), Turtleback) Turtleback Bks.
Peyo. Los Pitufos Vol. 1: La Flauta de los Pitufos. Díaz, Lorenzo, tr. from FRE. 2004. Orig. Title: Johan et Pirlouit: la Flute a Six Schtroumpfs. (SPA., Illus.). 66p. 14.95 (978-1-59497-050-4(5)) Public Square Bks.
Phelan, Matt. Around the World. Phelan, Matt, illus. 2011. (ENG., Illus.). 240p. (J). (gr. 4-7). 24.99 (978-0-7636-3619-7(3)) Candlewick Pr.
Pikachu Press, . Catch Oshawott! Set: A Pokémon Look & Listen. 2012. (Pokemon Pikachu Press Ser.). (ENG.). 32p. (J). (gr. 3-6). 12.99 (978-1-60438-158-0(2)) Pokemon, USA, Inc.
—Catch Snivy! A Pokémon Look & Listen Set. 2012. (Pokemon Pikachu Press Ser.). (ENG.). 32p. (J). (gr. 3-6). 12.99 (978-1-60438-157-3(4)) Pokemon, USA, Inc.
—Catch Tepig! Set: A Pokémon Look & Listen. 2012. (Pokemon Pikachu Press Ser.). (ENG.). 32p. (J). (gr. 3-6). 12.99 (978-1-60438-159-7(0)) Pokemon, USA, Inc.
—Pokémon Find 'Em All! Welcome to Unova! 2012. (Pokemon Pikachu Press Ser.). (ENG.). 42p. (J). (gr. 3-6). 9.99 (978-1-60438-161-0(2)) Pokemon, USA, Inc.
Pilkey, Dav. The Adventures of Ook & Gluk, Kung-Fu Cavemen from the Future. Pilkey, Dav, illus. (Captain Underpants Ser.). (ENG., Illus.). 176p. (J). (gr. 2-5). 2011. 5.99 (978-0-545-38577-0(6)) 2010. 9.99 (978-0-545-17530-2(5)) Scholastic, Inc.
—The Adventures of Ook & Gluk, Kung-Fu Cavemen from the Future. 2011. lib. bdg. 16.00 (978-0-606-16381-1(6), Turtleback) Turtleback Bks.
Pilkey, Dav & Beard, George. The Adventures of Ook & Gluk, Kung-Fu Cavemen from the Future. 2010. lib. bdg. 20.85 (978-0-606-15003-3(X), Turtleback) Turtleback Bks.
Poe, Edgar Allen. The Tell-Tale Heart & Other Stories. Grimly, Gris, illus. 2011. (ENG.). 144p. (J). (gr. 6-9). pap. 12.99 (978-1-4169-5026-4(5), Atheneum Bks. for Young Readers) Simon & Schuster Children's Publishing.
Poe, Marshall. Sons of Liberty. Purvis, Leland, illus. 2008. (Turning Points Ser.). (ENG.). 128p. (J). (gr. 3-7). pap. 8.99 (978-1-4169-5067-7(2), Aladdin) Simon & Schuster Children's Publishing.
Pokémon Adventures: Black & White, Vol. 5. 2014. (ENG., Illus.). 208p. (J). pap. 9.99 (978-1-4215-6181-3(6)) Viz Media.
Pokémon Adventures, Vol. 24. 2014. (ENG., Illus.). 216p. (J). pap. 9.99 (978-1-4215-3558-6(0)) Viz Media.
Pokémon Adventures, Vol. 25. 2014. (ENG., Illus.). 208p. (J). pap. 9.99 (978-1-4215-3559-3(9)) Viz Media.
Pope, Paul. Battling Boy. Pope, Paul, illus. 2013. (Battling Boy Ser.: 1). (ENG., Illus.). 208p. (J). (gr. 5-12). 24.99 (978-1-59643-805-7(3), 9781596438057); pap. 16.99 (978-1-59643-145-4(8), 9781596431454) Roaring Brook Pr. (First Second Bks.).
Pope, Paul & Petty, J. T. The Rise of Aurora West. Rubín, David, illus. 2014. (Battling Boy Ser.). (ENG.). 160p. (J). (gr. 5-12). pap. 9.99 (978-1-62672-009-1(6), 9781626720091, First Second Bks.) Roaring Brook Pr.
Porcellino, John. Thoreau at Walden. Porcellino, John, illus. 2009. (ENG., Illus.). 112p. (J). (gr. 5-18). pap. 9.99 (978-1-4231-0039-3(5)) Hyperion Pr.

C
D

Poryes, Michael, illus. The Trouble with Boys, 2 vols., Vol. 2. 2004. (That's So Raven Ser.). 96p. pap. 14.99 *(978-1-59182-807-5(4)*, Tokyopop Kids) TOKYOPOP, Inc.
Price, Pam. Cool Comics: Creating Fun & Fascinating Collections!, 1 vol. 2007. (Cool Collections Ser.). (ENG., Illus.). 32p. (YA). (gr. 2-5). 28.50 *(978-1-59679-769-7(X))* ABDO Publishing Co.
Publications International Ltd. Staff. Look & Find Smurfs. 2011. 24p. 7.98 *(978-1-4508-1180-4(9))* Phoenix International Publications, Inc.
Publishing, Arcturus. The Complete Guide to Drawing Comics. 2015. (ENG., Illus.). 128p. pap. 12.95 *(978-1-78404-512-8(8)*, 25dacec2-20ea-471f-b501-c878db71bbac) Arcturus Publishing GBR. Dist: Bookmasters Distribution.
Pullman, Philip. The Adventures of John Blake: Mystery of the Ghost Ship. Fordham, Fred, illus. 2017. (ENG.). 160p. (J). (gr. 3-7). 19.99 ***(978-1-338-14912-8(1)***, Graphix) Scholastic, Inc.
—The Adventures of John Blake: Mystery of the Ghost Ship. Fordham, Fred, illus. 2017. lib. bdg. 33.05 ***(978-0-606-40195-1(4))*** Turtleback Bks.
—The Golden Compass Graphic Novel, Complete Edition. 2017. (His Dark Materials Ser.). (ENG.). 224p. (J). (gr. 5). 21.99 ***(978-0-553-53516-7(1))***; pap. 12.99 ***(978-0-553-53517-4(X))***; lib. bdg. 24.99 ***(978-0-553-53518-1(8))*** Random Hse. Children's Bks. (Knopf Bks. for Young Readers).
Quino. Mafalda & Friends. 2004. (SPA., Illus.). 96p. *(978-950-515-760-0(6))*; *(978-950-515-759-4(2))* De La Flor.
Raum, Elizabeth, et al. True War Stories: Personal Accounts of History's Greatest Conflicts. Kinsella, Pat et al, illus. 2017. (J). *(978-1-4914-1965-6(2))* Capstone Press of Coughlan Cos.
Reger, Rob. Emily the Strange, Vol 1. Reger, Rob & Brooks, Brian, illus. 2006. (Emily the Strange (Spanish) Ser.). (SPA.). 64p. 19.95 *(978-1-59497-188-4(9))* Public Square Bks.
—El Libro Secreto de las Cosas Extranas. Reger, Rob, illus. 2006. (Emily the Strange (Spanish) Ser.). (SPA., Illus.). 64p. reprint ed. 19.95 *(978-1-59497-189-1(7))* Public Square Bks.
Reynolds, Aaron. The Pest Show on Earth, 1 vol. Lervold, Erik, illus. 2008. (Tiger Moth Ser.). (ENG.). 40p. (gr. 1-3). lib. bdg. 23.99 *(978-1-4342-0454-7(5)*, Graphic Sparks) Stone Arch Bks.
—The Pest Show on Earth: Tiger Moth, 1 vol. Lervold, Erik, illus. 2008. (Graphic Sparks Ser.). (ENG.). 40p. (gr. 1-3). per. 5.95 *(978-1-4342-0504-9(5)*, Graphic Sparks) Stone Arch Bks.
Ribeiro, Nelson & Spotlight Editors. Jughead with Archie in Fool Proof. Gorelick, Victor, illus. 2007. (Jughead with Archie Ser.). (ENG.). 80p. (J). (gr. 3-6). 24.21 *(978-1-59961-274-4(7))* Spotlight.
—Jughead with Archie in Pup-Ularity Contest. Gorelick, Victor, illus. 2007. (Jughead with Archie Ser.). (ENG.). 80p. (J). (gr. 3-6). 24.21 *(978-1-59961-276-8(3))* Spotlight.
—Jughead with Archie in Wish Fulfillment. Gorelick, Victor, illus. 2007. (Jughead with Archie Ser.). (ENG.). 80p. (J). (gr. 3-6). 24.21 *(978-1-59961-277-5(1))* Spotlight.
Ribeiro, Nelson, et al. Betty & Veronica in Color Blind. 2007. (Betty & Veronica Ser.). (ENG., Illus.). 80p. (J). (gr. 3-6). 24.21 *(978-1-59961-265-2(8))* Spotlight.
—Jughead with Archie in a Day to Remember. 2007. (Jughead with Archie Ser.). (ENG., Illus.). 80p. (J). (gr. 3-6). 24.21 *(978-1-59961-272-0(0))* Spotlight.
—Jughead with Archie in Family Photos. 2007. (Jughead with Archie Ser.). (ENG., Illus.). 80p. (J). (gr. 3-6). 24.21 *(978-1-59961-273-7(9))* Spotlight.
—Laugh with Fore! 2007. (Archie Digest Library). (ENG., Illus.). 80p. (J). (gr. 3-6). 24.21 *(978-1-59961-279-9(8))* Spotlight.
Richardson, Mike. Dark Horse Heroes, Vol. 1. Dark Horse Comics Staff & Warner, Christopher S., eds. Hughes, Adam, illus. 2008. (ENG.). 488p. pap. 24.95 *(978-1-59307-734-1(3))* Dark Horse Comics.
Riordan, Rick. The Red Pyramid, Bk. 1. Collar, Orpheus, illus. 2012. (Kane Chronicles Ser.). (ENG.). 192p. (J). (gr. 5-9). pap. 12.99 *(978-1-4231-5069-5(4))* Hyperion Pr.
Riordan, Rick & Venditti, Robert. Heroes of Olympus, Book One the Lost Hero: the Graphic Novel. Powell, Nathan, illus. 2014. (Heroes of Olympus Ser.). (ENG.). 192p. (J). (gr. 5-9). pap. 12.99 *(978-1-4231-6325-1(7))* Hyperion Bks. for Children.
—The Sea of Monsters. Futaki, Attila & Gaspar, Tamas, illus. 2013. (Percy Jackson & the Olympians Ser.). (ENG.). 128p. (J). (gr. 5-9). 19.99 *(978-1-4231-4529-5(1))*; pap. 12.99 *(978-1-4231-4550-9(X))* Hyperion Pr.
—The Titan's Curse. Futaki, Attila & Guilhaumond, Gregory, illus. 2013. (Percy Jackson & the Olympians Ser.). (ENG.). 128p. (J). (gr. 5-9). pap. 14.99 *(978-1-4231-4551-6(8))* Hyperion Pr.
—The Titan's Curse. 2013. (Percy Jackson & the Olympians Graphic Novels Ser.: 3). (J). lib. bdg. 26.95 *(978-0-606-32286-7(8)*, Turtleback) Turtleback Bks.
Ripley, Robert. Ripley's Believe It or Not! The Original Cartoons That Started It All! 2014. (ENG., Illus.). 328p. 39.99 *(978-1-61377-890-6(2)*, 9781613778906) Idea & Design Works, LLC.
Roba, Jean. Friends First. Roba, Jean, illus. 2012. (Billy & Buddy Ser.: 3). (ENG., Illus.). 48p. (J). (gr. 3-12). pap. 11.95 *(978-1-84918-124-2(1))* CineBook GBR. Dist: National Bk. Network.
Robbins, Trina. The Drained Brains Caper. Page, Tyler, illus. 2010. (Chicagoland Detective Agency Ser.: 1). (ENG.). 64p. (gr. 4-8). lib. bdg. 29.27 *(978-0-7613-4601-2(5))* Lerner Publishing Group.
Robert, Peters. Da Goodie Monsta. Robert, Peters, illus. 2010. (Illus.). 30p. (J). pap. 9.95 *(978-0-9823906-4-1(5))* Wiggles Pr.
Robertson, David. The Land of Os: John Ramsay. Tien, Wai, illus. 2014. (Tales from Big Spirit Ser.: 6). (ENG.). 32p. (J). (gr. 4-6). pap. *(978-1-55379-491-2(5)*, 71d193fb-9d6f-4711-9ca7-63e7716b3ed2, HighWater Pr.) Portage & Main Pr.
—The Poet: Pauline Johnson. Henderson, Scott B., illus. 2014. (Tales from Big Spirit Ser.: 6). (ENG.). 32p. (J). (gr. 4-6). pap. *(978-1-55379-481-3(8)*, ab04cc8e-58f6-479c-9f04-879c4a722ff3, HighWater Pr.) Portage & Main Pr.
Roche, Art. Art for Kids: Comic Strips - Create Your Own Comic Strips from Start to Finish. 2011. (Art for Kids Ser.). (ENG., Illus.). 112p. (J). (gr. 3-18). pap. 9.95 *(978-1-4027-8474-3(0))* Sterling Publishing Co., Inc.
Rock, Brian. Don't Play with Your Food! Moerner, John, illus. 2005. 32p. (J). 14.99 *(978-0-9754411-0-7(8))* First Light Publishing.
Roop, Peter & Roop, Connie. The Stormy Adventure of Abbie Burgess, Lighthouse Keeper. 2010. pap. 51.02 *(978-0-7613-6922-6(8))* Lerner Publishing Group.
Roques, Dominique. Anna Banana & the Chocolate Explosion. Dormal, Alexis, illus. 2015. (Anna Banana Ser.). (ENG.). 28p. (J). (gr. k-2). 15.99 *(978-1-62672-020-6(7)*, 9781626720206, First Second Bks.) Roaring Brook Pr.
Rosenstiehl, Agnes. Silly Lilly & the Four Seasons. Mouly, Francoise, ed. 2008. (ENG., Illus.). 36p. (J). (gr. -1-3). 12.95 *(978-0-9799238-1-4(6))* TOON Books / RAW Junior, LLC.
—Silly Lilly in What Will I Be Today? Mouly, Francoise, ed. 2011. (ENG., Illus.). 32p. (J). (gr. -1-3). 12.95 *(978-1-935179-08-5(X))* TOON Books / RAW Junior, LLC.
Royston, Angela. Paper: Let's Look at a Comic Book. 2005. (J). *(978-1-4109-1818-5(1))*; (ENG.). 24p. pap. *(978-1-4109-1827-7(0))* Steck-Vaughn.
Russell, Rachel Renée. Middle School Mayhem. Russell, Rachel Renée, illus. 2017. (Misadventures of Max Crumbly Ser.: 2). (ENG., Illus.). 240p. (J). (gr. 4-8). 13.99 ***(978-1-4814-6003-3(X)***, Aladdin) Simon & Schuster Children's Publishing.
Ruth, Greg. The Lost Boy. 2013. (ENG.). 192p. (J). (gr. 3-7). pap. 12.99 *(978-0-439-82332-6(3)*, Graphix) Scholastic, Inc.
Samanci, Özge. Dare to Disappoint: Growing up in Turkey. 2015. (ENG., Illus.). 200p. (YA). (gr. 9). pap. 16.99 *(978-0-374-31698-3(8)*, 9780374316983, Farrar, Straus & Giroux (BYR)) Farrar, Straus & Giroux.
Schmid, Katie Kelley. Nat Turner & Slave Life on a Southern Plantation. 2013. (Jr. Graphic African American History Ser.). 24p. (J). (gr. 3-6). pap. 63.60 *(978-1-4777-1454-6(5))*; (ENG., Illus.). pap. 10.60 *(978-1-4777-1453-9(7))*; (ENG., Illus.). lib. bdg. 25.25 *(978-1-4777-1314-3(X))* Rosen Publishing Group, Inc., The. (PowerKids Pr.).
Schneider, Maxwell. Do You Hear Me? Laughs for the Hard of Hearing by the Hard of Hearing, 1. 2003. (Illus.). 138p. per. 8.95 *(978-0-9727520-0-8(5)*, B555) Harris Communications, Inc.
Scholastic, Inc. Staff & Farshtey, Greg. Lego Ninjago. 2011. (Lego Ninjago Ser.). (ENG., Illus.). 112p. (J). (gr. 2-5). pap. 7.99 *(978-0-545-36258-0(X))* Scholastic, Inc.
Schreiber, Ellen. Blood Relatives, Vol. II. Rem, illus. 2008. (Vampire Kisses: Blood Relatives Ser.: Vol. 2). (ENG.). 192p. (YA). (gr. 8-18). pap. 9.99 *(978-0-06-134082-6(0)*, Tegen, Katherine Bks) HarperCollins Pubs.
—Blood Relatives, Vol. 3. Kwon, Elisa, illus. 2009. (Vampire Kisses: Blood Relatives Ser.: Vol. 3). (ENG.). 192p. (YA). (gr. 8-18). pap. 9.99 *(978-0-06-134083-3(9)*, Tegen, Katherine Bks) HarperCollins Pubs.
Schulz, Charles. Be My Valentine, Charlie Brown. (J). pap. 46.80 *(978-0-590-06610-5(2))* Scholastic, Inc.
Schulz, Charles & Pastis, Stephan. Happiness Is a Warm Blanket, Charlie Brown! Scott, Bob, illus. 2011. (Peanuts Ser.). (ENG.). 96p. (J). (gr. 3). 19.99 *(978-1-60886-682-3(3))* Boom! Studios.
Schulz, Charles M. Be Kind: Peanuts Wisdom to Carry You Through. 2013. (ENG., Illus.). 72p. (J). (gr. -1-17). 7.95 *(978-0-7624-4862-3(8)*, Running Pr. Kids) Running Pr. Bk. Pubs.
—Be Thankful: Peanuts Wisdom to Carry You Through. 2013. (ENG., Illus.). 72p. (J). (gr. -1-17). 7.95 *(978-0-7624-5045-9(2)*, Running Pr. Kids) Running Pr. Bk. Pubs.
—Peanuts: Be Friends. 2013. (ENG., Illus.). 72p. (J). (gr. -1-17). 7.95 *(978-0-7624-5044-2(4)*, Running Pr. Kids) Running Pr. Bk. Pubs.
Schulz, Charles M., creator. Be Yourself! 2013. (ENG., Illus.). 40p. (J). (gr. -1-17). 12.95 *(978-0-7624-4718-3(4)*, Running Pr. Kids) Running Pr. Bk. Pubs.
—Peanuts: Be Brave: Peanuts Wisdom to Carry You Through. 2013. (ENG., Illus.). 72p. (J). (gr. -1-17). 7.95 *(978-0-7624-4861-6(X)*, Running Pr. Kids) Running Pr. Bk. Pubs.
Schwartz, Simon. The Other Side of the Wall. Watkinson, Laura, tr. from GER. 2015. (ENG., Illus.). 112p. (J). (gr. 7-12). pap. 9.99 *(978-1-4677-6028-7(5)*, Graphic Universe™) Lerner Publishing Group.
Scott, Gwen. The Dog That Wore Glasses. 2012. 20p. pap. 24.95 *(978-1-4626-8268-3(5))* America Star Bks.
Seven, John & Christy, Jana. A Rule Is to Break: A Child's Guide to Anarchy. 2012. (Wee Rebel Ser.). (ENG., Illus.). 44p. (gr. -1). bds. 14.95 *(978-1-933149-25-7(6))* Manic D Pr.
Shakespeare, William. Macbeth: The Graphic Novel. 2010. (Classic Graphic Novel Collection). 144p. (YA). (gr. 7-12). 34.80 *(978-1-4205-0373-9(1))* Cengage Gale.
—A Midsummer Night's Dream. Bryant, Clive, ed. Nicholson, Kat & Cardy, Jason, illus. 2012. (ENG.). 144p. (gr. 6). lib. bdg. 24.95 *(978-1-907127-44-1(5))* Classical Comics GBR. Dist: Publishers Group West (PGW).
Shanower, Eric. Wonderful Wizard of Oz: Vol. 1, 1 vol. 2014. (ENG.). 24p. 24.21 *(978-1-61479-226-0(7))* ABDO Publishing Co.
—Wonderful Wizard of Oz: Vol. 2, 1 vol. 2014. (ENG.). 24p. 24.21 *(978-1-61479-227-7(5))* ABDO Publishing Co.
Shanower, Eric & Baum, L. Frank. The Marvelous Land of Oz: Adapted from the Novel by L. Frank Baum, 1 vol. Young, Skottie, illus. 2014. (ENG.). 24p. (J). *(978-1-61479-238-3(0))* Spotlight.
—The Wonderful Wizard of Oz, 1 vol. Young, Skottie, illus. 2014. (ENG.). 24p. (J). *(978-1-61479-229-1(1))* Spotlight.
Shealy, Dennis & Random House Staff. Heroes United! - Attack of the Robot! Doescher, Erik et al, illus. 2008. (Pictureback(R) Ser.). (ENG.). 32p. (J). (gr. -1-2). pap. 4.99 *(978-0-375-84409-6(0)*, Random Hse. Bks. for Young Readers) Random Hse. Children's Bks.
Shelley, Mary. Frankenstein. Irving, Frazer, illus. 2005. 176p. (gr. 3-7). 21.00 *(978-0-7569-5809-1(1))* Perfection Learning Corp.
—Frankenstein. abr. ed. 2010. (Dover Classic Stories Coloring Book Ser.). (ENG.). 48p. (J). (gr. 3-8). pap. 4.99 *(978-0-486-47415-1(1))* Dover Pubns., Inc.
—Frankenstein: The Graphic Novel. 2010. (Classic Graphic Novel Collection). (ENG., Illus.). 144p. (YA). (gr. 7-12). 34.80 *(978-1-4205-0374-6(X))* Cengage Gale.
—Gris Grimly's Frankenstein. Grimly, Gris, illus. 2013. (ENG.). 208p. (YA). (gr. 8). 24.99 *(978-0-06-186297-7(5))* HarperCollins Pubs.
Sherman, Susan & Poryes, Michael. That's So Raven, 2 vols., Vol. 1. 2004. (Illus.). 192p. pap. 14.99 *(978-1-59182-806-8(6)*, Tokyopop Kids) TOKYOPOP, Inc.
Shiga, Jason. Meanwhile: Pick Any Path. 3,856 Story Possibilities. 2010. (ENG., Illus.). 80p. (J). (gr. 3-7). 16.95 *(978-0-8109-8423-3(7)*, Amulet Bks.) Abrams, Inc.
Shin, Chi Sup. The Three Little Turtles & the Big Bad Pelican. 2003. (J). pap. 15.99 *(978-1-4134-3760-7(5))* Borders Personal Publishing.
Shipman, Gary, illus. Pakkins' Land: Tavitah, 4. 2003. (Pakkins' Land: 4). 128p. pap. 16.95 *(978-0-9700241-4-5(2))* Pakkins Presents.
Siegel, Mark & Siegel, Alexis. The Sand Warrior. Bouma, Xanthe et al, illus. 2017. (5 Worlds Ser.: 1). (ENG.). 256p. (J). (gr. 3-7). 18.99 ***(978-1-101-93586-6(3))***; pap. 12.99 ***(978-1-101-93588-0(X))***; lib. bdg. 21.99 ***(978-1-101-93587-3(1))*** Random Hse. Children's Bks. (Random Hse. Bks. for Young Readers).
—The Sand Warrior. Bouma, Xanthe et al, illus. 2017. (5 Worlds Ser.: 1). lib. bdg. 24.50 ***(978-0-606-40243-9(8))*** Turtleback Bks.
Singh, Asavari. How to Draw the Craziest, Creepiest Characters, 1 vol. James, Martin et al, illus. 2011. (Drawing Ser.). (ENG.). 48p. (gr. 3-4). lib. bdg. 31.99 *(978-1-4296-6595-7(5))* Capstone Press of Coughlan Cos.
—How to Draw the Darkest, Baddest Graphic Novels, 1 vol. Mudgal, Nishant et al, illus. 2011. (Drawing Ser.). (ENG.). 48p. (gr. 3-4). lib. bdg. 31.99 *(978-1-4296-6594-0(7))* Capstone Press of Coughlan Cos.
—How to Draw the Most Exciting, Awesome Manga, 1 vol. James, Martin et al, illus. 2011. (Drawing Ser.). (ENG.). 48p. (gr. 3-4). lib. bdg. 31.99 *(978-1-4296-6593-3(9))* Capstone Press of Coughlan Cos.
Smith, Jeff. Bone Vol. 2: La Gran Carrera de Vacas. 2007. (SPA., Illus.). 144p. reprint ed. 24.95 *(978-1-59497-347-5(4))* Public Square Bks.
—Bone Vol. 3: Los Ojos de la Tormenta. 2007. (SPA., Illus.). 144p. reprint ed. 24.95 *(978-1-59497-348-2(2))* Public Square Bks.
—Out from Boneville. Smith, Jeff & Hamaker, Steve, illus. 2005. (Bone Ser.: 1). (ENG.). 144p. (J). pap. 12.99 *(978-0-439-70640-7(8)*, Graphix) Scholastic, Inc.
Snider, Jesse Blaze. Toy Story: Toy Overboard. Watson, Nathan, illus. 2011. 128p. (J). pap. 9.99 *(978-1-60886-605-2(X))* Boom! Studios.
Soda, Masahito. Firefighter! Soda, Masahito, illus. 2005. (Firefighter Ser.: Vol. 12). (ENG., Illus.). 200p. pap. 9.95 *(978-1-59116-980-2(1))* Viz Media.
Solomons, David. My Brother Is a Superhero. (ENG.). (J). (gr. 3-7). 2017. 320p. 7.99 *(978-0-14-751605-3(6)*, Puffin Books) 2015. 304p. 16.99 *(978-0-451-47477-3(5)*, Viking Books for Young Readers) Penguin Young Readers Group.
Sonishi, Kenji. Leave It to PET!, Vol. 2. Sonishi, Kenji, illus. 2009. (ENG., Illus.). 196p. (J). pap. 7.99 *(978-1-4215-2650-8(6))* Viz Media.
Southgate, Anna & Li, Yishan. Drawing Manga Faces & Bodies. 2012. (Manga Mania Ser.). (ENG., Illus.). 80p. (YA). (gr. 5-8). 33.25 *(978-1-4488-9241-9(4))*; pap. 14.05 *(978-1-4488-9263-1(5))* Rosen Publishing Group, Inc., The. (Rosen Reference).
—Drawing Manga Mecha, Weapons, & Wheels. 2012. (Manga Mania Ser.). (ENG., Illus.). 80p. (YA). (gr. 5-8). 33.25 *(978-1-4488-9242-6(2))*; pap. 14.05 *(978-1-4488-9265-5(1))* Rosen Publishing Group, Inc., The. (Rosen Reference).
—Drawing Manga Men. 2012. (Manga Mania Ser.). (ENG., Illus.). 80p. (YA). (gr. 5-8). 33.25 *(978-1-4488-9240-2(6))*; pap. 14.05 *(978-1-4488-9261-7(9))* Rosen Publishing Group, Inc., The. (Rosen Reference).
—Drawing Manga Women. 2012. (Manga Mania Ser.). (ENG., Illus.). 80p. (YA). (gr. 5-8). 33.25 *(978-1-4488-9239-6(2))*; pap. 14.05 *(978-1-4488-9259-4(7))* Rosen Publishing Group, Inc., The. (Rosen Reference).
Southgate, Anna & Sparrow, Keith. Drawing Manga Boys. 2011. (J). 84.30 *(978-1-4488-4807-2(5))*; pap. 14.05 *(978-1-4488-4803-4(2))*; lib. bdg. 33.25 *(978-1-4488-4799-0(0))* Rosen Publishing Group, Inc., The. (Rosen Reference).
—Drawing Manga Expressions & Poses. 2011. (J). 84.30 *(978-1-4488-4808-9(3))*; pap. 14.05 *(978-1-4488-4804-1(0))*; lib. bdg. 33.25 *(978-1-4488-4800-3(8))* Rosen Publishing Group, Inc., The. (Rosen Reference).
—Drawing Manga Weapons, Vehicles, & Accessories. 2011. (Illus.). 80p. (J). 84.30 *(978-1-4488-4809-6(1))*; pap. 14.05 *(978-1-4488-4805-8(9))*; lib. bdg. 33.25 *(978-1-4488-4801-0(6))* Rosen Publishing Group, Inc., The. (Rosen Reference).
Spiegelman, Nadja. Lost in NYC: A Subway Adventure. Sánchez, Sergio García, illus. 2015. (ENG.). 52p. (J). (gr. 2-7). 16.95 *(978-1-935179-81-8(0))* TOON Books / RAW Junior, LLC.
—Zig & Wikki in Something Ate My Homework. Mouly, Francoise, ed. Loeffler, Trade, illus. 2010. (ENG.). 40p. (J). (gr. -1-3). 12.95 *(978-1-935179-02-3(0))* TOON Books / RAW Junior, LLC.
Stabenfeldt, prod. Starshine Legacy 2: Comic Book. 2007. (YA). *(978-1-933343-56-3(7))* Stabenfeldt Inc.
Stephens, Jay. Doc Phantom, Vol. 2. 2003. (ENG., Illus.). 80p. (gr. 12-18). pap. 12.95 *(978-1-929998-27-2(9)*, 9781929998272) Oni Pr., Inc.
Stevenson, Noelle. Nimona. Stevenson, Noelle, illus. 2015. (ENG., Illus.). 272p. (YA). (gr. 8). 17.99 *(978-0-06-227823-4(1))*; pap. 14.99 *(978-0-06-227822-7(3))* HarperCollins Pubs. (HarperTeen).
Stoker, Bram. Bram Stoker, Vol. 7. Pomplun, Tom, ed. 2003. (ENG., Illus.). 144p. pap. 9.95 *(978-0-9712464-7-8(5)*, 9780971246478) Eureka Productions.
—Dracula. Bryant, Clive, ed. Johnson, Staz et al, illus. 2012. (ENG.). 144p. (gr. 6). pap. 16.95 *(978-1-906332-68-6(1))*; pap. 16.95 *(978-1-906332-67-9(3)*, Classical Comics, Ltd.) Classical Comics GBR. Dist: Publishers Group West (PGW).
Stone, Adam. The Challenger Explosion. 2014. (Disaster Stories Ser.). (ENG., Illus.). 24p. (J). (gr. 3-8). 29.95 *(978-1-62617-151-0(3)*, Black Sheep) Bellwether Media.
Storck, Patrick. Muppet Sherlock Holmes. Mebberson, Amy, illus. 2011. (Muppet Show Ser.). 128p. pap. 9.99 *(978-1-60886-613-7(0))* Boom! Studios.
Sturm, James & Arnold, Andrew. Adventures in Cartooning: Characters in Action. 2013. (Adventures in Cartooning Ser.). (J). lib. bdg. 22.10 *(978-0-606-32306-2(6)*, Turtleback) Turtleback Bks.
—Adventures in Cartooning Christmas Special. 2012. (Adventures in Cartooning Ser.). (J). lib. bdg. 20.85 *(978-0-606-26709-0(3)*, Turtleback) Turtleback Bks.
Surhone, Lambert M., et al, eds. The Adventures of Tintin: Secret of the Unicorn. 2010. 124p. pap. *(978-613-0-99918-6(6))* AV Akademikerverlag GmbH & Co. KG.
Takahashi, Kazuki. Yu-Gi-Oh! Takahashi, Kazuki, illus. 2006. (Yu-Gi-oh! the Duelist Ser.: 14). (ENG., Illus.). 208p. pap. 7.95 *(978-1-4215-0339-4(5))* Viz Media.
—Yu-Gi-Oh!: Duelist, Vol. 13. 2006. (ENG., Illus.). 208p. pap. 9.99 *(978-1-4215-0277-9(1))* Viz Media.
Takahashi, Rumiko. Inuyasha Ani-Manga, Vol. 14. Takahashi, Rumiko, illus. 2006. (Inuyasha Ser.: 14). (ENG., Illus.). 208p. pap. 11.99 *(978-1-4215-0384-4(0))* Viz Media.
—Inuyasha, Vol. 44. Set. Takahashi, Rumiko, illus. 2003. (Inuyasha Ser.). (ENG., Illus.). 200p. (YA). pap. 39.98 *(978-1-59116-235-3(1)*, Viz Comics) Viz Media.
—Mermaid Saga. Takahashi, Rumiko, illus. 2004. (Mermaid Saga Ser.). (ENG., Illus.). (YA). 3. 176p. pap. 9.99 *(978-1-59116-483-8(4))* Vol. 4. 2nd ed. 192p. pap. 9.99 *(978-1-59116-482-1(6))* Viz Media.
Takase, Naoko, illus. Helen Keller: From Darkness to Light. 2011. (Biographical Comic Ser.). (ENG.). 152p. (J). (gr. 2-6). 18.99 *(978-1-4215-4238-6(2))*; pap. 9.99 *(978-1-4215-4239-3(0))* Shogakukan JPN. Dist: Simon & Schuster, Inc.
Takemoto, Novala. Kamikaze Girls, Vol. 1. Wegmuller, Akemi, tr. from JPN. 2006. (Kamikaza Girls Ser.). (ENG.). 208p. (YA). (gr. 10). 17.99 *(978-1-4215-0269-4(0))* Viz Media.
Tamaki, Mariko. This One Summer. Tamaki, Jillian, illus. 2014. (ENG.). 320p. (YA). (gr. 7). 21.99 *(978-1-62672-094-7(0)*, 9781626720947); pap. 18.99 *(978-1-59643-774-6(X)*, 9781596437746) Roaring Brook Pr. (First Second Bks.).
Tan, Shaun. The Arrival. Tan, Shaun, illus. 2007. (ENG., Illus.). 128p. (J). (gr. 7-12). 21.99 *(978-0-439-89529-3(4)*, Levine, Arthur A. Bks.) Scholastic, Inc.
—The Arrival. 2007. (J). *(978-0-439-89530-9(8)*, Levine, Arthur A. Bks.) Scholastic, Inc.
Tanabe, Yellow. Kekkaishi, Vol. 4. 2006. (ENG., Illus.). 208p. pap. 9.99 *(978-1-4215-0253-3(4))* Viz Media.
—Kekkaishi, Vol. 5. Tanabe, Yellow, illus. 2006. (ENG., Illus.). 208p. pap. 9.99 *(978-1-4215-0486-5(3))* Viz Media.
Taylor, Des. Cartoons & Manga. 2012. (Master This! Ser.). (Illus.). 32p. (J). lib. bdg. 25.25 *(978-1-4488-5283-3(8)*, PowerKids Pr.) Rosen Publishing Group, Inc., The.
Telgemeier, Raina. Drama. 2012. (ENG., Illus.). 240p. (J). (gr. 5-9). 24.99 *(978-0-545-32698-8(2))*; pap. 10.99 *(978-0-545-32699-5(0))* Scholastic, Inc. (Graphix).
—Ghosts. Telgemeier, Raina, illus. 2016. (ENG., Illus.). 256p. (J). (gr. 3-7). 24.99 *(978-0-545-54061-2(5)*, Graphix) Scholastic, Inc.
—Sisters. 2014. (ENG., Illus.). 208p. (J). (gr. 3-7). 24.99 *(978-0-545-54059-9(3))*; pap. 10.99 *(978-0-545-54060-5(7))* Scholastic, Inc. (Graphix).
—Sisters. 2014. lib. bdg. 22.10 *(978-0-606-36038-8(7))* Turtleback Bks.
—Smile. 2010. 21.00 *(978-1-60686-896-6(9))* Perfection Learning Corp.
—Smile. 2010. (ENG.). 224p. (J). (gr. 3-7). 24.99 *(978-0-545-13205-3(3))*; (Illus.). pap. 10.99 *(978-0-545-13206-0(1))* Scholastic, Inc. (Graphix).
—Smile. 2010. lib. bdg. 22.10 *(978-0-606-14082-9(4)*, Turtleback) Turtleback Bks.
Temple, Bob. A Nose for Danger, 1 vol. Harpster, Steve, illus. 2006. (Jimmy Sniffles Ser.). (ENG.). 40p. (gr. 1-3). lib. bdg. 23.99 *(978-1-59889-036-5(0)*, Graphic Sparks) Stone Arch Bks.
Thompson, Craig. Space Dumplins. 2015. (ENG.). 320p. (J). (gr. 3-7). 24.99 *(978-0-545-56541-7(3))*; pap. 14.99 *(978-0-545-56543-1(X))* Scholastic, Inc. (Graphix).
Tokyopop Staff, creator. Contents under Pressure, Vol. 3. 2005. (Lilo & Stitch Ser.). (Illus.). 89p. (gr. 3-7). pap. 14.99 *(978-1-59532-069-8(5)*, Tokyopop Kids) TOKYOPOP, Inc.
Tolstikova, Dasha. A Year Without Mom, 1 vol. 2015. (ENG., Illus.). 176p. (J). (gr. 4-9). 19.95 *(978-1-55498-692-7(3))* Groundwood Bks. CAN. Dist: Publishers Group West (PGW).
Tomita, Sukehiro. Young Love, Vol. 7. Yazawa, Nao, illus. 2004. (Wedding Peach Ser.). (ENG.). 200p. pap. 9.95 *(978-1-59116-450-0(8))* Viz Media.
Toriyama, Akira. Dragon Ball Z. Toriyama, Akira, illus. 2006. (Dragon Ball Z Ser.: 25). (ENG., Illus.). 208p. pap. 9.99 *(978-1-4215-0404-9(9))* Viz Media.
—Dragon Ball Z, Vol. 22. Toriyama, Akira, illus. 2005. (ENG., Illus.). 192p. pap. 9.99 *(978-1-4215-0051-5(5))* Viz Media.
—Dragon Ball Z, Vol. 24. Toriyama, Akira, illus. 2006. (ENG., Illus.). 208p. pap. 9.99 *(978-1-4215-0273-1(9))* Viz Media.
Torres, J. Charge of the Army Eternal, 1 vol. Davis, Dan & Suriano, Andy, illus. 2013. (Batman: the Brave & the Bold Ser.). (ENG.). 32p. (gr. 2-3). 22.60 *(978-1-4342-4706-3(6))* Stone Arch Bks.
Turner, Ginger & Shimpi, Shekhar. Gold Mine! The California Gold Rush Story. 2004. (Illus.). 44p. (J). pap. 15.95 *(978-0-9742502-3-6(6))* Gossamer Bks., LLC.
Turner, Michael. Michael Turner's Soulfire, Vol. 1. 2012. (ENG., Illus.). 376p. (YA). pap. 39.99 *(978-0-9823628-6-0(2)*, 9780982362860) Aspen MLT, Inc.
Uderzo, Albert. EL ESCUDO ARVERNO. 2009. (SPA., Illus.). 52p. 19.95 *(978-84-345-6729-0(6))* Grupo Anaya, S.A. ESP. Dist: Baker & Taylor Bks.
—LA HOZ DE ORO. 2009. (SPA., Illus.). 48p. 19.95 *(978-84-345-6720-7(2))* Grupo Anaya, S.A. ESP. Dist: Baker & Taylor Bks.
Ueda, Miwa. Peach Girl Vol. 11: Change of Heart. Ueda, Miwa, illus. 2004. (Illus.). (YA). pap. 9.99 *(978-1-59182-500-5(8))* TOKYOPOP, Inc.

UNESCO. Wangari Maathai. 2016. (ENG., Illus.). 112p. (J). (gr. 3-7). 13.95 *(978-0-00-814935-2(6))* HarperCollins Pubs. Ltd. GBR. Dist: Independent Pubs. Group.

Van Hamme, Jean. The Curse of the 30 Pieces of Silver, Pt. 1. Sterne, René & De Spiegeleer, Chantal, illus. 2012. (Blake & Mortimer Ser.: 13). (ENG.). 62p. (J). (gr. 5-12). pap. 15.95 *(978-1-84918-125-9(X))* CineBook GBR. Dist: National Bk. Network.

—Thorgal Vol. 4: La Galera Negra Rosinski, Grzegorz, illus. 2004. Orig. Title: Thorgal: la Galere Negra. (SPA.). 48p. pap. 16.95 *(978-1-59497-009-2(2))* Public Square Bks.

van Hamme, Jean. Thorgal - City of the Lost God, Vol. 6. Rosinski, Grzegorz, illus. 2009. (Thorgal Ser.: 6). (ENG.). 96p. pap. 19.95 *(978-1-84918-001-6(6))* CineBook GBR. Dist: National Bk. Network.

Vansant, Wayne. The Red Baron: The Graphic History of Richthofen's Flying Circus & the Air War in WWI. 2014. (Zenith Graphic Histories Ser.). (ENG., Illus.). 104p. pap. 19.99 *(978-0-7603-4602-0(X)*, 076034602X, Zenith Pr.) Quarto Publishing Group USA.

Various. Shrek TP Volume 1 Limited Edition Collection. 2012. (ENG., Illus.). 112p. pap. 14.95 *(978-1-934944-91-2(2)*, 9781934944912) Ape Entertainment.

Various Authors Staff. Fairy Tale Comics: Classic Tales Told by Extraordinary Cartoonists. Duffy, Chris, ed. Hernandez, Gilbert & Mazzucchellil, David, illus. 2013. (ENG.). 128p. (J). (gr. 1-7). 21.99 *(978-1-59643-823-1(1)*, 9781596438231, First Second Bks.) Roaring Brook Pr.

Vehlmann, Fabien. Green Manor Pt. 1: Assassins & Gentleman. Bodart, Denis, illus. 2008. (Expresso Collection). (ENG.). 56p. pap. 13.95 *(978-1-905460-53-3(8))* CineBook GBR. Dist: National Bk. Network.

Venditti, Robert & Riordan, Rick. The Sea of Monsters. 2013. (Percy Jackson & the Olympians Graphic Novels Ser.: 2). (J). lib. bdg. 24.50 *(978-0-606-23611-9(2)*, Turtleback) Turtleback Bks.

—The Titan's Curse. Futaki, Attila & Guilhaumond, Gregory, illus. 2013. (Percy Jackson & the Olympians Ser.). (ENG.). 128p. (J). (gr. 5-9). 19.99 *(978-1-4231-4530-1(5))* Disney Pr.

Wacholtz, Anthony. Mummies & Sound, 1 vol. Mallea, Cristian, illus. 2013. (Monster Science Ser.). (ENG.). 32p. (gr. 3-4). pap. 8.10 *(978-1-62065-818-5(6))*; 47.70 *(978-1-62065-819-2(4))*; 30.65 *(978-1-4296-9930-3(2))* Capstone Press of Coughlan Cos. (Graphic Library).

Waid, Mark. Fantastic Four, Vol. 1. Wieringo, Mike, illus. 2004. (Fantastic Four Ser.). 368p. (YA). 29.99 *(978-0-7851-1486-4(6))* Marvel Worldwide, Inc.

Wallis, Pete & Wilkins, Joseph. What Are You Staring At? A Comic about Restorative Justice in Schools. 2016. (ENG., Illus.). 36p. (J). 19.95 *(978-1-78592-016-5(2)*, 8283) Kingsley, Jessica Pubs. GBR. Dist: Macmillan Distribution Ltd.

Watase, Yû. Imadoki!, Vol. 4: Nowadays, 5 vols. Watase, Yû, illus. 2004. (ENG., Illus.). 200p. pap. 9.95 *(978-1-59116-618-4(7))* Viz Media.

Watase, Yuu. Imadoki!, Vol. 2, 5 vols. Watase, Yuu, illus. 2004. (ENG., Illus.). 200p. pap. 9.95 *(978-1-59116-469-2(9))* Viz Media.

—Imadoki!, Vol. 3. Watase, Yuu, illus. 2004. (ENG., Illus.). 200p. pap. 9.95 *(978-1-59116-504-0(0))* Viz Media.

—Imadoki!, Vol. 5, 5 vols. Watase, Yuu, illus. 2005. (ENG., Illus.). 200p. pap. 9.95 *(978-1-59116-619-1(5))* Viz Media.

—The Mysterious Play. Watase, Yuu, illus. 2nd ed. 2005. (Fushigi Yugi Ser.: 8). (ENG., Illus.). 200p. pap. 9.95 *(978-1-59116-087-8(1))* Viz Media.

Watson, Esther Pearl. Whatcha Mean, What's a Zine? The Art of Making Zines & Mini-Comics. Todd, Mark, illus. 2006. (ENG.). 112p. (YA). (gr. 7). pap. 13.99 *(978-0-618-56315-9(6))* Houghton Mifflin Harcourt Publishing Co.

Weiss, Lynne. Frederick Douglass & the Abolitionist Movement. 2013. (Jr. Graphic African American History Ser.). (Illus.). 24p. (J). (gr. 3-6). pap. 63.60 *(978-1-4777-1452-2(9))*; (ENG., pap. 10.60 *(978-1-4777-1451-5(0))*; (ENG., lib. bdg. 25.25 *(978-1-4777-1313-6(1))* Rosen Publishing Group, Inc., The. (PowerKids Pr.).

Weissman, Steven. The Kid Firechief. 2004. (ENG., Illus.). 96p. pap. 12.95 *(978-1-56097-596-0(2))* Fantagraphics Bks.

—White Flower Day. 2003. (ENG., Illus.). 112p. pap. 14.95 *(978-1-56097-514-4(8))* Fantagraphics Bks.

Welsh, C. E. L. Space Race. Jones, K. L., illus. 2011. (Campfire Graphic Novels Ser.). (ENG.). 68p. (YA). (gr. 5-12). pap. 9.99 *(978-93-80028-62-0(8)*, Campfire) Steerforth Pr.

West, David. Dawn Horse. Poluzzi, Alessandro, illus. 2017. (Graphic Prehistoric Animals Ser.). 32p. (gr. 3-7). lib. bdg. 31.35 *(978-1-62588-407-7(9))* Black Rabbit Bks.

—Woolly Mammoth. Poluzzi, Alessandro, illus. 2017. (Graphic Prehistoric Animals Ser.). 32p. (gr. 3-7). lib. bdg. 31.35 *(978-1-62588-414-5(1))* Black Rabbit Bks.

Which Pet Measures Up? 2003. (J). per. *(978-1-932524-02-4(9))* Region IV Education Service Ctr.

Whitaker-Taylor, Kandice. A Child Is Born. 2012. 20p. pap. 9.99 *(978-1-62419-090-2(1))* Salem Author Services.

Whitten, Samantha & Lee, Jeannie, illus. How to Draw Manga Chibis & Cute Critters. 2013. (Walter Foster Studio Ser.). 128p. (J). (gr. 3-8). 35.65 *(978-1-936309-93-1(9))* Quarto Publishing Group USA.

Wilson, Bob. Stanley Bagshaw & the Short-Sighted Football Trainer. 2006. (Stanley Bagshaw Ser.). (Illus.). 32p. (J). (gr. k-2). pap. 6.95 *(978-1-903015-26-1(X))* Barn Owl Bks, London GBR. Dist: Independent Pubs. Group.

Winick, Judd. The Boy Who Crashed to Earth. 2015. (Hilo Ser.: 1). (ENG., Illus.). 208p. (J). (gr. 3-7). 16.99 *(978-0-385-38618-0(4)*, Random Hse. Bks. for Young Readers) Random Hse. Children's Bks.

—The Great Big Boom. 2017. (Hilo Ser.: 3). (ENG., Illus.). 208p. (J). (gr. 3-7). 13.99 *(978-0-385-38620-3(6))*; lib. bdg. 16.99 *(978-0-385-38621-0(4))* Random Hse. Children's Bks. (Random Hse. Bks. for Young Readers).

—Saving the Whole Wide World. 2016. (Hilo Ser.: 2). (ENG., Illus.). 208p. (J). (gr. 3-7). 16.99 *(978-0-385-38624-1(9))*;Bk. 2. 13.99 *(978-0-385-38623-4(0))* Random Hse. Children's Bks. (Random Hse. Bks. for Young Readers).

Wohlrabe, Sarah C. A Visit to the Library. Thompson, Jeffrey, illus. (First Graphics: My Community Ser.). (ENG.). 24p. (gr. 1-2). 2011. pap. 35.70 *(978-1-4296-6404-2(5))* 2010. lib. bdg. 23.99 *(978-1-4296-5371-8(X))* Capstone Press of Coughlan Cos.

Woog, Adam. Robert Kirkman. 2015. (People in the News Ser.). (ENG., Illus.). 128p. (J). (gr. 7-10). 39.40 *(978-1-4205-1247-2(6)*, Lucent Bks.) Cengage Gale.

World Book, Inc Staff, contrib. by. The Circulatory System. 2013. (J). *(978-0-7166-1842-3(7))* World Bk., Inc.

—The Respiratory System. 2013. (Illus.). 32p. (J). *(978-0-7166-1847-8(8))* World Bk., Inc.

—Subtraction. 2013. (Illus.). 32p. (J). pap. *(978-0-7166-1478-4(2))* World Bk., Inc.

Wyss, Johann David. The Swiss Family Robinson. Tayal, Amit, illus. 2011. (Campfire Graphic Novels Ser.). (ENG.). 88p. (YA). (gr. 3-7). pap. 11.99 *(978-93-80028-47-7(4)*, Campfire) Steerforth Pr.

Yamamoto, Satoshi, illus. Pokemon Omega Ruby Alpha Sapphire, Vol. 2. 2016. (Pokemon Ser.: 2). (ENG.). 112p. (J). pap. 4.99 *(978-1-4215-9016-5(6))* Viz Media.

—Pokémon X*Y, Vol. 8. 2016. (Pokemon Ser.: 8). (ENG.). 96p. (J). pap. 4.99 *(978-1-4215-8779-0(3))* Viz Media.

Yang, Gene Luen. American Born Chinese. 2011. 10.04 *(978-0-7848-3435-0(0)*, Everbind) Marco Bk. Co.

—American Born Chinese. 2011. 20.00 *(978-1-60686-920-8(5))* 2007. 29.00 *(978-0-7569-7745-0(2))* Perfection Learning Corp.

—American Born Chinese. Yang, Gene Luen & Pien, Lark, illus. 2007. (ENG.). 240p. (YA). (gr. 7-18). 23.99 *(978-1-59643-373-1(6)*, 9781596433731, First Second Bks.) Roaring Brook Pr.

—American Born Chinese. Yang, Gene Luen, illus. rev. ed. 2006. (ENG., Illus.). 240p. (YA). (gr. 7-12). pap. 18.99 *(978-1-59643-152-2(0)*, 9781596431522, First Second Bks.) Roaring Brook Pr.

—American Born Chinese. Yang, Gene Luen, illus. 2008. (ENG., Illus.). 240p. (YA). (gr. 7-12). pap. 10.99 *(978-0-312-38448-7(3)*, 9780312384487) Square Fish.

—American Born Chinese. 2008. (YA). lib. bdg. 22.10 *(978-0-606-14484-1(6)*, Turtleback) Turtleback Bks.

—Boxers & Saints Boxed Set. 2013. (Boxers & Saints Ser.: 1). (YA). lib. bdg. 31.80 *(978-0-606-32304-8(X)*, Turtleback) Turtleback Bks.

—Saints. 2013. (Boxers & Saints Ser.: 2). (YA). lib. bdg. 28.15 *(978-0-606-32305-5(8)*, Turtleback) Turtleback Bks.

—Secret Coders. Holmes, Mike, illus. 2015. (Secret Coders Ser.: 1). (ENG.). 96p. (J). (gr. 3-7). 17.99 *(978-1-62672-276-7(5)*, 9781626722767); pap. 9.99 *(978-1-62672-075-6(4)*, 9781626720756) Roaring Brook Pr. (First Second Bks.).

—The Shadow Hero. Liew, Sonny, illus. 2014. (ENG.). 176p. (YA). (gr. 7-12). pap. 17.99 *(978-1-59643-697-8(2)*, 9781596436978, First Second Bks.) Roaring Brook Pr.

—The Shadow Hero. Liew, Sonny, illus. 2014. (YA). lib. bdg. 30.60 *(978-0-606-35521-6(9))* Turtleback Bks.

Yang, Gene Luen & Pien, Lark. Boxers & Saints Boxed Set. Yang, Gene Luen, illus. 2013. (Boxers & Saints Ser.: 1). (ENG., Illus.). (YA). (gr. 7). 512p. 34.99 *(978-1-59643-924-5(6)*, 9781596439245); 336p. pap. 18.99 *(978-1-59643-359-5(0)*, 9781596433595) Roaring Brook Pr. (First Second Bks.).

—Saints. Yang, Gene Luen, illus. 2013. (Boxers & Saints Ser.: 2). (ENG., Illus.). 176p. (YA). (gr. 7). pap. 15.99 *(978-1-59643-689-3(1)*, 9781596436893, First Second Bks.) Roaring Brook Pr.

Yomtov, Nel. The Apollo 11 Moon Landing: July 20 1969, 1 vol. 2014. (24-Hour History Ser.). (ENG.). 48p. (gr. 3-5). pap. 8.95 *(978-1-4329-9298-9(8)*, NA-h) Heinemann-Raintree.

—The Attack on Pearl Harbor: December 7 1941, 1 vol. 2014. (24-Hour History Ser.). (ENG.). 48p. (gr. 3-5). pap. 8.95 *(978-1-4329-9299-6(6)*, NA-h) Heinemann-Raintree.

—Night of Rebellion! Nickolas Flux & the Boston Tea Party, 1 vol. Ginevra, Dante, illus. 2014. (Nickolas Flux History Chronicles Ser.). (ENG.). 32p. (gr. 3-4). lib. bdg. 30.65 *(978-1-4765-3946-1(4)*, Graphic Library) Capstone Press of Coughlan Cos.

Yomtov, Nel, et al. 24-Hour History, 1 vol. 2014. (24-Hour History Ser.). (ENG.). 48p. (gr. 3-5). lib. bdg. 166.60 *(978-1-4329-9297-2(X)*, NA-h) Heinemann-Raintree.

Yomtov, Nelson. Courage on the Battlefield: True Tales of Survival in the Military. 2015. (True Stories of Survival Ser.). (ENG., Illus.). 32p. (gr. 3-4). lib. bdg. 30.65 *(978-1-4914-6571-4(9))* Capstone Press of Coughlan Cos.

—How to Write a Comic Book. Petelinsek, Kathleen, illus. 2013. (Explorer Junior Library: How to Write Ser.). (ENG.). 24p. (J). (gr. 1-4). lib. bdg. 25.64 *(978-1-62431-187-1(3)*, 203072) Cherry Lake Publishing.

—Terrors from the Deep: True Tales of Surviving Shark Attacks. 2015. (True Stories of Survival Ser.). (ENG., Illus.). 32p. (gr. 3-4). lib. bdg. 30.65 *(978-1-4914-6573-8(5))* Capstone Press of Coughlan Cos.

—Tracking an Assassin! Nickolas Flux & the Assassination of Abraham Lincoln, 1 vol. Pinelli, Amerigo, illus. 2014. (Nickolas Flux History Chronicles Ser.). (ENG.). 32p. (gr. 3-4). lib. bdg. 30.65 *(978-1-4914-0252-8(0)*, Graphic Library) Capstone Press of Coughlan Cos.

Yoshida, Tatsuo. Speed Racer Set: Mach Go Go Go, 2 vols. 2008. (ENG., Illus.). 700p. (YA). (gr. 8). 39.95 *(978-1-56970-731-9(6)*, 9781569707319) Digital Manga Publishing.

Young, J. E. Horror in Space. Huddleston, Courtney, illus. 2011. (Twisted Journeys (r) Ser.: 18). (ENG.). 112p. (J). (gr. 4-7). lib. bdg. 27.93 *(978-0-8225-9265-5(7)*, Graphic Universe™) Lerner Publishing Group.

Yudetamago. The Kinnikuman Legancy, Vol. 8. 2005. (Ultimate Muscle Ser.: 8). (ENG.). 224p. pap. 7.95 *(978-1-59116-997-0(6))* Viz Media.

Zatch Bell 1: The Lightning Boy From Another World. 2005. 24.98 *(978-1-4215-0215-1(1))* Viz Media.

COMIC BOOKS, STRIPS, ETC.—HISTORY AND CRITICISM

Bonser, Randall. Comics Graphic Novels & Manga. 2017. (It Happened to Me Ser.: 54). (ENG., Illus.). 326p. 45.00 ***(978-1-4422-6839-5(5))*** Rowman & Littlefield Publishers, Inc.

Comics: Investigate the History & Technology of American Cartooning. 2014. (Build It Yourself Ser.). (ENG., Illus.). 128p. (J). (gr. 3-7). pap. 17.95 *(978-1-61930-254-9(3))* Open City Bks.

Dorling Kindersley Publishing Staff & Snider, Brandon T. DC Comics Ultimate Character Guide. 2011. (ENG., Illus.). 208p. (J). (gr. 2-5). 16.99 *(978-0-7566-8261-3(4)*, DK Children) Dorling Kindersley Publishing, Inc.

Guillain, Charlotte. What Is a Graphic Novel? 2015. (Connect with Text Ser.). (ENG.). 32p. (gr. 2-4). 30.65 *(978-1-4109-6827-2(8)*, Raintree Perspectives) Heinemann-Raintree.

Harris, Ashley Rae. Graphic Novels, 1 vol. 2013. (Hot Topics in Media Ser.). (ENG.). 48p. (J). (gr. 3-6). lib. bdg. 32.79 *(978-1-61783-733-3(4))*; (Illus.). pap. 15.64 *(978-1-61783-783-8(0))* ABDO Publishing Co.

Kishimoto, Masashi. Naruto Illustration Book. Kishimoto, Masashi, illus. 2010. (ENG., Illus.). 100p. pap. 19.99 *(978-1-4215-3869-3(5))* Viz Media.

—Naruto: The Official Character Data Book. Kishimoto, Masashi, illus. 2012. (ENG., Illus.). 360p. pap. 16.99 *(978-1-4215-4125-9(4))* Viz Media.

Marcovitz, Hal. Comic Book Art. 2016. (ENG.). 80p. (J). 38.60 *(978-1-60152-944-2(9))* ReferencePoint Pr., Inc.

Nobleman, Marc Tyler. Boys of Steel: The Creators of Superman. MacDonald, Ross, illus. 2013. (ENG.). 40p. (J). (gr. 5-6). 7.99 *(978-0-449-81063-7(1)*, Dragonfly Bks.) Random Hse. Children's Bks.

Perkins, Chloe. The Great American Story of Charlie Brown, Snoopy, & the Peanuts Gang! Burroughs, Scott, illus. 2017. (History of Fun Stuff Ser.). (ENG.). 48p. (J). (gr. 1-3). pap. 3.99 ***(978-1-4814-9553-0(4)***, Simon Spotlight) Simon Spotlight.

Robson, Eddie. Comic Books & Manga. 2008. (ENG., Illus.). 32p. (J). (gr. 6-10). lib. bdg. *(978-0-7787-3813-8(2))* Crabtree Publishing Co.

Smith, David. History of Comic Books. 2016. (TIME for KIDS(r) Nonfiction Readers Ser.). (Illus.). 48p. (J). (gr. 6-6). 9.99 *(978-1-4938-3595-9(5))* Teacher Created Materials, Inc.

Smith, David. History of Comic Books. 2016. (Time for Kids Nonfiction Readers Ser.). (ENG.). (J). (gr. 6). lib. bdg. 20.85 ***(978-0-606-39531-1(8))*** Turtleback Bks.

Smith, Jeff. Bone. Hamaker, Steve, illus. 2010. (Bone Ser.). (ENG.). 128p. (J). (gr. 3-7). pap., instr.'s hndbk. ed. 9.99 *(978-0-545-21142-0(5)*, Graphix) Scholastic, Inc.

—Bone Handbook. 2010. (Bone Graphic Novels Ser.). lib. bdg. 20.85 *(978-0-606-15182-5(6)*, Turtleback) Turtleback Bks.

Superheroes of Science. 2015. (Superheroes of Science Ser.). (ENG.). 48p. (J). (gr. 6-6). pap., pap., pap. 84.30 *(978-1-4824-3506-1(3))* Stevens, Gareth Publishing LLLP.

Wallace, Daniel & Dorling Kindersley Publishing Staff. Batman - The World of the Dark Knight. 2012. (ENG., Illus.). 200p. (J). (gr. 1-4). 24.99 *(978-0-7566-9249-0(0)*, DK Children) Dorling Kindersley Publishing, Inc.

Zawisza, Doug. Hawkman Companion. 2008. (ENG., Illus.). 208p. pap. 24.95 *(978-1-893905-93-1(4)*, 9781893905931) TwoMorrows Publishing.

COMIC LITERATURE

see Comedy; Satire

COMIC OPERA

see Opera

COMMANDMENTS, TEN

see Ten Commandments

COMMENTARIES, BIBLICAL

see Bible—Commentaries

COMMERCE

see also Banks and Banking; Business; Markets; Merchants; Retail Trade; Statistics; Stock Exchanges; Stocks; Trade Routes; Transportation

ABDO Publishing Company Staff & Marcovitz, Hal. Fair Trade, 1 vol. 2011. (Essential Issues Set 2 Ser.). (ENG., Illus.). 112p. (J). (gr. 6-12). lib. bdg. 35.64 *(978-1-61714-772-2(9)*, Essential Library) ABDO Publishing Co.

Bow, James. Your Guide to Trade in the Middle Ages. 2017. (Destination: Middle Ages Ser.). (ENG., Illus.). 32p. (J). ***(978-0-7787-2996-9(6))***; pap. ***(978-0-7787-3052-1(2))*** Crabtree Publishing Co.

Bowden, Rob. Trade. 2009. (J). 32.80 *(978-1-59920-098-9(8))* Black Rabbit Bks.

Brezina, Corona. How Imports & Exports Work. 2011. (Real World Economics Ser.). (ENG.). 80p. (YA). lib. bdg. 33.25 *(978-1-4488-1274-5(7))* Rosen Publishing Group, Inc., The.

Buell, Tonya. Careers with Successful Dot-Com Companies. 2009. (Library of E-Commerce & Internet Careers Ser.). 64p. (gr. 5-5). 58.50 *(978-1-60853-584-2(3))* Rosen Publishing Group, Inc., The.

Burton, Margie, et al. Going Places. 2011. (Early Connections Ser.). (J). *(978-1-61672-490-0(0))* Benchmark Education Co.

Canino, Kate. How Trade Deficits Work. 2011. (Real World Economics Ser.). (ENG.). 80p. (YA). lib. bdg. 33.25 *(978-1-4488-1271-4(2))* Rosen Publishing Group, Inc., The.

Caraccilo, Dominic. E-Tailing: Careers Selling over the Web. 2009. (Library of E-Commerce & Internet Careers Ser.). 64p. (gr. 5-5). 58.50 *(978-1-60853-587-3(8))* Rosen Publishing Group, Inc., The.

Catel, Patrick. Money & Trade, 1 vol. 2011. (Understanding Money Ser.). (ENG.). 48p. (gr. 3-5). pap. 9.95 *(978-1-4329-4642-5(0))*; 33.32 *(978-1-4329-4635-7(8))* Heinemann-Raintree. (Heinemann InfoSearch).

Cefrey, Holly. The Interstate Commerce Act: The Government Takes Control of Trade Between States. 2009. (America's Industrial Society in the 19th Century Ser.). 32p. (gr. 4-4). 47.90 *(978-1-61511-342-2(8))* Rosen Publishing Group, Inc., The.

—The Interstate Commerce ACT: The Government Takes Control of Trade Between the States. 2004. (America's Industrial Society in the 19th Century Ser.). (ENG., Illus.). 32p. (gr. 5-8). pap. 10.00 *(978-0-8239-4282-4(1))* Rosen Publishing Group, Inc., The.

Connolly, Sean. International Trade. 2010. (World Economy Explained Ser.). 48p. (YA). (gr. 7-12). 35.65 *(978-1-60753-080-0(5))* Amicus Publishing.

—International Trade. 2012. (Illus.). 48p. (gr. 6-10). pap. 9.95 *(978-1-926722-78-8(7))* Saunders Bk. Co. CAN. Dist: RiverStream Publishing.

Connolly, Sean & Pipe, Jim. International Trade. 2011. (On the Edge Ser.). 32p. (YA). (gr. 3-6). lib. bdg. 28.50 *(978-1-59920-520-5(3))* Black Rabbit Bks.

Craig, Tom. Internet: Technology, People, Process. 2003. (Media Wise Ser.). 64p. (J). lib. bdg. 28.50 *(978-1-58340-257-3(8))* Black Rabbit Bks.

Davidson, Tish. Global Trade in the Ancient World, Vol. 7. 2016. (Understanding Global Trade & Commerce Ser.: Vol. 7). (ENG., Illus.). 80p. (J). (gr. 7-12). 24.95 *(978-1-4222-3666-6(8))* Mason Crest.

DeCarlo, Jacqueline. Fair Trade & How It Works. 2011. (Contemporary Issues Ser.). (Illus.). 166 ndash; 308p. (YA). (gr. 9-12). 37.95 *(978-1-4488-1865-5(6))* Rosen Publishing Group, Inc., The.

Earl, C. F. Building a Business in the Virtual World. Madrian, Brigitte, ed. 2013. (Young Adult Library of Small Business & Finance Ser.). (Illus.). 64p. (J). (gr. 7-18). pap. 12.95 *(978-1-4222-2980-4(7))* Mason Crest.

Eugster, Rachel & Lassieur, Allison. Trade & Commerce in the Early Islamic World. 2012. (Life in the Early Islamic World Ser.). (ENG., Illus.). 48p. (J). pap. *(978-0-7787-2179-6(5))* Crabtree Publishing Co.

Fitzgerald, Lee. Goods & Services. 2013. (InfoMax Readers Ser.). (ENG.). 24p. (J). (gr. 2-3). pap. 8.25 *(978-1-4777-2415-6(X))*; pap. 49.50 *(978-1-4777-2416-3(8))* Rosen Publishing Group, Inc., The. (Rosen Classroom).

Frost, Randall. The Globalization of Trade. 2004. (Understanding Global Issues Ser.). (Illus.). 56p. (J). (gr. 10-12). lib. bdg. 29.95 *(978-1-58340-363-1(9))* Black Rabbit Bks.

Gilbert, Sara. The Story of Amazon.com. 2012. (Built for Success Ser.). (Illus.). 48p. (J). (gr. 5-12). 23.95 *(978-1-60818-174-2(X)*, Creative Education) Creative Co., The.

Greathead, Helen. My Chocolate Bar & Other Foods. 2016. (Well Made, Fair Trade Ser.). (ENG., Illus.). 32p. (J). (gr. 5-8). *(978-0-7787-2714-9(9))* Crabtree Publishing Co.

Guidone, Lisa M. What Happens at a Museum? / ¿Qué pasa en un Museo? 2008. (Where People Work/Dónde Trabaja la Gente? Ser.). (SPA.). 24p. (gr. -1-3). pap. 8.15 *(978-0-8368-9381-6(6)*, Weekly Reader Leveled Readers) Stevens, Gareth Publishing LLLP.

—What Happens at a Museum?/¿Qué Pasa en un Museo? 2008. (Where People Work/Dónde Trabaja la Gente? Ser.). (ENG & SPA.). 24p. (J). (gr. -1-3). lib. bdg. 22.00 *(978-0-8368-9282-6(8)*, Weekly Reader Leveled Readers) Stevens, Gareth Publishing LLLP.

Harmon, Daniel E. The Global Community: Techniques & Strategies of Trade, Vol. 7. 2016. (Understanding Global Trade & Commerce Ser.: Vol. 7). (ENG., Illus.). 80p. (J). (gr. 7-12). 24.95 *(978-1-4222-3664-2(1))* Mason Crest.

Helweg, Laura. Global Trade in the Modern World, Vol. 7. 2016. (Understanding Global Trade & Commerce Ser.: Vol. 7). (ENG., Illus.). 80p. (J). (gr. 7-12). 24.95 *(978-1-4222-3667-3(6))* Mason Crest.

Herschbach, Elisabeth. Global Inequalities & the Fair Trade Movement, Vol. 7. 2016. (Understanding Global Trade & Commerce Ser.: Vol. 7). (ENG., Illus.). 80p. (J). (gr. 7-12). 24.95 *(978-1-4222-3665-9(X))* Mason Crest.

Houghton, Gillian. Goods & Services. 2009. (Invest Kids Ser.). 24p. (ENG., Illus.). (J). (gr. 2-5). pap. 8.25 *(978-1-4358-3210-7(8)*, 1291654); (gr. 2-3). 42.50 *(978-1-61513-617-9(7))*; (Illus.). (J). lib. bdg. 22.60 *(978-1-4358-2775-2(9)*, 1291654) Rosen Publishing Group, Inc., The. (PowerKids Pr.).

Hovanec, Erin. Careers as a Content Provider for the Web. 2009. (Library of E-Commerce & Internet Careers Ser.). 64p. (gr. 5-5). 58.50 *(978-1-60853-578-1(9))* Rosen Publishing Group, Inc., The.

Hutchings, Amy & Nations, Susan. What Happens at a Party Store?/¿Qué Pasa en una Tienda de Cosas para Fiestas? 2008. (Where People Work Ser.). 24p. (gr. -1-3). pap. 8.15 *(978-0-8368-9376-2(X))*; (SPA.). pap. 8.15 *(978-0-8368-9382-3(4))* Stevens, Gareth Publishing LLLP. (Weekly Reader Leveled Readers).

—What Happens at a Party Store?/¿Qué Pasa en una Tienda de Cosas para Fiestas. 2008. (Where People Work/Dónde Trabaja la Gente? Ser.). (ENG & SPA.). 24p. (J). (gr. -1-3). lib. bdg. 22.00 *(978-0-8368-9283-3(6)*, Weekly Reader Leveled Readers) Stevens, Gareth Publishing LLLP.

Jackson, Aurelia. Amazon(r): How Jeff Bezos Built the World's Largest Online Store. 2014. (Wizards of Technology Ser.: 10). 64p. (J). (gr. 7-18). 23.95 *(978-1-4222-3179-1(8))* Mason Crest.

Jones, Kari. A Fair Deal: Shopping for Social Justice, 1 vol. 2017. (Orca Footprints Ser.). (ENG., Illus.). 48p. (J). (gr. 3-7). 19.95 ***(978-1-4598-1043-3(0))*** Orca Bk. Pubs. USA.

Kallen, Stuart A. Internet Entrepreneurs. 2016. (ENG.). 80p. (J). (gr. 5-12). lib. bdg. *(978-1-68282-028-5(9))* ReferencePoint Pr., Inc.

La Bella, Laura. How Commodities Trading Works. 2011. (Real World Economics Ser.). (ENG.). 80p. (YA). lib. bdg. 33.25 *(978-1-4488-1273-8(9))* Rosen Publishing Group, Inc., The.

Larson, Jennifer S. Who's Buying? Who's Selling? Understanding Consumers & Producers. 2010. (Lightning Bolt Books — Exploring Economics Ser.). (ENG., Illus.). 32p. (gr. k-2). pap. 7.95 *(978-0-7613-5665-3(7))*; lib. bdg. 26.60 *(978-0-7613-3912-0(4))* Lerner Publishing Group.

Leppman, Elizabeth & Andrews, David. Business Without Borders: Globalization, 1 vol. 2010. (Global Marketplace Ser.). (ENG.). 56p. (gr. 6-9). 34.65 *(978-1-4329-3933-5(5)*, NA-h) Heinemann-Raintree.

MacDonald, Fiona. Travel & Trade in the Middle Ages. 2005. (World Almanac Library of the Middle Ages). (Illus.). 48p. (gr. 5-12). pap. 14.05 *(978-0-8368-5908-9(1))*; lib. bdg. 31.00 *(978-0-8368-5899-0(9))* Stevens, Gareth Publishing LLLP. (Gareth Stevens Secondary Library).

Mann, Charles. 1493 for Young People: From Columbus's Voyage to Globalization. 2016. (For Young People Ser.). (ENG., Illus.). 416p. (J). (gr. 7). pap. 18.95 *(978-1-60980-663-7(8)*, Triangle Square) Seven Stories Pr.

Mason, Helen. What Is Digital Entrepreneurship? 2016. (Your Start-Up Starts Now! a Guide to Entrepreneurship Ser.). (ENG.). 48p. (J). (gr. 5-8). *(978-0-7787-2740-8(8))* Crabtree Publishing Co.

Matthews, Sheelagh. Trade & Global Impact. 2010. (Illus.). 48p. *(978-1-55388-693-8(3))*; pap. *(978-1-55388-698-3(4))* Weigl Educational Pubs. Ltd.

Meyer, Susan. How Buying & Selling Futures Work. 2011. (Real World Economics Ser.). (ENG.). 80p. (YA). lib. bdg.

C
D

33.25 *(978-1-4488-1275-2(5))* Rosen Publishing Group, Inc., The.

Miller, Debra A. Fair Trade. 2010. (Current Controversies Ser.). (Illus.). 240p. (J). 40.95 *(978-0-7377-4703-4(X))*; pap. 28.45 *(978-0-7377-4704-1(8))* Cengage Gale. (Greenhaven Pr., Inc.).

Online Smarts. 2015. (Online Smarts Ser.). (ENG.). 32p. (J). (gr. 3-4). 151.62 *(978-0-7660-6684-7(3))* Enslow Pubs., Inc.

Oppedisano, Robert & McCoy, Lisa. Internet. 2nd rev. ed. 2011. (Career Launcher Ser.). 160p. (C). (gr. 9). 34.95 *(978-0-8160-7951-3(X)*, Ferguson Publishing Co.) Facts On File, Inc.

Penna, Christine. Careers in Network Engineering. 2009. (Library of E-Commerce & Internet Careers Ser.). 64p. (gr. 5-5). 58.50 *(978-1-60853-581-1(9))* Rosen Publishing Group, Inc., The.

Perritano, John. The Making of the Modern World: 1945 to the Present: Trade, Economic Life & Globalization, Vol. 9. van Dijk, Ruud, ed. 2016. (Making of the Modern World: 1945 to the Present Ser.: Vol. 9). (ENG., Illus.). 64p. (J). (gr. 7-12). 23.95 *(978-1-4222-3642-0(0))* Mason Crest.

Randolph, Ryan P. The Price You Pay: A Look at Supply & Demand. 2009. (Real Life Readers Ser.). 32p. (gr. 5-6). pap. 10.00 *(978-1-4358-0201-8(2)*, Rosen Classroom) Rosen Publishing Group, Inc., The.

Richardson, Hazel. Trade & Commerce in the Ancient World. Crabtree Publishing Staff, ed. 2011. (Life in the Ancient World Ser.: No. 6). (ENG.). 32p. (J). (gr. 5-8). pap. *(978-0-7787-1744-7(5))* Crabtree Publishing Co.

Scally, Robert. Jeff Bezos: Founder of Amazon & the Kindle. 2012. (Business Leaders Ser.). 112p. (YA). (gr. 7-12). 28.95 *(978-1-59935-178-0(1))* Reynolds, Morgan Inc.

Small, Cathleen. How to Start an Online Business. 2015. (J). lib. bdg. *(978-1-62713-541-2(3))* Cavendish Square Publishing.

Spilsbury, Richard. Global Economy, 1 vol. 2012. (Hot Topics Ser.). (ENG.). 64p. (gr. 7-8). 34.65 *(978-1-4329-6038-4(5)*, NA-h) Heinemann-Raintree.

Stinson, Paul. Sales, Marketing, Business & Finance. 2008. (Great Careers with a High School Diploma Ser.). 110p. (C). (gr. 9). 32.95 *(978-0-8160-7051-0(2)*, Ferguson Publishing Co.) Facts On File, Inc.

Suen, Anastasia. Downloading & Online Shopping Safety & Privacy. 2013. (21st Century Safety & Privacy Ser.). (Illus.). 64p. (J). (gr. 5-8). 31.95 *(978-1-4488-9571-7(5))*; pap. 77.70 *(978-1-4488-9583-0(9))*; pap. 12.95 *(978-1-4488-9582-3(0))* Rosen Publishing Group, Inc., The.

Sutherland, Adam. Amazon: The Business Behind the Everything Store. 2016. (Big Brands Ser.). (ENG., Illus.). 32p. (J). (gr. 4-6). 26.65 *(978-1-5124-0588-0(4))*; 39.99 *(978-1-5124-0592-7(2))* Lerner Publishing Group. (Lerner Pubns.).

Teichmann, Iris. Globalization. 2003. (In the News Ser.). (J). lib. bdg. 24.25 *(978-1-58340-397-6(3))* Black Rabbit Bks.

Uhl, Xina M. The Economics of Global Trade, Vol. 7. 2016. (Understanding Global Trade & Commerce Ser.: Vol. 7). (ENG., Illus.). 80p. (J). (gr. 7-12). 24.95 *(978-1-4222-3663-5(3))* Mason Crest.

Wright, Susan. Weapons of Mass Destruction: Illicit Trade & Trafficking. 2009. (Library of Weapons of Mass Destruction Ser.). 64p. (gr. 5-5). 58.50 *(978-1-60853-960-4(1))* Rosen Publishing Group, Inc., The.

Zodl, Joseph A. Export Import: Everything You & Your Company Need to Know to Compete in World Markets. 4th ed. 2005. (Illus.). 173p. (J). per. *(978-0-9773098-0-1(0))* IIEI Pr.

COMMERCIAL ART

see also Costume Design; Posters

Amidon Lusted, Marcia. Career Building Through Using Multimedia Art & Animation Tools. 2013. (Digital Career Building Ser.). 64p. (YA). (gr. 7-12). 31.95 *(978-1-4777-1725-7(0))*; pap. 12.95 *(978-1-4777-1743-1(9))* Rosen Publishing Group, Inc., The.

Career Building Through Using Multimedia Art & Animation Tools. 2013. (Digital Career Building Ser.). 64p. (YA). (gr. 7-12). pap. 77.70 *(978-1-4777-1745-5(5))* Rosen Publishing Group, Inc., The.

Mullins, Matt. Multimedia Artist & Animator. 2010. (21st Century Skills Library: Cool Careers Ser.). (ENG.). 32p. (gr. 4-8). lib. bdg. 28.50 *(978-1-60279-942-4(3)*, 200629) Cherry Lake Publishing.

COMMERCIAL AVIATION

see Aeronautics, Commercial

COMMERCIAL CORRESPONDENCE

see also English Language—Business English

Minden, Cecilia & Roth, Kate. How to Write a Business Letter. 2012. (Explorer Junior Library: Language Arts Explorer Junior Ser.). (ENG.). 24p. (gr. 1-4). pap. 12.79 *(978-1-61080-667-1(0)*, 202277) Cherry Lake Publishing.

—How to Write a Letter. 2011. (Explorer Junior Library: Language Arts Explorer Junior Ser.). (ENG.). 24p. (gr. 1-4). lib. bdg. 25.64 *(978-1-60279-991-2(1)*, 200982) Cherry Lake Publishing.

Roy, Jennifer Rozines & Gordon, Sherri Mabry. Sharpen Your Business Letter Writing Skills. 2011. (Sharpen Your Writing Skills Ser.). (Illus.). 64p. (J). (gr. 6-18). pap. 8.95 *(978-1-59845-377-5(7))*; lib. bdg. 29.27 *(978-0-7660-3972-8(2))* Enslow Pubs., Inc.

—You Can Write a Business Letter. 2003. (You Can Write Ser.). (Illus.). 64p. (J). (gr. 6-12). lib. bdg. 23.94 *(978-0-7660-2088-7(6))* Enslow Pubs., Inc.

COMMERCIAL EDUCATION

see Business Education

COMMERCIAL PRODUCTS

see also Manufactures; Marine Resources

Coad, John. Green Technology, 1 vol. 2011. (Sci-Hi: Science & Technology Ser.). (ENG., Illus.). 48p. (gr. 4-4). 33.32 *(978-1-4109-4272-2(4)*, Sci-Hi) Heinemann-Raintree.

Crabtree Publishing, creator. How Did That Get Here? 2007. (ENG.). 32p. (J). (gr. 4-8). pap. *(978-0-7787-2513-8(8))* Crabtree Publishing Co.

Fridell, Ron. Earth-Friendly Energy. 2009. pap. 58.95 *(978-0-7613-4692-0(9))* Lerner Publishing Group.

Scheunemann, Pam. Cool Stuff for Bath & Beauty: Creative Projects for Kids, 1 vol. 2012. (Cool Stuff Ser.). (ENG., Illus.). 32p. (J). (gr. 3-6). 28.50 *(978-1-61714-980-1(2))* ABDO Publishing Co.

Toth-Chernin, Jan. E-Textiles. 2013. (21st Century Skills Innovation Library: Makers As Innovators Ser.). (ENG., Illus.). 32p. (J). (gr. 4-8). lib. bdg. 28.50 *(978-1-62431-140-6(7)*, 202880) Cherry Lake Publishing.

Welsbacher, Anne. Earth-Friendly Design. 2009. pap. 58.95 *(978-0-7613-4693-7(7))* 2008. 72p. (YA). (gr. 4-7). lib. bdg. 30.60 *(978-0-8225-7564-1(7))* Lerner Publishing Group.

COMMERCIAL SCHOOLS

see Business Education

COMMERCIAL TRAVELERS

see Sales Personnel

COMMON MARKET

see European Economic Community

COMMON SCHOOLS

see Public Schools

COMMONWEALTH, THE

see Political Science

COMMONWEALTH OF NATIONS

Ganeri, Anita. All about the Commonwealth. 2016. (ENG., Illus.). 32p. (J). (gr. 4-7). pap. 10.99 *(978-1-4451-5005-5(0)*, Franklin Watts) Hachette Children's Group GBR. Dist: Hachette Bk. Group.

COMMUNAL LIVING

see Collective Settlements

COMMUNES

see Collective Settlements

COMMUNICABLE DISEASES

see also Bacteriology; Immunity; Insects As Carriers of Disease; Sexually Transmitted Diseases; Vaccination

Abramovitz, Melissa. Cystic Fibrosis. 2012. (Diseases & Disorders Ser.). (ENG., Illus.). 128p. (gr. 7-10). lib. bdg. 39.90 *(978-1-4205-0901-4(2)*, Lucent Bks.) Cengage Gale.

Adams, Jonathan S. Antibiotics. 2017. ***(978-1-5026-2873-2(2))*** Cavendish Square Publishing.

allman, toney. Infectious Disease Research. 2011. (Inside Science Ser.). (Illus.). 96p. (YA). (gr. 7-12). lib. bdg. 27.95 *(978-1-60152-177-4(4))* ReferencePoint Pr., Inc.

Allman, Toney, ed. Whooping Cough. 2012. (Diseases & Disorders Ser.). (ENG., Illus.). 128p. (J). (gr. 7-10). lib. bdg. 34.95 *(978-1-4205-0736-2(2)*, Lucent Bks.) Cengage Gale.

Asselin, Kristine Carlson. Dangerous Diseases: Scary Illnesses That Frighten the World, 1 vol. 2014. (Scary Science Ser.). (ENG.). 32p. (gr. 3-4). lib. bdg. 27.32 *(978-1-4765-3927-0(8)*, Fact Finders) Capstone Press of Coughlan Cos.

Asselin, Kristine Carlson & Lee, Sally. Scary Science, 1 vol. 2014. (Scary Science Ser.). (ENG.). 32p. (gr. 3-4). lib. bdg. 109.28 *(978-1-4765-7429-5(4)*, Fact Finders) Capstone Press of Coughlan Cos.

Ballard, Carol. Fighting Infectious Diseases. 2007. (Cutting Edge Medicine Ser.). (Illus.). 64p. (gr. 6-12). lib. bdg. 34.00 *(978-0-8368-7864-6(7)*, Gareth Stevens Secondary Library) Stevens, Gareth Publishing LLLP.

Bartoletti, Susan Campbell. Terrible Typhoid Mary: A True Story of the Deadliest Cook in America. 2015. (ENG., Illus.). 240p. (YA). (gr. 5-7). 18.99 *(978-0-544-31367-5(4)*, HMH Books For Young Readers) Houghton Mifflin Harcourt Publishing Co.

Bjorklund, Ruth. Cholera. 2010. (Health Alert 7 Ser.). 64p. (YA). (gr. 4-7). 32.79 *(978-0-7614-4820-4(9))* Marshall Cavendish Corp.

Brennan, Linda Crotta. Gulf Oil Spill Paperback. 2013. (J). 15.65 *(978-1-62403-022-2(X)*, Core Library) ABDO Publishing Co.

Brownlee, Christen. Cute, Furry, & Deadly: Diseases You Can Catch from Your Pet! 2007. (24/7: Science Behind the Scenes Ser.). (ENG., Illus.). 64p. (J). (gr. 9-12). pap. 7.95 *(978-0-531-18737-1(3)*, Watts, Franklin) Scholastic Library Publishing.

Cefrey, Holly. Yellow Fever. 2009. (Epidemics Ser.). 64p. (gr. 5-5). 58.50 *(978-1-61512-309-4(1))* Rosen Publishing Group, Inc., The.

Coleman, William. Cholera. 2nd rev. ed. 2008. (Deadly Diseases & Epidemics Ser.). (Illus.). 144p. (C). (gr. 9-18). 34.95 *(978-1-60413-232-8(9)*, Chelsea Hse.) Facts On File, Inc.

Colligan, L. H. Tick-Borne Illnesses. 2008. (Health Alert Ser.). 64p. (gr. 4-18). lib. bdg. 32.79 *(978-0-7614-2914-2(X)*, Benchmark Bks.) Marshall Cavendish Corp.

Cunningham, Kevin. Pandemics. 2011. (True Book(tm), A— Disasters Ser.). (Illus.). 48p. (J). lib. bdg. 31.00 *(978-0-531-25423-3(2))*; (ENG., pap. 6.95 *(978-0-531-26628-1(1))* Scholastic Library Publishing. (Children's Pr.).

Derkins, Susie. Legionnaire's Disease. 2009. (Epidemics Ser.). 64p. (gr. 5-5). 58.50 *(978-1-61512-289-9(3))* Rosen Publishing Group, Inc., The.

Diconsiglio, John. There's a Fungus among Us! True-Life Cases! 2007. (24/7: Science Behind the Scenes Ser.). (ENG., Illus.). 64p. (J). (gr. 9-12). pap. 7.95 *(978-0-531-17530-9(8)*, Watts, Franklin) Scholastic Library Publishing.

—There's a Fungus among Us! True Stories of Killer Molds. 2007. (24/7: Science Behind the Scenes Ser.). (ENG., Illus.). 64p. (J). (gr. 9-12). 29.00 *(978-0-531-12071-2(6)*, Watts, Franklin) Scholastic Library Publishing.

—When Birds Get Flu & Cows Go Mad! How Safe Are We? 2007. (24/7: Science Behind the Scenes Ser.). (ENG., Illus.). 64p. (J). (gr. 8-12). pap. 7.95 *(978-0-531-17528-6(6)*, Watts, Franklin) Scholastic Library Publishing.

Doeden, Matt. Can You Survive a Virus Outbreak? An Interactive Doomsday Adventure. 2015. (You Choose: Doomsday Ser.). (ENG., Illus.). 112p. (gr. 3-4). lib. bdg. 31.99 *(978-1-4914-5851-8(8)*, You Choose Bks.) Capstone Press of Coughlan Cos.

Drake, Jane & Love, Ann. Pandemic Survival: It's Why You're Alive. Slavin, Bill, illus. 2013. (ENG.). 124p. (J). (gr. 4-7). 22.95 *(978-1-77049-268-4(2)*, Tundra Bks.) Tundra Bks. CAN. Dist: Penguin Random Hse. LLC.

Emmeluth, Donald. Influenza. 2nd rev. ed. 2008. (Deadly Diseases & Epidemics Ser.). (Illus.). 152p. (C). (gr. 9-18). 34.95 *(978-1-60413-236-6(1)*, Chelsea Hse.) Facts On File, Inc.

Emmeluth, Donald, et al. Staphylococcus aureus Infections. 2nd rev. ed. 2011. (Deadly Diseases & Epidemics Ser.). (C). 34.95 *(978-1-61753-021-0(2)*, Chelsea Hse.) Facts On File, Inc.

Espejo, Roman. Do Infectious Diseases Pose a Threat? Greenhaven Press Editors, ed. 2013. (At Issue Ser.). (ENG.). 128p. (gr. 10-12). pap. 27.80 *(978-0-7377-6831-2(2))*; lib. bdg. 39.40 *(978-0-7377-6830-5(4))* Cengage Gale. (Greenhaven Pr., Inc.).

Farndon, John. Plague! Epidemics & Scourges Through the Ages. Dean, Venitia, illus. 2017. (Sickening History of Medicine Ser.). (ENG.). 32p. (J). (gr. 3-6). 26.65 *(978-1-5124-1557-5(X))*; 19.99 ***(978-1-5124-3634-1(8))***; 30.65 ***(978-1-5124-2709-7(8))***; 30.65 ***(978-1-5124-3632-7(1))*** Lerner Publishing Group.

Faulk, Michelle. The Case of the Flesh-Eating Bacteria: Annie Biotica Solves Skin Disease Crimes. 2013. (Body System Disease Investigations Ser.). 48p. (J). (gr. 5-12). pap. 8.95 *(978-1-4644-0224-1(8))*; lib. bdg. 25.27 *(978-0-7660-3945-2(5))* Enslow Pubs., Inc.

—The Case of the Infected Tick: Annie Biotica Solves Circulatory System Disease Crimes. 2013. (Body System Disease Investigations Ser.). 48p. (J). (gr. 5-12). pap. 8.95 *(978-1-4644-0226-5(4))*; lib. bdg. 25.27 *(978-0-7660-3948-3(X))* Enslow Pubs., Inc.

—The Case of the Sneezy Popcorn: Annie Biotica Solves Respiratory System Disease Crimes. 2013. (Body System Disease Investigations Ser.). 48p. (J). (gr. 5-12). pap. 8.95 *(978-1-4644-0228-9(0))* Enslow Pubs., Inc.

—The Case of the Undercooked Burger: Annie Biotica Solves Digestive System Disease Crimes. 2013. (Body System Disease Investigations Ser.). 48p. (J). (gr. 5-12). pap. 8.95 *(978-1-4644-0229-6(9))*; lib. bdg. 25.27 *(978-0-7660-3947-6(1))* Enslow Pubs., Inc.

Finer, Kim Renee. Smallpox. 2004. (Deadly Diseases & Epidemics Ser.). (Illus.). 112p. (C). (gr. 9-13). 34.95 *(978-0-7910-7594-4(X)*, Chelsea Hse.) Facts On File, Inc.

Forces of Nature. 2009. (Illus.). 47p. (J). *(978-0-7166-9822-7(6))* World Bk., Inc.

Friedman, Lauri S. Pandemics. 2008. (Writing the Critical Essay Ser.). (ENG., Illus.). 128p. (gr. 10-12). lib. bdg. 38.30 *(978-0-7377-4039-4(6)*, LML02109-240007) Cengage Gale.

Gallagher, Aileen. Hepatitis. 2004. (Epidemics Ser.). (Illus.). 64p. (YA). (gr. 7-12). lib. bdg. 31.95 *(978-1-4042-0255-9(2))* Rosen Publishing Group, Inc., The.

Geis, Patricia. Let's Get Well! Folch, Sergio, illus. 2009. (Good Habits with Coco & Tula Ser.). 16p. (J). (gr. -1-k). bds. 11.40 *(978-1-60754-407-4(5))* Windmill Bks.

Germ Theory. 2010. (Science Foundations Ser.). (Illus.). 128p. (gr. 6-12). 35.00 *(978-1-60413-041-6(5)*, Chelsea Hse.) Facts On File, Inc.

Gosman, Gillian. I Have Pinkeye. 2012. (Get Well Soon! Ser.). (ENG., Illus.). 24p. (J). (gr. 1-3). lib. bdg. 22.60 *(978-1-4488-7410-1(6)*, PowerKids Pr.) Rosen Publishing Group, Inc., The.

—I Have Strep Throat. 2012. (Get Well Soon! Ser.). (ENG., Illus.). 24p. (J). (gr. 1-3). lib. bdg. 22.60 *(978-1-4488-7412-5(2)*, PowerKids Pr.) Rosen Publishing Group, Inc., The.

—I Have the Flu. 2012. (Get Well Soon! Ser.). (ENG., Illus.). 24p. (J). (gr. 1-3). lib. bdg. 22.60 *(978-1-4488-7409-5(2)*, PowerKids Pr.) Rosen Publishing Group, Inc., The.

Green, Robert. Pandemics. 2008. (21st Century Skills Library: Global Perspectives Ser.). (ENG.). 32p. (gr. 4-8). lib. bdg. 29.93 *(978-1-60279-129-9(5)*, 200103) Cherry Lake Publishing.

Guilfoile, Patrick G. Human Papillomavirus. 2011. (Deadly Diseases & Epidemics Ser.). (C). 34.95 *(978-1-60413-467-4(4)*, Chelsea Hse.) Facts On File, Inc.

Hall, Linley Erin. Killer Viruses. 2010. (Doomsday Scenarios: Separating Fact from Fiction Ser.). 64p. (YA). (gr. 5-8). E-Book 58.50 *(978-1-4488-1207-3(0))* Rosen Publishing Group, Inc., The.

Hand, Carol. Epidemiology: The Fight Against Ebola & Other Diseases, 1 vol. 2014. (History of Science Ser.). (ENG., Illus.). 112p. (J). (gr. 6-12). lib. bdg. 35.64 *(978-1-62403-559-3(0)*, Essential Library) ABDO Publishing Co.

—Vaccines, 1 vol. 2013. (Medical Marvels Ser.). (ENG., Illus.). 112p. (YA). (gr. 6-12). lib. bdg. 35.64 *(978-1-61783-905-4(1)*, Essential Library) ABDO Publishing Co.

Hardyman, Robyn. Fighting the Flu. 2014. (Tiny Battlefields Ser.). 48p. (YA). (gr. 6-8). pap. 84.30 *(978-1-4824-1316-8(7))* Stevens, Gareth Publishing LLLP.

—The Race to End Epidemics. 2014. (World in Crisis Ser.). (Illus.). 48p. (J). (gr. 5-8). 30.25 *(978-1-4777-7840-1(3))* Rosen Publishing Group, Inc., The.

Haugen, David M. & Musser, Susan. Pandemics. 2007. (At Issue Ser.). (ENG.). 94p. (gr. 10-12). per. 22.50 *(978-0-7377-3604-5(6)*, Greenhaven Pr., Inc.) Cengage Gale.

Haugen, David M. & Musser, Susan, eds. Pandemics. 2007. (At Issue Ser.). (ENG., Illus.). 94p. (YA). (gr. 6-18). pap. 31.80 *(978-0-7377-3603-8(8)*, Greenhaven Pr., Inc.) Cengage Gale.

Hayhurst, Chris. Cholera. 2009. (Epidemics Ser.). 64p. (gr. 5-5). 58.50 *(978-1-61512-275-2(3))* Rosen Publishing Group, Inc., The.

Henry, Claire. The World's Deadliest Epidemics, 1 vol., 1. 2014. (World's Deadliest Ser.). (ENG.). 32p. (J). (gr. 3-6). 26.25 *(978-1-4777-6157-1(8)*, PowerKids Pr.) Rosen Publishing Group, Inc., The.

Herbst, Benjamin. What Happens When I Cough? 2013. (My Body Does Strange Stuff! Ser.). (ENG., Illus.). 24p. (J). (gr. 1-3). pap. 8.15 *(978-1-4339-9334-3(1))*; lib. bdg. 22.60 *(978-1-4339-9333-6(3))* Stevens, Gareth Publishing LLLP.

Hoffmann, Gretchen. The Flu. 2006. (Health Alert Ser.). (Illus.). 64p. (YA). (gr. 4-7). lib. bdg. 32.79 *(978-0-7614-2208-2(0))* Marshall Cavendish Corp.

Holt, Rinehart and Winston Staff. Decisions for Health Blue, Chptr. 17: Infectious Diseases. 4th ed. 2004. pap. 11.20 *(978-0-03-068052-6(2))* Holt McDougal.

—Decisions for Health Red Chptr. 14: Infectious Diseases. 4th ed. 2004. pap. 11.20 *(978-0-03-068041-0(7))* Holt McDougal.

Infectious Disease Workshop. 2003. cd-rom *(978-1-929524-02-0(1))* P K I Ds.

Isle, Mick. Malaria. 2009. (Epidemics Ser.). 64p. (gr. 5-5). 58.50 *(978-1-61512-293-6(1))* Rosen Publishing Group, Inc., The.

Karner, Julie. Plague & Pandemic Alert! Disaster Alert! 2004. (Disaster Alert! Ser.). (ENG., Illus.). 32p. (J). pap. *(978-0-7787-1612-9(0))* Crabtree Publishing Co.

Kelly, Evelyn B. & Wilker, Ian. Tuberculosis & Superbugs: Examining TB & Bacterial Infections. 2014. (Diseases, Disorders, Symptoms Ser.). (Illus.). 96p. (gr. 9-12). pap. 10.95 *(978-1-62293-086-9(X))* Enslow Pubs., Inc.

Kelly, Evelyn B. & Wilson, Claire. Influenza & Bird Flu: Examining the Flu. 2014. (Diseases, Disorders, Symptoms Ser.). (Illus.). 96p. (J). (gr. 9-12). 27.94 *(978-1-62293-075-3(4))* Enslow Pubs., Inc.

—Investigating Influenza & Bird Flu: Real Facts for Real Lives. 2010. (Investigating Diseases Ser.). 160p. (YA). (gr. 9-12). 35.94 *(978-0-7660-3341-2(4))* Enslow Pubs., Inc.

Klosterman, Lorrie. Meningitis. 2006. (Health Alert Ser.). (Illus.). 64p. (YA). (gr. 4-7). lib. bdg. 32.79 *(978-0-7614-2211-2(0))* Marshall Cavendish Corp.

Kneib, Martha. Meningitis. 2004. (Epidemics Ser.). (Illus.). 64p. (YA). (gr. 7-12). lib. bdg. 31.95 *(978-1-4042-0257-3(9))* Rosen Publishing Group, Inc., The.

Kopp, Megan. Parasites. 2011. (J). (gr. 4-6). pap. 12.95 *(978-1-61690-717-4(7)*, AV2 by Weigl); (Illus.). 24p. (YA). (gr. 2-5). 27.13 *(978-1-61690-711-2(8))* Weigl Pubs., Inc.

Krohn, Katherine. The 1918 Flu Pandemic, 1 vol. Williams, Keith et al, illus. 2007. (Disasters in History Ser.). (ENG.). 32p. (gr. 3-4). 30.65 *(978-1-4296-0158-0(2)*, Graphic Library) Capstone Press of Coughlan Cos.

Kupperberg, Paul. The Influenza Pandemic Of 1918-1919. 2008. (Great Historic Disasters Ser.). (Illus.). 120p. (gr. 5-8). lib. bdg. 35.00 *(978-0-7910-9640-6(8)*, Chelsea Hse.) Facts On File, Inc.

Landau, Elaine. The Common Cold. 2008. (Head-to-Toe Health Ser.). 32p. (gr. 2-7). lib. bdg. 28.50 *(978-0-7614-2844-2(5)*, Benchmark Bks.) Marshall Cavendish Corp.

—Strep Throat. 2010. (Head-to Toe Health 3 Ser.). 32p. (gr. 2). 28.50 *(978-0-7614-4834-1(9))* Marshall Cavendish Corp.

Langwith, Jacqueline. Pandemics. Greenhaven Press Editors, ed. 2011. (At Issue Ser.). (ENG.). 128p. (gr. 10-12). 39.40 *(978-0-7377-5588-6(1))*; pap. 27.80 *(978-0-7377-5589-3(X)*, Greenhaven Pr., Inc.) Cengage Gale.

Leone, Bruno. Disease in History. 2016. (ENG.). 104p. (J). (gr. 5-12). 38.60 *(978-1-60152-960-2(0))* ReferencePoint Pr., Inc.

Lew, Kristi. The Exterminator: Wiping Out the World's Most Infectious Diseases. 2009. (Current Science Ser.). 48p. (gr. 4-7). (YA). lib. bdg. 31.00 *(978-1-4339-2061-5(1))*; (ENG.). (J). pap. 8.95 *(978-1-4339-2132-2(4)*, Gareth Stevens Learning Library) Stevens, Gareth Publishing LLLP.

Marciniak, Kristin. Flu Pandemic Of 1918, 1 vol. 2013. (History's Greatest Disasters Ser.). (ENG., Illus.). 48p. (J). (gr. 3-6). lib. bdg. 32.79 *(978-1-61783-956-6(6))* ABDO Publishing Co.

—Flu Pandemic of 1918 Paperback. 2013. (Illus.). 48p. (J). pap. 15.64 *(978-1-62403-021-5(1)*, Core Library) ABDO Publishing Co.

McPartland, Randall. Tuberculosis. 2015. (Deadliest Diseases of All Time Ser.). (ENG., Illus.). 64p. (J). (gr. 8-8). 34.21 *(978-1-5026-0646-4(1))* Cavendish Square Publishing.

Micklos, John, Jr. The 1918 Flu Pandemic: Core Events of a Worldwide Outbreak. 2015. (What Went Wrong? Ser.). (ENG.). 32p. (gr. 3-4). lib. bdg. 27.32 *(978-1-4914-2045-4(6))* Capstone Press of Coughlan Cos.

Miller, Debra A. Pandemics. 2006. (Hot Topics Ser.). (ENG., Illus.). 128p. (J). (gr. 7-12). lib. bdg. 39.40 *(978-1-59018-965-8(5))* Cengage Gale.

Miller, Karen. Resurgent Diseases. 2008. (Opposing Viewpoints Ser.). (Illus.). 206p. (YA). (gr. 10-12). 29.45 *(978-0-7377-4229-9(1)*, LML01709-243148, Greenhaven Pr., Inc.) Cengage Gale.

—Resurgent Diseases. 2008. (Opposing Viewpoints Ser.). (ENG., Illus.). 224p. (gr. 10-12). 48.80 *(978-0-7377-4228-2(3)*, LML01709-243113, Greenhaven Pr., Inc.) Cengage Gale.

Miller, Madison. What Happens When I Sneeze? 2013. (My Body Does Strange Stuff! Ser.). (ENG., Illus.). 24p. (J). (gr. 1-3). pap. 8.15 *(978-1-4339-9343-5(0))*; lib. bdg. 22.60 *(978-1-4339-9342-8(2))* Stevens, Gareth Publishing LLLP.

Morgan, Philip. Fighting Diseases. 2010. (How Your Body Works). 32p. (YA). (gr. 4-7). 28.50 *(978-1-60753-052-7(X))* Amicus Publishing.

—Fighting Diseases. 2012. (Illus.). 32p. (gr. 4-7). pap. 8.95 *(978-1-926722-62-7(0))* Saunders Bk. Co. CAN. Dist: RiverStream Publishing.

Morgan, Philip & Martineau, Susan. Fighting Diseases. 2011. (Positive Steps Ser.). 32p. (gr. 2-5). lib. bdg. 31.35 *(978-1-59920-492-5(4))* Black Rabbit Bks.

Morley, Jacqueline. You Wouldn't Want to Meet Typhoid Mary! A Deadly Cook You'd Rather Not Know. Antram, David, illus. 2013. (You Wouldn't Want to... Ser.). (ENG.). 32p. (J). 29.00 *(978-0-531-25944-3(7))*; pap. 9.95 *(978-0-531-23041-1(4))* Scholastic Library Publishing. (Watts, Franklin).

Naff, Clayton Farris. Influenza. 2011. (Perspectives on Diseases & Disorders Ser.). 144p. (J). lib. bdg. 38.95 *(978-0-7377-5253-3(X)*, Greenhaven Pr., Inc.) Cengage Gale.

Nagle, Jeanne. Frequently Asked Questions about Avian Flu. 2009. (FAQ: Teen Life Ser.). 64p. (gr. 5-6). 58.50 *(978-1-61512-564-7(7))* Rosen Publishing Group, Inc., The.

Newman, Patricia. Ebola: Fears & Facts. 2015. (ENG., Illus.). 48p. (J). (gr. 4-8). 31.99 *(978-1-4677-9240-0(3))* Lerner Publishing Group.

Ollhoff, Jim. The Flu, 1 vol. 2009. (History of Germs Ser.). (ENG., Illus.). 32p. (YA). (gr. 5-9). 27.07 *(978-1-60453-498-6(2))* ABDO Publishing Co.

O'Neal, Claire. The Influenza Pandemic of 1918. 2007. (Natural Disasters Ser.). (Illus.). 32p. (J). (gr. 1-4). lib. bdg. 25.70 *(978-1-58415-569-0(8))* Mitchell Lane Pubs., Inc.

Orr, Tamra B. Avian Flu. 2007. (Coping in a Changing World Ser.). (Illus.). 112p. (YA). (gr. 7-12). lib. bdg. 34.60 *(978-1-4042-0950-3(6))* Rosen Publishing Group, Inc., The.

Peters, Marilee. Patient Zero: Solving the Mysteries of Deadly Epidemics. 2014. (ENG., Illus.). 168p. (J). (gr. 5-8). pap.

14.95 *(978-1-55451-670-4(6)*, 9781554516704) Annick Pr., Ltd. CAN. Dist: Publishers Group West (PGW).

Piddock, Charles. Outbreaks: Science Seeks Safeguards for Global Health. 2008. (National Geographic Investigates Science Ser.). (ENG., Illus.). 64p. (J). (gr. 5). 17.95 *(978-1-4263-0357-9(2))*; lib. bdg. 27.90 *(978-1-4263-0263-3(0))* National Geographic Society. (National Geographic Children's Bks.).

Platt, Richard. Plagues, Pox, & Pestilence. Kelly, John, illus. 2011. (ENG.). 48p. (J). (gr. 2-7). 15.99 *(978-0-7534-6687-2(2)*, 9780753466872, Kingfisher) Roaring Brook Pr.

Ridgway, Tom. Mad Cow Disease: Bovine Spongiform Encephalopathy. 2009. (Epidemics Ser.). 64p. (gr. 5-5). 58.50 *(978-1-61512-292-9(3))* Rosen Publishing Group, Inc., The.

Robert Green. Diseases & Disorders - SARS. 2004. (Illus.). 112p. 32.45 *(978-1-59018-529-2(3))* Cengage Gale.

Rodda, Geri. The flu & You. 2007. (J). 9.00 *(978-0-9793602-2-0(6))* Pumpkin Hill Productions.

Rolfes, Nina. Examining Pandemics. 2015. (ENG., Illus.). 48p. (J). lib. bdg. 24.95 net. *(978-1-934545-66-9(X))* Oliver Pr., Inc.

Rooney, Anne. World after Super-Plague. 2013. (World After Ser.). (ENG.). 56p. (gr. 7-8). pap. 9.95 *(978-1-4329-7626-2(5))* Heinemann-Raintree.

Rosaler, Maxine. Listeriosis. 2009. (Epidemics Ser.). 64p. (gr. 5-5). 58.50 *(978-1-61512-291-2(5))* Rosen Publishing Group, Inc., The.

Royston, Angela. Colds, the Flu, & Other Infections. 2009. (How's Your Health? Ser.). (J). (gr. 1-4). 28.50 *(978-1-59920-217-4(4))* Black Rabbit Bks.

—Fighting Smallpox. 2014. (Tiny Battlefields Ser.). 48p. (YA). (gr. 6-8). pap. 84.30 *(978-1-4824-1315-1(9))* Stevens, Gareth Publishing LLLP.

Rudolph, Jessica. The Flu of 1918: Millions Dead Worldwide! 2010. (Nightmare Plagues Ser.). 32p. (YA). (gr. 4-9). lib. bdg. 25.27 *(978-1-936088-05-8(3))* Bearport Publishing Co., Inc.

The Science of a Pandemic. 2014. (21st Century Skills Library: Disaster Science Ser.). (ENG., Illus.). 32p. (J). (gr. 4-8). 28.50 *(978-1-63137-625-2(X)*, 205283) Cherry Lake Publishing.

Scientific American Staff. Fighting Infectious Diseases. 2009. (Scientific American Cutting-Edge Science Ser.). 144p. (gr. 9-9). 63.90 *(978-1-60853-077-9(9))* Rosen Publishing Group, Inc., The.

Segall, Miriam. Pandemics: Epidemics in a Shrinking World. (In the News Ser.). 64p. 2009. (gr. 6-6). 58.50 *(978-1-61513-482-3(4))* 2007. (Illus.). (YA). (gr. 7-12). lib. bdg. 31.95 *(978-1-4042-0975-6(1))* Rosen Publishing Group, Inc., The.

Senior, Kathryn. You Wouldn't Want to Be Sick in the 16th Century! (Revised Edition) 2014. (You Wouldn't Want to... Ser.). (ENG.). 32p. (J). lib. bdg. 29.00 *(978-0-531-21176-2(2)*, Watts, Franklin) Scholastic Library Publishing.

Sheen, Barbara. Flu. 2006. (Diseases & Disorders Ser.). (ENG., Illus.). 128p. (gr. 7-12). lib. bdg. 39.90 *(978-1-59018-675-6(3))* Cengage Gale.

Sherman, Josepha. The War Against Germs. 2009. (Germs: the Library of Disease-Causing Organisms Ser.). 48p. (gr. 5-5). 53.00 *(978-1-61512-718-4(6))* Rosen Publishing Group, Inc., The.

Siderovski, Susan. Tularemia. Alcamo, I. Edward, ed. 2006. (Deadly Diseases & Epidemics Ser.). (Illus.). 112p. (C). (gr. 9-12). lib. bdg. 34.95 *(978-0-7910-8679-7(8)*, Chelsea Hse.) Facts On File, Inc.

Silverstein, Virginia. Handy Health Guide to Colds & Flu. 2013. (Handy Health Guides). 48p. (J). (gr. 5-12). pap. 8.95 *(978-1-4644-0491-7(7))* Enslow Pubs., Inc.

Somervill, Barbara A. Lice: Head Hunters. 2007. (Bloodsuckers Ser.). (Illus.). 24p. (J). (gr. 2-5). lib. bdg. 22.60 *(978-1-4042-3803-9(4))* Rosen Publishing Group, Inc., The.

Sommers, Michael A. Yeast Infections, Trichomoniasis, & Toxic Shock Syndrome. 2007. (Girls' Health Ser.). (Illus.). 48p. (YA). (gr. 7-12). lib. bdg. 29.25 *(978-1-4042-1951-9(X))* Rosen Publishing Group, Inc., The.

Squire, Ann O. Ebola. 2015. (ENG., Illus.). 48p. (J). lib. bdg. *(978-0-531-21469-5(9)*, Orchard Bks.) Scholastic, Inc.

Stille, Darlene R. Outbreak! The Science of Pandemics, 1 vol. 2010. (Headline Science Ser.). (ENG.). 48p. (gr. 7-8). lib. bdg. 29.32 *(978-0-7565-4374-7(6)*, Headline Science) Compass Point Bks.

Tilden, Thomasine E. Lewis & Lewis-Tilden, Thomasine E. Help! Whats Eating My Flesh? Runaway Staph & Strep Infections! 2007. (24/7: Science Behind the Scenes Ser.). (ENG., Illus.). 64p. (J). (gr. 9-12). 29.00 *(978-0-531-12073-6(2)*, Watts, Franklin) Scholastic Library Publishing.

Walker, Richard. Epidemics & Plagues. 2006. (Kingfisher Knowledge Ser.). (Illus.). 64p. (J). *(978-0-7534-1376-0(0)*, Kingfisher) Roaring Brook Pr.

West, Krista. Urinary Tract Infections. (Library of Sexual Health Ser.). 64p. 2009. (gr. 6-6). 58.50 *(978-1-60853-851-5(6))* 2006. (Illus.). (YA). (gr. 7-12). lib. bdg. 31.95 *(978-1-4042-0905-3(0))* Rosen Publishing Group, Inc., The.

Willett, Edward. Infectious Disease Specialists: Hunting down Disease. 2015. (Extreme Science Careers Ser.). (ENG.). 128p. (J). (gr. 7-7). lib. bdg. 37.27 *(978-0-7660-6970-1(2))* Enslow Pubs., Inc.

World Book, Inc Staff, contrib. by. Blizzards. 2nd ed. 2009. (Illus.). 47p. (J). *(978-0-7166-9817-3(X))* World Bk., Inc.

—Fighting Sickness. 2013. (J). *(978-0-7166-1845-4(1))* World Bk., Inc.

—Forces of Nature. 2007. (J). *(978-0-7166-9806-7(4))* World Bk., Inc.

—Pandemics. (J). 2007. *(978-0-7166-9811-1(0))* 2nd ed. 2009. (Illus.). 47p. *(978-0-7166-9827-2(7))* World Bk., Inc.

Yancey, Diane. Tuberculosis. 2008. (Twenty-First Century Medical Library Ser.). (Illus.). 128p. (YA). (gr. 7-12). lib. bdg. 30.60 *(978-0-8225-9190-0(1))* Lerner Publishing Group.

COMMUNICABLE DISEASES—FICTION

Choldenko, Gennifer. Chasing Secrets. 2015. (ENG.). 288p. (J). (gr. 4-7). lib. bdg. 19.99 *(978-0-375-99063-2(1)*, Lamb, Wendy Bks.) Random Hse. Children's Bks.

—Chasing Secrets. 2016. lib. bdg. 18.40 *(978-0-606-38879-5(6))* Turtleback Bks.

Harrison, Zac. Space Plague, 1 vol. 2014. (Hyperspace High Ser.). (ENG., Illus.). 288p. (gr. 4-8). 27.32 *(978-1-4342-6568-5(4))* Stone Arch Bks.

Nielsen, Jennifer A. The Scourge. 2016. (ENG.). 368p. (J). (gr. 4-7). 16.99 *(978-0-545-68245-9(2)*, Scholastic Pr.) Scholastic, Inc.

Plum-Ucci, Carol. Fire Will Fall. 2011. (ENG.). 492p. (YA). (gr. 9). pap. 25.99 *(978-0-547-55007-7(3))* Houghton Mifflin Harcourt Publishing Co.

Thomas, Lex. The Giant. 2016. (Quarantine Ser.: 4). (ENG.). 352p. (gr. 9-12). 17.99 *(978-1-5124-0103-5(X)*, Carolrhoda Bks.); (YA). 35.99 *(978-1-5124-0159-2(5)*, Carolrhoda Lab™) Lerner Publishing Group.

Wooding, Chris. Silver. 2014. (ENG.). 320p. (J). (gr. 7). 17.99 *(978-0-545-60392-8(7)*, Scholastic Pr.) Scholastic, Inc.

Woolston, Blythe. Troutzilla. 2012. (Carolrhoda YA Ser.). (ENG.). 216p. (YA). (gr. 9-12). 17.95 *(978-0-7613-7755-9(7)*, Carolrhoda Lab™) Lerner Publishing Group.

COMMUNICATION

see also Books and Reading; Language and Languages; Mass Media; Newspapers; Postal Service; Writing

Allen, Joy. Baby Signs. 2008. (ENG., Illus.). 16p. (J). (gr. -1 — 1). bds. 6.99 *(978-0-8037-3193-6(0)*, Dial Bks) Penguin Young Readers Group.

Amos, Janine & Spenceley, Annabel. Don't Do That! How Not to Act. 2009. (Best Behavior Ser.). (Illus.). 32p. (J). (gr. -1-2). lib. bdg. 22.60 *(978-1-60754-030-4(4))* Windmill Bks.

—Go Away! What Not to Say. 2009. (Best Behavior Ser.). (Illus.). 32p. (J). (gr. -1-2). pap. 10.55 *(978-1-60754-044-1(4))*; lib. bdg. 22.60 *(978-1-60754-026-7(6))* Windmill Bks.

Athans, Sandra K. & Parente, Robin W. Tips & Tricks for Evaluating Multimedia Content. 2014. (Common Core Readiness Guide to Reading Ser.). 80p. (YA). (gr. 5-8). 32.95 *(978-1-4777-7563-9(3)*, Rosen Reference) Rosen Publishing Group, Inc., The.

Berry, Joy. Help Me Be Good Tattling. Bartholomew, illus. 2010. (Help Me Be Good Ser.). (ENG.). 32p. (J). (gr. -1-2). pap. 4.99 *(978-0-60577-136-6(8))* Berry, Joy Enterprises.

Berry, Joy Wilt. A Book about Gossiping. 2005. (Illus.). (J). *(978-0-7172-8590-7(1))* Scholastic, Inc.

—A Book about Whining. 2005. (Illus.). (J). *(978-0-7172-7898-5(0))* Scholastic, Inc.

Bix, Cynthia Overbeck. Fad Mania! A History of American Crazes. 2014. 64p. (J). (gr. 6-12). lib. bdg. 34.60 *(978-1-4677-1034-3(2)*, Twenty-First Century Bks.) Lerner Publishing Group.

Blackstone, Stella. Hablando con Bebé. 2017. (ENG & SPA.). 14p. (J). (gr. -1 — 1). bds. 6.99 ***(978-1-78285-350-3(2))*** Barefoot Bks., Inc.

Bodden, Valerie. Analyze & Define the Assignment. 2015. (Info Wise Ser.). (ENG., Illus.). 40p. (gr. 4-6). 30.65 *(978-1-4677-5223-7(1)*, Lerner Pubns.) Lerner Publishing Group.

Boelts, Maribeth. Communication Past & Present. 2016. (Spring Forward Ser.). (J). (gr. 1). *(978-1-4900-9399-4(0))* Benchmark Education Co.

Bowers, Linda, et al. No Glamour Language & Reasoning. 2003. (J). per. 41.95 *(978-0-7606-0500-4(9))* LinguiSystems, Inc.

—Social Language Development Test Elementary. 2008. (J). spiral bd. 13.95 *(978-0-7606-0804-3(0))* LinguiSystems, Inc.

Braunius, Marlene J., et al. Exploring Language Arts Through Literature Birth - Grade 8. 2nd rev. ed. 2004. (ENG.). 332p. (gr. -1-8). 73.50 *(978-0-7575-0794-6(8)*, 0757507948) Kendall Hunt Publishing Co.

Brinkerhoff, Shirley. Folk Speech. 2004. (North American Folklore Ser.). (Illus.). 112p. (YA). (gr. 7-18). lib. bdg. 22.95 *(978-1-59084-345-1(2))* Mason Crest.

Bullard, Lisa. My Language, Your Language. 2015. (Cloverleaf Books (tm) — Alike & Different Ser.). (ENG., Illus.). 24p. (J). (gr. k-2). pap. 6.99 *(978-1-4677-6034-8(X))*; lib. bdg. 23.99 *(978-1-4677-4906-0(0))* Lerner Publishing Group. (Millbrook Pr.).

Burke, Sandra & Flebotte, Morrigan. The Crusading Communicator. Flebotte, Morrigan, ed. 2004. (Illus.). 2p. (J). per. *(978-0-9735303-8-4(3))* Black Castle Industries, Inc.

Cain, Marie Mowery. A Message for You. 2013. (Big Books, Blue Ser.). (ENG & SPA., Illus.). 16p. pap. 33.00 *(978-1-59246-013-7(5))* Big Books, by George!

Clapper, Nikki Bruno. Media Literacy for Kids. 2015. (Media Literacy for Kids Ser.). (ENG.). 24p. (gr. k-1). 53.30 *(978-1-4914-6947-7(1)*, Pebble Plus) Capstone Press of Coughlan Cos.

Communication, Education, & Travel. 2010. (Green Careers Ser.). (Illus.). 160p. (C). (gr. 9-18). 32.95 *(978-0-8160-8154-7(9)*, Ferguson Publishing Co.) Facts On File, Inc.

Communications. 2nd rev. ed. 2004. 73p. stu. ed., wbk. ed. *(978-0-86657-510-2(3))* Lab-Volt Systems, Inc.

Communications TCG. 2nd rev. ed. 2004. 72p. pap. *(978-0-86657-511-9(1))* Lab-Volt Systems, Inc.

CommunicationsAdvAddOn CELL Guide. 2nd rev. ed. 2004. 124p. pap. *(978-0-86657-495-2(6))* Lab-Volt Systems, Inc.

Cooper, Scott. Speak up & Get Along! Learn the Mighty Might, Thought Chop, & More Tools to Make Friends, Stop Teasing, & Feel Good about Yourself. 2005. (ENG., Illus.). 128p. (J). (gr. 4-7). pap. 12.99 *(978-1-57542-182-7(8))* Free Spirit Publishing, Inc.

Cosson, M. J. The Smart Kid's Guide to Knowing What to Say. Rooney, Ronnie, illus. 2014. (Smart Kid's Guide to Everyday Life Ser.). (ENG.). 32p. (J). (gr. 2-5). 28.50 *(978-1-62687-343-8(7)*, 207183) Child's World, Inc., The.

Donovan, Sandy. Communication Smarts: How to Express Yourself Best in Conversations, Texts, E-Mails, & More. 2012. (USA TODAY Teen Wise Guides: Lifestyle Choices Ser.). (ENG., Illus.). 64p. (gr. 8-12). lib. bdg. 31.93 *(978-0-7613-7024-6(2))* Lerner Publishing Group.

Doudna, Kelly. It's Not Too Late, Let's Communicate!, 1 vol. 2007. (Science Made Simple Ser.). (ENG., Illus.). 24p. (J). (gr. k-3). lib. bdg. 24.21 *(978-1-59928-606-8(8)*, SandCastle) ABDO Publishing Co.

—Speak Up!, 1 vol. 2007. (Character Concepts Ser.). (ENG., Illus.). 24p. (J). (gr. k-3). lib. bdg. 24.21 *(978-1-59928-741-6(2)*, SandCastle) ABDO Publishing Co.

Dow, Kathy & Dow, Danica, illus. Low-Down Dirty Words. 2004. 28p. (J). *(978-0-9749886-0-3(X))* KayStar Publishing.

Dugan, Christine. Tech World: The Language of Social Media (Level 5) 2017. (Exploring Reading Ser.). (Illus.). 48p. (J). (gr. 5-5). pap. 10.99 ***(978-1-4258-4989-4(X))*** Teacher Created Materials, Inc.

Eschbach, Andrea & Eschbach, Markus. How to Speak Horse: A Horse-Crazy Kid's Guide to Reading Body Language, Understanding Behavior, & Talking Back with Simple Groundwork Lessons. 2012. (ENG.). 32p. (J). (gr. 2-4). *(978-1-57076-532-2(4))* Verlhac Editions.

Espejo, Roman. Celebrity Culture. 2010. (Opposing Viewpoints Ser.). 176p. 42.95 *(978-0-7377-5213-7(0))*; 177p. pap. 29.45 *(978-0-7377-5214-4(9))* Cengage Gale. (Greenhaven Pr., Inc.).

Everly, Nita. Early Social Behavior Books Can You Talk to Your Friends. 2007. (J). spiral bd. 11.95 *(978-0-7606-0739-8(7))* LinguiSystems, Inc.

Fontichiaro, Kristin. Understanding & Creating Infographics. Petelinsek, Kathleen, illus. 2013. (Explorer Library: Information Explorer Ser.). (ENG.). 32p. (J). (gr. 4-8). 28.50 *(978-1-62431-126-0(1)*, 202824); pap. 14.21 *(978-1-62431-258-8(6)*, 202826) Cherry Lake Publishing.

Ford-Brown, Lisa A. & Dorling Kindersley Publishing Staff. DK Communication. 2016. (ENG., Illus.). 576p. (J). pap. 114.60 *(978-0-205-95657-9(2))* Prentice Hall PTR.

Fromm, Megan. Why the News Matters, 1 vol. 2015. (ENG.). 48p. (YA). 30.25 *(978-1-4777-8066-4(1)*, Rosen Reference) Rosen Publishing Group, Inc., The.

Gerber, Larry. Cited! Identifying Credible Information Online. 2010. (Digital & Information Literacy Ser.). (ENG.). 48p. (YA). pap. 11.75 *(978-1-4488-0599-0(6))*; lib. bdg. 29.25 *(978-1-4358-9430-3(8))* Rosen Publishing Group, Inc., The. (Rosen Reference).

Giglio, Judy. Communication Then & Now, 6, Set. 2004. (Phonics Readers Books 37-72 Ser.). (ENG.). 8p. (gr. k-1). pap. 35.70 *(978-0-7368-4063-7(X)*, Phonics Readers) Capstone Press of Coughlan Cos.

Greven, Alec. How to Talk to Girls. Acedera, Kei, illus. 2008. (ENG.). 48p. (J). (gr. 1-5). 9.99 *(978-0-06-170999-9(9)*, Collins) HarperCollins Pubs.

Hazen, Walter A. Communication. 2004. (Everyday Life Ser.). (Illus.). 96p. pap. 10.95 *(978-0-673-58664-3(2))* Good Year Bks.

Higgins, Nadia. US Culture Through Infographics. Thompson, Bryon & Kulihin, Vic, illus. 2014. (Super Social Studies Infographics Ser.). (ENG.). 32p. (gr. 3-5). lib. bdg. 26.60 *(978-1-4677-3464-6(0)*, Lerner Pubns.) Lerner Publishing Group.

Hobbs, Mike. Communications. 2013. (Young Entrepreneurs' Club Ser.). 48p. (gr. 5-11). 37.10 *(978-1-59920-920-3(9))* Black Rabbit Bks.

Hom, Susan & Richardson, Phillip. Message in a Bottle. Björkman, Steve, illus. 2009. (ENG.). 72p. (J). pap. 19.95 *(978-1-60433-001-4(5)*, Applesauce Pr.) Cider Mill Pr. Bk. Pubs., LLC.

Jackson, Donna M. & Goman, Carol Kinsey. Every Body's Talking: What We Say Without Words. 2014. (Illus.). 64p. (gr. 4-8). lib. bdg. 30.60 *(978-1-4677-0858-6(5)*, Twenty-First Century Bks.) Lerner Publishing Group.

Janssen-Mathes, Mieke M. E. Unlocking the Secret of Otherland: A Story & Activity Book for Children Living Abroad. Kwakkenbos, Frans, illus. 2007. 96p. pap. *(978-90-6832-587-4(6))* Royal Tropical Institute Pr. (KIT (Koninklijk Instituut voor de Tropen).

Jareaux, Marlena. 26 Things to Teach Your Parents. 2007. (Illus.). 76p. (YA). per. 10.95 *(978-0-9790415-1-8(1))* Inspired by the Beach Co.

Johnson, Robin. Above & Beyond with Communication. 2016. (Fueling Your Future! Going above & Beyond in the 21st Cent Ser.). (ENG.). 48p. (J). (gr. 5-8). *(978-0-7787-2830-6(7))* Crabtree Publishing Co.

Kalman, Bobbie. Body Talk. 2010. (My World Ser.). (ENG., Illus.). 16p. (J). (gr. k-3). *(978-0-7787-9511-7(X))*; pap. *(978-0-7787-9536-0(5))* Crabtree Publishing Co.

—Communication Then & Now. 2013. (ENG., Illus.). 24p. (J). *(978-0-7787-0114-9(X))*; pap. *(978-0-7787-0142-2(5))* Crabtree Publishing Co.

Khan, Hena. How to Say What You Mean, Mean What You Say, & Get What You Want. 2004. (Illus.). 80p. (J). *(978-0-439-57904-9(X))* Scholastic, Inc.

Kroll, Jennifer. A la Vanguardia: Adelantos en Tecnología. 2016. (TIME for Kids en Español - Level 5 Ser.). (SPA.). 64p. (gr. 5-5). lib. bdg. 31.99 *(978-1-5157-2927-3(3))* Time for Kids Inc AUS. Dist: Capstone Pub.

Landau, Jennifer. The Right Words: Knowing What to Say & How to Say It. 2011. (Communicating with Confidence Ser.). (ENG.). 80p. (YA). (gr. 7-12). pap. 14.15 *(978-1-4488-5637-4(X))*; lib. bdg. 33.25 *(978-1-4488-5519-3(5))* Rosen Publishing Group, Inc., The.

Leone, Laura. Choosing a Career in Information Science. 2009. (World of Work Ser.). 64p. (gr. 5-5). 58.50 *(978-1-60854-332-8(3))* Rosen Publishing Group, Inc., The.

Lewis, Clare. Entertainment Through the Years: How Having Fun Has Changed in Living Memory. 2015. (History in Living Memory Ser.). (ENG.). 24p. (gr. k-2). 23.32 *(978-1-4846-0923-1(9)*, Heinemann Read & Learn) Heinemann-Raintree.

—Shopping Around the World, 1 vol. 2014. (Around the World Ser.). (ENG., Illus.). 24p. (gr. -1-1). 22.65 *(978-1-4846-0373-4(7)*, Acorn) Heinemann-Raintree.

Library & Information Science. 2009. (Career Opportunities Ser.). 392p. (C). (gr. 9-18). pap. 18.95 *(978-0-8160-7547-8(6)*, Ferguson Publishing Co.) Facts On File, Inc.

Lindeen, Mary. Smart Online Communication: Protecting Your Digital Footprint. 2016. (Searchlight Books (tm) — What Is Digital Citizenship? Ser.). (ENG.). 40p. (J). (gr. 3-5). 30.65 *(978-1-4677-9487-9(2)*, Lerner Pubns.) Lerner Publishing Group.

Mabry-Gordon, Sherri. How to Create Digital Portfolios to Develop Communication Skills. 2017. (Project Learning Using Digital Portfolios Ser.). 64p. (J). (gr. 12-12). 34.45 ***(978-1-5081-7530-8(6)***, Rosen Young Adult) Rosen Publishing Group, Inc., The.

Marsico, Katie. Speak Up! 2012. (21st Century Basic Skills Library: Kids Can Make Manners Count Ser.). (ENG.). 24p. (gr. k-3). 22.79 *(978-1-61080-434-9(1)*, 202044); pap. 12.79 *(978-1-61080-608-4(5)*, 202218) Cherry Lake Publishing.

—Use Your Indoor Voice! 2012. (21st Century Basic Skills Library: Kids Can Make Manners Count Ser.). (ENG.). 24p. (gr. k-3). 22.79 *(978-1-61080-437-0(6)*, 202047); pap. 12.79 *(978-1-61080-611-4(5)*, 202221) Cherry Lake Publishing.

Martineau, Susan. Infographics for Kids. Barker, Vicky, illus. 2016. (ENG.). 48p. (J). (gr. 2-5). pap. 7.95 *(978-1-58089-723-5(1))* Charlesbridge Publishing, Inc.

Marx, Christy. Battlefield Command Systems of the Future. 2009. (Library of Future Weaponry Ser.). 64p. (gr. 6-6). 58.50 *(978-1-60853-636-8(X))* Rosen Publishing Group, Inc., The.

McCune, Susan. I Listen When You Speak, 01 vols., 1. 2016. (Rosen REAL Readers: Social Studies Nonfiction / Fiction: Family, Community, & the World Ser.). (ENG.). 8p. (J). pap. 5.46 *(978-1-5081-1632-5(6)*, Rosen Classroom) Rosen Publishing Group, Inc., The.

McDougal-Littell Publishing Staff, creator. Grammar, Usage, & Mechanics Book: Teaching, More Practice, Application. 2006. (Illus.). 219p. (gr. 7-18). per. *(978-0-618-15376-3(4)*, 2-04131) Holt McDougal.

Michelle Washington. Home & School Communication Journal: For Parents, Teachers & Students. 2005. 98p. pap. 10.00 *(978-1-4134-9969-8(4))* Xlibris Corp.

Miller, Reagan & Richardson, Hazel. Communication in the Ancient World. 2011. (ENG.). 32p. (J). lib. bdg. *(978-0-7787-1733-1(X))* Crabtree Publishing Co.

—Communication in the Ancient World. Crabtree Publishing Staff, ed. 2011. (Life in the Ancient World Ser.: No. 2). (ENG.). 32p. (J). (gr. 5-8). pap. *(978-0-7787-1740-9(2))* Crabtree Publishing Co.

Moore, Elizabeth. Let's Communicate. 2011. (Wonder Readers Emergent Level Ser.). (ENG.). (gr. -1-1). 16p. pap. 35.94 *(978-1-4296-8078-3(4))*; 32p. pap. 5.99 *(978-1-4296-7863-6(1))* Capstone Press of Coughlan Cos. (Wonder Readers).

Naik, Anita & Cronin, Ali. Read the Signals: The Body Language Handbook. 2009. (Really Useful Handbooks Ser.). (ENG., Illus.). 48p. (J). (gr. 5-11). lib. bdg. *(978-0-7787-4388-0(8))* Crabtree Publishing Co.

O'Dell. Elements of Language. 2003. (Elements of Language Ser.). (gr. 6-18). pupil's gde. ed. 64.73 *(978-0-03-052662-6(0))* Holt McDougal.

Offord, Alexander. Communication Inventions: The Talk of the Town. 2013. (Inventions That Shaped the World Ser.). (ENG., Illus.). 48p. (J). (gr. 5-8). pap. *(978-0-7787-0235-1(9))* Crabtree Publishing Co.

Parker, Vic. Buenas Relaciones, 1 vol. 2010. (Explorar el Civismo Ser.). (SPA & ENG.). 32p. (gr. 1-3). 27.32 *(978-1-4329-4463-6(0))*; pap. 8.29 *(978-1-4329-4471-1(1))* Heinemann-Raintree.

Patterson, Jacinta. Cambridge Checkpoints VCE Visual Communication Design Units 3 And 4 2014-16. 2013. (Cambridge Checkpoints Ser.). (ENG.). pap. *(978-1-107-67531-5(6))* Cambridge Univ. Pr.

—VCE Visual Communication Design Units 3 & 4 2014-17. 2013. (Cambridge Checkpoints Ser.). (ENG.). pap. *(978-1-107-68944-2(9))* Cambridge Univ. Pr.

Popek, Emily. Understanding the World of User-Generated Content. 2010. (Digital & Information Literacy Ser.). (ENG.). 48p. (YA). pap. 11.75 *(978-1-4488-0598-3(8))*; lib. bdg. 29.25 *(978-1-4358-9431-0(6))* Rosen Publishing Group, Inc., The. (Rosen Reference).

Rabbat, Suzy. Super Smart Information Strategies: Hit the Books. 2010. (Explorer Library: Information Explorer Ser.). (ENG.). 32p. (gr. 4-8). pap. 14.21 *(978-1-61080-258-1(6)*, 200906); lib. bdg. 28.50 *(978-1-60279-641-6(6)*, 200344) Cherry Lake Publishing.

Rissman, Rebecca. We All Communicate. 2016. (Disabilities & Differences Ser.). (ENG.). 24p. (gr. -1-1). pap. 6.29 *(978-1-4846-3625-1(2)*, Acorn) Heinemann-Raintree.

Rollins, Brenda. How to Write a Book Report: 80 Interactive Screen Pages. 2011. (Writing Skills Ser.). (J). (gr. 3-8). pap. 39.95 *(978-1-55319-506-1(X)*, Classroom Complete Pr.) Rainbow Horizons Publishing, Inc.

—How to Write an Essay: 80 Interactive Screen Pages. 2011. (Writing Skills Ser.). (J). (gr. 3-8). pap. 39.95 *(978-1-55319-507-8(8)*, Classroom Complete Pr.) Rainbow Horizons Publishing, Inc.

Rondina, Catherine. Gossip: Before Word Gets Around, 1 vol. Workman, Dan, illus. 2010. (Lorimer Deal with It Ser.). (ENG.). 32p. (J). (gr. 4-6). 24.95 *(978-1-55277-499-1(6)*, 9781552774991) Lorimer, James & Co., Ltd., Pubs. CAN. Dist: Casemate Pubs. & Bk. Distributors, LLC.

Rosen Publishing Staff. Digital & Information Literacy: Set 8, 1 vol. 2015. (Digital & Information Literacy Ser.). (ENG.). 48p. (YA). 181.50 *(978-1-4777-7954-5(X)*, Rosen Central) Rosen Publishing Group, Inc., The.

—Media Literacy, 1 vol. 2015. (Media Literacy Ser.). (ENG.). 48p. (YA). 181.50 *(978-1-4777-8072-5(6)*, Rosen Central) Rosen Publishing Group, Inc., The.

Rossi, Ann & National Geographic Learning Staff. Kids Communicate. 2007. (Nonfiction Reading & Writing Workshops Ser.). (ENG., Illus.). 32p. (J). pap. 17.95 *(978-0-7922-8689-9(8))* CENGAGE Learning.

Rustad, Martha E. H. Learning about Media Literacy. 2015. (Media Literacy for Kids Ser.). (ENG.). 24p. (gr. k-1). lib. bdg. 26.65 *(978-1-4914-1833-8(8)*, Pebble Plus) Capstone Press of Coughlan Cos.

—Media Literacy for Kids. 2015. (Media Literacy for Kids Ser.). (ENG.). 24p. (gr. k-1). 106.60 *(978-1-4914-1834-5(6)*, Pebble Plus) Capstone Press of Coughlan Cos.

Scholastic Library Publishing. A True Book—Information Literacy. 2012. (J). 116.00 *(978-0-531-28002-7(0)*, Children's Pr.) Scholastic Library Publishing.

Sévigny, Eric, illus. The Phone Call. 2003. (Clubhouse Ser.). (ENG.). 24p. (J). (gr. -1-1). pap. 3.99 *(978-2-89450-446-8(2))* Caillouet, Gerry.

Small, Cathleen. Make the Most of Facebook & Other Social Media. 2015. (J). lib. bdg. *(978-1-62713-535-1(9))* Cavendish Square Publishing.

Solway, Andrew. Communication: The Impact of Science & Technology. 2009. (Pros & Cons Ser.). (ENG.). 64p. (YA). (gr. 5-9). lib. bdg. 35.00 *(978-1-4339-1986-2(9))* Stevens, Gareth Publishing LLLP.

Sonneborn, Liz. Nonverbal Communication: The Art of Body Language. 2011. (Communicating with Confidence Ser.). (ENG.). 80p. (YA). (gr. 7-12). pap. 14.15

C
D

(978-1-4488-5629-9(9)); lib. bdg. 33.25 *(978-1-4488-5518-6(7))* Rosen Publishing Group, Inc., The.

Stein, Lee. Generation Communication: For Teens Who Want to Get Ahead in the World. 2011. 60p. (YA). per. 9.99 *(978-0-9786663-1-6(3))* Paradoxical Pr., The.

Taylor, Allan & Parish, James Robert. Library & Information Science. 2009. (Career Opportunities Ser.). (Illus.). 364p. (C). (gr. 9-18). 49.50 *(978-0-8160-7546-1(8)*, Ferguson Publishing Co.) Facts On File, Inc.

Transportation & Communication. (J). (gr. k-1). *(978-84-342-2418-6(6)*, PR30572) Parramon Ediciones S.A. ESP. Dist: Lectorum Pubns., Inc.

Velcro Interactive Phonic Lab. (Illus.). (J). (gr. 2-4). *(978-0-9673268-0-1(X))* Learning Fasten-Ations, Inc.

Weinick, Suzanne. Professional Connections: Learning How to Network. 2011. (Communicating with Confidence Ser.). (ENG.). 80p. (YA). (gr. 7-12). pap. 14.15 *(978-1-4488-5635-0(3))*; lib. bdg. 33.25 *(978-1-4488-5520-9(9))* Rosen Publishing Group, Inc., The.

Wells, James. Stuffy, the Short-Neck Giraffe Who Liked Peanut Butter. 2006. 9.00 *(978-0-8059-9174-1(3))* Dorrance Publishing Co., Inc.

whiting, jim. Online Communication & Social Networking. 2011. (Issues in the Digital Age Ser.). (Illus.). 96p. (J). (gr. 7-12). lib. bdg. 27.95 *(978-1-60152-190-3(1))* ReferencePoint Pr., Inc.

COMMUNICATION—FICTION

Allen, Kathryn Madeline. A Kiss Means I Love You. Futran, Eric, photos by. 2016. (ENG., Illus.). 16p. (J). (gr. -1 — 1). bds. 7.99 *(978-0-8075-4189-0(3))* Whitman, Albert & Co.

—A Kiss Means I Love You. Futran, Eric, illus. Futran, Eric, photos by. 2012. (ENG.). 24p. (J). (gr. -1-3). 15.99 *(978-0-8075-4186-9(9))* Whitman, Albert & Co.

—Show Me Happy. Futran, Eric, photos by. 2015. (ENG., Illus.). 24p. (J). (gr. -1-3). 15.99 *(978-0-8075-7349-5(3))* Whitman, Albert & Co.

Anderson, Linda. Let's Meet the Gickens. 2012. 104p. pap. 8.95 *(978-1-4575-1317-6(X))* Dog Ear Publishing, LLC.

Angus, Jennifer. In Search of Goliathus Hercules. 2013. (ENG.). 352p. (J). (gr. 3-7). 17.99 *(978-0-8075-2990-4(7))* Whitman, Albert & Co.

Baer, Edith. Words are like Faces, 1 vol. Teis, Kyra, illus. 2007. (ENG.). 32p. (J). 15.95 *(978-1-59572-108-2(8))* Star Bright Bks., Inc.

Bain, Michelle. The Adventures of Thumbs up Johnnie Reading Heart to Heart Thumbs up Johnnie, Little Digit & the Special Delivery: Reading Heart to Heart, Coloring & Activity Book. 2006. (Illus.). (J). pap. 7.95 *(978-0-9795832-5-4(X))* Pixie Stuff LLC.

—Las aventuras de Juanito el Pulgarcito Zipp, Pequeño Dígito, las señales y las Señas: Zipp, Pequeño Digito, las señales y las Señas. Lizana, Lorenzo, illus. 2007.Tr. of Zipp, Digit & the Happy Signs! (SPA.). 28p. (J). *(978-0-9795832-3-0(3))* Pixie Stuff LLC.

Barnett, Mac. Telephone. Corace, Jen, illus. 2014. (ENG.). 40p. (J). (gr. -1-3). 16.99 *(978-1-4521-1023-3(9))* Chronicle Bks. LLC.

Beard, Alex. The Jungle Grapevine. 2009. (ENG., Illus.). 48p. (J). (gr. k-2). 17.95 *(978-0-8109-8001-3(0)*, Abrams Bks. for Young Readers) Abrams, Inc.

Blackstone, Stella. Talk with Me! Mockford, Caroline, illus. 2009. (ENG.). 14p. (J). (gr. -1). 7.99 *(978-1-84686-180-2(2))* Barefoot Bks., Inc.

Brink Hull, Amanda. Maslyn: A Different Kind of Name for a Delightful Little Girl. 2009. (Illus.). 36p. pap. 16.99 *(978-1-4389-9338-6(2))* AuthorHouse.

Carter, Aimée. Simon Thorn & the Wolf's Den. 2016. (Simon Thorn Ser.). (ENG.). 320p. (YA). (gr. 3-6). 16.99 *(978-1-61963-704-7(9)*, 9781619637047, Bloomsbury USA Childrens) Bloomsbury Publishing USA.

Chandler, Susan. Welcome to Cuckooville. Durand, Delphine, illus. 2012. (ENG.). 24p. (J). (gr. k-3). 16.95 *(978-1-61608-665-7(3)*, 608665, Sky Pony Pr.) Skyhorse Publishing Co., Inc.

Charbonneau, Joelle. Need. 2015. (ENG.). 352p. (YA). (gr. 7). 17.99 *(978-0-544-41669-7(4)*, HMH Books For Young Readers) Houghton Mifflin Harcourt Publishing Co.

Cheng, Andrea, et al. Grandfather Counts. Zhang, Ange, illus. 2003. (Avenues Ser.). (ENG.). 32p. (C). pap. 11.95 *(978-1-58430-158-5(9))* National Geographic School Publishing, Inc.

Clements, Andrew. No Talking. 2014. (ENG.). 160p. (J). (gr. 3-7). 11.24 *(978-1-63245-298-6(7))* Lectorum Pubns., Inc.

—No Talking. (J). 2008. 78.75 *(978-1-4361-5835-0(4))* 2007. 54.75 *(978-1-4281-5418-6(3))* 2007. 51.75 *(978-1-4281-5424-7(8))* 2007. (SPA.). 54.75 *(978-1-4281-5422-3(1))* 2007. 52.75 *(978-1-4281-5420-9(5))* 2007. 1.25 *(978-1-4281-5415-5(9))* 2007. 209.75 *(978-1-4281-5419-3(1))* Recorded Bks., Inc.

—No Talking. Elliott, Mark, illus. (ENG.). 160p. (J). (gr. 3-7). 2009. pap. 7.99 *(978-1-4169-0984-2(2))* 2007. 18.99 *(978-1-4169-0983-5(4))* Simon & Schuster Children's Publishing. (Atheneum Bks. for Young Readers).

—No Talking. Elliott, Mark, illus. l.t. ed. 2007. (Literacy Bridge Middle Reader Ser.). 155p. (J). (gr. 3-7). 23.95 *(978-1-4104-0294-3(0))* Thorndike Pr.

—No Talking. 2009. (CHI., Illus.). 180p. (J). pap. 14.95 *(978-7-5309-5645-8(0))* Tianjin Education Pr.

—No Talking. 2009. lib. bdg. 18.40 *(978-0-606-14508-4(7)*, Turtleback) Turtleback Bks.

—Sin Hablar. 2009.Tr. of No Talking. (SPA.). 156p. (gr. 4-6). pap. 10.99 *(978-84-441-4100-8(3))* Everest Editora ESP. Dist: Lectorum Pubns., Inc.

Cohen, Penny L. Tapuchim & Dvash. Polsky, Beanie, illus. 2012. 36p. 24.95 *(978-1-4626-7769-6(X))*; pap. 24.95 *(978-1-4626-6667-6(1))* PublishAmerica, Inc.

Cole, Kathryn. Reptile Flu: A Story about Communication, 1 vol. Leng, Qin, illus. 2015. (I'm a Great Little Kid Ser.). (ENG.). 24p. (J). (gr. 1-3). 15.95 *(978-1-927583-61-6(6))* Second Story Pr. CAN. Dist: Orca Bk. Pubs. USA.

—A Tattle-Tell Tale: A Story about Getting Help, 1 vol. Leng, Qin, illus. 2016. (I'm a Great Little Kid Ser.). (ENG.). 24p. (J). (gr. 1-3). 15.95 *(978-1-927583-92-0(6))* Second Story Pr. CAN. Dist: Orca Bk. Pubs. USA.

Compagnucci, Veronica M. Emily Finds Her Voice. 2013. 40p. pap. 24.95 *(978-1-63004-288-2(9))* America Star Bks.

Cook, Julia. I Can't Believe You Said That! De Weerd, Kelsey, illus. 2014. (ENG.). 32p. (J). pap. 10.95 *(978-1-934490-67-9(9))* Boys Town Pr.

—My Mouth Is a Volcano! Hartman, Carrie, illus. 2008. 32p. (J). (gr. -1-3). pap. 9.95 *(978-1-931636-85-8(0))* National Ctr. For Youth Issues.

—Thanks for the Feedback, I Think. De Weerd, Kelsey & Dufalla, Anita, illus. 2013. (ENG.). 32p. (J). pap. 10.95 *(978-1-934490-49-5(0))* Boys Town Pr.

Cordell, Matthew. Hello! Hello! Cordell, Matthew, illus. 2012. (ENG., Illus.). 56p. (J). (gr. -1-4). 16.99 *(978-1-4231-5906-3(3))* Hyperion Pr.

Cosgrove, Stephen. Jalopy. 2011. (Orig.). (J). *(978-0-86592-797-1(9))* Rourke Enterprises, Inc.

Crompton, Laurie Boyle. Blaze (Or, Love in the Time of Supervillains) 2013. (ENG.). 320p. (YA). (gr. 7-12). pap. 8.99 *(978-1-4022-7343-8(6))* Sourcebooks, Inc.

Culbertson, Kim. The Wonder of Us. 2017. (ENG.). 336p. (J). (gr. 7). 17.99 ***(978-0-545-73151-5(8))*** Scholastic, Inc.

Diggle, David Mark. Lilly: The Crazy Little Van. Preuss, Sarah Louise, illus. 2011. 26p. (J). pap. *(978-0-9871658-4-8(4))* Diggle de Doo Productions Pty, Ltd.

Draper, Sharon M. Out of My Mind. 2009. 9.00 *(978-0-7848-3780-1(5)*, Everbind) Marco Bk. Co.

—Out of My Mind. (ENG., Illus.). (J). (gr. 5). 2012. 320p. pap. 9.99 *(978-1-4169-7171-9(8))* 2010. 304p. 18.99 *(978-1-4169-7170-2(X))* Simon & Schuster Children's Publishing. (Atheneum Bks. for Young Readers).

—Out of My Mind. 2012. lib. bdg. 20.85 *(978-0-606-25672-8(5)*, Turtleback) Turtleback Bks.

Edgar, Amy. Here, Kitty, Kitty. Tejido, Jomike, illus. 2017. (Scholastic Reader, Level 2 Ser.). (ENG.). 32p. (J). (gr. k-2). pap. 5.99 ***(978-1-338-04591-8(1))*** Scholastic, Inc.

Felix, Monique. The Rumor. Felix, Monique, illus. 2011. (ENG., Illus.). 24p. (J). (gr. 1-3). 19.99 *(978-1-56846-219-6(0)*, Creative Editions) Creative Co., The.

Fry, Sonali. Where Are You, Blue? Clifton-Brown, Holly, illus. 2015. (Dot Town Ser.). (ENG.). 32p. (J). (gr. -1 — 1). bds. 8.99 *(978-1-4814-3589-5(2)*, Little Simon) Little Simon.

Gould, M. & Gould, R. About Gossip: What Would Jesus Do, 1 vol. Hurst, Debbie, illus. 2009. 28p. pap. 24.95 *(978-1-60749-680-9(1))* America Star Bks.

Grant, Katy. Rumors. 2010. (Summer Camp Secrets Ser.). (ENG.). 256p. (J). (gr. 3-7). pap. 6.99 *(978-1-4169-9163-2(8)*, Aladdin) Simon & Schuster Children's Publishing.

Groeneweg, Nicole. One Word Pearl. Mitchell, Hazel, illus. 2013. (ENG.). 32p. (J). (gr. k-3). 17.95 *(978-1-934133-53-8(1))*; pap. 7.95 *(978-1-934133-54-5(X))* Charlesbridge Publishing, Inc.

Harmer, Wendy. I Lost My Mobile at the Mall. 2011. (ENG.). 272p. (YA). (gr. 7-18). 10.99 *(978-1-935279-97-6(1))* Kane Miller.

Hicks, Betty. The Worm Whisperer. Hatke, Ben, illus. 2013. (ENG.). 192p. (J). (gr. 3-7). 17.99 *(978-1-59643-490-5(2)*, 9781596434905) Roaring Brook Pr.

Lasky, Kathryn. Star Rise. 2014. (Horses of the Dawn Ser.: 2). (ENG., Illus.). 208p. (J). (gr. 3-7). 16.99 *(978-0-545-39717-9(0)*, Scholastic Pr.) Scholastic, Inc.

Lechner, John. The Clever Stick. Lechner, John, illus. 2009. (ENG., Illus.). 40p. (J). (gr. k-3). 14.99 *(978-0-7636-3950-1(8))* Candlewick Pr.

Lestrade, Agnès de & Frank-McNeil, Julia. Phileas's Fortune: A Story about Self-Expression. Docampo, Valeria, illus. 2010. 40p. (J). (gr. -1-3). 14.95 *(978-1-4338-0790-9(4))*; pap. 9.95 *(978-1-4338-0792-3(0))* American Psychological Assn. (Magination Pr.).

Lofting, Hugh. The Story of Doctor Dolittle: Animal Talk. Kanzler, John, illus. 2008. (Easy Reader Classics Ser.). (ENG.). 32p. (gr. 3-7). lib. bdg. 24.21 *(978-1-59961-338-3(7))* Spotlight.

Mammay, Judith. Ryan's Victory. Fargo, Todd, illus. 2009. 32p. (J). pap. 9.95 *(978-0-944727-53-9(0))*; lib. bdg. 15.95 *(978-0-944727-54-6(9))* Jason & Nordic Pubs. (Turtle Bks.).

Mason, Prue. Camel Rider. 2007. (ENG.). 208p. (J). (gr. 5-7). 15.95 *(978-1-58089-314-5(7))* Charlesbridge Publishing, Inc.

McCahan, Erin. Love & Other Foreign Words. 2014. (ENG.). 336p. (YA). (gr. 7). 17.99 *(978-0-8037-4051-8(4)*, Dial Bks) Penguin Young Readers Group.

McDonald, Megan. Hen Hears Gossip. Kim, Joung Un, illus. 2008. 32p. (J). (gr. -1-k). lib. bdg. 17.89 *(978-0-06-113877-5(0))*; (ENG.). 17.99 *(978-0-06-113876-8(2))* HarperCollins Pubs. (Greenwillow Bks.).

McSween, Michele. Gordon & Li Li Count in Mandarin. Nam, Doan, illus. 2010. 32p. 9.99 *(978-0-9820881-3-5(2))* McWong Ink.

—Gordon & Li Li Learn Animals in Mandarin. Nam, Doan, illus. 2010. 32p. 9.99 *(978-0-9820881-2-8(4))* McWong Ink.

Miller, Holly & Schwartzkopf, Jere. A Horse Named Princess: Hola Princess Adios Thistle. 2009. 48p. pap. 17.49 *(978-1-4343-6976-5(5))* AuthorHouse.

Mohammed, Khadra & Williams, Karen Lynn. My Name Is Sangoel. Stock, Catherine, illus. 2009. (ENG.). 36p. (J). (gr. 1-5). 17.00 *(978-0-8028-5307-3(2)*, Eerdmans Bks For Young Readers) Eerdmans, William B. Publishing Co.

Mueller, Dagmar H. David's World: A Picture Book about Living with Autism. Ballhaus, Verena, illus. 2012. (ENG.). 28p. (J). (gr. -1-k). 16.95 *(978-1-61608-962-7(8)*, 608962, Sky Pony Pr.) Skyhorse Publishing Co., Inc.

Ockler, Sarah. The Summer of Chasing Mermaids. 2015. (ENG., Illus.). 416p. (YA). (gr. 9). 17.99 *(978-1-4814-0127-2(0)*, Simon Pulse) Simon Pulse.

Owens, Greg. Rupert the Wrong-Word Pirate. Beaky, Suzanne, illus. 2006. (J). *(978-1-58987-143-4(X))* Kindermusik International.

Parsons, Garry. Krong! Parsons, Garry, illus. 2006. (Illus.). 32p. (J). (gr. -1-3). 15.95 *(978-1-58925-061-1(3))* Tiger Tales.

Rand, Ann & Rand, Paul. Sparkle & Spin: A Book about Words. 2006. (ENG., Illus.). 40p. (J). (gr. -1-3). 16.99 *(978-0-8118-5003-2(X))* Chronicle Bks. LLC.

Reynolds, Aaron. Pirates vs. Cowboys. Barneda, David, illus. 2013. (ENG.). 40p. (J). (gr. k-3). 16.99 *(978-0-375-85874-1(1)*, Knopf Bks. for Young Readers) Random Hse. Children's Bks.

Rigby Education Staff. Mickey Maloney's Mail. (Sails Literacy Ser.). (Illus.). 16p. (gr. 2-3). 27.00 *(978-0-7635-9939-3(5)*, 699395C99) Rigby Education.

Schraff, Anne. A Boy Called Twister, 1 vol. unabr. ed. 2010. (Urban Underground Ser.). (ENG.). 180p. (YA). (gr. 9-12). pap. 9.95 *(978-1-61651-002-2(1))* Saddleback Educational Publishing, Inc.

Seuss. Gerald Mcboing Boing. Crawford, Mel, illus. 2017. (Classic Seuss Ser.). (ENG.). 40p. (J). (gr. k-4). 16.99 ***(978-1-5247-1635-6(9))***; lib. bdg. 19.99 ***(978-1-5247-1757-5(6))*** Random Hse. Children's Bks. (Random Hse. Bks. for Young Readers).

Seuss, Dr. Gerald McBoing Boing. Seuss, Dr., illus. 2004. (Little Golden Book Ser.). (ENG., Illus.). 24p. (J). (gr. -1-2). 4.99 *(978-0-375-82721-1(8)*, Golden Bks.) Random Hse. Children's Bks.

Tidd, Louise Vitellaro. Ya Te Enteraste? Handelman, Dorothy, photos by. 2007. (Lecturas para niños de verdad - Nivel 2 (Real Kids Readers - Level 2) Ser.).Tr. of Did You Hear About Jake? (SPA., Illus.). 32p. (J). (gr. -1-3). per. 5.95 *(978-0-8225-7802-4(6)*, Ediciones Lerner) Lerner Publishing Group.

Trueman, Terry. Life Happens Next. 2012. (Stuck in Neutral Ser.: 3). (ENG.). 144p. (YA). (gr. 9). 17.99 *(978-0-06-202803-7(0)*, HarperTeen) HarperCollins Pubs.

Voake, Steve. Daisy Dawson at the Beach. Meserve, Jessica, illus. 2012. (Daisy Dawson Ser.: 4). (ENG.). 96p. (J). (gr. 1-4). pap. 5.99 *(978-0-7636-5946-2(0))* Candlewick Pr.

—Daisy Dawson on the Farm. Meserve, Jessica, illus. 2012. (Daisy Dawson Ser.: 5). (ENG.). 96p. (J). (gr. 1-4). 14.99 *(978-0-7636-5882-3(0))* Candlewick Pr.

Wallace, Nancy Elizabeth. Tell-A-Bunny, 0 vols. Wallace, Nancy Elizabeth, illus. 2007. (ENG., Illus.). 36p. (J). (gr. -1-1). 7.99 *(978-0-7614-5369-7(5)*, 9780761453697, Amazon Children's Publishing) Amazon Publishing.

Wells, Rosemary. Say Hello, Sophie! 2017. (ENG., Illus.). 32p. (J). (— 1). 17.99 *(978-1-101-99925-7(X)*, Viking Books for Young Readers) Penguin Young Readers Group.

—Use Your Words, Sophie! 2015. (ENG., Illus.). 24p. (J). (gr. -1 — 1). 16.99 *(978-0-670-01663-1(2)*, Viking Books for Young Readers) Penguin Young Readers Group.

Wise, Rachel. Digital Disaster! 2013. (Dear Know-It-All Ser.: 6). (ENG.). 160p. (J). (gr. 3-7). 15.99 *(978-1-4424-7218-1(9))*; pap. 5.99 *(978-1-4424-7217-4(0))* Simon Spotlight. (Simon Spotlight).

Young, T. M. My Ten Cents. Victoria Washington and Carla Watts, ed. Cromwell, Danielle, illus. 2013. 24p. pap. 24.95 *(978-1-4626-5790-2(7))* America Star Bks.

COMMUNICATION—HISTORY

Boothroyd, Jennifer. From Typewriters to Text Messages: How Communication Has Changed. 2011. (Comparing Past & Present Ser.). pap. 7.95 *(978-0-7613-7838-9(3))*; pap. 45.32 *(978-0-7613-8393-2(X))*; (ENG., Illus.). 32p. lib. bdg. 26.60 *(978-0-7613-6745-1(4))* Lerner Publishing Group.

Housel, Debra J. Inventions in Communications. 2012. (Time for Kids Nonfiction Readers: Level 3. 4 Ser.). (ENG., Illus.). 28p. (J). (gr. -1-3). pap. 8.99 *(978-1-4258-0557-9(4))* Shell Educational Publishing.

Jarnow, Jesse. Telegraph & Telephone Networks: Ground Breaking Developments in American Communications. 2004. (America's Industrial Society in the 19th Century Ser.). (ENG., Illus.). 32p. (gr. 5-8). pap. 10.00 *(978-0-8239-4279-4(1))* Rosen Publishing Group, Inc., The.

—Telegraph & Telephone Networks: Groundbreaking Developments in American Communications. 2009. (America's Industrial Society in the 19th Century Ser.). 32p. (gr. 4-4). 47.90 *(978-1-61511-341-5(X))* Rosen Publishing Group, Inc., The.

Mason, Prue. Camel Rider. 2011. 9.49 *(978-0-7848-3618-7(3)*, Everbind) Marco Bk. Co.

McCormick, Anita Louise. The Invention of the Telegraph & Telephone in American History. 2004. (In American History Ser.). (Illus.). 128p. (J). lib. bdg. 26.60 *(978-0-7660-1841-9(5))* Enslow Pubs., Inc.

O'Brien, Lindsy. Communication Long Ago & Today, 1 vol. 2014. (Long Ago & Today Ser.). (ENG.). 24p. (gr. 1-2). 25.32 *(978-1-4914-0295-5(4))*; pap. 6.95 *(978-1-4914-0303-7(9))* Capstone Press of Coughlan Cos.

Sundance/Newbridge LLC Staff. For Your Information. 2007. (Early Science Ser.). (gr. k-3). 18.95 *(978-1-4007-6567-6(6))*; pap. 6.10 *(978-1-4007-6563-8(3))* Sundance/Newbridge Educational Publishing.

Woods, Michael & Woods, Mary B. The History of Communication. 2005. (Major Inventions Through History Ser.). (Illus.). 56p. (J). (gr. 4-7). lib. bdg. 26.60 *(978-0-8225-3807-3(5)*, Twenty-First Century Bks.) Lerner Publishing Group.

World Book, Inc. Staff, contrib. by. Smoke Signals to Smartphones: A Timeline of Long-Distance Communication. 2016. (J). *(978-0-7166-3543-7(7))* World Bk., Inc.

COMMUNICATION AMONG ANIMALS

see Animal Communication

COMMUNICATIONS RELAY SATELLITES

see Artificial Satellites in Telecommunication

COMMUNISM

see also Anti-Communist Movements; Social Conflict; Socialism

Connolly, Sean. Communism. 2012. (Systems of Government Ser.). (Illus.). 48p. (gr. 6-12). lib. bdg. 37.10 *(978-1-59920-802-2(4))* Black Rabbit Bks.

Grant, R. G. Communism. 2005. (Systems of Government Ser.). (Illus.). 48p. (gr. 6-12). pap. 14.05 *(978-0-8368-5887-7(5))*; lib. bdg. 31.00 *(978-0-8368-5882-2(4))* Stevens, Gareth Publishing LLLP. (Gareth Stevens Secondary Library).

Heits, Rudolph T. Communism. Colton, Timothy J., ed. 2012. (Major Forms of World Government Ser.). 64p. (J). (gr. 5). 22.95 *(978-1-4222-2136-5(9))* Mason Crest.

Jarnow, Jesse. Socialism: A Primary Source Analysis. (Primary Sources of Political Systems Ser.). 64p. 2009. (gr. 5-8). 58.50 *(978-1-60851-839-5(6))* 2003. (Illus.). (J). lib. bdg. 31.95 *(978-0-8239-4521-4(9))* Rosen Publishing Group, Inc., The.

Keeley, Jennifer. Containing the Communists: America's Foreign Entanglements. 2003. (American War Library). (ENG., Illus.). 112p. (J). 30.85 *(978-1-59018-225-3(1)*, Lucent Bks.) Cengage Gale.

Lansford, Tom. Communism. 2007. (Political Systems of the World Ser.). (Illus.). 143p. (J). (gr. 4-7). lib. bdg. 42.79 *(978-0-7614-2628-8(0)*, Benchmark Bks.) Marshall Cavendish Corp.

Latchana Kenney, Karen. What Is Communism?, Vol. 1. 2014. (Understanding Political Systems Ser.). 48p. (gr. 6-8). (ENG.). (J). pap. 14.05 *(978-1-4824-0320-6(X))*; (YA). 31.95 *(978-1-4824-0319-0(6))* Stevens, Gareth Publishing LLLP.

Link, Theodore. Communism: A Primary Source Analysis. 2009. (Primary Sources of Political Systems Ser.). 64p. (gr. 5-8). 58.50 *(978-1-60851-835-7(3))* Rosen Publishing Group, Inc., The.

Malaspina, Ann. The Chinese Revolution & Mao Zedong in World History. 2004. (In World History Ser.). (Illus.). 128p. (J). lib. bdg. 27.94 *(978-0-7660-1935-5(7))* Enslow Pubs., Inc.

—Mao Zedong & the Chinese Revolution. 2016. (People & Events That Changed the World Ser.). (ENG., Illus.). 128p. (J). (gr. 7-8). lib. bdg. 37.27 *(978-0-7660-7292-3(4))* Enslow Pubs., Inc.

Murphy, John, ed. Socialism & Communism. 2014. (Political & Economic Systems Ser.). 312p. (YA). (gr. 9-12). 90.00 *(978-1-62275-336-9(4))*; 45.00 *(978-1-62275-335-2(6))* Rosen Publishing Group, Inc., The.

Porterfield, Jason. Communism: A Primary Source Analysis. 2003. (Primary Sources of Political Systems Ser.). (Illus.). 64p. (YA). (gr. 5-9). 31.95 *(978-0-8239-4517-7(0))* Rosen Publishing Group, Inc., The.

Riggs, Kate & Fandel, Jennifer. Communism. 2017. (Odysseys in Government Ser.). (ENG., Illus.). 80p. (J). (gr. 7-11). pap. 14.99 *(978-1-62832-319-1(1)*, Creative Paperbacks) Creative Co., The.

Rise & Fall of Communism. 2003. spiral bd. 16.95 *(978-1-56004-172-6(2))* Social Studies Schl. Service.

Vander Hook, Sue. Communism, 1 vol. 2011. (Exploring World Governments Ser.). (ENG., Illus.). 160p. (J). (gr. 9-12). lib. bdg. 37.07 *(978-1-61714-789-0(3)*, Essential Library) ABDO Publishing Co.

COMMUNISM—FICTION

Avi. Catch You Later, Traitor. (ENG.). 304p. (J). (gr. 3-7). 2016. pap. 7.95 *(978-1-61620-587-4(3))* 2015. 16.95 *(978-1-61620-359-7(5))* Algonquin Bks. of Chapel Hill.

Compestine, Ying Chang. Revolution Is Not a Dinner Party. 2009. (ENG.). 272p. (J). (gr. 5-9). pap. 9.99 *(978-0-312-58149-7(1)*, 9780312581497) Square Fish.

Dunivan, Dennis W. Escape from Communist Heaven. 2013. (ENG., Illus.). 392p. 17.99 *(978-1-59181-229-6(1))* Sentient Pubns.

Durbin, William. The Darkest Evening. 2011. (Fesler-Lampert Minnesota Heritage Ser.). (ENG.). 248p. pap. 11.95 *(978-0-8166-7568-5(6))* Univ. of Minnesota Pr.

Forbes, Dillon. Careful Enough? 2008. (YA). 8.99 *(978-1-59166-835-0(2))* BJU Pr.

Jiang, Ji-Li. Red Kite, Blue Kite. Ruth, Greg, illus. 2013. (ENG.). 32p. (J). (gr. 1-3). 17.99 *(978-1-4231-2753-6(6))* Hyperion Pr.

Levine, Kristin. The Paper Cowboy. (ENG.). (J). (gr. 5). 2016. 368p. 8.99 *(978-0-14-242715-6(2)*, Puffin Books) 2014. 352p. 16.99 *(978-0-399-16328-9(X)*, G.P. Putnam's Sons Books for Young Readers) Penguin Young Readers Group.

Lytton, Deborah. Silence. 2015. (ENG.). 320p. (YA). (gr. 7). 17.99 *(978-1-60907-945-1(0)*, Shadow Mountain) Shadow Mountain Publishing.

Nohrden, Patrick. The Crystal Monkey. 2014. 286p. (YA). pap. 16.99 *(978-1-4621-1481-8(4))* Cedar Fort, Inc./CFI Distribution.

Prozeller, Ellen Lucey. 32 Days: A Story of Faith & Courage. 2016. (J). pap. *(978-0-8198-0657-4(9))* Pauline Bks. & Media.

Yelchin, Eugene. Arcady's Goal. Yelchin, Eugene, illus. 2014. (ENG., Illus.). 240p. (J). (gr. 4-7). 15.99 *(978-0-8050-9844-0(5)*, 9780805098440, Holt, Henry & Co. Bks. For Young Readers) Holt, Henry & Co.

—Arcady's Goal. Yelchin, Eugene, illus. 2015. (ENG., Illus.). 256p. (J). (gr. 4-7). pap. 7.99 *(978-1-250-06814-9(2)*, 9781250068149) Square Fish.

—Breaking Stalin's Nose. Yelchin, Eugene, illus. 2011. (ENG., Illus.). 160p. (J). (gr. 4-7). 15.99 *(978-0-8050-9216-5(1)*, 9780805092165, Holt, Henry & Co. Bks. For Young Readers) Holt, Henry & Co.

—Breaking Stalin's Nose. Yelchin, Eugene, illus. 2013. (ENG., Illus.). 176p. (J). (gr. 4-7). pap. 7.99 *(978-1-250-03410-6(8)*, 9781250034106) Square Fish.

—Breaking Stalin's Nose. 2013. (J). lib. bdg. 18.40 *(978-0-606-32308-6(2)*, Turtleback) Turtleback Bks.

Yue, Gui & Farrow, Clare. Little Leap Forward: A Boy in Beijing. Cann, Helen, illus. 2011. (ENG.). 120p. (J). (gr. 3-6). pap. 12.99 *(978-1-84686-539-8(5))* Barefoot Bks., Inc.

Yue, Guo & Farrow, Clare. Little Leap Forward: A Boy in Beijing. Cann, Helen, illus. 2008. (ENG.). 128p. (YA). (gr. 4-7). 16.99 *(978-1-84686-114-7(4))* Barefoot Bks., Inc.

COMMUNISM—SOVIET UNION

The Collapse of the Soviet Union. 2010. (Milestones in World History Ser.). (Illus.). 128p. (C). (gr. 9-18). 35.00 *(978-1-60413-493-3(3)*, Chelsea Hse.) Facts On File, Inc.

Conklin, Wendy. Cold War Leaders, 1 vol. 2007. (Primary Source Readers Ser.). (ENG.). 32p. (J). (gr. 4-4). pap. 8.99 *(978-0-7439-0673-9(X))* Shell Educational Publishing.

COMMUNISM—UNITED STATES

Aronson, Marc. Master of Deceit: J. Edgar Hoover & America in the Age of Lies. 2012. (ENG., Illus.). 230p. (J). (gr. 9). 25.99 *(978-0-7636-5025-4(0))* Candlewick Pr.

COMMUNIST COUNTRIES

Keeley, Jennifer. Containing the Communists: America's Foreign Entanglements. 2003. (American War Library). (ENG., Illus.). 112p. (J). 30.85 *(978-1-59018-225-3(1)*, Lucent Bks.) Cengage Gale.

Richardson, Erik. NATO, the Warsaw Pact, & the Iron Curtain. 2017. (J). ***(978-1-5026-2727-8(2))*** Cavendish Square Publishing.

Small, Cathleen. The Collapse of Communism & the Break up of the Soviet Union. 2017. (J). ***(978-1-5026-2728-5(0))*** Cavendish Square Publishing.

COMMUNITY CHESTS

see Fund Raising

COMMUNITY LIFE

see also Cities and Towns

Ajmera, Maya & Ivanko, John D. Be My Neighbor. 2006. (ENG., Illus.). 32p. (J). (gr. k-3). per. 7.95 *(978-1-57091-685-4(3))* Charlesbridge Publishing, Inc.

Around the Neighborhood. 2005. (Lee Bennett Hopkins Worlds of Poetry Classroom Library). (YA). (gr. k-3). suppl. ed. 57.00 *(978-0-8215-0522-9(X))* Sadlier, William H. Inc.

Around the Neighborhood: Take-Home Book. 2005. (Lee Bennett Hopkins Worlds of Poetry Classroom Library). (YA). (gr. k-3). 13.50 *(978-0-8215-0567-0(X))* Sadlier, William H. Inc.

Aucoin, Lee. My Community, 1 vol. 2009. (Early Childhood Themes Ser.). (ENG., Illus.). 16p. (J). (gr. -1-2). pap. 6.99 *(978-1-4333-1473-5(8))* Teacher Created Materials, Inc.

Austen, Mary. Ayudantes de la Comunidad / Helping the Community Set. 2015. (Ayudantes de la Comunidad / Helping the Community Ser.). (ENG & SPA.). 24p. (J). (gr. 1-1). 141.60 *(978-1-4994-0609-2(6),* PowerKids Pr.) Rosen Publishing Group, Inc., The.

Becnel, Barbara, ed. Gangs & Your Neighborhood: Stanley Tookie Williams Street Peace Series, 8 bks., Vol. 1, Bk. 8. 2008. 24p. (J). 6.95 *(978-0-9753584-8-1(0))* Damamli Publishing Co.

Benchmark Education Company. Living in a Community (Teacher Guide) 2005. *(978-1-4108-4665-5(2))* Benchmark Education Co.

Benchmark Education Company, LLC Staff, compiled by. Living in Communities: Theme Set. 2006. (J). 305.00 *(978-1-4108-7067-4(7))* Benchmark Education Co.

—Social Studies Theme: Communities. 2005. spiral bd. 115.00 *(978-1-4108-5329-5(2))* Benchmark Education Co.

—19th Century Communities: Theme Set. 2006. (J). 121.00 *(978-1-4108-7099-5(5))* Benchmark Education Co.

Berendes, Mary. Neighborhood/el Barrio. Petelinsek, Kathleen, illus. 2008. (WordBooks/Libros de Palabras Ser.). (SPA & ENG.). 24p. (J). (gr. k-3). 25.64 *(978-1-59296-993-7(3),* 201096) Child's World, Inc., The.

Bishop, Celeste. Learning at Pre-K. 2016. (Places in My Community Ser.). 00024p. (J). (gr. 1-1). pap. 8.25 *(978-1-4994-2774-5(3),* PowerKids Pr.) Rosen Publishing Group, Inc., The.

Blankenship, LeeAnn. What Are Community Resources? 2017. (Let's Find Out! Communities Ser.). 32p. (J). (gr. 6-8). pap. 12.90 ***(978-1-68048-717-6(5),*** Britannica Educational Publishing) Rosen Publishing Group, Inc., The.

Boehm, Richard G., et al. Activity Books: Communities. 2003. (Harcourt Brace Social Studies). (gr. k-7). act. bk. ed. 13.80 *(978-0-15-310310-0(8))* Harcourt Schl. Pubs.

—Assessment Programs: Communities. 2003. (Harcourt Brace Social Studies). (gr. k-7). 50.60 *(978-0-15-310299-8(3))* Harcourt Schl. Pubs.

—Game Time! Communities. 2003. (Harcourt Brace Social Studies). (gr. k-7). 7.30 *(978-0-15-312355-9(9))* Harcourt Schl. Pubs.

Bullard, Lisa. This Is My Neighborhood. Conger, Holli, illus. 2016. (Cloverleaf Books (tm) — Where I Live Ser.). (ENG.). 24p. (J). (gr. k-2). 25.32 *(978-1-4677-9521-0(6),* Millbrook Pr.) Lerner Publishing Group.

Capstone Press. First Graphics: My Community, 1 vol. 2010. (First Graphics: My Community Ser.). (ENG.). 32p. lib. bdg. 106.60 *(978-1-4296-5935-2(1))* Capstone Press of Coughlan Cos.

Catalano, Angela. Community Needs: Meeting Needs & Wants in the Community. 2009. (Communities at Work Ser.). 24p. (gr. 2-2). 42.50 *(978-1-61511-889-2(6),* PowerKids Pr.) Rosen Publishing Group, Inc., The.

—Community Plans: Choices about Money Making in Communities. 2009. (Communities at Work Ser.). 24p. (gr. 2-2). 42.50 *(978-1-61511-890-8(X),* PowerKids Pr.) Rosen Publishing Group, Inc., The.

—Community Plans: Making Choices about Money in Communities. 2005. (Communities at Work Ser.). (Illus.). 24p. (J). (gr. 1-4). lib. bdg. 22.60 *(978-1-4042-2779-8(2));* (ENG., (gr. 2-3). pap. 8.25 *(978-1-4042-5014-7(X),* PowerKids Pr.) Rosen Publishing Group, Inc., The.

—Community Resources: The Land & the People in Communities. (Communities at Work Ser.). 24p. 2009. (gr. 2-2). 42.50 *(978-1-61511-891-5(8),* PowerKids Pr.) 2005. (Illus.). (J). (gr. 1-4). lib. bdg. 22.60 *(978-1-4042-2781-1(4))* 2005. (ENG., Illus.). (gr. 2-3). pap. 8.25 *(978-1-4042-5016-1(6),* PowerKids Pr.) Rosen Publishing Group, Inc., The.

Cavell-Clarke, Steffi. Sharing Our Global Community. 2017. (Illus.). 24p. (J). ***(978-0-7787-3264-8(9))*** Crabtree Publishing Co.

Chastain, Zachary. Passing the Time: Entertainment in The 1800s. 2009. (Daily Life in America in the 1800s Ser.). 64p. (YA). (gr. 7-18). pap. 9.95 *(978-1-4222-1858-7(9));* lib. bdg. 22.95 *(978-1-4222-1785-6(X))* Mason Crest.

Coldwell, Lamar. Our Community Is in a Valley. 2016. (Rosen REAL Readers: Social Studies Nonfiction / Fiction: Family, Community, & the World Ser.). 8p. (gr. 1-k). pap. 5.46 *(978-1-5081-2305-7(5),* Rosen Classroom) Rosen Publishing Group, Inc., The.

Community Helpers. 2016. (Community Helpers Ser.). 00024p. (J). (gr. 1-1). 94.40 *(978-1-4994-2633-5(X),* PowerKids Pr.) Rosen Publishing Group, Inc., The.

Community Helpers at Work. 2016. (Community Helpers at Work Ser.). (ENG.). 24p. (gr. 1-2). lib. bdg. 101.28 *(978-1-5157-4026-1(9),* First Facts) Capstone Press of Coughlan Cos.

Cordier, Claire. Nobody will hear Me... 2008. 32p. pap. 23.50 *(978-1-4092-1643-8(8))* Lulu Pr., Inc.

Cowen-Fletcher, Jane. Se Necesita Todo un Pueblo. 2003. (SPA., Illus.). (J). pap. 4.76 net. *(978-0-590-29394-5(X),* SO30915) Scholastic, Inc.

Cuthbert, Megan & Siemens, Jared. Bank. 2016. (J). ***(978-1-5105-1879-7(7))*** SmartBook Media, Inc.

Donnelly, Karen. Biomes of the Past & Future. 2003. (Earth's Changing Weather & Climate Ser.). (Illus.). 24p. (J). lib. bdg. 22.60 *(978-0-8239-6215-0(6),* PowerKids Pr.) Rosen Publishing Group, Inc., The.

Dumm, Brian Caleb, illus. Meet Your Community Workers, 6 vols., Set. Incl. Firefighters at Work. Kenney, Karen L. 28.50 *(978-1-60270-648-4(4));* Librarians at Work. Kenney, Karen Latchana. 28.50 *(978-1-60270-649-1(2));* Mail Carriers at Work. Kenney, Karen Latchana. 28.50 *(978-1-60270-650-7(6));* Nurses at Work. Kenney, Karen L. 28.50 *(978-1-60270-651-4(4));* Police Officers at Work. Kenney, Karen L. 28.50 *(978-1-60270-652-1(2));* Teachers at Work. Kenney, Karen L. 28.50 *(978-1-60270-653-8(0));* (J). (gr. -1-2). (Meet Your Community Workers Ser.). (Illus.). 32p. 2009. 171.00 *(978-1-60270-647-7(6),* Looking Glass Library- Nonfiction) Magic Wagon.

Durrie, Karen. Diversión. 2012. (SPA.). (J). 27.13 *(978-1-61913-209-2(5))* Weigl Pubs., Inc.

—Fun. 2011. (J). 27.13 *(978-1-61690-944-4(7))* Weigl Pubs., Inc.

—Fun: Arabic-English Bilingual Edition. 2016. (Community Helpers Ser.). (ENG.). (J). (gr. 3-7). 29.99 *(978-1-61913-902-2(2))* Weigl Pubs., Inc.

—Safety. 2011. (ENG.). (J). lib. bdg. 27.13 *(978-1-61690-951-2(X))* Weigl Pubs., Inc.

—Seguridad. 2012. (SPA & ENG.). (J). *(978-1-61913-211-5(7))* Weigl Pubs., Inc.

Edwards, Clint. Show Me Community Helpers: My First Picture Encyclopedia, 1 vol. 2013. (My First Picture Encyclopedias Ser.). (ENG.). 32p. (gr. 1-2). pap. 8.10 *(978-1-4765-3788-7(7),* Aplus Bks.); 7.95 *(978-1-62065-918-2(2));* lib. bdg. 27.32 *(978-1-62065-056-1(8))* Capstone Press of Coughlan Cos.

Exploring Community. 2005. (Exploring Community Ser.). 24p. 43.95 *(978-1-4042-5160-1(X),* Rosen Classroom) Rosen Publishing Group, Inc., The.

Fenner, M. On My Block: Learning the BL Sound. 2009. (PowerPhonics Ser.). 24p. (gr. 1-1). 39.90 *(978-1-60851-464-9(1),* PowerKids Pr.) Rosen Publishing Group, Inc., The.

First Graphics: My Community. 2010. (First Graphics: My Community Ser.). (ENG.). 24p. (gr. 1-2). pap. 142.80 *(978-1-4296-5618-4(2))* Capstone Press of Coughlan Cos.

Gillis, Jennifer Blizin. Puedes Ayudar/You Can Help. Alemián, Manuel, tr. 2006. (My Neighborhood Discovery Library). (SPA & ENG., Illus.). 24p. (J). (gr. 3-7). lib. bdg. 22.79 *(978-1-60044-295-7(1))* Rourke Educational Media.

Goodman, Polly. Communities Today & Tomorrow. 2011. (Earth Alert! Ser.). 32p. (YA). (gr. 3-6). lib. bdg. 26.60 *(978-1-4339-5999-8(2))* Stevens, Gareth Publishing LLLP.

Goodspeed, Horace. Will's Neighborhood. 2012. (InfoMax Readers Ser.). (ENG., Illus.). 16 pp.p. (J). (gr. k-1). pap. 7.00 *(978-1-4488-8881-8(6),* Rosen Classroom) Rosen Publishing Group, Inc., The.

Harcourt School Publishers Staff. Living in the Community, Bk. 1. 2nd ed. 2003. (Illus.). pap. 139.70 *(978-0-15-337563-7(9))* Harcourt Schl. Pubs.

Held, George. Neighbors: The Yard Critters Too. Kim, Joung Un, illus. 2013. (ENG.). 32p. 20.00 *(978-0-916754-26-6(X))* Filsinger & Co., Ltd.

Helping the Community. 2015. (Helping the Community Ser.). (ENG.). 24p. (J). (gr. 1-1). pap., pap., pap. 297.00 *(978-1-4994-1296-3(7),* PowerKids Pr.) Rosen Publishing Group, Inc., The.

Hill, Christina. Community Leaders Then & Now, 1 vol. 2006. (Primary Source Readers Ser.). (ENG., Illus.). 32p. (J). (gr. 1-1). pap. 8.99 *(978-0-7439-9385-2(3))* Shell Educational Publishing.

Holden, Pam. Close to Home. 2016. (ENG., Illus.). 16p. (-1). pap. *(978-1-77654-167-6(7),* Red Rocket Readers) Flying Start Bks.

—Close to Home - BIG BOOK. 2016. (ENG.). 16p. (-1). Beta *(978-1-77654-161-4(8),* Red Rocket Readers) Flying Start Bks.

Holland, Trish. Neighborhood Song. 2010. (J). *(978-1-60617-143-1(7))* Teaching Strategies, LLC.

Hord, Colleen. My Safe Community. 2011. (ENG., Illus.). 24p. (gr. k-2). pap. 8.95 *(978-1-61741-997-3(4))* Rourke Educational Media.

Idzikowski, Lisa. What Are Community Services? 2017. (Let's Find Out! Communities Ser.). 32p. (J). (gr. 6-8). 24.45 ***(978-1-68048-727-5(2));*** pap. 12.90 ***(978-1-68048-725-1(6))*** Rosen Publishing Group, Inc., The. (Britannica Educational Publishing).

James, Dawn. Neighborhood Math. 2015. (J). *(978-1-62713-447-7(6))* Cavendish Square Publishing.

James, Wayan. Our Community Is in the Desert. 2016. (Rosen REAL Readers: Social Studies Nonfiction / Fiction: Family, Community, & the World Ser.). 8p. (gr. 1-k). pap. 5.46 *(978-1-5081-2302-6(0),* Rosen Classroom) Rosen Publishing Group, Inc., The.

Johnson, J. Angelique. The Eco-Neighbor's Guide to a Green Community, 1 vol. Poling, Kyle, illus. 2010. (Point It Out! Tips for Green Living Ser.). (ENG.). 24p. (gr. 2-3). lib. bdg. 26.65 *(978-1-4048-6028-5(2))* Picture Window Bks.

Jones, Grace. My Community. 2017. 24p. (J). ***(978-0-7787-3702-5(0))*** Crabtree Publishing Co.

Jones, Tammy. I Like to Play Sports. 2009. (Sight Word Readers Set A Ser.). (J). 3.49 net. *(978-1-60719-135-3(0))* Newmark Learning LLC.

Kalman, Bobbie. Ayudantes de Mi Comunidad. 2010. (SPA.). 24p. (J). pap. *(978-0-7787-8589-7(0));* lib. bdg. *(978-0-7787-8563-7(7))* Crabtree Publishing Co.

—Community Helpers Then & Now. 2013. (ENG., Illus.). 24p. (J). pap. *(978-0-7787-0143-9(3))* Crabtree Publishing Co.

—Helpers in My Community. 2010. (My World Ser.). (ENG., Illus.). 24p. (J). (gr. k-2). *(978-0-7787-9444-8(X));* pap. *(978-0-7787-9488-2(1))* Crabtree Publishing Co.

—Places in My Community. 2010. (My World Ser.). (ENG., Illus.). 24p. (J). (gr. k-2). *(978-0-7787-9443-1(1));* pap. *(978-0-7787-9487-5(3))* Crabtree Publishing Co.

Katz, Welwyn W. Come Like Shadows. Springett, Martin, illus. 2005. 318p. (gr. 7-12). 7.95 *(978-1-55050-170-4(4))* Coteau Bks. CAN. Dist: Fitzhenry & Whiteside, Ltd.

Keogh, Josie. What Are Different Types of Communities? 2017. (Let's Find Out! Communities Ser.). 32p. (J). (gr. 6-8). 24.45 ***(978-1-68048-731-2(0));*** pap. 12.90 ***(978-1-68048-729-9(9))*** Rosen Publishing Group, Inc., The. (Britannica Educational Publishing).

Klein, Carol Swartout. Painting for Peace in Ferguson. 2nd ed. 2015. (ENG.). 54p. (J). (gr. 2-3). 25.95 *(978-0-9963901-0-1(3));* pap. 15.95 *(978-0-9892079-9-7(4))* TreeHse. Publishing Group.

Kreisman, Rachelle. Being a Good Citizen: A Kids' Guide to Community Involvement. Haggerty, Tim, illus. 2015. (Start Smart: Community Ser.). (ENG.). 32p. (gr. 1-3). 26.65 *(978-1-937529-50-5(9))* Red Chair Pr.

—People Who Help: A Kids' Guide to Community Heroes. Haggerty, Tim, illus. 2015. (Start Smart: Community Ser.). (ENG.). 32p. (gr. 1-3). 26.65 *(978-1-937529-35-2(5))* Red Chair Pr.

—Places We Go: A Kids' Guide to Community Sites. Haggerty, Tim, illus. 2015. (Start Smart: Community Ser.). (ENG.). 32p. (gr. 1-3). 26.65 *(978-1-937529-36-9(3))* Red Chair Pr.

—Things We Do: A Kids' Guide to Community Activity. Haggerty, Tim, illus. 2015. (Start Smart: Community Ser.). (ENG.). 32p. (gr. 1-3). 26.65 *(978-1-937529-51-2(7))* Red Chair Pr.

Lang, Glenna & Wunsch, Marjory. Genius of Common Sense: Jane Jacobs & the Story of the Death & Life of Great American Cities. 2012. pap. 15.95 *(978-1-56792-456-5(5))* Godine, David R. Pub.

Lang, Glenna W. & Wunsch, Marjory. Genius of Common Sense: Jane Jacobs & the Story of the Death & Life of Great American Cities. 2009. (ENG., Illus.). 128p. (YA). (gr. 5-18). 17.95 *(978-1-56792-384-1(4))* Godine, David R. Pub.

Let's Find Out! Communities. 2017. (Let's Find Out! Communities Ser.). 32p. (gr. 6-8). 146.70 ***(978-1-5081-0530-5(8));*** pap. 77.40 ***(978-1-5081-0532-9(4))*** Rosen Publishing Group, Inc., The. (Britannica Educational Publishing).

Linde, Barbara M. Living in a Community. 2005. (J). pap. *(978-1-4108-4617-4(2))* Benchmark Education Co.

Lusted, Marcia Amidon. America's Colonization & Settlement. 2011. (Explorer Library: Language Arts Explorer Ser.). (ENG.). 32p. (gr. 4-8). pap. 14.21 *(978-1-61080-282-6(9),* 201205); lib. bdg. 28.50 *(978-1-61080-194-2(6),* 201164) Cherry Lake Publishing.

Lyons, Shelly. My Neighborhood. 2013. (My Neighborhood Ser.). (ENG.). 24p. (gr. k-1). pap. 208.50 *(978-1-62065-894-9(1));* lib. bdg. 133.25 *(978-1-62065-103-2(3))* Capstone Press of Coughlan Cos. (Pebble Plus).

—People in My Neighborhood, 1 vol. 2013. (My Neighborhood Ser.). (ENG., Illus.). 24p. (gr. k-1). pap. 7.29 *(978-1-62065-883-3(6));* lib. bdg. 26.65 *(978-1-62065-099-8(1))* Capstone Press of Coughlan Cos. (Pebble Plus).

—Places in My Neighborhood, 1 vol. 2013. (My Neighborhood Ser.). (ENG.). 24p. (gr. k-1). pap. 7.29 *(978-1-62065-885-7(2));* lib. bdg. 26.65 *(978-1-62065-100-1(9))* Capstone Press of Coughlan Cos. (Pebble Plus).

Manhof, Errol. My Community. 2009. (Real Life Readers Ser.). 8p. (gr. k-1). pap. 5.15 *(978-1-4042-7991-9(1),* Rosen Classroom) Rosen Publishing Group, Inc., The.

Mason, Helen. Be an Active Citizen in Your Community. 2016. (Citizenship in Action Ser.). (ENG., Illus.). 24p. (J). (gr. 1-4). *(978-0-7787-2601-2(0))* Crabtree Publishing Co.

Miller, Jake. Community Needs: Meeting Needs & Wants in Communities. 2005. (Communities at Work Ser.). (ENG., Illus.). 24p. (gr. 2-3). pap. 8.25 *(978-1-4042-5012-3(3),* PowerKids Pr.) Rosen Publishing Group, Inc., The.

—Community Needs: Meeting Needs & Wants in the Communities. 2005. (Communities at Work Ser.). (Illus.). 24p. (J). (gr. 1-4). lib. bdg. 22.60 *(978-1-4042-2780-4(6))* Rosen Publishing Group, Inc., The.

—Who's Who in a Neighborhood. (Communities at Work Ser.). 24p. (gr. 2-2). 2009. 42.50 *(978-1-61511-897-7(7))* 2005. (Illus.). (J). lib. bdg. 22.60 *(978-1-4042-2785-9(7))* 2005. (ENG., Illus.). pap. 8.25 *(978-1-4042-5024-6(7))* Rosen Publishing Group, Inc., The. (PowerKids Pr.).

—Who's Who in a Public Housing Community. (Communities at Work Ser.). 24p. (gr. 2-2). 2009. 42.50 *(978-1-61511-898-4(5))* 2005. (Illus.). (J). lib. bdg. 22.60 *(978-1-4042-2786-6(5))* 2005. (ENG., Illus.). pap. 8.25 *(978-1-4042-5026-0(3))* Rosen Publishing Group, Inc., The. (PowerKids Pr.).

—Who's Who in a Rural Community. (Communities at Work Ser.). 24p. (gr. 2-2). 2009. 42.50 *(978-1-61511-899-1(3))* 2005. (Illus.). (J). lib. bdg. 22.60 *(978-1-4042-2787-3(3))* Rosen Publishing Group, Inc., The. (PowerKids Pr.).

—Who's Who in an Urban Community. (Communities at Work Ser.). 24p. (gr. 2-2). 2009. 42.50 *(978-1-61511-901-1(9))* 2005. (Illus.). (J). lib. bdg. 22.60 *(978-1-4042-2790-3(3))* Rosen Publishing Group, Inc., The. (PowerKids Pr.).

Moehn, Heather. Everything You Need to Know about Cliques. 2009. (Need to Know Library). 64p. (gr. 5-5). 58.50 *(978-1-60854-058-7(8))* Rosen Publishing Group, Inc., The.

Monroe Peterson, Judy. Who Are Community Workers? 2017. (Let's Find Out! Communities Ser.). 32p. (J). (gr. 6-8). 24.45 ***(978-1-68048-739-8(6));*** pap. 12.90 ***(978-1-68048-737-4(X))*** Rosen Publishing Group, Inc., The. (Britannica Educational Publishing).

Mortensen, Lori. A Visit to the Police Station Set. Thompson, Jeffrey, illus. Incl. Going to the Dentist. (ENG., Illus.). 24p. (gr. 1-2). 2010. 23.99 *(978-1-4296-4507-2(5));* (First Graphics: My Community Ser.). (ENG.). 24p. 2010. Set lib. bdg. 47.98 o.p. *(978-1-4296-4513-3(X))* Capstone Press of Coughlan Cos.

Nagle, Jeanne. What Is a Community? 2017. (Let's Find Out! Communities Ser.). 32p. (J). (gr. 6-8). 24.45 ***(978-1-68048-735-0(3));*** pap. 12.90 ***(978-1-68048-733-6(7))*** Rosen Publishing Group, Inc., The. (Britannica Educational Publishing).

Nelid, Piper. Our Neighborhood, 01 vols., 1. 2016. (Rosen REAL Readers: Social Studies Nonfiction / Fiction: Family, Community, & the World Ser.). (ENG.). 8p. (J). pap. 5.46 *(978-1-5081-1716-2(0),* Rosen Classroom) Rosen Publishing Group, Inc., The.

O'Neal, Claire. Ways to Help in Your Community: A Guide to Giving Back. 2010. (How to Help Ser.). (Illus.). 48p. (J). (gr. 4-8). lib. bdg. 29.95 *(978-1-58415-921-6(9))* Mitchell Lane Pubs., Inc.

Owens, L. L. Meet Your Neighborhood, 1 vol. Davidson, Chris, illus. 2010. (Let's Be Social Ser.). (ENG.). 32p. 28.50 *(978-1-60270-803-7(7),* Looking Glass Library- Nonfiction) Magic Wagon.

PowerKids Readers: My Community: Set 2. 2016. (PowerKids Readers: My Community Ser.). 00024p. (J). (gr. k-k). 141.60 *(978-1-4994-2676-2(3),* PowerKids Pr.) Rosen Publishing Group, Inc., The.

Publications International Ltd. Staff, ed. Sesame Street(r) Listen & Learn in Your Neighborhood. 2014. 19p. (J). bds. *(978-1-4508-7519-6(X),* 145087519X) Publications International, Ltd.

Rhatigan, Joe. People You Gotta Meet Before You Grow Up: Get to Know the Movers & Shakers, Heroes & Hotshots in Your Hometown. 2014. (ENG., Illus.). 128p. (J). (gr. 2-5). 14.95 *(978-1-62354-004-3(6))* Charlesbridge Publishing, Inc.

Rice, Dona Herweck. Trabajadores, 1 vol. 2nd rev. ed. 2011. (Nonfiction Readers Ser.). (SPA.). 12p. (J). (gr. 1-1). pap. 4.99 *(978-1-4333-4411-4(4))* Teacher Created Materials, Inc.

—Workers, 1 vol. 2nd rev. ed. 2011. (TIME for KIDS(r) Nonfiction Readers Ser.). (ENG.). 12p. (gr. 1-1). 4.99 *(978-1-4333-3572-3(7))* Teacher Created Materials, Inc.

Ritchie, Scot. Look Where We Live! A First Book of Community Building. Ritchie, Scot, illus. 2015. (ENG., Illus.). 32p. (J). (gr. -1-2). 16.95 *(978-1-77138-102-4(7))* Kids Can Pr., Ltd. CAN. Dist: Hachette Bk. Group.

Rodgers, Kelly. Doing Your Part: Serving Your Community, 1 vol. rev. ed. 2014. (Primary Source Readers Content & Literacy Ser.). (ENG., Illus.). 32p. (gr. 3-3). pap. 8.99 *(978-1-4333-7367-1(X))* Teacher Created Materials, Inc.

Salle, Katherine Talmadge. Daily Life Around the World: Text Pairs. 2008. (Bridges/Navigators Ser.). (J). (gr. 3). 94.00 *(978-1-4108-8357-5(4))* Benchmark Education Co.

Santos, Gloria. A Trip to the Town Hall. 2016. (PowerKids Readers: My Community Ser.). 00024p. (J). (gr. k-k). pap. 8.25 *(978-1-4994-2777-6(8),* PowerKids Pr.) Rosen Publishing Group, Inc., The.

Scholastic Library Publishing. Rookie Read: About Community. 2012. (J). 138.00 *(978-0-531-23450-1(9),* Children's Pr.) Scholastic Library Publishing.

Schuette, Sarah L. Communities. rev. ed. 2009. (People Ser.). (ENG.). 24p. (gr. k-1). 21.99 *(978-1-4296-2238-7(5),* Pebble Bks.) Capstone Press of Coughlan Cos.

Schuh, Mari. Community Helpers at a Fire. 2016. (Community Helpers on the Scene Ser.). (ENG., Illus.). 24p. (gr. k-1). lib. bdg. 21.99 *(978-1-5157-2399-8(2),* Pebble Bks.) Capstone Press of Coughlan Cos.

—Community Helpers on the Scene. 2016. (Community Helpers on the Scene Ser.). (ENG.). 24p. (gr. k-1). 87.96 *(978-1-5157-2433-9(6),* Pebble Bks.) Capstone Press of Coughlan Cos.

Scraper, Katherine, et al. Around Town: Things You Can Do in Your Community. 2011. (J). pap. *(978-1-4509-5327-6(1))* Benchmark Education Co.

Shores, Erika L. & Peterson, Megan Cooley. Here to There. 2016. (Here to There Ser.). (ENG.). 24p. (gr. k-1). 106.60 *(978-1-4914-8448-7(9),* Pebble Plus) Capstone Press of Coughlan Cos.

Sterling, Kristin. Living in Rural Communities. 2008. pap. 34.95 *(978-0-8225-9478-9(1))* Lerner Publishing Group.

—Living in Suburban Communities. 2008. pap. 34.95 *(978-0-8225-9479-6(X));* (ENG., Illus.). 24p. lib. bdg. 23.93 *(978-0-8225-8598-5(7),* Lerner Pubns.) Lerner Publishing Group.

—Living in Urban Communities. 2008. pap. 34.95 *(978-0-8225-9480-2(3))* Lerner Publishing Group.

Tan, Richard. New York City's Neighborhoods. 2011. (My Community Ser.). (ENG., Illus.). 12p. (gr. 2-2). pap. 6.95 *(978-1-4488-5718-0(X),* Rosen Classroom) Rosen Publishing Group, Inc., The.

Taylor, Chad. Our Community Is in the Mountains. 2016. (Rosen REAL Readers: Social Studies Nonfiction / Fiction: Family, Community, & the World Ser.). 8p. (gr. 1-k). pap. 5.46 *(978-1-5081-2299-9(7),* Rosen Classroom) Rosen Publishing Group, Inc., The.

Thomas, M. I Jog Around: Learning the J Sound. 2009. (PowerPhonics Ser.). 24p. (gr. 1-1). 39.90 *(978-1-60851-450-2(1),* PowerKids Pr.) Rosen Publishing Group, Inc., The.

Weiss, Ellen. Math in the Neighborhood. 2007. (Scholastic News Nonfiction Readers Ser.). (ENG., Illus.). 24p. (J). (gr. 1-2). 22.00 *(978-0-531-18532-2(X));* pap. 6.95 *(978-0-531-18785-2(3))* Scholastic Library Publishing.

World Book, Inc Staff, contrib. by. Community Helpers. 2010. (J). *(978-0-7166-7737-6(7))* World Bk., Inc.

COMMUNITY LIFE—FICTION

Absolutely Truly: A Pumpkin Falls Mystery. 2014. (Pumpkin Falls Mystery Ser.). (ENG., Illus.). 368p. (J). (gr. 3-7). 17.99 *(978-1-4424-2972-7(0),* Simon & Schuster Bks. For Young Readers) Simon & Schuster Bks. For Young Readers.

Alvarez, Julia. De Como la Tia Lola Aprendio a Ensenar. 2011. (Tia Lola Stories Ser.). (SPA & ENG.). 160p. (J). (gr. 3-7). 7.99 *(978-0-375-85793-5(1),* Yearling) Random Hse. Children's Bks.

—How Tia Lola Learned to Teach. 2011. (Tia Lola Stories Ser.). (ENG., Illus.). 144p. (J). (gr. 3-7). pap. 7.99 *(978-0-375-85792-8(3),* Yearling) Random Hse. Children's Bks.

Ayer, Jacqueline, creator. The Paper-Flower Tree. 2017. (ENG.). 40p. (J). (gr. -1-3). 16.95 *(978-1-59270-224-4(4))* Enchanted Lion Bks., LLC.

Berry, Julie. All the Truth That's in Me. 2013. (ENG.). 288p. (YA). (gr. 7). 17.99 *(978-0-670-78615-2(2),* Viking Books for Young Readers) Penguin Young Readers Group.

—All the Truth That's in Me. 2014. lib. bdg. 20.85 *(978-0-606-36191-0(X))* Turtleback Bks.

Boorman, Kate A. Winterkill. (Winterkill Ser.). (ENG.). (YA). (gr. 7-17). 2015. 352p. pap. 8.95 *(978-1-4197-1673-7(5))* 2014. 336p. 17.95 *(978-1-4197-1235-7(7))* Abrams, Inc. (Amulet Bks.).

Brashares, Ann. The Here & Now. 2014. 242p. (YA). *(978-0-385-39008-8(4),* Delacorte Pr) Random House Publishing Group.

—The Here & Now. (ENG.). 256p. (YA). (gr. 7). 2015. pap. 10.99 *(978-0-385-73683-1(5),* Ember) 2014. 18.99 *(978-0-385-73680-0(0),* Delacorte Pr.) Random Hse. Children's Bks.

Burger, Hamilton C. No Exit: The Apple Grove Gang #1. 2012. (ENG.). (J). pap. *(978-1-4675-3409-3(9))* Independent Pub.

Caine, Rachel, pseud. The Morganville Vampires, Vol. 4. 2011. (Morganville Vampires Ser.: Bks. 7-8). (ENG.). 464p. (YA). (gr. 9-18). 9.99 *(978-0-451-23426-1(X),* Berkley) Penguin Publishing Group.

Capstone Press Staff. Flood, 1 vol. Vila, Alvaro F., illus. 2013. (Fiction Picture Bks.). (ENG.). 32p. (gr. 1-3). 22.60

C D

(978-1-4048-8006-1(2), Fiction Picture Bks.) Picture Window Bks.

Carpenter, Tad. When I Grow Up. 2015. (Who's That? Ser.). (ENG., Illus.). 16p. (J). (— -1). bds. 7.95 (978-1-4549-1228-6(6)) Sterling Publishing Co., Inc.

Castro, Adam-Troy. Gustav Gloom & the Nightmare Vault #2. Margiotta, Kristen, illus. 2014. (Gustav Gloom Ser.: 2). (ENG.). 248p. (J). (gr. 3-7). 7.99 (978-0-448-48329-0(7), Grosset & Dunlap) Penguin Young Readers Group.

—Gustav Gloom & the People Taker. Margiotta, Kristen, illus. 2012. (Gustav Gloom Ser.: 1). (ENG.). 232p. (J). (gr. 3-7). 12.99 (978-0-448-45833-5(0), Grosset & Dunlap) Penguin Young Readers Group.

Chadwick, Katie. Meet Miss Molly. 2012. 44p. pap. (978-1-84961-134-3(3)) RealTime Publishing.

Chandler, Susan. Welcome to Cuckooville. Durand, Delphine, illus. 2012. (ENG.). 24p. (J). (gr. k-3). 16.95 (978-1-61608-665-7(3), 608665, Sky Pony Pr.) Skyhorse Publishing Co., Inc.

Choyce, Lesley. Thunderbowl, 1 vol. 2004. (Orca Soundings Ser.). (ENG.). 128p. (YA). (gr. 8-12). pap. 9.95 (978-1-55143-277-9(3)) Orca Bk. Pubs. USA.

Clinton, Hillary Rodham. It Takes a Village. Frazee, Marla, illus. 2017. (ENG.). 40p. (J). (gr. -1-3). 19.99 **(978-1-4814-3087-6(4)**, Simon & Schuster/Paula Wiseman Bks.) Simon & Schuster/Paula Wiseman Bks.

Cole, Penelope Anne. Magico Mateo. Collier, Kevin, illus. 2013. 24p. pap. 10.95 (978-1-61633-421-5(5)) Guardian Angel Publishing, Inc.

Crenshaw, Mills. The Christmas of 45. 2010. 176p. pap. 11.99 (978-1-59955-455-6(0)) Cedar Fort, Inc./CFI Distribution.

Cumpiano, Ina. Quinito's Neighborhood (El Vecindario de Quinito) Ramírez, José, illus. 2013. (ENG & SPA.). 32p. (J). (gr. -1-3). pap. 9.95 (978-0-89239-229-2(0)) Lee & Low Bks., Inc.

Cushman, Doug. Inspector Hopper's Mystery Year, No. 2. Cushman, Doug, illus. 2003. (I Can Read Bks.). (Illus.). 64p. (J). (gr. k-3). 16.89 (978-0-06-008963-4(6)); 15.99 (978-0-06-008962-7(8)) HarperCollins Pubs.

DeKeyser, Stacy. The Brixen Witch. Nickle, John, illus. (ENG.). 208p. (J). (gr. 3-7). 2013. pap. 6.99 (978-1-4424-3329-8(9)) 2012. 15.99 (978-1-4424-3328-1(0)) McElderry, Margaret K. Bks. (McElderry, Margaret K. Bks.).

DeLaCroix, Alice. How to Survive a Totally Boring Summer. Fisher, Cynthia, illus. 2007. (ENG.). 96p. (J). (gr. 1-4). 16.95 (978-0-8234-2024-7(8)) Holiday Hse., Inc.

Dillard, Sarah. Mouse Scouts: Make a Difference. 2016. (Mouse Scouts Ser.). (ENG., Illus.). 144p. (J). (gr. 2-5). 12.99 (978-0-385-75603-7(8), Knopf Bks. for Young Readers) Random Hse. Children's Bks.

Durango, Julia. The One-Day House. Diaz, Bianca, illus. 2017. (ENG.). 32p. (J). (gr. -1-2). lib. bdg. 16.99 (978-1-58089-709-9(6)) Charlesbridge Publishing, Inc.

Ehrenberg, Pamela. Tillmon County Fire. 2009. 192p. (YA). (gr. 9-18). pap. 9.00 (978-0-8028-5345-5(5), Eerdmans Bks For Young Readers) Eerdmans, William B. Publishing Co.

Fiedler, Lisa & Wallach, Anya. Showstopper! 2015. (Stagestruck Ser.). (ENG.). 280p. (J). (gr. 4-6). 11.99 (978-1-58536-925-6(X), 203948) Sleeping Bear Pr.

Foley, Lizzie K. & Foley, Elizabeth. Remarkable. 2012. (ENG.). 336p. (J). (gr. 3-7). 16.99 (978-0-8037-3706-8(8), Dial Bks) Penguin Young Readers Group.

Frederick, Heather Vogel. Absolutely Truly. 2015. (Pumpkin Falls Mystery Ser.). (ENG., Illus.). 368p. (J). (gr. 3-7). pap. 7.99 (978-1-4424-2973-4(9), Simon & Schuster Bks. For Young Readers) Simon & Schuster Bks. For Young Readers.

Friedman, Becky. Welcome to the Neighborhood! 2014. (Daniel Tiger's Neighborhood 8X8 Ser.). lib. bdg. 13.55 (978-0-606-35458-5(1)) Turtleback Bks.

Friedman, Laurie. Merry Christmas, Mary Christmas! Durst, Kathryn, illus. 2017. (ENG.). 32p. (J). (gr. -1-3). lib. bdg. 17.99 **(978-1-4677-9261-5(6)**, Carolrhoda Bks.) Lerner Publishing Group.

Graham, Bob. A Bus Called Heaven. Graham, Bob, illus. 2012. (ENG., Illus.). 40p. (J). (gr. -1-2). 16.99 (978-0-7636-5893-9(6)) Candlewick Pr.

Group/McGraw-Hill, Wright. The Bazaar, 6 vols. (D-Man Beans Ser.). 47p. (gr. 4-6). 42.50 (978-0-322-06260-3(8)) Wright Group/McGraw-Hill.

—Who Is Tuffy 2000?, 6 vols. (D-Man Beans Ser.). 47p. (gr. 4-6). 42.50 (978-0-322-06261-0(6)) Wright Group/McGraw-Hill.

Gutman, Dan. The Talent Show. 2010. (ENG.). 224p. (J). (gr. 3-7). 17.99 (978-1-4169-9003-1(8), Simon & Schuster Bks. For Young Readers) Simon & Schuster Bks. For Young Readers.

Hall, Kirsten. My New Town. Suzan, Gerardo, illus. 2005. (My First Reader Ser.). (ENG.). 32p. (J). (gr. k-1). lib. bdg. 18.50 (978-0-516-24877-6(4), Children's Pr.) Scholastic Library Publishing.

Hambrick, Sharon. Tommy's Clubhouse. Manning, Maurie J., tr. Manning, Maurie J., illus. 2003. (Fig Street Kids Ser.). 78p. (J). (gr. 1-2). pap. 7.49 (978-1-57924-993-9(0)) BJU Pr.

Harkey, Faith. Genuine Sweet. (ENG.). 288p. (J). (gr. 5-7). 2016. pap. 6.99 (978-0-544-66853-9(7), HMH Books For Young Readers) 2015. 16.99 (978-0-544-28366-4(X)) Houghton Mifflin Harcourt Publishing Co.

Harris, Erin & National Geographic Learning Staff. Elephant on My Roof. Harris, Erin, illus. 2010. (Rise & Shine Ser.). (ENG., Illus.). 32p. (C). (gr. -1-3). 26.95 (978-1-60108-002-8(6)) National Geographic School Publishing, Inc.

Heathfield, Lisa. Seed. 2015. (ENG.). 336p. (YA). (gr. 7). 16.95 (978-0-7624-5634-5(5), Running Pr. Kids) Running Pr. Bk. Pubs.

Helmer, Marilyn. One Splendid Tree. Eastman, Dianne, illus. 2007. (ENG.). 32p. (J). (gr. -1-3). 6.95 (978-1-55453-166-0(7)) Kids Can Pr., Ltd. CAN. Dist: Hachette Bk. Group.

Herrera, Juan Felipe. Grandma & Me at the Flea: Los Meros Meros Remateros. De Lucio-Brock, Anita, illus. 2013. (ENG & SPA.). 32p. (J). pap. 9.95 (978-0-89239-279-7(7), Children's Book Press) Lee & Low Bks., Inc.

Hoffman, Alice. Nightbird. (ENG., Illus.). 208p. (J). (gr. 5). 2016. pap. 7.99 (978-0-385-38961-7(2), Yearling) 2015. 16.99 (978-0-385-38958-7(2), Lamb, Wendy Bks.) Random Hse. Children's Bks.

—Nightbird. 2016. lib. bdg. 18.40 (978-0-606-38451-3(0)) Turtleback Bks.

Hulst, W. G. van de & Hulst, Willem G. van de, illus. The Little Wooden Shoe. 2014. (J). (978-1-928136-01-9(X)) Inheritance Pubns.

Hutchins, Hazel. Mattland. Petricic, Dusan, illus. 3rd ed. 2008. (ENG.). 32p. (J). (gr. -1-2). 19.95 (978-1-55451-121-1(6), 9781554511211); pap. 8.95 (978-1-55451-120-4(8), 9781554511204) Annick Pr., Ltd. CAN. Dist: Publishers Group West (PGW).

Kelsey, Marybeth. A Recipe for Robbery. 2009. (ENG.). 288p. (J). (gr. 3-7). 16.99 (978-0-06-128843-2(8), Greenwillow Bks.) HarperCollins Pubs.

King, Emiliya. Sara Sees Signs: Looking at Data. 2017. (Computer Science for the Real World Ser.). 8p. (gr. 5-6). pap. 6.20 **(978-1-5383-5008-9(4)**, Rosen Classroom) Rosen Publishing Group, Inc., The.

Knesek, Marian. Sage & the Peacock. Buehrle, Jackie, illus. 2011. 28p. pap. 24.95 (978-1-4512-2211-1(4)) America Star Bks.

Konigsburg, E. L. The Mysterious Edge of the Heroic World. 2009. (ENG.). 256p. (J). (gr. 5-9). pap. 7.99 (978-1-4169-5353-1(1), Atheneum Bks. for Young Readers) Simon & Schuster Children's Publishing.

Leblanc, Louise. Leo's Poster Challenge, 1 vol. Prud'homme, Jules & Cummins, Sarah, trs. from FRE. Prud'homme, Jules & Jules, Prud'homme, illus. 2003. (Formac First Novels Ser.). (ENG.). 64p. (J). (gr. 2-5). 4.95 (978-0-88780-608-7(2), 9780887806087); 14.95 (978-0-88780-609-4(0), 9780887806094) Formac Publishing Co., Ltd. CAN. Dist: Casemate Pubs. & Bk. Distributors, LLC.

Lee, Ingrid. Cat Found. 2013. (ENG.). 176p. (J). (gr. 3-7). pap. 6.99 (978-0-545-35108-9(1), Chicken Hse., The) Scholastic, Inc.

Lois, Lowry. Messenger. 2012. (Giver Quartet Ser.: 3). (ENG.). 192p. (YA). (gr. 7). 17.99 (978-0-547-99567-0(9)) Houghton Mifflin Harcourt Publishing Co.

—Messenger. (ENG.). (J). 2009. 176p. (gr. 3-7). mass mkt. 7.99 (978-0-385-73716-6(5), Bantam Bks. for Young Readers) 2006. 192p. (gr. 4-7). pap. 9.99 (978-0-385-73253-6(8), Ember) Random Hse. Children's Bks.

Lord, Janet. Albert the Fix-It Man, 1 vol. Paschkis, Julie, illus. (ENG.). 32p. (J). 2015. (gr. 1-3). pap. 7.95 (978-1-56145-830-1(9)) 2008. (gr. k-3). 15.95 (978-1-56145-433-4(8)) Peachtree Pubs.

Lupica, Mike. The Underdogs. (ENG.). (J). (gr. 5-18). 2012. 304p. pap. 7.99 (978-0-14-242139-0(1), Puffin Books) 2011. 288p. 17.99 (978-0-399-25001-9(8), Philomel Bks.) Penguin Young Readers Group.

Lynch, Casey. Mighty Mike Builds a Ball Field, 1 vol. Lynch, Kelly, illus. 2011. (Mighty Mike Ser.). (ENG.). 32p. (gr. -1-2). 28.50 (978-1-61641-128-2(7), Looking Glass Library) ABDO Publishing Co.

—Mighty Mike Builds a Library, 1 vol. Lynch, Kelly, illus. 2011. (Mighty Mike Ser.). (ENG.). 32p. (gr. -1-2). 28.50 (978-1-61641-129-9(5), Looking Glass Library) ABDO Publishing Co.

—Mighty Mike Repairs a Playground, 1 vol. Lynch, Kelly, illus. 2011. (Mighty Mike Ser.). (ENG.). 32p. (gr. -1-2). 28.50 (978-1-61641-132-9(5), Looking Glass Library) ABDO Publishing Co.

—Mighty Mike Saves a School Bus, 1 vol. Lynch, Kelly, illus. 2011. (Mighty Mike Ser.). (ENG.). 32p. (gr. -1-2). 28.50 (978-1-61641-133-6(3), Looking Glass Library) ABDO Publishing Co.

Lynch, Kelly. Mighty Mike Builds a Nature Trail, 1 vol. Lynch, Casey, illus. 2011. (Mighty Mike Ser.). (ENG.). 32p. (gr. -1-2). 28.50 (978-1-61641-130-5(9), Looking Glass Library) ABDO Publishing Co.

—Mighty Mike Does What's Right!, 1 vol. Lynch, Casey, illus. 2011. (Mighty Mike Ser.). (ENG.). 32p. (gr. -1-2). 28.50 (978-1-61641-131-2(7), Looking Glass Library) ABDO Publishing Co.

Mackall, Dandi Daley. The Secrets of Tree Taylor. 2014. (ENG.). 288p. (J). (gr. 5). 16.99 (978-0-375-86897-9(6), Knopf Bks. for Young Readers) Random Hse. Children's Bks.

Mann's Miracles, creator. When the Hurricane Blew. 2005. (Illus.). 34p. (J). (gr. 3-7). per. (978-0-9773569-0-4(6)) Clear Horizon.

Martinez, Claudia Guadalupe. Pig Park. 2014. (ENG.). 248p. (J). 15.95 (978-1-935955-76-4(4)) Cinco Puntos Pr.

Mighty Mike, 6 vols., Set. Incl. Mighty Mike Builds a Ball Field. Lynch, Casey. Lynch, Kelly, illus. 28.50 (978-1-61641-128-2(7)); Mighty Mike Builds a Library. Lynch, Casey. Lynch, Kelly, illus. 28.50 (978-1-61641-129-9(5)); Mighty Mike Builds a Nature Trail. Lynch, Kelly. Lynch, Casey, illus. 28.50 (978-1-61641-130-5(9)); Mighty Mike Does What's Right! Lynch, Kelly. Lynch, Casey, illus. 28.50 (978-1-61641-131-2(7)); Mighty Mike Repairs a Playground. Lynch, Casey. Lynch, Kelly, illus. 28.50 (978-1-61641-132-9(5)); Mighty Mike Saves a School Bus. Lynch, Casey. Lynch, Kelly, illus. 28.50 (978-1-61641-133-6(3)); (gr. -1-2). (Mighty Mike Ser.). 32p. 2011. 171.00 (978-1-61641-127-5(9), Looking Glass Library) ABDO Publishing Co.

Mills, David. Mei Ling's Hiccups. Brazell, Derek, illus. 2004. (J). 24p. (978-1-85269-559-0(5)); (ENG & BEN.). 32p. pap. (978-1-85269-554-5(4)); (ENG & ALB.). 32p. pap. (978-1-85269-552-1(8)); (ENG & CHI.). 32p. pap. (978-1-85269-555-2(2)); (ENG & ARA.). 32p. pap. (978-1-85269-553-8(6)); (ENG & CZE.). 32p. pap. (978-1-85269-682-5(6)); (ENG & POL.). 32p. pap. (978-1-85269-626-9(5)); (ENG & SPA.). 32p. pap. (978-1-85269-565-1(X)); (ENG & POR.). 32p. pap. (978-1-85269-562-0(5)); (ENG & JPN.). 32p. pap. (978-1-85269-560-6(9)); (ENG & URD.). 32p. pap. (978-1-85269-568-2(4)); (ENG.). 32p. pap. (978-1-85269-563-7(3)); (ENG & PAN.). 32p. pap. (978-1-85269-561-3(7)); (ENG & GUJ.). 32p. pap. (978-1-85269-558-3(7)); (ENG & KOR.). 32p. pap. (978-1-85269-704-4(0)); (ENG & VIE.). 32p. pap. (978-1-85269-569-9(2)); (ENG & TUR.). 32p. pap. (978-1-85269-567-5(6)); (ENG & TAM.). 32p. pap. (978-1-85269-566-8(8)); (ENG & FRE.). 32p. pap. (978-1-85269-557-6(9)); (ENG & PER.). 32p. pap. (978-1-85269-556-9(0)) Mantra Lingua.

Mills, Lauren A. Minna's Patchwork Coat. 2015. (ENG., Illus.). 288p. (J). (gr. 3-7). 17.00 (978-0-316-40621-5(X)) Little Brown & Co.

Murphy, Stuart J. Percy's Neighborhood. 2013. (I See I Learn Ser.). (ENG.). 32p. (J). (-k). lib. bdg. 14.95 (978-1-58089-480-7(1)); (Illus.). pap. 6.95 (978-1-58089-481-4(X)) Charlesbridge Publishing, Inc.

Murray, Eva & Hogan, Jamie. Island Birthday, 1 vol. 2015. (ENG., Illus.). 32p. (gr. 1-7). 16.95 (978-0-88448-425-7(4), 884425) Tilbury Hse. Pubs.

Nemukula, Zandile. I Am No Better Than You. 2012. 24p. pap. 15.99 (978-1-4691-7395-5(6)) Xlibris Corp.

Nolen, Jerdine. Bradford Street Buddies: Springtime Blossoms. Henninger, Michelle, illus. 2017. (Green Light Readers Level 3 Ser.). (ENG.). 48p. (J). (gr. 1-4). pap. 3.99 (978-0-544-87390-2(4), HMH Books For Young Readers) Houghton Mifflin Harcourt Publishing Co.

Oakes, Cory Putman. Witchtown. 2017. (ENG.). 320p. (YA). (gr. 7). 17.99 (978-0-544-76557-3(5), HMH Books For Young Readers) Houghton Mifflin Harcourt Publishing Co.

Ockler, Sarah. The Summer of Chasing Mermaids. 2015. (ENG., Illus.). 416p. (YA). (gr. 9). 17.99 (978-1-4814-0127-2(0), Simon Pulse) Simon Pulse.

Patron, Susan. Lucky for Good. McGuire, Erin, illus. 2012. (ENG.). 224p. (J). (gr. 3-7). pap. 6.99 (978-1-4169-9059-8(3), Atheneum Bks. for Young Readers) Simon & Schuster Children's Publishing.

—Lucky for Good. McGuire, Erin K., illus. 2011. (ENG.). 224p. (J). (gr. 3-7). 16.99 (978-1-4169-9058-1(5), Atheneum Bks. for Young Readers) Simon & Schuster Children's Publishing.

Peretti, Kim. Oodle Van Boodle & the Great Cake Adventure. 2010. (ENG., Illus.). 32p. (J). pap. 15.95 (978-0-9824461-4-0(4)) SDP Publishing.

Perkyns, Dorothy. Last Days in Africville. 2005. (Illus.). 144p. (YA). pap., tchr. ed. (978-0-88878-446-9(5), Sandcastle Bks.) Dundurn.

—Last Days in Africville. 2006. (ENG.). 120p. (J). (gr. 4-7). pap. 10.99 (978-1-55002-630-6(5), Dundurn Pr.) Dundurn CAN. Dist: Ingram Publisher Services.

Pinkowski, Vern V. A Twisted Pig's Tale. 2008. 144p. pap. 11.95 (978-0-595-46595-8(1), iUniverse, Inc.) iUniverse, Inc.

Pinkowski, Vernon V. A Twisted Pig's Tale. 2008. 148p. 21.95 (978-0-595-49022-6(0), iUniverse, Inc.) iUniverse, Inc.

Places in My Community. 2016. (Places in My Community Ser.). 00024p. (J). (gr. 1-1). 94.40 (978-1-4994-2659-5(3), PowerKids Pr.) Rosen Publishing Group, Inc., The.

Polacco, Patricia. The Mermaid's Purse. Polacco, Patricia, illus. 2016. (ENG., Illus.). 48p. (J). (gr. k-3). 17.99 (978-0-399-16692-1(0), G.P. Putnam's Sons Books for Young Readers) Penguin Young Readers Group.

Potter, Ellen. Piper Green & the Fairy Tree: Pie Girl. Leng, Qin, illus. 2017. (Piper Green & the Fairy Tree Ser.: 5). (ENG.). 144p. (J). (gr. 2-4). pap. 5.99 **(978-1-101-93968-0(0))**; lib. bdg. 17.99 **(978-1-101-93966-6(4))** Random Hse. Children's Bks. (Yearling).

Reichert, Paul. The Lemonade Ripple: A Sweet Story of Kindness & Charity. 2012. (ENG., Illus.). 40p. (J). (gr. -1-k). 12.95 (978-1-61608-701-2(3), 608701, Sky Pony Pr.) Skyhorse Publishing Co., Inc.

Reidy, Jean. All Through My Town. Timmers, Leo, illus. 2013. (ENG.). 32p. (J). (gr. -1-1). 14.99 (978-1-59990-785-7(2), 9781599907857); lib. bdg. 15.89 (978-1-61963-029-1(X), 9781619630291) Bloomsbury Publishing USA. (Bloomsbury USA Childrens).

Rey, H. A. & Rey, Margret. Curious George's Neighborhood. Weston, Martha, illus. 2004. (Curious George Ser.). (ENG.). 10p. (J). (gr. -1 — 1). bds. 11.95 (978-0-618-41203-7(4)) Houghton Mifflin Harcourt Publishing Co.

Rhodes, O. K. & Spencer, Octavia. The Case of the Time-Capsule Bandit. To, Vivienne, illus. 2013. (Randi Rhodes, Ninja Detective Ser.: 1). (ENG.). 224p. (J). (gr. 3-7). 16.99 (978-1-4424-7681-3(8), Simon & Schuster Bks. For Young Readers) Simon & Schuster Bks. For Young Readers.

Ritter, Joshua & Ellis-Ritter, Karen. Be It Every Day! 2012. 40p. pap. 20.99 (978-1-4634-5231-5(4)) AuthorHouse.

Rose, Naomi C. Tashi & the Tibetan Flower Cure. 2016. (ENG.). 40p. (J). (gr. 1-6). pap. 10.95 **(978-1-62014-318-6(6))** Lee & Low Bks., Inc.

Rosenfield, Kat. Amelia Anne Is Dead & Gone. 2013. (ENG.). 288p. (YA). (gr. 9). pap. 8.99 (978-0-14-242610-4(5), Speak) Penguin Young Readers Group.

Ruiz-Flores, Lupe & Rosales-Yeomans, Natalia. Let's Salsa. Rosales-Yeomans, Natalia, tr. Casilla, Robert, illus. 2013.Tr. of Bailemos Salsa. (SPA & ENG.). 32p. (J). 17.95 (978-1-55885-762-9(1), Piñata Books) Arte Publico Pr.

Salerni, Dianne K. The Caged Graves. 2014. (ENG.). 336p. (YA). (gr. 7). pap. 8.99 (978-0-544-33622-3(4), HMH Books For Young Readers) Houghton Mifflin Harcourt Publishing Co.

Santillo, LuAnn. Community Helpers, 6 vols. Santillo, LuAnn, ed. 2003. (Half-Pint Kids Readers Ser.). (Illus.). 42p. (J). (gr. -1-1). pap. 6.95 (978-1-59256-119-3(5)) Half-Pint Kids, Inc.

Say Please, Says Squeeze. 2009. (ENG.). 32p. pap. 3.99 (978-1-4231-1755-1(7)) Disney Pr.

Schindler, Holly. The Junction of Sunshine & Lucky. 2014. (ENG.). 240p. (J). (gr. 3-7). 16.99 (978-0-8037-3725-9(4), Dial Bks) Penguin Young Readers Group.

Silva, Sadie. Different Kinds of Communities: Putting Data in Order. 2017. (Computer Science for the Real World Ser.). 16p. (gr. 7-8). pap. 7.95 **(978-1-5383-5198-7(6)**, Rosen Classroom) Rosen Publishing Group, Inc., The.

Spinelli, Eileen. Cold Snap. Priceman, Marjorie, illus. 2012. (ENG.). 40p. (J). (gr. k-3). 17.99 (978-0-375-85700-3(1), Knopf Bks. for Young Readers) Random Hse. Children's Bks.

Staniszewski, Anna. Dogosaurus Rex. Hawkes, Kevin, illus. 2017. (ENG.). 40p. (J). 17.99 (978-0-8050-9706-1(6), 9780805097061, Holt, Henry & Co. Bks. For Young Readers) Holt, Henry & Co.

Travis, Lucille. The Far Journey. 2009. 160p. (J). (gr. 4-7). 8.99 (978-1-60682-023-0(0)) BJU Pr.

Turnage, Sheila. The Ghosts of Tupelo Landing. (ENG.). 368p. (J). (gr. 5). 2015. 7.99 (978-0-14-242571-8(0), Puffin Books) 2014. 16.99 (978-0-8037-3671-9(1), Kathy Dawson Books) Penguin Young Readers Group.

—The Ghosts of Tupelo Landing. 2015. lib. bdg. 18.40 (978-0-606-36773-8(X)) Turtleback Bks.

—The Odds of Getting Even. 2015. (ENG., Illus.). 352p. (J). (gr. 5). 16.99 (978-0-8037-3961-1(3), Kathy Dawson Books) Penguin Young Readers Group.

—Three Times Lucky. (ENG.). (J). (gr. 5). 2013. 336p. pap. 7.99 (978-0-14-242605-0(9), Puffin Books) 2012. 314p. 16.99 (978-0-8037-3670-2(3), Dial Bks) Penguin Young Readers Group.

—Three Times Lucky. 2013. lib. bdg. 18.40 (978-0-606-34168-4(4), Turtleback) Turtleback Bks.

Waber, Bernard. Betty's Day Off. Date not set. (J). (978-0-618-46875-1(7)) Houghton Mifflin Harcourt Publishing Co.

Walker, Nan. Follow That Clue! Palmisciano, Diane, illus. 2008. (Social Studies Connects Ser.). 32p. (J). (gr. -1-3). pap. 5.95 (978-1-57565-274-0(9)) Kane Press, Inc.

—Follow That Clue! Palmisciano, Diane, illus. 2009. (Social Studies Connects (r) Ser.). (ENG.). (gr. k-2). pap. 33.92 (978-0-7613-4805-4(0)) Lerner Publishing Group.

Watson, Renée. A Place Where Hurricanes Happen. Strickland, Shadra, illus. 2014. (ENG.). 40p. (J). (gr. k-4). 7.99 (978-0-385-37668-6(5), Dragonfly Bks.) Random Hse. Children's Bks.

White, Ruth. The Treasure of Way down Deep. 2013. (ENG.). 176p. (J). (gr. 5-9). 16.99 (978-0-374-38067-0(8), 9780374380670, Farrar, Straus & Giroux (BYR)) Farrar, Straus & Giroux.

—Way down Deep. 2011. (ENG.). 224p. (J). (gr. 5-8). pap. 7.99 (978-0-312-66096-3(0), 9780312660963) Square Fish.

COMMUNITY SCHOOLS

see Schools

COMMUNITY SONGBOOKS

see Songbooks

COMPACT DISC READ-ONLY MEMORY

see CD-ROMs

COMPACT DISCS

Here are entered works on small optical disks in general as well as audio compact discs.

see also CD-ROMs

Bernard, Yves & Fredette, Nathalie. Le Guide de la Musique du Monde. 2004. (FRE., Illus.). 230p. (J). pap. (978-2-89021-662-4(4)) Diffusion du livre Mirabel (DLM).

Sirrine, Carol. Cool Crafts with Old CDs: Green Projects for Resourceful Kids. 2010. (Green Crafts Ser.). (ENG.). 32p. (gr. 3-4). lib. bdg. 27.99 (978-1-4296-4007-7(3), Snap Bks.) Capstone Press of Coughlan Cos.

COMPANY UNIONS

see Management—Employee Participation

COMPARATIVE ANATOMY

see Anatomy, Comparative

COMPARATIVE PHYSIOLOGY

see Physiology, Comparative

COMPARATIVE PSYCHOLOGY

see Psychology, Comparative

COMPARATIVE RELIGION

see Religions

COMPETITION (PSYCHOLOGY)

Lynette, Rachel. How to Deal with Competitiveness. 2009. (Let's Work It Out Ser.). 24p. (gr. 2-3). 42.50 (978-1-61514-258-3(4), PowerKids Pr.); (Illus.). (J). lib. bdg. 22.60 (978-1-4042-4521-1(9)) Rosen Publishing Group, Inc., The.

Messier, Mireille. Competition: From Start to Finish, 1 vol. Murray, Steven, illus. 2004. (Lorimer Deal with It Ser.). (ENG.). 32p. (J). (gr. 4-6). 12.95 (978-1-55028-832-2(6), 9781550288322) Lorimer, James & Co., Ltd., Pubs. CAN. Dist: Casemate Pubs. & Bk. Distributors, LLC.

COMPETITION (PSYCHOLOGY)—FICTION

Arena, Felice & Kettle, Phil. Battle of the Games. Gordon, Gus, illus. 2004. (J). pap. (978-1-59336-372-7(9)) Mondo Publishing.

Arena, Felice, et al. Battle of the Games. Gordon, Gus & Vane, Mitch, illus. 2004. 48p. (J). pap. (978-0-7329-9254-5(0)) Mondo Publishing.

Awdry, Wilbert V. Fast Train, Slow Train. Stubbs, Tommy, illus. 2009. (Bright & Early Books(R) Ser.). (ENG.). 36p. (J). (gr. -1-2). 8.99 (978-0-375-85689-1(7), Golden Bks.) Random Hse. Children's Bks.

Barton, Chris. Shark vs. Train. Lichtenheld, Tom, illus. (ENG.). (J). (gr. -1 — 1). 2015. 20p. bds. 6.99 (978-0-316-37814-7(3)) 2010. 40p. 18.99 (978-0-316-00762-7(5)) Little, Brown Bks. for Young Readers.

Bateman, Teresa. Paul Bunyan vs. Hals Halson: The Giant Lumberjack Challenge! Canga, C. B, illus. 2012. (J). 34.28 (978-1-61913-126-2(9)) Weigl Pubs., Inc.

Beard, Alex. Monkey See, Monkey Draw. 2011. (ENG., Illus.). 48p. (J). (gr. k-2). 17.95 (978-0-8109-8970-2(0), Abrams Bks. for Young Readers) Abrams, Inc.

Behrens, Andy. The Fast & the Furriest. 2011. (ENG.). 256p. (J). (gr. 3-7). 7.99 (978-0-375-85900-7(4), Yearling) Random Hse. Children's Bks.

Benjamin, Brooks. My Seventh-Grade Life in Tights. 2016. (ENG.). 304p. (J). (gr. 4-7). 16.99 (978-0-553-51250-2(1), Delacorte Bks. for Young Readers) Random Hse. Children's Bks.

Bowe, Julie. Curve Ball. 2017. (Victoria Torres, Unfortunately Average Ser.). (ENG.). 160p. (gr. 4-4). pap. 5.95 (978-1-4965-3820-8(X)); lib. bdg. 26.65 (978-1-4965-3818-5(8)) Stone Arch Bks.

Bowen, Carl & Fuentes, Benny. BMX Breakthrough, 1 vol. Sandoval, Gerardo, illus. 2011. (Sports Illustrated Kids Graphic Novels Ser.). (ENG.). 56p. (gr. 2-3). pap. 7.19 (978-1-4342-3401-8(0)); lib. bdg. 26.65 (978-1-4342-2240-4(3)) Stone Arch Bks.

Bowen, Fred. Dugout Rivals, 1 vol. 2010. (Fred Bowen Sports Stories Ser.). (ENG.). 128p. (J). (gr. 2-7). pap. 6.95 (978-1-56145-515-7(6)) Peachtree Pubs.

—Out of Bounds, 1 vol. 2016. (Stanley Ser.). 132p. (J). (ENG.). (gr. -1-2). pap. 14.95 (978-1-56145-894-3(5)); (SPA & ENG.). (gr. 1-5). 17.95 (978-1-56145-845-5(7)) Peachtree Pubs.

Brege, K. B. Ghost Board Posse London Screaming! 2008. (Ghost Board Posse Ser.: No. 1). (Illus.). 207p. (YA). pap. 6.99 *(978-0-9774119-6-2(6))* Team B Creative LLC.

Brouwer, Sigmund. Timberwolf Tracks, 1 vol. Ross, Graham, illus. 2009. (Orca Echoes Ser.). (ENG.). 64p. (J). (gr. 2-3). pap. 6.95 *(978-1-55143-734-7(1))* Orca Bk. Pubs. USA.

Brown, Liz. Dark Ryder. Mclanson, Matt, illus. 2004. (New Series Canada). 91p. (J). pap. *(978-1-897039-02-1(6))* High Interest Publishing (HIP).

Burkhart, Jessica. Home Sweet Drama. 2010. (Canterwood Crest Ser.: 8). (ENG.). 240p. (J). (gr. 4-8). pap. 7.99 *(978-1-4169-9040-6(2),* Aladdin) Simon & Schuster Children's Publishing.

—Unfriendly Competition. 2011. (Canterwood Crest Ser.: 12). (ENG.). 192p. (J). (gr. 4-8). pap. 7.99 *(978-1-4424-0386-4(1),* Aladdin) Simon & Schuster Children's Publishing.

Callahan, Ann Marie. The Sun Tea Fish. Sponheimer, Katheryne, illus. 2008. 16p. pap. 24.95 *(978-1-60672-160-5(7))* America Star Bks.

Campbell, K. G. Dylan the Villain. Campbell, K. G., illus. 2016. (ENG., Illus.). 32p. (J). (gr. -1-1). 17.99 *(978-0-451-47642-5(5),* Viking Books for Young Readers) Penguin Young Readers Group.

Camper, Cathy. Low Riders in Space. Raúl, III, illus. 2014. (ENG & SPA.). 112p. (J). (gr. 3-7). pap. 9.99 *(978-1-4521-2869-6(3));*Bk. 1. 22.99 *(978-1-4521-2155-0(9))* Chronicle Bks. LLC.

Cascone, Gina & Cascone, Annette. Little Magic Shop of Horrors. 2012. (Deadtime Stories Ser.: 5). (ENG.). 192p. (J). (gr. 3-7). 14.99 *(978-0-7653-3075-8(X),* 9780765330758, Starscape) Doherty, Tom Assocs., LLC.

Chin, Oliver. The Belt of Fire. Chua, Charlene, illus. 2013. (Julie Black Belt Ser.). (ENG.). 36p. (J). (gr. -1-3). 15.95 *(978-1-59702-079-4(6))* Immedium.

Christopher, Matt. Out at Second. 2011. (Playaway Top Children's Picks Ser.). (J). 49.99 *(978-1-60941-973-8(1))* Findaway World, LLC.

—Out at Second. 2011. (ENG.). 144p. (J). (gr. 3-7). pap. 4.99 *(978-0-316-08481-9(6))* Little, Brown Bks. for Young Readers.

—QB Blitz. 2011. (ENG.). 144p. (J). (gr. 3-7). pap. 5.99 *(978-0-316-17682-8(6))* Little, Brown Bks. for Young Readers.

Ciencin, Scott & Maese, Fares. Avalanche Freestyle, 1 vol. Aburto, Jesus & Esparza, Andres, illus. 2010. (Sports Illustrated Kids Graphic Novels Ser.). (ENG.). 56p. (gr. 2-3). 26.65 *(978-1-4342-2009-7(5));* pap. 7.19 *(978-1-4342-2783-6(9))* Stone Arch Bks.

—BMX Blitz, 1 vol. Aburto, Jesus & Esparza, Andres, illus. 2011. (Sports Illustrated Kids Graphic Novels Ser.). (ENG.). 56p. (gr. 2-3). pap. 7.19 *(978-1-4342-3071-3(6))* Stone Arch Bks.

—BMX Blitz, 1 vol. Esparza, Andres & Aburto, Jesus, illus. 2011. (Sports Illustrated Kids Graphic Novels Ser.). (ENG.). 56p. (gr. 2-3). lib. bdg. 26.65 *(978-1-4342-2222-0(5))* Stone Arch Bks.

Ciencin, Scott, et al. Snowboard Standoff, 1 vol. Esparza, Andres et al, illus. 2011. (Sports Illustrated Kids Graphic Novels Ser.). (ENG.). 56p. (gr. 2-3). pap. 7.19 *(978-1-4342-3403-2(7))* Stone Arch Bks.

—Snowboard Standoff, 1 vol. Aburto, Jesus et al, illus. 2011. (Sports Illustrated Kids Graphic Novels Ser.). (ENG.). 56p. (gr. 2-3). lib. bdg. 26.65 *(978-1-4342-2242-8(X))* Stone Arch Bks.

Cobb, Amy. Dude, Where's My Saxophone?, 1 vol. Cattish, Anna, illus. 2015. (ENG.). 112p. (J). *(978-1-62402-073-5(9))* Magic Wagon.

—Swing Vote for Solo, 1 vol. Cattish, Anna, illus. 2015. (ENG.). 112p. (J). *(978-1-62402-078-0(X))* Magic Wagon.

Collins, Paul. Lucy in a Jam. Bocquée, Christian, illus. 2015. (Legends in Their Own Lunchbox Ser.). (ENG.). 48p. (gr. 1-2). pap. 7.99 *(978-1-4966-0248-0(X),* Legends in Their Own Lunchbox) Capstone Classroom.

Crawford, K. Michael, illus. The Munched-up Flower Garden. 2006. (Troublesome Creek Kids Story Ser.). (ENG.). 32p. (J). (gr. -1-3). 16.95 *(978-1-933176-04-8(0));* pap. 10.95 *(978-1-933176-06-2(7))* Red Rock Pr., Inc.

Dadey, Debbie. Books vs. Looks. Avakyan, Tatevik, illus. 2016. (Mermaid Tales Ser.: 15). (ENG.). 128p. (J). (gr. 1-4). pap. 5.99 *(978-1-4814-4081-3(0),* Aladdin) Simon & Schuster Children's Publishing.

—Twist & Shout. Avakyan, Tatevik, illus. 2016. (Mermaid Tales Ser.: 14). (ENG.). 112p. (J). (gr. 1-4). pap. 5.99 *(978-1-4814-4078-3(0),* Aladdin) Simon & Schuster Children's Publishing.

Davis, Izzy. The Croaks at Roaring River, 1 vol. 2009. 40p. pap. 24.95 *(978-1-60813-245-4(5))* America Star Bks.

Davis, Terry. Vision Quest. 2015. (ENG., Illus.). 240p. (YA). (gr. 7). 19.99 *(978-1-4814-5636-4(9),* Simon & Schuster Bks. For Young Readers) Simon & Schuster Bks. For Young Readers.

Denton, P. J. Girls Against Boys. Denos, Julia, illus. 2013. (Sleepover Squad Ser.: 7). (ENG.). 96p. (J). (gr. 1-4). pap. 4.99 *(978-1-4169-5933-5(5),* Simon & Schuster/Paula Wiseman Bks.) Simon & Schuster/Paula Wiseman Bks.

Depken, Kristen L. Here Comes Peter Cottontail. 2012. (Step into Reading Level 2 Ser.). lib. bdg. 13.55 *(978-0-606-23719-2(4),* Turtleback) Turtleback Bks.

—Here Comes Peter Cottontail (Peter Cottontail) Karl, Linda, illus. 2012. (Step into Reading Ser.). (ENG.). 32p. (J). (gr. -1-1). pap. 3.99 *(978-0-307-93032-3(7),* Random Hse. Bks. for Young Readers) Random Hse. Children's Bks.

DeVillers, Julia & Roy, Jennifer. Triple Trouble. 2014. (Mix Ser.). (ENG., Illus.). 240p. (J). (gr. 4-8). pap. 7.99 *(978-1-4424-3406-6(6),* Aladdin) Simon & Schuster Children's Publishing.

—Triple Trouble. 2013. (ENG.). 240p. (J). (gr. 4-8). 16.99 *(978-1-4424-3405-9(8),* Simon & Schuster/Paula Wiseman Bks.) Simon & Schuster/Paula Wiseman Bks.

Diersch, Sandra. False Start, 1 vol. 2005. (Lorimer Sports Stories Ser.: 78). (ENG.). 104p. (J). (gr. 4-8). 16.95 *(978-1-55028-873-5(3),* 9781550288735); 8.95 *(978-1-55028-872-8(5),* 9781550288728) Lorimer, James & Co., Ltd., Pubs. CAN. Dist: Casemate Pubs. & Bk. Distributors, LLC.

Dower, Laura. Kiki Takes the Cake. Lazuli, Lilly, illus. 2016. (Dessert Diaries). (ENG.). 160p. (gr. 4-5). lib. bdg. 26.65 *(978-1-4965-3120-9(5))* Stone Arch Bks.

Dzidrums, Christine. Princess Dessabelle: Tennis Star. Muths, Tohn Fayette, illus. 2013. 50p. pap. 10.99 *(978-1-938438-34-9(5))* Creative Media Publishing.

Earhart, Kristin. Rain Forest Relay. 2015. (Race the Wild Ser.: 1). lib. bdg. 14.75 *(978-0-606-37042-4(0))* Turtleback Bks.

Echols, Jennifer. The Ex Games. 2011. (Romantic Comedies Ser.). (ENG.). 240p. (YA). (gr. 7). pap. 11.99 *(978-1-4424-3083-9(4),* Simon Pulse) Simon Pulse.

Evans, Zoe. Pyramid of One. Barrager, Brigette, illus. 2011. (Cheer! Ser.: 2). (ENG.). 240p. (J). (gr. 3-7). pap. 6.99 *(978-1-4424-2239-1(4),* Simon Spotlight) Simon Spotlight.

Fairchild-Lenyo, Mary. When Winston Wins. Vigil, Cristina, illus. 2007. 36p. per. 14.95 *(978-1-59858-405-9(7))* Dog Ear Publishing, LLC.

Faris, Stephanie. 25 Roses. 2015. (Mix Ser.). (ENG., Illus.). 224p. (J). (gr. 4-8). pap. 7.99 *(978-1-4814-2420-2(3),* Aladdin) Simon & Schuster Children's Publishing.

Fein, Eric & Fuentes, Benny. Skateboard Breakdown, 1 vol. Sandoval, Gerardo, illus. 2010. (Sports Illustrated Kids Graphic Novels Ser.). (ENG.). 56p. (gr. 2-3). 26.65 *(978-1-4342-2011-0(7));* pap. 7.19 *(978-1-4342-2785-0(5))* Stone Arch Bks.

Fincher, Cecilia. Chandra's Adventure. 2012. 28p. pap. 19.99 *(978-1-4772-0137-4(8))* AuthorHouse.

Fitzgerald, Ruth. Emily Sparkes & the Competition Calamity. Cole, Allison, illus. 2017. (Emily Sparkes Ser.). (ENG.). 288p. (J). (gr. 4-6). pap. 8.99 ***(978-0-349-00184-5(7))*** Little, Brown Bks. for Young Readers.

Flack, Sophie. Bunheads. 2012. (ENG.). 320p. (YA). (gr. 7-17). pap. 10.99 *(978-0-316-12654-0(3),* Poppy) Little, Brown Bks. for Young Readers.

Freitas, Donna. Gold Medal Summer. (ENG.). 240p. (J). 2014. (gr. 5-9). pap. 6.99 *(978-0-545-32789-3(X))* 2012. (gr. 4-7). 16.99 *(978-0-545-32788-6(1))* Scholastic, Inc. (Levine, Arthur A. Bks.).

—Gold Medal Winter. 2014. (ENG.). 320p. (J). (gr. 4-7). 16.99 *(978-0-545-64377-1(5))* Scholastic, Inc.

Godin, Thelma Lynne. Hula-Hoopin' Queen. Brantley-Newton, Vanessa, illus. 2014. (ENG.). 40p. (J). 18.95 *(978-1-60060-846-9(9))* Lee & Low Bks., Inc.

Golden Books. Here Comes Peter Cottontail. Golden Books, illus. 2014. (Little Golden Book Ser.). (ENG., Illus.). 24p. (J). (-k). 4.99 *(978-0-385-37839-0(4),* Golden Bks.) Random Hse. Children's Bks.

GrandPré, Mary. Cleonardo, the Little Inventor. 2016. (ENG., Illus.). 48p. (J). (gr. -1-3). 18.99 *(978-0-439-35764-7(0))* Scholastic, Inc.

Green, D. L. Sweet Buttercup. Wallis, Emily, illus. 2016. (Silver Pony Ranch Ser.: 2). (ENG.). 96p. (J). (gr. 1-3). 15.99 *(978-0-545-79770-2(5))* Scholastic, Inc.

Green, Tim. Force Out. 2013. (ENG.). 288p. (J). (gr. 3-7). 16.99 *(978-0-06-208959-5(5))* HarperCollins Pubs.

Gurevich, Margaret. Chloe by Design, 4 vols. Hagel, Brooke, illus. 2015. (Chloe by Design Ser.). (ENG.). 96p. (gr. 5-8). 101.28 *(978-1-4965-1995-5(7))* Stone Arch Bks.

—Chloe by Design: Making the Cut, 1 vol. Hagel, Brooke, illus. 2014. (Chloe by Design Ser.). (ENG.). 384p. (gr. 4-8). 14.95 *(978-1-62370-112-3(0))* Capstone Young Readers of Coughlan Cos.

—Unraveling, 1 vol. Hagel, Brooke, illus. 2014. (Chloe by Design Ser.). (ENG.). 96p. (gr. 5-8). 25.32 *(978-1-4342-9179-0(0))* Stone Arch Bks.

Halliday, Susan. Quiz Champs. Jellett, Tom, illus. l.t. ed. 2014. 44p. pap. *(978-1-4596-7622-0(X))* ReadHowYouWant.com, Ltd.

Harrison, Lisi. Alphas. 2009. (Alphas Ser.: 1). (ENG.). 272p. (YA). (gr. 7-17). pap. 9.99 *(978-0-316-03579-8(3),* Poppy) Little, Brown Bks. for Young Readers.

—Movers & Fakers. 2010. (Alphas Ser.: 2). (ENG.). 240p. (YA). (gr. 7-17). pap. 9.99 *(978-0-316-03580-4(7),* Poppy) Little, Brown Bks. for Young Readers.

—Top of the Feud Chain. 2011. (Alphas Ser.: 4). (ENG.). 240p. (YA). (gr. 7-17). pap. 9.99 *(978-0-316-03582-8(3),* Poppy) Little, Brown Bks. for Young Readers.

Harvey, Alex. Dancing with the Star. 2013. (Spongebob Squarepants Step into Reading Ser.). lib. bdg. 13.55 *(978-0-606-23687-4(2),* Turtleback) Turtleback Bks.

Heos, Bridget. Mustache Baby. Ang, Joy, illus. 2015. (Mustache Baby Ser.). (ENG.). 40p. (J). (gr. -1-3). 16.99 *(978-0-544-36375-5(2),* Clarion Bks.) Houghton Mifflin Harcourt Trade & Reference Pubs.

Hutchins, Jennifer J. Just Plain Nora. 2012. 112p. (gr. 4-6). 28.95 *(978-1-4497-3318-6(2));* pap. 11.95 *(978-1-4497-3317-9(4))* Author Solutions, Inc. (WestBow Pr.).

Ihara, Shigekatsu. Pokémon: Diamond & Pearl Adventure!, Vol. 6. Ihara, Shigekatsu, illus. 2010. (ENG., Illus.). 192p. (J). pap. 9.99 *(978-1-4215-3170-0(4))* Viz Media.

Jones, Jen. Brooke's Quest for Captain, No. 2. 2011. (Team Cheer Ser.). (ENG.). 112p. (gr. 4-4). lib. bdg. 25.32 *(978-1-4342-2995-3(5),* Team Cheer) Stone Arch Bks.

—Brooke's Quest for Captain: # 2, 1 vol. 2012. (Team Cheer Ser.). (ENG.). 112p. (gr. 4-4). pap. 7.19 *(978-1-4342-4250-1(1),* Team Cheer) Stone Arch Bks.

—The Competition for Gaby, No. 4. 2011. (Team Cheer Ser.). (ENG.). 112p. (gr. 4-4). lib. bdg. 25.32 *(978-1-4342-2997-7(1),* Team Cheer) Stone Arch Bks.

—The Competition for Gaby: # 4, 1 vol. 2012. (Team Cheer Ser.). (ENG.). 112p. (gr. 4-4). pap. 7.19 *(978-1-4342-4252-5(8),* Team Cheer) Stone Arch Bks.

Jones, V. M. Out of Reach, 0 vols. unabr. ed. 2013. (ENG.). 272p. (J). (gr. 7-9). pap. 9.99 *(978-1-4778-1705-6(0),* 9781477817056, Amazon Children's Publishing) Amazon Publishing.

Joyner, Andrew. Boris for the Win. 2013. (Boris Ser.: 3). (ENG.). 80p. (J). (gr. k-2). pap. 4.99 *(978-0-545-48449-7(9))* Scholastic, Inc.

—Boris for the Win. 2013. (Boris Ser.: 3). lib. bdg. 14.75 *(978-0-606-31976-8(X),* Turtleback) Turtleback Bks.

Juby, Susan. The Fashion Committee. 2017. (ENG.). 320p. (YA). (gr. 7). 18.99 *(978-0-451-46878-9(3),* Viking Books for Young Readers) Penguin Young Readers Group.

Keller, Laurie. The Spinny Icky Showdown. Keller, Laurie, illus. 2015. (Adventures of Arnie the Doughnut Ser.: 3). (ENG., Illus.). 128p. (J). (gr. 2-5). 12.99 *(978-0-8050-9074-1(6),* 9780805090741, Holt, Henry & Co. Bks. For Young Readers) Holt, Henry & Co.

Kent, Renee Holmes. Cassie, You're a Winner! 2004. (Adventures in Misty Falls Ser.: Vol. 1). (Illus.). 100p. (gr. 4-7). pap. 2.99 *(978-1-56309-735-5(4),* N007116) New Hope Pubs.

Keplinger, Kody. Shut Out. 2012. (ENG.). 288p. (YA). (gr. 10-17). pap. 10.99 *(978-0-316-17555-5(2),* Poppy) Little, Brown Bks. for Young Readers.

Könnecke, Ole. Anton & the Battle. Chidgey, Catherine, tr. from GER. 2013.Tr. of Anton und der grosse Streit. (ENG., Illus.). 32p. (gr. -1-3). 17.95 *(978-1-877579-26-4(2))* Gecko Pr. NZL. Dist: Lerner Publishing Group.

Korman, Gordon. Everest Book One: the Contest. 2012. (Everest Ser.). (ENG.). 144p. (J). (gr. 3-7). pap. 6.99 *(978-0-545-39232-7(2))* Scholastic, Inc.

Kreie, Chris. Don't Wobble on the Wakeboard!, 1 vol. Santillan, Jorge H., illus. 2011. (Sports Illustrated Kids Victory School Superstars Ser.). (ENG.). 56p. (gr. 1-3). lib. bdg. 26.65 *(978-1-4342-2235-0(7))* Stone Arch Bks.

—I Couldn't Land a Bunny Hop, 1 vol. Santillan, Jorge H., illus. 2012. (Sports Illustrated Kids Victory School Superstars Ser.). (ENG.). 56p. (gr. 1-3). pap. 5.95 *(978-1-4342-3865-8(2));* lib. bdg. 26.65 *(978-1-4342-3762-0(1))* Stone Arch Bks.

Krosoczka, Jarrett J. Lunch Lady & the Mutant Mathletes. 2012. (Lunch Lady Ser.). (ENG., Illus.). 96p. (J). (gr. 2-5). pap. 6.99 *(978-0-375-87028-6(8));* lib. bdg. 12.99 *(978-0-375-97028-3(2))* Random Hse. Children's Bks. (Knopf Bks. for Young Readers).

—Lunch Lady & the Mutant Mathletes. 2012. (Lunch Lady Ser.: 7). lib. bdg. 17.20 *(978-0-606-23871-7(9),* Turtleback) Turtleback Bks.

Landry, Leo. What's up, Chuck? 2016. (ENG., Illus.). 48p. (J). (gr. k-3). lib. bdg. 12.95 *(978-1-58089-698-6(7))* Charlesbridge Publishing, Inc.

LeTourneau, Marie & Baty, Danielle Reed. The Mice of Bistrot des Sept Frères. 2008. (ENG & FRE.). 32p. (J). (gr. -1-3). pap. 7.95 *(978-1-933718-18-7(8))* Tanglewood Pr.

Lewis, Axel. Rain Forest Rampage, 1 vol. 2014. (Robot Racers Ser.). (ENG.). 160p. (gr. 2-4). 26.65 *(978-1-4342-6571-5(4))* Stone Arch Bks.

Lobe, Mira & Kovács, Cécilie. Hoppelpopp & the Best Bunny. Kaufmann, Angelika, illus. 2015. (ENG.). 32p. (J). (gr. -1-3). 16.95 *(978-0-8234-3287-5(4))* Holiday Hse., Inc.

Loughead, Deb. Sidetracked, 1 vol. 2012. (Orca Sports Ser.). (ENG.). 136p. (YA). (gr. 6-10). pap. 9.95 *(978-1-4598-0250-6(0))* Orca Bk. Pubs. USA.

Lucado, Max. Punchinello & the Most Marvelous Gift. Martinez, Sergio, illus. 2004. (Max Lucado's Wemmicks Ser.: 5). 32p. (J). 15.99 *(978-1-58134-546-9(1))* 2003. 28p. bds. 6.99 *(978-1-58134-562-9(3))* Crossway.

—Punchinello & the Most Marvelous Gift: And, Your Special Gift. Martinez, Sergio, illus. 2007. (J). *(978-1-58134-877-4(0))* Crossway.

Lupica, Mike. Long Shot, 1 vol. 2012. (Comeback Kids Ser.). (ENG.). 192p. (J). (gr. 4-8). lib. bdg. 27.07 *(978-1-59961-176-1(7))* Spotlight.

Mack, W. C. Athlete vs. Mathlete. 2013. (Athlete vs. Mathlete Ser.). (ENG.). (YA). (gr. 3-6). 192p. 16.99 *(978-1-61963-129-8(6),* 9781619631298); 192p. pap. 7.99 *(978-1-59990-938-7(3),* 9781599909387); 208p. 16.99 *(978-1-59990-915-8(4),* 9781599909158); (Illus.). 208p. pap. 7.99 *(978-1-59990-858-8(1),* 9781599908588) Bloomsbury Publishing USA. (Bloomsbury USA Childrens).

—Time-Out. 2014. (Athlete vs. Mathlete Ser.). (ENG.). 208p. (YA). (gr. 3-6). 16.99 *(978-1-61963-301-8(9),* 9781619633018, Bloomsbury USA Childrens) Bloomsbury Publishing USA.

Maddox, Jake. Basketball Breakdown. 2016. (Jake Maddox JV Girls Ser.). (ENG.). 96p. (gr. 3-4). lib. bdg. 25.99 *(978-1-4965-3166-7(3))* Stone Arch Bks.

—BMX Challenge, 1 vol. Tiffany, Sean, illus. 2011. (Jake Maddox Sports Stories Ser.). (ENG.). 72p. (gr. 2-3). pap. 5.95 *(978-1-4342-3423-0(1))* Stone Arch Bks.

—Cheer Challenge. Mourning, Tuesday, illus. 2008. (Jake Maddox Girl Sports Stories Ser.). (ENG.). 72p. (gr. 2-3). lib. bdg. 25.32 *(978-1-4342-0468-4(5));* per. 5.95 *(978-1-4342-0518-6(5))* Stone Arch Bks.

—Cheer Choice, 1 vol. Wood, Katie, illus. 2014. (Jake Maddox Girl Sports Stories Ser.). (ENG.). 72p. (gr. 2-3). 25.32 *(978-1-4342-4143-6(2))* Stone Arch Bks.

—Cycling Champion, 1 vol. Garcia, Eduardo, illus. 2012. (Jake Maddox Sports Stories Ser.). (ENG.). 72p. (gr. 2-3). pap. 5.95 *(978-1-4342-3904-4(7));* lib. bdg. 25.32 *(978-1-4342-3290-8(5))* Stone Arch Bks.

—Gold Medal Swim, 1 vol. Garcia, Eduardo, illus. 2012. (Jake Maddox Sports Stories Ser.). (ENG.). 72p. (gr. 2-3). pap. 5.95 *(978-1-4342-3902-0(0));* lib. bdg. 25.32 *(978-1-4342-3288-5(3))* Stone Arch Bks.

—Gymnastics Jitters, 1 vol. Wood, Katie, illus. 2012. (Jake Maddox Girl Sports Stories Ser.). (ENG.). 72p. (gr. 2-3). pap. 5.95 *(978-1-4342-3908-2(X));* lib. bdg. 25.32 *(978-1-4342-3293-9(X))* Stone Arch Bks.

—Kart Competition, 1 vol. Aburtov, Jesus Aburto, illus. 2013. (Jake Maddox Sports Stories Ser.). (ENG.). 72p. (gr. 2-3). pap. 5.95 *(978-1-4342-6209-7(X))* Stone Arch Bks.

—Kart Competition. 2013. (Jake Maddox Sports Stories Ser.). (ENG.). 72p. (gr. 2-3). pap. 35.70 *(978-1-4342-6236-3(7))* Stone Arch Bks.

—Kart Competition, 1 vol. Aburtov, Jesus, illus. 2013. (Jake Maddox Sports Stories Ser.). (ENG.). 72p. (gr. 2-3). lib. bdg. 25.32 *(978-1-4342-5976-9(5))* Stone Arch Bks.

—Lacrosse Attack. Tiffany, Sean, illus. 2008. (Jake Maddox Sports Stories Ser.). (ENG.). 72p. (gr. 2-3). 25.32 *(978-1-4342-0776-0(5));* pap. 5.95 *(978-1-4342-0872-9(9))* Stone Arch Bks.

—El Lanzador Bajo Presión. Heck, Claudia M., tr. from ENG. Tiffany, Sean, illus. 2012. (Jake Maddox en Español Ser.). (SPA.). 72p. (gr. 2-3). 25.32 *(978-1-4342-3815-3(6))* Stone Arch Bks.

—Motocross Double-Cross. Tiffany, Sean, illus. 2007. (Jake Maddox Sports Stories Ser.). (ENG.). 72p. (gr. 2-3). pap. 5.95 *(978-1-59889-897-2(3));* lib. bdg. 25.32 *(978-1-59889-845-3(0))* Stone Arch Bks.

—On Guard, 1 vol. Tiffany, Sean, illus. 2010. (Team Jake Maddox Sports Stories Ser.). (ENG.). 72p. (gr. 2-3). pap. 5.95 *(978-1-4342-2279-4(9));* lib. bdg. 25.32 *(978-1-4342-1920-6(8))* Stone Arch Bks.

—Outfield Outcast, 1 vol. Ray, Mike, illus. 2014. (Jake Maddox JV Ser.). (ENG.). 96p. (gr. 3-4). 25.99 *(978-1-4342-9153-0(7))* Stone Arch Bks.

—Power Play. 2016. (Jake Maddox JV Girls Ser.). (ENG.). 96p. (gr. 3-4). lib. bdg. 25.99 *(978-1-4965-3673-0(8))* Stone Arch Bks.

—Running Rivals. Mourning, Tuesday, illus. 2008. (Jake Maddox Girl Sports Stories Ser.). (ENG.). 72p. (gr. 2-3). 25.32 *(978-1-4342-0778-4(1))* Stone Arch Bks.

—Skateboard Idol. 2016. (Jake Maddox JV Ser.). (ENG.). 96p. (gr. 3-4). lib. bdg. 25.99 *(978-1-4965-2631-1(7))* Stone Arch Bks.

—Skating Showdown, 1 vol. Wood, Katie, illus. 2013. (Jake Maddox Girl Sports Stories Ser.). (ENG.). 72p. (gr. 2-3). pap. 5.95 *(978-1-4342-4204-4(8));* lib. bdg. 25.32 *(978-1-4342-4012-5(6))* Stone Arch Bks.

—Slap-Shot Slump. 2015. (Jake Maddox JV Ser.). (ENG.). 96p. (gr. 3-4). lib. bdg. 25.99 *(978-1-4342-9635-1(0))* Stone Arch Bks.

—Snowboard Duel, 1 vol. Tiffany, Sean, illus. 2007. (Jake Maddox Sports Stories Ser.). (ENG.). 72p. (gr. 2-3). pap. 5.95 *(978-1-59889-895-8(7))* Stone Arch Bks.

—Soccer Stand-Off. 2016. (Jake Maddox JV Ser.). (ENG.). 96p. (gr. 3-4). lib. bdg. 25.99 *(978-1-4965-3983-0(4))* Stone Arch Bks.

—Soccer Step-Up. 2016. (Jake Maddox JV Girls Ser.). (ENG.). 96p. (gr. 3-4). lib. bdg. 25.99 *(978-1-4965-3675-4(4))* Stone Arch Bks.

—Swimming the Distance. 2015. (Jake Maddox JV Ser.). (ENG.). 96p. (gr. 3-4). lib. bdg. 25.99 *(978-1-4342-9637-5(7))* Stone Arch Bks.

—Taekwondo Clash. 2016. (Jake Maddox JV Ser.). (ENG.). 96p. (gr. 3-4). lib. bdg. 25.99 *(978-1-4965-3981-6(8))* Stone Arch Bks.

—Track & Field Takedown, 1 vol. Garcia, Eduardo, illus. 2012. (Jake Maddox Sports Stories Ser.). (ENG.). 72p. (gr. 2-3). pap. 5.95 *(978-1-4342-3901-3(2));* lib. bdg. 25.32 *(978-1-4342-3287-8(5))* Stone Arch Bks.

Maddox, Jake & Anderson, Josh. Second Shot. Aburtov, Jesus Aburto, illus. 2016. (Jake Maddox Sports Stories Ser.). (ENG.). 72p. (gr. 2-3). lib. bdg. 25.32 *(978-1-4965-3052-3(7))* Stone Arch Bks.

Madonna, pseud. The New Girl, Vol. 3. Fulvimari, Jeffrey, illus. 2007. (English Roses Ser.: 3). (ENG.). 144p. (J). (gr. 3-7). 9.99 *(978-0-14-240884-1(0),* Puffin Books) Penguin Young Readers Group.

Mancusi, Mari. Golden Girl. 2015. (Mix Ser.). (ENG., Illus.). 336p. (J). (gr. 4-8). pap. 7.99 *(978-1-4814-3762-2(3),* Aladdin) Simon & Schuster Children's Publishing.

Martinez, Jessica. Virtuosity. (ENG.). (YA). (gr. 9). 2012. 320p. pap. 9.99 *(978-1-4424-2053-3(7))* 2011. 304p. 16.99 *(978-1-4424-2052-6(9))* Simon Pulse. (Simon Pulse).

Martino, Alfred C. Pinned: There Can Be Only One Winner... 2006. (ENG., Illus.). 320p. (YA). (gr. 7-12). reprint ed. pap. 8.99 *(978-0-15-205631-5(9))* Houghton Mifflin Harcourt Publishing Co.

McDonald, Megan. Frank Pearl in the Awful Waffle Kerfuffle. Madrid, Erwin, illus. 2014. (Judy Moody Ser.: 4). (ENG.). 64p. (J). (gr. -1-1). 12.99 *(978-0-7636-5717-8(4))* Candlewick Pr.

Metz, Melinda. S. M. A. R. T. S. & the Missing UFO. McKenzie, Heath, illus. 2015. (S. M. A. R. T. S. Ser.). (ENG.). 128p. (gr. 3-6). lib. bdg. 22.65 *(978-1-4965-0466-1(6))* S.M.A.R.T.S. Learning System.

Miles, Brenda & Sweet, Susan D. Chicken or Egg: Who Comes First? 2017. (J). ***(978-1-4338-2719-8(0))*** American Psychological Assn.

Mills, Claudia. Simon Ellis, Spelling Bee Champ. Shepperson, Rob, illus. 2015. (Franklin School Friends Ser.: 4). (ENG.). 144p. (J). (gr. 2-5). 15.99 *(978-0-374-30221-4(9),* 9780374302214, Farrar, Straus & Giroux (BYR)) Farrar, Straus & Giroux.

Misra, Michelle. Secrets & Sapphires. Chaffey, Samantha, illus. 2016. (Angel Wings Ser.: 3). (ENG.). 128p. (J). (gr. 1-4). 16.99 *(978-1-4814-5804-7(3),* Simon & Schuster/Paula Wiseman Bks.) Simon & Schuster/Paula Wiseman Bks.

Moceanu, Dominique & Thompson, Alicia. Reaching High. 2012. (Go-For-Gold Gymnasts Ser.). (ENG.). 224p. (J). (gr. 5-9). pap. 5.99 *(978-1-4231-3657-6(8))* Hyperion Pr.

Montgomery, Lewis B. The Case of the Missing Moose. Wummer, Amy, illus. 2011. (Milo & Jazz Mysteries Ser.). 96p. (J). 22.60 *(978-1-57565-331-0(1));* pap. 39.62 *(978-0-7613-7607-1(0));* (ENG.). (gr. 2-6). pap. 6.95 *(978-1-57565-322-8(2))* Kane Press, Inc.

Morgan, Winter. The Endermen Invasion: A Minecraft Gamer's Adventure, Book Three. 2014. (Unofficial Gamer's Adventure Ser.). (ENG.). 112p. (J). (gr. 1-7). pap. 7.99 *(978-1-63450-088-3(1),* Sky Pony Pr.) Skyhorse Publishing Co., Inc.

Moses, Antoinette. Vinnie's Vacation Level 1 Beginner/Elementary American English Edition. 2012. (ENG.). 48p. pap. 9.50 *(978-1-107-62130-5(5))* Cambridge Univ. Pr.

Mullarkey, Lisa. The Write Stuff: Book 7, 1 vol. Harris, Phyllis, illus. 2012. (Katharine the Almost Great Ser.). (ENG.). 80p. (J). (gr. 1-4). 27.07 *(978-1-61641-828-1(1))* Magic Wagon.

Nayeri, Daniel and Dina. Another Faust. 2010. (ENG., Illus.). 400p. (YA). (gr. 9). pap. 8.99 *(978-0-7636-4834-3(5))* Candlewick Pr.

Naylor, Phyllis Reynolds. The Girls Take Over. 2004. (Boys Against Girls Ser.: No. 8). 146p. (J). (gr. 4-7). 13.65 *(978-0-7569-2804-9(4))* Perfection Learning Corp.

—The Girls Take Over. 2004. (Boy/Girl Battle Ser.: No. 8). (ENG.). 160p. (J). (gr. 3-7). 6.99 *(978-0-440-41678-4(7),* Yearling) Random Hse. Children's Bks.

Nickel, Scott. Race on the River, 1 vol. Harpster, Steve, illus. 2011. (My First Graphic Novel Ser.). (ENG.). 32p. (gr. k-2). pap. 6.25 *(978-1-4342-3061-4(9));* lib. bdg. 24.65 *(978-1-4342-2521-4(6))* Stone Arch Bks. (My First Graphic Novel).

Noël, Alyson. Unrivaled: A Beautiful Idols Novel. 2016. 420p. (YA). *(978-0-06-245840-7(X))* HarperCollins Pubs.

C D

Norris, Shana. Troy High. 2009. (ENG.). 272p. (YA). (gr. 7-11). 16.95 *(978-0-8109-4647-7(5),* Amulet Bks.) Abrams, Inc.
O'Connell, Matthew J. The Adventures of Rick Cliff: The Almost Great Penguin Race. 2004. 80p. (J). pap. 6.95 *(978-1-932560-66-4(1),* Llumina Pr.) Aeon Publishing Inc.
O'Reilly, Sean. Science Fair Nightmare, 1 vol. (Mighty Mighty Monsters Ser.). (ENG., 48p. (gr. 2-3). 2013. Illus.). pap. 6.10 *(978-1-4342-4226-6(9))* 2012. lib. bdg. 23.99 *(978-1-4342-3891-7(1))* Stone Arch Bks.
O'Ryan, Ray. A Galactic Easter! Jack, Colin, illus. 2014. (Galaxy Zack Ser.: 7). (ENG.). 128p. (J). (gr. k-4). pap. 5.99 *(978-1-4424-9357-5(7),* Little Simon) Little Simon.
—A Galactic Easter! 2014. (Galaxy Zack Ser.: 7). lib. bdg. 16.00 *(978-0-606-35428-8(X))* Turtleback Bks.
—Ready, Set, Blast Off! Kraft, Jason, illus. 2017. (Galaxy Zack Ser.: 15). (ENG.). 128p. (J). (gr. k-4). pap. 5.99 *(978-1-4814-8595-1(4),* Little Simon) Little Simon.
Percival, Tom. Bubble Trouble. 2015. (ENG., Illus.). 32p. (J). (gr. -1-1). 17.99 *(978-1-61963-679-8(4),* 9781619636798, Bloomsbury USA Childrens) Bloomsbury Publishing USA.
Polak, Monique. Flip Turn, 1 vol. 2004. (Lorimer Sports Stories Ser.: 67). (ENG.). 104p. (J). (gr. 4-8). 16.95 *(978-1-55028-819-3(9),* 9781550288193) Lorimer, James & Co., Ltd., Pubs. CAN. Dist: Casemate Pubs. & Bk. Distributors, LLC.
Priebe, Val. Basketball Breakdown. 2016. (Jake Maddox JV Girls Ser.). (ENG.). 96p. (gr. 3-4). pap. 5.95 *(978-1-4965-3676-1(2))* Stone Arch Bks.
Raden, Tammy. Lucky Dime. 2011. 24p. 11.32 *(978-1-4567-2137-4(2))* AuthorHouse.
Rayner, Robert. Falling Star, 1 vol. 2007. (Lorimer Sports Stories Ser.). (ENG.). 136p. (J). (gr. 4-8). 16.95 *(978-1-55028-971-8(3),* 9781550289718) Lorimer, James & Co., Ltd., Pubs. CAN. Dist: Casemate Pubs. & Bk. Distributors, LLC.
—Just for Kicks, 1 vol. 2004. (Lorimer Sports Stories Ser.). (ENG.). 152p. (J). (gr. 4-8). 16.95 *(978-1-55028-825-4(3),* 9781550288254) Lorimer, James & Co., Ltd., Pubs. CAN. Dist: Casemate Pubs. & Bk. Distributors, LLC.
Reed, Liz & Reed, Jimmy. Sweet Competition. Reed, Liz & Reed, Jimmy, illus. 2016. (Illus.). 40p. (J). (gr. -1-3). 17.99 *(978-0-06-240359-9(1))* HarperCollins Pubs.
RH Disney. Back on Track. RH Disney, illus. 2017. (Step into Reading Ser.). (ENG., Illus.). 24p. (J). (gr. -1-1). pap. 4.99 ***(978-0-7364-3680-9(4))***; lib. bdg. 12.99 ***(978-0-7364-8198-4(2))*** Random Hse. Children's Bks. (RH/Disney).
Robins, Eleanor. Double-Cross, 1 vol. unabr. ed. 2011. (Choices Ser.). (ENG.). 51p. (YA). (gr. 9-12). 7.95 *(978-1-61651-595-9(3))* Saddleback Educational Publishing, Inc.
Rock, Nora. Fly Away, 1 vol. 2010. (Orca Sports Ser.). (ENG.). 192p. (YA). (gr. 6-10). pap. 9.95 *(978-1-55469-313-9(6))* Orca Bk. Pubs. USA.
Rodkey, Geoff. The Tapper Twins Run for President. 2016. (Tapper Twins Ser.: 3). (ENG., Illus.). 304p. (J). (gr. 3-7). 13.99 *(978-0-316-29785-1(2))* Little, Brown Bks. for Young Readers.
—The Tapper Twins Tear up New York. 2015. (Tapper Twins Ser.: 2). (ENG., Illus.). 288p. (J). (gr. 3-7). 13.99 *(978-0-316-29783-7(6))* Little Brown & Co.
—The Tapper Twins Tear up New York. 2016. (Tapper Twins Ser.: 2). (ENG., Illus.). 288p. (J). (gr. 3-7). pap. 5.99 *(978-0-316-31601-9(6))* Little, Brown Bks. for Young Readers.
Romay, Alexis, tr. OLIVIA Vende Galletas (OLIVIA Sells Cookies) Spaziante, Patrick, illus. 2013. (Olivia TV Tie-In Ser.). (SPA.). 24p. (J). (gr. -1-2). pap. 3.99 *(978-1-4424-5967-0(0),* Libros Para Ninos) Libros Para Ninos.
Ross, Tony. I Want to Win! Ross, Tony, illus. 2012. (Andersen Press Picture Bks). (ENG., Illus.). 32p. (J). (gr. -1-3). 16.95 *(978-0-7613-8993-4(8))* Lerner Publishing Group.
Rue, Nancy N. Totally Unfair, 1 vol. 2005. (Nama Beach High Ser.). (ENG.). 160p. (YA). pap. 6.99 *(978-0-310-25183-5(4))* Zondervan.
Sauer, Tammi. Ginny Louise & the School Field Day. Munsinger, Lynn, illus. 2016. (ENG.). 32p. (J). (gr. -1-k). 16.99 *(978-1-4847-3044-7(5))* Disney Pr.
Scott, Victoria. Fire & Flood. 2014. (ENG.). 320p. (J). (gr. 9). 17.99 *(978-0-545-53746-9(0),* Scholastic Pr.) Scholastic, Inc.
Serwacki, Kevin & Pallace, Chris. Joey & Johnny - The Ninjas - Get Mooned. Serwacki, Kevin & Pallace, Chris, illus. 2015. (Joey & Johnny, the Ninjas Ser.: 1). (ENG., Illus.). 320p. (J). (gr. 3-7). 12.99 *(978-0-06-229933-8(6))* HarperCollins Pubs.
Siciari, Theresa. The Case of the Missing Hairpin, 1 vol. 2009. 25p. pap. 24.95 *(978-1-60813-865-4(8))* America Star Bks.
Spalding, Amy. The New Guy (and Other Senior Year Distractions) 2016. (ENG.). 320p. (YA). (gr. 7-17). 17.99 *(978-0-316-38278-6(7),* Poppy) Little, Brown Bks. for Young Readers.
Sparks, Megan. Boot Camp Blues, 1 vol. 2014. (Roller Girls Ser.). (ENG.). 256p. (gr. 8-10). 12.95 *(978-1-62370-057-7(4))* Capstone Young Readers of Coughlan Cos.
Spaziante, Patrick, illus. OLIVIA Sells Cookies. 2013. (Olivia TV Tie-In Ser.). (ENG.). 24p. (J). (gr. -1-2). pap. 3.99 *(978-1-4424-5965-6(4),* Simon Spotlight) Simon Spotlight.
Stadelmann, Amy Marie. The Super-Smelly Moldy Blob. Stadelmann, Amy Marie, illus. 2016. (Olive & Beatrix Ser.: 2). (ENG., Illus.). 80p. (J). (gr. k-2). 15.99 *(978-0-545-81485-0(5))* Scholastic, Inc.
Steele, Michael Anthony. Fresh, 1 vol. Cano, Fernando, illus. 2014. (Tony Hawk: Live2Skate Ser.). (ENG.). 72p. (gr. 4-5). lib. bdg. 25.32 *(978-1-4342-9140-0(5))* Stone Arch Bks.
Stout, Shawn K. Miss Matched. Martini, Angela, illus. 2013. (Not-So-Ordinary Girl Ser.: 2). (ENG.). 176p. (J). (gr. 1-5). pap. 5.99 *(978-1-4424-7404-8(1),* Aladdin) Simon & Schuster Children's Publishing.
—Miss Matched. Martini, Angela, illus. 2013. (Not-So-Ordinary Girl Ser.: 2). (ENG.). 160p. (J). (gr. 1-5). 15.99 *(978-1-4424-7405-5(X),* Simon & Schuster/Paula Wiseman Bks.) Simon & Schuster/Paula Wiseman Bks.
Stuart, Janet. Something New in Cloverville? 2010. 20p. 12.49 *(978-1-4520-7701-7(0))* AuthorHouse.
TerKeurst, Lysa. Win or Lose, I Love You! Sometimes You Learn, 1 vol. 2015. (ENG., Illus.). 32p. (J). 15.99 *(978-0-529-10400-7(8))* Nelson, Thomas Inc.
Trussell-Cullen, Alan. The Twin Competition. Hurst, Elise, illus. 2009. (Rigby PM Stars Bridge Bks.). (ENG.). 16p. (gr. 2-3). pap. 8.70 *(978-1-4190-5510-2(0))* Rigby Education.
Tyler, Sandy. Herkimer's Big Day: Herkimer the Police Horse Meets a Young Girl Named Sammy. Williams, Brian, illus. 2012. (ENG.). 22p. (J). pap. 20.95 *(978-1-4327-9005-9(6))* Outskirts Pr., Inc.
Venning, Edward W. The Story of Pete & Ralph. 2008. 56p. pap. 16.95 *(978-1-4327-2237-1(9))* Outskirts Pr., Inc.
Wallace, Rich. Fast Company. 3rd ed. 2005. (Winning Season Ser.: Bk. 3). (ENG.). 128p. (J). (gr. 3-7). 5.99 *(978-0-14-240468-3(3),* Puffin Books) Penguin Young Readers Group.
—Game-Day Jitters. Holder, Jimmy, illus. 2012. (Kickers Ser.). (ENG.). 128p. (J). (gr. 2-5). 5.99 *(978-0-375-85095-0(3),* Yearling) Random Hse. Children's Bks.
Ward, Matthew. War of the World Records. 2nd ed. 2015. (Fantastic Family Whipple Ser.: 2). (ENG.). 384p. (J). (gr. 3-7). pap. 8.99 *(978-1-59514-692-2(X),* Razorbill) Penguin Young Readers Group.
Warner, Sally. Excellent Emma. Harper, Jamie, illus. 2010. (Emma Ser.). (ENG.). 144p. (J). (gr. 3-7). 6.99 *(978-0-14-241569-6(3),* Puffin Books) Penguin Young Readers Group.
Warner, Sally & Harper, Jamie. Excellent Emma. Harper, Jamie, illus. 2009. (Emma Ser.). (ENG., Illus.). 144p. (J). (gr. 3-7). 14.99 *(978-0-670-06310-9(X),* Viking Books for Young Readers) Penguin Young Readers Group.
Welton, Jude. Adam's Alternative Sports Day: An Asperger Story. 2004. (ENG., Illus.). 112p. (J). pap. 20.95 *(978-1-84310-300-4(1),* 5356) Kingsley, Jessica Pubs. GBR. Dist: Macmillan Distribution Ltd.
Wheeler, Lisa. Dino-Boarding. Gott, Barry, illus. 2014. (ENG.). 32p. (J). (gr. k-3). lib. bdg. 16.95 *(978-1-4677-0213-3(7),* Carolrhoda Bks.) Lerner Publishing Group.
Williams, Kathryn. Pizza, Love, & Other Stuff That Made Me Famous. 2013. (ENG.). 256p. (YA). (gr. 7-12). pap. 11.99 *(978-1-250-02745-0(4),* 9781250027450) Square Fish.
Wishinsky, Frieda. A Bee in Your Ear. Laliberte, Louise-Andree, illus. 2004. 64p. (J). lib. bdg. 20.00 *(978-1-4242-1255-2(3))* Fitzgerald Bks.
Wojciechowski, Susan. A Fine St. Patrick's Day. Curry, Tom, illus. 2008. (ENG.). 40p. (J). (gr. -1-2). pap. 7.99 *(978-0-385-73640-4(1),* Dragonfly Bks.) Random Hse. Children's Bks.
Woodrow, Allan. Unschooled. 2017. (ENG.). 288p. (J). (gr. 3-7). 16.99 ***(978-1-338-11688-5(6),*** Scholastic Pr.) Scholastic, Inc.
Wortche, Allison. Rosie Sprout's Time to Shine. Barton, Patrice, illus. 2011. (ENG.). 40p. (J). (gr. -1-2). 17.99 *(978-0-375-86721-7(X),* Knopf Bks. for Young Readers) Random Hse. Children's Bks.

COMPLEXION

see Beauty, Personal; Cosmetics

COMPOSERS

Allman, Barbara. Musical Genius: A Story about Wolfgang Amadeus Mozart. Hamlin, Janet, illus. 2004. (Creative Minds Biographies Ser.). (ENG.). 64p. (gr. 4-8). 22.60 *(978-1-57505-604-3(6))*; per. 8.95 *(978-1-57505-637-1(2))* Lerner Publishing Group.
Anderson, M. T. Handel, Who Knew What He Liked. Hawkes, Kevin, illus. 2013. (Candlewick Biographies Ser.). (ENG.). 48p. (J). (gr. 3-7). 14.99 *(978-0-7636-6599-9(1))*; pap. 4.99 *(978-0-7636-6600-2(9))* Candlewick Pr.
—Strange Mr. Satie: Composer of the Absurd. Mathers, Petra, illus. 2016. (ENG.). 48p. (J). (gr. 2-5). 7.99 *(978-0-7636-8775-5(8))* Candlewick Pr.
—Symphony for the City of the Dead: Dmitri Shostakovich & the Siege of Leningrad. 2015. (ENG., Illus.). 464p. (YA). (gr. 9). 25.99 *(978-0-7636-6818-1(4))* Candlewick Pr.
Babin, Pierre. Debussy, 1 vol. Voake, Charlotte, illus. 2012. (First Discovery Music Ser.). (ENG.). 28p. (J). (gr. 2-6). 19.99 *(978-1-85103-321-8(1))* Moonlight Publishing, Ltd. GBR. Dist: Independent Pubs. Group.
Bach, Nancy. Giuseppe Verdi, Compositore d'Opera Italiano - Giuseppe Verdi, Italian Opera Composer: A Bilingual Picture Book (Italian-English Text) Lätti, Leo, illus. 2013. 28p. pap. *(978-1-938712-12-8(9))* Roxby Media Ltd.
Bailey, Gerry & Foster, Karen. Mozart's Wig. 2008. (Stories of Great People Ser.). (ENG., Illus.). 40p. (J). (gr. 3-6). pap. *(978-0-7787-3718-6(7))* Crabtree Publishing Co.
—Mozart's Wig. Noyes, Leighton & Radford, Karen, illus. 2008. (Stories of Great People Ser.). (ENG.). 40p. (J). (gr. 3-6). lib. bdg. *(978-0-7787-3696-7(2))* Crabtree Publishing Co.
Bankston, John. The Life & Times of Duke Ellington. 2004. (Masters of Music Ser.). (Illus.). 48p. (gr. 4-8). lib. bdg. 20.95 *(978-1-58415-248-4(6))* Mitchell Lane Pubs., Inc.
—The Life & Times of Scott Joplin. 2004. (Masters of Music Ser.). (Illus.). 48p. (gr. 4-8). lib. bdg. 20.95 *(978-1-58415-270-5(2))* Mitchell Lane Pubs., Inc.
Bauer, Helen. Beethoven for Kids: His Life & Music with 21 Activities. 2011. (For Kids Ser.). (ENG., Illus.). 144p. (J). (gr. 4). pap. 16.95 *(978-1-56976-711-5(4))* Chicago Review Pr., Inc.
—Verdi for Kids: His Life & Music with 21 Activities. 2013. (For Kids Ser.). (ENG., Illus.). 144p. (J). (gr. 4). pap. 16.95 *(978-1-61374-500-7(1))* Chicago Review Pr., Inc.
Baumont, Olivier. Antonio Vivaldi, 1 vol. Voake, Charlotte, illus. 2012. (ENG.). 28p. (J). (gr. 2-6). 22.99 *(978-1-85103-323-2(8))* Moonlight Publishing, Ltd. GBR. Dist: Independent Pubs. Group.
Beth, Georgia. 18th Century Superstar: Mozart. 2017. (TIME for KIDS(r) Nonfiction Readers Ser.). (Illus.). 32p. (J). (gr. 7-7). pap. 8.99 *(978-1-4938-3631-4(5))* Teacher Created Materials, Inc.
Beyer, Mark. Stevie Wonder. 2009. (Rock & Roll Hall of Famers Ser.). 112p. (gr. 5-8). 63.90 *(978-1-60852-475-4(2),* Rosen Reference) Rosen Publishing Group, Inc., The.
Bobb, Barry L. Hero of Faith - Johann Sebastian Bach. 2011. 64p. pap. 7.99 *(978-0-7586-2829-9(3))* Concordia Publishing Hse.
Bodden, Valerie & Riggs, Kate. Wolfgang Amadeus Mozart. 2017. (Odysseys in Artistry Ser.). (ENG., Illus.). 80p. (J). (gr. 7-11). pap. 14.99 *(978-1-62832-318-4(3),* Creative Paperbacks) Creative Co., The.
Bryant, Jen. Music for the End of Time. Peck, Beth, illus. 2005. 32p. (J). (gr. 4-5). 17.00 *(978-0-8028-5229-8(7))* Eerdmans, William B. Publishing Co.
Carew-Miller, Anna. Ludwig Van Beethoven: Great Composer. 2013. (People of Importance Ser.: 21). (Illus.). 32p. (J). (gr. 4-18). 19.95 *(978-1-4222-2849-4(5))* Mason Crest.
Cook, Diane. Wolfgang Amadeus Mozart: World-Famous Composer. 2013. (People of Importance Ser.: 21). (Illus.). 32p. (J). (gr. 4-18). 19.95 *(978-1-4222-2860-9(6))* Mason Crest.
Du Bouchet, Paule. Franz Schubert, 1 vol. Voake, Charlotte, illus. 2013. (First Discovery Music Ser.). (ENG.). 28p. (J). (gr. 2-6). 19.99 *(978-1-85103-312-6(2))* Moonlight Publishing, Ltd. GBR. Dist: Independent Pubs. Group.
Ford, Carin T. George Gershwin: American Musical Genius. 2008. (People to Know Today Ser.). (Illus.). 112p. (J). (gr. k-6). lib. bdg. 33.27 *(978-0-7660-2887-6(9))* Enslow Pubs., Inc.
Gerstein, Mordicai. What Charlie Heard. Gerstein, Mordicai, illus. (Illus.). pap. incl. audio compact disk *(978-1-59112-525-9(1))*; pap. 16.95 incl. audio *(978-1-59112-484-9(0))*; pap. 18.95 incl. audio compact disk *(978-1-59112-277-7(5))*; pap. incl. audio *(978-1-59112-279-1(1))* Live Oak Media.
Getzinger, Donna & Felsenfeld, Daniel. Antonio Vivaldi & the Baroque Tradition. 2004. (Classical Composers Ser.). (Illus.). 144p. (gr. 6-12). lib. bdg. 28.95 *(978-1-931798-20-4(6))* Reynolds, Morgan Inc.
—George Frideric Handel & Music for Voices. 2004. (Classical Composers Ser.). (Illus.). 144p. (YA). (gr. 6-12). lib. bdg. 26.95 *(978-1-931798-23-5(0))* Reynolds, Morgan Inc.
—Johann Sebastian Bach & the Art of Baroque Music. 2004. (Classical Composers Ser.). (Illus.). 144p. (YA). (gr. 6-12). lib. bdg. 26.95 *(978-1-931798-22-8(2))* Reynolds, Morgan Inc.
—Johannes Brahms & the Twilight of Romanticism. 2004. (Classical Composers Ser.). (Illus.). 144p. (YA). (gr. 6-12). 26.95 *(978-1-931798-21-1(4))* Reynolds, Morgan Inc.
—Richard Wagner & German Opera. 2004. (Classical Composers Ser.). (Illus.). 144p. (YA). (gr. 6-12). 26.95 *(978-1-931798-24-2(9))* Reynolds, Morgan Inc.
Green, John & Negri, Paul. Great Composers. 2007. (Dover History Coloring Book Ser.). (ENG., Illus.). 32p. (gr. 3-5). 3.99 *(978-0-486-46214-1(5))* Dover Pubns., Inc.
Harrison, Kat. Lin-Manuel Miranda: Composer, Actor, & Creator of Hamilton. 2017. (Influential Lives Ser.). 128p. (J). (gr. 7-8). lib. bdg. 37.27 ***(978-0-7660-8505-3(8))*** Enslow Pubs., Inc.
Hoffman, Mary Ann. Scott Joplin: King of Ragtime. 2010. (Inspiring Lives Ser.). (Illus.). 32p. (J). (gr. 5-8). pap. 10.50 *(978-1-4339-3632-6(1))*; lib. bdg. 25.25 *(978-1-4339-3631-9(3),* 1309379) Stevens, Gareth Publishing LLLP.
Horowitz, Joseph. Dvoerak in America. 2003. (Illus.). x, 158p. (J). pap. 8.95 *(978-0-8126-2692-6(3))* Cricket Bks.
—Dvorak in America: In Search of the New World. 2003. (ENG., Illus.). 160p. (YA). 17.95 *(978-0-8126-2681-0(8))* Cricket Bks.
Hubbard-Brown, Janet. Scott Joplin: Composer. 2006. (Black Americans of Achievement Ser.). (Illus.). 103p. (YA). (gr. 7-12). lib. bdg. 35.00 *(978-0-7910-9211-8(9))* Facts On File, Inc.
Introducing Composers Set. Date not set. (Illus.). (YA). (gr. 8-18). 135.60 *(978-0-7910-6045-2(4),* Chelsea Hse.) Facts On File, Inc.
JOHANN SEBASTIAN BACH. 2007. (Descubrimos a Los Músicos Ser.). (ENG., Illus.). 24p. (J). (gr. 2-4). 14.95 *(978-84-9825-162-3(1))* Combel Editorial, S.A. ESP. Dist: Independent Pubs. Group.
Josephson, Judith Pinkerton. Bold Composer: A Story about Ludwig Van Beethoven. Kiwak, Barbara, illus. 2007. (Creative Minds Biographies Ser.). (ENG.). 64p. (gr. 4-8). lib. bdg. 22.60 *(978-0-8225-5987-0(0))* Lerner Publishing Group.
Khoury, Marielle D. & du Bouchet, Paule. Bach, 1 vol. Voake, Charlotte, illus. 2012. (ENG.). 28p. (J). (gr. 2-6). 22.99 *(978-1-85103-319-5(X))* Moonlight Publishing, Ltd. GBR. Dist: Independent Pubs. Group.
Lee, Lavina. Handel's World. 2009. (Music Throughout History Ser.). 64p. (gr. 5-6). 58.50 *(978-1-61514-684-0(9),* Rosen Reference) Rosen Publishing Group, Inc., The.
Leonard, Tom. Becoming Bach. 2017. (ENG., Illus.). 40p. (J). 17.99 *(978-1-62672-286-6(2),* 9781626722866) Roaring Brook Pr.
Loria, Laura. Wolfgang Amadeus Mozart, 1 vol. 2015. (ENG.). 32p. (J). 23.45 *(978-1-62275-681-0(9),* Britannica Educational Publishing) Rosen Publishing Group, Inc., The.
LUDWIG VAN BEETHOVEN. 2007. (Descubrimos a Los Músicos Ser.). (ENG., Illus.). 24p. (J). (gr. 2-4). 14.95 *(978-84-7864-959-4(X))* Combel Editorial, S.A. ESP. Dist: Independent Pubs. Group.
Malaspina, Ann. Chopin's World. 2009. (Music Throughout History Ser.). 64p. (gr. 5-6). 58.50 *(978-1-61514-683-3(0),* Rosen Reference) Rosen Publishing Group, Inc., The.
Mapua, Jeff. Ludwig Van Beethoven: Classical Composer of Passion & Power. 2015. (Britannica Beginner Bios Ser.). (ENG.). 32p. (J). 23.45 *(978-1-62275-931-6(1),* Britannica Educational Publishing) Rosen Publishing Group, Inc., The.
—Ludwig Van Beethoven: Composer of the Classical & Romantic Eras. 2015. (Britannica Beginner Bios Ser.). (ENG.). 32p. (J). (gr. 2-3). 46.90 *(978-1-62275-933-0(8),* Britannica Educational Publishing) Rosen Publishing Group, Inc., The.
Mattern, Joanne. Ludwig Van Beethoven: A Revolutionary Composer. 2017. (Rookie Biographies(tm) Ser.). (ENG., Illus.). 32p. (J). lib. bdg. 25.00 *(978-0-531-22289-8(6),* Children's Pr.) Scholastic Library Publishing.
McDonough, Yona Zeldis. Who Was Wolfgang Amadeus Mozart? Robbins, Carrie, illus. 2003. (Who Was? Ser.). (ENG.). 112p. (J). (gr. 3-7). pap. 5.99 *(978-0-448-43104-8(1),* Grosset & Dunlap) Penguin Young Readers Group.
—Who Was Wolfgang Amadeus Mozart? 2003. (Who Was... ? Ser.). (gr. 3-6). 16.00 *(978-0-613-61669-0(3),* Turtleback) Turtleback Bks.
Myers, Carrie Mieko. What If You'd Met Beethoven? 2004. (Illus.). 16p. (J). *(978-0-439-69713-2(1))* Scholastic, Inc.
Norton, James R. Haydn's World. (Music Throughout History Ser.). 64p. 2009. (gr. 5-6). 58.50 *(978-1-61514-685-7(7),* Rosen Reference) 2007. (Illus.). (J). (gr. 4-7). lib. bdg. 29.25 *(978-1-4042-0727-1(9))* Rosen Publishing Group, Inc., The.
The Primary Source Library of Famous Composers. (Illus.). (J). (gr. 3-5). 57.50 *(978-1-4042-3303-4(2))* Rosen Publishing Group, Inc., The.
Reef, Catherine. William Grant Still: African-American Composer. 2004. (Modern Music Masters Ser.). (Illus.). 112p. (YA). (gr. 6-12). 23.95 *(978-1-931798-11-2(7))* Reynolds, Morgan Inc.
Riggs, Kate. Wolfgang Amadeus Mozart. (Illus.). (J). 2016. 80p. *(978-1-60818-722-5(5))* 2008. 48p. (gr. 4-7). lib. bdg. 22.95 *(978-1-58341-664-8(1))* Creative Co., The. (Creative Education).
Roberto, Brother. Don't Push! a Story of Cesar Franck. Jagodits, Carolyn Lee, illus. 2011. 94p. 38.95 *(978-1-258-07305-3(6))* Literary Licensing, LLC.
—Music for Millions: A Story of Ignace Paderewski. Jagodits, Carolyn Lee, illus. 2011. 94p. 38.95 *(978-1-258-09336-5(7))* Literary Licensing, LLC.
Roberts, Russell. Scott Joplin. 2012. (J). lib. bdg. 29.95 *(978-1-61228-273-2(3))* Mitchell Lane Pubs., Inc.
Schoell, William. Giuseppe Verdi & Italian Opera. 2007. (Classical Composers Ser.). (Illus.). 128p. (J). (gr. 3-7). lib. bdg. 27.95 *(978-1-59935-041-7(6))* Reynolds, Morgan Inc.
Schwaeber, Barbie. Grand Old Flag. Nussbaum, Ben, ed. Pamintuan, Macky & Wang, Qi, illus. 2006. (Smithsonian American Favorites Ser.). (ENG.). 32p. (J). (gr. -1-3). 9.85 *(978-1-59249-650-1(4))* Soundprints.
Schwaeber, Barbie H. Grand Old Flag. Nussbaum, Ben, ed. Wang, Qi, illus. 2006. (Smithsonian American Favorites Ser.). (ENG.). 32p. (J). (gr. 3-7). 14.95 *(978-1-59249-649-5(0))* Soundprints.
Shefelman, Janice Jordan, et al. I, Vivaldi. Shefelman, Janice Jordan & Shefelman, Tom, illus. 2008. (ENG.). 32p. (J). (gr. 2-6). 18.00 *(978-0-8028-5318-9(8))* Eerdmans, William B. Publishing Co.
Shichtman, Sandra H. & Indenbaum, Dorothy. The Joy of Creation: The Story of Clara Schumann. 2011. (Classical Composers Ser.). (Illus.). 159p. lib. bdg. 28.95 *(978-1-59935-123-0(4))* Reynolds, Morgan Inc.
Sis, Peter. Play, Mozart, Play! Sis, Peter, illus. 2006. (Illus.). 32p. (J). (gr. -1-3). 16.99 *(978-0-06-112181-4(9),* Greenwillow Bks.) HarperCollins Pubs.
Snowman, Daniel. Giuseppe Verdi: Composer. 2016. (History Makers Ser.). 144p. (J). 45.64 *(978-1-5026-2449-9(4))* Cavendish Square Publishing.
Sombart, Elisabeth, et al. Doce Vidas para la Musica.Tr. of Twelve Composers. (SPA.). 118p. (J). 17.95 *(978-84-261-3115-7(8),* JV11155) Juventud, Editorial ESP. Dist: Lectorum Pubns., Inc.
Stanbridge, Joanne. The Extraordinary Music of Mr. Ives: The True Story of a Famous American Composer. 2012. (ENG., Illus.). 32p. (J). (gr. -1-3). 16.99 *(978-0-547-23866-1(5))* Houghton Mifflin Harcourt Publishing Co.
Stanley, Diane. Mozart: The Wonder Child - A Puppet Play in Three Acts. Stanley, Diane, illus. 2009. (ENG., Illus.). 48p. (J). (gr. 3-7). 17.99 *(978-0-06-072674-4(1),* Collins) HarperCollins Pubs.
Stéphane, Ollivier. PIOTR ILYCH TCHAIKOVSKI. 2010. (Descubrimos a Los Músicos Ser.). (SPA., Illus.). 24p. (J). (gr. 2-4). 15.95 *(978-84-9825-416-7(7))* Combel Editorial, S.A. ESP. Dist: Independent Pubs. Group.
Summerer, Eric. Wolfgang Amadeus Mozart. 2006. 36p. pap. 21.25 *(978-1-4358-3796-6(7),* PowerKids Pr.) Rosen Publishing Group, Inc., The.
Summerer, Eric Michael. Franz Joseph Haydn. (Primary Source Library of Famous Composers Ser.). 32p. 2009. (gr. 4-4). 42.50 *(978-1-60854-106-5(1))* 2006. (Illus.). (J). (gr. -1-3). lib. bdg. 23.95 *(978-1-4042-2767-5(9))* Rosen Publishing Group, Inc., The. (PowerKids Pr.).
—Franz Peter Schubert. (Primary Source Library of Famous Composers Ser.). 32p. 2009. (gr. 4-4). 42.50 *(978-1-60854-107-2(X))* 2006. (Illus.). (J). (gr. -1-3). lib. bdg. 23.95 *(978-1-4042-2768-2(7))* Rosen Publishing Group, Inc., The. (PowerKids Pr.).
—Frederic Chopin. 2006. (Primary Source Library of Famous Composers Ser.). (Illus.). 32p. (J). (gr. -1-3). lib. bdg. 23.95 *(978-1-4042-2769-9(5),* PowerKids Pr.) Rosen Publishing Group, Inc., The.
—Frédéric Chopin. 2009. (Primary Source Library of Famous Composers Ser.). 32p. (gr. 4-4). 42.50 *(978-1-60854-108-9(8),* PowerKids Pr.) Rosen Publishing Group, Inc., The.
—Johann Sebastian Bach. 2006. (Primary Source Library of Famous Composers). (Illus.). 32p. (J). (gr. -1-3). lib. bdg. 21.25 *(978-1-4042-2770-5(9),* PowerKids Pr.) Rosen Publishing Group, Inc., The.
—Ludwig van Beethoven. 2009. (Primary Source Library of Famous Composers Ser.). 32p. (gr. 4-4). 42.50 *(978-1-60854-112-6(6),* PowerKids Pr.) Rosen Publishing Group, Inc., The.
—Wolfgang Amadeus Mozart. (Primary Source Library of Famous Composers Ser.). 32p. 2009. (gr. 4-4). 42.50 *(978-1-60854-115-7(0))* 2006. (Illus.). (J). (gr. -1-3). lib. bdg. 21.25 *(978-1-4042-2772-9(5))* Rosen Publishing Group, Inc., The. (PowerKids Pr.).
Turner, Barrie Carson. Beethoven. 2003. (Famous Childhoods Ser.). (Illus.). (J). lib. bdg. 24.25 *(978-1-59389-112-1(1))* Chrysalis Education.
—Mozart. 2003. (Famous Childhoods Ser.). (Illus.). (J). lib. bdg. 24.25 *(978-1-59389-115-2(6))* Chrysalis Education.
Venezia, Mike. Frederic Chopin (Revised Edition) 2017. (Getting to Know the World's Greatest Composers Ser.). (ENG.). 40p. (J). pap. 7.95 ***(978-0-531-23035-0(X))***; lib. bdg. 29.00 ***(978-0-531-22657-5(3))*** Scholastic Library Publishing. (Children's Pr.).
—George Gershwin (Revised Edition) 2017. (Getting to Know the World's Greatest Composers Ser.). (ENG.). 40p. (J). pap. 7.95 ***(978-0-531-23037-4(6))***; lib. bdg. 29.00 ***(978-0-531-22659-9(X))*** Scholastic Library Publishing. (Children's Pr.).
—Johann Sebastian Bach (Revised Edition) 2017. (Getting to Know the World's Greatest Composers Ser.). (ENG., Illus.). 40p. (J). lib. bdg. 29.00 *(978-0-531-22060-3(5),* Children's Pr.) Scholastic Library Publishing.
—Ludwig Van Beethoven (Revised Edition) 2017. (Getting to Know the World's Greatest Composers Ser.). (ENG., Illus.).

40p. (J). lib. bdg. 29.00 *(978-0-531-22059-7(1),* Children's Pr.) Scholastic Library Publishing.

—Wolfgang Amadeus Mozart (Revised Edition) 2017. (Getting to Know the World's Greatest Composers Ser.). (ENG.). 40p. (J). lib. bdg. 29.00 *(978-0-531-22058-0(3),* Children's Pr.) Scholastic Library Publishing.

Vernon, Roland. Introducing Composers. 2005. (Introducing Composers Ser.). 32p. (gr. 5-8). 65.85 *(978-0-7910-8754-1(9),* Chelsea Hse.) Facts On File, Inc.

Viegas, Jennifer. Beethoven's World. 2009. (Music Throughout History Ser.). 64p. (gr. 5-6). 58.50 *(978-1-61514-682-6(2),* Rosen Reference) Rosen Publishing Group, Inc., The.

Walcker, Yann. Ludwig Van Beethoven, 1 vol. Voake, Charlotte, illus. 2012. (First Discovery Music Ser.). (ENG.). 28p. (J). (gr. 2-6). pap. 19.99 *(978-1-85103-310-2(6))* Moonlight Publishing, Ltd. GBR. Dist: Independent Pubs. Group.

Weeks, Marcus. World History Biographies: Mozart: The Boy Who Changed the World with His Music. 2013. (National Geographic World History Biographies Ser.). (ENG., Illus.). 64p. (J). (gr. 3-7). pap. 7.99 *(978-1-4263-1451-3(5),* National Geographic Children's Bks.) National Geographic Society.

White, Stephanie. Ludwig Van Beethoven: Famous Composer. 2013. (Rosen Readers Ser.). (ENG.). 24p. (J). (gr. 2-3). pap. 49.50 *(978-1-4777-2291-6(2));* pap. 8.25 *(978-1-4777-2290-9(4))* Rosen Publishing Group, Inc., The. (Rosen Classroom).

Whiting, Jim. The Life & Times of Antonio Lucio Vivaldi. 2004. (Masters of Music Ser.). (Illus.). 48p. (gr. 4-8). lib. bdg. 20.95 *(978-1-58415-241-5(9))* Mitchell Lane Pubs., Inc.

—The Life & Times of Franz Liszt. 2004. (Masters of Music Ser.). (Illus.). 48p. (gr. 4-8). lib. bdg. 20.95 *(978-1-58415-280-4(X))* Mitchell Lane Pubs., Inc.

—The Life & Times of Frederic Chopin. 2004. (Masters of Music Ser.). (Illus.). 48p. (gr. 4-8). lib. bdg. 20.95 *(978-1-58415-245-3(1))* Mitchell Lane Pubs., Inc.

—The Life & Times of Guiseppe Verdi. 2004. (Masters of Music Ser.). (Illus.). 48p. (gr. 4-8). lib. bdg. 20.95 *(978-1-58415-281-1(8))* Mitchell Lane Pubs., Inc.

—The Life & Times of Hector Berlioz. 2004. (Masters of Music Ser.). (Illus.). 48p. (gr. 4-8). lib. bdg. 20.95 *(978-1-58415-259-0(1))* Mitchell Lane Pubs., Inc.

—The Life & Times of Richard Wagner. 2004. (Masters of Music Ser.). (Illus.). 48p. (gr. 4-8). lib. bdg. 20.95 *(978-1-58415-278-1(8))* Mitchell Lane Pubs., Inc.

Wood, Susan. Esquivel! Space-Age Sound Artist. Tonatiuh, Duncan, illus. 2016. (ENG.). 32p. (J). (gr. 1-4). lib. bdg. 17.95 *(978-1-58089-673-3(1))* Charlesbridge Publishing, Inc.

Wood, Susan & Tonatiuh, Duncan. ¡Esquivel! Un Artista Del Sonido de la Era Espacial. Calvo, Carlos E., tr. from ENG. Tonatiuh, Duncan, illus. 2016. (SPA & ENG., Illus.). 32p. (J). (gr. 1-4). lib. bdg. 17.95 *(978-1-58089-733-4(9))* Charlesbridge Publishing, Inc.

COMPOSERS—FICTION

Celenza, Anna Harwell. Beethoven's Heroic Symphony. Kitchel, JoAnn E., illus. 2016. (Once upon a Masterpiece Ser.). (ENG.). 32p. (J). (gr. 1-4). lib. bdg. 16.95 *(978-1-58089-530-9(1))* Charlesbridge Publishing, Inc.

—The Farewell Symphony. Kitchel, JoAnn E., illus. 2016. (Once upon a Masterpiece Ser.). (ENG.). 32p. (J). (gr. 1-4). lib. bdg. 16.95 *(978-1-58089-527-9(1))* Charlesbridge Publishing, Inc.

—Pictures at an Exhibition. Kitchel, JoAnn E., illus. 2016. (Once upon a Masterpiece Ser.). (ENG.). 32p. (J). (gr. 1-4). lib. bdg. 16.95 *(978-1-58089-528-6(X))* Charlesbridge Publishing, Inc.

Collins Staff. Amazing Composers. 2014. (Collins English Readers Ser.). (ENG.). 80p. pap. 13.95 incl. audio compact disk *(978-0-00-754502-5(9))* HarperCollins Pubs. Ltd. GBR. Dist: Independent Pubs. Group.

Dunlap Cather, Katherine. Boyhood Stories of Famous Men. 2013. 292p. pap. *(978-3-95507-921-5(X))* DOGMA. in Europäischer Hochschulverlag GmbH & Co. KG.

Hamlisch, Marvin. Marvin Makes Music. Madsen, Jim, illus. 2012. (ENG.). 32p. (J). (gr. 1-3). 17.99 *(978-0-8037-3730-3(0),* Dial Bks) Penguin Young Readers Group.

Jones, Harmony. Girl vs. Boy Band: The Right Track. 2016. (ENG.). 240p. (J). 16.99 *(978-1-61963-947-8(5),* 9781619639478, Bloomsbury USA Childrens) Bloomsbury Publishing USA.

—The High Note. 2017. (ENG.). 240p. (J). 16.99 *(978-1-61963-949-2(1),* 9781619639492, Bloomsbury USA Childrens) Bloomsbury Publishing USA.

Lachenmeyer, Nathaniel. Scarlatti's Cat. Beccia, Carlyn, illus. 2014. (ENG.). 32p. (J). (gr. -1-3). 16.95 *(978-0-7613-5472-7(7),* Carolrhoda Bks.) Lerner Publishing Group.

Newman, Lesléa. Ketzel, the Cat Who Composed. Bates, Amy June, illus. 2015. (ENG.). 40p. (J). (gr. k-3). 16.99 *(978-0-7636-6555-5(X))* Candlewick Pr.

Perdue, Gillian. Conor's Concert. Connor, Michael, illus. 2003. (Pandas Ser.: 26). (ENG.). 64p. (J). pap. 9.95 *(978-0-86278-847-6(1))* O'Brien Pr., Ltd., The IRL. Dist: Dufour Editions, Inc.

Robinson, Fiona. What Animals Really Like. 2011. (ENG., Illus.). 24p. (J). (gr. k-2). 15.95 *(978-0-8109-8976-4(X),* Abrams Bks. for Young Readers) Abrams, Inc.

Swain, Gwenyth. I Wonder As I Wander. Himler, Ronald, illus. 2004. 32p. (J). (gr. 2-5). 16.00 *(978-0-8028-5214-4(9))* Eerdmans, William B. Publishing Co.

Weil, Cynthia. I'm Glad I Did. 2015. (ENG., Illus.). 272p. (YA). (gr. 9). 18.99 *(978-1-61695-356-0(X),* Soho Teen) Soho Pr., Inc.

Winter, Jonah. The Fabulous Feud of Gilbert & Sullivan. Egielski, Richard, illus. 2009. (J). pap. *(978-0-439-93051-2(0),* Levine, Arthur A. Bks.) Scholastic, Inc.

COMPOSITION (ART)

see also Painting

Markowitz-Meredith, Susan. What Is Form? 2009. (Get Art Smart Ser.). (ENG., Illus.). 24p. (J). (gr. k-3). pap. *(978-0-7787-5138-0(4));* lib. bdg. *(978-0-7787-5124-3(4))* Crabtree Publishing Co.

COMPOSITION (RHETORIC)

see Rhetoric

also names of languages with the subdivision Composition and exercises, e.g. English Language—Composition and exercises

COMPULSORY SCHOOL ATTENDANCE

see School Attendance

COMPUTER ART

Knapp-Grosz, Tamara & Loyd, Elizabeth. Some Things Are Made to Smoke. McCue, Patrick, illus. 2004. 20p. (J). pap. *(978-1-893974-23-4(5),* Design Pr. Bks.) Savannah College of Art & Design Exhibitions.

Rooney, Anne. Picture This. 2004. (QEB Learn Computing Ser.). (Illus.). 32p. (YA). (gr. 4-7). lib. bdg. 18.95 *(978-1-59566-039-8(9))* QEB Publishing Inc.

COMPUTER-ASSISTED INSTRUCTION

Mackay, Jennifer. Online Schools. Greenhaven Press, ed. 2013. (Technology 360 Ser.). (ENG., Illus.). 128p. (gr. 7-10). lib. bdg. 39.90 *(978-1-4205-0942-7(X),* Lucent Bks.) Cengage Gale.

COMPUTER CONTROL

see Automation

COMPUTER CRIMES

Bauchner, Elizabeth. Computer Investigation. Noziglia, Carla Miller & Siegel, Jay A., eds. 2013. (Solving Crimes with Science: Forensics Ser.: 12). (Illus.). 112p. (J). (gr. 7-18). 22.95 *(978-1-4222-2862-3(2))* Mason Crest.

—Computer Investigation. 2007. (Forensics Ser.). (Illus.). 112p. (YA). (gr. 3-7). lib. bdg. 22.95 *(978-1-4222-0035-3(3))* Mason Crest.

Brown, Tracy. Cyberbullying: Online Safety. 2013. (Illus.). 80p. (YA). (gr. 7-12). 33.25 *(978-1-4488-9450-5(6))* Rosen Publishing Group, Inc., The.

Colt, James P. & Rogers, Marcus K. Cyberpredators. 2011. (Cybersafety Ser.). (Illus.). 136p. (gr. 6-12). 39.95 *(978-1-60413-698-2(7))* Facts On File, Inc.

covaleski, john. Hacking. 2012. (Illus.). 96p. (J). lib. bdg. *(978-1-60152-268-9(1))* ReferencePoint Pr., Inc.

Di Piazza, Domenica. Google Cybersecurity Expert Parisa Tabriz. 2017. (J). ***(978-1-5415-0007-5(5))*** Lerner Publishing Group.

Etingoff, Kim. Bully on Campus & Online. Stephens, Ronald, ed. 2014. (Safety First Ser.: 11). 48p. (J). (gr. 5-18). 20.95 *(978-1-4222-3045-9(7))* Mason Crest.

—Navigating Cyberspace. Stephens, Ronald, ed. 2014. (Safety First Ser.: 11). 48p. (J). (gr. 5-18). 20.95 *(978-1-4222-3049-7(X))* Mason Crest.

Faust, Daniel R. Cyber Security Expert. 2017. (Behind the Scenes with Coders Ser.). 32p. (gr. 9-10). 60.00 ***(978-1-5081-5559-1(3),*** PowerKids Pr.) Rosen Publishing Group, Inc., The.

Gerdes, Louise. Cyberbullying. Greenhaven Press Editors, ed. 2011. (At Issue Ser.). (ENG.). 128p. (gr. 10-12). pap. 27.80 *(978-0-7377-5563-3(6),* Greenhaven Pr., Inc.) Cengage Gale.

Gerdes, Louise, ed. Cybercrime. 2013. (Opposing Viewpoints Ser.). (ENG., Illus.). 240p. (gr. 10-12). pap. 29.45 *(978-0-7377-6313-3(2));* lib. bdg. 42.95 *(978-0-7377-6312-6(4))* Cengage Gale. (Greenhaven Pr., Inc.).

Gitlin, Martin. Cyber Attack. 2015. (ENG., Illus.). 72p. (J). (gr. 8-12). lib. bdg. 33.32 *(978-1-4677-2512-5(9),* Twenty-First Century Bks.) Lerner Publishing Group.

Gitlin, Martin & Goldstein, Margaret J. Cyber Attack. 2015. (Illus.). 72p. (J). *(978-1-4677-6304-2(7))* Twenty First Century Bks.

Grant-Adamson, Andrew. Cyber Crime. 2004. (Crime & Detection Ser.). (Illus.). 96p. (YA). (gr. 7-18). lib. bdg. 22.95 *(978-1-59084-369-7(X))* Mason Crest.

—Cyber Crime, Vol. 20. Gomez, Manny, ed. 2016. (Crime & Detection Ser.). 96p. (J). (gr. 7). 24.95 *(978-1-4222-3471-6(1))* Mason Crest.

Gray, Leon. Cybercrime. 2013. (Crime Science Ser.). (Illus.). 48p. (J). (gr. 4-8). pap. 84.30 *(978-1-4339-9486-9(0));* pap. 14.05 *(978-1-4339-9485-2(2));* (ENG., lib. bdg. 31.95 *(978-1-4339-9484-5(4))* Stevens, Gareth Publishing LLLP.

—Virtual Crime! Solving Cybercrime. 2009. (Solve That Crime! Ser.). (Illus.). 48p. (J). (gr. 5-9). lib. bdg. 25.27 *(978-0-7660-3376-4(7))* Enslow Pubs., Inc.

Grayson, Robert. The FBI & Cyber Crimes. 2009. (FBI Story Ser.). 64p. (J). (gr. 4-7). lib. bdg. 22.95 *(978-1-4222-0568-6(1))* Mason Crest.

Greenhaven Press Editors, ed. Cyberbullying. 2011. (At Issue Ser.). 128p. (YA). (gr. 9-12). 34.45 *(978-0-7377-5562-6(8))* Cengage Gale.

Guillain, Charlotte. Coping with Bullying, 1 vol. 2011. (Real Life Issues Ser.). (ENG.). 48p. (gr. 6-8). 32.65 *(978-1-4329-4761-3(3))* Heinemann-Raintree.

Harmon, Daniel E. Cyber Attacks, Counterattacks, & Espionage. 2016. (Cryptography: Code Making & Code Breaking Ser.). 00064p. (J). (gr. 8-8). 34.45 *(978-1-5081-7316-8(8))* Rosen Publishing Group, Inc., The.

Henderson, Harry. Online Security. 2016. (ENG.). 80p. (J). (gr. 5-12). lib. bdg. *(978-1-60152-990-9(2))* ReferencePoint Pr., Inc.

Heos, Bridget. Be Safe on the Internet. Baroncelli, Silvia, illus. 2015. (Be Safe! Ser.). 24p. (J). 25.65 *(978-1-60753-445-7(2))* Amicus Publishing.

Hinton, Kerry. Hackathons. 2016. (Digital & Information Literacy Ser.). 00048p. (J). (gr. 6-6). pap. 11.75 *(978-1-5081-7322-9(2))* Rosen Publishing Group, Inc., The.

Hubbard, Ben. Hi Tech World: Code Breakers. 2010. (ENG., Illus.). 32p. (J). lib. bdg. *(978-0-7787-7528-7(3))* Crabtree Publishing Co.

Hunter, Nick. Cyber Bullying, 1 vol. 2011. (Hot Topics Ser.). (ENG.). 56p. (gr. 7-8). 34.65 *(978-1-4329-4869-6(5),* NA-h) Heinemann-Raintree.

—Internet Safety, 1 vol. 2011. (Hot Topics Ser.). (ENG.). 56p. (gr. 7-8). 34.65 *(978-1-4329-4871-9(7),* NA-h) Heinemann-Raintree.

Hurt, Avery Elizabeth. Everything You Need to Know about Sextortion. 2017. (Need to Know Library). 64p. (J). (gr. 12-11). 34.45 ***(978-1-5081-7408-0(3));*** pap. 12.95 ***(978-1-5081-7406-6(7))*** Rosen Publishing Group, Inc., The. (Rosen Young Adult).

Hynes, Patricia Freeland. Cyber Cop. 2007. (21st Century Skills Library: Cool Science Careers Ser.). (ENG.). 32p. (gr. 4-8). lib. bdg. 28.50 *(978-1-60279-056-8(6),* 200013) Cherry Lake Publishing.

Jacobs, Thomas A. Teen Cyberbullying Investigated: Where Do Your Rights End & Consequences Begin? 2010. (ENG.). 208p. (YA). (gr. 6-18). pap. 15.99 *(978-1-57542-339-5(1))* Free Spirit Publishing, Inc.

Jakubiak, David. A Smart Kid's Guide to Online Bullying. 2009. 24p. (YA). pap. 8.25 *(978-1-4358-3348-7(1))* Rosen Publishing Group, Inc., The.

Jakubiak, David J. A Smart Kid's Guide to Internet Privacy. (J). 2010. pap. 8.25 *(978-1-4358-3356-2(2))* 2009. (Illus.). 24p. (gr. 2-6). lib. bdg. 22.60 *(978-1-4042-8118-9(5))* Rosen Publishing Group, Inc., The. (PowerKids Pr.).

—A Smart Kid's Guide to Online Bullying. 2009. (Kids Online Ser.). (Illus.). 24p. (J). (gr. 2-6). 22.60 *(978-1-4042-8114-1(2),* PowerKids Pr.) Rosen Publishing Group, Inc., The.

Kamar, Haq. What Is Cybersecurity? 2017. (J). ***(978-1-5383-0036-7(2),*** Britannica Educational Publishing) Rosen Publishing Group, Inc., The.

Knittel, John. Everything You Need to Know about the Dangers of Computer Hacking. 2009. (Need to Know Library). 64p. (gr. 5-5). 58.50 *(978-1-60854-092-1(8))* Rosen Publishing Group, Inc., The.

Latta, Sara L. Cybercrime: Data Trails Do Tell Tales. 2011. (True Forensic Crime Stories Ser.). (Illus.). 104p. (J). (gr. 5-18). pap. 10.95 *(978-1-59845-361-4(0));* (gr. 7-12). lib. bdg. 33.27 *(978-0-7660-3668-0(5))* Enslow Pubs., Inc.

Levete, Sarah. Taking Action Against Internet Crime. 2010. (Taking Action Ser.). (Illus.). 48p. (J). pap. 11.75 *(978-1-4358-9669-7(6),* Rosen Reference); (YA). (gr. 5-9). lib. bdg. 29.25 *(978-1-4358-9667-3(X))* Rosen Publishing Group, Inc., The.

Loh-Hagan, Virginia. Ethical Hacker. 2015. (Illus.). 32p. (J). pap. *(978-1-63470-051-1(1))* Cherry Lake Publishing.

Lohmann, Raychelle Cassada & Taylor, Julia V. The Bullying Workbook for Teens: Activities to Help You Deal with Social Aggression & Cyberbullying. 2013. (ENG.). 152p. (YA). (gr. 6-12). pap. 17.95 *(978-1-60882-450-2(0),* Instant Help Books) New Harbinger Pubns.

MacEachern, Robyn. Cyberbullying: And Ctrl Alt Delete It, 1 vol. Charette, Geraldine, illus. 2009. (Lorimer Deal with It Ser.). (ENG.). 32p. (J). (gr. 5-12). pap. 12.95 *(978-1-55277-037-5(0),* 9781552770375) Lorimer, James & Co., Ltd., Pubs. CAN. Dist: Orca Bk. Pubs. USA.

Mapua, Jeff. Coping with Cyberbullying. 2017. (Coping Ser.). 112p. (gr. 12-12). 37.10 ***(978-1-5081-7393-9(1),*** Rosen Young Adult) Rosen Publishing Group, Inc., The.

Mara, Wil. Cyber Cop. 2015. (21st Century Skills Library: Cool STEAM Careers Ser.). (ENG., Illus.). 32p. (J). (gr. 4-7). 29.93 *(978-1-63362-557-0(5),* 206412) Cherry Lake Publishing.

Marzilli, Alan. The Internet & Crime. 2009. (Point/Counterpoint Ser.). (Illus.). 120p. (C). (gr. 9-18). 35.00 *(978-1-60413-506-0(9),* Chelsea Hse.) Facts On File, Inc.

Meyer, Terry Teague. Careers in Computer Forensics. 2013. (Careers in Computer Technology Ser.). (ENG., Illus.). 80p. (YA). (gr. 9-12). lib. bdg. 33.25 *(978-1-4488-9593-9(6),* Rosen Classroom) Rosen Publishing Group, Inc., The.

mooney, carla. Online Security. 2011. (Issues in the Digital Age Ser.). (Illus.). 96p. (YA). (gr. 7-12). lib. bdg. 27.95 *(978-1-60152-195-8(2))* ReferencePoint Pr., Inc.

Nelson, Drew. Dealing with Cyberbullies. 2012. (Cyberspace Survival Guide Ser.). (Illus.). 32p. (J). (gr. 3-6). 26.60 *(978-1-4339-7220-1(4));* pap. 10.50 *(978-1-4339-7221-8(2))* Stevens, Gareth Publishing LLLP. (Gareth Stevens Learning Library).

Parks, Peggy J. Computer Hacking. 2008. (Crime Scene Investigations Ser.). (ENG., Illus.). 104p. (J). (gr. 7-10). lib. bdg. 35.45 *(978-1-4205-0035-6(X),* LML02109-240022, Lucent Bks.) Cengage Gale.

Patchin, Justin W. & Hinduja, Sameer. Words Wound: Delete Cyberbullying & Make Kindness Go Viral. 2013. (ENG., Illus.). 208p. (YA). (gr. 7-12). pap. 15.99 *(978-1-57542-451-4(7))* Free Spirit Publishing, Inc.

Porterfield, Jason. White & Black Hat Hackers. 2016. (Cryptography: Code Making & Code Breaking Ser.). 00064p. (J). (gr. 8-8). 34.45 *(978-1-5081-7314-4(1))* Rosen Publishing Group, Inc., The.

Raatma, Lucia. Cyberbullying. 2013. (True Book™—Guides to Life Ser.). (ENG., Illus.). 48p. (J). pap. 6.95 *(978-0-531-23922-3(5));* lib. bdg. 29.00 *(978-0-531-25522-3(0))* Scholastic Library Publishing.

Rich, Mari. Cyber Spy Hunters!, Vol. 10. 2015. (Scientists in Action Ser.). (Illus.). 48p. (J). (gr. 5). 20.95 *(978-1-4222-3424-2(X))* Mason Crest.

Roleff, Tamara, ed. Cyberbullying. 2012. (Issues That Concern You Ser.). (ENG., Illus.). 144p. (gr. 7-10). lib. bdg. 36.95 *(978-0-7377-5692-0(6))* Cengage Gale.

Scherer, Lauri S. Cyber Bullying. Greenhaven Press Staff, ed. 2015. (Introducing Issues with Opposing Viewpoints Ser.). (ENG., Illus.). 144p. (J). (gr. 7-10). lib. bdg. 42.00 *(978-0-7377-7234-0(4),* Greenhaven Pr., Inc.) Cengage Gale.

Schwartz, Heather E. Cyberbullying, 6 vols. 2013. (Tech Safety Smarts Ser.). (ENG.). 32p. (gr. 3-4). 47.70 *(978-1-62065-799-7(6),* Fact Finders) Capstone Press of Coughlan Cos.

Shea, Therese. Avoiding Online Hoaxes. 2012. (Cyberspace Survival Guide Ser.). (Illus.). 32p. (J). (gr. 3-6). 26.60 *(978-1-4339-7207-2(7));* pap. 10.50 *(978-1-4339-7208-9(5))* Stevens, Gareth Publishing LLLP. (Gareth Stevens Learning Library).

Silverstein Gray, Judy & Baldwin Kiland, Taylor. Cyber Technology: Using Computers to Fight Terrorism. 2016. (Military Engineering in Action Ser.). 48p. (J). (gr. 6-5). pap. 11.70 *(978-0-7660-7535-1(4))* Enslow Pubs., Inc.

Spivet, Bonnie. Avoiding Predators Online. 2011. (CyberSmarts: Staying Safe Online Ser.). (ENG.). 24p. (J). (gr. 4-6). pap. 10.00 *(978-1-4488-6416-4(X));* lib. bdg. 21.25 *(978-1-4488-6411-9(9))* Rosen Publishing Group, Inc., The. (PowerKids Pr.).

Stefoff, Rebecca. Cybercrime. 2008. (Forensic Science Investigated Ser.). 80p. (gr. 5-18). lib. bdg. 34.21 *(978-0-7614-3084-1(9),* Benchmark Bks.) Marshall Cavendish Corp.

Timmons, Angie & Latta, Sara L. Investigating Cybercrime. 2017. (J). ***(978-0-7660-9183-2(X))*** Enslow Pubs., Inc.

Wiener, Gary. The Internet. 2010. (Global Viewpoints Ser.). (ENG.). 272p. 40.45 *(978-0-7377-4935-9(0));* 224p. (gr. 10-12). pap. 31.70 *(978-0-7377-4936-6(9))* Cengage Gale. (Greenhaven Pr., Inc.).

Wolinsky, Art. Safe Surfing on the Internet. 2003. (Internet Library). (Illus.). 64p. (YA). (gr. 4-12). lib. bdg. 22.60 *(978-0-7660-2030-6(4))* Enslow Pubs., Inc.

Yomtov, Nelson. Internet Security: From Concept to Consumer. 2015. (ENG.). 64p. (J). lib. bdg. *(978-0-531-21896-9(1),* Orchard Bks.) Scholastic, Inc.

COMPUTER ENGINEERING

Anniss, Matthew & Mason, Paul. Understanding Computing. 2015. (Understanding Computing Ser.). (ENG.). 48p. (gr. 3-6). lib. bdg. 133.28 *(978-1-4846-0905-7(0),* Heinemann InfoSearch) Heinemann-Raintree.

Career Building Through Using Digital Design Tools. 2013. (Digital Career Building Ser.). 64p. (YA). (gr. 7-12). pap. 77.70 *(978-1-4777-1740-0(4))* Rosen Publishing Group, Inc., The.

Coleman, Miriam. Share It: Using Digital Tools & Media. 2012. (Core Skills Ser.). (ENG., Illus.). 32p. (J). (gr. 3-6). pap. 10.00 *(978-1-4488-7526-9(9),* PowerKids Pr.) Rosen Publishing Group, Inc., The.

Halls, Kelly Milner. Virtual Reality Specialist. 2009. (21st Century Skills Library: Cool Science Careers Ser.). (ENG.). 32p. (gr. 4-8). lib. bdg. 28.50 *(978-1-60279-503-7(7),* 200307) Cherry Lake Publishing.

Harris, Patricia. Understanding Coding Through Debugging. 2016. (Spotlight on Kids Can Code Ser.). 00024p. (J). (gr. 4-5). pap. 11.75 *(978-1-4994-2796-7(4),* PowerKids Pr.) Rosen Publishing Group, Inc., The.

La Bella, Laura. Steve Jobs & Steve Wozniak, 01 vols., 1. 2016. (Tech Pioneers Ser.). (ENG.). 112p. (J). 35.60 *(978-1-4994-6286-9(7),* Rosen Young Adult) Rosen Publishing Group, Inc., The.

Mason, Paul. Understanding Computer Safety. 2015. (Understanding Computing Ser.). (ENG.). 48p. (gr. 3-6). 33.32 *(978-1-4846-0904-0(2),* Heinemann InfoSearch) Heinemann-Raintree.

Mattern, Joanne. Grace Hopper: Computer Pioneer. 2003. (Women Who Shaped History Ser.). (Illus.). 24p. (J). lib. bdg. 22.60 *(978-0-8239-6505-2(8),* PowerKids Pr.) Rosen Publishing Group, Inc., The.

Rajczak, Kristen. Instagram & Kevin Systrom & Mike Krieger, 1 vol. 2015. (ENG., Illus.). 128p. (J). lib. bdg. 35.60 *(978-1-4777-7917-0(5),* Rosen Young Adult) Rosen Publishing Group, Inc., The.

Staley, Erin. Grace Murray Hopper, 01 vols., 1. 2016. (Tech Pioneers Ser.). (ENG.). 112p. (J). 35.60 *(978-1-4994-6288-3(3),* Rosen Young Adult) Rosen Publishing Group, Inc., The.

Vescia, Monique. David Karp & Tumblr. 2013. (Internet Biographies Ser.). (ENG., Illus.). 128p. (YA). (gr. 7-12). lib. bdg. 34.60 *(978-1-4488-9528-1(6),* Rosen Classroom) Rosen Publishing Group, Inc., The.

Willett, Edward. Career Building Through Using Digital Design Tools. 2013. (Digital Career Building Ser.). 64p. (YA). (gr. 7-12). 31.95 *(978-1-4777-1723-3(4));* pap. 12.95 *(978-1-4777-1739-4(0))* Rosen Publishing Group, Inc., The.

COMPUTER GAMES

Anderson, Pamela. My New School. 2004. (J). cd-rom 12.95 *(978-1-932555-08-0(0))* Watch Me Grow Kids.

Austic, Greg. Game Design. 2013. (21st Century Skills Innovation Library: Makers As Innovators Ser.). (ENG., Illus.). 32p. (J). (gr. 4-8). 28.50 *(978-1-62431-142-0(3),* 202888); pap. 14.21 *(978-1-62431-274-8(8),* 202890) Cherry Lake Publishing.

Benson, Pete. Scratch. 2015. (21st Century Skills Innovation Library: Makers As Innovators Ser.). (Illus.). 32p. (J). (gr. 4-8). pap. 14.21 *(978-1-63362-405-4(6),* 206929) Cherry Lake Publishing.

Birlew, Dan. Resident Evil(r) 4 Official Strategy Guide. 2005. (Signature Ser.). (ENG., Illus.). 224p. (YA). pap. 16.99 *(978-0-7440-0346-8(6))* Pearson Education.

BradyGames Staff. GameCube/Game Boy Advance Secret Codes 2005, 1 vol., Vol. 1. 2004. (ENG., Illus.). 144p. pap. 7.99 *(978-0-7440-0490-8(X))* Pearson Education.

Burns, Jan. Shigeru Miyamoto: Nintendo Game Designer. 2006. (Inventors & Creators Ser.). (ENG., Illus.). 48p. (J). (gr. 3-7). lib. bdg. 29.95 *(978-0-7377-3534-5(1),* Greenhaven Pr., Inc.) Cengage Gale.

Cefrey, Holly. Career Building Through Machinima: Using Video Games to Make Movies. 2009. (Digital Career Building Ser.). 64p. (gr. 6-6). 58.50 *(978-1-61512-168-7(4))* Rosen Publishing Group, Inc., The.

Christian Founders 3D Adventure. 2004. (YA). cd-rom 19.95 *(978-1-931203-12-8(1))* Inspired Idea.

Cohen, Judith Love. You Can Be A Woman Video Game Producer. l.t. ed. 2005. (Illus.). 72p. (J). 17.95 *(978-1-880599-74-7(0));* pap. 12.95 *(978-1-880599-73-0(2))* Cascade Pass, Inc.

Cornell, Kari. Minecraft Creator Markus "Notch" Persson. 2016. (STEM Trailblazer Bios Ser.). (ENG.). 32p. (J). (gr. 2-5). 26.65 *(978-1-4677-9526-5(7),* Lerner Pubns.) Lerner Publishing Group.

Cuellar, Joey, et al. Capcom Fighting Evolution(R) Official Fighter's Guide. 2004. (ENG.). 128p. pap. 14.99 *(978-0-7440-0506-6(X))* Pearson Education.

Culp, Jennifer. Call of Duty: Vince Zampella, Grant Collier, & Jason West, 1 vol. 2015. (ENG., Illus.). 128p. (J). 35.60 *(978-1-4777-7923-1(X),* Rosen Young Adult) Rosen Publishing Group, Inc., The.

—Online Gaming Safety & Privacy. 2013. (21st Century Safety & Privacy Ser.). 64p. (J). (gr. 5-8). pap. 77.70 *(978-1-4488-9585-4(5));* pap. 12.95 *(978-1-4488-9584-7(7));* (Illus.). 31.95 *(978-1-4488-9570-0(7))* Rosen Publishing Group, Inc., The.

Culp, Jennifer. Using Computer Science in Digital Gaming Careers. 2017. (Coding Your Passion Ser.). 80p. (J). (gr. 12-12). 35.75 ***(978-1-5081-7522-3(5),*** Rosen Young Adult) Rosen Publishing Group, Inc., The.

Cunningham, Kevin. Video Game Designer. 2015. (21st Century Skills Library: Cool STEAM Careers Ser.). (ENG., Illus.). 32p. (J). (gr. 4-7). 29.93 *(978-1-63362-567-9(2),* 206452) Cherry Lake Publishing.

C
D

Darby, Jason. Creating Adventure Games for Teens. 2012. (ENG.). 363p. pap. 34.99 (978-1-133-72802-3(2)) Course Technology.

—Game Creation for Teens. 2008. (ENG., Illus.). 320p. pap. 29.99 (978-1-59863-500-3(X)) Course Technology.

Dorling Kindersley Publishing Staff. Disney Infinity Character Encyclopedia. 2015. (ENG., Illus.). 192p. (J). (gr. 1-4). 16.99 (978-1-4654-2895-0(X), DK Children) Dorling Kindersley Publishing, Inc.

Dorling Kindersley Publishing Staff & Woodcock, Jon. Coding Computer Games with Scratch. 2015. (Help Your Kids Ser.). (ENG.). 224p. (J). (gr. 3-7). pap. 19.99 (978-1-4654-3935-2(8), DK Children) Dorling Kindersley Publishing, Inc.

—Coding Projects in Scratch. 2016. (ENG., Illus.). 224p. (J). (gr. 4-7). pap. 19.99 (978-1-4654-5142-2(0), DK Children) Dorling Kindersley Publishing, Inc.

Edwards, Sue Bradford. Professional Gaming Careers. 2017. (ESports: Game On! Ser.). (ENG.). 48p. (J). (gr. 5-8). 29.27 **(978-1-59953-890-7(3))** Norwood Hse. Pr.

Farwell, Nick & Steer, Don. Minecraft Redstone Handbook. Burlinson, James et al, illus. 2015. 93p. (J). (978-0-545-82320-3(X)) Scholastic, Inc.

Featherstone, Mark. Computer Games Designer: The Coolest Jobs on the Planet, 1 vol. 2013. (Coolest Jobs on the Planet Ser.). (ENG.). 48p. (gr. 5-8). 32.65 (978-1-4109-5484-8(6)); pap. 8.99 (978-1-4109-5489-3(7)) Heinemann-Raintree.

Flanigan, Gertrude, et al. Finger Hockey: No Poke Checking! 2011. (Miniature Editions Ser.). (ENG.). 32p. pap. 9.95 (978-0-7624-4257-7(3)) Running Pr. Bk. Pubs.

Freedman, Jeri. Career Building Through Skinning & Modding. 2009. (Digital Career Building Ser.). 64p. (gr. 6-6). 58.50 (978-1-61512-171-7(4)) Rosen Publishing Group, Inc., The.

Gifford, Clive. Great Game Design. 2017. 32p. (J). **(978-0-7787-3622-6(9))** Crabtree Publishing Co.

Gill, Bill Pojo. Pojo's Unofficial Guide to Neopets. 2004. (Pojo's... Ser.). (ENG., Illus.). 80p. (J). pap. 9.95 (978-1-57243-628-2(X)) Triumph Bks.

Greenhaven Press Editors. Online Social Games. 2012. (Technology 360 Ser.). (ENG., Illus.). 128p. (YA). (gr. 7-12). lib. bdg. 34.60 (978-1-4205-0718-8(4)) Cengage Gale.

Hackett, Jennifer. Game Design. 2017. (True Book — Behind the Scenes Ser.). (ENG.). 48p. (J). pap. 7.95 **(978-0-531-24146-2(7))**; lib. bdg. 31.00 **(978-0-531-23503-4(3))** Scholastic Library Publishing. (Children's Pr.).

Harris, Patricia. Understanding Coding with Minecraft(tm), 01 vols., 1. 2016. (Kids Can Code Ser.). (ENG., Illus.). 24p. (J). pap. 11.75 (978-1-5081-4470-0(2), PowerKids Pr.) Rosen Publishing Group, Inc., The.

Heitkamp, Kristina Lyn. Getting Paid to Make Games & Apps. 2016. (Turning Your Tech Hobbies into a Career Ser.). 00080p. (J). (gr. 7-7). 35.75 (978-1-5081-7296-3(X)) Rosen Publishing Group, Inc., The.

Hutchison, Barry. Skylanders Universe. 2015. (Illus.). 79p. (J). (978-1-4806-9285-5(9), Grosset & Dunlap) Penguin Publishing Group.

Jakubiak, David J. A Smart Kid's Guide to Playing Online Games. 2009. (Kids Online Ser.). 24p. (J). (ENG.). pap. 8.25 (978-1-4358-3350-0(3)); (Illus.). (gr. 2-6). lib. bdg. 22.60 (978-1-4042-8115-8(0)) Rosen Publishing Group, Inc., The. (PowerKids Pr.).

Jozefowicz, Chris. Video Game Developer. 2009. (Cool Careers: Cutting Edge Ser.). (ENG., Illus.). 32p. (J). (gr. 5-8). pap. 10.50 (978-1-4339-2157-5(X)) Stevens, Gareth Publishing LLLP.

Koll, Hilary & Mills, Steve. A Math Journey Through Computer Games. 2016. (ENG.). 32p. (J). (978-0-7787-2311-0(9)) Crabtree Publishing Co.

Kuehl, William Aksel. Aksel's Field Guide to Monsters. 2004. cd-rom 9.99 (978-0-9752528-0-2(1)) William Askel Art.

La Bella, Laura. Careers for Tech Girls in Video Game Development. 2015. (Tech Girls Ser.). (ENG., Illus.). 80p. (J). (gr. 7-8). 34.25 (978-1-4994-6107-7(0), Rosen Young Adult) Rosen Publishing Group, Inc., The.

Lyons, Heather. Programming Games & Animation. Westgate, Alex, illus. 2017. (Kids Get Coding Ser.). (ENG.). 24p. (J). (gr. 1-4). 26.65 **(978-1-5124-3941-0(X))** Lerner Publishing Group.

Machajewski, Sarah. Mark Pincus & Zynga. 2013. (Internet Biographies Ser.). (ENG., Illus.). 128p. (YA). (gr. 7-12). lib. bdg. 34.60 (978-1-4488-9530-4(8), Rosen Classroom) Rosen Publishing Group, Inc., The.

marcovitz, hal. Online Gaming & Entertainment. 2011. (Issues in the Digital Age Ser.). (Illus.). 96p. (YA). (gr. 7-12). lib. bdg. 27.95 (978-1-60152-191-0(X)) ReferencePoint Pr., Inc.

Miko, Christopher & Romines, Garrett. The Unofficial Holy Bible for Minecrafters Box Set: Stories from the Bible Told Block by Block. 2016. (ENG., Illus.). 648p. (J). (gr. k). 29.99 (978-1-5107-1374-1(3), Sky Pony Pr.) Skyhorse Publishing Co., Inc.

Milton, Stephanie. Minecraft: the Survivors' Book of Secrets: An Official Mojang Book. 2016. (ENG., Illus.). 112p. (gr. 3-7). 9.99 (978-0-399-59320-8(9), Del Rey) Random House Publishing Group.

Milton, Stephanie & Soares, Paul. Minecraft Combat Handbook. Cordner, Theo & Bolder, Joe, illus. 2015. 95p. (J). (978-0-545-82319-7(6)) Scholastic, Inc.

Needler, Matthew & Southam, Phil. Minecraft Construction Handbook. Barker, James et al, illus. 2015. 87p. (J). (978-0-545-82321-0(8)) Scholastic, Inc.

Orr, Tamra. Markus (Notch) Persson. 2015. (ENG., Illus.). 32p. (J). 26.50 (978-1-62469-120-1(X)) Purple Toad Publishing, Inc.

Oxlade, Chris. Gaming Technology. 2011. (New Technology Ser.). 48p. (YA). (gr. 7-12). lib. bdg. 34.25 (978-1-59920-531-1(9)) Black Rabbit Bks.

Pratt, Gary Thomas. Code of Unaris: Chat Roleplaying LePorte, Christine, ed. 2004. (Illus.). 314p. per. 15.95 (978-0-9748757-0-5(8), GDL 1001) Goldleaf Games, LLC.

Rauf, Don & Vescia, Monique. Computer Game Designer. 2008. (Virtual Apprentice Ser.). (Illus.). 64p. (gr. 4-9). per. 9.95 (978-0-8160-7550-8(6), Checkmark Bks.) Facts On File, Inc.

Roy, Daniel. The Ultimate Survival Handbook. 2016. (Terraria Ser.). (ENG., Illus.). 80p. (J). (gr. 3-7). pap. 8.99 (978-0-399-54133-9(0), Grosset & Dunlap) Penguin Young Readers Group.

Scholastic. Go Gaming! The Ultimate Guide to the World's Greatest Mobile. 2016. (ENG.). 128p. (J). (gr. 3-7). pap. 8.99 (978-1-338-11811-7(0)) Scholastic, Inc.

Scholastic & Winters, Terra. Overwatch. 2017. (ENG., Illus.). 112p. (J). (gr. 7-7). pap. 8.99 (978-1-338-11280-1(5)) Scholastic, Inc.

Scholastic Inc, contrib. by. Now You See It! 2015. (Pokemon Ser.). (ENG., Illus.). 64p. (J). (gr. 2-5). pap. 5.99 (978-0-545-89237-7(6)) Scholastic, Inc.

Scholastic, Inc. Staff. Pirates Treasure. 2008. 29.99 (978-0-439-90349-3(1)) Scholastic, Inc.

Schrier, Allyson Valentine. Gaming Safely, 6 vols. 2013. (Tech Safety Smarts Ser.). (ENG.). 32p. (J). (gr. 3-4). 47.70 (978-1-62065-801-7(1), Fact Finders); (Illus.). pap. 8.10 (978-1-62065-800-0(3)); (Illus.). lib. bdg. 27.32 (978-1-4296-9946-4(9)) Capstone Press of Coughlan Cos.

Sethi, Maneesh. Game Programming for Teens. 3rd ed. 2008. (Computer Game & Simulation Programming Ser.). (ENG., Illus.). 349p. pap. 29.99 (978-1-59863-518-8(2)) Course Technology.

Sherman, Jill. All about Online Gaming. 2017. (Cutting-Edge Technology (hardcover) Ser.). (ENG., Illus.). 32p. (J). (gr. 4-7). lib. bdg. 28.50 **(978-1-63517-013-9(3)**, Focus Readers) North Star Editions.

Strom, Chris. 3D Game Programming for Kids: Create Interactive Worlds with JavaScript. 2013. (ENG., Illus.). 308p. pap. 36.00 (978-1-937785-44-4(0), 9781937785444, Pragmatic Bookshelf, The) Pragmatic Programmers, LLC, The.

Suen, Anastasia. Alternate Reality Game Designer Jane Mcgonigal. 2014. (STEM Trailblazer Bios Ser.). (ENG., Illus.). 32p. (gr. 2-5). lib. bdg. 26.60 (978-1-4677-2458-6(0), Lerner Pubns.) Lerner Publishing Group.

Swaine, Meg. Career Building Through Alternate Reality Gaming. 2008. (Digital Career Building Ser.). (Illus.). 64p. (YA). (gr. 8-12). lib. bdg. 31.95 (978-1-4042-1357-9(0)) Rosen Publishing Group, Inc., The.

—Career Building Through Interactive Online Games. 2009. (Digital Career Building Ser.). 64p. (gr. 6-6). 58.50 (978-1-61512-167-0(6)) Rosen Publishing Group, Inc., The.

Truthware. 2003. cd-rom 34.95 (978-1-931203-09-8(1)) Inspired Idea.

Vinopol, Corinne. Con-SIGN-tration 3: Computer Software Game in American Sign Language. 2003. (J). cd-rom 19.95 (978-0-9752933-6-2(2)) Institute for Disabilities Research & Training, Inc.

—Con-SIGN-tration 4: Computer Software Game in American Sign Language. 2003. (J). cd-rom (978-0-9752933-7-9(0)) Institute for Disabilities Research & Training, Inc.

Wainewright, Max. I'm a JavaScript Games Maker: Advanced Coding. 2017. 32p. (J). **(978-0-7787-3518-2(4))** Crabtree Publishing Co.

—I'm a JavaScript Games Maker: The Basics. 2017. 32p. (J). **(978-0-7787-3517-5(6))** Crabtree Publishing Co.

Wainewright, Max. 20 Games to Create with Scratch. 2017. (ENG., Illus.). 80p. (J). (gr. 1-6). spiral bd. 12.95 (978-1-4549-2331-2(8)) Sterling Publishing Co., Inc.

Watson, Stephanie. Video Game Designer. 2017. (ENG.). 64p. (YA). (gr. 5-12). **(978-1-68282-184-8(6))** ReferencePoint Pr., Inc.

Wilkinson, Colin. Gaming: Playing Safe & Playing Smart. 2011. (Digital & Information Literacy Ser.). (ENG.). 48p. (YA). (gr. 5-8). pap. 11.75 (978-1-4488-5611-4(6)); lib. bdg. 29.25 (978-1-4488-5552-0(7)) Rosen Publishing Group, Inc., The. (Rosen Reference).

Yogscast Staff. Yogscast: the Diggy Diggy Book. 2016. (ENG., Illus.). 112p. (J). (gr. 3-7). pap. 8.99 (978-0-545-95663-5(3)) Scholastic, Inc.

Zeiger, James. Minecraft Beginner's Guide. 2016. (21st Century Skills Innovation Library: Unofficial Guides). (ENG., Illus.). 32p. (J). (gr. 4-8). 29.93 (978-1-63470-520-2(3), 207811) Cherry Lake Publishing.

COMPUTER GAMES—FICTION

Adams, W. Royce. The Computer's Nerd. 2011. 154p. (gr. 4-7). 22.99 (978-0-9712206-9-0(7)) Rairarubia Bks.

Cheverton, Mark. Battle for the Nether. 2014. (Gameknight999 Ser.: Bk. 2). (ENG.). 336p. (J). (gr. 3). pap. 9.99 (978-1-63220-712-8(5), Sky Pony Pr.) Skyhorse Publishing Co., Inc.

—Confronting the Dragon. 2014. (ENG., Illus.). 352p. (J). (gr. 3). pap. 9.99 (978-1-63450-046-3(6), Sky Pony Pr.) Skyhorse Publishing Co., Inc.

—Invasion of the Overworld. 2013. (Gameknight999 Ser.: Bk. 1). (ENG.). 172p. pap. 7.99 (978-1-4909-3083-1(3)) CreateSpace Independent Publishing Platform.

—Invasion of the Overworld. 2014. (Gameknight999 Ser.: Bk. 1). (ENG.). 208p. (J). (gr. 3). pap. 9.99 (978-1-63220-711-1(7), Sky Pony Pr.) Skyhorse Publishing Co., Inc.

—The Jungle Temple Oracle. 2015. (Mystery of Herobrine Ser.: Bk. 2). (ENG.). 256p. (J). (gr. 3). pap. 9.99 (978-1-63450-096-8(2), Sky Pony Pr.) Skyhorse Publishing Co., Inc.

—Last Stand on the Ocean Shore. 2015. (ENG.). 272p. (J). (gr. 3). pap. 9.99 (978-1-63450-098-2(9), Sky Pony Pr.) Skyhorse Publishing Co., Inc.

—Mission to the Moon. 2017. (Mystery of Entity303 Ser.: 3). lib. bdg. 20.85 **(978-0-606-40314-6(0))** Turtleback Bks.

Cheverton, Mark. Trouble in Zombie-Town. 2015. (Mystery of Herobrine Ser.: Bk. 1). (ENG.). 288p. (J). (gr. 3). pap. 9.99 (978-1-63450-094-4(6), Sky Pony Pr.) Skyhorse Publishing Co., Inc.

Collins, Suzanne. When Charlie McButton Lost Power. Lester, Mike, illus. 2007. (ENG.). 32p. (J). (gr. -1-3). pap. 6.99 (978-0-14-240857-5(3), Puffin Books) Penguin Young Readers Group.

—When Charlie McButton Lost Power. Lester, Mike, illus. 2009. 32p. 16.00 (978-1-60686-529-3(3)) Perfection Learning Corp.

Cube Kid, Cube. Crafting Alliances: An Unofficial Minecraft Adventure. 2017. (Diary of an 8-Bit Warrior Ser.: 3). (ENG.). 256p. (J). 13.99 **(978-1-4494-8803-1(X))** Andrews McMeel Publishing.

—From Seeds to Swords: An Unofficial Minecraft Adventure. (Diary of an 8-Bit Warrior Ser.: 2). (ENG.). 192p. (J). 2017. 13.99 **(978-1-4494-8802-4(1))** 2016. (Illus.). (gr. 2-6). pap. 9.99 (978-1-4494-8008-0(X)) Andrews McMeel Publishing.

—An Unofficial Minecraft Adventure. 2017. (Diary of an 8-Bit Warrior Ser.: 1). (ENG.). 256p. (J). 13.99 **(978-1-4494-8801-7(3))** Andrews McMeel Publishing.

Dashner, James. The Eye of Minds. 2013. 310p. (YA). (978-0-385-38370-7(3), Delacorte Pr) Random House Publishing Group.

—The Eye of Minds. (Mortality Doctrine Ser.). (ENG.). (YA). (gr. 7). 2014. 342p. pap. 9.99 (978-0-385-74140-8(5), Ember) 2013. 320p. 18.99 (978-0-385-74139-2(1), Delacorte Pr.) Random Hse. Children's Bks.

—The Game of Lives. 2015. (Mortality Doctrine Ser.). (ENG.). 352p. (YA). (gr. 7). lib. bdg. 21.99 (978-0-375-99003-8(8)); 18.99 (978-0-385-74143-9(X)) Random Hse. Children's Bks. (Delacorte Pr.).

—The Rule of Thoughts. (Mortality Doctrine Ser.). (ENG.). (YA). (gr. 7). 2014. 336p. 18.99 (978-0-385-74141-5(3), Delacorte Pr.)Bk. 2. 2016. 352p. pap. 9.99 (978-0-385-74142-2(1), Ember) Random Hse. Children's Bks.

Doctorow, Cory. In Real Life. Wang, Jen, illus. 2014. (ENG.). 192p. (YA). (gr. 7). pap. 17.99 (978-1-59643-658-9(1), 9781596436589, First Second Bks.) Roaring Brook Pr.

Drake, Raelyn. Realm of Mystics. 2017. (Level Up Ser.). (ENG.). (YA). (gr. 6-12). 120p. pap. 7.99 **(978-1-5124-5359-1(5))**; lib. bdg. 26.65 **(978-1-5124-3989-2(4))** Lerner Publishing Group. (Darby Creek).

Eve, Carol. Tom Wallbank's Cat. 2015. (ENG.). 31p. (J). (gr. 3-4). mass mkt. 13.95 (978-1-78455-630-3(0), a5ab1896-bbe2-402d-8633-7159460e1903) Austin, Stan AUS. Dist: Bookmasters Distribution.

Guest, Jacqueline. War Games, 1 vol. 2008. (Lorimer SideStreets Ser.). (ENG.). 184p. (YA). (gr. 9-12). 9.95 (978-1-55277-035-1(4), 9781552770351); 16.95 (978-1-55277-036-8(2), 9781552770368) Lorimer, James & Co., Ltd., Pubs. CAN. Dist: Casemate Pubs. & Bk. Distributors, LLC.

Hill, Marvin. Playland. 2007. 96p. pap. 14.95 (978-1-84799-888-0(7)) Lulu Pr., Inc.

Hunter, Alex. Game Over. Rew, Jen, illus. 2012. 126p. pap. (978-1-78176-771-9(8)) FeedARead.com.

—Game over - Book Three. 2013. 268p. (J). pap. (978-1-78299-394-0(0)) FeedARead.com.

Keats, Israel. Labyrinth. 2017. (Level Up Ser.). (ENG.). 128p. (YA). (gr. 6-12). 26.65 **(978-1-5124-3987-8(8))**; pap. 7.99 **(978-1-5124-5357-7(9))** Lerner Publishing Group. (Darby Creek).

Keeper of the Colony. 2006. (Keeper Ser.). 246p. (J). (gr. 3-9). per. 10.95 (978-1-929976-35-5(6)) Top Pubns., Ltd.

Knoll, Amos. The Flower That Could Not Talk. 2010. 64p. pap. 28.99 (978-1-4490-7590-3(8)) AuthorHouse.

Kostick, Conor. Saga. 2009. (ENG.). 384p. (YA). (gr. 7-18). pap. 9.99 (978-0-14-241422-4(0), Firebird) Penguin Young Readers Group.

Mielcarek, David. Time for your Mind. Mielcarek, David, ed. 2006. (Illus.). 38p. (J). (978-0-9785480-0-1(0)) Mielcarek, David.

Morgan, Winter. Clash of the Creepers: An Unofficial Gamer's Adventure, Book Six. 2015. (Unofficial Gamer's Adventure Ser.). (ENG.). 112p. (J). (gr. 1-7). pap. 7.99 (978-1-63450-591-8(3), Sky Pony Pr.) Skyhorse Publishing Co., Inc.

—The Endermen Invasion: A Minecraft Gamer's Adventure, Book Three. 2014. (Unofficial Gamer's Adventure Ser.). (ENG.). 112p. (J). (gr. 1-7). pap. 7.99 (978-1-63450-088-3(1), Sky Pony Pr.) Skyhorse Publishing Co., Inc.

—The Griefer's Revenge: League of Griefers Series, Book Three. 2015. (League of Griefers Ser.: 3). (ENG.). 112p. (J). (gr. 1-7). pap. 7.99 (978-1-63450-597-0(2), Sky Pony Pr.) Skyhorse Publishing Co., Inc.

—The Hardcore War: Book Six in the League of Griefers Series. 2015. (League of Griefers Ser.: 6). (ENG.). 112p. (J). (gr. 1-7). pap. 7.99 (978-1-63450-540-6(9), Sky Pony Pr.) Skyhorse Publishing Co., Inc.

—The Mystery of the Griefer's Mark: A Minecraft Gamer's Adventure, Book Two. 2014. (Unofficial Gamer's Adventure Ser.). (ENG.). 112p. (J). (gr. 1-7). pap. 7.99 (978-1-63220-726-5(5), Sky Pony Pr.) Skyhorse Publishing Co., Inc.

—The Quest for the Diamond Sword: An Awesome Minecraft Adventure. 2014. (Minecraft Gamer's Adventure Ser.). (ENG.). 112p. (J). (gr. 1-7). pap. 7.99 (978-1-63220-442-4(8), Sky Pony Pr.) Skyhorse Publishing Co., Inc.

—The Return of the Rainbow Griefers: League of Griefers Series, Book Four. 2015. (League of Griefers Ser.: 4). (ENG.). 112p. (J). (gr. 1-7). pap. 7.99 (978-1-63450-599-4(9), Sky Pony Pr.) Skyhorse Publishing Co., Inc.

—The Skeletons Strike Back: An Unofficial Gamer's Adventure, Book Five. 2015. (Unofficial Gamer's Adventure Ser.). (ENG.). 112p. (J). (gr. 1-7). pap. 7.99 (978-1-63450-126-2(8), Sky Pony Pr.) Skyhorse Publishing Co., Inc.

Osa, Nancy. Spawn Point Zero: Defenders of the Overworld #3. 2015. (Defenders of the Overworld Ser.). (ENG.). 272p. (J). (gr. 6). pap. 9.99 (978-1-5107-0321-6(7), Sky Pony Pr.) Skyhorse Publishing Co., Inc.

Osterweil, Adam. The Amulet of Komondor. Thorpe, Peter, illus. 2003. (ENG.). 112p. (J). (gr. 4-6). 15.95 (978-1-886910-81-2(2), Lemniscaat) Boyds Mills Pr.

Paulsen, Gary. The Time Hackers. 2006. (ENG.). 96p. (J). (gr. 3-7). 5.99 (978-0-553-48788-6(4), Yearling) Random Hse. Children's Bks.

Poznanski, Ursula. Erebos: It's a Game. It Watches You. Pattinson, Judith, tr. from GER. 3rd ed. 2012. (ENG.). 440p. (YA). (gr. 6-18). 29.95 (978-1-55451-373-4(1), 9781554513734); pap. 19.95 (978-1-55451-372-7(3), 9781554513727) Annick Pr., Ltd. CAN. Dist: Publishers Group West (PGW).

Pratchett, Terry. Only You Can Save Mankind. 224p. (J). (gr. 3-7). 2006. (Johnny Maxwell Trilogy Ser.: 1). per. 6.99 (978-0-06-054187-3(3)) 2005. 15.99 (978-0-06-054185-9(7)) HarperCollins Pubs.

—Only You Can Save Mankind. 2006. (Johnny Maxwell Trilogy). 207p. (J). (gr. 3-7). 13.65 (978-0-7569-6933-2(6)) Perfection Learning Corp.

Stine, R. L. Battle of the Dum Diddys, 1 vol. Park, Trip, illus. 2011. (Rotten School Ser.: No. 12). (ENG.). 128p. (gr. 2-5). 24.21 (978-1-59961-836-4(2)) Spotlight.

Strange, Jason. Realm of Ghosts, 1 vol. Parks, Phil, illus. 2011. (Jason Strange Ser.). (ENG.). 72p. (gr. 2-3). pap. 6.25 (978-1-4342-3096-6(1)); 25.32 (978-1-4342-2962-5(9)) Stone Arch Bks.

Tabak, Lawrence. In Real Life. 2014. (ENG.). 288p. (J). (gr. 7-12). 16.99 (978-0-8048-4478-9(X)) Tuttle Publishing.

Thomas Nelson Publishing Staff. Camping the Bug-A-Boo Way: Go for the Gold Against Camp Hot Foot! 2008. cd-rom 19.95 (978-0-9754280-7-8(1)) Nelson, Thomas Inc.

Time for Your Mind. l.t. ed. 2006. (Illus.). 35p. (J). (978-0-9785480-1-8(9)) Mielcarek, David.

Vande Velde, Vivian. Deadly Pink. (ENG.). 288p. (J). (gr. 5-7). 2013. pap. 6.99 (978-0-544-02278-2(5)) 2012. 16.99 (978-0-547-73850-5(1)) Houghton Mifflin Harcourt Publishing Co.

Zucker, Jonny. Mission 1: Game On. Woodman, Ned, illus. 2013. (Max Flash Ser.: 1). (ENG.). 144p. (gr. 2-5). pap. 7.95 (978-1-4677-1465-5(8)); lib. bdg. 27.93 (978-1-4677-1207-1(8)) Lerner Publishing Group. (Darby Creek).

COMPUTER GRAPHICS

Bradley, Timothy. FX! Computer-Generated Imagery. 2017. (Time for Kids Nonfiction Readers Ser.). lib. bdg. 22.10 **(978-0-606-40284-2(5))** Turtleback Bks.

Centore, Michael. Entertainment Industry, Vol. 10. 2016. (Stem in Current Events Ser.). (Illus.). 64p. (J). (gr. 7). 23.95 (978-1-4222-3590-4(4)) Mason Crest.

Computer Graphic Design Module Guide. 4th rev. ed. 2004. 52p. pap. (978-0-86657-531-7(6)) Lab-Volt Systems, Inc.

Cunningham, Kevin. Computer Graphics: From Concept to Consumer. 2013. (Calling All Innovators). (ENG.). 64p. (J). pap. 8.95 (978-0-531-22008-5(7)); lib. bdg. 30.00 (978-0-531-26520-8(X)) Scholastic Library Publishing. (Children's Pr.).

Greek, Joe. A Career in Computer Graphics & Design, 1 vol. 2015. (ENG., Illus.). 80p. (J). 34.25 (978-1-4777-7888-3(8), Rosen Young Adult) Rosen Publishing Group, Inc., The.

Lovett, Amber. Coding with Blockly. 2017. (21st Century Skills Innovation Library: Makers As Innovators Junior Ser.). (ENG., Illus.). 24p. (J). (gr. 2-5). lib. bdg. 28.50 (978-1-63472-185-1(3), 209312) Cherry Lake Publishing.

QEB Let's Start! Computing National Book Stores Edition: Making Charts. 2006. (J). per. (978-1-59566-297-2(9)) QEB Publishing Inc.

Rauf, Don. Getting Paid to Work in 3D. 2016. (Turning Your Tech Hobbies into a Career Ser.). 00080p. (J). (gr. 7-7). 35.75 (978-1-5081-7298-7(6)) Rosen Publishing Group, Inc., The.

Red Bird Press Staff. Amazing 3D Magic. 2004. (Amazing Stereoscopic 3D Ser.). 24p. (J). pap. 5.95 (978-1-902626-64-2(8)) Red Bird Publishing GBR. Dist: Weatherhill, Inc.

Rose, John N. Direct Approach: Maya 5. l.t. ed. 2003. (Illus.). 302p. per. 49.95 (978-0-9742948-0-3(2), DA-Ma5) Platinum Rose Publishing.

Small, Cathleen. Computer Animation. 2015. (High-Tech Jobs Ser.). (ENG.). 96p. (J). (gr. 7-7). 42.79 (978-1-5026-0106-3(0)) Cavendish Square Publishing.

Totter, Donald. Architectural Presentation with DataCad 10. 2004. (YA). spiral bd. (978-0-9740796-3-9(4)) Technology Education Concepts Inc.

Zizka, Theo & Zizka, Theo. 3D Modeling. 2014. (21st Century Skills Innovation Library: Makers As Innovators Ser.). (ENG.). 32p. (J). (gr. 4-8). 28.50 (978-1-63137-772-3(8), 205331) Cherry Lake Publishing.

COMPUTER HARDWARE

see Computer Input-Output Equipment

COMPUTER INPUT-OUTPUT EQUIPMENT

Matthews, John. Interactive Whiteboards. 2008. (21st Century Skills Library: Global Products Ser.). (ENG.). 32p. (gr. 4-8). 28.50 (978-1-60279-254-8(2), 200121) Cherry Lake Publishing.

COMPUTER LITERACY

Here are entered works on the ability to use and understand computers, including their capabilities, applications, and social implications, in order to function in a computer-based society.

Computer Science Pure & Simple Book 1, 2. 2003. (Illus.). 126p. (gr. 5-18). spiral bd. 24.99 (978-0-9749653-0-7(8), 001) Motherboard Bks.

COMPUTER PROGRAMMING

Ambrosek, Renee. Shawn Fanning: The Founder of Napster. 2009. (Internet Career Biographies Ser.). 112p. (gr. 8-8). 63.90 (978-1-61513-600-1(2)) Rosen Publishing Group, Inc., The.

Anderson, Rane. Power of Patterns: Coding. 2017. (J). pap. 9.97 **(978-1-4938-3625-3(0))** Teacher Created Materials, Inc.

—Power of Patterns: Coding. 2017. (Time for Kids Nonfiction Readers Ser.). lib. bdg. 20.85 **(978-0-606-40277-4(2))** Turtleback Bks.

Anniss, Matthew. Understanding Programming & Logic. 2015. (Understanding Computing Ser.). (ENG., Illus.). 48p. (gr. 3-6). 33.32 (978-1-4846-0901-9(8), Heinemann InfoSearch) Heinemann-Raintree.

Bedell, Jane (J. M.). So, You Want to Be a Coder? Plug in to the World of Cyberspace, from Video Games to Robots. 2016. (Be What You Want Ser.). (ENG., Illus.). 256p. (J). (gr. 3-7). pap. 11.99 (978-1-58270-579-8(8)) Aladdin/Beyond Words.

Behind the Scenes with Coders. 2017. (Behind the Scenes with Coders Ser.). 32p. (gr. 9-10). 157.50 **(978-1-4994-3494-1(4))**; pap. 60.00 **(978-1-5081-5435-8(X))** Rosen Publishing Group, Inc., The. (PowerKids Pr.).

Benedict, Aaron & Gallaher, David. Using Computer Science in High-Tech Health & Wellness Careers. 2017. (Coding Your Passion Ser.). 80p. (J). (gr. 12-12). 35.75 **(978-1-5081-7515-5(2)**, Rosen Young Adult) Rosen Publishing Group, Inc., The.

Bitetto, Marco A. V. Theme Stream Vol. 10: Helicopters. l.t. ed. 2003. (Illus.). 128p. (YA). (gr. 9-12). pap. 22.00 (978-1-58578-483-7(4)) Institute of Cybernetics Research, Inc.

Blaine, Dalton. Tomás's Puzzle: Sticking to It. 2017. (Computer Science for the Real World Ser.). 12p. (gr. 6-7). pap. 7.05 ***(978-1-5383-5182-6(X)***, Rosen Classroom) Rosen Publishing Group, Inc., The.

Bonnice, Sherry. Computer Programmer. Riggs, Ernestine G. & Gholar, Cheryl, eds. 2013. (Careers with Character Ser.: 18). 96p. (J). (gr. 7-18). 22.95 *(978-1-4222-2754-1(5))* Mason Crest.

Braxton, Simone. Our Class Budget: Checking Your Work. 2017. (Computer Science for the Real World Ser.). 16p. (gr. 7-8). pap. 7.95 ***(978-1-5383-5239-7(7)***, Rosen Classroom) Rosen Publishing Group, Inc., The.

Brezina, Corona. Marc Andreessen, 01 vols., 1. 2016. (Tech Pioneers Ser.). (ENG.). 112p. (J). 35.60 *(978-1-4994-6284-5(0)*, Rosen Young Adult) Rosen Publishing Group, Inc., The.

Briggs, Jason R. Python for Kids: A Playful Introduction to Programming. 2012. (ENG., Illus.). 344p. (J). (gr. 5). pap. 34.95 *(978-1-59327-407-8(6)*, 9781593274078) No Starch Pr., Inc.

Carmichael, L. E. What Are Programs & Apps? 2015. (ENG., Illus.). 32p. (J). (gr. k-2). 26.65 *(978-1-4677-8076-6(6))* Lerner Publishing Group.

Code Power: a Teen Programmer's Guide: A Teen Programmer's Guide. 2014. (Code Power: a Teen Programmer's Guide Ser.). 64p. (YA). (gr. 5-8). 263.60 *(978-1-4777-7721-3(0)*, Rosen Reference) Rosen Publishing Group, Inc., The.

Coding Your Passion. 2017. (Coding Your Passion Ser.). 80p. (gr. 12-12). 214.50 ***(978-1-4994-6628-7(5)***, Rosen Young Adult) Rosen Publishing Group, Inc., The.

Computer-Free Coding. 2017. (Computer-Free Coding Ser.). 32p. (gr. 9-9). 114.00 ***(978-1-4994-8244-7(2))***; pap. 47.00 ***(978-1-4994-8382-6(1))*** Rosen Publishing Group, Inc., The. (Windmill Bks.).

Conway, Sommer. What I Do Every Day: Over & over Again. 2017. (Computer Science for the Real World Ser.). 8p. (gr. 5-6). pap. 6.20 ***(978-1-5383-5090-4(4)***, Rosen Classroom) Rosen Publishing Group, Inc., The.

Cornell, Kari. Minecraft Creator Markus "Notch" Persson. 2016. (STEM Trailblazer Bios Ser.). (ENG.). 32p. (J). (gr. 2-5). 26.65 *(978-1-4677-9526-5(7)*, Lerner Pubns.) Lerner Publishing Group.

Darby, Jason. Creating Adventure Games for Teens. 2012. (ENG.). 363p. pap. 34.99 *(978-1-133-72802-3(2))* Course Technology.

—Game Creation for Teens. 2008. (ENG., Illus.). 320p. pap. 29.99 *(978-1-59863-500-3(X))* Course Technology.

Di Piazza, Domenica. Google Cybersecurity Expert Parisa Tabriz. 2017. (J). ***(978-1-5415-0007-5(5))*** Lerner Publishing Group.

Dorling Kindersley Publishing Staff. Coding Projects in Python. 2017. (ENG.). 224p. (J). (gr. 4-7). pap. 19.99 ***(978-1-4654-6188-9(4)***, DK Children) Dorling Kindersley Publishing, Inc.

—Coding with Scratch. 2015. (ENG., Illus.). 40p. (J). (gr. 1-4). pap., wbk. ed. 5.99 *(978-1-4654-4392-2(4)*, DK Children) Dorling Kindersley Publishing, Inc.

—Computer Coding. 2014. (ENG.). 40p. (J). (gr. 1-4). pap., wbk. ed. 5.99 *(978-1-4654-2685-7(X)*, DK Children) Dorling Kindersley Publishing, Inc.

—DK Findout! Coding. 2017. (DK Find Out! Ser.). (ENG.). 64p. (J). (gr. 1-4). pap. 10.99 ***(978-1-4654-6233-6(3)***, DK Children) Dorling Kindersley Publishing, Inc.

—DK Workbooks: Raspberry Pi Projects Workbook. 2017. (ENG., Illus.). 40p. (J). (gr. 4-7). pap. 5.99 *(978-1-4654-5703-5(8)*, DK Children) Dorling Kindersley Publishing, Inc.

—DK Workbooks: Scratch Challenge Workbook. 2017. (ENG.). 40p. (J). (gr. 1-4). pap. 5.99 *(978-1-4654-5686-1(4)*, DK Children) Dorling Kindersley Publishing, Inc.

—Help Your Kids with Computer Coding. 2014. (Help Your Kids Ser.). (ENG., Illus.). 224p. (gr. 7). pap. 19.95 *(978-1-4654-1956-9(X)*, DK) Dorling Kindersley Publishing, Inc.

Dorling Kindersley Publishing Staff & Kelly, James Floyd. DK Readers L2: Story of Coding. 2017. (DK Readers Ser.). (ENG.). 48p. (J). (gr. k-2). 14.99 ***(978-1-4654-6231-2(7))***; pap. 3.99 ***(978-1-4654-6242-8(2))*** Dorling Kindersley Publishing, Inc. (DK Children).

Dorling Kindersley Publishing Staff & Prottsman, Kiki. My First Coding Book. 2017. (ENG., Illus.). 24p. (J). (gr. k-2). bds. 15.99 ***(978-1-4654-5973-2(1)***, DK Children) Dorling Kindersley Publishing, Inc.

Dorling Kindersley Publishing Staff & Woodcock, Jon. Coding Projects in Scratch. 2016. (ENG., Illus.). 224p. (J). (gr. 4-7). pap. 19.99 *(978-1-4654-5142-2(0)*, DK Children) Dorling Kindersley Publishing, Inc.

Dorling Kindersley Publishing Staff, et al. Computer Coding with Scratch: Games. 2016. (ENG., Illus.). 40p. (J). (gr. 1-4). pap., wbk. ed. 5.99 *(978-1-4654-4482-0(3)*, DK Children) Dorling Kindersley Publishing, Inc.

—DK Workbooks: Coding in Scratch: Projects Workbook. 2016. (ENG.). 40p. (J). (gr. 1-4). pap. 5.99 *(978-1-4654-4402-8(5)*, DK Children) Dorling Kindersley Publishing, Inc.

Edwards, Sue Bradford. Professional Gaming Careers. 2017. (ESports: Game On! Ser.). (ENG.). 48p. (J). (gr. 5-8). 29.27 ***(978-1-59953-890-7(3))*** Norwood Hse. Pr.

Ellis, Roman. Our Vegetable Garden: Working As a Team. 2017. (Computer Science for the Real World Ser.). 8p. (gr. 5-6). pap. 6.20 ***(978-1-5383-5068-3(8)***, Rosen Classroom) Rosen Publishing Group, Inc., The.

Fain, Yakov. Java Programming for Kids. 2004. (Illus.). 216p. per. *(978-0-9718439-5-0(3))* Smart Data Processing, Inc.

Fischer, James. Computer Math. 2013. (Math 24/7 Ser.: 10). 48p. (J). (gr. 5-18). 19.95 *(978-1-4222-2904-0(1))* Mason Crest.

Flores, Vanessa. My Pet Mouse: Step by Step. 2017. (Computer Science for the Real World Ser.). 8p. (gr. 5-6). pap. 6.20 ***(978-1-5383-5044-7(0)***, Rosen Classroom) Rosen Publishing Group, Inc., The.

Ford, Jerry Lee, Jr. Scratch 2. 0 Programming for Teens. 2nd ed. 2014. (For Teens Ser.). (ENG., Illus.). 336p. (YA). pap. 29.99 *(978-1-305-07519-1(6))* Course Technology.

—XNA 3. 1 Game Development for Teens. 2010. (For Teens Ser.). (ENG., Illus.). 336p. (J). pap. 34.99 *(978-1-4354-5438-5(3))* Course Technology.

Freedman, Jeri. Careers in Computer Science & Programming. 2011. (Careers in Computer Technology Ser.). (ENG.). 80p. (YA). lib. bdg. 33.25 *(978-1-4488-1318-6(2))* Rosen Publishing Group, Inc., The.

Furgang, Adam. For People Who Love Gaming. 2016. (Cool Careers Without College Ser.). 00104p. (J). (gr. 7-7). 38.45 *(978-1-5081-7282-6(X))* Rosen Publishing Group, Inc., The.

Gifford, Clive. Awesome Algorithms & Creative Coding. 2015. (ENG., Illus.). 32p. (J). *(978-0-7787-1508-5(6))* Crabtree Publishing Co.

Gifford, Clive. Computing & Coding in the Real World. 2017. 32p. (J). ***(978-0-7787-3621-9(0))*** Crabtree Publishing Co.

Harris, Patricia. Gareth's Guide to Becoming a Rock Star Coder. 2017. (Gareth Guides to an Extraordinary Life Ser.). 32p. (gr. 4-5). 26.60 ***(978-1-5382-0359-0(6))*** Stevens, Gareth Publishing LLLP.

—Understanding Coding Like a Programmer. 2016. (Spotlight on Kids Can Code Ser.). 00024p. (J). (gr. 4-5). pap. 11.75 *(978-1-4994-2795-0(6)*, PowerKids Pr.) Rosen Publishing Group, Inc., The.

—Understanding Coding Using Conditionals. (J). 2017. ***(978-1-4994-2814-8(6))*** 2016. 00024p. (gr. 4-5). pap. 11.75 *(978-1-4994-2807-0(3))* Rosen Publishing Group, Inc., The. (PowerKids Pr.).

—Understanding Coding with Lego Mindstorms(tm), 01 vols., 1. 2016. (Kids Can Code Ser.). (ENG., Illus.). 24p. (J). pap. 11.75 *(978-1-5081-4462-5(1)*, PowerKids Pr.) Rosen Publishing Group, Inc., The.

—Understanding Coding with Python, 01 vols., 1. 2016. (Kids Can Code Ser.). (ENG., Illus.). 24p. (J). pap. 11.75 *(978-1-5081-4474-8(5)*, PowerKids Pr.) Rosen Publishing Group, Inc., The.

—Understanding Coding with Ruby, 01 vols., 1. 2016. (Kids Can Code Ser.). (ENG., Illus.). 24p. (J). pap. 11.75 *(978-1-5081-4450-2(8)*, PowerKids Pr.) Rosen Publishing Group, Inc., The.

Harris, Patricia. Why Are There So Many Programming Languages? 2017. (Spotlight on Kids Can Code Ser.). 24p. (gr. 8-10). pap. 11.75 ***(978-1-5081-5520-1(8)***, PowerKids Pr.) Rosen Publishing Group, Inc., The.

Hatter, Clyde & Dojo, Coder. CoderDojo Nano: Building a Website - Create with Code. 2016. (ENG.). 96p. (J). (gr. 3-7). pap. 12.99 *(978-1-338-15676-8(4))* Scholastic, Inc.

Heitkamp, Kristina Lyn. Getting Paid to Make Games & Apps. 2016. (Turning Your Tech Hobbies into a Career Ser.). 00080p. (J). (gr. 7-7). 35.75 *(978-1-5081-7296-3(X))* Rosen Publishing Group, Inc., The.

Hixon, Rena. Mindstorms: Level 1. 2016. (21st Century Skills Innovation Library: Unofficial Guides). (ENG., Illus.). 32p. (J). (gr. 4-8). 29.93 *(978-1-63470-524-0(6)*, 207827) Cherry Lake Publishing.

—Mindstorms: Level 2. 2016. (21st Century Skills Innovation Library: Unofficial Guides). (ENG., Illus.). 32p. (J). (gr. 4-8). 29.93 *(978-1-63470-525-7(4)*, 207831) Cherry Lake Publishing.

—Mindstorms: Level 3. 2016. (21st Century Skills Innovation Library: Unofficial Guides). (ENG., Illus.). 32p. (J). (gr. 4-8). 29.93 *(978-1-63470-526-4(2)*, 207835) Cherry Lake Publishing.

—Mindstorms: Level 4. 2016. (21st Century Skills Innovation Library: Unofficial Guides). (ENG., Illus.). 32p. (J). (gr. 4-8). 29.93 *(978-1-63470-527-1(0)*, 207839) Cherry Lake Publishing.

Holland, Eva & Minnick, Chris. Adventures in Coding. 2016. (Adventures In ... Ser.). (ENG., Illus.). 320p. pap. 24.99 *(978-1-119-23268-1(6))* Wiley, John & Sons, Inc.

Hubbard, Ben. How Coding Works. 2017. (Our Digital Planet Ser.). (ENG., Illus.). 24p. (gr. k-2). lib. bdg. 23.32 *(978-1-4846-3599-5(X))* Heinemann-Raintree.

Huffman, Mindy. Use It Again! Sharing & Reusing. 2017. (Computer Science for the Real World Ser.). 8p. (gr. 5-6). pap. 6.20 ***(978-1-5383-5096-6(3)***, Rosen Classroom) Rosen Publishing Group, Inc., The.

Jackson, Aurelia. Tumblr(r): How David Karp Changed the Way We Blog. 2014. (Wizards of Technology Ser.: 10). (Illus.). 64p. (J). (gr. 7-18). 23.95 *(978-1-4222-3186-9(0))* Mason Crest.

Keppeler, Jill. The Inventors of Minecraft: Markus Notch Persson & His Coding Team. 2017. (Breakout Biographies Ser.). 32p. (J). (gr. 9-10). pap. 10.00 ***(978-1-5081-6062-5(7)***, PowerKids Pr.) Rosen Publishing Group, Inc., The.

La Bella, Laura. Building Apps. 2013. (Digital & Information Literacy Ser.). (Illus.). 48p. (J). (gr. 5-8). 29.25 *(978-1-4488-9515-1(4))* Rosen Publishing Group, Inc., The.

—Careers for Tech Girls in Video Game Development. 2015. (Tech Girls Ser.). (ENG., Illus.). 80p. (J). (gr. 7-8). 34.25 *(978-1-4994-6107-7(0)*, Rosen Young Adult) Rosen Publishing Group, Inc., The.

—Careers in Web Development. 2011. (Careers in Computer Technology Ser.). (ENG.). 80p. (YA). lib. bdg. 33.25 *(978-1-4488-1314-8(X))* Rosen Publishing Group, Inc., The.

Lent, Colleen Van. Web Design with Html5. 2014. (21st Century Skills Innovation Library: Makers As Innovators Ser.). (ENG., Illus.). 32p. (J). (gr. 4-8). 28.50 *(978-1-63137-773-0(6)*, 205335) Cherry Lake Publishing.

Levin, Judith. Careers Creating Search Engines. 2007. (Cutting-Edge Careers Ser.). (Illus.). 64p. (J). (gr. 3-7). lib. bdg. 31.95 *(978-1-4042-0957-2(3))* Rosen Publishing Group, Inc., The.

Levin, Judith N. Careers Creating Search Engines. 2009. (Cutting-Edge Careers Ser.). 64p. (gr. 7-7). 55.90 *(978-1-61512-097-0(1))* Rosen Publishing Group, Inc., The.

Lovett, Amber. Coding with Blockly. 2017. (21st Century Skills Innovation Library: Makers As Innovators Junior Ser.). (ENG., Illus.). 24p. (J). (gr. 2-5). lib. bdg. 28.50 *(978-1-63472-185-1(3)*, 209312) Cherry Lake Publishing.

Lyons, Heather. Coding in the Real World. Westgate, Alex, illus. 2017. (Kids Get Coding Ser.). (ENG.). 24p. (J). (gr. 1-4). 26.65 ***(978-1-5124-3943-4(6))***; pap. 7.99 ***(978-1-5124-5586-1(5))*** Lerner Publishing Group.

—Coding to Create & Communicate. Westgate, Alex, illus. 2017. (Kids Get Coding Ser.). (ENG.). 24p. (J). (gr. 1-4). 26.65 ***(978-1-5124-3944-1(4))***; pap. 7.99 ***(978-1-5124-5584-7(9))*** Lerner Publishing Group.

—Programming Awesome Apps. Westgate, Alex, illus. 2017. (Kids Get Coding Ser.). (ENG.). 24p. (J). (gr. 1-4). 26.65 ***(978-1-5124-3942-7(8))*** Lerner Publishing Group.

—Programming Games & Animation. Westgate, Alex, illus. 2017. (Kids Get Coding Ser.). (ENG.). 24p. (J). (gr. 1-4). 26.65 ***(978-1-5124-3941-0(X))*** Lerner Publishing Group.

Lyons, Heather & Tweedale, Elizabeth. Coding, Bugs, & Fixes. Westgate, Alex, illus. 2016. (Kids Get Coding Ser.). (ENG.). 24p. (J). (gr. 1-4). 26.65 *(978-1-5124-1359-5(3))* Lerner Publishing Group.

—Learn to Program. Westgate, Alex, illus. 2016. (Kids Get Coding Ser.). (ENG.). 24p. (J). (gr. 1-4). 26.65 *(978-1-5124-1360-1(7))* Lerner Publishing Group.

—A World of Programming. Westgate, Alex, illus. 2016. (Kids Get Coding Ser.). (ENG.). 24p. (J). (gr. 1-4). 26.65 *(978-1-5124-1362-5(3))* Lerner Publishing Group.

Mara, Wil. Software Development: Science, Technology, Engineering. 2016. (Calling All Innovators: a Career for You Ser.). (ENG., Illus.). 64p. (J). lib. bdg. 32.00 *(978-0-531-23003-9(1)*, Children's Pr.) Scholastic Library Publishing.

Marquardt, Meg. Coding. 2017. (Tech Bytes Ser.). (ENG.). 48p. (J). (gr. 4-6). 26.60 ***(978-1-59953-887-7(3))***; pap. 13.26 ***(978-1-68404-118-3(X))*** Norwood Hse. Pr.

Martinez, Manuel. The Lost Prince: Sticking to It. 2017. (Computer Science for the Real World Ser.). 8p. (gr. 5-6). pap. 6.20 ***(978-1-5383-5110-9(2)***, Rosen Classroom) Rosen Publishing Group, Inc., The.

Matteson, Adrienne. Coding with ScratchJr. 2017. (21st Century Skills Innovation Library: Makers As Innovators Junior Ser.). (ENG., Illus.). 24p. (J). (gr. 2-5). lib. bdg. 28.50 *(978-1-63472-186-8(1)*, 209316) Cherry Lake Publishing.

McCallum, Rory. A Career in Coding: Careers in Computers. 2017. (Computer Science for the Real World Ser.). 16p. (gr. 7-8). pap. 7.95 ***(978-1-5383-5251-9(6)***, Rosen Classroom) Rosen Publishing Group, Inc., The.

McClure, Leigh. My School Supplies: Sharing & Reusing. 2017. (Computer Science for the Real World Ser.). 8p. (gr. 5-6). pap. 6.20 ***(978-1-5383-5093-5(9)***, Rosen Classroom) Rosen Publishing Group, Inc., The.

McCue, Camille. Getting Started with Coding: Get Creative with Code! 2015. (Dummies Junior Ser.). (ENG., Illus.). 128p. (J). (gr. 2-6). pap. 9.99 *(978-1-119-17717-3(0)*, For Dummies) Wiley, John & Sons, Inc.

McGinty, Alice B. Software Designer. 2004. (Coolcareers. com Ser.). 48p. (YA). lib. bdg. 29.25 *(978-0-8239-4086-8(1))* Rosen Publishing Group, Inc., The.

McGuire, Erin K. Careers in Database Design. 2011. (Careers in Computer Technology Ser.). (ENG.). 80p. (YA). lib. bdg. 33.25 *(978-1-4488-1317-9(4))* Rosen Publishing Group, Inc., The.

McManus, Sean. How to Code in 10 Easy Lessons: Learn How to Design & Code Your Very Own Computer Game. 2015. (Super Skills Ser.). (ENG.). 64p. (J). (gr. 3-7). spiral bd. 12.95 *(978-1-63322-050-8(6)*, Walter Foster Jr) Quarto Publishing Group USA.

Minnick, Chris & Holland, Eva. JavaScript for Kids for Dummies. 2015. (ENG., Illus.). 384p. (YA). pap. 29.99 *(978-1-119-11986-9(3)*, For Dummies) Wiley, John & Sons, Inc.

—Writing Computer Code. 2016. (Dummies Junior Ser.). (ENG.). 128p. (J). (gr. 2-6). pap. 9.99 *(978-1-119-17730-2(8)*, For Dummies) Wiley, John & Sons, Inc.

Mooney, Carla. Online Privacy & Social Media. 2014. (Privacy in the Online World). (ENG., Illus.). 80p. (J). lib. bdg. *(978-1-60152-730-1(6))* ReferencePoint Pr., Inc.

Moore Niver, Heather. Getting to Know Ruby. 2014. (Code Power: a Teen Programmer's Guide Ser.). (Illus.). 64p. (J). (gr. 5-8). 32.95 *(978-1-4777-7713-8(X)*, Rosen Reference) Rosen Publishing Group, Inc., The.

Morgan, Nick. JavaScript for Kids: A Playful Introduction to Programming. 2014. (ENG., Illus.). 336p. (gr. 5). pap. 34.95 *(978-1-59327-408-5(4))* No Starch Pr., Inc.

Nagle, Jeanne. Getting to Know Alice. 2014. (Code Power: a Teen Programmer's Guide Ser.). (Illus.). 64p. (J). (gr. 5-8). 32.95 *(978-1-4777-7693-3(1)*, Rosen Reference) Rosen Publishing Group, Inc., The.

—Getting to Know Scratch. 2014. (Code Power: a Teen Programmer's Guide Ser.). 64p. (YA). (gr. 5-8). 32.95 *(978-1-4777-7697-1(4))*; pap. 12.95 *(978-1-4777-7699-5(0))* Rosen Publishing Group, Inc., The. (Rosen Reference).

Parks, Peggy J. Computer Animator. 2003. (Exploring Careers Ser.). (ENG., Illus.). 48p. (J). (gr. 4-8). lib. bdg. 27.50 *(978-0-7377-2065-5(4)*, Kidhaven) Cengage Gale.

Passantino, Claire. Itty Bitty Bytes of Space: For the TI 99-4A Computer. (Creative Pastimes Ser.). (J). 6.95 *(978-0-8359-3318-6(0))* Prentice Hall PTR.

Payment, Simone. Getting to Know Python. 2014. (Code Power: a Teen Programmer's Guide Ser.). (Illus.). 64p. (J). (gr. 5-8). pap. 77.70 *(978-1-4777-7720-6(2)*, Rosen Reference) Rosen Publishing Group, Inc., The.

Phillips, Miriam. Willa the Witch Makes Magic: Checking Your Work. 2017. (Computer Science for the Real World Ser.). 8p. (gr. 5-6). pap. 6.20 ***(978-1-5383-5072-0(6)***, Rosen Classroom) Rosen Publishing Group, Inc., The.

Poolos, Jamie. Designing, Building, & Maintaining Web Sites. 2010. (Digital & Information Literacy Ser.). (ENG.). 48p. (YA). pap. 11.75 *(978-1-4488-0594-5(5))*; lib. bdg. 29.25 *(978-1-4358-9424-2(3))* Rosen Publishing Group, Inc., The. (Rosen Reference).

Pratt, Mary K. What Is Computer Coding? 2015. (ENG., Illus.). 32p. (J). (gr. k-2). 26.65 *(978-1-4677-8077-3(4)*, Lerner Pubns.) Lerner Publishing Group.

QEB Let's Start! Computing National Book Stores Edition: Using Instructions. 2006. (J). per. *(978-1-59566-298-9(7))* QEB Publishing Inc.

Rauf, Don. Getting to Know Hackety Hack. 2014. (Code Power: a Teen Programmer's Guide Ser.). (Illus.). 64p. (J). (gr. 5-8). 32.95 *(978-1-4777-7705-3(9)*, Rosen Reference) Rosen Publishing Group, Inc., The.

Reed, Jennifer. Computer Scientist Jean Bartik. 2016. (STEM Trailblazer Bios Ser.). (ENG., Illus.). 32p. (J). (gr. 2-5). 26.65 *(978-1-5124-0789-1(5))* Lerner Publishing Group.

Roberts, Laura. Careers in Gaming. 2017. (ENG.). 80p. (YA). (gr. 5-12). *(978-1-68282-112-1(9))* ReferencePoint Pr., Inc.

Roff, Jason T. & Roff, Kimberly A. Careers in E-Commerce Software Development. 2005. (Library of E-Commerce & Internet Careers). (Illus.). 64p. (YA). (gr. 7-12). lib. bdg. 26.50 *(978-0-8239-3421-8(7))* Rosen Publishing Group, Inc., The.

Roffey, Chris. Building BIG Apps, Level 3. 2013. (ENG., Illus.). 132p. pap. 16.56 *(978-1-107-66687-0(2))* Cambridge Univ. Pr.

—Coding Club Python: Interactive Adventures Level 2. 2016. (ENG.). 106p. spiral bd. 16.56 *(978-1-316-63411-0(6))* Cambridge Univ. Pr.

—Python, Level 2: Next Steps. 2013. (ENG., Illus.). 106p. pap. 16.56 *(978-1-107-62325-5(1))* Cambridge Univ. Pr.

Sabatino, Michael. Understanding Coding with JavaScript. 2017. (Spotlight on Kids Can Code Ser.). 24p. (J). (gr. 8-10). 26.25 ***(978-1-5081-5513-3(5)***, PowerKids Pr.) Rosen Publishing Group, Inc., The.

Sande, Warren & Sande, Carter. Hello World! Computer Programming for Kids & Other Beginners. (ENG., Illus.). 2009. 440p. (J). pap. 34.99 *(978-1-933988-49-8(5)*, 9781933988498) 2nd ed. 2013. 435p. pap. 39.99 *(978-1-61729-092-3(0))* Manning Pubns. Co.

Saujani, Reshma. Girls Who Code: Learn to Code & Change the World. 2017. (Girls Who Code Ser.). (ENG., Illus.). 176p. (J). (gr. 5). 17.99 ***(978-0-425-28753-8(X)***, Viking Books for Young Readers) Penguin Young Readers Group.

Scott, Marc. A Beginner's Guide to Coding. Marston, Mick, illus. 2017. (ENG.). 64p. (J). 14.99 *(978-1-68119-540-7(2)*, 9781681195407, Bloomsbury USA Childrens) Bloomsbury Publishing USA.

Sethi, Maneesh. Game Programming for Teens. 3rd ed. 2008. (Computer Game & Simulation Programming Ser.). (ENG., Illus.). 349p. pap. 29.99 *(978-1-59863-518-8(2))* Course Technology.

Smibert, Angie. All about Coding. 2017. (Cutting-Edge Technology (paperback) Ser.). (ENG., Illus.). 32p. (J). (gr. 4-7). pap. 9.95 ***(978-1-63517-067-2(2)***, Focus Readers) North Star Editions.

Spilsbury, Richard. I'm Good with Computers... what Job Can I Get? 2012. (What's a Good Job for Me? Ser.). (ENG., Illus.). 32p. (J). (gr. 5-6). *(978-1-4488-6630-4(8)*, PowerKids Pr.) Rosen Publishing Group, Inc., The.

Stamo, Nancy. HTML 2 Student Activity Book. Matthews, Douglas L., ed. 2003. (Illus.). stu. ed., per., wbk. ed. *(978-1-931680-47-9(7)*, Expert Systems for Teachers) Teaching Point, Inc.

Sterling Children's, Sterling. C++ for Kids. 2016. (Code Babies Ser.). (ENG., Illus.). 26p. (J). (gr. -1). bds. 9.95 *(978-1-4549-2159-2(5))* Sterling Publishing Co., Inc.

—CSS for Babies. 2016. (Code Babies Ser.). (ENG., Illus.). 16p. (J). (gr. -1). bds. 6.95 *(978-1-4549-2156-1(0))* Sterling Publishing Co., Inc.

—HTML for Babies. 2016. (Code Babies Ser.). (ENG., Illus.). 16p. (J). (gr. -1). bds. 6.95 *(978-1-4549-2155-4(2))* Sterling Publishing Co., Inc.

—Javascript for Babies. 2016. (Code Babies Ser.). (ENG., Illus.). 16p. (J). (gr. -1). bds. 6.95 *(978-1-4549-2157-8(9))* Sterling Publishing Co., Inc.

—Web Colors. 2016. (Code Babies Ser.). (ENG., Illus.). 12p. (J). (gr. -1). bds. 9.95 *(978-1-4549-2158-5(7))* Sterling Publishing Co., Inc.

Strom, Chris. 3D Game Programming for Kids: Create Interactive Worlds with JavaScript. 2013. (ENG., Illus.). 308p. pap. 36.00 *(978-1-937785-44-4(0)*, 9781937785444, Pragmatic Bookshelf, The) Pragmatic Programmers, LLC, The.

Sweigart, Al. Scratch Programming Playground: Learn to Program by Making Cool Games. 2016. (ENG., Illus.). 288p. (J). (gr. 2). pap. 24.95 *(978-1-59327-762-8(8))* No Starch Pr., Inc.

Wainewright, Max. How to Code: A Step-By-Step Guide to Computer Coding. 2016. (ENG., Illus.). 128p. (J). (gr. 1-6). spiral bd. 14.95 *(978-1-4549-2177-6(3))* Sterling Publishing Co., Inc.

—I'm a JavaScript Games Maker: Advanced Coding. 2017. 32p. (J). ***(978-0-7787-3518-2(4))*** Crabtree Publishing Co.

—I'm a JavaScript Games Maker: The Basics. 2017. 32p. (J). ***(978-0-7787-3517-5(6))*** Crabtree Publishing Co.

—I'm a Python Programmer. 2017. 32p. (J). ***(978-0-7787-3519-9(2))*** Crabtree Publishing Co.

—I'm a Scratch Coder. 2017. 32p. (J). ***(978-0-7787-3515-1(X))*** Crabtree Publishing Co.

Wallmark, Laurie. Ada Byron Lovelace & the Thinking Machine. Chu, April, illus. 2015. (ENG.). 40p. (J). (gr. k). 17.99 *(978-1-939547-20-0(2))* Creston Bks.

Woodcock, Jon. Computer Coding Projects in Scratch: A Step-By-Step Visual Guide. 2016. lib. bdg. 33.05 *(978-0-606-38714-9(5))* Turtleback Bks.

COMPUTER SOFTWARE

see also names of specific computer software, e.g. Lotus 1-2-3 (Computer Program)

Brocklehurst, R. An Introduction to Powerpoint. 2004. (Computer Guides). (ENG.). 48p. (J). pap. 7.95 *(978-0-7945-0345-1(4))* EDC Publishing.

Brown, Jonatha A. Bill Gates. 2004. (Gente Que Hay Que Conocer Ser.). (SPA & ENG., Illus.). 24p. (gr. 1-4). pap. 8.15 *(978-0-8368-4359-0(2)*, Weekly Reader Leveled Readers) Stevens, Gareth Publishing LLLP.

—Bill Gates. Acosta, Tatiana & Gutierrez, Guillermo, trs. 2004. (Gente Que Hay Que Conocer Ser.). (SPA., Illus.). 24p. (gr. 1-4). lib. bdg. 22.00 *(978-0-8368-4352-1(5)*, Weekly Reader Leveled Readers) Stevens, Gareth Publishing LLLP.

Core HLE Tools for Pocket PC. 2004. (YA). cd-rom *(978-0-9762083-4-1(2))* GoKnow Learning.

Di Piazza, Domenica. NASA Computer Scientist Margaret Hamilton. 2017. (STEM Trailblazer Bios Ser.). (ENG.). 32p. (J). (gr. 2-5). 26.65 ***(978-1-5124-3450-7(7))*** Lerner Publishing Group.

Diction 2004. 2004. (J). cd-rom *(978-0-9764218-0-1(1))* Dawasoft.

Flath, Camden. Tomorrow's Enterprising Scientists: Computer Software Designers & Specialists. 2010. (New Careers for the 21st Century Ser.). 64p. (YA). (gr. 7-18). pap. 9.95 *(978-1-4222-2043-6(5))*; lib. bdg. 22.95 *(978-1-4222-1822-8(8))* Mason Crest.

Freedman, Jeri. Software Development. 2015. (J). lib. bdg. *(978-1-62713-399-9(2))* Musa Publishing.

Gardner, Jane P. Computer Science, Vol. 11. Lewin, Russ, ed. 2015. (Science 24/7 Ser.). (Illus.). 48p. (J). (gr. 5). lib. bdg. 20.95 *(978-1-4222-3407-5(X))* Mason Crest.

C
D

Gifford, Clive. Amazing Applications & Perfect Programs. 2015. (ENG., Illus.). 32p. (J). *(978-0-7787-1507-8(8))* Crabtree Publishing Co.

Harmon, Daniel E. Powering up a Career in Software Development & Programming. 2015. (Preparing for Tomorrow's Careers Ser.). (ENG., Illus.). 80p. (J). (gr. 7-8). 34.25 *(978-1-4994-6095-7(3),* Rosen Young Adult) Rosen Publishing Group, Inc., The.

Harris, Ashley Rae. Microsoft: The Company & Its Founders, 1 vol. 2012. (Technology Pioneers Set 2 Ser.). (ENG.). 112p. (J). (gr. 6-12). lib. bdg. 35.64 *(978-1-61783-333-5(9),* Essential Library) ABDO Publishing Co.

Image Pasters. 2004. (J). cd-rom *(978-0-9764218-1-8(X))* Dawasoft.

Jakubiak, David J. A Smart Kid's Guide to Internet Privacy. (J). 2010. pap. 8.25 *(978-1-4358-3356-2(2))* 2009. (Illus.). 24p. (gr. 2-6). lib. bdg. 22.60 *(978-1-4042-8118-9(5))* Rosen Publishing Group, Inc., The. (PowerKids Pr.).

Kuhn, Gerald. Cadkey V21 Cookbook. 2003. (Illus.). 197p. spiral bd. *(978-0-9740796-2-2(6))* Technology Education Concepts Inc.

Lauridsen, Craig. Stop Motion Handbook: Using GarageBand & IStopMotion. 2011. (ENG., Illus.). 192p. *(978-0-473-18921-1(6))* Acumen.

Lesinski, Jeanne M. Bill Gates. 2007. (Illus.). 112p. (J). (gr. 6-9). per. 7.95 *(978-0-8225-7027-1(0),* Lerner Pubns.) Lerner Publishing Group.

—Bill Gates: Entrepreneur & Philanthropist. 2008. (Lifeline Biographies Ser.). 112p. (YA). (gr. 7-12). lib. bdg. 33.26 *(978-1-58013-570-2(6))* Lerner Publishing Group.

Makerspaces. 2014. (Makerspaces Ser.). 64p. (YA). (gr. 6-12). 197.70 *(978-1-4777-7799-2(7))* Rosen Publishing Group, Inc., The.

Mara, Wil. Software Development: Science, Technology, Engineering. 2016. (Calling All Innovators: a Career for You Ser.). (ENG., Illus.). 64p. (J). lib. bdg. 32.00 *(978-0-531-23003-9(1),* Children's Pr.) Scholastic Library Publishing.

McGinty, Alice B. Software Designer. 2009. (Coolcareers. com Ser.). 48p. (gr. 5-8). 53.00 *(978-1-61511-984-4(1),* Rosen Reference) Rosen Publishing Group, Inc., The.

McKinney, Devon. A Day at Work with a Software Developer, 01 vols., 1. 2016. (Super STEM Careers Ser.). (ENG., Illus.). 24p. (J). pap. 8.25 *(978-1-5081-4414-4(1),* PowerKids Pr.) Rosen Publishing Group, Inc., The.

Mihaly, Christy. All about Apps. 2017. (Cutting-Edge Technology (hardcover) Ser.). (ENG., Illus.). 32p. (J). (gr. 4-7). lib. bdg. 28.50 ***(978-1-63517-010-8(9)***, Focus Readers) North Star Editions.

Roff, Jason T. Careers in E-Commerce: Software Development. 2009. (Library of E-Commerce & Internet Careers Ser.). 64p. (gr. 5-5). 58.50 *(978-1-60853-580-4(0))* Rosen Publishing Group, Inc., The.

Small, Cathleen. What Are Hardware & Software? 2017. (J). ***(978-1-5383-0035-0(4))*** Rosen Publishing Group, Inc., The.

Stagecast Creator 2.0: German Education Edition. 2004. (GER.). (YA). cd-rom 99.95 *(978-1-929721-15-3(3))* Stagecast Software, Inc.

Stagecast Creator 2.0 German Standard Edition. 2004. (GER.). (YA). cd-rom 49.95 *(978-1-929721-14-6(5))* Stagecast Software, Inc.

StudioLine Web Edition - English. 2004. cd-rom 279.00 *(978-1-885936-80-6(X))* H&M Systems Software, Inc.

StudioLine Web Edition - French. 2004. cd-rom 279.00 *(978-1-885936-82-0(6))* H&M Systems Software, Inc.

StudioLine Web Edition - German. 2004. cd-rom 279.00 *(978-1-885936-81-3(8))* H&M Systems Software, Inc.

StudioLine Web Edition - Italian. 2004. cd-rom 279.00 *(978-1-885936-83-7(4))* H&M Systems Software, Inc.

Truesdell, Ann. Present It! Creating & Sharing a Slide Show. 2014. (Explorer Junior Library: Information Explorer Junior Ser.). (ENG., Illus.). 24p. (J). (gr. 1-4). 28.50 *(978-1-63137-787-7(6),* 205391) Cherry Lake Publishing.

Van Lent, Colleen. More Web Design with HTML5. 2015. (21st Century Skills Innovation Library: Makers As Innovators Ser.). (ENG., Illus.). 32p. (J). (gr. 4-8). lib. bdg. 29.93 *(978-1-63188-868-7(4),* 206052) Cherry Lake Publishing.

Vargas, Daraciela. HyperStudio: Para Maestros y Estudiantes: 20 Ejercicios de Practica. 2003. ring bd. 14.99 *(978-0-9702021-8-5(0))* Conexion Educativa.

Winquist, Gloria & McCarthy, Matt. Coding iPhone Apps for Kids: A Playful Introduction to Swift. 2017. (ENG., Illus.). 336p. (J). (gr. 5). pap. 29.95 *(978-1-59327-756-7(3))* No Starch Pr., Inc.

Worldmanac 2004. 2004. (J). cd-rom *(978-0-9764218-2-5(8))* Dawasoft.

Zocchi, Judy. Curtain Up: Application Software. 2006. (Click & Squeak Ser.). (Illus.). 32p. (J). 20.65 *(978-1-891997-63-1(7))* Dingles & Co.

COMPUTER SOUND PROCESSING

Culp, Jennifer. Using Computer Science in Digital Music Careers. 2017. (Coding Your Passion Ser.). 80p. (gr. 12-12). 35.75 ***(978-1-5081-7517-9(9)***, Rosen Young Adult) Rosen Publishing Group, Inc., The.

COMPUTERS

see also Calculators; Cyberspace; Electronic Data Processing; Information Storage and Retrieval Systems

Abramovitz, Melissa. Cybersecurity Analyst. 2017. (ENG.). 64p. (YA). (gr. 5-12). ***(978-1-68282-182-4(X))*** ReferencePoint Pr., Inc.

Abramovitz, Melissa. How Do Computers Talk to One Another? 2015. (ENG., Illus.). 32p. (J). (gr. k-2). 26.65 *(978-1-4677-8075-9(8))* Lerner Publishing Group.

Allen, Mitchell. Our Class Lizard: Breaking down the Problem. 2017. (Computer Science for the Real World Ser.). 12p. (gr. 6-7). pap. 7.05 ***(978-1-5383-5140-6(4)***, Rosen Classroom) Rosen Publishing Group, Inc., The.

Aloian, Sam. How a Computer Is Made. 2016. (Engineering Our World Ser.). (ENG.). 24p. (J). (gr. 2-3). pap. 8.15 *(978-1-4824-3927-4(1))* Stevens, Gareth Publishing LLLP.

Ashley, Susan. I Can Use a Computer. 2004. (I Can Do It! Ser.). (Illus.). 24p. (gr. k-3). pap. 8.15 *(978-0-8368-4332-3(0))*; lib. bdg. 21.00 *(978-0-8368-4325-5(8))* Stevens, Gareth Publishing LLLP. (Weekly Reader Leveled Readers).

Bailey. Computer Science Tea Man. (J). (gr. 10-12). 42.00 *(978-0-669-95256-8(7))* Houghton Mifflin Harcourt School Pubs.

Bailey, Edward R. Computer Science: A Structure. (J). (gr. 10-12). 37.75 *(978-0-669-95104-2(8))* Houghton Mifflin Harcourt School Pubs.

Baum, L. Frank. Frank Baum: Oz Books. 2003. (J). cd-rom 19.00 *(978-0-931968-41-9(0))* Samizdat Express.

Baxter, Roberta. Computers. 2005. (Kidhaven Science Library). (Illus.). 48p. (J). (gr. 4-8). 26.20 *(978-0-7377-3053-1(6),* Greenhaven Pr., Inc.) Cengage Gale.

Beth, Georgia. On the Job: Podcast Producer: Multiplication (Grade 4) 2017. (Mathematics Readers Ser.). (Illus.). 32p. (gr. 4-4). pap. 9.99 ***(978-1-4258-5549-9(0))*** Teacher Created Materials, Inc.

Bitetto, Marco A. V. Journal of Amateur Computing: Spring/Summer 2003 Issue. Bitetto, Marco A. V., ed. l.t. ed. 2003. (Illus.). 120p. (YA). (gr. 9-12). pap. 22.00 *(978-1-58578-482-0(6))* Institute of Cybernetics Research, Inc.

Bodden, Valerie. Computers. 2008. (J). pap. 9.95 *(978-0-89812-529-0(4),* Creative Paperbacks); (Illus.). 24p. lib. bdg. 24.25 *(978-1-58341-556-6(4),* Creative Education) Creative Co., The.

Boritzke, Lauren. Working in Technology. 2018. (ENG.). 32p. (gr. 3-6). ***(978-1-63235-450-1(0)***, 12-Story Library) Pr. Room Editions LLC.

Burstein, John. Usar Computadoras: Una máquina con ratón. 2006. (Monstruos Matematicos Ser.). (ENG & SPA., Illus.). 24p. (J). (gr. k-4). lib. bdg. 21.00 *(978-0-8368-6679-7(7),* Weekly Reader Leveled Readers) Stevens, Gareth Publishing LLLP.

—Using Computers: Machine with a Mouse. Destiny Images Staff, illus. 2003. (Math Monsters Ser.). 24p. (J). (gr. k-4). lib. bdg. 21.00 *(978-0-8368-3817-6(3),* Weekly Reader Leveled Readers) Stevens, Gareth Publishing LLLP.

Carmichael, L. E. What Are Programs & Apps? 2015. (ENG., Illus.). 32p. (J). (gr. k-2). 26.65 *(978-1-4677-8076-6(6))* Lerner Publishing Group.

Chan, David. Meeting the Computer - One Byte at a Time (Chinese Edition) 2004. (CHI.). 296p. per. 25.00 *(978-0-9754302-1-7(1))* Chan, David.

Chandler, Fiona, et al. The Usborne First Encyclopedia of History. Hancock, David, illus. 2005. 64p. (J). *(978-0-439-78717-8(3))* Scholastic, Inc.

Coleman, Miriam. Share It: Using Digital Tools & Media. 2012. (Core Skills Ser.). (ENG., Illus.). 32p. (J). (gr. 3-6). 25.25 *(978-1-4488-7454-5(8),* PowerKids Pr.) Rosen Publishing Group, Inc., The.

Collier, Bruce & Maclachlan, James. Charles Babbage & the Engines of Perfection. 2006. (Illus.). 123p. reprint ed. pap. 12.00 *(978-1-4223-5040-9(1))* DIANE Publishing Co.

The Computer: KinderFacts Individual Title Six-Packs. (Kinderstarters Ser.). 8p. (gr. -1-1). 21.00 *(978-0-7635-8744-4(3))* Rigby Education.

Computer & You: Level Q, 6 vols. (Wonder Worldtm Ser.). 48p. 39.95 *(978-0-7802-3179-5(1))* Wright Group/McGraw-Hill.

Computer Pioneers. 2016. (Computer Pioneers Ser.). 32p. (gr. 5-4). 157.50 *(978-1-4994-1887-3(6))*; pap. 70.50 *(978-1-4994-2471-3(X))* Rosen Publishing Group, Inc., The. (PowerKids Pr.).

Computing: From the Abacus to the Ipad. 2011. (Computing & Connecting in the 21st Century Ser.). (ENG.). 168p. (YA). (gr. 10-12). 70.50 *(978-1-61530-772-2(9))* Rosen Publishing Group, Inc., The.

Conway, Sommer. Cultures in Our Class: Looking at Data. 2017. (Computer Science for the Real World Ser.). 16p. (gr. 7-8). pap. 7.95 ***(978-1-5383-5192-5(7)***, Rosen Classroom) Rosen Publishing Group, Inc., The.

—Our Class Clothing Drive: Sharing & Reusing. 2017. (Computer Science for the Real World Ser.). 12p. (gr. 6-7). pap. 7.05 ***(978-1-5383-5172-7(2)***, Rosen Classroom) Rosen Publishing Group, Inc., The.

Coolcareers.com, 8 bks. Incl. Hardware Engineer. Donelly, Karen. lib. bdg. 29.25 *(978-0-8239-3118-7(8),* CCHAEN); Multimedia & New Media Developer. Mazor, Barry. lib. bdg. 29.25 *(978-0-8239-3102-6(1),* CCMEDE); Software Designer. McGinty, Alice B. lib. bdg. 23.95 *(978-0-8239-3149-1(8),* CCSODE); Web Entrepreneur. Oleksy, Walter. lib. bdg. 29.25 *(978-0-8239-3103-3(X),* CCWEEN); Webmaster. Brown, Marty. lib. bdg. 23.95 *(978-0-8239-3111-8(0),* CCWEMA); 48p. (YA). (gr. 5-8). 2000. (Illus.). Set lib. bdg. 191.60 o.p. *(978-0-8239-9089-4(3),* CCCOCA, Rosen Reference) Rosen Publishing Group, Inc., The.

Cowan, Carla Romaine. E-Commerce Careers in Multimedia. 2005. (Library of e-Commerce & Internet Careers Ser.). (Illus.). 64p. (YA). (gr. 7-12). lib. bdg. 31.95 *(978-0-8239-3427-0(6))* Rosen Publishing Group, Inc., The.

Cunningham, Anne C., ed. Privacy & Security in the Digital Age. 2017. (Current Controversies Ser.). 224p. (J). (gr. 10-12). pap. 32.00 ***(978-1-5345-0032-7(4))***; lib. bdg. 46.40 ***(978-1-5345-0021-1(9))*** Greenhaven Publishing LLC. (Greenhaven Publishing).

Cunningham, Kevin. Computers. 2008. (21st Century Skills Library: Global Products Ser.). (ENG., Illus.). 32p. (gr. 4-8). 28.50 *(978-1-60279-251-7(8),* 200118) Cherry Lake Publishing.

Curatola Knowles, Carmela N. Piano & Laylee Go Online. 2011. (J). *(978-1-56484-292-3(4))* International Society for Technology in Education.

—Piano & Laylee Go Online. Lewellen, Emily, illus. 2011. (J). pap. *(978-1-56484-277-0(0))* International Society for Technology in Education.

Curley, Robert, ed. Computing: From the Abacus to the IPad. 2011. (Computing & Connecting in the 21st Century Ser.). (ENG.). 168p. (YA). (gr. 10-12). lib. bdg. 35.25 *(978-1-61530-660-2(9))* Rosen Publishing Group, Inc., The.

Dalton, James. The Computer Classroom. (Illus.). (J). (gr. 5-6). pap. *(978-1-876973-00-1(5))* Wizard Bks.

De Angelis, Gina & Bianco, David J. Computers: Processing the Data. 2005. (Innovators Ser.: Vol. 13). (Illus.). 144p. (J). (gr. 5-18). lib. bdg. 24.95 *(978-1-881508-87-8(0))* Oliver Pr., Inc.

De la Bédoyère, Guy & De la Bédoyère, Camilla. The First Computers. 2005. (Milestones in Modern Science Ser.). (Illus.). 48p. (gr. 6-12). lib. bdg. 31.00 *(978-0-8368-5854-9(9),* Gareth Stevens Secondary Library) Stevens, Gareth Publishing LLLP.

Dixon, Dale. Helping at the Library: Step by Step. 2017. (Computer Science for the Real World Ser.). 12p. (gr. 6-7). pap. 7.05 ***(978-1-5383-5144-4(7)***, Rosen Classroom) Rosen Publishing Group, Inc., The.

—Let's Track the Storm: What Will Happen? 2017. (Computer Science for the Real World Ser.). 8p. (gr. 5-6). pap. 6.20 ***(978-1-5383-5059-1(9)***, Rosen Classroom) Rosen Publishing Group, Inc., The.

Dorling Kindersley Publishing Staff. My Busy Computer Book. 2016. (Skills for Starting School Ser.). (ENG., Illus.). 10p. (J). (-k). bds. 13.99 *(978-1-4654-5129-3(3),* DK Children) Dorling Kindersley Publishing, Inc.

Dyan, Penelope. The Squeaky Wheel Gets to Greece — -A Kid's Guide to Athens, Greece. Weigand, John D., photos by. 2011. (Illus.). 36p. pap. 11.95 *(978-1-935630-58-6(X))* Bellissima Publishing, LLC.

Dymond, Kenneth. A Guide to the CMMI: Interpreting the Capability Maturity Model Integration. Dymond, Detta, ed. Faassen, Louis, illus. 2004. spiral bd. 20.00 *(978-0-9646008-4-3(6))* Process Transition International, Inc.

Edwards, Susan Denise. Computer Science Student Activity Book. 2003. (Illus.). stu. ed., per., wbk. ed. *(978-1-931680-28-8(0),* Expert Systems for Teachers) Teaching Point, Inc.

Endsley, Kezia, et al. Inventors of Computer Technology. 2015. 144p. (J). lib. bdg. *(978-1-5026-0654-9(2))* Musa Publishing.

Ennett, Jonathan. Clever Computers Turquoise Band. 2016. (Cambridge Reading Adventures Ser.). (ENG.). 24p. pap. 7.19 *(978-1-316-50331-7(3))* Cambridge Univ. Pr.

Espejo, Roman. Smartphones. 2013. (Opposing Viewpoints Ser.). (ENG., Illus.). 224p. (gr. 10-12). pap. 33.80 *(978-0-7377-6343-0(4))*; lib. bdg. 48.80 *(978-0-7377-6342-3(6))* Cengage Gale. (Greenhaven Pr., Inc.).

Faust, Daniel R. Building Computers: Computer Engineers, 01 vols., 1. 2016. (Engineers Rule Ser.). (ENG., Illus.). 32p. (J). pap. 11.75 *(978-1-5081-4536-3(9),* PowerKids Pr.) Rosen Publishing Group, Inc., The.

Festante, Dom. Computer Applications Student Activity Book. Matthews, Douglas L., ed. 2004. (Illus.). stu. ed., per., act. bk. ed. *(978-1-931680-98-1(1),* Expert Systems for Teachers) Teaching Point, Inc.

First Grade Technology: 32 lessons every First Grader can accomplish on a Computer. 2006. 18.99 net. *(978-0-9787800-1-2(9))* Structured Learning.

Fitzpatrick, Anne. The Computer. 2003. 24p. (J). lib. bdg. 21.35 *(978-1-58340-318-1(3))* Black Rabbit Bks.

Flores, Vanessa. Our Class Business: Working at the Same Time. 2017. (Computer Science for the Real World Ser.). 16p. (gr. 7-8). pap. 7.95 ***(978-1-5383-5247-2(8)***, Rosen Classroom) Rosen Publishing Group, Inc., The.

Freedman, Jeri. Intellectual Property. (Cyber Citizenship & Cyber Safety Ser.). 48p. (gr. 5-5). 2009. 53.00 *(978-1-61512-104-5(8),* Rosen Reference) 2008. (Illus.). (YA). lib. bdg. 29.25 *(978-1-4042-1348-7(1))* Rosen Publishing Group, Inc., The.

—Software Development. 2015. (High-Tech Jobs Ser.). (ENG., Illus.). 96p. (J). (gr. 7-7). 42.79 *(978-1-5026-0105-6(2))* Cavendish Square Publishing.

Gaming: From Atari to Xbox. 2011. (Computing & Connecting in the 21st Century Ser.). (ENG.). 144p. (YA). (gr. 10-12). 70.50 *(978-1-61530-780-7(X))* Rosen Publishing Group, Inc., The.

Gardner, Jane P. Computer Science, Vol. 11. Lewin, Russ, ed. 2015. (Science 24/7 Ser.). (Illus.). 48p. (J). (gr. 5). lib. bdg. 20.95 *(978-1-4222-3407-5(X))* Mason Crest.

Gerber, Larry. Cloud-Based Computing. 2013. (Digital & Information Literacy Ser.). 48p. (J). (gr. 5-8). 29.25 *(978-1-4488-9516-8(2))* Rosen Publishing Group, Inc., The.

Gifford, Clive. Awesome Algorithms & Creative Coding. 2015. (ENG., Illus.). 32p. (J). *(978-0-7787-1508-5(6))* Crabtree Publishing Co.

—Computer Networks. 2015. (ENG., Illus.). 32p. (J). *(978-0-7787-1509-2(4))* Crabtree Publishing Co.

—Computing & Coding in the Real World. 2017. 32p. (J). ***(978-0-7787-3621-9(0))*** Crabtree Publishing Co.

Gifford, Clive. The Science of Computers. 2015. (ENG., Illus.). 32p. (J). *(978-0-7787-1510-8(8))* Crabtree Publishing Co.

Gosman, Gillian. Express It: Sharing Your Media Online, 1 vol. 2015. (ENG.). 32p. (J). lib. bdg. 26.25 *(978-1-4777-7393-2(2),* PowerKids Pr.) Rosen Publishing Group, Inc., The.

Greathead, Helen. My Smartphone & Other Digital Accessories. 2016. (Illus.). 32p. (J). *(978-0-7787-2715-6(7))* Crabtree Publishing Co.

Gregoire, Maryellen. Computers. 2011. (Wonder Readers Early Level Ser.). (ENG.). (gr. -1-1). 16p. pap. 35.94 *(978-1-4296-8079-0(2))*; 32p. pap. 5.99 *(978-1-4296-7833-9(X))* Capstone Press of Coughlan Cos. (Wonder Readers).

Groves, Marsha. Inventing the Computer. rev. ed. 2007. (Breakthrough Inventions Ser.). (ENG., Illus.). 32p. (J). (gr. 4-7). pap. *(978-0-7787-2838-2(2))* Crabtree Publishing Co.

Haddon, Jean. Words: A Computer Lesson. Vargo, Sharon Hawkins, illus. 2003. (Silly Millies Ser.). 32p. (J). (gr. -1-1). pap. 4.99 *(978-0-7613-1797-5(X))*; lib. bdg. 17.90 *(978-0-7613-2870-4(X))* Lerner Publishing Group. (Millbrook Pr.).

Hagler, Gina. ADA Lovelace, 01 vols., 1. 2016. (Tech Pioneers Ser.). (ENG.). 112p. (J). 35.60 *(978-1-4994-6282-1(4),* Rosen Young Adult) Rosen Publishing Group, Inc., The.

Handheld Learning Environment (HLE) for Pocket PC. 2004. (YA). cd-rom *(978-0-9762083-1-0(8))* GoKnow Learning.

Harris, Patricia. Coding for Digital Security. 2017. (Spotlight on Kids Can Code Ser.). 24p. (J). (gr. 8-10). 26.25 ***(978-1-5081-5516-4(X)***, PowerKids Pr.) Rosen Publishing Group, Inc., The.

—What Is User Interface Design? 2017. (Spotlight on Kids Can Code Ser.). 24p. (gr. 8-10). pap. 11.75 ***(978-1-5081-5528-7(3)***, PowerKids Pr.) Rosen Publishing Group, Inc., The.

Henderson, Harry. Computer Viruses. 2003. (Lucent Library of Science & Technology Ser.). (ENG., Illus.). 128p. (YA). (gr. 7-10). lib. bdg. 30.85 *(978-1-59018-102-7(6),* Lucent Bks.) Cengage Gale.

—Encyclopedia of Computer Science & Technology. 2nd rev. ed. 2008. (Science Encyclopedia Ser.). (Illus.). 544p. (C). (gr. 9). 87.50 *(978-0-8160-6382-6(6))* Facts On File, Inc.

Hensley, Tana. Communities Work Together: Working As a Team. 2017. (Computer Science for the Real World Ser.). 16p. (gr. 7-8). pap. 7.95 ***(978-1-5383-5236-6(2)***, Rosen Classroom) Rosen Publishing Group, Inc., The.

Hicks, Keli L. I Use a Mouse. 2011. (ENG., Illus.). 24p. (gr. 1-2). pap. 8.95 *(978-1-61741-944-7(3))* Rourke Educational Media.

Hoare, Stephen. Computer World. (J). *(978-0-528-87857-2(3))* Checkerboard Pr., Inc.

How Do I... 2005. (YA). per. 24.95 *(978-0-9770372-0-9(7))* Brown, Samuel E.

Hubbard, Ben. How Computers Work. 2017. (Our Digital Planet Ser.). (ENG., Illus.). 24p. (gr. k-2). lib. bdg. 23.32 *(978-1-4846-3598-8(1))* Heinemann-Raintree.

Hughes, Lisa. Activators Computers Unlimited. (Illus.). 126p. (J). pap. 8.99 *(978-0-340-71520-8(0))* Hodder & Stoughton GBR. Dist: Trafalgar Square Publishing.

Informatik: Grundbegriffe der Informatik. (Duden-Schuelerduden Ser.). (GER., Illus.). 560p. (YA). *(978-3-411-04483-2(7))* Bibliographisches Institut & F. A. Brockhaus AG DEU. Dist: International Bk. Import Service, Inc.

Jackson, Cari. Revolution in Computers. 2009. (It Works! Ser.). 32p. (gr. 3). 28.50 *(978-0-7614-4375-9(4))* Marshall Cavendish Corp.

Jortberg, Charles A. The Big Machines: Kids & Computers. 2004. (Illus.). 39p. (J). (gr. k-4). reprint ed. 14.00 *(978-0-7567-8456-0(5))* DIANE Publishing Co.

Jouvet. Anne et L'Ordinateur. (FRE.). (J). 8.99 *(978-0-8219-1453-3(7),* 40332) EMC/Paradigm Publishing.

Kamberg, Mary-Lane. Becoming a Systems Administrator. 2017. (Tech Track: Building Your Career in IT Ser.). 80p. (J). (gr. 12-12). 35.75 ***(978-1-5081-7556-8(X)***, Rosen Young Adult) Rosen Publishing Group, Inc., The.

Kauffman, Dorothy. The Computer Age. 2005. (Oxford Picture Dictionary for the Content Areas Ser.). (ENG., Illus.). 22p. pap. 7.56 *(978-0-19-430960-8(6))* Oxford Univ. Pr., Inc.

Keranen, Rachel. Inventions in Computing: From the Abacus to Apple Computers. 2016. (Art & Invention Ser.). 112p. (J). 42.79 *(978-1-5026-2301-0(3))* Cavendish Square Publishing.

Koellhoffer, Tara, ed. Computers & Technology. 2006. (Science News for Kids Ser.). (Illus.). 144p. (gr. 4-6). lib. bdg. 30.00 *(978-0-7910-9120-3(1),* Chelsea Clubhouse) Facts On File, Inc.

Koontz, Robin. Computer Mouse. 2014. (ENG.). 24p. (gr. k-3). 28.50 *(978-1-62717-641-5(1))* Rourke Educational Media.

Kralovansky, Susan. What Would You Do with a Database?, 1 vol. 2013. (Library Resources Ser.). (ENG.). 32p. (J). (gr. k-4). lib. bdg. 27.07 *(978-1-61783-603-9(6),* Super SandCastle) ABDO Publishing Co.

Labrecque, Ellen. Ada Lovelace & Computer Algorithms. 2017. (21st Century Junior Library: Women Innovators Ser.). (ENG., Illus.). 24p. (J). (gr. 2-5). lib. bdg. 27.07 *(978-1-63472-177-6(2),* 209280) Cherry Lake Publishing.

Lesinski, Jeanne M. Bill Gates. (Biography Ser.). (Illus.). 112p. (gr. 6-12). 2005. lib. bdg. 27.93 *(978-0-8225-4949-9(2))* 2003. (J). pap. 7.95 *(978-0-8225-9689-9(X))* Lerner Publishing Group.

Lohr, Steve. Digital Revolutionaries: The Men & Women Who Brought Computing to Life. 2009. (New York Times Ser.). (ENG., Illus.). 176p. (YA). (gr. 5-9). pap. 16.99 *(978-1-59643-532-2(1),* 9781596435322) Roaring Brook Pr.

Lyons, Heather & Tweedale, Elizabeth. A World of Programming. Westgate, Alex, illus. 2016. (Kids Get Coding Ser.). (ENG.). 24p. (J). (gr. 1-4). 26.65 *(978-1-5124-1362-5(3))* Lerner Publishing Group.

Machajewski, Sarah. What Are Computers? 2017. (J). ***(978-1-5383-0034-3(6))*** Rosen Publishing Group, Inc., The.

Marsh, Carole. Let's Discover Georgia! 2004. (Georgia Experience! Ser.). (J). (gr. 2-8). cd-rom 14.95 *(978-0-7933-9488-3(0))* Gallopade International.

—Let's Discover Ohio! 2004. (Ohio Experience! Ser.). (J). (gr. 2-8). cd-rom 14.95 *(978-0-7933-9493-7(7))* Gallopade International.

Marsico, Katie. Working at a Computer Store. 2009. (21st Century Junior Library: Careers Ser.). (ENG.). 24p. (gr. 2-5). lib. bdg. 25.64 *(978-1-60279-513-6(4),* 200277) Cherry Lake Publishing.

Mattern, Joanne. The Computer: Passport to the Digital Age. (Technology That Changed the World Ser.). 24p. 2009. (gr. 2-3). 42.50 *(978-1-60853-275-9(5))* 2003. (Illus.). (J). lib. bdg. 22.60 *(978-0-8239-6492-5(2))* Rosen Publishing Group, Inc., The. (PowerKids Pr.).

Matthas, Seth. At the Hair Salon: Over & over Again. 2017. (Computer Science for the Real World Ser.). 12p. (gr. 6-7). pap. 7.05 ***(978-1-5383-5168-0(4)***, Rosen Classroom) Rosen Publishing Group, Inc., The.

McAlpine, Margaret. Working with Computers. 2004. (My Future Career Ser.). (Illus.). 64p. (gr. 3-7). lib. bdg. 27.00 *(978-0-8368-4242-5(1),* Gareth Stevens Learning Library) Stevens, Gareth Publishing LLLP.

McCallum, Rory. Why Do Things Fall? If... Then. 2017. (Computer Science for the Real World Ser.). 12p. (gr. 6-7). pap. 7.05 ***(978-1-5383-5180-2(3)***, Rosen Classroom) Rosen Publishing Group, Inc., The.

McClure, Leigh. Community Cultures: Looking at Data. 2017. (Computer Science for the Real World Ser.). 16p. (gr. 7-8). pap. 7.95 ***(978-1-5383-5194-9(3)***, Rosen Classroom) Rosen Publishing Group, Inc., The.

McDougal, Anna. Our Ant Farm: Working As a Team. 2017. (Computer Science for the Real World Ser.). 12p. (gr. 6-7). pap. 7.05 ***(978-1-5383-5154-3(4)***, Rosen Classroom) Rosen Publishing Group, Inc., The.

Miller, Deborah J. Careers with an Internet Service Provider. 2005. (Library of e-Commerce & Internet Careers Ser.). (Illus.). 64p. (J). (gr. 7-12). lib. bdg. 31.95 *(978-0-8239-3425-6(X))* Rosen Publishing Group, Inc., The.

Miller, Shannon. Keep Your Passwords Secret. 2013. (Internet DOs & DON'ts Ser.). (Illus.). 24p. (J). (gr. k-2). 22.60 *(978-1-4777-1537-6(1))*; (ENG., pap. 8.25

(978-1-4777-1562-8(2)); pap. 49.50 (978-1-4777-1563-5(0)) Rosen Publishing Group, Inc., The. (PowerKids Pr.).
Mooney, Carla. Careers in Computer Science. 2017. (ENG.). 80p. (YA). (gr. 5-12). **(978-1-68282-194-7(3))** ReferencePoint Pr., Inc.
—Using Computer Science in Fintech Careers. 2017. (Coding Your Passion Ser.). 80p. (J). (gr. 12-12). 35.75 **(978-1-5081-7513-1(6)**, Rosen Young Adult) Rosen Publishing Group, Inc., The.
Moore, Philip. How Can You Use A Computer? 2014. (Little Books of Answers: Level d Ser.). (Illus.). 16p. (gr. k-2). pap. 7.95 (978-1-927136-32-4(6)) Three Crows Media NZL. Dist: RiverStream Publishing.
Morretta, Alison. How to Buy & Share Files Safely Online. 2015. (J). lib. bdg. (978-1-62713-543-6(X)); (ENG.). 48p. (gr. 5-5). lib. bdg. 31.36 (978-1-5026-0189-6(3)) Cavendish Square Publishing.
A Mouse Sized Mystery: Navigating the Computer. 2004. (Click & Squeak Ser.). (978-1-891997-62-4(9)) Dingles & Co.
Nagelhout, Ryan. Digital ERA Encryption & Decryption. 2016. (Cryptography: Code Making & Code Breaking Ser.). 00064p. (YA). (gr. 8-8). 34.45 (978-1-5081-7308-3(7)) Rosen Publishing Group, Inc., The.
—The Problem with Early Computers. 2015. (Bloopers of Invention Ser.). (ENG., Illus.). 24p. (J). (gr. 2-3). 22.60 (978-1-4824-2774-5(5)) Stevens, Gareth Publishing LLLP.
Nakaya, Andrea C. Steve Jobs & Apple. 2015. (ENG., Illus.). 80p. (J). lib. bdg. (978-1-60152-880-3(9)) ReferencePoint Pr., Inc.
Napier, H. Albert, et al. Learning with Computers I. 2nd ed. 2011. (Middle School Solutions Ser.). (ENG & ABK., Illus.). 464p. (C). 70.95 (978-0-538-45070-6(3)) Cengage South-Western.
—Learning with Computers II. 2nd ed. 2011. (Middle School Solutions Ser.). (ENG & ABK., Illus.). 512p. (C). pap. 87.95 (978-0-538-45071-3(1)) Cengage South-Western.
Northrup, Mary. Pioneering American Computer Geniuses. 2013. (Inspiring Collective Biographies Ser.). 112p. (J). (gr. 5-12). pap. 10.95 (978-1-4644-0273-9(6)); lib. bdg. 33.27 (978-0-7660-4167-7(0)) Enslow Pubs., Inc.
Omoth, Tyler. Busting Boredom with Technology. 2017. (Boredom Busters Ser.). (ENG., Illus.). 32p. (gr. 3-4). lib. bdg. 27.99 (978-1-5157-4705-5(0)) Capstone Press of Coughlan Cos.
Otfinoski, Steven. Computers. 2007. (Great Inventions Ser.). (Illus.). 112p. (J). (gr. 9-18). lib. bdg. 39.93 (978-0-7614-2597-7(7), Benchmark Bks.) Marshall Cavendish Corp.
Oxlade, Chris. The History of Computers. 2017. (History of Technology Ser.). (ENG.). 32p. (gr. 2-5). pap. 8.29 **(978-1-4846-4041-8(1)**, Heinemann First Library) Heinemann-Raintree.
Oxlade, Chris & Ganeri, Anita. The Computer, 1 vol. 2010. (Tales of Invention Ser.). (ENG., Illus.). 32p. (gr. 3-5). 30.65 (978-1-4329-3829-1(0)); pap. 8.95 (978-1-4329-3836-9(3)) Heinemann-Raintree. (NA-h).
Passantino, Claire. Matilda, the Computer Cat: For the TI 99-4A. (Creative Pastimes Ser.). (J). 6.95 (978-0-8359-4324-6(0)) Prentice Hall PTR.
Pearlstein, Don. Make Your Own Laptop: Color & Build Your Own Computer! Stillerman, Robbie, illus. 2011. (Dover Children's Activity Bks.). (ENG.). 24p. (J). (gr. k-3). pap. 9.99 (978-0-486-48532-4(3)) Dover Pubns., Inc.
Pelton, Stephen, et al. Basic Computers for Beginners. 2003. per. 29.95 (978-0-9748237-0-6(8)) Web Wise Services, Inc.
Perritano, John. Apple. 2017. (J). **(978-1-5105-2358-6(8))** SmartBook Media, Inc.
Peterson, Megan Cooley & Rustad, Martha E. H. The First Computers, 1 vol. 2014. (Famous Firsts Ser.). (ENG., Illus.). 24p. (gr. k-1). 26.65 (978-1-4914-0575-8(9), Pebble Plus) Capstone Press of Coughlan Cos.
Petrie, Kristin. Computers, 1 vol. 2009. (Everyday Inventions Ser.). (ENG., Illus.). 32p. (gr. 3-6). 27.07 (978-1-60453-086-5(3), Checkerboard Library) ABDO Publishing Co.
Petrikowski, Nicki Peter. Getting to Know the Raspberry Pi. 2014. (Code Power: a Teen Programmer's Guide Ser.). (Illus.). 64p. (J). (gr. 5-8). pap. 77.70 (978-1-4777-7712-1(1), Rosen Reference) Rosen Publishing Group, Inc., The.
Phillips, Miriam. At the Recycling Center: Sharing & Reusing. 2017. (Computer Science for the Real World Ser.). 16p. (gr. 7-8). pap. 7.95 **(978-1-5383-5245-8(1)**, Rosen Classroom) Rosen Publishing Group, Inc., The.
Plotkin, Robert. Computers in the Workplace. 2012. (Computers, Internet, & Society Ser.). (Illus.). xvii, 172p. (C). (gr. 9). 45.00 (978-0-8160-7758-4(8)) Facts On File, Inc.
—Privacy, Security, & Cyberspace. 2012. (Computers, Internet, & Society Ser.). (Illus.). 224p. (C). (gr. 9). 45.00 (978-0-8160-7756-4(8)) Facts On File, Inc.
QEB Let's Start! Computing National Book Stores Edition: Finding Facts. 2006. (J). per. (978-1-59566-295-8(2)) QEB Publishing Inc.
QEB Let's Start! Computing National Book Stores Edition: Making Pictures. 2006. (J). per. (978-1-59566-293-4(6)) QEB Publishing Inc.
QEB Let's Start! Computing National Book Stores Edition: Starting with Words. 2006. (J). per. (978-1-59566-294-1(4)) QEB Publishing Inc.
QEB Let's Start! Computing National Book Stores Edition: Using Instructions. 2006. (J). per. (978-1-59566-298-9(7)) QEB Publishing Inc.
QEB Let's Start! Computing National Book Stores Edition: World Art. 2006. (J). per. (978-1-59566-300-9(2)) QEB Publishing Inc.
Rau, Dana Meachen. Bill & Melinda Gates. 2007. (21st Century Skills Library: Life Skills Biographies Ser.). (ENG., Illus.). 48p. (gr. 4-8). lib. bdg. 31.36 (978-1-60279-068-1(X), 200039) Cherry Lake Publishing.
Raum, Elizabeth. History of the Computer. 2008. (Illus.). 32p. 24.95 (978-0-431-19148-5(4)) Heinemann.
Reed, Jennifer. What Are Computer Networks & the Internet? 2017. (J). **(978-1-5383-0033-6(8))** Rosen Publishing Group, Inc., The.
Reeves, Diane Lindsey. Information Technology. 2017. (Bright Futures Press: World of Work Ser.). (ENG., Illus.). 32p. (J). (gr. 4-7). lib. bdg. 29.93 (978-1-63472-625-2(1), 209534) Cherry Lake Publishing.
Reeves, Diane Lindsey, et al. Career Ideas for Kids Who Like Computers. Bond, Nancy, illus. 2nd rev. ed. 2007. (Career Ideas for Kids Ser.). 208p. (gr. 4-9). 32.95 (978-0-8160-6543-1(8), Ferguson Publishing Co.) Facts On File, Inc.
Renaissance Learning, Inc. Staff. STAR Early Literacy Made EZ (v 2. 1) RP: Quick Guide to Software. 2004. 23p. spiral bd. 21.95 (978-1-931819-41-1(6)) Renaissance Learning, Inc.
Reyes, Sonja. Let's Learn Double Dutch! Working at the Same Time. 2017. (Computer Science for the Real World Ser.). 12p. (gr. 6-7). pap. 7.05 **(978-1-5383-5176-5(5)**, Rosen Classroom) Rosen Publishing Group, Inc., The.
Robinson, Fiona. Ada's Ideas: The Story of Ada Lovelace, the World's First Computer Programmer. 2016. (ENG., Illus.). 40p. (J). (gr. 1-4). 17.95 (978-1-4197-1872-4(X), Abrams Bks. for Young Readers) Abrams, Inc.
Rodriguez, Philippe L. All about Computers. 2012. 24p. (-18). pap. 17.99 (978-1-4772-7178-0(3)) AuthorHouse.
Rooney, Anne. Computers. 2005. (Technology All Around Us Ser.). (Illus.). 32p. (YA). (gr. 4-7). lib. bdg. 27.10 (978-1-58340-750-9(2)) Black Rabbit Bks.
—Finding Facts, 6 vols. 2005. (QEB Computer Tutors Ser.). (Illus.). 32p. (J). (gr. 1-4). lib. bdg. 18.95 (978-1-59566-109-8(3)) QEB Publishing Inc.
—Starting with Words, 6 vols. 2005. (QEB Computer Tutors Ser.). (Illus.). 32p. (J). (gr. 1-4). lib. bdg. 18.95 (978-1-59566-108-1(5)) QEB Publishing Inc.
—Take Control. 2004. (QEB Learn Computing Ser.). (Illus.). 32p. (YA). (gr. 4-7). lib. bdg. 18.95 (978-1-59566-040-4(2)) QEB Publishing Inc.
—Using Instructions, 6 vols. 2005. (QEB Learn Computing Ser.). (Illus.). 32p. (J). (gr. 1-4). lib. bdg. 18.95 (978-1-59566-112-8(3)) QEB Publishing Inc.
—What If? 2004. (QEB Learn Computing Ser.). (Illus.). 32p. (J). lib. bdg. 18.95 (978-1-59566-041-1(0)) QEB Publishing Inc.
Shand, Jennifer. Why Do Computers Know So Much? 2015. (Why Do... ? Ser.). lib. bdg. 19.65 (978-1-4867-0622-8(3)) Turtleback Bks.
Shea, John. Combating Computer Viruses. 2012. (Cyberspace Survival Guide Ser.). (Illus.). 32p. (J). (gr. 3-6). 26.60 (978-1-4339-7212-6(3)); pap. 10.50 (978-1-4339-7213-3(1)) Stevens, Gareth Publishing LLLP. (Gareth Stevens Learning Library).
Silva, Sadie. Finding My School: Sticking to It. 2017. (Computer Science for the Real World Ser.). 8p. (gr. 5-6). pap. 6.20 **(978-1-5383-5113-0(7)**, Rosen Classroom) Rosen Publishing Group, Inc., The.
—We Help Our Community: What's the Problem? 2017. (Computer Science for the Real World Ser.). 12p. (gr. 6-7). pap. 7.05 **(978-1-5383-5135-2(8)**, Rosen Classroom) Rosen Publishing Group, Inc., The.
SIRS Discoverer. 2005. (J). mass mkt. (978-0-89777-566-3(X)) SIRS Publishing, Inc.
SIRS Discoverer: Getting Started Manual Spring 2004. 2003. (YA). cd-rom 1425.00 (978-0-89777-542-7(2)) SIRS Publishing, Inc.
Small, Cathleen. What Are Hardware & Software? 2017. (J). **(978-1-5383-0035-0(4))** Rosen Publishing Group, Inc., The.
Stanley, Diane. Ada Lovelace. Hartland, Jessie, illus. 2016. (ENG.). 40p. (J). (gr. -1-3). 17.99 (978-1-4814-5249-6(5), Simon & Schuster Bks. For Young Readers) Simon & Schuster Bks. For Young Readers.
Stearns, Peggy Healy. Stationery Studio Writing Collection Deluxe CD-ROM Single Computer License: The Irresistible Tool to Encourage Writing. Reynolds, Peter H., illus. 2003. 112p. (J). 69.95 incl. cd-rom, cd-rom (978-1-891405-07-5(1)) FableVision Pr.
Steffens, Bradley. Real-World Stem: Securing Cyberspace. 2017. (Real-World Stem Ser.). (ENG.). 80p. (YA). (gr. 5-12). **(978-1-68282-249-4(4))** ReferencePoint Pr., Inc.
Stent, Amanda & Lewis, Philip. The Princess at the Keyboard: Why Girls Should Become Computer Scientists. 2009. 152p. pap. 14.90 (978-0-557-03851-0(0)) Lulu Pr., Inc.
Strother, Ruth. Bill Gates, 1 vol. 2007. (Essential Lives Set 1 Ser.). (ENG., Illus.). 112p. (J). (gr. 6-12). lib. bdg. 35.64 (978-1-59928-841-3(9)) ABDO Publishing Co.
Taylor-Butler, Christine. Computers. 2016. (True Book(tm), a — Greatest Discoveries & Discoverers Ser.). (ENG., Illus.). 48p. (J). lib. bdg. 31.00 (978-0-531-21862-4(7), Children's Pr.) Scholastic Library Publishing.
Thompson, Gary. Digital Photography & Your PC: A Guide to Using Your PC to Create Your Own Personalized Photo Albums. 2003. (Illus.). 166p. (YA). spiral bd. 29.95 (978-0-9749763-0-3(X)) Guiding Horizons.
Truesdell, Ann. Get to the Right Site. 2012. (Explorer Junior Library: Information Explorer Junior Ser.). (ENG., Illus.). 24p. (J). (gr. 1-4). pap. 12.79 (978-1-61080-390-8(6), 201327); lib. bdg. 28.50 (978-1-61080-365-6(5), 201264) Cherry Lake Publishing.
—Super Smart Information Strategies: Find the Right Site. 2010. (Explorer Library: Information Explorer Ser.). (ENG.). 32p. (gr. 4-8). lib. bdg. 28.50 (978-1-60279-638-6(6), 200341) Cherry Lake Publishing.
Vande Velde, Vivian. User Unfriendly. 2012. (ENG., Illus.). 400p. (J). (gr. 5-7). pap. 21.99 (978-0-15-216353-2(0)) Houghton Mifflin Harcourt Publishing Co.
Vargas, Daraciela, des. Internet en la Escuela y el Hogar. 2003. (SPA.). ring bd. 14.99 (978-0-9702021-7-8(2)) Conexion Educativa.
Ventura, Marne. The 12 Biggest Breakthroughs in Computer Technology. 2014. (ENG., Illus.). 32p. (J). (978-1-63235-012-1(2)) Pr. Room Editions LLC.
Wanniarachchi, Ruwan. Early Childhood Computer Learning Workbook - Level 1. 2007. 79p. pap. 18.50 (978-0-615-17026-8(9)) Wanniarachchige, Somiruwan.
Ward-Johnson, Chris. Computers: A Magic Mouse Guide. Laughing Gravy Design Staff, illus. 2003. (Magic Mouse Guides). 32p. (J). lib. bdg. 22.60 (978-0-7660-2263-8(3)) Enslow Pubs., Inc.
—E-Mail: A Magic Mouse Guide. Laughing Gravy Design Staff, illus. 2003. (Magic Mouse Guides). 32p. (J). lib. bdg. 23.94 (978-0-7660-2261-4(7)) Enslow Pubs., Inc.
Ward-Johnson, Chris & Gould, William. The Magic Mouse Dictionary of Computers & Information Technology. Laughing Gravy Design Staff, illus. 2003. (Magic Mouse Guides). 64p. (J). lib. bdg. 29.27 (978-0-7660-2264-5(1)) Enslow Pubs., Inc.
Weber, Sandra. Personal Computer. 2003. (Transforming Power of Technology Ser.). (Illus.). 112p. (C). (gr. 9-13). 30.00 (978-0-7910-7450-3(1), Chelsea Hse.) Facts On File, Inc.
Weinstein, Eric. Ruby Wizardry: An Introduction to Programming for Kids. 2014. (ENG., Illus.). 252p. (J). (gr. 5). pap. 29.95 (978-1-59327-566-2(8)) No Starch Pr., Inc.
Wentk, Richard. Raspberry Pi for Kids for Dummies. 2015. (For Kids for Dummies Ser.). (ENG., Illus.). 352p. (J). pap. 29.99 (978-1-119-04951-7(2), For Dummies) Wiley, John & Sons, Inc.
Wilkinson, Colin. Everything You Need to Know about Digital Privacy. 2017. (Need to Know Library). 64p. (J). (gr. 12-11). 34.45 **(978-1-5081-7400-4(8))**; pap. 12.95 **(978-1-5081-7398-4(2))** Rosen Publishing Group, Inc., The. (Rosen Young Adult).
Wilkinson, Colin. Mobile Platforms: Getting Information on the Go. 2011. (Digital & Information Literacy Ser.). (Illus.). 48p. (YA). 29.25 (978-1-4488-1320-9(4)); pap. 11.75 (978-1-4488-2291-1(2)) Rosen Publishing Group, Inc., The. (Rosen Reference).
Willis, Laurie. Electronic Devices in Schools. 2012. (Issues That Concern You Ser.). (ENG., Illus.). 144p. (gr. 7-10). lib. bdg. 42.00 (978-0-7377-6292-1(6)) Cengage Gale.
Wolinsky, Art. Internet Power Research Using the Big6 Approach. rev. ed. 2005. (Internet Library). (Illus.). 64p. (J). lib. bdg. 23.94 (978-0-7660-1563-0(7)) Enslow Pubs., Inc.
Wooster, Patricia. Flickr Cofounder & Web Community Creator Caterina Fake. 2014. (STEM Trailblazer Bios Ser.). (ENG., Illus.). 32p. (gr. 2-5). lib. bdg. 26.60 (978-1-4677-2460-9(2), Lerner Pubns.) Lerner Publishing Group.
Words & Images. (Illus.). (J). (gr. 4-6). pap. (978-1-876367-98-5(9)) Wizard Bks.
World Book, Inc. Staff, contrib. by. Counting Pebbles to Writing Code: A Timeline of Mathematics & Computers. 2016. (J). (978-0-7166-3541-3(0)) World Bk., Inc.
Yearling, Tricia. Computers: What They Are & How to Use Them. 2016. (Zoom in on Technology Ser.). (ENG., Illus.). 24p. (J). (gr. 2-2). pap. 9.35 (978-0-7660-7361-6(0)) Enslow Pubs., Inc.
Zocchi, Judy. Meet Click & Squeak: How Computers Work. 2006. (Click & Squeak Ser.). (Illus.). 32p. (J). lib. bdg. 20.65 (978-1-891997-61-7(0)) Dingles & Co.
—The Secret Diary: Saving Files. 2006. (Click & Squeak Ser.). (Illus.). 32p. (J). lib. bdg. 20.65 (978-1-891997-65-5(3)) Dingles & Co.
—Squeak for President: Printing Documents. 2006. (Click & Squeak Ser.). (Illus.). 32p. (J). lib. bdg. 20.65 (978-1-891997-66-2(1)) Dingles & Co.
Zuchora-Walske, Christine. What's Inside My Computer? 2015. (ENG., Illus.). 32p. (J). (gr. k-2). 26.65 (978-1-4677-8074-2(X), Lerner Pubns.) Lerner Publishing Group.

COMPUTERS, ELECTRONIC

see Computers

COMPUTERS—FICTION

Ackerman, Peter & Dalton, Max. The Lonely Typewriter. 2014. (Illus.). 32p. (J). 16.95 (978-1-56792-518-0(9)) Godine, David R. Pub.
Adams, W. Royce. The Computer's Nerd. 2004. 136p. (J). pap. 9.95 (978-0-9712206-4-5(6)) Rairarubia Bks.
Alexander, Alma. Spellspam. 2008. (Worldweavers Ser.: Bk. 2). (YA). (gr. 7-18). (ENG.). 448p. 17.99 (978-0-06-083958-1(9)); 437p. lib. bdg. 18.89 (978-0-06-083959-8(7)) HarperCollins Pubs. (Eos).
Barba, Rick. The Quantum Quandary. 2006. (Spy Gear Adventures Ser.: 3). (ENG.). 208p. (J). (gr. 3-7). pap. 10.99 (978-1-4169-0889-0(7), Aladdin) Simon & Schuster Children's Publishing.
Berenstain, Jan & Berenstain, Mike. The Berenstain Bears' Computer Trouble. Berenstain, Jan & Berenstain, Mike, illus. 2010. (Berenstain Bears Ser.). (ENG., Illus.). 32p. (J). (gr. -1-3). 10.99 (978-0-06-057410-9(0)); pap. 3.99 (978-0-06-057394-2(5)) HarperCollins Pubs. (HarperFestival).
Black, Peter Jay. Blackout. 2015. (Urban Outlaws Ser.: 2). (ENG.). 304p. (YA). (gr. 5-8). 16.99 (978-1-61963-592-0(5), 9781619635920, Bloomsbury USA Childrens) Bloomsbury Publishing USA.
—Urban Outlaws. 2014. (Urban Outlaws Ser.: Bk. 1). (ENG., Illus.). 288p. (J). (gr. 5-8). 16.99 (978-1-61963-400-8(7), 9781619634008, Bloomsbury USA Childrens) Bloomsbury Publishing USA.
Bourgeois, Paulette. Franklin & the Computer. Clark, Brenda, illus. 2003. (Franklin Ser.: Bk. 16). 32p. (J). pap. 4.50 (978-0-439-43121-7(2)) Scholastic, Inc.
Bourgeois, Paulette & Clark, Brenda. Franklin & the Computer. 2003. (Franklin TV Storybook Ser.). (ENG., Illus.). 32p. (J). (gr. -1-3). 4.95 (978-1-55337-363-6(4)) Kids Can Pr., Ltd. CAN. Dist: Hachette Bk. Group.
Brooks, Dominic, illus. Is It My Turn Yet? 2008. 30p. (J). per. (978-0-9795768-2-9(2)) Better Tomorrow Publishing, A.
Brouwer, Sigmund. Nowhere to Hide. 2015. (King & Co. Cyber Suspense Ser.: 2). (ENG.). 224p. (YA). pap. 9.99 (978-0-7369-1748-3(9)) Harvest Hse. Pubs.
Brown, Marc. Arthur's Computer Disaster. 2004. (Arthur Adventure Ser.). (J). (gr. k-3). spiral bd. (978-0-616-07220-2(1)); spiral bd. (978-0-616-07221-9(X)) Canadian National Institute for the Blind/Institut National Canadien pour les Aveugles.
Colfer, Eoin. The Eternity Code. rev. ed. 2009. (Artemis Fowl Ser.). (ENG.). 336p. (J). (gr. 5-9). pap. 8.99 (978-1-4231-2453-5(7)) Hyperion Pr.
Colfer, Eoin & Donkin, Andrew. Artemis Fowl the Opal Deception Graphic Novel. Rigano, Giovanni & Lamanna, Paolo, illus. 2014. (Artemis Fowl Ser.: 4). (ENG.). 112p. (J). (gr. 5-9). pap. 12.99 (978-1-4231-4549-3(6)) Hyperion Bks. for Children.
—Eternity Code. Rigano, Giovanni & Lamanna, Paolo, illus. 2013. (Artemis Fowl Ser.: 3). (ENG.). 112p. (J). (gr. 5-9). pap. 12.99 (978-1-4231-4577-6(1)) Hyperion Pr.
Cray, Jordan. Danger Com 4 Hot Pursuit. 2009. (Danger. com Ser.: 4). (ENG.). 192p. (YA). (gr. 7-7). pap. 9.99 (978-1-4169-9849-5(7), Simon Pulse) Simon Pulse.
—Firestorm. 2009. (Danger. com Ser.: 2). (ENG.). 208p. (YA). (gr. 7). pap. 9.99 (978-1-4169-9846-4(2), Simon Pulse) Simon Pulse.
—Gemini7. 2009. (Danger. com Ser.: 1). (ENG.). 192p. (YA). (gr. 7). pap. 9.99 (978-1-4169-9847-1(0), Simon Pulse) Simon Pulse.
—Shadow Man. 2009. (Danger. com Ser.: 3). (ENG.). 192p. (YA). (gr. 7). pap. 9.99 (978-1-4169-9848-8(9), Simon Pulse) Simon Pulse.
—Shiver. 2009. (Danger. com Ser.: 9). (ENG.). 224p. (YA). (gr. 7). pap. 10.99 (978-1-4169-9853-2(5), Simon Pulse) Simon Pulse.
—Stalker. 2009. (Danger. com Ser.: 5). (ENG.). 224p. (YA). (gr. 7). pap. 10.99 (978-1-4169-9850-1(0), Simon Pulse) Simon Pulse.
Cush, Don. School of the Future: The Dawning of Aquarius. 2013. 28p. pap. 16.95 (978-1-63004-619-4(1)) America Star Bks.
Davis, Regina & Spencer, Carolyn Royer. Señor Smarty Pantaloons & the Mystery of the Missing Teachers. 2011. 32p. (gr. 1-2). pap. 17.59 (978-1-4567-4557-8(3)) AuthorHouse.
Deering, Leta. Patriotic Samáand the Mendez Twins at the Alamo. 2008. 112p. pap. 19.95 (978-1-60610-689-1(9)) America Star Bks.
Deutsch, Stacia. The Friendship Code. Fernandez, Andrea, illus. 2017. (Girls Who Code Ser.: 1). (ENG.). 144p. (J). (gr. 3-7). 12.99 **(978-0-399-54251-0(5)**, Penguin Workshop) Penguin Young Readers Group.
Diamand, Emily. Raiders' Ransom. 2009. (Raiders' Ransom Ser.: 1). (ENG.). 368p. (J). (gr. 3-7). 17.99 (978-0-545-14297-7(0)) Scholastic, Inc.
Doctorow, Cory. Homeland. (ENG.). (YA). (gr. 8). 2014. 448p. pap. 12.99 (978-0-7653-3370-4(8), 9780765333704) 2013. 400p. 17.99 (978-0-7653-3369-8(4), 9780765333698) Doherty, Tom Assocs., LLC. (Tor Teen).
—Homeland. 2014. (YA). lib. bdg. 24.50 (978-0-606-38513-8(4)) Turtleback Bks.
Duane, Diane. High Wizardry, 7 vols. (Young Wizards Ser.: 3). (J). 2006. 90.75 (978-1-4025-9917-0(X)) 2004. 93.75 (978-1-4025-8355-1(9)) Recorded Bks., Inc.
Duckro, Rebecca S. Adventures of Charlie KeeperTechnobrat. 2006. 156p. per. 12.95 (978-0-595-40498-8(7)) iUniverse, Inc.
DuPrau, Jeanne. Car Trouble. 2005. 288p. (J). 15.99 (978-0-06-073672-9(0)); lib. bdg. 16.89 (978-0-06-073674-3(7)) HarperCollins Pubs.
Esmaili, Roza. Zagros & Nature Force: Coloring Book. Sun Rise Illustration and Computer Animation Staff, illus. Date not set. 74p. (J). (gr. k-8). pap. 2.49 (978-0-9656185-1-9(X)) Esmaili, Inc.
Fisher, Catherine. Sapphique. (ENG.). (YA). (gr. 7-18). 2011. 480p. 10.99 (978-0-14-241979-3(6), Firebird) 2010. 464p. 17.99 (978-0-8037-3397-8(6), Dial Bks) Penguin Young Readers Group.
Frid, Colt & Frid, Randy. Demons at the Door. 2009. (978-0-9811847-1-5(5)) Frid Enterprises, Inc.
Frith, Lilla. Jason's Talking Computer: Book Three. 2010. 36p. pap. 15.49 (978-1-4490-2337-9(1)) AuthorHouse.
Gioseffi, Anthony P. Mainframe. 2007. 144p. per. 11.95 (978-0-595-44953-8(0)) iUniverse, Inc.
Gutman, Dan. The Homework Machine. 2007. (ENG.). 176p. (J). (gr. 3-7). pap. 6.99 (978-0-689-87679-0(3), Simon & Schuster Bks. For Young Readers) Simon & Schuster Bks. For Young Readers.
Gutsche, Brigitte. The Intruder. 2006. (J). pap. (978-0-88092-743-7(7)) Royal Fireworks Publishing Co.
Haarsma, P. J. Awakening on Orbis 4. 2010. (Softwire Ser.: 4). (ENG., Illus.). 368p. (YA). (gr. 7-18). 16.99 (978-0-7636-2712-6(7)) Candlewick Pr.
—Betrayal on Orbis. 2008. (Softwire Ser.: 2). (ENG., Illus.). 272p. (YA). (gr. 7-12). 16.99 (978-0-7636-2710-2(0)) Candlewick Pr.
—The Softwire: Wormhole Pirates on Orbis 3. 2010. (Softwire Ser.: 3). (ENG., Illus.). 400p. (YA). (gr. 7). 8.99 (978-0-7636-4777-3(2)) Candlewick Pr.
—Wormhole Pirates on Orbis, Vol. 3. 2009. (Softwire Ser.: 3). (ENG., Illus.). 384p. (YA). (gr. 7). 16.99 (978-0-7636-2711-9(9)) Candlewick Pr.
Haddix, Margaret Peterson. The Always War. (ENG.). (YA). (gr. 7). 2012. 224p. pap. 8.99 (978-1-4169-9527-2(7)) 2011. 208p. 16.99 (978-1-4169-9526-5(9)) Simon & Schuster Bks. For Young Readers. (Simon & Schuster Bks. For Young Readers).
—Escape from Memory. (ENG.). (YA). (gr. 7). 2012. 272p. pap. 8.99 (978-1-4424-4602-1(1)) 2003. (Illus.). 224p. 17.99 (978-0-689-85421-7(8)) Simon & Schuster Bks. For Young Readers. (Simon & Schuster Bks. For Young Readers).
—Game Changer. 2012. (ENG.). 256p. (YA). (gr. 7). 16.99 (978-0-689-87380-5(8), Simon & Schuster Bks. For Young Readers) Simon & Schuster Bks. For Young Readers.
Hawking, Stephen & Hawking, Lucy. George & the Unbreakable Code. Parsons, Garry, illus. 2016. (George's Secret Key Ser.). (ENG.). 352p. (J). (gr. 3-7). 18.99 (978-1-4814-6627-1(5), Simon & Schuster Bks. For Young Readers) Simon & Schuster Bks. For Young Readers.
Hawking, Stephen W. & Hawking, Lucy. George's Secret Key to the Universe. Parsons, Garry, illus. 2009. (George's Secret Key Ser.). (ENG.). 336p. (J). (gr. 3-7). pap. 12.99 (978-1-4169-8584-6(0), Simon & Schuster Bks. For Young Readers) Simon & Schuster Bks. For Young Readers.
Hayes, Linda. Grandma's First Computer. 2008. 34p. pap. 17.95 (978-0-557-01609-9(6)) Lulu Pr., Inc.
Helgeson, Kat & Moskowitz, Hannah. Gena/Finn. 2016. (ENG., Illus.). (YA). (gr. 7-12). 17.99 (978-1-4521-3839-8(7)) Chronicle Bks. LLC.
Holl, Kristi. Chat Freak. 2004. 128p. (J). pap. 5.99 (978-1-4003-0326-7(5)) Nelson, Thomas Inc.
Hutton, Sam. Meltdown. 2005. (Special Agents Ser.: 6). (ENG., Illus.). 224p. (J). pap. 9.99 (978-0-00-714847-9(X), HarperCollins Children's Bks.) HarperCollins Pubs. Ltd. GBR. Dist: HarperCollins Pubs.
Jennings, Sharon, et al, adapted by. Franklin & the Computer. 2003. (Franklin TV Storybook Ser.). (ENG., Illus.). 32p. (J). (gr. -1-3). 10.95 (978-1-55337-362-9(6)) Kids Can Pr., Ltd. CAN. Dist: Hachette Bk. Group.

C
D

Johansen, K. V. The Black Box. 2010. (Illus.). 212p. (J). pap. 13.00 *(978-0-9864974-0-7(1))* Sybertooth, Inc. CAN. Dist: Lightning Source, Inc.

Johnson, Don. Tale of Billy the Bit. 2004. (Illus.). 80p. pap. *(978-1-84401-306-7(5))* Athena Pr.

Kindig, Tess. Luv @ First Site. 2004. 128p. (J). pap. 5.99 *(978-1-4003-0325-0(7))* Nelson, Thomas Inc.

Kogon, Stephen. Max Mooth — Cyber Sleuth & the Case of the Zombie Virus. 2005. 120p. (YA). 20.95 *(978-0-595-66843-4(7))* iUniverse, Inc.

Kubica, Jeremy. The CS Detective: An Algorithmic Tale of Crime, Conspiracy, & Computation. 2016. (ENG., Illus.). 256p. (YA). pap. 17.95 *(978-1-59327-749-9(0))* No Starch Pr., Inc.

Lancaster, Mike A. The Future We Left Behind. 2012. (ENG.). 384p. (J). (gr. 7). 16.99 *(978-1-60684-410-6(5)*, Carolrhoda Lab™) Lerner Publishing Group.

—Human. 4. 2012. (ENG.). 240p. (J). (gr. 7). pap. 8.99 *(978-1-60684-309-3(5)*, Carolrhoda Lab™) Lerner Publishing Group.

Liukas, Linda. Hello Ruby: Adventures in Coding. 2015. (Hello Ruby Ser.: 1). (ENG., Illus.). 112p. (J). (gr. -1-3). 16.99 *(978-1-250-06500-1(3)*, 9781250065001) Feiwel & Friends.

Manley, Craig. The Rammarg Files. 2006. (J). lib. bdg. *(978-0-88092-742-0(9))* Royal Fireworks Publishing Co.

Martin, Justin McCory. The Mega-Deluxe Capitalization Machine. Phillips, Matt, illus. 2004. (Grammar Tales Ser.). (ENG.). 16p. (J). (gr. 3-7). pap. 3.25 *(978-0-439-45821-4(8))* Scholastic, Inc.

Martinez, Manuel. Dev Plans a Food Drive: What's the Problem? 2017. (Computer Science for the Real World Ser.). 12p. (gr. 6-7). pap. 7.05 ***(978-1-5383-5132-1(3)***, Rosen Classroom) Rosen Publishing Group, Inc., The.

McClue-Tate, Brucetta. Jolly the Computer. 2011. 32p. pap. 21.99 *(978-1-4568-8151-1(5))* Xlibris Corp.

Pace, Marisa. Gina Goes to School: Over & over Again. 2017. (Computer Science for the Real World Ser.). 8p. (gr. 5-6). pap. 6.20 ***(978-1-5383-5086-7(6)***, Rosen Classroom) Rosen Publishing Group, Inc., The.

Pratchett, Terry. The Bromeliad Trilogy: Truckers, Diggers, & Wings. 2003. 512p. (J). (gr. 5-18). 18.89 *(978-0-06-054855-1(X))*; 19.99 *(978-0-06-009493-5(1))* HarperCollins Pubs.

Regan, Dian. Cyberpals According to Kaley. 2006. (Illus.). 128p. (J). (gr. 3-7). 15.95 *(978-1-58196-051-8(4)*, Darby Creek) Lerner Publishing Group.

Rosen, Marvin. Becca in Cyberland, 1 vol. 2010. 48p. pap. 16.95 *(978-1-4489-9831-9(X))* America Star Bks.

Santos, Penelope. Jayla & Her Tablet. 2015. (Rosen REAL Readers: STEM & STEAM Collection). (ENG.). 8p. pap. 5.46 *(978-1-4994-9568-3(4)*, Rosen Classroom) Rosen Publishing Group, Inc., The.

Seuling, Barbara. Robert Finds a Way. Brewer, Paul, illus. 2005. (Robert Bks.). (ENG.). 150p. (J). 15.95 *(978-0-8126-2734-3(2))* Cricket Bks.

Shambles, Shorty. The Computer Gangùconnie Computer. 2008. 36p. pap. 13.95 *(978-1-60693-213-1(6)*, Eloquent Bks.) Strategic Book Publishing & Rights Agency (SBPRA).

Smith, Lane. It's a Book. Smith, Lane, illus. 2010. (ENG., Illus.). 32p. (J). (gr. 1-5). 15.99 *(978-1-59643-606-0(9)*, 9781596436060) Roaring Brook Pr.

Sommer, Carl. Time Remote! Read-along. 2003. (Another Sommer-Time Story Ser.). (Illus.). 48p. (J). lib. bdg. 23.95 incl. audio *(978-1-57537-762-9(4))* Advance Publishing, Inc.

—Time Remote! Read-along. Budwine, Greg, illus. 2003. (Another Sommer-Time Story Ser.). (ENG.). 48p. (J). lib. bdg. 23.95 incl. audio compact disk *(978-1-57537-712-4(8))* Advance Publishing, Inc.

Stannard, Russell. www.Here-I-Am. Pugh, Jonathan, illus. 2011. (ENG.). 160p. (YA). (gr. 5-8). pap. 9.95 *(978-1-890151-85-0(8))* Templeton Pr.

Sugg, Zoe "Zoella". Girl Online. 2014. (ENG.). 352p. 17.99 *(978-1-4767-9745-8(5)*, Atria Bks.) Simon & Schuster.

Summers, Kim. Senor Mundo & Me: A Happy Birthday Story. Mariscal, Javier, illus. 2004. 31p. (J). (gr. k-4). 20.00 *(978-0-7567-7759-3(3))* DIANE Publishing Co.

Supercomputer Pizzas: Individual Title Six-Packs. (Bookweb Ser.). 32p. (gr. 3-18). 34.00 *(978-0-7635-3938-2(4))* Rigby Education.

Tashjian, Janet. Tru Confessions. 2007. (ENG., Illus.). 176p. (J). (gr. 4-7). per. 15.99 *(978-0-312-37273-6(6)*, 9780312372736) Square Fish.

Thaler, Mike. The Computer Teacher from the Black Lagoon. Lee, Jared, illus. 2007. (J). *(978-0-439-87133-4(6))* Scholastic, Inc.

—The Computer Teacher from the Black Lagoon, 1 vol. Lee, Jared, illus. 2012. (Black Lagoon Set 2 Ser.: No. 2). (ENG.). 32p. (J). (gr. 1-4). lib. bdg. 24.21 *(978-1-59961-955-2(5))* Spotlight.

Tinsley, P. S. A House with No Mouse. Deans, Nora L., ed. Castro, Luis F., illus. 2003. 28p. 14.95 *(978-0-9723213-1-0(4)*, Mousetime Bks.) Mousetime Media LLC.

Vega, Denise. Click Here: (To Find Out How I Survived Seventh Grade) 2006. (ENG., Illus.). 224p. (J). (gr. 5-17). reprint ed. per. 7.99 *(978-0-316-98559-8(7))* Little, Brown Bks. for Young Readers.

Whyman, Matt. Goldstrike: A Thriller. 2010. (ENG.). 272p. (YA). (gr. 7-18). 16.99 *(978-1-4169-9510-4(2)*, Atheneum Bks. for Young Readers) Simon & Schuster Children's Publishing.

Willis, Jeanne. Chicken Clicking. Ross, Tony, illus. 2015. (ENG.). 32p. (J). (gr. -1-k). pap. 9.99 *(978-1-78344-161-7(5))* Andersen Pr. GBR. Dist: Independent Pubs. Group.

Yang, Gene Luen. Secret Coders. Holmes, Mike, illus. 2015. (Secret Coders Ser.: 1). (ENG.). 96p. (J). (gr. 3-7). 17.99 *(978-1-62672-276-7(5)*, 9781626722767); pap. 9.99 *(978-1-62672-075-6(4)*, 9781626720756) Roaring Brook Pr. (First Second Bks.).

COMPUTERS—PROGRAMMING

see Computer Programming

COMPUTERS—VOCATIONAL GUIDANCE

Buell, Tonya. Cool Careers Without College for Web Surfers. (Cool Careers Without College Ser.). 2007. (Illus.). 144p. (J). (gr. 4-7). lib. bdg. 33.25 *(978-1-4042-0871-1(2))* 2005. (YA). (gr. 7-12). 35.95 *(978-1-4042-1092-9(X))* Rosen Publishing Group, Inc., The.

Careers in Computer Technology: Set 2. 2013. (Careers in Computer Technology Ser.). 80p. (YA). (gr. 9-12). 232.75 *(978-1-4488-9604-2(5))* Rosen Publishing Group, Inc., The.

Careers in Computer Technology: Sets 1 - 2. 2013. (Careers in Computer Technology Ser.). 80p. (YA). (gr. 9-12). 432.25 *(978-1-4777-0619-0(4))* Rosen Publishing Group, Inc., The.

Computers. 2011. (New Discovering Careers for Your Future Ser.). (Illus.). 128p. (gr. 4-9). 24.95 *(978-0-8160-8049-6(6)*, Ferguson Publishing Co.) Facts On File, Inc.

Cunningham, Kevin. Video Game Designer. 2008. (21st Century Skills Library: Cool Careers Ser.). (ENG., Illus.). 32p. (gr. 4-8). lib. bdg. 28.50 *(978-1-60279-305-7(0)*, 200144) Cherry Lake Publishing.

Ferguson. Computer & Video Game Design. 2nd rev. ed. 2009. (Careers in Focus Ser.). 224p. (gr. 6-12). 32.95 *(978-0-8160-7297-2(3)*, Ferguson Publishing Co.) Facts On File, Inc.

—Computers. 5th rev. ed. 2008. (Careers in Focus Ser.). 200p. (gr. 6-12). 32.95 *(978-0-8160-7285-9(X)*, Ferguson Publishing Co.) Facts On File, Inc.

Freedman, Jeri. Careers in Computer Support. 2013. 80p. (YA). (gr. 9-12). 33.25 *(978-1-4488-9594-6(4))* Rosen Publishing Group, Inc., The.

Furgang, Kathy. Careers in Digital Animation. 2013. 80p. (YA). (gr. 9-12). 33.25 *(978-1-4488-9591-5(X))* Rosen Publishing Group, Inc., The.

Gregory, Josh. Apps: From Concept to Consumer. 2015. (ENG., Illus.). 64p. (J). pap. 8.95 *(978-0-531-21236-3(X)*, Orchard Bks.) Scholastic Library Publishing.

Guillain, Charlotte. Computers, 1 vol. 2012. (Jobs If You Like... Ser.). (ENG.). 32p. (gr. 1-3). pap. 8.29 *(978-1-4329-6817-5(3))*; lib. bdg. 27.32 *(978-1-4329-6806-9(8))* Heinemann-Raintree. (Heinemann First Library).

Hayhurst, Chris. Careers in E-Commerce Security & Encryption. 2005. (Library of e-Commerce & Internet Careers Ser.). (Illus.). 64p. (YA). (gr. 7-12). lib. bdg. 31.95 *(978-0-8239-3420-1(9))* Rosen Publishing Group, Inc., The.

Internet. 3rd rev. ed. 2006. (Careers in Focus Ser.). (Illus.). 192p. (gr. 6-12). 32.95 *(978-0-8160-6564-6(0)*, Ferguson Publishing Co.) Facts On File, Inc.

JG Ferguson Publishing Company, creator. Computers. 2007. (What Can I Do Now? Ser.). 208p. (YA). (gr. 7-12). 32.95 *(978-0-8160-6027-6(4))* Facts On File, Inc.

Jozefowicz, Chris. Video Game Developer. 2009. (Cool Careers: Cutting Edge Ser.). (Illus.). 32p. (J). (gr. 5-8). lib. bdg. 26.00 *(978-1-4339-1958-9(3))* Stevens, Gareth Publishing LLLP.

King, Rachel. Technical Support. 2015. (High-Tech Jobs Ser.). (ENG.). 96p. (J). (gr. 7-7). 42.79 *(978-1-5026-0114-8(1))* Cavendish Square Publishing.

—Technical Support. 2015. (J). lib. bdg. *(978-1-62713-405-7(0))* Musa Publishing.

Mara, Wil. Information Security Analyst. 2013. (21st Century Skills Library: Cool STEM Careers Ser.). (ENG.). 32p. (J). (gr. 4-8). 28.50 *(978-1-62431-005-8(2)*, 202471) Cherry Lake Publishing.

Miller, Deborah J. Careers with an Internet Service Provider. 2005. (Library of e-Commerce & Internet Careers Ser.). (Illus.). 64p. (J). (gr. 7-12). lib. bdg. 31.95 *(978-0-8239-3425-6(X))* Rosen Publishing Group, Inc., The.

Niver, Heather Moore. Careers for Tech Girls in Computer Science. 2015. (Tech Girls Ser.). (ENG., Illus.). 80p. (J). (gr. 7-8). 34.25 *(978-1-4994-6105-3(4)*, Rosen Young Adult) Rosen Publishing Group, Inc., The.

Penna, Christina & Shook, Rachael. Careers in Network Engineering. 2005. (Library of e-Commerce & Internet Careers Ser.). (Illus.). 64p. (YA). (gr. 7-12). lib. bdg. 31.95 *(978-0-8239-3422-5(5))* Rosen Publishing Group, Inc., The.

Reeves, Diane Lindsey. Career Ideas for Teens in Information Technology. 2006. (Career Ideas for Teens Ser.). (Illus.). 192p. (gr. 8-12). per. 16.95 *(978-0-8160-6921-7(2)*, Checkmark Bks.) Facts On File, Inc.

Reeves, Diane Lindsey, et al. Career Ideas for Teens in Information Technology. 2005. (Career Ideas for Teens Ser.). (Illus.). 192p. (gr. 6-12). 40.00 *(978-0-8160-5293-6(X)*, Ferguson Publishing Co.) Facts On File, Inc.

Romano, Amy. Cool Careers Without College for People Who Love Everything Digital. (Cool Careers Without College Ser.). 144p. 2009. (gr. 6-6). 66.50 *(978-1-61511-965-3(5))* 2006. (Illus.). (YA). (gr. 7-12). lib. bdg. 35.95 *(978-1-4042-0748-6(1))* Rosen Publishing Group, Inc., The.

Smith, Jonathan. White Hat Hacking. 2015. (High-Tech Jobs Ser.). (ENG.). 96p. (J). (gr. 7-7). 42.79 *(978-1-5026-0272-5(5))* Cavendish Square Publishing.

—White Hat Hacking. 2015. (J). lib. bdg. *(978-1-62713-401-9(8))* Musa Publishing.

Teague Meyer, Terry. The Vo-Tech Track to Success in Information Technology. 2014. (Learning a Trade, Preparing for a Career Ser.). (Illus.). 80p. (J). (gr. 7-12). 34.25 *(978-1-4777-7724-4(5))* Rosen Publishing Group, Inc., The.

Weigant, Chris. Choosing a Career in Computers. rev. ed. 2005. (World of Work Ser.). (Illus.). 64p. (YA). (gr. 7-12). lib. bdg. 31.95 *(978-0-8239-3044-9(0)*, WWCOMP) Rosen Publishing Group, Inc., The.

COMPUTING MACHINES (ELECTRONIC)

see Computers

COMSTOCK LODE (NEV.)

Kraft, Eric. Gold Rush! & ¡la fiebre del Oro! 6 English, 6 Spanish Adaptations. 2011. (ENG & SPA.). (J). 97.00 net. *(978-1-4108-5699-9(2))* Benchmark Education Co.

CONCENTRATION CAMPS

Brandman, Bronia & Bierman, Carol. The Girl Who Survived: A True Story of the Holocaust. 2010. 91p. (J). pap. *(978-0-545-17574-6(7))* Scholastic, Inc.

Byers, Ann. Auschwitz, Bergen-Belsen, Treblinka: The Holocaust Camps. 2014. (Remembering the Holocaust Ser.). 96p. (J). (gr. 6-12). 27.94 *(978-0-7660-6212-2(0))*; pap. 10.95 *(978-0-7660-6213-9(9))* Enslow Pubs., Inc.

Currie, Stephen. Escapes from Nazi Persecution. 2003. (Great Escapes Ser.). (ENG., Illus.). 112p. (J). 30.85 *(978-1-59018-279-6(0)*, Lucent Bks.) Cengage Gale.

Deem, James M. Auschwitz: Voices from the Death Camp. 2011. (Holocaust Through Primary Sources Ser.). (Illus.). 128p. (J). (gr. 9-12). lib. bdg. 33.27 *(978-0-7660-3322-1(8))* Enslow Pubs., Inc.

—The Prisoners of Breendonk: Personal Histories from a World War II Concentration Camp. 2015. (ENG., Illus.). 352p. (YA). (gr. 9). 18.99 *(978-0-544-09664-6(9)*, HMH Books For Young Readers) Houghton Mifflin Harcourt Publishing Co.

Dooling, Sandra. Japanese Internment: Defining Moments in Canadian History. 2011. (Illus.). 32p. (gr. 5-8). *(978-1-77071-688-9(2))* Weigl Educational Pubs. Ltd.

Gruenbaum, Michael. Somewhere There Is Still a Sun: A Memoir of the Holocaust. 2015. (ENG., Illus.). 384p. (J). (gr. 5-9). 17.99 *(978-1-4424-8486-3(1)*, Aladdin) Simon & Schuster Children's Publishing.

Gruenbaum, Michael & Hasak-Lowy, Todd. Somewhere There Is Still a Sun: A Memoir of the Holocaust. 2017. (ENG., Illus.). 384p. (J). (gr. 5-9). pap. 8.99 *(978-1-4424-8487-0(X)*, Simon & Schuster/Paula Wiseman Bks.) Simon & Schuster/Paula Wiseman Bks.

Kacer, Kathy. The Magician of Auschwitz, 1 vol. Newland, Gillian, illus. 2014. (ENG.). 32p. (J). (gr. 3-5). 18.95 *(978-1-927583-46-3(2))* Second Story Pr. CAN. Dist: Orca Bk. Pubs. USA.

Lehman-Wilzig, Tami. Keeping the Promise: A Torah's Journey. Orback, Craig, illus. 2004. 32p. (J). (ENG.). (gr. k-3). pap. 9.95 *(978-1-58013-118-6(2))*; (gr. 1-5). 16.95 *(978-1-58013-117-9(4))* Lerner Publishing Group. (Kar-Ben Publishing).

Robson, David. Auschwitz. 2009. (World History Ser.). (ENG., Illus.). 128p. (J). (gr. 7-10). 34.95 *(978-1-4205-0131-5(3)*, Lucent Bks.) Cengage Gale.

CONCENTRATION CAMPS—FICTION

Aaron, Chester. Gideon. 2009. (ENG., Illus.). 190p. (YA). pap. 12.99 *(978-1-934841-62-4(5)*, Zumaya Thresholds) Zumaya Pubns. LLC.

Baraitser, Marion. Home Number One. 2006. (Illus.). 63p. (YA). pap. *(978-0-9529426-7-2(4))* Loki Books Ltd.

Boyne, John. The Boy in the Striped Pajamas. (ENG.). (YA). (gr. 7). 2006. 224p. 17.99 *(978-0-385-75106-3(0))* 2008. 240p. pap. 9.99 *(978-0-385-75189-6(3))* Fickling, David Bks. GBR. Dist: Penguin Random Hse. LLC.

—The Boy in the Striped Pajamas. 2011. 10.54 *(978-0-7848-3514-2(4)*, Everbind) Marco Bk. Co.

—The Boy in the Striped Pajamas. 2008. 215p. (gr. 7-12). 20.00 *(978-0-7569-8943-9(4))* Perfection Learning Corp.

—The Boy in the Striped Pajamas. 2007. (ENG.). 224p. (YA). (gr. 7-18). pap. 9.99 *(978-0-385-75153-7(2)*, Ember) Random Hse. Children's Bks.

—The Boy in the Striped Pajamas. rev. l.t. ed. 2007. (Thorndike Literacy Bridge Ser.). 247p. (YA). (gr. 7-12). 23.95 *(978-0-7862-9425-1(6))* Thorndike Pr.

—The Boy in the Striped Pajamas. 2007. 215p. (YA). (gr. 7-12). 20.85 *(978-1-4178-1823-5(9)*, Turtleback) Turtleback Bks.

—The Boy in the Striped Pajamas (Deluxe Illustrated Edition) Jeffers, Oliver, illus. 2016. (ENG.). 352p. (YA). (gr. 7). 18.99 *(978-0-399-55931-0(0)*, Knopf Bks. for Young Readers) Random Hse. Children's Bks.

Bunting, Eve. One Candle. Popp, K. Wendy, illus. 2004. (ENG.). 40p. (J). (gr. -1-3). pap. 6.99 *(978-0-06-008560-5(6))* HarperCollins Pubs.

Gallaz, Christophe. Rose Blanche. Innocenti, Roberto, illus. 2011. (ENG.). 32p. (J). (gr. 5-17). pap. 10.99 *(978-0-89812-385-2(2))* Creative Co., The.

Gruenbaum, Michael & Hasak-Lowy, Todd. Somewhere There Is Still a Sun. 2017. lib. bdg. 19.65 ***(978-0-606-40203-3(9))*** Turtleback Bks.

Hesse, Karen. Aleutian Sparrow. McGillivray, Kim & Zerbetz, Evon, illus. 2005. (ENG.). 160p. (J). (gr. 4-9). reprint ed. pap. 7.99 *(978-1-4169-0327-7(5)*, McElderry, Margaret K. Bks.) McElderry, Margaret K. Bks.

—Aleutian Sparrow. Zerbetz, Evon, illus. 2005. 156p. (J). (gr. 5-9). 13.65 *(978-0-7569-5589-2(0))* Perfection Learning Corp.

Jane, Yolen. The Devil's Arithmetic. 2014. (ENG.). 176p. (J). 11.24 *(978-1-63245-218-4(9))* Lectorum Pubns., Inc.

Kent, Trilby. Stones for My Father. 2011. (ENG.). 176p. (YA). (gr. 5-18). 19.95 *(978-1-77049-252-3(6)*, Tundra Bks.) Tundra Bks. CAN. Dist: Penguin Random Hse. LLC.

Polak, Monique. What World Is Left, 1 vol. 2008. (ENG.). 232p. (YA). (gr. 7-12). pap. 12.95 *(978-1-55143-847-4(X))* Orca Bk. Pubs. USA.

Schmidt, Gary D. Mara's Stories: Glimmers in the Darkness. 2008. (ENG.). 160p. (YA). (gr. 5-9). per. 14.99 *(978-0-312-37388-7(0)*, 9780312373887) Square Fish.

Smith, Icy. Half Spoon of Rice: A Survival Story of the Cambodian Holocaust. Nhem, Sopaul, illus. 2009. (J). (gr. 2-7). 19.95 *(978-0-9821675-8-8(X))* East West Discovery Pr.

Uchida, Yoshiko. Journey to Topaz. 2005. 160p. pap. 9.95 *(978-1-890771-91-1(0))* Heyday.

Wein, Elizabeth. Rose under Fire. 2013. (ENG.). 368p. (YA). (gr. 9-17). 17.99 *(978-1-4231-8309-9(6))* Hyperion Pr.

Wild, Margaret. Let the Celebrations Begin. Vivas, Julie, illus. 2014. (ENG.). 40p. (J). (gr. 2-5). 16.99 *(978-0-7636-7013-9(8))* Candlewick Pr.

Wiseman, Eva. Kanada. 2006. (ENG., Illus.). 264p. (YA). (gr. 5). pap. 9.95 *(978-0-88776-729-6(X)*, Tundra Bks.) Tundra Bks. CAN. Dist: Penguin Random Hse. LLC.

Wiviott, Meg. Paper Hearts. 2015. (ENG., Illus.). 352p. (YA). (gr. 7). 17.99 *(978-1-4814-3983-1(9)*, McElderry, Margaret K. Bks.) McElderry, Margaret K. Bks.

Yolen, Jane. The Devil's Arithmetic. 2004. (Puffin Modern Classics Ser.). (ENG.). 176p. (J). (gr. 5-3). pap. 7.99 *(978-0-14-240109-5(9)*, Puffin Books) Penguin Young Readers Group.

Zail, Suzy. Playing for the Commandant. 2014. (ENG.). 256p. (YA). (gr. 7). 16.99 *(978-0-7636-6403-9(0))* Candlewick Pr.

CONCEPTION—PREVENTION

see Birth Control

CONCERTS

Allen, Kathy. The Science of a Rock Concert: Sound in Action. 2010. (Action Science Ser.). (ENG.). 32p. (gr. 3-4). pap. 47.70 *(978-1-4296-5075-5(3)*, Fact Finders) Capstone Press of Coughlan Cos.

Dunn, Mary. My Adventure at a Concert Hall. 2006. 44p. (J). 8.99 *(978-1-59092-288-0(3))* Blue Forge Pr.

Hopkinson, Deborah. Sweet Land of Liberty, 1 vol. Jenkins, Leonard, illus. 2007. (ENG.). 32p. (J). (gr. 1-5). 16.95 *(978-1-56145-395-5(1))* Peachtree Pubs.

Pettiford, Rebecca. Concert. Fretland VanVoorst, Jenny, ed. 2016. (First Field Trips). 24p. (J). (gr. k-2). lib. bdg. 25.65 *(978-1-62031-294-0(8)*, Bullfrog Bks.) Jump! Inc.

—El Concierto. 2016. (Los Primeros Viajes Escolares (First Field Trips)).Tr. of Concert. (SPA.). 24p. (J). (gr. k-2). lib. bdg. 25.65 *(978-1-62031-329-9(4)*, Bullfrog Bks.) Jump! Inc.

Rissman, Rebecca. Going to a Concert, 1 vol. 2012. (World of Field Trips Ser.). (ENG.). 24p. (gr. -1-1). lib. bdg. 22.65 *(978-1-4329-6065-0(2)*, Acorn) Heinemann-Raintree.

CONCHOLOGY

see Mollusks; Shells

CONCORD, BATTLE OF, CONCORD, MASS., 1775

Brown, Don. Let It Begin Here! The Day the American Revolution Began April 19, 1775. Brown, Don, illus. 2010. (Actual Times Ser.: 1). (ENG., Illus.). 64p. (J). (gr. 1-5). pap. 9.99 *(978-1-59643-645-9(X)*, 9781596436459) Roaring Brook Pr.

Crewe, Sabrina & Uschan, Michael V. Lexington & Concord. 2004. (Events That Shaped America Ser.). (Illus.). 32p. (gr. 3-6). lib. bdg. 26.00 *(978-0-8368-3398-0(8)*, Gareth Stevens Learning Library) Stevens, Gareth Publishing LLLP.

—Lexington y Concord. 2006. (Hitos de la historia de Estados Unidos (Landmark Events in American History) Ser.). (SPA.). 48p. (gr. 5-12). pap. 11.70 *(978-0-8368-7474-7(9)*, Gareth Stevens Learning Library) Stevens, Gareth Publishing LLLP.

Fradin, Dennis Brindell & Day, Larry. Let It Begin Here! Lexington & Concord - First Battles of the American Revolution. 2009. (ENG., Illus.). 40p. (J). (gr. 2-4). pap. 8.99 *(978-0-8027-9711-7(3)*, 9780802797117, Bloomsbury USA Childrens) Bloomsbury Publishing USA.

Mara, Wil. The Battles of Lexington & Concord: Start of the American Revolution. 2017. (Major Battles in US History (hardcover) Ser.). (ENG., Illus.). 32p. (J). (gr. 4-7). lib. bdg. 28.50 ***(978-1-63517-023-8(0)***, Focus Readers) North Star Editions.

Niz, Xavier & Niz, Xavier W. Paul Revere's Ride. Bascle, Brian, illus. 2005. (Graphic History Ser.). (ENG.). 32p. (gr. 3-4). 30.65 *(978-0-7368-4965-4(3)*, Graphic Library) Capstone Press of Coughlan Cos.

Samuels, Charlie. The Battles of Lexington & Concord, Vol. 1. 2014. (Turning Points in US Military History Ser.). (ENG.). 48p. (J). (gr. 5-6). 31.95 *(978-1-4824-0417-3(6))* Stevens, Gareth Publishing LLLP.

Von Zumbusch, Amelie. The True Story of the Battle of Lexington & Concord. 2009. (What Really Happened? Ser.). (Illus.). 24p. (YA). (gr. 3-6). lib. bdg. 22.60 *(978-1-4042-4480-1(8))* Rosen Publishing Group, Inc., The.

von Zumbusch, Amelie. The True Story of the Battle of Lexington & Concord. 2009. (What Really Happened? Ser.). 24p. (gr. 2-3). 42.50 *(978-1-60854-767-8(1)*, PowerKids Pr.) Rosen Publishing Group, Inc., The.

Waldman, Scott P. The Battle of Lexington & Concord. (Atlas of Famous Battles of the American Revolution Ser.). 24p. 2009. (gr. 3-3). 42.50 *(978-1-60853-328-2(X))* 2003. (Illus.). (J). lib. bdg. 22.60 *(978-0-8239-6328-7(4))* Rosen Publishing Group, Inc., The. (PowerKids Pr.).

Whitelaw, Nancy. The Shot Heard Round the World: The Battles of Lexington & Concord. 2004. (First Battles Ser.). (Illus.). 112p. (J). (gr. 6-12). 23.95 *(978-1-883846-75-6(7)*, First Biographies) Reynolds, Morgan Inc.

Whitwell, Stephen. The Battles of Lexington & Concord: First Shots of the American Revolution. 2015. (Spotlight on American History Ser.). (ENG., Illus.). 24p. (J). (gr. 4-6). pap. 10.00 *(978-1-4994-1719-5(7)*, PowerKids Pr.) Rosen Publishing Group, Inc., The.

CONCORD, BATTLE OF, CONCORD, MASS., 1775—FICTION

Gunderson, Jessica. Secret Weapons: A Tale of the Revolutionary War, 1 vol. Aburto, Jesus, illus. 2008. (Historical Fiction Ser.). (ENG.). 56p. (gr. 2-3). pap. 6.25 *(978-1-4342-0848-4(6)*, Graphic Flash) Stone Arch Bks.

CONDOMINIUMS

see Apartment Houses

CONDORS

Becker, John E. The California Condor. 2004. (Returning Wildlife Ser.). (ENG., Illus.). 48p. (J). 27.50 *(978-0-7377-2292-5(4)*, Kidhaven) Cengage Gale.

Goldish, Meish. California Condors: Saved by Captive Breeding. 2007. (America's Animal Comebacks Ser.). (Illus.). 32p. (YA). (gr. 2-5). lib. bdg. 25.27 *(978-1-59716-741-3(X))* Bearport Publishing Co., Inc.

Harasymiw, N. D. Condors in Danger. 2013. (Animals at Risk Ser.). 24p. (J). (gr. 2-5). pap. 8.15 *(978-1-4339-9155-4(1))*; pap. 48.90 *(978-1-4339-9156-1(X))*; (ENG., Illus.). lib. bdg. 22.60 *(978-1-4339-9154-7(3))* Stevens, Gareth Publishing LLLP.

Macken, JoAnn Early. Condors. 2nd rev. ed. 2009. (Animals That Live in the Mountains Ser.). 24p. (J). (gr. -1-3). pap. 8.15 *(978-1-4339-2493-4(5))*; lib. bdg. 22.60 *(978-1-4339-2410-1(2))* Stevens, Gareth Publishing LLLP. (Weekly Reader Leveled Readers).

—Condors;Cóndor. 2nd rev. ed. 2009. (Animals That Live in the Mountains/Animales de las montañas Ser.). (ENG & SPA.). 24p. (J). (gr. -1-3). pap. 8.15 *(978-1-4339-2500-9(1))*; lib. bdg. 22.60 *(978-1-4339-2442-2(0))* Stevens, Gareth Publishing LLLP. (Weekly Reader Leveled Readers).

Martin, Patricia A. Fink & Fink-Martin, Patricia A. California Condors. 2003. (True Bks.). (ENG., Illus.). 48p. (J). (gr. 3-5). pap. 6.95 *(978-0-516-27470-6(8)*, Children's Pr.) Scholastic Library Publishing.

CONDUCT OF LIFE

see also Behavior; Obedience

ABDO Publishing Company Staff. Contemporary Lives Set 2, 1 vol. 2013. (Contemporary Lives Set 2 Ser.: 8). (ENG.). 112p. (J). (gr. 6-12). lib. bdg. 285.12 *(978-1-61783-615-2(X)*, Essential Library) ABDO Publishing Co.

Adams, Christine. Learning to Be a Good Friend: A Guidebook for Kids. Alley, R. W., illus. 2004. 32p. (J). per. 7.95 *(978-0-87029-388-7(5))* Abbey Pr.

Adams, M.H. Small Means & Great Ends (Illustrated. 2006. pap. *(978-1-4065-0478-1(5))* Dodo Pr.

Aikins, Anne Marie. Misconduct: Deal with It Without Bending the Rules, 1 vol. Murray, Steven, illus. 2005. (Lorimer Deal with It Ser.). (ENG.). 32p. (J). (gr. 4-6). 12.95 *(978-1-55028-871-1(7)*, 9781550288711) Lorimer, James & Co., Ltd., Pubs. CAN. Dist: Casemate Pubs. & Bk. Distributors, LLC.

Alexander, Kwame. The Playbook: 52 Rules to Aim, Shoot, & Score in This Game Called Life. Neave, Thai, photos by. 2017. (ENG., Illus.). 176p. (J). (gr. 5-7). 14.99 *(978-0-544-57097-9(9)*, HMH Books For Young Readers) Houghton Mifflin Harcourt Publishing Co.

—The Playbook: 52 Rules to Aim, Shoot, & Score in This Game Called Life. Neave, Thai, photos by. 2017. (ENG., Illus.). (J). (gr. 5-7). lib. bdg. 26.95 ***(978-0-606-39814-5(7))*** Turtleback Bks.

American Girl, creator. You Can Do It! A Kit to Help You Do Just about Anything. 2006. (American Girl Library). (ENG., Illus.). 48p. 9.95 *(978-1-59369-155-4(6)*, American Girl) American Girl Publishing, Inc.

Amoroso, Cynthia. Forgiveness. 2013. (Values to Live By Ser.). (ENG.). 24p. (J). (gr. -1-2). 25.64 *(978-1-62323-517-8(0)*, 206288) Child's World, Inc., The.

—Honesty. 2013. (Values to Live By Ser.). (ENG.). 24p. (J). (gr. -1-2). 25.64 *(978-1-62323-520-8(0)*, 206291) Child's World, Inc., The.

Amos, Janine. After You. 2009. (Best Behavior Ser.). (Illus.). 32p. (J). (gr. -1-2). pap. 10.55 *(978-1-60754-032-8(0))*; lib. bdg. 22.60 *(978-1-60754-020-5(7))* Windmill Bks.

—Don't Do That! How Not to Act. 2009. (Best Behavior Ser.). (Illus.). 32p. (J). (gr. -1-2). pap. 10.55 *(978-1-60754-052-6(5))* Windmill Bks.

—Hello! 2009. (Best Behavior Ser.). (Illus.). 32p. (J). (gr. -1-2). pap. 10.55 *(978-1-60754-034-2(7))*; lib. bdg. 22.60 *(978-1-60754-021-2(5))* Windmill Bks.

—I'm Sorry. 2009. (Best Behavior Ser.). (Illus.). 32p. (J). (gr. -1-2). pap. 10.55 *(978-1-60754-040-3(1))*; lib. bdg. 22.60 *(978-1-60754-024-3(X))* Windmill Bks.

—No, Thank You. 2009. (Best Behavior Ser.). (Illus.). 32p. (J). (gr. -1-2). pap. 10.55 *(978-1-60754-036-6(3))*; lib. bdg. 22.60 *(978-1-60754-022-9(3))* Windmill Bks.

—Please. 2009. (Best Behavior Ser.). (Illus.). 32p. (J). (gr. -1-2). pap. 10.55 *(978-1-60754-038-0(X))*; lib. bdg. 22.60 *(978-1-60754-023-6(1))* Windmill Bks.

—Thank You. 2009. (Best Behavior Ser.). (Illus.). 32p. (J). (gr. -1-2). pap. 10.55 *(978-1-60754-042-7(8))*; lib. bdg. 22.60 *(978-1-60754-025-0(8))* Windmill Bks.

Amos, Janine & Spenceley, Annabel. Don't Do That! How Not to Act. 2009. (Best Behavior Ser.). (Illus.). 32p. (J). (gr. -1-2). lib. bdg. 22.60 *(978-1-60754-030-4(4))* Windmill Bks.

—Don't Say That! Let's Talk Nicely. 2009. (Best Behavior Ser.). (Illus.). 32p. (J). (gr. -1-2). pap. 10.55 *(978-1-60754-054-0(1))*; lib. bdg. 22.60 *(978-1-60754-031-1(2))* Windmill Bks.

—Go Away! What Not to Say. 2009. (Best Behavior Ser.). (Illus.). 32p. (J). (gr. -1-2). pap. 10.55 *(978-1-60754-044-1(4))*; lib. bdg. 22.60 *(978-1-60754-026-7(6))* Windmill Bks.

—It Won't Work! Let's Try Again. 2009. (Best Behavior Ser.). (Illus.). 32p. (J). (gr. -1-2). pap. 10.55 *(978-1-60754-046-5(0))*; lib. bdg. 22.60 *(978-1-60754-027-4(4))* Windmill Bks.

—It's Mine! Let's Try to Share. 2009. (Best Behavior Ser.). (Illus.). 32p. (J). (gr. -1-2). pap. 10.55 *(978-1-60754-048-9(7))*; lib. bdg. 22.60 *(978-1-60754-028-1(2))* Windmill Bks.

—Let's Help Out! 2009. (Best Behavior Ser.). (Illus.). 32p. (J). (gr. -1-2). 22.60 *(978-1-60754-490-6(3))*; pap. 10.55 *(978-1-60754-491-3(1))* Windmill Bks.

—Let's Make Friends. 2009. (Best Behavior Ser.). (Illus.). 32p. (J). (gr. -1-2). 22.60 *(978-1-60754-500-2(4))*; pap. 10.55 *(978-1-60754-499-9(7))* Windmill Bks.

—Let's Own Up. 2009. (Best Behavior Ser.). (Illus.). 32p. (J). (gr. -1-2). 22.60 *(978-1-60754-503-3(9))*; pap. 10.55 *(978-1-60754-505-7(5))* Windmill Bks.

—Let's Share. 2009. (Best Behavior Ser.). (Illus.). 32p. (J). (gr. -1-2). 22.60 *(978-1-60754-508-8(X))*; pap. 10.55 *(978-1-60754-509-5(8))* Windmill Bks.

—Let's Take Turns. 2009. (Best Behavior Ser.). (Illus.). 32p. (J). (gr. -1-2). 22.60 *(978-1-60754-512-5(8))*; pap. 10.55 *(978-1-60754-513-2(6))* Windmill Bks.

—Move Over! Learning to Share Our Space. 2009. (Best Behavior Ser.). (Illus.). 32p. (J). (gr. -1-2). pap. 10.55 *(978-1-60754-050-2(9))*; lib. bdg. 22.60 *(978-1-60754-029-8(0))* Windmill Bks.

Amos, Janine & Spenceley, Annabel. Let's Be Kind. 2009. (Best Behavior Ser.). (Illus.). 32p. (J). (gr. -1-2). pap. 10.55 *(978-1-60754-494-4(6))*;1. 22.60 *(978-1-60754-493-7(8))* Windmill Bks.

Anderson, George William, ed. Achieving Success with Faith in God: The Concept of Faith - Based Perseverance. 2007. 128p. 15.95 *(978-0-9786565-0-8(4))* Naypree Enterprises, LLC.

Anderson, Joyce. Teen Discussion Guide - Your Parents. (Teen Discussion Guide Ser.). (Illus.). 64p. (YA). (gr. 7-18). pap. 9.95 *(978-0-937282-93-9(6))* Rainbow Pubs. & Legacy Pr.

Andries, Kathryn. Soul Choices: Six Paths to Find Your Life Purpose. Brill, Darlene, ed. 2003. (Illus.). 206p. (YA). pap. 19.95 *(978-0-9741334-0-9(X))* Intuitive Arts Pr.

Appreciation of Diversity. 2005. (Promoting Peace with the Friends from Sunshine Center Ser.). (Illus.). 32p. (J). 14.95 *(978-0-9768827-1-8(X))* Prevention Through Puppetry, Inc.

Armstrong, Susan. Just One?.. for Kids! 2008. 86p. pap. 9.95 *(978-1-4357-3844-7(6))* Lulu Pr., Inc.

Atkinson, Sue. Life Confidence for Kids. 2012. 240p. pap. *(978-0-9571138-0-0(3))* Harecroft Publishing.

Aunty Moose, Moose & Aunty Moose. The Gift of a Lifetime. 2009. 40p. pap. 18.49 *(978-1-4389-7868-0(5))* AuthorHouse.

Bad Guys [Capstone Sole Source]. 2010. (Bad Guys Ser.). 48p. lib. bdg. 122.60 *(978-1-4296-5844-7(4))* Capstone Press of Coughlan Cos.

Baden-Powell, Robert. Life's Snags & How to Meet Them. 2005. pap. 20.95 *(978-1-885529-81-7(3))* Stevens Publishing.

Bailey, Diane. Cyber Ethics. 2009. (Cyber Citizenship & Cyber Safety Ser.). 48p. (gr. 5-5). 53.00 *(978-1-61512-102-1(1)*, Rosen Reference) Rosen Publishing Group, Inc., The.

Banks, Jane Whelen. Liam Knows What to Do When Kids Act Snitty: Coping When Friends Are Tactless. 2008. (ENG., Illus.). 32p. 12.95 *(978-1-84310-902-0(6)*, 7167) Kingsley, Jessica Pubs. GBR. Dist: Macmillan Distribution Ltd.

Barraclough, Sue. Fair Play. 2016. (Exploring Citizenship Ser.). (ENG.). 32p. pap. 8.29 *(978-1-4846-3985-6(5)*, Heinemann First Library) Heinemann-Raintree.

—Jugar Limpio, 1 vol. 2010. (Explorar el Civismo Ser.). (SPA & ENG., Illus.). 32p. (gr. 1-3). 27.32 *(978-1-4329-4460-5(6))*; pap. 8.29 *(978-1-4329-4468-1(1))* Heinemann-Raintree.

Barrett, Selby. The Diva Code Diary. 2007. 152p. pap. 19.48 *(978-0-615-15832-7(3))* Pick Me Up N Go Publishing Co.

Barron, T. A. The Hero's Trail: A Guide for a Heroic Life. 2007. (ENG., Illus.). 192p. (J). (gr. 3-7). 8.99 *(978-0-14-240760-8(7)*, Puffin Books) Penguin Young Readers Group.

Beck, Randy. Teen Quest. l.t. ed. 2004. 80p. (YA). per. 12.95 *(978-1-59196-535-0(7))* Instant Pub.

Beckerman, Menucha. My Middos World: Where Is Michael?, 8. 2003. (My Middos World Ser.: Vol. 8). (Illus.). 24p. (J). 11.95 *(978-1-931681-16-2(3))* Israel Bookshop Pubns.

—My Middos World: Why Did Dina-dee's Face Shine, 6. Gaash, Elisheva, illus. 2003. (My Middos World Ser.: Vol. 6). 24p. (J). (gr. k-5). 11.95 *(978-1-931681-05-6(8))* Israel Bookshop Pubns.

—The Real Hero. (Illus.). 24p. (J). (gr. k-5). 4.95 *(978-1-931681-08-7(2))* Israel Bookshop Pubns.

—Who Dropped the Chick. 2003. (My Little World Ser.: Vol. 4). (Illus.). 32p. (J). (gr. k-5). 5.95 *(978-1-931681-09-4(0))* Israel Bookshop Pubns.

Benchmark Education Co., LLC. Show Respect Big Book. 2014. (Shared Reading Foundations Ser.). (J). (gr. -1). *(978-1-4509-9426-2(1))* Benchmark Education Co.

Benge, Janet & Benge, Geoff. Jacob Deshazer: Forgive Your Enemies. 2009. (ENG.). 224p. (YA). pap. 9.99 *(978-1-57658-475-0(5))* YWAM Publishing.

Bergeron, Pastor Susan "Suzy". A Preteens Mothers Best Friend. 2012. 16p. pap. 12.68 *(978-1-4669-5618-6(6))* Trafford Publishing.

Berman, Ron. Who's Got Next? Future Leaders of America. 2013. (Av2 Audio Chapter Bks.). (ENG., Illus.). 92p. (J). (gr. 4-7). lib. bdg. 27.13 *(978-1-62127-998-3(7)*, AV2 by Weigl) Weigl Pubs., Inc.

Bernson, Janet. Un-Masking the Soul: A Creative Approach to Working with the Masks in the Mirror, 1. 3rd ed. 2003. (Illus.). 134p. per. 17.95 *(978-0-9720509-4-4(9))* Bernson Pr.

Berry, Joy. Achieve Goals. 3rd ed. 2005. (Winning skills series, work It! Ser.). (ENG., Illus.). 48p. (J). pap. 3.95 *(978-1-57687-285-7(8)*, PowerHouse Kids) powerHouse Cultural Entertainment, Inc.

—Be a Star. 2005. (Winning skills series, go for It! Ser.). (ENG., Illus.). 48p. (J). pap. 3.95 *(978-1-57687-289-5(0)*, PowerHouse Kids) powerHouse Cultural Entertainment, Inc.

—Be a Winner. 2005. (Winning skills series, go for It! Ser.). (ENG., Illus.). 48p. (J). pap. 3.95 *(978-1-57687-290-1(4)*, PowerHouse Kids) powerHouse Cultural Entertainment, Inc.

—Be Assertive. 2005. (Winning skills series, work It! Ser.). (ENG., Illus.). 48p. (J). pap. 3.95 *(978-1-57687-295-6(5)*, PowerHouse Kids) powerHouse Cultural Entertainment, Inc.

—Be Beautiful. 2005. (Winning skills series, go for It! Ser.). (ENG., Illus.). 48p. (J). pap. 3.95 *(978-1-57687-286-4(6)*, PowerHouse Kids) powerHouse Cultural Entertainment, Inc.

—Be Happy. 2005. (Winning skills series, go for It! Ser.). (ENG., Illus.). 48p. (J). pap. 3.95 *(978-1-57687-288-8(2)*, PowerHouse Kids) powerHouse Cultural Entertainment, Inc.

—Be in Control. 2005. (Winning skills series, work It! Ser.). (ENG., Illus.). 48p. (J). pap. 3.95 *(978-1-57687-283-3(1)*, PowerHouse Kids) powerHouse Cultural Entertainment, Inc.

—Be Liked. 2005. (Winning skills series, go for It! Ser.). (ENG., Illus.). 48p. (J). pap. 3.95 *(978-1-57687-287-1(4)*, PowerHouse Kids) powerHouse Cultural Entertainment, Inc.

—Be Organized. 2005. (Winning skills series, work It! Ser.). (ENG., Illus.). 48p. (J). pap. 3.95 *(978-1-57687-284-0(X)*, PowerHouse Kids) powerHouse Cultural Entertainment, Inc.

—Be Smart. 2005. (Winning skills series, work It! Ser.). (ENG., Illus.). 48p. (J). pap. 3.95 *(978-1-57687-281-9(5)*, PowerHouse Kids) powerHouse Cultural Entertainment, Inc.

—Being Good. 2009. (ENG.). 40p. (J). (gr. -1-k). pap. 7.95 *(978-1-60577-213-4(5))* Berry, Joy Enterprises.

—Being Patient. 2009. (ENG.). 40p. (J). (gr. -1-k). pap. 7.95 *(978-1-60577-212-7(7))* Berry, Joy Enterprises.

—Criticism & Rejection. 2005. (Winning skills series, get over It! Ser.). (ENG., Illus.). 48p. (J). pap. 3.95 *(978-1-57687-277-2(7))* powerHouse Cultural Entertainment, Inc.

—Get over It! 2009. (ENG.). 304p. (J). (gr. 5-7). pap. 12.95 *(978-1-60577-603-3(3))* Berry, Joy Enterprises.

—Getting Dressed. 2009. (ENG.). 40p. (J). (gr. k — 1). bds. 7.95 *(978-1-60577-009-3(4))* Berry, Joy Enterprises.

—Good Answers to Tough Questions about Death. 2009. (ENG.). 52p. (J). (gr. k-7). pap. 7.95 *(978-1-60577-506-7(1))* Berry, Joy Enterprises.

—Good Answers to Tough Questions about Divorce. 2009. (ENG.). 52p. (J). (gr. k-7). pap. 7.95 *(978-1-60577-504-3(5))* Berry, Joy Enterprises.

—Good Answers to Tough Questions Divorce. Bartholomew, illus. 2010. (Good Answers to Tough Questions Ser.). (ENG.). 48p. (J). (gr. k-7). pap. 7.99 *(978-1-60577-509-8(6))* Berry, Joy Enterprises.

—Good Answers to Tough Questions Moving. Bartholomew, illus. 2010. (Good Answers to Tough Questions Ser.). (ENG.). 48p. (J). (gr. k-7). pap. 7.99 *(978-1-60577-508-1(8))* Berry, Joy Enterprises.

—Good Answers to Tough Questions Trauma. Bartholomew, illus. 2010. (Good Answers to Tough Questions Ser.). (ENG.). 48p. (J). (gr. k-7). pap. 7.99 *(978-1-60577-507-4(X))* Berry, Joy Enterprises.

—Have a Great Future. 3rd ed. 2005. (Winning skills series, go for It! Ser.). (ENG., Illus.). 48p. (J). pap. 3.95 *(978-1-57687-291-8(2)*, PowerHouse Kids) powerHouse Cultural Entertainment, Inc.

—Help Me Be Good about Being a Bad Sport. 2009. (Help Me Be Good Ser.). 40p. pap. 7.95 *(978-1-60577-108-3(2))* Berry, Joy Enterprises.

—Help Me Be Good about Being Bullied. 2009. (Help Me Be Good Ser.). 32p. pap. 7.95 *(978-1-60577-125-0(2))* Berry, Joy Enterprises.

—Help Me Be Good about Being Careless. 2009. (Help Me Be Good Ser.). 32p. pap. 7.95 *(978-1-60577-103-8(1))* Berry, Joy Enterprises.

—Help Me Be Good about Being Destructive. 2009. (Help Me Be Good Ser.). 32p. pap. 7.95 *(978-1-60577-127-4(9))* Berry, Joy Enterprises.

—Help Me Be Good about Being Forgetful. 2009. (Help Me Be Good Ser.). 32p. pap. 7.95 *(978-1-60577-102-1(3))* Berry, Joy Enterprises.

—Help Me Be Good about Being Greedy. 2009. (ENG.). 40p. (J). (gr. k-2). pap. 7.95 *(978-1-60577-110-6(4))* Berry, Joy Enterprises.

—Help Me Be Good about Being Lazy. 2009. (Help Me Be Good Ser.). 32p. pap. 7.95 *(978-1-60577-101-4(5))* Berry, Joy Enterprises.

—Help Me Be Good about Being Mean. 2009. (Help Me Be Good Ser.). 32p. pap. 7.95 *(978-1-60577-129-8(5))* Berry, Joy Enterprises.

—Help Me Be Good about Being Messy. 2009. (ENG.). 40p. (J). (gr. k-2). pap. 7.95 *(978-1-60577-104-5(X))* Berry, Joy Enterprises.

—Help Me Be Good about Being Rude. 2009. (ENG.). 40p. (J). (gr. k-2). pap. 7.95 *(978-1-60577-121-2(X))* Berry, Joy Enterprises.

—Help Me Be Good about Being Wasteful. 2009. (Help Me Be Good Ser.). 32p. pap. 7.95 *(978-1-60577-105-2(8))* Berry, Joy Enterprises.

—Help Me Be Good about Breaking Promises. 2009. (Help Me Be Good Ser.). 32p. pap. 7.95 *(978-1-60577-111-3(2))* Berry, Joy Enterprises.

—Help Me Be Good about Cheating. 2009. (Help Me Be Good Ser.). 32p. pap. 7.95 *(978-1-60577-123-6(6))* Berry, Joy Enterprises.

—Help Me Be Good about Complaining. 2009. (Help Me Be Good Ser.). 32p. pap. 7.95 *(978-1-60577-116-8(3))* Berry, Joy Enterprises.

—Help Me Be Good about Gossiping. 2009. (Help Me Be Good Ser.). 32p. pap. 7.95 *(978-1-60577-120-5(1))* Berry, Joy Enterprises.

—Help Me Be Good about Interrupting. 2009. (Help Me Be Good Ser.). 32p. pap. 7.95 *(978-1-60577-114-4(7))* Berry, Joy Enterprises.

—Help Me Be Good about Lying. 2009. (Help Me Be Good Ser.). 32p. pap. 7.95 *(978-1-60577-113-7(9))* Berry, Joy Enterprises.

—Help Me Be Good about Overdoing It. 2009. (Help Me Be Good Ser.). 32p. pap. 7.95 *(978-1-60577-106-9(6))* Berry, Joy Enterprises.

—Help Me Be Good about Showing Off. 2009. (Help Me Be Good Ser.). 32p. pap. 7.95 *(978-1-60577-107-6(4))* Berry, Joy Enterprises.

—Help Me Be Good about Snooping. 2009. (Help Me Be Good Ser.). 32p. pap. 7.95 *(978-1-60577-122-9(8))* Berry, Joy Enterprises.

—Help Me Be Good about Stealing. 2009. (Help Me Be Good Ser.). 32p. pap. 7.95 *(978-1-60577-124-3(4))* Berry, Joy Enterprises.

—Help Me Be Good about Tattling. 2009. (ENG.). 40p. (J). (gr. k-2). pap. 7.95 *(978-1-60577-119-9(8))* Berry, Joy Enterprises.

—Help Me Be Good about Teasing. 2009. (Help Me Be Good Ser.). 32p. pap. 7.95 *(978-1-60577-118-2(X))* Berry, Joy Enterprises.

—Help Me Be Good about Throwing Tantrums. 2009. (Help Me Be Good Ser.). 32p. pap. 7.95 *(978-1-60577-117-5(1))* Berry, Joy Enterprises.

—Help Me Be Good Being a Bad Sport. Bartholomew, illus. 2010. (Help Me Be Good Ser.). (ENG.). 32p. (J). (gr. -1-2). pap. 4.99 *(978-1-60577-139-7(2))* Berry, Joy Enterprises.

—Help Me Be Good Being Mean. Bartholomew, illus. 2010. (Help Me Be Good Ser.). (ENG.). 32p. (J). (gr. -1-2). pap. 4.99 *(978-1-60577-142-7(2))* Berry, Joy Enterprises.

—Help Me Be Good Being Selfish. Bartholomew, illus. 2010. (Help Me Be Good Ser.). (ENG.). 32p. (J). (gr. -1-2). pap. 4.99 *(978-1-60577-133-5(3))* Berry, Joy Enterprises.

—Help Me Be Good Bullying. Bartholomew, illus. 2010. (Help Me Be Good Ser.). (ENG.). 32p. (J). (gr. -1-2). pap. 4.99 *(978-1-60577-140-3(6))* Berry, Joy Enterprises.

—Help Me Be Good Showing Off. Bartholomew, illus. 2010. (Help Me Be Good Ser.). (ENG.). 32p. (J). (gr. -1-2). pap. 4.99 *(978-1-60577-143-4(0))* Berry, Joy Enterprises.

—Help Me Be Good Tattling. Bartholomew, illus. 2010. (Help Me Be Good Ser.). (ENG.). 32p. (J). (gr. -1-2). pap. 4.99 *(978-1-60577-136-6(8))* Berry, Joy Enterprises.

—Help Me Be Good Teasing. Bartholomew, illus. 2010. (Help Me Be Good Ser.). (ENG.). 32p. (J). (gr. -1-2). pap. 4.99 *(978-1-60577-141-0(4))* Berry, Joy Enterprises.

—Rude People. 2005. (Winning skills series, get over It! Ser.). (ENG., Illus.). 48p. (J). pap. 3.95 *(978-1-57687-278-9(5)*, PowerHouse Kids) powerHouse Cultural Entertainment, Inc.

—Stress. 2005. (Winning skills series, get over It! Ser.). (ENG., Illus.). 48p. (J). pap. 3.95 *(978-1-57687-276-5(9)*, PowerHouse Kids) powerHouse Cultural Entertainment, Inc.

—Substance Abuse. 2009. (ENG.). 52p. (J). (gr. k-7). pap. 7.95 *(978-1-60577-502-9(9))* Berry, Joy Enterprises.

—Trauma. 2009. (ENG.). 52p. (J). (gr. k-7). pap. 7.95 *(978-1-60577-501-2(0))* Berry, Joy Enterprises.

—Winning Skills You Can Work It! an Anthology of Six Books. Bartholomew, illus. 2010. (Winning Skills Ser.). (ENG.). 304p. (J). (gr. 5-7). pap. 9.95 *(978-1-60577-604-0(1))* Berry, Joy Enterprises.

—Work it! Set, 6 vols. 2005. (Winning skills series, work It! Ser.). (ENG., Illus.). 1p. (J). pap. 19.95 *(978-1-57687-293-2(9))* powerHouse Cultural Entertainment, Inc.

—You Can Go for It! 2009. (ENG.). 304p. (J). (gr. 5-7). pap. 12.95 *(978-1-60577-601-9(7))* Berry, Joy Enterprises.

—You Can... Work It! Being Smart, Being Creative, Being Assertive, Being in Control, Getting Organized & Attaining Goals! 2009. (ENG.). 304p. (J). (gr. 5-7). pap. 12.95 *(978-1-60577-602-6(5))* Berry, Joy Enterprises.

Berry, Joy Wilt. A Book about Being a Bad Sport. 2005. (Illus.). (J). *(978-0-7172-8588-4(X))* Scholastic, Inc.

—A Book about Being Bullied. 2005. (Illus.). (J). *(978-0-7172-8578-5(2))* Scholastic, Inc.

—A Book about Being Forgetful. 2005. (Illus.). (J). *(978-0-7172-8589-1(8))* Scholastic, Inc.

—A Book about Being Greedy. 2005. (Illus.). (J). *(978-0-7172-8598-3(7))* Scholastic, Inc.

—A Book about Being Lazy. 2005. (Illus.). (J). *(978-0-7172-7899-2(9))* Scholastic, Inc.

—A Book about Being Mean. 2005. (Illus.). (J). *(978-0-7172-8591-4(X))* Scholastic, Inc.

—A Book about Being Messy. 2005. (Illus.). (J). *(978-0-7172-8577-8(4))* Scholastic, Inc.

—A Book about Being Rude. 2005. (Illus.). (J). *(978-0-7172-8592-1(8))* Scholastic, Inc.

—A Book about Being Selfish. 2005. (Illus.). (J). *(978-0-7172-8579-2(0))* Scholastic, Inc.

—A Book about Breaking Promise. 2005. (Illus.). (J). *(978-0-7172-8600-3(2))* Scholastic, Inc.

—A Book about Cheating. 2005. (Illus.). (J). *(978-0-7172-8583-9(9))* Scholastic, Inc.

—A Book about Lying. 2005. (Illus.). (J). *(978-0-7172-8576-1(6))* Scholastic, Inc.

—A Book about Overdoing It. 2005. (Illus.). (J). *(978-0-7172-8575-4(8))* Scholastic, Inc.

—A Book about Showing Off. 2005. (Illus.). (J). *(978-0-7172-8597-6(9))* Scholastic, Inc.

—A Book about Stealing. 2005. (Illus.). (J). *(978-0-7172-8585-3(5))* Scholastic, Inc.

—A Book about Tattling. 2005. (Illus.). (J). *(978-0-7172-7897-8(2))* Scholastic, Inc.

—A Book about Teasing. 2005. (Illus.). (J). *(978-0-7172-8580-8(4))* Scholastic, Inc.

—A Children's Book about Being Destructive. 2005. (Illus.). (J). *(978-0-7172-8596-9(0))* Scholastic, Inc.

Berry, Ron. Rise & Shine! Sharp, Chris, illus. 2008. 14p. (J). bds. 12.99 *(978-0-8249-6735-2(6)*, Ideal Pubns.) Worthy Publishing.

Bishop, Jennie & Henson, Susan. Life Lessons from the Princess & the Kiss: Planting Seeds of Purity in Young Hearts. 2004. (Revive Our Hearts Ser.). (ENG., Illus.). 56p. pap. 9.99 *(978-0-940110-52-6(0))* Life Action Inc.

Blake, D M. Achieving Success with Faith in God: The Concept of Faith-Based Perserverance. 2007. 128p. per. 13.95 *(978-0-9786565-1-5(2))* Naypree Enterprises, LLC.

Blosser, Connie S. Destiny's Trouble: A True Story. 2013. 20p. pap. 24.95 *(978-1-4626-9341-2(5))* America Star Bks.

Blumenthal, Scott. A Kid's Mensch Handbook: Step by Step to a Lifetime of Jewish Values. 2004. (J). *(978-0-87441-700-5(7))* Behrman Hse., Inc.

Bockmann, Melanie. Just Plane Crazy: A Guide True Story Book. 2006. 128p. *(978-0-8280-1919-4(3))* Review & Herald Publishing Assn.

Bodden, Michelle. Well My Teacher Said. Williams, Brittney, illus. 2007. 32p. (J). 14.95 *(978-0-9753089-2-9(0))* Water Daughter Publishing.

Bohensky, Anita. Self Esteem Workbook for Teens. 2003. (ENG., Illus.). 101p. (YA). 54.00 *(978-1-893505-07-0(3))* Growth Publishing.

Born to Win. 2004. (J). 7.99 net. *(978-0-9763141-0-3(X))* G.S. Enterprises of America Inc.

Bottoms, James. Kid Ethics 2: From A to Z. 2007. (Illus.). 59p. (J). per. 12.95 *(978-0-9794863-1-9(9))* Summerland Publishing.

Boyd, Ervin D., Sr. Help for the Hurting: Getting Beyond This Veil of Tears! 2003. (Illus.). 200p. (YA). spiral bd. 22.00 *(978-0-9744024-0-6(0))* Anointed Word Pubns.

Boys to Men: A Christian Teen Survival Guide by Young Men Who Are Survivors. 2007. 165p. (J). *(978-0-929540-59-7(X))* Publishing Designs, Inc.

Breland, Cathy Easter. Choices! 2011. 24p. pap. 12.45 *(978-1-4497-1120-7(0)*, WestBow Pr.) Author Solutions, Inc.

Bremner, Shawn, compiled by. Aspire to Something Higher: A Pocket Book of Inspired Thoughts. 2003. 129p. per. *(978-0-9682738-0-7(7))* Happy Publishing.

Brereton, Erin. Real Girls' Guide to Everything: That Makes It Awesome to Be a Girl! Zalevskaya, Anastacia, illus. 2011. (ENG.). 192p. (J). pap. 12.95 *(978-1-60078-561-0(1))* Triumph Bks.

Buddhist Text Translation Society Staff, contrib. by. Standards for Students: Instructions in Virtue from the Chinese Heritage = [Di Zi Gui]. 2003. (ENG & CHI., Illus.). 41p. (J). *(978-0-88139-489-4(0))* Buddhist Text Translation Society.

Burns, Kylie. Live It: Perseverance. 2009. (ENG., Illus.). 32p. (J). (gr. 3-6). lib. bdg. *(978-0-7787-4884-7(7))* Crabtree Publishing Co.

Burton, Margie, et al. Growing Older. 2011. (Early Connections Ser.). (J). *(978-1-61672-491-7(9))* Benchmark Education Co.

—Rules. 2011. (Early Connections Ser.). (J). *(978-1-61672-505-1(2))* Benchmark Education Co.

Cabot, Meg. Princess Lessons. McLaren, Chesley, illus. 2003. (Princess Diaries Guidebook Ser.). (ENG.). 144p. (YA). (gr. 8-18). 15.99 *(978-0-06-052677-1(7)*, HarperTeen) HarperCollins Pubs.

Campbell, Hugh R. Goal Scoring Step-by-Step. 2011. 50p. pap. *(978-1-77067-493-6(4))* FriesenPress.

Candell, Arianna. Mind Your Manners: In School. Curto, Rosa M., illus. 2005. (Mind Your Manners Ser.). (ENG.). 36p. (J). pap. 6.99 *(978-0-7641-3166-0(4))* Barron's Educational Series, Inc.

Cap Compass Staff. Life after School, Explained. 2011. 164p. per. 13.95 *(978-0-9717366-0-3(X))* Cap & Compass, LLC.

Carbone, Courtney. How to Be a Princess (Disney Princess) RH Disney Staff, illus. 2015. (Ultimate Handbook Ser.). (ENG.). 64p. (J). (gr. 1-4). 9.99 *(978-0-7364-3415-7(1)*, RH/Disney) Random Hse. Children's Bks.

—Inside Out Guide to Life (Disney/Pixar Inside Out) RH Disney, illus. 2016. (ENG.). 80p. (J). (gr. -1-2). 9.99 *(978-0-7364-3559-8(X)*, RH/Disney) Random Hse. Children's Bks.

Carlson, Amie. My Princesses Learn to Share. Heyworth, Heather, illus. 2014. (ENG.). 24p. (J). 6.99 *(978-1-4143-9662-0(7))* Tyndale Hse. Pubs.

Carlson, Dale. Who Said What? Philosophy Quotes for Teens. Nicklaus, Carol, illus. 2003. (ENG.). 224p. (gr. 7-12). pap. 14.95 *(978-1-884158-28-5(5))* Team Kreskin Productions, LLC.

Carlson, Nancy. Think Happy! Carlson, Nancy, illus. (Nancy Carlson Picture Bks). (Illus.). 32p. (J). (gr. k-3). 2012. (ENG.). 9.95 *(978-0-7613-9175-3(4))* 2012. 56.72 *(978-0-7613-9312-2(9))* 2009. (ENG., 16.95

(978-0-8225-8940-2(0)) Lerner Publishing Group. (Carolrhoda Bks.).

Carr, Dan. God I Need to Talk Hurting Oth. 2004. 16p. (J). 1.19 (978-0-7586-0517-7(X)) Concordia Publishing Hse.

Carry the Sunshine in Your Heart. 2004. (J). pap. 7.99 net. (978-0-9763141-1-0(8)) G.S. Enterprises of America Inc.

Carson, Shonette. My Dear Child, I Have Gone to Heaven Let's Talk: A Child's Recovery Plan, 1 vol. Hearn, Marilyn, illus. 2010. 36p. 24.95 (978-1-4489-6341-6(9)) PublishAmerica, Inc.

Carter, Carol S., creator. Appreciation of Diversity. 2005. (Promoting Peace with the Friends from Sunshine Center Ser.). (J). pap. 12.95 (978-0-9768827-0-1(1)) Prevention Through Puppetry, Inc.

Catherman, Jonathan. The Manual to Middle School: The Do This, Not That Survival Guide for Guys. 2017. (ENG.). 224p. pap. 13.99 **(978-0-8007-2847-2(5))** Revell.

Chapus, Julie. The Blame Game. 2013. 62p. pap. 9.50 (978-1-935018-87-2(6)) International Localization Network.

Chobanian, Elizabeth, ed. Coconut's Guide to Life: Life Lessons from a Girl's Best Friend. Lukatz, Casey, illus. 2003. (Coconut Ser.). 32p. (J). 21.95 (978-1-58485-772-3(2)) American Girl Publishing, Inc.

Chobanian, Elizabeth & American Girl Publishing Staff, eds. Coconut's Guide to Life: Life Lessons from a Girl's Best Friend. Lukatz, Casey, illus. 2003. (Coconut Ser.). (ENG.). 32p. (J). 5.95 (978-1-58485-771-6(4)) American Girl Publishing, Inc.

Cleland, Jo. Achoo! 2012. (ENG.). 24p. (gr. k-2). pap. 8.95 (978-1-61810-214-0(1)) Rourke Educational Media.

Clinton, Chelsea. It's Your World: Get Informed, Get Inspired & Get Going! 2017. (ENG., Illus.). 432p. (J). (gr. 5). pap. 9.99 (978-0-399-54532-0(8), Puffin Books) Penguin Young Readers Group.

Clyde, Addie M. Sophie the Sofa. l.t. ed. 2004. 40p. (J). per. (978-1-59196-744-6(9)) Instant Pub.

Coan, Sharon. Good for Me: Love. 2015. (TIME for KIDS(r) Nonfiction Readers Ser.). (ENG., Illus.). 12p. (gr. k-k). 4.99 (978-1-4938-2153-2(9)) Teacher Created Materials, Inc.

Cody, Jacquelyne. How to Be Happy. 2008. 192p. 25.50 (978-1-60693-312-1(4), Strategic Bk. Publishing) Strategic Book Publishing & Rights Agency (SBPRA).

Coil, Carolyn. Becoming an Achiever. exp. rev. ed. 2004. (J). pap. 16.95 (978-1-931334-57-0(9)) Pieces of Learning.

Coleman-Cunningham, Carol D. Maria Was Touched by an Angel. 2012. 32p. pap. 10.00 (978-0-9849360-4-5(1)) G Publishing LLC.

Coleman, Patricia. What Mama Never Told Me! 2009. 80p. pap. 12.99 (978-1-60860-517-0(5), Strategic Bk. Publishing) Strategic Book Publishing & Rights Agency (SBPRA).

Concord, Juliet. I Am Kind. 2011. (Kids of Character Ser.). (Illus.). 24p. (J). (gr. 1-3). pap. 8.15 (978-1-4339-4869-5(9)); lib. bdg. 22.60 (978-1-4339-4868-8(0)) Stevens, Gareth Publishing LLLP.

Cook, Billie Montgomery. The Real Deal: A Spiritual Guide for Black Teen Girls. 2004. 144p. pap. 14.00 (978-0-8170-1458-2(6)) Judson Pr.

Cooper, Scott. Speak up & Get Along! Learn the Mighty Might, Thought Chop, & More Tools to Make Friends, Stop Teasing, & Feel Good about Yourself. 2005. (ENG., Illus.). 128p. (J). (gr. 4-7). pap. 12.99 (978-1-57542-182-7(8)) Free Spirit Publishing, Inc.

Cope Bowley, Tonia. From a Street Kid: Stephen Lungu's Incredible Life Journey. Petropouleas, Niko, illus. 2012. 192p. pap. (978-1-78003-380-8(X)) Pen Pr. Pubs., Ltd.

Coping in a Changing World, 6 bks., Set. Incl. Avian Flu. Orr, Tamra B. (Illus.). 2007. lib. bdg. 34.60 (978-1-4042-0950-3(6)); Body Piercing & Tattooing: The Hidden Dangers of Body Art. Sawyer, Sarah. 2006. lib. bdg. 34.60 (978-1-4042-0947-3(6)); HIV & AIDS. Johanson, Paula. (Illus.). 2007. lib. bdg. 34.60 (978-1-4042-0948-0(4)); Obesity. Harmon, Daniel E. 2006. lib. bdg. 34.60 (978-1-4042-0949-7(2)); Stress. Bickerstaff, Linda. (Illus.). 2007. lib. bdg. 34.60 (978-1-4042-0951-0(4)); Suicide. Giddens, Sandra. 2006. lib. bdg. 34.60 (978-1-4042-0952-7(2)); 112p. (YA). (gr. 7-12). 2007. Set lib. bdg. 191.70 (978-1-4042-1063-9(6)) Rosen Publishing Group, Inc., The.

Costanzo, Charlene A. & Costanzo, Charlene. The Twelve Gifts of Birth. Ackison, Wendy Wassink, illus. Reger, Jill, photos by. 2011. (Twelve Gifts Ser.: 1). (ENG.). 64p. 22.99 (978-0-06-621104-6(2), Morrow, William & Co.) HarperCollins Pubs.

Covey, Stephen R. & Covey, Sean. The 6 Most Important Decisions You'll Ever Make: A Guide for Teens. 2006. (ENG., Illus.). 336p. (gr. 8-18). pap. 16.99 (978-0-7432-6504-1(1), Touchstone) Touchstone.

Crist, James J. What to Do When You're Scared & Worried: A Guide for Kids. 2004. (ENG., Illus.). 128p. (YA). (gr. 4-8). pap. 10.99 (978-1-57542-153-7(4)) Free Spirit Publishing, Inc.

Crosson, Denise D. Mommy's Coming Home from Treatment. Motz, Mike, illus. 2009. (ENG.). 44p. (J). (gr. -1-3). pap. 14.95 (978-0-9799869-4-9(X)) Central Recovery Pr.

Crouch, Amie. Feng Shui Workbook for Teens. 2003. (ENG.). 19.95 (978-0-595-65513-7(0)); 128p. (YA). pap. 9.95 (978-0-595-26061-4(6)) iUniverse, Inc. (Writer's Showcase Pr.).

Cullen, Murray & O'Neill, Susan. Try: Treatment Readiness for Youth at Risk. 2005. (J). pap. 15.00 net. (978-1-56991-178-5(9)) American Correctional Assn.

Dahl, Gina M. Choices, Choices Everywhere! 2012. 24p. pap. 10.99 (978-1-4497-7547-6(0), WestBow Pr.) Author Solutions, Inc.

Deen, Marilyn. Share & Be Fair, 1 vol. (Wonder Readers: Mathematics Ser.). (ENG.). (gr. -1-2). 2012. 20p. lib. bdg. 22.65 (978-1-4296-9609-8(5)) 2011. 32p. pap. 5.99 (978-1-4296-7935-0(2)) Capstone Press of Coughlan Cos. (Wonder Readers).

Diamond, Kathryn. The Day I Almost Drowned: A Child's near-Death Experience. 2009. 84p. pap. 11.00 (978-0-557-06946-0(7)) Lulu Pr., Inc.

Dickow, Cheryl. All Things Girl. 2013. 84p. pap. 19.99 (978-1-936453-20-7(7)) Bezalel Bks.

DiOrio, Rana. What Does It Mean to Be Kind? Jorisch, Stephane, illus. 2015. (ENG.). 32p. (J). (gr. -1-3). 17.95 (978-1-939775-09-2(4)) March 4th, Inc.

Discovering Your Own... Teen Esteem. 2003. (Illus.). 345p. (YA). 24.95 (978-0-9753482-0-8(5)) Identity Pr.

Do You Have What It Takes. 2007. (YA). per. 35.00 (978-0-9661256-9-6(X)) Youth Communication - New York Center.

Donovan, Sandy. When Is It My Turn? A Book about Fairness. 2014. (Show Your Character Ser.). (ENG., Illus.). 32p. (gr. 1-3). lib. bdg. 26.60 (978-1-4677-1364-1(3), Lerner Pubns.) Lerner Publishing Group.

Doudna, Kelly. Right on Time!, 1 vol. 2007. (Character Concepts Ser.). (ENG., Illus.). 24p. (J). (gr. k-3). lib. bdg. 24.21 (978-1-59928-740-9(4), SandCastle) ABDO Publishing Co.

Dow, Kathy & Dow, Danica, illus. Low-Down Dirty Words. 2004. 28p. (J). (978-0-9749886-0-3(X)) KayStar Publishing.

Dranoel, Elttem. Elttem Dranoel:Judgement Day. 2003. 112p. 21.95 (978-0-595-65578-6(5), Writers Club Pr.) iUniverse, Inc.

Dromgoole, Glenn. What Puppies Teach Us: Life's Lessons Learned from Our Little Friends. 2003. (Illus.). 32p. tchr. ed. 12.95 (978-1-57223-684-4(1), 6841) Willow Creek Pr., Inc.

Dyer, Wayne & Tracy, Kristina. No Excuses! How What You Say Can Get in Your Way. Budnick, Stacy Heller, illus. 2009. (ENG.). 32p. 15.99 (978-1-4019-2583-3(9), 1060) Hay Hse., Inc.

Dyer, Wayne W. Unstoppable Me! 10 Ways to Soar Through Life. Budnick, Stacy Heller, illus. 2006. (ENG.). 32p. (gr. k-7). 15.99 (978-1-4019-1186-7(2)) Hay Hse., Inc.

East, Jacqueline, illus. Learn Good Habits with Jessica: Above All, Don't Behave Like Zoe! 2008. 28p. (J). (gr. -1-3). 6.95 (978-1-59496-163-2(8)) Teora USA LLC.

—Learn Good Manners with Charles: Above All, Don't Behave Like Trevor! 2008. 28p. (J). (gr. -1-3). 6.95 (978-1-59496-162-5(X)) Teora USA LLC.

Edwards, Josephine Cunnington. Children Can Be Taught. 2004. (Illus.). 84p. per. 9.95 (978-1-57258-293-4(6), 945-6145) TEACH Services, Inc.

Elkins, Stephen. Snuggle Time Devotions That End with a Hug! Jones, Mark, illus. 2015. (Share-A-Hug! Ser.). (ENG.). 168p. (J). 14.99 (978-1-4143-9948-5(0)) Tyndale Hse. Pubs.

The Encyclopedia of Danger. (Illus.). 112-128p. (gr. 5). pap. 19.90 (978-0-7910-3759-1(2), Chelsea Hse.) Facts On File, Inc.

Ennis, Pat. Becoming a Young Woman Who Pleases God: A Teen's Guide to Discovering Her Biblical Potential. 2009. (Illus.). 160p. pap. 14.99 (978-1-59669-240-4(5)) New Hope Pubs.

Espeland, Pamela. Knowing Me, Knowing You: The I-Sight Way to Understand Yourself & Others. 2004. (Illus.). 128p. (YA). (gr. 8-12). pap. 13.95 (978-1-57542-090-5(2)) Free Spirit Publishing, Inc.

Espeland, Pamela & Verdick, Elizabeth. Knowing & Doing What's Right: The Positive Values Assets. 2005. (Adding Assets Series for Kids Ser.). (ENG., Illus.). 80p. (J). (gr. 3-7). pap. 7.99 (978-1-57542-184-1(4)) Free Spirit Publishing, Inc.

—See You Later, Procrastinator! 2007. (Laugh & Learn Ser.). (ENG., Illus.). 112p. (J). (gr. 3-8). pap. 8.95 (978-1-57542-278-7(6)) Free Spirit Publishing, Inc.

Etingoff, Kim. All Around Good Habits. 2013. (Junior Martial Arts Ser.: 9). 32p. (J). (gr. 4-18). 19.95 (978-1-4222-2732-9(4)) Mason Crest.

Evans, Tony. A Kid's Guide to the Armor of God. 2015. (ENG., Illus.). 112p. (J). pap. 10.99 (978-0-7369-6056-4(2)) Harvest Hse. Pubs.

FAQ: Teen Life, 6 vols., Set. Incl. Frequently Asked Questions about Being Part of a Military Family. Hart, Joyce. lib. bdg. 31.95 (978-1-4358-5328-7(8)); Frequently Asked Questions about Emergency Lifesaving Techniques. Roza, Greg. lib. bdg. 31.95 (978-1-4358-5327-0(X)); Frequently Asked Questions about Everyday First Aid. Hasan, Heather. lib. bdg. 31.95 (978-1-4358-5326-3(1)); Frequently Asked Questions about How the Teen Brain Works. Wilson, Michael R. lib. bdg. 31.95 (978-1-4358-5324-9(5)); Frequently Asked Questions about Wii & Video Game Fitness & Injuries. Nagle, Jeanne. lib. bdg. 31.95 (978-1-4358-5329-4(6)); (Illus.). 64p. (J). (gr. 5-6). 2009. 2009. Set lib. bdg. 175.50 (978-1-4358-3311-1(2)); Set lib. bdg. 167.70 (978-1-4042-1062-2(8)) Rosen Publishing Group, Inc., The.

Fighting the Monster. 2004. (YA). ring bd. 59.95 (978-0-9661256-2-7(2)) Youth Communication - New York Center.

Finding Your Way: A Guidebook. 2004. pap. 12.00 (978-0-9744877-0-0(8)) Noller, Gail.

Fitzgerald, Sami & Caryn. Fish Sticks, Books & Blue Jeans. 2008. 48p. pap. 12.95 (978-0-615-17982-7(7)) Fitzgerald, Caryn.

Fone, Ann. Elf-help for Giving the Gift of You. 2005. per. 4.95 (978-0-87029-392-4(3)) Abbey Pr.

Fontes, Justine. Rude Ralph: A Rookie Reader. Jordan, Charles, illus. 2011. (Rookie Ready to Learn Ser.). 40p. (J). pap. 5.95 (978-0-531-26711-0(3)); (gr. -1-k). lib. bdg. 23.00 (978-0-531-26529-1(3)) Scholastic Library Publishing. (Children's Pr.).

Foote, Tracy. My Potty Reward Stickers for Boys: 126 Boy Stickers & Chart to Motivate Toilet Training. 2003. (J). 7.95 (978-0-9708226-6-6(9)) TracyTrends.

—My Potty Reward Stickers for Girls: 126 Girl Stickers & Chart to Motivate Toilet Training. 3rd rev. ed. 2003. (J). 7.95 (978-0-9708226-5-9(0)) TracyTrends.

Frazee, Randy. Believe Storybook: Think, Act, Be Like Jesus, 1 vol. Adams, Steve, illus. 2015. (ENG.). 256p. (J). 19.99 (978-0-310-74590-7(X)) Zonderkidz.

Frost, Shelley. I See Kindness Everywhere. 2009. (Illus.). 28p. pap. 12.99 (978-1-4490-0415-6(6)) AuthorHouse.

Galan, Alvaro. Billy Bully. Simpson, Steve, illus. 2009. (ENG.). 32p. (J). (gr. -1-3). pap. 3.99 (978-0-545-11012-9(2)) Scholastic, Inc.

Gallaudet, Thomas. The Child's Book on Repentance. 2005. pap. 12.99 (978-1-59925-020-5(9)) Solid Ground Christian Bks.

Gardner, Robert. How Big Is Big? Science Projects with Volume. 2015. (Hot Science Experiments Ser.). 48p. (J). (gr. 3-4). pap. 8.95 (978-0-7660-6621-2(5), Enslow Elementary) Enslow Pubs., Inc.

Garrett, Byron. The ABC's of Life. 2004. (YA). pap. 16.95 (978-0-9755938-0-6(3)) TRI LIFE Pr.

Garrett, Stephanie. A Girl's Guide to Wisdom & Virtue: Being a Lady in a Modern World. 2013. 86p. pap. 27.95 (978-1-4497-7221-5(8), WestBow Pr.) Author Solutions, Inc.

George, Liz. Thankfulness: A Gratitude Attitude! 2015. (Rookie Talk about It(tm) Ser.). (ENG., Illus.). 32p. (J). pap. 5.95 (978-0-531-21382-7(X), Children's Pr.) Scholastic Library Publishing.

Gerard, Franck J. Time Waits for No One! Prioritize to Change Your Life! 2005. (Illus.). 90p. per., training bk. ed. 14.99 net. (978-0-9772685-0-4(0)) ABC Pubs.

Gerety, Ed. Combinations: Opening the Door to Student Leadership. 2003. 160p. (YA). per. 14.95 (978-0-9725938-3-0(7)) Whaleback Publishing.

Get a Grip on Life: What Every Teen Must Know to Have a Great Life. 2004. 240p. (YA). per. 14.00 (978-0-9748994-0-4(2)) Youth Quest Institute.

Getting Through College. 2004. (YA). per. 13.95 (978-1-56870-507-1(7)) Hewell Publishing.

Gevinson, Tavi. Rookie Yearbook Three. 2014. (Rookie Ser.: 3). (ENG., Illus.). 358p. (J). (gr. 7). pap. 29.95 (978-1-59514-794-3(2), Razorbill) Penguin Young Readers Group.

Gibbons, Casey Hartley. A Girl's Life with God. 2006. 160p. pap. 8.99 (978-1-56309-757-7(5), N034115) New Hope Pubs.

Gifford, Clive. Teenage Kicks: 101 Things to Do Before You're 16. 2008. (ENG., Illus.). 160p. (J). (gr. 7-17). pap. 9.99 (978-0-340-95061-6(7)) Hodder & Stoughton GBR. Dist: Hachette Bk. Group.

Gilbert, Keith & Schuh, Leesa. TEENAGERS: Your Essential Guide to the Weird World of... Adults 2nd Edition. 2009. 180p. pap. 15.95 (978-1-4452-4859-2(X)) Lulu Pr., Inc.

Glassman, Bruce. Fairness. 2009. (Character Counts! Ser.). 48p. (gr. 4-5). 53.00 (978-1-61511-838-0(1)) Rosen Publishing Group, Inc., The.

—Respect. 2009. (Character Counts! Ser.). 48p. (gr. 4-5). 53.00 (978-1-61511-841-0(1)) Rosen Publishing Group, Inc., The.

—The Six Pillars of Character, 6 vols., Set. 2008. (J). (gr. 4-6). lib. bdg. 159.00 (978-1-4358-2556-7(X), PowerKids Pr.) Rosen Publishing Group, Inc., The.

—Trustworthiness. 2009. (Character Counts! Ser.). 48p. (gr. 4-5). 53.00 (978-1-61511-847-2(0)) Rosen Publishing Group, Inc., The.

Glassman, Bruce S. Responsibility. 2008. (Illus.). 48p. (J). pap. 9.95 (978-1-60108-509-2(5), Bearing Bks.); (YA). (gr. 3-6). lib. bdg. 29.25 (978-1-60108-508-5(7)) Red Cygnet Pr.

Gomez Seitz, M. Stella. The Master Cookie-Maker: A True Life Story for Children. 2003. 133p. (J). pap. 13.95 (978-0-595-26314-1(3), Writers Club Pr.) iUniverse, Inc.

Gonsalves, Samantha. The Magic Archive. 2009. 16p. pap. 12.50 (978-1-4490-2965-4(5)) AuthorHouse.

Gordon, Jon. The Energy Bus for Kids: A Story about Staying Positive & Overcoming Challenges. Scott, Korey, illus. 2012. (ENG.). 48p. (J). (gr. k-4). 17.00 (978-1-118-28735-4(5), Wiley) Wiley, John & Sons, Inc.

Gordon, Sharon. Compartimos: Listos para Ir a la Escuela. 2006. (Bookworms Ser.). (SPA & ENG., Illus.). 24p. (gr. k-1). lib. bdg. 15.95 (978-0-7614-2360-7(5), Benchmark Bks.) Marshall Cavendish Corp.

—Decimos la Verdad. 2006. (Bookworms Ser.). (SPA & ENG., Illus.). 24p. (gr. k-1). lib. bdg. 15.95 (978-0-7614-2362-1(1), Benchmark Bks.) Marshall Cavendish Corp.

—Respetamos las Reglas. 2006. (Bookworms Ser.). (SPA & ENG., Illus.). 24p. (gr. k-1). lib. bdg. 15.95 (978-0-7614-2358-4(3), Benchmark Bks.) Marshall Cavendish Corp.

—Somos Amables. 2006. (Bookworms Ser.). (SPA & ENG., Illus.). 24p. (gr. k-1). lib. bdg. 15.95 (978-0-7614-2356-0(7), Benchmark Bks.) Marshall Cavendish Corp.

—We Are Kind. 2007. (J). pap. 6.99 (978-0-7614-3270-8(1)) Marshall Cavendish Corp.

—We Are Kind/Somos Amables. 2006. (Bookworms Ser.). (ENG & SPA., Illus.). 24p. (gr. k-1). lib. bdg. 15.95 (978-0-7614-2435-2(0)) Marshall Cavendish Corp.

—We Follow the Rules. (Bookworms: Ready for School Ser.). (Illus.). (J). (gr. 3-7). 2007. 23p. pap. 6.99 (978-0-7614-3273-9(6)) 2005. (ENG & SPA., 24p. lib. bdg. (978-0-7614-1995-2(0)) Marshall Cavendish Corp. (Benchmark Bks.).

—We Follow the Rules/Respetamos Las Reglas. 2006. (Bookworms Ser.). (ENG & SPA., Illus.). 24p. (gr. k-1). lib. bdg. 15.95 (978-0-7614-2438-3(5)) Marshall Cavendish Corp.

—We Share. 2005. (Bookworms Ser.). (ENG & SPA., Illus.). 24p. (J). (gr. 3-7). lib. bdg. 22.79 (978-0-7614-1993-8(4), Benchmark Bks.) Marshall Cavendish Corp.

—We Share/Compartimos. 2006. (Bookworms Ser.). (ENG & SPA., Illus.). 24p. (gr. k-1). lib. bdg. 15.95 (978-0-7614-2441-3(5)) Marshall Cavendish Corp.

—We Tell the Truth. 2007. (J). pap. 6.99 (978-0-7614-3277-7(9)) Marshall Cavendish Corp.

—We Tell the Truth/Decimos la Verdad. 2006. (Bookworms Ser.). (ENG & SPA., Illus.). 24p. (gr. k-1). lib. bdg. 15.95 (978-0-7614-2442-0(3)) Marshall Cavendish Corp.

Green, Mischa. Wounded Voices Unwise Choices: The Truth from Our Youth. 2004. 90p. (YA). per. 10.00 (978-0-9754191-0-6(2)) Morals & Values Pr.

Grippo, Daniel. Playing Fair, Having Fun: A Kid's Guide to Sports & Games. Alley, R. W., illus. 2004. 32p. (J). per. 7.95 (978-0-87029-384-9(2)) Abbey Pr.

—When Mom or Dad Dies: A Book of Comfort for Kids. Alley, R. W., illus. 2008. (J). pap. 7.95 (978-0-87029-415-0(6)) Abbey Pr.

Hafiz, Dilara, et al. The American Muslim Teenager's Handbook. 2009. (ENG., Illus.). 192p. (YA). (gr. 7-18). pap. 13.99 (978-1-4169-8578-5(6), Atheneum Bks. for Young Readers) Simon & Schuster Children's Publishing.

Haley, Dennis & Brown, Marci. We Both Read-When I Grow Up. 2005. (We Both Read Ser.). (Illus.). 44p. (J). (gr. 1-18). 7.99 (978-1-891327-57-5(7)); pap. 4.99 (978-1-891327-58-2(5)) Treasure Bay, Inc.

Hall, LaMarcus J. I Refuse to Let You Give Up: To My Teens Who Feel All Hope Is Gone... 2009. 52p. pap. 15.95 (978-1-4327-3417-6(2)) Outskirts Pr., Inc.

Halper, Sharon. To Learn Is to Do: A Tikkun Olam Road Map. Koffsky, Ann D., illus. 2004. vi, 56p. (gr. 4-6). pap. 11.95 (978-0-8074-0729-5(1), 123935) URJ Pr.

Haltom, Cris. Stranger of the Table. 2004. (YA). per. 5.68 (978-1-56870-517-0(4)) Hewell Publishing.

Hamod, Rania. I Am Good. 2012. 52p. (-18). pap. 20.95 (978-1-4525-0807-8(0)) Balboa Pr.

Harris, Lisa Delmedico. The Official Princess Handbook: A Little Girl's Guide to Beauty, Poise, & Righteousness. 2010. (ENG.). 96p. (J). pap. 9.99 (978-1-60683-025-3(2)) Harrison House Pubs.

Hasenecz Calvert, Ellen. Nine Goldfish in David's Pond. 2009. 36p. pap. 17.99 (978-1-4490-3020-9(3)) AuthorHouse.

Hatch, Ines Amsberger. Marsha's Song: A Celebration of Life. 2004. 300p. (YA). per. 18.00 (978-1-932496-19-2(X)) Penman Publishing, Inc.

Hauser, Jill Frankel. The Kid's Guide to Becoming the Best You Can Be! Developing 5 Traits You Need to Achieve Your Personal Best. Kline, Michael, illus. (ENG.). 128p. (J). (gr. 3-7). 2008. pap. 14.25 (978-0-8249-6788-8(7)) 2006. 16.95 (978-0-8249-6789-5(5)) Worthy Publishing. (Ideal Pubns.).

Hay, Louise L. I Think, I Am! Teaching Kids the Power of Affirmations. Schwarz, Manuela, illus. 2008. (ENG.). 32p. (gr. -1-2). 15.99 (978-1-4019-2208-5(2)) Hay Hse., Inc.

Hayhurst, Chris. Stay Cool: A Guy's Guide to Handling Conflict. 2005. (Guys' Guides). (Illus.). 48p. (YA). (gr. 5-8). lib. bdg. 29.25 (978-0-8239-3159-0(5), GUSTCO) Rosen Publishing Group, Inc., The.

Heatherly, C. L. Chuck. My Piece of the Sky. 2012. (Illus.). 48p. (J). lib. bdg. 14.95 (978-0-9820576-4-3(4), Lighthouse for Leaders, A) Lighthouse for Leaders.

Herzog, Brad. Awesome Stories of Generosity in Sports. 2014. (Count on Me: Sports Ser.). (ENG., Illus.). 96p. (J). (gr. 4-7). pap. 9.99 (978-1-57542-477-4(0)) Free Spirit Publishing, Inc.

Hest, Amy. Tu Puedes Hacerlo, Sam. Jeram, Anita, illus. 2004.Tr. of You Can Do It, Sam. (SPA.). (J). 16.00 (978-1-930332-53-9(X)) Lectorum Pubns., Inc.

Hicks, Kelli L. Honesty. 2012. (ENG., Illus.). 24p. (gr. k-2). pap. 8.95 (978-1-61810-265-2(6)) Rourke Educational Media.

Higgins, Melissa. I Am Fair, 1 vol. 2014. (I Don't Bully Ser.). (ENG.). 24p. (gr. k-1). lib. bdg. 21.99 (978-1-4765-4069-6(1), Pebble Bks.) Capstone Press of Coughlan Cos.

—I Am Respectful, 1 vol. 2014. (I Don't Bully Ser.). (ENG.). 24p. (gr. k-1). lib. bdg. 21.99 (978-1-4765-4067-2(5), Pebble Bks.) Capstone Press of Coughlan Cos.

—I Am Responsible, 1 vol. 2014. (I Don't Bully Ser.). (ENG.). 24p. (gr. k-1). lib. bdg. 21.99 (978-1-4765-4068-9(3), Pebble Bks.) Capstone Press of Coughlan Cos.

—I Am Trustworthy, 1 vol. 2014. (I Don't Bully Ser.). (ENG.). 24p. (gr. k-1). lib. bdg. 21.99 (978-1-4765-4066-5(7), Pebble Bks.) Capstone Press of Coughlan Cos.

Hill-Sullivan, Shunice. Son, Do You Know How Truly Blessed You Are? 2009. 24p. pap. 12.95 (978-1-4490-0011-0(8)) AuthorHouse.

Hillery, Susie Moore. Count Your Blessings. 2003. pap. 20.00 (978-0-8059-6194-2(1)) Dorrance Publishing Co., Inc.

Hilliker, Amy Warren. Little One, God Loves You, 1 vol. Lovsin, Polona, illus. 2016. (ENG.). 14p. (J). bds. 6.99 (978-0-310-75307-0(4)) Zonderkidz.

—Little One, God Made You Special, 1 vol. Lovsin, Polona, illus. 2016. (ENG.). 14p. (J). bds. 6.99 (978-0-310-75300-1(7)) Zonderkidz.

Hollis, Randy. Meet Sneazle, 1. Rahn, Jess, illus. 2004. 20p. (J). 6.95 (978-0-9758815-0-7(7)) SNZ Publishing.

Holofcener, Mark. Evan's Earthly Adventure. l.t. ed. 2003. (Illus.). 202p. (YA). mass mkt. 11.00 (978-0-9718626-1-6(3)) Holofcener, Mark.

Holyoke, Nancy. Manners. 2013. (Smart Girl's Guide Ser.). lib. bdg. 24.50 (978-0-606-34733-4(X), Turtleback) Turtleback Bks.

—A Smart Girl's Guide to Manners: The Secrets to Grace, Confidence, & Being Your Best. Watkins, Michelle, ed. Mingus, Cathi, illus. 2005. (ENG.). 120p. (J). (gr. 3). per. 9.95 (978-1-58485-983-3(0), American Girl) American Girl Publishing, Inc.

Hong, K. L. Life Freaks Me Out: And Then I Deal with It. 2005. (ENG., Illus.). 168p. (YA). (gr. 7). per. 12.95 (978-1-57482-856-6(8)) Search Institute.

Hopkins, Cathy. The Mates, Dates Guide to Life, Love, & Looking Luscious. 2005. (Mates, Dates Ser.). (ENG., Illus.). 256p. (YA). (gr. 7). pap. 7.99 (978-1-4169-0279-9(1), Simon Pulse) Simon Pulse.

Horner, Randall. Navigating the Awkward Years: Useful Ideas & Concepts for Dealing with Life in High School & for Life after Graduation. 2008. 64p. pap. 9.95 (978-0-595-52930-8(5)) iUniverse, Inc.

Hsuan Hua. Dew Drops: Pearls of Wisdom by the Venerable Master Hua = [Zhao Lu: Xuanhuashangren Yi Li Ming Zhu]. 2003. (ENG & CHI., Illus.). 91p. (J). 5.00 (978-0-88139-862-5(4)) Buddhist Text Translation Society.

Human Relations Media. Good Character Adventure Pack: Adventures in Perseverance. 2006. (ENG.). (J). pap. 4.95 (978-1-55548-004-2(7), 4204) Human Relations Media.

—Good Character Adventure Pack: Adventures in Responsibility Workbook. 2006. (ENG.). (J). pap. 4.95 (978-1-55548-003-5(9), 4203) Human Relations Media.

Human Relations Media, prod. Good Character Adventure Pack: Adventures in Empathy. 2006. (ENG.). (J). pap., wbk. ed. 4.95 (978-1-55548-002-8(0), 4202) Human Relations Media.

Humphrey, Sandra McLeod & Barker, Dan. More-If You Had to Choose, What Would You Do? Strassburg, Brian, illus. 2003. (ENG.). 132p. (J). (gr. 4-7). pap. 14.99 (978-1-59102-077-6(8)) Prometheus Bks., Pubs.

Hyde, Natalie. Live It: Fairness. 2009. (ENG., Illus.). 32p. (J). (gr. 3-6). lib. bdg. (978-0-7787-4883-0(9)) Crabtree Publishing Co.

I Am Responsible. 2003. (Illus.). 48p. per. 9.00 (978-0-9726451-1-9(X)) Sheets, Judy.

I Can Do It Club. 2003. (J). mass mkt. (978-0-9747331-9-7(9)) Illusion Factory, The.

Ikeda, Daisaku. Soar into the Skies of Hope. 2015. (ENG., Illus.). 224p. (J). pap. 8.95 (978-1-935523-77-2(5)) World Tribune Pr.

Ingalls, Ann. Good Manners in Public. Rooney, Ronnie, illus. 2012. (Good Manners Ser.). (ENG.). 24p. (J). (gr. -1-2).

27.07 (978-1-61473-226-6(4), 204922) Child's World, Inc., The.

—Good Table Manners. Rooney, Ronnie, illus. 2012. (Good Manners Ser.). (ENG.). 24p. (J). (gr. -1-2). 27.07 (978-1-61473-230-3(2), 204925) Child's World, Inc., The.

It's Good 2b Good Staff & Zerner, Sandra. It's Good 2B Good: Why It's Not Bad to Be Good. 2011. (ENG., Illus.). 106p. (J). pap. 12.95 (978-0-615-51275-4(5)) It's Good 2B Good LLC.

Jackson, Sue Ann. The Gift of the Butterfly Box. 2nd ed. 2013. 84p. (J). pap. 15.00 (978-1-936688-56-2(5)) AKA:yoLa.

Jealousy Is Not for Me: A Guide for Freeing Yourself from Envy. 2008. (Elf-Help Books for Kids Ser.). (Illus.). 28p. (J). (gr. -1-3). per. 7.95 (978-0-87029-408-2(3)) Abbey Pr.

Jefferson, Anita. Climb Every Obstacle: Eliminate Your Limits! 2004. (Illus.). 216p. per. 19.95 (978-0-9743088-0-7(3)) RealWord Pubns.

Jensen, Diane Mastromarino. The Girl's Guide to Loving Yourself: A book about falling in love with the one person who matters most... you - UPDATED EDITION -, 1 vol. 2011. 64p. pap. 12.95 (978-1-59842-600-7(1)) Blue Mountain Arts Inc.

Johnson, Jason. How We See Things. 2012. 20p. pap. 17.99 (978-1-4685-5832-6(3)) AuthorHouse.

Johnson, Kevin. Total Devotion: 365 Days to Hang Tight with Jesus. 2004. (ENG.). 374p. (YA). reprint ed. pap. 16.00 (978-0-7642-2884-1(6)) Bethany Hse. Pubs.

Johnson, Spencer. ¿Quién Se Ha Llevado Mi Queso? Para Jovenes: ¡Una Forma Sorprendente de Cambiar y Ganar! 2003. (SPA., Illus.). 98p. (YA). 12.95 (978-84-7953-528-5(8), UO32376) Ediciones Urano S. A. ESP. Dist: Spanish Pubs., LLC.

Jones, Brenn. A Character Building Book: Set 4: Inspirational Role Models, 6 bks. Incl. Learning about Equal Rights from the Life of Ruth Bader Ginsburg. lib. bdg. 22.60 (978-0-8239-5781-1(0)); Learning about Love from the Life of Mother Teresa. lib. bdg. 22.60 (978-0-8239-5777-4(2)); Learning about Public Service from the Life of John F. Kennedy, Jr. lib. bdg. 22.60 (978-0-8239-5776-7(4)); Learning about Resilience from the Life of Lance Armstrong. lib. bdg. 22.60 (978-0-8239-5779-8(9)); Learning about Teamwork from the Lives of Sir Edmund Hillary & Tenzig Norgay. lib. bdg. 22.60 (978-0-8239-5778-1(0)); 24p. (J). (gr. 3). 2002. (Illus.). Set lib. bdg. 103.50 (978-0-8239-7136-7(8), PowerKids Pr.) Rosen Publishing Group, Inc., The.

Jones, Jen. Are You a Good Friend?, 1 vol. 2011. (Friendship Quizzes Ser.). (ENG.). 32p. (gr. 3-4). lib. bdg. 27.99 (978-1-4296-6541-4(6), Snap Bks.) Capstone Press of Coughlan Cos.

Joseph, Kurt. I Am Respectful. 2011. (Kids of Character Ser.). (Illus.). 24p. (J). (gr. 1-3). pap. 8.15 (978-1-4339-4875-6(3)); lib. bdg. 22.60 (978-1-4339-4874-9(5)) Stevens, Gareth Publishing LLLP.

Joy, Berry. Fun & Easy Way to Be Good. 2009. 48p. 12.95 (978-1-60577-612-5(2)) Berry, Joy Enterprises.

—Help Me Good about Being Messy. 2009. 32p. 7.95 (978-1-60577-112-0(0)) Berry, Joy Enterprises.

Just for Girls. 2008. (Amazing Body Growing Up Ser.). 96p. (978-1-4075-1571-7(3)) Parragon, Inc.

Kallmeyer-Mehlhorn, Margarete. The Wondrous Ball of Yarn: A Facsimile of the Previously Unpublished Manuscript. 2008.Tr. of Wunderknaul. (ENG & GER., Illus.). 40p. 41.00 (978-0-9745168-2-0(1)) Cotsen Occasional Pr.

Keller, Irene. Thingamajig Books of Do's & Don'ts. Keller, Dick, illus. 2005. (ENG.). 30p. (J). bds. 7.95 (978-0-8249-6591-4(4), Ideal Pubns.) Worthy Publishing.

Kelso, Susan. OUCH or AHHH - The Choice IS Easy!, 1 vol. Serpentelli, John, illus. 2009. 47p. pap. 24.95 (978-1-61546-148-6(5)) America Star Bks.

Kent, Susan. Learning How to Be Kind to Others. 2009. (Violence Prevention Library). 24p. (gr. 2-3). 42.50 (978-1-60854-264-2(5), PowerKids Pr.) Rosen Publishing Group, Inc., The.

Kerline-Nowak, Joni. Sebastian Breaks for Freedom, 1. aut. ed. 2006. (Illus.). 30p. (J). pap. 14.95 (978-0-9776772-1-4(4)) KidBookInk Publishing, LLC.

Kerr, Harold. Pout or Purpose? A Simple Approach for Understanding Your Purpose Pie & Improving Your Life. 2005. (Illus.). 120p. 19.95 (978-0-9767078-0-6(2)) K.C. Fox Publishing.

Kid Ethics: From A to Z. 2006. (Illus.). 56p. (J). (gr. -1-3). per. 12.95 (978-0-9794863-0-2(0)) Summerland Publishing.

Kiers, Erin L. I Have Chakras Just Like You. 2012. 24p. pap. (978-1-4602-0343-9(7)) FriesenPress.

King, Bart. The Pocket Guide to Boy Stuff, 1 vol. 2008. (ENG., Illus.). 272p. (J). (gr. 4-8). pap., instr.'s gde. ed. 9.99 (978-1-4236-0574-4(8)) Gibbs Smith, Publisher.

—The Pocket Guide to Girl Stuff, 1 vol. 2008. (ENG., Illus.). 272p. (J). (gr. 4-8). pap. 9.99 (978-1-4236-0573-7(X)) Gibbs Smith, Publisher.

Knight 6 Personal Growth Planbook: Extreme Quest. 2003. (Illus.). 48p. (J). pap. 4.95 (978-1-59312-047-4(8)) North American Mission Board, SBC.

Knowles, Jon. The Facts of Life: A Guide for Teens & Their Families. 2004. (YA). 2.00 (978-1-930996-72-4(1)) Planned Parenthood Federation of America, Inc.

Kozak, Diane, compiled by. The Kaleidoscope Project. 2012. 352p. pap. 16.95 (978-0-9841813-4-6(2)) Beagle Bks. Publishing, LLC.

Kristofer Says: Know Your Rules. 2006. (J). 5.95 (978-0-9777022-1-3(9)) Mother's Love Publishing, A.

Kuchler, B. L. That's Life. 2003. (ENG., Illus.). 112p. (J). tchr. ed. 14.95 (978-1-57223-709-4(0), 7090) Willow Creek Pr., Inc.

Kuchler, Bonnie Louise, compiled by. Just Kids: Pictures, Poems & Other Silly Animal Stuff Just for Kids! 2003. (ENG., Illus.). 32p. tchr. ed. 12.95 (978-1-57223-598-4(5), 5985) Willow Creek Pr., Inc.

Lad 1 Personal Growth Planbook: Clue Chasers. 2003. (Illus.). 48p. (J). pap. 4.95 (978-1-59312-042-9(7)) North American Mission Board, SBC.

Lad 2 Personal Growth Planbook: Everglade Explorers. 2003. (Illus.). 48p. (J). pap. 4.95 (978-1-59312-043-6(5)) North American Mission Board, SBC.

Lad 3 Personal Growth Planbook: Rawhide Wranglers. 2003. (Illus.). 48p. (J). pap. 4.95 (978-1-59312-044-3(3)) North American Mission Board, SBC.

Lamphere Slaughter, Sharyn. Anjelina Bobalina Concerto Juarez Small. 2009. 20p. pap. 11.99 (978-1-4490-4643-9(6)) AuthorHouse.

Larsen, Carolyn. Sharing with Others: A Book about Selfishness. O'Connor, Tim, illus. 2017. (Growing God's Kids Ser.). (ENG.). 32p. (J). pap. 4.99 (978-0-8010-0960-0(X)) Baker Bks.

Lavis, Rose Brenda. Christopher's New Suit. 2010. 24p. pap. 11.49 (978-1-4490-3606-5(6)) AuthorHouse.

Lazurek, Michelle S. Daddy, Am I Beautiful? Stott, Apryl, illus. 2015. 24p. (J). pap. (978-0-8198-1905-5(0)) Pauline Bks. & Media.

—Mommy, Am I Strong? Spinks, Scott, illus. 2015. 25p. (J). pap. (978-0-8198-4948-9(0)) Pauline Bks. & Media.

Leigh, Susan K. God, I Need to Talk to You about Disrespect. 2005. (J). 1.19 (978-0-7586-0810-9(1)) Concordia Publishing Hse.

—God, I Need to Talk to You about Greed. Clark, Bill, illus. 2005. 16p. (J). pap. 1.19 (978-0-7586-0795-9(4)) Concordia Publishing Hse.

—God, I Need to Talk to You about Laziness. 2005. (J). 1.19 (978-0-7586-0812-3(8)) Concordia Publishing Hse.

—God, I Need to Talk to You about Whining. Clark, Bill, illus. 2005. pap. 1.19 (978-0-7586-0794-2(6)) Concordia Publishing Hse.

Lennon, Liz. I Am Kind. 2012. (Little Stars: My Behavior Ser.). (ENG., Illus.). 24p. (J). (gr. k-3). lib. bdg. 25.65 (978-1-59771-409-9(7)) Sea-To-Sea Pubns.

Leventhal-Belfer, Laurie. Why Do I Have To? A Book for Children Who Find Themselves Frustrated by Everyday Rules. Montaini-Klovdahl, Luisa, illus. 2008. (ENG.). 80p. pap. 10.95 (978-1-84310-891-7(7), 5918) Kingsley, Jessica Pubs. GBR. Dist: Macmillan Distribution Ltd.

Lewis, Barbara A. What Do You Stand for? a Kid's Guide ToBuilding Character. 2014. 30.00 (978-1-63419-753-3(4)) Perfection Learning Corp.

Lewis, Barbara A. & Free Spirit Publishing Staff. What Do You Stand For? Character Building. 2006. (ENG., Illus.). 60p. (gr. 1-6). 13.99 (978-1-57542-217-6(4)) Free Spirit Publishing, Inc.

Lifeways - Group 5, 4 bks., Set. 136.86 (978-0-7614-1412-4(6), Benchmark Bks.) Marshall Cavendish Corp.

Lisbona, Margie Taylor. Rock & Rhino Learn Responsibility. Roberts, J. P., illus. 2011. 48p. pap. (978-1-77067-530-8(2)) FriesenPress.

Lishinski, Ann King. Let Your Light Shine. Morello, Charles, ed. Lishinski, Jamie, illus. 2003. (J). pap. 9.95 (978-0-9709575-0-4(5)) Singing River Pubns.

Llewellyn, Claire. Why Should I Listen? Gordon, Mike, illus. 2005. (Why Should I? Bks.). (ENG.). 32p. (J). pap. 7.99 (978-0-7641-3219-3(9)) Barron's Educational Series, Inc.

—Why Should I Share? Mike, Gordon, illus. 2005. (Why Should I? Bks.). (ENG.). 32p. (J). pap. 7.99 (978-0-7641-3220-9(2)) Barron's Educational Series, Inc.

Lorig, Steffanie & Jacobs, Jeanean. Chill & Spill: A Place to Put It down & Work It Out. 2005. (Illus.). 112p. (YA). (gr. 6-18). 20.00 (978-0-9715240-4-0(1)) Art With Heart Press.

Lublin, Nancy, et al. Do Something! A Handbook for Young Activists. 2010. (ENG., Illus.). 280p. (J). (gr. 4-7). pap. 13.95 (978-0-7611-5747-2(6), 15747) Workman Publishing Co., Inc.

Lucado, Max. Plunge! Come Thirsty, 1 vol. 2004. (ENG.). 128p. pap., stu. ed. 9.99 (978-1-4185-0028-3(3)) Nelson, Thomas Inc.

MacAdam, Lea. You & Rules in Your Family. 2009. (Family Matters Ser.). 48p. (gr. 5-8). 53.00 (978-1-61512-483-1(7), Rosen Reference) Rosen Publishing Group, Inc., The.

—You & the Rules in Your Family. 2005. (Family Matters Ser.). (Illus.). 48p. (YA). (gr. 5-8). lib. bdg. 29.25 (978-0-8239-3350-1(4)) Rosen Publishing Group, Inc., The.

MacAllister, Carol L. The Wisdom Tree & the Red Swing: Thinking Outside the Box for Preteens. 2009. (Wisdom Tree & the Red Swing Ser.). (ENG.). 116p. (J). pap. 3.99 (978-0-9815818-4-2(6), 9780981581842) Take Charge Bks.

MacDonald, Margaret. What to Do When You Are Lost. 2011. (Learn-Abouts: Level 10 Ser.). (Illus.). 16p. (J). pap. 7.95 (978-1-59920-600-4(5)) Black Rabbit Bks.

MacGregor, Cynthia. Think for Yourself: A Kid's Guide to Solving Life's Dilemmas & Other Sticky Problems. Farias, Susan Norberg, illus. 2004. (ENG.). 96p. (J). (gr. 4-7). pap. 7.95 (978-1-894222-73-0(3)) Lobster Pr. CAN. Dist: Univ. of Toronto Pr.

Mackall, Dandi Daley. Kids' Rules for Life: A Guide to Life's Journey from Those Just Starting Out. 2003. (Illus.). 176p. pap. 8.95 (978-1-57071-909-7(8)) Sourcebooks, Inc.

Mackenzie, Catherine. I Can Say to God, Please. 2015. (Prayer (Board Books) Ser.). (ENG.). 10p. (J). bds. 3.99 (978-1-85792-691-0(9), 4a46cdd3-be1d-48a9-bbee-7f9ad59ca112) Christian Focus Pubns. GBR. Dist: Bookmasters Distribution.

Marcovitz, Hal. Teens & Cheating. Developed in Association with the Gallup Organization Staff, ed. 2013. (Gallup Youth Survey: Major Issues & Trends Ser.: 14). 112p. (J). (gr. 7-18). 24.95 (978-1-4222-2951-4(3)) Mason Crest.

Marshall, Shelley. Super Ben Writes a Letter: A Book about Caring. Mahan, Ben, illus. 2010. (Character Education with Super Ben & Molly the Great Ser.). 24p. (J). 22.60 (978-0-7660-3516-4(6)); pap. 7.95 (978-0-7660-3741-0(X)) Enslow Pubs., Inc. (Enslow Elementary).

—Super Ben's Broken Cookie: A Book about Sharing. Mahan, Ben, illus. 2010. (Character Education with Super Ben & Molly the Great Ser.). 24p. (J). 22.60 (978-0-7660-3514-0(X)); pap. 7.95 (978-0-7660-3739-7(8)) Enslow Pubs., Inc. (Enslow Elementary).

Marsico, Katie. Play Fair! 2012. (21st Century Basic Skills Library: Kids Can Make Manners Count Ser.). (ENG.). 24p. (gr. k-3). 22.79 (978-1-61080-438-7(4), 202048); pap. 12.79 (978-1-61080-612-1(3), 202222) Cherry Lake Publishing.

Marston, Elsa. Santa Claus in Baghdad & Other Stories about Teens in the Arab World. 2008. (ENG.). 216p. (gr. 3-7). pap. 15.95 (978-0-253-22004-2(1), 0253220041) Indiana Univ. Pr.

Marston, Ralph S., Jr. Living the Wonder of It All: Positive, Empowering Messages from the Daily Motivator. 2003. 200p. (YA). pap. 14.50 (978-0-9664634-1-5(2)) Image Express Inc.

Matejko, Sonya. The Things We All Know but too Afraid to Say. 2004. 140p. (YA). 23.95 (978-0-595-66860-1(7)) iUniverse, Inc.

Mather, Anne D. & Weldon, Louise B. Character Building Day by Day: 180 Quick Read-Alouds for Elementary School & Home. Braun, Eric, ed. 2006. (ENG.). 240p. (gr. 3-6). pap. 15.99 (978-1-57542-178-0(X)) Free Spirit Publishing, Inc.

McCarnes, Kayla, et al. Bully-Proofing in Early Childhood: Building a Caring Community. 2004. (Illus.). 197p. 58.49 (978-1-59318-240-3(6)) Cambium Education, Inc.

McCloud, Carol. Have You Filled a Bucket Today? A Guide to Daily Happiness for Kids. Messing, David, illus. 2007. (ENG.). 32p. (J). 17.95 (978-1-933916-16-3(8)) Nelson Publishing & Marketing.

Mccloud, Carol. Have You Filled a Bucket Today: A Guide to Daily Happiness for Kids. 2015. lib. bdg. 20.80 (978-0-606-38236-6(4)) Turtleback Bks.

McCumbee, Stephie. The Garden in My Mind: Growing Through Positive Choices. Griffin, Lisa M., illus. 2014. (ENG.). 40p. (J). pap. 12.95 (978-1-934490-54-9(7)) Boys Town Pr.

—The Garden in My Mind Activity Guide: Lessons for Social Skill & Common Core Development. Griffin, Lisa M., illus. 2014. (ENG.). 48p. pap. 20.95 (978-1-934490-55-6(5)) Boys Town Pr.

McSpadden, Kay. A Child's Book of Virtues. 2010. (J). (978-1-58087-156-3(9)) Stampley, C. D. Enterprises, Inc.

Mead, David. Little Ben Franklin Learns a Lesson in Generosity: Generosity. Sharp, Chris, illus. 2003. (American Virtues for Kids Ser.). (J). bds. 6.95 (978-0-9746440-2-8(1), Ideal Pubns.) Worthy Publishing.

Mefford, David. How to Make A Friend in Three Days or Less. 2004. (YA). (978-0-9762143-0-4(X)) Mefford, David.

Meiners, Cheri J. Forgive & Let Go! A Book about Forgiveness. Allen, Elizabeth, illus. 2015. (Being the Best Me Ser.). (ENG.). 40p. (J). (gr. -1-3). pap. 9.99 (978-1-57542-487-3(8)) Free Spirit Publishing, Inc.

—Know & Follow Rules. Johnson, Meredith, illus. 2005. (Learning to Get Along(r) Ser.). (ENG.). 40p. (J). (gr. -1-3). pap. 10.95 (978-1-57542-130-8(5)) Free Spirit Publishing, Inc.

—The Learning to Get along Series Interactive Software. Johnson, Meredith, illus. 2008. (Learning to Get Along Ser.). (ENG.). 24p. (gr. k-3). cd-rom 99.99 (978-1-57542-281-7(6)) Free Spirit Publishing, Inc.

—Share & Take Turns. 2003. (Learning to Get Along(r) Ser.). (ENG., Illus.). 40p. (J). (gr. -1-3). pap. 11.99 (978-1-57542-124-7(0), 786) Free Spirit Publishing, Inc.

—Stand Tall! A Book about Integrity. Allen, Elizabeth, illus. 2015. (Being the Best Me Ser.). (ENG.). 40p. (J). (gr. -1-3). pap. 9.99 (978-1-57542-486-6(X)) Free Spirit Publishing, Inc.

—Understand & Care. 2003. (Learning to Get Along(r) Ser.). (ENG., Illus.). 40p. (J). (gr. -1-3). pap. 10.95 (978-1-57542-131-5(3)) Free Spirit Publishing, Inc.

—When I Feel Afraid. 2003. (Learning to Get Along(r) Ser.). (ENG., Illus.). 40p. (J). (gr. -1-3). pap. 10.95 (978-1-57542-138-4(0)) Free Spirit Publishing, Inc.

Meltzer, Brad. Heroes for My Daughter. 144p. (J). 2016. (gr. -1-3). 17.99 (978-0-06-243927-7(8)) 2012. (ENG., Illus.). 19.99 (978-0-06-190526-1(7)) HarperCollins Pubs.

—Heroes for My Son. 128p. 2016. (J). (gr. -1-3). 17.99 (978-0-06-243931-4(6)) 2010. (ENG., Illus.). 19.99 (978-0-06-190528-5(3)) HarperCollins Pubs.

Mercadante, Frank. Positively Dangerous: Live Loud, Be Real, Change the World. 2003. 117p. (YA). pap. 11.50 (978-0-88489-790-3(7)) St. Mary's Pr. of MN.

Metzger, Steve. The Way I Act. Cain, Janan, illus. 2011. (ENG.). 32p. (J). (gr. k-5). 16.95 (978-1-884734-99-1(5)) Parenting Pr., Inc.

Millennium Male: Separating the Men from the Boys. 2003. 88p. pap. 7.50 (978-0-9712585-6-3(2)) JuDe Publishing.

Miller, Marvin. Did You Know Did You: A Children's Book of Motivation & Inspiration. 2010. 68p. pap. 9.95 (978-1-4502-4656-9(7)) iUniverse, Inc.

Milne, A. A. Positively Pooh: Timeless Wisdom from Pooh. Shepard, Ernest H., illus. 2008. (Winnie-The-Pooh Ser.). (ENG.). 120p. (J). (gr. 3-7). 22.00 (978-0-525-47931-4(7), Dutton Books for Young Readers) Penguin Young Readers Group.

Monchamp, Genny. Shine: Choices to Make God Smile. Kaminski, Karol, illus. 2011. (J). 10.95 (978-0-8198-7149-7(4)) Pauline Bks. & Media.

Monckeberg, Paulina. Artilugia 2007 English. 2006. (Pascualina Family of Products Ser.). 274p. (J). spiral bd. 14.99 (978-956-8222-49-9(9)) Pascualina Producciones S.A.

—Pascoalina 2005 Portuguese. 2004. (Pascualina Family of Products Ser.). (ENG.). 272p. (J). spiral bd. 16.99 (978-956-8222-18-5(9)) Pascualina Producciones S.A.

Monson, Christy & Nawyn, Lori. Love, Hugs, & Hope: When Scary Things Happen. 2013. (ENG.). 32p. (J). (gr. k-5). 16.95 (978-1-938301-60-5(9)) Familius LLC.

Montalbano, Julie Williams. Middle School. 2014. (Smart Girl's Guide Ser.). lib. bdg. 24.50 (978-0-606-35213-0(9)) Turtleback Bks.

Moore, Andrew. Meditation. (Teen Mental Health Ser.). 48p. 2009. (gr. 5-6). 53.00 (978-1-60853-296-4(8)) 2008. (Illus.). (YA). (gr. 7-12). lib. bdg. 29.25 (978-1-4042-1799-7(1)) Rosen Publishing Group, Inc., The.

Morton, Emma. 18: Starting the Great Journey of Life on Your Eighteenth Birthday. 2008. 48p. 7.95 (978-0-86435-087-9(2)) Coniston Designs AUS. Dist: Independent Pubs. Group.

Moscattini, Alexander. The Classroom Chair: A True Story. 2007. 22p. pap. 24.95 (978-1-4241-9225-0(0)) America Star Bks.

Moss, Samantha. Where's My Stuff? The Ultimate Teen Organizing Guide. Wertz, Michael, illus. 2007. (ENG.). 96p. (YA). (gr. 8-12). pap. 16.95 (978-0-9772660-5-0(2)) Zest Bks.

Mullery Jr., Matthew W. Hanging Out with Happy Crackers, Fingers Baloo & Stinky Magoo: One Sunny Morning. 2008. 25p. pap. 24.95 (978-1-60672-136-0(4)) America Star Bks.

Mundy, Michaelene. One Caring Kid: A Book about You-and What Your Kindness Can Do! 2008. (Elf-Help Books for Kids Ser.). (Illus.). (J). per. 7.95 (978-0-87029-414-3(8)) Abbey Pr.

My Journey. 2005. (YA). spiral bd. 12.95 (978-0-9747181-1-8(4)) Jodan Collections.

Nagle, Jeanne. Great Lifelong Learning Skills. 2009. (Work Readiness Ser.). 64p. (gr. 6-6). 58.50 (978-1-60854-825-5(2)) Rosen Publishing Group, Inc., The.

National Geographic Kids. National Geographic Kids Thank You Cards. 2017. (ENG., Illus.). 32p. (J). (gr. 1-4). pap. 9.99 (978-1-4263-2769-8(2), National Geographic Children's Bks.) National Geographic Society.

The Need to Know Library: Unique Topics Covering Unique Issues, 8 bks. Incl. Everything You Need to Know about Down Syndrome. Bowman-Kruhm, Mary, ed. (gr. 4-6). 1999. lib. bdg. 25.25 (978-0-8239-2949-8(3), NTDOSY); Everything You Need to Know about Guns in Your Home. Croft, Jennifer. (gr. 7-12). 2005. lib. bdg. 31.95 (978-0-8239-3162-0(5), NTGUHO); Everything You Need to Know about Migraines & Other Headaches. Moe, Barbara. (gr. 7-12). 2005. lib. bdg. 31.95 (978-0-8239-3291-7(5), NTMIHE); Everything You Need to Know about Sexual Identity. Forbes, Jeff Donaldson. (gr. 7-12). 2005. lib. bdg. 31.95 (978-0-8239-3089-0(0), NTSEID); Everything You Need to Know about Sports Gambling. Willker, Joshua D. G. (gr. 7-12). 2005. lib. bdg. 31.95 (978-0-8239-3229-0(X), NTSPGA); Everything You Need to Know about Student-on-Student Sexual Harassment. Stanley, Debbie. (gr. 7-12). 2005. lib. bdg. 31.95 (978-0-8239-3281-8(8), NTSTHA); Everything You Need to Know about the Dangers of Computer Hacking. Knittel, John & Soto, Michael. (gr. 4-6). 2000. lib. bdg. 25.25 (978-0-8239-3034-0(3), NTHACK); Everything You Need to Know about the Goth Scene. Acker, Kerry. (gr. 7-12). 2005. lib. bdg. 31.95 (978-0-8239-3223-8(0), NTGOSC); 64p. (YA). (Illus.). Set lib. bdg. 202.00 (978-0-8239-9280-5(2)) Rosen Publishing Group, Inc., The.

Nelson, Maria. I Can Volunteer. 2013. (Kids of Character Ser.). 24p. (J). (gr. 1-3). pap. 48.90 (978-1-4339-9039-7(3)); (ENG., Illus.). pap. 8.15 (978-1-4339-9038-0(5)); (ENG., Illus.). lib. bdg. 22.60 (978-1-4339-9037-3(7)) Stevens, Gareth Publishing LLLP.

Nelson, Robin. Being Fair. 2003. (First Step Nonfiction - Citizenship Ser.). (ENG., Illus.). 24p. (gr. k-2). pap. 6.95 (978-0-8225-1322-3(6)); lib. bdg. 23.93 (978-0-8225-1285-1(8)) Lerner Publishing Group.

—Being Responsible. 2003. (First Step Nonfiction Ser.). (Illus.). 24p. (gr. k-2). (J). lib. bdg. 18.60 (978-0-8225-1288-2(2)); (ENG., pap. 6.95 (978-0-8225-1343-8(9), Lerner Pubns.) Lerner Publishing Group.

—Following Rules. 2003. (First Step Nonfiction - Citizenship Ser.). (ENG., Illus.). 24p. (gr. k-2). pap. 6.95 (978-0-8225-1321-6(8)); lib. bdg. 23.93 (978-0-8225-1284-4(X)) Lerner Publishing Group.

—Respecting Others. 2003. (First Step Nonfiction Ser.). (Illus.). 24p. (gr. k-2). (J). lib. bdg. 18.60 (978-0-8225-1286-8(6)); (ENG., pap. 6.95 (978-0-8225-1323-0(4)) Lerner Publishing Group.

—Respetar a los Demás. Translations.com Staff, tr. from ENG. 2005. (Mi Primer Paso Al Mundo Real - Civismo (First Step Nonfiction - Citizenship) Ser.). (SPA., Illus.). 24p. (gr. k-2). lib. bdg. 23.93 (978-0-8225-3187-6(9), Ediciones Lerner) Lerner Publishing Group.

—Ser Responsable. 2005. (Mi Primer Paso al Mundo Real (First Step Nonfiction) Ser.). (SPA., Illus.). 24p. (J). (gr. 3-7). lib. bdg. 17.27 (978-0-8225-3180-7(1), Ediciones Lerner) Lerner Publishing Group.

Novak, Robby & Montague, Brad. Kid President's Guide to Being Awesome. (J). (gr. 3-7). 2016. 256p. pap. 12.99 (978-0-06-243871-3(9)) 2015. (ENG., Illus.). 240p. 21.99 (978-0-06-235868-4(5)) HarperCollins Pubs.

Obama, Barack. Of Thee I Sing: A Letter to My Daughters. Long, Loren, illus. 2010. (ENG.). 40p. (J). (gr. k-12). 17.99 (978-0-375-83527-8(X), Knopf Bks. for Young Readers) Random Hse. Children's Bks.

Ochs, Tom. A Day on the Farm Playing Along, 1 vol. Dindar, Kubra, illus. 2009. 25p. pap. 24.95 (978-1-60749-405-8(1)) America Star Bks.

Odogbo, Fidelis C. Principles for Living: Inspiring & Motivating Stories for Overcoming Life's Storms. 2010. 176p. pap. 11.99 (978-1-4490-6051-0(X)) AuthorHouse.

Olson, Karen W. Healthy Choices, Healthy Lives. Hamelin, Marie-Micheline, illus. 2009. (Caring for Me Ser.). (ENG.). 20p. pap. 9.95 (978-1-894778-53-4(7)) Theytus Bks., Ltd. CAN. Dist: Univ. of Toronto Pr.

Orero, Maria Jesus. Nico y Sus Cosas. 2006. (Nico Collection). (SPA & ESP., Illus.). 12p. (gr. -1-2). per., bds. 6.99 (978-84-272-6151-8(9)) Molino, Editorial ESP. Dist: Santillana USA Publishing Co., Inc.

Osborne, Rick, et al. Creepy Creatures & Bizarre Beasts from the Bible, 1 vol. Carpenter, Anthony, illus. 2004. (2:52 Ser.). (ENG.). 128p. (J). pap. 7.99 (978-0-310-70654-0(8)) Zonderkidz.

Otto, Joanne. The You-Song. 2013. 56p. (J). pap. 19.95 (978-1-61933-374-1(0)) FastPrncil, Inc.

Paarmann, Al. Please Let Me Help: I Need Validation. Paarmann, Lesley, photos by. unabr. ed. 2003. (Illus.). 150p. (YA). pap. 12.95 (978-0-9715963-1-3(X)) Paarmann, Al International.

Page, Brenda. In the Hands of the Potter: Shaped for Purpose. Elum, Deborah, ed. 2004. (YA). per. 9.98 net. (978-0-9679441-6-6(3)) All That Productions, Inc.

Page, Nick. Amazing Academy Survival. 2008. (Illus.). 64p. (J). (gr. 4-7). (978-1-84610-817-4(9)) Make Believe Ideas.

Pagels, Douglas. What Every Teen Needs to Know. 2010. (ENG.). 60p. 13.95 (978-1-59842-494-2(7)) Blue Mountain Arts Inc.

Pagratis, Maggie & Pagratis, Illustrator Liliane, MaggieGrenier. With Their Tiny Hands. 2005. 19p. (J). 11.95 (978-1-4116-3763-4(1)) Lulu Pr., Inc.

Parker, Vic. Acting Responsibly. (Exploring Citizenship Ser.). (ENG.). 32p. 2016. pap. 8.29 (978-1-4846-3988-7(X)) 2009. (gr. 1-3). 26.65 (978-1-4329-3315-9(9)) Heinemann-Raintree. (Heinemann First Library).

Parkman, Tina. Show Me Some Love: Recipes of Survival for at Risk Teens & Young Adults. 2003. 96p. (YA). pap. 9.99 (978-1-56229-009-2(6), Christian Living Books, Inc.) Pneuma Life Publishing, Inc.

Payne, Timothy R. Payne Man. 2007. 52p. per. 7.95 (978-1-4327-0582-4(2)) Outskirts Pr., Inc.

Pears, Alison. Gus & Oliver-A Family Tale. 2012. 30p. pap. 13.99 (978-1-4525-5472-3(2)) Balboa Pr.

Perez, L. King. Primer dia en las Uvas. Casilla, Robert, illus. 2004. Orig. Title: First Day in Grapes. (SPA.). 32p. (J). (gr. 2-5). pap. 10.95 (978-1-58430-240-7(2)) Lee & Low Bks., Inc.

Perry, Janice Kapp. I'm Trying to Be Like Jesus. Abts, Stacey, illus. 2003. (J). (978-1-57008-843-8(8), Bookcraft, Inc.) Deseret Bk. Co.

Perry, Jason & Keels, Steve. You Are Not Your Own: Living Loud for God. 2004. (TruthQuest Ser.). 144p. (gr. 7-18). pap. 12.99 (978-0-8054-2591-8(8)) B&H Publishing Group.

Perry, M. Daily Pages to Create the Life You Want: A Companion Workbook to Pictures of My Days. 2005. pap. 13.00 (978-0-9759251-4-0(8), PlayGround) Forest Hill Publishing, LLC.

—Pictures of My Days: An Art & Writing Workbook for Creating the Life You Want. 2005. pap. 13.00 (978-0-9759251-3-3(X), PlayGround) Forest Hill Publishing, LLC.

Pitts, Wynter. For Girls Like You: A Devotional for Tweens. 2015. (ENG.). 144p. (J). pap. 10.99 (978-0-7369-6175-2(5)) Harvest Hse. Pubs.

Ponto, Joanna. Being Honest. 2015. (J). (978-0-7660-6633-5(9)) Enslow Pubs., Inc.

—Being Kind. 2015. (J). (978-0-7660-6637-3(1)) Enslow Pubs., Inc.

—Being Respectful. 2015. (All about Character Ser.). (ENG., Illus.). 24p. (J). (gr. -1-1). 22.60 (978-0-7660-7099-8(9)) Enslow Pubs., Inc.

—Being Responsible. 2015. (J). (978-0-7660-6629-8(0)) Enslow Pubs., Inc.

Pryor, Kimberley Jane. Courage. 2008. (Values Ser.). 32p. (gr. 1-2). lib. bdg. 18.56 (978-0-7614-3131-2(4), Benchmark Bks.) Marshall Cavendish Corp.

—Doing Your Best. 2010. (Values 2 Ser.). 32p. (gr. 1). 18.56 (978-1-60870-142-1(5)) Marshall Cavendish Corp.

—Fairness. 2010. (Values 2 Ser.). 32p. (gr. 1). 18.56 (978-1-60870-143-8(3)) Marshall Cavendish Corp.

—Helpfulness. 2010. (Values 2 Ser.). 32p. (gr. 1). 18.56 (978-1-60870-144-5(1)) Marshall Cavendish GBR. Dist: Marshall Cavendish Corp.

—Honesty. 2008. (Values Ser.). 32p. (gr. 1-2). lib. bdg. 18.56 (978-0-7614-3125-1(X), Benchmark Bks.) Marshall Cavendish Corp.

—Integrity. 2010. (Values 2 Ser.). 32p. (gr. 1). 18.56 (978-1-60870-145-2(X)) Marshall Cavendish GBR. Dist: Marshall Cavendish Corp.

—Kindness. 2008. (Values Ser.). 32p. (gr. 1-2). lib. bdg. 18.56 (978-0-7614-3126-8(8), Benchmark Bks.) Marshall Cavendish Corp.

—Respect. 2008. (Values Ser.). 32p. (J). (gr. 1-3). lib. bdg. 18.56 (978-0-7614-3128-2(4)) Marshall Cavendish Corp.

—Responsibility. 2010. (Values 2 Ser.). 32p. (gr. 1). 18.56 (978-1-60870-146-9(8)) Marshall Cavendish Corp.

—Self-Discipline. 2010. (Values 2 Ser.). 32p. (gr. 1). 18.56 (978-1-60870-147-6(6)) Marshall Cavendish GBR. Dist: Marshall Cavendish Corp.

—Tolerance. 2008. (Values Ser.). 32p. (J). (gr. 1-3). lib. bdg. 18.56 (978-0-7614-3129-9(2)) Marshall Cavendish Corp.

Pyle, Kevin C. & Cunningham, Scott. Bad for You: Exposing the War on Fun! Pyle, Kevin C., illus. 2014. (ENG., Illus.). 192p. (YA). (gr. 7). pap. 12.99 (978-0-8050-9289-9(7), Holt, Henry & Co. Bks. For Young Readers) Holt, Henry & Co.

Quaglia, Russell & Fox, Kristine M. Raising Student Aspirations Grades K-5: Classroom Activities. 2004. (ENG.). 122p. (gr. k-5). pap. 25.95 (978-0-87822-480-7(7), 5197) Research Pr.

Raatma, Lucia. Caring. 2009. (21st Century Junior Library: Character Education Ser.). (ENG.). 24p. (gr. 2-5). lib. bdg. 25.64 (978-1-60279-323-1(9), 200219) Cherry Lake Publishing.

—Fairness. 2009. (21st Century Junior Library: Character Education Ser.). (ENG.). 24p. (gr. 2-5). lib. bdg. 25.64 (978-1-60279-322-4(0), 200218) Cherry Lake Publishing.

—Respect. (21st Century Junior Library: Character Education Ser.). (ENG.). 24p. 2013. (J). (gr. 1-4). 25.64 (978-1-62431-156-7(3), 202944) 2013. (J). (gr. 1-4). pap. 12.79 (978-1-62431-288-5(8), 202946) 2009. (gr. 2-5). lib. bdg. 25.64 (978-1-60279-320-0(4), 200216) Cherry Lake Publishing.

—Sportsmanship. 2009. (21st Century Junior Library: Character Education Ser.). (ENG.). 24p. (gr. 2-5). lib. bdg. 25.64 (978-1-60279-325-5(5), 200221) Cherry Lake Publishing.

—Trustworthiness. (21st Century Junior Library: Character Education Ser.). (ENG.). 24p. 2013. (J). (gr. 1-4). 25.64 (978-1-62431-159-8(8), 202956) 2013. (J). (gr. 1-4). pap. 12.79 (978-1-62431-291-5(8), 202958) 2009. (gr. 2-5). lib. bdg. 25.64 (978-1-60279-319-4(0), 200215) Cherry Lake Publishing.

Radtke, Becky. People on the Go Mazes. 2008. (Dover Little Activity Bks.). (ENG.). 64p. (J). (gr. k-3). pap. 1.50 (978-0-486-46566-1(7)) Dover Pubns., Inc.

Rainey, Dennis, et al. So You're about to Be a Teenager: Godly Advice for Preteens on Friends, Love, Sex, Faith, & Other Life Issues, 1 vol. 2003. (ENG., Illus.). 176p. pap. 13.99 (978-0-7852-6279-4(2)) Nelson, Thomas Inc.

Rau, Dana Meachen. Kids Top 10 Pet Fish. 2015. (American Humane Association Top 10 Pets for Kids Ser.). 48p. (J). (gr. 3-4). pap. 8.95 (978-0-7660-6641-0(X), Enslow Elementary) Enslow Pubs., Inc.

Reed, Cristie. Problem Solving. 2012. (ENG., Illus.). 24p. (gr. k-2). pap. 8.95 (978-1-61810-266-9(4)) Rourke Educational Media.

Reed, Gregory J. Dear Mrs. Parks: A Dialogue with Today's Youth. 2013. (ENG., Illus.). 111p. (J). (gr. 3-7). reprint ed. per. 16.95 (978-1-880000-61-8(X)) Lee & Low Bks., Inc.

Rice, Ashley. Girls Rule: A Very Special Book Created Especially for Girls. Rice, Ashley, illus. (Illus.). 64p. (J). pap. 9.95 (978-0-88396-627-3(1), Blue Mountain Pr.) Blue Mountain Arts Inc.

Rich, C. & Richardson, Carla R. Completely You: 12 Things Every Girl Needs to Know. 2008. 60p. pap. 9.95 (978-0-595-51675-9(0)) iUniverse, Inc.

Ridge, Rachel Anne. Flash the Donkey Makes New Friends. Ridge, Rachel Anne, illus. 2016. (Flash the Donkey Ser.). (ENG., Illus.). 48p. (J). 12.99 (978-1-4964-1395-6(4), Tyndale Momentum) Tyndale Hse. Pubs.

Riley, Jim. Spiritual Grit: Pass It on to Kids 2004. (ENG., Illus.). 125p. per. 8.95 (978-1-57166-315-3(0)) Quixote Pr.

Rische, Stephanie. My Princesses Learn to Be Brave. Heyworth, Heather, illus. 2014. (ENG.). 24p. (J). 6.99 (978-1-4143-9661-3(9)) Tyndale Hse. Pubs.

Rissman, Rebecca. What Would You Do? 2013. (What Would You Do? Ser.). (ENG.). 24p. (gr. -1-1). pap. 35.94 (978-1-4329-7248-6(0)); lib. bdg. 135.90 (978-1-4329-7242-4(1)) Heinemann-Raintree. (Acorn).

Robinson, Sharon. Promises to Keep: How Jackie Robinson Changed America. 2004. (ENG., Illus.). 64p. (J). (gr. 3-7). 17.99 (978-0-439-42592-6(1)) Scholastic, Inc.

Robus, Debbie. What to Say & Do... When You Don't Know What to Say & Do. 2004. 7.95 (978-0-9762034-0-7(5)) Robus, Debbie.

Rondina, Catherine. Rudeness: Deal with It If You Please, 1 vol. Workman, Dan, illus. 2005. (Lorimer Deal with It Ser.). (ENG.). 32p. (J). (gr. 4-6). 12.95 (978-1-55028-870-4(9), 9781550288704) Lorimer, James & Co., Ltd., Pubs. CAN. Dist: Casemate Pubs. & Bk. Distributors, LLC.

Rose, Whitney. Woo Hoo, the Growing You'll Do. 2013. 24p. pap. 12.95 (978-0-9891694-6-2(4)) Barringer Publishing.

Rosen Publishing Group. FAQ: Teen Life, 6 bks., Set 1. 2007. (YA). lib. bdg. 167.70 (978-1-4042-1050-9(4)) Rosen Publishing Group, Inc., The.

Ross, Margaret. Casey & the Amazing Good Finder: Teaching Adults & Children How to Succeed in School, Work, Life & Relationships. l.t. ed. 2005. (Illus.). 32p. (J). 9.99 (978-0-9715713-5-8(X)) Kamaron Institute Pr.

Sabin, Ellen. The Hero Book: Learning Lessons from the People You Admire. Barbas, Kerren, illus. 2005. 64p. 19.95 (978-0-9759868-1-3(3)) Watering Can.

Sabin, Ellen & Driscoll, Patricia. The Healing Heroes Book: Braving the Changes When Someone You Love Is Wounded in Service. 2012. (ENG., Illus.). 64p. (J). spiral bd. 19.95 (978-0-9826416-0-6(5)) Watering Can.

Salas, Laura Purdie. Taking the Plunge. 2004. (Illus.). 250p. (J). pap. 12.95 (978-1-58760-012-8(9), 10129, Child & Family Pr.) Child Welfare League of America, Inc.

Salzmann, Mary Elizabeth. I Am Responsible. 2003. (Building Character Ser.). (ENG., Illus.). 24p. (J). (gr. k-3). lib. bdg. 24.21 (978-1-57765-830-6(2), SandCastle) ABDO Publishing Co.

Sanschagrin, Joceline. Caillou, Be Careful! Brignaud, Pierre, illus. 2nd ed. 2013. (Step by Step Ser.). (ENG.). 24p. (J). (gr. -1-k). bds. (978-2-89718-039-3(0)) Filmer Ltd.

Santorum, Karen. Everyday Graces: Child's Book of Good Manners. Torode, Sam, illus. 2003. (Foundations Ser.). 407p. (J). 25.00 (978-1-932236-09-5(0)) ISI Bks.

Sargent, Brian. Altruism: What's in It for Me? 2014. (ENG., Illus.). 32p. (J). pap. 9.50 (978-1-107-62262-3(X)) Cambridge Univ. Pr.

Schaefer, Lola M. Who Makes the Rules? 2011. (Early Connections Ser.). (J). (978-1-61672-657-7(1)) Benchmark Education Co.

Scherer, Lauri S. Recycling. Greenhaven Press Editors, ed. 2014. (Issues That Concern You Ser.). (ENG., Illus.). 144p. (gr. 7-10). lib. bdg. 42.00 (978-0-7377-6932-6(7), Greenhaven Pr., Inc.) Cengage Gale.

Scheunemann, Pam. Acting with Kindness, 1 vol. 2004. (Keeping the Peace Ser.). (ENG., Illus.). 24p. (J). (gr. k-3). lib. bdg. 24.21 (978-1-59197-557-1(3), SandCastle) ABDO Publishing Co.

—Being a Peacekeeper, 1 vol. 2004. (Keeping the Peace Ser.). (ENG., Illus.). 24p. (J). (gr. k-3). lib. bdg. 24.21 (978-1-59197-558-8(1), SandCastle) ABDO Publishing Co.

—Coping with Anger, 1 vol. 2004. (Keeping the Peace Ser.). (ENG., Illus.). 24p. (J). (gr. k-3). lib. bdg. 24.21 (978-1-59197-559-5(X), SandCastle) ABDO Publishing Co.

—Dealing with Bullies, 1 vol. 2004. (Keeping the Peace Ser.). (ENG., Illus.). 24p. (J). (gr. k-3). lib. bdg. 24.21 (978-1-59197-560-1(3), SandCastle) ABDO Publishing Co.

—Learning about Differences, 1 vol. 2004. (Keeping the Peace Ser.). (ENG., Illus.). 24p. (J). (gr. k-3). lib. bdg. 24.21 (978-1-59197-561-8(1), SandCastle) ABDO Publishing Co.

Scheunemann, Pam & ABDO Publishing Company Staff. Keeping the Peace. 2004. (Keeping the Peace Ser.: 6). (ENG., Illus.). 24p. (J). (gr. k-3). lib. bdg. 145.26 (978-1-59197-556-4(5), SandCastle) ABDO Publishing Co.

Schmidt, Nancy Li. The Little Spark That Grew. 2012. 28p. pap. 21.99 (978-1-4797-2166-5(2)) Xlibris Corp.

Scholastic, Inc. Staff, contrib. by. Can You Say Please? 2014. (Rookie Toddler(r) Ser.). (ENG.). 12p. (J). bds. 6.95 (978-0-531-20918-9(0)) Scholastic Library Publishing.

Segalove, Llene. List Your Self: Discover Your Own True Self by Making Lists. 2013. (ENG.). 128p. (J). pap. 12.99 (978-1-4494-3718-3(4)) Andrews McMeel Publishing.

Sevigny, Eric, illus. Caillou Gone Fishing. 2015. (Clubhouse Ser.). (ENG.). 24p. (J). (gr. -1-1). 3.99 (978-2-89718-183-3(4)) Caillouet, Gerry.

Sharp, Anna Layton. Taking Godly Care of My Money: Stewardship Lessons in Money Matters, Grades 2-5. Flint, Russ, illus. 2005. (Resource Bks.). 80p. (J). (gr. 2-5). per. 9.99 (978-1-59441-082-6(8), CD-204009) Carson-Dellosa Publishing, LLC.

Shaw, Holly & Gluck, Leanne. Mirror, Mirror: Discover Your Inner Beauty, a Guide for Girls 14-17. 2007. (Uniquely Me! Ser.: Vol. 4). (Illus.). 84p. (J). pap. (978-0-88441-706-4(9)) Girl Scouts of the USA.

Sheehan, Monica. Be Happy! Sheehan, Monica, illus. 2014. (ENG., Illus.). 68p. (J). (gr. -1-3). 14.99 (978-1-4424-9857-0(9), Little Simon) Little Simon.

Shepherd, Jodie. Kindness & Generosity: It Starts with Me! 2015. (Rookie Talk about It(tm) Ser.). (ENG., Illus.). 32p. (J). pap. 5.95 (978-0-531-21384-1(6), Children's Pr.) Scholastic Library Publishing.

—Perseverance: I Have Grit! 2015. (Rookie Talk about It(tm) Ser.). (ENG., Illus.). 32p. (J). pap. 5.95 (978-0-531-21379-7(X), Children's Pr.) Scholastic Library Publishing.

Shipp, Josh. The Teen's Guide to World Domination: Advice on Life, Liberty, & the Pursuit of Awesomeness. 2010. (ENG.). 304p. (YA). (gr. 8-18). pap., instr.'s gde. ed. 15.99 (978-0-312-64154-2(0), 9780312641542, St. Martin's Griffin) St. Martin's Pr.

Silverthorne, Sandy. Surviving When You're Home Alone: How to Avoid Being Grounded for Life. Silverthorne, Sandy, illus. 2006. (Illus.). 96p. (YA). (gr. 3-6). pap. 5.99 (978-0-7847-1434-8(7), 42176) Standard Publishing.

—Surviving Zits: How to Cope with Your Changing Self. Silverthorne, Sandy, illus. 2006. (Illus.). 96p. (YA). (gr. 3-6). pap. 5.99 (978-0-7847-1435-5(5), 42177) Standard Publishing.

Simon, Mary Manz, et al. I Love Fall! Nakata, Hiroe, illus. 2009. (ENG.). 12p. (J). (gr. -1-1). bds. 6.99 (978-1-4169-3609-1(2), Little Simon) Little Simon.

Skordy, Anne Marie. Start with Your Heart. Collier, Kevin, illus. 2011. 32p. (J). pap. 12.95 (978-1-60131-089-7(7)) Big Tent Bks.

Small, Mary. Being Responsible: A Book about Responsibility, 1 vol. Previn, Stacey, illus. 2005. (Way to Be! Ser.). (ENG.). 24p. (gr. k-2). lib. bdg. 26.65 (978-1-4048-1052-5(8)) Picture Window Bks.

—Ser Digno de Confianza. Previn, Stacey, illus. 2011. (¡Así Debemos Ser!/Way to Be! Ser.).Tr. of Being Trustworthy. (ENG, SPA & MUL.). 24p. (gr. -1-2). lib. bdg. 26.65 (978-1-4048-6691-1(4)) Picture Window Bks.

Smith, Brenda J. Where Did Mommy Go? A Spiritual Tool to Help Children Grow from Grief to Peace. Smith, Brenda J. & Cloud, Olivia, eds. Smith, Brock R. & Smith, Raissa B., illus. 2004. Orig. Title: Listed Above. 52p. (gr. 3-12). pap. 16.95 (978-0-9744549-0-0(7)) Tall Through Bks.

Smith, Tim. Buck Wilder's Animal Wisdom. Herrick, Mark, illus. 2006. 32p. (J). (gr. 3-7). (978-1-934133-02-6(7), Mackinac Island Press, Inc.) Charlesbridge Publishing, Inc.

Snow, Alan. How Kids Really Work. Snow, Alan, illus. 2013. (ENG., Illus.). 40p. (J). (gr. -1-5). 16.99 (978-0-689-85818-5(3), Atheneum Bks. for Young Readers) Simon & Schuster Children's Publishing.

Snow, Todd & Snow, Peggy. Kindness to Share from a to Z. Kirsten, Sevig, illus. 2008. (ENG.). 32p. (J). pap. 10.99 (978-1-934277-16-4(9)) Marn Green Publishing, Inc.

Snyder, Matthew. How to Survive in a World with Two or More People. 2008. 164p. pap. 15.95 (978-0-595-48948-0(6)) iUniverse, Inc.

Sprick, Randall S. The Solution Book. (Solution Book Ser.). (gr. k-8). 99.90 (978-0-07-568978-2(2)) SRA/McGraw-Hill.

Squire 5 Personal Growth Planbook: Daring Depths. 2003. (Illus.). 48p. (J). pap. 4.95 (978-1-59312-046-7(X)) North American Mission Board, SBC.

St. John, Patricia. A Young Person's Guide to Knowing God. 2014. (ENG.). 240p. (J). (gr. 8-13). pap. 10.99 (978-1-85792-558-6(0), 25eb103e-5706-4d05-ab4c-24ce869fd1b0) Christian Focus Pubns. GBR. Dist: Bookmasters Distribution.

Standing Tall & Respecting All. 2004. (J). pap. 7.99 net. (978-0-9763141-2-7(6)) G.S. Enterprises of America Inc.

Stein, Lee. Generation Communication: For Teens Who Want to Get Ahead in the World. 2011. 60p. (YA). per. 9.99 (978-0-9786663-1-6(3)) Paradoxical Pr., The.

Steinkraus, Kyla. May I Please? 2012. (ENG.). 24p. (gr. k-2). pap. 8.95 (978-1-61810-271-3(0)) Rourke Educational Media.

Stevens, Mitchell. Hey! Follow Your Dreams: 7 Steps to Dream Followin' 2013. (ENG.). 20.00 (978-0-9800123-2-3(5)) Anomaly Publishing.

Stewart, Ed & McDowell, Josh. Conflicts with Others. 2008. (Project 17:17 Ser.). (ENG.). 64p. (J). pap. 4.99 (978-1-84550-354-3(6), fb41ae66-973d-4060-8e31-2a08e1f62976) Christian Focus Pubns. GBR. Dist: Bookmasters Distribution.

—Finding True Love. 2008. (Project 17:17 Ser.). (ENG.). 64p. (J). pap. 4.99 (978-1-84550-356-7(2), d5fc11fa-99e7-4d6c-b4b5-7793875dbf44) Christian Focus Pubns. GBR. Dist: Bookmasters Distribution.

Stewart, Jan. Respecting Others. 2004. (ENG., Illus.). 32p. (J). pap. 9.95 (978-0-89793-313-1(3), Hunter Hse.) Turner Publishing Co.

Stock, Gregory. The Kids' Book of Questions. 2015. (ENG.). 216p. (J). (gr. 3-12). pap. 8.95 (978-0-7611-8464-5(3)) Workman Publishing Co., Inc.

Stormer, Kate. A Stranger in Casey's World. Lowes, Tom, illus. l.t. ed. 2004. 32p. (J). 16.95 (978-0-9647663-1-0(0)) Caseys World Bks.

Strauss, Ed. Devotions to Make You Smarter, 1 vol. 2007. (2:52 Ser.). (ENG., Illus.). 192p. (J). (gr. 3-7). pap. 9.99 (978-0-310-71312-8(9)) Zonderkidz.

Strazzabosco, Jeanne M. Learning about Responsibility. 2004. (Character Building Book Ser.). 24p. (J). lib. bdg. 22.60 (978-0-8239-6927-2(4), PowerKids Pr.) Rosen Publishing Group, Inc., The.

Strong, Terri. Wee Wisdom. 2007. 60p. per. 10.95 (978-1-933912-69-1(3)) Westview Publishing Co., Inc.

Stump, Chuck & Strawn, Jim. Another Sad Mad Glad Book: The Anatomy of Your Attitude. 2008. 104p. (J). pap. 14.50 (978-0-9799315-2-9(5)) Four Dolphins Pr., LLC.

Sullivan, James Kevin, illus. What Went RIght Today? Journal: WWRT Journal. 2007. 72p. (J). spiral bd. 12.95 (978-0-9766990-1-9(X)) Buz-Land Presentations, Inc.

Survivors: Ordinary People, Extraordinary Circumstances, 13 vols., Set. Incl. Danger in the Deep: Surviving Shark Attacks. Zoldak, Joyce. (YA). 24.95 (978-1-4222-0511-2(8)); Enemy Within: Overcoming Cancer & Other Life-Threatening Diseases. Therrien, Patricia. (YA). 24.95 (978-1-4222-0450-4(2)); In Defense of Our Country: Survivors of Military Conflict. Nelson, Sheila. (YA). 24.95 (978-1-4222-0452-8(9)); Nature's Wrath: Surviving Natural Disasters. Sanna, Ellyn. (YA). 24.95 (978-1-4222-0454-2(5)); Never Again: Survivors of the Holocaust. Nelson, Sheila. (J). 24.95 (978-1-4222-0459-7(6)); Those Who Remain: What It Means to Be a Survivor. Sanna, Ellyn. (Illus.). (J). 24.95 (978-1-4222-0457-3(X)); When Danger Hits Home: Survivors of Domestic Violence. Zoldak, Joyce. (YA). 24.95 (978-1-4222-0460-3(X)); 128p. (gr. 7-12). 2010. 2009. Set lib. bdg. 324.35 (978-1-4222-0449-8(9)) Mason Crest.

Swain, Claudia. What's a Girl to Do? 2004. 128p. pap. 6.99 (978-1-56309-440-8(1)) New Hope Pubs.

Swainston, Jeani. Grandma Stuff: ... it's what love Is made Of. 2006. (J). (978-0-9791384-0-9(X)) Rock Cliff Media.

Szumski, Bonnie. Cheating. rev. ed. 2014. (Matters of Opinion Ser.). (ENG.). 64p. (J). (gr. 4-6). pap. 14.60 (978-1-60357-585-0(5)); lib. bdg. 27.93 (978-1-59953-605-7(6)) Norwood Hse. Pr.

Tadder, Karen Mc. Donald. Picture Your Invisible Self: A Universal Lesson Plan for Learning Intrapersonal Skills. 2005. 20p. per. 8.00 (978-1-59196-911-2(5)) Instant Pub.

Tang, Greg. Math Fables. Cahoon, Heather, illus. 2004. (ENG.). 40p. (J). (gr. -1-3). 18.99 (978-0-439-45399-8(2)) Scholastic, Inc.

Team Dawg It's All about Respect, 1. 2004. (Illus.). 30p. (J). bds. 14.99 (978-0-9749378-0-9(0)) Team Dawg Productions, Inc.

Tebow, Tim. Shaken: Young Reader's Edition: Fighting to Stand Strong No Matter What Comes Your Way. 2017. (ENG.). 208p. (J). (gr. 5). 17.99 **(978-0-7352-8996-3(4)**, WaterBrook Pr.) Crown Publishing Group.

Telias, Ari. Tales of the Chocolate River: How to Make Your Dreams Come True. 2011. 48p. (J). pap. 10.00 (978-0-692-00612-2(5)) Justice Link Publishing.

There's Beauty in the Rainbow. 2006. (J). per. 12.00 (978-0-9786154-0-6(9)) Milestones Publishing.

Thomas, Isabel. Dealing with Feeling... Proud. 2013. (Dealing with Feeling... Ser.). (ENG.). 24p. (gr. 1-2). pap. 6.79 (978-1-4329-7116-8(6)); lib. bdg. 23.32 (978-1-4329-7107-6(7)) Heinemann-Raintree. (Heinemann Read & Learn).

Thomas, Kimberly. The Greatest Flag in the World: The Universal Family Flag. 2012. 24p. pap. 16.00 (978-1-4685-5659-9(2)) AuthorHouse.

Thomas, Patsy E. Why Not Me? 2011. 20p. pap. (978-1-4269-7417-5(5)) Trafford Publishing (UK) Ltd.

Thompson, Carol & Thompson, Carol. America the Good: Stories of Goodwill by Good Americans. 2003. (Illus.). 95p. bds. 15.95 (978-0-9744111-0-1(8)) Wren's Nest Publishing, Inc.

Tillman, Charles. The Middle School Rules of Charles Tillman. 2015. (Middle School Rules Ser.). (ENG., Illus.). 176p. (J). (gr. 4-8). 14.99 (978-1-4245-5101-9(3)) BroadStreet Publishing.

Titcomb, Timothy. Lessons in Life: a Series of Familiar Essays. 2007. pap. 31.95 (978-1-4304-7511-8(0)) Kessinger Publishing, LLC.

Todo lo Que Necesitas Saber Series, Set. 2003. (Todo lo Que Necesitas Saber Ser.). (SPA & ENG., Illus.). (J). lib. bdg. 238.50 (978-0-8239-9719-0(7), Editorial Buenas Letras) Rosen Publishing Group, Inc., The.

Tool Kits for Kids LLC Staff, creator. Build up Your Resilience - Tool Kit for Kids: Elementary School Edition. 2009. (J). 39.95 (978-0-9819483-4-8(0)) Tool Kits For Kids LLC.

—Build up Your Resilience - Tool Kit for Kids: High School / Middle School Edition. 2009. (J). 39.95 (978-0-9819483-5-5(9)) Tool Kits For Kids LLC.

—Outsmart Your Worry - Tool Kit for Kids: Elementary School Edition. 2008. (Illus.). 23p. (J). 39.95 (978-0-9819483-0-0(8)) Tool Kits For Kids LLC.

—Outsmart Your Worry - Tool Kit for Kids: High School / Middle School Edition. 2008. (Illus.). (J). 39.95 (978-0-9819483-1-7(6)) Tool Kits For Kids LLC.

Tousey, Ben. Acting Your Dreams: Using Acting Techniques to Interpret Your Dreams, 1. 2003. (C). per. 14.95 (978-0-9724292-0-7(4)) Yhabbut Publishing.

Towne, Isobel & MacAdam, Lea. Dealing with Family Rules, 01 vols., 1. 2016. (Family Issues & You Ser.). (ENG.). 48p. (J). pap. 11.75 (978-1-4994-3697-6(1), Rosen Central) Rosen Publishing Group, Inc., The.

Turk, Cynthia. My Daddy Stays at Home with Me. 2004. 27p. pap. 24.95 (978-1-4137-3363-1(8)) PublishAmerica, Inc.

Twin Talk: Advice from a TV Talk Show. 2005. (Illus.). 37p. (978-0-439-12406-5(9)) Scholastic, Inc.

Vaughn Loeffler. Love Makes the Green Grass Grow. 2006. (ENG.). 36p. per. 21.32 (978-1-4257-2781-9(6)) Xlibris Corp.

Veerman, David. Ready for Life. 2008. 400p. (J). pap. 16.99 (978-0-9724616-4-1(7)) Barton-Veerman Co.

Vining, Kathryn. You've Been Touched by the F. O. G. (Fingerprints of God) 2012. 142p. (gr. 4-6). 28.99 (978-1-4497-7622-0(1)); pap. 11.99 (978-1-4497-7621-3(3)) Author Solutions, Inc. (WestBow Pr.).

Vision, Mutiya & Vision, David. My Choices Make Me Who I Am. Alcantara, Ignacio, illus. 2009. 40p. (gr. 2-5). 17.00 (978-0-9659538-2-5(3)) Von Curtis Publishing.

Warlick, Sonya. A King's Love for His Daughter. 2010. 24p. pap. 7.99 (978-0-88144-511-4(8), Thorncrown Publishing) Yorkshire Publishing Group.

We are What We Do Staff. 31 Ways to Change the World. 2010. (ENG., Illus.). 80p. (J). (gr. 3-7). pap. 8.99 (978-0-7636-4506-9(0)) Candlewick Pr.

Wesbrooks, Linda. The New You: Lessons for Teenage Girls. (YA). pap. 7.99 (978-0-89098-406-2(9)) Twentieth Century Christian Bks.

Whelen-Banks, Jane. Liam Says "Hi" Learning to Greet a Friend. 2008. (ENG., Illus.). 32p. 12.95 (978-1-84310-901-3(8), 5372) Kingsley, Jessica Pubs. GBR. Dist: Macmillan Distribution Ltd.

White, Ellen Gould Harmon. The Ministry of Healing. 2005. reprint ed. pap. 42.95 (978-1-4191-4425-7(1)) Kessinger Publishing, LLC.

Whitfield, Kate. The Empowered Gal's 9 Life Lessons: Keys, Tips, Strategies, Advice & Everything You Need to Know to be a Confident, Successful, in Control Gal. 2008. 236p. pap. 18.95 (978-0-595-47829-3(8)) iUniverse, Inc.

Whitney, Brooks. How to Master the School Universe: Homework, Teachers, Tests, Bullies, & Other Ways to Survive the Classroom. Kennedy, Kelly, illus. 2004. 80p. (J). pap. (978-0-439-57902-5(3)) Scholastic, Inc.

Wiggin, Kate Douglas. The Story of Patsy. 2004. reprint ed. pap. 15.95 (978-1-4179-2620-6(1)) Kessinger Publishing, LLC.

—The Story of Patsy. 2009. (gr. 4-7). 108p. 22.95 (978-1-60664-686-1(9)); 104p. pap. 9.95 (978-1-60664-316-7(9)) Rodgers, Alan Bks.

Wilbur, Regina, ed. Keys to Success: Getting Control of Mr. & Mrs. Attitude & Temper (A. T.) Student Workbook Grades 6-12. 2003. (ENG.). 41p. (YA). stu. ed. 6.95 (978-0-9710925-2-5(4)) EniCare Consulting, Inc.

—Keys to Success: Getting Control of Mr. & Mrs Attitude & Temper (A. T.) Teacher's Guide/Students Assignments Grades 6-12. 2003. (ENG.). 48p. (YA). tchr. ed., spiral bd. 8.95 (978-0-9710925-1-8(6), 0-9710925-1-6) EniCare Consulting, Inc.

Wilkinson, Bruce & Thomas, Mack. A Life God Rewards: Guys Only. ltd. ed. 2006. 96p. bds. 9.99 *(978-1-60142-002-2(1),* Multnomah) Doubleday Religious Publishing Group, The.
Williams, Pharrell. Happy! (ENG., Illus.). (J). (gr. -1 — 1). 2016. 30p. bds. 6.99 *(978-0-399-54812-3(2))* 2015. 32p. 19.99 *(978-0-399-17643-2(8))* Penguin Young Readers Group. (G.P. Putnam's Sons Books for Young Readers).
Willis, Jaymie Janaye. The Deal. 2012. 72p. 19.95 *(978-1-4626-6857-1(7))* America Star Bks.
Wood, Kerry & Muskat, Carrie. All You Can Be: Learning & Growing Through Sports. 2012. (All You Can Be Ser.). (ENG., Illus.). 48p. (gr. 2-4). 16.95 *(978-1-60078-689-1(8))* Triumph Bks.
Woods, Earl & Tiger Woods Foundation Staff. Start Something: You Can Make a Difference. 2006. (ENG., Illus.). 144p. (gr. 4-7). pap. 14.00 *(978-1-4165-3704-5(X))* Simon & Schuster.
Wynn, Robbin. The Final Showdown under the Sun: You vs. Adversary. 2005. (YA). per. 13.00 incl. audio *(978-0-9770682-0-3(X))* Inner Circle Publishing.
Yonikus, Sandi. Dominga's Wonderful Year/El Año Maravilloso del Domingo. Nelson, Annika, illus. 2005. (SPA & ENG.). 32p. (J). 16.95 *(978-0-8146-2876-8(1))* Liturgical Pr.
You Choose Books Classroom Collection. 2011. (You Choose Bks.). (ENG.). 112p. (gr. 3-4). pap. 1626.30 *(978-1-4296-8026-4(1),* You Choose Bks.) Capstone Press of Coughlan Cos.
The Young Woman's Empowerment Journal: From Dreaming to Reaching Your Full Potential. 2004. (YA). per. 14.99 *(978-0-9748017-0-4(4))* Adelante Productions, Inc.
Yun, Hsing, et al. Prescription for the Heart: Between Ignorance & Enlightenment II, 7 vols., Vol. 2. 2003. (Between Ignorance & Enlightenment Ser.: Vol. 2). 131p. pap. 13.00 *(978-1-932293-02-9(7))* Buddha's Light Publications USA Corp.

CONDUCT OF LIFE—FICTION

A. L. O. E. The Triumph over Midian. 2006. 344p. per. 23.99 *(978-1-4255-3466-0(X))* Michigan Publishing.
Abbott, Jacob. Aunt Margaret; or, How John True Kept His Resolutions. 2013. 160p. pap. 19.95 *(978-1-4455-2937-0(8))* Research Pr.
—Rollo at Work. 2009. 148p. pap. 8.95 *(978-1-59915-342-1(4))* Yesterday's Classics.
—Rollo at Work & Rollo at Play. 2006. (Illus.). pap. 34.95 *(978-1-4286-4095-5(9))* Kessinger Publishing, LLC.
Abdul-Rauf, Muhammad. The Story of Tawaddud: A Brilliant & Beautiful Girl & a Model of Good Moral Conduct. 2005. xx, 185p. *(978-983-9184-66-2(0))* Institut Perkembangan Minda.
Adams, Carolyn Lee. Ruthless. 2015. (ENG., Illus.). 256p. (YA). (gr. 9). 17.99 *(978-1-4814-2262-8(6),* Simon Pulse) Simon Pulse.
Adhikary, Anita B. My Daughters Are Smart! D Is for Daughters & S Is for Smart. Russo, Blythe, illus. 2014. (ENG.). 24p. (J). (gr. -1-3). 14.95 *(978-1-62086-429-6(0))* Mascot Bks., Inc.
Adventures at Walnut Grove A Lesson about Teasing. l.t. ed. 2007. (ENG., Illus.). 32p. (J). 15.95 *(978-0-9792686-0-1(5),* 5,000) Lehman Publishing.
Adventures in Flatfrost. 2014. (Kingdom of Wrenly Ser.: 5). (ENG., Illus.). 128p. (J). (gr. k-4). pap. 5.99 *(978-1-4814-1388-6(0),* Little Simon) Little Simon.
Aguirre, Ann. The Queen of Bright & Shiny Things. 2015. (ENG.). 336p. (YA). (gr. 7). 17.99 *(978-1-250-04750-2(1),* 9781250047502) Feiwel & Friends.
Alam, Sarah H. Enchanting Fables. 2008. 48p. pap. 16.95 *(978-1-60441-768-5(4))* America Star Bks.
Alarid, Carilyn & Markel, Marilyn. Hits With His Fist Gives a Helping Hand: Mimbres Children Learn about Caring. 2012. (Illus.). 113p. (J). pap. 16.95 *(978-0-86534-508-9(2))* Sunstone Pr.
Alcott, Louisa May. A Garland for Girls. 2007. (ENG.). 182p. pap. 19.99 *(978-1-4264-2791-6(3))*; 198p. pap. 21.99 *(978-1-4264-2829-6(4))* Creative Media Partners, LLC.
—A Garland for Girls. l.t. ed. 2005. 376p. pap. *(978-1-84637-049-6(3))* Echo Library.
—Spinning-Wheel Stories. 2011. 202p. 27.95 *(978-1-4638-9494-8(5))* Rodgers, Alan Bks.
Alegria, Malin. Pueblo Fronterizo No. 2: Guerra de Quinceañeras. 2013. (Pueblo Fronterizo Ser.: 2). (SPA.). 208p. (J). (gr. 7). pap. 5.99 *(978-0-545-56565-3(0),* Scholastic en Espanol) Scholastic, Inc.
Alexander, Alma. Gift of the Unmage. 2007. (Worldweavers Ser.: Bk. 1). (ENG.). 400p. (YA). (gr. 7-12). 16.99 *(978-0-06-083955-0(4))* HarperCollins Pubs.
Alexander, Geoff. Toothbugs! Carole, Isaacs, illus. l.t. ed. 2005. 12p. (J). bds. 12.95 *(978-0-9760944-0-1(1))* Alexander-Marcus Publishing.
Alexander, Mary Helen. Please & Thank You. 2005. 23p. pap. 24.95 *(978-1-4137-6240-2(9))* PublishAmerica, Inc.
Alford, Doug. Ogs, Zogs & Useful Cogs. 2007. (J). pap. 5.99 net. *(978-1-933589-96-1(5))* Scripture Mastery Resources!
Alger, Horatio. Andy Grant's Pluck. 2006. 190p. pap. 19.99 *(978-1-4264-0879-3(X))*; (ENG.). 188p. pap. 21.99 *(978-1-4264-0860-1(9))* Creative Media Partners, LLC.
—Bound to Rise: Or: up the Ladder. 2007. (ENG.). 172p. per. 19.99 *(978-1-4346-5059-7(6))*; 188p. per. 21.99 *(978-1-4346-5060-3(X))* Creative Media Partners, LLC.
—Brave & Bold. 2005. 28.95 *(978-1-4218-1452-0(8))*; 280p. pap. 13.95 *(978-1-4218-1552-7(4))* 1st World Publishing, Inc. (1st World Library - Literary Society).
—Brave & Bold. 2006. 152p. per. 12.95 *(978-1-59818-652-9(3))*; 24.95 *(978-1-59818-570-6(5))* Aegypan.
—Brave & Bold: The Fortunes of Robert Rushton. 2007. (ENG.). 188p. per. 19.99 *(978-1-4346-4411-4(1))*; 208p. per. 22.99 *(978-1-4346-4412-1(X))* Creative Media Partners, LLC.
—Do & Dare: Or, A Brave Boy's Fight for Fortune. 2006. 182p. pap. 19.99 *(978-1-4264-0880-9(3))*; 170p. pap. 21.99 *(978-1-4264-0861-8(7))* Creative Media Partners, LLC.
—Do & Dare: Or, A Brave Boy's Fight for Fortune. 2006. pap. *(978-1-4065-0701-0(6))* Dodo Pr.
—Facing the World. 2006. pap. *(978-1-4065-0704-1(0))* Dodo Pr.
—Fame & Fortune: Or: the Progress of Richard Hunter. 2007. (ENG.). 160p. per. 19.99 *(978-1-4346-5061-0(8))*; 176p. per. 21.99 *(978-1-4346-5062-7(6))* Creative Media Partners, LLC.
—Five Hundred Dollars: Or: Jacob Marlowe's Secret. 2007. (ENG.). 192p. per. 19.99 *(978-1-4346-5063-4(4))*; 206p. per. 22.99 *(978-1-4346-5064-1(2))* Creative Media Partners, LLC.
—Frank & Fearless or the Fortunes of Jasper Kent. 2007. 228p. 20.99 *(978-1-4280-7465-1(1))*; per. 14.99 *(978-1-4280-7470-5(8))* IndyPublish.com.
—Frank's Campaign: Or, The Farm & the Camp. 2006. (ENG.). 196p. pap. 19.99 *(978-1-4264-0484-9(0))*; 188p. pap. 21.99 *(978-1-4264-0527-3(8))* Creative Media Partners, LLC.
—Frank's Campaign: Or, The Farm & the Camp. 2006. pap. *(978-1-4065-0705-8(9))* Dodo Pr.
—Hector's Inheritance: Or, The Boys of Smith Institute. 2006. pap. *(978-1-4065-0708-9(3))* Dodo Pr.
—Hector's Inheritance: Or: the Boys of Smith Institute. 2007. (ENG.). 186p. pap. 19.99 *(978-1-4346-5065-8(0))*; 192p. pap. 21.99 *(978-1-4346-5066-5(9))* Creative Media Partners, LLC.
—Helping Himself. 2006. 180p. pap. 19.99 *(978-1-4264-0881-6(1))*; (ENG.). 168p. pap. 21.99 *(978-1-4264-0862-5(5))* Creative Media Partners, LLC.
—Helping Himself. 2006. pap. *(978-1-4065-0709-6(1))* Dodo Pr.
—Herbert Carter's Legacy. 2006. pap. *(978-1-4065-0710-2(5))* Dodo Pr.
—Herbert Carter's Legacy: Or: the Inventor's Son. 2007. 174p. pap. 19.99 *(978-1-4346-5067-2(7))*; (ENG.). 188p. pap. 21.99 *(978-1-4346-5068-9(5))* Creative Media Partners, LLC.
—Jack's Ward. 2006. pap. *(978-1-4065-0711-9(3))* Dodo Pr.
—Jack's Ward: Or, The Boy Guardian. 2006. 176p. pap. 19.99 *(978-1-4264-0882-3(X))*; (ENG.). 168p. pap. 21.99 *(978-1-4264-0863-2(3))* Creative Media Partners, LLC.
—Joe the Hotel Boy. 2006. pap. *(978-1-4065-0712-6(1))* Dodo Pr.
—Joe the Hotel Boy: Or: Winning Out by Pluck. 2007. 164p. pap. 19.99 *(978-1-4346-5069-6(3))*; 172p. pap. 21.99 *(978-1-4346-5070-2(7))* Creative Media Partners, LLC.
—Joe's Luck: Or, Always Wide Awake. 2006. (ENG.). 172p. pap. 19.99 *(978-1-4264-6426-3(6))* 2006. (ENG.). 176p. pap. 19.99 *(978-1-4264-0883-0(8))* 2007. 186p. pap. 21.99 *(978-1-4264-6500-0(9))* 2006. (ENG.). 170p. pap. 21.99 *(978-1-4264-0864-9(1))* Creative Media Partners, LLC.
—Joe's Luck: Or, Always Wide Awake. 2006. pap. *(978-1-4065-0713-3(X))* Dodo Pr.
—Only an Irish Boy: Or, Andy Burke's Fortunes & Misfortunes. 2006. pap. *(978-1-4065-0716-4(4))* Dodo Pr.
—Risen from the Ranks. 2005. 28.95 *(978-1-4218-1458-2(7))*; 292p. pap. 13.95 *(978-1-4218-1558-9(3))* 1st World Publishing, Inc. (1st World Library - Literary Society).
—Risen from the Ranks: Or, Harry Walton's Success. 2006. (ENG.). 194p. pap. 19.99 *(978-1-4264-6391-4(X))*; 216p. pap. 22.99 *(978-1-4264-6465-2(7))* Creative Media Partners, LLC.
—Risen from the Ranks: Or, Harry Walton's Success. 2006. pap. *(978-1-4065-0721-8(0))* Dodo Pr.
—The Store Boy. 2005. 256p. 28.95 *(978-1-4218-0954-0(0),* 1st World Library - Literary Society) 1st World Publishing, Inc.
—The Store Boy. 2007. (ENG.). 170p. pap. 19.99 *(978-1-4264-4359-6(5))*; 182p. pap. 21.99 *(978-1-4264-4397-8(8))* Creative Media Partners, LLC.
—The Store Boy. 2006. pap. *(978-1-4065-0722-5(9))* Dodo Pr.
—The Store Boy. 2007. 116p. per. *(978-1-4068-1617-4(5))* Echo Library.
—Strive & Succeed. 2007. 172p. 24.95 *(978-1-4344-8359-1(2))*; per. 14.95 *(978-1-4344-8358-4(4))* Wildside Pr., LLC.
—Struggling Upward: Or, Luke Larkin's Luck. 2006. pap. *(978-1-4065-0723-2(7))* Dodo Pr.
—Struggling Upward; or, Luck Larkin's Luck. 2008. 104p. pap. 7.99 *(978-1-4209-3044-3(3))* Digireads.com Publishing.
—Timothy Crump's Ward. 2005. 27.95 *(978-1-4218-1451-3(X))*; 220p. pap. 12.95 *(978-1-4218-1551-0(6))* 1st World Publishing, Inc. (1st World Library - Literary Society).
—Tom Temple's Career. reprint ed. pap. 79.00 *(978-1-4047-3611-5(5))* Classic Textbooks.
—The Young Musician. reprint ed. pap. 79.00 *(978-1-4047-3629-0(8))* Classic Textbooks.
—The Young Musician. 2006. pap. *(978-1-4068-0673-1(0))* Echo Library.
—The Young Outlaw: Or, Adrift in the Streets. 2004. (Illus.). 15.90 *(978-1-4145-0294-6(X))* Pavilion Pr., Inc.
Alger Jr. Horatio Staff. Hector's Inheritance. rev. ed. 2006. 276p. 28.95 *(978-1-4218-1758-3(6))*; pap. 13.95 *(978-1-4218-1858-0(2))* 1st World Publishing, Inc. (1st World Library - Literary Society).
—Herbert Carter's Legacy. rev. ed. 2006. 264p. 28.95 *(978-1-4218-1756-9(X))*; pap. 13.95 *(978-1-4218-1856-6(6))* 1st World Publishing, Inc. (1st World Library - Literary Society).
—Only an Irish Boy. rev. ed. 2006. 284p. 28.95 *(978-1-4218-1759-0(4))*; pap. 13.95 *(978-1-4218-1859-7(0))* 1st World Publishing, Inc. (1st World Library - Literary Society).
Allen, Crystal. How Lamar's Bad Prank Won a Bubba-Sized Trophy. (ENG.). (J). (gr. 3-7). 2012. 304p. pap. 6.99 *(978-0-06-199273-5(9))* 2011. 288p. 16.99 *(978-0-06-199272-8(0))* HarperCollins Pubs.
Almond, David. The Fire-Eaters. 2010. (ENG.). 224p. (J). (gr. 3-7). mass mkt. 7.99 *(978-0-375-85751-5(6),* Laurel Leaf) Random Hse. Children's Bks.
—Raven Summer. 2011. (ENG.). 208p. (YA). (gr. 7). pap. 7.99 *(978-0-385-73807-1(2),* Ember) Random Hse. Children's Bks.
Amato, Mary. Sniff a Skunk!, Bk. 3. Jenkins, Ward, illus. 2015. (Good Crooks Ser.: Bk. 3). (ENG.). 128p. (gr. 2-4). 14.99 *(978-1-60684-598-1(5),* Darby Creek) Lerner Publishing Group.
Amerel. The Summer Holidays: A Story for Childre. 2006. pap. *(978-1-4065-0808-6(X))* Dodo Pr.
Amo, Montserrat del. La Piedra y el Agua. (SPA.). 119p. (J). *(978-84-279-3127-5(1),* NG1011) Noguer y Caralt Editores, S. A. ESP. Dist: Lectorum Pubns., Inc.
Amundson, Susan D. Three Little Lambs — Somewhere. Geiken, Brenda Joy, illus. 2006. 40p. (J). *(978-1-59984-002-4(2))* Bluedoor, llc.
Anderson, Jodi Lynn. Loser/Queen. Lee, Brittney, illus. 2010. (ENG.). 272p. (YA). (gr. 7-18). pap. 9.99 *(978-1-4169-9646-0(X),* Simon & Schuster Bks. For Young Readers) Simon & Schuster Bks. For Young Readers.
Anderson, R. J. Spell Hunter. 2009. (Faery Rebels Ser.). (ENG.). 336p. (J). (gr. 8-18). 16.99 *(978-0-06-155474-2(X))* HarperCollins Pubs.
—Wayfarer. 2010. (ENG.). 304p. (J). (gr. 8-18). 16.99 *(978-0-06-155477-3(4),* HarperTeen) HarperCollins Pubs.
Andrews, Andy. The Kid Who Changed the World, 1 vol. 2014. (ENG.). 40p. (J). 14.99 *(978-1-4003-2433-0(5))* Nelson, Thomas Inc.
Andrews, Jane. Each & All: The Seven Little Sisters Prove Their Sisterhood (Yesterday's Classics) 2009. 120p. pap. 8.95 *(978-1-59915-308-7(4))* Yesterday's Classics.
Andrews, Julie & Hamilton, Emma Walton. The Very Fairy Princess. Davenier, Christine, illus. 2010. (Very Fairy Princess Ser.). (ENG.). 32p. (J). (gr. -1-3). 18.00 *(978-0-316-04050-1(9))* Little, Brown Bks. for Young Readers.
—The Very Fairy Princess Takes the Stage. 2011. (Very Fairy Princess Ser.). (ENG., Illus.). 32p. (J). (gr. -1-3). 16.99 *(978-0-316-04052-5(5))* Little Brown & Co.
Angleberger, Tom. Horton Halfpott: Or, the Fiendish Mystery of Smugwick Manor - Or, the Loosening of M'Lady Luggertuck's Corset. (ENG., Illus.). (J). (gr. 3-7). 2012. 240p. pap. 7.99 *(978-1-4197-0169-6(X))* 2011. 224p. 16.95 *(978-0-8109-9715-8(0))* Abrams, Inc. (Amulet Bks.).
An Angry Day: Social/Emotional Lap Book. (Pebble Soup Explorations Ser.). (gr. -1-18). 16.00 *(978-0-7635-7572-4(0))* Rigby Education.
Annie S. Swan. Thankful Rest. 2007. 98p. pap. 16.99 *(978-1-4346-1978-5(8))*; (ENG.). 102p. pap. 19.99 *(978-1-4346-1888-7(9))* Creative Media Partners, LLC.
Applegate, Katherine. Never Swim in Applesauce. Biggs, Brian, illus. 2008. (Roscoe Riley Rules Ser.: 4). (ENG.). 96p. (J). (gr. 1-5). 15.99 *(978-0-06-114888-0(1))*; pap. 4.99 *(978-0-06-114887-3(3))* HarperCollins Pubs.
Arpaci, Halis. Eric & Derrick. 2011. (ENG.). 160p. (J). (gr. 3-7). 11.95 *(978-1-59784-232-7(X))* Tughra Bks.
Aryal, Aimee. Hello Big Al! Moore, Danny, illus. 2004. 24p. (J). lib. bdg. 19.95 *(978-1-932888-03-4(9))* Mascot Bks., Inc.
Ashman, Linda. Peace, Baby! Lew-Vriethoff, Joanne, illus. 2013. (ENG.). 32p. (J). (gr. -1-k). 15.99 *(978-1-4521-0613-7(4))* Chronicle Bks. LLC.
Atwood, Megan. Beat the Odds. 2016. (Contest Ser.: 2). (ENG.). 104p. (YA). (gr. 6-12). lib. bdg. 27.99 *(978-1-4677-7507-6(X),* Darby Creek) Lerner Publishing Group.
—Break the Code. 2016. (Contest Ser.: 4). (ENG.). 104p. (YA). (gr. 6-12). lib. bdg. 27.99 *(978-1-4677-7509-0(6),* Darby Creek) Lerner Publishing Group.
—Olive Finds Treasure (of the Most Precious Kind) Fleming, Lucy, illus. (Dear Molly, Dear Olive Ser.). (ENG.). 96p. (gr. 1-3). 2017. pap. 5.95 *(978-1-62370-615-9(7))* 2016. lib. bdg. 21.99 *(978-1-4795-8693-6(5))* Picture Window Bks.
—Raise the Stakes. 2016. (Contest Ser.: 3). (ENG.). 104p. (YA). (gr. 6-12). lib. bdg. 27.99 *(978-1-4677-7508-3(8),* Darby Creek) Lerner Publishing Group.
—Stay in the Game. 2016. (Contest Ser.: 1). (ENG.). 104p. (YA). (gr. 6-12). pap. 7.99 *(978-1-4677-8101-5(0))* Lerner Publishing Group.
—Turn the Tables. 2016. (Contest Ser.: 5). (ENG.). 112p. (J). (gr. 4-4). E-Book 20.99 *(978-1-4677-8835-9(X),* 9781467788359, Darby Creek) Lerner Publishing Group.
Avalon-Pai, Phyllis. Children's Stories from Around the World. Arrott, Nancy, illus. 2008. 70p. pap. 9.95 *(978-0-9788283-8-7(0))* Acacia Publishing, Inc.
Axelrod, Amy & Axelrod, David. The Bullet Catch. 2015. (ENG.). 320p. (J). (gr. 5-9). 17.95 *(978-0-8234-2858-8(3))* Holiday Hse., Inc.
Ayozie, Ben-EL. Ants Everywhere. 2011. 20p. 11.49 *(978-1-4520-3431-7(1))* AuthorHouse.
Babbitt, Natalie. The Devil's Storybooks: 20 Delightfully Wicked Stories. Babbitt, Natalie, illus. 2012. (ENG., Illus.). 224p. (J). (gr. 3-7). pap. 15.99 *(978-0-312-64158-0(3),* 9780312641580) Square Fish.
Bacigalupi, Paolo. The Drowned Cities. 2013. (ENG.). 464p. (J). (gr. 10-17). pap. 10.99 *(978-0-316-05622-9(7))* 2012. 448p. (YA). 17.99 *(978-0-316-20037-0(9))* Little, Brown Bks. for Young Readers.
—The Drowned Cities. 2012. 352p. *(978-1-59606-506-2(0))* Subterranean Pr.
—The Drowned Cities. 2013. (J). lib. bdg. 22.10 *(978-0-606-31749-8(X),* Turtleback) Turtleback Bks.
—Ship Breaker. 2011. (ENG.). 352p. (YA). (gr. 10-17). pap. 10.99 *(978-0-316-05619-9(7))* Little, Brown Bks. for Young Readers.
Backes, M. Molly. The Princesses of Iowa. (ENG.). 464p. (YA). (gr. 9). 2014. pap. 9.99 *(978-0-7636-7161-7(4))* 2012. (Illus.). 16.99 *(978-0-7636-5312-5(8))* Candlewick Pr.
Bad Boys. 2007. (J). (gr. k-3). 27.95 incl. audio *(978-0-8045-6956-9(8))*; 29.95 incl. audio compact disk *(978-0-8045-4179-4(5))* Spoken Arts, Inc.
Badger, Cynthia. Sara's Secret. 2009. 72p. pap. 24.99 *(978-1-4389-5999-3(0))* AuthorHouse.
Badger, Pearstina. Jessica's Journeys: Stories about Life's Lessons. 2006. 56p. pap. 16.95 *(978-1-4241-1576-1(0))* PublishAmerica, Inc.
Baird, Noah. Southpaw. McMaugh, Kimberly, illus. 2013. 40p. pap. 13.95 *(978-1-938101-35-9(9))* Indigo Sea Pr., LLC.
Baker, Ginger. Walking Home Alone. Levy, Pamela R., illus. 2003. (Books for Young Learners). (ENG.). 16p. (J). 5.75 net. *(978-1-57274-604-6(1),* 2534, Bks. for Young Learners) Owen, Richard C. Pubs., Inc.
Baker, Jason. People Are People. 2012. 80p. pap. 28.00 *(978-1-105-72519-7(7))* Lulu Pr., Inc.
Baker, Samuel White. Cast up by the Sea by Sir Samuel W Baker Complete with Ten Illustrations by Huard. 2006. 408p. per. 26.99 *(978-1-4255-4629-8(3))* Michigan Publishing.
Ballantyne, R. M. Blown to Bits; or, the Lonely Man of Rak. 2006. pap. *(978-1-4065-0515-3(3))* Dodo Pr.
—Red Rooney: Or, the Last of the Crew. 2007. (R. M. Ballantyne Collection). (Illus.). 408p. 22.00 *(978-1-934554-08-1(1))* Vision Forum, Inc., The.
—The Young Trawler. 2011. 250p. 27.95 *(978-1-4638-9496-2(1))* Rodgers, Alan Bks.
Ballantyne, Robert Michael. The Battery & the Boiler: Adventures in Laying of Submarine Electric Cables. 2007. 254p. pap. 21.99 *(978-1-4346-3754-3(9))*; (ENG.). 282p. pap. 23.99 *(978-1-4346-3768-0(9))* Creative Media Partners, LLC.
—My Doggie & I. 2007. 120p. pap. 18.99 *(978-1-4346-3682-9(8))*; (ENG.). 130p. pap. 19.99 *(978-1-4346-3730-7(1))* Creative Media Partners, LLC.
—Red Rooney: The Last of the Crew. 2007. (ENG.). 270p. pap. 21.99 *(978-1-4346-3693-5(3))*; 302p. pap. 24.99 *(978-1-4346-3741-3(7))* Creative Media Partners, LLC.
Ballart, Elisabet. Aprendamos a Convivir. Capdevila, Roser, illus.Tr. of Let's Learn to Get Along. (SPA.). 48p. (J). (gr. 3-5). 13.56 *(978-84-233-3109-3(1))* Ediciones Destino ESP. Dist: Lectorum Pubns., Inc.
Bancks, Tristan. On the Run. 2015. (ENG.). 240p. (J). (gr. 5-7). 16.99 *(978-0-374-30153-8(0),* 9780374301538, Farrar, Straus & Giroux (BYR)) Farrar, Straus & Giroux.
Banks, Celia. God Loves Me. 2007. (J). per. *(978-0-9764460-8-1(1))* BMCFerrell.
Banks, Erma. Fruit Cocktail. 2011. 28p. (gr. -1). pap. 13.00 *(978-1-4567-6222-3(2))* AuthorHouse.
Banks, Jane Whelen. Liam Knows What to Do When Kids Act Snitty: Coping When Friends Are Tactless. 2008. (ENG., Illus.). 32p. 12.95 *(978-1-84310-902-0(6),* 7167) Kingsley, Jessica Pubs. GBR. Dist: Macmillan Distribution Ltd.
—Liam Wins the Game, Sometimes: A Story about Losing with Grace. 2008. (ENG., Illus.). 32p. 12.95 *(978-1-84310-898-6(4),* 5374) Kingsley, Jessica Pubs. GBR. Dist: Macmillan Distribution Ltd.
Banks, Jane Whelen & Whelen-Banks, Jane. Liam Says "Sorry" Repairing an Encounter Gone Sour. 2008. (ENG., Illus.). 32p. 12.95 *(978-1-84310-903-7(4),* 5373) Kingsley, Jessica Pubs. GBR. Dist: Macmillan Distribution Ltd.
Bar-Lev, Rotem. No More Tears. 2009. (Illus.). 23p. (J). pap. 13.95 *(978-1-4327-3989-8(1))* Outskirts Pr., Inc.
Baras, Ronit. Be Special, Be Yourself: For Teenagers. 2005. 171p. (YA). per. *(978-0-9757976-0-0(3))* Be Happy in LIFE.
Barber, Tiki & Barber, Ronde. End Zone. (Barber Game Time Bks.). (ENG., Illus.). (J). (gr. 3-7). 2014. 192p. pap. 7.99 *(978-1-4169-9098-7(4))* 2012. 176p. 15.99 *(978-1-4169-9097-0(6))* Simon & Schuster/Paula Wiseman Bks. (Simon & Schuster/Paula Wiseman Bks.).
—Extra Innings. 2014. (Barber Game Time Bks.). (ENG., Illus.). 160p. (J). (gr. 3-7). 16.99 *(978-1-4424-5726-3(0),* Simon & Schuster/Paula Wiseman Bks.) Simon & Schuster/Paula Wiseman Bks.
Barnes, Derrick D. We Could Be Brothers. 2010. (J). *(978-0-545-13574-0(5),* Scholastic Pr.) Scholastic, Inc.
Barnett, Wm. Billy's Wish. Kiste, Tori Lynn, illus. 2008. 28p. pap. 24.95 *(978-1-60563-330-5(5))* America Star Bks.
Barnum, P. T. Dick Broadhead: A Story of Perilous Adve. 2006. pap. 30.95 *(978-1-4286-1959-3(3))* Kessinger Publishing, LLC.
Barone, Luisa T. Abby the Apple. 2012. 24p. pap. 24.95 *(978-1-4626-7901-0(3))* America Star Bks.
Barron, T. A. The Wisdom of Merlin: 7 Magical Words for a Meaningful Life. 2015. (ENG.). 80p. (J). (gr. 5). 12.99 *(978-0-399-17325-7(0),* Philomel Bks.) Penguin Young Readers Group.
Barry, Dave. The Worst Class Trip Ever. 2015. (Class Trip Ser.). (ENG.). 224p. (J). (gr. 3-7). 13.99 *(978-1-4847-0849-1(0))* Disney Pr.
Bartlett, Susan & Wrenn, Luanne. Opening Day, 1 vol. 2007. (ENG., Illus.). 32p. (gr. 1-4). 16.95 *(978-0-88448-288-8(X),* 884288) Tilbury Hse. Pubs.
Baskin, Nora Raleigh. The Summer Before Boys. (ENG.). 208p. (J). (gr. 4-7). 2012. pap. 6.99 *(978-1-4169-8674-4(X))* 2011. 16.99 *(978-1-4169-8673-7(1))* Simon & Schuster Bks. For Young Readers. (Simon & Schuster Bks. For Young Readers).
Bateman, Anya. I Just Got a Letter from Allyson Pringle. 2008. 256p. (YA). pap. 15.95 *(978-1-60641-028-8(8))* Deseret Bk. Co.
Bateson, Catherine. Stranded in Boringsville. (ENG.). 144p. (J). (gr. 5-9). 2007. pap. 6.95 *(978-0-8234-2113-8(9))* 2005. 16.95 *(978-0-8234-1969-2(X))* Holiday Hse., Inc.
Batkhuu, Kh. The Doll That Flew Away. Myagmardorj, Enkhtungalag, illus. 2007. 32p. (J). (POL & ENG.). pap. 12.95 *(978-1-60195-098-7(5))*; (ARA & ENG.). pap. 12.95 *(978-1-60195-092-5(6))* International Step by Step Assn.
Bauer, Marion Dane. On My Honor. 2012. lib. bdg. 18.40 *(978-0-606-24717-7(3),* Turtleback) Turtleback Bks.
Baum, L. Frank. The Wonderful Wizard of Oz: A Classic Story about Cooperation. 2003. (Illus.). 32p. per. 3.95 *(978-0-9747133-5-9(X),* Values to Live By Classic Stories) Thomas, Frederic Inc.
Baum, L. Frank & Bancroft, Laura. Twinkle & Chubbins. 2011. 106p. 22.95 *(978-1-4638-9604-1(2))* Rodgers, Alan Bks.
Be Kind, Be Friendly, Be Thankful: The Adventures of Brisky Bear & Trooper Dog. 2007. Orig. Title: Friends for Always. (J). pap. 7.95 incl. audio compact disk *(978-0-9795127-0-4(0))* Glory Be Collectibles.
Beck, Rachel. Bella & the Little Gray Kitten. 2011. 40p. (gr. -1). pap. 18.50 *(978-1-4567-3365-0(6))* AuthorHouse.
Bee, Clair. Dugout Jinx. (J). 17.95 *(978-0-8488-1247-8(6))* Amereon Ltd.
—Dugout Jinx: A Chip Hilton Sports Story. 2011. 222p. (gr. 4-7). 44.95 *(978-1-258-07860-7(0))* Literary Licensing, LLC.
Beers, Gary. Pumpkinroo. 2013. 32p. pap. 24.95 *(978-1-63004-258-5(7))* America Star Bks.
Beifus, Ruth. Shlavim Classics 2-in-1 Vol. 1: The Best Reward & the Taste of Truth. 2009. 32p. 14.99 *(978-1-59826-329-9(3))* Feldheim Pubs.
—Shlavim Classics 2-in-1 Vol.2: Goodbye to Miri's Mess & Half a Cup of Water. 2009. 32p. 14.99 *(978-1-59826-330-5(7))* Feldheim Pubs.
Bell, Anthea, tr. from FRE. Nicholas in Trouble. Sempé, Jean-Jacques, illus. 2008. (ENG.). 128p. (gr. 1-4). 19.95 *(978-0-7148-4813-6(1))* Phaidon Pr., Inc.
Bell, Hilari. Crown of Earth. Willis, Drew, illus. 2010. (Shield, Sword, & Crown Ser.: 3). (ENG.). 272p. (J). (gr. 3-7). pap.

C
D

5.99 *(978-1-4169-0599-8(5)*, Aladdin) Simon & Schuster Children's Publishing.

—Crown of Earth. Willis, Drew, illus. 2009. (Shield, Sword, & Crown Ser.: 3). (ENG.). 272p. (J). (gr. 3-7). 16.99 *(978-1-4169-0598-1(7)*, Simon & Schuster/Paula Wiseman Bks.) Simon & Schuster/Paula Wiseman Bks.

—Shield of Stars, No. 1. 2008. (Shield, Sword, & Crown Ser.: 1). (ENG.). 288p. (J). (gr. 3-7). pap. 13.99 *(978-1-4169-0595-0(2)*, Simon & Schuster/Paula Wiseman Bks.) Simon & Schuster/Paula Wiseman Bks.

—Sword of Waters. Willis, Drew, illus. 2009. (Shield, Sword, & Crown Ser.: 2). (ENG.). 384p. (J). (gr. 3-7). pap. 6.99 *(978-1-4169-0597-4(9)*, Aladdin) Simon & Schuster Children's Publishing.

—Sword of Waters, No. 2. Willis, Drew, illus. 2008. (Shield, Sword, & Crown Ser.: 2). (ENG.). 368p. (J). (gr. 3-7). 16.99 *(978-1-4169-0596-7(0)*, Simon & Schuster/Paula Wiseman Bks.) Simon & Schuster/Paula Wiseman Bks.

Belloc, Hilaire. Cautionary Tales for Children. 2009. 48p. (gr. 4-7). pap. 7.75 *(978-1-60459-576-5(0))* Wilder Pubns., Corp.

Benenfeld, Rikki. Let's Go to the Park. 2015. (ENG., Illus.). 36p. (J). 10.95 *(978-1-929628-82-7(X))* Hachai Publishing.

Benincasa, Sara. Great. 2014. (ENG.). 272p. (YA). (gr. 9). 17.99 *(978-0-06-222269-5(4)*, HarperTeen) HarperCollins Pubs.

Benoit, Charles. Snow Job. 2016. (ENG.). 288p. (YA). (gr. 7). 17.99 *(978-0-544-31886-1(2))* Houghton Mifflin Harcourt Publishing Co.

—You. 2012. (ENG.). 256p. (YA). (gr. 8). pap. 8.99 *(978-0-06-194706-3(7)*, HarperTeen) HarperCollins Pubs.

Bently, Peter & McPhillips, Robert, illus. Say Please, Little Bear. 2013. (J). *(978-1-4351-4727-0(8))* Barnes & Noble, Inc.

Berenstain, Jan, et al. The Berenstain Bears Get Involved, 1 vol. 2012. (Berenstain Bears/Living Lights Ser.). (ENG.). 32p. (J). pap. 3.99 *(978-0-310-72090-4(7))* Zonderkidz.

—Kindness Counts, 1 vol. 2010. (Berenstain Bears/Living Lights Ser.). (ENG.). 32p. (J). (gr. -1-2). pap. 3.99 *(978-0-310-71257-2(2))* Zonderkidz.

Berenstain, Mike. The Berenstain Bears Blessed Are the Peacemakers, 1 vol. 2014. (Berenstain Bears/Living Lights Ser.). (ENG.). 24p. (J). pap. 3.99 *(978-0-310-73481-9(9))* Zonderkidz.

Berenstain, Stan & Berenstain, Jan. The Berenstain Bears Play T-Ball. 2005. (Berenstain Bears Ser.). (Illus.). 32p. (J). 11.65 *(978-0-7569-5228-0(X))* Perfection Learning Corp.

Berenstain, Stan, et al. Berenstain Bears Love Their Neighbors, 1 vol. Berenstain, Stan, illus. 2009. (Berenstain Bears/Living Lights Ser.). (ENG., Illus.). 32p. (J). (gr. -1-2). pap. 3.99 *(978-0-310-71249-7(1))* Zonderkidz.

Berlin, Bill & Berlin, Susan Isakoff. The Kvetch Who Stole Hanukkah, 1 vol. Welling, Peter J., illus. 2010. (ENG.). 32p. (J). (gr. k-3). 16.99 *(978-1-58980-798-3(7))* Pelican Publishing Co., Inc.

Berman, Ali. Misdirected: A Novel. 2014. (ENG., Illus.). 290p. (YA). (gr. 7). 18.95 *(978-1-60980-573-9(9)*, Triangle Square) Seven Stories Pr.

Berman, Seryl. Around the Shabbos Table. Binus, Ari, illus. 2008. 40p. (J). (gr. -1-k). pap. 10.95 *(978-1-929628-44-5(7))* Hachai Publishing.

Bernabe, Victor. What to Be When I Grow Up. Bernabe, Tabitha Victoria, illus. 2008. 28p. pap. 24.95 *(978-1-60703-696-8(7))* America Star Bks.

Between the Lions - Early Literacy Kit - Help!, 1 cass., 1 bk. 2005. (Between the Lions Ser.). 24p. (J). VHS 29.95 *(978-1-59375-284-2(9)*, WG38623) WGBH Boston Video.

Bick, Ilsa J. The Sin-Eater's Confession. Elyum Studio, illus. 2014. (ENG.). 296p. (YA). (gr. 9-12). pap. 9.95 *(978-1-4677-3705-0(4)*, Carolrhoda Lab™) Lerner Publishing Group.

—The Sin-Eater's Confession. 2013. (ENG.). 296p. (YA). (gr. 9-12). 17.95 *(978-0-7613-5687-5(8))* Lerner Publishing Group.

Big Idea Entertainment, LLC. VeggieTales SuperComics: Vol 1. Jones, Cory, illus. 2015. (VeggieTales Super Comics Ser.: 1). (ENG.). 104p. (J). (gr. -1-3). pap. 12.99 *(978-1-4336-8534-7(5)*, B&H Kids) B&H Publishing Group.

—VeggieTales SuperComics: Vol 2. Jones, Cory, illus. 2015. (VeggieTales Super Comics Ser.). (ENG.). 104p. (J). (gr. -1-3). pap. 12.99 *(978-1-4336-8535-4(3)*, B&H Kids) B&H Publishing Group.

Bishop, Jennie. The Squire & the Scroll Coloring Book. 2005. (J). pap. 1.79 *(978-1-59317-085-1(8))* Warner Pr., Inc.

—The Three Gifts of Christmas. McDaniels, Preston, illus. 2009. 32p. (J). (gr. 3-18). 15.99 incl. audio compact disk *(978-1-59317-378-4(4))* Warner Pr., Inc.

Blabey, Aaron. Pig the Winner. 2017. (Pig the Pug Ser.). (ENG.). 32p. (J). (gr. -1-k). 14.99 *(978-1-338-13638-8(0)*, Scholastic Pr.) Scholastic, Inc.

Black Beauty: A Classic Story about Respect. 2003. (Illus.). 32p. per. 3.95 *(978-0-9747133-0-4(9)*, Values to Live By Classic Stories) Thomas, Frederic Inc.

Blackford. The Eskdale Herd-boy. l.t. ed. 2007. (ENG.). 146p. pap. 19.99 *(978-1-4264-8722-4(3))* Creative Media Partners, LLC.

—The Eskdale Herd-boy: The Eskdale Herd-boy. 2007. (ENG.). 134p. pap. 18.99 *(978-1-4264-8667-8(7))* Creative Media Partners, LLC.

—The Eskdale Herd Boy A Scottish Tale for the Instruction & Amusement of Young Persons. 2004. reprint ed. pap. 15.95 *(978-1-4191-6125-4(3))* Kessinger Publishing, LLC.

Blackman, Malorie. Black & White. 2007. (ENG.). 512p. (YA). (gr. 9-12). pap. 12.99 *(978-1-4169-0017-7(9)*, Simon & Schuster Bks. For Young Readers) Simon & Schuster Bks. For Young Readers.

Blackstone, Matt. Sorry You're Lost. 2014. (ENG.). 320p. (J). (gr. 5-9). 15.99 *(978-0-374-38065-6(1)*, 9780374380656, Farrar, Straus & Giroux (BYR)) Farrar, Straus & Giroux.

Blackwell, Paul E. Undercurrent. 2013. 320p. (YA). (gr. 9). 17.99 *(978-0-06-212350-3(5)*, HarperTeen) HarperCollins Pubs.

Blagden, Scott. Dear Life, You Suck: A Novel. 2015. (ENG.). 320p. (YA). (gr. 9). pap. 9.99 *(978-0-544-33621-6(6)*, HMH Books For Young Readers) Houghton Mifflin Harcourt Publishing Co.

Blessing, Victor. Santa Claus Got Sick Because. 2009. 24p. pap. 12.99 *(978-1-4490-1126-0(8))* AuthorHouse.

Blevins, James. The Crones. Whittaker, Stephen, illus. 2008. 36p. pap. 24.95 *(978-1-60610-259-6(1))* America Star Bks.

Blitz, Shmuel. Every Story Has a Soul. Katz, Tova, illus. 2006. 47p. (J). 15.99 *(978-1-4226-0224-9(9))* Mesorah Pubns., Ltd.

Blosser, Connie S. Donald Lionz Drought. 2013. 24p. pap. 24.95 *(978-1-4626-9346-7(6))* America Star Bks.

Blume, Judy. Are You There God? It's Me, Margaret. 149p. (J). (gr. 4-6). pap. 3.50 *(978-0-8072-1421-3(3))*; (YA). (gr. 5-18). pap. 4.99 *(978-0-8072-1508-1(2))* Random Hse. Audio Publishing Group. (Listening Library).

—Otherwise Known as Sheila the Great. 2007. (ENG.). 176p. (J). (gr. 3-7). 7.99 *(978-0-14-240879-7(4)*, Puffin Books) Penguin Young Readers Group.

—Otherwise Known as Sheila the Great. 2007. 154p. (gr. 4-7). 16.00 *(978-0-7569-7915-7(3))* Perfection Learning Corp.

—Otherwise Known as Sheila the Great. 2007. (Fudge Bks.: 2). 138p. (gr. 4-7). lib. bdg. 18.40 *(978-1-4177-8370-0(2)*, Turtleback) Turtleback Bks.

Blythe, Carolita. Revenge of a Not-So-Pretty Girl. 2013. (ENG.). 336p. (YA). (gr. 7). 19.99 *(978-0-375-99081-6(X)*, Delacorte Bks. for Young Readers) Random Hse. Children's Bks.

Bohlken, Robert L. Listening to the Mukies: And Their Character Building Adventures. Veasey, Michele, illus. 2003. (J). pap. 14.95 *(978-0-930643-15-7(1))* Images Unlimited Publishing.

—Listening to the Mukies & Their Character Building Adventures. Veasey, Michele, illus. 2003. (J). 24.95 *(978-0-930643-17-1(8))* Images Unlimited Publishing.

Bonin, Liane. Pretty on the Outside: Fame Unlimited. 2007. 288p. (YA). pap. 9.99 *(978-0-451-22122-3(2)*, N A L Trade) Penguin Publishing Group.

Boorman, Kate A. Winterkill. (Winterkill Ser.). (ENG.). (YA). (gr. 7-17). 2015. 352p. pap. 8.95 *(978-1-4197-1673-7(5))* 2014. 336p. 17.95 *(978-1-4197-1235-7(7))* Abrams, Inc. (Amulet Bks.).

Booth, Bradley. Noah: The Chosen One. 2009. (J). 19.99 *(978-0-8163-2344-9(5))* Pacific Pr. Publishing Assn.

—Noah: The End of the World. 2010. (J). pap. 19.99 *(978-0-8163-2407-1(7))* Pacific Pr. Publishing Assn.

—Shepherd Warrior. 2007. 127p. (J). *(978-0-8163-2161-2(2))* Pacific Pr. Pubns.

Boritzer, Etan. What Is Right? Sale, Graham, illus. l.t. ed. 2005. (What Is? Ser.: No. 6). 40p. (J). (gr. k-5). *(978-0-9762743-1-5(0))* Lane, Veronica Bks.

Bortner, Lynn A. Stanley's My Name Adventure's My Game. 2010. 28p. pap. 16.95 *(978-1-4269-3934-1(5))* Trafford Publishing.

Borton, Elizabeth. Pollyanna in Hollywood. (J). 17.95 *(978-0-8488-1448-9(7))* Amereon Ltd.

Bosak, Susan V. Dream: A Tale of Wonder, Wisdom & Wishes. Dillon, Leo et al, illus. 2004. 40p. (J). *(978-1-896232-04-1(3)*, TCP Pr.) Communication Project, The.

Bostic, Megan. Never Eighteen. 2012. (ENG.). 208p. (YA). (gr. 7). pap. 8.99 *(978-0-547-55076-3(6))* Houghton Mifflin Harcourt Publishing Co.

Boulden, James. Buddy Gets Angry: Student Involvement Pack. 2003. (Illus.). 21p. (J). 24.95 *(978-1-892421-73-9(9))* Boulden Publishing.

—Buddy Learns about Bullying Video Kit. 2003. (J). pap. 39.95 incl. VHS *(978-1-892421-89-0(5))* Boulden Publishing.

—Buddy Learns about Tattling: Student Involvement Pack. 2003. (Illus.). 21p. (J). 24.95 *(978-1-892421-80-7(1))* Boulden Publishing.

—Buddy learns about Teasing: Student Involvement Pack. 2003. (Illus.). 21p. (J). 24.95 *(978-1-892421-72-2(0)*, 720) Boulden Publishing.

Boyce, Frank Cottrell. Millions. 2005. 247p. (gr. 3-7). 19.00 *(978-0-7569-5439-0(8))* Perfection Learning Corp.

Bracken, Beth. Terrible, Awful, Horrible Manners, 1 vol. Watson, Richard, illus. 2012. (Little Boost Ser.). (ENG.). 32p. (gr. k-3). 7.95 *(978-1-4048-7419-0(4)*, Little Boost) Picture Window Bks.

Brashares, Ann. Forever in Blue: The Fourth Summer of the Sisterhood. 2008. (Sisterhood of the Traveling Pants Ser.: Bk. 4). (ENG.). 416p. (YA). (gr. 7-12). pap. 9.99 *(978-0-385-73401-1(8)*, Ember) Random Hse. Children's Bks.

—Girls in Pants. 2006. (Sisterhood of the Traveling Pants Ser.: Bk. 3). (ENG.). 384p. (YA). (gr. 7-12). reprint ed. per. 9.99 *(978-0-553-37593-0(8)*, Ember) Random Hse. Children's Bks.

—The Sisterhood of the Traveling Pants. 2003. (Sisterhood of the Traveling Pants Ser.: Bk. 1). (ENG.). 336p. (YA). (gr. 7-18). pap. 9.99 *(978-0-385-73058-7(6)*, Ember) Random Hse. Children's Bks.

—The Sisterhood of the Traveling Pants Set: The Sisterhood of the Traveling Pants - The Second Summer of the Sisterhood - Girls in Pants, 3 vols. 2006. (Sisterhood of the Traveling Pants Ser.: Vols. 1-3). (ENG.). (YA). pap., pap., pap. 26.85 *(978-0-385-73424-0(7)*, Ember) Random Hse. Children's Bks.

Bray, Pamela. The Day Lonyaie's Life Changed. 2008. 32p. pap. 24.95 *(978-1-60474-859-8(1))* America Star Bks.

Bredsdorff, Bodil. The Crow-Girl: The Children of Crow Cove. Ingwersen, Faith, tr. from DAN. 2007. (Illus.). 155p. (gr. 3-7). 18.00 *(978-0-7569-8186-0(7))* Perfection Learning Corp.

—The Crow-Girl: The Children of Crow Cove. Ingwersen, Faith, tr. 2006. (Children of Crow Cove Ser.: 1). (ENG., Illus.). 160p. (J). (gr. 3-7). reprint ed. pap. 8.99 *(978-0-374-40003-3(2)*, 9780374400033, Farrar, Straus & Giroux (BYR)) Farrar, Straus & Giroux.

Brenna, Beverley. Something to Hang on To. 2009. (ENG.). 176p. (J). pap. 12.95 *(978-1-897235-57-7(7))* Thistledown Pr., Ltd. CAN. Dist: Univ. of Toronto Pr.

Brian, Kate, pseud. Cruel Love. 2011. (Privilege Ser.). (ENG.). 224p. (YA). (gr. 9). pap. 9.99 *(978-1-4424-0788-6(3)*, Simon & Schuster Bks. For Young Readers) Simon & Schuster Bks. For Young Readers.

—Sweet 16. 2007. (ENG.). 288p. (YA). (gr. 7-12). pap. 9.99 *(978-1-4169-0033-7(0)*, Simon & Schuster Bks. For Young Readers) Simon & Schuster Bks. For Young Readers.

Brightwood, Laura, illus. Ka-ulu the Strong. Brightwood, Laura, 2006. (J). *(978-0-9789871-3-8(6))* 3-C Institute for Social Development.

Brisson, Pat. Melissa Parkington's Beautiful, Beautiful Hair. Bloom, Suzanne, illus. 2006. (ENG.). 32p. (J). (gr. 1-3). 16.95 *(978-1-59078-409-9(X))* Boyds Mills Pr.

Britt, Chris. Blabbering Bethann, 1 vol. 2014. (ENG., Illus.). 32p. (J). (gr. k-3). 16.99 *(978-1-4556-2004-3(1))* Pelican Publishing Co., Inc.

Brody, Jessica. The Karma Club. 2011. (ENG.). 288p. (YA). (gr. 7-12). pap. 10.99 *(978-0-312-67473-1(2)*, 9780312674731) Square Fish.

—52 Reasons to Hate My Father. 2013. (ENG.). 368p. (YA). (gr. 7-12). pap. 10.99 *(978-1-250-02459-6(5)*, 9781250024596) Square Fish.

Bromley, Anne C. & Casilla, Robert. The Lunch Thief, 1 vol. 2010. (ENG., Illus.). 32p. (gr. 3-7). 16.95 *(978-0-88448-311-3(8)*, 884311) Tilbury Hse. Pubs.

Brooks, George W. The Spirit of 1906. 2004. reprint ed. pap. 15.95 *(978-1-4191-8328-7(1))* Kessinger Publishing, LLC.

—The Spirit Of 1906. 2004. reprint ed. pap. 1.99 *(978-1-4192-8328-4(6))* Kessinger Publishing, LLC.

Brooks, Heather. Hercules: A Matter of Trust. 2009. (Running Horse Ridge Ser.: 2). (ENG.). 224p. (J). (gr. 5-18). pap. 6.99 *(978-0-06-142981-1(3))* HarperCollins Pubs.

Brooks, Kevin. The Bunker Diary. 2015. (ENG.). 264p. (YA). (gr. 8-12). 17.99 *(978-1-4677-5420-0(X))* Lerner Publishing Group.

A Brother's Sin. 2008. 84p. pap. 9.95 *(978-1-934335-21-5(5))* WordWright.biz, Inc.

Brouwer, Sigmund. Bug's Eye View: Annie Ant, Don't Cry! 2004. (Bug's-Eye View Bks.). (ENG., Illus.). 18p. (J). pap. 4.99 *(978-0-8499-7757-2(6))* Nelson, Thomas Inc.

—Daddy Ant, You Never Listen. 2004. (Bug's-Eye View Bks.). (ENG., Illus.). 18p. (J). pap. 4.99 *(978-0-8499-7755-8(X))* Nelson, Thomas Inc.

—Thunderbird Spirit, 1 vol. 2008. (Orca Sports Ser.). (ENG.). 192p. (YA). (gr. 6-10). pap. 9.95 *(978-1-55469-045-9(5))* Orca Bk. Pubs. USA.

Brown, Deborah Deal. My Typical Sunday. 2012. 20p. pap. 12.70 *(978-1-4669-4634-7(2))* Trafford Publishing.

Brown, Herman. A Cut Too Far. 2015. (ENG.). 96p. (YA). (gr. 6-12). 27.99 *(978-1-4677-5709-6(8))* Lerner Publishing Group.

—The Option. 2014. (Red Zone Ser.: 3). (ENG.). 104p. (YA). (gr. 6-12). pap. 7.95 *(978-1-4677-4473-7(5)*, Darby Creek); lib. bdg. 27.93 *(978-1-4677-2128-8(X))* Lerner Publishing Group.

Brown, Jennifer. Thousand Words. 2014. (YA). lib. bdg. 20.85 *(978-0-606-35311-3(9))* Turtleback Bks.

Brown, Leslie. Not Yet. 2008. 32p. pap. 12.99 *(978-1-4389-3218-7(9))* AuthorHouse.

Brown, Tryla. Pink Shirt - Blue Shirt. l.t. ed. 2005. (Illus.). 17p. (J). per. 13.99 *(978-1-59879-056-6(0))* Lifevest Publishing, Inc.

Brunstetter, Wanda E. Humble Pie. Madden, Colleen M., illus. 2014. 158p. (J). *(978-1-63058-967-7(5))* Barbour Publishing, Inc.

Bryant, Mary. Sped Spud: He May Be a Tater, but He's No Dud. 2008. 28p. pap. 24.95 *(978-1-60563-436-4(0))* America Star Bks.

Bucher, Charlotte. Cecil Learns to Smile. 2010. 26p. (J). pap. 19.95 *(978-1-4327-4992-7(7))* Outskirts Pr., Inc.

Buchholz, Chris. Beckett 81. 2010. 147p. pap. 10.00 *(978-0-557-27451-2(6))* Lulu Pr., Inc.

Bunny, Hull. The Hidden Treasure. Fleming, Kye, illus. 2007. (Young Masters Ser.). (J). (gr. -1). 13.95 incl. audio compact disk *(978-0-9721478-8-0(8))* BrassHeart Music.

Burchfield, Cindy. Gimme, Gimme Moocher Marmots. Burchfield, Cindy, illus. 2007. (Illus.). 48p. per. 18.95 *(978-1-59858-457-8(X))* Dog Ear Publishing, LLC.

Burk, Josh. The Summer of Saint Nick. 2007. (ENG.). 152p. (YA). per. 12.95 *(978-0-9768042-2-2(0))* Maven Of Memory Publishing.

Burnett, Frances Hodgson. Editha's Burglar. Sandham, Henry, illus. 2005. reprint ed. pap. 15.95 *(978-1-4179-0135-7(7))* Kessinger Publishing, LLC.

Burns, T. R. Watch Your Step. (Merits of Mischief Ser.: 3). (ENG., Illus.). (J). (gr. 3-7). 2015. 464p. pap. 7.99 *(978-1-4424-4036-4(8))* 2014. 480p. 16.99 *(978-1-4424-4035-7(X))* Simon & Schuster Children's Publishing. (Aladdin).

Bush, Penelope. Alice in Time. 2011. (ENG., Illus.). 208p. (YA). (gr. 7-18). 17.95 *(978-0-8234-2329-3(8))* Holiday Hse., Inc.

Bush, Rosetta Bowman. My Name Is Violet. 2013. 20p. pap. 24.95 *(978-1-63000-515-3(0))* America Star Bks.

Byrne, Marlene F. & Graber, Jesse. Just a Baseball Game. 2009. (Illus.). 52p. (J). 14.99 *(978-0-9777135-2-3(0))* Celtic Marketing Inc.

Cabot, Meg. Pants on Fire. (YA). 2008. (ENG.). 288p. (gr. 8). pap. 9.99 *(978-0-06-088017-0(1))* 2007. (ENG.). 272p. (gr. 7-10). 16.99 *(978-0-06-088015-6(5))* 2007. 260p. (gr. 7-10). lib. bdg. 17.89 *(978-0-06-088016-3(3))* HarperCollins Pubs. (HarperTeen).

—Teen Idol. 2005. 291p. (YA). 16.65 *(978-0-7569-5735-3(4))* Perfection Learning Corp.

Cadieux Davignon, Danielle. La Promesse. 2004. (Collection Impact Ado). (FRE.). 80p. (J). *(978-2-922762-48-8(3)*, Spotlight Poets) Academie Impact.

Cafaro, Phyllis. The Legend of Captain McFinn & Friends. 2012. (ENG.). 24p. (J). 17.99 *(978-0-9799283-3-8(8)*, 9780979928338) Cold River Pubns.

Caldwell, V. M. Runt: Story of a Boy. 2006. (ENG.). 208p. (J). (gr. 2-8). 16.95 *(978-1-57131-662-2(0))*; (gr. 3-7). per. 6.95 *(978-1-57131-661-5(2))* Milkweed Editions.

Callahan, Susan. Always Right. 2012. 20p. pap. 15.99 *(978-1-4772-0424-5(5))* AuthorHouse.

Cameron, Peter. Someday This Pain Will Be Useful to You. 2009. (ENG.). 240p. (YA). (gr. 9-13). pap. 16.00 *(978-0-312-42816-7(2)*, 9780312428167) Picador.

Cammuso, Frank. The Dragon Players. 2009. (Knights of the Lunch Table Ser.: 2). (ENG.). 128p. (J). (gr. 4-7). pap. 10.99 *(978-0-439-90323-3(8)*, Graphix) Scholastic, Inc.

Campbell, Angus Peter. Archie & the North Wind. 2010. (ENG.). 192p. pap. 17.95 *(978-1-906817-38-1(3)*, 9781906817381) Luath Pr. Ltd. GBR. Dist: Midpoint Trade Bks., Inc.

Capucilli, Alyssa Satin. Biscuit Is Thankful. Schories, Pat, illus. 2003. (Biscuit Ser.). (ENG.). 16p. (J). (gr. -1-1). bds. 4.99 *(978-0-694-01519-1(9)*, HarperFestival) HarperCollins Pubs.

Carbone, Peter W. Ben the Raindrop: Strength in Leadership. 2011. 40p. (gr. 4-6). pap. 18.49 *(978-1-4567-5994-0(9))* AuthorHouse.

Carlson, J. Kelley. Freeing Golden Eagle. 2007. 140p. 19.95 *(978-1-4327-0315-8(3))*; per. 10.95 *(978-1-4327-0302-8(1))* Outskirts Pr., Inc.

Carlson, Melody. Homecoming Queen, 1 vol. 2014. (Carter House Girls Ser.). (ENG.). 224p. (YA). pap. 9.99 *(978-0-310-74725-3(2))* Zondervan.

—It's a Green Thing. 2009. (Diary of a Teenage Girl Ser.: Bk. 15). (ENG.). 256p. pap. 14.99 *(978-1-60142-118-0(4)*, Multnomah) Doubleday Religious Publishing Group, The.

—Just Ask. 2005. (Diary of a Teenage Girl Ser.: Bk. 10). (ENG.). 256p. (J). (gr. 7-12). per. 14.99 *(978-1-59052-321-6(0)*, Multnomah Bks.) Crown Publishing Group.

—Last Dance, 1 vol. 2014. (Carter House Girls Ser.). (ENG.). 208p. (YA). pap. 9.99 *(978-0-310-74900-4(X))* Zondervan.

—Mixed Bags, 1 vol. 2014. (Carter House Girls Ser.). (ENG.). 224p. (YA). pap. 9.99 *(978-0-310-74756-7(2))* Zondervan.

—My Name Is Chloe. 2005. (Diary of a Teenage Girl: Bk. 5). 288p. (YA). mass mkt. 7.99 *(978-1-59052-736-8(4)*, Multnomah) Doubleday Religious Publishing Group, The.

—New York Debut, 1 vol. 2014. (Carter House Girls Ser.). (ENG.). 224p. (YA). pap. 9.99 *(978-0-310-74779-6(1))* Zondervan.

—Spring Breakdown, 1 vol. 2014. (Carter House Girls Ser.). (ENG.). 208p. (YA). pap. 9.99 *(978-0-310-74809-0(7))* Zondervan.

—Stealing Bradford, 1 vol. 2014. (Carter House Girls Ser.). (ENG.). 224p. (YA). pap. 9.99 *(978-0-310-74654-6(X))* Zondervan.

—Viva Vermont!, 1 vol. 2014. (Carter House Girls Ser.). (ENG.). 224p. (YA). pap. 9.99 *(978-0-310-74714-7(7))* Zondervan.

Carlson, Nancy. Life Is Fun. Carlson, Nancy, illus. 2012. (Nancy Carlson Picture Bks). (Illus.). 32p. (J). (gr. k-2). (ENG.). 9.95 *(978-0-7613-8945-3(8))*; 56.72 *(978-0-7613-9300-9(5))* Lerner Publishing Group. (Carolrhoda Bks.).

—Smile a Lot! Carlson, Nancy, illus. (Nancy Carlson Picture Bks). (Illus.). 32p. (J). (gr. k-2). 2012. 56.72 *(978-0-7613-9310-8(2))* 2012. (ENG.). 9.95 *(978-0-7613-9173-9(8))* 2003. 15.95 *(978-0-87614-869-3(0))* Lerner Publishing Group. (Carolrhoda Bks.).

—¡Sonríe! Translations.com Staff, tr. from ENG. Carlson, Nancy, illus. 2007. (Ediciones Lerner Single Titles Ser.).Tr. of Smile a Lot! (SPA., Illus.). 32p. (J). (gr. k-2). 15.95 *(978-0-8225-7817-8(4)*, Ediciones Lerner) Lerner Publishing Group.

Carman, Debby. Chewdalootie, Doing My Duty. Carman, Debby, illus. 2007. (Illus.). 28p. (J). (gr. -1-1). 14.99 *(978-0-9777340-3-0(X))* Faux Paw Media Group.

Carman, Patrick. The Walnut Cup. James, Steve, illus. 2009. (Elliot's Park Ser.: Bk. 3). 80p. (J). (gr. 1-5). 8.99 *(978-0-545-01932-3(X)*, Orchard Bks.) Scholastic, Inc.

Carmen, Indigo. Tee Hee. Diana, illus. 2008. 24p. pap. 24.95 *(978-1-4241-9959-4(X))* America Star Bks.

Carpenter, Ray. The Adventures of Benny Bell. 2004. 252p. 26.45 *(978-1-4140-8467-1(6))* AuthorHouse.

Carroll, Kathy. Rabbit & the Amazing Hopping Contest. 2007. (Illus.). 16p. (J). 9.99 *(978-0-9791401-6-7(1))* Abecedarian Bks.

Carson, Shonette. Ian's Bad Choices Turned His Life Around. Dupon-Martinez, Christopher, illus. 2011. 24p. pap. 24.95 *(978-1-4560-0965-6(6))* America Star Bks.

Carter, Scott William. The Last Great Getaway of the Water Balloon Boys. 2010. (ENG.). 208p. (YA). (gr. 7-18). 16.99 *(978-1-4169-7156-6(4)*, Simon & Schuster Bks. For Young Readers) Simon & Schuster Bks. For Young Readers.

Cartmell, C. J. The Magic Mailbox. 2011. 28p. pap. 15.99 *(978-1-4568-4525-4(X))* Xlibris Corp.

Casanova, Mary. Ice-Out. 2016. (ENG., Illus.). 264p. (YA). 16.95 *(978-0-8166-9417-4(6))* Univ. of Minnesota Pr.

Casella, Jody. Thin Space. 2013. (ENG.). 256p. (YA). (gr. 7). 16.99 *(978-1-58270-435-7(X))*; pap. 10.99 *(978-1-58270-392-3(2))* Simon Pulse. (Simon Pulse).

Casey & the See Through Head: Secrets for a Successful Life. 3rd ed. 2003. (Kamaron Concept Book:). (J). per. 9.99 *(978-0-9715713-3-4(3))* Kamaron Institute Pr.

Castan, Mike. Fighting for Dontae. 2012. (ENG.). 144p. (YA). 16.95 *(978-0-8234-2348-4(4))* Holiday Hse., Inc.

—The Price of Loyalty. 2011. (ENG., Illus.). 256p. (YA). (gr. 7-18). 17.95 *(978-0-8234-2268-5(2))* Holiday Hse., Inc.

Castlemon, Harry. Go-Ahead; or, the Fisher-Boy's Motto, by Harry Castlemon [Pseud.]. 2006. 308p. per. 23.99 *(978-1-4255-2946-8(1))* Michigan Publishing.

—No Moss; or, the Career of a Rolling Stone, by Harry Castlemon [Pseud.]. 2006. 328p. per. 23.99 *(978-1-4255-3290-1(X))* Michigan Publishing.

Cather, Willa. Willa Cather. Balkovek, James, illus. 2004. (Great American Short Stories Ser.). 80p. (gr. 4-7). lib. bdg. 24.00 *(978-0-8368-4251-7(0)*, Gareth Stevens Learning Library) Stevens, Gareth Publishing LLLP.

Cesena, Denise. Orderliness. Cesena, Denise & Perez, Maureen T., illus. l.t. ed. 2003. 28p. (J). 10.00 *(978-0-9740418-2-7(3))* Night Light Pubns., LLC.

—Orderliness - Companion Book. Cesena, Denise & Perez, Maureen T., illus. l.t. ed. 2003. 12p. (J). 2.00 *(978-0-9740418-3-4(1))* Night Light Pubns., LLC.

—Respect. Cesena, Denise & Perez, Maureen T., illus. l.t. ed. 2003. 28p. (J). *(978-0-9740418-4-1(X))* Night Light Pubns., LLC.

Chandler, Ann. Kootenay Silver. 2010. (ENG.). 216p. (YA). (gr. 9). pap. 12.99 *(978-1-55488-755-2(0))* Dundurn CAN. Dist: Ingram Publisher Services.

Chapman, Clay McLeod. Camp Cannibal. 2014. (Tribe Novel Ser.). (ENG.). 320p. (J). (gr. 3-7). 16.99 *(978-1-4231-5222-4(0))* Hyperion Bks. for Children.

Cheva, Cherry. She's So Money. 2009. (ENG.). 304p. (YA). (gr. 8). pap. 8.99 *(978-0-06-128853-1(5)*, HarperTeen) HarperCollins Pubs.

Child, Lauren. Clarice Bean Spells Trouble. Child, Lauren, illus. 2006. (Clarice Bean Ser.). (Illus.). 189p. (J). (gr. 3-6). 13.65 *(978-0-7569-7919-5(6))* Perfection Learning Corp.

—Spells Trouble. Child, Lauren, illus. 2006. (Clarice Bean Ser.). (ENG., Illus.). 192p. (J). (gr. 3-7). pap. 6.99 *(978-0-7636-2903-8(0))* Candlewick Pr.

Chin, Oliver. The Belt of Fire. Chua, Charlene, illus. 2013. (Julie Black Belt Ser.). (ENG.). 36p. (J). (gr. -1-3). 15.95 *(978-1-59702-079-4(6))* Immedium.

Chin, Oliver Clyde. Julie Black Belt: The Kung Fu Chronicles. Chua, Charlene, illus. 2008. (ENG.). 36p. (J). (gr. k-1). 15.95 *(978-1-59702-009-1(5))* Immedium.

Christiansen, Candace. The Mitten Tree. Greenstein, Elaine, illus. 2008. (ENG.). 32p. pap. 7.95 *(978-1-55591-698-5(8))* Fulcrum Publishing.

Christopher, Matt. Body Check. 2004. (Matt Christopher Sports Ser.). 138p. (gr. 3-7). 15.00 *(978-0-7569-2984-8(9))* Perfection Learning Corp.

—The Hit-Away Kid. Ulrich, George, illus. 2009. (New Peach Street Mudders Sports Library). 64p. (J). (gr. 2-4). lib. bdg. 23.93 *(978-1-59953-318-6(9))* Norwood Hse. Pr.

—Lacrosse Face-Off. 2010. (Matt Christopher Sports Library). 128p. (J). (gr. 4-6). lib. bdg. 26.60 *(978-1-59953-355-1(3))* Norwood Hse. Pr.

—Out at Second. 2011. (Playaway Top Children's Picks Ser.). (J). 49.99 *(978-1-60941-973-8(1))* Findaway World, LLC.

—Out at Second. 2011. (ENG.). 144p. (J). (gr. 3-7). pap. 4.99 *(978-0-316-08481-9(6))* Little, Brown Bks. for Young Readers.

Church, Alfred J. Three Greek Children. 2008. (Illus.). 160p. pap. 9.95 *(978-1-59915-081-9(6))* Yesterday's Classics.

Cirella-Mitts, Anne. The Candle. 2010. 32p. pap. 14.49 *(978-1-4520-0154-8(5))* AuthorHouse.

Cirrone, Dorian. Prom Kings & Drama Queens. 2008. 200p. (YA). (gr. 7). lib. bdg. 17.89 *(978-0-06-114373-1(1),* HarperTeen) HarperCollins Pubs.

Clampitt, Edward L. Team Dawg It's All about Respect. 2nd ed. 2012. (ENG., Illus.). 32p. (J). lib. bdg. 12.99 *(978-0-9749378-6-1(X))* Team Dawg Productions, Inc.

Clara Mulholland. Naughty Miss Bunny. 2007. 128p. per. 10.95 *(978-1-4218-3938-7(5),* 1st World Library - Literary Society) 1st World Publishing, Inc.

Clark, Clara Gillow. Hattie on Her Way. Thompson, John, illus. 2005. (ENG.). 208p. (J). (gr. 5-18). 15.99 *(978-0-7636-2286-2(9))* Candlewick Pr.

Clarke, Lyndia A. Tidy up Tommy. Clarke, Lyndia A., illus. 2005. (Illus.). (J). 1700.00 *(978-0-9762898-6-9(5))* LightHouse Pr.

Clements, Andrew. No Talking. 2014. (ENG.). 160p. (J). (gr. 3-7). 11.24 *(978-1-63245-298-6(7))* Lectorum Pubns., Inc.

—Troublemaker. Elliott, Mark, illus. 2013. (ENG.). 176p. (J). (gr. 3-7). pap. 7.99 *(978-1-4169-4932-9(1),* Atheneum Bks. for Young Readers) Simon & Schuster Children's Publishing.

Cloci, Gabriella. Minda's Happily Ever After. 2003. (J). pap. 9.95 *(978-0-7414-1501-1(1))* Infinity Publishing.

Coates, Doug. Pitching for Success: Character Lessons, the Joe Nuxhall Way. 2014. (ENG.). 16.95 *(978-1-939710-09-3(X))* Orange Frazer Pr.

Coleman, K. Showdown. 2017. (Gridiron Ser.). (ENG.). (YA). (gr. 6-12). 112p. pap. 7.99 ***(978-1-5124-5354-6(4))***; lib. bdg. 26.65 ***(978-1-5124-3978-6(9))*** Lerner Publishing Group. (Darby Creek).

Colin, Beatrice & Pinto, Sara. My Invisible Sister. Pinto, Sara, illus. 2011. (ENG., Illus.). 128p. (YA). (gr. 3-6). pap. 6.99 *(978-1-59990-678-2(3),* 9781599906782, Bloomsbury USA Childrens) Bloomsbury Publishing USA.

Coll-Seck, Jayden. Brianna's Best, 01 vols., 1. 2016. (Rosen REAL Readers: Social Studies Nonfiction / Fiction: Family, Community, & the World Ser.). (ENG.). 12p. (J). pap. 6.33 *(978-1-5081-1997-5(X),* Rosen Classroom) Rosen Publishing Group, Inc., The.

Collier, James Lincoln. Me & Billy, 0 vols. unabr. ed. 2013. (ENG.). 194p. (J). (gr. 5-7). pap. 9.99 *(978-1-4778-1706-3(9),* 9781477817063, Amazon Children's Publishing) Amazon Publishing.

Collier, Kevin Scott & Collier, Kristen. Dreamchaser. 2008. 64p. pap. 6.95 *(978-1-933090-93-1(6))* Guardian Angel Publishing, Inc.

Collingwood, Harry. The Log of a Privateersman. 2008. 216p. 26.95 *(978-1-60664-899-5(3))*; pap. 15.95 *(978-1-60664-018-0(6))* Aegypan.

Collins, Arda. Another Way of Life. Kiplinger Pandy, Lori, illus. l.t. ed. 2005. 30p. (J). (gr. -1-3). per. 9.99 *(978-1-59879-023-8(4))* Lifevest Publishing, Inc.

Collins, Paul. Lucy, the Boss. Bocquée, Christian, illus. 2015. (Legends in Their Own Lunchbox Ser.). (ENG.). 56p. (gr. 2-3). pap. 7.99 *(978-1-4966-0254-1(4),* Legends in Their Own Lunchbox) Capstone Classroom.

Coniglio, Rebecca Perlman. Lily's Little Life Lessons: Lily's Laces. Mundy, Jen, illus. 2013. (ENG.). 24p. (J). (gr. -1-3). 14.95 *(978-1-62086-408-1(8))* Mascot Bks., Inc.

Conner, Wendy Simpson. Stuff, Stuff, I Want More Stuff. (Illus.). (J). 16.95 *(978-1-889599-22-9(0))* Interstellar Publishing Co.

Connolly, C J. The Boomerang. 2010. (Illus.). 32p. (J). 16.95 *(978-0-9825559-1-0(1))* Crosswinds Pr., Inc.

—Wil, Fitz, & a Flea Named T. 2009. (Illus.). 32p. (J). 16.95 *(978-0-9825559-0-3(3))* Crosswinds Pr., Inc.

Conrad, Lauren. L. A. Candy. (L. A. Candy Ser.: 1). (ENG.). (YA). (gr. 9-18). 2010. 352p. pap. 9.99 *(978-0-06-176759-3(X))* 2009. 336p. 17.99 *(978-0-06-176758-6(1))* HarperCollins Pubs.

—Sugar & Spice. (YA). 2011. (L. A. Candy Ser.: 3). (ENG.). 288p. (gr. 9). pap. 9.99 *(978-0-06-176763-0(8))* 2010. (L. A. Candy Ser.: 3). (ENG.). 288p. (gr. 9-18). 17.99 *(978-0-06-176762-3(X))* 2010. 279p. 9.99 *(978-0-06-201148-0(0))* HarperCollins Pubs.

—Sweet Little Lies. 2010. (L. A. Candy Ser.: 2). (YA). (ENG.). 336p. (gr. 9). pap. 9.99 *(978-0-06-176761-6(1))*; 309p. 9.99 *(978-0-06-198572-0(4))* HarperCollins Pubs.

Conway, Celeste. When You Open Your Eyes. 2012. (ENG.). 320p. (YA). (gr. 9). 16.99 *(978-1-4424-4229-0(8))*; pap. 9.99 *(978-1-4424-3031-0(1))* Simon Pulse. (Simon Pulse).

Cook, Julia. Decibella & Her 6-Inch Voice. DuFalla, Anita, illus. 2014. (ENG.). 32p. (J). pap. 10.95 *(978-1-934490-58-7(X))* Boys Town Pr.

—El Peor Dia de TODA Mi Vida. DeWeerd, Kelsey, illus. 2012. (SPA.). 32p. (J). pap. 10.95 *(978-1-934490-34-1(2))* Boys Town Pr.

—Teamwork Isn't My Thing, & I Don't Like to Share! De Weerd, Kelsey, illus. 2012. (ENG.). 32p. (J). pap. 10.95 *(978-1-934490-35-8(0))* Boys Town Pr.

—Well, I Can Top That! Dufalla, Anita, illus. 2014. (ENG.). 32p. (J). pap. 10.95 *(978-1-934490-57-0(1))* Boys Town Pr.

—The Worst Day of My Life Ever! Cook, Julia & De Weerd, Kelsey, illus. 2011. (ENG.). 32p. (J). pap. 10.95 *(978-1-934490-20-4(2))* Boys Town Pr.

Cook, William. Worth the Wait. Kim, Jeehyun, illus. 2007. 32p. (J). per. 15.00 *(978-0-9791387-0-6(1))*; per. 15.00 *(978-0-9791387-1-3(X))* Yadda Yadda Pr.

Coolidge, Susan. What Katy Did. 2013. (ENG., Illus.). 200p. (J). 15.00 *(978-1-84135-843-7(6))* Award Pubns. Ltd. GBR. Dist: Parkwest Pubns., Inc.

—What Katy Did. Ledyard, Addie, illus. 2013. 132p. pap. *(978-1-909735-03-3(5))* Aziloth Bks.

—What Katy Did. 2012. 246p. pap. *(978-1-78139-262-1(5))* Benediction Classics.

—What Katy Did. 2012. 300p. pap. 29.75 *(978-1-286-00091-5(2))* 2012. 302p. pap. 29.75 *(978-1-286-07372-8(3))* 2011. 290p. (gr. 3-7). pap. 28.75 *(978-1-179-65265-8(7))* 2010. (ENG.). 300p. pap. 29.75 *(978-1-178-00783-1(9))* 2010. (ENG.). 282p. (gr. 3-7). pap. 28.75 *(978-1-177-27477-7(9))* 2010. 302p. pap. 29.75 *(978-1-145-74830-9(9))* 2008. 164p. (gr. 4-7). 25.99 *(978-0-554-28634-1(3))* 2008. 164p. (gr. 4-7). 22.99 *(978-0-554-37937-1(6))* 2007. (ENG.). 144p. pap. 18.99 *(978-1-4346-5943-9(7))* 2007. (ENG.). 160p. pap. 21.99 *(978-1-4346-5944-6(5))* Creative Media Partners, LLC.

—What Katy Did. 2007. (ENG.). 148p. per. *(978-1-4065-1527-5(2))* Dodo Pr.

—What Katy Did. 2006. (Dover Children's Classics Ser.). (ENG., Illus.). 160p. (J). (gr. 3-8). per. 6.95 *(978-0-486-44760-5(X))* Dover Pubns., Inc.

—What Katy Did. 2007. (ENG.). 104p. per. *(978-1-4068-4855-7(7))* Echo Library.

—What Katy Did. 2010. (Illus.). 92p. (gr. 3-7). pap. 19.99 *(978-1-153-74507-9(0))* 2009. 104p. pap. 6.40 *(978-0-217-53637-0(9))* General Bks. LLC.

—What Katy Did. 2010. 132p. pap. *(978-1-4076-5115-6(3))* HardPr.

—What Katy Did. Ledyard, Addie, illus. 284p. 2010. 35.16 *(978-1-163-85079-4(9))* 2010. pap. 23.16 *(978-1-163-77965-1(2))* 2007. 43.95 *(978-0-548-53870-8(0))* 2007. per. 28.95 *(978-0-548-48700-6(6))* Kessinger Publishing, LLC.

—What Katy Did. 2010. (Puffin Classics Ser.). (ENG., Illus.). 240p. (J). (gr. 5-7). pap. 5.99 *(978-0-14-132671-9(9),* Puffin Books) Penguin Young Readers Group.

—What Katy Did. 2013. (ENG., Illus.). 256p. (J). (gr. 4-7). pap. 12.99 *(978-0-09-957312-8(1))* Random Hse. GBR. Dist: Independent Pubs. Group.

—What Katy Did. 2007. (ENG.). 192p. pap. 12.45 *(978-1-60424-403-8(8),* Book Jungle) Standard Pubns., Inc.

—What Katy Did. 2011. 162p. (gr. 3-7). pap. *(978-3-8424-6664-7(1))* Tredition GmbH.

—What Katy Did. 2010. 144p. pap. 4.99 *(978-1-61720-100-4(6))* Wilder Pubns., Corp.

Coolidge, Susan & Ledyard, Addie. What Katy Did. 2010. (ENG.). 292p. pap. 28.75 *(978-1-172-34659-2(3))* Creative Media Partners, LLC.

Cooney, Caroline B. The Lost Songs. 2013. (ENG.). 256p. (YA). (gr. 7). pap. 8.99 *(978-0-385-73967-2(2),* Ember) Random Hse. Children's Bks.

Cooper, Ilene. The Golden Rule. Swiatowska, Gabi, illus. 2007. (ENG.). 40p. (J). (gr. -1-3). 17.95 *(978-0-8109-0960-1(X),* Abrams Bks. for Young Readers) Abrams, Inc.

—The Golden Rule. Swiatkowska, Gabi, illus. (J). (gr. k-4). 2008. 27.95 incl. audio *(978-0-8045-6968-2(1))* 2007. 29.95 incl. audio compact disk *(978-0-8045-4191-6(4))* Spoken Arts, Inc.

Corderoy, Tracey. No! Warnes, Tim, illus. 2015. (ENG.). 28p. (J). (gr. -1-2). bds. 7.99 *(978-1-58925-208-0(X))* Tiger Tales.

Correa, Shan. Gaff, 1 vol. 2010. (ENG.). 224p. (J). (gr. 3-7). 15.95 *(978-1-56145-526-3(1),* Peachtree Junior) Peachtree Pubs.

Corrigan, Eireann. Accomplice. 2010. (ENG.). 304p. (J). (gr. 7-7). 17.99 *(978-0-545-05236-8(X),* Scholastic Pr.) Scholastic, Inc.

Cosgrove, Stephen. The Bigg Family: Getting along with Others. Arroyo, Fian, illus. 2004. (J). *(978-1-58804-354-2(1))* P C I Education.

—The Grumpling. James, Robin, illus. 2003. (Serendipity Bks.). (Orig.). (J). (gr. k-4). 12.65 *(978-0-7569-5259-4(X))* Perfection Learning Corp.

—Hickory B. Hopp: Paying Attention. Arroyo, Fian, illus. 2004. (J). *(978-1-58804-379-5(7))* P C I Education.

Cotler, Steve. Cheesie Mack Is Not a Genius or Anything. McCauley, Adam, illus. (Cheesie Mack Ser.). (ENG.). 240p. (J). (gr. 3-7). 2012. 6.99 *(978-0-375-86394-3(X),* Yearling) 2011. 15.99 *(978-0-375-86437-7(7),* Random Hse. Bks. for Young Readers) Random Hse. Children's Bks.

Courtney, Suzanne Gene. Ride to the Stars, a Story for Children about Life, Loss, & Love. 2009. 32p. pap. 16.50 *(978-1-60860-164-6(1),* Eloquent Bks.) Strategic Book Publishing & Rights Agency (SBPRA).

Coven, Wanda. Heidi Heckelbeck Casts a Spell. Burris, Priscilla, illus. 2012. (Heidi Heckelbeck Ser.: 2). (ENG.). 128p. (J). (gr. k-4). 16.99 *(978-1-4424-4088-3(0))*; pap. 5.99 *(978-1-4424-3567-4(4))* Little Simon. (Little Simon).

—Heidi Heckelbeck Casts a Spell. 2012. (Heidi Heckelbeck Ser.: 2). lib. bdg. 16.00 *(978-0-606-26327-6(6),* Turtleback) Turtleback Bks.

Covey, Sean. The 7 Habits of Happy Kids. 2008. (Playaway Children Ser.). (J). (gr. -1-3). 39.99 *(978-1-60640-956-5(5))* Findaway World, LLC.

—The 7 Habits of Happy Kids. Curtis, Stacy, illus. 2008. (ENG.). 96p. (J). (gr. -1-3). 19.99 *(978-1-4169-5776-8(6),* Simon & Schuster Bks. For Young Readers) Simon & Schuster Bks. For Young Readers.

Cowling, Chani. Cookie Baker, Sweet & Sour. 2008. 24p. pap. 24.95 *(978-1-60703-021-8(7))* America Star Bks.

Crane, Cheri J. Moment of Truth: A Novel. 2005. 238p. (YA). *(978-1-59156-727-1(0))* Covenant Communications.

Crawford, Neil. The Journeyers. 2006. (ENG.). 248p. (J). per. *(978-0-9778205-4-2(8))* Helm Publishing.

Creech, Sharon. Replay. (J). (gr. 3-7). 2013. (ENG.). 224p. pap. 6.99 *(978-0-06-054021-0(4))* 2005. 240p. lib. bdg. 16.89 *(978-0-06-054020-3(6),* Cotler, Joanna Books) HarperCollins Pubs.

Crocker, Carter & Swift, Jonathan. The Last of the Gullivers. 2012. (ENG.). 224p. (J). (gr. 4-7). 16.99 *(978-0-399-24231-1(7),* Philomel Bks.) Penguin Young Readers Group.

Crompton, Laurie Boyle. Love & Vandalism. 2017. (ENG.). 336p. (YA). (gr. 8-12). pap. 10.99 *(978-1-4926-3605-2(3),* 9781492636052) Sourcebooks, Inc.

Crook, M. J. Village on Crooked Hill. 2008. 168p. pap. 11.99 *(978-1-4389-0486-3(X))* AuthorHouse.

Cummings, Priscilla. The Journey Back. 2013. (ENG.). 272p. (J). (gr. 5). pap. 7.99 *(978-0-14-242290-8(8),* Puffin Books) Penguin Young Readers Group.

—Red Kayak. 2006. (ENG.). 224p. (J). (gr. 5-18). 7.99 *(978-0-14-240573-4(6),* Puffin Books) Penguin Young Readers Group.

Curry, Kenneth. Chuka & the Drum. 2007. (Illus.). 22p. (J). 10.95 *(978-0-9798364-4-2(1))* Curry Brothers Publishing Group.

Curtis, Jamie Lee. Big Words for Little People. Cornell, Laura, illus. 2008. (ENG.). 40p. (J). (gr. -1-3). 16.99 *(978-0-06-112759-5(0))* HarperCollins Pubs.

—I'm Gonna Like Me: Letting off a Little Self-Esteem. Cornell, Laura, illus. 2007. (ENG.). 32p. (J). (gr. -1-3). 16.99 *(978-0-06-028761-0(6))* HarperCollins Pubs.

—Is There Really a Human Race? Cornell, Laura, illus. 2006. (ENG.). 40p. (J). (gr. -1-3). 16.99 *(978-0-06-075346-7(3))* HarperCollins Pubs.

—My Brave Year of Firsts: Tries, Sighs, & High Fives. Cornell, Laura, illus. 2012. (ENG.). 40p. (J). (gr. -1-3). 16.99 *(978-0-06-144155-4(4))* HarperCollins Pubs.

Curtis, Marci Lyn. The One Thing. 2015. (ENG., Illus.). 336p. (YA). (gr. 7-12). 17.99 *(978-1-4847-0902-3(0))* Hyperion Bks. for Children.

Cushman, Karen. Will Sparrow's Road. (ENG.). 224p. (J). (gr. 5-7). 2014. pap. 6.99 *(978-0-544-33632-2(1),* HMH Books For Young Readers) 2012. 16.99 *(978-0-547-73962-5(1))* Houghton Mifflin Harcourt Publishing Co.

Cuyler, Margery. Hooray for Reading Day! Howard, Arthur, illus. 2008. (J). (gr. k-1). 27.95 incl. audio *(978-0-8045-6969-9(X))*; 29.95 incl. audio compact disk *(978-0-8045-4194-7(9))* Spoken Arts, Inc.

Cyanne Bandanna Kindergartner always Tell the Truth. 2005. (YA). per. *(978-1-59872-133-1(X))* Instant Pub.

D' Almfras, Pauline H. Pisi the Cat & His Adventures. 2009. 16p. pap. 12.95 *(978-1-60860-111-0(0),* Strategic Bk. Publishing) Strategic Book Publishing & Rights Agency (SBPRA).

Dahl, Michael. Little Dinos Don't Bite, 1 vol. Record, Adam, illus. 2013. (Little Dinos Ser.). (ENG.). 20p. (gr. -1-k). bds. 7.99 *(978-1-4048-7536-4(0))* Picture Window Bks.

—Little Dinos Don't Hit, 1 vol. Record, Adam, illus. 2013. (Little Dinos Ser.). (ENG.). 20p. (gr. -1-k). bds. 7.99 *(978-1-4048-7533-3(6))* Picture Window Bks.

—Little Dinos Don't Push, 1 vol. Record, Adam, illus. 2013. (Little Dinos Ser.). (ENG.). 20p. (gr. -1-k). bds. 7.99 *(978-1-4048-7534-0(4))* Picture Window Bks.

Dale, Fanny. Golden Rule or Second Series of Househol. 2006. pap. 26.95 *(978-1-4286-5592-8(1))* Kessinger Publishing, LLC.

Daly, Niki. Thank You, Jackson: How One Little Boy Makes a Big Difference. Daly, Jude, illus. 2015. (ENG.). 32p. (J). (gr. -1-3). 17.99 *(978-1-84780-484-6(5),* Frances Lincoln) Quarto Publishing Group UK GBR. Dist: Hachette Bk. Group.

Damico, Gina. Hellhole. (ENG.). (YA). (gr. 9). 2016. 384p. pap. 9.99 *(978-0-544-54117-7(0))* 2015. 368p. 17.99 *(978-0-544-30710-0(0))* Houghton Mifflin Harcourt Publishing Co. (HMH Books For Young Readers).

Darby, Kim. I Wish I May I Wish I Might. 2009. 16p. pap. 8.49 *(978-1-4490-3404-7(7))* AuthorHouse.

Davey, Keith Peter. Squeaks Narrow Squeaks. Frost, Justine, illus. 2009. 32p. pap. 14.62 *(978-1-4120-4402-8(2))* Trafford Publishing.

Davies, Matt. Ben Rides On. 2013. (ENG., Illus.). 32p. (J). (gr. -1-2). 17.99 *(978-1-59643-794-4(4),* 9781596437944) Roaring Brook Pr.

Davis, Melissa. Denny the Duck. 2008. 25p. pap. 24.95 *(978-1-60672-712-6(5))* America Star Bks.

Davis, Tanita S. Peas & Carrots. 2016. (ENG.). 288p. (YA). (gr. 7). 17.99 *(978-0-553-51281-6(1))*; lib. bdg. 20.99 *(978-0-553-51282-3(X))* Random Hse. Children's Bks. (Knopf Bks. for Young Readers).

Dawson, Patricia. The Adventures of Farmer Bill. 2013. 28p. pap. 19.99 *(978-1-4817-0551-6(2))* AuthorHouse.

De felice, Cynthia. Lostman's River. 2008. (ENG.). 160p. (J). (gr. 3-7). pap. 8.99 *(978-1-4169-8690-4(1),* Simon & Schuster/Paula Wiseman Bks.) Simon & Schuster/Paula Wiseman Bks.

de Kinder, Jan. Red. 2015. (ENG., Illus.). 32p. (J). 16.00 *(978-0-8028-5446-9(X),* Eerdmans Bks For Young Readers) Eerdmans, William B. Publishing Co.

de Lint, Charles. The Blue Girl. 2006. (ENG.). 384p. (YA). (gr. 7-18). reprint ed. 7.99 *(978-0-14-240545-1(0),* Firebird) Penguin Young Readers Group.

Debbie Lamb & Michelle Villa. Luis Discovers the Lab N Earth. 2010. 24p. pap. 15.93 *(978-1-4269-2291-6(4))* Trafford Publishing.

Dee, Barbara. This Is Me from Now On. 2010. (Mix Ser.). (ENG.). 272p. (J). (gr. 4-8). pap. 7.99 *(978-1-4169-9414-5(9),* Aladdin) Simon & Schuster Children's Publishing.

DeLap, Mark. The Little Acorn, 1 vol. 2010. 40p. pap. 24.95 *(978-1-4489-9509-7(4))* PublishAmerica, Inc.

DeLoach, Kathleen. Daniel's World. Best, Cathy, illus. 2004. (J). pap. 15.95 *(978-0-9747440-5-6(0))* Three Moons Media.

Demas, Corinne & Roehrig, Artemis. Are Pirates Polite? Catrow, David, illus. 2016. (ENG.). 40p. (J). (gr. -1-k). 16.99 *(978-0-545-62874-7(1))* Scholastic, Inc.

Demers, Dominique. Today, Maybe, 1 vol. Grimard, Gabrielle, illus. 2011. (ENG.). 32p. (J). (gr. -1-3). 19.95 *(978-1-55469-400-6(0))* Orca Bk. Pubs. USA.

Denman, K. L. Destination Human, 1 vol. 2013. (Orca Currents Ser.). (ENG.). 136p. (J). (gr. 5-9). pap. 9.95 *(978-1-4598-0371-8(X))*; lib. bdg. 16.95 *(978-1-4598-0372-5(8))* Orca Bk. Pubs. USA.

Derby, Sally. Kyle's Island. (ENG.). 192p. (J). (gr. 5). 2014. pap. 7.95 *(978-1-58089-317-6(1))* 2010. 16.95 *(978-1-58089-316-9(3))* Charlesbridge Publishing, Inc.

DeRosa, Nancy. Lazy Robert. Verona Publishing, illus. 2006. (J). 5.95 *(978-0-9769031-0-9(5))* Verona (Bk.) Publishing, Inc.

Desbordes, Astrid & Martin, Pauline. Daydreams of a Solitary Hamster. 2010. (ENG., Illus.). 56p. (J). (gr. 1-2). 17.95 *(978-1-59270-093-6(4))* Enchanted Lion Bks., LLC.

Deseret Book Company Staff, contrib. by. A Story to Tell: The Classic Book of Virtues for Children. 2nd ed. 2004. 508p. (J). 16.95 *(978-1-59038-359-9(1))* Deseret Bk. Co.

Devries, Rachel. Teeny Tiny Tino's Fishing Story. 2008. 15p. pap. 6.00 *(978-1-884419-87-4(9))* Bordighera Incorporated.

Dierenfeldt, Jane. Grammy's Curtain Calls, 1 vol. Hanawalt, Josh, illus. 2010. 22p. 24.95 *(978-1-4512-1051-4(5))* PublishAmerica, Inc.

—A Time for Everything. Hanawalt, Josh, illus. 2012. 36p. 24.95 *(978-1-4626-6146-6(7))* America Star Bks.

Dietz, Irene Andrighetti. Clariss, Did You Do This? 2006. (J). pap. 8.00 *(978-0-8059-6968-9(3))* Dorrance Publishing Co., Inc.

Dillon, Leo & Dillon, Diane. If Kids Ran the World. Dillon, Leo & Dillon, Diane, illus. 2014. (ENG., Illus.). 32p. (J). 18.99 *(978-0-545-44196-4(X),* Blue Sky Pr., The) Scholastic, Inc.

Dockter, Toni. Percy & the Plod. (Illus.). 200p. (J). pap. 14.95 *(978-0-9712201-0-2(7))* Dockter, Toni.

Donovan, Kyle, Sr. CurBee Races the NasBee 500: The Do'Bees. 2008. (Illus.). 28p. (J). pap. 9.99 *(978-0-9767670-5-3(8))* WannaBees Media LLC.

—Introducing the Do'Bees: The Do'Bees. 2008. (Illus.). 28p. (J). pap. 9.99 *(978-0-9767670-6-0(6))* WannaBees Media LLC.

Don't Do That, Dexter! 2014. (Happy Day Ser.). (ENG., Illus.). 16p. (J). pap. 2.49 *(978-1-4143-9409-1(8))* Tyndale Hse. Pubs.

Dorfman, Joaquin. The Long Wait for Tomorrow. 2009. (YA). *(978-0-375-84696-0(4))* Random Hse., Inc.

Dougherty, Mary. Life Adventures with Fossy. 2004. 7p. (J). pap. 10.58 *(978-1-4116-1497-0(6))* Lulu Pr., Inc.

Douglas, Rachel. "You're a Meany!" Drewes, Dan, illus. 2011. 13p. pap. 10.19 *(978-1-4567-8643-4(1))* AuthorHouse.

Downs Webb, Michelle. What Color Is Love? 2005. 24p. 10.95 *(978-1-4116-2783-3(0))* Lulu Pr., Inc.

Doyen, Denise. Once upon a Twice. Moser, Barry, illus. 2013. (Picture Book Ser.). (ENG.). 32p. (J). (gr. -1-2). pap. 7.99 *(978-0-449-81794-0(6),* Dragonfly Bks.) Random Hse. Children's Bks.

Dreistadt, Jessica R. Ashley & Tiana. 2009. 96p. pap. 10.00 *(978-0-578-02239-0(7))* Dreistadt, Jessica R.

Dubison, Valentine. Willington Woods. 2008. 52p. pap. 7.95 *(978-1-4327-2153-4(4))* Outskirts Pr., Inc.

Duble, Kathleen Benner. Hearts of Iron. 2006. (ENG.). 256p. (J). (gr. 5-9). 15.95 *(978-1-4169-0850-0(1),* McElderry, Margaret K. Bks.) McElderry, Margaret K. Bks.

Dudley, David L. Caleb's Wars. 2011. (ENG.). 272p. (YA). (gr. 9). 17.99 *(978-0-547-23997-2(1))* Houghton Mifflin Harcourt Publishing Co.

Dungy, Tony & Dungy, Lauren. Here Comes the Parade! Newton, Vanessa Brantley, illus. 2014. (Tony & Lauren Dungy Ready-To-Reads Ser.). (ENG.). 32p. (J). (gr. k-2). pap. 3.99 *(978-1-4424-5469-9(5),* Simon Spotlight) Simon Spotlight.

DuPrau, Jeanne. The Prophet of Yonwood. 2007. (City of Ember Ser.: 4). (ENG.). 304p. (J). (gr. 3-7). 7.99 *(978-0-440-42124-5(1),* Yearling) Random Hse. Children's Bks.

—The Prophet of Yonwood. 2007. (City of Ember Ser.: 3). 289p. (gr. 4-8). lib. bdg. 18.40 *(978-1-4178-1984-3(7),* Turtleback) Turtleback Bks.

Durrant, George D. Sam's Christmas Wish. Burr, Dan, illus. 2014. (ENG.). 32p. (J). (gr. 3). 17.99 *(978-1-60907-606-1(0),* Shadow Mountain) Shadow Mountain Publishing.

Dyan, Penelope. Classy Nancy — A One of a Kind Girl. Dyan, Penelope, illus. 2009. (Illus.). 48p. pap. 11.95 *(978-1-935118-45-9(5))* Bellissima Publishing, LLC.

—Little Miss Chris & the Incredible Red Shoes. Dyan, Penelope, illus. 2009. (Illus.). 44p. pap. 11.95 *(978-1-935118-49-7(8))* Bellissima Publishing, LLC.

Easton, T. S. Boys Don't Knit. 2015. (ENG.). 272p. (YA). (gr. 8). 16.99 *(978-1-250-05331-2(5),* 9781250053312) Feiwel & Friends.

—Boys Don't Knit. 2016. (ENG.). 272p. (YA). pap. 9.99 *(978-1-250-07354-9(5),* 9781250073549) Square Fish.

Easton, Tom. Pirates Can Be Honest, 01 vols., 1. 2016. (Pirate Pals Ser.). (ENG.). 32p. (J). pap. 10.00 *(978-1-5081-9141-4(7),* Windmill Bks.) Rosen Publishing Group, Inc., The.

Echols, Jennifer. Going Too Far. 2009. (ENG.). 256p. pap. 16.99 *(978-1-4165-7173-5(6),* MTV Bks.) MTV Books.

Eddy, Daniel. Walter's Tours in the East: Walter in Je. 2005. pap. 16.95 *(978-1-59605-437-0(9),* Cosimo Classics) Cosimo, Inc.

Edgeworth, Maria. Moral Tales, by Maria Edgeworth Embellished with Original Designs, by Darley. 2006. 532p. per. 29.99 *(978-1-4255-5877-2(1))* Michigan Publishing.

—Parents Assistance or Stories for Child. 2006. 492p. (gr. 4-7). per. *(978-1-4067-9305-5(1),* Hesperides Pr.) Read Bks.

—Rosamond: With Other Tales. by Maria Edgeworth. 2006. 388p. per. 26.99 *(978-1-4255-4076-0(7))* Michigan Publishing.

Efaw, Amy. After. 2010. (ENG.). 368p. (YA). (gr. 7-18). 8.99 *(978-0-14-241590-0(1),* Speak) Penguin Young Readers Group.

Egan, Kate. Kate & Nate Are Running Late! Yaccarino, Dan, illus. 2012. (ENG.). 36p. (J). (gr. k-2). 16.99 *(978-1-250-00080-4(7),* 9781250000804) Feiwel & Friends.

Eisenberg, Kristy. When I Grow Up. Joslin, Irene, illus. 2009. 28p. pap. 12.49 *(978-1-4389-0183-1(6))* AuthorHouse.

Elise, Christy. Beez Take Flight. 2012. 56p. pap. 24.99 *(978-1-4685-6265-1(7))* AuthorHouse.

Elkeles, Simone. Better Than Perfect. 2014. (Wild Cards Ser.). (ENG.). 352p. (YA). (gr. 9). pap. 9.99 *(978-0-8027-3725-0(0),* 9780802737250, Bloomsbury USA Childrens) Bloomsbury Publishing USA.

Elliott, Ruth. Little Blossom, 1 disc. Culquipuma, Diana y. Jose, tr. Elliott, Ruth, illus. 2008. (ENG & SPA., Illus.). 26p. (J). per. 12.99 incl. DVD (978-0-9795017-2-2(5)) Edu Designs.
Ellis, Edward Sylvester. Through Forest & Fire. 2005. pap. 14.95 (978-1-59224-221-4(9)) Wildside Pr., LLC.
Ellis, Leanne Statland. Tree Huggers. 2010. (J). pap. (978-0-88092-521-1(3)) Royal Fireworks Publishing Co.
Ellsworth, Mark R. Boids of a Feather, 1 vol. 2010. 34p. 24.95 (978-1-4489-5142-0(9)) PublishAmerica, Inc.
Elster, Jean Alicia. I'll Do the Right Thing. Tadgell, Nicole, illus. 2010. (ENG.). 32p. (J). pap. 11.99 (978-0-8170-1658-6(9)) Judson Pr.
Elwood, Danielle. I Love Me, I Love You. 2009. 20p. pap. 10.49 (978-1-4490-2409-3(2)) AuthorHouse.
Ennis, Nancy. When Mommy & Daddy Say No, They Still Love You. Meadows, Cynthia, illus. 2014. (ENG.). 24p. (J). 14.95 net. (978-1-61254-198-3(4)) Brown Books Publishing Group.
Enright, Robert D. Rising above the Storm Clouds: What It's Like to Forgive. Finney, Kathryn Kunz, illus. 2004. 32p. (J). 14.95 (978-1-59147-075-5(7)); pap. 9.95 (978-1-59147-076-2(5)) American Psychological Assn. (Magination Pr.).
Ephron, Delia. The Girl with the Mermaid Hair. 2010. (ENG.). 320p. (YA). (gr. 8-18). 16.99 (978-0-06-154260-2(1), HarperTeen) HarperCollins Pubs.
Esdaille-Richardson, Eudora. Malcolm & the Money Tree. Williams, Christopher, illus. 2014. 31p. (J). pap. (978-1-934370-49-0(5)) Editorial Campana.
Ethier, Vicki. I Know My Nana Rosa Is an Alien. Ethier, Vicki, illus. 2003. (Illus.). 20p. (J). 6.00 (978-1-928972-10-5(1)) Critter Pubns.
Evans, Richard. The Christmas Candle. Collins, Jacob, illus. 2006. (ENG.). 32p. (J). (gr. -1-3). 8.99 (978-1-4169-2682-5(8), Simon & Schuster Bks. For Young Readers) Simon & Schuster Bks. For Young Readers.
—The Tower: A Story of Humility. Linton, Jonathan, illus. 2014. (ENG.). 32p. (J). (gr. -1-3). 16.99 (978-1-4814-3111-8(0), Simon & Schuster/Paula Wiseman Bks.) Simon & Schuster/Paula Wiseman Bks.
Everett Hale, Edward. Last of the Peterkins with Others of the. 2006. pap. (978-1-4068-1087-5(8)) Echo Library.
Ewing, Juliana Horatia. The Brownies & Other Tales. 2007. 140p. per. (978-1-4065-2523-6(5)) Dodo Pr.
—A Great Emergency & Other Tales. 2007. 188p. per. (978-1-4065-2525-0(1)) Dodo Pr.
—Mary's Meadow: And Other Tales of Fields & Flowers. 2007. (ENG.). 154p. pap. 19.99 (978-1-4346-3334-7(9)); 168p. pap. 21.99 (978-1-4346-3335-4(7)) Creative Media Partners, LLC.
—The Peace Egg & Other Tales. 2007. 108p. per. (978-1-4065-2534-2(0)) Dodo Pr.
Farrar, F. W. Eric, or, Little by Little. 2007. 276p. per. (978-1-4065-1686-9(4)) Dodo Pr.
Farrar, Frederic William. Eric; or, Little by Little. 2006. 372p. per. 26.99 (978-1-4255-3870-5(3)) Michigan Publishing.
Feld, Ellen F. Rimfire: The Barrel Racing Morgan Horse. Mellin, Jeanne, illus. 2009. (ENG.). 206p. (J). pap. 9.95 (978-0-9709002-1-0(X)) Willow Bend Publishing.
Feldman, Jody. The Gollywhopper Games. Jamieson, Victoria, illus. (Gollywhopper Games Ser.: 1). (ENG.). (J). (gr. 3-7). 2013. 336p. pap. 6.99 (978-0-06-121452-3(3)) 2008. 320p. 16.99 (978-0-06-121450-9(7)) HarperCollins Pubs. (Greenwillow Bks.).
—The Gollywhopper Games. 2013. (Gollywhopper Games Ser.: 1). (J). lib. bdg. 17.20 (978-0-606-35508-7(1)) Turtleback Bks.
—The Gollywhopper Games - Friend or Foe. Jamieson, Victoria, illus. 2015. (Gollywhopper Games Ser.: 3). (ENG.). 432p. (J). (gr. 3-7). 16.99 (978-0-06-221128-6(5), Greenwillow Bks.) HarperCollins Pubs.
—The Gollywhopper Games - The New Champion. Jamieson, Victoria, illus. 2015. (Gollywhopper Games Ser.: 2). (ENG.). 400p. (J). (gr. 3-7). pap. 6.99 (978-0-06-221126-2(9), Greenwillow Bks.) HarperCollins Pubs.
Fenn, G. Manville. Brownsmith's Boy. 2008. 260p. 29.95 (978-1-60664-780-6(6)); pap. 15.95 (978-1-60664-154-5(9)) Aegypan.
Fern, Fanny. Little Ferns for Fanny's Little Friends by the Author of Fern Leaves. 2006. 320p. per. 23.99 (978-1-4255-3132-4(6)) Michigan Publishing.
Ferrier, Charlotte. Goldilocks & the Three Bears. 2016. (Fairytale Cottages Ser.). (ENG., Illus.). 12p. (J). (gr. -1-k). bds. 8.99 (978-0-7641-6817-8(7)) Barron's Educational Series, Inc.
Ferrin, Wendy Wakefield. Germs on Their Fingers! Tono, Lucia, tr. Broyles, Beverly Ashley, illus. 2003.Tr. of Germenes en Tus Manos! (SPA & ENG.). 64p. (J). (gr. 1-7). 17.95 (978-0-9703632-1-3(4)); pap. 12.95 (978-0-9703632-0-6(6)) Wakefield Connection, The.
Fielding, Sarah. The Governess or the Little Female Academy. 2004. reprint ed. pap. 1.99 (978-1-4192-6442-9(7)); pap. 19.95 (978-1-4191-6442-2(2)) Kessinger Publishing, LLC.
Fields, Terri. One Good Deed. Melmon, Deborah, illus. 2015. (ENG.). 24p. (J). (gr. -1-3). pap. 7.99 (978-1-4677-3479-0(9), Kar-Ben Publishing) Lerner Publishing Group.
—One Good Deed. Melmon, Deborah, illus. 2015. (ENG.). 24p. (J). (gr. -1-3). 17.99 (978-1-4677-3478-3(0)) Lerner Publishing Group.
Finding Our Way: True Stories of Dilemmas, Difficulties & Discoveries. 2004. (J). pap. 15.00 net. (978-0-9710606-3-0(0)) Streetside Stories, Inc.
Finlay, Lizzie. Little Croc's Purse. 2011. (ENG., Illus.). 36p. (J). (gr. -1-2). 15.00 (978-0-8028-5392-9(7)) Eerdmans, William B. Publishing Co.
Fish, Thomas R. & Ober, Jillian. Lucky Dogs, Lost Hats, & Dating Don'ts: Hi-Lo Stories about Real Life. 2012. (ENG., Illus.). 216p. (YA). pap. 21.95 (978-1-60613-156-5(7)) Woodbine Hse.
Fisher, Kimball. Finding Baby Jesus. 2015. 12p. (J). pap. 3.99 (978-1-4621-1698-0(1)) Cedar Fort, Inc./CFI Distribution.
Fitzer, Robin. Summer Stories. 2008. 45p. pap. 24.95 (978-1-60563-742-6(4)) America Star Bks.
Fitzmaurice, Kathryn. The Year the Swallows Came Early. (ENG.). (J). (gr. 4-7). 2011. 304p. pap. 6.99 (978-0-06-162500-8(0)) 2009. 288p. 16.99 (978-0-06-162497-1(7)) HarperCollins Pubs.
Fitzpatrick, Huntley. My Life Next Door. 2012. (ENG.). 400p. (YA). (gr. 7-18). 18.99 (978-0-8037-3699-3(1), Dial Bks) Penguin Young Readers Group.
Flanagan, Artie & Licari, Peter J. The Birth of Buzzard Baby, 1 vol. 2009. (ENG.). 31p. 24.95 (978-1-60836-706-1(1)) America Star Bks.
Flannigan, Liz. Cara & the Wizard, 2 vols. Docampo, Valeria, illus. 2013. (Magic Stories Ser.). (ENG.). 48p. (J). (gr. 1-4). pap. 8.99 (978-1-84686-780-4(0)) Barefoot Bks., Inc.
—Starlight Grey. Docampo, Valeria, illus. 2013. (Magic Stories Ser.). (ENG.). 48p. (J). (gr. 1-4). pap. 8.99 (978-1-84686-778-1(9)) Barefoot Bks., Inc.
Fleming, Ligia Morales. The Very Special Princess. 2012. (ENG.). 25p. (J). pap. 14.95 (978-1-4327-9665-5(8)) Outskirts Pr., Inc.
Fluharty, Kristi & Fluharty, T. Lively. Fool Moon Rising. Fluharty, Kristi & Fluharty, T. Lively, illus. 2009. (Illus.). 40p. (J). 16.99 (978-1-4335-0682-6(3)) Crossway.
Fogliano, Julie. If You Want to See a Whale. Stead, Erin E., illus. 2013. (ENG.). 32p. (J). (gr. -1-2). 17.99 (978-1-59643-731-9(6), 9781596437319) Roaring Brook Pr.
Fontaine, Catherine Silliman. Have a Not for Christmas ... & Always. 2006. (Illus.). 44p. (J). 11.95 (978-0-9776958-0-5(8)) CyPress Pubns.
Forbush, Kyle. The Sourdoughs' Five Children. Forbush, Lisa, illus. 2004. (J). bds. 6.95 (978-1-57833-258-8(3)) Todd Communications.
Friedman, Laurie. Campfire Mallory. 2009. pap. 34.95 (978-0-7613-4787-3(9)) Lerner Publishing Group.
—Campfire Mallory. Kalis, Jennifer, illus. (Mallory Ser.: 9). (ENG.). 176p. (J). (gr. 2-5). 2009. pap. 5.95 (978-1-58013-841-3(1), First Avenue Editions) 2008. lib. bdg. 15.95 (978-0-8225-7657-0(0), Carolrhoda Bks.) Lerner Publishing Group.
Futch, Dorothy R. All about Life: A Collection of Children Stories. 2009. 40p. pap. 21.99 (978-1-4415-2848-3(2)) Xlibris Corp.
Gallagher, Diana G. Friends Forever? The Complicated Life of Claudia Cristina Cortez, 1 vol. Garvey, Brann, illus. 2008. (Claudia Cristina Cortez Ser.). (ENG.). 88p. (gr. 2-3). pap. 6.10 (978-1-4342-0868-2(0)); lib. bdg. 26.65 (978-1-4342-0772-2(2)) Stone Arch Bks. (Claudia Cristina Cortez).
Gallego Garcia, Laura & Bellm, Dan. The Legend of the Wandering King. 2005. (J). (978-0-439-58557-6(0), Levine, Arthur A. Bks.) Scholastic, Inc.
Gallo, Donald R. No Easy Answer. 2014. 17.50 (978-1-63419-721-2(6)) Perfection Learning Corp.
Galvin, Laura Gates & Studio Mouse Editorial. Cinderella & Belle: Kindness Counts. Williams, Tracee, ed. 2008. (ENG., Illus.). 24p. (J). (gr. -1). 4.99 (978-1-59069-652-1(2)) Studio Mouse LLC.
Gamble, Shanae. God's Dogs go to Heaven: Christian myths & Fables. 2011. 28p. pap. 15.99 (978-1-4520-5424-7(X)) AuthorHouse.
Gannon, Patty. Desdemona & the Eggs. 2011. 52p. pap. 23.00 (978-1-4567-1581-6(X)) AuthorHouse.
Gano, Debra. Beauty's Secret. Pitre, Dawn, illus. 2008. (Heartlight Girls Ser.). 54p. (J). 17.95 (978-0-9787689-0-4(6)) Heartlight Girls.
Garcia, Joan. Footsteps of Angels. 2003. 52p. (J). pap. 11.95 (978-0-7414-1602-5(6)) Infinity Publishing.
Gardner, Graham. Inventing Elliot. 2005. 181p. (YA). 13.65 (978-0-7569-5704-9(4)) Perfection Learning Corp.
Gaskins, Terry & Treigle, Jimmy. The Very Big Storm: Created by Terry Gaskins Inspired by Jimmy Treigle. 2009. 28p. pap. 13.99 (978-1-4389-4220-9(6)) AuthorHouse.
Gassman, Julie. Crabby Pants, 1 vol. Watson, Richard, illus. 2012. (Little Boost Ser.). (ENG.). 32p. (gr. k-3). 7.95 (978-1-4048-7416-9(X), Little Boost) Picture Window Bks.
Gates, Josephine Scribner. The Story of Live Dolls: Being an Account of How, on a Certain June Morning. unabr. ed. 2012. (Illus.). 104p. 39.99 (978-1-4622-8158-9(3)) Repressed Publishing LLC.
Geiger, J. C. Wildman. 2017. (ENG.). 1p. (YA). (gr. 9-17). 17.99 **(978-1-4847-4957-9(X))** Hyperion Bks. for Children.
Geldart, Thomas. Emilie the Peacemaker. 2004. reprint ed. pap. 15.95 (978-1-4191-1769-5(6)); pap. 1.99 (978-1-4192-1769-2(0)) Kessinger Publishing, LLC.
Genhart, Michael. Ouch Moments: When Words Hurt. Garófoli, Viviana, illus. 2015. (J). (978-1-4338-1961-2(9), Magination Pr.) American Psychological Assn.
Geraldi, Michele J. Pennies at Piper Park. 2009. 24p. pap. 12.99 (978-1-4389-2829-6(7)) AuthorHouse.
Geras, Adèle. Lizzie's Wish. 2009. (Historical House Ser.). 144p. (YA). (gr. 5-18). pap. 5.99 (978-0-7945-2337-4(4), Usborne) EDC Publishing.
Gerhardt, Paul L. The Diversity King. 2007. 35p. 19.50 (978-0-615-16208-9(8)) Gerhardt, Paul L.
Getti, C. Bear's Prayer. 2011. 28p. pap. 15.99 (978-1-4568-7228-1(1)) Xlibris Corp.
Ghigna, Charles. Cuddle Bunny. East, Jacqueline, illus. 2015. (Tiny Tales Ser.). (ENG.). 64p. (gr. -1-2). lib. bdg. 23.99 (978-1-4795-6528-3(8)) Tiny Tales.
Gibson, Amy. By Day, by Night. So, Meilo, illus. 2014. (ENG.). 32p. (J). (gr. -1). 16.95 (978-1-59078-991-9(1)) Boyds Mills Pr.
Gilbert, George. George, Candy, & the Raccoon. Perez-Torres, Juliana, illus. 2008. 40p. pap. 16.99 (978-1-4389-2848-7(3)) AuthorHouse.
Gill, David Macinnis. Soul Enchilada. (ENG.). (YA). (gr. 9). 2010. 384p. pap. 8.99 (978-0-06-167303-0(X)) 2009. 368p. 16.99 (978-0-06-167301-6(3)) HarperCollins Pubs. (Greenwillow Bks.).
Godbersen, Anna. The Luxe. (ENG.). (YA). (gr. 9). 2008. (Luxe Ser.: 1). 464p. pap. 9.99 (978-0-06-134568-5(7)) 2007. (Luxe Ser.: No. 1). 448p. 17.99 (978-0-06-134566-1(0), HarperTeen) HarperCollins Pubs.
—Rumors. 2009. (Luxe Ser.: 2). (ENG.). 448p. (YA). (gr. 9). pap. 9.99 (978-0-06-134571-5(7)) 2008. (Luxe Ser.: No. 2). 456p. (J). pap. 17.99 (978-0-06-170950-0(6)) HarperCollins Pubs.
—Splendor. 2010. (Luxe Ser.: 4). (ENG.). 416p. (YA). (gr. 9). pap. 9.99 (978-0-06-162633-3(3)) HarperCollins Pubs.
Godwin, Jane. Falling from Grace. 2007. (ENG.). 204p. (J). (gr. 6-12). 16.95 (978-0-8234-2105-3(8)) Holiday Hse., Inc.
Goethals, Angela. The Sisterhood of the Traveling Pants. 2004. (Sisterhood of the Traveling Pants Ser.: Bk. 1). 320p. (YA). (gr. 7-18). pap. 40.00 incl. audio (978-0-8072-2286-7(0), Listening Library) Random Hse. Audio Publishing Group.
Going, K. L. Saint Iggy. 2008. (ENG., Illus.). 272p. (YA). (gr. 9-18). pap. 9.99 (978-0-15-206248-4(3)) Houghton Mifflin Harcourt Publishing Co.
Goldblatt, Mark. Finding the Worm. 2015. (ENG.). 352p. (J). (gr. 4-7). 16.99 (978-0-385-39108-5(0), Random Hse. Bks. for Young Readers) Random Hse. Children's Bks.
—Finding the Worm (Twerp Sequel) 2016. (ENG.). 368p. (J). (gr. 4-7). 7.99 (978-0-385-39111-5(0), Yearling) Random Hse. Children's Bks.
—Twerp. 2013. (ENG.). 288p. (J). (gr. 4-7). 16.99 (978-0-375-97142-6(4), Random Hse. Bks. for Young Readers) Random Hse. Children's Bks.
Golding, Jacqueline. Healing Stories: Picture Books for the Big & Small Changes in a Child's Life. 2006. (ENG.). 336p. per. 17.95 (978-1-59077-097-9(8)) Evans, M. & Co., Inc.
Goldolphin, Mary. Sandford & Merton. 2005. reprint ed. pap. 15.95 (978-1-4191-0539-5(6)) Kessinger Publishing, LLC.
Goldston, Juli-Ette Robin. Bowtie Brownlee Goes to School. 2012. 16p. pap. 14.99 (978-1-4685-9456-0(7)) AuthorHouse.
Gologan, Trena. Esther's Younique Crown. 2008. 32p. pap. 16.25 (978-1-4357-3544-6(7)) Lulu Pr., Inc.
González, Rigoberto & Alvarez, Cecilia Concepcion. Antonio's Card/la Tarjeta de Antonio. 2013. (ENG & SPA., Illus.). 32p. (J). 17.95 (978-0-89239-204-9(5)) Lee & Low Bks., Inc.
Goon, Geraldine. Grandma Tells Dozens of Stories. 2008. 64p. pap. (978-1-84748-515-1(4)) Athena Pr.
Gorrell, Nancy. Anna Banana. 2006. (ENG., Illus.). 96p. (J). (gr. -1-2). per. 6.99 (978-1-84550-182-2(9), 5a21ceaa-6b5b-4fb6-b215-15915b289e40) Christian Focus Pubns. GBR. Dist: Bookmasters Distribution.
Gosselink, John. The Defense of Thaddeus A. Ledbetter. 2010. (ENG., Illus.). 240p. (J). (gr. 3-7). 14.95 (978-0-8109-8977-1(8), Amulet Bks.) Abrams, Inc.
Got, Yves. Chambre de Didou. pap. 12.95 (978-2-226-12991-8(X)) Albin-Michel, Editions FRA. Dist: Distribooks, Inc.
Goto, Scott. Perfect Sword. Goto, Scott, illus. 2010. (ENG., Illus.). 48p. (J). (gr. 1-4). pap. 8.95 (978-1-57091-698-4(5)) Charlesbridge Publishing, Inc.
Grace, Amanda. In Too Deep. 2012. (ENG.). 240p. (YA). pap. 9.95 (978-0-7387-2600-7(1), Flux) North Star Editions.
Grady, Karen. It's Not My Fault, She Started It. 2005. (Illus.). (J). (978-1-59975-127-6(5)) Independent Pub.
Grandpa & Little Guy. 2004. (J). 15.95 (978-0-9764012-0-9(7)) Rockmill Publishing Co.
Grateful Steps Publishing & Tipton, Angela. Butterflies Don't Crawl. Irvine, Wil, illus. 2009. 32p. (J). 16.95 (978-1-935130-14-7(5)) Grateful Steps.
Graves, Peter, tr. from SWE. Nils Holgersson's Wonderful Journey Through Sweden, 2 vols. 2013. (ENG., Illus.). 360p. pap. 32.00 (978-1-870041-96-6(8)); 382p. pap. 32.00 (978-1-870041-97-3(6)) Norvik Pr. GBR. Dist: Dufour Editions, Inc.
Graziano-Straus, Laura. The Happy Crabby Crying Happy Family's Blessing, 1 vol. 2009. 47p. pap. 24.95 (978-1-60672-710-2(9)) America Star Bks.
Green, D. L. Zeke Meeks vs the Annoying Princess Sing-Along, 1 vol. Alves, Josh, illus. 2014. (Zeke Meeks Ser.). (ENG.). 128p. (gr. 2-2). 22.65 (978-1-4795-4828-6(6), Zeke Meeks) Picture Window Bks.
Green, Jacqueline. Kiss & Tell. 2015. (Truth or Dare Ser.: 3). (ENG.). 288p. (YA). (gr. 10-17). 18.00 (978-0-316-22033-0(7), Poppy) Little, Brown Bks. for Young Readers.
—Secrets & Lies. 2014. (Truth or Dare Ser.: 2). (ENG.). 336p. (YA). (gr. 10-17). pap. 21.99 (978-0-316-22030-9(2), Poppy) Little, Brown Bks. for Young Readers.
—Truth or Dare. (Truth or Dare Ser.: 1). (ENG.). (YA). (gr. 10-17). 2014. 416p. pap. 10.99 (978-0-316-22035-4(3)) 2013. 400p. 18.00 (978-0-316-22036-1(1)) Little, Brown Bks. for Young Readers. (Poppy).
Green, Tim. Football Hero. (Football Genius Ser.: 2). (ENG.). (J). (gr. 3-7). 2009. 320p. pap. 6.99 (978-0-06-112276-7(9)) 2008. (Illus.). 304p. 16.99 (978-0-06-112274-3(2)) HarperCollins Pubs.
—Football Hero. l.t. ed. 2008. (YA). 23.95 (978-1-4104-1116-7(8)) Thorndike Pr.
—Force Out. 2013. (ENG.). 288p. (J). (gr. 3-7). 16.99 (978-0-06-208959-5(5)) HarperCollins Pubs.
Greenberg, Nicki. The Naughtiest Reindeer Goes South. 2017. (Naughtiest Reindeer Ser.: 3). (ENG.). 32p. (J). (gr. -1-1). 12.99 **(978-1-76029-311-6(3))** Allen & Unwin AUS. Dist: Independent Pubs. Group.
Greene, Bette. Summer of My German Soldier. 2006. (Puffin Modern Classics Ser.). (ENG.). 240p. (J). (gr. 5-18). 7.99 (978-0-14-240651-9(1), Puffin Books) Penguin Young Readers Group.
Greene, Thomas. Whacked Out Wrestling: Memorial - A tale of Headlocks, Hurricanranas, & High School. 2007. 228p. pap. 14.95 (978-1-60145-175-0(X)) Booklocker.com, Inc.
Greenwood, Grace. Stories from Famous Ballads for Children by Grace Greenwood [Pseud] with Illustrations by Billings. 2006. 160p. per. 18.99 (978-1-4255-1221-7(6)) Michigan Publishing.
Gribnau, Joe. Kick the Cowboy, 1 vol. Tans, Adrian, illus. 2009. (ENG.). 32p. (J). (gr. k-3). 16.99 (978-1-58980-605-4(0)) Pelican Publishing Co., Inc.
Griffin, Donna. Dani & the Beans. 2008. 28p. pap. 13.50 (978-1-4389-1175-5(0)) AuthorHouse.
Grime, L. L. Little Tree. 2007. 48p. pap. 22.95 (978-1-4357-0092-5(9)) Lulu Pr., Inc.
Grimes, Nikki. Almost Zero: A Dyamonde Daniel Book. Christie, R. Gregory, illus. 2010. (Dyamonde Daniel Book Ser.: 3). (ENG.). 128p. (J). (gr. 2-4). 11.99 (978-0-399-25177-1(4), G.P. Putnam's Sons Books for Young Readers) Penguin Young Readers Group.
Grindley, Sally. Hurricane Wills. 2012. (ENG.). 256p. (J). (gr. -1-k). pap. 6.95 (978-1-61608-732-6(3), 608732, Sky Pony Pr.) Skyhorse Publishing Co., Inc.
Grosso, Alissa. Ferocity Summer. 2012. (ENG., Illus.). 288p. (YA). pap. 9.95 (978-0-7387-3070-7(X), Flux) North Star Editions.
Grovet, Heather. Super Star Problems. 2008. (J). pap. 5.97 (978-0-8163-2255-8(4)) Pacific Pr. Publishing Assn.
Gruber, Yehudit. The Power of Giving. 2013. 38p. pap. (978-965-550-204-6(X)) Contento De Semrik.
Guerra, Stephanie. Torn, 0 vols. 2012. (ENG.). 272p. (YA). (gr. 10-12). 17.99 (978-0-7614-6272-9(4), 9780761462729, Amazon Children's Publishing) Amazon Publishing.
Guinan, Jack. I'm a Lot of Sometimes: A Growing-Up Story of Identity. Rudebjer, Lars, illus. 2017. (Growing Up Ser.). (ENG.). 24p. (gr. -1-1). lib. bdg. 19.99 (978-1-63440-177-7(8)); 30.65 **(978-1-63440-181-4(6))** Red Chair Pr.
Guinn, Dolores Hollyfield. Frederick Frog & His Family: Being a Bully. 2008. 16p. per. 24.95 (978-1-4241-9223-6(4)) America Star Bks.
Gummelt, Donna & Melchiorre, Dondino. Your Name Is Mud. Wall, Randy Hugh, ed. Varela, Carmen, tr. Varela, Juan D., illus. l.t. ed. 2006.Tr. of Tu nombre es Mud. 34p. (J). 14.95 (978-0-9764798-3-3(4)) Story Store Collection Publishing.
Gunn, Robin Jones. Mrs. Rosey Posey & the Fine China Plate, 1 vol. Schofield, Christina Diane, illus. 2008. (I Can Read! Ser.). (ENG.). 32p. (J). (gr. -1-3). pap. 3.99 (978-0-310-71578-8(4)) Zonderkidz.
—Open Your Heart Vol. 3, Vol. 3. 2006. (Sierra Jensen Collection: Bks. 7-9). (ENG.). 480p. (J). (gr. 7-12). 15.99 (978-1-59052-590-6(6), Multnomah) Doubleday Religious Publishing Group, The.
—Sierra Jensen Collection, Vol. 4. 2006. (Sierra Jensen Collection: Bks. 10-12). (ENG.). 464p. (J). (gr. 7-12). 15.99 (978-1-59052-591-3(4), Multnomah) Doubleday Religious Publishing Group, The.
—Sierra Jensen Collection, Vol 1, Vol. 1. 2006. (Sierra Jensen Collection: Bks. 1-3). (ENG.). 432p. (J). (gr. 7-12). 15.99 (978-1-59052-588-3(4), Multnomah) Doubleday Religious Publishing Group, The.
Gurtler, Janet. If I Tell. 2011. (ENG.). 256p. (YA). (gr. 7-12). pap. 12.99 (978-1-4022-6103-9(9)) Sourcebooks, Inc.
—Secrets Beneath the Sea. Wood, Katie, illus. 2015. (Mermaid Kingdom Ser.). (ENG.). 288p. (gr. 3-5). 12.95 (978-1-62370-187-1(2)) Capstone Young Readers of Coughlan Cos.
—The Truth about Us. 2015. (ENG.). 320p. (YA). (gr. 8-12). pap. 9.99 (978-1-4022-7800-6(4), 9781402278006) Sourcebooks, Inc.
Gustke, Carol Davis. An Angel's First Job. 2008. (Illus.). 24p. (J). lib. bdg. (978-0-9801376-2-0(4)); per. (978-0-9801376-3-7(2)) Dragonfly Publishing, Inc.
Gutman, Dan. Roberto & Me. (Baseball Card Adventures Ser.). (ENG.). 192p. (J). (gr. 5-9). 2012. pap. 5.99 (978-0-06-123486-6(9)) 2010. 16.99 (978-0-06-123484-2(2)) HarperCollins Pubs.
—Roberto & Me. 2012. (Baseball Card Adventures Ser.). (J). lib. bdg. 16.00 (978-0-606-23591-4(4), Turtleback) Turtleback Bks.
—Ted & Me. 2012. (Baseball Card Adventures Ser.). (Illus.). 208p. (J). (gr. 5-9). (ENG.). 15.99 (978-0-06-123487-3(7)); lib. bdg. 16.89 (978-0-06-123488-0(5)) HarperCollins Pubs.
Guzman, Stephanie. Oliver the Clownfish: The Invitation Slip-up. 2008. (ENG., Illus.). (J). 14.95 (978-1-59664-001-6(4)) R J Communications, LLC.
Haar, Jaap Ter & Mearns, Martha. Boris. Poortvliet, Rien, illus. 2009. (J). pap. (978-0-921100-72-0(8)) Inheritance Pubns.
Haber, Tiffany Strelitz. The Monster Who Lost His Mean. Edmunds, Kirstie, illus. 2012. (ENG.). 40p. (J). (gr. -1-3). 17.99 (978-0-8050-9375-9(3), 9780805093759, Holt, Henry & Co. Bks. For Young Readers) Holt, Henry & Co.
Haddix, Margaret Peterson. Among the Betrayed. 2003. (Shadow Children Ser.: 3). (ENG.). 176p. (J). (gr. 4-9). pap. 7.99 (978-0-689-83909-2(X), Simon & Schuster Bks. For Young Readers) Simon & Schuster Bks. For Young Readers.
—Among the Betrayed. 2003. (Shadow Children Ser.: 3). (gr. 5-8). lib. bdg. 18.40 (978-0-613-90190-1(8), Turtleback) Turtleback Bks.
—Among the Enemy. 2006. (Shadow Children Ser.: Bk. 6). (Illus.). 214p. (gr. 3-7). 17.00 (978-0-7569-6792-5(9)) Perfection Learning Corp.
—Among the Enemy. (Shadow Children Ser.: 6). (ENG., (J). (gr. 3-7). 2006. Illus.). 240p. pap. 7.99 (978-0-689-85797-3(7)) 2005. 224p. 17.99 (978-0-689-85796-6(9)) Simon & Schuster Bks. For Young Readers. (Simon & Schuster Bks. For Young Readers).
—Among the Free. 2007. (Shadow Children Ser.: Bk. 7). 194p. (gr. 3-7). 17.00 (978-0-7569-7953-9(6)) Perfection Learning Corp.
—Among the Free. (Shadow Children Ser.: Bk. 7). (ENG., Illus.). 208p. (J). (gr. 3-7). 2007. pap. 7.99 (978-0-689-85799-7(3)) 2006. 18.99 (978-0-689-85798-0(5)) Simon & Schuster Bks. For Young Readers. (Simon & Schuster Bks. For Young Readers).
—Among the Free. 2007. (Shadow Children Ser.: 7). lib. bdg. 18.40 (978-1-4178-1424-4(1), Turtleback) Turtleback Bks.
Hagan, Jeannine Marie. Bethany. 2009. 60p. pap. 21.99 (978-1-4389-7290-9(3)) AuthorHouse.
Hager, Robert. Saurcana: Terror from the Sea. 2004. (J). (978-0-9727676-1-3(4)); pap. (978-0-9727676-0-6(6)) Hager, Robert.
Hahn, Mary Downing. Where I Belong. 2014. (ENG.). 240p. (J). (gr. 5-7). 16.99 (978-0-544-23020-0(5)) Houghton Mifflin Harcourt Publishing Co.
Haines, Kathryn Miller. The Girl Is Trouble. 2012. (ENG.). 336p. (YA). (gr. 7-12). 17.99 (978-1-59643-610-7(7)) Roaring Brook Pr.
Hale, Kathleen. No One Else Can Have You. 2014. (Kippy Bushman Ser.). (ENG.). 384p. (YA). (gr. 9). 17.99 (978-0-06-221119-4(6)) HarperCollins Pubs.
Hale, Lucretia Peabody. The Last of the Peterkins: With Others of Their Kin. 2007. (ENG.). 142p. pap. 18.99 (978-1-4346-2126-9(X)); 154p. pap. 21.99 (978-1-4346-2145-0(6)) Creative Media Partners, LLC.
Hall, Annalisa. Blanket of Comfort. 2008. 20p. 11.95 (978-0-615-22113-7(0)) Hall, Annalisa.

Hall, Mary Lou. Wirewalker. 2016. (ENG.). 304p. (YA). (gr. 7). 17.99 *(978-0-670-01646-4(2)*, Viking Books for Young Readers) Penguin Young Readers Group.

Hall, Stephen M. The Shepherd's Son. 2013. 36p. 25.99 *(978-1-4808-0112-7(7))*; pap. 16.99 *(978-1-4808-0078-6(3))* Archway Publishing.

Hallinan, P. K. Heartprints. 2004. (ENG., Illus.). 26p. (J). bds. 6.95 *(978-0-8249-6564-8(7)*, Ideal Pubns.) Worthy Publishing.

—I'm Thankful Each Day!/Doy Gracias Cada Día! 2008. (ENG., Illus.). 32p. (J). (gr. -1-3). per. 4.99 *(978-0-8249-5583-0(8)*, Ideal Pubns.) Worthy Publishing.

—Let's Be Happy. Hallinan, P. K., illus. 2005. (ENG., Illus.). 26p. (J). (gr. -1-1). bds. 7.95 *(978-0-8249-6588-4(4)*, Ideal Pubns.) Worthy Publishing.

—Let's Be Helpful. 2008. (ENG., Illus.). 26p. (J). bds. 7.95 *(978-0-8249-6563-1(9)*, Ideal Pubns.) Worthy Publishing.

Hallmark, Danna G. How Do I Feel Happy? How Do I Feel Sad? 2008. 36p. pap. 24.95 *(978-1-4241-9178-9(5))* PublishAmerica, Inc.

Hammond, James F. Ski Challenge. 2008. 100p. pap. 16.95 *(978-1-60703-493-3(X))* PublishAmerica, Inc.

Hansen, Roland. Jingle Jangles Smith. 2007. (Illus.). (J). per. 9.95 *(978-0-9801297-0-0(2))* G Publishing LLC.

—Tim the Cat. Jackson, Brittany Janay, illus. 2008. (ARA.). 28p. per. 8.85 *(978-0-9814650-0-5(5))* G Publishing LLC.

—Tim the Cat. 2007. (Illus.). 28p. (J). 8.95 *(978-0-9796978-0-7(8))* G Publishing LLC.

Hardie, Jill. The Sparkle Box: The Story of a Very Special Christmas Gift. Kornacki, Christine, illus. 2012. 32p. (J). 19.99 *(978-0-8249-5647-9(8)*, Ideal Pubns.) Worthy Publishing.

—The Sparkle Egg. Kornacki, Christine, illus. 2014. 32p. (J). 16.99 *(978-0-8249-5664-6(8)*, Ideal Pubns.) Worthy Publishing.

Hardman, Christy. Against the Giant. 2008. 267p. (gr. 3-7). pap. 16.99 *(978-1-59955-117-3(9))* Cedar Fort, Inc./CFI Distribution.

Hargreaves, Roger. Mr. Wrong. 2010. (Mr. Men & Little Miss Ser.). (ENG.). 32p. (J). (gr. -1-2). mass mkt. 3.99 *(978-0-8431-3335-6(X)*, Price Stern Sloan) Penguin Young Readers Group.

harkins, charles. Naptime Adventures of Luksi the Turtle. 2010. 174p. pap. 20.96 *(978-0-557-28695-9(6))* Lulu Pr., Inc.

Hamer, Ron. Suck It up Tate! Surrey, Michael, illus. 2008. 36p. pap. 11.95 *(978-1-59858-512-4(6))* Dog Ear Publishing, LLC.

Harris, Amber. Wisteria Jane. Hoyt, Ard, illus. 2015. (Wisteria Jane Book Ser.). (ENG.). 32p. (J). (gr. -1-3). 16.95 *(978-1-60554-411-3(6))* Redleaf Pr.

Harris, Odis Clinton. Wee Willie & the Lonely Pine. 2008. 23p. pap. 24.95 *(978-1-60563-741-9(6))* America Star Bks.

Harris, Robie H. Who We Are! All about Being the Same & Being Different. Westcott, Nadine Bernard, illus. 2016. (Let's Talk about You & Me Ser.). (ENG.). 40p. (J). (-k). 15.99 *(978-0-7636-6903-4(2))* Candlewick Pr.

Harris, Virginia. Charlie's Cage. 2008. 28p. pap. 15.99 *(978-1-4343-6892-8(0))* AuthorHouse.

Harris, Wendy. Daniel Visits the Library. 2015. (Daniel Tiger's Neighborhood Ready-To-Read Ser.). lib. bdg. 13.55 *(978-0-606-37875-8(8))* Turtleback Bks.

Harrop, Isobel. The Isobel Journal, 1 vol. 2014. (ENG.). 208p. (gr. 10-12). 16.95 *(978-1-63079-003-5(6))* Switch Pr.

Hartnett, Sonya. The Silver Donkey. Powers, Don, illus. 2014. (ENG.). 272p. (J). (gr. 5). 16.99 *(978-0-7636-7211-9(4))* Candlewick Pr.

—The Silver Donkey. Spudvilas, Anne, illus. 2004. viii, 193p. (J). *(978-0-670-04240-1(4)*, Viking Adult) Penguin Publishing Group.

Harvey, Sharon M. Virginia's Travel Basket. 2008. 76p. pap. 10.95 *(978-1-4327-3424-4(5))* Outskirts Pr., Inc.

Haughton, Chris. Oh No, George! Haughton, Chris, illus. 2015. (ENG., Illus.). 32p. (J). (-k). bds. 7.99 *(978-0-7636-7652-0(7))* Candlewick Pr.

Hautman, Pete. Blank Confession. (ENG.). 176p. (YA). (gr. 7). 2011. pap. 10.99 *(978-1-4169-1328-3(9))* 2010. 16.99 *(978-1-4169-1327-6(0))* Simon & Schuster Bks. For Young Readers. (Simon & Schuster Bks. For Young Readers).

Haworth, Katie. Terrible Tim! Hughes, Laura, illus. 2016. (ENG.). 32p. (J). (gr. -1-3). 16.99 *(978-1-4998-0137-8(8))* Little Bee Books Inc.

Hawthorne, Nathaniel. The Scarlet Letter. Moliken, Paul, ed. 2005. 212p. per. 4.99 *(978-1-58049-595-0(8)*, 200132) Prestwick Hse., Inc.

Hayes, Sonia. Ms. Thang. 2009. (ENG.). 200p. (YA). per. 9.95 *(978-0-9777573-0-5(7))* NUA Multimedia.

—Urban Goddess. 2007. 224p. (YA). per. 9.95 *(978-0-9777573-1-2(5))* NUA Multimedia.

Hays, Helen Ashe. The Adventures of Prince Lazybones: And Other Stories. 2007. 152p. pap. 19.99 *(978-1-4264-8474-2(7))*; 168p. pap. 21.99 *(978-1-4264-8532-9(8))* Creative Media Partners, LLC.

Haywood, Ebony. There Was Once a Potato. 2009. 42p. (J). pap. 21.95 *(978-1-4327-3871-6(2))* Outskirts Pr., Inc.

Heaton, Maria. Kangaroos Say Sorry, Too. 2006. (Neighborhood Readers Ser.). (ENG.). 12p. (gr. 1-3). pap. 5.90 *(978-1-4042-7030-5(2)*, Rosen Classroom) Rosen Publishing Group, Inc., The.

Hedji, Charles. Fields of Discovery. 2006. 220p. pap. 24.95 *(978-1-4241-0605-9(2))* PublishAmerica, Inc.

Hege, Evelyn. A Letter for Titus. 2004. (Illus.). 24p. (gr. -1-5). 2.70 *(978-0-7399-2345-0(5)*, 2791) Rod & Staff Pubs., Inc.

Heide, Florence Parry. Tales for the Perfect Child. Ruzzier, Sergio, illus. 2017. (ENG.). 112p. (J). (gr. 1-5). 16.99 *(978-1-4814-6379-9(9))* Simon & Schuster Children's Publishing.

Heide, Florence Parry & Van Clief, Sylvia Worth. Fables You Shouldn't Pay Any Attention To. Ruzzier, Sergio, illus. 2017. (ENG.). 112p. (J). (gr. 1-5). 16.99 *(978-1-4814-6382-9(9))* Simon & Schuster Children's Publishing.

Heller, Alyson. Time for T-Ball. Björkman, Steve, illus. 2010. (After-School Sports Club Ser.). (ENG.). 32p. (J). (gr. -1-1). pap. 3.99 *(978-1-4169-9412-1(2)*, Simon Spotlight) Simon Spotlight.

Helping Hands. 2004. (J). per. 15.99 *(978-0-9753533-8-7(1))* Golden Eagle Publishing Hse., Inc.

Henn, Sophy. Pass It On. Henn, Sophy, illus. 2017. (ENG., Illus.). 32p. (J). (gr. -1-2). 16.99 *(978-0-399-54775-1(4)*, Philomel Bks.) Penguin Young Readers Group.

Hennessy, Claire. Afterwards. 2005. 188p. (YA). pap. *(978-1-84223-207-1(X))* Poolbeg Pr.

Hennessy, James. Shane's Game. 2003. 184p. 23.95 *(978-0-595-74739-9(6))*; pap. 13.95 *(978-0-595-28112-1(5))* iUniverse, Inc.

Henty, George Alfred. True to the Old Flag. 2007. 286p. pap. 21.99 *(978-1-4264-4288-9(2))*; (ENG.). 318p. pap. 24.99 *(978-1-4264-4352-7(8))* Creative Media Partners, LLC.

—With Wolfe in Canad: The Winning of a Continent. 2011. 378p. pap. 19.95 *(978-1-61179-149-5(9))* Fireship Pr.

—With Wolfe in Canada: The Winning of a Continent. 2006. per. 8.95 *(978-1-57646-980-4(8))* Quiet Vision Publishing.

Heos, Bridget. Mustache Baby. Ang, Joy, illus. 2016. (ENG.). 36p. (J). (— 1). bds. 7.99 *(978-0-544-78984-5(9)*, HMH Books For Young Readers) Houghton Mifflin Harcourt Publishing Co.

Herman, Alison & Grossman, Lynne. Dolly Goes on Vacation. Eve, Lealand, illus. 2007. 22p. (J). 24.95 *(978-0-9746153-2-5(3))* DMH Pr., Inc.

—Dolly Goes to the Beach. Eve, Lealand, illus. 2007. 24p. (J). 24.95 *(978-0-9746153-1-8(5))* DMH Pr., Inc.

—Dolly Goes to the Supermarket. Eve, Lealand, illus. 2007. 22p. (J). 24.96 *(978-0-9746153-0-1(7))* DMH Pr., Inc.

Herman, Carli. Good Graffiti Teen Talk on Tough Issues. 2009. 108p. pap. 10.00 *(978-0-578-01524-8(2))* Black Bart Bks.

Hermes, Patricia. Emma Dilemma & the Camping Nanny, 0 vols. Carter, Abby, illus. 2009. (Emma Dilemma Ser.: 4). (ENG.). 144p. (J). (gr. 3-6). 15.99 *(978-0-7614-5534-9(5)*, 9780761455349, Amazon Children's Publishing) Amazon Publishing.

Hernandez, David. No More Us for You. 2009. (YA). 281p. lib. bdg. 17.89 *(978-0-06-117334-9(7))*; (ENG.). 288p. (gr. 9-18). 16.99 *(978-0-06-117333-2(9))* HarperCollins Pubs. (HarperTeen).

Herron, Edward A. The Return of the Alaskan: Mailboat in the Outpost. Langley, Gene, illus. 2011. 190p. 42.95 *(978-1-258-09093-7(7))* Literary Licensing, LLC.

Hetzer, Michael. The Get Well Picture. Clayton, Kim, illus. 2005. (J). (2nd collector's ed. 32p. 18.95 *(978-0-9728222-5-1(9))* 3rd ed. 18.95 *(978-0-9728222-6-8(7))* Webster Henrietta Publishing.

Hewlett, Stefanie & Foulk, Allison. Heart Stockings. McCann, Caroline, illus. 2015. (J). pap. 7.99 *(978-1-62972-159-0(X))* Deseret Bk. Co.

Hickey, Caroline. Isabelle's Boyfriend. 2009. (ENG.). 192p. (J). (gr. 6-9). pap. 18.99 *(978-0-312-60273-4(1)*, 9780312602734) Square Fish.

Hicks-Alessi, Nicole. Raccoon Hollow: Marky's Troubles. 2011. 40p. pap. 16.95 *(978-1-4560-6541-6(6))* America Star Bks.

Hidden. 2014. (ENG., Illus.). 384p. (YA). (gr. 7). 17.99 *(978-1-4424-8300-2(8)*, Simon & Schuster/Paula Wiseman Bks.) Simon & Schuster/Paula Wiseman Bks.

Higgins, M. G. Fish Boy, 1 vol. 2015. (Red Rhino Ser.). (ENG.). 68p. (J). (gr. 4-6). pap. 7.95 *(978-1-62250-953-9(6))* Saddleback Educational Publishing, Inc.

Hillert, Margaret. It's a Good Game, Dear Dragon. Schimmell, David, illus. 2009. (BeginningtoRead Ser.). 32p. (J). (gr. k-2). lib. bdg. 22.60 *(978-1-59953-293-6(X))* Norwood Hse. Pr.

—It's a Good Game, Dear Dragon (Es un Buen Juego, Querido Dragon) Del Risco, Eida, tr. from ENG. Schimmell, David, illus. 2010. (BeginningtoRead Ser.). (SPA & ENG.). 32p. (J). (gr. k-2). lib. bdg. 22.60 *(978-1-59953-362-9(6))* Norwood Hse. Pr.

Hillhouse, Joanne C. With Grace: By Joanne C. Hillhouse. Ward, Cherise, illus. 2017. (J). pap. *(978-1-934370-62-9(2))* Editorial Campana.

Hilmo, Tess. With a Name Like Love. 2013. (ENG.). 272p. (J). (gr. 5-9). pap. 10.99 *(978-1-250-02733-7(0)*, 9781250027337) Square Fish.

Hindmarsh, Ted C. The Elf & the Magic Windows: A Christmas Fairy Tale. 2008. pap. 2.99 *(978-1-59955-179-1(9))* Cedar Fort, Inc./CFI Distribution.

Hoban, Russell. The Little Brute Family. Peck, Lillian Hoban, illus. 2004. (Sunburst Bks.). 17.00 *(978-0-7569-3301-2(3))* Perfection Learning Corp.

—The Little Brute Family. Hoban, Lillian, illus. 2011. (My Readers Ser.). (ENG.). 40p. (J). (gr. k-2). pap. 3.99 *(978-0-312-56373-8(6)*, 9780312563738) Square Fish.

Hockerman, Dennis, illus. The Little Seed: A Tale about Integrity. 2006. (J). *(978-1-59939-094-9(9)*, Reader's Digest Young Families, Inc.) Studio Fun International.

Hodge, A. D. Bubbles & Boundaries. 2013. 32p. *(978-1-4602-2858-6(8))* FriesenPress.

Hoffmeister, Peter Brown. This Is the Part Where You Laugh. 2016. (ENG.). 336p. (YA). (gr. 9). 17.99 *(978-0-553-53810-6(1)*, Knopf Bks. for Young Readers) Random Hse. Children's Bks.

Hofland. The Barbadoes Girl: A Tale for Young People. 2007. (ENG.). 106p. pap. 18.99 *(978-1-4346-4485-5(5))*; 118p. pap. 19.99 *(978-1-4346-4486-2(3))* Creative Media Partners, LLC.

Holland, Frances. Ryan's Praying Mantis, 1 vol. 2009. 19p. pap. 24.95 *(978-1-60749-432-4(9))* PublishAmerica, Inc.

Holm, H. R. Against an Amber Sky. 2007. 214p. (gr. 3-7). per. 14.99 *(978-1-55517-991-5(6))* Cedar Fort, Inc./CFI Distribution.

—Forever Santa. 2009. 14p. (J). pap. 2.99 *(978-1-59955-345-0(7))* Cedar Fort, Inc./CFI Distribution.

Holmes, Donna M. Jacob & Isabell, 1 vol. 2009. 18p. pap. 24.95 *(978-1-60813-826-5(7))* America Star Bks.

Holmes, Harold H. The Tale of the Purple Chicken & Orange Frog. 2010. 26p. pap. 12.00 *(978-1-60911-653-8(4)*, Eloquent Bks.) Strategic Book Publishing & Rights Agency (SBPRA).

Holmes, Kathryn. The Distance Between Lost & Found. 2015. (ENG.). 304p. (YA). (gr. 8). 17.99 *(978-0-06-231726-1(1))* HarperCollins Pubs.

Holt, Kimberly Willis. Piggy's Sweet Potato Pie Lesson. 2007. (Illus.). 22p. (J). per. 18.99 *(978-0-9759691-4-4(5))* Catch 22 Publishing Inc.

Hoopes, Sandra. Original Cin. 2013. 266p. pap. 15.95 *(978-1-300-61344-2(0))* Lulu Pr., Inc.

Hopkinson, Deborah. A Bandit's Tale: The Muddled Misadventures of a Pickpocket. 2016. (ENG.). 304p. (J). (gr. 3-7). lib. bdg. 19.99 *(978-0-385-75500-9(7)*, Knopf Bks. for Young Readers) Random Hse. Children's Bks.

Horatio Alger Jr. Cast upon the Breakers. l.t. ed. 2007. 226p. pap. 22.99 *(978-1-4264-8224-3(8))* Creative Media Partners, LLC.

Hotton, Rick. Holy Mole: Life Is What You Make It: Subtle Wisdom from an Unconventional Comic Strip. 2013. (ENG.). 96p. pap. *(978-1-62343-164-8(6))* Willow Creek Pr., Inc.

House, Brandy. Scorch the Dragon, 1 vol. 2009. 32p. pap. 24.95 *(978-1-60749-209-2(1))* America Star Bks.

—Under a Toadstool, 1 vol. 2009. 12p. pap. 24.95 *(978-1-60836-290-5(6))* America Star Bks.

House, Peggy. Prairie Anna. 2012. (J). *(978-1-60682-395-8(7))* BJU Pr.

Howard, Velma Swanston, tr. Wonderful Adventures of Nils. 2013. 354p. pap. *(978-1-78139-369-7(9))* Benediction Classics.

Howe, James. The Misfits. 2003. (gr. 7-12). lib. bdg. 18.40 *(978-0-613-66423-3(X)*, Turtleback) Turtleback Bks.

Howe, Norma. The Adventures of Blue Avenger. unabr. ed. 2004. (Blue Avenger Ser.). 240p. (J). (gr. 6-18). pap. 36.00 incl. audio *(978-0-8072-8423-0(8)*, YA167SP, Listening Library) Random Hse. Audio Publishing Group.

Howitt, Mary Botham. Strive & Thrive a Tale by Mary Howitt. 2006. 180p. per. 18.99 *(978-1-4255-1426-6(X))* Michigan Publishing.

Hueller, Andy. Skipping Stones at the Center of the Earth: A Middle Grade Novel. 2011. (J). pap. 8.99 *(978-1-59955-488-4(7)*, Bonneville Bks.) Cedar Fort, Inc./CFI Distribution.

Hughes, Dean. The Dean Hughes Collection: Soldier Boys; Search & Destroy; Missing in Action. 2015. (ENG., Illus.). 752p. (YA). (gr. 7). pap. 29.99 *(978-1-4814-3997-8(9)*, Atheneum Bks. for Young Readers) Simon & Schuster Children's Publishing.

—Soldier Boys. 2004. 230p. (gr. 7-12). 17.00 *(978-0-7569-4566-4(6))* Perfection Learning Corp.

—Soldier Boys. 2003. (ENG.). 240p. (YA). (gr. 7-12). mass mkt. 7.99 *(978-0-689-86021-8(8)*, Simon Pulse) Simon Pulse.

—Soldier Boys. 2015. (ENG., Illus.). 240p. (YA). (gr. 7). pap. 10.99 *(978-1-4814-2704-3(0)*, Atheneum Bks. for Young Readers) Simon & Schuster Children's Publishing.

Hughes, Patricia A. Tommy Learns a Great Secret. 2012. 48p. pap. 21.88 *(978-1-4669-1186-4(7))* Trafford Publishing.

Hull, Bunny. Young Masters: The Magic Eye. Fleming, Kye, illus. 2007. (Young Masters Ser.). (J). (gr. -1). 13.95 incl. audio compact disk *(978-0-9721478-7-3(X))* BrassHeart Music.

Humphrey, Anna. Mission (un)Popular. 2013. (ENG.). 416p. (J). (gr. 5-9). pap. 6.99 *(978-1-4231-2321-7(2))* Hyperion Pr.

Hunter, T. H. Car Key Elves. Gavrilovskiy, Olga, illus. 2008. 32p. (J). 16.95 *(978-0-9788085-1-8(7))* Tetoca Pr.

Hurley, Tonya. The Blessed. Watkins, Abbey, illus. 2012. (Blessed Ser.). (ENG.). 416p. (YA). (gr. 9). 17.99 *(978-1-4424-2951-2(8)*, Simon & Schuster Bks. For Young Readers) Simon & Schuster Bks. For Young Readers.

—Passionaries. (Blessed Ser.). (ENG., Illus.). 368p. (YA). (gr. 9). 2015. pap. 12.99 *(978-1-4424-2955-0(0))* 2014. 17.99 *(978-1-4424-2954-3(2))* Simon & Schuster Bks. For Young Readers. (Simon & Schuster Bks. For Young Readers).

—Precious Blood. Watkins, Abbey, illus. 2013. (Blessed Ser.). (ENG.). 432p. (YA). (gr. 9). pap. 9.99 *(978-1-4424-2952-9(6)*, Simon & Schuster Bks. For Young Readers) Simon & Schuster Bks. For Young Readers.

Hurwitz, Michele Weber. The Summer I Saved the World ... in 65 Days. 2015. (ENG.). 272p. (J). (gr. 5). pap. 9.99 *(978-0-385-37109-4(8)*, Ember) Random Hse. Children's Bks.

Hyatt, Patricia Rusch. The Quite Contrary Man: A True American Tale. Brown, Kathryn, illus. 2011. (ENG.). 32p. (J). (gr. 1-4). 16.95 *(978-0-8109-4065-9(5)*, Abrams Bks. for Young Readers) Abrams, Inc.

Idle, Molly. Flora & the Penguin. 2014. (ENG., Illus.). 40p. (J). (gr. -1-k). 16.99 *(978-1-4521-2891-7(X))* Chronicle Bks. LLC.

Ikeda, Daisaku. The Princess & the Moon. McCraughrean, Geraldine, tr. from JPN. Wildsmith, Brian, illus. 2013. 6.95 *(978-1-935523-58-1(9))* World Tribune Pr.

Ireland, Justina. Vengeance Bound. 2013. (ENG.). 320p. (YA). (gr. 9). 17.99 *(978-1-4424-4462-1(2)*, Simon & Schuster Bks. For Young Readers) Simon & Schuster Bks. For Young Readers.

Irwin, Kate. Alfie's Great Escape. Elsom, Clare, illus. 2016. (Reading Ladder Ser.). (ENG.). 48p. (J). (gr. k-2). 7.99 *(978-1-4052-8217-8(7))* Egmont Bks., Ltd. GBR. Dist: Independent Pubs. Group.

Jackson, Bobby L. Boon the Raccoon & Easel the Weasel. Rodriguez, Christina, illus. 2004. 32p. (J). pap. 11.95 *(978-1-884242-03-8(0)*, BREW2NED); 19.95 *(978-1-884242-02-1(2)*, BREW2NED) Multicultural Pubns.

Jackson, Kristina. The Plot Bunny. Winfield, Amy, illus. 2013. 24p. pap. *(978-1-909202-15-3(0))* Little Acorns Publishing.

Jacqueline, Thomas. Birthday Picnic. 2010. 24p. pap. 9.99 *(978-0-88144-493-3(6))* Yorkshire Publishing Group.

Jan, Young. Starting the Colt. 2014. (ENG.). 174p. (J). pap. 12.00 *(978-1-937849-10-8(4))* Raven Publishing Inc. of Montana.

Jean, Penny. Holding Grace. 2008. 28p. pap. 24.95 *(978-1-60441-692-3(0))* America Star Bks.

Jempsa, Alice B. Why Does Everything Happen to Me? 2011. 28p. (gr. -1). pap. 13.54 *(978-1-4269-5005-6(5))* Trafford Publishing.

Jenkins, A. M. Night Road, No. 1. 2008. (ENG.). 368p. (YA). (gr. 8-18). 16.99 *(978-0-06-054604-5(2)*, HarperTeen) HarperCollins Pubs.

—Repossessed. 2008. (ENG.). 240p. (YA). (gr. 8). pap. 9.99 *(978-0-06-083570-5(2)*, HarperTeen) HarperCollins Pubs.

Jenkins, Jerry B. & Fabry, Chris. The Author's Blood. 2008. (Wormling Ser.: 5). (ENG.). 368p. (J). (gr. 5-9). per. 7.99 *(978-1-4143-0159-4(6)*, Tyndale Kids) Tyndale Hse. Pubs.

—The Book of the King. 2007. (Wormling Ser.: 1). (ENG.). 288p. (J). (gr. 5-9). per. 7.99 *(978-1-4143-0155-6(3))* Tyndale Hse. Pubs.

—The Changeling. 2007. (Wormling Ser.: 3). (ENG.). 336p. (J). (gr. 5-9). per. 7.99 *(978-1-4143-0157-0(X))* Tyndale Hse. Pubs.

—El Libro del Rey. 2008. (Lombricero Ser.: 1).Tr. of Book of the King. (SPA.). 304p. (J). pap. 7.99 *(978-1-4143-2216-2(X)*, Tyndale Espanol) Tyndale Hse. Pubs.

Jennings, Patrick. Lucky Cap. 2011. (ENG.). 224p. (J). (gr. 4-7). 15.99 *(978-1-60684-054-2(1)*, Carolrhoda Bks.) Lerner Publishing Group.

Jesse, Mary. Abbey & Friends M Is for Manners. Cherif, Jennifer, illus. 2003. 48p. (J). 15.95 *(978-0-9729958-0-1(3))* Hexagon Blue.

Jo-Marie. Adi's World. 2013. 198p. 33.99 *(978-1-4497-9417-0(3))*; pap. 17.99 *(978-1-4497-9416-3(5))* Author Solutions, Inc. (WestBow Pr.).

Johansen, K. V. Treason in Eswy, 1 vol. 2008. (ENG., Illus.). 192p. (YA). (gr. 7-12). pap. 9.95 *(978-1-55143-888-7(7))* Orca Bk. Pubs. USA.

John, Jory. The Bad Seed. Oswald, Pete, illus. 2017. 40p. (J). (gr. -1-3). 17.99 ***(978-0-06-246776-8(X))*** HarperCollins Pubs.

Johnson, Angela. Sweet, Hereafter. 2010. (ENG.). 128p. (YA). (gr. 7-18). 16.99 *(978-0-689-87385-0(9)*, Simon & Schuster Bks. For Young Readers) Simon & Schuster Bks. For Young Readers.

Johnson, Antonia. Bianca's Light. 2009. 28p. pap. 14.99 *(978-1-4389-8951-8(2))* AuthorHouse.

Johnson-Choong, Shelly. The Jewelry Box. 2nd ed. 2004. (YA). reprint ed. pap. 10.95 *(978-1-932280-40-1(5)*, 80405) Granite Publishing & Distribution.

Johnson, Ken & Myers, Bill. The Big Lie: A Star in the Breaking / The Not-so-Great Escape. 2015. (McGee & Me! Ser.). (ENG.). 256p. (J). pap. 9.99 *(978-1-4964-0329-2(0))* Tyndale Hse. Pubs.

Johnson, Margaret. Selfish & the Blue Box. 2008. 28p. pap. 24.95 *(978-1-60563-992-5(3))* America Star Bks.

Johnson, Regan. Little Bunny Kung Fu. Johnson, Regan, illus. 2005. (ENG., Illus.). 32p. (J). (gr. -1 — 1). 14.95 *(978-0-9769417-8-1(3))* Blooming Tree Pr.

Johnston, Annie Fellows. The Little Colonel. 2004. reprint ed. pap. 1.99 *(978-1-4192-7020-8(6))* Kessinger Publishing, LLC.

Johri, Subia Ali. The Snackman & His Son, 1 vol. Johri, Shaan Mohammad, illus. 2010. 28p. 24.95 *(978-1-4512-0978-5(9))* America Star Bks.

Jones, Bryan E. Somebody Stole My Yawn! Embry, Stacey, illus. 2009. 28p. pap. 24.95 *(978-1-60749-877-3(4))* America Star Bks.

Jones, Juanita. Mr. Nice Guy. 2003. (YA). per. *(978-0-9740833-7-7(2))* Port Town Publishing.

Jones, Kimberly K. The Genie Scheme. (ENG.). 192p. (J). (gr. 3-7). 2010. pap. 6.99 *(978-1-4424-0304-8(7))* 2009. 15.99 *(978-1-4169-5554-2(2))* McElderry, Margaret K. Bks. (McElderry, Margaret K. Bks.).

Jones, Lara. Me Gusta Mi Orinal. (SPA.). 10p. 17.95 *(978-84-272-7865-3(9))* Molino, Editorial ESP. Dist: Distribooks, Inc.

Jones, Patrick. Controlled. 2014. (Alternative Ser.). (ENG.). 112p. (YA). (gr. 6-12). pap. 7.95 *(978-1-4677-4483-6(2)*, Darby Creek); lib. bdg. 27.93 *(978-1-4677-3902-3(2))* Lerner Publishing Group.

—Doing Right. 2015. (J). 27.99 *(978-1-4677-7691-2(2))*; (ENG.). 104p. (gr. 6-12). lib. bdg. 27.99 *(978-1-4677-5803-1(5))* Lerner Publishing Group.

—Guarding Secrets. 2015. (J). 9.99 *(978-1-4677-7694-3(7))*; (ENG.). 96p. (gr. 6-12). lib. bdg. 27.99 *(978-1-4677-5801-7(9))* Lerner Publishing Group.

—Out of the Tunnel. 2014. (Red Zone Ser.: 1). (ENG.). 104p. (YA). (gr. 6-12). pap. 7.95 *(978-1-4677-4471-3(9)*, Darby Creek); lib. bdg. 27.93 *(978-1-4677-2126-4(3))* Lerner Publishing Group.

—Returning to Normal. 2015. (J). 104p. 9.99 *(978-1-4677-7700-1(5))*; (ENG.). 112p. (gr. 6-12). lib. bdg. 27.99 *(978-1-4677-5799-7(3))* Lerner Publishing Group.

—Slammed: Honda Civic. 2013. (Turbocharged Ser.). (ENG.). 96p. (gr. 6-12). pap. 7.95 *(978-1-4677-1478-5(X))*; lib. bdg. 27.93 *(978-1-4677-1245-3(0))* Lerner Publishing Group. (Darby Creek).

—Target. 2014. (Alternative Ser.). (ENG.). 128p. (YA). (gr. 6-12). pap. 7.95 *(978-1-4677-4485-0(9)*, Darby Creek); lib. bdg. 27.93 *(978-1-4677-3900-9(6))* Lerner Publishing Group.

Jones, Patrick & Chartier, Brent. At All Costs. 2014. (Red Zone Ser.: 4). 104p. (YA). (gr. 6-12). (ENG.). pap. 7.95 *(978-1-4677-4475-1(1))*; lib. bdg. 27.93 *(978-1-4677-2129-5(8))* Lerner Publishing Group. (Darby Creek).

Jones, Pixy. Teen Dumb Come. 2008. 285p. pap. 17.50 *(978-0-557-00089-0(0))* Lulu Pr., Inc.

Jones, Shelley Lynn. The Story of Corey & Alice. 2005. (J). pap. 8.00 *(978-0-8059-6846-0(6))* Dorrance Publishing Co., Inc.

Jones, Traci L. Standing Against the Wind. 2010. (ENG.). 208p. (YA). (gr. 7-9). pap. 11.99 *(978-0-312-62293-0(7)*, 9780312622930) Square Fish.

Jones, Vickie E. The Many Worlds of Sachsawan. 2012. 62p. 19.95 *(978-1-4626-5957-9(8))* America Star Bks.

Joosse, Barbara M. Please Is a Good Word to Say. Plecas, Jennifer, illus. 2007. (J). *(978-1-4287-4649-7(8)*, Philomel) Penguin Publishing Group.

The Jupiter Pirates - Curse of the Iris. 2014. (Jupiter Pirates Ser.: 2). (ENG.). 352p. (J). (gr. 3-7). 16.99 *(978-0-06-223023-2(9))* HarperCollins Pubs.

Kalz, Jill. I Hate to Read: Belle Pepper. 2004. (Illus.). 32p. (J). pap. 9.95 *(978-0-89812-521-4(9)*, Creative Paperbacks) Creative Co., The.

Karst, Patrice. The Smile That Went Around the World. 2009. (Illus.). 32p. (J). (gr. -1-4). 15.95 *(978-0-87516-827-2(2)*, Devorss Pubns.) DeVorss & Co.

Kate Breding. The Revolution of Cool. 2010. 108p. 20.95 *(978-1-4502-0803-1(7))* iUniverse, Inc.

Kato, Etsuo. The King Who Saved the Dove. Yasui, Koji, illus. 2014. (J). 8.95 *(978-1-935523-68-0(6))* World Tribune Pr.

Kavasch, E. Barrie. Dream Catcher. Holland, Gay W., illus. 2003. (Books for Young Learners). (ENG.). 16p. (J). 5.75 net. *(978-1-57274-257-4(7)*, 2733, Bks. for Young Learners) Owen, Richard C. Pubs., Inc.

Keeling, Annie E. Andrew Golding A Tale of the Great Plague. 2004. reprint ed. pap. 15.95 *(978-1-4191-0694-1(5))*; pap. 1.99 *(978-1-4192-0694-8(X))* Kessinger Publishing, LLC.

C
D

Kellogg, Elijah. Charlie Bell, the Waif of Elm Island by Rev Elijah Kellogg. 2006. 352p. per. 23.99 (978-1-4255-3559-9(3)) Michigan Publishing.

—The Young Shipbuilders of Elm Island by Rev Elijah Kellogg. 2006. 316p. per. 23.99 (978-1-4255-3063-1(X)) Michigan Publishing.

Kelly, Dot Hutchinson. Meet Moses Mcrae. 2008. 112p. 21.49 (978-1-4389-1787-0(2)); pap. 10.99 (978-1-4389-1786-3(4)) AuthorHouse.

Kelly, Lynne. Chained, 1 vol. 2012. (ENG.). 256p. (J). (gr. 5-9). 17.99 (978-0-374-31237-4(0), 9780374312374, Farrar, Straus & Giroux (BYR)) Farrar, Straus & Giroux.

Kelly, Matthew. Why Am I Here? A Story about Becoming The-Best-Version-of-Yourself! Mitchell, Hazel, illus. 2009. 60p. (J). 17.99 (978-0-9841318-0-8(9)) Beacon Publishing.

Kemnitz, Dianna. King Eli Speaks to Jack. 2012. 38p. 24.95 (978-1-4626-6727-7(9)) America Star Bks.

Kenley, Holli. Another Way: A Novel. 2015. 155p. (YA). pap. (978-1-61599-259-1(6)) Loving Healing Pr., Inc.

Kenneally, Miranda. Things I Can't Forget. 2013. (Hundred Oaks Ser.: Bk. 3). (ENG.). 320p. (YA). (gr. 7-12). pap. 9.99 (978-1-4022-7190-8(5), 9781402271908) Sourcebooks, Inc.

Kennedy, Claire. After Hours. 2015. (ENG., Illus.). 256p. (YA). (gr. 9). 17.99 (978-1-4814-3016-6(5), Simon Pulse) Simon Pulse.

Kenney, Cindy. Cool Hand Cuke Vol. 5: A Lesson in Giving, 1 vol. Moore, Michael, illus. 2006. (Big Idea Books / VeggieTown Values Ser.: Bk. 5). (ENG.). 32p. (J). (gr. -1-3). pap. 3.99 (978-0-310-70738-7(2)) Zonderkidz.

Kenney, Cindy, et al. Frog Wars, 1 vol. 2005. (Big Idea Books / VeggieTown Values Ser.: Bk. 2). (ENG., Illus.). 32p. (J). pap. 3.99 (978-0-310-70627-4(0)) Zonderkidz.

—Veggietown Voyage, 1 vol. Moore, Michael, illus. 2013. (Big Idea Books / VeggieTales Ser.). (ENG.). 96p. (J). 7.99 (978-0-310-72352-3(3)) Zonderkidz.

Kephart, Beth. The Heart Is Not a Size. 2010. (ENG.). 256p. (YA). (gr. 8-18). 16.99 (978-0-06-147048-6(1), HarperTeen) HarperCollins Pubs.

Keplinger, Kody. A Midsummer's Nightmare. 2013. (ENG.). 304p. (YA). (gr. 10-17). pap. 9.99 (978-0-316-08421-5(2), Poppy) Little, Brown Bks. for Young Readers.

Kerline, Joni M. Sebastian Breaks for Freedom, 1. 2006. (Illus.). 30p. (J). 19.95 (978-0-9776772-0-7(6)) KidBookInk Publishing, LLC.

Kerr, M. E., pseud. Your Eyes in Stars. 2006. (YA). (gr. 7-12). (ENG.). 240p. 16.99 (978-0-06-075682-6(9)); 229p. lib. bdg. 17.89 (978-0-06-075683-3(7)) HarperCollins Pubs.

Kerrin, Jessica Scott. In High Gear! Kelly, Joseph, illus. 2008. (Martin Bridge Ser.). (ENG.). 112p. (J). (gr. 2-5). pap. 6.95 (978-1-55453-157-8(8)) Kids Can Pr., Ltd. CAN. Dist: Hachette Bk. Group.

Khan, Rukhsana. Big Red Lollipop. Blackall, Sophie, illus. 2010. (ENG.). 40p. (J). (gr. -1-3). 16.99 (978-0-670-06287-4(1), Viking Books for Young Readers) Penguin Young Readers Group.

Kidd, Dorothy. Tina's Tail, 1 vol. 2010. 20p. pap. 24.95 (978-1-4489-5974-7(8)) PublishAmerica, Inc.

Kidd, Ronald. The Year of the Bomb. 2009. (ENG.). 208p. (YA). (gr. 7). pap. 5.99 (978-1-4169-9625-5(7)); 16.99 (978-1-4169-5892-5(4)) Simon & Schuster Bks. For Young Readers. (Simon & Schuster Bks. For Young Readers).

—Year of the Bomb. 2009. 208p. 5.99 (978-1-4169-9504-3(8)) Studio Fun International.

Kiely, Brendan. The Gospel of Winter. 2015. (ENG., Illus.). 320p. (YA). (gr. 9). pap. 11.99 (978-1-4424-8490-0(X), McElderry, Margaret K. Bks.) McElderry, Margaret K. Bks.

Kijinski, Paul. Camp Limestone. 2006. (Illus.). 104p. (YA). per. 7.99 (978-1-59958-016-6(0)) Journey Stone Creations, LLC.

Kincaid, S. J. Catalyst. 2014. (Insignia Ser.: 3). (ENG.). 432p. (YA). (gr. 8). 17.99 (978-0-06-209305-9(3), Tegen, Katherine Bks) HarperCollins Pubs.

—Vortex. 2013. (Insignia Ser.: 2). (ENG.). 400p. (YA). (gr. 8). 17.99 (978-0-06-209302-8(9), Tegen, Katherine Bks) HarperCollins Pubs.

Kindl, Patrice. Don't You Trust Me? 2016. (ENG., Illus.). 256p. (YA). (gr. 7). 17.99 (978-1-4814-5910-5(4)) Simon & Schuster Children's Publishing.

Kingsbury, Karen. The Brave Young Knight, 1 vol. Grimard, Gabrielle, illus. 2011. (ENG.). 40p. (J). (gr. -1-2). 15.99 (978-0-310-71645-7(4)) Zonderkidz.

—The Princess & the Three Knights, 1 vol. Grimard, Gabrielle, illus. 2009. (ENG.). 40p. (J). (gr. -1-2). 15.99 (978-0-310-71641-9(1)) Zonderkidz.

Kingsbury, Karen & Smith, Alex. Go Ahead & Dream. Banning, Greg, illus. 2013. (ENG.). 32p. (J). (gr. -1-3). 17.99 (978-0-06-168625-2(5)) HarperCollins Pubs.

Kipling, Rudyard. The Jungle Book: A Classic Story about Uniqueness. 2003. (Illus.). 32p. per. 3.95 (978-0-9747133-1-1(7), Values to Live By Classic Stories) Thomas, Frederic Inc.

Kirby, Jessi. Golden. (ENG.). 288p. (YA). (gr. 7). 2014. pap. 9.99 (978-1-4424-5218-3(8)) 2013. 16.99 (978-1-4424-5216-9(1)) Simon & Schuster Bks. For Young Readers. (Simon & Schuster Bks. For Young Readers).

Kiss, Kay. Mr B T Bumblebee. 2007. 28p. per. 11.95 (978-1-4327-1744-5(8)) Outskirts Pr., Inc.

Kizer, Amber. Pieces of Me. 2014. (ENG.). 304p. (YA). (gr. 7). 16.99 (978-0-385-74116-3(2), Delacorte Pr.) Random Hse. Children's Bks.

Klass, David & Klass, Perri. Second Impact. 2013. (ENG.). 288p. (YA). (gr. 7). 16.99 (978-0-374-37996-4(3), 9780374379964, Farrar, Straus & Giroux (BYR)) Farrar, Straus & Giroux.

—Second Impact. 2014. (ENG.). 304p. (YA). (gr. 7). pap. 10.99 (978-1-250-04436-5(7), 9781250044365) Square Fish.

Klein, Abby. The Pumpkin Elf Mystery. McKinley, John, illus. 2007. (Ready, Freddy! Ser.: Bk. 11). 95p. (J). (gr. -1-3). 11.65 (978-0-7569-8301-7(0)) Perfection Learning Corp.

Klick, Kenn. Little Coyote Tales. 2007. 128p. pap. 12.95 (978-0-615-16770-1(5)) BlueCougar Studios.

Klise, Kate. Secrets of the Circus. Klise, M. Sarah, illus. 2016. (Three-Ring Rascals Ser.: 5). (ENG.). 128p. (J). (gr. 2-5). pap. 5.95 (978-1-61620-640-6(3)); 15.95 (978-1-61620-566-9(0)) Algonquin Bks. of Chapel Hill.

Koja, Kathe. Buddha Boy. 2004. (ENG.). 128p. (YA). (gr. 7-11). reprint ed. 6.99 (978-0-14-240209-2(5), Speak) Penguin Young Readers Group.

—Buddha Boy. 2004. 117p. (gr. 3-7). 16.00 (978-0-7569-3117-9(7)) Perfection Learning Corp.

Kormos, Lawrence A. The Fate of Old Joe Malone. 2007. (Illus.). (J). (978-1-55452-191-3(2)) Essence Publishing.

Kranz, Linda. Only One You. (ENG., Illus.). 32p. (J). (gr. -1-17). 2006. 12.95 (978-0-87358-901-7(7)) Vol. 2013. bds. 7.95 (978-1-58979-748-2(5)) Cooper Square Publishing Llc.

—Only One You. Mlawer, Teresa, tr. from ENG. 2014. (ENG & SPA., Illus.). 32p. (J). (gr. -1-1). 12.95 (978-1-63076-023-6(4)) Taylor Trade Publishing.

Kroll, Steven. Sweet America: An Immigrant's Story. 2004. 172p. (J). lib. bdg. 16.92 (978-1-4242-0773-2(8)) Fitzgerald Bks.

—When I Dream of Heaven: Angelina's Story. 2004. 156p. (J). lib. bdg. 16.92 (978-1-4242-0770-1(3)) Fitzgerald Bks.

Krulik, Nancy. Holly's Jolly Christmas. John and Wendy Staff, illus. 2009. (Katie Kazoo, Switcheroo Ser.: No. 8). (ENG.). 160p. (J). (gr. 2-4). pap. 4.99 (978-0-448-45218-0(9), Grosset & Dunlap) Penguin Young Readers Group.

Kulper, Kendall. Drift & Dagger. 2015. (ENG.). 368p. (YA). (gr. 7-17). 18.00 (978-0-316-40453-2(5)) Little, Brown Bks. for Young Readers.

Laboy, Gloria J. Freddie Learns Obedience. 2008. 24p. pap. 13.95 (978-1-4327-1906-7(8)) Outskirts Pr., Inc.

LaFaye, A. Stella Stands Alone. 2010. (ENG.). 256p. (YA). (gr. 7). pap. 7.99 (978-1-4169-8647-8(2), Simon & Schuster Bks. For Young Readers) Simon & Schuster Bks. For Young Readers.

Lafleur, Denis. Koal's Not Happy. 2012. 32p. pap. 21.99 (978-1-4771-5030-6(7)) Xlibris Corp.

Lagerlöf, Selma. The Wonderful Adventures of Nils. 2004. reprint ed. pap. 34.95 (978-1-4191-8845-9(3)); pap. 1.99 (978-1-4192-8845-6(8)) Kessinger Publishing, LLC.

—The Wonderful Adventures of Nils. 2009. 360p. (gr. 4-7). pap. 10.99 (978-1-60459-624-3(4)) Wilder Pubns., Corp.

—The Wonderful Adventures of Nils. Howard, Velma Swanston, tr. 2003. 284p. pap. 14.95 (978-1-59224-322-8(3)) Wildside Pr., LLC.

—The Wonderful Adventures of Nils. 2003. 32.95 (978-1-59224-745-5(8)) Wildside Pr., LLC.

Lallemand, Orianne & Strickland, Tessa. The Blue Bird's Palace. Hénaff, Carole, illus. 2016. (J). **(978-1-78285-308-4(1))** Barefoot Bks., Inc.

Lamonica, Lisa. You & Me As Big As the Se. 2008. 20p. pap. 24.95 (978-1-60563-390-9(9)) America Star Bks.

Lampkins, Antonia. My First Book Collection. 2009. 16p. pap. 24.95 (978-1-61546-538-5(3)) America Star Bks.

Lamplighter Staff. Stick to the Raft. 2004. 14.00 (978-1-58474-029-2(9)) Cornerstone Family Ministries/Lamplighter Publishing.

Lampshire Hayden, Gwendolen. Really Truly Stories #1/9, 9, Book 1. 2006. (ENG.). 128p. per. 13.95 (978-1-57258-433-4(5), 945-6294) TEACH Services, Inc.

—Really Truly Stories #2/9. 2006. (Illus.). 128p. per. 11.95 (978-1-57258-434-1(3), 945-6295) TEACH Services, Inc.

—Really Truly Stories #3/9. 2006. (Illus.). 128p. (J). per. 11.95 (978-1-57258-435-8(1), 945-6296) TEACH Services, Inc.

—Really Truly Stories #4/9. 2006. (Illus.). 128p. (YA). per. 12.95 (978-1-57258-436-5(X), 945-6297) TEACH Services, Inc.

Lanagan, Margo. White Time. 2006. 224p. (YA). (gr. 7-18). lib. bdg. 16.89 (978-0-06-074394-9(8)) HarperCollins Pubs.

Landers, Gail J. Late for the Race. 2008. 24p. pap. 24.95 (978-1-60441-371-7(9)) America Star Bks.

Lang, Diane & Buchanan, Michael. The Fat Boy Chronicles. 2010. (Fat Boy Chronicles Ser.). (ENG.). 224p. (J). (gr. 7-11). pap. 9.95 (978-1-58536-543-2(2), 202220) Sleeping Bear Pr.

Langteau, Scott. Sofa Boy. Vernon, Rion, illus. 2008. (ENG.). 40p. 14.95 (978-0-615-25125-7(0)) Shake the Moon Bks.

Lannin, Ann. A Child from Nowhere. 2011. 128p. (gr. 2-4). 21.95 (978-1-4620-2346-2(0)); pap. 11.95 (978-1-4620-2347-9(9)) iUniverse, Inc.

Larsen, Sharon G. The Parable of the Chocolate Chips. 2008. (J). (978-1-59038-912-6(3)) Deseret Bk. Co.

Larson, Kirby. The Friendship Doll. 2012. (ENG.). 208p. (J). (gr. 4-7). 6.99 (978-0-375-85089-9(9), Yearling) Random Hse. Children's Bks.

Larson, Melissa J. It's Your Ball after All. Larson, Caleb A., illus. 2007. 20p. per. 24.95 (978-1-4241-9046-1(0)) America Star Bks.

Law, Felicia. Florence the Flamingo: A Tale of Pride. Messina, Lilli, illus. 2010. (Animal Fair Values Ser.). (ENG.). 32p. (J). (gr. -1-3). pap. 10.55 (978-1-60754-907-9(7)); lib. bdg. 22.60 (978-1-60754-901-7(8)) Windmill Bks.

Lazewnik, Libby. Out of the Woods. Scheinberg, Shepsil, illus. 2011. 320p. (J). (978-1-4226-1176-0(0)) Mesorah Pubns., Ltd.

Lean, Sarah. Hero. 2015. (ENG.). 208p. (J). (gr. 3-7). 16.99 (978-0-06-212238-4(X)) HarperCollins Pubs.

—A Hundred Horses. (ENG.). (J). (gr. 3-7). 2015. 240p. pap. 6.99 (978-0-06-212230-8(4)) 2014. 224p. 16.99 (978-0-06-212229-2(0)) HarperCollins Pubs. (Tegen, Katherine Bks).

Leaney, Cindy. It's Your Turn Now: Politeness. Wilks, Peter, tr. Wilks, Peter, illus. 2003. 31p. (J). 28.50 (978-1-58952-735-5(6)) Rourke Educational Media.

Leaver, Trisha. The Secrets We Keep. 2015. (ENG.). 304p. (YA). (gr. 7). 17.99 (978-0-374-30046-3(1), Farrar, Straus & Giroux (BYR)) Farrar, Straus & Giroux.

LeBoutillier, Nate. A Running Back Can't Always Rush, 1 vol. Santillan, Jorge H., illus. 2010. (Sports Illustrated Kids Victory School Superstars Ser.). (ENG.). 56p. (gr. 1-3). 26.65 (978-1-4342-2055-4(9)); pap. 5.95 (978-1-4342-2805-5(3)) Stone Arch Bks.

Lee, Fonda. Zeroboxer. 2015. (ENG.). 360p. (YA). pap. 11.99 (978-0-7387-4338-7(0), Flux) North Star Editions.

Lee, Spike & Lee, Tonya Lewis. Giant Steps to Change the World. Qualls, Sean, illus. 2011. (ENG.). 40p. (J). (gr. -1). 18.99 (978-0-689-86815-3(4), Simon & Schuster Bks. For Young Readers) Simon & Schuster Bks. For Young Readers.

Lee, WonKyeong. The Chirping Band. Jang, EunJoo, illus. 2014. (MySELF Bookshelf Ser.). (ENG.). 32p. (J). (gr. k-2). pap. 11.94 (978-1-60357-698-7(3)); lib. bdg. 25.27 (978-1-59953-663-7(3)) Norwood Hse. Pr.

Legge, James. The Hsiao King or Classic of Filial Piet. 2004. reprint ed. pap. 15.95 (978-1-4191-6687-7(5)) Kessinger Publishing, LLC.

—The Hsiao King or Classic of Filial Piety. 2004. reprint ed. pap. 1.99 (978-1-4192-6687-4(X)) Kessinger Publishing, LLC.

Leslie, Emma. For Merrie England: A Tale of the Weavers of Norfolk. Taylor, R., illus. 2010. 168p. 20.95 (978-1-934671-38-2(X)); pap. 10.95 (978-1-934671-39-9(8)) Salem Ridge Press LLC.

Letría, José Jorge. If I Were a Book. Letria, Andre, illus. 2014. (ENG.). 64p. 12.95 (978-1-4521-2144-4(3)) Chronicle Bks. LLC.

Leveen, Tom. Random. 2014. (ENG., Illus.). 224p. (YA). (gr. 9). 17.99 (978-1-4424-9956-0(7), Simon Pulse) Simon Pulse.

Levine, Kristin. The Paper Cowboy. (ENG.). (J). (gr. 5). 2016. 368p. 8.99 (978-0-14-242715-6(2), Puffin Books) 2014. 352p. 16.99 (978-0-399-16328-9(X), G.P. Putnam's Sons Books for Young Readers) Penguin Young Readers Group.

Levithan, David. The Realm of Possibility. 2006. (ENG.). 224p. (YA). (gr. 7-12). reprint ed. pap. 9.99 (978-0-375-83657-2(8), Ember) Random Hse. Children's Bks.

Lewis, Beverly. SummerHill Secrets, Vol. 2. 2007. (Summerhill Secrets Ser.: Vols. 6-10). (ENG., Illus.). 544p. (gr. 11-12). pap. 17.00 (978-0-7642-0452-4(1)) Bethany Hse. Pubs.

Lewis, J. Patrick. Make the Earth Your Companion. Balbusso, Anna & Balbusso, Elena, illus. 2017. (ENG.). 32p. (J). (gr. 1-3). pap. 18.99 (978-1-56846-269-1(7), Creative Education) Creative Co., The.

Lewis, Regina N. The Smallest Schoolhouse. Moore, P. M., illus. 2007. 56p. (J). pap. 12.95 (978-0-9776958-3-6(2)) CyPress Pubns.

Licciardi, Paula. Wasting Calvin's Time. 2006. 9.00 (978-0-8059-8138-4(1)) Dorrance Publishing Co., Inc.

Licht, S. Goodbye, Thumb-Sucking! Edelstein, Racheli, illus. 2013. 24p. 10.95 (978-1-60091-266-5(4)) Israel Bookshop Pubns.

Lichtman, Wendy. The Writing on the Wall. 2008. (Do the Math Ser.: 2). (ENG.). 224p. (YA). (gr. 8-9). 16.99 (978-0-06-122958-9(X), Greenwillow Bks.) HarperCollins Pubs.

Lindemann, Lindy. A Cat's Tale, One Cat's Search for the Meaning of Life. Wheeler, Jody, illus. 2007. 28p. per. 12.95 (978-1-934246-03-0(4)) Peppertree Pr., The.

Lindsay, Elizabeth. Stardust Surprise. 2012. (Silverlake Fairy School Ser.). 100p. (J). pap. 4.99 (978-0-7945-3065-5(6), Usborne) EDC Publishing.

Ling, L. M. ZOEY LEE Schoolyard Scuffle. 2011. (ENG., Illus.). 160p. pap. 9.99 (978-1-937861-00-1(7)) Fear2love Pr.

Linseman, Daniel. Shroobear's First Swim: Book I of the Shroobear Short Stories. 2008. 36p. pap. 15.49 (978-1-4343-8252-8(4)) AuthorHouse.

Lipsyte, Robert. Center Field. 2010. (ENG.). 288p. (YA). (gr. 8-18). 17.99 (978-0-06-055704-1(4), HarperTeen) HarperCollins Pubs.

Littman, Sarah Darer. Confessions of a Closet Catholic. 2006. (ENG.). 208p. (J). (gr. 5-18). reprint ed. 7.99 (978-0-14-240597-0(3), Puffin Books) Penguin Young Readers Group.

Lois, Lowry. The Birthday Ball. Feiffer, Jules, illus. 2011. (ENG.). 192p. (J). (gr. 5-7). pap. 7.99 (978-0-547-57710-4(9)) Houghton Mifflin Harcourt Publishing Co.

Lombardo, Constance. Stunt Cat to the Stars. Lombardo, Constance, illus. 2015. (Mr. Puffball Ser.: 1). (ENG., Illus.). 240p. (J). (gr. 3-7). 12.99 (978-0-06-232065-0(3)) HarperCollins Pubs.

London, Jonathan. Froggy Goes to Hawaii. 2012. (Froggy Ser.). lib. bdg. 17.20 (978-0-606-26083-1(8), Turtleback) Turtleback Bks.

Look, Lenore. Ruby Lu, Star of the Show. Choi, Stef, illus. (ENG.). 144p. (J). (gr. 1-5). 2012. pap. 6.99 (978-1-4169-1776-2(4)) 2011. 15.99 (978-1-4169-1775-5(6)) Simon & Schuster Children's Publishing. (Atheneum Bks. for Young Readers).

Love, Jessica. In Real Life: A Novel. 2016. (ENG.). 240p. (YA). 18.99 (978-1-250-06471-4(6), 9781250064714, St. Martin's Griffin) St. Martin's Pr.

Lowe, Nakesha. Just Leave Me Alone. 2011. 16p. 10.70 (978-1-4567-2641-6(2)) AuthorHouse.

Lowrey, Chris. Wonec Adventures: The Gift of Giving. 2008. 26p. pap. 24.95 (978-1-60563-622-1(3)) America Star Bks.

Lowry, Brigid. Follow the Blue. 2006. (ENG.). 208p. (YA). (gr. 8-12). pap. 18.99 (978-0-312-34297-5(7), 9780312342975, St. Martin's Griffin) St. Martin's Pr.

Lubar, David. Sleeping Freshmen Never Lie. 2007. (ENG.). 288p. (YA). (gr. 7-18). 10.99 (978-0-14-240780-6(1), Speak) Penguin Young Readers Group.

—Sophomores & Other Oxymorons. 2015. (ENG.). 432p. (YA). (gr. 7). 17.99 (978-0-525-42970-8(0), Dutton Books for Young Readers) Penguin Young Readers Group.

Lucado, Max. Best of All. Martinez, Sergio, illus. 2003. (Max Lucado's Wemmicks Ser.: 4). 32p. (J). 16.99 (978-1-58134-501-8(1)) Crossway.

—A Max Lucado Children's Treasury: A Child's First Collection, 1 vol. 2007. (ENG., Illus.). 144p. (gr. -1-3). 19.99 (978-1-4003-1048-7(2)) Nelson, Thomas Inc.

Ludwig, Trudy. Confessions of a Former Bully. 2012. lib. bdg. 18.40 (978-0-606-26382-5(9), Turtleback) Turtleback Bks.

Lum, Kate. Princesses Are Not Just Pretty. Hellard, Sue, illus. 2014. (ENG.). 32p. (J). (gr. -1-1). 16.99 (978-1-59990-778-9(X), 9781599907789, Bloomsbury USA Childrens) Bloomsbury Publishing USA.

Lundy, Charlotte. Thank You, God. Waldrep, Evelyn L., ed. James, Margaret Ray, illus. 2004. 32p. (J). (gr. k-3). 15.95 (978-0-9670280-9-5(4)) Bay Light Publishing.

Lupica, Mike. True Legend. (ENG.). (J). (gr. 5). 2013. 320p. pap. 7.99 (978-0-14-242650-0(4), Puffin Books) 2012. 304p. 17.99 (978-0-399-25227-3(4), Philomel Bks.) Penguin Young Readers Group.

Luvd, U. R. Camp Gumbo. 2007. 113p. pap. 7.52 (978-1-4303-1322-9(6)) Lulu Pr., Inc.

Lyga, Barry. I Hunt Killers. (ENG.). (YA). (gr. 10-17). 2014. 464p. mass mkt. 8.00 (978-0-316-28363-2(0)) 2013. 384p. pap. 10.00 (978-0-316-12583-3(0)) Little, Brown Bks. for Young Readers.

Lynch, Chris. Angry Young Man. 2012. (ENG.). 192p. (YA). (gr. 7). pap. 10.99 (978-1-4424-5419-4(9), Simon & Schuster Bks. For Young Readers) Simon & Schuster Bks. For Young Readers.

—Irreversible. 2016. (ENG., Illus.). 352p. (YA). (gr. 7). 17.99 (978-1-4814-2985-6(X), Simon & Schuster Bks. For Young Readers) Simon & Schuster Bks. For Young Readers.

—Me, Dead Dad, & Alcatraz. 3rd ed. 2005. (ENG.). 240p. (J). 15.99 (978-0-06-059709-2(7)) HarperCollins Pubs.

Lyon, Nathan W. & Ellis, Kevin L. Sam the Clam. 2010. 28p. pap. 14.95 (978-1-4520-7784-0(3)) AuthorHouse.

Lyons, Stefanie. Dating Down. 2015. (ENG., Illus.). 312p. (YA). pap. 9.99 (978-0-7387-4337-0(2), Flux) North Star Editions.

Mac, Carrie. The Beckoners, 1 vol. 2007. (ENG.). 224p. (YA). (gr. 8-12). per. 14.95 (978-1-55143-729-3(5)) Orca Bk. Pubs. USA.

MacGregor, Doug, creator. Ochre the Smoker: A fantastic Fable. 2007. (Illus.). 48p. (J). per. 14.95 (978-0-9654843-2-9(7)) MacGregor, Doug.

Mack, Jeff. Clueless Mcgee Gets Famous. Mack, Jeff, illus. 2014. (Clueless Mcgee Ser.: 3). (ENG., Illus.). 288p. (J). (gr. 3-7). 12.99 (978-0-399-25751-3(9), Philomel Bks.) Penguin Young Readers Group.

MacKenzie, Lachlan. The Duke's Daughter: A Story of Faith & Love. Anderson, Jeff, illus. 2008. (Story Time Ser.). (ENG.). 24p. (J). (gr. -1-3). 7.99 (978-1-84550-326-0(0), de5339b0-1f9f-400d-8814-ce3da22de27c) Christian Focus Pubns. GBR. Dist: Bookmasters Distribution.

Mackler, Carolyn. Tangled. (ENG.). (YA). (gr. 9). 2011. 336p. pap. 9.99 (978-0-06-173106-8(4)) 2009. 320p. 16.99 (978-0-06-173104-4(8)) HarperCollins Pubs. (HarperTeen).

Maed, Mary Ann Graziani. Filled to Capacity. 2008. 56p. pap. 24.50 (978-0-615-16077-1(8)) Wishing Star Children's Bks.

Magaziner, Lauren. Pilfer Academy: A School So Bad It's Criminal. 2016. (ENG.). 272p. (J). (gr. 3-7). 16.99 (978-0-8037-3919-2(2), Dial Bks) Penguin Young Readers Group.

Magnason, Andri Snaer. The Story of the Blue Planet. D'Arcy, Julian Meldon, tr. Jonsdottir, Aslaug, illus. 2013. (ENG.). 136p. (J). (gr. 2-5). pap. 9.95 (978-1-60980-506-7(2), Triangle Square) Seven Stories Pr.

Magni, Aurora. The 10 Marys & the Little Gabriel. Vignaga, Francesca Dafne, illus. 2011. (J). (978-0-8091-6764-7(6)) Paulist Pr.

Magnin, Joyce. Carrying Mason, 1 vol. 2013. (ENG.). 176p. (J). pap. 6.99 (978-0-310-72682-1(4)) Zonderkidz.

Make Believe Ideas. Goldilocks & the Three Bears. 2014. (ENG.). 12p. (J). bds. 9.99 (978-1-78235-907-4(9)) Make Believe Ideas GBR. Dist: Nelson, Thomas Inc.

Malkin, Nina. Swear. (ENG.). 480p. (YA). (gr. 11). 2012. pap. 9.99 (978-1-4424-2111-0(8)) 2011. 17.99 (978-1-4424-2110-3(X)) Simon Pulse. (Simon Pulse).

—Swoon. 2010. (ENG.). 432p. (YA). (gr. 11). pap. 9.99 (978-1-4169-9801-3(2), Simon Pulse) Simon Pulse.

Malley, Gemma. The Returners. 2010. (Declaration Ser.). (ENG.). 256p. (YA). (gr. 7-18). 16.99 (978-1-59990-443-6(8), 9781599904436, Bloomsbury USA Childrens) Bloomsbury Publishing USA.

Manaster, Ilana. Doreen. 2016. (ENG.). 336p. (YA). (gr. 2-17). 16.95 (978-0-7624-5962-9(X), Running Pr. Kids) Running Pr. Bk. Pubs.

Manning, Sarra. Guitar Girl. 2005. 217p. (gr. 9-12). 17.00 (978-0-7569-5702-5(8)) Perfection Learning Corp.

Manushkin, Fran. Katie Woo & Her Big Ideas, 1 vol. Lyon, Tammie, illus. 2013. (Katie Woo Ser.). (ENG.). 96p. (gr. k-2). pap. 4.95 (978-1-4795-2026-8(8)) Picture Window Bks.

Marciano, John Bemelmans. The Nine Lives of Alexander Baddenfield. Blackall, Sophie, illus. 2013. (ENG.). 144p. (J). (gr. 5). 16.99 (978-0-670-01406-4(0), Viking Books for Young Readers) Penguin Young Readers Group.

Markey, Andrew C. The Afterlife Phenomenon. 2009. 107p. pap. 9.98 (978-0-615-19036-5(7)) Bug Boy Bks.

Marlow, Susan K. Andrea Carter & the Price of Truth, 1 vol. 2017. (Circle C Adventures Ser.: 6). 144p. (J). pap. 8.99 **(978-0-8254-4505-7(1))** Kregel Pubns.

—Heartbreak Trail: An Andrea Carter Book, 1 vol. 2015. (Circle C Milestones Ser.: 2). 168p. (YA). pap. 9.99 (978-0-8254-4368-8(7)) Kregel Pubns.

—Thick As Thieves: An Andrea Carter Book, 1 vol. 2015. (Circle C Milestones Ser.: 1). 176p. (YA). pap. 9.99 (978-0-8254-4367-1(9)) Kregel Pubns.

Marr, Nikki. Marty Misbehaves. 2008. 40p. pap. 17.99 (978-1-4389-3171-5(9)) AuthorHouse.

Marshall, Melanie. Ladybug. 2006. 25.00 (978-1-4122-0219-0(1)) Trafford Publishing.

Marston, Elsa. Figs & Fate: Stories about Growing up in the Arab World Today. 2005. (ENG.). 146p. (J). 22.50 (978-0-8076-1551-5(X)); pap. 15.95 (978-0-8076-1554-6(4)) Braziller, George Inc.

Martin, Ann M. Error de Stacey. (Club de las Canguro Misterios Ser.).Tr. of Stacey's Mistake. (SPA.). 142p. (J). 11.95 (978-84-272-3668-4(9)) Molino, Editorial ESP. Dist: AIMS International Bks., Inc.

Martin Ed.D., Pamela. Include Me. 2013. 48p. pap. (978-1-4602-2643-8(7)) FriesenPress.

Martin, Mabel. Days with Mary. Hoover, Charity, illus. 2015. 159p. (J). (978-0-7399-2515-7(6)) Rod & Staff Pubs., Inc.

Martínez, Jessica. Virtuosity. (ENG.). (YA). (gr. 9). 2012. 320p. pap. 9.99 (978-1-4424-2053-3(7)) 2011. 304p. 16.99 (978-1-4424-2052-6(9)) Simon Pulse. (Simon Pulse).

Mary Mccowski Was Not a Pretty Girl: About a Girl Who Isn't Pretty, & Never Will Be Pretty but Finds Success Anyway. 2005. (J). 3.99 (978-0-9754420-0-5(7)) www.underdogpublishing.com.

Maslin, Mirabelle. Tracy. 2007. 210p. pap. (978-0-9549551-0-6(2)) Augur Pr.

Mason, Albert. Ooshu, Dorothy, & the Old Lady. 2012. 40p. pap. 20.99 (978-1-4772-9314-0(0)) AuthorHouse.

Mass, Wendy. Jeremy Fink & the Meaning of Life. 2008. (ENG.). 304p. (J). (gr. 3-7). per. 8.99 (978-0-316-05849-0(1)) Little, Brown Bks. for Young Readers.

—13 Gifts. 2013. (ENG.). 352p. (J). (gr. 3-7). pap. 6.99 (978-0-545-31004-8(0)) Scholastic, Inc.

—13 Gifts. 2013. (Willow Falls Ser.: 3). lib. bdg. 17.20 (978-0-606-31957-7(3), Turtleback) Turtleback Bks.

Matheson, Dawn. Ruby Lee the Bumble Bee: A Bee's Bit of Wisdom. Cindy, Huffman, ed. Barcita, Pamela, illus. 2004.

40p. (J). 17.95 *(978-0-9754342-0-8(9))* Bumble Bee Publishing.

Matthews, Owen. How to Win at High School. 2015. (ENG.). 496p. (YA). (gr. 9). 17.99 *(978-0-06-233686-6(X)*, HarperTeen) HarperCollins Pubs.

McAllister O'Connell, Andrea. Jackson, Josie, & the (almost) Free Lunch. 2010. (J). 16.95 *(978-1-59298-300-1(6))* Beaver's Pond Pr., Inc.

McCarnes, Kayla, et al. Making a Happy Heart: A Storybook to Accompany Bully-Proofing in Early Childhood: Building a Caring Community. 2004. (Illus.). 28p. 27.49 *(978-1-59318-242-7(2))* Cambium Education, Inc.

McClure, Brian D. The Ants. Plumlee, Buddy, illus. 2009. (Brian D. Mcclure Childrens Book Collection). 57p. (J). (gr. -1-3). 16.95 *(978-1-933426-10-5(1))* Universal Flag Publishing.

—The Birds & the Frogs. Plumlee, Buddy, illus. 2009. (Brian D. Mcclure Childrens Book Collection). 37p. (J). (gr. -1-3). 16.95 *(978-1-933426-13-6(6))* Universal Flag Publishing.

McCombs, Margi. Dios es Bueno Todo el Tiempo. Ivanov, Aleksey & Ivanov, Olga, illus. 2012. (SPA.). 20p. (J). (gr. -1-k). bds. 9.99 *(978-0-545-45618-0(5)*, Scholastic en Espanol) Scholastic, Inc.

McCumbee, Stephie. Priscilla & the Perfect Storm. De Weerd, Kelsey, illus. 2014. (ENG.). 32p. (J). pap. 10.95 *(978-1-934490-60-0(1))* Boys Town Pr.

McCusker, Paul. Point of No Return. 2006. (Adventures in Odyssey Bks.). (ENG.). 336p. (J). (gr. 3-7). per. 15.99 *(978-1-58997-332-9(1))* Tyndale Hse. Pubs.

—Strange Journey Back. 2006. (Adventures in Odyssey Bks.: No. 1). (ENG., Illus.). 304p. (J). (gr. 3-7). per. 15.99 *(978-1-58997-325-1(9))* Tyndale Hse. Pubs.

McDonald, Ann-Eve. The Bad Day. 2004. (J). *(978-0-9770158-1-8(5))* BeachWalk Bks. Inc.

McDowell, Josh & Hostetler, Bob. The Truth Twisters. 2006. (Illus.). 167p. (YA). (gr. 8-12). per. 11.99 *(978-1-932587-84-5(5))* Practical Christianity Foundation.

McGhee, Holly M. Come with Me. Lemaître, Pascal, illus. 2017. (ENG.). 40p. (J). (gr. k-3). 17.99 ***(978-1-5247-3905-8(7)***, G.P. Putnam's Sons Books for Young Readers) Penguin Young Readers Group.

McGuirk, Leslie & Von Bidder, Alex. Wiggens Learns His Manners at the Four Seasons Restaurant. McGuirk, Leslie, illus. 2009. (ENG., Illus.). 32p. (J). (gr. -1-2). 16.99 *(978-0-7636-4014-9(X))* Candlewick Pr.

McHale, Remme. No Place for Niappy. 2010. 28p. pap. 12.85 *(978-1-4490-6900-1(2))* AuthorHouse.

McIntosh, Maria J. Florence Arnott; or, Is She Generous? by M J Mcintosh. 2006. 136p. per. 16.99 *(978-1-4255-0994-1(0))* Michigan Publishing.

McIntyre, Sharyn. Christmas Tea with the Angels. 2007. 112p. 24.95 *(978-1-4327-1457-4(0))* Outskirts Pr., Inc.

McIntyre, Will. Burning Midnight. 2016. (ENG.). 320p. (YA). (gr. 7). 17.99 *(978-0-553-53410-8(6)*, Delacorte Pr.) Random Hse. Children's Bks.

McKerley, Jennifer Guess. Rules of the Net, 1 vol. Duverne, Evelyne, illus. 2009. (Read-It! Readers: Character Education Ser.). (ENG.). 32p. (J). (gr. k-2). 21.32 *(978-1-4048-5240-2(9)*, Easy Readers) Picture Window Bks.

McKernan, Victoria. Son of Fortune. 2015. (ENG.). 448p. (YA). (gr. 7). pap. 9.99 *(978-0-375-85786-7(9)*, Ember) Random Hse. Children's Bks.

McKissack, Patricia C. Ol' Clip-Clop: A Ghost Story. Velasquez, Eric, illus. (ENG.). 32p. (J). 2014. (gr. 1-4). 6.99 *(978-0-8234-3186-1(X))* 2013. 16.95 *(978-0-8234-2265-4(8))* Holiday Hse., Inc.

McKissack, Patricia C., et al. The Honest-to-Goodness Truth. Potter, Giselle, illus. 2003. (ENG.). 40p. (J). (gr. -1-3). 7.99 *(978-0-689-85395-1(5)*, Aladdin) Simon & Schuster Children's Publishing.

McMullan, Kate & McMullan, Jim. I'm Dirty! 2011. (J). (gr. -1-2). 29.95 *(978-0-545-09456-6(9))* Weston Woods Studios, Inc.

McNamara, Margaret. Martin Luther King Jr. Day. Gordon, Mike, illus. 2007. (Robin Hill School Ser.). (ENG.). 32p. (J). (gr. -1-1). pap. 3.99 *(978-1-4169-3494-3(4)*, Simon Spotlight) Simon Spotlight.

McNeill, Audrey. From the Desk of a Three-Year-Old. Grondel, April, illus. 2009. 20p. pap. 24.95 *(978-1-60749-476-8(0))* America Star Bks.

McNichol, John. The Tripods Attack! 2008. (Young Chesterton Chronicles Ser.). 367p. (YA). (gr. 8-12). pap. 17.95 *(978-1-933184-26-5(4))* Sophia Institute Pr.

McNutt, William Slavens. Poor Little Eddie. 2004. reprint ed. pap. 1.99 *(978-1-4192-4260-1(1))* Kessinger Publishing, LLC.

McVicar, William E. Turtle Tries. 2008. 16p. pap. 24.95 *(978-1-60563-180-6(9))* America Star Bks.

Mebane-Walker, Vinita. Shareeka's Life. 2007. pap. 16.95 *(978-1-4241-8724-9(9))* America Star Bks.

Meister, Soizick & George, Kallie. Mr. M: The Exploring Dreamer. 2010. (ENG., Illus.). 54p. (J). 16.95 *(978-1-897476-51-2(5))* Simply Read Bks. CAN. Dist: Ingram Publisher Services.

Melcher, Rich. A Work in Progress. 2011. 148p. 29.99 *(978-1-4568-5192-7(6))*; pap. 15.99 *(978-1-4568-5191-0(8))* Xlibris Corp.

mendelsohn, martha. Bromley Girls. 2015. (ENG.). 192p. (YA). pap. 14.95 *(978-0-89672-922-3(2))* Texas Tech Univ. Pr.

Meng, Cece. Always Remember. Jago, Alison, illus. 2016. (ENG.). 32p. (J). (gr. -1-2). 17.99 *(978-0-399-16809-3(5)*, Philomel Bks.) Penguin Young Readers Group.

Menzie, Morgan. Diary of an Anorexic Girl, 1 vol. 2003. (ENG.). 192p. pap. 12.99 *(978-0-8499-4405-5(8))* Nelson, Thomas Inc.

Merkel, Ruth Vitrano. Hannah's Girls: Erin (Born 1988) 2009. (J). 9.99 *(978-0-8280-1956-9(8))* Review & Herald Publishing Assn.

Mermelstein, Yael. A Car That Goes Far. Rosenfeld, Dina, ed. Romanenko, Vitaliy & Romanenko, Vasilisa, illus. 2009. 30p. (J). (gr. 1-3). 12.95 *(978-1-929628-47-6(1))* Hachai Publishing.

Meron, Renato Mas. Why Corn Kernels Pop Up. 2012. 24p. pap. 24.95 *(978-1-62709-859-5(3))* America Star Bks.

Merrill, Jean. The Elephant Who Liked to Smash Small Cars. Solbert, Ronni, illus. 2015. (ENG.). 40p. (J). (gr. -1-2). 14.95 *(978-1-59017-872-0(6)*, NYR Children's Collection) New York Review of Bks., Inc., The.

Messer, Celeste M. The Boy Who Cried Wolf. Hoeffner, Deb, illus. 2004. 82-92p. 4.95 *(978-0-9702171-9-6(6))* AshleyAlan Enterprises.

—When Eagles Fly. Hoeffner, Deb, illus. 2004. 82-92p. 4.95 *(978-0-9702171-8-9(8))* AshleyAlan Enterprises.

Mezrich, Ben. Bringing down the Mouse. 2014. (ENG., Illus.). 336p. (J). (gr. 3-7). 16.99 *(978-1-4424-9626-2(6)*, Simon & Schuster Bks. For Young Readers) Simon & Schuster Bks. For Young Readers.

Michie, Sue. Possie & Neggie. 2011. (Illus.). 24p. pap. 12.99 *(978-1-4634-4174-6(6))* AuthorHouse.

Mikaelsen, Ben. Ghost of Spirit Bear. (Spirit Bear Ser.: 2). (ENG.). (J). (gr. 5). 2010. 176p. pap. 6.99 *(978-0-06-009009-8(X))* 2008. 160p. 16.99 *(978-0-06-009007-4(3))* HarperCollins Pubs.

Miles, Brenda & Sweet, Susan D. King Calm: Mindful Gorilla in the City. Langdo, Bryan, illus. 2016. (J). *(978-1-4338-2272-8(5)*, Magination Pr.) American Psychological Assn.

Milhander, Laura Aron. Not for All the Hamantaschen in Town. Chernyak, Inna, illus. 2016. (ENG.). 32p. (J). (gr. -1-3). 17.99 *(978-1-4677-5928-1(7)*, Kar-Ben Publishing) Lerner Publishing Group.

Miller, Pat. Squirrel's New Year's Resolution. Ember, Kathi, illus. 2012. (J). 34.28 *(978-1-61913-135-4(8))* Weigl Pubs., Inc.

—Squirrel's New Year's Resolution. Ember, Kathi, illus. (ENG.). 32p. (J). (gr. k-2). 2017. pap. 7.99 ***(978-0-8075-7592-5(5))*** 2010. 16.99 *(978-0-8075-7591-8(7))* Whitman, Albert & Co.

Miller, S. L. Yellow Kitty, Life in the Garden. 2008. 316p. pap. 18.95 *(978-0-615-22038-3(X))* Polar Club Publishing.

Millett, Melanie. CTR Boy. 2006. (Illus.). (J). *(978-1-59811-062-3(4))* Covenant Communications.

Mills, Claudia. Basketball Disasters. Francis, Guy, illus. 2013. (Mason Dixon Ser.). (ENG.). 176p. (J). (gr. 2-5). pap. 6.99 *(978-0-375-87276-1(0)*, Yearling) Random Hse. Children's Bks.

—Being Teddy Roosevelt. Alley, R. W., illus. 2007. (ENG.). 96p. (J). (gr. 2-5). 16.99 *(978-0-374-30657-1(5)*, 9780374306571, Farrar, Straus & Giroux (BYR)) Farrar, Straus & Giroux.

—Being Teddy Roosevelt. Alley, R. W., illus. 2012. (ENG.). 112p. (J). (gr. 2-5). pap. 8.99 *(978-0-312-64018-7(8)*, 9780312640187) Square Fish.

Mills, Joyce C. Little Tree: A Story for Children with Serious Medical Illness. Sebern, Brian, illus. 2nd ed. 2003. 32p. (J). pap. 9.95 *(978-1-59147-042-7(0))*; 14.95 *(978-1-59147-041-0(2))* American Psychological Assn. (Magination Pr.).

Mills, Wendy. All We Have Left. (ENG.). 368p. (YA). 2017. pap. 9.99 *(978-1-68119-432-5(5)*, 9781681194325) 2016. 17.99 *(978-1-61963-343-8(4)*, 9781619633438) Bloomsbury Publishing USA. (Bloomsbury USA Childrens).

Milz, Cynthia A. Waiting for the Last Leaf to Fall. 2008. 20p. per. 24.95 *(978-1-4241-8965-6(9))* America Star Bks.

Miner, Deb. I get Around. Miner, Deb, illus. 2007. (ENG., Illus.). 32p. (J). bds. 11.00 *(978-0-9794262-0-9(0))* do be you.

Minou: Evaluation Guide. 2006. (J). *(978-1-55942-416-5(8))* Witcher Productions.

Miranda, Megan. Soulprint. 2015. (ENG.). 368p. (YA). (gr. 7). 17.99 *(978-0-8027-3774-8(9)*, 9780802737748, Bloomsbury USA Childrens) Bloomsbury Publishing USA.

Mitchell, Laurence. Parents Don't Always Do the Right Things: Character Tales. 2009. 24p. pap. 12.00 *(978-1-4389-5407-3(7))* AuthorHouse.

Mitchell, Randall. Teenership: Leadership for Teens. 2013. 112p. 29.99 *(978-1-4797-7767-9(6))*; pap. 19.99 *(978-1-4797-7766-2(8))* Xlibris Corp.

Mlynowski, Sarah. Gimme a Call. 2011. (ENG.). 320p. (YA). (gr. 7). pap. 9.99 *(978-0-385-73589-6(8)*, Ember) Random Hse. Children's Bks.

Mlynowski, Sarah. Ten Things We Did (and Probably Shouldn't Have) (YA). (gr. 9). 2017. 384p. pap. 9.99 ***(978-0-06-268303-8(9))*** 2012. (ENG.). 368p. pap. 9.99 *(978-0-06-170126-9(2)*, HarperTeen) 2011. (ENG.). 368p. 16.99 *(978-0-06-170124-5(6)*, HarperTeen) HarperCollins Pubs.

Moffett, Elzater. Tenan & Colleen: I Don't Want to Go to Bed. Thibodeaux, Rebecca, illus. 2010. 36p. 15.49 *(978-1-4490-6633-8(X))* AuthorHouse.

Mohamoud, Ashlee. Brown Is Beautiful, 1 vol. 2010. 18p. 24.95 *(978-1-4512-0064-5(1))* PublishAmerica, Inc.

Mohler, Marie. Little Bird's Earth Nest. 2008. 32p. 18.95 *(978-1-4357-1711-4(2))* Lulu Pr., Inc.

Mohr, Janet. Flight of Change. 2007. 48p. pap. 16.95 *(978-1-4241-0793-3(8))* America Star Bks.

Molesworth & Molesworth, Mary Louisa S. Rosy. 2008. 120p. pap. 9.95 *(978-1-60664-226-9(X))* Rodgers, Alan Bks.

Mone, Gregory. Dangerous Waters: An Adventure on Titanic. 2012. (ENG.). 240p. (J). (gr. 4-7). 16.99 *(978-1-59643-673-2(5)*, 9781596436732) Roaring Brook Pr.

—Dangerous Waters: An Adventure on Titanic. 2013. (ENG.). 256p. (J). (gr. 4-7). pap. 7.99 *(978-1-250-01671-3(1)*, 9781250016713) Square Fish.

—Fish. 2010. (J). *(978-0-545-11631-2(7)*, Scholastic Pr.) Scholastic, Inc.

Monreal, Jeannie. What Will I Be? Asked Little Miss Christina Magee. 2010. 30p. pap. 12.99 *(978-1-60860-791-4(7)*, Eloquent Bks.) Strategic Book Publishing & Rights Agency (SBPRA).

Monteiro, Francelina. The Star That Couldn't Shine. 2009. 24p. pap. 12.99 *(978-1-4490-3775-8(5))* AuthorHouse.

Moore, Stephanie. Make Something of It. 2014. (Sharp Sisters Ser.: 1). (ENG.). 152p. (YA). (gr. 6-12). pap. 7.95 *(978-1-4677-4488-1(3)*, Darby Creek) Lerner Publishing Group.

Moore, Stephanie Perry. Back That Thing. 2015. (Illus.). 103p. (YA). 9.99 *(978-1-4677-7892-3(3))* Lerner Publishing Group.

—Forever Hot/Truly Fine. 2013. (Grovehill Giants Ser.). (YA). lib. bdg. 26.90 *(978-0-606-31877-8(1)*, Turtleback) Turtleback Bks.

—Give It Up. 2015. (YA). 9.99 *(978-1-4677-7886-2(9))*; (Swoop List Ser.: 1). (ENG., Illus.). 128p. (gr. 6-12). lib. bdg. 27.99 *(978-1-4677-5804-8(3))* Lerner Publishing Group.

—On Your Knees. 2015. (Swoop List Ser.: 2). (ENG., Illus.). 128p. (YA). (gr. 6-12). lib. bdg. 27.99 *(978-1-4677-5805-5(1))* Lerner Publishing Group.

—Sit on Top. 2015. (Swoop List Ser.: 4). (ENG., Illus.). 112p. (YA). (gr. 6-12). pap. 9.99 *(978-1-4677-6052-2(8))* Lerner Publishing Group.

—Turn up for Real. 2014. (Sharp Sisters Ser.: 3). (ENG.). 168p. (YA). (gr. 6-12). pap. 7.95 *(978-1-4677-4490-4(5)*, Darby Creek); lib. bdg. 27.93 *(978-1-4677-3726-5(7))* Lerner Publishing Group.

Moore, Stephanie Perry & Moore, Derrick. Forever Hot/Truly Fine, 1 vol. 2013. (Grovehill Giants Ser.: Bk. 1). (ENG.). 318p. (YA). (gr. 9-12). pap. 14.95 *(978-1-62250-683-5(9))* Saddleback Educational Publishing, Inc.

Moore, Wes & Goodman, Shawn. This Way Home. 2015. (ENG.). 256p. (YA). (gr. 9). 20.99 *(978-0-375-99019-9(4)*, Delacorte Pr.) Random Hse. Children's Bks.

Morel, John Henry. Mary Winkle Umperdinck. 2009. 48p. pap. 22.99 *(978-1-935436-38-6(4))* Rodaian Pr.

—Who Is Me? 2009. 48p. pap. 16.99 *(978-1-935436-80-5(5))* Rodaian Pr.

Morgenstern, Susie Hoch & Morgenstern, Susie. I Will Make Miracles. Chen, Jiang Hong, illus. 2008. (ENG.). 32p. (J). (gr. -1-3). 18.99 *(978-1-59990-189-3(7)*, 9781599901893, Bloomsbury USA Childrens) Bloomsbury Publishing USA.

Morty, Ducktor. Can Do & the Mall: A Story for Us All. 2005. (Illus.). 34p. (J). pap. *(978-0-9768384-0-1(0))* Can Do Duck Publishing.

Moss, Marissa, illus. Mira's Diary: Bombs over London. 2014. (ENG.). 190p. (J). (gr. 2-8). 12.99 *(978-1-939547-12-5(1))* Creston Bks.

Mulholland, Clara. Naughty Miss Bunny. 2007. 128p. 25.95 *(978-1-4218-3838-0(9)*, 1st World Library - Literary Society) 1st World Publishing, Inc.

Mullinax, Jerry. Enoree. 2009. (YA). pap. *(978-0-88092-646-1(5))* Royal Fireworks Publishing Co.

Murphy, Elspeth Campbell. God Makes It Right: Three Stories for Children Based on Favorite Bible Verses. Nelson, Jane E., illus. 72p. (J). *(978-1-55513-109-8(3))* Cook, David C.

Murphy, Stuart J. Freda Stops a Bully. Jones, Tim, illus. 2012. (I See I Learn Ser.). (ENG.). 32p. (J). (-k). 14.95 *(978-1-58089-466-1(6))*; pap. 6.95 *(978-1-58089-467-8(4))* Charlesbridge Publishing, Inc.

Muschla, Gary Robert. The Sword & the Cross. 2009. (YA). pap. *(978-0-88092-472-6(1))* Royal Fireworks Publishing Co.

Muth, Jon J. Zen Socks. 2015. (ENG., Illus.). 40p. (J). (gr. -1-3). 17.99 *(978-0-545-16669-0(1)*, Scholastic Pr.) Scholastic, Inc.

Myers, Bill. My Life As a Tarantula Toe Tickler, 1 vol., Vol. 22. 2003. (Incredible Worlds of Wally Mcdoogle Ser.: 22). (ENG., Illus.). 128p. pap. 6.99 *(978-0-8499-5993-6(4))* Nelson, Thomas Inc.

Myers, Laurie. Escape by Night: A Civil War Adventure. Bates, Amy June, illus. 2011. (ENG.). 128p. (J). (gr. 3-7). 14.99 *(978-0-8050-8825-0(3)*, 9780805088250, Holt, Henry & Co. Bks. For Young Readers) Holt, Henry & Co.

Myers, Tim J. The Christmas Stick: A Children's Story. Yilmaz, Necdet, illus. 2014. (ENG.). 32p. (J). pap. 13.99 *(978-1-61261-571-4(6))* Paraclete Pr., Inc.

Myers, Walter Dean. All the Right Stuff. (YA). (gr. 8). 2013. (ENG.). 240p. pap. 9.99 *(978-0-06-196089-5(6))* 2012. (ENG.). 224p. 17.99 *(978-0-06-196087-1(X))* 2012. 224p. lib. bdg. 18.89 *(978-0-06-196088-8(8))* HarperCollins Pubs. (Amistad).

—Dope Sick. (ENG.). 208p. (YA). (gr. 9). 2010. pap. 9.99 *(978-0-06-121479-0(5))* 2009. 17.99 *(978-0-06-121477-6(9))* HarperCollins Pubs. (Amistad).

—Handbook for Boys. 2003. (Amistad Ser.). (ENG.). 224p. (YA). (gr. 5-18). pap. 8.99 *(978-0-06-440930-8(9)*, Amistad) HarperCollins Pubs.

—Handbook for Boys. 2003. 19.00 *(978-0-7569-1459-2(0))* Perfection Learning Corp.

—Lockdown. (YA). (gr. 8). 2011. (ENG.). 272p. pap. 9.99 *(978-0-06-121482-0(5))* 2010. 256p. lib. bdg. 17.89 *(978-0-06-121481-3(7))* 2010. (ENG.). 256p. 16.99 *(978-0-06-121480-6(9))* HarperCollins Pubs. (Amistad).

Myers, Walter Dean & Workman, Ross. Kick. (ENG.). (YA). (gr. 9). 2012. 224p. pap. 9.99 *(978-0-06-200491-8(3))* 2011. 208p. 16.99 *(978-0-06-200489-5(1))* HarperCollins Pubs. (HarperTeen).

Myracle, Lauren. Rhymes with Witches. (ENG.). (YA). (gr. 8-17). 2006. 272p. pap. 7.95 *(978-0-8109-9215-3(9))* 2005. 224p. 16.95 *(978-0-8109-5859-3(7)*, Amulet Bks.) Abrams, Inc.

Nadin, Joanna. Wonderland. 2011. (ENG., Illus.). 224p. (YA). (gr. 9-18). 16.99 *(978-0-7636-4846-6(9))* Candlewick Pr.

Nambiar, Vinesh. Adventures in Human Values - Series 1: Courage, Kindness, Forgiveness, Teamwork, Compassion, Listening, Caring, Self-Confidence, Sharing. 2007. (Illus.). (J). pap. 9.99 *(978-0-9798986-0-0(9))* Human Values 4 Kids Foundation, The.

Namm, Diane. King Arthur & His Knights. Calo, Marcos, illus. 2014. (Silver Penny Stories Ser.). (ENG.). 48p. (J). (gr. -1-1). 4.95 *(978-1-4027-8432-3(5))* Sterling Publishing Co., Inc.

Napoli, Donna Jo. The Wager. 2010. (ENG.). 272p. (YA). (gr. 7-12). 16.99 *(978-0-8050-8781-9(8)*, 9780805087819, Holt, Henry & Co. Bks. For Young Readers) Holt, Henry & Co.

Narr, Rachel K. You're the Same As Me. Baker, David, illus. 2012. 26p. 24.95 *(978-1-60749-472-0(8))* America Star Bks.

Nash, Andy. Marcus & His Monkey: For Kids Blessed with Popularity. 2010. (J). *(978-0-8127-0452-5(5))* Autumn Hse. Publishing Co.

—Melinda & Her Mule: For Kids Blessed with a Strong Will. 2008. (J). *(978-0-8127-0453-2(3))* Autumn Hse. Publishing Co.

Nayeri, Daniel and Dina. Another Faust. 2010. (ENG., Illus.). 400p. (YA). (gr. 9). pap. 8.99 *(978-0-7636-4834-3(5))* Candlewick Pr.

Naylor, Phyllis Reynolds. All but Alice. 2011. (Alice Ser.: 4). (ENG.). 192p. (J). (gr. 5-9). pap. 6.99 *(978-1-4424-2756-3(6)*, Atheneum Bks. for Young Readers) Simon & Schuster Children's Publishing.

—Dangerously Alice. 2007. (Alice Ser.: 19). (ENG.). 304p. (YA). (gr. 9-12). 15.99 *(978-0-689-87094-1(9)*, Atheneum Bks. for Young Readers) Simon & Schuster Children's Publishing.

—Dangerously Alice. 2008. (Alice Ser.: No. 19). (ENG.). 320p. (YA). mass mkt. 6.99 *(978-0-689-87095-8(7)*, Simon Pulse) Simon Pulse.

Nelson, Blake. The New Rules of High School. 2004. (ENG.). 240p. (YA). (gr. 7-18). reprint ed. 7.99 *(978-0-14-240242-9(7)*, Speak) Penguin Young Readers Group.

—Paranoid Park. 2008. (ENG.). 192p. (YA). (gr. 7-18). 6.99 *(978-0-14-241156-8(6)*, Puffin Books) Penguin Young Readers Group.

Nelson, Valerie. I Can Do It Myself! 2008. (Illus.). 20p. (J). pap. *(978-0-9794171-1-5(2))* Nelson Publishing, LLC.

Nelson, Wendy Watson. The Not Even Once Club: My Promise to Heavenly Father. Dorman, Brandon, illus. 2013. 18.99 *(978-1-60907-337-4(1))* Deseret Bk. Co.

Nesbit, E. These Little Ones. 2006. 132p. per. 10.95 *(978-1-59818-961-2(1))*; 24.95 *(978-1-59818-175-3(0))* Aegypan.

Nesselrode, Sandra. Princess Kelsie & Her Special Gifts. 2008. 28p. pap. 19.95 *(978-1-4327-1708-7(1))* Outskirts Pr., Inc.

Newman, Lesléa. The Boy Who Cried Fabulous. Ferguson, Peter, illus. 2007. (ENG.). 32p. (J). (gr. -1-2). pap. 7.99 *(978-1-58246-224-0(0)*, Tricycle Pr.) Random Hse. Children's Bks.

Newman, Vivian. Tikkun Olam Ted. Mack, Steve, illus. 2013. (Life Cycle Ser.). (ENG.). 12p. (J). (gr. -1 — 1). pap. 5.95 *(978-0-7613-9040-4(5)*, Kar-Ben Publishing) Lerner Publishing Group.

Nicholson, William. Jango. 2007. 409p. (YA). *(978-1-4287-4812-5(1))* Harcourt Trade Pubs.

—Jango: Book Two of the Noble Warriors. 2008. (Noble Warriors Ser.: 2). (ENG., Illus.). 432p. (YA). (gr. 7). pap. 25.95 *(978-0-15-206160-9(6))* Houghton Mifflin Harcourt Publishing Co.

—Noman: Book Three of the Noble Warriors. 2009. (Noble Warriors Ser.: 3). (ENG., Illus.). 368p. (J). (gr. 7). pap. 15.95 *(978-0-15-206656-7(X))* Houghton Mifflin Harcourt Publishing Co.

—Noman: La Orden de los Guerreros Misticos. 2009. (SPA.). 352p. (YA). 18.95 *(978-84-666-4051-0(7))* Ediciones B ESP. Dist: Spanish Pubs., LLC.

—Seeker: Book One of the Noble Warriors. 2007. (Noble Warriors Ser.: 1). (ENG., Illus.). 448p. (YA). (gr. 7-12). pap. 23.99 *(978-0-15-205866-1(4))* Houghton Mifflin Harcourt Publishing Co.

Nienstedt, L. a. Phineas T Pudgepot & the Mysterious Flying Fish. 2009. 32p. pap. 14.49 *(978-1-4343-5123-4(8))* AuthorHouse.

Nigro, D. M. The Wolfman, the Shrink & the Eighth-Grade Election. 2006. 116p. (J). pap. 13.50 *(978-1-931201-66-7(8))* Twilight Times Bks.

Nobisso, Josephine. Take It to the Queen. 2009. 32p. 17.95 *(978-0-8146-3288-8(2)*, Liturgical Pr. Bks.) Liturgical Pr.

—Take It to the Queen: A Tale of Hope. Szegedi, Katalin, illus. 2008. (ENG.). 32p. (J). (gr. k-2). 17.95 *(978-0-940112-19-3(1))*; pap. 9.95 *(978-0-940112-21-6(3))* Gingerbread Hse.

Nolan, Allia Zobel. Fair & Squaresville: A Lesson in Playing Fair. Carter, Tod et al, illus. 2014. (VeggieTales (Big Idea) Ser.). (ENG.). 28p. (J). (gr. -1-3). pap. 6.99 incl. audio compact disk *(978-1-61795-333-0(4))* Worthy Publishing.

Numeroff, Laura Joffe. Happy Valentine's Day, Mouse! Bond, Felicia, illus. 2009. (If You Give... Ser.). (ENG.). 24p. (J). (gr. -1-3). bds. 6.99 *(978-0-06-180432-8(0))* HarperCollins Pubs.

Nunes, Rachel & Lindsley, David. Daughter of a King Board Book. 2004. bds. 10.95 *(978-1-59156-054-8(3))* Covenant Communications, Inc.

Nunes, Rachel Ann. Daughter of a King. 2004. (Illus.). 17.95 *(978-1-57734-935-8(0))* Covenant Communications, Inc.

Nyznyk, Darryl. Mary's Son: A Tale of Christmas. 2010. (ENG., Illus.). 176p. 15.95 *(978-0-9656513-5-6(5))* Cross Dove Publishing, LLC.

Oakes, Colleen. Blood of Wonderland. 2017. (Queen of Hearts Ser.: 2). (YA). (gr. 8). 352p. pap. 9.99 ***(978-0-06-240977-5(8))***; 336p. 17.99 *(978-0-06-240976-8(X))* HarperCollins Pubs. (HarperTeen).

O'Brien, Kathryn. I'd Be Your Princess: A Royal Tale of Godly Character. Garland, Michael, illus. 2007. 28p. (J). (gr. -1-3). 6.99 *(978-0-7847-1964-0(0))* Standard Publishing.

O'Connor, Barbara. How to Steal a Dog. 2009. (ENG.). 192p. (J). (gr. 3-7). pap. 6.99 *(978-0-312-56112-3(1)*, 9780312561123) Square Fish.

—Wish. 2016. (ENG.). 240p. (J). 16.99 *(978-0-374-30273-3(1)*, 9780374302733, Farrar, Straus & Giroux (BYR)) Farrar, Straus & Giroux.

O'Dell, Kathleen. Agnes Parker... Girl in Progress. 2004. (ENG.). 176p. (J). (gr. 2-5). reprint ed. 6.99 *(978-0-14-240228-3(1)*, Puffin Books) Penguin Young Readers Group.

Ogle-Graham, Laura. No-No Nona & No-No Nit. 2012. 30p. pap. 12.95 *(978-0-9853094-1-1(5))* Warren Publishing, Inc.

Oliver, Lauren. Before I Fall. (ENG.). (YA). (gr. 9). 2016. 544p. pap. 10.99 *(978-0-06-172681-1(8))* 2010. 480p. 17.99 *(978-0-06-172680-4(X))* HarperCollins Pubs.

—Before I Fall. 2010. 368p. pap. *(978-0-340-98090-3(7)*, Hodder Paperbacks) Hodder & Stoughton.

—Before I Fall. 2016. (YA). lib. bdg. 22.10 *(978-0-606-23576-1(0)*, Turtleback) Turtleback Bks.

Oliver, Lin. Two-Faced, No. 2. 2012. (Almost Identical Ser.: 2). (ENG.). 224p. (J). (gr. 3-7). pap. 7.99 *(978-0-448-45192-3(1)*, Grosset & Dunlap) Penguin Young Readers Group.

Oliver the Clownfish: The Invitation Slip-up. 2006. (J). 5.95 *(978-1-59664-000-9(6))* R J Communications, LLC.

Olmstead, Kathleen & Porter, Eleanor H. Pollyanna. Akib, Jamel, illus. 2007. (Classic Starts Ser.). 154p. (J). *(978-1-4287-4209-3(3))* Sterling Publishing Co., Inc.

Olson, Branden. Tuke the Noozle in... . Just in Case... 2011. 16p. pap. 8.32 *(978-1-4567-5809-7(8))* AuthorHouse.

O'Malley Cerra, Kerry. Just a Drop of Water. 2016. (ENG.). 320p. (J). (gr. 2-7). pap. 7.99 *(978-1-5107-1234-8(8)*, Sky Pony Pr.) Skyhorse Publishing Co., Inc.

On Thin Ice. 2005. per. *(978-0-9772505-2-3(0))* Adibooks.com.

O'Nan, Gerald D. The Adventures of Andy Ant: Lawn Mower on the Loose. McGary, Norman, illus. 2014. (ENG.). 28p. (gr. -1-4). pap. 9.95 *(978-1-61448-673-2(5))* Morgan James Publishing.

O'Neal, Shaquille. Little Shaq. Taylor, Theodore, III, illus. 2016. (ENG.). 80p. (J). 9.99 *(978-1-61963-879-2(7)*, 9781619638792, Bloomsbury USA Childrens) Bloomsbury Publishing USA.

C
D

O'Neill, Alexis & Sanchez, Enrique O. Estela's Swap, 1 vol. 2005. (ENG., Illus.). 32p. (J). (gr. -1-3). pap. 9.95 (978-1-60060-253-5(3)) Lee & Low Bks., Inc.

Optic, Oliver, pseud. Haste & Waste; or, the Young Pilot of Lake Champlain. 2007. 112p. (gr. 4-7). per. (978-1-4068-3636-3(2)) Echo Library.

—Northern Lands: Or, Young America in Russia & Prussia; A Story of Travel & Adventure / by William T. Adams (Oliver Optic). 2006. 384p. per. 26.99 (978-1-4255-4074-6(0)) Michigan Publishing.

—Northern Lands; or, Young America in Russia & Prussia a Story of Travel & Adventure. 2006. 376p. per. 26.99 (978-1-4255-3923-8(8)) Michigan Publishing.

—Outward Bound. 2007. 180p. (gr. 4-7). per. (978-1-4068-4343-9(1)) Echo Library.

—Outward Bound: Or Young America Afloat. l.t. ed. 2007. (ENG.). 274p. pap. 23.99 (978-1-4264-9153-5(0)) Creative Media Partners, LLC.

—Poor & Proud; or, the Fortunes of Katy Redburn a Story for Young Folks by Oliver Optic [Pseud.]. 2006. 280p. (gr. 4-7). per. 23.99 (978-1-4255-2551-4(2)) Michigan Publishing.

—Sunny Shores; or, Young America in Italy & Austria a Story of Travel & Adventure by William T Adams. 2006. 428p. per. 26.99 (978-1-4255-4627-4(7)) Michigan Publishing.

Oram, Hiawyn. Filbert, the Good Little Fiend. Liao, Jimmy, illus. 2013. (ENG.). 32p. (J). (gr. -1-2). 15.99 (978-0-7636-5870-0(7)) Candlewick Pr.

Orr, Peter. Now I Get It - Angry & Sharing: Social Stories for children with Autism. 2007. (Illus.). 20p. (J). 9.95 (978-0-9778866-2-3(X)) Natural Learning Concepts, Inc.

Orzechowski, Shawneen. Sarah's Secret: Civil War Deserter at Fredericksburg. 2011. 104p. (J). pap. 8.95 (978-1-57249-400-8(X), White Mane Kids) White Mane Publishing Co., Inc.

Osborne, Rick. Legend of the Christmas Stocking: An Inspirational Story of a Wish Come True, 1 vol. Griffin, Jim, illus. 2004. (ENG.). 32p. (J). 17.99 (978-0-310-70898-8(2)) Zonderkidz.

Osburn, Jacquelyn. Willy, the Worried Worm. 2008. 24p. pap. 12.99 (978-1-4343-8183-5(8)) AuthorHouse.

Otoshi, Kathryn. Zero. 2010. (ENG., Illus.). 32p. (J). (gr. -1-3). 17.95 (978-0-9723946-3-5(X)) KO Kids Bks.

Owens, L. L. Kendra's Big Decision. 2004. (Illus.). 26p. pap. (978-1-57021-031-0(4)) Comprehensive Health Education Foundation.

Padma, T. V. The Cleverest Thief. 2008. (Story Cove Ser.). (ENG., Illus.). 32p. (J). (gr. -1-3). pap. 4.95 (978-0-87483-882-4(7)) August Hse. Pubs., Inc.

Paige, D. M. Box-Office Smash. 2013. (Opportunity Ser.). (ENG.). 112p. (YA). (gr. 6-12). pap. 7.95 (978-1-4677-1494-5(1)); lib. bdg. 27.93 (978-1-4677-1371-9(6)) Lerner Publishing Group. (Darby Creek).

—Chart Topper. 2013. (Opportunity Ser.). (ENG.). 112p. (YA). (gr. 6-12). pap. 7.95 (978-1-4677-1493-8(3)); lib. bdg. 27.93 (978-1-4677-1370-2(8)) Lerner Publishing Group. (Darby Creek).

Painchaud, Michelle. Pretending to Be Erica. 2015. (ENG.). 272p. (YA). (gr. 7). 17.99 (978-0-670-01497-2(4), Viking Books for Young Readers) Penguin Young Readers Group.

Paladin, Frank. Hole in My Stocking. Amber, Holly & Lin, Melanie, illus. 2005. 24p. (J). per. 16.95 (978-0-9763635-4-5(2)) Beyond the Stars Pubns.

Palmer, Robin. Little Miss Red. 2010. (ENG.). 320p. (YA). (gr. 7-18). 9.99 (978-0-14-241123-0(X), Speak) Penguin Young Readers Group.

Paratore, Coleen Murtagh. Big. O'Malley, Judy, ed. Fennell, Clare, illus. 2012. (ENG.). 32p. (J). (gr. -1-2). 18.95 (978-0-9829938-5-9(4)) March 4th, Inc.

Parker, David. I Am a Leader! Walker, Sylvia, illus. 2005. (J). (978-0-439-73585-8(8)) Scholastic, Inc.

—I Will Keep Trying! Ramsey, Marcy Dunn, illus. 2005. (J). pap. (978-0-439-73588-9(2)) Scholastic, Inc.

Parker, Donald James. Reforming the Potter's Clay. 2008. 220p. pap. 12.95 (978-0-615-21223-4(9)) Sword of the Spirit Publishing.

Parnell, Fran & Fatus, Sophie. Grim, Grunt & Grizzle-Tail: A Story from Chile. Fatus, Sophie, illus. 2013. (Monster Stories Ser.: 6). (ENG., Illus.). 48p. (J). (gr. 1-4). pap. 8.99 (978-1-84686-910-5(2)) Barefoot Bks., Inc.

Pascal, Francine. Lucha por la Fama. Orig. Title: Claim to Fame. (SPA.). 128p. (J). 6.95 (978-84-272-3793-3(6)) Molino, Editorial ESP. Dist: AIMS International Bks., Inc.

A Pat on the Back. 2003. (J). per. (978-1-57657-879-7(8)) Paradise Pr., Inc.

Patience - Companion Book. 2003. (J). 2.00 (978-0-9740418-9-6(0)) Night Light Pubns., LLC.

Patterson, Horace. Ernie the Ermine. Parker, Jack, illus. 2007. 28p. per. 7.99 (978-1-58942-374-9(7)) R.H. Boyd Publishing Corp.

Patterson, James & Raymond, Emily. First Love. 2017. (ENG., Illus.). 384p. mass mkt. 7.99 **(978-1-4555-8500-7(9)**, Jimmy Patterson) Little Brown & Co.

—First Love. Illingworth, Sasha, photos by. 2015. (ENG., Illus.). 336p. (YA). (gr. 10-17). pap. 9.99 (978-0-316-20703-4(9), Jimmy Patterson) Little Brown & Co.

—First Love. 2014. (ENG.). 560p. (YA). pap. 16.00 (978-1-4555-8501-4(7), Jimmy Patterson) Little Brown & Co.

—First Love. 2014. (YA). lib. bdg. 28.20 (978-0-606-35894-1(3)) Turtleback Bks.

Paul, Marcy Beller. Underneath Everything. Davis, Bill, illus. 2015. (ENG.). 304p. (YA). (gr. 9). 17.99 (978-0-06-232721-5(6)) HarperCollins Pubs.

Paulsen, Gary. Flat Broke: The Theory, Practice & Destructive Properties of Greed. (ENG.). 128p. (J). (gr. 3-7). 2012. pap. 6.99 (978-0-375-86612-8(4), Yearling) 2011. 12.99 (978-0-385-74002-9(6), Lamb, Wendy Bks.) Random Hse. Children's Bks.

—The Tent: A Parable in One Sitting. 2006. (ENG., Illus.). 96p. (YA). (gr. 7-12). pap. 7.95 (978-0-15-205833-3(8)) Houghton Mifflin Harcourt Publishing Co.

—The Tent: A Parable in One Sitting. 2006. 86p. (gr. 7-12). 15.95 (978-0-7569-6891-5(7)) Perfection Learning Corp.

Pavón, Mar. A Very, Very Noisy Tractor. 2013. (ENG., Illus.). 28p. (J). (gr. -1-k). 16.95 (978-84-15619-65-9(0)) Eastern National.

Peacock, Hilda V. Eye-Jack & Hey-Oh. 2008. 20p. pap. 10.49 (978-1-4389-3239-2(1)) AuthorHouse.

Peck, Lisa J. Brittany to the Rescue: CTR Club - Book Two, 4 bks. 2005. (J). pap. 6.95 (978-0-9749241-6-8(4)) Golden Wings Enterprises.

—Meagan's Secret: CTR Club - Book Three, 4 bks. 2005. (J). pap. 6.95 (978-0-9749241-7-5(2)) Golden Wings Enterprises.

—Skating with Spencer: CTR Club - Book Four, 4 bks. 2005. (J). pap. 6.95 (978-0-9749241-8-2(0)) Golden Wings Enterprises.

Peet, Mal & Graham, Elspeth. Cloud Tea Monkeys. Wijngaard, Juan, illus. 2010. (ENG.). 56p. (J). (gr. -1-3). 17.99 (978-0-7636-4453-6(6)) Candlewick Pr.

Peirce, Lincoln. Big Nate Blasts Off. Peirce, Lincoln, illus. 2016. (Big Nate Ser.: 8). (ENG., Illus.). 224p. (J). (gr. 3-7). 13.99 (978-0-06-211111-1(6)) HarperCollins Pubs.

—Big Nate Goes for Broke. Peirce, Lincoln, illus. 2012. (Big Nate Ser.: 4). (Illus.). 224p. (J). (gr. 3-7). (ENG.). 12.99 (978-0-06-199661-0(0)); lib. bdg. 14.89 (978-0-06-199662-7(9)) HarperCollins Pubs.

—Big Nate Strikes Again. Peirce, Lincoln, illus. 2015. (Big Nate Ser.: 2). (ENG., Illus.). 224p. (J). (gr. 3-7). pap. 7.99 (978-0-06-228358-0(8)) HarperCollins Pubs.

—Big Nate's Greatest Hits. 2015. (ENG., Illus.). 376p. (J). pap. 12.99 (978-1-4494-6489-9(0)) Andrews McMeel Publishing.

Pellerin, Mona. Peetie, the Thinking Dabbler Duck. 2009. 32p. pap. 18.95 (978-1-4389-6303-7(3)) AuthorHouse.

Pelley, Kathleen T. The Sandal Artist, 1 vol. Sprague, Lois, illus. 2012. (ENG.). 32p. (J). (gr. k-3). 16.99 (978-1-58980-910-9(6)) Pelican Publishing Co., Inc.

Penn, Mw. Sidney the Silly Who Only Eats 6. Tommer, Sarah, illus. 2013. 36p. pap. 13.95 (978-0-9840425-7-9(1)) MathWord Pr., LLC.

Pentz, Jane A. Horatio's Magical Journeys - Horatio's New Book. 2007. 108p. pap. 10.00 (978-1-892426-10-9(2)) LMA Publishing.

Peterson, Donna. The Misadventures of Phillip Isaac Penn. 2011. 96p. pap. 7.99 (978-1-59955-893-6(9)) Cedar Fort, Inc./CFI Distribution.

—Pip Goes to Camp. 2012. 9.99 (978-1-4621-1077-3(0)) Cedar Fort, Inc./CFI Distribution.

Peterson, Doug. Ben Hurry: A Lesson in Patience, 1 vol. Moore, Michael, illus. 2006. (Big Idea Books / VeggieTown Values Ser.: Bk. 8). (ENG.). 32p. (J). (gr. -1-3). pap. 3.99 (978-0-310-70743-1(9)) Zonderkidz.

—Field of Beans: A Lesson in Faith, 1 vol. 2005. (Big Idea Books / VeggieTown Values Ser.: Bk. 3). (ENG., Illus.). 32p. (J). pap. 3.99 (978-0-310-70628-1(9)) Zonderkidz.

Peterson, Doug & Kenney, Cindy. Lost in Place: A Lesson in Overcoming Fear, 1 vol. Big Idea Productions Staff, illus. 2005. (Big Idea Books / VeggieTown Values Ser.: Bk. 4). (ENG.). 32p. (J). pap. 3.99 (978-0-310-70629-8(7)) Zonderkidz.

Peterson, Jim. The Summer House Kitten. 2007. 48p. pap. 16.95 (978-1-60441-914-6(8)) America Star Bks.

Peterson, M. E. You Are My Everything: Determined Little Maghara!!! Yang, Yi, illus. 2008. 43p. pap. 24.95 (978-1-60610-807-9(7)) America Star Bks.

Peterson, Matt. The Epic Tales of a Misfit Hero. 2012. pap. 8.99 (978-1-59955-999-5(4), Bonneville Bks.) Cedar Fort, Inc./CFI Distribution.

Pfaff, Eugene E. Guns at Guilford Court House. 2008. 132p. (YA). (gr. 6-9). pap. 14.95 (978-0-936389-97-4(4)) Tudor Pubs., Inc.

Phillips, Cynthia. The Way to Go! Emanuel, Effie Ann, illus. 2008. 17p. pap. 24.95 (978-1-60610-455-2(1)) America Star Bks.

Pichon, Liz. TOM GATES: EXCUSAS PERFECTAS (Y OTRAS COSILLAS GENIALES) 2013. (SPA.). 346p. (J). pap. 21.99 (978-84-216-8765-9(4)) Lectorum Pubns., Inc.

Pierre, Eileen. Why Is Life So Confusing? 2009. 40p. pap. 12.00 (978-1-60693-025-0(7), Eloquent Bks.) Strategic Book Publishing & Rights Agency (SBPRA).

Pike, Aprilynne. Life after Theft. 2013. (Life after Theft Ser.). (ENG.). 352p. (YA). (gr. 8). 17.99 (978-0-06-199900-0(6), HarperTeen) HarperCollins Pubs.

—Sleep No More. 2014. (ENG.). 352p. (YA). (gr. 8). 17.99 (978-0-06-199903-1(2), HarperTeen) HarperCollins Pubs.

Pincus, Gregory K. The Homework Strike. 2017. (ENG.). 272p. (J). (gr. 3-7). 16.99 (978-0-439-91301-0(2)) Scholastic, Inc.

Pinkney, Andrea Davis. Raven in a Dove House. 2014. (ENG.). 224p. (J). (gr. 5-7). pap. 8.99 (978-0-544-23016-3(7), HMH Books For Young Readers) Houghton Mifflin Harcourt Publishing Co.

Pinkowski, Vern V. A Twisted Pig's Tale. 2008. 144p. pap. 11.95 (978-0-595-46595-8(1), iUniverse, Inc.) iUniverse, Inc.

Pinkowski, Vernon V. A Twisted Pig's Tale. 2008. 148p. 21.95 (978-0-595-49022-6(0), iUniverse, Inc.) iUniverse, Inc.

Pittar, Gill. Milly, Molly & Beaky. Morrell, Cris, illus. 2005. 28p. (gr. -1). pap. (978-1-86972-048-3(2)) Milly Molly Bks.

—Milly, Molly & I Love You. 2005. (Illus.). 28p. pap. (978-1-86972-047-6(4)) Milly Molly Bks.

—Milly, Molly & the Bike Ride. 2005. 28p. (J). pap. (978-1-86972-046-9(6)) Milly Molly Bks.

—Milly, Molly & the Picnic. Morrell, Cris, illus. 2005. 28p. (gr. -1). pap. (978-1-86972-045-2(8)) Milly Molly Bks.

Pittar, Gill & Gill, Pittar. Basura No, Gracias! Rioja, Alberto Jimenez, tr. Morrell, Cris, illus. 2003. (Milly Molly Ser.). (SPA.). 24p. (J). pap. (978-84-241-8695-1(8)) Everest Editora ESP. Dist: Lectorum Pubns., Inc.

Pitts, Constance. Chulita the Blind Cat. 2007. (Illus.). 48p. (J). (978-0-9652902-2-7(0)) Beevinwood, Inc.

Please & Thank You. 2003. (J). per. (978-1-57657-820-9(8)) Paradise Pr., Inc.

Plonk, Michelle. Fritz, the Forgetful Frog. 2009. 40p. pap. 18.50 (978-1-60860-123-3(4), Eloquent Bks.) Strategic Book Publishing & Rights Agency (SBPRA).

Poage, Brenda. Ima Nobody Becomes Somebody! Book One in the Ima Nobody Series. 2009. 88p. pap. 10.99 (978-1-4490-0157-5(2)) AuthorHouse.

Porter, Eleanor H. Pollyanna. (J). 21.95 (978-0-8488-1445-8(2)) Amereon Ltd.

—Pollyanna. 2007. (ENG.). 184p. pap. 19.99 (978-1-4346-0972-4(3)) Creative Media Partners, LLC.

—Pollyanna. Date not set. (J). 14.99 (978-0-06-028226-4(6)); 32p. pap. 4.99 (978-0-06-443536-9(9)) HarperCollins Pubs.

—Pollyanna. 2016. (J). pap. (978-1-5124-2614-4(8)) Lerner Publishing Group.

—Pollyanna. McKowen, Scott, illus. 2013. (Sterling Unabridged Classics Ser.). (ENG.). 208p. (J). (gr. 5). 9.95 (978-1-4027-9718-7(4)) Sterling Publishing Co., Inc.

—Pollyanna. Akib, Jamel, illus. 2007. (Classic Starts(tm) Ser.). (ENG.). 160p. (J). (gr. 2-4). 6.95 (978-1-4027-3692-6(4)) Sterling Publishing Co., Inc.

—Pollyanna. abr. ed. 2006. 210p. (J). (gr. 3-7). per. 8.99 (978-1-59166-669-1(4)) BJU Pr.

—Pollyanna. l.t. ed. 2007. (ENG.). 206p. pap. 22.99 (978-1-4346-1071-3(3)) Creative Media Partners, LLC.

—Pollyanna. 2011. (Dover Children's Evergreen Classics Ser.). (ENG.). 208p. (J). (gr. 3-8). pap. 4.99 (978-0-486-43206-9(8)) Dover Pubns., Inc.

—Pollyanna Grows Up. Date not set. 216p. (J). 21.95 (978-0-8488-1447-2(9)) Amereon Ltd.

Posner, Tina. Rabbit Tricks. Corbett, Liza, illus. 2006. 8p. (J). pap. (978-0-439-73513-1(0)) Scholastic, Inc.

Potter, Noel Gyro. The Spoiled Sport, 1 vol. Cannon, Joseph, illus. 2010. (Adventures of Marshall & Art Set 2 Ser.). (ENG.). 32p. (gr. -1-4). 28.50 (978-1-60270-737-5(5), Looking Glass Library) ABDO Publishing Co.

Powell, Amy. Absolutely the Best. 2007. (J). per. 12.00 (978-0-9773608-6-4(5)) Shiny Red Ball Publishing.

Powers-Fish, Amy Rose. Ethics 4 Every Bunny. 2012. 78p. pap. 34.77 (978-1-105-50495-2(6)) Lulu Pr., Inc.

Pratchett, Terry. Dodger. 368p. (YA). (gr. 8). 2013. pap. 9.99 (978-0-06-200951-7(6)) 2012. 17.99 (978-0-06-200949-4(4)) 2012. lib. bdg. 18.89 (978-0-06-200950-0(8)) HarperCollins Pubs.

—Only You Can Save Mankind. 224p. (J). (gr. 3-7). 2006. (Johnny Maxwell Trilogy Ser.: 1). pap. 6.99 (978-0-06-054187-3(3)) 2005. 15.99 (978-0-06-054185-9(7)) HarperCollins Pubs.

—Only You Can Save Mankind. 2006. (Johnny Maxwell Trilogy). 207p. (J). (gr. 3-7). 13.65 (978-0-7569-6933-2(6)) Perfection Learning Corp.

Prater, Cindy. Kelsie's Potty Adventure. Williams, Denny, illus. 2006. 40p. per. 19.95 (978-1-59858-271-0(2)) Dog Ear Publishing, LLC.

Preller, James. Bystander. 2011. (ENG.). 256p. (YA). (gr. 5-9). pap. 8.99 (978-0-312-54796-7(X), 9780312547967) Square Fish.

Prendergast, Gabrielle. Capricious, 1 vol. 2014. (ENG.). 352p. (YA). (gr. 8-12). 19.95 (978-1-4598-0267-4(5)) Orca Bk. Pubs. USA.

PRESS, Celebration. Building a Winner. 2003. (ENG.). (J). (gr. 2-5). pap., stu. ed. 34.95 (978-0-673-62848-0(5), Celebration Pr.) Pearson Schl.

Price, Margaret Evans, illus. The Betty Fairy Book. 2006. (Shape Bks.). (ENG.). 16p. (J). pap. 9.95 (978-1-59583-092-0(8), Green Tiger Pr.) Laughing Elephant.

Primavera, Elise. Making Mistakes on Purpose. 2016. (Ms. Rapscott's Girls Ser.). (ENG., Illus.). 160p. (J). (gr. 3-7). 16.99 (978-0-8037-3824-9(2), Dial Bks) Penguin Young Readers Group.

Proud, Amy. Izzy the Very Bad Burglar. 2016. (ENG., Illus.). 32p. (J). (gr. -1-k). 16.99 (978-1-63450-174-3(8), Sky Pony Pr.) Skyhorse Publishing Co., Inc.

Provenzano, Stella Marie. How Rusty Rooster Found His Do. 2008. 16p. per. 24.95 (978-1-4241-9362-2(1)) America Star Bks.

Pryor, Bonnie. Perfect Percy. 2013. (ENG.). 28p. (J). (gr. -1-3). 12.99 (978-1-4424-8872-4(7), Atheneum Bks. for Young Readers) Simon & Schuster Children's Publishing.

Pyke, Helen Godfrey. Pinch River: Growing up Hard & Fast on the Michigan Frontier. 2008. (J). pap. 7.97 (978-0-8163-2250-3(3)) Pacific Pr. Publishing Assn.

Quarles, Patrice Michelle. Get up, & Start Your Day: Give Mommy & Daddy a Break. 2011. 28p. pap. 21.99 (978-1-4568-9186-2(3)) Xlibris Corp.

R. Friend Swallows Her Pride. 2003. (Down on Friendly Acres Ser.: No. 1). (J). per. 5.95 (978-0-9743627-0-0(0), 1179809) Sunflower Seeds Pr.

Radley, Gail. Kyle Jeffries, Pilgrim. Burns, Taurus, illus. 2010. (J). pap. (978-0-87743-712-3(2)) Baha'i Publishing Trust, U.S.

Rae, Milne. Geordie's Tryst. 2007. 72p. per. (978-1-4068-3682-0(6)) Echo Library.

Ramon, Elisa. Aquello Que Tanto Queria Susana. Lavarello, Jose Maria, illus. 2004.Tr. of What Susana Loved Dearly. (SPA.). (J). pap. 7.99 (978-84-236-6702-4(2)) Edebé ESP. Dist: Lectorum Pubns., Inc.

Ramos, Peregrina. The Little Clay Jar: La Vasijita de Barro. Graham, Dennis, illus. 2006.Tr. of vasijita de Barro. (SPA & ENG.). (J). per. 15.95 (978-0-9788381-0-2(6)) Word Gift Pubns.

Rand, Edward A. The Knights of the White Shield: Up-the-Ladder Club Series Round One Play. 2007. 166p. pap. 19.99 (978-1-4264-8273-1(6)); (ENG.). 184p. pap. 21.99 (978-1-4264-8310-3(4)) Creative Media Partners, LLC.

—The Knights of the White Shield; or, up-the-Ladder Club Series, Round One Play. 2007. 120p. per. (978-1-4068-3739-1(3)) Echo Library.

Rapp, Adam. The Children & the Wolves. Ering, Timothy Basil, illus. 2012. (ENG.). 160p. (YA). (gr. 9). 16.99 (978-0-7636-5337-8(3)) Candlewick Pr.

Ravel, Maurice, et al. The Boy & the Spell. Riglietti, Serena, illus. 2007. (Musical Stories Ser.). (ENG.). 36p. (J). (gr. 2-4). 16.95 (978-0-9646010-4-8(4)) Pumpkin Hse., Ltd.

Ray, Anna Chapin. Half a Dozen Girls. 2007. 148p. (gr. 4-7). per. (978-1-4068-3752-0(0)) Echo Library.

Rech, Lindsay Faith. It Started with a Dare. 2010. (ENG.). 312p. (YA). (gr. 7-18). pap. 17.99 (978-0-547-23558-5(5)) Houghton Mifflin Harcourt Publishing Co.

Reed, Amy Lynn. The Nowhere Girls. 2017. (YA). pap. **(978-1-4814-8174-8(6)**, Simon Pulse) Simon Pulse.

Reinhardt, Dana. Harmless. 2008. (ENG.). 240p. (YA). (gr. 9). pap. 8.99 (978-0-553-49497-6(X), Ember) Random Hse. Children's Bks.

Reintgen, Scott. Nyxia. 2017. (Nyxia Triad Ser.). (ENG.). 384p. (YA). (gr. 7). 17.99 **(978-0-399-55679-1(6))**; lib. bdg. 20.99 **(978-0-399-55680-7(X))** Random Hse. Children's Bks. (Crown Books For Young Readers).

Remenar, Kristen. Groundhog's Dilemma. Faulkner, Matt, illus. 2015. (ENG.). 32p. (J). (gr. -1-2). lib. bdg. 16.95 (978-1-58089-600-9(6)) Charlesbridge Publishing, Inc.

Renshaw, D. M. A Day to Remember. 2008. 100p. per. 23.95 (978-1-4327-0858-0(9)) Outskirts Pr., Inc.

Reynolds, Aaron. Here Comes Destructosaurus! Tankard, Jeremy, illus. 2014. (ENG.). 32p. (J). (gr. -1-k). 16.99 (978-1-4521-2454-4(X)) Chronicle Bks. LLC.

Reynolds, Jason. When I Was the Greatest. Frost, Michael, photos by. 2014. (ENG., Illus.). 240p. (YA). (gr. 7). 17.99 (978-1-4424-5947-2(6), Atheneum Bks. for Young Readers) Simon & Schuster Children's Publishing.

Reynolds, Peter H. The Best Kid in the World: A SugarLoaf Book. Reynolds, Peter H., illus. 2012. (ENG., Illus.). 48p. (J). (gr. -1-2). pap. 22.99 (978-1-4424-7178-8(6), Atheneum Bks. for Young Readers) Simon & Schuster Children's Publishing.

—So Few of Me. Reynolds, Peter H., illus. 2006. (ENG., Illus.). 32p. (J). (gr. k-12). 15.00 (978-0-7636-2623-5(6)) Candlewick Pr.

Rhuday-Perkovich, Olugbemisola. 8th Grade Super Zero. 2011. (ENG.). 336p. (J). (gr. 4-7). pap. 7.99 (978-0-545-09725-3(8), Levine, Arthur A. Bks.) Scholastic, Inc.

Ricchiuti, Paul B. Treasure on Spyglass Hill. 2015. 143p. (J). pap. (978-0-8163-5771-0(4)) Pacific Pr. Publishing Assn.

Rich, K. L. From Roaches to Riches. 2003. 107p. (YA). per. 15.95 (978-0-9728219-0-2(2)) Riches Publishing Co.

Richards, Anthony Lee. The Golden Bird, 1 vol. 2009. 56p. pap. 16.95 (978-1-60703-712-5(2)) America Star Bks.

Richards, Laura Elizabeth Howe. Queen Hildegarde. 2007. 92p. per. (978-1-4068-3867-1(5)) Echo Library.

Richter, Jutta. The Cat: Or, How I Lost Eternity. Brailovsky, Anna, tr. from GER. Berner, Rotraut Susanne, illus. 2007. (ENG.). 80p. (J). (gr. 1-6). 14.00 (978-1-57131-676-9(0)) Milkweed Editions.

Riley, Zach. Sacred Stick. Ricci, Andrés, illus. 2012. (Zach Riley Ser.). 80p. (J). (gr. 3-6). lib. bdg. 27.07 (978-1-61783-535-3(8)) Magic Wagon.

Ripken, Cal. Cal Ripken, Jr. 's All-Stars Out at Home. 2016. (Cal Ripken, Jr. 's All Stars Ser.). (ENG.). 224p. (J). (gr. 3-7). pap. 6.99 (978-1-4847-2789-8(4)) Hyperion Bks. for Children.

Ripken, Cal, Jr. Hothead. aut. ed. 2011. 16.99 (978-1-4231-5168-5(2)) Disney Pr.

—Hothead. 2011. (Playaway Children Ser.). (J). (gr. 4-6). 44.99 (978-1-61707-430-1(6)) Random Hse., Inc.

Ripken, Cal, Jr. & Cowherd, Kevin. Hothead. 2012. (ENG.). 160p. (J). (gr. 3-7). pap. 6.99 (978-1-4231-4003-0(6)) Hyperion Pr.

Ripken Jr., Cal. Cal Ripken, Jr. 's All-Stars Out at Home. 2015. (Cal Ripken, Jr. 's All Stars Ser.). (ENG.). 208p. (J). (gr. 3-7). 16.99 (978-1-4231-7867-5(X)) Hyperion Bks. for Children.

Rivera, Lilliam. The Education of Margot Sanchez. 2017. (ENG., Illus.). 304p. (YA). (gr. 9). 17.99 (978-1-4814-7211-1(9), Simon & Schuster Bks. For Young Readers) Simon & Schuster Bks. For Young Readers.

Roach, Tregenza A. The Lesson Box. Samuel, Karen L., illus. 2012. (J). (978-1-934370-25-4(8)) Editorial Campana.

Roberts, Emma Perry. Mrs. Murphy's Marvelous Mansion. Rogalski, Robert, illus. 2006. 32p. (J). (gr. -1-3). 15.95 (978-0-9740190-4-8(6), 888-210-8216) Illumination Arts Publishing Co., Inc.

Roberts, Justin. The Smallest Girl in the Smallest Grade. Robinson, Christian, illus. 2014. (ENG.). 32p. (J). (gr. -1-k). 16.99 (978-0-399-25743-8(8), G.P. Putnam's Sons Books for Young Readers) Penguin Young Readers Group.

Robertson, Elysia Hill. We Make the World A Special Place. Robertson, Elysia Hill & Bruce, Cindy, illus. 2005. 100p. (J). per. 12.95 (978-0-9764444-0-4(2), EJWV-001) E. J. Publishing.

Robins, E. Too Late. 2004. (Carter High Chronicles (High-Interest Readers) Ser.). (Illus.). 48p. (J). per. 3.95 (978-1-56254-693-9(7), SP6937) Saddleback Educational Publishing, Inc.

Robins, Eleanor. Broken Promise, 1 vol. unabr. ed. 2011. (Choices Ser.). (ENG.). 50p. (YA). (gr. 9-12). 7.95 (978-1-61651-591-1(0)) Saddleback Educational Publishing, Inc.

—Don't Get Caught, 1 vol. unabr. ed. 2011. (Choices Ser.). (ENG.). 52p. (YA). (gr. 9-12). 7.95 (978-1-61651-592-8(9)) Saddleback Educational Publishing, Inc.

—Just Be Yourself. (Carter High Chronicles Senior Year Ser.). 2005. (Illus.). 48p. (J). per. 3.95 (978-1-56254-772-1(0), SP7720) 2011. (ENG.). 50p. (YA). (gr. 9-12). pap. 7.95 (978-1-61651-325-2(X)) Saddleback Educational Publishing, Inc.

—The Last Time, 1 vol. unabr. ed. 2011. (Carter High Senior Year Ser.). (ENG.). 49p. (YA). (gr. 9-12). pap. 7.95 (978-1-61651-326-9(8)) Saddleback Educational Publishing, Inc.

—One More Chance. (Carter High Chronicles Senior Year Ser.). 2005. (Illus.). 48p. (J). per. 3.95 (978-1-56254-774-5(7), SP7747) 2011. (ENG.). 51p. (YA). (gr. 9-12). pap. 7.95 (978-1-61651-327-6(6)) Saddleback Educational Publishing, Inc.

—Pay Back, 1 vol. unabr. ed. 2011. (Choices Ser.). (ENG.). 52p. (YA). (gr. 9-12). 7.95 (978-1-61651-594-2(5)) Saddleback Educational Publishing, Inc.

—Someone to Count, 1 vol. unabr. ed. 2011. (Carter High Senior Year Ser.). (ENG.). 50p. (YA). (gr. 9-12). pap. 7.95 (978-1-61651-328-3(4)) Saddleback Educational Publishing, Inc.

—The Wrong Way, 1 vol. unabr. ed. 2011. (Carter High Senior Year Ser.). (ENG.). 52p. (YA). (gr. 9-12). pap. 7.95 (978-1-61651-331-3(4)) Saddleback Educational Publishing, Inc.

Robinson, Gary. Danny Blackgoat, Rugged Road to Freedom. 2014. (ENG.). (YA). pap. 9.95 (978-1-939053-05-3(6), 7th Generation) Book Publishing Co.

Robinson, Mark. Vile: A Cautionary Tale for Little Monsters. Home, Sarah, illus. 2011. (ENG.). 32p. (J). (gr. k-2). 14.99 (978-0-7459-6254-2(8)) Lion Hudson PLC GBR. Dist: Independent Pubs. Group.

Robshaw, Brandon. Big Wish. 2016. (ENG.). 240p. (J). (gr. 3-7). 16.99 (978-0-545-90410-0(2), Chicken Hse., The) Scholastic, Inc.

Rockliff, Mara. The Grudge Keeper, 1 vol. Wheeler, Eliza, illus. 2014. (ENG.). 32p. (J). (gr. -1-3). 16.95 (978-1-56145-729-8(9)) Peachtree Pubs.

Roddy, Lee. The Mystery of the Wild Surfer. 2006. (Ladd Family Adventure Ser.: Vol. 6). (Illus.). 135p. (J). (gr. 4-7). per. 7.99 (978-0-88062-255-4(5)) Mott Media.

Rodríguez, Orlando A. Valores Morales y Buenos Hábitos — Rangel, Mario Hugo, illus. (SPA.). 32p. (J). 2004. (978-0-311-38596-6(6)) 2004. (978-0-311-38597-3(4)) 2003. (978-0-311-38595-9(8)) Baptist Spanish Publishing Hse./Casa Bavtista de Publicaciones: Mundo Hispano.

Roman, Lisa. Boots. Steckler, Megan, illus. 2009. 24p. pap. 24.95 (978-1-60749-329-7(2)) America Star Bks.

Romano, Juliana. First There Was Forever. 2016. (ENG.). 416p. (YA). (gr. 9). pap. 10.99 (978-0-14-751391-5(X), Speak) Penguin Young Readers Group.

Rose, Sue. The Perfect Moment. 2007. (Unfabulous! Ser.). 120p. (J). (978-1-4287-1934-7(2)) Scholastic, Inc.

Rosenfeld, Dina. Yossi & Laibel Learn to Help. Wenkert, Norman, illus. 2012. 14p. (J). 6.95 (978-1-929628-62-9(5)) Hachai Publishing.

Rosenthal, Amy Krouse. One Smart Cookie: Bite-Size Lessons for the School Years & Beyond. Dyer, Jane & Dyer, Brooke, illus. 2010. (ENG.). 40p. (J). (gr. k-5). 12.99 (978-0-06-142970-5(8)) HarperCollins Pubs.

—Sugar Cookies: Sweet Little Lessons on Love. Dyer, Jane & Dyer, Brooke, illus. 2009. (ENG.). 40p. (J). (gr. k-5). 12.99 (978-0-06-174072-5(1)) HarperCollins Pubs.

—This Plus That: Life's Little Equations. Corace, Jen, illus. 2011. (ENG.). 40p. (J). (gr. -1-3). 14.99 (978-0-06-172655-2(9)) HarperCollins Pubs.

Ross, Barbara & Beatty, Nicholas. The Goops Circus: A Whimsical Telling of Do-Good Tales. Camille, Diana, illus. 2010. (Goops Ser.). 58p. (J). 19.95 incl. audio compact disk (978-0-9712368-4-4(4)) Goops Unlimited.

Ross, Betsy. Problem Solvers: Two Boys Solve Problems in Different Ways. 2012. 24p. pap. 15.00 (978-1-4669-4946-1(5)) Trafford Publishing.

Ross, Elizabeth. Belle Epoque. 2014. (ENG.). 352p. (YA). (gr. 7). pap. 9.99 (978-0-385-74147-7(2), Ember) Random Hse. Children's Bks.

Rottman, S. L. Hero, 1 vol. 2007. (ENG.). 144p. (YA). (gr. 7-18). (978-1-56145-427-3(3)) Peachtree Pubs.

Rouss, Sylvia. Sammy Spider's First Mitzvah. Janus Kahn, Katherine, illus. 2014. (ENG.). 24p. (J). (gr. -1-3). 17.95 (978-1-4677-1947-6(1), Kar-Ben Publishing) Lerner Publishing Group.

Rouss, Sylvia A. No Rules for Michael. Simon, Susan, illus. 2004. (ENG.). 24p. (J). (gr. -1-1). pap. 6.95 (978-1-58013-044-8(5), Kar-Ben Publishing) Lerner Publishing Group.

Rowley, Melissa. The Falcon Shield. 2009. (J). 6.99 (978-1-60641-103-2(9)) Deseret Bk. Co.

Rowley, M'lin. Knights of Right, BK 4: The Fiery Gloves. 2010. 80p. (J). pap. 6.99 (978-1-60641-241-1(8), Shadow Mountain) Shadow Mountain Publishing.

—The Silver Coat. 2009. (Knights of Right Ser.: Bk. 2). 71p. (J). (gr. 1-5). pap. 6.99 (978-1-60641-104-9(7), Shadow Mountain) Shadow Mountain Publishing.

Rowleym'Lin. Knights of Right, BK 3: The Warrior's Guard. 2010. 80p. (J). pap. 6.99 (978-1-60641-240-4(X), Shadow Mountain) Shadow Mountain Publishing.

Ruby, Laura. Good Girls. 2008. (ENG.). 304p. (YA). (gr. 9-12). pap. 8.99 (978-0-06-088225-9(5)) 2006. 288p. (J). lib. bdg. 17.89 (978-0-06-088224-2(7)) 2006. (ENG.). 288p. (YA). (gr. 9-12). 16.99 (978-0-06-088223-5(9)) HarperCollins Pubs. (HarperTeen).

Rue, Nancy N. Sophie's Drama, 1 vol. 2009. (Faithgirlz! Ser.: No. 11). (ENG.). 178p. (J). pap. 6.99 (978-0-310-71844-4(9)) Zonderkidz.

—Sophie's Friendship Fiasco. 2009. (Faithgirlz! Ser.: No. 7). (ENG.). 128p. (J). pap. 6.99 (978-0-310-71842-0(2)) Zonderkidz.

Russell, David O. & Auseon, Andrew. Alienated. 2010. (ENG.). 352p. (J). (gr. 3-7). pap. 5.99 (978-1-4169-8299-9(X), Aladdin) Simon & Schuster Children's Publishing.

Russell, Krista. Chasing the Nightbird, 1 vol. 2011. (ENG.). 192p. (YA). (gr. 5-9). 15.95 (978-1-56145-597-3(0), Peachtree Junior) Peachtree Pubs.

Russon, Penni. Breathe. 2007. (ENG., Illus.). 368p. (YA). (gr. 9-18). 16.99 (978-0-06-079393-7(7)) HarperCollins Pubs.

Ryan, P E. Saints of Augustine. 2007. 308p. (YA). (gr. 7-18). 16.99 (978-0-06-085810-0(9)); lib. bdg. 17.89 (978-0-06-085811-7(7)) HarperCollins Pubs. (HarperTeen).

Ryan, Pam Muñoz & McInerney, Kathleen. Paint the Wind. 2009. (ENG.). 352p. (J). (gr. 3-7). pap. 7.99 (978-0-545-10176-9(X), Scholastic Paperbacks) Scholastic, Inc.

Ryan, Shawn. Right Now I'm Small, & I Have a Long Time to Grow. 2010. 32p. pap. 17.95 (978-1-4269-3769-9(5)) Trafford Publishing.

Rylant, Cynthia. A Fine White Dust. 2006. (ENG.). 112p. (J). (gr. 5-9). pap. 6.99 (978-1-4169-2769-3(7), Atheneum Bks. for Young Readers) Simon & Schuster Children's Publishing.

Sabatini, Kimberly. Touching the Surface. 2012. (ENG.). 352p. (YA). (gr. 9). 16.99 (978-1-4424-4002-9(3), Simon Pulse) Simon Pulse.

Sacre, Antonio. A Mango in the Hand: A Story Told Through Proverbs. Serra, Sebastia, illus. 2011. (ENG.). 32p. (J). (gr. k-2). 16.95 (978-0-8109-9734-9(7), Abrams Bks. for Young Readers) Abrams, Inc.

Saffer, Sally. It's No Use Crying over Spilled Milk: A Lesson Within a Story from the Series, Learning to be Wise. 2012. (ENG.). 31p. (J). pap. 13.95 (978-1-4327-6981-9(2)) Outskirts Pr., Inc.

Saft, Lauren. Those Girls. 2016. (ENG.). 336p. (YA). (gr. 10-17). pap. 9.99 (978-0-316-26016-9(9), Poppy) Little, Brown Bks. for Young Readers.

Salerno, Tony. Where's Beeper? A Learning Adventure in Helpfulness, 4 vols. 2005. 56p. (J). 14.99 (978-0-89221-603-1(4)) New Leaf Pub. Group.

Sales, Leila. Tonight the Streets Are Ours. 2015. (ENG.). 352p. (YA). (gr. 7). 17.99 (978-0-374-37665-9(4), 9780374376659, Farrar, Straus & Giroux (BYR)) Farrar, Straus & Giroux.

Sandler, Steve. My Uncle Rob. Cunningham, Rob, illus. 2008. 32p. (J). pap. 12.95 (978-0-9715721-5-7(1)) Washington Pubs.

Sargent, Dave. Storky Stork: Be Trustworthy, 19 vols., Vol. 18. Lenoir, Jane, illus. 2003. (Feather Tales Ser.: 18). 42p. (J). pap. 10.95 (978-1-56763-754-0(X)) Ozark Publishing.

Sargent, Dave & Sargent, David, Jr. Kitty Hawk: Stealing, 20, 11. Lenoir, Jane, illus. 2003. (Feather Tales Ser.: 11). 42p. (J). pap. 6.95 (978-1-56763-740-3(X)) Ozark Publishing.

—Pinkie Flamingo: Leaving Home, 19 vols., Vol. 15. Lenoir, Jane, illus. 2003. (Feather Tales Ser.: 15). 42p. (J). pap. 10.95 (978-1-56763-748-9(5)) Ozark Publishing.

Sargent, Dave & Sargent, Pat. Bandit: I Help Others, 38 vols., Vol. 14. Huff, Jeane, illus. 2nd rev. ed. 2003. (Animal Pride Ser.: No. 14). 42p. (J). pap. 10.95 (978-1-56763-786-1(8)) Ozark Publishing.

Sargent, Dave, et al. Berry Picking Time Vol. 3: (Apache) Be Brave, 20 vols. Lenoir, Jane, illus. l.t. ed. 2003. (Story Keeper Ser.: 3). 42p. (J). Vol. 3. lib. bdg. 23.60 (978-1-56763-907-0(0), 1228136)vol. 3. pap. 6.95 (978-1-56763-908-7(9), 1228136) Ozark Publishing.

—Fields of Golden Corn Vol. 6: (Navajo) Be Energetic, 20 vols. Lenoir, Jane, illus. l.t. ed. 2003. (Story Keeper Ser.: 6). 42p. (J). pap. 10.95 (978-1-56763-914-8(3)); lib. bdg. 23.60 (978-1-56763-913-1(5)) Ozark Publishing.

—A Hole in the Sun: (Choctaw) Be Independent, 20, Vol. 1. Lenoir, Jane, illus. l.t. ed. 2003. (Story Keeper Ser.: 1). 42p. (J). pap. 6.95 (978-1-56763-904-9(6)); lib. bdg. 23.60 (978-1-56763-903-2(8)) Ozark Publishing.

—Knocking the Rice Vol. 9: (Chippewa) Be Powerful, 20 vols. Lenoir, Jane, illus. l.t. ed. 2003. (Story Keeper Ser.: 9). 42p. (J). lib. bdg. 23.60 (978-1-56763-919-3(4)) Ozark Publishing.

—Ladder at the Door Vol. 10: (Hopi) Be Curious, 20 vols. Lenoir, Jane, illus. l.t. ed. 2004. (Story Keeper Ser.: 10). 48p. (J). pap. 10.95 (978-1-56763-922-3(4)); lib. bdg. 23.60 (978-1-56763-921-6(6)) Ozark Publishing.

—Land of the Sun Vol. 11: (Ute) Respect Elders, 20 vols., Vol. 11. Lenoir, Jane, illus. l.t. ed. 2004. (Story Keeper Ser.: 11). 48p. (J). lib. bdg. 23.60 (978-1-56763-923-0(2)); pap. 10.95 (978-1-56763-924-7(0)) Ozark Publishing.

—Little One Vol. 12: (Cherokee) Be Inventive, 20 vols. Lenoir, Jane, illus. l.t. ed. 2003. (Story Keeper Ser.: Vol. 12). 42p. (J). pap. 10.95 (978-1-56763-926-1(7)); Vol. 12. lib. bdg. 23.60 (978-1-56763-925-4(9)) Ozark Publishing.

—On the Banks of the Wallowa River: (Nez Perce) Use Your Talent, 20 vols., Vol. 13. Lenoir, Jane, illus. l.t. ed. 2004. (Story Keeper Ser.: 13). 48p. (J). lib. bdg. 23.60 (978-1-56763-927-8(5)) Ozark Publishing.

Sasso, Emilie. Cystic Fibrosis & You. 2008. 23p. pap. 24.95 (978-1-60672-405-7(3)) America Star Bks.

Sazaklis, John. The Ferret Fiasco. Robinson, Lee, illus. 2016. (Billy Burger, Model Citizen Ser.). (ENG.). 96p. (gr. 2-3). lib. bdg. 22.65 (978-1-4965-2589-5(2)) Stone Arch Bks.

—Jumping for Junk Food. Robinson, Lee, illus. 2016. (Billy Burger, Model Citizen Ser.). (ENG.). 96p. (gr. 2-3). lib. bdg. 22.65 (978-1-4965-2586-4(8)) Stone Arch Bks.

—Recess Is Ruined. Robinson, Lee, illus. 2016. (Billy Burger, Model Citizen Ser.). (ENG.). 96p. (gr. 2-3). lib. bdg. 22.65 (978-1-4965-2588-8(4)) Stone Arch Bks.

Schaefer, Laura. Littler Women: A Modern Retelling. 2017. (ENG., Illus.). 224p. (J). (gr. 3-7). 16.99 **(978-1-4814-8761-0(2)**, Simon & Schuster/Paula Wiseman Bks.) Simon & Schuster/Paula Wiseman Bks.

Scheerger, Sarah Lynn. The Opposite of Love. 2014. (ENG.). 272p. (YA). (gr. 8-12). 16.99 (978-0-8075-6132-4(0)) Whitman, Albert & Co.

Scheie, Jesse. I'm Still Shinin' On. 2008. 24p. pap. 24.95 (978-1-60813-168-6(8)) America Star Bks.

Schertle, Alice. Little Blue Truck Leads the Way. McElmurry, Jill, illus. (Little Blue Truck Ser.). (ENG.). (J). 2012. 40p. (gr. -1-3). 26.99 (978-0-547-85060-3(3)) 2015. 38p. (— 1). bds. 7.99 (978-0-544-56805-1(2), HMH Books For Young Readers) Houghton Mifflin Harcourt Publishing Co.

Schraff, Anne. The Quality of Mercy, 1 vol. unabr. ed. 2011. (Urban Underground Ser.). (ENG.). 183p. (YA). (gr. 9-12). pap. 9.95 (978-1-61651-006-0(4)) Saddleback Educational Publishing, Inc.

—A Song to Sing. 2008. (Passages Ser.). 130p. (YA). (gr. 7-9). lib. bdg. 13.95 (978-0-7569-8384-0(3)) Perfection Learning Corp.

—Urban Underground Class Set. 2010. (J). pap. 119.50 (978-1-61651-012-1(9)) Saddleback Educational Publishing, Inc.

—Urban Underground Complete Set. 2010. (J). pap. 190.20 (978-1-61651-011-4(0)) Saddleback Educational Publishing, Inc.

—Wildflower, 1 vol. unabr. ed. 2011. (Urban Underground Ser.). (ENG.). 183p. (YA). (gr. 9-12). pap. 9.95 (978-1-61651-009-1(9)) Saddleback Educational Publishing, Inc.

Schreiber, Joe. Con Academy. 2016. (ENG.). 240p. (YA). (gr. 9). pap. 9.99 (978-0-544-81355-7(3), HMH Books For Young Readers) Houghton Mifflin Harcourt Publishing Co.

Schröder, Monika. Be Light Like a Bird. 2016. (Middle-Grade Novels Ser.). (ENG.). 240p. (gr. 4-7). 26.65 (978-1-4965-3301-2(1)) Stone Arch Bks.

Schroeder, Lisa. All We Have Is Now. 2015. (ENG.). 272p. (J). (gr. 7). 17.99 (978-0-545-80253-6(9)) Scholastic, Inc.

Schulkers, Robert. Stormie the Dog Stealer: Seckatary Hawkins. 2007. 307p. lib. bdg. 39.95 (978-0-8488-3253-7(1)) Amereon Ltd.

Schulz, Charles M., creator. Be Yourself! 2013. (ENG., Illus.). 40p. (J). (gr. -1-17). 12.95 (978-0-7624-4718-3(4), Running Pr. Kids) Running Pr. Bk. Pubs.

Schwartz, Howard. Gathering Sparks. Swarner, Kristina, illus. 2010. (ENG.). 32p. (J). (gr. -1-3). 16.99 (978-1-59643-280-2(2), 9781596432802) Roaring Brook Pr.

Scruggs, Stephanie. Deer Can't Dance. 2009. 36p. pap. 15.95 (978-1-4490-4535-7(9)) AuthorHouse.

Seamons, Karen. Child of Virtue: SamiTales Relationship Series. 2012. (ENG.). 190p. 49.95 (978-1-4327-8144-6(8)) Outskirts Pr., Inc.

Seok, Boln. Itchy! Itchy! My Wings Must Be Growing!, 1 vol. 2009. 33p. pap. 24.95 (978-1-61546-092-2(6)) America Star Bks.

Sepetys, Ruta. Out of the Easy. 2013. (ENG.). 352p. (YA). (gr. 9). 17.99 (978-0-399-25692-9(X), Philomel Bks.) Penguin Young Readers Group.

Seredy, Kate. The Chestry Oak. 2015. (Illus.). 253p. (J). pap. 12.95 (978-1-930900-81-3(3)) Purple Hse. Pr.

Seskin, Steve & Shamblin, Allen. A Chance to Shine. Christie, R. & Christie, Gregory, illus. 2006. (ENG.). 30p. (J). (gr. -1-2). 16.99 (978-1-58246-167-0(8), Tricycle Pr.) Random Hse. Children's Bks.

Seven, John & Christy, Jana. A Rule Is to Break: A Child's Guide to Anarchy. 2012. (Wee Rebel Ser.). (ENG., Illus.). 44p. (gr. -1). bds. 14.95 (978-1-933149-25-7(6)) Manic D Pr.

Shamblin, Seskin & National Geographic Learning Staff. A Chance to Shine. Christie, R. Gregory, illus. 2008. (ENG.). 32p. (C). (gr. -1-2). pap. 12.95 (978-1-58246-304-9(2)) National Geographic School Publishing, Inc.

Shams, K. The Piggle. Spears, Ashley E., illus. l.t. ed. 2004. 20p. (J). 9.99 (978-0-9728872-9-8(6)) Trent's Prints.

Shan, Darren, pseud. The Thin Executioner. 2011. (ENG.). 512p. (YA). (gr. 10-17). pap. 10.99 (978-0-316-07864-1(6)) Little, Brown Bks. for Young Readers.

Shaposhnik, Alina. A Warm Yellow Pancake, 1 vol. 2010. 22p. 24.95 (978-1-4489-7067-4(9)) PublishAmerica, Inc.

Sharp, Michael. Vayda Jane Bean - Chocolate. Van Tine, Laura, illus. 2007. 20p. pap. (978-1-897455-70-8(4)) Avatar Pubns., Inc.

Shaw, Natalie. A Guide to Life. Spaziante, Patrick, illus. 2015. (Olivia TV Tie-In Ser.). (ENG.). 16p. (J). (gr. -1-2). 5.99 (978-1-4814-2788-3(1), Simon Spotlight) Simon Spotlight.

Shaw, Tucker. The Girls. 2010. (ENG.). 224p. (YA). (gr. 7-11). pap. 7.95 (978-0-8109-8991-7(3), Amulet Bks.) Abrams, Inc.

Shaw, Tucker & Luce, Clare Boothe. The Girls. 2009. (ENG.). 208p. (YA). (gr. 7-11). 17.95 (978-0-8109-8348-9(6), Amulet Bks.) Abrams, Inc.

Shea, John & Harmon, Michael B. A Kid from Southie. 2011. 240p. (YA). (gr. 9-18). 16.95 (978-1-934813-53-9(2)) Westside Bks.

Sheehan, Monica. Be Happy! A Little Book for a Happy You. Sheehan, Monica, illus. 2010. (ENG., Illus.). 38p. (J). (gr. -1-k). bds. 7.99 (978-1-4424-0676-6(3), Little Simon) Little Simon.

Shefelman, Janice Jordan. Anna Maria's Gift. Papp, Robert, illus. 2011. (Stepping Stone Book Ser.). (ENG.). 112p. (J). (gr. 2-5). pap. 4.99 (978-0-375-85882-6(2), Random Hse. Bks. for Young Readers) Random Hse. Children's Bks.

Sheinmel, Courtney. All the Things You Are. (ENG.). 256p. (J). (gr. 4-8). 2012. pap. 6.99 (978-1-4169-9718-4(0)) 2011. 15.99 (978-1-4169-9717-7(2)) Simon & Schuster Bks. For Young Readers. (Simon & Schuster Bks. For Young Readers).

Sheldon, Dyan. The Moon Dragons. Blythe, Gary, illus. 2015. (J). 17.32 (978-1-4677-6318-9(7)) Lerner Publishing Group.

—Moon Dragons. Blythe, Gary, illus. 2015. (ENG.). 32p. (J). (gr. -1-3). 16.95 (978-1-4677-6314-1(4)) Lerner Publishing Group.

ShelFish. Dots Dots Polka Dots, 1 vol. 2010. 46p. 24.95 (978-1-4512-1427-7(8)) PublishAmerica, Inc.

Shepard, Sara. Burned. 2013. (Pretty Little Liars Ser.: 12). (ENG.). 352p. (YA). (gr. 9). pap. 9.99 (978-0-06-208193-3(4)) HarperCollins Pubs.

—Burned. 2013. (Pretty Little Liars Ser.: 12). (YA). lib. bdg. 20.85 (978-0-606-32177-8(2), Turtleback) Turtleback Bks.

—Crushed. 2014. (Pretty Little Liars Ser.: 13). (ENG.). 368p. (YA). (gr. 9). pap. 10.99 (978-0-06-219972-0(2), HarperTeen) HarperCollins Pubs.

—Crushed. 2014. (Pretty Little Liars Ser.: 13). (YA). lib. bdg. 20.85 (978-0-606-35497-4(2)) Turtleback Bks.

—Deadly. 2013. (Pretty Little Liars Ser.: No. 14). (ENG.). 320p. (YA). (gr. 9-12). 17.99 (978-0-06-219974-4(9), HarperTeen) HarperCollins Pubs.

—Flawless. (Pretty Little Liars Ser.: 2). (ENG.). (YA). (gr. 9-12). 2008. 352p. pap. 10.99 (978-0-06-088735-3(4)) 2007. 352p. 16.99 (978-0-06-088733-9(8)) 2010. 368p. pap. 8.99 (978-0-06-205987-1(4)) HarperCollins Pubs. (HarperTeen).

—Flawless. 2008. (Pretty Little Liars Ser.: 2). (YA). lib. bdg. 20.85 (978-0-606-12267-2(2), Turtleback) Turtleback Bks.

—Heartless. 2010. (Pretty Little Liars Ser.: 7). (ENG.). (YA). (gr. 9-18). 304p. pap. 10.99 (978-0-06-156616-5(0)); 288p. 16.99 (978-0-06-156614-1(4)) HarperCollins Pubs. (HarperTeen).

—Killer. (Pretty Little Liars Ser.: 6). (ENG.). (YA). (gr. 9). 2010. 352p. pap. 9.99 (978-0-06-156613-4(6))No. 6. 2009. 336p. 16.99 (978-0-06-156611-0(X)) HarperCollins Pubs. (HarperTeen).

—Killer. 2010. (Pretty Little Liars Ser.: 6). (YA). lib. bdg. 20.85 (978-0-606-12278-8(8), Turtleback) Turtleback Bks.

—Perfect. (Pretty Little Liars Ser.: No. 3). (ENG.). (YA). (gr. 9-12). 2007. 320p. 16.99 (978-0-06-088736-0(2))No. 3. 2008. 336p. pap. 9.99 (978-0-06-088738-4(9)) HarperCollins Pubs. (HarperTeen).

—Pretty Little Liars. (Pretty Little Liars Ser.: 1). (YA). (gr. 9-12). 2007. (ENG.). 304p. pap. 9.99 (978-0-06-088732-2(X)) 2010. (ENG.). 304p. pap. 9.99 (978-0-06-200954-8(0))Set, Bks. 1-4. 2009. pap. 29.99 (978-0-06-180131-0(3)) HarperCollins Pubs. (HarperTeen).

—Pretty Little Liars Bind-Up #2: Perfect & Unbelievable. 2014. (Pretty Little Liars Ser.). (ENG.). 672p. (YA). (gr. 9). pap. 10.99 (978-0-06-232293-7(1), HarperTeen) HarperCollins Pubs.

—Pretty Little Secrets. (Pretty Little Liars Companion Novel Ser.). (ENG.). (YA). (gr. 9). 2013. 480p. pap. 9.99 (978-0-06-212592-7(3)) 2012. 464p. 17.99 (978-0-06-212591-0(5)) HarperCollins Pubs. (HarperTeen).

—Ruthless. (Pretty Little Liars Ser.: 10). (ENG.). (YA). (gr. 9). 2012. 368p. pap. 10.99 (978-0-06-208187-2(X)) 2011. 352p. 17.99 (978-0-06-208186-5(1)) HarperCollins Pubs. (HarperTeen).

—Ruthless. 2012. (Pretty Little Liars Ser.: 10). (YA). lib. bdg. 20.85 (978-0-606-26873-8(1), Turtleback) Turtleback Bks.

—Twisted. (Pretty Little Liars Ser.: 9). (ENG.). (YA). (gr. 9). 2012. 336p. pap. 10.99 (978-0-06-208102-5(0)) 2011. 320p. 16.99 (978-0-06-208101-8(2)) HarperCollins Pubs. (HarperTeen).

—Twisted. 2012. (Pretty Little Liars Ser.: 9). (YA). lib. bdg. 20.85 (978-0-606-26288-0(1), Turtleback) Turtleback Bks.

—Unbelievable. 2008. (Pretty Little Liars Ser.: No. 4). (ENG.). 352p. (J). (gr. 9-18). 16.99 (978-0-06-088739-1(7), HarperTeen) HarperCollins Pubs.

—Wanted. (Pretty Little Liars Ser.: 8). (ENG.). (YA). (gr. 9). 2011. 288p. pap. 9.99 (978-0-06-156619-6(5)) 2010. 272p. 16.99 (978-0-06-156617-2(9)) HarperCollins Pubs. (HarperTeen).

—Wicked. 2009. (Pretty Little Liars Ser.: 5). (ENG.). 336p. (YA). (gr. 9). pap. 9.99 (978-0-06-156610-3(1), HarperTeen) HarperCollins Pubs.

Shephard, H. Ferebee. Jonathan & Roscoe. 2011. 24p. pap. 14.39 (978-1-4634-4881-3(3)) AuthorHouse.

Shields, Gillian. Elephantantrum! Johnson-Isaacs, Cally, illus. 2013. (ENG.). 32p. (J). (gr. -1-3). 14.99 (978-1-58925-126-7(1)) Tiger Tales.

Shoemaker, Tim. Below the Surface, 1 vol. 2015. (Code of Silence Novel Ser.). (ENG.). 416p. (J). pap. 9.99 (978-0-310-73765-0(6)) Zonderkidz.

The Short & the Tall of It, the Black & the White of It: A Very Important Experiment at Daylily Elementary. 2006. (J). mass mkt. 16.95 (978-0-9740410-4-9(1)) WordMaster Publishing.

Short M.S., Jeff. A Kid's World, 1 vol. 2009. (Illus.). 48p. pap. 24.95 (978-1-60836-760-3(6)) America Star Bks.

Showstack, Richard. The Gift of the Magic: And Other Enchanting Character-Building Stories for Smart Teenage Girls Who Want to Grow up to Be Strong Women. Eric, Whitfield, illus. 2004. 156p. (YA). per. 14.95 (978-1-888725-64-3(8), BeachHouse Bks.) Science & Humanities Pr.

—Peggy: And Other Enchanting Character-Building Stories for Smar Boys Who Want to Grow up to Be Strong Men. Whitfield, Eric, illus. 2004. 200p. (YA). per. 14.95 (978-1-888725-66-7(4), BeachHouse Bks.) Science & Humanities Pr.

Sileo, Frank J. Did You Hear? A Story about Gossip. Zivoin, Jennifer, illus. 2017. (J). **(978-1-4338-2720-4(4)**, Magination Pr.) American Psychological Assn.

Sileo, Frank J. Sally Sore Loser: A Story about Winning & Losing. Pillo, Cary, illus. 2012. (J). 14.95 (978-1-4338-1189-0(8)); pap. 9.95 (978-1-4338-1190-6(1)) American Psychological Assn. (Magination Pr.).

Simon, Francesca. Horrid Henry's Christmas. Ross, Tony, illus. 2009. (Horrid Henry Ser.: 0). (ENG.). 112p. (J). (gr. 2-5). pap. 5.99 (978-1-4022-1782-1(X), Sourcebooks Jabberwocky) Sourcebooks, Inc.

—Tricks the Tooth Fairy. Ross, Tony, illus. 2009. (Horrid Henry Ser.: 0). (ENG.). 112p. (J). (gr. 2-5). pap. 6.99 (978-1-4022-2275-7(0), 9781402222757, Sourcebooks Jabberwocky) Sourcebooks, Inc.

—Wakes the Dead. Ross, Tony, illus. 2011. (Horrid Henry Ser.: 0). (ENG.). 112p. (J). (gr. 2-5). pap. 4.99 (978-1-4022-5934-0(4), Sourcebooks Jabberwocky) Sourcebooks, Inc.

—Wakes the Dead, 1 vol. Ross, Tony, illus. 2012. (Horrid Henry Ser.). (ENG.). 112p. (J). (gr. 2-5). lib. bdg. 24.21 (978-1-59961-192-1(9)) Spotlight.

Simonds, William. Marcus; or, the Boy-Tamer by Walter Aimwell [Pseud.]. 2006. 336p. per. 23.99 (978-1-4255-3348-9(5)) Michigan Publishing.

—Whistler; or, the Manly Boy by Walter Aimwell [Pseud.]. 2006. 332p. per. 23.99 (978-1-4255-3293-2(4)) Michigan Publishing.

Sims, Tom. Repo Elf. Perri, Anthony F., illus. 2008. (ENG.). 104p. (J). 12.95 (978-0-9787213-4-3(9), Cambridge House Pr.) Sterling & Ross Pubs.

Sirowy, Alexandra. First We Were IV. 2017. (ENG., Illus.). 448p. (YA). (gr. 7). 18.99 **(978-1-4814-7842-7(7)**, Simon & Schuster Bks. For Young Readers) Simon & Schuster Bks. For Young Readers.

Sise, Katie. The Pretty App. 2015. (ENG.). 352p. (YA). (gr. 8). 17.99 (978-0-06-219529-6(8)) HarperCollins Pubs.

Skeers, Linda & National Geographic Learning Staff. The Impossible Patriotism Project. Hoyt, Ard, illus. 2010. (Rise & Shine Ser.). (ENG.). 32p. (C). (gr. -1-1). pap. 11.95 (978-0-14-241391-3(7)) National Geographic School Publishing, Inc.

Skinner, Daphne. Henry Lleva la Cuenta. O'Rourke, Page Eastburn, illus. 2007. (Math Matters Ser.). 32p. (J). (gr. -1-3). pap. 5.95 (978-1-57565-250-4(1)) Kane Press, Inc.

Skye, obert. Pinocula. Skye, obert, illus. 2013. (Creature from My Closet Ser.: 3). (ENG., Illus.). 256p. (J). (gr. 4-7). 12.99 (978-0-8050-9689-7(2), 9780805096897, Holt, Henry & Co. Bks. For Young Readers) Holt, Henry & Co.

—Potterwookiee. Skye, obert, illus. 2012. (Creature from My Closet Ser.: 2). (ENG., Illus.). 256p. (J). (gr. 4-7). 13.99 (978-0-8050-9451-0(2), 9780805094510, Holt, Henry & Co. Bks. For Young Readers) Holt, Henry & Co.

—Wonkenstein. Skye, obert, illus. 2011. (Creature from My Closet Ser.: 1). (ENG., Illus.). 240p. (J). (gr. 4-7). 12.99 (978-0-8050-9268-4(4), 9780805092684, Holt, Henry & Co. Bks. For Young Readers) Holt, Henry & Co.

—Wonkenstein. Skye, obert, illus. 2015. (Creature from My Closet Ser.: 1). (ENG., Illus.). 256p. (J). (gr. 4-7). pap. 6.99 (978-1-250-01022-3(5), 9781250010223) Square Fish.

Slate, Jenny & Fleischer-Camp, Dean. Marcel the Shell with Shoes On: Things about Me, 1 vol. 2011. (Marcel the Shell Ser.: 1). (ENG.). 42p. (J). (gr. k-3). 18.99 (978-1-59514-455-3(2), Razorbill) Penguin Young Readers Group.

Slegers, Liesbet. Laura Ayuda a Su Mama/ Laura Helps Her Mom. 2008. 28p. 10.95 (978-84-263-6492-0(6)) Vives, Luis Editorial (Edelvives) ESP. Dist: Baker & Taylor Bks.

Sleiman, Dina L. Dauntless. 2015. (Valiant Hearts Ser.: 1). (ENG.). 368p. (YA). pap. 13.99 (978-0-7642-1312-0(1)) Bethany Hse. Pubs.

Small, Lily. Penelope the Pony. 2017. (Fairy Animals of Misty Wood Ser.). (ENG., Illus.). 144p. (J). pap. 5.99 **(978-1-250-12700-6(9)**, 9781250127006, Holt, Henry & Co. Bks. For Young Readers) Holt, Henry & Co.

Smelcer, John. The Trap. 2007. (ENG.). 176p. (YA). (gr. 7-9). per. 9.99 (978-0-312-37755-7(X), 9780312377557) Square Fish.

The Smile of A Golden Child. 2004. (J). per. 16.99 (978-0-9753533-6-3(5)) Golden Eagle Publishing Hse., Inc.

Smith, Adam. Other People's Shoes. 2008. 36p. pap. 18.50 (978-1-60693-383-1(3), Eloquent Bks.) Strategic Book Publishing & Rights Agency (SBPRA).

Smith, Anya. Respect - Companion Book. Cesena, Denise, illus. l.t. ed. 2003. 12p. (J). 2.00 (978-0-9740418-5-8(8)) Night Light Pubns., LLC.

Smith, Bryan. Is There an App for That? Wish, Katia, illus. 2015. (ENG.). 32p. (J). pap. 10.95 (978-1-934490-74-7(1)) Boys Town Pr.

C
D

—Mindset Matters. Griffin, Lisa, illus. 2017. (Without Limits Ser.: 2). (ENG.). 32p. (J). (gr. k-5). pap. 10.95 **(978-1-944882-12-9(X))** Boys Town Pr.

—Of Course It's a Big Deal. Griffin, Lisa, illus. 2017. (Executive Function Ser.: 3). (ENG.). 32p. (J). (gr. k-5). pap. 10.95 **(978-1-944882-11-2(1))** Boys Town Pr.

Smith, Diana M. Every Sock Needs a Mate. 2009. 36p. pap. 17.49 (978-1-4389-2636-0(7)) AuthorHouse.

Smith, Harriet. Pollyanna's Debt of Honor. (J). 17.95 (978-1-56723-091-8(1)) Yestermorrow, Inc.

Smith, Harriet Lummis. Pollyanna's Debt of Honor. (J). 15.95 (978-0-8488-1446-5(0)) Amereon Ltd.

Smith, J. L. The Abominators: And My Amazing Panty Wanty Woos! Hearn, Sam, illus. 2013. (ENG.). 144p. (J). (gr. 2-4). pap. 7.99 (978-1-907411-62-5(3)) Little, Brown Book Group Ltd. GBR. Dist: Hachette Bk. Group.

Smith, Jennifer & Morgan, Andre. Zelza Zero. 2010. 20p. pap. 12.99 (978-1-4490-4546-3(4)) AuthorHouse.

Smith, Loretta. Bela & the Gold Medallion. Marconi, Gloria, illus. Preston, James, photos by. 2012. 32p. pap. 13.00 (978-1-930357-27-3(3)) Do The Write Thing Foundation of DC.

Smith, Roland. Storm Runners. (Storm Runners Ser.: Bk. 1). (ENG.). 160p. (J). (gr. 3-7). 2012. pap. 5.99 (978-0-545-08177-1(7), Scholastic Pr.) 2011. 16.99 (978-0-545-08175-7(0)) Scholastic, Inc.

Snedeker, Caroline. Downright Dencey. Barney, Maginel Wright, illus. 2003. (Young Adult Library). 268p. (YA). pap. 12.95 (978-1-883937-79-9(5)) Bethlehem Bks.

Soler, Michael. The Ladybug & Me. Eisenberg, Serge, illus. 2007. 24p. (J). per. 8.99 (978-0-9795469-0-7(7)) Soler, Michael.

Something Wise. 15 vols. 2004. (Illus.). 39p. (J). (gr. 1-2). per. 6.00 (978-0-9714844-2-9(2)) Zion Publishing.

Sommer, Carl. Can You Help Me Find My Smile? Me Puedes Ayudar a Encontrar Mi Sonrisa? Budwine, Greg, illus. 2009. (Another Sommer-Time Story Bilingual Ser.). (SPA & ENG.). 48p. (J). lib. bdg. 16.95 (978-1-57537-150-4(2)) Advance Publishing, Inc.

—Dare to Dream! Martinez, Jorge et al, illus. 2014. (J). pap. (978-1-57537-951-7(1)) Advance Publishing, Inc.

—Dare to Dream! Martinez, Jorge et al, illus. 2007. (Another Sommer-Time Story Ser.). (ENG.). 48p. (J). 23.95 incl. audio compact disk (978-1-57537-723-0(3)); (gr. -1-3). 16.95 incl. audio compact disk (978-1-57537-523-6(0)); (gr. -1-3). 9.95 (978-1-57537-024-8(7)); (gr. k-4). lib. bdg. 16.95 (978-1-57537-073-6(5)) Advance Publishing, Inc.

—Dare to Dream! ¡Atrévete a Soñar! Martinez, Jorge et al, illus. 2009. 48p. (J). 26.95 incl. audio compact disk (978-1-57537-176-4(6)) Advance Publishing, Inc.

—The Donkey, Fox, & the Lion. Noé, Ignacio, illus. 2016. (ENG.). 32p. (J). (gr. k-4). lib. bdg. 16.95 (978-1-57537-926-5(0), Another Sommer-Time Story) Advance Publishing, Inc.

—Dream. Martinez, Jorge et al, illus. 2009. (Quest for Success Ser.). (ENG.). 56p. (YA). pap. 4.95 (978-1-57537-276-1(2)); lib. bdg. 12.95 (978-1-57537-251-8(7)) Advance Publishing, Inc.

—Dream (Sueña) Martinez, Jorge et al, illus. 2009. (Quest for Success Bilingual Ser.). (SPA & ENG.). 104p. (YA). (gr. 6-18). lib. bdg. 14.95 (978-1-57537-226-6(6)) Advance Publishing, Inc.

—Fast Forward. Budwine, Greg, illus. 2009. (Quest for Success Ser.). (ENG.). 56p. (YA). pap. 4.95 (978-1-57537-277-8(0)); lib. bdg. 12.95 (978-1-57537-252-5(5)) Advance Publishing, Inc.

—Fast Forward(Avance Acelarado) Budwine, Greg, illus. 2009. (Quest for Success Bilingual Ser.). (SPA & ENG.). 104p. (YA). lib. bdg. 14.95 (978-1-57537-227-3(4)) Advance Publishing, Inc.

—Hopeless to Hopeful. Vignolo, Enrique, illus. 2009. (Quest for Success Ser.). (ENG.). 56p. (YA). pap. 4.95 (978-1-57537-278-5(9)); lib. bdg. 12.95 (978-1-57537-253-2(3)) Advance Publishing, Inc.

—King of the Pond. Budwine, Greg, illus. 2014. (J). pap. (978-1-57537-956-2(2)) Advance Publishing, Inc.

—Lost & Found. Budwine, Greg, illus. 2009. (Quest for Success Ser.). 56p. (YA). pap. 4.95 (978-1-57537-280-8(0)); lib. bdg. 12.95 (978-1-57537-255-6(X)) Advance Publishing, Inc.

—Lost & Found(Perdida y Encontrada) Budwine, Greg, illus. 2009. (Quest for Success Bilingual Ser.). (ENG & SPA.). 96p. (YA). lib. bdg. 14.95 (978-1-57537-229-7(0)) Advance Publishing, Inc.

—Mayor for a Day. Westbrook, Dick, illus. 2014. (J). pap. (978-1-57537-959-3(7)) Advance Publishing, Inc.

—Mayor for a Day: Alcalde Por un Día. Westbrook, Dick, illus. 2009. (Another Sommer-Time Story Bilingual Ser.). (SPA & ENG.). 48p. (J). lib. bdg. 16.95 (978-1-57537-159-7(6)) Advance Publishing, Inc.

—Miserable Millie. Vignolo, Enrique, illus. (J). 2014. pap. (978-1-57537-960-9(0)) 2007. (ENG.). 48p. 16.95 incl. audio compact disk (978-1-57537-521-2(4)) 2007. (ENG.). 48p. (gr. -1-3). 9.95 (978-1-57537-022-4(0)) 2007. (ENG.). 48p. (gr. -1-3). lib. bdg. 16.95 (978-1-57537-071-2(9)) Advance Publishing, Inc.

—Miserable Millie(La Pobrecita Mili) Vignolo, Enrique, illus. 2009. (Another Sommer-Time Story Bilingual Ser.). (SPA & ENG.). 48p. (J). lib. bdg. 16.95 (978-1-57537-160-3(X)) Advance Publishing, Inc.

—No Longer a Dilly Dally. James, Kennon, illus. 2014. (J). pap. (978-1-57537-961-6(9)) Advance Publishing, Inc.

—No Longer a Dilly Dally(Nunca Mas a Troche y Moche) James, Kennon, illus. 2009. (Another Sommer-Time Story Bilingual Ser.). (SPA & ENG.). 48p. (J). lib. bdg. 16.95 (978-1-57537-162-7(6)) Advance Publishing, Inc.

—No One Will Ever Know. Budwine, Greg, illus. 2014. (J). pap. (978-1-57537-962-3(7)) Advance Publishing, Inc.

—No One Will Ever Know(Nadie Se Va a Enterar) Westbrook, Dick, illus. 2009. (Another Sommer-Time Story Bilingual Ser.). (SPA & ENG.). 48p. (J). lib. bdg. 16.95 (978-1-57537-163-4(4)) Advance Publishing, Inc.

—The Rebel. Vignolo, Enrique, illus. 2009. (Quest for Success Ser.). (ENG.). 56p. (YA). pap. 4.95 (978-1-57537-282-2(7)); lib. bdg. 12.95 (978-1-57537-257-0(6)) Advance Publishing, Inc.

—The Rebel(El Rebelde) Vignolo, Enrique, illus. 2009. (Quest for Success Bilingual Ser.). (ENG & SPA.). 104p. (YA). lib. bdg. 14.95 (978-1-57537-231-0(2)) Advance Publishing, Inc.

—The Runaway(La Escapada) Vignolo, Enrique, illus. 2009. (Quest for Success Bilingual Ser.). (SPA & ENG.). 104p. (YA). lib. bdg. 14.95 (978-1-57537-234-1(7)) Advance Publishing, Inc.

—Spike the Rebel! Vignolo, Enrique, illus. (J). 2014. pap. (978-1-57537-967-8(8)) 2007. (ENG.). 48p. (gr. -1-3). lib. bdg. 16.95 (978-1-57537-072-9(7)) 2007. (ENG.). 48p. 23.95 incl. audio compact disk (978-1-57537-722-3(5)) 2007. (ENG.). 48p. 16.95 incl. audio compact disk (978-1-57537-522-9(2)) 2007. (ENG.). 48p. (gr. -1-3). lib. bdg. 9.95 (978-1-57537-023-1(9)) Advance Publishing, Inc.

—Spike the Rebel!(pua, el Rebelde!) Vignolo, Enrique, illus. 2009. (Another Sommer-Time Story Bilingual Ser.). (SPA & ENG.). 48p. (J). lib. bdg. 16.95 (978-1-57537-167-2(7)) Advance Publishing, Inc.

—Time Remote! Budwine, Greg, illus. 2014. (J). pap. (978-1-57537-970-8(8)) Advance Publishing, Inc.

—Time Remote! 2003. (Another Sommer-Time Story Ser.). (Illus.). 48p. (J). (gr. 1-4). 16.95 incl. audio (978-1-57537-561-8(3)) Advance Publishing, Inc.

—Time Remote! Budwine, Greg, illus. 2003. (Another Sommer-Time Story Ser.). (ENG.). 48p. (J). (gr. 1-4). 16.95 incl. audio compact disk (978-1-57537-512-0(5)) Advance Publishing, Inc.

—Time Remote!(El Control Del Tiempo!) Budwine, Greg, illus. 2009. (Another Sommer-Time Story Bilingual Ser.). (SPA & ENG.). 48p. (J). lib. bdg. 16.95 (978-1-57537-170-2(7)) Advance Publishing, Inc.

—The Ugly Caterpillar. Budwine, Greg, illus. 2014. (J). pap. (978-1-57537-971-5(6)) Advance Publishing, Inc.

—The Ugly Caterpillar(La Oruga Fea) Budwine, Greg, illus. 2009. (Another Sommer-Time Story Bilingual Ser.). (SPA & ENG.). 48p. (J). (gr. k-3). lib. bdg. 16.95 (978-1-57537-171-9(5)) Advance Publishing, Inc.

Soto, Gary. Facts of Life. 2012. (ENG.). 192p. (YA). (gr. 7-7). pap. 7.99 (978-0-547-57734-0(6)) Houghton Mifflin Harcourt Publishing Co.

Sowunmi, Lakeysha. Apple Leaves. 2009. 48p. pap. 17.49 (978-1-4490-2055-2(0)) AuthorHouse.

Spain, Susan. The Deep Cut. 0 vols. 2014. (ENG.). 228p. pap. 9.99 (978-1-4778-4768-8(5), 9781477847688, Amazon Children's Publishing) Amazon Publishing.

Spain, Susan Rosson. The Deep Cut. 1 vol. 2006. (ENG., Illus.). 224p. (J). (gr. 5-9). 16.99 (978-0-7614-5316-1(4)) Marshall Cavendish Corp.

Sparks, Favre. Katie. 2009. 28p. pap. 12.00 (978-1-60860-413-5(6), Eloquent Bks.) Strategic Book Publishing & Rights Agency (SBPRA).

Spears, Jr. Derek's Dilemm. 2009. 148p. pap. 24.95 (978-1-60836-387-2(2)) America Star Bks.

Speer, Laura Y. The Good Ground Seeds. 2008. 20p. pap. 10.95 (978-1-4343-7576-6(5)) AuthorHouse.

Spencer, Katherine. More Than Friends: A Saving Grace Novel. 2008. (Saving Grace Ser.). (ENG., Illus.). 224p. (YA). (gr. 7-12). pap. 14.95 (978-0-15-205746-6(3)) Houghton Mifflin Harcourt Publishing Co.

Spinelli, Eileen. Peace Week in Miss Fox's Class. Kennedy, Anne, illus. 2012. (J). (978-1-61913-155-2(2)) Weigl Pubs., Inc.

Spinelli, Jerry. Fourth Grade Rats. 2012. (ENG.). 160p. (J). (gr. 2-5). pap. 5.99 (978-0-545-46478-9(1), Levine, Arthur A. Bks.) Scholastic, Inc.

—Fourth Grade Rats. 2012. lib. bdg. 16.00 (978-0-606-26731-1(X), Turtleback) Turtleback Bks.

—Third Grade Angels. Bell, Jennifer, illus. 2014. (ENG.). 160p. (J). (gr. 2-5). pap. 5.99 (978-0-545-38773-6(6), Levine, Arthur A. Bks.) Scholastic, Inc.

—Zinkoff, el Inutil. (SPA.). (YA). 8.95 (978-958-04-7446-3(X)) Norma S.A. COL. Dist: Distribuidora Norma, Inc.

Spotlight Editors. Quiet Please. 2007. (Archie Digest Library). (Illus.). 80p. (J). (gr. 3-6). 24.21 (978-1-59961-260-7(7)) Spotlight.

Springman, I. C. More. Lies, Brian, illus. 2012. (ENG.). 40p. (J). (gr. -1-3). 16.99 (978-0-547-61083-2(1)) Houghton Mifflin Harcourt Publishing Co.

Squires, Mary L. Margaret Who Dared to Dream. l.t. ed. 2003. (Illus.). 45p. 12.95 (978-0-9631547-3-6(7)) Popular Truth, Inc.

Stahler, David, Jr. Doppelganger. (YA). 2008. (ENG.). 272p. (gr. 8). pap. 8.99 (978-0-06-087234-2(9), HarperTeen) 2006. (Illus.). 272p. (gr. 7-12). 16.99 (978-0-06-087232-8(2)) 2006. (Illus.). 258p. (gr. 7-12). lib. bdg. 17.89 (978-0-06-087233-5(0)) HarperCollins Pubs.

Stallings, Gary. Mario's Golden Locket. 2012. 38p. pap. 12.95 (978-0-9851659-0-1(1)) Flourish Publishing Hse.

Stampler, Ann Redisch. Afterparty. 2013. (ENG., Illus.). 416p. (YA). (gr. 9). 17.99 (978-1-4424-2324-4(2), Simon Pulse) Simon Pulse.

Standiford, Natalie. Confessions of the Sullivan Sisters. 2012. (ENG.). 320p. (J). (gr. 9). pap. 9.99 (978-0-545-10711-2(3), Scholastic Paperbacks) Scholastic, Inc.

Stanek, Robert, pseud. Break Their Bad Habits. deluxe ed. 2009. (Bugville Critters Ser.: No. 9). (Illus.). 24p. 9.99 (978-1-57545-213-5(8), Reagent Pr. Bks. for Young Readers) RP Media.

—Break Their Bad Habits: (the Bugville Critters, Lass's Adventures Series #2) 2009. (Bugville Critters Ser.: No. 9). (Illus.). 52p. (J). pap. 14.95 (978-1-57545-205-0(7), Reagent Pr. Bks. for Young Readers) RP Media.

Stanisha, Terésa (Tracey). Especially for Rachel - Butterflies Abound. 2009. 84p. pap. 16.97 (978-0-557-04450-4(2)) Lulu Pr., Inc.

Staniszewski, Anna. The Gossip File. 2015. (Dirt Diary Ser.: 3). (ENG.). 224p. (J). (gr. 5-9). pap. 6.99 (978-1-4926-0463-1(1), 9781492604631, Sourcebooks Jabberwocky) Sourcebooks, Inc.

Stanley, Diane. Saving Sky. 2010. (ENG.). 208p. (J). (gr. 3-7). 15.99 (978-0-06-123905-2(4)) HarperCollins Pubs.

Stanley, George E. Night Fires. 2009. (ENG.). 192p. (J). (gr. 3-7). 15.99 (978-1-4169-7559-5(4), Simon & Schuster/Paula Wiseman Bks.) Simon & Schuster/Paula Wiseman Bks.

Stanley, George Edward. Night Fires. 2011. (ENG.). 192p. (J). (gr. 3-7). pap. 6.99 (978-1-4169-1250-7(9), Simon & Schuster/Paula Wiseman Bks.) Simon & Schuster/Paula Wiseman Bks.

StarKidz: I Am Who I Am. l.t. ed. 2003. (Illus.). 28p. (J). 16.95 (978-0-9743964-1-5(9)) World of Angels, A.

Stein, David Ezra. Because Amelia Smiled. Stein, David Ezra, illus. 2012. (ENG., Illus.). 40p. (J). (gr. -1-2). 16.99 (978-0-7636-4169-6(3)) Candlewick Pr.

Steinkraus, Kyla. Los Problemas Del Intercambio. 2012. (SPA & ENG.). 24p. (gr. 2-3). pap. 8.95 (978-1-61810-543-1(4)) Rourke Educational Media.

Stephens, Sarah Hines. Creature of Chaos. Schoening, Dan, illus. 2013. (Wonder Woman Ser.). (ENG.). 56p. (gr. 2-3). pap. 4.95 (978-1-4342-2256-5(X), DC Super Heroes) Stone Arch Bks.

Stevenson, Robert Louis. Treasure Island: A Classic Story about Responsibility. 2003. (Illus.). 32p. per. 3.95 (978-0-9747133-4-2(1), Values to Live By Classic Stories) Thomas, Frederic Inc.

Stoddard, Jutta. Miss Elli. 2004. 28p. per. 18.65 (978-1-4134-3423-1(1)) Xlibris Corp.

Stokes, Paula. Liars, Inc. 2015. (ENG.). 368p. (YA). (gr. 8). 17.99 (978-0-06-232328-6(8), HarperTeen) HarperCollins Pubs.

Storer, Wendy. Bring Me Sunshine. 2013. 218p. pap. (978-0-9574812-8-2(4)) Applecore Bks.

Stork, Francisco X. The Last Summer of the Death Warriors. 2010. (ENG.). 352p. (J). (gr. 9-7). 18.99 (978-0-545-15133-7(3), Levine, Arthur A. Bks.) Scholastic, Inc.

Story, Rita. The Belly Garden. Galluzzo, Madeline, illus. 2008. 23p. pap. 24.95 (978-1-60610-035-6(1)) America Star Bks.

Stott, Ann. What to Do When You're Sent to Your Room. Gilpin, Stephen, illus. 2014. (ENG.). 32p. (J). (gr. -1-3). 15.99 (978-0-7636-6052-9(3)) Candlewick Pr.

Strasnick, Lauren. Then We Were Gone. (ENG., 272p. (YA). (gr. 9). 2014. Illus.). pap. 9.99 (978-1-4424-2716-7(7)) 2013. 16.99 (978-1-4424-2715-0(9)) Simon Pulse. (Simon Pulse).

Stromberg, Ronica. Living It up to Live It Down. 2009. (J). lib. bdg. (978-0-88092-752-9(6)) Royal Fireworks Publishing Co.

Stuart, Tara. Trees: A Tara's Tale about Being Yourself. 2006. (Illus.). (J). bds. 15.00 (978-0-9765060-3-4(3)) TouchSmart Publishing, LLC.

Studio Mouse, creator. Kindness Counts. rev. ed. 2008. (Learn-Aloud Bks.). (ENG., Illus.). (J). 12.99 (978-1-59069-627-9(1)) Studio Mouse LLC.

Studio Mouse Staff. Kindness Counts. rev. ed. 2004. (Kindness Counts Ser.). (Illus.). 36p. (J). (gr. -1-3). 12.99 (978-1-59069-364-3(7), 1A500) Studio Mouse LLC.

Sturey, James D. El and His Perfect Son, Justus: In the Land of Fell. 2011. 24p. pap. 12.45 (978-1-4497-2017-9(X), WestBow Pr.) Author Solutions, Inc.

Sturm, James, illus. Birdsong: a Story in Pictures: TOON Level 1. 2016. (ENG.). 60p. (J). (gr. k). 12.95 (978-1-935179-94-8(2)) TOON Books / RAW Junior, LLC.

Suen, Anastasia. Trust Me: A Loyalty Story. 1 vol. Ebbeler, Jeff, illus. 2008. (Main Street School - Kids with Character Ser.). (ENG.). 32p. (gr. -1-4). 28.50 (978-1-60270-273-8(X), Looking Glass Library) ABDO Publishing Co.

Suma, Nova Ren. Fade Out. 2012. (ENG.). 288p. (YA). (gr. 7). pap. 9.99 (978-1-4169-7565-6(9), Simon Pulse) Simon Pulse.

Summers, Courtney. All the Rage. (ENG.). 336p. (YA). 2016. pap. 10.99 (978-1-250-06915-3(7), 9781250069153) 2015. (gr. 9-13). 18.99 (978-1-250-02191-5(X), 9781250021915) St. Martin's Pr. (St. Martin's Griffin).

Summers, Susan. The Greatest Gift: The Story of the Other Wise Man. Morris, Jackie, illus. 2011. (ENG.). 30p. (J). 16.99 (978-1-84686-578-7(6)) Barefoot Bks., Inc.

Sundberg, Peggy. Okey-Dokey Oakie. Wiles, Pat, illus. 2008. (ENG.). 32p. (J). 17.95 (978-0-9721057-9-8(4)); pap. 11.95 (978-0-9721057-7-4(8)) Cowgirl Peg Enterprises. (Cowgirl Peg Bks.).

Surviving Southside. 6 vols., Set. Incl. Bad Deal. Korman, Susan. lib. bdg. 27.93 (978-0-7613-6152-7(9)); Beaten. Weyn, Suzanne. lib. bdg. 27.93 (978-0-7613-6150-3(2)); Benito Runs. Fontes, Justine. lib. bdg. 27.93 (978-0-7613-6151-0(0)); Plan B. Simon, Charnan. lib. bdg. 27.93 (978-0-7613-6149-7(9)); Recruited. Weyn, Suzanne. lib. bdg. 27.93 (978-0-7613-6153-4(7)); Shattered Star. Simon, Charnan. lib. bdg. 27.93 (978-0-7613-6154-1(5)); 104p. (YA). (gr. 6-12). (Surviving Southside Ser.). (ENG.). 2011. Set lib. bdg. 335.16 (978-0-7613-6148-0(0), Darby Creek) Lerner Publishing Group.

Sutcliffe, William. Concentr8. 2016. (ENG.). 256p. (YA). 17.99 (978-1-61963-919-5(X), 9781619639195, Bloomsbury USA Childrens) Bloomsbury Publishing USA.

Sutton, Kelsey. Where Silence Gathers. 2014. (ENG.). 360p. (YA). pap. 9.99 (978-0-7387-3947-2(2), Flux) North Star Editions.

Swallow, Pamela. It Only Looks Easy. 2009. (ENG.). 192p. (J). (gr. 3-7). pap. 9.99 (978-0-312-56114-7(8), 9780312561147) Square Fish.

Tagert-Paul, Kimberley. God's Ten Promises: Helping Children Understand the Ten Commandments. 2010. (J). 12.99 (978-0-8163-2379-1(8)) Pacific Pr. Publishing Assn.

Tague, James E. The Krankel Family. 2008. 32p. pap. 21.99 (978-1-4363-7170-4(8)) Xlibris Corp.

Tan, Shaun. Rules of Summer. 2014. (ENG.). 48p. (J). (gr. 3-7). 18.99 (978-0-545-63912-5(3), Levine, Arthur A. Bks.) Scholastic, Inc.

Tara. Knot Today. 2011. 28p. pap. 21.99 (978-1-4653-3764-1(4)) Xlibris Corp.

Tarkoff, Sarah. Eye of the Beholder - Revelation. 2018. (Eye of the Beholder Ser.: 1). 304p. pap. 15.99 (978-0-06-245638-0(5), Harper Voyager) HarperCollins Pubs.

Tate, Singleton M. Laugh a Little. Vorella2000, illus. 2012. 24p. pap. 24.95 (978-1-4560-9117-0(4)) America Star Bks.

Taylor-Gaines, Lonnetta. Fia & the Butterfly: 7 Stories for Character Education. 2005. 13.00 (978-0-8059-9848-1(9)) Dorrance Publishing Co., Inc.

Taylor, Jeannie. You Wouldnt Love Me If You Knew. 2009. 32p. (J). pap. 10.99 (978-0-687-65786-5(5)) Abingdon Pr.

Taylor, Jeannie St. John & St. John Taylor, Jeannie. Out at Home: A Novel. 2004. 144p. (J). pap. 7.99 (978-0-8254-3724-3(5)) Kregel Pubns.

Taylor, Kara. Prep School Confidential. 2013. (Prep School Confidential Novel Ser.: 1). (ENG.). 336p. (YA). (gr. 7). pap. 9.99 (978-1-250-01759-8(9), 9781250017598, St. Martin's Griffin) St. Martin's Pr.

Teague Sr., Charles R. The Right Way Family Meets Popper. 1 vol. 2010. 48p. 24.95 (978-1-4489-3934-3(8)) PublishAmerica, Inc.

Tekavec, Heather. Manners Are Not for Monkeys. Huyck, David, illus. 2016. (ENG.). 32p. (J). (gr. -1-2). 16.95 (978-1-77138-051-5(9)) Kids Can Pr., Ltd. CAN. Dist: Hachette Bk. Group.

Telle, Anita. A Little Different All Perfect. 2012. (ENG.). (J). pap. (978-1-4675-2559-6(6)) Independent Pub.

Terrell, Brandon. Take Away. 2014. (Red Zone Ser.: 5). (ENG.). 104p. (YA). (gr. 6-12). lib. bdg. 27.93 (978-1-4677-2130-1(1)) Lerner Publishing Group.

Terrell, Brandon, et al. Riptide Pride. 1 vol. 2011. (Sports Illustrated Kids Graphic Novels Ser.). (ENG., Illus.). 56p. (gr. 2-3). pap. 7.19 (978-1-4342-3399-8(5)); lib. bdg. 26.65 (978-1-4342-2238-1(1)) Stone Arch Bks.

Tewkesbury, Alexa. Benny's Barmy Bits. 2007. (Topz Secret Diaries). (ENG., Illus.). 128p. (J). (978-1-85345-431-8(1)) Crusade for World Revival.

—Danny's Daring Days. 1 vol. 2009. (Topz Secret Diaries). (ENG., Illus.). 128p. pap. (978-1-85345-502-5(4)) Crusade for World Revival.

Thank You, Meiling: Evaluation Guide. 2006. (J). (978-1-55942-423-3(0)) Witcher Productions.

Thomas, Cynthia. Promise Ring: The Promise. 2013. (ENG.). 82p. (YA). pap. 12.95 (978-1-4787-1008-0(X)) Outskirts Pr., Inc.

Thomas, Sean Michael. Sedikit-Sedikit Menjadi Bukit: Little by Little We Climb the Mountain. 2008. 37p. pap. 24.95 (978-1-60672-484-2(3)) America Star Bks.

Thompson, Tyler. Sneaker Freak. 1 vol. 2010. 164p. pap. 24.95 (978-1-4489-6191-7(2)) America Star Bks.

Thong, Roseanne Greenfield. Fly Free! Neilan, Eujin Kim, illus. 2010. (ENG.). 32p. (J). (gr. 2-4). 17.95 (978-1-59078-550-8(9)) Boyds Mills Pr.

Thunder Brook: Escape from the Land of Huffra, Adam & the Valley of the Weedgrass. 2005. (Illus.). 136p. (J). 14.95 (978-0-9768152-0-4(6)) Buttercup Media.

Tice, Kimberly & Litvack, Venita. Lou Knows What to Do: Supermarket. Kerry, Andre, illus. 2017. (Lou Knows What to Do Ser.: 1). (ENG.). 32p. (J). (gr. -1-6). pap. 10.95 **(978-1-944882-14-3(6))** Boys Town Pr.

Tidwell, Susan. Three Virtuous Brothers: A Story of the Three Acts of Goodness. Tidwell, Susan, illus. 2012. (Illus.). 47p. (J). pap. 9.95 (978-1-932293-63-0(9)) Buddha's Light Publications USA Corp.

Tiernan, Cate. Book of Shadows - The Coven - Blood Witch. 2010. (Sweep Ser.: 1). (ENG.). 592p. (YA). (gr. 7-18). 8.99 (978-0-14-241717-1(3), Speak) Penguin Young Readers Group.

—Immortal Beloved. (Immortal Beloved Ser.: 1). (ENG.). (YA). (gr. 7-17). 2012. 432p. pap. 9.99 (978-0-316-03591-0(2)) 2010. 416p. 16.99 (978-0-316-03592-7(0)) Little, Brown Bks. for Young Readers.

Tingle, Tim. Danny Blackgoat, Navajo Prisoner. 2013. (PathFinders Ser.). (ENG.). 151p. (YA). pap. 9.95 (978-1-939053-03-9(X), 7th Generation) Book Publishing Co.

Todd, John. Nuts for Boys to Crack: Earthly Stories with a Heavenly Meaning. 2009. 272p. pap. 20.00 (978-1-59925-232-2(5)) Solid Ground Christian Bks.

Toenies, Claudia. A Very Special Penguin. 2007. 36p. per. 16.99 (978-1-4343-3074-1(5)) AuthorHouse.

Tommy. Bubba & Cecil. 2009. 52p. pap. 16.95 (978-1-60836-860-0(2)) America Star Bks.

Tompert, Ann. The Errant Knight. Keith, Doug, illus. 2003. 32p. 15.95 (978-0-9701907-6-5(X)) Illumination Arts Publishing Co., Inc.

Toreeva, Natalia G. Greg & the Sea Monster. 2011. 34p. pap. 14.50 (978-1-61204-332-6(1), Eloquent Bks.) Strategic Book Publishing & Rights Agency (SBPRA).

Townsend, Peter. Shelly & Muffin's Big Lesson Learned. 2008. 11p. pap. 24.95 (978-1-60672-379-1(0)) America Star Bks.

Townsend, Una Belle. The Oklahoma Land Run. 1 vol. Henriquez, Emile, illus. 2008. (ENG.). 32p. (J). (gr. k-3). 16.99 (978-1-58980-566-8(6)) Pelican Publishing Co., Inc.

Tracy, Kristen. Camille McPhee Fell under the Bus. 2010. (ENG.). 304p. (J). (gr. 3-7). 7.99 (978-0-375-84546-8(1), Yearling) Random Hse. Children's Bks.

—Too Cool for This School. 2015. (ENG.). 288p. (J). (gr. 5). 6.99 (978-0-375-87296-9(5), Yearling) Random Hse. Children's Bks.

Traver, N. K. & Traver, N. K. Duplicity. 2015. (ENG.). 256p. (YA). (gr. 9-12). 18.99 (978-1-250-05914-7(3), 9781250059147, Dunne, Thomas Bks.) St. Martin's Pr.

Travis, Lucille. The Far Journey. 2009. 160p. (J). (gr. 4-7). 8.99 (978-1-60682-023-0(0)) BJU Pr.

Troeger, Virginia B. Secret along the St. Mary's. Swisher, Michael-Che, tr. Swisher, Michael-Che, illus. 2003. (Mysteries in Time Ser.). 92p. (gr. 4). 14.95 (978-1-893110-35-9(4)) Silver Moon Pr.

Troulis, Jennifer. Penelope & Prisilla & the Enchanted House of Whispers 2004. 240p. (YA). per. 13.95 (978-0-9741805-5-7(6)) American LaserTechnic.

Trusler, Heidi Jo. Firecracker the Miniature Donkey: Makes A Marvelous Choice! 2009. 25p. (J). pap. 13.95 (978-1-4327-4153-2(5)) Outskirts Pr., Inc.

Turner, Diane. Tangle-Leina? I'll Tangle-Leina Them. Mason, Roberta Black, illus. 2008. 48p. pap. 24.95 (978-1-60563-586-6(3)) America Star Bks.

Turner, Henry. Ask the Dark. (ENG.). 256p. (YA). (gr. 9). 2016. pap. 9.99 (978-0-544-81353-3(7), HMH Books For Young Readers) 2015. 17.99 (978-0-544-30827-5(1), Clarion Bks.) Houghton Mifflin Harcourt Publishing Co.

Twain, Mark, pseud. Advice to Little Girls. Radunsky, Vladimir, illus. 2013. (ENG.). 24p. (gr. k). 14.95 (978-1-59270-129-2(9)) Enchanted Lion Bks., LLC.

Ustinov, Pavla. Peggy Pots. 2008. 76p. pap. 33.32 (978-1-4257-1347-8(5)) Xlibris Corp.

Vail, Rachel. Brilliant. 2011. (Avery Sisters Trilogy Ser.: 3). (ENG., Illus.). 256p. (YA). (gr. 8). pap. 8.99 (978-0-06-089051-3(7)) HarperCollins Pubs.

Vaizey, George de Horne. Etheldreda the Ready. Horrell, Charles, illus. 2007. 200p. per. *(978-1-4065-4688-0(7))* Dodo Pr.

—Tom & Some Other Girls. Tarrant, Percy, illus. 2007. 208p. per. *(978-1-4065-4698-9(4))* Dodo Pr.

Van Draanen, Wendelin. Flipped. 2003. (ENG.). 256p. (YA). (gr. 7-9). pap. 9.99 *(978-0-375-82544-6(4),* Ember) Random Hse. Children's Bks.

—Sammy Keyes & the Kiss Goodbye. 2014. 236p. (J). pap. *(978-0-307-93063-7(7))* Knopf, Alfred A. Inc.

—Sammy Keyes & the Kiss Goodbye. 2014. (Sammy Keyes Ser.). (ENG.). 240p. (J). (gr. 5). 16.99 *(978-0-375-87055-2(5),* Knopf Bks. for Young Readers) Random Hse. Children's Bks.

—Sammy Keyes & the Night of Skulls. 2012. (Sammy Keyes Ser.: 14). (ENG.). 336p. (J). (gr. 5-7). 8.99 *(978-0-375-85457-6(6),* Yearling) Random Hse. Children's Bks.

Van Dyke, Henry. The Mansion: 100th Anniversary Edition. 100th ed. 2011. 32p. (J). 18.99 *(978-1-60641-845-1(9),* Shadow Mountain) Shadow Mountain Publishing.

VeggieTales, contrib. by. The Pirates Who Don't Do Anything. 2007. (VeggieTales (EMI-CMG Audio) Ser.). (J). (gr. -1-3). 12.99 *(978-5-557-52681-4(1))* Big Idea Productions.

Verma, Monika. My Storyland Animals. 2008. 29p. pap. 24.95 *(978-1-60563-010-6(1))* America Star Bks.

Villareal, Ray. On the Other Side of the Bridge. 2014. (ENG.). 227p. (J). pap. 11.95 *(978-1-55885-802-2(4),* Piñata Books) Arte Publico Pr.

Viorst, Judith. Just in Case. Bluthenthal, Diana Cain, illus. 2010. (ENG.). 40p. (J). (gr. -1-2). 6.99 *(978-1-4424-1282-6(8),* Atheneum Bks. for Young Readers) Simon & Schuster Children's Publishing.

Vision, David & Vision, Mutiya Sahar. Missing You. Alcantara, Ignacio, illus. 2009. 32p. 17.00 *(978-0-9659538-6-3(6))* Von Curtis Publishing.

Vollbracht, James. Mishan's Garden. Brooke, Janet, illus. 2013. (ENG.). 32p. (J). (gr. k-9). 16.95 *(978-1-61429-112-1(8))* Wisdom Pubns.

Volponi, Paul. Crossing Lines. 2011. (ENG.). 256p. (YA). (gr. 7). E-Book *(978-1-101-52904-1(0));* 16.99 *(978-0-670-01214-5(9))* Penguin Young Readers Group. (Viking Books for Young Readers).

—The Final Four. (ENG.). (YA). (gr. 7). 2013. 272p. pap. 9.99 *(978-0-14-242385-1(8),* Speak) 2012. 256p. 16.99 *(978-0-670-01264-0(5),* Viking Books for Young Readers) Penguin Young Readers Group.

—Rucker Park Setup. 2008. (ENG.). 160p. (YA). (gr. 7-18). 6.99 *(978-0-14-241207-7(4),* Speak) Penguin Young Readers Group.

Wade, Rebecca. The Theft & the Miracle. 2007. 351p. (J). (gr. 4-7). lib. bdg. 17.89 *(978-0-06-077495-0(9))* HarperCollins Pubs.

Wagner, Michael & Vanzet, Gaston. The Mess. 2008. (Rigby Focus Forward: Level E Ser.). (Illus.). 24p. (J). (gr. 4-7). pap. *(978-1-4190-3677-4(7),* Rigby) Pearson Education Australia.

Wahl, Leslea. The Perfect Blindside. 2015. 280p. (YA). pap. 10.95 *(978-0-8198-6013-2(1))* Pauline Bks. & Media.

Wahn, Udo. Cabo & Coral Go Surfing! Lyn, Jami, illus. 2007. 48p. (J). pap. 17.95 *(978-0-615-17598-0(8))* Caboandcoral.com.

Walker, Melissa. Small Town Sinners. (ENG.). (YA). (gr. 9-12). 2013. 304p. pap. 9.99 *(978-1-59990-982-0(0),* 9781599909820) 2011. 288p. 16.99 *(978-1-59990-527-3(2),* 9781599905273) Bloomsbury Publishing USA. (Bloomsbury USA Childrens).

Walker, Raynn. Toadina: The Story of a Lady Toad. 2005. (J). pap. 15.00 *(978-0-8059-6726-5(5))* Dorrance Publishing Co., Inc.

Wallace, Bill. Pick of the Litter. 2005. (ENG.). 160p. (J). (gr. 4-7). 16.95 *(978-0-8234-1921-0(5))* Holiday Hse., Inc.

—Pick of the Litter. 2006. (ENG.). 176p. (J). (gr. 3-7). pap. 5.99 *(978-1-4169-2511-8(2),* Aladdin) Simon & Schuster Children's Publishing.

Wallace, Jason. Out of Shadows. (ENG., Illus.). 272p. (J). (gr. 10). 2012. pap. 8.95 *(978-0-8234-2436-8(7))* 2011. 17.95 *(978-0-8234-2342-2(5))* Holiday Hse., Inc.

Wallace, Nancy Elizabeth. The Kindness Quilt. 0 vols. 2006. (ENG., Illus.). 48p. (J). (gr. -1-k). 16.99 *(978-0-7614-5313-0(X),* 9780761453130, Amazon Children's Publishing) Amazon Publishing.

Wallace, Sally. Three Parables & A Pickle. 2010. 60p. pap. 21.99 *(978-1-4520-4269-5(1))* AuthorHouse.

Waller, Barrett. New Feet for Old. 2013. (ENG., Illus.). 32p. (J). (gr. -1-3). 16.99 *(978-1-4814-2155-3(7),* Simon & Schuster Bks. For Young Readers) Simon & Schuster Bks. For Young Readers.

Waller, Linda. Hard Road to Manhood: I Ain't No Snitch. 2010. 128p. pap. 10.99 *(978-1-4490-6892-9(8))* AuthorHouse.

Walters, Eric. House Party. 1 vol. 2007. (Orca Soundings Ser.). (ENG.). (YA). (gr. 8-12). 112p. 14.95 *(978-1-55143-743-9(0));* 128p. pap. 9.95 *(978-1-55143-741-5(4))* Orca Bk. Pubs. USA.

Ward, Rachel. The Drowning. 2014. (ENG.). 272p. (J). (gr. 9). 17.99 *(978-0-545-62771-9(0),* Chicken Hse., The) Scholastic, Inc.

Warner, Sally. EllRay Jakes Is a Rock Star. 2 vols. Harper, Jamie, illus. 2012. (EllRay Jakes Ser.: 2). (ENG.). 128p. (J). (gr. 1-3). 5.99 *(978-0-14-241989-2(3),* Puffin Books) Penguin Young Readers Group.

—EllRay Jakes Is Not a Chicken. 1 vol. Harper, Jamie, illus. 2012. (EllRay Jakes Ser.: 1). (ENG.). 128p. (J). (gr. 1-3). 5.99 *(978-0-14-241988-5(5),* Puffin Books) Penguin Young Readers Group.

—EllRay Jakes the Dragon Slayer. 2013. (EllRay Jakes Ser.: 4). lib. bdg. 16.00 *(978-0-606-32136-5(5),* Turtleback) Turtleback Bks.

—EllRay Jakes Walks the Plank! 2013. (EllRay Jakes Ser.: 3). lib. bdg. 16.00 *(978-0-606-30188-6(7),* Turtleback) Turtleback Bks.

Warner, Susan & Wetherell, Elizabeth. Daisy in the Field. 2011. 272p. 29.95 *(978-1-4638-9964-6(5));* pap. 16.95 *(978-1-4638-0163-2(7))* Rodgers, Alan Bks.

Warren, Cynthia Marie. The Crazy Untamable, Tamable Tongue: Love with Your Words. 2012. 48p. pap. 20.45 *(978-1-4497-4322-2(6),* WestBow Pr.) Author Solutions, Inc.

Wasserman, Robin. Lust. 2005. (Seven Deadly Sins Ser.: 1). (ENG.). 256p. (YA). (gr. 9-12). pap. 9.99 *(978-0-689-87782-7(X),* Simon Pulse) Simon Pulse.

—Pride - Wrath Vol. 2. 2013. (Seven Deadly Sins Ser.: 2). (ENG., Illus.). 592p. (YA). (gr. 9). pap. 9.99 *(978-1-4424-7506-9(4),* Simon Pulse) Simon Pulse.

—Seven Deadly Sins Vol. 3: Sloth; Gluttony; Greed. 2013. (ENG., Illus.). 880p. (YA). (gr. 9). pap. 10.99 *(978-1-4424-7508-3(0),* Simon Pulse) Simon Pulse.

—Wrath. 2006. (Seven Deadly Sins Ser.: 4). (ENG., Illus.). 256p. (YA). (gr. 9-12). pap. 9.99 *(978-0-689-87785-8(4),* Simon Pulse) Simon Pulse.

Watkins, Rowboat. Rude Cakes. 2015. (ENG., Illus.). 40p. (J). (gr. -1-k). 16.99 *(978-1-4521-3851-0(6))* Chronicle Bks. LLC.

Watson, Jean. Onyx the Butterfly. 2007. 160p. pap. 58.25 *(978-1-4303-2408-9(2))* Lulu Pr., Inc.

Weber, Elka. One Little Chicken. Kleven, Elisa, illus. 2011. (ENG.). 32p. (J). (gr. -1-2). 16.99 *(978-1-58246-374-2(3),* Tricycle Pr.) Random Hse. Children's Bks.

Weigl Publishers, creator. The Farmer & His Sons: Why Should You Work Hard? 2013. (AV2 Animated Storytime Ser.: Vol. 13). (ENG., Illus.). 32p. (J). (gr. -1-3). lib. bdg. 29.99 *(978-1-62127-917-4(0),* AV2 by Weigl) Weigl Pubs., Inc.

Weil, Zoe. Claude & Medea: The Hellburn Dogs. 2007. (ENG., Illus.). 103p. (J). (gr. 2-7). per. 12.00 *(978-1-59056-105-8(8))* Lantern Bks.

Welborn, Amy. Adventures in Assisi: on the Path with St. Francis: On the Path with St. Francis. Engelhart, Ann Kissane, illus. 2014. (ENG.). 32p. (J). (gr. k-3). 15.99 *(978-1-61636-650-6(8))* Franciscan Media.

Weston Woods Staff, creator. Crow Boy. 2011. 38.75 *(978-0-545-23384-2(4));* 18.95 *(978-0-545-23383-5(6));* 29.95 *(978-0-545-23382-8(8))* Weston Woods Studios, Inc.

—Goldilocks & the Three Bears. 2011. 29.95 *(978-0-439-73471-4(1));* 18.95 *(978-0-439-72679-5(4));* 38.75 *(978-0-439-72682-5(4))* Weston Woods Studios, Inc.

Whelen-Banks, Jane. Liam Goes Poo in the Toilet: A Story about Trouble with Toilet Training. 2008. (ENG., Illus.). 32p. 12.95 *(978-1-84310-900-6(X),* 5371) Kingsley, Jessica Pubs. GBR. Dist: Macmillan Distribution Ltd.

—Liam Says "Hi" Learning to Greet a Friend. 2008. (ENG., Illus.). 32p. 12.95 *(978-1-84310-901-3(8),* 5372) Kingsley, Jessica Pubs. GBR. Dist: Macmillan Distribution Ltd.

Whidbee, Evelyn, told to. It's Called Blame. 2004. (J). pap. 8.00 *(978-0-8059-6361-8(8))* Dorrance Publishing Co., Inc.

Whitaker, Nathan. Snap Decision. 1 vol. 2015. (Game Face Ser.). (ENG.). 272p. (J). pap. 8.99 *(978-0-310-73703-2(6))* Zonderkidz.

White, Andrea. Window Boy. 2008. (ENG.). 256p. (J). (gr. 4-7). 17.95 *(978-1-933979-14-4(3),* 9781933979144) Bright Sky Pr.

White, Melissa. Purple Frogs, Imagine High. 2009. 131p. pap. 13.24 *(978-0-557-02960-0(0))* Lulu Pr., Inc.

White, Pauline. Jewel Baxter & Friends. 1 vol. 2009. 48p. pap. 16.95 *(978-1-60813-541-7(1))* America Star Bks.

Whitfield, Mary. Mrs. Adams Teaches a Lesson for a Lifetime. 2003. 14p. (J). 7.00 *(978-0-9720445-1-6(5))* Cathier Pr.

Whitley, David. The Midnight Charter. 2010. (Agora Trilogy Ser.: 1). (ENG.). 352p. (J). (gr. 6-9). pap. 19.99 *(978-0-312-62904-5(4),* 9780312629045) Square Fish.

Whitney, A. D. T. Patience Strong's Outings by Mrs A D T Whitney. 2006. 236p. per. 20.99 *(978-1-4255-2007-6(3))* Michigan Publishing.

Whitney, Kim Ablon. See You down the Road. 14.85 *(978-0-7569-5710-0(9))* Perfection Learning Corp.

Why Am I Special? (Peek A Boo Pockets Ser.). 12p. (J). bds. *(978-2-7643-0105-0(7))* Phidal Publishing, Inc./Editions Phidal, Inc.

Wilde, Oscar. The Picture of Dorian Gray. 2 vols. l.t. ed. (YA). (gr. 10-18). reprint ed. 10.00 *(978-0-89064-049-4(1))* National Assn. for Visually Handicapped.

Wilde, Oscar & Fisher, Eric Scott. The Picture of Dorian Gray. 1 vol. 2012. (Calico Illustrated Classics Ser.: No. 4). (ENG., Illus.). 112p. (J). (gr. 3-6). 27.07 *(978-1-61641-618-8(1),* Magic Wagon.

Wilks, Madeline Joan. Yellow Dot Red Dot. 2009. (Illus.). 24p. pap. 11.49 *(978-1-4490-1384-4(8))* AuthorHouse.

Williams, Bonnie. Say Cheese, Teddy Rex! Gordon, John, illus. 2016. (J). ***(978-1-5182-1896-5(2),*** Simon Spotlight) Simon Spotlight.

Williams, M. Ed. Friends in the Meadow - Squirrels the Frolics of Scamp & Scooter. 2013. 72p. pap. *(978-1-77067-429-5(2))* FriesenPress.

Wiseman, Rosalind. Boys, Girls & Other Hazardous Materials. 2011. (ENG.). 304p. (YA). (gr. 7-18). 8.99 *(978-0-14-241819-2(6),* Speak) Penguin Young Readers Group.

Withers, Pam. Les Casse-Cous: (Daredevil Club). 1 vol. 2010. (FRE.). 128p. (J). (gr. 5-9). pap. 9.95 *(978-1-55469-374-0(8))* Orca Bk. Pubs. USA.

Wolff, Ferida & Savitz, Harriet May. Is a Worry Worrying You? LeTourneau, Marie, illus. 2005. (ENG.). 32p. (J). (gr. -1-3). 15.95 *(978-0-9749303-2-9(6));* per. 7.95 *(978-1-933718-05-7(6))* Tanglewood Pr.

Wolff, Virginia Euwer. Make Lemonade. 2006. (ENG.). 208p. (YA). (gr. 5-9). pap. 8.99 *(978-0-8050-8070-4(8),* 9780805080704) Square Fish.

—This Full House. (ENG.). 496p. (YA). (gr. 9). 2011. pap. 9.99 *(978-0-06-158306-3(5))* 2009. (Make Lemonade Trilogy: No. 3). 17.99 *(978-0-06-158304-9(9))* HarperCollins Pubs. (HarperTeen).

—True Believer. 2004. (Make Lemonade Trilogy: No. 2). 272p. (J). (gr. 7-18). pap. 38.00 incl. audio *(978-0-8072-2283-6(6),* Listening Library) Random Hse. Audio Publishing Group.

Wolfson, Jill. What I Call Life. 2008. (ENG.). 288p. (J). (gr. 5-9). pap. 19.99 *(978-0-312-37752-6(5),* 9780312377526) Square Fish.

Wolk, Lauren. Wolf Hollow. 2016. (ENG.). 304p. (J). (gr. 5-7). 16.99 *(978-1-101-99482-5(7),* Dutton Books for Young Readers) Penguin Young Readers Group.

Wolnik, Charlotte. The Chocolate Chip Ghost. 2008. 40p. pap. 24.95 *(978-1-4241-8896-3(2))* America Star Bks.

Wood, Douglas. Old Turtle: Questions of the Heart. Ruth, Greg, illus. 2017. (ENG.). 56p. (J). (gr. -1-3). 19.99 *(978-0-439-32111-2(5),* Scholastic Pr.) Scholastic, Inc.

—The Secret of Saying Thanks. Shed, Greg, illus. 2005. (ENG.). 32p. (J). (gr. -1-3). 18.99 *(978-0-689-85410-1(2),* Simon & Schuster Bks. For Young Readers) Simon & Schuster Bks. For Young Readers.

Wood, Holly J. Invaluable. 2011. (YA). pap. 14.99 *(978-1-60908-835-4(2))* Deseret Bk. Co.

Wood, Nathaniel. Play Me Backwards. 2014. (ENG., Illus.). 288p. (YA). (gr. 9). 18.99 *(978-1-4814-0102-9(5),* Simon & Schuster Bks. For Young Readers) Simon & Schuster Bks. For Young Readers.

Wooden, John, et al. Inch & Miles: The Journey to Success. Cornelison, Sue, illus. 2003. 39p. (J). pap. *(978-0-7891-6073-7(0))* Perfection Learning Corp.

Woodford, Pamela. Ning. 2013. (Brighter Little Minds Ser.). (ENG., Illus.). 24p. (J). pap. 10.95 *(978-1-871305-81-4(0))* Orpen Pr. IRL. Dist: Dufour Editions, Inc.

—Watching Raindrops. 2013. (Brighter Little Minds Ser.). (ENG., Illus.). 24p. (J). pap. 9.99 *(978-1-871305-84-5(5))* Orpen Pr. IRL. Dist: M.H. Gill & Co. U. C.

Woods, Shirley. Planet of Success: An Inspirational Book about Attitude Adn Character. Lee, Haylen, illus. 2006. 41p. (J). per. 9.95 *(978-1-60002-183-1(2),* 4207) Mountain Valley Publishing, LLC.

Worthy Kids, creator. My Great Big Veggie Storybook: With Lessons from God's Word. 2014. (VeggieTales (Big Idea) Ser.). (ENG., Illus.). 254p. (J). 14.99 *(978-1-61795-334-7(2))* Worthy Publishing.

Wright, Caleb E. Marcus Blair A Story of Provincial Times. 2006. pap. 22.95 *(978-1-4286-6303-9(7))* Kessinger Publishing, LLC.

Wright, Gail. The Adventures of Alfred in Mom, I'm Growing up Now: Decision Making. 2012. 108p. (gr. 4-6). 28.95 *(978-1-4497-6639-9(0));* pap. 11.95 *(978-1-4497-6637-5(4))* Author Solutions, Inc. (WestBow Pr.).

Wullschleger Daldini, Elena. Ma tu, che Babbo Natale Sei? Caccia, Christiane, illus. 2004. (ITA.). 48p. (J). 19.00 *(978-88-87469-33-2(4),* gce) Gabriele Capelli Editore Sagl CHE. Dist: SPD-Small Pr. Distribution.

Xiong, Kim, illus. Kitchen God. 2008. 32p. (J). 18.95 *(978-1-60603-001-1(9))* Better Chinese LLC.

Yamanushi, Toshiko. The Deer King. Tani, Toshihiko, illus. 2014. (J). 8.95 *(978-1-935523-70-3(8))* World Tribune Pr.

Yancey, Rick. Alfred Kropp: the Seal of Solomon. 2015. (Alfred Kropp Ser.). (ENG.). 352p. (YA). (gr. 7). pap. 9.99 *(978-1-61963-917-1(3),* 9781619639171, Bloomsbury USA Childrens) Bloomsbury Publishing USA.

—Alfred Kropp: the Thirteenth Skull. 2015. (Alfred Kropp Ser.). (ENG.). 304p. (YA). (gr. 7). pap. 9.99 *(978-1-61963-918-8(1),* 9781619639188, Bloomsbury USA Childrens) Bloomsbury Publishing USA.

—The Thirteenth Skull. (Alfred Kropp Ser.). (ENG.). 304p. (YA). (gr. 7). 2009. mass mkt. 6.99 *(978-1-59990-363-7(6),* 9781599903637) 2008. 16.99 *(978-1-59990-114-5(5),* 9781599901145) Bloomsbury Publishing USA. (Bloomsbury USA Childrens).

Yazzie, Seraphine G. Beauty Beside Me: Stories of My Grandmother's Skirts. Ruffenach, Jessie Eve, ed. Whitethorne, Baje, Sr., illus. 2011. (NAV & ENG.). 32p. (J). (gr. -1-3). 17.95 *(978-1-893354-77-7(6))* Salina Bookshelf Inc.

Yeahpau, Thomas M. X-Indian Chronicles: The Book of Mausape. 2006. (ENG.). 240p. (YA). (gr. 9). 16.99 *(978-0-7636-2706-5(2))* Candlewick Pr.

Yerushalmi, Miriam. Feivel the Falafel Ball Who Wanted to Do a Mitzvah. Ginsberg, Dvora, illus. 2007. 28p. (J). 16.50 *(978-0-911643-37-4(0))* Aura Printing, Inc.

—Let's Go Camping & Discover Our Nature. Perez, Esther Ido, illus. 2007. 28p. (J). (gr. 2-4). 16.50 *(978-0-911643-38-1(9))* Aura Printing, Inc.

Yim, Natasha. Goldy Luck & the Three Pandas. Zong, Grace, illus. (ENG.). 32p. (J). (gr. -1-3). 2015. pap. 7.95 *(978-1-58089-653-5(7))* 2014. lib. bdg. 16.95 *(978-1-58089-652-8(9))* Charlesbridge Publishing, Inc.

Yokococo. Matilda & Hans. Yokococo, illus. 2013. (ENG., Illus.). 32p. (J). (gr. -1-2). 16.99 *(978-0-7636-6434-3(0),* Templar) Candlewick Pr.

Yolen, Jane. How Do Dinosaurs Say I Love You? Teague, Mark, illus. (J). 2011. pap. *(978-0-545-33076-3(9))* 2009. (ENG.). 40p. 16.99 *(978-0-545-14314-1(4),* Blue Sky Pr., The) Scholastic, Inc.

Yoo, David. The Detention Club. (ENG.). 304p. (J). (gr. 5). 2012. pap. 6.99 *(978-0-06-178380-7(3))* 2011. 16.99 *(978-0-06-178378-4(1))* HarperCollins Pubs.

Young, Ed & Mack, Jeff. The Cat from Hunger Mountain. Young, Ed, illus. 2016. (ENG., Illus.). 32p. (J). (gr. -1-3). bds. 17.99 *(978-0-399-17278-6(5),* Philomel Bks.) Penguin Young Readers Group.

Young, Jan. Starting the Colt. 2014. 173p. (J). *(978-1-937849-11-5(2))* Raven Publishing Inc. of Montana.

Young, Judy. Promise. 2016. (ENG.). 368p. (J). (gr. 4-6). pap. 8.99 *(978-1-58536-915-7(2),* 204079) Sleeping Bear Pr.

Yumel, Demain. Little Yellow Pear Tomatoes. Tamarin, Nicole, illus. 2005. 32p. (J). 15.95 *(978-0-9740190-2-4(X))* Illumination Arts Publishing Co., Inc.

Zadoff, Allen. Boy Nobody. 2013. (Unknown Assassin Ser.: 1). (ENG.). 352p. (YA). (gr. 10-17). 18.00 *(978-0-316-19968-1(0))* Little Brown & Co.

—I Am the Traitor. (ENG.). 304p. (YA). (gr. 10-17). 2016. pap. 10.99 *(978-0-316-19974-2(5))* 2015. (Unknown Assassin Ser.: 3). 18.00 *(978-0-316-19972-8(9))* Little, Brown Bks. for Young Readers.

Zafar, Nuzhat. Free Like a Bird. 2009. (Illus.). 28p. pap. 13.99 *(978-1-4389-7312-8(8))* AuthorHouse.

Ziglar, Christy. Must-Have Marvin! Martin, Luanne, illus. 2014. (Shine Bright Kids Ser.). 32p. (J). 14.99 *(978-0-8249-5657-8(5),* Ideal Pubns.) Worthy Publishing.

—Whatever Wanda. Billin-Frye, Paige, illus. 2015. (J). *(978-0-8249-5668-4(0),* Ideal Pubns.) Worthy Publishing.

Zimmer, Frank. Bird Singing Contest. 2008. 28p. pap. 13.99 *(978-1-4343-7971-9(X))* AuthorHouse.

Zink, Michelle. Lies I Told. 2015. (Lies I Told Ser.: 1). (ENG.). 352p. (YA). (gr. 8). pap. 9.99 *(978-0-06-232713-0(5),* HarperTeen); 17.99 *(978-0-06-232712-3(7))* HarperCollins Pubs.

—Promises I Made. 2015. (Lies I Told Ser.: 2). (ENG.). 304p. (YA). (gr. 8). 17.99 *(978-0-06-232715-4(1))* HarperCollins Pubs.

Zurcher, Corina. Growing up Claus. 2007. 188p. 21.99 *(978-1-60477-046-9(5));* per. 13.99 *(978-1-60266-917-8(1))* Salem Author Services.

Zuzo, Cheryl. Being Bella. Wellman, Megan, illus. 2008. (ENG.). 32p. pap. 9.95 *(978-1-933916-27-9(3))* Nelson Publishing & Marketing.

CONFECTIONERY

Abrams, Pam, et al. Candy 1 To 20. 2011. (ENG., Illus.). 20p. (J). (gr. -1 — 1). 8.99 *(978-1-4521-0293-1(7))* Chronicle Bks. LLC.

Besel, Jennifer M. Sugarcoat It! Desserts to Design, Decorate, & Devour. 1 vol. 2014. (Custom Confections Ser.). (ENG., Illus.). 48p. (gr. 4-5). lib. bdg. 31.99 *(978-1-4914-0861-2(8))* Capstone Press of Coughlan Cos.

Cacciatore, Stacy. Candy Around the World. 2008. 90p. pap. 7.95 *(978-0-9717119-4-5(1))* Consumer Pr., The.

Cohn, Jessica. 10 Fascinating Facts about Chewing Gum. 2016. (Rookie Star — Fact Finder Ser.). (ENG., Illus.). 32p. (J). lib. bdg. 25.00 *(978-0-531-22816-6(9),* Children's Pr.) Scholastic Library Publishing.

Dahlen, Noelle & Stickers. Glitter Candy Stickers. 2011. (Dover Little Activity Books Stickers Ser.). (ENG.). 2p. (J). (gr. 1-4). pap. 1.99 *(978-0-486-48282-8(0))* Dover Pubns., Inc.

Devore, Janna. Ballerina Cookbook. 2013. 94p. pap. *(978-1-4596-5916-2(3))* ReadHowYouWant.com, Ltd.

Dial Whitmore, Courtney. Candy Making for Kids. 2013. 80p. pap. *(978-1-4596-6159-2(1))* ReadHowYouWant.com, Ltd.

Eliot, Hannah. Sweet Treats. Ingham, Julie, illus. 2014. (Dream Doodle Draw! Ser.). (ENG.). 96p. (J). (gr. -1-2). pap. 7.99 *(978-1-4814-0452-5(0),* Little Simon) Little Simon.

Gilpin, Rebecca & Atkinson, Catherine. Yummy Little Cookbook. Taylor, Non et al, illus. rev. ed. 2007. (Children's Cooking Ser.). (ENG.). 96p. (J). (gr. -1-3). 7.99 *(978-0-7945-1655-0(6),* Usborne) EDC Publishing.

Greathouse, Lisa. Sweet: Inside a Bakery. 1 vol. 2nd rev. ed. 2011. (TIME for KIDS(r) Nonfiction Readers Ser.). (ENG.). 32p. (J). (gr. 3-3). pap. 8.99 *(978-1-4333-3663-8(4))* Teacher Created Materials, Inc.

Kihm, Steve. The Lost Candy Bar. 2004. (J). mass mkt. 6.95 *(978-0-9786794-0-8(7))* Lost Candy Bar Pr., LLC.

Leavitt, Loralee. Candy Experiments. 2013. (Candy Experiments Ser.: 1). (ENG., Illus.). 160p. (J). pap. 14.99 *(978-1-4494-1836-6(8))* Andrews McMeel Publishing.

—Candy Experiments 2. 2014. (Candy Experiments Ser.: 2). (ENG.). 160p. (J). pap. 14.99 *(978-1-4494-6103-4(4))* Andrews McMeel Publishing.

Love, Ann & Drake, Jane. Sweet! The Delicious Story of Candy. Dávila, Claudia, illus. 2009. (ENG.). 64p. (J). (gr. 4-7). pap. 12.95 *(978-0-88776-962-7(4),* Tundra Bks.) Tundra Bks. CAN. Dist: Penguin Random Hse. LLC.

Mattern, Joanne. Mars Family: M & M Mars Candy Makers. 1 vol. 2014. (Food Dudes Set 1 Ser.). (ENG.). 32p. (gr. 3-6). lib. bdg. 27.07 *(978-1-62403-497-8(7),* Checkerboard Library) ABDO Publishing Co.

McCarthy, Meghan. Pop! The Invention of Bubble Gum. McCarthy, Meghan, illus. 2010. (ENG., Illus.). 40p. (J). (gr. -1-3). 17.99 *(978-1-4169-7970-8(0),* Simon & Schuster/Paula Wiseman Bks.) Simon & Schuster/Paula Wiseman Bks.

Nelson, Robin. Fats, Oils, & Sweets. 2003. (First Step Nonfiction - Food Groups Ser.). (ENG., Illus.). 24p. (gr. k-2). lib. bdg. 23.93 *(978-0-8225-4634-4(5))* Lerner Publishing Group.

—From Cocoa Bean to Chocolate. (Illus.). 24p. (gr. k-3). 2012. (Start to Finish, Second Series: Food Ser.: No. 2). (ENG.). pap. 6.95 *(978-1-58013-965-6(5))* 2012. (Start to Finish, Second Series: Food Ser.: No. 2). (ENG.). lib. bdg. 23.93 *(978-0-7613-6560-0(5),* Lerner Pubns.) 2003. (Start to Finish Ser.). (J). lib. bdg. 18.60 *(978-0-8225-4665-8(5))* Lerner Publishing Group.

O'Ryan, Ellie. The Sugary Secrets Behind Candy. McClurkan, Rob, illus. 2015. (Science of Fun Stuff Ser.). (ENG.). 48p. (J). (gr. 1-3). pap. 3.99 *(978-1-4814-5626-5(1),* Simon Spotlight) Simon Spotlight.

Perelman, Helen. Cool Mint. Waters, Erica-Jane, illus. 2013. (Candy Fairies Ser.: 4). (ENG.). 128p. (J). (gr. 2-5). 15.99 *(978-1-4424-5923-6(9),* Simon & Schuster/Paula Wiseman Bks.) Simon & Schuster/Paula Wiseman Bks.

Rau, Dana Meachen. Eye Candy: Crafting Cool Candy Creations. 1 vol. 2012. (Dessert Designer Ser.). (ENG., Illus.). 32p. (gr. 3-4). lib. bdg. 27.99 *(978-1-4296-8620-4(0),* Snap Bks.) Capstone Press of Coughlan Cos.

Ridley, Sarah. A Chocolate Bar. 2006. (How It's Made Ser.). (Illus.). 32p. (gr. 1-4). lib. bdg. 26.00 *(978-0-8368-6293-5(7),* Gareth Stevens Learning Library) Stevens, Gareth Publishing LLLP.

Schuh, Mari. Sugars & Fats. 1 vol. 2012. (What's on Myplate? Ser.). (ENG., Illus.). 24p. (gr. k-1). pap. 7.29 *(978-1-4296-9422-3(X),* Pebble Plus) Capstone Press of Coughlan Cos.

Schuh, Mari C. Sugars & Fats. 1 vol. 2012. (What's on Myplate? Ser.). (ENG., Illus.). 24p. (gr. k-1). lib. bdg. 26.65 *(978-1-4296-8746-1(0),* Pebble Plus) Capstone Press of Coughlan Cos.

Smalley, Carol Parenzan. Fats, Oils, & Sweets. (Rookie Read-About Health Ser.). (ENG., Illus.). 32p. (J). (gr. k-2). 2006. pap. 5.95 *(978-0-516-24759-5(X))* 2005. lib. bdg. 20.50 *(978-0-516-25289-6(5))* Scholastic Library Publishing. (Children's Pr.).

Stadler, Charlotte. Penny Candy. 2011. (Early Connections Ser.). (J). *(978-1-61672-646-1(6))* Benchmark Education Co.

CONFEDERATE STATES OF AMERICA

Anderson, Dale. A Soldier's Life in the Civil War. 2004. (World Almanac Library of the Civil War). (Illus.). 48p. (gr. 5-12). pap. 14.05 *(978-0-8368-5595-1(7));* lib. bdg. 31.00 *(978-0-8368-5586-9(8))* Stevens, Gareth Publishing LLLP. (Gareth Stevens Secondary Library).

Anderson, Paul Christopher. Robert E. Lee: Legendary Commander of the Confederacy. (Library of American Lives & Times Ser.). 112p. 2009. (gr. 5-5). 69.20 *(978-1-60853-501-9(0))* 2005. (Illus.). (YA). (gr. 4-8). lib. bdg. 34.60 *(978-0-8239-5748-4(9))* Rosen Publishing Group, Inc., The.

Aretha, David A. Jefferson Davis. 2009. (Leaders of the Civil War Era Ser.). (Illus.). 144p. (gr. 6-12). 35.00 *(978-1-60413-297-7(3),* Chelsea Hse.) Facts On File, Inc.

Bader, Bonnie. Who Was Robert E. Lee? Harrison, Nancy & O'brien, John, illus. 2014. (Who Was? Ser.). (ENG.). 112p. (J). (gr. 3-7). 5.99 *(978-0-448-47909-5(5),* Grosset & Dunlap) Penguin Young Readers Group.

Bailey, Tom. Raphael Semmes: Commander of the Alabama. 2011. (Illus.). 120p. (J). *(978-1-59421-062-4(4))* Seacoast Publishing, Inc.

Baxter, Roberta. The Southern Home Front of the Civil War, 1 vol. (Why We Fought: the Civil War Ser.). (ENG.). 48p. (gr. 3-6). 2011. pap. 9.95 *(978-1-4329-3918-2(1))* 2010. 33.32 *(978-1-4329-3912-0(2))* Heinemann-Raintree. (Heinemann InfoSearch).

Beller, Susan Provost. Billy Yank & Johnny Reb: Soldiering in the Civil War. rev. ed. 2007. (Soldiers on the Battlefront Ser.). (ENG., Illus.). 112p. (gr. 6-8). lib. bdg. 33.26 *(978-0-8225-6803-2(9))* Lerner Publishing Group.

Brager, Bruce L. There He Stands: The Story of Stonewall Jackson. 2005. (Civil War Leaders Ser.). (Illus.). 176p. (J). (gr. 6-12). 26.95 *(978-1-931798-44-0(3))* Reynolds, Morgan Inc.

Brownell, Richard. The Civil War: The Fall of the Confederacy & the End of Slavery. 2005. (History's Great Defeats Ser.). (ENG., Illus.). 109p. (YA). (gr. 7-10). lib. bdg. 30.85 *(978-1-59018-429-5(7),* Lucent Bks.) Cengage Gale.

Collins, Terry. Robert E. Lee: The Story of the Great Confederate General. Mallea, Cristian, illus. (American Graphic Ser.). (ENG.). 32p. (gr. 3-4). 2011. pap. 47.70 *(978-1-4296-6436-3(3))* 2010. lib. bdg. 30.65 *(978-1-4296-5475-3(9))* Capstone Press of Coughlan Cos. (Graphic Library).

Conklin, Wendy. Civil War Leaders, 1 vol. 2005. (Primary Source Readers Ser.). (ENG.). 24p. (J). (gr. 5-5). pap. 8.99 *(978-0-7439-8917-6(1))* Shell Educational Publishing.

—Robert E. Lee, 1 vol. 2005. (Primary Source Readers Ser.). (ENG.). 24p. (J). (gr. 4-4). pap. 8.99 *(978-0-7439-8918-3(X))* Shell Educational Publishing.

Cooke, Tim. The Home Front. 2012. (American Civil War: the Right Answer Ser.). (Illus.). 48p. (J). (gr. 6-8). 31.95 *(978-1-4339-7543-1(2));* pap. 14.05 *(978-1-4339-7544-8(0))* Stevens, Gareth Publishing LLLP. (Gareth Stevens Secondary Library).

—Home Front, 1861-1865. 2012. (Civil War Highlights Ser.). (Illus.). 48p. (gr. 5-12). 37.10 *(978-1-59920-817-6(2))* Black Rabbit Bks.

—Key Figures. 2012. (American Civil War: the Right Answer Ser.). (Illus.). 48p. (J). (gr. 6-8). 31.95 *(978-1-4339-7547-9(5));* pap. 14.05 *(978-1-4339-7548-6(3))* Stevens, Gareth Publishing LLLP. (Gareth Stevens Secondary Library).

—Politics of the War: 1861-1865. 2012. (Civil War Highlights Ser.). (Illus.). 48p. (gr. 5-12). lib. bdg. 37.10 *(978-1-59920-818-3(0))* Black Rabbit Bks.

—Weapons & Tactics. 2012. (American Civil War: the Right Answer Ser.). (Illus.). 48p. (J). (gr. 6-8). 31.95 *(978-1-4339-7551-6(3));* pap. 14.05 *(978-1-4339-7552-3(1))* Stevens, Gareth Publishing LLLP. (Gareth Stevens Secondary Library).

Corrigan, Jim. General James Longstreet: Lee's "Old War Horse" 2012. (J). *(978-1-59556-043-8(2));* pap. *(978-1-59556-049-0(1))* OTTN Publishing.

Fein, Eric. Weapons, Gear, & Uniforms of the Civil War, 1 vol. 2012. (Equipped for Battle Ser.). (ENG.). 32p. (gr. 3-4). lib. bdg. 27.99 *(978-1-4296-7648-9(5),* Edge Bks.) Capstone Press of Coughlan Cos.

Gourley, Catherine. The Horrors of Andersonville: Life & Death Inside a Civil War Prison. 2010. (ENG.). 192p. (gr. 9-12). lib. bdg. 38.60 *(978-0-7613-4212-0(5))* Lerner Publishing Group.

Hale, Nathan. Big Bad Ironclad! 2012. (Nathan Hale's Hazardous Tales Ser.). (ENG., Illus.). 128p. (J). (gr. 3-7). 12.95 *(978-1-4197-0395-9(1),* Amulet Bks.) Abrams, Inc.

Hale, Sarah Elder, ed. Robert E. Lee: Duty & Honor. 2005. (ENG., Illus.). 48p. (J). (gr. 3-9). 17.95 *(978-0-8126-7905-2(9))* Cobblestone Publishing Co.

—Stonewall Jackson: Spirit of the South. 2005. (ENG., Illus.). 48p. (J). (gr. 3-9). 17.95 *(978-0-8126-7907-6(5))* Cobblestone Publishing Co.

Kerby, Mona. Robert E. Lee: Commander of the Confederate Army. 2015. (Legendary American Biographies Ser.). 96p. (J). (gr. 6-12). 27.94 *(978-0-7660-6490-4(5));* pap. 10.95 *(978-0-7660-6491-1(3))* Enslow Pubs., Inc.

Koestler-Grack, Rachel A. Stonewall Jackson. 2009. (Leaders of the Civil War Era Ser.). (Illus.). 136p. (gr. 6-12). 35.00 *(978-1-60413-299-1(X),* Chelsea Hse.) Facts On File, Inc.

Lieurance, Suzanne. Weapons & Strategies of the Civil War: A MyReportLinks. com Book. 2004. (American Civil War Ser.). (Illus.). 48p. (J). lib. bdg. 25.26 *(978-0-7660-5185-0(4),* MyReportLinks.com Bks.) Enslow Pubs., Inc.

Marsh, Carole. Jefferson Davis, Civil War Hero. 2004. 12p. (gr. k-4). 2.95 *(978-0-635-02366-7(0))* Gallopade International.

McCarthy, Pat. Famous Confederate Generals & Leaders of the South: A Myreportlinks. com Book. 2004. (American Civil War Ser.). (Illus.). 48p. (J). lib. bdg. 26.60 *(978-0-7660-5189-8(7),* MyReportLinks.com Bks.) Enslow Pubs., Inc.

McLeese, Don. Stonewall Jackson. 2005. (Civil War Military Leaders Ser.). (Illus.). 32p. (J). (gr. 3-6). lib. bdg. 19.95 *(978-1-59515-477-4(9))* Rourke Educational Media.

McNeese, Tim. Robert E. Lee. 2009. (Leaders of the Civil War Era Ser.). (Illus.). 152p. (gr. 6-12). lib. bdg. 35.00 *(978-1-60413-304-2(X),* Chelsea Hse.) Facts On File, Inc.

Miller, Reagan & Arthur, Martin. Great Leaders of the Civil War. 2011. (ENG.). 48p. (J). pap. *(978-0-7787-5359-9(X));* lib. bdg. *(978-0-7787-5342-1(5))* Crabtree Publishing Co.

Miller, Reagan & Claus, J. Matteson. Life on a Civil War Battlefield. 2011. (ENG.). 48p. (J). pap. *(978-0-7787-5357-5(3));* lib. bdg. *(978-0-7787-5340-7(9))* Crabtree Publishing Co.

Miller, Reagan & Doak, Melissa J. Life on the Homefront During the Civil War. 2011. (ENG.). 48p. (J). pap. *(978-0-7787-5361-2(1));* lib. bdg. *(978-0-7787-5344-5(1))* Crabtree Publishing Co.

Nardo, Don. The Civil War. 2009. (American History Ser.). pap. 24.10 *(978-1-4205-0302-9(2),* Lucent Bks.) Cengage Gale.

Ollhoff, Jim. The Civil War: Weapons, 1 vol. 2012. (Civil War Ser.). (ENG.). 32p. (J). (gr. 5-9). 27.07 *(978-1-61783-278-9(2))* ABDO Publishing Co.

Parker, Christi E. Civil War Is Coming, 1 vol. 2005. (Primary Source Readers Ser.). (ENG.). 24p. (J). (gr. 5-5). pap. 8.99 *(978-0-7439-8915-2(5))* Shell Educational Publishing.

Pflueger, Lynda. Stonewall Jackson: General of the Confederate Army. 2015. (J). *(978-0-7660-6495-9(6))* Enslow Pubs., Inc.

Phillips, Larissa. Women Civil War Spies of the Confederacy. (American Women at War Ser.). 112p. 2009. (gr. 8-8). 63.90 *(978-1-61511-402-3(5))* 2004. (Illus.). (gr. 7-12). lib. bdg. 34.60 *(978-0-8239-4451-4(4))* Rosen Publishing Group, Inc., The.

Pingry, Patricia A. Meet Robert E. Lee. Johnson, Meredith, illus. 2004. (J). 9.95 *(978-0-8249-5465-9(3),* Ideal Pubns.) Worthy Publishing.

—The Story of Robert E. Lee. Johnson, Meredith, illus. 2004. (ENG.). 26p. (J). (gr. -1-k). bds. 6.95 *(978-0-8249-6501-3(9),* Ideal Pubns.) Worthy Publishing.

Pittman, Rickey E. Confederate Alphabet, 1 vol. Ford, Stephanie A., illus. 2011. (ENG.). 32p. (J). (gr. k-3). 16.99 *(978-1-58980-760-0(X))* Pelican Publishing Co., Inc.

Power, J. Tracey. Stonewall Jackson: Hero of the Confederacy. 2009. (Library of American Lives & Times Ser.). 112p. (gr. 5-5). 69.20 *(978-1-60853-507-1(X))* Rosen Publishing Group, Inc., The.

Robertson, James I., Jr. Robert E. Lee: Virginian Soldier, American Citizen. 2005. (ENG., Illus.). 176p. (YA). (gr. 7-12). 29.99 *(978-0-689-85731-7(4),* Atheneum Bks. for Young Readers) Simon & Schuster Children's Publishing.

Roche, Tim. Soldiers of the Civil War, 1 vol. (Why We Fought: the Civil War Ser.). (ENG.). 48p. (gr. 3-6). 2011. pap. 9.95 *(978-1-4329-3920-5(3))* 2010. 33.32 *(978-1-4329-3914-4(9))* Heinemann-Raintree. (Heinemann InfoSearch).

Roppelt, Donna J. & DeAngelis, Therese. General A.P. Hill: Light Division Leader. 2011. (J). *(978-1-59556-042-1(4));* pap. *(978-1-59556-048-3(3))* OTTN Publishing.

Vonne, Mira. Gross Facts about the American Civil War. 2017. (Gross History Ser.). (ENG., Illus.). 32p. (gr. 1-2). lib. bdg. 26.65 *(978-1-5157-4155-8(9))* Capstone Press of Coughlan Cos.

Wilson, Camilla. Civil War Spies: Behind Enemy Lines. 2010. vii, 104p. (J). pap. *(978-0-545-13002-8(6))* Scholastic, Inc.

CONFEDERATE STATES OF AMERICA—FICTION

Connell, Kate. Yankee Blue or Rebel Grey? The Civil War Adventures of Sam Shaw. 2003. (I Am American Ser.). (ENG., Illus.). 40p. (J). (gr. 3-7). pap. 6.99 *(978-0-7922-5179-8(2),* National Geographic Children's Bks.) National Geographic Society.

Page, Thomas Nelson. Two Little Confederates. 2013. (Notable American Authors Ser.). reprint ed. lthr. 79.00 *(978-0-7812-4689-7(X))* Reprint Services Corp.

CONFEDERATION OF AMERICAN COLONIES

see United States—History—1783-1815

CONFLICT, SOCIAL

see Social Conflict

CONFUCIANISM

Buddhist Text Translation Society Staff, contrib. by. Standards for Students: Instructions in Virtue from the Chinese Heritage = [Di Zi Gui]. 2003. (ENG & CHI., Illus.). 41p. (J). *(978-0-88139-489-4(0))* Buddhist Text Translation Society.

Taylor, Rodney L. & Choy, Howard. The Illustrated Encyclopedia of Confucianism, 2 vols. 2003. (Illustrated Encyclopedia of Confucianism (2 Volume Set) Ser.). (Illus.). xxxvii, 869p. (J). 216.75 *(978-0-8239-4080-6(2));* 216.75 *(978-0-8239-4081-3(0))* Rosen Publishing Group, Inc., The.

CONFUCIUS

Carew-Miller, Anna. Confucius: Great Chinese Philosopher. 2004. (Great Names Ser.). (Illus.). 32p. (J). (gr. 3-18). lib. bdg. 19.95 *(978-1-59084-149-5(2))* Mason Crest.

Conklin, Wendy & Lee, Gisela. Confucius: Chinese Philosopher, 1 vol. 2007. (Primary Source Readers Ser.). (ENG.). 32p. (J). (gr. 4-4). pap. 8.99 *(978-0-7439-0437-7(0))* Shell Educational Publishing.

Miller, Anna Carew & Carew-Miller, Anna. Confucius: Great Chinese Philosopher. 2013. (People of Importance Ser.: 21). (Illus.). 32p. (J). (gr. 4-18). 19.95 *(978-1-4222-2845-6(2))* Mason Crest.

Tracy, Kathleen. The Life & Times of Confucius. 2004. (Biography from Ancient Civilizations Ser.). (Illus.). 48p. (J). (gr. 4-8). lib. bdg. 29.95 *(978-1-58415-246-0(X))* Mitchell Lane Pubs., Inc.

CONGO, BELGIAN

see Congo (Democratic Republic)

CONGO (BRAZZAVILLE)—FICTION

Whitmore, Andrew. Beast of the Jungle. 2007. 96p. (YA). pap. *(978-1-4207-0728-1(0))* Sundance/Newbridge Educational Publishing.

CONGO (DEMOCRATIC REPUBLIC)

DiPiazza, Francesca Davis. Democratic Republic of Congo in Pictures. 2008. (Visual Geography (Lerner) Ser.). (Illus.). 80p. (YA). (gr. 7-12). lib. bdg. 29.27 *(978-0-8225-8572-5(3))* Twenty First Century Bks.

Heale, Jay & Yong, Jui Lin. The Democratic Republic of the Congo. 2nd rev. ed. 2009. (Cultures of the World 17 Ser.). 144p. (gr. 6) 42.79 *(978-0-7614-4478-7(5))* Marshall Cavendish Corp.

Humphreys, Jessica Dee & Chikwanine, Michel. Child Soldier: When Boys & Girls Are Used in War. Dávila, Claudia, illus. 2015. (CitizenKid Ser.). (ENG.). 48p. (J). (gr. 5-9). 17.95 *(978-1-77138-126-0(4))* Kids Can Pr., Ltd. CAN. Dist: Hachette Bk. Group.

Milios, Rita. Democratic Republic of the Congo. Rotberg, Robert I., ed. 2012. (Evolution of Africa's Major Nations Ser.). (Illus.). 80p. (J). (gr. 7). 22.95 *(978-1-4222-2195-2(4))* Mason Crest.

—Democratic Republic of the Congo. 2011. (J). pap. *(978-1-4222-2223-2(3))* Mason Crest.

Oppong, Joseph R. & Woodruff, Tania. Democratic Republic of the Congo. 2007. (Modern World Nations Ser.). (Illus.). 104p. (YA). (gr. 7-12). lib. bdg. 35.00 *(978-0-7910-9249-1(6))* Facts On File, Inc.

Owhonda, John. Congo. 2003. (Modern Nations of the World Ser.). (ENG., Illus.). 112p. (J). 32.10 *(978-1-59018-111-9(5),* Lucent Bks.) Cengage Gale.

Pohl, Kathleen. Descubramos el Congo. 2008. (Descubramos Países Del Mundo Ser.). (SPA.). 32p. (gr. 1-5). pap. 10.50 *(978-0-8368-8787-7(5));* (Illus.). lib. bdg. 26.00 *(978-0-8368-8780-8(8))* Stevens, Gareth Publishing LLLP. (Gareth Stevens Learning Library).

—Looking at the Congo. 2008. (Looking at Countries Ser.). 32p. (gr. 1-5). pap. 10.50 *(978-0-8368-8773-0(5));* (Illus.). lib. bdg. 26.00 *(978-0-8368-8766-2(2))* Stevens, Gareth Publishing LLLP. (Gareth Stevens Learning Library).

Prentzas. Democratic Republic of Congo. 2012. (Explorer Library: Social Studies Explorer Ser.). (ENG.). 48p. (gr. 4-8). 31.36 *(978-1-61080-443-1(0),* 202053) Cherry Lake Publishing.

—It's Cool to Learn about Countries: Democratic Republic of Congo. 2012. (Explorer Library: Social Studies Explorer Ser.). (ENG.). 48p. (gr. 4-8). pap. 15.64 *(978-1-61080-617-6(4),* 202227) Cherry Lake Publishing.

Roberts, Mary Nooter & Roberts, Allen F. Luba. 2008. (Visions of Africa Ser.). (ENG., Illus.). 160p. (gr. 8-17). 39.95 *(978-88-7439-297-1(4))* 5 Continents ITA. Dist: Hachette Bk. Group.

Rodger, Ellen. A Refugee's Journey from the Democratic Republic of the Congo. 2017. (Leaving My Homeland Ser.). (ENG., Illus.). 32p. (J). pap. ***(978-0-7787-3156-6(1))*** Crabtree Publishing Co.

Uwiringiyimana, Sandra & Pesta, Abigail. How Dare the Sun Rise: Memoirs of a War Child. 2017. 304p. (YA). (gr. 8). 19.99 *(978-0-06-247014-0(0),* Tegen, Katherine Bks) HarperCollins Pubs.

Woolf, Alex. Trekking in the Congo Rainforest. 2014. (Traveling Wild Ser.). 32p. (J). (gr. 4-8). pap. 63.00 *(978-1-4824-1253-6(5))* Stevens, Gareth Publishing LLLP.

CONGO (DEMOCRATIC REPUBLIC)—FICTION

Anderson, Natalie C. City of Saints & Thieves. 2017. (ENG.). 432p. (YA). (gr. 7). 18.99 *(978-0-399-54758-4(4),* G.P. Putnam's Sons Books for Young Readers) Penguin Young Readers Group.

Briggs, Andy. The Savage Lands. 2013. (Tarzan Ser.). (ENG.). 212p. (J). (gr. 3-6). pap. 12.99 *(978-1-4804-0014-6(9),* Open Road Media E-riginal) Open Road Integrated Media, Inc.

—Tarzan: The Greystoke Legacy. 2011. (ENG.). 304p. pap. *(978-0-571-27238-9(X))* Faber & Faber, Ltd.

Hergé. Tintin au Congo. (FRE., Illus.). (J). (gr. 7-9). 24.95 *(978-0-8288-5090-2(9))* French & European Pubns., Inc.

—Tintin en el Congo. (SPA., Illus.). 62p. (J). 24.95 *(978-0-8288-5095-7(X))* French & European Pubns., Inc.

—Tintin im Kongo. (GER., Illus.). 62p. (J). pap. 24.95 *(978-0-8288-4998-2(6))* French & European Pubns., Inc.

Hergé & I, Herge-tintin Rustica. Tintin en el Congo. (Tintin Ser.). (SPA.). 64p. (J). 14.95 *(978-84-261-1401-3(6))* Juventud, Editorial ESP. Dist: Distribooks, Inc.

Howat, Irene. On His Majesty's Service. 2008. (Trailblazers Ser.). (ENG.). 176p. (J). (gr. 4-9). per. 8.99 *(978-1-84550-259-1(0),* bea45fc4-969e-4e89-84fe-2abf3d4baa6d) Christian Focus Pubns. GBR. Dist: Bookmasters Distribution.

Lewis, Gill. Gorilla Dawn. Meyer, Susan, illus. 2017. (J). pap. ***(978-1-4814-8658-3(6))*** Simon & Schuster Children's Publishing.

Luba Folk Tales. 2005. (YA). 10.00 *(978-1-59872-207-9(7))* Instant Pub.

Schrefer, Eliot. Endangered. 2014. (ENG.). 288p. (J). (gr. 7). pap. 9.99 *(978-0-545-16577-8(6),* Scholastic Paperbacks) Scholastic, Inc.

Shepard, Aaron. The Magic Flyswatter: A Superhero Tale of Africa, Retold from the Mwindo Epic. 2008. (Ancient Fantasy Ser.: 3). 44p. (J). pap. 6.00 *(978-0-938497-39-4(1));* lib. bdg. 15.00 *(978-0-938497-38-7(3))* Shepard Pubns. (Skyhook Pr.).

Whitney, Elliott. The Blind Lion of the Congo. 2011. 128p. pap. 9.99 *(978-1-61203-066-1(1))* Bottom of the Hill Publishing.

Yrjana, Colleen. Carry Me to Kinshasa Our Adoption Journey. Ulrich, Kelly, illus. 2012. 24p. pap. *(978-1-77097-655-9(8))* FriesenPress.

CONGRESS—UNITED STATES

see United States—Congress

CONGRESSMEN

see Legislators—United States; United States—Congress

CONJURING

see Magic Tricks

CONNECTICUT

Brown, Vanessa. Connecticut. (Bilingual Library of the United States of America Ser.). (ENG & SPA.). 32p. 2009. (gr. 2-2). 47.90 *(978-1-60853-349-7(2),* Editorial Buenas Letras) 2005. (Illus.). (J). (gr. 3-6). lib. bdg. 25.25 *(978-1-4042-3071-2(8))* Rosen Publishing Group, Inc., The.

dePaola, Tomie. Here We All Are. unabr. ed. 2004. (Fairmount Avenue Ser.: Vol. 2). 80p. (J). (gr. 2-5). pap. 17.00 incl. audio *(978-0-8072-0655-3(5),* LDTR 246 SP, Listening Library) Random Hse. Audio Publishing Group.

Elissa, Grodin. N Is for Nutmeg: A Connecticut Alphabet. Brookfield, Maureen, illus. 2003. (Discover America State by State Ser.). (ENG.). 40p. (J). 17.95 *(978-1-58536-124-3(0))* Sleeping Bear Pr.

Evento, Susan. Connecticut. Hamilton, Harriet, tr. (Rookie Español Geografía Ser.). (Illus.). 32p. (J). (gr. k-2). 2006. (SPA & ENG.). per. 5.95 *(978-0-516-25046-5(9))* 2005. (ENG & SPA., lib. bdg. 19.50 *(978-0-516-25245-2(3))* Scholastic Library Publishing. (Children's Pr.).

Gelman, Amy. Connecticut. 2012. (J). lib. bdg. 25.26 *(978-0-7613-4525-1(6),* Lerner Pubns.) Lerner Publishing Group.

George, Jean Craighead. Autumn Moon. 2003. (J). (gr. 3-7). 20.75 *(978-0-8446-7241-0(6))* Smith, Peter Pub., Inc.

Goldstein, Phyllis. Uniquely Connecticut, 1 vol. 2003. (State Studies). (ENG., Illus.). 48p. pap. 8.99 *(978-1-4034-4503-2(6),* Heinemann State Studies) Heinemann-Raintree.

Grodin, Elissa D. Yankee Doodle Numbers: A Connecticut Number Book. Brookfield, Maureen K., illus. rev. ed. 2007. (Count Your Way Across the U. S. A. Ser.). (ENG.). 40p. (J). (gr. 3-7). 17.95 *(978-1-58536-175-5(5))* Sleeping Bear Pr.

Kent, Zachary. Connecticut. 2014. (America the Beautiful Ser.: 3). (ENG.). 144p. (J). lib. bdg. 40.00 *(978-0-531-24879-9(8))* Scholastic Library Publishing.

Khanna, Rachel. Oh the Places to Know: A Guide to Greenwich for Kids. 2006. per. 18.95 *(978-0-9779568-0-7(6))* Khanna, Rachel.

Kirchner, Jason. Connecticut. 2016. (States Ser.). (ENG., Illus.). 32p. (gr. 3-4). lib. bdg. 27.32 *(978-1-5157-0393-8(2))* Next Page Pr., The.

Knapp, Ron. Connecticut: A MyReportLinks. Com Book. 2003. (States Ser.). (Illus.). 48p. (J). lib. bdg. 25.26 *(978-0-7660-5121-8(8),* MyReportLinks.com Bks.) Enslow Pubs., Inc.

Labairon, Cassandra Sharri. Connecticut. 2008. (This Land Called America Ser.). 32p. (YA). (gr. 3-6). 22.95 *(978-1-58341-632-7(3))* Creative Co., The.

Marsh, Carole. Connecticut Current Events Projects: 30 Cool, Activities, Crafts, Experiments & More for Kids to Do to Learn about Your State! 2003. (Connecticut Experience Ser.). 32p. (gr. k-8). pap. 5.95 *(978-0-635-02026-0(2),* Marsh, Carole Bks.) Gallopade International.

—The Connecticut Experience Pocket Guide. 2004. (Connecticut Experience! Ser.). (Illus.). 96p. (J). (gr. 3-8). pap. 6.95 *(978-0-7933-9578-1(X))* Gallopade International.

—Connecticut Geography Projects: 30 Cool, Activities, Crafts, Experiments & More for Kids to Learn about Your State! 2003. (Connecticut Experience Ser.). 32p. (gr. k-5). pap. 5.95 *(978-0-635-01826-7(8),* Marsh, Carole Bks.) Gallopade International.

—Connecticut Government Projects: 30 Cool, Activities, Crafts, Experiments & More for Kids to Do to Learn about Your State! 2003. (Connecticut Experience Ser.). 32p. (gr. k-5). pap. 5.95 *(978-0-635-01926-4(4),* Marsh, Carole Bks.) Gallopade International.

—Connecticut Jeopardy! Answers & Questions about Our State! 2004. (Connecticut Experience! Ser.). (Illus.). 32p. (J). (gr. 3-8). pap. 7.95 *(978-0-7933-9580-4(1))* Gallopade International.

—Connecticut "Jography" A Fun Run Thru Our State! 2004. (Connecticut Experience! Ser.). (Illus.). 32p. (J). (gr. 3-8). pap. 7.95 *(978-0-7933-9581-1(X))* Gallopade International.

—Connecticut People Projects: 30 Cool, Activities, Crafts, Experiments & More for Kids to Do to Learn about Your State! 2003. (Connecticut Experience Ser.). 32p. (gr. k-5). pap. 5.95 *(978-0-635-01976-9(0),* Marsh, Carole Bks.) Gallopade International.

—Connecticut Symbols & Facts Projects: 30 Cool, Activities, Crafts, Experiments & More for Kids to Learn about Your State! 2003. (Connecticut Experience Ser.). 32p. (gr. k-5). pap. 5.95 *(978-0-635-01876-2(4),* Marsh, Carole Bks.) Gallopade International.

—Connecticut's Big Activity Book. 2004. (Connecticut Experience! Ser.). (Illus.). 96p. (J). (gr. 2-6). pap. 9.95 *(978-0-7933-9582-8(8))* Gallopade International.

—The Cool Connecticut Coloring Book. 2004. (Connecticut Experience! Ser.). (Illus.). 32p. (J). (gr. k-2). pap. 3.95 *(978-0-7933-9583-5(5))* Gallopade International.

—My First Book about Connecticut. 2004. (Connecticut Experience! Ser.). (Illus.). 32p. (J). (gr. k-4). pap. 7.95 *(978-0-7933-9579-8(8))* Gallopade International.

McNeil, Niki, et al. Connecticut. 2007. (In the Hands of a Child: Project Pack Continent Study Ser.). (Illus.). 89p. spiral bd. 24.00 *(978-1-60308-141-2(0))* In the Hands of a Child.

Mezzanotte, Jim. Connecticut. 2006. (Portraits of the States Ser.). (Illus.). 32p. (gr. 2-6). pap. 10.50 *(978-0-8368-4682-9(6));* lib. bdg. 26.00 *(978-0-8368-4663-8(X))* Stevens, Gareth Publishing LLLP. (Gareth Stevens Learning Library).

Murray, Julie. Connecticut, 1 vol. 2006. (Buddy Book Ser.). (ENG., Illus.). 32p. (gr. k-4). 27.07 *(978-1-59197-666-0(9),* Buddy Bks.) ABDO Publishing Co.

Ollhoff, Jim. Connecticut, 1 vol. 2009. (United States Ser.). (ENG., Illus.). 48p. (YA). (gr. 2-5). 27.07 *(978-1-60453-642-3(X))* ABDO Publishing Co.

Quasha, Jennifer. How to Draw Connecticut's Sights & Symbols. 2009. (Kid's Guide to Drawing America Ser.). 32p. (gr. k-k). 50.50 *(978-1-61511-051-3(8),* PowerKids Pr.) Rosen Publishing Group, Inc., The.

Rissman, Rebecca. What's Great about Connecticut? 2015. (Our Great States Ser.). (ENG., Illus.). 32p. (J). (gr. 2-5). pap. 7.95 *(978-1-4677-6081-2(1),* Lerner Pubns.) Lerner Publishing Group.

Sherrow, Victoria. Connecticut. 2nd rev. ed. 2006. (Celebrate the States Ser.). (Illus.). 144p. (gr. 6-7). lib. bdg. 42.79 *(978-0-7614-2155-9(6),* Benchmark Bks.) Marshall Cavendish Corp.

Webster, Christine. Connecticut: The Constitution State. 2016. (J). *(978-1-4896-4833-4(X))* Weigl Pubs., Inc.

CONNECTICUT—FICTION

Acampora, Paul. Rachel Spinelli Punched Me in the Face. 2013. (ENG.). 192p. (J). (gr. 3-7). pap. 8.99 *(978-1-250-01669-0(X),* 9781250016690) Square Fish.

Amstel, Marsha. The Horse-Riding Adventure of Sybil Ludington, Revolutionary War Messenger. Hammond, Ted & Carbajal, Richard, illus. 2011. (History's Kid Heroes Ser.). (ENG.). 32p. (gr. 3-5). pap. 8.95 *(978-0-7613-7073-4(0),* Graphic Universe™) Lerner Publishing Group.

At Aunt Hattie's House. 2005. (YA). 12.00 net. *(978-0-9763793-1-7(7))* Mitchell, Karan.

Bacon, Josephine Daskam. While Caroline was Growing: Books about Children. 2007. (ENG.). 178p. pap. 19.99 *(978-1-4346-0447-7(0));* 196p. pap. 21.99 *(978-1-4346-0448-4(9))* Creative Media Partners, LLC.

Baratz-Logsted, Lauren. Red Girl, Blue Boy: An If Only Novel. 2015. (If Only... Ser.). (ENG.). 304p. (YA). (gr. 7). pap. 9.99 *(978-1-61963-685-9(9),* 9781619636859, Bloomsbury USA Childrens) Bloomsbury Publishing USA.

Barnholdt, Lauren. Aces Up. 2010. (ENG.). 288p. (YA). (gr. 7). pap. 9.99 *(978-0-385-73874-3(9),* Ember) Random Hse. Children's Bks.

Baskin, Nora Raleigh. Basketball (or Something Like It) 176p. (J). 2007. (ENG.). (gr. 4-7). pap. 6.99 *(978-0-06-059612-5(0))* 2005. (ENG.). 15.99 *(978-0-06-059610-1(4))* 2005. lib. bdg. 16.89 *(978-0-06-059611-8(2))* HarperCollins Pubs.

Biagiotti, Aldo. Escape from Death Valley: A Tale of Two Burros. Biagiotti, Aldo, photos by. 2003. (Books for Young Learners). (ENG., Illus.). 16p. (J). 5.75 net. *(978-1-57274-661-9(0),* 2737, Bks. for Young Learners) Owen, Richard C. Pubs., Inc.

Bianco, Margery Williams. Winterbound. Seredy, Kate, illus. 2014. (ENG.). 256p. (J). (gr. 5-9). pap. 5.99 *(978-0-486-49290-2(7))* Dover Pubns., Inc.

Bond, Douglas. Guns of Providence. 2010. (J). pap. (978-1-59638-156-8(6)) P & R Publishing.

Bradbury, Bianca. Flight into Spring. 2005. (Sally (Bethlehem Books) Ser.). 184p. (YA). (gr. 7). per. 11.95 (978-1-932350-01-2(2)) Bethlehem Bks.

Brian, Kate, pseud. Privilege. 2008. (Privilege Ser.: No. 1). (ENG.). 304p. (YA). (gr. 9-18). pap. 9.99 (978-1-4169-6759-0(1), Simon & Schuster Bks. For Young Readers) Simon & Schuster Bks. For Young Readers.

—Scandal. 2010. (Private Ser.: No. 11). (ENG., Illus.). 240p. (YA). (gr. 9-18). pap. 9.99 (978-1-4169-8470-2(4), Simon & Schuster Bks. For Young Readers) Simon & Schuster Bks. For Young Readers.

Burkhart, Jessica. Home for Christmas. 2013. (Canterwood Crest Ser.). lib. bdg. 18.40 (978-0-606-32322-2(8), Turtleback) Turtleback Bks.

Buyea, Rob. Because of Mr. Terupt. (ENG.). (J). (gr. 3-7). 2011. 304p. 7.99 (978-0-375-85824-6(5), Yearling) 2010. 288p. 16.99 (978-0-385-73882-8(X), Delacorte Bks. for Young Readers) Random Hse. Children's Bks.

Carlson, Melody. Lost in Las Vegas, 1 vol. 2014. (Carter House Girls Ser.). (ENG.). 208p. (YA). pap. 9.99 (978-0-310-74716-1(3)) Zondervan.

—Mixed Bags, 1 vol. 2014. (Carter House Girls Ser.). (ENG.). 224p. (YA). pap. 9.99 (978-0-310-74756-7(2)) Zondervan.

—Stealing Bradford, 1 vol. 2014. (Carter House Girls Ser.). (ENG.). 224p. (YA). pap. 9.99 (978-0-310-74654-6(X)) Zondervan.

—Viva Vermont!, 1 vol. 2014. (Carter House Girls Ser.). (ENG.). 224p. (YA). pap. 9.99 (978-0-310-74714-7(7)) Zondervan.

Cook, Kajsa C. The Untold Story: About the War of 1812. 2011. 84p. pap. 12.99 (978-1-4520-6557-1(8)) AuthorHouse.

Cooney, Caroline B. Diamonds in the Shadow. 2009. (ENG.). 240p. (YA). 9.99 (978-1-4000-7424-2(X), WaterBrook Pr.) Crown Publishing Group.

—Diamonds in the Shadow. 2009. (ENG.). 240p. (YA). (gr. 7). pap. 9.99 (978-0-385-73262-8(7), Delacorte Bks. for Young Readers) Random Hse. Children's Bks.

—If the Witness Lied. 2010. (ENG.). 224p. (YA). (gr. 7). pap. 8.99 (978-0-385-73449-3(2), Ember) Random Hse. Children's Bks.

—They Never Came Back. 2011. (ENG., Illus.). 208p. (YA). (gr. 7). pap. 7.99 (978-0-385-73809-5(9), Ember) Random Hse. Children's Bks.

Daniels, Sara. Pieces of the Sky. 2005. 135p. pap. 15.99 (978-1-4116-4291-1(0)) Lulu Pr., Inc.

Donovan, Rebecca. Barely Breathing, 0 vols. unabr. ed. 2013. (Breathing Ser.: 2). (ENG.). 512p. (YA). (gr. 10-12). pap. 9.99 (978-1-4778-1717-9(4), 9781477817179, Amazon Children's Publishing) Amazon Publishing.

—The Breathing Series: Books 1 And 2, 0 vols. 2013. (Breathing Ser.). (ENG.). 978p. (YA). (gr. 10-12). pap. 12.99 (978-1-4778-1695-0(X), 9781477816950, Skyscape) Amazon Publishing.

—Reason to Breathe, 0 vols. 2013. (Breathing Ser.: 1). (ENG.). 466p. (YA). (gr. 10-12). pap. 9.99 (978-1-4778-1714-8(X), 9781477817148, Amazon Children's Publishing) Amazon Publishing.

Fitzpatrick, Huntley. What I Thought Was True. 2014. (ENG.). 416p. (YA). (gr. 9). 17.99 (978-0-8037-3909-3(5), Dial Bks) Penguin Young Readers Group.

Fuller, Harvey. Tommy & the Island. Fuller, Harvey, illus. 2007. (Illus.). (J). pap. 18.95 (978-0-9773725-7-7(X)) Flat Hammock Pr.

Garant, Andre J. The Circus Kids. 2008. 140p. pap. 11.99 (978-1-4389-2833-3(5)) AuthorHouse.

Grabenstein, Chris. The Crossroads. 2009. (Haunted Mystery Ser.: 1). (ENG.). 352p. (J). (gr. 3-7). 7.99 (978-0-375-84698-4(0), Yearling) Random Hse. Children's Bks.

—The Hanging Hill. 2010. (Haunted Mystery Ser.: 2). (ENG.). 336p. (J). (gr. 3-7). pap. 6.99 (978-0-375-84700-4(6), Yearling) Random Hse. Children's Bks.

Greenwald, Lisa. My Summer of Pink & Green. 2013. (Pink & Green Ser.). (ENG.). 272p. (YA). (gr. 3-7). 17.95 (978-1-4197-0413-0(3), Amulet Bks.); (J). (gr. 5-9). 5.00 (978-1-4197-0932-6(1)) Abrams, Inc.

—My Summer of Pink & Green: Pink & Green Book Two. 2014. (Pink & Green Ser.). (ENG.). 288p. (YA). (gr. 3-7). pap. 7.95 (978-1-4197-0931-9(3), Amulet Bks.) Abrams, Inc.

Haight, Jessica & Robinson, Stephanie. The Secret Files of Fairday Morrow. Muradov, Roman, illus. 2015. (ENG.). 272p. (J). (gr. 4-7). 18.99 (978-0-375-99182-0(4), Delacorte Bks. for Young Readers) Random Hse. Children's Bks.

Hoberman, Mary Ann. Strawberry Hill. 2010. (ENG., Illus.). 240p. (J). (gr. 3-7). pap. 7.99 (978-0-316-04135-5(1)) Little, Brown Bks. for Young Readers.

Houston, Julian. New Boy. 2007. 282p. (gr. 7-12). 18.00 (978-0-7569-8139-6(5)) Perfection Learning Corp.

Hunt, Lynda Mullaly. One for the Murphys. (ENG.). (J). (gr. 5). 2013. 256p. pap. 7.99 (978-0-14-242652-4(0), Puffin Books) 2012. 288p. 16.99 (978-0-399-25615-8(6), Nancy Paulsen Books) Penguin Young Readers Group.

Jacobs, Lily. The Littlest Bunny in Connecticut: An Easter Adventure. 2015. (ENG.). 32p. (J). (-3). 9.99 (978-1-4926-1060-1(7), Sourcebooks Jabberwocky) Sourcebooks, Inc.

James, Eric. A Halloween Scare in Connecticut. Le Ray, Marina, illus. 2015. (ENG.). 32p. (J). (-5). 9.99 (978-1-4926-2370-0(9), 9781492623700, Sourcebooks Jabberwocky) Sourcebooks, Inc.

—Santa's Sleigh Is on Its Way to Connecticut: A Christmas Adventure. Dunn, Robert, illus. 2016. (ENG.). 32p. (J). (-2). 12.99 (978-1-4926-4325-8(4), 9781492643258, Sourcebooks Jabberwocky) Sourcebooks, Inc.

Kreitzer, Dora. Summer in Connecticut. 2012. 18p. pap. 16.95 (978-1-4626-8665-0(6)) America Star Bks.

Kuehnel, Judy Lyons. The Autumn of Aunt Charlotte. 2006. (ENG.). 132p. per. 9.95 (978-1-59800-688-9(6)) Outskirts Pr., Inc.

Latham, William. Scary Stories of Stamford. 2009. 51p. pap. 9.99 (978-1-4357-6032-5(8)) Lulu Pr., Inc.

Leite, Karen. A Miracle Named Angel. 2009. 24p. pap. 11.49 (978-1-4389-5246-8(5)) AuthorHouse.

Lenski, Lois. Bound Girl of Cobble Hill. (J). 23.95 (978-0-89190-632-2(0)) Amereon Ltd.

Littman, Sarah Darer. Want to Go Private? (ENG.). 336p. (J). 2013. (gr. 7). pap. 10.99 (978-0-545-15147-4(3)) 2011. (gr. 9-9). 17.99 (978-0-545-15146-7(5), Scholastic Pr.) Scholastic, Inc.

Logsted, Greg. Alibi Junior High. (ENG.). 256p. (J). (gr. 5-9). 2011. pap. 6.99 (978-1-4169-4814-8(7)) 2009. (Illus.). 16.99 (978-1-4169-7959-3(X)) Simon & Schuster/Paula Wiseman Bks. (Simon & Schuster/Paula Wiseman Bks.).

Lon Rogers. The Between Season. 2009. 280p. pap. 17.95 (978-1-4401-8368-3(6)) iUniverse, Inc.

Lynch, Brendan Denis. The Document. 2012. 218p. pap. 8.99 (978-0-9825243-2-9(3)) 1776 Pr.

Malkin, Nina. Swear. (ENG.). 480p. (YA). (gr. 11). 2012. pap. 9.99 (978-1-4424-2111-0(8)) 2011. 17.99 (978-1-4424-2110-3(X)) Simon Pulse. (Simon Pulse).

—Swoon. 2010. (ENG.). 432p. (YA). (gr. 11). pap. 9.99 (978-1-4169-9801-3(2), Simon Pulse) Simon Pulse.

Mason, Jane B. Without Annette. 2016. (ENG.). 336p. (YA). (gr. 7). 18.99 (978-0-545-81995-4(4), Scholastic Pr.) Scholastic, Inc.

Matson, Morgan. Since You've Been Gone. 2015. (ENG., Illus.). 480p. (YA). (gr. 7). pap. 9.99 (978-1-4424-3501-8(1), Simon & Schuster Bks. For Young Readers) Simon & Schuster Bks. For Young Readers.

McDougal-Littell Publishing Staff. Literature Connections English: Homecoming. 2004. (McDougal Littell Literature Connections Ser.). (ENG.). 480p. (gr. 8-8). 16.90 (978-0-395-85802-8(X), 2-70802) Great Source Education Group, Inc.

McPhail, J. A. Dawn of Day. Battis, Gwen, illus. 2012. 200p. pap. 10.99 (978-0-9851196-1-4(6)) Rowe Publishing and Design.

Mlynowski, Sarah. Ten Things We Did (and Probably Shouldn't Have) 2011. (ENG.). 368p. (YA). (gr. 9-18). 16.99 (978-0-06-170124-5(6), HarperTeen) HarperCollins Pubs.

Pakkala, Christine. Jasmine & Maddie. 2014. (ENG.). 192p. (J). (gr. 4-7). 16.95 (978-1-62091-739-8(4)) Boyds Mills Pr.

Peloquin, Lili. The Innocents. 2013. (Innocents Ser.: 1). (ENG.). 288p. (YA). (gr. 7). pap. 9.99 (978-1-59514-502-4(8), Razorbill) Penguin Young Readers Group.

Rand, Johnathan. American Chillers #28 Curse of the Connecticut Coyotes. 2010. 208p. (J). pap. 5.99 (978-1-893699-74-8(9)) AudioCraft Publishing, Inc.

Rice, Luanne. The Beautiful Lost. 2017. (ENG.). 304p. (J). (gr. 7). 18.99 **(978-1-338-11107-1(8))** Scholastic, Inc.

Rice, Luanne. The Secret Language of Sisters. 2016. (ENG.). 352p. (J). (gr. 7). 18.99 (978-0-545-83955-6(6)) Scholastic, Inc.

Rinaldi, Ann. The Education of Mary: A Little Miss of Color, 1832. 2005. 176p. (J). pap. (978-0-7868-1377-3(6)) Hyperion Pr.

Rogers, Lon. The Between Season. 2009. 280p. 27.95 (978-1-4401-8370-6(8)) iUniverse, Inc.

Schuck, Philip. A Ricochet from Circumstance. 2005. (YA). 19.95 (978-0-9764670-0-7(3)) Smithfield Capital Corp.

Silvano, Wendi. Love Is All Around Connecticut. Czernichowska, Joanna, illus. 2016. (ENG.). 32p. (J). (-6). 12.99 (978-1-4926-2915-3(4), Sourcebooks Jabberwocky) Sourcebooks, Inc.

Smallman, Steve. Santa Is Coming to Connecticut. Dunn, Robert, illus. 2014. (ENG.). 32p. (J). (-3). 9.99 (978-1-4926-0670-3(7), Sourcebooks Jabberwocky) Sourcebooks, Inc.

Specter, Baron. Chasing Whales Aboard the Charles W. Morgan, 1 vol., Bk. 2. Evans, Dustin, illus. 2010. (Ghostly Graphic Adventures Ser.). (ENG.). 32p. (gr. 4-6). 28.50 (978-1-60270-771-9(5), Graphic Planet- Fiction) ABDO Publishing Co.

Stegmaier, Laura J. Ling-Ling Turner, Ppi: Mystery of the Rising Island. 2013. 92p. pap. 10.95 (978-1-4575-2363-2(9)) Dog Ear Publishing, LLC.

Turetsky, Bianca. The Time-Traveling Fashionista at the Palace of Marie Antoinette. 2013. (Time-Traveling Fashionista Ser.: 2). (ENG., Illus.). 272p. (J). (gr. 3-7). pap. 9.00 (978-0-316-10535-4(X), Poppy) Little, Brown Bks. for Young Readers.

Vrba, Christina. Good Night Connecticut. Rosen, Anne, illus. 2009. (Good Night Our World Ser.). (ENG.). 20p. (J). (gr. k — 1). bds. 9.95 (978-1-60219-035-1(6)) Good Night Bks.

Wood, Maryrose. How I Found the Perfect Dress. 2008. (ENG.). 240p. (YA). (gr. 9-18). 11.00 (978-0-425-21939-3(9), Berkley) Penguin Publishing Group.

Wright, Bil. Sunday You Learn How to Box. 2013. (ENG., Illus.). (YA). (gr. 7). 224p. 16.99 (978-1-4424-7474-1(2)); 240p. pap. 9.99 (978-1-4424-7472-7(6)) Simon & Schuster Bks. For Young Readers. (Simon & Schuster Bks. For Young Readers).

Wright, Bill & Wright, Bil. When the Black Girl Sings. 2008. (ENG.). 272p. (YA). (gr. 7-12). 16.99 (978-1-4169-3995-5(4), Simon & Schuster Bks. For Young Readers) Simon & Schuster Bks. For Young Readers.

—When the Black Girl Sings. 2009. (ENG.). 272p. (YA). (gr. 7). mass mkt. 6.99 (978-1-4169-4003-6(0), Simon Pulse) Simon Pulse.

Yolen, Jane. Centaur Rising. 2014. (ENG.). 272p. (J). (gr. 3-7). 16.99 (978-0-8050-9664-4(7), 9780805096644, Holt, Henry & Co. Bks. For Young Readers) Holt, Henry & Co.

CONNECTICUT—HISTORY

Alexander, Richard. The Colony of Connecticut. 2015. (Spotlight on the 13 Colonies Ser.). (ENG., Illus.). 24p. (J). (gr. 4-5). pap. 8.25 (978-1-4994-0314-5(3), PowerKids Pr.) Rosen Publishing Group, Inc., The.

Boyd, John. Annals of Winchester, CT. 2004. Orig. Title: Annals & Family Records of Winchester, Conn. with Exercises of the Centennial Celebration on the 16th & 17th Days of August 1871. cd-rom 20.00 (978-0-9727403-5-7(X), EJ04-01) Between the Lakes Group, LLC.

Burgan, Michael. Connecticut, 1614-1776. 2007. (National Geographic Voices from ColonialAmerica Ser.). (ENG., Illus.). 112p. (J). (gr. 5-9). 21.95 (978-1-4263-0068-4(9)); lib. bdg. 32.90 (978-1-4263-0069-1(7)) National Geographic Society. (National Geographic Children's Bks.).

Burgan, Michael & Fitzgerald, Stephanie. Connecticut. 2nd rev. ed. 2010. (It's My State! Ser.). 80p. (gr. 3-18). lib. bdg. 31.36 (978-1-60870-047-9(X)) Marshall Cavendish Corp.

Cunningham, Kevin. The Connecticut Colony. 2011. (True Bk Ser.). (ENG., Illus.). 48p. (J). pap. 6.95 (978-0-531-26600-7(1)); lib. bdg. 29.00 (978-0-531-25387-8(2)) Scholastic Library Publishing. (Children's Pr.).

Davidson, Tish. Southern New England: Connecticut, Massachusetts, Rhode Island, Vol. 19. 2015. (Let's Explore the States Ser.). (Illus.). 64p. (J). (gr. 5). 23.95 (978-1-4222-3333-7(2)) Mason Crest.

dePaola, Tomie. Things Will Never Be the Same. 2014. 78p. pap. 7.00 (978-1-61003-321-3(3)) Center for the Collaborative Classroom.

—What a Year. dePaola, Tomie, illus. 2003. (26 Fairmount Avenue Bks.). (Illus.). 72p. (gr. 2-5). 16.00 (978-0-7569-1546-9(5)) Perfection Learning Corp.

—26 Fairmount Avenue. dePaola, Tomie, illus. 2005. (Illus.). 58p. (J). (gr. k-4). reprint ed. 14.00 (978-0-7567-8722-6(X)) DIANE Publishing Co.

Dodd, Marion. Mystic by the A,B, Sea. Dodd, Marion, illus. 2006. (Illus.). (J). 17.95 (978-0-9773725-2-2(9)) Flat Hammock Pr.

Doherty, Craig A. & Doherty, Katherine M. Connecticut. 2005. (Thirteen Colonies Ser.). (Illus.). 144p. (gr. 5-8). 35.00 (978-0-8160-5417-6(7)) Facts On File, Inc.

Durrie, Karen. Connecticut: The Constitution State. 2012. (J). (978-1-61913-333-4(4)); pap. (978-1-61913-334-1(2)) Weigl Pubs., Inc.

Furgang, Kathy. The Declaration of Independence & Roger Sherman of Connecticut. 2009. (Framers of the Declaration of Independence Ser.). 24p. (gr. 3-3). 42.50 (978-1-61512-632-3(5), PowerKids Pr.) Rosen Publishing Group, Inc., The.

Jerome, Kate B. Lucky to Live in Connecticut. 2017. (Arcadia Kids Ser.). (ENG., Illus.). 32p. (J). 16.99 **(978-0-7385-2796-3(3))** Arcadia Publishing.

Koontz, Robin Michal. Connecticut: The Constitution State. 2010. (Our Amazing States Ser.). (ENG.). 24p. (J). pap. 8.25 (978-1-4488-0726-0(3)); lib. bdg. 22.60 (978-1-4488-0647-8(X)) Rosen Publishing Group, Inc., The. (PowerKids Pr.).

Krebs, Laurie. A Day in the Life of a Colonial Miller. 2004. (Library of Living & Working in Colonial Times). (Illus.). 24p. (J). lib. bdg. 19.95 (978-0-8239-6230-3(X), PowerKids Pr.) Rosen Publishing Group, Inc., The.

La Bella, Laura. Connecticut: Past & Present. 2010. (United States: Past & Present Ser.). (ENG.). 48p. (YA). pap. 11.75 (978-1-4358-9505-8(3)); lib. bdg. 29.25 (978-1-4358-9478-5(2)) Rosen Publishing Group, Inc., The. (Rosen Reference).

Malaspina, Ann. A Primary Source History of the Colony of Connecticut. (Primary Sources of the Thirteen Colonies & the Lost Colony Ser.). 64p. 2009. (gr. 5-8). 58.50 (978-1-60851-876-0(0)) 2006. (ENG., Illus.). (gr. 4-8). per. 12.95 (978-1-4042-0665-6(5)) 2005. (Illus.). (YA). (gr. 4-7). lib. bdg. 31.95 (978-1-4042-0424-9(5)) Rosen Publishing Group, Inc., The.

Marsh, Carole. Connecticut History Projects: 30 Cool, Activities, Crafts, Experiments & More for Kids to Do to Learn about Your State! 2003. (Connecticut Experience Ser.). 32p. (gr. k-5). pap. 5.95 (978-0-635-01776-5(8), Marsh, Carole Bks.) Gallopade International.

—Exploring Connecticut Through Project-Based Learning. 2016. (Connecticut Experience Ser.). (ENG.). (J). pap. 9.99 (978-0-635-12331-2(2)) Gallopade International.

—I'm Reading about Connecticut. 2014. (Connecticut Experience Ser.). (ENG., Illus.). (J). pap., pap. 8.99 (978-0-635-11283-5(3)) Gallopade International.

Marsh, Carole & Marsh, Michael. Let's Discover Connecticut! 2003. (J). (gr. 2-8). cd-rom 14.95 (978-0-7933-9585-9(2)) Gallopade International.

Miller, Jake. The Colony of Connecticut: A Primary Source History. (Primary Source Library of the Thirteen Colonies & the Lost Colony Ser.). 24p. (gr. 3-4). 2009. 42.50 (978-1-60854-134-8(7)) 2006. (Illus.). (J). lib. bdg. 22.60 (978-1-4042-3030-9(0)) Rosen Publishing Group, Inc., The. (PowerKids Pr.).

Monson, Christy & Nawyn, Lori. Love, Hugs, & Hope: When Scary Things Happen. 2013. (ENG.). 32p. (J). (gr. k-5). 16.95 (978-1-938301-60-5(9)) Familius LLC.

O'Neill, Elizabeth. Alfred Visits Connecticut. 2009. 24p. (J). pap. 12.00 (978-0-9822288-9-0(9)) Global Business Information Strategies, Inc.

Otfinoski, Steven. Exploring the Connecticut Colony. 2016. (Exploring the 13 Colonies Ser.). (ENG., Illus.). 48p. (gr. 3-4). lib. bdg. 31.99 (978-1-5157-2240-3(6)) Capstone Press of Coughlan Cos.

Rissman, Rebecca. What's Great about Connecticut? 2015. (Our Great States Ser.). (ENG., Illus.). 32p. (J). (gr. 2-5). lib. bdg. 26.60 (978-1-4677-3857-6(3), Lerner Pubns.) Lerner Publishing Group.

Salzmann, Mary Elizabeth. Rachel's Home on Bear Mountain: A Story about Connecticut, 1 vol. Doucet, Bob, illus. 2011. (Fact & Fable: State Stories Set 3 Ser.). (ENG.). 24p. (J). (gr. -1-2). lib. bdg. 25.65 (978-1-61714-683-1(8)) ABDO Publishing Co.

Tieck, Sarah. Connecticut, 1 vol. 2012. (Explore the United States Ser.). (ENG.). 32p. (J). (gr. 2-5). lib. bdg. 28.50 (978-1-61783-345-8(2), Big Buddy Bks.) ABDO Publishing Co.

Webster, Christine. Connecticut. 2011. (Guide to American States Ser.). (Illus.). 48p. (YA). (gr. 3-6). 29.99 (978-1-61690-779-2(7)); (J). (978-1-61690-454-8(2)) Weigl Pubs., Inc.

—Connecticut: The Constitution State. 2016. (J). (978-1-5105-0665-7(9)) SmartBook Media, Inc.

Woollett, Laura A. Big Top Burning: The True Story of an Arsonist, a Missing Girl, & the Greatest Show on Earth. 2015. (ENG.). 176p. (J). (gr. 5). 18.95 (978-1-61373-114-7(0)) Chicago Review Pr., Inc.

Wyborny, Sheila. Connecticut. 2003. (Seeds of a Nation Ser.). (Illus.). 48p. (J). (gr. 3-5). 23.70 (978-0-7377-1445-6(X), Kidhaven) Cengage Gale.

CONNECTICUT—HISTORY—FICTION

Amstel, Marsha. The Horse-Riding Adventure of Sybil Ludington, Revolutionary War Messenger. Hammond, Ted & Carbajal, Richard, illus. 2011. (History's Kid Heroes Ser.). (ENG.). 32p. (gr. 3-5). 26.60 (978-0-7613-6181-7(2)) Lerner Publishing Group.

Bond, Douglas. Guns of Thunder. 2007. (Faith & Freedom Ser.). (Illus.). 261p. (J). (gr. 4-7). per. 11.99 (978-1-59638-013-4(6)) P & R Publishing.

Duble, Kathleen Benner. Hearts of Iron. 2006. (ENG.). 256p. (J). (gr. 5-9). 15.95 (978-1-4169-0850-0(1), McElderry, Margaret K. Bks.) McElderry, Margaret K. Bks.

Evan, Frances Y. The Forgotten Flag: Revolutionary Struggle in Connecticut. 2003. (Illus.). 92p. (J). 5.95 (978-1-57249-338-4(0), White Mane Kids) White Mane Publishing Co., Inc.

Kiely, Brendan. The Gospel of Winter. 2015. (ENG., Illus.). 320p. (YA). (gr. 9). pap. 11.99 (978-1-4424-8490-0(X), McElderry, Margaret K. Bks.) McElderry, Margaret K. Bks.

McPhail, J. A. Dawn of Day. Battis, Gwen, illus. 2012. 200p. 17.99 (978-0-9851196-2-1(4)) Rowe Publishing and Design.

Nelson, Marilyn. Pemba's Song. 2008. (ENG.). 112p. (J). (gr. 7-18). 16.99 (978-0-545-02076-3(X), Scholastic Pr.) Scholastic, Inc.

Speare, Elizabeth George. The Witch of Blackbird Pond. 2011. (ENG.). 272p. (J). (gr. 5-7). pap. 7.99 (978-0-547-55029-9(4)) Houghton Mifflin Harcourt Publishing Co.

CONQUISTADORES

see America—Discovery and Exploration

CONRAD, JOSEPH, 1857-1924

Johnson, Claudia, ed. Colonialism in Joseph Conrad's Heart of Darkness. 2012. (Social Issues in Literature Ser.). (ENG., Illus.). 224p. (gr. 10-12). pap. 32.00 (978-0-7377-5804-7(X)); lib. bdg. 40.95 (978-0-7377-5803-0(1)) Cengage Gale. (Greenhaven Pr., Inc.).

CONSCIENTIOUS OBJECTORS—FICTION

Kerr, M. E., pseud. Slap Your Sides. 2003. 198p. (YA). 13.65 (978-0-7569-4240-3(3)) Perfection Learning Corp.

CONSERVATION OF ENERGY

see Force and Energy

CONSERVATION OF FORESTS

see Forests and Forestry; Natural Resources

CONSERVATION OF NATURAL RESOURCES

see also Natural Resources

Baldwin, Christy. Care for Creation. Draven, Shelly, illus. 2010. (ENG.). 32p. (J). lib. bdg. 16.95 (978-0-9822565-6-5(6)) Tribute Bks.

Ball, Jacqueline A. Conservation & Natural Resources. 2004. (Discovery Channel School Science Ser.). (Illus.). 32p. (gr. 4-8). lib. bdg. 26.00 (978-0-8368-3377-5(5), Gareth Stevens Learning Library) Stevens, Gareth Publishing LLLP.

Bethune, Helen. Why Do Diamonds Sparkle? All about Earth's Resources. 2010. (Solving Science Mysteries Ser.). (Illus.). 24p. (J). pap. 8.25 (978-1-61531-919-0(0), PowerKids Pr.); (YA). (gr. 3-6). lib. bdg. 22.60 (978-1-61531-894-0(1)) Rosen Publishing Group, Inc., The.

Bullard, Lisa. Go Easy on Energy. Thomas, Wes, illus. 2011. (Planet Protectors Ser.). pap. 39.62 (978-0-7613-8653-7(X), Millbrook Pr.) Lerner Publishing Group.

—Go Easy on Energy. Thomas, Wes & Thomas, John, Jr., illus. 2011. (Cloverleaf Books (tm) — Planet Protectors Ser.). (ENG.). 24p. (J). (gr. k-2). lib. bdg. 23.93 (978-0-7613-6107-7(3)) Lerner Publishing Group.

—Go Easy on Energy. Thomas, Wes, illus. 2011. (Cloverleaf Books (tm) — Planet Protectors Ser.). (ENG.). 24p. (gr. k-2). pap. 6.95 (978-0-7613-8513-4(4), Millbrook Pr.) Lerner Publishing Group.

Castaldo, Nancy F. Keeping Our Earth Green. Caputo, Jim, illus. 2008. (ENG.). 128p. (J). (gr. 3-8). pap. 12.99 (978-0-8249-6825-0(5)); (gr. 8). 16.99 (978-0-8249-6824-3(7)) Worthy Publishing. (Ideal Pubns.).

Clare, Patricia. Living Green: Saving Our Earth. 2009. (Real Life Readers Ser.). 24p. (gr. 3-4). pap. 8.25 (978-1-4358-0121-9(0), Rosen Classroom); 24p. (gr. 3-3). 42.50 (978-1-61511-216-6(2), PowerKids Pr.); (J). lib. bdg. 22.60 (978-1-4358-2968-8(9), PowerKids Pr.) Rosen Publishing Group, Inc., The.

Claybourne, Anna. Saving the Earth. 2010. (Discovery of Life Ser.). 48p. (YA). lib. bdg. 19.95 (978-1-4222-1526-5(1)) Mason Crest.

Cleave, Rohan. Phasmid: Saving the Lord Howe Island Stick Insect. Tulloch, Coral, illus. 2015. (ENG.). 32p. (J). (gr. 2-2). 19.95 (978-1-4863-0112-6(6)) CSIRO Publishing AUS. Dist: Stylus Publishing, LLC.

Cohn, Jessica. Una Mano a la Tierra: Salvando el Medio Ambiente. 2017. (TIME for Kids en Español - Level 4 Ser.). (SPA., Illus.). 48p. (gr. 4-4). lib. bdg. 31.99 (978-1-5157-5149-6(X)) Time for Kids Inc AUS. Dist: Capstone Pub.

Colon De Mejias, Leticia. Dinero the Frog Learns to Save Energy. Tamara, Visco, illus. 2013. 32p. pap. 7.00 (978-0-9822168-9-7(0)) Independent Pub.

Davies, Leah. Kelly Bear Earth. Davies, Leah, ed. Hallett, Joy Davies, illus. 2008. 32p. (J). pap. 5.95 (978-0-9621054-3-2(0)) Kelly Bear Pr., Inc.

Enz, Tammy. Repurpose It: Invent New Uses for Old Stuff, 1 vol. 2012. (Invent It Ser.). (ENG.). 32p. (gr. 3-4). lib. bdg. 27.32 (978-1-4296-7636-6(1), Fact Finders) Capstone Press of Coughlan Cos.

Food and Agriculture Organization, ed. Youth Guide to Biodiversity. 2012. (ENG., Illus.). 261p. pap. 65.00 (978-92-5-107445-9(3)) Food & Agriculture Organization of the United Nations ITA. Dist: Rowman & Littlefield Publishers, Inc.

Gardner, Timothy. Oil. 2009. (Diminishing Resources Ser.). (Illus.). 111p. (J). lib. bdg. 28.95 (978-1-59935-117-9(X)) Reynolds, Morgan Inc.

George, Charles & Currie-McGhee, Leanne. Protecting Ecosystems. 2009. (21st Century Skills Library: Real World Science Ser.). (ENG.). 32p. (gr. 4-8). lib. bdg. 28.50 (978-1-60279-462-7(6), 200230) Cherry Lake Publishing.

Gillett, Jack & Gillett, Meg. Conservation-Area Maps. 2012. (Maps of the Environmental World Ser.). (ENG., Illus.). 32p. (J). (gr. 4-6). 26.50 (978-1-4488-8611-1(2)); pap. 10.60 (978-1-4488-8615-9(5)) Rosen Publishing Group, Inc., The. (PowerKids Pr.).

Green, Jen. Sustaining Our Natural Resources, 1 vol. 2011. (Environment Challenge Ser.). (ENG., Illus.). 48p. (gr. 5-6). pap. 9.49 (978-1-4109-4307-1(0)); 34.65 (978-1-4109-4300-2(3)) Heinemann-Raintree. (Raintree Freestyle).

—Why Should I Protect Nature? Gordon, Mike, illus. 2010. (Rise & Shine Ser.). (ENG.). 32p. (C). pap. 11.95 *(978-0-7641-3154-7(0))* National Geographic School Publishing, Inc.

Harper, Clay & Ingram, Jas. Are You Sure That Was a Rabbit?, 1 vol. 2012. (ENG., Illus.). 32p. (J). 12.99 *(978-0-7643-4007-9(7),* 9780764340079) Schiffer Publishing, Ltd.

Hirsch, Rebecca. Save the Planet: Protecting Our Natural Resources. 2010. (Explorer Library: Language Arts Explorer Ser.). (ENG.). 32p. (gr. 4-8). pap. 14.21 *(978-1-60279-670-6(X),* 200917); lib. bdg. 28.50 *(978-1-60279-661-4(0),* 200354) Cherry Lake Publishing.

Hunter, Nick. How Carbon Footprints Work. 2013. 32p. (J). (gr. 3-5). pap. 10.50 *(978-1-4339-9553-8(0));* pap. 63.00 *(978-1-4339-9554-5(9));* (ENG., Illus.). lib. bdg. 26.60 *(978-1-4339-9552-1(2))* Stevens, Gareth Publishing LLLP.

Jerome, Kate Boehm & National Geographic Learning Staff. Using Energy. 2007. (Rise & Shine Ser.). (ENG., Illus.). 32p. pap. 17.95 *(978-0-7922-8869-5(6))* CENGAGE Learning.

Kishel, Ann-Marie. Reuse. 2006. (First Step Nonfiction - Conservation Ser.). (ENG., Illus.). 8p. (gr. -1-1). pap. 4.95 *(978-0-8225-5675-6(8),* Lerner Pubns.) Lerner Publishing Group.

Lanz, Helen. Having the Energy. 2012. (Go Green Ser.). (Illus.). 32p. (J). (gr. 3-6). lib. bdg. 28.50 *(978-1-59771-301-6(5))* Sea-To-Sea Pubns.

Lepetit, Angie. Three Cheers for Trees! A Book about Our Carbon Footprint. 2013. (Earth Matters Ser.). (ENG.). 32p. (gr. 1-2). pap. 47.70 *(978-1-62065-742-3(2));* pap. 8.10 *(978-1-62065-741-6(4));* lib. bdg. 27.32 *(978-1-62065-048-6(7))* Capstone Press of Coughlan Cos. (Aplus Bks.).

Levy, Janey. Making Good Choices about Conservation. 2009. (J). 77.70 *(978-1-4358-5611-0(2),* Rosen Reference); (ENG.). 64p. (YA). pap. 12.95 *(978-1-4358-5610-3(4),* Rosen Reference); (Illus.). 64p. (YA). (gr. 5-9). lib. bdg. 31.95 *(978-1-4358-5314-0(8))* Rosen Publishing Group, Inc., The.

Lundgren, Julie K. How Do Humans Depend on Earth? 2012. (ENG., Illus.). 24p. (J). (gr. 4-5). pap. 8.95 *(978-1-61810-238-6(9))* Rourke Educational Media.

Mckay, Kim & Bonnin, Jenny. True Green Kids: 100 Things You Can Do to Save the Planet. 2008. (True Green Ser.). (ENG., Illus.). 144p. (J). (gr. 5-9). 27.90 *(978-1-4263-0443-9(9),* National Geographic Children's Bks.) National Geographic Society.

Mckay, Kim, et al. True Green Kids: 100 Things You Can Do to Save the Planet. 2008. (True Green Ser.). (ENG., Illus.). 144p. (J). (gr. 5-9). pap. 15.95 *(978-1-4263-0442-2(0),* National Geographic Children's Bks.) National Geographic Society.

Minden, Cecilia. Save the Planet: Reduce, Reuse, & Recycle. 2010. (Explorer Library: Language Arts Explorer Ser.). (ENG.). 32p. (gr. 4-8). pap. 14.21 *(978-1-60279-671-3(8),* 200918); lib. bdg. 28.50 *(978-1-60279-662-1(9),* 200355) Cherry Lake Publishing.

Morrison, Yvonne. Earth Matters. 2007. (Shockwave: People & Communities Ser.). (ENG., Illus.). 36p. (J). (gr. 4-6). lib. bdg. 25.00 *(978-0-531-17747-1(5),* Children's Pr.) Scholastic Library Publishing.

Nagle, Jeanne. Making Good Choices about Renewable Resources. 2009. (J). 77.70 *(978-1-4358-5603-5(1));* (ENG.). 64p. (YA). pap. 12.95 *(978-1-4358-5602-8(3));* (Illus.). 64p. (YA). (gr. 5-9). lib. bdg. 31.95 *(978-1-4358-5310-2(5))* Rosen Publishing Group, Inc., The.

Orme, Helen. Habitat Destruction. 2008. (Earth in Danger Ser.). (Illus.). 32p. (YA). (gr. 3-6). lib. bdg. 25.27 *(978-1-59716-725-3(8),* 1284353) Bearport Publishing Co., Inc.

Ravilious, Kate. Power: Ethical Debates about Resources & the Environment. 2009. (Dilemmas in Modern Science Ser.). (YA). (gr. 7-12). 34.25 *(978-1-59920-096-5(1))* Black Rabbit Bks.

—Power - Ethical Debates about Resources & the Environment. 2008. (Dilemmas in Modern Science Ser.). (ENG., Illus.). 48p. (J). 23.99 *(978-0-237-53369-4(3))* Evans Brothers, Ltd. GBR. Dist: Independent Pubs. Group.

Redlin, Janice L. Saving the Natural World. 2006. (Understanding Global Issues Ser.). (Illus.). 56p. per. 11.95 *(978-1-59036-510-6(0),* 1266440) Weigl Pubs., Inc.

Reynolds, Alison. Let's Save Water. Hopgood, Andrew, illus. 2009. (Save Our Planet! Ser.). 12p. (J). (gr. -1-3). bds. 11.40 *(978-1-60754-413-5(X))* Windmill Bks.

—Let's Turn It Off. Hopgood, Andrew, illus. 2009. (Save Our Planet! Ser.). 12p. (J). (gr. -1-3). bds. 11.40 *(978-1-60754-414-2(8))* Windmill Bks.

Rooney, Anne. Feeding the World. 2010. (World at Risk Ser.). (YA). (gr. 5-9). 34.25 *(978-1-59920-377-5(4))* Black Rabbit Bks.

Sawyer, Ava. Human Environmental Impact: How We Affect Earth. 2017. (Humans & Our Planet Ser.). (ENG.). 32p. (gr. 3-4). lib. bdg. 27.32 ***(978-1-5157-7196-8(2),*** Fact Finders) Capstone Press of Coughlan Cos.

Sollinger, Emily. This Is Our World: A Story about Taking Care of the Earth. Brown, Jo, illus. 2010. (Little Green Bks.). (ENG.). 12p. (J). (gr. -1-1). bds. 7.99 *(978-1-4169-7821-3(6),* Little Simon) Little Simon.

Solway, Andrew. Resources. 2010. (World at Risk Ser.). (YA). (gr. 5-9). 34.25 *(978-1-59920-378-2(2))* Black Rabbit Bks.

—Secrets of Pollution & Conservation. 2010. (Science Secrets Ser.). 32p. (gr. 4). 28.50 *(978-1-60870-140-7(9))* Marshall Cavendish Corp.

Ternier Gordon, Irene. Grey Owl (Junior Edition) 2007. (Amazing Stories Junior Ser.). (Illus.). 96p. pap. *(978-1-55439-723-5(5))* Altitude Publishing Canada Ltd.

Thomas, Elizabeth. Clean Water. 2011. (Go Green! Ser.). (ENG., Illus.). 32p. (J). (gr. 1-4). lib. bdg. 28.50 *(978-1-60973-171-7(9),* 201150) Child's World, Inc., The.

—Reduce, Reuse, Recycle. 2011. (Go Green! Ser.). (ENG., Illus.). 32p. (J). (gr. 1-4). lib. bdg. 28.50 *(978-1-60973-176-2(X),* 201155) Child's World, Inc., The.

Underwood, Deborah. 101 Ways to Save the Planet, 1 vol. 2011. (101 Ser.). (ENG., Illus.). 56p. (gr. 5-9). 34.65 *(978-1-4109-3898-5(0));* pap. 9.95 *(978-1-4109-4385-9(2))* Heinemann-Raintree. (NA-r).

Whiting, Karen & White, Rebecca. The Nature Girl: A Guide to Caring for God's Creation, 1 vol. 2014. (ENG.). 176p. (J). pap. 7.99 *(978-0-310-72500-8(3))* Zonderkidz.

Winters, Adam. Destruction of Earth's Resources: The Need for Sustainable Development. (Extreme Environmental Threats Ser.). 64p. 2009. (gr. 6-6). 58.50 *(978-1-61512-425-1(X))* 2006. (Illus.). (YA). (gr. 5-9). lib. bdg. 31.95 *(978-1-4042-0746-2(5))* Rosen Publishing Group, Inc., The.

CONSERVATION OF NATURAL RESOURCES—FICTION

Amara, Phil. The Treehouse Heroes: The Forgotten Beast. Chau, Alina, illus. 2012. (ENG.). 36p. (J). (gr. -1-3). 15.95 *(978-1-59702-034-3(6))* Immedium.

Barron, T. A. The Ancient One. 2003. (Illus.). 304p. 14.65 *(978-0-7569-6642-3(6))* Perfection Learning Corp.

Barron, Tom. The Ancient One. 2016. (ENG.). 320p. (J). (gr. 5). 8.99 *(978-1-101-99702-4(8),* Puffin Books) Penguin Young Readers Group.

Berthold, Joy. Peter on Patrol. 2011. 16p. 8.49 *(978-1-4567-1247-1(0))* AuthorHouse.

Breitrose, Prudence & Yue, Stephanie. Mousemobile: When Mice Hit the Road. 2014. (Mousenet Book Ser.). (ENG., Illus.). 288p. (J). (gr. 3-7). pap. 7.99 *(978-1-4231-7438-7(0))* Hyperion Bks. for Children.

Brooklyn. The Adventures of the Earth Saver Girl: Don't be a Litterbug. 2010. (Illus.). 24p. pap. 8.49 *(978-0-9822822-4-3(9))* Wright Bk. Publishing.

Cole, Henry. The Littlest Evergreen. Cole, Henry, illus. 2011. (ENG., Illus.). 32p. (J). (gr. -1-2). 16.99 *(978-0-06-114619-0(6),* Tegen, Katherine Bks) HarperCollins Pubs.

—The Littlest Evergreen. 2010. (J). lib. bdg. 18.89 *(978-0-06-114620-6(X))* HarperCollins Pubs.

Covey, Richard D. & Pappas, Diane H. I Always Turn off the Lights! 2009. (Planet Earth Patrol Ser.). (Illus.). (J). *(978-0-545-06101-8(6))* Scholastic, Inc.

—Let's All Be Water-Wise. 2009. (Planet Earth Patrol Ser.). (Illus.). (J). *(978-0-545-06100-1(8))* Scholastic, Inc.

Deedy, Carmen Agra. Un Colchón de Plumas para Ágata, 1 vol. De la Torre, Cristina, tr. from ENG. Seeley, Laura L., illus. 2007. (SPA.). 32p. (J). (gr. k-3). 15.95 *(978-1-56145-426-6(5))* Peachtree Pubs.

Eaton, Maxwell, III. The Flying Beaver Brothers & the Fishy Business. 2012. (Flying Beaver Brothers Ser.). (ENG.). 96p. (J). (gr. 1-4). pap. 7.99 *(978-0-375-86448-3(2),* Knopf Bks. for Young Readers) Random Hse. Children's Bks.

—The Flying Beaver Brothers & the Mud-Slinging Moles. 2013. (Flying Beaver Brothers Ser.). (ENG., Illus.). 96p. (J). (gr. 1-4). pap. 7.99 *(978-0-449-81019-4(4),* Knopf Bks. for Young Readers) Random Hse. Children's Bks.

—The Flying Beaver Brothers & the Mud-Slinging Moles. 2013. (Flying Beaver Brothers Ser.: 3). lib. bdg. 17.20 *(978-0-606-32233-1(7),* Turtleback) Turtleback Bks.

Engebretson, Monica fall. Lucky: Based on a true Story. 2008. (Illus.). 36p. (J). pap. 15.00 *(978-0-615-19395-3(1))* Avian Welfare Coalition, Inc.

Ghigna, Charles. We Need Water, 1 vol. Jatkowska, Ag, illus. 2012. (My Little Planet Ser.). (ENG.). 24p. (gr. -1 — 1). 6.95 *(978-1-4048-7227-1(2));* lib. bdg. 22.65 *(978-1-4048-6792-5(9))* Picture Window Bks. (My Little Planet).

Glennon, Michelle. My Big Green Teacher: Don't Rock the Boat: Saving Our Oceans. Glennon, Michelle, illus. 2008. (Illus.). 32p. (J). 19.95 *(978-0-9796625-2-2(4))* GDG Publishing.

—My Big Green Teacher: Please Turn off the Lights. Glennon, Michelle, illus. 2008. (ENG., Illus.). 32p. (J). 19.95 *(978-0-9796625-3-9(2))* GDG Publishing.

—My Big Green Teacher: Seven Generations from Now. Glennon, Michelle, illus. 2008. (Illus.). (J). 19.95 *(978-0-9797952-1-3(4))* GDG Publishing.

—My Big Green Teacher: Take a Deep Breath: Saving Our Rainforests. Glennon, Michelle, illus. 2008. (ENG., Illus.). 32p. (J). 19.95 *(978-0-9797952-0-6(6))* GDG Publishing.

—My Big Green Teacher: Taking the Green Road. Glennon, Michelle, illus. 2008. (Illus.). 32p. (J). 19.95 *(978-0-9796625-7-7(5))* GDG Publishing.

—My Big Green Teacher: Recycling: It's Easy Being Green. Glennon, Michelle, illus. 2007. (Illus.). 32p. (J). 19.95 *(978-0-9796625-6-0(7))* GDG Publishing.

Heim, Barbara. The Hudson Beavers & the New Neighbourhood. 2012. (ENG.). 42p. (J). pap. 11.95 *(978-1-938586-36-1(0))* Writer's Cramp, Inc.

Kauble, Christa. The Little Acorn. Natural Resources Conservation Service (U.S.), ed. Tannehill, Mary Jo, illus. 2008. (ENG.). 24p. (gr. -1-4). pap. 5.00 *(978-0-16-081701-4(3),* Forest Service) United States Government Printing Office.

Kylie's Concert: Evaluation Guide. 2006. (J). *(978-1-55942-413-4(3))* Witcher Productions.

Lloyd, Saci. The Carbon Diaries 2015. 2008. (ENG., Illus.). 384p. (YA). pap. *(978-0-340-97015-7(4),* Hodder Children's Books) Hachette Children's Group.

—The Carbon Diaries 2015. 2009. (ENG.). 384p. (YA). (gr. 9-18). 17.95 *(978-0-8234-2190-9(2))* Holiday Hse., Inc.

—The Carbon Diaries 2017. (ENG.). (YA). (gr. 6). 2011. 384p. pap. 8.95 *(978-0-8234-2390-3(5))* 2010. 352p. 17.95 *(978-0-8234-2260-9(7))* Holiday Hse., Inc.

Peters, Andrew. Ravenwood. 2011. (ENG.). 368p. (J). (gr. 5-9). 16.99 *(978-0-545-30550-1(0),* Chicken Hse., The) Scholastic, Inc.

Pfister, Marcus. Milo & the Magical Stones. Pfister, Marcus, illus. 2010. (Milo Ser.). (ENG., Illus.). 32p. (J). (gr. k-3). 17.95 *(978-0-7358-2253-5(0))* North-South Bks., Inc.

Pfitsch, Patricia Curtis. Riding the Flume. 2004. (Aladdin Historical Fiction Ser.). 232p. (gr. 5-9). 15.00 *(978-0-7569-2938-1(5))* Perfection Learning Corp.

Raffensperger. The Eagle Tree. 2013. 60p. (J). pap. 14.95 *(978-0-9896338-6-4(1))* Barringer Publishing.

Ramirez, Ken. You, Me, Naideen & a Bee. 2009. 278p. (YA). pap. 19.95 *(978-1-60619-208-5(6))* Twilight Times Bks.

Reader's Digest Staff. Let's Help the Earth. Brannon, Tom, illus. 2008. (Sesame Street Ser.). (ENG.). 12p. (J). (gr. -1-k). bds. 12.99 *(978-0-7944-1696-6(9))* Reader's Digest Assn., Inc., The.

Smalley, Ruth Ann. Sheila Says We're Weird, 1 vol. Emery, Jennifer, illus. 2011. (ENG.). 32p. (J). 16.95 *(978-0-88448-326-7(6))* Tilbury Hse. Pubs.

Stewart, Nancy. One Pelican at a Time: A Story of the Gulf Oil Spill. Bell, Samantha, illus. 2011. 26p. (J). 19.95 *(978-1-61633-138-2(0));* pap. 11.95 *(978-1-61633-139-9(9))* Guardian Angel Publishing, Inc.

CONSERVATION OF THE SOIL

see Soil Conservation

CONSERVATION OF WATER

see Water Conservation

CONSERVATION OF WILDLIFE

see Wildlife Conservation

CONSERVATISM

see also Right and Left (Political Science)

Steinberg, Arnold. Whiplash! From JFK to Donald Trump, a Political Odyssey. 2017. (J). ***(978-0-89803-180-5(X))*** Jameson Bks., Inc.

Storrs, Landon & Storrs, Landon R. Y. The Second Red Scare & the Unmaking of the New Deal Left. 2012. (Politics & Society in Modern America Ser.). (ENG., Illus.). 424p. (C). 47.95 *(978-0-691-15396-4(5))* Princeton Univ. Pr.

CONSPIRACIES—FICTION

Anaya, Rudolfo. ChupaCabra & the Roswell UFO. 2008. (ENG.). 144p. (YA). (gr. 9-18). 9.95 *(978-0-8263-4469-4(0))* Univ. of New Mexico Pr.

Arnold, Shari. Mystique. 2012. (YA). *(978-1-4521-0363-1(1))* Chronicle Bks. LLC.

Bailey, Kristin. Rise of the Arcane Fire. 2014. (Secret Order Ser.: 2). (ENG., Illus.). 464p. (YA). (gr. 9). 17.99 *(978-1-4424-6802-3(5),* Simon Pulse) Simon Pulse.

Bernard, Romily & Bolivar, Commander S. T., III. The Boy Who Knew Too Much. 2016. (Munchem Academy Ser.). (ENG.). 320p. (J). (gr. 3-7). 16.99 *(978-1-4847-5358-3(5))* Disney Pr.

Boie, Kirsten. The Princess Plot. 2010. (ENG.). 400p. (J). (gr. 3-7). 7.99 *(978-0-545-03221-6(0),* Chicken Hse., The) Scholastic, Inc.

—The Princess Plot. Wilson, David Henry, tr. from GER. 2009. (ENG.). 400p. (J). (gr. 3-7). 17.99 *(978-0-545-03220-9(2),* Chicken Hse., The) Scholastic, Inc.

Bowe, Kristine. Seers. 2013. (ENG.). 216p. (YA). (gr. 7). 16.95 *(978-1-934133-55-2(8));* pap. 8.95 *(978-1-934133-56-9(6))* Charlesbridge Publishing, Inc.

Bracken, Beth & Fraser, Kay. Believe, 1 vol. Sawyer, Odessa, illus. 2014. (Faerieground Ser.). (ENG.). 288p. (gr. 4-8). 12.95 *(978-1-62370-113-0(9))* Capstone Young Readers of Coughlan Cos.

Brambles, Lindsay. Becoming Darkness. 2015. (ENG.). 496p. 17.95 *(978-1-63079-017-2(6))* Switch Pr.

Bunting, Eve. Forbidden. 2015. (ENG.). 224p. (YA). (gr. 7). 17.99 *(978-0-544-39092-8(X))* Houghton Mifflin Harcourt Publishing Co.

Burns, Laura J. Bewitched in Oz, 1 vol. Peters, Liam, illus. 2014. (Bewitched in Oz Ser.). (ENG.). 256p. (gr. 4-8). 12.95 *(978-1-62370-129-1(5));* lib. bdg. 30.65 *(978-1-4342-9207-0(X))* Stone Arch Bks.

Cameron, Sharon. The Forgetting. (ENG.). 416p. (gr. 7-7). 2017. (J). pap. 9.99 ***(978-1-338-16071-0(0))*** 2016. (YA). 18.99 *(978-0-545-94521-9(6))* Scholastic, Inc. (Scholastic Pr.).

Carey, Benedict. Island of the Unknowns. 2011. (ENG., Illus.). 288p. (YA). (gr. 3-7). pap. 6.95 *(978-0-8109-9663-2(4),* Amulet Bks.) Abrams, Inc.

—The Unknowns: A Mystery. 2009. (ENG., Illus.). 272p. (YA). (gr. 3-7). 17.95 *(978-0-8109-7991-8(8),* Amulet Bks.) Abrams, Inc.

Carter, Ally. Take the Key & Lock Her Up. 2016. (Embassy Row Ser.: 3). (ENG.). 336p. (J). (gr. 7). 17.99 *(978-0-545-65495-1(5),* Scholastic Pr.) Scholastic, Inc.

Chima, Cinda Williams. The Enchanter Heir. 2013. 464p. 18.99 *(978-1-4231-8789-9(X))* Disney Pr.

—The Wizard Heir. 2008. (Heir Chronicles Ser.). (ENG.). 480p. (J). (gr. 5-9). pap. 9.99 *(978-1-4231-0488-9(9))* Hyperion Pr.

Colfer, Eoin. Half-Moon Investigations. 2006. 290p. (J). *(978-1-4156-7354-6(3))* Hyperion Bks. for Children.

Dashner, James. A Mutiny in Time. (Infinity Ring Ser.: 1). (ENG.). 192p. (J). (gr. 3-7). 2015. pap. 6.99 *(978-0-545-90016-4(6))* 2012. 12.99 *(978-0-545-38696-8(9))* 2012. 16.99 *(978-0-545-48321-6(2))* Scholastic, Inc.

Edge, Christopher. The Black Crow Conspiracy. 2015. (Penelope Tredwell Mysteries Ser.: 3). (ENG.). 272p. (J). (gr. 3-7). 16.99 *(978-0-8075-0780-3(6))* Whitman, Albert & Co.

Eldridge, Jim. The Invisible Assassin: The Malichea Quest. 2012. (Malichea Quest Ser.). (ENG.). 272p. (YA). (gr. 7). pap. 14.99 *(978-1-4088-1719-3(5),* 9781408817193, Bloomsbury USA Childrens) Bloomsbury Publishing USA.

Falksen, G. D. The Transatlantic Conspiracy. Iwata, Nat, illus. (ENG.). 240p. (YA). 2017. (gr. 9). pap. 10.99 *(978-1-61695-814-5(6))* 2016. (gr. 7). 18.99 *(978-1-61695-417-8(5))* Soho Pr., Inc. (Soho Teen).

Farrey, Brian. The Shadowhand Covenant. Helquist, Brett, illus. 2014. (Vengekeep Prophecies Ser.: 2). (ENG.). 400p. (J). (gr. 3-7). pap. 7.99 *(978-0-06-204932-2(1))* HarperCollins Pubs.

Fields, Jan. Track the Turtle Lake Monster, 1 vol. Brundage, Scott, illus. 2016. (ENG.). 80p. (J). lib. bdg. *(978-1-62402-155-8(7))* Magic Wagon.

Fry, Jason. The Jupiter Pirates: Hunt for the Hydra. 2013. (Jupiter Pirates Ser.: 1). (ENG.). 256p. (J). (gr. 3-7). 16.99 *(978-0-06-223020-1(4))* HarperCollins Pubs.

—The Jupiter Pirates: Hunt for the Hydra. 2014. (Jupiter Pirates Ser.: 1). (ENG.). 272p. (J). (gr. 3-7). pap. 6.99 *(978-0-06-223021-8(2))* HarperCollins Pubs.

Gabel, Claudia & Klam, Cheryl. Elusion. 2014. (Elusion Ser.: 1). (ENG.). 400p. (YA). (gr. 9). 17.99 *(978-0-06-212241-4(X),* Tegen, Katherine Bks) HarperCollins Pubs.

Gavin, Rohan. Knightley & Son - K-9. 2015. (Knightley & Son Ser.: 2). (ENG., Illus.). 304p. (YA). (gr. 4-6). 16.99 *(978-1-61963-494-7(5),* 9781619634947, Bloomsbury USA Childrens) Bloomsbury Publishing USA.

Gilbert, Julie. Fire & Ice: A Mermaid's Journey. Fagan, Kirbi, illus. 2017. (Dark Waters Ser.). (ENG.). 160p. (gr. 2-4). lib. bdg. 26.65 *(978-1-4965-4168-0(5))* Stone Arch Bks.

Giles, Lamar. Fake ID. 2014. (ENG.). 320p. (YA). (gr. 8). 17.99 *(978-0-06-212184-4(7),* Amistad) HarperCollins Pubs.

Girard, Geoffrey. Truthers. 2017. (ENG.). 360p. (YA). (gr. 7-12). 17.99 *(978-1-5124-2779-0(9))* Lerner Publishing Group.

Goodman, Alison. The Dark Days Club. 2016. (Lady Helen Novel Ser.: Bk. 1). (ENG.). 496p. (YA). (gr. 9). 18.99 *(978-0-670-78547-6(4),* Viking Books for Young Readers) Penguin Young Readers Group.

Hand, Cynthia, et al. My Lady Jane. 512p. (YA). (gr. 8). 2017. pap. 9.99 *(978-0-06-239176-6(3))* 2016. 17.99 *(978-0-06-239174-2(7))* HarperCollins Pubs. (HarperTeen).

Hirsch, Jeff. Magisterium. 2012. (ENG.). 320p. (J). (gr. 7). 17.99 *(978-0-545-29018-0(X),* Scholastic Pr.) Scholastic, Inc.

Jones, Frewin. The Seventh Daughter. 2009. (Faerie Path Ser.: 3). (ENG.). 352p. (YA). (gr. 8). pap. 9.99 *(978-0-06-087110-9(5),* HarperTeen) HarperCollins Pubs.

Kang, Lydia & Carey, Janet Lee. Catalyst. 2015. (Control Duology Ser.). (ENG.). 400p. (YA). (gr. 7). 17.99 *(978-0-8037-4093-8(X),* Kathy Dawson Books) Penguin Young Readers Group.

Korman, Gordon. The Dragonfly Effect. 2016. (Hypnotists Ser.: 3). lib. bdg. 17.20 *(978-0-606-38813-9(3))* Turtleback Bks.

—The Hypnotists. (ENG.). 240p. (J). (gr. 3-7). 2013. (Hypnotists Ser.: 1). 16.99 *(978-0-545-50322-8(1),* Scholastic Pr.)Bk. 1. 2014. pap. 6.99 *(978-0-545-50325-9(6),* Scholastic Paperbacks) Scholastic, Inc.

—The Hypnotists. 2014. (Hypnotists Ser.: 1). lib. bdg. 17.20 *(978-0-606-35808-8(0))* Turtleback Bks.

Kruger, Mark H. Overpowered. 2013. (ENG., Illus.). 432p. (YA). (gr. 7). 17.99 *(978-1-4424-3128-7(8),* Simon & Schuster Bks. For Young Readers) Simon & Schuster Bks. For Young Readers.

—Overtaken. 2016. (ENG.). 416p. (YA). (gr. 7). pap. 11.99 *(978-1-4424-3132-4(6))* Simon & Schuster Children's Publishing.

Landon, Kristen. The Limit. (ENG.). 304p. (J). (gr. 3-7). 2011. pap. 7.99 *(978-1-4424-0272-0(5))* 2010. (Illus.). 16.99 *(978-1-4424-0271-3(7))* Simon & Schuster Children's Publishing. (Aladdin).

Lane, Andrew. Knife Edge. 2015. (Sherlock Holmes: the Legend Begins Ser.: 6). (ENG.). 320p. (YA). (gr. 7). 18.99 *(978-0-374-38011-3(2),* 9780374380113, Farrar, Straus & Giroux (BYR)) Farrar, Straus & Giroux.

Larson, Kirby. Audacity Jones to the Rescue. 2016. (Audacity Jones Ser.: 1). (ENG.). 224p. (J). (gr. 3-7). pap. 6.99 *(978-0-545-84060-6(0));* 16.99 *(978-0-545-84056-9(2))* Scholastic, Inc. (Scholastic Pr.).

Larson, Sara B. Ignite. 2014. (Defy Trilogy: Bk. 2). (ENG.). 304p. (J). (gr. 7). 17.99 *(978-0-545-64474-7(7),* Scholastic Pr.) Scholastic, Inc.

Lasky, Kathryn. The River of Wind. 2007. (Guardians of Ga'Hoole Ser.: 13). lib. bdg. 17.20 *(978-1-4177-8261-1(7),* Turtleback) Turtleback Bks.

Lay, Kathryn. The Substitutes: An Up2U Action Adventure, 1 vol. Calo, Marcos, illus. 2015. (ENG.). 80p. (J). *(978-1-62402-095-7(X))* Magic Wagon.

Liss, David. Randoms. 2016. (Randoms Ser.: 1). (ENG., Illus.). 512p. (J). (gr. 5). pap. 8.99 *(978-1-4814-1780-8(0),* Simon & Schuster Bks. For Young Readers) Simon & Schuster Bks. For Young Readers.

—Rebels. 2016. (Randoms Ser.: 2). (ENG., Illus.). 400p. (J). (gr. 5). 18.99 *(978-1-4814-1782-2(7),* Simon & Schuster Bks. For Young Readers) Simon & Schuster Bks. For Young Readers.

Lo, Malinda. Adaptation. 2013. (ENG.). 416p. (YA). (gr. 10-17). pap. 10.00 *(978-0-316-19798-4(X))* Little, Brown Bks. for Young Readers.

—Inheritance. 2014. (ENG.). 480p. (YA). (gr. 10-17). pap. 25.99 *(978-0-316-19799-1(8))* Little, Brown Bks. for Young Readers.

MacHale, D. J. Storm. 2014. (SYLO Chronicles Ser.: 2). (ENG.). (J). (gr. 3-7). 512p. pap. 9.99 *(978-1-59514-668-7(7));* 2nd ed. 496p. 17.99 *(978-1-59514-667-0(9))* Penguin Young Readers Group. (Razorbill).

McKay, Kirsty. Unfed. 2013. (YA). *(978-0-545-53674-5(X));* (ENG.). 288p. (J). (gr. 9). 17.99 *(978-0-545-53672-1(3))* Scholastic, Inc. (Chicken Hse., The).

McNichol, John. The Tripods Attack! 2008. (Young Chesterton Chronicles Ser.). 367p. (YA). (gr. 8-12). pap. 17.95 *(978-1-933184-26-5(4))* Sophia Institute Pr.

Mitchell, Jack. The Roman Conspiracy. 2005. (ENG.). 176p. (J). (gr. 5-8). pap. 8.95 *(978-0-88776-713-5(3),* Tundra Bks.) Tundra Bks. CAN. Dist: Penguin Random Hse. LLC.

Neff, Henry H. Impyrium. (Impyrium Ser.: 1). 592p. (J). (gr. 3-7). 2017. pap. 7.99 ***(978-0-06-239206-0(9))*** 2016. (Illus.). 17.99 *(978-0-06-239205-3(0))* HarperCollins Pubs.

Nielsen, Jennifer A. Rise of the Wolf. 2016. (Mark of the Thief Ser.: 2). (ENG.). 352p. (J). (gr. 4-7). pap. 7.99 *(978-0-545-56205-8(8));* 17.99 *(978-0-545-56204-1(X))* Scholastic, Inc. (Scholastic Pr.).

—Rise of the Wolf. 2016. (Mark of the Thief Ser.: 2). lib. bdg. 18.40 ***(978-0-606-39707-0(8))*** Turtleback Bks.

—The Runaway King. (Ascendance Trilogy Ser.: 2). (ENG.). 352p. (J). (gr. 4-7). 2014. pap. 7.99 *(978-0-545-28416-5(3),* Scholastic Paperbacks) 2013. (Illus.). 17.99 *(978-0-545-28415-8(5),* Scholastic Pr.) Scholastic, Inc.

—The Runaway King. 2014. (Ascendance Trilogy Ser.: 2). lib. bdg. 18.40 *(978-0-606-35663-3(0))* Turtleback Bks.

—The Scourge. 2016. (ENG.). 368p. (J). (gr. 4-7). 16.99 *(978-0-545-68245-9(2),* Scholastic Pr.) Scholastic, Inc.

O'Neal, Eilis. The False Princess. 2012. (ENG.). 336p. (J). (gr. 7). pap. 8.99 *(978-1-60684-392-5(3),* Carolrhoda Lab™) Lerner Publishing Group.

Overpowered. 2014. (ENG., Illus.). 432p. (YA). (gr. 7). pap. 11.99 *(978-1-4424-3129-4(6),* Simon & Schuster Bks. For Young Readers) Simon & Schuster Bks. For Young Readers.

Paquette, Ammi-Joan & Mack, Jeff. Princess Juniper of the Hourglass. 2015. (Princess Juniper Ser.). (ENG., Illus.). 288p. (J). (gr. 3-7). bds. 16.99 *(978-0-399-17151-2(7),* Philomel Bks.) Penguin Young Readers Group.

Peacock, Kathleen. Willowgrove. 2015. (Hemlock Trilogy Ser.: 3). (ENG.). 384p. (YA). (gr. 9). 17.99 *(978-0-06-204871-4(6),* Tegen, Katherine Bks) HarperCollins Pubs.

Prose, Francine. After. 2003. 336p. (J). (gr. 5-18). lib. bdg. 17.89 *(978-0-06-008082-2(5),* Cotler, Joanna Books) 2004. (ENG.). 352p. (YA). (gr. 8). reprint ed. pap. 9.99 *(978-0-06-008083-9(3),* HarperTeen) HarperCollins Pubs.

Sacks, Nathan. The Big Fix. 2014. (Bareknuckle Ser.). 112p. (YA). (gr. 6-12). lib. bdg. 27.93 *(978-1-4677-1459-4(3)*, Darby Creek) Lerner Publishing Group.

Seven, John. The Outlaw of Sherwood Forest, 1 vol. Hans, Stephanie, illus. 2014. (Time-Tripping Faradays Ser.). (ENG.). 192p. (gr. 4-5). lib. bdg. 26.65 *(978-1-4342-9174-5(X))* Stone Arch Bks.

Shakespeare, William. Julius Caesar. Mahbab, Mustashrik, illus. 2008. (ENG.). 208p. (YA). (gr. 7-11). pap. 12.95 *(978-0-8109-7072-4(4)*, Amulet Bks.) Abrams, Inc.

Sleator, William. Test. 2010. (ENG.). 320p. (YA). (gr. 7-11). pap. 7.95 *(978-0-8109-8989-4(1)*, Amulet Bks.) Abrams, Inc.

Smith, Linda. The Broken Thread, 1 vol. 2008. (ENG.). 248p. (YA). (gr. 8-12). pap. 12.95 *(978-1-55050-398-2(7))* Coteau Bks. CAN. Dist: Orca Bk. Pubs. USA.

Vaughn, J. D. Second Guard. 2015. (Second Guard Novel Ser.). (ENG., Illus.). 424p. (J). (gr. 5-9). 16.99 *(978-1-4231-6909-3(3))* Disney Pr.

Wasserman, Robin. The Book of Blood & Shadow. 2012. (ENG.). 448p. (YA). (gr. 7). 17.99 *(978-0-375-86876-4(3))*; lib. bdg. 20.99 *(978-0-375-96876-1(8))* Random Hse. Children's Bks. (Knopf Bks. for Young Readers).

Weyn, Suzanne. The Bar Code Rebellion. 2012. (ENG.). 272p. (J). (gr. 7). pap. 9.99 *(978-0-545-47055-1(2)*, Scholastic Paperbacks) Scholastic, Inc.

Wick. Elfish Fantasy: The Great Chocolate Caper. 2003. 128p. (YA). pap. 11.95 *(978-0-595-29038-3(8))* iUniverse, Inc.

Williams, Sean. Twinmaker. 2013. (Twinmaker Ser.: 1). (ENG.). 496p. (YA). (gr. 8). 17.99 *(978-0-06-220321-2(5)*, HarperTeen) HarperCollins Pubs.

Zerfing, Robert A. The Silencer: A U. N. Conspiracy Novel. 2nd ed. 2003. 326p. (YA). per. 14.95 *(978-0-9747881-0-4(4))* Clawfoot Publishing.

CONSTANTINE I, EMPEROR OF ROME, -337

Baum, Margaux & Morgan, Julian. Constantine. 2016. (Leaders of the Ancient World Ser.). 00112p. (J). (gr. 6-6). 37.10 *(978-1-5081-7252-9(8))* Rosen Publishing Group, Inc., The.

Briere, Euphemia. Victor Constantinus, Maximus Augustus: The Life of Saint Constantine, the First Christian Emperor & His Mother, Saint Helena. 2003. (Illus.). (J). 4.00 *(978-0-913026-90-8(5)*, VC) St. Nectarios Pr.

Morgan, Julian. Constantine: Ruler of Christian Rome. (Ancient Leaders Ser.). 112p. (gr. 5-8). 2009. 66.50 *(978-1-61511-422-1(X))* 2003. (Illus.). (YA). lib. bdg. 34.60 *(978-0-8239-3592-5(2))* Rosen Publishing Group, Inc., The. (Rosen Reference).

Tracy, Kathleen. The Life & Times of Constantine. 2005. (Biography from Ancient Civilizations Ser.). (Illus.). 48p. (J). (gr. 4-8). lib. bdg. 29.95 *(978-1-58415-343-6(1))* Mitchell Lane Pubs., Inc.

CONSTELLATION (FRIGATE)

Myers, Walter Dean. USS Constellation: Pride of the American Navy. 2004. (ENG., Illus.). 96p. (J). (gr. 4-6). tchr. ed. 16.95 *(978-0-8234-1816-9(2))* Holiday Hse., Inc.

CONSTELLATIONS

see Astronomy; Stars

CONSTITUTION (FRIGATE)

Wachtel, Roger. Old Ironsides. 2003. (Cornerstones of Freedom Ser.). (ENG., Illus.). 48p. (YA). (gr. 4-7). 26.00 *(978-0-516-24207-1(5))* Scholastic Library Publishing.

CONSTITUTIONAL AMENDMENTS

The Bill of Rights. 2017. (Bill of Rights Ser.). 48p. (gr. 5-6). pap. 117.00 ***(978-0-7660-8803-0(0))*** Enslow Pubs., Inc.

Krull, Kathleen. A Kids' Guide to America's Bill of Rights. DiVito, Anna, illus. 2015. (ENG.). 240p. (J). (gr. 3-7). pap. 6.99 *(978-0-06-235230-9(X))* HarperCollins Pubs.

Leavitt, Amie Jane. The Bill of Rights in Translation: What It Really Means. 2016. (Kids' Translations Ser.). (ENG.). 32p. (gr. 3-4). pap. 8.10 *(978-1-5157-4218-0(0)*, Fact Finders) Capstone Press of Coughlan Cos.

Murray, Hallie. Limiting Federal Powers: The Tenth Amendment. 2017. (Bill of Rights Ser.). 48p. (gr. 5-6). 27.93 ***(978-0-7660-8567-1(8))*** Enslow Pubs., Inc.

—The Right to a Jury Trial: The Seventh Amendment. 2017. (Bill of Rights Ser.). 48p. (J). (gr. 5-6). lib. bdg. 27.93 ***(978-0-7660-8561-9(9))*** Enslow Pubs., Inc.

—The Rights of the Accused in Criminal Cases: The Sixth Amendment. 2017. (Bill of Rights Ser.). 48p. (gr. 5-6). 27.93 ***(978-0-7660-8559-6(7))*** Enslow Pubs., Inc.

Oatman, Eric. Amending the Constitution: Set Of 6. 2011. (Navigators Ser.). (J). pap. 48.00 net. *(978-1-4108-6257-0(7))* Benchmark Education Co.

CONSTITUTIONAL AMENDMENTS—UNITED STATES

Baxter, Roberta. The Bill of Rights, 1 vol. 2012. (Documenting U. S. History Ser.). (ENG.). 48p. (gr. 3-6). pap. 9.95 *(978-1-4329-6760-4(6)*, NA-h) Heinemann-Raintree.

The Bill of Rights. 2017. (Bill of Rights Ser.). 48p. (gr. 5-6). lib. bdg. 279.30 ***(978-0-7660-8587-9(2))*** Enslow Pubs., Inc.

Bozonelis, Helen Koutras. A Look at the Nineteenth Amendment: Women Win the Right to Vote. 2008. (Constitution of the United States Ser.). (Illus.). 128p. (J). (gr. 5-9). lib. bdg. 34.60 *(978-1-59845-067-5(0))* Enslow Pubs., Inc.

Brinkman, Patricia. Discover the Bill of Rights. 2006. (J). pap. *(978-1-4108-6455-0(3))* Benchmark Education Co.

Conway, John Richard. A Look at the First Amendment: Freedom of Speech & Religion. 2008. (Constitution of the United States Ser.). (Illus.). 128p. (J). (gr. 5-9). lib. bdg. 34.60 *(978-1-59845-069-9(7))* Enslow Pubs., Inc.

Cross, Nathaniel & Sommers, Michael A. Understanding Your Right to Bear Arms. 2011. (Personal Freedom & Civic Duty Ser.). (Illus.). 128p. (YA). (gr. 7-12). lib. bdg. 34.60 *(978-1-4488-4664-1(1))* Rosen Publishing Group, Inc., The.

Dils, Tracey E. 12 Questions about the Bill of Rights. 2017. (Examining Primary Sources Ser.). (ENG., Illus.). 32p. (J). (gr. 3-6). 21.95 *(978-1-63235-282-8(6))* Pr. Room Editions LLC.

Donnelly, Karen. The Bill of Rights. 2009. (Primary Source Library of American Citizenship Ser.). 32p. (gr. 5-5). 47.90 *(978-1-61511-221-0(9)*, Rosen Reference) Rosen Publishing Group, Inc., The.

Due Process DBA. 2003. spiral bd. 16.95 *(978-1-56004-148-1(X))* Social Studies Schl. Service.

Engdahl, Sylvia. Amendment XXVI — Lowering the Voting Age. 2009. (CONSTITUTIONAL AMENDMENTS Ser.). (ENG., Illus.). 144p. (YA). (gr. 9-12). 37.90 *(978-0-7377-4453-8(7))* Cengage Gale.

Fradin, Dennis Brindell. The Bill of Rights. 2008. (Turning Points in U. S. History Ser.). 48p. (gr. 3-18). lib. bdg. 31.36 *(978-0-7614-3009-4(1)*, Benchmark Bks.) Marshall Cavendish Corp.

Freedman, Russell. In Defense of Liberty: The Story of America's Bill of Rights. 2003. (ENG., Illus.). 208p. (J). (gr. 4-6). tchr. ed. 24.95 *(978-0-8234-1585-4(6))* Holiday Hse., Inc.

Furgang, Kathy. Ninth Amendment: Rights Retained by the People. 2011. (Amendments to the United States Constitution: the Bill of Rights Ser.). (ENG., Illus.). 64p. (J). pap. 12.95 *(978-1-4488-2310-9(2)*, Rosen Reference) Rosen Publishing Group, Inc., The.

—Seventh Amendment: The Right to a Jury Trial. 2011. (Amendments to the United States Constitution: the Bill of Rights Ser.). (ENG.). 64p. (YA). pap. 12.95 *(978-1-4488-2308-6(0)*, Rosen Reference) Rosen Publishing Group, Inc., The.

—The Seventh Amendment: The Right to a Jury Trial. 2011. (Amendments to the United States Constitution: the Bill of Rights Ser.). (Illus.). 64p. (YA). (gr. 5-9). lib. bdg. 31.95 *(978-1-4488-1262-2(3))* Rosen Publishing Group, Inc., The.

Galiano, Dean. Fourth Amendment: Unreasonable Search & Seizure. 2011. (Amendments to the United States Constitution: the Bill of Rights Ser.). (ENG., Illus.). 64p. (J). pap. 12.95 *(978-1-4488-2305-5(6)*, Rosen Reference) Rosen Publishing Group, Inc., The.

—The Fourth Amendment: Unreasonable Search & Seizure. 2011. (Amendments to the United States Constitution: the Bill of Rights Ser.). (Illus.). 64p. (YA). (gr. 5-9). lib. bdg. 31.95 *(978-1-4488-1259-2(3))* Rosen Publishing Group, Inc., The.

Gerber, Larry. Second Amendment: The Right to Bear Arms. 2011. (Amendments to the United States Constitution: the Bill of Rights Ser.). (ENG., Illus.). 64p. (J). pap. 12.95 *(978-1-4488-2303-1(X)*, Rosen Reference) Rosen Publishing Group, Inc., The.

—The Second Amendment: The Right to Bear Arms. 2011. (Amendments to the United States Constitution: the Bill of Rights Ser.). (Illus.). 64p. (YA). (gr. 5-9). lib. bdg. 31.95 *(978-1-4488-1253-0(4))* Rosen Publishing Group, Inc., The.

Harris, Nancy. What's the Bill of Rights? 2016. (First Guide to Government Ser.). (ENG.). 32p. (gr. 1-3). pap. 8.29 *(978-1-4846-3689-3(9)*, Heinemann First Library) Heinemann-Raintree.

Isaacs, Sally & Bedeksy, Baron. Understanding the Bill of Rights. 2008. (Documenting Early America Ser.). (ENG.). 32p. (J). (gr. 3-6). pap. *(978-0-7787-4379-8(9))* Crabtree Publishing Co.

Keller, Susanna. The Bill of Rights. 2016. (Let's Find Out! Primary Sources Ser.). 00032p. (J). (gr. 2-3). lib. bdg. 24.45 *(978-1-5081-0399-8(2))* Rosen Publishing Group, Inc., The.

Larson, Kirsten W. The Second Amendment: The Right to Bear Arms. 2017. (Cause & Effect: the Bill of Rights Ser.). (ENG.). 32p. (gr. 3-4). lib. bdg. 27.32 ***(978-1-5157-7165-4(2)***, Fact Finders) Capstone Press of Coughlan Cos.

Leavitt, Amie Jane. The Bill of Rights. 2011. (My Guide to the Constitution Ser.). (Illus.). 48p. (J). (gr. 3-6). lib. bdg. 29.95 *(978-1-58415-947-6(2))* Mitchell Lane Pubs., Inc.

—The Bill of Rights in Translation: What It Really Means. 2017. (Kids' Translations Ser.). (ENG.). 32p. (gr. 3-4). lib. bdg. 27.32 ***(978-1-5157-9138-6(6)***, Fact Finders) Capstone Press of Coughlan Cos.

Leavitt, Amie Jane. The Bill of Rights in Translation [Scholastic]: What It Really Means. 2010. (Kids' Translations Ser.). 32p. pap. 0.50 *(978-1-4296-5951-2(3)*, Fact Finders) Capstone Press of Coughlan Cos.

Lusted, Marcia Amidon. The Bill of Rights. 2016. (How America Works). (ENG.). 24p. (J). (gr. 3-6). 28.50 *(978-1-5038-0900-0(5)*, 210665) Child's World, Inc., The.

Micklos, John, Jr. The First Amendment: Freedom of Speech & Religion. 2017. (Cause & Effect: the Bill of Rights Ser.). (ENG.). 32p. (gr. 3-4). lib. bdg. 27.32 ***(978-1-5157-7164-7(4)***, Fact Finders) Capstone Press of Coughlan Cos.

Murray, Hallie. Preventing Cruel & Unusual Punishment: The Eighth Amendment. 2017. (Bill of Rights Ser.). 48p. (gr. 5-6). 27.93 ***(978-0-7660-8563-3(5))*** Enslow Pubs., Inc.

—The Right to Bear Arms: The Second Amendment. 2017. (Bill of Rights Ser.). 48p. (J). (gr. 5-6). pap. 11.70 ***(978-0-7660-8729-3(8))*** Enslow Pubs., Inc.

—Unreasonable Search & Seizure: The Fourth Amendment. 2017. (Bill of Rights Ser.). 48p. (J). (gr. 5-6). pap. 11.70 ***(978-0-7660-8733-0(6))*** Enslow Pubs., Inc.

Oatman, Eric. Amending the Constitution: Text Pairs. 2008. (Bridges/Navigators Ser.). (J). (gr. 5). 81.00 *(978-1-4108-8402-2(3))* Benchmark Education Co.

Orr, Tamra. Tenth Amendment: Limiting Federal Powers. 2011. (Amendments to the United States Constitution: the Bill of Rights Ser.). (ENG., Illus.). 64p. (YA). pap. 12.95 *(978-1-4488-2311-6(0))* Rosen Publishing Group, Inc., The.

—The Tenth Amendment: Limiting Federal Powers. 2011. (Amendments to the United States Constitution: the Bill of Rights Ser.). (Illus.). 64p. (YA). (gr. 5-9). lib. bdg. 31.95 *(978-1-4488-1265-3(8))* Rosen Publishing Group, Inc., The.

Pearl, Norman. The Bill of Rights, 1 vol. Skeens, Matthew, illus. 2007. (American Symbols Ser.). (ENG.). 24p. (gr. 1-2). 9.95 *(978-1-4048-2219-1(4))* Picture Window Bks.

Pearl, Norman & Picture Window Books Staff. The Bill of Rights, 1 vol. Skeens, Matthew, illus. 2007. (American Symbols Ser.). (ENG.). 24p. (gr. 1-2). 26.65 *(978-1-4048-2213-9(5))* Picture Window Bks.

Raum, Elizabeth. The Tenth Amendment: States' Rights. 2017. (Cause & Effect: the Bill of Rights Ser.). (ENG.). 32p. (gr. 3-4). lib. bdg. 27.32 ***(978-1-5157-7162-3(8)***, Fact Finders) Capstone Press of Coughlan Cos.

Rivera, Sheila. Bill of Rights, 1 vol. 2004. (American Moments Ser.). (ENG.). 48p. (gr. 4-8). 27.07 *(978-1-59197-279-2(5)*, Abdo & Daughters) ABDO Publishing Co.

Rokutani, John. Double Jeopardy, Self-Incrimination, & Due Process of Law: The Fifth Amendment. 2017. (Bill of Rights Ser.). 48p. (J). (gr. 5-6). lib. bdg. 27.93 ***(978-0-7660-8557-2(0))*** Enslow Pubs., Inc.

—The Right to Privacy in the Home: The Third Amendment. 2017. (Bill of Rights Ser.). 48p. (J). (gr. 5-6). lib. bdg. 27.93 ***(978-0-7660-8553-4(8))*** Enslow Pubs., Inc.

Roza, Greg. Eighth Amendment: Preventing Cruel & Unusual Punishment. 2011. (Amendments to the United States Constitution: the Bill of Rights Ser.). (ENG., Illus.). 64p. (J). pap. 12.95 *(978-1-4488-2309-3(9)*, Rosen Reference) Rosen Publishing Group, Inc., The.

—The Eighth Amendment: Preventing Cruel & Unusual Punishment. 2011. (Amendments to the United States Constitution: the Bill of Rights Ser.). (Illus.). 64p. (YA). (gr. 5-9). lib. bdg. 31.95 *(978-1-4488-1263-9(1))* Rosen Publishing Group, Inc., The.

Shea, Therese. Sixth Amendment: The Rights of the Accused in Criminal Cases. 2011. (Amendments to the United States Constitution: the Bill of Rights Ser.). (ENG.). 64p. (YA). pap. 12.95 *(978-1-4488-2307-9(2)*, Rosen Reference) Rosen Publishing Group, Inc., The.

—The Sixth Amendment: The Rights of the Accused in Criminal Cases. 2011. (Amendments to the United States Constitution: the Bill of Rights Ser.). (Illus.). 64p. (YA). (gr. 5-9). lib. bdg. 31.95 *(978-1-4488-1261-5(5))* Rosen Publishing Group, Inc., The.

Smith, Rich. The Bill of Rights, 10 vols., Set. Incl. Bill of Rights: Defining Our Freedoms. (gr. 4-8). 27.07 *(978-1-59928-913-7(X)*, Abdo & Daughters); Eighth Amendment: The Right to Mercy. (gr. 3-7). 27.07 *(978-1-59928-920-5(2)*, Abdo & Daughters); Fifth Amendment: The Right to Fairness. (gr. 4-8). 27.07 *(978-1-59928-917-5(2)*, Abdo & Daughters); First Amendment: The Right of Expression. (gr. 3-7). 27.07 *(978-1-59928-914-4(8)*, Abdo & Daughters); Fourth Amendment: The Right to Privacy. (gr. 4-8). 27.07 *(978-1-59928-916-8(4)*, Abdo & Daughters); How Amendments Are Adopted. (gr. 3-7). 27.07 *(978-1-59928-922-9(9)*, Abdo & Daughters); Ninth & Tenth Amendments: The Right to More Rights. (gr. 4-8). 27.07 *(978-1-59928-921-2(0)*, Abdo & Daughters); Second & Third Amendments: The Right to Security. (gr. 3-7). 27.07 *(978-1-59928-915-1(6)*, Abdo & Daughters); Seventh Amendment: The Right to a Trial by Jury. (J). (gr. 3-7). lib. bdg. 27.07 *(978-1-59928-919-9(9)*, Abdo & Daughter); Sixth Amendment: The Right to a Fair Trial. (gr. 4-8). 27.07 *(978-1-59928-918-2(0)*, Abdo & Daughters); (Bill of Rights Ser.). 32p. 2007. 270.70 *(978-1-59928-912-0(1)*, Abdo & Daughters) ABDO Publishing Co.

—The Bill of Rights: Defining Our Freedoms, 1 vol. 2007. (Bill of Rights Ser.). (ENG.). 32p. (gr. 4-8). 27.07 *(978-1-59928-913-7(X)*, Abdo & Daughters) ABDO Publishing Co.

—Eighth Amendment: The Right to Mercy, 1 vol. 2007. (Bill of Rights Ser.). (ENG.). 32p. (gr. 3-7). 27.07 *(978-1-59928-920-5(2)*, Abdo & Daughters) ABDO Publishing Co.

—Fifth Amendment: The Right to Fairness, 1 vol. 2007. (Bill of Rights Ser.). (ENG.). 32p. (gr. 4-8). 27.07 *(978-1-59928-917-5(2)*, Abdo & Daughters) ABDO Publishing Co.

—First Amendment: The Right of Expression, 1 vol. 2007. (Bill of Rights Ser.). (ENG.). 32p. (gr. 3-7). 27.07 *(978-1-59928-914-4(8)*, Abdo & Daughters) ABDO Publishing Co.

—Fourth Amendment: The Right to Privacy, 1 vol. 2007. (Bill of Rights Ser.). (ENG.). 32p. (gr. 4-8). 27.07 *(978-1-59928-916-8(4)*, Abdo & Daughters) ABDO Publishing Co.

—How Amendments Are Adopted, 1 vol. 2007. (Bill of Rights Ser.). (ENG.). 32p. (gr. 3-7). 27.07 *(978-1-59928-922-9(9)*, Abdo & Daughters) ABDO Publishing Co.

—Ninth & Tenth Amendments: The Right to More Rights, 1 vol. 2007. (Bill of Rights Ser.). (ENG.). 32p. (gr. 4-8). 27.07 *(978-1-59928-921-2(0)*, Abdo & Daughters) ABDO Publishing Co.

—Second & Third Amendments: The Right to Security, 1 vol. 2007. (Bill of Rights Ser.). (ENG.). 32p. (gr. 3-7). 27.07 *(978-1-59928-915-1(6)*, Abdo & Daughters) ABDO Publishing Co.

—Seventh Amendment: The Right to a Trial by Jury, 1 vol. 2007. (Bill of Rights Ser.). (ENG.). 32p. (J). (gr. 3-7). lib. bdg. 27.07 *(978-1-59928-919-9(9)*, Abdo & Daughter) ABDO Publishing Co.

—Sixth Amendment: The Right to a Fair Trial, 1 vol. 2007. (Bill of Rights Ser.). (ENG.). 32p. (gr. 4-8). 27.07 *(978-1-59928-918-2(0)*, Abdo & Daughters) ABDO Publishing Co.

Sobel, Syl & Sobel J. D., Syl. The Bill of Rights: Protecting Our Freedom Then & Now. 2008. (ENG., Illus.). 48p. (J). (gr. 3-7). pap. 6.99 *(978-0-7641-4021-1(3))* Barron's Educational Series, Inc.

Stanton, Terence M. The Bill of Rights: What It Means to You. 2009. (Real Life Readers Ser.). 32p. (gr. 4-5). pap. 10.00 *(978-1-4358-0169-1(5)*, Rosen Classroom); 32p. (gr. 4-4). 47.90 *(978-1-61511-370-5(3)*, PowerKids Pr.); (J). lib. bdg. 25.25 *(978-1-4358-2992-3(1)*, PowerKids Pr.) Rosen Publishing Group, Inc., The.

Streissguth, Tom. District of Columbia V. Heller: The Right to Bear Arms Case. 2010. (Landmark Supreme Court Cases, Gold Edition Ser.). (Illus.). 112p. (J). (gr. 7-12). 33.27 *(978-0-7660-3430-3(5))* Enslow Pubs., Inc.

Taylor-Butler, Christine. The Bill of Rights. 2007. (True Book(tm), a — American History Ser.). (ENG., Illus.). 48p. (J). (gr. 3-5). lib. bdg. 31.00 *(978-0-531-12627-1(7)*, Children's Pr.) Scholastic Library Publishing.

—The Bill of Rights: American History. 2008. (True Bks.). (ENG., Illus.). 48p. (J). (gr. 3-5). pap. 6.95 *(978-0-531-14777-1(0)*, Children's Pr.) Scholastic Library Publishing.

Wolny, Philip. Gun Rights: Interpreting the Constitution. 2014. (Understanding the United States Constitution Ser.). (Illus.). 112p. (J). (gr. 7-12). 35.60 *(978-1-4777-7516-5(1))* Rosen Publishing Group, Inc., The.

Yero, Judith Lloyd & National Geographic Learning Staff. The Bill of Rights. 2007. (Reading Expeditions Ser.). (ENG., Illus.). 32p. (J). pap. 17.95 *(978-0-7922-4552-0(0))* CENGAGE Learning.

CONSTITUTIONAL HISTORY

Bamaton, Paul. Elections: Choosing Our Leaders. 2009. (Explore Citizenship Ser.). 24p. (gr. 3-3). 42.50 *(978-1-61512-341-4(5)*, PowerKids Pr.) Rosen Publishing Group, Inc., The.

Barrington, Richard. The Magna Carta. 2016. (J). lib. bdg. *(978-1-68048-549-3(0))* Windmill Bks.

Baxter, Roberta. The Magna Carta: Cornerstone of the Constitution, 1 vol. 2012. (Documenting U. S. History Ser.). (ENG.). 48p. (gr. 3-6). pap. 9.95 *(978-1-4329-6765-9(7))*; lib. bdg. 32.65 *(978-1-4329-6756-7(8))* Heinemann-Raintree. (NA-h).

Belton, Blair. The Articles of Confederation. 2013. 32p. (J). (gr. 4-6). 26.60 *(978-1-4339-8993-3(X))*; pap. 10.50 *(978-1-4339-8994-0(8))*; pap. 63.00 *(978-1-4339-8995-7(6))* Stevens, Gareth Publishing LLLP.

Benchmark Education Company, LLC Staff, compiled by. The Constitution: Theme Set. 2006. (J). 173.00 *(978-1-4108-7126-8(6))* Benchmark Education Co.

Brinkman, Patricia. The Constitution. 2006. (J). pap. *(978-1-4108-6451-2(0))* Benchmark Education Co.

—Discover the Constitution. 2006. (J). pap. *(978-1-4108-6454-3(5))* Benchmark Education Co.

Darraj, Susan Muaddi. The Indian Independence Act Of 1947. 2011. (Milestones in Modern World History Ser.). (Illus.). 120p. (J). (gr. 9). 35.00 *(978-1-60413-496-4(8)*, Chelsea Hse.) Facts On File, Inc.

Dendy, Christina. Bringing Home the Constitution: Defining Moments in Canadian History. 2011. (Illus.). 32p. (gr. 5-8). *(978-1-77071-686-5(6))* Weigl Educational Pubs. Ltd.

Finkelman, Paul. The Constitution. 2005. (American Documents Ser.). (ENG., Illus.). 48p. (gr. k-3). 15.95 *(978-0-7922-7937-2(9))*; lib. bdg. 23.90 *(978-0-7922-7975-4(1))* National Geographic Society. (National Geographic Children's Bks.).

Giddens, Sandra. A Timeline of the Constitutional Convention. 2009. (Timelines of American History Ser.). 32p. (gr. 4-4). 47.90 *(978-1-60854-382-3(X)*, Rosen Reference) Rosen Publishing Group, Inc., The.

Judson, Karen. The United States Constitution: Its History, Bill of Rights, & Amendments. 2012. (Constitution & the United States Government Ser.). (Illus.). 104p. (J). (gr. 5-18). 33.27 *(978-0-7660-4067-0(4))* Enslow Pubs., Inc.

King, Margaret. Just Right Words: Revising the Constitution (Level 5) 2017. (Exploring Reading Ser.). (Illus.). 48p. (J). (gr. 5-5). pap. 10.99 ***(978-1-4258-4992-4(X))*** Teacher Created Materials, Inc.

Levy, Janey. The Magna Carta. 2013. 32p. (J). (gr. 4-6). 26.60 *(978-1-4339-9001-4(6))*; pap. 10.50 *(978-1-4339-9002-1(4))* Stevens, Gareth Publishing LLLP.

The Magna Carta. 2013. (Documents That Shaped America Ser.). 32p. (J). (gr. 4-6). pap. 63.00 *(978-1-4339-9003-8(2))* Stevens, Gareth Publishing LLLP.

McComb, Marianne. The Emancipation Proclamation. 2005. (American Documents Ser.). (ENG., Illus.). 48p. (gr. k-3). lib. bdg. 23.90 *(978-0-7922-7936-5(0)*, National Geographic Children's Bks.) National Geographic Society.

Metz, Lorijo. La Constitucin de los Estados Unidos y la Carta de Derechos / the United States Constitution & the Bill of Rights. Beullens-Maoui, Nathalie, ed. 2014. (¡Celebremos la Libertad! / Let's Celebrate Freedom! Ser.). (SPA & BYN.). 24p. (J). (gr. 3-6). 23.60 *(978-1-4777-3247-2(0)*, PowerKids Pr.) Rosen Publishing Group, Inc., The.

Mitchell Lane Publishers Inc. Staff, creator. My Guide to the Constitution Set. 2011. (ENG.). (J). (gr. 3-6). lib. bdg. 179.70 *(978-1-58415-948-3(0))* Mitchell Lane Pubs., Inc.

Otfinoski, Steven. The U. S. Constitution, Bill of Rights, & a New Nation. 2012. (Story of the American Revolution Ser.). (ENG.). 32p. (gr. 3-4). pap. 47.70 *(978-1-4296-9293-9(6)*, Fact Finders) Capstone Press of Coughlan Cos.

Otfinoski, Steven Anthony. The U. S. Constitution, Bill of Rights, & a New Nation, 1 vol. 2012. (Story of the American Revolution Ser.). (ENG.). 32p. (gr. 3-4). pap. 8.10 *(978-1-4296-9292-2(8)*, Fact Finders) Capstone Press of Coughlan Cos.

Rajczak Nelson, Kristen. U.S. Constitution. 2016. (Documents of American Democracy Ser.). (Illus.). 32p. (J). (gr. 5-5). pap. 10.00 *(978-1-4994-2089-0(7)*, PowerKids Pr.) Rosen Publishing Group, Inc., The.

Staunton, Ted. Confederation. Pilsworth, Graham, illus. 2004. (Dreadful Truth Ser.). (ENG.). 80p. (J). (gr. 3-8). *(978-0-88780-630-8(9))* Formac Publishing Co., Ltd.

Thompson, Gare. Shaping the Constitution: Set Of 6. 2011. (Navigators Ser.). (J). pap. 48.00 net. *(978-1-4108-6256-3(9))* Benchmark Education Co.

CONSTITUTIONAL HISTORY—UNITED STATES

Aloian, Molly. Constitution Day. 2008. (Celebrations in My World Ser.). (ENG., Illus.). 32p. (J). (gr. k-3). pap. *(978-0-7787-4304-0(7))* Crabtree Publishing Co.

Baxter, Roberta. The Bill of Rights, 1 vol. 2012. (Documenting U. S. History Ser.). (ENG.). 48p. (gr. 3-6). pap. 9.95 *(978-1-4329-6760-4(6)*, NA-h) Heinemann-Raintree.

—The Creation of the U. S. Constitution: A History Perspectives Book. 2014. (Perspectives Library). (ENG., Illus.). 32p. (J). (gr. 4-8). 28.50 *(978-1-63137-616-0(0)*, 205247) Cherry Lake Publishing.

Beckett, Leslie & Dunn, John M. The Story of the Constitution: Creating the U. S. Government. 2017. (American History Ser.). 104p. (J). (gr. 7-7). lib. bdg. 39.40 ***(978-1-5345-6044-4(0)***, Lucent Pr.) Greenhaven Publishing LLC.

Benoit, Peter. The Supreme Court. 2014. (Cornerstones of Freedom Ser.: 3). (ENG., Illus.). 64p. (J). lib. bdg. 30.00 *(978-0-531-21332-2(3))* Scholastic Library Publishing.

Buchanan, Shelly. The U. S. Constitution & You. rev. ed. 2014. (Primary Source Readers Content & Literacy Ser.). (ENG., Illus.). 32p. (gr. 3-3). pap. 8.99 *(978-1-4333-7364-0(5))* Teacher Created Materials, Inc.

Burgan, Michael. The Creation of the U. S. Constitution. Purcell, Gordon & Beatty, Terry, illus. 2006. (Graphic History Ser.). (ENG.). 32p. (gr. 3-4). pap. 8.10 *(978-0-7368-9653-5(8)*, Graphic Library) Capstone Press of Coughlan Cos.

—The U. S. Constitution. 2011. (Cornerstones of Freedom, Third Ser.). (ENG., Illus.). 64p. (J). pap. 8.95 *(978-0-531-26567-3(6)*, Children's Pr.) Scholastic Library Publishing.

—The U.S. Constitution/By Michael Burgan. 2011. (Cornerstones of Freedom, Third Ser.). (Illus.). 64p. (J). lib. bdg. 30.00 *(978-0-531-25042-6(3)*, Children's Pr.) Scholastic Library Publishing.

Burgan, Michael & Hoena, Blake A. The Creation of the U. S. Constitution, 1 vol. Purcell, Gordon & Beatty, Terry, illus. 2006. (Graphic History Ser.). (ENG.). 32p. (gr. 3-4). 30.65 (978-0-7368-6491-6(1), Graphic Library) Capstone Press of Coughlan Cos.

Cefrey, Holly. The United States Constitution & Early State Constitutions: Law & Order in the New Nation & States. 2009. (Life in the New American Nation Ser.). 32p. (gr. 4-4). 47.90 (978-1-61514-287-3(8)) Rosen Publishing Group, Inc., The.

Cheney, Lynne. We the People: The Story of Our Constitution. Harlin, Greg, illus. (ENG.). 40p. (J). (gr. k-4). 2012. 7.99 (978-1-4424-4422-5(3)) 2008. 17.99 (978-1-4169-5418-7(X)) Simon & Schuster/Paula Wiseman Bks. (Simon & Schuster/Paula Wiseman Bks.).

Clay, Kathryn. The U. S. Constitution: Introducing Primary Sources. 2016. (Introducing Primary Sources Ser.). (ENG., Illus.). 32p. (gr. 1-2). lib. bdg. 27.99 (978-1-4914-8225-4(7)) Capstone Press of Coughlan Cos.

Conklin, Wendy. Early Congresses, 1 vol. 2004. (Primary Source Readers Ser.). (ENG.). 24p. (J). (gr. 5-5). pap. 8.99 (978-0-7439-8750-9(0)) Shell Educational Publishing.

DeRubertis, Barbara. Let's Celebrate Constitution Day. 2015. (ENG., Illus.). 32p. (J). (gr. 1-4). pap. 7.95 (978-1-57565-749-3(X)) Kane Press, Inc.

Dunn, John M. The Constitution & Founding of America. 2007. (American History Ser.). (ENG., Illus.). 104p. (J). (gr. 3-7). lib. bdg. 34.80 (978-1-59018-956-6(6), Lucent Bks.) Cengage Gale.

Eck, Kristin. Drafting the Constitution: Weighing Evidence to Draw Sound Conclusions. 2006. (Critical Thinking in American History Ser.). (ENG., Illus.). 48p. (YA). (gr. 5-8). lib. bdg. 29.25 (978-1-4042-0412-6(1)) Rosen Publishing Group, Inc., The.

Elish, Dan. The U. S. Supreme Court. 2007. (Cornerstones of Freedom Ser.). (Illus.). 48p. (J). (gr. 4-6). 26.00 (978-0-516-23637-7(7), Children's Pr.) Scholastic Library Publishing.

Fradin, Dennis Brindell. The Bill of Rights. 2008. (Turning Points in U. S. History Ser.). 48p. (gr. 3-18). lib. bdg. 31.36 (978-0-7614-3009-4(1), Benchmark Bks.) Marshall Cavendish Corp.

—The U. S. Constitution. 2007. (Turning Points in U. S. History Ser.). (Illus.). 47p. (J). (gr. 4-7). lib. bdg. 31.36 (978-0-7614-2036-1(3), Benchmark Bks.) Marshall Cavendish Corp.

Fun Fact File: Founding Fathers. 2017. (Fun Fact File: Founding Fathers Ser.). 32p. (gr. 2-3). lib. bdg. 151.50 **(978-1-5382-0469-6(X))** Stevens, Gareth Publishing LLLP.

Graves, Kerry A. The Constitution: The Story Behind America's Governing Document. 2004. (America in Words & Song Ser.). (Illus.). 32p. (gr. 4-6). 23.00 (978-0-7910-7333-9(5), Chelsea Hse.) Facts On File, Inc.

Griffin, Maave. Constitution Day. 2009. (Explore Citizenship Ser.). 24p. (gr. 3-3). 42.50 (978-1-61512-340-7(7), PowerKids Pr.) Rosen Publishing Group, Inc., The.

Griffin, Maeve. Constitution Day. 2009. (Real Life Readers Ser.). 24p. (gr. 3-4). pap. 8.25 (978-1-4358-0139-4(3), Rosen Classroom); (J). 22.60 (978-1-4358-2978-7(6), PowerKids Pr.) Rosen Publishing Group, Inc., The.

Hubbard-Brown, Janet. How the Constitution Was Created. 2007. (U. S. Government Ser.). (Illus.). 104p. (YA). (gr. 5-9). lib. bdg. 30.00 (978-0-7910-9420-4(0)) Facts On File, Inc.

Hughes, Chris. The Constitutional Convention. 2005. (People at the Center of Ser.). (Illus.). 48p. (J). (gr. -1-7). lib. bdg. 24.95 (978-1-56711-918-3(2), Blackbirch Pr., Inc.) Cengage Gale.

Isaacs, Sally. Understanding the Articles of Confederation. 2008. (Documenting Early America Ser.). (ENG., Illus.). 32p. (J). (gr. 3-6). lib. bdg. (978-0-7787-4372-9(1)) Crabtree Publishing Co.

Isaacs, Sally & Bedeksy, Baron. Understanding the US Constitution. 2008. (Documenting Early America Ser.). (ENG.). 32p. (J). (gr. 3-6). pap. (978-0-7787-4378-1(0)) Crabtree Publishing Co.

Keegan, Anna. The United States Constitution & the Bill of Rights: The Law of the Land. 2015. (Spotlight on American History Ser.). (ENG., Illus.). 24p. (J). (gr. 4-6). pap. 10.00 (978-1-4994-1773-9(X), PowerKids Pr.) Rosen Publishing Group, Inc., The.

Krensky, Stephen. The Constitution. 2011. (Documents of Democracy Ser.). 96p. (gr. 8). 34.21 (978-0-7614-4917-1(5)) Marshall Cavendish Corp.

LearningExpress Staff. U. S. Constitution in 15 Minutes a Day. 2011. (15 Minutes a Day Ser.). (ENG.). 256p. pap. 14.95 (978-1-57685-767-0(0)) LearningExpress, LLC.

Maestro, Betsy & Maestro, Giulio. A More Perfect Union: The Story of Our Constitution. 2008. (Illus.). 48p. (J). (gr. -1-3). 18.40 (978-0-8335-6055-1(7), Turtleback) Turtleback Bks.

Manger, Katherine. The U.S. Constitution. 2016. (J). (978-1-5081-0455-1(7)) Rosen Publishing Group, Inc., The.

Marcovitz, Hal. The U. S. Constitution: Government by the People. Moreno, Barry, ed. 2014. (Patriotic Symbols of America Ser.: 20). (Illus.). 48p. (J). (gr. 4-18). lib. bdg. 20.95 (978-1-4222-3133-3(X)) Mason Crest.

Metz, Lorijo. The United States Constitution & the Bill of Rights, 1 vol., 1. 2014. (Let's Celebrate Freedom! Ser.). (ENG.). 24p. (J). (gr. 3-6). 23.60 (978-1-4777-2895-6(3), PowerKids Pr.) Rosen Publishing Group, Inc., The.

Micklos, John. The Making of the United States from Thirteen Colonies — Through Primary Sources. 2013. (American Revolution Through Primary Sources Ser.). 48p. (J). (gr. 4-18). 25.27 (978-0-7660-4133-2(6)) Enslow Pubs., Inc.

—The Making of the United States from Thirteen Colonies—Through Primary Sources. 2013. (American Revolution Through Primary Sources Ser.). 48p. (J). (gr. 4-10). pap. 8.95 (978-1-4644-0191-6(8)) Enslow Pubs., Inc.

Micklos, John & Micklos, John, Jr. From Thirteen Colonies to One Nation. 2008. (Revolutionary War Library). (Illus.). 48p. (J). (gr. 3-7). lib. bdg. 25.27 (978-0-7660-3015-2(6), Enslow Elementary) Enslow Pubs., Inc.

Mountjoy, Shane & McNeese, Tim. Marbury V. Madison. 2006. (Great Supreme Court Decisions Ser.). (Illus.). 144p. (YA). (gr. 5-9). 32.95 (978-0-7910-9240-8(2)) Facts On File, Inc.

New, David W. The Constitution for Beginners. 2003. 50p. (J). 4.95 (978-0-9721333-1-9(3)) Pocket Pubn., A.

Niver, Heather Moore. Articles of Confederation. 2016. (Documents of American Democracy Ser.). (Illus.). 32p. (J). (gr. 5-5). pap. 10.00 (978-1-4994-2069-2(2), PowerKids Pr.) Rosen Publishing Group, Inc., The.

Otfinoski, Steven. The U. S. Constitution, Bill of Rights, & a New Nation, 1 vol. 2012. (Story of the American Revolution Ser.). (ENG., Illus.). 32p. (gr. 3-4). lib. bdg. 27.32 (978-1-4296-8589-4(1)) Capstone Press of Coughlan Cos.

Pearl, Norman. The U. S. Constitution, 1 vol. Skeens, Matthew, illus. 2006. (American Symbols Ser.). (ENG.). 24p. (gr. 1-2). 9.95 (978-1-4048-2646-5(7)); lib. bdg. 26.65 (978-1-4048-2643-4(2)) Picture Window Bks.

Randolph, Joanne. What Is the US Constitution? 2003. (Rosen Real Readers Big Bookstm Ser.). (ENG.). 24p. (gr. 3-4). 43.95 (978-0-8239-8728-3(0)) Rosen Publishing Group, Inc., The.

Ransom, Candice. George Washington & the Story of the U. S. Constitution. Reeves, Jeni, illus. 2011. (History Speaks: Picture Books Plus Reader's Theater Ser.). 48p. pap. 56.72 (978-0-7613-7632-3(1)); (ENG.). (gr. 2-4). 27.93 (978-0-7613-5877-0(3), Millbrook Pr.); (ENG.). (gr. 2-4). pap. 9.95 (978-0-7613-7116-8(8)) Lerner Publishing Group.

—Who Wrote the U. S. Constitution? And Other Questions about the Constitutional Convention of 1787. 2010. (Six Questions of American History Ser.). (ENG.). (gr. 4-6). pap. 56.72 (978-0-7613-6949-3(X)); 48p. pap. 9.95 (978-0-7613-6126-8(X)); 48p. lib. bdg. 30.60 (978-1-58013-669-3(9)) Lerner Publishing Group.

Richmond, Benjamin. What Are the Three Branches of the Government? And Other Questions about the U. S. Constitution. 2015. (Good Question! Ser.). (ENG., Illus.). 32p. (J). (gr. 2). pap. 5.95 (978-1-4549-1244-6(8)) Sterling Publishing Co., Inc.

Roza, Greg. Evaluating the Articles of Confederation: Determining the Validity of Information & Arguments. 2009. (Critical Thinking in American History Ser.). 48p. (gr. 5-8). 53.00 (978-1-61512-092-5(0), Rosen Reference) Rosen Publishing Group, Inc., The.

Shea, Therese. The United States Constitution. 2013. (Documents That Shaped America Ser.). 32p. (J). (gr. 4-6). pap. 10.50 (978-1-4339-9010-6(5)); (ENG., Illus.). lib. bdg. 26.60 (978-1-4339-9009-0(1)) Stevens, Gareth Publishing LLLP.

—20 Fun Facts about the US Constitution. 2013. 32p. (J). (gr. 3-6). 25.25 (978-1-4339-9198-1(5)); pap. 63.00 (978-1-4339-9200-1(0)); pap. 10.50 (978-1-4339-9199-8(3)) Stevens, Gareth Publishing LLLP.

Smith, Robert W. The Constitution. 2004. (ENG.). 64p. pap. 9.99 (978-0-7439-3211-0(0)) Teacher Created Resources, Inc.

Sonneborn, Liz. The Articles of Confederation, 1 vol. 2012. (Documenting U. S. History Ser.). (ENG.). 48p. (gr. 3-6). pap. 9.95 (978-1-4329-6758-1(4)); lib. bdg. 32.65 (978-1-4329-6749-9(5)) Heinemann-Raintree. (NA-h).

—The United States Constitution, 1 vol. 2012. (Documenting U. S. History Ser.). (ENG.). 48p. (gr. 3-6). pap. 9.95 (978-1-4329-6761-1(4), NA-h) Heinemann-Raintree.

Steinagle, Jason. Understanding the Texas Constitution. 2014. (Spotlight on Texas Ser.). (ENG.). 32p. (J). (gr. 3-4). 26.25 (978-1-4777-4541-0(6), Rosen Classroom) Rosen Publishing Group, Inc., The.

Steinkraus, Kyla. Constitution. 2014. (ENG.). 24p. (gr. 3-5). 28.50 (978-1-62717-681-1(0)) Rourke Educational Media.

Taylor-Butler, Christine. The Constitution. 2007. (True Book(tm), a — American History Ser.). (ENG., Illus.). 48p. (J). (gr. 3-5). lib. bdg. 31.00 (978-0-531-12629-5(3), Children's Pr.) Scholastic Library Publishing.

—The Constitution of the United States. 2008. (True Bks.). (ENG., Illus.). 48p. (J). (gr. 3-5). pap. 6.95 (978-0-531-14779-5(7), Children's Pr.) Scholastic Library Publishing.

The United States Constitution. 2013. (Documents That Shaped America Ser.). 32p. (J). (gr. 4-6). pap. 63.00 (978-1-4339-9011-3(3)) Stevens, Gareth Publishing LLLP.

Waxman, Laura Hamilton. What Are the Articles of Confederation? And Other Questions about the Birth of the United States. 2012. (Six Questions of American History Ser.). (ENG.). 48p. (gr. 4-6). pap. 56.72 (978-0-7613-9238-5(6)); pap. 9.95 (978-0-7613-8564-6(9)); lib. bdg. 30.60 (978-0-7613-5330-0(5)) Lerner Publishing Group.

Weston Woods Staff, creator. Shh! We're Writing the Constitution. 2011. 38.75 (978-0-439-72886-7(X)) 2004. 29.95 (978-1-55592-682-3(7)) 2004. 18.95 (978-1-55592-681-6(9)) Weston Woods Studios, Inc.

Wolfe, James & Callahan, Kerry P. Understanding the Articles of Confederation. 2015. (Primary Sources of American Political Documents Ser.). (ENG.). 128p. (J). (gr. 7-7). 37.27 (978-0-7660-6866-7(8)) Enslow Pubs., Inc.

CONSTITUTIONAL LAW

see also Citizenship; Civil Rights; Constitutional Amendments; Democracy; Political Science; Suffrage

Brinkman, Patricia. Writing the Constitution. 2006. (J). pap. (978-1-4108-6450-5(2)) Benchmark Education Co.

Cefrey, Holly. The United States Constitution & Early State Constitutions: Law & Order in the New Nation & States. 2009. (Life in the New American Nation Ser.). 32p. (gr. 4-4). 47.90 (978-1-61514-287-3(8)) Rosen Publishing Group, Inc., The.

Hirsch, E. D., Jr., ed. Making the Constitution. 2003. tchr. ed. 9.95 (978-0-7690-5048-5(4)); stu. ed. 49.95 (978-0-7690-2953-5(1)) Pearson Learning.

Lansford, Tom. Voting Rights. 2008. (Opposing Viewpoints Ser.). (ENG., Illus.). 225p. (YA). (gr. 10-12). 29.45 (978-0-7377-4015-8(9), LML02109-239974, Greenhaven Pr., Inc.) Cengage Gale.

Lansford, Tom, ed. Voting Rights. 2008. (Opposing Viewpoints Ser.). (ENG., Illus.). 186p. (gr. 10-12). 46.45 (978-0-7377-4014-1(0), LML02109-239981, Greenhaven Pr., Inc.) Cengage Gale.

Latchana Kenney, Karen. What Is a Parliamentary Government?, Vol. 1. 2014. (Understanding Political Systems Ser.). (ENG.). 48p. (J). (gr. 6-8). pap. 14.05 (978-1-4824-0318-3(8)) Stevens, Gareth Publishing LLLP.

Levinson, Cynthia & Levinson, Sanford. Fault Lines in the Constitution: The Framers, Their Fights, & the Flaws That Affect Us Today. 2017. (ENG.). 192p. (J). (gr. 5-9). 19.95 **(978-1-56145-945-2(3))** Peachtree Pubs.

Malaspina, Ann. Heart on Fire: Susan B. Anthony Votes for President. James, Steven, illus. 2012. (ENG.). 32p. (J). (gr. 1-3). 16.99 (978-0-8075-3188-4(X)) Whitman, Albert & Co.

Murcia, Rebecca Thatcher. The Legislative Branch. 2011. (My Guide to the Constitution Ser.). 48p. (J). (gr. 3-6). pap. 16.50 (978-1-61228-184-1(2)) Mitchell Lane Pubs., Inc.

Pratt, Mary K. Parliaments, 1 vol. 2011. (Exploring World Governments Ser.). (ENG., Illus.). 160p. (J). (gr. 9-12). lib. bdg. 37.07 (978-1-61714-793-7(1), Essential Library) ABDO Publishing Co.

Rajczak Nelson, Kristen. U.S. Constitution. 2016. (Documents of American Democracy Ser.). (Illus.). 32p. (J). (gr. 5-5). pap. 10.00 (978-1-4994-2089-0(7), PowerKids Pr.) Rosen Publishing Group, Inc., The.

Slade, Suzanne. A Bill's Journey into Law, 1 vol. Trimmer, Tony, illus. 2011. (Follow It! Ser.). (ENG.). 24p. (gr. 1-3). pap. 7.49 (978-1-4048-7027-7(X)) Picture Window Bks.

Woog, Adam. Military Might & Global Intervention. 2011. (Controversy! 3 Ser.). (Illus.). 112p. (J). (gr. 7). 37.07 (978-1-60870-492-7(0)) Marshall Cavendish Corp.

CONSTITUTIONAL LAW—UNITED STATES

Bow, James. What Is the Legislative Branch? 2013. (ENG.). 32p. (J). (978-0-7787-0879-7(9)); pap. (978-0-7787-0905-3(1)) Crabtree Publishing Co.

Brannen, Daniel E., et al. Supreme Court Drama: Cases That Changed America. 2nd ed. 2011. (978-1-4144-8659-8(6)); (978-1-4144-8660-4(X)); (978-1-4144-8668-0(5)); (978-1-4144-8657-4(X)); (978-1-4144-8658-1(8));Set. (ENG.). 1119p. 458.00 (978-1-4144-8656-7(1)) Cengage Gale. (UXL).

Catrow, David. We the Kids: The Preamble to the Constitution of the United States. Catrow, David, illus. 2005. (ENG., Illus.). 32p. (J). (gr. k-3). pap. 7.99 (978-0-14-240276-4(1), Puffin Books) Penguin Young Readers Group.

Conklin, Wendy. Early Congresses, 1 vol. 2004. (Primary Source Readers Ser.). (ENG.). 24p. (J). (gr. 5-5). pap. 8.99 (978-0-7439-8750-9(0)) Shell Educational Publishing.

CQ Press Staff, ed. Understanding Constitutional Issues: Selections from the Cq Researcher, 00 vols. rev. ed. 2004. (ENG., Illus.). 432p. pap. 60.00 (978-1-56802-885-9(7)) CQ Pr.

Furgang, Kathy. Ninth Amendment: Rights Retained by the People. 2011. (Amendments to the United States Constitution: the Bill of Rights Ser.). (ENG., Illus.). 64p. (J). pap. 12.95 (978-1-4488-2310-9(2), Rosen Reference) Rosen Publishing Group, Inc., The.

—The Ninth Amendment: Rights Retained by the People. 2011. (Amendments to the United States Constitution: the Bill of Rights Ser.). (Illus.). 64p. (YA). (gr. 5-9). lib. bdg. 31.95 (978-1-4488-1264-6(X)) Rosen Publishing Group, Inc., The.

Furi-Perry, Ursula. Constitutional Law for Kids: Discovering the Rights & Privileges Granted by the U. S. Constitution. 2014. (ENG., Illus.). 148p. (J). (gr. 4-7). pap. 14.95 (978-1-62722-023-1(2)) American Bar Assn.

Graves, Kerry A. The Constitution: The Story Behind America's Governing Document. 2004. (America in Words & Song Ser.). (Illus.). 32p. (gr. 4-6). 23.00 (978-0-7910-7333-9(5), Chelsea Hse.) Facts On File, Inc.

Hand, Carol. Abortion: Interpreting the Constitution. 2014. (Understanding the United States Constitution Ser.). 112p. (YA). (gr. 7-12). 35.60 (978-1-4777-7510-3(2)) Rosen Publishing Group, Inc., The.

Harper, Leslie. What Are Checks & Balances? 2012. (Civics Q & A Ser.). (ENG., Illus.). 24p. (J). (gr. 3-6). 22.60 (978-1-4488-7433-0(5)); pap. 8.25 (978-1-4488-7506-1(4)) Rosen Publishing Group, Inc., The. (PowerKids Pr.).

Hirsch, E. D., Jr., ed. The United States Constitution, Level 4. 2003. tchr. ed. 9.95 (978-0-7690-5069-0(7)); stu. ed. 49.95 (978-0-7690-2846-0(2)) Pearson Learning.

Isaacs, Sally & Bedeksy, Baron. Understanding the Articles of Confederation. 2008. (Documenting Early America Ser.). (ENG., Illus.). 32p. (J). (gr. 3-6). pap. (978-0-7787-4377-4(2)) Crabtree Publishing Co.

Kukathas, Uma. The Minimum Wage. 2009. (EXAMINING ISS COURT DECSNS Ser.). (ENG., Illus.). 240p. (J). 42.15 (978-0-7377-4491-0(X), Greenhaven Pr., Inc.) Cengage Gale.

Linde, Barbara M. Thomas Jefferson Didn't Sign the Constitution: Exposing Myths about the Constitutional Convention. 2016. (Exposed! Myths about Early American History Ser.). 00032p. (J). pap. 10.50 **(978-1-4824-5735-3(0))** Stevens, Gareth Publishing LLLP.

Maddex, Robert L. State Constitutions of the United States, 00 vols. 2nd rev. ed. 2005. (ENG.). 592p. (gr. 9-18). 185.00 (978-1-933116-25-9(0)) CQ Pr.

Metz, Lorijo. La Constitucin de los Estados Unidos y la Carta de Derechos / the United States Constitution & the Bill of Rights. Beullens-Maoui, Nathalie, ed. 2014. (¡Celebremos la Libertad! / Let's Celebrate Freedom! Ser.). (SPA & BYN.). 24p. (J). (gr. 3-6). 23.60 (978-1-4777-3247-2(0), PowerKids Pr.) Rosen Publishing Group, Inc., The.

—The United States Constitution & the Bill of Rights, 1 vol., 1. 2014. (Let's Celebrate Freedom! Ser.). (ENG.). 24p. (J). (gr. 3-6). 23.60 (978-1-4777-2895-6(3), PowerKids Pr.) Rosen Publishing Group, Inc., The.

New, David W. The Constitution for Beginners. 2003. 50p. (J). 4.95 (978-0-9721333-1-9(3)) Pocket Pubn., A.

Panchyk, Richard. Our Supreme Court: A History with 14 Activities. 2006. (For Kids Ser.). (ENG., Illus.). 208p. (J). (gr. 5-7). pap. 18.95 (978-1-55652-607-7(5)) Chicago Review Pr., Inc.

Pearl, Norman. The U. S. Constitution, 1 vol. Skeens, Matthew, illus. 2006. (American Symbols Ser.). (ENG.). 24p. (gr. 1-2). 9.95 (978-1-4048-2646-5(7)); lib. bdg. 26.65 (978-1-4048-2643-4(2)) Picture Window Bks.

Randolph, Joanne. What Is the US Constitution? 2003. (Rosen Real Readers Big Bookstm Ser.). (ENG.). 24p. (gr. 3-4). 43.95 (978-0-8239-8728-3(0)) Rosen Publishing Group, Inc., The.

Randolph, Ryan. Marbury V. Madison: The New Supreme Court Gets More Powers. 2009. (Life in the New American Nation Ser.). 32p. (gr. 4-4). 47.90 (978-1-61514-277-4(0)) Rosen Publishing Group, Inc., The.

Shea, Therese. The United States Constitution. 2013. (Documents That Shaped America Ser.). 32p. (J). (gr. 4-6). pap. 10.50 (978-1-4339-9010-6(5)); (ENG., Illus.). lib. bdg. 26.60 (978-1-4339-9009-0(1)) Stevens, Gareth Publishing LLLP.

—20 Fun Facts about the US Constitution. 2013. 32p. (J). (gr. 3-6). 25.25 (978-1-4339-9198-1(5)); pap. 10.50 (978-1-4339-9199-8(3)); pap. 63.00 (978-1-4339-9200-1(0)) Stevens, Gareth Publishing LLLP.

Slade, Suzanne. A Bill's Journey into Law, 1 vol. Trimmer, Tony, illus. 2011. (Follow It! Ser.). (ENG.). 24p. (gr. 1-3). lib. bdg. 26.65 (978-1-4048-6831-1(3)) Picture Window Bks.

Steinkraus, Kyla. Constitution. 2014. (ENG.). 24p. (gr. 3-5). 28.50 (978-1-62717-681-1(0)) Rourke Educational Media.

Tallarico, Tony J., Jr. U. S. A. Constitution Activity Book. 2016. (Dover Children's Activity Bks.). (ENG.). 48p. (J). (gr. 3-6). pap. 4.99 (978-0-486-80934-2(X)) Dover Pubns., Inc.

Thomas, William David. What Is a Constitution? 2008. (My American Government Ser.). 32p. (gr. 3-7). pap. 10.50 (978-0-8368-8868-3(5)); (Illus.). lib. bdg. 26.00 (978-0-8368-8863-8(4)) Stevens, Gareth Publishing LLLP. (Gareth Stevens Learning Library).

Turner, Juliette. Our Constitution Rocks! 2012. 224p. pap. 15.99 (978-0-310-73520-5(3)) Zondervan Bks.

The United States Constitution. 2013. (Documents That Shaped America Ser.). 32p. (J). (gr. 4-6). pap. 63.00 (978-1-4339-9011-3(3)) Stevens, Gareth Publishing LLLP.

Way, Jennifer. What Is the Constitution? 2015. (Let's Find Out! Government Ser.). (ENG., Illus.). 32p. (J). (gr. 2-3). 23.45 (978-1-62275-971-2(0), Britannica Educational Publishing) Rosen Publishing Group, Inc., The.

CONSTRUCTION

see Architecture; Building; Engineering

CONSTRUCTION EQUIPMENT

ABDO Publishing Company Staff & Lennie, Charles. Construction Machines. 2014. (Construction Machines Ser.: 6). (ENG.). 24p. (J). (gr. 4-8). lib. bdg. 171.00 (978-1-62970-014-4(2)) ABDO Publishing Co.

Addison, D. R. Cement Mixers at Work. 2009. (Big Trucks Ser.). (J). lib. bdg. 22.60 (978-1-4358-2701-1(5), PowerKids Pr.) Rosen Publishing Group, Inc., The.

—Diggers at Work. 2009. (Big Trucks Ser.). 24p. (Illus.). (J). (gr. k-2). pap. 8.25 (978-1-4358-3086-8(5)); (gr. 1-1). 42.50 (978-1-61511-584-6(6)) Rosen Publishing Group, Inc., The. (PowerKids Pr.).

—Tractors at Work. 2009. (Big Trucks Ser.). (Illus.). 24p. (J). (gr. k-2). pap. 8.25 (978-1-4358-3090-5(3), PowerKids Pr.) Rosen Publishing Group, Inc., The.

Allen, Kenny. Earthmovers. 2012. (Monster Machines Ser.). (Illus.). 24p. (J). (gr. 1-3). pap. 8.15 (978-1-4339-7168-6(2)); lib. bdg. 22.60 (978-1-4339-7167-9(4)) Stevens, Gareth Publishing LLLP.

Askew, Amanda. Loaders. 2010. (Mighty Machines Ser.). (ENG., Illus.). 24p. (J). (gr. -1-2). pap. 5.95 (978-1-55407-706-9(0), 9781554077069) Firefly Bks., Ltd.

—Mighty Machines: Diggers. 2010. (Mighty Machines Ser.). (ENG., Illus.). 24p. (J). (gr. -1-2). pap. 5.95 (978-1-55407-705-2(2), 9781554077052) Firefly Bks., Ltd.

Bridges, Sarah. Yo Manejo Una Niveladora. Alderman, Derrick & Shea, Denise, illus. 2010. (Vehículos de Trabajo/Working Wheels Ser.).Tr. of I Drive a Bulldozer. (MUL & SPA.). 24p. (gr. -1-2). lib. bdg. 26.65 (978-1-4048-6300-2(1)) Picture Window Bks.

Butterfield, Moira. Bulldozers & Other Construction Machines. Lyon, Chris & Biggin, Gary, illus. 32p. (J). mass mkt. 8.99 (978-0-590-24556-2(2)) Scholastic, Inc.

Cerato, Mattia. You Can Draw Construction Vehicles, 1 vol. Cerato, Mattia, illus. 2011. (You Can Draw Ser.). (ENG., Illus.). 24p. (gr. 1-2). lib. bdg. 26.65 (978-1-4048-6807-6(0)) Picture Window Bks.

Clay, Kathryn. Construction Vehicles. 2015. (Wild about Wheels Ser.). (ENG.). 24p. (gr. k-1). lib. bdg. 26.65 (978-1-4914-2117-8(7), Pebble Plus) Capstone Press of Coughlan Cos.

—Construction Vehicles at Work. 2016. (Construction Vehicles at Work Ser.). (ENG.). 24p. (gr. k-1). 87.96 (978-1-5157-2548-0(0), Pebble Bks.) Capstone Press of Coughlan Cos.

Dayton, Connor. Asphalt Pavers. 2012. (J). 49.50 (978-1-4488-5075-4(4)); pap. 8.25 (978-1-4488-5074-7(6)); lib. bdg. 22.60 (978-1-4488-4962-8(4)) Rosen Publishing Group, Inc., The. (PowerKids Pr.).

Doman, Mary Kate. Earthmovers & Diggers. 2011. (All about Big Machines Ser.). (Illus.). 24p. (J). (gr. -1-18). pap. 7.95 (978-1-59845-245-7(2), Enslow Elementary); (gr. k-3). lib. bdg. 22.60 (978-0-7660-3931-5(5)) Enslow Pubs., Inc.

Dorling Kindersley Publishing Staff. Feel & Find Fun: Building Site: Building Site. 2015. (ENG., Illus.). 14p. (J). (gr. -1 — 1). bds. 9.99 (978-1-4654-3627-6(8), DK Children) Dorling Kindersley Publishing, Inc.

Goldish, Meish. Huge Earthmovers. 2009. (World's Biggest Ser.). (Illus.). 24p. (J). (gr. 1-6). lib. bdg. 22.61 (978-1-59716-955-4(2)) Bearport Publishing Co., Inc.

Greathouse, Lisa. Big Digs: Construction Site, 1 vol. 2nd rev. ed. 2014. (TIME for KIDS(r) Nonfiction Readers Ser.). (ENG., Illus.). 32p. (J). (gr. 3-3). pap. 25.96 (978-1-4807-1077-1(6)) Shell Educational Publishing.

Greathouse, Lisa E. Excavar: Una Obra de Construcción. 2017. (TIME for Kids en Español - Level 3 Ser.). (SPA.). 32p. (gr. 3-3). lib. bdg. 31.99 **(978-1-5157-5175-5(9))** Time for Kids Inc AUS. Dist: Capstone Pub.

Hill, Lee Sullilvan. Earthmovers on the Move. 2010. (Lightning Bolt Books Vroom-Vroom Ser.). (ENG.). 32p. (gr. k-2). pap. 7.95 (978-0-7613-6116-9(2)) Lerner Publishing Group.

Hill, Lee Sullivan. Earthmovers on the Move. 2010. pap. 45.32 (978-0-7613-6936-3(8)); (ENG., Illus.). 32p. lib. bdg. 26.60 (978-0-7613-3918-2(3)) Lerner Publishing Group.

Jennings, Terry J. Construction Vehicles. 2009. (How Machines Work Ser.). (J). 28.50 (978-1-59920-293-8(X)) Black Rabbit Bks.

Kalman, Bobbie & MacAulay, Kelley. Fantásticos Vehiculos para la Construccion. 2007. (Vehículos en Acción Ser.). (SPA & ENG., Illus.). 32p. (J). lib. bdg. (978-0-7787-8304-6(9)) Crabtree Publishing Co.

Kawa, Katie. Diggers. 2011. (Big Machines Ser.). (Illus.). 24p. (gr. k-2). (J). pap. 8.15 (978-1-4339-5560-0(1)); (J). lib. bdg. 22.60 (978-1-4339-5558-7(X)); 69.20 (978-1-4339-6888-4(6)) Stevens, Gareth Publishing LLLP.

Kilby, Don. At a Construction Site. Kilby, Don, illus. 2006. (Wheels at Work Ser.). (ENG., Illus.). 24p. (J). (gr. -1-2). 6.95 *(978-1-55337-987-4(X))* Kids Can Pr., Ltd. CAN. Dist: Hachette Bk. Group.

Langley, Andrew. Diggers. 2010. (Machines on the Move Ser.). 32p. (J). 28.50 *(978-1-60753-058-9(9))* Amicus Publishing.

Lovitt, Chip. My Big Dump Truck. LaPadula, Thomas, illus. 2011. (Diecut Vehicles Ser.). (ENG.). 12p. (J). (gr. -1-1). bds. 5.99 *(978-0-7944-2272-1(1),* Reader's Digest Children's Bks.) Studio Fun International.

MacAulay, Kelley & Kalman, Bobbie. Cool Construction Vehicles. 2007. (Vehicles on the Move Ser.). (ENG., Illus.). 32p. (J). (gr. 3-7). lib. bdg. *(978-0-7787-3042-2(5))*; (gr. 1-5). pap. *(978-0-7787-3056-9(5))* Crabtree Publishing Co.

—Fantasticos Vehiculos para la Construccion. 2007. (Vehículos en Acción Ser.). (SPA & ENG., Illus.). 32p. (J). (gr. 6-10). pap. *(978-0-7787-8314-5(6))* Crabtree Publishing Co.

Marshall, Jane. Trucks & Diggers. 2013. (Wild Rides Ser.). 32p. (J). (gr. k-2). *(978-1-84898-623-7(8),* TickTock Books) Octopus Publishing Group.

Masters, Nancy Robinson. Heavy Equipment Operator. 2010. (21st Century Skills Library: Cool Careers Ser.). (ENG.). 32p. (gr. 4-8). lib. bdg. 28.50 *(978-1-60279-941-7(5),* 200627) Cherry Lake Publishing.

Osier, Dan. Cement Mixers, 1 vol., 1. 2014. (Construction Site Ser.). (ENG.). 24p. (J). (gr. k-2). 23.60 *(978-1-4777-2861-1(9),* PowerKids Pr.) Rosen Publishing Group, Inc., The.

—Dump Trucks, 1 vol., 1. 2014. (Construction Site Ser.). (ENG.). 24p. (J). (gr. k-2). 23.60 *(978-1-4777-2862-8(7),* PowerKids Pr.) Rosen Publishing Group, Inc., The.

—Forklifts, 1 vol., 1. 2014. (Construction Site Ser.). (ENG.). 24p. (J). (gr. k-2). pap. 8.25 *(978-1-4777-2956-4(9),* PowerKids Pr.) Rosen Publishing Group, Inc., The.

Pallotta, Jerry. The Construction Alphabet Book. Bolster, Rob, illus. 2006. (Jerry Pallotta's Alphabet Bks.). (ENG.). 32p. (J). (gr. -1-3). lib. bdg. 17.95 *(978-1-57091-437-9(0))*; per. 7.95 *(978-1-57091-438-6(9))* Charlesbridge Publishing, Inc.

Pallotta, Jerry & Bolster, Rob. The Construction Alphabet. 2017. (ENG., Illus.). 28p. (J). (— 1). bds. 7.99 *(978-1-57091-799-8(X))* Charlesbridge Publishing, Inc.

Perritano, John. Construction Machines. 2013. (Machines in Motion Ser.). 48p. (J). (gr. 3-5). pap. 14.05 *(978-1-4339-9601-6(4))*; pap. 84.30 *(978-1-4339-9602-3(2))*; (ENG., Illus.). lib. bdg. 31.95 *(978-1-4339-9600-9(6))* Stevens, Gareth Publishing LLLP.

Priddy, Roger. Playtown Chunky Pack: Construction. 2017. (Playtown Ser.). (ENG., Illus.). 10p. (J). bds. 7.99 *(978-0-312-52196-7(0),* 9780312521967, Priddy Bks.) St. Martin's Pr.

Randolph, Joanne. Concrete Mixers. 2009. (Road Machines Ser.). 24p. (gr. k-1). 37.50 *(978-1-60852-461-7(2),* PowerKids Pr.) Rosen Publishing Group, Inc., The.

—Road Milling Machines. 2009. (Road Machines Ser.). 24p. (gr. k-1). 37.50 *(978-1-60852-462-4(0),* PowerKids Pr.) Rosen Publishing Group, Inc., The.

—Road Pavers. 2009. (Road Machines Ser.). 24p. (gr. k-1). 37.50 *(978-1-60852-463-1(9),* PowerKids Pr.) Rosen Publishing Group, Inc., The.

—Road Rollers. 2009. (Road Machines Ser.). 24p. (gr. k-1). 37.50 *(978-1-60852-464-8(7),* PowerKids Pr.) Rosen Publishing Group, Inc., The.

—Road Scrapers. 2009. (Road Machines Ser.). 24p. (gr. k-1). 37.50 *(978-1-60852-465-5(5),* PowerKids Pr.) Rosen Publishing Group, Inc., The.

Reinke, Beth. Concrete Mixers Stir! 2017. (Bumba Books (tm) — Construction Zone Ser.). (ENG.). (J). (gr. -1-1). pap. 6.99 ***(978-1-5124-5541-0(5))***; (Illus.). lib. bdg. 25.32 ***(978-1-5124-3357-9(8))*** Lerner Publishing Group.

Riggs, Kate. Dig It! Kubinyi, Laszlo, illus. 2013. (ENG.). 14p. (J). (gr. -1-k). bds. 7.99 *(978-1-56846-237-0(9),* Creative Editions) Creative Co., The.

Schuh, Mari. Las Mezcladoras de Concreto (Concrete Mixers) 2017. (Spot Mighty Machines Ser.). (ENG & SPA.). 16p. (J). (gr. k-3). 17.95 ***(978-1-68151-265-5(3),*** Amicus Readers) Amicus Publishing.

Smith, Derek. Bob the Builder Manual. 2011. (ENG., Illus.). 40p. (J). (gr. -1-1). 12.95 *(978-0-85733-115-1(9),* 0857331159) Haynes Publishing PLC GBR. Dist: Hachette Bk. Group.

Smith, Sian. Machines on a Construction Site, 1 vol. 2013. (Machines at Work Ser.). (ENG.). 24p. (gr. 1-2). pap. 6.95 *(978-1-4329-7505-0(6),* Heinemann Read & Learn) Heinemann-Raintree.

Suen, Anastasia & O'Rourke, Ryan. Up! up! up! Skyscraper. 2017. (ENG., Illus.). 32p. (J). (gr. -1-2). lib. bdg. 16.99 *(978-1-58089-710-5(X))* Charlesbridge Publishing, Inc.

Sutton, Sally. Construction. Lovelock, Brian, illus. 2015. (ENG.). 32p. (J). (-k). bds. 6.99 *(978-0-7636-7975-0(5))* Candlewick Pr.

Toth, Henrietta. A Career As a Heavy Equipment Operator, 01 vols., 1. 2016. (Essential Careers Ser.). (ENG.). 80p. (J). 34.25 *(978-1-4994-6215-9(8),* Rosen Young Adult) Rosen Publishing Group, Inc., The.

Tuxworth, Nicola. Diggers & Dumpers. 2015. (ENG., Illus.). 20p. (J). (gr. -1 — 1). bds. 6.99 *(978-1-86147-383-7(4),* Armadillo) Anness Publishing GBR. Dist: National Bk. Network.

Veitch, Catherine. Big Machines Build!, 1 vol. 2014. (Big Machines Ser.). (ENG.). 24p. (gr. k-1). 23.32 *(978-1-4846-0584-4(5),* Heinemann Read & Learn) Heinemann-Raintree.

Weber, Rebecca. Making a House. 2011. (Early Connections Ser.). (J). *(978-1-61672-326-2(2))* Benchmark Education Co.

Wiseman, Blaine. Excavators. 2010. (J). pap. 9.95 *(978-1-61690-134-9(9))* Weigl Pubs., Inc.

—Extreme Excavators. 2010. (World of Wonder Ser.). 24p. (J). (gr. 2-4). lib. bdg. 25.70 *(978-1-61690-133-2(0))* Weigl Pubs., Inc.

Zemlicka, Shannon. From Rock to Road. 2004. (Start to Finish Ser.). (J). pap. 4.95 *(978-0-8225-2146-4(6))*; 18.60 *(978-0-8225-1391-9(9),* Lerner Pubns.) Lerner Publishing Group.

CONSTRUCTION EQUIPMENT—FICTION

AZ Books Staff. Sam the Constructor. Boroda, Janna, ed. 2012. (Little Master Ser.). (ENG.). 10p. (J). (gr. -1-k). bds. 10.95 *(978-1-61889-149-5(9))* AZ Bks. LLC.

Bentley, Peter. Push-Pull-Turn! Construction Site. Bucco, Joe, illus. 2017. (ENG.). 20p. (J). (gr. -1). 15.99 *(978-1-62686-837-3(9),* Silver Dolphin Bks.) Readerlink Distribution Services, LLC.

Braun, Sebastien. Digger & Tom! Braun, Sebastien, illus. 2013. (Illus.). 32p. (J). (gr. -1-3). 16.99 *(978-0-06-207752-3(X))* HarperCollins Pubs.

Clement, Nathan. Job Site. Clement, Nathan, illus. 2011. (ENG., Illus.). 32p. (J). (gr. -1-1). 16.95 *(978-1-59078-769-4(2))* Boyds Mills Pr.

Clement, Nathan, illus. Job Site. 2015. (ENG.). 32p. (J). (— 1). bds. 7.99 *(978-1-62979-407-5(4))* Boyds Mills Pr.

Copeland, Cynthia L. What Are You Waiting For? Gordon, Mike, illus. 2003. (Silly Millies Ser.: 1). 32p. lib. bdg. 17.90 *(978-0-7613-2804-9(1),* Millbrook Pr.) Lerner Publishing Group.

Copeland, Cynthia L. & Gordon, Mike. What Are You Waiting For? 2003. (Silly Millies Ser.: Vol.1). (Illus.). 32p. (J). (gr. -1-1). pap. 4.99 *(978-0-7613-1828-6(3))* Lerner Publishing Group.

Dale, Penny. Dinosaur Dig! Dale, Penny, illus. 2012. (ENG., Illus.). 14p. (J). (gr. k-k). bds. 6.99 *(978-0-7636-6270-7(4),* Nosy Crow) Candlewick Pr.

Dean, James. Construction Destruction. Dean, James, illus. 2015. (Pete the Cat Ser.). (ENG., Illus.). 24p. (J). (gr. -1-3). pap. 4.99 *(978-0-06-219861-7(0),* HarperFestival) HarperCollins Pubs.

Dewdney, Anna. Little Excavator. 2017. (ENG., Illus.). 44p. (J). (-k). 17.99 *(978-1-101-99920-2(9),* Viking Books for Young Readers) Penguin Young Readers Group.

Fleming, Candace. Bulldozer Helps Out. Rohmann, Eric, illus. 2017. (Bulldozer Bks.). (ENG.). 40p. (J). (gr. -1-2). 17.99 *(978-1-4814-5894-8(9))* Simon & Schuster Children's Publishing.

—Bulldozer's Big Day. Rohmann, Eric, illus. 2015. (Bulldozer Bks.). (ENG.). 40p. (J). (gr. -1-2). 17.99 *(978-1-4814-0097-8(5),* Atheneum Bks. for Young Readers) Simon & Schuster Children's Publishing.

Fritz, Betty. Bang Bang Bang, Hammers in the Morning. 2009. (J). 16.95 *(978-1-61623-624-3(8))* Independent Pub.

Greene, Rhonda Gowler. Push! Dig! Scoop! A Construction Counting Rhyme. Kirk, Daniel, illus. (ENG.). (J). 2017. 26p. bds. 7.99 *(978-1-68119-085-3(0),* 9781681190853) 2016. 32p. 16.99 *(978-0-8027-3506-5(1),* 9780802735065) Bloomsbury Publishing USA. (Bloomsbury USA Childrens).

Hannigan, Paula & Accord Publishing Staff. Under Construction. Brown, Heather, illus. 2012. (ENG.). 12p. (J). bds. 14.99 *(978-1-4494-0498-7(7))* Andrews McMeel Publishing.

Harper, Charise Mericle. Go! Go! Go! Stop! 2015. (ENG.). 32p. (J). (-k). bds. 7.99 *(978-0-553-53391-0(6),* Knopf Bks. for Young Readers) Random Hse. Children's Bks.

Holub, Joan. Dig, Scoop, Ka-Boom! Gordon, David, illus. 2013. (Step into Reading Ser.). (ENG.). 24p. (J). (gr. -1-1). pap. 3.99 *(978-0-375-86910-5(7),* Random Hse. Bks. for Young Readers) Random Hse. Children's Bks.

—Mighty Dads. Dean, James, illus. 2014. (ENG.). 40p. (J). (gr. -1-k). 16.99 *(978-0-545-60968-5(2),* Scholastic Pr.) Scholastic, Inc.

Horvath, James. Build, Dogs, Build: A Tall Tail. Horvath, James, illus. 2013. (ENG., Illus.). 40p. (J). (gr. -1-3). 15.99 *(978-0-06-218967-7(0))* HarperCollins Pubs.

Katz, Karen. Vroom, Vroom, Trucks! Katz, Karen, illus. 2016. (ENG., Illus.). 14p. (J). (gr. -1 — 1). bds. 6.99 *(978-1-4814-4209-1(0),* Little Simon) Little Simon.

King, Trey. Training Academy: Contruction. 2016. (Transformers Passport to Reading Ser.). (J). lib. bdg. 13.55 *(978-0-606-38322-6(0))* Turtleback Bks.

Leman, Nora. The Alpha Building Crew. Hartmann, April, illus. 2005. (J). *(978-1-58987-110-6(3))* Kindermusik International.

Light, Steve. Diggers Go. 2013. (ENG., Illus.). 16p. (J). (gr. -1 — 1). bds. 9.99 *(978-1-4521-1864-2(7))* Chronicle Bks. LLC.

Litton, Jonathan. Noisy Noisy Digger. Galloway, Fhiona, illus. 2017. (My Little World Ser.). (ENG.). 10p. (J). (gr. -1-2). bds. 12.99 ***(978-1-58925-242-4(X))*** Tiger Tales.

Lund, Deb. Monsters on Machines. Neubecker, Robert, illus. 2017. (ENG.). 40p. (J). (gr. -1-3). pap. 6.99 *(978-0-544-92783-4(4),* HMH Books For Young Readers) Houghton Mifflin Harcourt Publishing Co.

—Monsters on Machines. Neubecker, Robert, illus. 2017. (ENG.). (J). (gr. -1-3). lib. bdg. 17.20 ***(978-0-606-39815-2(5))*** Turtleback Bks.

Mattel. Bob the Builder: Alien Mix-Up. 2016. (Passport to Reading Level 1 Ser.). (ENG., Illus.). 32p. (J). (gr. -1-3). pap. 3.99 *(978-0-316-35683-1(2))* Little, Brown Bks. for Young Readers.

—Bob the Builder: All about Scoop! 2016. (ENG.). 10p. (J). (gr. -1-1). bds. 6.99 *(978-0-316-39445-1(9))* Little, Brown Bks. for Young Readers.

—Bob the Builder: Bob's Big Builds! 2016. (ENG., Illus.). 12p. (J). (gr. -1-1). bds. 9.99 *(978-0-316-39444-4(0))* Little, Brown Bks. for Young Readers.

—Bob the Builder: Can We Build It? Yes, We Can! 2016. (ENG., Illus.). 24p. (J). (gr. -1-3). pap. 5.99 *(978-0-316-35681-7(6))* Little, Brown Bks. for Young Readers.

—Bob the Builder: Welcome to Spring City! 2016. (ENG., Illus.). 16p. (J). (gr. -1-1). bds. 8.99 *(978-0-316-39449-9(1))* Little, Brown Bks. for Young Readers.

Meltzer, Lynn. The Construction Crew. Eko-Burgess, Carrie, illus. (ENG.). (J). 2017. 32p. bds. 7.99 *(978-1-250-11267-5(2),* 9781250112675) 2011. 40p. (gr. -1-k). 15.99 *(978-0-8050-8884-7(9),* 9780805088847) Holt, Henry & Co. (Holt, Henry & Co. Bks. For Young Readers).

Mighty Mike, 6 vols., Set. Incl. Mighty Mike Builds a Ball Field. Lynch, Casey. Lynch, Kelly, illus. 28.50 *(978-1-61641-128-2(7))*; Mighty Mike Builds a Library. Lynch, Casey. Lynch, Kelly, illus. 28.50 *(978-1-61641-129-9(5))*; Mighty Mike Builds a Nature Trail. Lynch, Kelly. Lynch, Casey, illus. 28.50 *(978-1-61641-130-5(9))*; Mighty Mike Does What's Right! Lynch, Kelly. Lynch, Casey, illus. 28.50 *(978-1-61641-131-2(7))*; Mighty Mike Repairs a Playground. Lynch, Casey. Lynch, Kelly, illus. 28.50 *(978-1-61641-132-9(5))*; Mighty Mike Saves a School Bus. Lynch, Casey. Lynch, Kelly, illus. 28.50 *(978-1-61641-133-6(3))*; (gr. -1-2). (Mighty Mike Ser.). 32p. 2011. 171.00 *(978-1-61641-127-5(9),* Looking Glass Library) ABDO Publishing Co.

My Day at a Construction Site. 2004. (J). ring bd. 4.50 *(978-0-9762740-8-7(6))* Smart Smiles Co., The.

Nakagawa, Chihiro. Who Made This Cake? Koyose, Junji, illus. 2008. (ENG.). 32p. (J). (gr. -1-2). 16.95 *(978-1-59078-595-9(9),* Front Street) Boyds Mills Pr.

Nevius, Carol. Building with Dad, 0 vols. Thomson, Bill, illus. 2012. (ENG.). 32p. (J). (gr. k-3). pap. 9.99 *(978-0-7614-5984-2(7),* 9780761459842, Amazon Children's Publishing) Amazon Publishing.

Nosy Crow Staff. Bizzy Bear: Let's Get to Work! Davies, Benji, illus. 2012. (Bizzy Bear Ser.). (ENG.). 8p. (J). (gr. k — 1). bds. 6.99 *(978-0-7636-5899-1(5),* Nosy Crow) Candlewick Pr.

Parragon Publishing Staff. Busy Day at the Construction Site. (Busy Books Large Ser.). *(978-1-4054-7874-8(8))* Parragon, Inc.

Prince, April Jones. Dig In! Berg, Michelle, illus. 2013. (ENG.). 14p. (J). (gr. -1 — 1). bds. 7.95 *(978-1-4197-0522-9(9))* Abrams, Inc.

—Dive In! Berg, Michelle, illus. 2013. (ENG.). 14p. (J). (gr. -1 — 1). bds. 7.95 *(978-1-4197-0523-6(7))* Abrams, Inc.

Publications International Ltd. Staff, ed. Construction: (Play-a-Sound Book) 2010. 12p. (J). bds. 12.98 *(978-1-4508-0111-9(0))* Phoenix International Publications, Inc.

Rinker, Sherri Duskey. Goodnight, Goodnight, Construction Site. Lichtenheld, Tom, illus. (ENG.). (J). 2017. 30p. bds. 7.99 *(978-1-4521-1173-5(1))* 2016. 32p. (gr. -1 — 1). 18.99 *(978-1-4521-5215-8(2))* 2016. 20p. (gr. -1-7). 12.99 *(978-1-4521-5463-3(5))* 2015. 66p. (gr. -1 — 1). 15.99 *(978-1-4521-4698-0(5))* 2011. 32p. (gr. -1-1). 16.99 *(978-0-8118-7782-4(5))* Chronicle Bks. LLC.

—Goodnight, Goodnight, Construction Site: Let's Go! Lichtenheld, Tom, illus. 2017. (ENG.). 10p. (J). (gr. -1 — 1). bds. 8.99 ***(978-1-4521-6476-2(2))*** Chronicle Bks. LLC.

—Goodnight, Goodnight Construction Site Sound Book. Lichtenheld, Tom, illus. 2014. (ENG.). 12p. (J). (gr. -1 — 1). 12.99 *(978-1-4521-2824-5(3))* Chronicle Bks. LLC.

—Mighty, Mighty Construction Site. Lichtenheld, Tom, illus. 2017. (ENG.). 40p. (J). 16.99 *(978-1-4521-5216-5(0))* Chronicle Bks. LLC.

Rinker, Sherri Duskey & Lichtenheld, Tom. Goodnight, Goodnight, Construction Site. 2012. 12.95 *(978-0-545-50222-1(5))* Scholastic, Inc.

Robinson, Michelle. Goodnight Digger: The Perfect Bedtime Book! 2015. (Goodnight Ser.). (ENG., Illus.). 32p. (J). (gr. -1 — 1). pap. 7.99 *(978-1-4380-0661-1(6))* Barron's Educational Series, Inc.

Scieszka, Jon. Zoom! Boom! Bully. Shannon, David et al, illus. 2008. (Jon Scieszka's Trucktown Ser.). (ENG.). 24p. (J). (gr. -1-1). pap. 3.99 *(978-1-4169-4139-2(8),* Simon Spotlight) Simon Spotlight.

Sobel, June. B Is for Bulldozer: A Construction ABC. Iwai, Melissa, illus. 2006. 28p. (gr. -1-k). 17.00 *(978-0-7569-7037-6(7))* Perfection Learning Corp.

—B Is for Bulldozer: A Construction ABC. Iwai, Melissa, illus. 2006. (ENG.). 32p. (J). (gr. -1-3). pap. 7.99 *(978-0-15-205774-9(9))* Houghton Mifflin Harcourt Publishing Co.

Sobel, June & Iwai, Melissa. B Is for Bulldozer: A Construction ABC. Iwai, Melissa, illus. 2013. (ENG., Illus.). 32p. (J). (— 1). bds. 7.99 *(978-0-544-10808-0(6))* Houghton Mifflin Harcourt Publishing Co.

Springstubb, Tricia. Phoebe & Digger. Newman, Jeff, illus. 2013. (ENG.). 32p. (J). (gr. -1-2). 16.99 *(978-0-7636-5281-4(4))* Candlewick Pr.

Steers, Billy. Tractor Mac Teamwork. 2016. (Tractor Mac Ser.). (ENG., Illus.). 32p. (J). 8.99 *(978-0-374-30113-2(1),* 9780374301132, Farrar, Straus & Giroux (BYR)) Farrar, Straus & Giroux.

Sterling Children's, Sterling. Builders. Finn, Rebecca, illus. 2015. (Busy Bks.). (ENG.). 10p. (J). (— 1). bds. 8.95 *(978-1-4549-1733-5(4))* Sterling Publishing Co., Inc.

Sutton, Sally. Construir una Carretera (Roadwork) Lovelock, Brian, illus. 2013. (SPA.). 28p. (J). (-k). bds. 6.99 *(978-0-7636-6494-7(4))* Candlewick Pr.

—Demolicion. Lovelock, Brian, illus. 2014. (SPA.). 22p. (J). (-k). bds. 6.99 *(978-0-7636-7031-3(6))* Candlewick Pr.

—Demolition. Lovelock, Brian, illus. (ENG.). (J). 2014. 22p. (-k). bds. 6.99 *(978-0-7636-6493-0(6))* 2012. 32p. (gr. -1-2). 16.99 *(978-0-7636-5830-4(8))* Candlewick Pr.

Taplin, Sam. Noisy Building Site Board Book. 2008. (Busy Sounds Board Bks). 10p. (J). bds. 18.99 *(978-0-7945-2076-2(6),* Usborne) EDC Publishing.

Whiting, Sue. Machine Mates. Townsend, Peter, illus. 2003. 12p. (J). (gr. k-3). 22.00 *(978-0-7567-6650-4(8))* DIANE Publishing Co.

Wojtowycz, David. Scoop, the Digger! 2003. (Illus.). (J). *(978-0-439-74269-6(2))* Scholastic, Inc.

CONSTRUCTION OF ROADS

see Roads

CONSULS

see Diplomats

CONSUMER EDUCATION

Here are entered works on the selection and most efficient use of consumer goods and services, including methods of educating the consumer. Works on the economic theory of consumption are entered under Consumption (Economics).

see also Shopping

Berry, Joy. Help Me Be Good about Being Destructive. 2009. (Help Me Be Good Ser.). 32p. pap. 7.95 *(978-1-60577-127-4(9))* Berry, Joy Enterprises.

—Help Me Be Good about Being Wasteful. 2009. (Help Me Be Good Ser.). 32p. pap. 7.95 *(978-1-60577-105-2(8))* Berry, Joy Enterprises.

Berry, Joy Wilt. A Book about Being Wasteful. 2005. (Illus.). (J). *(978-0-7172-8587-7(1))* Scholastic, Inc.

—A Children's Book about Being Destructive. 2005. (Illus.). (J). *(978-0-7172-8596-9(0))* Scholastic, Inc.

Bullard, Lisa. Gabriel Gets a Great Deal. Moran, Mike, illus. 2013. (Cloverleaf Books — Money Basics Ser.). (ENG.). 24p. (gr. k-2). pap. 6.95 *(978-1-4677-1512-6(3))*; lib. bdg. 23.93 *(978-1-4677-0766-4(X))* Lerner Publishing Group. (Millbrook Pr.).

Gagne, Tammy. Teen Guide to Buying Goods & Services. 2014. (Illus.). 48p. (gr. 4-8). lib. bdg. 29.95 *(978-1-61228-472-9(8))* Mitchell Lane Pubs., Inc.

Garey, Marita & National Geographic Learning Staff. Kids Are Consumers. 2007. (Reading Expeditions Ser.). (ENG., Illus.). 32p. (J). pap. 17.95 *(978-0-7922-8700-1(2))* CENGAGE Learning.

Kowalski, Kathiann M. Be Smart about Shopping: The Critical Consumer & Civic Financial Responsibility. 2014. (Be Smart about Money & Financial Literacy Ser.). 48p. (J). lib. bdg. 22.60 *(978-0-7660-4283-4(9))* Enslow Pubs., Inc.

Lusted, Marcia Amidon. Advertising to Children, 1 vol. 2008. (Essential Viewpoints Set 3 Ser.). (ENG.). 112p. (J). (gr. 6-12). lib. bdg. 35.64 *(978-1-60453-107-7(X))* ABDO Publishing Co.

Mason, Paul. How Big Is Your Shopping Footprint? 2009. (Environmental Footprints Ser.). 32p. (gr. 4). 28.50 *(978-0-7614-4414-5(9))* Marshall Cavendish Corp.

Minden, Cecilia. Smart Shopping. 2015. (21st Century Skills Library: Real World Math Ser.). (ENG., Illus.). 32p. (J). (gr. 4-7). 29.93 *(978-1-63362-575-4(3),* 206484) Cherry Lake Publishing.

Moran, Katherine J. Diabetes: The Ultimate Teen Guide. 2004. (It Happened to Me Ser.: 7). (ENG., Illus.). 208p. (gr. 9). 55.00 *(978-0-8108-4806-1(6))* Scarecrow Pr., Inc.

Nagle, Jeanne. Smart Shopping: Shopping Green. 2009. (Your Carbon Footprint Ser.). 48p. (gr. 5-5). 53.00 *(978-1-60854-914-6(3),* Rosen Reference) Rosen Publishing Group, Inc., The.

Reynolds, Mattie. Super-Smart Shopping: An Introduction to Financial Literacy. 2013. (Start Smart: Money Ser.). (Illus.). 24p. (gr. k-2). (J). lib. bdg. 17.95 net. *(978-1-937529-43-7(6))*; (ENG., pap. 5.95 *(978-1-937529-39-0(8))* Red Chair Pr.

Scheff, Anna. Shopping Smarts: How to Choose Wisely, Find Bargains, Spot Swindles, & More. 2012. (USA TODAY Teen Wise Guides: Time, Money, & Relationships Ser.). (ENG.). 64p. (gr. 8-12). lib. bdg. 31.93 *(978-0-7613-7017-8(X))* Lerner Publishing Group.

Schwartz, Heather E. Spend Wisely. 2015. (Money Smarts Ser.). (ENG.). 32p. (gr. 2-4). 19.95 *(978-1-60753-795-3(8),* Amicus High Interest) Amicus Publishing.

Stefoff, Rebecca. Smart Spending. 2015. (J). lib. bdg. *(978-1-62713-387-6(9))*; (ENG., Illus.). 48p. (gr. 4-4). 31.36 *(978-1-5026-0281-7(4))* Cavendish Square Publishing.

Tardiff, Joseph. Consumer Debt. 2010. (Current Controversies Ser.). (Illus.). 240p. (J). pap. 28.45 *(978-0-7377-4702-7(1),* Greenhaven Pr., Inc.) Cengage Gale.

Wittekind, Erika. The Big Push: How Popular Culture Is Always Selling, 1 vol. 2012. (Exploring Media Literacy Ser.). (ENG.). 80p. (gr. 6-7). pap. 9.10 *(978-0-7565-4535-2(8))*; lib. bdg. 34.65 *(978-0-7565-4518-5(8))* Compass Point Bks. (CPB Grades 4-8).

World Book, Inc Staff, contrib. by. Consumable Goods. 2008. (J). *(978-0-7166-1407-4(3))* World Bk., Inc.

—Durable Goods. 2008. 64p. (J). *(978-0-7166-1408-1(1))* World Bk., Inc.

CONSUMER GOODS

see Manufactures

CONSUMER PROTECTION

Furgang, Kathy. Internet Surveillance & How to Protect Your Privacy. 2016. (Digital & Information Literacy Ser.). 00048p. (J). (gr. 6-6). pap. 11.75 *(978-1-4994-6519-8(X))* Rosen Publishing Group, Inc., The.

Mooney, Carla. Online Privacy & Business. 2014. (Privacy in the Online World). (ENG., Illus.). 80p. (J). lib. bdg. *(978-1-60152-724-0(1))* ReferencePoint Pr., Inc.

Nelson, Maria. Gross Things about Your Food. 2012. (That's Gross! Ser.). (Illus.). 24p. (J). (gr. 2-5). 22.60 *(978-1-4339-7115-0(1))*; pap. 8.15 *(978-1-4339-7116-7(X))* Stevens, Gareth Publishing LLLP. (Gareth Stevens Learning Library).

Scheff, Anna. Shopping Smarts: How to Choose Wisely, Find Bargains, Spot Swindles, & More. 2012. (USA TODAY Teen Wise Guides: Time, Money, & Relationships Ser.). (ENG.). 64p. (gr. 8-12). lib. bdg. 31.93 *(978-0-7613-7017-8(X))* Lerner Publishing Group.

Ullmann, Carol. Copyright Infringmnt. Greenhaven Press Editors, ed. 2014. (Opposing Viewpoints Ser.). (ENG.). 224p. (gr. 10-12). lib. bdg. 48.80 *(978-0-7377-6650-9(6),* Greenhaven Pr., Inc.) Cengage Gale.

—Copyright Infringmnt. Greenhaven Press Editors & Gale Editors, eds. 2014. (Opposing Viewpoints Ser.). (ENG., Illus.). 224p. (gr. 7-12). pap. 33.80 *(978-0-7377-6651-6(4),* Greenhaven Pr., Inc.) Cengage Gale.

CONSUMERS' GUIDES

see Consumer Education

CONSUMPTION (ECONOMICS)

Andrews, Carolyn. What Are Goods & Services? 2008. (Economics in Action Ser.). (ENG., Illus.). 32p. (J). (gr. 3-7). pap. *(978-0-7787-4260-9(1))* Crabtree Publishing Co.

Bullard, Lisa. Lily Learns about Wants & Needs. Schneider, Christine M., illus. 2013. (Cloverleaf Books — Money Basics Ser.). (ENG.). 24p. (gr. k-2). pap. 6.95 *(978-1-4677-1509-6(3))*; lib. bdg. 23.93 *(978-1-4677-0764-0(3))* Lerner Publishing Group. (Millbrook Pr.).

Donovan, Sandra. Budgeting Smarts: How to Set Goals, Save Money, Spend Wisely, & More. 2012. (USA TODAY Teen Wise Guides: Time, Money, & Relationships Ser.). (ENG.). 64p. (gr. 8-12). lib. bdg. 31.93 *(978-0-7613-7016-1(1))* Lerner Publishing Group.

Dutton, Michael. Amazing Carbon Footprint Facts. 2010. (Dover Nature Coloring Book Ser.). (ENG., Illus.). 32p. (J). (gr. 2-5). pap. 3.99 *(978-0-486-47552-3(2))* Dover Pubns., Inc.

Eagen, Rachel. What Do I Want? What Do I Need? 2016. (Money Sense: an Introduction to Financial Literacy Ser.). (ENG., Illus.). 24p. (J). (gr. 1-4). *(978-0-7787-2664-7(9))* Crabtree Publishing Co.

Espejo, Roman. Consumerism. 2009. (Opposing Viewpoints Ser.). (ENG., Illus.). 224p. (gr. 10-12). 48.80 *(978-0-7377-4506-1(1))*; pap. 33.80 *(978-0-7377-4507-8(X))* Cengage Gale.

Hollander, Barbara. Top 10 Secrets for Spending Your Money Wisely. 2013. (Student's Guide to Financial Empowerment

C D

Ser.). (Illus.). 64p. (YA). (gr. 7-12). pap. 12.95 (978-1-4488-9380-5(1)); pap. 77.70 (978-1-4488-9381-2(X)) Rosen Publishing Group, Inc., The.

Hollander, Barbara & Gottfried Hollander, Barbara. Top 10 Secrets for Spending Your Money Wisely. 2013. (Illus.). 64p. (YA). (gr. 7-12). 31.95 (978-1-4488-9361-4(5)) Rosen Publishing Group, Inc., The.

Hudak, Heather C. Spending. 2017. (J). **(978-1-5105-1949-7(1))** SmartBook Media, Inc.

—Spending. 2009. (Everyday Economics Ser.). (Illus.). 32p. (J). (gr. 4-6). pap. 9.95 (978-1-60596-654-0(1)); lib. bdg. 26.00 (978-1-60596-653-3(3)) Weigl Pubs., Inc.

Kirk, Ellen. Human Footprint: Everything You Will Eat, Use, Wear, Buy, & Throw Out in Your Lifetime. 2011. (ENG., Illus.). 32p. (J). (gr. 3-7). pap. 6.95 (978-1-4263-0767-6(5), National Geographic Children's Bks.) National Geographic Society.

Larson, Jennifer S. What Can You Do with Money? Earning, Spending, & Saving. 2010. (Lightning Bolt Books — Exploring Economics Ser.). (ENG., Illus.). 32p. (gr. k-2). pap. 7.95 (978-0-7613-5666-0(5)); lib. bdg. 26.60 (978-0-7613-3910-6(8)) Lerner Publishing Group.

—Who's Buying? Who's Selling? Understanding Consumers & Producers. 2010. (Lightning Bolt Books — Exploring Economics Ser.). (ENG., Illus.). 32p. (gr. k-2). pap. 7.95 (978-0-7613-5665-3(7)); lib. bdg. 26.60 (978-0-7613-3912-0(4)) Lerner Publishing Group.

Meachen Rau, Dana. Gastando el dinero (Spending Money) 2010. (Dinero y los Bancos (Money & Banks) Ser.). (SPA., Illus.). 24p. (gr. 2-5). pap. 8.15 (978-1-4339-3724-8(7)) Stevens, Gareth Publishing LLLP.

—Spending Money. 2010. (Money & Banks Ser.). (Illus.). 24p. (gr. 2-5). pap. 8.15 (978-1-4339-3390-5(X)) Stevens, Gareth Publishing LLLP.

Moore, Elizabeth. Wants or Needs, 1 vol. 2013. (Wonder Readers Next Steps: Social Studies). (ENG.). 20p. (gr. -1-1). 22.65 (978-1-4765-2365-1(7), Wonder Readers) Capstone Press of Coughlan Cos.

Mulder, Michelle. Pocket Change: Pitching in for a Better World, 1 vol. 2016. (Orca Footprints Ser.). (ENG., Illus.). 48p. (J). (gr. 3-7). 19.95 (978-1-4598-0966-6(1)) Orca Bk. Pubs. USA.

Nelson, Robin. What Do We Buy? A Look at Goods & Services. 2010. (Lightning Bolt Books — Exploring Economics Ser.). (ENG., Illus.). 32p. (gr. k-2). pap. 7.95 (978-0-7613-5667-7(3)); lib. bdg. 26.60 (978-0-7613-3913-7(2)) Lerner Publishing Group.

Perritano, John. The Making of the Modern World: 1945 to the Present: Trade, Economic Life & Globalization, Vol. 9. van Dijk, Ruud, ed. 2016. (Making of the Modern World: 1945 to the Present Ser.: Vol. 9). (ENG., Illus.). 64p. (J). (gr. 7-12). 23.95 (978-1-4222-3642-0(0)) Mason Crest.

Rau, Dana Meachen. Gastar el Dinero. 2010. (Dinero y los Bancos Ser.). (SPA., Illus.). 24p. (J). (gr. 2-5). lib. bdg. 22.00 (978-1-4339-3723-1(9)) Stevens, Gareth Publishing LLLP.

—Spending Money. 2010. (Money & Banks Ser.). (Illus.). 24p. (J). (gr. 2-5). lib. bdg. 22.00 (978-1-4339-3389-9(6)) Stevens, Gareth Publishing LLLP.

Seba, Jaime A. Smashing the Stereotypes: What Does It Mean to Be Gay, Lesbian, Bisexual, or Transgender? 2009. (Gallup's Guide to Modern Gay, Lesbian, & Transgender Lifestyle Ser.). 64p. (YA). (gr. 7-18). pap. 9.95 (978-1-4222-1874-7(0)) Mason Crest.

Simons, Rae. Spending Money. 2010. (Junior Library of Money). 64p. (YA). (gr. 7-18). lib. bdg. 22.95 (978-1-4222-1770-2(1)) Mason Crest.

Staniford, Linda. Clothes. 2015. (Wants vs Needs Ser.). (ENG., Illus.). 24p. (gr. k-2). 23.32 (978-1-4846-0944-6(1), Heinemann Read & Learn) Heinemann-Raintree.

Thompson, Helen. Cost of Living. 2010. (Junior Library of Money). 64p. (YA). (gr. 7-18). lib. bdg. 22.95 (978-1-4222-1762-7(0)) Mason Crest.

The True Cost of Food. 2014. (ENG., Illus.). 48p. (J). (978-0-7787-0484-3(X)) Crabtree Publishing Co.

The True Cost of Technology. 2014. (ENG., Illus.). 48p. (J). (978-0-7787-0485-0(8)) Crabtree Publishing Co.

CONTACT LENSES

see Eyeglasses

CONTAGION AND CONTAGIOUS DISEASES

see Communicable Diseases

CONTAGIOUS DISEASES

see Communicable Diseases

CONTESTS

Kids, National Geographic. How to Ace the National Geographic Bee. 2017. (ENG.). 176p. (J). (gr. 3-7). pap. 13.99 **(978-1-4263-3080-3(4)**, National Geographic Children's Bks.) National Geographic Society.

CONTESTS—FICTION

Ackelsberg, Amy. Berry Bitty Bakers. MJ Illustrations Staff, illus. 2011. (Strawberry Shortcake Ser.). (ENG.). 24p. (J). (gr. -1-k). pap. 4.99 (978-0-448-45695-9(8), Grosset & Dunlap) Penguin Young Readers Group.

Adler, David A. Cam Jansen & the Joke House Mystery. Allen, Joy, illus. 2014. (Cam Jansen Ser.: 34). (ENG.). 64p. (J). (gr. 2-5). 14.99 (978-0-670-01262-6(9), Viking Books for Young Readers) Penguin Young Readers Group.

Aisha. Parsley, Sage, Rosemary & Thyme. 2012. 24p. 24.95 (978-1-4626-5122-1(4)) America Star Bks.

Alexan, Julie. Nolia Fasolia: Read-Along Book: Arabic & English. El-Ahraf, Amer, ed. Ceasar, Fady, illus. 2011. (ARA & ENG.). 48p. pap. 5.99 (978-0-9844310-1-4(2)) BigKids Bilingual Bks.

Alexander, Kwame. Acoustic Rooster & His Barnyard Band. Bowers, Tim, illus. 2011. (ENG.). 32p. (gr. k-5). lib. bdg. 15.95 (978-1-58536-688-0(9)) Sleeping Bear Pr.

Allison, Jennifer. The Ghost Sonata. 2008. (Gilda Joyce Ser.). (ENG.). 352p. (J). (gr. 3-7). 8.99 (978-0-14-241232-9(5), Puffin Books) Penguin Young Readers Group.

Applegate, Katherine. Don't Swap Your Sweater for a Dog. Biggs, Brian, illus. 2008. (Roscoe Riley Rules Ser.: 3). (ENG.). 96p. (J). (gr. 1-5). 15.99 (978-0-06-114886-6(5)); pap. 4.99 (978-0-06-114885-9(7)) HarperCollins Pubs.

—Don't Swap Your Sweater for a Dog. 2016. (Roscoe Riley Rules Ser.: 3). (J). lib. bdg. 14.75 (978-0-606-38736-1(6)) Turtleback Bks.

Aretha, David. The Treasure Hunt Stunt at Fenway Park: The Baseball Geeks Adventures Book 3. 2014. (Baseball Geeks Adventures Ser.). (Illus.). 96p. (J). (gr. 4-9). 17.95 (978-1-62285-128-7(5)) Enslow Pubs., Inc.

Atwood, Megan. Beat the Odds. 2016. (Contest Ser.: 2). (ENG.). 104p. (YA). (gr. 6-12). lib. bdg. 27.99 (978-1-4677-7507-6(X), Darby Creek) Lerner Publishing Group.

—Break the Code. 2016. (Contest Ser.: 4). (ENG.). 104p. (YA). (gr. 6-12). lib. bdg. 27.99 (978-1-4677-7509-0(6), Darby Creek) Lerner Publishing Group.

—Raise the Stakes. 2016. (Contest Ser.: 3). (ENG.). 104p. (YA). (gr. 6-12). lib. bdg. 27.99 (978-1-4677-7508-3(8), Darby Creek) Lerner Publishing Group.

—Stay in the Game. 2016. (Contest Ser.: 1). (ENG.). 104p. (YA). (gr. 6-12). pap. 7.99 (978-1-4677-8101-5(0)) Lerner Publishing Group.

—Turn the Tables. 2016. (Contest Ser.: 5). (ENG.). 112p. (J). (gr. 4-4). E-Book 20.99 (978-1-4677-8835-9(X), 9781467788359, Darby Creek) Lerner Publishing Group.

Auerbach, Annie. Scooby-Doo in the Coolsville Contraption Contest, 1 vol. 2016. (Scooby-Doo! Set 3 Ser.). (ENG., Illus.). 32p. (J). (gr. k-4). lib. bdg. 24.21 (978-1-61479-409-7(X)) Spotlight.

Awdry, W. The Good Sport. Courtney, Richard, illus. 2016. 24p. (J). **(978-1-5182-1481-3(9))** Random Hse., Inc.

Azose, Elana & Amancio, Brandon. Never Insult a Killer Zucchini. Clark, David, illus. 2016. (ENG.). 32p. (J). (gr. 2-5). lib. bdg. 16.95 (978-1-58089-618-4(9)) Charlesbridge Publishing, Inc.

Baker, Keith. Gumballs: A Mr. & Mrs. Green Adventure. 2014. (Green Light Readers Level 2 Ser.). (ENG., Illus.). 32p. (J). (gr. -1-3). 12.99 (978-0-544-23605-9(X), HMH Books For Young Readers) Houghton Mifflin Harcourt Publishing Co.

Barkley, Callie. Amy Is a Little Bit Chicken. Bishop, Tracy, illus. 2015. (Critter Club Ser.: 13). (ENG.). 128p. (J). (gr. k-4). pap. 5.99 (978-1-4814-5174-1(X), Little Simon) Little Simon.

—Liz & the Sand Castle Contest. Riti, Marsha, illus. 2015. (Critter Club Ser.: 11). (ENG.). 128p. (J). (gr. k-4). pap. 5.99 (978-1-4814-2405-9(X), Little Simon) Little Simon.

—Marion Strikes a Pose. Riti, Marsha, illus. 2014. (Critter Club Ser.: 8). (ENG.). 128p. (J). (gr. k-4). 16.99 (978-1-4424-9529-6(4), Little Simon) Little Simon.

Barnes, Derrick D. Trivia Queen/Supreme. Newton, Vanessa Brantley, illus. 2008. (Ruby & the Booker Boys Ser.: 2). (ENG.). 144p. (J). (gr. 2-5). pap. 5.99 (978-0-545-01761-9(0)) Scholastic, Inc.

Bates, Michelle. Midnight Horse. rev. ed. 2011. (Sandy Lane Stables Ser.). 128p. (J). pap. 4.99 (978-0-7945-2529-3(6), Usborne) EDC Publishing.

Bateson, Maggie. My Fairy Fashion Show: A Pop-up & Play Book. Comfort, Louise, illus. 2008. (ENG.). 20p. (J). (gr. 4-8). 23.95 (978-0-230-53035-5(4), Macmillan) Pan Macmillan GBR. Dist: Trans-Atlantic Pubns., Inc.

Bee, William. Worst in Show. Hindley, Kate, illus. 2015. (ENG.). 40p. (J). (gr. -1-2). 15.99 (978-0-7636-7318-5(8)) Candlewick Pr.

Belgue, Nancy. Casey Little, Yo-Yo Queen, 1 vol. 2005. (Orca Young Readers Ser.). (ENG., Illus.). 128p. (J). (gr. 3-6). per. 5.95 (978-1-55143-357-8(5)) Orca Bk. Pubs. USA.

Benton, Jim. You Can Bet on That. Benton, Jim, illus. 2014. (Dear Dumb Diary Year Two Ser.: 5). (ENG., Illus.). 160p. (J). (gr. 3-7). pap. 5.99 (978-0-545-64257-6(4), Scholastic Paperbacks) Scholastic, Inc.

Berlin, Eric. The Potato Chip Puzzles. 2010. (Puzzling World of Winston Breen Ser.: 2). (ENG.). 272p. (J). (gr. 3-7). 7.99 (978-0-14-241637-2(1), Puffin Books) Penguin Young Readers Group.

Best, Cari. Ava & the Real Lucille, 1 vol. Valentine, Madeline, illus. 2012. (ENG.). 32p. (J). (gr. -1-3). 16.99 (978-0-374-39903-0(4), 9780374399030, Farrar, Straus & Giroux (BYR)) Farrar, Straus & Giroux.

Bildner, Phil. Tournament of Champions. Probert, Tim, illus. 2017. (Rip & Red Ser.: 3). (ENG.). 256p. (J). 16.99 (978-0-374-30507-9(2), 9780374305079, Farrar, Straus & Giroux (BYR)) Farrar, Straus & Giroux.

Birtha, Becky. Lucky Beans. Tadgell, Nicole, illus. 2012. (J). 34.28 (978-1-61913-129-3(3)) Weigl Pubs., Inc.

—Lucky Beans. Tadgell, Nicole, illus. 2010. (ENG.). 32p. (J). (gr. 2-3). 16.99 (978-0-8075-4782-3(4)) Whitman, Albert & Co.

Blake, Kendare. Three Dark Crowns. (YA). (gr. 9). 2018. (Three Dark Crowns Ser.: 1). 432p. pap. 10.99 **(978-0-06-238544-4(5))** 2016. (ENG.). 416p. 17.99 (978-0-06-238543-7(7)) HarperCollins Pubs. (HarperTeen).

—Three Dark Crowns. 2018. lib. bdg. 22.10 **(978-0-606-40404-4(X))** Turtleback Bks.

Blake, Stephanie J. The Marble Queen, 0 vols. 2012. (ENG.). 192p. (YA). (gr. 5-9). 16.99 (978-0-7614-6227-9(9), 9780761462279, Amazon Children's Publishing) Amazon Publishing.

Bliss, Emily. Flash's Dash. Hanson, Sydney, illus. 2017. (Unicorn Princesses Ser.). (ENG.). 128p. (J). 15.99 (978-1-68119-329-8(9), 9781681193298, Bloomsbury USA Childrens) Bloomsbury Publishing USA.

Booth, Tom. Don't Blink! Booth, Tom, illus. 2017. (ENG., Illus.). 40p. (J). 17.99 (978-1-250-11736-6(4), 9781250117366) Feiwel & Friends.

Bourgeois, Paulette & Clark, Brenda. Franklin & the Contest. 2004. (Kids Can Read Ser.). (ENG., Illus.). 32p. (J). (gr. 1-2). 3.95 (978-1-55337-492-3(4)); 14.95 (978-1-55337-491-6(6)) Kids Can Pr., Ltd. CAN. Dist: Hachette Bk. Group.

Bradfield, Roger, illus. The Pickle-Chiffon Pie Olympics. 2011. 64p. (J). (gr. -1-3). 18.95 (978-1-930900-52-3(X)) Purple Hse. Pr.

Braver, Vanita. Madison & the Two-Wheeler, 1 vol. DiRocco, Carl, illus. 2007. (ENG.). 32p. (J). (gr. -1-3). 14.95 (978-1-59572-109-9(6)) Star Bright Bks., Inc.

Bray, Libba. Beauty Queens. (ENG.). 400p. (J). (gr. 7). 2012. pap. 10.99 (978-0-439-89598-9(7), Scholastic Paperbacks) 2011. 18.99 (978-0-439-89597-2(9), Scholastic Pr.) Scholastic, Inc.

Brett, Jan. The Easter Egg. Brett, Jan, illus. (ENG., Illus.). 32p. (J). 2017. (-k). bds. 8.99 (978-0-399-54733-1(9)) 2010. (gr. -1-k). 17.99 (978-0-399-25238-9(X)) Penguin Young Readers Group. (G.P. Putnam's Sons Books for Young Readers).

Bricker, Chris. The Leaping Frogs of Calameris County. 2006. 48p. pap. 16.95 (978-1-4241-2408-4(5)) PublishAmerica, Inc.

Bruce, Sheila. Todos Ganan! Billin-Frye, Paige, illus. 2006. (Math Matters en Espanol Ser.). (SPA.). 32p. (J). (gr. -1-3). pap. 5.95 (978-1-57565-162-0(9)) Kane Press, Inc.

Brun, Laura. Frosty the Craft Maker. 2012. 24p. pap. 24.95 (978-1-62709-700-0(7)) America Star Bks.

The Bubble Gum Contest. 2007. (Spaceboy Chapter Ser.). (J). per. 7.67 (978-1-932570-62-5(4)) Pioneer Valley Bks.

Burgard, Anna Marlis. Flying Feet: A Story of Irish Dance. Dees, Leighanne, illus. 2006. 31p. (J). (gr. 4-8). 16.00 (978-1-4223-5255-7(2)) DIANE Publishing Co.

Burkhart, Jessica. Comeback. 2012. (Canterwood Crest Ser.: 15). lib. bdg. 18.40 (978-0-606-26312-2(8), Turtleback) Turtleback Bks.

Caffrey, Jaye Andras. First Star I See. Adamson, Lynne, illus. 2nd ed. 2010. (ENG.). 164p. (J). (gr. 2-7). pap. 12.95 (978-1-936290-01-7(4)) Central Recovery Pr.

Callahan, Sean. Shannon & the World's Tallest Leprechaun. Kemly, Kathleen, illus. 2008. (ENG.). 32p. (J). (gr. 2-3). lib. bdg. 15.95 (978-0-8075-7326-6(4)) Whitman, Albert & Co.

Calmenson, Stephanie & Cole, Joanna. No Dogs Allowed. Ross, Heather, illus. 2014. (Ready, Set, Dogs! Ser.: 1). (ENG.). 144p. (J). (gr. 1-4). pap. 5.99 (978-1-250-04414-3(6), 9781250044143) Square Fish.

Cammuso, Frank. The Dragon Players. 2009. (Knights of the Lunch Table Ser.: 2). (ENG.). 128p. (J). (gr. 4-7). pap. 10.99 (978-0-439-90323-3(8), Graphix) Scholastic, Inc.

Capucilli, Alyssa Satin & Cole, Henry. Katy Duck Is a Caterpillar. 2009. (Katy Duck Ser.). (ENG., Illus.). 32p. (J). (gr. -1-k). 14.99 (978-1-4169-6061-4(9), Little Simon) Little Simon.

Carmi, Rebecca. Amazing Magnetism. Speirs, John, illus. 2003. (Magic School Bus Science Chapter Bks.). 76p. (gr. 2-4). 15.00 (978-0-7569-1576-6(7)) Perfection Learning Corp.

Carroll, Kathy. Rabbit & the Amazing Hopping Contest. 2007. (Illus.). 16p. (J). 9.99 (978-0-9791401-6-7(1)) Abecedarian Bks.

Carter, Aubrey Smith. The Enchanted Lizard: La Lagartijita Mágica. Nelson, Esther Whitt, ed. Branton, Molly, illus. 2006. (ENG & SPA.). 96p. (J). 18.95 (978-1-893271-38-8(2), Maverick Bks.) Trinity Univ. Pr.

Cass, Kiera. The Crown. 2016. (Selection Ser.: 5). (ENG.). 288p. (YA). (gr. 8). 19.99 (978-0-06-239217-6(4), HarperTeen) HarperCollins Pubs.

—The Elite. (Selection Ser.: 2). (ENG.). (YA). (gr. 8). 2014. 352p. pap. 9.99 (978-0-06-205997-0(1)) 2013. 336p. 17.99 (978-0-06-205996-3(3)) HarperCollins Pubs. (HarperTeen).

—LA ÉLITE. 2013. (SPA.). 224p. pap. 20.95 (978-84-9918-613-9(0)) Roca Editorial ESP. Dist: Spanish Pubs., LLC.

—La Elite. 2017. (SPA.). 224p. (YA). (gr. 7-12). pap. 12.95 **(978-84-16240-61-6(2))** Roca Bolsillo ESP. Dist: Spanish Pubs., LLC.

—The Elite. 2014. (Selection Ser.: 2). (YA). lib. bdg. 20.85 (978-0-606-35489-9(1)) Turtleback Bks.

—Happily Ever After. 2015. (Selection Novella Ser.). (ENG., Illus.). 416p. (YA). (gr. 8). 18.99 (978-0-06-241408-3(9), HarperTeen) HarperCollins Pubs.

—Happily Ever After: Companion to the Selection Series. 2016. (Selection Ser.). (YA). lib. bdg. 20.85 (978-0-606-38919-8(9)) Turtleback Bks.

—The Heir. 2015. (ENG.). 368p. (YA). (Selection Ser.: 4). (gr. 8). 18.99 (978-0-06-234985-9(6), HarperTeen); pap. (978-0-06-239130-8(5)) HarperCollins Pubs.

—The One. (Selection Ser.: 3). (ENG.). (gr. 8). 2015. 368p. (YA). pap. 9.99 (978-0-06-206000-6(7)) 2014. 352p. (J). 17.99 (978-0-06-205999-4(8)) HarperCollins Pubs. (HarperTeen).

—The Selection. (Selection Ser.: 1). (ENG.). (YA). (gr. 8). 2013. 352p. pap. 9.99 (978-0-06-205994-9(7)) 2012. 336p. 17.99 (978-0-06-205993-2(9)) HarperCollins Pubs. (HarperTeen).

—The Selection, 1. (ENG.). 272p. pap. (978-0-00-746669-6(2), HarperCollins Children's Bks.) HarperCollins Pubs. Ltd.

—The Selection. 2013. (Selection Ser.: 1). (YA). lib. bdg. 20.85 (978-0-606-35488-2(3)) Turtleback Bks.

—The Selection Stories: The Prince & the Guard. 2014. (Selection Ser.). (ENG.). 240p. (J). (gr. 8). pap. 9.99 (978-0-06-231832-9(2)) HarperCollins Pubs.

Catalanotto, Peter. Emily's Art. Catalanotto, Peter, illus. 2006. (ENG., Illus.). 32p. (J). (gr. k-3). 7.99 (978-1-4169-2688-7(7), Atheneum Bks. for Young Readers) Simon & Schuster Children's Publishing.

Cervantes, Angela. Allie, First at Last. 2016. (ENG.). 208p. (J). (gr. 3-7). 16.99 (978-0-545-81223-8(2), Scholastic Pr.) Scholastic, Inc.

Child, Lauren. Utterly Me, Clarice Bean. Child, Lauren, illus. 2005. (Clarice Bean Ser.). (ENG., Illus.). 208p. (J). (gr. 3-7). reprint ed. pap. 5.99 (978-0-7636-2788-1(7)) Candlewick Pr.

—Utterly Me, Clarice Bean. Child, Lauren, illus. 2006. (Clarice Bean Ser.). (Illus.). 16.00 (978-0-7569-6567-9(5)) Perfection Learning Corp.

Child, Lauren, et al. Fi'n Hollol, Carys Blodyn. 2005. (WEL., Illus.). 192p. pap. (978-1-85596-675-8(1)) Dref Wen.

Clark, Sherryl. Kim's Fake Cake Bake. McKenzie, Heath, illus. 2015. (J). pap. (978-1-4966-0256-5(0)) Capstone Classroom.

—Kim's Super Science Day. McKenzie, Heath, illus. 2015. (J). pap. (978-1-4966-0250-3(1)) Capstone Classroom.

—Kim's Tug of War. McKenzie, Heath, illus. 2015. (J). pap. (978-1-4966-0244-2(7)) Capstone Classroom.

Clements, Andrew. No Talking. 2014. (ENG.). 160p. (J). (gr. 3-7). 11.24 (978-1-63245-298-6(7)) Lectorum Pubns., Inc.

—No Talking. (J). 2008. 78.75 (978-1-4361-5835-0(4)) 2007. 54.75 (978-1-4281-5418-6(3)) 2007. 52.75 (978-1-4281-5420-9(5)) 2007. (SPA.). 54.75 (978-1-4281-5422-3(1)) 2007. 51.75 (978-1-4281-5424-7(8)) 2007. 1.25 (978-1-4281-5415-5(9)) 2007. 209.75 (978-1-4281-5419-3(1)) Recorded Bks., Inc.

—No Talking. Elliott, Mark, illus. (ENG.). 160p. (J). (gr. 3-7). 2009. pap. 7.99 (978-1-4169-0984-2(2)) 2007. 18.99 (978-1-4169-0983-5(4)) Simon & Schuster Children's Publishing. (Atheneum Bks. for Young Readers).

—No Talking. Elliott, Mark, illus. l.t. ed. 2007. (Literacy Bridge Middle Reader Ser.). 155p. (J). (gr. 3-7). 23.95 (978-1-4104-0294-3(0)) Thorndike Pr.

—No Talking. 2009. (CHI., Illus.). 180p. (J). pap. 14.95 (978-7-5309-5645-8(0)) Tianjin Education Pr.

—No Talking. 2009. lib. bdg. 18.40 (978-0-606-14508-4(7), Turtleback) Turtleback Bks.

—Sin Hablar. 2009.Tr. of No Talking. (SPA.). 156p. (gr. 4-6). pap. 10.99 (978-84-441-4100-8(3)) Everest Editora ESP. Dist: Lectorum Pubns., Inc.

Cobb, Amy. Swing Vote for Solo, 1 vol. Cattish, Anna, illus. 2015. (ENG.). 112p. (J). (978-1-62402-078-0(X)) Magic Wagon.

Collins, Suzanne. Catching Fire. 2009. (Hunger Games Trilogy: Bk. 2). (YA). 74.99 (978-1-61574-572-2(6)) Findaway World, LLC.

—Catching Fire. 2009. 12.04 (978-0-7848-3842-6(9), Everbind) Marco Bk. Co.

—Catching Fire. 2011. 480p. pap. (978-1-4071-3209-9(1)) Scholastic.

—Catching Fire. (Hunger Games Ser.: 2). (ENG.). (gr. 7). 2014. 448p. (YA). pap. 12.99 (978-0-545-79188-5(X), Tangerine Pr.) 2013. 400p. (YA). pap. 12.99 (978-0-545-58617-7(8), Scholastic Pr.) 2010. (Illus.). 400p. (J). lib. bdg. 22.99 (978-0-545-31059-8(8), Scholastic Pr.) 2009. 400p. (J). 18.99 (978-0-439-02349-8(1), Scholastic Pr.) 2013. 400p. (J). pap. 12.99 (978-0-545-60368-3(4), Scholastic Paperbacks) Scholastic, Inc.

—Catching Fire. l.t. ed. (Hunger Games Trilogy: 2). (ENG.). (YA). 2012. 498p. (gr. 7-12). pap. 14.99 (978-1-59413-585-9(1), Large Print Pr.) 2009. 500p. 23.95 (978-1-4104-2044-2(2)) Thorndike Pr.

—Catching Fire. 2013. (Hunger Games Trilogy Ser.: 2). lib. bdg. 24.50 (978-0-606-32025-2(3), Turtleback) Turtleback Bks.

—Catching Fire. 2011. (Hunger Games Trilogy: Bk. 2). (CHI.). 344p. (YA). (gr. 7-12). pap. (978-7-5063-5566-7(3)) Writers' Publishing Hse.

—EN LLAMAS. 2012. (Hunger Games Trilogy: Bk. 2). (SPA.). 416p. (J). pap. 19.99 (978-84-272-0213-9(X)) Molino, Editorial ESP. Dist: Lectorum Pubns., Inc.

—En Llamas, Bk. 2. 2010. (Hunger Games Trilogy: Bk. 2).Tr. of Catching Fire. (SPA.). 416p. (J). (gr. 8-12). pap. 19.99 (978-84-272-0000-5(5)) Lectorum Pubns., Inc.

—The Hunger Games. 2009. (Hunger Games Trilogy: Bk. 1). 10.85 (978-0-7848-3801-3(1), Everbind) Marco Bk. Co.

—The Hunger Games. 2010. (Hunger Games Trilogy: Bk. 1). (ENG.). 374p. (gr. 7-12). 21.00 (978-1-60686-581-1(1)) Perfection Learning Corp.

—The Hunger Games. Fournier, Guillaume, tr. 2011. (Hunger Games Trilogy: Bk. 1). (FRE.). 398p. (YA). (gr. 7-12). pap. (978-2-266-18269-0(2)) Presses Pocket.

—The Hunger Games. 2011. (Hunger Games Trilogy: 1). (YA). 69.75 (978-1-4561-3196-8(6)) Recorded Bks., Inc.

—The Hunger Games. 2010. (Hunger Games Ser.: 1). (ENG.). 384p. (J). (gr. 7-18). pap. 10.99 (978-0-439-02352-8(1), Scholastic Pr.) Scholastic, Inc.

—The Hunger Games. O'Brien, Tim, illus. 2009. 448p. pap. (978-1-4071-0908-4(1), Scholastic) Scholastic, Inc.

—The Hunger Games. (Hunger Games Ser.: 1). (ENG.). (gr. 7). 2008. 384p. (J). 18.99 (978-0-439-02348-1(3), Scholastic Pr.) 2012. 384p. (J). pap. 12.99 (978-0-545-42511-7(5))Set. 2014. (YA). pap. 38.97 (978-0-545-79191-5(X), Scholastic Pr.) Scholastic, Inc.

—The Hunger Games. l.t. ed. (Hunger Games Trilogy: Bk. 1). (ENG.). (YA). 2012. 484p. (gr. 7-12). pap. 14.99 (978-1-59413-587-3(8), Large Print Pr.) 2009. 486p. 23.95 (978-1-4104-1986-6(X)) Thorndike Pr.

—The Hunger Games. 2010. (Hunger Games Trilogy Ser.: 1). lib. bdg. 22.10 (978-1-4178-3173-9(1), Turtleback) Turtleback Bks.

—The Hunger Games. 2010. (Hunger Games Trilogy: Bk. 1). (CHI.). 324p. (YA). (gr. 7-12). pap. (978-7-5063-5153-9(6)) Writers' Publishing Hse.

—The Hunger Games: Foil Edition. 2014. (Hunger Games Ser.: 1). (ENG.). 448p. (YA). (gr. 7). pap. 12.99 (978-0-545-79187-8(1), Scholastic Pr.) Scholastic, Inc.

—The Hunger Games Trilogy Set: The Hunger Games; Catching Fire; Mockingjay. 2010. (Hunger Games Ser.: 1). (ENG.). (J). (gr. 7-18). 53.97 (978-0-545-26535-5(5), Scholastic Pr.) Scholastic, Inc.

—The Hunger Games Trilogy Collection. 2014. (Hunger Games Ser.). (ENG.). (J). (gr. 9). pap. 36.97 (978-0-545-67031-9(4), Scholastic Pr.) Scholastic, Inc.

—Los Juegos del Hambre. 2009. (Hunger Games Trilogy: Bk. 1).Tr. of Hunger Games. (SPA.). pap. 19.99 (978-84-9867-539-9(1)) RBA Libros, S.A. ESP. Dist: Lectorum Pubns., Inc.

—Los Juegos del Hambre. 2012. (Hunger Games Trilogy Spanish Ser.: 1).Tr. of Hunger Games. (SPA.). lib. bdg. 33.05 (978-0-606-26447-1(7), Turtleback) Turtleback Bks.

—LOS JUEGOS DEL HAMBRE. 2012. (Hunger Games Trilogy: Bk. 1). (SPA.). 400p. (J). pap. 19.99 (978-84-272-0212-2(1)) Molino, Editorial ESP. Dist: Lectorum Pubns., Inc.

—Mockingjay. 2011. (Hunger Games Trilogy: Bk. 3). (CHI.). 435p. (YA). (gr. 7-12). pap. (978-986-213-216-6(7)) Locus Publishing Co.

—Mockingjay. (Hunger Games Trilogy: 3). (YA). 2011. 77.75 (978-1-4561-3203-3(2)) 2010. 1.25 (978-1-4640-2636-2(X)) 2010. 75.75 (978-1-4561-3205-7(9)) Recorded Bks., Inc.

—Mockingjay. 2011. (Hunger Games Ser.: Vol. 3). (ENG.). 448p. (YA). (gr. 8-12). pap. (978-1-4071-3210-5(5)) Scholastic Canada, Ltd.

—Mockingjay. 2014. (Hunger Games Ser.: 3). (ENG.). 400p. (YA). (gr. 7). pap. 12.99 (978-0-545-78829-8(3), Scholastic Paperbacks) 2014. (Hunger Games Ser.: 3). (ENG.). 448p. (YA). (gr. 7). pap. 12.99 (978-0-545-79190-8(1), Scholastic Pr.) 2014. (Hunger Games Ser.: 3). (ENG.). 400p. (J). (gr. 7). pap. 12.99 (978-0-545-66326-7(1), Scholastic Pr.) 2010. (Hunger Games Ser.: 3). (ENG.). 400p. (J). (gr. 7-7). lib. bdg. 22.99 (978-0-545-31060-4(1), Scholastic Pr.) 2010. (Hunger Games Ser.: 3). (ENG.). 400p. (J). (gr. 7-18). 18.99 (978-0-439-02351-1(3), Scholastic Pr.) 2010. pap. (978-0-439-02354-2(8), Scholastic Pr.) Scholastic, Inc.

—Mockingjay. l.t. ed. (Hunger Games Trilogy: Bk. 3). (ENG.). (YA). 2012. 502p. (gr. 7-12). pap. 14.99

(978-1-59413-586-6(X), Large Print Pr.) 2010. 503p. 23.99 (978-1-4104-2841-7(9)) Thorndike Pr.

—Mockingjay. 2014. (Hunger Games Trilogy Ser.: 3). lib. bdg. 24.50 (978-0-606-36328-0(9)); lib. bdg. 24.50 (978-0-606-35133-1(7)) Turtleback Bks.

Cooper, Elisha. Homer. Cooper, Elisha, illus. 2012. (ENG., Illus.). 32p. (J). (gr. -1-3). 16.99 (978-0-06-201248-7(7), Greenwillow Bks.) HarperCollins Pubs.

Cooper, Ilene. Look at Lucy! Merrell, David, illus. 2009. (Lucy Ser.: No. 3). (ENG.). 112p. (J). (gr. 1-4). 4.99 (978-0-375-85558-0(0), Random Hse. Bks. for Young Readers) Random Hse. Children's Bks.

Cosgrove, Stephen. Mizz Buggly: Doing Your Best. Arroyo, Fian, illus. 2004. (J). (978-1-58804-380-1(0)) P C I Education.

Costain, Meredith. Stella & the Pet Parade. McGowan, Shane, illus. 2015. (Legends in Their Own Lunchbox Ser.). (ENG.). 48p. (gr. 1-2). pap. 7.99 (978-1-4966-0243-5(9), Legends in Their Own Lunchbox) Capstone Classroom.

Cotler, Steve. Cheesie Mack Is Cool in a Duel. McCauley, Adam, illus. (Cheesie Mack Ser.). (ENG.). 240p. (J). (gr. 3-7). 2013. 6.99 (978-0-375-86395-0(8), Yearling) 2012. 15.99 (978-0-375-86438-4(5), Random Hse. Bks. for Young Readers) Random Hse. Children's Bks.

Courtenay, L. A. Space Penguins Galaxy Race! Davies, James, illus. 2015. (Space Penguins Ser.). (ENG.). 112p. (gr. 2-3). lib. bdg. 22.65 (978-1-4342-9783-9(7)) Stone Arch Bks.

Cousins, Dave. 15 Days Without a Head. 2013. (ENG.). 312p. (YA). pap. 9.99 (978-0-7387-3642-6(2), Flux) North Star Editions.

Coven, Wanda. Heidi Heckelbeck & the Cookie Contest. Burris, Priscilla, illus. 2012. (Heidi Heckelbeck Ser.: 3). (ENG.). 128p. (J). (gr. k-2). 16.99 (978-1-4424-4166-8(6)); pap. 5.99 (978-1-4424-4165-1(8)) Little Simon. (Little Simon).

—Heidi Heckelbeck & the Cookie Contest. 2012. (Heidi Heckelbeck Ser.: 3). lib. bdg. 16.00 (978-0-606-26328-3(4), Turtleback) Turtleback Bks.

—Heidi Heckelbeck Has a Secret - Heidi Heckelbeck Casts a Spell - Heidi Heckelbeck & the Cookie Contest. Burris, Priscilla, illus. 2014. (Heidi Heckelbeck Ser.). (ENG.). 384p. (J). (gr. k-4). pap. 8.99 (978-1-4814-2771-5(7), Little Simon) Little Simon.

Cronin, Doreen. Dooby Dooby Moo. Lewin, Betsy, illus. 2010. (Click, Clack Book Ser.). (ENG.). 40p. (J). (gr. -1-k). bds. 7.99 (978-1-4424-0890-6(1), Little Simon) Little Simon.

—Dooby Dooby Moo. Lewin, Betsy, illus. 2006. (Click, Clack Book Ser.). (ENG.). 40p. (J). (gr. -1-3). 17.99 (978-0-689-84507-9(3), Atheneum Bks. for Young Readers) Simon & Schuster Children's Publishing.

—Dooby Dooby Moo, 1 vol. Lewin, Betsy, illus. 2008. (Doreen Cronin: Click-Clack & More Ser.). (ENG.). 40p. (gr. -1-3). lib. bdg. 24.21 (978-1-59961-423-6(5)) Spotlight.

—Dooby Dooby Moo. Lewin, Betsy, illus. 2011. (J). (gr. -1-3). 29.95 (978-0-545-04281-9(X)) Weston Woods Studios, Inc.

Croteau, Marie-Danielle. Fred & the Pig Race. Cummins, Sarah, tr. from FRE. St-Aubin, Bruno, illus. 2007. (Formac First Novels Ser.). (ENG.). 64p. (gr. 2-5). 14.95 (978-0-88780-733-6(X), 9780887807336); (J). 4.95 (978-0-88780-731-2(3), 9780887807312) Formac Publishing Co., Ltd. CAN. Dist: Casemate Pubs. & Bk. Distributors, LLC.

Danziger, Paula. Segundo Grado Es Increible, Ambar Dorado. Ross, Tony, illus. 2007. (de Ámbar / a Is for Amber Easy-To-Read Ser.).Tr. of Second Grade Rules, Amber Brown. (SPA.). 48p. (gr. k-3). pap. 8.95 (978-1-59820-594-7(3)) Santillana USA Publishing Co., Inc.

David, Erica. The Great Ice Engine. RH Disney Staff et al, illus. 2015. (Stepping Stone Book(TM) Ser.: 4). (ENG.). 128p. (J). (gr. 1-4). 9.99 (978-0-7364-3431-7(3), RH/Disney) Random Hse. Children's Bks.

David, Lawrence. The Terror of the Pink Dodo Balloons. Gott, Barry, illus. 2003. (Horace Splattly Ser.). 153p. (J). (gr. 4-7). 12.65 (978-0-7569-2816-2(8)) Perfection Learning Corp.

Davidowitz, Stacy. Camp Rolling Hills. 2017. (Camp Rolling Hills Ser.: 3). (ENG., Illus.). 240p. (J). (gr. 3-7). pap. 8.95 (978-1-4197-2291-2(3), Amulet Bks.) Abrams, Inc.

De felice, Cynthia. Devil's Bridge. 2008. (ENG.). 96p. (YA). (gr. 7). pap. 9.99 (978-1-4169-8307-1(4), Atheneum Bks. for Young Readers) Simon & Schuster Children's Publishing.

De Witt, Peter. Toaster Pond. 2006. (ENG.). 248p. (YA). (gr. 7-12). per. (978-1-933255-21-7(8)) DNA Pr.

Denman, K. L. & Fernández, Queta. La Guerra de las Bandas, 1 vol. 2008. (Spanish Soundings Ser.). (SPA.). 112p. (YA). (gr. 8-12). pap. 9.95 (978-1-55143-998-3(0)) Orca Bk. Pubs. USA.

Derubertis, Barbara. Jeremy Jackrabbit's Jumping Journey. 2010. pap. 45.32 (978-0-7613-6512-9(5)) Kane Press, Inc.

deRubertis, Barbara. Jeremy Jackrabbit's Jumping Journey. Alley, R. W., illus. 2010. (Animal Antics A to Z Ser.). 32p. (J). (gr. -1-3). pap. 7.95 (978-1-57565-314-3(1)); lib. bdg. 22.60 (978-1-57565-321-1(4)) Kane Press, Inc.

deRubertis, Barbara & DeRubertis, Barbara. Jeremy Jackrabbit's Jumping Journey. Alley, R. W., illus. 2012. (Animal Antics A to Z Ser.). 32p. (J). (gr. 2 — 1). cd-rom 7.95 (978-1-57565-403-4(2)) Kane Press, Inc.

DiCamillo, Kate. Raymie Nightingale. 2016. (ENG.). 272p. (J). (gr. 5-7). 16.99 (978-0-7636-8117-3(2)) Candlewick Pr.

—Raymie Nightingale. 2016. (J). lib. bdg. 29.40 (978-0-606-37935-9(5)) Turtleback Bks.

Disney & Sisler, Celeste. Disney Fairies: Pixie Hollow Bake Off. 2014. (ENG., Illus.). 24p. (J). (gr. -1-3). 4.99 (978-0-316-28332-8(0)) Little, Brown Bks. for Young Readers.

Disney Book Group Staff & Higginson, Sheila Sweeny. Minnie: Minnie's Costume Contest. Disney Storybook Artists Staff, illus. 2014. (ENG.). 12p. (J). (gr. -1-k). bds. 7.99 (978-1-4231-9427-9(6)) Disney Pr.

Disney Editors. Cinderella Takes the Stage. 2017. (Disney Princess Beginnings Ser.). lib. bdg. 17.20 **(978-0-606-39857-2(0))** Turtleback Bks.

Dorros, Arthur. Julio's Magic. Date not set. 32p. (gr. -1-1). mass mkt. 5.99 (978-0-06-443686-1(1)) HarperCollins Pubs.

—Julio's Magic. Grifalconi, Ann, illus. 2005. (ENG.). 32p. (J). (gr. -1-4). 15.99 (978-0-06-029004-7(8)) HarperCollins Pubs.

dos Santos, Steven. The Culling. 2013. (Torch Keeper Ser.: 1). (ENG.). 432p. (YA). pap. 9.99 (978-0-7387-3537-5(X), Flux) North Star Editions.

Doudna, Kelly. Doggie Pants, 1 vol. Haberstroh, Anne, illus. 2006. (Animal Tales Ser.). 24p. (J). (gr. k-3). (ENG.). lib. bdg. 24.21 (978-1-59679-931-8(5), SandCastle); pap. 48.42 (978-1-59679-932-5(3)) ABDO Publishing Co.

Dower, Laura. Kiki Takes the Cake. Lazuli, Lilly, illus. 2016. (Dessert Diaries). (ENG.). 160p. (gr. 4-5). lib. bdg. 26.65 (978-1-4965-3120-9(5)) Stone Arch Bks.

Doyle, Bill. The Prizewinners of Piedmont Place. Jack, Colin, illus. 2016. (Prizewinners of Piedmont Place Ser.: 1). (ENG.). 192p. (J). (gr. 3-7). 15.99 (978-0-553-52177-1(2), Random Hse. Bks. for Young Readers) Random Hse. Children's Bks.

Doyle, Bill H. Extreme Home Takeover/C by Bill Doyle; Illustrated by Colin Jack. Jack, Colin, illus. 2017. (Prizewinners of Piedmont Place Ser.). (ENG.). 208p. (J). (gr. 3-7). 15.99 (978-0-553-52181-8(0), Random Hse. Bks. for Young Readers) Random Hse. Children's Bks.

Draper, Sharon M. Double Dutch. 2004. 183p. (gr. 6-9). 17.00 (978-0-7569-2934-3(2)) Perfection Learning Corp.

Driscoll, Laura. The Blast off Kid! Thornburgh, Rebecca McKillip, illus. 2003. (Math Matters Ser.). (ENG.). 32p. (J). pap. 5.95 (978-1-57565-130-9(0)) Kane Press, Inc.

—El Chico del Despegue. Ramirez, Alma, tr. from ENG. Thornburgh, Rebecca McKillip, illus. 2009. (Math Matters en Espanol Ser.). (SPA.). 32p. (J). (gr. k-2). pap. 5.95 (978-1-57565-267-2(6)) Kane Press, Inc.

—El Chico Del Despegue (the Blast-off Kid) 2009. (SPA.). pap. 34.95 (978-0-7613-4789-7(5)) Lerner Publishing Group.

Duane, Diane. Games Wizards Play. (Young Wizards Ser.: 10). (ENG.). 640p. (YA). (gr. 7). 2017. pap. 8.99 (978-0-544-81323-6(5)) 2016. 17.99 (978-0-547-41806-3(X)) Houghton Mifflin Harcourt Publishing Co. (HMH Books For Young Readers).

Duble, Kathleen Benner. Bravo Zulu, Samantha!, 1 vol. 2007. (ENG.). 144p. (J). (gr. 3-7). 14.95 (978-1-56145-401-3(X)) Peachtree Pubs.

Dunston, Marc. The Magic of Giving, 1 vol. Cantrell, Katie, illus. 2010. (ENG.). 32p. (J). (gr. k-3). 16.99 (978-1-58980-805-8(3)) Pelican Publishing Co., Inc.

Earhart, Kristin. Outback All-Stars (Race the Wild #5) 2016. (Race the Wild Ser.: 5). (ENG., Illus.). 144p. (J). (gr. 2-5). pap. 4.99 (978-0-545-94064-1(8), Scholastic Paperbacks) Scholastic, Inc.

Earhart, Kristin. Savanna Showdown. 2016. (Illus.). 138p. (J). **(978-1-5182-0302-2(7))** Scholastic, Inc.

—Savanna Showdown. 2015. (Race the Wild Ser.: 4). (ENG., Illus.). 144p. (J). (gr. 2-5). lib. bdg. 14.75 (978-0-606-38080-5(9)) Turtleback Bks.

Echols, Jennifer. The Ex Games. 2011. (Romantic Comedies Ser.). (ENG.). 240p. (YA). (gr. 7). pap. 11.99 (978-1-4424-3083-9(4), Simon Pulse) Simon Pulse.

Egan, Kate. The Hunger Games - Catching Fire. 2013. (ENG., Illus.). 160p. (J). (gr. 7-12). pap. 18.99 (978-0-545-59933-7(4)) Scholastic, Inc.

Elliott, Kate, pseud. Court of Fives. 2015. (Court of Fives Ser.: Bk. 1). (ENG., Illus.). 448p. (YA). (gr. 7-17). 18.00 (978-0-316-36419-5(3)) Little Brown & Co.

—Court of Fives. 2016. (Court of Fives Ser.: 1). (ENG., Illus.). 464p. (YA). (gr. 7-17). pap. 10.99 (978-0-316-36430-0(4)) Little, Brown Bks. for Young Readers.

—Poisoned Blade. 2016. (Court of Fives Ser.: 2). (ENG., Illus.). 480p. (YA). (gr. 7-17). 17.99 (978-0-316-34437-1(0)) Little, Brown Bks. for Young Readers.

Enriquez, Jose. Saving the Mango Farm. 2006. 23p. (J). 10.98 (978-1-4116-5917-9(1)) Lulu Pr., Inc.

Estep, Jennifer. Bright Blaze of Magic. 2016. (Black Blade Ser.). (ENG.). 368p. (YA). (gr. 9). pap. 9.95 (978-1-61773-828-9(X)) Kensington Publishing Corp.

Evans, Douglas. MVP. Shelley, John, illus. 2004. (ENG.). 232p. (J). (gr. 4-6). 16.95 (978-1-932425-13-0(6), Lemniscaat) Boyds Mills Pr.

Eveleigh, Victoria. Katy's Pony Challenge. 2016. (Katy's Exmoor Ponies Ser.). (ENG., Illus.). 144p. (J). (gr. 2-4). 7.99 (978-1-4440-1451-8(X), Orion Children's Bks.) Hachette Children's Group GBR. Dist: Hachette Bk. Group.

Feldman, Jody. The Gollywhopper Games. Jamieson, Victoria, illus. (Gollywhopper Games Ser.: 1). (ENG.). (J). (gr. 3-7). 2013. 336p. pap. 6.99 (978-0-06-121452-3(3)) 2008. 320p. 16.99 (978-0-06-121450-9(7)) HarperCollins Pubs. (Greenwillow Bks.).

—The Gollywhopper Games. 2013. (Gollywhopper Games Ser.: 1). (J). lib. bdg. 17.20 (978-0-606-35508-7(1)) Turtleback Bks.

—The Gollywhopper Games - Friend or Foe. Jamieson, Victoria, illus. 2015. (Gollywhopper Games Ser.: 3). (ENG.). 432p. (J). (gr. 3-7). 16.99 (978-0-06-221128-6(5), Greenwillow Bks.) HarperCollins Pubs.

—The Gollywhopper Games - The New Champion. Jamieson, Victoria, illus. 2015. (Gollywhopper Games Ser.: 2). (ENG.). 400p. (J). (gr. 3-7). pap. 6.99 (978-0-06-221126-2(9), Greenwillow Bks.) HarperCollins Pubs.

Finn, Perdita. Equestria Girls: Friendship Games. 2015. (Equestria Girls Ser.: 5). (ENG., Illus.). 208p. (J). (gr. 3-7). 9.99 (978-0-316-41080-9(2)) Little, Brown Bks. for Young Readers.

Fisch, Sarah. The Smallest Snowman. Durk, Jim, illus. 2006. (J). (978-0-439-81616-8(5)) Scholastic, Inc.

Fontes, Justine. Please Say Please, Grumpy Bunny! McQueen, Lucinda, illus. 2007. (J). (978-0-439-02012-1(3)) Scholastic, Inc.

Franklin, Shirley A. Emma's Fantastique Word Play. 2009. 80p. pap. 8.95 (978-1-4401-3824-9(9)) iUniverse, Inc.

Frazier, Sundee T. The Other Half of My Heart. 2011. (ENG.). 304p. (J). (gr. 3-7). 7.99 (978-0-440-24006-8(9), Yearling) Random Hse. Children's Bks.

Frey, James & Johnson-Shelton, Nils. The Calling. (Endgame Ser.: 1). (ENG.). (gr. 9). 2015. 496p. (YA). pap. 10.99 (978-0-06-233259-2(7)) 2014. 464p. (J). 19.99 (978-0-06-233258-5(9), HarperTeen) HarperCollins Pubs.

—The Complete Training Diaries. 2015. (Endgame: the Training Diaries: Nos. 1-3). (ENG.). 416p. (YA). (gr. 9). pap. 9.99 (978-0-06-233276-9(7)) HarperCollins Pubs.

—Sky Key. 2015. (Endgame Ser.: 2). (ENG.). 512p. (YA). (gr. 9). 19.99 (978-0-06-233261-5(9)) HarperCollins Pubs.

Friedman, Laurie. Mallory & Mary Ann Take New York. Kalis, Jennifer, illus. (Mallory Ser.: 19). (ENG.). 160p. (J). (gr. 2-5). 2014. pap. 5.95 (978-1-4677-0935-4(2), Darby Creek) 2013. 15.95 (978-0-7613-6074-2(3)) Lerner Publishing Group.

Fry, Erin. The Benefactor, 0 vols. 2014. (ENG.). 318p. (YA). (gr. 7-9). pap. 9.99 (978-1-4778-1742-1(5), 9781477817421, Amazon Children's Publishing) Amazon Publishing.

Furgang, Kathy. The Cooking Contest. 2011. (Early Connections Ser.). (J). (978-1-61672-673-7(3)) Benchmark Education Co.

—The Cooking Contest: Set Of 6. 2011. (Early Connections Ser.). (J). pap. 39.00 net. (978-1-4108-1560-6(9)) Benchmark Education Co.

Fussell, Sandy. White Crane. James, Rhian Nest, illus. 2010. (Samurai Kids Ser.: 1). (ENG.). 256p. (J). (gr. 4-7). 15.99 (978-0-7636-4503-8(6)) Candlewick Pr.

Gallagher, Diana G. Guilty! The Complicated Life of Claudia Cristina Cortez, 1 vol. Garvey, Brann, illus. 2007. (Claudia Cristina Cortez Ser.). (ENG.). 88p. (gr. 2-3). per. 6.10 (978-1-59889-881-1(7), Claudia Cristina Cortez) Stone Arch Bks.

—The Pet Store Pet Show, 1 vol. Puglisi, Adriana, illus. 2014. (Pet Friends Forever Ser.). (ENG.). 88p. (gr. 1-3). 25.32 (978-1-4795-2177-7(9)) Picture Window Bks.

Gantos, Jack. Best in Show for Rotten Ralph. Rubel, Nicole, illus. 2008. (Rotten Ralph Rotten Readers Ser.). (J). 25.95 incl. audio (978-1-4301-0448-3(1)); 28.95 incl. audio compact disk (978-1-4301-0451-3(1)) Live Oak Media.

Garber, Stephanie. Caraval. 2017. (SPA.). 432p. pap. 16.95 **(978-607-07-4044-2(0))** Editorial Planeta, S. A. ESP. Dist: Two Rivers Distribution.

—Caraval. 2017. (Caraval Ser.). (ENG.). (YA). 416p. 18.99 (978-1-250-09525-1(5), 9781250095251); (gr. 8-12). pap. 11.99 **(978-1-250-14149-1(4))** Flatiron Bks.

Giusti, Katiuscia. The Clean-Up Contest. 2014. (AV2 Animated Storytime Ser.: Vol. 29). (ENG., Illus.). 32p. (J). (gr. -1-3). lib. bdg. 29.99 (978-1-4896-2299-0(3), AV2 by Weigl) Weigl Pubs., Inc.

Goerzen, Christy. Farmed Out, 1 vol. 2011. (Orca Currents Ser.). (ENG.). 128p. (J). (gr. 5-9). pap. 9.95 (978-1-55469-910-0(X)); lib. bdg. 16.95 (978-1-55469-911-7(8)) Orca Bk. Pubs. USA.

Gowar, Mick. The Pie-Eating Contest. Hall, Francois, illus. 2013. (Start Reading Ser.). (ENG.). 24p. (gr. k-1). pap. 7.95 (978-1-4765-4127-3(2)) Capstone Press of Coughlan Cos.

Grabenstein, Chris. Mr. Lemoncello's Library Olympics. (ENG., (J). (gr. 3-7). 2017. Illus.). 320p. 7.99 **(978-0-553-51042-3(8)**, Yearling) 2016. 288p. 16.99 (978-0-553-51040-9(1), Random Hse. Bks. for Young Readers) 2016. 288p. lib. bdg. 19.99 (978-0-553-51041-6(X), Random Hse. Bks. for Young Readers) Random Hse. Children's Bks.

—Mr. Lemoncello's Library Olympics. 2017. lib. bdg. 18.40 **(978-0-606-39875-6(9))** Turtleback Bks.

Grace, N. B. Battle of the Bands. 2007. (High School Musical Stories from East High Ser.). 142p. (J). (gr. 3-7). 12.65 (978-0-7569-8337-6(1)) Perfection Learning Corp.

Graff, Lisa. Double Dog Dare. (ENG.). (J). (gr. 3-7). 2013. 320p. pap. 7.99 (978-0-14-242412-4(9), Puffin Books) 2012. 304p. 16.99 (978-0-399-25516-8(8), Philomel Bks.) Penguin Young Readers Group.

GrandPré, Mary. Cleonardo, the Little Inventor. 2016. (ENG., Illus.). 48p. (J). (gr. -1-3). 18.99 (978-0-439-35764-7(0)) Scholastic, Inc.

Grau, Sheila. Dr. Critchlore's School for Minions: Polar Distress. Sutphin, Joe, illus. 2017. (Dr. Critchlore's School for Minions Ser.). (ENG.). 288p. (J). (gr. 3-7). 14.95 (978-1-4197-2294-3(8), Amulet Bks.) Abrams, Inc.

Green, Tim. Home Run. 2016. (Baseball Great Ser.: 4). 352p. (J). (gr. 3-7). 16.99 (978-0-06-231711-7(3)) HarperCollins Pubs.

Grigsby, Susan. First Peas to the Table: How Thomas Jefferson Inspired a School Garden. Tadgell, Nicole, illus. 2012. (ENG.). 32p. (J). (gr. 1-3). 16.99 (978-0-8075-2452-7(2)) Whitman, Albert & Co.

Guess, R. J. The Frog That Would Not Jump. 2011. 20p. pap. 24.95 (978-1-4560-0977-9(X)) America Star Bks.

Gurevich, Margaret. Gina's Balance. 2016. (What's Your Dream? Ser.). (ENG., Illus.). 96p. (gr. 3-4). lib. bdg. 25.32 (978-1-4965-3443-9(3)) Capstone Press of Coughlan Cos.

Gutknecht, Allison. Never Wear Red Lipstick on Picture Day: And Other Lessons I've Learned. Lewis, Stevie, illus. 2014. (ENG.). 176p. (J). (gr. 2-5). 16.99 (978-1-4814-2959-7(0)); pap. 6.99 (978-1-4814-2958-0(2)) Simon & Schuster Children's Publishing. (Aladdin).

Gutman, Dan. The Million Dollar Putt. 2007. 69p. (J). (gr. 3-7). 13.65 (978-0-7569-8281-2(2)) Perfection Learning Corp.

—The Million Dollar Shot. 2nd rev. ed. 2006. (ENG.). 128p. (J). (gr. 3-7). pap. 5.99 (978-1-4231-0084-3(0)) Hyperion Pr.

—Miss Brown Is Upside Down! Paillot, Jim, illus. 2015. (My Weirdest School Ser.: 3). (ENG.). 112p. (J). (gr. 1-5). pap. 4.99 (978-0-06-228427-3(4)) HarperCollins Pubs.

Hambrick, Sharon. Brain Games. 2009. (J). 8.99 (978-1-59166-954-8(5)) BJU Pr.

Hamburg, Jennifer. Monkey & Duck Quack Up! Fotheringham, Edwin, illus. 2015. (ENG.). 32p. (J). (gr. -1-3). 17.99 (978-0-545-64514-0(X), Scholastic Pr.) Scholastic, Inc.

Hapka, Cathy, pseud. Lights, Camera, Girl Power! 2013. (ENG.). 64p. (J). (gr. 2-5). pap. 4.99 (978-0-545-51654-9(4)) Math Solutions.

—Lights, Camera, Girl Power! 2013. (LEGO Friends Chapter Bks.: 2). lib. bdg. 14.75 (978-0-606-31550-0(0), Turtleback) Turtleback Bks.

Harkrader, Lisa. The Adventures of Beanboy. 2012. (ENG., Illus.). 240p. (J). (gr. 5-7). 12.99 (978-0-547-55078-7(2)) Houghton Mifflin Harcourt Publishing Co.

Harper, Charise Mericle. Lights, Camera, Cook! Blard-Quintard, Aurélie, illus. 2017. (Next Best Junior Chef Ser.: 1). (ENG.). 192p. (J). (gr. 2-5). 12.99 **(978-0-544-91260-1(8)**, HMH Books For Young Readers) Houghton Mifflin Harcourt Publishing Co.

Harrison, Zac. Robot Warriors, 1 vol. 2013. (Hyperspace High Ser.). (ENG.). 288p. (gr. 4-8). pap. 8.95 (978-1-4342-6312-4(6)); 27.32 (978-1-4342-6308-7(8)) Stone Arch Bks.

Harvey, Pam & Panckridge, Michael. In the Deep End. 2007. 224p. (978-0-207-20064-9(5)) HarperCollins Pubs. Australia.

Herman, Charlotte. My Chocolate Year: A Novel with 12 Recipes. Pham, LeUyen, illus. 2008. (ENG.). 176p. (J). (gr. 3-7). 15.99 (978-1-4169-3341-0(7), Simon & Schuster Bks. For Young Readers) Simon & Schuster Bks. For Young Readers.

Herman, Gail. Scooby-Doo in up, up, & Away!, 1 vol. 2016. (Scooby-Doo! Set 3 Ser.). (ENG., Illus.). 32p. (J). (gr. k-4). lib. bdg. 24.21 (978-1-61479-412-7(X)) Spotlight.

Himes, Rachel. Princess & the Peas. Himes, Rachel, illus. 2017. (ENG., Illus.). 32p. (J). (gr. k-3). 16.99 (978-1-58089-718-1(5)) Charlesbridge Publishing, Inc.

Hockerman, Dennis, illus. The Little Seed: A Tale about Integrity. 2006. (J). (978-1-59939-094-9(9), Reader's Digest Young Families, Inc.) Studio Fun International.

Holm, Jennifer L. & Holm, Matthew. Dragonslayer. Holm, Jennifer L. & Holm, Matthew, illus. 2009. (Babymouse Ser.: 11). (ENG., Illus.). 96p. (J). (gr. 2-5). pap. 6.99 (978-0-375-85712-6(5)); lib. bdg. 12.99 (978-0-375-95712-3(X)) Random Hse. Children's Bks. (Random Hse. Bks. for Young Readers).

Hopkins, Cathy. The Princess of Pop. 2012. (Truth or Dare Ser.). (ENG.). 224p. (YA). (gr. 7). pap. 10.99 (978-1-4424-6057-7(1), Simon Pulse) Simon Pulse.

Ishida, Sanae. Little Kunoichi, the Ninja Girl. 2015. (Little Kunoichi, the Ninja Girl Ser.). (ENG., Illus.). 32p. (J). (gr. -1-2). 16.99 (978-1-57061-954-0(9), Little Bigfoot) Sasquatch Bks.

Jacob, Bill & Fosnot, Catherine Twomey. The California Frog-Jumping Contest - Algebra. 2008. (ENG.). 80p. (gr. 4-5). pap. 31.25 (978-0-325-01024-3(2), E01024, Firsthand) Heinemann.

Jane, Pamela. Winky Blue Goes Wild! Tilley, Debbie, illus. 2003. 64p. (J). 13.95 (978-1-59034-588-7(6)); pap. (978-1-59034-589-4(4)) Mondo Publishing.

Jones, Jen. Maren Loves Luke Lewis. Franco, Paula, illus. 2014. (Sleepover Girls Ser.). (ENG.). 128p. (gr. 3-5). lib. bdg. 22.65 (978-1-4342-9755-6(1)) Stone Arch Bks.

Jones, Melanie Davis. Field Day. Molnar, Albert, illus. 2011. (Rookie Ready to Learn — Out & about: in My Community Ser.). 40p. (J). (gr. -1-k). lib. bdg. 25.00 (978-0-531-27176-6(5)); (ENG.). pap. 5.95 (978-0-531-26826-1(8)) Scholastic Library Publishing. (Children's Pr.).

Joyce, William. Billy's Booger. Joyce, William, illus. 2015. (ENG., Illus.). 40p. (J). (gr. -1-3). 17.99 (978-1-4424-7351-5(7)) Simon & Schuster Children's Publishing.

Kade, Stacey. Project Paper Doll the Trials. 2016. (Project Paper Doll Ser.). (ENG.). 336p. (YA). (gr. 7-12). pap. 9.99 (978-1-4231-9474-3(8)) Hyperion Bks. for Children.

—The Trials. 2015. (Project Paper Doll Ser.). (ENG., Illus.). 336p. (YA). (gr. 7-12). 17.99 (978-1-4231-8463-8(7)) Hyperion Bks. for Children.

Kanellos, Nicolás. El Torneo de Trabalenguas / the Tongue Twister Tournament. Vega, Anne, illus. 2016. (SPA & ENG.). 32p. (J). (gr. k-4). 17.95 (978-1-55885-832-9(6), Piñata Books) Arte Publico Pr.

Kann, Victoria. Tickled Pink. Kann, Victoria, illus. 2010. (Pinkalicious Ser.). (ENG., Illus.). 24p. (J). (gr. -1-3). pap. 3.99 (978-0-06-192877-2(1), HarperFestival) HarperCollins Pubs.

—Tickled Pink. Kann, Victoria, illus. 2010. (Pinkalicious Ser.). (Illus.). (J). lib. bdg. 13.55 (978-0-606-14869-6(8), Turtleback) Turtleback Bks.

Karalius, Kimberly. Love Charms & Other Catastrophes. 2016. (Grimbaud Ser.). (ENG.). 384p. (YA). pap. 10.99 (978-1-250-08404-0(0), 9781250084040) Feiwel & Friends.

Katcher, Brian. The Improbable Theory of Ana & Zak. (YA). (gr. 8). 2016. 352p. pap. 9.99 (978-0-06-227278-2(0)) 2015. (ENG.). 336p. 17.99 (978-0-06-227277-5(2)) HarperCollins Pubs. (Tegen, Katherine Bks).

Keene, Carolyn. Designed for Disaster. Pamintuan, Macky, illus. 2011. (Nancy Drew & the Clue Crew Ser.: 29). (ENG.). 96p. (J). (gr. 1-4). pap. 5.99 (978-1-4169-9439-8(4), Aladdin) Simon & Schuster Children's Publishing.

—Princess Mix-Up Mystery, No. 24. Pamintuan, Macky, illus. 2009. (Nancy Drew & the Clue Crew Ser.: 24). (ENG.). 96p. (J). (gr. 1-4). pap. 5.99 (978-1-4169-7811-4(9), Aladdin) Simon & Schuster Children's Publishing.

Kelley, Marty. Lucky Break. Kelley, Marty, illus. 2017. (Molly Mac Ser.). (ENG., Illus.). 56p. (gr. k-2). lib. bdg. 22.65 (978-1-5158-0837-4(8)) Picture Window Bks.

Kennedy, J. Aday. Stella, the Fire Farting Dragon. Foster, Jack, illus. 2011. 20p. pap. 10.95 (978-1-61633-149-8(6)) Guardian Angel Publishing, Inc.

Kenney, Cindy. Project Precious Paws, Bk. 3. 2009. 86p. (J). pap. 5.99 (978-0-9817159-4-0(X)) Precious Moments, Inc.

Kerr, Philip. The Most Frightening Story Ever Told. 2016. (ENG.). 320p. (J). (gr. 3-7). 16.99 (978-0-553-52209-9(4), Knopf Bks. for Young Readers) Random Hse. Children's Bks.

King, Trey & Kiernan, Kenny. Cops, Crocs, & Crooks! 2015. (Lego City Ser.). (ENG., Illus.). 24p. (J). (gr. -1-3). pap. 3.99 (978-0-545-78525-9(1)) Scholastic, Inc.

Kingsbury, Karen. The Brave Young Knight, 1 vol. Grimard, Gabrielle, illus. 2011. (ENG.). 40p. (J). (gr. -1-2). 15.99 (978-0-310-71645-7(4)) Zonderkidz.

—The Princess & the Three Knights, 1 vol. Grimard, Gabrielle, illus. 2009. (ENG.). 40p. (J). (gr. -1-2). 15.99 (978-0-310-71641-9(1)) Zonderkidz.

Kinra, Richa, illus. The Princess Panda Tea Party: A Cerebral Palsy Fairy Tale. 2014. 45p. (J). pap. 14.95 (978-1-61599-219-5(7)) Loving Healing Pr., Inc.

Klein, Abby. The Reading Race. McKinley, John, illus. 2013. (Ready, Freddy! Ser.: 27). (ENG.). 96p. (J). (gr. 2-5). pap. 5.99 (978-0-545-55044-4(0)) Scholastic, Inc.

Kline, Suzy. Horrible Harry & the Scarlet Scissors. Wummer, Amy, illus. (Horrible Harry Ser.). (ENG.). 80p. (J). (gr. 2-4). 2013. pap. 4.99 (978-0-14-242671-5(7), Puffin Books) 2012. 14.99 (978-0-670-01306-7(4), Viking Books for Young Readers) Penguin Young Readers Group.

Klise, Kate & Klise, M. Sarah. The Greatest Star on Earth. Klise, M. Sarah, illus. 2014. (Three-Ring Rascals Ser.: 2). (ENG., Illus.). 144p. (J). (gr. 2-5). 15.95 (978-1-61620-245-3(9), 73245) Algonquin Bks. of Chapel Hill.

Knight, Richard, et al. Finn at Clee Point. Hurst, Oliver, illus. 2012. (ENG.). 128p. (J). pap. 12.99 *(978-1-84686-401-8(1))* Barefoot Bks., Inc.

Kompelien, Tracy. Leap Frog, 1 vol. Haberstroh, Anne, illus. (Critter Chronicles Ser.). 24p. (J). (gr. k-3). 2007. (ENG.). lib. bdg. 24.21 *(978-1-59928-448-4(0),* SandCastle) 2006. 48.42 *(978-1-59928-449-1(9))* ABDO Publishing Co.

Korelitz, Jean Hanff. Interference Powder, 0 vols. 2006. (ENG.). 146p. (J). (gr. 4-7). pap. 7.99 *(978-0-7614-5275-1(3),* 9780761452751, Amazon Children's Publishing) Amazon Publishing.

—Interference Powder, 1 vol. 2003. (ENG.). 300p. (J). 15.95 *(978-0-7614-5139-6(0))* Marshall Cavendish Corp.

Kroll, Steven. The Biggest Snowman Ever. Bassett, Jeni, illus. 2005. (ENG.). 32p. (J). (gr. -1-3). 4.99 *(978-0-439-62768-9(0),* Cartwheel Bks.) Scholastic, Inc.

—Super-Dragon, 0 vols. Holgate, Doug, illus. 2011. (ENG.). 32p. (J). (gr. -1-2). 16.99 *(978-0-7614-5819-7(0),* 9780761458197, Amazon Children's Publishing) Amazon Publishing.

Krulik, Nancy. Any Way You Slice It. John and Wendy Staff, illus. 9th ed. 2003. (Katie Kazoo, Switcheroo Ser.: 9). (ENG.). 80p. (J). (gr. 2-4). pap. 4.99 *(978-0-448-43204-5(8),* Grosset & Dunlap) Penguin Young Readers Group.

—How Do You Pee in Space? 2014. (George Brown, Class Clown Ser.: 13). lib. bdg. 14.75 *(978-0-606-36163-7(4))* Turtleback Bks.

—What's Black & White & Stinks All Over? Blecha, Aaron, illus. 2011. (George Brown, Class Clown Ser.: 4). (ENG.). 128p. (J). (gr. 2-4). pap. 5.99 *(978-0-448-45370-5(3),* Grosset & Dunlap) Penguin Young Readers Group.

Kulling, Monica & Walker, Nan. The Messiest Room on the Planet. Smath, Jerry, illus. 2009. (Social Studies Connects Ser.). 32p. (J). (gr. k-2). pap. 5.95 *(978-1-57565-282-5(X))* Kane Press, Inc.

Lawrence, Maggie. An Element of Fun. 2008. 76p. pap. 27.95 *(978-1-4092-4969-6(7))* Lulu Pr., Inc.

Leedy, Loreen. The Great Graph Contest. Leedy, Loreen, illus. 2006. (ENG., Illus.). 32p. (J). (gr. -1-3). 7.99 *(978-0-8234-2029-2(9))* Holiday Hse., Inc.

Lin, Grace. The Year of the Dog. 2007. (Pacy Lin Novel Ser.). (ENG., Illus.). 160p. (J). (gr. 3-7). per. 6.99 *(978-0-316-06002-8(X))* Little, Brown Bks. for Young Readers.

—The Year of the Dog. 2007. (Illus.). 134p. (gr. 3-7). 16.00 *(978-0-7569-8143-3(3))* Perfection Learning Corp.

Lindsay, Elizabeth. Bugs & Butterflies. 2012. (Silverlake Fairy School Ser.). 100p. (J). pap. 4.99 *(978-0-7945-3066-2(4),* Usborne) EDC Publishing.

Little, Robert. Fun Day in Mrs. Walker's Class. Galey, Chuck, illus. 2005. 32p. (J). *(978-0-9701863-6-2(3))* Relde Publishing.

Littlewood, Kathryn. A Dash of Magic: A Bliss Novel. McGuire, Erin, illus. 2013. (Bliss Bakery Trilogy Ser.: 2). (ENG.). 368p. (J). (gr. 3-7). 16.99 *(978-0-06-208429-3(1),* Tegen, Katherine Bks) HarperCollins Pubs.

London, Jonathan. Froggy Plays in the Band. Remkiewicz, Frank, illus. 2004. (Froggy Ser.). (J). (gr. -1-3). 13.65 *(978-0-7569-2955-8(5))* Perfection Learning Corp.

Long, Loren & Bildner, Phil. Great Balls of Fire. Long, Loren, illus. 2009. (Sluggers Ser.: 3). (ENG., Illus.). 224p. (J). (gr. 3-7). pap. 7.99 *(978-1-4169-1889-9(2),* Simon & Schuster Bks. For Young Readers) Simon & Schuster Bks. For Young Readers.

Lord, Cynthia. Hot Rod Hamster & the Haunted Halloween Party. Anderson, Derek & Paprocki, Greg, illus. 2015. (Scholastic Reader, Level 2 Ser.). (ENG.). 32p. (J). (gr. k-2). pap. 3.99 *(978-0-545-81528-4(2),* Scholastic Pr.) Scholastic, Inc.

—Hot Rod Hamster & the Haunted Halloween Party! Anderson, Derek, illus. 2015. (ENG.). 32p. (J). (gr. -1-3). 16.99 *(978-0-545-81529-1(0),* Scholastic Pr.) Scholastic, Inc.

Lundquist, Jenny. Plastic Polly. 2013. (Mix Ser.). (ENG.). 256p. (J). (gr. 4-8). pap. 6.99 *(978-1-4424-5248-0(X),* Aladdin) Simon & Schuster Children's Publishing.

Luper, Eric. Jeremy Bender vs. the Cupcake Cadets. 2011. (ENG.). 240p. (J). (gr. 3-7). 16.99 *(978-0-06-201512-9(5))* HarperCollins Pubs.

Lupica, Mike. Million-Dollar Throw. 2010. (ENG.). 272p. (J). (gr. 5-18). 7.99 *(978-0-14-241558-0(8),* Puffin Books) Penguin Young Readers Group.

—Million-Dollar Throw. 2010. (Million Dollar Sports Ser.). lib. bdg. 18.40 *(978-0-606-25316-1(5),* Turtleback) Turtleback Bks.

Maddox, Jake. Skateboard Idol. 2016. (Jake Maddox JV Ser.). (ENG.). 96p. (gr. 3-4). lib. bdg. 25.99 *(978-1-4965-2631-1(7))* Stone Arch Bks.

—Snowboard Hero. 2015. (Jake Maddox JV Ser.). (ENG.). 96p. (gr. 3-4). lib. bdg. 25.99 *(978-1-4342-9636-8(9))* Stone Arch Bks.

Magoon, Kekla. Rebellion of Thieves. 2016. (Robyn Hoodlum Adventure Ser.). (ENG.). 256p. (J). 16.99 *(978-1-61963-655-2(7),* 9781619636552, Bloomsbury USA Childrens) Bloomsbury Publishing USA.

—Rebellion of Thieves. 2017. (Robyn Hoodlum Ser.: 2). (J). lib. bdg. 18.40 ***(978-0-606-40596-6(8))*** Turtleback Bks.

Mahony, Mary. Harry Scores A Hat Trick, Pawns, Pucks, & Scoliosis: The Sequel to Stand Tall, Harry. Pasternack, Susan, ed. Larkin, Catherine, illus. 2003. 130p. (YA). (gr. 5-8). per. 14.95 *(978-0-9658879-3-9(6))* Redding Pr.

Makura, Sho. Panda Man & the Treasure Hunt. Kato, Haruhi, illus. 2011. (ENG.). 96p. (J). (gr. 1-4). pap. 7.99 *(978-1-4215-3521-0(1))* Viz Media.

Mann, Seymour. The Purple Automobile & the Newspaper Girl. 2003. 112p. 20.95 *(978-0-595-66076-6(2));* pap. 10.95 *(978-0-595-29907-2(5))* iUniverse, Inc.

Marshall, Carly. The Babysitter & Little Miss Bossy. 2013. 26p. 24.95 *(978-1-63000-618-1(1));* 28p. pap. 24.95 *(978-1-63000-541-2(X))* America Star Bks.

Marwood, Lorraine. Jamie Wins Again. Hocking, Geoff, illus. 2004. iv, 36p. (J). pap. *(978-0-7608-6743-3(7))* Sundance/Newbridge Educational Publishing.

Mass, Wendy. The Candymakers. (ENG.). (J). (gr. 3-7). 2011. 480p. pap. 9.99 *(978-0-316-00259-2(3))* 2010. 464p. 16.99 *(978-0-316-00258-5(5))* 2015. 480p. 12.99 *(978-0-316-26499-0(7))* Little, Brown Bks. for Young Readers.

—The Candymakers. 2011. (J). lib. bdg. 20.85 *(978-0-606-23448-1(9),* Turtleback) Turtleback Bks.

Mawter, J. A. Launched! 2007. 256p. *(978-0-207-20073-1(4))* HarperCollins Pubs. Australia.

May, Eleanor. The Real Me. Gott, Barry, illus. 2006. (Social Studies Connects). 32p. (J). (gr. k-2). pap. 5.95 *(978-1-57565-186-6(6))* Kane Press, Inc.

May, Kyla. Lulu: My Glamorous Life. 2013. (Lotus Lane Ser.: 3). (ENG.). 96p. (J). (gr. 1-3). 15.99 *(978-0-545-49618-6(7));* pap. 4.99 *(978-0-545-44516-0(7));* E-Book *(978-0-545-49682-7(9))* Scholastic, Inc.

—My Glamorous Life. 2013. (Lotus Lane Ser.: 3). lib. bdg. 14.75 *(978-0-606-32364-2(3),* Turtleback) Turtleback Bks.

Mayer, Mercer. Just a Kite. Mayer, Mercer, illus. 2014. (My First I Can Read Ser.). (ENG., Illus.). 32p. (J). (gr. -1-3). 16.99 *(978-0-06-207197-2(1))* HarperCollins Pubs.

—Little Critter: Just a Kite. Mayer, Mercer, illus. 2014. (My First I Can Read Ser.). (ENG., Illus.). 32p. (J). (gr. -1-3). pap. 3.99 *(978-0-06-147814-7(8))* HarperCollins Pubs.

—Little Critter: Just a Kite 6c Clip Strip. 2014. (ENG.). 100p. (J). 23.94 *(978-0-06-230135-2(7))* HarperCollins Pubs.

McDonald, Kirsten. The Costume Contest. 2016. (Carlos & Carmen Set 3 Ser.). (ENG.). (J). (gr. -1-3). lib. bdg. 27.07 ***(978-1-62402-182-4(4))*** ABDO Publishing Co.

McDonald, Megan. Judy Moody Saves the World! Reynolds, Peter H., illus. 2004. (Judy Moody Ser.: Bk. 3). 144p. (J). (gr. 1-5). 13.65 *(978-0-7569-2588-8(6))* Perfection Learning Corp.

—Judy Moody Saves the World! Reynolds, Peter H., illus. 2010. (Judy Moody Ser.: 3). (ENG.). 160p. (J). (gr. 1-4). 15.99 *(978-0-7636-4860-2(4))* Candlewick Pr.

—Judy Moody Saves the World! 2010. (Judy Moody Ser.: 3). lib. bdg. 16.00 *(978-0-606-12340-2(7),* Turtleback) Turtleback Bks.

—Judy Moody Saves the World!, Bk. 3. Reynolds, Peter H., illus. 2010. (Judy Moody Ser.: 3). (ENG.). 160p. (J). (gr. 1-4). pap. 5.99 *(978-0-7636-4859-6(0))* Candlewick Pr.

—Stink & the World's Worst Super-Stinky Sneakers, Bk. 3. Reynolds, Peter H., illus. 2013. (Stink Ser.: 3). (ENG.). 144p. (J). (gr. 1-4). pap. 4.99 *(978-0-7636-6424-4(3));*Bk. 3. 12.99 *(978-0-7636-6390-2(5))* Candlewick Pr.

—Stink & the World's Worst Super-Stinky Sneakers. Reynolds, Peter H., illus. 2010. (Stink Ser.: No. 3). 144p. (J). (gr. k-4). 24.21 *(978-1-59961-685-8(8))* Spotlight.

—Stink & the World's Worst Super-Stinky Sneakers. 2013. (Stink Ser.: 3). lib. bdg. 14.75 *(978-0-606-31589-0(6),* Turtleback) Turtleback Bks.

—Stink y los Tenis Más Apestosos del Mundo. 2008. (SPA.). 208p. (J). (gr. 3-5). pap. 7.95 *(978-1-60396-195-0(X),* Alfaguara) Santillana USA Publishing Co., Inc.

—The Wishbone Wish. Reynolds, Peter H., illus. 2016. (Judy Moody & Stink Ser.: 4). (ENG.). 116p. (J). (gr. 1-4). lib. bdg. 18.40 *(978-0-606-39093-4(6))* Turtleback Bks.

McLean, Hope. Battle of the Brightest. 2013. 140p. (J). *(978-0-545-48292-9(5))* Scholastic, Inc.

—Jewel Society #4: Battle of the Brightest. 2013. (Jewel Society Ser.: 4). (ENG.). 144p. (J). (gr. 3-7). pap. 5.99 *(978-0-545-60765-0(5),* Scholastic Paperbacks) Scholastic, Inc.

McMahon-Dumas, Carmen E. The Grammie Award, 1 vol. 2009. 38p. pap. 24.95 *(978-1-60836-365-0(1))* America Star Bks.

McMahon, P. J. Case of the Singing Sea Dragons. Manders, John, illus. 2005. 153p. (J). lib. bdg. 15.38 *(978-1-4242-0406-9(2))* Fitzgerald Bks.

McMullan, Kate. Wheel of Misfortune. Basso, Bill, illus. 2003. (Dragon Slayers' Academy Ser.: 7). (ENG.). 112p. (J). (gr. 2-5). pap. 5.99 *(978-0-448-43507-7(1),* Grosset & Dunlap) Penguin Young Readers Group.

—Wheel of Misfortune, 1 vol. Basso, Bill, illus. 2007. (Dragon Slayers' Academy Ser.: No. 7). (ENG.). 109p. (gr. 2-5). 24.21 *(978-1-59961-381-9(6))* Spotlight.

McNamara, Margaret. Clara & the Magical Charms. Denos, Julia, illus. 2013. (Fairy Bell Sisters Ser.: 4). (ENG.). 128p. (J). (gr. 1-5). 15.99 *(978-0-06-222811-6(0));* pap. 4.99 *(978-0-06-222810-9(2))* HarperCollins Pubs.

—The Counting Race. Gordon, Mike, illus. 2003. (Robin Hill School Ser.). (ENG.). 32p. (J). (gr. -1-1). pap. 3.99 *(978-0-689-85539-9(7),* Simon Spotlight) Simon Spotlight.

—The Fairy Bell Sisters No. 3: Golden at the Fancy-Dress Party. Denos, Julia, illus. 2013. (Fairy Bell Sisters Ser.: 3). (ENG.). 144p. (J). (gr. 1-5). pap. 4.99 *(978-0-06-222807-9(2))* HarperCollins Pubs.

—The Fairy Bell Sisters #3: Golden at the Fancy-Dress Party. Denos, Julia, illus. 2013. (Fairy Bell Sisters Ser.: 3). (ENG.). 144p. (J). (gr. 1-5). 15.99 *(978-0-06-222808-6(0))* HarperCollins Pubs.

—Golden at the Fancy-Dress Party. 2013. (Fairy Bell Sisters Ser.: 3). (J). lib. bdg. 14.75 *(978-0-606-32154-9(3),* Turtleback) Turtleback Bks.

Meister, Cari. Buzz Beaker & the Putt-Putt Contest. McGuire, Bill, illus. 2010. (Buzz Beaker Bks.). (ENG.). 32p. (gr. 2-3). pap. 6.25 *(978-1-4342-2799-7(5));* 22.65 *(978-1-4342-2062-2(1))* Stone Arch Bks.

—Ora at the Monster Contest, 1 vol. Messner, Dennis, illus. 2010. (Monster Friends Ser.). (ENG.). 32p. (gr. 2-3). pap. 6.25 *(978-1-4342-2305-0(1));* lib. bdg. 22.65 *(978-1-4342-1875-9(9))* Stone Arch Bks.

Menard, Lucille R. & Menard, Michele R. Inky the Talent Scout. 2013. 38p. pap. 12.75 *(978-0-9891734-2-1(9))* Four Menards, The.

Merola, Caroline. Toni Biscotti's Magic Trick. Cummins, Sarah, tr. from FRE. Merola, Caroline, illus. 2006. (Formac First Novels Ser.: 60). (ENG., Illus.). 64p. (J). (gr. 2-5). 14.95 *(978-0-88780-719-0(4),* 9780887807190); 4.95 *(978-0-88780-715-2(1),* 9780887807152) Formac Publishing Co., Ltd. CAN. Dist: Casemate Pubs. & Bk. Distributors, LLC.

Metzger, Steve. The Great Turkey Race. Paillot, Jim, illus. 2006. (J). *(978-0-439-85930-1(1))* Scholastic, Inc.

Mia's Recipe for Disaster. 2014. (Cupcake Diaries: 22). (ENG., Illus.). 160p. (J). (gr. 3-7). pap. 6.99 *(978-1-4814-1864-5(5),* Simon Spotlight) Simon Spotlight.

Miller, Jennifer. Run, Rasputin, Run! Trials & Friendships (Book 2) 2006. (ENG., Illus.). 172p. per. 14.85 *(978-1-4120-8494-9(6))* Trafford Publishing.

Miller, Sibley. Hungry as a Horse. 2009. (Wind Dancers Ser.: 8). (ENG., Illus.). 80p. (J). (gr. 1-4). pap. 6.99 *(978-0-312-56403-2(1),* 9780312564032) Feiwel & Friends.

Mills, Claudia. Annika Riz, Math Whiz. Shepperson, Rob, illus. 2014. (Franklin School Friends Ser.: 2). (ENG.). 128p. (J). (gr. 2-5). 15.99 *(978-0-374-30335-8(5),* 9780374303358, Farrar, Straus & Giroux (BYR)) Farrar, Straus & Giroux.

—Kelsey Green, Reading Queen, 1 vol. Shepperson, Rob, illus. 2013. (Franklin School Friends Ser.: 1). (ENG.). 128p. (J). (gr. 2-5). 15.99 *(978-0-374-37485-3(6),* 9780374374853, Farrar, Straus & Giroux (BYR)) Farrar, Straus & Giroux.

—Kelsey Green, Reading Queen. Shepperson, Rob, illus. 2014. (Franklin School Friends Ser.: 1). (ENG.). 144p. (J). (gr. 2-5). pap. 5.99 *(978-1-250-03405-2(1),* 9781250034052) Square Fish.

Mongredien, Sue. Oliver Moon & the Broomstick Battle. 2011. (Oliver Moon Ser.). 94p. (J). pap. 4.99 *(978-0-7945-3038-9(9),* Usborne) EDC Publishing.

Moulton, Erin E. Chasing the Milky Way. 2014. (ENG.). 288p. (J). (gr. 3-7). 16.99 *(978-0-399-16449-1(9),* Philomel Bks.) Penguin Young Readers Group.

Munsch, Robert. More Pies. Martchenko, Michael, illus. 2004. (J). (gr. k-3). spiral bd. *(978-0-616-14590-6(X))* Canadian National Institute for the Blind/Institut National Canadien pour les Aveugles.

—The Sandcastle Contest. 2007. 15.00 *(978-0-7569-7690-3(1))* Perfection Learning Corp.

Myers, Kate Kae. Inherit Midnight. (ENG.). (YA). 2016. 416p. pap. 9.99 *(978-1-61963-936-2(X),* 9781619639362) 2015. 400p. (gr. 7). 17.99 *(978-1-61963-219-6(5),* 9781619632196) Bloomsbury Publishing USA. (Bloomsbury USA Childrens).

Nance, Andrew. Return to Daemon Hall: Evil Roots. Polhemus, Coleman, illus. 2011. (ENG.). 256p. (YA). (gr. 7-12). 18.99 *(978-0-8050-8748-2(6),* Holt, Henry & Co. Bks. For Young Readers) Holt, Henry & Co.

Nathan, Sarah. Blue-Ribbon Bunny. 2014. (Sofia the First World of Reading Ser.). (J). lib. bdg. 13.55 *(978-0-606-35264-2(3))* Turtleback Bks.

Nathan, Sarah & Disney Book Group Staff. Blue Ribbon Bunny, Level 1. Disney Storybook Art Team, illus. 2014. (World of Reading Ser.). (ENG.). 32p. (J). (gr. -1-k). pap. 3.99 *(978-1-4231-7158-4(6))* Disney Pr.

Nelson, Suzanne. Cake Pop Crush. (J). 2016. (ENG.). 256p. (gr. 4-7). pap. 6.99 *(978-0-545-85734-5(1),* Scholastic Paperbacks) 2013. 247p. *(978-0-545-50389-1(2))* Scholastic, Inc.

Nolan, Allia Zobel. Fair & Squaresville: A Lesson in Playing Fair. Carter, Tod et al, illus. 2014. (VeggieTales (Big Idea) Ser.). (ENG.). 28p. (J). (gr. -1-3). pap. 6.99 incl. audio compact disk *(978-1-61795-333-0(4))* Worthy Publishing.

Ocean, Davy. Splash Dance. Blecha, Aaron, illus. 2015. (Shark School Ser.: 6). (ENG.). 128p. (J). (gr. 1-4). pap. 5.99 *(978-1-4814-0694-9(9),* Aladdin) Simon & Schuster Children's Publishing.

O'Connor, Barbara. Fame & Glory in Freedom, Georgia. 2008. (ENG.). 112p. (J). (gr. 3-7). pap. 8.99 *(978-0-374-40018-7(0),* 9780374400187) Square Fish.

O'Connor, Jane. Fancy Nancy's Fashion Parade! Reusable Sticker Book. Glasser, Robin Preiss & Bracken, Carolyn, illus. 2008. (Fancy Nancy Ser.). (ENG.). 12p. (J). (gr. -1-2). pap. 6.99 *(978-0-06-123601-3(2),* HarperFestival) HarperCollins Pubs.

Pankhurst, Kate. Mariella Mystery Investigates a Cupcake Conundrum. 2014. (Mariella Mysteries Ser.). (ENG., Illus.). 176p. (J). (gr. 2-6). pap. 5.99 *(978-1-4380-0459-4(1))* Barron's Educational Series, Inc.

Parish, Herman. Amelia Bedelia Bakes Off. Sweat, Lynn, illus. 2010. (I Can Read Level 2 Ser.). 64p. (J). (gr. k-3). (ENG.). pap. 3.99 *(978-0-06-084360-1(8));* (ENG.). 17.99 *(978-0-06-084358-8(6));* lib. bdg. 18.89 *(978-0-06-084359-5(4))* HarperCollins Pubs. (Greenwillow Bks.).

Park, Linda Sue. The Kite Fighters. 2010. (ENG., Illus.). 144p. (J). (gr. 2-5). pap. 7.99 *(978-0-547-32863-8(X))* Houghton Mifflin Harcourt Publishing Co.

Parker, Emma & Renaud, Marguerite. The Honey Bee Race. 2010. (Illus.). 16p. pap. *(978-1-877561-78-8(9))* First Edition Ltd.

Pass, Erica. Hooray for Dads! 2014. (SpongeBob Squarepants 8X8 Ser.). lib. bdg. 14.75 *(978-0-606-35560-5(X))* Turtleback Bks.

Pastis, Stephan. Now Look What You've Done. 2016. (Timmy Failure Ser.: 2). lib. bdg. 18.40 *(978-0-606-37947-2(9))* Turtleback Bks.

Patterson, James & Grabenstein, Chris. I Even Funnier: A Middle School Story. Park, Laura, illus. 2013. (I Funny Ser.: 2). (ENG.). 368p. (J). (gr. 3-7). 13.99 *(978-0-316-20697-6(0),* Jimmy Patterson) Little Brown & Co.

—I Totally Funniest: A Middle School Story. Park, Laura, illus. 2015. (J). 320p. *(978-0-316-26161-6(0));* (ENG.). 336p. (gr. 3-7). 13.99 *(978-0-316-40593-5(0),* Jimmy Patterson) Little Brown & Co.

Peirce, Lincoln. Big Nate on a Roll. Peirce, Lincoln, illus. 2011. (Big Nate Ser.: 3). (Illus.). 224p. (J). (gr. 3-7). (ENG.). 12.99 *(978-0-06-194438-3(6));* lib. bdg. 14.89 *(978-0-06-194439-0(4))* HarperCollins Pubs.

—What Could Possibly Go Wrong? Peirce, Lincoln, illus. 2012. (Big Nate Comix Ser.: 1). (ENG., Illus.). 224p. (J). (gr. 3-7). pap. 9.99 *(978-0-06-208694-5(4))* HarperCollins Pubs.

Perelman, Helen. Sweet Secrets. Waters, Erica-Jane, illus. 2015. (Candy Fairies Ser.: 15). (ENG.). 128p. (J). (gr. 2-5). pap. 5.99 *(978-1-4814-0610-9(8),* Aladdin) Simon & Schuster Children's Publishing.

Peschke, Marci. Cooking Queen. Mourning, Tuesday, illus. 2017. (Kylie Jean Ser.). (ENG.). 112p. (gr. 2-3). lib. bdg. 22.65 ***(978-1-4795-9899-1(2),*** Kylie Jean) Picture Window Bks.

—Hoop Queen, 1 vol. Mourning, Tuesday, illus. 2011. (Kylie Jean Ser.). (ENG.). 112p. (gr. 2-3). lib. bdg. 22.65 *(978-1-4048-5962-3(4),* Kylie Jean) Picture Window Bks.

—Hoop Queen, 1 vol. Mourning, Tuesday, illus. 2011. (Kylie Jean Ser.). (ENG.). 112p. (gr. 2-3). pap. 5.95 *(978-1-4048-6617-1(5),* Kylie Jean) Picture Window Bks.

—Rodeo Queen, 1 vol. Mourning, Tuesday, illus. 2011. (Kylie Jean Ser.). (ENG.). 112p. (gr. 2-3). pap. 5.95 *(978-1-4048-6618-8(3));* lib. bdg. 22.65 *(978-1-4048-5961-6(6))* Picture Window Bks. (Kylie Jean).

Petrucha, Stefan & Kinney, Sarah. High School Musical Mystery. 2010. (Nancy Drew Graphic Novels: Girl Detective Ser.). (ENG., Illus.). 96p. (J). (gr. 3-7). pap. 8.99 *(978-1-59707-178-9(1),* 9781597071789) Papercutz.

—Nancy Drew: High School Musical Mystery II - "The Lost Verse" 2010. (Nancy Drew Graphic Novels: Girl Detective Ser.). (ENG., Illus.). 96p. (J). (gr. 3-7). pap. 8.99 *(978-1-59707-195-6(1),* 9781597071956) Papercutz.

Pierce, Seth J. The Day the School Blew Up. 2009. (J). pap. 12.99 *(978-0-8163-2329-6(1))* Pacific Pr. Publishing Assn.

Polacco, Patricia. Picnic at Mudsock Meadow. 2009. (ENG.). 32p. (J). (gr. k-3). pap. 7.99 *(978-0-14-241392-0(5),* Puffin Books) Penguin Young Readers Group.

—Rotten Richie & the Ultimate Dare. Polacco, Patricia, illus. 2006. (ENG., Illus.). 48p. (J). (gr. k-3). 17.99 *(978-0-399-24531-2(6),* Philomel Bks.) Penguin Young Readers Group.

Posner-Sanchez, Andrea. The Pirate Games. Random House Disney Staff, illus. 2012. (Little Golden Book Ser.). (ENG.). 24p. (J). (-k). 4.99 *(978-0-7364-3028-9(8),* Golden/Disney) Random Hse. Children's Bks.

Pounder, Sibéal. Witch Wars. Anderson, Laura Ellen, illus. 2016. (Witch Wars Ser.). (ENG.). 272p. (J). 16.99 *(978-1-61963-925-6(4),* 9781619639256, Bloomsbury USA Childrens) Bloomsbury Publishing USA.

—Witch Wars. Anderson, Laura Ellen, illus. 2017. (Witch Wars Ser.). (ENG.). 288p. (J). pap. 7.99 *(978-1-68119-296-3(9),* 9781681192963, Bloomsbury USA Childrens) Bloomsbury Publishing USA.

Prineas, Sarah. Summerkin. 2013. (Summerlands Ser.: 2). (ENG.). (J). (gr. 3-7). 288p. pap. 6.99 *(978-0-06-192108-7(4));* 272p. 16.99 *(978-0-06-192106-3(8))* HarperCollins Pubs.

Pulver, Robin. Nouns & Verbs Have a Field Day. Reed, Lynn Rowe, illus. 2007. (ENG.). 32p. (J). (gr. -1-3). 7.99 *(978-0-8234-2097-1(3))* Holiday Hse., Inc.

—Nouns & Verbs Have a Field Day. Reed, Lynn Rowe, illus. 2013. pap. 18.95 incl. audio compact disk *(978-1-4301-1115-3(1))* Live Oak Media.

Random House. Hooray for Dads! (SpongeBob SquarePants) Random House, illus. 2014. (Pictureback(R) Ser.). (ENG., Illus.). 24p. (J). (gr. -1-2). 4.99 *(978-0-385-37607-5(3),* Random Hse. Bks. for Young Readers) Random Hse. Children's Bks.

Random House Staff. SpongeBob's Easter Parade (SpongeBob SquarePants) Random House Staff, illus. 2013. (Pictureback(R) Ser.). (ENG., Illus.). 24p. (J). (gr. -1-2). pap. 3.99 *(978-0-449-81444-4(0),* Random Hse. Bks. for Young Readers) Random Hse. Children's Bks.

Rebecca, Rebecca. The Turtle Who Did His Best. 2016. (ENG., Illus.). 26p. pap. 5.99 *(978-1-61984-471-1(0))* Price World Publishing.

Reynolds, Aaron. Tiger Moth & the Dragon Kite Contest. Lervold, Erik, illus. 2006. (Tiger Moth Ser.). (ENG.). 40p. (gr. 1-3). per. 5.95 *(978-1-59889-229-1(0),* Graphic Sparks) Stone Arch Bks.

Reynolds, Paul A. & Reynolds, Peter H. Going Places. Reynolds, Peter H., illus. 2014. (ENG., Illus.). 40p. (J). (gr. -1-3). 17.99 *(978-1-4424-6608-1(1),* Atheneum Bks. for Young Readers) Simon & Schuster Children's Publishing.

Riddell, Chris. Goth Girl & the Wuthering Fright. 2017. (Goth Girl Ser.: 3). (ENG., Illus.). 224p. (J). (gr. 2-6). 14.99 *(978-1-4472-7789-7(9))* Pan Macmillan GBR. Dist: Independent Pubs. Group.

Rosenberg, Aaron. Case of the Topsy-Turvy Toy. Harrington, David, illus. 2011. (Pete & Penny's Pizza Puzzles Ser.: 2). (ENG.). 64p. (J). (gr. 1-3). pap. 3.99 *(978-0-8431-9929-1(6),* Price Stern Sloan) Penguin Young Readers Group.

Roy, James. Chaz, Superbarf Surprise. Gorissen, Dean, illus. 2015. (J). pap. *(978-1-4966-0239-8(0))* Capstone Classroom.

—Chaz, TV Superstar? Gorissen, Dean, illus. 2015. (J). pap. *(978-1-4966-0257-2(9))* Capstone Classroom.

Rucker, Mike. Terry & the Elephant. pap. *(978-1-56002-746-1(0))* Univ. Editions.

Salem, Iosi, illus. The Mr. Mentch Coloring Book. 2008. (J). (gr. -1-3). 6.95 *(978-1-934440-37-7(X),* Pitspopany Pr.) Simcha Media Group.

Salzmann, Mary Elizabeth. Goldfish Bowl, 1 vol. Chawla, Neena, illus. 2006. (Animal Tales Ser.). (ENG.). 24p. (J). (gr. k-3). lib. bdg. 24.21 *(978-1-59679-939-4(0),* SandCastle) ABDO Publishing Co.

—Goldfish Bowl (6-pack) Chawla, Neena, illus. 2006. (Fact & Fiction Ser.). 24p. (J). pap. 59.57 *(978-1-59679-940-0(4))* ABDO Publishing Co.

—Presidential Seal, 1 vol. 2007. (Critter Chronicles Ser.). (ENG., Illus.). 24p. (J). (gr. k-3). lib. bdg. 24.21 *(978-1-59928-464-4(2),* SandCastle) ABDO Publishing Co.

Schaefer, Laura. The Secret Ingredient. Rim, Sujean, illus. (ENG.). 240p. (J). (gr. 4-8). 2012. pap. 6.99 *(978-1-4424-1960-5(1))* 2011. 15.99 *(978-1-4424-1959-9(8))* Simon & Schuster/Paula Wiseman Bks. (Simon & Schuster/Paula Wiseman Bks.).

Scheunemann, Pam. El Bolígrafo del Cerdo, 1 vol. Nobens, C. A., illus. 2007. (Cuentos de Animales Ser.). (SPA & ENG.). 24p. (J). (gr. k-3). lib. bdg. 24.21 *(978-1-59928-659-4(9),* SandCastle) ABDO Publishing Co.

—Pig Pens, 1 vol. Nobens, Cheryl A., illus. 2006. (Animal Tales Ser.). (ENG.). 24p. (J). (gr. k-3). lib. bdg. 24.21 *(978-1-59679-959-2(5),* SandCastle) ABDO Publishing Co.

—Pig Pens. Nobens, C. A., illus. 2006. (Fact & Fiction Ser.). 24p. (J). pap. 48.42 *(978-1-59679-960-8(9))* ABDO Publishing Co.

Scholastic, Inc. Staff & Simon, Jenne. Welcome to Shopville. Scholastic, Inc. Staff, illus. 2015. (Shopkins Ser.). (ENG., Illus.). 24p. (J). (gr. -1-3). pap. 3.99 *(978-0-545-84228-0(X))* Scholastic, Inc.

Schraff, Anne. The Fairest. 2011. (Urban Underground — Harriet Tubman High School Ser.). (YA). lib. bdg. 20.80 *(978-0-606-14813-9(2),* Turtleback) Turtleback Bks.

Schroeder, Lisa. It's Raining Cupcakes. (ENG., Illus.). 208p. (J). (gr. 3-7). 2011. pap. 6.99 *(978-1-4169-9085-7(2))* 2010. 17.99 *(978-1-4169-9084-0(4))* Simon & Schuster Children's Publishing. (Aladdin).

Scott, Victoria. Fire & Flood. 2014. (ENG.). 320p. (J). (gr. 9). 17.99 *(978-0-545-53746-9(0),* Scholastic Pr.) Scholastic, Inc.
—Salt & Stone. 2015. (ENG.). 320p. (J). (gr. 7). 17.99 *(978-0-545-53748-3(7),* Scholastic Pr.) Scholastic, Inc.
Self, Jeffery. Drag Teen. 2016. (ENG.). 272p. (YA). (gr. 9). 17.99 *(978-0-545-82993-9(3),* PUSH) Scholastic, Inc.
Sharpe, Luke. Billy Sure, Kid Entrepreneur. Ross, Graham, illus. 2015. (Billy Sure Kid Entrepreneur Ser.: 1). (ENG.). 160p. (J). (gr. 3-7). pap. 6.99 *(978-1-4814-3947-3(2),* Simon Spotlight) Simon Spotlight.
Siegal, Ida. Party Drama! (Emma Is on the Air #2) 2015. (Emma Is on the Air Ser.: 2). (ENG.). 128p. (J). (gr. 2-5). pap. 4.99 *(978-0-545-68695-2(4),* Scholastic Paperbacks) Scholastic, Inc.
Simon, Coco. Mia's Recipe for Disaster. 2014. (Cupcake Diaries: 22). lib. bdg. 17.20 *(978-0-606-36098-2(0))* Turtleback Bks.
Simon, Francesca. Horrid Henry & the Abominable Snowman, 1 vol. Ross, Tony, illus. 2012. (Horrid Henry Ser.). (ENG.). 112p. (J). (gr. 2-5). lib. bdg. 24.21 *(978-1-59961-186-0(4))* Spotlight.
Sise, Katie. The Boyfriend App. 2013. (ENG.). 320p. (YA). (gr. 8). 17.99 *(978-0-06-219526-5(3))* HarperCollins Pubs.
—The Pretty App. 2015. (ENG.). 352p. (YA). (gr. 8). 17.99 *(978-0-06-219529-6(8))* HarperCollins Pubs.
Sividious Stark & the Stadium Between Worlds. 2013. (ENG.). 236p. (YA). pap. 12.99 *(978-1-62108-273-6(3))* Covenant Communications, Inc.
Sky Koster, Amy & Tillworth, Mary. The Knight Night Guard. Random House Disney Staff, illus. 2016. (Step into Reading Ser.). (ENG.). 24p. (J). (gr. -1-1). 4.99 *(978-0-7364-3450-8(X),* RH/Disney) Random Hse. Children's Bks.
Small, Lily. Penelope the Pony. 2017. (Fairy Animals of Misty Wood Ser.). (ENG., Illus.). 144p. (J). pap. 5.99 ***(978-1-250-12700-6(9),*** 9781250127006, Holt, Henry & Co. Bks. For Young Readers) Holt, Henry & Co.
Spohn, Kate. Turtle & Snake's Day at the Beach. Spohn, Kate, illus. 2004. (Penguin Young Readers, Level 2 Ser.). (ENG., Illus.). 32p. (J). (gr. 1-2). mass mkt. 3.99 *(978-0-14-240157-6(9),* Penguin Young Readers) Penguin Young Readers Group.
—Turtle & Snake's Day at the Beach. Spohn, Kate, illus. 2004. (Puffin Easy-to-Read Ser.). (Illus.). 32p. (gr. k-3). 14.00 *(978-0-7569-2826-1(5))* Perfection Learning Corp.
Staunton, Ted. Power Chord, 1 vol. 2011. (Orca Currents Ser.). (ENG.). 128p. (J). (gr. 5-9). pap. 9.95 *(978-1-55469-903-2(7));* lib. bdg. 16.95 *(978-1-55469-904-9(5))* Orca Bk. Pubs. USA.
Stellings, Caroline. The Contest, 1 vol. 2009. (ENG.). 160p. (J). (gr. 4-7). pap. 9.95 *(978-0-9779183-5-5(1),* 7th Generation) Book Publishing Co.
Stern, Ricki & Worcester, Heidi P. Adventure: Lonely Leader. Bates, Amy, illus. 2003. (Beryl E. Bean Ser.: No. 3). 64p. (J). lib. bdg. 16.89 *(978-0-06-028774-0(8))* HarperCollins Pubs.
Stilton, Geronimo. Don't Wake the Dinosaur! 2014. (Geronimo Stilton Cavemice Ser.: 6). (ENG.). 128p. (J). (gr. 2-5). pap. 7.99 *(978-0-545-65603-0(6),* Scholastic Paperbacks) Scholastic, Inc.
—Don't Wake the Dinosaur! 2014. (Geronimo Stilton Cavemice Ser.: 6). lib. bdg. 18.40 *(978-0-606-36057-9(3))* Turtleback Bks.
—Fright Night. 2013. (Creepella Von Cacklefur Ser.: 5). (ENG.). 128p. (J). (gr. 2-5). pap. 7.99 *(978-0-545-39349-2(3),* Scholastic Paperbacks) Scholastic, Inc.
—Super Chef Contest. 2014. (ENG., Illus.). 128p. (J). (gr. 2-5). pap. 7.99 *(978-0-545-65600-9(1),* Scholastic Paperbacks) Scholastic, Inc.
—The Super Chef Contest. 2014. (Geronimo Stilton Ser.: 58). lib. bdg. 18.40 *(978-0-606-36056-2(5))* Turtleback Bks.
Stine, R. L. The Big Blueberry Barf-Off! Park, Trip, illus. 2005. (Rotten School Ser.: No. 1). 128p. (J). (ENG.). 6.99 *(978-0-06-078586-4(1));* lib. bdg. 14.89 *(978-0-06-078587-1(X))* HarperCollins Pubs.
—The Big Blueberry Barf-Off! Park, Trip, illus. 2008. (Rotten School Ser.: 1). (ENG.). 128p. (J). (gr. 3-7). pap. 5.99 *(978-0-06-078588-8(8))* HarperCollins Pubs.
—Night of the Creepy Things. Park, Trip, illus. (Rotten School Ser.: Bk. 14). 4.99 *(978-0-06-123274-9(2))* HarperCollins Pubs.
—Punk'd & Skunked, 1 vol. Park, Trip, illus. 2011. (Rotten School Ser.: No. 11). (ENG.). 128p. (gr. 2-5). 24.21 *(978-1-59961-835-7(4))* Spotlight.
—Rotten School #15: Calling All Birdbrains. Park, Trip, illus. 4.99 *(978-0-06-123277-0(7))* HarperCollins Pubs.
—Shake, Rattle, & Hurl! Park, Trip, illus. 2008. (Rotten School Ser.: 5). (ENG.). 128p. (J). (gr. 3-7). pap. 5.99 *(978-0-06-078813-1(5))* HarperCollins Pubs.
—The Teacher from Heck, 1 vol. Park, Trip, illus. 2011. (Rotten School Ser.: No. 8). (ENG.). 128p. (gr. 2-5). 24.21 *(978-1-59961-832-6(X))* Spotlight.
Style Guide, Style, illus. The Dragon Games. 2015. (How to Train Your Dragon TV Ser.). (ENG.). 24p. (J). (gr. -1-3). pap. 3.99 *(978-1-4814-3288-7(5),* Simon Spotlight) Simon Spotlight.
The Sugar Cup. 2014. (Candy Fairies Ser.: 14). (ENG., Illus.). 128p. (J). (gr. 2-5). pap. 5.99 *(978-1-4814-0607-9(8),* Aladdin) Simon & Schuster Children's Publishing.
The Sugar Cup. 2014. (Candy Fairies Ser.: 14). (ENG., Illus.). 128p. (J). (gr. 2-5). 16.99 *(978-1-4814-0608-6(6),* Simon & Schuster/Paula Wiseman Bks.) Simon & Schuster/Paula Wiseman Bks.
Sullivan, Dana. Ozzie & the Art Contest. Sullivan, Dana, illus. 2013. (ENG., Illus.). 15.99 *(978-1-58536-820-4(2))* Sleeping Bear Pr.
Sylvester, Kevin. Neil Flambé & the Crusader's Curse. Sylvester, Kevin, illus. (Neil Flambe Capers Ser.: 3). (ENG., Illus.). (J). (gr. 3-7). 2014. 320p. pap. 7.99 *(978-1-4424-4287-0(5))* 2012. 304p. 13.99 *(978-1-4424-4286-3(7))* Simon & Schuster Bks. For Young Readers. (Simon & Schuster Bks. For Young Readers).
Tabor, Corey R. Fox & the Jumping Contest. Tabor, Corey R., illus. 2016. (Illus.). 32p. (J). (gr. -1-3). 17.99 *(978-0-06-239874-1(1))* HarperCollins Pubs.
Tanen, Sloane. Are You Going to Kiss Me Now? 2011. (ENG.). 368p. (YA). (gr. 8-12). pap. 8.99 *(978-1-4022-5461-1(X))* Sourcebooks, Inc.
Terrell, Brandon. Fearless, 1 vol. Cano, Fernando, illus. 2014. (Tony Hawk: Live2Skate Ser.). (ENG.). 72p. (gr. 4-5). 25.32 *(978-1-4342-9141-7(3),* Tony Hawk's 900 Revolution) Stone Arch Bks.
—Science Fair Sabotage. Epelbaum, Mariano, illus. 2017. (Snoops, Inc Ser.). (ENG.). 112p. (gr. 4-6). lib. bdg. 26.65 *(978-1-4965-4347-9(5))* Stone Arch Bks.
—The Vanishing Treasure. Epelbaum, Mariano, illus. 2017. (Snoops, Inc Ser.). (ENG.). 112p. (gr. 4-6). lib. bdg. 26.65 *(978-1-4965-4345-5(9))* Stone Arch Bks.
Thaler, Mike. The Field Day from the Black Lagoon. Lee, Jared, illus. 2008. (From the Black Lagoon Ser.). 64p. (gr. 2-5). 14.00 *(978-0-7569-8801-2(2))* Perfection Learning Corp.
—The Field Day from the Black Lagoon. Lee, Jared, illus. 2008. (Black Lagoon Adventures Ser.: 6). (ENG.). 64p. (J). (gr. 2-5). pap. 4.99 *(978-0-439-68076-9(X))* Scholastic, Inc.
—The Reading Challenge from the Black Lagoon. Lee, Jared D., illus. 2015. 64p. (J). pap. *(978-0-545-78521-1(9))* Scholastic, Inc.
Thompson, Colin. The Floods #2: School Plot. Scrambly, Crab, illus. 2008. (Floods Ser.). (J). (ENG.). 224p. 15.99 *(978-0-06-113861-4(4));* 256p. lib. bdg. 16.89 *(978-0-06-113855-3(X))* HarperCollins Pubs.
Thorpe, Kiki. A Pinch of Magic. Christy, Jana, illus. 2014. (Never Girls Ser.: No. 7). (ENG.). 128p. (J). (gr. 1-4). 5.99 *(978-0-7364-3097-5(0),* RH/Disney) Random Hse. Children's Bks.
—A Pinch of Magic. 2014. (Never Girls Ser.: 7). lib. bdg. 16.00 *(978-0-606-36008-1(5))* Turtleback Bks.
Tidwell, Susan. Little Lotus & the Loving-Kindness Cup. Lee, Wei-Chun, illus. 2012. 77p. (J). 6.95 *(978-1-932293-72-2(8))* Buddha's Light Publications USA Corp.
TJ & the Mysterious Stranger. 2004. (J). bds. 16.95 *(978-0-9710487-2-0(X))* Highlights of Chicago Pr.
Tolan, Stephanie S. & Tolan, R. J. Applewhites Coast to Coast. 2017. 320p. (J). (gr. 3-7). 16.99 ***(978-0-06-213320-5(9))*** HarperCollins Pubs.
Trailblazers! Individual Title Six-Packs. (Action Packs Ser.). 104p. (gr. 3-5). 44.00 *(978-0-7635-2992-5(3))* Rigby Education.
Viguié, Debbie. Violet Eyes. 2010. (Once upon a Time Ser.). (ENG.). 224p. (YA). (gr. 7-18). mass mkt. 7.99 *(978-1-4169-8676-8(6),* Simon Pulse) Simon Pulse.
Walker, Nan & Kulling, Monica. The Messiest Room on the Planet. 2009. (Social Studies Connects (r) Ser.). (ENG.). (gr. k-2). pap. 33.92 *(978-0-7613-4803-0(4))* Lerner Publishing Group.
Watts, Frances. Heroes of the Year. Watson, Judy, illus. 2012. (ENG.). 80p. (J). pap. 6.00 *(978-0-8028-5412-4(5),* Eerdmans Bks For Young Readers) Eerdmans, William B. Publishing Co.
Wheeler, Lisa. Dino-Dancing. Gott, Barry, illus. 2017. (ENG.). 32p. (J). (gr. k-3). lib. bdg. 17.99 ***(978-1-5124-0316-9(4),*** Carolrhoda Bks.) Lerner Publishing Group.
White, Andrea. Surviving Antarctica: Reality TV 2083. 2006. (ENG.). 448p. (YA). (gr. 8). pap. 8.99 *(978-0-06-055456-9(8),* HarperTeen) 2005. 336p. (J). (gr. 7-18). 16.99 *(978-0-06-055454-5(1),* HarperCollins) HarperCollins Pubs.
Whittemore, Jo. Colonial Madness. 2015. (ENG., Illus.). 240p. (J). (gr. 4-8). 17.99 *(978-1-4814-0508-9(X),* Aladdin) Simon & Schuster Children's Publishing.
Wittlinger, Ellen. This Means War! 2010. (ENG.). 224p. (J). (gr. 5-9). 16.99 *(978-1-4169-7101-6(7),* Simon & Schuster Bks. For Young Readers) Simon & Schuster Bks. For Young Readers.
Wolitzer, Meg. The Fingertips of Duncan Dorfman. 2012. (ENG.). 304p. (J). (gr. 3-7). pap. 7.99 *(978-0-14-242204-5(5),* Puffin Books) Penguin Young Readers Group.
Young, Jessica. Original Recipe. Secheret, Jessica, illus. 2015. (Finley Flowers Ser.). (ENG.). 128p. (J). (gr. 2-3). 8.95 *(978-1-4795-5878-0(8),* Finley Flowers) Picture Window Bks.
Zail, Suzy. Lulu. Hill, Trish, illus. 2004. iv, 36p. (J). pap. *(978-0-7608-6741-9(0))* Sundance/Newbridge Educational Publishing.
Zimmer, Frank. Bird Singing Contest. 2008. 28p. pap. 13.99 *(978-1-4343-7971-9(X))* AuthorHouse.

CONTINENTAL DRIFT

Harris, Nicolas. Dinosaurs Through Time. Dennis, Peter, illus. 2009. (Fast Forward Ser.). 32p. (YA). (gr. 2-5). lib. bdg. 25.25 *(978-1-4358-2802-5(X))* Rosen Publishing Group, Inc., The.

CONTRACEPTION

see Birth Control

CONTRACTIONS

see Ciphers

CONUNDRUMS

see Riddles

CONVICTS

see Criminals; Prisons

COOK, JAMES, 1728-1779

Beales, R. A. James Cook: The Pacific Coast & Beyond. 2005. (In the Footsteps of Explorers Ser.). (ENG., Illus.). 32p. (J). (gr. 4-5). pap. *(978-0-7787-2451-3(4));* lib. bdg. *(978-0-7787-2415-5(8))* Crabtree Publishing Co.
Bowen, Richard. Captain James Cook: British Explorer. (Illus.). 32p. (J). 2013. (People of Importance Ser.: 21). (gr. 4-18). 19.95 *(978-1-4222-2843-2(6))* 2004. (Great Names Ser.). (gr. 3-18). lib. bdg. 19.95 *(978-1-59084-147-1(6))* Mason Crest.
Dalrymple, Lisa. Explore with James Cook. 2015. (Travel with the Great Explorers Ser.). (ENG., Illus.). 32p. (J). (gr. 3-6). *(978-0-7787-1701-0(1))* Crabtree Publishing Co.
Feinstein, Stephen. Captain Cook: Great Explorer of the Pacific. 2010. (Great Explorers of the World Ser.). (Illus.). 112p. (J). (gr. 7-12). 33.27 *(978-1-59845-102-3(2))* Enslow Pubs., Inc.
Lace, William W. Captain James Cook. 2009. (Great Explorers Ser.). (Illus.). 112p. (gr. 6-12). 30.00 *(978-1-60413-416-2(X),* Chelsea Hse.) Facts On File, Inc.
Meyer, Susan. James Cook. 2016. (Spotlight on Explorers & Colonization Ser.). 00048p. (J). (gr. 6-6). pap. 11.75 *(978-1-5081-7232-1(3))* Rosen Publishing Group, Inc., The.
Morriss, Roger. Captain Cook & His Exploration of the Pacific. 2010. (History of Exploration Ser.). 48p. 32.80 *(978-1-84898-303-8(4))* Black Rabbit Bks.
Ollhoff, Jim. Captain Cook. 2013. (Great Explorers Ser.). 32p. (gr. 5-9). lib. bdg. 27.07 *(978-1-61783-965-8(5),* Abdo & Daughters) ABDO Publishing Co.
Petrie, Kristin. James Cook, 1 vol. 2004. (Explorers Set 1 Ser.). (ENG., Illus.). 32p. (gr. k-6). 27.07 *(978-1-59197-596-0(4),* Checkerboard Library) ABDO Publishing Co.
Rosen, Michael J. Sailing the Unknown. Pritelli, Maria Cristina, illus. 2014. (ENG.). 40p. (J). (gr. 1-3). pap. 12.00 *(978-0-89812-976-2(1),* Creative Paperbacks) Creative Co., The.

COOK, JAMES, 1728-1779—FICTION

Eyre, David & Kalahele, Imaikalani. Floating Islands. 2009. 35p. 14.95 *(978-0-87336-216-0(0))* Kamehameha Publishing.
Hesse, Karen. Stowaway. unabr. ed. 2004. 328p. (J). (gr. 5-9). pap. 48.00 incl. audio *(978-0-8072-8760-6(1),* LYA 259 SP, Listening Library) Random Hse. Audio Publishing Group.
Rosen, Michael J. Sailing the Unknown: Around the World with Captain Cook. Pritelli, Maria Cristina, illus. 2012. (ENG.). 40p. (J). (gr. 1-3). 19.99 *(978-1-56846-216-5(6),* Creative Editions) Creative Co., The.

COOK BOOKS

see Cooking

COOKBOOKS

see Cooking

COOKERY

see Cooking

COOKIES

Besel, Jennifer M. Baking Bliss! Baked Desserts to Make & Devour, 1 vol. 2014. (Custom Confections Ser.). (ENG., Illus.). 48p. (gr. 4-5). lib. bdg. 31.99 *(978-1-4914-0859-9(6))* Capstone Press of Coughlan Cos.
Blake, Susannah. Cookies & Cakes. 2009. (Make & Eat Ser.). (ENG.). 24p. (J). (gr. 3-5). pap. 9.40 *(978-1-4358-2933-6(6),* PowerKids Pr.) Rosen Publishing Group, Inc., The.
—Cookies & Cakes. Crawford, Andy, photos by. 2009. (Make & Eat Ser.). (Illus.). 24p. (J). (gr. 3-5). 25.25 *(978-1-4358-2859-9(3),* PowerKids Pr.) Rosen Publishing Group, Inc., The.
Boon, Fiona, ed. The Great Fairy Baking Competition. Ede, Lara, illus. Snaith, Andy, photos by. 2013. (ENG.). 64p. (J). 12.99 *(978-1-78235-591-5(X))* Make Believe Ideas GBR. Dist: Nelson, Thomas Inc.
Cornell, Kari. Sweet Cookies & Bars. Cohen, Brie, photos by. 2013. (You're the Chef Ser.). (ENG., Illus.). 32p. (gr. 3-5). lib. bdg. 26.60 *(978-0-7613-6638-6(5),* Millbrook Pr.) Lerner Publishing Group.
Goodman, Susan E. All in Just One Cookie. Bush, Timothy, illus. 2006. (ENG.). 32p. (J). (gr. -1-4). 17.99 *(978-0-06-009092-0(8),* Greenwillow Bks.) HarperCollins Pubs.
Haste, Dianne. C C Cookie Bear's Cookbook. 2009. 68p. pap. 24.49 *(978-1-4389-5450-9(6))* AuthorHouse.
Holloway, Jamie. We Make Art for Christmas. 2015. (Rosen REAL Readers: STEM & STEAM Collection). (ENG.). 8p. pap. 5.46 *(978-1-4994-9739-7(3),* Rosen Classroom) Rosen Publishing Group, Inc., The.
Joyal, Kristen. Baking with Mommy Cookbook: Recipes for Kid-Size Ovens 10th Anniversary Edition. 2011. 121p. (J). spiral bd. 13.95 *(978-0-9718515-6-6(5))* Straight Forward Technologies.
Kuskowski, Alex. Super Simple Classic Cookies: Easy Cookie Recipes for Kids!, 1 vol. 2016. (Super Simple Cookies Ser.). (ENG., Illus.). 32p. (J). (gr. k-4). 27.07 *(978-1-62403-947-8(2))* ABDO Publishing Co.
—Super Simple Healthy Cookies: Easy Cookie Recipes for Kids!, 1 vol. 2016. (Super Simple Cookies Ser.). (ENG., Illus.). 32p. (J). (gr. k-4). 27.07 *(978-1-62403-948-5(0))* ABDO Publishing Co.
—Super Simple Holiday Cookies: Easy Cookie Recipes for Kids!, 1 vol. 2016. (Super Simple Cookies Ser.). (ENG., Illus.). 32p. (J). (gr. k-4). 27.07 *(978-1-62403-949-2(9))* ABDO Publishing Co.
—Super Simple No-Bake Cookies: Easy Cookie Recipes for Kids!, 1 vol. 2016. (Super Simple Cookies Ser.). (ENG., Illus.). 32p. (J). (gr. k-4). 27.07 *(978-1-62403-950-8(2))* ABDO Publishing Co.
—Super Simple Specialty Cookies: Easy Cookie Recipes for Kids!, 1 vol. 2016. (Super Simple Cookies Ser.). (ENG., Illus.). 32p. (J). (gr. k-4). 27.07 *(978-1-62403-951-5(0))* ABDO Publishing Co.
LaPenta, Marilyn. Cool Cookies. 2011. (Yummy Tummy Recipes Ser.). 24p. (J). (gr. 1-4). lib. bdg. 22.61 *(978-1-61772-308-7(8))* Bearport Publishing Co., Inc.
Larrew, Brekka Hervey. Apple Pie Calzones & Other Cookie Recipes, 1 vol. 2008. (Fun Foods for Cool Cooks Ser.). (ENG., Illus.). 32p. (gr. 3-4). 27.99 *(978-1-4296-1336-1(X),* Snap Bks.) Capstone Press of Coughlan Cos.
Meachen Rau, Dana. Cookies. 2008. (What's Cooking? Ser.). 24p. (gr. k-1). lib. bdg. 15.95 *(978-0-7614-2890-9(9),* Benchmark Bks.) Marshall Cavendish Corp.
—Galletas. 2008. (Qué Preparamos Hoy? Ser.). (SPA.). 24p. (gr. k-1). lib. bdg. 15.95 *(978-0-7614-3435-1(6),* Benchmark Bks.) Marshall Cavendish Corp.
Nathan, Helen. Flossie Crums & the Enchanted Cookie Tree: A Flossie Crums Baking Adventure. Stevenson, Daryl, illus. 2012. (Flossie Crums Ser.). (ENG.). 56p. (J). (gr. k-2). pap. 8.99 *(978-1-84365-197-0(1),* Pavilion Children's Books) Pavilion Bks. GBR. Dist: Independent Pubs. Group.
Nettles, Granny Sarah A. I Baked Cookies at Granny's House. 2012. 16p. pap. 15.99 *(978-1-4772-6695-3(X))* AuthorHouse.
Price, Pamela S. Cool Cookies & Bars: Easy Recipes for Kids to Bake, 1 vol. 2010. (Cool Baking Ser.). (ENG.). 32p. (gr. 3-6). 28.50 *(978-1-60453-775-8(2),* Checkerboard Library) ABDO Publishing Co.
Rau, Dana Meachen. Smart Cookie: Designing Creative Cookies, 1 vol. 2012. (Dessert Designer Ser.). (ENG., Illus.). 32p. (gr. 3-4). lib. bdg. 27.99 *(978-1-4296-8619-8(7),* Snap Bks.) Capstone Press of Coughlan Cos.
Shannon, George. Who Put the Cookies in the Cookie Jar? Paschkis, Julie, illus. 2013. (ENG.). 32p. (J). (gr. -1-1). 17.99 *(978-0-8050-9197-7(1),* 9780805091977, Holt, Henry & Co. Bks. For Young Readers) Holt, Henry & Co.
Sullivan, Erin. Cookie Count! 2011. (Early Connections Ser.). (J). *(978-1-61672-632-4(6))* Benchmark Education Co.
Wellington, Monica. Color & Cook CHRISTMAS COOKIES. 2009. (Dover Coloring Bks.). (ENG., Illus.). 32p. (J). (gr. -1-3). pap. 4.99 *(978-0-486-47448-9(8))* Dover Pubns., Inc.
Young, Bev. Presidential Cookies. 2nd ed. 2005. Orig. Title: Presidential Cookies the Lure & the Lore. (ENG., Illus.). 168p. (YA). 23.95 *(978-0-9729095-3-2(2),* SAN 255-1077) Presidential Publishing.

COOKING

see also Baking; Bread; Coffee; Confectionery; Desserts; Diet; Food; Menus; Outdoor Cooking; Pastry; Salads; Sandwiches; Soups

Abdo Publishing. Cool Recipes for Your Health, 1 vol. 2013. (Cool Recipes for Your Health Ser.: 6). (ENG.). 32p. (J). (gr. 3-6). lib. bdg. 171.00 *(978-1-61783-580-3(3),* Checkerboard Library) ABDO Publishing Co.
ABDO Publishing Company Staff. Cool Cupcakes & Muffins. 2014. (Cool Cupcakes & Muffins Ser.: 6). (ENG.). 32p. (gr. 8-12). lib. bdg. 171.00 *(978-1-62403-298-1(2),* Checkerboard Library) ABDO Publishing Co.
—Cool Young Chefs. 2014. (Cool Young Chefs Ser.: 6). (ENG.). 32p. (gr. 3-6). lib. bdg. 171.00 *(978-1-62403-084-0(X),* Checkerboard Library) ABDO Publishing Co.
—Food Dudes Set 2. 2014. (Food Dudes Set 2 Ser.: 6). (ENG.). 32p. (gr. 8-12). lib. bdg. 162.42 *(978-1-62403-313-1(X),* Checkerboard Library) ABDO Publishing Co.
Allegri, Natasha. Easy Eats: a Bee & PuppyCat Cookbook. 2016. (Bee & PuppyCat Ser.: 1). (ENG., Illus.). 96p. 16.95 *(978-1-4215-8805-6(6))* Viz Media.
Allred, Erin. 5-Alarm Cookbook: For Those Who Just Can't Get It Hot Enough. 2003. (YA). spiral bd. 9.95 *(978-1-885027-22-1(2))* Apricot Pr.
American Girl Editorial Staff. Coconut Cookbook: Fun & Fluffy Treats to Eat. 2004. (ENG., Illus.). 32p. (J). 7.95 *(978-1-58485-892-8(3))* American Girl Publishing, Inc.
American Girl Editors & Richards, Mary, eds. Oodles of Sweet Stuff. 2011. (ENG.). 80p. (J). spiral bd. 12.95 *(978-1-59369-826-3(7))* American Girl Publishing, Inc.
Ancona, George. Mis Comidas - My Foods. 2005. (Somos Latinos (We Are Latinos) Ser.). (ENG & SPA., Illus.). 32p. (J). (gr. 1-3). lib. bdg. 21.00 *(978-0-516-25292-6(5),* Children's Pr.) Scholastic Library Publishing.
Anderson, Joanna. Cooking with My Dad: Number Names & Count Sequence. 2013. (InfoMax Math Readers Ser.). (ENG.). 16p. (J). (gr. k-1). pap. 42.00 *(978-1-4777-1998-5(9));* (Illus.). pap. 7.00 *(978-1-4777-1997-8(0))* Rosen Publishing Group, Inc., The. (Rosen Classroom).
Anderson, Sara. Sara's Kitchen. 2009. (Illus.). 32p. (J). 16.95 *(978-0-8118-6684-2(X))* Chronicle Bks. LLC.
Andrews McMeel Publishing Staff & Broadhurst, Lucy. Ready, Steady, Spaghetti: Cooking for Kids & with Kids. 2009. (ENG.). 192p. pap. 19.99 *(978-0-7407-8087-5(5))* Andrews McMeel Publishing.
Arroyo, Sheri, et al. How Chefs Use Math. 2009. (Math in the Real World Ser.). 32p. (gr. 4-6). 28.00 *(978-1-60413-608-1(1),* Chelsea Clubhouse) Facts On File, Inc.
Askew, Amanda & Crowson, Andrew. Chef. 2012. (Illus.). 24p. (gr. 1-3). pap. 7.95 *(978-1-926853-46-8(6))* Saunders Bk. Co. CAN. Dist: RiverStream Publishing.
Auld, Mary. Sharing a Meal. 2011. (My Family & Me Ser.). (Illus.). 24p. (J). lib. bdg. 24.25 *(978-1-59771-231-6(0))* Sea-To-Sea Pubns.
Austin, Judi. Making My Breakfast: Learning the Sequential Steps of a Process. 2009. (Math for the REAL World Ser.). 12p. (gr. 1-2). pap. 5.90 *(978-0-8239-8889-1(9),* Rosen Classroom) Rosen Publishing Group, Inc., The.
Baines, Emily Ansara. The Unofficial Hunger Games Cookbook: From Lamb Stew to Groosling - More Than 150 Recipes Inspired by the Hunger Games Trilogy. 2011. (Unofficial Cookbook Ser.). (ENG.). 256p. 12.99 *(978-1-4405-2658-9(3))* Adams Media Corp.
Baker, Linda R. Using Math in Cooking. 2017. (Math You Will Actually Use Ser.). 48p. (J). (gr. 10-10). pap. 11.75 ***(978-1-4994-3856-7(7),*** Rosen Central) Rosen Publishing Group, Inc., The.
Baking Day: Individual Title Six-Packs. (gr. 1-2). 22.00 *(978-0-7635-9168-7(8))* Rigby Education.
Barasch, Lynne. Hiromi's Hands, 1 vol. Barasch, Lynne, illus. 2007. (ENG., Illus.). 40p. (J). (gr. k-6). 18.95 *(978-1-58430-275-9(5))* Lee & Low Bks., Inc.
Barlow, Melissa. Noodlemania! 50 Playful Pasta Recipes. 2013. (ENG., Illus.). 112p. (J). (gr. 1-4). pap. 15.95 *(978-1-59474-617-8(6))* Quirk Bks.
Barrett, Judi. Grandpa's Cloudy with a Chance of Meatballs Cookbook. Barrett, Ronald, illus. 2013. (ENG.). 64p. (J). (gr. -1-3). spiral bd. 17.99 *(978-1-4424-4475-1(4),* Atheneum Bks. for Young Readers) Simon & Schuster Children's Publishing.
Batmanglij, Najmieh. Happy Nowruz: Cooking with Children to Celebrate the Persian New Year. 2008. (ENG., Illus.). 120p. spiral bd. 40.00 *(978-1-933823-16-4(X))* Mage Pubs., Inc.
Beach, Mark. Simply in Season Children's Cookbook: A World Community Cookbook. 2006. (World Community Cookbook Ser.). (ENG., Illus.). 88p. (J). (gr. 3-7). 24.99 *(978-0-8361-9336-7(9))* Herald Pr.
Beaton, Clare. My Book of Things to Make & Do. 2007. (ENG., Illus.). 96p. (J). (gr. 1-4). pap. 15.99 *(978-1-902915-95-1(X))* B Small Publishing GBR. Dist: Independent Pubs. Group.
Beckett, Leslie. Native American Recipes. 2017. (J). (gr. 3-3). 24p. 27.25 ***(978-1-5345-2094-3(5));*** 24p. pap. 10.60 ***(978-1-5345-2092-9(9));*** pap. 63.60 ***(978-1-5345-2093-6(7))*** Greenhaven Publishing LLC. (KidHaven Publishing).
Bedell, J. M. So, You Want to Be a Chef? How to Get Started in the World of Culinary Arts. 2013. (Be What You Want Ser.). (ENG., Illus.). 224p. (J). (gr. 3-7). pap. 9.99 *(978-1-58270-436-4(8))* Aladdin/Beyond Words.
Beery, Barbara. Barbara Beery's Pink Princess Party Cookbook. Williams, Zac, photos by. 2011. (ENG., Illus.). 64p. (J). (gr. 2-7). spiral bd. 15.99 *(978-1-4424-1231-6(3),*

C
D

Simon & Schuster Bks. For Young Readers) Simon & Schuster Bks. For Young Readers.

—Fairies Cookbook, 1 vol. 2007. (ENG., Illus.). 64p. (J). (gr. 4-7). 14.99 *(978-1-4236-0290-3(0))* Gibbs Smith, Publisher.

—Mermaid Cookbook, 1 vol. Shultz, Kirsten, photos by. 2008. (ENG., Illus.). 64p. (J). (gr. 1). spiral bd. 14.99 *(978-1-4236-0417-4(2))* Gibbs Smith, Publisher.

—Spa Princess Cookbook, 1 vol. 2008. (ENG., Illus.). 64p. (J). (gr. 1). spiral bd. 14.99 *(978-1-4236-0502-7(0))* Gibbs Smith, Publisher.

Behnke, Alison. Cooking the Middle Eastern Way. 2nd rev. ed. 2005. (Easy Menu Ethnic Cookbooks 2nd Edition Ser.). (ENG., Illus.). 72p. (gr. 5-12). lib. bdg. 25.26 *(978-0-8225-1238-7(6)*, Lerner Pubns.) Lerner Publishing Group.

Behnke, Alison & Duro, Karin L. Cooking the Brazilian Way. 2nd rev. ed. 2004. (Easy Menu Ethnic Cookbooks 2nd Edition Ser.). (ENG., Illus.). 72p. (gr. 5-12). lib. bdg. 25.26 *(978-0-8225-4111-0(4))* Lerner Publishing Group.

Behnke, Alison, et al. Cooking the Mediterranean Way. 2nd rev. ed. 2005. (Easy Menu Ethnic Cookbooks 2nd Edition Ser.). (ENG., Illus.). 72p. (gr. 5-12). 25.26 *(978-0-8225-1237-0(8)*, Lerner Pubns.) Lerner Publishing Group.

Bellisario, Gina. Choose Good Food! My Eating Tips. Conger, Holli, illus. 2014. (Cloverleaf Books — My Healthy Habits Ser.). (ENG.). 24p. (gr. k-2). lib. bdg. 23.93 *(978-1-4677-1350-4(3)*, Millbrook Pr.) Lerner Publishing Group.

Bennett, Meagan, des. Pancakes! Pancakes!, an Interactive Recipe Book. 2016. (Cook in a Book Ser.). (ENG., Illus.). 16p. 14.95 *(978-0-7148-7282-7(2))* Phaidon Pr., Inc.

Berenstain, Mike. The Berenstain Bears' Country Cookbook: Cub-Friendly Cooking with an Adult, 1 vol. 2015. (Berenstain Bears/Living Lights Ser.). (ENG., Illus.). 96p. (J). 12.99 *(978-0-310-74720-8(1))* Zonderkidz.

Besel, Jennifer M. Baking Bliss! Baked Desserts to Make & Devour, 1 vol. 2014. (Custom Confections Ser.). (ENG., Illus.). 48p. (gr. 4-5). lib. bdg. 31.99 *(978-1-4914-0859-9(6))* Capstone Press of Coughlan Cos.

Better Homes and Gardens Books Staff. New Junior Cookbook. 8th ed. 2012. (Better Homes & Gardens Cooking Ser.: 66). (ENG., Illus.). 128p. spiral bd. 16.99 *(978-1-118-14606-4(9))* Houghton Mifflin Harcourt Publishing Co.

Betty Crocker, Betty. Betty Crocker Kids Cook. 2015. (Betty Crocker Cooking Ser.). (ENG., Illus.). 160p. spiral bd. 19.99 *(978-0-544-57002-3(2)*, Betty Crocker) Houghton Mifflin Harcourt Publishing Co.

Betty Crocker Editors. Betty Crocker's Cookbook for Boys & Girls. fac. ed. 2003. (Betty Crocker Cooking Ser.). (ENG., Illus.). 192p. 16.95 *(978-0-7645-2634-3(0))* Houghton Mifflin Harcourt Publishing Co.

Bird, Fiona. Kids' Kitchen: 40 Fun & Healthy Recipes to Make & Share. Arenson, Roberta, illus. 2009. (ENG.). 40p. (J). (gr. 3-18). 19.99 *(978-1-84686-176-5(4))* Barefoot Bks., Inc.

Black, Rosemary. Sweet Celebrations: A Holiday Dessert Book for Kids. (Illus.). (J). pap. *(978-0-312-31023-3(4))*; mass mkt. *(978-0-312-98759-6(5))* St. Martin's Pr. (St. Martin's Paperbacks).

Blackstone, Stella. Making Minestrone. Brooks, Nan, illus. 2006. 32p. (J). (gr. k-4). reprint ed. 16.00 *(978-0-7567-9926-7(0))* DIANE Publishing Co.

Blake, Susannah. Vegetarian Dishes. 2009. (Make & Eat Ser.). (ENG., Illus.). 24p. (J). (gr. 3-5). pap. 9.40 *(978-1-4358-2934-3(4)*, PowerKids Pr.) Rosen Publishing Group, Inc., The.

—Vegetarian Food. Crawford, Andy, photos by. 2009. (Make & Eat Ser.). (Illus.). 24p. (J). (gr. 3-5). 25.25 *(978-1-4358-2860-5(7)*, PowerKids Pr.) Rosen Publishing Group, Inc., The.

Bolte, Mari. Awesome Recipes You Can Make & Share, 1 vol. Franco, Paula, illus. 2014. (Sleepover Girls Crafts Ser.). (ENG.). 32p. (gr. 3-4). 27.99 *(978-1-4914-1733-1(1)*, Snap Bks.) Capstone Press of Coughlan Cos.

—In Good Taste: Great Gifts to Make, Eat, & Share. 2015. (Make It, Gift It Ser.). (ENG., Illus.). 32p. (gr. 3-4). lib. bdg. 27.99 *(978-1-4914-5200-4(5)*, Snap Bks.) Capstone Press of Coughlan Cos.

Boothroyd, Jennifer. How I Pack My Lunch. 2014. (First Step Nonfiction - Responsibility in Action Ser.). (ENG., Illus.). 24p. (gr. k-2). lib. bdg. 23.93 *(978-1-4677-3635-0(X)*, Lerner Pubns.) Lerner Publishing Group.

—Taste Something New! Giving Different Foods a Try. 2016. (Lightning Bolt Books — Healthy Eating Ser.). (ENG., Illus.). 32p. (J). (gr. 1-3). 26.65 *(978-1-4677-9472-5(4)*, Lerner Pubns.) Lerner Publishing Group.

Boyee, Claire & Hains, Harriet. First Cook Book. 2003. (J). bds. 5.98 *(978-0-7525-8921-3(0))* Parragon, Inc.

Brash, Lorna. Professor Cook's Dynamite Dinners. 2013. (Professor Cook's... Ser.). 32p. (J). (gr. 4-12). pap. 7.95 *(978-1-4644-0547-1(6))*; (Illus.). lib. bdg. 23.94 *(978-0-7660-4301-5(0))* Enslow Pubs., Inc.

—Professor Cook's Fruity Desserts. 2013. (Professor Cook's... Ser.). 32p. (J). lib. bdg. 23.94 *(978-0-7660-4302-2(9))* Enslow Pubs., Inc.

—Professor Cook's Mind-Blowing Baking. 2013. (Professor Cook's... Ser.). (Illus.). 32p. (J). lib. bdg. 23.94 *(978-0-7660-4303-9(7))* Enslow Pubs., Inc.

—Professor Cook's Smashing Snacks. 2013. (Professor Cook's... Ser.). 32p. (J). lib. bdg. 23.94 *(978-0-7660-4304-6(5))*; (gr. 4-12). pap. 7.95 *(978-1-4644-0553-2(0))* Enslow Pubs., Inc.

Bugni, Alice. Beluga Whales, Grizzly Tales, & More Alaska Kidsnacks: Fun Recipes for Cooking with Kids. Brooks, Erik, illus. 2016. (Paws IV Ser.). (ENG.). 32p. (J). (gr. -1-2). pap. 10.99 *(978-1-57061-999-1(9)*, Little Bigfoot) Sasquatch Bks.

Bulloch, Ivan. Watch It Cook. James, Diane, illus. 2004. (I Can Do It Ser.). 32p. (J). (gr. 2-5). 12.95 *(978-1-58728-510-3(X)*, Two-Can Publishing) T&N Children's Publishing.

Butler, Daphne. What Happens When Food Cooks? 2004. (Illus.). 31p. (J). (gr. k-4). reprint ed. 10.00 *(978-0-7567-7561-2(2))* DIANE Publishing Co.

Butterworth, Chris. How Did That Get in My Lunchbox? The Story of Food. Gaggiotti, Lucia, illus. 2013. (Exploring the Everyday Ser.). (ENG.). 32p. (J). (gr. k-3). 5.99 *(978-0-7636-6503-6(7))* Candlewick Pr.

Canas-Jovel, Lourdes E. & Acock, Anthony W. Little Vegan Monsters' Cookbook. Schiller, Caitlin, ed. 2006. (J). per. 19.95 *(978-0-9787590-3-2(6))* Little Vegan Monsters Publishing.

Carew-Miller, Anna. Native American Cooking. Johnson, Troy, ed. 2013. (Native American Life Ser.: 15). 64p. (J). (gr. 5-18). 19.95 *(978-1-4222-2968-2(8))* Mason Crest.

Carle, Meghan, et al. Teens Cook: How to Cook What You Want to Eat. 2004. (ENG., Illus.). 160p. (YA). (gr. 7). 19.99 *(978-1-58008-584-7(9)*, Ten Speed Pr.) Potter/TenSpeed/Harmony.

Carlota's Cooking Class: Fourth Grade Guided Comprehension Level K. (On Our Way to English Ser.). (gr. 4-18). 34.50 *(978-0-7578-7147-4(X))* Rigby Education.

Celebrity Chefs: Set 2. 2016. (Celebrity Chefs Ser.). 128p. (gr. 6-6). lib. bdg. 149.08 *(978-0-7660-7509-2(5))* Enslow Pubs., Inc.

Chanko, Pamela. Follow-The-Directions Flip Chart: No-Cook Recipes: 12 Healthy, Month-By-Month Recipes with Fun Activities That Teach Young Learners How to Listen & Follow Directions. 2013. (ENG., Illus.). 24p. (-1). pap. 25.99 *(978-0-545-44270-1(2)*, Teaching Resources) Scholastic, Inc.

Chilson, Martin. Carmen Cooks Healthy! Represent & Solve Problems Involving Division. 2014. (Math Masters: Operations & Algebraic Thinking Ser.). 24p. (J). (gr. 3-4). 23.60 *(978-1-4777-6410-7(0))*; (ENG.). pap. 8.25 *(978-1-4777-4965-4(9))* Rosen Publishing Group, Inc., The. (Rosen Classroom).

CICO Kidz Staff, compiled by. My First Cookbook: 35 Fun & Easy Recipes for Children 7 Years + 2014. (ENG., Illus.). 128p. (J). (gr. 7-11). pap. 14.95 *(978-1-78249-102-6(3)*, CICO Books) Ryland Peters & Small GBR. Dist: WIPRO.

Clegg, Holly. Holly Clegg's Trim & Terrific Freezer Friendly Meals: Quick & Healthy Recipes You Can Make in Advance. Humphreys, David, photos by. 2006. (ENG., Illus.). 304p. 19.95 *(978-0-7624-2597-6(0))* Running Pr. Bk. Pubs.

Cobb, Vicki. Science Experiments You Can Eat. Carpenter, Tad, illus. 2016. 256p. (J). (gr. 3-7). pap. 9.99 *(978-0-06-237729-6(9))* HarperCollins Pubs.

Cohn, Jessica. On the Job in a Restaurant. Scheuer, Lauren, illus. 2016. (Core Content Social Studies — on the Job Ser.). (ENG.). 32p. (J). (gr. 2-5). lib. bdg. 26.65 *(978-1-63440-110-4(7))* Red Chair Pr.

Collister, Linda. Cooking with Kids. Davies, Vanessa, photos by. (Illus.). 128p. 2007. per. *(978-1-84597-488-6(3))* 2003. (ENG., (gr. 6-11). tchr. ed. *(978-1-84172-498-0(X))* Ryland Peters & Small.

Conger, Holli, intro. Little Chef. 2007. 5p. bds. 8.95 *(978-1-58117-597-4(3)*, Intervisual/Piggy Toes) Bendon, Inc.

Cook, Deanna F. Cooking Class: 50 Fun Recipes Kids Will Love to Make (and Eat!) 2015. (ENG., Illus.). 144p. (J). (gr. 3-6). spiral bd. 18.95 *(978-1-61212-400-1(3)*, 622400) Storey Publishing, LLC.

—The Kids' Multicultural Cookbook: Food & Fun Around the World. Kline, Michael P., illus. 2008. (ENG.). 160p. (J). (gr. k). per. 12.99 *(978-0-8249-6818-2(2)*, Ideal Pubns.) Worthy Publishing.

Cooking Around the World. 2013. (Cooking Around the World Ser.). 32p. (J). (gr. 3-6). 159.00 *(978-1-4777-1552-9(5))*; pap. 70.50 *(978-1-4777-2697-6(7))*; pap. 423.00 *(978-1-4777-2698-3(5))* Rosen Publishing Group, Inc., The. (PowerKids Pr.).

Cooking Books for Children, 6 bks. (J). lib. bdg. 104.70 *(978-1-56674-903-9(4))* Forest Hse. Publishing Co., Inc.

Cooking with Mickey & Friends Cookbook. 2005. (ENG., Illus.). 32p. pap. 9.99 *(978-0-7868-4425-8(6))* Disney Pr.

Cornell, Kari. Marvelous Muffins, Breads, & Pancakes. Cohen, Brie, photos by. 2013. (You're the Chef Ser.). (ENG., Illus.). 32p. (gr. 3-5). lib. bdg. 26.60 *(978-0-7613-6636-2(9)*, Millbrook Pr.) Lerner Publishing Group.

Cornell, Kari & Thomas, Peter. Cooking the Southern African Way. 2nd rev. ed. 2005. (Easy Menu Ethnic Cookbooks 2nd Edition Ser.). (ENG., Illus.). 72p. (gr. 5-12). 25.26 *(978-0-8225-1239-4(4)*, Lerner Pubns.) Lerner Publishing Group.

Cosgrove, Stephen & Higgins, Kitty, told to. The Tasty Tort Trial. 2004. (Reader's Theater Ser.). (J). pap. *(978-1-4108-1144-8(1))* Benchmark Education Co.

CQ Products Staff. Candy Creations: Sweet Treats to Build & Eat! 2012. (ENG., Illus.). 60p. (J). spiral bd. 12.00 *(978-1-56383-421-9(9))* G & R Publishing.

—Fake-Out Food: Wacky Treats to Fool Your Friends! 2010. (ENG.). 64p. spiral bd. 12.00 *(978-1-56383-383-0(2))* G & R Publishing.

Crabtree, Marc. Meet My Neighbor, the Chef. 2009. (Meet my Neighbor Ser.). (ENG., Illus.). 24p. (J). (gr. k-2). pap. *(978-0-7787-4581-5(3))*; lib. bdg. *(978-0-7787-4571-6(6))* Crabtree Publishing Co.

Cramer, Lisa. My Kids Can't Cook Book. 2005. spiral bd. 24.95 *(978-1-932252-47-7(9))* Creative Continuum, Inc.

Cruz, Abel. Juguitos para Ninos.Tr. of Juices for Kids. (SPA.). 9.98 *(978-970-643-350-3(3))* Selector, S.A. de C.V. MEX. Dist: AIMS International Bks., Inc.

Curry, Ella I. Ella's Little Cookbook. 2003. 71p. (YA). pap. 9.95 *(978-0-7414-1536-3(4))* Infinity Publishing.

Dale, Jay. Cooking in Class, 1 vol. Robledo, Emilia, illus. 2012. (Wonder Words Ser.). (ENG.). 32p. (gr. k-2). pap. 5.99 *(978-1-4296-8922-9(6)*, Engage Literacy) Capstone Press of Coughlan Cos.

Dambra, Marianne E. Cooking Is Cool: Heat-Free Recipes for Kids to Cook. 2013. (ENG., Illus.). 144p. pap. 24.95 *(978-1-60554-158-7(3))* Redleaf Pr.

Dann, Penny. My Big Rainy Day Activity Book. Smee, Nicola, illus. 2004. 96p. (J). act. bk. ed. 7.99 *(978-1-85854-554-7(4))* Brimax Books Ltd. GBR. Dist: Byeway Bks.

David C. Cook Publishing Company Staff. The Shooting Star Drive-in Snack Guide. 2007. (Vacation Bible School Ser.). 24p. (J). (gr. 3-12). pap. 6.99 *(978-1-4347-9958-6(1))* Cook, David C.

Davis, Robin & Starr, Lara. Wookiee Pies, Clone Scones, & Other Galactic Goodies. 2012. (ENG., Illus.). 64p. (J). (gr. -1-17). 22.99 *(978-1-4521-0466-9(2))* Chronicle Bks. LLC.

Davis, Tina. Look & Cook: A Cookbook for Children. 2004. (ENG., Illus.). 160p. (gr. 8-17). 24.95 *(978-1-58479-358-8(9))* Stewart, Tabori & Chang.

Dawson, Emily C. Cooking. 2010. (Everyday Science Ser.). 24p. (J). (gr. k-3). 25.65 *(978-1-60753-020-6(1))* Amicus Publishing.

de Las Casas, Dianne & Eliana, Kid. Cool Kids Cook: Fresh & Fit, 1 vol. Lisette, Soleil, illus. 2014. (ENG.). 64p. (J). (gr. 3-7). 14.95 *(978-1-4556-1892-7(6))* Pelican Publishing Co., Inc.

de Mariaffi, Elisabeth. Eat It Up! Lip-Smacking Recipes for Kids. Stephens, Jay, illus. 2004. 88p. 15.95 *(978-2-89507-549-3(2))* Bayard Canada Livres CAN. Dist: Univ. of Toronto Pr.

Deen, Paula. Paula Deen's Cookbook for the Lunch-Box Set. Mitchell, Susan, illus. 2009. (ENG.). 192p. (J). (gr. 2-7). spiral bd. 21.99 *(978-1-4169-8268-5(X)*, Simon & Schuster Bks. For Young Readers) Simon & Schuster Bks. For Young Readers.

—Paula Deen's My First Cookbook. Mitchell, Susan, illus. 2008. (ENG.). 176p. (J). (gr. -1-3). spiral bd. 21.99 *(978-1-4169-5033-2(8)*, Simon & Schuster Bks. For Young Readers) Simon & Schuster Bks. For Young Readers.

Della Casa, Chef Luca. No Egg on Your Face! Easy & Delecious Egg-Free Recipes for Kids with Allergies. 2016. (Allergy Aware Cookbooks Ser.). (ENG.). 32p. (gr. 3-4). lib. bdg. 27.99 *(978-1-4914-8055-7(6)*, Edge Bks.) Capstone Press of Coughlan Cos.

Della Casa, Chef Luca, contrib. by. Beat the Wheat! Easy & Delecious Wheat-Free Recipes for Kids with Allergies. 2016. (Allergy Aware Cookbooks Ser.). (ENG., Illus.). 32p. (gr. 3-4). lib. bdg. 27.99 *(978-1-4914-8057-1(2)*, Edge Bks.) Capstone Press of Coughlan Cos.

—Enjoy Without Soy: Easy & Delecious Soy-Free Recipes for Kids with Allergies. 2016. (Allergy Aware Cookbooks Ser.). (ENG., Illus.). 32p. (gr. 3-4). lib. bdg. 27.99 *(978-1-4914-8056-4(4)*, Edge Bks.) Capstone Press of Coughlan Cos.

—No Peanuts, No Problem! Easy & Delecious Nut-Free Recipes for Kids with Allergies. 2016. (Allergy Aware Cookbooks Ser.). (ENG.). 32p. (gr. 3-4). lib. bdg. 27.99 *(978-1-4914-8054-0(8)*, Edge Bks.) Capstone Press of Coughlan Cos.

Dennis, Yvonne Wakim & Hirschfelder, Arlene. A Kid's Guide to Native American History: More Than 50 Activities. 2009. (Kid's Guide Ser.). (ENG.). 256p. (J). (gr. 2-4). pap. 16.95 *(978-1-55652-802-6(7))* Chicago Review Pr., Inc.

Denzer, Barbara & Denzer, Missy. The Crazy Kids Guide to Cooking for Your Pet: Recipes, Jokes, Pet Care Tips & Fun Things to Do with Your Pet Featuring the Back Bones of Character. Rodriguez, Manny, illus. 2004. 64p. (J). (gr. k-7). 12.95 *(978-0-9744749-0-8(8))* Crazy Pet Pr., The.

DePietro, Frank. Latino American Cuisine. 2012. (Illus.). 64p. (J). pap. *(978-1-4222-2337-6(X))* Mason Crest.

—Latino American Cuisine. Limón, José E., ed. 2012. (Hispanic Americans: Major Minority Ser.). (Illus.). 64p. (J). (gr. 4). 22.95 *(978-1-4222-2320-8(5))* Mason Crest.

Di Vecchio, Jerry Anne & Kirkman, Françoise Dudal. You've Got Recipes: A cookbook for a Lifetime. 2009. 106p. pap. 31.50 *(978-1-4251-6855-1(8))* Trafford Publishing.

Dickinson, Gill. Creative Crafts for Kids. 2013. (ENG.). 256p. pap. 14.99 *(978-0-600-62710-4(1)*, Hamlyn) Octopus Publishing Group GBR. Dist: Hachette Bk. Group.

Dingles, Molly. Crescent Kitchen: Cocina de Medialuna. Brodie, Neale, illus. 2006. (ENG & SPA.). (J). 21.65 *(978-1-59646-050-8(4))* Dingles & Co.

Disney Book Group Staff. The Disney Princess Cookbook. Disney Storybook Art Team, illus. 2013. (ENG.). 144p. (J). (gr. 1-3). 15.99 *(978-1-4231-6324-4(9))* Disney Pr.

Dolbear, Emily. How Did That Get to My Table? Ketchup. 2009. (Community Connections: How Did That Get to My Table? Ser.). (ENG.). 24p. (gr. 2-5). lib. bdg. 25.64 *(978-1-60279-471-9(5)*, 200264) Cherry Lake Publishing.

—How Did That Get to My Table? Pasta. 2009. (Community Connections: How Did That Get to My Table? Ser.). (ENG.). 24p. (gr. 2-5). lib. bdg. 25.64 *(978-1-60279-470-2(7)*, 200266) Cherry Lake Publishing.

Dooley, Norah. Everybody Cooks Rice. Thornton, Peter J., illus. 2015. 32p. pap. 7.00 *(978-1-61003-603-0(4))* Center for the Collaborative Classroom.

Dorling Kindersley Publishing Staff. Children Just Like Me Food Like Mine. 2017. (ENG.). 80p. (J). (gr. 1-4). 16.99 ***(978-1-4654-6135-3(3)***, DK Children) Dorling Kindersley Publishing, Inc.

—Complete Children's Cookbook. 2015. (ENG., Illus.). 304p. (J). (gr. 2-5). 24.99 *(978-1-4654-3546-0(8)*, DK Children) Dorling Kindersley Publishing, Inc.

—Cook It: Learn to Cook 100 Easy Recipes. 2013. (ENG.). 128p. (J). (gr. 3-7). 19.99 *(978-1-4654-0254-7(3)*, DK Children) Dorling Kindersley Publishing, Inc.

—The Cookbook for Girls. 2009. (ENG.). 128p. (J). (gr. 2-5). 17.99 *(978-0-7566-4500-7(X)*, DK Children) Dorling Kindersley Publishing, Inc.

Dorling Kindersley Publishing Staff. Look I'm a Cook. 2017. (ENG.). 48p. (J). (gr. -1-2). 12.99 ***(978-1-4654-5964-0(2)***, DK Children) Dorling Kindersley Publishing, Inc.

Dorling Kindersley Publishing Staff & Ibbs, Katharine. DK Children's Cookbook. Shooter, Howard, photos by. 2004. (ENG., Illus.). 128p. (J). (gr. 3-7). 17.99 *(978-0-7566-0597-1(0)*, 1235962, DK Children) Dorling Kindersley Publishing, Inc.

Duffy, Kate & McRedmond, Sarah. Fit Kids Cookbook. Bagley, Pat, illus. 2004. 94p. (J). (gr. 4-7). spiral bd. 19.95 *(978-0-9709301-6-3(X))* Fit Kids.

Dummies Technical Press Staff, et al. IBS Cookbook for Dummies(r). 2009. (ENG., Illus.). 360p. pap. 22.99 *(978-0-470-53072-6(3)*, For Dummies) Wiley, John & Sons, Inc.

Dunn, Mary R. I Want to Be a Chef. 2009. (Dream Jobs Ser.). 24p. (gr. 2-3). 42.50 *(978-1-61512-205-9(2)*, PowerKids Pr.); (Illus.). (YA). lib. bdg. 22.60 *(978-1-4042-4471-9(9))* Rosen Publishing Group, Inc., The.

—Quiero Ser Chef. 2009.Tr. of I Want to Be a Chef. (SPA., Illus.). 24p. pap. 8.25 *(978-1-4358-3427-9(5))*; (J). (gr. 2-4). lib. bdg. 22.60 *(978-1-4042-8156-1(8))* Rosen Publishing Group, Inc., The. (Editorial Buenas Letras).

Dyer, Janice. Get into Smart Snacks. 2017. (Illus.). 32p. (J). ***(978-0-7787-3642-4(3))*** Crabtree Publishing Co.

Dymock, Christina. Young Chefs. 2013. 16.99 *(978-1-4621-1195-4(5)*, Horizon Pubs.) Cedar Fort, Inc./CFI Distribution.

Elliott, Lynne. Food & Feasts in the Middle Ages. 2004. (Medieval World Ser.). (ENG., Illus.). 32p. (J). pap. *(978-0-7787-1380-7(6))* Crabtree Publishing Co.

Ellison, Virginia H. The Winnie-the-Pooh Cookbook. Shepard, Ernest H., illus. 2010. (Winnie-The-Pooh Ser.). (ENG.). 112p. (J). (gr. 3-7). 19.99 *(978-0-525-42359-1(1)*, Dutton Books for Young Readers) Penguin Young Readers Group.

Elton, Sarah. Starting from Scratch: What You Should Know about Food & Cooking, 0 vols. Kulak, Jeff & Owlkids Books Inc. Staff, illus. 2014. (ENG.). 96p. (J). (gr. 4-6). 18.95 *(978-1-926973-96-8(8)*, Owlkids) Owlkids Bks. Inc. CAN. Dist: Publishers Group West (PGW).

Encyclopaedia Britannica, Inc. Staff, compiled by. What Happens to a Hamburger? 2008. 49.95 *(978-1-59339-662-6(7))* Encyclopaedia Britannica, Inc.

Enviornment Canada Staff. Oil, Water & Chocolate Mousse. (Illus.). 28p. (J). pap. *(978-0-660-15503-6(6))* Canadian Government Publishing.

Eudy, P. D. PB & J Delight. 2010. 32p. pap. 14.78 *(978-1-4520-0676-5(8))* AuthorHouse.

Fejtö, Raphaël. French Fries. 2016. (Little Inventions Ser.). (ENG., Illus.). 32p. (J). (gr. 3-5). 9.95 *(978-1-77085-746-9(X)*, 9781770857469) Firefly Bks., Ltd.

—Pizza. 2016. (Little Inventions Ser.). (ENG., Illus.). 32p. (J). (gr. 3-5). 9.95 *(978-1-77085-749-0(4)*, 9781770857490) Firefly Bks., Ltd.

Festive Foods for the Holidays. (Illus.). (J). (gr. k-5). 119.70 *(978-0-8239-7182-4(1))* Rosen Publishing Group, Inc., The.

Fischer, James. Computer Math. 2014. (Illus.). 48p. (J). *(978-1-4222-2901-9(7))* Mason Crest.

Fishbein, Susie. Kosher by Design Kids in the Kitchen. Uher, John, photos by. 2005. (Illus.). 192p. (J). (gr. 4-12). 22.99 *(978-1-57819-071-3(1))* Mesorah Pubns., Ltd.

Flaherty, Liz. Cooking up a Storm. 2007. (Action Numeracy Middle Primary Ser.). 32p. pap. 9.95 *(978-0-86431-670-7(4))* ACER Pr. AUS. Dist: ISBS Publisher Services.

Ford, Jean. Latino Cuisine & Its Influence on American Foods: The Taste of Celebration. 2007. (Hispanic Heritage Ser.). (Illus.). 112p. (YA). (gr. 4-7). lib. bdg. 22.95 *(978-1-59084-935-4(3)*, 1234497) Mason Crest.

Fortuna, Lois. Helping with Dinner. 2016. (We Can Do It! Ser.). (ENG., Illus.). 24p. (J). (gr. k-k). pap. 8.15 *(978-1-4824-3811-6(9))* Stevens, Gareth Publishing LLLP.

French, Deborah. The Cookbook for Children with Special Needs: Learning a Life Skill with Fun, Tasty, Healthy Recipes. Ehrlich, Leah, illus. 2015. (ENG.). 200p. 24.95 *(978-1-84905-538-3(6)*, 3467) Kingsley, Jessica Pubs. GBR. Dist: Macmillan Distribution Ltd.

Fulcher, Roz. Be Good to Your Body: Healthy Eating & Fun Recipes. 2012. (Dover Children's Activity Bks.). (ENG.). 80p. (J). (gr. 3-5). pap. 6.99 *(978-0-486-48643-7(5))* Dover Pubns., Inc.

Galvin, Laura Gates. My First Cookbook: Family Fun in the Kitchen. 2005. (Family Fun Ser.). (ENG., Illus.). 40p. (J). (gr. -1-3). 12.99 *(978-1-59069-451-0(1)*, 1A702) Studio Mouse LLC.

Gay, Kathlyn. Anne Burrell. 2016. (Celebrity Chefs Ser.). 128p. (J). (gr. 6-6). 37.27 *(978-0-7660-7757-7(8))* Enslow Pubs., Inc.

Gedzyk, Emily, illus. Paleo Cooking for Cavekids. 2012. (ENG.). 102p. (J). pap. 19.75 *(978-0-9855541-2-5(6))* Firestorm Editions.

Geography Collective Staff. Mission Explore Food. Morgan-Jones, Tom, illus. 2012. (Mission Explore Ser.). (ENG.). 272p. (J). (gr. 4-7). 32.95 *(978-1-904872-44-3(1)*, Can of Worms Kids Pr.) Can of Worms Pr. GBR. Dist: Independent Pubs. Group.

Germaine, Elizabeth & Burckhardt, Ann. Cooking the Australian Way. 2nd rev. ed. 2003. (Easy Menu Ethnic Cookbooks 2nd Edition Ser.). (ENG., Illus.). 72p. (gr. 5-12). 25.26 *(978-0-8225-4101-1(7))* Lerner Publishing Group.

Gifford, Clive. Food & Cooking in Ancient Egypt. 2010. (Cooking in World Cultures Ser.). (Illus.). 32p. (J). (ENG.). pap. 10.60 *(978-1-61532-359-3(7))*; (gr. 3-5). lib. bdg. 26.50 *(978-1-61532-337-1(6))* Rosen Publishing Group, Inc., The. (PowerKids Pr.).

—Food & Cooking in Viking Times. 2010. (Cooking in World Cultures Ser.). (Illus.). 32p. (J). (ENG.). pap. 10.60 *(978-1-61532-365-4(1))*; (gr. 3-5). lib. bdg. 26.50 *(978-1-61532-354-8(6))* Rosen Publishing Group, Inc., The. (PowerKids Pr.).

Gilpin, Rebecca. Little Children's Cookbook. Sage, Molly & Larkum, Adam, illus. Allman, Howard, photos by. 2005. (ENG.). 96p. (J). (gr. 4-7). 7.95 *(978-0-7945-1113-5(9)*, Usborne) EDC Publishing.

Gilpin, Rebecca & Atkinson, Catherine. Easter Cooking. 2003. (ENG.). 32p. (J). pap. 6.95 *(978-0-7945-0412-0(4)*, Usborne) EDC Publishing.

—Fairy Cooking. 2004. (Children's Cooking Ser.). (ENG., Illus.). 32p. (Orig.). (J). pap. 6.95 *(978-0-7945-0633-9(X)*, Usborne) EDC Publishing.

—Yummy Little Cookbook. 2004. (Children's Cooking Ser.). (ENG.). 96p. (J). 7.95 *(978-0-7945-0676-6(3)*, Usborne) EDC Publishing.

Giulieri, Anne. Cooking Pancakes, 1 vol. Meldrum, Ned, photos by. 2012. (Engage Literacy Red Ser.). (ENG., Illus.). 32p. (gr. k-2). pap. 5.99 *(978-1-4296-8950-2(1)*, Engage Literacy) Capstone Press of Coughlan Cos.

—Surprise Pancakes for Mom, 1 vol. Boyer, Susy, illus. 2012. (Engage Literacy Red Ser.). (ENG.). 32p. (gr. k-2). pap. 5.99 *(978-1-4296-8948-9(X)*, Engage Literacy) Capstone Press of Coughlan Cos.

Gleeson, Erin. The Forest Feast for Kids: Colorful Vegetarian Recipes That Are Simple to Make. 2016. (ENG., Illus.). 112p. (J). (gr. 3-7). 19.95 *(978-1-4197-1886-1(X)*, Abrams Bks. for Young Readers) Abrams, Inc.

Glock, Beverley. 200 Healthy Kids Recipes. 2016. (200 Ser.). (Illus.). 96p. pap. 10.95 *(978-1-4162-4574-2(X))* Sellers Publishing, Inc.

Gold, Rozanne & Mansfield, Phil. Eat Fresh Food: Awesome Recipes for Teen Chefs. 2009. (ENG., Illus.). 160p. (J). (gr. 9-12). pap. 19.99 *(978-1-59990-445-0(4)*, 9781599904450, Bloomsbury USA Childrens) Bloomsbury Publishing USA.

Golosi, Rosanne. Best Friends Forever! Martini, Angela, illus. 2005. 64p. (J). *(978-0-439-80072-3(2))* Scholastic, Inc.

Good, Phyllis Pellman. Fix-It & Forget-It Kids' Cookbook: 50 Favorite Recipes to Make in a Slow Cooker. 2012. (Fix-It &

Forget-It Ser.). (ENG.). 128p. (J). (gr. 3-18). 19.99 *(978-1-56148-704-2(X)*, Good Bks.) Skyhorse Publishing Co., Inc.
Goodman, Polly. Food in the Carribbean. 2008. (Food Around the World Ser.). (Illus.). 30p. (J). (gr. 3-7). lib. bdg. 25.25 *(978-1-4042-4299-9(6)*, PowerKids Pr.) Rosen Publishing Group, Inc., The.
Gooseberry Patch. Kids in the Kitchen Cookbook: Recipes for Fun! 2006. (Everyday Cookbook Collection). (ENG., Illus.). 80p. 16.95 *(978-1-933494-04-3(2)*, Gooseberry Patch) Rowman & Littlefield Publishers, Inc.
Gordon, Sherri Mabry. Tyler Florence. 2016. (Celebrity Chefs Ser.). 128p. (J). (gr. 6-6). 37.27 *(978-0-7660-7756-0(X))* Enslow Pubs., Inc.
Goss, Gary. Blue Moon Soup: A Family Cookbook. Dyer, Jane, illus. 2013. (ENG.). 72p. (J). (gr. 1-4). 16.95 *(978-1-62087-990-0(5)*, 620990, Sky Pony Pr.) Skyhorse Publishing Co., Inc.
Gourmet with Google. 2004. (YA). per. *(978-0-9754307-2-9(6))* The Publishing Place LLC.
Graham, Gillian. The Rainbow Cookbook for Kids. 2011. 64p. pap. 26.49 *(978-1-4567-5209-5(X))* AuthorHouse.
Graimes, Nicola. Kids' Fun & Healthy Cookbook. Shooter, Howard, photos by. 2007. (ENG., Illus.). 128p. (J). (gr. 2-5). 17.99 *(978-0-7566-2916-8(0)*, DK Children) Dorling Kindersley Publishing, Inc.
Grant, Amanda & Yorke, Francesca. Kids' Kitchen: Good Food Made Easy. 2006. (ENG., Illus.). 336p. (gr. -1-17). pap. 14.95 *(978-1-84533-316-4(0)*, Mitchell Beazley) Octopus Publishing Group GBR. Dist: Hachette Bk. Group.
Greathouse, Lisa. Make It Healthy, 1 vol. 2011. (Science Readers: a Closer Look Ser.). (ENG.). 32p. (J). (gr. 2-2). pap. 8.99 *(978-1-4333-3088-9(1))* Teacher Created Materials, Inc.
Green, Jen. The Caribbean. 2010. (World of Food Ser.). 32p. (YA). (gr. 4-7). lib. bdg. 24.95 *(978-1-934545-15-7(5))* Oliver Pr., Inc.
Greenfield, Tonya. Nonnie's Kitchen: Fun & Food in the Kitchen with Kids. 2nd ed. 2005. (Illus.). 132p. (J). reprint ed. per. 16.95 *(978-0-9768884-1-3(6))* M2M Partners.
Greenfield, Tonya G. Nonnies Kitchen Fun & Food in the Kitchen with Kids. 2005. 132p. (YA). spiral bd. 16.95 *(978-0-9768884-0-6(8)*, 65,000) M2M Partners.
Greenhaven Press Editors & Busby, Barbara Sheen. Foods of Indonesia. 2012. (Taste of Culture Ser.). (ENG., Illus.). 64p. (gr. 3-6). lib. bdg. 35.20 *(978-0-7377-5950-1(X)*, Kidhaven) Cengage Gale.
Gregory, Helen. Bread Around the World, 1 vol. 2011. (Wonder Readers Early Level Ser.). (ENG.). 32p. (gr. -1-1). pap. 5.99 *(978-1-4296-7798-1(8)*, Wonder Readers) Capstone Press of Coughlan Cos.
Gregory, Josh. Chef. 2011. (21st Century Skills Library: Cool Careers Ser.). (ENG.). 32p. (gr. 4-8). lib. bdg. 28.50 *(978-1-60279-985-1(7)*, 200976) Cherry Lake Publishing.
Greve, Tom. How to Make Ice Cream. 2015. (ENG.). 24p. (gr. k-3). 28.50 *(978-1-63430-353-8(9))* Rourke Educational Media.
Groner, Judye & Wikler, Madeline. Maccabee Meals: Food & Fun for Hanukkah. Roma, Ursula, illus. 2012. (Hanukkah Ser.). (ENG.). 64p. (J). (gr. 2-5). pap. 8.95 *(978-0-7613-5144-3(2)*, Kar-Ben Publishing) Lerner Publishing Group.
Gunderson, Jessica & Gunderson, Mary. Pioneer Farm Cooking. 2016. (Exploring History Through Food Ser.). (ENG., Illus.). 32p. (gr. 3-4). lib. bdg. 27.32 *(978-1-5157-2355-4(0))* Capstone Press of Coughlan Cos.
Hadley and Delaney. Twice As Good: Cookbook for Kids. 2014.Tr. of Twice As Good Cookbook for Kids. (ENG., Illus.). 96p. (J). 17.95 *(978-0-9960696-0-1(7))* Twice As Good Productions, LLC.
Hamilton-Fairley, Fiona. Little Cooks: 30 Delicious Recipes to Make & Enjoy. 2008. (ENG., Illus.). 96p. *(978-1-84537-984-1(5))* New Holland Pubs., Ltd.
Hamlyn. Princess Cupcakes, Kit. 2012. (ENG., Illus.). 64p. (gr. -1-17). pap. 19.99 *(978-0-600-62194-2(4)*, Hamlyn) Octopus Publishing Group GBR. Dist: Hachette Bk. Group.
Hankin, Rosemary. An Indian Cookbook for Kids. 2013. (Cooking Around the World Ser.). 32p. (J). (gr. 3-6). pap. 70.50 *(978-1-4777-1525-3(8))*; pap. 11.75 *(978-1-4777-1524-6(X))*; lib. bdg. 26.50 *(978-1-4777-1338-9(7))* Rosen Publishing Group, Inc., The. (PowerKids Pr.).
Hankin, Rosie. A Mediterranean Cookbook for Kids. 2013. (Cooking Around the World Ser.). 32p. (J). (gr. 3-6). 26.50 *(978-1-4777-1339-6(5))*; pap. 11.75 *(978-1-4777-1526-0(6))* Rosen Publishing Group, Inc., The. (PowerKids Pr.).
Hartland, Jessie. Bon Appétit! The Delicious Life of Julia Child. Hartland, Jessie, illus. 2012. (ENG., Illus.). 48p. (J). (gr. k-12). 17.99 *(978-0-375-86944-0(1))*; 20.99 *(978-0-375-96944-7(6))* Random Hse. Children's Bks. (Schwartz & Wade Bks.).
Harvey, Gill. Starting Cooking - Internet Linked. 2005. 32p. (J). pap. 4.95 *(978-0-7945-0666-7(6)*, Usborne) EDC Publishing.
—Starting Cooking Kid Kit. 2005. 32p. (J). 14.99 *(978-1-58086-744-3(8)*, Usborne) EDC Publishing.
Hawkins, Linda J. Catering to Children: With Recipes for Memorable Tea Parties. Yonts, Barbara, photos by. 2003. (Illus.). 56p. (J). (gr. k-5). 19.99 *(978-0-9742806-0-8(7))* Heart to Heart Publishing, Inc.
Head, Honor. Dairy. 2006. (QEB What's for Lunch? Ser.). (Illus.). 32p. (YA). (gr. 1-4). lib. bdg. 19.95 *(978-1-59566-197-5(2))* QEB Publishing Inc.
Hengel, Katherine. Cool Basil from Garden to Table: How to Plant, Grow, & Prepare Basil, 1 vol. 2012. (Cool Garden to Table Ser.). (ENG.). 32p. 28.50 *(978-1-61783-182-9(4)*, Checkerboard Library) ABDO Publishing Co.
—Garden to Table: A Kid's Guide to Planting, Growing, & Preparing Food. 2014. (ENG., Illus.). 144p. (J). (gr. 2-7). pap. 15.95 *(978-1-938063-42-8(2)*, Mighty Media Junior Readers) Mighty Media Pr.
Hershberger, Fannie. Kinder Kookin' Amish Children Share Their Own Recipes. 216p. spiral bd. 7.95 *(978-0-9725806-0-1(3))* Hershberger, Ivan & Fannie.
Hewitt, Sally. Fruit. 2008. (Good for Me Ser.). (Illus.). 24p. (J). (gr. -1-3). lib. bdg. 22.60 *(978-1-4042-4267-8(8)*, PowerKids Pr.) Rosen Publishing Group, Inc., The.
Hinton, Kerry. Cool Careers Without College for People Who Love Food. 2009. (Cool Careers Without College Ser.). 144p. (gr. 6-6). 66.50 *(978-1-61511-966-0(3))*; (Illus.). (J). lib. bdg. 35.95 *(978-1-4358-5246-4(X))* Rosen Publishing Group, Inc., The.
Hoffmann, Peggy. Miss B's First Cookbook: Twenty Family-Sized Recipes for for the Youngest Cook. Hunter, Gerald, illus. 2011. 48p. pap. 35.95 *(978-1-258-08433-2(3))* Literary Licensing, LLC.
Hood, Karen Jean Matsko. Grandma Bert's Favorite Christmas Sweets Recipes: A Collection of Recipes from Grandma Bert, Vol. 8. Whispering Pine Press International, ed. Artistic Design Services, illus. 2014. 324p. 34.95 *(978-1-59210-538-0(6))* Whispering Pine Pr. International, Inc.
Hopkinson, Deborah. Fannie in the Kitchen: The Whole Story from Soup to Nuts of How Fannie Farmer Invented Recipes with Precise Measurements. Carpenter, Nancy, illus. 2004. (ENG.). 40p. (J). (gr. -1-4). reprint ed. 7.99 *(978-0-689-86997-6(5)*, Simon & Schuster/Paula Wiseman Bks.) Simon & Schuster/Paula Wiseman Bks.
Hughes, Helga. Cooking the Austrian Way. 2nd rev. ed. 2003. (Easy Menu Ethnic Cookbooks 2nd Edition Ser.). (ENG., Illus.). 72p. (gr. 5-12). 25.26 *(978-0-8225-4102-8(5))* Lerner Publishing Group.
Hughes, Meredith Sayles. Green Power: Leaf & Flower Vegetables. 2005. (Plants We Eat Ser.). (Illus.). 104p. (gr. 6-9). 26.60 *(978-0-8225-2839-5(8))* Lerner Publishing Group.
—Hard to Crack: Nut Trees. 2005. (Plants We Eat Ser.). (Illus.). 104p. (gr. 6-9). 26.60 *(978-0-8225-2838-8(X))* Lerner Publishing Group.
Hupp, Abby. A Wizard in the Kitchen: Magical recipes for Kids of All Ages. 2006. (YA). spiral bd. 13.99 *(978-0-9785798-0-7(1))* Plan B Bks.
I'm a Chef, 6 Packs. (Literatura 2000 Ser.). (gr. 2-3). 33.00 *(978-0-7635-0263-8(4))* Rigby Education.
In Nonna's Kitchen: Individual Title Six-Packs. (gr. -1-2). 23.00 *(978-0-7635-8996-7(9))* Rigby Education.
Indovino, Shaina C. Rachael Ray: From Candy Counter to Cooking Show. 2012. (Extraordinary Success with a High School Diploma or Less Ser.). (Illus.). 64p. (J). (gr. 7-8). 22.95 *(978-1-4222-2300-0(0))* Mason Crest.
Indovino, Shaina Carmel. Rachael Ray: From Candy Counter to Cooking Show. 2012. (Illus.). 64p. (J). pap. *(978-1-4222-2311-6(6))* Mason Crest.
Ipcizade, Catherine. The Dish on Mac & Cheese, 1 vol. 2011. (Favorite Food Facts Ser.). (ENG.). 24p. (gr. k-1). 26.65 *(978-1-4296-6660-2(9)*, Pebble Plus) Capstone Press of Coughlan Cos.
—Favorite Food Facts. 2011. (Favorite Food Facts Ser.). (ENG.). 24p. (gr. k-1). lib. bdg. 53.30 *(978-1-4296-6512-4(2)*, Pebble Plus) Capstone Press of Coughlan Cos.
—The Skinny on Hot Dogs, 1 vol. 2011. (Favorite Food Facts Ser.). (ENG.). 24p. (gr. k-1). 26.65 *(978-1-4296-6661-9(7)*, Pebble Plus) Capstone Press of Coughlan Cos.
Iselin, Tom. The Bread of Life: For the Table ... for Eternity 2004. 300p. pap. 25.00 *(978-0-9649139-7-4(6)*, 964913976) Pelican Lake Pr.
Jacques, Brian. The Redwall Cookbook. Denise, Christopher, illus. 2005. (Redwall Ser.). (ENG.). 104p. (J). (gr. 5-5). pap. 24.99 *(978-0-399-23791-1(7)*, Philomel Bks.) Penguin Young Readers Group.
John, Margaret. Little Belly Monster Makes French Toast. Kim, Sarah, illus. 2012. 40p. pap. *(978-0-9869424-2-6(1))* Belly Productions, Inc.
Johnson, Kristi. Grilled Pizza Sandwich & Other Vegetarian Recipes. 2008. (Fun Foods for Cool Cooks Ser.). (ENG.). 32p. (gr. 3-4). 27.99 *(978-1-4296-2018-5(8)*, Snap Bks.) Capstone Press of Coughlan Cos.
Jorgensen, Katrina. Football Cookbooks. 2015. (Football Cookbooks Ser.). (ENG.). 48p. (gr. 3-6). lib. bdg. 93.96 *(978-1-4914-2560-2(1))* Capstone Press of Coughlan Cos.
—Football Fuel: Recipes for Before, During, & after the Big Game. 2015. (Football Cookbooks Ser.). (ENG.). 48p. (gr. 3-6). lib. bdg. 31.32 *(978-1-4914-2135-2(5))* Capstone Press of Coughlan Cos.
—This Is Not Cheesy! Easy & Delecious Dairy-Free Recipes for Kids with Allergies. 2016. (Allergy Aware Cookbooks Ser.). (ENG., Illus.). 32p. (gr. 3-4). lib. bdg. 27.99 *(978-1-4914-8053-3(X)*, Edge Bks.) Capstone Press of Coughlan Cos.
Joyal, Kristen. Baking with Mommy Cookbook: Recipes for Kid-Size Ovens 10th Anniversary Edition. 2011. 121p. (J). spiral bd. 13.95 *(978-0-9718515-6-6(5))* Straight Forward Technologies.
Junior League of Tyler, Texas Staff, contrib. by. Ring Around the Rosie: A Collection of Children's Recipes. 2007. (Illus.). 176p. (J). *(978-0-9607122-2-9(4))* Junior League of Tyler, Inc., The.
Kallen, Stuart A. Medieval Food & Customs. 2014. (The Library of Medieval Times Ser.). (ENG., Illus.). 80p. (J). lib. bdg. *(978-1-60152-718-9(7))* ReferencePoint Pr., Inc.
Kalman, Bobbie. Delicious Desserts. 2003. (Kid Power Ser.). (ENG., Illus.). 32p. (J). pap. *(978-0-7787-1276-3(1))*; (gr. 3). lib. bdg. *(978-0-7787-1254-1(0))* Crabtree Publishing Co.
—Lunch Munch: Step-by-Step Recipes. 2003. (Kid Power Ser.). (ENG., Illus.). 32p. (J). (gr. 3). pap. *(978-0-7787-1273-2(7))*; lib. bdg. *(978-0-7787-1251-0(6))* Crabtree Publishing Co.
—Super Snacks: Step-by-Step Recipes. 2003. (Kid Power Ser.). (ENG., Illus.). 32p. (J). (gr. 3). pap. *(978-0-7787-1274-9(5))* Crabtree Publishing Co.
Kann, Bob. A Recipe for Success: Lizzie Kander & Her Cookbook. 2006. (Badger Biographies Ser.). (ENG., Illus.). 144p. (J). (gr. 3-7). per. 12.95 *(978-0-87020-373-2(8))* Wisconsin Historical Society.
Kann, Victoria. Pinkalicious Cupcake Cookbook. Kann, Victoria, illus. 2013. (Pinkalicious Ser.). (ENG., Illus.). 64p. (J). (gr. 1-5). 14.99 *(978-0-06-202357-5(8)*, HarperFestival) HarperCollins Pubs.
Karmel, Annabel. Mom & Me Cookbook: Have Fun in the Kitchen! 2005. (ENG.). 48p. (J). (gr. -1-3). 12.99 *(978-0-7566-1006-7(0)*, DK Children) Dorling Kindersley Publishing, Inc.
—My Favorite Recipes. 2011. (ENG.). 96p. (J). (gr. 2-5). 15.99 *(978-0-7566-7195-2(7)*, DK Children) Dorling Kindersley Publishing, Inc.
Karpinske, Stephanie & Chihak, Sheena, eds. Disney the Magic Kitchen Cookbook. 2007. (Illus.). 128p. (J). (gr. 4-7). 16.95 *(978-0-696-23732-4(6))* Meredith Bks.
Katzen, Mollie. Honest Pretzels: And 64 Other Amazing Recipes for Kids Who Love to Cook. 2009. (ENG., Illus.). 192p. (J). (gr. 3-7). pap. 17.99 *(978-1-58246-305-6(0)*, Tricycle Pr.) Random Hse. Children's Bks.
—Salad People & More Real Recipes: A New Cookbook for Preschoolers & Up. 2005. (ENG., Illus.). 96p. (J). (gr. -1-2). 17.99 *(978-1-58246-141-0(4)*, Tricycle Pr.) Random Hse. Children's Bks.
Keedle, Jayne. Rachael Ray. 2009. (People We Should Know Ser.). (ENG., Illus.). 48p. (J). (gr. 3-5). pap. 10.50 *(978-1-4339-2149-0(9))*; lib. bdg. 31.00 *(978-1-4339-2189-6(8))* Stevens, Gareth Publishing LLLP. (Gareth Stevens Learning Library).
Kelly, Tracey. The Culture & Recipes of India. 2016. (Let's Cook! Ser.). 00048p. (J). (gr. 4-4). pap. 11.75 *(978-1-4994-3179-7(1)*, PowerKids Pr.) Rosen Publishing Group, Inc., The.
—The Culture & Recipes of Japan. 2016. (Let's Cook! Ser.). 00048p. (J). (gr. 4-4). pap. 11.75 *(978-1-4994-3183-4(X)*, PowerKids Pr.) Rosen Publishing Group, Inc., The.
Kennedy, Marge. Time to Eat at the White House. 2009. (Scholastic News Nonfiction Readers Ser.). 24p. (J). (gr. 1-2). 22.00 *(978-0-531-21098-7(7))* Scholastic Library Publishing.
Kids Can Cook! 2008. 64p. *(978-1-4075-3392-6(4))* Parragon, Inc.
Kishel, Ann-Marie. Cook. 2007. (First Step Nonfiction Ser.). (J). pap. 3.95 *(978-0-8225-6844-5(6))* Lerner Publishing Group.
Knowlden, Martin. The Kids' Cookbook: Over 50 Fun Recipes for Kids to Cook. Heap, Will & Dunne, Kevin, photos by. 2006. (Illus.). 128p. *(978-1-85626-626-0(5))* Cathie, Kyle Ltd. GBR. Dist: Independent Pubs. Group.
KociendaGenevieve. SUSHI NATION LOW INTERMEDIATE BOOK WITH ONLINE ACCESS. 2014. (ENG., Illus.). 28p. (J). pap. 9.50 *(978-1-107-63147-2(5))* Cambridge Univ. Pr.
Koosmann, Melissa. Recipe & Craft Guide to South Africa. 2011. (World Crafts & Recipes Ser.). (ENG., Illus.). 64p. (J). (gr. 4-7). lib. bdg. 33.95 *(978-1-61228-080-6(3))* Mitchell Lane Pubs., Inc.
Korman, Susan. Rachael Ray. 2012. (J). *(978-1-61900-025-4(3))*; pap. *(978-1-61900-026-1(1))* Eldorado Ink.
Kovalev, Neil. Kaylee Can Cook: Number Names & Count Sequence. 2013. (Rosen Math Readers Ser.). (ENG.). 16p. (J). (gr. k-1). pap. 42.00 *(978-1-4777-1612-0(2))*; (Illus.). pap. 7.00 *(978-1-4777-1611-3(4))* Rosen Publishing Group, Inc., The. (Rosen Classroom).
Kozlowski, Bryan. Cook Me a Rhyme: In the Kitchen with Mother Goose. 2017. (Cook Me A... Ser.). (ENG., Illus.). 80p. (J). (gr. k-6). spiral bd. 16.95 *(978-1-63322-218-2(7)*, Walter Foster Jr) Quarto Publishing Group USA.
Kuhn, Kate. The Budding Chef. 2011. (Budding Ser.). (ENG., Illus.). 72p. (gr. -1-5). pap. 9.95 *(978-0-87659-372-1(4)*, Gryphon House Inc) Gryphon Hse., Inc.
Kushner, Malcolm. California Squisine: Healthy Food That's Fast & Fun for Kids. 2010. (ENG., Illus.). 112p. per. 11.95 *(978-1-931741-67-5(0))* Reed, Robert D. Pubs.
Kuskowski, Alex. Cool Breads & Biscuits, 1 vol. 2014. (Cool Home Cooking Ser.). (ENG.). 32p. (gr. 3-6). 28.50 *(978-1-62403-500-5(0))* ABDO Publishing Co.
—Cool Dips & Drinks, 1 vol. 2014. (Cool Home Cooking Ser.). (ENG.). 32p. (gr. 3-6). 28.50 *(978-1-62403-501-2(9))* ABDO Publishing Co.
—Cool Home Cooking, 1 vol. 2014. (Cool Home Cooking Ser.: 6). (ENG.). 32p. (gr. 3-6). lib. bdg. 171.00 *(978-1-62403-499-2(3)*, Checkerboard Library) ABDO Publishing Co.
—Cool Main Dishes, 1 vol. 2014. (Cool Home Cooking Ser.). (ENG.). 32p. (gr. 3-6). 28.50 *(978-1-62403-502-9(7))* ABDO Publishing Co.
—Cool Sides & Salads, 1 vol. 2014. (Cool Home Cooking Ser.). (ENG.). 32p. (gr. 3-6). 28.50 *(978-1-62403-503-6(5))* ABDO Publishing Co.
—Cool Soups & Stews, 1 vol. 2014. (Cool Home Cooking Ser.). (ENG.). 32p. (gr. 3-6). 28.50 *(978-1-62403-504-3(3))* ABDO Publishing Co.
—Cool Treats & Sweets, 1 vol. 2014. (Cool Home Cooking Ser.). (ENG.). 32p. (gr. 3-6). 28.50 *(978-1-62403-505-0(1))* ABDO Publishing Co.
—Super Simple Cookies. 2016. (Super Simple Cookies Ser.: 6). (ENG.). 32p. (J). (gr. k-4). lib. bdg. 162.42 *(978-1-62403-945-4(6)*, Super SandCastle) ABDO Publishing Co.
—Super Simple No-Bake Cookies: Easy Cookie Recipes for Kids!, 1 vol. 2016. (Super Simple Cookies Ser.). (ENG., Illus.). 32p. (J). (gr. k-4). 27.07 *(978-1-62403-950-8(2))* ABDO Publishing Co.
Labat, Yancey C., illus. It's Party Time! 2006. 56p. (J). *(978-0-439-83227-4(6))* Scholastic, Inc.
—Pizza-Zazz & Lotsa Pasta. 2006. 56p. (J). *(978-0-439-83187-1(3))* Scholastic, Inc.
—S'mores, Shakes & Chocolate Cakes: Chocolate, Chocolate All Day Long. 2006. 56p. (J). *(978-0-439-83226-7(8))* Scholastic, Inc.
Labrecque, Ellen. Chef. 2016. (21st Century Skills Library: Cool Vocational Careers Ser.). (ENG., Illus.). 32p. (J). (gr. 4-7). 29.93 *(978-1-63471-060-2(6)*, 208320) Cherry Lake Publishing.
Lagasse, Emeril. Emeril's There's a Chef in My Soup! Recipes for the Kid in Everyone. Yuen, Charles, illus. 2005. (ENG.). 256p. (J). 28.99 *(978-0-688-17706-5(9))* HarperCollins Pubs.
Landau, Elaine. Popcorn! Lies, Brian, illus. 2003. (ENG.). 32p. (J). (gr. 1-4). pap. 7.95 *(978-1-57091-443-0(5))* Charlesbridge Publishing, Inc.
Langston, Laura. Abuelita, te Acuerdas? Gardiner, Lindsey, illus. 2004.Tr. of Mile High Apple Pie. (SPA.). (J). 18.99 *(978-84-488-1911-8(X))* Beascoa, Ediciones S.A. ESP. Dist: Lectorum Pubns., Inc.
LaPenta, Marilyn. Artful Snacks. 2011. (Yummy Tummy Recipes Ser.). 24p. (J). (gr. 1-4). lib. bdg. 22.61 *(978-1-61772-307-0(X))* Bearport Publishing Co., Inc.
—Cool Cookies. 2011. (Yummy Tummy Recipes Ser.). 24p. (J). (gr. 1-4). lib. bdg. 22.61 *(978-1-61772-308-7(8))* Bearport Publishing Co., Inc.
Lapenta, Marilyn. Fall Shakes to Harvest Bakes. 2013. (Yummy Tummy Recipes: Seasons Ser.). 24p. (J). (gr. 1-6). lib. bdg. 23.93 *(978-1-61772-742-9(3))* Bearport Publishing Co., Inc.
—Spring Spreads to Nutty Breads. 2013. (Yummy Tummy Recipes: Seasons Ser.). 24p. (J). (gr. 1-6). lib. bdg. 23.93 *(978-1-61772-744-3(X))* Bearport Publishing Co., Inc.
—Summer Sips to Chill Dips. 2013. (Yummy Tummy Recipes: Seasons Ser.). 24p. (J). (gr. 1-6). lib. bdg. 23.93 *(978-1-61772-741-2(5))* Bearport Publishing Co., Inc.
LaPenta, Marilyn. Super 'Wiches. 2011. (Yummy Tummy Recipes Ser.). 24p. (J). (gr. 1-4). lib. bdg. 22.61 *(978-1-61772-306-3(1))* Bearport Publishing Co., Inc.
—Way Cool Drinks. 2011. (Yummy Tummy Recipes Ser.). 24p. (J). (gr. 1-4). lib. bdg. 22.61 *(978-1-61772-163-2(8))* Bearport Publishing Co., Inc.
Lapenta, Marilyn. Winter Punches to Nut Crunches. 2013. (Yummy Tummy Recipes: Seasons Ser.). 24p. (J). (gr. 1-6). lib. bdg. 23.93 *(978-1-61772-743-6(1))* Bearport Publishing Co., Inc.
Larrew, Brekka Hervey. Banana-Berry Smoothies & Other Breakfast Recipes, 1 vol. 2008. (Fun Foods for Cool Cooks Ser.). (ENG.). 32p. (gr. 3-4). 27.99 *(978-1-4296-2015-4(3)*, Snap Bks.) Capstone Press of Coughlan Cos.
Larson, Jennifer S. Delicious Vegetarian Main Dishes. Cohen, Brie, photos by. 2013. (You're the Chef Ser.). (ENG., Illus.). 32p. (gr. 3-5). lib. bdg. 26.60 *(978-0-7613-6635-5(0)*, Millbrook Pr.) Lerner Publishing Group.
—Perfect Pizza Recipes. Cohen, Brie, photos by. 2013. (You're the Chef Ser.). (ENG., Illus.). 32p. (gr. 3-5). lib. bdg. 26.60 *(978-0-7613-6637-9(7)*, Millbrook Pr.) Lerner Publishing Group.
—Super Pasta & Rice Dishes. Cohen, Brie, photos by. 2013. (You're the Chef Ser.). (ENG., Illus.). 32p. (gr. 3-5). lib. bdg. 26.60 *(978-0-7613-6641-6(5)*, Millbrook Pr.) Lerner Publishing Group.
—Tasty Sandwiches. Cohen, Brie, photos by. 2013. (You're the Chef Ser.). (ENG., Illus.). 32p. (J). (gr. 3-5). lib. bdg. 26.60 *(978-0-7613-6643-0(1)*, Millbrook Pr.) Lerner Publishing Group.
—Yummy Soup & Salad Recipes. Cohen, Brie, photos by. 2013. (You're the Chef Ser.). (ENG., Illus.). 32p. (gr. 3-5). lib. bdg. 26.60 *(978-0-7613-6633-1(4)*, Millbrook Pr.) Lerner Publishing Group.
Lasslett, Sally & Collins, Chrissy. Recipes for Food Technology. 2013. (ENG.). 198p. pap., wbk. ed. 33.95 *(978-1-107-68219-1(3))* Cambridge Univ. Pr.
—Recipes for Food Technology: Middle Secondary. 2013. (ENG.). pap., wbk. ed. 33.95 *(978-1-107-69230-5(X))* Cambridge Univ. Pr.
Lehman-Wilzig, Tami. Tasty Bible Stories: A Menu of Tales & Matching Recipes. Kahn, Katherine Janus, illus. 2003. (ENG.). 64p. (J). (gr. 3-5). pap. 10.95 *(978-1-58013-080-6(1)*, Kar-Ben Publishing) Lerner Publishing Group.
Let's Cook! 2016. (Let's Cook! Ser.). 00048p. (J). (gr. 4-4). 181.50 *(978-1-5081-5344-3(2)*, PowerKids Pr.) Rosen Publishing Group, Inc., The.
Let's Get Cooking!, 4 vols., Set. Incl. Fun with French Cooking. Gioffrè, Rosalba. lib. bdg. 26.50 *(978-1-4358-3454-5(2))*; Fun with Italian Cooking. Gioffrè, Rosalba. lib. bdg. 26.50 *(978-1-4358-3451-4(8))*; Fun with Mexican Cooking. Ward, Karen. lib. bdg. 26.50 *(978-1-4358-3452-1(6))*; (Illus.). 32p. (J). (gr. 3-6). 2009. 2009. Set lib. bdg. 101.00 *(978-1-4358-3502-3(6)*, PowerKids Pr.) Rosen Publishing Group, Inc., The.
Levy, Janey. Recipes for a Medieval Feast: Medieval Feast: Working Flexibly with Fractions. 2009. (PowerMath: Advanced Proficiency Plus Ser.). 32p. (gr. 5-5). 47.90 *(978-1-60851-364-2(5)*, PowerKids Pr.) Rosen Publishing Group, Inc., The.
—Recipes for a Medieval Feast: Working Flexibly with Fractions. (Math for the Real World Ser.). (Illus.). 32p. 2009. (ENG.). (gr. 6-7). pap. 10.00 *(978-1-4042-6061-0(7))* 2006. (YA). (gr. 5-9). lib. bdg. 25.25 *(978-1-4042-3354-6(7))* Rosen Publishing Group, Inc., The.
Levy, Robert. Not Just Mustard & Ketchup/ No Solo Mostaza y Salsa de Tomate. 2007. 58p. pap. 9.95 *(978-0-7414-4304-5(X))* Infinity Publishing.
Lewis, Carole. New First Place Favorites. 2004. 19.99 *(978-0-8307-3231-9(4)*, Gospel Light) Gospel Light Pubns.
Lewis, Rachel. Cook's Coloring Book: Simple Recipes for Beginners, 1 vol. Lewis, Rachel, illus. 2015. (ENG., Illus.). 144p. pap. 12.99 *(978-1-4236-3845-2(X))* Gibbs Smith, Publisher.
Liddy, Michael. Kid's Cooking in the Kitchen. 2006. 80p. 6.95 *(978-1-58581-019-2(3)*, Golden West Publishers) American Traveler Pr.
Liebman, Dan. I Want to Be a Chef. 2014. 24p. pap. 4.00 *(978-1-61003-349-7(3))* Center for the Collaborative Classroom.
—I Want to Be a Chef. 2013. (I Want to Be Ser.). (ENG., Illus.). 24p. (J). (gr. -1-2). 14.95 *(978-1-77085-003-3(1)*, 9781770850033); pap. 3.99 *(978-1-77085-004-0(X)*, 9781770850040) Firefly Bks., Ltd.
Linder, Dorothy Perillo. A Vegetable Collection: Recipes & Rhymes to Conquer Kids of All Ages. 2008. (Illus.). (J). 35.00 *(978-0-9753334-2-6(9))* Sanctuary Bks.
Liversidge, Cassie, illus. Ice Cream! Grow Your Own Ingredients. 2015. (ENG.). 40p. (J). (gr. -1-3). 12.99 *(978-1-63220-405-9(3)*, Sky Pony Pr.) Skyhorse Publishing Co., Inc.
Llanas, Sheila Griffin. Ettore Boiardi: Chef Boyardee Manufacturer, 1 vol. 2014. (Food Dudes Set 2 Ser.). (ENG.). 32p. (J). (gr. 8-12). lib. bdg. 27.07 *(978-1-62403-314-8(8)*, Checkerboard Library) ABDO Publishing Co.
Locricchio, Matthew. The International Cookbook for Kids, 0 vols. 2012. (ENG.). 176p. (YA). (gr. 7-9). pap. 12.99 *(978-0-7614-6313-9(5)*, 9780761463139, Amazon Children's Publishing) Amazon Publishing.
Lunis, Natalie. Making Ice Cream. 2011. (Early Connections Ser.). (J). *(978-1-61672-562-4(1))* Benchmark Education Co.
Lustig, Harriet & Lustig, Laurence. The Young Folks' Cook Book. 2011. 32p. pap. 35.95 *(978-1-258-10342-2(7))* Literary Licensing, LLC.
Lynette, Rachel. Let's Throw a St. Patrick's Day Party! 2011. (J). 49.50 *(978-1-4488-2738-1(8))*; pap. 8.25

(978-1-4488-2737-4(X)); lib. bdg. 22.60 (978-1-4488-2574-5(1)) Rosen Publishing Group, Inc., The. (PowerKids Pr.).

—Let's Throw a Thanksgiving Party! 2011. (J). 49.50 (978-1-4488-2736-7(1)); pap. 8.25 (978-1-4488-2735-0(3)); lib. bdg. 22.60 (978-1-4488-2573-8(3)) Rosen Publishing Group, Inc., The. (PowerKids Pr.).

—Let's Throw a Valentine's Day Party! 2011. (J). 49.50 (978-1-4488-2730-5(2)); pap. 8.25 (978-1-4488-2729-9(9)); lib. bdg. 22.60 (978-1-4488-2570-7(9)) Rosen Publishing Group, Inc., The. (PowerKids Pr.).

MacLeod, Elizabeth. Chock Full of Chocolate. Bradford, June, illus. 2005. (Kids Can Do It Ser.). (ENG.). 40p. (J). (gr. 3-7). 6.95 (978-1-55337-763-4(X)) Kids Can Pr., Ltd. CAN. Dist: Hachette Bk. Group.

Madavan, Vijay. Cooking the Indian Way. 2nd ed. 2003. (Easy Menu Ethnic Cookbooks). (Illus.). 72p. (J). (gr. 5-12). pap. 7.95 (978-0-8225-0534-1(7)) Lerner Publishing Group.

Make your own Cakes & Cookies. 2004. (How 2 Kits Ser.). (Illus.). 48p. (J). (978-1-84229-936-4(0)) Top That! Publishing PLC.

Malam, John. Grow Your Own Smoothie, 1 vol. 2011. (Grow It Yourself! Ser.). (ENG.). 32p. (gr. k-2). 27.32 (978-1-4329-5111-5(4), Heinemann First Library) Heinemann-Raintree.

Manning, Ella L. Macaretti. 2012. 16p. pap. 15.99 (978-1-4685-6602-4(4)) AuthorHouse.

Markle, Sandra. Chocolate: A Sweet History. Harper, Charise Mericle, illus. 2004. (Smart about History Ser.). (ENG.). 32p. (J). (gr. k-4). mass mkt. 5.99 (978-0-448-43480-3(6), Grosset & Dunlap) Penguin Young Readers Group.

Marlowe, Christie. Chef. 2013. (Earning $50,000 - $100,000 with a High School Diploma or Less Ser.: 14). 64p. (J). (gr. 7-18). 22.95 (978-1-4222-2890-6(8)) Mason Crest.

Marsico, Katie. Kitchen Math. 2014. (Math Everywhere! Ser.). (Illus.). 32p. (gr. 3-4). (J). lib. bdg. 26.60 (978-1-4677-1883-7(1), Lerner Pubns.); pap. 7.95 (978-1-4677-4513-0(8)) Lerner Publishing Group.

Mason, Helen. Chef. 2014. (Creative Careers Ser.). 48p. (J). (gr. 4-8). pap. 84.30 (978-1-4824-1187-4(3)) Stevens, Gareth Publishing LLLP.

Matt, F. Cooking, Vegetarian Cooking, Pizza & Pasta, Cakes & Cookies. 2004. (Cooking School Ser.). (Illus.). 195p. (J). pap. 19.95 (978-0-7945-0353-6(5)) EDC Publishing.

—Pasta & Pizza for Beginners. rev. ed. 2004. (Cooking School Ser.). (Illus.). 48p. (J). pap. 7.95 (978-0-7945-0555-4(4)) EDC Publishing.

Mattern, Joanne. Chefs. 2009. (Working Together Ser.). 24p. (gr. 1-2). 42.50 (978-1-60854-829-3(5), PowerKids Pr.) Rosen Publishing Group, Inc., The.

—Cocineros. 2004. (Trabajo en Grupo (Working Together) Ser.). (SPA & ENG., Illus.). 24p. (J). (gr. 1-4). lib. bdg. 22.60 (978-0-8239-6841-1(3)) Rosen Publishing Group, Inc., The.

—Cocineros (Chefs) 2009. (Trabajo en grupo (Working Together) Ser.). (SPA.). 24p. (gr. 1-2). 42.50 (978-1-60854-576-6(8), Editorial Buenas Letras) Rosen Publishing Group, Inc., The.

—I Use Math in the Kitchen. 2005. (I Use Math Ser.). (Illus.). 24p. (gr. k-3). pap. 8.15 (978-0-8368-4864-9(0)); lib. bdg. 22.00 (978-0-8368-4857-1(8)) Stevens, Gareth Publishing LLLP. (Weekly Reader Leveled Readers).

Mattern, Joanne, et al. I Use Math in the Kitchen (USO las Matematicas en la Cocina) 2005. (I Use Math/ Uso las matematicas Ser.). (ENG & SPA., Illus.). 24p. (gr. k-3). lib. bdg. 22.00 (978-0-8368-6002-3(0), Weekly Reader Leveled Readers) Stevens, Gareth Publishing LLLP.

Maurer, Daniel D. Do You Really Want to Burn Your Toast? A Book about Heat. Alberini, Teresa, illus. 2016. (Adventures in Science Ser.). (ENG.). 24p. (J). (gr. k-3). 20.95 (978-1-60753-961-2(6)) Amicus Publishing.

Maxwell, Sarah. I Can Cook: Recipes for Kids Shown Step by Step. 2014. (Show Me How Ser.). (ENG., Illus.). 48p. (J). (gr. -1-6). 7.99 (978-1-84322-755-7(X), Armadillo) Anness Publishing GBR. Dist: National Bk. Network.

Mayo Clinic Center for Social Media Staff. Mayo Clinic Kids' 50 Favorite Recipes for Fun & Healthy Eating. 2012. (ENG., Illus.). 128p. (gr. -1-7). 19.95 (978-1-56148-751-6(1), Da Capo Lifelong) Da Capo Pr., Inc.

Mayo Clinic Staff, contrib. by. 20 Tasty Recipes for People with Diabetes. 2004. (Mayo Clinic on Health Ser.). (Illus.). 36,52p. (YA). (gr. 8-18). lib. bdg. 15.95 (978-1-59084-247-8(2)) Mason Crest.

Mayo, Gretchen Will. Applesauce. 2004. (Weekly Reader Early Learning Library). (Illus.). 24p. (gr. 1-4). pap. 8.15 (978-0-8368-4071-1(2)); lib. bdg. 21.00 (978-0-8368-4064-3(X)) Stevens, Gareth Publishing LLLP. (Weekly Reader Leveled Readers).

McCallum, Ann. Eat Your Math Homework: Recipes for Hungry Minds. Hernandez, Leeza, illus. 2011. (Eat Your Homework Ser.). (ENG.). 48p. (J). (gr. 2-5). pap. 7.95 (978-1-57091-780-6(9)) Charlesbridge Publishing, Inc.

—Eat Your Science Homework: Recipes for Inquiring Minds. Hernandez, Leeza, illus. 2014. (Eat Your Homework Ser.). (ENG.). 48p. (J). (gr. 2-5). 16.95 (978-1-57091-298-6(X)) Charlesbridge Publishing, Inc.

McConnell, S. Let's Bring Mom Breakfast: Learning the BR Sound. 2009. (PowerPhonics Ser.). 24p. (gr. 1-1). 39.90 (978-1-60851-455-7(2), PowerKids Pr.) Rosen Publishing Group, Inc., The.

McCord, Marianne. Gilbert! Front & Center! Maginn, Traci, illus. 2003. 24p. (J). per. 5.95 (978-0-9743352-0-9(7)) Jades Publishing.

McCrary, Greta. Kidz in the Kitchen. 2007. 132p. per. 19.95 (978-1-4137-9081-8(X)) America Star Bks.

McDougall, Nancy. Kids Can Cook! Fun in the Kitchen: Learn How to Cook with over 100 Great Recipes: Illustrated Step by Step with 175 Photographs. 2016. (ENG., Illus.). 160p. pap. 9.99 (978-0-85723-871-9(X), Southwater) Anness Publishing GBR. Dist: National Bk. Network.

—The Ultimate Step-by-Step Kid's First Cookbook - How to Cook More Than 150 Irresistible Dishes, Shown Step-by-Step in over 1000 Fantastic Photographs: Delicious Recipe Ideas for 5-12 Year Olds, from Lunch Boxes & Picnics to Quick & Easy Meals, Sweet Treats, Desserts, Drinks & Party Food. 2014. (ENG., Illus.). 256p. (J). (gr. -1-7). pap. 13.99 (978-1-78019-324-3(6), Southwater) Anness Publishing GBR. Dist: National Bk. Network.

—We Can Cook! Kids in the Kitchen. 2012. (ENG., Illus.). 160p. pap. 17.99 (978-1-78019-030-3(1)) Anness Publishing GBR. Dist: National Bk. Network.

McDougall, Nancy & Shehzad, Husain. The Best-Ever Step-by-Step Kid's First Cookbook: Delicious Recipe Ideas for 5-12 Year Olds, from Lunch Boxes & Picnics to Quick & Easy Meals, Sweet Treats, Desserts, Drinks & Party Food. 2017. (ENG., Illus.). 256p. (J). (gr. -1-12). pap. 11.99 **(978-0-85723-197-0(9)**, Southwater) Anness Publishing GBR. Dist: National Bk. Network.

Meachen Rau, Dana. Applesauce. 2008. (What's Cooking? Ser.). 24p. (gr. k-1). lib. bdg. 15.95 (978-0-7614-2894-7(1), Benchmark Bks.) Marshall Cavendish Corp.

—Chefs. 2007. (Tools We Use Ser.). (Illus.). 32p. (gr. k-2). lib. bdg. 15.95 (978-0-7614-2657-8(4), Benchmark Bks.) Marshall Cavendish Corp.

—Chefs/Los Chefs. 2007. (Tools We Use/Instrumentos de Trabajo Ser.). (SPA & ENG., Illus.). 32p. (gr. k-2). lib. bdg. 15.95 (978-0-7614-2822-0(4), Benchmark Bks.) Marshall Cavendish Corp.

—Los Chefs. 2007. (Instrumentos de Trabajo Ser.). (SPA & ENG., Illus.). 32p. (gr. k-2). lib. bdg. 15.95 (978-0-7614-2798-8(8), Benchmark Bks.) Marshall Cavendish Corp.

—Puré de Manzana. 2008. (Qué Preparamos Hoy? Ser.). (SPA.). 24p. (gr. k-1). lib. bdg. 15.95 (978-0-7614-3440-5(2), Benchmark Bks.) Marshall Cavendish Corp.

—What's Cooking?, 6 bks., Set. Incl. Applesauce. lib. bdg. 15.95 (978-0-7614-2894-7(1)); Bread. lib. bdg. 15.95 (978-0-7614-2892-3(5)); Cake. lib. bdg. 15.95 (978-0-7614-2896-1(8)); Cookies. lib. bdg. 15.95 (978-0-7614-2890-9(9)); Ice Cream. lib. bdg. 15.95 (978-0-7614-2893-0(3)); Pizza. lib. bdg. 15.95 (978-0-7614-2891-6(7)); 24p. (gr. k-1). (Benchmark Rebus: What's Cooking? Ser.). 2008. Set lib. bdg. 95.70 (978-0-7614-2889-3(5), Benchmark Bks.) Marshall Cavendish Corp.

A Mediterranean Cookbook for Kids. 2013. (Cooking Around the World Ser.). 32p. (J). (gr. 3-6). pap. 70.50 (978-1-4777-1527-7(4), PowerKids Pr.) Rosen Publishing Group, Inc., The.

Meredith Books Staff, ed. Cooking for Kids. 2004. (Illus.). 200p. 19.95 (978-0-696-22227-6(2), Food Network Kitchens) Meredith Bks.

Meyer, Susan. A Career As a Chef. 2012. (Essential Careers Ser.). (ENG., Illus.). 80p. (YA). (gr. 7-12). lib. bdg. 33.25 (978-1-4488-8236-6(2)) Rosen Publishing Group, Inc., The.

Miller, Brandon Marie. Benjamin Franklin, American Genius: His Life & Ideas with 21 Activities. 2009. (For Kids Ser.). (ENG., Illus.). 144p. (J). (gr. 4-7). pap. 16.95 (978-1-55652-757-9(8)) Chicago Review Pr., Inc.

Miller, Connie Colwell. I'll Be a Chef. Baroncelli, Silvia, illus. 2016. (When I Grow Up Ser.). (ENG.). 24p. (J). (gr. k-3). 20.95 (978-1-60753-759-5(1)) Amicus Publishing.

Minden, Cecilia. Cooking by the Numbers. 2007. (21st Century Skills Library: Real World Math Ser.). (ENG., Illus.). 32p. (gr. 4-8). lib. bdg. 28.50 (978-1-60279-007-0(8), 200061) Cherry Lake Publishing.

—Dinner by the Numbers. 2007. (21st Century Skills Library: Real World Math Ser.). (ENG., Illus.). 32p. (gr. 4-8). lib. bdg. 28.50 (978-1-60279-013-1(2), 200062) Cherry Lake Publishing.

Mitchell, James. Kids' Cookbook. 2007. (Illus.). 64p. (J). (gr. 4-7). (978-1-57215-465-0(9), JG Pr.) World Pubns. Group, Inc.

Mix, Make & Munch: Individual Title Six-Packs. (gr. k-1). 23.00 (978-0-7635-8833-5(4)) Rigby Education.

Mofford, Juliet. Recipe & Craft Guide to the Caribbean. 2010. (World Crafts & Recipes Ser.). (Illus.). 48p. (J). (gr. 4-8). lib. bdg. 29.95 (978-1-58415-935-3(9)) Mitchell Lane Pubs., Inc.

Mohan, et al. Parties with Pizzazz: A Complete Resource for Holiday Classroom Parties. 2004. (Illus.). 128p. pap. 19.95 (978-0-9744936-0-2(0)) Pizzazz Publishing.

Mommy & Me Start Cooking. 2014. (ENG.). 80p. (J). (gr. k-4). 15.99 (978-1-4654-1690-2(0), DK Children) Dorling Kindersley Publishing, Inc.

Montgomery, L. M. Anne of Green Gables Cookbook. 22.95 (978-0-8488-2657-4(4)) Amereon Ltd.

Montoya, Carina Monica. Let's Cook Adobo!, 1 vol. Silva, Eliseo Art, illus. 2010. 22p. pap. 24.95 (978-1-4489-9022-1(X)) PublishAmerica, Inc.

Mooney, Carla. Amazing Africa Projects. Sterns, Megan, illus. 2010. (Build It Yourself Ser.). (ENG.). 128p. (J). (gr. 3-7). pap. 15.95 (978-1-934670-41-5(3)) Octavio Publishing.

Mooney, Carla & Stearns, Megan. Amazing Africa Projects. 2010. (Build It Yourself Ser.). (ENG., Illus.). 128p. (J). (gr. 3-7). 21.95 (978-1-934670-42-2(1)) Octavio Publishing.

Morado, Leah. What's on My Plate? Develop Understanding of Fractions & Numbers, 1 vol. 2015. (InfoMax Common Core Math Readers Ser.). (ENG.). 24p. (J). pap. 8.25 (978-1-4777-4609-7(9), Rosen Classroom) Rosen Publishing Group, Inc., The.

My Recipe Keeper. 2008. 144p. (978-1-4075-2448-1(8)) Parragon, Inc.

My Tea Party: Incl. 9 Piece Tea Set, Cookie Cutter & Carrying Case. (J). (gr. 3-18). pap. (978-1-56021-299-7(3), 200) W.J. Fantasy, Inc.

Nagle, Jeanne. Giada de Laurentiis. 2016. (Celebrity Chefs Ser.). 128p. (J). (gr. 6-6). 37.27 (978-0-7660-7759-1(4)) Enslow Pubs., Inc.

Nelson, Robin. Los Productos Lacteos. Castañer, Mercedes & Fitzpatrick, Julia, trs. 2003. (Mi Primer Paso Al Mundo Real - Los Grupos de Alimentos (First Step Nonfiction - Food Groups) Ser.). (SPA., Illus.). 24p. (gr. k-2). lib. bdg. 23.93 (978-0-8225-5060-0(1)) Lerner Publishing Group.

—Strawberries. 2009. (First Step Nonfiction - Plant Life Cycles Ser.). (ENG.). 24p. (gr. k-2). 23.93 (978-0-7613-4074-4(2), Lerner Pubns.) Lerner Publishing Group.

Nieminen, Lotta. Pancakes! An Interactive Recipe Book. 2016. (Cook in a Book Ser.). (ENG., Illus.). 16p. (gr. -1 — 1). 14.95 (978-0-7148-7283-4(0)) Phaidon Pr., Inc.

Nieminen, Lotta. Pizza! An Interactive Recipe Book. 2017. (Cook in a Book Ser.). (ENG., Illus.). 16p. bds. 14.95 **(978-0-7148-7410-4(8))** Phaidon Pr., Inc.

Nieminen, Lotta, contrib. by. Pizza! An Interactive Recipe Book. 2017. (Cook in a Book Ser.). (ENG., Illus.). 16p. (gr. -1 — 1). bds. 14.95 **(978-0-7148-7409-8(4))** Phaidon Pr. Ltd. GBR. Dist: Hachette Bk. Group.

Norton, Frances Maree. The Victorian Tea Spirit: A Girl's Guide to Her Secret Self, 1. 100th ed. 2003. (Illus.). 230p. (YA). per. 19.95 (978-0-9632938-1-7(8)) Norton, Frances M.

Numeroff, Laura Joffe. If You Give a Bear a Brownie Recipes. Bond, Felicia, illus. Date not set. 32p. (J). (gr. -1-2). 12.99 (978-0-06-028559-3(1)) HarperCollins Pubs.

—If You Give a Cat a Cupcake Recipes. Bond, Felicia, illus. Date not set. 32p. (J). (gr. -1-2). 12.99 (978-0-06-028560-9(5)) HarperCollins Pubs.

—If You Give a Moose a Muffin Recipe Book. Bond, Felicia, illus. Date not set. 32p. (J). (gr. -1-2). 12.99 (978-0-06-028562-3(1)) HarperCollins Pubs.

—Pig Pancakes. Bond, Felicia, illus. Date not set. 32p. (J). (gr. -1-2). 1.00 (978-0-06-028563-0(X)) HarperCollins Pubs.

Ofanansky, Allison. How It's Made Matzah. Alpern, Andrew, photos by. 2017. (Illus.). (J). (978-1-68115-524-1(9)) Behrman Hse., Inc.

Omoth, Tyler. Campfire Chef: Mouthwatering Campfire Recipes. 2017. (Kids Can Cook! Ser.). (ENG., Illus.). 32p. (gr. 3-4). lib. bdg. 27.99 (978-1-5157-3813-8(2)) Capstone Press of Coughlan Cos.

Owen, Ruth. Halloween Sweets & Treats. 2012. (Holiday Cooking for Kids! Ser.). (ENG., Illus.). 32p. (J). (gr. 3-6). 26.50 (978-1-4488-8079-9(3)); pap. 11.75 (978-1-4488-8126-0(9)) Windmill Bks.

—Valentine's Day Sweets & Treats. 2012. (Holiday Cooking for Kids! Ser.). (ENG., Illus.). 32p. (J). (gr. 3-6). 26.50 (978-1-4488-8080-5(7)); pap. 11.75 (978-1-4488-8127-7(7)) Windmill Bks.

Owens, Chef David. Brocklee & the Little Chef. 2010. pap. 19.95 (978-0-578-05417-9(5)) Owens, David A.

Paré, Jean. Kids Cook! 2010. (3-In-1 Cookbook Collection). (ENG., Illus.). 208p. (J). spiral bd. 16.99 (978-1-896891-63-7(2), 9781896891637) Company's Coming Publishing, Ltd. CAN. Dist: Lone Pine Publishing USA.

—Kids Do Snacks, 1 vol. 2007. (Original Ser.). (ENG., Illus.). 160p. (J). spiral bd. 16.99 (978-1-897069-27-1(8), 1897069278) Company's Coming Publishing, Ltd. CAN. Dist: Lone Pine Publishing USA.

—Kids Healthy Cooking. 2006. (Original Ser.). (ENG., Illus.). 160p. (J). spiral bd. 16.99 (978-1-897069-02-8(2), 1897069022) Company's Coming Publishing, Ltd. CAN. Dist: Lone Pine Publishing USA.

—Kitchen Fun for Kids. 2011. (2-In-1 Cookbook Collection). (ENG.). 256p. (J). spiral bd. 19.99 (978-1-897069-85-1(5), 9781897069851) Company's Coming Publishing, Ltd. CAN. Dist: Lone Pine Publishing USA.

Parrini, Sabrina. Little Kitchen: 40 Delicious & Simple Things That Children Can Really Make. Melville, Jacqui, photos by. 2010. (Illus.). 128p. pap. (978-1-74066-743-2(3)) Hardie Grant Bks. AUS. Dist: Independent Pubs. Group.

—Little Kitchen: 40 Delicious & Simple Things That Children Can Really Make. 2011. (ENG., Illus.). 128p. (J). (gr. 1-5). pap. 17.95 (978-1-61608-188-1(0), 608188) Skyhorse Publishing Co., Inc.

Patchett, Fiona. The Usborne Healthy Cookbook. Dreidemy, Joëlle, illus. Allman, Howard, photos by. 2008. (Children's Cooking Ser.). (ENG.). 64p. (J). (gr. 4-7). pap. 16.99 (978-0-7945-2062-5(6), Usborne) EDC Publishing.

—30 Yummy Things to Bake. 2008. (Activity Cards Ser.). (Illus.). 30p. (J). 9.99 (978-0-7945-2169-1(X), Usborne) EDC Publishing.

Paul, Aileen. Kids Cooking Without a Stove: A Cookbook for Young Children. Inouye, Carol, illus. rev. ed. 2005. 64p. (J). pap. 10.95 (978-0-86534-060-2(9)) Sunstone Pr.

Peters, Rosalind. Midnight Feast Magic: Sleepover Fun & Food. Pankhurst, Kate, illus. Boursnell, Clive, photos by. 2009. (ENG.). 64p. (J). (gr. 3-6). pap. 15.95 (978-1-84507-783-9(0), Frances Lincoln) Quarto Publishing Group UK GBR. Dist: Hachette Bk. Group.

Peterseil, Tamar. Zap It! A Microwave Cookbook Just for Kids. 2003. (Illus.). 32p. (YA). (gr. 4-7). 12.95 (978-0-943706-13-9(0), Pitspopany Pr.) Simcha Media Group.

Phaidon Press Editors. The Silver Spoon for Children: Favorite Italian Recipes. Grant, Amanda, ed. 2009. (ENG.). 100p. (gr. 5-17). 19.95 (978-0-7148-5756-5(4)) Phaidon Pr., Inc.

Pillsbury Editors, ed. Pillsbury Kids Cookbook: Food Fun for Boys & Girls. 2005. (Pillsbury Cooking Ser.). (ENG., Illus.). 160p. (gr. 3-7). 19.95 (978-0-7645-7861-8(8)) Houghton Mifflin Harcourt Publishing Co.

PopPopPopcorn! Individual Title Six-Packs. (gr. -1-2). 23.00 (978-0-7635-8992-9(6)) Rigby Education.

Powell, Jillian & O'Shea, Clare. Cooking with Cereals & Grains. 2011. (Cooking Healthy Ser.). (J). lib. bdg. 29.25 (978-1-4488-4842-3(3), Rosen Reference) Rosen Publishing Group, Inc., The.

Publications International Ltd. Staff, ed. Beth Logan la Cuisine. 2011. bds. 10.98 (978-1-4508-1359-4(3)) Publications International, Ltd.

—Biscuit Magic Cook Book. 2011. 96p. 7.98 (978-1-4508-1721-9(1)) Publications International, Ltd.

—Disney Princess: Cupcakes & More. 2011. (Illus.). 48p. (J). bds. 10.98 (978-1-4127-6435-3(1)) Publications International, Ltd.

Raab, Evelyn. Clueless in the Kitchen: A Cookbook for Teens. Walker, George, illus. 2nd rev. ed. 2011. (Clueless Ser.). (ENG.). 216p. pap. 14.95 (978-1-55407-824-0(5), 9781554078240) Firefly Bks., Ltd.

Raab, Evelyn. Clueless in the Kitchen: Cooking for Beginners. 3rd enl. ed. 2017. (ENG., Illus.). 208p. pap. 16.95 **(978-1-77085-933-3(0)**, 9781770859333) Firefly Bks., Ltd.

Rajczak, Kristen. Creative Cocoa Recipes. 2014. (Ingredients for a Healthy Life Ser.). (Illus.). 24p. (J). (gr. 2-5). 22.60 (978-1-4824-0559-0(8)) Stevens, Gareth Publishing LLLP.

—Fantastic Fruit Recipes. 2014. (Ingredients for a Healthy Life Ser.). (Illus.). 24p. (J). (gr. 2-5). 22.60 (978-1-4824-0565-1(2)) Stevens, Gareth Publishing LLLP.

—Great Grain Recipes. 2014. (Ingredients for a Healthy Life Ser.). (Illus.). 24p. (J). (gr. 2-5). 22.60 (978-1-4824-0569-9(5)) Stevens, Gareth Publishing LLLP.

—Perfect Pasta Recipes. 2014. (Ingredients for a Healthy Life Ser.). (Illus.). 24p. (J). (gr. 2-5). 22.60 (978-1-4824-0571-2(7)) Stevens, Gareth Publishing LLLP.

Randall, Ronne. Hanukkah Sweets & Treats. 2012. (Holiday Cooking for Kids! Ser.). (ENG., Illus.). 32p. (J). (gr. 3-6). 26.50 (978-1-4488-8083-6(1)); pap. 11.75 (978-1-4488-8130-7(7)) Windmill Bks.

—Thanksgiving Sweets & Treats. 2012. (Holiday Cooking for Kids! Ser.). (ENG., Illus.). 32p. (J). (gr. 3-6). 26.50 (978-1-4488-8082-9(3)); pap. 11.75 (978-1-4488-8129-1(3)) Windmill Bks.

Rao, Nikhil & Wolf, Gita. All about Indian Food. 2005. (Illus.). 146p. 10.99 (978-81-86211-79-3(9)) Penguin Publishing Group.

Rau, Dana Meachen. Cooking Around the World, 1 vol. 2014. (Cooking Around the World Ser.). (ENG.). 48p. (gr. 5-8). lib. bdg. 119.96 (978-1-4109-5975-1(9)) Heinemann-Raintree.

Rauf, Don. Emeril Lagasse. 2016. (Celebrity Chefs Ser.). (ENG., Illus.). 128p. (J). (gr. 7-8). 37.27 (978-0-7660-7197-1(9)) Enslow Pubs., Inc.

—Rachael Ray. 2016. (Celebrity Chefs Ser.). (ENG., Illus.). 128p. (J). (gr. 7-8). 37.27 (978-0-7660-7330-2(0)) Enslow Pubs., Inc.

Ray, Rachael. Rachael Ray's 30-Minute Meals for Kids: Cooking Rocks! Kalb, Chris, illus. 2004. (ENG.). 192p. spiral bd. 16.95 (978-1-891105-15-9(9)) Lake Isle Pr., Inc.

Redinger, Anne. Chow Now Brown Cow: Storybook Cooking. 2012. 60p. pap. 24.99 (978-1-4772-1114-4(4)) AuthorHouse.

Rees, Rob. Backyard Cookbook. 2010. (Crabtree Connections Ser.). (ENG.). 24p. (J). (gr. 3-6). (978-0-7787-9939-9(5)); pap. (978-0-7787-9961-0(1)) Crabtree Publishing Co.

Reynolds, Wendy A. & Hayes, Amy. Turning Apples into Applesauce. 2015. (Step-By-Step Transformations Ser.). (ENG., Illus.). 24p. (J). (gr. 1-1). pap. 8.22 (978-1-5026-0442-2(6)) Cavendish Square Publishing.

Rissman, Rebecca. Cooking & Eating: Comparing Past & Present, 1 vol. 2014. (Comparing Past & Present Ser.). (ENG.). 24p. (gr. -1-1). lib. bdg. 22.65 (978-1-4329-8990-3(1), Acorn) Heinemann-Raintree.

—Eat, 1 vol. 2013. (Say What You See Ser.). (ENG.). 24p. (gr. -1-1). 22.65 (978-1-4109-5047-5(6)); pap. 7.10 (978-1-4109-5052-9(2)) Heinemann-Raintree.

Roholt, Christine VeLure. Foods of Brazil. 2014. (Cook with Me Ser.). (ENG., Illus.). 24p. (J). (gr. 3-7). lib. bdg. 25.95 (978-1-62617-115-2(7), Express Bks.) Bellwether Media.

—Foods of India. 2014. (Cook with Me Ser.). (ENG., Illus.). 24p. (J). (gr. 3-7). lib. bdg. 25.95 (978-1-62617-118-3(1), Express Bks.) Bellwether Media.

—Foods of Japan. 2014. (Cook with Me Ser.). (ENG.). 24p. (J). (gr. 3-7). 25.95 (978-1-62617-120-6(3), Express Bks.) Bellwether Media.

Romero, Libby. Discover Kitchen Chemistry. 2006. (J). pap. (978-1-4108-6501-4(0)) Benchmark Education Co.

—Kitchen Chemistry. 2006. (J). pap. (978-1-4108-6498-7(7)) Benchmark Education Co.

Rooney, Ronnie. Thanksgiving Recipes, 1 vol. Rooney, Ronnie, illus. 2010. (Thanksgiving Ser.). (ENG., Illus.). 24p. (gr. 1-2). lib. bdg. 27.32 (978-1-4048-6283-8(8)) Picture Window Bks.

Rosario, Miguel. Kitchen Math. 2015. (J). pap. (978-1-62713-452-1(2)) Cavendish Square Publishing.

Rosenbaum, Stephanie. Fun Food. Williams, Chuck, ed. Lowe, Jason, photos by. 2006. (ENG., Illus.). 128p. 19.95 (978-0-7432-7856-0(9), Free Pr.) Free Pr.

Rosenberg, Pam. How Did That Get to My Table? Ice Cream. 2009. (Community Connections: How Did That Get to My Table? Ser.). (ENG.). 24p. (gr. 2-5). lib. bdg. 25.64 (978-1-60279-467-2(7), 200263) Cherry Lake Publishing.

Rosman, Jessica. Kindy Kitchen: Where Fruit & Vegies Come to Life. Lodge, Nettie, illus. 2016. 128p. pap. 19.99 (978-0-7333-3438-2(5)) ABC Bks. AUS. Dist: HarperCollins Pubs.

Roth, Ruby. The Help Yourself Cookbook for Kids: 60 Easy Plant-Based Recipes Kids Can Make to Make to Stay Healthy & Save the Earth. 2016. (ENG., Illus.). 144p. (J). pap. 19.99 (978-1-4494-7187-3(0)) Andrews McMeel Publishing.

Rouss, Sylvia A. & Turndorf, Genene Levy. Sammy Spider's First Taste of Hanukkah: A Cookbook. Kahn, Katherine Janus, illus. 2015. (ENG.). 32p. (J). (gr. -1-3). 16.99 (978-1-4677-5237-4(1), Kar-Ben Publishing) Lerner Publishing Group.

Rumsey, Frances. My Very Own Organic Cookbook: Bananas. 2013. 20p. pap. 7.95 (978-1-61170-112-8(0)) Robertson Publishing.

Rustad, Alan & Isaac, Andrew. Cooks & Kids: 11 Top Chefs & Children Cook up a Storm in the Kitchen with Their Favourite Recipes. 2011. (ENG., Illus.). 96p. 15.99 (978-1-905582-55-6(2)) Graffeg Limited GBR. Dist: Independent Pubs. Group.

Rustad, Martha E. H. Fall Apples: Crisp & Juicy. Enright, Amanda, illus. 2011. (Fall's Here! Ser.). pap. 39.62 (978-0-7613-8644-5(0), Millbrook Pr.); (ENG.). 24p. pap. 6.95 (978-0-7613-8507-3(X), Millbrook Pr.); (ENG.). 24p. lib. bdg. 23.93 (978-0-7613-5064-4(0)) Lerner Publishing Group.

Sanders, Moira. Gastro Blast: Make Tasty Treats & Learn Great Science: Comics, Quizzes & Questions Answered! Get Ready to Make Science Delicious! 2016. (ENG., Illus.). 128p. (J). (gr. 1-7). pap. 24.95 (978-1-4595-0462-2(3), 9781459504622) Formac Publishing Co., Ltd. CAN. Dist: Casemate Pubs. & Bk. Distributors, LLC.

Sanger, Amy Wilson. Mangia! Mangia! 2005. (World Snacks Ser.). (ENG., Illus.). 20p. (J). (gr. k — 1). bds. 6.99 (978-1-58246-144-1(9), Tricycle Pr.) Random Hse. Children's Bks.

Sanner, Catie. Cooking with Catie: The 3ABN Kids Time Cookbook. Walsh, Brenda, ed. 2004. 86p. (J). ring bd. (978-0-9720888-4-8(9)) Three Angels Broadcasting Network.

Schloss, Andrew & Joachim, David. Mastering the Grill: The Owner's Manual for Outdoor Cooking. Miksch, Alison, photos by. 2007. (ENG., Illus.). 416p. (gr. 8-17). pap. 24.95 (978-0-8118-4964-7(3)) Chronicle Bks. LLC.

Schuette, Sarah L. A Ballerina Cookbook: Simple Recipes for Kids, 1 vol. 2012. (First Cookbooks Ser.). (ENG.). 24p. (gr. 1-2). lib. bdg. 25.32 (978-1-4296-7622-9(1), First Facts) Capstone Press of Coughlan Cos.

—A Dinosaur Cookbook: Simple Recipes for Kids, 1 vol. 2012. (First Cookbooks Ser.). (ENG.). 24p. (gr. 1-2). lib. bdg. 25.32

(978-1-4296-7621-2(3), First Facts) Capstone Press of Coughlan Cos.

—First Cookbooks. (First Cookbooks Ser.). (ENG.). 24p. (gr. 1-2). 2012. lib. bdg. 101.28 (978-1-4296-8154-4(3)) 2012. lib. bdg. 177.24 (978-1-4296-8155-1(1)) 2011. lib. bdg. 50.64 (978-1-4296-6134-8(8)) Capstone Press of Coughlan Cos. (First Facts).

—First Cookbooks, 6 vols., Set. Incl. Christmas Cookbook: Simple Recipes for Kids. 2011. lib. bdg. 25.32 (978-1-4296-5999-4(8)); Princess Cookbook: Simple Recipes for Kids. 2010. lib. bdg. 25.32 (978-1-4296-5374-9(4)); Superhero Cookbook: Simple Recipes for Kids. 2011. lib. bdg. 25.32 (978-1-4296-5998-7(X)); (gr. 1-2). (First Cookbooks Ser.). (ENG.). 24p. 2011. Set lib. bdg. 75.96 (978-1-4296-6135-5(6), First Facts) Capstone Press of Coughlan Cos.

—A Football Cookbook: Simple Recipes for Kids, 1 vol. 2012. (First Cookbooks Ser.). (ENG.). 24p. (gr. 1-2). lib. bdg. 25.32 (978-1-4296-7620-5(5), First Facts) Capstone Press of Coughlan Cos.

—A Halloween Cookbook: Simple Recipes for Kids, 1 vol. 2012. (First Cookbooks Ser.). (ENG., Illus.). 24p. (gr. 1-2). lib. bdg. 25.32 (978-1-4296-7619-9(1), First Facts) Capstone Press of Coughlan Cos.

—A Princess Cookbook: Simple Recipes for Kids, 1 vol. 2010. (First Cookbooks Ser.). (ENG.). 24p. (gr. 1-2). lib. bdg. 25.32 (978-1-4296-5374-9(4), First Facts) Capstone Press of Coughlan Cos.

—A Superhero Cookbook: Simple Recipes for Kids, 1 vol. 2011. (First Cookbooks Ser.). (ENG.). 24p. (gr. 1-2). lib. bdg. 25.32 (978-1-4296-5998-7(X), First Facts) Capstone Press of Coughlan Cos.

Scotti, Alberto Douglas. Cocina y Ciencia. 2012. 44p. (J). (gr. 3-5). pap. 23.99 (978-958-30-3715-3(X)) Juventud, Editorial ESP. Dist: Lectorum Pubns., Inc.

Seaver, Barton. National Geographic Kids Cookbook: A Year-Round Fun Food Adventure. 2014. (ENG., Illus.). 160p. (J). (gr. 3-7). pap. 19.99 (978-1-4263-1717-0(4), National Geographic Children's Bks.) National Geographic Society.

Segarra, Mercedes. Fun Party Food: Little Chef Recipes. 2013. (Little Chef Ser.). 36p. (J). lib. bdg. 23.94 (978-0-7660-4262-9(6), Enslow Elementary) Enslow Pubs., Inc.

—Pizza & Pasta: Little Chef Recipes. 2013. (Little Chef Ser.). 36p. (J). lib. bdg. 23.94 (978-0-7660-4263-6(4)); pap. 7.95 (978-1-4644-0469-6(0)) Enslow Pubs., Inc. (Enslow Elementary).

—Tasty Desserts: Little Chef Recipes. 2013. (Little Chef Ser.). (Illus.). 36p. (J). lib. bdg. 23.94 (978-0-7660-4261-2(8), Enslow Elementary) Enslow Pubs., Inc.

—Yummy Snacks: Little Chef Recipes. 2013. (Little Chef Ser.). 36p. (J). lib. bdg. 23.94 (978-0-7660-4264-3(2)); pap. 7.95 (978-1-4644-0471-9(2)) Enslow Pubs., Inc. (Enslow Elementary).

Seltzer, Donna Lee & Thorne, Lawrence R., creators. The Carnival Cookbook: From the Kitchen of the Hurricane Grille. 2nd ed. 2004. spiral bd. 15.00 (978-0-9747072-3-5(6)) Bon Tiki Bks.

Sesame Workshop, Sesame & McQuillan, Susan. Sesame Street Let's Cook! 2015. (Sesame Street Ser.). (ENG., Illus.). 128p. (gr. -1-k). spiral bd. 17.99 (978-0-544-45436-1(7)) Houghton Mifflin Harcourt Publishing Co.

Shah, Kieran. Math in the Kitchen. 2016. (Math Is Everywhere! Ser.). 00024p. (J). pap. 8.15 (978-1-4824-5447-5(5)) Stevens, Gareth Publishing LLLP.

Shea, Mary Molly. Foods of India. 2011. (Culture in the Kitchen Ser.). 24p. (J). (gr. 2-5). pap. 8.15 (978-1-4339-5708-6(6)); lib. bdg. 22.60 (978-1-4339-5706-2(X)) Stevens, Gareth Publishing LLLP. (Gareth Stevens Learning Library).

Sheen, Barbara. Chile. 2010. (Taste of Culture Ser.). (ENG.). 64p. lib. bdg. 30.45 (978-0-7377-5421-6(4), Kidhaven) Cengage Gale.

—Foods of Afghanistan. 2011. (Taste of Culture Ser.). 64p. (J). lib. bdg. 30.45 (978-0-7377-5420-9(6), Kidhaven) Cengage Gale.

—Foods of Australia. 2010. (Taste of Culture Ser.). (Illus.). 64p. (J). 30.45 (978-0-7377-4812-3(5), Kidhaven) Cengage Gale.

—Foods of Egypt. 2010. (Taste of Culture Ser.). (Illus.). 64p. (J). 30.45 (978-0-7377-4843-7(5), Kidhaven) Cengage Gale.

—Foods of Ethiopia. 2007. (Taste of Culture Ser.). (ENG., Illus.). 64p. (J). (gr. 3-7). lib. bdg. 30.45 (978-0-7377-3775-2(1), Kidhaven) Cengage Gale.

—Foods of Iran. 2006. (Taste of Culture Ser.). (ENG., Illus.). 64p. (J). (gr. 3-7). lib. bdg. 28.75 (978-0-7377-3453-9(1), Greenhaven Pr., Inc.) Cengage Gale.

—Foods of Kenya. 2010. (Taste of Culture Ser.). (Illus.). 64p. (J). 30.45 (978-0-7377-4813-0(3), Kidhaven) Cengage Gale.

—Foods of the Caribbean. 2007. (Taste of Culture Ser.). (ENG., Illus.). 64p. (J). (gr. 3-7). lib. bdg. 28.75 (978-0-7377-3774-5(3), Kidhaven) Cengage Gale.

Sheen, Barbara, ed. Foods of Canada. 2012. (Taste of Culture Ser.). (ENG., Illus.). 64p. (J). (gr. 3-6). lib. bdg. 30.45 (978-0-7377-5947-1(X), Kidhaven) Cengage Gale.

—Foods of Colombia. 2012. (Taste of Culture Ser.). (ENG., Illus.). 64p. (J). (gr. 3-6). lib. bdg. 30.45 (978-0-7377-5948-8(8), Kidhaven) Cengage Gale.

—Foods of Ghana. 2012. (Taste of Culture Ser.). (ENG., Illus.). 64p. (gr. 3-6). lib. bdg. 35.20 (978-0-7377-5949-5(6), Kidhaven) Cengage Gale.

—Foods of Morocco. 2011. (Taste of Culture Ser.). (Illus.). 64p. (J). lib. bdg. 30.45 (978-0-7377-5865-8(1), Kidhaven) Cengage Gale.

—Foods of Poland. 2011. (Taste of Culture Ser.). (ENG.). 64p. (gr. 3-6). lib. bdg. 35.20 (978-0-7377-5951-8(8), Kidhaven) Cengage Gale.

Short, Deborah J., et al. An Old Family Recipe. (Avenues Ser.). (ENG.). (C). 2004. pap. 65.95 (978-0-7362-2165-8(4)) 2003. pap. 10.95 (978-0-7362-1757-6(6)) CENGAGE Learning.

Siemens, Jared. Chefs. 2015. (J). (978-1-4896-4213-4(7)) Weigl Pubs., Inc.

Silate, Jennifer. Planning & Preparing Healthy Meals & Snacks: A Day-to-Day Guide to a Healthier Diet. (Library of Nutrition Ser.). 48p. 2009. (gr. 5-8). 53.00 (978-1-60853-776-1(5), Rosen Reference) 2008. (ENG., Illus.). (gr. 5-8). per. 11.75 (978-1-4042-1634-1(0)) 2004. (Illus.). (J). lib. bdg. 26.50 (978-1-4042-0302-0(8)) Rosen Publishing Group, Inc., The.

Sinish, Peter. Your Cookbook with Chef Peter. 2013. 122p. 26.99 (978-1-62839-004-9(2)); pap. 15.99 (978-1-62839-002-5(6)) Salem Author Services.

Skaug, Joshua. Kooking for Kids. Skaug, Terry, ed. 2004. (Illus.). 82p. (J). 11.50 (978-0-9764323-0-2(7)) Prickly Pear Pr.

Smithyman, Kathryn & Kalman, Bobbie. Native North American Foods & Recipes. 2005. (Native Nations of North America Ser.). (ENG., Illus.). 32p. (J). (gr. 4-7). pap. (978-0-7787-0475-1(0)); lib. bdg. (978-0-7787-0383-9(5)) Crabtree Publishing Co.

Snyder, Inez. Berries to Jelly. 2005. (How Things Are Made Ser.). (ENG., Illus.). 24p. (J). (gr. -1-1). per. 4.95 (978-0-516-25526-2(6), Children's Pr.) Scholastic Library Publishing.

Solis, Lisa V. Classroom Cupboard: Lessons, Activities & Culinary Concoctions for Kids, 1 vol. 2003. (Illus.). 160p. (C). pap. 28.00 (978-1-56308-957-2(2), LU9572, Libraries Unlimited) ABC-CLIO, LLC.

Solway, Andrew. The Science of a Loaf of Bread: The Science of Changing Properties. 2009. (Science of... Ser.). (Illus.). 32p. (YA). (gr. 3-6). lib. bdg. 26.00 (978-1-4339-0043-3(2)) Stevens, Gareth Publishing LLLP.

Speregen, Debra Newberger. Party Girl: How to Throw a Fab Fest. Tallardy, Laura, illus. 2008. 48p. pap. (978-0-545-04093-8(0)) Scholastic, Inc.

Springer, David. Samhain in the Kitchen. 2005. 52p. (J). spiral bd. 9.00 (978-1-4116-3670-5(8)) Lulu Pr., Inc.

Start to Cook. 2017. (Start to Cook Ser.). (ENG.). (J). spiral bd. 19.99 **(978-0-7945-3743-2(X)**, Usborne) EDC Publishing.

Stern, Sam & Stern, Susan. Get Cooking. Campbell, Lorne, photos by. 2009. (ENG., Illus.). 144p. (J). (gr. 5-18). pap. 17.99 (978-0-7636-3926-6(5)) Candlewick Pr.

Stiefel, Chana. There's a Rat in My Soup: Could You Survive Medieval Food? Kelley, Gerald, illus. 2011. (Ye Yucky Middle Ages Ser.). 48p. (J). (gr. 5-18). pap. 8.95 (978-1-59845-375-1(0)); (gr. 7-12). lib. bdg. 25.27 (978-0-7660-3785-4(1)) Enslow Pubs., Inc.

Strauss, Holden. A Chef's Tools. 2015. (Community Helpers & Their Tools Ser.). (ENG., Illus.). 24p. (J). (gr. 2-3). pap. 8.25 (978-1-4994-0834-8(X), PowerKids Pr.) Rosen Publishing Group, Inc., The.

Students of Dorsey High School Staff. From the Couch to the Kitchen: A Book to Indulge In. 2011. (ENG.). 144p. (gr. k). 15.00 (978-1-934750-24-7(7)) 826 Valencia.

Studio Mouse Staff. Sesame Street Rosita Reads a Recipe. rev. ed. 2008. (ENG.). 24p. 4.99 (978-1-59069-619-4(0)) Studio Mouse LLC.

Suen, Anastasia. How to Bake a Cake. 2015. (ENG.). 24p. (gr. k-3). 28.50 (978-1-63430-357-6(1)) Rourke Educational Media.

Sullivan, Laura. The Colonial Cook. 2015. (Colonial People Ser.). (ENG.). 48p. (J). (gr. 4-4). lib. bdg. 31.36 (978-1-5026-0488-0(4)) Cavendish Square Publishing.

Superchef: Group 2, 4 Bks, Set. 2004. (J). 119.71 (978-0-7614-1728-6(1)) Marshall Cavendish Corp.

Superchef Series, 4 bks., Set. 119.71 (978-0-7614-1213-7(1), Benchmark Bks.) Marshall Cavendish Corp.

Sweetser, Wendy. How to Cook in 10 Easy Lessons: Learn How to Prepare Food & Cook Like a Pro. 2015. (Super Skills Ser.). (ENG.). 64p. (J). (gr. 3-7). spiral bd. 12.95 (978-1-63322-039-3(7), Walter Foster Jr) Quarto Publishing Group USA.

Therrien, Patricia. Amish & Mennonite Cooking. (American Regional Cooking Library). (Illus.). 72p. 2006. (YA). lib. bdg. 19.95 (978-1-59084-612-4(5)) 2005. (J). lib. bdg. 299.25 (978-1-59084-609-4(5)) Mason Crest.

—Hawaiian. 2006. (American Regional Cooking Library). (Illus.). 72p. (YA). lib. bdg. 19.95 (978-1-59084-614-8(1)) Mason Crest.

Thomas, Danita & Thomas, John E. The Ultimate Book of Holiday Kid Concoctions: More Than 50 Wacky, Wild, & Crazy Concoctions for All Occasions. 2006. (Ultimate Book of Kid Concoctions Ser.). (Illus.). 80p. (J). (gr. 4-7). per. 14.99 (978-0-8054-4445-2(9)) B&H Publishing Group.

—The Ultimate Book of Kid Concoctions. 2006. (Illus.). 80p. (J). (gr. 4-7). per. 14.99 (978-0-8054-4443-8(2)) B&H Publishing Group.

Thomas, John E. & Thomas, Danita. The Ultimate Book of Kid Concoctions 2. 2006. (Illus.). 80p. (J). (gr. 4-7). per. 14.99 (978-0-8054-4444-5(0)) B&H Publishing Group.

Thompson, Helen. Culinary Math. 2013. (Math 24/7 Ser.: 10). 48p. (J). (gr. 5-18). 19.95 (978-1-4222-2905-7(X)) Mason Crest.

Tirone, Lisa & TIRONE, Lisa. Chef It Up! 2009. 48p. pap. 12.50 (978-0-557-04286-9(0)) Lulu Pr., Inc.

Tjernagel, Kelsi Turner. Gross Recipes, 1 vol. 2013. (Gross Guides). (ENG.). 32p. (gr. 3-4). lib. bdg. 27.99 (978-1-4296-9925-9(6), Edge Bks.) Capstone Press of Coughlan Cos.

Tomnay, Susan & Australian Women's Weekly Staff. Kids in the Kitchen: More Than 90 Fabulous Recipes for Kids to Make. 2006. (ENG., Illus.). 216p. (gr. -1-17). pap. 24.95 (978-1-86396-518-7(1), Australian Women's Weekly) Bauer Media Bks. AUS. Dist: Hachette Bk. Group.

Top That Publishing Editors, ed. Ghastly Grub. Dahl, Roald, illus. 2005. 24p. (J). pap. (978-1-905359-54-7(3)) Top That! Publishing PLC.

Top That Publishing Staff, ed. Favorite Recipes. 2005. 120p. (978-1-84510-560-0(5)) Top That! Publishing PLC.

Tullet, Hervé. Doodle Cook. Barbour, Susan, tr. from FRE. 2011. (ENG., Illus.). 48p. (gr. k-3). pap. 14.95 (978-0-7148-6227-9(4)) Phaidon Pr., Inc.

Tuminelly, Nancy. Cool Creepy Food Art: Easy Recipes That Make Food Fun to Eat!, 1 vol. 2011. (Cool Food Art Ser.). (ENG.). 32p. (gr. 3-6). 28.50 (978-1-61613-363-4(5), Checkerboard Library) ABDO Publishing Co.

—Cool Fruit & Veggie Food Art: Easy Recipes That Make Food Fun to Eat!, 1 vol. 2011. (Cool Food Art Ser.). (ENG.). 32p. (gr. 3-6). 28.50 (978-1-61613-364-1(3), Checkerboard Library) ABDO Publishing Co.

—Cool Nut-Free Recipes: Delicious & Fun Foods Without Nuts, 1 vol. 2013. (Cool Recipes for Your Health Ser.). (ENG.). 32p. (J). (gr. 3-6). lib. bdg. 28.50 (978-1-61783-583-4(8), Checkerboard Library) ABDO Publishing Co.

—Cool Sugar-Free Recipes: Delicious & Fun Foods Without Refined Sugar, 1 vol. 2013. (Cool Recipes for Your Health Ser.). (ENG.). 32p. (J). (gr. 3-6). lib. bdg. 28.50 (978-1-61783-585-8(4), Checkerboard Library) ABDO Publishing Co.

—Cool Wheat-Free Recipes: Delicious & Fun Foods Without Gluten, 1 vol. 2013. (Cool Recipes for Your Health Ser.). (ENG.). 32p. (J). (gr. 3-6). lib. bdg. 28.50 (978-1-61783-586-5(2), Checkerboard Library) ABDO Publishing Co.

—Let's Cook with Apples! Delicious & Fun Apple Dishes Kids Can Make, 1 vol. 2012. (Super Simple Recipes Ser.). (ENG.). 32p. (J). (gr. k-4). lib. bdg. 27.07 (978-1-61783-418-9(1), Super SandCastle) ABDO Publishing Co.

—Let's Cook with Cereal! Delicious & Fun Cereal Dishes Kids Can Make, 1 vol. 2012. (Super Simple Recipes Ser.). (ENG.). 32p. (J). (gr. k-4). lib. bdg. 27.07 (978-1-61783-419-6(X), Super SandCastle) ABDO Publishing Co.

—Let's Cook with Cheese! Delicious & Fun Cheese Dishes Kids Can Make, 1 vol. 2012. (Super Simple Recipes Ser.). (ENG.). 32p. (J). (gr. k-4). lib. bdg. 27.07 (978-1-61783-420-2(3), Super SandCastle) ABDO Publishing Co.

—Let's Cook with Eggs! Delicious & Fun Egg Dishes Kids Can Make, 1 vol. 2012. (Super Simple Recipes Ser.). (ENG.). 32p. (J). (gr. k-4). 27.07 (978-1-61783-421-9(1)) ABDO Publishing Co.

—Let's Cook with Noodles! Delicious & Fun Noodle Dishes Kids Can Make, 1 vol. 2012. (Super Simple Recipes Ser.). (ENG.). 32p. (J). (gr. k-4). lib. bdg. 27.07 (978-1-61783-422-6(X), Super SandCastle) ABDO Publishing Co.

—Let's Cook with Popcorn! Delicious & Fun Popcorn Dishes Kids Can Make, 1 vol. 2012. (Super Simple Recipes Ser.). (ENG.). 32p. (J). (gr. k-4). lib. bdg. 27.07 (978-1-61783-423-3(8), Super SandCastle) ABDO Publishing Co.

—Super Simple Breakfasts: Easy No-Bake Recipes for Kids, 1 vol. 2010. (Super Simple Cooking Ser.). (ENG.). 32p. (gr. k-4). 27.07 (978-1-61613-383-2(X), Super SandCastle) ABDO Publishing Co.

—Super Simple Desserts: Easy No-Bake Recipes for Kids, 1 vol. 2010. (Super Simple Cooking Ser.). (ENG.). 32p. (gr. k-4). 27.07 (978-1-61613-384-9(8), Super SandCastle) ABDO Publishing Co.

—Super Simple Dinners: Easy No-Bake Recipes for Kids, 1 vol. 2010. (Super Simple Cooking Ser.). (ENG.). 32p. (gr. k-4). 27.07 (978-1-61613-385-6(6), Super SandCastle) ABDO Publishing Co.

—Super Simple Lunches: Easy No-Bake Recipes for Kids, 1 vol. 2010. (Super Simple Cooking Ser.). (ENG.). 32p. (gr. k-4). 27.07 (978-1-61613-387-0(2), Super SandCastle) ABDO Publishing Co.

—Super Simple Snacks: Easy No-Bake Recipes for Kids, 1 vol. 2010. (Super Simple Cooking Ser.). (ENG.). 32p. (gr. k-4). 27.07 (978-1-61613-388-7(0), Super SandCastle) ABDO Publishing Co.

Turnbull, Stephanie. A Chef. 2016. (How to Be... Ser.). 24p. (gr. 2-6). 28.50 (978-1-62588-366-7(8), Smart Apple Media) Black Rabbit Bks.

—Cooking Skills. 2012. (Super Skills Ser.). (Illus.). 32p. (gr. 3-6). lib. bdg. 31.35 (978-1-59920-800-8(8)) Black Rabbit Bks.

—Fabulous Food. 2016. (Sleepover Secrets Ser.). 24p. (gr. 2-6). 28.50 (978-1-62588-379-7(X), Smart Apple Media) Black Rabbit Bks.

—Fun with Friends: Style Secrets for Girls. 2013. (Girl Talk Ser.). 32p. (gr. 4-7). 31.35 (978-1-59920-946-3(2)) Black Rabbit Bks.

Usborne Books Staff, creator. Starting Cooking Kid Kit. 2005. (Usborne Kid Kits Ser.). (Illus.). 32p. (J). (gr. -1). 14.99 (978-1-58086-873-0(8), Usborne) EDC Publishing.

Van der Linde, Polly & Van der Linde, Tasha. Around the World in Eighty Dishes. Lemke, Horst, illus. 88p. (J). (gr. k-7). 12.95 (978-0-87592-007-8(1)) Scroll Pr., Inc.

Vega, Ali. Brains, Brains, & Other Horrifying Breakfasts. 2017. (Little Kitchen of Horrors Ser.). (ENG.). 32p. (J). (gr. 2-5). 12.99 **(978-1-5124-3765-2(4)**, Lerner Pubns.); 39.99 **(978-1-5124-3764-5(6)**, Lerner Pubns.); 39.99 **(978-1-5124-2804-9(3)**, Lerner Pubns.); (Illus.). 26.65 (978-1-5124-2578-9(8)) Lerner Publishing Group.

—Cat Litter Cake & Other Horrifying Desserts. 2017. (Little Kitchen of Horrors Ser.). (ENG.). 32p. (J). (gr. 2-5). 12.99 **(978-1-5124-3768-3(9)**, Lerner Pubns.); 39.99 **(978-1-5124-2805-6(1)**, Lerner Pubns.); 39.99 **(978-1-5124-3767-6(0)**, Lerner Pubns.); (Illus.). 26.65 (978-1-5124-2574-1(5)) Lerner Publishing Group.

—Mummy Dogs & Other Horrifying Snacks. 2017. (Little Kitchen of Horrors Ser.). (ENG.). 32p. (J). (gr. 2-5). lib. bdg. 26.65 (978-1-5124-2575-8(3)); 12.99 **(978-1-5124-3771-3(9)**, Lerner Pubns.); 39.99 **(978-1-5124-3770-6(0)**, Lerner Pubns.); 39.99 **(978-1-5124-2806-3(X)**, Lerner Pubns.) Lerner Publishing Group.

—Tombstone Sandwiches & Other Horrifying Lunches. 2017. (Little Kitchen of Horrors Ser.). (ENG.). 32p. (J). (gr. 2-5). 12.99 **(978-1-5124-3774-4(3)**, Lerner Pubns.); 39.99 **(978-1-5124-3773-7(5)**, Lerner Pubns.); 39.99 **(978-1-5124-2807-0(8)**, Lerner Pubns.); (Illus.). 26.65 (978-1-5124-2577-2(X)) Lerner Publishing Group.

—Zombie-Gut Chili & Other Horrifying Dinners. 2017. (Little Kitchen of Horrors Ser.). (ENG.). 32p. (J). (gr. 2-5). 12.99 **(978-1-5124-3780-5(8)**, Lerner Pubns.); 39.99 **(978-1-5124-3779-9(4)**, Lerner Pubns.); 39.99 **(978-1-5124-2809-4(4)**, Lerner Pubns.); (Illus.). 26.65 (978-1-5124-2573-4(7)) Lerner Publishing Group.

Ventura, Marne. Bacon Artist: Savory Bacon Recipes. 2017. (Kids Can Cook! Ser.). (ENG., Illus.). 32p. (gr. 3-4). lib. bdg. 27.99 (978-1-5157-3814-5(0)) Capstone Press of Coughlan Cos.

—Disgusting Eats: Nasty, but Tasty Recipes. 2017. (Kids Can Cook! Ser.). (ENG., Illus.). 32p. (gr. 3-4). lib. bdg. 27.99 (978-1-5157-3812-1(4)) Capstone Press of Coughlan Cos.

Vize, Dania. High Chair Buddy Silly Snacks. 2006. (High Chair Buddy Ser.). (Illus.). 10p. (gr. -1 — 1). per., bds. (978-1-84610-016-1(X)) Make Believe Ideas.

Wagner, Lisa. Cool African Cooking: Fun & Tasty Recipes for Kids, 1 vol. 2011. (Cool World Cooking Ser.). (ENG., Illus.). 32p. (J). (gr. 3-6). 28.50 (978-1-61714-658-9(7), Checkerboard Library) ABDO Publishing Co.

—Cool Cuisine for Super Sleepovers: Easy Recipes for Kids to Cook, 1 vol. 2007. (Cool Cooking Ser.). (ENG., Illus.). 32p. (gr. 4-6). 28.50 (978-1-59928-721-8(8), Checkerboard Library) ABDO Publishing Co.

—Cool Foods for Fun Fiestas: Easy Recipes for Kids to Cook, 1 vol. 2007. (Cool Cooking Ser.). (ENG., Illus.). 32p. (gr. 4-7). 28.50 (978-1-59928-722-5(6), Checkerboard Library) ABDO Publishing Co.

—Cool Lunches to Make & Take: Easy Recipes for Kids to Cook, 1 vol. 2007. (Cool Cooking Ser.). (ENG., Illus.). 32p. (gr. 4-7). 28.50 (978-1-59928-723-2(4), Checkerboard Library) ABDO Publishing Co.

—Cool Meals to Start Your Wheels: Easy Recipes for Kids to Cook, 1 vol. 2007. (Cool Cooking Ser.). (ENG., Illus.). 32p. (gr. 4-7). 28.50 (978-1-59928-724-9(2), Checkerboard Library) ABDO Publishing Co.

—Cool Pizza to Make & Bake, 1 vol. 2007. (Cool Cooking Ser.). (ENG., Illus.). 32p. (gr. 4-7). 28.50 (978-1-59928-725-6(0), Checkerboard Library) ABDO Publishing Co.

Walberg, Anders. The Sport Fishermen's Cookbook. 2004. (Complete Guide to Fishing Ser.). (Illus.). 64p. (YA). (gr. 7-18). lib. bdg. 24.95 (978-1-59084-498-4(X)) Mason Crest.

Waldendorf, Kurt. Hooray for Chefs! 2016. (Bumba Books (tm) — Hooray for Community Helpers! Ser.). (ENG., Illus.). 24p. (J). (gr. -1-1). 25.32 (978-1-5124-1439-4(5)) Lerner Publishing Group.

Waldendorf, Kurt. ¡Que Vivan los Chefs! 2017. (Bumba Books (tm) en Español — ¡Que Vivan Los Ayudantes Comunitarios! (Hooray for Community Helpers!) Ser.). (SPA.). 24p. (J). (gr. -1-1). 25.32 **(978-1-5124-4134-5(1))** Lerner Publishing Group.

Walker, Kathryn. See How Cats Grow. 2009. (See How They Grow Ser.). (SPA & ENG., Illus.). 24p. (J). (gr. k-3). pap. 8.25 (978-1-4358-2875-9(5), PowerKids Pr.) Rosen Publishing Group, Inc., The.

Walton, Sally & Painter, Lucy. 100 Fantastic Things to Make, Do & Play: Simple, Fun Projects That Use Easy Everyday Materials. 2008. (ENG., Illus.). 256p. (J). (gr. -1-2). pap. 24.99 (978-1-84476-473-0(7)) Anness Publishing GBR. Dist: National Bk. Network.

Watt, Fiona & Cartwright, Stephen. Children's Cookbook. 2004. (Children's Cooking Ser.). (ENG., Illus.). 48p. (J). spiral bd. 12.95 (978-0-7945-0361-1(6), Usborne) EDC Publishing.

Webster, Penny. Allergy Free for All Ages: Milk-Free, Egg-Free, Nut-Free Recipes. 2005. 124p. pap. 19.95 (978-1-4137-9852-4(7)) PublishAmerica, Inc.

Weiss, Ellen. Math in the Kitchen. 2007. (Scholastic News Nonfiction Readers Ser.). (ENG., Illus.). 24p. (J). (gr. 1-2). 22.00 (978-0-531-18531-5(1)) Scholastic Library Publishing.

Wellington, Monica. Color & Cook BREAKFAST. 2010. (Dover Coloring Bks.). (ENG., Illus.). 32p. (J). (gr. -1-3). pap. 4.99 (978-0-486-47763-3(0)) Dover Pubns., Inc.

—Color & Cook CUPCAKES. 2009. (Dover Coloring Bks.). (ENG., Illus.). 32p. (J). (gr. -1-3). pap. 4.99 (978-0-486-47113-6(6)) Dover Pubns., Inc.

—Color & Cook HALLOWEEN. 2011. (Dover Coloring Bks.). (ENG., Illus.). 30p. (J). (gr. -1-3). pap. 4.99 (978-0-486-48106-7(9)) Dover Pubns., Inc.

—Color & Cook HEALTHY SNACKS. 2010. (Dover Coloring Bks.). (ENG., Illus.). 32p. (J). (gr. -1-3). pap. 4.99 (978-0-486-47449-6(6)) Dover Pubns., Inc.

—Color & Cook PIZZA. 2009. (Dover Coloring Bks.). (ENG., Illus.). 32p. (J). (gr. -1-3). pap. 4.99 (978-0-486-47114-3(4)) Dover Pubns., Inc.

—Color & Cook Story Coloring Book. 2014. (ENG.). 160p. (J). (gr. -1-5). pap. 5.99 (978-0-486-77967-6(X)) Dover Pubns., Inc.

—Color & Cook TEA PARTY! 2013. (ENG.). 32p. (J). (gr. -1-3). pap. 4.99 (978-0-486-49270-4(2)) Dover Pubns., Inc.

Wellington, Monica & Activity Books. What's Cooking? Stickers. 2012. (Dover Little Activity Bks.). (ENG.). 8p. (J). (gr. k-3). pap. 1.50 (978-0-486-48881-3(0)) Dover Pubns., Inc.

Wheeler, Jill C. Simple Solutions with Rachael Ray, 1 vol. 2016. (ENG.). 32p. (J). (978-1-62403-820-4(4)) ABDO Publishing Co.

Wick, Jacque. A to Z Cookbook. 2013. (Illus.). xi, 67p. (J). 15.99 (978-1-4621-1213-5(7), Horizon Pubs.) Cedar Fort, Inc./CFI Distribution.

—Colorful Cooking. 2014. spiral bd. 17.99 (978-1-4621-1520-4(9)) Cedar Fort, Inc./CFI Distribution.

Wildot Press. Amanda Patricia's Kitchen. 2007. (Illus.). 35p. (J). spiral bd. 12.95 (978-0-9797933-0-1(0)) Wildot Pr.

Wilkes, Angela. Children's Quick & Easy Cookbook. 2006. (ENG., Illus.). 96p. (J). (gr. k-3). pap. 9.99 (978-0-7566-1814-8(2), DK Children) Dorling Kindersley Publishing, Inc.

—Mi Primer Libro de Cocina. (SPA.). 48p. (J). (gr. 3-5). (978-84-272-1700-3(5), ML4524) Molino, Editorial ESP. Dist: Lectorum Pubns., Inc.

Wilkes, Angela & Cartwright, Stephen. The Usborne First Cookbook. Gilpin, Rebecca, ed. 2007. (ENG., Illus.). 72p. (J). (gr. 4-7). 18.99 (978-0-7945-1479-2(0), Usborne) EDC Publishing.

Williams, Judy. 50 Recipes for Kids to Cook: Tasty Food to Make Yourself Shown in Step-By-Step Pictures. 2014. (ENG., Illus.). 96p. (J). (gr. -1-12). pap. 13.99 (978-1-86147-219-9(6), Armadillo) Anness Publishing GBR. Dist: National Bk. Network.

Williams, Nancy Noel. Rice Is Nice. 2010. (J). (978-1-60617-144-8(5)) Teaching Strategies, LLC.

Williams-Sonoma Staff. Junior Chef Cookbook. 2016. (ENG., Illus.). 56p. 14.95 (978-1-68188-024-2(5)) Weldon Owen, Inc.

Wilson, Lia. Class Treats: Take-To-School Goodies for Every Occasion: All Nut-Free Recipes. 2003. (Illus.). 125p. (J). (978-1-931294-58-4(5)) Cookbook Resources, LLC.

Winget, Mary. Cooking the North African Way. 2nd rev. ed. 2003. (Easy Menu Ethnic Cookbooks 2nd Edition Ser.).

(ENG., Illus.). 72p. (gr. 5-12). 25.26 *(978-0-8225-4169-1(6),* Lerner Pubns.) Lerner Publishing Group.

Wolf, Laurie Goldrich. The Do It Myself Kids' Cookbook: Nothing Hot, Nothing Sharp. 2010. (ENG.). 128p. (J). (gr. k). 17.99 *(978-1-935703-09-9(9))* Downtown Bookworks.

Worthington, Niles. A Chef's Job. 2015. (Community Workers Ser.). (ENG., Illus.). 24p. (J). (gr. 1-1). pap. 8.22 *(978-1-5026-0439-2(6))* Cavendish Square Publishing.

Yolen, Jane. Fairy Tale Breakfasts: A Cookbook for Young Readers & Eaters. Béha, Philippe, illus. 2009. (Fairy Tale Cookbooks Ser.). 32p. (J). (gr. 2-5). 22.60 *(978-1-60754-573-6(X));* pap. 10.55 *(978-1-60754-574-3(8))* Windmill Bks.

—Fairy Tale Desserts: A Cookbook for Young Readers & Eaters. Béha, Philippe, illus. 2009. (Fairy Tale Cookbooks Ser.). 32p. (J). (gr. 2-5). 22.60 *(978-1-60754-583-5(7));* pap. 10.55 *(978-1-60754-584-2(5))* Windmill Bks.

—Fairy Tale Dinners: A Cookbook for Young Readers & Eaters. Béha, Philippe, illus. 2009. (Fairy Tale Cookbooks Ser.). 32p. (J). (gr. 2-5). 22.60 *(978-1-60754-580-4(2));* pap. 10.55 *(978-1-60754-582-8(9))* Windmill Bks.

—Fairy Tale Lunches: A Cookbook for Young Readers & Eaters. Béha, Philippe, illus. 2009. (Fairy Tale Cookbooks Ser.). 32p. (J). (gr. 2-5). 22.60 *(978-1-60754-576-7(4));* pap. 10.55 *(978-1-60754-577-4(2))* Windmill Bks.

Yolen, Jane & Stemple, Heidi E. Y. Fairy Tale Feasts: A Literary Cookbook for Young Readers & Eaters. Beha, Philippe, illus. 2009. (ENG.). 264p. (J). (gr. -1-3). pap. 20.00 *(978-1-56656-751-0(3),* Crocodile Bks.) Interlink Publishing Group, Inc.

(Your Child's Name Here) Cookbook: 100 Fun to Cook Recipes. 2007. (J). 10.00 *(978-0-9766756-6-2(8))* Shively, Lisa Cookbooks.

826 Valencia Writing Project Student Staff. A Time to Eat Cake. 2012. (ENG., Illus.). 73p. (J). (gr. k). pap. 12.00 *(978-1-934750-27-8(1))* 826 Valencia.

COOKING (APPETIZERS)

see Appetizers

COOKING (BEEF)

Sullivan, Jaclyn. What's in Your Hamburger? 2012. (What's in Your Fast Food Ser.). (ENG., Illus.). 24p. (J). (gr. 2-5). pap. 8.25 *(978-1-4488-6381-5(3),* PowerKids Pr.); lib. bdg. 22.60 *(978-1-4488-6211-5(6))* Rosen Publishing Group, Inc., The.

COOKING (CHICKEN)

Sullivan, Jaclyn. What's in Your Chicken Nugget? 2012. (What's in Your Fast Food Ser.). (ENG., Illus.). 24p. (J). (gr. 2-5). pap. 8.25 *(978-1-4488-6375-4(9),* PowerKids Pr.); lib. bdg. 22.60 *(978-1-4488-6208-5(6))* Rosen Publishing Group, Inc., The.

COOKING (DAIRY PRODUCTS)

Head, Honor. Milk, Cheese, & Eggs. 2010. (J). 24.25 *(978-1-59920-335-5(9))* Black Rabbit Bks.

Powell, Jillian & O'Shea, Clare. Cooking with Eggs & Dairy. 2011. (Cooking Healthy Ser.). (J). lib. bdg. 29.25 *(978-1-4488-4843-0(1),* Rosen Reference) Rosen Publishing Group, Inc., The.

Rajczak, Kristen. Delicious Dairy Recipes. 2014. (Ingredients for a Healthy Life Ser.). (Illus.). 24p. (J). (gr. 2-5). 22.60 *(978-1-4824-0561-3(X))* Stevens, Gareth Publishing LLLP.

COOKING—FICTION

Adams, Alison. The Gingerbread Man: Classic Tales Edition. Rogers, Jacqueline, illus. 2011. (Classic Tales Ser.). (J). *(978-1-936258-67-3(6))* Benchmark Education Co.

Akin, Sara Laux. Three Scoops & a Fig, 1 vol. Hartung, Susan Kathleen, illus. 2010. (ENG.). 32p. (J). (gr. -1-3). 15.95 *(978-1-56145-522-5(9))* Peachtree Pubs.

Animal Cookies: Individual Title Six-Pack. (Story Steps Ser.). (gr. k-2). 23.00 *(978-0-7635-9822-8(4))* Rigby Education.

Argueta, Jorge. La Fiesta de las Tortillas: The Fiesta of the Tortillas. Hayes, Joe & Franco, Sharon, trs. from SPA. Alvarez, Maria Jesus, illus. 2006. (Bilingual Bks). (ENG & SPA.). 32p. (gr. 3-5). 15.95 *(978-1-59820-094-2(1),* Alfaguara) Santillana USA Publishing Co., Inc.

Armstrong-Ellis, Carey F. I Love You More Than Moldy Ham. 2015. (ENG., Illus.). 32p. (J). (gr. -1-3). 14.95 *(978-1-4197-1646-1(8),* Abrams Bks. for Young Readers) Abrams, Inc.

Auch, Mary Jane. The Princess & the Pizza. Auch, Herm, illus. 2003. (ENG.). 32p. (J). (gr. k-3). 7.99 *(978-0-8234-1798-8(0))* Holiday Hse., Inc.

Bailey, Mark & Oatman, Michael. Tiny Pie. Hemingway, Edward, illus. 2013. (ENG.). 32p. (J). (gr. -1-17). 15.95 *(978-0-7624-4482-3(7),* Running Pr. Kids) Running Pr. Bk. Pubs.

Baker, Alan. Brown Rabbit's Busy Day. 2017. (Little Rabbit Bks.). (ENG.). 24p. (J). 12.99 *(978-0-7534-7337-5(2),* 9780753473375, Kingfisher) Roaring Brook Pr.

Barrett, Judi & Barrett, Ron. The Marshmallow Incident. Barrett, Ron, illus. 2009. (Illus.). (J). pap. *(978-0-545-04654-1(8),* Scholastic Pr.) Scholastic, Inc.

Bastianich, Lidia Matticchio. Lidia's Family Kitchen: Nonna's Birthday Surprise. Graef, Renee, illus. 2013. (ENG.). 60p. (J). (gr. -1-17). 16.95 *(978-0-7624-4655-1(2),* Running Pr. Kids) Running Pr. Bk. Pubs.

Benchmark Education Co., LLC. What Is Papa Cooking? Big Book. 2014. (Shared Reading Foundations Ser.). (J). (gr. -1). *(978-1-4509-9438-5(5))* Benchmark Education Co.

Benton, Jim. Dumbness Is a Dish Best Served Cold. Benton, Jim, illus. 2016. (Dear Dumb Diary Ser.). (ENG., Illus.). 224p. (J). (gr. 3-7). 12.99 *(978-0-545-93228-8(9),* Scholastic Pr.) Scholastic, Inc.

Berenstain, Mike, illus. The Berenstain Bears' Holiday Cookbook: Cub-Friendly Cooking with an Adult, 1 vol. 2016. (Berenstain Bears/Living Lights Ser.). (ENG.). 96p. (J). 12.99 *(978-0-310-75399-5(6))* Zonderkidz.

Bertrand, Diane Gonzales. Sip, Slurp, Soup Soup/Caldo Caldo Caldo: CD & Book Set. DeLange, Alex Pardo, illus. 2008. 32p. (J). pap. 19.95 *(978-0-9815686-1-4(0))* Lorito Bks., Inc.

Birkett, Georgie, illus. Cook It!/¡A Cocinar! 2009. (Helping Hands English/Spanish Edition Ser.). (ENG & SPA.). 24p. (J). (gr. -1-k). pap. *(978-1-84643-568-3(4))* Child's Play International Ltd.

Blake, Colleen H. Robley. Don't You Wish Your Momma Could Cook Like Mine? Jennings, Randy, illus. 2012. 40p. pap. 16.97 *(978-1-61204-876-5(5),* Strategic Bk. Publishing) Strategic Book Publishing & Rights Agency (SBPRA).

Blane, Francisco. The Muffin Man. Hammond, Andy, illus. 2010. (Rising Readers Ser.). (J). 3.49 *(978-1-60719-691-4(3))* Newmark Learning LLC.

Bonasia, Steve. Dominic & the Secret Ingredient. Van Norstrand, Kain, illus. 2012. (ENG.). 39p. (J). pap. 24.95 *(978-1-4327-9805-5(7))* Outskirts Pr., Inc.

Brennan, Frank. Tasty Tales Level 4, 1 vol. 2009. (ENG.). 96p. pap. 16.50 incl. audio compact disk *(978-84-8323-545-4(5))* Cambridge Univ. Pr.

Burgess, Lisa Maria. Juma Cooks Chapati. Gugu, Abdul M., illus. 2013. 32p. 19.95 *(978-1-939604-08-8(7));* pap. 9.99 *(978-1-939604-04-0(4))* Barranca Pr.

Burnette, Margarette. Counting in the Crazy Garden. Henson, Brooke, illus. 2008. (Chipper Kids Ser.). 30p. (J). (gr. -1-2). 15.95 *(978-0-9653791-3-7(2))* JenPrint Pubns., LLC.

Carle, Eric. Pancakes, Pancakes! Carle, Eric, illus. 2005. (ENG., Illus.). 36p. (J). (gr. -1-3). reprint ed. 4.99 *(978-0-689-87833-6(8),* Simon & Schuster/Paula Wiseman Bks.) Simon & Schuster/Paula Wiseman Bks.

—Pancakes, Pancakes! Carle, Eric, illus. 2013. (World of Eric Carle Ser.). (ENG., Illus.). 24p. (J). (gr. -1-1). 16.99 *(978-1-4424-7275-4(8));* pap. 3.99 *(978-1-4424-7274-7(X))* Simon Spotlight. (Simon Spotlight).

—Pancakes, Pancakes! 2013. (Eric Carle Ready-To-Read Ser.). lib. bdg. 13.55 *(978-0-606-32064-1(4),* Turtleback) Turtleback Bks.

Chaos in the Kitchen: Individual Title Six-Packs. (gr. k-1). 23.00 *(978-0-7635-9076-5(2))* Rigby Education.

Chef Jeff. Do Cows Eat Cake? 2008. 28p. pap. 13.99 *(978-1-4389-0494-8(0))* AuthorHouse.

Chen, Shan-Shan & Goodman, Heidi. Mei-Mei's Lucky Birthday Noodles: A Loving Story of Adoption, Chinese Culture & a Special Birthday Treat. 2014. (ENG., Illus.). 32p. (J). (gr. -1-3). 13.95 *(978-0-8048-4461-1(5))* Tuttle Publishing.

Church, Peggy Pond. The Pancake Stories: Cuentos Del Panqueque. Chilton, Noel, tr. Church, Elizabeth Comfort, illus. 2013. (ENG & SPA.). 96p. (J). 12.95 *(978-0-8263-5387-0(8))* Univ. of New Mexico Pr.

Ciminera, Siobhan & Testa, Maggie. So Yummy! So Yummy! Yoe! Studio Staff, illus. 2009. (Yo Gabba Gabba! Ser.). (ENG.). 32p. (J). (gr. -1-1). 4.99 *(978-1-4169-8494-8(1),* Simon Scribbles) Simon Scribbles.

Colman, Michelle Sinclair. Foodie Babies Wear Bibs. Dion, Nathalie, illus. 2008. (Urban Babies Wear Black Book Ser.). (ENG.). 20p. (J). (— 1). bds. 6.99 *(978-1-58246-254-7(2),* Tricycle Pr.) Random Hse. Children's Bks.

Compestine, Ying. The Story of Chopsticks: Amazing Chinese Inventions. Xuan, YongSheng, illus. 2016. (ENG & CHI.). 40p. (J). (gr. -1-3). 15.95 *(978-1-59702-120-3(2))* Immedium.

—The Story of Noodles: Amazing Chinese Inventions. Xuan, YongSheng, illus. 2016. (ENG & CHI.). 40p. (J). (gr. -1-3). 15.95 *(978-1-59702-121-0(0))* Immedium.

Compestine, Ying Chang. Boy Dumplings. Yamasaki, James, illus. 2009. (ENG.). 32p. (J). (gr. -1-3). 16.95 *(978-0-8234-1955-5(X))* Holiday Hse., Inc.

—Boy Dumplings: A Chinese Food Tale. Yamaski, James, illus. 2016. (ENG & CHI.). 40p. (J). (gr. -1-3). 15.95 *(978-1-59702-119-7(9))* Immedium.

Conford, Ellen. What's Cooking, Jenny Archer? Palmisciano, Diane & Brooks, Erik, illus. 2006. (ENG.). 80p. (J). (gr. 1-4). per. 13.99 *(978-0-316-01488-5(5))* Little, Brown Bks. for Young Readers.

Cooper, Helen S. Pumpkin Soup. braille ed. 2004. (J). (gr. k-3). spiral bd. *(978-0-616-07224-0(4))* Canadian National Institute for the Blind/Institut National Canadien pour les Aveugles.

—Pumpkin Soup, Set. unabr. ed. 2009. (ENG., Illus.). 32p. (J). (gr. -1-3). 9.99 *(978-1-4272-0740-1(2),* 9781427207401) Macmillan Audio.

Creech, Sharon. Granny Torrelli Makes Soup. Raschka, Chris, illus. 2012. (ENG.). 160p. (J). (gr. 3-7). reprint ed. pap. 6.99 *(978-0-06-440960-5(0))* HarperCollins Pubs.

—Granny Torrelli Makes Soup. Raschka, Chris, illus. 2004. (Joanna Cotler Bks.). 141p. (gr. 3-7). 17.00 *(978-0-7569-4604-3(2))* Perfection Learning Corp.

Dad cooks Breakfast: Individual Title Six-Packs. (gr. 1-2). 25.00 *(978-0-7635-9135-9(1))* Rigby Education.

Dairman, Tara. All Four Stars. 2014. (All Four Stars Ser.: Bk. 1). (ENG.). 288p. (J). (gr. 3-7). 16.99 *(978-0-399-16252-7(6),* G.P. Putnam's Sons Books for Young Readers) Penguin Young Readers Group.

—The Stars of Summer. 2015. (All Four Stars Ser.: Bk. 2). (ENG.). 336p. (J). (gr. 3-7). 16.99 *(978-0-399-17069-0(3),* G.P. Putnam's Sons Books for Young Readers) Penguin Young Readers Group.

Daley, Michael J. Pinch & Dash Make Soup. Yezerski, Thomas F., illus. 2012. (ENG.). 48p. (J). (gr. k-3). 12.95 *(978-1-58089-346-6(5));* pap. 5.95 *(978-1-58089-347-3(3))* Charlesbridge Publishing, Inc.

Davis, Jacky. Black Belt Bunny. Fleck, Jay, illus. 2017. (ENG.). 40p. (J). (-k). 16.99 ***(978-0-525-42902-9(6),*** Dial Bks) Penguin Young Readers Group.

De Laurentiis, Giada. Naples! Gambatesa, Francesca, illus. 2013. (Recipe for Adventure Ser.: 1). (ENG.). 144p. (J). (gr. 2-5). 6.99 *(978-0-448-46256-1(7));*No. 1. 16.99 *(978-0-448-47853-1(6))* Penguin Young Readers Group. (Grosset & Dunlap).

DeLuise, Dom & Carter, Derek. Pouch Potato. 2007. 33p. pap. 9.95 *(978-0-9717952-0-4(7))* Bacchus Bks.

deRubertis, Barbara & National Geographic Learning Staff. Lulu's Lemonade. Billin-Frye, Paige, illus. 2010. (Rise & Shine Ser.). (ENG.). 32p. (C). (gr. -1-3). pap. 10.95 *(978-1-57565-093-7(2))* National Geographic School Publishing, Inc.

Dompierre, Judith. Unleashing Fruits & Vegetables. 2012. 38p. 29.95 *(978-1-4512-2614-0(4))* America Star Bks.

Dompierre, Judith E. Unleashing Fruits & Vegetables. 2012. 36p. pap. 24.95 *(978-1-4626-9335-1(0))* America Star Bks.

Dooley, Norah. Everybody Brings Noodles. Thornton, Peter J., illus. 40p. (J). 2005. (ENG.). (gr. k-3). pap. 6.95 *(978-1-57505-916-7(9))* 2003. (gr. -1-3). 15.95 *(978-0-87614-455-8(5),* Carolrhoda Bks.) Lerner Publishing Group.

Dowell, Frances O'Roark. Phineas L. MacGuire ... Gets Cooking! McDaniels, Preston, illus. 2015. (From the Highly Scientific Notebooks of Phineas L. MacGuire Ser.). (ENG.). 224p. (J). (gr. 3-7). pap. 6.99 *(978-1-4814-0100-5(9))* Simon & Schuster Children's Publishing.

Downing, Johnette. Today Is Monday in Louisiana, 1 vol. Kadair, Deborah Ousley, illus. 2006. (ENG.). 32p. (J). (gr. k-k). 16.99 *(978-1-58980-406-7(6))* Pelican Publishing Co., Inc.

Duley, Wayla C. Strawberry Soup & Other Crazy Things. 2013. 28p. pap. 24.95 *(978-1-63000-952-6(0))* America Star Bks.

Dunbar, Fiona. Chocolate Wishes. 2009. (Jinx,the Lulu Baker Trilogy Ser.: Bk. 3). (ENG.). 256p. (J). (gr. 4-6). pap. 9.99 *(978-1-4083-0746-5(4))* Hodder & Stoughton GBR. Dist: Hachette Bk. Group.

—The Truth Cookie. 2009. (Jinx,the Lulu Baker Trilogy Ser.: Bk. 1). (ENG.). 208p. (J). (gr. 4-6). pap. 9.99 *(978-1-4083-0744-1(8))* Hodder & Stoughton GBR. Dist: Hachette Bk. Group.

Edwards, Amelia. It's Good Enough to Eat!, 1 vol. rev. ed. 2013. (Fiction Readers Ser.). (ENG., Illus.). 20p. (J). (gr. 1-1). pap. 15.96 *(978-1-4807-1149-5(7));* pap. 4.99 *(978-1-4333-5493-9(4))* Shell Educational Publishing.

Eismann, Sheila F. & Putz, Ali F. The Christmas Tin. Richardson, Cathie, illus. 2013. 40p. pap. 9.95 *(978-0-9897133-8-2(5))* Desert Sage Pr.

Emmett, Jonathan. The Conjuror's Cookbook Vol. I: Goblin Stew. (ENG., Illus.). 64p. (J). pap. 7.99 *(978-0-7475-4403-6(4))* Bloomsbury Publishing Plc GBR. Dist: Trafalgar Square Publishing.

—The Conjuror's Cookbook Vol. II: Serpent Soup. (ENG., Illus.). 64p. (J). pap. 7.99 *(978-0-7475-4408-1(5))* Bloomsbury Publishing Plc GBR. Dist: Trafalgar Square Publishing.

—The Conjuror's Cookbook Vol. III: Ghostly Goulash. (ENG., Illus.). 64p. (J). pap. 7.99 *(978-0-7475-4413-5(1))* Bloomsbury Publishing Plc GBR. Dist: Trafalgar Square Publishing.

Enderle, Dotti. The Library Gingerbread Man. Madden, Colleen M., illus. 2010. 32p. (J). (gr. -1). 17.95 *(978-1-60213-048-7(5),* Upstart Bks.) Highsmith Inc.

Fajardo, Renee & Ruby, Carl. Chili Today, Hot Tamale & Other Tummy Tales. Fajardo, Renee & Ruby, Carl, eds. 2004. (Illus.). 110p. (YA). (gr. 4-8). pap. 14.00 *(978-0-9724472-2-5(9))* Just Enjoyable Memorable Story Bks.

Falwell, Cathryn. Feast for 10, 1 vol. Falwell, Cathryn, illus. (Read along Book & CD Ser.). (ENG., Illus.). (J). (gr. -1-3). 2008. 32p. audio compact disk 10.99 *(978-0-547-06431-4(4))* 2003. 28p. bds. 4.95 *(978-0-618-38226-2(7))* Houghton Mifflin Harcourt Publishing Co.

Feuerbach, Jennifer. Chef Philip Has Autism. Wroth, Dean, illus. 2014. 32p. (J). pap. 10.49 *(978-0-944727-61-4(1),* Turtle Bks.) Jason & Nordic Pubs.

Finch, Mary & Slater, Kate. La Gallinita Roja. Slater, Kate, illus. 2013. (SPA., Illus.). 32p. (J). pap. 7.99 *(978-1-84686-753-8(3))* Barefoot Bks., Inc.

Fisher, Carolyn. The Snow Show. 2008. (ENG., Illus.). 48p. (J). (gr. k-5). 17.00 *(978-0-15-206019-0(7))* Houghton Mifflin Harcourt Publishing Co.

Fisher, Meaghan. Giuseppe's Famous Pizza Pies. Barrett, Diana, illus. 2013. 24p. 17.99 *(978-1-938768-34-7(5))* Gypsy Pubns.

Florence, Debbi Michiko. Jasmine Toguchi, Mochi Queen. 2017. (J). pap. ***(978-0-374-30411-9(4))*** Farrar, Straus & Giroux.

Florence, Tyler. Tyler Makes Spaghetti! Frazier, Craig, illus. 2013. (ENG.). 40p. (J). (gr. -1-3). 17.99 *(978-0-06-204756-4(6))* HarperCollins Pubs.

Florence, Tyler & Frazier, Craig. Tyler Makes Pancakes! Florence, Tyler & Frazier, Craig, illus. 2012. (ENG., Illus.). 40p. (J). (gr. -1-2). 16.99 *(978-0-06-204752-6(3))* HarperCollins Pubs.

Freund, William C. The Cookie That Saved My Family. Mikle, Toby, illus. 2011. (J). *(978-0-9846346-7-5(3))* Adibooks.com.

Fuchs, Menucha. The Little Helpers. 2004. (Illus.). 20p. (J). 6.95 *(978-1-932443-14-1(2),* TLHH) Judaica Pr., Inc., The.

Furgang, Kathy. The Cooking Contest. 2011. (Early Connections Ser.). (J). *(978-1-61672-673-7(3))* Benchmark Education Co.

—The Cooking Contest: Set Of 6. 2011. (Early Connections Ser.). (J). pap. 39.00 net. *(978-1-4108-1560-6(9))* Benchmark Education Co.

Ganeshram, Ramin. Stir It Up! 2011. (J). *(978-0-545-16583-9(0));* (ENG.). 176p. (gr. 5-9). 16.99 *(978-0-545-16582-2(2),* Scholastic Pr.) Scholastic, Inc.

Garcia, Nasario. Grandma Lale's Tamales: A Christmas Story. Aragon, Dolores, illus. 2014. (SPA & ENG.). 58p. (J). *(978-1-936744-26-8(0),* Rio Grande Bks.) LPD Pr.

García, Nasario & Aragon, Dolores, illus. Grandpa Lolo's Matanza: A New Mexican Tradition = la Matanza de Abuelito Lolo: Una Tradición Nuevo Mexicana. 2015. (SPA & ENG.). 70p. (J). *(978-1-936744-47-3(3),* Rio Grande Bks.) LPD Pr.

Garland, Sarah. Eddie's Kitchen. 2014. (ENG., Illus.). 40p. (J). (gr. -1-2). pap. 8.99 *(978-1-84780-003-9(3),* Frances Lincoln) Quarto Publishing Group UK GBR. Dist: Hachette Bk. Group.

Gaskins, Melda. Anit: The Chef. Kauffin, Karlynn, illus. 2011. 24p. pap. 24.95 *(978-1-4626-4485-8(6))* America Star Bks.

Gershenson, Harold P. Noodles from Scratch. Mills, Christopher, illus. 2006. (J). *(978-1-58987-007-9(7))* Kindermusik International.

Giff, Patricia Reilly. Gingersnap. 2014. (ENG.). 160p. (J). (gr. 3-7). 6.99 *(978-0-440-42178-8(0),* Yearling) Random Hse. Children's Bks.

Gil, Lydia. Letters from Heaven. 2014.Tr. of Cartas Del Cielo. (ENG & SPA.). 128p. (J). pap. 9.95 *(978-1-55885-798-8(2),* Piñata Books) Arte Publico Pr.

Gomes, Filomena. My Mom Loves Me More Than Sushi. Spires, Ashley, illus. 2006. 24p. (J). pap. *(978-1-897187-13-5(0))* Second Story Pr.

—My Mom Loves Me More Than Sushi, 1 vol. Spires, Ashley, illus. 2006. (ENG.). 32p. (J). (gr. -1-3). 15.95 *(978-1-897187-09-8(2))* Second Story Pr. CAN. Dist: Orca Bk. Pubs. USA.

Gourley, Robbin. Bring Me Some Apples & I'll Make You a Pie: A Story about Edna Lewis. (ENG., Illus.). 48p. (J). (gr. -1-3). 2016. pap. 6.99 *(978-0-544-80901-7(7),* HMH Books For Young Readers) 2008. 17.99 *(978-0-618-15836-2(7))* Houghton Mifflin Harcourt Publishing Co.

Grim, Katie. Gingerbread Land. Johnson, Jake, illus. 2007. (ENG.). 24p. (J). (gr. 1-18). 19.95 *(978-1-58117-635-3(X),* Intervisual/Piggy Toes) Bendon, Inc.

Gutknecht, Allison. Pizza Is the Best Breakfast: And Other Lessons I've Learned. Lewis, Stevie, illus. 2015. (ENG.). 176p. (J). (gr. 2-5). pap. 6.99 *(978-1-4814-2961-0(2),* Aladdin) Simon & Schuster Children's Publishing.

Harper, Charise Mericle. Lights, Camera, Cook! Blard-Quintard, Aurélie, illus. 2017. (Next Best Junior Chef Ser.: 1). (ENG.). 192p. (J). (gr. 2-5). 12.99 ***(978-0-544-91260-1(8),*** HMH Books For Young Readers) Houghton Mifflin Harcourt Publishing Co.

Hechtman, Betty Jacobson. Blue Schwartz & Nefertiti's Necklace: A Mystery with Recipes. 2006. 152p. (J). (gr. 5-9). per. 8.95 *(978-0-9768126-3-0(0))* Brown Barn Bks.

Heppermann, Christine & Koertge, Ron. Jess's Story. Marcero, Deborah, illus. 2016. (Backyard Witch Ser.: 2). 192p. (J). (gr. 3-7). 16.99 *(978-0-06-233841-9(2),* Greenwillow Bks.) HarperCollins Pubs.

Hester, Denia Lewis. Grandma Lena's Big Ol' Turnip. Urbanovic, Jackie, illus. 2005. (ENG.). 32p. (J). (gr. -1-3). 6.99 *(978-0-8075-3023-8(9))* Whitman, Albert & Co.

—Grandma Lena's Big Ol'turnip. Urbanovic, Jackie, illus. 2014. (AV2 Fiction Readalong Ser.: Vol. 138). (ENG.). 32p. (J). (gr. -1-3). lib. bdg. 34.28 *(978-1-4896-2329-4(9),* AV2 by Weigl) Weigl Pubs., Inc.

Himes, Rachel. Princess & the Peas. Himes, Rachel, illus. 2017. (ENG., Illus.). 32p. (J). (gr. k-3). 16.99 *(978-1-58089-718-1(5))* Charlesbridge Publishing, Inc.

Hippely, Hilary Horder. A Song for Lena. Baker, Leslie, illus. 2011. (ENG.). 40p. (J). (gr. -1-3). 19.99 *(978-1-4424-2946-8(1),* Simon & Schuster Bks. For Young Readers) Simon & Schuster Bks. For Young Readers.

Hoffman, Mary Ann. Bananas for Breakfast! 2006. (Neighborhood Readers Ser.). (ENG.). 16p. (gr. 1-3). pap. 6.50 *(978-1-4042-7034-3(5),* Rosen Classroom) Rosen Publishing Group, Inc., The.

—Molly Makes a Milkshake. 2006. (Neighborhood Readers Ser.). (ENG.). 12p. (gr. -1-3). pap. 5.90 *(978-1-4042-5768-9(3),* Rosen Classroom) Rosen Publishing Group, Inc., The.

Holden, Pam. Stone Soup, 6 pack. Hawley, Kelvin, illus. 2009. (Red Rocket Readers Ser.). (ENG.). 16p. (gr. 2-2). pap. *(978-1-877363-84-9(7))* Flying Start Bks.

I Love to Cook. 2003. (Illus.). (J). per. *(978-1-57657-959-6(X))* Paradise Pr., Inc.

Imholtz, August & Tannenbaum, Alison. Alice Eats Wonderland. Carr, A. E. K., illus. 2009. (ENG.). 120p. pap. 14.95 *(978-1-4290-9106-0(1))* Applewood Bks.

Ingalls, Ann. Ice Cream Soup. 2013. (Penguin Young Readers, Level 1 Ser.). (ENG.). 32p. (J). (gr. k-1). 14.99 *(978-0-448-46571-5(X));* pap. 3.99 *(978-0-448-46265-3(6))* Penguin Young Readers Group. (Penguin Young Readers).

—Ice Cream Soup. 2013. (Penguin Young Readers Level 1 Ser.). lib. bdg. 13.55 *(978-0-606-31704-7(X),* Turtleback) Turtleback Bks.

Iwai, Melissa. Soup Day. Iwai, Melissa, illus. 2010. (ENG., Illus.). 40p. (J). (gr. -1-k). 15.99 *(978-0-8050-9004-8(5),* 9780805090048, Holt, Henry & Co. Bks. For Young Readers) Holt, Henry & Co.

Jan, Romero Stevens. Carlos Digs to China Carlos Excava Hasta la China. Jeanne, Arnold, illus. 2004. (Carlos Digs to China / Carlos Excava Hasta la China Ser.). (SPA, MUL & ENG.). 32p. (J). (gr. k-3). pap. 7.95 *(978-0-87358-870-6(3))* Cooper Square Publishing Llc.

Jarman, Julia. The Magic Backpack. Gon, Adriano, illus. 2003. (Flying Foxes Ser.). (ENG.). 48p. (J). lib. bdg. *(978-0-7787-1487-3(X))* Crabtree Publishing Co.

Jenkins, Emily. A Fine Dessert: Four Centuries, Four Families, One Delicious Treat. Blackall, Sophie, illus. 2015. (ENG.). 44p. (J). (gr. -1-3). 17.99 *(978-0-375-86832-0(1));* 20.99 *(978-0-375-96832-7(6))* Random Hse. Children's Bks. (Schwartz & Wade Bks.).

Jensen, Patricia & Demar, Regier. Good Food. Clar, David Austin & Hantel, Johanna, illus. 2006. (My First Reader Ser.). (ENG.). 32p. (J). (gr. k-1). per. 3.95 *(978-0-516-24969-8(X),* Children's Pr.) Scholastic Library Publishing.

Johnson, Vincent L. Daddy's Good Cookin' Pavlova, Vera, illus. 2006. 32p. (J). 16.95 *(978-0-9657033-3-8(9))* Marzetta Bks.

Jorden, Edwin W. Cookie Paws. Waywell, Valerie J., illus. 2nd ed. 2007. (ENG.). 32p. (J). (gr. -1-3). 9.95 *(978-0-9793483-0-3(7))* Gilded Dog Enterprises LLC.

Jules, Jacqueline. The Secret Recipe. Smith, Kim, illus. 2016. (Sofia Martinez Ser.). (ENG.). 32p. (gr. k-2). lib. bdg. 21.32 *(978-1-4795-8717-9(6),* Sofia Martinez) Picture Window Bks.

Kaplan, Bruce Eric. Monsters Eat Whiny Children. Kaplan, Bruce Eric, illus. 2010. (ENG., Illus.). 40p. (J). (gr. -1-3). 17.99 *(978-1-4169-8689-8(8),* Simon & Schuster Bks. For Young Readers) Simon & Schuster Bks. For Young Readers.

Kaplan, Michael B. Betty Bunny Loves Chocolate Cake. Jorisch, Stéphane, illus. 2011. (Betty Bunny Ser.). (ENG.). 36p. (J). (gr. -1-k). 17.99 *(978-0-8037-3407-4(7),* Dial Bks) Penguin Young Readers Group.

Kariya, Tetsu. Oishinbo: Izakaya — Pub Food, Vol. 7. Hanasaki, Akira, illus. 2010. (ENG.). 276p. pap. 12.99 *(978-1-4215-2145-9(8))* Viz Media.

Katzler, Eva. Florentine & Pig. Mikhail, Jess, illus. 2012. (ENG.). 32p. (J). 17.89 *(978-1-59990-949-3(9),* 9781599909493); (gr. -1-6). 16.99 *(978-1-59990-847-2(6),* 9781599908472) Bloomsbury Publishing USA. (Bloomsbury USA Childrens).

Kaus, Cathy. The Bean Bandit, 1 vol. 2010. 24p. 24.95 *(978-1-4489-2202-4(X))* PublishAmerica, Inc.

Keenan, Penny. Cooking with Ginger: Ginger Gets Lost Book I. Murray, Carol, illus. 2005. (J). per. 19.95 *(978-1-932604-23-8(5))* Tennessee Valley Publishing.

Keene, Carolyn. Cooking Camp Disaster. Pamintuan, Macky, illus. 2013. (Nancy Drew & the Clue Crew Ser.: 35). (ENG.). 96p. (J). (gr. 1-4). pap. 4.99 *(978-1-4169-9466-4(1),* Aladdin) Simon & Schuster Children's Publishing.

—Scream for Ice Cream, 1 vol. Pamintuan, Macky, illus. 2007. (Nancy Drew & the Clue Crew Ser.). (ENG.). 89p. (gr. 1-4). 24.21 *(978-1-59961-347-5(6))* Spotlight.

Kenah, Katharine. The Best Chef in Second Grade. Carter, Abby, illus. (I Can Read Level 2 Ser.). 48p. (J). 2008. (ENG.). (gr. k-3). pap. 3.99 *(978-0-06-053563-6(6))* 2007. (gr. -1-3). lib. bdg. 16.89 *(978-0-06-053562-9(8))* HarperCollins Pubs.

Kephart, Beth. Small Damages. 2013. (ENG., Illus.). 304p. (YA). (gr. 9). pap. 8.99 *(978-0-14-242641-8(5)*, Speak) Penguin Young Readers Group.

Kimmel, Eric A. Jack & the Giant Barbecue, 0 vols. Manders, John, illus. 2012. (ENG.). 32p. (J). (gr. 1-3). 17.99 *(978-0-7614-6128-9(0)*, 9780761461289, Amazon Children's Publishing) Amazon Publishing.

—The Three Little Tamales, 0 vols. Docampo, Valeria, illus. 2009. (ENG.). 32p. (J). (gr. -1-3). 17.99 *(978-0-7614-5519-6(1)*, 9780761455196, Amazon Children's Publishing) Amazon Publishing.

King, Jane. Creepy Cafeteria. 2013. (Ghoul School Ser.: 2). (ENG.). 80p. (J). (gr. 1-4). pap. 13.99 *(978-1-4814-2163-8(8)*, Simon & Schuster/Paula Wiseman Bks.) Simon & Schuster/Paula Wiseman Bks.

King, Zelda. Let's Bake a Cake. 2006. (Neighborhood Readers Ser.). (ENG.). 16p. (gr. 1-3). pap. 6.50 *(978-1-4042-7260-6(7)*, Rosen Classroom) Rosen Publishing Group, Inc., The.

Kladstrup, Kristin. The Gingerbread Pirates. Tavares, Matt, illus. gif. ed. 2012. (ENG.). 32p. (J). (gr. -1-3). 9.99 *(978-0-7636-6233-2(X))* Candlewick Pr.

Komura, Ayumi. Mixed Vegetables, Vol. 8. Komura, Ayumi, illus. 2010. (Mixed Vegetables Ser.: 8). (ENG., Illus.). 208p. pap. 9.99 *(978-1-4215-3235-6(2))* Viz Media.

Krause, Ute. Oscar & the Very Hungry Dragon. Krause, Ute, illus. 2015. (ENG., Illus.). 40p. (J). 8.95 *(978-0-7358-4230-4(2))* North-South Bks., Inc.

Kudo, Maki. The Pokémon Cookbook: Easy & Fun Recipes. 2016. (Pokemon Ser.: 1). (ENG., Illus.). 80p. 14.99 *(978-1-4215-8989-3(3))* Viz Media.

Kurup, Sindhu. Baby Bear's Favorite Food Pyramid. 2011. 28p. pap. 11.99 *(978-1-935268-91-8(0))* Halo Publishing International.

Kyle, Tracey C. Gazpacho for Nacho, 0 vols. 2014. (ENG.). 32p. (J). (gr. 1-3). 16.99 *(978-1-4778-1727-8(1)*, 9781477817278, Amazon Children's Publishing) Amazon Publishing.

Laird, Donivee Martin. The Magic Shark Learns to Cook. Johnson, Carol Ann, illus. 2004. 48p. (J). 9.95 *(978-1-57306-233-6(2))* Bess Pr., Inc.

Lawrence, Mike. The Macaroni Disaster! 2006. 44p. pap. 12.00 *(978-1-4116-8613-7(6))* Lulu Pr., Inc.

Lazo Gilmore, Dorina K. Cora Cooks Pancit. Valiant, Kristi, illus. 2014. (ENG.). 32p. (J). pap. 9.95 *(978-1-885008-48-0(1))*; (gr. -1-3). 17.95 *(978-1-885008-35-0(X))* Lee & Low Bks., Inc. (Shen's Bks.).

Lesynski, Loris. Boy Soup. Martchenko, Michael, illus. 2nd ed. 2008. (ENG.). 32p. (J). (gr. -1-2). 18.95 *(978-1-55451-143-3(7)*, 9781554511433); pap. 6.95 *(978-1-55451-142-6(9)*, 9781554511426) Annick Pr., Ltd. CAN. Dist: Publishers Group West (PGW).

Levine, Deborah A. & Riley, JillEllyn. The Icing on the Cake. 2015. (Saturday Cooking Club Ser.: 2). (ENG., Illus.). 304p. (J). (gr. 4-9). 17.99 *(978-1-4424-9942-3(7)*, Aladdin) Simon & Schuster Children's Publishing.

—Kitchen Chaos. 2015. (Saturday Cooking Club Ser.: 1). (ENG., Illus.). 336p. (J). (gr. 4-9). pap. 7.99 *(978-1-4424-9940-9(0)*, Aladdin) Simon & Schuster Children's Publishing.

—Kitchen Chaos. Espinosa, Leo, illus. 2015. (Saturday Cooking Club Ser.: 1). (ENG.). 336p. (J). (gr. 4-9). 17.99 *(978-1-4424-9939-3(7)*, Aladdin) Simon & Schuster Children's Publishing.

Lewis, Stewart. The Secret Ingredient. 2013. (ENG.). 256p. (YA). (gr. 7). 17.99 *(978-0-385-74331-0(9)*, Delacorte Bks. for Young Readers) Random Hse. Children's Bks.

Lin, Grace. Dim Sum for Everyone! Lin, Grace, illus. 2014. (ENG., Illus.). 24p. (J). (gr. -1-2). bds. 6.99 *(978-0-385-75488-0(4)*, Knopf Bks. for Young Readers) Random Hse. Children's Bks.

Littlewood, Kathryn. Bite-Sized Magic: A Bliss Novel. McGuire, Erin, illus. 2014. (Bliss Bakery Trilogy Ser.: 3). (ENG.). 432p. (J). (gr. 3-7). 16.99 *(978-0-06-208426-2(7)*, Tegen, Katherine Bks) HarperCollins Pubs.

—A Dash of Magic: A Bliss Novel. McGuire, Erin, illus. 2013. (Bliss Bakery Trilogy Ser.: 2). (ENG.). 368p. (J). (gr. 3-7). 16.99 *(978-0-06-208429-3(1)*, Tegen, Katherine Bks) HarperCollins Pubs.

Loehr, Patrick. Mucumber McGee & the Half-Eaten Hot Dog. Loehr, Patrick, illus. 2007. (Illus.). 32p. (J). (gr. -1-3). lib. bdg. 16.89 *(978-0-06-082328-3(3)*, Tegen, Katherine Bks) HarperCollins Pubs.

Lowell, Jax Peters. No More Cupcakes & Tummy Aches. 2004. (Illus.). 38p. (J). 22.99 *(978-1-4134-6255-5(3))* Xlibris Corp.

Lynch, Diane M., ed. Now You're Cooking! Ten Short Stories with Recipes. 2009. (J). (gr. 4-7). pap. 7.95 *(978-0-8198-5167-3(1))* Pauline Bks. & Media.

Lyons, Fergus. Shoestring Soup. 2004. (Pandas Ser.: 30). (ENG., Illus.). 64p. (J). pap. 9.95 *(978-0-86278-871-1(4))* O'Brien Pr., Ltd., The IRL. Dist: Dufour Editions, Inc.

Maccarone, Grace. The Gingerbread Family: A Scratch-and-Sniff Book. Gardner, Louise, illus. 2010. (ENG.). 14p. (J). (gr. -1-k). bds. 7.99 *(978-1-4424-0678-0(X)*, Little Simon) Little Simon.

Magden, Loretta. The Treetop Bird Family. Barringer, J. M., illus. 2007. 28p. (J). 15.95 *(978-0-9788771-0-1(1))* Level Green Bks.

Mahy, Margaret. Stop That Stew! Rigby, Deborah, illus. 2009. (Treasure Chest Readers Ser.). 24p. (J). (gr. -1-2). pap. 8.15 *(978-1-60754-683-2(3))*; lib. bdg. 22.60 *(978-1-60754-682-5(5))* Windmill Bks.

Make Believe Ideas. Annie the Apple Pie Fairy. 2013. (ENG.). 32p. (J). pap. 6.99 *(978-1-78235-588-5(X))* Make Believe Ideas GBR. Dist: Nelson, Thomas Inc.

Manushkin, Fran. Katie in the Kitchen, 1 vol. Lyon, Tammie, illus. 2010. (Katie Woo Ser.). (ENG.). 32p. (gr. k-2). lib. bdg. 21.32 *(978-1-4048-5724-7(9))* Picture Window Bks.

Manzano, Sonia. Miracle on 133rd Street. Priceman, Marjorie, illus. 2015. (ENG.). 48p. (J). (gr. -1-3). 17.99 *(978-0-689-87887-9(7))* Simon & Schuster Children's Publishing.

Marcucci, Vince. Tutti Frutti. St Anthony, Gus, illus. 2005. 32p. (J). (gr. -1-3). pap. 8.99 *(978-0-9769198-0-3(X))* Chick Light Publishing.

Markowitz, Susan Meredith. Maggie Makes Macaroni & Maggie hace Macarrones: 6 English, 6 Spanish Adaptations. 2011. (ENG & SPA.). (J). 75.00 net. *(978-1-4108-5649-4(6))* Benchmark Education Co.

McAlister, Caroline. Holy Mole! A Folktale from Mexico. Czernecki, Stefan, illus. 2006. (ENG.). 32p. (J). (gr. k-3). 16.95 *(978-0-87483-775-9(8))* August Hse. Pubs., Inc.

McDaniels, Preston, illus. Phineas L. MacGuire ... Gets Cooking! 2014. (From the Highly Scientific Notebooks of Phineas L. MacGuire Ser.). (ENG.). 208p. (J). (gr. 3-7). 16.99 *(978-1-4814-0099-2(1)*, Atheneum Bks. for Young Readers) Simon & Schuster Children's Publishing.

McElligott, Matthew. Even Aliens Need Snacks. McElligott, Matthew, illus. 2014. (ENG., Illus.). 40p. (J). (gr. k-3). pap. 7.99 *(978-0-8027-3652-9(1)*, 9780802736529, Bloomsbury USA Childrens) Bloomsbury Publishing USA.

McGinty, Alice B. Rabbi Benjamin's Buttons. Reinhardt, Jennifer Black, illus. (ENG.). 32p. (J). (gr. -1-3). 2017. pap. 7.99 *(978-1-58089-433-3(X))* 2014. lib. bdg. 17.95 *(978-1-58089-432-6(1))* Charlesbridge Publishing, Inc.

McLeod, Kimberly. Cooking Is for Girls! 2012. 28p. 25.00 *(978-0-9829825-4-9(2))* Creative Energy, LLC.

McNamara, Margaret & Thompson, Kay. Eloise Breaks Some Eggs. Lyon, Tammie, illus. 2005. (Eloise Ser.). (ENG.). 32p. (J). (gr. -1-1). pap. 3.99 *(978-0-689-87368-3(9)*, Simon Spotlight) Simon Spotlight.

Meredith-Markowitz, Susan. Maggie Makes Macaroni: Set Of 6. 2011. (Early Connections Ser.). (J). pap. 37.00 net. *(978-1-4108-1369-5(X))* Benchmark Education Co.

Meredith, Susan Markowitz. Maggie Makes Macaroni. 2011. (Early Connections Ser.). (J). *(978-1-61672-587-7(7))* Benchmark Education Co.

Michiko Florence, Debbi. Jasmine Toguchi, Mochi Queen. Vukovic, Elizabet, illus. 2017. (Jasmine Toguchi Ser.). (ENG.). 128p. (J). 15.99 *(978-0-374-30410-2(6)*, 9780374304102, Farrar, Straus & Giroux (BYR)) Farrar, Straus & Giroux.

Miller, Pat Zietlow. Sharing the Bread: An Old-Fashioned Thanksgiving Story. McElmurry, Jill, illus. 2015. (ENG.). 32p. (J). (gr. -1-3). 17.99 *(978-0-307-98182-0(7)*, Schwartz & Wade Bks.) Random Hse. Children's Bks.

Miller, Sibley. Hungry as a Horse. 2009. (Wind Dancers Ser.: 8). (ENG., Illus.). 80p. (J). (gr. 1-4). pap. 6.99 *(978-0-312-56403-2(1)*, 9780312564032) Feiwel & Friends.

Mills, Charles. The Great Sleepy-Time Stew Rescue. 2004. (Honors Club Story Ser.: Vol. 4). (Illus.). 127p. (J). 7.99 *(978-0-8163-2009-7(8))* Pacific Pr. Publishing Assn.

Mitsui Brown, Janet, illus. Oshogatsu with Obaachan. 2005. (J). *(978-1-879965-24-9(0))* Polychrome Publishing Corp.

Monkeys Can't Cook! 2004. (J). 10.95 *(978-0-9761350-3-6(5))* Murphey, Hiromi.

Monroe, Chris. Monkey with a Tool Belt & the Maniac Muffins. Monroe, Chris, illus. 2016. (ENG., Illus.). 32p. (gr. -1-2). (J). 17.99 *(978-1-4677-2155-4(7))*; 35.99 *(978-1-4677-9562-3(3))* Lerner Publishing Group. (Carolrhoda Bks.).

Mothershead, Martha Fulford. Petoskey Stone Soup. Clarkson, Janet M., illus. 2006. 32p. (J). 18.95 *(978-0-9785465-0-2(4))* Leelanau Pr.

Muldrow, Diane. Stirring It Up. Pollak, Barbara, illus. 2007. (Dish Ser.: 1). (ENG.). 160p. (J). (gr. 4-7). pap. 4.99 *(978-0-448-44526-7(3)*, Grosset & Dunlap) Penguin Young Readers Group.

—Turning up the Heat. No. 2. Pollak, Barbara, illus. 2nd ed. 2007. (Dish Ser.: 2). (ENG.). 160p. (J). (gr. 4-7). pap. 4.99 *(978-0-448-44527-4(1)*, Grosset & Dunlap) Penguin Young Readers Group.

Nasser, Sarah. Busy Ben Make Stir Fry. 2012. 24p. pap. 28.03 *(978-1-4797-0475-0(X))* Xlibris Corp.

Neuschwander, Cindy. Pastry School in Paris: An Adventure in Capacity. Langdo, Bryan, illus. 2009. (ENG.). 32p. (J). (gr. 2-6). 18.99 *(978-0-8050-8314-9(6)*, 9780805083149, Holt, Henry & Co. Bks. For Young Readers) Holt, Henry & Co.

North, Laura. Jack & the Bean Pie. 2014. (ENG., Illus.). 32p. (J). *(978-0-7787-0441-6(6))*; pap. *(978-0-7787-0449-2(1))* Crabtree Publishing Co.

Numeroff, Laura Joffe. Mouse Cookies & More: A Treasury. Bond, Felicia, illus. 2015. (If You Give... Ser.). (ENG.). 224p. (J). (gr. -1-3). 24.99 *(978-0-06-113763-1(4))* HarperCollins Pubs.

Odanaka, Barbara. A Crazy Day at the Critter Café. White, Lee, illus. 2009. (ENG.). 32p. (J). (gr. -1-3). 17.99 *(978-1-4169-3914-6(8)*, McElderry, Margaret K. Bks.) McElderry, Margaret K. Bks.

Odell, Carol. Once upon a Time in the Kitchen. Pignataro, Anna, illus. 2010. (Myths, Legends, Fairy & Folktales Ser.). (ENG.). 48p. (J). (gr. 1-4). 12.95 *(978-1-58536-518-0(1)*, 202208) Sleeping Bear Pr.

Olin, Marilyn. Mom, Mac & Cheese, Please! Pantic, Dunja, illus. 2013. (ENG.). 28p. (J). (gr. -1-k). 16.95 *(978-1-62087-995-5(6)*, 620995, Sky Pony Pr.) Skyhorse Publishing Co., Inc.

Osterhold, Jared, illus. Cooks up a Surprise. 2011. (Olivia TV Tie-In Ser.). (ENG.). 24p. (J). (gr. -1-2). pap. 3.99 *(978-1-4424-1384-9(0)*, Simon Spotlight) Simon Spotlight.

Palazzo, Christine. Josephina & Her Terrific Tomato Soup. 2011. 24p. pap. 14.59 *(978-1-4634-0704-9(1))* AuthorHouse.

Palmer, Jennie. The Wompananny Witches Make One Mean Pizza. 2017. (ENG., Illus.). 40p. (J). (gr. -1-2). 16.95 ***(978-1-4197-2642-2(0)**,* Abrams Bks. for Young Readers) Abrams, Inc.

Papp, Robert, illus. The Cupcake Caper. 2010. (Boxcar Children Mysteries Ser.: 125). (ENG.). 128p. (J). (gr. 1-5). 14.99 *(978-0-8075-1373-6(3))*;No. 125. pap. 5.99 *(978-0-8075-1374-3(1))* Whitman, Albert & Co.

Park, Frances, et al. Where on Earth Is My Bagel? Lin, Grace, illus. 2003. (Avenues Ser.). (ENG.). 32p. (C). (gr. -1-4). pap. 22.95 *(978-0-58430-033-5(7))* National Geographic School Publishing, Inc.

Park, Linda Sue. Bee-Bim Bop! Lee, Ho Baek, illus. (ENG.). 32p. (J). (gr. -1-3). 2008. pap. 7.99 *(978-0-547-07671-3(1))* 2005. 17.99 *(978-0-618-26511-4(2))* Houghton Mifflin Harcourt Publishing Co.

Paschkis, Julie. Apple Cake: A Recipe for Love. 2012. (ENG., Illus.). 32p. (J). (gr. -1-3). 16.99 *(978-0-547-80745-4(7))* Houghton Mifflin Harcourt Publishing Co.

Payne, C. C. The Thing about Leftovers. 2016. (ENG.). 288p. (J). (gr. 5). 16.99 *(978-0-399-17204-5(1)*, Nancy Paulsen Books) Penguin Young Readers Group.

Perelman-Bernstein, Helen. Feel the Noise! Tips & Tricks to Rockin' Camp. 2009. (ENG.). 40p. (J). 4.99 *(978-1-4231-2219-7(4))* Disney Pr.

Perelman, Helen. Rainbow Swirl. Waters, Erica-Jane, illus. 2010. (Candy Fairies Ser.: 2). (ENG.). 128p. (J). (gr. 2-5). pap. 5.99 *(978-1-4169-9455-8(6)*, Aladdin) Simon & Schuster Children's Publishing.

Perrenot, Christine. Jackson & Julie the Twelve-Month Chefs: A Holiday Cookbook for Families & Children. Voltz, Ralph, illus. 2011. 32p. (J). 16.95 *(978-1-61254-028-3(7))* Brown Books Publishing Group.

Peschke, Marci. Cooking Queen. Mourning, Tuesday, illus. 2017. (Kylie Jean Ser.). (ENG.). 112p. (gr. 2-3). lib. bdg. 22.65 ***(978-1-4795-9899-1(2)**,* Kylie Jean) Picture Window Bks.

Petrella, Angela, et al. Recipe. Althea, Erin & Bertino, Mike, illus. 2013. (ENG.). 48p. (J). (gr. -1-3). 17.95 *(978-1-936365-84-5(7))* McSweeney's Publishing.

Pitt, Roosevelt, Jr. A Day at the Four Seasons: "Finding the Ingredients" Kuumba, Mshindo, illus. 2005. (Food Adventures with Charles the Chef Ser.). (J). per. 12.95 *(978-0-9760745-0-2(8))* AMARA Entertainment.

Poon, Janice. Claire & the Bakery Thief. Poon, Janice, illus. 2008. (ENG., Illus.). 104p. (J). (gr. 2-5). 15.95 *(978-1-55453-286-5(8))*; pap. 7.95 *(978-1-55453-245-2(0))* Kids Can Pr., Ltd. CAN. Dist: Hachette Bk. Group.

Previn, Stacey. If Snowflakes Tasted Like Fruitcake. 2016. (ENG., Illus.). 40p. (J). (gr. -1-3). 17.99 *(978-1-4998-0180-4(7))* Little Bee Books Inc.

Price, Marilyn. Grandma's Cookies. 2011. 32p. pap. 12.95 *(978-1-934527-28-3(9))* Torah Aura Productions.

Publications International Ltd. Staff, ed. Nickelodeon Dora the Explorer: Cook with Dora: Abuela's Birthday Fiesta. 2010. 14p. (J). bds. 16.98 *(978-1-4508-0842-2(5))* Phoenix International Publications, Inc.

Quihuis, Albert. The Search for the Lost Art of Making Tortillas. 2012. 38p. pap. 16.95 *(978-0-9884576-0-7(1))* Perfect Bound Marketing.

Ray, Christie Jones & Ray, Christie Jones. Eliza Celebrates a Royal Wedding. 2012. (Illus.). 48p. pap. 15.00 *(978-0-9853223-6-6(5))* Rose Water Cottage Pr.

Reich, Susanna. Minette's Feast: The Delicious Story of Julia Child & Her Cat. Bates, Amy, illus. 2012. (ENG.). 40p. (J). (gr. -1-k). 17.95 *(978-1-4197-0177-1(0)*, Abrams Bks. for Young Readers) Abrams, Inc.

Reid Banks, Lynne & Stephenson, Omri. The Spice Rack. 2010. 40p. pap. 23.50 *(978-1-4461-3229-6(3))* Lulu Pr., Inc.

Reynolds, Aaron. Chicks & Salsa. Bogan, Paulette, illus. 2007. (ENG.). 32p. (J). (gr. 1-3). pap. 7.99 *(978-1-59990-099-5(8)*, 9781599900995, Bloomsbury USA Childrens) Bloomsbury Publishing USA.

Richards, Kitty & RH Disney Staff. Run, Remy, Run! Disney Storybook Artists Staff, illus. 2007. (Step into Reading Ser.). (ENG.). 32p. (J). (gr. k-3). pap. 3.99 *(978-0-7364-2476-9(8)*, RH/Disney) Random Hse. Children's Bks.

Rigby Education Staff. Dad's Pasta. (Sails Literacy Ser.). (Illus.). 16p. (gr. 2-3). 27.00 *(978-0-7635-9951-5(4)*, 699514C99) Rigby Education.

Rog&eacute. The French Fry King. Rog&eacute, illus. 2012. (ENG., Illus.). 32p. (J). (gr. -1-1). 17.95 *(978-1-77049-350-6(6)*, Tundra Bks.) Tundra Bks. CAN. Dist: Penguin Random Hse. LLC.

Rosenthal, Amy Krouse. Spoon. Magoon, Scott, illus. 2009. (Spoon Ser.). (ENG.). 40p. (J). (gr. -1-k). 16.99 *(978-1-4231-0685-2(7))* Hyperion Pr.

Rosenthal, Sally. Matzo Frogs. Sheldon, David, illus. 2014. (ENG.). 32p. (J). 17.95 *(978-1-58838-302-0(4)*, NewSouth Bks.) NewSouth, Inc.

Roy, James. Chaz & the Missing Mayo. Gorissen, Dean, illus. 2015. (J). pap. *(978-1-4966-0245-9(5))* Capstone Classroom.

—Chaz, Superbarf Surprise. Gorissen, Dean, illus. 2015. (J). pap. *(978-1-4966-0239-8(0))* Capstone Classroom.

—Chaz, TV Superstar? Gorissen, Dean, illus. 2015. (J). pap. *(978-1-4966-0257-2(9))* Capstone Classroom.

Ruiz, Jackson. It's Cool in the Furnace: The first graphic novel by Jackson Ruiz. 2010. 32p. pap. 16.99 *(978-1-4520-2634-3(3))* AuthorHouse.

Rylant, Cynthia. Mr. Putter & Tabby Spill the Beans. Howard, Arthur, illus. 2010. (Mr. Putter & Tabby Ser.). (ENG.). 44p. (J). (gr. 1-4). pap. 5.99 *(978-0-547-41433-1(1))* Houghton Mifflin Harcourt Publishing Co.

Sager, Ryan K. The World's Greatest Chocolate-Covered Pork Chops. 2017. (ENG.). 256p. (J). (gr. 3-7). 16.99 ***(978-1-4847-6761-0(6))*** Hyperion Bks. for Children.

Sanders, Addie Meyer. I Don't Want to Go. l.t. ed. 2012. 43p. (J). pap. *(978-1-4596-3449-7(7))* ReadHowYouWant.com, Ltd.

Sanger, Amy Wilson. Yum Yum Dim Sum. Sanger, Amy Wilson, illus. 2003. (ENG., Illus.). 22p. (J). (gr. k — 1). bds. 6.99 *(978-1-58246-108-3(2)*, Knopf Bks. for Young Readers) Random Hse. Children's Bks.

Sanger, Amy Wilson & Wilson Sanger, Amy. A Little Bit of Soul Food. Wilson Sanger, Amy, illus. 2004. (World Snacks Ser.). (ENG., Illus.). 20p. (J). (— 1). bds. 6.99 *(978-1-58246-109-0(0)*, Tricycle Pr.) Random Hse. Children's Bks.

Sargent, Dave, et al. Rays of the Sun Vol. 15: (shoshone) Learn Lessons, 20 vols. Lenoir, Jane, illus. l.t. ed. 2004. (Story Keeper Ser.: 15). 48p. (J). pap. 10.95 *(978-1-56763-932-2(1))* Ozark Publishing.

—Rays of the Sun Vol. 15: (Shoshone) Learn Lessons, 20 vols. Lenoir, Jane, illus. l.t. ed. 2004. (Story Keeper Ser.: 15). 48p. (J). lib. bdg. 23.60 *(978-1-56763-931-5(3))* Ozark Publishing.

Sateren, Shelley Swanson. Max & Zoe Celebrate Mother's Day, 1 vol. Sullivan, Mary, illus. 2012. (Max & Zoe Ser.). (ENG.). 32p. (gr. k-2). lib. bdg. 21.32 *(978-1-4048-6214-2(5)*, Max & Zoe) Picture Window Bks.

Saxon, Victoria & RH Disney Staff. Ratatouille. Tilley, Scott & Orpinas, Jean-Paul, illus. 2007. (Little Golden Book Ser.). (ENG.). 24p. (J). (gr. -1-2). 3.99 *(978-0-7364-2423-3(7)*, RH/Disney) Random Hse. Children's Bks.

Schubert, Ingrid & Schubert, Dieter. Elephant Soup. 2010. (ENG., Illus.). 32p. (J). (gr. -1-3). 17.95 *(978-1-59078-807-3(9)*, 9781590788073) Lemniscaat USA.

Secret Soup: Individual Title Six-Packs. (Literatura 2000 Ser.). (gr. 1-2). 28.00 *(978-0-7635-0111-2(5))* Rigby Education.

Selfors, Suzanne. Kiss & Spell. 2015. (Ever after High Ser.: Bk. 2). (ENG., Illus.). 224p. (J). (gr. 3-7). 13.99 *(978-0-316-40131-9(5))* Little, Brown Bks. for Young Readers.

Sherrard, Valerie. Miss Wondergem's Dreadfully Dreadful Pie, 1 vol. Whittingham, Wendy, illus. 2011. (ENG.). 32p. (J). (gr. k-5). pap. 9.95 *(978-1-897174-81-4(0)*, Tuckamore Bks) Creative Bk. Publishing CAN. Dist: Orca Bk. Pubs. USA.

Simon, Coco. Alexis & the Missing Ingredient. 2013. (Cupcake Diaries: 16). (ENG., Illus.). 160p. (J). (gr. 3-7). 17.99 *(978-1-4424-8588-4(4))*; pap. 5.99 *(978-1-4424-8587-7(6))* Simon Spotlight. (Simon Spotlight).

—Alexis & the Perfect Recipe. (Cupcake Diaries: 4). (ENG., Illus.). 160p. (J). (gr. 3-7). 2013. 15.99 *(978-1-4424-7493-2(9))* 2011. pap. 6.99 *(978-1-4424-2901-7(1))* Simon Spotlight. (Simon Spotlight).

—Katie's New Recipe. 2013. (Cupcake Diaries: 13). (ENG., Illus.). 160p. (J). (gr. 3-7). pap. 5.99 *(978-1-4424-7168-9(9)*, Simon Spotlight) Simon Spotlight.

Smith, Carrie. Stone Soup: Classic Tales Edition. Rogers, Jacqueline, illus. 2011. (Classic Tales Ser.). (J). *(978-1-936258-72-7(2))* Benchmark Education Co.

Specht, Judy. Appetizers, Please. 2011. pap. 14.95 *(978-0-7414-6587-0(6))* Infinity Publishing.

Stead, Philip C. Creamed Tuna Fish & Peas on Toast. Stead, Philip C., illus. 2009. (ENG., Illus.). 32p. (J). (gr. -1-1). 16.99 *(978-1-59643-401-1(5)*, 9781596434011) Roaring Brook Pr.

Steadman, Ralph. The Jelly Book. Steadman, Ralph, illus. (Illus.). 32p. (J). (gr. -1-3). 14.95 *(978-0-87592-026-9(8))* Scroll Pr., Inc.

Stevenson, Robin. Dead in the Water, 1 vol. 2008. (Orca Sports Ser.). (ENG.). 176p. (YA). (gr. 6-10). pap. 9.95 *(978-1-55143-962-4(X))* Orca Bk. Pubs. USA.

Stremanos, A. M., illus. Rosemary's Taken over My Potatoes. 2008. 20p. (J). 5.00 *(978-0-9801372-0-0(9))* Benedetti, Jef.

Stutson, Caroline. Blue Corn Soup. Weidner, Teri, illus. 2017. (ENG.). 32p. (J). (gr. k-2). 16.99 ***(978-1-58536-967-6(5)**,* 204325) Sleeping Bear Pr.

Sylvester, Kevin. Neil Flambé & the Bard's Banquet. Sylvester, Kevin, illus. 2015. (Neil Flambe Capers Ser.: 5). (ENG., Illus.). 320p. (J). (gr. 3-7). 12.99 *(978-1-4814-1038-0(5)*, Simon & Schuster Bks. For Young Readers) Simon & Schuster Bks. For Young Readers.

—Neil Flambé & the Crusader's Curse. Sylvester, Kevin, illus. (Neil Flambe Capers Ser.: 3). (ENG., Illus.). (J). (gr. 3-7). 2014. 320p. pap. 7.99 *(978-1-4424-4287-0(5))* 2012. 304p. 13.99 *(978-1-4424-4286-3(7))* Simon & Schuster Bks. For Young Readers. (Simon & Schuster Bks. For Young Readers).

—Neil Flambé & the Duel in the Desert. Sylvester, Kevin, illus. (Neil Flambe Capers Ser.: 6). (ENG., Illus.). 304p. (J). (gr. 3-7). 2017. pap. 7.99 *(978-1-4814-1042-7(3))* 2016. 13.99 *(978-1-4814-1041-0(5))* Simon & Schuster Bks. For Young Readers. (Simon & Schuster Bks. For Young Readers).

—Neil Flambé & the Marco Polo Murders. 2010. (Neil Flambé Capers Ser.: No. 1). (Illus.). 304p. (YA). (gr. 5-9). *(978-1-55470-266-4(6))* Me to We.

—Neil Flambé & the Marco Polo Murders. Sylvester, Kevin, illus. 2012. (Neil Flambe Capers Ser.: 1). (ENG., Illus.). 304p. (J). (gr. 3-7). 14.99 *(978-1-4424-4604-5(8)*, Simon & Schuster Bks. For Young Readers) Simon & Schuster Bks. For Young Readers.

—Neil Flambé & the Tokyo Treasure. Sylvester, Kevin, illus. (Neil Flambe Capers Ser.: 4). (ENG., Illus.). (J). (gr. 3-7). 2014. 368p. pap. 7.99 *(978-1-4424-4289-4(1))* 2012. 352p. 13.99 *(978-1-4424-4288-7(3))* Simon & Schuster Bks. For Young Readers. (Simon & Schuster Bks. For Young Readers).

Templeton, Donna L. Mother's Surprise. Berlinger, Nancy A., illus. 2009. (ENG.). 32p. (J). pap. 9.99 *(978-0-9764336-6-8(4))* MJS Publishing Group LLC.

Thong, Roseanne Greenfield. Noodle Magic. So, Meilo, illus. 2014. (ENG.). 32p. (J). (gr. -1-3). 17.99 *(978-0-545-52167-3(X))* Scholastic, Inc.

Toretto, Jordana. The Runaway Children. 2013. 30p. pap. 16.95 *(978-1-63004-706-1(6))* America Star Bks.

Travers, P. L. Mary Poppins in the Kitchen: A Cookery Book with a Story. Shepard, Mary, illus. 2006. (Mary Poppins Ser.: No. 6). (ENG.). 88p. (J). (gr. 5-7). 16.99 *(978-0-15-206080-0(4))* Houghton Mifflin Harcourt Publishing Co.

Two Smart Cookies. 2005. 44p. (J). 3.99 *(978-0-9763213-5-4(1))* OHC Group LLC.

Urbanovic, Jackie. Duck Soup. Urbanovic, Jackie, illus. 2008. (Max the Duck Ser.: 2). (Illus.). 32p. (J). (gr. -1-2). (ENG.). 17.99 *(978-0-06-121441-7(8))*; lib. bdg. 18.89 *(978-0-06-121442-4(6))* HarperCollins Pubs.

Vamos, Samantha R. The Cazuela That the Farm Maiden Stirred. López, Rafael, illus. (ENG & SPA.). 32p. (J). (gr. k-3). 2013. pap. 8.95 *(978-1-58089-243-8(4))* 2011. 17.95 *(978-1-58089-242-1(6))* Charlesbridge Publishing, Inc.

Walsh, Ann. Whatever. 2013. (ENG.). 200p. pap. 11.95 *(978-1-55380-259-4(4))* Ronsdale Pr. CAN. Dist: SPD-Small Pr. Distribution.

Wax, Wendy. Picnic Day! Artful Doodlers, illus. 2006. 24p. (J). lib. bdg. 15.00 *(978-1-4242-0952-1(8))* Fitzgerald Bks.

Weeks, Sarah. Pie. 2013. (ENG.). 192p. (J). (gr. 3-7). pap. 6.99 *(978-0-545-27012-0(X)*, Scholastic Paperbacks) Scholastic, Inc.

Wellington, Monica. Mr. Cookie Baker (Board Book Edition) 2011. (ENG.). 26p. (J). (gr. -1 — 1). bds. 5.99 *(978-0-525-42372-0(9)*, Dutton Books for Young Readers) Penguin Young Readers Group.

—Pizza at Sally's. Wellington, Monica, illus. 2006. (ENG., Illus.). 32p. (J). (gr. -1-2). 15.99 *(978-0-525-47715-0(2)*, Dutton Books for Young Readers) Penguin Young Readers Group.

Welsh, Karen Leis. The Gingerbread Class. 2012. 32p. pap. 17.99 *(978-1-4772-7488-0(X))* AuthorHouse.

C
D

Weston Woods Staff, creator. Too Many Tamales. 2004. (J). (gr. -1-3). 29.95 *(978-1-55592-137-8(X))* Weston Woods Studios, Inc.

Whytock, Cherry. My Scrumptious Scottish Dumplings: The Life of Angelica Cookson Potts. Whytock, Cherry, illus. 2006. (ENG., Illus.). 192p. (YA). mass mkt. 5.99 *(978-0-689-86552-7(X),* Simon Pulse) Simon Pulse.

Williams, Kathryn. Pizza, Love, & Other Stuff That Made Me Famous. 2013. (ENG.). 256p. (YA). (gr. 7-12). pap. 11.99 *(978-1-250-02745-0(4),* 9781250027450) Square Fish.

Winkler, Henry & Oliver, Lin. Holy Enchilada! Heyer, Carol et al, illus. 2004. (Hank Zipzer Ser.: 6). (ENG.). 160p. (J). (gr. 3-7). pap. 5.99 *(978-0-448-43353-0(2),* Grosset & Dunlap) Penguin Young Readers Group.

—The Zippity Zinger, 4 vols. Heitz, Tim, illus. 2004. (Hank Zipzer Ser.: 4). (ENG.). 160p. (J). (gr. 3-7). mass mkt. 5.99 *(978-0-448-43193-2(9),* Grosset & Dunlap) Penguin Young Readers Group.

Winner, Ramana Moreno. Freaky Foods from Around the World: Platillos Sorprendentes de todo el Mundo. Haake, Susana, tr. Borsan, Luis, illus. 2004. (ENG & SPA.). (J). (gr. 1-5). pap. 15.95 *(978-0-9651174-2-5(1))* BrainStorm 3000.

Winslow, Marjorie. Mud Pies & Other Recipes: A Cookbook for Dolls. Blegvad, Erik, illus. 2010. (ENG.). 56p. (J). (gr. k-4). 14.95 *(978-1-59017-368-8(6),* NYR Children's Collection) New York Review of Bks., Inc., The.

Wong, Janet S. Apple Pie Fourth of July. Chodos-Irvine, Margaret, illus. 2006. (ENG.). 40p. (J). (gr. -1-3). pap. 7.99 *(978-0-15-205708-4(0))* Houghton Mifflin Harcourt Publishing Co.

Wood, Nancy. Mr. & Mrs. God in the Creation Kitchen. Ering, Timothy Basil, illus. 2006. (ENG.). 32p. (J). (gr. k-4). 16.99 *(978-0-7636-1258-0(8))* Candlewick Pr.

Worth, Bonnie. The Cat in the Hat - Cooking with the Cat. Moroney, Christopher, illus. 2003. (Step into Reading Ser.). (ENG.). 32p. (J). (gr. -1-1). pap. 3.99 *(978-0-375-82494-4(4),* 53560581, Random Hse. Bks. for Young Readers) Random Hse. Children's Bks.

Yanisko, Thomas. What You Eat It's up to You. Hoyes, Kerry, illus. 2012. 36p. pap. 9.99 *(978-1-937260-26-2(7))* Sleepytown Pr.

Yolen, Jane. How Do Dinosaurs Eat Cookies? Teague, Mark, illus. 2012. (How Do Dinosaurs... Ser.). (ENG.). 14p. (J). (gr. -1-k). bds. 7.99 *(978-0-545-38253-3(X),* Cartwheel Bks.) Scholastic, Inc.

Yolen, Jane & Stemple, Heidi E. Y. Fairy Tale Feasts: A Literary Cookbook for Young Readers & Eaters. Beha, Philippe, illus. 2006. (ENG.). 264p. (J). (gr. 4-7). 24.95 *(978-1-56656-643-8(6))* Interlink Publishing Group, Inc.

Young, Jessica. Original Recipe. Secheret, Jessica, illus. 2015. (Finley Flowers Ser.). (ENG.). 128p. (gr. 2-3). 8.95 *(978-1-4795-5878-0(8),* Finley Flowers) Picture Window Bks.

Zepeda, Gwendolyn & Ventura, Gabriela Baeza. Growing up with Tamales: Los Tamales de Ana. Ward, April, illus. 2008. (SPA & ENG.). 32p. (J). (gr. -1-2). 16.95 *(978-1-55885-493-2(2),* Piñata Books) Arte Publico Pr.

Zibart, Rosemary. I Have a Grandma Who ... Herzlich, Valori, illus. 2014. (J). *(978-1-929115-25-9(3))* Azro Pr., Inc.

Zolkower, Edie Stoltz. When It's Purim. Bjornson, Barb, illus. 2009. (Very First Board Bks.). (ENG.). 12p. (J). (gr. -1 — 1). 5.95 *(978-0-8225-8947-1(8),* Kar-Ben Publishing) Lerner Publishing Group.

COOKING (FISH)

Deering, Alison. Fish & Fowl: Easy & Awesome Sandwiches for Kids. Lentz, Bob, illus. 2017. (Between the Bread Ser.). (ENG.). 48p. (gr. 4-5). lib. bdg. 31.32 ***(978-1-5157-3920-3(1))*** Capstone Press of Coughlan Cos.

Dilkes, D. H. Meat & Fish. 2011. (All about Good Foods We Eat Ser.). (Illus.). 24p. (J). (gr. -1-18). pap. 7.95 *(978-1-59845-254-9(1),* Enslow Elementary); (gr. k-3). lib. bdg. 22.60 *(978-0-7660-3925-4(0))* Enslow Pubs., Inc.

Hewitt, Sally. Meat & Fish. 2008. (Good for Me Ser.). (Illus.). 24p. (J). (gr. -1-3). lib. bdg. 22.60 *(978-1-4042-4266-1(X),* PowerKids Pr.) Rosen Publishing Group, Inc., The.

Llewellyn, Claire & O'Shea, Clare. Cooking with Meat & Fish. 2011. (Cooking Healthy Ser.). (J). lib. bdg. 29.25 *(978-1-4488-4845-4(8),* Rosen Reference) Rosen Publishing Group, Inc., The.

COOKING (MEAT)

Alexander, Heather. Easy Main Dishes from Around the World. 2011. (Easy Cookbooks for Kids Ser.). (Illus.). 48p. (J). lib. bdg. 25.27 *(978-0-7660-3766-3(5));* (gr. 3-18). pap. 8.95 *(978-1-59845-273-0(8))* Enslow Pubs., Inc. (Enslow Elementary).

Burstein, John. Marvelous Meats & More. 2009. (Slim Goodbody's Nutrition Edition Ser.). (ENG., Illus.). 24p. (J). (gr. k-3). pap. *(978-0-7787-5059-8(0));* lib. bdg. *(978-0-7787-5044-4(2))* Crabtree Publishing Co.

Dilkes, D. H. Meat & Fish. 2011. (All about Good Foods We Eat Ser.). (Illus.). 24p. (J). (gr. -1-18). pap. 7.95 *(978-1-59845-254-9(1),* Enslow Elementary); (gr. k-3). lib. bdg. 22.60 *(978-0-7660-3925-4(0))* Enslow Pubs., Inc.

Goldish, Meish. Mammal Menu. 2009. (Extreme Cuisine Ser.). (Illus.). 24p. (J). (gr. 1-4). lib. bdg. 22.61 *(978-1-59716-760-4(6))* Bearport Publishing Co., Inc.

Hewitt, Sally. Meat & Fish. 2008. (Good for Me Ser.). (Illus.). 24p. (J). (gr. -1-3). lib. bdg. 22.60 *(978-1-4042-4266-1(X),* PowerKids Pr.) Rosen Publishing Group, Inc., The.

Larson, Jennifer S. Meaty Main Dishes. Cohen, Brie, photos by. 2013. (You're the Chef Ser.). (ENG., Illus.). 32p. (gr. 3-5). lib. bdg. 26.60 *(978-0-7613-6634-8(2),* Millbrook Pr.) Lerner Publishing Group.

Llewellyn, Claire & O'Shea, Clare. Cooking with Meat & Fish. 2011. (Cooking Healthy Ser.). (J). lib. bdg. 29.25 *(978-1-4488-4845-4(8),* Rosen Reference) Rosen Publishing Group, Inc., The.

Sylver, Adrienne. Hot Diggity Dog: The History of the Hot Dog. Smith, Elwood H., illus. 2010. (ENG.). 32p. (J). (gr. k-3). 16.99 *(978-0-525-47897-3(3),* Dutton Books for Young Readers) Penguin Young Readers Group.

COOKING (NATURAL FOODS)

Fordham, Henrietta. Healthy Food for Young Children Internet-Referenced. 2010. (Parent's Guides). 128p. (J). pap. 12.99 *(978-0-7945-1925-4(3),* Usborne) EDC Publishing.

Gilpin, Rebecca. 30 Healthy Things to Cook & Eat. 2010. (Children's Cooking Ser.). (ENG., Illus.). 30p. (J). (gr. 1). 9.99 *(978-0-7945-2396-1(X),* Usborne) EDC Publishing.

Karmel, Annabel. The Toddler Cookbook. 2008. (ENG., Illus.). 48p. (J). (gr. -1-k). 12.99 *(978-0-7566-3505-3(5),* DK Children) Dorling Kindersley Publishing, Inc.

Tuminelly, Nancy. Cool Raw Food Recipes: Delicious & Fun Foods Without Cooking, 1 vol. 2013. (Cool Recipes for Your Health Ser.). (ENG.). 32p. (J). (gr. 3-6). lib. bdg. 28.50 *(978-1-61783-584-1(6),* Checkerboard Library) ABDO Publishing Co.

COOKING (POULTRY)

see also Cooking (Chicken)

Deering, Alison. Fish & Fowl: Easy & Awesome Sandwiches for Kids. Lentz, Bob, illus. 2017. (Between the Bread Ser.). (ENG.). 48p. (gr. 4-5). lib. bdg. 31.32 ***(978-1-5157-3920-3(1))*** Capstone Press of Coughlan Cos.

COOKING (SEAFOOD)

Williams, Dinah. Shocking Seafood. 2009. (Extreme Cuisine Ser.). (Illus.). 24p. (J). (gr. 1-4). lib. bdg. 22.61 *(978-1-59716-761-1(4))* Bearport Publishing Co., Inc.

COOKING (VEGETABLES)

Berkes, Marianne. What's in the Garden?, 1 vol. Arbo, Cris, illus. 2013. (ENG.). 32p. (J). (gr. -1-4). 16.95 *(978-1-58469-189-1(1));* pap. 8.95 *(978-1-58469-190-7(5))* Dawn Pubns.

Cornell, Kari & Turkoglu, Nurcay. Cooking the Turkish Way. 2nd rev. ed. 2004. (Easy Menu Ethnic Cookbooks 2nd Edition Ser.). (ENG., Illus.). 72p. (gr. 5-12). 25.26 *(978-0-8225-4123-3(8),* Carolrhoda Bks.) Lerner Publishing Group.

Grant, Amanda. Grow It, Cook It with Kids. 2010. (ENG., Illus.). 128p. (J). *(978-1-84597-969-0(9))* Ryland Peters & Small.

Head, Honor. Beans & Nuts: On Your Plate. 2010. (J). 24.25 *(978-1-59920-336-2(7))* Black Rabbit Bks.

Hengel, Katherine. Cool Carrots from Garden to Table: How to Plant, Grow, & Prepare Carrots, 1 vol. 2012. (Cool Garden to Table Ser.). (ENG.). 32p. 28.50 *(978-1-61783-183-6(2),* Checkerboard Library) ABDO Publishing Co.

—Cool Green Beans from Garden to Table: How to Plant, Grow, & Prepare Green Beans, 1 vol. 2012. (Cool Garden to Table Ser.). (ENG.). 32p. 28.50 *(978-1-61783-184-3(0),* Checkerboard Library) ABDO Publishing Co.

—Cool Potatoes from Garden to Table: How to Plant, Grow, & Prepare Potatoes, 1 vol. 2012. (Cool Garden to Table Ser.). (ENG.). 32p. 28.50 *(978-1-61783-186-7(7),* Checkerboard Library) ABDO Publishing Co.

—Cool Tomatoes from Garden to Table: How to Plant, Grow, & Prepare Tomatoes, 1 vol. 2012. (Cool Garden to Table Ser.). (ENG.). 32p. 28.50 *(978-1-61783-187-4(5),* Checkerboard Library) ABDO Publishing Co.

Hewitt, Sally. Vegetables. 2008. (Good for Me Ser.). (Illus.). 24p. (J). (gr. -1-3). lib. bdg. 22.60 *(978-1-4042-4265-4(1),* PowerKids Pr.) Rosen Publishing Group, Inc., The.

Houbre, Gilbert. Vegetables. Houbre, Gilbert, illus. 2012. (ENG., Illus.). 36p. (J). (gr. -1-k). 12.99 *(978-1-85103-402-4(1))* Moonlight Publishing, Ltd. GBR. Dist: Independent Pubs. Group.

Liversidge, Cassie. Pasta Sauce! Grow Your Own Ingredients. 2013. (ENG., Illus.). 40p. (J). (gr. k-3). 14.95 *(978-1-62087-533-9(0),* 620533, Sky Pony Pr.) Skyhorse Publishing Co., Inc.

Llanas, Sheila Griffin. Easy Vegetarian Foods from Around the World. 2011. (Easy Cookbooks for Kids Ser.). (Illus.). 48p. (J). (gr. 3-18). pap. 8.95 *(978-1-59845-271-6(1),* Enslow Elementary) Enslow Pubs., Inc.

Llewellyn, Claire & O'Shea, Clare. Cooking with Fruits & Vegetables. 2011. (Cooking Healthy Ser.). (Illus.). 48p. (J). lib. bdg. 29.25 *(978-1-4488-4844-7(X),* Rosen Reference) Rosen Publishing Group, Inc., The.

Malam, John. Grow Your Own Sandwich, 1 vol. 2011. (Grow It Yourself! Ser.). (ENG.). 32p. (gr. k-2). pap. 8.29 *(978-1-4329-5115-3(7));* 27.32 *(978-1-4329-5108-5(4))* Heinemann-Raintree. (Heinemann First Library).

—Grow Your Own Snack, 1 vol. 2011. (Grow It Yourself! Ser.). (ENG.). 32p. (gr. k-2). 27.32 *(978-1-4329-5107-8(6),* Heinemann First Library) Heinemann-Raintree.

—Grow Your Own Soup, 1 vol. 2011. (Grow It Yourself! Ser.). (ENG.). 32p. (gr. k-2). 27.32 *(978-1-4329-5106-1(8),* Heinemann First Library) Heinemann-Raintree.

McDougall, Nancy & Hendy, Jenny. 300 Step-By-Step Cooking & Gardening Projects for Kids: The Ultimate Book for Budding Gardeners & Super Chefs with Amazing Things to Grow & Cook Yourself, Shown in over 2300 Photographs. 2012. (ENG., Illus.). 512p. 25.00 *(978-0-7548-2383-4(0))* Anness Publishing GBR. Dist: National Bk. Network.

—300 Step-By-Step Cooking & Gardening Projects for Kids: The Ultimate Book for Budding Gardeners & Super Chefs, with Amazing Things to Grow & Cook Yourself, Shown in over 2300 Photographs. 2015. (ENG., Illus.). 512p. pap. 14.99 *(978-1-86147-707-1(4),* Armadillo) Anness Publishing GBR. Dist: National Bk. Network.

Nelson, Robin. Tomatoes. 2009. (First Step Nonfiction - Plant Life Cycles Ser.). (ENG.). 24p. (gr. k-2). 23.93 *(978-0-7613-4070-6(X),* Lerner Pubns.) Lerner Publishing Group.

Rajczak, Kristen. Very Tasty Vegetable Recipes. 2014. (Ingredients for a Healthy Life Ser.). (Illus.). 24p. (J). (gr. 2-5). 22.60 *(978-1-4824-0575-0(X))* Stevens, Gareth Publishing LLLP.

Robinson, Fay. Baked Potatoes. 2016. (Spring Forward Ser.). (J). (gr. 2). *(978-1-4900-9420-5(2))* Benchmark Education Co.

Rumsey, Frances. My Very Own Organic Cookbook: Potatoes. 2013. 20p. pap. 7.95 *(978-1-61170-110-4(4))* Robertson Publishing.

—My Very Own Organic Cookbook: The Teen, Book 1. 2013. 40p. pap. 9.95 *(978-1-61170-123-4(6))* Robertson Publishing.

Tuminelly, Nancy. Cool Meat-Free Recipes: Delicious & Fun Foods Without Meat, 1 vol. 2013. (Cool Recipes for Your Health Ser.). (ENG.). 32p. (J). (gr. 3-6). lib. bdg. 28.50 *(978-1-61783-582-7(X),* Checkerboard Library) ABDO Publishing Co.

Vaughn, Inés. Chiles. 2009. (Native Foods of Latin America / Alimentos indígenas de Latino América Ser.). (ENG & SPA.). 24p. (gr. 2-3). 42.50 *(978-1-61514-795-3(0),* Editorial Buenas Letras) Rosen Publishing Group, Inc., The.

—Potatoes: Papas. 2009. (Native Foods of Latin America / Alimentos Indígenas de Latinoamérica Ser.). (SPA & ENG.). (J). 22.60 *(978-1-4358-2728-8(7),* PowerKids Pr.) Rosen Publishing Group, Inc., The.

COOKING, AFRICAN AMERICAN

see African American Cooking

COOKING, AMERICAN

Albright, Sawyer. Emeril Lagasse. 2012. (J). *(978-1-61900-016-2(4));* pap. *(978-1-61900-017-9(2))* Eldorado Ink.

American Girl Editors. Molly's Cooking Studio. Backes, Nick, illus. 2004. 54p. (gr. 3-18). 15.95 *(978-1-59369-265-0(X))* American Girl Publishing, Inc.

—Samantha's Cooking Studio. Backes, Nick, illus. 2005. 54p. (gr. 3-18). 15.95 *(978-1-59369-268-1(4))* American Girl Publishing, Inc.

Athan, Polly, et al. Felicity's Cooking Studio. Mahal, Susan, illus. 2007. (American Girl Ser.). 55p. (J). (gr. 3-7). 15.95 *(978-1-59369-266-7(8))* American Girl Publishing, Inc.

Behnke, Alison, et al. Cooking the Central American Way. 2nd rev. ed. 2005. (Easy Menu Ethnic Cookbooks 2nd Edition Ser.). (ENG., Illus.). 72p. (gr. 5-12). 25.26 *(978-0-8225-1236-3(X),* Lerner Pubns.) Lerner Publishing Group.

Bradley, Barbara. Hawaiian Kids Cook & Color Book. pap. 5.95 *(978-0-930492-43-4(9))* Hawaiian Service, Inc.

Burtwell, Ross & Celeste Rosenfeld, Julia. Texas Hill Country Cuisine: Flavors from the Cabernet Grill Texas Wine Country Restaurant. Whitney, Jennifer, photos by. 2014. (ENG., Illus.). 196p. 34.95 *(978-0-9899450-0-4(6))* Creative Noggin.

D'Amico, Joan & Drummond, Karen Eich. The U. S. History Cookbook: Delicious Recipes & Exciting Events from the Past. Cline, Jeff & Cash-Walsh, Tina, illus. 2003. (ENG.). 192p. (J). (gr. 3-7). pap. 16.00 *(978-0-471-13602-6(6),* Jossey-Bass) Wiley, John & Sons, Inc.

D'Amico, Joan & Drumond, Karen Eich. The US History Cook Book: Delicious Recipes & Exciting Events from the Past. 2006. (Illus.). 180p. (J). (gr. 4-8). reprint ed. pap. 15.00 *(978-1-4223-5809-2(7))* DIANE Publishing Co.

Dosier, Susan. Civil War Cooking: The Confederacy. 2016. (Exploring History Through Food Ser.). (ENG., Illus.). 32p. (gr. 3-4). lib. bdg. 27.32 *(978-1-5157-2354-7(2))* Capstone Press of Coughlan Cos.

—Civil War Cooking: The Union. 2016. (Exploring History Through Food Ser.). (ENG., Illus.). 32p. (gr. 3-4). lib. bdg. 27.32 *(978-1-5157-2353-0(4))* Capstone Press of Coughlan Cos.

—Colonial Cooking. 2016. (Exploring History Through Food Ser.). (ENG., Illus.). 32p. (gr. 3-4). lib. bdg. 27.32 *(978-1-5157-2356-1(9))* Capstone Press of Coughlan Cos.

Drummond, Karen Eich & D'Amico, Joan. The Coming to America Cookbook: Delicious Recipes & Fascinating Stories from America's Many Cultures. 2005. (ENG., Illus.). 192p. (J). (gr. 3-7). pap. 16.95 *(978-0-471-48335-9(4),* Wiley) Wiley, John & Sons, Inc.

Florence, Sarah. Pilgrim Foods & Recipes. 2009. (Reading Room Collection 2 Ser.). 24p. (gr. 3-4). 42.50 *(978-1-60851-983-5(X),* PowerKids Pr.) Rosen Publishing Group, Inc., The.

Gammon, Shana B. The Great State Cookbook: Recipes from Around the Country-for Kids. 2003. (Illus.). 62p. (J). spiral bd., act. bk. ed. 8.95 *(978-0-9743795-0-0(6))* Little Willow Tree Bks.

George, Lynn. Civil War Recipes: Adding & Subtracting Simple Fractions. (PowerMath Ser.). (ENG., 24p. (gr. 3-4). 2009. Illus.). (J). pap. 8.25 *(978-0-8239-8896-9(1),* PowerKids Pr.) 2004. 43.95 *(978-0-8239-7643-0(2))* Rosen Publishing Group, Inc., The.

Gilbert, Sara. American Food. 2015. (J). *(978-1-60818-500-9(1),* Creative Education) Creative Co., The.

—Cooking School: American Food. 2015. (Cooking School Ser.). (ENG.). 24p. (J). (gr. 1-3). pap. 9.99 *(978-1-62832-094-7(X),* Creative Paperbacks) Creative Co., The.

Group, Brown Reference. Festive Foods: United States. 2008. (Festive Foods Ser.). 48p. (gr. 4-6). 28.00 *(978-0-7910-9758-8(7),* Chelsea Clubhouse) Facts On File, Inc.

Hamilton, Robert M. Recipes of the American Revolution. 2017. (Cooking Your Way Through American History Ser.). 24p. (J). (gr. 3-3). 27.25 ***(978-1-5345-2106-3(2));*** pap. 63.60 ***(978-1-5345-2105-6(4));*** pap. 10.60 ***(978-1-5345-2104-9(6))*** Greenhaven Publishing LLC. (KidHaven Publishing).

Hirsch, Jennifer & Jones, Michelle. Kit's Cooking Studio. Witkowski, Teri, ed. McAliley, Susan et al, illus. 2007. (American Girl Ser.). 55p. (J). (gr. 3-7). 15.95 *(978-1-59369-267-4(6))* American Girl Publishing, Inc.

Houts, Amy. Cooking Around the Country with Kids: USA Regional Recipes & Fun Activities. 2009. (J). 19.95 *(978-0-930643-20-1(8))* Images Unlimited Publishing.

Ichord, Loretta Frances & Millbrook Press. Skillet Bread, Sourdough, & Vinegar Days: Cooking in Pioneer Days. Ellis, Jan Davey, illus. 2005. 64p. (J). (gr. 4-8). per. 8.95 *(978-0-7613-9521-8(0),* First Avenue Editions) Lerner Publishing Group.

Jeffries, Joyce. Recipes of the Thirteen Colonies. 2017. (J). (gr. 3-3). 24p. pap. 10.60 ***(978-1-5345-2108-7(9));*** pap. 63.60 ***(978-1-5345-2109-4(7));*** 24p. lib. bdg. 27.25 ***(978-1-5345-2110-0(0))*** Greenhaven Publishing LLC. (KidHaven Publishing).

Jones, Emma. Recipes of the Pilgrims. 2017. (Cooking Your Way Through American History Ser.). (J). (gr. 3-3). pap. 63.60 ***(978-1-5345-2097-4(X));*** 24p. pap. 10.60 ***(978-1-5345-2096-7(1));*** 24p. lib. bdg. 27.25 ***(978-1-5345-2098-1(8))*** Greenhaven Publishing LLC. (KidHaven Publishing).

Jorgensen, Katrina. Ballpark Cookbooks: Recipes Inspired by Baseball Stadium Foods. 2016. (Ballpark Cookbooks Ser.). (ENG.). 64p. (gr. 3-4). 63.98 *(978-1-4914-8697-9(X))* Capstone Press of Coughlan Cos.

—Ballpark Eats: Recipes Inspired by America's Baseball Stadiums. 2016. (Sports Illustrated Kids Ser.). (ENG., Illus.). 144p. (gr. 3-4). pap. 15.95 *(978-1-62370-647-0(5))* Capstone Press of Coughlan Cos.

Jorgensen, Katrina & Hoena, Blake. Ballpark Cookbook - The American League: Recipes Inspired by Baseball Stadium Foods. 2016. (Ballpark Cookbooks Ser.). (ENG., Illus.). 64p. (gr. 3-4). lib. bdg. 31.99 *(978-1-4914-8232-2(X))* Capstone Press of Coughlan Cos.

—Ballpark Cookbook - The National League: Recipes Inspired by Baseball Stadium Foods. 2016. (Ballpark Cookbooks Ser.). (ENG., Illus.). 64p. (gr. 3-4). lib. bdg. 31.99 *(978-1-4914-8233-9(8))* Capstone Press of Coughlan Cos.

Kalman, Bobbie. Breakfast Blast: Step-by-Step Recipes. 2003. (Kid Power Ser.). (ENG., Illus.). 32p. (J). (gr. 3). pap. *(978-0-7787-1272-5(9));* lib. bdg. *(978-0-7787-1250-3(8))* Crabtree Publishing Co.

Kuskowski, Alex. Cool East Coast Cooking: Easy & Fun Regional Recipes, 1 vol. 2013. (Cool USA Cooking Ser.). (ENG.). 32p. (J). (gr. 3-6). lib. bdg. 28.50 *(978-1-61783-828-6(4),* Checkerboard Library) ABDO Publishing Co.

—Cool Gulf Coast Cooking: Easy & Fun Regional Recipes, 1 vol. 2013. (Cool USA Cooking Ser.). (ENG.). 32p. (J). (gr. 3-6). lib. bdg. 28.50 *(978-1-61783-829-3(2),* Checkerboard Library) ABDO Publishing Co.

—Cool Midwest Cooking: Easy & Fun Regional Recipes, 1 vol. 2013. (Cool USA Cooking Ser.). (ENG.). 32p. (J). (gr. 3-6). lib. bdg. 28.50 *(978-1-61783-830-9(6),* Checkerboard Library) ABDO Publishing Co.

—Cool Pacific Coast Cooking: Easy & Fun Regional Recipes, 1 vol. 2013. (Cool USA Cooking Ser.). (ENG.). 32p. (J). (gr. 3-6). lib. bdg. 28.50 *(978-1-61783-831-6(4),* Checkerboard Library) ABDO Publishing Co.

—Cool Southern Cooking: Easy & Fun Regional Recipes, 1 vol. 2013. (Cool USA Cooking Ser.). (ENG.). 32p. (J). (gr. 3-6). lib. bdg. 28.50 *(978-1-61783-832-3(2),* Checkerboard Library) ABDO Publishing Co.

—Cool Western Cooking: Easy & Fun Regional Recipes, 1 vol. 2013. (Cool USA Cooking Ser.). (ENG.). 32p. (J). (gr. 3-6). lib. bdg. 28.50 *(978-1-61783-833-0(0),* Checkerboard Library) ABDO Publishing Co.

Larkin, Tanya. Cooking Throughout American History Set 2, 6 bks. Incl. What Was Cooking in Abigail Adam's White House? lib. bdg. 22.60 *(978-0-8239-5607-4(5));* What Was Cooking in Dolly Madison's White House? lib. bdg. 21.25 *(978-0-8239-5608-1(3));* What Was Cooking in Edith Roosevelt's White House? lib. bdg. 22.60 *(978-0-8239-5610-4(5));* What Was Cooking in Julia Grant's White House? lib. bdg. 22.60 *(978-0-8239-5611-1(3));* What Was Cooking in Martha Washington's Presidential Mansion? lib. bdg. 21.25 *(978-0-8239-5606-7(7));* What Was Cooking in Mary Todd Lincoln's White House? lib. bdg. 21.25 *(978-0-8239-5609-8(1));* 24p. (J). (gr. 3). 2001. (Illus.). Set lib. bdg. 117.00 *(978-0-8239-7062-9(0),* PowerKids Pr.) Rosen Publishing Group, Inc., The.

—What Was Cooking in Abigail Adams' White House? 2009. (Cooking Throughout American History Ser.). 24p. (gr. 3-3). 42.50 *(978-1-61511-949-3(3),* PowerKids Pr.) Rosen Publishing Group, Inc., The.

—What Was Cooking in Dolley Madison's White House? 2009. (Cooking Throughout American History Ser.). 24p. (gr. 3-3). 42.50 *(978-1-61511-950-9(7),* PowerKids Pr.) Rosen Publishing Group, Inc., The.

—What Was Cooking in Edith Roosevelt's White House? 2009. (Cooking Throughout American History Ser.). 24p. (gr. 3-3). 42.50 *(978-1-61511-951-6(5),* PowerKids Pr.) Rosen Publishing Group, Inc., The.

—What Was Cooking in Julia Grant's White House? 2009. (Cooking Throughout American History Ser.). 24p. (gr. 3-3). 42.50 *(978-1-61511-952-3(3),* PowerKids Pr.) Rosen Publishing Group, Inc., The.

—What Was Cooking in Martha Washington's Presidential Mansion? 2009. (Cooking Throughout American History Ser.). 24p. (gr. 3-3). 42.50 *(978-1-61511-953-0(1),* PowerKids Pr.) Rosen Publishing Group, Inc., The.

—What Was Cooking in Mary Todd Lincoln's White House? 2009. (Cooking Throughout American History Ser.). 24p. (gr. 3-3). 42.50 *(978-1-61511-954-7(X),* PowerKids Pr.) Rosen Publishing Group, Inc., The.

Leavitt, Amie Jane. Southwestern Recipes. 2011. (Kids Can Cook Ser.). (ENG., Illus.). 64p. (YA). (gr. 4-7). lib. bdg. 33.95 *(978-1-61228-069-1(2))* Mitchell Lane Pubs., Inc.

—Western Recipes. 2011. (Kids Can Cook Ser.). (ENG., Illus.). 64p. (YA). (gr. 4-7). lib. bdg. 33.95 *(978-1-61228-070-7(6))* Mitchell Lane Pubs., Inc.

Libal, Autumn. Cuban Americans: Exiles from an Island Home, 16 vols. 2006. (Illus.). 112p. (J). lib. bdg. *(978-1-59084-924-8(8),* 1234500) Mason Crest.

Libal, Joyce. California. 2006. (American Regional Cooking Library). (Illus.). 72p. (YA). lib. bdg. 19.95 *(978-1-59084-613-1(3))* Mason Crest.

—Southern. 2006. (American Regional Cooking Library). (Illus.). 72p. (YA). lib. bdg. 19.95 *(978-1-59084-621-6(4))* Mason Crest.

—Texas. 2005. (American Regional Cooking Library). (Illus.). 72p. (J). lib. bdg. *(978-1-59084-623-0(0))* Mason Crest.

Libal, Joyce, compiled by. Mid-Atlantic Cooking. 2006. (American Regional Cooking Library). (Illus.). 72p. (YA). lib. bdg. 19.95 *(978-1-59084-618-6(4))* Mason Crest.

Mattern, Joanne. Mid-Atlantic Recipes. 2011. (Kids Can Cook Ser.). (ENG., Illus.). 64p. (YA). (gr. 4-7). lib. bdg. 33.95 *(978-1-61228-068-4(4))* Mitchell Lane Pubs., Inc.

McCallum, Ann. Eat Your U. S. History Homework: Recipes for Revolutionary Minds. Hernandez, Leeza, illus. 2015. (Eat Your Homework Ser.). (ENG.). 48p. (J). (gr. 2-5). lib. bdg. 15.95 *(978-1-57091-923-7(2))* Charlesbridge Publishing, Inc.

Meachen Rau, Dana. La Comida y la Cocina: en la historia de América. 2006. (Como era la vida en America (How People Lived in America) Ser.). (SPA., Illus.). 24p. (gr. 1-4). lib. bdg. 22.00 *(978-0-8368-7430-3(7),* Weekly Reader Leveled Readers) Stevens, Gareth Publishing LLLP.

—La Comida y la Cocina en la Historia de América. 2006. (Como era la vida en America (How People Lived in America) Ser.). (SPA., Illus.). 24p. (gr. 1-4). pap. 8.15 *(978-0-8368-7437-2(4),* Weekly Reader Leveled Readers) Stevens, Gareth Publishing LLLP.

—Food & Cooking in American History. 2006. (How People Lived in America Ser.). (Illus.). 24p. (gr. 1-4). lib. bdg. 22.00 *(978-0-8368-7206-4(1),* Weekly Reader Leveled Readers) Stevens, Gareth Publishing LLLP.

—Food & Cooking in American History. 2006. (How People Lived in America Ser.). (Illus.). 24p. (gr. 1-4). pap. 8.15 *(978-0-8368-7213-2(4)*, Weekly Reader Leveled Readers) Stevens, Gareth Publishing LLLP.

Moore, Sharon. Native American Foods & Recipes. 2009. (Reading Room Collection 2 Ser.). 24p. (gr. 3-4). 42.50 *(978-1-60851-982-8(1)*, PowerKids Pr.) Rosen Publishing Group, Inc., The.

Rogers, Amy B. Recipes of the Civil War. 2017. (Cooking Your Way Through American History Ser.). 24p. (J). (gr. 3-3). pap. 10.60 *(978-1-5345-2088-2(0)*, KidHaven Publishing) Greenhaven Publishing LLC.

Sampson, Sally. The Chop Chop: The Kids' Guide to Cooking Real Food with Your Family. Tremblay, Carl, photos by. 2013. (ENG., Illus.). 208p. pap. 19.99 *(978-1-4516-8587-9(4))* Simon & Schuster.

Vaughn, Inés. Chiles. 2009. (Native Foods of Latin America / Alimentos Indígenas de Latinoamérica Ser.). (SPA & ENG.). (J). 22.60 *(978-1-4358-2725-7(2)*, PowerKids Pr.) Rosen Publishing Group, Inc., The.

—Chocolate. 2009. (Native Foods of Latin America / Alimentos Indígenas de Latinoamérica Ser.). (SPA & ENG.). (J). 22.60 *(978-1-4358-2726-4(0)*, PowerKids Pr.) Rosen Publishing Group, Inc., The.

Williams-Sonoma. American Girl Cooking: Recipes for Delicious Snacks, Meals & More. 2016. (ENG., Illus.). 128p. (J). 19.95 *(978-1-68188-101-0(2)*, 3039364) Weldon Owen, Inc.

Yerdon, Joe. America's Oddest Foods. 2016. (Weird America Ser.). (ENG., Illus.). 32p. (J). (gr. 3-4). pap. 10.50 *(978-1-4824-4012-6(1))* Stevens, Gareth Publishing LLLP.

COOKING, AMERICAN—NEW ENGLAND STYLE

Libal, Joyce. New England. 2006. (American Regional Cooking Library). (Illus.). 72p. (YA). lib. bdg. 19.95 *(978-1-59084-617-9(6))* Mason Crest.

COOKING, ASIAN

Cornell, Kari & Anwar, Merry. Cooking the Indonesian Way: Includes Low-Fat & Vegetarian Recipes. 2nd rev. ed. 2004. (Easy Menu Ethnic Cookbooks 2nd Edition Ser.). (ENG., Illus.). 72p. (J). (gr. 5-12). 25.26 *(978-0-8225-4127-1(0)*, Carolrhoda Bks.) Lerner Publishing Group.

Ejaz, Khadija. Recipe & Craft Guide to India. 2010. (World Crafts & Recipes Ser.). (Illus.). 48p. (J). (gr. 4-8). lib. bdg. 29.95 *(978-1-58415-938-4(3))* Mitchell Lane Pubs., Inc.

Goodman, Polly. Food in India. 2008. (Food Around the World Ser.). (Illus.). 30p. (J). (gr. 3-7). lib. bdg. 25.25 *(978-1-4042-4296-8(1)*, PowerKids Pr.) Rosen Publishing Group, Inc., The.

Group, Brown Reference. Festive Foods: India. 2008. (Festive Foods Ser.). 48p. (gr. 4-6). 28.00 *(978-0-7910-9757-1(9)*, Chelsea Clubhouse) Facts On File, Inc.

—Festive Foods: Japan. 2008. (Festive Foods Ser.). 48p. (gr. 4-6). 28.00 *(978-0-7910-9754-0(4)*, Chelsea Clubhouse) Facts On File, Inc.

Mofford, Juliet. Recipe & Craft Guide to Japan. 2010. (World Crafts & Recipes Ser.). (Illus.). 48p. (J). (gr. 4-8). lib. bdg. 29.95 *(978-1-58415-933-9(2))* Mitchell Lane Pubs., Inc.

Nguyen, Chi & Monroe, Judy. Cooking the Vietnamese Way: Includes New Low-Fat & Vegetarian Recipes. rev. expurg. ed. 2003. (Easy Menu Ethnic Cookbooks). (Illus.). 72p. pap. 7.95 *(978-0-8225-0513-6(4))* Lerner Publishing Group.

Rau, Dana Meachen. Recipes from India, 1 vol. 2014. (Cooking Around the World Ser.). (ENG., Illus.). 48p. (gr. 5-8). lib. bdg. 29.99 *(978-1-4109-5972-0(4))* Heinemann-Raintree.

Reusser, Kayleen. Recipe & Craft Guide to Indonesia. 2010. (World Crafts & Recipes Ser.). (Illus.). 48p. (J). (gr. 4-8). lib. bdg. 29.95 *(978-1-58415-934-6(0))* Mitchell Lane Pubs., Inc.

Sanmugam, Devagi. Fun with Asian Food: A Kids' Cookbook. Ouden, Marijke Den, illus. 2005. (ENG.). 32p. (J). (gr. -1-3). 15.95 *(978-0-7946-0339-7(4))* Periplus Editions (HK), Ltd. HKG. Dist: Simon & Schuster, Inc.

Senker, Cath. Lebanon. 2010. (World of Food Ser.). 32p. (YA). (gr. 4-7). lib. bdg. 24.95 *(978-1-934545-12-6(0))* Oliver Pr., Inc.

Sheen, Barbara. Foods of India. 2006. (Taste of Culture Ser.). (ENG., Illus.). 64p. (J). (gr. 3-6). lib. bdg. 30.45 *(978-0-7377-3553-6(8))* Cengage Gale.

Sheen, Barbara, ed. Foods of Pakistan. 2011. (Taste of Culture Ser.). (Illus.). 67p. (YA). (gr. 9-12). 30.45 *(978-0-7377-5883-2(X))* Cengage Gale.

Wagner, Lisa. Cool Chinese & Japanese Cooking: Fun & Tasty Recipes for Kids, 1 vol. 2011. (Cool World Cooking Ser.). (ENG., Illus.). 32p. (J). (gr. 3-6). 28.50 *(978-1-61714-659-6(5)*, Checkerboard Library) ABDO Publishing Co.

COOKING, CHINESE

A Chinese Cookbook for Kids. 2013. (Cooking Around the World Ser.). 32p. (J). (gr. 3-6). pap. 70.50 *(978-1-4777-1519-2(3)*, PowerKids Pr.) Rosen Publishing Group, Inc., The.

Clickard, Carrie. Dumpling Dreams: How Joyce Chen Brought the Dumpling from Beijing to Cambridge. Wu, Katy, illus. 2017. (ENG.). 48p. (J). (gr. -1-3). 17.99 ***(978-1-4814-6707-0(7)***, Simon & Schuster Bks. For Young Readers) Simon & Schuster Bks. For Young Readers.

Fauchald, Nick. Wrap-N-Bake Egg Rolls: And Other Chinese Dishes. Rooney, Ronnie, illus. 2009. (Kids Dish Ser.). (ENG.). 32p. (gr. 1-3). lib. bdg. 27.32 *(978-1-4048-5183-2(6))* Picture Window Bks.

Gilbert, Sara. Chinese Food. 2015. (J). *(978-1-60818-501-6(X)*, Creative Education) Creative Co., The.

—Cooking School: Chinese Food. 2015. (Cooking School Ser.). (ENG.). 24p. (J). (gr. 1-3). pap. 9.99 *(978-1-62832-095-4(8)*, Creative Paperbacks) Creative Co., The.

Goodman, Polly. Food in China. 2008. (Food Around the World Ser.). (Illus.). 30p. (J). (gr. 3-7). lib. bdg. 25.25 *(978-1-4042-4297-5(X)*, PowerKids Pr.) Rosen Publishing Group, Inc., The.

Group, Brown Reference. Festive Foods: China. 2008. (Festive Foods Ser.). 48p. (gr. 4-6). 28.00 *(978-0-7910-9751-9(X)*, Chelsea Clubhouse) Facts On File, Inc.

Hankin, Rosemary. A Chinese Cookbook for Kids. 2013. (Cooking Around the World Ser.). (ENG., Illus.). 32p. (J). (gr. 3-6). lib. bdg. 26.50 *(978-1-4777-1335-8(2)*, PowerKids Pr.) Rosen Publishing Group, Inc., The.

Hankin, Rosie. A Chinese Cookbook for Kids. 2013. (Cooking Around the World Ser.). 32p. (J). (gr. 3-6). pap. 11.75 *(978-1-4777-1518-5(5)*, PowerKids Pr.) Rosen Publishing Group, Inc., The.

Hibbert, Clare. China. 2010. (World of Food Ser.). 32p. (YA). (gr. 4-7). lib. bdg. 24.95 *(978-1-934545-09-6(0))* Oliver Pr., Inc.

Kelly, Tracey. The Culture & Recipes of China. 2016. (Let's Cook! Ser.). 00048p. (J). (gr. 4-4). pap. 11.75 *(978-1-4994-3175-9(9)*, PowerKids Pr.) Rosen Publishing Group, Inc., The.

Lee, Frances. Fun with Chinese Cooking. 2009. (Let's Get Cooking! Ser.). (Illus.). 32p. (J). (ENG.). pap. 11.75 *(978-1-4358-3475-0(5))*; (gr. 3-6). lib. bdg. 26.50 *(978-1-4358-3453-8(4))* Rosen Publishing Group, Inc., The. (PowerKids Pr.).

Maher, Erin. Chinese Foods & Recipes. 2009. (Reading Room Collection 2 Ser.). 24p. (gr. 3-4). 42.50 *(978-1-60851-961-3(9)*, PowerKids Pr.) Rosen Publishing Group, Inc., The.

Marshall Cavendish. The Cooking of China. 2nd rev. ed. 2011. (Superchef, Second Edition Ser.). (Illus.). 96p. (J). (gr. 6). 35.64 *(978-1-60870-550-4(1))* Marshall Cavendish Corp.

Matter, Joanne. Recipe & Craft Guide to China. 2010. (World Crafts & Recipes Ser.). (Illus.). 48p. (J). (gr. 4-8). lib. bdg. *(978-1-58415-937-7(5))* Mitchell Lane Pubs., Inc.

Rau, Dana Meachen. Recipes from China, 1 vol. 2014. (Cooking Around the World Ser.). (ENG.). 48p. (gr. 5-8). lib. bdg. 29.99 *(978-1-4109-5971-3(6))* Heinemann-Raintree.

Roholt, Christine VeLure. Foods of China. 2014. (Cook with Me Ser.). (ENG., Illus.). 24p. (J). (gr. 3-7). lib. bdg. 25.95 *(978-1-62617-116-9(5)*, Express Bks.) Bellwether Media.

Shea, Therese. Foods of China. 2011. (Culture in the Kitchen Ser.). 24p. (J). (gr. 2-5). pap. 8.15 *(978-1-4339-5704-8(3))*; lib. bdg. 22.60 *(978-1-4339-5702-4(7))* Stevens, Gareth Publishing LLLP. (Gareth Stevens Learning Library).

Sheen, Barbara. Foods of China. 2006. (Taste of Culture Ser.). (ENG., Illus.). 64p. (J). (gr. 3-7). lib. bdg. 35.20 *(978-0-7377-3031-9(5)*, Greenhaven Pr., Inc.) Cengage Gale.

Wang, Shaoli, illus. Chinese Fairy Tale Feasts: A Literary Cookbook. 2014. 160p. (J). 25.00 *(978-1-56656-993-4(1)*, Crocodile Bks.) Interlink Publishing Group, Inc.

Yu, Ling. Cooking the Chinese Way. 2nd rev. exp. ed. 2003. (Easy Menu Ethnic Cookbooks). (Illus.). 72p. (J). (gr. 5-12). pap. 7.95 *(978-0-8225-4160-8(2))* Lerner Publishing Group.

COOKING, ENGLISH

Bucholz, Dinah. The Unofficial Harry Potter Cookbook: From Cauldron Cakes to Knickerbocker Glory — More Than 150 Magical Recipes for Muggles & Wizards. 2010. (Unofficial Cookbook Ser.). (ENG.). 256p. 19.95 *(978-1-4405-0325-2(7))* Adams Media Corp.

Sheen, Barbara, ed. Foods of England. 2011. (Taste of Culture Ser.). (ENG.). 64p. (J). (gr. 3-6). 30.45 *(978-0-7377-5881-8(3)*, Kidhaven) Cengage Gale.

COOKING, FRENCH

Blaxland, Wendy. French Food. 2011. (I Can Cook ! Ser.). 32p. (YA). (gr. 2-5). 28.50 *(978-1-59920-669-1(2))* Black Rabbit Bks.

Crump, A. K., ed. Chocolate French: Recipes, Language, & Directions to Francais Au Chocolat. 2004. (Illus.). 192p. (gr. 10). pap. *(978-0-9674898-4-1(9))* Temmen, Edition, Horst Temmen.

Elgin, Kathy. France. 2010. (World of Food Ser.). 32p. (YA). (gr. 4-7). lib. bdg. 24.95 *(978-1-934545-10-2(4))* Oliver Pr., Inc.

A French Cookbook for Kids. 2013. (Cooking Around the World Ser.). 32p. (J). (gr. 3-6). pap. 70.50 *(978-1-4777-1523-9(1)*, PowerKids Pr.) Rosen Publishing Group, Inc., The.

Gilbert, Sara. Cooking School: French Food. 2015. (Cooking School Ser.). (ENG.). 24p. (J). (gr. 1-3). pap. 9.99 *(978-1-62832-096-1(6)*, Creative Paperbacks) Creative Co., The.

—French Food. 2015. (J). *(978-1-60818-502-3(8)*, Creative Education) Creative Co., The.

Gioffrè, Rosalba. Fun with French Cooking. 2009. (Let's Get Cooking! Ser.). (Illus.). 32p. (J). (ENG.). pap. 11.75 *(978-1-4358-3473-6(9))*; (gr. 3-6). lib. bdg. 26.50 *(978-1-4358-3454-5(2))* Rosen Publishing Group, Inc., The. (PowerKids Pr.).

Group, Brown Reference. Festive Foods: France. 2008. (Festive Foods Ser.). 48p. (gr. 4-6). 28.00 *(978-0-7910-9752-6(8)*, Chelsea Clubhouse) Facts On File, Inc.

Hankin, Rosemary. A French Cookbook for Kids. 2013. (Cooking Around the World Ser.). (ENG., Illus.). 32p. (J). (gr. 3-6). lib. bdg. 26.50 *(978-1-4777-1337-2(9)*, PowerKids Pr.) Rosen Publishing Group, Inc., The.

Hankin, Rosie. A French Cookbook for Kids. 2013. (Cooking Around the World Ser.). 32p. (J). (gr. 3-6). pap. 11.75 *(978-1-4777-1522-2(3)*, PowerKids Pr.) Rosen Publishing Group, Inc., The.

Kelly, Tracey. The Culture & Recipes of France. 2016. (Let's Cook! Ser.). 00048p. (J). (gr. 4-4). 30.25 *(978-1-4994-3257-2(7)*, PowerKids Pr.) Rosen Publishing Group, Inc., The.

LaRoche, Amelia. Recipe & Craft Guide to France. 2010. (World Crafts & Recipes Ser.). (Illus.). 48p. (J). (gr. 4-8). lib. bdg. 29.95 *(978-1-58415-936-0(7))* Mitchell Lane Pubs., Inc.

Marshall Cavendish Benchmark Staff. The Cooking of France. 2nd rev. ed. 2011. (Superchef, Second Edition Ser.). (Illus.). 96p. (gr. 6). 35.64 *(978-1-60870-551-1(X))* Marshall Cavendish Corp.

Murphy, Frank. Thomas Jefferson's Feast. Walz, Richard, illus. 2004. (Step into Reading Ser.). 48p. 14.00 *(978-0-7569-3235-0(1))* Perfection Learning Corp.

—Thomas Jefferson's Feast. Walz, Richard, illus. 2003. (Step into Reading Ser.). (ENG.). 48p. (J). (gr. 2-4). pap. 3.99 *(978-0-375-82289-6(5)*, Random Hse. Bks. for Young Readers) Random Hse. Children's Bks.

Parks, Peggy J. Foods of France. 2005. (Taste of Culture Ser.). (ENG., Illus.). 64p. (gr. 3-6). lib. bdg. 35.20 *(978-0-7377-3032-6(3))* Cengage Gale.

Roholt, Christine VeLure. Foods of France. 2014. (Cook with Me Ser.). (ENG., Illus.). 24p. (J). (gr. 3-7). lib. bdg. 25.95 *(978-1-62617-117-6(3)*, Express Bks.) Bellwether Media.

Wagner, Lisa. Cool French Cooking: Fun & Tasty Recipes for Kids, 1 vol. 2011. (Cool World Cooking Ser.). (ENG., Illus.). 32p. (J). (gr. 3-6). 28.50 *(978-1-61714-660-2(9)*, Checkerboard Library) ABDO Publishing Co.

Waters, Alice. Fanny in France: With French Adventures & French Recipes. Arnold, Ann, illus. 2016. (ENG.). 184p. (J). (gr. 5). 19.99 *(978-0-670-01666-2(7)*, Viking Books for Young Readers) Penguin Young Readers Group.

COOKING, GERMAN

Group, Brown Reference. Festive Foods: Germany. 2008. (Festive Foods Ser.). 48p. (gr. 4-6). 28.00 *(978-0-7910-9756-4(0)*, Chelsea Clubhouse) Facts On File, Inc.

COOKING, GREEK

Gifford, Clive. Food & Cooking in Ancient Greece. 2010. (Cooking in World Cultures Ser.). (Illus.). 32p. (J). (ENG.). pap. 10.60 *(978-1-61532-361-6(9))*; (gr. 3-5). lib. bdg. 26.50 *(978-1-61532-338-8(4))* Rosen Publishing Group, Inc., The. (PowerKids Pr.).

Marshall Cavendish. The Cooking of Greece. 2nd rev. ed. 2011. (Superchef, Second Edition Ser.). (Illus.). 96p. (J). (gr. 6). 35.64 *(978-1-60870-552-8(8))* Marshall Cavendish Corp.

Villios, Lynne W. Cooking the Greek Way. 2003. (Easy Menu Ethnic Cookbooks). (Illus.). 72p. pap. 7.95 *(978-0-8225-0533-4(9))* Lerner Publishing Group.

COOKING, INTERNATIONAL

see International Cooking

COOKING, ITALIAN

Bisignano, Alphonse. Cooking the Italian Way. 2nd rev. exp. ed. 2003. (Easy Menu Ethnic Cookbooks). (Illus.). 72p. (J). (gr. 5-12). pap. 7.95 *(978-0-8225-4161-5(0))* Lerner Publishing Group.

Cappellino, Marilyn. Mangia! Macaroni. 2009. 32p. pap. 18.60 *(978-0-557-05215-8(7))* Lulu Pr., Inc.

Fauchald, Nick. Roly-Poly Ravioli: And Other Italian Dishes, 1 vol. Rooney, Ronnie, illus. 2009. (Kids Dish Ser.). (ENG.). 32p. (gr. 1-3). lib. bdg. 27.32 *(978-1-4048-5186-3(0))* Picture Window Bks.

Franklin, Liz. Cooking Italian with Kids. 2008. (ENG., Illus.). 128p. *(978-1-84597-698-9(3))* Ryland Peters & Small.

Garfield, Yvette. Handstand Kids Italian Cookbook. 2007. (Illus.). 52p. (J). 25.00 *(978-0-9792107-0-9(4))* Handstand Kids.

Gifford, Clive. Food & Cooking in Ancient Rome. 2010. (Cooking in World Cultures Ser.). (Illus.). 32p. (J). (ENG.). pap. 10.60 *(978-1-61532-363-0(5))*; (gr. 3-5). lib. bdg. 26.50 *(978-1-61532-339-5(2))* Rosen Publishing Group, Inc., The. (PowerKids Pr.).

Gilbert, Sara. Cooking School: Italian Food. 2015. (Cooking School Ser.). (ENG.). 24p. (J). (gr. 1-3). pap. 9.99 *(978-1-62832-097-8(4)*, Creative Paperbacks) Creative Co., The.

—Italian Food. 2015. (J). *(978-1-60818-503-0(6)*, Creative Education) Creative Co., The.

Gioffrè, Rosalba. Fun with Italian Cooking. 2009. (Let's Get Cooking! Ser.). (Illus.). 32p. (J). (ENG.). pap. 11.75 *(978-1-4358-3489-7(5))*; (gr. 3-6). lib. bdg. 26.50 *(978-1-4358-3451-4(8))* Rosen Publishing Group, Inc., The. (PowerKids Pr.).

Goodman, Polly. Food in Italy. 2008. (Food Around the World Ser.). (Illus.). 30p. (J). (gr. 3-7). lib. bdg. 25.25 *(978-1-4042-4298-2(8)*, PowerKids Pr.) Rosen Publishing Group, Inc., The.

Group, Brown Reference. Festive Foods: Italy. 2008. (Festive Foods Ser.). 48p. (gr. 4-6). 28.00 *(978-0-7910-9753-3(6)*, Chelsea Clubhouse) Facts On File, Inc.

Hankin, Rosemary. An Italian Cookbook for Kids. 2013. (Cooking Around the World Ser.). (ENG., Illus.). 32p. (J). (gr. 3-6). lib. bdg. 26.50 *(978-1-4777-1336-5(0)*, PowerKids Pr.) Rosen Publishing Group, Inc., The.

Hankin, Rosie. An Italian Cookbook for Kids. 2013. (Cooking Around the World Ser.). 32p. (J). (gr. 3-6). pap. 11.75 *(978-1-4777-1520-8(7)*, PowerKids Pr.) Rosen Publishing Group, Inc., The.

Harms, Julia. Recipe & Craft Guide to Italy. 2011. (World Crafts & Recipes Ser.). (ENG., Illus.). 64p. (J). (gr. 4-7). lib. bdg. 33.95 *(978-1-61228-083-7(8))* Mitchell Lane Pubs., Inc.

An Italian Cookbook for Kids. 2013. (Cooking Around the World Ser.). 32p. (J). (gr. 3-6). pap. 70.50 *(978-1-4777-1521-5(5)*, PowerKids Pr.) Rosen Publishing Group, Inc., The.

Kelly, Tracey. The Culture & Recipes of Italy. 2016. (Let's Cook! Ser.). 00048p. (J). (gr. 4-4). pap. 11.75 *(978-1-4994-3181-0(3)*, PowerKids Pr.) Rosen Publishing Group, Inc., The.

Locricchio, Matthew. The Cooking of Italy. 2nd rev. ed. 2011. (Superchef, Second Edition Ser.). (Illus.). 96p. (J). (gr. 6). 35.64 *(978-1-60870-554-2(4))* Marshall Cavendish GBR. Dist: Marshall Cavendish Corp.

Matthew, John. Foods of Italy. 2011. (Culture in the Kitchen Ser.). 24p. (J). (gr. 2-5). pap. 8.15 *(978-1-4339-5712-3(4))*; lib. bdg. 22.60 *(978-1-4339-5710-9(8))* Stevens, Gareth Publishing LLLP. (Gareth Stevens Learning Library).

Rau, Dana Meachen. Recipes from Italy, 1 vol. 2014. (Cooking Around the World Ser.). (ENG., Illus.). 48p. (gr. 5-8). lib. bdg. 29.99 *(978-1-4109-5973-7(2))* Heinemann-Raintree.

Roholt, Christine VeLure. Foods of Italy. 2014. (Cook with Me Ser.). (ENG.). 24p. (J). (gr. 3-7). lib. bdg. 25.95 *(978-1-62617-119-0(X)*, Express Bks.) Bellwether Media.

Wagner, Lisa. Cool Italian Cooking: Fun & Tasty Recipes for Kids, 1 vol. 2011. (Cool World Cooking Ser.). (ENG., Illus.). 32p. (J). (gr. 3-6). 28.50 *(978-1-61714-661-9(7)*, Checkerboard Library) ABDO Publishing Co.

Watt, Fiona. Pasta & Pizza: For Beginners. Lane, Kim, illus. Allman, Howard, photos by. rev. ed. 2004. (Cooking School Ser.). 48p. (J). (gr. 5). lib. bdg. 15.95 *(978-1-58086-567-8(4))* EDC Publishing.

COOKING, JEWISH

see Jewish Cooking

COOKING, MEXICAN

Barker, Geoff. The World of Food - Mexico. 2010. (World of Food Ser.). 32p. (YA). (gr. 4-7). lib. bdg. 24.95 *(978-1-934545-13-3(9))* Oliver Pr., Inc.

Blaxland, Wendy. Mexican Food. 2011. (I Can Cook ! Ser.). 32p. (YA). (gr. 2-5). 28.50 *(978-1-59920-668-4(4))* Black Rabbit Bks.

Dawson, Imogen. Food & Feasts with the Aztecs. 2004. (Illus.). 32p. (J). (gr. 4-8). reprint ed. 14.00 *(978-0-7567-7143-0(9))* DIANE Publishing Co.

Fauchald, Nick. Funky Chicken Enchiladas: And Other Mexican Dishes, 1 vol. Rooney, Ronnie, illus. 2009. (Kids Dish Ser.). (ENG.). 32p. (gr. 1-3). lib. bdg. 27.32 *(978-1-4048-5189-4(5))* Picture Window Bks.

Garfield, Yvette & Azima, Cricket. Handstand Kids Mexican Cookbook. DeRose, Kim, illus. 2008. 52p. (J). (gr. -1-3). 28.00 *(978-0-9792107-2-3(0))* Handstand Kids.

Gilbert, Sara. Cooking School: Mexican Food. 2015. (Cooking School Ser.). (ENG.). 24p. (J). (gr. 1-3). pap. 9.99 *(978-1-62832-098-5(2)*, Creative Paperbacks) Creative Co., The.

—Mexican Food. 2015. (J). *(978-1-60818-504-7(4)*, Creative Education) Creative Co., The.

Group, Brown Reference. Festive Foods: Mexico. 2008. (Festive Foods Ser.). 48p. (gr. 4-6). 28.00 *(978-0-7910-9755-7(2)*, Chelsea Clubhouse) Facts On File, Inc.

Hankin, Rosie. A Mexican Cookbook for Kids. 2013. (Cooking Around the World Ser.). 32p. (J). (gr. 3-6). 26.50 *(978-1-4777-1334-1(4))*; pap. 11.75 *(978-1-4777-1516-1(9))* Rosen Publishing Group, Inc., The. (PowerKids Pr.).

Kelly, Tracey. The Culture & Recipes of Mexico. 2016. (Let's Cook! Ser.). 00048p. (J). (gr. 4-4). pap. 11.75 *(978-1-4994-3185-8(6)*, PowerKids Pr.) Rosen Publishing Group, Inc., The.

Locricchio, Matthew. The Cooking of Mexico. 2nd rev. ed. 2011. (Superchef, Second Edition Ser.). (Illus.). 96p. (J). (gr. 6). 35.64 *(978-1-60870-555-9(2))* Marshall Cavendish Corp.

McDaniel, Jan. The Food of Mexico. 2009. (Mexico: Beautiful Land, Diverse People Ser.). (Illus.). 64p. (YA). (gr. 7-12). 21.95 *(978-1-4222-0655-3(6))* Mason Crest.

Mexican. 2008. (Everyday Ser.). 240p. *(978-1-4075-3022-2(4))* Parragon, Inc.

Mexican Cookbook. 2008. 96p. *(978-1-4075-3942-3(6))* Parragon, Inc.

A Mexican Cookbook for Kids. 2013. (Cooking Around the World Ser.). 32p. (J). (gr. 3-6). pap. 70.50 *(978-1-4777-1517-8(7)*, PowerKids Pr.) Rosen Publishing Group, Inc., The.

Pearce, Kevin. Foods of Mexico. 2011. (Culture in the Kitchen Ser.). 24p. (J). (gr. 2-5). pap. 8.15 *(978-1-4339-5716-1(7))*; lib. bdg. 22.60 *(978-1-4339-5714-7(0))* Stevens, Gareth Publishing LLLP. (Gareth Stevens Learning Library).

Rau, Dana Meachen. Recipes from Mexico, 1 vol. 2014. (Cooking Around the World Ser.). (ENG., Illus.). 48p. (gr. 5-8). lib. bdg. 29.99 *(978-1-4109-5974-4(0))* Heinemann-Raintree.

Roholt, Christine VeLure. Foods of Mexico. 2014. (Cook with Me Ser.). (ENG.). 24p. (J). (gr. 3-7). 25.95 *(978-1-62617-121-3(1)*, Express Bks.) Bellwether Media.

Wagner, Lisa. Cool Mexican Cooking: Fun & Tasty Recipes for Kids, 1 vol. 2011. (Cool World Cooking Ser.). (ENG., Illus.). 32p. (J). (gr. 3-6). 28.50 *(978-1-61714-662-6(5)*, Checkerboard Library) ABDO Publishing Co.

Ward, Karen. Fun with Mexican Cooking. 2009. (Let's Get Cooking! Ser.). (Illus.). 32p. (J). (ENG.). pap. 11.75 *(978-1-4358-3477-4(1))*; (gr. 3-6). lib. bdg. 26.50 *(978-1-4358-3452-1(6))* Rosen Publishing Group, Inc., The. (PowerKids Pr.).

Wood, Ira. A Mexican Feast: The Foods & Recipes of Mexico. 2009. (Reading Room Collection 2 Ser.). 24p. (gr. 3-4). 42.50 *(978-1-60851-953-8(8)*, PowerKids Pr.) Rosen Publishing Group, Inc., The.

COOKING, MIDDLE EASTERN

Blaxland, Wendy. Middle-Eastern Food. 2011. (I Can Cook ! Ser.). 32p. (YA). (gr. 2-5). 28.50 *(978-1-59920-672-1(2))* Black Rabbit Bks.

Cornell, Kari & Turkoglu, Nurcay. Cooking the Turkish Way. 2nd rev. ed. 2004. (Easy Menu Ethnic Cookbooks 2nd Edition Ser.). (ENG., Illus.). 72p. (gr. 5-12). 25.26 *(978-0-8225-4123-3(8)*, Carolrhoda Bks.) Lerner Publishing Group.

Fauchald, Nick. On-the-Go Schwarmas: And Other Middle-Eastern Dishes. Rooney, Ronnie, illus. 2009. (Kids Dish Ser.). (ENG.). 32p. (gr. 1-3). lib. bdg. 27.32 *(978-1-4048-5192-4(5))* Picture Window Bks.

Gilbert, Sara. Cooking School: Middle-Eastern Food. 2015. (Cooking School Ser.). (ENG.). 24p. (J). (gr. 1-3). pap. 9.99 *(978-1-62832-099-2(0)*, Creative Paperbacks) Creative Co., The.

—Middle Eastern Food. 2015. (J). *(978-1-60818-505-4(2)*, Creative Education) Creative Co., The.

Saul, Laya. Recipe & Craft Guide to Israel. 2011. (World Crafts & Recipes Ser.). (ENG., Illus.). 64p. (J). (gr. 4-7). lib. bdg. 33.95 *(978-1-61228-081-3(1))* Mitchell Lane Pubs., Inc.

Wagner, Lisa. Cool Middle Eastern Cooking: Fun & Tasty Recipes for Kids, 1 vol. 2011. (Cool World Cooking Ser.). (ENG., Illus.). 32p. (J). (gr. 3-6). 28.50 *(978-1-61714-663-3(3)*, Checkerboard Library) ABDO Publishing Co.

COOKING, SCANDINAVIAN

Sheen, Barbara. Foods of Scandinavia. 2010. (Taste of Culture Ser.). (Illus.). 64p. (J). 30.45 *(978-0-7377-4814-7(1)*, Kidhaven) Cengage Gale.

COOKING, THAI

Locricchio, Matthew. The Cooking of Thailand. 2004. (Superchef Ser.). (Illus.). 80p. (J). 29.93 *(978-0-7614-1731-6(1)*, Benchmark Bks.) Marshall Cavendish Corp.

Roholt, Christine VeLure. Foods of Thailand. 2014. (Cook with Me Ser.). (ENG.). 24p. (J). (gr. 3-7). 25.95 *(978-1-62617-122-0(X)*, Express Bks.) Bellwether Media.

Sheen, Barbara. Foods of Thailand. 2006. (Taste of Culture Ser.). (ENG., Illus.). 64p. (J). (gr. 3-7). lib. bdg. 28.75 *(978-0-7377-3037-1(4)*, Greenhaven Pr., Inc.) Cengage Gale.

COOKING UTENSILS

see Household Equipment and Supplies

C D

COOLIDGE, CALVIN, 1872-1933

Elston, Heidi. Calvin Coolidge, 1 vol. 2016. (ENG., Illus.). 40p. (J). *(978-1-68078-090-1(5))* ABDO Publishing Co.

Elston, Heidi M. D. Calvin Coolidge, 1 vol. 2009. (United States Presidents Ser.). (ENG., Illus.). 40p. (YA). (gr. 3-6). 27.07 *(978-1-60453-448-1(6))* ABDO Publishing Co.

Feldman, Ruth Tenzer. Calvin Coolidge. 2005. (Presidential Leaders Ser.). (Illus.). 112p. (J). (gr. 3-7). lib. bdg. 29.27 *(978-0-8225-1496-1(6))* Lerner Publishing Group.

Johansen, H. L. How to Draw the Life & Times of Calvin Coolidge. 2009. (Kid's Guide to Drawing the Presidents of the United States of America Ser.). 32p. (gr. 4-4). 50.50 *(978-1-61511-134-3(4),* PowerKids Pr.) Rosen Publishing Group, Inc., The.

Johansen, Heidi Leigh. How to Draw the Life & Times of Calvin Coolidge. 2007. (Kid's Guide to Drawing the Presidents of the United States of America Ser.). (Illus.). 32p. (YA). (gr. 2-5). 26.50 *(978-1-4042-3006-4(8))* Rosen Publishing Group, Inc., The.

Otfinoski, Steven. Calvin Coolidge. 2008. (Presidents & Their Times Ser.). 96p. (gr. 6-18). lib. bdg. 34.21 *(978-0-7614-2836-7(4),* Benchmark Bks.) Marshall Cavendish Corp.

COOLING APPLIANCES

see Refrigeration and Refrigerating Machinery

COOPER, JAMES FENIMORE, 1789-1851

Saddleback Educational Publishing Staff, ed. The Last of the Mohicans. 2011. (Timeless Classics Ser.). (ENG.). 48p. (YA). (gr. 9-12). pupil's gde. ed. 19.95 incl. cd-rom *(978-1-61651-142-5(7))* Saddleback Educational Publishing, Inc.

COOPERATION, INTERNATIONAL

see International Cooperation

COPE, E. D. (EDWARD DRINKER), 1840-1897

Goldish, Meish. The Fossil Feud: Marsh & Cope's Bone Wars. 2006. (Fossil Hunters Ser.). (Illus.). 32p. (YA). (gr. 2-5). lib. bdg. 25.27 *(978-1-59716-256-2(6))* Bearport Publishing Co., Inc.

COPERNICUS, NICOLAUS, 1473-1543

Andronik, Catherine M. Copernicus: Founder of Modern Astronomy. 2009. (Great Minds of Science Ser.). (Illus.). 128p. (J). (gr. 5). lib. bdg. 33.27 *(978-0-7660-3013-8(X))* Enslow Pubs., Inc.

—Copernicus: Genius of Modern Astronomy. 2015. (Genius Scientists & Their Genius Ideas Ser.). 96p. (J). (gr. 5-12). 27.94 *(978-0-7660-6550-5(2))*; pap. 10.95 *(978-0-7660-6551-2(0))* Enslow Pubs., Inc.

Boerst, William J. Nicholas Copernicus & the Founding of Modern Astronomy. 2004. (Profiles in Science Ser.). (Illus.). 144p. (YA). (gr. 6-12). lib. bdg. 26.95 *(978-1-883846-99-2(4),* First Biographies) Reynolds, Morgan Inc.

Bortz, Fred. The Sun-Centered Universe & Nicolaus Copernicus. 2013. (Revolutionary Discoveries of Scientific Pioneers Ser.). 80p. (YA). (gr. 7-12). 33.25 *(978-1-4777-1801-8(X))* Rosen Publishing Group, Inc., The.

Fradin, Dennis Brindell. Nicolaus Copernicus: The Earth Is a Planet. von Buhler, Cynthia, tr. von Buhler, Cynthia, illus. 2003. 32p. (J). (gr. 2-6). 15.95 *(978-1-59336-006-1(1))*; pap. *(978-1-59336-007-8(X))* Mondo Publishing.

Ingram, Scott. Nicolaus Copernicus: Father of Modern Astronomy. 2004. (Illus.). 64p. (J). 26.20 *(978-1-56711-489-8(X),* Blackbirch Pr., Inc.) Cengage Gale.

Ridley, Sarah. Nicolaus Copernicus. 2017. (Super Scientists Ser.). (ENG., Illus.). 24p. (J). (gr. 1-3). pap. 9.99 ***(978-1-4451-5356-8(4),*** Franklin Watts) Hachette Children's Group GBR. Dist: Hachette Bk. Group.

Sakolsky, Josh. Copernicus & Modern Astronomy. (Primary Sources of Revolutionary Scientific Discoveries & Theories Ser.). 64p. 2009. (gr. 5-5). 58.50 *(978-1-60851-840-1(X))* 2004. (Illus.). (J). lib. bdg. 31.95 *(978-1-4042-0305-1(2))* Rosen Publishing Group, Inc., The.

COPPER

Perritano, John. Copper, Vol. 12. 2015. (North American Natural Resources Ser.). (Illus.). 64p. (J). (gr. 7). 23.95 *(978-1-4222-3380-1(4))* Mason Crest.

COPPER ENGRAVING

see Engraving

COPPER MINES AND MINING

Aronson, Marc. Trapped: How the World Rescued 33 Miners from 2,000 Feet below the Chilean Desert. 2012. (ENG., Illus.). 144p. (J). pap. 6.99 *(978-1-4424-4025-8(2),* Atheneum Bks. for Young Readers) Simon & Schuster Children's Publishing.

Lusted, Marcia Amidon. The Chilean Miners' Rescue, 1 vol. 2011. (Essential Events Set 7 Ser.). (ENG., Illus.). 112p. (J). (gr. 6-12). lib. bdg. 35.64 *(978-1-61783-097-6(6))* ABDO Publishing Co.

Perritano, John. Copper, Vol. 12. 2015. (North American Natural Resources Ser.). (Illus.). 64p. (J). (gr. 7). 23.95 *(978-1-4222-3380-1(4))* Mason Crest.

Scott, Elaine. Buried Alive! How 33 Miners Survived 69 Days Deep under the Chilean Desert. 2012. (ENG., Illus.). 80p. (J). (gr. 5-7). 18.99 *(978-0-547-70778-5(9))* Houghton Mifflin Harcourt Publishing Co.

CORAL REEFS AND ISLANDS

Banting, Erinn. The Great Barrier Reef. 2004. (Illus.). 32p. (J). lib. bdg. 26.00 *(978-1-59036-272-3(1))* Weigl Pubs., Inc.

Belcher, Andy. Life on the Reef. 2016. (Cambridge Reading Adventures Ser.). (ENG.). 24p. pap. 7.19 *(978-1-107-56022-2(5))* Cambridge Univ. Pr.

Benchmark Education Company. Coral Reefs (Teacher Guide) 2005. *(978-1-4108-4656-3(3))* Benchmark Education Co.

Berger, Melvin & Berger, Gilda. Life on a Coral Reef. 2013. (Illus.). 16p. (J). pap. *(978-0-545-35173-7(1))* Scholastic, Inc.

Boyle, Doe. Coral Reef Hideaway: The Story of a Clown Anemonefish. (ENG., Illus.). 32p. (J). (gr. -1-2). 8.95 *(978-1-59249-489-7(7),* SC4008) Soundprints.

Brannon, Barbara. Discover Coral Reefs. 2005. (J). pap. *(978-1-4108-5131-4(1))* Benchmark Education Co.

Brenneman, Kimberly. Let's Visit a Coral Reef. 2016. (Illus.). 32p. (J). pap. *(978-0-87659-708-8(8))* Gryphon Hse., Inc.

Brinkworth, Brian. Life in a Coral Reef. (Reading Room Collection 1 Ser.). 16p. 2009. (gr. 2-3). 37.50 *(978-1-60851-946-0(5))* 2006. (Illus.). (J). (gr. 3-7). lib. bdg. 17.25 *(978-1-4042-3342-3(3))* Rosen Publishing Group, Inc., The. (PowerKids Pr.).

Brooke, Samantha. Coral Reefs in Danger. Bull, Peter, illus. 2008. (Penguin Young Readers, Level 3 Ser.). (ENG.). 48p. (J). (gr. 1-3). mass mkt. 3.99 *(978-0-448-44872-5(6),* Penguin Young Readers) Penguin Young Readers Group.

Butterfield, Moira & Collins UK Staff. Coral Reefs. 2016. (ENG.). 80p. (J). (gr. 5-6). pap. 9.95 *(978-0-00-816403-4(7))* HarperCollins Pubs. Ltd. GBR. Dist: Independent Pubs. Group.

Chin, Jason. Coral Reefs. Chin, Jason, illus. 2011. (ENG., Illus.). 40p. (J). (gr. k-4). 17.99 *(978-1-59643-563-6(1),* 9781596435636) Roaring Brook Pr.

Collard, Sneed B., III. On the Coral Reefs. 2005. (Science Adventures Ser.). (Illus.). 43p. (YA). (gr. 3-6). lib. bdg. 29.93 *(978-0-7614-1953-2(5))* Marshall Cavendish Corp.

Creature Color & Discover Coral Reef. (Illus.). 28p. (J). (gr. 1-8). reprint ed. *(978-1-881469-42-1(5))* Safari, Ltd.

De la Bédoyère, Camilla. Coral Reef. 2010. (Unpredictable Nature Ser.). (Illus.). 48p. (J). (gr. 3-18). lib. bdg. 19.95 *(978-1-4222-1995-9(X))* Mason Crest.

Dorling Kindersley Publishing Staff. DK Readers L0: Fishy Tales. 2015. (DK Readers Ser.). (ENG., Illus.). 32p. (J). (gr. -1-1). pap. 3.99 *(978-1-4654-3494-4(1),* DK Children) Dorling Kindersley Publishing, Inc.

Dunphy, Madeleine. Here Is the Coral Reef. Leonard, Tom, illus. 2006. (Web of Life Ser.). (ENG.). 32p. (J). (gr. -1-3). 16.95 *(978-0-9773795-5-2(8))*; pap. 9.95 *(978-0-9773795-4-5(X))* Web of Life Children's Bks.

Earle, Sylvia A. Coral Reefs. (Jump into Science Ser.). (ENG., Illus.). 32p. (J). (gr. -1-3). 2016. pap. 7.99 *(978-1-4263-2364-5(6))* 2009. 7.95 *(978-1-4263-0475-0(7))* National Geographic Society. (National Geographic Children's Bks.).

—Coral Reefs. Matthews, Bonnie, illus. 2003. (Jump into Science Ser.). (ENG.). 32p. (J). (gr. -1-3). 16.95 *(978-0-7922-6953-3(5),* National Geographic Children's Bks.) National Geographic Society.

Fishy Tales. 12p. (J). *(978-2-7643-0193-7(6))* Phidal Publishing, Inc./Editions Phidal, Inc.

Franchino, Vicky. Great Barrier Reef. 2016. (Community Connections: Getting to Know Our Planet Ser.). (ENG., Illus.). 24p. (J). (gr. 2-5). 27.07 *(978-1-63470-517-2(3),* 207799) Cherry Lake Publishing.

Frisch, Aaron. Coral Reefs. 2008. (Our World Ser.). (Illus.). 24p. (J). lib. bdg. 24.25 *(978-1-58341-570-2(X),* Creative Education) Creative Co., The.

Ganeri, Anita. Exploring Coral Reefs: A Benjamin Blog & His Inquisitive Dog Investigation, 1 vol. 2014. (Exploring Habitats with Benjamin Blog & His Inquisitive Dog Ser.). (ENG., Illus.). 32p. (gr. 1-3). pap. 8.95 *(978-1-4329-8787-9(9))*; lib. bdg. 29.99 *(978-1-4329-8780-0(1))* Heinemann-Raintree. (NA-h).

—Exploring Habitats, with Benjamin Blog & His Inquisitive Dog, 1 vol. 2014. (Exploring Habitats with Benjamin Blog & His Inquisitive Dog Ser.). (ENG.). 32p. (gr. 1-3). lib. bdg. 179.94 *(978-1-4329-8781-7(X),* NA-h) Heinemann-Raintree.

George, Lynn. Coral: Reef Builders. 2010. (Animal Architects Ser.). (ENG.). 24p. (J). pap. 8.25 *(978-1-4488-1349-0(2))*; lib. bdg. 22.60 *(978-1-4488-0694-2(1))* Rosen Publishing Group, Inc., The. (PowerKids Pr.).

Gibbons, Gail. Coral Reefs. Gibbons, Gail, illus. (ENG., Illus.). 32p. (J). (gr. -1-3). 2009. pap. 7.99 *(978-0-8234-2278-4(X))* 2007. 16.95 *(978-0-8234-2080-3(9))* Holiday Hse., Inc.

Green, Jen. Life in a Coral Reef. 2010. (Nature in Focus Ser.). (Illus.). 32p. (gr. 2-5). (J). pap. 10.50 *(978-1-4339-3424-7(8),* Gareth Stevens Learning Library); (YA). lib. bdg. 26.00 *(978-1-4339-3423-0(X))* Stevens, Gareth Publishing LLLP.

Hanson, Krista Finstad. Great Barrier Reef. 2004. (Natural Wonders of the World Ser.). (Illus.). 32p. (J). lib. bdg. 18.95 *(978-1-58341-324-1(3),* Creative Education) Creative Co., The.

Haugen, Hayley Mitchell. Life in a Coral Reef. 2003. (Ecosystems Library). (Illus.). 48p. (J). 23.70 *(978-0-7377-1370-1(4),* Greenhaven Pr., Inc.) Cengage Gale.

Heos, Bridget. Do You Really Want to Visit a Coral Reef? Fabbri, Daniele, illus. 2014. (Do You Really Want to Visit... ? Ser.). (ENG.). 24p. (J). (gr. 1-4). 27.10 *(978-1-60753-449-5(5))* Amicus Publishing.

Hyde, Natalie. Great Barrier Reef Research Journal. 2017. (Illus.). 32p. (J). ***(978-0-7787-3470-3(6))***; pap. ***(978-0-7787-3495-6(1))*** Crabtree Publishing Co.

Kids: Discover Coral Reefs. 2005. (J). 1.00 *(978-1-888631-32-6(5))* Project WET Foundation.

Kopp, Megan. What Do You Find in a Coral Reef? 2016. (ENG., Illus.). 24p. (J). *(978-0-7787-2257-1(0))* Crabtree Publishing Co.

Lantz, Peggy Sias & Hale, Wendy A. The Coral Reefs of Florida. 2014. (Florida Water Story Ser.). (ENG., Illus.). 34p. (J). (gr. 4). pap. 6.95 *(978-1-56164-703-3(9),* 9781561647033) Pineapple Pr., Inc.

Levy, Janey. Discovering Coral Reefs. (World Habitats Ser.). 32p. 2009. (gr. 4-5). 47.90 *(978-1-60854-834-7(1),* PowerKids Pr.) 2007. (Illus.). (YA). (gr. 3-6). lib. bdg. 25.25 *(978-1-4042-3786-5(0))* Rosen Publishing Group, Inc., The.

MacAulay, Kelley. Les Récifs Coralliens. 2009. (Petit Monde Vivant Ser.). (FRE., Illus.). 32p. (J). pap. 9.95 *(978-2-89579-229-1(1))* Bayard Canada Livres CAN. Dist: Crabtree Publishing Co.

Macken, JoAnn Early. Coral Reefs (Arrecifes de Coral) 2005. (Water Habitats/ Habitats acuaticos Ser.). (SPA., Illus.). 24p. (gr. k-3). pap. 8.15 *(978-0-8368-6035-1(7),* Weekly Reader Leveled Readers) Stevens, Gareth Publishing LLLP.

Macken, JoAnn Early & Early Macken, JoAnn. Coral Reefs/Arrecifes de Coral. 2005. (Water Habitats/ Habitats acuaticos Ser.). (SPA., Illus.). 24p. (gr. k-3). lib. bdg. 22.00 *(978-0-8368-6028-3(4),* Weekly Reader Leveled Readers) Stevens, Gareth Publishing LLLP.

Meachen Rau, Dana. Los Arrecifes de Coral. 2007. (Maravillas de la Naturaleza Ser.). (SPA & ENG., Illus.). 32p. (gr. 1-2). lib. bdg. 15.95 *(978-0-7614-2805-3(4),* Benchmark Bks.) Marshall Cavendish Corp.

—Coral Reefs. 2007. (Wonders of Nature Ser.). (SPA & ENG.). 32p. (gr. 1-2). lib. bdg. 15.95 *(978-0-7614-2666-0(3),* Benchmark Bks.) Marshall Cavendish Corp.

—Coral Reefs/Los Arrecifes de Coral. 2007. (Wonders of Nature/Maravillas de la Naturaleza Ser.). (SPA & ENG., Illus.). 32p. (gr. 1-2). lib. bdg. 15.95 *(978-0-7614-2829-9(1),* Benchmark Bks.) Marshall Cavendish Corp.

—Undersea City: A Story of a Caribbean Coral Reef. 2005. (Soundprints' Wild Habitats Ser.). (ENG., Illus.). 32p. (J). (gr. 1-4). 8.95 *(978-1-59249-090-5(5),* SC7002) Soundprints.

Medina, Nico. Where Is the Great Barrier Reef? Hinderliter, John, illus. 2016. 108p. (J). lib. bdg. ***(978-1-4844-9197-3(1),*** Grosset & Dunlap) Penguin Publishing Group.

Meister, Cari. Corals. 2013. (ENG., Illus.). 24p. (J). lib. bdg. 25.65 *(978-1-62031-031-1(7))* Jump! Inc.

Meltzer Kleinhenz, Sydnie. Coral Reefs. 2004. (ENG., Illus.). 32p. (J). (gr. 4-4). pap. 12.29 *(978-0-7652-5223-4(6),* Celebration Pr.) Pearson Schl.

Montag, Emily. Coral Reefs. 2011. (Illus.). 16p. (J). pap. *(978-0-545-24790-0(X))* Scholastic, Inc.

Moore Niver, Heather. Viaje Dentro de un Arrecife de Coral (a Trip Through a Coral Reef) 2015. (Maravillosos Viajes a Través de la Ciencia (Fantastic Science Journeys) Ser.). (SPA.). 32p. (J). (gr. 2-3). 25.25 *(978-1-4824-2019-7(8))* Stevens, Gareth Publishing LLLP.

O'Neill, Michael Patrick, photos by. Ocean Magic. O'Neill, Michael Patrick, . 2008. (Illus.). 48p. (J). (gr. 1-4). 19.95 *(978-0-9728653-5-7(7))* Batfish Bks.

Peterson, Megan Cooley & Rustad, Martha E. H. Coral Reefs, 1 vol. 2013. (Little Scientist Ser.). (ENG., Illus.). 32p. (gr. 1-2). 6.95 *(978-1-4765-3541-8(8))*; 27.99 *(978-1-4765-0247-2(1))*; pap. 6.95 *(978-1-4765-3547-0(7))* Capstone Press of Coughlan Cos.

Phillips, Dee. Find It on a Coral Reef. 2006. (Can You Find It? Ser.). (Illus.). 24p. (J). (gr. k-3). lib. bdg. 23.00 *(978-0-8368-6302-4(X),* Gareth Stevens Learning Library) Stevens, Gareth Publishing LLLP.

Priddy, Roger. Coral Reef. 2014. (Smart Kids Ser.). (ENG.). 30p. (J). (gr. -1-2). 9.99 *(978-0-312-51677-2(0),* 9780312516772, Priddy Bks.) St. Martin's Pr.

Pyers, Greg. Biodiversity of Coral Reefs. 2010. (Biodiversity Ser.). 32p. (gr. 4-18). 28.50 *(978-1-60870-070-7(4))* Marshall Cavendish Corp.

Rattini, Kristin. National Geographic Readers: Coral Reefs. 2015. (Readers Ser.). (ENG.). 32p. (J). (gr. k-3). pap. 3.99 *(978-1-4263-2113-9(9),* National Geographic Children's Bks.) National Geographic Society.

Romero, Libby. Coral Reefs. 2005. (J). pap. *(978-1-4108-4608-2(3))* Benchmark Education Co.

Rose, Simon. Coral Reefs. 2017. (J). ***(978-1-5105-2169-8(0))*** SmartBook Media, Inc.

—Coral Reefs. 2014. (Illus.). 32p. (J). *(978-1-62127-484-1(5))* Weigl Pubs., Inc.

Roumanis, Alexis. Coral Reefs. 2014. (Illus.). 24p. (J). *(978-1-4896-2998-2(X))* Weigl Pubs., Inc.

Schomp, Virginia. 24 Hours on a Coral Reef. 2013. (Day in an Ecosystem Ser.). 48p. (J). (gr. 4-8). pap. 12.93 *(978-1-62712-065-4(3))* Cavendish Square Publishing.

Schuetz, Kari. Life in a Coral Reef. 2016. (Biomes Alive! Ser.). (ENG., Illus.). 24p. (J). (gr. k-3). lib. bdg. 25.95 *(978-1-62617-315-6(X),* Blastoff! Readers) Bellwether Media.

Sexton, Colleen. Coral Reefs. 2008. (Learning about the Earth Ser.). (ENG., Illus.). 24p. (J). (gr. k-3). lib. bdg. 25.95 *(978-1-60014-228-4(1))* Bellwether Media.

Simon, Seymour. Coral Reefs. 2013. (ENG.). 32p. (J). (gr. 1-5). pap. 6.99 *(978-0-06-191496-6(7))* HarperCollins Pubs.

—Coral Reefs. 2013. (ENG.). 32p. (J). (gr. 1-5). 17.99 *(978-0-06-191495-9(9),* Collins) HarperCollins Pubs. Ltd. GBR. Dist: HarperCollins Pubs.

Stewart, Melissa. Extreme Coral Reef! 2008. (Smithsonian Q & A Ser.). (Illus.). 48p. (J). (gr. k-4). 16.99 *(978-0-06-111577-6(0))* Smithsonian Institution Pr.

Walker, Sally M. Reefs. 2008. pap. 52.95 *(978-0-8225-9346-1(7))* 2007. (ENG., Illus.). 48p. (gr. 2-5). lib. bdg. 26.60 *(978-0-8225-6738-7(5),* Lerner Pubns.) Lerner Publishing Group.

World Book, Inc Staff, contrib. by. Treasures of the Ocean. 2017. (J). ***(978-0-7166-3370-9(1))*** World Bk., Inc.

CORALS

Collard, Sneed B., III. One Night in the Coral Sea. Brickman, Robin, illus. 2006. (ENG.). 32p. (J). (gr. 1-4). pap. 7.95 *(978-1-57091-390-7(0))* Charlesbridge Publishing, Inc.

—One Night in the Coral Sea. Brickman, Robin, illus. 2006. 32p. (gr. 3-7). 17.95 *(978-0-7569-6969-1(7))* Perfection Learning Corp.

Fiedler, Heidi. Coral: A Close-Up Photographic Look Inside Your World. 2017. (Up Close Ser.). (ENG., Illus.). (J). (gr. k-6). lib. bdg. 27.99 ***(978-1-942875-35-2(5),*** Walter Foster Jr) Quarto Publishing Group USA.

George, Lynn. Coral: Reef Builders. 2010. (Animal Architects Ser.). (ENG.). 24p. (J). pap. 8.25 *(978-1-4488-1349-0(2))*; lib. bdg. 22.60 *(978-1-4488-0694-2(1))* Rosen Publishing Group, Inc., The. (PowerKids Pr.).

Herriges, Ann. Corals. 2006. (Oceans Alive Ser.). (ENG., Illus.). 24p. (J). (gr. k-3). lib. bdg. 25.95 *(978-1-60014-049-5(1))* Bellwether Media.

Hirschmann, Kris. Coral. 2007. (Creatures of the Sea Ser.). (ENG., Illus.). 48p. (J). (gr. 4-8). 27.50 *(978-0-7377-3007-4(2),* Greenhaven Pr., Inc.) Cengage Gale.

Leggitt, Marjorie & Padilla-Gamino, Jacqueline L. Kupe & the Coral (Kupe e te To'a) 2014. (Long Term Ecological Research Ser.). (ENG & TAH., Illus.). 32p. (J). (gr. 3-7). pap. 8.95 *(978-1-58979-780-2(9))* Taylor Trade Publishing.

Meister, Cari. Corals. 2013. (ENG., Illus.). 24p. (J). lib. bdg. 25.65 *(978-1-62031-031-1(7))* Jump! Inc.

Padilla-Gamino, Jacqueline L. Kupe & the Corals (Kupe y los Corales) 2014. (Long Term Ecological Research Ser.). (ENG & SPA., Illus.). 32p. (J). (gr. 3-7). pap. 8.95 *(978-1-58979-776-5(0))* Taylor Trade Publishing.

Rose, Simon. Coral Reefs. 2017. (J). ***(978-1-5105-2169-8(0))*** SmartBook Media, Inc.

Schuh, Mari. Corals. 2017. (Ocean Life up Close Ser.). (ENG., Illus.). 24p. (J). (gr. k-3). lib. bdg. 25.95 *(978-1-62617-569-3(1),* Blastoff! Readers) Bellwether Media.

CORDUROY (FICTITIOUS CHARACTER)—FICTION

Don, Freeman. Corduroy. 2014. (Corduroy Ser.). (ENG.). 32p. (J). (gr. k-12). 11.24 *(978-1-63245-291-7(X))* Lectorum Pubns., Inc.

Freeman, Don. Corduroy. 2014. (Corduroy Ser.). (ENG., Illus.). 32p. (J). (gr. -1 — 1). bds. 7.99 *(978-0-451-47079-9(6),* Viking Books for Young Readers) Penguin Young Readers Group.

—Corduroy. Freeman, Don, illus. 40th anniv. ed. 2008. (Corduroy Ser.). (ENG., Illus.). 48p. (J). (gr. -1-k). 19.99 *(978-0-670-06336-9(3),* Viking Books for Young Readers) Penguin Young Readers Group.

—Corduroy's Tiny Treasury, 5 bks., Set. McCue, Lisa, illus. 2010. (Corduroy Ser.). (ENG.). 10p. (J). (gr. -1 — 1). 9.99 *(978-0-670-01230-5(0),* Viking Books for Young Readers) Penguin Young Readers Group.

—A Pocket for Corduroy. 2015. (Corduroy Ser.). (ENG.). 32p. (J). (— 1). bds. 7.99 *(978-0-451-47113-0(X),* Viking Books for Young Readers) Penguin Young Readers Group.

Freeman, Don & McCue, Lisa. Corduroy Series Boxed Set: Corduroy; A Pocket for Corduroy; Corduroy's Busy Street; Corduroy Goes to the Doctor; Corduroy's Day; Corduroy's Party, Set. Freeman, Don & McCue, Lisa, illus. (Corduroy Ser.). (Illus.). (J). (gr. k-1). pap. 30.95 incl. audio *(978-0-87499-471-1(3))* Live Oak Media.

Scott, MaryJo. Corduroy's Seasons. McCue, Lisa, illus. 2016. (Corduroy Ser.). (ENG.). 14p. (J). (— 1). bds. 5.99 *(978-0-451-47249-6(7),* Viking Books for Young Readers) Penguin Young Readers Group.

—Corduroy's Shapes. McCue, Lisa, illus. 2016. (Corduroy Ser.). (ENG.). 14p. (J). (— 1). bds. 5.99 *(978-0-451-47250-2(0),* Viking Books for Young Readers) Penguin Young Readers Group.

Weston Woods Staff, creator. Corduroy. 2011. 38.75 *(978-0-545-14080-5(3))*; 29.95 *(978-0-545-14916-7(9))*; 18.95 *(978-0-545-14078-2(1))* Weston Woods Studios, Inc.

CORN

Brannon, Cecelia H. Corn. 2017. (All about Food Crops Ser.). 24p. (gr. k-1). lib. bdg. 22.60 ***(978-0-7660-8579-4(1))*** Enslow Pubs., Inc.

Etingoff, Kim. Corn. 2013. (Feeding the World Ser.: 8). (Illus.). 48p. (J). (gr. 4-18). 19.95 *(978-1-4222-2742-8(1))* Mason Crest.

Franks, Katie. Corn up Close. (Nature up Close Ser.). 24p. 2009. (gr. k-1). 42.50 *(978-1-61514-826-4(4))* 2008. (Illus.). (J). (gr. 3-7). lib. bdg. 22.60 *(978-1-4042-4142-8(6))* Rosen Publishing Group, Inc., The. (PowerKids Pr.).

—Corn up Close / el Maiz. 2009. (Nature up Close / la naturaleza de cerca Ser.). (ENG & SPA.). 24p. (gr. k-1). 42.50 *(978-1-61514-832-5(9),* Editorial Buenas Letras) Rosen Publishing Group, Inc., The.

—Corn up Close/el Maiz. Sanz, Pilar, tr. from ENG. 2008. (Nature up Close / la Naturaleza de Cerca Ser.). (Illus.). 24p. (J). (gr. -1-3). lib. bdg. 22.60 *(978-1-4042-7677-2(7),* Editorial Buenas Letras) Rosen Publishing Group, Inc., The.

Gibbons, Gail. Corn. Gibbons, Gail, illus. (ENG., Illus.). 32p. (J). (gr. -1-3). 2009. pap. 7.99 *(978-0-8234-2245-6(3))* 2008. 16.95 *(978-0-8234-2169-5(4))* Holiday Hse., Inc.

Gonzales, Doreen. Corn/Maíz. 2009. (Native Foods of Latin America / Alimentos indígenas de Latino América Ser.). (ENG & SPA.). 24p. (gr. 2-3). 42.50 *(978-1-61514-797-7(7),* Editorial Buenas Letras) Rosen Publishing Group, Inc., The.

Gonzales, Doreen & Sanz, Ma Pilar. Corn: Maíz. 2009. (Native Foods of Latin America / Alimentos Indígenas de Latinoamérica Ser.). (SPA & ENG.). (J). lib. bdg. 22.60 *(978-1-4358-2723-3(6),* PowerKids Pr.) Rosen Publishing Group, Inc., The.

Heos, Bridget. So You Want to Grow a Taco? Fabbri, Daniele, illus. 2015. (Grow Your Food Ser.). (ENG.). 24p. (gr. 1-3). 19.95 *(978-1-60753-742-7(7))* Amicus Publishing.

Hipp, Andrew. Corn. 2004. (Getting into Nature Ser.). (Illus.). 32p. (YA). (gr. 3-6). lib. bdg. 25.25 *(978-0-8239-4205-3(8))* Rosen Publishing Group, Inc., The.

—Corn: Inside & Out. 2009. (Getting into Nature Ser.). 32p. (gr. 3-4). 47.90 *(978-1-61512-721-4(6),* PowerKids Pr.) Rosen Publishing Group, Inc., The.

—El Maiz: Por Dentro y Por Fuera. González, Thomas, tr. di Gaudesi, Andrea Ricciardi, illus. 2004. (Explora la Naturaleza (Getting into Nature) Ser.). (SPA.). 27p. lib. bdg. 25.25 *(978-1-4042-2863-4(2))* Rosen Publishing Group, Inc., The.

—El Maiz: Por dentro y por fuera (Corn: Inside & Out) 2009. (Explora la Naturaleza (Getting into Nature) Ser.). (SPA.). 32p. (gr. 3-4). 47.90 *(978-1-61512-337-7(7),* Editorial Buenas Letras) Rosen Publishing Group, Inc., The.

Landau, Elaine. Popcorn! Lies, Brian, illus. 2003. (ENG.). 32p. (J). (gr. 1-4). pap. 7.95 *(978-1-57091-443-0(5))* Charlesbridge Publishing, Inc.

Lindeen, Mary. The Story of Corn, 1 vol. 2011. (Wonder Readers: Social Studies). (ENG.). (gr. -1-2). 20p. lib. bdg. 22.65 *(978-1-4296-8641-9(3))*; 16p. pap. 35.94 *(978-1-4296-8175-9(6))*; 32p. pap. 5.99 *(978-1-4296-7971-8(9))* Capstone Press of Coughlan Cos. (Wonder Readers).

Malam, John. Bowl of Cornflakes. 2012. (Journey of A... Ser.). (ENG.). 32p. (gr. 1-3). pap. 8.29 *(978-1-4329-6608-9(1),* Heinemann First Library) Heinemann-Raintree.

—Journey of a Bowl of Cornflakes, 1 vol. 2012. (Journey of A... Ser.). (ENG.). 32p. (gr. 1-3). lib. bdg. 27.32 *(978-1-4329-6601-0(4),* Heinemann First Library) Heinemann-Raintree.

Mattern, Joanne. How Corn Grows. 2006. (How Plants Grow Ser.). (Illus.). 24p. (gr. k-2). (ENG.). pap. 8.15 *(978-0-8368-6337-6(2))*; lib. bdg. 22.00 *(978-0-8368-6330-7(5))* Stevens, Gareth Publishing LLLP. (Weekly Reader Leveled Readers).

—How Corn Grows (Cómo Crece el Maíz) 2006. (How Plants Grow/ Como crecen las plantas Ser.). (ENG & SPA., Illus.). 24p. (gr. k-3). pap. 8.15 *(978-0-8368-6468-7(9),* Weekly Reader Leveled Readers) Stevens, Gareth Publishing LLLP.

—How Corn Grows (Cómo crece el Maíz) 2006. (How Plants Grow/ Como crecen las plantas Ser.). (ENG & SPA., Illus.). 24p. (gr. k-3). lib. bdg. 22.00 *(978-0-8368-6461-8(1),* Weekly Reader Leveled Readers) Stevens, Gareth Publishing LLLP.

Mexico's Marvelous Corn: Six-Pack. (Greetings Ser.: Vol. 2). (gr. 3-5). 31.00 *(978-0-7635-1809-7(3))* Rigby Education.

Micucci, Charles. The Life & Times of Corn. Micucci, Charles, illus. 2009. (ENG., Illus.). 32p. (J). (gr. -1-3). 16.99 *(978-0-618-50751-1(5))* Houghton Mifflin Harcourt Publishing Co.

Murray, Julie. Corn, 1 vol. 2007. (Life Cycles Ser.). (ENG.). 24p. (gr. 4-7). 25.65 *(978-1-59928-705-8(6),* Buddy Bks.) ABDO Publishing Co.

Murray, Laura K. Corn. 2015. (Illus.). 32p. (J). *(978-1-60818-561-0(3),* Creative Education) Creative Co., The.

—Corn: Grow with Me. 2016. (Grow with Me Ser.). (ENG.). 32p. (J). (gr. 3-5). pap. 9.99 *(978-1-62832-162-3(8),* Creative Paperbacks) Creative Co., The.

Nelson, Robin. From Kernel to Corn. 2012. (Start to Finish, Second Series: Nature's Cycles Ser.). (ENG.). 24p. (gr. k-3). pap. 39.62 *(978-0-7613-9294-1(7));* pap. 6.95 *(978-0-7613-8674-2(2));* lib. bdg. 23.93 *(978-0-7613-8673-5(4))* Lerner Publishing Group.

Nielsen, L. Michelle & Nielson, L. Michelle. The Biography of Corn. 2007. (How Did That Get Here? Ser.). (ENG., Illus.). 32p. (J). (gr. 3-7). lib. bdg. *(978-0-7787-2491-9(3));* (gr. 2-9). pap. *(978-0-7787-2527-5(8))* Crabtree Publishing Co.

Powell, Patricia Hruby. Zinnia: How the Corn Was Saved. Ruffenach, Jessie, ed. Thomas, Peter, tr. from NAV. Benally, Kendrick, illus. 2004. (ENG & NAV.). 32p. (J). (gr. -1-3). 17.95 *(978-1-893354-38-8(5))* Salina Bookshelf Inc.

Rajczak, Kristen. Watch Corn Grow. 2011. (Watch Plants Grow! Ser.). 24p. (gr. k-2). 69.20 *(978-1-4339-6155-7(5));* (Illus.). (J). pap. 8.15 *(978-1-4339-4823-7(0));* (Illus.). (J). lib. bdg. 22.60 *(978-1-4339-4822-0(2))* Stevens, Gareth Publishing LLLP.

—Watch Corn Grow / ¡Mira cómo crece el Maíz! 2011. (Watch Plants Grow! / ¡Mira cómo crecen las plantas! Ser.). (SPA & ENG., Illus.). 24p. (J). (gr. -1-2). 22.60 *(978-1-4339-4826-8(5))* Stevens, Gareth Publishing LLLP.

—Watch Grass Grow. 2011. (Watch Plants Grow! Ser.). (Illus.). 24p. (J). (gr. k-2). pap. 8.15 *(978-1-4339-4828-2(1));* lib. bdg. 22.60 *(978-1-4339-4827-5(3))* Stevens, Gareth Publishing LLLP.

Tate, Kelly. Selling Popcorn: Understand Place Value. 2013. (InfoMax Math Readers Ser.). (ENG.). 24p. (J). (gr. 1-2). pap. 49.50 *(978-1-4777-2196-4(7));* (Illus.). pap. 8.25 *(978-1-4777-2195-7(9))* Rosen Publishing Group, Inc., The. (Rosen Classroom).

Trumbauer, Lisa. Corn, Set. 2005. (Yellow Umbrella Fluent Level Ser.). (ENG.). 16p. (gr. k-1). pap. 35.70 *(978-0-7368-5312-5(X),* Yellow Umbrella Bks.) Capstone Press of Coughlan Cos.

Weiss, Ellen. From Kernel to Corncob. 2007. (Scholastic News Nonfiction Readers Ser.). (ENG., Illus.). 24p. (J). (gr. 1-2). 22.00 *(978-0-531-18536-0(2))* Scholastic Library Publishing.

CORN—FICTION

Abbott, Jacob. Rollo at Work. 2009. 124p. 23.95 *(978-1-60664-636-6(2));* pap. 10.95 *(978-1-60664-261-0(8))* Rodgers, Alan Bks.

Anaya, Rudolfo. The First Tortilla: A Bilingual Story. Lamadrid, Enrique R., tr. Córdova, Amy, illus. 2012. (ENG & SPA.). 32p. (J). pap. 16.95 *(978-0-8263-4215-7(9))* Univ. of New Mexico Pr.

Anaya, Rudolfo A. & Anaya, Rudolfo. The First Tortilla: A Bilingual Story. Lamadrid, Enrique R., tr. from ENG. Córdova, Amy, illus. 2007. (SPA & ENG.). 32p. (J). (gr. 4-7). 16.95 *(978-0-8263-4214-0(0))* Univ. of New Mexico Pr.

Cotes, Gilles. OGM et Chant de Mais. Begin, Jean-Guy, illus. 2004. (FRE.). 112p. (J). *(978-2-89599-002-4(6))* Editions de la Paix CAN. Dist: World of Reading, Ltd.

Lenard, Steve. The Mysterious Maze #1: The Search for the Skeleton Key. 2009. 60p. pap. 21.99 *(978-1-4389-5029-7(2))* AuthorHouse.

McQueen, Todd. Bob & Rob & Corn on the Cob. McQueen, Todd, illus. 2014. (ENG., Illus.). 32p. (J). (gr. -1-k). 16.95 *(978-1-62873-591-8(0),* Sky Pony Pr.) Skyhorse Publishing Co., Inc.

Meierhenry, Mark V. & Volk, David. The Mystery of the Maize. Two Bulls, Marty Grant, illus. 2010. (J). *(978-0-9822749-1-0(2),* South Dakota State Historical Society Pr.) South Dakota State Historical Society Pr.

Pugliano-Martin, Carol. Quetzacoatl Brings Corn to His People: A Legend from Mexico. 2006. (J). pap. *(978-1-4108-7168-8(1))* Benchmark Education Co.

Rau, Dana Meachen. Corn Aplenty. Iwai, Melissa, illus. 2009. (Step into Reading Ser.). (ENG.). 32p. (J). (gr. -1-1). 3.99 *(978-0-375-85575-7(0),* Random Hse. Bks. for Young Readers) Random Hse. Children's Bks.

Robey, Stephanie. My Favorite Food. Loeffelholz, Sarah, illus. 2006. (J). 14.95 *(978-0-9786850-0-3(8))* Overdue Bks.

Ross, Mandy. Dominic Grows Sweetcorn. Bartlett, Alison, illus. 2014. (ENG.). 32p. (J). (gr. 1-5). 17.99 *(978-1-84780-327-6(X),* Frances Lincoln) Quarto Publishing Group UK GBR. Dist: Hachette Bk. Group.

Viguié, Debbie. The Fall of Candy Corn, 1 vol. 2008. (Sweet Seasons Novel Ser.). (ENG.). 224p. (YA). (gr. 8-11). pap. 9.99 *(978-0-310-71559-7(8))* Zondervan.

Watson, Gayle. Catie Corn & the Corn Cops. Fautsch, Jackie, illus. l.t. ed. 22p. (J). 2006. 15.99 *(978-1-59879-098-6(6))* 2005. per. 9.99 *(978-1-59879-079-5(X))* Lifevest Publishing, Inc.

CORNWALL (ENGLAND: COUNTY)—FICTION

Caine, Paul. Jake's Journey. 2010. 68p. pap. 10.49 *(978-1-4520-0508-9(7))* AuthorHouse.

Cooper, Susan. The Dark Is Rising. 2009. 7.64 *(978-0-7848-2212-8(3),* Everbind) Marco Bk. Co.

—The Dark Is Rising. 15.85 *(978-0-7569-8464-9(5))* Perfection Learning Corp.

—The Dark Is Rising. (Dark Is Rising Sequence Ser.). 244p. (YA). (gr. 5-18). pap. 4.99 *(978-0-8072-1533-3(3),* Listening Library) Random Hse. Audio Publishing Group.

—Over Sea, under Stone. 2013. (Dark Is Rising Sequence Ser.: 1). (ENG., Illus.). 288p. (J). (gr. 3-7). 17.99 *(978-1-4424-9592-0(8),* McElderry, Margaret K. Bks.) McElderry, Margaret K. Bks.

Coughlin, Shirley. Toby & the Pirates. 2012. 58p. pap. 13.00 *(978-1-61204-745-4(9),* Strategic Bk. Publishing) Strategic Book Publishing & Rights Agency (SBPRA).

Dunmore, Helen. Ingo. 2008. (Ingo Ser.: 1). 336p. (YA). (gr. 5). per. 7.99 *(978-0-06-081854-8(9))* HarperCollins Pubs.

—The Tide Knot. 2008. 330p. (J). 5.99 *(978-0-06-081857-9(3));* (Ingo Ser.: 2). (ENG.). 336p. (YA). (gr. 5-8). 16.99 *(978-0-06-081855-5(7))* HarperCollins Pubs.

Elgert, C. J. The Elder Brothers & the Padstow Crystals. 2013. 208p. *(978-1-4602-1788-7(8));* pap. *(978-1-4602-1789-4(6))* FriesenPress.

Green, Julia. Hunter's Heart. 2007. 264p. (YA). (gr. 7-12). 16.95 *(978-0-7613-9493-8(1),* Carolrhoda Bks.) Lerner Publishing Group.

Guerra, Elisa Puricelli. The Forest of Talking Trees. Zeni, Marco, tr. from ITA. Bernstein, Gabriel León, illus. 2015. (Minerva Mint Ser.). (ENG.). 160p. (gr. 2-4). lib. bdg. 25.32 *(978-1-4342-9673-3(3))* Stone Arch Bks.

—The Legend of Black Bart, 1 vol. Pernigotti, Chiara, tr. from ITA. Bernstein, Gabo León, illus. 2014. (Minerva Mint Ser.). (ENG.). 160p. (gr. 2-4). pap. 7.99 *(978-1-4342-6515-9(3))* Capstone Young Readers of Coughlan Cos.

—The Legend of Black Bart, 1 vol. Pernigotti, Chiara, tr. from ITA. Bernstein, Gabo León, illus. 2014. (Minerva Mint Ser.). (ENG.). 160p. (gr. 2-4). 25.32 *(978-1-4342-6512-8(9))* Stone Arch Bks.

—Merlin's Island, 1 vol. Pernigotti, Chiara, tr. from ITA. Bernstein, Gabo León, illus. 2014. (Minerva Mint Ser.). (ENG.). 160p. (gr. 2-4). pap. 7.99 *(978-1-4342-6514-2(5))* Capstone Young Readers of Coughlan Cos.

—Merlin's Island, 1 vol. Pernigotti, Chiara, tr. from ITA. Bernstein, Gabo León, illus. 2014. (Minerva Mint Ser.). (ENG.). 160p. (gr. 2-4). 25.32 *(978-1-4342-6511-1(0))* Stone Arch Bks.

—Minerva Mint, 1 vol. 2014. (Minerva Mint Ser.). (ENG.). 160p. (gr. 2-4). 75.96 *(978-1-4342-8932-2(X))* Stone Arch Bks.

—The Night of the Blue Turtles. Zeni, Marco, tr. from ITA. Bernstein, Gabriel León, illus. 2015. (Minerva Mint Ser.). (ENG.). 160p. (gr. 2-4). lib. bdg. 25.32 *(978-1-4342-9672-6(5))* Stone Arch Bks.

—The Order of the Owls, 1 vol. Bernstein, Gabo León, illus. 2014. (Minerva Mint Ser.). (ENG.). 160p. (gr. 2-4). 9.95 *(978-1-62370-038-6(8))* Capstone Young Readers of Coughlan Cos.

Harris, J. Henry & Everson, Michael. Phyllis in Piskie-Land: A Tale of Cornwall, Inspired by Lewis Carroll's Wonderland. 2012. (Illus.). 102p. pap. *(978-1-904808-84-8(0))* Evertype.

Hopkins, Cathy & Hopkins, Cathy. All Mates Together. 2007. (Truth or Dare Ser.: No. 8). (ENG.). 240p. (YA). (gr. 7-18). mass mkt. 11.99 *(978-1-4169-2722-8(0),* Simon Pulse) Simon Pulse.

Hosken, John. Sophie Storme. 2011. (Illus.). 268p. (gr. -1). 32.12 *(978-1-4567-7596-4(0));* pap. 17.23 *(978-1-4567-7595-7(2))* AuthorHouse.

Hussey, Charmian. The Valley of Secrets. Crump, Christopher, illus. 2006. (ENG.). 400p. (J). (gr. 7-12). per. 17.99 *(978-1-4169-0015-3(2),* Simon Pulse) Simon Pulse.

Jones, Allan Frewin. The Wreckers. 2003. (ENG.). 163p. (J). mass mkt. *(978-0-330-36810-0(9),* Pan) Pan Macmillan.

Kent, Trilby. Medina Hill. 2009. (ENG.). 176p. (YA). (gr. 5-9). 19.95 *(978-0-88776-888-0(1),* Tundra Bks.) Tundra Bks. CAN. Dist: Penguin Random Hse. LLC.

Mendes, Valerie. The Drowning. 2005. (ENG.). 256p. (J). (gr. 7). per. 8.99 *(978-1-4169-0127-3(2))* Simon & Schuster, Ltd. GBR. Dist: Simon & Schuster, Inc.

O'Rourke, Tim. Flashes. 2015. (ENG.). 320p. (J). (gr. 9). 16.99 *(978-0-545-82959-5(3))* Scholastic, Inc.

Overington, Marcus. Lost on Bodmin Moor. 2012. (Illus.). 50p. pap. *(978-1-909039-36-0(5))* Legend Pr.

Priestley, Chris. Tales of Terror from the Black Ship. Roberts, David, illus. 2008. (Tales of Terror Ser.: 1). (ENG.). 256p. (YA). (gr. 3-6). 12.99 *(978-1-59990-290-6(7),* 9781599902906, Bloomsbury USA Childrens) Bloomsbury Publishing USA.

Quiller-Couch, Mabel. Kitty Trenire. 2006. (ENG.). 210p. pap. 20.99 *(978-1-4264-7475-0(X))* 2007. 230p. pap. 22.99 *(978-1-4264-7552-8(7))* Creative Media Partners, LLC.

Roy, Lillian Elizabeth. Alice in Beeland: A Tale of Cornwall, Inspired by Lewis Carroll's Wonderland. 2nd ed. 2012. (Illus.). 128p. pap. *(978-1-78201-018-0(1))* Evertype.

Sargeant, Theresa. The Drainpipe Gang - the Adventures of Chris & Andy Smy. 2011. 112p. pap. *(978-1-907256-80-6(6))* Abela Publishing.

CORONADO, FRANCISCO VASQUEZ DE, 1510-1554

Cantor, Carrie Nichols. Francisco Vásquez de Coronado: The Search for Cities of Gold. 2003. (Proud Heritage: the Hispanic Library). (ENG., Illus.). 40p. (J). (gr. 3-6). 29.93 *(978-1-56766-210-8(2),* 200007) Child's World, Inc., The.

Cooke, Tim. Explore with Francisco Vazquez de Coronado. 2016. (Travel with the Great Explorers Ser.). (ENG., Illus.). 32p. (J). (gr. 3-6). *(978-0-7787-2847-4(1))* Crabtree Publishing Co.

Hazleton, Amie. Francisco Vasquez de Coronado: An Explorer of the Southwest. 2017. (World Explorers Ser.). (ENG., Illus.). 32p. (gr. 3-4). lib. bdg. 27.32 *(978-1-5157-4203-6(2))* Capstone Press of Coughlan Cos.

Herr, Melody. Exploring the New World: An Interactive History Adventure. 2016. (You Choose: History Ser.). (ENG.). 112p. (gr. 3-4). pap. 6.95 *(978-1-5157-4258-6(X),* You Choose Bks.) Capstone Press of Coughlan Cos.

Kallen, Stuart A. A Journey with Francisco Vázquez de Coronado. 2017. (Primary Source Explorers Ser.). (ENG.). 40p. (J). (gr. 3-5). 30.65 *(978-1-5124-0773-0(9))* Lerner Publishing Group.

Mountjoy, Shane. Francisco Coronado & the Seven Cities of Gold. Goetzmann, William H., ed. 2005. (Explorers of New Lands Ser.). (Illus.). 160p. (gr. 5-8). lib. bdg. 30.00 *(978-0-7910-8631-5(3))* Facts On File, Inc.

Peppas, Lynn. Why Francisco Coronado Matters to Texas. 2014. (Illus.). 32p. (J). lib. bdg. 26.25 *(978-1-4777-0909-2(6))* Rosen Publishing Group, Inc., The.

Petrie, Kristin. Francisco Vasquez de Coronado, 1 vol. 2004. (Explorers Set 1 Ser.). (ENG.). 32p. (gr. k-6). 27.07 *(978-1-59197-597-7(2),* Checkerboard Library) ABDO Publishing Co.

Roberts, Steven. Francisco Vasquez de Coronado. 2013. (Jr. Graphic Famous Explorers Ser.). (ENG., Illus.). 24p. (J). (gr. 3-6). pap. 10.60 *(978-1-4777-0125-6(7));* lib. bdg. 25.25 *(978-1-4777-0070-9(6))* Rosen Publishing Group, Inc., The. (PowerKids Pr.).

Two Worlds Meet: the Travels of Francisco de Coronado: Fourth Grade Guided Comprehension Level R. (On Our Way to English Ser.). (gr. 4-18). 34.50 *(978-0-7578-7184-9(4))* Rigby Education.

Uhl, Xina M. Francisco de Vasquez Coronado. 2016. (Spotlight on Explorers & Colonization Ser.). 00048p. (J). (gr. 6-6). pap. 11.75 *(978-1-5081-7214-7(5))* Rosen Publishing Group, Inc., The.

Weisberg, Barbara & Haley, Alex. Coronado's Golden Quest. Eagle, Mike, illus. 2009. (Steck-Vaughn Stories of America Ser.). (ENG.). 88p. (gr. 3-8). pap. 14.20 *(978-0-8114-8072-7(0))* Houghton Mifflin Harcourt Publishing Co.

CORONARY HEART DISEASES

see Heart—Diseases

CORRECTIONAL INSTITUTIONS

see Prisons

CORRESPONDENCE

see Commercial Correspondence; Letter Writing; Letters

CORRUPTION (IN POLITICS)

see Political Corruption

CORSAIRS

see Pirates

CORTES, HERNANDO, 1485-1547

Abnett, Dan. Hernan Cortes & the Fall of the Aztec Empire. (Jr. Graphic Biographies Ser.). (ENG.). 24p. 2009. (J). (gr. 2-3). 47.90 *(978-1-61513-819-7(6),* PowerKids Pr.) 2007. (Illus.). (J). (gr. 2-5). lib. bdg. 25.25 *(978-1-4042-3391-1(1))* 2007. (Illus.). (gr. 3-8). pap. 10.60 *(978-1-4042-2144-4(1),* PowerKids Pr.) Rosen Publishing Group, Inc., The.

—Hernán Cortés y la Caída Del Imperio Azteca. 2009. (Historietas Juveniles: Biografías (Jr. Graphic Biographies) Ser.). (SPA., Illus.). 24p. (gr. 3-8). pap. 10.60 *(978-1-4358-3314-2(7))* Rosen Publishing Group, Inc., The.

—Hernán Cortés y la Caída Del Imperio Azteca. Abregón, José María, tr. 2009. (Historietas Juveniles: Biografías (Jr. Graphic Biographies) Ser.). (SPA., Illus.). 24p. (J). (gr. 2-5). 25.25 *(978-1-4358-8560-8(0))* Rosen Publishing Group, Inc., The.

Angelis, Gina De. Hernando Cortes & the Conquest of Mexico. 2007. (Illus.). 63p. (J). 25.00 *(978-1-4223-6717-9(7))* DIANE Publishing Co.

Blanch, Carmen Soler. HERNÁN CORTÉS. (SPA., Illus.). 160p. (YA). 11.95 *(978-84-7281-174-4(3),* AF1174) Auriga, Ediciones S.A. ESP. Dist: Continental Bk. Co., Inc.

Gaff, Jackie. Hernan Cortes: The Life of a Spanish Conquistador. 2005. (Graphic Nonfiction Biographies Ser.). (ENG., Illus.). 48p. (YA). (gr. 4-7). lib. bdg. 31.95 *(978-1-4042-0244-3(7))* Rosen Publishing Group, Inc., The.

Green, Carl R. Cortes: Conquering the Powerful Aztec Empire. 2010. (Great Explorers of the World Ser.). (Illus.). 112p. (J). (gr. 7-12). 33.27 *(978-1-59845-099-6(9))* Enslow Pubs., Inc.

Koestler-Grack, Rachel A. Hernando Cortes & the Fall of the Aztecs. Goetzmann, William H., ed. 2005. (Explorers of New Lands Ser.). (Illus.). 176p. (gr. 5-8). lib. bdg. 30.00 *(978-0-7910-8609-4(7))* Facts On File, Inc.

Loria, Laura. Malinche: Indigenous Translator for Hernán Cortés in Mexico. 2017. (Women Who Changed History Ser.). 48p. (gr. 10-12). pap. 14.05 ***(978-1-68048-649-0(7),*** Britannica Educational Publishing) Rosen Publishing Group, Inc., The.

Petrie, Kristin. Hernan Cortes, 1 vol. 2004. (Explorers Set 1 Ser.). (ENG., Illus.). 32p. (gr. k-6). 27.07 *(978-1-59197-598-4(0),* Checkerboard Library) ABDO Publishing Co.

Ramen, Fred. Hernán Cortés: The Conquest of Mexico & the Aztec Empire. 2015. (Incredible Explorers Ser.). (ENG., Illus.). 64p. (J). (gr. 7-7). 34.21 *(978-1-5026-0129-2(X))* Cavendish Square Publishing.

—Hernán Cortés: The Conquest of Mexico & the Aztec Empire. 2009. (Library of Explorers & Exploration Ser.). 112p. (gr. 5-8). 66.50 *(978-1-60853-606-1(8),* Rosen Reference) Rosen Publishing Group, Inc., The.

Serrano, Francisco. La Malinche: The Princess Who Helped Cortés Conquer the Aztec Empire, 1 vol. Ouriou, Susan, tr. from SPA. Serrano, Pablo, illus. 2012. (ENG.). 36p. (J). (gr. 3-7). 18.95 *(978-1-55498-111-3(5))* Groundwood Bks. CAN. Dist: Publishers Group West (PGW).

West, David. Hernán Cortés: The Life of a Spanish Conquistador. 2009. (Graphic Nonfiction Biographies Ser.). (ENG.). 48p. (YA). (gr. 4-5). 58.50 *(978-1-61513-019-1(5),* Rosen Reference) Rosen Publishing Group, Inc., The.

Zronik, John Paul & Zronik, John. Hernando Cortés: Spanish Invader of Mexico. 2006. (In the Footsteps of Explorers Ser.). (ENG., Illus.). 32p. (J). (gr. 4-7). pap. *(978-0-7787-2470-4(0))* Crabtree Publishing Co.

COSBY, BILL, 1937-

Bill Cosby: Entertainer & Activist. 2nd rev. ed. 2010. (Black Americans of Achievement Legacy Edition Ser.). (Illus.). 104p. (gr. 6-12). 35.00 *(978-1-60413-711-8(8))* Facts On File, Inc.

COSMETICS

see also Perfumes

Beery, Barbara. Spa Princess Cookbook, 1 vol. 2008. (ENG., Illus.). 64p. (J). (gr. 1). spiral bd. 14.99 *(978-1-4236-0502-7(0))* Gibbs Smith, Publisher.

Blake, Susannah. Crafts for Pampering Yourself. 2013. (Eco Chic Ser.). 32p. (J). lib. bdg. 23.94 *(978-0-7660-4314-5(2));* (gr. 4-12). pap. 7.95 *(978-1-4644-0573-0(5))* Enslow Pubs., Inc.

Eagen, Rachel. Body Care Chemistry. 2011. (Chemtastrophe! Ser.). (ENG.). 32p. (J). (gr. 5-8). pap. *(978-0-7787-5288-2(7));* lib. bdg. *(978-0-7787-5282-0(8))* Crabtree Publishing Co.

Higgins, Nadia. Brilliant Beauty Inventions. 2013. (Awesome Inventions You Use Every Day Ser.). (ENG., Illus.). 32p. (gr. 3-6). lib. bdg. 26.60 *(978-1-4677-1089-3(X),* Lerner Pubns.) Lerner Publishing Group.

Kenney, Karen Latchana. Skin Care & Makeup Tips & Tricks. Heschke, Elena, illus. 2015. (ENG.). 32p. (J). (gr. 4-8). lib. bdg. 26.65 *(978-1-4677-5219-0(3),* Lerner Pubns.) Lerner Publishing Group.

Kent, Jacqueline C. Business Builders in Cosmetics. 2003. (Business Builders Ser.: Vol. 7). (Illus.). 160p. (gr. 5-18). lib. bdg. 22.95 *(978-1-881508-82-3(X))* Oliver Pr., Inc.

Krohn, Katherine E. Madam C. J. Walker & New Cosmetics, 1 vol. Dominguez, Richard et al, illus. 2006. (Inventions & Discovery Ser.). (ENG.). 32p. (gr. 3-4). 30.65 *(978-0-7368-6485-5(7),* Graphic Library) Capstone Press of Coughlan Cos.

Larson, Jessica. FX! Costumes & Makeup. 2017. (Time for Kids Nonfiction Readers Ser.). lib. bdg. 22.10 ***(978-0-606-40270-5(5))*** Turtleback Bks.

Lasky, Kathryn. Vision of Beauty: The Story of Sarah Breedlove Walker. Bennett, Nneka, illus. 2012. (Candlewick Biographies Ser.). (ENG.). 56p. (J). (gr. 3-7). 14.99 *(978-0-7636-6428-2(6));* pap. 4.99 *(978-0-7636-6092-5(2))* Candlewick Pr.

McDonald, Fiona. Jewelry & Makeup Through History. 2006. (Why Do We Wear? Ser.). (Illus.). 32p. (gr. 2-6). lib. bdg. 26.00 *(978-0-8368-6856-2(0),* Gareth Stevens Learning Library) Stevens, Gareth Publishing LLLP.

Mooney, Carla. Sunscreen for Plants. 2009. (Great Idea Ser.). (Illus.). 48p. (J). (gr. 4-6). lib. bdg. 26.60 *(978-1-59953-344-5(8))* Norwood Hse. Pr.

Nichols, Catherine. Madam C.J. Walker. 2005. (Scholastic News Nonfiction Readers Ser.). (Illus.). 24p. (J). pap. 6.95 *(978-0-516-24784-7(0),* Children's Pr.) Scholastic Library Publishing.

Stille, Darlene R. Madam C. J. Walker: The Inspiring Life Story of the Hair Care Entrepreneur. 2016. (Inspiring Stories Ser.). (ENG., Illus.). 112p. (gr. 5-7). lib. bdg. 35.99 *(978-0-7565-5165-0(X),* CPB Grades 4-8) Compass Point Bks.

Wood, Alix. Hair & Makeup Design. 2017. (Design It! Ser.). 32p. (gr. 3-4). pap. 63.00 ***(978-1-5382-0783-3(4))*** Stevens, Gareth Publishing LLLP.

COSMETICS—FICTION

Berke, Lindsey Jensen. Am I Pretty? 2013. 28p. 22.99 *(978-1-4808-0106-6(2));* pap. 16.99 *(978-1-4808-0108-0(9))* Archway Publishing.

Blumenthal, Deborah. A Different Me. 2014. (ENG.). 272p. (YA). (gr. 8-12). 16.99 *(978-0-8075-1573-0(6))* Whitman, Albert & Co.

Carol White-Hill. Mommy & Her Makeup. 2009. 12p. pap. 8.49 *(978-1-4389-6013-5(1))* AuthorHouse.

Chartrand, Lili. The Smelly Story of Hazel the Weasel. Eid, Jean-Paul, illus. 2009. (Rainy Day Readers Ser.). 32p. (J). (gr. -1-3). 22.60 *(978-1-60754-379-4(6));* pap. 10.55 *(978-1-60754-380-0(X))* Windmill Bks.

Fowler, Elle & Fowler, Blair. Beneath the Glitter. 2013. (Sophia & Ava London Ser.: 1). (ENG.). 288p. (YA). (gr. 7). pap. 17.99 *(978-1-250-01715-4(7),* 9781250017154, St. Martin's Griffin) St. Martin's Pr.

Greenwald, Lisa. My Life in Pink & Green. (Pink & Green Ser.). (ENG.). (gr. 3-7). 2010. 288p. (J). pap. 7.95 *(978-0-8109-8984-9(0))* 2009. 272p. (YA). 17.95 *(978-0-8109-8352-6(4))* Abrams, Inc. (Amulet Bks.).

—My Summer of Pink & Green. 2013. (Pink & Green Ser.). (ENG.). 272p. (YA). (gr. 3-7). 17.95 *(978-1-4197-0413-0(3),* Amulet Bks.); (J). (gr. 5-9). 5.00 *(978-1-4197-0932-6(1))* Abrams, Inc.

—My Summer of Pink & Green: Pink & Green Book Two. 2014. (Pink & Green Ser.). (ENG.). 288p. (YA). (gr. 3-7). pap. 7.95 *(978-1-4197-0931-9(3),* Amulet Bks.) Abrams, Inc.

—Pink & Green Is the New Black: Pink & Green Book Three. (Pink & Green Ser.). (ENG.). 280p. (J). (gr. 3-7). 2015. pap. 7.95 *(978-1-4197-1679-9(4))* 2014. 16.95 *(978-1-4197-1225-8(X))* Abrams, Inc. (Amulet Bks.).

Grime, L. L. The Make up Story. 2007. 36p. 17.50 *(978-1-4357-0585-2(8))* Lulu Pr., Inc.

Horowitz, Anthony. The Switch. 2010. (ENG.). 192p. (J). (gr. 5-18). 7.99 *(978-0-14-241547-4(2),* Puffin Books) Penguin Young Readers Group.

Meadows, Daisy. Frankie the Makeup Fairy. 2013. (Rainbow Magic — the Superstar Fairies Ser.: 5). lib. bdg. 14.75 *(978-0-606-31517-3(9),* Turtleback) Turtleback Bks.

Munro, Marija. Mardi Loves Lipstick. 2009. 24p. pap. 11.49 *(978-1-60693-754-9(5),* Eloquent Bks.) Strategic Book Publishing & Rights Agency (SBPRA).

Munsch, Robert. Makeup Mess. 2004. (Illus.). (J). (gr. k-3). spiral bd. *(978-0-616-11125-3(8))* Canadian National Institute for the Blind/Institut National Canadien pour les Aveugles.

—Makeup Mess. Martchenko, Michael, illus. 2004. (J). (gr. k-3). spiral bd. *(978-0-616-11124-6(X))* Canadian National Institute for the Blind/Institut National Canadien pour les Aveugles.

O'Connor, Jane. Ooh La La! It's Beauty Day. Glasser, Robin Preiss, illus. 2010. (Fancy Nancy Ser.). (ENG.). 40p. (J). (gr. -1-2). 12.99 *(978-0-06-191525-3(4))* HarperCollins Pubs.

Summy, Barrie. I So Don't Do Makeup. 2011. (ENG.). 288p. (J). (gr. 3-7). 7.99 *(978-0-385-73789-0(0),* Yearling) Random Hse. Children's Bks.

Vail, Rachel. Gorgeous. 2010. (Avery Sisters Trilogy Ser.: 2). (ENG.). 304p. (YA). (gr. 8). pap. 9.99 *(978-0-06-089048-3(7))* HarperCollins Pubs.

Wells, Rosemary. Ruby's Beauty Shop. Wells, Rosemary, illus. 2004. (Max & Ruby Ser.). (ENG., Illus.). 32p. (J). (gr. -1-k). pap. 6.99 *(978-0-14-240194-1(3),* Puffin Books) Penguin Young Readers Group.

COSMOGONY

see Universe

COSMOGONY, BIBLICAL

see Creation

COSMOGRAPHY

see Universe

COSMOLOGY

see Universe

COSMOLOGY, BIBLICAL

see Creation

COSMONAUTS

see Astronauts

COSTA RICA

Bartell, Jim. Costa Rica. 2011. (Exploring Countries Ser.). (ENG., Illus.). 32p. (J). (gr. 3-7). lib. bdg. 26.95 *(978-1-60014-572-8(8),* Blastoff! Readers) Bellwether Media.

Cerullo, Mary M. Journey to Shark Island: A Shark Photographer's Close Encounters, 1 vol. Rotman, Jeffrey L., illus. Rotman, Jeffrey L., photos by. 2014. (Shark Expedition Ser.). (ENG.). 40p. (gr. 5-7). lib. bdg. 31.99 *(978-0-7565-4887-2(X))* Compass Point Bks.

Cooper, Sharon Katz. Costa Rica ABCs: A Book about the People & Places of Costa Rica, 1 vol. Eitzen, Allan, illus. 2007. (Country ABCs Ser.). (ENG.). 32p. (gr. k-5). lib. bdg. 27.99 *(978-1-4048-2249-8(6))* Picture Window Bks.

Cox, Vicki. Oscar Arias Sanchez: Bringing Peace to Central America. 2007. (Modern Peacemakers Ser.). (Illus.). 118p.

C D

(YA). (gr. 9-12). lib. bdg. 30.00 *(978-0-7910-8999-6(1))* Facts On File, Inc.
Deady, Kathleen W. Costa Rica. 2005. (True Bks.). (ENG., Illus.). 48p. (J). (gr. 3-5). pap. 6.95 *(978-0-516-25831-7(1),* Children's Pr.) Scholastic Library Publishing.
Foley, Erin & Cooke, Barbara. Costa Rica. 2nd rev. ed. 2007. (Cultures of the World Ser.). 144p. (gr. 6). lib. bdg. 42.79 *(978-0-7614-2079-8(7),* Benchmark Bks.) Marshall Cavendish Corp.
Foley, Erin, et al. Costa Rica. 2017. (J). ***(978-1-5026-2610-3(1))*** Cavendish Square Publishing.
Fox, Mary Virginia. Costa Rica, 1 vol. 2nd ed. 2008. (Visit To Ser.). (ENG., Illus.). 32p. (gr. k-2). lib. bdg. 26.65 *(978-1-4329-1281-9(X),* Heinemann First Library) Heinemann-Raintree.
Kopp, Megan. Costa Rica. 2016. (J). ***(978-1-4896-5405-2(4))*** Weigl Pubs., Inc.
Marcus, Amy. Exploring Costa Rica with the Five Themes of Geography. (Library of the Western Hemisphere Ser.). 24p. 2009. (gr. 4-4). 42.50 *(978-1-60853-925-3(3),* PowerKids Pr.) 2005. (Illus.). (J). (gr. 5-7). lib. bdg. 22.60 *(978-1-4042-2672-2(9),* PowerKids Pr.) 2005. (Illus.). (gr. 3-8). pap. 8.25 *(978-0-8239-4632-7(0))* Rosen Publishing Group, Inc., The.
Pratt-Serafini, Kristin Joy & Crandell, Rachel. The Forever Forest: Kids Save a Tropical Treasure, 1 vol. Pratt-Serafini, Kristin Joy, illus. 2008. (ENG., Illus.). 32p. (J). (gr. k-5). 16.95 *(978-1-58469-101-3(8))* Dawn Pubns.
—The Forever Forest: Kids Save a Tropical Treasure. 2008. (Illus.). 32p. (J). (gr. k-5). pap. 8.95 *(978-1-58469-102-0(6))* Dawn Pubns.
Raum, Elizabeth. Costa Rica, 1 vol. 2011. (Countries Around the World Ser.). (ENG.). 48p. (J). (gr. 3-6). pap. 9.95 *(978-1-4329-5223-5(4));* 33.32 *(978-1-4329-5198-6(X))* Heinemann-Raintree. (NA-h).
Scimone, Diana. Adventures with Pawpaw: Costa Rica. Wiedemer, Leah, illus. 2003. 32p. (J). 8.95 *(978-0-9729507-2-5(9))* Peapod Publishing, Inc.
Shields, Charles J. Costa Rica. 2010. (Central America Today Ser.). 63p. (YA). (gr. 7-18). pap. 9.95 *(978-1-4222-0713-0(7));* (Illus.). (gr. 9-12). 21.95 *(978-1-4222-0646-1(7))* Mason Crest.
—Costa Rica, Vol. 8. Henderson, James D., ed. 2015. (Discovering Central America: History, Politics, & Culture Ser.). (Illus.). 64p. (J). (gr. 7). lib. bdg. 22.95 *(978-1-4222-3287-3(5))* Mason Crest.
West, Tracey. Costa Rica. 2009. pap. 52.95 *(978-0-7613-4726-2(7))* 2008. (ENG.). 48p. (gr. 2-4). 29.27 *(978-0-8225-9416-1(1))* Lerner Publishing Group.
Yomtov, Nel. Costa Rica. 2014. (Enchantment of the World Ser.: 2). (ENG.). 144p. (J). lib. bdg. 40.00 *(978-0-531-22014-6(1))* Scholastic Library Publishing.

COSTA RICA—FICTION

Barr, Brady & Curtis, Jennifer Keats. After a While Crocodile: Alexa's Diary, 1 vol. Detwiler, Susan, illus. 2016. (ENG & SPA.). 32p. (J). (gr. k-3). 17.95 *(978-1-62855-834-0(2))* Arbordale Publishing.
Cronin, Susan L. Gidget Goes Away. 2006. 54p. pap. 16.95 *(978-1-4137-9878-4(0))* PublishAmerica, Inc.
Cunningham, Elaine. Ethan, a Soccer Player for Jesus. Valliant, Kristi, illus. 2010. 32p. (J). *(978-0-8341-2486-8(6))* Beacon Hill Pr. of Kansas City.
Eisele, Barbara. Curious Cozy. 2011. 48p. pap. 9.99 *(978-1-4567-1746-9(4))* AuthorHouse.
Haidar, Hanna. Earl's Big Adventure in Costa Rica. Hutcheson, Meredith, ed. Newton, Kimberly, illus. 2007. 22p. (J). per. 7.99 *(978-0-9800975-0-4(9))* Old Silver Pr.
—Earl's Big Adventure in Costa Rica. Newton, Kimberly, illus. 2nd ed. 2012. 22p. (J). *(978-0-9800975-2-8(5))* Old Silver Pr.
Keene, Carolyn. Green with Envy: Book Two in the Eco Mystery Trilogy. 2010. (Nancy Drew (All New) Girl Detective Ser.: 40). (ENG.). 160p. (J). (gr. 3-7). pap. 6.99 *(978-1-4169-7842-8(9),* Aladdin) Simon & Schuster Children's Publishing.
—Trails of Treachery. 2008. (Nancy Drew: Girl Detective Ser.). 136p. (gr. 3-7). 15.00 *(978-0-7569-8295-9(2))* Perfection Learning Corp.
Keister, Douglas. El Regalo de Fernando. Keister, Douglas, photos by. 2004.Tr. of Fernando's Gift. (SPA., Illus.). 32p. (J). (gr. 3-3). reprint ed. 16.95 *(978-0-87156-414-6(9))* Sierra Club Bks. for Children.
Lopez, Maria Lorena. The Bird's Party, Birds in the Tropical Dry Forest. 2009. 28p. pap. 13.00 *(978-1-60860-156-1(0),* Eloquent Bks.) Strategic Book Publishing & Rights Agency (SBPRA).
Messner, Kate. Hide & Seek. (ENG.). 256p. (J). (gr. 3-7). 2015. pap. 7.99 *(978-0-545-79910-2(4),* Scholastic Paperbacks) 2013. (Illus.). 16.99 *(978-0-545-41975-8(1),* Scholastic Pr.) Scholastic, Inc.
Pierson, Rich. Adventures of Fred the Donkey. 2012. 48p. pap. 21.99 *(978-1-4691-7343-6(3))* Xlibris Corp.
Skinner, J. C. Ringo & the Fruit Tree. 2008. 24p. pap. 24.95 *(978-1-60441-028-0(0))* America Star Bks.
Spady, Angela & Thomas Nelson Publishing Staff. Channing O'Banning & the Rainforest Rescue, 1 vol. 2015. (ENG., Illus.). 112p. (J). pap. 6.99 *(978-0-7180-3262-3(4))* Nelson, Thomas Inc.
Stubben, Michael. Clark vs. the Rainforest. 2012. 110p. pap. 9.99 *(978-1-105-54615-0(2))* Lulu Pr., Inc.
Walters, Eric. Skye Above, 1 vol. Parkins, David, illus. 2014. (Orca Echoes Ser.). (ENG.). 64p. (J). (gr. 2-3). pap. 6.95 *(978-1-4598-0701-3(4))* Orca Bk. Pubs. USA.

COSTUME

Here are entered descriptive and historical works on the costume of particular countries or periods and for works on fancy costume. Works dealing with clothing from a practical standpoint, including the art of dress, are entered under Clothing and Dress. Works describing the prevailing mode or style in dress are entered under Fashion.

see also Clothing and Dress; Cosmetics; Dressmaking; Fashion; Hats; Indians of North America—Clothing; Jewelry; Theatrical Makeup; Weapons

Aikman, Louise. North American Dress. 2004. (Twentieth-Century Developments in Fashion & Costume Ser.). (Illus.). 64p. (YA). (gr. 7-18). lib. bdg. 19.95 *(978-1-59084-425-0(4))* Mason Crest.
Bernhardt, Carolyn. Duct Tape Costumes. 2017. (Create with Duct Tape Ser.). (ENG.). 32p. (J). (gr. 2-5). 12.99 ***(978-1-5124-3849-9(9),*** Lerner Pubns.); 39.99 ***(978-1-5124-2764-6(0),*** Lerner Pubns.); 39.99 ***(978-1-5124-3848-2(0),*** Lerner Pubns.); (Illus.). 26.65 *(978-1-5124-2667-0(9))* Lerner Publishing Group.
Boase, Petra & Graham, Bettina. Dressing Up! 50 Step-By-Step Amazing Outfits to Make & Faces to Paint. 2014. (ENG., Illus.). 96p. (J). (gr. 3-8). 13.99 *(978-1-84322-914-8(5),* Armadillo) Anness Publishing GBR. Dist: National Bk. Network.
Bolte, Mari. Unique Accessories You Can Make & Share. 2015. (Sleepover Girls Crafts Ser.). (ENG.). 32p. (gr. 3-4). lib. bdg. 27.99 *(978-1-62065-176-6(9),* Snap Bks.) Capstone Press of Coughlan Cos.
Bone, Emily. 1920's Fashion IR. 2013. (Historical Sticker Dolly Dressing Ser.). 224p. (J). pap. 9.99 *(978-0-7945-3355-7(8),* Usborne) EDC Publishing.
Bonnice, Sherry. Folk Fashion. 2004. (North American Folklore Ser.). (Illus.). 112p. (YA). (gr. 7-18). lib. bdg. 22.95 *(978-1-59084-338-3(X))* Mason Crest.
Brown, Mike. Rescue Services. 2004. (Twentieth-Century Developments in Fashion & Costume Ser.). (Illus.). 64p. (YA). (gr. 7-18). lib. bdg. 19.95 *(978-1-59084-428-1(9))* Mason Crest.
Brown, Tessa. Costume Crafts. 2010. (Creative Crafts for Kids Ser.). 32p. (J). (gr. 2-5). lib. bdg. 28.00 *(978-1-4339-3555-8(4));* (Illus.). pap. 10.50 *(978-1-4339-3556-5(2))* Stevens, Gareth Publishing LLLP. (Gareth Stevens Learning Library).
Croll, Jennifer. Bad Girls of Fashion: Style Rebels Through the Ages. Buchholc, Ada, illus. 2016. (ENG.). 208p. (J). pap. 14.95 *(978-1-55451-785-5(0))* Annick Pr., Ltd. CAN. Dist: Publishers Group West (PGW).
Culp, Jennifer. Cosplay, 01 vols., 1. 2016. (Role-Playing for Fun & Profit Ser.). (ENG.). 48p. (J). pap. 11.75 *(978-1-4777-8761-8(5),* Rosen Central) Rosen Publishing Group, Inc., The.
Doudna, Kelly. Clothing Around the World, 1 vol. 2004. (Around the World Ser.). (ENG., Illus.). 24p. (J). (gr. k-3). lib. bdg. 24.21 *(978-1-59197-565-6(4),* SandCastle) ABDO Publishing Co.
Fancy Dress Princess. 2004. (Fun Kits Ser.). (Illus.). 48p. (J). *(978-1-84229-733-9(3))* Top That! Publishing PLC.
Fremont, Eleanor. Picture Me As a Dinosaur. 2003. (Baby Costume Minis Ser.). (Illus.). 10p. (J). (gr. -1-18). bds. 4.99 *(978-1-57151-568-1(2))* Playhouse Publishing.
Galford, Ellen. Festivals. 2004. (Twentieth-Century Developments in Fashion & Costume Ser.). (Illus.). 64p. (YA). (gr. 7-18). lib. bdg. 19.95 *(978-1-59084-423-6(8))* Mason Crest.
—Religious Costumes. 2004. (Twentieth-Century Developments in Fashion & Costume Ser.). (Illus.). 64p. (YA). (gr. 7-18). lib. bdg. 19.95 *(978-1-59084-429-8(7))* Mason Crest.
Harris, Carol & Brown, Mike. Accessories. 2004. (Twentieth-Century Developments in Fashion & Costume Ser.). (Illus.). 64p. (YA). (gr. 7-18). lib. bdg. 19.95 *(978-1-59084-419-9(X))* Mason Crest.
—Ceremonial Costumes. 2004. (Twentieth-Century Developments in Fashion & Costume Ser.). (Illus.). 64p. (YA). (gr. 7-18). lib. bdg. 19.95 *(978-1-59084-424-3(6))* Mason Crest.
—Children's Costumes. 2004. (Twentieth-Century Developments in Fashion & Costume Ser.). (Illus.). 64p. (YA). (gr. 7-18). lib. bdg. 19.95 *(978-1-59084-420-5(3))* Mason Crest.
—Women's Costumes. 2004. (Twentieth-Century Developments in Fashion & Costume Ser.). (Illus.). 64p. (YA). (gr. 7-18). lib. bdg. 19.95 *(978-1-59084-421-2(1))* Mason Crest.
Heiter, Celeste. Costumes of Asia: A Connoisseur's Coloring Book. Pulido, Rene, illus. 2010. (ENG.). 48p. (J). (gr. k-5). pap. 4.95 *(978-1-934159-20-0(4))* ThingsAsian Pr.
—Fashion Asia: Patterns & Designs of Traditional Cultures. Pulido, Rene, illus. 2010. (ENG.). 224p. (J). (gr. -1-3). pap. 9.95 *(978-1-934159-19-4(0))* ThingsAsian Pr.
Jones, Jen. Costume Parties: Planning a Party That Makes Your Friends Say Wow!, 1 vol. 2014. (Perfect Parties Ser.). (ENG.). 32p. (gr. 3-4). lib. bdg. 27.99 *(978-1-4765-4007-8(1),* Snap Bks.) Capstone Press of Coughlan Cos.
Kenney, Karen Latchana. Cool Costumes: How to Stage Your Very Own Show, 1 vol. 2010. (Cool Performances Ser.). (ENG., Illus.). 32p. (gr. 3-6). 28.50 *(978-1-60453-714-7(0),* Checkerboard Library) ABDO Publishing Co.
Larson, Jessica. FX! Costumes & Makeup. 2017. (Time for Kids Nonfiction Readers Ser.). lib. bdg. 22.10 ***(978-0-606-40270-5(5))*** Turtleback Bks.
—FX! Makeup & Costumes (Grade 7) 2017. (TIME for KIDS(r) Nonfiction Readers Ser.). (Illus.). 64p. (gr. 7-7). pap. 10.99 ***(978-1-4938-3613-0(7))*** Teacher Created Materials, Inc.
Lee Humphrey, Robert, ed. Culture & Costumes: Symbols of Their Period, 13 vols., Set. (Illus.). 64p. (YA). (gr. 7-18). lib. bdg. *(978-1-59084-430-4(0))* Mason Crest.
Madan, Fredric C. Greer Garson Paper Dolls. Madan, Fredric C. & Ernst, Clara, illus. 2007. (ENG.). 16p. pap. 12.00 *(978-0-9790668-6-3(7))* Paper Studio Pr.
McNab, Chris. Everyday Dress. 2004. (Twentieth-Century Developments in Fashion & Costume Ser.). (Illus.). 64p. (YA). (gr. 7-18). lib. bdg. 19.95 *(978-1-59084-427-4(0))* Mason Crest.
Mingo, Norman. Rita Hayworth Paper Dolls. Taliadoros, Jenny, ed. Mingo, Norman & Ernst, Clara, illus. 2006. 16p. pap. 12.00 *(978-0-9790668-0-1(8))* Paper Studio Pr.
Mitchell, Alycen. The Performing Arts. 2004. (Twentieth-Century Developments in Fashion & Costume Ser.). (Illus.). 64p. (YA). (gr. 7-18). lib. bdg. 19.95 *(978-1-59084-426-7(2))* Mason Crest.
Nelson, Robin. Clothing. 2004. (First Step Nonfiction - Basic Human Needs Ser.). (ENG., Illus.). 8p. (gr. -1-1). pap. 4.95 *(978-0-8225-3927-8(6),* Lerner Pubns.) Lerner Publishing Group.
Olsen, Mary-Kate & Olsen, Ashley. Mary-Kate & Ashley Style Secrets. 2005. (ENG., Illus.). 160p. *(978-0-00-720982-8(7))* HarperCollins Pubs. Australia.
Ross, Timothy & Whitt, Shannon. Clever Costumes. 2013. (Crafty Pants Ser.: 4). (ENG.). 64p. (J). (gr. 1). 16.99 *(978-1-935703-31-0(5))* Downtown Bookworks.
Rowland-Warne, L. Trajes. (Coleccion Biblioteca Visual).Tr. of Costumes. (SPA.). 64p. (YA). (gr. 5-8). *(978-84-372-3768-8(8))* Altea, Ediciones, S.A. - Grupo Santillana.
Shirley, Rebekah Joy. Dressing up Fun: Make Your Own Costumes at Home. Fairclough, Chris, photos by. 2012. (ENG., Illus.). 128p. (J). pap. 9.95 *(978-1-84837-915-2(3))* Arcturus Publishing GBR. Dist: Bookmasters Distribution.
—I Want to Be a Fairy. 2011. (Let's Play Dress up Ser.). (ENG., Illus.). 24p. (J). (gr. k-3). pap. 10.60 *(978-1-61533-396-7(7));* lib. bdg. 25.25 *(978-1-61533-358-5(4))* Windmill Bks.
—I Want to Be a Knight. 2011. (Let's Play Dress up Ser.). (ENG., Illus.). 24p. (J). (gr. k-3). lib. bdg. 25.25 *(978-1-61533-354-7(1))* Windmill Bks.
—I Want to Be a Pirate. 2011. (Let's Play Dress up Ser.). (ENG., Illus.). 24p. (J). (gr. k-3). pap. 10.60 *(978-1-61533-393-6(2));* lib. bdg. 25.25 *(978-1-61533-355-4(X))* Windmill Bks.
—I Want to Be a Princess. 2011. (Let's Play Dress up Ser.). (ENG., Illus.). 24p. (J). (gr. k-3). pap. 10.60 *(978-1-61533-394-3(0));* lib. bdg. 25.25 *(978-1-61533-356-1(8))* Windmill Bks.
—I Want to Be a Robot. 2011. (Let's Play Dress up Ser.). (ENG., Illus.). 24p. (J). (gr. k-3). pap. 10.60 *(978-1-61533-395-0(9));* lib. bdg. 25.25 *(978-1-61533-357-8(6))* Windmill Bks.
—I Want to Be an Astronaut. 2011. (Let's Play Dress up Ser.). (ENG., Illus.). 24p. (J). (gr. k-3). pap. 10.60 *(978-1-61533-397-4(5));* lib. bdg. 25.25 *(978-1-61533-359-2(2))* Windmill Bks.
Skillicorn, Helen. Spooky Crafts. 2010. (Creative Crafts for Kids Ser.). 32p. (J). (gr. 2-5). lib. bdg. 28.00 *(978-1-4339-3564-0(3));* (Illus.). pap. 10.50 *(978-1-4339-3565-7(1))* Stevens, Gareth Publishing LLLP. (Gareth Stevens Learning Library).
Svitil, Torene & Dunkleburger, Amy. So You Want to Work in Set Design, Costuming, or Make-Up? 2008. (Careers in Film & Television Ser.). (Illus.). 128p. (J). (gr. 6-9). lib. bdg. 33.27 *(978-0-7660-2740-4(6))* Enslow Pubs., Inc.
Taliadoros, Jenny, ed. The Lollypop Crowd Stand-up Paper Dolls. 2007. (Illus.). 8p. pap. 12.00 *(978-0-9795053-1-7(3))* Paper Studio Pr.
Thomas, Mark & National Geographic Learning Staff. Clothes in Colonial America. 2012. (ENG., Illus.). 24p. (C). (gr. -1-2). pap. 7.95 *(978-0-516-23490-8(0))* National Geographic School Publishing, Inc.
Tierney, Tom. Fashions from India. 2013. (Dover Fashion Coloring Book Ser.). (ENG., Illus.). 48p. (J). (gr. 3-12). pap. 4.99 *(978-0-486-43040-9(5))* Dover Pubns., Inc.
—Mexican Folk Dance Paper Dolls. 2013. (Dover Paper Dolls Ser.). (ENG.). 32p. (gr. 3-8). pap. 9.99 *(978-0-486-48831-8(4))* Dover Pubns., Inc.
Valliant, Regina. Judy Garland Cut-Out Dolls. Valliant, Regina & Lunzer, Lee, illus. 2007. (ENG.). 16p. pap. 12.00 *(978-0-9790668-9-4(1))* Paper Studio Pr.
Wolf, Jackie. Picture Me Easter Baby (mini Bunny) 2003. (Baby Costume Minis Ser.). (Illus.). 10p. (J). (gr. -1-18). bds. 2.99 *(978-1-57151-566-7(6))* Playhouse Publishing.
—Picture Me Easter Baby (mini Chick) 2003. (Illus.). 10p. (J). (gr. -1-18). bds. 2.99 *(978-1-57151-565-0(8))* Playhouse Publishing.

COSTUME—HISTORY

Brooke, Iris. English Costume of the Early Middle Ages. Landes, William-Alan, ed. 3rd rev. exp. ed. 2003. (Illus.). 96p. (gr. 4-12). pap. 23.00 *(978-0-88734-945-4(5))* Players Pr., Inc.
Fischell, Emma. Northern Europe. 2004. (Cultures & Costumes Ser.). (Illus.). 64p. (YA). (gr. 7-18). lib. bdg. 19.95 *(978-1-59084-439-7(4))* Mason Crest.
Greig, Charlotte. Oceania. 2004. (Cultures & Costumes Ser.). (Illus.). 64p. (YA). (gr. 7-18). lib. bdg. 19.95 *(978-1-59084-432-8(7))* Mason Crest.
Hammond, Paula. Italy & Switzerland. 2004. (Cultures & Costumes Ser.). (Illus.). 64p. (YA). (gr. 7-18). lib. bdg. 19.95 *(978-1-59084-438-0(6))* Mason Crest.
Harris, Carol & Brown, Mike. Men's Costumes. 2004. (Twentieth-Century Developments in Fashion & Costume Ser.). (Illus.). 64p. (YA). (gr. 7-18). lib. bdg. 19.95 *(978-1-59084-422-9(X))* Mason Crest.
Mitchell, Alycen. France. 2004. (Cultures & Costumes Ser.). (Illus.). 64p. (YA). (gr. 7-18). lib. bdg. 19.95 *(978-1-59084-442-7(4),* 1247999) Mason Crest.
Peacock, John. The Story of Costume. 2006. (ENG., Illus.). 48p. 19.95 *(978-0-500-51309-5(0),* 551309) Thames & Hudson.
Reid, Struan & Halstead, Rachel. Clothes: Discover How People Dressed Around the World With 30 Great Step-by-Step Projects. 2008. (ENG.). 64p. (J). (gr. 4-7). pap. 7.99 *(978-1-84476-523-2(7))* Anness Publishing GBR. Dist: National Bk. Network.
Scott, Margaret. Medieval Clothing & Costumes. 2004. (Library of the Middle Ages Ser.). (Illus.). 64p. (gr. 5-8). lib. bdg. 31.95 *(978-0-8239-3991-6(X),* Rosen Reference) Rosen Publishing Group, Inc., The.
Skinner, Tina. Fashionable Clothing from the Sears Catalogs, Mid-1940s. 2003. (ENG., Illus.). 160p. (gr. 10-13). pap. 29.95 *(978-0-7643-1858-0(6),* 9780764318580) Schiffer Publishing, Ltd.
Twentieth-Century Developments in Fashion & Costume, 12 vols., Set. (Illus.). 64p. (YA). (gr. 7-18). lib. bdg. *(978-1-59084-417-5(3))* Mason Crest.

COSTUME DESIGN

Anton, Carrie, ed. Paper Doll Fashion Fun: Make paper doll clothes with the supplies Inside! Decaire, Camela, illus. 2007. 54p. (J). (gr. 4-7). pap. 17.95 *(978-1-59369-284-1(6))* American Girl Publishing, Inc.
Bjorklund, Ruth. Costume Design in Theater. 2016. (Exploring Theater Ser.). 96p. (J). lib. bdg. 42.79 *(978-1-5026-2277-8(7))* Cavendish Square Publishing.
Blumenthal, Deborah. Fancy Party Gowns: The Story of Ann Cole Lowe. Freeman, Laura, illus. 2017. (ENG.). 40p. (J). (gr. -1-3). 17.99 *(978-1-4998-0239-9(0))* Little Bee Books Inc.
Claybourne, Anna. Customize Your Clothes. 2013. (Illus.). 32p. (J). lib. bdg. 27.10 *(978-1-59920-693-6(5))* Black Rabbit Bks.
Dunn, Mary R. I Want to Be a Fashion Designer. 2009. (Dream Jobs Ser.). 24p. (gr. 2-3). 42.50 *(978-1-61512-206-6(0),* PowerKids Pr.) Rosen Publishing Group, Inc., The.
—Quiero Ser Diseñador de Modas. 2009.Tr. of I Want to Be a Fashion Designer. (SPA., Illus.). 24p. pap. 8.25 *(978-1-4358-3433-0(X),* Editorial Buenas Letras) Rosen Publishing Group, Inc., The.
Hilton, Lisa. Inventions in Fashion: From Rawhide to Rayon. 2016. (Art & Invention Ser.). 112p. (YA). lib. bdg. 42.79 *(978-1-5026-2305-8(6))* Cavendish Square Publishing.
Klutz Editors, ed. My Style Studio: Design & Trace Your Own Fashions. 2014. (ENG.). 48p. (J). (gr. 3). 21.99 *(978-0-545-65053-3(4))* Klutz.
Kuskowski, Alex. Cool Refashioned Odds & Ends: Fun & Easy Fashion Projects, 1 vol. 2016. (ENG.). 32p. (J). *(978-1-62403-702-3(X))* ABDO Publishing Co.
—Cool Refashioned Scarves & Ties: Fun & Easy Fashion Projects, 1 vol. 2016. (ENG.). 32p. (J). *(978-1-62403-703-0(8))* ABDO Publishing Co.
—Cool Refashioned Sweaters: Fun & Easy Fashion Projects, 1 vol. 2016. (ENG.). 32p. (J). *(978-1-62403-704-7(6))* ABDO Publishing Co.
—Cool Refashioned T-Shirts: Fun & Easy Fashion Projects, 1 vol. 2016. (ENG.). 32p. (J). *(978-1-62403-705-4(4))* ABDO Publishing Co.
Lambert, Nancy. Clothes Designer: Cut, Color, Make & Create! Feyer, Diane Le, illus. 2016. (My Fashion Studio Ser.). (ENG.). 144p. (J). (gr. 3). pap. 12.99 *(978-1-78445-642-9(X))* Top That! Publishing PLC GBR. Dist: Independent Pubs. Group.
LeLarge, Blandine. Fashion Design Lookbook: More Than 50 Creative Tips & Techniques for the Fashion-Forward Artist. 2014. (ENG., Illus.). 128p. (J). (gr. 5-11). pap. 16.95 *(978-1-60058-436-7(5))* Quarto Publishing Group USA.
Low, Rachel. Girl's Guide to DIY Fashion: Design & Sew 5 Complete Outfits * Mood Boards * Fashion Sketching * Choosing Fabric * Adding Style. 2015. (ENG., Illus.). 192p. (J). (gr. 2-8). pap. 19.95 *(978-1-60705-995-0(9),* FunStitch Studio) C & T Publishing.
Mason, Helen. Costume Designer. 2014. (Creative Careers Ser.). 48p. (J). (gr. 4-8). pap. 84.30 *(978-1-4824-1289-5(6))* Stevens, Gareth Publishing LLLP.
Matthews, Elizabeth. Different Like Coco. Matthews, Elizabeth, illus. 2007. (ENG., Illus.). 40p. (J). (gr. k-4). 16.99 *(978-0-7636-2548-1(5))* Candlewick Pr.
Menten, Ted. Paper Doll Design Studio. 2013. (Dover Paper Dolls Ser.). (ENG.). 48p. (J). (gr. 2-5). pap. 9.99 *(978-0-486-49004-5(1))* Dover Pubns., Inc.
Mihaly, Christy. Getting Paid to Make Cosplay Costumes & Props. 2016. (Turning Your Tech Hobbies into a Career Ser.). 00080p. (J). (gr. 7-7). 35.75 *(978-1-5081-7302-1(8))* Rosen Publishing Group, Inc., The.
Morreale, Marie. Bethany Mota. 2016. (Real Bios Ser.). (ENG., Illus.). 48p. (J). lib. bdg. 29.00 *(978-0-531-22378-9(7),* Children's Pr.) Scholastic Library Publishing.
Niven, Felicia Lowenstein. Fabulous Fashions of The 1920s. 2011. (Fabulous Fashions of the Decades Ser.). (Illus.). 48p. (J). (gr. 5-9). lib. bdg. 25.27 *(978-0-7660-3551-5(4))* Enslow Pubs., Inc.
—Fabulous Fashions of The 1930s. 2011. (Fabulous Fashions of the Decades Ser.). (Illus.). 48p. (J). (gr. 5-9). lib. bdg. 25.27 *(978-0-7660-3824-0(6))* Enslow Pubs., Inc.
—Fabulous Fashions of The 1940s. 2011. (Fabulous Fashions of the Decades Ser.). (Illus.). 48p. (J). (gr. 5-9). lib. bdg. 25.27 *(978-0-7660-3552-2(2))* Enslow Pubs., Inc.
—Fabulous Fashions of The 1950s. 2011. (Fabulous Fashions of the Decades Ser.). (Illus.). 48p. (J). (gr. 5-9). lib. bdg. 25.27 *(978-0-7660-3825-7(4))* Enslow Pubs., Inc.
—Fabulous Fashions of The 1960s. 2011. (Fabulous Fashions of the Decades Ser.). (Illus.). 48p. (J). (gr. 5-9). lib. bdg. 25.27 *(978-0-7660-3553-9(0))* Enslow Pubs., Inc.
—Fabulous Fashions of The 1970s. 2011. (Fabulous Fashions of the Decades Ser.). (Illus.). 48p. (J). (gr. 5-9). lib. bdg. 25.27 *(978-0-7660-3826-4(2))* Enslow Pubs., Inc.
—Fabulous Fashions of The 1980s. 2011. (Fabulous Fashions of the Decades Ser.). (Illus.). 48p. (J). (gr. 5-9). lib. bdg. 25.27 *(978-0-7660-3554-6(9))* Enslow Pubs., Inc.
—Fabulous Fashions of The 1990s. 2011. (Fabulous Fashions of the Decades Ser.). (Illus.). 48p. (J). (gr. 5-9). lib. bdg. 25.27 *(978-0-7660-3827-1(0))* Enslow Pubs., Inc.
Parot, Annelore, illus. Kokeshi Style: Design Your Own Kokeshi Fashions. 2012. (ENG.). 120p. 14.99 *(978-1-4521-1372-2(6))* Chronicle Bks. LLC.
Petrillo, Lisa. Vera Wang. 2011. (Profiles in Fashion Ser.). (Illus.). 112p. 28.95 *(978-1-59935-150-6(1))* Reynolds, Morgan Inc.
Roshell, Starshine & Kelley, K. C. A Day with a Fashion Designer. 2008. (Reading Rocks! Ser.). (ENG., Illus.). 32p. (J). (gr. 2-5). 28.50 *(978-1-60253-096-6(3),* 200759) Child's World, Inc., The.
Rubin, Susan Goldman. Hot Pink: The Life & Fashions of Elsa Schiaparelli. 2015. (ENG., Illus.). 56p. (J). (gr. 5-9). 21.95 *(978-1-4197-1642-3(5),* Abrams Bks. for Young Readers) Abrams, Inc.
Sanchez Vegara, Isabel & Albero, Ana. Coco Chanel. 2016. (Little People, Big Dreams Ser.). (ENG.). 32p. (J). (gr. k-3). 14.99 *(978-1-84780-784-7(4));* (Illus.). 14.99 *(978-1-84780-771-7(2))* Quarto Publishing Group UK GBR. (Frances Lincoln Children's Bks.). Dist: Hachette Bk. Group, Littlehampton Bk Services, Ltd.
Scott-Smith, Louise. Fashion Rebel Outfit Maker: Mix & Mismatch Styles. 2015. (ENG., Illus.). 100p. (J). (gr. 3-6). 17.95 *(978-0-500-65045-5(4),* 565045) Thames & Hudson.
Scott-Smith, Louise & Vaux, Georgia. I Can Make My Own Accessories: Easy-To-follow Patterns to Make & Customize Fashion Accessories. 2016. (ENG., Illus.). 176p. (J). (gr. 2-7). 19.95 *(978-0-500-65082-0(9),* 565082) Thames & Hudson.
Senker, Cath. Fashion Designers. 2012. (Celebrity Secrets Ser.). (ENG., Illus.). 24p. (J). (gr. 5-8). pap. 8.25 *(978-1-4488-7082-0(8));* lib. bdg. 22.60 *(978-1-4488-7036-3(4))* Rosen Publishing Group, Inc., The. (PowerKids Pr.).
Slee, Natasha. Style Guide - Fashion from Head to Toe: 35 Prints to Colour. Stadtlander, Becca, illus. 2015. (ENG.). 72p. (J). pap. 19.99 *(978-1-84780-734-2(8),* Wide Eyed Editions) Quarto Publishing Group UK GBR. Dist: Littlehampton Bk Services, Ltd.

—Style Guide: Fashion from Head to Toe. Stadtlander, Becca, illus. 2016. (ENG.). 72p. (J). (gr. 1-4). pap. 19.99 *(978-1-84780-830-1(1),* Wide Eyed Editions) Quarto Publishing Group UK GBR. Dist: Hachette Bk. Group.

Sun, Jennie. Fashion. 2011. (Dover Doodle Bks.). (ENG.). 64p. (J). (gr. 3-5). pap. 5.99 *(978-0-486-48050-3(X))* Dover Pubns., Inc.

Tierney, Tom. Southern Belle Ball Gowns Paper Dolls. 2006. (Dover Paper Dolls Ser.). (ENG., Illus.). 32p. (gr. 3-8). per. 6.95 *(978-0-486-45365-1(0))* Dover Pubns., Inc.

Van Haeringen, Annemarie. Coco & the Little Black Dress. 2015. (ENG., Illus.). 32p. (J). 16.95 *(978-0-7358-4239-7(6))* North-South Bks., Inc.

Vargas, Constanza Orozco. Coco Chanel: Una Mujer Salida del Molde. 2005. (100 Personajes Ser.). (SPA.). 152p. (YA). *(978-958-30-1765-0(5))* Panamericana Editorial.

Ward, Wendy. My One-of-a-Kind Fashion Design. Neild, Robyn, illus. 2014. (ENG.). 128p. (J). (gr. 4-8). pap. 14.99 *(978-1-4022-9541-6(3),* Sourcebooks Jabberwocky) Sourcebooks, Inc.

Watt, Fiona. Fashion Designer Summer Collection. Baggott, Stella & Miller, Antonia, illus. 2013. (Sticker Dolly Dressing Ser.). (ENG.). 24p. (J). (gr. -1-3). 8.99 *(978-0-7945-3008-2(7),* Usborne) EDC Publishing.

Wood, Alix. Fashion Design. 2017. (Design It! Ser.). 32p. (gr. 3-4). pap. 63.00 ***(978-1-5382-0781-9(8))*** Stevens, Gareth Publishing LLLP.

Wood, Anita. Fashion Doodles, 1 vol. Kalis, Jennifer, illus. 2014. (ENG.). 240p. (J). pap. 16.99 *(978-1-4236-3607-6(4))* Gibbs Smith, Publisher.

Worth, Richard. Vera Wang: Fashion Designer. 2016. (Influential Asians Ser.). 128p. (J). (gr. 7-6). 37.27 *(978-0-7660-7903-8(1))* Enslow Pubs., Inc.

COSTUME DESIGN—FICTION

Berk, Sheryl & Berk, Carrie. Fashion Academy. 2015. (Fashion Academy Ser.: 1). (ENG.). 160p. (J). (gr. 5-8). pap. 6.99 *(978-1-4926-0162-3(4),* Sourcebooks Jabberwocky) Sourcebooks, Inc.

—Model Madness. 2017. (Fashion Academy Ser.: 4). (ENG.). 192p. (J). (gr. 5-8). pap. 7.99 *(978-1-4926-4496-5(X),* 9781492644965, Sourcebooks Jabberwocky) Sourcebooks, Inc.

A Change of Lace. 2014. (Sew Zoey Ser.: 9). (ENG., Illus.). 176p. (J). (gr. 3-7). pap. 6.99 *(978-1-4814-1961-1(7),* Simon Spotlight) Simon Spotlight.

Child, Lauren. But I Am an Alligator. 2008. (Charlie & Lola Ser.). (ENG.). 24p. (J). (gr. -1-k). mass mkt. 3.99 *(978-0-448-44697-4(9),* Grosset & Dunlap) Penguin Young Readers Group.

Christelow, Eileen. Five Little Monkeys Trick-Or-Treat. 2013. (Five Little Monkeys Story Ser.). (ENG., Illus.). 40p. (J). (gr. -1-3). 16.99 *(978-0-547-85893-7(0))* Houghton Mifflin Harcourt Publishing Co.

Couteaud, Cheryl. A Monster for Halloween. Couteaud, Cheryl, illus. 2009. (Illus.). 24p. pap. 10.96 *(978-1-4251-8563-3(0))* Trafford Publishing.

Coven, Wanda. Heidi Heckelbeck in Disguise. Burris, Priscilla, illus. 2012. (Heidi Heckelbeck Ser.: 4). (ENG.). 128p. (J). (gr. k-2). 16.99 *(978-1-4424-4169-9(0));* pap. 5.99 *(978-1-4424-4168-2(2))* Little Simon. (Little Simon).

Davis, Jacky & Soman, David. Ladybug Girl & the Dress-Up Dilemma. Soman, David, illus. 2014. (Ladybug Girl Ser.). (ENG., Illus.). 40p. (J). (gr. -1-k). 17.99 *(978-0-8037-3584-2(7),* Dial Bks) Penguin Publishing Group.

Friedman, Laurie. Mallory & Mary Ann Take New York. Kalis, Jennifer, illus. 2014. (Mallory Ser.: 19). (ENG.). 160p. (J). (gr. 2-5). pap. 5.95 *(978-1-4677-0935-4(2),* Darby Creek) Lerner Publishing Group.

Gallion, Sue Lowell. Pug & Pig Trick-or-Treat. Wan, Joyce, illus. 2017. (Pug & Pig Ser.). (ENG.). 40p. (J). (gr. -1-3). 17.99 ***(978-1-4814-4977-9(X),*** Beach Lane Bks.) Beach Lane Bks.

Gurevich, Margaret. Balancing ACT. Hagel, Brooke, illus. 2015. (Chloe by Design Ser.). (ENG.). 384p. (gr. 4-8). 14.95 *(978-1-62370-258-8(5))* Capstone Young Readers of Coughlan Cos.

—Chloe by Design. 4 vols. Hagel, Brooke, illus. 2015. (Chloe by Design Ser.). (ENG.). 96p. (gr. 5-8). 101.28 *(978-1-4965-1995-5(7))* Stone Arch Bks.

—Design Destiny, 1 vol. Hagel, Brooke, illus. 2014. (Chloe by Design Ser.). (ENG.). 96p. (gr. 5-8). 25.32 *(978-1-4342-9180-6(4))* Stone Arch Bks.

—Design Disaster. Hagel, Brooke, illus. 2015. (Chloe by Design Ser.). (ENG.). 96p. (gr. 5-8). 25.32 *(978-1-4965-0505-7(0))* Stone Arch Bks.

—Design Diva, 1 vol. Hagel, Brooke, illus. 2014. (Chloe by Design Ser.). (ENG.). 96p. (gr. 5-8). 25.32 *(978-1-4342-9177-6(4))* Stone Arch Bks.

—Fashion Week Finale. Hagel, Brooke, illus. 2015. (Chloe by Design Ser.). (ENG.). 96p. (gr. 5-8). 25.32 *(978-1-4965-0507-1(7))* Stone Arch Bks.

—The First Cut, 1 vol. Hagel, Brooke, illus. 2014. (Chloe by Design Ser.). (ENG.). 96p. (gr. 5-8). 25.32 *(978-1-4342-9178-3(2))* Stone Arch Bks.

—Intern Ambition. Hagel, Brooke, illus. 2015. (Chloe by Design Ser.). (ENG.). 96p. (gr. 5-8). 25.32 *(978-1-4965-0504-0(2))* Stone Arch Bks.

—Runway Rundown. Hagel, Brooke, illus. 2015. (Chloe by Design Ser.). (ENG.). 96p. (gr. 5-8). 25.32 *(978-1-4965-0506-4(9))* Stone Arch Bks.

—Unraveling, 1 vol. Hagel, Brooke, illus. 2014. (Chloe by Design Ser.). (ENG.). 96p. (gr. 5-8). 25.32 *(978-1-4342-9179-0(0))* Stone Arch Bks.

Hills, Tad & Hills, Tad. Duck & Goose, Honk! Quack! Boo! 2017. (Duck & Goose Ser.). (ENG., Illus.). 40p. (J). (gr. -1-2). 16.99 ***(978-1-5247-0175-8(0));*** lib. bdg. 19.99 ***(978-1-5247-0176-5(9))*** Random Hse. Children's Bks. (Schwartz & Wade Bks.).

Kushner, Elisabeth. The Purim Superhero. Byrne, Mike, illus. 2013. (Purim Ser.). (ENG.). 32p. (J). (gr. -1-3). 7.95 *(978-0-7613-9062-6(6),* Kar-Ben Publishing) Lerner Publishing Group.

Landry, Leo. Trick or Treat. 2012. (ENG., Illus.). 32p. (J). (gr. -1-3). 12.99 *(978-0-547-24969-8(1))* Houghton Mifflin Harcourt Publishing Co.

Marsoli, Lisa Ann & Disney Book Group Staff. The Halloween Ball. Disney Storybook Art Team, illus. 2013. (ENG.). 24p. (J). (gr. -1-k). pap. 5.99 *(978-1-4231-7144-7(6))* Disney Pr.

McGrath, Barbara Barbieri. Halloween Colors. Tagel, Peggy, illus. 2016. (First Celebrations Ser.). (ENG.). 12p. (J). (— 1). bds. 6.95 *(978-1-58089-533-0(6))* Charlesbridge Publishing, Inc.

Mia's Recipe for Disaster. 2014. (Cupcake Diaries: 22). (ENG., Illus.). 160p. (J). (gr. 3-7). pap. 6.99 *(978-1-4814-1864-5(5),* Simon Spotlight) Simon Spotlight.

Muncaster, Harriet. Happy Halloween, Witch's Cat! Muncaster, Harriet, illus. 2015. (ENG., Illus.). 32p. (J). (gr. -1-3). 15.99 *(978-0-06-222916-8(8))* HarperCollins Pubs.

Norriss, Andrew. Friends for Life. 2015. (ENG.). 240p. (J). (gr. 3-7). 17.99 *(978-0-545-85186-2(6))* Scholastic, Inc.

Perkins, Stephanie. Lola & the Boy Next Door. (ENG.). (YA). (gr. 9). 2013. 368p. pap. 10.99 *(978-0-14-242201-4(0),* Speak) 2011. 352p. 16.99 *(978-0-525-42328-7(1),* Dutton Books for Young Readers) Penguin Young Readers Group.

Reeve, Penny. The Back Leg of a Goat: A Tania Abbey Adventure. Apps, Fred, illus. 2008. (Tania Abbey Adventure Ser.). (ENG.). 96p. (J). pap. 6.99 *(978-1-84550-340-6(6),* c8e23bb3-9904-4201-971e-e57faa66b8f3) Christian Focus Pubns. GBR. Dist: Bookmasters Distribution.

RH Disney. A Paw-Some Costume Party! (Disney Palace Pets Whisker Haven Tales) RH Disney, illus. 2017. (Little Golden Book Ser.). (ENG., Illus.). 24p. (J). (-k). 4.99 ***(978-0-7364-3723-3(1),*** Golden/Disney) Random Hse. Children's Bks.

Ricci, Christine. Dora's Costume Party! Saunders, Zina, illus. 2005. (Dora the Explorer Ser.). (ENG.). 24p. (J). (gr. -1-2). pap. 3.99 *(978-1-4169-0010-8(1),* Simon Spotlight/Nickelodeon) Simon Spotlight/Nickelodeon.

Rim, Sujean. Birdie's Happiest Halloween. 2016. (ENG., Illus.). 40p. (J). (gr. -1-3). 16.99 *(978-0-316-40746-5(1))* Little Brown & Co.

Scollon, William. The Case of the Missing Sparkle-Izer. 2013. (Mickey & Friends World of Reading Ser.). (J). lib. bdg. 13.55 *(978-0-606-32292-8(2),* Turtleback) Turtleback Bks.

Scollon, William & Parent, Nancy. Blooming Bows. Disney Storybook Artists Staff, illus. 2013. (ENG.). 32p. (J). (gr. -1-1). pap. 3.99 *(978-1-4231-6691-7(4))* Disney Pr.

Silvano, Wendi J. Turkey Claus, 0 vols. Harper, Lee, illus. 2012. (ENG.). 40p. (J). (gr. -1-3). 16.99 *(978-0-7614-6239-2(2),* 9780761462392, Two Lions) Amazon Publishing.

Simon, Coco. Mia's Recipe for Disaster. 2014. (Cupcake Diaries: 22). lib. bdg. 17.20 *(978-0-606-36098-2(0))* Turtleback Bks.

Sticker Dolly Dressing Fashion Designer Paris Collection. 2017. (Sticker Dolly Dressing Fashion Designer Ser.). (ENG.). (J). pap. 9.99 ***(978-0-7945-3945-0(9),*** Usborne) EDC Publishing.

Stone, Phoebe. Paris for Two. 2016. (ENG.). 272p. (J). (gr. 3-7). 16.99 *(978-0-545-44362-3(8),* Levine, Arthur A. Bks.) Scholastic, Inc.

Stonebraker Wright, Susan. Enchanted Costume Shop. 2004. 73p. pap. 19.95 *(978-1-4137-3862-9(1))* America Star Bks.

Tate, Nancy. Grandmother Ellie's Attic. 2010. 232p. pap. 32.50 *(978-1-60976-033-5(6),* Eloquent Bks.) Strategic Book Publishing & Rights Agency (SBPRA).

Taylor, Chloe. Cute As a Button. Zhang, Nancy, illus. 2014. (Sew Zoey Ser.: 5). (ENG.). 176p. (J). (gr. 3-7). pap. 5.99 *(978-1-4814-0248-4(X),* Simon Spotlight) Simon Spotlight.

Taylor, Chloe. On Pins & Needles. Christy, Jana & Zhang, Nancy, illus. 2013. (Sew Zoey Ser.: 2). (ENG.). 160p. (J). (gr. 3-7). 15.99 *(978-1-4424-7937-1(X));* pap. 6.99 *(978-1-4424-7936-4(1))* Simon Spotlight. (Simon Spotlight).

—Ready to Wear. Christy, Jana & Zhang, Nancy, illus. 2013. (Sew Zoey Ser.: 1). (ENG.). 176p. (J). (gr. 3-7). pap. 6.99 *(978-1-4424-7933-3(7),* Simon Spotlight) Simon Spotlight.

—Swatch Out! Zhang, Nancy, illus. 2014. (Sew Zoey Ser.: 8). (ENG.). 176p. (J). (gr. 3-7). pap. 5.99 *(978-1-4814-1535-4(2),* Simon Spotlight) Simon Spotlight.

Wojciechowski, Susan. The Best Halloween of All. Meddaugh, Susan, illus. 2012. (ENG.). 24p. (J). (gr. -1-3). pap. 3.99 *(978-0-7636-6008-6(6))* Candlewick Pr.

COTE D'IVOIRE

Habeeb, William Mark. Ivory Coast. Rotberg, Robert I., ed. 2012. (Evolution of Africa's Major Nations Ser.). (Illus.). 80p. (J). (gr. 7). 22.95 *(978-1-4222-2197-6(0))* Mason Crest.

—Ivory Coast. 2011. (J). pap. *(978-1-4222-2225-6(X))* 2006. (Illus.). 79p. (YA). lib. bdg. 21.95 *(978-1-59084-808-1(X))* Mason Crest.

Hamilton, Janice. Ivory Coast in Pictures. 2nd rev. expurg. ed. 2004. (Visual Geography Ser.). (Illus.). 80p. (J). (gr. 5-12). 27.93 *(978-0-8225-1992-8(5))* Lerner Publishing Group.

Weber, Valerie J. I Come from Ivory Coast. 2006. (This Is My Story Ser.). (Illus.). 24p. (gr. 1-4). pap. 8.15 *(978-0-8368-7243-9(6));* lib. bdg. 22.00 *(978-0-8368-7236-1(3))* Stevens, Gareth Publishing LLLP. (Weekly Reader Leveled Readers).

COTTAGES

see Houses

COTTON

see also Fibers

Alonso, Manuel L. Algodon.Tr. of Cotton. (SPA.). 56p. (J). (gr. 2-3). 7.96 *(978-84-321-2743-4(4))* Rialp, Ediciones, S.A. ESP. Dist: Lectorum Pubns., Inc.

Gleason, Carrie. The Biography of Cotton. 2005. (How Did That Get There?). (ENG., Illus.). 32p. (J). (gr. 4-5). pap. *(978-0-7787-2516-9(2));* lib. bdg. *(978-0-7787-2480-3(8))* Crabtree Publishing Co.

Hayes, Amy. Turning Cotton into Clothes. 2015. (Step-By-Step Transformations Ser.). (ENG., Illus.). 24p. (J). (gr. 1-1). pap. 8.22 *(978-1-5026-0448-4(5))* Cavendish Square Publishing.

Malam, John. Journey of a T-Shirt, 1 vol. 2012. (Journey of A... Ser.). (ENG.). 32p. (gr. 1-3). pap. 8.29 *(978-1-4329-6611-9(1),* Heinemann First Library) Heinemann-Raintree.

Nelson, Robin. From Cotton to T-Shirt. 2003. (Start to Finish Ser.). (ENG., Illus.). 24p. (gr. k-3). lib. bdg. 19.93 *(978-0-8225-4661-0(2))* Lerner Publishing Group.

Ridley, Sarah. A Cotton T-Shirt. 2006. (How It's Made Ser.). (Illus.). 32p. (gr. 1-4). lib. bdg. 26.00 *(978-0-8368-6294-2(5),* Gareth Stevens Learning Library) Stevens, Gareth Publishing LLLP.

Schaefer, Lola M. Cotton Plant to Cotton Shirt. 2011. (Early Connections Ser.). (J). *(978-1-61672-633-1(4))* Benchmark Education Co.

COTTON MANUFACTURE

Hayes, Amy. Turning Cotton into Clothes. 2015. (Step-By-Step Transformations Ser.). (ENG., Illus.). 24p. (J). (gr. 1-1). pap. 8.22 *(978-1-5026-0448-4(5))* Cavendish Square Publishing.

Huff, Regan A. Eli Whitney: The Cotton Gin & American Manufacturing. 2005. (Library of American Lives & Times). (Illus.). 112p. (J). (gr. 4-8). lib. bdg. 34.60 *(978-0-8239-6628-8(3))* Rosen Publishing Group, Inc., The.

Nelson, Robin. From Cotton to T-Shirt. 2013. (Start to Finish, Second Series: Everyday Products Ser.). (ENG., Illus.). 24p. (gr. k-3). lib. bdg. 23.93 *(978-0-7613-6561-7(3),* Lerner Pubns.) Lerner Publishing Group.

COUGAR

see Puma

COUNSELING

see also Educational Counseling; Vocational Guidance

Coping: Help & Guidance for Teens in Need, 4 bks. Incl. Coping with Homelessness. Hurwitz, Sue & Hurwitz, Eugene. (YA). 1997. lib. bdg. 34.60 *(978-0-8239-2072-3(0),* COHOME); Coping with Sleep Disorders. Simpson, Carolyn. (J). 1996. lib. bdg. 34.60 *(978-0-8239-2068-6(2),* COSLDI); 192p. (gr. 7-12). (Illus.). Set lib. bdg. 101.00 *(978-0-8239-8042-0(1))* Rosen Publishing Group, Inc., The.

Flath, Camden. 21st-Century Counselors: New Approaches to Mental Health & Substance Abuse. 2010. (New Careers for the 21st Century Ser.). 64p. (YA). (gr. 7-18). pap. 9.95 *(978-1-4222-2046-7(X))* Mason Crest.

Landau, Elaine. Family Therapy. 2004. (Life Balance Ser.). (ENG.). 80p. (J). 20.50 *(978-0-531-12216-7(6),* Watts, Franklin) Scholastic Library Publishing.

Stewart, Jan. Getting along with Others. 2004. (ENG., Illus.). 32p. (J). pap. 9.95 *(978-0-89793-312-4(5),* Hunter Hse.) Turner Publishing Co.

COUNSELING—VOCATIONAL GUIDANCE

Smead, Rosemarie. Skills for Living-Adolescent Vol. 2 Vol. 2: Group Counseling Activities for Young Adolescents. 2004. (ENG., Illus.). 298p. pap. 37.99 *(978-0-87822-420-3(3),* 3185) Research Pr.

COUNTER-REFORMATION

see Reformation

COUNTERFEITS AND COUNTERFEITING—FICTION

Abdo, Kenny. Comic Relief, 1 vol. Doucet, Bob, illus. 2013. (Haven't Got a Clue! Ser.). (ENG.). 80p. (J). (gr. 3-6). lib. bdg. 27.07 *(978-1-61641-951-6(2),* Calico Chapter Bks) Magic Wagon.

Alger, Horatio. Jack's Ward. 2005. 28.95 *(978-1-4218-1454-4(4));* 260p. pap. 13.95 *(978-1-4218-1554-1(0))* 1st World Publishing, Inc. (1st World Library - Literary Society).

—Jack's Ward. 2006. pap. *(978-1-4065-0711-9(3))* Dodo Pr.

—Jack's Ward: Or, The Boy Guardian. 2006. 176p. pap. 19.99 *(978-1-4264-0882-3(X));* (ENG.). 168p. pap. 21.99 *(978-1-4264-0863-2(3))* Creative Media Partners, LLC.

—Timothy Crump's Ward. 2005. 27.95 *(978-1-4218-1451-3(X));* 220p. pap. 12.95 *(978-1-4218-1551-0(6))* 1st World Publishing, Inc. (1st World Library - Literary Society).

Baum, L. Frank. Mary Louise in the Country. 2011. 188p. pap. 14.95 *(978-1-4638-0069-7(X))* Rodgers, Alan Bks.

Baum, L. Frank & van Dyne, Edith. Mary Louise in the Country. 2011. 188p. 26.95 *(978-1-4638-9605-8(0))* Rodgers, Alan Bks.

Bollback, Anthony G. Mystery of the Counterfeit Money. 2012. 170p. (gr. 4-7). pap. 8.99 *(978-0-9849359-2-5(4))* Finding the Cause, LLC.

Bossley, Michele Martin. Cracked, 1 vol. 2007. (Orca Currents Ser.). (ENG.). (J). (gr. 5-9). 112p. lib. bdg. 14.95 *(978-1-55143-702-6(3));* 128p. per. 9.95 *(978-1-55143-700-2(7))* Orca Bk. Pubs. USA.

Kelly, David A. The Rangers Rustlers. Meyers, Mark, illus. 2016. (Ballpark Mysteries Ser.: Bk. 12). (ENG.). 112p. (J). (gr. 1-4). pap. 4.99 *(978-0-385-37881-9(5),* Random Hse. Bks. for Young Readers) Random Hse. Children's Bks.

Pierce, Tamora. Bloodhound. 2010. (Beka Cooper Ser.: Bk. 2). (ENG., Illus.). 576p. (YA). (gr. 7-11). pap. 10.99 *(978-0-375-83817-0(1),* Random Hse. Bks. for Young Readers) Random Hse. Children's Bks.

Roberts, Willo Davis. Rebel. 2005. 153p. (J). (gr. 3-7). 13.65 *(978-0-7569-5076-7(7))* Perfection Learning Corp.

—Rebel. 2012. (ENG., Illus.). 160p. (J). (gr. 3-7). pap. 8.99 *(978-0-689-85081-3(6),* Aladdin) Simon & Schuster Children's Publishing.

Sutton, Margaret. The Ghost Parade. Doane, Pelagie, illus. 2008. (Judy Bolton Mysteries Ser.). (ENG.). 240p. (J). (gr. 4-7). pap. 14.95 *(978-1-4290-9025-4(1))* Applewood Bks.

Timberlake, Amy. One Came Home. 2013. (ENG., Illus.). 272p. (J). (gr. 4-7). 16.99 *(978-0-375-86925-9(5),* Knopf Bks. for Young Readers) Random Hse. Children's Bks.

Van Draanen, Wendelin. Sammy Keyes & the Cold Hard Cash. 2010. (Sammy Keyes Ser.: Bk. 12). (ENG.). 320p. (J). (gr. 5-7). 8.99 *(978-0-440-42113-9(6),* Yearling) Random Hse. Children's Bks.

Van Dyne, Edith. Mary Louise. 2007. (ENG.). 148p. pap. 18.99 *(978-1-4264-1952-2(X));* 144p. pap. 19.99 *(978-1-4264-2063-4(3))* Creative Media Partners, LLC.

COUNTING BOOKS

Abignale, Michelle. The School Food Drive: Extend the Counting Sequence. 2013. (InfoMax Math Readers Ser.). (ENG.). 24p. (J). (gr. 1-2). pap. 49.50 *(978-1-4777-2161-2(4));* (Illus.). pap. 8.25 *(978-1-4777-2160-5(6))* Rosen Publishing Group, Inc., The. (Rosen Classroom).

Abrams, Pam. Can I Push the Button. 2009. 14p. 10.95 *(978-1-58117-903-0(0),* Intervisual/Piggy Toes) Bendon, Inc.

Abrams, Pam, et al. Candy 1 To 20. 2011. (ENG., Illus.). 20p. (J). (gr. -1 — 1). 8.99 *(978-1-4521-0293-1(7))* Chronicle Bks. LLC.

Acacia Publishing, creator. My Little Black Book of Numbers/Mi Libro Chiquito Negro de Numeros: Coutning from/Contar de 0 To 20. 2007. (ENG & SPA.). pap. 19.95 incl. audio compact disk *(978-0-9790826-7-2(6))* Acacia Publishing, Inc.

—My Little White Book of Numbers/Mi Libro Chiquito Blanco de Numeros: Counting from/Contar de 20 To 40. 2007. (ENG & SPA.). pap. 19.95 incl. audio compact disk *(978-0-9790826-8-9(4))* Acacia Publishing, Inc.

Accord Publishing Staff & Andrews McMeel Publishing, LLC Staff. Numbers: A Silly Slider Book. Cole, Jeff, illus. 2011. (ENG.). 12p. (J). (gr. -1-k). bds. 10.99 *(978-1-4494-0174-0(0))* Andrews McMeel Publishing.

Adamson, Thomas K. and Heather. 2, 4, Skip Count Some More. 2012. (Fun with Numbers Ser.). (ENG.). 32p. (gr. 1-2). pap. 47.70 *(978-1-4296-8303-6(1),* Aplus Bks.) Capstone Press of Coughlan Cos.

Adly, Muhammad S. Let's Count in Arabic, Bk. 1. 24p. *(978-1-894264-46-4(0))* Al-Attique Pubs., Inc.

Affaya, Colett & Affaya, Otman. Arkam, Numero & Numbers, 1 vol. Affaya, Colette, illus. 2009. 16p. pap. 24.95 *(978-1-60749-929-9(0))* America Star Bks.

Aigner-Clark, Julie. Asomate Y Ve Los Numeros. Zaidi, Nadeem, illus. 2004. (Baby Einstein Ser.). (SPA.). 16p. (J). bds. *(978-970-718-150-2(8),* Silver Dolphin en Español) Advanced Marketing, S. de R. L. de C. V.

Ainsworth, Kimberly. Hootenanny! A Festive Counting Book. Brown, Jo, illus. 2011. (ENG.). 32p. (J). (gr. -1-k). 12.99 *(978-1-4424-2273-5(4),* Little Simon) Little Simon.

Alaina, Maria. Counting Money, 1 vol. 2011. (Wonder Readers Early Level Ser.). (ENG.). (gr. -1-1). 32p. pap. 5.99 *(978-1-4296-7801-8(1));* 16p. pap. 35.94 *(978-1-4296-8081-3(4))* Capstone Press of Coughlan Cos. (Wonder Readers).

—You Can Count! 2011. (Wonder Readers Early Level Ser.). (ENG.). 16p. (gr. -1-1). pap. 35.94 *(978-1-4296-8210-7(8),* Wonder Readers) Capstone Press of Coughlan Cos.

Albee, Sarah. Elmo's 12 Days of Christmas. Swanson, Maggie, illus. 2015. (Little Golden Book Ser.). (ENG.). 24p. (J). (-k). 4.99 *(978-0-553-52430-7(5),* Golden Bks.) Random Hse. Children's Bks.

Alexander, Richard. Counting To 10: Number Names & Count Sequence. 2013. (InfoMax Math Readers Ser.). (ENG.). 16p. (J). (gr. k-1). pap. 42.00 *(978-1-4777-1968-8(7));* (Illus.). pap. 7.00 *(978-1-4777-1967-1(9))* Rosen Publishing Group, Inc., The. (Rosen Classroom).

Allan, Nicholas. Father Christmas Needs a Wee! Allan, Nicholas, illus. 2009. (ENG., Illus.). 32p. (J). (gr. -1-k). pap. 13.99 *(978-1-86230-825-1(X),* Red Fox) Random House Children's Books GBR. Dist: Independent Pubs. Group.

Allum, Margaret & Watson, Judy. How Many Peas in a Pod? 2006. (Illus.). 16p. pap. *(978-1-921049-43-9(X))* Little Hare Bks. AUS. Dist: HarperCollins Pubs. Australia.

American Museum of Natural History Staff. 1-2-3 Dinosaurs Bite: A Prehistoric Counting Book. 2012. (ENG., Illus.). 18p. (J). (gr. -1-2). bds. 6.95 *(978-1-4027-7722-6(1),* 1350121) Sterling Publishing Co., Inc.

Amery, Heather. What's Happening on the Farm? Cartwright, Stephen, illus. rev. ed. 2006. (What's Happening? Ser.). 32p. (J). (gr. -1-3). 5.99 *(978-0-7945-1288-0(7),* Usborne) EDC Publishing.

Anderson, Airlie, illus. Ten Little Ducks. 2008. (Activity Bks.). (ENG.). 24p. (J). (gr. -1-1). *(978-1-84643-182-1(4))* Child's Play International Ltd.

Anderson, Debby. Kindness Counts! Anderson, Debby, illus. 2007. (Illus.). 32p. (J). (gr. -1-3). 9.99 *(978-1-58134-861-3(4))* Crossway.

Anderson, Derek. Ten Pigs: An Epic Bath Adventure. Anderson, Derek, illus. 2015. (ENG., Illus.). 40p. (J). (gr. -1-k). 16.99 *(978-0-545-16846-5(5))* Scholastic, Inc.

Anderson, Jill. Counting with Sebastian Pig & Friends on the Farm. Amy Huntington, illus. 2013. (Math Fun with Sebastian Pig & Friends! Ser.). 32p. (J). (gr. k-3). pap. 7.95 *(978-0-7660-5980-1(4),* Enslow Elementary) Enslow Pubs., Inc.

—Counting with Sebastian Pig & Friends on the Farm. Huntington, Amy, illus. 2009. (Math Fun with Sebastian Pig & Friends! Ser.). 32p. (J). (gr. k-3). lib. bdg. 23.94 *(978-0-7660-3359-7(7))* Enslow Pubs., Inc.

—Money Math with Sebastian Pig & Friends at the Farmer's Market. Amy Huntington, illus. 2013. (Math Fun with Sebastian Pig & Friends! Ser.). 32p. (J). (gr. k-3). pap. 7.95 *(978-0-7660-5983-2(9),* Enslow Elementary) Enslow Pubs., Inc.

—Money Math with Sebastian Pig & Friends at the Farmer's Market. Huntington, Amy, illus. 2009. (Math Fun with Sebastian Pig & Friends! Ser.). 32p. (J). (gr. k-3). lib. bdg. 23.94 *(978-0-7660-3364-1(3))* Enslow Pubs., Inc.

Anderson, Lynne. The Aquarium Adds Up. 2011. (Early Connections Ser.). (J). *(978-1-61672-599-0(0))* Benchmark Education Co.

Andreae, Giles. Giraffes Can't Dance: Number Rumba. Parker-Rees, Guy, illus. 2014. (ENG.). 12p. (J). (gr. -1 — 1). bds. 7.99 *(978-0-545-63996-5(4),* Cartwheel Bks.) Scholastic, Inc.

Ant, Exupery. Imparo a Contare con il Picco. pap. 13.95 *(978-88-451-2268-2(9))* Fabbri Editori - RCS Libri ITA. Dist: Distribooks, Inc.

Appelt, Kathi. Counting Crows. Dunlavey, Rob, illus. 2015. (ENG.). 40p. (J). (gr. -1-3). 17.99 *(978-1-4424-2327-5(7))* Simon & Schuster Children's Publishing.

Arcturus Publishing Staff. Santa's Sleigh. 2013. (ENG., Illus.). 10p. (J). bds. 9.95 *(978-1-78212-186-2(2))* Arcturus Publishing GBR. Dist: Bookmasters Distribution.

Armadillo. Let's Count 123: A Very First Number Book. 2015. (ENG., Illus.). 48p. bds. 9.99 *(978-1-86147-659-3(0),* Armadillo) Anness Publishing GBR. Dist: National Bk. Network.

Armadillo Press. Dog & Friends! A Box of Exciting Picture Books, 6 vols. 2017. (ENG., Illus.). 54p. (J). (gr. -1-12). bds. 14.99 *(978-1-86147-640-1(X),* Armadillo) Anness Publishing GBR. Dist: National Bk. Network.

Armstrong-Ellis, Carey F. Ten Creepy Monsters. (ENG., Illus.). 32p. (J). (gr. k-2). 2017. pap. 4.95 ***(978-1-4197-2741-2(9))*** 2012. 15.95 *(978-1-4197-0433-8(8))* Abrams, Inc. (Abrams Bks. for Young Readers).

Arnold, Connie. Count 1, 2, 3 with Me. Nielson, Ginger, illus. 2013. 24p. pap. 12.99 *(978-1-940310-12-1(1))* 4RV Publishing, LLC.

C
D

Arps, Melissa. Numbers. 2006. (Illus.). (J). (978-0-7364-2380-9(X)) Random Hse., Inc.

Atinuke. Baby Goes to Market. Brooksbank, Angela, illus. 2017. (ENG.). 32p. (J). (gr. -1-2). 16.99 **(978-0-7636-9570-5(X))** Candlewick Pr.

Atlas, Ron. Ten Pigs Fiddling. Flint, Stacie, illus. 2nd rev. ed. 2006. (ENG.). 32p. (J). (gr. -1-k). 17.95 (978-0-9630243-3-6(7)) Amberwood Pr.

Atwood, Megan. Busy Beavers: Counting By 5s, 1 vol. Holm, Sharon, illus. 2012. (Count the Critters Ser.). (ENG.). 24p. (J). (gr. k-3). 27.07 (978-1-61641-852-6(4)) Magic Wagon.

—Monarch Migration: Counting by 10s, 1 vol. Holm, Sharon, illus. 2012. (Count the Critters Ser.). (ENG.). 24p. (J). (gr. k-3). 27.07 (978-1-61641-854-0(0)) Magic Wagon.

—Piglets Playing: Counting from 11 To 20, 1 vol. Holm, Sharon, illus. 2012. (Count the Critters Ser.). (ENG.). 24p. (J). (gr. k-3). 27.07 (978-1-61641-855-7(9)) Magic Wagon.

Auerbach, Annie. Where's the Chick? Counting Book. Whitehead, Paul, illus. 2005. (J). bds. 14.99 (978-0-9767325-5-6(6)) Toy Quest.

Austen, Elizabeth. Baby Animals, 1 vol. rev. ed. 2014. (Science Readers: Content & Literacy Ser.). (ENG., Illus.). 24p. (gr. k-k). pap. 8.99 (978-1-4807-4521-6(9)) Teacher Created Materials, Inc.

Austin, Richard. Pocket Piggies Numbers! Featuring the Teacup Pigs of Pennywell Farm. Austin, Richard, photos by. 2014. (ENG., Illus.). 22p. (J). bds. 5.95 (978-0-7611-7979-5(8), 17979) Workman Publishing Co., Inc.

Autumn Publishing Staff, illus. Adding Up. 2004. (Wall Charts Ser.). (J). pap. 4.99 (978-1-85997-319-6(1)) Byeway Bks.

—Numbers 1-100. 2004. (Wall Charts Ser.). (J). pap. 4.99 (978-1-85997-285-4(3)) Byeway Bks.

Avril, Lynne, illus. Five Little Monkeys. 2010. (Favorite Children's Songs Ser.). (ENG.). 16p. (J). (gr. -1-2). 25.64 (978-1-60253-530-5(2), 200112) Child's World, Inc., The.

AWARD & Award, Anna. Dot to Dot Count & Colour Fun. 2015. (ENG.). 16p. (J). pap. 3.99 (978-1-78270-124-8(9)); pap. 3.99 (978-1-78270-125-5(7)); pap. 3.99 (978-1-78270-123-1(0)) Award Pubns. Ltd. GBR. Dist: Parkwest Pubns., Inc.

Award, Anna. My First 123. 2012. (ENG., Illus.). 10p. (J). bds. 9.95 (978-1-84135-500-9(3)); bds. 6.50 (978-1-84135-417-0(1)) Award Pubns. Ltd. GBR. Dist: Parkwest Pubns., Inc.

Award Publications Limited Staff, creator. My First Bumper Colouring Fun: ABC & 1 2 3. 2013. (ENG., Illus.). 32p. (J). (gr. -1-3). pap. 6.50 (978-1-84135-997-7(1)) Award Pubns. Ltd. GBR. Dist: Parkwest Pubns., Inc.

Award Publications Staff. My First Counting. 2012. (ENG., Illus.). 24p. (J). pap. 4.95 (978-1-84135-575-7(5)) Award Pubns. Ltd. GBR. Dist: Parkwest Pubns., Inc.

Ayers, Amy. Contando en el Zoologico. 2007. (Las matimaticas en nuestro mundo (Spanish- Math in Our World) Ser.). (SPA.). 24p. (gr. 1-2). pap. 8.15 (978-0-8368-8496-8(5), Weekly Reader Leveled Readers) Stevens, Gareth Publishing LLLP.

—Counting at the Zoo. 2007. (Math in Our World Ser.). (Illus.). 24p. (gr. 1-2). lib. bdg. 22.00 (978-0-8368-8469-2(8), Weekly Reader Leveled Readers) Stevens, Gareth Publishing LLLP.

—Using Money at the Lemonade Stand. 2007. (Math in Our World Ser.). 24p. (gr. 1-2). pap. 8.15 (978-0-8368-8481-4(7), Weekly Reader Leveled Readers) Stevens, Gareth Publishing LLLP.

AZ Books Staff. Counting. Petrovskaya, Olga, ed. 2012. (Matching Game Ser.). (ENG.). 18p. (J). (gr. -1-k). spiral bd. 4.95 (978-1-61889-200-3(2)) AZ Bks. LLC.

—Numeros - Count the Toys: Count the Toys. Gorbachenok, Ekaterina, ed. 2012. (Spanish for Kids Ser.). (ENG & SPA.). 10p. (J). (-k). bds. 11.95 (978-1-61889-137-2(5)) AZ Bks. LLC.

Azadi, Azita. Thank You Sun. 2009. 32p. pap. 16.50 (978-1-4269-2197-1(7)) Trafford Publishing.

Baby's First Counting Book. 2004. 10p. (J). bds. 4.99 (978-1-85854-924-8(8)) Brimax Books Ltd. GBR. Dist: Byeway Bks.

Bader, Bonnie. 100 Monsters in My School. Hendrix, Bryan, illus. 2003. (All Aboard Math Reader Ser.). 48p. (gr. -1-3). 14.00 (978-0-7569-1648-0(8)) Perfection Learning Corp.

Bailey, Linda & Masse, Josée. Goodnight, Sweet Pig. Masse, Josée, illus. 2007. (ENG., Illus.). 32p. (J). (gr. -1-k). 18.95 (978-1-55337-844-0(X)) Kids Can Pr., Ltd. CAN. Dist: Hachette Bk. Group.

Bak, Jenny. Ten Gifts from Santa Claus: A Counting Book. Harding, Niall, illus. 2011. (ENG.). 22p. (J). (gr. -1-k). 14.99 (978-1-4052-5127-3(1)) Egmont Bks., Ltd. GBR. Dist: Independent Pubs. Group.

Baker, Alan. Gray Rabbit's 1,2,3. 2017. (Little Rabbit Bks.). (ENG.). 24p. (J). 12.99 (978-0-7534-7324-5(0), 9780753473245, Kingfisher) Roaring Brook Pr.

Baker, Keith. Peas in a Pod! Baker, Keith, illus. 2013. (ENG., Illus.). 80p. (J). (gr. -1-3). 33.99 (978-1-4424-9991-1(5), Beach Lane Bks.) Beach Lane Bks.

—Quack & Count. (ENG., Illus.). (J). 2004. 24p. (gr. -1 — 1). pap. 7.99 (978-0-15-205025-2(6)) 2003. 22p. (gr. k — 1). bds. 6.95 (978-0-15-204751-1(4)) Houghton Mifflin Harcourt Publishing Co.

—1-2-3 Peas. Baker, Keith, illus. 2012. (Peas Ser.). (ENG., Illus.). 40p. (J). (gr. -1-3). 17.99 (978-1-4424-4551-2(3), Beach Lane Bks.) Beach Lane Bks.

—1-2-3 Peas. Baker, Keith, illus. 2014. (Peas Ser.). (ENG., Illus.). 36p. (J). (gr. -1 — 1). bds. 7.99 (978-1-4424-9928-7(1), Little Simon) Little Simon.

Baker, Mary. English - Spanish Counting Book. Mason, Alfonso & Mason, Ruth, illus. 2008. 24p. pap. 24.95 (978-1-60672-035-6(X)) America Star Bks.

Baker, Mary E. English - French Counting Book, 1 vol. Mason, Alfonso & Mason, Ruth, illus. 2010. 28p. pap. 24.95 (978-1-4489-4347-0(7)) PublishAmerica, Inc.

Baldyga, Steve. In the Pond. 2009. 36p. pap. 24.95 (978-1-60749-473-7(6)) America Star Bks.

Balloon Books Staff. Dot to Dot Count to 50. 2003. (ENG.). 64p. (J). pap. 4.95 (978-1-4027-0631-8(6), Balloon Bks.) Sterling Publishing Co., Inc.

Balsley, Tilda. Soo's Boo-Boos: She's Got 10! McNicholas, Shelagh, illus. 2013. (ENG.). 32p. (J). (gr. -1-2). 12.95 (978-1-58925-118-2(0)) Tiger Tales.

Balsley, Tilda & Fischer, Ellen. The Count's Hanukkah Countdown. Leigh, Tom, illus. 2012. (Hanukkah Ser.). (SPA & ENG.). 24p. (J). (gr. -1-1). 6.95 (978-0-7613-7557-9(0), Kar-Ben Publishing) Lerner Publishing Group.

Bang, Molly. Ten, Nine, Eight. Bang, Molly, illus. 2003. (ENG., Illus.). 24p. (J). (gr. -1-3). reprint ed. pap. 6.99 (978-0-688-10480-1(0)); 20th ed. 16.99 (978-0-688-00906-9(9)) HarperCollins Pubs. (Greenwillow Bks.).

Banner, Angela. Ant & Bee Count 123. 2015. (Ant & Bee Ser.). (ENG., Illus.). 96p. (J). (gr. -1-k). 7.99 (978-1-4052-7513-2(8)) Egmont Bks., Ltd. GBR. Dist: Independent Pubs. Group.

Bardwell, Yvett. My Little Green Book of Numbers. 2007. (ENG & SPA.). (J). 19.95 (978-0-9792531-1-9(X)) Acacia Publishing, Inc.

—My Little Red Book of Numbers. 2007. (ENG & SPA.). (J). 19.95 (978-0-9790826-9-6(2)) Acacia Publishing, Inc.

—My Little Yellow Book of Numbers. 2007. (ENG & SPA.). (J). 19.95 (978-0-9792531-0-2(1)) Acacia Publishing, Inc.

Barlow, Amanda. 1 2 3. 2004. (Baby Board Bks.). (ENG., Illus.). 1p. (J). (gr. -1-18). bds. 4.95 (978-0-7460-4099-7(7)) EDC Publishing.

Barr, Bitsy. Zock's Counting Book. 2013. (Illus.). 40p. pap. 16.00 (978-1-300-51038-3(2)) Lulu Pr., Inc.

Barry, Cotter. By the Numbers. 2010. 16p. 12.99 (978-1-4520-1476-0(0)) AuthorHouse.

Basaluzzo, Constanza & Stanford, Elisa. The Baby Bible 1,2,3, 1 vol. 2009. (Baby Bible Ser.). (ENG.). 48p. (J). bds. 12.99 (978-1-4347-6540-6(7)) Cook, David C.

Base, Graeme. Uno's Garden. 2006. (ENG., Illus.). 44p. (J). (gr. -1-3). 19.95 (978-0-8109-5473-1(7)) Abrams, Inc.

—The Water Hole. Base, Graeme, illus. 2004. (ENG., Illus.). 32p. (J). (gr. k-3). reprint ed. pap. 8.99 (978-0-14-240197-2(8), Puffin Books) Penguin Young Readers Group.

Bass, Jennifer Vogel. Edible Numbers. (ENG., Illus.). (J). 2016. 30p. bds. 8.99 (978-1-62672-285-9(4), 9781626722859) 2015. 32p. (gr. -1-k). 12.99 (978-1-62672-003-9(7), 9781626720039) Roaring Brook Pr.

Bataille, Marion. 10. 2011. (ENG., Illus.). 22p. (J). (gr. -1 — 1). 14.99 (978-1-59643-682-4(4), 9781596436824) Roaring Brook Pr.

Bateman, Donna M. Deep in the Swamp. Lies, Brian, illus. 2007. (ENG.). 32p. (J). (gr. -1-3). 16.95 (978-1-57091-596-3(2)); pap. 7.95 (978-1-57091-597-0(0)) Charlesbridge Publishing, Inc.

Bathala, Neeti & Curtis, Jennifer Keats. Contando Los Cangrejos Herradura a la Luz de la Luna. Jones, Veronica V., illus. 2017. (SPA.). 32p. (J). (gr. k-3). pap. 9.95 (978-1-62855-932-3(2)) Arbordale Publishing.

—Moonlight Crab Count. Jones, Veronica V., illus. 2017. (ENG & SPA.). 32p. (J). (gr. k-3). 17.95 (978-1-62855-930-9(6)) Arbordale Publishing.

Baxter, Nicola. Learn to Count. Elliott, Rebecca, illus. 2013. (ENG.). 16p. (J). (gr. -1-2). bds. 17.99 (978-1-84322-984-1(6), Armadillo) Anness Publishing GBR. Dist: National Bk. Network.

Beaty, Andrea. Hide & Sheep. Mayer, Bill, illus. 2011. (ENG.). 32p. (J). (gr. -1-3). 15.99 (978-1-4169-2544-6(9), McElderry, Margaret K. Bks.) McElderry, Margaret K. Bks.

Beaumont, Karen. Doggone Dogs! Catrow, David, illus. 2008. (ENG.). 40p. (J). (gr. -1-k). 16.99 (978-0-8037-3157-8(4), Dial Bks) Penguin Young Readers Group.

Beckstrand, Karl. Crumbs on the Stairs - Migas en Las Escaleras: A Mystery. Beckstrand, Karl, illus. 2011. (Mini-Mysteries for Minors Ser.: 2).Tr. of Migas en Las Escaleras. (ENG & SPA., Illus.). 24p. (J). pap. 14.95 (978-0-9776065-9-7(7), Gozo Bks.) Premio Publishing & Gozo Bks., LLC.

Bee, William. Stanley's Numbers, 1 vol. Bee, William, illus. 2017. (Stanley Ser.). (ENG., Illus.). 20p. (J). (gr. -1 — 1). bds. 6.95 **(978-1-56145-976-6(3))** Peachtree Pubs.

Behrens, Janice. Letters/Numbers, 4 bks., Set. Michael, Joan, illus. Incl. Let's Make Letters: ABC Kids. (Illus.). 32p. (J). (gr. -1-3). 2007. 18.00 (978-0-531-14867-9(X), Children's Pr.); (Let's Find Out Early Learning Bks.). 2007. 72.00 o.p. (978-0-531-17599-6(5), Children's Pr.) Scholastic Library Publishing.

Beil, Karen Magnuson. Mooove Over! A Book about Counting by Twos. Meisel, Paul, tr. Meisel, Paul, illus. 2004. (ENG.). 32p. (J). (gr. k-3). tchr. ed. 16.95 (978-0-8234-1736-0(0)) Holiday Hse., Inc.

Bell, Hilary & Pesenti, Antonia. Numerical Street. 2016. (ENG., Illus.). 32p. (J). (gr. -1-3). 24.99 (978-1-74223-228-7(0), UNSW Press) NewSouth Publishing AUS. Dist: Independent Pubs. Group.

Bell, Liz. Ten Little Babies Bouncing on My Knee. 2012. 28p. pap. 24.95 (978-1-4626-8029-0(1)) America Star Bks.

Bellefontaine, Kim. Canada 123. Gürth, Per-Henrik, illus. 2008. (ENG.). 24p. (J). (gr. -1 — 1). bds. 8.95 (978-1-55453-235-3(3)) Kids Can Pr., Ltd. CAN. Dist: Hachette Bk. Group.

—Canada 123. Gürth, Per-Henrik, illus. 2006. (ENG.). 24p. (J). (gr. -1-1). 15.95 (978-1-55337-897-6(0)) Kids Can Pr., Ltd. CAN. Dist: Hachette Bk. Group.

Benchmark Education Company, LLC Staff, compiled by. Counting. 2006. (J). 317.00 (978-1-4108-7048-3(0)) Benchmark Education Co.

—Estimation. 2006. (J). 91.00 (978-1-4108-7054-4(5)) Benchmark Education Co.

Benzwie, Teresa. Numbers on the Move. 2011. (ENG., Illus.). 32p. (J). pap. 16.95 (978-1-4399-0342-1(5)) Temple Univ. Pr.

Berenstain, Stan & Berenstain, Jan. Bears on Wheels. 2014. (Step into Reading Level 1 Ser.). lib. bdg. 13.55 (978-0-606-35994-8(X)) Turtleback Bks.

Berkes, Marianne. Over in Australia: Amazing Animals down Under, 1 vol. Dubin, Jill, illus. 2011. (ENG.). 32p. (J). (gr. -1-3). 16.95 (978-1-58469-135-8(2)); pap. 8.95 (978-1-58469-136-5(0)) Dawn Pubns.

—Over in the Arctic: Where the Cold Winds Blow, 1 vol. Dubin, Jill, illus. 2008. (ENG.). 32p. (J). (gr. -1-2). 16.95 (978-1-58469-109-9(3)); pap. 8.95 (978-1-58469-110-5(7)) Dawn Pubns.

—Over in the Forest: Come & Take a Peek, 1 vol. Dubin, Jill, illus. 2012. (ENG.). 32p. (J). 16.95 (978-1-58469-162-4(X)); pap. 8.95 (978-1-58469-163-1(8)) Dawn Pubns.

—Over in the Grasslands: On an African Savanna, 1 vol. Dubin, Jill, illus. 2016. (ENG.). 32p. (J). (gr. -1-2). 16.95 (978-1-58469-567-7(6)) Dawn Pubns.

—Over in the Jungle: A Rainforest Rhyme. Canyon, Jeanette, illus. 2007. 32p. (J). (gr. -1-2). 16.95 (978-1-58469-091-7(7)) Dawn Pubns.

—Over in the Jungle: A Rainforest Rhyme, 1 vol. Canyon, Jeanette, illus. 2007. (Sharing Nature with Children Book Ser.). (ENG.). 32p. (J). (gr. -1-3). 8.95 (978-1-58469-092-4(5)) Dawn Pubns.

—Over in the Ocean: In a Coral Reef. Canyon, Jeanette, illus. (Simply Nature Bks.). (J). (gr. -1). 2006. (ENG.). 26p. bds. 7.95 (978-1-58469-082-5(8)) 2004. (ENG.). 36p. 16.95 (978-1-58469-063-4(1)) 2004. 36p. pap. 8.95 (978-1-58469-062-7(3)) Dawn Pubns.

—Over on a Mountain: Somewhere in the World, 1 vol. Dubin, Jill, illus. 2015. (ENG.). 32p. (J). (gr. -1-3). 16.95 (978-1-58469-518-9(8)) Dawn Pubns.

Berkes, Marianne Collins. Over on the Farm. Morrison, Cathy, illus. 2016. (ENG.). 32p. (J). (gr. -1-2). 16.95 (978-1-58469-548-6(X)) Dawn Pubns.

—Seashells by the Seashore. Noreika, Robert, illus. 2004. (Sharing Nature with Children Book Ser.). 32p. (J). (gr. -1-5). 16.95 (978-1-58469-035-1(6)); pap. 8.95 (978-1-58469-034-4(8)) Dawn Pubns.

Bestselling Counting Books: Ten Little Ladybugs; Eight Silly Monkeys; This Little Piggy. (J). 29.99 (978-1-58117-380-2(6), Intervisual/Piggy Toes) Bendon, Inc.

Beswick, Clare. 30 Fun Ways to Learn about Counting. 2011. (30 Fun Ways to Learn Ser.). (ENG., Illus.). 80p. pap. 12.95 (978-0-87659-367-7(8), Gryphon House Inc) Gryphon Hse., Inc.

Bianchi, Mike & Novak, Marisol. Swampmeet: A Gator Counting Book. Marlette, Andy, illus. 2004. 32p. (J). (gr. -1-k). 6.95 (978-1-58261-780-0(5)) Sports Publishing, LLC.

Bickico Enterprises Staff, concept. BabyKids Bk. 2: The Counting Book. 2003. 16p. (J). pap. 2.95 (978-0-9746508-1-4(1)) Bickico Enterprises, Inc.

Bicknell, J. Buby Baby 123_Padded. 2010. 12p. (978-1-84879-163-3(1)) Make Believe Ideas.

Bicknell, Joanna. My First BK of Animals. 2010. 16p. (J). bds. 8.99 (978-1-84879-361-3(8)) Make Believe Ideas GBR. Dist: Nelson, Thomas Inc.

Big Bear Books Staff. 1, 2, 3 Baylor: A Little Bear Counting Book. Wiede, Matt, illus. 2012. (Big Bear Bks.). (ENG.). 18p. (gr. 17). bds. 9.95 (978-1-60258-660-4(8)) Baylor Univ. Pr.

Biggs, Brian. 123 Beep Beep Beep! Biggs, Brian, illus. 2012. (ENG., Illus.). 24p. (J). (gr. -1 — 1). bds. 7.99 (978-0-06-195812-0(3)) HarperCollins Pubs.

Bird, Benjamin. Scooby-Doo's 1-2-3 Mystery. 2015. (Scooby-Doo! Little Mysteries Ser.). (ENG., Illus.). 20p. (gr. -1 — 1). bds. 7.99 (978-1-62370-177-2(5)) Capstone Press of Coughlan Cos.

Blackstone, Stella. Bear's Birthday. Harter, Debbie, illus. 2011.Tr. of El Cumpleanos de Oso. (ENG.). 24p. (J). (gr. -1-1). pap. 6.99 (978-1-84686-515-2(8)) Barefoot Bks., Inc.

—Bear's Birthday (L'Anniversaire de l'Ours) Harter, Debbie, illus. 2013. (ENG & FRE.). 24p. (J). (gr. k-1). pap. 6.99 (978-1-84686-944-0(7)) Barefoot Bks., Inc.

—Bear's Birthday/El Cumpleanos de Oso. Harter, Debbie, illus. 2013. (ENG & SPA.). 24p. (J). (gr. k-1). 6.99 (978-1-84686-943-3(9)) Barefoot Bks., Inc.

—Cleo's Counting Book. Mockford, Caroline, illus. 2003. (Cleo the Cat Ser.). (ENG.). 24p. (J). (gr. -1-3). 15.99 (978-1-84148-207-1(2)) Barefoot Bks., Inc.

—Counting Cockatoos. Bauer, Stephanie, illus. 2007. (ENG.). 32p. (J). (gr. -1-k). 8.99 (978-1-84686-061-4(X)) Barefoot Bks., Inc.

Blackstone, Stella & Bauer, Stephanie. Counting Cockatoos. 2006. (ENG., Illus.). 32p. (J). (gr. -1-3). 16.99 (978-1-905236-31-2(X)) Barefoot Bks., Inc.

Blackstone, Stella & Corr, Christopher. My Granny Went to Market: A Round-the-World Counting Rhyme. 2006. (ENG., Illus.). 24p. (J). (gr. -1-2). 6.99 (978-1-905236-62-6(X)) Barefoot Bks., Inc.

Blackstone, Stella & Mockford, Caroline. Cleo's Counting Book. 2003. (ENG., Illus.). 32p. (J). pap. 6.99 (978-1-84148-174-6(2)) Barefoot Bks., Inc.

Blake, Quentin. Ten Frogs: A Book about Counting in English & French. Blake, Quentin, illus. 2008. (FRE & ENG., Illus.). 32p. (J). (gr. -1-k). 14.95 (978-1-84365-104-8(1)) Pavilion Bks. GBR. Dist: Independent Pubs. Group.

Blechman, Nicholas. Night Light. 2013. (ENG.). 48p. (J). (gr. -1-k). 16.99 (978-0-545-46263-1(0)) Scholastic, Inc.

Blechmann, R. O. The One & Only 1, 2, 3 Book. Blechmann, R. O., illus. 2013. (ENG., Illus.). 24p. (J). (gr. -1-k). 15.99 (978-1-56846-245-5(X), Creative Editions) Creative Co., The.

Bleiman, Andrew & Eastland, Chris. 1-2-3 ZooBorns! 2015. (ZooBorns Ser.). (ENG., Illus.). 32p. (J). (gr. -1-3). 14.99 (978-1-4814-3103-3(X), Beach Lane Bks.) Beach Lane Bks.

Blevins, Wiley. Count on It. Kreloff, Elliott, illus. 2016. (Basic Concepts Ser.). (ENG.). 24p. (J). (gr. -1-1). lib. bdg. 14.99 (978-1-63440-081-7(X)) Red Chair Pr.

Bloom, Suzanne, illus. Number Slumber. 2016. (ENG.). 40p. (J). (gr. -1-k). 16.95 (978-1-62979-557-7(7)) Boyds Mills Pr.

Blyton, Enid, et al. My First 123 & Nursery Rhymes. 2013. (ENG., Illus.). 20p. (J). bds. 11.50 (978-1-84135-759-1(6)) Award Pubns. Ltd. GBR. Dist: Parkwest Pubns., Inc.

—Out in Space. 2013. (ENG.). 10p. (J). bds. 9.95 (978-1-84135-726-3(X)) Award Pubns. Ltd. GBR. Dist: Parkwest Pubns., Inc.

Bodach, Vijaya. Ten Easter Eggs. Logan, Laura, illus. 2015. (ENG.). 22p. (J). (gr. -1-k). bds. 8.99 (978-0-545-74730-1(9), Cartwheel Bks.) Scholastic, Inc.

Bolam, Emily, illus. Counting. 2009. 10p. (J). (gr. -1-k). 5.95 (978-1-58925-846-4(0)) Tiger Tales.

Bolton, Bill, illus. My Magnetic Counting Book: Ten Dancing Dinosaurs. 2006. (Magnix Learning Fun Ser.). 12p. (J). (gr. -1-3). 9.95 (978-1-932915-16-7(8)) Sandvik Innovations, LLC.

Bond, Michael. Paddington at the Beach. Alley, R. W., illus. 2015. (Paddington Ser.). 32p. (J). (gr. -1-3). 17.99 (978-0-06-231720-9(2)) HarperCollins Pubs.

Book Company Staff. Counting. 2003. (Bug Chunkie Board Bks.). (Illus.). (J). bds. 2.95 (978-1-74047-346-0(9)) Book Co. Publishing Pty, Ltd., The AUS. Dist: Penton Overseas, Inc.

Boothroyd, Jennifer. Counting. 2007. (First Step Nonfiction - Early Math Ser.). (ENG.). 8p. (gr. -1-1). pap. 4.95 (978-0-8225-6827-8(6)) Lerner Publishing Group.

—Skip Counting. 2007. (First Step Nonfiction - Early Math Ser.). (ENG.). 8p. (gr. -1-1). pap. 4.95 (978-0-8225-6828-5(4)) Lerner Publishing Group.

Borja, Richard. Flash! Alphabet Enigma. 2009. 48p. pap. 14.92 (978-1-84728-659-8(3)) Lulu Pr., Inc.

Bousquet, Anthea. Counting St. Lucian Style: A delightfully illustrated counting rhyme set in the Caribbean island of St. Lucia. Sandiford, Ted, illus. 2011. 16p. (J). pap. (978-976-8238-01-6(1)) Maryli Pubs.

Boynton, Sandra. Hippos Go Berserk! Boynton, Sandra, illus. 2009. (ENG., Illus.). 32p. (J). 9.99 (978-1-4169-9619-4(2), Little Simon) Little Simon.

Brainy Baby Quad Book. 2005. (Brainy Baby Ser.). 40p. (J). bds. 10.39 (978-1-59394-240-3(0)) Bendon, Inc.

Brendler, Carol. The Pickwicks' Picnic: A Counting Adventure. Kurilla, Renée, illus. 2017. (ENG.). 40p. (J). (gr. -1-3). 16.99 **(978-0-544-83958-8(7)**, Clarion Bks.) Houghton Mifflin Harcourt Trade & Reference Pubs.

Brexel, Bernadette. Counting with Crayons. 2015. (Rosen REAL Readers: STEM & STEAM Collection). (ENG.). 8p. pap. 5.46 (978-1-4994-9705-2(9), Rosen Classroom) Rosen Publishing Group, Inc., The.

Brimner, Larry Dane. Monkey Math. Kulka, Joe, illus. 2007. (Rookie Reader Skill Set Ser.). (ENG.). 32p. (J). (gr. k-2). pap. 4.95 (978-0-531-13850-2(X)) Scholastic Library Publishing.

Brinker, Spencer. Counting to Add with Baron Von Madd. 2015. (Spooky Math Ser.). (ENG., Illus.). 32p. (J). (gr. -1-3). lib. bdg. 26.60 (978-1-62724-867-9(6)) Bearport Publishing Co., Inc.

—The Ghost of Skip-Count Castle. 2015. (Illus.). 32p. (J). lib. bdg. (978-1-62724-332-2(1)) Bearport Publishing Co., Inc.

—More or Less & a Vampire's Guess. 2015. (Illus.). 32p. (J). lib. bdg. (978-1-62724-330-8(5)) Bearport Publishing Co., Inc.

—The Witch's Things: A Counting to 20 Rhyme. 2015. (Illus.). 32p. (J). lib. bdg. (978-1-62724-333-9(X)) Bearport Publishing Co., Inc.

Brocket, Jane. 1 Cookie, 2 Chairs, 3 Pears: Numbers Everywhere. 2013. 32p. 26.60 (978-1-4677-1702-1(9)) Lerner Publishing Group.

Brocklehurst, Ruth. 1001 Animals to Spot. 2004. (1001 Things to Spot Ser.). (SPA., Illus.). 32p. (J). (gr. -1-18). pap. 6.95 (978-0-7945-0149-5(4), Usborne) EDC Publishing.

Broekstra, Lorette. Baby Bbear Goes to the Farm. 2004. (Baby-Bear Ser.). (Illus.). 32p. (J). 5.99 (978-1-85854-488-5(2)) Brimax Books Ltd. GBR. Dist: Byeway Bks.

Brooks, David. You Can Count in the Jungle. 2005. (You Can Count Ser.). (ENG., Illus.). 24p. (J). (gr. -1 — 1). bds. 6.95 (978-1-55971-931-5(1)) Cooper Square Publishing Llc.

Brooks, Felicity. Lift-the-Flap Counting Book. 2011. (Lift-the-Flap Bks). 14p. (J). ring bd. 11.99 (978-0-7945-2916-1(X), Usborne) EDC Publishing.

—Very First Numbers. 2009. (First Words Board Bks). 18p. (J). bds. 6.99 (978-0-7945-2354-1(4), Usborne) EDC Publishing.

Brooks, Felicity & Fearn, Katrina. First Dot-To-Dot Animals. 2013. (First Dot-To-Dot Ser.). 16p. (J). pap. 5.99 (978-0-7945-3198-0(9), Usborne) EDC Publishing.

Brooks, Felicity & Litchfield, Jo. First Numbers. 2004. (First Numbers Ser.). (SPA., Illus.). 28p. (J). pap. 7.95 (978-0-7945-0092-4(7), Usborne) EDC Publishing.

Brooks, Felicity & Tyler, Jenny. The Usborne 1,2,3 Jigsaw Book. Cartwright, Stephen, illus. 2006. (Usborne Jigsaw Bks.). 12p. (J). (gr. -1-k). bds. 15.95 (978-0-7945-1168-5(6), Usborne) EDC Publishing.

Brown, Margaret Wise. Goodnight Moon. Hurd, Clement, illus. 2007. (ENG.). 32p. (J). (gr. -1-3). pap. 24.99 (978-0-06-111977-4(6), HarperFestival) HarperCollins Pubs.

—Goodnight Moon 1 2 3: A Counting Book. Hurd, Clement, illus. 2008. (ENG.). 30p. (J). (gr. -1-k). bds. 8.99 (978-0-06-112597-3(0), HarperFestival) HarperCollins Pubs.

—Goodnight Moon 123: A Counting Book. Hurd, Clement, illus. (J). 2013. (ENG.). 30p. (gr. -1-k). bds. 9.99 (978-0-06-224405-5(1), HarperFestival) 2007. (ENG.). 32p. (gr. -1-k). 16.99 (978-0-06-112593-5(8)) 2007. 32p. (gr. -1-k). lib. bdg. 17.89 (978-0-06-112594-2(6)) 2007. (978-1-4287-4853-8(9)) HarperCollins Pubs.

—Goodnight Moon 123/Buenas Noches, Luna 123: A Counting Book/un Libro para Contar. Hurd, Clement, illus. 2007. (ENG & SPA.). 32p. (J). (gr. -1-k). 16.99 (978-0-06-117325-7(8), Rayo) HarperCollins Pubs.

Brown, Ruth. Ten Seeds. 2013. (ENG., Illus.). 24p. (J). (gr. -1-k). 10.99 (978-1-84939-251-8(X)) Andersen Pr. GBR. Dist: Independent Pubs. Group.

Browne, Anthony. One Gorilla. Browne, Anthony, illus. 2013. (ENG., Illus.). 32p. (J). (gr. -1-2). 17.99 (978-0-7636-6352-0(2)) Candlewick Pr.

Browne, Eileen. Handa's Hen. 2011. (ENG., Illus.). 32p. (J). (gr. -1-2). pap. 6.99 (978-0-7636-5361-3(6)) Candlewick Pr.

—Handa's Hen. 2004. (J). (ENG & SOM.). (978-1-84444-187-7(3)); (ENG & URD.). (978-1-84444-196-9(2)); (ENG & HIN.). (978-1-84444-193-8(8)); (ENG & GUJ.). (978-1-84444-192-1(X)); (ENG & FRE.). (978-1-84444-191-4(1)); (CRO & ENG.). (978-1-84444-190-7(3)); (CHI & ENG.). (978-1-84444-185-3(7)); (BEN & ENG.). (978-1-84444-189-1(X)); (ARA & ENG.). (978-1-84444-184-6(9)); (ALB & ENG.). (978-1-84444-188-4(1)); (ENG & VIE.). (978-1-84444-197-6(0)); (ENG & RUS.). (978-1-84444-195-2(4)) Mantra Lingua.

—Handa's Hen. Browne, Eileen, illus. 2004. (ENG & PAN., Illus.). 32p. (J). bds. (978-1-84444-194-5(6)) Mantra Lingua.

Bruna, Dick. I Can Count. 2012. (ENG., Illus.). 28p. 7.95 (978-1-84976-076-8(4)) Tate Publishing, Ltd. GBR. Dist: Abrams, Inc.

Bryant-Mole, Karen. Dot-to-Dot on Seashore. Round, Graham, illus. 2003. 24p. (J). pap. 3.99 (978-0-7945-0494-6(9), Usborne) EDC Publishing.

Bugbird, T. My Pretty Pink School Purse. Horne, J., illus. 2010. 16p. (J). 12.99 (978-1-84879-379-8(0)) Make Believe Ideas GBR. Dist: Nelson, Thomas Inc.

Bulloch, Ivan & James, Diane. Learn with Me 123. Pangbourne, Daniel, illus. Pangbourne, Daniel, photos by. 2007. (ENG.). 46p. (J). (gr. -1 — 1). pap. 6.95 *(978-1-58728-622-3(X))* Cooper Square Publishing Llc.

Burg, Ann E. Times Square: A New York State Number Book. Brookfield, Maureen K., illus. 2005. (Count Your Way Across the USA Ser.). (ENG.). 40p. (J). (gr. k-6). 16.95 *(978-1-58536-195-3(X))* Sleeping Bear Pr.

Burnett, James & Irons, Calvin. Stella's Store: Book about Skip Counting by Five. 2012. (J). *(978-1-921358-61-6(0))* Origo Education.

—Sweet Dreams: A Book about Counting Quantities to Ten. 2012. (J). *(978-1-921358-96-8(3))* Origo Education.

Burnette, Margarette. Counting in the Crazy Garden. Henson, Brooke, illus. 2008. (Chipper Kids Ser.). 30p. (J). (gr. -1-2). 15.95 *(978-0-9653791-3-7(2))* JenPrint Pubns., LLC.

Burstein, John. Hacer Decenas: Grupos de Gollyluvas. 2006. (Monstruos Matematicos Ser.). (SPA., Illus.). 24p. (J). (gr. k-4). lib. bdg. 21.00 *(978-0-8368-6672-8(X)*, Weekly Reader Leveled Readers) Stevens, Gareth Publishing LLLP.

—Making Tens: Groups of Gollywomples. Destiny Images Staff, illus. 2003. (Math Monsters Ser.). 24p. (J). (gr. k-4). lib. bdg. 21.00 *(978-0-8368-3812-1(2)*, Weekly Reader Leveled Readers) Stevens, Gareth Publishing LLLP.

Burton, Margie, et al. Guess How Many I Have. 2011. (Early Connections Ser.). (J). *(978-1-61672-292-0(4))* Benchmark Education Co.

—Sorting My Money. 2011. (Early Connections Ser.). (J). *(978-1-61672-538-9(9))* Benchmark Education Co.

Bussiere, Desireé. Tennis by the Numbers, 1 vol. 2013. (Sports by the Numbers Ser.). (ENG.). 24p. (J). (gr. k-3). lib. bdg. 24.21 *(978-1-61783-847-7(0)*, SandCastle) ABDO Publishing Co.

Butler, John. Bedtime in the Jungle. Butler, John, illus. 2009. (Illus.). 32p. (J). (gr. -1-1). 16.95 *(978-1-56145-486-0(9))* Peachtree Pubs.

Byeway Wall Charts Staff. Counting to 20. Autumn Publishing Staff, illus. 2004. (Wall Charts Ser.). (J). pap. 4.99 *(978-1-85997-282-3(9))* Byeway Bks.

Cabral, Jeane. Count My Blessing 1 to 10. Kolanovic, Dubravka, illus. 2007. (Magnetic Counting Book Ser.). 10p. *(978-1-84666-360-4(1)*, Tide Mill Pr.) Top That! Publishing PLC.

Calino & Abbeville Press Staff. 123 Caterpillar. Calino, illus. 2008. (ENG., Illus.). 30p. (J). (gr. k-k). 8.95 *(978-0-7892-0304-5(9)*, Abbeville Kids) Abbeville Pr., Inc.

Canetti, Yanitzia. Canta y Cuenta Las Arañas. 2010. (J). *(978-1-59835-226-9(1))* Cambridge BrickHouse, Inc.

—Canta y Cuenta Las Hormigas. 2010. (J). *(978-1-59835-150-7(8))* Cambridge BrickHouse, Inc.

—Canta y Cuenta Las Ovejas. 2010. (J). *(978-1-59835-224-5(5))* Cambridge BrickHouse, Inc.

—1-2-3 Do, Re, Mi Ants. 2010. (J). *(978-1-59835-154-5(0))* Cambridge BrickHouse, Inc.

—1-2-3, Do, Re, Mi Elephants. 2010. (J). *(978-1-59835-151-4(6))* Cambridge BrickHouse, Inc.

—1-2-3 Do, Re, Mi Sheep. 2010. (J). *(978-1-59835-223-8(7))* Cambridge BrickHouse, Inc.

—1-2-3 Do, Re, Mi Spiders. 2010. (J). *(978-1-59835-225-2(3))* Cambridge BrickHouse, Inc.

Capote, Lori. Monster Knows Numbers, 1 vol. Wass, Chip, illus. 2013. (Monster Knows Math Ser.). (ENG.). 24p. (gr. 3-4). lib. bdg. 24.65 *(978-1-4048-7946-1(3))* Picture Window Bks.

Capucilli, Alyssa Satin. Biscuit's 123. Schories, Pat & Berlin, Rose Mary, illus. 2012. (Biscuit Ser.). (ENG.). 16p. (J). (gr. -1-1). pap. 6.99 *(978-0-06-162523-7(X)*, HarperFestival) HarperCollins Pubs.

—Mrs. McTats & Her Houseful of Cats. Rankin, Joan E. & Rankin, Joan, illus. 2004. (ENG.). 32p. (J). (gr. -1-3). 7.99 *(978-0-689-86991-4(6)*, Aladdin) Simon & Schuster Children's Publishing.

Cardenas, Ernesto A. Two by Two. 2009. 19.95 *(978-1-60698-014-9(9))*; pap. 3.95 *(978-1-60698-012-5(2))* Milo Educational Bks. & Resources.

Carle, Eric. Count with the Very Hungry Caterpillar. Carle, Eric, illus. 2006. (World of Eric Carle Ser.). (ENG., Illus.). 16p. (J). (gr. -1-k). pap. 6.99 *(978-0-448-44420-8(8)*, Grosset & Dunlap) Penguin Young Readers Group.

—My First Busy Book. Carle, Eric, illus. 2015. (World of Eric Carle Ser.). (ENG., Illus.). 12p. (J). bds. 14.99 *(978-1-4814-5791-0(8)*, Little Simon) Little Simon.

—My Very First Book of Numbers. Carle, Eric, illus. 2006. (ENG., Illus.). 20p. (J). (gr. -1 — 1). bds. 5.99 *(978-0-399-24509-1(X)*, Philomel Bks.) Penguin Young Readers Group.

—My Very First Book of Numbers (Mi Primer Libro de Numeros) Carle, Eric, illus. 2013. (SPA & ENG., Illus.). 20p. (J). (gr. -1 — 1). bds. 5.99 *(978-0-399-16141-4(4)*, Philomel Bks.) Penguin Young Readers Group.

—Rooster Is off to See the World. Carle, Eric, illus. 2013. (World of Eric Carle Ser.). (ENG., Illus.). 24p. (J). (gr. -1-1). 16.99 *(978-1-4424-7270-9(7))*; pap. 3.99 *(978-1-4424-7269-3(3))* Simon Spotlight. (Simon Spotlight).

—Rooster Is off to See the World. 2013. (Eric Carle Ready-To-Read Ser.). lib. bdg. 13.55 *(978-0-606-32063-4(6)*, Turtleback) Turtleback Bks.

Carle, Eric & Chronicle Books Staff. 1, 2, 3, to the Zoo Train Flash Cards. 2013. (ENG., Illus.). 21p. (J). (gr. -1 — 1). 14.99 *(978-1-4521-1341-8(6))* Chronicle Bks. LLC.

Carr, Aaron. Magents with Code. 2012. (Science Kids Ser.). (ENG., Illus.). 24p. (J). (gr. -1-3). lib. bdg. 27.13 *(978-1-61913-086-9(6)*, AV2 by Weigl) Weigl Pubs., Inc.

—Magnets, with Code. 2012. (Science Kids Ser.). (ENG., Illus.). 24p. (J). (gr. -1-1). pap. 12.95 *(978-1-61913-756-1(9)*, AV2 by Weigl) Weigl Pubs., Inc.

—Números. 2013. (SPA.). (J). *(978-1-62127-609-8(0))* Weigl Pubs., Inc.

Carroll, Danielle. Is It Odd or Even? 2005. (Yellow Umbrella Fluent Level Ser.). (ENG., Illus.). 16p. (gr. k-1). pap. 35.70 *(978-0-7368-5321-7(9)*, Yellow Umbrella Bks.) Capstone Press of Coughlan Cos.

—What Is a Hundred? 2005. (Yellow Umbrella Fluent Level Ser.). (ENG., Illus.). 16p. (gr. k-1). pap. 35.70 *(978-0-7368-5326-2(X)*, Yellow Umbrella Bks.) Capstone Press of Coughlan Cos.

Carson-Dellosa Publishing Staff. Numbers 1 to 26, Grades PK - 1. 2006. (ENG., Illus.). 54p. (gr. -1-1). 2.99 *(978-0-7696-4739-5(1)*, Brighter Child) Carson-Dellosa Publishing, LLC.

Carter, David. David Carter's 100: Lift the Flaps & Learn to Count! 2013. (ENG., Illus.). 20p. (J). (gr. -1-2). bds. 17.95 *(978-1-4027-8738-6(3))* Sterling Publishing Co., Inc.

Carter, David A. Counting: A Bugs Pop-Up Concept Book. Carter, David A., illus. 2010. (David Carter's Bugs Ser.). (ENG., Illus.). 16p. (J). (gr. -1-1). 7.99 *(978-1-4424-0828-9(6)*, Little Simon) Little Simon.

—How Many Bugs in a Box? Carter, David A., illus. 2006. (David Carter's Bugs Ser.). (ENG., Illus.). 20p. (J). (gr. -1-1). 11.99 *(978-1-4169-0804-3(8)*, Little Simon) Little Simon.

—School Bugs. Carter, David A., illus. 2009. (David Carter's Bugs Ser.). (ENG., Illus.). 20p. (J). (gr. -1-2). 12.99 *(978-1-4169-5056-1(7)*, Little Simon) Little Simon.

—The 12 Bugs of Christmas: A Pop-Up Christmas Counting Book. Carter, David A., illus. 2011. (David Carter's Bugs Ser.). (ENG., Illus.). 24p. (J). (gr. -1-1). 12.99 *(978-1-4424-2649-8(7)*, Little Simon) Little Simon.

Cartwright, Shannon. Alaska 1 2 3: Colors & Numbers. 2005. (Illus.). (J). *(978-0-9772297-0-3(X))* Taku Graphics.

Cassels, Jean. The Twelve Days of Christmas in Louisiana. Cravath, Lynne Avril, illus. 2007. (Twelve Days of Christmas in America Ser.). (ENG.). 40p. (J). (gr. k-3). 12.95 *(978-1-4027-3814-2(5))* Sterling Publishing Co., Inc.

Cassilly, Barbara. Numbers from the Bible. 2007. 16p. per. 24.95 *(978-1-4241-8876-5(8))* America Star Bks.

Casteel, Seth. Underwater Doggies 1,2,3. 2014. (ENG., Illus.). 18p. (J). (gr. -1 — 1). bds. 6.99 *(978-0-316-33175-3(9))* Little, Brown Bks. for Young Readers.

Castro, Shirley. The Pelican Family Counting Book. Castro, Christopher, illus. 2006. (ENG.). (J). 15.00 *(978-0-9790307-0-3(6))* Castro, Shirley.

—The Pelican Family Series — Telly's Story. Castro, Christopher, illus. 2008. 36p. (J). 15.00 *(978-0-9790307-1-0(4))* Castro, Shirley.

Catalanotto, Peter. Daisy 1, 2, 3. Catalanotto, Peter, illus. 2003. (ENG., Illus.). 32p. (J). (gr. -1-1). 17.99 *(978-0-689-85457-6(9)*, Atheneum/Richard Jackson Bks.) Simon & Schuster Children's Publishing.

Celebrations Grade Level Libraries: Anno's Counting Book. 2005. (Little Celebrations Ser.). (J). (gr. k-3). 82.95 *(978-0-673-75780-7(3))* Celebration Pr.

Chall, Marsha Wilson. One Pup's Up. Cole, Henry, illus. 2010. (ENG.). 32p. (J). (gr. -1 — 1). 16.99 *(978-1-4169-7960-9(3)*, McElderry, Margaret K. Bks.) McElderry, Margaret K. Bks.

Chamberlin-Calamar, Pat. Alaska's 12 Days of Summer. Cartwright, Shannon, illus. 2003. (Paws IV Ser.). (ENG.). 32p. (J). (gr. -1-2). pap. 10.99 *(978-1-57061-341-8(9)*, Little Bigfoot) Sasquatch Bks.

Chaplain, Dawn. One Red Apple. 2008. 23p. pap. 24.95 *(978-1-60703-020-1(9))* America Star Bks.

Chapman, Joan. Count the Ways to Get Around: Learning to Count To 5. 2009. (Math for the Real World Ser.). (ENG., Illus.). 8p. (gr. k-1). pap. 5.15 *(978-0-8239-8841-9(4))* Rosen Publishing Group, Inc., The.

Chapman, Sherill, et al, adapted by. More Numbers. 2004. (Kids Can Learn with Franklin Ser.). (ENG., Illus.). 32p. (J). (gr. k-1). 3.95 *(978-1-55337-598-2(X))* Kids Can Pr., Ltd. CAN. Dist: Hachette Bk. Group.

Charles, Faustin. The Selfish Crocodile Counting Book. Terry, Michael, illus. I.t. ed. 2008. (ENG.). 12p. (J). (gr. k-k). bds. 8.95 *(978-0-7475-9238-9(1))* Bloomsbury Publishing Plc GBR. Dist: Independent Pubs. Group.

Charles, Faustin & Beynon-Davies, Paul. The Selfish Crocodile Book of Numbers. Terry, Michael, illus. 2012. (Selfish Crocodile Ser.). (ENG.). 12p. (J). (gr. -1-k). bds. 10.99 *(978-1-4088-1451-2(X)*, 9781408814512, Bloomsbury USA Childrens) Bloomsbury Publishing USA.

Charlesworth, Liza & Scholastic Canada Ltd. Staff. Eight Legs Are Great! Snider, Jackie, illus. 2005. (Number Tales Ser.). (ENG.). 16p. (J). (gr. -1-1). pap. 2.99 *(978-0-439-69019-5(6))* Scholastic, Inc.

Charlesworth, Liza & Scholastic, Inc. Staff. 100 Wacky Wishes. Kennedy, Kelly, illus. 2005. (Number Tales Ser.). (ENG.). 16p. (J). (gr. -1-1). pap. 2.99 *(978-0-439-69030-0(7))* Scholastic, Inc.

Cheng, Andrea. Grandfather Counts. 2004. (Illus.). (J). (gr. k-3). spiral bd. *(978-0-616-07253-0(8))* Canadian National Institute for the Blind/Institut National Canadien pour les Aveugles.

Chichester Clark, Emma. Mimi's Book of Counting. Chichester Clark, Emma, illus. 2004. (Illus.). 24p. (J). 9.95 *(978-1-57091-573-4(3))* Charlesbridge Publishing, Inc.

Childrens Press Staff & Scholastic, Inc. Staff, contrib. by. 5 Busy Ducklings. 2010. (Rookie Toddler: First Concepts Ser.). (ENG.). 12p. (J). bds. 6.95 *(978-0-531-25232-1(9)*, Children's Pr.) Scholastic Library Publishing.

Chilek, Laurie. Counting at the Zoo: Learning to Add 1 to One-Digit Numbers. 2004. (Math Big Booksm Ser.). (ENG., Illus.). 8p. (gr. k-1). 29.95 *(978-0-8239-7628-7(9))* Rosen Publishing Group, Inc., The.

Christelow, Eileen. Five Little Monkeys Jumping on the Bed. Ortiz, Victoria, tr. 2014. (Five Little Monkeys Story Ser.). (ENG & SPA., Illus.). 30p. (J). (— 1). bds. 7.99 *(978-0-544-08900-6(6)*, HMH Books For Young Readers) Houghton Mifflin Harcourt Publishing Co.

—Five Little Monkeys Sitting in a Tree. 2014. (Five Little Monkeys Story Ser.). (ENG & SPA., Illus.). 28p. (J). (— 1). bds. 7.99 *(978-0-544-30218-1(4)*, HMH Books For Young Readers) Houghton Mifflin Harcourt Publishing Co.

—Five Little Monkeys Sitting in a Tree Book & CD, 1 vol. 2007. (Five Little Monkeys Story Ser.). (ENG., Illus.). 32p. (J). (gr. -1-3). 10.99 *(978-0-618-85284-0(0))* Houghton Mifflin Harcourt Publishing Co.

—Five Little Monkeys Wash the Car. 2004. (Five Little Monkeys Story Ser.). (ENG., Illus.). 40p. (J). (gr. -1-3). 6.99 *(978-0-618-48602-1(X))* Houghton Mifflin Harcourt Publishing Co.

Christian, Cheryl. How Many? (English/Haitian Creole), 1 vol. Dwight, Laura, photos by. 2005. (ENG., Illus.). 12p. (J). 5.95 *(978-1-59572-024-5(3))* Star Bright Bks., Inc.

—How Many? (English/Russian), 1 vol. Dwight, Laura, photos by. 2005. (Photo Flap Bks.). (RUS & ENG., Illus.). 12p. (J). 5.95 *(978-1-932065-88-6(1))* Star Bright Bks., Inc.

—How Many? (Korean), 1 vol. Choi, Jin, tr. Dwight, Laura, photos by. 2004. (KOR & ENG., Illus.). 12p. (J). 5.95 *(978-1-932065-82-4(2))* Star Bright Bks., Inc.

—How Many? (Portuguese/English), 1 vol. Dwight, Laura, photos by. 2009. (ENG & POR., Illus.). 12p. (J). 5.95 *(978-1-59572-190-7(8))* Star Bright Bks., Inc.

—How Many? (Simplified Mandarin), 1 vol. Dwight, Laura, photos by. 2004. (CHI & ENG., Illus.). 12p. (J). 5.95 *(978-1-932065-70-1(9))* Star Bright Bks., Inc.

—How Many? (Traditional Cantonese) Dwight, Laura, photos by. 2004. (CHI., Illus.). 12p. (J). bds. 5.95 *(978-1-932065-64-0(4))* Star Bright Bks., Inc.

Churchill, Jill. Five Little Ducks. Yaccarino, Dan, illus. 2005. 26p. (J). (gr. -1 — 1). bds. 5.99 *(978-0-06-073465-7(5)*, HarperFestival) HarperCollins Pubs.

Chwast, Seymour & Moskof, Martin. Still Another Number Book. 2014. (ENG., Illus.). 64p. (J). (gr. -1). pap. 9.99 *(978-0-486-49201-8(X))* Dover Pubns., Inc.

Cisner, Naftali. Count with Mendel. Cisner, Naftali, illus. 2003. (Illus.). 10p. (J). bds. 5.95 *(978-1-880582-84-8(8)*, CWMH) Judaica Pr., Inc., The.

Clarke, Jacqueline & Rhodes, Immacula A. Shoe Box Learning Centers: Counting: 30 Instant Centers with Reproducible Templates & Activities That Help Kids Practice Important Literacy Skills-Independently! 2012. (ENG.). 80p. (gr. k-2). pap. 12.99 *(978-0-545-46867-1(1)*, Teaching Resources) Scholastic, Inc.

Class P3 in Scoil Chiarain Staff. 10 Scary Monsters. 2007. (ENG., Illus.). 32p. (J). pap. 12.95 *(978-1-84717-002-6(1))* O'Brien Pr., Ltd., The IRL. Dist: Dufour Editions, Inc.

Claybourne, Anna. 1001Things to Spot in the Town. 2009. (1001 Things to Spot Ser.). 32p. (J). 9.99 *(978-0-7945-2514-9(8)*, Usborne) EDC Publishing.

Clish, Marian L. I Wonder What a Fish Would Wish For? Swaim, Mike, illus. 2009. 29p. pap. 24.95 *(978-1-60836-289-9(2))* America Star Bks.

Clissold, Caroline. Wild Animals. 2007. (Trackers-Math Ser.). (gr. 2-5). pap. 5.00 *(978-1-59055-916-1(9))* Pacific Learning, Inc.

Coan, Sharon. Birds & Bugs. 2015. (TIME for KIDS(r) Nonfiction Readers Ser.). (ENG., Illus.). 12p. (gr. k-k). 4.99 *(978-1-4938-2061-0(3))* Teacher Created Materials, Inc.

—Cuantos Juguetes? (How Many Toys?) 2016. (TIME for KIDS(r) Nonfiction Readers Ser.). (SPA., Illus.). 12p. (J). (gr. k-k). 4.99 *(978-1-4938-2971-2(8))* Teacher Created Materials, Inc.

—How Many Toys? 2015. (TIME for KIDS(r) Nonfiction Readers Ser.). (ENG., Illus.). 12p. (gr. k-k). 4.99 *(978-1-4938-2062-7(1))* Teacher Created Materials, Inc.

—Pajaros e Insectos (Birds & Bugs) 2016. (Nonfiction Readers Ser.). (SPA., Illus.). 12p. (J). (gr. k-k). pap. 4.99 *(978-1-4938-2970-5(X))* Teacher Created Materials, Inc.

Cobb, Rebecca. Spooky Sums & Counting Horrors. 2006. (ENG., Illus.). 32p. (J). (gr. -1-3). 14.95 *(978-0-7145-3307-0(6))* Boyars, Marion Pubs., Inc.

Cohn, Scotti. One Wolf Howls, 1 vol. Detwiler, Susan, illus. 2009. (ENG.). 32p. (J). (gr. -1-3). 16.95 *(978-1-934359-92-1(0))* Arbordale Publishing.

Coirault, Christine. Numbers: Learn to Count in Five Languages (English, Spanish, French, German, Italian) 2008. (Gymboree Play & Music Ser.). (ENG., Illus.). 24p. (J). (gr. -1). bds. *(978-1-55470-032-5(9))* Magma.

Cole, Carol A. La Dama de Los Pingüinos, 1 vol. Rogers, Sherry, illus. 2012. (SPA & ENG.). 32p. (J). (gr. -1-3). 17.95 *(978-1-60718-697-7(7))* Arbordale Publishing.

—The Penguin Lady, 1 vol. Rogers, Sherry, illus. 2012. (SPA.). 32p. (J). (gr. -1-3). pap. 9.95 *(978-1-62855-420-5(7))* Arbordale Publishing.

Collins Easy Learning & HarperCollins UK Staff. Counting Practice. 2008. (Collins Easy Learning Age 5-7 Ser.). (ENG.). 32p. (J). pap. 6.99 *(978-0-00-730095-2(6))* HarperCollins Pubs. Ltd. GBR. Dist: Independent Pubs. Group.

Collisin, Shauna. Heavenites Learning to Count on God Board Book with audio CD. Nelson, Christine, illus. 2007. 22p. (J). 15.95 *(978-0-9792510-1-6(X))* Revelation Products LLC.

Connelly, Neil O. Numbers. Thornburgh, Rebecca, illus. (Cuddly Beasties Ser.). 10p. (J). (gr. -1). bds. 3.95 *(978-1-58989-001-5(9))* Thurman Hse., LLC.

Cooper, Elisha. 8: An Animal Alphabet. 2015. (ENG., Illus.). 40p. (J). (gr. -1-k). 17.99 *(978-0-545-47083-4(8))* Scholastic, Inc.

Corbett, Sue. The Twelve Days of Christmas in Virginia. Cole, Henry, illus. 2009. (Twelve Days of Christmas in America Ser.). (ENG.). 40p. (J). (gr. k-3). 12.95 *(978-1-4027-6344-1(1))* Sterling Publishing Co., Inc.

Corcorane, Ann. Counting at the Parade, 1 vol. 2011. (Wonder Readers Emergent Level Ser.). (ENG.). (gr. -1-1). 32p. pap. 5.99 *(978-1-4296-7864-3(X))*; 16p. pap. 35.94 *(978-1-4296-8080-6(6))* Capstone Press of Coughlan Cos. (Wonder Readers).

—Counting to Ten, 1 vol. 2011. (Wonder Readers Emergent Level Ser.). (ENG.). (gr. -1-1). 32p. pap. 5.99 *(978-1-4296-7842-1(9))*; 8p. pap. 35.94 *(978-1-4296-8224-4(8))* Capstone Press of Coughlan Cos. (Wonder Readers).

—Numbers Are Everywhere. 2011. (Wonder Readers Emergent Level Ser.). (ENG.). 8p. (gr. -1-1). pap. 35.94 *(978-1-4296-8233-6(7)*, Wonder Readers) Capstone Press of Coughlan Cos.

Cornell, Kari. Goldilocks & the Three Pancakes: A Story of Shapes, Numbers, & Friendship. Sevig, Kirsten, illus. 2016. 32p. (J). pap. *(978-0-87659-706-4(1))* Gryphon Hse., Inc.

Corrigan, Kathleen. 123, 1 vol. 2014. (Canadian Board Bks.). (ENG & FRE.). 20p. bds. 7.99 *(978-1-62370-224-3(0))* Capstone Young Readers of Coughlan Cos.

Coss, Lauren. Let's Sort Money. 2014. (21st Century Basic Skills Library: Sorting Ser.). (ENG.). 24p. (J). (gr. k-3). 22.79 *(978-1-63137-633-7(0)*, 205315) Cherry Lake Publishing.

Cotton, Katie. Counting Lions: Portraits from the Wild. Walton, Stephen, illus. 2015. (ENG.). 40p. (J). (gr. k-12). 22.00 *(978-0-7636-8207-1(1))* Candlewick Pr.

Count & Color (Pre-K) 2003. (J). *(978-1-58232-042-7(X))* ECS Learning Systems, Inc.

Count To 100. 2017. (ENG.). (J). bds. 15.99 ***(978-0-7945-3797-5(9)***, Usborne) EDC Publishing.

Count to Ten. (J). 26.20 *(978-0-8136-8411-6(0))*; 26.20 *(978-0-8136-8410-9(2))*; (gr. -1-3). 59.50 *(978-0-8136-7942-6(7))* Modern Curriculum Pr.

Counting, Bk. 2. 2005. (J). per. 8.95 *(978-1-59566-157-9(3))* QEB Publishing Inc.

Counting Animals. (Illus.). 12p. (J). *(978-2-7643-0149-4(9))* Phidal Publishing, Inc./Editions Phidal, Inc.

Counting Book 1. 2005. (J). per. 8.95 *(978-1-59566-153-1(0))* QEB Publishing Inc.

Counting Puzzles. Date not set. (Illus.). 96p. (J). 2.98 *(978-0-7525-7519-3(8))* Parragon, Inc.

Counting the Seasons. 2010. (Counting Bks.). 32p. lib. bdg. 103.96 *(978-1-4296-5199-8(7)*, Aplus Bks.) Capstone Press of Coughlan Cos.

Counting with Fish. 2006. (J). bds. *(978-0-9771117-4-9(1))* JMG Studio.

Cousins, Lucy. Maisy Goes Camping. Cousins, Lucy, illus. 2009. (Maisy Ser.). (ENG., Illus.). 32p. (J). (gr. k-k). pap. 6.99 *(978-0-7636-4368-3(8))* Candlewick Pr.

—Maisy Goes Camping. 2009. (Maisy First Experiences Ser.). lib. bdg. 17.20 *(978-0-606-06667-9(5)*, Turtleback) Turtleback Bks.

Cox, Judy. Sheep Won't Sleep: Counting by 2s, 5s, And 10s. Cuneo, Nina, illus. 2017. (ENG.). 32p. (J). 16.95 ***(978-0-8234-3701-6(9))*** Holiday Hse., Inc.

Cox, Katie. Learn on the Go Sticker Activity - 123. 2010. 20p. pap. *(978-1-84879-397-2(9))* Make Believe Ideas.

Coyle, Carmela Lavigna. Do Princesses Count? Gordon, Mike & Gordon, Carl, illus. 2006. (ENG.). 24p. (J). (gr. -1-3). bds. 6.95 *(978-0-87358-916-1(5))* Cooper Square Publishing Llc.

Crane, Carol. Discover Florida, 2 bks. Monroe, Michael Glenn & Monroe Donovan, Jane, illus. 2003. (ENG.). 40p. (J). 27.95 *(978-1-58536-226-4(3))* Sleeping Bear Pr.

—Discover Texas, 2 bks. Stacy, Alan, illus. 2003. (ENG.). 40p. (J). 27.95 *(978-1-58536-227-1(1))* Sleeping Bear Pr.

—A Peck of Peaches: A Georgia Number Book. Braught, Mark, illus. rev. ed. 2007. (State Counting Ser.). (ENG.). 40p. (J). (gr. 1-3). 17.95 *(978-1-58536-177-9(1))* Sleeping Bear Pr.

—Round Up: A Texas Number Book. Stacey, Alan, illus. 2003. (America by the Numbers Ser.). (ENG.). 40p. (J). (gr. k-6). 16.95 *(978-1-58536-133-5(X))* Sleeping Bear Pr.

—Wright Numbers: A North Carolina Number Book. Palmer, Gary, illus. 2005. (Count Your Way Across the USA Ser.). (ENG.). 40p. (J). (gr. k-5). 16.95 *(978-1-58536-196-0(8))* Sleeping Bear Pr.

Crews, Donald. Los Diez Puntos Negros, 1 vol. Crews, Donald, illus. 2009. (SPA & ENG., Illus.). 32p. (J). (gr. -1-k). 16.99 *(978-0-06-177138-5(4))* HarperCollins Pubs.

—Ten Black Dots Board Book. Crews, Donald, illus. 2010. (ENG., Illus.). 32p. (J). (gr. -1-3). bds. 7.99 *(978-0-06-185779-9(3)*, Greenwillow Bks.) HarperCollins Pubs.

Crimi, Carolyn. Pugs in a Bug. Buscema, Stephanie, illus. 2012. (ENG.). 32p. (J). (gr. -1-k). 16.99 *(978-0-8037-3320-6(8)*, Dial Bks) Penguin Young Readers Group.

Crisp, Dan, illus. The Ants Go Marching! 2013. (Classic Books with Holes 8x8 with CD Ser.). (ENG.). 16p. (J). (gr. -1). pap. incl. audio compact disk *(978-1-84643-622-2(2))* Child's Play International Ltd.

Cronin, Doreen. Click, Clack, 123. Lewin, Betsy, illus. 2010. (Click, Clack Book Ser.). (ENG.). 24p. (J). (gr. -1 — 1). bds. 7.99 *(978-1-4169-9125-0(5)*, Little Simon) Little Simon.

Cronin, Doreen & Lewin, Betsy. Click, Clack, Splish, Splash: A Counting Adventure, 1 vol. 2006. (Doreen Cronin: Click-Clack & More Ser.). (ENG.). 24p. (gr. -1-3). lib. bdg. 24.21 *(978-1-59961-090-0(6))* Spotlight.

Crossley, David, illus. Baby's First Learning Book: 123. 2004. 10p. (J). bds. 2.99 *(978-0-681-03556-0(0))* Autumn Publishing Group, LLC.

—123. 2004. (Baby's First Learning Ser.). 12p. (J). bds. 4.99 *(978-1-85854-891-3(8))* Brimax Books Ltd. GBR. Dist: Byeway Bks.

Crowther, Robert. The Most Amazing Hide-and-Seek Numbers Book. Crowther, Robert, illus. 2010. (ENG., Illus.). 12p. (J). (gr. -1-2). pap. 12.99 *(978-0-7636-5029-2(3))* Candlewick Pr.

Cuento Hasta Diez. 2003. 63.50 *(978-0-8136-8067-5(0))*; suppl. ed. 8.95 *(978-0-8136-8064-4(6))* Modern Curriculum Pr.

Cummings, Priscilla. Chesapeake 1-2-3, 1 vol. Aiken, David, illus. 2009. (ENG.). 32p. (J). (gr. -1-2). 11.95 *(978-0-87033-542-6(1)*, 9780870335426, Cornell Maritime Pr./Tidewater Pubs.) Schiffer Publishing, Ltd.

Dahl, Michael. Una Bandera a Cuadros: Un Libro para Contar Sobre Carreras de Autos. Alderman, Derrick & Shea, Denise, illus. 2010. (Apréndete Tus Números/Know Your Numbers Ser.).Tr. of One Checkered Flag - A Counting Book about Racing. (SPA & MUL.). 24p. (gr. -1-2). lib. bdg. 26.65 *(978-1-4048-6295-1(1))* Picture Window Bks.

—¡Córrele, Córrele Ciempiés! Cuenta de Diez en Diez. Trover, Zachary, illus. 2010. (Apréndete Tus Números/Know Your Numbers Ser.).Tr. of Speed, Speed Centipede! - Counting by Tens. (SPA & MUL.). 24p. (gr. -1-2). lib. bdg. 26.65 *(978-1-4048-6299-9(4))* Picture Window Bks.

—Downhill Fun: A Counting Book about Winter, 1 vol. Ouren, Todd, illus. 2004. (Know Your Numbers Ser.). (ENG.). 24p. (gr. -1-2). per. 8.95 *(978-1-4048-1092-1(7))* Picture Window Bks.

—Eggs & Legs: Counting by Twos, 1 vol. Ouren, Todd, illus. 2005. (Know Your Numbers Ser.). (ENG.). 24p. (gr. -1-2). 26.65 *(978-1-4048-0945-1(7))* Picture Window Bks.

—Un Gran Edificio: Un Libro para Contar Sobre Construcción. Ouren, Todd, illus. 2010. (Apréndete Tus Números/Know Your Numbers Ser.).Tr. of One Big Building - A Counting Book about Construction. (ENG, SPA & MUL.). 24p. (gr. -1-2). lib. bdg. 26.65 *(978-1-4048-6294-4(3))* Picture Window Bks.

—Huevos y Patas: Cuenta de Dos en Dos. Ouren, Todd, illus. 2010. (Apréndete Tus Números/Know Your Numbers Ser.).Tr. of Eggs & Legs/Counting by Twos. (MUL & SPA.). 24p. (gr. -1-2). lib. bdg. 26.65 *(978-1-4048-6296-8(X))* Picture Window Bks.

—Lots of Ladybugs! Counting by Fives, 1 vol. Ouren, Todd, illus. 2005. (Know Your Numbers Ser.). (ENG.). 24p. (gr. -1-2). 26.65 *(978-1-4048-0944-4(9))* Picture Window Bks.

C
D

—¡Montones de Mariquitas! Cuenta de Cinco en Cinco. Ouren, Todd, illus. 2010. (Aprêndete Tus Números/Know Your Numbers Ser.).Tr. of Lots of Ladybugs! - Counting by Fives. (SPA & MUL.). 24p. (gr. -1-2). lib. bdg. 26.65 *(978-1-4048-6297-5(8))* Picture Window Bks.

—On the Launch Pad: A Counting Book about Rockets, 1 vol. Alderman, Derrick & Shea, Denise, illus. 2004. (Know Your Numbers Ser.). (ENG.). 24p. (gr. -1-2). per. 8.95 *(978-1-4048-1119-5(2))* Picture Window Bks.

Dale, Penny. Dinosaur Dig! Dale, Penny, illus. 2012. (ENG., Illus.). 14p. (J). (gr. k-k). bds. 6.99 *(978-0-7636-6270-7(4),* Nosy Crow) Candlewick Pr.

—Ten in the Bed. Dale, Penny, illus. 2007. (ENG., Illus.). 24p. (J). (— 1). bds. 5.99 *(978-0-7636-3514-5(6))* Candlewick Pr.

Dalmatian Press Staff. Maggie Can Count. 2008. (ENG.). 5p. (J). bds. 4.95 *(978-1-58117-728-2(3),* Intervisual/Piggy Toes) Bendon, Inc.

Dalton, Julie. Counting Money. 2006. (Rookie Read-About Math Ser.). (ENG., Illus.). 32p. (J). (gr. 1-2). per. 5.95 *(978-0-516-25361-9(1),* Children's Pr.) Scholastic Library Publishing.

—Look & Count. 2006. (Rookie Read-About Math Ser.). (ENG., Illus.). 32p. (J). (gr. 1-2). lib. bdg. 20.50 *(978-0-516-24958-2(4),* Children's Pr.) Scholastic Library Publishing.

—Making Change at the Fair. 2006. (Rookie Read-About Math Ser.). (ENG., Illus.). 32p. (J). (gr. 1-2). lib. bdg. 20.50 *(978-0-516-24960-5(6),* Children's Pr.) Scholastic Library Publishing.

Davenport, Maxine & Roberts, Cindy, illus. 1 2 3 Counting: First Freeze. 2015. (ENG.). 10p. (J). 7.00 *(978-1-61067-421-8(9))* Kane Miller.

David. Counting Nifty from One to Fifty. 2011. 72p. pap. 31.99 *(978-1-4568-4719-7(8))* Xlibris Corp.

David C. Cook Publishing Company Staff. Learning to Count. 2004. (My Jesus Pocket Bks.). (Illus.). 32p. (J). pap., pap. 8.90 *(978-1-55513-097-8(6),* 1555130976) Cook, David C.

Davies, Ann. Fun Adding. (Illus.). 10p. (J). 9.95 *(978-1-85479-246-4(6))* O'Mara, Michael Bks., Ltd. GBR. Dist: Trans-Atlantic Pubns., Inc.

Davies, Becky. Peekaboo Pals 123. Lucas, Gareth, illus. 2016. (Peekaboo Pals Ser.). (ENG.). 20p. (J). (gr. -1). bds. 14.95 *(978-1-62686-521-1(3),* Silver Dolphin Bks.) Readerlink Distribution Services, LLC.

Davies, Gill. Ten in a Bed: A Pop-up Counting Book. Guile, Gill, illus. 20p. (J). *(978-1-59394-120-8(X))* Bendon, Inc.

Davis, Darren. Atlas 123S for Superheroes. 2006. (ENG.). 16p. (J). (gr. -1-12). bds. 5.99 *(978-1-59559-117-3(6))* Left Field,Angel Gate.

Davis, David. Ten Redneck Babies: A Southern Counting Book, 1 vol. Ward, Sue Marshall, illus. 2004. (ENG.). 32p. (J). (gr. k-k). 16.99 *(978-1-58980-232-2(2))* Pelican Publishing Co., Inc.

Davis, Rebecca F. Playas y Bicicletas: Un Libro para Contar en el Verano. 2012. (Vamos a Contar / Counting Bks.).Tr. of Beaches & Bicycles - A Summer Counting Book. (ENG, SPA & MUL.). 32p. (gr. 1-2). lib. bdg. 27.32 *(978-1-4296-8250-3(7),* A+ Bilingue/Bilingual) Capstone Press of Coughlan Cos.

Day, Nancy Raines. What in the World? Sets in Nature. Cyrus, Kurt, illus. 2015. (ENG.). 32p. (J). (gr. -1-3). 17.99 *(978-1-4814-0060-2(6),* Beach Lane Bks.) Beach Lane Bks.

Daynes, Katie. 1001 Things to Spot in the Sea. Gower, Teri, illus. 2009. (1001 Things to Spot Ser.). 32p. (J). (gr. 1). 9.99 *(978-0-7945-2615-3(2),* Usborne) EDC Publishing.

de Brunhoff, Laurent. Babar's Counting Book. rev. ed. 2012. (ENG., Illus.). 40p. (J). (gr. k-2). 16.95 *(978-1-4197-0341-6(2),* Abrams Bks. for Young Readers) Abrams, Inc.

de Klerk, Roger, illus. Foxy Learns to Add. 2009. (Foxy Learns Ser.). 16p. (J). pap. 4.95 *(978-1-59496-178-6(6))* Teora USA LLC.

Dealey, Erin. Little Bo Peep Can't Get to Sleep. Wakiyama, Hanako, illus. 2010. (ENG.). 40p. (J). (gr. -1-2). 13.99 *(978-1-4424-0935-4(5),* Atheneum Bks. for Young Readers) Simon & Schuster Children's Publishing.

Deen, Marilyn. From 1 To 100, 1 vol. 2011. (Wonder Readers Fluent Level Ser.). (ENG.). (gr. -1-2). 32p. pap. 5.99 *(978-1-4296-7789-9(9));* 16p. pap. 35.94 *(978-1-4296-7790-5(2))* Capstone Press of Coughlan Cos. (Wonder Readers).

Delessert, Etienne. Hungry for Numbers. 2006. (ENG., Illus.). 32p. (J). (gr. 1-3). 19.95 *(978-1-56846-198-4(4))* Creative Co., The.

Dempsey, Kristy. Ten Little Fingers, Two Small Hands. Massey, Jane, illus. 2016. (ENG.). 32p. (J). (gr. -1-2). 16.99 *(978-1-4998-0229-0(3))* Little Bee Books Inc.

—Ten Little Toes, Two Small Feet. Massey, Jane, illus. 2016. (ENG.). 32p. (J). (gr. -1-2). 16.99 *(978-1-4998-0236-8(6))* Little Bee Books Inc.

Dena, Anael. Los Numbers. (SPA.). 46p. (J). *(978-84-263-3289-9(7))* Vives, Luis Editorial (Edelvives) ESP. Dist: Lectorum Pubns., Inc.

Deneux, Xavier. Numbers. 2014. (ENG., Illus.). 22p. (J). (gr. -1 — 1). bds. 14.99 *(978-1-4521-1724-9(1))* Chronicle Bks. LLC.

Derke, Connie Butterfield. Mommy Has 1 Foot: Learning about Numbers - Learning about People. Smith, Tracy, illus. 2003. (Kayla's Learning Books). 24p. (J). (gr. 1-6). pap. 5.95 *(978-0-9747063-0-6(2))* Derke, Connie.

deRubertis, Barbara. Bobby Baboon's Banana Be-Bop. Alley, R. W., illus. 2010. (Animal Antics A to Z Ser.). 32p. (J). lib. bdg. 22.60 *(978-1-57565-305-1(2));* (ENG.). (gr. -1-3). pap. 7.95 *(978-1-57565-301-3(X))* Kane Press, Inc.

deRubertis, Barbara & DeRubertis, Barbara. Bobby Baboon's Banana Be-Bop. Alley, R. W., illus. 2012. (Animal Antics A to Z Ser.). 32p. (J). (gr. 2 — 1). cd-rom 7.95 *(978-1-57565-395-2(8))* Kane Press, Inc.

Dicmas, Courtney. Numbers. Dicmas, Courtney, illus. 2017. (Wild! Concepts Ser.: 4). (ENG., Illus.). 14p. (J). bds. ***(978-1-84643-993-3(0))*** Child's Play International Ltd.

Dils, Tracey E. Around the Moon 1,2,3: A Space Counting Book. 2015. (1, 2, 3... Count with Me Ser.). (ENG., Illus.). 24p. (J). (gr. k-2). 19.95 *(978-1-60753-714-4(1))* Amicus Publishing.

—Down in the Jungle 1,2,3: A Rainforest Counting Book. 2015. (1, 2, 3... Count with Me Ser.). (ENG., Illus.). 24p. (J). (gr. k-2). 19.95 *(978-1-60753-715-1(X))* Amicus Publishing.

—Down on the Farm 1,2,3: A Farm Counting Book. 2015. (1, 2, 3... Count with Me Ser.). (ENG., Illus.). 24p. (J). (gr. k-2). 19.95 *(978-1-60753-718-2(4))* Amicus Publishing.

—Falling Leaves 1,2,3: A Fall Counting Book. 2015. (1, 2, 3... Count with Me Ser.). (ENG., Illus.). 24p. (J). (gr. k-2). 19.95 *(978-1-60753-719-9(2))* Amicus Publishing.

—My Pet & Me, 1,2,3: A Pets Counting Book. 2015. (1, 2, 3... Count with Me Ser.). (ENG., Illus.). 24p. (J). (gr. k-2). 19.95 *(978-1-60753-716-8(8))* Amicus Publishing.

—Under the Sea 1,2,3: An Ocean Counting Book. 2015. (1, 2, 3... Count with Me Ser.). (ENG., Illus.). 24p. (J). (gr. k-2). 19.95 *(978-1-60753-717-5(6))* Amicus Publishing.

Dingles, Molly. Number 10 Where Is the Hen? Wallis, Rebecca, illus. 2005. (Community of Counting Ser.). (ENG.). 32p. (J). lib. bdg. 21.65 *(978-1-891997-90-7(4))* Dingles & Co.

—Number 2 Let's Go to the Zoo! Wallis, Rebecca, illus. 2005. (Community of Counting Ser.). 32p. (J). pap. 10.95 *(978-1-59646-276-2(0))* Dingles & Co.

—Number 2 Let's Go to the Zoo!/Número 2 Vamos al Zoologico! Wallis, Rebecca, illus. 2005. (Community of Counting Ser.).Tr. of Número 2 Vamos al Zoologico! (ENG & SPA.). 32p. (J). pap. 10.95 *(978-1-59646-278-6(7));* lib. bdg. 21.65 *(978-1-891997-88-4(2))* Dingles & Co.

—Number 3 What's in the Sea? 2005. (Community of Counting Ser.). (ENG., Illus.). 32p. (J). lib. bdg. 21.65 *(978-1-891997-97-6(1))* Dingles & Co.

—Number 3 What's in the Sea? Wallis, Rebecca, illus. 2005. (Community of Counting Ser.). 32p. (J). pap. 10.95 *(978-1-59646-280-9(9))* Dingles & Co.

—Number 3 What's in the Sea?/Número 3 Qué hay en el Mar? Wallis, Rebecca, illus. 2005. (Community of Counting Ser.).Tr. of Número 3 Qué hay en el Mar? (ENG & SPA.). 32p. (J). pap. 10.95 *(978-1-59646-282-3(5));* lib. bdg. 21.65 *(978-1-891997-87-7(4))* Dingles & Co.

—Number 4 Shop at the Store! Wallis, Rebecca, illus. (Community of Counting Ser.). 32p. (J). 2005. pap. 10.95 *(978-1-59646-284-7(1))* 2004. (ENG.). lib. bdg. 21.65 *(978-1-891997-96-9(3))* Dingles & Co.

—Number 4 Shop at the Store!/Número 4 Vamos de compras a la Tienda! Wallis, Rebecca, illus. 2005. (Community of Counting Ser.).Tr. of Número 4 Vamos de compras a la Tienda! (ENG & SPA.). 32p. (J). pap. 10.95 *(978-1-59646-286-1(8));* lib. bdg. 21.65 *(978-1-891997-86-0(6))* Dingles & Co.

—Number 5 Let's Go for a Drive! Wallis, Rebecca, illus. 2005. (Community of Counting Ser.). 32p. (J). pap. 10.95 *(978-1-59646-288-5(4));* (ENG.). lib. bdg. 21.65 *(978-1-891997-95-2(5))* Dingles & Co.

—Number 5 Let's Go for a Drive!/Número 5 Vamos a viajar en Coche! Wallis, Rebecca, illus. 2005. (Community of Counting Ser.).Tr. of Número 5 Vamos a viajar en Coche! (ENG & SPA.). 32p. (J). pap. 10.95 *(978-1-59646-290-8(6));* lib. bdg. 21.65 *(978-1-891997-85-3(8))* Dingles & Co.

—Number 6 What Can We Mix? Wallis, Rebecca, illus. 2005. (Community of Counting Ser.). 32p. (J). pap. 10.95 *(978-1-59646-292-2(2))* Dingles & Co.

—Number 6 What Can We Mix ? Wallis, Rebecca, illus. 2005. (Community of Counting Ser.). 32p. (J). lib. bdg. 21.65 *(978-1-891997-94-5(7))* Dingles & Co.

—Number 6 What Can We Mix?/Número 6 Qué podemos Mezclar? Wallis, Rebecca, illus. 2005. (Community of Counting Ser.).Tr. of Número 6 Qué podemos Mezclar? (ENG & SPA.). 32p. (J). pap. 10.95 *(978-1-59646-294-6(9));* lib. bdg. 21.65 *(978-1-891997-84-6(X))* Dingles & Co.

—Number 7 Stars in the Heaven. Wallis, Rebecca, illus. (Community of Counting Ser.). 32p. (J). 2005. pap. 10.95 *(978-1-59646-296-0(5))* 2004. lib. bdg. 21.65 *(978-1-891997-93-8(9))* Dingles & Co.

—Number 7 Stars in the Heaven/Número 7 Estrellas en el Cielo. Wallis, Rebecca, illus. (Community of Counting Ser.).Tr. of Número 7 Estrellas en el Cielo. (ENG & SPA.). 32p. (J). 2005. pap. 10.95 *(978-1-59646-298-4(1))* 2004. lib. bdg. 21.65 *(978-1-891997-83-9(1))* Dingles & Co.

—Number 8 Let's Stay up Late! Wallis, Rebecca, illus. 2005. (Community of Counting Ser.). 32p. (J). pap. 10.95 *(978-1-59646-300-4(7))* Dingles & Co.

—Number 8 Let's Stay up Late!/Número 8 Vamos a quedarnos en vela hasta muy Noche! Wallis, Rebecca, illus. (Community of Counting Ser.).Tr. of Número 8 Vamos a quedarnos en vela hasta muy Noche! (ENG & SPA.). 32p. (J). 2005. pap. 10.95 *(978-1-59646-302-8(3))* 2004. lib. bdg. 21.65 *(978-1-891997-82-2(3))* Dingles & Co.

—Number 9 Dress up to Dine! Wallis, Rebecca, illus. (Community of Counting Ser.). 32p. (J). 2005. pap. 10.95 *(978-1-59646-304-2(X))* 2004. lib. bdg. 21.65 *(978-1-891997-91-4(2))* Dingles & Co.

—Number 9 Dress up to Dine!/Número 9 Vestirse con elegancia para Cenar! Wallis, Rebecca, illus. 2005. (Community of Counting Ser.).Tr. of Número 9 Vestirse con elegancia para Cenar! (ENG & SPA.). 32p. (J). pap. 10.95 *(978-1-59646-306-6(6));* lib. bdg. 21.65 *(978-1-891997-81-5(5))* Dingles & Co.

Disney, Princesses, ed. ClubHouse ABCs. 2009. 24p. 7.99 *(978-1-59069-770-2(7))* Studio Mouse LLC.

DiTerlizzi, Tony. G Is for One Gzonk! An Alpha-Number-Bet Book. DiTerlizzi, Tony, illus. 2006. (ENG., Illus.). 80p. (J). (gr. -1-2). 29.99 *(978-0-689-85290-9(8),* Simon & Schuster Bks. For Young Readers) Simon & Schuster Bks. For Young Readers.

Dobbins, Jan. Driving My Tractor. Sim, David, illus. 2009. (ENG.). 32p. (J). (gr. -1-3). 16.99 incl. audio compact disk *(978-1-84686-358-5(9))* Barefoot Bks., Inc.

Dobson, Christina. The Pizza Counting. Holmes, Matthew, illus. 2003. (ENG.). 32p. (J). (gr. 1-4). pap. 7.95 *(978-0-88106-339-4(8))* Charlesbridge Publishing, Inc.

Dodd, Emma. Counting. 2017. (ENG., Illus.). 12p. (J). (gr. -1-12). bds. 9.99 ***(978-1-86147-839-9(9),*** Armadillo) Anness Publishing GBR. Dist: National Bk. Network.

Dodd, Emma. Dog's Colorful Day: A Messy Story about Colors & Counting. Dodd, Emma, illus. 2003. (ENG., Illus.). 32p. (J). (gr. k-k). 6.99 *(978-0-14-250019-4(4),* Puffin Books) Penguin Young Readers Group.

—Dog's Colorful Day: A Messy Story about Colors & Counting. 2003. (gr. k-3). 16.00 *(978-0-613-57720-5(5),* Turtleback) Turtleback Bks.

Doherty, Gillian. 1001 Animals to Spot. 2010. (1001 Things to Spot Ser.). 32p. (J). 9.99 *(978-0-7945-2704-4(3),* Usborne) EDC Publishing.

—1001 Cosas Que Buscar en el Psia de las Hadas. Gower, Teri, illus. 2007. (Titles in Spanish Ser.). 32p. (J). 9.99 *(978-0-7460-8346-8(7),* Usborne) EDC Publishing.

Domeniconi, David. Golden Numbers: A California Number Book. Carroll, Pam, illus. 2008. (Count Your Way Across the U. S. A. Ser.). (ENG.). 40p. (J). 17.95 *(978-1-58536-173-1(9))* Sleeping Bear Pr.

Donaldson, Julia. My First 123 Sticker Book. Sharratt, Nick, illus. 2016. (ENG.). 30p. (J). (gr. -1-2). pap. 8.99 *(978-1-5098-1621-7(6))* Pan Macmillan GBR. Dist: Independent Pubs. Group.

—One Mole Digging A Hole. Sharratt, Nick, illus. 2015. (ENG.). 22p. (J). (-k). bds. 9.99 *(978-1-4472-8790-2(8))* Pan Macmillan GBR. Dist: Independent Pubs. Group.

—One Mole Digging a Hole, 2. Sharratt, Nick, illus. 2010. (ENG.). 32p. (J). (gr. k-k). pap. 8.99 *(978-0-230-70647-7(9))* Macmillan Pubs., Ltd. GBR. Dist: Independent Pubs. Group.

—One Ted Falls Out of Bed. Currey, Anna, illus. 2014. (ENG.). 12p. (J). (gr. -1 — 1). bds. 8.99 *(978-1-4472-0995-9(8))* Pan Macmillan GBR. Dist: Independent Pubs. Group.

Donaldson, Julia. Spinderella. Braun, Sebastian, illus. 2017. (ENG.). 32p. (J). (gr. -1-k). pap. 9.99 ***(978-1-4052-8272-7(X))*** Egmont Bks., Ltd. GBR. Dist: Independent Pubs. Group.

Donoghue, Stella. Lift & Learn 123. Snaith, Andy, photos by. 2006. (Illus.). 24p. (gr. -1). per., bds. *(978-1-84610-030-7(5))* Make Believe Ideas.

Dorling Kindersley Publishing Staff. Counting. 2016. (DK Braille Ser.). (ENG.). 18p. (J). (-k). bds. 14.99 *(978-1-4654-3613-9(8),* DK Children) Dorling Kindersley Publishing, Inc.

—My First 123. 2015. (My First Bks.). (ENG.). 36p. (J). (gr. -1 — 1). bds. 5.99 *(978-1-4654-2903-2(4),* DK Children) Dorling Kindersley Publishing, Inc.

—My First Numbers: Let's Get Counting! 2008. (Tab Board Bks.). (ENG.). 28p. (J). (gr. -1-k). bds. 9.99 *(978-0-7566-3604-3(3),* DK Children) Dorling Kindersley Publishing, Inc.

—Pull the Tab: Numbers. 2015. (ENG., Illus.). 10p. (J). (— 1). bds. 6.99 *(978-1-4654-3857-7(2),* DK Children) Dorling Kindersley Publishing, Inc.

—Skills for Starting School I Can Count. 2017. (Skills for Starting School Ser.). (ENG.). 18p. (J). (-k). bds. 12.99 ***(978-1-4654-5676-2(7),*** DK Children) Dorling Kindersley Publishing, Inc.

Dorling Kindersley Publishing Staff. Touch & Feel 123. 2013. (Touch & Feel Ser.). (ENG.). 12p. (J). (gr. -1-k). bds. 6.99 *(978-1-4654-0917-1(3),* DK Children) Dorling Kindersley Publishing, Inc.

Dotlich, Rebecca Kai. Race Car Count. Slack, Michael, illus. 2017. (ENG.). 32p. (J). bds. 7.99 *(978-1-62779-934-8(6),* 9781627799348, Holt, Henry & Co. Bks. For Young Readers) Holt, Henry & Co.

Dowdy, Penny. Money. 2008. (My Path to Math Ser.). (ENG., Illus.). 24p. (J). (gr. k-3). pap. *(978-0-7787-4360-6(8))* Crabtree Publishing Co.

—Place Value. 2008. (My Path to Math Ser.). (ENG., Illus.). 24p. (J). (gr. k-3). pap. *(978-0-7787-4361-3(6));* lib. bdg. *(978-0-7787-4343-9(8))* Crabtree Publishing Co.

Doxey, Heidi. 1, 2, 3 with Nephi & Me! Konopasek, Emily, illus. 2015. 9.99 *(978-1-4621-1636-2(1),* Horizon Pubs.) Cedar Fort, Inc./CFI Distribution.

Drews, Judith. The Zoo's Grand Opening: An ABC & Counting Book. 2014. (ENG., Illus.). 64p. 16.95 *(978-3-89955-714-5(X))* Die Gestalten Verlag DEU. Dist: Penguin Random Hse. LLC.

Driscoll, Laura. El Chico Del Despegue (the Blast-off Kid) 2009. (SPA.). pap. 34.95 *(978-0-7613-4789-7(5))* Lerner Publishing Group.

Dugan, Joanne. 123 Nyc: A Counting Book of New York City. 2007. (ENG., Illus.). 52p. (J). (gr. -1-1). 17.95 *(978-0-8109-1381-3(X),* Abrams Bks. for Young Readers) Abrams, Inc.

Duke, Shirley. Money Counts. 2012. (ENG.). 24p. (gr. -1-1). pap. 8.95 *(978-1-61810-209-6(5))* Rourke Educational Media.

—What's the Place Value? 2012. (ENG.). 24p. (gr. -1-1). pap. 8.95 *(978-1-61810-208-9(7))* Rourke Educational Media.

Dunn, Opal. Number Rhymes to Say & Play! Gon, Adriano, illus. 2005. (ENG.). 32p. (J). (gr. -1 — 1). per. 7.95 *(978-1-84507-441-8(6),* Frances Lincoln) Quarto Publishing Group UK GBR. Dist: Hachette Bk. Group.

Durango, Julia. Cha-Cha Chimps. Taylor, Eleanor, illus. 2010. (ENG.). 32p. (J). (gr. -1-3). 7.99 *(978-1-4169-9574-6(9),* Simon & Schuster Bks. For Young Readers) Simon & Schuster Bks. For Young Readers.

DuTemple, Leslie A. One Little Balsam Fir: A Northwoods Counting Book. Robinson, Susan, illus. 2006. 32p. (J). per. *(978-1-892384-37-9(X))* Avery Color Studios, Inc.

Dyan, Penelope. Jump Frog, Funny Frog — -Because Frogs Are Funny. Dyan, Penelope, illus. 2008. (Illus.). 44p. pap. 11.95 *(978-1-935118-19-0(6))* Bellissima Publishing, LLC.

—Olympic Gold — Because Everyone Loves a Winner! Dyan, Penelope, illus. 2008. (Illus.). 44p. pap. 11.95 *(978-1-935118-20-6(X))* Bellissima Publishing, LLC.

Early Days Counting. 2007. (Jigsaw Book Ser.). (Illus.). 16p. (gr. -1-k). bds. *(978-1-84666-367-3(9))* Top That! Publishing PLC.

Edwards, Pamela Duncan. Roar! A Noisy Counting Book. Cole, Henry, illus. Date not set. 32p. (J). (gr. -1-2). pap. 5.99 *(978-0-06-443572-7(5))* HarperCollins Pubs.

Electric Confetti. Neon Baby: Numbers. 2017. (Neon Baby Ser.). (ENG.). (J). 20p. (J). (— 1). bds. 12.99 ***(978-1-76012-931-6(3))*** Hardie Grant Egmont Pty, Ltd. AUS. Dist: Independent Pubs. Group.

Elig, Jennifer. One Lord, Two People — un Señor, Dos Personas: A Bible Counting Book — una Biblia para Contar. 2012. (Illus.). 30p. pap. 15.95 *(978-1-4497-6271-1(9),* WestBow Pr.) Author Solutions, Inc.

Elissa Grodin. Everyone Counts: A Citizens' Number Book. Juhasz, Victor, illus. rev. ed. 2006. (Count Your Way Across the U. S. A. Ser.). (ENG.). 40p. (J). (gr. -1-3). 17.95 *(978-1-58536-295-0(6))* Sleeping Bear Pr.

Ellens, Brenda L. The Duckling Pond. 2008. 32p. pap. 16.49 *(978-1-4343-9566-5(9))* AuthorHouse.

Elliott, David. One Little Chicken: A Counting Book. Long, Ethan, illus. 2007. (ENG.). 24p. (J). (gr. -1-3). 16.95 *(978-0-8234-1983-8(5))* Holiday Hse., Inc.

Ellis, Greg & BeachHouse Publishing. Baby's First 1-2-3 in Hawaii. 2008. (ENG.). 20p. (J). (gr. -1-1). bds. 7.95 *(978-1-933067-24-7(1))* Beachhouse Publishing, LLC.

Emberley, Rebecca. My Numbers (Mis Numeros) braille ed. 2004. (ENG & SPA.). (J). (gr. 1). spiral bd., bds. *(978-0-616-07272-1(4))* Canadian National Institute for the Blind/Institut National Canadien pour les Aveugles.

Emma Treehouse Ltd. My Babies. Davis, Caroline, illus. 2007. (Easy Flaps Ser.). 10p. (J). (gr. -1). bds. 6.95 *(978-1-58925-822-8(3))* Tiger Tales.

Engel, Christiane & Songs, Steve. Knick Knack Paddy Whack. Engel, Christiane, illus. 2011. (ENG., Illus.). 24p. (J). (gr. -1-2). 9.99 *(978-1-84686-659-3(6))* Barefoot Bks., Inc.

Engel, Steve. Tracks Count: A Guide to Counting Animal Prints. Petersen, Alexander, illus. 2014. (Little Naturalist Ser.). (ENG.). 32p. (J). (gr. -1-k). 17.99 *(978-1-940052-07-6(6))* Craigmore Creations.

Enslow, Brian. Counting Ants 1-2-3. 2011. (All about Counting Bugs 1-2-3 Ser.). (Illus.). 24p. (J). (gr. -1-18). pap. 7.95 *(978-1-59845-249-5(5),* Enslow Elementary) Enslow Pubs., Inc.

—Counting Bees 1-2-3. 2011. (All about Counting Bugs 1-2-3 Ser.). (Illus.). 24p. (J). (gr. -1-18). pap. 7.95 *(978-1-59845-247-1(9),* Enslow Elementary) Enslow Pubs., Inc.

—Counting Butterflies 1-2-3. 2011. (All about Counting Bugs 1-2-3 Ser.). (Illus.). 24p. (J). (gr. -1-18). pap. 7.95 *(978-1-59845-246-4(0),* Enslow Elementary) Enslow Pubs., Inc.

—Counting Ladybugs 1-2-3. 2011. (All about Counting Bugs 1-2-3 Ser.). (Illus.). 24p. (J). (gr. -1-18). pap. 7.95 *(978-1-59845-251-8(7),* Enslow Elementary); (gr. k-3). lib. bdg. 22.60 *(978-0-7660-3922-3(6))* Enslow Pubs., Inc.

Entin, Cindy. My First Counting Book: Coast Guard. 2014. (ENG.). 10p. (J). bds. 5.99 *(978-1-60433-460-9(6),* Applesauce Pr.) Cider Mill Pr. Bk. Pubs., LLC.

—My First Counting Book: Firefighters. Boldman, Craig, illus. 2014. (ENG.). 10p. (J). bds. 5.99 *(978-1-60433-470-8(3),* Applesauce Pr.) Cider Mill Pr. Bk. Pubs., LLC.

—My First Counting Book: Marines. 2013. (ENG.). 10p. (J). (-k). bds. 5.99 *(978-1-60433-322-0(7),* Applesauce Pr.) Cider Mill Pr. Bk. Pubs., LLC.

—My First Counting Book: Police. Boldman, Craig, illus. 2014. (ENG.). 10p. (J). bds. 5.99 *(978-1-60433-456-2(8),* Applesauce Pr.) Cider Mill Pr. Bk. Pubs., LLC.

Esmay, Gabriel. The History of Number Systems. 2017. (Mathematics Readers Ser.). 32p. (gr. 3-3). 8.99 ***(978-1-4807-5794-3(2))*** Teacher Created Materials, Inc.

Esplanie, Kevin. Counting Pennies: Number Names & Count Sequence. 2013. (InfoMax Math Readers Ser.). (ENG.). 16p. (J). (gr. k-1). pap. 42.00 *(978-1-4777-1995-4(4));* (Illus.). pap. 7.00 *(978-1-4777-1994-7(6))* Rosen Publishing Group, Inc., The. (Rosen Classroom).

Eubank, Patricia Reeder. Countdown to Christmas. 2003. (ENG., Illus.). 14p. (J). (gr. -1-k). bds. 9.95 *(978-0-8249-6505-1(1),* Ideal Pubns.) Worthy Publishing.

—Halloween 123s. Eubank, Patricia Reeder, illus. 2011. (Illus.). 22p. (J). bds. 6.99 *(978-0-8249-1868-2(1),* Ideal Pubns.) Worthy Publishing.

Evans, Lezlie. Can You Count Ten Toes? Count to 10 in 10 Different Languages. Roche, Denis, illus. 2004. (J). (gr. -1-3). 13.60 *(978-0-7569-5182-5(8))* Perfection Learning Corp.

—Can You Count Ten Toes? Count to 10 in 10 Different Languages. Roche, Denis, illus. 2004. (ENG.). 32p. (J). (gr. -1-3). pap. 6.99 *(978-0-618-49487-3(1))* Houghton Mifflin Harcourt Publishing Co.

Evanson, Ashley. San Francisco: A Book of Numbers. Evanson, Ashley, illus. 2015. (Hello, World Ser.). (ENG., Illus.). 14p. (J). (— 1). bds. 6.99 *(978-0-448-48914-8(7),* Grosset & Dunlap) Penguin Young Readers Group.

Evensen, Rachelle. Finn's Marching Band: A Story of Counting, Colors, & Playing Together. 2009. 32p. (J). 14.95 *(978-0-8091-6749-4(2),* Ambassador Bks.) Paulist Pr.

Falconer, Ian. Olivia Cuenta. 2006. (Olivia Ser.).Tr. of Olivia Counts. (SPA.). (J). (gr. -1-k). bds. 6.99 *(978-1-930332-89-8(0),* LC33420) Lectorum Pubns., Inc.

Falwell, Cathryn. Feast for 10, 1 vol. Falwell, Cathryn, illus. (Read along Book & CD Ser.). (ENG., Illus.). (J). (gr. -1-3). 2008. 32p. audio compact disk 10.99 *(978-0-547-06431-4(4))* 2003. 28p. bds. 4.95 *(978-0-618-38226-2(7))* Houghton Mifflin Harcourt Publishing Co.

—Feast For 10. 2017. (ENG., Illus.). 32p. (J). (gr. -1-3). 26.99 *(978-0-544-93030-8(4),* HMH Books For Young Readers) Houghton Mifflin Harcourt Publishing Co.

—Turtle Splash! Countdown at the Pond. Falwell, Cathryn, illus. 2008. (ENG., Illus.). 32p. (J). (gr. -1-3). pap. 6.99 *(978-0-06-142927-9(9),* Greenwillow Bks.) HarperCollins Pubs.

Feelings, Muriel L. Moja Means One: A Swahili Counting Book. Feelings, Tom, illus. 2004. 20p. (J). (gr. k-4). reprint ed. pap. 5.00 *(978-0-7567-7108-9(0))* DIANE Publishing Co.

Feldman, Jean R. & Karapetkova, Holly. Chant & Write (Tune, Sound off Cadence) Lap Book. 2010. (ENG., Illus.). 12p. (gr. -1-k). 9.95 *(978-1-61590-192-0(2))* Rourke Educational Media.

Feldman, Thea. ASPCA Mix & Match Pets: A Colors & Counting Book. 2015. (Mix & Match Ser.: 1). (ENG.). 12p. (J). (gr. -1-k). 8.99 *(978-0-7944-3299-7(9),* Reader's Digest Children's Bks.) Studio Fun International.

Felix, Monique. The Numbers. Felix, Monique, illus. 2013. (ENG., Illus.). 32p. (J). (gr. -1-k). 12.99 *(978-1-56846-235-6(2),* Creative Editions) Creative Co., The.

Ferrante, Joanne. R. G.'s on Vacation! 2003. (Illus.). 32p. (J). 15.95 *(978-0-9721949-1-4(4))* Window Seat Publishing.

Filipek, Nina. Counting. O'Toole, Jeanette, illus. 2009. (Bright Basics Ser.). 12p. (J). (gr. -1-k). bds. 11.40 *(978-1-60754-686-3(8))* Windmill Bks.

First, Rachel. Count It! Fun with Counting & Comparing, 1 vol. 2016. (Math Beginnings Ser.). (ENG., Illus.). 24p. (J). (gr. k-3). 24.21 *(978-1-62403-933-1(2))* ABDO Publishing Co.

Fish, Sandra Palmer. S E W for Peace. 2007. 48p. pap. 19.05 *(978-0-9722839-7-7(8))* Just Write Bks.

Fisher, Doris & Sneed, Dani. One Odd Day, 1 vol. Lee, Karen, illus. 2006. (Basic Math Numbers Ser.). (ENG.). 32p. (J). (gr. -1-3). 15.95 *(978-0-9768823-3-6(7))* Arbordale Publishing.

Fladd, Jane. 1-2-3 Jump! 2009. 32p. pap. 12.99 *(978-1-4389-3272-9(3))* AuthorHouse.

Flaherty, Liz. Action Numeracy: Bikes. 2008. (Action Numeracy Upper Primary Ser.). 32p. pap. 9.95 *(978-0-86431-800-8(6))* ACER Pr. AUS. Dist: ISBS Publisher Services.

Flatt, Lizann. Counting on Fall. Barron, Ashley, illus. 2017. (Math in Nature Ser.: 1). (ENG.). 32p. (J). (gr. k-2). pap. 7.95 ***(978-1-77147-310-1(X))*** Owlkids Bks. Inc. CAN. Dist: Publishers Group West (PGW).

Fleming, Candace. Who Invited You? Booth, George, illus. 2009. (ENG.). 36p. (J). (gr. -1-3). 10.99 *(978-1-4424-0219-5(9)*, Atheneum Bks. for Young Readers) Simon & Schuster Children's Publishing.

Fleming, Maria. Five Shiny Apples. Sexton, Brenda, illus. 2005. (Number Tales Ser.). (ENG.). 16p. (J). (gr. -1-1). pap. 2.99 *(978-0-439-69014-0(5))* Scholastic, Inc.

Flintham, Thomas. Animal Numbers. Flintham, Thomas, illus. 2016. (ENG., Illus.). 24p. (J). (gr. -1 — 1). bds. 7.99 *(978-1-4814-6937-1(1)*, Little Simon) Little Simon.

Flip along Fun. (Illus.). 22p. (J). (gr. -1-k). spiral bd. *(978-1-56021-374-1(4)*, #221) W.J. Fantasy, Inc.

Flores, Cory, illus. Bugs on Parade: A Counting Book. 2006. 8p. (J). *(978-1-58970-400-8(2))* Lakeshore Learning Materials.

Flowerpot Press Staff, contrib. by. Sockheadz: Counting. 2013. (ENG., Illus.). 20p. (J). (gr. -1-k). 6.99 *(978-1-77093-594-5(0))* Flowerpot Children's Pr. Inc. CAN. Dist: Cardinal Pubs. Group.

Fontes, Justine. Cheerios Count to 100. Croll, Carolyn, illus. 2005. (J). *(978-0-439-70341-3(7))* Scholastic, Inc.

Food - Set 3: Foods That Count. 2004. (J). spiral bd. 23.40 *(978-0-9770248-3-4(0))* Sidedoor Publishing LLC.

Formento, Alison. These Bees Count! Snow, Sarah, illus. 2012. (These Things Count! Ser.). (ENG.). 32p. (J). (gr. -1-3). 16.99 *(978-0-8075-7868-1(1))* Whitman, Albert & Co.

—This Tree Counts!, 1 vol. Snow, Sarah, illus. 2010. (These Things Count! Ser.). (ENG.). 32p. (J). (gr. -1-3). 16.99 *(978-0-8075-7890-2(8))* Whitman, Albert & Co.

Forrester, Anna. Bat Count: A Citizen Science Story, 1 vol. Detwiler, Susan, illus. 2017. (ENG & SPA.). 32p. (J). (gr. k-3). 17.95 *(978-1-62855-894-4(6))* Arbordale Publishing.

—Contando Los Murciélagos: Una Historia de Ciencias para Los Ciudadanos. Detwiler, Susan, illus. 2017. (SPA.). 32p. (J). (gr. k-3). pap. 9.95 *(978-1-62855-896-8(2))* Arbordale Publishing.

Forsythe, Demming. The Ten Little Menehunes: A Hawaiian Counting Book. l.t. ed. 2005. (ENG., Illus.). 40p. (J). (gr. -1-2). 18.95 *(978-0-932529-75-6(5))* Oldcastle Publishing.

Foster, Jane. Jane Foster's 123. 2015. (Jane Foster Bks.). (ENG., Illus.). 24p. (J). (gr. -1 — 1). bds. 7.99 *(978-1-4998-0073-9(8))* Little Bee Books Inc.

Fox, Mem. Let's Count Goats! Thomas, Jan, illus. 2010. (ENG.). 40p. (J). (gr. -1-1). 16.99 *(978-1-4424-0598-1(8)*, Beach Lane Bks.) Beach Lane Bks.

Franceschelli, Christopher & Peskimo. Countablock. 2014. (Alphablock Ser.). (ENG., Illus.). 94p. (J). (gr. -1 — 1). bds. 16.95 *(978-1-4197-1374-3(4)*, Abrams Appleseed) Abrams, Inc.

Franco, Betsy & Franco-Feeney, Betsy. Birdsongs. Jenkins, Steve, illus. 2007. (ENG.). 40p. (J). (gr. -1-3). 17.99 *(978-0-689-87777-3(3)*, McElderry, Margaret K. Bks.) McElderry, Margaret K. Bks.

Freeman, Marcia S. More Ice Cream: Words for Math Comparisons. 2007. (Illus.). 24p. (J). pap. 7.95 *(978-1-60044-685-6(X))*; (gr. 3-7). lib. bdg. 22.79 *(978-1-60044-641-2(8))* Rourke Educational Media.

Fried, Miriam. My Jelly Bean Book. 2005. (Illus.). (J). *(978-1-57400-049-8(7))* Data Trace Publishing, Co.

Friedman, Maya. Three Falafels in My Pita. Mack, Steve, illus. 2015. (ENG.). 12p. (J). (gr. -1 — 1). bds. 5.95 *(978-1-4677-3472-1(1)*, Kar-Ben Publishing) Lerner Publishing Group.

Froeb, Lori & Brown, Jo. Zoo! A Big Fold-Out Counting Book. 2007. (Big Fold-Out Flap Ser.). (ENG., Illus.). 10p. (J). (gr. -1-k). bds. 12.99 *(978-0-7944-1361-3(7))* Reader's Digest Assn., Inc., The.

Frost, Jayson. Picking Pears: Count to Tell the Number of Objects. 2013. (Rosen Math Readers Ser.). (ENG.). 16p. (J). (gr. k-1). pap. 42.00 *(978-1-4777-1639-7(4))*; (Illus.). pap. 7.00 *(978-1-4777-1638-0(6))* Rosen Publishing Group, Inc., The. (Rosen Classroom).

Fyffe, Brian, illus. Christmas Counting: Count & Create with 42 Holiday Stickers. 2003. 10p. (J). (gr. -1-18). bds. 4.99 *(978-1-57151-722-7(7))* Playhouse Publishing.

Galloway, Fhiona, illus. 123 Counting Sticker Book. 2014. (My Little World Ser.). (ENG.). 14p. (J). (gr. -1). pap. 3.99 *(978-1-58925-444-2(9))* Tiger Tales.

Galvin, Laura Gates. Handy Manny: 1,2,3 Amigos. Parisi, Anthony, ed. 2011. (Learning Library). (ENG., Illus.). 24p. (gr. -1-k). 8.99 *(978-1-60727-268-7(7))* Studio Mouse LLC.

—Handy Manny Counting on Friends. 2008. (ENG.). 32p. (J). (gr. -1-3). 4.99 *(978-1-59069-735-1(9))* Studio Mouse LLC.

—Mickey Mouse Clubhouse Fun with Numbers & Shapes. 2008. (ENG.). 20p. (J). (gr. -1-3). 9.99 *(978-1-59069-655-2(7))* Studio Mouse LLC.

—Princess Counting Fun. Parisi, Anthony, ed. 2011. (Learning Library). (ENG., Illus.). 24p. (gr. -1). 8.99 *(978-1-60727-265-6(2))* Studio Mouse LLC.

—Take-with-Me Numbers. 2006. (ENG., Illus.). 36p. (J). (gr. -1). 12.99 *(978-1-59069-481-7(3))* Studio Mouse LLC.

Gamble, Adam & Jasper, Mark. Count to Sleep America. Veno, Joe, illus. 2015. (Count to Sleep Ser.). (ENG.). 20p. (J). (— 1). bds. 7.95 *(978-1-60219-231-7(6))* Good Night Bks.

—Count to Sleep California. Veno, Joe, illus. 2014. (Count to Sleep Ser.). (ENG.). 20p. (J). (— 1). bds. 7.95 *(978-1-60219-200-3(6))* Good Night Bks.

—Count to Sleep Florida. Veno, Joe, illus. 2014. (Count to Sleep Ser.). (ENG.). 20p. (J). (— 1). bds. 7.95 *(978-1-60219-202-7(2))* Good Night Bks.

—Count to Sleep Michigan. Veno, Joe, illus. 2014. (Count to Sleep Ser.). (ENG.). 20p. (J). (— 1). bds. 7.95 *(978-1-60219-327-7(4))* Good Night Bks.

—Count to Sleep Minnesota. Veno, Joe, illus. 2014. (Count to Sleep Ser.). (ENG.). 20p. (J). (— 1). bds. 7.95 *(978-1-60219-205-8(7))* Good Night Bks.

—Count to Sleep Wisconsin. Veno, Joe, illus. 2014. (Count to Sleep Ser.). (ENG.). 20p. (J). (— 1). bds. 7.95 *(978-1-60219-328-4(2))* Good Night Bks.

Gant, Robert, illus. My Big Box of Numbers. gif. ed. 2005. 64p. (J). cd-rom 24.95 *(978-1-57791-194-4(6))* Brighter Minds Children's Publishing.

Garza, Xavier, illus. The Great & Mighty Nikko. 2015. (ENG.). 32p. (J). pap. 7.95 *(978-1-935955-83-2(7))*; (gr. -1-4). 16.95 *(978-1-935955-82-5(9))* Cinco Puntos Pr.

Gateman, Ryan, creator. Spelling the Number Words: From a Child's View. 2004. (Illus.). 24p. (J). 8.95 *(978-1-932226-23-2(0))* Wizard Academy Pr.

Gayzagian, Doris K. One White Wishing Stone: A Beach Day Counting Book. Swarner, Kristina, illus. 2006. (ENG.). 32p. (J). (gr. -1-2). 25.90 *(978-0-7922-5573-4(9))*; 16.95 *(978-0-7922-5110-1(5))* National Geographic Society. (National Geographic Children's Bks.).

George, Patrick & PatrickGeorge. Numeros. 2012. (SPA.). 26p. (J). (gr. -1-1). pap. 19.99 *(978-84-261-3883-5(7))* Juventud, Editorial ESP. Dist: Lectorum Pubns., Inc.

Gerber, Carole. 10 Busy Brooms. Fleming, Michael, illus. 2016. (ENG.). 32p. (J). (gr. -1-2). 12.99 *(978-0-553-53341-5(X)*, Doubleday Bks. for Young Readers) Random Hse. Children's Bks.

Gerth, Melanie. Ten Little Ladybugs. Huliska-Beith, Laura, illus. 2007. (ENG.). 22p. (J). (gr. -1-3). bds. 15.95 *(978-1-58117-578-3(7)*, Intervisual/Piggy Toes) Bendon, Inc.

Gevry, Claudine, illus. One Little Penguin & His Friends: A Pushing, Turning, Counting Book. 2012. (ENG.). 10p. (J). bds. *(978-1-84956-027-6(7))* Top That! Publishing PLC.

Ghahremani, Susie. Stack the Cats. 2017. (ENG., Illus.). 32p. (J). (gr. -1-k). 14.95 *(978-1-4197-2349-0(9)*, Abrams Appleseed) Abrams, Inc.

Ghigna, Charles. Count by 10 To 100. Saburi, Misa, illus. 2017. (Winter Math Ser.). (ENG.). 24p. (gr. k-2). 33.99 ***(978-1-68410-017-0(8))*** Cantata Learning.

—Even Numbers. Saburi, Misa, illus. 2017. (Winter Math Ser.). (ENG.). 24p. (gr. k-2). 33.99 ***(978-1-68410-023-1(2))*** Cantata Learning.

—Making 10. Saburi, Misa, illus. 2017. (Winter Math Ser.). (ENG.). 24p. (gr. k-2). 33.99 ***(978-1-68410-037-8(2))*** Cantata Learning.

—Odd Numbers. Saburi, Misa, illus. 2017. (Winter Math Ser.). (ENG.). 24p. (gr. k-2). 33.99 ***(978-1-68410-043-9(7))*** Cantata Learning.

Gibbs, Edward. I Spy under the Sea. Gibbs, Edward, illus. 2012. (ENG., Illus.). 32p. (J). (gr. k-k). 14.99 *(978-0-7636-5952-3(5)*, Templar) Candlewick Pr.

Gibson, R. Contar y Estampar. 2004.Tr. of I Can Count. (SPA., Illus.). 32p. (J). lib. bdg. 12.95 *(978-1-58086-395-7(7))* EDC Publishing.

Giles, Angela & Picthall, Chez. 123. Calver, Paul, illus. 2015. (ENG.). 6p. (J). 9.99 *(978-1-909763-29-6(2))* Award Pubns. Ltd. GBR. Dist: Parkwest Pubns., Inc.

Gillian, Chelsea, et al. Princess ABCs And 123s. rev. ed. 2007. (Illus.). 24p. (J). (gr. -1-1). 4.99 *(978-1-59069-560-9(7))* Studio Mouse LLC.

Ginkel, Anne. I've Got an Elephant, 1 vol. Bynum, Janie, illus. 2006. (ENG.). 32p. (J). (gr. k-3). 16.95 *(978-1-56145-373-3(0))* Peachtree Pubs.

Giogas, Valarie. In My Backyard, 1 vol. Zecca, Katherine, illus. 2007. (ENG.). 32p. (J). (gr. -1-3). 15.95 *(978-0-9777423-1-8(8))*; pap. 8.95 *(978-1-934359-17-4(3))* Arbordale Publishing.

Gliori, Debi. Tobermory Cat 1, 2, 3. 2015. (ENG., Illus.). 32p. (J). (gr. -1-k). *(978-1-78027-199-6(9))* Birlinn, Ltd.

Gobo, creator. Little Learners Ready to Read & Write. 2007. (Magnix Little Learners Ser.). (Illus.). 40p. (J). (gr. -1-3). 14.95 *(978-1-932915-44-0(3))* Sandvik Innovations, LLC.

Gobo Books Staff. Ready for Numbers: Little Learners. 2007. (Magnix Little Learners Ser.). 42p. (J). (gr. -1-1). bds., act. bk. ed. 14.95 *(978-1-932915-45-7(1))* Sandvik Innovations, LLC.

Golden Books. Mighty Adventures (Team Umizoomi) Fruchter, Jason, illus. 2012. (Super Color with Stickers Ser.). (ENG.). 96p. (J). (gr. -1-2). pap. 3.99 *(978-0-307-93085-9(8)*, Golden Bks.) Random Hse. Children's Bks.

Gollub, Matthew. Ten Oni Drummers. Stone, Kazuko G., illus. 2013. (JPN & ENG.). 32p. (J). (gr. -1-3). 16.95 *(978-1-58430-011-3(6))* Lee & Low Bks., Inc.

—Ten Oni Drummers. Stone, Kazuko G., illus. 2017. (J). *(978-1-889910-51-2(1))* Tortuga Pr.

Gomi, Taro. I Know Numbers! 2017. (ENG., Illus.). 40p. (J). (gr. -1-k). 15.99 ***(978-1-4521-5918-8(1))*** Chronicle Bks. LLC.

Gonyea, Mark. Counting on Letters: From A to Z & 1 to 26. 2014. (ENG., Illus.). 28p. (J). (gr. -1-1). bds. 10.95 *(978-1-57687-702-9(7)*, powerHouse Bks.) powerHouse Cultural Entertainment, Inc.

Goodrum, L. E. Counting with G & Me. 2009. 20p. pap. 24.95 *(978-1-60749-615-1(1))* America Star Bks.

Gordon, Bob. Giant See a Shape My Giant 123 Book. 2005. (Giant See a Shape Ser.). (Illus.). 44p. (gr. -1-k). *(978-1-84610-023-9(2))* Make Believe Ideas.

Gordon, Bob, et al. Wipe Clean 123. 2009. 16p. (J). 9.99 *(978-1-84610-998-0(1))* Make Believe Ideas GBR. Dist: Nelson, Thomas Inc.

Gould, Ellen. The Blue Number Counting Book. Kelly, Cathy, illus. 13p. (J). (gr. -1-2). pap. 6.00 *(978-0-938017-01-1(2))* Learning Tools Co.

Gould, Jane. At the Pond. rev. ed. 2011. (Mathematics Readers Ser.). (ENG.). 32p. (J). (gr. k-k). pap. 8.99 *(978-1-4333-3430-6(5))* Teacher Created Materials, Inc.

Govan, Nina & Olive and Moss Staff. Margot & Mo. 2014. (Olive & Moss Ser.). (ENG., Illus.). 10p. (J). (— 1). bds. 8.99 *(978-1-4052-6002-2(5))* Egmont Bks., Ltd. GBR. Dist: Independent Pubs. Group.

Gowan, Barbara. Desert Digits: An Arizona Number Book. Toddy, Irving, illus. 2006. (Count Your Way Across the U. S. A. Ser.). (ENG.). 40p. (J). (gr. -1-3). 17.95 *(978-1-58536-162-5(3))* Sleeping Bear Pr.

Graham, Judith A. The Didley-Doo's, 1 vol. 2009. 36p. pap. 24.95 *(978-1-60836-035-2(0))* America Star Bks.

Graire, Virginie, illus. 123. 2016. (ENG.). 12p. (J). (gr. -1 — 1). bds. 6.99 *(978-1-4998-0295-5(1))* Little Bee Books Inc.

Gravelle, Karen. Eight Little Legs. Davis, Nelle, illus. 2004. (ENG.). 20p. (gr. k-2). pap. 8.95 *(978-1-57874-042-0(8)*, Kaeden Bks.) Kaeden Corp.

Gravett, Emily. The Rabbit Problem. Gravett, Emily, illus. 2010. (ENG., Illus.). 32p. (J). (gr. -1-3). 17.99 *(978-1-4424-1255-2(0)*, Simon & Schuster Bks. For Young Readers) Simon & Schuster Bks. For Young Readers.

Gray, Kes. How Many Legs? Field, Jim, illus. 2015. (ENG.). 32p. (J). (gr. -1-k). pap. 8.99 *(978-1-4380-0684-0(5))* Barron's Educational Series, Inc.

Greathouse, Lisa. Count Me In! - School Carnival, 1 vol. 2nd rev. ed. 2014. (TIME for KIDS(r) Nonfiction Readers Ser.). (ENG., Illus.). 28p. (J). (gr. 2-2). pap. 23.96 *(978-1-4807-1058-0(X))* Shell Educational Publishing.

—Farm Animals: Classifying & Sorting. rev. ed. 2011. (Mathematics Readers Ser.). (ENG.). 32p. (J). (gr. k-k). pap. 8.99 *(978-1-4333-3442-9(9))* Teacher Created Materials, Inc.

—The Pet Store. rev. ed. 2011. (Mathematics Readers Ser.). (ENG.). 32p. (J). (gr. k-k). pap. 8.99 *(978-1-4333-3428-3(3))* Teacher Created Materials, Inc.

—The Toy Store. rev. ed. 2011. (Mathematics Readers Ser.). (ENG.). 32p. (J). (gr. k-k). pap. 8.99 *(978-1-4333-3429-0(1))* Teacher Created Materials, Inc.

Green, Kate. A Number of Animals. Wormell, Christopher, illus. 2012. (ENG.). 32p. (J). (gr. -1-k). 15.99 *(978-1-56846-222-6(0)*, Creative Editions) Creative Co., The.

Green, Shayla. What's in My House? 2013. (InfoMax Math Readers Ser.). (ENG.). 16p. (J). (gr. k-1). pap. 7.00 *(978-1-4777-1900-8(8)*, Rosen Classroom) Rosen Publishing Group, Inc., The.

—What's in My House? Number Names & Count Sequence. 2013. (InfoMax Math Readers Ser.). (ENG.). 16p. (J). (gr. k-1). pap. 42.00 *(978-1-4777-1911-4(3)*, Rosen Classroom) Rosen Publishing Group, Inc., The.

Green-Warren, Loretta M. Counting, Rhyming & Body Parts. 2010. 24p. 12.99 *(978-1-4490-8408-0(7))* AuthorHouse.

Greene, Rhonda Gowler. Push! Dig! Scoop! A Construction Counting Rhyme. Kirk, Daniel, illus. 2017. (ENG.). 26p. (J). bds. 7.99 *(978-1-68119-085-3(0)*, 9781681190853, Bloomsbury USA Childrens) Bloomsbury Publishing USA.

Gregoire, Maryellen. Contar Crayones (Counting Crayons) 2012. (Wonder Readers Spanish Emergent Ser.). (SPA.). 8p. (gr. -1-1). pap. 35.94 *(978-1-62065-569-6(1))* Capstone Press of Coughlan Cos.

Grey, Cristina. My Messy Room: Count to Tell the Number of Objects. 2013. (InfoMax Math Readers Ser.). (ENG.). 16p. (J). (gr. k-1). pap. 42.00 *(978-1-4777-2010-3(3))*; (Illus.). pap. 7.00 *(978-1-4777-2009-7(X))* Rosen Publishing Group, Inc., The. (Rosen Classroom).

Griffin, Keith. Carry-Me 123. 2009. (Carry-Me Ser.). (ENG., Illus.). 12p. (J). (gr. -1-k). 7.99 *(978-1-84610-872-3(1))* Make Believe Ideas GBR. Dist: Nelson, Thomas Inc.

Grodin, Elissa D. Yankee Doodle Numbers: A Connecticut Number Book. Brookfield, Maureen K., illus. rev. ed. 2007. (Count Your Way Across the U. S. A. Ser.). (ENG.). 40p. (J). (gr. 3-7). 17.95 *(978-1-58536-175-5(5))* Sleeping Bear Pr.

Gross, Sandra & Busch, Leah. Toast to Counting: Toast to Baby. Hutton, John, ed. 2012. (Toast to Baby Ser.). (ENG., Illus.). 14p. (J). (— 1). bds. 7.99 *(978-1-936669-09-7(9))* Blue Manatee Press.

Group/McGraw-Hill, Wright. And the Winner Is: Level N, 6 vols. 128p. (gr. 3-6). 36.95 *(978-0-322-05885-9(6))* Wright Group/McGraw-Hill.

—How not to Catch the Moon: Level L, 6 vols. (Summer Skies Ser.). 128p. (gr. 3-6). 36.95 *(978-0-322-05886-6(4))* Wright Group/McGraw-Hill.

Gunzi, Christiane. 1 2 3. 2015. (ENG., Illus.). 34p. (J). 7.99 *(978-1-906572-18-1(6))* Award Pubns. Ltd. GBR. Dist: Parkwest Pubns., Inc.

Gunzi, Christiane. Let's Count Noisy Kittens. 2015. (ENG., Illus.). 10p. (J). 9.99 *(978-1-905503-19-3(9))* Award Pubns. Ltd. GBR. Dist: Parkwest Pubns., Inc.

—Let's Count Noisy Puppies. 2015. (ENG., Illus.). 10p. (J). 9.99 *(978-1-905503-18-6(0))* Award Pubns. Ltd. GBR. Dist: Parkwest Pubns., Inc.

—Numbers. 2015. (ENG., Illus.). 6p. (J). 7.99 *(978-1-907604-94-2(4))* Award Pubns. Ltd. GBR. Dist: Parkwest Pubns., Inc.

Gupta, Jennifer. Silly Turtle! That's Not on the Menu! 2008. 28p. pap. 13.99 *(978-1-4343-9183-4(3))* AuthorHouse.

Gurule, Jennifer. Look at Aunt Clare's Hair. Gurule, Jennifer, illus. 2005. (Daddy's Collection). (Illus.). (J). pap. 11.50 *(978-1-59134-033-1(0))* Maval Publishing, Inc.

Gutman, Anne & Hallensleben, Georg. Mommy Loves. 2005. (ENG., Illus.). 14p. (J). (gr. -1 — 1). bds. 5.99 *(978-0-8118-4616-5(4))* Chronicle Bks. LLC.

Gutman, Anne, et al. Numeros. 2003. (Collection Mira Mira Ser.). (SPA., Illus.). 16p. (J). (gr. -1-k). bds. 9.99 *(978-84-261-3328-1(2))* Juventud, Editorial ESP. Dist: Lectorum Pubns., Inc.

Guy, Ginger Foglesong. Fiesta! Moreno, Rene King, illus. 2007. (SPA.). 32p. (J). (gr. -1-3). 6.99 *(978-0-06-088226-6(3)*, Greenwillow Bks.) HarperCollins Pubs.

Haeick, Noah. Welcome to My Class! Count to Tell the Number of Objects. 2013. (InfoMax Math Readers Ser.). (ENG.). 16p. (J). (gr. k-1). pap. 42.00 *(978-1-4777-1920-6(2))*; pap. 7.00 *(978-1-4777-1919-0(9))* Rosen Publishing Group, Inc., The. (Rosen Classroom).

Haines, Genny, illus. Five Little Ducks. 2016. (ENG.). 10p. (J). (gr. -1 — 1). bds. 8.99 *(978-1-4998-0217-7(X))* Little Bee Books Inc.

Hall, Kirsten. Birthday Beastie: All about Counting. Luedecke, Bev, illus. 2003. (Beastieville Ser.). 32p. (J). 19.50 *(978-0-516-22891-4(9)*, Children's Pr.) Scholastic Library Publishing.

Hall, Pam. The Odds Get Even. Chapman, Lynne, illus. 2005. 16p. (J). 12.95 *(978-1-58117-216-4(8)*, Intervisual/Piggy Toes) Bendon, Inc.

Halsey, Megan. 3 Pandas Planting, 0 vols. Halsey, Megan, illus. rev. ed. 2011. (ENG., Illus.). 34p. (J). (gr. -1-3). pap. 6.99 *(978-0-7614-5844-9(1)*, 9780761458449, Amazon Children's Publishing) Amazon Publishing.

Handa's Hen. 2004. (PER & ENG.). (J). *(978-1-84444-186-0(5))* Mantra Lingua.

Hanes, Kathleen & Bonfield, Chloe. Seagrass Dreams: A Counting Book. 2017. (ENG., Illus.). 32p. (J). (gr. -1-2). 17.95 *(978-1-63322-125-3(3)*, Seagrass) Quarto Publishing Group USA.

Hansen, Nichole. Kids Count. Hansen, Tevin, illus. 2015. 44p. (J). pap. 9.49 *(978-1-941429-18-1(1))* Handersen Publishing.

Harley, Bill. Sitting down to Eat. 2005. (ENG., Illus.). 32p. (J). (gr. -1-3). pap. 8.95 *(978-0-87483-603-5(4))* August Hse. Pubs., Inc.

Harper, Charley. 123's. Harper, Charley, illus. 2008. (ENG., Illus.). 20p. (J). (gr. -1-3). bds. 9.95 *(978-1-934429-22-8(8))* AMMO Bks., LLC.

Harris, Marian. Ten Little Kittens. Harris, Jim, illus. 2010. (ENG.). 28p. (J). (gr. k). 15.99 *(978-0-7407-9197-0(4))* Andrews McMeel Publishing.

Harris, Marian & Harris, Jim. Ten Little Kittens. 2011. (ENG., Illus.). 26p. (J). (gr. -1-k). bds. 9.99 *(978-1-4494-0175-7(9))* Andrews McMeel Publishing.

Harris, Marie. Primary Numbers: A New Hampshire Numbers Book. Holman, Karen Busch, illus. 2004. (Count Your Way Across the U. S. A. Ser.). (ENG.). 40p. (J). 16.95 *(978-1-58536-192-2(5))* Sleeping Bear Pr.

Harris, Nancy. Sticky Fingers: Exploring the Number 5. 2007. (Illus.). 24p. (ENG.). (gr. k-3). 28.95 *(978-1-60472-045-7(X))*; (J). (gr. 3-7). lib. bdg. 22.79 *(978-1-60044-639-9(6))* Rourke Educational Media.

Harris, Stephen. Ballroom Bonanza: A Hidden Pictures ABC Book. Rycroft, Nina, illus. 2010. (ENG.). 40p. (J). (gr. k-2). 16.95 *(978-0-8109-8842-2(9)*, Abrams Bks. for Young Readers) Abrams, Inc.

Harris, Trudy. Splitting the Herd: A Corral of Odds & Evens. Julian, Russell, illus. 2008. (Math Is Fun! Ser.). (ENG.). 32p. (gr. k-2). 16.95 *(978-0-8225-7466-8(7)*, Millbrook Pr.) Lerner Publishing Group.

—Tally Cat Keeps Track. Harris, Andrew, illus. 2010. (Math Is Fun! Ser.). (ENG.). 32p. (gr. k-2). lib. bdg. 22.60 *(978-0-7613-4451-3(9)*, Millbrook Pr.) Lerner Publishing Group.

Harte, May. 1, 2, 3 in My House. 2004. (Look-And-Learn Books). (Illus.). (J). lib. bdg. 8.95 *(978-1-4042-2823-8(3)*, PowerKids Pr.) Rosen Publishing Group, Inc., The.

Haskins, James & Benson, Kathleen. Count Your Way Through Afghanistan. Moore, Megan, illus. 2006. (Count Your Way Ser.). 40p. (J). (gr. -1-3). lib. bdg. 19.93 *(978-1-57505-880-1(4)*, Millbrook Pr.) Lerner Publishing Group.

—Count Your Way Through Egypt. Rama, Sue, illus. 2006. (Count Your Way Ser.). 24p. (J). (gr. -1-3). lib. bdg. 19.93 *(978-1-57505-882-5(0)*, Millbrook Pr.) Lerner Publishing Group.

—Count Your Way Through Iran. Zaman, Farida, illus. 2006. (Count Your Way Ser.). 40p. (J). (gr. -1-3). lib. bdg. 19.93 *(978-1-57505-881-8(2)*, Millbrook Pr.) Lerner Publishing Group.

—Count Your Way Through Kenya. Leveque, Lyne, illus. 2006. (Count Your Way Ser.). 24p. (J). (gr. -1-3). lib. bdg. 19.93 *(978-1-57505-884-9(7)*, Millbrook Pr.) Lerner Publishing Group.

Haskins, Jim & Benson, Kathleen. Count Your Way Through South Africa. Neibert, Alissa, illus. 2006. (Count Your Way Ser.). (ENG.). 24p. (gr. 2-5). lib. bdg. 19.93 *(978-1-57505-883-2(9)*, Millbrook Pr.) Lerner Publishing Group.

—Count Your Way Through Zimbabwe. Park, Janie Jaehyun, illus. 2006. (Count Your Way Ser.). (ENG.). 24p. (gr. 2-5). lib. bdg. 19.93 *(978-1-57505-885-6(5)*, Millbrook Pr.) Lerner Publishing Group.

Hauber, Jennifer. Just Like Om. 2008. 20p. pap. 12.49 *(978-1-4389-0992-9(6))* AuthorHouse.

Hawcock, David. 0-20. Hawcock, David, illus. 2015. (ENG., Illus.). 52p. (J). (gr. -1-k). 14.99 *(978-1-85707-898-5(5))* Tango Bks. GBR. Dist: Independent Pubs. Group.

Hayes, Larry E. My Name Starts with S (Library Version) Anderson, Airlie, illus. 2004. (My Name Starts With Ser.). 32p. (J). lib. bdg. 12.95 *(978-0-9725292-8-0(4))* Inspire Pubns.

Hayes, Trudie L. & Perkins, Kenneth B. Of All the People in the World to Be I Am Glad That I Am Me! 2008. 24p. pap. 14.95 *(978-1-59858-853-8(2))* Dog Ear Publishing, LLC.

Hays, Ethel. One, Two, Buckle My Shoe: an Alphabet & Counting Book. 2012. (Shape Bks.). (ENG., Illus.). 16p. (J). pap. 9.95 *(978-1-59583-624-3(1))* Laughing Elephant.

Head, Debby & Pollett, Libby. Bby Practice Pages: 03-Choosing Coins. 2004. (ENG., Illus.). spiral bd. 37.00 *(978-1-885775-18-4(0))* bby Publications at The University of West Alabama.

Heath, Beverly C. Counting with Colors. Floyd, John, Jr., illus. 2005. 8p. (J). (gr. -1). bds. 5.95 *(978-0-9752860-0-5(5))* OurRainbow Pr., LLC.

Heling, Kathryn & Hembrook, Deborah. Ten Lucky Leprechauns. 2013. lib. bdg. 13.55 *(978-0-606-31493-0(8)*, Turtleback) Turtleback Bks.

Helman, Andrea. 1, 2, 3 Moose. Wolfe, Art, photos by. 2016. (ENG., Illus.). 20p. (J). (— 1). bds. 9.99 *(978-1-63217-032-3(9)*, Little Bigfoot) Sasquatch Bks.

Hensley, Tana. Keesha Counts Money: Putting Data in Order. 2017. (Computer Science for the Real World Ser.). 12p. (gr. 6-7). pap. 7.05 ***(978-1-5383-5127-7(7))***, Rosen Classroom) Rosen Publishing Group, Inc., The.

Henson, Laura J. & Grooms, Duffy. Ten Little Elvi. Gorissen, Dean, illus. 2004. (ENG.). 30p. (J). (gr. -1-2). 12.99 *(978-1-58246-124-3(4)*, Tricycle Pr.) Random Hse. Children's Bks.

Heos, Bridget. Counting Change. Longhi, Katya, illus. 2015. (Math World Ser.). 24p. (J). lib. bdg. 27.10 *(978-1-60753-462-4(2))* Amicus Publishing.

Hierlmaier Nelson, Christine M. Green Yellow Go! Nat Knows Bananas. Hierlmaier, Joy, illus. 2004. 26p. (J). spiral bd. 14.95 *(978-0-9759362-0-7(4))* Expressive Ink.

Hilderbrand, Karen Mitzo & Thompson, Kim Mitzo. Essential Preschool Skills. 2008. (J). 44.99 *(978-1-59922-321-6(X))* Findaway World, LLC.

C
D

Hill, Emma. My First Book of Numbers: A Pull-Out Toddler Book. 2014. (My First Book Ser.). (ENG., Illus.). 12p. (J). (gr. -1 — 1). bds. 6.99 (978-1-77085-312-6(X), 9781770853126) Firefly Bks., Ltd.

Hill, Eric. Spot Can Count. 2009. (Spot (Chinese) Ser.). (CHI., Illus.). 22p. (978-957-762-468-0(5)) Hsin Yi Pubns.

—Spot Can Count. Hill, Eric, illus. 2003. (Spot Ser.). (ENG., Illus.). 24p. (J). (gr. -1-k). 6.99 (978-0-14-250121-4(2), Warne) Penguin Young Readers Group.

—Spot Counts to 10. 2013. (Spot Ser.). (ENG.). 10p. (J). (gr. -1-k). bds. 6.99 (978-0-7232-7020-1(1), Warne) Penguin Young Readers Group.

Hill, Merle Roddy. Let's Count Again! 2011. 32p. pap. 24.95 (978-1-4626-1251-2(2)) America Star Bks.

Hillert, Margaret. Dear Dragon's Colors 1 ,2, 3. Schimmell, David, illus. 2010. (BeginningtoRead Ser.). 32p. (J). (gr. k-2). lib. bdg. 22.60 (978-1-59953-376-6(6)) Norwood Hse. Pr.

—Querido Dragón, Los Colores y 1, 2, 3 /Dear Dragon's Colors 1, 2, 3. del Risco, Eida, tr. Schimmell, David, illus. 2011. (BeginningtoRead Ser.). 32p. (J). (-2). pap. 11.94 (978-1-60357-554-6(5)) Norwood Hse. Pr.

—Querido Dragón, los Colores y 1, 2, 3 /Dear Dragon's Colors 1, 2, 3. del Risco, Eida, tr. from ENG. Schimmell, David, illus. 2011. (BeginningtoRead Ser.). 32p. (J). (gr. k-2). lib. bdg. 22.60 (978-1-59953-470-1(3)) Norwood Hse. Pr.

Hillmerle Roddy. All under the Bright Yellow Sun. 2011. 28p. pap. 24.95 (978-1-4489-2602-2(5)) America Star Bks.

Hinkler Studios Staff., ed. Disney Princess: Counting & Spelling. 2011. 12p. 9.99 (978-1-74183-871-8(1)) Hinkler Bks. Pty, Ltd. AUS. Dist: Ideals Pubns.

Hinton, Stephanie, illus. Busy Book for Boys: 550 Things to Find. 2014. (J). (978-1-4351-5358-5(8)) Barnes & Noble, Inc.

—Busy Book for Girls: 550 Things to Find. 2014. (J). (978-1-4351-5359-2(6)) Barnes & Noble, Inc.

Hirsch, Esther. Counting on Friends. 2005. 13p. (J). 10.00 (978-1-4116-3620-0(1)) Lulu Pr., Inc.

Hodgekiss, Jo. Libro de los Numeros (Book of Numbers) (SPA.). (J). 12.95 (978-84-243-2795-8(0)) Publicaciones Fher, S.A. ESP. Dist: AIMS International Bks., Inc.

Hoffman, Don. A Counting Book with Billy & Abigail. Dakins, Todd, illus. 2nd ed. 2016. (Billy & Abby Ser.). (ENG.). 24p. (J). (gr. -1-k). pap. 3.99 (978-1-943154-08-1(2)) Peek-A-Boo Publishing.

Hogan, Martina, illus. 123 under the Sea. 2016. (Early Birds Ser.). (ENG.). 12p. (J). (gr. -1 — 1). bds. 6.99 (978-1-4998-0208-5(0)) Little Bee Books Inc.

Holden, Arianne. It's Fun to Count & Learn: A Busy Picture Book Full of Fabulous Facts & Things to Do! 2016. (ENG., Illus.). 32p. 9.99 (978-1-86147-702-6(3), Armadillo) Anness Publishing GBR. Dist: National Bk. Network.

Holland, Gill. Louisvile Counts! A Children's Counting & Art Book. Brothers, Stephanie, ed. 2009. (ENG., Illus.). (J). 20.00 (978-0-9797006-2-0(0)) Holland Brown.

Holland, Trish. Trees: Count. 2010. (J). (978-1-60617-128-8(3)) Teaching Strategies, LLC.

Holliday, Patricia. A Is for Anjelina: an Introduction to ABC's And 123's. 2005. 29p. (J). 12.26 (978-1-4116-4471-7(9)) Lulu Pr., Inc.

Holloway, Ethan. Numbers at the Market: Number Names & Count Sequence. 2013. (Rosen Math Readers Ser.). (ENG.). 16p. (J). (gr. k-1). pap. 42.00 (978-1-4777-1576-5(2)); (Illus.). pap. 7.00 (978-1-4777-1575-8(4)) Rosen Publishing Group, Inc., The. (Rosen Classroom).

Holloway, Jamie. Adding with Animals. 2015. (Rosen REAL Readers: STEM & STEAM Collection). (ENG.). 8p. pap. 5.46 (978-1-4994-9639-0(7), Rosen Classroom) Rosen Publishing Group, Inc., The.

Holmes, Stephen. Number Farm. 2003. (J). bds. 5.98 (978-0-7525-8920-6(2)) Parragon, Inc.

Holub, Joan. Apple Countdown. Smith, Jan, illus. 2012. (J). (978-1-61913-117-0(X)) Weigl Pubs., Inc.

—Apple Countdown. Smith, Jan, illus. 2009. (ENG.). 32p. (J). (gr. -1-3). 16.99 (978-0-8075-0398-0(3)) Whitman, Albert & Co.

Honey, Elizabeth. Ten Blue Wrens & What a Lot of Wattle! An Absolutely Australian Counting Book. Honey, Elizabeth, illus. (ENG., Illus.). 32p. (J). (gr. -1-3). 2016. pap. 10.99 (978-1-76029-051-1(3)) 2012. 19.99 (978-1-74237-787-2(4)) Allen & Unwin AUS. Dist: Independent Pubs. Group.

Horne, Jane. Busy Baby Sparklies 4 Volume Boxed Set: Baby's First Box of Books. 2007. (Illus.). 12p. (gr. -1-k). bds., bds. (978-1-84610-565-4(X)) Make Believe Ideas.

—Flip & Find 123. 2008. (Illus.). 12p. (J). (gr. -1-3). bds. (978-1-84610-731-3(8)) Make Believe Ideas.

Horowitz, Dave. Five Little Gefiltes. Horowitz, Dave, illus. 2007. (ENG., Illus.). 32p. (J). (gr. -1-3). 15.99 (978-0-399-24608-1(8), G.P. Putnam's Sons Books for Young Readers) Penguin Young Readers Group.

How Many Are There? (Peek A Boo Pockets Ser.). 12p. (J). bds. (978-2-89393-979-7(1)) Phidal Publishing, Inc./Editions Phidal, Inc.

Hughes, Jennifer L. The Nature of Numbers. 2008. 23p. pap. 24.95 (978-1-60672-827-7(X)) America Star Bks.

Hughes, Shirley. Alphie's Numbers. 2015. (Alfie Ser.). (ENG., Illus.). 32p. (J). (gr. -1-k). pap. 9.99 (978-1-84941-846-1(2), Red Fox) Random House Children's Books GBR. Dist: Independent Pubs. Group.

Hulin, Pamela. Down under in Australia. Mendoza, Carlos, illus. 2007. 20p. per. 24.95 (978-1-4241-8929-8(2)) America Star Bks.

Humphreys, Patrick B. Love of Tin Robots. 2011. 28p. pap. 24.95 (978-1-4626-3355-5(2)) America Star Bks.

—1-2-3 Kitties: A Cat Counting Book. 2008. 25p. pap. 24.95 (978-1-60610-804-8(2)) America Star Bks.

Hunt, Darleen L. Ellen Elizabeth's Peanut Butter Jar: Counting. Komarck, Michael, illus. 2003. (Sherman's Math Corner Ser.). (J). (gr. -1-3). (978-1-929591-11-4(X)) Reading Rock, Inc.

—Lyle & Mildred Are a Pair: Counting by 2's. Komarck, Michael, illus. 2003. (Sherman's Math Corner Ser.). (J). (gr. -1-3). (978-1-929591-00-8(4)) Reading Rock, Inc.

—Spider Inventories: Count & Record. Komarck, Michael, illus. 2003. (Sherman's Math Corner Ser.). (J). (gr. -1-3). (978-1-929591-05-3(5)) Reading Rock, Inc.

Hvass & Hannibal. Technicolor Treasure Hunt: Learn to Count with Nature. 2016. (ENG.). 14p. (J). (gr. -1-k). bds. 12.99 (978-1-84780-780-9(1), Wide Eyed Editions) Quarto Publishing Group UK GBR. Dist: Hachette Bk. Group.

Hvass, Nan Na & Hannibal, Sofie, illus. Technicolour Treasure Hunt: Learn to Count with Nature. 2016. (ENG.). 14p. (J). bds. 12.99 (978-1-84780-744-1(5), Wide Eyed Editions) Quarto Publishing Group UK GBR. Dist: Littlehampton Bk Services, Ltd.

I Can Count. (First Bks.: No. S808-2). (Illus.). (J). (gr. -1). pap. 3.95 (978-0-7214-5053-7(9), Dutton Juvenile) Penguin Publishing Group.

Ideals Publications Inc. Staff. Thomas & Friends Write, Slide & Learn: Numbers. 2011. (Write, Slide & Learn Ser.). 14p. (J). pap. (978-1-74184-161-9(5)) Hinkler Bks. Pty, Ltd.

Idle, Molly. Flora & the Chicks. 2017. (ENG., Illus.). 20p. (J). bds. 9.99 (978-1-4521-4657-7(8)) Chronicle Bks. LLC.

Ikids Staff. Little Turtles. Larranaga, Ana, illus. 2008. (iBaby Float-Alongs Ser.). (ENG.). 6p. (J). (gr. -1). 12.99 (978-1-58476-808-1(8)) Innovative Kids.

—Tiny Tugboats. Larranaga, Ana, illus. 2008. (iBaby Float-Alongs Ser.). (ENG.). 6p. (J). (gr. -1). 12.99 (978-1-58476-807-4(X)) Innovative Kids.

—10 Little Monkeys. King, Travis, illus. 2009. (ENG.). 20p. (J). (gr. -1-k). 14.99 (978-1-58476-938-5(6)) Innovative Kids.

Imperato, Teresa. How Many Ducks in a Row? A Turn & Pop Book. Petrone, Valeria, illus. 2005. 10p. (J). bds. 5.95 (978-1-58117-278-2(8), Intervisual/Piggy Toes) Bendon, Inc.

—Ten Christmas Lights: Count the Lights from One to Ten! Parry, Jo, illus. 2005. (ENG.). 20p. (J). 10.95 (978-1-58117-321-5(0), Intervisual/Piggy Toes) Bendon, Inc.

Inkpen, Mick. Wibbly Pig Has 10 Balloons. 2012. (ENG., Illus.). 32p. (J). (gr. -1-k). pap. 9.99 (978-1-4449-0267-9(9)) Hodder & Stoughton GBR. Dist: Hachette Bk. Group.

Innovative Kids Staff. Counting: E-Z Page Turners. Larrañaga, Ana Martin, illus. 2008. (ENG.). 12p. (J). (gr. -1 — 1). bds. 5.99 (978-1-58476-657-5(3)) Innovative Kids.

Innovative Kids Staff, creator. Soft Shapes - Counting. 2010. (ENG.). 8p. (J). (gr. -1 — 1). 10.99 (978-1-58476-962-0(9)) Innovative Kids.

Iossa, Federica, illus. Peekaboo Bunny. 2016. (Peekaboo Bks.). (ENG.). 8p. (J). (gr. -1 — 1). bds. 7.99 (978-0-7641-6861-1(4)) Barron's Educational Series, Inc.

Irwin-Ayotte, Tracy. Bilingual Songs: English-French. 2003. 48p. (J). pap. 14.95 incl. audio (978-1-894262-77-4(8), JMP F24K) Jordan Music Productions, Inc.

—Bilingual Songs Vol. 1: English-French. 2003. 48p. (J). pap. 14.95 incl. audio (978-1-894262-72-9(7), JMP F23K) Jordan Music Productions, Inc.

Ivanke, illus. Sparkling Easter Eggs: A Glittery Counting Book. 2008. (ENG.). 10p. (J). bds. 7.95 (978-1-58117-685-8(6), Intervisual/Piggy Toes) Bendon, Inc.

Jackson, Ellen. Octopuses One to Ten. Page, Robin, illus. 2016. (ENG.). 32p. (J). (gr. -1-3). 17.99 (978-1-4814-3182-8(X), Beach Lane Bks.) Beach Lane Bks.

Jacobs, Paul DuBois & Swender, Jennifer. Count on the Subway. Yaccarino, Dan, illus. 2014. (ENG.). 32p. (J). (-k). 14.99 (978-0-307-97923-0(7)); lib. bdg. 17.99 (978-0-307-97924-7(5)) Random Hse. Children's Bks. (Knopf Bks. for Young Readers).

James, Dawn. Neighborhood Math. 2015. (J). (978-1-62713-447-7(6)) Cavendish Square Publishing.

—Playground Math. 2015. (Math Around Us Ser.). (ENG.). 24p. (J). (gr. 1-1). pap. 24.21 (978-1-5026-0152-0(4)) Cavendish Square Publishing.

—Store Math. 2015. (Math Around Us Ser.). (ENG.). 24p. (J). (gr. 1-1). pap. 8.22 (978-1-5026-0165-0(6)) Cavendish Square Publishing.

Jane, Pamela. Little Elfie One. Manning, Jane, illus. 2015. (ENG.). 32p. (J). (gr. -1-3). 17.99 (978-0-06-220673-2(7)) HarperCollins Pubs.

—Little Goblins Ten. Jane, Pamela & Manning, Jane, illus. 2011. (ENG.). 32p. (J). (gr. -1-3). 16.99 (978-0-06-176798-2(0)) HarperCollins Pubs.

Jansson, Tove. Moomin's Little Book of Numbers. 2011. (Moomins Ser.). (ENG., Illus.). 16p. (J). (gr. -1 — 1). bds. 6.99 (978-0-374-35047-5(7), 9780374350475, Farrar, Straus & Giroux (BYR)) Farrar, Straus & Giroux.

Jocelyn, Marthe. One Some Many. Slaughter, Tom, illus. (ENG.). (J). (gr. k-k). 2006. 16p. bds. 7.95 (978-0-88776-789-0(3)) 2004. 32p. 11.95 (978-0-88776-675-6(7)) Tundra Bks. CAN. (Tundra Bks.). Dist: Penguin Random Hse. LLC.

Jocelyn, Marthe & Jocelyn, Nell. Ones & Twos. 2011. (ENG., Illus.). 24p. (J). (gr. -1-k). 15.95 (978-1-77049-220-2(8), Tundra Bks.) Tundra Bks. CAN. Dist: Penguin Random Hse. LLC.

Johnson, Stephen T. & Johnson, Stephen. City by Numbers. Johnson, Stephen T., illus. 2003. (ENG., Illus.). 32p. (J). (gr. k-3). 7.99 (978-0-14-056636-9(8), Puffin Books) Penguin Young Readers Group.

—City by Numbers. 2003. (gr. k-3). lib. bdg. 18.40 (978-0-613-67534-5(7), Turtleback) Turtleback Bks.

Johnston, Tony. 10 Fat Turkeys. Deas, Rich, illus. 2009. (ENG.). 28p. (J). (gr. -1-k). bds. 6.99 (978-0-545-16469-6(9), Cartwheel Bks.) Scholastic, Inc.

Jones, Stephanie, des. 1-2-3 Look & Say Chunky Flashcards. 2007. (Look & Say Flashcards Ser.). (Illus.). 30p. (J). (gr. -1-k). 9.99 (978-0-7945-1462-4(6), Usborne) EDC Publishing.

Jones, Tammy. Count Around the Room. 2009. (Sight Word Readers Set A Ser.). (J). 3.49 net. (978-1-60719-157-5(1)) Newmark Learning LLC.

—Count at the Baseball Field. 2009. (Sight Word Readers Set A Ser.). (J). 3.49 net. (978-1-60719-156-8(3)) Newmark Learning LLC.

—Count on Me. 2009. (Sight Word Readers Set A Ser.). (J). (978-1-60719-154-4(7)) Newmark Learning LLC.

Jordan, Christopher. Hockey 123: My First NHL Book. 2010. (My First NHL Bks.). (ENG., Illus.). 30p. (J). (gr. -1). bds. (978-1-55168-367-6(9)) Me to We.

—NASCAR 123. 2012. (My First NASCAR Racing Ser.). (ENG., Illus.). 24p. (J). (gr. k-k). bds. 7.95 (978-1-77049-428-2(6), Fenn-Tundra) Tundra Bks. CAN. Dist: Penguin Random Hse. LLC.

Jugran, Jan. Three Little Duckies. Parsons, Jackie & Larranaga, Ana Martin, illus. 2006. (ENG.). 6p. (J). (gr. -1 — 1). 14.99 (978-1-58476-352-9(3), IKIDS) Innovative Kids.

Julian, Alison, illus. The 12 Days of Christmas. 2005. (J). (978-1-74157-281-0(9)) Hinkler Bks. Pty, Ltd.

Kalman, Bobbie. I Can Count. 2010. (ENG., Illus.). 16p. (J). (gr. k-2). (978-0-7787-9411-0(3)); pap. (978-0-7787-9455-4(5)) Crabtree Publishing Co.

—I Can Count: Sé Contar. 2010. (SPA, ENG & MUL.). 16p. (J). pap. (978-0-7787-8262-9(X)); lib. bdg. (978-0-7787-8269-8(7)) Crabtree Publishing Co.

—Sé Contar. 2010. (SPA.). 16p. (J). pap. (978-0-7787-8577-4(7)); lib. bdg. (978-0-7787-8551-4(3)) Crabtree Publishing Co.

Kander, Beth & Kenyon, Bret. Glubbery Gray, the Knight-Eating Beast, 1 vol. Labbé, Jesse, illus. 2010. (ENG.). 40p. (J). (gr. k-3). 17.99 (978-1-58980-867-6(3)) Pelican Publishing Co., Inc.

Katz, Karen. Counting Christmas. Katz, Karen, illus. 2003. (ENG., Illus.). 32p. (J). (gr. -1-1). 16.99 (978-0-689-84925-1(7), McElderry, Margaret K. Bks.) McElderry, Margaret K. Bks.

—Counting Kisses. Katz, Karen, illus. 2003. (Classic Board Bks.). (ENG., Illus.). 32p. (J). (gr. -1-k). bds., bds. 7.99 (978-0-689-85658-7(X), Little Simon) Little Simon.

—Counting Kisses: Lap Edition. Katz, Karen, illus. 2010. (ENG., Illus.). 26p. (J). (gr. -1 — 1). bds. 12.99 (978-1-4424-0792-3(1), Little Simon) Little Simon.

—Daddy Hugs. Katz, Karen, illus. 2007. (Classic Board Bks.). (ENG., Illus.). 32p. (J). (gr. -1 — 1). bds. 7.99 (978-1-4169-4120-0(7), Little Simon) Little Simon.

—Daddy Hugs 1 2 3. Katz, Karen, illus. 2005. (ENG., Illus.). 32p. (J). (gr. -1-1). 18.99 (978-0-689-87771-1(4), McElderry, Margaret K. Bks.) McElderry, Margaret K. Bks.

—Mommy Hugs: Lap Edition. Katz, Karen, illus. 2010. (ENG., Illus.). 26p. (J). (gr. -1 — 1). bds. 12.99 (978-1-4424-0791-6(3), Little Simon) Little Simon.

—Ten Tiny Babies. Katz, Karen, illus. 2011. (Classic Board Bks.). (ENG., Illus.). 32p. (J). (gr. -1-k). bds. 7.99 (978-1-4424-1394-8(8), Little Simon) Little Simon.

—Ten Tiny Tickles. Katz, Karen, illus. 2008. (Classic Board Bks.). (ACE & ENG., Illus.). 32p. (J). (gr. -1-k). bds. 7.99 (978-1-4169-5101-8(6), Little Simon) Little Simon.

—Ten Tiny Tickles. Katz, Karen, illus. 2005. (ENG., Illus.). 32p. (J). (gr. -1-k). 15.99 (978-0-689-85976-2(7), McElderry, Margaret K. Bks.) McElderry, Margaret K. Bks.

Keiser, Melissa. My Airplane Book-Counting. 2005. (Board Book Ser.). (ENG., Illus.). 12p. (J). (gr. -1-12). bds. 6.95 (978-1-59373-041-3(1)) Bunker Hill Publishing, Inc.

Kelly, Mij. One More Sheep. Ayto, Russell, illus. 2006. (ENG.). 32p. (J). (gr. k-3). 16.95 (978-1-56145-378-8(1)) Peachtree Pubs.

Kenison, Misti, illus. The Tiny Traveler: Italy: A Book of Numbers. 2016. (ENG.). 24p. (J). (— 1). bds. 5.99 (978-1-5107-0466-4(3), Sky Pony Pr.) Skyhorse Publishing Co., Inc.

Kennedy, Anne Vittur. One Big Turkey, 1 vol. 2016. (ENG., Illus.). 20p. (J). bds. 8.99 (978-0-7180-8711-1(9)) Nelson, Thomas Inc.

Kennedy, Anne Vittur & Kennedy, Anne V. One Shining Star, 1 vol. 2006. (ENG., Illus.). 22p. (J). (gr. -1). bds. 6.99 (978-0-310-71029-5(4)) Zonderkidz.

Kent, Lorna, illus. Baby's First Counting Book. 2004. 12p. (J). bds. 7.99 (978-1-85854-616-2(8)) Brimax Books Ltd. GBR. Dist: Byeway Bks.

Kernan, Elizabeth. Counting at the Store: Learning to Count from 6 To 10. 2009. (Math for the Real World: Early Emergent Ser.). (ENG., Illus.). 8p. (gr. k-1). pap. 5.15 (978-0-8239-8842-6(2)) Rosen Publishing Group, Inc., The.

Kids Can Press Staff. Numbers. 2003. (Kids Can Learn with Franklin Ser.). (ENG., Illus.). 32p. (J). (gr. -1 — 1). 3.95 (978-1-55337-591-3(2)) Kids Can Pr., Ltd. CAN. Dist: Hachette Bk. Group.

Klemm, Rebecca & Rebecca Klemm Charitable Foundation. NumbersAlive! Books for Young Travelers. 2012. (ENG.). pap. 13.95 (978-0-9853667-0-4(2)) NumbersAlive! Pr.

Kompelein, Tracy. Skip Count by 2, Now Can You?, 1 vol. 2007. (Math Made Fun Ser.). (ENG., Illus.). 24p. (J). (gr. k-3). lib. bdg. 24.21 (978-1-59928-545-0(2), SandCastle) ABDO Publishing Co.

—Skip Count by 5, Its No Jive!, 1 vol. 2007. (Math Made Fun Ser.). (ENG., Illus.). 24p. (J). (gr. k-3). lib. bdg. 24.21 (978-1-59928-543-6(6), SandCastle) ABDO Publishing Co.

—1, 2, 3, It's Easy for Me!, 1 vol. 2007. (Math Made Fun Ser.). (ENG., Illus.). 24p. (J). (gr. k-3). lib. bdg. 24.21 (978-1-59928-505-4(3), SandCastle) ABDO Publishing Co.

Kompelien, Tracy. Can You Count More Than Before?, 1 vol. 2007. (Math Made Fun Ser.). (ENG., Illus.). 24p. (J). (gr. k-3). lib. bdg. 24.21 (978-1-59928-511-5(8), SandCastle) ABDO Publishing Co.

—Skip Count by 10, Lets Do It Again!, 1 vol. 2007. (Math Made Fun Ser.). (ENG., Illus.). 24p. (J). (gr. k-3). lib. bdg. 24.21 (978-1-59928-541-2(X), SandCastle) ABDO Publishing Co.

Kono, Erin Eitter, illus. The Twelve Days of Christmas in Wisconsin. (Twelve Days of Christmas in America Ser.). (ENG.). (J). 2017. 22p. (— 1). bds. 7.95 **(978-1-4549-2286-5(9))** 2007. 40p. (gr. -1-3). 12.95 (978-1-4027-3815-9(3)) Sterling Publishing Co., Inc.

Kovalev, Neil. Kaylee Can Cook: Number Names & Count Sequence. 2013. (Rosen Math Readers Ser.). (ENG.). 16p. (J). (gr. k-1). pap. 42.00 (978-1-4777-1612-0(2)); (Illus.). pap. 7.00 (978-1-4777-1611-3(4)) Rosen Publishing Group, Inc., The. (Rosen Classroom).

Kramer, Alan. Counting at the Zoo. 2004. (Reader's Theater Ser.). (J). pap. (978-1-4108-0692-5(8)) Benchmark Education Co.

Krans, Kim. 123 Dream. 2016. (ENG., Illus.). 48p. (J). (gr. -1-2). 16.99 (978-0-553-53932-5(9), Random Hse. Bks. for Young Readers) Random Hse. Children's Bks.

Krause, Robert. The President's Counting Book: The Future Generations of America. 2011. 36p. pap. 18.41 (978-1-4269-6049-9(2)) Trafford Publishing.

Krebs, Laurie. We All Went on Safari: A Counting Journey Through Tanzania. Cairns, Julia, illus. 2003. (ENG & SWA.). 32p. (J). (gr. k-3). 16.99 (978-1-84148-478-5(4)) Barefoot Bks., Inc.

Krejewski, Sandra. Numbers with Attitude. 2009. 14p. 12.50 (978-1-60695-027-2(4)) Callanish Pr.

Kreloff, Elliot, illus. Counting Duckies. 2010. 16p. (J). bds. (978-1-60906-007-7(5)) Begin Smart LLC.

Krishnaswami, Uma. Hooray! 100 Days. 2006. (Early Explorers Ser.). (J). pap. (978-1-4108-6114-6(7)) Benchmark Education Co.

Kroll, Olivia. Riley's Vegetable Garden: Count to Tell the Number of Objects. 2013. (Rosen Math Readers Ser.). (ENG.). 16p. (J). (gr. k-1). pap. 42.00 (978-1-4777-1579-6(7)); (Illus.). pap. 7.00 (978-1-4777-1578-9(9)) Rosen Publishing Group, Inc., The. (Rosen Classroom).

Kumon. My Book of Numbers 1-120. 2004. (Kumon Ser.). (ENG., Illus.). 80p. (J). per. 6.95 (978-4-7743-0704-6(1)) Kumon Publishing North America, Inc.

—My Book of Numbers 1-30. 2004. (Kumon Ser.). (ENG., Illus.). 80p. (J). per. 6.95 (978-4-7743-0703-9(3)) Kumon Publishing North America, Inc.

Kumon Publishing North America, creator. Numbers 1-30 Write & Wipe! 2006. (Kumon Flash Cards Ser.). 32p. (J). 9.95 (978-1-933241-08-1(X)) Kumon Publishing North America, Inc.

Kunhardt, Katharine. Let's Count the Puppies. 2004. (Illus.). 32p. (J). (gr. -1-1). 13.89 (978-0-06-054337-2(X)) HarperCollins Pubs.

Kuskowski, Alex. Know Your Numbers: School, 1 vol. 2014. (Numbers 1-20 Ser.). (ENG.). 24p. (J). (gr. k-3). lib. bdg. 24.21 (978-1-62403-267-7(2), SandCastle) ABDO Publishing Co.

—Know Your Numbers: Sports, 1 vol. 2014. (Numbers 1-20 Ser.). (ENG.). 24p. (J). (gr. k-3). lib. bdg. 24.21 (978-1-62403-268-4(0), SandCastle) ABDO Publishing Co.

La Coccinella. Look & See: Let's Count! 2008. (Look & See! Ser.). (ENG., Illus.). 26p. (J). (gr. -1-1). bds. 6.95 (978-1-4027-5825-6(1)) Sterling Publishing Co., Inc.

Ladybird Books Staff. My Counting Book. (Early Readers Ser.: No. S8711-6). (Illus.). 24p. (J). (gr. -1-2). 3.95 (978-0-7214-5146-6(2), Dutton Juvenile) Penguin Publishing Group.

Lalley, Kristine. How Many Legs? Learning to Multiply Using Repeated Addition. 2006. (Rosen Publishing Group's Reading Room Collection). (Illus.). 16p. (J). (gr. 3-7). lib. bdg. 18.75 (978-1-4042-3336-2(9), PowerKids Pr.) Rosen Publishing Group, Inc., The.

—How Many Legs? Learning to Multiply Using Repeated Action. 2009. (Math for the REAL World Ser.). 16p. (gr. 2-3). pap. 7.05 (978-0-8239-8929-4(1), Rosen Classroom) Rosen Publishing Group, Inc., The.

Lamb, Stacey, illus. 123 Sticker Book. 2009. (Sticker Bks). 24p. (J). pap. 6.99 (978-0-7945-2361-9(7), Usborne) EDC Publishing.

Langham, Tony. Creepy Crawly Calypso. Harter, Debbie, illus. (ENG.). 32p. (J). 2007. pap. 6.99 (978-1-84686-133-8(0)) 2004. 16.99 (978-1-84148-699-4(X)) Barefoot Bks., Inc.

Langham, Tony & Harter, Debbie. Creepy Crawly Calypso. 2005. (ENG.). 32p. (J). pap. 9.99 (978-1-902283-46-3(5)) Barefoot Bks., Inc.

—Mira Quien Toca Calipso! Harter, Debbie, illus. 2009. (SPA., Illus.). 32p. (J). (gr. -1-2). pap. 7.99 (978-1-84686-281-6(7)) Barefoot Bks., Inc.

Laval, Thierry. Numbers. 2011. (ENG., Illus.). 10p. (J). (gr. -1 — 1). bds. 6.99 (978-0-8118-7953-8(4)) Chronicle Bks. LLC.

Law, Felicia & Way, Steve. The Mystery of Nine: Number Place & Value in Action. Spoor, Mike & Mostyn, David, illus. 2010. (Mandrill Mountain Math Mysteries Ser.). 32p. (J). (gr. 2-6). 22.60 (978-1-60754-819-5(4)); pap. 10.55 (978-1-60754-824-9(0)) Windmill Bks.

Layne, Steven L. Number 1 Teacher: A School Counting Book. Ettlinger, Doris & Layne, Deborah, illus. 2008. (ENG.). 40p. (J). (gr. k-6). 17.95 (978-1-58536-307-0(3)) Sleeping Bear Pr.

Lazar, Tara. 7 Ate 9. MacDonald, Ross, illus. 2017. (ENG.). 32p. (J). (gr. -1-k). 17.99 **(978-1-4847-1779-0(1))** Hyperion Bks. for Children.

LeapFrog Staff. Imagination Desk Counting Day at the Beach. 2003. (Illus.). 9.99 (978-1-59319-025-5(5)) LeapFrog Enterprises, Inc.

—Lots & Lots of Honeypots. 2003. (Illus.). (J). spiral bd. 14.99 (978-1-59319-002-6(6)) LeapFrog Enterprises, Inc.

Learn to Count. 2004. (Alphabet & Counting Ser.). 12p. (J). bds. 5.99 (978-1-85997-810-8(X)) Byeway Bks.

Learning Company Books Staff, ed. Reader Rabbit Fun with Crayons: 1-2-3. 2004. (Illus.). 32p. (J). pap. (978-0-7630-7736-5(4)) Magma.

Learning Numbers. (Learning Ser.). 22p. (J). bds. (978-2-7643-0110-4(3)) Phidal Publishing, Inc./Editions Phidal, Inc.

Lebron, Karen. My Big Book of Numbers. Lonsdale, Mary, illus. 2004. 48p. (J). 5.99 (978-1-85854-317-8(7)) Brimax Books Ltd. GBR. Dist: Byeway Bks.

Lee, Mark. Twenty Big Trucks in the Middle of the Street. Cyrus, Kurt, illus. 2013. (ENG.). 32p. (J). (gr. -1-2). 15.99 (978-0-7636-5809-0(X)) Candlewick Pr.

Leech, Bonnie. The Names of Numbers: Learning How Numbers Are Represented with Words. 2009. (Math for the Real World: Early Emergent Ser.). (ENG., Illus.). 8p. (gr. k-1). pap. 5.15 (978-0-8239-8884-6(8)) Rosen Publishing Group, Inc., The.

Leigh, Autumn. On the Ball: Learning to Identify the Place Values of Ones & Tens. 2009. (Math for the Real World: Early Emergent Ser.). (ENG., Illus.). 8p. (gr. k-1). pap. 5.15 (978-0-8239-8859-4(7)) Rosen Publishing Group, Inc., The.

Lenore, Vikki. I Can Count To 100. 2009. 40p. pap. 8.10 (978-0-557-05462-6(1)) Lulu Pr., Inc.

LernerClassroom Editors. Count Your Way Teaching Guide. 2009. pap. 7.95 (978-0-8225-6886-5(1)) Lerner Publishing Group.

Lessac, Frané. Island Counting 1 2 3. Lessac, Frané, illus. 2007. (ENG., Illus.). 24p. (J). (— 1). bds. 6.99 (978-0-7636-3518-3(9)) Candlewick Pr.

Let's Say Our Numbers. 2007. (Simple First Words Ser.). (Illus.). 14p. (J). (978-1-84332-520-8(9)) Priddy Bks.

Letters & Numbers. (Early Learning Ser.). (J). incl. audio NewSound, LLC.

Letters & Numbers. 2004. 12.99 incl. audio compact disk (978-1-57583-300-2(X)) Twin Sisters IP, LLC.

Levine, Arthur A. Monday Is One Day. Hector, Julian, illus. 2015. (ENG.). 32p. (J). (gr. -1-k). 6.99 (978-0-439-78925-7(7)) Scholastic, Inc.

Levine, Julia Pimsleur. Little Pim: Numbers. 2012. (ENG.). 10p. (J). (gr. -1-k). bds. 8.95 *(978-1-4197-0175-7(4))* Abrams, Inc.

Lewis, Jan, illus. Look & Learn with Little Dino: Count 123. 2014. (ENG.). 24p. (J). (gr. -1-1). bds. 6.99 *(978-1-86147-381-3(8)*, Armadillo) Anness Publishing GBR. Dist: National Bk. Network.

—My First 123. 2014. (ENG.). 24p. (J). (gr. -1-k). bds. 6.99 *(978-1-86147-371-4(0)*, Armadillo) Anness Publishing GBR. Dist: National Bk. Network.

—My First 123: Learn to Count from 1 To 100! 2015. (ENG.). 48p. pap. 9.99 *(978-1-86147-425-4(3)*, Armadillo) Anness Publishing GBR. Dist: National Bk. Network.

—My First Learning Library: 3 Great Books: First Abc First 123 First Words, 3 vols. 2014. (ENG.). 72p. (J). (gr. -1-1). bds., bds., bds. 9.99 *(978-1-86147-387-5(7)*, Armadillo) Anness Publishing GBR. Dist: National Bk. Network.

—123: Turn the Wheels - Learn to Count! 2015. (ENG.). 10p. (J). (gr. -1-12). bds. 14.99 *(978-1-86147-661-6(2)*, Armadillo) Anness Publishing GBR. Dist: National Bk. Network.

Liddiard, Merrilee. Fairy Friends: a Counting Primer, 1 vol. 2016. (ENG., Illus.). 22p. (J). bds. 9.99 *(978-1-4236-4534-4(0))* Gibbs Smith, Publisher.

Lift & See 123. (Baby Goldstars Lift Out Eva Ser.). 5p. *(978-1-4054-9312-3(7))* Parragon, Inc.

Lin, Chris. Mandy & Pandy Play Let's Count. Villalta, Ingrid, illus. 2008. 18p. (J). (gr. -1-3). bds. 9.99 *(978-0-9800156-5-2(0))* Mandy & Pandy Bks., LLC.

Lionni, Leo. Colors, Numbers, Letters. 2010. (ENG., Illus.). 40p. (J). (gr. k — 1). bds. 10.99 *(978-0-375-85474-3(6)*, Knopf Bks. for Young Readers) Random Hse. Children's Bks.

Lisa Darby And Rachel Darby. When Balloons Go Bye-Bye. 2008. 28p. pap. 21.99 *(978-1-4257-7068-6(1))* Xlibris Corp.

Lisi, Branden. Count on the Farm. Lisi, Margaret, illus. 2006. (J). lib. bdg. 15.95 *(978-0-9771472-0-5(7))* Count On Learning.

Litchfield, J. Very First Numbers. 2004. (First Words Board Bks.). 10p. (J). 4.95 *(978-0-7945-0095-5(1)*, Usborne) EDC Publishing.

Litchfield, Jo & Jones, Stephanie, illus. First 1,2,3. Allman, Howard, photos by. 2006. (Usborne Look & Say Ser.). 20p. (J). (gr. -1-k). bds. 14.95 *(978-0-7945-1219-4(4)*, Usborne) EDC Publishing.

Litchfield, Jo & Sanchez Gallego, Maria Isabel. 123. Jones, Stephanie, illus. Allman, Howard & MMStudios, photos by. 2007. (Dime lo Que Ves Ser.). 22p. (J). bds. 14.99 *(978-0-7460-8354-3(8)*, Usborne) EDC Publishing.

little bee books, little bee & Seal, Julia. Jungle. 2016. (ENG., Illus.). 12p. (J). (gr. -1 — 1). bds. 6.99 *(978-1-4998-0259-7(5))* Little Bee Books Inc.

Little Bee Books Staff & Blake, Carly. Baby's First 123. Max and Sid Staff, illus. 2015. (Baby's First Ser.). (ENG.). 12p. (J). (gr. -1 — 1). bds. 4.99 *(978-1-4998-0051-7(7))* Little Bee Books Inc.

Little Dragon Counts 1, 2, 3, 4, 5. 2008. (Little Dragon Flying Board Ser.). 7p. bds. *(978-1-4075-2665-2(0))* Parragon, Inc.

Litton, Jonathan. Moo. Galloway, Fhiona, illus. 2016. (My Little World Ser.). (ENG.). 24p. (J). (gr. -1-k). mass mkt. 3.99 *(978-1-58925-484-8(8))* Tiger Tales.

—Peek-Through Forest. Nowowiejska, Kasia, illus. 2015. (Little Snappers Ser.). (ENG.). 12p. (J). (gr. -1-2). bds. 9.99 *(978-1-68010-508-7(6))* Tiger Tales.

Litwin, Eric. Pete the Cat & His Four Groovy Buttons. 2013. (CHI & ENG.). (J). (gr. -1-2). ***(978-957-570-982-2(9))*** Eastern Publishing Co., Ltd., The.

—Pete the Cat & His Four Groovy Buttons. Dean, James, illus. 2012. (Pete the Cat Ser.). 40p. (J). (gr. -1-2). (ENG.). 17.99 *(978-0-06-211058-9(6))*; lib. bdg. 17.89 *(978-0-06-211059-6(4))* HarperCollins Pubs.

Litz, Amanda. Sam & Pam Can & You Can Too! We Can Count. Garcia, Cynthia, illus. 2011. 32p. (J). pap. 3.99 *(978-0-9841496-3-6(5))* Traveler's Trunk Publishing LLC.

Lloyd, Sam. Shape Sorters - Numbers, 2. Lloyd, Sam, illus. 2011. (Shape Sorters Ser.). (ENG., Illus.). 12p. (J). (gr. k-k). bds. 7.99 *(978-0-230-70962-1(1))* Macmillan Pubs., Ltd. GBR. Dist: Independent Pubs. Group.

Lluch, Alex A. Animal Numbers: Slide & Seek Counting. 2012. (ENG.). 14p. (J). bds. 7.95 *(978-1-936061-90-7(2))* WS Publishing.

—Animal Numbers: Slide & Seek The 123s. 2014. (ENG., Illus.). 14p. (J). bds. 12.99 *(978-1-61351-042-1(X))* WS Publishing.

—Numbers - I Like to Count from 1 to 10! Defenbaugh, David, illus. 2014. (ENG.). 30p. (J). bds. 8.95 *(978-1-61351-078-0(0))* WS Publishing.

Lobel, Anita. 10 Hungry Rabbits. 2015. (ENG., Illus.). 20p. (J). (-k). bds. 7.99 *(978-0-553-49828-8(2)*, Knopf Bks. for Young Readers) Random Hse. Children's Bks.

Long, Ethan. One Drowsy Dragon. 2010. (Illus.). (J). *(978-0-545-23412-2(3)*, Orchard Bks.) Scholastic, Inc.

—The Wing Wing Brothers: Carnival de Math. Long, Ethan, illus. 2013. (ENG., Illus.). 32p. (J). 15.95 *(978-0-8234-2604-1(1))* Holiday Hse., Inc.

—The Wing Wing Brothers Carnival de Math. Long, Ethan, illus. 2014. (ENG., Illus.). 32p. (J). (gr. -1-1). 6.99 *(978-0-8234-3062-8(6))* Holiday Hse., Inc.

Look & Count. 2005. (J). pap. 3.99 *(978-1-933200-19-4(7))* Family Bks. at Home.

Loughran, Donna. Herding a Hundred: Counting the Sheep. 2013. (IMath Ser.). (Illus.). 24p. (J). (gr. k-2). lib. bdg. 21.27 *(978-1-59953-547-0(5))* Norwood Hse. Pr.

—Herding a Hundred: Counting the Sheep. 2013. (IMath Ser.). (Illus.). 24p. (J). (gr. k-2). pap. 11.94 *(978-1-60357-486-0(7))* Norwood Hse. Pr.

Luna, Tom. The Spots on the Jaguar: A Counting Book. Luna, Tom & Alvarez, Laura, illus. 2005. (SPA & ENG.). 20p. (J). *(978-0-9716580-4-2(8))* Lectura Bks.

MacCarthy, Patricia. Ocean Parade: A Counting Book. MacCarthy, Patricia, illus. 2005. (Illus.). 24p. (J). (gr. -1-3). reprint ed. 12.00 *(978-0-7567-8983-1(4))* DIANE Publishing Co.

MacDonald, Margaret Read & Taibah, Nadia Jameel. How Many Donkeys? An Arabic Counting Tale. Liddiment, Carol, illus. 2012. (J). 34.28 *(978-1-61913-148-4(X))* Weigl Pubs., Inc.

MacDonald, Suse. Fish, Swish! Splash, Dash! Counting Round & Round. MacDonald, Suse, illus. 2007. (ENG., Illus.). 30p. (J). (gr. -1-k). 12.99 *(978-1-4169-3605-3(X)*, Little Simon) Little Simon.

MacGregor, Bailey. What's for Lunch? Classify & Count Objects in Each Category. 2013. (InfoMax Math Readers Ser.). (ENG.). 16p. (J). (gr. k-1). pap. 42.00 *(978-1-4777-1944-2(X))*; pap. 7.00 *(978-1-4777-1943-5(1))* Rosen Publishing Group, Inc., The. (Rosen Classroom).

Make Believe Ideas, creator. Touch & Learn 123 Casebound. 2007. per. *(978-1-84610-507-4(2))* Make Believe Ideas.

Make Believe Ideas Staff. Baby Fun 123. 2005. (Illus.). 10p. (gr. -1 — 1). per. *(978-1-905051-18-2(2))* Make Believe Ideas.

Maltby, Robert I. My Money Got Gobbled, 1 vol. 2010. 36p. 24.95 *(978-1-4489-6407-9(5))* PublishAmerica, Inc.

Manolessou, Katherina. Zoom Zoom Zoom. 2014. (ENG., Illus.). 32p. (J). (gr. -1-k). 19.99 *(978-0-230-76378-4(2))* Pan Macmillan GBR. Dist: Independent Pubs. Group.

Mansfield, Andy. One Lonely Fish. Flintham, Thomas & Mansfield, Andy, illus. 2017. (ENG.). 22p. (J). 15.99 *(978-1-68119-201-7(2)*, 9781681192017, Bloomsbury USA Childrens) Bloomsbury Publishing USA.

Mara, Nichole. All Aboard! Let's Ride a Train. Kolb, Andrew, illus. 2017. (ENG.). 10p. (J). (gr. -1 — 1). bds. 9.95 ***(978-1-4197-2567-8(X)***, Abrams Appleseed) Abrams, Inc.

Markle, Sandra. How Many Baby Pandas? / Scholastic Book Fair Edition. 2009. (Illus.). 32p. (J). pap. 4.99 *(978-0-8027-2070-2(6))* Walker & Co.

Marrewa, Jennifer. Using Money on a Shopping Trip. 2008. (Math in Our World - Level 2 Ser.). 24p. (gr. 1-4). pap. 8.15 *(978-0-8368-9013-6(2)*, Weekly Reader Leveled Readers) Stevens, Gareth Publishing LLLP.

—Using Money on a Shopping Trip. McKinley, Kay, photos by. 2008. (Math in Our World: Level 2 Ser.). (Illus.). 24p. (gr. 1-4). lib. bdg. 22.00 *(978-0-8368-9004-4(3)*, Weekly Reader Leveled Readers) Stevens, Gareth Publishing LLLP.

—Vamos a Usar Dinero en un Viaje de Compras. McKinley, Kay, photos by. 2008. (Matemáticas en Nuestro Mundo - Nivel 2 (Math in Our World - Level 2) Ser.). (SPA., Illus.). 24p. (gr. 1-4). lib. bdg. 22.00 *(978-0-8368-9022-8(1)*, Weekly Reader Leveled Readers) Stevens, Gareth Publishing LLLP.

—Vamos a USAR DINERO en un Viaje de Compras. 2008. (Las Matemáticas en Nuestro Mundo Ser.). (SPA.). 24p. (gr. 1-4). pap. 8.15 *(978-0-8368-9031-0(0)*, Weekly Reader Leveled Readers) Stevens, Gareth Publishing LLLP.

Martin, Bill, Jr. & Archambault, John. Chicka Chicka Boom Boom. Ehlert, Lois, illus. 2012. (Classic Board Bks.). (ENG.). 36p. (J). (gr. -1 — 1). bds. 7.99 *(978-1-4424-5070-7(3)*, Little Simon) Little Simon.

Martin, Bill, Jr. & Sampson, Michael. Chicka Chicka 1, 2, 3. Ehlert, Lois, illus. 2014. (Chicka Chicka Book Ser.). (ENG.). 36p. (J). (gr. -1 — 1). bds. 7.99 *(978-1-4814-0056-5(8)*, Little Simon) Little Simon.

—Chicka Chicka 1, 2, 3. Ehlert, Lois, illus. 2004. (Chicka Chicka Book Ser.). (ENG.). 40p. (J). (gr. -1-2). 17.99 *(978-0-689-85881-9(7)*, Simon & Schuster Bks. For Young Readers) Simon & Schuster Bks. For Young Readers.

—Chicka Chicka 1, 2, 3. Ehlert, Lois, illus. 2005. (J). (gr. -1-3). 29.95 *(978-0-439-76677-7(X)*, WHCD669) Weston Woods Studios, Inc.

—Chicka Chicka 1, 2, 3: Lap Edition. Ehlert, Lois, illus. 2013. (Chicka Chicka Book Ser.). (ENG.). 36p. (J). (gr. -1-1). bds. 12.99 *(978-1-4424-6613-5(8)*, Little Simon) Little Simon.

Martin, Bill, Jr., et al. Chicka Chicka Box Box! Chicka Chicka Boom Boom; Chicka Chicka 1, 2, 3. Ehlert, Lois, illus. 2013. (Chicka Chicka Book Ser.). (ENG.). 80p. (J). (gr. -1-3). 35.99 *(978-1-4814-0223-1(4)*, Beach Lane Bks.) Beach Lane Bks.

Martin, Susi. Animal 123. 2014. (ENG., Illus.). 32p. (J). (gr. -1-2). 9.95 *(978-1-77085-454-3(1)*, 9781770854543) Firefly Bks., Ltd.

Martinez, Jeny. A Walk in the Park. 2011. 32p. pap. 21.99 *(978-1-4568-5229-0(9))* Xlibris Corp.

Marzollo, Jean. Help Me Learn Numbers 0-20. Phillips, Chad, photos by. 2012. (ENG., Illus.). 32p. (J). (gr. -1-k). pap. 6.99 *(978-0-8234-2542-6(8))* Holiday Hse., Inc.

—I Spy Numbers. Wick, Walter, illus. 2012. (I Spy Ser.). (ENG.). 32p. (J). (gr. -1-k). pap. 3.99 *(978-0-545-41585-9(3))* Scholastic, Inc.

—I Spy Numbers. 2012. (I Spy — Scholastic Ser.). lib. bdg. 13.55 *(978-0-606-23971-4(5)*, Turtleback) Turtleback Bks.

Mathieu, Joe, et al. Big Bird's Big Book: Counting Colors Country City Opposites Playing. Mathieu, Joe, illus. 2009. (Sesame Street Ser.). (ENG., Illus.). 14p. (J). (gr. k — 1). bds. 45.00 *(978-0-394-89128-6(7)*, Random Hse. Bks. for Young Readers) Random Hse. Children's Bks.

Matthias, Catherine & Sharp, Gene. Demasiados Globos. Sharp, Gene, illus. 2011. (Rookie Ready to Learn Español Ser.). (SPA., Illus.). 40p. (J). pap. 5.95 *(978-0-531-26792-9(X))*; lib. bdg. 23.00 *(978-0-531-26124-8(7))* Scholastic Library Publishing. (Children's Pr.).

May, Eleanor. Albert Helps Out: Counting Money. Melmon, Deborah, illus. 2017. (Mouse Math (r) Ser.). (ENG.). 32p. (gr. -1-1). 7.95 *(978-1-57565-860-5(7))* Kane Press, Inc.

—Albert Helps Out: Counting Money. Melmon, Deborah, illus. 2017. (Mouse Math (r) Ser.). (ENG.). 32p. (gr. -1-1). lib. bdg. 22.65 *(978-1-57565-857-5(7))*; 34.65 ***(978-1-57565-863-6(1))*** Kane Press, Inc.

—Mac & Cheese, Pleeeeeeze! 2008. pap. 34.95 *(978-1-58013-780-5(6))* Kane Press, Inc.

—The Mousier the Merrier. Melmon, Deborah, illus. 2012. (Mouse Math Ser.). (ENG.). 32p. (J). (gr. -1-1). 22.60 *(978-1-57565-447-8(4))*; pap. 7.95 *(978-1-57565-440-9(7))* Kane Press, Inc.

—Where's Albert? Counting & Skip Counting. Melmon, Deborah, illus. 2017. (Mouse Math (r) Ser.). (ENG.). 32p. (gr. -1-1). lib. bdg. 22.65 *(978-1-57565-855-1(0))* Kane Press, Inc.

May, Eleanor. Where's Albert? Counting Skip Counting. Melmon, Deborah, illus. 2017. (Mouse Math (r) Ser.). (ENG.). 32p. (gr. -1-1). 34.65 ***(978-1-57565-861-2(5))*** Kane Press, Inc.

McBratney, Sam. Guess How Much I Love You: Look What I Can Do: A First Concepts Book. Jeram, Anita, illus. 2014. (Guess How Much I Love You Ser.). (ENG.). 16p. (J). (— 1). bds. 9.99 *(978-0-7636-7064-1(2))* Candlewick Pr.

McCurry, Kristen. Counting. Banks, Timothy, illus. 2013. (Wizard of Oz Ser.). (ENG.). 24p. (gr. 1-2). 27.99 *(978-1-4765-3766-5(6))* Capstone Press of Coughlan Cos.

McDonald, Caryl. On the Team: Count to Tell the Number of Objects. 2013. (Rosen Math Readers Ser.). (ENG.). 16p. (J). (gr. k-1). pap. 42.00 *(978-1-4777-1585-7(1))*; (Illus.). pap. 7.00 *(978-1-4777-1584-0(3))* Rosen Publishing Group, Inc., The. (Rosen Classroom).

McDonald, Jill. Over in the Meadow. 2012. (ENG., Illus.). 24p. (J). (gr. -1-2). 9.99 *(978-1-84686-747-7(9))* Barefoot Bks., Inc.

McGehee, Claudia. A Woodland Counting Book. 2006. (Bur Oak Book Ser.). (Illus.). 32p. (J). (gr. 3-7). 17.95 *(978-0-87745-989-7(4))* Univ. of Iowa Pr.

McGrath, Barbara Barbieri. Birthday Counting. Tagel, Peggy, illus. 2017. (First Celebrations Ser.). (ENG.). 12p. (J). (— 1). bds. 6.99 *(978-1-58089-537-8(9))* Charlesbridge Publishing, Inc.

—Christmas Colors & Counting. Tagel, Peggy, illus. 2016. (First Celebrations Ser.). (ENG.). 12p. (J). (— 1). bds. 6.95 *(978-1-58089-531-6(X))* Charlesbridge Publishing, Inc.

—Easter Counting. Tagel, Peggy, illus. 2017. (First Celebrations Ser.). (ENG.). 12p. (J). (— 1). bds. 6.99 *(978-1-58089-535-4(2))* Charlesbridge Publishing, Inc.

—M & M's(r) Brand Count Around the Circle. 2004. (Illus.). 24p. (J). bds. 7.95 *(978-1-57091-436-2(2))* Charlesbridge Publishing, Inc.

—The M & M's(r) Brand Count to One Hundred Book. 2004. (Illus.). 32p. (J). 16.95 *(978-1-57091-570-3(9))*; pap. 6.95 *(978-1-57091-571-0(7))* Charlesbridge Publishing, Inc.

—The M & M's(r) Brand Counting Book. Glass, Roger, illus. rev. ed. 2004. 32p. (J). 16.95 *(978-1-57091-367-9(6))*; pap. 6.95 *(978-1-57091-368-6(4))* Charlesbridge Publishing, Inc.

—Mas Matematicas con los Chocolates de M & M's Brand. Mlawer, Teresa, tr. Glass, Roger, illus. 2004. (SPA.). 32p. (J). pap. 6.95 *(978-1-57091-481-2(8)*, CH30498) Charlesbridge Publishing, Inc.

—Teddy Bear Counting. Nihoff, Tim, illus. 2010. (McGrath Math Ser.). (ENG.). 32p. (J). (gr. -1-2). 16.95 *(978-1-58089-215-5(9))*; pap. 7.95 *(978-1-58089-216-2(7))* Charlesbridge Publishing, Inc.

—Teddy Bear Subtraction. Nihoff, Tim, illus. (McGrath Math Ser.). (J). 2016. (ENG.). 32p. (gr. -1-3). pap. 7.95 *(978-1-58089-427-2(5))* 2016. (ENG.). 32p. (gr. -1-3). lib. bdg. 17.95 *(978-1-58089-426-5(7))* 2014. *(978-1-60734-652-4(4))* Charlesbridge Publishing, Inc.

—Teddy Bear, Teddy Bear, School Day Math. Nihoff, Tim, illus. 2012. (McGrath Math Ser.). (ENG.). 32p. (J). (gr. -1-3). 16.95 *(978-1-58089-420-3(8))*; pap. 7.95 *(978-1-58089-421-0(6))* Charlesbridge Publishing, Inc.

McGrath, Barbara Barbieri & Alderman, Peter. Soccer Counts! Estrada, Pau, illus. 2003. (ENG.). 32p. (J). (gr. -1-3). pap. 7.95 *(978-1-57091-554-3(7))* Charlesbridge Publishing, Inc.

—Soccer Counts! (El Futbol Cuenta!) Estrada, Pau, illus. 2011. (SPA & ENG.). 32p. (J). (gr. -1-3). pap. 7.95 *(978-1-57091-794-3(9))* Charlesbridge Publishing, Inc.

McGuckin, Mitchelle. Bullfrog Henry. 2010. 60p. pap. 23.99 *(978-1-4490-9547-5(X))* AuthorHouse.

McKee, David. Elmer's First Counting Book. McKee, David, ed. 2012. (Andersen Press Board Bks). (ENG., Illus.). 10p. (J). (gr. -1-2). bds. 7.95 *(978-0-7613-8999-6(7))* Lerner Publishing Group.

McKellar, Danica. Goodnight, Numbers! Padrón, Alicia, illus. 2017. (ENG.). 40p. (J). (-k). 16.99 *(978-1-101-93378-7(X)*, Crown Books For Young Readers) Random Hse. Children's Bks.

McKissack, Fredrick L. & McKissack, Lisa Beringer. Chinese New Year-Count & Celebrate! 2009. (Holidays—Count & Celebrate! Ser.). (Illus.). 32p. (J). (gr. k-3). lib. bdg. 23.94 *(978-0-7660-3101-2(2))* Enslow Pubs., Inc.

—Christmas. 2009. (Holidays—Count & Celebrate! Ser.). (Illus.). 32p. (J). (gr. k-3). lib. bdg. 23.94 *(978-0-7660-3103-6(9))* Enslow Pubs., Inc.

—Cinco de Mayo-Count & Celebrate! 2009. (Holidays—Count & Celebrate! Ser.). (Illus.). 32p. (J). (gr. k-3). lib. bdg. 23.94 *(978-0-7660-3104-3(7))* Enslow Pubs., Inc.

—Counting in the Desert. 2008. (Counting in the Biomes Ser.). (Illus.). 32p. (J). (gr. 3-7). lib. bdg. 23.94 *(978-0-7660-2988-0(3)*, Enslow Elementary) Enslow Pubs., Inc.

—Counting in the Grasslands. 2008. (Counting in the Biomes Ser.). (Illus.). 32p. (J). (gr. 1-3). lib. bdg. 23.94 *(978-0-7660-2991-0(3)*, Enslow Elementary) Enslow Pubs., Inc.

—Counting in the Oceans. 2009. (Counting in the Biomes Ser.). (Illus.). 32p. (J). (gr. 1-3). lib. bdg. 23.94 *(978-0-7660-2994-1(8)*, Enslow Elementary) Enslow Pubs., Inc.

—Counting in the Rain Forest. 2008. (Counting in the Biomes Ser.). (Illus.). 32p. (J). (gr. 1-3). lib. bdg. 23.94 *(978-0-7660-2992-7(1)*, Enslow Elementary) Enslow Pubs., Inc.

—Counting in the Taiga. 2009. (Counting in the Biomes Ser.). (Illus.). 32p. (J). (gr. 1-3). lib. bdg. 23.94 *(978-0-7660-2995-8(6)*, Enslow Elementary) Enslow Pubs., Inc.

—Counting in the Temperate Forest. 2008. (Counting in the Biomes Ser.). (Illus.). 32p. (J). (gr. 1-3). lib. bdg. 23.94 *(978-0-7660-2990-3(5)*, Enslow Elementary) Enslow Pubs., Inc.

—Counting in the Tundra. 2008. (Counting in the Biomes Ser.). (Illus.). 32p. (J). (gr. 3-7). lib. bdg. 23.94 *(978-0-7660-2989-7(1)*, Enslow Elementary) Enslow Pubs., Inc.

—Counting in the Wetlands. 2008. (Counting in the Biomes Ser.). (Illus.). 32p. (J). (gr. 1-3). lib. bdg. 23.94 *(978-0-7660-2993-4(X)*, Enslow Elementary) Enslow Pubs., Inc.

—Kwanzaa-Count & Celebrate! 2009. (Holidays—Count & Celebrate! Ser.). (Illus.). 32p. (J). (gr. k-3). lib. bdg. 23.94 *(978-0-7660-3102-9(0))* Enslow Pubs., Inc.

—Martin Luther King, Jr. Count & Celebrate! 2009. (Holidays—Count & Celebrate! Ser.). (Illus.). 32p. (J). (gr. k-3). lib. bdg. 23.94 *(978-0-7660-3105-0(5))* Enslow Pubs., Inc.

McKown, Hunter. Sand Castle Bash: Counting from 1 To 10. Shannon, David et al, illus. 2009. (Jon Scieszka's Trucktown Ser.). (ENG.). 26p. (J). (gr. -1-k). bds. 5.99 *(978-1-4169-4179-8(7)*, Little Simon) Little Simon.

McLaughlin, Julie. Hungry Mr. Gator. McKay, Ann Marie, illus. 2005. (J). 15.99 *(978-0-933101-24-1(4))* Legacy Pubns.

McNamara, Margaret. The Counting Race. Gordon, Mike, illus. 2005. 32p. (J). lib. bdg. 15.00 *(978-1-59054-967-4(8))* Fitzgerald Bks.

—The Counting Race. Gordon, Mike, illus. 2003. (Robin Hill School Ser.). (ENG.). 32p. (J). (gr. -1-1). pap. 3.99 *(978-0-689-85539-9(7)*, Simon Spotlight) Simon Spotlight.

—How Many Seeds in a Pumpkin? Karas, G. Brian, illus. 2007. (Mr. Tiffin's Classroom Ser.). (ENG.). 40p. (J). (gr. -1-2). 17.99 *(978-0-375-84014-2(1)*, Schwartz & Wade Bks.) Random Hse. Children's Bks.

—One Hundred Days (Plus One) Gordon, Mike, illus. 2008. (Robin Hill School Ser.). (J). (gr. -1-3). pap. 16.95 *(978-1-4301-0616-6(6))* Live Oak Media.

—One Hundred Days (Plus One) Gordon, Mike, illus. 2003. (Robin Hill School Ser.). (ENG.). 32p. (J). (gr. -1-1). pap. 3.99 *(978-0-689-85535-1(4)*, Simon Spotlight) Simon Spotlight.

McOmber, Rachel B., ed. McOmber Phonics Storybooks: Number Fun. rev. ed. (Illus.). (J). *(978-0-944991-58-9(0))* Swift Learning Resources.

McSween, Michele. Gordon & Li Li Count in Mandarin. Nam, Doan, illus. 2010. 32p. 9.99 *(978-0-9820881-3-5(2))* McWong Ink.

McTaggart, Stephen & McTaggart, Debra. Bookee Presents 1, 2, 3 Count with Me. Nord, Mary, illus. (Talking Book Adventures Ser.). 14p. (J). (gr. -1-18). 16.95 *(978-0-9627001-3-2(4))* Futech Educational Products, Inc.

Meachen Rau, Dana. Count on It!, 6 bks., Set. Incl. Five. lib. bdg. 15.95 *(978-0-7614-2970-8(0))*; Four. lib. bdg. 15.95 *(978-0-7614-2969-2(7))*; One. lib. bdg. 15.95 *(978-0-7614-2966-1(2))*; Ten. lib. bdg. 15.95 *(978-0-7614-2971-5(9))*; Three. lib. bdg. 15.95 *(978-0-7614-2968-5(9))*; Two. lib. bdg. 15.95 *(978-0-7614-2967-8(0))*; 24p. (gr. k-1). (Bookworms: Count on It! Ser.). 2004. Set lib. bdg. 95.70 *(978-0-7614-2965-4(4)*, Benchmark Bks.) Marshall Cavendish Corp.

—Count on It! ¡Cuenta con Ello!, 6 bks., Set. Incl. Five/Cinco. lib. bdg. 15.95 *(978-0-7614-3477-1(1))*; Four/Cuatro. lib. bdg. 15.95 *(978-0-7614-3476-4(3))*; One/Uno. lib. bdg. 15.95 *(978-0-7614-3472-6(0))*; Ten/Diez. lib. bdg. 15.95 *(978-0-7614-3478-8(X))*; Three/Tres. lib. bdg. 15.95 *(978-0-7614-3475-7(5))*; Two/Dos. lib. bdg. 15.95 *(978-0-7614-3474-0(7))*; 24p. (gr. k-1). (Bookworms — Bilingual Editions: Count on It!/¡Cuenta con Ello! Ser.). (ENG & SPA.). 2008. Set lib. bdg. 95.70 *(978-0-7614-3471-9(2)*, Benchmark Bks.) Marshall Cavendish Corp.

Medcalf, Carol & Hempstock, Becky. Letts Monster Practice e Counting Age 3-5. 2014. (Letts Monster Practice Ser.). (ENG.). 32p. (J). (gr. -1-k). pap. 6.99 *(978-1-84419-771-2(9))* HarperCollins Pubs. Ltd. GBR. Dist: Independent Pubs. Group.

Medcalf, Carol, et al. Numbers, Age 3-5. 2014. (Letts Monster Practice Ser.). (ENG.). 32p. (J). (gr. -1-k). pap. 6.99 *(978-1-84419-770-5(0))* HarperCollins Pubs. Ltd. GBR. Dist: Independent Pubs. Group.

Medlock-Adams, Michelle. Counting Cows. Meyers, Mark, illus. 2010. 26p. (J). (gr. -1-k). 7.99 *(978-0-8249-1836-1(3)*, Ideal Pubns.) Worthy Publishing.

Mellark, Kat. Our Zoo Adventure: Compare Numbers. 2013. (Rosen Math Readers Ser.). (ENG.). 16p. (J). (gr. k-1). pap. 42.00 *(978-1-4777-1600-7(9))*; (Illus.). pap. 7.00 *(978-1-4777-1599-4(1))* Rosen Publishing Group, Inc., The. (Rosen Classroom).

Melling, David. Splish, Splash, Splosh! Melling, David, illus. 2013. (ENG., Illus.). 22p. (J). (gr. -1). bds. 8.95 *(978-1-58925-643-9(3))* Tiger Tales.

Melling, David. Splosh! 2017. (Splosh Ser.). (ENG., Illus.). 32p. (J). (gr. -1-k). pap. 7.99 ***(978-1-4449-0847-3(2))*** Hachette Children's Group GBR. Dist: Hachette Bk. Group.

Melmed, Laura Krauss. This First Thanksgiving Day: A Counting Story. Buehner, Mark, illus. 2003. (ENG.). 32p. (J). (gr. -1-3). pap. 6.99 *(978-0-06-054184-2(9))* HarperCollins Pubs.

Menotti, Andrea. How Many Jelly Beans? A Giant Book of Giant Numbers! Labat, Yancey, illus. 2012. (ENG.). 28p. (J). (gr. -1-1). 18.99 *(978-1-4521-0206-1(6))* Chronicle Bks. LLC.

Merberg, Julie & Bober, Suzanne. Quiet Time with Cassatt. 2006. (Mini Masters Ser.: MINI). (ENG., Illus.). 22p. (J). (gr. -1 — 1). bds. 6.99 *(978-0-8118-5504-4(X))* Chronicle Bks. LLC.

Mercer, Erin. How Do You Count To 10? 2011. 16p. pap. 9.95 *(978-1-4634-3296-6(8))* AuthorHouse.

Metsola, Aino-Maija. Counting. (Learning Garden Ser.). (ENG.). 14p. (J). 2016. (gr. -1-k). bds. 9.99 *(978-1-84780-706-9(2))* 2015. (Illus.). bds. 9.99 *(978-1-84780-610-9(4))* Quarto Publishing Group UK GBR. (Wide Eyed Editions). Dist: Hachette Bk. Group, Littlehampton Bk Services, Ltd.

Metzger, Steve. Five Spooky Ghosts Playing Tricks at School. Harrald-Pilz, Marilee, illus. 2005. (J). *(978-0-439-80381-6(0))* Scholastic, Inc.

Meza, Martin. Martin Meza's story time Volume 5. 2007. 54p. pap. 25.95 *(978-0-615-16571-4(0))* Meza, Marti.

Micklos, John. One Leaf, Two Leaves, Count with Me! McFarland, Clive, illus. 2017. (ENG.). 32p. (J). (— 1). 16.99 ***(978-0-399-54471-2(2)***, Nancy Paulsen Books) Penguin Young Readers Group.

Milbourne, Anna. How Big Is a Million? Doherty, Gillian, ed. Riglietti, Serena, illus. 2008. (Picture Books Ser.). 32p. (J). (gr. -1-3). 10.99 *(978-0-7945-1924-7(5)*, Usborne) EDC Publishing.

—How Big Is a Million? Riglietti, Serena, illus. 2008. (J). *(978-0-545-11519-3(1))* Scholastic, Inc.

Miles, L. Empiezo a Contar. 2005. (Computer Guide Ser.). Orig. Title: Starting to Count Sticker Book. (SPA.). 18p. (J). pap. 6.95 *(978-0-7460-4530-5(1))* EDC Publishing.

Milet Publishing Staff. My First Bilingual Book - Numbers. (My First Bilingual Book Ser.). (Illus.). 24p. (J). (gr. k — 1). 2011. (JPN & ENG.). bds. 7.99 *(978-1-84059-573-4(6))* 2011. (PER & ENG., bds. 7.99 *(978-1-84059-572-7(8))* 2011. (CHI & ENG., bds. 8.99 *(978-1-84059-571-0(X))* 2011. (KOR &

ENG., bds. 7.99 *(978-1-84059-574-1(4))* 2011. (POR & ENG., bds. 7.99 *(978-1-84059-575-8(2))* 2011. (URD, ENG & RUS., bds. 8.99 *(978-1-84059-578-9(7))* 2011. (VIE & ENG., bds. 8.99 *(978-1-84059-579-6(5))* 2010. (ENG & TUR., bds. 7.99 *(978-1-84059-546-8(9))* 2010. (SPA & ENG., bds. 8.99 *(978-1-84059-545-1(0))* 2010. (ENG & GER., bds. 7.99 *(978-1-84059-542-0(6))* Milet Publishing.

—Numbers. 2011. (My First Bilingual Book Ser.). (Illus.). 24p. (J). (gr. k — 1). (ARA & ENG.). bds. 7.99 *(978-1-84059-570-3(1))*; (SOM & ENG., bds. 8.99 *(978-1-84059-577-2(9))* Milet Publishing.

—Numbers - My First Bilingual Book. (My First Bilingual Book Ser.). (Illus.). 24p. (J). (gr. k — 1). 2011. (RUS & ENG.). bds. 7.99 *(978-1-84059-576-5(0))* 2010. (ENG & ITA., bds. 7.99 *(978-1-84059-543-7(4))* 2010. (FRE & ENG., bds. 7.99 *(978-1-84059-541-3(8))* 2010. (ENG & POL., bds. 8.99 *(978-1-84059-544-4(2))* Milet Publishing.

Milich, Zoran. City 123. 0 vols. (ENG., Illus.). 32p. (J). (gr. -1-k). 2014. bds. 12.95 *(978-1-77138-120-8(5))* 2005. 16.95 *(978-1-55337-540-1(8))* Kids Can Pr., Ltd. CAN. Dist: Hachette Bk. Group.

Mills, Nathan & Honders, Jamie. I Can Count My Blocks. 2012. (Rosen Readers Ser.). (ENG., Illus.). 16p. (J). (gr. k-1). pap. 7.00 *(978-1-4488-8652-4(X),* Rosen Classroom) Rosen Publishing Group, Inc., The.

Mills, Nathan & Rau, Heather. I Can Count To 50! 2012. (Rosen Readers Ser.). (ENG., Illus.). 16p. (J). (gr. k-1). pap. 7.00 *(978-1-4488-8734-7(8),* Rosen Classroom) Rosen Publishing Group, Inc., The.

Milne, A. A. Winnie the Pooh's 1,2,3. Shepard, Ernest H., illus. 2009. (Winnie-The-Pooh Ser.). (ENG.). 18p. (J). (gr. -1 — 1). bds. 6.99 *(978-0-525-42084-2(3),* Dutton Books for Young Readers) Penguin Young Readers Group.

Mishica, Clare. Here Comes the Parade. Richard, Ilene, illus. 2005. (Rookie Readers Ser.). (ENG.). 24p. (J). (gr. k-2). lib. bdg. 19.50 *(978-0-516-24857-8(X),* Children's Pr.) Scholastic Library Publishing.

—Vamos al Desfile. 2006. (Rookie Reader Español Ser.). (ENG & SPA., Illus.). 32p. (J). (gr. k-2). lib. bdg. 19.50 *(978-0-516-25309-1(3))* Scholastic Library Publishing.

Modern Publishing Staff. Counting! 2007. (Disney Bath Time Bubble Bks.). (Illus.). (J). (gr. -1-k). 4.99 *(978-0-7666-2555-6(9))* Modern Publishing.

Monica, Carol. Elmo's Easy as 1 2 3. 2006. (Sesame Street Ser.). (ENG., Illus.). 10p. (J). (gr. -1-2). 15.99 *(978-0-7944-1018-6(9))* Reader's Digest Assn., Inc., The.

Montague-Smith, Ann. Counting Book 1. 2004. (QEB Start Math Ser.). (Illus.). 24p. (J). Vol. 1. lib. bdg. 15.95 *(978-1-59566-024-4(0))* Vol. 2. lib. bdg. 15.95 *(978-1-59566-028-2(3))* QEB Publishing Inc.

Moon, Jo, illus. Counting. 2014. (Wipe-Clean Buggy Buddies Ser.). (ENG.). 10p. (J). (— 1). 9.99 *(978-1-4472-6779-9(6))* Pan Macmillan GBR. Dist: Independent Pubs. Group.

Moore, Karen. Everybody Counts. Reed, Lisa, illus. 2012. (Roma Downey's Little Angels Ser.). 24p. (J). bds. 7.99 *(978-0-8249-5643-1(5),* Ideal Pubns.) Worthy Publishing.

Moore, Lilian. My First Counting Book. Williams, Garth, illus. 2015. (Little Golden Board Book Ser.). (ENG.). 26p. (J). (-k). bds. 7.99 *(978-0-553-52223-5(X),* Golden Bks.) Random Hse. Children's Bks.

Moore, Phillip. When Did People Start to Count? 2014. (Little Books of Answers: Level e Ser.). (Illus.). 16p. (gr. k-2). pap. 7.95 *(978-1-927136-42-3(3))* Three Crows Media NZL. Dist: RiverStream Publishing.

Morales, Yuyi. Just a Minute: A Trickster Tale & Counting Book. (Illus.). 36p. (J). 2016. (ENG.). (gr. k-3). 7.99 *(978-0-8118-6483-1(9))* 2003. (SPA & ENG., (gr. -1-7). 15.99 *(978-0-8118-3758-3(0))* Chronicle Bks. LLC.

Moritz, S. Dianne & Mitchell, Hazel. 1, 2, 3 ... by the Sea. 2013. (ENG., Illus.). 36p. (J). pap. 6.99 *(978-1-935279-94-5(7))* Kane Miller.

Mortensen, Lori. Mousequerade Ball: A Counting Tale. Lewin, Betsy, illus. 2016. (ENG.). 32p. (J). 16.99 *(978-1-61963-422-0(8),* 9781619634220, Bloomsbury USA Childrens) Bloomsbury Publishing USA.

Moshel, Eluzer. My Number Book, Vol. 1. 2004. pap. 8.50 *(978-0-9728849-6-9(3))* Cong Bais Tziporah.

Moss, Lloyd. Zin! Zin! Zin! A Violin. Priceman, Marjorie, illus. 2005. (Stories to Go! Ser.). (ENG.). 32p. (J). (gr. -1-3). 4.99 *(978-1-4169-0838-8(2),* Simon & Schuster/Paula Wiseman Bks.) Simon & Schuster/Paula Wiseman Bks.

Msmh. Learning to Count, Alphabets a-J & Colours. 2013. 16p. pap. 12.68 *(978-1-4669-7416-6(8))* Trafford Publishing.

Murphy, Patricia J. Counting Puppies & Kittens. 2007. (Puppy & Kitten Math Ser.). (Illus.). 32p. (J). (gr. 1-2). lib. bdg. 23.94 *(978-0-7660-2724-4(4),* Enslow Elementary) Enslow Pubs., Inc.

Murphy, Stuart J. Coyotes All Around. Björkman, Steve, illus. 2003. (MathStart 2 Ser.). (ENG.). 40p. (J). (gr. 1-18). pap. 5.99 *(978-0-06-051531-7(7))* HarperCollins Pubs.

—Coyotes All Around. Björkman, Steve, illus. 2003. (MathStart Level 2 Ser.). 32p. (J). (gr. -1-3). 16.00 *(978-0-613-68415-6(X),* Turtleback) Turtleback Bks.

—Jack the Builder. Rex, Michael, illus. 2006. (MathStart 1 Ser.). (ENG.). 40p. (J). (gr. -1-3). pap. 5.99 *(978-0-06-055775-1(3))* HarperCollins Pubs.

—Leaping Lizards. Adinolfi, JoAnn, illus. 2005. (MathStart 1 Ser.). (ENG.). 40p. (J). (gr. -1). pap. 5.99 *(978-0-06-000132-2(1))* HarperCollins Pubs.

—Leaping Lizards. Adinolfi, JoAnn, illus. 2005. (MathStart Level 1 Ser.). 33p. (J). (gr. -1-3). lib. bdg. 16.00 *(978-1-4176-7758-0(9),* Turtleback) Turtleback Bks.

—Mall Mania. Andriani, Renee W., illus. 2006. (MathStart Ser.). (ENG.). 40p. (J). (gr. 1-4). 15.99 *(978-0-06-055776-8(1))*; pap. 5.99 *(978-0-06-055777-5(X))* HarperCollins Pubs.

—100 Days of Cool. Bendall-Brunello, John, illus. 2003. (MathStart 2 Ser.). (ENG.). 40p. (J). (gr. 1-18). pap. 5.99 *(978-0-06-000123-0(2))* HarperCollins Pubs.

Murphy, Stuart J. & Andriani, Renee. Mall Mania. 2006. (Mathstart Ser.). (Illus.). 33p. (gr. 1-4). 16.00 *(978-0-7569-6666-9(3))* Perfection Learning Corp.

Murphy, Stuart J. & Rex, Michael. Jack the Builder. 2006. (Mathstart Ser.). (Illus.). 33p. (gr. -1-3). 16.00 *(978-0-7569-6667-6(1))* Perfection Learning Corp.

Murray, Aaron R. Counting in the Desert 1-2-3. 2012. (All about Counting in the Biomes Ser.). 24p. (J). (gr. -1-1). 22.60 *(978-0-7660-4051-9(8))* Enslow Pubs., Inc.

—Counting in the Forest 1-2-3. 2012. (All about Counting in the Biomes Ser.). (Illus.). 24p. (J). (gr. -1-1). 22.60 *(978-0-7660-4053-3(4))* Enslow Pubs., Inc.

—Counting in the Grasslands 1-2-3. 2012. (All about Counting in the Biomes Ser.). (Illus.). 24p. (J). (gr. -1-1). 22.60 *(978-0-7660-4054-0(2))* Enslow Pubs., Inc.

—Counting in the Oceans 1-2-3. 2012. (All about Counting in the Biomes Ser.). (Illus.). 24p. (J). (gr. -1-1). 22.60 *(978-0-7660-4052-6(6))* Enslow Pubs., Inc.

—Counting in the Rain Forest 1-2-3. 2012. (All about Counting in the Biomes Ser.). (Illus.). 24p. (J). (gr. -1-1). 22.60 *(978-0-7660-4055-7(0))* Enslow Pubs., Inc.

—Counting in the Tundra 1-2-3. 2012. (All about Counting in the Biomes Ser.). (Illus.). 24p. (J). (gr. -1-1). 22.60 *(978-0-7660-4056-4(9))* Enslow Pubs., Inc.

Murray, Alison. One Two That's My Shoe! Murray, Alison, illus. 2012. (ENG., Illus.). 32p. (J). (gr. -1-1). 16.99 *(978-1-4231-4329-1(9))* Hyperion Pr.

Musselwhite, Helen. Little Houses: A Counting Book. 2015. (ENG., Illus.). 32p. (J). (gr. -1-k). 15.95 *(978-1-78067-613-5(1))* King, Laurence Publishing GBR. Dist: Hachette Bk. Group.

My First 1 2 3. Date not set. (Illus.). (J). bds. 5.98 *(978-0-7525-7983-2(5))* Parragon, Inc.

My First 123. (Punched Foam Book Ser.). 6p. *(978-1-4075-0416-2(9))* Parragon, Inc.

Nadja. Cinco Deditos. 2004. (SPA.). 12p. (gr. -1-k). bds. 16.99 *(978-84-8470-019-7(4))* Corimbo, Editorial S.L. ESP. Dist: Lectorum Pubns., Inc.

Nagara, Innosanto. Counting on Community. 2015. (ENG., Illus.). 24p. (J). (gr. -1-2). bds. 9.99 *(978-1-60980-632-3(8),* Triangle Square) Seven Stories Pr.

Napier, Matt. Hockey Numbers. Rose, Melanie, illus. (Numbers & Counting Ser.). (ENG.). 2009. 14p. 11.75 *(978-1-58536-495-4(9))* 2007. 22p. (J). (gr. -1-1). 7.99 *(978-1-58536-346-9(4))* Sleeping Bear Pr.

National Geographic Staff. Count! No. 1,2,3. 2011. (ENG., Illus.). 24p. (J). (gr. k-k). bds. 6.99 *(978-1-4263-0891-8(4),* National Geographic Children's Bks.) National Geographic Society.

Neubecker, Robert. Too Many Monsters! A Halloween Counting Book. Neubecker, Robert, illus. 2010. (ENG., Illus.). 26p. (J). (gr. -1-k). bds. 7.99 *(978-1-4424-0172-3(9),* Little Simon) Little Simon.

Neuschwander, Cindy. Sir Cumference & All the King's Tens. Geehan, Wayne, illus. 2009. (ENG.). 32p. (J). (gr. 3-7). 16.95 *(978-1-57091-727-1(2))* Charlesbridge Publishing, Inc.

—Sir Cumference & the Roundabout Battle. Geehan, Wayne, illus. 2015. (ENG.). 32p. (J). (gr. 3-7). lib. bdg. 16.95 *(978-1-57091-765-3(5))* Charlesbridge Publishing, Inc.

Newhouse, Maxwell. Counting on Snow. 2010. (ENG., Illus.). 24p. (J). (gr. k-k). 14.99 *(978-0-88776-985-6(3),* Tundra Bks.) Tundra Bks. CAN. Dist: Penguin Random Hse. LLC.

Newman, Lesléa. Dogs, Dogs, Dogs! Oller, Erika, illus. 2011. (ENG.). 30p. (J). (gr. -1-3). pap. 16.99 *(978-1-4424-5228-2(5),* Simon & Schuster Bks. For Young Readers) Simon & Schuster Bks. For Young Readers.

Nguyen, An Mai. Let's Learn How to Count in Vietnamese. 2006. (VIE & ENG., Illus.). (J). bds. 6.95 *(978-0-9776482-2-1(2))* Viet Baby, LLC.

Nickelodeon Staff, ed. 1-2-3 - Go Diego Go! 2010. (Write, Slide & Learn Ser.). 14p. (J). (gr. -1-1). 9.99 *(978-1-74184-521-1(1))* Hinkler Bks. Pty, Ltd. AUS. Dist: Ideals Pubns.

Nobisso, Josephine. The Numbers Dance: A Counting Comedy. Ziborova, Dasha, illus. 2005. (ENG.). 32p. (J). (gr. k-2). 16.95 *(978-0-940112-11-7(6))*; pap. 8.95 *(978-0-940112-12-4(4))* Gingerbread Hse.

Noble, Trinka Hakes. One for All: A Pennsylvania Number Book. Papp, Lisa, illus. 2005. (Count Your Way Across the USA Ser.). (ENG.). 40p. (J). (gr. k-5). 16.95 *(978-1-58536-200-4(X))* Sleeping Bear Pr.

Norma Staff, ed. Numeros. 2005. 14p. *(978-958-04-8069-3(9))* Norma S.A.

Norman, Kimberly. Ten on the Sled. Woodruff, Liza, illus. 2010. (ENG.). 26p. (J). (gr. -1). 14.95 *(978-1-4027-7076-0(6))* Sterling Publishing Co., Inc.

Norton, George. Ten Buttermilk Pancakes. Hutcherson, Darren, illus. Date not set. (J). 9.95 *(978-1-889506-10-4(9))* Kendar Publishing, Inc.

Novit, Renee Z. Counting by Tens & Fives. (Kidz & Katz Educational Learning Book Ser.). (Illus.). 16p. (J). (gr. -1). pap. 7.95 *(978-1-883371-02-9(3))* Kidz & Katz Publishing Co.

—Counting One to Twenty. (Kidz & Katz Educational Learning Book Ser.). (Illus.). 16p. (J). (gr. -1). pap. 7.95 *(978-1-883371-01-2(5))* Kidz & Katz Publishing Co.

Numbers. (Butterfly Bks.). (ARA., Illus.). 15p. (J). 11.95 *(978-0-86685-614-0(5),* LDL6164) International Bk. Ctr., Inc.

Nunn, Daniel. Counting 1 To 10, 1 vol. 2012. (Math Every Day Ser.). (ENG., Illus.). 24p. (gr. -1-k). pap. 9.95 *(978-1-4329-5735-3(X))*; lib. bdg. 25.99 *(978-1-4329-5730-8(9))* Heinemann-Raintree.

—Numbers in French: Les Chiffres - 1 2 3. 2012. (World Languages - Numbers Ser.). (ENG & MUL.). 24p. (gr. 1-3). pap. 6.29 *(978-1-4329-6679-9(0),* Acorn) Heinemann-Raintree.

—Numbers in French - Les Chiffres: Un, Deux, Trois... 2012. (World Languages - Numbers Ser.). (ENG & MUL.). 24p. (gr. 1-3). lib. bdg. 22.65 *(978-1-4329-6672-0(3),* Acorn) Heinemann-Raintree.

O'Brady, Terry, et al. Count the Animals. 2007. (Windows on Literacy Ser.). (ENG., Illus.). 12p. (J). pap. 10.95 *(978-0-7922-8484-0(4))* CENGAGE Learning.

O'Keefe, Susan Heyboer. Un Esperpento Hambriento: Un Libro Rimado Para Contar. (SPA., Illus.). (J). pap. *(978-0-590-50705-9(2),* SO7981) Scholastic Canada, Ltd. CAN. Dist: Lectorum Pubns., Inc.

Oldland, Nicholas. Dinosaur Countdown. Oldland, Nicholas, illus. 2012. (ENG., Illus.). 24p. (J). (gr. -1-1). 15.95 *(978-1-55453-834-8(3))* Kids Can Pr., Ltd. CAN. Dist: Hachette Bk. Group.

Oliver, Ilanit. Ten Flying Brooms. Poling, Kyle, illus. 2015. (ENG.). 24p. (J). (gr. -1-k). 3.99 *(978-0-545-81336-5(0),* Cartwheel Bks.) Scholastic, Inc.

Olson, K. C. Construction Countdown. Gordon, David, illus. rev. ed. 2004. (ENG.). 24p. (J). (gr. -1-1). 18.99 *(978-0-8050-6920-4(8),* 9780805069204, Holt, Henry & Co. Bks. For Young Readers) Holt, Henry & Co.

Omoto, Garrett, illus. Tutu Books Preschool Library, 3 bks. 2006. (ENG & HAW.). 48p. (YA). 29.95 *(978-1-933835-04-4(4))* Partners in Development Foundation.

—'Umi Keiki Li'i Li'i - Ten Little Children. 2006. Orig. Title: 'Umi Keiki Li'i Li'i. (HAW.). 16p. (J). 8.95 *(978-1-933835-01-3(X))* Partners in Development Foundation.

One, Two, Three, Four: KinderWords Individual Title Six-Packs. (Kinderstarters Ser.). 8p. (gr. -1-1). 21.00 *(978-0-7635-8705-5(2))* Rigby Education.

Orozco, Jose-Luis. Rin, Rin, Rin - Do, Re, Mi. Diaz, David, illus. 2005. (Lee y Seras Ser.). (ENG.). 32p. (J). (gr. -1-k). 3.99 *(978-0-439-75531-3(X),* Orchard Bks.) Scholastic, Inc.

Ortiz, Associate Professor Enrique. Ten Elephants & a Spider's Web: A Traditional Latin American Counting Rhyme & Other Activities: Spanish/English. 2009. 20p. 10.80 *(978-0-615-26124-9(8))* Ortiz, Enrique Publishing.

Otoshi, Kathryn. Zero. 2010. (ENG., Illus.). 32p. (J). (gr. -1-3). 17.95 *(978-0-9723946-3-5(X))* KO Kids Bks.

Owl's Forest Numbers. 2015. (Illus.). (J). *(978-1-58865-882-1(1))* Kidsbooks, LLC.

P, N., illus. & text. Down on the Ranch: A Counting Book, 1. P, N., text. 2011. 24p. (J). spiral bd. 9.00 *(978-0-615-50973-0(8))* Easy Reach Corp.

Page, Claire. Five Noisy Ducks: An Action-Packed Counting Book. 2008. (Illus.). 18p. (J). (gr. -1-k). bds. *(978-1-84610-587-6(0))* Make Believe Ideas.

Pallotta, Jerry. Butterfly Colors & Counting. Bersani, Shennen, illus. 2013. (ENG.). 10p. (J). (— 1). bds. 5.95 *(978-1-57091-899-5(6))* Charlesbridge Publishing, Inc.

—Butterfly Counting. Bersani, Shennen, illus. 2015. (ENG.). 32p. (J). (gr. -1-2). 17.95 *(978-1-57091-414-0(1))* Charlesbridge Publishing, Inc.

—Count by Fives. Bolster, Rob, illus. 2008. 32p. (J). *(978-0-545-00245-5(1))* Scholastic, Inc.

—Count by Tens. Bolster, Rob, illus. 2008. 32p. (J). *(978-0-545-07068-3(6))* Scholastic, Inc.

—The Icky Bug Counting Book. Masiello, Ralph, illus. 2004. (ENG.). 30p. (J). (-k). bds. 7.95 *(978-1-57091-624-3(1))* Charlesbridge Publishing, Inc.

—Ocean Counting: Odd Numbers. Bersani, Shennen, illus. 2005. (ENG.). 32p. (J). (gr. -1-3). pap. 7.95 *(978-0-88106-150-5(6))* Charlesbridge Publishing, Inc.

Pallotta, Jerry & Newton, Joy. The Very Berry Counting Book. 2017. (ENG., Illus.). 10p. (J). (— 1). bds. 6.99 *(978-1-58089-784-6(3))* Charlesbridge Publishing, Inc.

Panec, D. J. How Many? A Counting Book. Blackmore, Katherine, illus. 2016. 41p. (J). **(978-1-4844-8056-4(2))** Treasure Bay, Inc.

—How Many? Cuantos Hay? A Counting Book: Spanish/English Bilingual Edition (We Both Read - Level Pk-K) Blackmore, Katherine, illus. 2016. (We Both Read - Level Pk -K Ser.). (ENG & SPA.). 41p. (J). pap. 4.99 *(978-1-60115-074-5(1))* Treasure Bay, Inc.

—How Many? (We Both Read - Level Pk-K) A Counting Book. Blackmore, Katherine, illus. 2016. (We Both Read - Level Pk -K Ser.). (ENG.). 41p. (J). 9.95 *(978-1-60115-291-6(4))* Treasure Bay, Inc.

Pankova, Yuliya, ed. Numbers - Guess What? 2013. (Guess What? Ser.). (ENG.). 10p. (J). (— 1). bds. 5.95 *(978-1-61889-317-8(3))* AZ Bks. LLC.

Paradis, Anne. Caillou, My Big Search & Count Book, 2 bks. in 1. Sévigny, Eric, illus. 2016. (Coloring & Activity Book Ser.). (ENG.). 32p. (gr. -1-k). bds. 9.99 *(978-2-89718-252-6(0))* Caillouet, Gerry.

Paré, Roger. Les Chiffres. 2004. (Livres-jeux Ser.). (FRE.). 12p. (J). (gr. -1). pap. *(978-2-89021-654-9(3))* Diffusion du livre Mirabel (DLM).

Parenteau, Shirley. One Frog Sang. Jabar, Cynthia, illus. 2007. (ENG.). 32p. (J). (gr. -1-2). 15.99 *(978-0-7636-2394-4(6))* Candlewick Pr.

Park, Margaret. Now for My Next Number! Songs for Multiplying Fun. Esterman, Sophia, illus. 2007. 48p. (J). (gr. -1-3). 16.95 *(978-0-915556-38-0(3))* Great River Bks.

Parker, Ant, illus. Amazing Machines First Concepts: Numbers. 2015. (ENG.). 12p. (J). (gr. -1-1). bds. 5.99 *(978-0-7534-7231-6(7),* 9780753472316, Kingfisher) Roaring Brook Pr.

Parker, Emma. Bill Hides Acorns. 2010. (Illus.). 24p. pap. *(978-1-877561-33-7(9))* First Edition Ltd.

—The Monkey in the Tree. 2010. (Illus.). pap. *(978-1-877547-91-1(3))* First Edition Ltd.

Parker, Sandy. What Month Is It? Hofner, Cathy, illus. l.t. ed. 2004. 32p. 15.95 *(978-0-9643462-5-3(7),* Just Think Bks.) Canary Connect Pubns.

Parry, Jo. Blast Off! 2009. (Wow! Bks.). (Illus.). (J). bds. 12.99 *(978-1-934650-26-4(9))* Just For Kids Pr., LLC.

Pastor Fernández, Andrea. Contar. (Coleccion Mundo Maravilloso). (SPA., Illus.). (J). (gr. 2-7). *(978-84-348-4320-2(X),* SM0098) SM Ediciones ESP. Dist: Lectorum Pubns., Inc.

Patnaude, Jeffrey. Penny. 2003. (ENG., Illus.). 32p. (J). (gr. -1-3). 19.95 *(978-0-9704122-2-5(3))* White Rhino Pr.

Patricia Pierce. Numbers in a Row: An Iowa Number Book. Rohner, Dorothia, illus. 2006. (Count Your Way Across the U. S. A. Ser.). (ENG.). 40p. (J). (gr. -1-3). 17.95 *(978-1-58536-164-9(X))* Sleeping Bear Pr.

Paul, Ann Whitford. Count on Culebra. Long, Ethan, illus. 2010. (ENG.). 40p. (J). (gr. -1-3). pap. 6.95 *(978-0-8234-2310-1(7))* Holiday Hse., Inc.

—Count on Culebra: Go from 1 to 10 in Spanish. Long, Ethan, illus. 2008. (ENG.). 40p. (J). (gr. -1-3). 16.95 *(978-0-8234-2124-4(4))* Holiday Hse., Inc.

Paul, Miranda. 10 Little Ninjas. Wragg, Nate, illus. 2016. (ENG.). 32p. (J). (-k). 14.99 *(978-0-553-53497-9(1),* Knopf Bks. for Young Readers) Random Hse. Children's Bks.

Pavey, Peter. One Dragon's Dream. Pavey, Peter, illus. 2009. (ENG., Illus.). 40p. (J). (gr. -1-2). 17.99 *(978-0-7636-4470-3(6))* Candlewick Pr.

Pearlman, Carly. Ana Goes Apple Picking: Count to Tell the Number of Objects. 2013. (InfoMax Math Readers Ser.). (ENG.). 16p. (J). (gr. k-1). pap. 42.00 *(978-1-4777-1929-9(6))*; (Illus.). pap. 7.00 *(978-1-4777-1928-2(8))* Rosen Publishing Group, Inc., The. (Rosen Classroom).

Penn, M. W. Counting Money!, 1 vol. 2012. (Pebble Math Ser.). (ENG.). 24p. (gr. k-1). pap. 6.29 *(978-1-4296-7875-9(5))*; lib. bdg. 21.99 *(978-1-4296-7562-8(4))* Capstone Press of Coughlan Cos. (Pebble Bks.).

Phillips, Dee. Big Zoo. 2009. (Flip Flap Fun Bks.). (ENG.). 5p. (J). (gr. -1-k). bds. 5.95 *(978-1-84696-086-4(X),* TickTock Books) Octopus Publishing Group GBR. Dist: Independent Pubs. Group.

—What Can I Be? 2010. (Look at Me! Ser.). (ENG.). 5p. (J). (gr. -1-k). bds. 6.95 *(978-1-84696-199-1(8),* TickTock Books) Octopus Publishing Group GBR. Dist: Independent Pubs. Group.

Phillips, Sarah. Touch & Learn 123. 2005. (Illus.). 12p. (J). (gr. -1-1). per., bds. *(978-1-905051-76-2(X))* Make Believe Ideas.

Phillips, Sarah & Wallace, Bruce. Flip Flaps Counting. 2005. (Flip Flaps (Make Believe Ideas) Ser.). (Illus.). 12p. (gr. -1-k). per., bds. *(978-1-905051-94-6(8))* Make Believe Ideas.

Picayo, Mario. Fun, Fun, One Crab on the Run. Byer, Stacey, illus. 2012. (J). *(978-1-934370-27-8(4))* Editorial Campana.

Picthall, Chez & Gunzl, Christiane. Numbers. 2014. (ENG., Illus.). 20p. 8.95 *(978-1-907604-32-4(4))* Award Pubns. Ltd. GBR. Dist: Parkwest Pubns., Inc.

Piggy Toes Press, creator. Giggle & Grow Baby Counts! 2007. (ENG., Illus.). 12p. (gr. -1-k). bds. 7.99 *(978-1-58117-584-4(1),* Intervisual/Piggy Toes) Bendon, Inc.

Pistoia, Sara. Counting. 2013. (Simply Math Ser.). (ENG.). 24p. (J). (gr. -1-2). 27.07 *(978-1-62323-528-4(6),* 206334) Child's World, Inc., The.

—Counting. 2016. (J). *(978-1-4896-5101-3(2))* Weigl Pubs., Inc.

Pitman, Sandra. 10 Busy Bumble Bees, 1 vol. Sizemore, Carmen, illus. 2009. 20p. pap. 24.95 *(978-1-60749-683-0(6))* America Star Bks.

Pluckrose, Henry. How Many Are There? 2006. (Let's Explore, Maths Set Ser.). (Illus.). 32p. (J). (gr. -1-3). lib. bdg. 27.10 *(978-1-59771-037-4(7))* Sea-To-Sea Pubns.

Poke-A-Dot: Wheels on the Bus. 2017. (ENG.). (J). 15.99 ***(978-1-60169-420-1(2))*** Innovative Kids.

Pomaska, Anna. Fun with Numbers. 2012. (Dover Coloring Bks.). (ENG., Illus.). 48p. (J). (gr. -1-2). pap. 4.99 *(978-0-486-24707-6(4))* Dover Pubns., Inc.

Pooh & Friends Numbers & Counting. 2007. (ENG., Illus.). 26p. (J). (gr. -1-1). 16.99 *(978-1-59069-502-9(X),* 1A1000) Studio Mouse LLC.

Poplawska, Yolanda, illus. Halifax Harbour 123 (BB) A Counting Book about Halifax Harbour, 1 vol. 2014. (ENG.). 12p. (J). (gr. -1-k). bds. 9.95 *(978-1-77108-002-6(7))* Nimbus Publishing, Ltd. CAN. Dist: Orca Bk. Pubs. USA.

Porter, Matthew. Count the Birdies. 2007. (ENG., Illus.). 22p. (J). (gr. -1 — 1). bds. 8.95 *(978-1-894965-73-6(6))* Simply Read Bks. CAN. Dist: Ingram Publisher Services.

Practice Pals Bilingual Practice Book: Counting. 2006. (ENG & FRE., Illus.). 16p. (J). (gr. -1-1). spiral bd. *(978-1-930355-53-8(X))* Bright of America.

Practice Power Bilingual Practice Pals: Counting. 2003. (Illus.). 16p. (J). (gr. -1-1). spiral bd. *(978-1-930355-49-1(1))* Bright of America.

Press, Applesauce & Entin, Cindy. My First Counting Book - Airforce: A Celebration of the United States Air Forces from 1 to 10! 2013. (ENG.). 10p. (J). bds. 5.99 *(978-1-60433-320-6(0),* Applesauce Pr.) Cider Mill Pr. Bk. Pubs., LLC.

—My First Counting Book - Army. 2013. (ENG.). 10p. (J). bds. 5.99 *(978-1-60433-321-3(9),* Applesauce Pr.) Cider Mill Pr. Bk. Pubs., LLC.

Press, Cider Mill & Entin, Cindy. Navy. 2013. (ENG.). 10p. (J). bds. 5.99 *(978-1-60433-323-7(5),* Applesauce Pr.) Cider Mill Pr. Bk. Pubs., LLC.

Preston-Gannon, Frann. Deep Deep Sea. 2015. (ENG., Illus.). 14p. (J). (— 1). bds. 7.99 *(978-1-84365-268-7(4),* Pavilion) Pavilion Bks. GBR. Dist: Independent Pubs. Group.

Priddy Books Staff. First Concepts: Numbers. 2003. (Illus.). (J). bds. *(978-0-312-49232-8(4),* Priddy Bks.) St. Martin's Pr.

Priddy, Roger. Baby's First 123. 2016. (Baby's First Ser.). (ENG., Illus.). 8p. (J). bds. 7.99 *(978-0-312-51951-3(6),* 9780312519513, Priddy Bks.) St. Martin's Pr.

—Bright Baby Touch & Feel Numbers. 2008. (Bright Baby Touch & Feel Ser.). (ENG.). 12p. (J). (gr. -1 — 1). bds. 4.95 *(978-0-312-50423-6(3),* 9780312504236, Priddy Bks.) St. Martin's Pr.

—Counting Colors. 2007. (ENG., Illus.). 20p. (J). (gr. -1-1). 8.95 *(978-0-312-50137-2(4),* 9780312501372, Priddy Bks.) St. Martin's Pr.

—First 100 Board Books First 100 Numbers. 2012. (First 100 Ser.). (ENG., Illus.). 14p. (J). (gr. -1 — 1). bds. 8.95 *(978-0-312-51376-4(3),* 9780312513764, Priddy Bks.) St. Martin's Pr.

—First 100 Numbers. 2017. (First 100 Ser.). (ENG.). 24p. (J). bds. 5.99 *(978-0-312-52282-7(7),* 9780312522827, Priddy Bks.) St. Martin's Pr.

—Lift-the-Flap First 100 Numbers. 2014. (First 100 Ser.). (ENG.). 14p. (J). (gr. -1 — 1). bds. 9.99 *(978-0-312-51674-1(6),* 9780312516741, Priddy Bks.) St. Martin's Pr.

—Little Alphaprints: Numbers. 2015. (Alphaprints Ser.). (ENG., Illus.). 10p. (J). (gr. -1 — 1). bds. 5.99 *(978-0-312-51830-1(7),* 9780312518301, Priddy Bks.) St. Martin's Pr.

—My Little Numbers Book. 2012. (My Little Bks.). (ENG., Illus.). 24p. (J). (gr. -1-k). bds. 8.99 *(978-0-312-51463-1(8),* 9780312514631, Priddy Bks.) St. Martin's Pr.

—Numbers 1 2 3. rev. ed. 2004. (Wipe Clean Learning Bks.). (ENG., Illus.). 24p. (J). (gr. -1-1). 8.95 *(978-0-312-49264-9(2),* 9780312492649, Priddy Bks.) St. Martin's Pr.

—Numbers Colors Shapes. 2011. (First 100 Ser.). (ENG., Illus.). 26p. (J). (gr. -1 — 1). bds. 5.99 *(978-0-312-51081-7(0),* 9780312510817, Priddy Bks.) St. Martin's Pr.

—Numbers (Números) English-Spanish Bilingual. 2008. (Bright Baby Touch & Feel Ser.). (ENG & SPA., Illus.). 12p. (J). (gr. -1 — 1). bds. 4.95 *(978-0-312-50215-7(X),* 9780312502157, Priddy Bks.) St. Martin's Pr.

—Picture Fit Board Books: a Parade of Animals: A Counting Book. 2017. (Picture Fit Ser.). (ENG., Illus.). 14p. (J). bds.

8.99 (978-0-312-52173-8(1), 9780312521738, Priddy Bks.) St. Martin's Pr.

—Picture Fit Board Books: a Parade of Animals (Large) A Counting Book. 2017. (Picture Fit Ser.). (ENG., Illus.). 14p. (J). bds. 12.99 (978-0-312-52174-5(X), 9780312521745, Priddy Bks.) St. Martin's Pr.

—Play & Learn 123. 2013. (Play & Learn Ser.). (ENG.). 10p. (J). (gr. -1-k). bds. 12.99 (978-0-312-51639-0(8), 9780312516390, Priddy Bks.) St. Martin's Pr.

—Trace, Write & Learn 123. 2017. (Alphaprints Ser.). (ENG.). 14p. (J). bds. 9.99 (978-0-312-52151-6(0), 9780312521516, Priddy Bks.) St. Martin's Pr.

—Tracing & Pen Control. 2010. (ENG.). 28p. (J). (gr. -1-1). spiral bd., wbk. ed. 6.99 (978-0-312-50870-8(0), 9780312508708, Priddy Bks.) St. Martin's Pr.

—Wipe Clean Workbook Numbers 1-20. 2010. (ENG.). 28p. (J). (gr. -1-1). spiral bd., wbk. ed. 6.99 (978-0-312-50869-2(7), 9780312508692, Priddy Bks.) St. Martin's Pr.

—123. 2014. (Alphaprints Ser.). (ENG.). 20p. (J). (gr. -1 — 1). bds. 9.99 (978-0-312-51736-6(X), 9780312517366, Priddy Bks.) St. Martin's Pr.

—123 - Happy Baby. 2004. (Happy Baby Ser.). (SPA & ENG., Illus.). 28p. (J). (gr. -1 — 1). bds. 6.99 (978-0-312-49235-9(9), 9780312492359, Priddy Bks.) St. Martin's Pr.

Princess Adjepong. My First Shapes & Numbers Colouring Book. 2013. 52p. pap. 27.45 (978-1-4817-9519-7(8)) AuthorHouse.

Prochovnic, Dawn Babb. The Best Day in Room A: Sign Language for School Activities, 1 vol. Bauer, Stephanie, illus. 2009. (Story Time with Signs & Rhymes Ser.). (ENG.). 32p. (gr. -1-3). 28.50 (978-1-60270-667-5(0), Looking Glass Library) ABDO Publishing Co.

—One Trick for One Treat: Sign Language for Numbers, 1 vol. Bauer, Stephanie, illus. 2012. (ENG.). 32p. 28.50 (978-1-61641-838-0(9), Looking Glass Library) Magic Wagon.

Publications International Ltd. Staff, creator. Tonka Wipe-off Activity Kit: ABCs And 123s. 2007. (Wipe off Activity Kit Ser.). 14.98 (978-1-4127-7443-7(8)) Publications International, Ltd.

Publications International Ltd. Staff, ed. Baby's 123. 2010. 18p. (J). bds. 7.98 (978-1-60553-960-7(0)) Publications International, Ltd.

—Counting. 2011. 12p. (J). spiral bd. (978-1-4508-1449-2(2)) Publications International, Ltd.

—Counting Bilingual. 2005. 12p. (J). 9.60 (978-1-4127-3475-2(4)) Publications International, Ltd.

—Counting Fun. 2010. (My Wipe-off Book Ser.). 18p. (J). spiral bd. 10.98 (978-1-4127-0525-7(8), 7218500) Publications International, Ltd.

—Eric Carle Counting Write & Erase Sound. 2011. 16p. (J). bds. 16.98 (978-1-4508-1373-0(9), 89ea66b2-f0ff-4240-b53e-290c676c9925) Phoenix International Publications, Inc.

—Mickey Mouse Clubhouse: Count To 10. 2010. 16p. (J). bds. 16.98 (978-1-60553-568-5(0)) Phoenix International Publications, Inc.

—10 Tiny Puppies: A Counting Book. 2010. (J). bds. 7.98 (978-1-60553-436-7(6)) Phoenix International Publications, Inc.

Puck. One to Ten L. A. Puck, illus. 2016. (ENG., Illus.). 22p. (J). (gr. k-k). bds. 9.95 (978-1-938093-49-4(6), Duo Pr. Llc (US)) Duo Pr. LLC.

—123 Beach. 2012. (Cool Counting Bks.). (ENG., Illus.). 22p. (J). (gr. k — 1). bds. 7.95 (978-0-9838121-1-1(X)) Duo Pr. LLC.

—123 California. Somers, Kevin, illus. 2008. (Cool Counting Bks.). (ENG.). 22p. (J). (gr. k — 1). bds. 7.95 (978-0-9796213-3-8(X)) Duo Pr. LLC.

—123 Chicago. Somers, Kevin, illus. 2009. (Cool Counting Bks.). (ENG.). 22p. (J). (gr. k — 1). bds. 8.95 (978-0-9796213-5-2(6)) Duo Pr. LLC.

—123 Minnesota: A Cool Counting Book. 2012. (Cool Counting Bks.). (ENG.). 22p. (J). (gr. k — 1). bds. 8.95 (978-0-9838121-2-8(8)) Duo Pr. LLC.

—123 San Francisco. Somers, Kevin, illus. 2009. (Cool Counting Bks.). (ENG.). 22p. (J). (gr. k — 1). bds. 8.95 (978-0-9796213-8-3(0)) Duo Pr. LLC.

—123 Texas. Somers, Kevin, illus. 2009. (Cool Counting Bks.). (ENG.). 22p. (J). (gr. k — 1). bds. 8.95 (978-0-9796213-6-9(4)) Duo Pr. LLC.

—123 USA: A Cool Counting Book. Somers, Kevin, illus. 2008. (Cool Counting Bks.). (SPA & ENG.). 22p. (J). (gr. k — 1). bds. 7.95 (978-0-9796213-1-4(3)) Duo Pr. LLC.

—123 Washington, D. C. 2012. (Cool Counting Bks.). (ENG.). 22p. (J). (gr. k — 1). bds. 8.95 (978-0-9838121-0-4(1)) Duo Pr. LLC.

Pulley, Kelly. Ten Unusual Features of Lulu McDunn. Pulley, Kelly, illus. 2010. (Illus.). 32p. (J). (gr. -1). 16.95 (978-0-9820812-7-3(8), Frog Legs Ink) Gauthier Pubns. Inc.

Q. Dani-L's Counting Alphabet Book. 2009. 28p. pap. 14.99 (978-1-4343-7927-6(2)) AuthorHouse.

QEB Start Math Book Stores Edition: Counting - Book 2. 2006. (J). per. (978-1-59566-275-0(8)) QEB Publishing Inc.

QEB Start Maths National Book Stores Edition: Counting - Book 1. 2006. (J). per. (978-1-59566-271-2(5)) QEB Publishing Inc.

Queen Octavia. 10 Silly Duckies: Counting Book. 2010. 28p. pap. 15.49 (978-1-4490-5521-9(4)) AuthorHouse.

Radford, Tracey. Animal Fun! Count to 10: Lift the Flaps & Find the Number! 2016. (ENG., Illus.). 10p. (J). (gr. 1-4). 6.95 (978-1-78249-400-3(6), 1782494006, CICO Books) Ryland Peters & Small GBR. Dist: WIPRO.

Rae, Philippa. Count the Sheep to Sleep. Röhr, Stéphanie, illus. 2012. (ENG.). 28p. (J). (gr. -1-k). 12.95 (978-1-61608-660-2(2), 608660, Sky Pony Pr.) Skyhorse Publishing Co., Inc.

Rainy Day Counting: Big Book: Level C. 8p. 20.95 (978-0-322-00368-2(7)) Wright Group/McGraw-Hill.

Ramos, Mario. Mama! 2004.Tr. of Mom! (SPA., Illus.). 28p. (J). (gr. -1-k). 17.99 (978-84-8470-145-3(X)) Corimbo, Editorial S.L. ESP. Dist: Lectorum Pubns., Inc.

Ranchetti, Sebastiano. Counting with Animals. 2008. (Learn with Animals Ser.). (Illus.). 24p. (gr. -1-2). lib. bdg. 22.00 (978-0-8368-8823-2(5), Weekly Reader Leveled Readers) Stevens, Gareth Publishing LLLP.

—Counting with Animals/Cuenta con los Animales. 2008. (Learn with Animals/Aprende con los Animales Ser.). (SPA & ENG., Illus.). 24p. (gr. -1-2). lib. bdg. 22.00 (978-0-8368-9039-6(6), Weekly Reader Leveled Readers) Stevens, Gareth Publishing LLLP.

Ranchetti, Sebastiano & Nations, Susan. Counting with Animals. 2008. (Learn with Animals Ser.). (Illus.). 24p. (gr. -1-2). pap. 8.15 (978-0-8368-8828-7(6), Weekly Reader Leveled Readers) Stevens, Gareth Publishing LLLP.

Random House. Elmo's 123. 2015. (Pictureback(R) Ser.). (ENG., Illus.). 24p. (J). (gr. -1-2). 4.99 (978-0-553-53679-9(6), Random Hse. Bks. for Young Readers) Random Hse. Children's Bks.

Raschka, Chris. Five for a Little One. Raschka, Chris, illus. 2006. (ENG., Illus.). 48p. (J). (gr. -1-2). 17.99 (978-0-689-84599-4(5), Atheneum/Richard Jackson Bks.) Simon & Schuster Children's Publishing.

Rathmann, Peggy. 10 Minutos Antes de Dormir. 2004. (SPA.). 46p. (J). (gr. k-18). pap. 6.99 (978-980-257-276-2(4)) Ekare, Ediciones VEN. Dist: Lectorum Pubns., Inc.

Rauen, Amy. Counting at the Market. Pickering, Russell, photos by. 2008. (Getting Started with Math Ser.). (Illus.). 16p. (gr. -1-2). lib. bdg. 19.00 (978-0-8368-8981-9(9), Weekly Reader Leveled Readers) Stevens, Gareth Publishing LLLP.

—Usamos Dinero en el Puesto de Limonada. 2007. (Las matimaticas en nuestro mundo (Spanish- Math in Our World) Ser.). (SPA.). 24p. (gr. 1-2). pap. 8.15 (978-0-8368-8499-9(X), Weekly Reader Leveled Readers) Stevens, Gareth Publishing LLLP.

—Using Math at the Class Party. McKinley, Kay, photos by. 2007. (Math in Our World Ser.). (Illus.). 24p. (gr. 1-2). lib. bdg. 22.00 (978-0-8368-8475-3(2), Weekly Reader Leveled Readers) Stevens, Gareth Publishing LLLP.

—Using Math Outdoors. Walter, Lorin, illus. 2008. (Getting Started with Math Ser.). 16p. (gr. -1-2). pap. 5.30 (978-0-8368-8989-5(4)); lib. bdg. 19.00 (978-0-8368-8984-0(3)) Stevens, Gareth Publishing LLLP. (Weekly Reader Leveled Readers).

—Vamos a Contar en el Mercado. 2008. (Matemáticas para empezar (Getting Started with Math) Ser.).Tr. of Counting at the Market. (SPA., Illus.). 16p. (gr. -1-2). pap. 5.30 (978-0-8368-8996-3(7), Weekly Reader Leveled Readers) Stevens, Gareth Publishing LLLP.

—Vamos a Contar en el Mercado. Pickering, Russell, photos by. 2008. (Matemáticas para Empezar (Getting Started with Math) Ser.).Tr. of Counting at the Market. (SPA., Illus.). 16p. (gr. -1-2). lib. bdg. 19.00 (978-0-8368-8991-8(6), Weekly Reader Leveled Readers) Stevens, Gareth Publishing LLLP.

—Vamos a Usar las Matematicas al Aire Libre. Walter, Lorin, illus. 2008. (Matemáticas para Empezar (Getting Started with Math) Ser.). (SPA.). 16p. (gr. -1-2). lib. bdg. 19.00 (978-0-8368-8994-9(0), Weekly Reader Leveled Readers) Stevens, Gareth Publishing LLLP.

Rauen, Amy & Ayers, Amy. Counting at the Zoo. Andersen, Gregg, photos by. 2007. (Math in Our World Ser.). (Illus.). 24p. (gr. 1-2). pap. 8.15 (978-0-8368-8478-4(7), Weekly Reader Leveled Readers) Stevens, Gareth Publishing LLLP.

—Usamos Dinero en el Puesto de Limonada. Pickering, Russell, photos by. 2007. (Matimáticas en Nuestro Mundo (Math in Our World) Ser.). (SPA., Illus.). 24p. (gr. 1-2). lib. bdg. 22.00 (978-0-8368-8490-6(6), Weekly Reader Leveled Readers) Stevens, Gareth Publishing LLLP.

—Usamos Matemáticas en la Fiesta Del Salón. 2007. (Las matimaticas en nuestro mundo (Spanish- Math in Our World) Ser.). (SPA.). 24p. (gr. 1-2). pap. 8.15 (978-0-8368-8502-6(3), Weekly Reader Leveled Readers) Stevens, Gareth Publishing LLLP.

—Usamos Matematicas en la Fiesta del Salon. McKinley, Kay, photos by. 2007. (Matimáticas en Nuestro Mundo (Math in Our World) Ser.). (SPA., Illus.). 24p. (gr. 1-2). lib. bdg. 22.00 (978-0-8368-8493-7(0), Weekly Reader Leveled Readers) Stevens, Gareth Publishing LLLP.

—Using Money at the Lemonade Stand. Pickering, Russell, photos by. 2007. (Math in Our World Ser.). (Illus.). 24p. (gr. 1-2). lib. bdg. 22.00 (978-0-8368-8472-2(8), Weekly Reader Leveled Readers) Stevens, Gareth Publishing LLLP.

Rayner, Catherine. Counting Stars. Rayner, Catherine, illus. 2016. (ENG., Illus.). 28p. (J). (gr. -1-k). bds. 7.99 (978-1-58925-225-7(X)) Tiger Tales.

Really Big Coloring Books Staff. ABC 123 Learn My Letters & Numbers. l.t. ed. 2003. Orig. Title: 123-ABC Learn My Letters & Numbers. (Illus.). 321p. (J). (978-0-9729753-1-5(4)) Really Big Coloring Bks., Inc.

Reich, Dale. Graham's Shiny Things. 2016. (ENG., Illus.). 36p. (J). pap. (978-1-55571-825-1(6), Grid Pr.) L & R Publishing, LLC.

Reid, Camilla. Lulu Loves Numbers. Busby, Ailie, illus. 2015. (ENG.). 12p. (J). (gr. -1-1). bds. 8.99 (978-1-4088-4957-6(7), 9781408849576, Bloomsbury USA Childrens) Bloomsbury Publishing USA.

Reidy, Hannah. Crazy Creatures Counting. Mackie, Clare, illus. 2003. (Crazy Creatures Ser.). 26p. (J). pap. (978-1-84089-220-8(X)) Zero to Ten, Ltd.

Rey, H. A. Curious Baby Counting. 2009. (Curious Baby Curious George Ser.). (ENG., Illus.). 12p. (J). (gr. -1 — 1). bds. 8.99 (978-0-547-21521-1(5)) Houghton Mifflin Harcourt Publishing Co.

—Curious George Learns to Count from 1 To 100. 2011. (Curious George Ser.). (ENG., Illus.). 80p. (J). (gr. -1-3). pap. 8.99 (978-0-547-13841-1(5)) Houghton Mifflin Harcourt Publishing Co.

—Learns to Count from 1 to 100: Counting, Grouping, Mapping, & More! Hines, Anna Grossnickle, illus. 2005. (Curious George Ser.). (ENG.). 64p. (J). (gr. -1-3). 16.99 (978-0-618-47602-2(4)) Houghton Mifflin Harcourt Publishing Co.

—Music Play. 2009. (Curious Baby Curious George Ser.). (ENG., Illus.). 10p. (J). (gr. -1 — 1). bds. 8.99 (978-0-547-23876-0(2)) Houghton Mifflin Harcourt Publishing Co.

Rey, H. A., et al. Curious George Discovery Day. 2007. (Curious George Ser.). (ENG., Illus.). 14p. (J). (gr. k — 1). bds. 13.95 (978-0-618-73761-1(8)) Houghton Mifflin Harcourt Publishing Co.

Reynolds, Cynthia Furlong. Fishing for Numbers: A Maine Number Book. Brett, Jeannie, illus. 2005. (Count Your Way Across the USA Ser.). (ENG.). 40p. (J). (gr. k-5). 16.95 (978-1-58536-035-2(X)) Sleeping Bear Pr.

Rhodes, Karen. Numeros en la Biblia. 2004. (SPA., Illus.). 16p. (J). pap. 1.89 (978-1-59317-062-2(9)) Warner Pr., Inc.

Rice, Adrienne. How Many? 2013. 24p. pap. 24.95 (978-1-62709-548-8(9)) America Star Bks.

Rice, Dona. Use Math: Compare It. 2015. (TIME for KIDS(r) Nonfiction Readers Ser.). (ENG., Illus.). 12p. (gr. k-k). 4.99 (978-1-4938-2143-3(1)) Teacher Created Materials, Inc.

Rice, Dona Herweck. USA Las Matematicas (Use Math - Compare It) 2016. (TIME for KIDS(r) Nonfiction Readers Ser.). (SPA.). 12p. (J). (gr. k-k). 4.99 (978-1-4938-3024-4(4)) Teacher Created Materials, Inc.

Rigol, Francesc, illus. Dan & Din Learn Numbers. 2009. (Learning with Dan & Din Ser.). 12p. (J). (gr. -1-k). bds. 11.40 (978-1-60754-402-9(4)) Windmill Bks.

Ringler, Matt. One Little, Two Little, Three Little Apples. Kennedy, Anne, illus. 2005. (J). pap. (978-0-439-77500-7(0)) Scholastic, Inc.

Rissman, Rebecca. Counting at Home, 1 vol. 2012. (I Can Count! Ser.). (ENG.). 24p. (gr. -1-k). pap. 9.95 (978-1-4329-6699-7(5)); lib. bdg. 25.32 (978-1-4329-6694-2(4)) Heinemann-Raintree.

—Counting at the Park, 1 vol. 2012. (I Can Count! Ser.). (ENG.). 24p. (gr. -1-k). pap. 9.95 (978-1-4329-6700-0(2)); lib. bdg. 25.32 (978-1-4329-6695-9(2)) Heinemann-Raintree.

—Counting in the Forest, 1 vol. 2012. (I Can Count! Ser.). (ENG.). 24p. (gr. -1-k). pap. 9.95 (978-1-4329-6698-0(7)); lib. bdg. 25.32 (978-1-4329-6693-5(6)) Heinemann-Raintree.

—Counting in the Ocean, 1 vol. 2012. (I Can Count! Ser.). (ENG.). 24p. (gr. -1-k). pap. 9.95 (978-1-4329-6701-7(0)); lib. bdg. 25.32 (978-1-4329-6696-6(0)) Heinemann-Raintree.

Robbins, Becky. Creature Teacher. 2016. (ENG., Illus.). 25p. (J). pap. 10.95 (978-1-78612-354-1(1), 9b9495a8-cc78-438c-ac17-3ade2a4a0aac) Austin, Stan AUS. Dist: Bookmasters Distribution.

Roddick, Melissa. Time for Gym Class: Count to Tell the Number of Objects. 2013. (Rosen Math Readers Ser.). (ENG.). 16p. (J). (gr. k-1). pap. 42.00 (978-1-4777-1624-3(6)); (Illus.). pap. 7.00 (978-1-4777-1623-6(8)) Rosen Publishing Group, Inc., The. (Rosen Classroom).

Roffey, Maureen, illus. 1 2 3 Count with Me! 2014. (ENG.). 26p. (J). (gr. -1 — 1). bds. 5.99 (978-0-7944-3016-0(3), Reader's Digest Children's Bks.) Studio Fun International.

Rogers, Kate. I Can Count To 10! Number Names & Count Sequence. 2013. (Rosen Math Readers Ser.). (ENG.). 16p. (J). (gr. k-1). pap. 42.00 (978-1-4777-1582-6(7)); (Illus.). pap. 7.00 (978-1-4777-1581-9(9)) Rosen Publishing Group, Inc., The. (Rosen Classroom).

Roll Over: Individual Title Six-Packs. (Literatura 2000 Ser.). (gr. 1-2). 28.00 (978-0-7635-0150-1(6)) Rigby Education.

Rolle, Elvy P. Five Little Children at the Zoo. Stasuyk, Max, illus. 2016. (ENG.). 26p. (J). pap. 13.95 (978-1-4796-0534-7(4), Aspect) Grand Central Publishing.

Roop, Peter & Roop, Connie. Down East in the Ocean: A Maine Counting Book. 2011. (ENG., Illus.). 32p. (J). (gr. -1-3). 16.95 (978-0-89272-709-4(8)) Down East Bks.

Root, Phyllis. One Duck Stuck. 2003. (gr. k-3). 17.20 (978-0-613-60361-4(3), Turtleback) Turtleback Bks.

—One Duck Stuck: A Mucky Ducky Counting Book. Chapman, Jane, illus. 2003. (ENG.). 40p. (J). (gr. k-k). pap. 6.99 (978-0-7636-1566-6(8)) Candlewick Pr.

—One Duck Stuck: A Mucky Ducky Counting Book. Chapman, Jane, illus. 2008. (Candlewick Press Big Book Ser.). (ENG.). 40p. (J). (gr. k-k). pap. 24.99 (978-0-7636-3817-7(X)) Candlewick Pr.

Roper, Dawn. 30 Fun Ways to Learn about Time & Money. 2011. (30 Fun Ways to Learn Ser.). (ENG.). 80p. (gr. -1-k). pap. 12.95 (978-0-87659-370-7(8), Gryphon House Inc) Gryphon Hse., Inc.

Rosario, Miguel. Backyard Math. 2015. (J). lib. bdg. (978-1-62713-439-2(5)) Cavendish Square Publishing.

—Car Math. 2015. (J). lib. bdg. (978-1-62713-442-2(5)) Cavendish Square Publishing.

—Kitchen Math. 2015. (J). pap. (978-1-62713-452-1(2)) Cavendish Square Publishing.

Rosas, Heather. 1-2-3 Count with Me! 2009. (ENG.). 10p. (J). 7.95 (978-1-58117-774-9(7), Intervisual/Piggy Toes) Bendon, Inc.

Rose, Deborah Lee. The Twelve Days of Kindergarten: A Counting Book. Armstrong-Ellis, Carey F., illus. 2017. (ENG.). 32p. (J). (gr. -1-1). pap. 4.95 **(978-1-4197-2742-9(7)**, Abrams Bks. for Young Readers) Abrams, Inc.

—The Twelve Days of Kindergarten: A Counting Book. Armstrong-Ellis, Carey, illus. 2003. (ENG.). 30p. (J). (gr. -1-1). 16.95 (978-0-8109-4512-8(6)) Abrams, Inc.

—The Twelve Days of Springtime: A School Counting Book. Armstrong-Ellis, Carey, illus. 2009. (ENG.). 32p. (J). (gr. -1-3). 15.95 (978-0-8109-8330-4(3), Abrams Bks. for Young Readers) Abrams, Inc.

Rosen, Michael J. Chanukah Lights. Sabuda, Robert, illus. 2011. (ENG.). 16p. (J). (gr. k-4). 34.99 (978-0-7636-5533-4(3)) Candlewick Pr.

—Chanukah Lights Everywhere. 2010. (ENG.). 22p. (J). pap. 6.00 (978-1-4379-7172-9(5)) DIANE Publishing Co.

—Chanukah Lights Everywhere. Iwai, Melissa, illus. 2006. (ENG.). 32p. (J). (gr. -1-3). pap. 7.99 (978-0-15-205675-9(0)) Houghton Mifflin Harcourt Publishing Co.

Roth, Carol. Ten Dirty Pigs: An Upside-Down Turn Around. Paparone, Pamela, illus. 2008. (ENG.). 22p. (J). (gr. -1-k). bds. 7.95 (978-0-7358-2213-9(1)) North-South Bks., Inc.

Rothstein, Gloria L. Sheep Asleep. Date not set. 224p. (J). (gr. -1-1). pap. 4.99 (978-0-06-443717-2(5)) HarperCollins Pubs.

Rovetch, L. Bob. 1,2,3 Octopus & Me. Gévry, Claudine, illus. 2006. (J). (978-1-58987-011-6(5)) Kindermusik International.

Rowe, Jeanette. First 1, 2, 3. 2016. (I Spy with My Little Eye... Bks.). (ENG.). 16p. (J). (gr. -1-k). bds. 9.99 (978-0-7641-6815-4(0)) Barron's Educational Series, Inc.

Roy, Jennifer Rozines & Roy, Gregory. Money at the Store. 2006. (Math All Around Ser.). (Illus.). 32p. (gr. 2-7). lib. bdg. 29.93 (978-0-7614-2264-8(1), Benchmark Bks.) Marshall Cavendish Corp.

—Numbers on the Street. 2005. (Math All Around Ser.). (Illus.). 32p. (gr. 2-7). lib. bdg. 29.93 (978-0-7614-2002-6(9), Benchmark Bks.) Marshall Cavendish Corp.

Rubin, Susan Goldman. Counting with Wayne Thiebaud. 2007. (ENG., Illus.). 26p. (J). (gr. -1 — 1). bds. 6.99 (978-0-8118-5720-8(4)) Chronicle Bks. LLC.

Rubinger, Ami, illus. Dog Number 1, Dog Number 10. 2011. (ENG.). 28p. (J). (gr. k-k). 13.95 (978-0-7892-1066-1(5), Abbeville Kids) Abbeville Pr., Inc.

Ruble, Eugene. Counting 1 to 10 with Professor Hoot. Ruble, Eugene, illus. 2008. (Illus.). 24p. pap. 10.95 (978-1-935137-47-4(6)) Guardian Angel Publishing, Inc.

Ruffenach, Jessie, ed. Baby Learns to Count. Thomas, Peter, tr. Blacksheep, Beverly, illus. l.t. ed. 2003. (NAV & ENG.). 16p. (J). (gr. -1-12). 7.95 (978-1-893354-47-0(4)) Salina Bookshelf Inc.

Running Press Staff & Texier, Ophelie. Numbers. 2003. (Illus.). 8p. (J). pap. 4.95 (978-0-7624-1525-0(8)) Running Pr. Bk. Pubs.

Rustad, Martha E. H. Across the Country 18, 19, 20: A Transportation Counting to 20 Book. 2017. (1, 2, 3 Count with Me Ser.). (ENG., Illus.). 24p. (J). (gr. k-2). pap. 8.99 (978-1-68152-110-7(5)) Amicus.

—Across the Country 18, 19, 20: A Transportation Counting to 20 Book. 2016. (1, 2, 3 Count with Me Ser.). (ENG., Illus.). 24p. (J). (gr. k-3). 20.95 (978-1-60753-919-3(5)) Amicus Publishing.

—Chicks 2, 4, 6: A Baby Animals Counting by Twos Book. 2017. (1, 2, 3 Count with Me Ser.). (ENG., Illus.). 24p. (J). (gr. k-2). pap. 8.99 (978-1-68152-111-4(3)) Amicus.

—Chicks 2, 4, 6: A Baby Animals Counting by Twos Book. 2016. (1, 2, 3 Count with Me Ser.). (ENG., Illus.). 24p. (J). (gr. k-3). 20.95 (978-1-60753-920-9(9)) Amicus Publishing.

—Down the Field 10, 20, 30: A Football Counting by Tens Book. 2017. (1, 2, 3 Count with Me Ser.). (ENG., Illus.). 24p. (J). (gr. k-2). pap. 8.99 (978-1-68152-112-1(1)) Amicus.

—Down the Field 10, 20, 30: A Football Counting by Tens Book. 2016. (1, 2, 3 Count with Me Ser.). (ENG., Illus.). 24p. (J). (gr. k-3). 20.95 (978-1-60753-921-6(7), Amicus Readers) Amicus Publishing.

—On a Safari 5, 10, 15: A Counting by Fives Book. 2017. (1, 2, 3 Count with Me Ser.). (ENG., Illus.). 24p. (J). (gr. k-2). pap. 8.99 (978-1-68152-113-8(X)) Amicus.

—On a Safari 5, 10, 15: A Counting by Fives Book. 2016. (1, 2, 3 Count with Me Ser.). (ENG., Illus.). 24p. (J). (gr. k-3). 20.95 (978-1-60753-922-3(5)) Amicus Publishing.

—100 Snowflakes: A Winter Counting Book. 2017. (1, 2, 3 Count with Me Ser.). (ENG., Illus.). 24p. (J). (gr. k-2). pap. 8.99 (978-1-68152-109-1(1)) Amicus.

—100 Snowflakes: A Winter Counting Book. 2016. (1, 2, 3 Count with Me Ser.). (ENG., Illus.). 24p. (J). (gr. k-3). 20.95 (978-1-60753-918-6(7)) Amicus Publishing.

Salzano, Tammi. One Little Blueberry. Whelan, Kat, illus. 2011. (ENG.). 22p. (J). (gr. -1-k). 12.95 (978-1-58925-859-4(2)) Tiger Tales.

—One Snowy Day. Wood, Hannah, illus. 2010. (ENG.). 24p. (J). (gr. -1-k). bds. 8.95 (978-1-58925-857-0(6)) Tiger Tales.

Salzmann, Mary Elizabeth. Know Your Numbers: Animals, 1 vol. 2014. (Numbers 1-20 Ser.). (ENG.). 24p. (J). (gr. k-3). lib. bdg. 24.21 (978-1-62403-264-6(8), SandCastle) ABDO Publishing Co.

—Know Your Numbers: Food, 1 vol. 2014. (Numbers 1-20 Ser.). (ENG.). 24p. (J). (gr. k-3). lib. bdg. 24.21 (978-1-62403-265-3(6), SandCastle) ABDO Publishing Co.

—Know Your Numbers: Nature, 1 vol. 2014. (Numbers 1-20 Ser.). (ENG.). 24p. (J). (gr. k-3). lib. bdg. 24.21 (978-1-62403-266-0(4), SandCastle) ABDO Publishing Co.

—Know Your Numbers: Toys, 1 vol. 2014. (Numbers 1-20 Ser.). (ENG.). 24p. (J). (gr. k-3). lib. bdg. 24.21 (978-1-62403-269-1(9), SandCastle) ABDO Publishing Co.

San Diego Zoo Staff. Count to 10 & Back Again: San Diego Zoo. 2004. (ENG., Illus.). 24p. (J). 7.95 (978-0-8249-6552-5(3), Ideal Pubns.) Worthy Publishing.

Sanchez, Richard. Numeros (Numbers) (SPA.). (J). 4.95 (978-84-243-2190-1(1)) Publicaciones Fher, S.A. ESP. Dist: AIMS International Bks., Inc.

Sanrio Company, Ltd. Staff. I Heart Hello Kitty Activity Book: Read, Write, Count, & Draw with Hello Kitty & Friends! 2012. (ENG.). 224p. (J). (gr. k-2). pap. 10.95 (978-1-4197-0551-9(2), Abrams Bks. for Young Readers) Abrams, Inc.

Santillo, LuAnn. Liz. Santillo, LuAnn, ed. 2003. (Half-Pint Kids Readers Ser.). (Illus.). 7p. (J). (gr. -1-1). pap. 1.00 (978-1-59256-083-7(0)) Half-Pint Kids, Inc.

Sargent, Brian. Guess the Order. 2006. (Rookie Read-About Math Ser.). (ENG., Illus.). 32p. (J). (gr. 1-2). lib. bdg. 20.50 (978-0-516-24963-6(0), Children's Pr.) Scholastic Library Publishing.

—Pen Pals Compare. (Rookie Read-About Math Ser.). (ENG., Illus.). 32p. (J). (gr. 1-2). 2006. per. 5.95 (978-0-516-25363-3(8)) 2005. lib. bdg. 20.50 (978-0-516-25262-9(3)) Scholastic Library Publishing. (Children's Pr.).

Saunders, Katie & Little Bee Books Staff. Counting Fun! An Abacus Book. Saunders, Katie, illus. 2015. (Baby Steps Ser.). (ENG., Illus.). 14p. (J). (gr. -1 — 1). bds. 7.99 (978-1-4998-0005-0(3)) Little Bee Books Inc.

Saviola, Ava. Dinosaurs Count! 2012. (Dinosaur School Ser.). (Illus.). 24p. (J). (gr. -1-1). pap. 8.15 (978-1-4339-7152-5(6)); lib. bdg. 22.60 (978-1-4339-7151-8(8)) Stevens, Gareth Publishing LLLP.

Sayre, April Pulley & Sayre, Jeff. One Is a Snail, Ten Is a Crab: A Counting by Feet Book. Cecil, Randy, illus. 2006. (ENG.). 40p. (J). (gr. k-3). 6.99 (978-0-7636-2631-0(7)) Candlewick Pr.

Sayre, Jeff & Sayre, April Pulley. One Is a Snail, Ten Is a Crab Big Book: A Counting by Feet Book. Cecil, Randy, illus. 2010. (ENG.). 40p. (J). (gr. k-3). pap. 24.99 (978-0-7636-4790-2(X)) Candlewick Pr.

Scarry, Richard. Richard Scarry's Best Counting Book Ever. Scarry, Richard, illus. 2004. (SPA, ENG & MUL., Illus.). 40p. (J). (gr. -1-2). 14.95 (978-0-87358-875-1(4)); pap. 8.95 (978-0-87358-876-8(2)) Cooper Square Publishing Llc.

—Richard Scarry's Best Counting Book Ever. 2010. (ENG., Illus.). 44p. (J). (gr. -1-2). 12.95 (978-1-4027-7217-7(3)) Sterling Publishing Co., Inc.

—School Bus Box Set. 2014. (Illus.). (J). (978-0-7641-6690-7(5)) Barron's Educational Series, Inc.

Scarry, Richard, illus. Counting to Ten Jigsaw Book: With Six 24-Piece Jigsaws Inside. 2004. 12p. (J). bds. (978-1-74124-406-9(4)) Bonnier Publishing Australia.

Schachner, Judy. Shape Up. 2008. (Skippyjon Jones Ser.). (ENG., Illus.). 14p. (J). (gr. -1 — 1). bds. 6.99 (978-0-525-47957-4(0), Dutton Books for Young Readers) Penguin Young Readers Group.

—Skippyjon Jones 1-2-3. 2008. (Skippyjon Jones Ser.). (ENG., Illus.). 12p. (J). (gr. -1 — 1). bds. 6.99 (978-0-525-47956-7(2), Dutton Books for Young Readers) Penguin Young Readers Group.

Schaefer, Ted. Harvest Time. 2006. (My First Math Discovery Library). (Illus.). 24p. (J). (gr. k-2). lib. bdg. 22.79 (978-1-59515-975-5(4)) Rourke Educational Media.

Schafer, Kevin. Penguins 123. 2004. (Penguins Ser.). (ENG., Illus.). 32p. (J). (gr. -1 — 1). bds. 6.95 (978-1-55971-906-3(0)) Cooper Square Publishing Llc.

Schertle, Alice. Little Blue Truck's Christmas. McElmurry, Jill, illus. 2014. (Little Blue Truck Ser.). (ENG.). 24p. (J). (— 1). 14.99 (978-0-544-32041-3(7), HMH Books For Young Readers) Houghton Mifflin Harcourt Publishing Co.

Schieber, Jennifer. Counting at the Olympics. 2004. (Shared Connections Ser.). (J). pap. (978-1-4108-1632-0(X)); pap., instr.'s gde. ed. 27.00 (978-1-4108-1608-5(7)) Benchmark Education Co.

Schmidt, Julie. My Piggy Bank: Number Names & Count Sequence. 2013. (Rosen Math Readers Ser.). (ENG., Illus.). 16p. (J). (gr. k-1). pap. 7.00 (978-1-4777-1608-3(4), Rosen Classroom) Rosen Publishing Group, Inc., The.

Schmidt, Julie & Schmidt, Jessica. My Piggy Bank: Number Names & Count Sequence. 2013. (Rosen Math Readers Ser.). (ENG.). 16p. (J). (gr. k-1). pap. 42.00 (978-1-4777-1609-0(2), Rosen Classroom) Rosen Publishing Group, Inc., The.

Scholastic, Inc. Staff. Carry & Learn Numbers. Ward, Sarah G., illus. 2015. (ENG.). 10p. (J). (— 1). bds. 7.99 (978-0-545-79790-0(X), Cartwheel Bks.) Scholastic, Inc.

—Counting to 100. 2005. (ENG.). 5.99 (978-0-439-73282-6(4), Teaching Resources) Scholastic, Inc.

—Write & Wipe Early Math 123. 2016. (Scholastic Early Learners Ser.). (ENG.). 28p. (J). (gr. -1-k). bds. 8.99 (978-0-545-90339-4(4)) Scholastic, Inc.

Scholastic, Inc. Staff, contrib. by. Counting 1 to 10. 2012. (Rookie Toddler Ser.). (ENG., Illus.). 12p. (J). bds. 6.95 (978-0-531-20851-9(6), Children's Pr.) Scholastic Library Publishing.

—Counting 1 To 20. 2014. (Rookie Toddler(r) Ser.). (ENG.). 12p. (J). bds. 6.95 (978-0-531-20913-4(X)) Scholastic Library Publishing.

—Counting Cars & Trucks. 2016. (Rookie Toddlers Ser.). (ENG.). 12p. (J). bds. 6.95 (978-0-531-22453-3(8), Children's Pr.) Scholastic Library Publishing.

—Counting in the Garden Dog: Magalina the Dog Plush. 2006. (ENG.). (J). 11.99 (978-0-439-84307-2(3), Scholastic) Scholastic, Inc.

—Counting Machines. 2015. (Rookie Toddler(tm) Ser.). (ENG., Illus.). 12p. (J). bds. 6.95 (978-0-531-21268-4(8), Children's Pr.) Scholastic Library Publishing.

—Counting Tools 1 to 10. 2013. (Rookie Toddler(r) Ser.). (ENG.). 12p. (J). bds. 6.95 (978-0-531-21578-4(4), Children's Pr.) Scholastic Library Publishing.

—Romeo Rabbit Counting in the Garden. 2006. (ENG.). (J). 11.99 (978-0-439-84309-6(X), Scholastic) Scholastic, Inc.

—Rudy Cat Counting in the Garden. 2006. (ENG.). (J). 11.99 (978-0-439-84308-9(1), Scholastic) Scholastic, Inc.

Scholastic, Inc. Staff, ed. Comptons les Animaux Grandeur Nature.Tr. of Lifesize Animal Counting Book. (FRE., Illus.). (J). 16.99 (978-0-590-24358-2(6)) Scholastic, Inc.

—Lifesize Animal Counting Book. (Illus.). (J). (gr. -1). pap. 16.95 (978-0-590-24270-7(9)) Scholastic, Inc.

Scholastic Teaching Resources Staff. Kindergarten Basic Skills: Numbers & Counting. 2012. (Kindergarten Basic Skills Ser.). (ENG.). 48p. pap. 6.99 (978-0-545-42965-8(X)) Teacher's Friend Pubns., Inc.

Schonberg, Marcia. Discover Ohio, 2 bks. Langton, Bruce, illus. 2003. (ENG.). 40p. (J). 27.95 (978-1-58536-225-7(5)) Sleeping Bear Pr.

School Zone Interactive Staff. Flash Action Software Go Fish / Old Maid. 2005. (ENG.). (J). cd-rom 12.99 (978-1-58947-830-5(4)) School Zone Publishing Co.

School Zone Publishing Company Staff. Bilingual Counting 1-10. 2007. (ENG.). 64p. (J). pap. 3.99 (978-1-58947-973-9(4)) School Zone Publishing Co.

—Counting 1-10. (Illus.). (J). 19.99 incl. audio compact disk (978-0-88743-925-4(X)) School Zone Publishing Co.

School Zone Staff. Old Maid. 2004. (ENG.). (J). 2.79 (978-1-58947-992-0(0)) School Zone Publishing Co.

School Zone Staff, ed. Preschool Counting Farm. 2006. (ENG.). 8p. (J). (gr. k). 5.99 (978-1-58947-846-6(0)) School Zone Publishing Co.

Schrier, Allyson Valentine. How Many Baby Animals? 2008. (Discovering & Exploring Science Ser.). (Illus.). 16p. (J). (gr. -1-3). lib. bdg. 12.95 (978-0-7569-8436-6(X)) Perfection Learning Corp.

Schuepbach, Lynnette. Froggy Hollow. Schuepbach, Lynnette, illus. l.t. ed. 2004. (Illus.). 32p. (J). 7.00 net. (978-0-9759613-0-8(6)) Creative Sources.

Schuette, Sarah L. Eating Pairs (Comer Pares) Counting Fruits & Vegetables by Two (Contar Frutas y Vegetales de DOS en DOS) 2012. (Vamos a Contar / Counting Bks.). (ENG, SPA & MUL.). 32p. (gr. 1-2). lib. bdg. 27.32 (978-1-4296-8251-0(5), A+ Bilingue/Bilingual) Capstone Press of Coughlan Cos.

—3, 2, 1 ¡Vamos!/3, 2, 1, Go! Contemos Hacia Atrás Usando el Transporte. 2012. (Vamos a Contar / Counting Bks.).Tr. of Transportation Countdown. (ENG, SPA & MUL.). 32p. (gr. 1-2). lib. bdg. 27.32 (978-1-4296-8249-7(3), A+ Bilingue/Bilingual) Capstone Press of Coughlan Cos.

Schuette, Sarah L. & Davis, Rebecca F. Counting Books (Vamos a Contar) 2012. (Vamos a Contar / Counting Bks.). (MUL.). 32p. (gr. 1-2). 81.96 (978-1-4296-9594-7(3), A+ Bilingue/Bilingual) Capstone Press of Coughlan Cos.

—Vamos a Contar / Counting Books. 2012. (Vamos a Contar / Counting Bks.). (MUL.). 32p. (gr. 1-2). 81.96 (978-1-4296-8252-7(3), A+ Bilingue/Bilingual) Capstone Press of Coughlan Cos.

Schuh, Mari. Counting Money. 2015. (Money Matters Ser.). (ENG., Illus.). 24p. (J). (gr. k-3). lib. bdg. 25.95 (978-1-62617-245-6(5), Blastoff! Readers) Bellwether Media.

Schuh, Mari C. The Crayola Counting Book. 2017. (Crayola (r) Concepts Ser.). (ENG.). 24p. (J). (gr. -1-3). 26.65 **(978-1-5124-3288-6(1))** Lerner Publishing Group.

Schulman, Janet. 10 Easter Egg Hunters: A Holiday Counting Book. Davick, Linda, illus. (ENG.). (J). 2015. 32p. (— 1). 4.99 (978-0-553-50784-3(2), Dragonfly Bks.) 2012. 26p. (gr. -1 — 1). bds. 6.99 (978-0-375-86637-1(X), Knopf Bks. for Young Readers) 2011. 32p. (gr. -1 — 1). 8.99 (978-0-375-86787-3(2), Knopf Bks. for Young Readers) Random Hse. Children's Bks.

—10 Trick-or-Treaters: A Halloween Counting Book. Davick, Linda, illus. (ENG.). (J). (gr. -1-2). 2009. 26p. bds. 6.99 (978-0-375-85347-0(2), Knopf Bks. for Young Readers) 2008. 32p. pap. 7.99 (978-0-385-73614-5(2), Dragonfly Bks.) Random Hse. Children's Bks.

—10 Valentine Friends. Davick, Linda, illus. 2012. (ENG.). 26p. (J). (gr. -1 — 1). bds. 6.99 (978-0-375-87130-6(6), Knopf Bks. for Young Readers) Random Hse. Children's Bks.

Schumacher, Bev. Count on Me! 2004. 20p. (J). lib. bdg. 9.95 (978-0-9741549-6-1(2)) Learning Props.

Schwartz, Betty & Seresin, Lynn. Ten Playful Tigers: A Touch-And-Feel Counting Book. Powell, Luciana Navarro, illus. 2015. (Back-And-Forth Bks.). (ENG.). 22p. (gr. -1 — 1). bds. 9.99 (978-1-62370-233-5(X)) Capstone Young Readers of Coughlan Cos.

Schwartz, Betty Ann. One to Ten... & Back Again. Shakir, Susie, illus. 2009. 24p. bds. 12.99 (978-0-8249-1436-3(8), Ideal Pubns.) Worthy Publishing.

Schwartz, David M. Cuanto Es un Millon? Kellogg, Steven, illus. 2003. (SPA.). (J). (gr. k-3). pap. 3.96 net. (978-0-590-47393-4(X), SO30942) Scholastic, Inc.

—How Much Is a Million? Kellogg, Steven, illus. 20th anniv. ed. 2004. (Reading Rainbow Bks.). (ENG.). 40p. (J). (gr. -1-3). pap. 7.99 (978-0-688-09933-6(5)) HarperCollins Pubs.

—How Much Is a Million? 2004. (J). (gr. k-3). 18.40 (978-0-8085-7914-4(2), Turtleback) Turtleback Bks.

Schwarz, Viviane. Counting with Tiny Cat. Schwarz, Viviane, illus. 2017. (ENG., Illus.). 32p. (J). (-k). 14.99 **(978-0-7636-9462-3(2))** Candlewick Pr.

Scillian, Devin. One Nation: America by the Numbers. Carroll, Pam, illus. 2004. (ENG.). 40p. (J). (gr. k-6). pap. 7.95 (978-1-58536-249-3(2)) Sleeping Bear Pr.

Scillian, Devin & Scillian, Corey. One Kansas Farmer: A Kansas Number Book. Bowles, Doug, illus. 2009. (Discover America State by State Ser.). (ENG.). 40p. (J). (gr. k-6). 16.95 (978-1-58536-182-3(8)) Sleeping Bear Pr.

Scott, Ron. Latte's Counting Book, 1 vol. 2009. 24p. pap. 24.95 (978-1-60813-992-7(1)) America Star Bks.

Scott, Winston. We Can Count! 2012. (InfoMax Readers Ser.). (ENG., Illus.). 16 pp.p. (J). (gr. k-1). pap. 7.00 (978-1-4488-8887-0(5), Rosen Classroom) Rosen Publishing Group, Inc., The.

Sebe, Masayuki. Let's Count to 100! Sebe, Masayuki, illus. 2011. (ENG., Illus.). 24p. (J). (gr. -1-2). 16.95 (978-1-55453-661-0(8)) Kids Can Pr., Ltd. CAN. Dist: Hachette Bk. Group.

—Let's Count To 100! Sebe, Masayuki, illus. 2014. (ENG., Illus.). 24p. (J). (gr. -1-2). 7.95 (978-1-55453-813-3(0)) Kids Can Pr., Ltd. CAN. Dist: Hachette Bk. Group.

—100 Animals on Parade! Sebe, Masayuki, illus. 2013. (ENG., Illus.). 24p. (J). (gr. -1-2). 16.95 (978-1-55453-871-3(8)) Kids Can Pr., Ltd. CAN. Dist: Hachette Bk. Group.

Secor, Julie. Counting Flowers Is Fun: Number Names & Count Sequence. 2013. (Rosen Math Readers Ser.). (ENG.). 16p. (J). (gr. k-1). pap. 42.00 (978-1-4777-1660-1(2)); (Illus.). pap. 7.00 (978-1-4777-1659-5(9)) Rosen Publishing Group, Inc., The. (Rosen Classroom).

Seeger, Laura Vaccaro. One Boy. Seeger, Laura Vaccaro, illus. 2016. (ENG., Illus.). 48p. (J). 14.99 (978-1-62672-252-1(8), 9781626722521) Roaring Brook Pr.

Sesame Street, Sesame. Sesame Street Elmo's 1 2 3. 2015. (Lift-The-Flap Ser.). (ENG.). 10p. (J). (gr. -1-k). bds. 11.99 (978-0-7944-3476-2(2)) Studio Fun International.

Sesame Street Staff. Sesame Street Count with Elmo! A Look, Lift, & Learn Book. 2013. (Look, Lift & Learn Bks.: 1). (ENG.). 10p. (J). (gr. -1-k). 10.99 (978-0-7944-2861-7(4)) Reader's Digest Assn., Inc., The.

Sesame Street Staff, creator. Sesame Street: Early Learning Boxed Set. 2011. 72p. (J). bds. 12.99 (978-1-60745-237-9(5)) Flying Frog Pubs.

Sévigny, Eric, illus. Caillou Around Town. 2nd ed. 2013. (Coloring & Activity Book Ser.). (ENG.). 16p. (J). (gr. -1-1). bds. 9.99 (978-2-89718-045-4(5)) Caillouet, Gerry.

—Caillou, Search & Count: Fun Adventures! 2013. (Coloring & Activity Book Ser.). (ENG.). 16p. (J). (gr. -1-1). bds. 9.99 (978-2-89718-034-8(X)) Caillouet, Gerry.

Shahan, Sherry. Cool Cats Counting. Barragán, Paula, illus. (ENG.). (J). (gr. -1-2). 2016. 28p. pap. 8.95 (978-1-941460-42-9(9)) 2005. 24p. 16.95 (978-0-87483-757-5(X)) August Hse. Pubs., Inc.

Shannon, George. One Family. Gomez, Blanca, illus. 2015. (ENG.). 32p. (J). (gr. -1-3). 17.99 (978-0-374-30003-6(8), 9780374300036, Farrar, Straus & Giroux (BYR)) Farrar, Straus & Giroux.

Shapiro, David R. Flowers by Number. Vair, Hayley, illus. 2013. (Little Naturalist Ser.). (ENG.). 32p. (J). 14.99 (978-0-9844422-8-7(6)) Craigmore Creations.

Sharp, Jean. Contando Por la Ciudad. Walter, Lorin, illus. 2007. (Matimáticas en Nuestro Mundo (Math in Our World) Ser.). (SPA.). 24p. (gr. 1-2). lib. bdg. 22.00 (978-0-8368-8486-9(8), Weekly Reader Leveled Readers) Stevens, Gareth Publishing LLLP.

—Counting in the City. Walter, Lorin, illus. 2007. (Math in Our World Ser.). 24p. (gr. 1-2). pap. 8.15 (978-0-8368-8477-7(9)); lib. bdg. 22.00 (978-0-8368-8468-5(X)) Stevens, Gareth Publishing LLLP. (Weekly Reader Leveled Readers).

Sherab, Chodzin & Langham, Tony. Creepy Crawly Calypso. 2012. (ENG., Illus.). 32p. (J). (gr. -1-2). 9.99 (978-1-84686-828-3(9)) Barefoot Bks., Inc.

Sherman, Janice. Colorful Critters. 2007. (ENG., Illus.). 10p. (J). pap. 4.99 (978-0-9797139-2-7(7)) Jan's Bks.

—Colorful Critters Color Match Coloring Book. 2007. (ENG., Illus.). 10p. (J). pap. 1.99 (978-0-9797139-3-4(5)) Jan's Bks.

—Counting Critters. 2007. (ENG., Illus.). 10p. (J). pap. 4.99 (978-0-9797139-1-0(9)) Jan's Bks.

—Critters A-Z. 2007. (ENG., Illus.). 26p. (J). pap. 5.99 (978-0-9797139-0-3(0)) Jan's Bks.

Shields, Carol Diggory. Wombat Walkabout. Blackall, Sophie, illus. 2009. (ENG.). 32p. (J). (gr. -1-k). 16.99 (978-0-525-47865-2(5), Dutton Books for Young Readers) Penguin Young Readers Group.

Shiring, Jeff. Pizza by the Numbers. 2008. 32p. pap. 17.49 (978-1-4363-0289-0(7)) Xlibris Corp.

Shostak, Myra. Rainbow Candles: A Hanukkah Counting Book. Springer, Sally, illus. 2003. 12p. (J). (gr. -1-18). 4.95 (978-1-58013-031-8(3), Kar-Ben Publishing) Lerner Publishing Group.

Shoulders, Michael. Count on Us: A Tennessee Number Book. Langton, Bruce, illus. 2003. (Count Your Way Across the U. S. A. Ser.). (ENG.). 40p. (J). 16.95 (978-1-58536-131-1(3)) Sleeping Bear Pr.

—Discover Tennessee: Count on Us; V is for Volunteer, 2 bks. Langton, Bruce, illus. 2003. (ENG.). 40p. (J). 27.95 (978-1-58536-228-8(X)) Sleeping Bear Pr.

—Natural Numbers: An Arkansas Number Book. Anderson, Rick, illus. 2008. (Count Your Way Across the U. S. A. Ser.). (ENG.). 40p. (J). 17.95 (978-1-58536-172-4(0)) Sleeping Bear Pr.

—1 Mississippi 2 Mississippi: A Mississippi Number Book. Anderson, Rick, illus. 2004. (Count Your Way Across the U. S. A. Ser.). (ENG.). 40p. (J). 16.95 (978-1-58536-188-5(7)) Sleeping Bear Pr.

Shulman, Mark. I'll Take a Dozen! Milne, Bill, photos by. 2006. (Illus.). 12p. (J). (gr. k-4). reprint ed. 6.00 (978-1-4223-5725-5(2)) DIANE Publishing Co.

Sim, David. Matt's Mat: A Touch & Feel Counting Book, 2 vols. Sim, David, illus. 2003. (Illus.). 10p. (J). 7.95 (978-1-58117-198-3(6), Intervisual/Piggy Toes) Bendon, Inc.

Simson, Dana. Numbers. 2003. (Dana Simson Chunky Books Ser.). 10p. (J). bds. 2.95 (978-1-74047-259-3(4)) Book Co. Publishing Pty, Ltd., The AUS. Dist: Penton Overseas, Inc.

Sing along Rhymes Five Little Ducks. 2010. (J). (978-85-312-5232-7(6)) Children's Pr., Ltd.

Sing to Baby Jesus. 2013. (Illus.). 32p. (J). 14.99 (978-1-62108-071-8(4)) Covenant Communications, Inc.

Singer, Marilyn. City Lullaby. Cneut, Carll, illus. 2007. (ENG.). 32p. (J). (gr. -1-3). 16.99 (978-0-618-60703-7(X)) Houghton Mifflin Harcourt Publishing Co.

Singhal, Sheetal. Counting. Sona & Jacob, illus. 2007.Tr. of Ginti. (ENG, HIN, GUJ & PAN.). 24p. (J). pap. 8.00 (978-0-9773645-8-9(5)) MeeraMasi, Inc.

Singleton, Debbie. The King Who Wouldn't Sleep. Swain, Holly, illus. 2012. (Andersen Press Picture Bks). (ENG.). 32p. (J). (gr. -1-3). 16.95 (978-0-7613-8997-2(0)) Lerner Publishing Group.

Sirotich, Erica & Sirotich, Erica. Found Dogs. 2017. (ENG., Illus.). 32p. (J). (-k). 16.99 **(978-0-399-18641-7(7)**, Dial Bks) Penguin Young Readers Group.

Siwak, Brenda S. Counting on the Bay. Dodge, Barbara A., illus. 2006. (J). per. 14.95 (978-0-9790906-0-8(1)) Pleasant Plains Pr.

Sly, Alexandra. One Tractor. Rogers, Jacqueline, illus. 2009. (ENG.). 32p. (J). (gr. -1-k). pap. 6.95 (978-0-8234-2188-6(0)) Holiday Hse., Inc.

Slade, Suzanne & Waites, Joan. What's New at the Zoo? An Animal Adding Adventure, 1 vol. 2009. (Basic Math Operations Ser.). (ENG., Illus.). 32p. (J). (gr. -1-3). 16.95 (978-1-934359-93-8(9)); pap. 8.95 (978-1-60718-038-8(3), 9781607180388) Arbordale Publishing.

Slater, Teddy. Four Fiddlers. Kennedy, Kelly, illus. 2005. (Number Tales Ser.). (ENG.). 16p. (J). (gr. -1-1). pap. 2.99 (978-0-439-69008-9(0)) Scholastic, Inc.

Slater, Teddy & Scholastic, Inc. Staff. Nine Bright Pennies. Lewis, Stephen, illus. 2005. (Number Tales Ser.). (ENG.). 16p. (J). (gr. -1-1). pap. 2.99 (978-0-439-69020-1(X)) Scholastic, Inc.

Slaughter, Tom. One, Two, Three. 2003. (ENG., Illus.). 24p. (J). (gr. k-k). 12.95 (978-0-88776-664-0(1), Tundra Bks.) Tundra Bks. CAN. Dist: Penguin Random Hse. LLC.

—1 2 3. 2006. (ENG., Illus.). 16p. (J). (gr. k-k). bds. 7.95 (978-0-88776-788-3(5), Tundra Bks.) Tundra Bks. CAN. Dist: Penguin Random Hse. LLC.

—1 2 3. Slaughter, Tom, illus. 2006. (FRE., Illus.). 24p. (J). (gr. k-k). pap. 7.95 (978-0-88776-802-6(4)) Tundra Bks. CAN. Dist: Penguin Random Hse. LLC.

Sloat, Teri. Zip! Zoom! on a Broom. Bonnet, Rosalinde, illus. 2017. (ENG.). 40p. (J). (gr. -1-3). 16.99 **(978-0-316-25673-5(0))** Little Brown & Co.

Smallman, Steve. Spot a Lot Animal Escape. Slater, Nicola, illus. 2014. (ENG.). (J). (gr. -1-3). (978-1-4723-5096-1(0)) Parragon Bk. Service Ltd.

Smart Kidz, creator. The 123s of How I Love You. 2013. (Parent Love Letters Ser.). (ENG., Illus.). 12p. (gr. -1). bds. 12.99 (978-1-891100-31-4(9), Smart Kids) Penton Overseas, Inc.

Smith, Danna. Dos en el Zoológico: Un Libro para Contar. Petrone, Valeria, illus. 2011.Tr. of Two at the Zoo - A Counting Book. (ENG & SPA.). 30p. (J). (gr. k — 1). bds. 4.99 (978-0-547-58137-8(8)) Houghton Mifflin Harcourt Publishing Co.

—Swallow the Leader. Sherry, Kevin, illus. 2016. (ENG.). 32p. (J). (gr. -1-3). 16.99 (978-0-544-10518-8(4), Clarion Bks.) Houghton Mifflin Harcourt Trade & Reference Pubs.

Smith, Maggie. Counting Our Way to Maine. 2008. (ENG., Illus.). 32p. (J). (gr. -1-3). 15.95 (978-0-89272-775-9(6)) Down East Bks.

Smith, R. M. Peep in the Deep - Sea Creature Counting Book: Sea Creature Counting Book. 2012. (ENG., Illus.). 28p. (J). pap. 7.95 (978-0-615-42297-8(7)) Clarence-Henry Bks.

Smith, Sherri. Counting with Mike the Tiger. Walsh, D. T., illus. 2013. (ENG.). (J). (gr. -1-k). 14.95 (978-1-62086-349-7(9)) Mascot Bks., Inc.

Snyder, Jane. Days of the Week: Learning Ordinal Numbers. 2009. (Math for the REAL World Ser.). 12p. (gr. 1-2). pap. 5.90 (978-0-8239-8913-3(5), Rosen Classroom) Rosen Publishing Group, Inc., The.

Somers, Kevin & Puck. 1 2 3 New York. Somers, Kevin, illus. 2008. (Cool Counting Bks.). (ENG., Illus.). 22p. (J). (gr. k — 1). bds. 7.95 (978-0-9796213-0-7(5)) Duo Pr. LLC.

Spelvin, Justin. Deep-Sea Countdown. McGee, Warner, illus. 2006. (Backyardigans Ser.). (ENG.). 26p. (J). (gr. -1). bds. 5.99 (978-1-4169-1484-6(6), Simon Spotlight/Nickelodeon) Simon Spotlight/Nickelodeon.

Spencer, Alison Hill. Bird Count, 1 vol. 2013. (Adventure Boardbook Ser.). (ENG.). 24p. (J). (gr. -1-k). bds. 6.95 (978-1-59193-427-1(3)) Adventure Pubns.

Spinelli, Eileen. Counting Blessings, 1 vol. Holland, Lee, illus. 2016. (ENG.). 20p. (J). bds. 9.99 (978-0-310-75072-7(5)) Zonderkidz.

—Together at Christmas. Lee, Bin, illus. 2012. (ENG.). 24p. (J). (gr. -1-3). 15.99 (978-0-8075-8010-3(4)) Whitman, Albert & Co.

Spurr, Elizabeth. The Farm Life. Björkman, Steve, illus. 2005. (ENG.). 32p. (J). (gr. k-3). tchr. ed. 16.95 (978-0-8234-1777-3(8)) Holiday Hse., Inc.

Steck-Vaughn Staff. Skip-Count by Threes. 2003. pap. 4.10 (978-0-7398-7660-2(0)) Steck-Vaughn.

Steckel, Richard & Steckel, Michele, photos by. My Teeth. 2008. (Milestones Project Chewables Ser.). (ENG., Illus.). 20p. (J). (gr. k — 1). bds. 6.99 (978-1-58246-212-7(7), Tricycle Pr.) Random Hse. Children's Bks.

Steffora, Tracey. Adding with Ants, 1 vol. 2013. (Animal Math Ser.). (ENG.). 24p. (gr. -1-1). 22.65 (978-1-4329-7558-6(7)); pap. 6.95 (978-1-4329-7565-4(X)) Heinemann-Raintree. (NA-h).

—Animal Math. 2013. (Animal Math Ser.). (ENG.). 24p. (gr. -1-1). pap. 29.95 (978-1-4329-7571-5(4)); lib. bdg. 113.25 (978-1-4329-7564-7(1)) Heinemann-Raintree. (NA-h).

—Animal Math: Adding, Taking Away, & Skip Counting, 1 vol. 2014. (Animal Math Ser.). (ENG.). 32p. (gr. -1-1). 29.99 (978-1-4846-0061-0(4), NA-h) Heinemann-Raintree.

—Counting in the City, 1 vol. 2011. (Math Around Us Ser.). (ENG.). 24p. (gr. -1-1). pap. 6.29 (978-1-4329-4929-7(2), Acorn) Heinemann-Raintree.

—Skip Counting with Meerkats, 1 vol. 2013. (Animal Math Ser.). (ENG.). 24p. (gr. -1-1). 22.65 (978-1-4329-7561-6(7)); pap. 6.95 (978-1-4329-7568-5(4)) Heinemann-Raintree. (NA-h).

Stemple, Heidi E. Y. One If by Land: A Massachusetts Number Book. Brett, Jeannie, illus. 2006. (Count Your Way Across the U. S. A. Ser.). (ENG.). 40p. (J). 17.95 (978-1-58536-186-1(0)) Sleeping Bear Pr.

Sterling Children's, Sterling. A Day at the Beach: A Book Of 123s. 2016. (ENG., Illus.). 28p. (J). (— 1). bds. 6.95 (978-1-4114-7588-5(7), Spark Publishing Group) Sterling Publishing Co., Inc.

Sterling Editors, creator. Dot to Dot Count To 30. 2008. (ENG., Illus.). 64p. (J). (gr. -1). per. 4.95 (978-1-4027-5134-9(6)) Sterling Publishing Co., Inc.

Sterling, Kristin. Money. 2008. (First Step Nonfiction - Early Math Set II Ser.). (ENG.). 8p. (gr. -1-1). pap. 4.95 (978-0-8225-8848-1(X)) Lerner Publishing Group.

Sterling Publishing Company Staff, creator. Dot to Dot Count To 25. 2007. (ENG., Illus.). 64p. (J). (gr. -1). per. 4.95 (978-1-4027-4626-0(1)) Sterling Publishing Co., Inc.

Stiegemeyer, Julie. Seven Little Bunnies, 0 vols. Bryant, Laura J., illus. 2010. (ENG.). 24p. (J). (gr. -1-3). 15.99 (978-0-7614-5600-1(7), 9780761456001, Amazon Children's Publishing) Amazon Publishing.

Stihler, Chérie B. Wiggle-Waggle Woof: Counting Sled Dogs in Alaska. Bania, Michael, illus. 2009. (Paws IV Ser.). (ENG.). 32p. (J). (gr. -1-2). pap. 10.99 (978-1-57061-559-7(4), Little Bigfoot) Sasquatch Bks.

—Wiggle-Waggle Woof 1, 2, 3. Bania, Michael, illus. 2015. (Paws IV Ser.). (ENG.). 20p. (J). (— 1). bds. 8.99 (978-1-57061-978-6(6), Little Bigfoot) Sasquatch Bks.

Stott, Dorothy, illus. Ten in the Bed. 2010. (Padded Board Book W/CD Ser.). 8p. (J). (gr. k-2). bds. 10.99 incl. audio compact disk (978-1-59922-578-4(6)) Twin Sisters IP, LLC.

Stuart, Carrie. Kinds of Coins: Learning the Values of Pennies, Nickels, Dimes & Quarters. 2009. (Math for the REAL World Ser.). 12p. (gr. 1-2). pap. 5.90 (978-0-8239-8862-4(7), Rosen Classroom) Rosen Publishing Group, Inc., The.

Studio Mouse. Sesame Street: Counting All Around: Zip & Carry Book & CD. rev. ed. 2007. (ENG.). 36p. 12.99 (978-1-59069-571-5(2)) Studio Mouse LLC.

Studio Mouse, creator. Mother Goose Counting Rhymes. rev. ed. 2006. (ENG., Illus.). 80p. (J). (gr. 4-7). 14.99 (978-1-59069-485-5(6)) Studio Mouse LLC.

Studio Mouse Staff. First Concepts, Pack. rev. ed. 2003. (ENG., Illus.). 60p. (J). (gr. -1-k). 12.99 (978-1-59069-363-6(9), 1A502) Studio Mouse LLC.

—Five Little Monkeys: And Other Counting Rhymes. Elliott, Rebecca et al, illus. rev. ed. 2007. (ENG.). 24p. (J). (gr. -1-k). 4.99 (978-1-59069-608-8(5)) Studio Mouse LLC.

—Mickey Mouse Clubhouse Count Along. rev. ed. 2007. (ENG.). 36p. 12.99 (978-1-59069-613-2(1)) Studio Mouse LLC.

—Pooh & Friends ABCs & 123s: First Concepts. rev. ed. 2007. (ENG., Illus.). 24p. (J). (gr. -1-3). 4.99 (978-1-59069-606-4(9)) Studio Mouse LLC.

—Take-with-Me Counting. rev. ed. 2007. (ENG.). 36p. 12.99 (978-1-59069-568-5(2)) Studio Mouse LLC.

—Wedding Countdown. 2008. 36p. (J). (gr. -1). 12.99 (978-1-59069-740-5(5)) Studio Mouse LLC.

Sturgis, Brenda Reeves. 10 Turkeys in the Road, 0 vols. Slonim, David, illus. 2011. (ENG.). 32p. (J). (gr. -1-1). 16.99 (978-0-7614-5847-0(6), 9780761458470, Amazon Children's Publishing) Amazon Publishing.

Stutson, Caroline. Cats' Night Out. Klassen, Jon, illus. 2010. (ENG.). 32p. (J). (gr. -1-3). 17.99 (978-1-4169-4005-0(7), Simon & Schuster/Paula Wiseman Bks.) Simon & Schuster/Paula Wiseman Bks.

Sugita, Yutaka. Goodnight, One, Two, Three. Sugita, Yutaka, illus. (Illus.). 32p. (J). (gr. -1-2). 14.95 (978-0-87592-022-1(5)) Scroll Pr., Inc.

Sullivan, Erin Ash. Counting Clues: Set Of 6. 2011. (Early Connections Ser.). (J). pap. 37.00 net. (978-1-4108-1094-6(1)) Benchmark Education Co.

Sullivan, Mary C. Bugs! a Counting Book. Sullivan, Mary C., illus. 2013. (Illus.). 32p. 18.95 (978-0-9859986-6-0(0)) Nectar Pubns.

Surplice, Holly. Guinea Pig Party. Surplice, Holly, illus. 2015. (ENG., Illus.). 24p. (J). (— 1). bds. 7.99 (978-0-7636-7604-9(7), Nosy Crow) Candlewick Pr.

Suttle, Darlene. On that Mountain So Hilly! 2011. 28p. (gr. -1). pap. 16.95 *(978-1-4497-1529-8(X)*, WestBow Pr.) Author Solutions, Inc.

Swarbrick, David E. Twenty Goofy Gumballs: Counting Made Fun. 2012. 26p. 24.95 *(978-1-4626-6248-7(X))* America Star Bks.

Swenson, Jamie A. Boom! Boom! Boom! Walker, David, illus. 2013. (ENG.). 32p. (J). (gr. -1-1). 16.99 *(978-0-374-30868-1(3)*, 9780374308681, Farrar, Straus & Giroux (BYR)) Farrar, Straus & Giroux.

Tabletop Pocket Chart Counting & Numbers Card Set. 2004. (J). pap. 8.95 *(978-1-56911-169-7(3))* Learning Resources, Inc.

Tafuri, Nancy. The Big Storm: A Very Soggy Counting Book. Tafuri, Nancy, illus. 2013. (Classic Board Bks.). (ENG., Illus.). 34p. (J). (gr. -1 — 1). bds. 7.99 *(978-1-4424-8179-4(X)*, Little Simon) Little Simon.

—The Big Storm: A Very Soggy Counting Book. Tafuri, Nancy, illus. 2009. (ENG., Illus.). 32p. (J). (gr. -1-2). 18.99 *(978-1-4169-6795-8(8)*, Simon & Schuster Bks. For Young Readers) Simon & Schuster Bks. For Young Readers.

Tai, Elise See. Farm Animal Counting. 2014. (Lumpy Bumpy Ser.). (ENG., Illus.). 10p. (J). (gr. -1 — 1). 5.99 *(978-0-7641-6708-9(1))* Barron's Educational Series, Inc.

Talarico Msn, Karen M. My New Brother: A Counting Book. 2008. 32p. pap. 13.75 *(978-1-4389-3522-5(6))* AuthorHouse.

Tang, Greg. Math Fables. Cahoon, Heather, illus. 2004. (ENG.). 40p. (J). (gr. -1-3). 18.99 *(978-0-439-45399-8(2))* Scholastic, Inc.

—Math-Terpieces: The Art of Problem-Solving. Paprocki, Greg, illus. 2003. (ENG.). 32p. (J). (gr. 2-5). 18.99 *(978-0-439-44388-3(1))* Scholastic, Inc.

Tang, Greg & Greg, Tang. Come una y Cuenta Veinte. Briggs, Harry, illus. 2003.Tr. of Grapes of Math. (SPA.). 40p. (J). (gr. 3-4). 14.99 *(978-84-241-8075-1(5))* Everest Editora ESP. Dist: Lectorum Pubns., Inc.

Taplin, Sam. Easter Bunny Flap Book. 2012. (Flap Bks). 10p. (J). ring bd. 7.99 *(978-0-7945-3256-7(X)*, Usborne) EDC Publishing.

Tata. I Smile. 2009. 20p. pap. 10.89 *(978-1-4389-2627-8(8))* AuthorHouse.

Taylor-Butler, Christine. Ah-Choo. Koeller, Carol, illus. 2005. (My First Reader Ser.). (ENG.). 32p. (J). (gr. k-1). 18.50 *(978-0-516-25175-2(9)*, Children's Pr.) Scholastic Library Publishing.

Ten Toads, Eleven Lizards: Consonants l, t. 2003. (J). 38.50 *(978-0-8136-9129-9(X))* Modern Curriculum Pr.

Tengan, G. Shay. Marching Dinosaur Parade. 2012. (Illus.). 60p. 17.99 *(978-0-9883478-0-9(6))* Tengan, G. Shay Service Group.

Texier, Ophélie & Baumann, Anne-Sophie. Numbers. 2009. (Little Discoveries: Ser.). (ENG., Illus.). 6p. (J). (gr. -1-k). bds. 8.95 *(978-0-7892-0983-2(7)*, Abbeville Kids) Abbeville Pr., Inc.

Thayer, Tanya. Counting Money. 2005. (First Step Nonfiction Ser.). (Illus.). 24p. (gr. k-2). lib. bdg. 17.27 *(978-0-8225-1258-5(0))* Lerner Publishing Group.

Thomas & Friends, Thomas &. Thomas & Friends: Thomas Speeds Along. 2015. (Lift-The-Flap Ser.: 1). (ENG.). 10p. (J). (gr. -1-k). 11.99 *(978-0-7944-3480-9(0)*, Reader's Digest Children's Bks.) Studio Fun International.

Thomas, Isabel. Number Fun: Making Numbers with Your Body, 1 vol. 2014. (ENG., Illus.). 24p. (gr. -1-1). 25.99 *(978-1-4846-0409-0(1))* Heinemann-Raintree.

Thomas, Jan. Is That Wise, Pig? Thomas, Jan, illus. 2016. (ENG., Illus.). 40p. (J). (gr. -1-3). 15.99 *(978-1-4169-8582-2(4)*, Beach Lane Bks.) Beach Lane Bks.

Thomas Nelson. Flip Flap Fun Counting. 2015. (ENG.). 62p. (J). (gr. -1-7). *(978-1-78393-712-7(2))* Make Believe Ideas.

—My Awesome Counting. 2016. (ENG.). 30p. (gr. -1). bds. *(978-1-78598-465-5(9))* Make Believe Ideas.

Thomas Nelson. Petite Boutique Counting. 2017. (ENG.). (J). (gr. -1-7). bds. ***(978-1-78692-113-0(8))*** Make Believe Ideas.

Thompson, Kim Mitzo & Hilderbrand, Karen Mitzo. Counting. 2010. 12p. (J). (gr. k-2). bds. 8.99 *(978-1-59922-570-8(0))* Twin Sisters IP, LLC.

Thompson, Kim Mitzo, et al. Trace & Learn Sticker Fun: Numbers & Counting. 2014. (I'm Learning the Bible Activity Book Ser.). (ENG.). 16p. (J). pap. 6.99 *(978-1-63058-441-2(X))* Barbour Publishing, Inc.

Thompson, Lauren. Cuaquito (Little Quack) Anderson, Derek, illus. 2010. (SPA.). 34p. (J). (gr. -1-1). bds. 7.99 *(978-1-4169-9894-5(2)*, Libros Para Ninos) Libros Para Ninos.

—Little Quack Counts. Anderson, Derek, illus. 2009. (Super Chubbies Ser.). (ENG.). 26p. (J). (gr. -1 — 1). bds. 5.99 *(978-1-4169-6093-5(7)*, Little Simon) Little Simon.

Thompson, Lauren & Anderson, Derek. Little Quack's Hide & Seek. 2007. (Classic Board Bks.). (ENG., Illus.). 34p. (J). (gr. -1-k). bds. 7.99 *(978-1-4169-0325-3(9)*, Little Simon) Little Simon.

Thompson, Richard & Thompson, Ofa. Ko'eku Tohi Lau Fika. Lee, Bill, illus. l.t. ed. 2003. (TON.). 24p. (J). (gr. -1-18). 5.00 *(978-0-9678979-1-2(2))* Friendly Isles Pr.

Thong, Roseanne Greenfield. One Is a Drummer: A Book of Numbers. 2014. (Multicultural Shapes & Colors Ser.). (Illus.). 40p. (J). lib. bdg. 28.50 *(978-1-60753-567-6(X))* Amicus Publishing.

Thorne-Thomsen, Kathleen. A Shaker's Dozen: Counting Book. Thorne-Thomsen, Kathleen, illus. Rocheleau, Paul, photos by. 2003. (Illus.). 27p. (J). (gr. k-13). reprint ed. 16.00 *(978-0-7567-9041-7(7))* DIANE Publishing Co.

Thornhill, Jan. The Wildlife 123: A Nature Counting Book. 2012. (ENG., Illus.). 32p. (J). (gr. -1-2). pap. 7.95 *(978-1-926973-46-3(1)*, Owlkids) Owlkids Bks. Inc. CAN. Dist: Publishers Group West (PGW).

Three Bear Family: Counting & Numbers Activity Book. 2003. (J). pap. 4.95 *(978-1-56911-102-4(2))* Learning Resources, Inc.

Ticktock Media, Ltd. Staff. Kittens & Puppies: Counting. 2008. (Tab Bks.). (ENG.). 10p. (J). (gr. -1-k). bds. 4.95 *(978-1-84696-822-8(4)*, TickTock Books) Octopus Publishing Group GBR. Dist: Independent Pubs. Group.

Tiger Tales, ed. 1 2 3 Count with Me. Birkett, Georgie, illus. 2011. (ENG.). 26p. (J). bds. 7.95 *(978-1-58925-873-0(8))* Tiger Tales.

Tiger Tales Staff, creator. Count 123. 2013. (My First Touch & Trace Ser.). (ENG., Illus.). 26p. (gr. -1). bds. 7.99 *(978-1-58925-625-5(5))* Tiger Tales.

—First Numbers. 2013. (My First Lift & Learn Ser.). (ENG., Illus.). 10p. (gr. -1). bds. 7.99 *(978-1-58925-630-9(1))* Tiger Tales.

—123 Counting Fun. 2014. (My First Touch & Feel Bks.). (ENG., Illus.). 22p. (J). bds. 12.99 *(978-1-58925-591-3(7))* Tiger Tales.

Tiger Tales Staff & Mantle, Ben. Five Little Pumpkins. Tiger Tales Staff, ed. 2010. (ENG., Illus.). 24p. (J). (gr. -1-k). bds. 8.95 *(978-1-58925-856-3(8))* Tiger Tales.

Tofts, Hannah. One Cool Watermelon. 2007. (One Cool Watermelon Ser.). (Illus.). 24p. (gr. -1-2). lib. bdg. 23.00 *(978-0-8368-7488-4(9)*, Gareth Stevens Learning Library) Stevens, Gareth Publishing LLLP.

—One Cool Watermelon. Tofts, Hannah, illus. 2008. (Things I Eat Ser.). (ENG., Illus.). 24p. (J). (gr. -1-k). *(978-1-84089-555-1(1))* Zero to Ten, Ltd.

—Una Sandia Bien Fria. 2007. (sandia bien fria (One Cool Watermelon) Ser.). (SPA.). 24p. (gr. -1-2). pap. 8.15 *(978-0-8368-8144-8(3))*; (Illus.). lib. bdg. 23.00 *(978-0-8368-7489-1(7))* Stevens, Gareth Publishing LLLP. (Gareth Stevens Learning Library).

Top That Publishing Staff. How Many. 2006. 10p. *(978-1-84666-099-3(8))* Top That! Publishing PLC.

Top That Publishing Staff, ed. Counting. 2004. (Magnetic Play & Learn Ser.). (Illus.). 12p. (J). *(978-1-84510-050-6(6))* Top That! Publishing PLC.

—Counting on the Farm. Sapp, Karen, illus. 2007. (Magnetic Fun Ser.). 16p. (J). (gr. -1). *(978-1-84666-270-6(2)*, Tide Mill Pr.) Top That! Publishing PLC.

—In My Little Blue Bed. Henley, Claire, illus. 2007. 11p. (J). (gr. -1-k). bds. *(978-1-84666-280-5(X)*, Tide Mill Pr.) Top That! Publishing PLC.

—In My Little Pink Bed: A Counting Book. Henley, Claire, illus. 2007. (In My Bed Book Ser.). 11p. (J). (gr. -1-k). bds. *(978-1-84666-285-0(0)*, Tide Mill Pr.) Top That! Publishing PLC.

—Jungle Numbers. Parry, Jo, illus. 2007. (Magnetic - Numbers Ser.). 10p. (J). (gr. -1). bds. *(978-1-84666-163-1(3)*, Tide Mill Pr.) Top That! Publishing PLC.

—There Were Ten Bears in a Bed: A Count-and-Feel Book. Atkins, Alison, illus. 2007. (Story Book Ser.). 22p. (J). (gr. -1). bds. *(978-1-84666-130-3(7)*, Tide Mill Pr.) Top That! Publishing PLC.

Top That! Jungle Numbers (large Version) Parry, Jo, illus. 2007. 10p. (J). (gr. -1). *(978-1-84666-552-3(3)*, Tide Mill Pr.) Top That! Publishing PLC.

Top That!, creator. Counting with Billy the Bear. 2012. (Learn with Magnets Ser.). (ENG., Illus.). 10p. (gr. -1-k). *(978-1-84956-669-8(0))* Top That! Publishing PLC.

—123 Train. 2007. (Jigsaw Book Ser.). (Illus.). 18p. (J). (gr. -1-3). bds. *(978-1-84666-097-9(1))* Top That! Publishing PLC.

Topek, Susan Remick. Ten Good Rules: A Counting Book. Cohen, Tod, photos by. 2007. (ENG., Illus.). 24p. (J). (gr. -1-1). lib. bdg. 15.95 *(978-0-8225-7293-0(1)*, Kar-Ben Publishing) Lerner Publishing Group.

Torres, J. Checkers & Dot at the Beach. Lum, J., illus. 2013. (J). E-Book *(978-1-77049-448-0(0))* Tundra Bks.

Touchable Counting Books. 2005. (ENG.). (J). bds. 14.95 *(978-1-58117-284-3(2)*, Intervisual/Piggy Toes) Bendon, Inc.

Tourville, Amanda Doering. Hiding Hippos: Counting from 1 To 10, 1 vol. Holm, Sharon Lane, illus. 2008. (Count the Critters Ser.). (ENG.). 24p. (J). (gr. k-3). 27.07 *(978-1-60270-263-9(2))* Magic Wagon.

—Lions Leaving: Counting from 10 To 1, 1 vol. Holm, Sharon Lane, illus. 2008. (Count the Critters Ser.). (ENG.). 24p. (J). (gr. k-3). 27.07 *(978-1-60270-264-6(0))* Magic Wagon.

—Penguin Pairs: Counting By 2s, 1 vol. Holm, Sharon Lane, illus. 2008. (Count the Critters Ser.). (ENG.). 24p. (J). (gr. k-3). 27.07 *(978-1-60270-265-3(9))* Magic Wagon.

—Prairie Dogs Perching: Counting By 3s, 1 vol. Holm, Sharon Lane, illus. 2008. (Count the Critters Ser.). (ENG.). 24p. (J). (gr. k-3). 27.07 *(978-1-60270-266-0(7))* Magic Wagon.

—Sunning Sea Lions: Discovering Even Numbers, 1 vol. Holm, Sharon Lane, illus. 2008. (Count the Critters Ser.). (ENG.). 24p. (J). (gr. k-3). 27.07 *(978-1-60270-267-7(5))* Magic Wagon.

Trapani, Iza. Haunted Party. Trapani, Iza, illus. 2010. (ENG., Illus.). 28p. (J). (gr. -1-2). pap. 7.95 *(978-1-58089-247-6(7))* Charlesbridge Publishing, Inc.

Trawick, Renee. Mrs. T's Day of Numbers, 1 vol. 2010. 16p. pap. 24.95 *(978-1-4489-5998-3(5))* PublishAmerica, Inc.

Trinity University Press Staff & Budnick, Madeleine. 123 Si! An Artistic Counting Book in English & Spanish. 2011. (ArteKids Ser.). (SPA & ENG., Illus.). 16p. (gr. k-k). bds. 7.95 *(978-1-59534-080-1(7))* Trinity Univ. Pr.

Trottier, Maxine. One Is Canada. 2004. (Illus.). (J). (gr. 1-5). spiral bd. *(978-0-616-01797-5(9))* Canadian National Institute for the Blind/Institut National Canadien pour les Aveugles.

Tsong, Jing Jing. Counting Birds. 2012. (ENG.). 28p. (J). bds. 8.95 *(978-1-58925-638-5(7))* Tiger Tales.

Tucker, Sian. My Book of First Numbers. Tucker, Sian, illus. 2003. (My Book of. . . Ser.). (Illus.). 48p. (YA). *(978-1-85602-482-2(2)*, Pavilion Children's Books) Pavilion Bks.

Tulip, Jenny, illus. Sticker & Color-In Playbook: Teddy Bear Counting. 2016. (ENG.). 16p. (J). (gr. -1-12). pap. 4.99 *(978-1-86147-750-7(3)*, Armadillo) Anness Publishing GBR. Dist: National Bk. Network.

Tuxworth, Nicola. Numbers. (Learn-a-Word Book Ser.). (ENG., Illus.). (J). (gr. -1-2). 2015. 20p. bds. 6.99 *(978-1-84322-750-2(9)*, Armadillo) 2005. 12p. bds. 6.99 *(978-0-7548-1419-1(X))* Anness Publishing GBR. Dist: National Bk. Network.

Twin Sisters(r) Staff, prod. Alphabet & Counting: Songs That Teach. 2009. (J). per. 10.99 *(978-1-57583-819-9(2))* Twin Sisters IP, LLC.

Twine, Alice. My Favorite Book of Numbers. 2008. (Board Bks.). (Illus.). 14p. (J). (gr. -1-k). bds. 11.95 *(978-1-4042-4256-2(2))* Rosen Publishing Group, Inc., The.

Twinem, Neecy. Baby Coyote Counts. 2004. (New Board Book Ser.).Tr. of Bebe Coyote cuenta. (ENG., Illus.). 12p. (J). (gr. -1-k). bds. 5.95 *(978-0-87358-852-2(5))* Cooper Square Publishing Llc.

Tyler, Jenny & Gee, R. Counting up to Ten. 2004. (First Learning Ser.). (ENG.). 24p. (J). pap., act. bk. ed. 4.95 *(978-0-7945-0499-1(X))* EDC Publishing.

Tyre, Greg R. Fun with Sockie. 2009. 28p. pap. 14.99 *(978-1-4490-0105-6(X))* AuthorHouse.

Ulmer, Mike. Loonies & Toonies: A Canadian Number Book. Rose, Melanie, illus. rev. ed. 2006. (ENG.). 40p. (J). (gr. k-6). 18.95 *(978-1-58536-239-4(5))* Sleeping Bear Pr.

Ulmer, Wendy K. Zero, Zilch, Nada: Counting to None. Knorr, Laura, illus. 2010. (ENG.). 32p. (J). (gr. -1-3). 16.95 *(978-1-58536-461-9(4))* Sleeping Bear Pr.

Ungerer, Tomi. One, Two, Where's My Shoe? 2014. (ENG., Illus.). 32p. (gr. -1-k). 14.95 *(978-0-7148-6798-4(5))* Phaidon Pr., Inc.

Unknown & Grosset and Dunlap Staff. Let's Count! A First Book of Numbers. Aikins, Dave, illus. 2014. (Sassy Ser.). (ENG.). 10p. (J). (gr. -1 — 1). bds. 6.99 *(978-0-448-48012-1(3)*, Grosset & Dunlap) Penguin Young Readers Group.

Urbansky, Edward. Caroline Counting. 2007. 28p. 22.50 *(978-1-4303-2040-1(0))* Lulu Pr., Inc.

Utarid, Anjana. Count Me In. 2008. 24p. pap. 12.95 *(978-1-60264-281-2(8))* Virtualbookworm.com Publishing, Inc.

Valer, Frantisek, illus. The Buffalo & the Boat: Thathánka na Wáta. 2004. (DAK, ENG & SIO.). 18p. (J). 9.95 *(978-0-9761082-3-8(2))* Lakota Language Consortium, Inc.

—Pispiza WAN Wayawa Iyaye/Prairie Dog Goes to School. 2006. (DAK, ENG & SIO.). 24p. (J). (gr. -1-3). pap. 9.95 *(978-0-9761082-4-5(0))* Lakota Language Consortium, Inc.

Valério, Geraldo. Jump, Leap, Count Sheep! A Canadian Wildlife 123. 2017. (ENG., Illus.). 24p. (J). (gr. -1-2). 16.95 ***(978-1-77147-289-0(8))*** Owlkids Bks. Inc. CAN. Dist: Publishers Group West (PGW).

Van Fleet, Matthew. Tails. 2017. (ENG., Illus.). 20p. (J). (— 1). 14.99 ***(978-1-328-88685-9(9)***, HMH Books For Young Readers) Houghton Mifflin Harcourt Publishing Co.

Van Hoven, Constance. The Twelve Days of Christmas in Minnesota. Wohnoutka, Mike, illus. 2016. (Twelve Days of Christmas in America Ser.). (ENG.). 22p. (J). (— 1). bds. 7.95 *(978-1-4549-2057-1(2))* Sterling Publishing Co., Inc.

van Lieshout, Maria. Flight 1-2-3. 2015. (ENG., Illus.). 32p. (J). (gr. -1 — 1). bds. 7.99 *(978-1-4521-4291-3(2))* Chronicle Bks. LLC.

—Flight 1-2-3. van Lieshout, Maria, illus. 2013. (ENG., Illus.). 40p. (J). (gr. -1 — 1). 14.99 *(978-1-4521-1662-4(8))* Chronicle Bks. LLC.

Vanwye, Karissa. 1 2 3 Count with Me, 1 vol. 2009. 23p. pap. 24.95 *(978-1-60474-740-9(4))* America Star Bks.

Verdick, Elizabeth. Peep Leap, 0 vols. Bendall-Brunello, John, illus. 2013. (ENG.). 32p. (J). (gr. -1-2). 16.99 *(978-1-4778-1640-0(2)*, 9781477816400, Amazon Children's Publishing) Amazon Publishing.

Very First Numbers Kid Kit. 2004. 10p. (J). (gr. -1-18). 11.95 *(978-1-58086-448-0(1))* EDC Publishing.

Viner, Callie Lee. Pebbles Loves Counting. Viner, Callie Lee, photos by. 2013. (Illus.). 24p. pap. 12.95 *(978-1-61493-213-0(1))* Peppertree Pr., The.

Volke, Gordon & Book Company Staff. Disco Fish. 2004. (Novelty Bks.). 10p. (J). (gr. 3-5). bds. *(978-1-74047-496-2(1))* Book Co. Publishing Pty, Ltd., The.

Waber, Bernard. Lyle, Lyle, Crocodile Storybook Treasury. 2012. (Lyle the Crocodile Ser.). (ENG., Illus.). 192p. (J). (gr. -1-3). 11.99 *(978-0-547-51618-9(5))* Houghton Mifflin Harcourt Publishing Co.

—Lyle Walks the Dogs. Waber, Paulis, illus. 2010. (ENG.). 24p. (J). (gr. -1-3). 17.99 *(978-0-547-22323-0(4))* Houghton Mifflin Harcourt Publishing Co.

Wadsworth, Olive A. Over in the Meadow: A Counting Rhyme. Vojtech, Anna, illus. 2003. (Cheshire Studio Book Ser.). (ENG.). 32p. (J). pap. 7.95 *(978-0-7358-1871-2(1))* North-South Bks., Inc.

Wahman, Joe. Snowboy 1, 2, 3. Wahman, Wendy, illus. 2012. (ENG.). 32p. (J). (gr. -1-1). 14.99 *(978-0-8050-8732-1(X)*, 9780805087321, Holt, Henry & Co. Bks. For Young Readers) Holt, Henry & Co.

Waldrep, Susan. Papa Ant's Picnic. 2008. 24p. 15.00 *(978-1-4357-1129-7(7))* Lulu Pr., Inc.

Walker, Nan. The Yum-Yum House. Pilz, M. H., illus. 2009. (Math Matters Complete Set Ser.). 32p. (J). (gr. 3-5). pap. 5.95 *(978-1-57565-290-0(0))* Kane Press, Inc.

Walling, Sandy Seeley. A Day at the Beach: A Seaside Counting Book from One to Ten. Walling, Sandy Seeley, illus. 2003. (Illus.). 28p. (J). 6.95 *(978-0-9741940-0-4(X))* Abernathy Hse. Publishing.

Wallis, Rebecca, illus. Number 1 What Grows in the Sun? 2005. (Community of Counting Ser.). 32p. (J). pap. 10.95 *(978-1-59646-272-4(8))* Dingles & Co.

—Number 1 What Grows in the Sun?/Número 1 Qué crece en el Sol? 2005. (Community of Counting Ser.). (ENG & SPA.). 32p. (J). pap. 10.95 *(978-1-59646-274-8(4))*; lib. bdg. 21.65 *(978-1-891997-89-1(0))* Dingles & Co.

—Number 10 Where Is the Hen? 2005. (Community of Counting Ser.). 32p. (J). pap. 10.95 *(978-1-59646-308-0(2))* Dingles & Co.

—Number 10 Where Is the Hen?/Número 10 en dónde está la Gallina? 2005. (Community of Counting Ser.).Tr. of Número 10 en dónde está la Gallina? (ENG & SPA.). 32p. (J). pap. 10.95 *(978-1-59646-310-3(4))*; lib. bdg. 21.65 *(978-1-891997-80-8(7))* Dingles & Co.

Wallis, Rebecca, intro. Number 1 What Grows in the Sun? 2005. (Community of Counting Ser.). (ENG., Illus.). 32p. (J). lib. bdg. 21.65 *(978-1-891997-99-0(8))* Dingles & Co.

—Number 2 Let's Go to the Zoo! 2005. (Community of Counting Ser.). (Illus.). 32p. (J). lib. bdg. 21.65 *(978-1-891997-98-3(X))* Dingles & Co.

Walters, Eric. Bedtime 123, 1 vol. Bisaillon, Josée, illus. 2017. (ENG.). 26p. (J). (gr. -1-k). bds. 9.95 ***(978-1-4598-1073-0(2))*** Orca Bk. Pubs. USA.

Wang, Margaret. Eency Weency Spider. Rueda, Claudia, illus. 2006. (ENG.). 12p. (J). bds. 5.95 *(978-1-58117-505-9(1)*, Intervisual/Piggy Toes) Bendon, Inc.

—Five Little Puppies. Haines, Genny, illus. 2006. (ENG.). 12p. (J). (gr. -1-k). 9.95 *(978-1-58117-487-8(X)*, Intervisual/Piggy Toes) Bendon, Inc.

Ward, Jennifer. Way up in the Arctic. Spengler, Kenneth J., illus. 2007. (SPA & ENG.). 32p. (J). (gr. -1-3). 15.95 *(978-0-87358-928-4(9))* Cooper Square Publishing Llc.

Wargin, Kathy-jo. North Star Numbers: A Minnesota Number Book. Caple, Laurie, illus. 2008. (Count Your Way Across the U. S. A. Ser.). (ENG.). 40p. (J). (gr. -1-3). 17.95 *(978-1-58536-187-8(9))* Sleeping Bear Pr.

—Prairie Numbers: An Illinois Number Book. O'Malley, Kathy, illus. 2006. (Count Your Way Across the U. S. A. Ser.). (ENG.). 40p. (J). (gr. -1-3). 17.95 *(978-1-58536-180-9(1))* Sleeping Bear Pr.

Wasikhongo, Odalo Magruder. My First Book of Numbers. Wasikhongo, Odalo Magruder, illus. 2012. (Illus.). 24p. pap. 5.00 *(978-0-9845203-2-9(5))* WasiWorks Studio LLC.

Watson, Craig. Maddie Counts Marbles: Number Names & Count Sequence. 2013. (InfoMax Math Readers Ser.). (ENG.). 16p. (J). (gr. k-1). pap. 42.00 *(978-1-4777-1950-3(4))*; (Illus.). pap. 7.00 *(978-1-4777-1949-7(0))* Rosen Publishing Group, Inc., The. (Rosen Classroom).

Watson, Jane Werner. The Fuzzy Duckling. Provensen, Martin & Provensen, Alice, illus. 2015. (Little Golden Book Ser.). (ENG.). 24p. (J). (-k). 4.99 *(978-0-553-52213-6(2)*, Golden Bks.) Random Hse. Children's Bks.

Watt, Fiona. 123 Touchy Feely (Farmyard Tales) 2008. (Luxury Touchy-Feely Board Bks). 18p. (J). bds. 15.99 *(978-0-7945-2081-6(2)*, Usborne) EDC Publishing.

Watt, Mélanie. Numbers. Watt, Mélanie, illus. 2005. (Learning with Animals Ser.). (ENG., Illus.). 24p. (J). (gr. -1 — 1). bds. 5.95 *(978-1-55337-831-0(8))* Kids Can Pr., Ltd. CAN. Dist: Hachette Bk. Group.

Weakland, Mark. Hockey Counting, 1 vol. 2013. (SI Kids Rookie Bks.). (ENG.). 32p. (gr. 1-2). 27.32 *(978-1-4765-0226-7(9))* Capstone Press of Coughlan Cos.

Weatherill, Steve & So, Sungwan. Shanyi Goes to China. 2009. (Children Return to Their Roots Ser.). (ENG., Illus.). 40p. (J). (gr. 1-4). pap. 8.95 *(978-1-84507-705-1(9)*, Frances Lincoln) Quarto Publishing Group UK GBR. Dist: Hachette Bk. Group.

Webb, Mary & Ni Laoghaire, Ide. My Ireland Counting Book. Ryan, Eoin, illus. (ENG.). 32p. (J). 2012. pap. 12.95 *(978-1-84717-278-5(4))* 2nd rev. ed. 2017. pap. 12.00 ***(978-1-84717-931-9(2))*** O'Brien Pr., Ltd., The IRL. Dist: Dufour Editions, Inc.

Weekly Reader Early Learning Library Staff, contrib. by. I Know Numbers/Los Números. 2006. (I'm Ready for Math/ Ya puedo aprender matematicas Ser.). (ENG & SPA., Illus.). 16p. (gr. -1-2). pap. 5.30 *(978-0-8368-6490-8(5)*, Weekly Reader Leveled Readers) Stevens, Gareth Publishing LLLP.

Weekly Reader Editorial Staff. I Know Numbers. 2006. (I'm Ready for Math Ser.). (Illus.). 16p. (gr. -1-2). lib. bdg. 19.00 *(978-0-8368-6475-5(1)*, Weekly Reader Leveled Readers) Stevens, Gareth Publishing LLLP.

—Los Numeros. 2006. (I'm Ready for Math/YA Puedo Aprender Matematicas Ser.). (ENG & SPA., Illus.). 16p. (gr. -1-2). lib. bdg. 19.00 *(978-0-8368-6485-4(9)*, Weekly Reader Leveled Readers) Stevens, Gareth Publishing LLLP.

Weekly Reader Editorial Staff, contrib. by. I Know Numbers. 2006. (I'm Ready for Math Ser.). (Illus.). 16p. (gr. -1-2). pap. 5.30 *(978-0-8368-6480-9(8)*, Weekly Reader Leveled Readers) Stevens, Gareth Publishing LLLP.

Wegman, William. 3... 2... 1... Circus! 2014. (ENG., Illus.). 24p. (J). (— 1). bds. 6.99 *(978-0-8037-3934-5(6)*, Dial Bks) Penguin Young Readers Group.

Weill, Cynthia. Count Me In: A Parade of Mexican Folk Art Numbers in English & Spanish. Aguilar Sisters Staff, illus. 2012. (First Concepts in Mexican Folk Art Ser.). (ENG & SPA.). 32p. (J). (gr. k-k). 14.95 *(978-1-935955-39-9(X))* Cinco Puntos Pr.

Weisenfluh, C. C. In the Garden with the LittleWeeds: A Counting Book for Little Ones. Freeman, Julie, illus. 2004. 26p. (J). 11.95 *(978-0-9746782-0-7(1))* B'Squeak Productions.

Wells, Rosemary. Emily's First 100 Days of School. Wells, Rosemary, illus. 2005. (ENG., Illus.). 64p. (J). (gr. -1-1). pap. 9.99 *(978-0-7868-1354-4(7))* Hyperion Pr.

—Emily's First 100 Days of School. 2006. (Illus.). (J). (gr. -1-4). 18.95 *(978-0-439-84903-6(9)*, WPCD654) Weston Woods Studios, Inc.

—Max's Toys: A Counting Book. 2004. (Max & Ruby Ser.). (ENG.). 12p. (J). (gr. 1 — 1). bds. 6.99 *(978-0-670-88720-0(X)*, Viking Books for Young Readers) Penguin Young Readers Group.

Wen, Dref. Fy Llyfr Rhifau Cyntaf. 2005.Tr. of My First Numbers. (WEL., Illus.). 34p. *(978-1-85596-672-7(7))* Dref Wen.

Wenger, Shaunda. How Many Muffins? 2006. (Early Explorers Ser.). (J). pap. *(978-1-4108-6120-7(1))* Benchmark Education Co.

Werner, Sharon & Forss, Sarah. Bugs by the Numbers Counting Cards. 2011. (ENG., Illus.). 27p. (J). (gr. k-12). 24.99 *(978-1-60905-101-3(7))* Blue Apple Bks.

Werner Watson, Jane. The Fuzzy Duckling. Provensen, Alice & Provensen, Martin, illus. 2012. (Golden Baby Ser.). (ENG.). 24p. (J). (gr. k — 1). bds. 6.99 *(978-0-307-92966-2(3)*, Golden Bks.) Random Hse. Children's Bks.

Weston Woods Staff, creator. Emily's First 100 Days of School. 2011. 38.75 *(978-0-439-84892-3(X))* Weston Woods Studios, Inc.

—Inch by Inch. 2011. 38.75 *(978-0-439-90543-5(5))* Weston Woods Studios, Inc.

—Over in the Meadow. 2004. 38.75 *(978-1-55592-759-2(9))*; 18.95 *(978-1-55592-809-4(9))*; 29.95 *(978-1-55592-852-0(8))* Weston Woods Studios, Inc.

Wheeler, Lisa. Uncles & Antlers. Floca, Brian, illus. 2014. (ENG.). 40p. (J). (gr. -1-3). 17.99 *(978-1-4814-3018-0(1)*, Atheneum Bks. for Young Readers) Simon & Schuster Children's Publishing.

Wheldon, Nicole. The 1, 2, 3 Bees: A Counting Book. Zourelias-Noro, Diane, illus. 2005. 24p. (J). (gr. -1-7). 17.95 *(978-0-9744792-1-7(7))* Acmon Blue Publishing.

White, Ella. I Can Write Numbers! Number Names & Count Sequence. 2013. (Rosen Math Readers Ser.). (ENG., Illus.). 16p. (J). (gr. k-1). pap. 7.00 *(978-1-4777-1590-1(8)*, Rosen Classroom) Rosen Publishing Group, Inc., The.

White, Ella & White, Emma. I Can Write Numbers! Number Names & Count Sequence. 2013. (Rosen Math Readers Ser.). (ENG.). 16p. (J). (gr. k-1). pap. 42.00 *(978-1-4777-1591-8(6)*, Rosen Classroom) Rosen Publishing Group, Inc., The.

White, Teagan. Counting with Barefoot Critters. 2016. (ENG., Illus.). 32p. (J). (gr. -1-3). 16.99 *(978-1-101-91771-8(7)*, Tundra Bks.) Tundra Bks. CAN. Dist: Penguin Random Hse. LLC.

Whiten, Jan. Chooky-Doodle-Doo. Hanley, Sinéad, illus. 2015. (ENG.). 32p. (J). (-k). 12.99 *(978-0-7636-7327-7(7))* Candlewick Pr.

Whitman, Nancy C. Counting Petals: Using Flowers of Hawaii. Chong, Luther, photos by. 2009. (Illus.). 31p. (J). *(978-1-4363-8562-6(8))* Xlibris Corp.

Whittington, Melanie & Holtz, Lara Tankel, eds. Counting Book. King, Dave, photos by. 2003. (Illus.). 32p. (J). *(978-0-681-62667-6(4))* Dorling Kindersley.

Wildsmith, Brian. Animals to Count. Wildsmith, Brian, illus. (Illus.). 16p. (J). 2004. (PER.). bds. 4.99 *(978-1-932065-43-5(1))* 2003. (CHI., bds. 4.99 *(978-1-932065-17-6(2)*, 1718-784-9112) Star Bright Bks., Inc.

—Brian Wildsmith's Animals to Count, 1 vol. Wildsmith, Brian, illus. 2009. (ENG., Illus.). 32p. (J). bds. 4.99 *(978-1-59572-128-0(2))* Star Bright Bks., Inc.

—Brian Wildsmith's Animals to Count, 1 vol. 2004. (NAV., Illus.). 16p. (J). 4.99 *(978-1-932065-25-1(3))* Star Bright Bks., Inc.

—Brian Wildsmith's Animals to Count, 1 vol. Wildsmith, Brian, illus. 2003. (Illus.). 16p. (J). (TAG.). 4.99 *(978-1-932065-31-2(8)*, 1-718-784-9112); (KOR., 4.99 *(978-1-932065-13-8(X)*, 1718-784-9112); (POR., bds. 4.95 *(978-1-932065-15-2(6)*, 17187849112) Star Bright Bks., Inc.

—Brian Wildsmith's Opposites, 1 vol. 2009. (ENG., Illus.). 32p. (J). bds. 4.99 *(978-1-59572-139-6(8))* Star Bright Bks., Inc.

Wildsmith, Brian, illus. Brian Wildsmith's Animal Colors. 2004. (ARA.). 16p. (J). bds. 4.95 *(978-1-932065-44-2(X)*, 718-784-9112) Star Bright Bks., Inc.

—Brian Wildsmith's Animals to Count. 16p. (J). 2004. (ARA.). bds. 4.95 *(978-1-932065-45-9(8)*, 718-784-9112) 2003. (VIE.). bds. 4.95 *(978-1-932065-16-9(4)*, 17187849112) Star Bright Bks., Inc.

Wildsmith, Brian, illus. Brian Wildsmith's Animals to Count (Traditional Cantonese), 1 vol. Wildsmith, Brian, . 2003. (CHI & ENG.). 16p. (J). 4.99 *(978-1-932065-18-3(0)*, 1-718-784-9112) Star Bright Bks., Inc.

Williams, Becky. Ten Little Mermaids. East, Jacqueline, illus. 2007. (Story Book Ser.). 22p. (J). (gr. -1). bds. *(978-1-84666-375-8(X)*, Tide Mill Pr.) Top That! Publishing PLC.

Williams, Emma Louise. 30 Sheep & One Cow. Williams, Emma Louise, illus. 2012. (Illus.). 24p. pap. 8.99 *(978-1-939076-05-2(6))* Wiggies, Piggy.

Williams, Rozanne Lanczak. Crayola Counting. Jarrett, Michael, illus. Jarrett, Michael, photos by. 2004. (I Can Do Math Ser.). 24p. (gr. k-3). lib. bdg. 22.00 *(978-0-8368-4109-1(3)*, Gareth Stevens Learning Library) Stevens, Gareth Publishing LLLP.

—Learning about Coins. Jarrett, Michael, photos by. 2004. (I Can Do Math Ser.). (Illus.). 24p. (gr. k-3). lib. bdg. 22.00 *(978-0-8368-4110-7(7)*, Gareth Stevens Learning Library) Stevens, Gareth Publishing LLLP.

Williams, Sue. Let's Go Visiting. Vivas, Julie, illus. 2003. (ENG.). 32p. (J). (gr. k — 1). bds. 6.95 *(978-0-15-204638-5(0))* Houghton Mifflin Harcourt Publishing Co.

Williams, Suzanne. Ten Naughty Little Monkeys. Watts, Suzanne, illus. 2007. 32p. (J). (gr. -1-3). lib. bdg. 17.89 *(978-0-06-059905-8(7))* HarperCollins Pubs.

Williams, Zachary. Cleaning up the Park: Learning to Count by Fives. 2009. (Math for the REAL World Ser.). 12p. (gr. 1-2). pap. 5.90 *(978-0-8239-8892-1(9)*, Rosen Classroom) Rosen Publishing Group, Inc., The.

Wilson, Anne, illus. My First Box of Books: 1 2 3 Colours Animals, 3 vols. 2016. (ENG.). 72p. (J). (gr. -1-2). bds. 9.99 *(978-1-86147-416-2(4)*, Armadillo) Anness Publishing GBR. Dist: National Bk. Network.

Wilson, Karma. Bear Counts. Chapman, Jane, illus. 2015. (Bear Bks.). (ENG.). 32p. (J). (gr. -1-2). 16.99 *(978-1-4424-8092-6(0)*, McElderry, Margaret K. Bks.) McElderry, Margaret K. Bks.

Wilson, Zachary. Number One Puppy. Pertile, Paula, illus. 2011. (Rookie Ready to Learn Ser.). 40p. (J). pap. 5.95 *(978-0-531-26748-6(2))*; (gr. -1-k). lib. bdg. 23.00 *(978-0-531-26448-5(3))* Scholastic Library Publishing. (Children's Pr.).

Wingard-Nelson, Rebecca. How Many Pennies Make a Dollar? 2009. (I Like Money Math! Ser.). (Illus.). 24p. (J). pap. 7.95 *(978-0-7660-3656-7(1)*, Enslow Elementary); (gr. 1-3). lib. bdg. 22.60 *(978-0-7660-3141-8(1))* Enslow Pubs., Inc.

—I Can Count Money. 2009. (I Like Money Math! Ser.). (Illus.). 24p. (J). pap. 7.95 *(978-0-7660-3658-1(8)*, Enslow Elementary); (gr. 1-3). lib. bdg. 22.60 *(978-0-7660-3142-5(X))* Enslow Pubs., Inc.

Wise, William. Ten Sly Piranhas: A Counting Story in Reverse (A Tale of Wickedness - And Worse!) Chess, Victoria, illus. 2004. (ENG.). 32p. (J). (gr. -1-k). pap. 5.99 *(978-0-14-240074-6(2)*, Puffin Books) Penguin Young Readers Group.

Witcher, John. 123 & Me. 2009. 28p. pap. 13.99 *(978-1-4389-6896-4(5))* AuthorHouse.

Witty One Creature Count Number Book. 2003. (J). per. *(978-1-932435-21-4(2))* Cardinal Brands, Inc.

Wolf, Jackie. Sparkle Basket. 2003. (Illus.). 10p. (J). (gr. -1-18). bds. 6.99 *(978-1-57151-713-5(8))* Playhouse Publishing.

Wood, Audrey. Ten Little Fish. Wood, Bruce, illus. 2004. (ENG.). 40p. (J). (gr. -1-k). 17.99 *(978-0-439-63569-1(1)*, Blue Sky Pr., The) Scholastic, Inc.

Wood, Jakki. March of the Dinosaurs: A Dinosaur Counting Book. (Illus.). 30p. (J). (gr. -1-1). pap. *(978-0-7112-1456-9(5))* ReiseArt Buchhandlung GmbH.

—Moo Moo, Brown Cow. 2004. (Illus.). (J). (gr. -1-18). spiral bd., bds. *(978-0-616-14613-2(2))* Canadian National Institute for the Blind/Institut National Canadien pour les Aveugles.

Woods, Michael & Woods, Mary B. Ancient Computing Technology: From Abacuses to Water Clocks. 2011. (Technology in Ancient Cultures Ser.). (ENG.). 96p. (gr. 6-12). lib. bdg. 31.93 *(978-0-7613-6528-0(1))* Lerner Publishing Group.

Wormell, Chris. A Number of Animals. 2003. (Illus.). 24p. (J). (gr. -1-3). pap. 7.95 *(978-0-89812-384-5(4)*, Creative Paperbacks) Creative Co., The.

Wormell, Christopher. Teeth, Tails & Tentacles: An Animal Counting Book. 2004. (Illus.). 64p. 18.95 *(978-0-7624-2085-8(5))* Running Pr. Bk. Pubs.

Write on, Wipe off Numbers. 2007. (Early Days: Copy & Learn Ser.). (Illus.). 40p. *(978-1-84666-392-5(X))* Top That! Publishing PLC.

Wyatt, Leslie. Noah Learns His Numbers: Number Names & Count Sequence. 2013. (InfoMax Math Readers Ser.). (ENG.). 16p. (J). (gr. k-1). pap. 42.00 *(978-1-4777-1977-0(6))*; (Illus.). pap. 7.00 *(978-1-4777-1976-3(8))* Rosen Publishing Group, Inc., The. (Rosen Classroom).

Yang, Belle. A Nest in Springtime: A Bilingual Book of Numbers. Yang, Belle, illus. 2012. (CHI & ENG., Illus.). 24p. (J). (gr. k — 1). bds. 6.99 *(978-0-7636-5279-1(2))* Candlewick Pr.

Yarbray Brucke, Candice & Moore, Dawnyelle. Wrappers Wanted: A Mathematical Adventure in Surface Area. 2009. 32p. pap. 15.00 *(978-1-4389-7468-2(X))* AuthorHouse.

Yates, Gene. The Giraffe Numbers Book. 2003. (Illus.). 18p. (J). *(978-1-58865-107-5(X))* Kidsbooks, LLC.

Yates, Gene, illus. The Giraffe Numbers Book. 2006. (J). *(978-1-58865-364-2(1))* Kidsbooks, LLC.

Yates, Louise. Dog Loves Counting. 2013. (ENG.). 32p. (J). (gr. -1-3). 17.99 *(978-0-449-81342-3(8)*, Knopf Bks. for Young Readers) Random Hse. Children's Bks.

Yearling, Tricia & Summers, Portia. One Dollar: How Many Pennies? 2016. (Value of Money Ser.). (Illus.). 24p. (J). (gr. 2-1). pap. 9.35 *(978-0-7660-7685-3(7))* Enslow Pubs., Inc.

Yolen, Jane. How Do Dinosaurs Count to Ten? Teague, Mark, illus. 2004. (How Do Dinosaurs... Ser.). (ENG.). 12p. (J). (gr. -1-k). bds. 6.99 *(978-0-439-64949-0(8)*, Blue Sky Pr., The) Scholastic, Inc.

Yoon, Salina. One Halloween Night: A Spooky Seek-and-Count Book. 2011. (ENG., Illus.). 14p. (J). bds. 6.95 *(978-1-4027-8413-2(9))* Sterling Publishing Co., Inc.

Yorke, Jane & Dorling Kindersley Publishing Staff. My First Numbers & Counting: Touch & Feel Picture Cards. Thomson, Maria & Hester, Elizabeth, eds. 2005. (My 1st T&F Picture Cards Ser.). (ENG., Illus.). 16p. (J). (gr. -1 — 1). 9.99 *(978-0-7566-1517-8(8)*, DK Children) Dorling Kindersley Publishing, Inc.

Young, Cybèle. Ten Birds. Young, Cybèle, illus. 2011. (Ten Birds Ser.). (ENG., Illus.). 32p. (J). (gr. 1-6). 16.95 *(978-1-55453-568-2(9))* Kids Can Pr., Ltd. CAN. Dist: Hachette Bk. Group.

Young, Judy. Show Me the Number: A Missouri Number Book. Young, Ross, illus. rev. ed. 2007. (State Counting Ser.). (ENG.). 40p. (J). (gr. 1-7). 17.95 *(978-1-58536-156-4(9))* Sleeping Bear Pr.

Your Baby Can Learn! Numbers, Vol. 1. 2007. (J). 7.95 *(978-1-931026-14-7(9))* Infant Learning Co., The.

Yoyo Books, creator. Numbers. 2011. (Baby's First Library). (ENG., Illus.). 40p. (gr. -1-k). bds. *(978-94-6033-702-4(3))* YoYo Bks.

Yoyo Books Staff, creator. Maxi Peekaboo Learning to Count. 2006. (Illus.). 40p. (J). (gr. -1-7). *(978-90-5843-889-8(9))* YoYo Bks.

Zaidi, Ishan, illus. Keep Counting. 2010. (J). *(978-1-60617-145-5(3))* Teaching Strategies, LLC.

Ziefert, Harriet. Two Little Witches: A Halloween Counting Story. Taback, Simms, illus. 2007. (ENG.). 32p. (J). (gr. k-k). pap. 3.99 *(978-0-7636-3309-7(7))* Candlewick Pr.

Zubek, Adeline. Counting Lions. 2011. (Animal Math Ser.). 24p. (J). (gr. 1-3). pap. 8.15 *(978-1-4339-5664-5(0))*; lib. bdg. 22.60 *(978-1-4339-5662-1(4))* Stevens, Gareth Publishing LLLP.

Zuckerman, Rory. Counting Sleepy Sheep. Roos, Maryn, illus. 2004. (J). bds. 12.95 *(978-0-9749305-0-3(4))* Castle Pacific Publishing.

—Counting Sleepy Sheep. Roos, Maryn, illus. 2007. (Sleepy Sheep Ser.). 16p. (J). (gr. -1). bds. 7.95 incl. audio compact disk *(978-0-9796393-3-3(6))* Little Lion Pr.

1 2 3. 2003. (First Concepts Book Ser.). 32p. (J). 3.98 *(978-0-7525-8891-9(5))* Parragon, Inc.

123. 2004. (Illus.). (J). *(978-1-59060-333-8(8))* Waldman Publishing Corp.

COUNTING-OUT RHYMES

Cabrera, Jane. Ten in the Bed. Cabrera, Jane, illus. 2006. (ENG., Illus.). 32p. (J). (gr. -1-3). 16.95 *(978-0-8234-2027-8(2))* Holiday Hse., Inc.

Crisp, Dan, illus. The Ants Go Marching. 2007. (Classic Books with Holes Board Book Ser.). (ENG.). (J). 14p. bds. *(978-1-84643-109-8(3))*; 16p. (gr. 1-2). pap. *(978-1-84643-105-0(0))* Child's Play International Ltd.

Downtain, C.J. 1 2 3 Count with Me. 2013. 48p. pap. 8.10 *(978-1-4907-0538-5(4))* Trafford Publishing.

Fox, Mem. Ten Little Fingers & Ten Little Toes. Oxenbury, Helen, illus. (ENG.). (J). 2010. 38p. (gr. k — 1). bds. 8.99 *(978-0-547-36620-3(5))* 2008. 40p. (gr. -1 — 1). 17.99 *(978-0-15-206057-2(X))* Houghton Mifflin Harcourt Publishing Co.

Murray, Alison. One Two That's My Shoe! Murray, Alison, illus. 2012. (ENG., Illus.). 32p. (J). (gr. -1-1). 16.99 *(978-1-4231-4329-1(9))* Hyperion Pr.

Rešcek, Sanja, illus. One Elephant Went Out to Play. 2007. (Classic Books with Holes Board Book Ser.). (ENG.). (J). 14p. (gr. -1-1). bds. *(978-1-84643-111-1(5))*; 16p. (gr. 1-1). pap. *(978-1-84643-107-4(7))* Child's Play International Ltd.

Studio Mouse, creator. Mother Goose Counting Rhymes. rev. ed. 2006. (ENG., Illus.). 80p. (J). (gr. 4-7). 14.99 *(978-1-59069-485-5(6))* Studio Mouse LLC.

Yolen, Jane. Count Me a Rhyme: Animal Poems by the Numbers. Stemple, Jason, illus. Stemple, Jason, photos by. 2006. (ENG.). 32p. (J). (gr. 5-7). 18.95 *(978-1-59078-345-0(X)*, Wordsong) Boyds Mills Pr.

COUNTRY HOUSES

see Architecture, Domestic

COUNTRY LIFE

Here are entered descriptive, popular and literary works on living in the country. Works dealing with social organization and conditions in rural communities are entered under Sociology, Rural.

see also Farm Life; Outdoor Life; Sociology, Rural

Alatalo, Jaakko. Iina-Marja's Day: From Dawn to Dusk in Lapland. 2011. (Child's Day Ser.). (ENG., Illus.). 32p. (J). (gr. k-3). pap. 8.95 *(978-1-84507-993-2(0)*, Frances Lincoln) Quarto Publishing Group UK GBR. Dist: Hachette Bk. Group.

Austen, Mary. We Live in the Country, 01 vols., 1. 2016. (American Communities Ser.). (ENG., Illus.). 24p. (J). pap. 8.25 *(978-1-5081-4205-8(X)*, PowerKids Pr.) Rosen Publishing Group, Inc., The.

Barber, Nicola. Village Homes. 2007. (Homes Around the World Ser.). (ENG., Illus.). 32p. (J). (gr. 3-7). pap. *(978-0-7787-3558-8(3))* Crabtree Publishing Co.

Barbour, Karen. Mr. Williams. Barbour, Karen, illus. rev. ed. 2005. (ENG., Illus.). 32p. (J). (gr. 1-5). 18.99 *(978-0-8050-6773-6(6)*, 9780805067736, Holt, Henry & Co. Bks. For Young Readers) Holt, Henry & Co.

Bodden, Valerie. A Farming Town. 2011. (My First Look At Ser.). (ENG.). 24p. (J). (gr. 1-17). pap. 7.99 *(978-1-926722-30-6(2)*, Creative Paperbacks) Creative Co., The.

Cane, Ella. Communities in My World, 1 vol. 2013. (My World Ser.). (ENG.). 24p. (gr. k-1). 21.99 *(978-1-4765-3120-5(X))*; pap. 6.95 *(978-1-4765-3462-6(4))* Capstone Press of Coughlan Cos. (Pebble Bks.).

Collard, Sneed B., III. The World Famous Miles City Bucking Horse Sale. 2010. 64p. 18.00 *(978-0-9844460-0-1(1))* Bucking Horse Bks.

Country Insights, 11 bks., Set. (Illus.). (J). (gr. 4-7). lib. bdg. 325.44 *(978-0-8172-4799-7(8))* Heinemann-Raintree.

Dendrites, Waymore. Branton's Blossoms. 2006. per. 5.95 *(978-0-9769715-3-5(4))* Pangus Publishing.

Guin, Valerie. In the Country. 2005. (One World (Smart Apple Media) Ser.). (Illus.). 30p. (J). (gr. 3-6). lib. bdg. 27.10 *(978-1-58340-695-3(6))* Black Rabbit Bks.

Hinds, Kathryn. The Countryside. (Life in Elizabethan England Ser.). (Illus.). 2007. 80p. (J). (gr. 4-7). lib. bdg. 32.79 *(978-0-7614-2543-4(8))* 2006. 70p. (J). (gr. 4-7). lib. bdg. 32.79 *(978-0-7614-2185-6(8))* 2004. 80p. (gr. 6). 34.21 *(978-0-7614-1656-2(0))* Marshall Cavendish Corp. (Benchmark Bks.).

Holland, Gini. I Live in the Country. 2004. (Where I Live Ser.). (Illus.). 24p. (gr. k-3). lib. bdg. 22.00 *(978-0-8368-4079-7(8)*, Weekly Reader Leveled Readers) Stevens, Gareth Publishing LLLP.

—I Live in the Country/Vivo en el Campo. Coffey, Colleen & Carrillo, Consuelo, trs. 2004. (Weekly Reader Early Learning Library). (SPA & ENG., Illus.). 24p. (gr. k-3). lib. bdg. 22.00 *(978-0-8368-4127-5(1)*, Weekly Reader Leveled Readers) Stevens, Gareth Publishing LLLP.

Lane, Allison. The Countryside in the Roman Empire. 2016. (Life in the Roman Empire Ser.). 80p. (J). 35.64 *(978-1-5026-2261-7(0))* Cavendish Square Publishing.

McDonald, Caryl. Rural Life, Urban Life. 2013. (InfoMax Readers Ser.). (ENG.). 24p. (J). (gr. 2-3). pap. 8.25 *(978-1-4777-2346-3(3))*; pap. 49.50 *(978-1-4777-2347-0(1))* Rosen Publishing Group, Inc., The. (Rosen Classroom).

McDowell, Pamela. Small Town. 2016. (Illus.). 24p. (J). pap. *(978-1-4896-3614-0(5))* Weigl Pubs., Inc.

My Cousin Jake: Individual Title Six-Packs. (gr. -1-2). 27.00 *(978-0-7635-9463-3(6))* Rigby Education.

North, Sterling. Rascal. 2004. (Puffin Modern Classics Ser.). (ENG., Illus.). 192p. (J). (gr. 3-7). 5.99 *(978-0-14-240252-8(4)*, Puffin Books) Penguin Young Readers Group.

—Rascal, Mi Tremendo Mapache. 2003. (Cuatro Vientos Ser.: Vol. 9). (SPA.). 168p. (gr. 5-12). pap. 13.99 *(978-84-279-3109-1(3)*, NG3492) Lectorum Pubns., Inc.

Rolbin, Cyrus. Art & Life in Rural Japan: Toho Village Throught the Eyes of Its Youth. 2011. 176p. (J). (gr. 3-6). pap. 24.95 *(978-0-9815595-3-7(0))* Next Generation Pr.

Schomp, Virginia. The Countryside. 2010. (Life in Victorian England Ser.). 80p. (gr. 6). 34.21 *(978-1-60870-030-1(5))* Marshall Cavendish GBR. Dist: Marshall Cavendish Corp.

Schwartz, Heather E. Marjorie Kinnan Rawlings: Writing in Rural Florida. 2016. (Primary Source Readers Ser.). 32p. (J). (gr. 4-4). pap. 8.99 *(978-1-4938-3543-0(2))* Teacher Created Materials, Inc.

Shaffer, Jody Jensen. City & Country. 2017. (Readers Ser.). (ENG.). 48p. (J). (-k). lib. bdg. 14.90 ***(978-1-4263-2887-9(7)***, National Geographic Children's Bks.) National Geographic Society.

Shaffer, Jody Jensen & National Geographic Kids Staff. City & Country, Level 1. 2017. (Readers Ser.). (ENG., Illus.). 48p. (J). (-k). pap. 4.99 ***(978-1-4263-2886-2(9)***, National Geographic Children's Bks.) National Geographic Society.

Sterling, Kristin. Living in Rural Communities. 2008. pap. 34.95 *(978-0-8225-9478-9(1))*; (ENG., Illus.). 24p. lib. bdg. 23.93 *(978-0-8225-8599-2(5)*, Lerner Pubns.) Lerner Publishing Group.

Watson, Danielle. The Countryside in Medieval Europe. 2016. (Life in Medieval Europe Ser.). (Illus.). 80p. (J). (gr. 6-6). 35.64 *(978-1-5026-1882-5(6))* Cavendish Square Publishing.

COUNTRY LIFE—FICTION

Abbott, Jacob. Aunt Margaret; or, How John True Kept His Resolutions. 2013. 160p. pap. 19.95 *(978-1-4455-2937-0(8))* Research Pr.

—Rollo at Play. 2004. reprint ed. pap. 1.99 *(978-1-4192-4527-5(9))*; pap. 15.95 *(978-1-4191-4527-8(4))* Kessinger Publishing, LLC.

Alger, Horatio. Herbert Carter's Legacy. 2006. pap. *(978-1-4065-0710-2(5))* Dodo Pr.

—Herbert Carter's Legacy: Or: the Inventor's Son. 2007. 174p. pap. 19.99 *(978-1-4346-5067-2(7))*; (ENG.). 188p. pap. 21.99 *(978-1-4346-5068-9(5))* Creative Media Partners, LLC.

Ashley-Hollinger, Mika. Precious Bones. 2013. (ENG.). 352p. (J). (gr. 4-7). 8.99 *(978-0-307-93070-5(X)*, Yearling) Random Hse. Children's Bks.

Bailey, Linda. When Addie Was Scared. 2004. (Illus.). (J). (gr. k-3). spiral bd. *(978-0-616-01537-7(2))*; spiral bd. *(978-0-616-01535-3(6))* Canadian National Institute for the Blind/Institut National Canadien pour les Aveugles.

Barklem, Jill. Autumn Story. Barklem, Jill, illus. 2011. (Brambly Hedge Ser.). (ENG., Illus.). 32p. (J). 9.99 *(978-0-00-183739-3(7)*, HarperCollins Children's Bks.) HarperCollins Pubs. Ltd. GBR. Dist: HarperCollins Pubs.

Bauer, Joan. Close to Famous. 2012. (ENG.). 272p. (J). (gr. 5-18). 7.99 *(978-0-14-242017-1(4)*, Puffin Books) Penguin Young Readers Group.

—Squashed. 2005. (ENG.). 208p. (YA). (gr. 7-7). pap. 7.99 *(978-0-14-240426-3(8)*, Speak) Penguin Young Readers Group.

—Squashed. 2005. 194p. (gr. 7-12). 18.00 *(978-0-7569-5781-0(8))* Perfection Learning Corp.

Baum, L. Frank. Mary Louise in the Country. 2011. 188p. pap. 14.95 *(978-1-4638-0069-7(X))* Rodgers, Alan Bks.

Baum, L. Frank & van Dyne, Edith. Mary Louise in the Country. 2011. 188p. 26.95 *(978-1-4638-9605-8(0))* Rodgers, Alan Bks.

Beha, Eileen. Tango: The Tale of an Island Dog. 2010. (ENG.). 256p. (YA). (gr. 3-6). pap. 7.99 *(978-1-59990-485-6(3)*, 9781599904856, Bloomsbury USA Childrens) Bloomsbury Publishing USA.

Bentley, Sue. A Summer Spell. Swan, Angela & Farley, Andrew, illus. 2008. (Magic Kitten Ser.: 1). (ENG.). 128p. (J). (gr. 1-3). pap. 5.99 *(978-0-448-44998-2(6)*, Grosset & Dunlap) Penguin Young Readers Group.

Berning, Terri J. Grace Alone Is Enough, 1 vol. Arling, Jackie L., illus. 2010. 34p. 24.95 *(978-1-4512-9045-5(4))* PublishAmerica, Inc.

Betancourt, Jeanne. Penny & Pepper. Riley, Kellee, illus. 2011. (Scholastic Reader Level 3 Ser.). (ENG.). 48p. (J). (gr. 1-4). pap. 3.99 *(978-0-545-11508-7(6)*, Cartwheel Bks.) Scholastic, Inc.

Birney, Betty G. The Seven Wonders of Sassafras Springs. Phelan, Matt, illus. 2007. 210p. 17.00 *(978-0-7569-8075-7(5))* Perfection Learning Corp.

—The Seven Wonders of Sassafras Springs. Phelan, Matt, illus. (ENG.). 224p. (J). (gr. 3-7). 2007. pap. 7.99 *(978-1-4169-3489-9(8))* 2005. 16.95 *(978-0-689-87136-8(8))* Simon & Schuster Children's Publishing. (Atheneum Bks. for Young Readers).

Blume, Lesley M. M. The Rising Star of Rusty Nail. 2009. (ENG.). 288p. (J). (gr. 3-7). 7.99 *(978-0-440-42111-5(X)*, Yearling) Random Hse. Children's Bks.

Broach, Elise. Wet Dog! Catrow, David, illus. 2007. (ENG.). 32p. (J). (gr. k-3). pap. 5.99 *(978-0-14-240855-1(7)*, Puffin Books) Penguin Young Readers Group.

Brown, Palmer. Cheerful. 2012. (ENG., Illus.). 72p. (J). (gr. -1-2). 12.95 *(978-1-59017-501-9(8)*, NYR Children's Collection) New York Review of Bks., Inc., The.

Burton, Virginia Lee. The Little House. Burton, Virginia Lee, illus. 2009. (ENG., Illus.). 42p. (J). (gr. -1 — 1). bds. 7.99 *(978-0-547-13104-7(6))* Houghton Mifflin Harcourt Publishing Co.

Carter, Alden R. Up Country. 2004. (ENG.). 256p. (YA). (gr. 7-5). 7.99 *(978-0-14-240243-6(5)*, Speak) Penguin Young Readers Group.

Chronicles of Avonlea. 2004. 142p. (YA). pap. 7.95 *(978-1-57646-893-7(3))* Quiet Vision Publishing.

Chwast, Seymour. Tall City, Wide Country. Chwast, Seymour, illus. 2013. (ENG., Illus.). 32p. (J). (gr. -1-k). 15.99 *(978-1-56846-228-8(X)*, Creative Editions) Creative Co., The.

Correa, Alvaro. Mountain Miracle: A Navtivity Story. Lorenzo, Gloria, illus. 2008. 94p. (J). (gr. -1). pap. 14.95 *(978-1-933271-23-1(X))* Circle Pr.

Corum, Stephanie J. Goats with Coats. 2008. 32p. pap. 12.99 *(978-1-4343-9302-9(X))* AuthorHouse.

Creech, Sharon. Moo. 288p. (J). (gr. 3-7). 2017. pap. 6.99 ***(978-0-06-241526-4(3))*** 2016. 16.99 *(978-0-06-241524-0(7))* 2016. lib. bdg. 17.89 *(978-0-06-241525-7(5))* HarperCollins Pubs.

—Moo. 2017. lib. bdg. 17.20 ***(978-0-606-40402-0(3))*** Turtleback Bks.

Creech, Sharon. Ruby Holler. 2012. (ENG.). 288p. (J). (gr. 3-7). pap. 6.99 *(978-0-06-056015-7(0))* HarperCollins Pubs.

—Ruby Holler. 2004. (Joanna Cotler Bks.). 310p. (gr. 3-7). 17.00 *(978-0-7569-1940-5(1))* Perfection Learning Corp.

—Ruby Holler. 2012. (J). (gr. 3-6). 17.20 *(978-0-613-86272-1(4)*, Turtleback) Turtleback Bks.

Cregan, Mairin. Old John. Sewell, Helen, illus. 2012. 198p. 44.95 *(978-1-258-23306-8(1))*; pap. 29.95 *(978-1-258-24727-0(5))* Literary Licensing, LLC.

Croza, Laurel. From There to Here, 1 vol. James, Matt, illus. 2014. (ENG.). 36p. (J). (gr. -1-2). 18.95 *(978-1-55498-365-0(7))* Groundwood Bks. CAN. Dist: Publishers Group West (PGW).

Crumly, Billie Lang. The Best of Country Living. 2004. (Illus.). 171p. per. *(978-0-9760577-0-3(0))* Crumly, Billie.

Cumyn, Alan. The Secret Life of Owen Skye. 2nd ed. 2008. (ENG.). 176p. (J). (gr. 3-7). pap. 9.95 *(978-0-88899-867-5(8))* Groundwood Bks. CAN. Dist: Publishers Group West (PGW).

Cupper, Karin. More Adventures from Eidland. 2013. 128p. (J). pap. *(978-1-78148-603-0(4))* Grosvenor Hse. Publishing Ltd.

Curtin, Judi. Eva's Holiday. 2012. (Eva Ser.). (ENG.). 272p. (J). pap. 12.95 *(978-1-84717-280-8(6))* O'Brien Pr., Ltd., The IRL. Dist: Dufour Editions, Inc.

Davis, Heather. The Clearing. 2010. (ENG., Illus.). 224p. (YA). (gr. 9). pap. 8.99 *(978-0-547-26367-0(8))* Houghton Mifflin Harcourt Publishing Co.

Day, Alexandra. Carl's Summer Vacation. Day, Alexandra, illus. 2008. (Carl Ser.). (ENG., Illus.). 32p. (J). (gr. -1-1). 15.99 *(978-0-374-31085-1(8)*, 9780374310851, Farrar, Straus & Giroux (BYR)) Farrar, Straus & Giroux.

DeFelice, Cynthia C. Signal. 2011. (ENG.). 176p. (J). (gr. 5-8). pap. 8.99 *(978-0-312-61776-9(3)*, 9780312617769) Square Fish.

Dennard, Deborah. Hedgehog Haven: A Story of a British Hedgerow Community. 2005. (Soundprints' Wild Habitats Ser.). (ENG., Illus.). 32p. (J). (gr. 1-4). 8.95 *(978-1-59249-108-7(1)*, SC7020) Soundprints.

—Hedgehog Haven: The Story of an English Hedgerow Community. Hynes, Robert, illus. 2005. (ENG.). (J). (gr. 1-4). 32p. 19.95 *(978-1-56899-989-0(5)*, BC7020); 36p. 15.95

(978-1-56899-987-6(9), B7020); 36p. pap. 6.95 (978-1-56899-988-3(7), S7020) Soundprints.

Drummond, Ree. Little Ree. Rogers, Jacqueline, illus. 2017. (Little Ree Ser.). 40p. (J). (gr. -1-3). 17.99 (978-0-06-245318-1(1)) HarperCollins Pubs.

Dunmore, Helen. Tara's Tree House. Littlewood, Karin, illus. 2005. (Yellow Go Bananas Ser.). (ENG.). 48p. (J). (gr. 3-4). (978-0-7787-2743-9(2)); lib. bdg. (978-0-7787-2721-7(1)) Crabtree Publishing Co.

Ellis, Edward Sylvester. Through Forest & Fire. 2005. pap. 14.95 (978-1-59224-221-4(9)) Wildside Pr., LLC.

Fiona Fox Staff, ed. The Railway Children. 2012. (ENG., Illus.). 64p. (J). 15.00 (978-1-84135-840-6(1)) Award Pubns. Ltd. GBR. Dist: Parkwest Pubns., Inc.

Fisher, Dorothy Canfield. Understood Betsy. 2004. reprint ed. pap. 1.99 (978-1-4192-9201-9(3)); pap. 24.95 (978-1-4179-0955-1(2)) Kessinger Publishing, LLC.

Frazier, Craig. Stanley Goes for a Drive. 2004. (Stanley Ser.: STAN). (ENG., Illus.). 40p. (J). (gr. -1-7). 15.95 (978-0-8118-4429-1(3)) Chronicle Bks. LLC.

Gaines, Ernest J. A Long Day in November. 2013. (ENG., Illus.). 160p. (gr. 2). pap. 11.95 (978-1-939601-02-5(9)) Ig Publishing, Inc.

Garis, Howard Roger. Uncle Wiggily in the Country. Date not set. 192p. (J). 20.95 (978-0-8488-2282-8(X)) Amereon Ltd.

Garland, Michael. King Puck. Garland, Michael, illus. 2007. (Illus.). 32p. (J). (gr. -1-3). (ENG.). 16.99 (978-0-06-084809-5(X)); lib. bdg. 18.99 (978-0-06-084810-1(3)) HarperCollins Pubs.

Gibbons, Faye. Full Steam Ahead. Meidell, Sherry, illus. 2003. (ENG.). 32p. (J). (gr. k-2). 15.95 (978-1-56397-858-6(X)) Boyds Mills Pr.

Godwin, Laura. One Moon, Two Cats. Tanaka, Yoko, illus. 2011. (ENG.). 32p. (J). (gr. -1-1). 16.99 (978-1-4424-1202-6(X), Atheneum Bks. for Young Readers) Simon & Schuster Children's Publishing.

Grab, Daphne. Alive & Well in Prague, New York. 2008. (Laura Geringer Bks.). 247p. (YA). (gr. 7-18). lib. bdg. 17.89 (978-0-06-125671-4(4), Geringer, Laura Book) HarperCollins Pubs.

Green, Connie Jordan. Emmy. 2nd ed. 2007. (J). pap. 15.00 (978-1-60454-000-0(1)) Iris Publishing Group, Inc., The.

Guest, Elissa Haden. Iris & Walter. 2012. (Iris & Walter — Green Light Reader Ser.). lib. bdg. 13.55 (978-0-606-24229-5(5), Turtleback) Turtleback Bks.

—Iris & Walter Book & CD. Davenier, Christine, illus. 2015. (Green Light Readers Level 3 Ser.). (ENG.). 44p. (J). (gr. -1-3). audio compact disk 6.99 (978-0-544-45604-4(1), HMH Books For Young Readers) Houghton Mifflin Harcourt Publishing Co.

Hadley, Caroline. Woodside; or, Look, Listen & Learn. 2007. (ENG., Illus.). 80p. per. (978-1-4065-1557-2(4)) Dodo Pr.

Hamilton, Virginia. M. C. Higgins, the Great. 2006. 271p. (gr. 8-12). 18.00 (978-0-7569-6809-0(7)) Perfection Learning Corp.

Harrar, George. The Trouble with Jeremy Chance. Thayer, Elizabeth, illus. 2007. (Historical Fiction for Young Readers Ser.). (ENG.). 168p. (J). (gr. 2-8). per. 6.95 (978-1-57131-669-1(8)) Milkweed Editions.

Haywood, Carolyn. Two & Two Are Four. 2005. (ENG., Illus.). 160p. (J). (gr. 1-4). pap. 10.95 (978-0-15-205231-7(3)) Houghton Mifflin Harcourt Publishing Co.

Hedrick, Helen Groves. Tails, Trails & Pies: An Appalachian Cattle Drive. Spiker, Sue Ann Maxwell, illus. 2008. 32p. 15.95 (978-0-929915-87-6(9)) Headline Bks., Inc.

Helldorfer, M. C. Anne of Green Gables. Beier, Ellen, illus. 2003. (ENG.). 40p. (J). (gr. -1-2). pap. 7.99 (978-0-440-41614-2(0), Dragonfly Bks.) Random Hse. Children's Bks.

Henry, Beresford. The Gaulin & the Dove. 2008. 128p. (J). pap. (978-0-435-89938-7(4)) Pearson Education, Ltd.

Henson, Heather. Grumpy Grandpa. MacDonald, Ross, illus. 2009. (ENG.). 40p. (J). (gr. -1-3). 16.99 (978-1-4169-0811-1(0), Atheneum Bks. for Young Readers) Simon & Schuster Children's Publishing.

Herrick, Steven. Cold Skin. 2009. (ENG.). 279p. (YA). (gr. 9-18). 18.95 (978-1-59078-572-0(X), Front Street) Boyds Mills Pr.

Hilmo, Tess. With a Name Like Love. 2013. (ENG.). 272p. (J). (gr. 5-9). pap. 10.99 (978-1-250-02733-7(0), 9781250027337) Square Fish.

Hobbs, Constance. Bugsy's Special Event. 2008. 64p. pap. 10.50 (978-0-9556783-7-0(4)) Hobbs, Constance GBR. Dist: Lulu Pr., Inc.

Hoberman, Mary Ann. Strawberry Hill. 2010. (ENG., Illus.). 240p. (J). (gr. 3-7). pap. 7.99 (978-0-316-04135-5(1)) Little, Brown Bks. for Young Readers.

Hope, Laura Lee. The Bobbsey Twins at Meadow Brook. 2005. 200p. 27.95 (978-1-4218-0653-2(3), 1st World Library - Literary Society) 1st World Publishing, Inc.

—The Bobbsey Twins at the Seashore. 2005. 26.95 (978-1-4218-1070-6(0)); 176p. pap. 11.95 (978-1-4218-1170-3(7)) 1st World Publishing, Inc. (1st World Library - Literary Society).

—The Bobbsey Twins in the Country. 2005. 208p. 27.95 (978-1-4218-0655-6(X), 1st World Library - Literary Society) 1st World Publishing, Inc.

—The Bobbsey Twins in the Great West. 2005. 27.95 (978-1-4218-0365-4(8), 1st World Library - Literary Society) 1st World Publishing, Inc.

Howard, Vera. My Gran: Country Stories for Young Children. 2004. 88p. pap. (978-1-84401-331-9(6)) Athena Pr.

Jeffers, Sunni. Eyes on the Prize. 2009. (Tales from Grace Chapel Inn Ser.). (ENG.). 328p. pap. 13.99 (978-0-8249-4787-3(8), Ideal Pubns.) Worthy Publishing.

Johnson, Sandi. Cowgirls Dream. Perritt, Jordona, illus. Date not set. (Kooky Kountry Ser.). (J). (gr. -1-6). 8.99 (978-1-929063-56-7(3)) Moons & Stars Publishing For Children.

Jon Scieszkas Trucktown, et al. Take a Trip with Trucktown! Gordon, David et al, illus. 2011. (Jon Scieszka's Trucktown Ser.). (ENG.). 24p. (J). (gr. -1-3). pap. 3.99 (978-1-4169-4181-1(9), Simon & Schuster Bks. For Young Readers) Simon & Schuster Bks. For Young Readers.

Jones, Judith. You're from Where Grandma? 2011. 24p. pap. 12.99 (978-1-4568-8150-4(7)) Xlibris Corp.

Kessler, Deirdre & Montgomery, L. M. Anne of Green Gables, 1 vol. Smith, David Preston, illus. 2008. (ENG.). 46p. (J). (gr. k-5). pap. 10.95 (978-1-55109-662-9(5)) Nimbus Publishing, Ltd. CAN. Dist: Orca Bk. Pubs. USA.

Lawrence, Mary. Que Es Ese Sonido? Adams, Lynn, illus. 2008. (Science Solves It! en Espanol Ser.). (SPA.). 32p. (J). (gr. -1-3). pap. 5.95 (978-1-57565-266-5(8)) Kane Press, Inc.

—¿Qué es Ese Sonido? (What's That Sound?) Adams, Lynn, illus. 2009. (Science Solves It! (r) en Espanol Ser.). (SPA.). (gr. k-2). pap. 33.92 (978-0-7613-4801-6(8)) Lerner Publishing Group.

Les Becquets, Diane. The Stones of Mourning Creek, 0 vols. 2005. (ENG.). 320p. (YA). (gr. 7-9). reprint ed. pap. 9.99 (978-0-7614-5238-6(9), 9780761452386, Amazon Children's Publishing) Amazon Publishing.

Levine, Kristin. The Best Bad Luck I Ever Had. 2010. (ENG.). 272p. (J). (gr. 5-18). 7.99 (978-0-14-241648-8(7), Puffin Books) Penguin Young Readers Group.

Lewis, Beverly. SummerHill Secrets, Vol. 2. 2007. (Summerhill Secrets Ser.: Vols. 6-10). (ENG., Illus.). 544p. (gr. 11-12). pap. 17.00 (978-0-7642-0452-4(1)) Bethany Hse. Pubs.

MacDonald, George. Ranald Bannermans Boyhood. 2006. 168p. per. 13.95 (978-1-59818-238-5(2)) Aegypan.

MacLachlan, Patricia. The Boxcar Children Beginning. Jessell, Tim, illus. (Boxcar Children Mysteries Ser.). (ENG.). 144p. (J). (gr. 1-5). 2013. 6.99 (978-0-8075-6617-6(9)) 2012. 16.99 (978-0-8075-6616-9(0)) Whitman, Albert & Co.

—Just Dance. 2017. (ENG., Illus.). 128p. (J). (gr. 2). 15.99 **(978-1-4814-7252-4(6)**, McElderry, Margaret K. Bks.) McElderry, Margaret K. Bks.

MacLachlan, Patricia. What You Know First. 2007. 17.00 (978-0-7569-7908-9(0)) Perfection Learning Corp.

Magnin, Joyce. Carrying Mason, 1 vol. 2013. (ENG.). 176p. (J). pap. 6.99 (978-0-310-72682-1(4)) Zonderkidz.

Mansfield, Creina. My Nutty Neighbours. 2006. (ENG., Illus.). 192p. (J). pap. 12.95 (978-0-86278-788-2(2)) O'Brien Pr., Ltd., The IRL. Dist: Dufour Editions, Inc.

Marsh, Barry. Good Harbor Bay. 2009. (J). 14.95 (978-0-9767268-1-4(5)) Crofton Creek Pr.

McCormick, Wendy. Daniel & His Walking Stick, 1 vol. Bergum, Constance R., illus. 2005. (ENG.). 32p. (J). (gr. k-3). 15.95 (978-1-56145-330-6(7)) Peachtree Pubs.

McQuinn, Anna. A Rosette for Maeve? Young, Paul, illus. 2014. (ENG.). 32p. (J). pap. 13.95 (978-1-84717-340-9(3)) O'Brien Pr., Ltd., The IRL. Dist: Dufour Editions, Inc.

Merkel, Ruth Vitrano. Hannah's Girls: Erin (Born 1988) 2009. (J). 9.99 (978-0-8280-1956-9(8)) Review & Herald Publishing Assn.

Meyer, Carolyn. Loving Will Shakespeare. 2008. (ENG., Illus.). 272p. (YA). (gr. 7-12). pap. 6.95 (978-0-15-206221-7(1)) Houghton Mifflin Harcourt Publishing Co.

Montgomery, L. M. Anne of Green Gables. 400p. 2005. 33.95 (978-1-4218-0660-0(6), 1st World Library - Literary Society) 2004. per. 16.95 (978-1-59540-110-6(5)) 1st World Publishing, Inc.

—Anne of Green Gables. 2009. 292p. 27.99 (978-1-60512-375-2(7)); pap. 14.99 (978-1-60512-475-9(3)) Akasha Publishing, LLC. (Akasha Classics).

—Anne of Green Gables. 2008. 316p. 29.99 (978-0-554-23545-5(5)) 2008. 316p. 28.99 (978-0-554-32848-5(8)) 2007. (ENG.). 312p. pap. 24.99 (978-1-4264-4662-7(4)) Creative Media Partners, LLC.

—Anne of Green Gables. 2008. (Anne of Green Gables Ser.). (ENG.). 366p. (J). (gr. 4-7). pap. 9.95 (978-0-9782552-6-8(7)) Davenport Pr. CAN. Dist: Independent Pubs. Group.

—Anne of Green Gables. 2007. per. 6.99 (978-1-4209-2922-5(4)) Digireads.com Publishing.

—Anne of Green Gables. 2007. 284p. per. (978-1-4065-6399-3(4)) Dodo Pr.

—Anne of Green Gables. 2007. 572p. (978-1-84702-773-3(3)) 2006. pap. (978-1-4068-2170-3(5)) Echo Library.

—Anne of Green Gables. 2008. 316p. pap. 16.95 (978-1-60096-565-4(2)); pap. 16.95 (978-1-60096-101-4(0)) Editorium, The.

—Anne of Green Gables. 2009. 242p. pap. 8.58 (978-0-217-43952-7(7)) General Bks. LLC.

—Anne of Green Gables. 2005. (My First Classics Ser.). 112p. (J). (gr. k-3). pap., pap. 4.99 (978-0-06-079147-6(0), HarperFestival) HarperCollins Pubs.

—Anne of Green Gables. 2005. 21.99 (978-1-4142-5125-7(4)) IndyPublish.com.

—Anne of Green Gables. 2008. (ENG.). 376p. (gr. k-12). pap. 14.95 (978-0-7710-9368-5(3), New Can Library) McClelland & Stewart CAN. Dist: Penguin Random Hse. LLC.

—Anne of Green Gables, 1 vol. 2016. (ENG.). 352p. (J). (gr. 2-5). pap. 10.95 (978-1-55109-249-2(2)) Nimbus Publishing, Ltd. CAN. Dist: National Bk. Network.

—Anne of Green Gables. Rubio, Mary Henley & Waterston, Elizabeth, eds. 2007. (Norton Critical Editions Ser.: 0). (ENG., Illus.). 464p. (C). (gr. 9-12). per. 15.02 (978-0-393-92695-8(8), 92695) Norton, W. W. & Co., Inc.

—Anne of Green Gables. 2003. (ENG.). 320p. (gr. 5-7). 5.95 (978-0-451-52882-7(4), Signet) Penguin Publishing Group.

—Anne of Green Gables. 2008. (Puffin Classics Ser.). (ENG., Illus.). 464p. (J). (gr. 3-7). 5.99 (978-0-14-132159-2(8), Puffin Books) Penguin Young Readers Group.

—Anne of Green Gables. 2003. 320p. (J). (gr. 4-7). 12.60 (978-0-7569-1848-4(0)) Perfection Learning Corp.

—Anne of Green Gables. 2013. (Word Cloud Classics Ser.). (ENG.). 264p. pap. 14.99 (978-1-60710-728-6(7), Thunder Bay Pr.) Readerlink Distribution Services, LLC.

—Anne of Green Gables. 2009. 224p. pap. 15.45 (978-1-4385-1847-3(1), Book Jungle) Standard Pubns., Inc.

—Anne of Green Gables. McKowen, Scott, illus. 2004. (Sterling Unabridged Classics Ser.). (ENG.). 312p. (J). (gr. 5). 9.95 (978-1-4027-1451-1(3)) Sterling Publishing Co., Inc.

—Anne of Green Gables. Corvino, Lucy, illus. 2005. (Classic Starts(tm) Ser.). (ENG.). 160p. (J). (gr. 2-4). 6.95 (978-1-4027-1130-5(1)) Sterling Publishing Co., Inc.

—Anne of Green Gables. 2008. (Modern Library Classics Ser.). (ENG.). 320p. pap. 9.00 (978-0-8129-7903-9(6), Modern Library) Random House Publishing Group.

—Anne of Green Gables. 2012. (World Classics Ser.). (ENG.). 260p. pap. 19.99 (978-1-909438-96-5(0), Sovereign) Bollinger, Max GBR. Dist: Lightning Source UK, Ltd.

—Anne of Green Gables. rev. ed. 2007. 280p. pap. 21.99 (978-1-4264-4611-5(X)) Creative Media Partners, LLC.

—Anne of Green Gables. l.t. ed. 2006. pap. (978-1-4068-3174-0(3)) Echo Library.

—Anne of Green Gables. 2004. reprint ed. pap. 27.95 (978-1-4191-0717-7(8)); pap. 1.99 (978-1-4192-0717-4(2)) Kessinger Publishing, LLC.

—Anne of Green Gables. l.t. ed. 2009. (World Classics Ser.). 288p. pap. 21.95 (978-1-59688-123-5(2)) Large Print Bk. Co., The.

—The Anne of Green Gables Collection: Six Complete & Unabridged Novels in One Volume. 2013. 1140p. (978-1-78139-344-4(3)) Benediction Classics.

—Anne of the Green Gables. 2014. (Anne of Green Gables Ser.: 1). (ENG.). 352p. (YA). (gr. 5-12). pap. 9.99 (978-1-4022-8894-4(8)) Sourcebooks, Inc.

Montgomery, L. M & Castelao, Patricia. Anne of Green Gables, 1 vol. 2012. (Calico Illustrated Classics Ser.: No. 4). (ENG., Illus.). 112p. (J). (gr. 3-6). 27.07 (978-1-61641-612-6(2)) Magic Wagon.

Moverley, Richard. The Reluctant Rajput. Dean, David, illus. 2005. (Yellow Go Bananas Ser.). (ENG.). 48p. (J). (gr. 3-4). lib. bdg. (978-0-7787-2723-1(8)) Crabtree Publishing Co.

Napoli, Donna Jo. Alligator Bayou. 2010. (ENG.). 288p. (YA). (gr. 7). pap. 8.99 (978-0-553-49417-4(1), Lamb, Wendy Bks.) Random Hse. Children's Bks.

Nesbit, E. The Railway Children. 2007. 236p. per. 12.95 (978-1-4218-3945-5(8)); (ENG.). (gr. 4-7). 27.95 (978-1-4218-3845-8(1)) 1st World Publishing, Inc. (1st World Library - Literary Society).

—The Railway Children. 2006. (ENG.). 228p. (gr. 4-7). per. 14.95 (978-1-59818-933-9(6)); 26.95 (978-1-59818-179-1(3)) Aegypan.

—The Railway Children. 2013. 140p. pap. (978-1-908388-94-0(3)) Aziloth Bks.

—The Railway Children. 2008. (J). 8.99 (978-1-59166-924-1(3)) BJU Pr.

—The Railway Children. Brock, C. E., illus. (YA). 14.95 (978-0-8118-4933-3(3)) Chronicle Bks. LLC.

—The Railway Children. 2012. (ENG.). 234p. pap. 14.99 (978-1-4812-4818-1(9)) CreateSpace Independent Publishing Platform.

—The Railway Children. 2008. 204p. (gr. 4-7). 24.99 (978-0-554-36009-6(8)); 27.99 (978-0-554-26706-7(3)) Creative Media Partners, LLC.

—The Railway Children. 2008. (gr. 4-7). pap. 5.99 (978-1-4209-3105-1(9)) Digireads.com Publishing.

—The Railway Children. Brock, C. E., illus. 2008. (ENG.). 248p. per. (978-1-4065-9815-5(1)) Dodo Pr.

—The Railway Children. 2007. (ENG.). 204p. per. (978-1-4065-3083-4(2)) Dodo Pr.

—The Railway Children. 2006. pap. (978-1-4068-3505-2(6)) 2005. 348p. pap. (978-1-84637-205-6(4)) Echo Library.

—The Railway Children. Brock, Charles Edmund, illus. 2012. 232p. pap. (978-1-78201-004-3(1)) Evertype.

—The Railway Children. 2010. (Illus.). 118p. pap. 19.99 (978-1-153-71841-7(3)) General Bks. LLC.

—The Railway Children. Dryhurst, Dinah, tr. Dryhurst, Dinah, illus. 2004. 184p. 18.95 (978-1-56792-261-5(9)) Godine, David R. Pub.

—The Railway Children. 2010. 184p. pap. (978-1-4076-1891-3(1)) HardPr.

—The Railway Children. (J). (978-0-340-71497-3(2)) Hodder & Stoughton.

—The Railway Children. 2010. 194p. 30.36 (978-1-169-28328-2(4)) 2010. 194p. pap. 18.36 (978-1-162-70632-0(5)) 2010. 194p. 37.95 (978-1-161-47496-1(X)) 2004. reprint ed. pap. 22.95 (978-1-4191-7972-3(1)) 2004. reprint ed. pap. 1.99 (978-1-4192-7972-0(6)) Kessinger Publishing, LLC.

—The Railway Children. 2006. (Twelve-Point Ser.). lib. bdg. 25.00 (978-1-58287-399-2(2)); lib. bdg. 26.00 (978-1-58287-890-4(0)) North Bks.

—The Railway Children. 2012. (Oxford Children's Classics Ser.). (ENG.). 240p. 9.95 (978-0-19-275819-4(5)) Oxford Univ. Pr., Inc.

—The Railway Children. unabr. ed. 2004. (Chrysalis Childrens Classics Ser.). (Illus.). 128p. (YA). pap. (978-1-84365-050-8(9), Pavilion Children's Books) Pavilion Bks.

—The Railway Children. 2nd ed. 2008. (ENG., Illus.). 48p. pap. 11.99 (978-1-4058-6964-5(X)) Pearson Education.

—The Railway Children. 2nd ed. 2011. (Puffin Classics Ser.). (ENG., Illus.). 304p. (J). (gr. 5-7). pap. 5.99 (978-0-14-132160-8(1), Puffin Books) Penguin Young Readers Group.

—The Railway Children. (ENG.). (J). (gr. 4-7). 2013. 320p. pap. 10.99 (978-0-09-957299-2(0)) 2012. 290p. 10.99 (978-0-09-957715-7(1)) Random Hse. GBR. Dist: Independent Pubs. Group.

—The Railway Children. 2010. 146p. (gr. 4-7). pap. 8.95 (978-1-61104-337-2(9)) ReadaClassic.com.

—The Railway Children. 2004. (ENG.). 580p. (978-0-9548401-2-9(7)) Shoes & Ships & Sealing Wax Ltd.

—The Railway Children. 2011. 200p. (gr. 4-7). pap. (978-3-8424-4120-0(7)) Tredition GmbH.

—The Railway Children. 2009. 156p. (gr. 4-7). pap. 6.99 (978-1-60459-698-4(8)) Wilder Pubns., Corp.

Newman, Gerry. Nellie, the Scarecrow: A Dorset Fable. 2003. (Illus.). 188p. pap. 12.50 (978-1-84426-184-0(0)) Upfront Publishing Ltd. GBR. Dist: Printondemand-worldwide.com.

Nolan, Lucy. The Lizard Man of Crabtree County, 1 vol. Kastner, Jill, illus. 2003. (ENG.). 32p. (J). (gr. 1-4). pap. 5.95 (978-0-7614-5144-0(7)) Marshall Cavendish Corp.

Paulsen, Gary. Fishbone's Song. 2016. (ENG., Illus.). 160p. (J). (gr. 5). 16.99 (978-1-4814-5226-7(6), Simon & Schuster Bks. For Young Readers) Simon & Schuster Bks. For Young Readers.

Pavlicin, Karen. Perch, Mrs. Sackets, & Crow's Nest. 2007. (J). (ENG.). 160p. 16.95 (978-1-934617-00-7(8)); pap. (978-1-934617-01-4(6)) Elva Resa Publishing, LLC. (Alma Little).

—Summer of Courage. 2014. (ENG.). 160p. (J). pap. 12.95 (978-1-934617-24-3(5), Alma Little) Elva Resa Publishing, LLC.

Peck, Richard. Here Lies the Librarian. 2007. (ENG.). 160p. (J). (gr. 5-18). 7.99 (978-0-14-240908-4(1), Puffin Books) Penguin Young Readers Group.

—Here Lies the Librarian. 2007. 145p. (J). (gr. 4-7). 14.65 (978-0-7569-8193-8(X)) Perfection Learning Corp.

—Here Lies the Librarian. rev. l.t. ed. 2007. (Thorndike Literacy Bridge Ser.). 173p. (J). (gr. 5-9). 23.95 (978-0-7862-9183-0(4)) Thorndike Pr.

—A Long Way from Chicago. 2004. (Puffin Modern Classics Ser.). (ENG.). 160p. (J). (gr. 5-7). pap. 7.99 (978-0-14-240110-1(2), Puffin Books) Penguin Young Readers Group.

—The Teacher's Funeral. 2006. (ENG.). 224p. (J). (gr. 3-7). reprint ed. 7.99 (978-0-14-240507-9(8), Puffin Books) Penguin Young Readers Group.

—A Year down Yonder. unabr. ed. 2004. (Middle Grade Cassette Librariestm Ser.). 144p. (J). (gr. 5-9). pap. 29.00 incl. audio (978-0-8072-0991-2(0), S YA 256 SP, Listening Library) Random Hse. Audio Publishing Group.

Pelletier, Cathie. The Summer Experiment. 2014. (ENG.). 288p. (J). (gr. 4-7). 16.99 (978-1-4022-8578-3(7), 9781402285783, Sourcebooks Jabberwocky) Sourcebooks, Inc.

Plastow, Joan. Adventures of Joe. 2003. (Illus.). 68p. pap. (978-1-84401-144-5(5)) Athena Pr.

Polacco, Patricia. Meteor! 2014. 32p. pap. 7.00 (978-1-61003-312-1(4)) Center for the Collaborative Classroom.

Polette, Keith. Moon over the Mountain. Russik, Michael, illus. 2010. (ENG.). 32p. (J). (gr. -1-3). pap. 7.95 (978-1-934960-08-0(X), Raven Tree Pr.,Csi) Continental Sales, Inc.

Randles, Slim & Montoya, Jerry, illus. Ol' Jimmy Dollar. 2015. 42p. (J). (978-1-936744-40-4(6)) LPD Pr.

Ransom, Candice. Finding Day's Bottom. 2006. 176p. (J). (gr. 3-7). lib. bdg. 15.95 (978-1-57505-933-4(9), Carolrhoda Bks.) Lerner Publishing Group.

—Rebel Mckenzie. 2013. (ENG.). 288p. (J). (gr. 3-7). pap. 7.99 (978-1-4231-6388-6(5)) Hyperion Pr.

—Seeing Sky-Blue Pink. 2007. (Exceptional Reading & Language Arts Titles for Intermediate Grades Ser.). 122p. (J). (gr. 4-7). 16.95 (978-0-8225-7142-1(0), Carolrhoda Bks.) Lerner Publishing Group.

Raye, Rebekah. Bear-Ly There. Raye, Rebekah, illus. 2009. (ENG., Illus.). 32p. (gr. 3-6). 16.95 (978-0-88448-314-4(2), 884314) Tilbury Hse. Pubs.

Resau, Laura. What the Moon Saw. 2008. (ENG.). 272p. (J). (gr. 3-7). pap. 7.99 (978-0-440-23957-4(5), Yearling) Random Hse. Children's Bks.

Reynolds, Jason. As Brave As You. (ENG.). 432p. (J). (gr. 5). 2017. pap. 7.99 (978-1-4814-1591-0(3), Atheneum Bks. for Young Readers) 2016. (Illus.). 16.99 (978-1-4814-1590-3(5), Atheneum/Caitlyn Dlouhy Books) Simon & Schuster Children's Publishing.

Rosen, Michael J. A Drive in the Country. Burckhardt, Marc, illus. 2007. (ENG.). 32p. (J). (gr. k-4). 16.99 (978-0-7636-2140-7(4)) Candlewick Pr.

Rylant, Cynthia. Night in the Country. Szilagyi, Mary, illus. 2014. 32p. pap. 7.00 (978-1-61003-359-6(0)) Center for the Collaborative Classroom.

Salisbury, Linda G. Trouble in Contrary Woods: A Bailey Fish Adventure. Tornatore, Carol, illus. 2009. (J). 8.85 (978-1-881539-46-9(6)) Tabby Hse. Bks.

Santillan, Suzanne. Grandma's Pear Tree. Pernisco, Atilio, illus. 2010. (ENG.). 32p. (J). (gr. 4-7). 16.95 (978-1-934960-82-0(9), Raven Tree Pr.,Csi) Continental Sales, Inc.

—Grandma's Pear Tree/El Peral de Abuela. Pernisco, Atilio, illus. 2010. (ENG & SPA.). 32p. (J). (gr. 4-7). 16.95 (978-1-934960-80-6(2), Raven Tree Pr.,Csi) Continental Sales, Inc.

Selden, George. Tucker's Countryside. Williams, Garth, illus. 2012. (ENG.). 192p. (J). (gr. 3-7). pap. 7.99 (978-1-250-00256-3(7), 9781250002563) Square Fish.

Slayton, Fran. When the Whistle Blows. 2010. (ENG.). 176p. (J). (gr. 5-18). 6.99 (978-0-14-241732-4(7), Puffin Books) Penguin Young Readers Group.

Smith, Alex T. Claude in the Country, 1 vol. Smith, Alex T., illus. 2016. (Claude Ser.). (ENG., Illus.). 96p. (J). (gr. 1-3). 12.95 (978-1-56145-918-6(6)) Peachtree Pubs.

Smith, Ronald L. Hoodoo. 2015. (ENG.). 224p. (J). (gr. 5-7). 16.99 (978-0-544-44525-3(2), Clarion Bks.) Houghton Mifflin Harcourt Trade & Reference Pubs.

—Hoodoo. 2017. (ENG.). (J). (gr. 5-7). lib. bdg. 18.40 **(978-0-606-39820-6(1))** Turtleback Bks.

Snyder, Laurel. Penny Dreadful. Halpin, Abigail, illus. 2011. (ENG.). 320p. (J). (gr. 3-7). 8.99 (978-0-375-86169-7(6), Yearling) Random Hse. Children's Bks.

Stone, Phoebe. Deep down Popular. 2010. (ENG.). 288p. (J). (gr. 4-7). 6.99 (978-0-439-80244-4(X), Levine, Arthur A. Bks.) Scholastic, Inc.

Sullivan, Sarah. Passing the Music Down. Root, Barry, illus. 2011. (ENG.). 32p. (J). (gr. k-3). 17.99 (978-0-7636-3753-8(X)) Candlewick Pr.

Supplee, Suzanne. Somebody Everybody Listens To. 2011. (ENG.). 288p. (YA). (gr. 7-18). 8.99 (978-0-14-241886-4(2), Speak) Penguin Young Readers Group.

Thomas, Cynthia. Little Mountain Princess. 2008. 32p. pap. 12.95 (978-1-933912-84-4(7)) Westview Publishing Co., Inc.

Tonatiuh, Duncan. Dear Primo: A Letter to My Cousin. 2010. (ENG., Illus.). 32p. (J). (gr. k-2). 16.95 (978-0-8109-3872-4(3), Abrams Bks. for Young Readers) Abrams, Inc.

Townsend, Wendy. Lizard Love. 2013. 198p. 18.95 (978-1-60898-151-9(7)) namelos llc.

Trimble, Tonya. Curiosity, with a Capital S. Enik, Ted, illus. 2011. 144p. (J). pap. 9.95 (978-0-9816453-9-1(9)); 16.95 (978-0-9829421-5-4(X)) Tell Me Pr., LLC.

Uttley, Alison & Singh, Mahendra. A Traveller in Time. Bray, Phyllis, illus. 2011. (ENG.). 336p. (J). (gr. 4-7). 17.95 (978-1-59017-388-6(0), NYR Children's Collection) New York Review of Bks., Inc., The.

Van Dyne, Edith. Mary Louise. 2007. (ENG.). 148p. pap. 18.99 (978-1-4264-1952-2(X)); 144p. pap. 19.99 (978-1-4264-2063-4(3)) Creative Media Partners, LLC.

Van Stockum, Hilda. A Day on Skates: The Story of a Dutch Picnic. Van Stockum, Hilda, illus. 2007. (Illus.). 40p. (J). (gr. 1). 19.95 *(978-1-932350-18-0(7))* Bethlehem Bks.

Wallace, Sandra Neil. Little Joe. Elliott, Mark, illus. 2011. (ENG.). 192p. (J). (gr. 3-7). 6.99 *(978-0-375-85450-7(9)*, Yearling) Random Hse. Children's Bks.

Wax, Wendy. City Witch, Country Switch, 0 vols. Gibala-Broxholm, Scott, illus. 2013. (ENG.). 42p. (J). (gr. -1-3). pap. 9.99 *(978-1-4778-1676-9(3)*, 9781477816769, Amazon Children's Publishing) Amazon Publishing.

Wells, Helen. Cherry Ames, Rural Nurse. 2007. (Cherry Ames Nurse Stories Ser.). 224p. (J). (gr. 3-7). 14.95 *(978-0-8261-0425-0(8))* Springer Publishing Co., Inc.

Where the Red Fern Grows. 8.97 *(978-0-673-58326-0(0))* Addison-Wesley Longman, Inc.

White, Ruth. A Month of Sundays. 2013. (ENG.). 192p. (YA). (gr. 5-9). pap. 6.99 *(978-1-250-02730-6(6)*, 9781250027306) Square Fish.

Wyatt, Melissa. Funny How Things Change. 2009. (ENG.). 208p. (YA). (gr. 9-13). 26.99 *(978-0-374-30233-7(2)*, Farrar, Straus & Giroux (BYR)) Farrar, Straus & Giroux.

Zentner, Jeff. The Serpent King. 2016. (ENG.). 384p. (YA). (gr. 9). 17.99 *(978-0-553-52402-4(X)*, Crown Books For Young Readers) Random Hse. Children's Bks.

COUPS D'ETAT

see Revolutions

COURAGE

see also Fear; Heroes

Amoroso, Cynthia. Courage. 2013. (Values to Live By Ser.). (ENG.). 24p. (J). (gr. -1-2). 25.64 *(978-1-62323-516-1(2)*, 206287) Child's World, Inc., The.

Arnaldo, Monica. The Little Book of Big Fears. 2015. (ENG., Illus.). 40p. (J). (gr. k-4). 16.95 *(978-1-77147-047-6(X)*, Owlkids) Owlkids Bks. Inc. CAN. Dist: Publishers Group West (PGW).

Burns, Heidi A., contrib. by. U. S. Army True Stories: Tales of Bravery. 2014. (Courage under Fire Ser.). (ENG.). 32p. (gr. 3-4). lib. bdg. 27.99 *(978-1-4765-9938-0(6))* Capstone Press of Coughlan Cos.

Character Ed Says Courtesy Is Contagious. 2006. (J). 4.95 *(978-1-55548-055-4(1)*, 676) Human Relations Media.

Dowswell, Paul. True Stories of Heroes. rev. ed. 2004. (True Stories Ser.). 144p. (J). pap. 4.99 *(978-0-7945-0094-8(3))* EDC Publishing.

Doyle, Bill H. Behind Enemy Lines. 2009. 135p. (J). pap. *(978-0-545-14705-7(0))* Scholastic, Inc.

—Behind Enemy Lines: Under Fire in the Middle East. 2011. 136p. (J). pap. *(978-0-545-33463-1(2))* Scholastic, Inc.

Edgar, Kathleen J., et al. Courage. 2003. (J). *(978-1-59203-056-9(4))* Learning Challenge, Inc.

Edgar, Susan E. & Edgar, Kathleen J. 50 American Women of Courage & Vision. 2007. (Illus.). 288p. (J). *(978-1-58865-391-8(9))* Kidsbooks, LLC.

Francis, Dorothy Brenner. Courage on the Oregon Trail. 2003. (Reading Essentials in Social Studies). (Illus.). 40p. pap. 8.00 *(978-0-7891-5872-7(8))* Perfection Learning Corp.

Frankel, Erin. Dare!, Bk. 2. Heaphy, Paula, illus. 2012. (Weird! Ser.). (ENG.). 48p. (J). (gr. k-4). 15.99 *(978-1-57542-399-9(5))* Free Spirit Publishing, Inc.

Greive, Bradley Trevor. A Teaspoon of Courage for Kids: A Little Book of Encouragement for Whenever You Need It. 2007. (ENG., Illus.). 48p. (gr. 1-7). 9.99 *(978-0-7407-6949-8(9))* Andrews McMeel Publishing.

Gunderson, Jessica. U. S. Navy True Stories: Tales of Bravery. 2014. (Courage under Fire Ser.). (ENG.). 32p. (gr. 3-4). lib. bdg. 27.99 *(978-1-4765-9937-3(8))* Capstone Press of Coughlan Cos.

Hamilton, Elizabeth L. & Hamilton, David E. Courage. 2003. (Character Builder Ser.: No. 2). 64p. per. 5.95 *(978-0-9713749-8-0(8)*, Character-in-Action) Quiet Impact, Inc.

Hanson, Anders. Stand up for Yourself: The Kids' Book of Courage, 1 vol. 2014. (What We Stand For Ser.). (ENG.). 24p. (gr. 5-10). lib. bdg. 25.65 *(978-1-62403-297-4(4)*, Super SandCastle) ABDO Publishing Co.

HarperCollins UK Staff. Real Heroes Vol. 2: Courage under Fire. 2011. (ENG., Illus.). 192p. 19.95 *(978-0-00-737903-3(X))* HarperCollins Pubs. Ltd. GBR. Dist: Independent Pubs. Group.

Hernandez, Daniel. They Call Me a Hero: A Memoir of My Youth. 2013. (ENG., Illus.). 240p. (YA). (gr. 7). 17.99 *(978-1-4424-6228-1(0)*, Simon & Schuster Bks. For Young Readers) Simon & Schuster Bks. For Young Readers.

Herzog, Brad. Incredible Stories of Courage in Sports. 2014. (Count on Me: Sports Ser.). (ENG., Illus.). 96p. (J). (gr. 4-7). pap. 9.99 *(978-1-57542-478-1(9))* Free Spirit Publishing, Inc.

Human relations Media. Good Character Adventure Pack: Adventures in Courage. 2006. (ENG.). (J). pap. 4.95 *(978-1-55548-005-9(5)*, 4205) Human Relations Media.

Humphrys-Dunne, Deanie. Tails of Sweetbrier. Humphrys-Bajaj, Holly, illus. 2013. 82p. pap. 9.95 *(978-1-61286-182-1(2))* Avid Readers Publishing Group.

Hyde, Natalie. Live It: Courage. 2009. (ENG., Illus.). 32p. (J). (gr. 3-6). lib. bdg. *(978-0-7787-4885-4(5))* Crabtree Publishing Co.

Jensen, Hay R. Home with Honor Vol. 1: A Vietnam P.O.W. Tells How to Conquer Adversity Through Courage, Honor & Faith. (Illus.). 171p. (Orig.). (YA). pap. 14.95 *(978-1-877898-15-0(5))* P.O.W. (Pubns. of Worth).

Lewis, Simon. Desperate Escapes. 2009. (Difficult & Dangerous Ser.). (Illus.). 32p. (J). (gr. 4-7). pap. *(978-1-897563-23-6(X))* Saunders Bk. Co.

MacKenzie, Carine. David the Shepherd: A Man of Courage. 2009. (Bible Alive Ser.). (ENG., Illus.). 24p. (J). 3.99 *(978-1-84550-486-1(0)*, 9781845504861) Christian Focus Pubns. GBR. Dist: Bookmasters Distribution.

Markovics, Joyce L. & Pushies, Fred J. Today's Army Heroes. 2012. (Acts of Courage: Inside America's Military Ser.). 32p. (J). (gr. 2-7). lib. bdg. 25.27 *(978-1-61772-445-9(9))* Bearport Publishing Co., Inc.

Marshall, Shelley. Super Ben's Brave Bike Ride: A Book about Courage. Mahan, Ben, illus. 2010. (Character Education with Super Ben & Molly the Great Ser.). 24p. (J). 22.60 *(978-0-7660-3515-7(8))*; pap. 7.95 *(978-0-7660-3740-3(1)*, Enslow Elementary) Enslow Pubs., Inc.

Mead, David. Little Teddy Roosevelt Learns a Lesson in Courage: Courage. Sharp, Chris, illus. 2003. (American Virtues for Kids Ser.). (J). bds. 6.95 *(978-0-9746440-3-5(X)*, Ideal Pubns.) Worthy Publishing.

Meiners, Cheri J. & Allen, Elizabeth. Have Courage! 2014. (Being the Best Me Ser.). (ENG., Illus.). 40p. (J). (gr. -1-3). 14.99 *(978-1-57542-458-3(4))* Free Spirit Publishing, Inc.

Miller, Adam. U. S. Air Force True Stories: Tales of Bravery. 2014. (Courage under Fire Ser.). (ENG.). 32p. (gr. 3-4). lib. bdg. 27.99 *(978-1-4765-9936-6(X))* Capstone Press of Coughlan Cos.

—U. S. Marines True Stories: Tales of Bravery. 2014. (Courage under Fire Ser.). (ENG.). 32p. (gr. 3-4). lib. bdg. 27.99 *(978-1-4765-9935-9(1))* Capstone Press of Coughlan Cos.

Miller, Adam, et al. Courage under Fire: Tales of Bravery, 1 vol. 2014. (Courage under Fire Ser.). (ENG.). 32p. (gr. 3-4). 111.96 *(978-1-4765-9939-7(4)*, Edge Bks.) Capstone Press of Coughlan Cos.

—Courage under Fire: True Stories of Bravery from the U. S. Army, Navy, Air Force, & Marines, 1 vol. 2014. (Courage under Fire Ser.). (ENG., Illus.). 112p. (gr. 3-4). pap. 9.95 *(978-1-4914-1065-3(5))* Capstone Press of Coughlan Cos.

Pryor, Kimberley Jane. Courage. 2008. (Values Ser.). 32p. (gr. 1-2). lib. bdg. 18.56 *(978-0-7614-3131-2(4)*, Benchmark Bks.) Marshall Cavendish Corp.

Rinaldo, Denise. Amelia Earhart: With a Discussion of Courage. 2004. (Values in Action Ser.). (J). *(978-1-59203-068-2(8))* Learning Challenge, Inc.

—Rosa Parks: With a Discussion of Courage. 2003. (Values in Action Ser.). (J). *(978-1-59203-061-3(0))* Learning Challenge, Inc.

Rische, Stephanie. My Princesses Learn to Be Brave. Heyworth, Heather, illus. 2014. (ENG.). 24p. (J). 6.99 *(978-1-4143-9661-3(9))* Tyndale Hse. Pubs.

Roth, Irene. Courage. Turchan, Monique, illus. 2012. 24p. pap. 11.95 *(978-1-61244-068-2(1))* Halo Publishing International.

Scheunemann, Pam. Courage. 2003. (United We Stand Ser.). (ENG., Illus.). 24p. (J). (gr. k-3). lib. bdg. 24.21 *(978-1-57765-877-1(9))* ABDO Publishing Co.

Seguin, Marilyn. Young & Courageous: American Girls Who Made History. 2012. (J). pap. *(978-0-8283-2463-2(8))* Branden Bks.

Snow, Todd. You Are Brave. Strong, Melodee, illus. 2007. (ENG.). 24p. (J). bds. 7.99 *(978-1-934277-08-9(8))* Marn Green Publishing, Inc.

—You Are Brave (PB) Strong, Melodee, illus. 2008. (ENG.). 24p. (J). pap. 8.99 *(978-1-934277-19-5(3))* Marn Green Publishing, Inc.

Sundem, Garth. Real Kids, Real Stories, Real Change: Courageous Actions Around the World. 2010. (ENG.). 176p. (J). (gr. 4-8). pap. 9.99 *(978-1-57542-350-0(2))* Free Spirit Publishing, Inc.

—Real Kids, Real Stories, Real Character: Choices That Matter Around the World. 2016. (ENG., Illus.). 176p. (J). (gr. 3-8). pap. 9.99 *(978-1-63198-026-8(2))* Free Spirit Publishing, Inc.

Waldman, Neil. A Land of Big Dreamers: Voices of Courage in America. Waldman, Neil, illus. 2011. (Single Titles Ser.). (ENG., Illus.). 32p. (gr. 3-5). lib. bdg. 16.95 *(978-0-8225-6810-0(1))* Lerner Publishing Group.

Washington-Gattis, Ishia L. Meet Camden: Living with Sickle Cell Anemia. 2010. 36p. 18.99 *(978-1-4490-8616-9(0))* AuthorHouse.

Zullo, Allan. The Rescuers: Kids Who Risked Everything to Save Others. 2006. 135p. pap. *(978-0-439-85483-2(0))* Scholastic, Inc.

COURAGE—FICTION

Alexander, Carol. When My Name Was Keoko. Friedland, Joyce & Kessler, Rikki, eds. 2008. (Novel-Ties Ser.). 29p. pap. 16.95 *(978-0-7675-1520-7(X))* Learning Links Inc.

Allred, Chris Ross. Sir E. Bobbo! 2004. 21p. pap. 24.95 *(978-1-4137-2785-2(9))* PublishAmerica, Inc.

Amateau, Gigi. Macadoo of the Maury River. 2013. (Horses of the Maury River Ser.). (ENG.). 192p. (J). (gr. 4-7). 15.99 *(978-0-7636-3766-8(1))* Candlewick Pr.

Amestoy, Jennifer. Junkyard Junction: The Story of the Magic Microwave. 2008. 32p. pap. 14.75 *(978-1-4389-1755-9(4))* AuthorHouse.

Anaya, Rudolfo. The First Tortilla: A Bilingual Story. Lamadrid, Enrique R., tr. Córdova, Amy, illus. 2012. (ENG & SPA.). 32p. (J). pap. 16.95 *(978-0-8263-4215-7(9))* Univ. of New Mexico Pr.

Anaya, Rudolfo A. & Anaya, Rudolfo. The First Tortilla: A Bilingual Story. Lamadrid, Enrique R., tr. from ENG. Córdova, Amy, illus. 2007. (SPA & ENG.). 32p. (J). (gr. 4-7). 16.95 *(978-0-8263-4214-0(0))* Univ. of New Mexico Pr.

Aparici Martin, Irene. Mom Goes to War. 2013. (ENG., Illus.). 24p. (J). (gr. 2-4). 15.95 *(978-84-15503-20-0(2))* Eastern National.

Asare, Meshack. Sosu's Call. Asare, Meshack, illus. 2006. (ENG., Illus.). 40p. (J). (gr. k-4). 11.99 *(978-1-929132-21-8(2))* Kane Miller.

Asrani, Megan. The Cat on the Windowsill. 2012. 58p. (gr. 1-2). pap. 8.99 *(978-1-4624-0088-1(4)*, Inspiring Voices) Author Solutions, Inc.

Austin, Karen D. Jay Jay & the Broken Picture Frame. 2009. 20p. pap. 10.49 *(978-1-4389-9003-3(0))* AuthorHouse.

Averill, Esther. Jenny's Moonlight Adventure. 32p. (J). pap. 12.95 *(978-0-553-15145-9(2))* Random House Publishing Group.

—Jenny's Moonlight Adventure: A Jenny's Cat Club Book. Averill, Esther, illus. 2005. (New York Review Children's Collection). (ENG., Illus.). 32p. (J). (gr. -1-2). 14.00 *(978-1-59017-160-8(8)*, NYR Children's Collection) New York Review of Bks., Inc., The.

Awdry, W. Thomas & the Monster (Thomas & Friends) 2014. (Color Plus Chunky Crayons Ser.). (ENG.). 48p. (J). (gr. -1-2). pap. 3.99 *(978-0-385-38511-4(0)*, Golden Bks.) Random Hse. Children's Bks.

Bailey, Linda. The Farm Team. Slavin, Bill, illus. 2008. (ENG.). 32p. (J). (gr. -1-2). pap. 7.95 *(978-1-55453-317-6(1))* Kids Can Pr., Ltd. CAN. Dist: Hachette Bk. Group.

Balazy, Elizabeth M. Prince to the Rescue. 2008. 48p. pap. 24.95 *(978-1-60474-812-3(5))* America Star Bks.

Barchers, Suzanne. Bunyip in the Moon: A Tale from Australia. Clarke, Peter, illus. 2015. (Tales of Honor Ser.). (ENG.). 32p. (gr. 1-3). lib. bdg. 26.60 *(978-1-939656-77-3(X))* Red Chair Pr.

—The Wounded Lion: A Tale from Spain. 2013. pap. 26.60 *(978-1-936163-89-2(6))* Red Chair Pr.

Barchers, Suzanne I. The Tale of the Oki Islands: A Tale from Japan. Yokota, Hiromitsu, illus. 2013. (Tales of Honor Ser.). (ENG.). 32p. (gr. 1-3). pap. 8.95 *(978-1-937529-62-8(2))* Red Chair Pr.

Bardhan-Quallen, Sudipta. The Adventures of Caveboy. Wight, Eric, illus. 2017. (Caveboy Ser.). (ENG.). 80p. (J). 9.99 *(978-1-61963-986-7(6)*, 9781619639867, Bloomsbury USA Childrens) Bloomsbury Publishing USA.

Barron, T. A. Ghost Hands. Low, William, illus. 2011. (ENG.). 40p. (J). (gr. k-3). 18.99 *(978-0-399-25083-5(2)*, Philomel Bks.) Penguin Young Readers Group.

Bartoletti, Susan Campbell. The Boy Who Dared. 2008. (ENG., Illus.). 192p. (J). (gr. 3-7). 17.99 *(978-0-439-68013-4(1)*, Scholastic Pr.) Scholastic, Inc.

Barulich-Liederbach, Terri & Liederbach, Tom. The Memory Chair. 2010. 48p. pap. 19.49 *(978-1-4520-5672-2(2))* AuthorHouse.

Basoff, Kathleen. Merdove Cove. 2008. 28p. pap. 14.95 *(978-1-4389-2095-5(4))* AuthorHouse.

Becq, Cecile. Once upon a Timeless Tale: Cinderella. 2016. (Once upon a Timeless Tale Ser.). (ENG.). 32p. (J). (gr. k-2). 9.99 *(978-1-74297-403-3(1))* Little Hare Bks. AUS. Dist: Independent Pubs. Group.

Beitler, Stacey Ann. Willy Helps a Friend. 2010. 30p. pap. 14.50 *(978-1-60911-355-1(1)*, Eloquent Bks.) Strategic Book Publishing & Rights Agency (SBPRA).

Bell, Krista & Smith, Craig. If the Shoe Fits. 2008. (ENG., Illus.). 64p. (Orig.). (J). (gr. 4-7). pap. 5.95 *(978-1-58089-339-8(2))* Charlesbridge Publishing, Inc.

Berenstain, Jan & Berenstain, Mike. Berenstain Bears & the Gift of Courage, 1 vol. Berenstain, Stan, illus. 2010. (Berenstain Bears/Living Lights Ser.). (ENG.). 32p. (J). (gr. -1-2). pap. 3.99 *(978-0-310-71256-5(4))* Zonderkidz.

Berkowitz, Barbara. The Talent Show. 2009. 108p. 21.49 *(978-1-4389-9826-8(0))*; pap. 10.99 *(978-1-4389-9825-1(2))* AuthorHouse.

Big Idea Entertainment, LLC. VeggieTales SuperComics: Vol 1. Jones, Cory, illus. 2015. (VeggieTales Super Comics Ser.: 1). (ENG.). 104p. (J). (gr. -1-3). pap. 12.99 *(978-1-4336-8534-7(5)*, B&H Kids) B&H Publishing Group.

—VeggieTales SuperComics: Vol 2. Jones, Cory, illus. 2015. (VeggieTales Super Comics Ser.). (ENG.). 104p. (J). (gr. -1-3). pap. 12.99 *(978-1-4336-8535-4(3)*, B&H Kids) B&H Publishing Group.

Booth, Bradley. Shepherd Warrior. 2007. 127p. (J). *(978-0-8163-2161-2(2))* Pacific Pr. Pubns.

Bowman, Crystal. Little David's Brave Day, 1 vol. Hartung, Susan Kathleen & Endersly, Frank, illus. 2010. (I Can Read! / Little David Ser.). (ENG.). 32p. (J). pap. 3.99 *(978-0-310-71709-6(4))* Zonderkidz.

Bradman, Tony. Mr. Giant & the Beastly Baron, 1 vol. Warburton, Sarah, illus. 2014. (After Happily Ever After Ser.). (ENG.). 56p. (gr. 2-3). lib. bdg. 25.32 *(978-1-4342-7949-1(9)*, After Happily Ever After) Stone Arch Bks.

Brent, Alexander Michael. Play Date with T-Rex: The Adventures of Jake & Sammy Wiggles. 2010. 52p. pap. 19.50 *(978-1-4520-7531-0(X))* AuthorHouse.

Brice, Ginny. Princess Maddy & Her Blankie. Gary Ripper, illus. 2011. 20p. pap. 24.95 *(978-1-4560-7745-7(7))* America Star Bks.

Briceno, Carole. Turtle's Journey, 1 vol. White, Tina Jorgenson, illus. 2009. 28p. pap. 24.95 *(978-1-60813-934-7(4))* America Star Bks.

Brightwood, Laura, illus. King's New Suit. Brightwood, Laura, . 2007. (J). DVD *(978-1-934409-05-3(7))* 3-C Institute for Social Development.

Brinegar, R. L. Ron. Pokey: The Fastest Horse on the Ranch. 2007. 33p. pap. 8.95 *(978-0-7414-4078-5(4))* Infinity Publishing.

Bromley, Nick. Open Very Carefully: A Book with Bite. O'Byrne, Nicola, illus. 2013. (ENG.). 32p. (J). (gr. -1-2). 15.99 *(978-0-7636-6163-2(5)*, Nosy Crow) Candlewick Pr.

Brooks, Donna. The Magic Amphor. 2009. 100p. pap. 30.00 *(978-1-60693-027-4(3)*, Eloquent Bks.) Strategic Book Publishing & Rights Agency (SBPRA).

Brown, Sam. Herbert: I Am - I Can. 2009. (Illus.). 48p. pap. 10.95 *(978-1-4327-4842-5(4))* Outskirts Pr., Inc.

Brown, Skila. Caminar. 2016. (ENG.). 208p. (J). (gr. 5-9). pap. 7.99 *(978-0-7636-9094-6(5))* Candlewick Pr.

—Caminar. 2016. (ENG.). 208p. (J). (gr. 5-9). 18.40 *(978-0-606-39096-5(0))* Turtleback Bks.

Bruel, Nick. Bad Kitty Scaredy-Cat. 2016. (Bad Kitty Ser.). (ENG., Illus.). 32p. (J). 16.99 *(978-1-59643-978-8(5)*, 9781596439788) Roaring Brook Pr.

Bryce, Conor. Wesco P. Mcsnaffle & the Great Brave Quest. 2008. 127p. pap. 22.50 *(978-1-4092-1273-7(4))* Lulu Pr., Inc.

Buckley, Michael. Kel Gilligan's Daredevil Stunt Show. Santat, Dan, illus. 2012. (ENG.). 40p. (J). (gr. k-2). 17.95 *(978-1-4197-0379-9(X)*, Abrams Bks. for Young Readers) Abrams, Inc.

Cai, Ning & Bosco, Don. Magicienne: A Novel. 2017. (ENG.). 192p. pap. 11.99 ***(978-981-4771-40-5(6))*** Marshall Cavendish International (Asia) Private Ltd. SGP. Dist: National Bk. Network.

Carlson, Nancy. Arnie & the Skateboard Gang. Carlson, Nancy, illus. 2012. (Nancy Carlson Picture Bks). (Illus.). 32p. (J). (gr. k-2). (ENG.). 9.95 *(978-0-7613-8948-4(2))*; 56.72 *(978-0-7613-9303-0(X))* Lerner Publishing Group. (Carolrhoda Bks.).

—Harriet & the Roller Coaster. 20th anniv. ed. (Nancy Carlson's Neighborhood Ser.). (Illus.). 32p. (gr. k-2). 2005. 15.95 *(978-1-57505-053-9(6))* 2003. (ENG., (J). 6.95 *(978-1-57505-202-1(4))* Lerner Publishing Group.

Carnes, Daphane. Grace. 2009. 48p. (J). pap. 12.95 *(978-1-4327-3380-3(X))* Outskirts Pr., Inc.

Carr, Matt. Superbat. 2017. (ENG.). 32p. (J). (gr. -1-k). 16.99 ***(978-1-338-16052-9(4)**, Scholastic Pr.)* Scholastic, Inc.

Carter, Caela. My Life with the Liars. 2016. 288p. (J). (gr. 3-7). 16.99 *(978-0-06-238571-0(2))* HarperCollins Pubs.

Castillo, Lauren. Nana in the City. 2014. (ENG., Illus.). 40p. (J). (gr. -1-3). 16.99 *(978-0-544-10443-3(9))* Houghton Mifflin Harcourt Publishing Co.

Cazet, Denys. Snail & Slug. Cazet, Denys, illus. 2016. (ENG., Illus.). 32p. (J). (gr. -1-3). 17.99 *(978-1-4814-4506-1(5)*, Atheneum/Richard Jackson Bks.) Simon & Schuster Children's Publishing.

Chin, Oliver. The Year of the Horse: Tales from the Chinese Zodiac. Wood, Jennifer, illus. 2013. (Tales from the Chinese Zodiac Ser.: 8). (ENG.). 36p. (J). (gr. -1-3). 15.95 *(978-1-59702-080-0(X))* Immedium.

Choi, JeongIm. Who's Coming Tonight? Gang, MinJeong, illus. rev. ed. 2014. (MySELF Bookshelf Ser.). (ENG.). 32p. (J). (gr. k-2). lib. bdg. 25.27 *(978-1-59953-653-8(6))* Norwood Hse. Pr.

Choyce, Lesley. Skate Freak, 1 vol. 2008. (Orca Currents Ser.). (ENG.). (J). (gr. 5-9). 112p. 16.95 *(978-1-55469-043-5(9))*; 128p. pap. 9.95 *(978-1-55469-042-8(0))* Orca Bk. Pubs. USA.

Christopher, Matt. Rock On. Koelsch, Michael, illus. 5th ed. 2004. (ENG.). 64p. (J). (gr. 1-4). pap. 13.99 *(978-0-316-76265-6(2))* Little, Brown Bks. for Young Readers.

Clark, Eleanor. Victoria Grace: Courageous Patriot. 2007. (Eleanor Ser.: Bk. 2). 209p. (J). (gr. 4-7). 14.99 *(978-0-9753036-8-9(6))* HonorNet.

Clark, Kathy. Guardian Angel House, 1 vol. 2009. (Holocaust Remembrance Ser.). (ENG., Illus.). 180p. (J). (gr. 4-8). pap. 14.95 *(978-1-897187-58-6(0))* Second Story Pr. CAN. Dist: Orca Bk. Pubs. USA.

Cohen, Deborah Bodin. Nachshon, Who Was Afraid to Swim: A Passover Story. Jago, illus. 2008. (Passover Ser.). (ENG.). 32p. (J). (gr. -1-3). 17.95 *(978-0-8225-8764-4(5)*, Kar-Ben Publishing) Lerner Publishing Group.

Coleman, K. R. Truth or Dare. 2017. (Midnight Ser.). (ENG.). 104p. (YA). (gr. 6-12). lib. bdg. 26.65 *(978-1-5124-2768-4(3))*; 12.99 ***(978-1-5124-3495-8(7))***; 39.99 ***(978-1-5124-2788-2(8))***; 39.99 ***(978-1-5124-3494-1(9))*** Lerner Publishing Group. (Darby Creek).

Condie, Ally. Reached. 2013. (Matched Trilogy Ser.: 3). lib. bdg. 20.85 *(978-0-606-34456-2(X)*, Turtleback) Turtleback Bks.

Conley, Deane W. Angelino Courage to Fly. 2007. (J). lib. bdg. 19.95 *(978-1-933732-27-5(X))* Big Ransom Studio.

Cooney, Caroline B. Goddess of Yesterday. 2009. (ENG.). 272p. (YA). (gr. 7). pap. 8.99 *(978-0-385-73865-1(X)*, Ember) Random Hse. Children's Bks.

Cornfield, Lynda Ellis. Rocks for Clean Oceans. 2009. 28p. pap. 13.99 *(978-1-4389-8417-9(0))* AuthorHouse.

Cornwall, Gaia. Jabari Jumps. Cornwall, Gaia, illus. 2017. (ENG., Illus.). 32p. (J). (gr. -1-3). 15.99 *(978-0-7636-7838-8(4))* Candlewick Pr.

Cote, Nancy. Watch the Cookie! Cote, Nancy, illus. 2014. (ENG., Illus.). 32p. (J). (gr. -1-k). 16.95 *(978-1-62914-630-0(7)*, Sky Pony Pr.) Skyhorse Publishing Co., Inc.

Coughlin, Denise. Dragon in My Pocket. Kastan, Bill, illus. 2005. (J). *(978-0-9765905-0-7(6))* Rose Valley Publishing.

Courtney, Kateri. Welby & the Knobby King. 2003. pap. 14.95 *(978-0-9743588-0-2(0))* Castlegate Pr.

Crum, Shutta. Thomas & the Dragon Queen. Wildish, Lee, illus. 2011. (ENG.). 272p. (J). (gr. 3-7). 6.99 *(978-0-375-84634-2(4)*, Yearling) Random Hse. Children's Bks.

Curtis, Jamie Lee. My Brave Year of Firsts: Tries, Sighs, & High Fives. Cornell, Laura, illus. 2012. (ENG.). 40p. (J). (gr. -1-3). 16.99 *(978-0-06-144155-4(4))* HarperCollins Pubs.

Darlison, Aleesah. Ellabeth's Test. Brailsford, Jill, illus. 2016. (Unicorn Riders Ser.). (ENG.). 112p. (gr. 3-5). lib. bdg. 22.65 *(978-1-4795-6547-4(4))* Picture Window Bks.

—Ellabeth's Test Cancelled. Brailsford, Jill, illus. 2017. (Unicorn Riders Ser.). (ENG.). 112p. (gr. 3-5). pap. 5.95 *(978-1-4795-6555-9(5))* Picture Window Bks.

Davie, Jan. Stairway to the Stars. 2005. 76p. pap. *(978-1-84401-569-6(6))* Athena Pr.

Davies, Gill. Brave Little Owl. Twinney, Dick, illus. 2006. (ENG.). 24p. (J). *(978-1-55168-279-2(6))* Fenn, H. B. & Co., Ltd.

Demi & Demi Staff. The Boy Who Painted Dragons. Demi & Demi Staff, illus. 2007. (ENG., Illus.). 52p. (J). (gr. 2-5). 21.99 *(978-1-4169-2469-2(8)*, McElderry, Margaret K. Bks.) McElderry, Margaret K. Bks.

Denman, K. L. Spiral, 1 vol. 2008. (Orca Soundings Ser.). (ENG.). 128p. (YA). (gr. 8-12). pap. 9.95 *(978-1-55143-930-3(1))* Orca Bk. Pubs. USA.

Desbordes, Astrid. The Thing. Boutavant, Marc, illus. 2017. (ENG.). 32p. (J). (gr. -1-3). 17.95 ***(978-1-59270-217-6(1))*** Enchanted Lion Bks., LLC.

Disney Book Group & Sutherland, Kari. The Story of Moana Moana: A Tale of Courage & Adventure. 2016. (ENG., Illus.). 304p. (J). (gr. 3-7). 10.99 *(978-1-4847-4358-4(X))* Disney Pr.

Donovan, Anna. A Dragon's Tale. 2003. (ENG., Illus.). 12p. (J). pap. 7.95 *(978-0-86278-845-2(5))* O'Brien Pr., Ltd., The IRL. Dist: Dufour Editions, Inc.

Dubosarsky, Ursula. The Terrible Plop. Joyner, Andrew, illus. 2009. (ENG.). 40p. (J). (gr. -1-1). 17.99 *(978-0-374-37428-0(7)*, 9780374374280, Farrar, Straus & Giroux (BYR)) Farrar, Straus & Giroux.

Dugin, Andrei. Dragon Feathers. Dugina, Olga, illus. 2010. Orig. Title: Die Drachenfedern. 24p. (J). (gr. k-3). 17.95 *(978-0-86315-774-5(2))* Floris Bks. GBR. Dist: SteinerBooks, Inc.

Eason, Sarah. Chin up, Charlie: Be Brave. 2013. (You Choose Ser.). 32p. (J). (gr. k-3). pap. 7.95 *(978-1-4644-0555-6(7)*, Enslow Elementary) Enslow Pubs., Inc.

Eliotte, Lisa J. The Adventures of Derby Doodle. 2009. 640p. pap. 25.99 *(978-1-4389-3058-9(5))* AuthorHouse.

Elisabeth, Megan. A Star's Journey from Twinkle to Shine. 2012. 28p. pap. 24.95 *(978-1-62709-789-5(9))* America Star Bks.

Ellis, Deborah. Mud City. 2013. 156p. pap. *(978-1-4596-6445-6(0))* ReadHowYouWant.com, Ltd.

Enderle, Dotti. Crosswire. 2010. (ENG.). 144p. (J). (gr. 4-6). 17.95 *(978-1-59078-751-9(X)*, Calkins Creek) Boyds Mills Pr.

Engelbreit, Mary. Queen of Halloween. Engelbreit, Mary, illus. 2008. (Illus.). 32p. (J). (gr. -1-3). lib. bdg. 17.89 *(978-0-06-008191-1(0))*; (ENG., 16.99 *(978-0-06-008190-4(2))* HarperCollins Pubs.

Errico, Daniel. The Journey of the Marmabill. Turrill, Tiffany, illus. 2013. (ENG.). 32p. (J). (gr. -1-k). 16.95

(978-1-62087-736-4(8), 620736, Sky Pony Pr.) Skyhorse Publishing Co., Inc.
Eskye, Tony. The Adventures of Fojo the Frog. 2009. (Illus.). 224p. pap. 14.49 (978-1-4389-9530-4(X)) AuthorHouse.
Everett, George W. G. W. Frog & the Circus Lion. 2010. 32p. 16.95 (978-1-4497-0443-8(3), WestBow Pr.) Author Solutions, Inc.
Flanagan, John. The Ghostfaces. 2016. (Brotherband Chronicles Ser.: 6). (ENG.). 400p. (J). (gr. 5). 18.99 (978-0-399-16357-9(3), Philomel Bks.) Penguin Young Readers Group.
—The Hunters. (Brotherband Chronicles Ser.: 3). (ENG.). (J). (gr. 5). 2014. 448p. pap. 8.99 (978-0-14-242664-7(4), Puffin Books) 2012. 416p. 18.99 (978-0-399-25621-9(0), Philomel Bks.) Penguin Young Readers Group.
—The Hunters. 2014. (Brotherband Chronicles Ser.: 3). lib. bdg. 19.65 (978-0-606-35708-1(4)) Turtleback Bks.
—The Invaders. (Brotherband Chronicles Ser.: 2). (ENG.). (J). (gr. 5). 2013. 448p. pap. 8.99 (978-0-14-242663-0(6), Puffin Books) 2012. 432p. 18.99 (978-0-399-25620-2(2), Philomel Bks.) Penguin Young Readers Group.
—The Invaders. 2013. (Brotherband Chronicles Ser.: 2). lib. bdg. 19.65 (978-0-606-26637-6(2), Turtleback) Turtleback Bks.
—The Outcasts. 2011. (Brotherband Chronicles: Bk. 1). (ENG.). (J). (gr. 3-7). 54.99 (978-1-61657-043-9(1)) Findaway World, LLC.
—The Outcasts. (Brotherband Chronicles Ser.: 1). (ENG.). (J). (gr. 5). 2012. 464p. pap. 8.99 (978-0-14-242194-9(4), Puffin Books) 2011. 448p. 18.99 (978-0-399-25619-6(9), Philomel Bks.) Penguin Young Readers Group.
—The Outcasts. 2012. (Brotherband Chronicles Ser.: 1). lib. bdg. 19.65 (978-0-606-26636-9(4), Turtleback) Turtleback Bks.
—Slaves of Socorro. 2014. (Brotherband Chronicles Ser.: Bk. 4). (ENG., Illus.). 480p. (J). 18.99 (978-0-399-16355-5(7), Philomel Bks.) Penguin Publishing Group.
—Slaves of Socorro. 2015. (Brotherband Chronicles Ser.: 4). (ENG.). 496p. (J). (gr. 5). pap. 8.99 (978-0-14-242726-2(8), Puffin Books) Penguin Young Readers Group.
—Slaves of Socorro. 2015. (Brotherband Chronicles Ser.: 4). lib. bdg. 19.65 (978-0-606-36771-4(3)) Turtleback Bks.
Ford, Lorry. Goodnight Red: A Lesson in Courage. 2007. 20p. per. 12.90 (978-1-4343-0477-3(9)) AuthorHouse.
Forte, Joyce. The Brave Little Girl. 2004. 37p. pap. 24.95 (978-1-4137-1833-1(7)) PublishAmerica, Inc.
Francesca, Sieglinde De. A Donsy of Gnomes. 2009. pap. (978-1-61623-243-6(9)) Independent Pub.
Froeber, Sarah & Mosher, Kim. Pelican & Pelicant. 2003. (Illus.). 36p. (J). 17.99 (978-0-9744926-0-5(4)) Toucan Pr., Inc.
Frye, Timea Csonka. Wishing Star: Lost in the Woods. 2013. 32p. pap. 24.95 (978-1-63000-931-1(8)) America Star Bks.
Funke, Cornelia. Igraine the Brave. Bell, Anthea, tr. Funke, Cornelia, illus. l.t. ed. 2008. (Thorndike Literacy Bridge Middle Reader Ser.). (Illus.). 259p. (J). (gr. 4-7). 23.95 (978-1-4104-0341-4(6)) Thorndike Pr.
Fusek Peters, Andrew. The Ant & the Big Bad Bully Goat. Wadham, Anna, illus. 2010. (Traditional Tales with a Twist Ser.). (ENG.). 32p. (J). (gr. -1-2). audio compact disk (978-1-84643-348-1(7)) Child's Play International Ltd.
Gantos, Jack. Desire Lines. 2006. (ENG.). 144p. (YA). (gr. 7-12). reprint ed. pap. 15.99 (978-0-374-41703-1(2), Farrar, Straus & Giroux (BYR)) Farrar, Straus & Giroux.
Gardner, Sally. Maggot Moon. Crouch, Julian, illus. (ENG.). 288p. (YA). (gr. 7). 2014. pap. 8.99 (978-0-7636-7169-3(X)) 2013. 16.99 (978-0-7636-6553-1(3)) Candlewick Pr.
Gawade, Akansha A. This Is Who I Am. 2006. (J). pap. 8.00 (978-0-8059-6886-6(5)) Dorrance Publishing Co., Inc.
Gayle, Sherri. Bubbles of Faith. 2013. 48p. pap. 11.95 (978-1-61244-076-7(2)) Halo Publishing International.
Gee, Maurice. Gool, 1 vol. 2012. (Salt Trilogy Ser.: 2). (ENG.). 240p. (YA). (gr. 7-12). pap. 12.95 (978-1-4598-0196-7(2)) Orca Bk. Pubs. USA.
—Salt, 1 vol. 2011. (Salt Trilogy Ser.: 1). (ENG., Illus.). 272p. (J). (gr. 7-12). pap. 12.95 (978-1-55469-369-6(1)) Orca Bk. Pubs. USA.
Gemeinhart, Dan. Some Kind of Courage. 2016. lib. bdg. 17.20 **(978-0-606-39703-2(5))** Turtleback Bks.
Giff, Patricia Reilly. Willow Run. 2007. 149p. (J). 13.65 (978-0-7569-7769-6(X)) Perfection Learning Corp.
—Willow Run. 2007. (ENG.). 160p. (J). (gr. 3-7). per. 5.99 (978-0-440-23801-0(3), Yearling) Random Hse. Children's Bks.
—Winter Sky. 2014. (ENG.). 160p. (J). (gr. 3-7). 15.99 (978-0-375-83892-7(9), Lamb, Wendy Bks.) Random Hse. Children's Bks.
Gipson, Mary Willene. The Tattered Feather. 2012. 28p. pap. 13.95 (978-1-4525-5036-7(0)) Balboa Pr.
Glover, Darryl. The Pirate Kitty. Austin, Britta, ed. Kosir, Ana, illus. 2008. 24p. (J). 16.95 (978-0-9821387-0-0(9)) MagicStar Inc.
Glynn, Eoin. Mischief at Se. 2009. 232p. pap. 14.49 (978-1-4389-4919-2(7)) AuthorHouse.
Gottesfeld, Jeff. The Code. 2014. (Red Rhino Ser.). (J). lib. bdg. 18.40 (978-0-606-36199-6(5)) Turtleback Bks.
Gummelt, Donna & Melchiorre, Dondino. My Sunshine Friend. Wall, Randy Hugh, ed. Varela, Juan D., tr. from ENG. Varela, Juan D., illus. 2006. (SPA.). 32p. (J). 14.95 (978-0-9764798-2-6(6)) Story Store Collection Publishing.
Gunderson, Jessica. A Rebel among Redcoats: A Revolutionary War Novel. 2015. (Revolutionary War Ser.). (ENG., Illus.). 96p. (gr. 4-4). lib. bdg. 26.65 (978-1-4342-9701-3(2)) Stone Arch Bks.
Hall, Kirsten. I'm Not Scared. Holub, Joan, illus. 2003. (My First Reader Ser.). (ENG.). 32p. (J). 18.50 (978-0-516-22929-4(X), Children's Pr.) Scholastic Library Publishing.
Hallagin, Janet. The Way of Courage. 2006. 30.99 (978-1-4257-1249-5(5)); pap. 20.99 (978-1-4257-1248-8(7)) Xlibris Corp.
Hamilton, Laura, reader. Sheila Rae, the Brave. 2003. (Illus.). (J). (gr. -1-2). 28.95 incl. audio compact disk (978-1-59112-550-1(2)) Live Oak Media.
Han, Yu-Mei, illus. The Brave Servant: A Tale from China. 2013. (Tales of Honor Ser.). (ENG.). 32p. (J). (gr. 1-4). pap. 8.95 (978-1-937529-57-4(6)); lib. bdg. 26.60 (978-1-937529-73-4(8)) Red Chair Pr.
Hanson, Martina D. & Benchmark Education Co. Staff. Analytical Arguments about Courage. 2014. (Text Connections Ser.). (J). (gr. 6). (978-1-4900-1530-9(2)) Benchmark Education Co.
Hardwell, Gary D. A Boo Bears' Story: Stormy Night. 2007. (Illus.). 36p. per. 10.00 (978-0-9792016-9-1(1)) Professional Publishing Hse. LLC.
Hardy, Gary D. Pj the Water Breathing Dragon: In Being Different Is a Good Thing. 2012. 28p. pap. 15.99 (978-1-4691-7742-7(0)) Xlibris Corp.
A Hare, a Hound & Shy Mousey Brown. 2013. (J). (978-1-4351-4729-4(4)) Barnes & Noble, Inc.
Hartry, Nancy. Watching Jimmy. 2009. (ENG.). 160p. (YA). (gr. 4-7). 16.95 (978-0-88776-871-2(7), Tundra Bks.) Tundra Bks. CAN. Dist: Penguin Random Hse. LLC.
Hayes, Geoffrey. Benny & Penny in Just Pretend, 1 vol. 2013. (Toon Bks). (ENG.). 36p. (J). (gr. 1-2). lib. bdg. 27.07 (978-1-61479-148-5(1)) Spotlight.
—Benny & Penny in Just Pretend. Hayes, Geoffrey, illus. 2008. (Benny & Penny Ser.). (ENG., Illus.). 32p. (J). (gr. -1-3). 12.95 (978-0-9799238-0-7(8)) TOON Books / RAW Junior, LLC.
Healy, Reneé. You Are Safe in the Universe. 2011. 28p. pap. 25.00 (978-1-936688-07-4(7)) AKA:yoLa.
Hearne, Betsy. Seven Brave Women. Andersen, Bethanne, illus. 2006. (gr. -1-3). 17.00 (978-0-7569-6669-0(8)) Perfection Learning Corp.
Heffernan, Colleen. A Kind of Courage, 1 vol. 2005. (ENG.). 160p. (YA). (gr. 8-12). per. 12.00 (978-1-55143-358-5(3)) Orca Bk. Pubs. USA.
Henkes, Kevin. Sheila Rae, the Brave. Henkes, Kevin, illus. (Illus.). 9.95 (978-1-59112-865-6(X)) Live Oak Media.
Henty, George Alfred. At Agincourt: A Tale of the White Hoods of Paris. 2011. 332p. pap. 19.95 (978-1-61179-111-2(1)) Fireship Pr.
Hernandez, David. The Mighty Armor, 1 vol., Vol. 2. 2003. (Adventures of Toby Digz Ser.: 2). (ENG., Illus.). 96p. pap. 5.99 (978-1-4003-0196-6(3)) Nelson, Thomas Inc.
Hiiasen, Carl. Hoot. 2014. 17.00 (978-1-63419-707-6(0)) Perfection Learning Corp.
Hodgson, Julie. The Mothaich. 2008. 185p. 41.95 (978-1-4092-3819-5(9)) Lulu Pr., Inc.
Hodgson, Mona. The Princess Twins & the Puppy, 1 vol. Olson, Julie, illus. 2015. (I Can Read! / Princess Twins Ser.). (ENG.). 32p. (J). pap. 3.99 (978-0-310-75064-2(4)) Zonderkidz.
—The Princess Twins Play in the Garden, 1 vol. Olson, Julie, illus. 2015. (I Can Read! / Princess Twins Ser.). (ENG.). 32p. (J). pap. 3.99 (978-0-310-75050-5(4)) Zonderkidz.
Holm, Jennifer L. & Holm, Matthew. Super Amoeba. Holm, Jennifer L. & Holm, Matthew, illus. 2011. (Squish Ser.: No. 1). (ENG., Illus.). 96p. (J). (gr. 3-7). pap. 6.99 (978-0-375-84389-1(2)); lib. bdg. 12.99 (978-0-375-93783-5(8)) Random Hse. Children's Bks. (Random Hse. Bks. for Young Readers).
Holub, Joan & Williams, Suzanne. Artemis the Brave. (Goddess Girls Ser.: 4). (ENG.). 240p. (J). (gr. 3-7). 2013. 17.99 (978-1-4424-6139-0(X)) 2010. pap. 7.99 (978-1-4169-8274-6(4)) Simon & Schuster Children's Publishing. (Aladdin).
Holyoke, Polly. The Neptune Project. 2014. (ENG.). 352p. (J). (gr. 3-7). pap. 7.99 (978-1-4231-5979-7(9)) Hyperion Bks. for Children.
Hoppey, Tim. The Good Fire Helmet. McElrath-Eslick, Lori, illus. 2010. (ENG.). 32p. (J). 16.95 (978-1-934617-06-9(7), Alma Little) Elva Resa Publishing, LLC.
Horowitz, Dave. Humpty Dumpty Climbs Again. Horowitz, Dave, illus. 2011. (ENG., Illus.). 32p. (J). (gr. -1-k). pap. 6.99 (978-0-14-241932-8(X), Puffin Books) Penguin Young Readers Group.
Houran, Lori Haskins. Earth's Got Talent! Warrick, Jessica, illus. 2016. (How to Be an Earthling (r) Ser.: 4). (ENG.). 64p. (gr. 1-3). lib. bdg. 22.65 (978-1-57565-827-8(5)) Kane Press, Inc.
—Earth's Got Talent! Courage. Warrick, Jessica, illus. 2016. (How to Be an Earthling (r) Ser.: 4). (ENG.). 64p. (gr. 1-3). 34.65 (978-1-57565-829-2(1)) Kane Press, Inc.
Howarth, Heidi. The Otter Who Loved to Hold Hands. Howarth, Daniel, illus. 2014. (J). (978-1-4351-5537-4(8)) Barnes & Noble, Inc.
Hunter, Erin. The Forgotten Warrior. Richardson, Owen & Douglas, Allen, illus. 2012. (Warriors: Omen of the Stars Ser.: 5). (ENG.). 384p. (J). (gr. 3-7). pap. 6.99 (978-0-06-155526-8(6)) HarperCollins Pubs.
—Into the Wild. Richardson, Owen & Stevenson, Dave, illus. 2015. (Warriors: the Prophecies Begin Ser.: 1). (ENG.). 320p. (J). (gr. 3-7). pap. 7.99 (978-0-06-236696-2(3)) HarperCollins Pubs.
—Into the Wild. 2015. (Warriors Ser.: 1). (J). lib. bdg. 18.40 (978-0-606-36494-2(3)) Turtleback Bks.
Husby, Greg. The Zoebirds. 2008. 40p. pap. 21.99 (978-1-4363-4941-3(9)) Xlibris Corp.
Jacobsen, Annie. Ivar, the Short, but Brave Viking. Hanson, Susan Jo, illus. 2007. (J). lib. bdg. 16.95 (978-0-9778276-1-9(5)) Pickled Herring Pr.
Jenkins, Amanda. Tornado! 2005. (J). pap. (978-1-4108-4212-1(6)) Benchmark Education Co.
Jennewein, Lenore. Chick-O-Saurus Rex. Jennewein, Daniel, illus. 2013. (ENG.). 32p. (J). (gr. -1-3). 16.99 (978-1-4424-5186-5(6), Simon & Schuster Bks. For Young Readers) Simon & Schuster Bks. For Young Readers.
Jerry, Spinelli. Wringer. 2014. (ENG.). 256p. (J). (gr. 8-12). 13.24 (978-1-63245-323-5(1)) Lectorum Pubns., Inc.
Joe, O'Brien. Alfie Green & the Magical Gift. Jean, Texier, illus. 2007. (Alfie Green Ser.). (ENG.). 80p. (J). pap. 10.95 (978-1-84717-041-5(2)) O'Brien Pr., Ltd., The IRL. Dist: Dufour Editions, Inc.
Johnson, Dwayne. My Angel. 2013. (Illus.). 12p. pap. 18.30 (978-1-4817-8188-6(X)) AuthorHouse.
Jonell, Lynne. Bravemole. 2004. (Illus.). (J). (gr. k-3). spiral bd. (978-0-616-14579-1(9)) Canadian National Institute for the Blind/Institut National Canadien pour les Aveugles.
—Grasshopper Magic. Dorman, Brandon, illus. (Magical Mix-Ups Ser.: 3). (ENG.). 112p. (J). (gr. 1-4). 2014. pap. 4.99 (978-0-307-93123-8(4)) 2013. 12.99 (978-0-375-87084-2(9)) Random Hse. Children's Bks. (Random Hse. Bks. for Young Readers).
Jones, Marcia Thornton. Woodford Brave. Whipple, Kevin, illus. 2015. (ENG.). 200p. (J). (gr. 3-7). 16.95 (978-1-62979-305-4(1), Calkins Creek) Boyds Mills Pr.
Jordan, Apple. Oh, Brother! 2012. (Disney Princess Step into Reading Ser.). lib. bdg. 13.55 (978-0-606-26560-7(0), Turtleback) Turtleback Bks.
Jordan, Christopher. The Little Beaver. Boey, Stephanie, illus. 2008. (ENG.). 24p. (J). (gr. k-3). (978-1-55168-249-5(4)) Magma.
Jordan, Mark. Courage the Monkey. 2006. (Illus.). 40p. (J). 13.95 (978-0-9717013-7-3(7)) Decere Publishing.
Judge, Chris. The Brave Beast. 2013. (ENG., Illus.). 32p. (J). (gr. -1-k). pap. 12.99 (978-1-84939-561-8(6)) Andersen Pr. GBR. Dist: Independent Pubs. Group.
Kafer, Kathy & Benchmark Education Co. Staff. Analytical Arguments about Folklore. 2014. (Text Connections Ser.). (J). (gr. 6). (978-1-4900-1522-4(1)) Benchmark Education Co.
Kay, Kimberly. Courage to Face an Ogre. 2012. 28p. pap. 21.99 (978-1-4691-5436-7(6)) Xlibris Corp.
Kerrin, Jessica Scott. Martin Bridge: Onwards & Upwards! Kelly, Joseph, illus. 2009. (Martin Bridge Ser.). (ENG.). 112p. (J). (gr. 2-5). 6.95 (978-1-55453-161-5(6)) Kids Can Pr., Ltd. CAN. Dist: Hachette Bk. Group.
Kingsbury, Karen. The Brave Young Knight, 1 vol. Grimard, Gabrielle, illus. 2011. (ENG.). 40p. (J). (gr. -1-2). 15.99 (978-0-310-71645-7(4)) Zonderkidz.
Kirk, Daniel. Library Mouse: A World to Explore. 2010. (ENG., Illus.). 32p. (J). (gr. 1-4). 17.95 (978-0-8109-8968-9(9), Abrams Bks. for Young Readers) Abrams, Inc.
Kirk, David. Oh So Brave Dragon. Kirk, David, illus. 2014. (ENG., Illus.). 40p. (J). (gr. -1-1). 17.99 (978-1-250-01689-8(4), 9781250016898) Feiwel & Friends.
Kishimoto, Masashi. Naruto: Chapter Book, Vol. 1. Kishimoto, Masashi, illus. 2008. (ENG., Illus.). 80p. (J). (gr. 1-5). pap. 4.99 (978-1-4215-2056-8(7)) Viz Media.
Kiss, Kay. Mr B T Bumblebee. 2007. 28p. per. 11.95 (978-1-4327-1744-5(8)) Outskirts Pr., Inc.
Krensky, Stephen. I Am So Brave! Gillingham, Sara, illus. 2014. (Empowerment Ser.). (ENG.). 12p. (J). (gr. -1 — 1). bds. 6.95 (978-1-4197-0937-1(2), Abrams Appleseed) Abrams, Inc.
Kriszt, Ann Marie. Bestis Friends. 2008. 276p. pap. 27.95 (978-1-60703-154-3(X)) PublishAmerica, Inc.
Kropp, Paul. Against All Odds. Melanson, Matt, illus. 2004. (New Series Canada). 87p. (J). pap. (978-1-897039-06-9(9)) High Interest Publishing (HIP).
Landry, Cristy. Snowboarding with Courage. 2016. 98p. (YA). (gr. 8-12). pap. 10.95 (978-0-9963756-0-3(0)) All About Kids Publishing.
Lansky, Bruce, ed. Hidden Courage: 10 Inspiring Stories about Clever & Courageous Girls from Around the World. 2013. (Girls to the Rescue Ser.: 3). (ENG.). 112p. (J). (gr. 3-6). pap. 4.99 (978-1-4424-9195-3(7)) Meadowbrook Pr.
Lasky, Kathryn. Lone Wolf. 2011. (Wolves of the Beyond Ser.: 1). (ENG.). 240p. (J). (gr. 3-7). pap. 6.99 (978-0-545-09311-8(2)) Scholastic, Inc.
Law, Felicia. Darwin the Dolphin: A Tale of Bravery & Courage. Danson, Lesley, illus. 2010. (Animal Fair Values Ser.). 32p. (J). (gr. -1-3). pap. 10.55 (978-1-60754-810-2(0)); lib. bdg. 22.60 (978-1-60754-806-5(2)) Windmill Bks.
Leblanc, Louise. Leo's Midnight Rescue. Prud'homme, Jules, illus. 2004. 62p. (J). lib. bdg. 12.00 (978-1-4242-1217-0(0)) Fitzgerald Bks.
—Leo's Midnight Rescue, 1 vol. Cummins, Sarah, tr. from FRE. Prud'homme, Jules & Jules, Prud'homme, illus. 2004. (Formac First Novels Ser.: 53). (ENG.). 64p. (J). (gr. 2-5). 4.95 (978-0-88780-640-7(6), 9780887806407); 14.95 (978-0-88780-641-4(4), 9780887806414) Formac Publishing Co., Ltd. CAN. Dist: Casemate Pubs. & Bk. Distributors, LLC.
Lee, Hoseok M. A Different Kind of Fle. 2009. 28p. pap. 12.49 (978-1-4490-1545-9(X)) AuthorHouse.
Lewis, Kelly. Johan & the Dragon. 2011. 44p. pap. 21.99 (978-1-4628-7149-0(6)) Xlibris Corp.
Lionni, Leo. Swimmy. 2013. (ENG., Illus.). 32p. (J). (gr. -1-2). 17.99 (978-0-385-75358-6(6)); lib. bdg. 20.99 (978-0-385-75366-1(7)) Random Hse. Children's Bks. (Knopf Bks. for Young Readers).
Lore, Pittacus. The Rise of Nine. (Lorien Legacies Ser.: 3). (ENG.). 416p. (YA). (gr. 9). 2013. pap. 9.99 (978-0-06-197460-1(9)) 2012. 17.99 (978-0-06-197458-8(7)) HarperCollins Pubs.
—The Rise of Nine. 2013. (Lorien Legacies Ser.: 3). (YA). lib. bdg. 20.85 (978-0-606-31830-3(5), Turtleback) Turtleback Bks.
Lustig, Lindsey Beth. Snail's Trail. 2008. 21p. pap. 24.95 (978-1-60610-310-4(5)) America Star Bks.
Maddox, Jake. BMX Bravery. 2016. (Jake Maddox JV Ser.). (ENG.). 96p. (gr. 3-4). lib. bdg. 25.99 (978-1-4965-2630-4(9)) Stone Arch Bks.
Magness, Robert. Silent Knife, Holy Knife. Glon, Nancy, illus. 2003. 345p. 10.00 (978-0-9774577-0-0(2)) Magness, Robert Pubns., LLC.
Mangskau, Monica. My Grandpa the Super Hero. 2010. 16p. 9.49 (978-1-4343-8088-3(2)) AuthorHouse.
Marien, Donna. Waiting at the Bay: A Young Woman's Reflections on Journeys in the Sea of Life. 2003. 108p. (YA). pap. 10.95 (978-0-595-26304-2(6), Writers Club Pr.) iUniverse, Inc.
Marlow, Layn. The Witch with a Twitch. Dreidemy, Joëlle, illus. (Tiger Tales Ser.). (J). (gr. -1-2). 2006. 28p. pap. 6.95 (978-1-58925-400-8(7)) 2005. 32p. 15.95 (978-1-58925-052-9(4)) Tiger Tales.
Marshall, Melanie. Ladybug. 2006. 25.00 (978-1-4122-0219-0(1)) Trafford Publishing.
Marshall, Stacey A. Captain Courage & the World's Most Shocking Secret Book 2. Morse, Michelle, illus. 2013. 24p. 19.95 (978-1-61633-431-4(2)) Guardian Angel Publishing, Inc.
Martin, Rafe. The Banyan Deer: A Parable of Courage & Compassion. Wehrman, Richard, illus. 2010. (ENG.). 48p. (J). (gr. 4). 15.00 (978-0-86171-625-8(6)) Wisdom Pubns.
McCrimmon, Linda. Can You Please tie My Shoes? 2007. (J). 10.95 (978-0-9796978-2-1(4)) G Publishing LLC.
McDonald, Megan. Beetle Mcgrady Eats Bugs! Manning, Jane K., illus. 2005. (ENG.). 32p. (J). (gr. k-5). 17.99 (978-0-06-001354-7(0), Greenwillow Bks.) HarperCollins Pubs.
McGhee, Holly M. Come with Me. Lemaître, Pascal, illus. 2017. (ENG.). 40p. (J). (gr. k-3). 17.99 **(978-1-5247-3905-8(7)**, G.P. Putnam's Sons Books for Young Readers) Penguin Young Readers Group.
McGrath, Milo & McGrath, Chris. South Pole Santa. 2007. 68p. pap. 12.50 (978-1-84799-221-5(8)) Lulu Pr., Inc.
McKay, Sharon E. & Lafrance, Daniel. War Brothers: The Graphic Novel. Lafrance, Daniel, illus. 2013. (ENG., Illus.). 176p. (YA). (gr. 9-12). 2nd ed. 27.95 (978-1-55451-489-2(4), 9781554514892) 3rd ed. pap. 18.95 (978-1-55451-488-5(6), 9781554514885) Annick Pr., Ltd. CAN. Dist: Publishers Group West (PGW).
McKissack, Patricia C. & Moss, Onawumi Jean. Precious & the Boo Hag. Brooker, Kyrsten, illus. 2005. (ENG.). 40p. (J). (gr. -1-3). 17.99 (978-0-689-85194-0(4), Atheneum Bks. for Young Readers) Simon & Schuster Children's Publishing.
McMullan, Kate. Revenge of the Dragon Lady. 2005. (Dragon Slayers Academy Ser.: No. 2). (J). 28.75 (978-1-4193-1910-5(8)) Recorded Bks., Inc.
McNamara, Margaret. Sylva & the Fairy Ball. Denos, Julia, illus. 2013. (Fairy Bell Sisters Ser.: 1). (ENG.). 128p. (J). (gr. 1-5). 15.99 (978-0-06-222802-4(1)); pap. 4.99 (978-0-06-222801-7(3)) HarperCollins Pubs.
—Sylva & the Fairy Ball. 2013. (Fairy Bell Sisters Ser.: 1). (J). lib. bdg. 14.75 (978-0-606-31796-2(1), Turtleback) Turtleback Bks.
McQuestion, Karen. Celia & the Fairies, 0 vols. unabr. ed. 2010. (ENG.). 142p. (gr. 4-6). pap. 7.95 (978-1-935597-28-5(0), 9781935597285, Two Lions) Amazon Publishing.
McSwigan, Marie. Snow Treasure. Reardon, Mary, illus. 2006. (ENG.). 208p. (J). (gr. 3-7). 6.99 (978-0-14-240224-5(9), Puffin Books) Penguin Young Readers Group.
Meade, Holly. If I Never Forever Endeavor. Meade, Holly, illus. 2011. (ENG., Illus.). 32p. (J). (gr. -1-3). 16.99 (978-0-7636-4071-2(9)) Candlewick Pr.
Meister, Cari. The Brave Puffer Fish, 1 vol. Harpster, Steve, illus. 2011. (Ocean Tales Ser.). (ENG.). 32p. (gr. 2-3). pap. 6.25 (978-1-4342-3389-9(8)) Stone Arch Bks.
Merialdo, Lee K. Kidnapped. 2006. 112p. pap. 10.95 (978-0-7414-3407-4(5)) Infinity Publishing.
Meyer, Ken, Jr., illus. Lucky Lionel. 2009. (J). (978-1-60108-020-2(4)) Red Cygnet Pr.
Mittal, Anjali. The Convent Rules. 2009. (Illus.). 80p. pap. 10.49 (978-1-4389-8575-6(4)) AuthorHouse.
Montgomery, R. A. Always Picked Last. 2009. 64p. (J). pap. 7.99 (978-1-933390-38-3(7)) Chooseco LLC.
Morgan-Cole, Trudy J. Esther: Courage to Stand. 2010. 144p. (J). pap. 12.99 (978-0-8280-2430-3(8)) Review & Herald Publishing Assn.
Morino, Sakana. Becoming a Dragon. Morino, Sakana, illus. 2014. (Illus.). (J). 8.95 (978-1-935523-67-3(8)) World Tribune Pr.
Moses, Tammy. The Prophecy. 2006. 288p. per. 19.99 (978-1-58169-194-8(7)) Genesis Communications, Inc.
Moss, Anne H. The Amazing, True-To-Life Tale of Me Do It. 2012. 28p. pap. 19.99 (978-1-4772-2072-6(0)) AuthorHouse.
Myhre, J. A. A Bird, a Girl, & a Rescue. 2016. (Illus.). ix, 133p. (J). pap. 15.99 (978-1-942572-69-5(7)) New Growth Pr.
Nanette. Sunny the Orange Puppy. 2004. (Life on Granny's Farm Ser.). (J). 12.95 (978-0-9741269-6-8(9)) St. Bernard Publishing, LLC.
Narsimhan, Mahtab. The Third Eye. 2007. (Tara Trilogy Ser.: 1). (ENG.). 240p. (YA). (gr. 5-7). pap. 12.99 (978-1-55002-750-1(6), Boardwalk Bks.) Dundurn CAN. Dist: Ingram Publisher Services.
Neil, Deanna. The Land of Curiosities (Book 2)) Lost in Yellowstone, 1872-1873. 2009. 320p. (J). pap. 12.95 (978-0-9798800-2-5(5)) EcoSeekers, The.
Nobleman, Marc Tyler. Brave Like My Brother. 2016. (ENG.). 112p. (J). (gr. 2-5). 15.99 (978-0-545-88035-0(1), Scholastic Pr.) Scholastic, Inc.
Norris, Christine. The Talisman of Zandria. 2013. 240p. pap. 14.99 (978-1-61271-220-8(7)) Zumaya Pubns. LLC.
Nye, Barry. Hannah & the Magic Blanket - Land of the Dinosaurs. 2009. 40p. pap. 18.50 (978-0-557-03682-0(8)) Lulu Pr., Inc.
Ohi, Ruth. Chicken, Pig, Cow. Ohi, Ruth, illus. 2008. (ENG., Illus.). 32p. (J). (gr. -1-k). 2nd ed. 19.95 (978-1-55451-157-0(7), 9781554511570) 6th ed. pap. 6.95 (978-1-55451-156-3(9), 9781554511563) Annick Pr., Ltd. CAN. Dist: Publishers Group West (PGW).
Orietta, Susan. The Day Tyson Became a Hero. 2011. 24p. pap. 15.99 (978-1-4628-6823-0(1)) Xlibris Corp.
Otoshi, Kathryn. One. pap. (978-0-9723946-5-9(6)); 2008. (ENG., Illus.). 32p. (J). (gr. -1). 17.95 (978-0-9723946-4-2(8)) KO Kids Bks.
—Two. 2014. (ENG., Illus.). 40p. (J). (gr. -1). 18.95 (978-0-9723946-6-6(4)) KO Kids Bks.
Parish, Alex. Peter & the Flying Sergeant. 2009. 30p. 21.50 (978-0-9561613-0-7(8)) Parish, Alex GBR. Dist: Lulu Pr., Inc.
Park, Linda Sue. When My Name Was Keoko. 2004. 199p. (J). (gr. 5). 14.65 (978-0-7569-2928-2(8)) Perfection Learning Corp.
—When My Name Was Keoko. 2012. lib. bdg. 18.40 (978-0-606-24716-0(5), Turtleback) Turtleback Bks.
Parsons, Wendelin Van Draanen. The Secret Life of Lincoln Jones. 2016. (ENG.). 272p. (J). (gr. 3-7). 16.99 (978-1-101-94040-2(9), Knopf Bks. for Young Readers) Random Hse. Children's Bks.
Pascal, Francine. Fearless 2: Twisted; Kiss; Payback. 2013. (Fearless Ser.). (ENG.). 656p. (YA). (gr. 9). pap. 12.99 (978-1-4424-6860-3(2), Simon Pulse) Simon Pulse.
Paton, Doug. Terror 911. 90p. pap. (978-0-9731237-6-0(1)) High Interest Publishing (HIP).
Pearson, Yvonne. Sadie Braves the Wilderness. Ritz, Karen, illus. 2017. (ENG.). 32p. (J). (gr. -1-2). 16.95 **(978-1-68134-038-8(0))** Minnesota Historical Society Pr.
Peck, Lisa J. Skating with Spencer: CTR Club - Book Four, 4 bks. 2005. (J). pap. 6.95 (978-0-9749241-8-2(0)) Golden Wings Enterprises.

C D

Penn, Audrey. Chester the Brave. Gibson, Barbara Leonard, illus. 2012. (Kissing Hand Ser.). (ENG.). 32p. (J). (gr. -1-3). 16.95 *(978-1-933718-79-8(X))* Tanglewood Pr.

Perez, Annette. My Brain Won't Float Away / Mi cerebro no va a salir Flotando. Herranz Brooks, Jacqueline, tr. Fundora, Yolanda V., illus. 2007. (ENG & SPA.). 32p. (J). 19.95 *(978-0-9725611-2-9(9)*, Campanita Bks.) Editorial Campana.

Peters, Andrew Fusek. The Ant & the Big Bad Bully Goat. Wadham, Anna, illus. 2007. (Traditional Tales with a Twist Ser.). (ENG.). 32p. (J). (gr. 2-2). pap. *(978-1-84643-079-4(8))* Child's Play International Ltd.

Pierce, Seth J. Camporee of Doom. 2009. (J). pap. 12.99 *(978-0-8163-2364-7(X))* Pacific Pr. Publishing Assn.

Pilkington, Linda Rash. Arthur Collins & the Three Wishes: Arthur the Brave! 322p. (YA). (gr. 4-18). 2009. pap. 13.95 *(978-0-615-26743-2(2))* 2008. 20.95 *(978-0-615-22213-4(7))* City Castles Publishing.

Pinkney, Andrea Davis. Sojourner Truth's Step-Stomp Stride. Pinkney, Brian, illus. 2009. (ENG.). 32p. (J). (gr. k-4). 16.99 *(978-0-7868-0767-3(9)*, Jump at the Sun) Hyperion Bks. for Children.

Porter, Jen. I Am Brave. Saunders, Katie, illus. 2016. (ENG.). 16p. (J). (-3). bds. 7.99 *(978-1-4926-4165-0(0)*, 9781492641650, Sourcebooks Jabberwocky) Sourcebooks, Inc.

Price, Margaret Evans, illus. The Betty Fairy Book. 2006. (Shape Bks.). (ENG.). 16p. (J). pap. 9.95 *(978-1-59583-092-0(8)*, Green Tiger Pr.) Laughing Elephant.

Priddy, Roger. Little Friends: Splish Splash. 2014. (Little Friends Ser.). (ENG.). 6p. (J). (gr. -1 — 1). 7.99 *(978-0-312-51682-6(7)*, 9780312516826, Priddy Bks.) St. Martin's Pr.

Pritchett, Georgia. Wilf the Mighty Worrier: Battles a Pirate. 2016. (Wilf the Mighty Worrier Ser.: 2). (ENG., Illus.). 208p. (J). 16.99 *(978-1-68144-320-1(1))* Quercus NA.

Prose, Francine. Rhino, Rhino, Sweet Potato. Armstrong, Matthew S., illus. 2009. 32p. (J). (gr. -1-1). lib. bdg. 18.89 *(978-0-06-008079-2(5))* HarperCollins Pubs.

Pryce, Denise. Alexander & the Ring of Destiny. 2009. 72p. pap. 24.99 *(978-1-4251-8887-0(7))* Trafford Publishing.

Puzzuoli, Jon. Wishing to Whistle. 2009. 32p. pap. 17.50 *(978-0-557-10420-8(3))* Lulu Pr., Inc.

The Quest for Courage. 2006. (Amazing Travels of Wannabeb Ser.). (Illus.). 32p. (J). (gr. -1-3). 8.99 *(978-0-7847-1801-8(6)*, 04127) Standard Publishing.

Reid, Janet. Granny Rags. 2012. 194p. pap. *(978-1-922120-25-0(1)*, IP Kidz) Interactive Pubns. Pty, Ltd.

—Granny Rags. 2013. 200p. pap. *(978-1-4596-6125-7(7))* ReadHowYouWant.com, Ltd.

Ressy-Nieves, Cynthia Ann. Keek-A-Poo's Adventures. 2010. 48p. pap. 24.99 *(978-1-4535-1479-5(1))* Xlibris Corp.

Reynolds, Jason. As Brave As You. (ENG.). 432p. (J). (gr. 5). 2017. pap. 7.99 *(978-1-4814-1591-0(3)*, Atheneum Bks. for Young Readers) 2016. (Illus.). 16.99 *(978-1-4814-1590-3(5)*, Atheneum/Caitlyn Dlouhy Books) Simon & Schuster Children's Publishing.

—As Brave As You. 2017. (J). lib. bdg. 18.40 ***(978-0-606-39930-2(5))*** Turtleback Bks.

Richmond, Marianne. Be Brave Little One. 2017. (ENG.). 40p. (J). (-2). 17.99 ***(978-1-4926-5883-2(9)***, Sourcebooks Jabberwocky) Sourcebooks, Inc.

Ridley, R. W. Delon City: Book Two of the Oz Chronicles. 2006. (YA). per. 9.99 *(978-0-9792067-0-2(7))* Middleburry Hse. Publishing.

Rinaldi, Ann. Keep Smiling Through. 2005. (ENG.). 208p. (J). (gr. 2-5). pap. 13.95 *(978-0-15-205399-4(9))* Houghton Mifflin Harcourt Publishing Co.

Rix, Jamie. Bendro Bach. Williams, Dylan, tr. from ENG. Chapman, Lynne, illus. 2005. (WEL.). 36p. *(978-1-902416-84-7(8))* Cymdeithas Lyfrau Ceredigion.

Robinson, Sharon. Testing the Ice: A True Story about Jackie Robinson. Nelson, Kadir, illus. 2009. (ENG.). 40p. (J). (gr. 2-5). 18.99 *(978-0-545-05251-1(3)*, Scholastic Pr.) Scholastic, Inc.

Roscoe, Charlie. The Red Prince. Cole, Tom Clohosy, illus. 2016. (ENG.). 32p. (J). (-k). 16.99 *(978-0-7636-8912-4(2)*, Templar) Candlewick Pr.

Roth, Veronica. Allegiant. (Divergent Ser.: 3). (YA). (gr. 9). 2016. 592p. pap. 12.99 *(978-0-06-242009-1(7))* 2016. 592p. pap. 12.99 *(978-0-06-202407-7(8))* 2013. (ENG.). 544p. 19.99 *(978-0-06-202406-0(X))* 2016. 592p. 19.99 *(978-0-06-242008-4(9))* HarperCollins Pubs. (Tegen, Katherine Bks).

—Allegiant. l.t. ed. 2016. (Divergent Ser.: 3). (ENG.). 580p. pap. 12.99 *(978-1-59413-960-4(1)*, Large Print Pr.) Thorndike Pr.

—Allegiant. 2016. (Divergent Ser.: 3). lib. bdg. 24.50 *(978-0-606-38141-3(4))*; lib. bdg. 24.50 *(978-0-606-38182-6(1))* Turtleback Bks.

—Divergent. 2013. (KOR.). ***(978-89-5660-710-8(9))*** Eunhaeng Namu Publishing Co.

—Divergent. Delort, Nicolas, photos by. 2014. (Divergent Ser.: 1). (ENG., Illus.). 576p. (YA). (gr. 9). pap. 12.99 *(978-0-06-238724-0(3)*, Tegen, Katherine Bks) HarperCollins Pubs.

—Divergent. 2012. (ENG.). 512p. pap. *(978-0-06-219406-0(2))* HarperCollins Pubs.

—Divergent, 3 vols. Delort, Nicolas, photos by. (Divergent Ser.: 1). (ENG., Illus.). (YA). (gr. 9-18). 2011. 496p. 17.99 *(978-0-06-202402-2(7))* 2014. 576p. 19.99 *(978-0-06-235217-0(2))* HarperCollins Pubs. (Tegen, Katherine Bks).

—Divergent. movie tie-in ed. 2014. (Divergent Ser.: Bk. 1). (ENG.). 496p. (YA). (gr. 9). 17.99 *(978-0-06-228984-1(5)*, Tegen, Katherine Bks) HarperCollins Pubs.

—Divergent, 1. 2012. (ENG.). 496p. *(978-0-00-742042-1(0))* HarperCollins Pubs. Ltd.

—Divergent. 2009. (Divergent Ser.: Bk. 1). 11.04 *(978-0-7848-3786-3(4)*, Everbind) Marco Bk. Co.

—Divergent. 2014. (Divergent Trilogy Ser.). (ENG.). (YA). (gr. 9). lib. bdg. 23.60 ***(978-1-62765-593-4(X))*** Perfection Learning Corp.

—Divergent. l.t. ed. 2014. (Divergent Ser.: Bk. 1). (ENG.). 530p. pap. 12.99 *(978-1-59413-745-7(5)*, Large Print Pr.) Thorndike Pr.

—Divergent. 2014. (Divergent Ser.: 1). (YA). lib. bdg. 24.50 *(978-0-606-36515-4(X))* Turtleback Bks.

—Divergent; Insurgent; Allegiant, 3 vols., Set. 2013. (Divergent Ser.: Bks. 1-3). (ENG.). (YA). (gr. 9). 55.97 *(978-0-06-227878-4(9)*, Tegen, Katherine Bks) HarperCollins Pubs.

—Divergente. 2013. (Divergent Ser.: Bk. 1).Tr. of Divergent. (SPA.). 464p. (YA). pap. 21.99 *(978-84-272-0118-7(4))* Molino, Editorial ESP. Dist: Lectorum Pubns., Inc.

—Four: A Divergent Collection: The Transfer; The Initiate; The Son; The Traitor. 2014. (Divergent Ser.). (ENG.). 304p. (J). (gr. 9). 17.99 *(978-0-06-234521-9(4))* HarperCollins Pubs.

Roth, Veronica. Insurgent. 2014. (KOR.). ***(978-89-5660-758-0(3))*** Eunhaeng Namu Publishing Co.

—Insurgent. 2015. pap. *(978-0-06-238845-2(2))* 2015. (Divergent Ser.: 2). (ENG.). 592p. (J). (gr. 9). pap. 12.99 *(978-0-06-202405-3(1))* 2012. (Divergent Ser.: 2). (ENG.). 544p. (YA). (gr. 9). 17.99 *(978-0-06-202404-6(3))* 2012. (Divergent Ser.: 2). 544p. (YA). (gr. 9). pap. 12.00 *(978-0-06-212784-6(5))* 2012. (Divergent Ser.: 2). (ENG.). 592p. (YA). (gr. 9). 19.99 *(978-0-06-223493-3(5))* 2015. (Divergent Ser.: 2). (ENG.). 544p. (YA). (gr. 9). 17.99 *(978-0-06-237284-0(X))* 2015. (Divergent Ser.: Bk. 2). (ENG.). 592p. (YA). (gr. 9). pap. 12.99 *(978-0-06-237285-7(8))* HarperCollins Pubs. (Tegen, Katherine Bks).

—Insurgent. 2015. (Divergent Trilogy Ser.). (ENG.). (YA). (gr. 9). lib. bdg. 23.60 ***(978-1-62765-988-8(9))*** Perfection Learning Corp.

—Insurgent. 2015. (Divergent Ser.: 2). (YA). lib. bdg. 24.50 *(978-0-606-36475-1(7))* Turtleback Bks.

Rotstein, Adira. Little Jane & the Nameless Isle: A Little Jane Silver Adventure (Large Print 16pt) 2013. 324p. pap. *(978-1-4596-6322-0(5))* ReadHowYouWant.com, Ltd.

Scheel, Morgan Lee. The Fabulous Glitter Girl. Sbandelli, Angela, illus. 2017. (ENG.). 54p. (J). pap. 9.95 *(978-1-63047-998-5(5))* Morgan James Publishing.

Schraff, Anne. I Am Underdog. 2014. (Red Rhino Ser.). (J). lib. bdg. 18.40 *(978-0-606-36198-9(7))* Turtleback Bks.

Scott, Rosanna. Peter & Friends at Camp. Fargo, Todd, illus. l.t. ed. 2006. (Turtle Books). 32p. (J). (gr. k-4). pap. 9.95 *(978-0-944727-51-5(4))*; lib. bdg. 15.95 *(978-0-944727-52-2(2))* Jason & Nordic Pubs. (Turtle Bks.).

Shannon, George. Tippy-Toe Chick, Go! Dronzek, Laura, illus. 2003. (ENG.). 32p. (J). (gr. -1-3). 17.99 *(978-0-06-029823-4(5)*, Greenwillow Bks.) HarperCollins Pubs.

Shepherd, Keith D., illus. Kumba & Kambili: A Tale from Mali. 2013. (Tales of Honor Ser.). (ENG.). 32p. (J). (gr. 1-4). pap. 8.95 *(978-1-937529-58-1(4))* Red Chair Pr.

Shepherd, Keith D., illus. & retold by. Kumba & Kambili: A Tale from Mali. Shepherd, Keith D., retold by. 2013. (Tales of Honor (Red Chair Press) Ser.). (ENG.). 32p. (J). (gr. 1-4). lib. bdg. 26.60 *(978-1-937529-74-1(6))* Red Chair Pr.

Sherman, M. Zachary. Blood Brotherhood, 1 vol. Casas, Fritz, illus. 2011. (Bloodlines Ser.). (ENG.). 88p. (gr. 4-8). pap. 6.95 *(978-1-4342-3098-0(8))*; 26.65 *(978-1-4342-2559-7(3))* Stone Arch Bks.

—The Heart of War. 2013. (Bloodlines Ser.). (ENG.). 240p. (gr. 4-8). pap. 7.95 *(978-1-62370-002-7(7))* Stone Arch Bks.

—A Time for War, 1 vol. Casas, Fritz, illus. 2011. (Bloodlines Ser.). (ENG.). 88p. (gr. 4-8). pap. 6.95 *(978-1-4342-3097-3(X))*; 26.65 *(978-1-4342-2558-0(5))* Stone Arch Bks.

Shlasko, Robert. Molly & the Sword Diamond, Donna, illus. 2004. 32p. (J). 15.95 *(978-0-9745077-4-3(1))* Jane & Street Pubs. Ltd.

Silverberry, A. R. Wyndano's Cloak. 2010. 424p. 21.95 *(978-0-9841037-6-8(7))* Tree Tunnel Pr.

Sinke, Janet Mary. Priscilla Mcdoodlenut Doodle Mcmae Asks, Why? Pennington, Craig, illus. 2007. 40p. (J). 17.95 *(978-0-9742732-8-0(7))* My Grandma & Me Pubs.

Skrbina, Daniel William. A Knight to Remember: Gulliver's Journey Continues, 1 vol. 2009. 74p. pap. 19.95 *(978-1-60836-737-5(1))* America Star Bks.

Sky Koster, Amy & Tillworth, Mary. The Knight Night Guard. Random House Disney Staff, illus. 2016. (Step into Reading Ser.). (ENG.). 24p. (J). (gr. -1-1). 4.99 *(978-0-7364-3450-8(X)*, RH/Disney) Random Hse. Children's Bks.

Slote, Alfred. Hang Tough, Paul Mather. 2013. 146p. pap. 11.99 *(978-0-9886988-3-3(8))* Arborville Bks.

Smith, Mary P. Wells. The Young Puritans in King Philip's War. Bridgman, L. J., illus. 2011. 396p. 54.95 *(978-1-258-05550-9(3))* Literary Licensing, LLC.

Smith, Shirleen L. Not All Heroes Are on TV. 2011. 24p. (gr. -1). pap. 12.45 *(978-1-4497-1721-6(7)*, WestBow Pr.) Author Solutions, Inc.

Smucker, Anna Egan. To Keep the South Manitou Light. (Great Lakes Books Ser.). (ENG., Illus.). 144p. (J). 2006. (gr. 3-7). per. 15.99 *(978-0-8143-3236-8(6)*, 1147) 2004. 23.95 *(978-0-8143-3235-1(8)*, 1148, Painted Turtle) Wayne State Univ. Pr.

Sperry, Armstrong. Call It Courage. 2008. (ENG.). 128p. (YA). (gr. 7). mass mkt. 6.99 *(978-1-4169-5368-5(X)*, Simon Pulse) Simon Pulse.

—Call It Courage. 2008. 17.20 *(978-1-4178-1178-6(1)*, Turtleback) Turtleback Bks.

Spoon, Cynthia. The Ice Angel. Harr, Lynn, illus. 2006. 24p. (J). (gr. -1-3). per. 8.50 *(978-1-60002-280-7(4)*, 4233) Mountain Valley Publishing, LLC.

Sretaw. Aussie Animal Friends. 2010. 36p. pap. 32.70 *(978-1-4500-7415-5(4))* Xlibris Corp.

Stein, Peter. Little Red's Riding 'Hood. Gall, Chris, illus. 2015. (ENG.). 40p. (J). (gr. -1-k). 16.99 *(978-0-545-60969-2(0))* Scholastic, Inc.

Stengel, Joyce A. St. Patrick & the Three Brave Mice, 1 vol. Leonhard, Herb, illus. 2009. (ENG.). 32p. (J). (gr. k-3). 16.99 *(978-1-58980-663-4(8))* Pelican Publishing Co., Inc.

Stevenson, Robert Louis. Treasure Island: With a Discussion of Courage. 2003. (Values in Action Illustrated Classics Ser.). (J). *(978-1-59203-054-5(8))* Learning Challenge, Inc.

Stimson, Joan. Brave Lion, Scared Lion. Rubio, Esther, tr. Rutherford, Meg, illus. (J). (gr. k-1). pap. *(978-0-590-90985-3(1)*, SO3690) Scholastic, Inc.

Stingley, Tanya. Jonas & the Pride of Fiona. 2008. pap. 9.00 *(978-0-8059-8685-3(5))* Dorrance Publishing Co., Inc.

Stoddard, Jeffery. Skid & the Too Tiny Tunnel: A Story of Courage Based on Deuteronomy 31:6. Fogle, Robin & Rhodes, Karen, eds. Stoddard, Jeffery, illus. 2009. (ENG., Illus.). 32p. (J). (gr. -1-2). 12.99 *(978-1-59317-355-5(5))* Warner Pr., Inc.

Studio Mouse Editorial. Ariel: The Brave Little Mermaid. 2008. (ENG., Illus.). 36p. (gr. -1-k). 7.99 *(978-1-59069-434-3(1))* Studio Mouse LLC.

Suhajcik, Andrea. Mommy, I Did Nothing Wrong! 2012. 16p. pap. 15.99 *(978-1-4772-1192-2(6))* AuthorHouse.

Sullivan, Deirdre. Ming Goes to School. Löfdahl, Maja, illus. 2016. (ENG.). 32p. (J). (gr. -1-k). 16.99 *(978-1-5107-0050-5(1)*, Sky Pony Pr.) Skyhorse Publishing Co., Inc.

Sun Edit and Book Design, ed. Abraham Lincoln & the Forest of Little Pigeon Creek. 2007. (Illus.). 56p. (J). 19.95 *(978-0-9798739-0-4(8))* AmeriTales Entertainment, LLC.

Susko, Mark D. Sally Sassafras, the Girl with Monster Hair. 2011. 50p. pap. 16.95 *(978-1-4560-5521-9(6))* America Star Bks.

Taylor, Sean. A Brave Bear. Hughes, Emily, illus. 2016. (ENG.). 32p. (J). (-k). 16.99 *(978-0-7636-8224-8(1))* Candlewick Pr.

Thompson, Lauren. Cuaquito (Little Quack) Anderson, Derek, illus. 2010. (SPA.). 34p. (J). (gr. -1-1). bds. 7.99 *(978-1-4169-9894-5(2)*, Libros Para Ninos) Libros Para Ninos.

—Little Quack. Anderson, Derek, illus. 2005. (Classic Board Bks.). (ENG.). 32p. (J). (gr. -1-k). bds. 7.99 *(978-0-689-87645-5(9)*, Little Simon) Little Simon.

—Little Quack's Bath Book. Anderson, Derek, illus. 2006. (ENG.). 8p. (J). (gr. -1 — 1). 8.99 *(978-1-4169-0803-6(X)*, Little Simon) Little Simon.

Thompson, Lauren & Anderson, Derek. Little Quack. 2003. (ENG., Illus.). 32p. (J). (gr. -1-3). 17.99 *(978-0-689-84723-3(8)*, Simon & Schuster Bks. For Young Readers) Simon & Schuster Bks. For Young Readers.

Tillworth, Mary. The Puppy & the Ring (Bubble Guppies) Random House Staff & MJ Illustrations Staff, illus. 2014. (Pictureback Ser.). (ENG.). 24p. (J). (gr. -1-2). 3.99 *(978-0-385-38408-7(4)*, Random Hse. Bks. for Young Readers) Random Hse. Children's Bks.

Toh, Irene. Kumi the Bear. Hagan, Stacy, illus. 2008. (ENG.). 24p. pap. 12.75 *(978-1-4389-1368-1(0))* AuthorHouse.

Vere, Ed. Max the Brave. 2017. (ENG.). 30p. (J). bds. 7.99 ***(978-1-4926-5706-4(9)***, Sourcebooks Jabberwocky) Sourcebooks, Inc.

Vermeulen, Thomas. Gabangani Guinea Fowl & Huzu the Bird Eating Spider. 2009. 50p. pap. 19.50 *(978-1-60693-741-9(3)*, Eloquent Bks.) Strategic Book Publishing & Rights Agency (SBPRA).

Vernon, Ursula. Nurk: The Strange, Surprising Adventures of a (Somewhat) Brave Shrew. 2008. (ENG., Illus.). 144p. (J). (gr. 3-7). 16.00 *(978-0-15-206375-7(7))* Houghton Mifflin Harcourt Publishing Co.

Wales, Dirk. Jack London's Dog. Moser, Barry, illus. 2008. 64p. (YA). (gr. 5-9). 17.95 *(978-0-9632459-3-9(7))* Great Plains Pr.

Wallace, Bill. Danger on Panther Peak. 2008. (ENG., Illus.). 176p. (J). (gr. 3-7). pap. 6.99 *(978-1-4169-4110-1(X)*, Simon & Schuster/Paula Wiseman Bks.) Simon & Schuster/Paula Wiseman Bks.

Watt, Mélanie. Scaredy Squirrel. Watt, Mélanie, illus. 2008. (ENG., Illus.). 40p. (J). (gr. -1-3). pap. 7.95 *(978-1-55453-023-6(7))* Kids Can Pr., Ltd. CAN. Dist: Hachette Bk. Group.

—Scaredy Squirrel. 2011. (J). (gr. -1-3). 18.95 *(978-0-545-32752-7(0))*; 29.95 *(978-0-545-32740-4(7))*;Set. 38.75 *(978-0-545-32759-6(8))* Weston Woods Studios, Inc.

Weinberger, Kimberly. Dolphin's Big Leap. Ziss, Debra, illus. 2003. (Hello Reader! Ser.). 30p. (J). *(978-0-439-44159-9(5))* Scholastic, Inc.

Wendling, Peter. Caterpillars Never Lie, 1 vol. 2010. 26p. pap. 24.95 *(978-1-4489-4676-1(X))* PublishAmerica, Inc.

Weston Woods Staff, creator. Brave Irene. 2011. 38.75 *(978-0-439-72666-5(2))*; 18.95 *(978-0-439-72665-8(4))*; 29.95 *(978-0-439-73468-4(1))* Weston Woods Studios, Inc.

Whelan, Gloria. Homeless Bird. unabr. ed. 2004. 240p. (J). (gr. 5-9). pap. 29.00 incl. audio *(978-0-8072-8859-7(4)*, Listening Library) Random Hse. Audio Publishing Group.

Wigger, Sherry. Scary Stories for Brave Kids, 1 vol. 2009. 73p. pap. 16.95 *(978-1-61582-308-6(5))* PublishAmerica, Inc.

Willard, Claudette. Chloe & Banana Island. 2008. 40p. pap. 16.99 *(978-1-4343-8756-1(9))* AuthorHouse.

Wood, Steve & Fox, Woody. Courageous Cats Compete. 2006. (ENG., Illus.). 174p. (J). (gr. 2-4). pap. 8.99 *(978-0-7459-6011-1(1))* Lion Hudson PLC GBR. Dist: Independent Pubs. Group.

World Almanac Editors. Great Stories of Courage: The Call of the Wild; the Red Badge of Courage; Treasure Island. 2007. (Bank Street Graphic Novels Ser.). (Illus.). 56p. (gr. 5-8). lib. bdg. 31.00 *(978-0-8368-7926-1(0))* Stevens, Gareth Publishing LLLP.

World Almanac Editors, creator. Great Stories of Courage: The Call of the Wild, the Red Badge of Courage, Treasure Island. 2007. (Bank Street Graphic Novels Ser.). (Illus.). 56p. (gr. 5-8). pap. 14.05 *(978-0-8368-7933-9(3))* Stevens, Gareth Publishing LLLP.

Wright-McAdoo, Joyce & Wright-Mcadoo, Joyce. Zimb: Believe. 2009. (Illus.). 28p. pap. 15.99 *(978-1-4415-8051-1(4))* Xlibris Corp.

Wyley, Enda. Boo & Bear. Massardier, Greg, tr. Massardier, Greg, illus. 2003. (Panda Cubs Ser.: 01). (ENG.). 48p. (J). pap. 9.95 *(978-0-86278-806-3(4))* O'Brien Pr., Ltd., The IRL. Dist: Dufour Editions, Inc.

Yamada, Shale. Rainbow Kitty Saves the Day. Riedler, Amelia, ed. 2013. (Story Lines Ser.). (ENG.). 24p. (J). (gr. -1-3). 9.95 *(978-1-935414-92-6(5))* Compendium, Inc., Publishing & Communications.

Yep, Laurence. The Earth Dragon Awakes: The San Francisco Earthquake of 1906. (ENG., Illus.). 128p. (J). (gr. 3-7). 2008. pap. 6.99 *(978-0-06-000846-8(6))* 2006. 14.99 *(978-0-06-027524-2(3))* HarperCollins Pubs.

Yogananda, Paramahansa. Due Rane Nei Guai. 2011. 30p. 22.00 *(978-0-87612-125-2(3))* Self-Realization Fellowship Pubs.

Yokota, Hiromitsu, illus. The Tale of the Oki Islands: A Tale from Japan. 2013. (Tales of Honor (Red Chair Press) Ser.). (ENG.). 32p. (J). (gr. 1-4). lib. bdg. 26.60 *(978-1-937529-78-9(9))* Red Chair Pr.

Zullo, Allan. Kid Pirates: Their Battles, Shipwrecks, & Narrow Escapes. 2007. 147p. (J). pap. *(978-0-439-91813-8(8))* Scholastic, Inc.

COURTESY

see also Behavior; Etiquette

Amos, Janine. After You. 2009. (Best Behavior Ser.). (Illus.). 32p. (J). (gr. -1-2). pap. 10.55 *(978-1-60754-032-8(0))*; lib. bdg. 22.60 *(978-1-60754-020-5(7))* Windmill Bks.

—No, Thank You. 2009. (Best Behavior Ser.). (Illus.). 32p. (J). (gr. -1-2). pap. 10.55 *(978-1-60754-036-6(3))*; lib. bdg. 22.60 *(978-1-60754-022-9(3))* Windmill Bks.

—Please. 2009. (Best Behavior Ser.). (Illus.). 32p. (J). (gr. -1-2). pap. 10.55 *(978-1-60754-038-0(X))*; lib. bdg. 22.60 *(978-1-60754-023-6(1))* Windmill Bks.

Amos, Janine & Spenceley, Annabel. Let's Take Turns. 2009. (Best Behavior Ser.). (Illus.). 32p. (J). (gr. -1-2). 22.60 *(978-1-60754-512-5(8))*; pap. 10.55 *(978-1-60754-513-2(6))* Windmill Bks.

Berry, Joy. Help Me Be Good about Being Mean. 2009. (Help Me Be Good Ser.). 32p. pap. 7.95 *(978-1-60577-129-8(5))* Berry, Joy Enterprises.

—Help Me Be Good about Being Rude. 2009. (ENG.). 40p. (J). (gr. k-2). pap. 7.95 *(978-1-60577-121-2(X))* Berry, Joy Enterprises.

—Help Me Be Good Being Mean. Bartholomew, illus. 2010. (Help Me Be Good Ser.). (ENG.). 32p. (J). (gr. -1-2). pap. 4.99 *(978-1-60577-142-7(2))* Berry, Joy Enterprises.

—Help Me Be Good Being Rude. Bartholomew, illus. 2010. (Help Me Be Good Ser.). (ENG.). 32p. (J). (gr. -1-2). pap. 4.99 *(978-1-60577-138-0(4))* Berry, Joy Enterprises.

—Help Me Be Good Teasing. Bartholomew, illus. 2010. (Help Me Be Good Ser.). (ENG.). 32p. (J). (gr. -1-2). pap. 4.99 *(978-1-60577-141-0(4))* Berry, Joy Enterprises.

Berry, Joy Wilt. A Book about Being Mean. 2005. (Illus.). (J). *(978-0-7172-8591-4(X))* Scholastic, Inc.

—A Book about Being Rude. 2005. (Illus.). (J). *(978-0-7172-8592-1(8))* Scholastic, Inc.

—A Book about Teasing. 2005. (Illus.). (J). *(978-0-7172-8580-8(4))* Scholastic, Inc.

Brown, Marcy & Haley, Dennis. We Both Read Bilingual Edition-The Well-Mannered Monster/el Monstruo Debuenos Modales. Raglin, Tim, illus. 2011. (ENG & SPA.). 44p. (J). pap. 4.99 *(978-1-60115-044-8(X))* Treasure Bay, Inc.

Brown, Marcy, et al. The Well-Mannered Monster: Monstruo de Buenos Modales. Raglin, Tim, illus. 2010. 41p. (J). *(978-1-60115-043-1(1))* Treasure Bay, Inc.

Chancellor, Deborah. Good Manners. 2009. (Now We Know About... Ser.). (ENG., Illus.). 24p. (J). (gr. k-3). pap. *(978-0-7787-4736-9(0))*; lib. bdg. *(978-0-7787-4719-2(0))* Crabtree Publishing Co.

Chomet, Natalie. Coping with Body Shaming. 2017. (J). ***(978-1-5081-7687-9(6))*** Rosen Publishing Group, Inc., The.

Ciovacco, Justine. Etiquette As a Guest & at Parties. 2016. (Etiquette Rules! Ser.). 00048p. (J). (gr. 6-6). lib. bdg. 31.75 *(978-1-4994-6486-3(X))* Rosen Publishing Group, Inc., The.

Heos, Bridget. Manners at the Store. Longhi, Katya, illus. 2015. (Monstrous Manners Ser.). (ENG.). 24p. (J). (gr. 1-3). 19.95 *(978-1-60753-746-5(X))* Amicus Publishing.

—Manners on Vacation. Longhi, Katya, illus. 2015. (Monstrous Manners Ser.). (ENG.). 24p. (J). (gr. 1-3). 19.95 *(978-1-60753-747-2(8))* Amicus Publishing.

Jones, Grace. My Manners. 2017. (Illus.). 24p. (J). ***(978-0-7787-3260-0(6))*** Crabtree Publishing Co.

Larsen, Carolyn. Being Nice to Others: A Book about Rudeness. O'Connor, Tim, illus. 2016. (Growing God's Kids Ser.). (ENG.). 32p. (J). pap. 4.99 *(978-0-8010-0957-0(X))* Baker Bks.

Marsico, Katie. Taking Turns! 2012. (21st Century Basic Skills Library: Kids Can Make Manners Count Ser.). (ENG.). 24p. (gr. k-3). 22.79 *(978-1-61080-432-5(5)*, 202042); pap. 12.79 *(978-1-61080-606-0(9)*, 202216) Cherry Lake Publishing.

Nelson, Maria. I Am Polite. 2013. (Kids of Character Ser.). 24p. (J). (gr. 1-3). 22.60 *(978-1-4339-9025-0(3))*; pap. 48.90 *(978-1-4339-9027-4(X))* Stevens, Gareth Publishing LLLP.

—Saying Please & Thank You. 2015. (J). *(978-1-4824-1728-9(6))* Stevens, Gareth Publishing LLLP.

Nunn, Daniel & Smith, Sian. Manners at Home, 1 vol. 2012. (Oh, Behave! Ser.). (ENG.). 24p. (gr. -1-1). lib. bdg. 22.65 *(978-1-4329-6636-2(7)*, Acorn) Heinemann-Raintree.

Plattner, Josh. Manners Out & About, 1 vol. 2016. (ENG., Illus.). 24p. (J). *(978-1-62403-717-7(8))* ABDO Publishing Co.

Steinkraus, Kyla. May I Please? 2012. (ENG.). 24p. (gr. k-2). pap. 8.95 *(978-1-61810-271-3(0))* Rourke Educational Media.

COURTESY—FICTION

Antony, Steve. Please, Mr. Panda. 2014. (ENG.). 32p. (J). (gr. -1-k). 16.99 *(978-0-545-78892-2(7)*, Scholastic Pr.) Scholastic, Inc.

Banks, Jane Whelen. Liam Knows What to Do When Kids Act Snitty: Coping When Friends Are Tactless. 2008. (ENG., Illus.). 32p. 12.95 *(978-1-84310-902-0(6)*, 7167) Kingsley, Jessica Pubs. GBR. Dist: Macmillan Distribution Ltd.

Bently, Peter & McPhillips, Robert, illus. Say Please, Little Bear. 2013. (J). *(978-1-4351-4727-0(8))* Barnes & Noble, Inc.

Bradman, Tony. Snow White & the Magic Mirror, 1 vol. Warburton, Sarah, illus. 2014. (After Happily Ever After Ser.). (ENG.). 56p. (gr. 2-3). lib. bdg. 25.32 *(978-1-4342-7950-7(2)*, After Happily Ever After) Stone Arch Bks.

Cook, Julia. Sorry, I Forgot to Ask! My Story about Asking Permission & Making an Apology! De Weerd, Kelsey, illus. 2012. (ENG.). 32p. 16.95 *(978-1-934490-29-7(6))*; pap. 10.95 *(978-1-934490-28-0(8))* Boys Town Pr.

Crews, G. S. Ellen G Goes to the Haunted Planetarium. Designs, Marion, photos by. 2009. (Illus.). 50p. pap. 20.00 *(978-0-9795236-4-9(8))* Crews Pubns., LLC.

Dahl, Michael. Hippo Says "Excuse Me" Vidal, Oriol, illus. 2011. (Hello Genius Ser.). (ENG.). 20p. (gr. 1-2). bds. 7.99 *(978-1-4048-6787-1(2))* Picture Window Bks.

—Mouse Says Sorry, 1 vol. Vidal, Oriol, illus. 2011. (Hello Genius Ser.). (ENG.). 20p. (gr. 1-2). bds. 7.99 *(978-1-4048-6789-5(9))* Picture Window Bks.

—Penguin Says Please, 1 vol. Vidal, Oriol, illus. 2011. (Hello Genius Ser.). (ENG.). 20p. (gr. 1-2). bds. 7.99 *(978-1-4048-6788-8(0))* Picture Window Bks.

Daly, Niki. Thank You, Jackson: How One Little Boy Makes a Big Difference. Daly, Jude, illus. 2015. (ENG.). 32p. (J). (gr.

-1-3). 17.99 *(978-1-84780-484-6(5),* Frances Lincoln) Quarto Publishing Group UK GBR. Dist: Hachette Bk. Group.

Demas, Corinne & Roehrig, Artemis. Are Pirates Polite? Catrow, David, illus. 2016. (ENG.). 40p. (J). (gr. -1-k). 16.99 *(978-0-545-62874-7(1))* Scholastic, Inc.

Easton, Tom. Pirates Can Be Polite, 01 vols., 1. 2016. (Pirate Pals Ser.). (ENG.). 32p. (J). pap. 10.00 *(978-1-5081-9149-0(2),* Windmill Bks.) Rosen Publishing Group, Inc., The.

Fenske, Jonathan. Plankton Is Pushy. Fenske, Jonathan, illus. 2017. (ENG., Illus.). 40p. (J). (gr. -1-k). 14.99 *(978-1-338-09896-9(9),* Scholastic Pr.) Scholastic, Inc.

Higginson, Sheila Sweeny & Disney Book Group Staff. Loud Louie. Disney Storybook Artists Staff, illus. 2013. (World of Reading Ser.). (ENG.). 32p. (J). (gr. -1-k). pap. 3.99 *(978-1-4231-6456-2(3))* Disney Pr.

Hoban, Russell. The Little Brute Family. Hoban, Lillian, illus. 2011. (My Readers Ser.). (ENG.). 40p. (J). (gr. k-2). pap. 3.99 *(978-0-312-56373-8(6),* 9780312563738) Square Fish.

Kipling, Rudyard. How the Rhinoceros Got His Skin: The Graphic Novel, 1 vol. Rodriguez, Pedro, illus. 2012. (Graphic Spin Ser.). (ENG.). 40p. (gr. 1-3). pap. 5.95 *(978-1-4342-3882-5(2),* Graphic Revolve) Stone Arch Bks.

—How the Rhinoceros Got His Skin: The Graphic Novel, 1 vol. Rodríguez, Pedro, illus. 2012. (Graphic Spin Ser.). (ENG.). 40p. (gr. 1-3). lib. bdg. 23.99 *(978-1-4342-3025-6(2),* Graphic Revolve) Stone Arch Bks.

MacDonald, Alan. Worms!, 1 vol. Roberts, David, illus. 2013. (Dirty Bertie Ser.). (ENG.). 112p. (gr. 1-3). pap. 4.95 *(978-1-4342-4823-7(2));* lib. bdg. 25.32 *(978-1-4342-4619-6(1))* Stone Arch Bks.

Morel, John Henry. Is It True. 2009. 144p. 24.99 *(978-1-935436-40-9(6))* Rodaian Pr.

Murphy, Stuart J. Freda Says Please. Jones, Tim, illus. 2013. (I See I Learn Ser.). (ENG.). 32p. (J). (-k). pap. 6.95 *(978-1-58089-475-3(5))* Charlesbridge Publishing, Inc.

Pinckney, Julia. Am I Big Enough? A Fun Little Book on Manners, 1 vol. Young, Timothy, illus. 2016. (ENG.). 32p. (J). 16.99 *(978-0-7643-5053-5(6),* 9780764350535) Schiffer Publishing, Ltd.

Publications International Ltd. Staff, ed. Disney Princess: Please & Thank You. 2011. 12p. (J). bds. *(978-1-4508-0399-1(7))* Phoenix International Publications, Inc.

—Please & Thank You. 2010. 20p. (J). bds. 10.98 *(978-1-60553-439-8(0),* PIL Kids) Publications International, Ltd.

Ricci, Christine. Be Nice, Swiper! Aikins, Dave & Miller, Victoria, illus. 2007. (J). pap. *(978-1-4127-8925-7(7))* Publications International, Ltd.

Robinson, Mark. Vile: A Cautionary Tale for Little Monsters. Home, Sarah, illus. 2011. (ENG.). 32p. (J). (gr. k-2). 14.99 *(978-0-7459-6254-2(8))* Lion Hudson PLC GBR. Dist: Independent Pubs. Group.

Slater, Teddy & Rescek, Sanja, illus. I Can Say Please. 2012. (J). *(978-0-545-47249-4(0))* Scholastic, Inc.

Style Guide Staff, illus. Everyone Is Different: Why Being Different Is Great! 2012. (Yo Gabba Gabba! Ser.). (ENG.). 24p. (J). (gr. -1-2). pap. 3.99 *(978-1-4424-5443-9(1),* Simon Spotlight) Simon Spotlight.

Watkins, Rowboat. Rude Cakes. 2015. (ENG., Illus.). 40p. (J). (gr. -1-k). 16.99 *(978-1-4521-3851-0(6))* Chronicle Bks. LLC.

Webster, Kyle T. Please Say Please! Webster, Kyle T., illus. 2016. (ENG., Illus.). 32p. (J). (gr. -1-k). 17.99 *(978-0-545-84485-7(1),* Scholastic Pr.) Scholastic, Inc.

COURTING

see Dating (Social Customs)

COURTS

see also Judges; Jury; Justice, Administration of

Cuthbert, Megan & Siemens, Jared. Courthouse. 2016. (J). ***(978-1-5105-1883-4(5))*** SmartBook Media, Inc.

Harris, Nancy. What's the State Judicial Branch? 2016. (First Guide to Government Ser.). (ENG.). 32p. (gr. 1-3). pap. 8.29 *(978-1-4846-3691-6(0),* Heinemann First Library) Heinemann-Raintree.

Hiber, Amanda. Should Cameras Be Allowed in Courtrooms? 2008. (At Issue Ser.). (ENG., Illus.). 128p. (gr. 10-12). 39.40 *(978-0-7377-3928-2(2));* pap. 27.80 *(978-0-7377-3929-9(0),* Greenhaven Pr., Inc.) Cengage Gale.

Hunt, Santana. What Does the U.S. Supreme Court Do? 2017. (Look at Your Government Ser.). 32p. (gr. 2-2). pap. 10.50 *(978-1-4824-6059-9(9))* Stevens, Gareth Publishing LLLP.

Jacobs, Thomas A. They Broke the Law - You Be the Judge: True Cases of Teen Crime. 2003. (ENG.). 224p. (YA). (gr. 7-18). pap. 15.99 *(978-1-57542-134-6(8))* Free Spirit Publishing, Inc.

Kowalski, Kathiann M. Judges & Courts: A Look at the Judicial Branch. 2012. (Searchlight Books How Does Government Work Ser.). (ENG., Illus.). 40p. (gr. 3-5). pap. 51.01 *(978-0-7613-9233-0(5));* pap. 8.95 *(978-0-7613-8562-2(2));* lib. bdg. 27.93 *(978-0-7613-6516-7(8))* Lerner Publishing Group.

—Order in the Court: A Look at the Judicial Branch. 2003. (How Government Works). (ENG., Illus.). 56p. (gr. 4-8). lib. bdg. 25.26 *(978-0-8225-4698-6(1))* Lerner Publishing Group.

Krygier, Leora. Juvenile Court: A Judge's Guide for Young Adults & Their Parents, Vol. 2008. (ENG., Illus.). 196p. (gr. 9-18). 45.00 *(978-0-8108-6127-5(5))* Scarecrow Pr., Inc.

Lange, Donna. The Juvenile Court System. Albers, Lisa et al, eds. 2014. (Living with a Special Need Ser.: 16). 128p. (J). (gr. 7-18). 25.95 *(978-1-4222-3038-1(4))* Mason Crest.

LeVert, Suzanne. State Courts. 2003. (Kaleidoscope Ser.). (Illus.). 48p. (gr. 3-18). lib. bdg. 20.95 *(978-0-7614-1594-7(7),* Benchmark Bks.) Marshall Cavendish Corp.

Loria, Laura. What Is the Judicial Branch? 2015. (Let's Find Out! Government Ser.). (ENG.). 32p. (J). (gr. 2-3). 23.45 *(978-1-62275-961-3(3),* Britannica Educational Publishing) Rosen Publishing Group, Inc., The.

Madani, Hamed. The Judicial Branch: Interpreting America's Laws. 2008. (Federal Government Ser.). (Illus.). 128p. (J). (gr. 6-18). lib. bdg. 34.60 *(978-1-59845-059-0(X),* MyReportLinks.com Bks.) Enslow Pubs., Inc.

—The Supreme Court & the Judicial Branch: How the Federal Courts Interpret Our Laws. 2012. (Constitution & the United States Government Ser.). (Illus.). 104p. (J). (gr. 5-18). 33.27 *(978-0-7660-4065-6(8))* Enslow Pubs., Inc.

Marreel, Anne M. Kids in Court. 2011. 24p. pap. 15.99 *(978-1-4568-5735-6(5))* Xlibris Corp.

Morris, Kimberly & Burke, Kathleen. Just for Now: Kids & the People of the Court. Sansevero, Tony, illus. 2007. 48p. (J). (gr. k-4). 16.95 *(978-0-9754953-9-1(9))* Child Advocates, Inc.

Nagle, Cristen. Your Legal Rights As a Juvenile Being Tried As an Adult, 1 vol. 2015. (ENG., Illus.). 64p. (J). 33.25 *(978-1-4777-8016-9(5),* Rosen Reference) Rosen Publishing Group, Inc., The.

Petersen, Christine. How the Judicial Branch Works, 1 vol. 2014. (How the US Government Works). (ENG.). 48p. (gr. 3-6). lib. bdg. 32.79 *(978-1-62403-636-1(8))* ABDO Publishing Co.

Rodger, Ellen. What Is the Judicial Branch? 2013. (ENG.). 32p. (J). *(978-0-7787-0880-3(2));* pap. *(978-0-7787-0906-0(X))* Crabtree Publishing Co.

Salyers, Wendy. The Verdict Is In: Destination Reality. 2003. (YA). pap. 14.99 *(978-0-89265-966-1(1))* Randall Hse. Pubns.

Stewart, Sheila. Kids Have Troubles Too, 13 vols., Set. Incl. House Between Homes: Kids in the Foster Care System. Flath, Camden, told to. pap. 7.95 *(978-1-4222-1905-8(4));* I Don't Keep Secrets. Simons, Rae, told to. pap. 7.95 *(978-1-4222-1911-9(9));* I Like Me. Simons, Rae, told to. pap. 7.95 *(978-1-4222-1912-6(7));* I Live in Two Homes: Adjusting to Divorce & Remarriage. Simons, Rae, told to. pap. 7.95 *(978-1-4222-1907-2(0));* Place Called Dead. Simons, Rae, told to. (Illus.). pap. 7.95 *(978-1-4222-1914-0(3));* Sometimes My Mom Drinks Too Much. Simons, Rae, told to. (Illus.). pap. 7.95 *(978-1-4222-1917-1(8));* What's Going to Happen Next? Kids in the Juvenile Court System. Flath, Camden. pap. 7.95 *(978-1-4222-1906-5(2));* When Daddy Hit Mommy. Simons, Rae, told to. pap. 7.95 *(978-1-4222-1909-6(7));* When Life Makes Me Mad. Simons, Rae, told to. pap. 7.95 *(978-1-4222-1913-3(5));* When My Brother Went to Prison. Simons, Rae, told to. (Illus.). pap. 7.95 *(978-1-4222-1908-9(9));* When My Dad Lost His Job. Simons, Rae, told to. (Illus.). pap. 7.95 *(978-1-4222-1916-4(X));* (YA). (gr. 5-18). 2009. (Illus.). 48p. 2011. Set pap. 103.35 *(978-1-4222-1904-1(6));* Set lib. bdg. 259.35 *(978-1-4222-1691-0(8))* Mason Crest.

Stewart, Sheila & Flath, Camden. What's Going to Happen Next? Kids in the Juvenile Court System. (Kids Have Troubles Too Ser.). 48p. (YA). (gr. 5-18). 2010. (Illus.). lib. bdg. 19.95 *(978-1-4222-1693-4(4))* 2009. pap. 7.95 *(978-1-4222-1906-5(2))* Mason Crest.

Supreme Court Milestones, 5 bks., Group 2. Incl. Bakke Case: Challenge to Affirmative Action. Stefoff, Rebecca. 128p. (gr. 7). lib. bdg. 42.79 *(978-0-7614-1939-6(X));* Engel V. Vitale: Prayer in the Schools. Gold, Susan Dudley. 160p. (J). (gr. 3-7). lib. bdg. *(978-0-7614-1940-2(3));* Korematsu V. United States: Japanese-American Internment. Gold, Susan Dudley. 160p. (J). (gr. 4-7). lib. bdg. *(978-0-7614-1943-3(8));* Miranda Law: The Right to Remain Silent. Fridell, Ron. 144p. (J). (gr. 4-7). lib. bdg. *(978-0-7614-1942-6(X));* Vernonia School District V. Action: Drug Testing in the Schools. Gold, Susan Dudley. 142p. (J). (gr. 3-7). lib. bdg. *(978-0-7614-1941-9(1));* (Illus.). 2005. *(978-0-7614-1938-9(1),* Benchmark Bks.) Marshall Cavendish Corp.

Supreme Court Milestones Series, 5 Bks, Set. 2004. (J). 185.35 *(978-0-7614-1838-2(5))* Marshall Cavendish Corp.

The Supreme Court of the United States, 6 vols. (gr. 2-5). 39.95 *(978-0-7368-8925-4(6))* Red Brick Learning.

Weiss, Carrie & Lukes, Jessica. Step into the Courtroom: An Overview of Laws, Courts & Jury Trials. 2003. (J). per. 10.95 *(978-1-883055-61-5(X),* 152) Dandy Lion Pubns.

COURTS—FICTION

Grisham, John. The Accused. (Theodore Boone Ser.: 3). (ENG.). (J). (gr. 3-7). 2013. 304p. pap. 8.99 *(978-0-14-242613-5(X),* Puffin Books) 2012. 288p. 16.99 *(978-0-525-42576-2(4),* Dutton Books for Young Readers) Penguin Young Readers Group.

—The Accused. 2013. (Theodore Boone Ser.: 3). lib. bdg. 18.40 *(978-0-606-31696-5(5),* Turtleback) Turtleback Bks.

—The Activist. 2014. (Theodore Boone Ser.: Bk. 4). (ENG.). 304p. (J). (gr. 4). pap. 8.99 *(978-0-14-242309-7(2),* Puffin Books) Penguin Publishing Group.

Grisham, John. The Scandal. 2017. (Theodore Boone Ser.: 6). lib. bdg. 19.65 ***(978-0-606-40086-2(9))*** Turtleback Bks.

Jackson, Ellen. The Cupcake Thief. 2008. pap. 34.95 *(978-1-58013-765-2(2))* Kane Press, Inc.

—The Cupcake Thief. Sims, Blanche, illus. 2007. (Social Studies Connects). 32p. (J). (gr. -1-3). pap. 5.95 *(978-1-57565-247-4(1))* Kane Press, Inc.

Miller, Marvin. You Be the Jury: Courtroom Collection. Roper, Bob, illus. 2005. 361p. pap. *(978-0-439-77480-2(2))* Scholastic, Inc.

Proulx-Willis, Dana. Cinderella vs. the Stepfamily: A Fairy Tale Courtroom Event. 2007. 28p. pap. 7.00 *(978-0-88734-696-5(0))* Players Pr., Inc.

COURTS AND COURTIERS

Goldberg, Enid & Itzkowitz, Norman. Grigory Rasputin: Holy Man or Mad Monk? 2008. (ENG.). 128p. (J). (gr. 6-12). pap. 5.95 *(978-0-531-13896-0(8),* Watts, Franklin) Scholastic Library Publishing.

Layne, Deborah & Layne, Steven. P Is for Princess: A Royal Alphabet. Papp, Robert & Papp, Lisa, illus. rev. ed. 2007. (ENG.). 40p. (J). (gr. k-6). 17.95 *(978-1-58536-306-3(5))* Sleeping Bear Pr.

Roshell, Starshine. Real-Life Royalty. 2007. (Reading Rocks! Ser.). (ENG., Illus.). 32p. (J). (gr. 2-5). 28.50 *(978-1-59296-869-5(4),* 200749) Child's World, Inc., The.

Scott, Margaret. Medieval Clothing & Costumes. 2004. (Library of the Middle Ages Ser.). (Illus.). 64p. (gr. 5-8). lib. bdg. 31.95 *(978-0-8239-3991-6(X),* Rosen Reference) Rosen Publishing Group, Inc., The.

—Medieval Clothing & Costumes: Displaying Wealth & Class in Medieval Times. 2009. (Library of the Middle Ages Ser.). 64p. (gr. 5-8). 58.50 *(978-1-60853-900-0(8),* Rosen Reference) Rosen Publishing Group, Inc., The.

Wheeler, Opal. Handel: at the Court of Kings. Greenwalt, Mary, illus. 2006. 166p. per. 13.95 *(978-1-933573-03-8(1),* 4481) Zeezok Publishing, LLC.

COURTS AND COURTIERS—FICTION

Aveyard, Victoria. King's Cage. 2017. (Red Queen Ser.: 3). (Illus.). 528p. (YA). (gr. 8). 19.99 *(978-0-06-231069-9(0),* HarperTeen) HarperCollins Pubs.

Bell, Hilari. Sword of Waters. Willis, Drew, illus. 2009. (Shield, Sword, & Crown Ser.: 2). (ENG.). 384p. (J). (gr. 3-7). pap. 6.99 *(978-1-4169-0597-4(9),* Aladdin) Simon & Schuster Children's Publishing.

—Sword of Waters, No. 2. Willis, Drew, illus. 2008. (Shield, Sword, & Crown Ser.: 2). (ENG.). 368p. (J). (gr. 3-7). 16.99 *(978-1-4169-0596-7(0),* Simon & Schuster/Paula Wiseman Bks.) Simon & Schuster/Paula Wiseman Bks.

Bridges, Robin. The Katerina Trilogy, Vol. I: the Gathering Storm. 2012. (ENG.). 400p. (YA). (gr. 7). pap. 9.99 *(978-0-385-74023-4(9),* Ember) Random Hse. Children's Bks.

Dickerson, Melanie. The Princess Spy, 1 vol. 2014. (Fairy Tale Romance Ser.). (ENG.). 304p. (YA). pap. 12.99 *(978-0-310-73098-9(8))* Zondervan.

Elliott, L. M. Da Vinci's Tiger. (YA). (gr. 8). 2017. 320p. pap. 9.99 ***(978-0-06-074426-7(X))*** 2015. (ENG.). 304p. 17.99 *(978-0-06-074424-3(3))* HarperCollins Pubs. (Tegen, Katherine Bks).

Ewing, Amy. The Black Key. 2017. (Lone City Trilogy Ser.: 3). 304p. (YA). (gr. 9). pap. 9.99 ***(978-0-06-223585-5(0),*** HarperTeen) 2016. (Lone City Trilogy Ser.: 3). 304p. (YA). (gr. 9). 17.99 *(978-0-06-223584-8(2),* HarperTeen) 2016. 295p. (J). ***(978-0-06-256581-5(8))*** HarperCollins Pubs.

—The Jewel. (Lone City Trilogy Ser.: 1). (ENG.). (YA). (gr. 9). 2015. 400p. pap. 9.99 *(978-0-06-223578-7(8))* 2014. 368p. 17.99 *(978-0-06-223579-4(6))* HarperCollins Pubs. (HarperTeen).

—The White Rose. 2016. (Lone City Trilogy Ser.: 2). 336p. (YA). (gr. 9). pap. 9.99 *(978-0-06-223582-4(6),* HarperTeen) 2015. (Lone City Trilogy Ser.: 2). (ENG.). 320p. (YA). (gr. 9). 17.99 *(978-0-06-223581-7(8),* HarperTeen) 2015. 320p. pap. 17.99 *(978-0-06-241475-5(5))* HarperCollins Pubs.

Fantaskey, Beth. Jessica Rules the Dark Side. 2012. (ENG.). 320p. (YA). (gr. 9). 16.99 *(978-0-547-39309-4(1))* Houghton Mifflin Harcourt Publishing Co.

Friesner, Esther M. Deception's Pawn. 2015. (ENG.). 336p. (YA). (gr. 7). 17.99 *(978-0-449-81867-1(5),* Random Hse. Bks. for Young Readers) Random Hse. Children's Bks.

Gaughen, A. C. Lady Thief. 2015. (Scarlet Ser.: No. 2). (ENG.). 336p. (YA). (gr. 7). pap. 9.99 *(978-0-8027-3788-5(9),* 9780802737885, Bloomsbury USA Childrens) Bloomsbury Publishing USA.

—Lion Heart. 2015. (Scarlet Trilogy: No. 3). (ENG.). 352p. (YA). 17.99 *(978-0-8027-3616-1(5),* 9780802736161, Bloomsbury USA Childrens) Bloomsbury Publishing USA.

—Lion Heart: A Scarlet Novel. 2016. (Scarlet Ser.). (ENG.). 352p. (YA). pap. 9.99 *(978-1-61963-928-7(9),* 9781619639287, Bloomsbury USA Childrens) Bloomsbury Publishing USA.

Goodman, Alison. The Dark Days Club. 2016. (Lady Helen Novel Ser.: Bk. 1). (ENG.). 496p. (YA). (gr. 9). 18.99 *(978-0-670-78547-6(4),* Viking Books for Young Readers) Penguin Young Readers Group.

—The Dark Days Pact. 2017. (Lady Helen Novel Ser.: 2). (ENG.). 496p. (YA). (gr. 9). 18.99 *(978-0-670-78548-3(2),* Viking Books for Young Readers) Penguin Young Readers Group.

Greenwood, Grace. Stories from Famous Ballads for Children by Grace Greenwood [Pseud.] with Illustrations by Billings. 2006. 160p. per. 18.99 *(978-1-4255-1221-7(6))* Michigan Publishing.

Hand, Cynthia, et al. My Lady Jane. 512p. (YA). (gr. 8). 2017. pap. 9.99 *(978-0-06-239176-6(3))* 2016. 17.99 *(978-0-06-239174-2(7))* HarperCollins Pubs. (HarperTeen).

Hartman, Rachel. Seraphina. (ENG.). (YA). (gr. 7). 2014. 528p. pap. 10.99 *(978-0-375-86622-7(1),* Ember) 2012. 512p. lib. bdg. 20.99 *(978-0-375-96656-9(0),* Random Hse. Bks. for Young Readers) Random Hse. Children's Bks.

—Shadow Scale. 2015. (ENG., Illus.). 608p. (J). (gr. 7). 18.99 *(978-0-375-86657-9(4),* Random Hse. Bks. for Young Readers) Random Hse. Children's Bks.

Herbert, Bethany Zohner. The Perfect Fool. 2015. 279p. (YA). pap. 17.99 *(978-1-4621-1620-1(5))* Cedar Fort, Inc./CFI Distribution.

Kincaid, S. J. The Diabolic. (Diabolic Ser.). (ENG.). (YA). (gr. 9). 2017. 432p. pap. 10.99 ***(978-1-4814-7268-5(2))*** 2016. (Illus.). 416p. 17.99 *(978-1-4814-7267-8(4))* Simon & Schuster Bks. For Young Readers. (Simon & Schuster Bks. For Young Readers).

LaFevers, Robin. Grave Mercy. (His Fair Assassin Ser.: 1). (ENG., Illus.). (YA). (gr. 9). 2013. 576p. pap. 9.99 *(978-0-544-02249-2(1))* 2012. 560p. 17.99 *(978-0-547-62834-9(X))* Houghton Mifflin Harcourt Publishing Co.

—Grave Mercy, 10 vols. 2012. (His Fair Assassin Trilogy: Bk. 1). (YA). 132.75 *(978-1-4640-2388-0(3));* 130.75 *(978-1-4640-2390-3(5));* 130.75 *(978-1-4640-2387-3(5));* 287.75 *(978-1-4640-2386-6(7))* Recorded Bks., Inc.

Longshore, Katherine. Gilt. (ENG.). (YA). (gr. 7). 2013. 432p. pap. 9.99 *(978-0-14-242619-7(9),* Speak) 2012. 416p. 17.99 *(978-0-670-01399-9(4),* Viking Books for Young Readers) Penguin Young Readers Group.

Lough, Amber. The Blind Wish. 2015. (Jinni Wars Ser.: 2). (ENG.). 320p. (YA). (gr. 7). 17.99 *(978-0-385-36980-0(8),* Random Hse. Bks. for Young Readers) Random Hse. Children's Bks.

Maas, Sarah J. Crown of Midnight. (Throne of Glass Ser.: 2). (ENG.). (YA). (gr. 9). 2014. 448p. pap. 10.99 *(978-1-61963-064-2(8),* 9781619630642) 2013. (Illus.). 432p. 18.99 *(978-1-61963-062-8(1),* 9781619630628) Bloomsbury Publishing USA. (Bloomsbury USA Childrens).

—Crown of Midnight. 2014. (Throne of Glass Ser.: 2). (YA). lib. bdg. 22.10 *(978-0-606-36441-6(2))* Turtleback Bks.

—Throne of Glass. (Throne of Glass Ser.: 1). (ENG., Illus.). (YA). (gr. 9). 2013. 432p. pap. 10.99 *(978-1-61963-034-5(6),* 9781619630345) 2012. 416p. 18.99 *(978-1-59990-695-9(3),* 9781599906959) Bloomsbury Publishing USA. (Bloomsbury USA Childrens).

—Throne of Glass. 2013. (Throne of Glass Ser.: 1). (YA). lib. bdg. 22.10 *(978-0-606-31888-4(7),* Turtleback) Turtleback Bks.

Maid of Deception. 2014. (Maids of Honor Ser.). (ENG., Illus.). 416p. (YA). (gr. 7). 17.99 *(978-1-4424-4141-5(0),* Simon & Schuster Bks. For Young Readers) Simon & Schuster Bks. For Young Readers.

Marsh, Katherine. Jepp, Who Defied the Stars. 2013. (ENG.). 400p. (J). (gr. 5-9). pap. 9.99 *(978-1-4231-3786-3(8))* Hyperion Pr.

McGowan, Jennifer. Maid of Secrets. (Maids of Honor Ser.). (ENG.). (YA). (gr. 7). 2014. 432p. pap. 9.99 *(978-1-4424-4139-2(9))* 2013. 416p. 17.99 *(978-1-4424-4138-5(0))* Simon & Schuster Bks. For Young Readers. (Simon & Schuster Bks. For Young Readers).

—Maid of Wonder. 2015. (Maids of Honor Ser.). (ENG., Illus.). 336p. (YA). (gr. 7). 17.99 *(978-1-4814-1826-3(2))* Simon & Schuster Children's Publishing.

Meyer, Carolyn. The Bad Queen: Rules & Instructions for Marie-Antoinette. 2011. (Young Royals Ser.). (ENG.). 432p. (YA). (gr. 7). pap. 9.99 *(978-0-547-48249-1(3))* Houghton Mifflin Harcourt Publishing Co.

—Victoria Rebels. (ENG., Illus.). 272p. (YA). (gr. 7). 2014. pap. 9.99 *(978-1-4169-8730-7(4))* 2013. 16.99 *(978-1-4169-8729-1(0))* Simon & Schuster/Paula Wiseman Bks. (Simon & Schuster/Paula Wiseman Bks.).

Murdock, Catherine Gilbert. Princess Ben. 2009. (ENG.). 352p. (YA). (gr. 7). pap. 9.99 *(978-0-547-22325-4(0))* Houghton Mifflin Harcourt Publishing Co.

Nielsen, Jennifer A. The False Prince. 2012. (Ascendance Trilogy: Bk. 1). (ENG.). (J). (gr. 5-8). 64.99 *(978-1-61707-596-4(5))* Findaway World, LLC.

—The False Prince. 2013. (False Prince Ser.: Bk. 1). (ENG.). 352p. (J). (gr. 5-9). pap. 7.99 *(978-0-545-28414-1(7),* Scholastic Paperbacks) 2012. (Ascendance Trilogy Ser.: 1). (ENG., Illus.). 352p. (J). (gr. 4-7). 17.99 *(978-0-545-28413-4(9),* Scholastic Pr.) 2012. (Ascendance Trilogy: Bk. 1). 352p. pap. 17.99 *(978-0-545-39249-5(7))* 2012. (Ascendance Trilogy: Bk. 1). (Illus.). 342p. (J). pap. *(978-0-545-43347-1(9),* Scholastic Pr.) Scholastic, Inc.

—The False Prince. 2013. (Ascendance Trilogy Ser.: 1). lib. bdg. 18.40 *(978-0-606-31491-6(1),* Turtleback) Turtleback Bks.

—The Runaway King. (Ascendance Trilogy Ser.: 2). (ENG.). 352p. (J). (gr. 4-7). 2014. pap. 7.99 *(978-0-545-28416-5(3),* Scholastic Paperbacks) 2013. (Illus.). 17.99 *(978-0-545-28415-8(5),* Scholastic Pr.) Scholastic, Inc.

—The Runaway King. 2014. (Ascendance Trilogy Ser.: 2). lib. bdg. 18.40 *(978-0-606-35663-3(0))* Turtleback Bks.

Pacat, C. S. Kings Rising. 2016. (Captive Prince Trilogy Ser.: 3). (ENG., Illus.). 368p. pap. 16.00 *(978-0-425-27399-9(7),* Berkley) Penguin Publishing Group.

Pike, Aprilynne. Glitter. 2016. (ENG., Illus.). 384p. (YA). (gr. 9). 17.99 *(978-1-101-93370-1(4),* Random Hse. Bks. for Young Readers) Random Hse. Children's Bks.

Roberts, Constance. Sigil in Shadow. 2016. (ENG.). (J). pap. 15.99 *(978-1-4621-1873-1(9),* Sweetwater Bks.) Cedar Fort, Inc./CFI Distribution.

Rose, Kathryn. Avalon Rising. 2015. (Metal & Lace Novel Ser.: 2). (ENG., Illus.). 360p. (YA). pap. 11.99 *(978-0-7387-4489-6(1),* Flux) North Star Editions.

Schmid, Susan Maupin. If the Magic Fits. (100 Dresses Ser.: 1). (ENG.). (J). (gr. 3-7). 2017. 320p. 7.99 ***(978-0-553-53369-9(X),*** Yearling) 2016. (Illus.). 304p. 16.99 *(978-0-553-53366-8(5),* Random Hse. Bks. for Young Readers) Random Hse. Children's Bks.

Somper, Justin. Allies & Assassins. 2014. (Allies & Assassins Ser.). (ENG.). 496p. (YA). (gr. 7-17). 18.00 *(978-0-316-25393-2(6))* Little, Brown Bks. for Young Readers.

—A Conspiracy of Princes. 2015. (Allies & Assassins Ser.: 2). (ENG., Illus.). 496p. (J). (gr. 7-17). 18.00 *(978-0-316-25397-0(9))* Little, Brown Bks. for Young Readers.

Stanley, Diane. The Princess of Cortova. (J). 2015. (Silver Bowl Ser.: 3). (ENG.). 336p. (gr. 3-7). pap. 6.99 *(978-0-06-204732-8(9))* 2013. 311p. lib. bdg. *(978-0-06-204731-1(0))* HarperCollins Pubs.

Sullivan, Laura L. Ladies in Waiting. 2013. (ENG.). 336p. (YA). (gr. 9). pap. 18.99 *(978-0-544-02220-1(3))* Houghton Mifflin Harcourt Publishing Co.

Thomas, Rhiannon. A Wicked Thing. (YA). (gr. 9). 2016. 368p. pap. 9.99 *(978-0-06-230354-7(6))* 2015. (ENG.). 352p. 17.99 *(978-0-06-230353-0(8))* HarperCollins Pubs. (HarperTeen).

Trent, Tiffany. The Unnaturalists. (ENG., (YA). (gr. 7). 2013. Illus.). 336p. pap. 9.99 *(978-1-4424-2207-0(6))* 2012. 320p. 16.99 *(978-1-4424-2206-3(8))* Simon & Schuster Bks. For Young Readers. (Simon & Schuster Bks. For Young Readers).

Turetsky, Bianca. The Time-Traveling Fashionista at the Palace of Marie Antoinette. 2013. (Time-Traveling Fashionista Ser.: 2). (ENG., Illus.). 272p. (J). (gr. 3-7). pap. 9.00 *(978-0-316-10535-4(X),* Poppy) Little, Brown Bks. for Young Readers.

Zettel, Sarah. Assassin's Masque. 2017. (Palace of Spies Ser.: 3). (ENG.). 432p. (YA). (gr. 7). pap. 8.99 *(978-0-544-81317-5(0),* HMH Books For Young Readers) Houghton Mifflin Harcourt Publishing Co.

—Palace of Spies. 2013. (Palace of Spies Ser.: 1). (ENG.). 368p. (YA). (gr. 7). 16.99 *(978-0-544-07411-8(4))* Houghton Mifflin Harcourt Publishing Co.

COURTSHIP

see Dating (Social Customs)

COUSTEAU, JACQUES-YVES, 1910-1997

Berne, Jennifer. Manfish: A Story of Jacques Cousteau. Puybaret, Éric, illus. 2008. (ENG.). 40p. (J). (gr. 1-4). 16.99 *(978-0-8118-6063-5(9))* Chronicle Bks. LLC.

—Manfish: The Story of Jacques Cousteau. Puybaret, Éric, illus. 2015. (ENG.). 38p. (J). (gr. k-3). 9.99 *(978-1-4521-4123-7(1))* Chronicle Bks. LLC.

DuTemple, Lesley A. Jacques Cousteau. 2005. (Biography Ser.). (Illus.). 112p. (gr. 6-12). lib. bdg. 27.93 *(978-0-8225-4979-6(4))* Lerner Publishing Group.

Knowles, Johanna. Jacques Cousteau. 2011. (Conservation Heroes Ser.). (Illus.). 120p. (YA). (gr. 6-12). 35.00 *(978-1-60413-947-1(1),* Chelsea Hse.) Facts On File, Inc.

Medina, Nico & Putra, Dede. Who Was Jacques Cousteau? 2015. (Who Was...? Ser.). lib. bdg. 16.00 *(978-0-606-36599-4(0))* Turtleback Bks.

C D

Medina, Nico & Tomie, dePaola. Who Was Jacques Cousteau? Putra, Dede & Harrison, Nancy, illus. 2015. (Who Was? Ser.). (ENG.). 112p. (J). (gr. 3-7). 5.99 *(978-0-448-48234-7(7),* Grosset & Dunlap) Penguin Young Readers Group.

Ollhoff, Jim. Jacques Cousteau. 2013. (Great Explorers Ser.). (Illus.). 32p. (J). (gr. 5-9). lib. bdg. 27.07 *(978-1-61783-966-5(3),* Abdo & Daughters) ABDO Publishing Co.

Petrie, Kristin. Jacques Cousteau, 1 vol. 2004. (Explorers Set 1 Ser.). (ENG.). 32p. (gr. k-6). 27.07 *(978-1-59197-599-1(9),* Checkerboard Library) ABDO Publishing Co.

Yaccarino, Dan. The Fantastic Undersea Life of Jacques Cousteau. 2012. (ENG.). 40p. (J). (gr. 1-4). pap. 7.99 *(978-0-375-84470-6(8),* Dragonfly Bks.) Random Hse. Children's Bks.

Zronik, John Paul & Zronik, John. Jacques Cousteau: Conserving Underwater Worlds. 2007. (In the Footsteps of Explorers Ser.). (ENG., Illus.). 32p. (J). (gr. 3-7). lib. bdg. *(978-0-7787-2419-3(0));* pap. *(978-0-7787-2455-1(7))* Crabtree Publishing Co.

COW

see Cows

COWBOYS

see also Rodeos

Adkins, Jan. What If You Met a Cowboy? Adkins, Jan, illus. 2013. (ENG., Illus.). 48p. (J). (gr. 1-4). 17.99 *(978-1-59643-149-2(0),* 9781596431492) Roaring Brook Pr.

Bone, Emily. Cowboy Things to Make & Do. Harrison, Erica, illus. 2008. (Activity Bks). 34p. (J). (gr. 1). pap. 6.99 *(978-0-7945-2077-9(4),* Usborne) EDC Publishing.

Braun, Eric. If I Were a Cowboy, 1 vol. Reid, Mick, illus. 2010. (Dream Big! Ser.). (ENG.). 24p. (gr. k-3). lib. bdg. 26.65 *(978-1-4048-5531-1(9))* Picture Window Bks.

Cefrey, Holly. From Slave to Cowboy: The Nat Love Story. 2009. (Great Moments in American History Ser.). 32p. (gr. 3-3). 47.90 *(978-1-61513-142-6(6))* Rosen Publishing Group, Inc., The.

Cooke, Tim. Go West with Cowboys & Ranchers. 2016. (ENG.). 32p. (J). *(978-0-7787-2322-6(4))* Crabtree Publishing Co.

Cowboys. (Awesome Adventures Ser.). 16p. (J). *(978-2-7643-0118-0(9))* Phidal Publishing, Inc./Editions Phidal, Inc.

Drinkard, Lawson. Riding on a Range: Western Activities for Kids. Lee, Fran, illus. 2003. (ENG.). 64p. (YA). pap. 9.99 *(978-1-58685-036-4(9))* Gibbs Smith, Publisher.

Gartland, Robert A. Cowboys & Cattle. 2011. 50p. 35.95 *(978-1-258-06963-6(6))* Literary Licensing, LLC.

Gibbons, Gail. Cowboys & Cowgirls. Gibbons, Gail, illus. 2003. (ENG., Illus.). 32p. (J). (gr. 1-4). pap. 8.00 *(978-0-316-16859-5(9))* Little, Brown Bks. for Young Readers.

—Cowboys & Cowgirls. Gibbons, Gail, illus. 2003. (Illus.). (J). (gr. 1-4). 18.45 *(978-0-613-71749-6(X),* Turtleback) Turtleback Bks.

Granfield, Linda. Cowboy: An Album. (J). 9.99 *(978-1-55054-230-1(3))* Da Capo Pr., Inc.

Herweck, Dona. A Day in the Life of a Cowhand, 1 vol. 2nd rev. ed. 2014. (TIME for KIDS(r) Nonfiction Readers Ser.). (ENG., Illus.). 28p. (J). (gr. 3-3). pap. 25.96 *(978-1-4807-1064-1(4))* Shell Educational Publishing.

—A Day in the Life of a Cowhand, 1 vol. 2nd rev. ed. 2011. (Nonfiction Readers Ser.). (ENG.). 28p. (J). (gr. 3-3). pap. 8.99 *(978-1-4333-3649-2(9))* Teacher Created Materials, Inc.

I Want to Be a Cowboy. 2008. (Magnetic Board Books Ser.). 7p. bds. *(978-1-4075-1416-1(4))* Parragon, Inc.

James, Will. The Will James Cowboy Book, Vol. 1. rev. ed. (Illus.). 128p. (J). (gr. 4). *(978-0-87842-469-6(5),* 816) Mountain Pr. Publishing Co., Inc.

Kovacs, Vic. A Cowboy's Life. 2015. (True History of the Wild West Ser.). (ENG., Illus.). 32p. (J). (gr. 5-5). pap. 10.00 *(978-1-4994-1169-0(3),* PowerKids Pr.) Rosen Publishing Group, Inc., The.

Kubke, Jane & Kubke, Jessica. Bull Riding. 2006. (World of Rodeo Ser.). (Illus.). 48p. (YA). (gr. 4-7). lib. bdg. 29.25 *(978-1-4042-0544-4(6))* Rosen Publishing Group, Inc., The.

Landau, Elaine. Bill Pickett: Wild West Cowboy. 2004. (Best of the West Biographies Ser.). (Illus.). 48p. (J). lib. bdg. 25.27 *(978-0-7660-2215-7(3))* Enslow Pubs., Inc.

Lickens, Alice. How to Be a Cowboy. Lickens, Alice, illus. 2016. (ENG., Illus.). 32p. (J). (gr. -1-2). 16.99 *(978-1-84365-241-0(2),* Pavilion) Pavilion Bks. GBR. Dist: Independent Pubs. Group.

Moran, Margaret. Cowhands & Cattle Trails & Los vaqueros y el arreo de Ganado: 6 English, 6 Spanish Adaptations. 2011. (ENG & SPA.). (J). 97.00 net. *(978-1-4108-5700-2(X))* Benchmark Education Co.

Munro, Roxie. Wild West Trail Ride Maze. 2006. (ENG., Illus.). 50p. (J). (gr. k-2). 16.95 *(978-1-931721-67-7(X),* c7606323-9d58-4d30-ad89-d1aee1920627) Bright Sky Pr.

Nat Love. 2010. (Legends of the Wild West Ser.). (Illus.). 104p. (gr. 6-12). 35.00 *(978-1-60413-599-2(9),* Chelsea Hse.) Facts On File, Inc.

The New South & the Old West, 1866-1890. 2010. (Discovering U. S. History Ser.). (Illus.). 136p. (gr. 5-8). 35.00 *(978-1-60413-354-7(6),* Chelsea Hse.) Facts On File, Inc.

Oatman, Eric. Cowboys & Cattle Drives: Life on the Western Trail. 2007. (Reading Expeditions Ser.). (ENG., Illus.). 40p. (J). pap. 19.95 *(978-0-7922-4550-6(4))* CENGAGE Learning.

Penn, Sarah. Nat Love: African American Cowboy. (Primary Sources of Famous People in American History Ser.). 32p. 2009. (gr. 2-3). 47.90 *(978-1-60851-706-0(3))* 2004. (ENG., Illus.). (gr. 4-8). pap. 10.00 *(978-0-8239-4188-9(4))* Rosen Publishing Group, Inc., The.

—Nat Love: African American Cowboy / Vaquero Afroamericano. 2009. (Famous People in American History/Grandes personajes en la historia de los Estados Unidos Ser.). (ENG & SPA.). 32p. (gr. 2-3). 47.90 *(978-1-61512-551-7(5),* Editorial Buenas Letras) Rosen Publishing Group, Inc., The.

—Nat Love: Vaquero Afroamericano. 2004. (Grandes personajes en la historia de los Estados Unidos Ser.). (SPA.). 32p. (gr. 4-8). pap. 10.00 *(978-0-8239-4234-3(1),* Rosen Classroom) Rosen Publishing Group, Inc., The.

—Nat Love: Vaquero afroamericano (Nat Love: African American Cowboy) 2009. (Grandes personajes en la historia de los Estados Unidos (Famous People in American History) Ser.). (SPA.). 32p. (gr. 2-3). 47.90 *(978-1-61512-804-4(2),* Editorial Buenas Letras) Rosen Publishing Group, Inc., The.

Peppas, Lynn. Why Charles Goodnight Matters to Texas. 2014. (Illus.). 32p. (J). lib. bdg. 26.25 *(978-1-4777-0907-8(X))* Rosen Publishing Group, Inc., The.

Petruccio, Steven James. Cowboy Tattoos. 2003. (Dover Tattoos Ser.). (ENG., Illus.). 2p. (J). (gr. 1-4). pap. 1.99 *(978-0-486-43028-7(6))* Dover Pubns., Inc.

Pirk, Wendy & Radford, Duane. Rodeo Roundup, 1 vol. 2017. (ENG., Illus.). 64p. (J). pap. 6.99 ***(978-1-896124-63-6(1),*** 9781896124636) Dragon Hill Publishing CAN. Dist: Lone Pine Publishing USA.

Plourde, Lynn. Storytime Stickers: Cowboy Dreams. Kulka, Joe, illus. 2010. (Storytime Stickers Ser.). (ENG.). 16p. (J). (gr. k-2). pap. 5.95 *(978-1-4027-7128-6(2))* Sterling Publishing Co., Inc.

Randolph, Ryan P. Black Cowboys. (Library of the Westward Expansion Ser.). 24p. 2009. (gr. 3-4). 42.50 *(978-1-60853-933-8(4),* PowerKids Pr.) 2003. (Illus.). (J). lib. bdg. 22.60 *(978-0-8239-6294-5(6))* Rosen Publishing Group, Inc., The.

Sanford, William R. & Green, Carl R. Bill Pickett: Courageous African-American Cowboy. 2012. (Courageous Heroes of the American West Ser.). (Illus.). 48p. (J). (gr. 5-18). 22.60 *(978-0-7660-4001-4(1))* Enslow Pubs., Inc.

Savage, Jeff. American Cowboys: True Tales of the Wild West. 2012. (True Tales of the Wild West Ser.). (Illus.). 48p. (J). (gr. 5-18). pap. 8.95 *(978-1-4644-0027-8(X));* lib. bdg. 22.60 *(978-0-7660-4019-9(4))* Enslow Pubs., Inc.

Schwartz, Heather. War, Cattle, & Cowboys: Texas as a Young State, 1 vol. 2012. (Primary Source Readers Ser.). (ENG.). 32p. (J). (gr. 4-4). pap. 8.99 *(978-1-4333-5050-4(5))* Teacher Created Materials, Inc.

Sullivan, Laura L. Life As a Cowboy in the American West. 2016. (Life As... Ser.). (ENG., Illus.). 32p. (J). (gr. 3-3). pap. 10.58 *(978-1-5026-1072-0(8))* Cavendish Square Publishing.

Underwood, Deborah. Nat Love. 2008. pap. 52.95 *(978-0-8225-9395-9(5));* (ENG., Illus.). 48p. (gr. 3-6). lib. bdg. 27.93 *(978-0-8225-7171-1(4),* Lerner Pubns.) Lerner Publishing Group.

West, David. Lots of Things You Want to Know about Cowboys: ... & Some You Don't! 2015. (Lots of Things You Want to Know About Ser.). (Illus.). 24p. (J). 28.50 *(978-1-62588-089-5(8))* Black Rabbit Bks.

Whitney, Gleaves & Whitney, Louise Doak. B Is for Buckaroo: A Cowboy Alphabet. Guy, Susan, illus. 2006. (Sleeping Bear Alphabets Ser.). (ENG.). 40p. (J). (gr. -1-3). pap. 7.95 *(978-1-58536-336-0(7))* Sleeping Bear Pr.

—B Is for Buckaroo: A Cowboy Alphabet. Guy, Sue & Guy, Susan, illus. rev. ed. 2003. (Sports Ser.). (ENG.). 40p. (J). (gr. 1-4). 17.95 *(978-1-58536-139-7(9),* 202000) Sleeping Bear Pr.

Wood, Anita. Cowboy Doodles, 1 vol. 2013. (ENG., Illus.). 240p. (J). pap. 9.99 *(978-1-4236-3392-1(X))* Gibbs Smith, Publisher.

COWBOYS—DICTIONARIES

Kalman, Bobbie. A Visual Dictionary of the Old West. 2007. (Crabtree Visual Dictionaries Ser.). (ENG., Illus.). 32p. (J). (gr. 3-7). lib. bdg. *(978-0-7787-3503-8(6))* Crabtree Publishing Co.

COWBOYS—FICTION

Ames, Joseph B. Pete Cow Puncher a Story of the Texas Plains. Perard, Victor, illus. 2005. reprint ed. pap. 31.95 *(978-0-7661-9421-2(3))* Kessinger Publishing, LLC.

Andrews, Neva. Stormy & Stub. 2008. 108p. pap. 10.95 *(978-0-595-52854-7(6),* iUniverse, Inc.) iUniverse, Inc.

Anglund, Joan Walsh. The Cowboy's Christmas. Anglund, Joan Walsh, illus. 2004. (ENG., Illus.). 40p. (J). 8.95 *(978-0-7407-4675-8(8))* Andrews McMeel Publishing.

Arena, Felice & Kettle, Phil. Bull Riding. Cox, David, illus. 2004. (J). pap. *(978-1-59336-370-3(2))* Mondo Publishing.

Bain, Michelle. The Adventures of Thumbs up Johnnie Johnnie Finds A Buddy: Johnnie Finds A Buddy Color Version 2. Lizana, Lorenzo, illus. 2007. (J). 14.95 *(978-0-9761421-6-4(3))* Pixie Stuff LLC.

—The Adventures of Thumbs up Johnnie Reading Heart to Heart Thumbs up Johnnie, Little Digit & the Special Delivery: Reading Heart to Heart, Coloring & Activity Book. 2006. (J). pap. 7.95 *(978-0-9761421-5-7(5))* Pixie Stuff LLC.

—Las aventuras de Juanito el Pulgarcito Juanito encuentra un Compañerito: Juanito encuentra un Compañerito. Lizana, Lorenzo, illus. 2006.Tr. of Johnnie Finds a Buddy. (SPA.). (J). 16.95 *(978-0-9761421-4-0(7))* Pixie Stuff LLC.

—Las aventuras de Juanito el Pulgarcito Liborio el Microbio y el apretón de Manos: Liborio el Microbio y el apretón de Manos. Lizana, Lorenzo, illus. 2007.Tr. of Jimmy Jam Germ & the Happy Handshake! (SPA.). (J). pap. 16.95 *(978-0-9795832-1-6(7))* Pixie Stuff LLC.

Baker, Willard F. The Boy Ranchers among the Indians. 2007. 180p. 25.96 *(978-1-4218-3920-2(2),* 1st World Library - Literary Society) 1st World Publishing, Inc.

Banda, Lo Hartog Van. Fingers. Morris Publishing Company Staff, illus. 2013. (Lucky Luke Ser.: 37). (ENG.). 48p. (J). (gr. 3-12). pap. 11.95 *(978-1-84918-138-9(1))* CineBook GBR. Dist: National Bk. Network.

Bedford, Annie North. Roy Rogers & the New Cowboy. Helweg, Hans & Crawford, Mel, illus. 2011. 30p. 35.95 *(978-1-258-03516-7(2))* Literary Licensing, LLC.

Beecher, Elizabeth. Roy Rogers & Cowboy Toby. Crawford, Mel, illus. 2011. 30p. 35.95 *(978-1-258-03514-3(6))* Literary Licensing, LLC.

—Roy Rogers & the Sure 'Nough Cowpoke. Steffen, Randy, illus. 2011. 32p. pap. 35.95 *(978-1-258-03587-7(1))* Literary Licensing, LLC.

—Roy Rogers on the Double-R Ranch. Nordli, Ernest, illus. 2011. 78p. 37.95 *(978-1-258-03590-7(1))* Literary Licensing, LLC.

Bell, Marion R. & Geyer, Donna M. Young Cowboys at the Broken Arrow. Stein, Harve, illus. 2011. 256p. 47.95 *(978-1-258-10205-0(6))* Literary Licensing, LLC.

Blair, Eric. Pecos Bill, 1 vol. Chambers-Goldberg, Micah, illus. 2013. (My First Classic Story Ser.).Tr. of Pecos Bill. (ENG.). 32p. (gr. k-3). pap. 7.10 *(978-1-4795-1860-9(3),* My First Classic Story) Picture Window Bks.

Blanchet, Deborah A. The Hat. 2009. 122p. 29.99 *(978-1-4415-4624-1(3));* pap. 19.99 *(978-1-4415-4623-4(5))* Xlibris Corp.

Bowman, James Cloyd. Pecos Bill: The Greatest Cowboy of All Time. Bannon, Laura, illus. 2017. (ENG.). 384p. (J). (gr. 4-7). pap. 9.99 ***(978-0-8075-6376-2(5))*** Whitman, Albert & Co.

Brian, Kate, pseud. Untouchable. 2006. (Private Ser.: No. 3). (ENG.). 256p. (YA). (gr. 9). pap. 9.99 *(978-1-4169-1875-2(2),* Simon & Schuster Bks. For Young Readers) Simon & Schuster Bks. For Young Readers.

Brooks, Walter R. Freddy the Cowboy. Wiese, Kurt, illus. 2014. (ENG.). 240p. (gr. 4-13). pap. 10.99 *(978-1-4683-0830-3(0),* 460830) Overlook Pr., The.

Burton, Virginia Lee. Calico the Wonder Horse. gif. ed. 2016. (ENG., Illus.). 64p. (J). (gr. -1-3). 14.99 *(978-0-547-57572-8(6),* HMH Books For Young Readers) Houghton Mifflin Harcourt Publishing Co.

Capstone Press Staff. Pecos Bill, Colossal Cowboy. Weber, Lisa K., illus. 2010. (Graphic Spin Ser.). (ENG.). 40p. (gr. 1-3). lib. bdg. 25.32 *(978-1-4342-1896-4(1),* Graphic Revolve) Stone Arch Bks.

Cash, John Carter. The Cat in the Rhinestone Suit. Nash, Scott, illus. 2012. (ENG.). 32p. (J). (gr. -1-3). 17.99 *(978-1-4169-7483-3(0),* Little Simon Inspirations) Little Simon Inspirations.

Catlow, Nikalas. Trolls vs. Cowboys in the Arctic. Wesson, Tim, illus. 2012. (Mega Mash-Up Ser.). (ENG.). 96p. (J). (gr. 2-5). pap. 6.99 *(978-0-7636-6271-4(2),* Nosy Crow) Candlewick Pr.

Caviezel, Giovanni. Cowboy. Mesturini, C., illus. 2011. (Mini People Shape Bks.). (ENG.). 10p. (J). bds. 5.99 *(978-0-7641-6438-5(4))* Barron's Educational Series, Inc.

Charlip, Remy. Little Old Big Beard & Big Young Little Beard: A Short & Tall Tale, 1 vol. Charlip, Remy & Rettenmund, Tamara, illus. (ENG.). (J). 2006. 300p. (gr. -1-3). pap. 5.95 *(978-0-7614-5288-1(5))* 2003. 32p. 16.95 *(978-0-7614-5142-6(0))* Marshall Cavendish Corp.

Councilman, Janet H. Rocky & His Responsible Band of Cowboys, 1 vol. 2009. pap. 24.95 *(978-1-60749-384-6(5))* America Star Bks.

Cousins Camp. 2010. 32p. pap. 12.99 *(978-1-4490-8387-8(0))* AuthorHouse.

Cunningham, Kay. Bucky: The Adventures of the Dinosaur Cowboy. Wilson, Mary Ann, illus. 2004. 32p. (J). 18.99 *(978-1-57860-173-8(8))* Clerisy Pr.

Dahl, Michael. Dragon Cowboy, 1 vol. Piatti, Federico, illus. 2010. (Dragonblood Ser.). (ENG.). 40p. (gr. 1-3). lib. bdg. 23.99 *(978-1-4342-1927-5(5),* Zone Bks.) Stone Arch Bks.

Dahlstrom, S. J. Green Colt, No. 4. 2016. (Adventures of Wilder Good Ser.). (ENG.). 162p. (J). (gr. 3). pap. 8.95 *(978-1-58988-114-3(1))* Dry, Paul Bks., Inc.

—Texas Grit: the Adventures of Wilder Good #2. 2014. (Adventures of Wilder Good Ser.). (ENG.). 141p. (J). (gr. 3). pap. 7.95 *(978-1-58988-094-8(3))* Dry, Paul Bks., Inc.

Dailey, Reid. The Legend of Ross the Reader: A Story of How a Smart Cowboy Saved the Prairie One Book at a Time. Edgerley, Ross, illus. 2007. 32p. per. 15.95 *(978-1-59858-483-7(9))* Dog Ear Publishing, LLC.

Davis, David. Texas Zeke & the Longhorn, 1 vol. Stacy, Alan, illus. 2006. (ENG.). 32p. (J). (gr. k-3). 16.99 *(978-1-58980-348-0(5))* Pelican Publishing Co., Inc.

Day, Jan. Kissimmee Pete & the Hurricane, 1 vol. Mason, Janeen, illus. 2008. (ENG.). 32p. (J). (gr. 1-3). 16.99 *(978-1-58980-544-6(5))* Pelican Publishing Co., Inc.

de Groot, Bob & Morris Publishing Company Staff. The One-Armed Bandits, Vol. 33. 2012. (Lucky Luke Ser.: 33). (ENG., Illus.). 48p. (J). (gr. 3-12). pap. 11.95 *(978-1-84918-111-2(X))* CineBook GBR. Dist: National Bk. Network.

Deering, Freemont B. The Border Boys Across the Frontier. I.t. ed. 2007. (ENG.). 174p. pap. 21.99 *(978-1-4264-9949-4(3))* Creative Media Partners, LLC.

Erickson, John R. Slim's Good-Bye. Holmes, Gerald L., illus. 2011. (Hank the Cowdog Ser.). (ENG.). 132p. (J). (gr. 3-6). pap. 5.99 *(978-1-59188-134-6(X))* Maverick Bks., Inc.

Fleming, Bryn. Cassie & Jasper: Cattle Drive Danger. 2016. (Range Riders Ser.). (ENG.). 147p. (J). pap. 10.99 *(978-1-941821-95-4(2),* West Winds Pr.) Graphic Arts Ctr. Publishing Co.

—Cassie & Jasper to the Rescue. 2014. (Range Riders Ser.). (ENG.). 128p. (YA). (gr. 3-7). 23.99 *(978-1-941821-04-6(9));* pap. 9.99 *(978-0-88240-992-4(1))* Graphic Arts Ctr. Publishing Co. (West Winds Pr.).

Fowler, Frank. The Broncho Rider Boys with Funston at Vera Cruz: Or, Upholding the Honor of the Stars & Stripes. 2007. (ENG.). 190p. pap. 19.99 *(978-1-4346-3206-7(1));* 202p. pap. 22.99 *(978-1-4346-3207-4(5))* Creative Media Partners, LLC.

Frank, John. The Toughest Cowboy: Or How the Wild West Was Tamed. Pullen, Zachary, illus. 2004. (ENG.). 48p. (J). (gr. 1-3). 17.95 *(978-0-689-83461-5(6),* Simon & Schuster Bks. For Young Readers) Simon & Schuster Bks. For Young Readers.

Frank, John & Pullen, Zachary. The Toughest Cowboy: Or How the Wild West Was Tamed. Pullen, Zachary, illus. 2008. (ENG., Illus.). 48p. (J). (gr. 1-3). 7.99 *(978-0-689-83462-2(4),* Aladdin) Simon & Schuster Children's Publishing.

Fraser, Jess, illus. The Legend of the Cosmic Cowboy. 2007. (J). cd-rom 12.99 *(978-0-9795190-7-9(1))* Color & Learn.

Fretz, Denette. Conrad & the Cowgirl Next Door, 1 vol. Barretta, Gene, illus. 2014. (Next Door Ser.). (ENG.). 40p. (J). 12.99 *(978-0-310-72349-3(3))* Zonderkidz.

Frisch, Aaron. A Night on the Range. Sheban, Chris, illus. (ENG.). 32p. (J). 2013. (gr. -1-17). pap. 7.99 *(978-0-89812-829-1(3),* Creative Paperbacks) 2010. (gr. 1-3). 19.99 *(978-1-56846-205-9(0),* Creative Editions) Creative Co., The.

—Pirates at the Plate. Summers, Mark, illus. 2012. (ENG.). 32p. (J). (gr. 1-3). 17.99 *(978-1-56846-210-3(7),* Creative Editions) Creative Co., The.

Gallagher, Diana G. Monica & the Crushworthy Cowboy, 1 vol. 2011. (Monica Ser.). (ENG.). 88p. (gr. 2-3). lib. bdg. 26.65 *(978-1-4342-2554-2(2))* Stone Arch Bks.

Gamble, Adam & Jasper, Mark. Good Night Cowboys. Veno, Joe, illus. 2017. (Good Night Our World Ser.). (ENG.). 20p. (J). (— 1). bds. 9.95 *(978-1-60219-509-7(9))* Good Night Bks.

Garst, Shannon. Silver Spurs for Cowboy Boots. Hargens, Charles, illus. 2011. 194p. 42.95 *(978-1-258-08454-7(6))* Literary Licensing, LLC.

Gerra, Laurent. The Man from Washington. 2013. (Lucky Luke Ser.: 39). (ENG., Illus.). 48p. pap. 11.95 *(978-1-84918-149-5(7))* CineBook GBR. Dist: National Bk. Network.

—Tying the Knot, Vol. 45. 2014. (Lucky Luke Ser.: 45). (ENG., Illus.). 48p. pap. 11.95 *(978-1-84918-188-4(8))* CineBook GBR. Dist: National Bk. Network.

Goodman, Larry. The Cowboy & Other Stories. 2008. 36p. pap. 24.95 *(978-1-60813-546-2(2))* America Star Bks.

Goscinny, René. The Bounty Hunter, Vol. 26. Morris Publishing Company Staff, illus. 2011. (Lucky Luke Ser.: 26). (ENG.). 48p. pap. 11.95 *(978-1-84918-059-7(8))* CineBook GBR. Dist: National Bk. Network.

—A Cure for the Daltons, Vol. 23. Morris, Alfred, illus. 2010. (Lucky Luke Ser.: 23). (ENG.). 48p. (J). (gr. 3-17). pap. 11.95 *(978-1-84918-034-4(2))* CineBook GBR. Dist: National Bk. Network.

—The Daltons Always on the Run. Morris, illus. 2012. (Lucky Luke Ser.: 34). (ENG.). 48p. (J). (gr. 3-12). pap. 11.95 *(978-1-84918-119-8(5))* CineBook GBR. Dist: National Bk. Network.

—Daltons in the Blizzard. 2009. (Lucky Luke Ser.: 15). (ENG., Illus.). 48p. (gr. 3-17). pap. 11.95 *(978-1-905460-76-2(7))* CineBook GBR. Dist: National Bk. Network.

—The Dashing White Cowboy. Morris, illus. 2009. (Lucky Luke Ser.: 14). (ENG.). 46p. (J). (gr. -1-17). pap. 11.95 *(978-1-905460-66-3(X))* CineBook GBR. Dist: National Bk. Network.

—In the Shadow of the Derricks. 2007. (Lucky Luke Ser.: 5). (ENG., Illus.). 48p. (gr. -1). per. 11.95 *(978-1-905460-17-5(1))* CineBook GBR. Dist: National Bk. Network.

—Jesse James. Morris, Alfred, illus. 2007. (Lucky Luke Ser.: 4). (ENG.). 48p. (J). (gr. 4-7). per. 11.95 *(978-1-905460-14-4(7))* CineBook GBR. Dist: National Bk. Network.

—Lucky Luke Versus Joss Jamon. Morris, illus. 27th ed. 2011. (Lucky Luke Ser.: 27). (ENG.). 48p. (gr. 3-17). pap. 11.95 *(978-1-84918-071-9(7))* CineBook GBR. Dist: National Bk. Network.

—Ma Dalton. 2007. (Lucky Luke Ser.: 6). (ENG., Illus.). 48p. (J). (gr. 4-7). pap. 11.95 *(978-1-905460-18-2(X))* CineBook GBR. Dist: National Bk. Network.

—The Rivals of Painful Gulch. Morris Publishing Company Staff, illus. 2009. (Lucky Luke Ser.: 12). (ENG.). 48p. pap. 11.95 *(978-1-905460-60-1(0))* CineBook GBR. Dist: National Bk. Network.

—The Stagecoach. Morris Publishing Company Staff, illus. 2011. (Lucky Luke Ser.: 25). (ENG.). 48p. (J). (gr. 3-17). pap. 11.95 *(978-1-84918-052-8(0))* CineBook GBR. Dist: National Bk. Network.

—The Tenderfoot. Morris, Alfred, illus. 2008. (Lucky Luke Ser.: 13). (ENG.). 48p. (J). (gr. -1-17). pap. 11.95 *(978-1-905460-65-6(1))* CineBook GBR. Dist: National Bk. Network.

—Tortillas for the Daltons. Spear, Luke, tr. from FRE. Morris, Ting, illus. 2008. (Lucky Luke Ser.: 10). (ENG.). 48p. pap. 11.95 *(978-1-905460-49-6(X))* CineBook GBR. Dist: National Bk. Network.

—The Wagon Train. Morris, Jean, illus. 2008. (Lucky Luke Ser.: 9). (ENG.). 48p. pap. 11.95 *(978-1-905460-40-3(6))* CineBook GBR. Dist: National Bk. Network.

—Western Circus. Morris, Alfred, illus. 2008. (Lucky Luke Ser.: 11). (ENG.). 48p. pap. 11.95 *(978-1-905460-55-7(4))* CineBook GBR. Dist: National Bk. Network.

Goscinny, René & Morris Publishing Company Staff. Billy the Kid. 2009. (Lucky Luke Ser.: 1). (ENG., Illus.). 46p. (J). (gr. 4-7). pap. 11.95 *(978-1-905460-11-3(2))* CineBook GBR. Dist: National Bk. Network.

—The Dalton Cousins. 2011. (Lucky Luke Ser.: 28). (ENG., Illus.). 48p. (J). (gr. 3-17). pap. 11.95 *(978-1-84918-076-4(8))* CineBook GBR. Dist: National Bk. Network.

—The Daltons Redeem Themselves. 2012. (Lucky Luke Ser.: 36). (ENG., Illus.). 48p. (J). (gr. 3-12). pap. 11.95 *(978-1-84918-132-7(2))* CineBook GBR. Dist: National Bk. Network.

—Emperor Smith. 2010. (Lucky Luke Ser.: 22). (ENG., Illus.). 47p. (J). (gr. 4-7). pap. 11.95 *(978-1-84918-026-9(1))* CineBook GBR. Dist: National Bk. Network.

—The Grand Duke. 2011. (Lucky Luke Ser.: 29). (ENG., Illus.). 48p. (gr. 3-17). pap. 11.95 *(978-1-84918-083-2(0))* CineBook GBR. Dist: National Bk. Network.

—Rails on the Prairie. 2012. (Lucky Luke Ser.: 32). (ENG., Illus.). 48p. (J). (gr. 3-12). pap. 11.95 *(978-1-84918-104-4(7))* CineBook GBR. Dist: National Bk. Network.

—The Singing Wire. 2012. (Lucky Luke Ser.: 35). (ENG., Illus.). 48p. (J). (gr. 3-9). pap. 11.95 *(978-1-84918-123-5(3))* CineBook GBR. Dist: National Bk. Network.

Goscinny, René & Spear, Luke. Barbed Wire on the Prairie. Spear, Luke, tr. from FRE. Morris, Ting, illus. 2007. (Lucky Luke Ser.: 7). (ENG.). 48p. (J). (gr. 4-7). pap. 11.95 *(978-1-905460-24-3(4))* CineBook GBR. Dist: National Bk. Network.

Goscinny, René, et al. Lucky Luke: The Dashing White Cowboy. 2008. (ENG.). 48p. (J). (gr. 2-4). pap. *(978-81-8386-014-7(1))* India Research Pr. IND. Dist: Independent Pubs. Group.

—Lucky Luke - Jesse James. 2008. (ENG.). 48p. (J). (gr. 2-4). pap. *(978-81-8386-016-1(8))* India Research Pr. IND. Dist: Independent Pubs. Group.

—Lucky Luke - Ma Dalton. 2008. (ENG.). 48p. (J). (gr. 2-4). pap. *(978-81-8386-015-4(X))* India Research Pr. IND. Dist: Independent Pubs. Group.

—Lucky Luke - the Tender Foot. 2008. (ENG.). 48p. (J). (gr. 2-4). pap. *(978-81-8386-017-8(6))* India Research Pr. IND. Dist: Independent Pubs. Group.

Gribnau, Joe. Kick the Cowboy, 1 vol. Tans, Adrian, illus. 2009. (ENG.). 32p. (J). (gr. k-3). 16.99 *(978-1-58980-605-4(0))* Pelican Publishing Co., Inc.

Gruskin, Edward I. Roy Rogers: Robin Hood of the Range. Hess, Erwin L., illus. 2011. 420p. 54.95 *(978-1-258-04369-8(6))* Literary Licensing, LLC.
Harman, Fred. Bronc Peeler: The Lone Cowboy. 2011. 422p. 56.95 *(978-1-258-06724-3(2))* Literary Licensing, LLC.
Harper, Jo. Mayor Jalapeno Hal from Presidio, Texas. 2003. (Illus.). (J). *(978-1-57168-767-8(X)*, Eakin Pr.) Eakin Pr.
Harper, Jo & Harper, Josephine. Whistling Willie from Amarillo, Texas, 1 vol. Harrington, David, illus. 2015. (ENG.). 32p. (J). (gr. k-3). 16.99 *(978-1-4556-2056-2(4))* Pelican Publishing Co., Inc.
Heaton, Layce D. The Many Tracks of Lap'n Tap, 1. Heaton, Layce D., illus. 2006. (Illus.). 32p. (J). lib. bdg. 18.95 *(978-0-9761128-3-9(3))* KB Bks. & More.
Hemphill, Helen. The Adventurous Deeds of Deadwood Jones. (ENG.). 232p. (J). 2011. (gr. 6-9). pap. 7.95 *(978-1-59078-896-7(6))* 2008. (gr. 5-18). 16.95 *(978-1-59078-637-6(8)*, Front Street) Boyds Mills Pr.
Henty, George Alfred. A Tale of the Western Plains. Pearse, Alfred, illus. 2006. (Dover Children's Classics Ser.). (ENG.). 352p. (YA). (gr. 3-8). per. 8.95 *(978-0-486-45261-6(1))* Dover Pubns., Inc.
Hiebert, Elfrieda H. & Juel, Connie. The Three Silly Cowboys. (Little Book Practice Reader Ser.). (J). *(978-0-8136-0889-1(9))* Modern Curriculum Pr.
High, Linda Oatman. Tenth Avenue Cowboy. Farnsworth, Bill, illus. 2008. 32p. (J). (gr. 4-7). 17.00 *(978-0-8028-5330-1(7)*, Eerdmans Bks For Young Readers) Eerdmans, William B. Publishing Co.
Hill, Monica. Dale Evans & the Lost Gold Mine. Crawford, Mel, illus. 2011. 32p. pap. 35.95 *(978-1-258-01715-6(6))* Literary Licensing, LLC.
Hillert, Margaret. The Little Cowboy & the Big Cowboy. Clark, Bradley, illus. 2016. (BeginningtoRead Ser.). (ENG.). 32p. (J). (gr. -1-2). pap. 11.94 *(978-1-60357-940-7(0))*; (gr. 1-2). 22.60 *(978-1-59953-799-3(0))* Norwood Hse. Pr.
Hoefler, Kate. Real Cowboys. Bean, Jonathan, illus. 2016. (ENG.). 32p. (J). (gr. -1-3). 16.99 *(978-0-544-14892-5(4)*, HMH Books For Young Readers) Houghton Mifflin Harcourt Publishing Co.
Hope, Lee Laura. Six Little Bunkers at Cowboy Jack's. 2007. 156p. 95.99 *(978-1-4280-7668-6(9))*; per. 89.99 *(978-1-4280-7677-8(8))* IndyPublish.com.
Hubbard, L. Ron, contrib. by. The Toughest Ranger: Literature Guide for Teachers & Librarians, Based on Common Core ELA Standards for Classrooms 6-9. 2013. (Stories from the Golden Age Ser.). (ENG.). 35p. (gr. 6-9). pap., tchr. ed. 14.95 *(978-1-61986-220-3(4))* Galaxy Pr., LLC.
Hurt-Newton, Tania. Yee-Ha Harvey. 2007. (ENG., Illus.). 14p. (J). (gr. k — 1). 14.95 *(978-0-00-724414-0(2))* HarperCollins Pubs. Ltd. GBR. Dist: Independent Pubs. Group.
Icenoggle, Jodi. 'Til the Cows Come Home. Chartier, Normand, illus. 2010. (ENG.). 32p. (J). (gr. k-2). pap. 9.95 *(978-1-59078-800-4(1))* Boyds Mills Pr.
James, Will. Cowboy in the Making. rev. ed. (Illus.). 104p. (J). (gr. 4-6). pap. 15.00 *(978-0-87842-439-9(3)*, 811) Mountain Pr. Publishing Co., Inc.
—Look-See with Uncle Bill. rev. ed. (Illus.). 190p. (J). (gr. 4). pap. *(978-0-87842-458-0(X)*, 814) Mountain Pr. Publishing Co., Inc.
—My First Horse, Vol. 1. rev. ed. (Illus.). 48p. (J). (gr. 4). 16.00 *(978-0-87842-488-7(1)*, 819) Mountain Pr. Publishing Co., Inc.
—Smoky, the Cow Horse. 2003. (J). (gr. 3-8). 20.50 *(978-0-8446-7247-2(5))* Smith, Peter Pub., Inc.
—Uncle Bill: A Tale of Two Kids & a Cowboy. rev. ed. (Tumbleweed Ser.). (Illus.). 185p. (J). (gr. 4-12). pap. 14.00 *(978-0-87842-380-4(X)*, 694) Mountain Pr. Publishing Co., Inc.
—Young Cowboy. rev. ed. 2004. (Illus.). 88p. (J). (gr. 4-7). 15.00 *(978-0-87842-419-1(9)*, 806) Mountain Pr. Publishing Co., Inc.
Jan, Young. Starting the Colt. 2014. (ENG.). 174p. (J). pap. 12.00 *(978-1-937849-10-8(4))* Raven Publishing Inc. of Montana.
Jones, Buck. Buck Jones in Ride 'Em Cowboy. 2011. 228p. 46.95 *(978-1-258-06725-0(0))* Literary Licensing, LLC.
—Buck Jones Rangers-Cowboys Collection. 2011. 68p. 36.95 *(978-1-258-07141-7(X))* Literary Licensing, LLC.
Justice, Tonya. Millie Mathison's Imagination: Cowboys, Indians, & no Red Cards. 2009. 24p. pap. 11.99 *(978-1-4389-9519-9(9))* AuthorHouse.
Kelso, Mary Jean. Cowboy James. Snider, K. C., illus. 2011. 24p. pap. 10.95 *(978-1-61633-174-0(7))*; 19.95 *(978-1-61633-178-8(X))* Guardian Angel Publishing, Inc.
Knight, Barbara. The Cowboys with penny the mustang Pony. 2006. (Penny the Mustang Pony Ser.). (Illus.). 16p. (J). 14.95 net. *(978-0-9766270-1-2(9))* Mustang BKS.
Krensky, Stephen. Pecos Bill. Tong, Paul, illus. 2007. (On My Own Folklore Ser.). (ENG.). 48p. (gr. 2-4). per. 6.95 *(978-0-8225-6475-1(0)*, First Avenue Editions) Lerner Publishing Group.
Kroll, Francis Lynde. Young Sand Hills Cowboy: Young Heroes Library. Geer, Charles H., illus. 2011. 188p. 42.95 *(978-1-258-09908-4(X))* Literary Licensing, LLC.
Kyne, Peter B. The Three Godfathers. 2005. reprint ed. pap. 15.95 *(978-1-4179-0351-1(1))* Kessinger Publishing, LLC.
Lawson, Dorie McCullough. Tex: A Book for Little Dreamers. 2011. (ENG., Illus.). 44p. (J). (gr. -1-k). 15.95 *(978-1-57076-501-8(4))* Trafalgar Square Bks.
Lenski, Lois. Cowboy Small. Lenski, Lois, illus. 2006. (Lois Lenski Bks.). (ENG., Illus.). 32p. (J). (gr. -1-2). bds. 6.99 *(978-0-375-83570-4(9)*, Random Hse. Bks. for Young Readers) Random Hse. Children's Bks.
Léturgie, Jean & Fauche, Xavier. The Daily Star. Morris, illus. 2013. (Lucky Luke Ser.: 41). (ENG.). 48p. pap. 11.95 *(978-1-84918-160-0(8))* CineBook GBR. Dist: National Bk. Network.
Lukas, Catherine & Artifact Group, The. Trouble on the Train. 2007. (Backyardigans Ser.: 6). (ENG., Illus.). 24p. (J). (gr. -1-1). pap. 3.99 *(978-1-4169-2818-8(9)*, Simon Spotlight/Nickelodeon) Simon Spotlight/Nickelodeon.
Maccarone, Grace. The Cowboy. Müller, Hildegard, illus. 2015. (I Like to Read(r) Ser.). (ENG.). 24p. (J). (gr. -1-3). 14.95 *(978-0-8234-3202-8(5))* Holiday Hse., Inc.
MacPhee, Bill. Stella, Nothing Has Changed. 2008. 312p. 28.50 *(978-1-60693-230-8(6)*, Strategic Bk. Publishing) Strategic Book Publishing & Rights Agency (SBPRA).
Maddox, Jake. Cowboy Up, 1 vol. Tiffany, Sean, illus. 2011. (Jake Maddox Sports Stories Ser.). (ENG.). 72p. (gr. 2-3). pap. 5.95 *(978-1-4342-3425-4(8))*; lib. bdg. 25.32 *(978-1-4342-2989-2(0))* Stone Arch Bks.
The Many Tracks of Lap'n Tap. 2007. (J). per. 10.95 *(978-0-9761128-4-6(1))* KB Bks. & More.
Marsh, Carole. The Case of the Crybaby Cowboy. 2006. (Carole Marsh Mysteries Ser.). (Illus.). 54p. (J). (gr. 4-7). per. 4.99 *(978-0-635-06166-9(X)*, Marsh, Carole Bks.); 14.95 *(978-0-635-06199-7(6))* Gallopade International.
McBride, Earvin, Jr. The Bowdery Rodeo Cowboys of Texas. McBride, Earvin, Jr., illus. 2nd unabr. ed. 2003. (Earvin MacBride's Amazing Sci-Fi & Adventure Heroes Ser.). (Illus.). 329p. (J). (gr. 7-12). pap. 4.95 *(978-1-892511-07-2(X))* MacBride, E. J. Pubn., Inc.
McKay, Sindy. We Read Phonics-I Want to Be a Cowboy! Raglin, Tim, illus. 2012. 32p. (J). 9.95 *(978-1-60115-351-7(1))*; pap. 4.99 *(978-1-60115-352-4(X))* Treasure Bay, Inc.
McKenzie, Tim A. Baxter Barret Brown's Cowboy Band. Atkinson, Elaine, illus. 2006. (ENG.). 28p. (gr. 2-4). 19.95 *(978-1-931721-77-6(7)*, a4a22ca5-3fa1-4c8b-8248-2efe0591d9b2) Bright Sky Pr.
Melton, Jelina Guffey. Carson the Cowboy: A Little Boy Waiting to Be a Cowboy. 2012. 66p. 24.99 *(978-1-4771-5592-9(9))*; pap. 15.99 *(978-1-4771-5591-2(0))* Xlibris Corp.
Miller, Peggy Reiff. The Seagoing Cowboy. Ewart, Claire, illus. 2016. 39p. (J). *(978-0-87178-212-0(X))* Brethren Pr.
Montijo, Rhode. The Halloween Kid. Montijo, Rhode, illus. 2010. (ENG., Illus.). 40p. (J). (gr. -1-3). 14.99 *(978-1-4169-3575-9(4)*, Simon & Schuster Bks. For Young Readers) Simon & Schuster Bks. For Young Readers.
Morgan, Leon. Tom: The Fighting Cowboy. Arbo, Hal, illus. 2011. 426p. 56.95 *(978-1-258-10103-9(3))* Literary Licensing, LLC.
Morris, illus. The Bluefeet Are Coming! 2014. (Lucky Luke Ser.: 43). (ENG.). 48p. pap. 11.95 *(978-1-84918-173-0(X))* CineBook GBR. Dist: National Bk. Network.
—Doc Doxey's Elixir. 2013. (Lucky Luke Ser.: 38). (ENG.). 48p. pap. 11.95 *(978-1-84918-141-9(1))* CineBook GBR. Dist: National Bk. Network.
—Lucky Luke Versus Pat Poker. 2014. (Lucky Luke Ser.: 44). (ENG.). 48p. pap. 11.95 *(978-1-84918-179-2(9))* CineBook GBR. Dist: National Bk. Network.
—Phil Wire. 2013. (Lucky Luke Ser.: 40). (ENG.). 48p. pap. 11.95 *(978-1-84918-155-6(1))* CineBook GBR. Dist: National Bk. Network.
Morris & Goscinny, René. Dalton City. 2007. (Lucky Luke Ser.: 3). (ENG., Illus.). 48p. (J). (gr. 4-7). pap. 11.95 *(978-1-905460-13-7(9))* CineBook GBR. Dist: National Bk. Network.
Morris, Alfred, illus. The Judge. 2010. (Lucky Luke Ser.: 24). (ENG.). 46p. (J). (gr. 3-17). pap. 11.95 *(978-1-84918-045-0(8))* CineBook GBR. Dist: National Bk. Network.
Morris Publishing Company Staff & Goscinny, René. The Daltons' Escape, Vol. 30. 2011. (Lucky Luke Ser.: 30). (ENG., Illus.). 48p. pap. 11.95 *(978-1-84918-091-7(1))* CineBook GBR. Dist: National Bk. Network.
Mortensen, Lori. Cowpoke Clyde & Dirty Dawg. Austin, Michael Allen, illus. 2013. (ENG.). 32p. (J). (gr. -1-3). 16.99 *(978-0-547-23993-4(9))* Houghton Mifflin Harcourt Publishing Co.
Müller, Hildegard. The Cowboy. Müller, Hildegard, illus. 2015. (I Like to Read(r) Ser.). (ENG., Illus.). 24p. (J). (gr. -1-3). 6.99 *(978-0-8234-3316-2(1))* Holiday Hse., Inc.
Nislick, June Levitt. Zayda Was a Cowboy. 2005. (ENG.). 88p. pap. 11.95 *(978-0-8276-0817-7(9))* Jewish Pubn. Society.
Nusz, Janean. The Littlest Cowboy. 2005. 26p. 12.30 *(978-1-4116-4019-1(5))* Lulu Pr., Inc.
Nuzum, K. A. A Small White Scar. 2008. (ENG.). 208p. (J). (gr. 5). pap. 8.99 *(978-0-06-075641-3(1))* HarperCollins Pubs.
Paris, Stephanie. Pecos Bill & Slue-Foot Sue, 1 vol. 2009. (Building Fluency Through Reader's Theater Ser.). (ENG.). 24p. (J). (gr. 2-4). pap. 6.99 *(978-1-4333-0991-5(2))* Teacher Created Materials, Inc.
Patchin, Frank Gee. The Pony Rider Boys in Texas: Or- the Veiled Riddle of the Plains. 2007. (ENG.). 166p. pap. 19.99 *(978-1-4346-3536-5(8))*; 182p. pap. 21.99 *(978-1-4346-3537-2(6))* Creative Media Partners, LLC.
Pennac, D. & Benacquista, E. Lone Riders. 2013. (Lucky Luke Ser.: 42). (ENG., Illus.). 48p. (J). (gr. 3-12). pap. 11.95 *(978-1-84918-168-6(3))* CineBook GBR. Dist: National Bk. Network.
Pennac, Daniel & Benacquista, Tonino. Lucky Luke Versus the Pinkertons. Achdé, illus. 2012. (Lucky Luke Ser.: 31). (ENG.). 48p. pap. 11.95 *(978-1-84918-098-6(9))* CineBook GBR. Dist: National Bk. Network.
Perdue, Gillian. An Buachaill Bo. Connor, Michael, illus. 2006. (Sraith Sos Ser.: 13). (IRI, ENG & GLE.). 64p. (J). pap. 9.95 *(978-1-84717-006-4(4))* O'Brien Pr., Ltd., The IRL. Dist: Dufour Editions, Inc.
Poulsen, David A. Cowboy Cool. 2008. (Lawrence High Yearbook Ser.). (ENG.). 96p. (YA). (gr. 7-18). pap. *(978-1-55470-099-8(X))* Me to We.
Punter, Russell. Stories of Cowboys. Fiorin, Fabiano, illus. 2008. (Usborne Young Reading: Series One Ser.). 48p. (J). 8.99 *(978-0-7945-1822-6(2)*, Usborne) EDC Publishing.
Redmond, Mark L. Arty's Long Day. Ury, Laura, illus. 2003. 102p. pap. *(978-0-87398-042-5(5))* Sword of the Lord Pubs.
Reed, Sharon. Tara: Prairie Horse Series. 2006. pap. 14.00 *(978-0-8059-7091-3(6))* Dorrance Publishing Co., Inc.
Reynolds, Aaron. Pirates vs. Cowboys. Barneda, David, illus. 2013. (ENG.). 40p. (J). (gr. k-3). 16.99 *(978-0-375-85874-1(1)*, Knopf Bks. for Young Readers) Random Hse. Children's Bks.
Rice, James. Gaston(r) Goes to Texas, 1 vol. Rice, James, illus. 2007. (Gaston(r) Ser.). (ENG., Illus.). 32p. (J). (gr. 1-3). 16.99 *(978-1-58980-531-6(3))* Pelican Publishing Co., Inc.
—Too Tall Thomas Rides the Grub Line, 1 vol. Rice, James, illus. 2004. (ENG., Illus.). 32p. (J). (gr. k-3). 16.99 *(978-1-58980-177-6(6))* Pelican Publishing Co., Inc.
Rice, James, tr. & illus. Trail Boss: J. M. Daugherty. Rice, James, illus. 2003. (J). *(978-1-57168-769-2(6)*, Eakin Pr.) Eakin Pr.
Roach, Joyce Gibson. Horned Toad Canyon. Shaw, Charles, illus. 2003. (ENG.). 48p. (J). (gr. 2-4). 17.95 *(978-1-931721-01-1(7)*, c2d211ff-dcbc-4d55-8600-9edaa91d316d) Bright Sky Pr.
Rogers-Barnett, Cheryl, et al. The All-American Cowboy Grill: Sizzlin' Recipes from the World's Greatest Cowboys, 1 vol. 2005. (ENG., Illus.). 240p. 16.99 *(978-1-4016-0200-0(2))* Nelson, Thomas Inc.
Rogers, Roy. Roy Rogers & the Deadly Treasure. 2011. 286p. 48.95 *(978-1-258-03926-4(5))* Literary Licensing, LLC.
Rossi, Joyce. The Gullywasher: El Chaparron Torrencial. 2004. (ENG, SPA & MUL., Illus.). 32p. (J). (gr. k-3). pap. 7.95 *(978-0-87358-728-0(6))* Cooper Square Publishing Llc.
Sanders, Rob. Cowboy Christmas. Manders, John, illus. 2012. (ENG.). 32p. (J). (gr. k-k). 10.99 *(978-0-375-86985-3(9)*, Golden Bks.) Random Hse. Children's Bks.
Sankey, Alice. Roy Rogers & the Desert Treasure. Souza, Paul, illus. 2011. 26p. 35.95 *(978-1-258-03927-1(3))* Literary Licensing, LLC.
Santillo, LuAnn. The Ball. Santillo, LuAnn, ed. 2003. (Half-Pint Kids Readers Ser.). (Illus.). 7p. (J). (gr. -1-1). pap. 1.00 *(978-1-59256-081-3(4))* Half-Pint Kids, Inc.
—The Best Tricks. Santillo, LuAnn, ed. 2003. (Half-Pint Kids Readers Ser.). (Illus.). 7p. (J). (gr. -1-1). pap. 1.00 *(978-1-59256-082-0(2))* Half-Pint Kids, Inc.
Sargent, Dave & Denton, Ivan. Blizzard No. 5: Don't Give Up. Denton, Ivan, illus. 2004. (Illus.). 36p. (J). pap. 10.95 *(978-1-59381-009-2(1))* Ozark Publishing.
—My Grandpa Is a Cowboy: Learning Is Fun #1, 6 vols. Denton, Ivan, illus. 2004. (Illus.). 36p. (J). pap. 10.95 *(978-1-59381-001-6(6))* Ozark Publishing.
Sargent, Dave & Sargent, Pat. The Chuck Wagon: Don't Be Stubborn, 10 vols., Vol. 7. Lenoir, Jane, illus. 2005. (Colorado Cowboys Ser.: 10). 32p. (J). pap. 10.95 *(978-1-59381-099-3(7))*; lib. bdg. 23.60 *(978-1-59381-098-6(9))* Ozark Publishing.
—The Colorado Blizzard: Be Determined, 10 vols., Vol. 8. Lenoir, Jane, illus. (Colorado Cowboys Ser.: 10). 32p. (J). 2005. pap. 10.95 *(978-1-59381-027-6(X))* 2004. (gr. 3-8). lib. bdg. 23.60 *(978-1-59381-026-9(1))* Ozark Publishing.
—The Drought: Have Faith, 10 vols., Vol. 9. Lenoir, Jane, illus. 2005. (Colorado Cowboys Ser.: 10). 32p. (J). pap. 10.95 *(978-1-59381-103-7(9))*; lib. bdg. 23.60 *(978-1-59381-102-0(0))* Ozark Publishing.
—The Fire: A Second Chance, 10 vols., Vol. 10. Lenoir, Jane, illus. 2005. (Colorado Cowboys Ser.: 10). 32p. (J). pap. 10.95 *(978-1-59381-105-1(5))* Ozark Publishing.
—Rusty: (Red Roan) Be Strong & Brave, 30 vols., Vol. 52. Lenoir, Jane, illus. 2003. (Saddle up Ser.: Vol. 52). 42p. (J). pap. 10.95 *(978-1-56763-804-2(X))*; lib. bdg. 23.60 *(978-1-56763-803-5(1))* Ozark Publishing.
Sauer, Tammi. Cowboy Camp. Reed, Mike, illus. (ENG.). (J). (gr. -1-k). 2015. 24p. bds. 6.95 *(978-1-4549-1389-4(4))* 2014. 32p. pap. 6.95 *(978-1-4549-1360-3(6))* 2005. 32p. 14.95 *(978-1-4027-2224-0(9))* Sterling Publishing Co., Inc.
Schaefer, Jack. Stubby Pringle's Christmas. Bjorklund, Lorence, illus. 2017. (ENG.). 48p. pap. 16.95 ***(978-0-8263-5865-3(9))*** Univ. of New Mexico Pr.
Schnetzler, Pattie L. Widdermaker. Sealock, Rick, illus. 2005. 32p. (gr. k-2). 15.95 *(978-0-87614-647-7(7))* Lerner Publishing Group.
Scieszka, Jon. The Good, the Bad, & the Goofy. Smith, Lane, illus. 2004. (Time Warp Trio Ser.: 3). (ENG.). 80p. (J). (gr. 2-4). pap. 5.99 *(978-0-14-240046-3(7)*, Puffin Books) Penguin Young Readers Group.
—The Good, the Bad, & the Goofy. Smith, Lane, illus. 2005. (Time Warp Trio Ser.: No. 3). 70p. (gr. 4-7). 15.00 *(978-0-7569-5876-3(8))* Perfection Learning Corp.
Scott, Elizabeth M. It's Rodeo Time! With Mamma Scottie & the Kids. 2009. 52p. pap. 24.99 *(978-1-4490-1750-7(9))* AuthorHouse.
Shaver, Susan M. Flying Cowboys. 2011. 32p. pap. 14.99 *(978-1-4567-9450-7(7))* AuthorHouse.
Shoopman, Jim. Cowboy Zack & the Monkey from the Muggletown Zoo. 2013. 50p. pap. 13.98 *(978-0-9887836-2-1(2))* Taylor and Seale Publishing, LLC.
Sonneborn, Scott. The Good, the Bad, & the Monkeys, 1 vol. Bradley, Jessica, illus. 2013. (Comics Land Ser.). (ENG.). 32p. (gr. k-2). 7.95 *(978-1-4342-6283-7(9))*; lib. bdg. 25.32 *(978-1-4342-4945-6(X))* Stone Arch Bks.
Steig, Jeanne. Tales from Gizzard's Grill. Turner, Sandy, illus. 2004. 80p. (J). 17.89 *(978-0-06-000960-1(8)*, Cotler, Joanna Books) HarperCollins Pubs.
Stein, David Ezra. Cowboy Ned & Andy. Stein, David Ezra, illus. (ENG., Illus.). 32p. (J). (gr. -1-1). 2011. 6.99 *(978-1-4424-3619-0(0))* 2006. 16.99 *(978-1-4169-0041-2(1))* Simon & Schuster/Paula Wiseman Bks. (Simon & Schuster/Paula Wiseman Bks.).
Stilton, Geronimo. The Wild, Wild West. 2005. (Geronimo Stilton Ser.: 21). (ENG., Illus.). 128p. (J). (gr. 2-5). pap. 7.99 *(978-0-439-69144-4(3)*, Scholastic Paperbacks) Scholastic, Inc.
Stoddard, Jack. Cowboy Dreams. 2006. 144p. pap. 15.95 *(978-1-60047-002-8(5))* Wasteland Pr.
Stone Arch Books Staff. Pecos Bill: Colossal Cowboy. Weber, Lisa K., illus. 2010. (Graphic Spin Ser.). (ENG.). 40p. (gr. 1-3). pap. 5.95 *(978-1-4342-2267-1(5)*, Graphic Revolve) Stone Arch Bks.
Stratemeyer, Edward. Dave Porter at Star Ranch. 2007. 260p. 28.95 *(978-1-4218-4144-1(4)*, 1st World Library - Literary Society) 1st World Publishing, Inc.
Strauss, Kevin. Pecos Bill Invents the Ten-Gallon Hat, 1 vol. Harrington, David, illus. 2012. (ENG.). 32p. (J). (gr. k-3). 16.99 *(978-1-4556-1502-5(1))* Pelican Publishing Co., Inc.
Stuart, Pamela Haught. Just like my Papa. 2008. 40p. per. 16.99 *(978-1-4343-5369-6(9))* AuthorHouse.
Sylvester, Merrill. Ho-Ho Where Did All My Reindeer Go? The Chicken Leg Detective Service. 2011. 72p. pap. 19.95 *(978-1-4626-0794-5(2))* America Star Bks.
Thomas, Jan. Let's Sing a Lullaby with the Brave Cowboy. Thomas, Jan, illus. 2012. (ENG., Illus.). 40p. (J). (gr. -1-3). 12.99 *(978-1-4424-4276-4(X)*, Beach Lane Bks.) Beach Lane Bks.
Timberlake, Amy. The Dirty Cowboy. Rex, Adam, illus. 2003. (ENG.). 32p. (J). (gr. -1-3). 18.99 *(978-0-374-31791-1(7)*, 9780374317911, Farrar, Straus & Giroux (BYR)) Farrar, Straus & Giroux.
Townsend, Tom. The Ballad of Ol' Hook. 2006. (YA). pap. 9.95 *(978-1-932196-91-7(9))* WordWright.biz, Inc.
Toy Box Innovations, creator. Disney/Pixar: Volume 2. abr. ed. 2006. (Disney's Read along Collection Ser.). (ENG.). 24p. (J). (gr. -1-3). pap. *(978-0-7634-2181-6(2))* Walt Disney Records.
Trent, Shanda. Giddy-Up Buckaroos! Knight, Tom, illus. 2016. (ENG.). 32p. (J). (gr. -1-2). 16.99 *(978-1-68010-008-2(4))* Tiger Tales.
Van Riper, Guernsey, Jr. Will Rogers, Young Cowboy. 2011. 196p. 42.95 *(978-1-258-06291-0(7))* Literary Licensing, LLC.
Vens, William D. Alias Pecos Bill. 2003. per. 13.95 *(978-1-891929-92-2(5))* Four Seasons Pubs.
Waites, Joan C., illus. How-to Cowboy: 22 Secret, Magic How-to Fun Tricks. 2003. 96p. (J). pap. 5.95 *(978-0-9716911-1-7(8))* IM Pr.
Wallace, Sharolyn. The Adventures of Bruce, Ben & Gerry: Bruce's Dream. 2012. 28p. pap. 17.99 *(978-1-4772-0249-4(8))* AuthorHouse.
—The Adventures of Bruce, Ben & Gerry: The Surprise. 2013. 24p. pap. 17.99 *(978-1-4772-9489-5(9))* AuthorHouse.
Webster, Frank V. Comrades of the Saddle. 2007. 176p. 26.95 *(978-1-4218-3229-6(1)*, 1st World Library - Literary Society); (ENG.). per. 11.95 *(978-1-4218-3329-3(8))* 1st World Publishing, Inc.
—Comrades of the Saddle or the Young Rough Riders of the Plains. 2004. reprint ed. pap. 1.99 *(978-1-4192-1372-4(5))* Kessinger Publishing, LLC.
—Cowboy Dave. 2007. 176p. 26.95 *(978-1-4218-3230-2(5)*, 1st World Library - Literary Society); (ENG.). per. 11.95 *(978-1-4218-3330-9(1))* 1st World Publishing, Inc.
White, Chris. The Great Jammy Adventures: The Flying Cowboy. 2010. (J). pap. 14.99 *(978-0-9827705-6-6(1))* StoneHouse Ink.
Willard F. Baker. The Boy Ranchers among the Indians. 2007. 180p. per. 11.95 *(978-1-4218-4020-8(0)*, 1st World Library - Literary Society) 1st World Publishing, Inc.
Wilson, John. Ghost Moon, 1 vol. 2011. (Desert Legend Trilogy Ser.: 2). (ENG.). 192p. (YA). (gr. 8-12). pap. 12.95 *(978-1-55469-879-0(0))* Orca Bk. Pubs. USA.
Wilson, Mark A. The Legend of Crawley Creek. 2008. 104p. pap. 9.95 *(978-1-60693-423-4(6)*, Eloquent Bks.) Strategic Book Publishing & Rights Agency (SBPRA).
Wissinger, Tamera Will. This Old Band. Loveridge, Matt, illus. 2014. (ENG.). 32p. (J). (gr. -1-k). 16.95 *(978-1-62873-595-6(3)*, Sky Pony Pr.) Skyhorse Publishing Co., Inc.
Wooten, Sherry. Cowboy Connor. 2009. 20p. pap. 10.49 *(978-1-4389-5064-8(0))* AuthorHouse.
Young, Jan. Starting the Colt. 2014. 173p. (J). *(978-1-937849-11-5(2))* Raven Publishing Inc. of Montana.

COWBOYS—SONGS AND MUSIC

Ketteman, Helen. There Once Was a Cowpoke Who Swallowed an Ant. Terry, Will, illus. 2014. (ENG.). 32p. (J). (gr. -1-3). 16.99 *(978-0-8075-7850-6(9))* Whitman, Albert & Co.

COWS

see also Dairying; Milk

Amoroso, Cynthia & Noyed, Bob. Cows. 2016. (In the Barnyard Ser.). (ENG.). 24p. (J). (gr. k-3). 27.07 *(978-1-5038-0825-6(4)*, 210669) Child's World, Inc., The.
Amstutz, Lisa J. American Crows. 2016. (Backyard Birds Ser.). (ENG., Illus.). 24p. (J). (gr. k-1). lib. bdg. 26.65 *(978-1-4914-8511-8(6)*, Pebble Plus) Capstone Press of Coughlan Cos.
Aspen-Baxter, Linda & Kissock, Heather. Vacas. 2012. (SPA.). (J). *(978-1-61913-186-6(2))* Weigl Pubs., Inc.
Boynton, Sandra. Amazing Cows: Udder Absurdity for Children. 2010. (ENG., Illus.). 96p. (J). (gr. -1-3). pap. 10.95 *(978-0-7611-6214-8(3)*, 16214); (gr. 1-4). 15.95 *(978-0-7611-6371-8(9))* Workman Publishing Co., Inc.
Carraway, Rose. Cows on the Farm. 2012. (Farm Animals Ser.). (Illus.). 24p. (gr. k-2). 69.20 *(978-1-4339-8053-4(3))*; (J). 22.60 *(978-1-4339-7348-2(0))*; (J). pap. 8.15 *(978-1-4339-7349-9(9))* Stevens, Gareth Publishing LLLP.
—Cows on the Farm: Vacas de Granja? 2012. (Farm Animals / Animales de granja Ser.). (SPA & ENG., Illus.). 24p. (J). (gr. k-2). lib. bdg. 22.60 *(978-1-4339-7396-3(0))* Stevens, Gareth Publishing LLLP.
Cows. Date not set. (Old MacDonald Stickers Ser.). (Illus.). 16p. (J). 2.98 *(978-0-7525-7057-0(9))*; 5.98 *(978-0-7525-9966-3(6))* Parragon, Inc.
Cows (for Doubleday Entertainment USA) Down on the Farm. 2006. (J). per. 6.95 *(978-1-59566-225-5(1))* QEB Publishing Inc.
Deedy, Carmen Agra. 14 Cows for America, 1 vol. González, Thomas, illus. 2009. (ENG.). 36p. (J). (gr. 1-5). 17.95 *(978-1-56145-490-7(7))* Peachtree Pubs.
—14 Cows for America. Gonzalez, Thomas, illus. 2016. (ENG.). 36p. (J). (gr. -1-3). lib. bdg. 19.60 *(978-0-606-39065-1(0))* Turtleback Bks.
—14 Vacas para América, 1 vol. González, Thomas, illus. 2010.Tr. of 14 Cows for America. (SPA.). 36p. (J). pap. 8.95 *(978-1-56145-555-3(5))* Peachtree Pubs.
—14 Vacas para América, 1 vol. De la Torre, Cristina, tr. from ENG. González, Thomas, illus. 2010.Tr. of 14 Cows for America. (SPA.). 36p. (J). (gr. 1-5). 17.95 *(978-1-56145-550-8(4))* Peachtree Pubs.
Deedy, Carmen Agra & Naiyomah, Wilson Kimeli. 14 Cows for America, 1 vol. González, Thomas, illus. 2016. (ENG.). 36p. (J). (gr. 1-5). pap. 8.95 *(978-1-56145-961-2(5))* Peachtree Pubs.
Dicker, Katie. Cows. 2014. (Farm Animals Ser.). (Illus.). 24p. (gr. 2-5). 28.50 *(978-1-62588-019-2(7))* Black Rabbit Bks.
Diemer, Lauren. Cows. 2010. pap. 9.95 *(978-1-60596-920-6(6))*; 24p. (J). (gr. 2-4). lib. bdg. 25.70 *(978-1-60596-919-0(2))* Weigl Pubs., Inc.
Dolphin, Colleen. Casual Cows, 1 vol. 2011. (Farm Pets Ser.). (ENG., Illus.). 24p. (J). (gr. k-3). lib. bdg. 24.21 *(978-1-61613-369-6(4))* ABDO Publishing Co.
Donlon, Bridget. Got Milk? How? Chelsey, Emily, illus. 2012. 28p. (-18). pap. 24.95 *(978-1-4626-8033-7(X))* America Star Bks.

Doyle, Sheri. Cows, 1 vol. 2012. (Farm Animals Ser.). (ENG., Illus.). 24p. (gr. k-1). lib. bdg. 26.65 (978-1-4296-8646-4(4), Pebble Plus) Capstone Press of Coughlan Cos.

Gibbs, Maddie. Cows, 1 vol. 2015. (ENG., Illus.). 24p. (J). lib. bdg. 23.60 (978-1-4994-0082-3(9), PowerKids Pr.) Rosen Publishing Group, Inc., The.

—Las Vacas / Cows, 1 vol. 2015. (Amigos de la Granja / Farmyard Friends Ser.). (ENG & SPA.). 24p. (J). 23.60 (978-1-4994-0265-0(1), PowerKids Pr.) Rosen Publishing Group, Inc., The.

Gish, Melissa. A Dairy Farm. 2003. (Field Trips Ser.). 24p. (J). lib. bdg. 14.95 (978-1-58340-325-9(6)) Black Rabbit Bks.

Glaser, Rebecca Stromstad. Cows Moo. 2016. (ENG., Illus.). 14p. (J). (gr. -1 — 1). bds. 7.99 (978-1-68152-125-1(3)) Amicus.

Green, Emily K. Cows. 2007. (Farm Animals Ser.). (ENG., Illus.). 24p. (J). (gr. k-3). lib. bdg. 25.95 (978-1-60014-065-5(3)) Bellwether Media.

Group/McGraw-Hill, Wright. Fibonacci's Cows: Level O, 6 vols. (Mountain Peaks Ser.). 128p. (gr. 6-18). 36.95 (978-0-322-06737-0(5)) Wright Group/McGraw-Hill.

Hall, Margaret. Cows & Their Calves [Scholastic]. 2011. (Animal Offspring Ser.). 24p. pap. 0.50 (978-1-4296-6296-3(4), Pebble Plus) Capstone Press of Coughlan Cos.

Holley, Rebecca L. Cow-racter A Lesson in Kindness: Barnyard Blessings. 2011. 24p. pap. 10.95 (978-1-4497-1164-1(2), WestBow Pr.) Author Solutions, Inc.

Kishel, Ann-Marie. Cows & Calves. 2006. (First Step Nonfiction - Animal Families Ser.). (ENG., Illus.). 8p. (gr. -1-1). pap. 4.95 (978-0-8225-5649-7(9), Lerner Pubns.) Lerner Publishing Group.

Kissock, Heather & Aspen-Baxter, Linda. Cows. 2011. (J). (978-1-61690-571-2(9)); (978-1-61690-925-3(0)) Weigl Pubs., Inc.

Lapsley, Sarah. Learning about Cows. Williams, Glenn, illus. Williams, Glenn, photos by. 2008. 20p. (J). pap. (978-1-935289-10-4(1)) Spalding Education International.

Macken, JoAnn Early. Cows. 2nd rev. ed. 2009. (Animals That Live on the Farm Ser.). (ENG.). 24p. (J). (gr. -1-3). pap. 8.15 (978-1-4339-2465-1(X)); lib. bdg. 22.60 (978-1-4339-2396-8(3)) Stevens, Gareth Publishing LLLP. (Weekly Reader Leveled Readers).

—Cows;Las Vacas. 2nd rev. ed. 2009. (Animals That Live on the Farm/Animales que viven en la granja Ser.). (ENG & SPA.). 24p. (J). (gr. -1-3). pap. 8.15 (978-1-4339-2472-9(2)); lib. bdg. 22.60 (978-1-4339-2428-6(5)) Stevens, Gareth Publishing LLLP. (Weekly Reader Leveled Readers).

Madema, Victoria. Crazy Cows Stickers. 2010. (Dover Little Activity Books Stickers Ser.). (ENG., Illus.). 4p. (J). (gr. -1-5). 1.50 (978-0-486-47445-8(3)) Dover Pubns., Inc.

Meister, Cari. Cows. 2012. (ENG., Illus.). 24p. (J). lib. bdg. 25.65 (978-1-62031-001-4(5)) Jump! Inc.

Mercer, Abbie. Cows on a Farm. 2009. (Illus.). 24p. (J). 49.50 (978-1-4042-8059-5(6)); (ENG., pap. 8.25 (978-1-4042-8055-7(3)); (ENG., lib. bdg. 22.60 (978-1-4042-8047-2(2)) Rosen Publishing Group, Inc., The. (PowerKids Pr.).

Meredith, Susan. Cows on the Farm. 2010. (Farm Animals Ser.). (Illus.). 24p. (J). (gr. k-3). 22.79 (978-1-61590-265-1(1)) Rourke Educational Media.

Metz, Lorijo. Cattle: Cows, Bulls, & Calves. 2010. (On the Farm Ser.). (Illus.). 24p. (J). 22.60 (978-1-4488-0687-4(9)); pap. 8.25 (978-1-4488-1335-3(2)) Rosen Publishing Group, Inc., The. (PowerKids Pr.).

Minden, Cecilia. Farm Animals: Cows. 2009. (21st Century Junior Library: Farm Animals Ser.). (ENG., Illus.). 24p. (gr. 2-4). lib. bdg. 25.64 (978-1-60279-540-2(1), 200271) Cherry Lake Publishing.

Murray, Julie. Cows, 1 vol. (ENG., Illus.). 24p. 2015. (J). 27.07 (978-1-62970-939-0(5), 1391178) 2005. 25.65 (978-1-59197-310-2(4), Buddy Bks.) ABDO Publishing Co.

—Grass to Milk, 1 vol. 2006. (Beginning to End Ser.). (ENG., Illus.). 24p. (gr. k-4). 25.65 (978-1-59679-837-3(8), Buddy Bks.) ABDO Publishing Co.

Nelson, Robin. Cows. 2009. pap. 34.95 (978-0-7613-4091-1(2)); (ENG.). 24p. 23.93 (978-0-7613-4057-7(2), Lerner Pubns.) Lerner Publishing Group.

Owen, Ruth. Milk! Life on a Dairy Farm. 2012. (Food from Farmers Ser.). (ENG.). 32p. (J). (gr. k-3). pap. 11.75 (978-1-61533-534-3(X)); lib. bdg. 26.50 (978-1-61533-528-2(5)) Windmill Bks.

Peterson, Cris. Clarabelle: Making Milk & So Much More. Lundquist, David R., photos by. 2013. (ENG., Illus.). 32p. (J). (gr. 4-6). pap. 7.95 (978-1-62091-590-5(1)) Boyds Mills Pr.

Pohl, Kathleen. What Happens at a Dairy Farm? 2006. (Where People Work Ser.). (Illus.). 24p. (gr. -1-3). pap. 8.15 (978-0-8368-6893-7(5)); lib. bdg. 22.00 (978-0-8368-6886-9(2)) Stevens, Gareth Publishing LLLP. (Weekly Reader Leveled Readers).

—What Happens at a Dairy Farm? (¿Qué pasa en una granja Lechera?) 2006. (Where People Work/Dónde Trabaja la Gente? Ser.). (ENG & SPA., Illus.). 24p. (gr. -1-3). pap. 8.15 (978-0-8368-7394-8(7), Weekly Reader Leveled Readers) Stevens, Gareth Publishing LLLP.

—What Happens at a Dairy Farm?/¿Qué Pasa en Una Granja Lechera? 2006. (Where People Work/Dónde Trabaja la Gente? Ser.). (SPA & ENG., Illus.). 24p. (J). (gr. -1-3). lib. bdg. 22.00 (978-0-8368-7387-0(4), Weekly Reader Leveled Readers) Stevens, Gareth Publishing LLLP.

Ray, Hannah. Cows. 2006. (Down on the Farm Ser.). (Illus.). 24p. (J). (gr. 4-7). lib. bdg. 15.95 (978-1-59566-180-7(8)) QEB Publishing Inc.

Rebman, Renee C. Cows. 2009. (Animals Animals Ser.). 48p. (gr. 3). 29.93 (978-0-7614-3977-6(3)) Marshall Cavendish Corp.

Sexton, Colleen. The Life Cycle of a Cow. 2010. (Life Cycles Ser.). (ENG., Illus.). 24p. (J). (gr. k-3). lib. bdg. 25.95 (978-1-60014-451-6(9), Blastoff! Readers) Bellwether Media.

Silverman, Buffy. Meet a Baby Cow. 2016. (Lightning Bolt Books (tm) — Baby Farm Animals Ser.). (ENG., Illus.). 32p. (J). (gr. 1-3). 26.65 (978-1-5124-0798-3(4)); 39.99 (978-1-5124-1026-6(8), Lerner Pubns.) Lerner Publishing Group.

Stiefel, Chana. Cows on the Family Farm. 2013. (Animals on the Family Farm Ser.). 24p. (J). (gr. k-3). pap. 7.95 (978-1-4644-0353-8(8), Enslow Elementary); lib. bdg. 22.60 (978-0-7660-4205-6(7)) Enslow Pubs., Inc.

Taus-Bolstad, Stacy. From Grass to Milk. (ENG., Illus.). 24p. (gr. k-3). 2012. (Start to Finish, Second Series: Food Ser.: No. 2). pap. 6.95 (978-1-58013-966-3(3)) 2012. (Start to Finish, Second Series: Food Ser.: No. 2). lib. bdg. 23.93 (978-0-7613-9179-1(7), Lerner Pubns.) 2003. (Start to Finish Ser.). 19.93 (978-0-8225-4664-1(7), Lerner Pubns.) Lerner Publishing Group.

Ticktock Media, Ltd. Staff. What Do Cows Do? 2008. (What Do Animals Do? Ser.). (ENG.). 10p. (J). (gr. k — 1). bds. 4.95 (978-1-84696-796-2(1), TickTock Books) Octopus Publishing Group GBR. Dist: Independent Pubs. Group.

Top That Publishing Staff, ed. Wacky Cow. 2004. (Wacky Animals Ser.). (Illus.). 10p. (J). pap. (978-1-84510-088-9(3)) Top That! Publishing PLC.

Wolfman, Judy. Life on a Cattle Farm. Winston, David Lorenz, photos by. 2005. (Life on a Farm Ser.). (Illus.). 48p. (gr. 2-5). lib. bdg. 23.93 (978-1-57505-516-9(3)) Lerner Publishing Group.

—Life on a Dairy Farm. Winston, David Lorenz, illus. Winston, David Lorenz, photos by. 2004. (Life on a Farm Ser.). (ENG.). 48p. (gr. 2-5). lib. bdg. 23.93 (978-1-57505-190-1(7)) Lerner Publishing Group.

Wood, Alix. Dexter Cattle. 2016. (Mini Animals Ser.). 00032p. (J). (gr. 2-3). pap. 10.00 (978-1-4994-8152-5(7), Windmill Bks.) Rosen Publishing Group, Inc., The.

Yoon, Salina. Do Cows Meow? 2012. (Lift-The-Flap Book Ser.). (ENG., Illus.). 18p. (J). (gr. k — 1). bds. 9.95 (978-1-4027-8956-4(4)) Sterling Publishing Co., Inc.

COWS—FICTION

Alan E. And Lisa J. Laird. Cows Can Be Scary. 2009. 40p. pap. 18.49 (978-1-4389-8150-5(3)) AuthorHouse.

Anderson, D. M. Killer Cows. 2010. 274p. (YA). pap. 13.99 (978-1-59080-686-9(7), Quake) Echelon Press Publishing.

Antillano, Laura. Una Vaca Querida. Ochoa, Ana, illus. (Literary Encounters Ser.). (SPA.). (J). (gr. 3-5). pap. (978-968-494-077-2(7), CI7709) Centro de Informacion y Desarrollo de la Comunicacion y la Literatura MEX. Dist: Lectorum Pubns., Inc.

Applegate, Katherine. Home of the Brave. 2008. (ENG.). 272p. (J). (gr. 5-9). pap. 7.99 (978-0-312-53563-6(5), 9780312535636) Square Fish.

Arena, Felice & Kettle, Phil. On the Farm/By Felice Arena & Phil Kettle; Illustrated by Susy Boyer. Boyer, Susy, illus. 2004. (J). pap. (978-1-59336-363-5(X)) Mondo Publishing.

Arkangel, Brian. Cow Story. Moffat, Ross, illus. 2009. 24p. pap. 24.95 (978-1-60703-272-4(4)) America Star Bks.

Arkin, Alan. Cassie Loves Beethoven. l.t. ed. 2003. (Children's Large Print Ser.). 28.95 (978-1-58118-108-1(6)) LRS.

Atherton, Isabel. Ruby Moo's Deep-Sea Adventure! Straker, Bethany, illus. 2014. (ENG.). 32p. (J). (gr. -1-k). 14.95 (978-1-62914-625-6(0), Sky Pony Pr.) Skyhorse Publishing Co., Inc.

Baker, Ken. Cow Can't Sleep, 0 vols. Gray, Steve, illus. 2012. (ENG.). 24p. (J). (gr. -1-3). 12.99 (978-0-7614-6198-2(1), 9780761461982, Amazon Children's Publishing) Amazon Publishing.

Balmer, Fred. Festus & His New Job. Newcomb, Kristene, illus. 2004. 26p. (J). per. 7.00 (978-0-9760790-1-9(1)) Folsom Fallies Pr.

—Festus & the Hole in the Fence Gang. Newcomb, Kristene, illus. 2005. 33p. (J). per. 7.00 (978-0-9760790-3-3(8)) Folsom Fallies Pr.

—Festus & the Missing Bag of Feed. Newcomb, Kristene, illus. 2004. 26p. (J). per. 7.00 (978-0-9760790-0-2(3)) Folsom Fallies Pr.

—Festus & the Stranger. Miller, Callie, ed. Newcomb, Kristene, illus. 2007. 30p. (J). per. 7.00 (978-0-9760790-4-0(6)) Folsom Fallies Pr.

Banicki, Patsy & Staige, Pat. Farmer Carpenter's Barn & the Cow's Saturday Night Dance. Staige, Pat & Stanton, Janet, illus. Date not set. (Orig.). (J). (gr. k-4). pap. (978-0-9641375-1-6(8)) Staige Productions.

Bar-el, Dan. Audrey (Cow) Mai-Wyss, Tatjana, illus. 2014.Tr. of Cow. (ENG.). 240p. (J). (gr. 2-5). 17.99 (978-1-77049-602-6(5), Tundra Bks.) Tundra Bks. CAN. Dist: Penguin Random Hse. LLC.

Bar-El, Dan. Audrey (Cow) Mai-Wyss, Tatjana, illus. 2016. (ENG.). 240p. (J). (gr. 2-4). pap. 9.99 (978-1-77049-603-3(3), Tundra Bks.) Tundra Bks. CAN. Dist: Penguin Random Hse. LLC.

Barnett, Susanne. Pink & the Mystery of the Stable Room Monster. 2012. 34p. pap. 19.99 (978-1-4772-0921-9(2)) AuthorHouse.

Barry, Marian. Baby Moo. 2012. 24p. pap. 15.99 (978-1-4771-3264-7(3)) Xlibris Corp.

Beach, John, reader. Moo Cow Kaboom! unabr. ed. 2005. (Picture Book Readalong Ser.). (J). (gr. -1-2). 28.95 incl. audio compact disk (978-1-59519-502-9(5)) Live Oak Media.

Bean, Margo Cronbaugh. Brutus the Bull. Perry, Aumi Kauffman, illus. 2013. 24p. 19.95 (978-1-61633-373-7(1)); pap. 11.95 (978-1-61633-374-4(X)) Guardian Angel Publishing, Inc.

Beil, Karen Magnuson. Mooove Over! A Book about Counting by Twos. Meisel, Paul, tr. Meisel, Paul, illus. 2004. (ENG.). 32p. (J). (gr. k-3). tchr. ed. 16.95 (978-0-8234-1736-0(0)) Holiday Hse., Inc.

Bellehumeur, Johanne G. Zilch to Zenith. 2007. (Illus.). 66p. (J). pap. 9.00 (978-0-8059-7263-4(3)) Dorrance Publishing Co., Inc.

Benson, P. Bryn. Josefina, the Christmas Cow: A Tale of Hope & Faith. Cinelli, Lisa, illus. 2005. 35p. (J). (gr. -1-3). per. 9.95 (978-0-929636-47-4(3)) Syren Bk. Co.

Bester, Maryanne. The Long Trousers. Bester, Shayle, illus. 2009. (Cool Nguni Ser.). (ENG.). 32p. (J). (gr. 2-4). pap. 12.00 (978-1-77009-499-4(7)) Jacana Media ZAF. Dist: Independent Pubs. Group.

Blair, Eric. El Ninito de Jengibre, 1 vol. Abello, Patricia, tr. from ENG. Peterson, Ben, illus. 2006. (Read-It! Readers en Español: Cuentos Folclóricos Ser.).Tr. of Gingerbread Man. (SPA.). 32p. (gr. k-3). 21.32 (978-1-4048-1647-3(X), Easy Readers) Picture Window Bks.

Boddy, Gary. This Cow These Cows. 2007. 31p. 21.00 (978-1-84799-960-3(3)) Lulu Pr., Inc.

Bowater, Alan. A Pig Called Pete Meets a Cow Called Carlotta. Pascoe, Pete, illus. 2009. (Pig Called Pete Ser.). 32p. (J). (gr. -1-2). 22.60 (978-1-60754-567-5(5)); pap. 10.55 (978-1-60754-568-2(3)) Windmill Bks.

Boychuk, Bryan. The Sword: A Story of Medieval Times. 2010. 24p. 14.95 (978-1-4269-3842-9(X)) Trafford Publishing.

Buchwald, Emilie. Floramel & Esteban. Robinson, Charles, illus. 2009. (ENG.). 80p. (J). (gr. 1-6). 16.95 (978-1-57131-688-2(4)) Milkweed Editions.

Bunting, Eve. The Baby Shower. Love, Judy, illus. 2007. (ENG.). 28p. (J). (gr. -1-2). 15.95 (978-1-58089-139-4(X)) Charlesbridge Publishing, Inc.

Burchard, Patti. Cows Really Do Fly Kites: Patti Burchard. 2012. 24p. pap. 15.00 (978-1-4685-7627-6(5)) AuthorHouse.

Busch, Miriam. Raisin, the Littlest Cow. Day, Larry, illus. 2017. 40p. (J). (gr. -1-3). 17.99 (978-0-06-242763-2(6)) HarperCollins Pubs.

Cabral, Jeane. Good Night Little Moo. Howarth, Daniel, illus. 2007. (Night Light Book Ser.). 10p. (gr. -1-k). (978-1-84666-128-0(5), Tide Mill Pr.) Top That! Publishing PLC.

Carlin, Pat. Cow Visits Chicago. 2010. 32p. 17.25 (978-1-4269-2841-3(6)) Trafford Publishing.

Cazet, Denys. Minnie & Moo: Hooves of Fire. Cazet, Denys, illus. 2014. (ENG., Illus.). 208p. (J). (gr. k-6). 15.95 (978-1-939547-08-8(3)) Creston Bks.

—Minnie & Moo: The Attack of the Easter Bunnies. Cazet, Denys, illus. 2004. (I Can Read Bks.). (Illus.). 48p. (J). (gr. k-3). (ENG.). 15.99 (978-0-06-000506-1(8)); lib. bdg. 17.89 (978-0-06-000507-8(6)) HarperCollins Pubs.

—Minnie & Moo: The Case of the Missing Jelly Donut. Cazet, Denys, illus. 2006. (I Can Read Bks.). (ENG., Illus.). 48p. (J). (gr. k-3). pap. 3.99 (978-0-06-073009-3(9)) HarperCollins Pubs.

—Minnie & Moo: The Case of the Missing Jelly Donut. Cazet, Denys, illus. 2007. (Minnie & Moo Ser.). (Illus.). 45p. (J). (gr. -1-3). pap. 29.95 incl. audio (978-1-4301-0088-1(5)) Live Oak Media.

—Minnie & Moo: The Case of the Missing Jelly Donut, 4 bks., Set. 2007. (J). (gr. k-2). pap. 31.95 incl. audio compact disk (978-1-4301-0091-1(5)) Live Oak Media.

—Minnie & Moo: The Night Before Christmas. Cazet, Denys, illus. 2004. (Readalongs for Beginning Readers Ser.). (Illus.). 25.95 incl. audio (978-1-59112-884-7(6)) Live Oak Media.

—Minnie & Moo: The Night of the Living Bed. Cazet, Denys, illus. 2003. (I Can Read Bks.). (Illus.). 48p. (J). (gr. k-3). lib. bdg. 16.89 (978-0-06-000504-7(1)) HarperCollins Pubs.

—Minnie & Moo - The Night of the Living Bed. Cazet, Denys, illus. 2004. (I Can Read Level 3 Ser.). (ENG., Illus.). 48p. (J). (gr. k-3). pap. 3.99 (978-0-06-000505-4(X)) HarperCollins Pubs.

—Minnie & Moo & the Haunted Sweater. Cazet, Denys, illus. 2007. (I Can Read Level 3 Ser.). (ENG., Illus.). 48p. (J). (gr. k-3). 16.99 (978-0-06-073016-1(1)) HarperCollins Pubs.

—Minnie & Moo & the Seven Wonders of the World. Cazet, Denys, illus. 2003. (ENG., Illus.). 144p. (J). (gr. 2-5). 19.99 (978-0-689-85330-2(0), Atheneum/Richard Jackson Bks.) Simon & Schuster Children's Publishing.

—Minnie & Moo Holiday Series. Cazet, Denys, illus. 2004. (Illus.). pap. 45.95 incl. audio (978-1-59112-851-9(X)); pap. 51.95 incl. audio compact disk (978-1-59112-852-6(8)) Live Oak Media.

—Minnie & Moo Meet Frankenswine. Cazet, Denys, illus. 2004. (Readalongs for Beginning Readers Ser.). (Illus.). 28.95 incl. audio compact disk (978-1-59112-876-2(5)); (J). 25.95 incl. audio (978-1-59112-262-3(7)); (J). pap. 29.95 incl. audio (978-1-59112-263-0(5)) Live Oak Media.

—Minnie & Moo Meet Frankenswine, 4 bks. 2004. (Readalongs for Beginning Readers Ser.). (Illus.). 48p. (J). (gr. -1-2). pap. 31.95 incl. audio compact disk (978-1-59112-877-9(3)) Live Oak Media.

—The Night of the Living Bed. Cazet, Denys, illus. unabr. ed. 2005. (Minnie & Moo Ser.). (Illus.). (J). (gr. k-4). 25.95 incl. audio (978-1-59519-389-6(8));Set. pap. 29.95 incl. audio (978-1-59519-390-2(1));Set. pap. 31.95 incl. audio compact disk (978-1-59519-394-0(4)) Live Oak Media.

—Wanted Dead or Alive. Cazet, Denys, illus. (I Can Read Level 3 Ser.). (Illus.). 48p. (J). 2007. (ENG.). (gr. k-3). pap. 3.99 (978-0-06-073012-3(9)) 2006. (ENG., (gr. -1-3). 15.99 (978-0-06-073010-9(2)) 2006. (gr. -1-3). lib. bdg. 16.89 (978-0-06-073011-6(0)) HarperCollins Pubs.

—Wanted Dead or Alive. Cazet, Denys, illus. 2008. (Minnie & Moo Ser.). (Illus.). (J). (gr. -1-3). pap. 16.95 incl. audio (978-1-4301-0471-1(6)) Live Oak Media.

—Wanted Dead or Alive. 2008. (Minnie & Moo Ser.). (J). (gr. k-2). 25.95 incl. audio (978-1-4301-0472-8(4)) Live Oak Media.

Cazet, Denys, reader. Minnie & Moo: Will You Be My Valentine? 2004. (Read-Alongs for Beginning Readers Ser.). (Illus.). (J). (gr. -1-3). 25.95 incl. audio (978-1-59112-892-2(7)); pap. 31.95 incl. audio compact disk (978-1-59112-897-7(8)); pap. 29.95 incl. audio (978-1-59112-893-9(5)) Live Oak Media.

Celeste, Ruby. Millie, the Miracle Baby. 2008. 48p. pap. 24.95 (978-1-60563-574-3(X)) America Star Bks.

Chambers, Linda Kandelin. The Littlest Bull. 2009. 48p. pap. 25.32 (978-1-4363-7450-7(2)) Xlibris Corp.

Charlip, Remy. Little Old Big Beard & Big Young Little Beard: A Short & Tall Tale, 1 vol. Charlip, Remy & Rettenmund, Tamara, illus. 2006. (ENG.). 300p. (J). (gr. -1-3). pap. 5.95 (978-0-7614-5288-1(5)) Marshall Cavendish Corp.

Chenous, Brad. Stories from Farmer Ready's. 2011. 52p. (gr. 4-6). pap. 9.99 (978-1-4634-0001-9(2)) AuthorHouse.

Chloe Cow & the Party. 2004. (Play Pals Ser.). (Illus.). 12p. (J). bds. (978-1-84229-644-8(2)) Top That! Publishing PLC.

Clarissa - Evaluation Guide: Evaluation Guide. 2006. (J). (978-1-55942-402-8(8)) Witcher Productions.

Cohen, Melissa. PuzzlePal Books: Cuddly Cow. Magnayon, Megan Coy, illus. 2013. (PuzzlePal Bks.). (ENG.). 10p. (J). (gr. -1). bds. 14.95 (978-1-60710-700-2(7), Silver Dolphin Bks.) Readerlink Distribution Services, LLC.

Cole, Burton. Bash & the Chocolate Milk Cows. Lewis, Buddy, illus. 2015. (ENG.). 224p. (J). (gr. 3-7). pap. 8.99 (978-1-4336-8530-9(2), B&H Kids) B&H Publishing Group.

Coulman, Valerie. When Pigs Fly. l.t. ed. 2012. 63p. (J). pap. (978-1-4596-3455-8(1)) ReadHowYouWant.com, Ltd.

Coulson-Staak, Louise. Clarisse the Cow: A Circus Adventure. 2012. 28p. pap. 12.50 (978-1-61897-735-9(0), Strategic Bk. Publishing) Strategic Book Publishing & Rights Agency (SBPRA).

A Cow Had a Wish. l.t. ed. Date not set. (Illus.). 32p. (J). (gr. 1-6). (978-0-9653327-1-2(3)) BF Publishing.

Cow up a Tree, 6 vols., Pack. (Story Steps Ser.). (gr. k-2). 23.00 (978-0-7635-9807-5(0)) Rigby Education.

Cowley, Joy. Mrs. Wishy-Washy's Farm. Fuller, Elizabeth, illus. (ENG.). 32p. (J). (gr. -1-k). 2006. 5.99 (978-0-14-240299-3(0), Puffin Books) 2003. 16.99 (978-0-399-23872-7(7), Philomel Bks.) Penguin Young Readers Group.

Creech, Sharon. Moo. 288p. (J). (gr. 3-7). 2017. pap. 6.99 **(978-0-06-241526-4(3))** 2016. 16.99 (978-0-06-241524-0(7)) 2016. lib. bdg. 17.89 (978-0-06-241525-7(5)) HarperCollins Pubs.

—Moo. 2017. lib. bdg. 17.20 **(978-0-606-40402-0(3))** Turtleback Bks.

Crockett, Johns. Click Clack Meuuh. 29.95 (978-2-87142-345-4(8)) Mijade Editions BEL. Dist: Distribooks, Inc.

Cronin, Doreen. Click, Clack, Moo. 2016. (Simon & Schuster Ready-To-Read Level 2 Ser.). (Illus.). (J). lib. bdg. 13.55 **(978-0-606-39751-3(5))** Turtleback Bks.

—Click, Clack, Moo: Cows That Type. braille ed. 2004. (Illus.). (J). (gr. k-3). spiral bd. (978-0-616-07228-8(7)); spiral bd. (978-0-616-07227-1(9)) Canadian National Institute for the Blind/Institut National Canadien pour les Aveugles.

—Click, Clack, Moo: Cows That Type. Lewin, Betsy, illus. (Click, Clack Book Ser.). (ENG.). (J). (gr. -1-3). 2011. 32p. pap. 9.99 (978-1-4424-3370-0(1)) 2010. 34p. bds. 7.99 (978-1-4424-0889-0(8))Set. 2009. 16p. bds. 14.99 (978-1-4169-5516-0(X)) Little Simon. (Little Simon).

—Click, Clack, Moo: Cows That Type. 2004. 29.95 (978-1-55592-104-0(3)) Weston Woods Studios, Inc.

—Teque, Teque, Muu: Vacas que Escrevem à Máquina. pap. 26.95 (978-85-325-1566-7(5)) Rocco, Editora, Ltda BRA. Dist: Distribooks, Inc.

Cronin, Doreen & Lewin, Betsy. Click, Clack, Moo: Cows That Type. 2014. 32p. pap. 8.00 (978-1-61003-342-8(6)) Center for the Collaborative Classroom.

Cronin, Doreen & Simon and Schuster/LeapFrog Staff. Click, Clack, Moo: Cows That Type. Lewin, Betsy, illus. 2008. (J). 13.99 (978-1-59319-936-4(8)) LeapFrog Enterprises, Inc.

Cutbill, Andy. The Cow That Laid an Egg. Ayto, Russell, illus. 2008. (ENG.). 32p. (J). (gr. -1-3). 17.99 (978-0-06-137295-7(1)) HarperCollins Pubs.

Dahl, Michael. Snack Time for Cow, 1 vol. Vidal, Oriol, illus. 2011. (Hello Genius Ser.). (ENG.). 20p. (gr. 1-2). bds. 7.99 (978-1-4048-6496-2(2)) Picture Window Bks.

d'Allancé, Mireille. No, No Y No! 2005. (SPA., Illus.). (J). 15.99 (978-84-8470-114-9(X)) Corimbo, Editorial S.L. ESP. Dist: Iaconi, Mariuccia Bk. Imports.

David, Juliet. The Midnight Visitors, 1 vol. Parry, Jo, illus. 2015. 32p. (J). 14.99 (978-1-78128-233-5(1), Candle Bks.) Lion Hudson PLC GBR. Dist: Kregel Pubns.

Davies, Lewis. Tai, Troll & the Black & White Cow. 2009. (ENG., Illus.). 30p. (J). pap. 7.95 (978-1-905762-64-4(X)) Parthian Bks. GBR. Dist: Independent Pubs. Group.

Dawson, Joy. Maggie, the Color-Blind Cow: A loving heart — -that didn't see Color. 2006. (ENG., Illus.). 36p. (J). per. 12.95 (978-1-59800-892-0(7)) Outskirts Pr., Inc.

Day, Jan. Kissimmee Pete, Cracker Cow Hunter, 1 vol. Mason, Janeen, illus. 2005. (ENG.). 32p. (J). (gr. k-3). 16.99 (978-1-58980-325-1(6)) Pelican Publishing Co., Inc.

Dickinson, Donald J. A Bird's Eye View of the Civil War in Loudon County & Campbell's Station, TN: A Book for Children. 2003. (Illus.). 251p. (J). per. (978-0-9637951-3-7(9)) Hart-Whitlow Pubs.

Disney Book Group Staff & Weinberg, Jennifer Liberts. World of Reading: Doc Mcstuffins Blame It on the Rain: Level 1. Disney Storybook Artists Staff & Disney Storybook Art Team, illus. 2014. (World of Reading Ser.). (ENG.). 32p. (J). (gr. -1-k). pap. 3.99 (978-1-4847-0676-3(5)) Disney Pr.

Dogiakis, Helen. Captain Terry the Pirate Cow's Adventure to Italy. 2011. 32p. pap. 14.99 (978-1-4567-3131-1(9)) AuthorHouse.

Don't Eat the Bluebonnets. 2006. (J). lib. bdg. 17.95 (978-0-9645493-3-3(6)) Bluebonnets, Boots & Bks. Pr.

Doscher, E. L. M. S. Emmy Sue & the Blue Moo. Doscher, Susan, illus. 2010. 20p. pap. 9.99 (978-1-935125-92-1(3)) Robertson Publishing.

Dreher, Gidge. Gus, Scruffy, Clara & Friends. 2007. 80p. per. 9.95 (978-1-933912-24-0(3)) Westview Publishing Co., Inc.

Drummond, Ree. Charlie & the New Baby. deGroat, Diane, illus. 2014. (Charlie the Ranch Dog Ser.). (ENG.). 40p. (J). (gr. -1-3). 17.99 (978-0-06-229750-1(3)) HarperCollins Pubs.

—Charlie the Ranch Dog: Stuck in the Mud. deGroat, Diane & Whipple, Rick, illus. 2015. (I Can Read Level 1 Ser.). (ENG.). 32p. (J). (gr. -1-3). 16.99 (978-0-06-234775-6(6)); pap. 3.99 (978-0-06-234774-9(8)) HarperCollins Pubs.

Dunsmuir, Tom. You Can't Milk a Dancing Cow. Jones, Brian T., illus. 2005. (ENG.). 24p. (J). (gr. -1-3). 14.95 (978-0-9749303-3-6(4)) Tanglewood Pr.

Dwire, Joyann. What Kind of Cow Are You? Being Content with How God Made You. Dickson, Bill, illus. 2006. 24p. (J). per. 2.99 (978-1-59958-006-7(3)) Journey Stone Creations, LLC.

Edmond, Wally. Cuddles the Chocolate Cow & Friends. Melinda, Sheffler, illus. 2006. 39p. (J). 14.95 (978-1-59879-108-2(7)); per. 9.99 (978-1-59879-125-9(7)) Lifevest Publishing, Inc.

Egan, Tim. Metropolitan Cow. 2004. (J). (gr. k-3). spiral bd. (978-0-616-07231-8(7)) Canadian National Institute for the Blind/Institut National Canadien pour les Aveugles.

Elchgar, Yasmin. Noonoo the Doctor. 2013. 20p. pap. 13.77 (978-1-4907-1037-2(X)) Trafford Publishing.

Elkhatib, Tristan & Anthony. The Determined Cow. 2012. 40p. pap. 20.99 (978-1-4772-5717-3(9)) AuthorHouse.

Esbaum, Jill. I Am Cow, Hear Me Moo! Gordon, Gus, illus. 2014. (ENG.). 32p. (J). (gr. -1-k). 16.99 (978-0-8037-3524-8(3), Dial Bks) Penguin Young Readers Group.

Fajerman, Deborah. How to Speak Moo! 2014. (ENG.). 32p. (J). (gr. -1-k). bds. 7.99 (978-0-7641-6752-2(9)) Barron's Educational Series, Inc.

Fleming, Denise. The Cow Who Clucked. Fleming, Denise, illus. rev. ed. 2006. (ENG., Illus.). 40p. (J). (gr. -1-2). 18.99

(978-0-8050-7265-5(9), 9780805072655, Holt, Henry & Co. Bks. For Young Readers) Holt, Henry & Co.
—The Cow Who Clucked. 2007. (J). (gr. -1-1). 27.95 incl. audio *(978-0-8045-6951-4(7))* Spoken Arts, Inc.
Fletcher, Susan. Dadblamed Union Army Cow. Root, Kimberly Bulcken, illus. 2016. (ENG.). 32p. (J). (gr. k-3). 7.99 *(978-0-7636-8770-0(7))* Candlewick Pr.
Flora, James, creator. The Day the Cow Sneezed. 2010. (ENG., Illus.). 48p. (J). (gr. -1-3). 16.95 *(978-1-59270-097-4(7))* Enchanted Lion Bks., LLC.
Fort, Jean Jacobs. Trouble. 2011. 24p. pap. 14.49 *(978-1-4634-0597-7(9))* AuthorHouse.
Freeman, Martha. Mrs. Wow Never Wanted a Cow. Salerno, Steven, illus. 2006. (Beginner Books(R) Ser.). (ENG.). 48p. (J). (gr. -1-2). 9.99 *(978-0-375-83418-9(4)*, Random Hse. Bks. for Young Readers) Random Hse. Children's Bks.
French, Jackie. Too Many Pears!, 1 vol. Whatley, Bruce, illus. 2003. (ENG.). 32p. (J). 16.95 *(978-1-932065-47-3(4)*, 718-784-9112) Star Bright Bks., Inc.
—Too Many Pears! (Japanese/English), 1 vol. Whatley, Bruce, illus. 2007. (JPN & ENG.). 32p. (J). (gr. -1). pap. 5.95 *(978-1-59572-112-9(6))* Star Bright Bks., Inc.
—Too Many Pears! (Portuguese/English), 1 vol. 2009. (ENG., Illus.). 32p. (J). pap. 6.95 *(978-1-59572-197-6(5))* Star Bright Bks., Inc.
—Too Many Pears! (Spanish/English), 1 vol. Whatley, Bruce, illus. 2005. 32p. (J). (ABK, SPA & ENG.). 16.95 *(978-1-59572-012-2(X))*; (SPA & ENG.). pap. 6.95 *(978-1-59572-013-9(8))* Star Bright Bks., Inc.
The Goose Who Acted Like a Cow. (Early Intervention Levels Ser.). 31.86 *(978-0-7362-0627-3(2))* CENGAGE Learning.
Greenleaf, E. Who Wants to Nap? (Illus.). 32p. (J). (gr. 2-3). lib. bdg. 9.95 *(978-0-87783-050-4(9))* Oddo Publishing, Inc.
Grimm, Jacob & Grimm, Wilhelm K. Hut in the Forest, 1 vol. Lawson, Polly, tr. from GER. Stietencron, Bettina, illus. 2007. (Grimm's Fairy Tales Ser.). (ENG.). 28p. (J). *(978-0-86315-615-1(0))* Floris Bks.
Guibert, Emmanuel. Where's Petula? 2015. (Ariol Ser.: 7). (J). lib. bdg. 20.85 *(978-0-606-37284-8(9))* Turtleback Bks.
Haase Wittler, Penny S. Emma, the Big Red Cow. 2011. 16p. pap. 9.99 *(978-1-4520-1959-8(2))* AuthorHouse.
Haile, Carol J. Christmas Cows. Haile, Carol J., illus. 2012. (ENG., Illus.). 40p. (J). 19.95 *(978-0-9711236-5-6(9))* Firenze Pr.
Hall, Lisa. Burton the Sneezing Cow. Keaton, Pam, illus. 2012. 28p. (-18). pap. 9.95 *(978-1-939289-06-3(8)*, Little Creek Bks.) Jan-Carol Publishing, INC.
Hamilton, Arlene. Only a Cow, 1 vol. Griffiths, Dean, illus. 2006. (ENG.). 32p. (J). (gr. -1-2). *(978-1-55041-871-2(8))* Fitzhenry & Whiteside, Ltd.
Hart, Janice. Henry & the Oranges: Henry's Wild Adventures. McDonald, Suzi, illus. 2010. 32p. pap. 13.00 *(978-1-60860-911-6(1)*, Eloquent Bks.) Strategic Book Publishing & Rights Agency (SBPRA).
Hastings, Leon. Trixie - the Christmas Cow. McLeod, David, illus. 2012. 18p. pap. *(978-1-84903-192-9(4))* Schiel & Denver Publishing Ltd.
Hayden, Gwendolen Lampshire. Mary Martha's Really Truly Stories: Book 1. 2nd ed. 2013. 130p. pap. 11.95 *(978-1-4796-0099-1(7))* TEACH Services, Inc.
—Mary Martha's Really Truly Stories: Book 2. 2nd ed. 2013. (Illus.). 136p. pap. 11.95 *(978-1-4796-0102-8(0))* TEACH Services, Inc.
—Mary Martha's Really Truly Stories: Book 4. 2nd ed. 2013. 130p. pap. 11.95 *(978-1-4796-0108-0(X))* TEACH Services, Inc.
—Mary Martha's Really Truly Stories: Book 5. 2nd ed. 2013. 130p. pap. 11.95 *(978-1-4796-0111-0(X))* TEACH Services, Inc.
—Mary Martha's Really Truly Stories: Book 6. 2nd ed. 2013. 130p. pap. 11.95 *(978-1-4796-0114-1(4))* TEACH Services, Inc.
—Mary Martha's Really Truly Stories: Book 7. 2nd ed. 2013. 130p. pap. 11.95 *(978-1-4796-0117-2(9))* TEACH Services, Inc.
—Mary Martha's Really Truly Stories: Book 8. 2nd ed. 2013. 130p. pap. 11.95 *(978-1-4796-0120-2(9))* TEACH Services, Inc.
The Healthy Way with Wow the Cow. 2006. (Illus.). 32p. (J). 4.95 *(978-0-9668611-4-3(0))* Kimberly Pr., LLC.
Heller, Maryellen. My Favorite Place. Friar, Joanne, illus. 2005. (ENG.). 16p. (J). 5.75 *(978-1-57274-535-3(5)*, 2771, Bks. for Young Learners) Owen, Richard C. Pubs., Inc.
Hill, Ros. Shamoo: A Whale of a Cow. 2005. (ENG., Illus.). 32p. (J). (gr. -1-3). 15.95 *(978-1-59687-188-5(1))* IBks., Inc.
—Shamoo: A Whale of a Cow (Lib) 2017. (ENG., Illus.). (J). (gr. k-3). 19.95 ***(978-1-59687-536-4(4)***, ipicturebooks) ibooks, Inc.
—Shamoo, a Whale of a Cow. 2013. (Illus.). 34p. pap. 12.95 *(978-1-59687-941-6(6)*, Milk & Cookies) ibooks, Inc.
—Shamooo: A Whale of a Cow. Hill, Ros, illus. 2005. (Illus.). 32p. (J). 15.95 *(978-0-689-04634-6(0)*, Milk & Cookies) ibooks, Inc.
Hillert, Margaret. The Cow That Got Her Wish. (J). 4.95 *(978-0-87895-694-4(8))* Modern Curriculum Pr.
—The Cow That Got Her Wish. Prater, Linda, illus. 2016. (BeginningtoRead Ser.). (ENG.). 32p. (J). (gr. -1-2). pap. 11.94 *(978-1-60357-938-4(9))*; (gr. 1-2). 22.60 *(978-1-59953-797-9(4))* Norwood Hse. Pr.
Himmelman, John. The Cow Said Meow. Himmelman, John, illus. 2016. (ENG., Illus.). 32p. (J). 16.99 *(978-1-62779-378-0(X)*, 9781627793780, Holt, Henry & Co. Bks. For Young Readers) Holt, Henry & Co.
—Cows to the Rescue. Himmelman, John, illus. 2011. (Barnyard Rescue Ser.). (ENG., Illus.). 32p. (J). (gr. -1-3). 17.99 *(978-0-8050-9249-3(8)*, 9780805092493, Holt, Henry & Co. Bks. For Young Readers) Holt, Henry & Co.
Hogan, Jayne. Callie Cow. Reiter, Cheryl, ed. Solheim, Kermit, illus. (J). (gr. -1). mass mkt. 12.99 *(978-1-887327-55-8(X))* TOMY International, Inc.
Hunter, Skillman "Kim". El Becerrito en Valle Grande. Ritthaler, Sarah Pilcher, tr. Sundstrom, Mary, illus. 2006.Tr. of Little Cow in Valle Grande. (SPA & ENG.). 32p. (J). (gr. -1-k). 16.95 *(978-0-8263-4044-3(X))* Univ. of New Mexico Pr.
ImageBooks Staff. Little Cow. 2007. (Little Finger Puppet Board Bks.: FING). (ENG., Illus.). 12p. (J). (gr. -1 — 1). bds. 6.95 *(978-0-8118-6109-0(0))* Chronicle Bks. LLC.
Isaacs, Latricia. Mason & Hayden Visit Grandma. 2011. 16p. 8.32 *(978-1-4567-0170-3(3))* AuthorHouse.
—Mason & Lilly Visit Grandpa. 2011. 16p. 8.32 *(978-1-4567-2788-8(5))* AuthorHouse.
Ivey, Douglas G. The Three Cows. 2010. 28p. pap. 13.99 *(978-1-4520-4272-5(1))* AuthorHouse.
Jay, Larsen. What If Cows Could... ? 2005. (J). lib. bdg. 19.95 *(978-1-933732-01-5(6))* Big Ransom Studio.
Jumbo & the Mean Tenant. 2004. (J). per. 15.99 *(978-0-9744205-9-2(X))* Golden Eagle Publishing Hse., Inc.
Kinerk, Robert. Clorinda. Kellogg, Steven, illus. 2007. (ENG.). 40p. (J). (gr. -1-3). 7.99 *(978-1-4169-3964-1(4)*, Simon & Schuster/Paula Wiseman Bks.) Simon & Schuster/Paula Wiseman Bks.
—Clorinda Plays Baseball! Kellogg, Steven, illus. 2012. (ENG.). 40p. (J). (gr. -1-3). 16.99 *(978-0-689-86865-8(0)*, Simon & Schuster/Paula Wiseman Bks.) Simon & Schuster/Paula Wiseman Bks.
—Clorinda Takes Flight. Kellogg, Steven, illus. 2007. (ENG.). 40p. (J). (gr. -1-3). 17.99 *(978-0-689-86864-1(2)*, Simon & Schuster/Paula Wiseman Bks.) Simon & Schuster/Paula Wiseman Bks.
Kinerk, Robert & Kellogg, Steven. Clorinda. Kellogg, Steven, illus. 2003. (ENG., Illus.). 40p. (J). (gr. -1-3). 17.99 *(978-0-689-86449-0(3)*, Simon & Schuster/Paula Wiseman Bks.) Simon & Schuster/Paula Wiseman Bks.
Koch, Dorothy Clarke. When the Cows Got Out. 2016. (Illus.). 32p. (J). ***(978-0-7399-2535-5(0))*** Rod & Staff Pubs., Inc.
Laguatan, Alwen & Buada, Joselito. Kobi. 2013. 40p. pap. 24.95 *(978-1-63000-853-6(2))* America Star Bks.
Lane, Nickel. Maggy, the Cow that Jumped over the Moon. 2004. 15p. (J). pap. 7.47 *(978-1-4116-1728-5(2))* Lulu Pr., Inc.
LaRochelle, David. Moo! Wohnoutka, Mike, illus. 2014. (ENG.). 32p. (J). (gr. -1-3). bds. 7.99 *(978-0-8027-3802-8(8)*, 9780802738028, Bloomsbury USA Childrens) Bloomsbury Publishing USA.
Laurence, Margaret & James Lorimer and Company Ltd. Staff. Six Darn Cows, 1 vol. Blades, Ann, illus. 2nd rev. ed. 2011. (Kids of Canada Ser.). (ENG.). 32p. (J). (gr. k-3). 14.95 *(978-1-55277-719-0(7)*, 9781552777190) Lorimer, James & Co., Ltd., Pubs. CAN. Dist: Casemate Pubs. & Bk. Distributors, LLC.
Leavy, Una. Tomas No Quiere Zapatos. 2005. (SPA., Illus.). 64p. (J). (gr. k-1). 6.95 *(978-84-348-6355-2(3))* SM Ediciones ESP. Dist: Iaconi, Mariuccia Bk. Imports.
Lee Coy, Amy. Duke Devlin the Daring Dogie. 2007. 48p. pap. 19.00 *(978-0-615-14380-4(6))* Z Pr.
Leech, Carlyle & Leech, Thirma. Ha-Ha Farm. 2009. (ENG., Illus.). 24p. (J). (gr. -1-1). 14.95 *(978-1-59583-396-9(X)*, 9781595833969, Green Tiger Pr.) Laughing Elephant.
LeLeu, Lisa. Miss Moo-Moo the Cow Story Starter: Puppet Book Story Starter. 2004. (Puppet Show Bks.). (Illus.). 14p. 1.50 *(978-0-9710537-1-7(5))* LeLeu, Lisa Studios! Inc.
Linkowski, Tami Leli. Lynn Can Fly, 1 vol. Selover, Lisa & Selover, Arthur, illus. 2009. 15p. pap. 24.95 *(978-1-60749-611-3(9))* America Star Bks.
—Lynn Was a Cow Who Could Ski. 2008. 20p. pap. 24.95 *(978-1-4241-9626-5(4))* America Star Bks.
Litwin, Mike. The Amazing IncrediBull. Litwin, Mike, illus. 2015. (Welcome to Bermooda! Ser.: 4). (ENG., Illus.). 160p. (J). (gr. 1-5). 14.99 *(978-0-8075-8713-3(3))* Whitman, Albert & Co.
—The Big Cowhuna. Litwin, Mike, illus. 2015. (Welcome to Bermooda! Ser.: 3). (ENG., Illus.). 160p. (J). (gr. 1-5). 14.99 *(978-0-8075-8720-1(6))* Whitman, Albert & Co.
—Crown of the Cowibbean. Litwin, Mike, illus. 2014. (Welcome to Bermooda! Ser.: 2). (ENG., Illus.). 144p. (J). (gr. 1-5). 14.99 *(978-0-8075-8719-5(2))* Whitman, Albert & Co.
Lock, Brian. Chicken Lips & Rocket Ships, 1 vol. 2009. 56p. pap. 16.95 *(978-1-61582-205-8(4))* America Star Bks.
Lovelace, Kelley. Ready Set Go Organic. 2006. 7.99 *(978-0-9791029-0-5(1))* KelleyGreenworks Publishing.
Macaulay, David. Black & White. 2005. (ENG., Illus.). 32p. (J). (gr. -1-3). 7.99 *(978-0-618-63687-7(0))* Houghton Mifflin Harcourt Publishing Co.
MacLachlan, Patricia. Fly Away. 2014. (ENG., Illus.). 128p. (J). (gr. 2). 15.99 *(978-1-4424-6008-9(3)*, McElderry, Margaret K. Bks.) McElderry, Margaret K. Bks.
—The True Gift. Floca, Brian, illus. 2013. (ENG.). 112p. (J). (gr. 2-6). pap. 6.99 *(978-1-4424-8858-8(1)*, Atheneum Bks. for Young Readers) Simon & Schuster Children's Publishing.
—The True Gift: A Christmas Story. Floca, Brian, illus. 2009. (ENG.). 96p. (J). (gr. 2-6). 14.99 *(978-1-4169-9081-9(X)*, Atheneum Bks. for Young Readers) Simon & Schuster Children's Publishing.
MacLean, Kerry Lee. Moody Cow Learns Compassion. 2012. (ENG., Illus.). 32p. (J). (gr. -1-3). 16.95 *(978-1-61429-033-9(4))* Wisdom Pubns.
Magaro, Dan. The Adventures of Fred & Daisymae. 2010. 48p. pap. 10.99 *(978-1-60957-407-9(9))* Salem Author Services.
Make Believe Ideas, creator. Udderly Book & Cow Plush. 2007. (Illus.). (J). (gr. -1-3). *(978-1-84610-690-3(7))* Make Believe Ideas.
Mallet, C. Claire. Disparition Chez les Lutins. Begin, Jean-Guy, illus. 2003. (Collection des 6 Ans: Vol. 21). (FRE.). 64p. (J). 7.95 *(978-2-922565-64-5(5))* Editions de la Paix CAN. Dist: World of Reading, Ltd.
Markowitz, Krista. Mrs Tipperwillow's Afterlife Adventures. 2008. 316p. 28.95 *(978-0-595-49079-0(4))*; pap. 18.95 *(978-0-595-44671-1(X))* iUniverse, Inc.
Marunowski, Barbara L. My Cow Book. 2009. 56p. pap. 21.99 *(978-1-4490-0254-1(4))* AuthorHouse.
Mayfield, Mary. Snowbank, the Great Texas Cow. 2005. (Illus.). 18p. (J). per. 7.99 *(978-1-932338-98-0(5))* Lifevest Publishing, Inc.
McManis, Margaret. Olé! Cinco de Mayo!, 1 vol. Harrington, David, illus. 2013. (ENG.). 32p. (J). (gr. k-3). 16.99 *(978-1-4556-1754-8(7))* Pelican Publishing Co., Inc.
McNaughton, Colin. Cushie Butterfield. 2004. (ENG., Illus.). 24p. (J). (gr. -1-k). pap. 8.99 *(978-0-00-715466-1(6)*, HarperSport) HarperCollins Pubs. Ltd. GBR. Dist: Independent Pubs. Group.
McQuinn, Anna. A Rosette for Maeve? Young, Paul, illus. 2014. (ENG.). 32p. (J). pap. 13.95 *(978-1-84717-340-9(3))* O'Brien Pr., Ltd., The IRL. Dist: Dufour Editions, Inc.
Medlock-Adams, Michelle. Counting Cows. Meyers, Mark, illus. 2010. 26p. (J). (gr. -1-k). 7.99 *(978-0-8249-1836-1(3)*, Ideal Pubns.) Worthy Publishing.
Milgrim, David. Moo Bird. 2016. (Illus.). 32p. (J). ***(978-1-5182-0400-5(7))*** Scholastic, Inc.
—Moo Bird. Milgrim, David, illus. 2015. (Scholastic Reader, Level 1 Ser.). (ENG., Illus.). 32p. (J). (gr. -1-1). pap. 3.99 *(978-0-545-82502-3(4))* Scholastic, Inc.
Mill, Fran. Harriet's Hunt for the Sun. 2010. 28p. pap. 12.49 *(978-1-4520-1491-3(4))* AuthorHouse.
Millton, Jane. Moo & Moo & the Little Calf Too. Hinde, Deborah, illus. 2017. (ENG.). 32p. (J). (-3). pap. 14.99 ***(978-1-877505-92-8(7))*** Allen & Unwin AUS. Dist: Independent Pubs. Group.
Mindes, Erin. Missy Moo, Where Are You off to? Surfing Adventure. Harston, David, illus. 2011. (J). 14.95 *(978-0-9841558-8-0(0))* Tasty Minstrel Games.
Mortensen, Lori. Cindy Moo. Mack, Jeff, illus. 2012. (ENG.). 32p. (J). (gr. -1-2). 16.99 *(978-0-06-204393-1(5))* HarperCollins Pubs.
Morton, Jane & Dreier, Ted. Moozie's Cow Wisdom for Loving to the "Uddermost" Royse, Jane, illus. 2003. (J). pap. 4.95 *(978-0-9662268-3-6(6))* Children's Kindness Network.
Most, Bernard. La Vaca Que Decia Oink. Mlawer, Teresa, tr. from ENG.Tr. of Cow That Went Oink. (SPA., Illus.). (J). (gr. k-2). pap. 6.99 *(978-1-880507-66-7(8)*, LC4889) Lectorum Pubns., Inc.
Muscia, Marilena Carrubba. Misses Cowy to the Rescue. 2011. 24p. (gr. -1). 12.99 *(978-1-4567-3582-1(9))* AuthorHouse.
Mustaine Hettinger, Cynthia. Casey the Confused Cow. Ramsey, Jayne, illus. 2003. (Electra's Acres Ser.). 32p. (J). per. 14.95 *(978-0-9746330-1-5(1))* Anton Berkshire Publishing.
Newlin-Chase, Edith. El Ternero Recien Nacido. Reid, Barbara, illus. (SPA.). 32p. (J). (gr. -1-1). pap. 4.99 *(978-0-590-46106-1(0)*, SO30492) Scholastic, Inc.
Nicoll, David. Bean on the Farm. 2012. 24p. pap. 15.99 *(978-1-4691-7837-0(0))* Xlibris Corp.
Ohi, Ruth. Chicken, Pig, Cow & the Purple Problem. Ohi, Ruth, illus. 2010. (Chicken, Pig, Cow Ser.). (ENG., Illus.). 32p. (J). (gr. -1-k). 19.95 *(978-1-55451-219-5(0)*, 9781554512195); 2nd ed. pap. 6.95 *(978-1-55451-218-8(2)*, 9781554512188) Annick Pr., Ltd. CAN. Dist: Publishers Group West (PGW).
—Chicken, Pig, Cow Horse Around. Ohi, Ruth, illus. 2010. (Chicken, Pig, Cow Ser.). (ENG., Illus.). 32p. (J). (gr. -1-k). 19.95 *(978-1-55451-245-4(X)*, 9781554512454) Annick Pr., Ltd. CAN. Dist: Publishers Group West (PGW).
—Chicken, Pig, Cow on the Move. Ohi, Ruth, illus. 3rd ed. 2009. (Chicken, Pig, Cow Ser.). (ENG., Illus.). 32p. (J). (gr. -1-k). 19.95 *(978-1-55451-194-5(1)*, 9781554511945); pap. 6.95 *(978-1-55451-193-8(3)*, 9781554511938) Annick Pr., Ltd. CAN. Dist: Publishers Group West (PGW).
Ohi, Ruth, illus. Chicken, Pig, Cow Horse Around. 3rd ed. 2010. (Chicken, Pig, Cow Ser.). (ENG.). 32p. (J). (gr. -1-k). pap. 6.95 *(978-1-55451-244-7(1)*, 9781554512447) Annick Pr., Ltd. CAN. Dist: Publishers Group West (PGW).
P. Cats & Cows & Moos & Meows. 2011. 28p. (gr. -1). pap. 13.50 *(978-1-4567-3464-0(4))* AuthorHouse.
Palatini, Margie. Boo-Hoo Moo. Graves, Keith, illus. 2009. 32p. (J). (gr. -1-3). lib. bdg. 18.89 *(978-0-06-114376-2(6))* HarperCollins Pubs.
—Moo Who? Graves, Keith, illus. (ENG.). 40p. (J). (gr. -1-2). 2007. pap. 6.99 *(978-0-06-000107-0(0))* 2004. 16.99 *(978-0-06-000105-6(4))* HarperCollins Pubs. (Tegen, Katherine Bks).
Parker, Jo Ann. The Cow That Could, & Did! (with a Little Help from Her Friends) 2012. 32p. pap. 19.99 *(978-1-4772-2909-5(4))* AuthorHouse.
Parks, M. Elizabeth. The Sea Cow. 2013. (Illus.). 44p. pap. 16.95 *(978-0-9824565-2-1(2))* Sibyl Merritt.
Pat Carlin, Carlin & Carlin, Patricia. A Cow & her Car. 2010. 24p. 12.95 *(978-1-4269-2788-1(6))* Trafford Publishing.
Paull, John W. The Great Stampede: A Jimmy James Story. 2010. 28p. 16.09 *(978-1-4269-4698-1(8))* Trafford Publishing.
Pereira, William. The Adventures of LC, the Lucky Calf. Bowlsby, Tina Marie, illus. 2005. (J). 18.95 *(978-0-9773133-0-3(1))* Little Tule Bks.
Posner-Sanchez, Andrea. Toby the Cowsitter (Disney Junior: Sheriff Callie's Wild West) RH Disney Staff & Fruchter, Jason, illus. 2015. (Little Golden Book Ser.). (ENG.). 24p. (J). (-k). 4.99 *(978-0-7364-3299-3(X)*, Golden/Disney) Random Hse. Children's Bks.
Prichard, Diana. The Cow in Patrick O'Shanahan's Kitchen. Knopf, Heather, illus. 2013. (ENG.). 32p. (J). (gr. -1-3). 17.95 *(978-1-939775-01-6(9))* March 4th, Inc.
Priddy, Roger. Cow - Animal Buddies. 2015. (Animal Buddies Ser.). (ENG.). 8p. (J). (gr. -1 — 1). bds. 5.99 *(978-0-312-51854-7(4)*, 9780312518547, Priddy Bks.) St. Martin's Pr.
Pritchett, Andy. Stick! 2013. (ENG., Illus.). 32p. (J). (gr. -1-2). 15.99 *(978-0-7636-6616-3(5))* Candlewick Pr.
Probert, Mitzi. Esther's Miracle at the Manger. 2010. 44p. pap. 19.99 *(978-1-60957-503-8(2))* Salem Author Services.
Punter, Russell. Cow Takes a Bow. Blunt, Fred, illus. 2014. (Usborne Phonics Readers Ser.). (ENG.). (J). pap. 6.99 *(978-0-7945-3368-7(X)*, Usborne) EDC Publishing.
Purkapile, Susan. Nosy Noodles: The Curious Cow. Ducommon, Barbara, illus. 2006. 15p. (J). (gr. k-5). 13.95 *(978-1-930596-34-4(0))* Amherst Pr.
Ranganathan, Babu G. The Selfish Apple Tree. 2010. 12p. 7.95 *(978-1-4497-0312-7(7)*, WestBow Pr.) Author Solutions, Inc.
Raschka, Chris. Cowy Cow. 2014. (Thingy Things Ser.). (ENG., Illus.). 24p. (J). (gr. -1-k). 6.95 *(978-1-4197-1055-1(9)*, Abrams Appleseed) Abrams, Inc.
Reasoner, Charles. I'm Just a Little Cow. Orkrania, Alexia, illus. 2014. (ENG.). 12p. (gr. -1). *(978-1-78244-588-3(9))* Top That! Publishing PLC.
—Number Munch! 2009. (Bite Bks.). (Illus.). (J). bds. 7.99 *(978-1-934650-14-1(5))* Just For Kids Pr., LLC.
Remphry, Martin. Pirates Are Stealing Our Cows. 2014. (ENG., Illus.). 32p. (J). *(978-0-7787-1330-2(X))* Crabtree Publishing Co.
Rena, Regina. Where Do Cows Moo? 2010. 20p. pap. 12.99 *(978-1-4490-8204-8(1))* AuthorHouse.
Rex, Adam. XO, OX: A Love Story. Campbell, Scott, illus. 2017. (ENG.). 40p. (J). 17.99 *(978-1-62672-288-0(9)*, 9781626722880) Roaring Brook Pr.
Rigg, Jo. Millie Moo. 2007. (Illus.). 10p. (J). *(978-1-84332-473-7(3))* Priddy Bks.
Rigo, L. Little Cow. 2011. (Look at Me Bks.). (ENG., Illus.). 10p. (J). bds. 7.99 *(978-0-7641-6446-0(5))* Barron's Educational Series, Inc.
Rising, Morgan. Maggie Moo the Holstein Cow. 2011. 20p. (gr. 1-2). pap. 11.99 *(978-1-4634-0689-9(4))* AuthorHouse.
Robinson, Hilary. Over the Moon. Abbott, Jane, illus. 2009. (Tadpoles Ser.). (ENG.). 24p. (J). (gr. k-2). pap. *(978-0-7787-3899-2(X))*; lib. bdg. *(978-0-7787-3868-8(X))* Crabtree Publishing Co.
Rodriguez, Grisell. Chaka the Cow. 2010. 32p. pap. 13.99 *(978-1-60844-153-2(9))* Dog Ear Publishing, LLC.
Romig, Hilary. Meet Ruby & Louise. 2009. 16p. pap. 8.49 *(978-1-4389-4609-2(0))* AuthorHouse.
Roop, James Q. Billy Brahman: The Story of A Calf. Pomerantz, Norman, illus. 2011. 28p. 35.95 *(978-1-258-01757-6(1))* Literary Licensing, LLC.
Root, Phyllis. Kiss the Cow! Hillenbrand, Will, illus. 2003. (ENG.). 32p. (J). (gr. -1-3). pap. 6.99 *(978-0-7636-2003-5(3))* Candlewick Pr.
—Kiss the Cow! 2003. (gr. k-3). 17.20 *(978-0-613-60357-7(5)*, Turtleback) Turtleback Bks.
Ross, Fiona. Chilly Milly Moo. 2011. (ENG., Illus.). 32p. (J). (gr. -1-2). 15.99 *(978-0-7636-5693-5(3))* Candlewick Pr.
Russell, Natalie. Hamish the Highland Cow. 2003. (J). 7.99 *(978-1-58234-818-6(9))* Bloomsbury Publishing USA.
Sazaklis, John. Barnyard Brainwash, 1 vol. Baltazar, Art, illus. 2012. (DC Super-Pets Ser.). (ENG.). 56p. (gr. 2-2). pap. 4.95 *(978-1-4048-7213-4(2))*; lib. bdg. 23.99 *(978-1-4048-6483-2(0))* Picture Window Bks. (DC Super-Pets).
Schermbrucker, Reviva. Taking the Cows Home. Lomofsky, Lynne & Laubscher, André, illus. 2011. (ENG.). 24p. (J). (gr. k-2). pap. 6.95 *(978-1-77009-862-6(3))* Jacana Media ZAF. Dist: Independent Pubs. Group.
Scheunemann, Pam. Cow Licks, 1 vol. Haberstroh, Anne, illus. 2006. (Animal Tales Ser.). 24p. (J). (gr. k-3). (ENG.). lib. bdg. 24.21 *(978-1-59679-929-5(3)*, SandCastle); pap. 48.42 *(978-1-59679-930-1(7))* ABDO Publishing Co.
Shaffer, Jody Jensen. Prudence the Part-Time Cow. Laberis, Stephanie, illus. 2017. (ENG.). 32p. (J). 16.99 *(978-1-62779-615-6(0)*, 9781627796156, Holt, Henry & Co. Bks. For Young Readers) Holt, Henry & Co.
Silverman, Erica. Cowgirl Kate & Cocoa: Partners. Lewin, Betsy, illus. 2007. (Cowgirl Kate & Cocoa Ser.). (ENG.). 44p. (J). (gr. 1-4). pap. 5.95 *(978-0-15-206010-7(3))* Houghton Mifflin Harcourt Publishing Co.
—Favorite Stories from Cowgirl Kate & Cocoa: Rain or Shine. Lewin, Betsy, illus. 2013. (Green Light Readers Level 2 Ser.). (ENG.). 24p. (J). (gr. 1-4). pap. 3.99 *(978-0-544-10502-7(8))* Houghton Mifflin Harcourt Publishing Co.
—Partners. Lewin, Betsy, illus. 2007. (Cowgirl Kate & Cocoa Ser.). pap. 7.93 *(978-1-4189-5237-2(0))* Houghton Mifflin Harcourt Trade & Reference Pubs.
—Partners. Lewin, Betsy, illus. 2007. (Cowgirl Kate & Cocoa Ser.). (gr. 1-4). 15.95 *(978-0-7569-8042-9(9))* Perfection Learning Corp.
Simmons, Lynn Sheffield. Sugar Lump, the Orphan Calf, 1 vol. 2003. (ENG., Illus.). 50p. (J). (gr. k-5). 12.95 *(978-1-58980-216-2(0))* Pelican Publishing Co., Inc.
Simone, Yve. Little Valentine. 2013. 72p. pap. 28.99 *(978-1-4817-0496-0(6))* AuthorHouse.
Sleepy Brown Cow. (J). (gr. 2-3). 75.00 *(978-0-669-13450-6(3))*; pap. 9.90 *(978-0-669-15892-2(5))*; pap. 9.90 *(978-0-669-15292-0(7))* Houghton Mifflin Harcourt School Pubs.
Smith, Richard G. When the Moon Fell Down. Date not set. 32p. (J). (gr. -1-18). pap. 4.99 *(978-0-06-443550-5(4))* HarperCollins Pubs.
Snellenberger, Tracy. Tyler the Toddler Feeds the Cows. 2010. 28p. 13.99 *(978-1-4520-5169-7(0))* AuthorHouse.
Solomon, Michelle & Pereira, Lavinia. Cow Cake. Faust, Laurie A., illus. 2009. 24p. pap. 10.96 *(978-1-4251-8951-8(2))* Trafford Publishing.
Spinelli, Eileen. Something to Tell the Grandcows. Slavin, Bill, illus. 2004. 32p. (J). (gr. -1-3). 8.00 *(978-0-8028-5304-2(8)*, Eerdmans Bks For Young Readers) Eerdmans, William B. Publishing Co.
St. Jean, Alan. The Legend of OinkADoodleMoo. St. Jean, Alan, ed. Krock, Libby Carruth, illus. 2013. 32p. 19.95 *(978-0-9777272-9-2(7))* Oren Village, LLC.
Stevens, Janet & Crummel, Susan Stevens. Find a Cow Now! Stevens, Janet, illus. 2012. (ENG., Illus.). 32p. (J). (gr. -1-3). 16.95 *(978-0-8234-2218-0(6))* Holiday Hse., Inc.
Stripland, Rubye Weldon. Lucy Bell, Queen of the Pasture. 2008. 92p. pap. 10.95 *(978-1-4357-1472-4(5))* Lulu Pr., Inc.
—Lucy Bell, Queen of the Pasture Book Four. 2009. 94p. pap. 10.96 *(978-1-4357-4742-5(9))* Lulu Pr., Inc.
—Lucy Bell, Queen of the Pasture, Book Three. 2008. 90p. pap. 10.95 *(978-1-4357-3418-0(1))* Lulu Pr., Inc.
—Lucy Bell, Queen of the Pasture Book Two. 2008. 100p. pap. 10.95 *(978-1-4357-1895-1(X))* Lulu Pr., Inc.
Thomas, Jan. Is Everyone Ready for Fun? Thomas, Jan, illus. 2011. (ENG., Illus.). 40p. (J). (gr. -1-3). 14.99 *(978-1-4424-2364-0(1)*, Beach Lane Bks.) Beach Lane Bks.
Thompson, Kate. I'm Just a Little Cow. Green, Barry, illus. 2017. (Googley-Eye Bks.). (ENG.). 12p. (J). (gr. -1-k). bds. 7.99 *(978-1-78445-870-6(8))* Top That! Publishing PLC GBR. Dist: Independent Pubs. Group.
Toms, Kate. I Udderly Love You! 2007. (Illus.). 25p. (gr. -1). *(978-1-84610-680-4(X))* Make Believe Ideas.
—I Udderly Love You! 2007. (Kate Toms Ser.). (Illus.). 26p. (gr. -1). bds. 7.95 *(978-1-84610-460-2(2))* Make Believe Ideas GBR. Dist: Nelson, Thomas Inc.
Townsend, Una Belle. Grady's in the Silo, 1 vol. Artley, Bob, illus. 2003. (ENG.). 32p. (J). (gr. k-3). 16.99 *(978-1-58980-098-4(2))* Pelican Publishing Co., Inc.
Twin Sister Productions & Shepherd, Jodie. Sesame Street Rosita & the Beanstalk. 2010. (J). (gr. k-2). 14.99 *(978-1-59922-634-7(0))* Twin Sisters IP, LLC.
Twin Sister Prodtions Staff & Shepherd, Jodie. Sesame Street Rosita & the Beanstalk. 2010. (J). (gr. k-2). 14.99 *(978-1-59922-525-8(5))* Twin Sisters IP, LLC.

C
D

Uihlein, Mary. Hello Little Owl, I Am Hermit Crab! Uihlein, Mary, illus. 2013. (Illus.). 28p. 24.95 *(978-1-61493-159-1(3))*; pap. 12.95 *(978-1-61493-158-4(5))* Peppertree Pr., The.

Vermeulen, Mariska. Bella & Clara Finger Puppet Book. van de Leijgraaf, Deborah, illus. 2016. (My Best Friend & Me Ser.). (ENG.). 10p. (J). (gr. -1-k). bds. 6.99 *(978-0-7641-6829-1(0))* Barron's Educational Series, Inc.

Watt, Fiona. That's Not My Cow. 2015. (Touchy-Feely Board Bks.). (ENG.). 10p. (J). 9.99 *(978-0-7945-3544-5(5),* Usborne) EDC Publishing.

Weidt, Maryann N. Daddy Played Music for the Cows. Sorensen, Henri, illus. 2nd ed. 2004. 32p. (J). pap. 7.95 *(978-0-89317-060-8(7),* WW-0607, Windward Publishing) Finney Co., Inc.

Weinberg, Jennifer Liberts. Doc Mcstuffins: Blame It on the Rain. 2014. (World of Reading Ser.). (J). lib. bdg. 13.55 *(978-0-606-35909-2(5))* Turtleback Bks.

Weis, Carol. When the Cows Got Loose. Hoyt, Ard, illus. 2006. (ENG.). 40p. (J). (gr. -1-1). 17.99 *(978-0-689-85166-7(9),* Simon & Schuster Bks. For Young Readers) Simon & Schuster Bks. For Young Readers.

Wheeler, Lisa. Sixteen Cows. Cyrus, Kurt, illus. 2006. (ENG.). 32p. (J). (gr. -1-3). reprint ed. pap. 6.99 *(978-0-15-205592-9(4))* Houghton Mifflin Harcourt Publishing Co.

Widmayer, Paul E. Bessie & Bo: The Story of a Mother's Love. 2013. 20p. pap. 12.45 *(978-1-4908-0300-5(9),* WestBow Pr.) Author Solutions, Inc.

Williamson, Pam. Sweet & Sour Milk. 2011. 24p. pap. 12.79 *(978-1-4634-0725-4(4))* AuthorHouse.

Wilson, Karma. The Cow Loves Cookies. Hall, Marcellus, illus. 2010. (ENG.). 40p. (J). (gr. -1-3). 17.99 *(978-1-4169-4206-1(8),* McElderry, Margaret K. Bks.) McElderry, Margaret K. Bks.

Wise, Alicia. Myrtle's True Friend. Wise, Jesse D., illus. 2008. 15p. pap. 24.95 *(978-1-60610-626-6(0))* America Star Bks.

COYOTES

Avett, Harper. Coyotes. 2016. (Wild Canines Ser.). (Illus.). 24p. (J). (gr. 3-3). pap. 8.25 *(978-1-4994-2015-9(3),* PowerKids Pr.) Rosen Publishing Group, Inc., The.

Berne, Emma Carlson. Coyotes. 2014. (Scavengers: Eating Nature's Trash Ser.). (Illus.). 24p. (J). (gr. k-5). lib. bdg. 23.60 *(978-1-4777-6607-1(3),* PowerKids Pr.) Rosen Publishing Group, Inc., The.

Bowman, Chris. Coyotes. 2015. (North American Animals Ser.). (ENG., Illus.). 24p. (J). (gr. k-3). lib. bdg. 25.95 *(978-1-62617-259-3(5),* Blastoff! Readers) Bellwether Media.

Bradley, James V. The Coyote. 2006. (Nature Walk Ser.). (Illus.). 64p. (gr. 4-6). lib. bdg. 28.00 *(978-0-7910-9114-2(7),* Chelsea Hse.) Facts On File, Inc.

Bronson, Wilfrid. Coyotes. 2007. 68p. (J). (gr. 3-7). per. 16.95 *(978-0-86534-624-6(0))* Sunstone Pr.

Bruchac, Joseph. Buffalo Song. Farnsworth, Bill, illus. 2013. (ENG.). 40p. (C). pap. 15.95 *(978-1-60060-990-9(2))* National Geographic School Publishing, Inc.

The Coyote, 6 vols. (gr. 4-18). 39.95 *(978-0-7368-8497-6(1))* Red Brick Learning.

Coyotes: Level J, Group 2. (Story Box Ser.). 16p. 31.50 *(978-0-322-02461-8(7))* Wright Group/McGraw-Hill.

Gagne, Tammy. Coyotes. 2017. (Animals of North America (paperback) Ser.). (ENG., Illus.). 32p. (J). (gr. 3-5). pap. 9.95 ***(978-1-63517-090-0(7),*** Focus Readers) North Star Editions.

Gianferrari, Maria. Coyote Moon. Ibatoulline, Bagram, illus. 2016. (ENG.). 32p. (J). 17.99 *(978-1-62672-041-1(X),* 9781626720411) Roaring Brook Pr.

Green, Emily. Coyotes. 2010. (Backyard Wildlife Ser.). (ENG., Illus.). 24p. (J). (gr. k-3). lib. bdg. 25.95 *(978-1-60014-439-4(X),* Blastoff! Readers) Bellwether Media.

Hyman, Teresa L. Coyotes. 2003. (Nature's Predators Ser.). (Illus.). 48p. (J). 26.20 *(978-0-7377-1886-7(2),* Greenhaven Pr., Inc.) Cengage Gale.

Jackson, Tom. Coyote. 2008. (Nature's Children Ser.). (Illus.). 52p. *(978-0-7172-6221-2(9))* Grolier, Ltd.

Linde, Barbara. Coyotes & Wolves Are Not Pets! 2013. (When Pets Attack! Ser.). 32p. (J). (gr. 3-6). pap. 10.50 *(978-1-4339-9294-0(9))*; pap. 63.00 *(978-1-4339-9295-7(7))* Stevens, Gareth Publishing LLLP.

Linde, Barbara & Linde, Barbara M. Coyotes & Wolves Are Not Pets! 2013. 32p. (J). (gr. 3-6). 26.60 *(978-1-4339-9293-3(0))* Stevens, Gareth Publishing LLLP.

Llanas, Sheila Griffin. Coyotes, 1 vol. 2013. (Animal Icons Ser.). (ENG.). 32p. (J). (gr. 3-6). lib. bdg. 27.07 *(978-1-61783-570-4(6),* Checkerboard Library) ABDO Publishing Co.

Lunis, Natalie. Coyote: The Barking Dog. 2011. (Animal Loudmouths: Noisy Animals Ser.). 24p. (J). (gr. k-3). lib. bdg. 22.61 *(978-1-61772-279-0(0))* Bearport Publishing Co., Inc.

Macken, JoAnn Early. Coyotes. 2nd rev. ed. 2009. (Animals That Live in the Desert Ser.). (ENG.). 24p. (J). (gr. -1-3). pap. 8.15 *(978-1-4339-2448-4(X))*; lib. bdg. 22.60 *(978-1-4339-2190-2(1))* Stevens, Gareth Publishing LLLP. (Weekly Reader Leveled Readers).

—Coyotes;Coyotes. 2nd rev. ed. 2009. (Animals That Live in the Desert/Animales del desierto Ser.). (ENG & SPA.). 24p. (J). (gr. -1-3). pap. 8.15 *(978-1-4339-2456-9(0))*; lib. bdg. 22.60 *(978-1-4339-2060-8(3))* Stevens, Gareth Publishing LLLP. (Weekly Reader Leveled Readers).

Mara, Wil. Coyotes. 2008. (Animals Animals Ser.). (Illus.). 48p. (J). (gr. 3-18). lib. bdg. 29.93 *(978-0-7614-2928-9(X),* Benchmark Bks.) Marshall Cavendish Corp.

Marsico, Katie. How Do We Live Together? Coyotes. 2010. (Community Connections: How Do We Live Together? Ser.). (ENG.). 24p. (gr. 2-5). lib. bdg. 25.64 *(978-1-60279-621-8(1),* 200325) Cherry Lake Publishing.

Mattern, Joanne. Coyotes. 2012. (North American Animals Ser.). (ENG.). 24p. (gr. k-1). pap. 41.70 *(978-1-4296-8359-3(7))*; pap. 7.29 *(978-1-4296-7923-7(9))*; lib. bdg. 26.65 *(978-1-4296-7700-4(7))* Capstone Press of Coughlan Cos. (Pebble Plus).

—Coyotes Are Night Animals. 2007. (Night Animals Ser.). (Illus.). 24p. (gr. k-3). lib. bdg. 22.00 *(978-0-8368-7847-9(7),* Weekly Reader Leveled Readers) Stevens, Gareth Publishing LLLP.

—Coyotes Are Night Animals (Los Coyotes Son Animales Nocturnos) 2007. (Night Animals/ Animales Nocturnos Ser.). (ENG & SPA., Illus.). 24p. (gr. k-3). pap. 8.15 *(978-0-8368-8051-9(X),* Weekly Reader Leveled Readers) Stevens, Gareth Publishing LLLP.

—Coyotes Are Night Animals/Los Coyotes Son Animales Nocturnos. 2007. (Night Animals/ Animales Nocturnos Ser.). (ENG & SPA., Illus.). 24p. (gr. k-3). lib. bdg. 22.00 *(978-0-8368-8044-1(7),* Weekly Reader Leveled Readers) Stevens, Gareth Publishing LLLP.

McGill, Jordan. Coyotes. (J). 2012. (SPA.). *(978-1-61913-192-7(7))* 2011. *(978-1-61690-935-2(8))* 2011. *(978-1-61690-581-1(6))* Weigl Pubs., Inc.

McKinnon, Elaine. Watch Out for Coyotes!, 01 vols., 1. 2016. (Wild Backyard Animals Ser.). (ENG., Illus.). 24p. (J). pap. 8.25 *(978-1-5081-4259-1(9),* PowerKids Pr.) Rosen Publishing Group, Inc., The.

Moore Niver, Heather. Coyotes after Dark. 2016. (Animals of the Night Ser.). (ENG.). 32p. (J). (gr. 3-3). pap. 10.52 *(978-0-7660-7181-0(2))* Enslow Pubs., Inc.

Murphy, Stuart J. Coyotes All Around. Björkman, Steve, illus. 2003. (MathStart 2 Ser.). (ENG.). 40p. (J). (gr. 1-18). pap. 5.99 *(978-0-06-051531-7(7))* HarperCollins Pubs.

—Coyotes All Around. Björkman, Steve, illus. 2003. (MathStart Level 2 Ser.). 32p. (J). (gr. -1-3). 16.00 *(978-0-613-68415-6(X),* Turtleback) Turtleback Bks.

Niver, Heather Moore. Coyotes after Dark. 2016. (Animals of the Night Ser.). (ENG., Illus.). 32p. (J). (gr. 3-3). 25.27 *(978-0-7660-7183-4(9))* Enslow Pubs., Inc.

Read, Tracy C. Exploring the World of Coyotes. 2011. (Exploring the World Of Ser.). (ENG., Illus.). 24p. (J). (gr. 3-7). 16.95 *(978-1-55407-795-3(8),* 9781554077953); pap. 6.95 *(978-1-55407-796-0(6),* 9781554077960) Firefly Bks., Ltd.

Roza, Greg. Your Neighbor the Coyote. 2011. (City Critters Ser.). (ENG., Illus.). 24p. (J). (gr. k-5). pap. 8.25 *(978-1-4488-5131-7(9))*; lib. bdg. 22.60 *(978-1-4488-5001-3(0))* Windmill Bks.

Silverman, Buffy. Can You Tell a Coyote from a Wolf? 2012. (Lightning Bolt Books (tm) — Animal Look-Alikes Ser.). 32p. (gr. k-2). (ENG.). pap. 7.95 *(978-0-7613-8557-8(6))*; pap. 45.32 *(978-0-7613-9253-8(X))*; (ENG., Illus.). lib. bdg. 26.60 *(978-0-7613-6739-0(X),* Lerner Pubns.) Lerner Publishing Group.

Spilsbury, Louise. Coyote, 1 vol. 2011. (Day in the Life: Grassland Animals Ser.). (ENG., Illus.). 24p. (gr. k-2). 23.32 *(978-1-4329-4729-3(X))*; pap. 6.79 *(978-1-4329-4739-2(7))* Heinemann-Raintree. (Heinemann Read & Learn).

Strother, Ruth & Van Valkenburgh, Blaire. Coyote. 2013. (Wild Canine Pups Ser.). 24p. (J). (gr. -1-3). lib. bdg. 21.32 *(978-1-61772-928-7(0))* Bearport Publishing Co., Inc.

Vogel, Julia. Coyotes. Recher, Andrew, illus. 2007. (Our Wild World Ser.). (ENG.). 48p. (J). (gr. 2-5). 10.95 *(978-1-55971-982-7(6))* Cooper Square Publishing Llc.

Webster, Christine. Coyotes. (J). 2012. *(978-1-61913-065-4(3))* 2012. *(978-1-61913-262-7(1))* 2007. (Illus.). 24p. (gr. -1-3). lib. bdg. 24.45 *(978-1-59036-673-8(5))* Weigl Pubs., Inc.

—Coyotes. Hudak, Heather C., ed. 2007. (Backyard Animals Ser.). (Illus.). 24p. (J). (gr. -1-3). pap. 8.95 *(978-1-59036-674-5(3))* Weigl Pubs., Inc.

Wolves & Coyotes. (Eyes on Nature Ser.). 32p. (J). (gr. 1). pap. *(978-1-882210-57-2(3))* Action Publishing, Inc.

Wolves & Coyotes. (Eyes on Nature Ser.). (Illus.). 32p. (J). (gr. 1-18). 7.95 *(978-1-56156-424-8(9))* Kidsbooks, LLC.

COYOTES—FICTION

Appelt, Kathi. When Otis Courted Mama. Szekeres, Cyndy & McElmurry, Jill, illus. 2015. (ENG.). 40p. (J). (gr. -1-3). 16.99 *(978-0-15-216688-5(2),* HMH Books For Young Readers) Houghton Mifflin Harcourt Publishing Co.

Beaumont, Karen. Duck, Duck, Goose! (A Coyote's on the Loose!) Aruego, Jose & Dewey, Ariane, illus. 2004. 32p. (J). (gr. -1-2). lib. bdg. 18.89 *(978-0-06-050804-3(3))* HarperCollins Pubs.

—Duck, Duck, Goose! A Coyote's on the Loose! Aruego, Jose & Dewey, Ariane, illus. 2004. (ENG.). 32p. (J). (gr. -1-2). 17.99 *(978-0-06-050802-9(7))* HarperCollins Pubs.

Blackford, Cheryl. Hungry Coyote. Caple, Laurie, illus. 2015. (ENG.). 32p. (J). (gr. -1-2). 16.95 *(978-0-87351-964-9(7))* Minnesota Historical Society Pr.

Burgess, Thornton W. Bowser the Hound. 2007. 128p. (gr. 4-7). per. 10.95 *(978-1-60312-295-5(8))*; 23.95 *(978-1-60312-713-4(5))* Aegypan.

—Bowser the Hound. 2011. 128p. 24.95 *(978-1-4638-9566-2(6))* Rodgers, Alan Bks.

Edmonds, Lin. Patric the Pony & the Flash of Lightning. 2009. 34p. pap. 13.99 *(978-1-4389-6302-0(5))* AuthorHouse.

—Patric the Pony & the Race for Freedom. 2011. 32p. pap. 15.50 *(978-1-4670-3662-7(5))* AuthorHouse.

Erickson, John R. The Case of the Coyote Invasion. Holmes, Gerald L., illus. 2011. (Hank the Cowdog Ser.: No. 56). (ENG.). 132p. (J). (gr. 3-6). pap. 5.99 *(978-1-59188-156-8(0))* Maverick Bks., Inc.

—The Case of the Deadly Ha-Ha Game. Holmes, Gerald L., illus. 2011. (Hank the Cowdog Ser.). (ENG.). 128p. (J). (gr. 3-6). pap. 5.99 *(978-1-59188-137-7(4))* Maverick Bks., Inc.

—The Ghost of Rabbits Past. Holmes, Gerald L., illus. 2013. 128p. (J). pap. *(978-1-59188-162-9(5))* Maverick Bks., Inc.

García, Nasario. Grandpa Lolo & Trampa: A Story of Surprise & Mystery = Abuelito Lolo y Trampa: Un Cuento de Sorpresa y Misterio. Montoya, Jeremy, illus. 2014. (SPA & ENG.). (J). 9.99 *(978-1-936744-30-5(9))* LPD Pr.

Garrido, Felipe. El Coyote Tonto. Gonzalez, Francisco, illus. 2003. (Infantil Alfaguara Ser.).Tr. of Dumb Coyote. (SPA.). 60p. (J). (gr. 3-5). pap. 8.95 *(978-968-19-0277-3(7))* Santillana USA Publishing Co., Inc.

Hazelwood, K. D. Coyotebat. Mathis, Leslie, illus. 2010. 68p. pap. 14.99 *(978-1-935105-52-7(3))* Avid Readers Publishing Group.

Hiscock, Bruce. Coyote & Badger: Desert Hunters of the Southwest. 2003. (ENG., Illus.). 32p. (J). (gr. 2-4). 15.95 *(978-1-56397-848-7(2))* Boyds Mills Pr.

Janowski, Alice & Boyer, Colleen McKinnon. Dakota & the Magical Gardens. 2008. 28p. pap. 12.95 *(978-1-59858-711-1(0))* Dog Ear Publishing, LLC.

Jenkins, Amanda. Leaf Monster: A Spanish American Tale. 2006. (J). pap. *(978-1-4108-6176-4(7))* Benchmark Education Co.

King, Thomas. A Coyote Columbus Story, 1 vol. Monkman, William Kent, illus. 2007. (ENG.). 32p. (J). (gr. -1-k). pap. 8.95 *(978-0-88899-830-9(9))* Groundwood Bks. CAN. Dist: Publishers Group West (PGW).

—Coyote Sings to the Moon. Wales, Johnny, illus. 2008. (ENG.). 36p. (J). pap. *(978-1-55263-868-2(5))* Magma.

—A Coyote Solstice Tale, 1 vol. Clement, Gary, illus. 2009. (ENG.). 64p. (gr. -1). 14.95 *(978-0-88899-929-0(1))* Groundwood Bks. CAN. Dist: Publishers Group West (PGW).

Lewis, J. M. The Adventures of Gabby & Coyote Girl. 2007. 64p. per. 7.95 *(978-1-4327-1511-3(9))* Outskirts Pr., Inc.

Lowell, Susan. Los Tres Pequenos Jabalies: The Three Little Javelinas. Harris, Jim, illus. 2004. (SPA, ENG & MUL.). 32p. (J). (gr. -1-3). 15.95 *(978-0-87358-661-0(1),* NP611) Rowman & Littlefield Publishers, Inc.

—A Very Hairy Christmas. Harris, Jim, illus. 2012. (J). *(978-1-933855-80-6(0))* Rio Nuevo Pubs.

Mattern, Joanne. The Tricky Garden. 2005. (J). pap. *(978-1-4108-4191-9(X))* Benchmark Education Co.

Meredith, Susan Markowitz. Coyote Brings Back Spring. 2016. (Spring Forward Ser.). (J). (gr. 2). *(978-1-4900-9421-2(0))* Benchmark Education Co.

Morrison, Kevin. Frank Is a Chihuahua. De La Cruz, Erin Harris, illus. 2007. 32p. (J). (gr. 1-4). *(978-1-929039-43-2(3))* Ambassador Bks., Inc.

Paris, Stephanie. Pecos Bill & Slue-Foot Sue, 1 vol. 2009. (Building Fluency Through Reader's Theater Ser.). (ENG.). 24p. (J). (gr. 2-4). pap. 6.99 *(978-1-4333-0991-5(2))* Teacher Created Materials, Inc.

Polette, Keith. Isabel & the Hungry Coyote. 2009. (ENG.). 32p. (J). (gr. 4-7). 16.95 *(978-1-934960-72-1(1),* Raven Tree Pr.,Csi) Continental Sales, Inc.

—Isabel & the Hungry Coyote/ Isabel y el Coyote Hambriento. Raven Tree Press Staff, ed. Szegedy, Esther, illus. 2004.Tr. of Isabel y el coyote Hambriento. (SPA & ENG.). 32p. (J). (gr. -1-3). 16.95 *(978-0-9724973-0-5(7),* 626999, Raven Tree Pr.) Continental Sales, Inc.

Rand, Johnathan. American Chillers #28 Curse of the Connecticut Coyotes. 2010. 208p. (J). pap. 5.99 *(978-1-893699-74-8(9))* AudioCraft Publishing, Inc.

Rubino, Tony. Animal Farm. 2013. 24p. pap. 24.95 *(978-1-62709-615-7(9))* America Star Bks.

Solod, Margo. Coyote Summer: A Summerhood Island Book. 2014. 1. (Illus.). 118p. (J). pap. 15.00 *(978-1-939930-18-7(9))* Brandylane Pubs., Inc.

Swinford, Betty. Cry of the Wild. 2003. (Flamingo Fiction 9-13s Ser.). (ENG.). 192p. (J). mass mkt. 6.99 *(978-1-85792-853-2(9),* 57f373c8-3223-4d9d-9e0d-40a9937df740) Christian Focus Pubns. GBR. Dist: Bookmasters Distribution.

Tireman, Loyd. 3 Toes. Douglass, Ralph, illus. 2015. (Mesaland Ser.). (ENG.). 48p. (J). 12.95 *(978-0-8263-5610-9(9))* Univ. of New Mexico Pr.

Tonatiuh, Duncan. Pancho Rabbit & the Coyote: A Migrant's Tale. 2013. (ENG., Illus.). 32p. (J). (gr. 1-4). 17.95 *(978-1-4197-0583-0(0),* Abrams Bks. for Young Readers) Abrams, Inc.

Twinem, Neecy. Baby Coyote Counts. 2004. (New Board Book Ser.).Tr. of Bebe Coyote cuenta. (ENG., Illus.). 12p. (J). (gr. -1-k). bds. 5.95 *(978-0-87358-852-2(5))* Cooper Square Publishing Llc.

Vaughan, Marcia. The Treasure of Ghostwood Gully: A Southwest Mystery. Terry, Will, illus. 2004. (ENG.). 32p. (J). (gr. 1-3). 15.95 *(978-0-87358-858-4(4))* Cooper Square Publishing Llc.

Wadsworth, Ginger. Yosemite's Songster: One Coyote's Story. San Souci, Daniel, illus. 2013. (ENG.). 32p. (J). (gr. -1-2). 15.95 *(978-1-930238-34-3(7))* Yosemite Assn.

Wilson, Elizabeth & Wilson, Betty. Song Dogs. 2005. (ENG., Illus.). 150p. (J). pap. 8.95 *(978-1-55050-216-9(6))* Coteau Bks. CAN. Dist: Fitzhenry & Whiteside, Ltd.

Yeoman, John. Quentin Blake's Amazing Animal Stories. Blake, Quentin, illus. 2012. (ENG.). 124p. (J). (gr. 2-4). 19.99 *(978-1-84365-195-6(5),* Pavilion Children's Books) Pavilion Bks. GBR. Dist: Independent Pubs. Group.

Zafar, Anas. The Leader of the Pack. 2010. 24p. pap. 14.99 *(978-1-4389-5725-8(4))* AuthorHouse.

CRABS

Alessi, Jolene. Zombie Crabs. 2015. (Zombie Animals: Parasites Take Control! Ser.). (ENG., Illus.). 24p. (J). (gr. 2-3). pap. 8.15 *(978-1-4824-2836-0(9))* Stevens, Gareth Publishing LLLP.

Armentrout, David & Armentrout, Patricia. Help! I Have a Hermit Crab. 2010. (Let's Talk about Pets Ser.). (Illus.). 24p. (J). (gr. k-4). 28.50 *(978-1-61590-250-7(3))* Rourke Educational Media.

Bathala, Neeti & Curtis, Jennifer Keats. Contando Los Cangrejos Herradura a la Luz de la Luna. Jones, Veronica V., illus. 2017. (SPA.). 32p. (J). (gr. k-3). pap. 9.95 *(978-1-62855-932-3(2))* Arbordale Publishing.

—Moonlight Crab Count. Jones, Veronica V., illus. 2017. (ENG & SPA.). 32p. (J). (gr. k-3). 17.95 *(978-1-62855-930-9(6))* Arbordale Publishing.

Baxter, Bethany. King Crabs. 2013. (Awesome Armored Animals Ser.). 24p. (J). (gr. k-5). 22.60 *(978-1-4777-0793-7(X))*; pap. 8.25 *(978-1-4777-0958-0(4))* Rosen Publishing Group, Inc., The. (PowerKids Pr.).

Binns, Tristan Boyer. Hermit Crabs, 1 vol. 2nd ed. 2010. (Keeping Unusual Pets Ser.). (ENG.). 48p. (gr. 3-6). 32.65 *(978-1-4329-3854-3(1),* NA-h) Heinemann-Raintree.

Bodden, Valerie. Amazing Animals: Crabs. 2017. (Amazing Animals Ser.). (ENG.). 24p. (J). (gr. 1-3). pap. 8.99 ***(978-1-62832-360-3(4),*** Creative Paperbacks) Creative Co., The.

Bodden, Valerie. Crabs. 2017. (J). *(978-1-60818-752-2(7),* Creative Education) Creative Co., The.

Carr, Aaron. Hermit Crab. 2014. (J). *(978-1-4896-3098-8(8))* Weigl Pubs., Inc.

Carraway, Rose. Happy Hermit Crabs. 2012. (Pet Corner Ser.). (ENG.). 24p. (J). (gr. k-2). pap. 8.15 *(978-1-4339-6295-0(0))*; lib. bdg. 22.60 *(978-1-4339-6293-6(4))* Stevens, Gareth Publishing LLLP.

—Happy Hermit Crabs: Cangrejos Ermitaños Felices. 2012. (Pet Corner / RincóN de Las Mascotas Ser.). (SPA & ENG.). 24p. (J). (gr. k-3). lib. bdg. 22.60 *(978-1-4339-6641-5(7))* Stevens, Gareth Publishing LLLP.

Caviezel, Giovanni, illus. Little Crab. 2014. (Mini-Creatures Ser.). (ENG.). 8p. (J). (gr. -1 — 1). bds. 4.99 *(978-0-7641-6714-0(6))* Barron's Educational Series, Inc.

Cooper, Sharon Katz. When Crabs Cross the Sand: The Christmas Island Crab Migration. Wald, Christina, illus. 2015. (Extraordinary Migrations Ser.). (ENG.). 24p. (gr. 2-3). lib. bdg. 26.65 *(978-1-4795-6077-6(4))* Picture Window Bks.

Crabs: Level M, 6 vols. (Wonder Worldtm Ser.). 16p. 34.95 *(978-0-7802-2893-1(6))* Wright Group/McGraw-Hill.

Doudna, Kelly. Hidden Hermit Crabs, 1 vol. 2007. (Perfect Pets Ser.). (ENG., Illus.). 24p. (J). (gr. k-3). lib. bdg. 24.21 *(978-1-59928-751-5(X),* SandCastle) ABDO Publishing Co.

Douglas, Lloyd G. Crab. 2005. (Ocean Life Ser.). (ENG., Illus.). 24p. (J). (gr. -1-2). per. 4.95 *(978-0-516-23740-4(3),* Children's Pr.) Scholastic Library Publishing.

Fredericks, Anthony D. In One Tidepool: Crabs, Snails, & Salty Tails. DiRubbio, Jennifer, illus. 2004. (Sharing Nature with Children Book Ser.). 32p. (J). (gr. -1-2). 16.95 *(978-1-58469-039-9(9))*; pap. 7.95 *(978-1-58469-038-2(0))* Dawn Pubns.

Gish, Melissa. Crabs. 2015. (Illus.). 46p. (J). *(978-1-60818-565-8(6),* Creative Education) Creative Co., The.

—Crabs: Living Wild. 2016. (Living Wild Ser.). (ENG.). 48p. (J). (gr. 5-9). pap. 12.00 *(978-1-62832-166-1(0),* Creative Paperbacks) Creative Co., The.

Green, Jen. Crabs. 2009. (Illus.). 52p. (J). *(978-0-7172-8062-9(4))* Grolier, Ltd.

Hollenbeck, Kathleen M. Dancing on the Sand: A Story of an Atlantic Blue Crab. Popeo, Joanie, illus. 2004. (ENG.). 32p. (J). (gr. -1-2). 15.95 *(978-1-56899-730-8(2),* B4017) Soundprints.

Howse, Jennifer. Crabs. 2011. (J). (gr. 2-4). pap. 12.95 *(978-1-61690-694-8(4),* AV2 by Weigl); (Illus.). 24p. (gr. 3-6). 27.13 *(978-1-61690-690-0(1))* Weigl Pubs., Inc.

Jones, Tammy. At the Shore. 2009. (Sight Word Readers Set A Ser.). (J). 3.49 net. *(978-1-60719-137-7(7))* Newmark Learning LLC.

King Crabs. 2013. (Awesome Armored Animals Ser.). 24p. (J). (gr. k-5). pap. 49.50 *(978-1-4777-0959-7(2),* PowerKids Pr.) Rosen Publishing Group, Inc., The.

Lewis, Brenda Ralph. Crabs & Mollusks. 2006. (Nature's Monsters: Water Creatures Ser.). (Illus.). 32p. (J). (gr. 2-6). lib. bdg. 26.00 *(978-0-8368-6176-1(0),* Gareth Stevens Learning Library) Stevens, Gareth Publishing LLLP.

Lunis, Natalie. Crawling Crabs. (No Backbone! Marine Invertebrates Ser.). 24p. (J). (gr. k-3). 2016. (ENG.). pap. 7.95 *(978-1-944998-76-9(4))* 2007. (Illus.). lib. bdg. 21.28 *(978-1-59716-509-9(3))* Bearport Publishing Co., Inc.

Macheske, Felicia. Blue & Bumpy: Blue Crab. 2016. (Guess What Ser.). (ENG., Illus.). 24p. (J). (gr. k-2). 28.50 *(978-1-63470-717-6(6),* 207579) Cherry Lake Publishing.

Mason, Janeen. Ocean Commotion: Life on the Reef, 1 vol. Mason, Janeen, illus. 2010. (ENG., Illus.). 32p. (J). (gr. k-3). 16.99 *(978-1-58980-783-9(9))* Pelican Publishing Co., Inc.

Meister, Cari. Crabs. 2013. (ENG.). 24p. (J). lib. bdg. 25.65 *(978-1-62031-032-8(5))* Jump! Inc.

Metz, Lorijo. Discovering Crabs. 2012. (Along the Shore Ser.). (Illus.). 24p. (J). (gr. k-3). lib. bdg. 22.60 *(978-1-4488-4993-2(4))* Rosen Publishing Group, Inc., The.

Murray, Julie. Hermit Crabs, 1 vol. 2015. (ENG., Illus.). 24p. (J). 27.07 *(978-1-62970-903-1(4))* ABDO Publishing Co.

Nagelhout, Ryan. Crabs. 2013. (Underwater World Ser.). (Illus.). 24p. (J). (gr. k-2). pap. 8.15 *(978-1-4339-8568-3(3))*; lib. bdg. 22.60 *(978-1-4339-8567-6(5))* Stevens, Gareth Publishing LLLP.

—Crabs: Cangrejos. 2013. (Underwater World / el Mundo Submarino Ser.). (SPA & ENG., Illus.). 24p. (J). (gr. k-2). lib. bdg. 22.60 *(978-1-4339-8780-9(5))* Stevens, Gareth Publishing LLLP.

Nagle, Kerry. Crabs. 2010. (Weird, Wild, & Wonderful Ser.). 24p. (J). (gr. 2-5). lib. bdg. 22.00 *(978-1-4339-3574-9(0),* Gareth Stevens Learning Library) Stevens, Gareth Publishing LLLP.

Pallotta, Jerry. Lobster vs. Crab. Bolster, Rob, illus. 2014. 32p. (J). pap. *(978-0-545-68121-6(9))* Scholastic, Inc.

Perkins, Wendy. Japanese Spider Crabs. 2017. (Weird & Unusual Animals Ser.). (ENG.). 24p. (gr. 1-4). 20.95 ***(978-1-68151-158-0(4))*** Amicus Publishing.

Pettiford, Rebecca. Crabs. 2016. (Ocean Life up Close Ser.). (ENG., Illus.). 24p. (J). (gr. k-3). 25.95 *(978-1-62617-415-3(6),* Blastoff! Readers) Bellwether Media.

Randolph, Joanne. My Friend the Hermit Crab. 2010. (Curious Pet Pals Ser.). (ENG., Illus.). 24p. (J). (gr. k-3). pap. 8.15 *(978-1-60754-987-1(5))*; lib. bdg. 22.60 *(978-1-60754-978-9(6))* Windmill Bks.

Rober, Harold. I Love Hermit Crabs. 2016. (Bumba Books (tm) — Pets Are the Best Ser.). (ENG.). 24p. (J). (gr. -1-1). lib. bdg. 25.32 *(978-1-5124-1418-9(2))* Lerner Publishing Group.

Silverstein, Alvin, et al. Hermit Crabs: Cool Pets! Kelley, Gerald, illus. 2011. (Far-Out & Unusual Pets Ser.). 48p. (J). (gr. 2-5). lib. bdg. 25.27 *(978-0-7660-3684-0(7))* Enslow Pubs., Inc.

Stevens, Kathryn. Hermit Crabs. 2015. (Pet Care Ser.). (ENG.). 24p. (J). (gr. -1-2). 25.64 *(978-1-63143-729-8(1),* 208547) Child's World, Inc., The.

Sullivan, Jody. Crabs [Scholastic]. 2010. (Under the Sea Ser.). 24p. pap. 0.52 *(978-1-4296-5062-5(1),* Pebble Plus) Capstone Press of Coughlan Cos.

Thomson, Ruth. The Life Cycle of a Crab. 2009. (Learning about Life Cycles Ser.). 24p. (J). (ENG., Illus.). (gr. k-5). pap. 8.25 *(978-1-4358-2884-1(4),* PowerKids Pr.); (gr. 2-5). lib. bdg. 22.60 *(978-1-4358-2834-6(8))* Rosen Publishing Group, Inc., The.

Wittrock, Jeni. Pet Hermit Crabs up Close. 2015. (Pets up Close Ser.). (ENG.). 24p. (gr. k-1). lib. bdg. 26.65 *(978-1-4914-2109-3(6),* Pebble Plus) Capstone Press of Coughlan Cos.

World Book, Inc Staff, contrib. by. Purple Pinchers & Other Hermit Crabs. 2007. (World Book's Animals of the World Ser.). (Illus.). 64p. (J). *(978-0-7166-1333-6(6))* World Bk., Inc.

Zappa, Marcia. Coconut Crabs, 1 vol. 2016. (ENG., Illus.). 32p. (J). *(978-1-62403-772-6(0))* ABDO Publishing Co.

CRABS—FICTION

Alfano, Doreen D. The Adventures of Hermie the Hermit Crab: Finding a New Shell. 2012. 24p. pap. 14.99 *(978-1-4685-5492-2(1))* AuthorHouse.

Aloha Potter! Evaluation Guide: Evaluation Guide. 2006. (J). *(978-1-55942-397-7(8))* Witcher Productions.
Amdahl Elco, Anita & Weikert Stelmach, Katherine. Who Is in That Shell? Patch, Michael, illus. 2012. 130p. (J). pap. 13.50 *(978-0-9883568-0-1(5))* Inkwell Books LLC.
Baker, Grandma Grace. Charlie Crab's Day at the Beach. 2012. 40p. pap. 20.99 *(978-1-4772-6975-6(4))* AuthorHouse.
Barr, Margy. The Big Adventure of Claire & Carmela Crab. 2009. 44p. pap. 18.95 *(978-1-4490-4949-2(4))* AuthorHouse.
Benoit, Brian. Crustacean Vacation, 1 vol. Kelley, Marty, illus. 2012. (ENG.). 36p. (J). 17.95 *(978-1-934031-95-7(X)*, 14581bf9-2b61-42b1-8413-13cac209cd63) Islandport Pr., Inc.
Blumenthal, Bliss & Alarcon, Claudia. Wiley's Way: El Camino de Wiley. Gonzalez, Ricky & Gonzalez, Crysol, illus. 2004. (ENG & SPA.). 96p. mass mkt. 9.95 *(978-0-292-70615-6(4))* Univ. of Texas Pr.
Burgess, Karin Whiting. It's Always a Good Day for Crabbing. 2005. (J). 16.95 *(978-0-9718303-4-9(7))* Flat Hammock Pr.
Calfee, Pat. Issy Books Set 1, 5 bks. Gee, Isybilla, illus. 2013. 60p. (J). pap. 24.95 *(978-1-938406-13-3(3)*, Compass) Raphel Marketing, Inc.
The Careful Crab. 2003. (J). per. *(978-1-57657-935-0(2))* Paradise Pr., Inc.
Carle, Eric. A House for Hermit Crab. Carle, Eric, illus. (World of Eric Carle Ser.). (ENG., Illus.). 32p. (J). 2013. (gr. -1-2). pap. 9.99 *(978-1-4424-7224-2(3))* 2004. (gr. k-3). bds. 8.99 *(978-0-689-87064-4(7))* Little Simon. (Little Simon).
—A House for Hermit Crab. Carle, Eric, illus. 2005. (ENG., Illus.). 32p. (J). (gr. -1-3). 4.99 *(978-1-4169-0309-3(7)*, Simon & Schuster/Paula Wiseman Bks.) Simon & Schuster/Paula Wiseman Bks.
—A House for Hermit Crab. Carle, Eric, illus. 2014. (World of Eric Carle Ser.). (ENG., Illus.). 32p. (J). (gr. k-2). pap. 3.99 *(978-1-4814-0915-5(8)*, Simon Spotlight) Simon Spotlight.
Clarke, Jane. Sherman Swaps Shells. Parker, Ant, illus. 2003. (Flying Foxes Ser.). (ENG.). 48p. (J). lib. bdg. *(978-0-7787-1485-9(3))* Crabtree Publishing Co.
Cogdill, Jill K., illus. Cracker the Crab & the Sideways Afternoon. 2003. 40p. (J). lib. bdg. 19.95 *(978-0-9725560-0-2(1))* Cracker the Crab LLC.
Cooper, Ross Gordon. Craig the Crab. 2010. 35p. pap. 21.95 *(978-0-557-30897-2(6))* Lulu Pr., Inc.
Cooper, Stephanie. Crab the Traveler. 2012. (Curious Eyes Ser.). (ENG., Illus.). 12p. (J). (gr. -1 — 1). bds. 12.95 *(978-1-61889-105-1(7))* AZ Bks. LLC.
COX, Margaret. The Soul-pearl. 2010. 169p. pap. 11.50 *(978-1-4457-5679-0(X))* Lulu Pr., Inc.
Cummings, Priscilla. Chadwick & the Garplegrungen, 1 vol. Cohen, Allen R., illus. 2009. (ENG.). 30p. (J). (gr. 2-18). 8.95 *(978-0-87033-377-4(1)*, 9780870333774, Cornell Maritime Pr./Tidewater Pubs.) Schiffer Publishing, Ltd.
—Chadwick's Wedding, 1 vol. Cohen, A. R., illus. 2009. (ENG.). 30p. (J). (gr. 2-18). 8.95 *(978-0-87033-390-3(9)*, 9780870333903, Cornell Maritime Pr./Tidewater Pubs.) Schiffer Publishing, Ltd.
Donaldson, Julia. Sharing a Shell Jigsaw Book. Monks, Lydia, illus. 2008. (ENG.). 14p. (J). (gr. 3-6). 23.95 *(978-0-230-01640-8(5)*, Macmillan) Pan Macmillan GBR. Dist: Trans-Atlantic Pubns., Inc.
Doudna, Kelly. Crab Cakes, 1 vol. Haberstroh, Anne, illus. 2007. (Critter Chronicles Ser.). (ENG.). 24p. (J). (gr. k-3). lib. bdg. 24.21 *(978-1-59928-434-7(0)*, SandCastle) ABDO Publishing Co.
Downing, Johnette. Why the Crawfish Lives in the Mud, 1 vol. Downing, Johnette, illus. 2009. (ENG., Illus.). 32p. (J). (gr. k-3). 16.99 *(978-1-58980-678-8(6))* Pelican Publishing Co., Inc.
Draeger, Manuela. In the Time of the Blue Ball. Evenson, Brian, tr. 2011. 134p. pap. 16.00 *(978-0-9844693-3-8(8))* Dorothy, a publishing project.
Ellis, Julie. Shark & Crab Big Book Edition. Hawley, Kelvin, illus. 2014. (ENG.). 16p. (gr. 1-1). Beta *(978-1-77654-094-5(8)*, Red Rocket Readers) Flying Start Bks.
Enderlin, Darlene C. Pathways of Hermie. 2008. 48p. pap. 16.95 *(978-1-60672-086-8(4))* America Star Bks.
Fisk, Scott. Herman the Homeless Hermit Crab. 2004. 17p. 7.99 *(978-1-4116-1770-4(3))* Lulu Pr., Inc.
Galloway, Ruth. Clumsy Crab. Galloway, Ruth, illus. (Tiger Tales Ser.). (Illus.). 32p. (J). (gr. -1-2). 2007. pap. 6.95 *(978-1-58925-402-2(3))* 2005. 15.95 *(978-1-58925-050-5(8))* Tiger Tales.
Garrett, Lyn. Horatio & the Sea Tornado. 2012. 28p. (-18). pap. 12.50 *(978-1-62212-615-6(7)*, Strategic Bk. Publishing) Strategic Book Publishing & Rights Agency (SBPRA).
Gillingham, Sara. On My Beach. Siminovich, Lorena, illus. 2015. (ENG.). 12p. (J). (gr. -1 — 1). bds. 8.99 *(978-1-4521-0640-3(1))* Chronicle Bks. LLC.
Giulieri, Anne. Little Sea Horse & the Big Crab, 1 vol. Aranda, Omar, illus. 2012. (Engage Literacy Yellow Ser.). (ENG.). 32p. (gr. k-2). pap. 5.99 *(978-1-4296-8968-7(4)*, Engage Literacy) Capstone Press of Coughlan Cos.
Goodrich, Carter. The Hermit Crab. Goodrich, Carter, illus. 2009. (ENG., Illus.). 40p. (J). (gr. 1-5). 16.99 *(978-1-4169-3892-7(3)*, Simon & Schuster Bks. For Young Readers) Simon & Schuster Bks. For Young Readers.
Gray, Laurel. The Selfish Shellfish. 2012. 16p. pap. *(978-1-909039-83-4(7))* Legend Pr.
Halfmann, Janet. Hermit Crab's Home: Safe in a Shell. Dacey, Bob & Bandelin, Debra, illus. 2011. (Smithsonian Oceanic Collection Ser.). (ENG.). 32p. (J). (gr. -1-3). 19.95 *(978-1-60727-650-0(X))* Soundprints.
—Hermit Crab's Home: Safe in a Shell. Dacey, Bob, illus. 2007. (ENG.). 32p. 8.95 *(978-1-59249-736-2(5))*; 19.95 *(978-1-59249-735-5(7))*; (J). pap. 6.95 *(978-1-59249-733-1(0))* Soundprints.
—Hermit Crab's Home: Safe in a Shell. Dacey, Bob & Bandelin, Debra, illus. 2007. (Smithsonian Oceanic Collection). (ENG.). 32p. (J). (gr. -1-3). 16.95 *(978-1-59249-732-4(2))*; 4.95 *(978-1-59249-734-8(9))*; 9.95 *(978-1-59249-737-9(3))* Soundprints.
Halter, Loretta. Lacy's Journey: The Life of a Decorator Crab. 2010. (ENG.). 64p. (J). 19.95 *(978-0-9822942-1-5(2))* Nature's Hopes & Heroes.
Hohenthal, K. D. Herman Goes Home: A Duffy Family Adventure. 2003. (Illus.). 46p. (J). per. 15.95 *(978-0-9716907-3-8(1)*, Ridgewood Publishing) Ridgewood Group, The.
Hollenbeck, Kathleen M. Dancing on the Sand: A Story of an Atlantic Blue Crab. 2005. (ENG., Illus.). 32p. (J). (gr. -1-2). 8.95 *(978-1-59249-234-3(7)*, SC4017) Soundprints.
—Dancing on the Sand: A Story of an Atlantic Blue Crab. Popeo, Joanie, illus. 2005. (Smithsonian Oceanic Collection). (ENG.). 32p. (J). (gr. -1-2). per. 6.95 *(978-1-59249-194-0(4)*, S4017) Soundprints.
Horowitz, Ruth. Crab Moon. Kiesler, Kate, illus. 2004. (Read & Wonder Ser.). (ENG.). 32p. (J). (gr. -1-3). pap. 6.99 *(978-0-7636-2313-5(X))* Candlewick Pr.
ImageBooks Staff & Chronicle Books Staff. Little Crab Finger Puppet Book. 2010. (Little Finger Puppet Board Bks.). (ENG., Illus.). 12p. (J). (gr. -1 — 1). bds. 6.99 *(978-0-8118-7340-6(4))* Chronicle Bks. LLC.
Inglis, Lillian. The One That Caught Away. 2012. 52p. pap. 31.99 *(978-1-4691-8622-1(5))* Xlibris Corp.
Itoh, Shimpei. Hyper Dolls, Vol. 5. 2003. (Illus.). 208p. pap. 15.95 *(978-1-929090-67-9(6))* International Comics & Entertainment L.L.C.
Jimmie the Crab: An Adventure in the Chesapeake Bay. 2013. (Illus.). 28p. pap. 13.97 *(978-1-62516-364-6(9)*, Strategic Bk. Publishing) Strategic Book Publishing & Rights Agency (SBPRA).
Jones, Jeannelle. Henry's Adventure. 2011. 36p. pap. 18.00 *(978-1-4634-1664-5(4))* AuthorHouse.
Joyce, S. E. Silas Saves the Friendly Crab: A Low Country Tale. 2011. 28p. (gr. 1-2). pap. 14.99 *(978-1-4634-0285-3(6))* AuthorHouse.
KING, R. O. N. S. The Soul-pearl. 2010. 169p. pap. 11.50 *(978-1-4457-5542-7(4))* Lulu Pr., Inc.
Kline, Trish & Donev, Mary. It's a Party! KA Reader 2. 2007. (Illus.). 32p. (J). per. 20.00 *(978-0-9717234-3-6(5))* Ghost Hunter Productions.
Kremer, Shelly. Coco the Coconut Crab. 2010. 27p. (J). pap. 17.95 *(978-1-4327-3043-7(6))* Outskirts Pr., Inc.
Krosoczka, Jarrett J. Peanut Butter & Jellyfish. 2014. (ENG.). 40p. (J). (gr. -1-2). 16.99 *(978-0-375-87036-1(9)*, Knopf Bks. for Young Readers) Random Hse. Children's Bks.
Kucej, Kristine. Sheldon Zab the Crab. Lester, Roseanna, illus. 2009. 24p. pap. 11.49 *(978-1-4389-6204-7(5))* AuthorHouse.
Larsen, Kirsten. Dora & the Baby Crab. Roper, Robert, illus. 2008. (Dora the Explorer Ser.: 17). (ENG.). 24p. (J). (gr. -1-1). pap. 3.99 *(978-1-4169-5451-4(1)*, Simon Spotlight/Nickelodeon) Simon Spotlight/Nickelodeon.
Lesley, Sharon. The Red Scarf & Other Stories. 2010. 165p. pap. 14.95 *(978-1-4457-6720-8(1))* Lulu Pr., Inc.
Lindsey, Stephanie. Crabs in a Bucket. 2013. 28p. pap. 24.95 *(978-1-63000-538-2(X))* America Star Bks.
Loughran, Kelley. A Crab Called Mouse. 2006. (Illus.). (J). (gr. -1-3). pap. 9.50 *(978-0-9787995-2-6(6))* High-Pitched Hum Inc.
Lyday, Kevin J. Albert's Shell. 2004. 32p. pap. 24.95 *(978-1-4137-3158-3(9))* PublishAmerica, Inc.
Maranhas, Jayne Ellen. Claude's Shrinking Shell. Baker, David, illus. 2011. 28p. pap. 24.95 *(978-1-4512-8144-6(7))* America Star Bks.
Marsh, Naomi Fawn. Mr. Crabby Pants the Crab. 2008. 36p. pap. 24.95 *(978-1-60474-092-9(2))* PublishAmerica, Inc.
Moore, Sherry. The Crab Is Back in Town. 2007. (ENG.). 100p. (J). per. *(978-1-894936-78-1(7))* Saga Bks.
—Dude; You're a Crab! 2006. (YA). per. *(978-1-894936-41-5(8))* Saga Bks.
Mucha, Mark. Adventures with Edison & His Friends Vol. 1: "Crab in a Bucket" 2008. 58p. pap. 11.95 *(978-1-934449-29-5(6))* Legacy Publishing Services, Inc.
Painted Daisies Inc. Staff & Borgatti, Katherine. Shermit's Adventure to Sprinkle Island. Painted Daisies Inc. Staff, illus. 2010. (ENG., Illus.). 32p. (J). 15.95 *(978-0-615-34491-1(7))* Painted Daisies Inc.
Patterson, Christine. Calvin Crab's Magical Wish. 2004. 9p. (J). per. 8.88 *(978-1-4116-0673-9(6))* Lulu Pr., Inc.
Patterson, Sandra Jean. Crabby Crab. 2006. bds. 12.95 *(978-1-59700-246-2(1))* Island Heritage Publishing.
Posnock, Michael A. The Adventures of Wilbur the Wave. 2013. 44p. pap. 17.99 *(978-1-4808-0132-5(1))* Archway Publishing.
Raschka, Chris. Crabby Crab. 2014. (Thingy Things Ser.). (ENG., Illus.). 24p. (J). (gr. -1-k). 6.95 *(978-1-4197-1056-8(7)*, Abrams Appleseed) Abrams, Inc.
Reasoner, Charles. I'M Just a Crab! Reasoner, Charles, illus. 2007. (Large Googley-Eye Bks.). (ENG., Illus.). 12p. (J). (gr. -1). 9.99 *(978-1-84666-291-1(5)*, Tide Mill Pr.) Top That! Publishing PLC GBR. Dist: Independent Pubs. Group.
Rouse, W. H. D. The Giant Crab & Other Tales from Old Indi. 2011. 90p. 20.95 *(978-1-4638-9898-4(3))* Rodgers, Alan Bks.
Rouse, W. H. D., ed. The Giant Crab & Other Tales from Old Indi. 2011. 90p. pap. 9.95 *(978-1-4638-0139-7(4))* Rodgers, Alan Bks.
Rouss, Sylvia & Avalone, C. The Littlest Fish. 2008. 32p. 12.95 *(978-1-934440-53-7(1)*, Pitspopany Pr.) Simcha Media Group.
Safley, Beverly M. A Tale of a Crab. 2012. 28p. pap. 19.99 *(978-1-4685-6632-1(6))* AuthorHouse.
Santillo, LuAnn. The Bad Crab. Santillo, LuAnn, ed. 2003. (Half-Pint Kids Readers Ser.). (Illus.). 7p. (J). (gr. -1-1). pap. 1.00 *(978-1-59256-094-3(6))* Half-Pint Kids, Inc.
Sayers, Mary. Franky: The Cranky Crab. 2012. 40p. pap. 20.99 *(978-1-4772-6040-1(4))* AuthorHouse.
Shimberg, Elaine Fantle. Herman, the Hermit Crab. Walling, Sandy Seeley, illus. l.t. ed. 2007. 28p. (J). 7.95 *(978-0-9741940-2-8(6))* Abernathy Hse. Publishing.
Slate, Kelly. The Adventures of Santa Claws: At Amelia Island. 2012. 28p. pap. 16.99 *(978-1-4772-2093-1(3))* AuthorHouse.
St. Aubyn, Douglas. Caribbean Fables. 2007. 72p. pap. *(978-976-8054-72-2(7))* Paria Publishing Co., Ltd.
Sullivan, Carolyn. Cutter the Crab: Spring Break. 2012. pap. 11.95 *(978-0-7414-7391-2(7))* Infinity Publishing.
Talley, Linda. Aloha Potter! - hardcover Book. Chase, Andra, illus. 2004. 30p. (J). *(978-1-55942-200-0(9))* Witcher Productions.
Thames, Bob, illus. Hermy the Hermit Crab Goes Shrimping. 2007. 44p. (J). 16.99 *(978-0-933101-05-0(8))* Legacy Pubns.
Ticktock Media, Ltd. Staff. At the Beach with the Snappy Little Crab. 2009. (Touch & Feel Fun Ser.). (ENG.). 10p. (J). (gr. k — 1). bds. 5.95 *(978-1-84696-809-9(7)*, TickTock Books) Octopus Publishing Group GBR. Dist: Independent Pubs. Group.
ToyBox Innovations, creator. Disney's the Little Mermaid. abr. ed. 2006. (Disney's Read along Collection). (ENG.). (J). (gr. -1-3). pap. *(978-0-7634-2184-7(7))* Walt Disney Records.
Tristen And Tahleez. Bubba & Tata the Hermit Crabs. 2011. 32p. pap. 16.19 *(978-1-4634-1898-4(1))* AuthorHouse.
—Bubba & Tata the Hermit Crabs: New Shells. 2011. 24p. pap. 14.60 *(978-1-4634-2351-3(9))* AuthorHouse.
Voyage to Shelter Cove. 2006. (Illus.). (J). pap., act. bk. ed. 2.00 *(978-0-9724425-5-8(3)*, White Tiger Pr.) Homes for the Homeless Institute, Inc.
Walton, William J. Polly. Walton, William J., illus. 2013. (Illus.). 88p. 20.00 *(978-0-615-79808-0(X))* Awkward Labs.
Weathers, Andrea. Hermy the Hermit Crab: The Adventure Begins. 2004. (J). pap. 15.99 *(978-0-933101-22-7(8))* Legacy Pubns.
Weigl Publishers, creator. The Crab & Its Mother: What Is the Best Way to Teach Others? 2013. (AV2 Animated Storytime Ser.: Vol. 11). (ENG., Illus.). 32p. (J). (gr. -1-3). lib. bdg. 29.99 *(978-1-62127-915-0(4)*, AV2 by Weigl) Weigl Pubs., Inc.
Wheeler-Cribb, Peggy. Madeline Becomes a Star. Bensch, April, illus. 2013. 50p. 29.95 *(978-0-9886194-1-8(5))* ProsePress.
Whitehead, Jenny. You're a Crab! A Moody Day Book. Whitehead, Jenny, illus. 2015. (ENG., Illus.). 32p. (J). (gr. -1-2). 16.99 *(978-0-8050-9361-2(3)*, 9780805093612, Holt, Henry & Co. Bks. For Young Readers) Holt, Henry & Co.
Williams, Jonnie. Harry the Hopetown Hermit Crab. Kanitsch, Christine, illus. Date not set. (Abaco Ser.). (J). (gr. -1-3). pap. 5.97 *(978-0-9657849-1-7(6))* Island Ink.

CRADLE SONGS

see Lullabies

CRAFTS

see Handicraft

CRANDALL, PRUDENCE, 1803-1890

Jurmain, Suzanne. The Forbidden Schoolhouse: The True & Dramatic Story of Prudence Crandall & Her Students. 2005. (ENG., Illus.). 160p. (J). (gr. 5-7). 19.00 *(978-0-618-47302-1(5))* Houghton Mifflin Harcourt Publishing Co.

CRANE, STEPHEN, 1871-1900

Bickerstaff, Linda. The Red Badge of Courage & the Civil War. 2009. (Looking at Literature Through Primary Sources Ser.). 64p. (gr. 5-8). 58.50 *(978-1-61514-307-8(6))* Rosen Publishing Group, Inc., The.

CRANES (BIRDS)

Becker, Ann. Cranes. 2009. (Amazing Machines Ser.). 32p. (gr. 2). 28.50 *(978-0-7614-4401-5(7))* Marshall Cavendish GBR. Dist: Marshall Cavendish Corp.
Benchmark Education Company, compiled by. Bringing Back the Whooping Crane & ¡Vamos a Rescatar a la Grulla Blanca! 2005. (J). 62.00 net. *(978-1-4108-4494-1(3))* Benchmark Education Co.
Borgert-Spaniol, Megan. Cranes. 2015. (Animal Safari Ser.). (ENG., Illus.). 24p. (J). (gr. k-3). lib. bdg. 25.95 *(978-1-62617-211-1(0)*, Blastoff! Readers) Bellwether Media.
Campbell, Jane & Hartley, Susan. Bringing Back the Whooping Crane. 2004. (Shared Connections Ser.). (J). pap. *(978-1-4108-1641-2(9))*; instr.'s gde. ed. 27.00 *(978-1-4108-1617-7(6))* Benchmark Education Co.
Cook, Jean G. & Jimmie, Elsie. How the Crane Got Its Blue Eyes. (Illus.). (J). pap. 11.00 *(978-1-55036-505-4(3))* Todd Communications.
Craats, Rennay. Whooping Cranes. 2003. (Endangered Plants & Animals of the United States Ser.). (J). pap. *(978-1-58417-211-6(8))*; lib. bdg. *(978-1-58417-210-9(X))* Lake Street Pubs.
Cranes: Big Book: Level M, 6 vols. (Take-Twostm Ser.). 32p. 36.95 *(978-0-322-03400-6(0))* Wright Group/McGraw-Hill.
Goodman, Susan E. Saving the Whooping Crane. 2009. pap. 40.95 *(978-0-7613-4821-4(2))* Lerner Publishing Group.
—Saving the Whooping Crane. Saroff, Phyllis V., illus. 2007. (On My Own Science Ser.). (ENG.). 48p. (gr. 2-4). lib. bdg. 25.26 *(978-0-8225-6748-6(2)*, Millbrook Pr.) Lerner Publishing Group.
Gray, Susan H. Whooping Crane. 2007. (21st Century Skills Library: Road to Recovery Ser.). (ENG., Illus.). 32p. (gr. 4-8). lib. bdg. 28.50 *(978-1-60279-034-6(5)*, 200087) Cherry Lake Publishing.
Imbriaco, Alison. The Whooping Crane: Help Save This Endangered Species! 2006. (Saving Endangered Species Ser.). (Illus.). 128p. (J). (gr. 4-10). lib. bdg. 34.60 *(978-1-59845-032-3(8)*, MyReportLinks.com Bks.) Enslow Pubs., Inc.
Orr, Tamra B. Battling Extinction. 2014. (Explorer Library: Follow the Clues Ser.). (ENG., Illus.). 32p. (J). (gr. 4-8). 28.50 *(978-1-62431-780-4(4)*, 203316) Cherry Lake Publishing.
Otfinoski, Steven. Storks & Cranes. 2009. (Animals Animals 10 Ser.). 48p. (gr. 3). 29.93 *(978-0-7614-3973-8(0))* Marshall Cavendish Corp.

CRANES, DERRICKS, ETC.

Addison, D. R. Cranes at Work. 2009. (Big Trucks Ser.). (Illus.). 24p. (J). (gr. k-2). pap. 8.25 *(978-1-4358-3089-9(X))*; 24p. (gr. 1-1). 42.50 *(978-1-61511-579-2(X))*; (J). lib. bdg. 22.60 *(978-1-4358-2703-5(1))* Rosen Publishing Group, Inc., The. (PowerKids Pr.).
Allen, Kenny. Drilling Rigs. 2012. (Monster Machines Ser.). (Illus.). 24p. (J). (gr. 1-3). pap. 8.15 *(978-1-4339-7164-8(X))*; lib. bdg. 22.60 *(978-1-4339-7163-1(1))* Stevens, Gareth Publishing LLLP.
—Giant Cranes. 2012. (Monster Machines Ser.). (Illus.). 24p. (J). (gr. 1-3). pap. 8.15 *(978-1-4339-7172-3(0))*; lib. bdg. 22.60 *(978-1-4339-7171-6(2))* Stevens, Gareth Publishing LLLP.
Askew, Amanda. Cranes. 2010. (Mighty Machines Ser.). (ENG., Illus.). 24p. (J). (gr. -1-2). pap. 5.95 *(978-1-55407-704-5(4)*, 9781554077045) Firefly Bks., Ltd.
Bowman, Chris. Cranes. 2017. (Mighty Machines in Action Ser.). (ENG., Illus.). 24p. (J). (gr. k-3). lib. bdg. 25.95 *(978-1-62617-602-7(7)*, Blastoff! Readers) Bellwether Media.
Bullard, Lisa. Cranes. 2006. (Pull Ahead Bks.). (Illus.). 32p. (J). (gr. -1-3). lib. bdg. 22.60 *(978-0-8225-6007-4(0)*, Lerner Pubns.); (ENG., (gr. k-3). pap. 7.95 *(978-0-8225-5895-8(5)*, First Avenue Editions) Lerner Publishing Group.
Clay, Kathryn. Cranes. 2016. (Construction Vehicles at Work Ser.). (ENG.). 24p. (gr. k-1). lib. bdg. 21.99 *(978-1-5157-2528-2(6))* Capstone Press of Coughlan Cos.
Dayton, Connor. Cranes. 2012. (Illus.). 24p. (J). pap. 8.25 *(978-1-4488-5068-6(1))*; lib. bdg. 22.60 *(978-1-4488-4959-8(4))* Rosen Publishing Group, Inc., The. (PowerKids Pr.).
Dieker, Wendy. Cranes. 2012. (ENG., Illus.). 24p. (J). lib. bdg. 25.65 *(978-1-62031-018-2(X))* Jump! Inc.
Frisch, Aaron. Cranes. 2013. 24p. 23.09 *(978-1-60818-339-5(4))* Creative Co., The.
—Seedlings: Cranes. 2014. (Seedlings Ser.). (ENG.). 24p. (J). (gr. -1-k). pap. 7.99 *(978-0-89812-884-0(6)*, Creative Paperbacks) Creative Co., The.
Gifford, Clive. Diggers & Cranes. 2013. (ENG.). 24p. (J). *(978-0-7787-1003-5(3))*; pap. *(978-0-7787-1006-6(8))* Crabtree Publishing Co.
Gilbert, Sara. Cranes. 2009. (Machines That Build Ser.). (gr. 1-5). 24.25 *(978-1-58341-727-0(3)*, Creative Education) Creative Co., The.
Glover, David & Glover, Penny. Cranes. 2005. (Big Machines Ser.). (Illus.). 30p. (J). (gr. 1-4). lib. bdg. 24.25 *(978-1-58340-700-4(6))* Black Rabbit Bks.
Gordon, Nick. Monster Cranes. 2013. (Monster Machines Ser.). (ENG., Illus.). 24p. (J). (gr. k-3). lib. bdg. 25.95 *(978-1-60014-936-8(7)*, Blastoff! Readers) Bellwether Media.
Gregory, Josh. What Does It Do? Crane. 2011. (Community Connections: What Does It Do? Ser.). (ENG.). 24p. (gr. 2-5). lib. bdg. 25.64 *(978-1-60279-967-7(9)*, 200958) Cherry Lake Publishing.
Hayes, Amy. Big Cranes. 2015. (Machines That Work Ser.). (ENG., Illus.). 24p. (J). (gr. 1-1). 24.21 *(978-1-5026-0404-0(3))* Cavendish Square Publishing.
Kawa, Katie. Cranes. 2011. (Big Machines Ser.). (Illus.). 24p. (gr. k-2). (J). pap. 8.15 *(978-1-4339-5556-3(3))*; (J). lib. bdg. 22.60 *(978-1-4339-5554-9(7))*; 69.20 *(978-1-4339-6887-7(8))* Stevens, Gareth Publishing LLLP.
—Cranes: Grúas. 2011. (Big Machines / Grandes MáQuinas Ser.). (SPA & ENG., Illus.). 24p. (J). (gr. k-3). lib. bdg. 22.60 *(978-1-4339-5576-1(8))* Stevens, Gareth Publishing LLLP.
Lennie, Charles. Cranes, 1 vol. 2014. (Construction Machines Ser.). (ENG.). 24p. (J). (gr. 4-8). lib. bdg. 28.50 *(978-1-62970-017-5(7))* ABDO Publishing Co.
Martin, M. T. Cranes. 2006. (Mighty Machines Ser.). (ENG., Illus.). 24p. (J). (gr. k-3). lib. bdg. 25.95 *(978-1-60014-045-7(9))* Bellwether Media.
Osier, Dan. Cranes, 1 vol., 1. 2014. (Construction Site Ser.). (ENG.). 24p. (J). (gr. k-2). 23.60 *(978-1-4777-2863-5(5)*, PowerKids Pr.) Rosen Publishing Group, Inc., The.
Peppas, Lynn. Cranes. 2012. (ENG.). 32p. (J). *(978-0-7787-3018-7(2))*; pap. *(978-0-7787-3023-1(9))* Crabtree Publishing Co.
Reinke, Beth. Cranes Lift! 2017. (Bumba Books (tm) — Construction Zone Ser.). (ENG.). (J). (gr. -1-1). pap. 6.99 ***(978-1-5124-5542-7(3))***; (Illus.). lib. bdg. 25.32 ***(978-1-5124-3356-2(X))*** Lerner Publishing Group.
Schuh, Mari. Las Grúas (Cranes) 2017. (Spot Mighty Machines Ser.). (ENG & SPA.). 16p. (J). (gr. k-3). 17.95 ***(978-1-68151-266-2(1)***, Amicus Readers) Amicus Publishing.
Schuh, Mari C. Cranes. 2017. (Spot Mighty Machines Ser.). (ENG.). 16p. (gr. k-3). 17.95 ***(978-1-68151-100-9(2))*** Amicus Publishing.
Tourville, Amanda Doering. Cranes, 1 vol. Trover, Zachary, illus. 2009. (Mighty Machines Ser.). (ENG.). 32p. (J). (gr. -1-3). 28.50 *(978-1-60270-622-4(0))* Magic Wagon.
Troupe, Thomas Kingsley. Knock It Down! 2013. (Destruction Ser.). (ENG.). 24p. (gr. k-1). lib. bdg. 26.65 *(978-1-4765-2087-2(9)*, Pebble Plus) Capstone Press of Coughlan Cos.
Young, Caroline. Diggers & Cranes. Lyon, Chris et al, illus. rev. ed. 2006. (Usborne Big Machines Ser.). 32p. (J). (gr. k-3). per. 6.95 *(978-0-7945-0840-1(5)*, Usborne) EDC Publishing.

CRANES, DERRICKS, ETC.—FICTION

Dalton, Kippy. The Fox & the Crane. 2016. (Spring Forward Ser.). (J). (gr. 1). *(978-1-4900-9392-5(3))* Benchmark Education Co.
Iverson, Gregory. Katie's Day. Fritz, Siegfried, illus. 2006. 48p. (J). *(978-0-9755184-1-0(0))* Sandbox Bks.
Kai Dotlich, Rebecca. What Can a Crane Pick Up? Lowery, Mike, illus. 2012. (ENG.). 32p. (J). (gr. k-k). 16.99 *(978-0-375-86726-2(0)*, Knopf Bks. for Young Readers) Random Hse. Children's Bks.
—What Can a Crane Pick Up? Lowery, Mike, illus. 2014. (ENG.). 28p. (J). (-k). bds. 6.99 *(978-0-385-75383-8(7)*, Knopf Bks. for Young Readers) Random Hse. Children's Bks.
Rey, H. A. Curious George's Crane (mini Movers Shaped Board Books) 2014. (Curious George Ser.). (ENG., Illus.). 12p. (J). (— 1). bds. 8.99 *(978-0-544-32359-9(9)*, HMH Books For Young Readers) Houghton Mifflin Harcourt Publishing Co.
Sturges, Philemon. I Love Cranes! Halpern, Shari, illus. Date not set. 32p. (J). (gr. -1-1). 5.99 *(978-0-06-443666-3(7))* HarperCollins Pubs.
—I Love Planes! Halpern, Shari, illus. 2003. (ENG.). 32p. (J). (gr. -1-1). 16.99 *(978-0-06-028898-3(1))* HarperCollins Pubs.

CRAYON DRAWING

see also Pastel Drawing

Big Bear & the Dentist. 2004. (Play Pals Ser.). (Illus.). 12p. (J). bds. *(978-1-84229-638-7(8))* Top That! Publishing PLC.
Gibson, Ray. Crayon Activities Pack. 2004. (Activity Kits Ser.). 24p. (J). act. bk. ed. 14.95 *(978-0-7945-0457-1(4))* EDC Publishing.
Nelson, Robin. From Wax to Crayon. 2003. (Start to Finish Ser.). (ENG., Illus.). 24p. (gr. k-3). 19.93 *(978-0-8225-4660-3(4)*, Lerner Pubns.) Lerner Publishing Group.
Schuh, Mari C. The Crayola Patterns Book. 2017. (Crayola (r) Concepts Ser.). (ENG.). 24p. (J). (gr. -1-3). 26.65 ***(978-1-5124-3285-5(7))*** Lerner Publishing Group.

C
D

CRAYON DRAWING—FICTION

Chapman, Joan. The Lonely Crayon. 2006. (Neighborhood Readers Ser.). (ENG.). 16p. (gr. 1-3). pap. 6.50 (978-1-4042-7212-5(7), Rosen Classroom) Rosen Publishing Group, Inc., The.

Crockett, Johns. Harold et le crayon Rose. pap. 13.95 (978-2-266-09592-1(7)) Presses Pocket FRA. Dist: Distribooks, Inc.

Cyr, Joe. Magical Trees & Crayons: Great Stories. 2006. (Illus.). pap. 9.95 (978-0-9778525-6-7(3)) Peppertree Pr., The.

Daywalt, Drew. The Day the Crayons Quit. 2014. (CHI.). 32p. (J). (978-7-5448-3406-3(9)) Jieli Publishing Hse.

—The Day the Crayons Quit, 2 vols. Jeffers, Oliver, illus. (ENG.). (J). (gr. -1-2). 2016. 88p. 40.00 (978-0-399-54892-5(0)) 2013. 40p. 17.99 (978-0-399-25537-3(0)) Penguin Young Readers Group. (Philomel Bks.).

Johnson, Crockett. Harold & the Purple Crayon. Johnson, Crockett, illus. 50th anniv. ed. 2015. (ENG., Illus.). 64p. (J). (gr. -1-3). pap. 6.99 (978-0-06-443022-7(7)); 16.99 (978-0-06-022935-1(7)) HarperCollins Pubs.

Owen, Rob. Spy Boy, Cheyenne, & Ninety-Six Crayons: A "Mardi Gras" Indian's Story, 1 vol. Owen, Rob, illus. 2013. (ENG., Illus.). 32p. (J). (gr. k-3). 16.99 (978-1-4556-1799-9(7)) Pelican Publishing Co., Inc.

Patterson, Christine D. Conversation in the Crayon Box. 2008. 24p. per. 12.95 (978-1-4327-1469-7(4)) Outskirts Pr., Inc.

Piggy Toes Press, creator. Animals: Colors & Animals. 2011. (Crayola (Piggy Toes Press) Ser.). (Illus.). 6p. (J). (gr. -1-3). bds. 5.95 (978-1-61524-286-3(4), Intervisual/Piggy Toes) Bendon, Inc.

—Dinosaurs: Guess the Dinosaur. 2011. (Crayola (Piggy Toes Press) Ser.). (Illus.). 6p. (J). (gr. -1-3). 5.95 (978-1-61524-287-0(2), Intervisual/Piggy Toes) Bendon, Inc.

Rivera, Monica O. Lola the Spider & the Purple Crayon. 2009. 20p. pap. 15.00 (978-1-4389-7487-3(6)) AuthorHouse.

Ruprecht, Jennifer L. The Crayon Kids' Art Adventure. Shaw-Peterson, Kimberly, illus. 2007. (ENG.). 32p. (J). per. 9.95 (978-1-933916-10-1(9)) Nelson Publishing & Marketing.

Weston Woods Staff, creator. Harold & the Purple Crayon. 2011. 38.75 (978-0-439-72693-1(X)); 18.95 (978-0-439-72691-7(3)); 29.95 (978-0-439-73474-5(6)) Weston Woods Studios, Inc.

—Harold's Fairy Tale. 2011. 18.95 (978-0-439-72704-4(9)); 38.75 (978-0-439-72706-8(5)) Weston Woods Studios, Inc.

—A Picture for Harold's Room. 2011. 18.95 (978-0-439-72871-3(1)); 38.75 (978-0-439-72872-0(X)) Weston Woods Studios, Inc.

CRAZY HORSE, APPROXIMATELY 1842-1877

Brimner, Larry Dane. Chief Crazy Horse: Following a Vision. 2008. (American Heroes Ser.). 48p. (gr. 3-18). lib. bdg. 29.93 (978-0-7614-3061-2(X), Benchmark Bks.) Marshall Cavendish Corp.

Crazy Horse. 2010. (Legends of the Wild West Ser.). (Illus.). 144p. (gr. 6-12). 35.00 (978-1-60413-526-8(3), Chelsea Hse.) Facts On File, Inc.

Cunningham, Chet. Chief Crazy Horse. 2005. (Biography Ser.). (Illus.). 112p. (gr. 6-12). lib. bdg. 27.93 (978-0-8225-4978-9(6)) Lerner Publishing Group.

Landau, Elaine. Crazy Horse: American Indian Leader. 2004. (Best of the West Biographies Ser.). (Illus.). 48p. (J). lib. bdg. 23.93 (978-0-7660-2216-4(1)) Enslow Pubs., Inc.

Sanford, William R. Oglala Sioux Chief Crazy Horse. 2013. (Native American Chiefs & Warriors Ser.). 48p. (J). (gr. 5-18). 22.60 (978-0-7660-4094-6(1)); pap. 8.95 (978-1-4644-0261-6(2)) Enslow Pubs., Inc.

Sterngass, Jon. Crazy Horse: The Wild West for Kids. 2014. (ENG., Illus.). 160p. (J). (gr. 2-7). pap. 12.95 (978-1-62636-159-1(2), 263159, Sky Pony Pr.) Skyhorse Publishing Co., Inc.

CREATION

see also Earth (Planet); Evolution; Geology; God; Human Beings; Mythology; Theology; Universe

Alexander, Cecil Frances & Hudson, Katy, illus. All Things Bright & Beautiful. 2016. (J). (978-0-8249-5676-9(1), Ideal Pubns.) Worthy Publishing.

All Things Bright & Beautiful. 2006. 16p. (J). pap. 1.99 (978-0-7847-1588-8(2), 22135) Standard Publishing.

Anderson, Debby. Let's Explore God's World. Anderson, Debby, illus. 2009. (Illus.). 32p. (J). (gr. -1-1). 10.99 (978-1-4335-0708-3(0)) Crossway.

The Answer Book for Kids: 25 Questions on Dinosaurs & the Flood of Noah. 2008. 60p. (J). pap. 7.99 (978-0-89051-527-3(1)) Master Bks.

Apologetics Press, creator. Creation Cards: Exploring God's Creation. 2007. (ENG., Illus.). (J). (gr. 4-7). 9.95 (978-0-932859-75-4(5)) Apologetics Pr., Inc.

Audia, John P. The Creation Story: In Words & Sign Language. Spohn, David, illus. 2007. (ENG.). 16p. (gr. 3-7). 9.95 (978-0-8146-3174-4(6)) Liturgical Pr.

Bates, Delphine Branon. Help Me Remember the Days of Creation. Bates, Delphine Branon & EsDesignStudio, illus. 2010. 24p. (J). 11.95 (978-0-9799116-3-7(X)) LifeSong Pubs.

Bicknell, Joanna. All Things Bright & Beautiful. 2008. 14p. (978-1-84610-728-3(8)) Make Believe Ideas.

Blaivas, C. & Z. Our Beautiful World: The Six Days of Creation. 2006. (J). bds. 6.95 (978-1-931681-91-9(0)) Israel Bookshop Pubns.

Bostrom, Kathleen Long. Who Made the World? Kucharik, Elena, illus. 2009. (Little Blessings Ser.). (ENG.). 80p. (J). (gr. -1-1). 9.99 (978-1-4143-2011-3(6), Tyndale Kids) Tyndale Hse. Pubs.

Breems, Beau A. La Gran Historia: The Illustrated Gospel from Creation to Resurrection. Breems, Beau A., illus. 2005.Tr. of His Story. (SPA., Illus.). (J). 10.99 (978-0-9768680-5-7(9)) Burning Bush Creation.

Breems, Beau Alan. His Story: The Illustrated Gospel from Creation to Resurrection. Breems, Beau Alan, illus. 2005. (Illus.). (J). per. 14.95 (978-0-9768680-2-6(4)) Burning Bush Creation.

Bruno, Bonnie. God Thought of Everything Strange & Slimy. Brown, Kevin, illus. 2006. 128p. (YA). (gr. 3-6). pap. 8.99 (978-0-7847-1448-5(7), 04084) Standard Publishing.

—God Thought of Everything Weird & Wacky. Brown, Kevin, illus. 2006. 128p. (YA). (gr. 3-6). pap. 8.99 (978-0-7847-1447-8(9), 04083) Standard Publishing.

Butt, Kyle. God Made Plants. 2007. (ENG., Illus.). (J). 3.00 (978-0-932859-85-3(2)) Apologetics Pr., Inc.

Butterworth, Nick & Inkpen, Mick. Wonderful Earth. 2003. (Illus.). 32p. 14.99 (978-1-85608-005-7(6)) Hunt, John Publishing Ltd. GBR. Dist: Send The Light Distribution LLC.

Byous, Shawn. 7 Days of Awesome: A Creation Tale, 1 vol. Jack, Colin, illus. 2016. (ENG.). 40p. (J). 16.99 (978-0-310-74349-1(4)) Zonderkidz.

Caduto, Michael J. In the Beginning: The Story of Genesis & Earth Activities for Children. 2004. 48p. 16.95 (978-0-8091-6717-3(4), 6717-4) Paulist Pr.

Clausman, Rachel. Who Made the World? 2011. 44p. (gr. 1-2). pap. 16.59 (978-1-4634-0784-1(X)) AuthorHouse.

Collins, Sarah Jean. God Made the World. 2017. (ENG.). 20p. bds. 7.99 **(978-1-4964-2648-2(7))** Tyndale Hse. Pubs.

Cooper, Gilly Cameron. How the World Began: Creation in Myths & Legends. Ludlow, Patricia, illus. 2006. (ENG.). 48p. (J). (gr. 3-7). pap. 11.99 (978-1-84476-246-0(7)) Anness Publishing GBR. Dist: National Bk. Network.

Cope, Dorothy. The Day Star: A Love Spirit, 1 vol. 2009. 30p. pap. 24.95 (978-1-60749-729-5(8)) America Star Bks.

Davis, Rebecca. God's Special Creation. de Papenbrock, Dervy Romero, tr. Clement, Stacy, illus. unabr. ed. 2003. (ENG & SPA.). 30p. (J). (gr. k-3). spiral bd. 8.00 (978-0-9720881-3-8(X), B004) His Hands, Inc.

Delace Wofford Canada. Smiles for God from a Sunflower & You. 2013. (Illus.). 32p. pap. 16.99 (978-1-4497-8695-3(2), WestBow Pr.) Author Solutions, Inc.

dePaola, Tomie. Let the Whole Earth Sing Praise. dePaola, Tomie, illus. 2011. (ENG., Illus.). 28p. (J). (gr. -1-k). 15.99 (978-0-399-25478-9(1), G.P. Putnam's Sons Books for Young Readers) Penguin Young Readers Group.

Engdahl, Sharon & Engdahl, Terry. The Evolution of Creation: A Children's Primer on the Evolution of God's Creation, 1 vol. 2010. 30p. 24.95 (978-1-4489-4228-2(4)) PublishAmerica, Inc.

Exploring Creation Marine Biology. 2006. cd-rom 58.50 (978-1-932012-66-8(4)) Apologia Educational Ministries, Inc.

Exploring Creation Marine Biology Companion CD-ROM. 2006. cd-rom 13.50 (978-1-932012-67-5(2)) Apologia Educational Ministries, Inc.

Fawcett, Cheryl & Newman, Robert C. Kids' Questions about the Bible & Creation. 2003. 64p. pap. (978-1-59402-082-7(5)) Regular Baptist Pr.

Fleischman, Paul. First Light, First Life: A Worldwide Creation Story. Paschkis, Julie, illus. 2016. (ENG.). 32p. (J). 17.99 (978-1-62779-101-4(9), 9781627791014, Holt, Henry & Co. Bks. For Young Readers) Holt, Henry & Co.

Forche, Carolyn A. Colors Come from God ... Just Like Me! 2015. 32p. pap. 9.99 (978-1-5018-0838-8(9)) Abingdon Pr.

Fritz, Greg. God Made You Special! Reed, Lisa, illus. 2015. (J). (978-0-8249-1947-4(5), Ideal Pubns.) Worthy Publishing.

Froeb, Lori C. God's Creation, 1 vol. Rinaldo, Luana, illus. 2008. 12p. (J). bds. 7.99 (978-0-8254-5545-2(6)) Kregel Pubns.

Fulbright, Jeannie. Exploring Creation with Botany. Wile, Jay L., ed. 2004. 35.00 (978-1-932012-49-1(4)) Apologia Educational Ministries, Inc.

—Exploring Creation with Zoology 1: The Flying Creatures of Day Five. Wile, Jay L., ed. 2005. (Illus.). xvi, 240p. (J). 35.00 (978-1-932012-61-3(3)) Apologia Educational Ministries, Inc.

Garcia, Emmett Shkeme & Garcia, Emmett. Coyote & the Sky: How the Sun, Moon, & Stars Began. Pringle, Victoria, illus. 2006. (ENG.). 32p. (J). (gr. 6-18). 19.95 (978-0-8263-3730-6(9)) Univ. of New Mexico Pr.

Gardener, Ryan. Thank You God for Making the Sun. 2008. 28p. pap. 12.95 (978-1-4389-1488-6(1)) AuthorHouse.

Goble, Paul. The Earth Made New: Plains Indian Stories of Creation. 2009. (ENG.). 40p. (J). (gr. 4-7). 17.95 (978-1-933316-67-3(5)) World Wisdom, Inc.

—Song of Creation. Goble, Paul, illus. 2004. (ENG., Illus.). 32p. (J). 17.00 (978-0-8028-5271-7(8)) Eerdmans, William B. Publishing Co.

God Made Everything Good. 3.50 (978-0-8054-5878-7(6)) B&H Publishing Group.

God Made Me. 3.50 (978-0-8054-5887-9(5)) B&H Publishing Group.

God Made the World (for Four-Year-Olds) 2004. (gr. -1-18). tchr. ed. 23.95 (978-0-8294-0818-8(5)) Loyola Pr.

Godfrey, Jan. God's Wonderful World. Adderley, Peter, illus. 2008. Orig. Title: Wonderful World. (J). (gr. k-3). 12.95 (978-0-8198-8317-9(4)) Pauline Bks. & Media.

Goodings, Christina. In the Beginning. Carletti, Emanuela, illus. 2015. (ENG.). 16p. (J). (gr. -1-k). pap. 6.99 (978-0-7459-6568-0(7)) Lion Hudson PLC GBR. Dist: Independent Pubs. Group.

Greene, Carol. Why Boys & Girls Are Different. Dorankamp, Michelle, illus. 2008. pap. 12.99 (978-0-7586-1409-4(8)) Concordia Publishing Hse.

Grimes, Nikki. At Break of Day. Collier, John & Morin, Paul, illus. 2004. 32p. (J). (gr. -1-3). 17.00 (978-0-8028-5104-8(5)) Eerdmans, William B. Publishing Co.

Haidle, Helen & Haidle, David. Creation Story for Children. Haidle, Helen & Haidle, David, illus. 2009. (Illus.). 32p. (J). 14.99 (978-0-89051-565-5(4)) Master Bks.

Ham, Ken. The Answer Book for Kids: 25 Questions on Creation & the Fall. 2008. 60p. (J). pap. 7.99 (978-0-89051-526-6(3)) Master Bks.

—Six Days or Millions of Years? 2004. 48p. pap. 0.75 (978-1-893345-23-2(8)) Answers in Genesis Ministries.

Ham, Ken & Davis, Buddy. It's Designed to Do What It Does Do. 2006. (Illus.). 22p. (J). bds. 9.99 (978-0-89051-484-9(4)) Master Bks.

Hansen, Janis. Creation: God's Wonderful Gift, 5 vols. Fransisco, Wendy, illus. 2003. (Bible Adventure Club Ser.). 36p. wbk. ed. 19.99 incl. audio, cd-rom (978-1-58134-292-5(6)) Crossway.

Harrub, Brad. God Made Fish. 2007. (ENG., Illus.). (J). 3.00 (978-0-932859-87-7(9)) Apologetics Pr., Inc.

Henning, Heather. Creation. Bull, Nicola, ed. Chapman, Gillian, illus. 2007. (Touch & Feel Ser.). 14p. (J). (gr. -1-3). bds. 10.49 (978-0-7586-1384-4(9)) Concordia Publishing Hse.

—When God Created the World. 2006. (Illus.). 22p. (J). (gr. -1-3). 10.95 (978-1-59325-077-5(0)) Word Among Us Pr.

Hilton, Jennifer Sue & McCurry, Kristen. El Mundo Maravilloso de Dios. Rimmington, Natasha, illus. 2016. (SPA.). (J). (978-1-5064-2094-3(X)) Augsburg Fortress, Pubs.

Icilda. God Made Me Perfect & Wonderful: To Do What? 2009. 28p. pap. 13.99 (978-1-4490-4545-6(6)) AuthorHouse.

In the Beginning. 2006. 16p. (J). pap. 1.99 (978-0-7847-1352-5(9), 22129) Standard Publishing.

Jensen, Rebecca Ridges & Jensen, Daniel Loran. The Creation-From the Book of Moses. 2007. (Illus.). 32p. (J). 15.99 (978-1-55517-894-9(4)) Cedar Fort, Inc./CFI Distribution.

Keener, Joan N. God Thought of It First. Petrova, Valeria, illus. 2006. 28p. (J). 14.99 (978-0-7847-1432-4(0), 04016) Standard Publishing.

Kessler, Tim. When God Made the Dakotas. Morin, Paul, illus. 2006. 32p. (J). (gr. k). 17.00 (978-0-8028-5275-5(0), Eerdmans Bks For Young Readers) Eerdmans, William B. Publishing Co.

Kovacs, Victoria. Creation/Noah Flip-Over Book. Krome, Mike, illus. 2015. (Little Bible Heroes(tm) Ser.). (ENG.). 32p. (J). (gr. k-2). pap. 3.99 (978-1-4336-8712-9(7), B&H Kids) B&H Publishing Group.

Laflamme, Sonia K. & Delezenne, Christine. Les Hommes de Maïs. (FRE., Illus.). 71p. (J). pap. 9.95 (978-2-923234-58-8(8)) Editions de l'"Isatis CAN. Dist: Crabtree Publishing Co.

Leah, Carole. God's World: Book 1 A Biblebased Reading Project, 8 vols. 2009. (ENG., Illus.). 24p. 3.99 (978-1-84550-529-5(8)) Christian Focus Pubns. GBR. Dist: Send The Light Distribution LLC.

Lee, Otha. Mrs. Lee's Stories about God's First People. 2013. 268p. pap. 19.95 (978-1-58427-387-5(9)) Guardian of Truth Foundation.

Lehmann, Charles. God Made It for You! The Story of Creation. Kemly, Kathleen, illus. 2007. 32p. (J). (gr. -1-3). 14.99 (978-0-7586-1287-8(7)) Concordia Publishing Hse.

Leunk, Thea. Fossils & Faith: Finding Our Way Through the Creation Controversy. (Other Beliefs Ser.). (gr. 11-12). pap., stu. ed. 4.95 (978-1-59255-198-9(X), 130700); pap. 12.95 (978-1-59255-199-6(8), 130705) Faith Alive Christian Resources.

Lyons, Eric. God Made Insects. 2007. (ENG., Illus.). (J). 3.00 (978-0-932859-86-0(0)) Apologetics Pr., Inc.

Mackenzie, Catherine. God's Little Guidebooks - Creation: God Creates a Day of Rest. 2003. (ENG., Illus.). 16p. (J). pap. 0.99 (978-1-85792-847-1(4), Christian Focus) Christian Focus Pubns. GBR. Dist: Send The Light Distribution LLC.

—God's Little Guidebooks - Creation: God Creates Animals & People. 2003. (ENG., Illus.). 16p. (J). pap. 0.99 (978-1-85792-846-4(6), Christian Focus) Christian Focus Pubns. GBR. Dist: Send The Light Distribution LLC.

—God's Little Guidebooks - Creation: God Creates New Life in Me. 2003. (ENG., Illus.). 16p. (J). pap. 0.99 (978-1-85792-848-8(2), Christian Focus) Christian Focus Pubns. GBR. Dist: Send The Light Distribution LLC.

—God's Little Guidebooks - Creation: God Creates the Fish & Birds. 2003. (ENG., Illus.). 16p. (J). pap. 0.99 (978-1-85792-845-7(8), Christian Focus) Christian Focus Pubns. GBR. Dist: Send The Light Distribution LLC.

—God's Little Guidebooks - Creation: God Creates the Land, Seas & Plants. 2003. (ENG., Illus.). 16p. (J). pap. 0.99 (978-1-85792-843-3(1), Christian Focus) Christian Focus Pubns. GBR. Dist: Send The Light Distribution LLC.

—God's Little Guidebooks - Creation: God Creates the Sun, Moon & Stars. 2003. (ENG., Illus.). 16p. (J). pap. 0.99 (978-1-85792-844-0(X), Christian Focus) Christian Focus Pubns. GBR. Dist: Send The Light Distribution LLC.

—God's Little Guidebooks - Creation: God Creates the Water & the Sky. 2003. (ENG., Illus.). 16p. (J). pap. 0.99 (978-1-85792-842-6(3), Christian Focus) Christian Focus Pubns. GBR. Dist: Send The Light Distribution LLC.

MacKenzie, Catherine. What God Says: Creation. 2006. (Bible Art Ser.). (ENG.). 16p. (J). pap. 1.99 (978-1-84550-219-5(1), 9781845502195) Christian Focus Pubns. GBR. Dist: Bookmasters Distribution.

Maier, Paul L. The Real Story of the Creation. Barrett, Robert T., illus. 2007. 28p. (J). (gr. -1-18). 16.99 (978-0-7586-1265-6(6)) Concordia Publishing Hse.

McCurry, Kristen & Hilton, Jennifer. Dios No Creo Todos. Garton, Michael, illus. 2016. (SPA.). (J). **(978-1-5064-2092-9(3))** Augsburg Fortress, Pubs.

Miller, Bryan. Dinosaur Fun: With Letters. 2008. (Illus.). 24p. (J). (gr. -1). bds. 11.99 (978-0-89051-488-7(7)) Master Bks.

Miller, Dave. Birds, Bugs, & Bees. 2006. (ENG., Illus.). (J). 3.00 (978-0-932859-90-7(9)) Apologetics Pr., Inc.

—Dogs, Frogs, & Hogs. 2006. (ENG., Illus.). (J). 3.00 (978-0-932859-88-4(7)) Apologetics Pr., Inc.

Natus, Uwe. The Creation of the World. Geisler, Dagmar, illus. 2016. (ENG.). 28p. (J). (gr. -1-3). 14.99 (978-1-5064-0883-5(4), Sparkhouse Family) Augsburg Fortress, Pubs.

Novaskshonoff, Varlaarm. Creation of the World: For Young People. Date not set. (Illus.). 27p. (YA). (gr. 7-12). pap. 3.00 (978-1-879038-44-8(7), 9012) Synaxis Pr.

Parker, Gary & Parker, Mary. The Complete Zoo Adventure: A Field Trip in a Book. 2008. (Illus.). 160p. (J). (gr. -1). 18.99 (978-0-89051-500-6(X)) Master Bks.

—The Fossil Book. 2006. (Wonders of Creation Ser.). 36p. (J). (gr. 4-7). pap. 3.99 (978-1-60092-007-3(1)) Master Bks.

Pickett, Cheryl. Creation Inspirations: A New View of Your Neighborhood. 2013. 126p. pap. 14.95 (978-0-9841855-1-1(8)) Brighter Day Publishing.

Pingry, Patricia A. & Venturi-Pickett, Stacy, trs. The Story of Creation. Venturi-Pickett, Stacy, illus. 2003. (Illus.). 26p. (J). bds. 7.95 (978-0-8249-6504-4(3), Ideal Pubns.) Worthy Publishing.

Prestofillipo, Mary Nazarene, tr. The Story of Creation. Flamini, Lorella, illus. 2005. Orig. Title: Piccola storia della Creazione. (ITA.). 36p. (J). pap. 12.95 (978-0-8198-7093-3(5)) Pauline Bks. & Media.

Pridham, Caroline. Twilight & Dawn: Simple Talks on the Six Days of Creation. 2007. (ENG.). 286p. pap. 21.99 (978-1-4264-2599-8(6)); 310p. pap. 24.99 (978-1-4264-2640-7(2)) Creative Media Partners, LLC.

Ridley, Yvonne. God Made Me! Who Made You? 2009. (Illus.). 32p. (J). pap. 24.95 (978-1-4327-3315-5(X)) Outskirts Pr., Inc.

Rivers-Moore, Debbie. God Made the World, 1 vol. Haines, Emma, illus. 2017. 4p. 11.99 **(978-0-8254-4520-0(5))** Kregel Pubns.

Rubino, Michael. Bang! How We Came to Be. 2011. (ENG.). 69p. (J). (gr. 4-7). pap. 17.00 (978-1-61614-472-2(6)) Prometheus Bks., Pubs.

Rylant, Cynthia. Creation. Rylant, Cynthia, illus. 2016. (ENG., Illus.). 40p. (J). (gr. -1). 17.99 (978-1-4814-7039-1(6), Beach Lane Bks.) Beach Lane Bks.

Schlitt, D. Celebrate the World God Made. 2004. 52p. 6.99 (978-0-8054-0826-3(6)) B&H Publishing Group.

Scott-Brown, Anna. Creation Song. Gomez, Elena, illus. 2008. 32p. (J). (gr. k-2). 12.99 (978-0-8254-6263-4(0)) Kregel Pubns.

Scott, Cassandra. Boys & Girls Are Created2Produce. 2013. 40p. pap. 17.99 (978-0-9882936-2-5(5)) Scott, Cassandra Dr Ministries.

Shaw, Luci. The Genesis of It All. Miao, Huai-Kuang, Sr. & Miao, Huai-Kuang, illus. 2006. 32p. (J). (gr. -1-3). 17.95 (978-1-55725-480-1(X)) Paraclete Pr., Inc.

Silverstru, Emil. The Cave Book. 2008. 80p. (J). 15.99 (978-0-89051-496-2(8)) Master Bks.

Sinclair, Mehded Maryam. A Trust of Treasures. Desira, Angela, illus. 2010. (ENG.). 29p. (J). (gr. k). 14.95 (978-0-86037-462-6(9)) Kube Publishing Ltd. GBR. Dist: Consortium Bk. Sales & Distribution.

Smith, Martina. La Historia de la Creacion: Un Relato de la Biblia Chispita. Grosshauser, Peter & Temple, Ed, illus. 2016. (SPA.). (J). (978-1-5064-2100-1(8)) Augsburg Fortress, Pubs.

Snyder, Bernadette McCarver. 110 Fun Facts about God's Creation: Is It Animal, Vegetable, or Mineral? 2010. (J). 12.99 (978-0-7648-1861-5(9)) Liguori Pubns.

Stevens, Noel. In the Never-Never-Converse with an Archangel. 2008. 132p. pap. 13.95 (978-0-595-52727-4(2)) iUniverse, Inc.

Stewart, Henry. He Created Me. 2007. (Illus.). (J). 28.99 (978-1-59879-345-1(4)); per. 20.99 (978-1-59879-269-0(5)) Lifevest Publishing, Inc.

Stoop, Naoko, illus. All Creatures Great & Small. 2012. (ENG.). 22p. (J). (gr. k — 1). bds. 6.95 (978-1-4027-8581-8(X)) Sterling Publishing Co., Inc.

Sumner, Tracy M. & Landreth, Jane. Big Bible Guide: Kids' Guide to Creation & Bible Animals: Fun & Fascinating Bible Reference for Kids Ages 8-12. 2014. (ENG., Illus.). 320p. (J). pap. 14.99 (978-1-62416-868-0(X), Barbour Bks.) Barbour Publishing, Inc.

Tanner, Earnest D., Jr. Creation the Sixth Day. 2006. per. 11.95 (978-1-59872-563-6(7)) Instant Pub.

Taylor, Jane & Macleod, Una. God Made Me. Matthews, Derek, illus. 2015. (Board Books God Made Ser.). (ENG.). 16p. (J). bds. 3.99 (978-1-85792-289-9(1), 03f5af1b-96db-40aa-997a-68a2c4d74abd) Christian Focus Pubns. GBR. Dist: Bookmasters Distribution.

Taylor, Jane, et al. God Made the World. 2015. (Board Books God Made Ser.). (ENG., Illus.). 16p. (J). (gr. -1-k). bds. 3.99 (978-1-85792-292-9(1), 4833da61-2487-4961-8495-ce76e356ada2) Christian Focus Pubns. GBR. Dist: Bookmasters Distribution.

Tutu, Desmond. Let There Be Light, 1 vol. Tillman, Nancy, illus. 2014. (ENG.). 30p. (J). bds. 7.99 (978-0-310-73396-6(0)) Zonderkidz.

Tyndale, prod. The Gigantic Coloring Book of God's World. 2014. (ENG.). 320p. (J). pap. 5.99 (978-1-4143-9499-2(3)) Tyndale Hse. Pubs.

Vander Klipp, Michael. God Made Animals, 1 vol. 2008. (God Made... Ser.). 14p. (J). bds. 3.99 (978-0-8254-3911-7(6)) Kregel Pubns.

—God Made Food, 1 vol. 2008. (God Made... Ser.). 14p. (J). bds. 3.99 (978-0-8254-3913-1(2)) Kregel Pubns.

—God Made My Body, 1 vol. 2008. (God Made... Ser.). 14p. (J). bds. 3.99 (978-0-8254-3912-4(4)) Kregel Pubns.

—God Made the World, 1 vol. 2008. (God Made... Ser.). 14p. (J). bds. 3.99 (978-0-8254-3914-8(0)) Kregel Pubns.

Walker, Joni. Tell Me What God Made. Walker, Joni, illus. 2007. (Illus.). 20p. (J). (gr. -1-3). bds. 6.49 (978-0-7586-1247-2(8)) Concordia Publishing Hse.

Watson, Lori Ann. Beginnings. Bersani, Shennen, illus. 2009. 32p. (J). (gr. -1-1). 12.95 (978-0-8198-1172-1(6)) Pauline Bks. & Media.

West, Edith. A World Just for Me. 2009. 32p. pap. 13.99 (978-1-4389-7083-7(8)) AuthorHouse.

Wile, Jay L. & Durnell, Marilyn F. Exploring Creation with Biology, 2 Bks., Set. 2nd ed. 2005. 85.00 (978-1-932012-57-6(5)) Apologia Educational Ministries, Inc.

Wright, Carolyn. In the Beginning. 2013. 24p. pap. 12.45 (978-1-4624-0736-1(6), Inspiring Voices) Author Solutions, Inc.

Yasuda, Anita. N Gua Mends the Sky: A Chinese Flood Myth. 2014. (Short Tales Chinese Myths Ser.). 32p. (J). (gr. 3-6). lib. bdg. 24.21 (978-1-62402-033-9(X), Short Tales) Magic Wagon.

—Pangu Separates the Sky from the Earth: A Chinese Creation Myth. 2014. (Short Tales Chinese Myths Ser.). (Illus.). 32p. (J). (gr. 3-6). lib. bdg. 24.21 (978-1-62402-034-6(8), Short Tales) Magic Wagon.

Zondervan. The Beginner's Bible Wild about Creation Sticker & Activity Book, 1 vol. 2015. (Beginner's Bible Ser.). (ENG., Illus.). 16p. (J). pap. 3.99 (978-0-310-74705-5(8)) Zonderkidz.

—Wonders of Creation: Illustrations to Color & Inspire, 1 vol. 2016. (ENG., Illus.). 96p. (YA). pap. 15.99 (978-0-310-75739-9(8)) Zondervan.

Zondervan Staff. God's Great Creation, 1 vol. Miles, David, illus. 2014. (I Can Read! / Adventure Bible Ser.). (ENG.). 32p. (J). pap. 3.99 (978-0-310-73238-9(7)) Zondervan.

—Jungle Beasts, 1 vol. 2011. (I Can Read! / Made by God Ser.). (ENG.). 32p. (J). pap. 3.99 (978-0-310-72191-8(1)) Zonderkidz.

—Polar Pals, 1 vol. 2011. (I Can Read! / Made by God Ser.). (ENG.). 32p. (J). pap. 3.99 (978-0-310-72188-8(1)) Zonderkidz.

—Sea Creatures, 1 vol. 2011. (I Can Read! / Made by God Ser.). (ENG., Illus.). 32p. (J). (gr. -1-2). pap. 3.99 (978-0-310-72183-3(0)) Zonderkidz.

—Wilderness Discoveries, Volume 1: Sand, Snakes, & Screeching Birds, 1 vol. 2013. (Nature of God Ser.). (ENG.). (J). 7.99 *(978-0-310-88834-5(4))* Zonderkidz.
Zondervan Staff & Schriemer, Peter. Ocean Adventures, Volume 3: Winged Creatures, Waterfalls, & Wild Reptiles, 1 vol. 2013. (Nature of God Ser.). (ENG.). (J). 7.99 *(978-0-310-88833-8(6))* Zonderkidz.
—Wilderness Discoveries, Volume 2: Forest, Frogs, & Feisty Critters, 1 vol. 2013. (Nature of God Ser.). (ENG.). (J). 7.99 *(978-0-310-88835-2(2))* Zonderkidz.
—Wilderness Discoveries, Volume 3: Bugs, Bogs, & Spiky Beasts, 1 vol. 2013. (Nature of God Ser.). (ENG.). (J). 7.99 *(978-0-310-88836-9(0))* Zonderkidz.

CREATION (LITERARY, ARTISTIC, ETC.)

Ajmera, Maya & Ivanko, John D. To Be an Artist. 2004. (ENG., Illus.). 32p. (J). (gr. -1-3). 16.95 *(978-1-57091-503-1(2))* Charlesbridge Publishing, Inc.
Ashman, Sarah & Parent, Nancy. Holly Bloom's Garden. Mitchell, Lori, illus. 2008. (ENG.). 32p. (J). (gr. k-3). pap. 7.95 *(978-0-9799746-0-1(7))* Flashlight Pr.
Bao, Julie. A Loving Teacher Forever: A True Story of Loving Children, Defying Fate & Achieving Teaching Excellence. 2004. (Illus.). 32p. (J). 15.00 *(978-0-9748890-0-9(8))* Dings Bks.
Berry, Joy. Be Creative. 2005. (Winning skills series, work It! Ser.). (ENG., Illus.). 48p. (J). pap. 3.95 *(978-1-57687-282-6(3),* PowerHouse Kids) powerHouse Cultural Entertainment, Inc.
Creative Careers. 2014. (Creative Careers Ser.). 48p. (J). (gr. 4-8). 191.70 *(978-1-4824-1184-3(9))* Stevens, Gareth Publishing LLLP.
Edgar, Susan E. & Edgar, Kathleen J. 50 American Women of Courage & Vision. 2007. (Illus.). 288p. (J). *(978-1-58865-391-8(9))* Kidsbooks, LLC.
Glenn, Lexi & Nia. My Invention: How Lexi Glenn, a fourth grader, came up with an idea & got it in toy stores all over the world. A story of how you must first believe in Yourself. 2011. 32p. 12.99 *(978-1-4389-3949-0(3))* AuthorHouse.
Green, Marilyn. My Anytime Anywhere Autograph Book. 2003. (ENG., Illus.). 66p. (J). (gr. 3-18). 12.95 *(978-1-57054-954-0(0))* Klutz.
Haas, Carolyn B. Big Book of Fun: Creative Learning Activities for Home & School. Phillips, Jane B., illus. 2nd ed. 2003. 288p. (J). (gr. -1-7). reprint ed. pap. 14.95 *(978-1-55652-020-4(4))* Chicago Review Pr., Inc.
Kenney, Sean. Cool Creations in 35 Pieces. Kenney, Sean, illus. 2013. (ENG., Illus.). 32p. (J). (gr. -1-3). 14.99 *(978-0-8050-9692-7(2),* 9780805096927, Holt, Henry & Co. Bks. For Young Readers) Holt, Henry & Co.
Mahaney, Ian F. Author, 1 vol. 2015. (Best Job Ever Ser.). (ENG.). 24p. (J). 23.60 *(978-1-4994-0106-6(X),* PowerKids Pr.) Rosen Publishing Group, Inc., The.
Marsh, Carole. Heroes & Helpers. 2004. (Heroes & Helper Ser.). 48p. (J). (gr. 2-6). pap., act. bk. ed. 9.95 *(978-0-635-01094-0(1))* Gallopade International.
Murphy, Patricia J. Creative Minds. 2005. (Real Deal Ser.). (Illus.). 32p. (J). *(978-0-7608-9637-2(2))* Sundance/Newbridge Educational Publishing.
Nobisso, Josephine. Show; Don't Tell! Secrets of Writing. Montanari, Eva, illus. 2004. (ENG.). 40p. (J). (gr. 2-6). 28.95 *(978-0-940112-13-1(2))* Gingerbread Hse.
Ortega, Julian G. Warrior Inspiration. 2010. 152p. pap. 11.95 *(978-1-59330-659-5(8))* Aventine Pr.
Phillips, Karen. Doodle Journal: My Life in Scribbles. 2010. (ENG., Illus.). 76p. (J). (gr. 3-18). 16.95 *(978-1-59174-736-9(8))* Klutz.
Phillips, Vivian A. Show & Tell: Education. Date not set. (Illus.). 10p. (Orig.). (J). pap. *(978-1-888413-00-7(X))* Seasoning Quilting (Arts & Crafts).
Polar (Gr. PreK-5) 2003. (J). *(978-1-58232-025-0(X))* ECS Learning Systems, Inc.
Schuller, Kathleen. How to Be a Hero - for Boys: Inspiration from Classic Heroes. 2013. 72p. 19.95 *(978-1-4575-1796-9(5))* Dog Ear Publishing, LLC.
—How to Be a Heroine — -For Girls: Inspiration from Classic Heroines. 2013. 68p. pap. 9.95 *(978-1-4575-1906-2(2))* Dog Ear Publishing, LLC.
Snow, Todd. You Are Creative. Strong, Melodee, illus. 2007. (ENG.). 24p. (J). bds. 7.99 *(978-1-934277-07-2(X))* Mam Green Publishing, Inc.
Soley, Liesel. Can You Be an Artist? Soley, Liesel, illus. 2011. (Illus.). 28p. (J). (gr. -1-3). 16.95 *(978-1-935359-69-2(X))* Book Pubs. Network.
Sterling, Kristin. Mary Mcleod Bethune. 2008. pap. 40.95 *(978-0-8225-9474-1(9))* Lerner Publishing Group.

CREATION—POETRY

Alexander, Cecil F. All Things Bright & Beautiful. Bryan, Ashley, illus. 2010. (ENG.). 40p. (J). (gr. -1-3). 17.99 *(978-1-4169-8939-4(0),* Atheneum Bks. for Young Readers) Simon & Schuster Children's Publishing.
Brady, Janeen. The Creation. Oswald, Bonnie, illus. 2008. (J). 16.99 *(978-1-59955-139-5(X))* Cedar Fort, Inc./CFI Distribution.
Carlstrom, Nancy White. Glory. Jenkins, Debra Reid, illus. 2004. 32p. (J). (gr. -1-3). 17.00 *(978-0-8028-5143-7(6))* Eerdmans, William B. Publishing Co.

CREATIVENESS

see Creation (Literary, Artistic, etc.)

CREDIBILITY

see Truthfulness and Falsehood

CREDIT

see also Banks and Banking

Blohm, Craig E. Teen Guide to Credit & Debt. 2016. (ENG.). 64p. (J). (gr. 5-12). lib. bdg. *(978-1-68282-080-3(7))* ReferencePoint Pr., Inc.
Challen, Paul & Cipriano, Jeri. How Do Mortgages, Loans, & Credit Work? 2009. (ENG., Illus.). 32p. (J). (gr. 2-5). lib. bdg. *(978-0-7787-4445-0(0))* Crabtree Publishing Co.
Connolly, Sean. Insurance. 2010. (World Economy Explained Ser.). (Illus.). 48p. (YA). (gr. 7-12). 35.65 *(978-1-60753-078-7(3))* Amicus Publishing.
—Insurance. 2012. (Illus.). 48p. (gr. 6-10). pap. 9.95 *(978-1-926722-76-4(0))* Saunders Bk. Co. CAN. Dist: RiverStream Publishing.
—Money & Credit. 2010. (World Economy Explained Ser.). 48p. (YA). (gr. 7-12). 35.65 *(978-1-60753-081-7(3))* Amicus Publishing.
—Money & Credit. 2012. (Illus.). 48p. (gr. 6-10). pap. 9.95 *(978-1-926722-79-5(5))* Saunders Bk. Co. CAN. Dist: RiverStream Publishing.
Connolly, Sean & Claybourne, Anna. Insurance. 2011. (On the Edge Ser.). 32p. (YA). (gr. 3-6). 28.50 *(978-1-59920-519-9(X))* Black Rabbit Bks.
Donovan, Sandra. Budgeting Smarts: How to Set Goals, Save Money, Spend Wisely, & More. 2012. (USA TODAY Teen Wise Guides: Time, Money, & Relationships Ser.). (ENG.). 64p. (gr. 8-12). lib. bdg. 31.93 *(978-0-7613-7016-1(1))* Lerner Publishing Group.
Flatt, Andy. Penny Wise Finds Out about Borrowing - Pupil's Book: Penny Is Ten & Wants to Know What Money Is All about & Why Grown-Ups Make Such a Fuss about It. 2014. (ENG.). 24p. (C). pap. 4.50 *(978-1-85741-102-7(1))* Parkwest Pubns., Inc.
Fradin, Dennis Brindell & Fradin, Judith Bloom. Borrowing. 2010. (Money Smart Ser.). 64p. (gr. 4). 32.79 *(978-1-60870-122-3(0))* Marshall Cavendish Corp.
Hollander, Barbara. How Credit Crises Happen. 2010. (Real World Economics Ser.). (ENG.). 80p. (YA). lib. bdg. 33.25 *(978-1-4358-9461-7(8))* Rosen Publishing Group, Inc., The.
—What Are Saving & Spending? 2016. (Let's Find Out! Ser.). (ENG.). 32p. (J). (gr. 3-2). lib. bdg. 24.45 *(978-1-68048-405-2(2))* Rosen Publishing Group, Inc., The.
Houghton, Gillian. How Credit Cards Work. 2009. (Invest Kids Ser.). 24p. (gr. 2-3). 42.50 *(978-1-61513-623-0(1),* PowerKids Pr.) Rosen Publishing Group, Inc., The.
Kowalski, Kathiann M. Be Smart about Credit: Credit & Debt Management. 2014. (Be Smart about Money & Financial Literacy Ser.). 48p. (J). lib. bdg. 22.60 *(978-0-7660-4282-7(0))* Enslow Pubs., Inc.
Lynette, Rachel. What to Do When Your Family Is in Debt. 2010. (Let's Work It Out Ser.). 24p. (J). (ENG.). pap. 8.25 *(978-1-4358-9770-0(6),* PowerKids Pr.); (Illus.). (gr. 2-5). lib. bdg. 22.60 *(978-1-4358-9341-2(7))* Rosen Publishing Group, Inc., The.
Marsico, Katie. Using Credit Wisely. 2015. (21st Century Skills Library: Real World Math Ser.). (ENG., Illus.). 32p. (J). (gr. 4-7). 29.93 *(978-1-63362-578-5(8),* 206496) Cherry Lake Publishing.
McGuire, Kara. Smart Spending: The Teens' Guide to Cash, Credit, & Life's Costs, 1 vol. 2014. (Financial Literacy for Teens Ser.). (ENG.). 64p. (gr. 6-7). lib. bdg. 33.99 *(978-0-7565-4923-7(X),* CPB Grades 4-8) Compass Point Bks.
Minden, Cecilia. Using Credit Wisely. 2007. (21st Century Skills Library: Real World Math Ser.). (ENG., Illus.). 32p. (gr. 4-8). lib. bdg. 28.50 *(978-1-60279-002-5(7),* 200074) Cherry Lake Publishing.
Mooney, Carla. Understanding Credit. 2015. (Searchlight Books (tm) — How Do We Use Money? Ser.). (ENG., Illus.). 40p. (gr. 3-5). 39.99 *(978-1-4677-8917-2(8),* Lerner Digital); (J). pap. 8.99 *(978-1-4677-6106-2(0),* Lerner Pubns.); (J). lib. bdg. 27.99 *(978-1-4677-5229-9(0),* Lerner Pubns.) Lerner Publishing Group.
Morgan, Sally. Earth's Energy Sources. 2011. (Earth Cycles Ser.). 32p. (YA). (gr. 3-6). lib. bdg. 28.50 *(978-1-59920-522-9(X))* Black Rabbit Bks.
Randolph, Ryan P. How to Use Credit. 2013. (Smart Kid's Guide to Personal Finance Ser.). 24p. (J). (gr. 3-6). 22.60 *(978-1-4777-0744-9(1));* pap. 8.25 *(978-1-4777-0829-3(4));* pap. 49.50 *(978-1-4777-0830-9(8))* Rosen Publishing Group, Inc., The. (PowerKids Pr.).
Shea, Therese. Top 10 Secrets for Managing Credit Cards & Paying Bills Successfully. 2013. (Student's Guide to Financial Empowerment Ser.). (ENG., Illus.). 64p. (YA). (gr. 7-12). pap. 12.95 *(978-1-4488-9376-8(3));* lib. bdg. 31.95 *(978-1-4488-9358-4(5))* Rosen Publishing Group, Inc., The. (Rosen Classroom).
Thompson, Helen. Understanding Credit. 2010. (Junior Library of Money). 64p. (YA). (gr. 7-18). lib. bdg. 22.95 *(978-1-4222-1772-6(8))* Mason Crest.
Tomljanovic, Tatiana. Borrowing. 2009. (Everyday Economics Ser.). (Illus.). 32p. (J). (gr. 4-6). pap. 9.95 *(978-1-60596-646-5(0));* lib. bdg. 26.00 *(978-1-60596-645-8(2))* Weigl Pubs., Inc.
Top 10 Secrets for Managing Credit Cards & Paying Bills Successfully. 2013. (Student's Guide to Financial Empowerment Ser.). 64p. (YA). (gr. 7-12). pap. 77.70 *(978-1-4488-9377-5(1))* Rosen Publishing Group, Inc., The.

CREEDS—COMPARATIVE STUDIES

Baynes, Pauline, illus. I Believe: The Nicene Creed. 2004. 32p. (YA). (gr. 3-18). 16.00 *(978-0-8028-5258-8(0))* Eerdmans, William B. Publishing Co.

CRESTS

see Heraldry

CRETE (GREECE)—FICTION

O'Neill, Katrina. Protecting the Sunken City. 2007. (Illus.). 52p. (J). pap. *(978-1-4207-0724-3(8))* Sundance/Newbridge Educational Publishing.
Shepherd, Deborah. A Thread Through Time. 2013. 102p. pap. *(978-0-9571756-5-5(5))* Shepline Words.

CREWE, SARA (FICTITIOUS CHARACTER)—FICTION

Burnett, Frances Hodgson. A Little Princess. 2008. 156p. 25.95 *(978-1-60664-768-4(7));* pap. 13.95 *(978-1-60664-141-5(7))* Aegypan.
—A Little Princess. 2008. 212p. (gr. 2-4). 27.99 *(978-0-554-29155-0(X));* 24.99 *(978-0-554-38458-0(2))* Creative Media Partners, LLC.
—A Little Princess. Aldous, Kate, illus. 2005. 62p. (J). (gr. 4-7). 8.95 *(978-0-7945-1123-4(6),* Usborne) EDC Publishing.
—A Little Princess. 2012. (ENG., Illus.). 280p. *(978-1-905716-04-3(4),* Collector's Library, The) Pan Macmillan.
—A Little Princess. Gill, Margery, illus. 2008. (Puffin Classics Ser.). (ENG.). 320p. (J). (gr. 5-7). 5.99 *(978-0-14-132112-7(1),* Puffin Books) Penguin Young Readers Group.
—A Little Princess. 188p. 2009. pap. 13.95 *(978-1-4385-0876-4(X))* 2008. pap. 13.45 *(978-1-4385-0194-9(3))* Standard Pubns., Inc. (Book Jungle).
—A Little Princess. McKowen, Scott, illus. 2004. (Sterling Unabridged Classics Ser.). (ENG.). 208p. (J). (gr. 5). 9.95 *(978-1-4027-1454-2(8))* Sterling Publishing Co., Inc.
—A Little Princess. Engelbreit, Mary, illus. 2007. (Mary Engelbreit's Classic Library). (ENG.). 304p. (J). (gr. 3-7). 9.99 *(978-0-06-008137-9(6),* HarperFestival) HarperCollins Pubs.
—A Little Princess. 2012. (Children's Classics Ser.). (ENG.). 186p. pap. 19.99 *(978-1-909438-52-1(9),* Sovereign) Bollinger, Max GBR. Dist: Lightning Source UK, Ltd.
—A Little Princess. Kliros, Thea, illus. abr. ed. 2012. (Dover Children's Thrift Classics Ser.). (ENG.). 96p. (J). (gr. 3-8). pap. 3.00 *(978-0-486-29171-0(5))* Dover Pubns., Inc.
—A Little Princess: Being the whole story of Sara Crewe now told for T. 2007. 196p. per. 19.99 *(978-1-4346-7028-1(7));* (ENG.). 210p. per. 22.99 *(978-1-4346-7029-8(5))* Creative Media Partners, LLC.
—A Little Princess: The Story of Sara Crewe. (J). 16.95 *(978-0-8488-1253-9(0))* Amereon Ltd.
—A Little Princess: The Story of Sara Crewe. Warren, Eliza, ed. Marcos, Pablo, illus. 2006. 239p. (YA). reprint ed. 10.00 *(978-0-7567-9835-2(3))* DIANE Publishing Co.
—A Little Princess: The Story of Sara Crewe. 2005. 112p. per. 4.95 *(978-1-4209-2529-6(6))* Digireads.com Publishing.
—A Little Princess: The Story of Sara Crewe. 2006. pap. *(978-1-4065-0559-7(5))* Dodo Pr.
—A Little Princess: The Story of Sara Crewe. l.t. ed. 2005. 376p. pap. *(978-1-84637-117-2(1))* Echo Library.
—A Little Princess: The Story of Sara Crewe. 2004. reprint ed. pap. 22.95 *(978-1-4191-0213-4(3));* pap. 1.99 *(978-1-4192-0213-1(8))* Kessinger Publishing, LLC.
—A Little Princess: The Story of Sara Crewe. 2006. 204p. (YA). 19.95 *(978-1-934169-20-9(X));* pap. 7.95 *(978-1-934169-21-6(8))* Norilana Bks.
—A Little Princess: The Story of Sara Crewe. 2005. (Twelve-Point Ser.). lib. bdg. 25.00 *(978-1-58287-320-6(8));* lib. bdg. 26.00 *(978-1-58287-814-0(5))* North Bks.
—A Little Princess: The Story of Sara Crewe. Rust, Graham, illus. (J). pap. 22.95 *(978-0-590-24079-6(X))* Scholastic, Inc.
—A Little Princess: The Story of Sara Crewe. l.t. ed. 2003. 342p. pap. 10.95 *(978-0-7862-6247-2(8))* Thorndike Pr.
—A Little Princess: With a Discussion of Generosity. Gribbon, Sean & Jael, trs. Gribbon, Sean & Jael, illus. 2003. (Values in Action Illustrated Classics Ser.). (J). *(978-1-59203-050-7(5))* Learning Challenge, Inc.
Zamorsky, Tania & Burnett, Frances Hodgson. A Little Princess. Corvino, Lucy, illus. 2005. (Classic Starts(tm) Ser.). (ENG.). 160p. (J). (gr. 2-4). 6.95 *(978-1-4027-1275-3(8))* Sterling Publishing Co., Inc.

CRICKET

Bodden, Valerie. Crickets. 2011. (Creepy Creatures Ser.). (ENG.). 24p. (J). (gr. 1-3). pap. 8.99 *(978-0-89812-566-5(9),* Creative Paperbacks) Creative Co., The.
Gifford, Clive. Cricket. 2016. (Great Sporting Events Ser.). (ENG., Illus.). 32p. (J). (gr. 4-6). pap. 11.99 *(978-1-4451-4962-2(1),* Franklin Watts) Hachette Children's Group GBR. Dist: Hachette Bk. Group.
Greenwood, Mark. Boomerang & Bat: The Story of the Real First Eleven. Denton, Terry, illus. 2016. (ENG.). 32p. (J). (gr. 2-7). 24.99 *(978-1-74331-924-6(X))* Allen & Unwin AUS. Dist: Independent Pubs. Group.
Hunter, Nick & Collins UK Staff. Greatest Ashes Moments. 2017. (ENG., Illus.). 48p. (J). (gr. 3-4). pap. 9.95 *(978-0-00-816387-7(1))* HarperCollins Pubs. Ltd. GBR. Dist: Independent Pubs. Group.
Oxlade, Chris. Cricket. 2017. (Sports Skills Ser.). (ENG., Illus.). 32p. (J). (gr. 4-6). pap. 12.99 ***(978-1-4451-5243-1(6),*** Franklin Watts) Hachette Children's Group GBR. Dist: Hachette Bk. Group.
Ricketts, Harry. How to Catch a Cricket Match. 9th ed. 2006. (Ginger Ser.). (ENG., Illus.). 160p. per. 16.95 *(978-0-9582629-0-3(X))* Awa Pr. NZL. Dist: Independent Pubs. Group.
Sellers, Luke. Complete Skills - Cricket. 2015. (Know the Game Ser.). (ENG., Illus.). 96p. pap. 16.00 *(978-1-4729-1958-8(0),* 9781472919588) Bloomsbury Publishing USA.
Vass, Coral. Meet... Don Bradman. Howe, Brad, illus. 2016. (ENG.). 32p. (J). (gr. k-2). 22.99 *(978-1-925324-89-1(3))* Random Hse. Australia AUS. Dist: Independent Pubs. Group.
Way, Edward. Cricket. 2017. (Get Sporty Ser.). (ENG., Illus.). 32p. (J). (gr. 2-4). pap. 11.99 *(978-0-7502-9488-1(4),* Wayland) Hachette Children's Group GBR. Dist: Hachette Bk. Group.

CRICKET—FICTION

Bishop, Clive. Trophy Trouble. 2009. 74p. pap. 9.99 *(978-1-60860-547-7(7),* Strategic Bk. Publishing) Strategic Book Publishing & Rights Agency (SBPRA).
Brashear-Hopper, Celia. The Curious Cricket. 2005. (J). lib. bdg. 15.95 *(978-0-9765467-8-8(7))* Creative Bk. Pubs.
Buckeridge, Anthony. Jennings in Particular. 2008. (Jennings Ser.: 17). (ENG.). 164p. (J). (gr. -1-12). pap. 12.95 *(978-0-7551-0160-3(X))* House of Stratus, Inc. GBR. Dist: Gardners Bks. Ltd.
Carbon, Sally & Langer, Justin. I Want to Be a Cricketer. Gollan, Stewart, illus. 2008. 32p. (J). pap. 16.95 *(978-1-921361-24-1(7))* Fremantle Pr. AUS. Dist: Independent Pubs. Group.
Cattell, Bob & Agard, John. Butter-Finger. Smy, Pam, illus. 2006. (ENG.). 128p. (J). (gr. 2-17). per. 7.95 *(978-1-84507-376-3(2),* Frances Lincoln) Quarto Publishing Group UK GBR. Dist: Hachette Bk. Group.
Christi, C. C. Gorge the Fart. 2012. 16p. pap. 15.99 *(978-1-4772-5401-1(3))* AuthorHouse.
Crandell, Bethany. Summer on the Short Bus. 2014. (ENG.). 256p. (YA). (gr. 2-17). pap. 9.95 *(978-0-7624-4951-4(9),* Running Pr. Kids) Running Pr. Bk. Pubs.
English, David. Confessions of a Dedicated Englishman, 1. unabr. ed. 2006. (ENG., Illus.). 352p. 44.50 *(978-1-4050-5361-7(5))* Macmillan Pubs., Ltd. GBR. Dist: Trans-Atlantic Pubns., Inc.
Hennessey, David G. A Cricket's Christmas: the Bethlehem Story. 2009. 151p. pap. 15.30 *(978-0-557-04685-0(8))* Lulu Pr., Inc.
Kuperman, Joshua & Kuperman, Laura. The Little Lost Cricket. 2011. 20p. 11.59 *(978-1-4269-5486-3(7))* Trafford Publishing.
Loughlin, Patrick/Maxwell. Glenn Maxwell 1 & 2 Bindup. 2016. (Glenn Maxwell Ser.). (ENG., Illus.). 384p. (J). (gr. 3-6). pap. 17.99 *(978-0-85798-886-7(7))* Random Hse. Australia AUS. Dist: Independent Pubs. Group.
—Glenn Maxwell 3 & 4 Bindup. 2016. (Glenn Maxwell Ser.). (ENG., Illus.). 384p. (J). (gr. 3-6). pap. 17.99 *(978-0-85798-888-1(3))* Random Hse. Australia AUS. Dist: Independent Pubs. Group.
Lutterbach, Johanna. Little Orly & the Cricket. Polchlopek, Mary Ann, illus. 2008. 24p. pap. 11.49 *(978-1-4389-0656-0(0))* AuthorHouse.
Marks, Jeannette. The Cheerful Cricket & Others. 2004. reprint ed. pap. 1.99 *(978-1-4192-5649-3(1));* pap. 15.95 *(978-1-4191-5649-6(7))* Kessinger Publishing, LLC.
May, Chris. A Cricketing Dream. 2012. 64p. pap. 15.99 *(978-1-4797-1498-8(4))* Xlibris Corp.
Mayfield, Marilee Joy. The Golden Cricket: A Story of Luck & Prosperity. 2004. 48p. (J). lib. bdg. 19.95 *(978-0-9659222-7-2(8))* Leaping Antelope Productions.
Mooring, John L. Cricket's Chronicles: The Third Grade Science Fair. 2010. 24p. pap. 12.99 *(978-1-4490-3278-4(8))* AuthorHouse.
Moxilada, J. L. Jonty Jones Takes Guard. 2005. 242p. pap. 16.88 *(978-1-4116-4126-6(4))* Lulu Pr., Inc.
Panckridge, Michael & Lee, Brett. Toby Jones & the Clash with Father Time. 5th ed. 2007. 208p. *(978-0-207-20047-2(5))* HarperCollins Pubs. Australia.
Parkinson, Helen. How Well Can Wombats Bat? 2012. 28p. pap. 32.70 *(978-1-4797-2235-8(9))* Xlibris Corp.
Thomas, G. D. Keep Your Head Down. 2012. 160p. pap. 11.00 *(978-1-78035-281-7(6),* Fastprint Publishing) Upfront Publishing Ltd. GBR. Dist: Printondemand-worldwide.com.
Walker, Cindy, illus. Serenade of the Cricket. 2nd ed. 2004. (J). 12.95 *(978-1-59655-000-1(7))* Cooper Publishing.
Wodehouse, P. G. Mike at Wrykyn. 2013. 189p. reprint ed. lthr. 69.00 *(978-0-7426-3265-3(2))* Classic Bks.
Wunsch, Andrew. Let's Play Cricket! 2011. 32p. pap. 32.70 *(978-1-4568-5409-6(7))* Xlibris Corp.

CRICKETS

Bluemel Oldfield, Dawn. Inside the Cricket's Burrow. 2013. (Science Slam: Snug As a Bug-Where Bugs Live Ser.). 24p. (J). (gr. -1-3). lib. bdg. 23.93 *(978-1-61772-906-5(X))* Bearport Publishing Co., Inc.
Bodden, Valerie. Crickets. 2011. (Creepy Creatures Ser.). 24p. (J). (gr. 1-3). 24.25 *(978-1-58341-993-9(4),* Creative Education) Creative Co., The.
—Crickets. 2010. (ENG., Illus.). 24p. (J). *(978-1-926853-73-4(3))* Saunders Bk. Co. CAN. Dist: Creative Co., The.
Clapper, Nikki Bruno. Crickets. 2015. (Creepy Crawlers Ser.). (ENG., Illus.). 24p. (J). (gr. k-1). lib. bdg. 26.65 *(978-1-4914-6217-1(5))* Capstone Press of Coughlan Cos.
Collins, Nancy. All about Tree Crickets. 2013. (ENG.). 52p. 14.95 *(978-1-4787-0134-7(X))* Outskirts Pr., Inc.
Glaser, Linda. Singing Crickets. Feltes, Tess, illus. 2009. (Linda Glaser's Classic Creatures Ser.). (ENG.). 32p. (gr. k-3). 22.60 *(978-0-8225-8806-1(4),* Millbrook Pr.) Lerner Publishing Group.
Gonzales, Doreen. Crickets in the Dark. 2009. 24p. (YA). pap. 8.25 *(978-1-4358-3253-4(1));* (Illus.). (J). (gr. 1-3). 22.60 *(978-1-4042-8098-4(7))* Rosen Publishing Group, Inc., The.
Loewen, Nancy. Chirp, Chirp! Crickets in Your Backyard. Peterson, Rick, illus. 2005. (Backyard Bugs Ser.). (ENG.). 24p. (gr. -1-3). lib. bdg. 26.65 *(978-1-4048-1141-6(9))* Picture Window Bks.
Murray, Laura K. Crickets. 2015. (Illus.). 32p. (J). *(978-1-60818-580-1(X),* Creative Education) Creative Co., The.
—Crickets: Seedlings. 2016. (Seedlings Ser.). (ENG.). 24p. (J). (gr. k-2). pap. 7.99 *(978-1-62832-185-2(7),* Creative Paperbacks) Creative Co., The.
Schuh, Mari. Crickets. 2013. (ENG., Illus.). 24p. (J). lib. bdg. 25.65 *(978-1-62031-054-0(6))* Jump! Inc.
Shoulders, Michael. Katydid. 2015. (21st Century Junior Library: Creepy Crawly Critters Ser.). (ENG., Illus.). 24p. (J). (gr. k-3). 27.07 *(978-1-63362-592-1(3),* 206552) Cherry Lake Publishing.
Shusterman, Danielle. Grasshoppers & Crickets. 2015. (1G Bugs Ser.). (ENG., Illus.). 28p. (J). pap. 5.99 *(978-1-63437-111-7(9))* American Reading Co.
Silverman, Buffy. Can You Tell a Cricket from a Grasshopper? 2012. (Animal Look-Alikes Ser.). 32p. (gr. k-2). pap. 45.32 *(978-0-7613-9254-5(8));* (ENG.). pap. 7.95 *(978-0-7613-8553-0(3));* (ENG.). lib. bdg. 26.60 *(978-0-7613-6736-9(5),* Lerner Pubns.) Lerner Publishing Group.
Squire, Ann O. Crickets & Grasshoppers. 2004. (True Bks.). (ENG.). 48p. (J). (gr. 3-5). pap. 6.95 *(978-0-516-29357-8(5),* Children's Pr.) Scholastic Library Publishing.
Woodward, John. Cricket. 2010. (Garden Minibeasts up Close Ser.). 32p. (gr. 2-4). 30.00 *(978-1-60413-902-0(1),* Chelsea Clubhouse) Facts On File, Inc.

CRICKETS—FICTION

Carle, Eric. The Very Quiet Cricket. Carle, Eric, illus. 2014. (Penguin Young Readers, Level 3 Ser.). (ENG., Illus.). 32p. (J). (gr. 1-3). pap. 3.99 *(978-0-448-48138-8(3),* Penguin Young Readers) Penguin Young Readers Group.
Delessert, Etienne. Yok-Yok, 12 bks., Set. Delessert, Etienne, illus. Incl. At Home. lib. bdg. 14.60 *(978-0-88682-646-8(2),* 97934-098); Best Friends. lib. bdg. 14.60 *(978-0-88682-639-0(X),* 97927-098); For the Birds. lib. bdg. 14.60 *(978-0-88682-638-3(1),* 97926-098); Moonlight. lib. bdg. 14.60 *(978-0-88682-648-2(9),* 97936-098); Nonsense. lib. bdg. 14.60 *(978-0-88682-641-3(1),* 97929-098); Nuts! lib. bdg. 14.60 *(978-0-88682-644-4(6),* 97932-098); Surprises. lib. bdg. 14.60 *(978-0-88682-643-7(8),* 97931-098); Weird? lib. bdg. 14.60 *(978-0-88682-645-1(4),* 97933-098); What a Circus! lib. bdg. 14.95 *(978-0-88682-640-6(3),* 97928-098); 32p. (J). (gr. 1-5). 1993. (Illus.). lib. bdg. o.p. *(978-0-88682-637-6(3),* Creative Education) Creative Co., The.
Elliott, David. The Cool Crazy Crickets to the Rescue. Meisel, Paul, illus. 2010. (ENG.). 48p. (J). (gr. 1-4). 5.99 *(978-0-7636-4658-5(X))* Candlewick Pr.
Holman, Felice. The Cricket Winter. Thomas, Robyn, illus. 2006. 91p. (J). (gr. 3-7). 15.00 *(978-0-8028-5289-2(0),*

C D

Eerdmans Bks For Young Readers) Eerdmans, William B. Publishing Co.

Moghee, Alison. Firefly Hollow. Denise, Christopher, illus. 2015. (ENG.). 304p. (J). (gr. 3-7). 16.99 *(978-1-4424-2336-7(6),* Atheneum Bks. for Young Readers) Simon & Schuster Children's Publishing.

Moulton, Mark Kimball. A Cricket's Carol. Blowers, Lisa, illus. 2004. 32p. (J). 14.95 *(978-0-8249-5488-8(2),* Ideal Pubns.) Worthy Publishing.

Perry, Ellyse;Clark. Double Time. 2017. (Ellyse Perry Ser.: 4). (ENG.). 160p. (J). (gr. 4-7). 12.99 *(978-0-14-378130-1(8))* Random Hse. Australia AUS. Dist: Independent Pubs. Group.

Phanton, Rick. Boston & the Bean. 2012. 112p. pap. 19.95 *(978-1-4626-4809-2(6))* America Star Bks.

Pritchard, Gabby. Lost! Blue Band. Stuart, Jon, illus. 2016. (Cambridge Reading Adventures Ser.). (ENG.). 16p. pap. 6.56 *(978-1-316-60078-8(5))* Cambridge Univ. Pr.

Regnew, Tera. Christopher Cricket's Christmas. 2011. 16p. pap. *(978-1-4269-9687-0(X))* Trafford Publishing (UK) Ltd.

Russell-Gilmer, Phyllis A. Where Do Crickets Go When Winter Comes? Jones, Chamira, illus. 2009. 32p. (J). 16.95 *(978-1-934363-10-2(3))* Zoe Life Publishing.

Selden, George. The Cricket in Times Square. Williams, Garth, illus. (Chester Cricket Ser.). 151p. (J). (gr. 3-6). pap. 5.50 *(978-0-8072-8311-0(8),* Listening Library) Random Hse. Audio Publishing Group.

—The Cricket in Times Square. unabr. ed. 2004. (Chester Cricket Ser.). 151p. (J). (gr. 3-7). pap. 29.00 incl. audio *(978-0-8072-8310-3(X),* S YA 158 SP, Listening Library) Random Hse. Audio Publishing Group.

—The Cricket in Times Square. Williams, Garth, illus. 2008. (Chester Cricket & His Friends Ser.: 1). (ENG.). 144p. (J). (gr. 1-4). pap. 6.99 *(978-0-312-38003-8(8),* 9780312380038) Square Fish.

—Tucker's Countryside. Williams, Garth, illus. 2012. (ENG.). 192p. (J). (gr. 3-7). pap. 7.99 *(978-1-250-00256-3(7),* 9781250002563) Square Fish.

Smith, Sindy. Ervin & Alma's Little Mouse House. 2013. 38p. 24.95 *(978-1-63004-209-7(9));* 40p. pap. 24.95 *(978-1-62709-189-3(0))* America Star Bks.

Stevens, A. P. The Volcano: The Adventures of Antboy & Mr Cricket. Finn, N. K., ed. Deskcube, illus. 2008. (ENG.). 29p. pap. 9.95 *(978-0-9798886-0-1(3))* Mugsy and Sugar Pressed.

Tarr, Rebecca M. My Cricket & Me. 2008. 32p. pap. 24.95 *(978-1-60474-622-8(X))* America Star Bks.

Waring, Geoff. Oscar & the Cricket: A Book about Moving & Rolling. Waring, Geoff, illus. 2009. (Start with Science Ser.). (ENG., Illus.). 32p. (J). (gr. -1-3). pap. 6.99 *(978-0-7636-4512-0(5))* Candlewick Pr.

Wheeler, Lisa. Old Cricket. Goembel, Ponder, illus. (ENG.). 32p. (J). (gr. -1-1). 2003. 18.99 *(978-0-689-84510-9(3),* Atheneum/Richard Jackson Bks.) 2006. reprint ed. 7.99 *(978-1-4169-1855-4(8),* Atheneum Bks. for Young Readers) Simon & Schuster Children's Publishing.

Williams, Mavis E. A Cricket. 2009. 24p. pap. 11,99 *(978-1-4389-7714-0(X))* AuthorHouse.

CRIME

see also Computer Crimes; Criminal Law; Criminals; Justice, Administration of; Juvenile Delinquency; Sex Crimes

Allman, Toney. Poisoning. 2008. (Crime Scene Investigations Ser.). (ENG., Illus.). 128p. (gr. 7-10). lib. bdg. 40.40 *(978-1-4205-0064-6(3),* LML02109-241678, Lucent Bks.) Cengage Gale.

Anderson, Dale. The FBI & Organized Crime. 2009. (FBI Story Ser.). 64p. (J). (gr. 4-7). lib. bdg. 22.95 *(978-1-4222-0565-5(7))* Mason Crest.

—The FBI & White-Collar Crime. 2009. (FBI Story Ser.). 64p. (J). (gr. 4-7). lib. bdg. 22.95 *(978-1-4222-0566-2(5))* Mason Crest.

Anderson, Judith & Vaughan, Jenny. Crime. 2011. (Inside Crime Ser.). 48p. (YA). (gr. 5-9). lib. bdg. 34.25 *(978-1-59920-400-0(2))* Black Rabbit Bks.

Bage, Grant. Crime & Punishment Through the Ages: Band 18/Pearl. 2017. (ENG., Illus.). 80p. (J). pap. 9.99 ***(978-0-00-820899-8(9))*** HarperCollins Pubs. Ltd. GBR. Dist: Independent Pubs. Group.

Ballard, Carol. Crimebusting! Identifying Criminals & Victims. 2009. (Solve That Crime! Ser.). (Illus.). 48p. (J). (gr. 5-9). lib. bdg. 25.27 *(978-0-7660-3375-7(9))* Enslow Pubs., Inc.

Banks, Jewelene. Don't Give That Boy No Gun. 2010. pap. 12.00 *(978-1-61658-990-5(6))* Independent Pub.

Becnel, Barbara, ed. Gangs & Violence: Stanley Tookie Williams Street Peace Series, 8 bks., Vol. 1, Bk. 3. 2008. 24p. (J). 6.95 *(978-0-9753584-4-3(8))* Damamli Publishing Co.

Behnke, Alison. Up for Sale: Human Trafficking & Modern Slavery. 2014. (Illus.). 72p. (gr. 6-12). lib. bdg. 34.60 *(978-1-4677-1611-6(1),* Twenty-First Century Bks.) Lerner Publishing Group.

Berlatsky, Noah. America's Prisons. 2010. (Opposing Viewpoints Ser.). (Illus.). 176-240p. (J). 42.95 *(978-0-7377-4956-4(3));* pap. 29.45 *(978-0-7377-4957-1(1))* Cengage Gale. (Greenhaven Pr., Inc.).

Biskup, Agnieszka. The Science Behind Batman's Tools. Vecchio, Luciano, illus. 2016. (Science Behind Batman Ser.). (ENG.). 24p. (gr. 1-2). lib. bdg. 25.32 *(978-1-5157-2038-6(1),* DC Super Heroes) Stone Arch Bks.

—The Science Behind Batman's Uniform. Vecchio, Luciano, illus. 2016. (Science Behind Batman Ser.). (ENG.). 24p. (gr. 1-2). lib. bdg. 25.32 *(978-1-5157-2031-7(4),* DC Super Heroes) Stone Arch Bks.

Bjorklund, Ruth. Gun Control. 2012. (J). 32.79 *(978-0-7614-4974-4(4))* Marshall Cavendish Corp.

—Gun Control. 2014. (Illus.). 80p. (J). *(978-1-62712-416-4(0))* Musa Publishing.

Blumenthal, Karen. Bootleg: Murder, Moonshine, & the Lawless Years of Prohibition. 2013. (ENG., Illus.). 176p. (YA). (gr. 7-12). pap. 13.99 *(978-1-250-03427-4(2),* 9781250034274) Square Fish.

Bodden, Valerie. Odysseys in Crime Scene Science: at the Scene. 2017. (Odysseys in Crime Scene Science Ser.). (ENG.). 80p. (J). (gr. 7-11). pap. 14.99 ***(978-1-62832-468-6(6),*** Creative Paperbacks) Creative Co., The.

Bontrager, Stephanie. Social Threat or Social Justice? 2007. 164p. per. *(978-3-8364-2950-4(0))* AV Akademikerverlag GmbH & Co. KG.

Brimner, Larry Dane. Birmingham Sunday. 2010. (ENG., Illus.). 48p. (J). (gr. 5-18). 17.95 *(978-1-59078-613-0(0),* Calkins Creek) Boyds Mills Pr.

Brook, Henry. True Stories of Gangsters. McNee, Ian, illus. 2004. (True Adventure Stories Ser.). 144p. (J). pap. 4.95 *(978-0-7945-0722-0(0),* Usborne) EDC Publishing.

Broyles, Janell. Hate Crimes. 2009. (In the News Ser.). 64p. (gr. 6-6). 58.50 *(978-1-61513-468-7(9))* Rosen Publishing Group, Inc., The.

Bruce, Judith. Hate Crimes. 2009. (Issues on Trial Ser.). (ENG., Illus.). 240p. (gr. 10-12). 48.30 *(978-0-7377-4177-3(5),* Greenhaven Pr., Inc.) Cengage Gale.

Bryfonski, Dedria. Human Trafficking. Greenhaven Press Editors, ed. 2013. (Current Controversies Ser.). (ENG., Illus.). 224p. (gr. 10-12). pap. 32.00 *(978-0-7377-6232-7(2));* lib. bdg. 46.40 *(978-0-7377-6231-0(4))* Cengage Gale. (Greenhaven Pr., Inc.).

Campbell, Marilyn & Columbus, Curt. Crime & Punishment. 2004. (YA). pap. 6.50 *(978-1-58342-225-0(0),* CB8) Dramatic Publishing Co.

Coleman, Wim & Perrin, Pat. Racism on Trial: From the Medgar Evers Murder Case to Ghosts of Mississippi. 2009. (Famous Court Cases That Became Movies Ser.). (Illus.). 112p. (J). (gr. 7-12). lib. bdg. 33.27 *(978-0-7660-3059-6(8))* Enslow Pubs., Inc.

Cooke, Tim. Butch Cassidy & the Sundance Kid: Notorious Outlaws of the West. 2016. (Wanted! Famous Outlaws Ser.). (ENG., Illus.). 48p. (J). (gr. 6-8). pap. 14.05 *(978-1-4824-4255-7(8))* Stevens, Gareth Publishing LLLP.

Currie, Stephen. Medieval Punishment & Torture. 2014. (The Library of Medieval Times Ser). (ENG., Illus.). 80p. (J). lib. bdg. *(978-1-60152-658-8(X))* ReferencePoint Pr., Inc.

Diker, Katie. Unsolved Crimes. 2015. (ENG., Illus.). 24p. (J). pap. 8.95 *(978-1-77092-236-5(9))* RiverStream Publishing.

Doeden, Matt. Whistle-Blowers: Exposing Crime & Corruption. 2015. (Illus.). 96p. (J). *(978-1-4677-6312-7(8))* Twenty First Century Bks.

Dowswell, Paul & Fleming, Fergus. Spies. 2008. (Usborne True Stories Ser.). (Illus.). 139p. (J). pap. 4.99 *(978-0-7945-1842-4(7),* Usborne) EDC Publishing.

Dunkell, Barbara & Broyles, Janell. Frequently Asked Questions about Hate Crimes. 2011. (FAQ: Teen Life Ser.). (ENG.). 64p. (YA). (gr. 7-12). lib. bdg. 31.95 *(978-1-4488-5562-9(4))* Rosen Publishing Group, Inc., The.

Dupont, Ellen. Criminal Terminology, Vol. 20. Gomez, Manny, ed. 2016. (Crime & Detection Ser.). (Illus.). 96p. (J). (gr. 7). 24.95 *(978-1-4222-3470-9(3))* Mason Crest.

Durrie, Karen. Safety. 2011. (ENG.). (J). lib. bdg. 27.13 *(978-1-61690-951-2(X))* Weigl Pubs., Inc.

—Seguridad. 2012. (SPA & ENG.). (J). *(978-1-61913-211-5(7))* Weigl Pubs., Inc.

Ellis, Carol & Grayson, Robert. Drug Cartels & Smugglers. 2013. (J). *(978-1-61900-029-2(6))* Eldorado Ink.

Espejo, Roman. Urban America. 2011. (Opposing Viewpoints Ser.). 240p. (J). lib. bdg. 42.95 *(978-0-7377-5249-6(1),* Greenhaven Pr., Inc.) Cengage Gale.

Farrell, Courtney. The Mexican Drug War, 1 vol. 2011. (Essential Issues Set 3 Ser.). (ENG., Illus.). 112p. (J). (gr. 6-12). lib. bdg. 35.64 *(978-1-61783-136-2(0))* ABDO Publishing Co.

Ford, Jean Otto. Rural Crime & Poverty: Violence, Drugs, & Other Issues. 2009. (Youth in Rural North America Ser.). (Illus.). 96p. (YA). (gr. 3-7). lib. bdg. 22.95 *(978-1-4222-0016-2(7))* Mason Crest.

Forrest, Glen C. Police Technology: 21st Century Crime Fighting Tools. 2016. (Law Enforcement & Intelligence Gathering Ser.). 00104p. (YA). (gr. 8-8). lib. bdg. 36.25 *(978-1-5081-0379-0(8))* Rosen Publishing Group, Inc., The.

Friedman, Lauri S. Crime. 2008. (Introducing Issues with Opposing Viewpoints Ser.). (ENG., Illus.). 144p. (gr. 10-12). 42.00 *(978-0-7377-4167-4(8),* Greenhaven Pr., Inc.) Cengage Gale.

—Prisons. Des Chenes, Elizabeth, ed. 2007. (Introducing Issues with Opposing Viewpoints Ser.). (ENG., Illus.). 144p. (gr. 10-12). lib. bdg. 42.00 *(978-0-7377-3578-9(3))* Cengage Gale.

Furgang, Adam. Everything You Need to Know about Gun Violence. 2017. (Need to Know Library). 64p. (J). (gr. 12-11). pap. 12.95 ***(978-1-5081-7402-8(4),*** Rosen Young Adult) Rosen Publishing Group, Inc., The.

Furgang, Kathy. Defeating School Violence, 01 vols., 1. 2016. (Effective Survival Strategies Ser.). (ENG.). 64p. (J). 32.95 *(978-1-4994-6149-7(6),* Rosen Young Adult) Rosen Publishing Group, Inc., The.

Gelletly, LeeAnne. Modern-Day Pirates. 2013. (J). 34.95 *(978-1-61900-037-7(7))* Eldorado Ink.

Gerdes, Louise. Guns & Crime. 2008. (At Issue Ser.). (ENG., Illus.). 91p. (gr. 10-12). pap. 22.50 *(978-0-7377-3919-0(3),* Greenhaven Pr., Inc.); 80-128p. (YA). (gr. 9-12). pap. 31.80 *(978-0-7377-3918-3(5))* Cengage Gale.

Gold, Susan Dudley. Parody of Public Figures: Hustler Magazine V. Falwell. 2014. pap. *(978-1-62712-391-4(1));* lib. bdg. *(978-1-62712-390-7(3))* Cavendish Square Publishing.

Graves, Renee. The Scopes Trial. 2003. (Cornerstones of Freedom Ser.). (ENG., Illus.). 48p. (YA). (gr. 4-7). 26.00 *(978-0-516-24221-7(0))* Scholastic Library Publishing.

Haerens, Margaret. War Crimes. 2010. (Opposing Viewpoints Ser.). (ENG., Illus.). 240p. pap. 29.45 *(978-0-7377-4997-7(0));* 224p. (gr. 10-12). 48.80 *(978-0-7377-4996-0(2))* Cengage Gale. (Greenhaven Pr., Inc.).

Hamilton, Sue L. Forensic Artist: Solving the Case with a Face, 1 vol. 2008. (Crime Scene Investigation Ser.). (ENG.). 32p. (gr. 4-8). 27.07 *(978-1-59928-989-2(X),* Abdo & Daughters) ABDO Publishing Co.

Harvey, Gill. Crime & Detection. rev. ed. 2008. (True Stories Ser.). 144p. (J). pap. 4.99 *(978-0-7945-1981-0(4),* Usborne) EDC Publishing.

Head, Honor. Being Safe with People. 2017. (Keep Yourself Safe Ser.). (ENG., Illus.). 24p. (J). (gr. k-2). 16.99 *(978-1-4451-4429-0(8),* Franklin Watts) Hachette Children's Group GBR. Dist: Hachette Bk. Group.

Heinemann Educational Ltd. Publishing Staff. True Crime Package 6-Pack. 2004. pap. 275.40 *(978-1-4109-1392-0(9))* Harcourt Schl. Pubs.

Heits, Rudolph T. Mass Murderers. 2013. (J). *(978-1-61900-035-3(0))* Eldorado Ink.

Hermsen, Sarah, et al. American Reference Library. 2004. (Crime & Punishment in America Ser.). (ENG.). 39p. (J). 5.00 *(978-0-7876-9174-5(7),* UXL) Cengage Gale.

Hiber, Amanda. Sexual Violence. Greenhaven Press Editors, ed. 2014. (Opposing Viewpoints Ser.). (ENG.). 224p. (gr. 10-12). lib. bdg. 48.80 *(978-0-7377-6340-9(X),* Greenhaven Pr., Inc.) Cengage Gale.

—Sexual Violence. Greenhaven Press Editors & Gale Editors, eds. 2014. (Opposing Viewpoints Ser.). (ENG., Illus.). 224p. (gr. 7-12). pap. 33.80 *(978-0-7377-6341-6(8),* Greenhaven Pr., Inc.) Cengage Gale.

Higgins, Melissa. Night Dad Went to Jail: What to Expect When Someone You Love Goes to Jail. Kirwan, Wednesday, illus. 2013. (Life's Challenges Ser.). (ENG.). 24p. (gr. 2-3). 8.99 *(978-1-4795-2142-5(6))* Picture Window Bks.

Hile, Lori. Gangs, 1 vol. 2012. (Teen Issues Ser.). (ENG.). 56p. (gr. 6-10). pap. 9.99 *(978-1-4329-6540-2(9));* lib. bdg. 34.65 *(978-1-4329-6535-8(2))* Heinemann-Raintree.

Hudson, David L., Jr. Prisoners' Rights. 2007. (Point/Counterpoint Ser.). (Illus.). 107p. (YA). (gr. 9-12). lib. bdg. 35.00 *(978-0-7910-9277-4(1))* Facts On File, Inc.

Ibrahim, Zafar Y. Folie a Deux: Shared Psychosis. Ibrahim, Zafar Y. & Ibrahim, Idore, eds. 2003. 116p. (YA). pap. *(978-0-9640389-7-4(8))* Crispus Medical Pr.

Innes, Brian. Major Unsolved Crimes. 2004. (Crime & Detection Ser.). (Illus.). 96p. (YA). (gr. 7-18). lib. bdg. 22.95 *(978-1-59084-382-6(7))* Mason Crest.

—Unsolved Crimes, Vol. 20. Gomez, Manny, ed. 2016. (Crime & Detection Ser.). 96p. (J). (gr. 7). 24.95 *(978-1-4222-3482-2(7))* Mason Crest.

Jacobs, Thomas A. They Broke the Law - You Be the Judge: True Cases of Teen Crime. 2003. (ENG.). 224p. (YA). (gr. 7-18). pap. 15.99 *(978-1-57542-134-6(8))* Free Spirit Publishing, Inc.

Kerrigan, Michael. Police Crime Prevention. 2004. (Rescue & Prevention Ser.). (Illus.). 96p. (J). (gr. 6-18). lib. bdg. 22.95 *(978-1-59084-406-9(8))* Mason Crest.

Kuklin, Susan. No Choirboy: Murder, Violence, & Teenagers on Death Row. 2014. (ENG., Illus.). 240p. (YA). (gr. 9-13). pap. 12.99 *(978-1-250-04445-7(6),* 9781250044457) Square Fish.

La Bella, Laura. Stalking. 2015. (Confronting Violence Against Women Ser.). (ENG., Illus.). 64p. (J). (gr. 6-7). 32.95 *(978-1-4994-6046-9(5),* Rosen Young Adult) Rosen Publishing Group, Inc., The.

Lane, Brian, et al. Eyewitness Books - Crime & Detection. Crawford, Andy, photos by. 2005. (DK Eyewitness Bks.). (ENG., Illus.). 72p. (J). (gr. 3-7). 16.99 *(978-0-7566-1386-0(8),* DK Children) Dorling Kindersley Publishing, Inc.

Lankford, Ronnie D. Gun Violence. 2010. (Social Issues Firsthand Ser.). (Illus.). 192p. (J). 33.75 *(978-0-7377-4797-3(8),* Greenhaven Pr., Inc.) Cengage Gale.

Lassieur, Allison. Violent Crime, 1 vol. 2011. (Hot Topics Ser.). (ENG.). 56p. (gr. 7-8). 34.65 *(978-1-4329-4874-0(1),* NA-h) Heinemann-Raintree.

Lawrence, Sandra. Murder & Mayhem. 2016. (Hideous History Ser.). (ENG., Illus.). 64p. (J). (gr. 5-9). 11.99 *(978-1-4998-0082-1(7))* Little Bee Books Inc.

Lock, Joan. Protecting Yourself Against Criminals, Vol. 20. Gomez, Manny, ed. 2016. (Crime & Detection Ser.). (Illus.). 96p. (J). (gr. 7). 24.95 *(978-1-4222-3484-6(3))* Mason Crest.

Loveless, Antony. Bodyguards. 2009. (World's Most Dangerous Jobs Ser.). (ENG., Illus.). 32p. (J). (gr. 3-6). pap. *(978-0-7787-5108-3(2));* lib. bdg. *(978-0-7787-5094-9(9))* Crabtree Publishing Co.

MacDonald, Fiona. Meet a Body Snatcher! Criminals & Murderers You'D Rather Avoid. 2009. (You Wouldn't Want to Ser.). (ENG., Illus.). 32p. (J). (gr. 3-18). 29.00 *(978-0-531-20822-9(2),* Watts, Franklin) Scholastic Library Publishing.

—You Wouldn't Want to Meet a Body Snatcher! Criminals & Murderers You'd Rather Avoid. 2009. (You Wouldn't Want to... Ser.). (ENG., Illus.). 32p. (J). (gr. 3-18). pap. 9.95 *(978-0-531-21046-8(4),* Children's Pr.) Scholastic Library Publishing.

Marcovitz, Hal. Exposing Torture: Centuries of Cruelty. 2015. (ENG., Illus.). 112p. (J). (gr. 8-12). lib. bdg. 34.65 *(978-1-4677-5049-3(2),* Twenty-First Century Bks.) Lerner Publishing Group.

—Exposing Torture: Centuries of Cruelty. 2015. (Illus.). 112p. (J). *(978-1-4677-6306-6(3))* Twenty First Century Bks.

Marriott, Emma. Violence Against Women. 2016. (Illus.). 48p. (J). *(978-0-7787-2590-9(1))* Crabtree Publishing Co.

Matthews, Rupert. You Wouldn't Want to Be a Chicago Gangster! Some Dangerous Characters You'd Better Avoid. Bergin, Mark, illus. 2010. (You Wouldn't Want to Ser.). (ENG.). 32p. (J). (gr. 3-18). pap. 9.95 *(978-0-531-22825-8(8))* Scholastic Library Publishing.

Matthews, Rupert & Salariya, David. You Wouldn't Want to Be a Chicago Gangster! Some Dangerous Characters You'd Better Avoid. Bergin, Mark, illus. 2010. (You Wouldn't Want to Ser.). (ENG.). 32p. (J). 29.00 *(978-0-531-20470-2(7))* Scholastic Library Publishing.

Mauro, Paul & Melton, H. Keith. Crime Scene & Surveillance Photography. 2004. (Detective Academy Ser.). (Illus.). 48p. (J). *(978-0-439-57182-1(0))* Scholastic, Inc.

Merino, Noël. Prison. 2009. (Issues on Trial Ser.). (ENG., Illus.). 240p. (gr. 10-12). 48.30 *(978-0-7377-4344-9(1),* Greenhaven Pr., Inc.) Cengage Gale.

Mooney, Carla. Your Legal Rights Regarding Misdemeanor Prosecution, 1 vol. 2015. (ENG., Illus.). 64p. (J). 33.25 *(978-1-4777-8028-2(9),* Rosen Reference) Rosen Publishing Group, Inc., The.

Murray, Elizabeth A. Overturning Wrongful Convictions: Science Serving Justice. 2015. (ENG., Illus.). 120p. (J). (gr. 8-12). lib. bdg. 33.32 *(978-1-4677-2513-2(7),* Twenty-First Century Bks.) Lerner Publishing Group.

Nakaya, Andrea C. Thinking Critically Mass Shootings. 2015. (Illus.). 80p. (J). lib. bdg. 28.95 *(978-1-60152-822-3(1))* ReferencePoint Pr., Inc.

Nardo, Don. Bernie Madoff. 2011. (People in the News Ser.). (ENG.). 128p. (gr. 10-10). lib. bdg. 39.40 *(978-1-4205-0353-1(7))* Cengage Gale.

Netzley, Patricia D. Video Games, Violence & Crime. 2014. (Video Games & Society Ser.). (ENG., Illus.). 80p. (J). lib. bdg. *(978-1-60152-752-3(7))* ReferencePoint Pr., Inc.

O'Brien, Susan. Child Abduction & Kidnapping. 2008. (Criminal Investigations Ser.). (Illus.). 160p. (J). (gr. 9-12). 35.00 *(978-0-7910-9403-7(0),* Chelsea Hse.) Facts On File, Inc.

Orr, Tamra. Egyptian Islamic Jihad. 2009. (Inside the World's Most Infamous Terrorist Organizations Ser.). 64p. (gr. 5-5). 58.50 *(978-1-61513-574-5(X))* Rosen Publishing Group, Inc., The.

Parker, Christi E. Pioneer Trails, 1 vol. 2005. (Primary Source Readers Ser.). (ENG.). 24p. (J). (gr. 5-5). pap. 8.99 *(978-0-7439-8909-1(0))* Shell Educational Publishing.

Parker, Janice. Crime. 2009. (Science Q & A Ser.). (Illus.). 48p. (YA). (gr. 5-8). pap. 10.95 *(978-1-60596-069-2(1));* lib. bdg. 29.05 *(978-1-60596-068-5(3))* Weigl Pubs., Inc.

—Crime Q & A. 2014. (Science Discovery Ser.). (ENG., Illus.). 48p. (J). (gr. 5-8). pap. 13.95 *(978-1-4896-0685-3(8),* AV2 by Weigl) Weigl Pubs., Inc.

Parks, Peggy. Street Crime. 2007. (Ripped from the Headlines Ser.). (Illus.). 64p. (YA). (gr. 7-12). 23.95 *(978-1-60217-007-0(X))* Erickson Pr.

Peppas, Lynn. Piracy. 2013. (ENG.). 48p. (J). *(978-0-7787-1103-2(X));* pap. *(978-0-7787-1123-0(4))* Crabtree Publishing Co.

Price, Sean. Unsolved Crime Mysteries. 2015. (Unsolved Mystery Files Ser.). (ENG., Illus.). 32p. (gr. 3-4). lib. bdg. 27.99 *(978-1-4914-4263-0(8))* Capstone Press of Coughlan Cos.

Raatma, Lucia. Staying Safe Around Strangers, 1 vol. 2011. (Staying Safe Ser.). (ENG.). 24p. (gr. 1-2). lib. bdg. 25.32 *(978-1-4296-6821-7(0),* First Facts) Capstone Press of Coughlan Cos.

Rauf, Don & Cawthorne, Nigel. The World's Worst Acts of Brutality. 2016. (Making Headlines Ser.). 160p. (J). lib. bdg. 39.93 *(978-0-7660-8370-7(5))* Enslow Pubs., Inc.

Ridenour, Melissa Harker. What Would You Do? A Kid's Guide to Staying Safe in a World of Strangers. Fehling, Leslie, illus. 2011. (J). *(978-0-938467-11-3(5))* Headline Bks., Inc.

Rosenthal, Beth. Cheating. 2007. (Introducing Issues with Opposing Viewpoints Ser.). (Illus.). 141p. (YA). (gr. 7-12). lib. bdg. 36.95 *(978-0-7377-3802-5(2))* Cengage Gale.

Schauer, Pete, ed. Homelessness & Street Crime. 2017. (Current Controversies Ser.). (ENG.). (YA). (gr. 10-12). pap. 32.00 ***(978-1-5345-0093-8(6))*** Greenhaven Publishing LLC.

Schauer, Peter J. Homelessness & Street Crime. 2017. (J). ***(978-1-5345-0095-2(2))*** Greenhaven Publishing LLC.

Schauer, Peter J. What You Need to Know about Violent Crimes, Felonies, & the Law, 1 vol. 2015. (ENG., Illus.). 64p. (J). 33.25 *(978-1-4777-8024-4(6),* Rosen Reference) Rosen Publishing Group, Inc., The.

Sherman, Benjamin. Gregory's Paper Airplane. 2010. 32p. 11.95 *(978-1-4497-0719-4(X),* WestBow Pr.) Author Solutions, Inc.

Shone, Rob. Solving Crimes Through Criminal Profiling. Spender, Nick, illus. 2008. (Graphic Forensic Science Ser.). (ENG.). 48p. (gr. 5-8). per. 14.05 *(978-1-4042-1438-5(0));* (YA). lib. bdg. 31.95 *(978-1-4042-1437-8(2))* Rosen Publishing Group, Inc., The.

Smith, Roger. Prison Conditions: Overcrowding, Disease, Violence, & Abuse. 2008. (Incarceration Issues Ser.). (Illus.). 111p. (YA). (gr. 7-18). lib. bdg. 22.95 *(978-1-59084-986-6(8))* Mason Crest.

Smith, Roger & McIntosh, Marsha & Smith. Youth in Prison. 2008. (Incarceration Issues Ser.). (Illus.). 111p. (YA). (gr. 7-18). lib. bdg. 22.95 *(978-1-59084-990-3(6))* Mason Crest.

Somervill, Barbara A. Graphing Crime, 1 vol. 2010. (Real World Data Ser.). (ENG., Illus.). 32p. (gr. 3-5). lib. bdg. 29.99 *(978-1-4329-2623-6(3),* NA-h) Heinemann-Raintree.

Spence, David. Crime & Punishment. 2004. (Illus.). 32p. (J). (gr. 4-7). pap. 5.95 *(978-1-86007-010-5(8),* TickTock Books) Octopus Publishing Group GBR. Dist: Independent Pubs. Group.

Spilsbury, Richard. Zoom in on Crime Scenes. 2013. (Zoom in on... Ser.). 32p. (J). lib. bdg. 23.94 *(978-0-7660-4311-4(8))* Enslow Pubs., Inc.

Staunton, Ted. The Dreadful Truth: Canadian Crime. Geoffroi, Remie, illus. 2006. (Dreadful Truth Ser.). (ENG.). 104p. (J). (gr. 3-8). *(978-0-88780-705-3(4))* Formac Publishing Co., Ltd.

Steele, Philip. Race & Crime. 2016. (Illus.). 48p. (J). *(978-0-7787-2588-6(X))* Crabtree Publishing Co.

Stuckey, Rachel. Digital Dangers. 2015. (ENG., Illus.). 48p. (J). *(978-0-7787-2202-1(3))* Crabtree Publishing Co.

Sutherland, Jonathan & Canwell, Diane. Violent Crimes. 2010. (Solve It with Science Ser.). (YA). (gr. 5-9). 34.25 *(978-1-59920-334-8(0))* Black Rabbit Bks.

Swift, Richard. Gangs, 1 vol. 2012. (Groundwork Guides). (ENG., Illus.). 144p. (gr. 8). pap. 10.00 *(978-0-88899-978-8(X))* Groundwood Bks. CAN. Dist: Publishers Group West (PGW).

T R Thomas & Thomas, T. R. Celebrity Cases: True Crime, 1 vol. unabr. ed. 2010. (True Crime Ser.). (ENG.). 64p. (YA). (gr. 9-12). pap. 8.95 *(978-1-59905-435-3(3))* Saddleback Educational Publishing, Inc.

Taylor, Robert & MacKay, Jennifer. Profiling. 2008. (Crime Scene Investigations Ser.). (ENG., Illus.). 128p. (gr. 7-12). lib. bdg. 40.40 *(978-1-59018-990-0(6),* LML02109-234471) Cengage Gale.

Tonge, Neil. Banished, Beheaded, or Boiled in Oil: A Hair-Raising History of Crime & Punishment Throughout the Ages! 2015. (Awfully Ancient Ser.). (ENG.). 32p. (J). (gr. 5-5). pap. 10.50 *(978-1-4824-3121-6(1))* Stevens, Gareth Publishing LLLP.

Townsend, John. Robberies & Heists. 2010. (Solve It with Science Ser.). (Illus.). 48p. (YA). (gr. 5-9). lib. bdg. 34.25 *(978-1-59920-333-1(2))* Black Rabbit Bks.

—Unsolved Crimes. 2010. (Amazing Mysteries Ser.). (YA). (gr. 3-6). 28.50 *(978-1-59920-367-6(7))* Black Rabbit Bks.

Turner, Queen of England Patrenia. Queen Patrenialla - A Canadian Story Poem. Turner, Keeng of England Troyius, ed. 2015. (Illus.). pap. *(978-0-578-18000-7(6))* Royalty Patrenia Turner Publications.

Uschan, Michael V. Hate Crimes. 2007. (Hot Topics Ser.). (ENG., Illus.). 128p. (gr. 7-12). lib. bdg. 39.40 *(978-1-56006-661-3(X))* Cengage Gale.

Valdez, Jannay. Bonnie & Clyde - Villains or Victims? (Illus.). 120p. (YA). *(978-1-886709-09-6(2))* Outlaw Pubns.

Winters, Robert. What Is a Hate Crime? 2007. (At Issue Ser.). (ENG., Illus.). 128p. (gr. 10-12). 39.40 *(978-0-7377-2436-3(6))* Cengage Gale.

Winters, Robert, ed. What Is a Hate Crime? 2007. (At Issue Ser.). (ENG.). 121p. (gr. 10-12). 24.45 *(978-0-7377-2437-0(4),* Greenhaven Pr., Inc.) Cengage Gale.

Wolny, Philip. Understanding Financial Frauds & Scams. 2012. (Real World Economics Ser.). (ENG., Illus.). 80p. (J). (gr. 7-12). 33.25 *(978-1-4488-6784-4(3))* Rosen Publishing Group, Inc., The.

Wright, Cynthia. Everything You Need to Know about Dealing with Stalking. 2005. (Need to Know Library). (Illus.). 64p. (YA). (gr. 7-12). lib. bdg. 31.95 *(978-0-8239-2841-5(1),* NTSTAL) Rosen Publishing Group, Inc., The.

Wright, John D. Hate Crimes, Vol. 20. Gomez, Manny, ed. 2016. (Crime & Detection Ser.). (Illus.). 96p. (J). (gr. 7). 24.95 *(978-1-4222-3479-2(7))* Mason Crest.

—Race & Crime. 2004. (Crime & Detection Ser.). (Illus.). 96p. (YA). (gr. 7-18). lib. bdg. 22.95 *(978-1-59084-378-9(9))* Mason Crest.

—Race & Crime, Vol. 20. Gomez, Manny, ed. 2016. (Crime & Detection Ser.). (Illus.). 96p. (J). (gr. 7). 24.95 *(978-1-4222-3485-3(1))* Mason Crest.

Yancey, Diane. The Zodiac Killer. 2008. (Crime Scene Investigations Ser.). (Illus.). 112p. (YA). (gr. 7-10). lib. bdg. 35.45 *(978-1-4205-0063-9(5),* LML02109-240733, Lucent Bks.) Cengage Gale.

Yomtov, Nel. Illegal Animal Traffickers. 2016. (True Book(tm), a — The New Criminals Ser.). (ENG., Illus.). 48p. (J). lib. bdg. 31.00 *(978-0-531-21464-0(8),* Children's Pr.) Scholastic Library Publishing.

CRIME—FICTION

Alender, Katie. Marie Antoinette, Serial Killer. 2013. (ENG.). 304p. (J). (gr. 7). 18.99 *(978-0-545-46809-1(4))* Scholastic, Inc.

Alger, Horatio. Joe the Hotel Boy: Or: Winning Out by Pluck. 2007. 164p. pap. 19.99 *(978-1-4346-5069-6(3));* 172p. pap. 21.99 *(978-1-4346-5070-2(7))* Creative Media Partners, LLC.

Anderson, Jennifer. Spider. 2013. 174p. pap. 10.99 *(978-1-62237-146-4(1))* Turquoise Morning Pr.

Anonymous. Calling Maggie May. 2015. (ENG., Illus.). 272p. (YA). (gr. 9). pap. 10.99 *(978-1-4814-3901-5(4),* Simon Pulse) Simon Pulse.

Avi. The Seer of Shadows. 2009. (ENG.). 224p. (J). (gr. 4-7). pap. 6.99 *(978-0-06-000017-2(1))* HarperCollins Pubs.

Ayarbe, Heidi. Wanted. 2012. (ENG.). 400p. (YA). (gr. 9). 17.99 *(978-0-06-199388-6(3))* HarperCollins Pubs.

Bacigalupi, Paolo. The Doubt Factory. 2014. (ENG.). 496p. (YA). (gr. 10-17). 18.00 *(978-0-316-22075-0(2))* Little Brown & Co.

Barchers, Suzanne I. Mike Makes up His Mind, 1 vol. 2011. (Targeted Phonics Ser.). (ENG.). 16p. (J). (gr. k-2). pap. 5.99 *(978-1-4333-2911-1(5))* Teacher Created Materials, Inc.

Barker, M. P. A Difficult Boy. 2009. (ENG.). 272p. (YA). (gr. 5-18). pap. 7.95 *(978-0-8234-2244-9(5))* Holiday Hse., Inc.

Barnes, Charlotte. Stella Ducktropolis. 2008. 36p. pap. 11.95 *(978-1-4327-1806-0(1))* Outskirts Pr., Inc.

Barnes, Jennifer Lynn. All in ((the Naturals #3)) 2016. (Naturals Ser.). (ENG.). 400p. (YA). (gr. 7-12). pap. 9.99 *(978-1-4847-2367-8(8))* Hyperion Bks. for Children.

Barnett, Mac. The Ghostwriter Secret. Rex, Adam, illus. (Brixton Brothers Ser.: 2). (ENG.). (J). (gr. 3-7). 2011. 256p. pap. 7.99 *(978-1-4169-7818-3(6))* 2010. 240p. 17.99 *(978-1-4169-7817-6(8))* Simon & Schuster Bks. For Young Readers. (Simon & Schuster Bks. For Young Readers).

Barratt, Mark. The Wild Man. 2010. (ENG.). 352p. (YA). (gr. 6-18). pap. 9.00 *(978-0-8028-5377-6(3),* Eerdmans Bks For Young Readers) Eerdmans, William B. Publishing Co.

Barth, Amy. Annabelle's Secret: A Story about Sexual Abuse. Kinra, Richa, illus. 2011. 24p. (gr. 3-7). 28.95 *(978-1-61599-099-3(2))* Loving Healing Pr., Inc.

Barwin, Steven. Desert Slam. 2017. (Orca Soundings Ser.). lib. bdg. 20.80 ***(978-0-606-40453-2(8))*** Turtleback Bks.

Battista, Mary Jane. Danny's Day at the Children's Museum. 2009. 24p. pap. 11.49 *(978-1-4389-4396-1(2))* AuthorHouse.

Beil, Michael D. The Mistaken Masterpiece. 2011. (Red Blazer Girls Ser.). (ENG.). 320p. (J). (gr. 3-7). 16.99 *(978-0-375-86740-8(6),* Knopf Bks. for Young Readers) Random Hse. Children's Bks.

Belasen, Amy & Osborn, Jacob. Jenny Green's Killer Junior Year. 2008. (ENG.). 304p. (YA). (gr. 9-18). pap. 14.99 *(978-1-4169-6792-7(3),* Simon Pulse) Simon Pulse.

Berry, Julie. All the Truth That's in Me. 2014. (ENG.). 304p. (YA). (gr. 7). pap. 9.99 *(978-0-14-242730-9(6),* Speak) Penguin Young Readers Group.

Bick, Ilsa J. Draw the Dark. (Carolrhoda YA Ser.). (ENG.). 344p. (YA). (gr. 9-12). 2011. pap. 9.95 *(978-0-7613-8131-0(7))* 2010. 16.95 *(978-0-7613-5686-8(X))* Lerner Publishing Group. (Carolrhoda Lab™).

—The Sin-Eater's Confession. Elyum Studio, illus. 2014. (ENG.). 296p. (YA). (gr. 9-12). pap. 9.95 *(978-1-4677-3705-0(4),* Carolrhoda Lab™) Lerner Publishing Group.

Black, Holly. Red Glove. 2011. (Curse Workers Ser.: 2). (ENG.). 336p. (YA). (gr. 9-18). 17.99 *(978-1-4424-0339-0(X),* McElderry, Margaret K. Bks.) McElderry, Margaret K. Bks.

Bock, Caroline. Lie. 2011. (ENG.). 224p. (YA). (gr. 7-18). pap. 18.99 *(978-0-312-66832-7(5),* 9780312668327, St. Martin's Griffin) St. Martin's Pr.

Bowen, Carl & Fuentes, Benny. Sniper Shield, 1 vol. Tortosa, Wilson, illus. 2013. (Shadow Squadron Ser.). (ENG.). 112p. (gr. 4-8). lib. bdg. 26.65 *(978-1-4342-4607-3(8))* Stone Arch Bks.

Brackett, Leigh & Coppel, Jr., Alfred. Planet Stories - Summer 1949. 2008. 128p. (YA). pap. 14.95 *(978-1-59798-181-1(8))* Adventure Hse.

Brezenoff, Steve. The Symphony That Was Silent, 1 vol. Calo, Marcos, illus. 2011. (Field Trip Mysteries Ser.). (ENG.). 88p. (gr. 2-3). pap. 6.10 *(978-1-4342-3429-2(0));* lib. bdg. 25.32 *(978-1-4342-3226-7(3))* Stone Arch Bks.

Brezenoff, Steven. The Case of the Stolen Space Suit. Weber, Lisa K., illus. 2016. (Museum Mysteries Ser.). (ENG.). 128p. (gr. 2-3). 26.65 *(978-1-4965-2516-1(7))* Stone Arch Bks.

Broad, Michael. Spooky Ballet!, No. 4. Broad, Michael, illus. 2011. (Agent Amelia Ser.: 4). (ENG., Illus.). 144p. (J). (gr. 2-5). pap. 5.95 *(978-0-7613-8064-1(7),* Darby Creek) Lerner Publishing Group.

—#4 Spooky Ballet! 2011. (Agent Amelia Ser.). pap. 33.92 *(978-0-7613-8344-4(1),* Darby Creek) Lerner Publishing Group.

Bronstein, S. N. Private Eye Cats Book Two: The Case of the Kidnapped Dog. 2013. 116p. (gr. 4-6). 23.99 *(978-1-4817-2421-0(5));* pap. 14.95 *(978-1-4817-2422-7(3))* AuthorHouse.

Brooks, Kevin. Martyn Pig. 2003. 230p. (J). (gr. 5-9). 15.65 *(978-0-7569-7217-2(5))* Perfection Learning Corp.

Burkhart, Kiersi. Honor Code. 2017. (ENG.). 320p. (YA). ***(978-1-5124-2996-1(1),*** Carolrhoda Bks.) Lerner Publishing Group.

Burns, A. M. Finding the Sky. 2016. (ENG., Illus.). (YA). 24.99 ***(978-1-63533-014-4(9));*** 180p. (J). pap. 14.99 *(978-1-63476-336-3(X))* Dreamspinner Pr. (Harmony Ink Pr.).

Cage, Elizabeth. License to Thrill. 2013. (Spy Girls Ser.: 1). (ENG., Illus.). 192p. (YA). (gr. 7). pap. 13.99 *(978-1-4814-2078-5(X),* Simon Pulse) Simon Pulse.

—Live & Let Spy. 2013. (Spy Girls Ser.: 2). (ENG., Illus.). 192p. (YA). (gr. 7). pap. 13.99 *(978-1-4814-2079-2(8),* Simon Pulse) Simon Pulse.

Cameron, Sam. Mystery of the Tempest: A Fisher Key Adventure. 2011. (ENG.). 288p. (J). (gr. 7). pap. 13.95 *(978-1-60282-579-6(3))* Bold Strokes Bks.

Carman, Patrick. Shantorian, Bk. 2. 2011. (Trackers Ser.: 2). (ENG.). 176p. (J). (gr. 3-7). 14.99 *(978-0-545-16501-3(6),* Scholastic Pr.) Scholastic, Inc.

—Trackers, Bk. 1. 2010. (Trackers Ser.: 1). (ENG.). 224p. (J). (gr. 3-7). 14.99 *(978-0-545-16500-6(8),* Scholastic Pr.) Scholastic, Inc.

Carroll, Jenny, pseud & Cabot, Meg. Sanctuary. 2007. (1-800-Where-R-You Ser.: No. 4). (ENG., Illus.). 240p. (YA). (gr. 9-12). mass mkt. 6.99 *(978-1-4169-2707-5(7),* Simon Pulse) Simon Pulse.

Carter, Ally. Heist Society. 2011. (Heist Society Novel Ser.). (ENG.). 304p. (J). (gr. 5-9). pap. 9.99 *(978-1-4231-1661-5(5))* Hyperion Pr.

—Perfect Scoundrels. 2014. (Heist Society Novel Ser.). (ENG.). 336p. (YA). (gr. 7-12). pap. 9.99 *(978-1-4231-6681-8(7))* Hyperion Bks. for Children.

—Perfect Scoundrels. 2013. (Heist Society Novel Ser.). (ENG.). 336p. (YA). (gr. 7-17). 17.99 *(978-1-4231-6600-9(0))* Hyperion Pr.

—Uncommon Criminals. 2011. (Playaway Children Ser.). (YA). (gr. 7-12). 69.99 *(978-1-4558-2483-0(6))* Findaway World, LLC.

—Uncommon Criminals. 2012. (Heist Society Novel Ser.). (ENG.). 304p. (J). (gr. 5-9). pap. 9.99 *(978-1-4231-4807-4(X))* Hyperion Pr.

Carter, Scott William. The Last Great Getaway of the Water Balloon Boys. 2010. (ENG.). 208p. (YA). (gr. 7-18). 16.99 *(978-1-4169-7156-6(4),* Simon & Schuster Bks. For Young Readers) Simon & Schuster Bks. For Young Readers.

Casanova, Mary. Moose Tracks. 2nd ed. 2010. (J). *(978-0-9793444-3-5(3))* Quercus Pr.

Casey, Jane. How to Fall. 2014. (Jess Tennant Mysteries Ser.: 1). (ENG.). 352p. (YA). (gr. 8-11). 18.99 *(978-1-250-04065-7(5),* 9781250040657, St. Martin's Griffin) St. Martin's Pr.

Caygill, Ronald. Scrope Hall. 2009. 48p. pap. 11.49 *(978-1-4490-5078-8(6))* AuthorHouse.

Choldenko, Gennifer. Al Capone Does My Homework. 2014. (ENG.). 240p. (J). (gr. 5). pap. 7.99 *(978-0-14-242522-0(2),* Puffin Books) Penguin Young Readers Group.

—Al Capone Does My Homework. 2014. (Tale from Alcatraz (Al Capone) Ser.: 3). lib. bdg. 18.40 *(978-0-606-35714-2(9))* Turtleback Bks.

Choyce, Lesley. Scam, 1 vol. 2016. (Orca Soundings Ser.). (ENG.). 144p. (YA). (gr. 8-12). pap. 9.95 *(978-1-4598-1174-4(7))* Orca Bk. Pubs. USA.

Collier, James Lincoln. Me & Billy, 0 vols. unabr. ed. 2013. (ENG.). 194p. (J). (gr. 5-7). pap. 9.99 *(978-1-4778-1706-3(9),* 9781477817063, Amazon Children's Publishing) Amazon Publishing.

Coman, Carolyn. The Big House. Shepperson, Rob, illus. 2004. (ENG.). 224p. (J). (gr. 4-6). 16.95 *(978-1-932425-09-3(8),* Lemniscaat) Boyds Mills Pr.

Cook, Eileen. The Hanging Girl. 2017. (ENG.). 320p. (YA). (gr. 9). 17.99 ***(978-0-544-82982-4(4),*** HMH Books For Young Readers) Houghton Mifflin Harcourt Publishing Co.

Corley, Sandra Y. The Crochet Detective Case #101: The Case of the Missing African Treasure. 2011. 36p. (gr. 4-6). pap. 16.86 *(978-1-4567-4678-0(2))* AuthorHouse.

Cormier, Robert. I Am the Cheese. 2007. (ENG.). 256p. (YA). (gr. 7). pap. 9.99 *(978-0-375-84039-5(7),* Ember) Random Hse. Children's Bks.

Cosimano, Elle & Carey, Janet Lee. Nearly Found. 2015. (Nearly Boswell Mysteries Ser.). (ENG.). 384p. (YA). (gr. 7-12). 17.99 *(978-0-8037-3927-7(3),* Kathy Dawson Books) Penguin Young Readers Group.

Cox, Suzy. The Dead Girls Detective Agency. 2012. (ENG.). 368p. (YA). (gr. 9). pap. 9.99 *(978-0-06-202064-2(1),* HarperTeen) HarperCollins Pubs.

Crime & Detection, 10 vols. rev. ed. 2005. (Fastback Ser.). 32p. (J). (gr. 6-12). pap. 44.95 *(978-0-13-024445-1(7))* Globe Fearon Educational Publishing.

Croall, Marie. Ali Baba: Fooling the Forty Thieves [an Arabian Tale]. Hilinski, Clint, illus. 2009. (Graphic Myths & Legends Ser.). (ENG.). 48p. (gr. 4-8). pap. 8.95 *(978-1-58013-887-1(X))* Lerner Publishing Group.

Crummel, Susan Stevens. Sherlock Bones & the Missing Cheese, 0 vols. Donohue, Dorothy, illus. 2012. (ENG.). 40p. (J). (gr. k-3). 17.99 *(978-0-7614-6186-9(8),* 9780761461869, Amazon Children's Publishing) Amazon Publishing.

DAVIS, Tamika. Now i Know. 2010. 152p. pap. 17.00 *(978-0-557-58446-8(9))* Lulu Pr., Inc.

De Grift Stevenson, Fanny Van & Stevenson, Robert Louis. The Dynamiter. 2007. (ENG.). 200p. pap. 19.99 *(978-1-4346-4611-8(4));* 222p. pap. 22.99 *(978-1-4346-4612-5(2))* Creative Media Partners, LLC.

Dean, Carolee. Take Me There. 2010. (ENG.). 336p. (YA). (gr. 9-18). pap. 8.99 *(978-1-4169-8950-9(1),* Simon Pulse) Simon Pulse.

Dekker, James C. Scum, 1 vol. 2008. (Orca Soundings Ser.). (ENG.). 112p. (YA). (gr. 8-12). 16.95 *(978-1-55143-926-6(3))* Orca Bk. Pubs. USA.

Delashmit, Margaret V. Thief! 2012. 148p. (gr. 4-6). pap. 12.99 *(978-1-4624-0348-6(4),* Inspiring Voices) Author Solutions, Inc.

Deluca, Laura. Hyde. 2013. 320p. pap. 12.95 *(978-1-938397-56-1(8),* Pagan Writers Pr.) Mroczka Media.

Demetrios, Heather. Exquisite Captive. 2014. (Dark Caravan Cycle Ser.: 1). (ENG., Illus.). 480p. (YA). (gr. 8). 17.99 *(978-0-06-231856-5(X))* HarperCollins Pubs.

Derting, Kimberly. The Last Echo. 2013. (Body Finder Ser.: 3). (ENG.). 384p. (YA). (gr. 9). pap. 9.99 *(978-0-06-208220-6(5))* HarperCollins Pubs.

Descoteaux, Chad. Once upon A Crime Syndicate: A mafia fairy Tale. 2006. 151p. pap. 24.95 *(978-1-4241-0893-0(4))* PublishAmerica, Inc.

Dickens, Charles. Oliver Twist. 2009. (Foundation Classics Ser.). (Illus.). 56p. (J). (gr. 5-9). lib. bdg. 27.95 *(978-1-60754-542-2(X))* Windmill Bks.

—Oliver Twist. Ablett, Barry, illus. 2007. (Young Reading Series 3 Gift Bks.). 63p. (J). (gr. 3). 8.99 *(978-0-7945-1459-4(6),* Usborne) EDC Publishing.

—Oliver Twist. 2007. (Oxford Bookworms Ser.). (Illus.). 120p. pap. 10.00 *(978-0-19-423763-5(X))* Oxford Univ. Pr., Inc.

—Oliver Twist. 2nd ed. 2008. (ENG.). 136p. pap. 11.99 *(978-1-4058-6525-8(3))* Pearson Education.

—Oliver Twist. 2008. (Puffin Classics Ser.). (ENG.). 416p. (J). (gr. 5-7). 5.99 *(978-0-14-132243-8(8),* Puffin Books) Penguin Young Readers Group.

—Oliver Twist. 2006. 516p. (gr. 3-3). per. *(978-1-4067-9405-2(8),* Hesperides Pr.) Read Bks.

—Oliver Twist. Johnson, Cynthia Brantley, ed. annot. ed. 2007. (Enriched Classics Ser.). (ENG.). 672p. (gr. 3). mass mkt. 4.95 *(978-1-4165-3475-4(X))* Simon & Schuster.

—Oliver Twist. McKowen, Scott, illus. 2008. (Sterling Unabridged Classics Ser.). (ENG.). 464p. (J). 14.95 *(978-1-4027-5425-8(6))* Sterling Publishing Co., Inc.

—Oliver Twist, 3 cass.; set. 2004. (Masterpiece Theatre Ser.). (gr. 7-18). tchr. ed. 59.95 incl. VHS *(978-1-57807-576-8(9),* WG1062) WGBH Boston Video.

Dillon, Elena. Breathe. 2013. 190p. pap. 9.99 *(978-0-9886353-2-6(1))* Dillon, Elena.

Dixon, Franklin W. Comic con Artist. 21st ed. 2008. (Hardy Boys (All New) Undercover Brothers Ser.: 21). (ADY & ENG., Illus.). 192p. (J). (gr. 3-7). pap. 5.99 *(978-1-4169-5498-9(8),* Aladdin) Simon & Schuster Children's Publishing.

—Murder House, Bk. 3. 24th ed. 2008. (Hardy Boys (All New) Undercover Brothers Ser.: 24). (ENG.). 160p. (J). (gr. 3-7). pap. 6.99 *(978-1-4169-6409-4(6),* Aladdin) Simon & Schuster Children's Publishing.

Doty, Jean Slaughter. The Valley of the Ponies. 2012. (ENG.). 96p. (YA). (gr. 7-7). pap. 6.99 *(978-1-4424-8607-2(4),* Simon & Schuster Bks. For Young Readers) Simon & Schuster Bks. For Young Readers.

Doyle, Malachy & Philpot, Graham. Jack the Giant-Killer. 2009. (Hopscotch Adventures Ser.). (Illus.). 31p. (J). (gr. 1). lib. bdg. 25.65 *(978-1-59771-184-5(5))* Sea-To-Sea Pubns.

Draper, Sharon M. Panic. 2013. (ENG., Illus.). 272p. (YA). (gr. 9). 17.99 *(978-1-4424-0896-8(0),* Atheneum Bks. for Young Readers) Simon & Schuster Children's Publishing.

Duncan, Lois. Killing Mr. Griffin. 2009. 7.61 *(978-0-7848-3597-5(7),* Everbind) Marco Bk. Co.

Edmondson, Nathan. Who Is Jake Ellis?, Vol. 1. 2011. (ENG., Illus.). 136p. (YA). pap. 16.99 *(978-1-60706-459-6(6),* 9781607064596) Image Comics.

Ehrenberg, Pamela. Tillmon County Fire. 2009. 192p. (YA). (gr. 9-18). pap. 9.00 *(978-0-8028-5345-5(5),* Eerdmans Bks For Young Readers) Eerdmans, William B. Publishing Co.

Eisenstein, Ann E. Hiding Carly, a Sean Gray Junior Special Agent Mystery. 2013. 162p. pap. 9.99 *(978-1-935711-27-8(X))* Peak City Publishing, LLC.

Electric Chair or Taser Fried: Malicious Murder; Good Cop, Bad Cop. 2004. (YA). per. 25.00 *(978-0-9760909-0-8(2))* Yost-Haynes, Melissa.

Farmer, Nancy. The Lord of Opium. 2013. (ENG., Illus.). 432p. (YA). (gr. 7). 17.99 *(978-1-4424-8254-8(0))* Simon & Schuster Children's Publishing.

Farrell-Whelan, Max. Something Fishy Aboard the Red Herring: Can You Catch the Killer? 2013. 130p. pap. 11.95 *(978-1-61204-239-8(2),* Strategic Bk. Publishing) Strategic Book Publishing & Rights Agency (SBPRA).

Ferguson, Alane. The Christopher Killer. 2008. (Forensic Mystery Ser.). 274p. (gr. 7-12). 17.00 *(978-0-7569-8930-9(2))* Perfection Learning Corp.

Ferris, Jean. Love among the Walnuts. 2008. (ENG., Illus.). 228p. (J). (gr. 5-7). pap. 7.99 *(978-0-15-206227-9(0))* Houghton Mifflin Harcourt Publishing Co.

Fickey, Brenda. Beckoning Shadows, 1 vol. 2009. (ENG.). 179p. pap. 24.95 *(978-1-61546-330-5(5))* America Star Bks.

Galante, Cecilia. Stealing Our Way Home. 2017. (ENG.). 304p. (J). (gr. 3-7). 17.99 ***(978-1-338-04296-2(3),*** Scholastic Pr.) Scholastic, Inc.

Gavin, Rohan. K-9. 2016. (Knightley & Son Ser.: 2). (ENG.). 320p. (J). pap. 7.99 *(978-1-61963-687-3(5),* 9781619636873, Bloomsbury USA Childrens) Bloomsbury Publishing USA.

Gibson, Jo. Twisted. 2014. (ENG.). 560p. (YA). (gr. 13). pap. 9.95 *(978-1-61773-240-9(0),* K-Teen) Kensington Publishing Corp.

Gilbert, Kelly Loy. Conviction. 2017. (YA). lib. bdg. 20.85 ***(978-0-606-39170-2(3))*** Turtleback Bks.

Giles, Gail. What Happened to Cass McBride? 2007. (ENG.). 240p. (J). (gr. 10-17). per. 9.99 *(978-0-316-16639-3(1))* Little, Brown Bks. for Young Readers.

—What Happened to Cass McBride? 2007. 211p. 18.00 *(978-0-7569-8178-5(6))* Perfection Learning Corp.

Giles, Lamar. Overturned. 2017. (ENG.). 352p. (J). (gr. 7). 17.99 *(978-0-545-81250-4(X),* Scholastic Pr.) Scholastic, Inc.

Gray, Jennifer. Atticus Claw Settles a Score. Ecob, Mark, illus. 2016. (Atticus Claw Ser.). (ENG.). 240p. (gr. 1-4). 7.95 *(978-0-571-28681-2(X))* Faber & Faber, Inc.

Green, Jacqueline. Kiss & Tell. 2015. (Truth or Dare Ser.: 3). (ENG.). 288p. (YA). (gr. 10-17). 18.00 *(978-0-316-22033-0(7),* Poppy) Little, Brown Bks. for Young Readers.

Grogan, Shannon. From Where I Watch You. 2015. (ENG.). 304p. (YA). (gr. 9). 18.99 *(978-1-61695-554-0(6),* Soho Teen) Soho Pr., Inc.

Guerra, Stephanie. Betting Blind, 0 vols. 2014. (ENG.). 256p. (gr. 9-12). pap. 9.99 *(978-1-4778-4785-5(5),* 9781477847855, Skyscape) Amazon Publishing.

Haesche, Richard, Sr. The Mystery of Monster Manor. 2007. (ENG.). 306p. (YA). 11.99 *(978-0-9798536-6-1(4))* Kreative X-Pressions Pubns.

Hale, Kathleen. Nothing Bad Is Going to Happen. 2017. (Kippy Bushman Ser.). 272p. (YA). (gr. 9). pap. 9.99 *(978-0-06-221123-1(4),* HarperTeen) HarperCollins Pubs.

Harris, Loretta. A Gangsta's Life. 2007. 26p. (YA). 1.99 *(978-0-9786681-4-3(6))* Triumphant Living Enterprises, Inc.

Harvey, Sarah N. Shattered, 1 vol. 2011. (Orca Soundings Ser.). (ENG.). 128p. (YA). (gr. 8-12). pap. 9.95 *(978-1-55469-845-5(6));* lib. bdg. 16.95 *(978-1-55469-846-2(4))* Orca Bk. Pubs. USA.

Hautman, Pete. All-In. 2012. (ENG.). 208p. (YA). (gr. 7). pap. 8.99 *(978-1-4424-3335-9(3),* Simon & Schuster Bks. For Young Readers) Simon & Schuster Bks. For Young Readers.

Healey, Karen. The Shattering. 2013. (ENG.). 336p. (YA). (gr. 7-17). pap. 8.99 *(978-0-316-12573-4(3))* Little, Brown Bks. for Young Readers.

Hearn, Julie. Ivy. 2008. (ENG.). 368p. (YA). (gr. 7-18). 17.99 *(978-1-4169-2506-4(6),* Atheneum Bks. for Young Readers) Simon & Schuster Children's Publishing.

Heflick, LaMonte. The Story of Boney & Clyde. 2004. (Illus.). 64p. pap. 3.99 *(978-1-56175-911-8(2))* Remedia Pubns.

Heneghan, Judith. The Magician's Apprentice. 2008. (Illus.). 168p. (J). (gr. 3-7). 16.95 *(978-0-8234-2150-3(3))* Holiday Hse., Inc.

Henry, April. The Girl I Used to Be. 2017. (YA). lib. bdg. 20.85 ***(978-0-606-39999-9(2))*** Turtleback Bks.

Hieber, Leanna Renee. Darker Still. 2011. (Magic Most Foul Ser.: 1). (ENG.). 336p. (YA). (gr. 7-12). pap. 8.99 *(978-1-4022-6052-0(0))* Sourcebooks, Inc.

Hobbs, Will. Take Me to the River. 2011. (ENG.). 192p. (J). (gr. 5-18). 15.99 *(978-0-06-074144-0(9))* HarperCollins Pubs.

Hubbard, L. Ron, contrib. by. Common Core Literature Guide: Dead Men Kill: Literature Guide for Teachers & Librarians Based on Common Core ELA Standards for Classrooms 6-9. 2013. (Stories from the Golden Age Ser.). (ENG.). 35p. (gr. 6-9). pap., tchr. ed. 14.95 *(978-1-61986-218-0(2))* Galaxy Pr., LLC.

Hutton, Sam. Kiss & Kill. 2004. (Special Agents Ser.: 4). (ENG.). 240p. (J). (gr. 4-7). pap. 9.99 *(978-0-00-714845-5(3))* HarperCollins Pubs. Ltd. GBR. Dist: HarperCollins Pubs.

Inspector Grub & the Jelly Bean Robber: Individual Title Six-Packs. (Bookweb Ser.). 32p. (gr. 3-18). 34.00 *(978-0-7635-3934-4(1))* Rigby Education.

Jackson, Melanie. High Wire, 1 vol. 2012. (Orca Currents Ser.). (ENG.). 128p. (J). (gr. 5-9). pap. 9.95 *(978-1-4598-0236-0(5));* lib. bdg. 16.95 *(978-1-4598-0237-7(3))* Orca Bk. Pubs. USA.

Jakobsen, Lars. The Mysterious Manuscript. Jakobsen, Lars, illus. 2012. (Mortensen's Escapades Ser.: 1). (ENG., Illus.). 48p. (gr. 6-12). pap. 6.95 *(978-0-8225-9409-3(9));* lib. bdg. 27.93 *(978-0-7613-7883-9(9))* Lerner Publishing Group. (Graphic Universe™).

Jayne, Hannah. The Escape. 2015. (ENG., Illus.). 256p. (YA). (gr. 8-12). pap. 9.99 *(978-1-4926-1654-2(0),* 9781492616542) Sourcebooks, Inc.

Jenkins, Jerry B. & Fabry, Chris. Double Fault. 2005. (Red Rock Mysteries Ser.: 7). (ENG.). 272p. (YA). pap. 6.99 *(978-1-4143-0146-4(4),* Tyndale Kids) Tyndale Hse. Pubs.

—Hidden Riches. 2006. (Red Rock Mysteries Ser.: 13). (ENG.). 262p. (YA). (gr. 3-7). per. 6.99 *(978-1-4143-0152-5(9),* Tyndale Kids) Tyndale Hse. Pubs.

Jinks, Catherine. Evil Genius. 2007. 486p. (J). *(978-1-4287-3510-1(0))* Harcourt Trade Pubs.

—Evil Genius. 2008. (ENG., Illus.). 496p. (YA). (gr. 7). pap. 9.99 *(978-0-15-206185-2(1))* Houghton Mifflin Harcourt Publishing Co.

—Genius Squad. 2009. (ENG., Illus.). 448p. (J). (gr. 7). pap. 8.99 *(978-0-15-206650-5(0))* Houghton Mifflin Harcourt Publishing Co.

—The Genius Wars. 2011. (ENG.). 384p. (YA). (gr. 7). pap. 8.99 *(978-0-547-57727-2(3))* Houghton Mifflin Harcourt Publishing Co.

Johnston, Wayne M. North Fork. 2016. (ENG.). 210p. (YA). (gr. 7-12). pap. 14.95 *(978-1-936364-20-6(4))* Black Heron Pr.

Jones, Patrick. Fight or Flee. 2016. (Unbarred Ser.). (ENG.). 120p. (YA). (gr. 6-12). lib. bdg. 27.99 *(978-1-5124-0004-5(1),* Darby Creek) Lerner Publishing Group.

—Fight or Flee. 2016. (Unbarred Ser.). (ENG.). 120p. (YA). (gr. 6-12). pap. 7.99 *(978-1-5124-0093-9(9),* Darby Creek) Lerner Publishing Group.

—Fight or Flee. 2016. (Unbarred Ser.). (ENG.). 120p. (YA). (gr. 6-12). 42.65 *(978-1-5124-0094-6(7),* Darby Creek) Lerner Publishing Group.

Jones, T. W. Derth. 2006. 165p. pap. 24.95 *(978-1-4241-0806-0(3))* PublishAmerica, Inc.

Karas, Phyllis. The Hate Crime. 2004. 190p. (YA). pap. 13.95 *(978-0-595-33138-3(6),* Authors Choice Pr.) iUniverse, Inc.

Kay, Elizabeth. Fury. 2012. (Stoke Books Titles Ser.). (ENG.). 80p. (YA). (gr. 8-12). pap. 6.95 *(978-1-78112-097-2(8));* lib. bdg. 22.60 *(978-1-78112-098-9(6))* Lerner Publishing Group.

Keene, Carolyn. Sabotage Surrender: Book Three in the Sabotage Mystery Trilogy. 2011. (Nancy Drew (All New) Girl Detective Ser.: 44). (ENG.). 128p. (J). (gr. 3-7). pap. 6.99 *(978-1-4169-9071-0(2),* Aladdin) Simon & Schuster Children's Publishing.

Kehoe, Tim. Furious Jones & the Assassin's Secret. 2014. (ENG., Illus.). 336p. (J). (gr. 3-7). 16.99 *(978-1-4424-7337-9(1),* Simon & Schuster Bks. For Young Readers) Simon & Schuster Bks. For Young Readers.

C
D

Kehret, Peg. Bone Breath & the Vandals. 2008. (Frightmares Ser.: 2). (ENG.). 128p. (YA). (gr. 7). pap. 8.99 *(978-1-4169-8484-9(4)*, Simon & Schuster Bks. For Young Readers) Simon & Schuster Bks. For Young Readers.
Kidd, Rob. Day of the Shadow. 4th ed. 2009. (Pirates of the Caribbean Ser.: No. 5). 256p. (YA). (gr. 5-18). pap. 6.99 *(978-1-4231-1041-5(2))* Disney Pr.
Kimmel, Elizabeth Cody. Lily B. on the Brink of Cool. 2005. 245p. (J). (gr. 5-9). 14.65 *(978-0-7569-5653-0(6))* Perfection Learning Corp.
Kimpton, Diana. Princess Ellie Solves a Mystery. Finlay, Lizzie, illus. 8th rev. ed. 2007. (ENG.). 96p. (gr. 1-4). pap. 3.99 *(978-1-4231-0901-3(5))* Hyperion Pr.
Kirby, Matthew J. Last Descendants. 2016. (Last Descendants Ser.: 1). (ENG.). 320p. (J). (gr. 7). pap. 9.99 *(978-0-545-85551-8(9))* Scholastic, Inc.
—A Taste for Monsters. 2016. (ENG.). 352p. (YA). (gr. 7). 18.99 *(978-0-545-81784-4(6)*, Scholastic Pr.) Scholastic, Inc.
Korman, Gordon. Dragonfly Effect, Bk. 3. 2016. (Hypnotists Ser.: 3). (ENG.). 256p. (J). (gr. 3-7). pap. 6.99 *(978-0-545-50338-9(8)*, Scholastic Pr.) Scholastic, Inc.
—Swindle. 2009. (ENG.). 256p. (J). (gr. 3-7). 6.99 *(978-0-439-90345-5(9)*, Scholastic Paperbacks) Scholastic, Inc.
Korman, Susan. Bad Deal. 2011. (Surviving Southside Ser.). (ENG.). 104p. (YA). (gr. 6-12). lib. bdg. 27.93 *(978-0-7613-6152-7(9))* Lerner Publishing Group.
Kowitt, Holly, illus. The Loser List. 2011. 213p. (J). pap. *(978-0-545-32900-2(0)*, Scholastic Pr.) Scholastic, Inc.
Krailing, Tessa. El Ladron de Gatos. (Club de las Mascotas Coleccion). (SPA.). 96p. (J). (gr. 3). *(978-84-88061-89-8(7))* Serres, Ediciones, S. L. ESP. Dist: Lectorum Pubns., Inc.
Kramer, Paul. Louie the Lobster Mobster. 2012. (ENG.). 48p. (J). (gr. 1-7). 15.95 *(978-0-9819745-2-1(X))* Aloha Wellness Pubs.
Kraus, Daniel. The Death & Life of Zebulon Finch Vol. 1: At the Edge of Empire. 2015. (Zebulon Finch Ser.: 1). (ENG., Illus.). 656p. (YA). (gr. 9). 21.99 *(978-1-4814-1139-4(X)*, Simon & Schuster Bks. For Young Readers) Simon & Schuster Bks. For Young Readers.
Krensky, Stephen. The Great Moon Hoax. Bisaillon, Josée, illus. 2011. (Carolrhoda Picture Bks.). (ENG.). 32p. (J). (gr. 2-5). lib. bdg. 16.95 *(978-0-7613-5110-8(8))* Lerner Publishing Group.
Kropp, Paul. The Edge Is Burning. Doherty, Catherine, illus. 2008. 112p. (YA). (gr. 7-18). pap. *(978-1-897039-33-5(6))* High Interest Publishing (HIP).
Larkin, Jillian. Ingenue. 2012. (Flappers Ser.). (ENG.). 368p. (YA). (gr. 7). pap. 9.99 *(978-0-385-74037-1(9)*, Ember) Random Hse. Children's Bks.
Leavitt, Martine. My Book of Life by Angel. 2014. (ENG.). 272p. (YA). (gr. 9-13). pap. 11.99 *(978-1-250-04003-9(5)*, 9781250040039) Square Fish.
Lee, Helen. Guide's Greatest Escape from Crime Stories. 2003. (Pathfinder Junior Book Club Ser.). 141p. (J). pap. 10.99 *(978-0-8280-1753-4(0)*, 79-967) Review & Herald Publishing Assn.
Leonard, Julia Platt. Cold Case. 2012. (ENG.). 288p. (J). (gr. 3-7). pap. 5.99 *(978-1-4424-2010-6(3)*, Simon & Schuster/Paula Wiseman Bks.) Simon & Schuster/Paula Wiseman Bks.
Lerangis, Peter. Wtf. 2009. (ENG.). 272p. (YA). (gr. 9-18). pap. 8.99 *(978-1-4169-1360-3(2)*, Simon Pulse) Simon Pulse.
Lewman, David. The Case of the Ruined Ram. 2012. (Club CSI Ser.: 4). (ENG.). 160p. (J). (gr. 3-7). 15.99 *(978-1-4424-4672-4(2))*; pap. 5.99 *(978-1-4424-3397-7(3))* Simon Spotlight. (Simon Spotlight).
Linn, Laurent. Draw the Line. Linn, Laurent, illus. 2016. (ENG., Illus.). 528p. (YA). (gr. 7). 17.99 *(978-1-4814-5280-9(0)*, McElderry, Margaret K. Bks.) McElderry, Margaret K. Bks.
Liss, David. Renegades. 2017. (Randoms Ser.: 3). (ENG., Illus.). 352p. (J). (gr. 5). 18.99 ***(978-1-4814-1785-3(1)***, Simon & Schuster Bks. For Young Readers) Simon & Schuster Bks. For Young Readers.
The Lord of Opium. 2014. (ENG., Illus.). 448p. (YA). (gr. 7). pap. 12.99 *(978-1-4424-8255-5(6)*, Atheneum Bks. for Young Readers) Simon & Schuster Children's Publishing.
Ludwig, Elisa. Pretty Sly. 2014. (Pretty Crooked Trilogy Ser.: 2). (ENG.). 336p. (YA). (gr. 8). 17.99 *(978-0-06-206609-1(9)*, Tegen, Katherine Bks) HarperCollins Pubs.
Lynch, Chris. Little Blue Lies. 2014. (ENG.). 224p. (YA). (gr. 7). 17.99 *(978-1-4424-4008-1(2)*, Simon & Schuster Bks. For Young Readers) Simon & Schuster Bks. For Young Readers.
Mack, Tracy & Citrin, Michael. Fall of the Amazing Zalindas. 2009. (Sherlock Holmes & the Baker St. Irregulars Ser.: 1). (ENG.). 272p. (J). (gr. 3-7). 6.99 *(978-0-545-06939-7(4)*, Scholastic Paperbacks) Scholastic, Inc.
Manley, Francis G. Tellin Twins: The Great Art Scam. 2004. (Illus.). 132p. pap. *(978-1-84401-292-3(1))* Athena Pr.
Marr, Melissa. Made for You. 2014. (ENG.). 368p. (YA). (gr. 8). 17.99 *(978-0-06-201119-0(7))* HarperCollins Pubs.
Marz, Ron. Witchblade Redemption, Vol. 4. 2012. (ENG., Illus.). 160p. pap. 19.99 *(978-1-60706-424-4(3)*, 9781607064244) Image Comics.
Mayowa-Harrison, Lady Paula Merry. The Buckaroos. 2006. (J). pap. 8.00 *(978-0-8059-6978-8(0))* Dorrance Publishing Co., Inc.
McBride, Susan. Very Bad Things. 2014. (ENG.). 240p. (YA). (gr. 7). lib. bdg. 20.99 *(978-0-385-90704-0(4)*, Delacorte Pr.) Random Hse. Children's Bks.
McClintock, Norah. Bang, 1 vol. 2007. (Orca Soundings Ser.). (ENG.). 112p. (YA). (gr. 8-12). per. 9.95 *(978-1-55143-654-8(X))* Orca Bk. Pubs. USA.
McCormack, Devon. Hideous. 2016. (ENG., Illus.). (J). 24.99 ***(978-1-63533-028-1(9)***, Harmony Ink Pr.) Dreamspinner Pr.
McCormick, Patricia. Sold. 2011. 10.36 *(978-0-7848-3420-6(2)*, Everbind) Marco Bk. Co.
—Sold. 2008. 263p. (J). (gr. 7-12). 19.65 *(978-1-4178-1810-5(7)*, Turtleback) Turtleback Bks.
Mcgill, Leslie. Break & Enter. 2016. (White Lightning Ser.). (J). lib. bdg. 19.60 *(978-0-606-37965-6(7))* Turtleback Bks.
McIntosh, Kenneth. Close-Up: Forensic Photography. 2009. (J). pap. 24.95 *(978-1-4222-1455-8(9))* Mason Crest.
—Devil's Canyon: Forensic Geography. 2009. (J). 24.95 *(978-1-4222-1450-3(8))* Mason Crest.
—Devil's Canyon: Forensic Geography. Miller, Justin, illus. 2007. (Crime Scene Club Ser.: Bk. 1). 144p. (YA). (gr. 9-12). 24.95 *(978-1-4222-0247-0(X))* Mason Crest.
—The Earth Cries Out: Forensic Chemistry & Environmental Science. 2009. (J). pap. 24.95 *(978-1-4222-1457-2(5))* Mason Crest.
—The Earth Cries Out: Forensic Chemistry & Environmental Science, 8 vols. Miller, Justin, illus. 2007. (Crime Scene Club Ser.: Bk. 9). 144p. (YA). (gr. 9-12). lib. bdg. 24.95 *(978-1-4222-0254-8(2))* Mason Crest.
—Face from the Past: Skull Reconstruction. 2009. (J). pap. 24.95 *(978-1-4222-1454-1(0))* Mason Crest.
—If the Shoe Fits: Footwear Analysis. 2009. (J). pap. 24.95 *(978-1-4222-1456-5(7))* Mason Crest.
—If the Shoe Fits: Footwear Analysis, 7 vols. Miller, Justin, illus. 2007. (Crime Scene Club Ser.). 144p. (YA). (gr. 9-12). lib. bdg. 24.95 *(978-1-4222-0253-1(4))* Mason Crest.
—Monsoon Murder: Forensic Meteorology. 2009. (J). pap. 24.95 *(978-1-4222-1461-9(3))* Mason Crest.
—Monsoon Murder: Forensic Meteorology, 12 vols. Holland, Joe, illus. 2007. (Crime Scene Club Ser.). 144p. (YA). (gr. 9-12). lib. bdg. 24.95 *(978-1-4222-0258-6(5))* Mason Crest.
—Numbering the Crime: Forensic Mathematics, 11 vols. Golden, John Ashton, illus. 2007. (Crime Scene Club Ser.). 144p. (YA). (gr. 9-12). lib. bdg. 24.95 *(978-1-4222-0257-9(7))* Mason Crest.
—Over the Edge: Forensic Accident Reconstruction. 2009. (J). pap. 24.95 *(978-1-4222-1451-0(6))* Mason Crest.
—Over the Edge: Forensic Accident Reconstruction, 2 vols. Sanborn, Casey, illus. 2007. (Crime Scene Club Ser.: Bk. 2). 144p. (YA). (gr. 9-12). lib. bdg. 24.95 *(978-1-4222-0248-7(8))* Mason Crest.
—Poison & Peril: Forensic Toxicology. 2009. (J). pap. 24.95 *(978-1-4222-1453-4(2))* Mason Crest.
—Poison & Peril: Forensic Toxicology, 4 vols. Miller, Justin, illus. 2007. (Crime Scene Club Ser.). 144p. (YA). (gr. 9-12). lib. bdg. 24.95 *(978-1-4222-0250-0(X))* Mason Crest.
—A Stranger's Voice: Forensic Speech Identification, 9 vols. Golden, John Ashton, illus. 2007. (Crime Scene Club Ser.). 144p. (YA). (gr. 9-12). lib. bdg. 24.95 *(978-1-4222-0255-5(0))* Mason Crest.
—Things Fall Apart: Forensic Engineering. 2009. (J). pap. 24.95 *(978-1-4222-1459-6(1))* Mason Crest.
—Things Fall Apart: Forensic Engineering, 10 vols. Golden, John Ashton, illus. 2007. (Crime Scene Club Ser.). 144p. (YA). (gr. 9-12). lib. bdg. 24.95 *(978-1-4222-0256-2(9))* Mason Crest.
—The Trickster's Image: Forensic Art. 2007. (Crime Scene Club: Fact & Fiction Ser.). (Illus.). 144p. (YA). (gr. 8-12). pap. 9.95 *(978-1-4222-0873-1(7))* Mason Crest.
—The Trickster's Image: Forensic Art, 3 vols. Miller, Justin, illus. 2007. (Crime Scene Club Ser.). 144p. (YA). (gr. 9-12). lib. bdg. 24.95 *(978-1-4222-0249-4(6))* Mason Crest.
McNicoll, Sylvia. Crush. Candy. Corpse, 1 vol. 2012. (ENG.). 224p. (YA). (gr. 7-12). pap. 12.95 *(978-1-4594-0062-7(3)*, 9781459400627) Lorimer, James & Co., Ltd., Pubs. CAN. Dist: Casemate Pubs. & Bk. Distributors, LLC.
McRae, David. Blood of the Donnellys. 2007. (ENG.). 144p. (J). (gr. 8). pap. 11.99 *(978-1-55002-754-9(9))* Dundurn CAN. Dist: Ingram Publisher Services.
Meyer, Kai. Arcadia Awakens. 2012. (Arcadia Ser.: 1). (ENG.). 464p. (YA). (gr. 9). 17.99 *(978-0-06-200606-6(1))* HarperCollins Pubs.
Miller, Kirsten. The Darkness Dwellers. 2013. (Kiki Strike Ser.). (ENG., Illus.). 416p. (YA). (gr. 7-12). 17.99 *(978-1-59990-736-9(4)*, 9781599907369, Bloomsbury USA Childrens) Bloomsbury Publishing USA.
—The Empress's Tomb. 2013. (Kiki Strike Ser.). (ENG.). 384p. (YA). (gr. 7-12). pap. 9.99 *(978-1-59990-921-9(9)*, 9781599909219, Bloomsbury USA Childrens) Bloomsbury Publishing USA.
—Inside the Shadow City. (Kiki Strike Ser.). (ENG.). 400p. (YA). 2013. (gr. 7-12). pap. 9.99 *(978-1-59990-920-2(0)*, 9781599909202) 2006. (gr. 4-8). 16.95 *(978-1-58234-960-2(6)*, 9781582349602) Bloomsbury Publishing USA. (Bloomsbury USA Childrens).
Molnar, Gwen. Hate Cell: A Casey Templeton Mystery. 2009. (Casey Templeton Mystery Ser.: 1). (ENG.). 184p. (YA). (gr. 5). pap. 11.99 *(978-1-55002-850-8(2))* Dundurn CAN. Dist: Ingram Publisher Services.
Moloney, James. Black Taxi. 2005. 272p. (J). (gr. 7-18). 15.99 *(978-0-06-055937-3(3))* HarperCollins Pubs.
—Black Taxi. 2003. 288p. *(978-0-207-19989-9(2))* HarperCollins Pubs. Australia.
Monir, Alexandra. The Girl in the Picture. 2016. (ENG.). 272p. (YA). (gr. 7). 17.99 *(978-0-385-74390-7(4)*, Delacorte Pr.) Random Hse. Children's Bks.
Moore, Stephanie Perry. Truth & Nothing But. 2014. (Sharp Sisters Ser.: 4). (ENG.). 160p. (YA). (gr. 6-12). pap. 7.95 *(978-1-4677-4489-8(1)*, Darby Creek); lib. bdg. 27.93 *(978-1-4677-3727-2(5))* Lerner Publishing Group.
Morgan, Lori. Healing the Bruises, 1 vol. Kaulbach, Kathy R., illus. 2013. (ENG.). 32p. (J). (gr. 1-4). 16.95 *(978-1-4595-0283-3(3)*, 9781459502833) Formac Publishing Co., Ltd. CAN. Dist: Casemate Pubs. & Bk. Distributors, LLC.
Morgenroth, Kate. Jude. 2006. (ENG., Illus.). 288p. (YA). (gr. 7-12). reprint ed. mass mkt. 7.99 *(978-1-4169-1267-5(3)*, Simon Pulse) Simon Pulse.
Morphew, Chris. The Man in the Shadows. 2017. (Phoenix Files Ser.: 1). (ENG.). 512p. (YA). (gr. 7). pap. 12.99 ***(978-1-76012-425-0(7))*** Hardie Grant Egmont Pty, Ltd. AUS. Dist: Independent Pubs. Group.
Morris, Paula. Unbroken. 2014. (ENG.). 304p. (J). (gr. 7). pap. 9.99 *(978-0-545-41642-9(6))* Scholastic, Inc.
Moser, Elise. Lily & Taylor, 1 vol. 2013. (ENG.). 224p. (J). (gr. 8). 16.95 *(978-1-55498-334-6(7))* Groundwood Bks. CAN. Dist: Publishers Group West (PGW).
Myers, Walter Dean & Sims, Guy A. Monster. Anyabwile, Dawud, illus. 2015. (YA). lib. bdg. 20.85 *(978-0-606-37629-7(1))* Turtleback Bks.
Mystery of the Phantom Heist. 2013. (Hardy Boys Adventures Ser.: 2). (ENG.). 160p. (J). (gr. 3-7). 15.99 *(978-1-4424-6586-2(7))*; pap. 6.99 *(978-1-4424-2237-7(8))* Simon & Schuster Children's Publishing. (Aladdin).
Nabors, V. L. Mad Craze Middle School; the Case of the Crumpled Balls. 2010. 215p. pap. 16.95 *(978-0-557-44140-2(4))* Lulu Pr., Inc.
Narsimhan, Mahtab. The Deadly Conch: Tara Trilogy. 2011. (Tara Trilogy Ser.: 3). (ENG.). 288p. (YA). (gr. 9). pap. 12.99 *(978-1-55488-794-1(1))* Dundurn CAN. Dist: Ingram Publisher Services.
Nobel, Zack. The Twisted Teenage Mysteries. 2009. 48p. pap. 17.49 *(978-1-4389-1127-4(0))* AuthorHouse.
Nonenmacher, Dawn Marie. Piccolo's Personal Case: The Talented Trio Series Story #2, 1 vol. 2009. 73p. pap. 19.95 *(978-1-61582-622-3(X))* America Star Bks.
Norris, Zack. Tunnel of Bones. 2012. (Double Detectives Ser.). (ENG.). 144p. (J). (gr. 3-7). pap. 4.95 *(978-1-4027-9147-5(X))* Sterling Publishing Co., Inc.
Northrop, Michael. Gentlemen. 2009. (ENG.). 256p. (J). (gr. 9-18). 17.99 *(978-0-545-09749-9(5)*, Scholastic Pr.) Scholastic, Inc.
Oakes, Cory Putman. Witchtown. 2017. (ENG.). 320p. (YA). (gr. 7). 17.99 *(978-0-544-76557-3(5)*, HMH Books For Young Readers) Houghton Mifflin Harcourt Publishing Co.
O'Brien, Anne Sibley. In the Shadow of the Sun. 2017. (ENG.). 304p. (J). (gr. 3-7). 17.99 ***(978-0-545-90574-9(5))*** Scholastic, Inc.
O'Brien, Johnny. Day of the Assassins: A Jack Christie Novel. Hardcastle, Nick, illus. 2009. (Jack Christie Adventure Ser.: 1). (ENG.). 224p. (J). (gr. 4-7). 15.99 *(978-0-7636-4595-3(8)*, Templar) Candlewick Pr.
Oliver, Lauren & Chester, H. C. The Fearsome Firebird. 2017. (Curiosity House Ser.: 3). 336p. (J). (gr. 3-7). 16.99 *(978-0-06-227087-0(7))* HarperCollins Pubs.
Ormerod, Nicola. Roxy May, Help My Boyfriend Is a Fairy. 2012. 224p. pap. *(978-1-909402-03-4(6))* Vamptasy Publishing.
Parker, Amy Christine. Smash & Grab. 2016. (ENG.). 384p. (YA). (gr. 7). 17.99 *(978-0-553-53382-8(7)*, Random Hse. Bks. for Young Readers) Random Hse. Children's Bks.
Parker, S. M. The Girl Who Fell. (ENG., Illus.). (YA). (gr. 11). 2017. 384p. pap. 10.99 *(978-1-4814-3724-0(0))* 2016. 368p. 17.99 *(978-1-4814-3725-7(9))* Simon Pulse. (Simon Pulse).
Parkhurst, Johanna. Every Inferno. 2016. (ENG., Illus.). (J). 24.99 ***(978-1-63533-009-0(2)***, Harmony Ink Pr.) Dreamspinner Pr.
Peralta, Joaquin. An Almost Private Eye: Mystery of the Starfighter. 2008. 260p. (YA). (gr. 8-18). per. 17.00 *(978-1-934376-17-1(5))* Balona Bks.
Pluth, Lisa Anderson. A Haunting in Little River. 2011. 94p. pap. 19.95 *(978-1-4560-9700-4(8))* America Star Bks.
Promitzer, Rebecca. The Pickle King. 2010. (ENG.). 416p. (J). (gr. 3-7). 17.99 *(978-0-545-17087-1(7)*, Chicken Hse., The) Scholastic, Inc.
Pullman, Philip. Two Crafty Criminals! And How They Were Captured by the Daring Detectives of the New Cut Gang. (ENG.). 288p. (J). (gr. 3-7). 2013. 7.99 *(978-0-307-93035-4(1)*, Yearling) 2012. (Illus.). 16.99 *(978-0-375-87029-3(6)*, Knopf Bks. for Young Readers) Random Hse. Children's Bks.
Rae, Kimberly. Capturing Jasmina. 2014. (YA). *(978-1-60682-853-3(3))* BJU Pr.
Reilly, Carmel & Ashforth, Kate. The Jewelry Story Robbery. 2008. (Rigby Focus Forward: Level F Ser.). (Illus.). 24p. (J). (gr. 4-7). pap. *(978-1-4190-3685-9(8)*, Rigby) Pearson Education Australia.
Restivo, Andrea E. Arabella & the Perilous Pantheon. 2010. 28p. pap. 12.99 *(978-1-60693-790-7(1)*, Strategic Bk. Publishing) Strategic Book Publishing & Rights Agency (SBPRA).
Rilla, Donald. The Three Italian Foster Kids. 2012. 68p. pap. 15.99 *(978-1-4797-1582-4(4))* Xlibris Corp.
Roberts, Daniel. Young Pep Squad Mysteries. 2011. 36p. pap. 16.99 *(978-1-4567-9640-2(2))* AuthorHouse.
Roberts, Willo Davis. The View from the Cherry Tree. 2015. (ENG., Illus.). 256p. (J). (gr. 3-7). pap. 6.99 *(978-1-4814-3994-7(4)*, Aladdin) Simon & Schuster Children's Publishing.
Robinson, Nikia. The Lock-in. 2009. 38p. pap. 13.40 *(978-0-557-18567-2(X))* Lulu Pr., Inc.
Roderman, Anna Marie. Two Tales of Courage. 2004. 116p. (YA). pap. 7.95 *(978-0-87714-318-5(8))* i-5 Publishing LLC.
Rosenfield, Kat. Amelia Anne Is Dead & Gone. 2013. (ENG.). 288p. (YA). (gr. 9). pap. 8.99 *(978-0-14-242610-4(5)*, Speak) Penguin Young Readers Group.
Ross, Jeff. Coming Clean, 1 vol. 2012. (Orca Soundings Ser.). (ENG.). 128p. (YA). (gr. 8-12). pap. 9.95 *(978-1-4598-0331-2(0))* Orca Bk. Pubs. USA.
Ryan, Patrick. In Mike We Trust. 2009. 321p. (J). lib. bdg. 17.89 *(978-0-06-085814-8(1)*, HarperTeen) HarperCollins Pubs.
Salane, Jeffrey. Mayhem. 2016. (Lawless Ser.: 3). (ENG.). 304p. (J). (gr. 3-7). 17.99 *(978-0-545-45033-1(0)*, Scholastic Pr.) Scholastic, Inc.
Salin-Pascual, Rafael. El espectro del seÑor Amok. 2008. 151p. pap. 20.49 *(978-1-4357-4508-7(6))* Lulu Pr., Inc.
S.C.A.M. 170p. (J). pap. *(978-1-4114-0441-0(6)*, SparkNotes) Barnes & Noble, Inc.
Scarlett Giblin, Alison. Children of Conygre & the Time Capsule. 2006. 220p. per. *(978-1-905529-41-4(4))* Grosvenor Hse. Publishing Ltd.
Schraff, Anne. Once upon a Crime (Mystery), 1 vol. 2017. (Pageturners Ser.). (ENG.). 76p. (YA). (gr. 9-12). 8.95 ***(978-1-68021-388-1(1))*** Saddleback Educational Publishing, Inc.
—The Quality of Mercy. 2011. (Urban Underground — Harriet Tubman High School Ser.). (YA). lib. bdg. 20.80 *(978-0-606-14800-9(0)*, Turtleback) Turtleback Bks.
—Sounds of Terror, 1 vol. unabr. ed. 2010. (Q Reads Ser.). (ENG.). 32p. (YA). (gr. 9-12). pap. 6.95 *(978-1-61651-206-4(7))* Saddleback Educational Publishing, Inc.
Schraff, Anne E. Guilt Trip. 2014. (Urban Underground — Cesar Chavez High School Ser.). (YA). lib. bdg. 20.80 *(978-0-606-35592-6(8))* Turtleback Bks.
Seaman, John E. The Captain's Secret: A Lost Boy's Odyssey in Old New York. 2008. 220p. pap. 15.95 *(978-0-595-51753-4(6))* iUniverse, Inc.
Secret of the Red Arrow. 2013. (Hardy Boys Adventures Ser.: 1). (ENG.). 176p. (J). (gr. 3-7). 15.99 *(978-1-4424-6585-5(9))*; pap. 6.99 *(978-1-4424-4615-1(3))* Simon & Schuster Children's Publishing. (Aladdin).
Sedgwick, Marcus. Saint Death. 2017. (ENG.). 240p. (YA). 17.99 *(978-1-62672-549-2(7)*, 9781626725492) Roaring Brook Pr.
Shadows at Predator Reef. 2014. (Hardy Boys Adventures Ser.: 7). (ENG., Illus.). 128p. (J). (gr. 3-7). 17.99 *(978-1-4814-0010-7(X))*; pap. 6.99 *(978-1-4814-0009-1(6))* Simon & Schuster Children's Publishing. (Aladdin).
Shaw, Murray & Cosson, M. J. Sherlock Holmes & the Adventure at the Abbey Grange. Rohrbach, Sophie, illus. 2010. (On the Case with Holmes & Watson Ser.: 2). (ENG.). 48p. (J). (gr. 4-6). pap. 6.95 *(978-0-7613-6200-5(2)*, Graphic Universe™) Lerner Publishing Group.
—Sherlock Holmes & the Adventure of the Speckled Band. Rohrbach, Sophie, illus. 2010. (On the Case with Holmes & Watson Ser.: 5). (ENG.). 48p. (J). (gr. 4-6). pap. 6.95 *(978-0-7613-6198-5(7)*, Graphic Universe™) Lerner Publishing Group.
Shaw, Susan. Tunnel Vision. (ENG.). 272p. (YA). (gr. 7). 2012. pap. 8.99 *(978-1-4424-0840-1(5))* 2011. 16.99 *(978-1-4424-0839-5(1))* McElderry, Margaret K. Bks. (McElderry, Margaret K. Bks.).
Shea, John & Harmon, Michael B. A Kid from Southie. 2011. 240p. (YA). (gr. 9-18). 16.95 *(978-1-934813-53-9(2))* Westside Bks.
Sherry, Kevin. Attack of the Kraken (the Yeti Files #3) 2016. (Yeti Files Ser.: 3). (ENG.). 128p. (J). (gr. 2-5). 8.99 *(978-0-545-85781-9(3)*, Scholastic Pr.) Scholastic, Inc.
Silvey, Craig. Jasper Jones. 2012. 20.00 *(978-1-61383-806-8(9))* Perfection Learning Corp.
—Jasper Jones. 2012. (ENG.). 320p. (YA). (gr. 7). pap. 9.99 *(978-0-375-86627-2(2)*, Ember) Random Hse. Children's Bks.
Simmons, Lynn. Bo & the Christmas Bandit, 1 vol. Lyne, Alison, illus. 2009. (Bo Ser.). (ENG.). 128p. (J). (gr. 3-6). pap. 8.95 *(978-1-58980-723-5(5))* Pelican Publishing Co., Inc.
Skillchecks for Crime & Detection. rev. ed. 2005. (Fastback Ser.). 32p. (J). (gr. 6-12). pap. 5.95 *(978-0-13-024453-6(8))* Globe Fearon Educational Publishing.
Smiley, Jane. A Good Horse. 2011. (Horses of Oak Valley Ranch Ser.: Bk. 2). (ENG.). 256p. (J). (gr. 5). 6.99 *(978-0-375-86230-4(7)*, Yearling) Random Hse. Children's Bks.
Smith, Dan. Boy X. 2017. (J). ***(978-1-338-17150-1(X))*** Scholastic, Inc.
Smith, Roland. Beneath. 2015. (ENG., Illus.). 272p. (J). (gr. 4-7). 16.99 *(978-0-545-56486-1(7)*, Scholastic Pr.) Scholastic, Inc.
Smith, Sherri L. Pasadena. 2016. (ENG.). 240p. (YA). (gr. 9). 17.99 *(978-1-101-99625-6(0)*, G.P. Putnam's Sons Books for Young Readers) Penguin Young Readers Group.
Snicket, Lemony, pseud & Stookey, Nathaniel. The Composer Is Dead. Ellis, Carson, illus. 2009. (ENG.). 40p. (J). (gr. k-5). 17.99 *(978-0-06-123627-3(6))* HarperCollins Pubs.
Stassen, Jean-Philippe. Deogratias. 2006. (Illus.). 96p. (J). pap. *(978-0-330-44467-5(0)*, First Second Bks.) Roaring Brook Pr.
Staunton, Ted. Coda, 1 vol. 2014. (Seven Sequels Ser.). (ENG., Illus.). 224p. (J). (gr. 5-10). pap. 10.95 *(978-1-4598-0549-1(6))* Orca Bk. Pubs. USA.
Stevens, Serita. The Adventure Begins. 2004. (Illus.). 182p. *(978-0-9753548-1-0(7))* Palm Publishing LLC.
Stewart, Michael F. Assured Destruction. 2013. 188p. pap. *(978-0-9812699-4-8(X))* Non Sequitur Pr.
Stine, R. L. Broken Hearts. 2011. (Fear Street Superchillers Ser.: Bk. 3). (ENG.). 224p. (YA). (gr. 7). pap. 10.99 *(978-1-4424-4273-3(5)*, Simon Pulse) Simon Pulse.
—The Lost Girl: A Fear Street Novel. 2015. (Fear Street Ser.). (ENG.). 272p. (YA). 17.99 *(978-1-250-05163-9(0)*, 9781250051639, St. Martin's Griffin) St. Martin's Pr.
Stone, Danika. Internet Famous. 2017. (ENG.). 336p. (YA). pap. 10.99 *(978-1-250-11437-2(3)*, 9781250114372) Feiwel & Friends.
Strasser, Todd. Famous. 2013. (ENG.). 272p. (YA). (gr. 7). pap. 9.99 *(978-1-4424-5418-7(0)*, Simon & Schuster Bks. For Young Readers) Simon & Schuster Bks. For Young Readers.
—Stolen Kisses, Secrets, & Lies. 2007. (Mob Princess Ser.: 2). (ENG., Illus.). 224p. (YA). (gr. 9-12). pap. 10.99 *(978-1-4169-3541-4(X)*, Simon Pulse) Simon Pulse.
Sutherland, Tui T. & Sutherland, Kari. Dragon on Trial. 2015. (Menagerie Ser.: 2). (ENG.). 320p. (J). (gr. 3-7). pap. 6.99 *(978-0-06-085145-3(7))* HarperCollins Pubs.
Sylvester, Kevin. The Neil Flambé Capers Collection: Neil Flambé & the Marco Polo Murders; Neil Flambé & the Aztec Abduction; Neil Flambé & the Crusader's Curse; Neil Flambé & the Tokyo Treasure. Sylvester, Kevin, illus. 2014. (Neil Flambe Capers Ser.). (ENG., Illus.). 1344p. (J). (gr. 3-7). pap. 31.99 *(978-1-4814-3238-2(9)*, Simon & Schuster Bks. For Young Readers) Simon & Schuster Bks. For Young Readers.
Taylor, Billy. Thieving Weasels. 2016. (ENG.). 256p. (YA). (gr. 7). 17.99 *(978-0-525-42924-1(7)*, Dial Bks) Penguin Young Readers Group.
Taylor, Jo-Ann. The Alchemist's Secret. 2011. 268p. pap. *(978-1-907652-87-5(6))* Grosvenor Hse. Publishing Ltd.
Taylor, Kara. Deadly Little Sins. 2014. (Prep School Confidential Novel Ser.: 3). (ENG.). 288p. (YA). (gr. 7). pap. 19.99 *(978-1-250-03363-5(2)*, 9781250033635, St. Martin's Griffin) St. Martin's Pr.
Teer, Robert & Demartino, Damian. Gloom & Dread. 2013. 38p. pap. 18.86 *(978-1-300-64200-8(9))* Lulu Pr., Inc.
Tharp, Tim. Mojo. 2014. (ENG.). 288p. (YA). (gr. 7). pap. 8.99 *(978-0-375-86402-5(4)*, Ember) Random Hse. Children's Bks.
Tillit, L. B. Unchained. 2012. (Gravel Road Ser.). (YA). lib. bdg. 20.80 *(978-0-606-25250-8(9)*, Turtleback) Turtleback Bks.
Tome. Spirou & Fantasio in New York. Janry, illus. 2011. (Spirou & Fantasio Ser.: 2). (ENG.). 48p. (J). (gr. 3-17). pap. 11.95 *(978-1-84918-054-2(7))* CineBook GBR. Dist: National Bk. Network.
Trevayne, Emma. Chorus. 2014. (ENG.). 288p. (YA). (gr. 2-17). pap. 9.95 *(978-0-7624-4950-7(0)*, Running Pr. Kids) Running Pr. Bk. Pubs.

Trionfo, Nikki. Shatter. 2017. (YA). pap. 18.99 (978-1-4621-2013-0(X), Horizon Pubs.) Cedar Fort, Inc./CFI Distribution.

Turnage, Sheila. The Odds of Getting Even. 2015. (ENG., Illus.). 352p. (J). (gr. 5). 16.99 (978-0-8037-3961-1(3), Kathy Dawson Books) Penguin Young Readers Group.

Turnbull, Peter. Aftermath. l.t. ed. 2013. (Hennessey & Yellich Mystery Ser.: 21). (ENG.). 288p. (978-0-7278-9602-5(4)) Severn Hse. Pubs., Ltd.

Tzvieli, Neta. The Private Eyes & the Mysterious Submarine. 2009. 149p. 17.99 (978-1-59826-286-5(6)) Feldheim Pubs.

Updale, Eleanor. Johnny Swanson. 2012. (ENG.). 384p. (J). (gr. 3-7). 8.99 (978-0-385-75228-2(8), Yearling) Random Hse. Children's Bks.

Uwuigiaren, Omoruyi. The Adventures of Nihu. Ayalomeh, Shedrach, illus. 2007. 158p. (J). (gr. 2-8). 16.95 (978-1-934138-15-1(0)) Bouncing Ball Bks., Inc.

van Diepen, Allison. Run the Risk. 2017. 288p. (YA). (gr. 9). 17.99 (978-0-06-243335-0(0), HarperTeen) HarperCollins Pubs.

Volponi, Paul. Response. 2010. (ENG.). 176p. (YA). (gr. 7-18). 6.99 (978-0-14-241603-7(7), Speak) Penguin Young Readers Group.

Vrettos, Adrienne Maria. Sight. 2008. (ENG.). 272p. (YA). (gr. 7). pap. 8.99 (978-1-4169-0658-2(4), McElderry, Margaret K. Bks.) McElderry, Margaret K. Bks.

Wahl, Leslea. The Perfect Blindside. 2015. 280p. (YA). pap. 10.95 (978-0-8198-6013-2(1)) Pauline Bks. & Media.

Waid, Mark. City of Incredibles, Vol. 2. Takara, Marcio, illus. 2010. (Incredibles Ser.). (ENG.). 112p. (J). 24.99 (978-1-60886-529-1(0)) Boom! Studios.

Ward, Rachel. Numbers. 2010. (Numbers Ser.: 1). (ENG.). 336p. (J). (gr. 7-12). 17.99 (978-0-545-14299-1(7), Chicken Hse., The) Scholastic, Inc.

Welvaert, Scott R. The Alabaster Ring. 2014. (ENG.). 96p. (J). (978-1-63235-052-7(1)) Pr. Room Editions LLC.

Whitman, Sylvia. The Milk of Birds. (ENG., Illus.). 384p. (YA). (gr. 9). 2014. pap. 10.99 (978-1-4424-4683-0(8)) 2013. 16.99 (978-1-4424-4682-3(X), Atheneum Bks. for Young Readers) Simon & Schuster Children's Publishing.

Whyte, June. Murder Sucks. 2008. (ENG., Illus.). 192p. (J). pap. 12.99 (978-1-934841-12-9(9), Zumaya Thresholds) Zumaya Pubns. LLC.

Wiggins, Thalia. Greg's Game Dilemma, 1 vol. Tate, Don, illus. 2012. (Making Choices: the Mcnair Cousins Ser.). (ENG.). 64p. 27.07 (978-1-61641-632-4(7), Calico Chapter Bks) Magic Wagon.

—James Makes a Choice, 1 vol. Tate, Don, illus. 2012. (Making Choices: the Mcnair Cousins Ser.). (ENG.). 64p. 27.07 (978-1-61641-634-8(3), Calico Chapter Bks) Magic Wagon.

Wynne-Jones, Tim. Blink & Caution. (ENG., Illus.). 352p. (YA). (gr. 9). 2012. pap. 8.99 (978-0-7636-5697-3(6)) 2011. 16.99 (978-0-7636-3983-9(4)) Candlewick Pr.

You Came for Me. 2013. (ENG.). 240p. pap. 14.99 (978-1-60861-221-5(X)) Covenant Communications, Inc.

Zadoff, Allen. I Am the Mission. 2015. (Unknown Assassin Ser.: 2). (ENG.). 448p. (YA). (gr. 10-17). pap. 10.99 (978-0-316-19971-1(0)) Little, Brown Bks. for Young Readers.

Zevin, Gabrielle. In the Age of Love & Chocolate. 2014. (Birthright Ser.: 3). (ENG.). 320p. (YA). (gr. 7). pap. 10.99 (978-1-250-05071-7(5), 9781250050717) Square Fish.

CRIME AND CRIMINALS

see Crime; Criminals

CRIMEAN WAR, 1853-1856

Howell, Izzi. Mary Seacole. 2016. (Fact Cat: History Ser.). (ENG., Illus.). 24p. (J). (gr. k-2). 14.99 (978-0-7502-9854-4(5), Wayland) Hachette Children's Group GBR. Dist: Hachette Bk. Group.

Howell, Izzi & Wayland Publishers Staff. Florence Nightingale. 2016. (Fact Cat: History Ser.). (ENG., Illus.). 24p. (J). (gr. k-2). 14.99 (978-1-5263-0168-0(7), Wayland) Hachette Children's Group GBR. Dist: Hachette Bk. Group.

Ross, Stewart. Don't Say No to Flo: The Story of Florence Nightingale. Shields, Susan, illus. 32p. (J). pap. (978-0-7502-3273-9(0), Wayland) Hachette Children's Group.

CRIMEAN WAR, 1853-1856—FICTION

Cook, Norman. Sam in the Crimea: A Victorian Adventure Based on the Work of Lord Shaftesbury. 2007. (Illus.). 128p. (J). (gr. 4-7). per. 9.00 (978-1-84625-045-3(5)) DayOne Pubns. GBR. Dist: Send The Light Distribution LLC.

Dunlap, Susanne. In the Shadow of the Lamp. 2012. (ENG., Illus.). 320p. (YA). (gr. 7). pap. 9.99 (978-1-59990-753-6(4), 9781599907536, Bloomsbury USA Childrens) Bloomsbury Publishing USA.

CRIMES, POLITICAL

see Political Crimes and Offenses

CRIMINAL INVESTIGATION

see also Criminals—Identification; Detectives; Forensic Sciences; Police

Allman, Toney. The Homicide Detective. 2009. (Crime Scene Investigations Ser.). (ENG., Illus.). 128p. (YA). (gr. 7-12). 35.45 (978-1-4205-0109-4(7)) Cengage Gale.

Anderson, Dale. The FBI & Civil Rights. 2009. (FBI Story Ser.). 64p. (J). (gr. 4-7). lib. bdg. 22.95 (978-1-4222-0569-3(X)) Mason Crest.

—The FBI & White-Collar Crime. 2009. (FBI Story Ser.). 64p. (J). (gr. 4-7). lib. bdg. 22.95 (978-1-4222-0566-2(5)) Mason Crest.

—The FBI Files: Successful Investigations. 2009. (FBI Story Ser.). 64p. (J). (gr. 4-7). lib. bdg. 22.95 (978-1-4222-0561-7(4)) Mason Crest.

Anniss, Matt. Cold Cases. 2013. (Crime Science Ser.). (Illus.). 48p. (J). (gr. 4-8). pap. 14.05 (978-1-4339-9477-7(1)); pap. 84.30 (978-1-4339-9478-4(X)); (ENG., lib. bdg. 31.95 (978-1-4339-9476-0(3)) Stevens, Gareth Publishing LLLP.

—Criminal Profiling. 2013. (Crime Science Ser.). (Illus.). 48p. (J). (gr. 4-8). pap. 84.30 (978-1-4339-9482-1(8)); pap. 14.05 (978-1-4339-9481-4(X)); (ENG., lib. bdg. 31.95 (978-1-4339-9480-7(1)) Stevens, Gareth Publishing LLLP.

Ballard, Carol. At the Crime Scene! Collecting Clues & Evidence. 2009. (Solve That Crime! Ser.). (Illus.). 48p. (J). (gr. 5-9). lib. bdg. 25.27 (978-0-7660-3373-3(2)) Enslow Pubs., Inc.

—Crime under the Microscope! In the Forensics Lab. 2009. (Solve That Crime! Ser.). (Illus.). 48p. (J). (gr. 5-9). lib. bdg. 25.27 (978-0-7660-3374-0(0)) Enslow Pubs., Inc.

Bauchner, Elizabeth. Document Analysis. 2007. (Forensics Ser.). (Illus.). 112p. (YA). (gr. 3-7). lib. bdg. 22.95 (978-1-4222-0029-2(9)) Mason Crest.

Beak, Nick Huckleberry. How to Be a Detective! Crack the Case with 25 Devious Disguises & Devices! 2014. (ENG., Illus.). 64p. (J). (gr. 3-7). 9.99 (978-1-84322-890-5(4), Armadillo) Anness Publishing GBR. Dist: National Bk. Network.

Beck, Esther. Cool Biological Clues: What Hair, Bones, & Bugs Tell Us, 1 vol. 2009. (Cool CSI Ser.). (ENG., Illus.). 32p. (YA). (gr. 3-6). 28.50 (978-1-60453-483-2(4)) ABDO Publishing Co.

—Cool Crime Scene Basics: Securing the Scene, 1 vol. 2009. (Cool CSI Ser.). (ENG., Illus.). 32p. (YA). (gr. 3-6). 28.50 (978-1-60453-484-9(2)) ABDO Publishing Co.

—Cool Eyewitness Encounters: How's Your Memory?, 1 vol. 2009. (Cool CSI Ser.). (ENG., Illus.). 32p. (YA). (gr. 3-6). 28.50 (978-1-60453-485-6(0)) ABDO Publishing Co.

—Cool Forensic Tools: Technology at Work, 1 vol. 2009. (Cool CSI Ser.). (ENG., Illus.). 32p. (YA). (gr. 3-6). 28.50 (978-1-60453-486-3(9)) ABDO Publishing Co.

—Cool Physical Evidence: What's Left Behind, 1 vol. 2009. (Cool CSI Ser.). (ENG., Illus.). 32p. (YA). (gr. 3-6). 28.50 (978-1-60453-487-0(7)) ABDO Publishing Co.

—Cool Written Records: The Proof Is in the Paper, 1 vol. 2009. (Cool CSI Ser.). (ENG., Illus.). 32p. (YA). (gr. 3-6). 28.50 (978-1-60453-488-7(5)) ABDO Publishing Co.

Benson, Michael. Cons & Frauds. 2008. (Criminal Investigations Ser.). (Illus.). 112p. (C). (gr. 9-12). 35.00 (978-0-7910-9404-4(9), Chelsea Hse.) Facts On File, Inc.

Beres, D. B. Sticky Evidence: Burglar Caught on Tape. 2011. (J). pap. (978-0-545-32803-6(9)) Scholastic, Inc.

Beres, D. B. & Franklin, Watts. Dusted & Busted! The Science of Fingerprinting. 2007. (24/7: Science Behind the Scenes Ser.). (ENG., Illus.). 64p. (YA). (gr. 9-12). 29.00 (978-0-531-11822-1(3), Watts, Franklin) Scholastic Library Publishing.

Bickerstaff, Linda. Careers in Undercover Narcotics Investigation. 2013. (Extreme Law Enforcement Ser.). 112p. (YA). (gr. 7-12). 34.60 (978-1-4777-1707-3(2)) Rosen Publishing Group, Inc., The.

Blohm, Craig E. The O. J. Simpson Case. 2008. (Crime Scene Investigations Ser.). (ENG., Illus.). 104p. (YA). (gr. 7-10). lib. bdg. 35.45 (978-1-4205-0038-7(4), LML02109-240025, Lucent Bks.) Cengage Gale.

Bodden, Valerie. At the Scene. 2017. (J). (978-1-60818-679-2(2), Creative Education) Creative Co., The.

—Identification. 2016. (J). (978-1-60818-681-5(4), Creative Education) Creative Co., The.

—Lab Analysis. 2016. (J). (978-1-60818-682-2(2), Creative Education) Creative Co., The.

—Medical Examination. 2016. (J). (978-1-60818-683-9(0), Creative Education) Creative Co., The.

—Mind of a Criminal. 2016. (J). (978-1-60818-684-6(9), Creative Education) Creative Co., The.

—Odysseys in Crime Scene Science: Identification. 2017. (Odysseys in Crime Scene Science Ser.). (ENG.). 80p. (J). (gr. 7-11). pap. 14.99 (978-1-62832-470-9(8), Creative Paperbacks) Creative Co., The.

—Odysseys in Crime Scene Science: Medical Examination. 2017. (Odysseys in Crime Scene Science Ser.). (ENG.). 80p. (J). (gr. 7-11). pap. 14.99 (978-1-62832-472-3(4), Creative Paperbacks) Creative Co., The.

—Odysseys in Crime Scene Science: Mind of a Criminal. 2017. (Odysseys in Crime Scene Science Ser.). (ENG.). 80p. (J). (gr. 7-11). pap. 14.99 (978-1-62832-473-0(2), Creative Paperbacks) Creative Co., The.

Boudreau, Hélène & Aksomitis, Linda. Crimebusting & Detection. 2008. (Science Solves It Ser.). (ENG., Illus.). 32p. (J). (gr. 3-7). pap. (978-0-7787-4174-9(5)); lib. bdg. (978-0-7787-4167-1(2)) Crabtree Publishing Co.

Brian, Sarah Jane. Forensics Chemistry & Crime: Set Of 6. 2010. (Navigators Ser.). (J). pap. 48.00 net. (978-1-4108-6234-1(8)) Benchmark Education Co.

—Forensics: Chemistry & Crime: Text Pairs. 2008. (Bridges/Navigators Ser.). (J). (gr. 5). 81.00 (978-1-4108-8417-6(1)) Benchmark Education Co.

Careers in Focus: Forensics. 2010. (Careers in Focus Ser.). (Illus.). 208p. (gr. 6-12). 32.95 (978-0-8160-8020-5(8), Ferguson Publishing Co.) Facts On File, Inc.

Collins, Terry. The FBI. Brown, Kelly, illus. 2008. (Cartoon Nation Ser.). (ENG.). 32p. (gr. 3-4). 30.65 (978-1-4296-1982-0(1), Graphic Library) Capstone Press of Coughlan Cos.

Cooper, Chris & Dorling Kindersley Publishing Staff. Forensic Science. 2008. (DK Eyewitness Bks.). (ENG., Illus.). 72p. (J). (gr. 3-7). 16.99 (978-0-7566-3383-7(4), DK Children) Dorling Kindersley Publishing, Inc.

Crewe, Sabrina. A History of the FBI. 2009. (FBI Story Ser.). 64p. (J). (gr. 4-7). lib. bdg. 22.95 (978-1-4222-0563-1(0)) Mason Crest.

Crime Solvers. 2017. (Crime Solvers Ser.). 48p. (gr. 6-6). pap. 84.30 (978-1-5382-0611-9(0)); lib. bdg. 191.70 (978-1-5382-0609-6(9)) Stevens, Gareth Publishing LLLP.

Croce, Nicholas. Detectives: Life Investigating Crime. 2009. (Extreme Careers Ser.). 64p. (gr. 5-5). 58.50 (978-1-61512-390-2(3), Rosen Reference) Rosen Publishing Group, Inc., The.

—Detectives: Life of Investigating Crime. 2005. (Extreme Careers Ser.). (Illus.). 64p. (YA). (gr. 5-9). 31.95 (978-0-8239-3796-7(8)) Rosen Publishing Group, Inc., The.

Dicker, Katie. Unsolved Crimes. 2015. (Mystery! Ser.). 24p. (gr. 3-6). 28.50 (978-1-62588-205-9(X)) Black Rabbit Bks.

Dupont, Ellen. Criminal Terminology, Vol. 20. Gomez, Manny, ed. 2016. (Crime & Detection Ser.). (Illus.). 96p. (J). (gr. 7). 24.95 (978-1-4222-3470-9(3)) Mason Crest.

Eldridge, Stephen. Investigating Trace Evidence. 2017. (J). (978-0-7660-9187-0(2)) Enslow Pubs., Inc.

Engdahl, Sylvia. Forensic Technology. Gale Editors, ed. 2010. (Current Controversies Ser.). (ENG.). 240p. 40.95 (978-0-7377-4911-3(3)); pap. 28.45 (978-0-7377-4912-0(1)) Cengage Gale. (Greenhaven Pr., Inc.).

Engdahl, Sylvia Louise. Domestic Wiretapping. 2008. (Current Controversies Ser.). (ENG., Illus.). 246p. (YA). (gr. 7-12). pap. 40.95 (978-0-7377-3958-9(4), Greenhaven Pr., Inc.) Cengage Gale.

Engdahl, Sylvia Louise, ed. Domestic Wiretapping. 2008. (Current Controversies Ser.). (ENG., Illus.). 224p. (gr. 10-12). pap. 32.00 (978-0-7377-3959-6(2), Greenhaven Pr., Inc.) Cengage Gale.

Evans, Colin. Crime Scene Investigation. 2009. (Criminal Investigations Ser.). (Illus.). 120p. (J). (gr. 9-18). 35.00 (978-0-7910-9405-1(7), Chelsea Hse.) Facts On File, Inc.

Faulk, Michelle. Gun Crimes: Dead People Do Tell Tales. 2011. (True Forensic Crime Stories Ser.). (Illus.). 104p. (J). (gr. 5-18). pap. 10.95 (978-1-59845-365-2(3)); (gr. 7-12). lib. bdg. 33.27 (978-0-7660-3763-2(0)) Enslow Pubs., Inc.

FBI Agent. 2009. (Virtual Apprentice Ser.). 64p. (gr. 4-9). 29.95 (978-0-8160-6758-9(9), Ferguson Publishing Co.) Facts On File, Inc.

Fearon Staff. Crime & Detection: Skillchecks, 10 bks. (YA). (gr. 6-12). pap. 5.95 (978-0-8224-3550-1(0)) Globe Fearon Educational Publishing.

Ford, Jean. Explosives & Arson Investigation. Noziglia, Carla Miller & Siegel, Jay A., eds. 2013. (Solving Crimes with Science: Forensics Ser.: 12). (Illus.). 112p. (J). (gr. 7-18). 22.95 (978-1-4222-2867-8(3)) Mason Crest.

—Forensics in American Culture. 2013. (J). (978-1-4222-2861-6(4)) Mason Crest.

—Forensics in American Culture. Noziglia, Carla Miller & Siegel, Jay A., eds. 2013. (Solving Crimes with Science: Forensics Ser.: 12). (Illus.). 112p. (J). (gr. 7-18). 22.95 (978-1-4222-2870-8(3)) Mason Crest.

Forensic Files, 12 vols., Set. Incl. Bullet Proof! The Evidence That Guns Leave Behind. Joyce, Jaime. (YA). 29.00 (978-0-531-11820-7(7)); Do You Read Me? Famous Cases Solved by Handwriting Analysis! Webber, Diane. (YA). 29.00 (978-0-531-12066-8(X)); Dusted & Busted! The Science of Fingerprinting. Beres, D. B. & Franklin, Watts. (YA). 29.00 (978-0-531-11822-1(3)); Guilty by a Hair! Real-Life DNA Matches! Prokos, Anna. (J). 29.00 (978-0-531-11821-4(5)); Killer Wallpaper: True Cases of Deadly Poisonings. Prokos, Anna. (YA). 29.00 (978-0-531-12061-3(9)); Right Bite: Dentists As Detectives. Winchester, Elizabeth Siris & Siris-Winchester, Elizabeth. (YA). 29.00 (978-0-531-12062-0(7)); Shot & Framed: Photographers at the Crime Scene. Webber, Diane. (YA). 29.00 (978-0-531-12063-7(5)); Skulls & Skeletons: True-Life Stories of Bone Detectives. Denega, Danielle M. & Denega, Danielle. (YA). 29.00 (978-0-531-12064-4(3)); 64p. (gr. 9-12). 2007. (24/7: Science Behind the Scenes Ser.). (Illus.). 2007. 300.00 o.p. (978-0-531-12476-5(2), Watts, Franklin) Scholastic Library Publishing.

Forensic Science Investigated, 5 bks., Set. Incl. Careers in Forensics. Williams, Linda D. lib. bdg. 34.21 (978-0-7614-3080-3(6)); Cybercrime. Stefoff, Rebecca. lib. bdg. 34.21 (978-0-7614-3084-1(9)); Famous Forensic Cases. Stefoff, Rebecca. lib. bdg. 34.21 (978-0-7614-3082-7(2)); Forensic Techniques. Stefoff, Rebecca. lib. bdg. 34.21 (978-0-7614-3083-4(0)); Solving History's Mysteries. Stefoff, Rebecca. lib. bdg. 34.21 (978-0-7614-3081-0(4)); 80p. (gr. 5-18). (Forensic Science Investigated Ser.). 2008. Set lib. bdg. 171.05 (978-0-7614-3078-0(4), Benchmark Bks.) Marshall Cavendish Corp.

Forensics: The Science of Crime-Solving, 12 vols., Set. Incl. Computer Investigation. Bauchner, Elizabeth. (gr. 3-7). lib. bdg. 22.95 (978-1-4222-0035-3(3)); DNA Analysis. Hunter, William. (gr. 7-18). lib. bdg. 22.95 (978-1-4222-0026-1(4)); Document Analysis. Bauchner, Elizabeth. (gr. 3-7). lib. bdg. 22.95 (978-1-4222-0029-2(9)); Mark & Trace Analysis. Hunter, William. (gr. 3-7). lib. bdg. 22.95 (978-1-4222-0027-8(2)); Pathology. Walker, Maryalice. (gr. 3-7). lib. bdg. 22.95 (978-1-4222-0033-9(7), 1248056); Solving Crimes with Physics. Hunter, William. (gr. 7-18). lib. bdg. 22.95 (978-1-4222-0036-0(1)); (YA). 2007. (Forensics Ser.). (Illus.). 112p. 2006. Set lib. bdg. 275.40 (978-1-4222-0025-4(6), 1248051) Mason Crest.

French, John L. Criminal Investigations Set, 14-Volumes. 2009. (Criminal Investigations Ser.). (C). (gr. 9-18). 490.00 (978-0-7910-9908-7(3), Chelsea Hse.) Facts On File, Inc.

Fridell, Ron. Forensic Science. 2006. (Cool Science Ser.). (ENG., Illus.). 48p. (gr. 4-8). lib. bdg. 27.93 (978-0-8225-5935-1(8), Lerner Pubns.) Lerner Publishing Group.

Friedlander, Mark P., Jr. & Phillips, Terry M. When Objects Talk: Solving a Crime with Science. 2005. (Discovery! Ser.). (Illus.). 120p. (gr. 5-12). lib. bdg. 27.93 (978-0-8225-0649-2(1)) Lerner Publishing Group.

Frith, Alex. Forensic Science. Chen, Kuo Kan et al, illus. 2007. (Forensic Science Ser.). 96p. (J). (gr. 4-7). pap. 10.99 (978-0-7945-1689-5(0), Usborne) EDC Publishing.

Gaensslen, Robert E. Blood, Bugs, & Plants. 2008. (Essentials of Forensic Science Ser.). (Illus.). 174p. (gr. 6-12). 35.00 (978-0-8160-5509-8(2)) Facts On File, Inc.

Gardner, Robert. Crime Lab 101: 25 Different Experiments in Crime Detection. 2012. (Dover Children's Science Bks.). (ENG., Illus.). 128p. (J). (gr. 6-8). pap. 6.99 (978-0-486-48864-6(0)) Dover Pubns., Inc.

—Forensic Science Projects with a Crime Lab You Can Build. 2007. (Build-A-Lab! Science Experiments Ser.). (Illus.). 128p. (J). (gr. 3-7). lib. bdg. 33.27 (978-0-7660-2806-7(2)) Enslow Pubs., Inc.

Giordano, Geraldine. The Oklahoma City Bombing. 2009. (Terrorist Attacks Ser.). 64p. (gr. 5-5). 58.50 (978-1-60853-318-3(2)) Rosen Publishing Group, Inc., The.

Graham, Ian. Forensic Technology. 2011. (New Technology Ser.). 48p. (YA). (gr. 7-12). lib. bdg. 34.25 (978-1-59920-532-8(7)) Black Rabbit Bks.

Gray, Leon. Cybercrime. 2013. (Crime Science Ser.). (Illus.). 48p. (J). (gr. 4-8). pap. 84.30 (978-1-4339-9486-9(0)); pap. 14.05 (978-1-4339-9485-2(2)); (ENG., lib. bdg. 31.95 (978-1-4339-9484-5(4)) Stevens, Gareth Publishing LLLP.

—Virtual Crime! Solving Cybercrime. 2009. (Solve That Crime! Ser.). (Illus.). 48p. (J). (gr. 5-9). lib. bdg. 25.27 (978-0-7660-3376-4(7)) Enslow Pubs., Inc.

Greenberg, Keith Elliot. Forensics. 2003. (Science on the Edge Ser.). 48p. (J). 23.70 (978-1-56711-785-1(6), Blackbirch Pr., Inc.) Cengage Gale.

Hamilton, John. The FBI, 1 vol. 2007. (Defending the Nation Ser.). (ENG., Illus.). 32p. (gr. 4-7). 27.07 (978-1-59679-757-4(6), Checkerboard Library) ABDO Publishing Co.

Hamilton, Sue L. Crime Scene Investigation, 6 vols., Set. Incl. DNA Analysis: Forensic Fluids & Follicles. 27.07 (978-1-59928-987-8(3)); Fingerprint Analysis: Hints from Prints. 27.07 (978-1-59928-988-5(1)); Forensic Artist: Solving the Case with a Face. 27.07 (978-1-59928-989-2(X)); Forensic Ballistics: Styles of Projectiles. 27.07 (978-1-59928-990-8(3)); Forensic Entomology: Bugs & Bodies. 27.07 (978-1-59928-991-5(1)); 32p. (gr. 4-8). (Crime Scene Investigation Ser.). 2008. 162.42 (978-1-59928-986-1(5), Abdo & Daughters) ABDO Publishing Co.

—Fingerprint Analysis: Hints from Prints, 1 vol. 2008. (Crime Scene Investigation Ser.). (ENG.). 32p. (gr. 4-8). 27.07 (978-1-59928-988-5(1), Abdo & Daughters) ABDO Publishing Co.

—Forensic Ballistics: Styles of Projectiles, 1 vol. 2008. (Crime Scene Investigation Ser.). (ENG.). 32p. (gr. 4-8). 27.07 (978-1-59928-990-8(3), Abdo & Daughters) ABDO Publishing Co.

Harding, Lauri R., ed. DNA Databases. 2007. (At Issue Ser.). (ENG., Illus.). 100p. (YA). (gr. 8-12). 22.50 (978-0-7377-3600-7(3), Greenhaven Pr., Inc.); (gr. 9-12). pap. 31.80 (978-0-7377-3599-4(6)) Cengage Gale.

Harmon, Daniel E. Careers in Explosives & Arson Investigation. 2009. (Careers in Forensics Ser.). 64p. (gr. 5-5). 58.50 (978-1-61511-803-8(9), Rosen Reference) Rosen Publishing Group, Inc., The.

Harris, Nathaniel. Crime Fighting: The Impact of Science & Technology. 2009. (Pros & Cons Ser.). (ENG.). 64p. (YA). (gr. 5-9). lib. bdg. 35.00 (978-1-4339-1985-5(0)) Stevens, Gareth Publishing LLLP.

Harvey, Gill. Crime & Detection. rev. ed. 2008. (True Stories Ser.). 144p. (J). pap. 4.99 (978-0-7945-1981-0(4), Usborne) EDC Publishing.

—True Stories of Crime & Detection. 2004. (True Adventure Stories Ser.). 144p. (J). lib. bdg. 12.95 (978-1-58086-644-6(1), Usborne) EDC Publishing.

—True Stories of Crime & Detection. Chisholm, Jane, ed. 2004. (True Adventure Stories Ser.). 144p. (J). pap. 4.95 (978-0-7945-0613-1(5), Usborne) EDC Publishing.

Heinrichs, Ann. Fire Investigator. 2009. (21st Century Skills Library: Cool Science Careers Ser.). (ENG.). 32p. (gr. 4-8). lib. bdg. 28.50 (978-1-60279-310-1(7), 200206) Cherry Lake Publishing.

Herweck, Diana. On the Scene: A CSI's Life, 1 vol. 2nd rev. ed. 2012. (Nonfiction Readers Ser.). (ENG.). 48p. (J). (gr. 4-4). pap. 9.99 (978-1-4333-4825-9(X)) Teacher Created Materials, Inc.

Hook, Sue Vander & Kamisar, Yale. Miranda v. Arizona: An Individual's Rights When under Arrest, 1 vol. 2012. (Landmark Supreme Court Cases Ser.). (ENG., Illus.). 160p. (J). (gr. 6-12). 37.07 (978-1-61783-474-5(2)) ABDO Publishing Co.

Horn, Geoffrey M. Crime Scene Investigator. 2008. (Cool Careers: Adventure Careers Ser.). (Illus.). 32p. (gr. 5-8). pap. 10.50 (978-0-8368-8887-4(1)); lib. bdg. 26.00 (978-0-8368-8880-5(4)) Stevens, Gareth Publishing LLLP.

Hunter, William. Mark & Trace Analysis. Siegel, Jay A., ed. 2013. (Solving Crimes with Science: Forensics Ser.: 12). (Illus.). 112p. (J). (gr. 7-18). 22.95 (978-1-4222-2871-5(1)) Mason Crest.

—Mark & Trace Analysis. 2007. (Forensics Ser.). (Illus.). 112p. (YA). (gr. 3-7). lib. bdg. 22.95 (978-1-4222-0027-8(2)) Mason Crest.

—Solving Crimes with Physics. Noziglia, Carla Miller & Siegel, Jay A., eds. 2013. (Solving Crimes with Science: Forensics Ser.: 12). (Illus.). 112p. (J). (gr. 7-18). 22.95 (978-1-4222-2873-9(8)) Mason Crest.

Innes, Brian. Forensic Science. 2004. (Crime & Detection Ser.). (Illus.). 96p. (YA). (gr. 7-18). lib. bdg. 22.95 (978-1-59084-373-4(8)) Mason Crest.

—Forensic Science, Vol. 20. Gomez, Manny, ed. 2016. (Crime & Detection Ser.). (Illus.). 96p. (J). (gr. 7). 24.95 (978-1-4222-3477-8(0)) Mason Crest.

—Major Unsolved Crimes. 2004. (Crime & Detection Ser.). (Illus.). 96p. (YA). (gr. 7-18). lib. bdg. 22.95 (978-1-59084-382-6(7)) Mason Crest.

—Unsolved Crimes, Vol. 20. Gomez, Manny, ed. 2016. (Crime & Detection Ser.). 96p. (J). (gr. 7). 24.95 (978-1-4222-3482-2(7)) Mason Crest.

Jeffrey, Gary. Solving Crimes with Trace Evidence. 2009. (Graphic Forensic Science Ser.). (ENG.). 48p. (YA). (gr. 5-5). 58.50 (978-1-61512-955-3(3), Rosen Reference) Rosen Publishing Group, Inc., The.

—Solving Crimes with Trace Evidence. Richardson, Peter, illus. 2008. (Graphic Forensic Science Ser.). (ENG.). 48p. (gr. 5-8). per. 14.05 (978-1-4042-1432-3(1)); (YA). lib. bdg. 31.95 (978-1-4042-1431-6(3)) Rosen Publishing Group, Inc., The.

Joyce, Jaime. Going Ballistic: Who Pulled the Trigger in a Gangland Massacre? 2011. (J). pap. (978-0-545-32801-2(2)) Scholastic, Inc.

Juettner, Bonnie. Blackmail & Bribery. 2009. (Crime Scene Investigations Ser.). (ENG., Illus.). 128p. (gr. 7-10). lib. bdg. 40.40 (978-1-4205-0068-4(6), LML02109-242072, Lucent Bks.) Cengage Gale.

Karlitz, Gail. Virtual Apprentice: FBI Agent. 2009. (Virtual Apprentice Ser.). 64p. (gr. 4-9). pap. 9.95 (978-0-8160-7894-3(7), Checkmark Bks.) Facts On File, Inc.

Kawa, Katie. Forensic Detectives, 01 vols., 1. 2016. (Out of the Lab: Extreme Jobs in Science Ser.). (ENG., Illus.). 32p. (J). pap. 10.00 (978-1-5081-4521-9(0), PowerKids Pr.) Rosen Publishing Group, Inc., The.

Kiesbye, Stefan, ed. DNA Databases. 2011. (At Issue Ser.). 128p. (J). pap. 24.45 (978-0-7377-5891-7(0), Greenhaven Pr., Inc.); (gr. 9-12). 34.45 (978-0-7377-5890-0(2)) Cengage Gale.

Lane, Brian, et al. Eyewitness Books - Crime & Detection. Crawford, Andy, photos by. 2005. (DK Eyewitness Bks.). (ENG., Illus.). 72p. (J). (gr. 3-7). 16.99 (978-0-7566-1386-0(8), DK Children) Dorling Kindersley Publishing, Inc.

Latta, Sara L. DNA & Blood: Dead People Do Tell Tales. 2011. (True Forensic Crime Stories Ser.). (Illus.). 104p. (J). (gr. 7-12). lib. bdg. 33.27 (978-0-7660-3667-3(7)) Enslow Pubs., Inc.
—DNA & Blood: Dead People DO Tell Tales. 2011. (True Forensic Crime Stories Ser.). (Illus.). 104p. (J). (gr. 5-18). pap. 10.95 (978-1-59845-362-1(9)) Enslow Pubs., Inc.
Leimbach, Judy & Eckert, Sharon. Detective Club: Mysteries for Young Thinkers. 2005. (ENG.). 64p. (gr. 2-4). pap. 11.95 (978-1-59363-065-2(4)) Prufrock Pr.
Levy, Janey. Careers in Criminal Profiling. 2009. (Careers in Forensics Ser.). 64p. (gr. 5-5). 58.50 (978-1-61511-801-4(2), Rosen Reference) Rosen Publishing Group, Inc., The.
Libal, Angela. Fingerprints, Bite Marks, Ear Prints. Noziglia, Carla Miller & Siegel, Jay A., eds. 2013. (Solving Crimes with Science: Forensics Ser.: 12). (Illus.). 112p. (J). (gr. 7-18). 22.95 (978-1-4222-2868-5(1)) Mason Crest.
—Forensic Anthropology. Noziglia, Carla Miller & Siegel, Jay A., eds. 2013. (Solving Crimes with Science: Forensics Ser.: 12). (Illus.). 112p. (J). (gr. 7-18). 22.95 (978-1-4222-2869-2(X)) Mason Crest.
Litmanovich, Ellina & Latta, Sara L. Investigating Bones. 2017. (J). **(978-0-7660-9182-5(1))** Enslow Pubs., Inc.
Lockwood, Brad. Domestic Spying & Wiretapping. 2009. (In the News Ser.). 64p. (gr. 6-6). 58.50 (978-1-61513-465-6(4)) Rosen Publishing Group, Inc., The.
MacKay, Jennifer. Forensic Art. 2009. (Crime Scene Investigations Ser.). (ENG., Illus.). 128p. (YA). (gr. 7-10). lib. bdg. 35.45 (978-1-4205-0069-1(4), LML02109-242073, Lucent Bks.) Cengage Gale.
MacKay, Jenny. Fingerprints & Impression Evidence. 2007. (Crime Scene Investigations Ser.). (ENG., Illus.). 128p. (gr. 3-7). lib. bdg. 40.40 (978-1-4205-0037-0(6), Lucent Bks.) Cengage Gale.
Mara, Wil. Cyber Cop. 2015. (21st Century Skills Library: Cool STEAM Careers Ser.). (ENG., Illus.). 32p. (J). (gr. 4-7). 29.93 (978-1-63362-557-0(5), 206412) Cherry Lake Publishing.
Mauro, Paul & Melton, H. Keith. Collecting & Handling Evidence. 2004. (Illus.). 48p. (J). (978-0-439-57178-4(2)) Scholastic, Inc.
—Crime Scene Investigation. 2003. (Detective Academy Ser.). (Illus.). 48p. (J). (978-0-439-57175-3(8)) Scholastic, Inc.
—Detective Mastery. 2004. (Detective Academy Ser.). (Illus.). 48p. (J). pap. (978-0-439-57185-2(5)) Scholastic, Inc.
—Interviews & Interrogations. 2003. (Detective Academy Ser.). (Illus.). 48p. (J). pap. (978-0-439-57176-0(6)) Scholastic, Inc.
—Undercover Operations. Aycock, Daniel et al, illus. 2004. (Detective Academy Ser.). 48p. (J). (978-0-439-57183-8(9)) Scholastic, Inc.
Mooney, Carla. Forensics: Uncover the Science & Technology of Crime Scene Investigation. Carbaugh, Samuel, illus. 2013. (Inquire & Investigate Ser.). (ENG.). 128p. (YA). (gr. 6-10). 21.95 (978-1-61930-188-7(1)); pap. 16.95 (978-1-61930-184-9(9)) Open City Bks.
Moran, Lisa & Hawley, Mary. Making a Difference Let the Evidence Decide. 2010. (Connect to Literacy Ser.). 8p. pap. (978-1-4334-0506-8(7)) Millmark Education.
Murley, Leon. Working the Case: Law Enforcement, Police Work, & Police Organizations. 2016. (Law Enforcement & Intelligence Gathering Ser.). 00104p. (YA). (gr. 8-8). lib. bdg. 36.25 (978-1-5081-0380-6(1), Britannica Educational Publishing) Rosen Publishing Group, Inc., The.
Murray, Hallie & Stiefel, Chana. Investigating Fingerprints. 2017. (J). **(978-0-7660-9185-6(6))** Enslow Pubs., Inc.
Nardo, Don. Nazi War Criminals. 2015. (Illus.). 80p. (J). (978-1-60152-850-6(7)) ReferencePoint Pr., Inc.
Newcomb, Tim. FBI Agent, Vol. 12. 2015. (On a Mission Ser.). 48p. (J). (gr. 5). 20.95 (978-1-4222-3394-8(4)) Mason Crest.
Newton, Michael. Gangs & Gang Crimes. 2008. (Criminal Investigations Ser.). (Illus.). 120p. (C). (gr. 9-12). 35.00 (978-0-7910-9408-2(1), Chelsea Hse.) Facts On File, Inc.
—Serial Killers. 2008. (Criminal Investigations Ser.). (Illus.). 120p. (J). (gr. 9-12). 35.00 (978-0-7910-9411-2(1), Chelsea Hse.) Facts On File, Inc.
O'Brien, Susan. Child Abduction & Kidnapping. 2008. (Criminal Investigations Ser.). (Illus.). 160p. (J). (gr. 9-12). 35.00 (978-0-7910-9403-7(0), Chelsea Hse.) Facts On File, Inc.
Orr, Tamra. Crime Scene Investigator. 2007. (21st Century Skills Library: Cool Science Careers Ser.). (ENG., Illus.). 32p. (gr. 4-8). lib. bdg. 28.50 (978-1-60279-057-5(4), 200012) Cherry Lake Publishing.
—Forensic Science Investigator. 2007. (21st Century Skills Library: Cool Science Careers Ser.). (ENG., Illus.). 32p. (gr. 4-8). lib. bdg. 28.50 (978-1-60279-055-1(8), 200014) Cherry Lake Publishing.
Orr, Tamra B. Crime Scene Investigator. 2015. (21st Century Skills Library: Cool STEAM Careers Ser.). (ENG., Illus.). 32p. (J). (gr. 4-7). 29.93 (978-1-63362-556-3(7), 206408) Cherry Lake Publishing.
—Forensic Science Investigator. 2015. (21st Century Skills Library: Cool STEAM Careers Ser.). (ENG., Illus.). 32p. (J). (gr. 4-7). 29.93 (978-1-63362-560-0(5), 206424) Cherry Lake Publishing.
—Investigating a Crime Scene. 2014. (Explorer Library: Follow the Clues Ser.). (ENG.). 32p. (J). (gr. 4-8). 28.50 (978-1-62431-777-4(4), 203304) Cherry Lake Publishing.
Parker, Janice. Crime. 2009. (Science Q & A Ser.). (Illus.). 48p. (YA). (gr. 5-8). pap. 10.95 (978-1-60596-069-2(1)); lib. bdg. 29.05 (978-1-60596-068-5(3)) Weigl Pubs., Inc.
—Crime Q & A. 2014. (Science Discovery Ser.). (ENG., Illus.). 48p. (J). (gr. 5-8). pap. 13.95 (978-1-4896-0685-3(8), AV2 by Weigl) Weigl Pubs., Inc.
Parks, Peggy J. DNA Evidence & Investigation. 2010. (Compact Research Ser.). 96p. (YA). (gr. 7-12). lib. bdg. 25.95 (978-1-60152-102-6(2)) ReferencePoint Pr., Inc.
Perritano, John. Science Beats Crime. 2010. (Cool Science Ser.). 48p. (J). (gr. 3-6). 28.50 (978-1-60870-078-3(X)) Marshall Cavendish Corp.
Rainis, Kenneth G. Fingerprints: Crime-Solving Science Experiments. 2006. (Forensic Science Projects Ser.). (Illus.). 128p. (J). (gr. 5-18). lib. bdg. 33.27 (978-0-7660-1960-7(8)) Enslow Pubs., Inc.
—Hair, Clothing, & Tire Track Evidence: Crime-Solving Science Experiments. 2006. (Forensic Science Projects Ser.). (Illus.). 128p. (J). (gr. 5-18). lib. bdg. 33.27 (978-0-7660-2729-9(5)) Enslow Pubs., Inc.
Ricciuti, Edward R. Federal Bureau of Investigation. 2010. (Law Enforcement Agencies Ser.). (Illus.). 144p. (gr. 6-12). 35.00 (978-1-60413-636-4(7), Chelsea Hse.) Facts On File, Inc.
Rogers, Kate. The Zodiac Killer: Terror in California. 2017. (J). **(978-1-5345-6085-7(8))** Greenhaven Publishing LLC.
Romero, Libby. Discover Forensic Chemistry. 2006. (J). pap. (978-1-4108-6503-8(7)) Benchmark Education Co.
—Forensic Chemistry. 2006. (J). pap. (978-1-4108-6500-7(2)) Benchmark Education Co.
Rosen Central, creator. Careers in Forensics. 2008. (J). 175.50 (978-1-4042-1476-7(3), Rosen Reference) Rosen Publishing Group, Inc., The.
Royston, Angela. Homicide. 2013. (Crime Science Ser.). (Illus.). 48p. (J). (gr. 4-8). pap. 14.05 (978-1-4339-9493-7(3), 1358485); pap. 84.30 (978-1-4339-9494-4(1), 1358485); (ENG., lib. bdg. 31.95 (978-1-4339-9492-0(5), 1358485) Stevens, Gareth Publishing LLLP.
—Science vs. Crime. 2013. (Science Fights Back Ser.). (Illus.). 48p. (J). (gr. 4-6). 31.95 (978-1-4339-8683-3(3)); pap. 14.05 (978-1-4339-8684-0(1)) Stevens, Gareth Publishing LLLP. (Gareth Stevens Learning Library).
—Science vs. Natural Disasters. 2013. (Science Fights Back Ser.). (Illus.). 48p. (J). (gr. 4-6). 31.95 (978-1-4339-8691-8(4)); pap. 14.05 (978-1-4339-8692-5(2)) Stevens, Gareth Publishing LLLP. (Gareth Stevens Learning Library).
Sawyer, Sarah. Careers in DNA Analysis. (Careers in Forensics Ser.). 64p. 2009. (gr. 5-5). 58.50 (978-1-61511-802-1(0), Rosen Reference) 2008. (Illus.). (J). (gr. 3-7). lib. bdg. 31.95 (978-1-4042-1343-2(0)) Rosen Publishing Group, Inc., The.
Schulz, Karen. Crime Scene Detective: Using Science & Critical Thinking to Solve Crimes. 2003. (J). per. 12.95 (978-1-883055-58-5(X), 150) Dandy Lion Pubns.
—Crime Scene Detective: Using Science & Critical Thinking to Solve Crimes. 2005. (ENG.). 80p. (gr. 5-8). pap. 14.95 (978-1-59363-063-8(8)) Prufrock Pr.
Schulz, Karen K. Csi Expert! Forensic Science for Kids. Parker, David, illus. 2008. (ENG.). 160p. (gr. 5-8). pap. 19.95 (978-1-59363-312-7(2)) Prufrock Pr.
Shone, Rob. Crime Scene Investigators. 2009. (Graphic Forensic Science Ser.). (ENG.). 48p. (YA). (gr. 5-5). 58.50 (978-1-61512-947-8(2), Rosen Reference) Rosen Publishing Group, Inc., The.
—Crime Scene Investigators. Saraceni, Claudia, illus. 2008. (Graphic Forensic Science Ser.). (ENG.). 48p. (YA). (gr. 5-8). lib. bdg. 31.95 (978-1-4042-1443-9(7)) Rosen Publishing Group, Inc., The.
Siegel, Jay. Forensic Science at Work. 2011. (Contemporary Issues Ser.). (Illus.). 166 ndash; 308p. (YA). (gr. 9-12). 37.95 (978-1-4488-1864-8(8)) Rosen Publishing Group, Inc., The.
Sohn, Emily & Townsend, Laura. Patterns & Textures: Who Took the Pets? 2011. (IScience Readers Ser.). 32p. (J). (gr. 3-4). lib. bdg. 22.60 (978-1-59953-414-5(2)) Norwood Hse. Pr.
Spaulding, Jeffrey. Careers in Fingerprint & Trace Analysis. 2009. (Careers in Forensics Ser.). 64p. (gr. 5-5). 58.50 (978-1-61511-804-5(7), Rosen Reference) Rosen Publishing Group, Inc., The.
Spilsbury, Richard. Zoom in on Crime Scenes. 2013. (Zoom in on... Ser.). 32p. (J). (gr. 4-12). pap. 7.95 (978-1-4644-0567-9(0)) Enslow Pubs., Inc.
Stefoff, Rebecca. Criminal Profiling. 2010. (Forensic Science Investigated 2 Ser.). (Illus.). 80p. (J). (gr. 5). lib. bdg. 34.21 (978-0-7614-4141-0(7)) Marshall Cavendish Corp.
—Cybercrime. 2008. (Forensic Science Investigated Ser.). 80p. (gr. 5-18). lib. bdg. 34.21 (978-0-7614-3084-1(9), Benchmark Bks.) Marshall Cavendish Corp.
—Famous Forensic Cases. 2008. (Forensic Science Investigated Ser.). 80p. (gr. 5-18). lib. bdg. 34.21 (978-0-7614-3082-7(2), Benchmark Bks.) Marshall Cavendish Corp.
—Forensic Techniques. 2008. (Forensic Science Investigated Ser.). 80p. (gr. 5-18). lib. bdg. 34.21 (978-0-7614-3083-4(0), Benchmark Bks.) Marshall Cavendish Corp.
—Forensics & Modern Disasters. 2010. (Forensic Science Investigated 2 Ser.). (Illus.). 80p. (J). (gr. 5). lib. bdg. 34.21 (978-0-7614-4144-1(1)) Marshall Cavendish Corp.
—Solving History's Mysteries. 2008. (Forensic Science Investigated Ser.). 80p. (gr. 5-18). lib. bdg. 34.21 (978-0-7614-3081-0(4), Benchmark Bks.) Marshall Cavendish Corp.
Sterling Casil, Amy. Bomb Scares. 2009. (Violence & Society Ser.). 64p. (gr. 6-6). 58.50 (978-1-60854-723-4(X)) Rosen Publishing Group, Inc., The.
Stewart, Gail B. Cold Cases. Gale Editors, ed. 2010. (Crime Scene Investigations Ser.). (ENG.). 128p. (YA). (gr. 7-12). 35.45 (978-1-4205-0323-4(5)) Cengage Gale.
—The Crime Scene Photographer. 2008. (Crime Scene Investigations Ser.). (ENG., Illus.). 128p. (gr. 7-10). lib. bdg. 40.40 (978-1-4205-0036-3(8), LML02109-240023, Lucent Bks.) Cengage Gale.
—Identity Theft. 2007. (Crime Scene Investigations Ser.). (ENG., Illus.). 103p. (J). (gr. 4-7). lib. bdg. 33.45 (978-1-59018-977-1(9), Lucent Bks.) Cengage Gale.
Stiefel, Chana. Fingerprints: Dead People Do Tell Tales. 2011. (True Forensic Crime Stories Ser.). (Illus.). 104p. (J). (gr. 5-18). pap. 10.95 (978-1-59845-364-5(5)); (gr. 7-12). lib. bdg. 33.27 (978-0-7660-3689-5(8)) Enslow Pubs., Inc.
Stille, Darlene R. Forensic Evidence: Blood. 2008. (ENG., Illus.). 32p. (J). (gr. 6-10). lib. bdg. (978-0-7787-3815-2(9)) Crabtree Publishing Co.
Storrs, Landon & Storrs, Landon R. Y. The Second Red Scare & the Unmaking of the New Deal Left. 2012. (Politics & Society in Modern America Ser.). (ENG., Illus.). 424p. (C). 47.95 (978-0-691-15396-4(5)) Princeton Univ. Pr.
Sutherland, Adam. Police Forensics. 2012. (On the Radar: Defend & Protect Ser.). (ENG., Illus.). 32p. (gr. 4-8). lib. bdg. 26.60 (978-0-7613-7774-0(3), Lerner Pubns.) Lerner Publishing Group.
T R Thomas & Thomas, T. R. Cold Cases, 1 vol. unabr. ed. 2010. (True Crime Ser.). (ENG.). 64p. (YA). (gr. 9-12). pap. 8.95 (978-1-59905-437-7(X)) Saddleback Educational Publishing, Inc.
Thomas, William David. How to Become an FBI Agent. 2009. (FBI Story Ser.). 64p. (J). (gr. 4-7). lib. bdg. 22.95 (978-1-4222-0571-6(1)) Mason Crest.
Timmons, Angie & Latta, Sara L. Investigating Cybercrime. 2017. (J). **(978-0-7660-9183-2(X))** Enslow Pubs., Inc.
Townsend, John. Bone Dectectives. 2008. (Crabtree Contact Ser.). (ENG., Illus.). 32p. (J). (gr. 3-7). lib. bdg. (978-0-7787-3806-0(X)) Crabtree Publishing Co.
—Famous Forensic Cases. 2011. (Amazing Crime Scene Science Ser.). 32p. (YA). (gr. 4-7). 19.95 (978-1-60753-169-2(0)) Amicus Publishing.
—Robberies & Heists. 2010. (Solve It with Science Ser.). (Illus.). 48p. (YA). (gr. 5-9). lib. bdg. 34.25 (978-1-59920-333-1(2)) Black Rabbit Bks.
Wachtel, Alan. Investigative Techniques of the FBI. 2009. (FBI Story Ser.). 64p. (J). (gr. 4-7). lib. bdg. 22.95 (978-1-4222-0572-3(X)) Mason Crest.
Wagner, Heather Lehr. The Federal Bureau of Investigation. 2007. (U. S. Government Ser.). (Illus.). 104p. (YA). (gr. 5-9). lib. bdg. 30.00 (978-0-7910-9281-1(X)) Facts On File, Inc.
Walker, Maryalice. Entomology & Palynology. Noziglia, Carla Miller & Siegel, Jay A., eds. 2013. (Solving Crimes with Science: Forensics Ser.: 12). (Illus.). 112p. (J). (gr. 7-18). 22.95 (978-1-4222-2866-1(5)) Mason Crest.
—Pathology. Noziglia, Carla Miller & Siegel, Jay A., eds. 2013. (Solving Crimes with Science: Forensics Ser.: 12). (Illus.). 112p. (J). (gr. 7-18). 22.95 (978-1-4222-2872-2(X)) Mason Crest.
—Pathology. 2007. (Forensics Ser.). (Illus.). 112p. (YA). (gr. 3-7). lib. bdg. 22.95 (978-1-4222-0033-9(7), 1248056) Mason Crest.
Webber, Diane. Shot & Framed: Photographers at the Crime Scene. 2007. (24/7: Science Behind the Scenes Ser.). (ENG., Illus.). 64p. (YA). (gr. 9-12). 29.00 (978-0-531-12063-7(5), Watts, Franklin) Scholastic Library Publishing.
Wicker, R. Doug. The Bombing of Pan Am Flight 103. 2009. (Terrorist Attacks Ser.). 64p. (gr. 5-5). 58.50 (978-1-60853-315-2(8)) Rosen Publishing Group, Inc., The.
Williams, Linda D. Careers in Forensics. 2008. (Forensic Science Investigated Ser.). 80p. (gr. 5-18). lib. bdg. 34.21 (978-0-7614-3080-3(6), Benchmark Bks.) Marshall Cavendish Corp.
—Forensics & Medicine. 2008. (J). (978-0-7614-3079-7(2)) Marshall Cavendish.
Wood, Alix. The Body in the Woods: Be a Crime Scene Investigator. 2017. (Crime Solvers Ser.). 48p. (gr. 6-6). pap. 84.30 **(978-1-5382-0617-1(X))** Stevens, Gareth Publishing LLLP.
—Chasing a Serial Killer: Be a Criminal Profiler. 2017. (Crime Solvers Ser.). 48p. (gr. 6-6). pap. 84.30 **(978-1-5382-0618-8(8))** Stevens, Gareth Publishing LLLP.
—Killer Evidence: Be a Police Detective. 2017. (Crime Solvers Ser.). 48p. (gr. 6-6). pap. 84.30 **(978-1-5382-0620-1(X))** Stevens, Gareth Publishing LLLP.
Woog, Adam. Careers in Forensic Science. 2012. (J). 34.21 (978-0-60870-958-8(2)) Marshall Cavendish Corp.
—Careers in the ATF. 2014. 96p. 39.92 (978-1-62712-428-7(4)) Cavendish Square Publishing.
—Careers in the ATF. 2012. (J). 34.21 (978-1-60870-956-4(6)) Marshall Cavendish Corp.
Wright, John D. & Singer, Jane. DNA & Body Evidence, 4 bks., Set. Incl. Hair & Fibers. (ENG., Illus.). 96p. (C). (gr. 6-18). 2008. lib. bdg. 158.00 (978-0-7656-8116-4(1), Y182555); (ENG., Illus.). 96p. 2007. Set lib. bdg. 158.00 (978-0-7656-8113-3(7), Y182327) Routledge.
Yancey, Diane. The Forensic Anthropologist. 2006. (Crime Scene Investigations Ser.). (ENG.). 104p. (YA). (gr. 7-12). lib. bdg. 35.45 (978-1-59018-618-3(4)) Cengage Gale.
—The Forensic Entomologist. 2008. (Crime Scene Investigations Ser.). (ENG., Illus.). 128p. (gr. 7-10). lib. bdg. 40.40 (978-1-4205-0070-7(8), LML02109-242074, Lucent Bks.) Cengage Gale.
—Murder. 2006. (Crime Scene Investigations Ser.). (ENG., Illus.). 128p. (gr. 7-12). lib. bdg. 40.40 (978-1-59018-619-0(2)) Cengage Gale.
—Tracking Serial Killers. 2007. (Crime Scene Investigations Ser.). (ENG., Illus.). 104p. (YA). (gr. 7-12). lib. bdg. 35.45 (978-1-59018-985-6(X)) Cengage Gale.
Young, Karen Romano. Crime Scene Science: 20 A+ Projects & Experiments - Want to Rock Your Science Fair & Score an A? Goldin, David, illus. 2009. (Science Fair Winners Ser.). (ENG.). 80p. (J). (gr. 5-9). pap. 12.95 (978-1-4263-0521-4(4), National Geographic Children's Bks.) National Geographic Society.
—Crime Scene Science: 20 Projects & Experiments about Clues, Crimes, Criminals, & Other Mysterious Things. Goldin, David, illus. 2009. (Science Fair Winners Ser.). (ENG.). 80p. (J). (gr. 5-9). 24.90 (978-1-4263-0522-1(2), National Geographic Children's Bks.) National Geographic Society.
Yount, Lisa. Forensic Science: From Fibers to Fingerprints. 2006. (Milestones in Discovery & Invention Ser.). (Illus.). 224p. (YA). (gr. 7-12). 35.00 (978-0-8160-5751-1(6)) Facts On File, Inc.
Zullo, Allan. Crime Scene Investigators. 2008. 149p. (J). pap. (978-0-439-93406-0(0)) Scholastic, Inc.
—Ten True Stories - FBI Heroes. 2014. (10 True Tales Ser.). (ENG.). 192p. (J). (gr. 3-7). pap. 5.99 (978-0-545-81812-4(5), Scholastic Nonfiction) Scholastic, Inc.

CRIMINAL LAW

see also Capital Punishment; Jury; Kidnapping; Trials

Bursztyn, Alberto M., ed. Childhood Psychological Disorders: Current Controversies, 1 vol. 2011. (Making Sense of Psychology Ser.). 206p. (C). 49.00 (978-0-313-33696-6(2), GR3696, Greenwood) ABC-CLIO, LLC.
Campbell, Marilyn & Columbus, Curt. Crime & Punishment. 2004. (YA). pap. 6.50 (978-1-58342-225-0(0), CB8) Dramatic Publishing Co.
Criminal Justice, 6 vols., Set. 2010. (Criminal Justice Ser.). (gr. 6-12). 210.00 (978-1-60413-955-6(2), Chelsea Hse.) Facts On File, Inc.
Ferguson, creator. Public Safety. 3rd rev. ed. 2007. (Careers in Focus Ser.). (Illus.). 224p. (gr. 6-12). 32.95 (978-0-8160-6594-3(2), Ferguson Publishing Co.) Facts On File, Inc.
Furi-Perry, Ursula. Going to Court: An Introduction to the U.S. Justice System. 2015. (ENG., Illus.). 266p. (J). (gr. 6-8). pap. 14.95 (978-1-62722-620-2(6)) American Bar Assn.
Gold, Susan Dudley. Parody of Public Figures: Hustler Magazine Inc. V. Falwell. 2013. (J). 42.79 (978-1-60870-906-9(X)) Marshall Cavendish Corp.
Haerens, Margaret. Mandatory Minimum Sentencing. 2010. (Opposing Viewpoints Ser.). (Illus.). 240p. 42.95 (978-0-7377-4775-1(7)); pap. 29.45 (978-0-7377-4776-8(5)) Cengage Gale. (Greenhaven Pr., Inc.).
Hand, Carol. Using Computer Science in High Tech Criminal Justice Careers. 2017. (Coding Your Passion Ser.). 80p. (J). (gr. 12-12). 35.75 **(978-1-5081-7511-7(X)**, Rosen Young Adult) Rosen Publishing Group, Inc., The.
Hermsen, Sarah, et al. American Reference Library. 2004. (Crime & Punishment in America Ser.). (ENG.). 39p. (J). 5.00 (978-0-7876-9174-5(7), UXL) Cengage Gale.
Hunter, David. Unequal Justice. 2017. (J). **(978-1-4222-3789-2(3))** Mason Crest.
Hurt, Avery Elizabeth. Trial by Internet. 2017. (J). pap. **(978-1-5345-0067-9(7))** Greenhaven Publishing LLC.
Jones, Molly. Frequently Asked Questions about Slander & Libel in the Digital Age. 2012. (FAQ: Teen Life Ser.). (ENG., Illus.). 64p. (YA). (gr. 7-12). lib. bdg. 31.95 (978-1-4488-8332-5(6)) Rosen Publishing Group, Inc., The.
Kanefield, Teri. Guilty? Crime, Punishment, & the Changing Face of Justice. 2014. (ENG., Illus.). 144p. (YA). (gr. 7-9). 16.99 (978-0-544-14896-3(7), HMH Books For Young Readers) Houghton Mifflin Harcourt Publishing Co.
Kerrigan, Michael. The History of Punishment, Vol. 20. Gomez, Manny, ed. 2016. (Crime & Detection Ser.). (Illus.). 96p. (J). (gr. 7). 24.95 (978-1-4222-3487-7(8)) Mason Crest.
The Law. 2010. (Criminal Justice Ser.). (Illus.). 168p. (gr. 6-12). 35.00 (978-1-60413-634-0(0), Chelsea Hse.) Facts On File, Inc.
Mara, Wil. Law & Order. 2016. (21st Century Skills Library: a Citizen's Guide Ser.). (ENG., Illus.). 32p. (J). (gr. 4-7). 29.93 (978-1-63471-069-5(X), 208355) Cherry Lake Publishing.
Mooney, Carla. Your Legal Rights Regarding Misdemeanor Prosecution, 1 vol. 2015. (ENG., Illus.). 64p. (J). 33.25 (978-1-4777-8028-2(9), Rosen Reference) Rosen Publishing Group, Inc., The.
Moran, Lisa & Hawley, Mary. Making a Difference Let the Evidence Decide. 2010. (Connect to Literacy Ser.). 8p. pap. (978-1-4334-0506-8(7)) Millmark Education.
Murray, Hallie. The Rights of the Accused in Criminal Cases: The Sixth Amendment. 2017. (Bill of Rights Ser.). 48p. (gr. 5-6). 27.93 **(978-0-7660-8559-6(7))** Enslow Pubs., Inc.
Nagle, Cristen. Your Legal Rights As a Juvenile Being Tried As an Adult, 1 vol. 2015. (ENG., Illus.). 64p. (J). 33.25 (978-1-4777-8016-9(5), Rosen Reference) Rosen Publishing Group, Inc., The.
Orr, Tamra B. The Vo-Tech Track to Success in Law, Public Safety, Corrections, & Security. 2014. (Learning a Trade, Preparing for a Career Ser.). (Illus.). 80p. (J). (gr. 7-12). 34.25 (978-1-4777-7736-7(9)) Rosen Publishing Group, Inc., The.
Perl, Lila. Torture. 2011. (Controversy! 3 Ser.). 112p. (gr. 7). 37.07 (978-1-60870-495-8(5)) Marshall Cavendish Corp.
Riley, Gail Blasser. And Justice for All. 2003. (Illus.). 60p. (J). 11.60 net. (978-0-7398-5175-3(6)) Steck-Vaughn.
Roleff, Tamara. Is Torture Ever Justified? 2010. (At Issue Ser.). (ENG.). 128p. (gr. 10-12). 39.40 (978-0-7377-5091-1(X)); pap. 27.80 (978-0-7377-5092-8(8)) Cengage Gale. (Greenhaven Pr., Inc.).
Shea, Therese. Sixth Amendment: The Rights of the Accused in Criminal Cases. 2011. (Amendments to the United States Constitution: the Bill of Rights Ser.). (ENG.). 64p. (YA). pap. 12.95 (978-1-4488-2307-9(2), Rosen Reference) Rosen Publishing Group, Inc., The.
—The Sixth Amendment: The Rights of the Accused in Criminal Cases. 2011. (Amendments to the United States Constitution: the Bill of Rights Ser.). (Illus.). 64p. (YA). (gr. 5-9). lib. bdg. 31.95 (978-1-4488-1261-5(5)) Rosen Publishing Group, Inc., The.
Spence, David. Crime & Punishment. 2004. (Illus.). 32p. (J). (gr. 4-7). pap. 5.95 (978-1-86007-010-5(8), TickTock Books) Octopus Publishing Group GBR. Dist: Independent Pubs. Group.
Swan, Bill. Real Justice: Jailed for Life for Being Black: The Story of Rubin Hurricane Carter, 1 vol. 2014. (Lorimer Real Justice Ser.). (ENG., Illus.). 144p. (YA). (gr. 8-12). pap. 12.95 (978-1-4594-0665-0(6), 9781459406650) Lorimer, James & Co., Ltd., Pubs. CAN. Dist: Casemate Pubs. & Bk. Distributors, LLC.

CRIMINALS

see also Gangs; Impostors and Imposture

Bad Guys [Capstone Sole Source]. 2010. (Bad Guys Ser.). 48p. lib. bdg. 122.60 (978-1-4296-5844-7(4)) Capstone Press of Coughlan Cos.
Barr, Linda. Captured, 1 vol. unabr. ed. 2012. (Astonishing Headlines Ser.). (ENG.). 92p. (YA). (gr. 9-12). 8.95 (978-1-61651-919-3(3)) Saddleback Educational Publishing, Inc.
Barrington, Richard. The Juvenile Court System: Your Legal Rights. 2015. (J). (978-1-4777-8042-8(4)) Rosen Publishing Group, Inc., The.
Bascomb, Neal. The Nazi Hunters: How a Team of Spies & Survivors Captured the World's Most Notorious Nazi. 2013. (ENG., Illus.). 256p. (J). (gr. 7). 17.99 (978-0-545-43099-9(2), Levine, Arthur A. Bks.) Scholastic, Inc.
Bearce, Stephanie. Top Secret Files: Gangsters & Bootleggers: Secrets, Strange Tales, & Hidden Facts about the Roaring 20s. rev. ed. 2015. (Top Secret Files Ser.: 0). (ENG., Illus.). 125p. (J). (gr. 4-7). 8.95 (978-1-61821-461-4(6)) Prufrock Pr.
Brook, Henry. True Stories of Gangsters. McNee, Ian, illus. 2004. (True Adventure Stories Ser.). 144p. (J). pap. 4.95 (978-0-7945-0722-0(0), Usborne) EDC Publishing.
Burlingame, Jeff. Prisons: Rehabilitate or Severely Punish? 2011. (Controversy! 3 Ser.). 112p. (gr. 7). 37.07 (978-1-60870-493-4(9)) Marshall Cavendish Corp.
Cooke, Tim. Bonnie & Clyde: Notorious Outlaws of the Great Depression. 2016. (Wanted! Famous Outlaws Ser.). (ENG.). 48p. (J). (gr. 6-8). pap. 14.05 (978-1-4824-4251-9(5)) Stevens, Gareth Publishing LLLP.

Cope Bowley, Tonia. From a Street Kid: Stephen Lungu's Incredible Life Journey. Petropouleas, Niko, illus. 2012. 192p. pap. *(978-1-78003-380-8(X))* Pen Pr. Pubs., Ltd.

Costain, Meredith. You Wouldn't Want to Be an 18th-Century British Convict! A Trip to Australia You'd Rather Not Take. Antram, David, illus. 2006. (You Wouldn't Want to Ser.). (ENG.). 32p. (J). (gr. 2-5). pap. 9.95 *(978-0-531-16998-8(7),* Watts, Franklin) Scholastic Library Publishing.

Ellis, Carol & Grayson, Robert. Drug Cartels & Smugglers. 2013. (J). *(978-1-61900-029-2(6))* Eldorado Ink.

Esherick, Joan. Prisoner Rehabilitation: Success Stories & Failures. 2006. (Incarceration Issues Ser.). (Illus.). 111p. (YA). (gr. 7-18). lib. bdg. 22.95 *(978-1-59084-994-1(9))* Mason Crest.

Ganeri, Anita & West, David. Outlaws & Villains from History. 2012. (Illus.). 32p. (J). 70.50 *(978-1-4488-5237-6(4));* pap. 11.75 *(978-1-4488-5236-9(6));* lib. bdg. 26.50 *(978-1-4488-5199-7(8))* Rosen Publishing Group, Inc., The. (PowerKids Pr.).

Gantos, Jack. Hole in My Life. 2004. 18.10 *(978-0-7569-3197-1(5))* Farrar, Straus & Giroux.

—Hole in My Life. 2009. 8.89 *(978-0-7848-2463-4(0),* Everbind) Marco Bk. Co.

—Hole in My Life. 2012. (ENG.). 224p. (YA). (gr. 9-13). pap. 9.99 *(978-0-312-64157-3(5),* 9780312641573) Square Fish.

Heits, Rudolph T. Mass Murderers. 2013. (J). *(978-1-61900-035-3(0))* Eldorado Ink.

Henry, Nathan L. Good Behavior. 2011. 256p. pap. 9.99 *(978-1-59990-470-2(5),* Bloomsbury USA Childrens) Bloomsbury Publishing USA.

Hermsen, Sarah, et al. American Reference Library. 2004. (Crime & Punishment in America Ser.). (ENG.). 39p. (J). 5.00 *(978-0-7876-9174-5(7),* UXL) Cengage Gale.

Higgins, Melissa. The Night Dad Went to Jail: What to Expect When Someone You Love Goes to Jail, 1 vol. Kirwan, Wednesday, illus. 2011. (Life's Challenges Ser.). (ENG.). 24p. (gr. 2-3). lib. bdg. 25.99 *(978-1-4048-6679-9(5))* Picture Window Bks.

History's Most Murderous Villains. 2016. (History's Most Murderous Villains Ser.). 32p. (gr. 5-4). pap. 63.00 *(978-1-4824-5323-2(1));* lib. bdg. 159.60 *(978-1-4824-4607-4(3))* Stevens, Gareth Publishing LLLP.

Hoblin, Paul. The Boston Strangler, 1 vol. 2012. (Unsolved Mysteries (el) Ser.). (ENG.). 112p. (J). (gr. 6-12). lib. bdg. 35.64 *(978-1-61783-299-4(5),* Essential Library) ABDO Publishing Co.

Hubbard, Ben. Hi Tech World: Code Breakers. 2010. (ENG., Illus.). 32p. (J). lib. bdg. *(978-0-7787-7528-7(3))* Crabtree Publishing Co.

Innes, Brian. Forensic Science, Vol. 20. Gomez, Manny, ed. 2016. (Crime & Detection Ser.). (Illus.). 96p. (J). (gr. 7). 24.95 *(978-1-4222-3477-8(0))* Mason Crest.

Keppeler, Jill. Elizabeth Báthory: The Blood Countess. 2016. (History's Most Murderous Villains Ser.). (Illus.). 32p. (J). (gr. 5-4). pap. 10.50 *(978-1-4824-4785-9(1))* Stevens, Gareth Publishing LLLP.

Kiesbye, Stefan, ed. DNA Databases. 2011. (At Issue Ser.). 128p. (J). pap. 24.45 *(978-0-7377-5891-7(0),* Greenhaven Pr., Inc.); (gr. 9-12). 34.45 *(978-0-7377-5890-0(2))* Cengage Gale.

La Bella, Laura. The Nuremberg Trials. 2014. (Documentary History of the Holocaust Ser.). (Illus.). 80p. (J). (gr. 7-12). 34.25 *(978-1-4777-7607-0(9))* Rosen Publishing Group, Inc., The.

Landau, Elaine. Assassins, Traitors, & Spies. 2015. (ShockZone (tm) — Villains Ser.). (ENG., Illus.). 32p. (gr. 5-8). 21.32 *(978-1-4677-6000-3(5),* Lerner Digital) Lerner Publishing Group.

Langston-George, Rebecca. The Booth Brothers: Drama, Fame, & the Death of President Lincoln. 2017. (Encounter: Narrative Nonfiction Stories Ser.). (ENG.). 112p. (gr. 3-5). lib. bdg. 30.65 ***(978-1-5157-7338-2(8))*** Encounter Bks.

Latta, Sara L. Medical Serial Killers. 2016. (J). *(978-0-7660-7297-8(5))* Enslow Pubs., Inc.

Lusted, Marcia Amidon. Capture & Killing of Osama Bin Laden, 1 vol. 2011. (Essential Events Set 7 Ser.). (ENG.). 112p. (J). (gr. 6-12). lib. bdg. 35.64 *(978-1-61783-180-5(8))* ABDO Publishing Co.

Marcovitz, Hal. Should Juveniles Be Tried As Adults? 2011. (In Controversy Ser.). (YA). (gr. 7-12). lib. bdg. 27.95 *(978-1-60152-230-6(4))* ReferencePoint Pr., Inc.

Miller, Shannon. Don't Share Your Address Online. 2013. (Internet DOs & DON'ts Ser.). (Illus.). 24p. (J). (gr. k-2). 22.60 *(978-1-4777-1536-9(3));* (ENG., pap. 8.25 *(978-1-4777-1558-1(4));* pap. 49.50 *(978-1-4777-1559-8(2))* Rosen Publishing Group, Inc., The. (PowerKids Pr.).

—Don't Talk to Strangers Online. 2013. (Internet DOs & DON'ts Ser.). (Illus.). 24p. (J). (gr. k-2). 22.60 *(978-1-4777-0755-5(7));* (ENG., pap. 8.25 *(978-1-4777-1564-2(9));* pap. 49.50 *(978-1-4777-1565-9(7))* Rosen Publishing Group, Inc., The. (PowerKids Pr.).

Mockaitis, Thomas R. Osama Bin Laden: A Biography, 1 vol. 2010. (Greenwood Biographies Ser.). (Illus.). 141p. (C). 39.00 *(978-0-313-35374-1(3),* GR5374, Greenwood) ABC-CLIO, LLC.

Nardo, Don. Nazi War Criminals. 2015. (Illus.). 80p. (J). *(978-1-60152-850-6(7))* ReferencePoint Pr., Inc.

Netzley, Patricia D. What Impact Does Mental Illness Have on Crime? 2014. (In Controversy Ser.). (ENG., Illus.). 96p. (J). lib. bdg. *(978-1-60152-660-1(1))* ReferencePoint Pr., Inc.

Newton, Michael. Bank Robbery. 2008. (Criminal Investigations Ser.). (Illus.). 120p. (C). (gr. 9-12). 35.00 *(978-0-7910-9401-3(4),* Chelsea Hse.) Facts On File, Inc.

Petrikowski, Nicki Peter. Cannibal Serial Killers. 2016. (Psychology of Serial Killers Ser.). (ENG.). 128p. (J). (gr. 9-9). 37.27 *(978-0-7660-7282-4(7))* Enslow Pubs., Inc.

Pizzoli, Greg. The Impossibly True Story of Tricky Vic: The Man Who Sold the Eiffel Tower. 2015. (ENG., Illus.). 42p. (J). (gr. 2-4). 17.99 *(978-0-670-01652-5(7),* Viking Books for Young Readers) Penguin Young Readers Group.

The Psychology of Mass Murderers. 2016. (Psychology of Mass Murderers Ser.). 128p. (gr. 8-8). lib. bdg. 149.08 *(978-0-7660-7508-5(7))* Enslow Pubs., Inc.

Rauf, Don. Female Serial Killers. 2016. (Psychology of Serial Killers Ser.). (ENG.). 128p. (J). (gr. 9-9). lib. bdg. 37.27 *(978-0-7660-7288-6(6))* Enslow Pubs., Inc.

—Historical Serial Killers. 2016. (Psychology of Serial Killers Ser.). (ENG., Illus.). 128p. (J). (gr. 9-9). lib. bdg. 37.27 *(978-0-7660-7290-9(8))* Enslow Pubs., Inc.

—Modern-Day Serial Killers. 2016. (Psychology of Serial Killers Ser.). (ENG.). 128p. (J). (gr. 9-9). lib. bdg. 37.27 *(978-0-7660-7298-5(3))* Enslow Pubs., Inc.

Rice, Dona. Chicas y Chicos Malos Del Mundo Antiguo. 2016. (TIME for Kids en Español - Level 5 Ser.). (SPA.). 64p. (gr. 5-5). lib. bdg. 31.99 *(978-1-5157-2953-2(2))* Time for Kids Inc AUS. Dist: Capstone Pub.

Rice, Dona Herweck. Bad Guys & Gals of the Ancient World, 1 vol. 2nd rev. ed. 2013. (Nonfiction Readers Ser.). (ENG.). 64p. (J). (gr. 5-5). pap. 10.99 *(978-1-4333-4904-1(3));* (Illus.). pap. 31.96 *(978-1-4333-7427-2(7))* Teacher Created Materials, Inc.

—Bad Guys & Gals of the Wild West, 1 vol. 2nd rev. ed. 2013. (Nonfiction Readers Ser.). (ENG.). 64p. (J). (gr. 5-5). pap. 10.99 *(978-1-4333-4903-4(5))* Teacher Created Materials, Inc.

Scandiffio, Laura. Outlaws, Spies, & Gangsters: Chasing Notorious Criminals. Williams, Gareth, illus. 2014. (ENG.). 148p. (J). (gr. 4-7). 24.95 *(978-1-55451-621-6(8),* 9781554516216); pap. 14.95 *(978-1-55451-620-9(X),* 9781554516209) Annick Pr., Ltd. CAN. Dist: Publishers Group West (PGW).

Schwartz, Heather E. Gangsters, Bootleggers, & Bandits. (ShockZone (tm) — Villains Ser.). (ENG., Illus.). 32p. (gr. 5-8). 2015. 21.32 *(978-1-4677-6001-0(3),* Lerner Digital) 2013. pap. 8.95 *(978-1-4677-0895-1(X))* 2013. lib. bdg. 26.60 *(978-1-4677-0604-9(3),* Lerner Pubns.) Lerner Publishing Group.

Scott, Caitlin. Condemned, 1 vol. unabr. ed. 2012. (Astonishing Headlines Ser.). (ENG.). 92p. (YA). (gr. 9-12). 8.95 *(978-1-61651-920-9(7))* Saddleback Educational Publishing, Inc.

Shone, Rob & Spender, Nick. Solving Crimes Through Criminal Profiling. 2008. (Graphic Forensic Science Ser.). (ENG., Illus.). 48p. (YA). 58.50 *(978-1-4488-1666-8(1),* Rosen Reference) Rosen Publishing Group, Inc., The.

Smith, Roger. Political Prisoners. 2008. (Incarceration Issues Ser.). (Illus.). 111p. (YA). (gr. 7-18). lib. bdg. 22.95 *(978-1-59084-987-3(6))* Mason Crest.

Staunton, Ted. The Dreadful Truth: Canadian Crime. Geoffroi, Remie, illus. 2006. (Dreadful Truth Ser.). (ENG.). 104p. (J). (gr. 3-8). *(978-0-88780-705-3(4))* Formac Publishing Co., Ltd.

Stewart, Sheila. When My Brother Went to Prison. (Kids Have Troubles Too Ser.). (Illus.). 48p. (YA). (gr. 5-18). 2010. lib. bdg. 19.95 *(978-1-4222-1695-8(0))* 2009. pap. 7.95 *(978-1-4222-1908-9(9))* Mason Crest.

T R Thomas & Thomas, T. R. Celebrity Cases: True Crime, 1 vol. unabr. ed. 2010. (True Crime Ser.). (ENG.). 64p. (YA). (gr. 9-12). pap. 8.95 *(978-1-59905-435-3(3))* Saddleback Educational Publishing, Inc.

—Serial Killers, 1 vol. unabr. ed. 2010. (True Crime Ser.). (ENG.). 64p. (YA). (gr. 9-12). 8.95 *(978-1-59905-436-0(1))* Saddleback Educational Publishing, Inc.

Tallman, Dylan. A Blessing in Disguise. 2013. 154p. (gr. 10-12). pap. 14.95 *(978-1-4759-6568-1(0))* iUniverse, Inc.

Torres, John Albert. The People Behind Murderous Crime Sprees. 2016. (Psychology of Mass Murderers Ser.). 144p. (J). (gr. 8-8). 37.27 *(978-0-7660-7612-9(1))* Enslow Pubs., Inc.

—The People Behind School Shootings & Public Massacres. 2016. (Psychology of Mass Murderers Ser.). (Illus.). 144p. (J). (gr. 8-8). 37.27 *(978-0-7660-7615-0(6))* Enslow Pubs., Inc.

U. S. National Geographic Society Staff. Weird but True: Stupid Criminals: 100 Brainless Baddies Busted, Plus Wacky Facts. Cocotos, Tom Nick, illus. 2012. (ENG.). 176p. (J). (gr. 3-7). pap. 7.95 *(978-1-4263-0861-1(2),* National Geographic Children's Bks.) National Geographic Society.

Wachtel, Alan. The FBI's Most Wanted. 2009. (FBI Story Ser.). 64p. (J). (gr. 4-7). lib. bdg. 22.95 *(978-1-4222-0562-4(2))* Mason Crest.

Watson, Stephanie. The Escape from Alcatraz, 1 vol. 2012. (Unsolved Mysteries (el) Ser.). (ENG.). 112p. (J). (gr. 6-12). lib. bdg. 35.64 *(978-1-61783-303-8(7),* Essential Library) ABDO Publishing Co.

Yancey, Diane. The Zodiac Killer. 2008. (Crime Scene Investigations Ser.). (Illus.). 112p. (YA). (gr. 7-10). lib. bdg. 35.45 *(978-1-4205-0063-9(5),* LML02109-240733, Lucent Bks.) Cengage Gale.

Yolen, Jane & Stemple, Heidi E. Y. Bad Girls: Sirens, Jezebels, Murderesses, Thieves & Other Female Villains. Guay, Rebecca, illus. 2015. (ENG.). 172p. (J). (gr. 4-7). pap. 9.95 *(978-1-58089-186-8(1))* Charlesbridge Publishing, Inc.

—Bad Girls: Sirens, Jezebels, Murderesses, Thieves & Other Female Villains. 2015. lib. bdg. 20.80 *(978-0-606-37602-0(X))* Turtleback Bks.

Yomtov, Nelson. Tracking an Assassin! Nickolas Flux & the Assassination of Abraham Lincoln, 1 vol. Pinelli, Amerigo, illus. 2014. (Nickolas Flux History Chronicles Ser.). (ENG.). 32p. (gr. 3-4). lib. bdg. 30.65 *(978-1-4914-0252-8(0),* Graphic Library) Capstone Press of Coughlan Cos.

Zehr, Howard & Amstutz, Lorraine Stutzman. "What Will Happen to Me?" Every Night, Approximately Three Million Children Go to Bed with a Parent in Prison or Jail. Here Are Their Thoughts & Stories. 2010. (ENG.). 94p. pap. 14.95 *(978-1-56148-689-2(2),* Good Bks.) Skyhorse Publishing Co., Inc.

CRIMINALS—FICTION

Adams, Carolyn Lee. Ruthless. 2015. (ENG., Illus.). 256p. (YA). (gr. 9). 17.99 *(978-1-4814-2262-8(6),* Simon Pulse) Simon Pulse.

Alender, Katie. Famous Last Words. 2014. (ENG.). 320p. (J). (gr. 7). 18.99 *(978-0-545-63997-2(2))* Scholastic, Inc.

Alger, Horatio. Joe the Hotel Boy: Or, Winning Out by Pluck. 2007. 164p. pap. 19.95 *(978-1-4346-5069-6(3));* 172p. pap. 21.99 *(978-1-4346-5070-2(7))* Creative Media Partners, LLC.

Alphin, Elaine Marie. Counterfeit Son. 2010. (ENG., Illus.). 192p. (YA). (gr. 9). pap. 7.99 *(978-0-547-25853-9(4))* Houghton Mifflin Harcourt Publishing Co.

Amowitz, Lisa. Vision. 2014. (ENG.). 264p. (YA). (gr. 10-12). pap. 9.95 *(978-1-937053-99-4(7))* Spencer Hill Pr.

Anderson, John David. Minion. 2014. (ENG.). 288p. (J). (gr. 3-7). 16.99 *(978-0-06-213311-3(X),* Walden Pond Pr.) HarperCollins Pubs.

Angelique, A. J. Rose Petals & Ash: Curse of the Red Rose Killer, 1 vol. 2010. 94p. pap. 19.95 *(978-1-4489-5316-5(2))* America Star Bks.

Angleberger, Tom. Fake Mustache: Or, How Jodie o'Rodeo & Her Wonder Horse (and Some Nerdy Kid) Saved the U. S. Presidential Election from a Mad Genius Criminal Mastermind. 2012. (ENG., Illus.). 208p. (J). (gr. 3-7). 14.95 *(978-1-4197-0194-8(0),* Amulet Bks.) Abrams, Inc.

Atwood, Megan. Turn the Tables. 2016. (Contest Ser.: 5). (ENG.). 112p. (YA). (gr. 6-12). lib. bdg. 27.99 *(978-1-4677-7510-6(X));* (J). (gr. 4-4). E-Book 20.99 *(978-1-4677-8835-9(X),* 9781467788359) Lerner Publishing Group. (Darby Creek).

Auborn, Jodi. Secrets of the North Country: The Hobo's Story. 2012. 210p. pap. 24.95 *(978-1-4626-7898-3(X))* America Star Bks.

Avi. The Mayor of Central Park. Floca, Brian, illus. 2005. 193p. (J). (gr. 3-7). 13.65 *(978-0-7569-5125-2(9))* Perfection Learning Corp.

—The Seer of Shadows. 2009. (ENG.). 224p. (J). (gr. 4-7). pap. 6.99 *(978-0-06-000017-2(1))* HarperCollins Pubs.

Bach, Ari. Valhalla. 2nd ed. 2016. (ENG., Illus.). (YA). (gr. 9-12). 29.99 ***(978-1-63477-990-6(8))*** 2014. 330p. pap. 17.99 *(978-1-62798-718-9(5))* Dreamspinner Pr. (Harmony Ink Pr.).

Bancks, Tristan. On the Run. 2015. (ENG.). 240p. (J). (gr. 5-7). 16.99 *(978-0-374-30153-8(0),* 9780374301538, Farrar, Straus & Giroux (BYR)) Farrar, Straus & Giroux.

Barba, Rick. The Delta Anomaly. 2010. (ENG.). 224p. (YA). (gr. 7). pap. 7.99 *(978-1-4424-1241-5(0));* 14.99 *(978-1-4424-1409-9(X))* Simon Spotlight. (Simon Spotlight).

Barker, M. P. A Difficult Boy. 2009. (ENG.). 272p. (YA). (gr. 5-18). pap. 7.95 *(978-0-8234-2244-9(5))* Holiday Hse., Inc.

Bell, Juliet. Kepler's Dream. 2013. (ENG.). 256p. (J). (gr. 5). pap. 6.99 *(978-0-14-242648-7(2),* Puffin Books) Penguin Young Readers Group.

Bergstrom, Scott. The Cruelty. 2017. (Cruelty Ser.). (ENG.). 384p. (YA). 18.99 *(978-1-250-10818-0(7),* 9781250108180) Feiwel & Friends.

Bernard, Romily. Find Me. (Find Me Ser.: 1). (ENG.). (YA). (gr. 8). 2014. 336p. pap. 9.99 *(978-0-06-222904-5(4))* 2013. 320p. 17.99 *(978-0-06-222903-8(6))* HarperCollins Pubs. (HarperTeen).

—Trust Me. 2016. (Find Me Ser.: 3). 336p. (YA). (gr. 8). 17.99 *(978-0-06-222909-0(5),* HarperTeen) HarperCollins Pubs.

Black, Holly. Black Heart. (Curse Workers Ser.: 3). (ENG.). (YA). (gr. 9). 2013. 320p. pap. 11.99 *(978-1-4424-0347-5(0))* 2012. 304p. 17.99 *(978-1-4424-0346-8(2))* McElderry, Margaret K. Bks. (McElderry, Margaret K. Bks.).

—Red Glove. (Curse Workers Ser.: 2). (ENG.). (YA). (gr. 9). 2012. 352p. pap. 12.99 *(978-1-4424-0340-6(3))* 2011. 336p. 17.99 *(978-1-4424-0339-0(X))* McElderry, Margaret K. Bks. (McElderry, Margaret K. Bks.).

—White Cat. (Curse Workers Ser.: 1). (ENG.). (YA). (gr. 9). 2011. 336p. pap. 8.99 *(978-1-4169-6397-4(9))* 2010. 320p. 17.99 *(978-1-4169-6396-7(0))* McElderry, Margaret K. Bks. (McElderry, Margaret K. Bks.).

Black, Peter Jay. Lockdown. 2016. (Urban Outlaws Ser.: 3). (ENG.). 272p. (J). 16.99 *(978-1-61963-834-1(7),* 9781619638341, Bloomsbury USA Childrens) Bloomsbury Publishing USA.

—Urban Outlaws. 2014. (Urban Outlaws Ser.: Bk. 1). (ENG., Illus.). 288p. (J). (gr. 5-8). 16.99 *(978-1-61963-400-8(7),* 9781619634008, Bloomsbury USA Childrens) Bloomsbury Publishing USA.

Blair, Eric. The Bremen Town Musicians: A Retelling of the Grimm's Fairy Tale, 1 vol. Dickson, Bill, illus. 2013. (My First Classic Story Ser.). (ENG.). 32p. (gr. k-3). pap. 7.10 *(978-1-4795-1848-7(4),* My First Classic Story) Picture Window Bks.

Blair, Jamie. Leap of Faith. 2013. (ENG., Illus.). 240p. (YA). (gr. 9). 16.99 *(978-1-4424-4713-4(3),* Simon & Schuster Bks. For Young Readers) Simon & Schuster Bks. For Young Readers.

Blundell, Judy. Strings Attached. 2012. (ENG.). 320p. (J). (gr. 7). pap. 9.99 *(978-0-545-22127-6(7),* Scholastic Paperbacks) Scholastic, Inc.

Bradley, F. T. Double Vision - Code Name 711. 2015. (Double Vision Ser.: 2). (ENG.). 272p. (J). (gr. 3-7). pap. 6.99 *(978-0-06-210441-0(1))* HarperCollins Pubs.

Bross, Lee. Tangled Webs. 2016. (Tangled Webs Ser.). (ENG., Illus.). 400p. (YA). (gr. 9-17). pap. 9.99 *(978-1-4231-9467-5(5))* Hyperion Bks. for Children.

Butler, Dori H. Campus Attack, Sabotage! 2011. (Readers' & Writers' Genre Workshop Ser.). (YA). pap. *(978-1-4509-3018-5(2))* Benchmark Education Co.

Card, Melanie. Ward Against Darkness. 2013. (Necromancer Ser.: 2). (ENG.). 326p. (YA). (gr. 7). pap. 9.99 *(978-1-62061-303-0(4),* 9781620613030) Entangled Publishing, LLC.

Carman, Patrick. Shantorian, Bk. 2. 2011. (Trackers Ser.: 2). (ENG.). 176p. (J). (gr. 3-7). 14.99 *(978-0-545-16501-3(6),* Scholastic Pr.) Scholastic, Inc.

Carter, Ally. Perfect Scoundrels. 2013. (Heist Society Novel Ser.). (ENG.). 336p. (YA). (gr. 7-17). 17.99 *(978-1-4231-6600-9(0))* Hyperion Pr.

—Uncommon Criminals. 2012. (Heist Society Novel Ser.). (ENG.). 304p. (J). (gr. 5-9). pap. 9.99 *(978-1-4231-4807-4(X))* Hyperion Pr.

Chapman, Elsie. Divided (Dualed Sequel) 2015. (ENG.). 336p. (YA). (gr. 7). pap. 9.99 *(978-0-449-81298-3(7),* Ember) Random Hse. Children's Bks.

Charles, Valerie. The Dancing Light. 2013. 118p. pap. *(978-1-84944-167-4(7))* UKUnpublished.

Chilton, Claire. Shattered. 2012. 268p. pap. *(978-1-908822-10-9(4))* Ragz Bks.

Choksi, Sean. The Theft of Time. 2010. 67p. pap. 14.95 *(978-1-4327-6598-9(1))* Outskirts Pr., Inc.

Choldenko, Gennifer. Al Capone Does My Homework. 2013. Bk. 3. (ENG.). 224p. (J). (gr. 5). 17.99 *(978-0-8037-3472-2(7),* Dial Bks) Penguin Publishing Group.

—Al Capone Does My Homework. 2014. (ENG.). 240p. (J). (gr. 5). pap. 7.99 *(978-0-14-242522-0(2),* Puffin Books) Penguin Young Readers Group.

—Al Capone Does My Homework. 2014. (Tale from Alcatraz (Al Capone) Ser.: 3). lib. bdg. 18.40 *(978-0-606-35714-2(9))* Turtleback Bks.

Clark, Joan. Penny Nichols & the Black Imp. 2012. 136p. pap. *(978-1-78139-156-3(4))* Benediction Classics.

Colfer, Eoin. The Forever Man. 2016. (Warp Ser.). (ENG.). 368p. (YA). (gr. 7-12). pap. 9.99 *(978-1-4847-2616-7(2))* Hyperion Bks. for Children.

—The Hangman's Revolution. 2015. (Warp Ser.). (ENG.). 400p. (YA). (gr. 7-12). pap. 9.99 *(978-1-4231-6498-2(9))* Hyperion Bks. for Children.

Collier, James Lincoln. Me & Billy, 0 vols. unabr. ed. 2013. (ENG.). 194p. (J). (gr. 5-7). pap. 9.99 *(978-1-4778-1706-3(9),* 9781477817063, Amazon Children's Publishing) Amazon Publishing.

Crider, Mike. Gonzo & the Almost Invisible Man. 2012. (ENG.). 140p. (J). (gr. 3-7). pap. 8.99 *(978-1-4424-8128-2(5),* Simon & Schuster/Paula Wiseman Bks.) Simon & Schuster/Paula Wiseman Bks.

Cypess, Leah. Death Sworn. 2014. (ENG.). 352p. (YA). (gr. 8). 17.99 *(978-0-06-222121-6(3),* Greenwillow Bks.) HarperCollins Pubs.

Daly, Stuart. The Final Battle. 2016. (Brotherhood of Thieves Ser.: 3). (ENG.). 336p. (J). (gr. 4-7). pap. 9.99 *(978-0-85798-538-5(8))* Random Hse. Australia AUS. Dist: Independent Pubs. Group.

D'Andra, Anastasia. In the Shadows: Book 2 Rosegrove Series. 2012. 186p. pap. 24.95 *(978-1-4626-5920-3(9))* America Star Bks.

Dawson, Delilah S. Hit. 2015. (ENG., Illus.). 336p. (YA). (gr. 9). 17.99 *(978-1-4814-2339-7(8),* Simon Pulse) Simon Pulse.

—Strike. 2016. (ENG., Illus.). 480p. (YA). (gr. 9). 17.99 *(978-1-4814-2342-7(8),* Simon Pulse) Simon Pulse.

de Fombelle, Timothée. Vango: Between Sky & Earth. Ardizzone, Sarah, tr. 2016. (ENG.). 432p. (YA). (gr. 7). pap. 9.99 *(978-0-7636-8781-6(2))* Candlewick Pr.

De la Cruz, Melissa. Return to the Isle of the Lost: A Descendants Novel. 2016. (Descendants Ser.). (ENG.). 320p. (J). (gr. 4-7). 17.99 *(978-1-4847-8521-8(5));* 17.99 *(978-1-4847-8522-5(3));* 17.99 *(978-1-4847-8520-1(7));* (Illus.). 17.99 *(978-1-4847-5071-1(3))* Hyperion Bks. for Children.

Delaney, Joseph. Grimalkin the Witch Assassin, Bk. 9. Arrasmith, Patrick, illus. 2013. (Last Apprentice Ser.: 9). (ENG.). 416p. (YA). (gr. 8). pap. 9.99 *(978-0-06-208208-4(6),* Greenwillow Bks.) HarperCollins Pubs.

Dickens, Charles. Oliver Twist. Volpari, Daniela, illus. 2014. (Big Picture Book Ser.). (ENG.). 48p. (J). (gr. 1). 16.95 *(978-2-7338-2529-7(1))* Auzou, Philippe Editions FRA. Dist: Consortium Bk. Sales & Distribution.

—Oliver Twist. 2014. (Graphic Classics Ser.). 48p. (gr. 2-7). pap. 8.95 *(978-1-905087-97-6(7))* Book Hse. GBR. Dist: Black Rabbit Bks.

—Oliver Twist. 2013. 274p. pap. 14.99 *(978-1-4837-0319-0(3))* Bottom of the Hill Publishing.

—Oliver Twist. Belli, Alfredo, illus. 2008. (Green Apple Step Two Ser.). (ENG.). 96p. (J). (gr. 5). pap. incl. audio compact disk *(978-88-530-0580-9(7))* Cideb.

—Oliver Twist. 2013. (ENG., Illus.). 722p. (J). (gr. 4-7). pap. 12.99 *(978-0-09-958263-2(5))* Random Hse. GBR. Dist: Independent Pubs. Group.

Diederich, Phillippe. Playing for the Devil's Fire. 2016. (ENG.). 232p. (J). (gr. 6-10). 16.95 *(978-1-941026-29-8(X))* Cinco Puntos Pr.

Dillon, Elena. Crushing. 2013. 368p. (YA). pap. 13.99 *(978-0-9886353-4-0(8))* Dillon, Elena.

Dionne, Erin. Moxie & the Art of Rule Breaking: A 14-Day Mystery. (ENG.). (J). (gr. 5). 2014. 288p. pap. 6.99 *(978-0-14-242614-2(8),* Puffin Books) 2013. 256p. 16.99 *(978-0-8037-3871-3(4),* Dial Bks) Penguin Young Readers Group.

Doctorow, Cory. Homeland. (ENG.). (YA). (gr. 8). 2014. 448p. pap. 12.99 *(978-0-7653-3370-4(8),* 9780765333704) 2013. 400p. 17.99 *(978-0-7653-3369-8(4),* 9780765333698) Doherty, Tom Assocs., LLC. (Tor Teen).

—Homeland. 2014. (YA). lib. bdg. 24.50 *(978-0-606-38513-8(4))* Turtleback Bks.

Dunn, Pintip. Before Tomorrow. 2016. (ENG., Illus.). (YA). pap. 12.99 ***(978-1-68281-336-2(3))*** Entangled Publishing, LLC.

Easton, Tom. Seven Second Delay. 2015. (ENG.). 240p. (J). (gr. 7-12). 16.95 *(978-0-8234-3209-7(2))* Holiday Hse., Inc.

Falkner, Brian. Brain Jack. 2011. (ENG.). 368p. (YA). (gr. 7). pap. 9.99 *(978-0-375-84367-9(1),* Ember) Random Hse. Children's Bks.

Fardell, John. Manfred the Baddie. Fardell, John, illus. 2009. (ENG., Illus.). 32p. (J). (gr. -1-k). pap. 11.99 *(978-1-84916-044-5(9))* Quercus GBR. Dist: Hachette Bk. Group.

Fields, Jan. Hack Attack: A Trip to Wonderland, 1 vol. Altmann, Scott, illus. 2013. (Adventures in Extreme Reading Ser.). (ENG.). 112p. (J). (gr. 3-6). 27.07 *(978-1-61641-919-6(9))* Magic Wagon.

—Lightning Strikes Twice: Escaping Great Expectations, 1 vol. Altmann, Scott, illus. 2013. (Adventures in Extreme Reading Ser.). (ENG.). 112p. (J). (gr. 3-6). 27.07 *(978-1-61641-922-6(9))* Magic Wagon.

—Trapped in Stormy Seas: Sailing to Treasure Island, 1 vol. Altmann, Scott, illus. 2013. (Adventures in Extreme Reading Ser.). (ENG.). 112p. (J). (gr. 3-6). 27.07 *(978-1-61641-921-9(0))* Magic Wagon.

Figley, Marthy Rhodes & Figley, Marty Rhodes. The Prison-Ship Adventure of James Forten, Revolutionary War Captive. Hammond, Ted & Carbajal, Richard, illus. 2011. (History's Kid Heroes Ser.). (ENG.). 32p. (gr. 3-5). 26.60 *(978-0-7613-6183-1(9));* pap. 8.95 *(978-0-7613-7075-8(7),* Graphic Universe™) Lerner Publishing Group.

Figley, Marty Rhodes. The Prison-Ship Adventure of James Forten, Revolutionary War Captive. Hammond, Ted & Carbajal, Richard, illus. 2011. (History's Kid Heroes Ser.). 32p. pap. 51.02 *(978-0-7613-7637-8(2),* Graphic Universe™) Lerner Publishing Group.

Fox, Janet. Sirens. 2012. (ENG.). 384p. (YA). (gr. 7). pap. 9.99 *(978-0-14-242430-8(7),* Speak) Penguin Young Readers Group.

Freeman, Martha. The Orphan & the Mouse. McPhail, David, illus. 2014. (ENG.). 176p. (J). (gr. 3-7). 16.95 *(978-0-8234-3167-0(3))* Holiday Hse., Inc.

C
D

Geesey, Kathleen. Black Fog. 2011. 200p. pap. 24.95 *(978-1-4560-7000-7(2))* America Star Bks.

Giles, Gail. Dark Song. 2011. (ENG.). 320p. (gr. 10-17). pap. 8.99 *(978-0-316-06887-1(X))* Little, Brown Bks. for Young Readers.

Girard, Geoffrey. Project Cain. 2013. (ENG., Illus.). 368p. (YA). (gr. 9). 17.99 *(978-1-4424-7696-7(6)*, Simon & Schuster Bks. For Young Readers) Simon & Schuster Bks. For Young Readers.

Goodman, Shawn. Kindness for Weakness. 2015. (ENG.). 272p. (YA). (gr. 9). pap. 9.99 *(978-0-385-74325-9(4)*, Ember) Random Hse. Children's Bks.

Gosling, Sharon. The Ruby Airship. 2015. (Diamond Thief Ser.). (ENG.). 496p. (gr. 9-12). 16.95 *(978-1-63079-004-2(4))* Switch Pr.

Grant, Vicki. Res Judicata, 1 vol. 2008. (ENG.). 184p. (YA). (gr. 7-12). pap. 9.95 *(978-1-55143-940-2(9))* Orca Bk. Pubs. USA.

Graves, Judith. Exposed, 1 vol. 2015. (Retribution Ser.). (ENG.). 144p. (YA). (gr. 8-12). pap. 9.95 *(978-1-4598-0722-8(7))* Orca Bk. Pubs. USA.

Green, Roger Lancelyn & Green, Richard. Adventures of Robin Hood. Hall, Arthur & Terrazzini, Daniela Jaglenka, illus. 2010. (Puffin Classics Ser.). (ENG.). 320p. (J). (gr. 5-7). 16.99 *(978-0-14-133489-9(4)*, Puffin Books) Penguin Young Readers Group.

Green, S. E. Killer Instinct. 2014. (ENG., Illus.). 272p. (YA). (gr. 9). 17.99 *(978-1-4814-0285-9(4)*, Simon Pulse) Simon Pulse.

—Killer Within. 2015. (ENG.). 304p. (YA). (gr. 9). 17.99 *(978-1-4814-0288-0(9)*, Simon Pulse) Simon Pulse.

Green, Tim. The Big Time. (Football Genius Ser.: 4). (ENG.). (J). (gr. 3-7). 2011. 304p. pap. 6.99 *(978-0-06-168621-4(2))* 2010. 288p. 16.99 *(978-0-06-168619-1(0))* HarperCollins Pubs.

Guerra, Elisa Puricelli. The Legend of Black Bart, 1 vol. Pernigotti, Chiara, tr. from ITA. Bernstein, Gabo León, illus. 2014. (Minerva Mint Ser.). (ENG.). 160p. (gr. 2-4). pap. 7.99 *(978-1-4342-6515-9(3))* Capstone Young Readers of Coughlan Cos.

—The Legend of Black Bart, 1 vol. Pernigotti, Chiara, tr. from ITA. Bernstein, Gabo León, illus. 2014. (Minerva Mint Ser.). (ENG.). 160p. (gr. 2-4). 25.32 *(978-1-4342-6512-8(9))* Stone Arch Bks.

—The Night of the Blue Turtles. Zeni, Marco, tr. from ITA. Bernstein, Gabriel León, illus. 2015. (Minerva Mint Ser.). (ENG.). 160p. (gr. 2-4). lib. bdg. 25.32 *(978-1-4342-9672-6(5))* Stone Arch Bks.

Gutman, Dan. Mission Unstoppable. 2011. (Genius Files Ser.: 1). (ENG.). 304p. (J). (gr. 3-7). pap. 6.99 *(978-0-06-182766-2(5))*; (Illus.). 16.99 *(978-0-06-182764-8(9))* HarperCollins Pubs.

—Mission Unstoppable. 2011. (Genius Files Ser.: 1). (J). lib. bdg. 17.20 *(978-0-606-23559-4(0)*, Turtleback) Turtleback Bks.

—Never Say Genius. 2012. (Genius Files Ser.: 2). (J). (gr. 3-7). (ENG.). 304p. pap. 6.99 *(978-0-06-182769-3(X))*; (ENG.). 288p. 16.99 *(978-0-06-182767-9(3))*; 288p. lib. bdg. 17.89 *(978-0-06-182768-6(1))* HarperCollins Pubs.

—You Only Die Twice. 2013. (Genius Files Ser.: 3). (J). (gr. 3-7). (ENG.). 320p. pap. 6.99 *(978-0-06-182772-3(X))*; (ENG., Illus.). 304p. 16.99 *(978-0-06-182770-9(3))*; (Illus.). 304p. lib. bdg. 17.89 *(978-0-06-182771-6(1))* HarperCollins Pubs.

Haddix, Margaret Peterson. Full Ride. (ENG.). (YA). (gr. 7). 2014. 368p. pap. 12.99 *(978-1-4424-4279-5(4))* 2013. 352p. 16.99 *(978-1-4424-4278-8(6))* Simon & Schuster Bks. For Young Readers. (Simon & Schuster Bks. For Young Readers).

Halliday, John. Shooting Monarchs. 2007. (ENG.). 144p. (YA). (gr. 8). pap. 8.95 *(978-1-4169-5559-7(3)*, McElderry, Margaret K. Bks.) McElderry, Margaret K. Bks.

Hamilton, Peter F. The Hunting of the Princes. 2016. (Queen of Dreams Ser.: 2). (ENG., Illus.). 320p. (J). (gr. 4-7). pap. 11.99 *(978-1-4472-9114-5(X))* Pan Macmillan GBR. Dist: Independent Pubs. Group.

Hardy, Janice. The Healing Wars: Book II: Blue Fire. 2011. (Healing Wars Ser.: II). (ENG.). 400p. (J). (gr. 5). pap. 7.99 *(978-0-06-174744-1(0))* HarperCollins Pubs.

Harmon, Michael B. Under the Bridge. 2013. (ENG.). 272p. (YA). (gr. 9). pap. 8.99 *(978-0-375-85930-4(6)*, Ember) Random Hse. Children's Bks.

Hautman, Pete. Blank Confession. 2011. (ENG.). 176p. (YA). (gr. 7). pap. 10.99 *(978-1-4169-1328-3(9)*, Simon & Schuster Bks. For Young Readers) Simon & Schuster Bks. For Young Readers.

Hearn, Julie. Ivy. 2009. (ENG.). 384p. (YA). (gr. 7). pap. 9.99 *(978-1-4169-2507-1(4)*, Atheneum Bks. for Young Readers) Simon & Schuster Children's Publishing.

Heath, Jack. Money Run. 2013. (ENG.). 256p. (J). (gr. 7). 17.99 *(978-0-545-51266-4(2))* Scholastic, Inc.

Heflick, LaMonte. The Story of Boney & Clyde. 2004. (Illus.). 64p. pap. 3.99 *(978-1-56175-911-8(2))* Remedia Pubns.

Horowitz, Anthony. Russian Roulette: The Story of an Assassin. 2014. (Alex Rider Ser.). (ENG.). 432p. (J). (gr. 5). pap. 8.99 *(978-0-14-751231-4(X)*, Puffin Books) Penguin Young Readers Group.

—The Switch. 2010. (ENG.). 192p. (J). (gr. 5-18). 7.99 *(978-0-14-241547-4(2)*, Puffin Books) Penguin Young Readers Group.

Hotchkiss, Gerry. Emily & the Lost City of Urgup: An Adventure in Arabia. 2012. 112p. 20.95 *(978-1-4759-3764-0(4))*; pap. 10.95 *(978-1-4759-3762-6(8))* iUniverse, Inc.

Humphries, Jessie. Killing Ruby Rose, 0 vols. 2014. (Ruby Rose Ser.: 1). (ENG.). 304p. (YA). (gr. 9-12). pap. 9.99 *(978-1-4778-2006-3(X)*, 9781477820063, Amazon Children's Publishing) Amazon Publishing.

Hyder, M. A. Donia: Stolen Raindrops or Honour among Thieves. 2011. (Illus.). 364p. pap. 20.53 *(978-1-4567-7428-8(X))* AuthorHouse.

Jakobsen, Lars. The Secret Mummy. Jakobsen, Lars, illus. 2013. (Mortensen's Escapades Ser.: 4). (ENG., Illus.). 48p. (gr. 6-12). pap. 6.95 *(978-1-4677-0730-5(9))*; lib. bdg. 27.93 *(978-0-7613-7915-7(0))* Lerner Publishing Group. (Graphic Universe™).

Jakubowski, Michele. Tour of Trouble. Pinelli, Amerigo, illus. 2016. (Sleuths of Somerville Ser.). (ENG.). 144p. (gr. 4-6). lib. bdg. 25.99 *(978-1-4965-3176-6(0))* Stone Arch Bks.

—Tour of Trouble. Pinelli, Amerigo, illus. 2017. (Sleuths of Somerville Ser.). (ENG.). 144p. (gr. 4-6). pap. 6.95 *(978-1-4965-3180-3(9))* Stone Arch Bks.

Johnson, Denise Donna. The Veridical Circle. 2011. 78p. pap. 19.95 *(978-1-4626-0472-2(2))* America Star Bks.

Jones, Patrick. Fight or Flee. 2016. (Unbarred Ser.). (ENG.). 120p. (YA). (gr. 6-12). lib. bdg. 27.99 *(978-1-5124-0004-5(1)*, Darby Creek) Lerner Publishing Group.

—Fight or Flee. 2016. (Unbarred Ser.). (ENG.). 120p. (YA). (gr. 6-12). pap. 7.99 *(978-1-5124-0093-9(9)*, Darby Creek) Lerner Publishing Group.

—Fight or Flee. 2016. (Unbarred Ser.). (ENG.). 120p. (YA). (gr. 6-12). 42.65 *(978-1-5124-0094-6(7)*, Darby Creek) Lerner Publishing Group.

—Target. 2014. (Alternative Ser.). (ENG.). 128p. (YA). (gr. 6-12). lib. bdg. 27.93 *(978-1-4677-3900-9(6))* Lerner Publishing Group.

Kehoe, Tim. Furious Jones & the Assassin's Secret. 2014. (ENG., Illus.). 336p. (J). (gr. 3-7). 16.99 *(978-1-4424-7337-9(1)*, Simon & Schuster Bks. For Young Readers) Simon & Schuster Bks. For Young Readers.

Kelly, Mark. Mousetronaut Goes to Mars. Payne, C. F., illus. 2013. (ENG.). 40p. (J). (gr. -1-3). 16.99 *(978-1-4424-8426-9(8)*, Simon & Schuster/Paula Wiseman Bks.) Simon & Schuster/Paula Wiseman Bks.

Kimmel, Elizabeth Cody. Lily B. on the Brink of Cool. 2005. 245p. (J). (gr. 5-9). 14.65 *(978-0-7569-5653-0(6))* Perfection Learning Corp.

King, Trey. Detective Chase McCain- Save That Cargo! Primeau, Chuck, illus. 2013. (Lego City Ser.). (ENG.). 24p. (J). (gr. -1-3). 3.99 *(978-0-545-51573-3(4))* Scholastic, Inc.

Korman, Gordon. Criminal Destiny. 2016. (Masterminds Ser.: 2). 320p. (J). (gr. 3-7). 16.99 *(978-0-06-230002-7(4))* HarperCollins Pubs.

—Criminal Destiny. 2017. (Masterminds Ser.: 2). (J). lib. bdg. 18.40 ***(978-0-606-39612-7(8))*** Turtleback Bks.

—Masterminds. (Masterminds Ser.: 2). (J). (gr. 3-7). 2017. 336p. 7.99 *(978-0-06-230003-4(2))* 2016. 352p. pap. 7.99 *(978-0-06-229999-4(9))* 2015. 336p. 16.99 *(978-0-06-229996-3(4))* HarperCollins Pubs.

—Masterminds. 2016. (Masterminds Ser.: 1). (J). lib. bdg. 18.40 *(978-0-606-38138-3(4))* Turtleback Bks.

—Swindle. 2009. (ENG.). 256p. (J). (gr. 3-7). 6.99 *(978-0-439-90345-5(9)*, Scholastic Paperbacks) Scholastic, Inc.

—Titanic. 2011. (Titanic Ser.: 3). (ENG.). 176p. (J). (gr. 3-7). pap. 6.99 *(978-0-545-12333-4(X)*, Scholastic Paperbacks) Scholastic, Inc.

LaBree Stute, Lela. Wonder Pugs. 2010. 36p. pap. 19.99 *(978-0-557-42611-9(1))* Lulu Pr., Inc.

Lacey, Josh. The Sultan's Tigers. 2014. (ENG.). 304p. (J). (gr. 5-7). pap. 6.99 *(978-0-544-33629-2(1)*, HMH Books For Young Readers) Houghton Mifflin Harcourt Publishing Co.

LaFevers, Robin. Dark Triumph. (His Fair Assassin Ser.: 2). (ENG.). 400p. (YA). (gr. 9). 2014. pap. 9.99 *(978-0-544-22720-0(4)*, HMH Books For Young Readers) 2013. 17.99 *(978-0-547-62838-7(2))* Houghton Mifflin Harcourt Publishing Co.

—Dark Triumph, 10 vols. 2013. (His Fair Assassin Ser.: 2). (YA). *(978-1-4640-2397-2(2))* Recorded Bks., Inc.

—Grave Mercy. (His Fair Assassin Ser.: 1). (ENG., Illus.). (YA). (gr. 9). 2013. 576p. pap. 9.99 *(978-0-544-02249-2(1))* 2012. 560p. 17.99 *(978-0-547-62834-9(X))* Houghton Mifflin Harcourt Publishing Co.

—Grave Mercy, 10 vols. 2012. (His Fair Assassin Trilogy: Bk. 1). (YA). 132.75 *(978-1-4640-2388-0(3))*; 287.75 *(978-1-4640-2386-6(7))*; 130.75 *(978-1-4640-2387-3(5))*; 130.75 *(978-1-4640-2390-3(5))* Recorded Bks., Inc.

—Mortal Heart. 2014. (His Fair Assassin Ser.: 3). (ENG.). 464p. (YA). (gr. 9). 17.99 *(978-0-547-62840-0(4)*, HMH Books For Young Readers) Houghton Mifflin Harcourt Publishing Co.

Laird, Elizabeth. The Betrayal of Maggie Blair. 2011. (ENG.). 432p. (YA). (gr. 7-18). 16.99 *(978-0-547-34126-2(1))* Houghton Mifflin Harcourt Publishing Co.

Lange, Erin Jade. Rebel, Bully, Geek, Pariah. 2016. (ENG.). 320p. (YA). 17.99 *(978-1-61963-498-5(8)*, 9781619634985, Bloomsbury USA Childrens) Bloomsbury Publishing USA.

LaPorte, Tom. Hembree Heiroglyphs. 2008. 98p. pap. 9.42 *(978-1-4357-5970-1(2))* Lulu Pr., Inc.

Larbalestier, Justine. Razorhurst. 2016. (ENG.). 336p. (YA). (gr. 9). pap. 10.99 *(978-1-61695-625-7(9)*, Soho Teen) Soho Pr., Inc.

Lee, Y. S. The Agency: A Spy in the House. 2016. (Agency Ser.). (ENG.). 352p. (YA). (gr. 7). pap. 7.99 *(978-0-7636-8748-9(0))* Candlewick Pr.

Leonard, Niall. Shredder. 2015. (ENG.). 384p. (YA). (gr. 9). 17.99 *(978-0-385-74365-5(3)*, Delacorte Pr.) Random Hse. Children's Bks.

Lerangis, Peter. Wtf. 2013. (ENG., Illus.). 288p. (YA). (gr. 9). 17.99 *(978-1-4424-9369-8(0))*; pap. 9.99 *(978-1-4424-9368-1(2))* Simon Pulse. (Simon Pulse).

Lim, Rebecca. The Sweet Life. 2012. (ENG.). 196p. (YA). (gr. 7). pap. 11.99 *(978-1-74237-770-4(X))* Allen & Unwin AUS. Dist: Independent Pubs. Group.

Lisle, Janet Taylor. Black Duck. 2007. (ENG.). 256p. (J). (gr. 5-18). 7.99 *(978-0-14-240902-2(2)*, Puffin Books) Penguin Young Readers Group.

Lockwood, Vicki. The Magnificent Lizzie Brown & the Mysterious Phantom, 1 vol. 2014. (Magnificent Lizzie Brown Ser.). (ENG., Illus.). 200p. (gr. 5-9). 10.95 *(978-1-62370-069-0(8))*; lib. bdg. 26.65 *(978-1-4342-7940-8(5))* Stone Arch Bks.

—The Magnificent Lizzie Brown & the Mysterious Phantom, 1 vol. Hans, Stephanie, illus. 2014. (ENG.). 200p. (J). pap. *(978-1-4342-7942-2(1))* Stone Arch Bks.

Lu, Marie. Legend. aut. ltd. collector's ed. 2013. (Legend Trilogy: Bk. 1). (Illus.). 306p. (YA). mass mkt. 100.00 net. *(978-1-934267-38-7(4))* Gauntlet, Inc.

—Legend. 2011. (Legend Trilogy: Bk. 1). (ENG.). (YA). (gr. 8-12). 54.99 *(978-1-61657-044-6(X)*, Penguin AudioBooks) Penguin Publishing Group.

—Legend. (Legend Ser.: 1). (ENG.). (YA). (gr. 7). 2013. 352p. pap. 9.99 *(978-0-14-242207-6(X)*, Speak) 2011. 320p. 17.99 *(978-0-399-25675-2(X)*, G.P. Putnam's Sons Books for Young Readers) Penguin Young Readers Group.

—Legend. l.t. ed. 2012. (Legend Trilogy: Bk. 1). (ENG.). 394p. (J). (gr. 7-12). 23.99 *(978-1-4104-4606-0(9))* Thorndike Pr.

—Legend. (Legend Graphic Novels Ser.: 1). 2015. lib. bdg. 26.95 *(978-0-606-38424-7(3))* 2013. lib. bdg. 20.85 *(978-0-606-31701-6(5)*, Turtleback) Turtleback Bks.

—Prodigy. 2013. (Legend Trilogy: Bk. 2). (ENG.). 384p. (YA). (gr. 7). 18.99 *(978-0-399-25676-9(8)*, G.P. Putnam's Sons Books for Young Readers) Penguin Publishing Group.

—Prodigy. 2014. (Legend Ser.: 2). (ENG., Illus.). 416p. (YA). (gr. 7). pap. 10.99 *(978-0-14-242755-2(1)*, Speak) Penguin Young Readers Group.

—Prodigy. l.t. ed. 2013. (Legend Trilogy: Bk. 2). (ENG.). 486p. 23.99 *(978-1-4104-5512-3(2))* Thorndike Pr.

—Prodigy. 2014. (Legend Ser.: 2). lib. bdg. 20.85 *(978-0-606-35716-6(5))* Turtleback Bks.

—Prodigy: The Graphic Novel. 2016. (Legend Trilogy: Bk. 2). (ENG.). 160p. (YA). (gr. 7). pap. 14.99 *(978-0-399-17190-1(8)*, G.P. Putnam's Sons Books for Young Readers) Penguin Young Readers Group.

Lyga, Barry. Blood of My Blood. 2014. (ENG.). 480p. (YA). (gr. 10-17). 18.00 *(978-0-316-19870-7(6))* Little, Brown Bks. for Young Readers.

—Game. 2014. (ENG.). 544p. (YA). (gr. 10-17). pap. 10.99 *(978-0-316-12585-7(7))* Little, Brown Bks. for Young Readers.

Maas, Sarah J. Crown of Midnight. (Throne of Glass Ser.: 2). (ENG.). (YA). (gr. 9). 2014. 448p. pap. 10.99 *(978-1-61963-064-2(8)*, 9781619630642) 2013. (Illus.). 432p. 18.99 *(978-1-61963-062-8(1)*, 9781619630628) Bloomsbury Publishing USA. (Bloomsbury USA Childrens).

—Crown of Midnight. 2014. (Throne of Glass Ser.: 2). (YA). lib. bdg. 22.10 *(978-0-606-36441-6(2))* Turtleback Bks.

—Heir of Fire. (Throne of Glass Ser.: 3). (ENG.). (YA). (gr. 9). 2015. 592p. pap. 10.99 *(978-1-61963-067-3(2)*, 9781619630673) 2014. (Illus.). 576p. 18.99 *(978-1-61963-065-9(6)*, 9781619630659) Bloomsbury Publishing USA. (Bloomsbury USA Childrens).

—Queen of Shadows. 2015. (Throne of Glass Ser.: Vol. 4). (ENG., Illus.). 656p. (YA). (gr. 9). 18.99 *(978-1-61963-604-0(2)*, 9781619636040, Bloomsbury USA Childrens) Bloomsbury Publishing USA.

—Throne of Glass. (Throne of Glass Ser.: 1). (ENG., Illus.). (YA). (gr. 9). 2013. 432p. pap. 10.99 *(978-1-61963-034-5(6)*, 9781619630345) 2012. 416p. 18.99 *(978-1-59990-695-9(3)*, 9781599906959) Bloomsbury Publishing USA. (Bloomsbury USA Childrens).

—Throne of Glass. 2013. (Throne of Glass Ser.: 1). (YA). lib. bdg. 22.10 *(978-0-606-31888-4(7)*, Turtleback) Turtleback Bks.

Macauley, Jo. Inferno, 1 vol. 2014. (Secrets & Spies Ser.). (ENG.). 224p. (gr. 4-7). 26.65 *(978-1-4342-9595-8(8))* Stone Arch Bks.

—New World, 1 vol. 2014. (Secrets & Spies Ser.). (ENG.). 224p. (gr. 4-7). 26.65 *(978-1-4342-9596-5(6))* Stone Arch Bks.

MacKenzie, Carine. How God Changes People: Conversion Stories from the Bible. 2012. (ENG., Illus.). 48p. (J). 9.99 *(978-1-84550-822-7(X)*, e5e27b55-010c-4952-912d-4d962f516ac6) Christian Focus Pubns. GBR. Dist: Bookmasters Distribution.

Maniscalco, Kerri. Stalking Jack the Ripper. (ENG., Illus.). (YA). (gr. 10-17). 2017. 352p. pap. 10.99 ***(978-0-316-27351-0(1))*** 2016. 336p. 18.99 *(978-0-316-27349-7(X))* 2016. 464p. 20.99 *(978-0-316-46428-4(7))* Little Brown & Co. (Jimmy Patterson).

Manley, Francis G. Tellin Twins: The Great Art Scam. 2004. (Illus.). 132p. pap. *(978-1-84401-292-3(1))* Athena Pr.

Martin, Bob. James' Night of Terror. Salinas, Alex, illus. 2010. 120p. (gr. 4-6). 20.95 *(978-1-4502-6500-3(6))*; pap. 10.95 *(978-1-4502-6498-3(0))* iUniverse, Inc.

Mass, Wendy & Brawer, Michael. The Galactic B. U. R. P. 2016. (Space Taxi Ser.: 4). (ENG., Illus.). 128p. (J). (gr. 1-5). 14.99 *(978-0-316-24331-5(0))*; pap. 5.99 *(978-0-316-24330-8(2))* Little, Brown Bks. for Young Readers.

McBay, Bruce. Angels Inc., 1 vol. LaFave, Kim, illus. 2008. (ENG.). 71p. (J). (gr. 1-3). pap. 7.95 *(978-1-896580-30-2(0))* Tradewind Bks. CAN. Dist: Orca Bk. Pubs. USA.

McCaffrey, Laura Williams. Marked. 2017. (ENG.). 368p. (YA). (gr. 7). pap. 9.99 *(978-0-544-93884-7(4)*, HMH Books For Young Readers) Houghton Mifflin Harcourt Publishing Co.

McClintock, Norah. El Regreso, 1 vol. 2011. (Spanish Soundings Ser.).Tr. of Back. (SPA.). 112p. (YA). (gr. 8-12). pap. 9.95 *(978-1-55469-973-5(8))* Orca Bk. Pubs. USA.

McKay, Kirsty. The Assassin Game. 2016. (ENG.). 336p. (YA). (gr. 6-12). pap. 10.99 *(978-1-4926-3275-7(9)*, 9781492632757) Sourcebooks, Inc.

McLaughlin, Lauren. The Free. 2017. (ENG.). 288p. (YA). (gr. 9). 18.99 *(978-1-61695-731-5(X)*, Soho Teen) Soho Pr., Inc.

McLean, Hope. Jewel Society #3: Keep Friends Close, Emeralds Closer. 2013. (Jewel Thieves Ser.: 3). (ENG.). 144p. (J). (gr. 3-7). pap. 5.99 *(978-0-545-60764-3(7))* Scholastic, Inc.

McNamee, Graham. Acceleration. 2012. (ENG.). 240p. (YA). (gr. 7). pap. 9.99 *(978-0-307-97595-9(9)*, Ember) Random Hse. Children's Bks.

Messner, Kate. Hide & Seek. (ENG.). 256p. (J). (gr. 3-7). 2015. pap. 7.99 *(978-0-545-79910-2(4)*, Scholastic Paperbacks) 2013. (Illus.). 16.99 *(978-0-545-41975-8(1)*, Scholastic Pr.) Scholastic, Inc.

Meyer, L. A. Wild Rover No More: Being the Last Recorded Account of the Life & Times of Jacky Faber. 2014. (Bloody Jack Adventures Ser.: 12). (ENG.). 368p. (YA). (gr. 9). 17.99 *(978-0-544-21777-5(2)*, HMH Books For Young Readers) Houghton Mifflin Harcourt Publishing Co.

Miranda, Megan. Soulprint. 2015. (ENG.). 368p. (YA). (gr. 7). 17.99 *(978-0-8027-3774-8(9)*, 9780802737748, Bloomsbury USA Childrens) Bloomsbury Publishing USA.

Montijo, Rhode. Chews Your Destiny. 2017. (Gum Girl Ser.: 1). (J). lib. bdg. 16.00 ***(978-0-606-39969-2(0))*** Turtleback Bks.

Morgan, Angie. Sedric & the Hairy Troll Invasion. 2015. (ENG., Illus.). 192p. (J). (gr. 2-6). pap. 10.99 *(978-1-4052-7512-5(X))* Egmont Bks., Ltd. GBR. Dist: Independent Pubs. Group.

Myers, Walter Dean. Somewhere in the Darkness. 2008. 18.00 *(978-0-7569-9060-2(2))* Perfection Learning Corp.

Neighbors, Jolene. Nobody's Dog. 2010. 107p. pap. 14.95 *(978-1-4327-5957-5(4))* Outskirts Pr., Inc.

Nelson, James Gary. Dientecito y la Placa Peligros. Burnstead, Debbie, illus. 2011. 16p. pap. 9.95 *(978-1-61633-132-0(1))* Guardian Angel Publishing, Inc.

Norris, Zack. The Secret of Skull Island. 2012. (Double Detectives Ser.). (ENG.). 144p. (J). (gr. 3-7). pap. 4.95 *(978-1-4027-7912-1(7))* Sterling Publishing Co., Inc.

Oaks, J. Adams. Why I Fight. (ENG.). 240p. (YA). (gr. 7). 2010. pap. 9.99 *(978-1-4424-0254-6(7)*, Atheneum Bks. for Young Readers) 2009. 17.99 *(978-1-4169-1177-7(4)*, Atheneum/Richard Jackson Bks.) Simon & Schuster Children's Publishing.

O'Rourke, Tim. Flashes. 2015. (ENG.). 320p. (J). (gr. 9). 16.99 *(978-0-545-82959-5(3))* Scholastic, Inc.

Pass, Emma. Acid. 2014. (ENG.). 384p. (YA). (gr. 9). 17.99 *(978-0-385-74387-7(4)*, Delacorte Pr.) Random Hse. Children's Bks.

Patterson, James. The Dangerous Days of Daniel X. 2014. lthr. 79.00 *(978-1-62715-506-9(6))* Leatherbound Bestsellers.

—The Dangerous Days of Daniel X. (Daniel X Ser.: 1). (ENG.). 2010. 272p. (J). (gr. 3-7). pap. 8.00 *(978-0-316-11970-2(9)*, Jimmy Patterson) 2008. 304p. pap. 20.99 *(978-0-316-03025-0(2))* Little Brown & Co.

—The Dangerous Days of Daniel X. 2010. (Daniel X Ser.: 1). (J). lib. bdg. 18.45 *(978-0-606-14720-0(9)*, Turtleback) Turtleback Bks.

—Demons & Druids. 2011. (Daniel X Ser.: 3). (ENG.). 304p. (J). (gr. 3-7). pap., pap. 8.00 *(978-0-316-03830-0(X)*, Jimmy Patterson) Little Brown & Co.

Patterson, James & Ledwidge, Michael. The Dangerous Days of Daniel X. 2009. (Daniel X Ser.: 1). (ENG.). 288p. mass mkt. 7.99 *(978-0-446-50913-8(2)*, Jimmy Patterson) Little Brown & Co.

Patterson, James & Sadler, Adam. Demons & Druids. l.t. ed. 2010. (Daniel X Ser.: 3). (ENG.). 320p. 29.99 *(978-0-316-08731-5(9)*, Jimmy Patterson) Little Brown & Co.

Paul, Naomi. Code Name Komiko. 2014. (Illus.). 288p. (YA). (gr. 6-12). pap. 10.95 *(978-1-62324-024-0(7))* Enslow Pubs., Inc.

Polan, Alex. Catching the Jigglypuff Thief: PokéStop Stories, Book One. 2016. (ENG.). 112p. (J). (gr. 1-7). pap. 7.99 *(978-1-5107-2157-9(6)*, Sky Pony Pr.) Skyhorse Publishing Co., Inc.

Porter, Kevin Don. Missing. 2013. 166p. pap. 11.99 *(978-0-9857014-7-5(1))* Artists' Orchard, LLC, The.

Project Cain. 2014. (ENG., Illus.). 384p. (YA). (gr. 9). pap. 11.99 *(978-1-4424-7698-1(2)*, Simon & Schuster Bks. For Young Readers) Simon & Schuster Bks. For Young Readers.

Pryor, Bonnie. Mr. Munday & the Rustlers. 2013. (ENG.). 32p. (J). (gr. -1-3). 16.99 *(978-1-4424-8876-2(X)*, Atheneum Bks. for Young Readers) Simon & Schuster Children's Publishing.

Purdie, Kathryn. Burning Glass. (Burning Glass Ser.: 1). (YA). (gr. 9). 2017. 528p. pap. 9.99 *(978-0-06-241237-9(X))* 2016. (Illus.). 512p. 17.99 *(978-0-06-241236-2(1))* HarperCollins Pubs. (Tegen, Katherine Bks).

Quick, Matthew. Boy21. 2013. (ENG.). 272p. (YA). (gr. 7-17). pap. 10.99 *(978-0-316-12796-7(5))* Little, Brown Bks. for Young Readers.

Reid, Roger. Time. 2011. (ENG.). 152p. (J). 19.95 *(978-1-58838-262-7(1)*, NewSouth Bks.) NewSouth, Inc.

Ripley, Esther. Heroes to the Rescue. 2016. (DK Reader Level 2 Ser.). lib. bdg. 13.55 *(978-0-606-38711-8(0))* Turtleback Bks.

Ritter, William. Jackaby. (Jackaby Ser.: 1). (ENG.). 304p. (YA). (gr. 9-12). 2015. pap. 9.95 *(978-1-61620-546-1(6))* 2014. 16.95 *(978-1-61620-353-5(6)*, 73353) Algonquin Bks. of Chapel Hill.

Rodman, Sean. Final Crossing, 1 vol. 2014. (Orca Soundings Ser.). (ENG.). 112p. (YA). (gr. 8-12). pap. 9.95 *(978-1-4598-0552-1(6))* Orca Bk. Pubs. USA.

Rohan, Margaret de. Celia & Granny Meg go to Paris: A survival Guide. 2011. (ENG., Illus.). 184p. pap. *(978-1-84876-650-1(5))* Troubador Publishing Ltd.

—Celia & Granny Meg Return to Paris: The man with no Face. 2012. (ENG., Illus.). 176p. pap. *(978-1-78088-243-7(2))* Troubador Publishing Ltd.

Ryan, Patrick. In Mike We Trust. 2009. 321p. (J). lib. bdg. 17.89 *(978-0-06-085814-8(1)*, HarperTeen) HarperCollins Pubs.

Salane, Jeffrey. Justice. (ENG.). 288p. (J). (gr. 3-7). 2016. (Lawless Ser.: 2). pap. 6.99 *(978-0-545-45032-4(2))* 2015. 16.99 *(978-0-545-45031-7(4))* Scholastic, Inc. (Scholastic Pr.).

—Lawless. (J). 2013. 277p. *(978-0-545-54882-3(9))*Bk. 1. 2015. (ENG.). 288p. (gr. 3-7). pap. 6.99 *(978-0-545-45030-0(6))* Scholastic, Inc. (Scholastic Pr.).

—Lawless: Book 1. 2013. (Lawless Ser.). (ENG.). 288p. (J). (gr. 5-9). 16.99 *(978-0-545-45029-4(2)*, Scholastic Pr.) Scholastic, Inc.

—Mayhem. 2016. (Lawless Ser.: 3). (ENG.). 304p. (J). (gr. 3-7). 17.99 *(978-0-545-45033-1(0)*, Scholastic Pr.) Scholastic, Inc.

Sazaklis, John. Batman Classic - Eternal Enemies. Tong, Andie, illus. 2013. (ENG.). 24p. (J). (gr. -1-3). pap. 3.99 *(978-0-06-220997-9(3)*, HarperFestival) HarperCollins Pubs.

Scholastic Editors & Marsham, Liz. Harley Quinn: Wild Card. 2016. (Backstories Ser.). (ENG., Illus.). 128p. (J). (gr. 3-7). 16.00 *(978-0-606-39148-1(7))* Turtleback Bks.

Schreiber, Joe. Perry's Killer Playlist. 2013. (ENG.). 224p. (YA). (gr. 9). pap. 8.99 *(978-0-544-10489-1(7))* Houghton Mifflin Harcourt Publishing Co.

Shakespeare, William. Julius Caesar, 1 vol. Garcia, Eduardo, illus. 2011. (Shakespeare Graphics Ser.). (ENG.). 88p. (gr. 2-3). pap. 7.15 *(978-1-4342-3450-6(9))*; lib. bdg. 27.99 *(978-1-4342-2631-0(X))* Stone Arch Bks. (Shakespeare Graphics).

Shankman, Adam & Sullivan, Laura L. Girl about Town. 2016. (ENG., Illus.). 336p. (YA). (gr. 9). 17.99 *(978-1-4814-4787-4(4)*, Atheneum Bks. for Young Readers) Simon & Schuster Children's Publishing.

Sheehan, Anna. A Long, Long Sleep. 2011. (ENG., Illus.). 352p. (YA). (gr. 9). 16.99 *(978-0-7636-5260-9(1))* Candlewick Pr.

Shepard, Sara. Crushed. 2014. (Pretty Little Liars Ser.: 13). (ENG.). 368p. (YA). (gr. 9). pap. 10.99 *(978-0-06-219972-0(2),* HarperTeen) HarperCollins Pubs.
Shepherd, Megan. Her Dark Curiosity. 2014. (Madman's Daughter Ser.: 2). (ENG.). 432p. (YA). (gr. 8). 17.99 *(978-0-06-212805-8(1))* HarperCollins Pubs.
Sherman, M. Zachary. Control under Fire, 1 vol. Casas, Fritz, illus. 2011. (Bloodlines Ser.). (ENG.). 88p. (gr. 4-8). pap. 6.95 *(978-1-4342-3100-0(3));* lib. bdg. 26.65 *(978-1-4342-2561-0(5))* Stone Arch Bks.
Shields, Breeana. Poison's Kiss. 2017. (Serpent's Promise Ser.). (ENG.). 304p. (YA). (gr. 7). 17.99 *(978-1-101-93782-2(3),* Random Hse. Bks. for Young Readers) Random Hse. Children's Bks.
Shinoda, Anna. Learning Not to Drown. 2014. (ENG., Illus.). 352p. (YA). (gr. 9). 17.99 *(978-1-4169-9393-3(2),* Atheneum Bks. for Young Readers) Simon & Schuster Children's Publishing.
Simmons, Michael. Pool Boy. 2005. 164p. (gr. 7). 17.95 *(978-0-7569-5064-4(3))* Perfection Learning Corp.
Skidmore, Lauren. The Fairest Poison. 2016. (YA). pap. 16.99 *(978-1-4621-1792-5(9))* Cedar Fort, Inc./CFI Distribution.
Skuse, C. J. Pretty Bad Things. 2011. (ENG.). 256p. (J). (gr. 7-7). 17.99 *(978-0-545-28973-3(4),* Chicken Hse., The) Scholastic, Inc.
Slott, Dan, et al. Playing with Matches, 1 vol. Burchett, Rick, illus. 2013. (Batman Adventures Ser.). (ENG.). 32p. (gr. 2-3). 22.60 *(978-1-4342-6034-5(8))* Stone Arch Bks.
Smiley, Jane. A Good Horse. 2011. (Horses of Oak Valley Ranch Ser.: Bk. 2). (ENG.). 256p. (J). (gr. 5). 6.99 *(978-0-375-86230-4(7),* Yearling) Random Hse. Children's Bks.
Smith, Emilie & Tejada, Marguerita. Viva Zapata!, 1 vol. Czernecki, Stefan, illus. 2009. (ENG.). 32p. (J). (gr. -1-3). 14.95 *(978-1-896580-55-5(6))* Tradewind Bks. CAN. Dist: Orca Bk. Pubs. USA.
Smith, Roland. Shatterproof. 2012. (39 Clues: Cahills vs. Vespers Ser.: 4). (ENG.). 192p. (J). (gr. 3-7). 12.99 *(978-0-545-29842-1(3));*Bk. 4. (Illus.). lib. bdg. 12.99 *(978-0-545-32413-7(0))* Scholastic, Inc.
—Zach's Lie. 2003. (ENG.). 224p. (J). (gr. 5-9). pap. 6.99 *(978-0-7868-1440-4(3))* Hyperion Pr.
—Zach's Lie. 2003. (J). (gr. 5-8). lib. bdg. 17.20 *(978-0-613-63491-5(8),* Turtleback) Turtleback Bks.
Somper, Justin. Allies & Assassins. 2014. (Allies & Assassins Ser.). (ENG.). 496p. (YA). (gr. 7-17). 18.00 *(978-0-316-25393-2(6))* Little, Brown Bks. for Young Readers.
Sonnebom, Scott. The Computer Meltdown. Lozano, Omar, illus. 2015. (North Police Ser.). (ENG.). 32p. (J). (gr. k-2). lib. bdg. 21.32 *(978-1-4795-6485-9(0))* Picture Window Bks.
Soria, Destiny. Iron Cast. 2016. (ENG.). 384p. (YA). (gr. 8-17). 17.95 *(978-1-4197-2192-2(5),* Amulet Bks.) Abrams, Inc.
Springer, Michael. The Bootlegger's Secret. 2010. (Illus.). 164p. pap. 15.95 *(978-1-4327-5792-2(X))* Outskirts Pr., Inc.
Staunton, Ted. Jump Cut, 1 vol. 2012. (Seven (the Series) Ser.). (ENG., Illus.). 232p. (J). (gr. 5-10). pap. 9.95 *(978-1-55469-947-6(9))* Orca Bk. Pubs. USA.
Stephens, Berin L. Time Gangsters. 2012. pap. 14.99 *(978-1-59955-966-7(8))* Cedar Fort, Inc./CFI Distribution.
Stewart, Dianne C. Season of the Cold Moon. 2011. (ENG.). 108p. (J). (gr. 2). pap. 8.95 *(978-0-9831032-0-2(8),* BeanPole Bks.) Harren Communications, LLC.
Stohl, Margaret. Black Widow: Forever Red. (Black Widow Novel Ser.). (ENG.). (YA). (gr. 7-12). 2016. 432p. pap. 9.99 *(978-1-4847-7645-2(3))* 2015. 416p. 17.99 *(978-1-4847-2643-3(X))* Disney Publishing Worldwide. (Marvel Pr.).
Stone, David Lee. The Shadewell Shenanigans. 2006. (Illus.). 308p. (J). *(978-1-4156-8147-3(3))* Hyperion Bks. for Children.
Storti, Kara. Tripping Back Blue. 2016. (ENG.). 368p. (YA). (gr. 9-12). 35.99 *(978-1-5124-0444-9(6),* Carolrhoda Lab™) Lerner Publishing Group.
Stratford, Jordan. The Case of the Counterfeit Criminals (the Wollstonecraft Detective Agency, Book 3) Murphy, Kelly, illus. 2017. (Wollstonecraft Detective Agency Ser.). (ENG.). 208p. (J). (gr. 3-7). 16.99 *(978-0-385-75448-4(5),* Knopf Bks. for Young Readers) Random Hse. Children's Bks.
Striker, Fran. The Lone Ranger Traps the Smugglers. Laune, Paul, illus. 2011. 224p. 44.95 *(978-1-258-09845-2(8))* Literary Licensing, LLC.
Styles, Walker. The Big Bad Woof. Whitehouse, Ben, illus. 2017. (Rider Woofson Ser.: 8). (ENG.). 128p. (J). (gr. k-4). pap. 5.99 ***(978-1-4814-9188-4(1),*** Little Simon) Little Simon.
Surget, Alain & Yeardley, Glynne. Cleopatra Must Be Saved! Parme, Fabrice, illus. 2014. 95p. (J). *(978-1-4351-5329-5(4))* Barnes & Noble, Inc.
Taylor, Billy. Thieving Weasels. 2016. (ENG.). 256p. (YA). (gr. 7). 17.99 *(978-0-525-42924-1(7),* Dial Bks) Penguin Young Readers Group.
Torres, J., et al. Demo, 1 vol. 2014. (Teen Titans GO! Ser.). (ENG., Illus.). 32p. (gr. 2-3). 22.60 *(978-1-4342-4789-6(9))* Stone Arch Bks.
Trine, Greg. Wyatt Burp Rides Again. Dormer, Frank W., illus. 2012. (Adventures of Jo Schmo Ser.: 2). (ENG.). 112p. (J). (gr. 1-4). 12.99 *(978-0-547-80795-9(3))* Houghton Mifflin Harcourt Publishing Co.
Updale, Eleanor. Montmorency's Revenge. 2007. 289p. (J). 25.66 *(978-1-4287-3312-1(4),* Follettbound) Follett School Solutions.
van Diepen, Allison. Street Pharm. 2013. (ENG., Illus.). 320p. (YA). (gr. 8). pap. 10.99 *(978-1-4424-8166-4(8),* Simon Pulse) Simon Pulse.
Volponi, Paul. Rikers High. 2011. (ENG.). 272p. (YA). (gr. 7-18). 7.99 *(978-0-14-241778-2(5),* Speak) Penguin Young Readers Group.
Waid, Mark. City of Incredibles, Vol. 2. Takara, Marcio, illus. 2010. (Incredibles Ser.). (ENG.). 112p. (J). 24.99 *(978-1-60886-529-1(0))* Boom! Studios.
Walden, Mark. Deadlock. 2015. (H. I. V. E. Ser.: 8). (ENG., Illus.). 304p. (J). (gr. 3-7). 16.99 *(978-1-4424-9470-1(0),* Simon & Schuster Bks. For Young Readers) Simon & Schuster Bks. For Young Readers.
—Escape Velocity. (H. I. V. E. Ser.: 3). (ENG.). (J). (gr. 3-7). 2012. 368p. pap. 8.99 *(978-1-4424-1367-2(0))* 2011. 352p. 16.99 *(978-1-4424-2185-1(1))* Simon & Schuster Bks. For Young Readers. (Simon & Schuster Bks. For Young Readers).
—Zero Hour. (H. I. V. E. Ser.: 6). (ENG.). 304p. (J). (gr. 3-7). 2013. pap. 7.99 *(978-1-4424-1373-3(5))* 2012. 18.99 *(978-1-4424-2188-2(6))* Simon & Schuster Bks. For Young Readers. (Simon & Schuster Bks. For Young Readers).
Whyman, Matt. Goldstrike: A Thriller. 2010. (ENG.). 272p. (YA). (gr. 7-18). 16.99 *(978-1-4169-9510-4(2),* Atheneum Bks. for Young Readers) Simon & Schuster Children's Publishing.
Will Mcallister. Sam Rivers & the Night Rustlers. 2009. 88p. pap. 9.95 *(978-0-595-46287-2(1))* iUniverse, Inc.
Wolfe, Bradley W. Upside Downside Up. 2009. 144p. 27.99 *(978-0-557-11670-6(8))* Lulu Pr., Inc.
Zadoff, Allen. Boy Nobody. 2013. (Unknown Assassin Ser.: 1). (ENG.). 352p. (YA). (gr. 10-17). 18.00 *(978-0-316-19968-1(0))* Little Brown & Co.
—I Am the Traitor. (ENG.). 304p. (YA). (gr. 10-17). 2016. pap. 10.99 *(978-0-316-19974-2(5))* 2015. (Unknown Assassin Ser.: 3). 18.00 *(978-0-316-19972-8(9))* Little, Brown Bks. for Young Readers.
—I Am the Weapon. 2014. (Unknown Assassin Ser.: 1). (ENG.). 368p. (YA). (gr. 10-17). pap. 10.99 *(978-0-316-19967-4(2))* Little, Brown Bks. for Young Readers.
Zephaniah, Benjamin. Being Cool. Bellemare, Paule Trudel, illus. 2014. (Collins Big Cat Progress Ser.). (ENG.). 32p. (J). (gr. 5-6). pap. 7.99 *(978-0-00-751929-3(X))* HarperCollins Pubs. Ltd. GBR. Dist: Independent Pubs. Group.

CRIMINALS—IDENTIFICATION

Ballard, Carol. Crimebusting! Identifying Criminals & Victims. 2009. (Solve That Crime! Ser.). (Illus.). 48p. (J). (gr. 5-9). lib. bdg. 25.27 *(978-0-7660-3375-7(9))* Enslow Pubs., Inc.
Bodden, Valerie. Odysseys in Crime Scene Science: Identification. 2017. (Odysseys in Crime Scene Science Ser.). (ENG.). 80p. (J). (gr. 7-11). pap. 14.99 ***(978-1-62832-470-9(8),*** Creative Paperbacks) Creative Co., The.
Hamilton, Sue L. Forensic Artist: Solving the Case with a Face, 1 vol. 2008. (Crime Scene Investigation Ser.). (ENG.). 32p. (gr. 4-8). 27.07 *(978-1-59928-989-2(X),* Abdo & Daughters) ABDO Publishing Co.
Holzer, David. Prime Suspect: Suspect Identification System. 2004. (Illus.). 48p. (J). pap. *(978-0-439-68027-1(1))* Scholastic, Inc.
Libal, Angela. Fingerprints, Bite Marks, Ear Prints. Noziglia, Carla Miller & Siegel, Jay A., eds. 2013. (Solving Crimes with Science: Forensics Ser.: 12). (Illus.). 112p. (J). (gr. 7-18). 22.95 *(978-1-4222-2868-5(1))* Mason Crest.

CRIMINOLOGY

see Crime; Criminals

CRIPPLES

see People with Disabilities

CRITICISM

see also Book Reviews; Style, Literary
also literature and music subjects with the subdivision History and Criticism, e.g. English Literature—History and Criticism; English Poetry—History and Criticism; Music—History and Criticism

ABDO Publishing Company Staff. Essential Critiques Set 4, 1 vol. 2013. (Essential Critiques Set 4 Ser.: 8). (ENG.). 112p. (J). (gr. 6-12). lib. bdg. 285.12 *(978-1-61783-641-1(9),* Essential Library) ABDO Publishing Co.
Becnel, Kim E. Bloom's How to Write about F. Scott Fitzgerald. 2007. (Bloom's How to Write about Literature Ser.). 232p. (C). (gr. 9-18). 45.00 *(978-0-7910-9482-2(0),* Chelsea Hse.) Facts On File, Inc.
Chomet, Natalie. Coping with Body Shaming. 2017. (J). ***(978-1-5081-7687-9(6))*** Rosen Publishing Group, Inc., The.
Gleed, Paul. Bloom's How to Write about William Shakespeare. 2007. (Bloom's How to Write about Literature Ser.). 244p. (C). (gr. 9-18). 45.00 *(978-0-7910-9484-6(7),* Chelsea Hse.) Facts On File, Inc.
Kerr, Christine. Bloom's How to Write about J. D. Salinger. 2007. (Bloom's How to Write about Literature Ser.). 280p. (C). (gr. 9-12). 45.00 *(978-0-7910-9483-9(9),* Chelsea Hse.) Facts On File, Inc.
Priddy, Anna. Bloom's How to Write about Emily Dickinson. 2007. (Bloom's How to Write about Literature Ser.). 262p. (C). (gr. 9-18). 45.00 *(978-0-7910-9492-1(8),* Chelsea Hse.) Facts On File, Inc.
Sterling, Laurie A. Bloom's How to Write about Nathaniel Hawthorne. 2007. (Bloom's How to Write about Literature Ser.). 344p. (C). (gr. 9-18). 45.00 *(978-0-7910-9481-5(2),* Chelsea Hse.) Facts On File, Inc.

CROCHETING

see also Beadwork

Annie's Staff. I Can Crochet. Ellison, Connie, ed. 2012. (I Can Ser.). (ENG., Illus.). 32p. (J). (gr. 4-7). pap. 7.95 *(978-1-59635-641-2(3),* Annie's) Annie's Publishing, LLC.
Blakley Kinsler, Gwen & Young, Jackie. Crocheting. Melo, Esperança, illus. 2003. (Kids Can Do It Ser.). (ENG.). 40p. (J). (gr. 3-7). 6.95 *(978-1-55337-177-9(1))* Kids Can Pr., Ltd. CAN. Dist: Hachette Bk. Group.
Burger, Deborah. Creative Kids Photo Guide to Crochet. 2015. (Creative Kids Ser.). (ENG., Illus.). 128p. (gr. 3-7). pap. 24.99 *(978-1-58923-855-8(9),* 1387833, Creative Publishing International) Quarto Publishing Group USA.
Crochet a Quick & Easy Fashion Doll Wardrobe. 2003. (Illus.). 55p. spiral bd. 14.95 *(978-0-9742848-0-4(7))* Mostats, Marie C.
DRG, D. R. G. Kids Learn to Knit, Quilt & Crochet, 1 vol. 2009. (Workshop Ser.). (ENG., Illus.). 128p. (J). spiral bd. 16.99 *(978-1-897477-13-7(9),* 9781897477137) Company's Coming Publishing, Ltd. CAN. Dist: Lone Pine Publishing USA.
Fryer, Jane Eayre. The Mary Frances Knitting & Crocheting Book 100th Anniversary Edition: A Childrens Story-Instruction Book with Doll Clothes Patterns for American Girl & Other 18-Inch Dolls. 2011. (ENG., Illus.). 208p. (J). pap. 19.95 *(978-1-937564-05-6(3),* Classic Bookwrights) Lindaloo Enterprises.
Grabowski, Angela. Encyclopedia of Tunisian Crochet. 2004. (Illus.). 148p. spiral bd. 24.95 *(978-0-974725-5-8(X),* Lonestar Abilene Publishing) LoneStar Abilene Publishing, LLC.
Heidenreich, Franziska. Crochet for Kids: Basic Techniques & Great Projects That Kids Can Make Themselves, 1 vol. 2014. (ENG., Illus.). 132p. pap. 16.95 *(978-0-8117-1417-4(9))* Stackpole Bks.
Kuskowski, Alex. Cool Crocheting for Kids: A Fun & Creative Introduction to Fiber Art, 1 vol. 2014. (Cool Fiber Art Ser.). (ENG.). 32p. (gr. 8-12). lib. bdg. 28.50 *(978-1-62403-306-3(7),* Checkerboard Library) ABDO Publishing Co.
Rau, Dana Meachen. Learning to Crochet. Petelinsek, Kathleen, illus. 2016. (How-To Library). (ENG.). 32p. (J). (gr. 3-6). lib. bdg. 29.93 *(978-1-63471-418-1(0),* 208451) Cherry Lake Publishing.
Ronci, Kelli. Kids Crochet: Projects for Kids of All Ages. Corwin, Lena, illus. Gruen, John, photos by. 2005. (ENG.). 128p. (gr. 8-17). 21.95 *(978-1-58479-413-4(5))* Stewart, Tabori & Chang.
Warwick, Ellen. Fully Woolly. Lum, Bernice, illus. 2007. (Planet Girl Ser.). (ENG.). 80p. (J). (gr. 5-9). 12.95 *(978-1-55337-798-6(2))* Kids Can Pr., Ltd. CAN. Dist: Hachette Bk. Group.
Wolfensberger Singer, Beth. Sweet & Simple Granny Squares: 8 Irresistible Crochet Projects. 2015. (ENG., Illus.). 32p. 9.95 *(978-1-63186-315-8(0),* 9781631863158) Taunton Pr., Inc.

CROCKERY

see Pottery

CROCKETT, DAVY, 1786-1836

Allen, Charles F. David Crockett: Scout, Small Boy, Pilgrim, Mountaineer, Soldier, Bear-Hunter, & Congressman, Defender of the Alamo. (Illus.). 308p. reprint ed. lib. bdg. 98.00 *(978-0-7222-4856-0(3))* Library Reprints, Inc.
Alphin, Elaine Marie. Davy Crockett. 2003. (History Maker Bios Ser.). (Illus.). 48p. (J). (gr. 3-5). lib. bdg. 26.60 *(978-0-8225-0393-4(X))* Lerner Publishing Group.
Benge, Janet & Benge, Geoff. Davy Crockett: Ever Westward. 2011. (ENG.). 192p. (YA). pap. 9.99 *(978-1-932096-67-5(1))* Emerald Bks.
Capek, Michael. Davy Crockett. 2017. 25.70 *(978-1-61228-974-8(6))* Mitchell Lane Pubs., Inc.
Chemerka, William R. Davy Crockett from a to Z, 1 vol. Dillon, Wade, illus. 2013. (ENG.). 32p. (J). (gr. k-3). 16.99 *(978-1-4556-1835-4(7))* Pelican Publishing Co., Inc.
Coddington, Andrew. Davy Crockett. Lapegüe, Matias, illus. 2016. (American Legends & Folktales Ser.). 32p. (J). (gr. 28.50 *(978-1-5026-2193-1(2))* Cavendish Square Publishing.
Collard, Sneed B., III. David Crockett: Fearless Frontiersman. 2006. (American Heroes Ser.). (Illus.). 40p. (J). (gr. 3-7). lib. bdg. 28.50 *(978-0-7614-2160-3(2),* Benchmark Bks.) Marshall Cavendish Corp.
Davy Crockett. 2010. (Legends of the Wild West Ser.). (Illus.). 120p. (gr. 6-12). 35.00 *(978-1-60413-592-3(1),* Chelsea Hse.) Facts On File, Inc.
Devillier, Christy. Davy Crockett, 1 vol. 2004. (First Biographies Set Iv Ser.). (ENG., Illus.). 32p. (gr. k-4). 27.07 *(978-1-59197-512-0(3),* Buddy Bks.) ABDO Publishing Co.
Fein, Eric. Outnumbered: Davy Crockett's Final Battle at the Alamo. 2009. (Great Moments in American History Ser.). 32p. (gr. 3-3). 47.90 *(978-1-61513-148-8(5))* Rosen Publishing Group, Inc., The.
Ford, Anne. Davy Crockett. Vosburgh, Leonard, illus. 2011. 48p. 35.95 *(978-1-258-06913-1(X))* Literary Licensing, LLC.
Furstinger, Nancy. Davy Crockett. 2003. (Folk Heroes Ser.). (Illus.). 24p. (J). lib. bdg. 24.45 *(978-1-59036-073-6(7))* Weigl Pubs., Inc.
Haldy, Emma E. Davy Crockett. Bane, Jeff, illus. 2017. (My Early Library: My Itty-Bitty Bio Ser.). (ENG.). 24p. (J). (gr. k-1). lib. bdg. 28.50 *(978-1-63472-151-6(9),* 209176) Cherry Lake Publishing.
Herman, Gail. Who Was Davy Crockett? Squier, Robert & Harrison, Nancy, illus. 2013. (Who Was? Ser.). (ENG.). 112p. (J). (gr. 3-7). 5.99 *(978-0-448-46704-7(6),* Grosset & Dunlap) Penguin Young Readers Group.
—Who Was Davy Crockett? 2013. (Who Was... ? Ser.). lib. bdg. 16.00 *(978-0-606-32133-4(0),* Turtleback) Turtleback Bks.
Herweck, Diana. Davy Crockett, 1 vol. 2009. (Building Fluency Through Reader's Theater Ser.). (ENG.). 24p. (J). (gr. 2-4). pap. 6.99 *(978-1-4333-0996-0(3))* Teacher Created Materials, Inc.
Jarnow, Jesse. Davy Crockett: Defensor de la frontera (Davy Crockett: Frontier Hero) 2009. (Grandes personajes en la historia de los Estados Unidos (Famous People in American History) Ser.). (SPA.). 32p. (gr. 2-3). 47.90 *(978-1-61512-797-9(6),* Editorial Buenas Letras) Rosen Publishing Group, Inc., The.
—Davy Crockett: Frontier Hero / Defensor de la Frontera. 2009. (Famous People in American History/Grandes personajes en la historia de los Estados Unidos Ser.). (ENG & SPA.). 32p. (gr. 2-3). 47.90 *(978-1-61512-543-2(4),* Editorial Buenas Letras) Rosen Publishing Group, Inc., The.
Johnston, Marianne. Davy Crockett. 2009. (American Legends Ser.). 24p. (gr. 3-3). 42.50 *(978-1-61511-381-1(9),* PowerKids Pr.) Rosen Publishing Group, Inc., The.
Krensky, Stephen. Davy Crockett: A Life on the Frontier. Bandelin, Debra & Dacey, Bob, illus. 2004. (Ready-To-read SOFA Ser.). (ENG.). 48p. (J). (gr. 1-3). pap. 3.99 *(978-0-689-85944-1(9),* Simon Spotlight) Simon Spotlight.
Kunstler, James Howard. Davy Crockett, 1 vol. Brodner, Steve, illus. 2004. (Rabbit Ears-A Classic Tale Ser.). (ENG.). 36p. (gr. k-5). 25.65 *(978-1-59197-762-9(2))* Spotlight.
Moriarty, J. T. Davy Crockett: Defensor de la Frontera. 2004. (Grandes personajes en la historia de los Estados Unidos Ser.). (SPA.). 32p. (gr. 3-6). pap. 10.00 *(978-0-8239-4226-8(0),* Rosen Classroom) Rosen Publishing Group, Inc., The.
—Davy Crockett: Frontier Hero. (Primary Sources of Famous People in American History Ser.). 32p. 2009. (gr. 2-3). 47.90 *(978-1-60851-670-4(9))* 2004. (ENG., Illus.). (gr. 4-8). pap. 10.00 *(978-0-8239-4180-3(9))* Rosen Publishing Group, Inc., The.
Nichols, Kaitlyn. Davey Crockett. 2009. pap. 13.25 *(978-1-60559-057-8(6))* Hameray Publishing Group, Inc.
Roberts, Russell. Davy Crockett. 2006. (What's So Great About... ? Ser.). (Illus.). 32p. (J). (gr. 2-4). lib. bdg. 25.70 *(978-1-58415-476-1(4))* Mitchell Lane Pubs., Inc.
Saddleback Educational Publishing Staff, ed. Davy Crockett, 1 vol. unabr. ed. 2008. (Graphic Biographies Ser.). (ENG., Illus.). 25p. (YA). (gr. 9-12). pap. 7.95 *(978-1-59905-220-5(2))* Saddleback Educational Publishing, Inc.
Sanford, William R. & Green, Carl R. Davy Crockett: Courageous Hero of the Alamo. 2012. (Courageous Heroes of the American West Ser.). (Illus.). 48p. (J). pap. 8.95 *(978-1-4644-0086-5(5));* (gr. 5-18). 22.60 *(978-0-7660-4005-2(4))* Enslow Pubs., Inc.
Santillana U. S. A. Publishing Co, Inc. Staff. David Crockett. Alvarez, Jose M. & Alonso, Jesus, illus. 2003. (Historias de Siempre Ser.). (SPA.). 95p. (J). (gr. 5-8). pap. 12.95 *(978-84-204-5703-1(5))* Santillana USA Publishing Co., Inc.
Smith, Andrea P. Davy Crockett. 2012. (Illus.). 24p. (J). 63.60 *(978-1-4488-5223-9(4));* lib. bdg. 25.25 *(978-1-4488-5192-8(0))* Rosen Publishing Group, Inc., The. (PowerKids Pr.).
Wade, Mary Dodson. David Crockett: Creating a Legend. Hein, Joy Fisher, illus. 2009. (ENG.). 24p. (J). (gr. k-2). 16.95 *(978-1-933979-12-0(7),* 9781933979120) Bright Sky Pr.
Wade, Mary Dodson & Collins, Don. David Crockett: Hero & Legend. Collins, Don, illus. 2009. (ENG., Illus.). 63p. (J). (gr. 4-7). 16.95 *(978-1-933979-24-3(0),* 9781933979243) Bright Sky Pr.
Winders, Richard Bruce. Davy Crockett: The Legend of the Wild Frontier. (Library of American Lives & Times Ser.). 112p. 2009. (gr. 5-5). 69.20 *(978-1-60853-476-0(6))* 2005. (Illus.). (YA). (gr. 4-8). lib. bdg. 34.60 *(978-0-8239-5747-7(0))* Rosen Publishing Group, Inc., The.

CROCKETT, DAVY, 1786-1836—FICTION

Krensky, Stephen. Davy Crockett A Life on the Frontier. Dacey, Bob & Bandelin, Debra, illus. 2005. (Ready-to-Read Ser.). 48p. (J). lib. bdg. 15.00 *(978-1-59054-959-9(7))* Fitzgerald Bks.
Meadows, Melissa. What's the Word, Thunderbird? 2008. (ENG., Illus.). 80p. (J). *(978-1-934517-01-7(1))* Firelight Press, Inc.
—What's the Word, Thunderbird? Book A: the Alamo. 2007. (Wishing Well Ser.). (Illus.). 81p. (J). (gr. k-3). per. 4.99 *(978-1-934517-00-0(3))* Firelight Press, Inc.
Santrey, Laurence & Macken, JoAnn Early. Davy Crockett: Young Pioneer. Livingston, Francis, illus. 2008. 55p. (J). pap. *(978-0-439-02048-0(4))* Scholastic, Inc.

CROCODILES

Antill, Sara. A Crocodile's Life. 2012. (Illus.). 24p. (J). 49.50 *(978-1-4488-5103-4(3),* PowerKids Pr.); pap. 8.25 *(978-1-4488-5100-3(9),* PowerKids Pr.); lib. bdg. 22.60 *(978-1-4488-4976-5(4))* Rosen Publishing Group, Inc., The.
Arnosky, Jim. Crocodile Safari. 2009. (ENG.). 40p. (J). (gr. 2-5). 22.99 *(978-0-439-90356-1(4))* Scholastic, Inc.
Barr, Brady. Crocodile Encounters! And More True Stories of Adventures with Animals. 2012. (NGK Chapters Ser.). (ENG., Illus.). 112p. (J). (gr. 2-5). pap. 5.99 *(978-1-4263-1028-7(5),* National Geographic Children's Bks.) National Geographic Society.
Barr, Brady & Zoehfeld, Kathleen Weidner. Crocodile Encounters: And More True Stories of Adventures with Animals. 2012. (NGK Chapters Ser.). (ENG., Illus.). 112p. (J). (gr. 2-5). lib. bdg. 14.90 *(978-1-4263-1029-4(3),* National Geographic Children's Bks.) National Geographic Society.
Bodden, Valerie. Amazing Animals - Crocodiles. 2010. (Amazing Animals Ser.). 24p. (J). (gr. -1-3). 16.95 *(978-1-58341-806-2(7),* Creative Education) Creative Co., The.
—Amazing Animals: Crocodiles. 2011. (ENG.). 24p. (J). (gr. 1-17). pap. 5.99 *(978-0-89812-750-8(5));* pap. 8.99 *(978-0-89812-749-2(1))* Creative Co., The. (Creative Paperbacks).
Buckingham, Suzanne. Meet the Crocodile. 2009. (Scales & Tails Ser.). 24p. (gr. 2-3). 42.50 *(978-1-60852-982-7(7));* (Illus.). (J). lib. bdg. 22.60 *(978-1-4042-4504-4(9))* Rosen Publishing Group, Inc., The. (PowerKids Pr.).
Bull, Schuyler. Crocodile Crossing. Male, Alan, illus. 2005. (Amazing Animal Adventures Ser.). (ENG.). 36p. (J). (gr. -1-2). 15.95 *(978-1-59249-051-6(4),* B7104); (gr. -1-2). pap. 6.95 *(978-1-59249-052-3(2),* S7104); (gr. -1-2). 19.95 *(978-1-59249-390-6(4),* BC7104); (gr. 2-2). 8.95 *(978-1-59249-391-3(2),* SC7104) Soundprints.
Bull, Schuyler M. Crocodile Crossing. Male, Alan, illus. 2003. (Soundprints' Amazing Animal Adventures! Ser.). (ENG.). 36p. (J). (gr. -1-3). 9.95 *(978-1-59249-060-8(3),* PS7154); 2.95 *(978-1-59249-053-0(0),* S7154) Soundprints.
Calhoun, Kelly. Nadadores Escamosos (Scaly Swimmers) Cocodrilo (Crocodile) 2016. (Adivina (Guess What) Ser.). (SPA.). 24p. (J). (gr. k-2). 28.50 *(978-1-63471-451-8(2),* 208867) Cherry Lake Publishing.
—Scaly Swimmers: Crocodile. 2015. (Guess What Ser.). (ENG., Illus.). 24p. (J). (gr. k-2). 28.50 *(978-1-63362-629-4(6),* 206692) Cherry Lake Publishing.
Charles, Faustin. The Selfish Crocodile Counting Book. Terry, Michael, illus. I.t. ed. 2008. (ENG.). 12p. (J). (gr. k-k). bds. 8.95 *(978-0-7475-9238-9(1))* Bloomsbury Publishing Plc GBR. Dist: Independent Pubs. Group.
Clark, Willow. Crocodile! 2010. (Animal Danger Zone Ser.). (ENG.). 24p. (J). (gr. k-3). lib. bdg. 22.60 *(978-1-60754-956-7(5));* (Illus.). pap. 8.15 *(978-1-60754-962-8(X))* Windmill Bks.
Los Cocodrilos (Crocodiles) 2006. (J). pap. 7.95 *(978-0-8225-6629-8(X),* Ediciones Lerner) Lerner Publishing Group.
Cole, Hannah. Crocodiles. 2009. (Wild Reads Ser.). (ENG., Illus.). 32p. (YA). pap. 4.95 *(978-0-19-911926-4(0))* Oxford Univ. Pr., Inc.
Crocodiles, 6 bks. 2005. (Animal Predators Ser.). (Illus.). 40p. (J). (gr. 3-6). pap. 46.95 *(978-0-8225-5493-6(3))* Lerner Publishing Group.
Crocodiles & Alligators. 2005. (J). per. 4.99 *(978-1-933581-23-1(9))* Byeway Bks.
Dennard, Deborah. Alligators & Crocodiles. Dewey, Jennifer Owings, illus. (Our Wild World Ser.). (ENG.). 48p. (J). (gr. 2-5). 2008. pap. 8.95 *(978-1-55971-859-2(5))* 2003. 10.95 *(978-1-55971-860-8(9))* Cooper Square Publishing Llc.
Dorling Kindersley Publishing Staff & Foreman, Niki. Snappy Crocodile Tale. 2014. (DK Readers Ser.). (ENG.). 64p. (J). (gr. 2-4). pap. 3.99 *(978-1-4654-2837-0(2),* DK Children) Dorling Kindersley Publishing, Inc.

C D

Duhaime, Darla. Crocodiles. 2017. (Reptiles! Ser.). (ENG.). (J). (gr. k-1). 28.51 ***(978-1-68342-155-9(8))*** Rourke Educational Media.

Fishman, Jon M. Meet a Baby Crocodile. 2017. (Lightning Bolt Books (tm) — Baby Australian Animals Ser.). (ENG.). 24p. (J). (gr. 1-3). 25.32 ***(978-1-5124-3390-6(X))*** Lerner Publishing Group.

Gagne, Tammy. Crocodile, 1 vol. 2013. (Great Predators Ser.). (ENG., Illus.). 48p. (J). (gr. 3-6). lib. bdg. 32.79 *(978-1-61783-946-7(9))* ABDO Publishing Co.

—Crocodile Paperback. 2013. (ENG., Illus.). 48p. (J). pap. 15.64 *(978-1-62403-011-6(4),* Core Library) ABDO Publishing Co.

—Crocodiles: Built for the Hunt. 2015. (Predator Profiles Ser.). (ENG., Illus.). 24p. (gr. 1-2). lib. bdg. 25.32 *(978-1-4914-5038-3(X))* Capstone Press of Coughlan Cos.

Gallagher, Debbie. Alligators & Crocodiles. 2009. (Zoo Animals 2 Ser.). 32p. (gr. 2). lib. bdg. 18.56 *(978-0-7614-4743-6(1))* Marshall Cavendish GBR. Dist: Marshall Cavendish Corp.

Gambino, Karlie. A Float of Crocodiles. 2013. (Animal Groups Ser.). (Illus.). 24p. (J). (gr. 1-3). pap. 8.15 *(978-1-4339-8195-1(5));* lib. bdg. 22.60 *(978-1-4339-8194-4(7))* Stevens, Gareth Publishing LLLP.

—A Float of Crocodiles / una Manada de Cocodrilos. 2013. (Animal Groups / Grupos de Animales Ser.). (ENG & SPA., Illus.). 24p. (gr. 1-3). 22.60 *(978-1-4339-8802-8(X))* Stevens, Gareth Publishing LLLP.

Gareth Stevens Publishing Staff, contrib. by. Crocodiles. 2004. (All about Wild Animals Ser.). (Illus.). 32p. (gr. k-4). lib. bdg. 26.00 *(978-0-8368-4182-4(4),* Gareth Stevens Learning Library) Stevens, Gareth Publishing LLLP.

Gibbons, Gail. Alligators & Crocodiles. Gibbons, Gail, illus. (ENG., Illus.). 32p. (J). 2011. pap. 7.99 *(978-0-8234-2343-9(3))* 2010. (gr. -1-3). 17.95 *(978-0-8234-2234-0(8))* Holiday Hse., Inc.

Gibbs, Maddie. Crocodiles. 2011. (Safari Animals Ser.). (ENG.). 24p. (J). pap. 8.25 *(978-1-4488-2594-3(6));* lib. bdg. 22.60 *(978-1-4488-2504-2(0))* Rosen Publishing Group, Inc., The. (PowerKids Pr.).

—Crocodiles: Cocodrilos. 2011. (Safari Animals / Animales de Safari Ser.). (ENG & SPA.). 24p. (J). (gr. -1-2). lib. bdg. 22.60 *(978-1-4488-3118-0(0))* Rosen Publishing Group, Inc., The.

Gish, Melissa. Crocodiles. 2009. (Living Wild Ser.). (Illus.). 48p. (J). 22.95 *(978-1-58341-738-6(9),* Creative Education) Creative Co., The.

Green, Jen. Crocodiles. 2009. (Illus.). 52p. (J). *(978-0-7172-6291-5(X))* Grolier, Ltd.

Hamilton, Sue. Attacked by a Crocodile, 1 vol. 2010. (Close Encounters of the Wild Kind Ser.). (ENG.). 32p. (YA). (gr. 4-7). 27.07 *(978-1-60453-929-5(1))* ABDO Publishing Co.

Harris, Tim. Crocodiles & Alligators. 2010. (Slimy, Scaly, Deadly Reptiles & Amphibians Ser.). (Illus.). 32p. (J). (gr. 2-6). pap. 10.50 *(978-1-4339-3436-0(1));* lib. bdg. 26.00 *(978-1-4339-3435-3(3))* Stevens, Gareth Publishing LLLP. (Gareth Stevens Learning Library).

Heos, Bridget. What to Expect When You're Expecting Hatchlings: A Guide for Crocodilian Parents (and Curious Kids) Jorisch, Stéphane, illus. 2012. (Expecting Animal Babies Ser.). (ENG.). 32p. (gr. 2-5). lib. bdg. 25.26 *(978-0-7613-5860-2(9))* Lerner Publishing Group.

Herrington, Lisa M. Crocodiles & Alligators. 2015. (Rookie Read-About(tm) Science: What's the Difference? Ser.). (ENG., Illus.). 32p. (J). lib. bdg. 25.00 *(978-0-531-21483-1(4),* Children's Pr.) Scholastic Library Publishing.

Hoff, Mary. Crocodiles. 2006. (Wild World of Animals (Creative Education) Ser.). (Illus.). 31p. (J). 18.95 *(978-1-58341-431-6(2),* Creative Education) Creative Co., The.

Hudak, Heather C. Alligators. 2008. (Backyard Animals Ser.). (Illus.). 24p. (J). (gr. 4-7). lib. bdg. 24.45 *(978-1-60596-001-2(2))* Weigl Pubs., Inc.

Hudak, Heather C., ed. Alligators. 2008. (Backyard Animals Ser.). (Illus.). 24p. (J). (gr. 4-7). pap. 8.95 *(978-1-60596-007-4(1))* Weigl Pubs., Inc.

Jackson, Tom. Monster Crocs. 2008. (Crabtree Contact Ser.). (ENG., Illus.). 32p. (J). (gr. 3-7). lib. bdg. *(978-0-7787-3763-6(2))* Crabtree Publishing Co.

—Saltwater Crocodile. 2013. (Science Slam: the Deep End-Animal Life Underwater Ser.). 24p. (J). (gr. -1-3). lib. bdg. 23.93 *(978-1-61772-923-2(X))* Bearport Publishing Co., Inc.

Kaufman, Gabriel. Saltwater Crocodile: The World's Biggest Reptile. 2007. (SuperSized! Ser.). (Illus.). 24p. (J). (gr. k-3). lib. bdg. 21.28 *(978-1-59716-396-5(1),* 1265941) Bearport Publishing Co., Inc.

Kralovansky, Susan. Crocodile or Alligator?, 1 vol. 2014. (This or That? Ser.). (ENG.). 24p. (gr. 5-10). lib. bdg. 25.65 *(978-1-62403-285-1(0),* Super SandCastle) ABDO Publishing Co.

Kulka, Joe, illus. My Crocodile Does Not Bite. 2013. (ENG.). 32p. (J). (gr. k-3). lib. bdg. 16.95 *(978-0-7613-8937-8(7),* Carolrhoda Bks.) Lerner Publishing Group.

Landau, Elaine. Alligators & Crocodiles: Hunters of the Night. 2007. (Animals after Dark Ser.). (Illus.). 32p. (J). (gr. 2-4). lib. bdg. 23.94 *(978-0-7660-2771-8(6),* Enslow Elementary) Enslow Pubs., Inc.

Linde, Barbara M. The Life Cycle of a Crocodile. 2011. (Nature's Life Cycles Ser.). (Illus.). 24p. (J). (gr. 2-5). pap. 8.15 *(978-1-4339-4672-1(6));* lib. bdg. 22.60 *(978-1-4339-4671-4(8))* Stevens, Gareth Publishing LLLP. (Gareth Stevens Learning Library).

Lodge, Jo. Colour & Stick, Mr Croc. 2013. (ENG.). 24p. (J). (gr. -1-k). pap. 5.99 *(978-1-4449-1308-8(5))* Hodder & Stoughton GBR. Dist: Hachette Bk. Group.

Lunis, Natalie & Sereno, Paul C. Supercroc: Paul Sereno's Dinosaur Eater. 2006. (Fossil Hunters Ser.). (Illus.). 32p. (YA). (gr. 2-5). lib. bdg. 25.27 *(978-1-59716-255-5(8))* Bearport Publishing Co., Inc.

Markle, Sandra. Los Cocodrilos. 2006. (Animales Depredadores (Animal Predators) Ser.). (SPA., Illus.). 39p. (J). (gr. 4). lib. bdg. 25.26 *(978-0-8225-6492-8(0),* Ediciones Lerner) Lerner Publishing Group.

—Crocodiles. (Animal Predators Ser.). 40p. 2005. (J). (gr. 4-6). pap. 7.95 *(978-1-57505-742-2(5))* 2004. (ENG., Illus.). (gr. 3-6). lib. bdg. 26.60 *(978-1-57505-726-2(3))* Lerner Publishing Group.

—Los Cocodrilo; Crocodiles. 2008. pap. 46.95 *(978-0-8225-7088-2(2))* Lerner Publishing Group.

Marsh, Laura. National Geographic Readers: Alligators & Crocodiles. 2015. (Readers Ser.). (ENG., Illus.). 32p. (J). (gr. k-3). pap. 3.99 *(978-1-4263-1947-1(9),* National Geographic Children's Bks.) National Geographic Society.

Marsico, Katie. Saltwater Crocodiles. 2013. (ENG.). 48p. (J). 28.00 *(978-0-531-23361-0(8));* pap. 6.95 *(978-0-531-25159-1(4))* Scholastic Library Publishing.

Meachen Rau, Dana. When Crocodiles Attack! 2006. (When Wild Animals Attack! Ser.). (Illus.). 48p. (J). (gr. 4-10). lib. bdg. 25.27 *(978-0-7660-2666-7(3))* Enslow Pubs., Inc.

Meinking, Mary. Crocodile vs. Wildebeest, 1 vol. 2011. (Predator vs. Prey Ser.). (ENG., Illus.). 32p. (gr. 1-2). 29.99 *(978-1-4109-3935-7(9));* pap. 8.29 *(978-1-4109-3944-9(8))* Heinemann-Raintree. (Read Me!).

Meister, Cari. Crocodiles. 2015. (Illus.). 24p. (J). lib. bdg. *(978-1-62031-195-0(X),* Bullfrog Bks.) Jump! Inc.

—Do You Really Want to Meet a Crocodile? Fabbri, Daniele, illus. 2015. (Do You Really Want to Meet... ? Ser.). 24p. (J). 27.10 *(978-1-60753-457-0(6))* Amicus Publishing.

Morgan, Sally. Alligators & Crocodiles. 2011. (Amazing Animal Hunters Ser.). (Illus.). 32p. (J). 28.50 *(978-1-60753-043-5(0))* Amicus Publishing.

—Alligators & Crocodiles. 2006. (QEB Animal Lives Ser.). (Illus.). 32p. (J). (gr. 4-7). lib. bdg. 19.95 *(978-1-59566-205-7(7))* QEB Publishing Inc.

—Alligators & Crocodiles. 2012. (Illus.). 32p. (gr. 3-5). pap. 8.95 *(978-1-926722-47-4(7))* Saunders Bk. Co. CAN. Dist: RiverStream Publishing.

Morgan, Sally & Teacher Created Resources Staff. Alligators & Crocodiles. 2007. (Animal Lives (QEB Publishing) Ser.). (ENG., Illus.). 32p. (gr. 2-9). pap. 7.99 *(978-1-4206-8114-7(1))* Teacher Created Resources, Inc.

Murray, Julie. Crocodiles, 1 vol. (Life Cycles Ser.). (ENG.). 24p. 2007. (gr. -1-3). 25.65 *(978-1-59928-706-5(4))* 2005. (Illus.). (gr. k-4). 25.65 *(978-1-59197-311-9(2))* ABDO Publishing Co. (Buddy Bks.).

Niver, Heather Moore. 20 Fun Facts about Crocodiles. 2012. (Fun Fact File: Animals! Ser.). (ENG.). 32p. (J). (gr. 2-5). pap. 10.50 *(978-1-4339-6511-1(9));* lib. bdg. 25.25 *(978-1-4339-6509-8(7))* Stevens, Gareth Publishing LLLP. (Gareth Stevens Learning Library).

Norton, Liss. Crocodile!, 1 vol. McCann, Emma, illus. 2013. (Start Reading Ser.). (ENG.). 24p. (gr. k-1). pap. 7.95 *(978-1-4765-4093-1(4))* Capstone Press of Coughlan Cos.

O'Shaughnessy, Ruth. Crocodiles & Alligators after Dark, 2015. (Animals of the Night Ser.). (ENG.). 32p. (J). (gr. 3-4). pap. 10.52 *(978-0-7660-6754-7(8));* (Illus.). 25.27 *(978-0-7660-6756-1(4))* Enslow Pubs., Inc.

Parker, Steve. Crocodiles. Roberts, Steve, illus. 2010. (I Love Animals Ser.). (ENG.). 24p. (gr. 1-5). 22.60 *(978-1-61533-247-2(2));* pap. 8.15 *(978-1-61533-255-7(3))* Windmill Bks.

—10 Things You Should Know about Crocodiles. Gallagher, Belinda & Borton, Paula, eds. Roberts, Steve, illus. 2004. (10 Things You Should Know Ser.). 24p. (J). 6.99 *(978-1-84236-121-4(X))* Miles Kelly Publishing, Ltd. GBR. Dist: Independent Pubs. Group.

Peyrols, Sylvaine. Crocodile. Peyrols, Sylvaine, illus. 2012. (ENG., Illus.). 34p. (J). (gr. k-3). pap. 11.99 *(978-1-85103-317-1(3))* Moonlight Publishing, Ltd. GBR. Dist: Independent Pubs. Group.

Pohl, Kathleen. Crocodiles. 2007. (Let's Read about Animals Ser.). (Illus.). 24p. (gr. k-3). pap. 8.15 *(978-0-8368-7822-6(1));* lib. bdg. 22.00 *(978-0-8368-7815-8(9))* Stevens, Gareth Publishing LLLP. (Weekly Reader Leveled Readers).

—Crocodiles/Cocodrilos. 2007. (Let's Read about Animals/ Conozcamos a los animales Ser.). (ENG & SPA., Illus.). 24p. (gr. k-3). pap. 8.15 *(978-0-8368-8011-3(0));* lib. bdg. 22.00 *(978-0-8368-8004-5(8))* Stevens, Gareth Publishing LLLP. (Weekly Reader Leveled Readers).

Polydoros, Lori. Crocodiles: On the Hunt. 2016. (Killer Animals Ser.). (ENG.). 32p. (gr. 1-2). pap. 7.95 *(978-1-5157-6254-6(8),* Blazers) Capstone Press of Coughlan Cos.

PRESS, Celebration. Hunting Crocodiles with Steve Irwin. 2003. (ENG.). (J). (gr. 2-5). pap., stu. ed. 34.95 *(978-0-673-62080-4(8),* Celebration Pr.) Pearson Schl.

Pringle, Laurence. Alligators & Crocodiles! Henderson, Meryl, illus. 2009. (Strange & Wonderful Ser.). (ENG.). 32p. (J). (gr. 2-4). 16.95 *(978-1-59078-256-9(9))* Boyds Mills Pr.

Rafferty, John P. Meat Eaters: Raptors, Sharks, & Crocodiles. 2011. (Britannica Guide to Predators & Prey Ser.). (Illus.). 208p. (YA). (gr. 9-12). lib. bdg. 51.70 *(978-1-61530-342-7(1))* Rosen Publishing Group, Inc., The.

Rake, Matthew. Scaly, Slippery Creatures. Mendez, Simon, illus. 2015. (Real-Life Monsters Ser.). (ENG.). 32p. (J). (gr. 3-6). pap. 7.99 *(978-1-4677-7645-5(9),* Lerner Pubns.) Lerner Publishing Group.

Read, Tracy. Exploring the World of Alligators & Crocodiles. 2017. (Exploring the World Of Ser.). (ENG., Illus.). 24p. (J). (gr. 4-7). 16.95 ***(978-1-77085-942-5(X),*** 9781770859425); pap. 6.95 ***(978-1-77085-943-2(8),*** 9781770859432) Firefly Bks., Ltd.

Reher, Matt. Come in Here, Crocs! 2016. (1G Science Ser.). (ENG., Illus.). 32p. (J). pap. 5.99 ***(978-1-63437-670-9(6))*** American Reading Co.

Robak, Raelinda. Cruzer the Crocodile. 2008. (SPA & ENG., Illus.). 32p. (J). 2.99 *(978-0-8127-0467-9(3))* Autumn Hse. Publishing Co.

Rockwood, Leigh. Tell Me the Difference Between an Alligator & a Crocodile. 2013. (How Are They Different? Ser.). (ENG., Illus.). 24p. (J). (gr. k-5). pap. 8.25 *(978-1-4488-9728-5(9));* lib. bdg. 22.60 *(978-1-4488-9635-6(5))* Rosen Publishing Group, Inc., The. (PowerKids Pr.).

Royston, Angela. Alligators & Crocodiles. (Amazing Animals Ser.). (Illus.). 24p. (J). 2009. (gr. 2-4). pap. 8.95 *(978-1-60596-153-8(1))* 2009. (gr. 2-4). lib. bdg. 24.45 *(978-1-60596-152-1(3))* 2003. lib. bdg. 24.45 *(978-1-58340-225-2(X))* Weigl Pubs., Inc.

Rushby, Pamela. Discovering SuperCroc. 2007. (Science Chapters Ser.). (ENG., Illus.). 48p. (J). (gr. 1-4). lib. bdg. 17.90 *(978-1-4263-0186-5(3),* National Geographic Children's Bks.) National Geographic Society.

Ryndak, Rob. Alligator or Crocodile? 2015. (Animal Look-Alikes Ser.). (ENG., Illus.). 24p. (J). (gr. 1-2). pap. 8.15 *(978-1-4824-2708-0(7))* Stevens, Gareth Publishing LLLP.

—Crocodiles. 2015. (Jungle Animals Ser.). (ENG., Illus.). 24p. (J). (gr. k-k). 22.60 *(978-1-4824-1748-7(0))* Stevens, Gareth Publishing LLLP.

Sabatino, Michael. T. Rex vs. Crocodile. 2015. (Bizarre Beast Battles Ser.). (ENG., Illus.). 24p. (J). (gr. 2-3). lib. bdg. 22.60 *(978-1-4824-2802-5(4))* Stevens, Gareth Publishing LLLP.

Saia, Stephanie. Hunting with Crocodiles. 2012. (Animal Attack! Ser.). (Illus.). 24p. (J). (gr. 2-5). pap. 8.15 *(978-1-4339-7068-9(6));* lib. bdg. 22.60 *(978-1-4339-7067-2(8))* Stevens, Gareth Publishing LLLP.

Schafer, Susan. Saltwater Crocodiles. 2014. (J). pap. *(978-1-62712-958-9(8))* Cavendish Square Publishing.

Scherer, Glenn & Fletcher, Marty. The American Crocodile: Help Save This Endangered Species! 2007. (Saving Endangered Species Ser.). (Illus.). 128p. (J). (gr. 4-7). lib. bdg. 34.60 *(978-1-59845-041-5(7),* MyReportLinks.com Bks.) Enslow Pubs., Inc.

Scholastic, Inc. Staff, contrib. by. Is Your Smile Like a Crocodile's? 2016. (Rookie Toddlers Ser.). (ENG.). 12p. (J). bds. 6.95 *(978-0-531-22454-0(6),* Children's Pr.) Scholastic Library Publishing.

Schuetz, Kari & Borgert-Spaniol, Megan. Crocodiles. 2014. (Animal Safari Ser.). (ENG., Illus.). 24p. (J). (gr. k-3). lib. bdg. 25.95 *(978-1-62617-063-6(0),* Blastoff! Readers) Bellwether Media.

Sexton, Colleen. The Saltwater Crocodile. 2011. (Nature's Deadliest Ser.). (ENG., Illus.). 24p. (YA). (gr. 3-8). lib. bdg. 25.95 *(978-1-60014-669-5(4),* Pilot Bks.) Bellwether Media.

Shea, Therese. Crocodiles, 1 vol. 2015. (ENG., Illus.). 24p. (J). lib. bdg. 23.60 *(978-1-4777-5820-5(8),* PowerKids Pr.) Rosen Publishing Group, Inc., The.

—Crocodiles & Alligators. (Big Bad Biters Ser.). 24p. 2009. (gr. 2-3). 42.50 *(978-1-61511-562-4(5))* 2006. (Illus.). (J). (gr. 3-7). lib. bdg. 22.60 *(978-1-4042-3523-6(X))* Rosen Publishing Group, Inc., The. (PowerKids Pr.).

Shofner, Melissa Raé. Crocodiles Lived with the Dinosaurs! 2016. (Living with the Dinosaurs Ser.). 00024p. (J). pap. 8.15 ***(978-1-4824-5645-5(1))*** Stevens, Gareth Publishing LLLP.

Silverman, Buffy. Can You Tell an Alligator from a Crocodile? 2011. (Lightning Bolt Books (tm) — Animal Look-Alikes Ser.). (ENG.). 32p. (gr. k-2). pap. 7.95 *(978-0-7613-7846-4(4))* Lerner Publishing Group.

—Can You Tell an Alligator from A Crocodile? 2011. (Animal Look-Alikes Ser.). pap. 45.32 *(978-0-7613-8381-9(6))* Lerner Publishing Group.

Snyder, Trish. Alligator & Crocodile Rescue: Changing the Future for Endangered Wildlife. 2006. (Firefly Animal Rescue Ser.). (ENG., Illus.). 64p. (J). (gr. 5-12). 19.95 *(978-1-55297-920-4(2),* 9781552979204); pap. 9.95 *(978-1-55297-919-8(9),* 9781552979198) Firefly Bks., Ltd.

Stewart, Melissa. Alligator or Crocodile? How Do You Know? 2011. (Which Animal Is Which? Ser.). (Illus.). 24p. (J). (gr. k-18). pap. 7.95 *(978-1-59845-234-1(7),* Enslow Elementary); lib. bdg. 22.60 *(978-0-7660-3677-2(4))* Enslow Pubs., Inc.

TAYLOR, Barbara. Incredible Crocodiles: Look at the Fascinating World of Crocodiles, Alligators, Caimans And Gharials, Shown in over 180 Exciting Images. 2014. (ENG., Illus.). 64p. (J). (gr. -1-12). 12.99 *(978-1-86147-367-7(2),* Armadillo) Anness Publishing GBR. Dist: National Bk. Network.

Taylor, Trace. Nile Crocodiles. Taylor, Trace, illus. 2007. (1-3Y Reptiles Ser.). (ENG., Illus.). 24p. (J). (gr. k-2). pap. 5.99 *(978-1-59301-655-5(7))* American Reading Co.

Thapaliya, Bishnu Prasad & Karki, Ajay. Distribution & Status of Gharials. 2012. 56p. pap. *(978-3-8484-0571-8(7))* Lap Lambert Academic Publishing GmbH & Co. KG.

Troupe, Thomas Kingsley. I Want to Be a Crocodile. Wald, Christina, illus. 2015. (I Want to Be... Ser.). (ENG.). 24p. (gr. k-3). lib. bdg. 26.65 *(978-1-4795-6857-4(0))* Capstone Press of Coughlan Cos.

Tyler, Gemma. Crocodile. 2016. (J). lib. bdg. *(978-1-62724-818-1(8))* Bearport Publishing Co., Inc.

Walker, Sally M. Crocodiles. 2003. (Nature Watch Ser.). (ENG., Illus.). 48p. (gr. 4-8). lib. bdg. 27.93 *(978-1-57505-345-5(4))* Lerner Publishing Group.

—Supercroc Found. Hood, Philip, illus. 2005. (On My Own Science Ser.). 48p. (J). (gr. 3-7). lib. bdg. 25.26 *(978-1-57505-760-6(3))* Lerner Publishing Group.

—SuperCroc Found. Hood, Philip, illus. 2006. (On My Own Science Ser.). 48p. (J). (gr. 3-7). per. 6.95 *(978-1-57505-852-8(9),* First Avenue Editions) Lerner Publishing Group.

Wexo, John Bonnett. Alligators & Crocodiles. rev. ed. 2003. (Illus.). 24p. (J). (gr. 1-7). 10.95 *(978-1-932396-03-4(9),* Zoo Bks.) Wildlife Education, Ltd.

CROCODILES—FICTION

ABDO Publishing Company Staff. Mr. & Mrs. Green - 4 Titles. 2007. (Mr. & Mrs. Green Ser.). (ENG., Illus.). 70p. 108.28 *(978-1-59961-299-7(2))* Spotlight.

Adkins, Patricia. Jeremy & the Crocodile Dentist. 2013. 24p. pap. 10.99 *(978-1-4908-0883-3(3),* WestBow Pr.) Author Solutions, Inc.

Alligator Tails & Crocodile Cakes: Level L, 6 vols. 128p. (gr. 2-3). 49.95 *(978-0-7699-0985-1(X))* Shortland Pubns. (U. S. A.) Inc.

Angel, Ido. Vipo in Brazil: The Crocodile Who Lost His Teeth. 2015. (AV2 Animated Storytime Ser.). (ENG.). (J). lib. bdg. 29.99 *(978-1-4896-3896-0(2),* AV2 by Weigl) Weigl Pubs., Inc.

Anholt, Laurence. A Kiss Like This. Anholt, Catherine, illus. 2009. (ENG.). 32p. (J). (gr. -1-1). pap. 7.95 *(978-1-84507-862-1(4),* Frances Lincoln) Quarto Publishing Group UK GBR. Dist: Hachette Bk. Group.

Balzola, Asun. Munia y el Cocolilo Naranja. (SPA.). 32p. (J). *(978-84-233-1335-8(2))* Ediciones Destino ESP. Dist: Lectorum Pubns., Inc.

Bannerman, Helen. The Story of Little Black Mingo (Illustr. 2006. pap. *(978-1-4065-0770-6(9))* Dodo Pr.

Barr, Brady & Curtis, Jennifer Keats. After a While Crocodile: Alexa's Diary, 1 vol. Detwiler, Susan, illus. 2016. (ENG & SPA.). 32p. (J). (gr. k-3). 17.95 *(978-1-62855-834-0(2))* Arbordale Publishing.

—Hasta la Vista, Cocodrilo: El Diario de Alexa. Detwiler, Susan, illus. 2016. (SPA.). 32p. (J). (gr. k-3). pap. 9.95 *(978-1-62855-836-4(9))* Arbordale Publishing.

Barsy, Kalman. El Cocodrilo Lloron. Gastaldo, Walter, illus. 2004. (Yellow Ser.). (SPA.). 31p. (J). (gr. k-3). pap. 5.95 *(978-1-57581-433-9(1))* Santillana USA Publishing Co., Inc.

Bedford, David. The Copy Crocs, 1 vol. Bolam, Emily, illus. 2015. (ENG.). 32p. (J). (gr. -1-3). pap. 7.95 *(978-1-56145-885-1(6))* Peachtree Pubs.

—The Copy Crocs. Bolam, Emily, tr. Bolam, Emily, illus. 2004. (ENG.). 32p. (J). (gr. k-3). 15.95 *(978-1-56145-304-7(8))* Peachtree Pubs.

Benchmark Education Co., LLC. Happy Hippo Holiday Big Book. 2014. (Shared Reading Foundations Ser.). (J). (gr. -1). *(978-1-4509-9425-5(3))* Benchmark Education Co.

Bromley, Nick. Open Very Carefully: A Book with Bite. O'Byrne, Nicola, illus. 2013. (ENG.). 32p. (J). (gr. -1-2). 15.99 *(978-0-7636-6163-2(5),* Nosy Crow) Candlewick Pr.

Brown, Jo. Where's My Mommy? Brown, Jo, illus. 2006. (Storytime Board Bks.). (Illus.). 18p. (J). (gr. -1-3). bds. 6.95 *(978-1-58925-795-5(2))* Tiger Tales.

—Where's My Mommy? 2004. (Illus.). 32p. (J). tchr. ed. 14.95 *(978-1-58925-019-2(2))* Tiger Tales.

Browne, Anthony. The Little Bear Book. Browne, Anthony, illus. 2014. (ENG., Illus.). 24p. (J). (gr. -1-2). 15.99 *(978-0-7636-7007-8(3))* Candlewick Pr.

Burch, Sharon. Freddie the Frog & the Thump in the Night: 1st Adventure - Treble Clef Island. 2010. (ENG., Illus.). 46p. 24.99 incl. audio compact disk *(978-0-9747454-9-7(9),* 0974745499) Mystic Publishing.

Burton, Lynne. Charlotte's Crocodile. 2012. 22p. pap. *(978-1-909395-00-8(5))* Legend Pr.

Calopisis, Dennis. The Hungry Little Crocodile. 2009. 17p. 9.98 *(978-0-557-05963-8(1))* Lulu Pr., Inc.

Carrington, Jim. Sang Kancil & Crocodile Orange Band. Oliver, Juanbjuan, illus. 2016. (Cambridge Reading Adventures Ser.). (ENG.). 16p. pap. 6.56 *(978-1-107-57604-9(0))* Cambridge Univ. Pr.

Charles, Faustin. The Selfish Crocodile. Terry, Michael, illus. 2010. (Selfish Crocodile Ser.). (ENG.). 32p. (J). (gr. -1-k). pap. 9.99 *(978-0-7475-4193-6(0),* 9780747541936, Bloomsbury USA Childrens) Bloomsbury Publishing USA.

—The Selfish Crocodile Book of Sounds. Terry, Michael, illus. 2012. (Selfish Crocodile Ser.). (ENG.). 14p. (J). (gr. -1-3). bds. 10.99 *(978-1-4088-1450-5(1),* 9781408814505, Bloomsbury USA Childrens) Bloomsbury Publishing USA.

Charles, Faustin & Terry, Michael. The Selfish Crocodile Book of Nursery Rhymes. Terry, Michael, illus. 2008. (ENG., Illus.). 1p. (J). (gr. -1-k). 25.95 *(978-0-7475-9523-6(2))* Bloomsbury Publishing Plc GBR. Dist: Independent Pubs. Group.

Chichester Clark, Emma. Friends for Life. Chichester Clark, Emma, illus. 2006. (Melrose & Croc Ser.). (ENG., Illus.). 32p. (J). (gr. -1-2). pap. 8.95 *(978-0-00-718242-8(2),* HarperCollins Children's Bks.) HarperCollins Pubs. Ltd. GBR. Dist: HarperCollins Pubs.

Christelow, Eileen. Five Little Monkeys Sitting in a Tree. 2014. (Five Little Monkeys Story Ser.). (ENG & SPA., Illus.). 28p. (J). (— 1). bds. 7.99 *(978-0-544-30218-1(4),* HMH Books For Young Readers) Houghton Mifflin Harcourt Publishing Co.

—Five Little Monkeys Sitting in a Tree Book & CD, 1 vol. 2007. (Five Little Monkeys Story Ser.). (ENG., Illus.). 32p. (J). (gr. -1-3). 10.99 *(978-0-618-85284-0(0))* Houghton Mifflin Harcourt Publishing Co.

—Five Little Monkeys Wash the Car. 2004. (Five Little Monkeys Story Ser.). (ENG., Illus.). 40p. (J). (gr. -1-3). 6.99 *(978-0-618-48602-1(X))* Houghton Mifflin Harcourt Publishing Co.

Costamagna, Beatrice, illus. Crocodile Snap! 2016. (Crunchy Board Bks.). (ENG.). 12p. (J). (gr. -1-1). bds. 6.99 *(978-1-4998-0201-6(3))* Little Bee Books Inc.

Dahl, Michael. The Fantastic Flexy Frog, 1 vol. Baltazar, Art, illus. 2012. (DC Super-Pets Ser.). (ENG.). 56p. (gr. 2-2). pap. 4.95 *(978-1-4048-7666-8(9));* 23.99 *(978-1-4048-6494-8(6))* Picture Window Bks. (DC Super-Pets).

—The Worm Tunnel: Finnegan Zwake #2. 2008. (Finnegan Zwake Ser.: 2). (ENG.). 176p. (YA). (gr. 7). pap. 9.99 *(978-1-4169-8667-6(7),* Simon Pulse) Simon Pulse.

Dahl, Roald. The Enormous Crocodile. 2009. (ENG.). 32p. (J). (gr. 2-5). pap. 7.99 *(978-0-14-241453-8(0),* Puffin Books) Penguin Young Readers Group.

—The Enormous Crocodile. 2009. (gr. k-3). lib. bdg. 18.40 *(978-0-613-87826-5(4),* Turtleback) Turtleback Bks.

Dale, Jay. Big Green Crocodile, 1 vol. Hancock, Anna, illus. 2012. (Engage Literacy Blue Ser.). (ENG.). 32p. (gr. k-2). pap. 5.99 *(978-1-4296-8984-7(6),* Engage Literacy) Capstone Press of Coughlan Cos.

David, Erica. Extreme Rescue: Crocodile Mission. McGee, Warner, illus. 2009. (Go, Diego, Go! Ser.). (ENG.). 24p. (J). pap. 3.99 *(978-1-4169-8515-0(8),* Simon Spotlight/Nickelodeon) Simon Spotlight/Nickelodeon.

De Gieter, Lucien. Imhotep's Transformation. Spear, Luke, tr. from FRE. 2008. (Papyrus Ser.: 2). (ENG., Illus.). 48p. pap. 11.95 *(978-1-905460-50-2(3))* CineBook GBR. Dist: National Bk. Network.

The Deer & the Crocodile: Individual Title Six-Packs. (Literatura 2000 Ser.). (gr. 1-2). 28.00 *(978-0-7635-0130-3(1))* Rigby Education.

Derrick, David G., Jr., illus. I'm the Scariest Thing in the Jungle! 2013. (ENG.). 36p. (J). (gr. -1-3). 15.95 *(978-1-59702-087-9(7))* Immedium.

Donnio, Sylviane. I'd Really Like to Eat a Child. 2012. (ENG., Illus.). 32p. (J). (gr. -1-2). pap. 7.99 *(978-0-307-93008-8(4),* Dragonfly Bks.) Random Hse. Children's Bks.

—I'd Really Like to Eat a Child. 2012. lib. bdg. 18.40 *(978-0-606-23845-8(X),* Turtleback) Turtleback Bks.

Dorémus, Gaëtan, illus. My Baby Crocodile. 2016. (ENG.). 56p. (J). (gr. -1-3). 18.95 *(978-1-59270-192-6(2))* Enchanted Lion Bks., LLC.

Dorling Kindersley Publishing Staff & Foreman, Niki. DK Readers L3: Snappy Crocodile Tale: Snappy Crocodile Tale. 2014. (DK Readers Ser.). (ENG.). 64p. (J). (gr. 2-4). 14.99 *(978-1-4654-2835-6(6),* DK Children) Dorling Kindersley Publishing, Inc.

Douglas, Marjory Stoneman & Milkweed Editions Staff. Alligator Crossing. Nicholson, Trudy, illus. 2003. (ENG.).

192p. (J). (gr. 3-8). pap. 7.95 *(978-1-57131-644-8(2))* Milkweed Editions.
Easterling, Anne S. Ozzie the Great Christmas Crocodile. 2006. (Illus.). 12p. (J). 3.95 *(978-0-9768890-4-5(8))* ASE Media.
Easton, Marilyn. Eris to the Rescue. 2013. (LEGO Legends of Chima: Comic Reader Ser.: 3). lib. bdg. 13.55 *(978-0-606-32398-7(8),* Turtleback) Turtleback Bks.
Ellerson, Terryann. The Rappin' Tappin Alphabet. 2011. 24p. pap. 11.99 *(978-1-4567-6733-4(X))* AuthorHouse.
Emberley, Rebecca. The Crocodile & the Scorpion. Emberley, Ed, illus. 2013. (ENG.). 32p. (J). (gr. -1-2). 17.99 *(978-1-59643-494-3(5),* 9781596434943) Roaring Brook Pr.
Farshtey, Greg. Beware of the Wolves. 2013. (LEGO Legends of Chima Chapter Bks.: 2). lib. bdg. 14.75 *(978-0-606-32014-6(8),* Turtleback) Turtleback Bks.
Fenn, G. Manville. The Rajah of Dah. 2011. 194p. 26.95 *(978-1-4638-9697-3(2))* Rodgers, Alan Bks.
Finlay, Lizzie. Little Croc's Purse. 2011. (ENG., Illus.). 36p. (J). (gr. -1-2). 15.00 *(978-0-8028-5392-9(7))* Eerdmans, William B. Publishing Co.
Fisher, Teresa. Croc on the Rock. 2012. 20p. pap. 13.77 *(978-1-4669-1936-5(1))* Trafford Publishing.
Fortunato, Mike. Later Gator, in a While Crocodile. 2013. (ENG.). 40p. (J). pap. 14.95 *(978-1-4787-1285-5(6))* Outskirts Pr., Inc.
François, André, creator. Crocodile Tears. 2017. (ENG.). 44p. (J). (-3). 16.95 *(978-1-59270-227-5(9))* Enchanted Lion Bks., LLC.
Friden, Chris. Toothtime with Chomper. 2008. (Illus.). 27p. (J). bds. 14.99 *(978-0-9758785-7-6(3))* Haydenburri Lane.
—Toothtime with Chomper. Rodriguez Braojos, Alberto et al, illus. 2008. (J). *(978-0-9801849-3-8(2))* Haydenburri Lane.
Fulton-Vengco, Aletha. A Crocodile Farm in the City. 2009. 28p. 22.40 *(978-0-578-00613-0(8))* Vengco, Aletha Fulton.
Golden, Kathleen M. Cleopatra's Big Birthday BBQ. Golden, Kathleen M., illus. 2003. (Illus.). 18p. (J). (gr. -1-k). mass mkt. 14.95 *(978-0-9726418-0-7(7))* Happyland Media.
Gordon, Gus. Herman & Rosie. Gordon, Gus, illus. 2013. (ENG., Illus.). 32p. (J). (gr. 2-5). 17.99 *(978-1-59643-856-9(8),* 9781596438569) Roaring Brook Pr.
Graham, Bob. Tales from the Waterhole. Graham, Bob, illus. 2004. (ENG., Illus.). 64p. (J). (gr. -1-3). 16.99 *(978-0-7636-2324-1(5))* Candlewick Pr.
Hamilton, Linda. The Big-Hearted Monkey & the Crocodile. 2005. (J). *(978-1-933248-01-1(7))* World Quest Learning.
Hamish, Jeannette. The Duck Who Drove a Boat. Hamish, Alexander, illus. 2008. 31p. pap. 24.95 *(978-1-60610-665-5(1))* America Star Bks.
Hawthorne, Rachel. The Crocodile Who Was Afraid of the Water. 2009. (Illus.). 16p. pap. 8.49 *(978-1-4389-9674-5(8))* AuthorHouse.
Heidbreder, Robert. Crocodiles Play! Mate, Rae, illus. 2009. (ENG.). 32p. (J). (gr. -1-3). 16.95 *(978-1-894965-86-6(8))* Simply Read Bks. CAN. Dist: Ingram Publisher Services.
—Crocodiles Say... Mate, Rae, illus. 2005. (ENG.). 32p. (J). (gr. -1-3). 16.95 *(978-1-894965-42-2(6))* Simply Read Bks. CAN. Dist: Ingram Publisher Services.
Hoffman, Beth Greiner. Animal Gym. Gergely, Tibor, illus. 2009. (Little Golden Book Ser.). (ENG.). 24p. (J). (gr. -1-2). 4.99 *(978-0-375-84751-6(0),* Golden Bks.) Random Hse. Children's Bks.
Hovland, Henrik & Bartlett, Don. John Jensen Feels Different. Kove, Torill, illus. 2011. (ENG.). 40p. (J). 16.00 *(978-0-8028-5399-8(4),* Eerdmans Bks For Young Readers) Eerdmans, William B. Publishing Co.
Hughes, Mónica. Little Mouse Deer & the Crocodile. Moricuchi, Mique, illus. 2004. 24p. (J). lib. bdg. 23.65 *(978-1-59646-684-5(7))* Dingles & Co.
Irly, I. R. Why Crocodile Does Not Smile. 2004. (Illus.). (J). bds. *(978-0-9753075-4-0(1))* M-Graphics Publishing.
Irwin, Bindi & Kunz, Chris. Croc Capers: Bindi Wildlife Adventures. 2012. (Bindi's Wildlife Adventures Ser.: 7). (ENG.). 112p. (J). (gr. 3-6). pap. 4.99 *(978-1-4022-7373-5(8),* Sourcebooks Jabberwocky) Sourcebooks, Inc.
James, Jake. Jake s Short Stories. 2010. 64p. pap. 10.99 *(978-1-60957-640-0(3))* Salem Author Services.
Johnson, Rebecca. The Cranky Crocodile. Parish, Steve, illus. 2005. (Animal Storybooks Ser.). 24p. (gr. k-3). lib. bdg. 22.00 *(978-0-8368-5970-6(7),* Gareth Stevens Learning Library) Stevens, Gareth Publishing LLLP.
Kerr, Judith. The Crocodile under the Bed. 2014. (ENG., Illus.). 32p. (J). 17.99 *(978-0-00-758675-2(2),* HarperCollins Children's Bks.) HarperCollins Pubs. Ltd. GBR. Dist: HarperCollins Pubs.
Ketteman, Helen. The Three Little Gators. Terry, Will, illus. 2012. (J). 34.28 *(978-1-61913-140-8(4))* Weigl Pubs., Inc.
King, Trey. The Legend Begins. 2013. (LEGO Legends of Chima: Comic Reader Ser.: 1). lib. bdg. 13.55 *(978-0-606-32012-2(1),* Turtleback) Turtleback Bks.
Kipling, Rudyard. Crocodile, Crocodile. Mogensen, Jan & Schroeder, Binnette, illus. 2003. Orig. Title: Krokodil, Krokodil. pap. 7.95 *(978-1-56656-512-7(X))* Interlink Publishing Group, Inc.
Kok, Gemma. Scribble. 2008. 42p. pap. 17.94 *(978-1-4092-2060-2(5))* Lulu Pr., Inc.
—Scribble (Printed in black & White) 2008. 42p. pap. 7.96 *(978-1-4092-2531-7(3))* Lulu Pr., Inc.
La Rose, Melinda. Jake & the Neverland Pirates: X Marks the Croc!, 1 vol. Batson, Alan, illus. 2014. (World of Reading Pre-1 Ser.). (ENG.). 32p. (J). (gr. 3-5). lib. bdg. 24.21 *(978-1-61479-247-5(X))* Spotlight.
Lamb. Bianca the Dancing Crocodile. Skon, Sandy, illus. 2008. 30p. pap. 24.95 *(978-1-60563-447-0(6))* America Star Bks.
LaRose, Melinda & Disney Book Group Staff. The Croc Takes the Cake. Disney Storybook Artists Staff, illus. 2012. (World of Reading Ser.). (ENG.). 32p. (J). (gr. -1-k). pap. 3.99 *(978-1-4231-5543-0(2))* Disney Pr.
Levy, Didier & Rapaport, Gilles. Ernesto. (SPA., Illus.). 32p. (J). (gr. k-2). 5.56 *(978-84-95150-80-6(8),* COR1529) Corimbo, Editorial S.L. ESP. Dist: Distribooks, Inc.
Lewis, J. Patrick. Good Ship Crocodile. Felix, Monique, illus. 2013. (ENG.). 32p. (J). (gr. 1-3). 18.99 *(978-1-56846-238-7(7),* Creative Editions) Creative Co., The.
Lodge, Jo. La Casa del Senor Coc/ The House of Mr Coc. 2007. 8p. bds. 36.95 *(978-84-263-6454-8(3))* Vives, Luis Editorial (Edelvives) ESP. Dist: Baker & Taylor Bks.
—Flip Flap, Mr Croc: A Mix & Match Book. 2014. (ENG., Illus.). 14p. (J). (gr. -1-k). 8.99 *(978-1-4449-0992-0(4))* Hodder & Stoughton GBR. Dist: Hachette Bk. Group.
—Imita Al Senor Coc/ Imitate Mr Coc. 2007. 22p. bds. 18.95 *(978-84-263-6221-6(4))* Vives, Luis Editorial (Edelvives) ESP. Dist: Baker & Taylor Bks.
Lofting, Hugh. The Story of Doctor Dolittle: The Circus Crocodile. Kanzler, John, illus. 2008. (Easy Reader Classics Ser.). (ENG.). 32p. (gr. 3-7). lib. bdg. 24.21 *(978-1-59961-339-0(5))* Spotlight.
MacKinnon, Mairi. Croc Gets a Shock. Blunt, Fred, illus. 2014. (Usborne Phonics Readers Ser.). (ENG.). (J). (gr. -1-3). pap. 6.99 *(978-0-7945-3395-3(7),* Usborne) EDC Publishing.
Marion, L. K. Summer Holiday with Funny Bunny. 2012. 32p. pap. 17.25 *(978-1-4669-6475-4(8))* Trafford Publishing.
McDermott, Gerald. Monkey: A Trickster Tale from India. 2011. (ENG., Illus.). 32p. (J). (gr. -1-3). 16.99 *(978-0-15-216596-3(7))* Houghton Mifflin Harcourt Publishing Co.
McKendry, Sam. Are You Ticklish? Mitchell, Melanie, illus. 2006. (ENG.). 12p. (J). (gr. -1-18). bds. 10.95 *(978-1-58117-376-5(8),* Intervisual/Piggy Toes) Bendon, Inc.
McOmber, Rachel B., ed. McOmber Phonics Storybooks: The Invisible Crocodiles. rev. ed. (Illus.). (J). *(978-0-944991-80-0(7))* Swift Learning Resources.
—McOmber Phonics Storybooks: Yellow Crocodile. rev. ed. (Illus.). (J). *(978-0-944991-76-3(9))* Swift Learning Resources.
Merino, Gemma. The Crocodile Who Didn't Like Water. 2014. (ENG., Illus.). 32p. (J). (gr. k-3). 17.95 *(978-0-7358-4163-5(2))* North-South Bks., Inc.
Miller, John. Winston & George. Cucco, Giuliano, illus. 2014. (ENG.). 56p. (J). (gr. k-3). 17.95 *(978-1-59270-145-2(0))* Enchanted Lion Bks., LLC.
Moncure, Jane Belk. 'Smile,' Says Little Crocodile: A Book about Good Habits. DeSantis, Susan, illus. 2013. (Magic Castle Readers Ser.). (ENG.). 32p. (J). (gr. -1-2). 25.64 *(978-1-62323-570-3(7),* 206305) Child's World, Inc., The.
Nancee Jean. The Boomerang Babies Club. 2012. 36p. pap. 13.95 *(978-1-4525-5243-9(6))* Balboa Pr.
Noel, Genevieve. Que Amor de Cocodrilo!/Al Agua, Leo. (Torre de Papel Ser.). (SPA., Illus.). (J). 7.95 *(978-958-04-5039-9(0))* Norma S.A. COL. Dist: Distribuidora Norma, Inc.
Ormerod, Jan. The Baby Swap. Joyner, Andrew, illus. 2015. (ENG.). 32p. (J). (gr. -1-1). 16.99 *(978-1-4814-1914-7(5),* Little Simon) Little Simon.
Panzieri, Lucia. The Kindhearted Crocodile. Ferrari, Antongionata, illus. 2013. (ENG.). 32p. (J). (gr. -1). 16.95 *(978-0-8234-2767-3(6))* Holiday Hse., Inc.
Parker, Vic, compiled by. The Hare-Brained Crocodiles & Other Silly Stories. 2016. (Silly Stories Ser.). (ENG.). 40p. (J). (gr. 2-3). pap. 14.05 *(978-1-4824-4202-1(7))* Stevens, Gareth Publishing LLLP.
Pastis, Stephan. Beginning Pearls. 2013. lib. bdg. 20.85 *(978-0-606-31764-1(3),* Turtleback) Turtleback Bks.
Patton, Jack. The Dragonfly Defense. 2016. (Battle Bugs Ser.: 7). (ENG.). 128p. (J). (gr. 2-5). pap. 4.99 *(978-0-545-94509-7(7),* Scholastic Paperbacks) Scholastic, Inc.
Paye, Won-Ldy & Lippert, Margaret H. Mrs. Chicken & the Hungry Crocodile. Paschkis, Julie, illus. 2014. (ENG.). 32p. (J). (gr. -1-2). pap. 7.99 *(978-1-250-04673-4(4),* 9781250046734) Square Fish.
Perret, Delphine. Pedro & George. Perret, Delphine, illus. 2015. (ENG., Illus.). 32p. (J). (gr. -1-3). 17.99 *(978-1-4814-2925-2(6))* Simon & Schuster Children's Publishing.
Pittman, Seth. Raggy's Island. 2010. 124p. pap. 9.95 *(978-0-557-59557-0(6))* Lulu Pr., Inc.
Pizzoli, Greg. The Watermelon Seed. Pizzoli, Greg, illus. 2013. (ENG., Illus.). 40p. (J). (gr. -1-k). 16.99 *(978-1-4231-7101-0(2))* Disney Pr.
Polhemus, Coleman. The Crocodile Blues. Polhemus, Coleman, illus. 2007. (ENG., Illus.). 48p. (J). (gr. -1-2). 16.99 *(978-0-7636-3543-5(X))* Candlewick Pr.
Postgate, Daniel. Richest Crocodile in the World. 2004. (ENG., Illus.). 32p. (J). (gr. k-2). pap. 8.95 *(978-0-00-710387-4(5),* HarperCollins Children's Bks.) HarperCollins Pubs. Ltd. GBR. Dist: Independent Pubs. Group.
—The Richest Crocodile in the World. 2003. (ENG., Illus.). 32p. (J). (gr. k-2). 17.95 *(978-0-00-710388-1(3))* HarperCollins Pubs. Ltd. GBR. Dist: Independent Pubs. Group.
Pugliano-Martin, Carol. Kanchil Outsmarts Crocodile: A Folktale from Malaysia & Indonesia. 2006. (J). pap. *(978-1-4108-7165-7(7))* Benchmark Education Co.
Pundir, Annie. Gauri & the Crocodile: Smiley Crocodiley. 2009. 28p. pap. 12.50 *(978-1-4389-8611-1(4))* AuthorHouse.
Ramoutar, Tagore. Eric Boyle the Crocodile Chooses a New Car. 2010. (Illus.). pap. *(978-1-907837-03-6(5))* Longshot Ventures, Ltd.
Robinson, Hilary. Croc by the Rock. Gordon, Mike, illus. 2005. 32p. (J). lib. bdg. 9.00 *(978-1-4242-0885-2(8))* Fitzgerald Bks.
—A Croc Shock! Gordon, Mike, illus. 2009. (Get Set Readers Ser.). 32p. (J). (gr. -1-2). lib. bdg. 22.60 *(978-1-60754-265-0(X))* Windmill Bks.
Rolt, Molly. The Chocci-Croc & Other Stories. 2006. 64p. pap. *(978-1-84401-890-1(3))* Athena Pr.
Scheunemann, Pam. Crocodile Tears, 1 vol. Chawla, Neena, illus. 2007. (Critter Chronicles Ser.). (ENG.). 24p. (J). (gr. k-3). lib. bdg. 24.21 *(978-1-59928-436-1(7),* SandCastle) ABDO Publishing Co.
Schlitz, Laura Amy. Princess Cora & the Crocodile. Floca, Brian, illus. 2017. (ENG.). 80p. (J). (gr. -1-3). 16.99 *(978-0-7636-4822-0(1))* Candlewick Pr.
Siefker, Eunice. The Crocodile Song. Grimm, Debi & Eadie, Inger Sommer, illus. 2009. 40p. (J). (gr. -1-3). 19.95 *(978-1-60227-476-1(2))* Above the Clouds Publishing.
Sierra, Judy. What Time Is It, Mr. Crocodile? Cushman, Doug, illus. 2007. (ENG.). 32p. (J). (gr. -1-3). pap. 7.99 *(978-0-15-205850-0(8))* Houghton Mifflin Harcourt Publishing Co.
Sithole, Thelma. The Little Monkey & the Crocodile. Montague, Christine, illus. 2007. 32p. per. 12.00 *(978-1-59858-204-8(6))* Dog Ear Publishing, LLC.
—Little Shoko & the Crocodile. Holmes, Rebecca, illus. 2007. 36p. per. 12.00 *(978-1-59858-330-4(1))* Dog Ear Publishing, LLC.
Sloan, William. Of Bees & Bats of Crocodiles & Cats. 2009. 73p. pap. 14.95 *(978-1-4092-9470-2(6))* Lulu Pr., Inc.
Smith, Marvelyn A. The Kangaroo & the Crocodile. 2008. 28p. pap. 12.49 *(978-1-4343-9650-1(9))* AuthorHouse.
Taylor, Sean. Crocodiles Are the Best Animals of All! Shaw, Hannah, illus. 2009. (Time to Read Ser.). (ENG.). 32p. (J). (gr. -1-k). *(978-1-84507-904-8(3))* Rough Guides, Ltd.
Thomas, Warren. The Adventures of Mu-Mu Lost in the Outback. 2012. 44p. pap. 8.99 *(978-1-60746-566-9(3))* FastPencil, Inc.
Thomassie, Tynia. Feliciana Feydra Leroux: A Cajun Tall Tale, 1 vol. Smith, Cat Bowman, illus. 2005. (ENG.). 32p. (J). (gr. -1-3). 16.99 *(978-1-58980-286-5(1))* Pelican Publishing Co., Inc.
Trevethan, Glenn A. The Adventures of Sammi Snake: Sammi's Coat. 2012. 24p. pap. 13.97 *(978-1-61897-926-1(4),* Strategic Bk. Publishing) Strategic Book Publishing & Rights Agency (SBPRA).
Tye, Peter. Crocodile Tours. Howe, Norma, illus. 2012. 80p. pap. *(978-1-78176-536-4(7))* FeedARead.com.
Usui, Kanako. Fantastic Mr Wani. Usui, Kanako, illus. 2006. (Illus.). 32p. (J). 15.95 *(978-1-58925-054-3(0))* Tiger Tales.
Vermeulen, Mariska. James & Cooper Finger Puppet Book. van de Liejgraaf, Deborah, illus. 2016. (My Best Friend & Me Ser.). (ENG.). 10p. (J). (gr. -1-k). bds. 6.99 *(978-0-7641-6830-7(4))* Barron's Educational Series, Inc.
Vilarino, Andres Garcia. Un Cocodrilo en Mi Habitacion. 6th ed. 2003. (SPA., Illus.). 56p. *(978-84-236-3696-9(8),* ED0976) Edebé ESP. Dist: Lectorum Pubns., Inc.
Voelkel, Jon & Voelkel, Pamela. The End of the World Club, Bk. 2. 2010. (Jaguar Stones Ser.: Bk. 2). (ENG.). 384p. (gr. 5-6). 16.99 *(978-1-60684-072-6(X),* Darby Creek) Lerner Publishing Group.
Waber, Bernard. Lyle, Lyle, Crocodile, 1 vol. 2008. (Read along Book & CD Ser.). (ENG., Illus.). 48p. (J). (gr. -1-3). audio compact disk 10.99 *(978-0-618-95968-6(8))* Houghton Mifflin Harcourt Publishing Co.
—Lyle, Lyle, Crocodile Storybook Treasury. 2012. (Lyle the Crocodile Ser.). (ENG., Illus.). 192p. (J). (gr. -1-3). 11.99 *(978-0-547-51618-9(5))* Houghton Mifflin Harcourt Publishing Co.
—Lyle Walks the Dogs. Waber, Paulis, illus. 2010. (ENG.). 24p. (J). (gr. -1-3). 17.99 *(978-0-547-22323-0(4))* Houghton Mifflin Harcourt Publishing Co.
West, Colin. Have You Seen the Crocodile? Read & Share. West, Colin, illus. 2003. (Reading & Math Together Ser.). (ENG., Illus.). 32p. (J). (gr. -1-3). pap. 3.99 *(978-0-7636-0862-0(9))* Candlewick Pr.
Whitmore, Gary. Prince Luna & the Space Dreamers. 2011. (ENG.). 204p. pap. 8.50 *(978-1-4565-8438-2(3))* CreateSpace Independent Publishing Platform.
Widdowson, Kay, illus. Please, Mr. Crocodile. 2006. (Lift-the-Flap Books (Child's Play) Ser.). (ENG.). 24p. (J). (gr. -1-1). *(978-1-84643-025-1(9))* Child's Play International Ltd.
William H. Sadlier Staff. How to Make a Crocodile. 2005. (Early Library). (gr. k-2). 24.00 net. *(978-0-8215-8952-6(0))* Sadlier, William H. Inc.
Zoboli, Giovanna. Professional Crocodile. Di Giorgio, Mariachiara, illus. 2017. (ENG.). 32p. (J). (gr. k-3). 17.99 ***(978-1-4521-6506-6(8))*** Chronicle Bks. LLC.

CROMWELL, OLIVER, 1599-1658

Ashworth, Leon. Oliver Cromwell. (Illus.). 32p. *(978-0-7451-5287-5(2));* pap. *(978-0-7540-9010-6(8))* Cherrytree Bks.
Lace, William W. Oliver Cromwell & the English Civil War in World History. 2003. (In World History Ser.). (Illus.). 128p. (J). (gr. 5-12). lib. bdg. 27.94 *(978-0-7660-1937-9(3))* Enslow Pubs., Inc.

CROPS

see Farm Produce

CROSS-COUNTRY RUNNING

see Track and Field

CROSSWORD PUZZLES

Andrews McMeel Publishing Staff. Go Fun! Big Book of Crosswords 2. 2016. (Go Fun! Ser.: 13). (ENG.). 128p. (J). pap. 8.99 *(978-1-4494-7882-7(4))* Andrews McMeel Publishing.
Clifton, Chuck & Clifton, Joyce. A Crossword Walk with Lewis & Clark. 2003. 56p. (J). 9.95 *(978-0-9669760-6-9(1))* Maple Canyon Co.
—Fundamentals of Freedom Crossword Puzzles - Volume 1. 2004. 50p. (YA). 9.95 *(978-0-9669760-7-6(X))* Maple Canyon Co.
Crossword Puzzles: Bible Characters from the Old Testament. (Illus.). 32p. (YA). (gr. 5-18). pap. 2.25 *(978-0-87162-608-0(X),* E4452) Warner Pr., Inc.
Crossword Puzzles: New Testament. (Illus.). 32p. (YA). (gr. 5-18). pap. 2.25 *(978-0-87162-495-6(8),* E4451) Warner Pr., Inc.
Crossword Puzzles: Old Testament. (Illus.). 32p. (YA). (gr. 5-18). pap. 2.25 *(978-0-87162-494-9(X),* E4450) Warner Pr., Inc.
David, Edward. When Time for Poetry, vol. 2. 2016. (ENG.). 116p. pap. *(978-0-9728118-8-0(5),* 29) Inkwell Books LLC.
Doherty, Brian. Search-a-Words. 2011. (Dover Children's Activity Bks.). (ENG., Illus.). 96p. (gr. 3). pap. 4.00 *(978-0-486-27853-7(0))* Dover Pubns., Inc.
Dunn, Kevin Ikim. In Search of Yourself Word Search Puzzles: Explorations into the Black Experience. Sedalia, Rajan, illus. 2005. (ENG.). 92p. per. 9.95 *(978-0-9767337-0-6(6))* Invision Pubns.
DynaNotes Lab Measurement & Equipment Workbook. 2007. (J). pap. *(978-1-933854-72-4(3))* DynaStudy, Inc.
Elite Crossword Puzzle Digest. 2003. per. *(978-1-884907-18-0(0))* Paradise Pr., Inc.
Fremont, Victoria. Quick Crossword Puzzles. 2011. (Dover Children's Activity Bks.). (ENG., Illus.). 64p. (gr. 3). pap. 2.50 *(978-0-486-28969-4(9))* Dover Pubns., Inc.
Gogna, Ruth M. Hollywood Nineteen Eighty Crossword Puzzle. 80p. (Orig.). (J). (gr. 7-18). pap. 9.95 *(978-0-931290-36-7(8))* Alchemy Bks.
Hartman, Randall J. Cakewalk Crosswords. 2013. (Easy Crosswords Ser.). (ENG.). 96p. spiral bd. 8.95 *(978-1-4549-0654-4(5),* Puzzlewright) Sterling Publishing Co., Inc.
Hemminger, Marcia. Comprehension Crosswords Grade 4, 6 vols. McAskin, Denice, illus. 2003. 32p. (J). 4.99 *(978-1-56472-188-4(4))* Edupress, Inc.
—Comprehension Crosswords Grade 6, 6 vols. Adams Marks, Elizabeth, illus. 2003. 32p. (J). 4.99 *(978-1-56472-190-7(6))* Edupress, Inc.
Hoffman, Joan. Crosswords. 2003. (ENG.). 64p. (J). pap., wbk. ed. 3.99 *(978-1-58947-075-0(3),* 02352) School Zone Publishing Co.
Hovanec, Helene. Easy First Puzzles. Shems, Ed, illus. 2011. (First Puzzles Ser.). (ENG.). 64p. (J). pap. 4.95 *(978-1-4027-7810-0(4))* Sterling Publishing Co., Inc.
Kellaher, Karen. Grammar Games & Activities Kids Can't Resist! 40 Super-Cool Crosswords, Codes, Mazes & More That Teach the Essential Rules of Grammar. 2003. (ENG., Illus.). 64p. (J). pap. 10.95 *(978-0-439-07756-9(7))* Scholastic, Inc.
Koumpouras, Sally. Comprehension Crosswords Grade 5, 6 vols. Adams Marks, Elizabeth, illus. 2003. 32p. (J). 4.99 *(978-1-56472-189-1(2))* Edupress, Inc.
Lawrence, Linda. Crosswords for Kids, Vol. 2. Reardon, Will, ed. 2004. (Illus.). 56p. (J). (gr. 4-7). per. 10.95 *(978-0-9716039-1-2(X))* Lawrence Publishing.
McCoy, Heather. French Crossword Puzzles for Practice & Fun. 2012. (Dover Language Guides French Ser.). (FRE & ENG.). 120p. pap. 8.95 *(978-0-486-48585-0(4))* Dover Pubns., Inc.
My First Crosswords (Gr. 1-2) 2003. (J). *(978-1-58232-096-0(9))* ECS Learning Systems, Inc.
Newman-D'Amico, Fran. ABC Crosswords. 2005. (Dover Little Activity Bks.). (ENG., Illus.). 64p. (J). (gr. k-2). pap. 1.99 *(978-0-486-44115-3(6))* Dover Pubns., Inc.
—BOOST My First Book of Puzzle Fun. 2013. (BOOST Educational Ser.). (ENG.). 64p. (J). (gr. -1-k). pap. 5.99 *(978-0-486-49401-2(2))* Dover Pubns., Inc.
Payne, Trip. Awesome Crosswords for Kids. 2004. (ENG., Illus.). 96p. (J). pap. 6.95 *(978-1-4027-1038-4(0),* Puzzlewright) Sterling Publishing Co., Inc.
—Crossword Puzzles for Clever Kids. 2017. (ENG.). 96p. (J). (gr. 3-7). pap. 6.95 ***(978-1-4549-2482-1(9),*** Puzzlewright) Sterling Publishing Co., Inc.
—Crossword Puzzles for Smart Kids. 2017. (ENG.). 96p. (J). (gr. 3-7). pap. 6.95 ***(978-1-4549-2483-8(7),*** Puzzlewright) Sterling Publishing Co., Inc.
Peterson, Doug. Easy As ABC Crosswords. 2013. (Easy Crosswords Ser.). (ENG.). 96p. spiral bd. 8.95 *(978-1-4549-0422-9(4),* Puzzlewright) Sterling Publishing Co., Inc.
Pomaska, Anna & Newman-D'Amico, Fran. Crazy Crosswords Activity Book. 2014. (ENG.). 64p. (J). (gr. -1-3). pap. 3.99 *(978-0-486-77963-8(7))* Dover Pubns., Inc.
Price, Roger & Stern, Leonard. World's Greatest Word Game. 2005. (Mad Libs Ser.). (ENG.). 48p. (J). (gr. 3-7). mass mkt. 4.99 *(978-0-8431-1349-5(9),* Mad Libs) Penguin Young Readers Group.
Puzzle Society Staff. Girl Crosswords: 75 Puzzles. 2011. (ENG.). 176p. pap. 7.99 *(978-1-4494-0736-0(6))* Andrews McMeel Publishing.
—Pocket Posh Girl Crosswords: 75 Puzzles. 2010. (ENG.). 176p. pap. 7.99 *(978-0-7407-9862-7(6))* Andrews McMeel Publishing.
Puzzler's Giant Book of Crosswords. 2003. (YA). Vol. 10. per. 9.45 *(978-1-55956-869-2(0))* Vol. 11. per. 9.45 *(978-1-55956-872-2(0))* Penny Pubns., LLC. (Penny Pr.).
School Zone Publishing Company Staff. Big Activity Ages 8-Up: Word Searches, Crosswords, Puzzles, & Codes. 2004. (ENG.). 320p. (J). pap. 9.99 *(978-1-58947-422-2(8))* School Zone Publishing Co.
School Zone Staff, ed. Crosswords Challenges. 2006. (ENG.). 32p. (J). pap. 2.99 *(978-1-58947-396-6(5),* 02198) School Zone Publishing Co.
Shiotsu, Vicky. Comprehension Crosswords Grade 1, 6 vols. McMahon, Kelly, illus. 2003. 32p. (J). 4.99 *(978-1-56472-185-3(X))* Edupress, Inc.
—Comprehension Crosswords Grade 2, 6 vols. McMahon, Kelly, illus. 2003. 32p. (J). 4.99 *(978-1-56472-186-0(8))* Edupress, Inc.
—Comprehension Crosswords Grade 3, 6 vols. Tunell, Ken, illus. 2003. 32p. (J). 4.99 *(978-1-56472-187-7(6))* Edupress, Inc.
Taliarico, Tony J., Jr. Baseball Activity Book. 2010. (Dover Little Activity Bks.). (ENG., Illus.). 64p. (J). (gr. k-3). 1.99 *(978-0-486-47387-1(2))* Dover Pubns., Inc.
Top That Publishing Staff, ed. 101 Crossword Search Puzzles. 2005. (Illus.). 48p. pap. *(978-1-84510-200-5(2))* Top That! Publishing PLC.
—101 Wordsearch Puzzles. 2005. (Illus.). 48p. pap. *(978-1-84510-199-2(5))* Top That! Publishing PLC.
University Games Staff. Crosswords for Kids. 2004. (Spinner Bks.). (ENG.). pap. 7.95 *(978-1-57528-841-3(9))* Univ. Games.
—Word Searches for Kids. 2007. (Spinner Books for Kids Ser.). (ENG.). 128p. (J). (gr. -1-3). pap. 7.95 *(978-1-57528-840-6(0))* Univ. Games.
Ward, Mike. Scratch & Solve Hangman, Vol. 2. 2005. (Scratch & Solve(r) Ser.). (ENG., Illus.). 96p. pap. 6.95 *(978-1-4027-2580-7(9))* Sterling Publishing Co., Inc.
—Scratch & Solve Hangman #1, No. 1. 2005. (Scratch & Solve(r) Ser.). (ENG., Illus.). 96p. pap. 6.95 *(978-1-4027-2579-1(5),* Puzzlewright) Sterling Publishing Co., Inc.
Woodworth, Viki. The 50 States: Facts & Fun. 2010. (Dover Little Activity Bks.). (ENG., Illus.). 64p. (J). (gr. 1-5). 1.99 *(978-0-486-47524-0(7))* Dover Pubns., Inc.

CROWS

Bradley, James V. Crows & Ravens. 2006. (Nature Walk Ser.). (Illus.). 64p. (gr. 4-6). lib. bdg. 28.00 *(978-0-7910-9115-9(5),* Chelsea Hse.) Facts On File, Inc.
Jacobs, Lee. Crow. 2003. (Wild America Ser.). (Illus.). 24p. (J). 24.94 *(978-1-56711-567-3(5),* Blackbirch Pr., Inc.) Cengage Gale.
Johnson, Sylvia A. Crows. 2004. (Nature Watch Ser.). (ENG., Illus.). 48p. (gr. 4-8). lib. bdg. 27.93 *(978-1-57505-628-9(3))* Lerner Publishing Group.

Keenan, Sheila. As the Crow Flies. Duggan, Kevin, illus. 2012. (ENG.). 40p. (J). (gr. k-1). 16.99 *(978-0-312-62156-8(6)*, 9780312621568) Feiwel & Friends.

Otfinoski, Steven. Crows. 2014. (Backyard Safari Ser.). 32p. (J). (gr. 3-5). 28.50 *(978-1-62712-831-5(X))* Cavendish Square Publishing.

Owen, Ruth. Crows. 2011. (World's Smartest Animals Ser.). (ENG., Illus.). 32p. (J). (gr. k-5). 26.50 *(978-1-61533-376-9(2))*; pap. 11.75 *(978-1-61533-414-8(9))* Windmill Bks.

Petrie, Kristin. American Crows, 1 vol. 2014. (Backyard Animals Ser.). (ENG.). 32p. (gr. 3-6). 27.07 *(978-1-62403-658-3(9))* ABDO Publishing Co.

Pringle, Laurence. Crows! Strange & Wonderful. Robert, Marstall & Marstall, Bob, illus. 2010. (Strange & Wonderful Ser.). (ENG.). 32p. (J). (gr. 2-4). pap. 9.95 *(978-1-59078-724-3(2))* Boyds Mills Pr.

Roza, Greg. A Murder of Crows. 2013. (Animal Groups Ser.). (Illus.). 24p. (J). (gr. 1-3). pap. 8.15 *(978-1-4339-8205-7(6))*; lib. bdg. 22.60 *(978-1-4339-8204-0(8))* Stevens, Gareth Publishing LLLP.

—A Murder of Crows / una Bandada de Cuervos. 2013. (Animal Groups / Grupos de Animales Ser.). (ENG & SPA., Illus.). 24p. (gr. 1-3). 22.60 *(978-1-4339-8806-6(2))* Stevens, Gareth Publishing LLLP.

Turner, Pamela S. Crow Smarts: Inside the Brain of the World's Brightest Bird. Comins, Andy, photos by. 2016. (Scientists in the Field Ser.). (ENG., Illus.). 80p. (J). (gr. 5-7). 18.99 *(978-0-544-41619-2(8)*, HMH Books For Young Readers) Houghton Mifflin Harcourt Publishing Co.

CROWS—FICTION

Aesop. The Crow & the Pitcher: A Tale about Problem Solving. Heyer, Carol, illus. 2006. (J). *(978-1-59939-096-3(5)*, Reader's Digest Young Families, Inc.) Studio Fun International.

Anastasio, Dina. How Raven Became Black & Owl Got Its Spots & Por qué el cuervo es negro y el búho tiene Manchitas: 6 English, 6 Spanish Adaptations. 2011. (ENG & SPA.). (J). 75.00 net. *(978-1-4108-5626-5(7))* Benchmark Education Co.

Appelt, Kathi. Counting Crows. Dunlavey, Rob, illus. 2015. (ENG.). 40p. (J). (gr. -1-3). 17.99 *(978-1-4424-2327-5(7))* Simon & Schuster Children's Publishing.

Applegate, Katherine. Wishtree. 2017. (ENG., Illus.). 224p. (J). 16.99 ***(978-1-250-04322-1(0)***, 9781250043221) Feiwel & Friends.

Awdry, W. Thomas Scares the Crows (Thomas & Friends) 2016. (Pictureback(R) Ser.). (ENG.). 24p. (J). (gr. -1-2). 4.99 *(978-1-101-93831-7(5)*, Random Hse. Bks. for Young Readers) Random Hse. Children's Bks.

Bailey, Arthur Scott. Tuck-Me-in Tales: The Tale of Old Mr Cro. 2006. pap. *(978-1-4065-0450-7(5))* Dodo Pr.

Bauer, A. C. E. & Shakespeare, William. Come Fall. 2011. (ENG.). 240p. (J). (gr. 3-7). pap. 6.99 *(978-0-375-85826-0(1)*, Yearling) Random Hse. Children's Bks.

Bendoly, Lynne Anne. Tabetha's Crow. 2009. 32p. pap. 24.95 *(978-1-60749-851-3(0))* America Star Bks.

Bennicke, Rune Brandt. The Mystery Hat. Jensen, Jakob Hjort, illus. 2014. (ENG.). 32p. (J). (gr. -1-k). 16.95 *(978-1-62914-621-8(8)*, Sky Pony Pr.) Skyhorse Publishing Co., Inc.

Bird, J. K. Shadow the Dog. 2010. 28p. 13.99 *(978-1-4520-3476-8(1))* AuthorHouse.

Blair, Eric. El Cuervo y la Jarra: Versión de la Fábula de Esopo. Abello, Patricia, tr. Silverman, Dianne, illus. 2006. (Read-It! Readers en Español: Fábulas Ser.).Tr. of Crow & the Pitcher - A Retelling of Aesop's Fable. (SPA.). 24p. (gr. k-3). 21.32 *(978-1-4048-1618-3(6)*, Easy Readers) Picture Window Bks.

Burgess, Thornton W. The Adventures of Poor Mrs Quack. 2008. 124p. (gr. 4-7). per. 10.95 *(978-1-60312-417-1(9))* Aegypan.

—Blacky the Crow. 2006. 136p. per. 10.95 *(978-1-59818-116-6(5))*; 24.95 *(978-1-59818-470-9(9))* Aegypan.

—Blacky the Crow. (J). 18.95 *(978-0-8488-0394-0(9))* Amereon Ltd.

—Blacky the Crow. 2004. reprint ed. pap. 15.95 *(978-1-4191-1030-6(6))*; pap. 1.99 *(978-1-4192-1030-3(0))* Kessinger Publishing, LLC.

—Blacky the Crow. 2011. 132p. 25.95 *(978-1-4638-9575-4(5))* Rodgers, Alan Bks.

Burggraaf, Deborah. Crow No More. Lumsden, Matt, illus. 2011. 28p. (J). pap. 10.95 *(978-0-9845161-8-6(2))* Protective Hands Communications.

Campbell, Judy. Gizmo the Little Crow: Written & Illustrated By. 2012. 38p. 17.95 *(978-1-4327-8389-1(0))* Outskirts Pr., Inc.

Cann, Kate. Crow Girl. 2012. (Stoke Books Titles Ser.). (ENG.). 80p. (YA). (gr. 8-12). pap. 6.95 *(978-1-78112-121-4(4))*; lib. bdg. 22.60 *(978-1-78112-122-1(2))* Lerner Publishing Group.

Clark, Patricia Nikolina. In the Shadow of the Mammoth. LeTourneau, Anthony Alex, illus. (J). 2005. 14.99 *(978-0-9674602-8-4(X))* 2003. 190p. pap. 6.99 *(978-0-9674602-4-6(7))* Blue Marlin Pubns.

Croskerry, Frank J. Our Land Is the Sky: The Adventures of Jimmy Fastwing. 2011. 88p. (gr. 4-6). pap. 9.95 *(978-1-4620-2839-9(X))* iUniverse, Inc.

Devereux, Jan. Poe the Crow. Devereux, Jan, ed. Vansiette, Roxy, illus. 2004. 139p. (J). per. *(978-0-9749677-0-7(X))* Lakeview Pr.

Dillon, Jana. Jeb Scarecrow's Pumpkin Patch, 1 vol. 2016. (ENG., Illus.). 32p. (J). (gr. k-3). pap. 8.99 *(978-1-4556-2181-1(1))* Pelican Publishing Co., Inc.

Faulk, Terry. Joe the Roadside Crow. 2010. 20p. 12.99 *(978-1-4490-7006-9(X))* AuthorHouse.

Fort, Jean Jacobs. Trouble. 2011. 24p. pap. 14.49 *(978-1-4634-0597-7(9))* AuthorHouse.

Fox, Culpeo S., illus. The Fox & the Crow. 2014. (ENG.). 28p. (J). (gr. -1). 17.95 *(978-81-8190-303-7(X))* Karadi Tales Co. Pvt. Ltd. IND. Dist: Consortium Bk. Sales & Distribution.

Fox, Helen. George the Orphan Crow & the Creatures of Blossom Valley. 2016. (ENG., Illus.). (J). (gr. 4-6). pap. ***(978-1-78538-505-6(4))*** Andrews UK Ltd.

Freeman, David. The Scarecrow. Beers, Robert Lee, illus. 2012. 24p. 24.95 *(978-1-4626-9609-3(0))*; 20p. pap. 24.95 *(978-1-4137-9543-1(9))* PublishAmerica, Inc.

George, Ben W. Wanda the Witch's Broom: How an Old School Witch Learns New Tricks. 2011. 24p. pap. 12.99 *(978-1-4634-4380-1(3))* AuthorHouse.

George, Jean Craighead. Crowbar, the Smartest Bird in the World. Minor, Wendell, illus. 2015. (J). *(978-0-06-000257-2(3))* HarperCollins Pubs.

Grey, Jacob. Ferals #2: the Swarm Descends. 2016. (Ferals Ser.: 2). 288p. (J). (gr. 3-7). 16.99 *(978-0-06-232106-0(4))* HarperCollins Pubs.

Griver, Jeanette A. Curio, a Shetland Sheepdog Meets the Crow: A Story of Friendship For Children of All Ages 2004. (Illus.). 44p. (J). pap. 6.95 *(978-0-929948-04-1(1))* Compsych Systems, Inc., Pubns. Div.

Haak, Rieneke. Kari, Meraai en Die Rollende, Tollende Lemoene. 2012. (ZUL, AFR & ENG., Illus.). 24p. pap. 15.99 *(978-1-4691-9637-4(9))* Xlibris Corp.

Hamilton, Martha & Weiss, Mitch. Two Fables of Aesop. MacDonald, Bruce, illus. 2005. (ENG.). 16p. (J). 5.75 *(978-1-57274-718-0(8)*, 2788, Bks. for Young Learners) Owen, Richard C. Pubs., Inc.

Hanson, Thor. Bartholomew Quill: A Crow Learns to Tell Who's Who in the Animal World. Amim, Dana, illus. 2016. (ENG.). 32p. (J). (gr. -1-3). 17.99 *(978-1-63217-046-0(9))*, Little Bigfoot) Sasquatch Bks.

Hardy, Edward. Where Is Fred? Pye, Ali, illus. 2013. (ENG.). 32p. (J). (gr. -1-k). pap. 9.99 *(978-1-4052-5403-8(3))* Egmont Bks., Ltd. GBR. Dist: Independent Pubs. Group.

Hellberg, Joanne S. Soltee's Indian. 2011. 36p. (J). pap. 15.14 *(978-1-4520-8681-1(8))* AuthorHouse.

Hines, Amber. Maggie & the Moo Bully. 2012. 20p. pap. 17.99 *(978-1-4685-4312-4(1))* AuthorHouse.

Hobbs, Valerie. Carolina Crow Girl. 2013. 146p. pap. 12.95 *(978-1-62352-008-3(8))* IntoPrint Publishing LLC.

Holden, Pam & Aesop. Clever Crow. Hatam, Samer, illus. (ENG.). 24p. (gr. 3-3). pap. *(978-1-927197-34-9(1)*, Red Rocket Readers) Flying Start Bks.

Howarth, Naomi. The Crow's Tale. 2015. (ENG., Illus.). 32p. (J). (gr. -1-2). 18.99 *(978-1-84780-614-7(7)*, Frances Lincoln) Quarto Publishing Group UK GBR. Dist: Littlehampton Bk Services, Ltd.

Howe, James. Bunnicula Meets Edgar Allan Crow. Fortune, Eric, illus. (Bunnicula & Friends Ser.). (ENG.). 160p. (J). (gr. 3-7). 2008. pap. 6.99 *(978-1-4169-1473-0(0))* 2006. 15.95 *(978-1-4169-1458-7(7))* Simon & Schuster Children's Publishing. (Atheneum Bks. for Young Readers).

Huxley, Aldous. The Crows of Pearblossom. Blackall, Sophie, illus. 2011. (ENG.). 40p. (J). (gr. k-2). 17.95 *(978-0-8109-9730-1(4)*, Abrams Bks. for Young Readers) Abrams, Inc.

—The Crows of Pearblossom. (J). 15.95 *(978-0-89190-167-9(1))* Amereon Ltd.

Joy, Christine. The Dream Quest. 2013. 162p. pap. *(978-1-78148-790-7(1))* Grosvenor Hse. Publishing Ltd.

Kaplan, Kathy Walden. Crow Story: A Tale from the Oak Grove. 2012. (Illus.). 46p. (J). *(978-1-879571-10-5(2))* Librado Pr.

Keithly, Bryan. Princess Tarang. 2009. 24p. pap. 11.49 *(978-1-4343-7601-5(X))* AuthorHouse.

Kerven, Rosalind. Sparrow, the Crow & the Pearl. Williamson, Melanie, illus. 2005. (ENG.). 24p. (J). lib. bdg. 23.65 *(978-1-59646-754-5(1))* Dingles & Co.

Kubler, Annie. Dingle Dangle Scarecrow. 2003. (Baby Board Bks.). (ENG., Illus.). 12p. (J). (gr. 1-1). bds. *(978-0-85953-626-4(2))* Child's Play International Ltd.

Kwaymullina, Ambelin. The Disappearance of Ember Crow: the Tribe, Book Two. 2016. (Tribe Ser.). (ENG.). 432p. (YA). (gr. 7). 17.99 *(978-0-7636-7843-2(0))* Candlewick Pr.

Lionni, Leo. Six Crows. 2010. (ENG.). 32p. (J). (gr. -1-2). 16.99 *(978-0-375-84550-5(X)*, Knopf Bks. for Young Readers) Random Hse. Children's Bks.

Lois, Lowry. Crow Call. Ibatoulline, Bagram, illus. 2009. (ENG.). 32p. (J). (gr. 3-7). 19.99 *(978-0-545-03035-9(8)*, Scholastic Pr.) Scholastic, Inc.

—Crow Call. 2011. (J). (gr. -1-2). 29.95 incl. audio compact disk *(978-0-545-29674-8(9))* Weston Woods Studios, Inc.

Loux, Lynn Crosbie. The Day I Could Fly. Porfirio, Guy, illus. 2003. (ENG.). 32p. (J). (gr. k-3). 15.95 *(978-1-55971-866-0(8))* Cooper Square Publishing Llc.

Lowrey, Becky. Chirps. 2004. 45p. pap. 24.95 *(978-1-4137-2984-9(3))* PublishAmerica, Inc.

Marcolina, P. J. My Friend Grows Feathers - the True Story of Jackie the Crow. 2009. 52p. pap. 24.60 *(978-0-557-02706-4(3))* Lulu Pr., Inc.

Martinez, Rocio, illus. The Fox & the Crow. 2007. (First Reading Level 1 Ser.). 32p. (J). (gr. -1-3). 8.99 *(978-0-7945-1813-4(3)*, Usborne) EDC Publishing.

Martini, Clem. The Judgment. 2007. (Feather & Bone: the Crow Chronicles Ser.). (ENG., Illus.). 304p. (J). (gr. 5-9). 7.95 *(978-1-55337-757-3(5))* Kids Can Pr., Ltd. CAN. Dist: Hachette Bk. Group.

—The Mob. 2005. (Feather & Bone: the Crow Chronicles Ser.). (ENG.). 240p. (J). (gr. 5-9). 7.95 *(978-1-55337-664-4(1))* Kids Can Pr., Ltd. CAN. Dist: Hachette Bk. Group.

—The Plague. 2006. (Feather & Bone: the Crow Chronicles Ser.). (ENG., Illus.). 272p. (J). (gr. 5-9). 7.95 *(978-1-55337-667-5(6))* Kids Can Pr., Ltd. CAN. Dist: Hachette Bk. Group.

Marwood, Diane. The Fox & the Crow. 2012. (ENG., Illus.). 24p. (J). *(978-0-7787-7892-9(4))*; pap. *(978-0-7787-7904-9(1))* Crabtree Publishing Co.

Mcallister, Herb West. Doo West to Toadstool. 2011. 44p. pap. 21.99 *(978-1-4628-5530-8(X))* Xlibris Corp.

Menzin, Marit. Song for Papa Crow, 1 vol. 2012. (ENG., Illus.). 32p. (J). 16.99 *(978-0-7643-4131-1(6)*, 9780764341311) Schiffer Publishing, Ltd.

Mirhady, Irandought. Thorn-Bush Boy: Pesare Tigh. Mirhady, Irandought, illus. 2004. Orig. Title: Pesare Tigh. (PEO., Illus.). 63p. (YA). per. *(978-0-9760323-0-4(9))* Mirhady, Farhad.

The Mysterious Secret. 2013. (Illus.). 30p. pap. 14.99 *(978-1-940426-03-7(0))* Love Ink LLC.

Newman, Marlene. Myron's Magic Cow. 2005. (Illus.). 40p. (J). 16.99 *(978-1-84148-495-2(4))* Barefoot Bks., Inc.

Niemela, JoAnn Huston. The Crows of Hidden Creek. Bradley, Sandy, illus. 2003. 109p. (YA). 20.00 *(978-0-9716786-0-6(X))* Ten Minas Publishing.

Ocker, Christa Holder. A Crow Named Robin. 2006. (J). per. *(978-1-59872-712-8(5))* Instant Pub.

Peot, Margaret. Crow Made a Friend. 2015. (I Like to Read(r) Ser.). (ENG., Illus.). 24p. (J). (gr. -1-3). 14.95 *(978-0-8234-3297-4(1))* Holiday Hse., Inc.

Raschka, Chris. Little Black Crow. Raschka, Chris, illus. 2010. (ENG., Illus.). 40p. (J). (gr. -1-2). 16.99 *(978-0-689-84601-4(0)*, Atheneum/Richard Jackson Bks.) Simon & Schuster Children's Publishing.

Rath, Tom H. Donkey Oatie's Field Trip. Gaudet, Christine, illus. 2013. 26p. pap. *(978-0-9918033-4-7(5))* Wood Islands Prints.

Rex, Annmarie. Black's Adventure in the Big, Scary, Hairy World. 2007. (Illus.). 46p. (J). 19.99 *(978-1-59879-365-9(9)*, Lifevest) Lifevest Publishing, Inc.

—Black's Adventure in the Big, Scary, Hairy World. Rex, Annmarie, illus. 2007. (Illus.). 46p. (J). (gr. -1-3). per. 15.99 *(978-1-59879-364-2(0)*, Lifevest) Lifevest Publishing, Inc.

Rice, Dona Herwick. The Fox & the Crow, 1 vol. 2008. (Building Fluency Through Reader's Theater Ser.). (ENG.). 24p. (J). (gr. 1-3). pap. 6.99 *(978-1-4333-0295-4(0))* Teacher Created Materials, Inc.

Roberts, Shelly. Sissy & the Old Crow. 2006. (Illus.). 36p. (J). per. 18.00 *(978-0-9789798-2-9(6)*, 978-9789798-2-9) Blackbird's World Publishing Co.

—Sissy & the Old Crow (Coloring Book) 2006. (Illus.). 36p. (J). per. 6.50 *(978-0-9789798-3-6(4)*, 978-0-9789798-3-6) Blackbird's World Publishing Co.

Sargent, Dave. Blackie Crow: Tell the Truth, 20 vols. Lenoir, Jane, illus. 2003. (Feather Tales Ser.: No. 2). 42p. (J). Vol. 2. lib. bdg. 20.95 *(978-1-56763-721-2(3))*vol. 2. pap. 6.95 *(978-1-56763-722-9(1))* Ozark Publishing.

Simmons, Lynn Sheffield. Jack Crow Said Hello, 1 vol. Lopez, Willie, illus. 2003. (ENG.). 128p. (J). (gr. 3-7). 10.95 *(978-1-58980-218-6(7))* Pelican Publishing Co., Inc.

Smith, Carrie. The Crow & the Pitcher: Classic Tales Series. Greenhead, Bill, illus. 2011. (Classic Tales Ser.). (J). *(978-1-936258-73-4(0))* Benchmark Education Co.

Sophia Hansen, Hansen & Hansen, Sophia. The Crow & the Raven. 2010. 20p. 9.50 *(978-1-4269-2752-2(5))* Trafford Publishing.

Stauffacher, Sue. Animal Rescue Team: Special Delivery! Lamont, Priscilla, illus. 2011. (Animal Rescue Team Ser.). (ENG.). 176p. (J). (gr. 3-7). 6.99 *(978-0-375-85132-2(1)*, Yearling) Random Hse. Children's Bks.

—Special Delivery! Lamont, Priscilla, illus. 2010. (Animal Rescue Team Ser.: No. 2). (ENG.). 176p. (J). (gr. 3-7). 12.99 *(978-0-375-85848-2(2)*, Knopf Bks. for Young Readers) Random Hse. Children's Bks.

Stephens, Sarah Hines. Night of the Scaredy Crows, 1 vol. Baltazar, Art, illus. 2012. (DC Super-Pets Ser.). (ENG.). 56p. (gr. 2-2). pap. 4.95 *(978-1-4048-7663-7(4))*; lib. bdg. 23.99 *(978-1-4048-6492-4(X))* Picture Window Bks. (DC Super-Pets).

Stilton, Geronimo. The Dragon of Fortune: An Epic Kingdom of Fantasy Adventure. 2017. (Geronimo Stilton & the Kingdom of Fantasy Ser.: 2). (ENG.). 592p. (J). (gr. 2-5). 19.99 ***(978-1-338-15939-4(9)***, Scholastic Paperbacks) Scholastic, Inc.

Strelkoff, Tatiana. Jeremy & the Crow Nation. Martin, Bobi, ed. 2003. (Changer Ser.: Vol. 2). (Illus.). 128p. (Orig.). (J). (gr. 7-12). pap. 6.95 *(978-0-945522-04-1(5)*, 2204-5) Rebecca Hse.

Swallow, Pamela Curtis & Swallow, Pamela C. Groundhog Gets a Say. Bunkus, Denise, illus. 2007. (ENG.). 40p. (J). (gr. k-3). pap. 6.99 *(978-0-14-240896-4(4)*, Puffin Books) Penguin Young Readers Group.

Talbot, Amy. Deer & His Dear Friends: A Tale from India. 2006. (J). pap. *(978-1-4108-6173-3(2))* Benchmark Education Co.

Trottier, Doug. The Crow & His Boy. 2011. 382p. pap. 19.00 *(978-1-60976-469-2(2)*, Eloquent Bks.) Strategic Book Publishing & Rights Agency (SBPRA).

VanDerwest, Steven M. Reuben's First Christmas Crow. 2012. 40p. pap. 13.95 *(978-1-4497-5164-7(4)*, WestBow Pr.) Author Solutions, Inc.

Varley, Dax. The Crow. Proctor, Jon, illus. 2016. (ENG.). 48p. (J). lib. bdg. *(978-1-62402-160-2(3))* Magic Wagon.

Villasenor, Victor. Little Crow to the Rescue/el Cuervito al Rescate. Munoz, Elizabeth Cummins, tr. Alcantara, Felipe Ugalde, illus. 2005. (SPA & ENG.). 32p. (J). (gr. -1-3). pap. 16.95 *(978-1-55885-430-7(4)*, Piñata Books) Arte Publico Pr.

Vos, Sharon. Neddy the Nutty Acorn. Rosenfelder, Cheryl, illus. 2008. 40p. per. 24.95 *(978-1-60441-232-1(1))* America Star Bks.

Weeks, Sarah. Angel Face. Diaz, David, illus. 2014. (ENG.). 32p. (J). (gr. -1-2). 13.99 *(978-1-4814-5045-4(X)*, Atheneum Bks. for Young Readers) Simon & Schuster Children's Publishing.

Weston Woods Staff, creator. Crow Boy. 2011. 29.95 *(978-0-545-23382-8(8))*; 18.95 *(978-0-545-23383-5(6))*; 38.75 *(978-0-545-23384-2(4))* Weston Woods Studios, Inc.

—Crow Call. 2011. 18.95 *(978-0-545-37493-4(6))*; 38.75 *(978-0-545-37494-1(4))* Weston Woods Studios, Inc.

Wheeler, Lisa. Old Cricket. Goembel, Ponder, illus. 2006. 28p. (gr. -1-1). 18.00 *(978-0-7569-6795-6(3))* Perfection Learning Corp.

—Old Cricket. Goembel, Ponder, illus. (ENG.). 32p. (J). (gr. -1-1). 2003. 18.99 *(978-0-689-84510-9(3)*, Atheneum/Richard Jackson Bks.) 2006. reprint ed. 7.99 *(978-1-4169-1855-4(8)*, Atheneum Bks. for Young Readers) Simon & Schuster Children's Publishing.

Wiley, Melissa. Fox & Crow Are Not Friends. Braun, Sebastien, illus. 2012. (Step into Reading Ser.). (ENG.). 48p. (J). (gr. k-3). pap. 3.99 *(978-0-375-86982-2(4)*, Random Hse. Bks. for Young Readers) Random Hse. Children's Bks.

—Fox & Crow Are Not Friends. 2012. (Step into Reading Level 3 Ser.). lib. bdg. 13.55 *(978-0-606-26806-6(5)*, Turtleback) Turtleback Bks.

Yepes, Rebecca. It Might Be A Crow. 2011. 12p. 8.95 *(978-1-4567-1849-7(5))* AuthorHouse.

CRUELTY TO ANIMALS

see Animals—Treatment

CRUSADES

see also Chivalry

Coddington, Andrew. Strategic Inventions of the Crusades. 2016. (Tech in the Trenches Ser.). 112p. (YA). lib. bdg. 42.79 *(978-1-5026-2353-9(6))* Cavendish Square Publishing.

Crompton, Samuel Willard. The Third Crusade: Richard the Lionhearted vs. Saladin. 2003. (Great Battles Through the Ages Ser.). (Illus.). 112p. (J). (gr. 6-12). 30.00 *(978-0-7910-7437-4(4)*, Chelsea Hse.) Facts On File, Inc.

Currie, Stephen. Medieval Crusades. 2009. (World History Ser.). (ENG., Illus.). 128p. (gr. 7-10). 39.90 *(978-1-4205-0062-2(7)*, Lucent Bks.) Cengage Gale.

Davenport, John C. Saladin. 2003. (Ancient World Leaders Ser.). (Illus.). 112p. (gr. 6-12). 30.00 *(978-0-7910-7223-3(1)*, Chelsea Hse.) Facts On File, Inc.

DeCarlo, Carolyn. The Crusades. 2017. pap. ***(978-1-68048-860-9(0))***; lib. bdg. ***(978-1-68048-781-7(7))*** Rosen Publishing Group, Inc., The.

Grant, Neil. Medieval Europe. 2003. (Uncovering History Ser.). 46p. (J). lib. bdg. 28.50 *(978-1-58340-254-2(3))* Black Rabbit Bks.

Harkins, Susan Sales & Harkins, William H. The Life & Times of Richard the Lionheart. 2008. (Biography from Ancient Civilizations Ser.). (Illus.). 48p. (J). (gr. 4-8). lib. bdg. 29.95 *(978-1-58415-699-4(6))* Mitchell Lane Pubs., Inc.

Hilliam, David. Richard the Lionheart & the Third Crusade: The English King Confronts Saladin in AD 1191. 2009. (Library of the Middle Ages Ser.). 64p. (gr. 5-8). 58.50 *(978-1-60853-902-4(4)*, Rosen Reference) Rosen Publishing Group, Inc., The.

—Richard the Lionhearted & the Third Crusade: The English King Confronts Saladin, AD 1191. 2004. (Library of the Middle Ages Ser.). (Illus.). 64p. (YA). (gr. 5-8). lib. bdg. 31.95 *(978-0-8239-4213-8(9)*, Rosen Reference) Rosen Publishing Group, Inc., The.

Hoggard, Brian. Crusader Castles: Christian Fortresses in the Middle East. (Library of the Middle Ages Ser.). 64p. (gr. 5-8). 2009. 58.50 *(978-1-60853-897-3(4)*, Rosen Reference) 2004. (Illus.). (YA). lib. bdg. 31.95 *(978-0-8239-4212-1(0))* Rosen Publishing Group, Inc., The.

Jeffrey, Gary. Crusades. 2014. (ENG., Illus.). 48p. (J). *(978-0-7787-0397-6(5))* Crabtree Publishing Co.

Jones, J. Sydney, et al. The Crusades Biography. 2004. (Crusades Reference Library). (ENG., Illus.). 256p. (J). lib. bdg. 106.00 *(978-0-7876-9177-6(1)*, UXL) Cengage Gale.

—The Crusades Primary Sources. 2004. (Crusades Reference Library). (ENG., Illus.). 208p. lib. bdg. 106.00 *(978-0-7876-9178-3(X))* Cengage Gale.

Kallen, Stuart A. Life During the Crusades. 2014. (Living History Ser). (ENG., Illus.). 80p. (J). lib. bdg. *(978-1-60152-720-2(9))* ReferencePoint Pr., Inc.

Kelman, Janet Harvey. Stories from the Crusades (Yesterday's Classics) 2005. (Illus.). 92p. (J). per. 7.95 *(978-1-59915-054-3(9))* Yesterday's Classics.

Lace, William W. The Unholy Crusade: The Ransacking of Medieval Constantinople. 2006. (Lucent Library of Historical Eras). (ENG., Illus.). 104p. (J). (gr. 3-7). lib. bdg. 33.45 *(978-1-59018-846-0(2)*, Lucent Bks.) Cengage Gale.

Lloyd Jones, Rob. Crusaders. 2007. (Young Reading Series 3 Gift Bks). (Illus.). 63p. (J). 8.99 *(978-0-7945-1617-8(3))* EDC Publishing.

Macdonald, Fiona. You Wouldn't Want to Be a Crusader! (Revised Edition) 2017. (You Wouldn't Want to... History of the World Ser.). (ENG., Illus.). 32p. (J). lib. bdg. 29.00 *(978-0-531-23831-8(8)*, Watts, Franklin) Scholastic Library Publishing.

Murrell, Deborah Jane. Fighting a Battle. 2008. (Medieval Warfare Ser.). 32p. (gr. 5-8). (J). lib. bdg. 26.00 *(978-0-8368-9209-3(7)*, Gareth Stevens Secondary Library); pap. 10.50 *(978-0-8368-9336-6(0))* Stevens, Gareth Publishing LLLP.

O'Neal, Michael J., et al. The Crusades Almanac. 2004. (Crusades Reference Library). (ENG.). 240p. lib. bdg. 106.00 *(978-0-7876-9176-9(3)*, UXL) Cengage Gale.

Streissguth, Tom. Richard the Lionheart: Crusader King of England. 2007. (Rulers of the Middle Ages Ser.). (Illus.). 160p. (YA). (gr. 6-12). lib. bdg. 35.94 *(978-0-7660-2714-5(7))* Enslow Pubs., Inc.

West, David. Richard the Lionheart: The Life of a King & Crusader. 2009. (Graphic Nonfiction Biographies Ser.). (Illus.). 48p. (YA). (gr. 4-5). 58.50 *(978-1-61513-025-2(X)*, Rosen Reference) Rosen Publishing Group, Inc., The.

West, David & Gaff, Jackie. Richard the Lionheart: The Life of a King & Crusader. 2005. (Graphic Nonfiction Biographies Ser.). (ENG., Illus.). 48p. (YA). (gr. 4-7). lib. bdg. 31.95 *(978-1-4042-0241-2(2))* Rosen Publishing Group, Inc., The.

Wilson, John. Crusade Pt. 1: The Heretic's Secret. 2009. (ENG.). 304p. (J). (gr. 7). 12.95 *(978-1-55470-096-7(5))* Leaf Storm Pr.

Worth, Richard. Saladin: Sultan of Egypt & Syria. 2007. (Rulers of the Middle Ages Ser.). (Illus.). 160p. (YA). (gr. 6-12). lib. bdg. 35.94 *(978-0-7660-2712-1(0))* Enslow Pubs., Inc.

CRUSADES—FICTION

Grant, K. M. Blood Red Horse. 2006. (DeGranville Trilogy Ser.). (ENG.). 320p. (YA). (gr. 5-9). per. 10.99 *(978-0-8027-7734-8(1)*, 9780802777348, Bloomsbury USA Childrens) Bloomsbury Publishing USA.

Henty, George Alfred. The Boy Knight: A Tale of the Crusades. 2006. (Dover Children's Classics Ser.). (ENG., Illus.). 272p. (YA). (gr. 3-8). per. 6.95 *(978-0-486-44803-9(7))* Dover Pubns., Inc.

Jewett, Eleanore M. Big John's Secret. Chapman, Frederick T., illus. 2nd ed. 2004. 203p. (J). pap. 12.95 *(978-1-883937-89-8(2))* Bethlehem Bks.

Laird, Elizabeth. Crusade. 2016. (ENG.). 400p. (J). (gr. 4-7). pap. 8.99 *(978-1-5098-0296-8(7))* Pan Macmillan GBR. Dist: Independent Pubs. Group.

Muschla, Gary Robert. Crusader. 2006. (YA). pap. *(978-0-88092-491-7(8))* Royal Fireworks Publishing Co.

—Crusaders. 2006. (YA). lib. bdg. 9.99 *(978-0-88092-490-0(X))* Royal Fireworks Publishing Co.

Spradlin, Michael P. Keeper of the Grail, Bk. 1. 2009. (Youngest Templar Ser.: 1). (ENG.). 272p. (J). (gr. 5-6). 7.99 *(978-0-14-241461-3(1)*, Puffin Books) Penguin Young Readers Group.

Stein, Evaleen. Our Little Crusader Cousin of Long Ago. Meister, Charles E., illus. 2007. 136p. per. 8.95 *(978-1-59915-243-1(6))* Yesterday's Classics.

Viguié, Debbie. Scarlet Moon. 2004. (Once upon a Time Ser.). (ENG.). 176p. (YA). (gr. 9). mass mkt. 6.99 *(978-0-689-86716-3(6)*, Simon Pulse) Simon Pulse.

Weil, Sylvie. Elvina's Mirror. 2009. (ENG.). 150p. (gr. 5-18). pap. 14.00 *(978-0-8276-0885-6(3))* Jewish Pubn. Society.
—My Guardian Angel. Rosner, Gillian, tr. from FRE. 2014. (ENG., Illus.). 208p. (J). pap. 14.95 *(978-0-8276-1211-2(7))* Jewish Pubn. Society.
Wilson, John. Crusade, Bk. 1. 2010. (Heretic's Secret Ser.). (ENG., Illus.). 304p. (YA). (gr. 7-18). pap. *(978-1-55470-322-7(0))* Me to We.

CRUSOE, ROBINSON (FICTITIOUS CHARACTER)—FICTION

Allison, Samuel B. An American Robinson Crusoe. 2005. 136p. pap. 10.95 *(978-1-4218-0186-5(6))*; 26.95 *(978-1-4218-0086-8(1))* 1st World Publishing, Inc. (1st World Library - Literary Society).
—An American Robinson Crusoe. 2004. reprint ed. pap. 15.95 *(978-1-4191-0613-2(9))*; pap. 1.99 *(978-1-4192-0613-9(3))* Kessinger Publishing, LLC.
Defoe, Daniel. Robinson Crusoe. Elphinstone, Katy, illus. 2014. (Travel & Adventure Ser.). (ENG.). 64p. pap. 6.95 *(978-1-906230-71-5(4))* Real Reads Ltd. GBR. Dist: Casemate Pubs. & Bk. Distributors, LLC.
—Robinson Crusoe. 2012. 338p. pap. 10.99 *(978-1-61382-256-2(1))* Simon & Brown.
—Robinson Crusoe: The Complete Story of Robinson Crusoe. 2004. (SPA., Illus.). 284p. (YA). (gr. -1-7). pap. *(978-958-30-0091-1(4))* Panamericana Editorial.
—Robinson Crusoe: The Complete Story of Robinson Crusoe. 2nd ed. 2003. (Historias de Siempre Ser.). (SPA., Illus.). 92p. (J). (gr. 5-8). pap. 12.95 *(978-84-204-5723-9(X))* Santillana USA Publishing Co., Inc.
—Robinson Crusoe, Level 4. 2009. (ENG.). 96p. pap. 12.75 *(978-84-8323-553-9(6))* Cambridge Univ. Pr.
—ROBINSON CRUSOE LEVEL 4 INTERMEDIATE BOOK WITH CD-ROM AND AUDIO CD, 1 vol. 2009. (ENG.). 96p. pap. 16.50 incl. cd-rom, audio compact disk *(978-84-8323-550-8(1))* Cambridge Univ. Pr.
Defoe, Daniel, et al. Robinson Crusoe: The Complete Story of Robinson Crusoe. (Classics Illustrated Ser.). (Illus.). 52p. (YA). pap. 4.95 *(978-1-57209-021-7(9))* Classics International Entertainment, Inc.
Kerr, Gordon. Story of Robinson Crusoe. 2006. 100p. per. *(978-1-4067-2131-7(X))*, Hesperides Pr.) Read Bks.
Wilkes, Angela & Rawson, Christopher. Robinson Crusoe. 2004. (Young Reading Ser.). (Illus.). 64p. (J). (gr. 2-18). pap. 5.95 *(978-0-7945-0410-6(8))*, Usborne) EDC Publishing.

CRYOGENICS

see Low Temperatures

CRYPTOGRAPHY

see also Ciphers

Anderson, Rane. Cryptography. 2017. (J). pap. 9.97 ***(978-1-4938-3624-6(2))*** Teacher Created Materials, Inc.
—Power of Patterns: Cryptography. 2017. (Time for Kids Nonfiction Readers Ser.). lib. bdg. 20.85 ***(978-0-606-40278-1(0))*** Turtleback Bks.
Barber, Nicola. Who Broke the Wartime Codes?, 1 vol. 2014. (Primary Source Detectives Ser.). (ENG., Illus.). 64p. (gr. 7-8). lib. bdg. 35.99 *(978-1-4329-9606-2(1))* Heinemann-Raintree.
Beatty, Ken & Pearson Education Staff. Secret Codes. 2007. (ENG.). 80p. pap. 17.32 incl. cd-rom *(978-1-4058-5222-7(4))* Pearson Education.
Beissinger, Janet & Pless, Vera. The Cryptoclub: Using Mathematics to Make & Break Secret Codes. 2006. (ENG., Illus.). 200p. (C). pap. 43.95 *(978-1-56881-223-6(X))*, K00700) AK Peters, Ltd.
Bow, James. Secret Signs. 2013. (ENG.). 32p. (J). *(978-0-7787-1125-4(0))*; pap. *(978-0-7787-1129-2(3))* Crabtree Publishing Co.
Burrows, Terry. Codes, Ciphers, & Cartography: Math Goes to War. 2017. (STEM on the Battlefield Ser.). (ENG., Illus.). 48p. (J). (gr. 4-6). 31.99 ***(978-1-5124-3927-4(4))***, Lerner Pubns.) Lerner Publishing Group.
Byers, Ann. Uncracked Codes & Cyphers. 2016. (Cryptography: Code Making & Code Breaking Ser.). 00064p. (J). (gr. 8-8). 34.45 *(978-1-5081-7310-6(9))* Rosen Publishing Group, Inc., The.
Capstone Press. Making & Breaking Codes, 1 vol. 2010. (Making & Breaking Codes Ser.). (ENG.). 32p. lib. bdg. 79.95 *(978-1-4296-5943-7(2))*, Edge Bks.) Capstone Press of Coughlan Cos.
Colson, Mary. Destroy after Reading: The World of Secret Codes. 2010. (Culture in Action Ser.). (ENG.). 32p. (gr. 3-6). 30.65 *(978-1-4109-3927-2(8))*, NA-r) Heinemann-Raintree.
Cryptography: Code Making & Code Breaking. 2016. (Cryptography: Code Making & Code Breaking Ser.). 00064p. (YA). (gr. 8-8). 241.15 *(978-1-5081-7363-2(X))*, Rosen Young Adult) Rosen Publishing Group, Inc., The.
Freedman, Jeri. Famous Cryptographers. 2016. (Cryptography: Code Making & Code Breaking Ser.). 00064p. (J). (gr. 8-8). 34.45 *(978-1-5081-7312-0(5))* Rosen Publishing Group, Inc., The.
Fun with Map Skills. 2014. (Fun with Map Skills Ser.). 32p. (J). (gr. 3-6). pap. 60.00 *(978-1-4777-7222-5(7))*, PowerKids Pr.) Rosen Publishing Group, Inc., The.
Gregory, Jillian. Breaking Secret Codes, 1 vol. 2010. (Making & Breaking Codes Ser.). (ENG.). 32p. (gr. 3-4). lib. bdg. 27.99 *(978-1-4296-4568-3(7))*, Edge Bks.) Capstone Press of Coughlan Cos.
—Making Secret Codes, 1 vol. 2010. (Making & Breaking Codes Ser.). (ENG.). 32p. (gr. 3-4). lib. bdg. 27.99 *(978-1-4296-4567-6(9))*, Edge Bks.) Capstone Press of Coughlan Cos.
Gutner, Howard. America's Secret Weapon: The Navajo Code Talkers of World War II. 2003. (ENG., Illus.). 32p. (J). (gr. 6-8). pap. 7.97 net. *(978-0-7652-3266-3(9))*, Celebration Pr.) Pearson Schl.
Hall, Kirsten. Top Secret. Simard, Remy, illus. 2003. 64p. (J). *(978-0-439-50133-0(4))* Scholastic, Inc.
Hubbard, Ben. Hi Tech World: Code Breakers. 2010. (ENG., Illus.). 32p. (J). lib. bdg. *(978-0-7787-7528-7(3))* Crabtree Publishing Co.
Johnson, Bud. Break the Code: Cryptography for Beginners. 2013. (Dover Children's Activity Bks.). (ENG., Illus.). 84p. (Orig.). (J). (gr. 3-12). pap. 6.99 *(978-0-486-29146-8(4))* Dover Pubns., Inc.
La Bella, Laura. Ciphers, Codes, Algorithms, & Keys. 2016. (Cryptography: Code Making & Code Breaking Ser.). 00064p. (J). (gr. 8-8). 34.45 *(978-1-5081-7306-9(0))* Rosen Publishing Group, Inc., The.
Levy, Janey. Breaking the Code with Cryptography: Analyzing Patterns. (Math for the Real World Ser.). (Illus.). 32p. 2009. (ENG.). (gr. 6-7). pap. 10.00 *(978-1-4042-6089-4(7))* 2007. (YA). (gr. 5-9). lib. bdg. 25.25 *(978-1-4042-3368-3(7))* Rosen Publishing Group, Inc., The.
Mackay, Jenny. Cryptology. 2009. (Crime Scene Investigations Ser.). (Illus.). 128p. (YA). (gr. 7-12). 35.45 *(978-1-4205-0140-7(2))* Cengage Gale.
Making & Breaking Codes, 1 vol. 2010. (Making & Breaking Codes Ser.). (ENG.). 32p. (gr. 3-4). lib. bdg. 83.97 *(978-1-4296-4570-6(9))*, Edge Bks.) Capstone Press of Coughlan Cos.
McCune, Susan. I Like Making Maps, 01 vols., 1. 2016. (Rosen REAL Readers: Social Studies Nonfiction / Fiction: Family, Community, & the World Ser.). (ENG.). 8p. (J). pap. 5.46 *(978-1-5081-1701-8(2))*, Rosen Classroom) Rosen Publishing Group, Inc., The.
McFadzean, Lesley. Creating & Cracking Codes. 2013. (Discovery Education: Discoveries & Inventions Ser.). 32p. (J). (gr. 3-6). pap. 10.00 *(978-1-4777-1500-0(2))*; pap. 60.00 *(978-1-4777-1501-7(0))*; lib. bdg. 25.25 *(978-1-4777-1329-7(8))* Rosen Publishing Group, Inc., The. (PowerKids Pr.).
Meyer, Susan. The History of Cryptography. 2016. (Cryptography: Code Making & Code Breaking Ser.). 00064p. (J). (gr. 8-8). 34.45 *(978-1-5081-7304-5(4))* Rosen Publishing Group, Inc., The.
Mitchell, Susan K. Spy Codes & Ciphers. 2011. (Secret World of Spies Ser.). (Illus.). 48p. (J). (gr. 2-5). lib. bdg. 25.27 *(978-0-7660-3709-0(6))*; (gr. 4-18). pap. 8.95 *(978-1-59845-353-9(X))* Enslow Pubs., Inc.
Rosenberg, Aaron. Cryptologists: Life Making & Breaking Codes. (Extreme Careers Ser.). 64p. (gr. 5-5). 2009. 58.50 *(978-1-61512-388-9(1))*, Rosen Reference) 2004. (Illus.). (YA). lib. bdg. 31.95 *(978-0-8239-3965-7(0))* Rosen Publishing Group, Inc., The.
Throp, Claire. Spies & Codebreakers. 2015. (Heroes of World War II Ser.). (ENG., Illus.). 48p. (gr. 4-6). 32.65 *(978-1-4109-8047-2(2))* Heinemann-Raintree.

CRYPTOGRAPHY—FICTION

see Code and Cipher Stories

CRYSTAL GAZING

see Divination

CRYSTALLINE ROCKS

see Rocks

CRYSTALLIZATION

see Crystallography

CRYSTALLOGRAPHY

see also Mineralogy

Aloian, Molly. What Are Crystals? 2012. (ENG., Illus.). 32p. (J). pap. *(978-0-7787-7218-7(7))*; (gr. 3-6). lib. bdg. *(978-0-7787-7213-2(6))* Crabtree Publishing Co.
Crystal Kids Balance the World. 2003. (Illus.). (J). pap. *(978-0-9745496-0-6(6))* Kid by Kid, Incorporated.
Crystal Messages from the Crystal Kids. 2003. (J). pap. *(978-0-9745496-1-3(4))* Kid by Kid, Incorporated.
Dayton, Connor. Crystals. (Rocks & Minerals Ser.). 24p. (gr. 2-3). 2009. 42.50 *(978-1-60852-498-3(1))*, PowerKids Pr.) 2007. (Illus.). (YA). lib. bdg. 22.60 *(978-1-4042-3687-5(2))* Rosen Publishing Group, Inc., The.
Hirsch, Rebecca. Crystals, 1 vol. 2014. (Rocks & Minerals Ser.). (ENG.). 48p. (gr. 8-12). lib. bdg. 32.79 *(978-1-62403-384-1(9))* ABDO Publishing Co.
Hoffman, Steven M. Gems, Crystals, & Precious Rocks. 2011. (Rock It! Ser.). (Illus.). 24p. (J). 22.60 *(978-1-4488-2561-5(X))*; pap. 8.25 *(978-1-4488-2708-4(6))* Rosen Publishing Group, Inc., The. (PowerKids Pr.).
Lembo, Margaret Ann. Color Your Life with Crystals! Your First Guide to Crystals, Colors & Chakras. 2013. (ENG., Illus.). 112p. (gr. k-9). pap. *(978-1-84409-605-3(X))* Me to We.
Martin, Bobi. What Are Gems?, 01 vols., 1. 2016. (Junior Geologist Ser.). (ENG., Illus.). 32p. (J). pap. 12.90 *(978-1-5081-0050-8(0))*, Britannica Educational Publishing) Rosen Publishing Group, Inc., The.
McConnell, William. Crystals & Gems. 2009. (Real Life Readers Ser.). 16p. (gr. 1-3). pap. 7.05 *(978-1-4358-0107-3(5))*, Rosen Classroom) Rosen Publishing Group, Inc., The.
Mooney, Carla. Crystals. 2016. (Geology Rocks! Ser.). (ENG.). 24p. (J). (gr. 3-6). 28.50 *(978-1-5038-0799-0(1))*, 210635) Child's World, Inc., The.
Pellant, Chris & Pellant, Helen. Crystals & Gemstones. 2008. (Rock Stars Ser.). (Illus.). 24p. (J). (gr. 1-4). lib. bdg. 23.00 *(978-0-8368-9222-2(4))* Stevens, Gareth Publishing LLLP.
Reynolds, Toby & Calver, Paul. Rocks, Crystals, & Gems. 2016. (Visual Explorers Ser.). (ENG., Illus.). 32p. (J). (gr. 3-7). pap. 6.99 *(978-1-4380-0828-8(7))* Barron's Educational Series, Inc.
Spilsbury, Louise. Cristales. 2011. (Las Rocas Ser.). (SPA.). 32p. (gr. 3-5). pap. 8.29 *(978-1-4329-5657-8(4))*; lib. bdg. 33.32 *(978-1-4329-5649-3(3))* Heinemann-Raintree. (Heinemann InfoSearch).
Spilsbury, Louise & Spilsbury, Richard. Crystals, 1 vol. 2011. (Let's Rock Ser.). (ENG.). 32p. (gr. 3-6). pap. 8.29 *(978-1-4329-4692-0(7))*, Heinemann InfoSearch) Heinemann-Raintree.
Symes, R. F. Crystal & Gem. 2014. (DK Eyewitness Bks.). (ENG., Illus.). 72p. (J). (gr. 3-7). pap. 9.99 *(978-1-4654-2052-7(5))*, DK Children) Dorling Kindersley Publishing, Inc.
Symes, R. F. & Harding, Robert. Crystal & Gem: Eyewitness Books. Keates, Colin, photos by. 2004. (Illus.). 63p. (J). (gr. 4-8). reprint ed. 19.00 *(978-0-7567-7687-9(2))* DIANE Publishing Co.

CRYSTALS

see Crystallography

CUB SCOUTS

see Boy Scouts

CUBA

Campbell, Kumari. Cuba in Pictures. 2nd ed. 2005. (Visual Geography Ser.). (Illus.). 80p. (YA). (gr. 7-12). 27.93 *(978-0-8225-1167-0(3))* Lerner Publishing Group.
Catel, Patrick & Collins, Frank. Cuba, 1 vol. 2011. (Countries Around the World Ser.). (ENG.). 48p. (gr. 3-6). 33.32 *(978-1-4329-5199-3(8))*, NA-h) Heinemann-Raintree.
Cavallo, Anna. Cuba. 2010. pap. 51.02 *(978-0-7613-6973-8(2))* Lerner Publishing Group.
Dunn, John M. Life in Castro's Cuba. 2004. (Way People Live Ser.). (ENG., Illus.). 112p. (J). (gr. 7-10). 30.85 *(978-1-59018-464-6(5))* Cengage Gale.
Harkrader, Lisa. Cuba: A MyReportLinks.com Book. 2004. (Top Ten Countries of Recent Immigrants Ser.). (Illus.). 48p. (J). lib. bdg. 25.26 *(978-0-7660-5178-2(1))*, MyReportLinks.com Bks.) Enslow Pubs., Inc.
Hughes, Christopher. Cuba. 2003. (Nations in Conflict Ser.). 48p. (J). 26.19 *(978-1-56711-511-6(X))*, Blackbirch Pr., Inc.) Cengage Gale.
Hughes, Susan & Fast, April. Cuba: The Culture. 2004. (Lands, Peoples & Cultures Ser.). (ENG., Illus.). 32p. (J). lib. bdg. *(978-0-7787-9326-7(5))* Crabtree Publishing Co.
—Cuba - The Culture. 2004. (Lands, Peoples & Cultures Ser.). (ENG., Illus.). 32p. (J). pap. *(978-0-7787-9694-7(9))* Crabtree Publishing Co.
—Cuba - The Land. 2004. (Lands, Peoples & Cultures Ser.). (ENG., Illus.). 32p. (J). lib. bdg. *(978-0-7787-9324-3(9))* Crabtree Publishing Co.
Kent, Deborah. Cuba. 2015. (ENG., Illus.). 144p. (J). lib. bdg. *(978-0-531-21694-1(2))*, Orchard Bks.) Scholastic, Inc.
Lazaro, Georgina. Jose. Sanchez, Maria, illus. 2007. (J). 14.99 *(978-1-933032-08-5(1))* Lectorum Pubns., Inc.
Marx, Trish. Reaching for the Sun: Kids in Cuba. 2003. (Single Titles Ser.: 6). (ENG., Illus.). 48p. (gr. 2-4). lib. bdg. 26.60 *(978-0-7613-2261-0(2))*, Millbrook Pr.) Lerner Publishing Group.
Pohl, Kathleen. Descubramos Cuba. 2008. (Descubramos países del mundo (Looking at Countries) Ser.). (SPA., Illus.). 32p. (gr. 1-5). pap. 10.50 *(978-0-8368-9061-7(2))*, Gareth Stevens Learning Library) Stevens, Gareth Publishing LLLP.
—Looking at Cuba. 2008. (Looking at Countries Ser.). (Illus.). 32p. (J). (gr. 1-5). lib. bdg. 26.00 *(978-0-8368-9058-7(2))*, Gareth Stevens Learning Library) Stevens, Gareth Publishing LLLP.
Pohl, Kathleen & Nations, Susan. Descubramos Cuba. 2008. (Descubramos países del mundo (Looking at Countries) Ser.). (SPA.). 32p. (J). (gr. 1-5). lib. bdg. 26.00 *(978-0-8368-9060-0(4))*, Gareth Stevens Learning Library) Stevens, Gareth Publishing LLLP.
Wright, David K. Cuba. 2008. (Enchantment of the World Ser.). (ENG.). 144p. (J). (gr. 5-9). 40.00 *(978-0-531-12096-5(1))* Scholastic Library Publishing.
Zimmerman, W. Frederick. Cool Maps of Cub: An Atlas of History, Population, Resources Before & after Fidel Castro. 2007. 32p. per. 17.36 *(978-1-934840-15-3(7))* Nimble Bks. LLC.
Zocchi, Judy. In Cuba/en Cuba. Brodie, Neale, illus. 2005. (Global Adventures II Ser.).Tr. of En Cuba. (ENG & SPA.). 32p. (J). per. 10.95 *(978-1-59646-163-5(2))* Dingles & Co.

CUBA—FICTION

Aldridge, Janet. The Meadow-Brook Girls by the Sea, or Th. 2006. pap. *(978-1-4065-0693-8(1))* Dodo Pr.
Bowen, Carl. Black Anchor, 1 vol. Tortosa, Wilson & Fuentes, Benny, illus. 2013. (Shadow Squadron Ser.). (ENG.). 112p. (gr. 4-8). lib. bdg. 26.65 *(978-1-4342-4605-9(1))* Stone Arch Bks.
Colon, Edie. Good-Bye, Havana! Hola, New York! Colón, Raúl, illus. 2011. (ENG.). 32p. (J). (gr. -1-3). 17.99 *(978-1-4424-0674-2(7))*, Simon & Schuster/Paula Wiseman Bks.) Simon & Schuster/Paula Wiseman Bks.
Crosshill, Tom. The Cat King of Havana. 2016. 368p. (YA). (gr. 8). 17.99 *(978-0-06-242283-5(9))*, Tegen, Katherine Bks) HarperCollins Pubs.
Cuenca, Hector. La Cucarachita Martina. 2008. (SPA., Illus.). 32p. (J). (gr. -1-3). 14.99 *(978-1-933032-36-8(7))* Lectorum Pubns., Inc.
Deedy, Carmen Agra. Martina the Beautiful Cockroach: A Cuban Folktale, 1 vol. Austin, Michael, illus. 2007. (ENG.). 32p. (J). (gr. k-3). 16.95 *(978-1-56145-399-3(4))* Peachtree Pubs.
—Martina una Cucarachita Muy Linda: Un Cuento Cubano, 1 vol. Austin, Michael, illus. 2010. (SPA.). 32p. (J). pap. 8.95 *(978-1-56145-532-4(6))* Peachtree Pubs.
—Martina una Cucarachita Muy Linda: Un Cuento Cubano. De la Torre, Cristina, tr. Austin, Michael, illus. 2007. (SPA.). 32p. (J). (gr. -1-3). 17.95 *(978-1-56145-425-9(7))* Peachtree Pubs.
Engle, Margarita. All the Way to Havana. Curato, Mike, illus. 2017. (ENG.). 40p. (J). 17.99 *(978-1-62779-642-2(8))*, 9781627796422, Holt, Henry & Co. Bks. For Young Readers) Holt, Henry & Co.
—Drum Dream Girl: How One Girl's Courage Changed Music. López, Rafael, illus. 2015. (ENG.). 48p. (J). (gr. -1-3). 16.99 *(978-0-544-10229-3(0))*, HMH Books For Young Readers) Houghton Mifflin Harcourt Publishing Co.
—Forest World. 2017. (ENG., Illus.). 208p. (J). (gr. 5). 16.99 ***(978-1-4814-9057-3(5))***, Atheneum Bks. for Young Readers) Simon & Schuster Children's Publishing.
—The Lightning Dreamer: Cuba's Greatest Abolitionist. 2013. (ENG.). 192p. (YA). (gr. 7). 16.99 *(978-0-547-80743-0(0))* Houghton Mifflin Harcourt Publishing Co.
—Lion Island: Chinese Cuba's Warrior of Words. 2017. (ENG.). 192p. (J). (gr. 5). pap. 7.99 *(978-1-4814-6113-9(3))* Simon & Schuster Children's Publishing.
—Lion Island: Cuba's Warrior of Words. 2016. (ENG., Illus.). 176p. (J). (gr. 5). 16.99 *(978-1-4814-6112-2(5))*, Atheneum Bks. for Young Readers) Simon & Schuster Children's Publishing.
—Tropical Secrets: Holocaust Refugees in Cuba. 2009. (ENG.). 208p. (YA). (gr. 7-12). 23.99 *(978-0-8050-8936-3(5))*, 9780805089363, Holt, Henry & Co. Bks. For Young Readers) Holt, Henry & Co.
—The Wild Book. 2014. (ENG., Illus.). 144p. (J). (gr. 5-7). pap. 7.99 *(978-0-544-02275-1(0))* Houghton Mifflin Harcourt Publishing Co.
Figueredo, D. H. The Road to Santiago. Torrecilla, Pablo, illus. 2003. (ENG.). 32p. (J). 16.95 *(978-1-58430-059-5(0))* Lee & Low Bks., Inc.
Figueredo, Dan & Torrecilla, Pablo. The Road to Santiago. 2016. (ENG., Illus.). 32p. (J). (gr. 1-4). 9.95 ***(978-1-62014-317-9(8))*** Lee & Low Bks., Inc.
Flores-Galbis, Enrique. 90 Miles to Havana. 2010. (ENG.). 304p. (J). (gr. 4-7). 18.99 *(978-1-59643-168-3(7))*, 9781596431683) Roaring Brook Pr.
—90 Miles to Havana. 2012. (ENG.). 304p. (J). (gr. 4-7). pap. 7.99 *(978-1-250-00559-5(0))*, 9781250005595) Square Fish.
Garcia, Cristina. The Dog Who Loved the Moon. Serra, Sebastia, illus. 2011. (ENG.). 32p. (J). (gr. -1-3). 16.99 *(978-1-4424-3089-1(3))*, Atheneum Bks. for Young Readers) Simon & Schuster Children's Publishing.
Gonzalez, Christina Diaz. The Red Umbrella. 2011. (ENG.). 304p. (J). (gr. 3-7). 7.99 *(978-0-375-85489-7(4))*, Yearling) Random Hse. Children's Bks.
Hayes, Joe. Baila, Nana, Baila: Cuban Folktales in English & Spanish. Trenard Sayago, Mauricio, illus. 2008.Tr. of Dance, Nana, Dance. (SPA & ENG.). 96p. (J). (gr. 3-6). 20.95 *(978-1-933693-17-0(7))* Cinco Puntos Pr.
Lacamara, Laura. Dalia's Wondrous Hair / el Maravilloso Cabello de Dalia. Baeza Ventura, Gabriela, tr. from SPA. Lacamara, Laura, illus. 2014. (ENG & SPA., Illus.). (J). 17.95 *(978-1-55885-789-6(3))*, Piñata Books) Arte Publico Pr.
Lantigua, Lizette M. Mission Libertad. 2012. (ENG.). 192p. (YA). pap. 9.95 *(978-0-8198-4900-7(6))* Pauline Bks. & Media.
Martinez, Raul. Rooly & Flora's Reunion: A Story of Cuba. Prieto, Antonio, illus. 2006. (ENG.). 32p. (J). pap. 6.95 *(978-1-59249-658-7(X))* Soundprints.
Rodriguez, Lourdes. Mandy, Princess of la la Land: The Green Monster. 2013. 52p. pap. 24.99 *(978-1-4817-0077-1(4))* AuthorHouse.
Rosengren, Gayle. Cold War on Maplewood Street. 2015. (ENG.). 192p. (J). (gr. 3-7). 16.99 *(978-0-399-17183-3(5))*, G.P. Putnam's Sons Books for Young Readers) Penguin Publishing Group.
Sacre, Antonio. A Mango in the Hand: A Story Told Through Proverbs. Serra, Sebastia, illus. 2011. (ENG.). 32p. (J). (gr. k-2). 16.95 *(978-0-8109-9734-9(7))*, Abrams Bks. for Young Readers) Abrams, Inc.
Sánchez-Korrol, Virginia. Feminist & Abolitionist: The Story of Emilia Casanova. 2013. (ENG.). 248p. (YA). pap. 12.95 *(978-1-55885-765-0(6))*, Piñata Books) Arte Publico Pr.
Shorack, Todd. Hero in the Mirror. 2010. 176p. pap. 13.95 *(978-1-60844-506-6(2))* Dog Ear Publishing, LLC.
The Troubles of Johnny Cannon. 2014. (ENG., Illus.). 304p. (J). (gr. 3-7). 16.99 *(978-1-4814-0003-9(7))*, Simon & Schuster Bks. For Young Readers) Simon & Schuster Bks. For Young Readers.
Volponi, Paul & Wells, Rosemary. Game Seven. 2015. (ENG.). 256p. (YA). (gr. 7). bds. 17.99 *(978-0-670-78518-6(0))*, Viking Books for Young Readers) Penguin Young Readers Group.
Wells, Rosemary, et al. My Havana: Memories of a Cuban Boyhood. Ferguson, Peter, illus. 2010. (ENG.). 72p. (J). (gr. 2-5). 17.99 *(978-0-7636-4305-8(X))* Candlewick Pr.

CUBA—HISTORY

Anderson, Dale. Cuban Americans. 2006. (World Almanac Library of American Immigration). (Illus.). 48p. (gr. 5-12). pap. 14.05 *(978-0-8368-7322-1(X))*; lib. bdg. 31.00 *(978-0-8368-7309-2(2))* Stevens, Gareth Publishing LLLP. (Gareth Stevens Secondary Library).
Berlatsky, Noah. Cuba. 2013. (Opposing Viewpoints Ser.). (ENG., Illus.). 224p. (gr. 10-12). pap. 33.80 *(978-0-7377-6309-6(4))*; lib. bdg. 48.80 *(978-0-7377-6308-9(6))* Cengage Gale. (Greenhaven Pr., Inc.).
Bodden, Valerie. Che Guevara: Political Activist & Revolutionary, 1 vol. 2011. (Essential Lives Set 6 Ser.). (ENG., Illus.). 112p. (J). (gr. 6-12). lib. bdg. 35.64 *(978-1-61714-780-7(X))*, Essential Library) ABDO Publishing Co.
Bryan, Bethany. The Bay of Pigs & the Cuban Missile Crisis. 2017. (J). ***(978-1-5026-2863-3(5))*** Cavendish Square Publishing.
Burns, Kylie. Cultural Traditions in Cuba. 2017. 32p. (J). ***(978-0-7787-8094-6(5))*** Crabtree Publishing Co.
Butts, Ellen R. & Schwartz, Joyce R. Fidel Castro. 2005. (Biography Ser.). (Illus.). 112p. (J). 29.27 *(978-0-8225-2371-0(X))*, Lerner Pubns.); (gr. 6-18). pap. 7.95 *(978-0-8225-9524-3(9))* Lerner Publishing Group.
Cantor, Rachel Anne. Cuba. 2016. (Countries We Come From Ser.). (ENG., Illus.). 32p. (J). (gr. -1-3). 19.95 *(978-1-943553-35-8(1))* Bearport Publishing Co., Inc.
Catel, Patrick & Collins, Frank. Cuba, 1 vol. 2011. (Countries Around the World Ser.). (ENG.). 48p. (gr. 3-6). pap. 9.95 *(978-1-4329-5224-2(2))*, NA-h) Heinemann-Raintree.
Cavallo, Anna. Cuba. 2010. (Country Explorers Ser.). (ENG.). 48p. (gr. 2-4). pap. 9.95 *(978-0-7613-6033-9(6))*; lib. bdg. 29.27 *(978-0-7613-5317-1(8))* Lerner Publishing Group.
Conley, Kate. Cuba. 2015. (One World, Many Countries Ser.). (ENG.). 32p. (J). (gr. 1-4). 28.50 *(978-1-63407-041-6(0))*, 208890) Child's World, Inc., The.
Crompton, Samuel. Che Guevara: The Making of a Revolutionary. 2009. (Life Portraits Ser.). (Illus.). 112p. (J). (gr. 7-12). lib. bdg. 36.00 *(978-1-4339-0053-2(X))* Stevens, Gareth Publishing LLLP.
Cuba. 2nd rev. ed. 2010. (Modern World Nations Ser.). (Illus.). 128p. (gr. 6-12). 35.00 *(978-1-60413-622-7(7))*, Chelsea Hse.) Facts On File, Inc.
Engfer, Lee. Cubans in America. 2005. (In America Ser.). (ENG., Illus.). 80p. (gr. 5-8). lib. bdg. 27.93 *(978-0-8225-4870-6(4))*, Lerner Pubns.) Lerner Publishing Group.
Ernesto Che Guevara. 2010. (Great Hispanic Heritage Ser.). (Illus.). 128p. (gr. 6-12). 35.00 *(978-1-60413-732-3(0))*, Chelsea Hse.) Facts On File, Inc.
Fabiny, Sarah. Who Was Fidel Castro? Hammond, Ted, illus. 2017. (Who Was? Ser.). (ENG.). 112p. (J). (gr. 3-7). 5.99 ***(978-0-451-53333-3(X))***; lib. bdg. 15.99 ***(978-0-451-53335-7(6))*** Penguin Young Readers Group. (Penguin Workshop).
Flor Ada, Alma. Island Treasures: Growing up in Cuba: Includes Where the Flame Trees Bloom, under the Royal Palms, & Five Brand New Stories. Martorell, Antonio &

C
D

Rodriguez, Edel, illus. 2015. (ENG.). 240p. (J). (gr. 3-7). pap. 7.99 *(978-1-4814-2900-9(0))* Simon & Schuster Children's Publishing.

—Where the Flame Trees Bloom. 2007. (ENG.). 80p. (J). (gr. 4-6). pap. 9.95 *(978-1-4169-6840-5(7)*, Simon & Schuster/Paula Wiseman Bks.) Simon & Schuster/Paula Wiseman Bks.

Francis, Amy. The U. S. Policy on Cuba. 2008. (At Issue Ser.). (ENG., Illus.). 128p. (gr. 10-12). 39.40 *(978-0-7377-4108-7(2))*; pap. 27.80 *(978-0-7377-4109-4(0))* Cengage Gale. (Greenhaven Pr., Inc.).

Gitlin, Martin. U. S. Sanctions on Cuba, 1 vol. 2010. (Essential Viewpoints Set 5 Ser.). (ENG., Illus.). 112p. (J). (gr. 6-12). lib. bdg. 35.64 *(978-1-61613-525-6(5)*, 1315619, Essential Library) ABDO Publishing Co.

Green, Jen. National Geographic Countries of the World - Cuba. 2007. (National Geographic Countries of the World Ser.). (ENG., Illus.). 64p. (J). (gr. 5-9). lib. bdg. 27.90 *(978-1-4263-0057-8(3)*, National Geographic Children's Bks.) National Geographic Society.

Gregory, Joy. Cuba. 2016. (Illus.). 32p. (J). *(978-1-4896-4605-7(1))* Weigl Pubs., Inc.

Hernandez, Roger. Cuba, Vol. 11. Henderson, James D., ed. 2015. (Discovering the Caribbean: History, Politics, & Culture Ser.). (Illus.). 64p. (J). (gr. 7). lib. bdg. 22.95 *(978-1-4222-3310-8(3))* Mason Crest.

Hernández, Roger E. Cuba. (Caribbean Today Ser.). 64p. (YA). 2010. (Illus.). (gr. 9-12). 21.95 *(978-1-4222-0623-2(8))* 2006. (gr. 7-18). pap. 9.95 *(978-1-4222-0690-4(4))* Mason Crest.

—Cuban Immigration. 2005. (Changing Face of North America Ser.). (Illus.). 112p. (YA). lib. bdg. 24.95 *(978-1-59084-681-0(8))* Mason Crest.

Hinman, Bonnie. The Battle of San Juan Hill: Famous Battle of the Spanish-American War. 2017. (Major Battles in US History (hardcover) Ser.). (ENG., Illus.). 32p. (J). (gr. 4-7). lib. bdg. 28.50 ***(978-1-63517-022-1(2)**,* Focus Readers) North Star Editions.

Hughes, Susan & Fast, April. Cuba: The People. 2004. (Lands, Peoples & Cultures Ser.). (ENG., Illus.). 32p. (J). lib. bdg. *(978-0-7787-9325-0(7))* Crabtree Publishing Co.

Immell, Myra, ed. The Cuban Revolution. 2013. (Perspectives on Modern World History Ser.). (ENG., Illus.). 224p. (J). (gr. 10-12). lib. bdg. 42.45 *(978-0-7377-6366-9(3)*, Greenhaven Pr., Inc.) Cengage Gale.

Jeffrey, Gary & Riley, Terry, illus. The Cuban Missile Crisis. 2013. (ENG.). 48p. (J). *(978-0-7787-1233-6(8))*; pap. *(978-0-7787-1237-4(0))* Crabtree Publishing Co.

Kallen, Stuart A. Che Guevara: You Win or You Die. 2012. (Single Titles Ser.). (ENG., Illus.). 88p. (gr. 6-12). lib. bdg. 33.27 *(978-0-8225-9035-4(2))* Lerner Publishing Group.

Levy, Patricia, et al. Cuba. 2016. (ENG., Illus.). 144p. (J). 47.07 *(978-1-5026-0800-0(6))* Cavendish Square Publishing.

Markel, Rita J. Fidel Castro's Cuba. 2007. (Dictatorships Ser.). (ENG., Illus.). 160p. (J). (gr. 9-12). lib. bdg. 38.60 *(978-0-8225-7284-8(2))* Lerner Publishing Group.

Marsico, Katie. Fidel Castro: Cuban President & Revolutionary, 1 vol. 2009. (Essential Lives Set 3 Ser.). (ENG., Illus.). 112p. (J). (gr. 6-12). lib. bdg. 35.64 *(978-1-60453-522-8(9))* ABDO Publishing Co.

Marti, Jose. Jose Marti: Cuatro cuentos Infantiles. Martinez, Enrique & Graullera, Fabiola, illus. (SPA.). 28p. (J). (gr. 3-5). 9.95 *(978-970-29-0522-6(2))* Santillana, Editorial, S.A. de C.V. MEX. Dist: Santillana USA Publishing Co., Inc.

Mason, Paul. Cuba. 2009. (Global Hotspots Ser.). 32p. (gr. 5-18). lib. bdg. 18.56 *(978-0-7614-4760-3(1))* Marshall Cavendish Corp.

McNeese, Tim. Remember the Maine! The Spanish-American War Begins. 2004. (First Battles Ser.). (Illus.). 112p. (YA). (gr. 6-12). 23.95 *(978-1-883846-79-4(X)*, First Biographies) Reynolds, Morgan Inc.

Miller, Calvin Craig. Che Guevara: In Search of Revolution. 2006. (World Leaders Ser.). (Illus.). 192p. (J). (gr. 6-12). lib. bdg. 26.95 *(978-1-931798-93-8(1))* Reynolds, Morgan Inc.

Moon, Walt K. Let's Explore Cuba. 2017. (Bumba Books (tm) — Let's Explore Countries Ser.). (ENG.). 24p. (J). (gr. -1-1). 12.99 ***(978-1-5124-3732-4(8)**,* Lerner Pubns.); 38.65 ***(978-1-5124-3731-7(X)**,* Lerner Pubns.); 38.65 ***(978-1-5124-3016-5(1)**,* Lerner Pubns.); (Illus.). 25.32 *(978-1-5124-3007-3(2))* Lerner Publishing Group.

Murray, Julie. Cuba, 1 vol. 2013. (Explore the Countries Ser.). (ENG.). 40p. (J). (gr. 2-5). lib. bdg. 29.93 *(978-1-61783-808-8(X)*, Big Buddy Bks.) ABDO Publishing Co.

Naden, Corinne J. & Blue, Rose. Fidel Castro & the Cuban Revolution. 2006. (World Leaders Ser.). (Illus.). 144p. (J). (gr. 3-7). lib. bdg. 27.95 *(978-1-59935-029-5(7))* Reynolds, Morgan Inc.

Pohl, Kathleen. Descubramos Cuba. 2008. (Looking at Countries Ser.). (Illus.). 32p. (gr. 1-5). pap. 10.50 *(978-0-8368-9059-4(0)*, Gareth Stevens Learning Library) Stevens, Gareth Publishing LLLP.

Prentzas, G. S. The Cuban Revolution. 2011. (Milestones in Modern World History Ser.). (Illus.). 144p. (J). (gr. 9). 35.00 *(978-1-60413-921-1(8)*, Chelsea Hse.) Facts On File, Inc.

Roque-Velasco, Ismael. Cuba for Kids: Illustrated History Book/Libro de Historia Ilustrado. Montes de Oca, Gonzalo, illus. (SPA & ENG.). (J). (gr. 3-5). 16.00 net. *(978-0-9706319-0-9(1))* Roque-Velasco, Dr. Ismael.

Sexton, Colleen & Simmons, Walter. Cuba. 2010. (Exploring Countries Ser.). (ENG., Illus.). 32p. (J). (gr. 3-7). lib. bdg. 26.95 *(978-1-60014-477-6(2)*, Blastoff! Readers) Bellwether Media.

Sheehan, Sean & Jermyn, Leslie. Cuba. 2nd rev. ed. 2005. (Cultures of the World Ser.). (Illus.). 144p. (gr. 6-10). lib. bdg. 42.79 *(978-0-7614-1965-5(9)*, Benchmark Bks.) Marshall Cavendish Corp.

Sheen, Barbara. Cuba. 2010. (Taste of Culture Ser.). (ENG., Illus.). 64p. (J). 30.45 *(978-0-7377-5113-0(4)*, Kidhaven) Cengage Gale.

Smith-Llera, Danielle. Che Guevara's Face: How a Cuban Photographer's Image Became a Cultural Icon. 2016. (Captured World History Ser.). (ENG., Illus.). 64p. (gr. 5-7). lib. bdg. 34.65 *(978-0-7565-5440-8(3)*, CPB Grades 4-8) Compass Point Bks.

Tracy, Kathleen. We Visit Cuba. 2010. (Your Land & My Land Ser.). (Illus.). 64p. (J). (gr. 3-6). lib. bdg. 33.95 *(978-1-58415-890-5(5))* Mitchell Lane Pubs., Inc.

Ziff, John. Arts & Literature of Cuba. 2017. (Exploring Cuba Ser.: Vol. 6). (ENG.). (YA). (gr. 7-12). 24.95 ***(978-1-4222-3809-7(1))*** Mason Crest.

—Cuba: Facts & Figures. 2017. (Exploring Cuba Ser.: Vol. 6). (ENG.). (YA). (gr. 7-12). 24.95 ***(978-1-4222-3810-3(5))*** Mason Crest.

—Cuba under the Castros. 2017. (Exploring Cuba Ser.: Vol. 6). (ENG.). (YA). (gr. 7-12). 24.95 ***(978-1-4222-3811-0(3))*** Mason Crest.

—Cuban Music, Dance, & Celebrations. 2017. (Exploring Cuba Ser.: Vol. 6). (ENG.). (YA). (gr. 7-12). 24.95 ***(978-1-4222-3812-7(1))*** Mason Crest.

—The Culture & People of Cuba. 2017. (Exploring Cuba Ser.: Vol. 6). (ENG.). (YA). (gr. 7-12). 24.95 ***(978-1-4222-3813-4(X))*** Mason Crest.

—The Opening of Cuba, 2008-Present. 2017. (Exploring Cuba Ser.: Vol. 6). (ENG.). (YA). (gr. 7-12). 24.95 ***(978-1-4222-3814-1(8))*** Mason Crest.

Zocchi, Judy. In Cuba. Brodie, Neale, illus. 2005. (Global Adventures II Ser.). 32p. (J). pap. 10.95 *(978-1-59646-160-4(8))*; lib. bdg. 21.65 *(978-1-59646-079-9(2))* Dingles & Co.

—In Cuba/en Cuba. Brodie, Neale, illus. 2005. (Global Adventures II Ser.).Tr. of En Cuba. (ENG & SPA.). 32p. (J). pap. 10.95 *(978-1-59646-162-8(4))*; lib. bdg. 21.65 *(978-1-59646-080-5(6))* Dingles & Co.

CUBAN AMERICANS

Anderson, Dale. Cuban Americans. 2006. (World Almanac Library of American Immigration). (Illus.). 48p. (gr. 5-12). pap. 14.05 *(978-0-8368-7322-1(X))*; lib. bdg. 31.00 *(978-0-8368-7309-2(2))* Stevens, Gareth Publishing LLLP. (Gareth Stevens Secondary Library).

Bryan, Nichol. Cuban Americans, 1 vol. 2004. (One Nation Set 1 Ser.). (ENG.). 32p. (gr. k-6). 27.07 *(978-1-57765-980-8(5)*, Checkerboard Library) ABDO Publishing Co.

DePietro, Frank. Cuban Americans. 2013. (Illus.). 64p. pap. *(978-1-4222-2335-2(3))*; (J). *(978-1-4222-2332-1(9))*; (J). *(978-1-4222-2315-4(9))* Mason Crest.

—Cuban Americans. Limón, José E., ed. 2012. (Hispanic Americans: Major Minority Ser.). (Illus.). 64p. (J). (gr. 4). 22.95 *(978-1-4222-2318-5(3))* Mason Crest.

Engfer, Lee. Cubans in America. 2005. (In America Ser.). (ENG., Illus.). 80p. (gr. 5-8). lib. bdg. 27.93 *(978-0-8225-4870-6(4)*, Lerner Pubns.) Lerner Publishing Group.

Engle, Margarita. Enchanted Air: Two Cultures, Two Wings: A Memoir. Rodriguez, Edel, illus. (ENG.). (YA). (gr. 7). 2016. 224p. pap. 10.99 *(978-1-4814-3523-9(X))* 2015. 208p. 18.99 *(978-1-4814-3522-2(1))* Simon & Schuster Children's Publishing.

Flor Ada, Alma. Where the Flame Trees Bloom. 2007. (ENG.). 80p. (J). (gr. 4-6). pap. 9.95 *(978-1-4169-6840-5(7)*, Simon & Schuster/Paula Wiseman Bks.) Simon & Schuster/Paula Wiseman Bks.

Hernández, Roger E. Cuban Immigration. 2005. (Changing Face of North America Ser.). (Illus.). 112p. (YA). lib. bdg. 24.95 *(978-1-59084-681-0(8))* Mason Crest.

Kent, Deborah. Cuban Refugees: Cuban Roots, American Freedoms. 2005. (Proud Heritage: the Hispanic Library). (ENG., Illus.). 40p. (J). (gr. 3-6). 29.93 *(978-1-59296-382-9(X)*, 200004) Child's World, Inc., The.

Marcovitz, Hal. Cuban Americans. (Successful Americans Ser.). 64p. (YA). 2009. (gr. 9-12). 22.95 *(978-1-4222-0523-5(1))* 2007. (gr. 7-18). pap. 9.95 *(978-1-4222-0856-4(7))* Mason Crest.

Moreno, Barry. The Cuban Americans. (Major American Immigration Ser.). (YA). 2010. (Illus.). 64p. (gr. 9-12). 22.95 *(978-1-4222-0606-5(8))* 2007. pap. 9.95 *(978-1-4222-0673-7(4))* Mason Crest.

National Geographic Learning. From Cuba to the United States. 2009. (Inside the USA Ser.). (ENG., Illus.). 16p. (C). pap. 13.95 *(978-0-7362-7056-4(6))* CENGAGE Learning.

Parker-Rock, Michelle. Alma Flor Ada: An Author Kids Love. 2008. (Authors Kids Love Ser.). (Illus.). 48p. (J). (gr. 3-4). lib. bdg. 25.27 *(978-0-7660-2760-2(0)*, Enslow Elementary) Enslow Pubs., Inc.

CUBAN AMERICANS—FICTION

Cartaya, Pablo. The Epic Fail of Arturo Zamora. 2017. (ENG.). 256p. (J). (gr. 5). 16.99 *(978-1-101-99723-9(0)*, Viking Books for Young Readers) Penguin Young Readers Group.

Colon, Edie. Good-Bye, Havana! Hola, New York! Colón, Raúl, illus. 2011. (ENG.). 32p. (J). (gr. -1-3). 17.99 *(978-1-4424-0674-2(7)*, Simon & Schuster/Paula Wiseman Bks.) Simon & Schuster/Paula Wiseman Bks.

Corbett, Sue. Free Baseball. 2008. (ENG.). 160p. (J). (gr. 3-7). 6.99 *(978-0-14-241080-6(2)*, Puffin Books) Penguin Young Readers Group.

Dole, Mayra L. Drum, Chavi, Drum! Tonel, illus. 2013.Tr. of ¡Toca, Chavi, Toca! (ENG & SPA.). 32p. (J). pap. 9.95 *(978-0-89239-302-2(5)*, Children's Book Press) Lee & Low Bks., Inc.

—Toca, Chavi, Toca! Tonel, illus. 2003.Tr. of Drum, Chavi, Drum! (ENG & SPA.). 32p. (J). 16.95 *(978-0-89239-186-8(3))* Lee & Low Bks., Inc.

Dole, Mayra Lazara. Down to the Bone. 2008. 384p. (J). (gr. 9). lib. bdg. 17.89 *(978-0-06-084311-3(X)*, HarperTeen) HarperCollins Pubs.

Gil, Lydia. Letters from Heaven. 2014.Tr. of Cartas Del Cielo. (ENG & SPA.). 128p. (J). pap. 9.95 *(978-1-55885-798-8(2)*, Piñata Books) Arte Publico Pr.

Hijuelos, Óscar. Dark Dude. 2009. (ENG., Illus.). 464p. (YA). (gr. 8-18). pap. 12.99 *(978-1-4169-4945-9(3)*, Atheneum Bks. for Young Readers) Simon & Schuster Children's Publishing.

Hijuelos, Óscar & Óscar, Hijuelos. Dark Dude. Roja, Alberto Jimenenz, tr. 2010. (SPA.). 430p. (YA). (gr. 9-18). 19.99 *(978-84-441-4316-3(2))* Everest Editora ESP. Dist: Lectorum Pubns., Inc.

Milanes, Janelle. The Victoria in My Head. 2017. (ENG., Illus.). 400p. (YA). (gr. 7). 17.99 ***(978-1-4814-8089-5(8)**,* Simon Pulse) Simon Pulse.

Osa, Nancy. Cuba 15. 2011. 10.54 *(978-0-7848-3376-6(1)*, Everbind) Marco Bk. Co.

Sacre, Antonio. La Noche Buena: A Christmas Story. Dominguez, Angela, illus. 2010. (ENG.). 32p. (J). (gr. k-2). 17.95 *(978-0-8109-8967-2(0)*, Abrams Bks. for Young Readers) Abrams, Inc.

Volponi, Paul. Game Seven. 2016. lib. bdg. 20.85 *(978-0-606-38392-9(1))* Turtleback Bks.

Volponi, Paul & Wells, Rosemary. Game Seven. 2015. (ENG.). 256p. (YA). (gr. 7). bds. 17.99 *(978-0-670-78518-6(0)*, Viking Books for Young Readers) Penguin Young Readers Group.

CUBAN MISSILE CRISIS, 1962

Bryan, Bethany. The Bay of Pigs & the Cuban Missile Crisis. 2017. (J). ***(978-1-5026-2863-3(5))*** Cavendish Square Publishing.

Edwards, Sue Bradford. 12 Incredible Facts about the Cuban Missile Crisis. 2015. (Turning Points in US History Ser.). (ENG., Illus.). 32p. (J). (gr. 3-5). *(978-1-63235-127-2(7)*, 12-Story Library) Pr. Room Editions LLC.

Hanes, Sharon M., et al. Cold War: Almanac, 2 vols. 2003. (U-X-L Cold War Reference Library). (Illus.). (J). *(978-0-7876-9087-8(2))*; (ENG., 376p. lib. bdg. 191.00 *(978-0-7876-9089-2(9))* Cengage Gale. (UXL).

Hyde, Natalie. The Cold War & the Cuban Missile Crisis. 2016. (ENG., Illus.). 48p. (J). *(978-0-7787-2570-1(7))* Crabtree Publishing Co.

Jeffrey, Gary & Riley, Terry, illus. The Cuban Missile Crisis. 2013. (ENG.). 48p. (J). *(978-0-7787-1233-6(8))*; pap. *(978-0-7787-1237-4(0))* Crabtree Publishing Co.

Roxburgh, Ellis. John F. Kennedy vs. Nikita Khrushchev. 2015. (History's Greatest Rivals Ser.). (ENG., Illus.). 48p. (J). (gr. 6-8). lib. bdg. 31.95 *(978-1-4824-2221-4(2))* Stevens, Gareth Publishing LLLP.

Samuels, Charlie. The Cuban Missile Crisis, Vol. 1. 2014. (Turning Points in US Military History Ser.). (ENG.). 48p. (J). (gr. 5-6). pap. 14.05 *(978-1-4824-0430-2(3))* Stevens, Gareth Publishing LLLP.

Schier, Helga. The Cuban Missile Crisis, 1 vol. 2008. (Essential Events Set 2 Ser.). (ENG., Illus.). 112p. (J). (gr. 6-12). lib. bdg. 35.64 *(978-1-60453-046-9(4))* ABDO Publishing Co.

Senker, Cath. Kennedy & the Cuban Missile Crisis: Days of Decision, 1 vol. 2013. (Days of Decision Ser.). (ENG.). 64p. (gr. 7-8). 35.99 *(978-1-4329-7637-8(0))* Heinemann-Raintree.

Stein, R. Conrad. Cuban Missile Crisis: In the Shadow of Nuclear War. 2008. (America's Living History Ser.). (Illus.). 128p. (J). (gr. 5-9). lib. bdg. 33.27 *(978-0-7660-2905-7(0))* Enslow Pubs., Inc.

Wagner, Heather Lehr. The Cuban Missile Crisis: Cold War Confrontation. 2nd rev. ed. 2011. (Milestones in American History Ser.). (Illus.). 128p. (gr. 6-12). 35.00 *(978-1-60413-762-0(2)*, Chelsea Hse.) Facts On File, Inc.

Whiting, Jim. The Cuban Missile Crisis: The Cold War Goes Hot. 2005. (Monumental Milestones Ser.). (Illus.). 48p. (YA). (gr. 4-7). lib. bdg. 29.95 *(978-1-58415-404-4(7))* Mitchell Lane Pubs., Inc.

CUBANS—UNITED STATES—FICTION

Bernardo, Anilu. Quedando Bien. Sanmiguel, Rosario, tr. from ENG. 2006. (SPA., Illus.). 236p. (J). (gr. 6). per. 9.95 *(978-1-55885-474-1(6)*, Piñata Books) Arte Publico Pr.

Lantigua, Lizette M. Mission Libertad. 2012. (ENG.). 192p. (YA). pap. 9.95 *(978-0-8198-4900-7(6))* Pauline Bks. & Media.

CUCKOOS

Linde, Barbara M. The Bizarre Life Cycle of a Cuckoo. 2012. (Strange Life Cycles Ser.). (Illus.). 24p. (J). (gr. 2-5). pap. 8.15 *(978-1-4339-7044-3(9))*; lib. bdg. 22.60 *(978-1-4339-7043-6(0))* Stevens, Gareth Publishing LLLP.

CUCKOOS—FICTION

Brooke, Samantha. Unikitty: A Cuckoo Adventure. 2014. lib. bdg. 13.55 *(978-0-606-36365-5(3))* Turtleback Bks.

Jasper, Elizabeth. The Golden Cuckoo. 2013. 102p. (J). pap. *(978-1-78299-195-3(6))* FeedARead.com.

Molesworth. The Cuckoo Clock. 2007. 172p. per. 12.99 *(978-1-59986-835-6(0))* Filiquarian Publishing, LLC.

Stead, Philip C. A Home for Bird. Stead, Philip C., illus. 2012. (ENG., Illus.). 32p. (J). (gr. -1-3). 17.99 *(978-1-59643-711-1(1)*, 9781596437111) Roaring Brook Pr.

CULPEPPER, DUNC (FICTITIOUS CHARACTER)—FICTION

Paulsen, Gary. Culpepper's Cannon; Dunc Gets Tweaked. unabr. ed. (Culpepper Adventures Ser.: Nos. 3-4). (gr. 3-5). lib. bdg. 16.95 *(978-1-55656-185-6(7)*, DAB 076) Dercum Audio.

CULTS AND SECTS

see Sects

CULTURAL CHANGE

see Social Change

CULTURE

see also Civilization; Education; Humanism; Learning and Scholarship; Self-Culture

Adamson, Heather. Homes in Many Cultures. 2016. (Life Around the World Ser.). (ENG.). 24p. (gr. k-1). pap. 7.29 *(978-1-5157-4238-8(5)*, Pebble Plus) Capstone Press of Coughlan Cos.

Ancient Cultures & Civilizations. 2016. (Ancient Cultures & Civilizations Ser.). 32p. (gr. 5-5). 157.50 *(978-1-4994-2247-4(4))*; pap. 60.00 *(978-1-5081-5247-7(0))* Rosen Publishing Group, Inc., The. (PowerKids Pr.).

Anemone, Robert L. Race Biology & Culture: A Reader. 2nd rev. ed. 2011. (ENG.). 166p. spiral bd. 89.25 *(978-0-7575-8887-7(5))* Kendall Hunt Publishing Co.

Benchmark Education Company, LLC Staff, compiled by. Arts & Culture: Theme Set. 2006. (J). 195.00 *(978-1-4108-7101-5(0))*; 173.00 *(978-1-4108-7117-6(7))* Benchmark Education Co.

The Big Picture. (Big Picture Ser.). (ENG.). 24p. (gr. 1-2). 2010. pap. 333.60 *(978-1-4296-5829-4(0))*Pack. 2011. pap. 667.20 *(978-1-4296-6737-1(0))* Capstone Press of Coughlan Cos. (First Facts).

Big Picture Press, Big Picture. Walk This World at Christmastime. Powell, Debbie, illus. 2016. (ENG.). 24p. (J). (gr. k-3). 17.99 *(978-0-7636-8921-6(1)*, Big Picture Press) Candlewick Pr.

The Big Picture Set: People & Culture. 2010. (Big Picture: People & Culture Ser.). (ENG.). 24p. (gr. 1-2). pap. 166.80 *(978-1-4296-5826-3(6)*, First Facts) Capstone Press of Coughlan Cos.

Boehm, Richard G., et al. World Geography & Cultures. 2007. (Illus.). 853p. (J). 98.00 *(978-0-07-874529-4(2)*, 9780078745294) Glencoe/McGraw-Hill.

Capstone Press. People & Culture. 2010. (Big Picture Ser.). (ENG.). 32p. lib. bdg. 95.96 *(978-1-4296-5928-4(9)*, First Facts) Capstone Press of Coughlan Cos.

Cave, Kathryn. W Is for World Big Book: A Round-the-World ABC. Oxfam Staff, illus. 2004. 32p. (J). pap. *(978-1-84507-026-7(7)*, Frances Lincoln) Quarto Publishing Group UK.

Challen, Paul. The Culture & Crafts of Canada. 2015. (Cultural Crafts Ser.). (ENG.). 32p. (J). (gr. 4-6). pap. 11.75 *(978-1-4994-1118-8(9)*, PowerKids Pr.) Rosen Publishing Group, Inc., The.

Colson, Mary. Chinese Culture, 1 vol. 2012. (Global Cultures Ser.). (ENG.). 48p. (gr. 4-6). pap. 9.95 *(978-1-4329-6786-4(X))*; 32.65 *(978-1-4329-6777-2(0))* Heinemann-Raintree. (NA-h).

Corrick, James A., et al. Disgusting History: The Smelliest, Dirtiest Eras of the Past 10,000 Years. 2014. (Disgusting History Ser.). (ENG.). 240p. pap. 12.95 *(978-1-4765-7745-6(5)*, Fact Finders) Capstone Press of Coughlan Cos.

Culturas Antiguas, 6 vols., Vol. 3. (Explorers. Exploradores Nonfiction Sets Ser.). (SPA.). (gr. 3-6). *(978-0-7699-0659-1(1))* Shortland Pubns. (U. S. A.) Inc.

Culture Encyclopedia, 8 vols., Set. (Illus.). 40p. (YA). (gr. 5-18). lib. bdg. *(978-1-59084-474-8(2))* Mason Crest.

Cultures of the World - Group 15, 6 bks., Set. 2nd rev. ed. Incl. Georgia. Spilling, Michael & Wong, Winnie. lib. bdg. 42.79 *(978-0-7614-3033-9(4))*; Hong Kong. Kagda, Falaq & Koh, Magdalene. lib. bdg. 42.79 *(978-0-7614-3034-6(2))*; Laos. Mansfield, Stephen & Koh, Magdalene. lib. bdg. 42.79 *(978-0-7614-3035-3(0))*; Madagascar. Heale, Jay & Latif, Zawiah Abdul. lib. bdg. 42.79 *(978-0-7614-3036-0(9))*; Tunisia. Brown, Roslind Varghese & Spilling, Michael. (Illus.). (J). lib. bdg. 42.79 *(978-0-7614-3037-7(7))*; Zambia. Holmes, Timothy & Wong, Winnie. lib. bdg. 42.79 *(978-0-7614-3039-1(3))*; 144p. (gr. 6-18). (Cultures of the World 15 Ser.). 2008. Set lib. bdg. 256.74 *(978-0-7614-3032-2(6)*, Benchmark Bks.) Marshall Cavendish Corp.

Cultures of the World - Group 23, 6 Bks. 2004. (J). 222.43 *(978-0-7614-1851-1(2))* Marshall Cavendish Corp.

Cultures of the World - Group 27, 6 bks., Set. Incl. Andorra. Augustin, Byron. (Illus.). lib. bdg. 42.79 *(978-0-7614-3122-0(5))*; Bermuda. Orr, Tamra. (Illus.). lib. bdg. 42.79 *(978-0-7614-3115-2(2))*; Brunei. Orr, Tamra. lib. bdg. 42.79 *(978-0-7614-3121-3(7))*; Greenland. King, David C. lib. bdg. 42.79 *(978-0-7614-3118-3(7))*; Mauritania. Blauer, Ettagale & Lauré, Jason. (Illus.). lib. bdg. 42.79 *(978-0-7614-3116-9(0))*; Oman. King, David C. (Illus.). lib. bdg. 42.79 *(978-0-7614-3120-6(9))*; 144p. (gr. 6-18). (Cultures of the World 27 Ser.). 2008. Set lib. bdg. 256.74 *(978-0-7614-3113-8(6)*, Benchmark Bks.) Marshall Cavendish Corp.

Diaz, Natalia & Owens, Melissa. A Ticket Around the World. Smith, Kim, illus. 2015. (ENG.). 32p. (J). (gr. 2-5). 16.95 *(978-1-77147-051-3(8)*, Owlkids) Owlkids Bks. Inc. CAN. Dist: Publishers Group West (PGW).

Discovering Cultures - Group 2, 6 vols. 2003. 288p. (YA). (gr. 2-18). lib. bdg. 158.86 *(978-0-7614-1514-5(9))* Marshall Cavendish Corp.

Dorling Kindersley Publishing Staff. Ultimate Sticker Book: Children Just Like Me. 2016. (Ultimate Sticker Bks.). (ENG.). 32p. (J). (gr. 1-4). pap. 6.99 *(978-1-4654-5395-2(4)*, DK Children) Dorling Kindersley Publishing, Inc.

Doudna, Kelly. Boys & Girls Around the World, 1 vol. 2004. (Around the World Ser.). (ENG., Illus.). 24p. (J). (gr. k-3). lib. bdg. 24.21 *(978-1-59197-564-9(6)*, SandCastle) ABDO Publishing Co.

—People Around the World, 1 vol. 2004. (Around the World Ser.). (ENG., Illus.). 24p. (J). (gr. k-3). lib. bdg. 24.21 *(978-1-59197-567-0(0)*, SandCastle) ABDO Publishing Co.

DuBois, J., et al. Cultures of the World - Group 7, 6 Bks, Set. 2nd rev. ed. 2004. (Cultures of the World 7 Ser.). (gr. 6). 256.74 *(978-0-7614-1783-5(4))* Marshall Cavendish Corp.

Dustman, Jeanne. Cultures Around the World. rev. ed. 2014. (Primary Source Readers Content & Literacy Ser.). (ENG., Illus.). 32p. (gr. 3-3). pap. 8.99 *(978-1-4333-7361-9(0))* Teacher Created Materials, Inc.

Espejo, Roman. Celebrity Culture. 2010. (Opposing Viewpoints Ser.). 176p. 42.95 *(978-0-7377-5213-7(0))*; 177p. pap. 29.45 *(978-0-7377-5214-4(9))* Cengage Gale. (Greenhaven Pr., Inc.).

Exploring World Cultures. 2015. (Exploring World Cultures Ser.). (ENG.). 32p. (J). (gr. 3-4). pap., pap., pap. 63.48 *(978-1-5026-0691-4(7))* Cavendish Square Publishing.

Gagne, Tammy & Willis, John. Migration & Settlement. 2017. (J). ***(978-1-5105-2179-7(8)**,* Berkley) Penguin Publishing Group.

Gale. Bwlng Btnks Bell Btms 2, 6 vols. 2nd ed. 2012. (Bowling, Beatniks, & Bell-Bottoms Ser.). (ENG., Illus.). 1650p. lib. bdg. 522.00 *(978-1-4144-1165-1(0)*, UXL) Cengage Gale.

Ganeri, Anita. Cultures & Customs. 2015. (Cultures & Customs Ser.). (ENG.). 32p. (gr. 3-3). 122.60 *(978-1-4109-8019-9(7)*, Raintree Perspectives) Heinemann-Raintree.

Gay, Kathlyn. Bigotry & Intolerance: The Ultimate Teen Guide. 2015. (It Happened to Me Ser.: 35). (ENG., Illus.). 182p. pap. 30.00 *(978-1-4422-5659-0(1))* Rowman & Littlefield Publishers, Inc.

George, Enzo. The Age of Exploration. 2016. (Primary Sources in World History Ser.). (ENG.). 48p. (YA). (gr. 6-6). 31.36 *(978-1-5026-1814-6(1))* Cavendish Square Publishing.

Glencoe McGraw-Hill Staff. World Geography & Cultures, Interactive Tutor Self-Assessment. 2007. (Glencoe World Geography Ser.). (ENG.). (gr. 9-12). cd-rom 107.12 *(978-0-07-878573-3(1)*, 0078785731) McGraw-Hill Higher Education.

—World Geography & Cultures, Standardized Test Practice Workbook. 2007. (Glencoe World Geography Ser.). (ENG.). (gr. 9-12). pap. 9.00 *(978-0-07-878564-1(2)*, 0078785642) McGraw-Hill Higher Education.

Gregory, Helen. Celebrations Around the World. 2011. (Wonder Readers Early Level Ser.). (ENG.). 16p. (gr. -1-1). pap. 35.94 *(978-1-4296-8075-2(X)*, Wonder Readers) Capstone Press of Coughlan Cos.

Haugen, David M. Popular Culture. 2010. (Opposing Viewpoints Ser.). (ENG.). 240p. pap. 29.45 *(978-0-7377-4981-6(4)*, Greenhaven Pr., Inc.) Cengage Gale.

Heapy, Teresa. Japanese Culture, 1 vol. 2012. (Global Cultures Ser.). (ENG., Illus.). 48p. (gr. 4-6). pap. 9.95 *(978-1-4329-6789-5(4))*; 32.65 *(978-1-4329-6780-2(0))* Heinemann-Raintree. (NA-h).

Higgins, Nadia. US Culture Through Infographics. Thompson, Bryon & Kulihin, Vic, illus. 2014. (Super Social Studies Infographics Ser.). (ENG.). 32p. (gr. 3-5). lib. bdg. 26.60 *(978-1-4677-3464-6(0)*, Lerner Pubns.) Lerner Publishing Group.

Holidays & Culture [Really Good Stuff]. 2011. (Holidays & Culture Ser.). 24p. pap. 41.70 *(978-1-4296-6087-7(2)*, First Facts) Capstone Press of Coughlan Cos.

Johnson, Cynthia & Baker, Lawrence W. Bowling, Beatniks, & Bell-Bottoms: Pop Culture of 20th- & 21st-Century America, 6 vols. 2nd ed. 2012. (Illus.). (J). *(978-1-4144-1171-2(5))*; *(978-1-4144-1170-5(7))*; *(978-1-4144-1169-9(3))*; *(978-1-4144-1168-2(5))*; *(978-1-4144-1166-8(9))*; *(978-1-4144-1167-5(7))* Cengage Gale. (UXL).

Jones, Tammy. I Like to Play Sports. 2009. (Sight Word Readers Set A Ser.). (J). 3.49 net. *(978-1-60719-135-3(0))* Newmark Learning LLC.

Kallen, Stuart A. Postmodern Art. 2008. (Eye on Art Ser.). (ENG., Illus.). 112p. (YA). (gr. 7-10). lib. bdg. 34.80 *(978-1-4205-0075-2(9)*, LML02109-242079, Lucent Bks.) Cengage Gale.

—A Travel Guide to Harlem Renaissance. 2003. (Travel Guide To Ser.). (ENG.). (J). 30.85 *(978-1-59018-358-8(4)*, Lucent Bks.) Cengage Gale.

Kalman, Bobbie. I Can Write a Book about Culture. 2012. (ENG.). 32p. (J). *(978-0-7787-7989-6(0))*; pap. *(978-0-7787-7998-8(X))* Crabtree Publishing Co.

—My Culture. 2010. (My World Ser.). (ENG.). 24p. (J). (gr. k-3). *(978-0-7787-9518-6(7))*; pap. *(978-0-7787-9543-8(8))* Crabtree Publishing Co.

—What Is Culture? 2009. (Our Multicultural World Ser.). (ENG., Illus.). 32p. (J). (gr. 1-4). pap. *(978-0-7787-4650-8(X))* Crabtree Publishing Co.

Lampkins, Antonia. Global Friends. 2009. 36p. pap. 24.95 *(978-1-61546-370-1(4))* PublishAmerica, Inc.

Lewis, Clare. Around the World, 1 vol. 2014. (Around the World Ser.). (ENG.). 24p. (gr. -1-1). 135.90 *(978-1-4846-0375-8(3)*, Acorn) Heinemann-Raintree.

MacDonald, Fiona. Design. 2004. (Culture Encyclopedia Ser.). (Illus.). 40p. (YA). (gr. 5-18). lib. bdg. 19.95 *(978-1-59084-476-2(9))* Mason Crest.

—History of Culture. 2004. (Culture Encyclopedia Ser.). (Illus.). 40p. (YA). (gr. 5-18). lib. bdg. 19.95 *(978-1-59084-477-9(7))* Mason Crest.

Mason, Antony. Art. 2004. (Culture Encyclopedia Ser.). (Illus.). 40p. (YA). (gr. 5-18). lib. bdg. 19.95 *(978-1-59084-475-5(0))* Mason Crest.

McGraw-Hill Education. World Geography & Cultures, Spanish Reading Essentials & Note-Taking Guide. 2007. (Glencoe World Geography Ser.). (ENG & SPA.). (gr. 9-12). pap. 11.68 *(978-0-07-878391-3(7)*, 0078783917) McGraw-Hill Higher Education.

McGraw-Hill Staff. World Geography & Cultures, StudentWorks Plus. 2007. (Glencoe World Geography Ser.). (ENG.). (gr. 9-12). cd-rom 168.08 *(978-0-07-878394-4(1)*, 0078783941) McGraw-Hill Higher Education.

Miller, Reagan & Richardson, Hazel. Arts & Culture in the Ancient World. 2011. (ENG., Illus.). 32p. (J). *(978-0-7787-1732-4(1))* Crabtree Publishing Co.

—Arts & Culture in the Ancient World. Crabtree Publishing Co. Staff, ed. 2011. (Life in the Ancient World Ser.: No. 1). (ENG., Illus.). 32p. (J). (gr. 5-8). pap. *(978-0-7787-1739-3(9))* Crabtree Publishing Co.

MoonRattles. Heritage Holiday Activity Guide: Chinese New Year 2007, 1 vol. 2006. (Illus.). 52p. (J). spiral bd. *(978-0-9790920-8-0(0))* MoonRattles.

Phillips, Clifton C. We Are Children of Eden. 2011. 28p. pap. 9.99 *(978-1-61286-010-7(9))* Avid Readers Publishing Group.

Pop Culture: A View from the Paparazzi, 15 vols., Set. Incl. Ashlee & Jessica Simpson. Kaminsky, Kristy & Dornboski, Brian. (gr. 3-7). lib. bdg. 22.95 *(978-1-4222-0208-1(9))*; Hilary Duff. Whiting, Jim. (gr. 3-7). lib. bdg. 22.95 *(978-1-4222-0201-2(1))*; Jake Gyllenhaal. Snyder, Gail. (gr. 3-7). lib. bdg. 22.95 *(978-1-4222-0203-6(8))*; John Legend. Magram, Clara. (gr. 4-7). lib. bdg. 22.95 *(978-1-4222-0076-6(0))*; Johnny Depp. Graziano, Jim. (gr. 3-7). lib. bdg. 22.95 *(978-1-4222-0200-5(3))*; Kelly Clarkson. Lawlor, Michelle. (gr. 3-7). lib. bdg. 22.95 *(978-1-4222-0199-2(6))*; LeBron James. Marcovitz, Hal. (gr. 3-7). lib. bdg. 22.95 *(978-1-4222-0205-0(4))*; Lindsay Lohan. Marcovitz, Hal. (gr. 3-7). lib. bdg. 22.95 *(978-1-4222-0206-7(2))*; Mandy Moore. Whiting, Jim. (gr. 3-7). lib. bdg. 22.95 *(978-1-4222-0207-4(0))*; Orlando Bloom. Mattern, Joanne. (gr. 3-7). lib. bdg. 22.95 *(978-1-4222-0198-5(8))*; Owen & Luke Wilson. Marcovitz, Hal. (gr. 3-7). lib. bdg. 22.95 *(978-1-4222-0210-4(0))*; Paris & Nicky Hilton. Berne, Emma Carlson. (gr. 3-7). lib. bdg. 22.95 *(978-1-4222-0204-3(6))*; Tiger Woods. Gallagher, Jim. (gr. 3-7). lib. bdg. 22.95 *(978-1-4222-0211-1(9))*; Will Ferrell. Clark, Travis. (gr. 3-7). lib. bdg. 22.95 *(978-1-4222-0202-9(X))*; (Illus.). 64p. (YA). 2008. 2007. Set lib. bdg. 344.25 *(978-1-4222-0197-8(X))* Mason Crest.

Ruland, Patty J. From Painted Scrolls to Anime: Literature & the Arts of Japan. 2007. (Lucent Library of Historical Eras:Twentieth-Century Japan Ser.). (ENG., Illus.). 96p. (J). (gr. 4-7). lib. bdg. 34.80 *(978-1-4205-0026-4(0)*, Lucent Bks.) Cengage Gale.

Rustad, Martha E. H. Transportation in Many Cultures. 2016. (Life Around the World Ser.). (ENG.). 24p. (gr. k-1). pap. 7.29 *(978-1-5157-4241-8(5)*, Pebble Plus) Capstone Press of Coughlan Cos.

Smith, Daniel. World Cultures Explained, 1 vol. 2015. (ENG.). 136p. (J). 38.25 *(978-1-4777-8130-2(7)*, Rosen Young Adult) Rosen Publishing Group, Inc., The.

Spangenburg, Ray & Moser, Kit. Teen Fads: Fun, Foolish, or Fatal? 2003. (Teen Issues Ser.). (Illus.). 64p. (J). (gr. 6-12). lib. bdg. 22.60 *(978-0-7660-1665-1(X))* Enslow Pubs., Inc.

Sundance/Newbridge LLC Staff. One World, Many Cultures. 2004. (Reading PowerWorks Ser.). (gr. 1-3). 37.50 *(978-0-7608-8952-7(X))*; pap. 6.10 *(978-0-7608-8953-4(8))* Sundance/Newbridge Educational Publishing.

Understanding Differences. 2010. (Understanding Differences Ser.). (ENG.). 24p. (gr. k-1). pap. 29.75 *(978-1-4296-5770-9(7)*, Pebble Bks.) Capstone Press of Coughlan Cos.

Unglick, Richard. Journey Around the World. 2016. (Playmobil Ser.). (ENG., Illus.). 64p. (J). (gr. 1-7). 19.95 *(978-1-63322-079-9(6)*, Walter Foster Jr) Quarto Publishing Group USA.

Vickers, Rebecca. Every Possession Has a History, 1 vol. 2014. (Everything Has a History Ser.). (ENG., Illus.). 64p. (gr. 7-8). pap. 10.95 *(978-1-4329-9591-1(X))*; lib. bdg. 35.99 *(978-1-4329-9586-7(3))* Heinemann-Raintree.

Williams, Brian. How We Live. 2010. (What About... Ser.). (Illus.). 40p. (J). (gr. 6-8). lib. bdg. 19.95 *(978-1-4222-1560-9(1))* Mason Crest.

—What about How We Live. 2008. 40p. pap. *(978-1-84810-069-5(8))* Miles Kelly Publishing, Ltd.

CUMBERLAND MOUNTAINS—FICTION

Murfree, Mary N. The Mystery of Witch-Face Mountain & Other Stories. 2013. (Notable American Authors Ser.). reprint ed. lthr. 79.00 *(978-0-7812-4601-9(6))* Reprint Services Corp.

CUMMINGS, E. E. (EDWARD ESTLIN), 1894-1962

Berry, S. L. E. E. Cummings. 2014. (J). *(978-1-60818-325-8(4)*, Creative Education) Creative Co., The.

—Voices in Poetry: E. E. Cummings. 2015. (Voices in Poetry Ser.). (ENG.). 48p. (J). (gr. 5-8). pap. 12.00 *(978-1-62832-053-4(2)*, Creative Paperbacks) Creative Co., The.

Burgess, Matthew. Enormous Smallness: The Story of e. e. Cummings. Di Giacomo, Kris, illus. 2015. (ENG.). 64p. (J). (gr. -1-3). 17.95 *(978-1-59270-171-0(X))* Enchanted Lion Bks., LLC.

CURIE, MARIE, 1867-1934

Ardagh, Philip. Marie Curie. 7th ed. 2003. (ENG., Illus.). 64p. (J). pap. 6.99 *(978-0-330-37571-9(7)*, Pan) Pan Macmillan GBR. Dist: Trafalgar Square Publishing.

Borzendowski, Janice. Marie Curie: Mother of Modern Physics. 2009. (Sterling Biographies(r) Ser.). (ENG., Illus.). 128p. (J). (gr. 5-18). pap. 5.95 *(978-1-4027-5318-3(7))* Sterling Publishing Co., Inc.

Cobb, Vicki & Dorling Kindersley Publishing Staff. Marie Curie. 2008. (DK Biography Ser.). (ENG., Illus.). 128p. (J). (gr. 5-12). pap. 6.99 *(978-0-7566-3831-3(3)*, DK Children) Dorling Kindersley Publishing, Inc.

Cregan, Elizabeth. 20th Century Superstar: Curie. 2017. (Time for Kids Nonfiction Readers Ser.). lib. bdg. 19.65 ***(978-0-606-40267-5(5))*** Turtleback Bks.

—20th Century Superstar: Curie (Grade 7) 2017. (TIME for KIDS(r) Nonfiction Readers Ser.). (Illus.). 32p. (gr. 7-7). pap. 8.99 ***(978-1-4258-5159-0(2))*** Teacher Created Materials, Inc.

Cregan, Elizabeth R. C. Marie Curie: Pioneering Physicist, 1 vol. 2007. (Science Readers Ser.). (ENG., Illus.). 32p. (J). (gr. 3-3). pap. 8.99 *(978-0-7439-0570-1(9))* Shell Educational Publishing.

Edison, Erin. Marie Curie, 1 vol. 2014. (Great Women in History Ser.). (ENG.). 24p. (gr. k-1). lib. bdg. 21.99 *(978-1-4765-4216-4(3)*, Pebble Bks.) Capstone Press of Coughlan Cos.

Gordon, Fernando. Marie Curie, 1 vol. 2016. (ENG., Illus.). 24p. (J). 25.65 *(978-1-68078-154-0(5))* ABDO Publishing Co.

Gormley, Beatrice. Marie Curie: Young Scientist. 2007. (Childhood of World Figures Ser.). (ENG.). 240p. (J). (gr. 3-7). pap. 11.99 *(978-1-4169-1545-4(1)*, Simon & Schuster/Paula Wiseman Bks.) Simon & Schuster/Paula Wiseman Bks.

Hardyman, Robyn. Pierre & Marie Curie. 2014. (Dynamic Duos of Science Ser.). 48p. (YA). (gr. 5-8). pap. 84.30 *(978-1-4824-1287-1(X))* Stevens, Gareth Publishing LLLP.

Hasday, Judy L. Marie Curie: Pioneer on the Frontier of Radioactivity. 2004. (Nobel Prize-Winning Scientists Ser.). (Illus.). 112p. (J). lib. bdg. 27.94 *(978-0-7660-2440-3(7))* Enslow Pubs., Inc.

Healy, Nick. Marie Curie. 2005. (Genius Ser.). (Illus.). 48p. (J). (gr. 5-9). lib. bdg. 21.95 *(978-1-58341-332-6(4)*, Creative Education) Creative Co., The.

Henderson, Harry. The Curie Family. 2012. (Trailblazers in Science & Technology Ser.). 136p. (gr. 6-12). 35.00 *(978-1-60413-675-3(8)*, Chelsea Hse.) Facts On File, Inc.

Koestler-Grack, Rachel A. Marie Curie: Scientist. 2009. (Women of Achievement Ser.). (Illus.). 136p. (gr. 6-12). 35.00 *(978-1-60413-086-7(5)*, Chelsea Hse.) Facts On File, Inc.

Krieg, Katherine. Marie Curie: Physics & Chemistry Pioneer, 1 vol. 2014. (Great Minds of Science Ser.). (ENG., Illus.). 48p. (J). (gr. 8-12). lib. bdg. 32.79 *(978-1-62403-377-3(6))* ABDO Publishing Co.

Krull, Kathleen. Marie Curie. 2009. (Giants of Science Ser.). (ENG.). 144p. (J). (gr. 3-7). pap. 7.99 *(978-0-14-241265-7(1)*, Puffin Books) Penguin Young Readers Group.

Lin, Yoming S. The Curies & Radioactivity. 2012. (Eureka! Ser.). (Illus.). 24p. (YA). (gr. 3-6). lib. bdg. 22.60 *(978-1-4488-5033-4(9))* Rosen Publishing Group, Inc., The.

Lindeen, Mary. Marie Curie: Scientist, 1 vol. Soud, illus. 2008. (Beginner Biographies Ser.). (ENG.). 32p. (gr. -1-3). 28.50 *(978-1-60270-248-6(9)*, Looking Glass Library- Nonfiction) Magic Wagon.

MacLeod, Elizabeth. Marie Curie. Mantha, John, illus. 2009. (Kids Can Read Ser.). (ENG.). 32p. (J). (gr. 1-3). 3.95 *(978-1-55453-297-1(3))*; 14.95 *(978-1-55453-296-4(5))* Kids Can Pr., Ltd. CAN. Dist: Hachette Bk. Group.

—Marie Curie: A Brilliant Life. 2004. (Snapshots: Images of People & Places in History Ser.). (ENG., Illus.). 32p. (J). (gr. 3-7). 7.95 *(978-1-55337-571-5(8))* Kids Can Pr., Ltd. CAN. Dist: Hachette Bk. Group.

Marsh, Carole. Marie Curie, Nobel Prize Winning Scientist. 2004. 12p. (gr. k-4). 2.95 *(978-0-635-02374-2(1))* Gallopade International.

Mattern, Joanne & Brandt, Keith. Marie Curie, Brave Scientist. Dugan, Karen, illus. 2005. 45p. (J). *(978-0-439-80153-9(2))* Scholastic, Inc.

McKown, Robin. Marie Curie. Rethi, Lili, illus. 2012. 128p. 40.95 *(978-1-258-23532-1(3))*; pap. 25.95 *(978-1-258-24675-4(9))* Literary Licensing, LLC.

Miller, Connie Colwell. Marie Curie & Radioactivity, 1 vol. Larson, Scott & Heike, Mark, illus. 2006. (Inventions & Discovery Ser.). (ENG.). 32p. (gr. 3-4). 30.65 *(978-0-7368-6486-2(5)*, Graphic Library) Capstone Press of Coughlan Cos.

Mortensen, Lori. Marie Curie: Prize-Winning Scientist, 1 vol. Jaekel, Susan, illus. 2008. (Biographies Ser.). (ENG.). 24p. (gr. k-3). lib. bdg. 26.65 *(978-1-4048-3731-7(0))* Picture Window Bks.

Ogilvie, Marilyn Bailey. Marie Curie: A Biography, 1 vol. 2004. (Greenwood Biographies Ser.). (Illus.). 184p. (C). 43.00 *(978-0-313-32529-8(4)*, GR2529, Greenwood) ABC-CLIO, LLC.

O'Quinn, Amy M. Marie Curie for Kids: Her Life & Scientific Discoveries, with 21 Activities & Experiments. 2016. (For Kids Ser.). (ENG.). 144p. (J). (gr. 4). pap. 16.99 *(978-1-61373-320-2(8))* Chicago Review Pr., Inc.

Orr, Tamra. Marie Curie. 2003. (World Was Never the Same Ser.). (J). pap. *(978-1-58417-263-5(0))*; lib. bdg. *(978-1-58417-262-8(2))* Lake Street Pubs.

Poynter, Margaret. Marie Curie: Genius Researcher of Radioactivity. 2015. (Genius Scientists & Their Genius Ideas Ser.). 96p. (J). (gr. 5-12). 27.94 *(978-0-7660-6580-2(4))*; pap. 10.95 *(978-0-7660-6581-9(2))* Enslow Pubs., Inc.

Rubin, Elizabeth. The Curies & Radium. Moyler, Alan, illus. 2011. 122p. 40.95 *(978-1-258-09479-9(7))* Literary Licensing, LLC.

Saddleback Educational Publishing Staff, ed. Marie Curie, 1 vol. unabr. ed. 2008. (Graphic Biographies Ser.). (ENG., Illus.). 25p. (YA). (gr. 9-12). pap. 7.95 *(978-1-59905-226-7(1))* Saddleback Educational Publishing, Inc.

Sanchez Vegara, Isabel. Marie Curie. Isa, Frau, illus. 2017. (Little People, Big Dreams Ser.). (ENG.). 32p. (J). (gr. k-3). 14.99 ***(978-1-84780-962-9(6)***, Frances Lincoln Children's Bks.) Quarto Publishing Group UK GBR. Dist: Hachette Bk. Group.

Steele, Philip. Marie Curie: La Mujer Que Cambio el Curso de la Ciencia. 2007. (World History Biographies Ser.). (Illus.). 64p. (J). (gr. -1-3). *(978-84-372-2469-5(1))* Altea, Ediciones, S.A. - Grupo Santillana.

—Marie Curie: The First Great Woman Scientist. 2006. (National Geographic World History Biographies Ser.). (ENG., Illus.). 64p. (J). (gr. 3-7). 17.95 *(978-0-7922-5387-7(6))*; lib. bdg. 27.90 *(978-0-7922-5388-4(4))* National Geographic Society. (National Geographic Children's Bks.).

—Marie Curie: The Woman Who Changed the Course of Science. 2008. (National Geographic World History Biographies Ser.). (ENG., Illus.). 64p. (J). (gr. 3-7). pap. 7.99 *(978-1-4263-0249-7(5)*, National Geographic Children's Bks.) National Geographic Society.

Stine, Megan. Who Was Marie Curie? Hammond, Ted & Harrison, Nancy, illus. 2014. (Who Was? Ser.). (ENG.). 112p. (J). (gr. 3-7). 5.99 *(978-0-448-47896-8(X)*, Grosset & Dunlap) Penguin Young Readers Group.

—Who Was Marie Curie? 2014. (Who Was... ? Ser.). lib. bdg. 16.00 *(978-0-606-35698-5(3))* Turtleback Bks.

Thrap, Claire. Marie Curie. 2015. (Against the Odds Biographies Ser.). (ENG., Illus.). 48p. (gr. 3-6). 33.32 *(978-1-4846-2467-8(X))* Heinemann-Raintree.

Tracy, Kathleen. Pierre & Marie Curie & the Discovery of Radium. 2004. (Uncharted, Unexplored, & Unexplained Ser.). (Illus.). 48p. (J). (gr. 4-8). lib. bdg. 29.95 *(978-1-58415-310-8(5))* Mitchell Lane Pubs., Inc.

Venezia, Mike. Marie Curie: Scientist Who Made Glowing Discoveries. Venezia, Mike, illus. (Getting to Know the World's Greatest Inventors & Scientists Ser.). (ENG., Illus.). 32p. (J). 2009. (gr. 3-4). pap. 6.95 *(978-0-531-22208-9(X)*, Children's Pr.) 2008. (gr. 2-5). 28.00 *(978-0-531-14977-5(3))* Scholastic Library Publishing.

Waxman, Laura Hamilton. Marie Curie. 2003. (History Maker Biographies Ser.). (ENG., Illus.). 48p. (gr. 3-6). 27.93 *(978-0-8225-0300-2(X)*, Lerner Pubns.) Lerner Publishing Group.

CURIE, PIERRE, 1859-1906

Hardyman, Robyn. Pierre & Marie Curie. 2014. (Dynamic Duos of Science Ser.). 48p. (YA). (gr. 5-8). pap. 84.30 *(978-1-4824-1287-1(X))* Stevens, Gareth Publishing LLLP.

Henderson, Harry. The Curie Family. 2012. (Trailblazers in Science & Technology Ser.). 136p. (gr. 6-12). 35.00 *(978-1-60413-675-3(8)*, Chelsea Hse.) Facts On File, Inc.

Rubin, Elizabeth. The Curies & Radium. Moyler, Alan, illus. 2011. 122p. 40.95 *(978-1-258-09479-9(7))* Literary Licensing, LLC.

Tracy, Kathleen. Pierre & Marie Curie & the Discovery of Radium. 2004. (Uncharted, Unexplored, & Unexplained Ser.). (Illus.). 48p. (J). (gr. 4-8). lib. bdg. 29.95 *(978-1-58415-310-8(5))* Mitchell Lane Pubs., Inc.

CURIOUS GEORGE (FICTITIOUS CHARACTER)—FICTION

ABDO Publishing Company Staff. Curious George, 12 titles, Set. 2008. (Curious George Ser.: 12). (ENG., Illus.). 24p. lib. bdg. 290.52 *(978-1-59961-409-0(X))* Spotlight.

Anderson, R. P. Sweet Dreams, Curious George. Obrero, Rudy, illus. 2005. (J). (gr. -1-k). pap. *(978-0-618-69493-8(5))* Houghton Mifflin Harcourt Trade & Reference Pubs.

Houghton Mifflin and Company Publishing Staff & Rey, H. A. The Family Christmas Treasury with CD & Downloadable Audio. 2013. (ENG., Illus.). 288p. (J). (gr. -1-3). 18.99 *(978-0-544-09249-5(X))* Houghton Mifflin Harcourt Publishing Co.

Houghton Mifflin Company Staff. Birthday Fun with Curious George. 2005. (J). (gr. -1-k). pap. *(978-0-618-69654-3(7))* Houghton Mifflin Harcourt Trade & Reference Pubs.

—Fire Truck Fun with Curious George. 2005. (J). (gr. -1-k). pap. *(978-0-618-70499-6(X))* Houghton Mifflin Harcourt Trade & Reference Pubs.

—Splish, Splash, Curious George. 2005. (J). (gr. -1-k). pap. *(978-0-618-70498-9(1))* Houghton Mifflin Harcourt Trade & Reference Pubs.

Houghton Mifflin Harcourt Publishing Company Staff & Rey, H. A. Start Your Engines 5-Minute Stories. 2014. (5-Minute Stories Ser.). (ENG., Illus.). 224p. (J). (gr. -1-3). 12.99 *(978-0-544-15881-8(4)*, HMH Books For Young Readers) Houghton Mifflin Harcourt Publishing Co.

Margaret. Curious George im Schokolade. 20.95 *(978-3-8157-2329-6(9))* Coppenrath, F. Verlag KG DEU. Dist: Distribooks, Inc.

—Curious George und der Lastwa. 20.95 *(978-3-8157-2327-2(2))* Coppenrath, F. Verlag KG DEU. Dist: Distribooks, Inc.

—Curious George und der Seltsa. 20.95 *(978-3-8157-2330-2(2))* Coppenrath, F. Verlag KG DEU. Dist: Distribooks, Inc.

—Curious George und die Hundelb. 20.95 *(978-3-8157-2328-9(0))* Coppenrath, F. Verlag KG DEU. Dist: Distribooks, Inc.

Moscovich, Rotem, et al. Curious George Snowy Day. 2007. (Curious George Ser.). (ENG., Illus.). 24p. (J). (gr. -1-3). 3.99 *(978-0-618-80043-8(3))* Houghton Mifflin Harcourt Publishing Co.

Perez, Monica & Houghton Mifflin Company Editors. Curious George & Me! Paprocki, Greg & Hines, Anna Grossnickle, illus. 2007. (Curious George Ser.). (ENG.). 56p. (J). (gr. -1-3). 9.95 *(978-0-618-73762-8(6))* Houghton Mifflin Harcourt Publishing Co.

Rey, H. A. Apple Harvest: Curious about Harvest Time. 2012. (Curious George TV Tie-In 8x8 Ser.). lib. bdg. 13.55 *(978-0-606-23984-4(7)*, Turtleback) Turtleback Bks.

—Awake-Asleep Cloth Book & Door Hanger. 2010. (Curious Baby Curious George Ser.). (ENG., Illus.). 4p. (J). (gr. -1 — 1). 8.99 *(978-0-547-23897-5(5))* Houghton Mifflin Harcourt Publishing Co.

—Builds a Home. 2011. (Curious George Ser.). (ENG., Illus.). 24p. (J). (gr. -1-3). 6.99 *(978-0-547-59410-1(0))* Houghton Mifflin Harcourt Publishing Co.

—Builds a Tree House. 2017. (Curious George Ser.). (SPA & ENG., Illus.). 24p. (J). (gr. -1-3). 12.99 *(978-0-544-97461-6(1)*, HMH Books For Young Readers) Houghton Mifflin Harcourt Publishing Co.

—Builds an Igloo. 2013. (Curious George Ser.). (ENG., Illus.). 24p. (J). (gr. -1-3). pap. 3.99 *(978-0-544-09666-0(5))* Houghton Mifflin Harcourt Publishing Co.

—C Is for Curious. 2014. (Curious George Ser.). (ENG., Illus.). 14p. (J). (— 1). 13.99 *(978-0-544-15911-2(X)*, HMH Books For Young Readers) Houghton Mifflin Harcourt Publishing Co.

—Car Wash. 2013. (Curious George Ser.). (ENG., Illus.). 24p. (J). (gr. -1-3). pap. 3.99 *(978-0-547-94086-1(6))* Houghton Mifflin Harcourt Publishing Co.

—Christmas Countdown. 2009. (Curious George Ser.). (ENG., Illus.). 14p. (J). (gr. k — 1). bds. 7.99 *(978-0-547-23863-0(0))* Houghton Mifflin Harcourt Publishing Co.

—Curious about Christmas. 2011. (Curious Baby Curious George Ser.). (ENG., Illus.). 12p. (J). (gr. k — 1). bds. 8.99 *(978-0-547-58841-4(0))* Houghton Mifflin Harcourt Publishing Co.

—Curious Baby Counting. 2009. (Curious Baby Curious George Ser.). (ENG., Illus.). 12p. (J). (gr. -1 — 1). bds. 8.99 *(978-0-547-21521-1(5))* Houghton Mifflin Harcourt Publishing Co.

—Curious George a Home for Honeybees (CGTV Early Reader) 2014. (Curious George Ser.). (ENG., Illus.). 24p. (J). (gr. -1-3). 12.99 *(978-0-544-23777-3(3)*, HMH Books For Young Readers) Houghton Mifflin Harcourt Publishing Co.

—Curious George & the Dump Truck. 2010. (Curious George Ser.). (ENG., Illus.). 24p. (J). (gr. -1-3). pap. 4.99 *(978-0-547-50425-4(X))* Houghton Mifflin Harcourt Publishing Co.

—Curious George & the Ice Cream Surprise. 2011. (Curious George Ser.). (ENG., Illus.). 24p. (J). (gr. -1-3). 13.99 *(978-0-547-24284-2(0))*; pap. 4.99 *(978-0-547-24285-9(9))* Houghton Mifflin Harcourt Publishing Co.

—Curious George & the Sleepover. 2017. (Curious George Ser.). (ENG., Illus.). 24p. (J). (gr. -1-3). 14.99 *(978-0-544-76346-3(7)*, HMH Books For Young Readers) Houghton Mifflin Harcourt Publishing Co.

—Curious George at the Baseball Game (Jorge el Curioso en el Partido de Beisbol) 2011. (Curious George Ser.). (SPA & ENG., Illus.). 24p. (J). (gr. -1-3). pap. 4.99 *(978-0-547-51500-7(6))* Houghton Mifflin Harcourt Publishing Co.

—Curious George Boxcar Derby (CGTV 8x8) 2016. (Curious George Ser.). (ENG., Illus.). 24p. (J). (gr. -1-3). 4.99 *(978-0-544-38077-6(0)*, HMH Books For Young Readers) Houghton Mifflin Harcourt Publishing Co.

—Curious George Builds a Tree House (CGTV Reader) 2017. (Curious George Ser.). (ENG., Illus.). 24p. (J). (gr. -1-3). pap. 3.99 *(978-0-544-86704-8(1)*, HMH Books For Young Readers) Houghton Mifflin Harcourt Publishing Co.

—Curious George Builds an Igloo (CGTV Reader) 2013. (Curious George Ser.). (ENG., Illus.). 24p. (J). (gr. -1-3). 12.99 *(978-0-544-09570-0(7))* Houghton Mifflin Harcourt Publishing Co.

—Curious George Car Wash. 2013. (Curious George Ser.). (ENG., Illus.). 24p. (J). (gr. -1-3). 12.99 *(978-0-544-03251-4(9))* Houghton Mifflin Harcourt Publishing Co.

—Curious George Classic Collection. 2015. (Curious George Ser.). (ENG., Illus.). 416p. (J). (gr. -1-3). 39.99 *(978-0-544-56239-4(9)*, HMH Books For Young Readers) Houghton Mifflin Harcourt Publishing Co.

—Curious George Cleans Up. Canetti, Yanitzia, tr. 2007. (Curious George Ser.). (SPA & ENG., Illus.). 24p. (J). (gr. -1-3). mass mkt. 3.99 *(978-0-618-89687-5(2))* Houghton Mifflin Harcourt Publishing Co.

—Curious George Colors Eggs. 2012. (Curious George Ser.). (ENG., Illus.). 24p. (J). (gr. -1-3). pap. 3.99 *(978-0-547-31585-0(6))* Houghton Mifflin Harcourt Publishing Co.

—Curious George Colors Eggs (CGTV Reader) 2012. (Curious George Ser.). (ENG., Illus.). 24p. (J). (gr. -1-3). 12.99 *(978-0-547-55904-9(6))* Houghton Mifflin Harcourt Publishing Co.

—Curious George Curious about Learning Boxed Set. 2012. (Curious George Ser.). (ENG., Illus.). 144p. (J). (gr. -1-3).

C
D

16.99 (978-0-547-58209-2(9)) Houghton Mifflin Harcourt Publishing Co.

—Curious George Dance Party CGTV Reader. 2013. (Curious George Ser.). (ENG., Illus.). 24p. (J). (gr. -1-3). 12.99 (978-0-547-96819-3(1)) Houghton Mifflin Harcourt Publishing Co.

—Curious George Discovers Germs (Science Storybook) 2015. (Curious George Ser.). (ENG., Illus.). 32p. (J). (gr. -1-3). 6.99 (978-0-544-43066-2(2), HMH Books For Young Readers) Houghton Mifflin Harcourt Publishing Co.

—Curious George Discovers Plants (science Storybook) 2016. (Curious George Ser.). (ENG., Illus.). 32p. (J). (gr. -1-3). 14.99 (978-0-544-65142-5(1), HMH Books For Young Readers) Houghton Mifflin Harcourt Publishing Co.

—Curious George Discovers Recycling (science Storybook) 2017. (Curious George Ser.). (ENG., Illus.). 32p. (J). (gr. -1-3). 14.99 (978-0-544-88035-1(8), HMH Books For Young Readers) Houghton Mifflin Harcourt Publishing Co.

—Curious George Discovers Space (science Storybook) 2015. (Curious George Ser.). (ENG., Illus.). 32p. (J). (gr. -1-3). 6.99 (978-0-544-50028-0(8), HMH Books For Young Readers) Houghton Mifflin Harcourt Publishing Co.

—Curious George Discovers the Ocean (Science Storybook) 2015. (Curious George Ser.). (ENG., Illus.). 32p. (J). (gr. -1-3). 6.99 (978-0-544-43065-5(4), HMH Books For Young Readers) Houghton Mifflin Harcourt Publishing Co.

—Curious George Discovers the Rainbow (Science Storybook) 2015. (Curious George Ser.). (ENG., Illus.). 32p. (J). (gr. -1-3). 6.99 (978-0-544-43068-6(9), HMH Books For Young Readers) Houghton Mifflin Harcourt Publishing Co.

—Curious George Discovers the Seasons (science Storybook) 2016. (Curious George Ser.). (ENG., Illus.). 32p. (J). (gr. -1-3). 14.99 (978-0-544-78586-1(X), HMH Books For Young Readers) Houghton Mifflin Harcourt Publishing Co.

—Curious George Discovers the Senses. 2015. (Curious George Ser.). (ENG., Illus.). 32p. (J). (gr. -1-3). 6.99 (978-0-544-50023-5(7), HMH Books For Young Readers) Houghton Mifflin Harcourt Publishing Co.

—Curious George Discovers the Stars (science Storybook) 2016. (Curious George Ser.). (ENG., Illus.). 32p. (J). (gr. -1-3). 14.99 (978-0-544-65162-3(6), HMH Books For Young Readers) Houghton Mifflin Harcourt Publishing Co.

—Curious George Discovers the Sun (Science Storybook) 2015. (Curious George Ser.). (ENG., Illus.). 32p. (J). (gr. -1-3). 6.99 (978-0-544-43067-9(0), HMH Books For Young Readers) Houghton Mifflin Harcourt Publishing Co.

—Curious George Dragon Dance (CGTV 8x8) 2016. (Curious George Ser.). (ENG., Illus.). 24p. (J). (gr. -1-3). 4.99 (978-0-544-78499-4(5), HMH Books For Young Readers) Houghton Mifflin Harcourt Publishing Co.

—Curious George Farm to Table. 2016. (Curious George TV Tie-In 8x8 Ser.). lib. bdg. 14.75 (978-0-606-37991-5(6)) Turtleback Bks.

—Curious George Farm to Table (CGTV 8x8) 2016. (Curious George Ser.). (ENG., Illus.). 24p. (J). (gr. -1-3). 12.99 (978-0-544-65220-0(7), HMH Books For Young Readers) Houghton Mifflin Harcourt Publishing Co.

—Curious George Fire Dog Rescue (CGTV Reader) 2015. (Curious George Ser.). (ENG., Illus.). 24p. (J). (gr. -1-3). 12.99 (978-0-544-50202-4(7), HMH Books For Young Readers) Houghton Mifflin Harcourt Publishing Co.

—Curious George Flies a Kite. 2004. (J). (gr. k-3). spiral bd. (978-0-616-01770-8(7)); spiral bd. (978-0-616-01771-5(5)) Canadian National Institute for the Blind/Institut National Canadien pour les Aveugles.

—Curious George Gets a Medal. 2004. (J). (gr. -1-2). spiral bd. (978-0-616-01773-9(1)); spiral bd. (978-0-616-01772-2(3)) Canadian National Institute for the Blind/Institut National Canadien pour les Aveugles.

—Curious George Goes to a Bookstore. 2017. (Curious George Ser.). (ENG., Illus.). 24p. (J). (gr. -1-3). pap. 4.99 (978-0-544-93204-3(8), HMH Books For Young Readers) Houghton Mifflin Harcourt Publishing Co.

—Curious George Goes to a Bookstore. 2017. (Curious George 8x8 Ser.). (ENG.). (J). (gr. -1-3). lib. bdg. 14.75 **(978-0-606-39823-7(6))** Turtleback Bks.

—Curious George Goes to the Zoo. 2014. (Curious George 8x8 Ser.). lib. bdg. 14.75 (978-0-606-23335-4(0), Turtleback) Turtleback Bks.

—Curious George Grows a Garden. 2012. (Curious George Ser.). (ENG., Illus.). 48p. (J). (gr. -1-3). pap. 4.99 (978-0-547-64304-5(7)) Houghton Mifflin Harcourt Publishing Co.

—Curious George Harvest Hoedown (CGTV 8 X 8) 2017. (Curious George Ser.). (ENG., Illus.). 24p. (J). (gr. -1-3). 12.99 **(978-1-328-69596-3(4)**, HMH Books For Young Readers) Houghton Mifflin Harcourt Publishing Co.

—Curious George Haunted Halloween. 2014. (Curious George Ser.). (ENG., Illus.). 24p. (J). (gr. -1-3). pap. 3.99 (978-0-544-32079-6(4), HMH Books For Young Readers) Houghton Mifflin Harcourt Publishing Co.

—Curious George Haunted Halloween (CGTV Reader) 2014. (Curious George Ser.). (ENG., Illus.). 24p. (J). (gr. -1-3). 12.99 (978-0-544-32077-2(8), HMH Books For Young Readers) Houghton Mifflin Harcourt Publishing Co.

—Curious George Home Run (Jorge el Curioso el Jonrón) 2012. (Curious George Ser.). (ENG & SPA., Illus.). 24p. (J). (gr. -1-3). pap. 3.99 (978-0-547-69114-5(9)) Houghton Mifflin Harcourt Publishing Co.

—Curious George Joins the Team. 2016. (Curious George Ser.). (ENG., Illus.). 24p. (J). (gr. -1-3). 13.99 (978-0-544-46500-8(8), HMH Books For Young Readers) Houghton Mifflin Harcourt Publishing Co.

—Curious George Learns the Alphabet, 1 vol. 2009. (Curious George Ser.). (ENG., Illus.). 80p. (J). (gr. -1-3). audio compact disk 10.99 (978-0-618-95966-2(1)) Houghton Mifflin Harcourt Publishing Co.

—Curious George Learns to Count from 1 To 100. 2011. (Curious George Ser.). (ENG., Illus.). 80p. (J). (gr. -1-3). pap. 8.99 (978-0-547-13841-1(5)) Houghton Mifflin Harcourt Publishing Co.

—Curious George Lemonade Stand (CGTV Reader) 2016. (Curious George Ser.). (ENG., Illus.). 24p. (J). (gr. -1-3). 12.99 (978-0-544-65221-7(5), HMH Books For Young Readers) Houghton Mifflin Harcourt Publishing Co.

—Curious George Magnetic Maze Book. 2012. (Curious George Ser.). (ENG., Illus.). 10p. (J). (gr. -1-3). 12.99 (978-0-547-64302-1(0)) Houghton Mifflin Harcourt Publishing Co.

—Curious George Makes Maple Syrup (CGTV 8x8) 2014. (Curious George Ser.). (ENG., Illus.). 24p. (J). (gr. -1-3). 12.99 (978-0-544-10494-5(3)) Houghton Mifflin Harcourt Publishing Co.

—Curious George Museum Mystery (CGTV 8x8) 2017. (Curious George Ser.). (ENG., Illus.). 24p. (J). (gr. -1-3). 12.99 (978-0-544-85992-0(8), HMH Books For Young Readers) Houghton Mifflin Harcourt Publishing Co.

—Curious George Neighborhood Friends. 2010. (Curious George Ser.). (ENG., Illus.). 12p. (J). (gr. -1 — 1). bds. 6.99 (978-0-547-23875-3(4)) Houghton Mifflin Harcourt Publishing Co.

—Curious George Parade Day. 2011. (Curious George Ser.). (ENG., Illus.). 14p. (J). (gr. -1 — 1). bds. 7.99 (978-0-547-47282-9(X)) Houghton Mifflin Harcourt Publishing Co.

—Curious George Pat-A-Cake. 2011. (Curious George Ser.). (ENG., Illus.). 8p. (J). (gr. k — 1). bds. 9.99 (978-0-547-51689-9(4)) Houghton Mifflin Harcourt Publishing Co.

—Curious George Plants a Seed. 2007. (Curious George Ser.). (ENG., Illus.). 24p. (J). (gr. -1-3). 4.99 (978-0-618-77710-5(5)) Houghton Mifflin Harcourt Publishing Co.

—Curious George Plays Soccer. 2017. (Curious George Ser.). (ENG., Illus.). 24p. (J). (gr. -1-3). 14.99 (978-0-544-91246-5(2), HMH Books For Young Readers) Houghton Mifflin Harcourt Publishing Co.

—Curious George Saves His Pennies. 2013. (Curious George Ser.). (ENG., Illus.). 32p. (J). (gr. -1-3). 12.99 (978-0-547-63231-5(2)) Houghton Mifflin Harcourt Publishing Co.

—Curious George Subway Train Adventure. 2016. (Curious George Ser.). (ENG., Illus.). 24p. (J). (gr. 1-4). 12.99 (978-0-544-78585-4(1), HMH Books For Young Readers) Houghton Mifflin Harcourt Publishing Co.

—Curious George Tool Time (CGTV Board Book) 2013. (Curious George Ser.). (ENG., Illus.). 12p. (J). (gr. -1 — 1). bds. 6.99 (978-0-547-96818-6(3)) Houghton Mifflin Harcourt Publishing Co.

—Curious George Travel Activity Kit. 2010. (Curious George Ser.). (ENG., Illus.). 64p. (J). (gr. -1-3). 12.99 (978-0-547-25875-1(5)) Houghton Mifflin Harcourt Publishing Co.

—Curious George Visits the Dentist. 2015. (Curious George 8x8 Ser.). lib. bdg. 14.75 (978-0-606-36555-0(9)) Turtleback Bks.

—Curious George's 5-Minute Stories. 2013. (Curious George Ser.). (ENG., Illus.). 192p. (J). (gr. -1-3). 12.99 (978-0-544-10793-9(4)) Houghton Mifflin Harcourt Publishing Co.

—Curious George's Crane (mini Movers Shaped Board Books) 2014. (Curious George Ser.). (ENG., Illus.). 12p. (J). (— 1). bds. 8.99 (978-0-544-32359-9(9), HMH Books For Young Readers) Houghton Mifflin Harcourt Publishing Co.

—Curious George's Dump Truck. 2014. (Curious George Ser.). (ENG., Illus.). 12p. (J). (— 1). bds. 8.99 (978-0-544-14686-0(7), HMH Books For Young Readers) Houghton Mifflin Harcourt Publishing Co.

—Curious George's Fire Truck. 2014. (Curious George Ser.). (ENG., Illus.). 12p. (J). (— 1). bds. 8.99 (978-0-544-14709-6(X), HMH Books For Young Readers) Houghton Mifflin Harcourt Publishing Co.

—Curious George's Train (mini Movers Shaped Board Books) 2014. (Curious George Ser.). (ENG., Illus.). 12p. (J). (— 1). bds. 8.99 (978-0-544-32074-1(3), HMH Books For Young Readers) Houghton Mifflin Harcourt Publishing Co.

—Dance Party. 2013. (Curious George Ser.). (ENG., Illus.). 24p. (J). (gr. -1-3). pap. 3.99 (978-0-547-96820-9(5)) Houghton Mifflin Harcourt Publishing Co.

—Day at the Farm. 2017. (Curious George Ser.). (ENG., Illus.). 16p. (J). (— 1). bds. 8.99 **(978-0-544-98874-3(4)**, HMH Books For Young Readers) Houghton Mifflin Harcourt Publishing Co.

—Dinosaur Tracks. 2011. (Curious George Ser.). (ENG., Illus.). 24p. (J). (gr. -1-3). pap. 3.99 (978-0-547-43888-7(5)) Houghton Mifflin Harcourt Publishing Co.

—Get Well, Curious George. 2017. (Curious George Ser.). (ENG., Illus.). 24p. (J). (gr. -1-3). 14.99 **(978-0-544-97750-1(5)**, HMH Books For Young Readers) Houghton Mifflin Harcourt Publishing Co.

—Happy Birthday, Curious George! 2016. (Curious George Ser.). (ENG., Illus.). 14p. (J). (— 1). bds. 7.99 (978-0-544-75050-0(0), HMH Books For Young Readers) Houghton Mifflin Harcourt Publishing Co.

—Happy St. Patrick's Day. 2014. (Curious George Ser.). (ENG., Illus.). 14p. (J). (— 1). bds. 7.99 (978-0-544-08888-7(3)) Houghton Mifflin Harcourt Publishing Co.

—Happy Thanksgiving. 2010. (Curious George Ser.). (ENG., Illus.). 14p. (J). (gr. -1 — 1). bds. 7.99 (978-0-547-13106-1(2)) Houghton Mifflin Harcourt Publishing Co.

—Happy Valentine's Day. Young, Mary O'Keefe, illus. 2011. (Curious George Ser.). (ENG.). 14p. (J). (gr. -1-3). 8.99 (978-0-547-13107-8(0)) Houghton Mifflin Harcourt Publishing Co.

—Home Run. 2012. (Curious George Ser.). (ENG., Illus.). 24p. (J). (gr. -1-3). pap. 3.99 (978-0-547-69118-3(1)) Houghton Mifflin Harcourt Publishing Co.

—Jorge el Curioso el Baile. 2013. (Curious George Ser.). (SPA & ENG., Illus.). 24p. (J). (gr. -1-3). pap. 3.99 (978-0-547-96822-3(1)) Houghton Mifflin Harcourt Publishing Co.

—Jorge el Curioso en el Partido de Beisbol. 2011. (Curious George Ser.).Tr. of Curious George at the Baseball Game. (SPA & ENG., Illus.). 24p. (J). (gr. -1-3). 12.99 (978-0-547-54746-6(3)) Houghton Mifflin Harcourt Publishing Co.

—Jorge el Curioso Huellas de Dinosaurio. 2011. (Curious George Ser.). (ENG & SPA., Illus.). 24p. (J). (gr. -1-3). pap. 3.99 (978-0-547-55798-4(1)) Houghton Mifflin Harcourt Publishing Co.

—Jorge el Curioso Va a una Fiesta de Disfraces/Curious George Goes to a Costume Party (Bilingual) 2012. (Curious George Ser.). (ENG & SPA., Illus.). 24p. (J). (gr. -1-3). pap. 3.99 (978-0-547-86575-1(9)) Houghton Mifflin Harcourt Publishing Co.

—Jorge el Curioso y la Piñata. 2009. (Curious George Ser.).Tr. of Curious George Pinata Party. (SPA & ENG., Illus.). 24p. (J). (gr. -1-3). pap. 3.99 (978-0-547-23830-2(4)) Houghton Mifflin Harcourt Publishing Co.

—Keep Curious & Carry a Banana: Words of Wisdom from the World of Curious George. 2016. (Curious George Ser.). (ENG., Illus.). 80p. (YA). (gr. 7). 12.99 (978-0-544-65648-2(2), HMH Books For Young Readers) Houghton Mifflin Harcourt Publishing Co.

—Learns to Count from 1 to 100: Counting, Grouping, Mapping, & More! Hines, Anna Grossnickle, illus. 2005. (Curious George Ser.). (ENG.). 64p. (J). (gr. -1-3). 16.99 (978-0-618-47602-2(4)) Houghton Mifflin Harcourt Publishing Co.

—Lemonade Stand. 2016. (Curious George TV Tie-In Early Reader Ser.). lib. bdg. 13.55 (978-0-606-37993-9(2)) Turtleback Bks.

—Librarian for a Day. 2012. (Curious George Ser.). (ENG., Illus.). 24p. (J). (gr. -1-3). pap. 3.99 (978-0-547-85281-2(9)) Houghton Mifflin Harcourt Publishing Co.

—Music Play. 2009. (Curious Baby Curious George Ser.). (ENG., Illus.). 10p. (J). (gr. -1 — 1). bds. 8.99 (978-0-547-23876-0(2)) Houghton Mifflin Harcourt Publishing Co.

—My Curious World. 2009. (Curious Baby Curious George Ser.). (ENG., Illus.). 10p. (J). (gr. -1 — 1). 14.99 (978-0-547-21520-4(7)) Houghton Mifflin Harcourt Publishing Co.

—My Favorite Things. 2011. (Curious Baby Curious George Ser.). (ENG., Illus.). 14p. (J). (gr. -1 — 1). bds. 8.99 (978-0-547-42893-2(6)) Houghton Mifflin Harcourt Publishing Co.

—My Little Boat. 2009. (Curious Baby Curious George Ser.). (ENG., Illus.). 8p. (J). (gr. -1 — 1). 12.99 (978-0-547-21541-9(X)) Houghton Mifflin Harcourt Publishing Co.

—On the Go! 2011. (Curious George Ser.). (ENG., Illus.). 10p. (J). (gr. -1 — 1). bds. 6.99 (978-0-547-55151-7(7)) Houghton Mifflin Harcourt Publishing Co.

—The Perfect Carrot. 2010. (Curious George Ser.). (ENG., Illus.). 24p. (J). (gr. -1-3). pap. 3.99 (978-0-547-24299-6(9)) Houghton Mifflin Harcourt Publishing Co.

—Pinata Party. 2009. (Curious George Ser.). (ENG., Illus.). 24p. (J). (gr. -1-3). pap. 3.99 (978-0-547-11962-5(3)) Houghton Mifflin Harcourt Publishing Co.

—Plumber's Helper. Meyer, Emily, ed. 2010. (Curious George Ser.). (ENG., Illus.). 24p. (J). (gr. -1-3). pap. 4.99 (978-0-547-23589-9(5)) Houghton Mifflin Harcourt Publishing Co.

—Race Day. 2010. (Curious George Ser.). (ENG., Illus.). 24p. (J). (gr. -1-3). pap. 3.99 (978-0-547-39361-2(X)) Houghton Mifflin Harcourt Publishing Co.

—Sight Words. 2017. (Curious George Ser.). (ENG., Illus.). 160p. (J). (gr. -1-k). 14.99 (978-0-544-89824-0(9), HMH Books For Young Readers) Houghton Mifflin Harcourt Publishing Co.

—Storybook Collection. 2010. (Curious George Ser.). (ENG., Illus.). 208p. (J). (gr. -1-3). 10.99 (978-0-547-39631-6(7)) Houghton Mifflin Harcourt Publishing Co.

—Sweet Dreams, Curious George. 2016. (Curious George Ser.). (ENG., Illus.). 24p. (J). (gr. -1-3). 4.99 (978-0-544-50321-2(X), HMH Books For Young Readers) Houghton Mifflin Harcourt Publishing Co.

—Tadpole Trouble. 2007. (Curious George Ser.). (ENG., Illus.). 24p. (J). (gr. -1-3). 4.99 (978-0-618-77712-9(1)) Houghton Mifflin Harcourt Publishing Co.

—Three Tales for a Winter's Night. 2012. (Curious George Ser.). (ENG., Illus.). 72p. (J). (gr. -1-3). pap. 7.99 (978-0-547-83936-3(7)) Houghton Mifflin Harcourt Publishing Co.

—Time for School. 2011. (Curious George Ser.). (ENG., Illus.). 16p. (J). (gr. -1-3). 5.99 (978-0-547-42230-5(X)) Houghton Mifflin Harcourt Publishing Co.

—Visits the Library / Jorge el Curioso Va a la Biblioteca. 2011. (Curious George Ser.). (ENG & SPA., Illus.). 24p. (J). (gr. -1-3). pap. 3.99 (978-0-547-55075-6(8)) Houghton Mifflin Harcourt Publishing Co.

—Windy Delivery. 2014. (Curious George Ser.). (ENG., Illus.). 24p. (J). (gr. -1-3). 12.99 (978-0-544-32075-8(1)); pap. 4.99 (978-0-544-32076-5(X)) Houghton Mifflin Harcourt Publishing Co. (HMH Books For Young Readers).

Rey, H. A. & Hapka, Catherine. Merry Christmas, Curious George (with Stickers) Young, Mary O'Keefe, illus. 2017. (Curious George Ser.). (ENG.). 24p. (J). (gr. -1-3). pap. 5.99 **(978-1-328-69558-1(1)**, HMH Books For Young Readers) Houghton Mifflin Harcourt Publishing Co.

Rey, H. A. & Khan, Hena. It's Ramadan, Curious George. 2016. (Curious George Ser.). (ENG., Illus.). 14p. (J). (— 1). bds. 7.99 (978-0-544-65226-2(6), HMH Books For Young Readers) Houghton Mifflin Harcourt Publishing Co.

Rey, H. A. & Margaret. Curious George Visits the Dentist. 2014. (Curious George Ser.). (ENG., Illus.). 24p. (J). (gr. -1-3). 13.99 (978-0-544-14611-2(5), HMH Books For Young Readers) Houghton Mifflin Harcourt Publishing Co.

Rey, H. A. & Rey, Margret. At the Zoo. 2007. (Curious George Ser.). (ENG., Illus.). 10p. (J). (gr. k — 1). bds. 6.99 (978-0-618-80042-1(5)) Houghton Mifflin Harcourt Publishing Co.

—Before & After. 2007. (Curious George Ser.). (ENG., Illus.). 12p. (J). (gr. -1 — 1). bds. 6.99 (978-0-618-72399-7(4)) Houghton Mifflin Harcourt Publishing Co.

—Big Book of Adventures: 12 Beginning Readers in One. 2013. (Curious George Ser.). (ENG., Illus.). 296p. (J). (gr. -1-3). 15.99 (978-0-544-08463-6(2)) Houghton Mifflin Harcourt Publishing Co.

—Cecily G. & the 9 Monkeys. 2009. (Curious George Ser.). (ENG., Illus.). 48p. (J). (gr. -1-3). pap. 6.99 (978-0-618-99794-7(6), HMH Books For Young Readers) Houghton Mifflin Harcourt Publishing Co.

—Chasing Waves. 2014. (Curious George Ser.). (ENG., Illus.). 24p. (J). (gr. -1-3). pap. 4.99 (978-0-544-24004-9(9), HMH Books For Young Readers) Houghton Mifflin Harcourt Publishing Co.

—Circus Act. 2008. (Curious George Ser.). (ENG., Illus.). 16p. (J). (gr. -1-3). 5.99 (978-0-618-99909-5(4)) Houghton Mifflin Harcourt Publishing Co.

—The Complete Adventures of Curious George: 75th Anniversary Edition. 75th ed. 2016. (Curious George Ser.). (ENG., Illus.). 432p. (J). (gr. -1-3). 34.99 (978-0-544-64448-9(4), HMH Books For Young Readers) Houghton Mifflin Harcourt Publishing Co.

—Curious Baby My Growing World. 2011. (Curious Baby Curious George Ser.). (ENG., Illus.). 14p. (J). (gr. k — 1). bds. 9.99 (978-0-547-27939-8(6)) Houghton Mifflin Harcourt Publishing Co.

—Curious George, 1 vol. 2005. (Curious George Ser.). (ENG., Illus.). 64p. (J). (gr. -1-3). act. bk. ed. 10.99 incl. audio compact disk (978-0-618-60922-2(9)) Houghton Mifflin Harcourt Publishing Co.

—Curious George & the Birthday Surprise. Weston, Martha, illus. 2003. (Curious George Ser.). (ENG.). 24p. (J). (gr. -1-3). pap. 4.99 (978-0-618-34687-5(2)) Houghton Mifflin Harcourt Publishing Co.

—Curious George & the Birthday Surprise. 2003. (Curious George 8x8 Ser.). (gr. k-3). lib. bdg. 14.75 (978-0-613-90050-8(2), Turtleback) Turtleback Bks.

—Curious George & the Pizza Party. 2013. (Curious George Ser.). (ENG., Illus.). 24p. (J). (gr. -1-3). pap. 4.99 (978-0-544-10988-9(0)) Houghton Mifflin Harcourt Publishing Co.

—Curious George & the Puppies. 2007. (Curious George Ser.). (ENG., Illus.). 24p. (J). (gr. -1-3). audio compact disk 10.99 (978-0-618-80065-0(4)) Houghton Mifflin Harcourt Publishing Co.

—Curious George Feeds the Animals. 2005. (J). (gr. k-3). 9.95 (978-0-618-55520-8(X)) Houghton Mifflin Harcourt Trade & Reference Pubs.

—Curious George Flies a Kite, 1 vol. 2008. (Curious George Ser.). (ENG., Illus.). 80p. (J). (gr. -1-3). audio compact disk 10.99 (978-0-618-99884-5(5)) Houghton Mifflin Harcourt Publishing Co.

—Curious George Goes Bowling (CGTV Lift-The-Flap 8x8) 2009. (Curious George Ser.). (ENG., Illus.). 18p. (J). (gr. -1-3). 5.99 (978-0-618-80041-4(7)) Houghton Mifflin Harcourt Publishing Co.

—Curious George Goes to a Bookstore. 2014. (Curious George Ser.). (ENG., Illus.). 32p. (J). (gr. -1-3). 13.99 (978-0-544-32073-4(5), HMH Books For Young Readers) Houghton Mifflin Harcourt Publishing Co.

—Curious George Goes to the Hospital (Special Edition) 2017. (Curious George Ser.). (ENG., Illus.). 56p. (J). (gr. -1-3). 17.99 (978-0-544-76408-8(0), HMH Books For Young Readers) Houghton Mifflin Harcourt Publishing Co.

—Curious George Goes to the Movies. 2005. (J). (gr. k-3). 9.95 (978-0-618-55521-5(8)) Houghton Mifflin Harcourt Trade & Reference Pubs.

—Curious George Hide-and-Seek. 2008. (Curious George Ser.). (ENG., Illus.). 10p. (J). (gr. -1 — 1). bds. 6.99 (978-0-618-89199-3(4)) Houghton Mifflin Harcourt Publishing Co.

—Curious George Learns the Alphabet. 50th ed. 2013. (Curious George Ser.). (ENG., Illus.). 80p. (J). (gr. -1-3). 12.99 (978-0-544-10523-2(0)) Houghton Mifflin Harcourt Publishing Co.

—Curious George Makes Maple Syrup. 2014. (Curious George Ser.). (ENG., Illus.). 24p. (J). (gr. -1-3). pap. 3.99 (978-0-544-03252-1(7)) Houghton Mifflin Harcourt Publishing Co.

—Curious George Saves His Pennies. 2014. (Curious George Ser.). (ENG., Illus.). 24p. (J). (gr. -1-3). pap. 4.99 (978-0-547-81853-5(X)) Houghton Mifflin Harcourt Publishing Co.

—Curious George Says Thank You. 2012. (Curious George Ser.). (ENG., Illus.). 24p. (J). (gr. -1-3). pap. 4.99 (978-0-547-81852-8(1)) Houghton Mifflin Harcourt Publishing Co.

—Curious George Says Thank You. 2012. (Curious George 8x8 Ser.). lib. bdg. 14.75 (978-0-606-26601-7(1), Turtleback) Turtleback Bks.

—Curious George Stories to Share. 2011. (Curious George Ser.). (ENG., Illus.). 208p. (J). (gr. -1-3). 10.99 (978-0-547-59529-0(8)) Houghton Mifflin Harcourt Publishing Co.

—Curious George Super Sticker Coloring Book. 2008. (Curious George Ser.). (ENG., Illus.). 64p. (J). (gr. -1-3). 12.99 (978-0-618-99877-7(2)) Houghton Mifflin Harcourt Publishing Co.

—Curious George Takes a Job. 2007. (Curious George Ser.). (ENG., Illus.). 48p. (J). (gr. -1-3). audio compact disk 10.99 (978-0-618-72406-2(0)) Houghton Mifflin Harcourt Publishing Co.

—Curious George to the Rescue. 2007. (Curious George Ser.). (ENG., Illus.). 12p. (J). (gr. -1-3). 8.99 (978-0-618-72401-7(X)) Houghton Mifflin Harcourt Publishing Co.

—Curious George Visits the Library. Weston, Martha, illus. 2013. (Curious George Ser.). (ENG.). 24p. (J). (gr. -1-3). pap. 4.99 (978-0-544-11450-0(7)) Houghton Mifflin Harcourt Publishing Co.

—Curious George's Neighborhood. Weston, Martha, illus. 2004. (Curious George Ser.). (ENG.). 10p. (J). (gr. -1 — 1). bds. 11.95 (978-0-618-41203-7(4)) Houghton Mifflin Harcourt Publishing Co.

—George O Curioso. pap. 23.95 (978-85-336-0916-7(7)) Livraria Martins Editora BRA. Dist: Distribooks, Inc.

—Goes to the Beach. 2014. (Curious George Ser.). (ENG., Illus.). 24p. (J). (gr. -1-3). pap. 4.99 (978-0-544-25001-7(X), HMH Books For Young Readers) Houghton Mifflin Harcourt Publishing Co.

—Happy Hanukkah. 2012. (Curious George Ser.). (ENG., Illus.). 14p. (J). (gr. k — 1). bds. 7.99 (978-0-547-75731-5(X)) Houghton Mifflin Harcourt Publishing Co.

—Home Run. 2012. (Curious George TV Tie-In Early Reader Ser.). lib. bdg. 13.55 (978-0-606-23985-1(5), Turtleback) Turtleback Bks.

—Jorge el Curioso. Català, Josep Maria & Tusquets, Eugenia, trs. 2008. (Curious George Ser.).Tr. of Curious George. (SPA & ENG., Illus.). 64p. (J). (gr. -1-3). pap. 7.99 (978-0-618-88411-7(4)) Houghton Mifflin Harcourt Publishing Co.

—Jorge el Curioso Vuela Una Cometa. 2012. (Curious George Ser.). (ENG & SPA., Illus.). 80p. (J). (gr. -1-3). pap. 7.99 *(978-0-547-69162-6(9))* Houghton Mifflin Harcourt Publishing Co.

—Librarian for a Day. 2012. (Curious George TV Tie-In Early Reader Ser.). lib. bdg. 13.55 *(978-0-606-26602-4(X),* Turtleback) Turtleback Bks.

—My First Words at the Zoo, Set. gif. ed. 2010. (Curious Baby Curious George Ser.). (ENG., Illus.). 12p. (J). (gr. -1 — 1). 14.99 *(978-0-618-99953-8(1))* Houghton Mifflin Harcourt Publishing Co.

—Plays Mini Golf. 2008. (Curious George Ser.). (ENG., Illus.). 24p. (J). (gr. -1-3). pap. 3.99 *(978-0-618-99986-6(8))* Houghton Mifflin Harcourt Publishing Co.

—Roller Coaster. 2007. (Curious George Ser.). (ENG., Illus.). 24p. (J). (gr. -1-3). pap. 3.99 *(978-0-618-80040-7(9))* Houghton Mifflin Harcourt Publishing Co.

—Seasons. 2008. (Curious George Ser.). (ENG., Illus.). 10p. (J). (gr. -1 — 1). bds. 6.99 *(978-0-618-99848-7(9))* Houghton Mifflin Harcourt Publishing Co.

—Shapes. 2008. (Curious George Ser.). (ENG., Illus.). 10p. (J). (gr. k — 1). bds. 6.99 *(978-0-618-89198-6(6))* Houghton Mifflin Harcourt Publishing Co.

—The Surprise Gift. gif. ed. 2008. (Curious George Ser.). (ENG., Illus.). 24p. (J). (gr. -1-3). pap. 4.99 *(978-0-618-99864-7(0))* Houghton Mifflin Harcourt Publishing Co.

—Takes a Trip. 2007. (Curious George Ser.). (ENG., Illus.). 24p. (J). (gr. -1-3). pap. 3.99 *(978-0-618-88403-2(3))* Houghton Mifflin Harcourt Publishing Co.

—Three Tales for a Winter's Night. 2012. (Curious George TV Tie-In 8x8 Ser.). lib. bdg. 18.40 *(978-0-606-26603-1(8),* Turtleback) Turtleback Bks.

—Where Is Curious George? A Look & Find Book. 2013. (Curious George Ser.). (ENG., Illus.). 32p. (J). (gr. -1-3). 9.99 *(978-0-547-91416-9(4))* Houghton Mifflin Harcourt Publishing Co.

Rey, H. A. & Rey, Margret, creators. Curious George Loves to Ride. 2016. (Curious George Ser.). (ENG., Illus.). 20p. (J). (gr. -1-3). bds. 6.99 *(978-0-544-61102-3(0),* HMH Books For Young Readers) Houghton Mifflin Harcourt Publishing Co.

Rey, H. A. & Rey, Margret, illus. Curious George's 1 to 10 & Back Again. 2003. (J). bds. 9.95 *(978-0-618-27711-7(0))* Houghton Mifflin Harcourt Trade & Reference Pubs.

Rey, H. A. & Young, Mary OKeefe. Ready for School. 2017. (Curious George Ser.). (ENG., Illus.). 14p. (J). (— 1). bds. 7.99 *(978-0-544-93120-6(3),* HMH Books For Young Readers) Houghton Mifflin Harcourt Publishing Co.

Rey, H. A., et al. Curious George & the Firefighters. (Curious George Ser.). (ENG., Illus.). 24p. (J). (gr. -1-3). 2007. bds. 11.99 *(978-0-618-89194-8(3))* 2004. 14.99 *(978-0-618-49497-2(9))* 2004. 4.99 *(978-0-618-49496-5(0))* Houghton Mifflin Harcourt Publishing Co.

—Curious George Cleans Up. 2007. (Curious George Ser.). (ENG., Illus.). 24p. (J). (gr. -1-3). 3.99 *(978-0-618-73759-8(6))* Houghton Mifflin Harcourt Publishing Co.

—Curious George Discovery Day. 2007. (Curious George Ser.). (ENG., Illus.). 14p. (J). (gr. k — 1). bds. 13.95 *(978-0-618-73761-1(8))* Houghton Mifflin Harcourt Publishing Co.

—Curious George the Movie. movie tie-in ed. 2006. (Curious George Ser.). (ENG., Illus.). 10p. (J). (gr. -1 — 1). bds. 6.99 *(978-0-618-60587-3(8))* Houghton Mifflin Harcourt Publishing Co.

Rey, Margret & Rey, H. A. Curious about Phonics. 2008. (Curious George Ser.). (ENG., Illus.). 192p. (J). (gr. -1-3). 12.95 *(978-0-618-95670-8(0))* Houghton Mifflin Harcourt Publishing Co.

—Curious George Goes to the Beach. 2014. (Curious George 8x8 Ser.). (gr. k-3). lib. bdg. 13.55 *(978-0-613-21392-9(0),* Turtleback) Turtleback Bks.

—Curious George's First Day of School. Hines, Anna Grossnickle, illus. 2005. (Curious George Ser.). (ENG.). 24p. (J). (gr. -1-3). 13.99 *(978-0-618-60563-7(0));* pap. 4.99 *(978-0-618-60564-4(9))* Houghton Mifflin Harcourt Publishing Co.

—The New Adventures of Curious George. Vipah Interactive Staff, illus. 2006. (Curious George Ser.). (ENG.). 208p. (J). (gr. -1-3). 10.99 *(978-0-618-66373-6(8))* Houghton Mifflin Harcourt Publishing Co.

—Takes a Train. Weston, Martha, illus. 2010. (Curious George Ser.). (ENG.). 24p. (J). (gr. -1-3). pap. 4.99 *(978-0-547-50424-7(1))* Houghton Mifflin Harcourt Publishing Co.

CURIOSITIES AND WONDERS

see also Disasters; Monsters; Unidentified Flying Objects; World Records

Abdo Publishing. Record Breakers. 2015. (Record Breakers Ser.: Vol. 6). (ENG.). 48p. (J). (gr. 4-7). lib. bdg. 196.74 *(978-1-62403-844-0(1))* ABDO Publishing Co.

ABDO Publishing Company Staff. World of Horror: Set Of 12. 2007. (World of Horror Ser.). 324.84 *(978-1-59928-765-2(X),* Abdo & Daughters) ABDO Publishing Co.

Acampora, Courtney. Smithsonian First Discoveries: Young Explorer. Riggs, Jenna, illus. 2016. (Smithsonian First Discoveries Ser.). (ENG.). 48p. (J). 16.95 *(978-1-62686-481-8(0),* Silver Dolphin Bks.) Readerlink Distribution Services, LLC.

Acer, David. Gotcha! 18 Amazing Ways to Freak Out Your Friends. MacEachern, Stephen, illus. 2008. (ENG.). 48p. (J). (gr. 3-7). 16.95 *(978-1-55453-194-3(2));* pap. 8.95 *(978-1-55453-195-0(0))* Kids Can Pr., Ltd. CAN. Dist: Hachette Bk. Group.

Adamson, Thomas K. & Adamson, Heather. The World's Tallest House of Cards & Other Number Records, 1 vol. 2013. (Wow! Ser.). (ENG.). 24p. (gr. k-1). lib. bdg. 26.65 *(978-1-4765-0240-3(4),* Pebble Plus) Capstone Press of Coughlan Cos.

AIO Team. The Official Guide: A Behind-the-Scenes Look at the World's Favorite Family Audio Drama. 25th ed. 2012. (Adventures in Odyssey Bks.). (ENG.). 680p. (J). pap. 24.99 *(978-1-58997-719-8(X))* Tyndale Hse. Pubs.

Aladdin Books. The Really Big Awesome Book: Monsters of the Deep, the Universe, Volcanoes, Prehistoric Animals, & Tornadoes. Paiva, Johannah Gilman, ed. Various, illus. 2014. (ENG.). 160p. (J). (gr. 3-7). 24.95 *(978-1-77093-928-8(8))* Flowerpot Children's Pr. Inc. CAN. Dist: Cardinal Pubs. Group.

—The Really Big I Didn't Know That Book: Bugs, Sharks, Dinosaurs, Cars, & Trains. Paiva, Johannah Gilman, ed. Various, illus. 2014. (ENG.). 160p. (J). (gr. 2). 24.95 *(978-1-77093-927-1(X))* Flowerpot Children's Pr. Inc. CAN. Dist: Cardinal Pubs. Group.

Almanac, Old Farmer's. The Old Farmer's Almanac for Kids, Vol. 7. 2017. (ENG., Illus.). 192p. pap. 9.95 ***(978-1-57198-743-3(6),*** Old Farmer's Almanac) Yankee Publishing, Inc.

Amazing Feats. 2014. (Ripleys Believe It or Not! Dare to Look Ser.: 8). 36p. (J). (gr. 4-18). lib. bdg. 20.95 *(978-1-4222-3139-5(9))* Mason Crest.

Anastasio, Dina. Where Is the Eiffel Tower? Foley, Tim, illus. 2017. (Where Is? Ser.). (ENG.). 112p. (J). (gr. 3-7). pap. 5.99 *(978-0-451-53384-5(4),* Grosset & Dunlap) Penguin Young Readers Group.

Anderson, Kirsten. Who Was Robert Ripley? 2015. (Who Was... ? Ser.). lib. bdg. 16.00 *(978-0-606-36596-3(6))* Turtleback Bks.

Anderson, Kirsten & dePaola, Tomie. Who Was Robert Ripley? Foley, Tim & Harrison, Nancy, illus. 2015. (Who Was? Ser.). (ENG.). 112p. (J). (gr. 3-7). 5.99 *(978-0-448-48298-9(3),* Grosset & Dunlap) Penguin Young Readers Group.

Aronson, Marc & Newquist, H. P. For Boys Only: The Biggest, Baddest Book Ever. Headcase Design, illus. 2007. (ENG.). 160p. (J). (gr. 5-8). 16.99 *(978-0-312-37706-9(1),* 9780312377069) Feiwel & Friends.

Ash, Russell. Boring, Botty & Spong. 2012. (ENG., Illus.). 320p. (J). (gr. 4-7). pap. 7.99 *(978-1-84941-192-9(1),* Red Fox) Random House Children's Books GBR. Dist: Independent Pubs. Group.

Ash, Russell & Terry, Paul. Top 10 for Boys. 2nd ed. 2013. (ENG., Illus.). 320p. (J). (gr. 4-7). 24.95 *(978-1-77085-223-5(9),* 9781770852235) Firefly Bks., Ltd.

Astronomy Now!, 9 vols., Set. Incl. Look at Earth. Dunn, Mary R. (J). (gr. 3-7). lib. bdg. 21.25 *(978-1-4042-3827-5(1),* PowerKids Pr.); Look at Jupiter. Slade, Suzanne. (J). (gr. 2-5). lib. bdg. 22.60 *(978-1-4042-3829-9(8));* Look at Mars. Dunn, Mary R. (YA). (gr. 2-5). lib. bdg. 21.25 *(978-1-4042-3828-2(X));* Look at Mercury. Dunn, Mary R. (YA). (gr. 2-5). lib. bdg. 22.60 *(978-1-4042-3825-1(5));* Look at Neptune. Slade, Suzanne. (YA). (gr. 2-5). lib. bdg. 22.60 *(978-1-4042-3832-9(8));* Look at Pluto & Other Dwarf Planets. Kaspar, Anna. (YA). (gr. 2-5). lib. bdg. 22.60 *(978-1-4042-3824-4(7));* Look at Saturn. Slade, Suzanne. (J). (gr. 2-5). lib. bdg. 22.60 *(978-1-4042-3830-5(1));* Look at Uranus. Slade, Suzanne. (J). (gr. 2-5). lib. bdg. 22.60 *(978-1-4042-3831-2(X));* Look at Venus. Dunn, Mary R. (YA). (gr. 2-5). lib. bdg. 22.60 *(978-1-4042-3826-8(3));* (Illus.). 24p. 2007. 2007. Set lib. bdg. 191.25 *(978-1-4042-3863-3(8))* Rosen Publishing Group, Inc., The.

Awesome Animal Trivia. 2013. (Ultimate Trivia Challenge Ser.). 32p. (J). (gr. 2-5). pap. 63.00 *(978-1-4339-8290-3(0))* Stevens, Gareth Publishing LLLP.

Awesome Arts. 2014. (Ripleys Believe It or Not! Download the Weird Ser.: 8). 36p. (J). (gr. 4-18). lib. bdg. 20.95 *(978-1-4222-3148-7(8))* Mason Crest.

Bathroom Readers' Institute Staff. The Haunted Outhouse: Science, History, Horror, Mystery, and... Eerily Twisted Tales. 2013. (ENG., Illus.). 288p. (J). (gr. 1-6). pap. 12.95 *(978-1-60710-784-2(8),* Portable Pr.) Readerlink Distribution Services, LLC.

—Ogre Drool: 36 Tear-Off Placemats - Puzzles, Mazes, Brainteasers, Weird Facts, Jokes, & More! Merrell, Patrick & Schuna, Sam, illus. 2014. (ENG.). 72p. (gr. k-4). pap. 10.95 *(978-1-62686-070-4(X),* Portable Pr.) Readerlink Distribution Services, LLC.

—Scrambled Brains: 36 Tear-Off Placemats - Puzzles, Mazes, Brainteasers, Weird Facts, Jokes, & More! Merrell, Patrick & Schuna, Sam, illus. 2014. (ENG.). 72p. (gr. k-4). pap. 10.95 *(978-1-62686-039-1(4),* Portable Pr.) Readerlink Distribution Services, LLC.

—Uncle John's InfoMania Bathroom Reader for Kids Only! 2013. (ENG., Illus.). 272p. (gr. 2-7). pap. 9.95 *(978-1-60710-561-9(6),* Portable Pr.) Readerlink Distribution Services, LLC.

—Uncle John's the Enchanted Toilet Bathroom Reader for Kids Only! 2012. (ENG., Illus.). 288p. (J). (gr. 1-6). pap. 12.95 *(978-1-60710-558-9(6),* Portable Pr.) Readerlink Distribution Services, LLC.

—Uncle John's Top Secret Bathroom Reader for Kids Only! Collectible Edition. 2014. (ENG., Illus.). 288p. (J). (gr. 2-7). 14.95 *(978-1-62686-047-6(5),* Portable Pr.) Readerlink Distribution Services, LLC.

—Uncle John's Totally Quacked Bathroom Reader for Kids Only! 2014. (ENG., Illus.). 288p. (J). (gr. 2-7). 14.95 *(978-1-62686-175-6(7),* Portable Pr.) Readerlink Distribution Services, LLC.

Bathroom Readers' Institute Staff, creator. Uncle John's Bathroom Reader for Kids Only! Collectible Edition. 2014. (ENG., Illus.). 288p. (J). (gr. 2-7). 14.95 *(978-1-62686-045-2(9),* Portable Pr.) Readerlink Distribution Services, LLC.

—Uncle John's Electrifying Bathroom Reader for Kids Only! 2014. (ENG., Illus.). 288p. (J). (gr. 2-7). 14.95 *(978-1-62686-046-9(7),* Portable Pr.) Readerlink Distribution Services, LLC.

Beer, Julie. Weird but True Food. 2015. lib. bdg. 18.40 *(978-0-606-36426-3(9))* Turtleback Bks.

Behnke, Alison. Can Rats Swim from Sewers into Toilets? And Other Questions about Your Home. 2010. (Is That a Fact? Ser.). (ENG.). 40p. (gr. 4-6). lib. bdg. 26.60 *(978-0-7613-4914-3(6))* Lerner Publishing Group.

Believe It Or Not, Ripley's. One Zany Day! 2015. (Fun Facts Ser.: 2). (ENG., Illus.). 144p. (J). 18.95 *(978-1-60991-138-6(5))* Ripley Entertainment, Inc.

Believe It Or Not, Ripley's Staff, compiled by. Ripley's Fun Facts & Silly Stories 4. 2015. (Fun Facts Ser.: 4). (ENG., Illus.). 224p. (J). pap. 8.99 *(978-1-60991-142-3(3))* Ripley Entertainment, Inc.

Bell-Rehwoldt, Sheri. Ripley's Believe It or Not! Totally Bizarre. 2008. (Illus.). 384p. *(978-1-893951-30-3(8))* Ripley Entertainment, Inc.

Bingham, Jane. Crop Circles, 1 vol. 2013. (Solving Mysteries with Science Ser.). (ENG., Illus.). 48p. (gr. 5-5). pap. 9.95 *(978-1-4109-4993-6(1))* Heinemann-Raintree.

Bizarre World. 2014. (Ripleys Believe It or Not! Dare to Look Ser.: 8). 36p. (J). (gr. 4-18). lib. bdg. 20.95 *(978-1-4222-3140-1(2))* Mason Crest.

Blackwood, Gary L. Enigmatic Events. 2005. (Unsolved History Ser.). (Illus.). 80p. (gr. 6-7). lib. bdg. 23.95 *(978-0-7614-1889-4(X),* Benchmark Bks.) Marshall Cavendish Corp.

—Unsolved History, 4 bks., Set. Incl. Debatable Deaths. 80p. (gr. 6). lib. bdg. 23.95 *(978-0-7614-1888-7(1));* Enigmatic Events. 80p. (gr. 6-7). lib. bdg. 23.95 *(978-0-7614-1889-4(X));* Legends or Lies. 72p. lib. bdg. *(978-0-7614-1891-7(1));* Perplexing People. 80p. (gr. 6-7). lib. bdg. 23.95 *(978-0-7614-1890-0(3));* (Illus.). 2005. *(978-0-7614-1892-4(X),* Benchmark Bks.) Marshall Cavendish Corp.

Blackwood, Gary L. & Follett, Katherine. Enigmatic Events. 2009. (Benchmark Rockets: History's Mysteries Ser.). 32p. (gr. 3). 28.50 *(978-0-7614-4358-2(4))* Marshall Cavendish GBR. Dist: Marshall Cavendish Corp.

The Book for Clever Kids. 2016. (ENG., Illus.). 256p. (J). (gr. 3-7). 16.99 *(978-1-78055-316-0(1))* O'Mara, Michael Bks., Ltd. GBR. Dist: Independent Pubs. Group.

The Book of Amazing Curiosities. 2015. (Illus.). 704p. *(978-1-4508-8842-4(9))* Publications International, Ltd.

The Book of Incredible Information. 2015. (Illus.). 704p. *(978-1-4508-8843-1(7))* Publications International, Ltd.

Borgenicht, David & Heimberg, Justin. The Worst-Case Scenario Survival Handbook. 2014. (Worst Case Scenario Survival Handbook Ser.). 128p. (gr. 4-7). 41.35 *(978-1-59920-974-6(8))* Black Rabbit Bks.

Borgenicht, David, et al. The Worst-Case Scenario Survival Handbook - Weird. 2010. (Worst Case Scenario Ser.). (ENG., Illus.). 128p. (J). (gr. 4-17). pap. 10.99 *(978-0-8118-7438-0(9))* Chronicle Bks. LLC.

Bortz, Alfred B. Seven Wonders of Exploration Technology. 2010. (Seven Wonders Ser.). (YA). (gr. 5-9). lib. bdg. 33.26 *(978-0-7613-4241-0(9))* Twenty First Century Bks.

Botham, Noel. How Fast Can You Fart? And Other Weird, Gross & Disgusting Facts. 2014. (Dr. Dino's Learnatorium Ser.: 1). (ENG., Illus.). 122p. (J). (gr. 4-7). pap. 8.99 *(978-1-78219-766-9(4))* Blake, John Publishing, Ltd. GBR. Dist: Independent Pubs. Group.

Boyer, Crispin. Famous Fails! 2016. (ENG., Illus.). 128p. (J). (gr. 3-7). pap. 12.99 *(978-1-4263-2548-9(7),* National Geographic Children's Bks.) National Geographic Society.

—National Geographic Kids Why? 1,111 Answers to Everything. 2015. (ENG., Illus.). 192p. (J). (gr. 3-7). 19.99 *(978-1-4263-2096-5(5),* National Geographic Children's Bks.) National Geographic Society.

—That's Creepy: Spine-Tingling Facts That Will Test Your Creep-Out Factor. 2013. (ENG.). 176p. (J). (gr. 3-7). lib. bdg. 21.95 *(978-1-4263-1367-7(5),* National Geographic Children's Bks.) National Geographic Society.

—That's Deadly! 2015. (Illus.). 176p. (J). *(978-0-545-88319-1(9))* National Geographic Society.

Boyer, Crispin. What Would Happen? Serious Answers to Silly Questions. 2017. (ENG.). 176p. (J). (gr. 3-7). lib. bdg. 24.90 ***(978-1-4263-2771-1(4));*** (Illus.). pap. 14.99 ***(978-1-4263-2770-4(6))*** National Geographic Society. (National Geographic Children's Bks.).

Boyer, Crispin & National Geographic Kids Staff. That's Creepy: Spine-Tingling Facts That Will Test Your Creep-Out Factor. 2013. (ENG., Illus.). 176p. (J). (gr. 3-7). pap. 12.95 *(978-1-4263-1366-0(7),* National Geographic Children's Bks.) National Geographic Society.

—That's Deadly! Fatal Facts That Will Test Your Fearless-Factor. 2015. (ENG., Illus.). 176p. (J). (gr. 3-7). pap. 12.99 *(978-1-4263-2078-1(7),* National Geographic Children's Bks.) National Geographic Society.

—That's Sneaky! Stealthy Secrets & Devious Data That Will Test Your Lie Detector. 2014. (ENG., Illus.). 176p. (J). (gr. 3-7). pap. 12.99 *(978-1-4263-1783-5(2));* lib. bdg. 21.95 *(978-1-4263-1784-2(0))* National Geographic Society. (National Geographic Children's Bks.).

Brant, Cherie. Legends of Ventura County. 2003. per. 9.99 *(978-0-9722936-4-8(7),* Legends1) Del Sol Pubns.

Brill, Calista. Guinness World Records: Wacky & Wild! 2016. (J). lib. bdg. 24.50 *(978-0-606-38194-9(5))* Turtleback Bks.

Bunnell, James. Night Orbs. 2003. (Illus.). 296p. per. 22.00 *(978-0-9709249-2-6(5))* Lacey Publishing Co.

Burke, Kathy & Pearson Education Staff. Mysteries of the Unexplained. 2007. (ENG., Illus.). iv, 44p. pap. 17.32 *(978-1-4058-5212-8(7))* Pearson Education.

Burns, Jan. Crop Circles. 2008. (Mysterious Encounters Ser.). (ENG., Illus.). 48p. (gr. 4-8). lib. bdg. 33.60 *(978-0-7377-4047-9(7),* Kidhaven) Cengage Gale.

Calkhoven, Laurie & Herndon, Ryan. Fearless Feats: Incredible Records of Human Achievement. 2006. (Guinness World Records Ser.). (ENG., Illus.). 96p. (J). (gr. 5-9). per. 5.99 *(978-0-439-71565-2(2))* Scholastic, Inc.

Campbell, Rod. Who's That? 2003. (Illus.). 10p. (J). pap. 7.99 *(978-1-85292-031-9(9),* Campbell Bks.) Pan Macmillan GBR. Dist: Trafalgar Square Publishing.

Carangelo, Audrey. How Unusual! 2006. (Illus.). 16p. *(978-0-439-75712-6(6))* Scholastic, Inc.

Carney, Elizabeth & National Geographic Kids Staff. Little Kids First Big Book of the World. 2015. (National Geographic Little Kids First Big Bks.). (ENG., Illus.). 128p. (J). (gr. -1-3). 14.99 *(978-1-4263-2050-7(7),* National Geographic Children's Bks.) National Geographic Society.

Cerulean, Susan I., et al, eds. Between Two Rivers: Stories from the Red Hills to the Gulf. Meyer, Nancy, illus. 2004. 352p. (YA). per. 21.95 *(978-0-9759339-0-9(6))* Red Hills Writers Project.

Chandler, Matt, et al. All-Star Goofball Trivia: Weird & Wild Sports Trivia. 2017. (Sports Illustrated Kids Ser.). (ENG., Illus.). 144p. (gr. 3-4). pap. 9.95 *(978-1-62370-778-1(1))* Capstone Press of Coughlan Cos.

Chanko, Pamela. Totally Wacky Roadside Attractions. 2017. (Rookie Amazing America(tm) Ser.). (ENG., Illus.). 32p. (J). pap. 5.95 *(978-0-531-22592-9(5),* Children's Pr.) Scholastic Library Publishing.

Chesire, Gerald. People & Places. Antram, David, illus. 2008. (World of Wonder Ser.). (ENG.). 32p. (J). (gr. 1-4). 29.00 *(978-0-531-24028-1(2),* Children's Pr.) Scholastic Library Publishing.

—People & Places. Antram, David et al, illus. 2008. (World of Wonder Ser.). (ENG.). 32p. (J). (gr. 1-4). pap. 9.95 *(978-0-531-23824-0(5),* Children's Pr.) Scholastic Library Publishing.

A Child's First Library of Learning, 30 bks. Incl. Animal Friends. Time-Life Staff. (Illus.). 88p. (gr. -1-4). 1999. 14.95 *(978-0-8094-4849-4(1));* Animals in Action. (Illus.). 88p. (gr. -1-2). 1999. 14.95 *(978-0-8094-4869-2(6));* Dangerous Animals. Time-Life Books Editors. Kinney, Karin, ed. (Illus.). 88p. (gr. -1-3). 1996. 16.00 *(978-0-8094-9480-4(9));* Everyday Life. Cfl. (Illus.). 88p. (gr. -1-4). 1999. 14.95 *(978-0-8094-4865-4(3));* Explorers & Adventurers. Time-Life Books Editors. Fallow, Allan, ed. (Illus.). 88p. (gr. -1-3). 1996. lib. bdg. *(978-0-8094-9482-8(5));* Famous Places. Gakken Co. Ltd. Editors. Time-Life Books Editors, tr. (Illus.). 88p. (gr. 1-4). 1999. 14.95 *(978-0-8094-4893-7(9));* Feelings & Manners. Time-Life Books Editors. Fallow, Allan, ed. (Illus.). 88p. (gr. -1-3). 1997. 14.95 *(978-0-8094-9483-5(3));* Flowers & Trees. Time-Life Staff. (Illus.). 88p. (gr. 1-4). 1999. 14.95 *(978-0-8094-4857-9(2));* Health & Safety. Time-Life Books Editors. 1996. *(978-0-8094-9479-8(5));* How Things Work in Your Home. Time-Life Books Editors. (Illus.). 88p. (gr. 1-4). 1999. 14.95 *(978-0-8094-4873-9(4));* Insect World. Time-Life Books Editors. (Illus.). 88p. (gr. -1-3). 1999. 14.95 *(978-0-8094-4841-8(6));* Science Starter. Time-Life Books Editors. (Illus.). 88p. (gr. 1-4). 1999. 14.95 *(978-0-8094-4881-4(5));* Sky & Earth. Time-Life Books Editors. (Illus.). 88p. (gr. 1-4). 1999. 14.95 *(978-0-8094-4837-1(8));* Things Around Us. Time-Life Staff. (Illus.). 88p. (gr. -1-2). 1999. 14.95 *(978-0-8094-4845-6(9));* Things to Do. Gakken Co. Ltd. Editors & Time-Life Books Editors. (Illus.). 88p. (gr. 1-4). 1999. 14.95 *(978-0-8094-4897-5(1));* Wheels & Wings. Gakken Co. Ltd. Editors. Time-Life Books Editors, tr. (Illus.). 88p. (gr. 1-4). 1999. 14.95 *(978-0-8094-4861-6(0));* Where Things Come From. Time-Life Books Editors. Fallow, Allan, ed. (Illus.). 88p. (gr. -1-3). 1997. *(978-0-8094-9484-2(1));* Wind & Weather. Gakken Co. Ltd. Editors. Time-Life Books Editors, tr. (Illus.). 88p. (gr. 1-4). 1999. 14.95 *(978-0-8094-4829-6(7));* World We Live In. Gakken Co. Ltd. Editors. Time-Life Books Editors, tr. (Illus.). 88p. (gr. 1-4). 1999. 14.95 *(978-0-8094-4885-2(8));* (J). 403.88 *(978-0-8094-9499-6(X))* Time-Life, Inc.

Child's World Staff & Watson, S. B. Weird Sports of the World. 2011. (Weird Sports Ser.). (ENG., Illus.). 24p. (J). (gr. 2-5). lib. bdg. 28.50 *(978-1-60954-378-5(5),* 201056) Child's World, Inc., The.

Child's World Staff, The & Kelley, K. C. Weird Sports Moments. 2011. (Weird Sports Ser.). (ENG., Illus.). 24p. (J). (gr. 2-5). lib. bdg. 28.50 *(978-1-60954-377-8(7),* 201055) Child's World, Inc., The.

Child's World Staff, The & Watson, S. B. Weird Animal Sports. 2011. (Weird Sports Ser.). (ENG., Illus.). 24p. (J). (gr. 2-5). lib. bdg. 28.50 *(978-1-60954-375-4(0),* 201053) Child's World, Inc., The.

Clay, Kathryn & Vonne, Mira. Top 10 Unsolved Mysteries, 1 vol. 2012. (Top 10 Unexplained Ser.). (ENG.). 32p. (gr. 1-2). 26.65 *(978-1-4296-7637-3(X),* Blazers) Capstone Press of Coughlan Cos.

Clay, Kathryn, et al. Top 10 Unexplained. 2012. (Top 10 Unexplained Ser.). (ENG.). 32p. (gr. 1-2). lib. bdg. 106.60 *(978-1-4296-8185-8(3),* Blazers) Capstone Press of Coughlan Cos.

Claybourne, Anna. 100 Most Awesome Things on the Planet. 2011. (ENG.). 112p. (J). (gr. 3-7). pap. 7.99 *(978-0-545-26848-6(6),* Scholastic Paperbacks) Scholastic, Inc.

—100 Most Dangerous Things on the Planet. 2008. (ENG.). 112p. (J). (gr. 3-7). pap. 7.99 *(978-0-545-06927-4(0),* Scholastic Reference) Scholastic, Inc.

—100 Scariest Things on the Planet. 2011. (ENG.). 112p. (J). (gr. 3-7). pap. 7.99 *(978-0-545-37444-6(8),* Scholastic Paperbacks) Scholastic, Inc.

Clifford, Clive. Atlas of Oddities. Worrall, Tracy, illus. 2016. (ENG.). 96p. (J). (gr. 2). 16.95 *(978-1-4549-2176-9(5))* Sterling Publishing Co., Inc.

Coddington, Andrew. The Bermuda Triangle, Stonehenge, & Unexplained Places. 2017. (J). ***(978-1-5026-2843-5(0))*** Cavendish Square Publishing.

Collins. Collins Fascinating Facts - Amazing Places. rev. ed. 2016. (Collins Fascinating Facts Ser.). (ENG.). 72p. (J). (gr. 1-3). pap. 10.99 *(978-0-00-816919-0(5))* HarperCollins Pubs. Ltd. GBR. Dist: Independent Pubs. Group.

Collins, Terry Lee & Weakland, Mark Andrew. Scooby-Doo! & the Truth Behind Zombies. 2016. (Illus.). 24p. (J). *(978-1-4062-8894-0(2))* Capstone Press of Coughlan Cos.

—Scooby Doo Unmasks the Truth Behind Ghosts. 2016. (Illus.). 24p. (J). *(978-1-4062-8899-5(3))* Capstone Press of Coughlan Cos.

—Scooby Doo Unmasks the Truth Behind Sea Monsters. 2016. (Illus.). 24p. (J). *(978-1-4062-8898-8(5))* Capstone Press of Coughlan Cos.

Cornsweet, Tom. Why Is Everything! Doing Science. 2009. 260p. 29.95 *(978-0-595-51834-0(6));* pap. 19.95 *(978-0-595-52871-4(6))* iUniverse, Inc.

Crabtree Publishing Co. Staff & Burns, Kylie. What's the Problem? How to Start Your Scientific Investigation. 2009. (Step into Science Ser.). (ENG., Illus.). 32p. (J). (gr. 3-6). pap. *(978-0-7787-5173-1(2));* lib. bdg. *(978-0-7787-5158-8(9))* Crabtree Publishing Co.

Crazy Animals. 2014. (Ripleys Believe It or Not! Download the Weird Ser.: 8). 36p. (J). (gr. 4-18). lib. bdg. 20.95 *(978-1-4222-3149-4(6))* Mason Crest.

Curiosidades y Ejemplos.Tr. of Curiosities & Examples. (SPA.). (J). (gr. 4-5). 29.95 *(978-968-416-014-9(3),* 204U) Fernandez USA Publishing.

Curious Critters. 2014. (Ripleys Believe It or Not! Dare to Look Ser.: 8). 36p. (J). (gr. 4-18). lib. bdg. 20.95 *(978-1-4222-3141-8(0))* Mason Crest.

Dalby, L. Mysteries & Marvels of Nature. 2004. 128p. (J). lib. bdg. 27.95 *(978-1-58086-610-1(7),* Usborne) EDC Publishing.

Dalgleish, Sharon. It's a Mystery. 2003. (Real Deal Ser.). (Illus.). 32p. (J). pap. *(978-0-7608-6692-4(9))* Sundance/Newbridge Educational Publishing.

Davies, Gill. 365 Awesome Facts & Records about Everything. McRae, Anne, ed. Ravaglia, Paola et al, illus. 2008. (365 Awesome Facts & Records Ser.). (ENG.). 176p. (J). (gr. 1-18). 19.95 (978-88-6098-001-4(1)) McRae Bks. Srl ITA. Dist: Independent Pubs. Group.

Davies, Gill & Morris, Neil. 365 Awesome Facts & Records about Nature. 2008. (365 Awesome Facts & Records Ser.). (ENG., Illus.). 176p. (J). (gr. 1-18). 19.95 (978-88-6098-112-7(3)) McRae Bks. Srl ITA. Dist: Independent Pubs. Group.

Dicker, Katie. Missing! 2015. (Mystery! Ser.). (Illus.). 24p. (gr. 3-6). 28.50 (978-1-62588-201-7(7)) Black Rabbit Bks.

—Mysterious Creatures. 2015. (Mystery! Ser.). 24p. (gr. 3-6). 28.50 (978-1-62588-202-8(5)) Black Rabbit Bks.

—Mysterious Messages. 2015. (Mystery! Ser.). 24p. (gr. 3-6). 28.50 (978-1-62588-203-5(3)) Black Rabbit Bks.

—Mysterious Places. 2015. (Mystery! Ser.). (Illus.). 24p. (gr. 3-6). 28.50 (978-1-62588-204-2(1)) Black Rabbit Bks.

Digging into History, 6 bks., Set. Incl. Solving the Mysteries of Ancient Rome. Hanbury-Murphy, Trudy. lib. bdg. 29.93 (978-0-7614-3101-5(2)); Solving the Mysteries of Aztec Cities. Croy, Anita. lib. bdg. 29.93 (978-0-7614-3102-2(0)); Solving the Mysteries of Machu Picchu. Croy, Anita. lib. bdg. 29.93 (978-0-7614-3103-9(9)); Solving the Mysteries of Pompeii. Samuel, Charlie. lib. bdg. 29.93 (978-0-7614-3105-3(5)); Solving the Mysteries of Stonehenge. Gray, Leon. lib. bdg. 29.93 (978-0-7614-3110-7(1)); Solving the Mysteries of the Pyramids. MacDonald, Fiona. lib. bdg. 29.93 (978-0-7614-3106-0(3)); 32p. (gr. 4-18). (Digging into History Ser.). 2008. Set lib. bdg. 179.58 (978-0-7614-3100-8(4), Benchmark Bks.) Marshall Cavendish Corp.

Diker, Katie. Missing! 2015. (ENG., Illus.). 24p. (J). pap. 8.95 (978-1-77092-232-7(6)) RiverStream Publishing.

—Mysterious Creatures. 2015. (ENG., Illus.). 24p. (J). pap. 8.95 (978-1-77092-233-4(4)) RiverStream Publishing.

—Mysterious Messages. 2015. (ENG., Illus.). 24p. (J). pap. 8.95 (978-1-77092-234-1(2)) RiverStream Publishing.

—Mysterious Places. 2015. (ENG., Illus.). 24p. (J). pap. 8.95 (978-1-77092-235-8(0)) RiverStream Publishing.

DiPerna, Kaitlyn. Smithsonian First Discoveries: Little Learner. Riggs, Jenna, illus. 2016. (Smithsonian First Discoveries Ser.). (ENG.). 48p. (J). 16.95 (978-1-62686-482-5(9), Silver Dolphin Bks.) Readerlink Distribution Services, LLC.

Discovery Education. 2013. (Discovery Education Ser.). 32p. (J). (gr. 3-6). 1035.25 (978-1-4777-1555-0(X)); pap. 410.00 (978-1-4777-2736-2(1)); pap. 2460.00 (978-1-4777-2737-9(X)) Rosen Publishing Group, Inc., The. (PowerKids Pr.).

Discovery Education: Discoveries & Inventions. 2013. (Discovery Education: Discoveries & Inventions Ser.). 32p. (J). (gr. 3-6). 151.50 (978-1-4777-1551-2(7)); pap. 360.00 (978-1-4777-2700-3(0)); pap. 60.00 (978-1-4777-2699-0(3)) Rosen Publishing Group, Inc., The. (PowerKids Pr.).

Dompierre, Judith. Read It Whichever Direction You Want. 2011. 50p. pap. 24.95 (978-1-4512-6625-2(1)) America Star Bks.

Dorling Kindersley Publishing Staff. All about Everything. 2014. (ENG., Illus.). 304p. (J). (gr. 4-7). pap. 12.99 (978-1-4654-1746-6(X), DK Children) Dorling Kindersley Publishing, Inc.

—I Can't Believe It! 2017. (ENG., Illus.). 352p. (J). (gr. 4-7). pap. 12.99 (**978-1-4654-6236-7(8)**, DK Children) Dorling Kindersley Publishing, Inc.

—It Can't Be True. 2016. (DK Braille Ser.). (ENG.). 72p. (J). (gr. 4-7). 29.99 (978-1-4654-4406-6(8), DK Children) Dorling Kindersley Publishing, Inc.

—Strange but True! 2015. (ENG., Illus.). 192p. (J). (gr. 3-7). 19.99 (978-1-4654-3911-6(0), DK Children) Dorling Kindersley Publishing, Inc.

—Wonders of the World. 2014. (DK Eyewitness Bks.). (ENG.). 72p. (J). (gr. 3-7). pap. 9.99 (978-1-4654-2249-1(8), DK Children) Dorling Kindersley Publishing, Inc.

Dorling Kindersley Publishing Staff. 131/2 Incredible Things You Need to Know about Everything. 2017. (ENG.). 176p. (J). (gr. 3-7). 24.99 (**978-1-4654-6112-4(4)**, DK Children) Dorling Kindersley Publishing, Inc.

Dorling Kindersley Publishing Staff & Bingham, Caroline. My Encyclopedia of Very Important Things. 2016. (ENG., Illus.). 224p. (J). (**978-0-241-22493-9(4)**) Dorling Kindersley Publishing, Inc.

Dover & Hourglass Press, Hourglass. Art Smart: Spot the Details & Find Out the Facts! 2015. (ENG., Illus.). 64p. (J). (gr. 1-6). pap. 9.99 (978-0-486-79220-0(X)) Dover Pubns., Inc.

Doyle, Oliver. Strange Mysteries of the Unexplained. 2012. (ENG.). 96p. (J). (gr. 3-7). pap. 6.99 (978-0-545-47824-3(3)) Scholastic, Inc.

Drake, Carol. The 10 Most Incredible Ancient Wonders. 2007. (J). 14.99 (978-1-55448-467-6(7)) Scholastic Library Publishing.

Dutton, Michael. Fantastic Facts! Tantalizing Trivia from Around the World! 2009. (Dover Coloring Bks.). (ENG., Illus.). 32p. (J). (gr. 1-5). pap. 3.99 (978-0-486-47249-2(3)) Dover Pubns., Inc.

Editors of TIME For Kids Magazine. Time for Kids Big Book of Answers: 1,001 Facts Kids Want to Know. 2015. (TIME for Kids Big Bks.). (ENG., Illus.). 192p. (J). (gr. 3-17). 19.95 (978-1-61893-150-4(4)) Time Inc. Bks.

—Time for Kids Big Book of How: 501 Facts Kids Want to Know. 2011. (TIME for Kids Big Bks.). (ENG., Illus.). 192p. (J). (gr. 3-7). 19.95 (978-1-60320-184-1(X)) Time Inc. Bks.

—Time for Kids Big Book of Where. 2013. (TIME for Kids Big Bks.). (ENG., Illus.). 192p. (J). (gr. 3-17). 19.95 (978-1-61893-042-2(7)) Time Inc. Bks.

—Top 5 of Everything: Tallest, Tastiest, Fastest! 2013. (ENG., Illus.). 144p. (J). (gr. 3-17). pap. 11.99 (978-1-60320-953-3(0)) Time Inc. Bks.

Eggleton, Jill. Fact or Fiction? 2007. (Connectors Ser.). (gr. 2-5). pap. (978-1-877453-22-9(6)) Global Education Systems Ltd.

Extraordinary Bodies. 2014. (Ripleys Believe It or Not! Download the Weird Ser.: 8). 36p. (J). (gr. 4-18). lib. bdg. 20.95 (978-1-4222-3150-0(X)) Mason Crest.

Forty, Sandra. Wonders of the World. 2009. (Illus.). 158p. (YA). (978-1-84406-127-3(2)) Taj Bks., Ltd.

From the Earth to the Moon / 100 Facts You Should Know: Space Paired Set. 2016. (LitLinks Ser.). (gr. 8-6). 61.27 (978-1-4824-5384-3(3)) Stevens, Gareth Publishing LLLP.

From the Earth to the Moon / 100 Facts You Should Know: Space Reader Resource Guide. 2016. (LitLinks Ser.). (gr. 8-6). pap. (978-1-4824-5409-3(2)) Stevens, Gareth Publishing LLLP.

Frost, Adam. The Awesome Book of Awesomeness. Bramall, Dan, illus. 2015. (ENG.). 112p. (J). (gr. 2-4). pap. 9.99 (978-1-61963-793-1(6), 9781619637931, Bloomsbury USA Childrens) Bloomsbury Publishing USA.

Fun Fact File: Complete Set. 2016. (Fun Fact File Ser.). 32p. (gr. 3-2). lib. bdg. 1363.50 (978-1-4824-5278-5(2)) Stevens, Gareth Publishing LLLP.

Fun Fact File (August 2014) 2014. (Fun Fact File Ser.). 32p. (J). (gr. 2-5). 909.00 (978-1-4824-1514-8(3)); pap. 378.00 (978-1-4824-1605-3(0)) Stevens, Gareth Publishing LLLP.

Gaarder, Jostein. Questions Asked. Bartlett, Don, tr. from NOR. Duezakin, Akin, illus. 2017. (ENG.). 72p. (J). (gr. -1-2). 14.00 (978-0-914671-66-4(9), Elsewhere Editions) Steerforth Pr.

Ganeri, Anita. The Book of World Facts Purple Band. 2016. (Cambridge Reading Adventures Ser.). (ENG.). 24p. pap. 7.19 (978-1-316-60080-1(7)) Cambridge Univ. Pr.

Ganeri, Anita & West, David. Lost in the Bermuda Triangle & Other Mysteries. 2011. (Incredible True Adventures Ser.). (ENG.). 48p. (YA). (gr. 5-8). pap. 11.75 (978-1-4488-6662-5(6)); lib. bdg. 29.25 (978-1-4488-6658-8(8)) Rosen Publishing Group, Inc., The. (Rosen Reference).

Garbe, Suzanne. The World's Craziest Records. 2015. (Library of Weird Ser.). (ENG., Illus.). 32p. (gr. 3-4). lib. bdg. 27.99 (978-1-4914-2015-7(4)) Capstone Press of Coughlan Cos.

Gareth Guides to an Extraordinary Life. 2017. (Gareth Guides to an Extraordinary Life Ser.). 32p. (gr. 4-5). pap. 63.00 (**978-1-5382-0485-6(1)**); lib. bdg. 159.60 (**978-1-5382-0471-9(1)**) Stevens, Gareth Publishing LLLP.

Gifford, Clive. 100 Grossest Facts. 2014. (Illus.). 112p. (J). pap. (978-1-4351-5524-4(6)) Barnes & Noble, Inc.

—100 Weirdest Facts. 2014. (Illus.). 112p. (J). pap. (978-1-4351-5525-1(4)) Barnes & Noble, Inc.

Gilpin, Daniel. Record-Breaking Animals. 2012. (Record Breakers Ser.). (Illus.). 32p. lib. bdg. 26.50 (978-1-4488-5287-1(0), PowerKids Pr.) Rosen Publishing Group, Inc., The.

Goodman, Michael E. Dark Labyrinths. (Scary Places Ser.). 32p. (gr. 4-8). 2017. (ENG.) (J). 8.95 (**978-1-68402-607-4(5)**) 2010. (Illus.). (YA). lib. bdg. 25.27 (978-1-936087-56-3(1)) Bearport Publishing Co., Inc.

Gordon, Sharon. Adivina Quién, 6 bks., Set. Incl. Adivina Quien Atrapa. lib. bdg. 15.95 (978-0-7614-2383-6(4)); Adivina Quien Baja en Picada. lib. bdg. 15.95 (978-0-7614-2387-4(7)); Adivina Quien Cambia. lib. bdg. 15.95 (978-0-7614-2380-5(X)); Adivina Quien Ruge. lib. bdg. 15.95 (978-0-7614-2386-7(9)); Adivina Quien Se Esconde. lib. bdg. 15.95 (978-0-7614-2385-0(0)); Adivina Quien Se Zambulle. lib. bdg. 15.95 (978-0-7614-2381-2(8)); (Illus.). (gr. k-2). (Bookworms — Spanish Editions: Adivina Quien Ser.). (SPA.). 32p. 2006. Set lib. bdg. 95.70 (978-0-7614-2379-9(6)) Marshall Cavendish Corp.

—Guess Who (Adivina Quién), 6 bks., Set. Incl. Guess Who Changes/Adivina Quien Cambia. lib. bdg. 15.95 (978-0-7614-2461-1(X)); Guess Who Dives/Adivina Quien Se Zambulle. lib. bdg. 15.95 (978-0-7614-2462-8(8)); Guess Who Grabs/Adivina Quien Atrapa. lib. bdg. 15.95 (978-0-7614-2464-2(4)); Guess Who Hides/Adivina Quien Se Esconde. lib. bdg. 15.95 (978-0-7614-2465-9(2)); Guess Who Roars/Adivina Quien Ruge. lib. bdg. 15.95 (978-0-7614-2466-6(0)); Guess Who Swoops/Adivina Quien Baja en Picada. lib. bdg. 15.95 (978-0-7614-2468-0(7)); (Illus.). 32p. (gr. k-2). (Bookworms — Bilingual Editions: Guess Who/Adivina Quien Ser.). (ENG & SPA.). 2006. Set lib. bdg. 95.70 (978-0-7614-2459-8(8)) Marshall Cavendish Corp.

Gors, Steven E. The Secret Files of Professor L. Otto Funn: Or, Stop Being a Slug, Open This Book, & Make Your Brain Happy. Carrington, Matt, illus. 2013. 159p. (J). pap. (978-0-7166-1324-4(7)) World Bk., Inc.

Gould, Francesca. Why Fish Fart: Gross but True Things You'll Wish You Didn't Know. Coovert, J. P., illus. 2014. (ENG.). 144p. (J). (gr. 3-7). pap. 8.99 (978-0-399-16598-6(3), G.P. Putnam's Sons Books for Young Readers) Penguin Young Readers Group.

Graham, Ian. Extreme Comparisons: Fastest, Tallest, Strongest, Biggest Record Breakers. Bergin, Mark, illus. 2014. (Big Book Of... Ser.). 64p. (gr. 3-6). 37.10 (**978-1-907184-91-8(0)**) Book Hse. GBR. Dist: Black Rabbit Bks.

Graziano, John, illus. Woof! Funny Pet Stories. 2012. 96p. (J). pap. (978-0-545-38687-6(X)) Ripley Entertainment, Inc.

Greathouse, Lisa & Kuligowski, Stephanie. Unsolved! Mysterious Events, 1 vol. 2nd rev. ed. 2012. (Nonfiction Readers Ser.). (ENG., Illus.). 48p. (J). (gr. 4-4). pap. 9.99 (978-1-4333-4827-3(6)) Teacher Created Materials, Inc.

—Unsolved! Mysterious Places, 1 vol. 2nd rev. ed. 2012. (Nonfiction Readers Ser.). (ENG., Illus.). 48p. (J). (gr. 4-4). pap. 9.99 (978-1-4333-4828-0(4)) Teacher Created Materials, Inc.

Greathouse, Lisa E. & Kuligowski, Stephanie. ¡Sin Resolver! Casos Misteriosos. 2017. (TIME for Kids en Español - Level 4 Ser.). (SPA.). 48p. (gr. 4-4). lib. bdg. 31.99 (978-1-5157-5132-8(5)) Time for Kids Inc AUS. Dist: Capstone Pub.

—¡Sin Resolver! Lugares Misteriosos. 2017. (TIME for Kids en Español - Level 4 Ser.). (SPA.). 48p. (gr. 4-4). lib. bdg. 31.99 (978-1-5157-5133-5(3)) Time for Kids Inc AUS. Dist: Capstone Pub.

Greene, Janice. Strange but True, 1 vol., Bk. 5. unabr. ed. 2011. (Strange but True Ser.). (ENG.). 75p. (YA). (gr. 9-12). pap. 8.95 (978-1-61651-769-4(7)) Saddleback Educational Publishing, Inc.

—Strange but True Book 1, 1 vol. unabr. ed. 2011. (Strange but True Ser.). (ENG.). 76p. (YA). (gr. 9-12). pap. 8.95 (978-1-61651-765-6(4)) Saddleback Educational Publishing, Inc.

—Strange but True Stories Book 1: The Presidential Ghost, Mystery Spots on Earth, UFO or Weather Balloon? ... & More. 2006. (Strange but True Ser.). 76p. (YA). (gr. 8-12). per. (978-1-59905-010-2(2)) Saddleback Educational Publishing, Inc.

—Strange but True Stories Book 5. 2006. (Strange but True Ser.). 75p. (J). per. 6.95 (978-1-59905-014-0(5), SA0145) Saddleback Educational Publishing, Inc.

Guest, John. Amazing True Facts. 2012. (Illus.). 224p. (978-1-4351-4353-1(1)) Barnes & Noble, Inc.

Guinness Editors. Guinness World Records 2016, Gamers Edition. 2015. lib. bdg. 26.95 (978-0-606-38494-0(4)) Turtleback Bks.

Hamilton, John. Fantasy & Folklore. 2004. (Fantasy & Folklore Ser.). (gr. 4-8). 162.42 (978-1-59197-710-0(X), Abdo & Daughters) ABDO Publishing Co.

Hamilton, Sue. Unsolved Mysteries, 6 vols., Set. Incl. Air & Sea Mysteries. (gr. 3-7). 27.07 (978-1-59928-837-6(0), Abdo & Daughters); Bermuda Triangle. (J). (gr. 3-7). lib. bdg. 27.07 (978-1-59928-834-5(6), Abdo & Daughter); Creatures of the Abyss. (gr. 3-7). 27.07 (978-1-59928-836-9(2), Abdo & Daughters); Lost Cities. (gr. 4-7). 27.07 (978-1-59928-832-1(X), Abdo & Daughters); Monsters of Mystery. (gr. 3-7). 27.07 (978-1-59928-835-2(4), Abdo & Daughters); (Unsolved Mysteries Ser.). 32p. 2007. 162.42 (978-1-59928-831-4(1), Abdo & Daughters) ABDO Publishing Co.

Hammelef, Danielle S., et al. Super Trivia Collection. 2012. (Super Trivia Collection). (ENG.). 32p. (gr. 3-4). lib. bdg. 83.97 (978-1-4296-9145-1(X), Edge Bks.) Capstone Press of Coughlan Cos.

Hansen, Grace. Places to Amaze You!, 1 vol. 2014. (Seeing Is Believing Ser.). (ENG., Illus.). 24p. (J). lib. bdg. 28.50 (978-1-62970-733-4(3)) ABDO Publishing Co.

—Seeing Is Believing, 1 vol. 2014. (Seeing Is Believing Ser.: 6). (ENG.). 24p. (J). (gr. 2-4). lib. bdg. 171.00 (978-1-62970-730-3(9)) ABDO Publishing Co.

Hard to Believe. 2014. (Ripleys Believe It or Not! Dare to Look Ser.: 8). 36p. (J). (gr. 4-18). lib. bdg. 20.95 (978-1-4222-3143-2(7)) Mason Crest.

Harrison, Kathryn & Hall, Allan. The World's Most Shocking Secrets & Mysteries. 2016. (Making Headlines Ser.). 160p. (J). lib. bdg. 39.93 (978-0-7660-8372-1(1)) Enslow Pubs., Inc.

Hawkins, John. The World's Strangest Unexplained Mysteries. 2012. (Mystery Hunters Ser.). (ENG.). 32p. (J). (gr. 4-6). pap. 10.60 (978-1-4488-6443-0(7)); lib. bdg. 25.25 (978-1-4488-6430-0(5)) Rosen Publishing Group, Inc., The. (PowerKids Pr.).

Helstrom, Kraig. Crop Circles. 2011. (Unexplained Ser.). (ENG., Illus.). 24p. (J). (gr. 3-7). lib. bdg. 25.95 (978-1-60014-583-4(3), Torque Bks.) Bellwether Media.

Hennessy, B. G. The Scary Places Map Book: Seven Terrifying Tours. Madrid, Erwin, illus. 2012. (ENG.). 32p. (J). (gr. k-4). 15.99 (978-0-7636-4541-0(9)) Candlewick Pr.

Herbst, Judith. Hoaxes. 2004. (Unexplained Ser.). (Illus.). 48p. (J). pap. 7.95 (978-0-8225-2406-9(6), Lerner Pubns.); (ENG., (gr. 5-12). lib. bdg. 26.60 (978-0-8225-1629-3(2)) Lerner Publishing Group.

—Lands of Mystery. 2004. (Unexplained Ser.). (Illus.). 48p. (J). pap. 7.95 (978-0-8225-2407-6(4)); (ENG., (gr. 5-12). lib. bdg. 26.60 (978-0-8225-1630-9(6)) Lerner Publishing Group.

Herndon, Ryan, compiled by. 3-D Extreme! 2006. (Illus.). 31p. (J). pap. (978-0-439-79190-8(1)) Scholastic, Inc.

Herweck Rice, Dona. ¡Sin Resolver! Misterios de la Historia. 2017. (TIME for Kids en Español - Level 4 Ser.). (SPA., Illus.). 48p. (gr. 4-4). lib. bdg. 31.99 (978-1-5157-5134-2(1)) Time for Kids Inc AUS. Dist: Capstone Pub.

Hibbert, Adam. World Wonders. 2010. (Unpredictable Nature Ser.). 48p. (J). (gr. 3-18). lib. bdg. 19.95 (978-1-4222-2008-5(7)) Mason Crest.

Higgins, Nadia. UFOs. 2014. (Unexplained Mysteries Ser.). (ENG., Illus.). 24p. (J). (gr. 3-7). lib. bdg. 25.95 (978-1-62617-107-7(6), Epic Bks.) Bellwether Media.

Hill, Nancy S. The One Year Did You Know Devotions 2. 2009. (ENG., Illus.). 416p. (J). pap. 13.99 (978-1-4143-2014-4(0), Tyndale Kids) Tyndale Hse. Pubs.

Hinman, Bonnie. Fascinating History. 2018. (ENG.). 32p. (gr. 3-6). 31.35 (**978-1-63235-420-4(9)**, 12-Story Library) Pr. Room Editions LLC.

Hirschmann, Kris & Herndon, Ryan, compiled by. Guinness World Records. 2011. (Illus.). 80p. (J). (978-0-545-30851-9(8)) Scholastic, Inc.

—Guinness World Records: Records of Overwhelming Size. 2007. (Illus.). 90p. (J). pap. (978-0-439-89829-4(3)) Scholastic, Inc.

History of the Bizarre. 2015. (History of the Bizarre Ser.). (ENG.). 32p. (gr. 3-4). 111.96 (978-1-4914-6662-9(6), Edge Bks.) Capstone Press of Coughlan Cos.

History's Mysteries. 2015. (History's Mysteries Ser.). (ENG.). 32p. (J). (gr. 4-5). 159.60 (978-1-4824-1648-0(4)) Stevens, Gareth Publishing LLLP.

Hobbs, Pamela. The Secret Elf. 2012. 26p. 24.95 (978-1-4626-7234-9(5)) America Star Bks.

Horn, Randy & Workman Publishing Company Staff. You Gotta Be Kidding! The Crazy Book of Would You Rather... ? Questions. 2006. (ENG., Illus.). 416p. (J). (gr. 4-12). pap. 8.95 (978-0-7611-4365-9(3), 14365) Workman Publishing Co., Inc.

How It Is Made. 2016. (How It Is Made Ser.). 24p. (J). lib. bdg. 145.26 (978-1-5026-2394-2(3)) Cavendish Square Publishing.

Hughes-Odgers, Kyle. Can a Skeleton Have an X-Ray? Hughes-Odgers, Kyle, illus. 2016. (ENG., Illus.). 32p. (J). (gr. -1-k). 16.99 (978-1-925162-69-1(9)) Fremantle Pr. AUS. Dist: Independent Pubs. Group.

Hunter, Nick. Top Secret! 2016. (Top Secret! Ser.). (ENG.). 48p. (gr. 5-8). 133.28 (978-1-4109-8171-4(1)) Heinemann-Raintree.

Hyde, Natalie. History Mysteries Revealed. 2010. (ENG., Illus.). 32p. (J). pap. (978-0-7787-7429-7(5)); (gr. 4-7). lib. bdg. (978-0-7787-7414-3(7)) Crabtree Publishing Co.

I Want to Know. 2016. (I Want to Know Ser.). 32p. (J). pap. 63.12 (978-0-7660-8396-7(9)) Enslow Pubs., Inc.

Incredible World. 2014. (Ripleys Believe It or Not! Download the Weird Ser.: 8). 36p. (J). (gr. 4-18). lib. bdg. 20.95 (978-1-4222-3151-7(8)) Mason Crest.

Jaffé, Laura. The Book of When. Cointe, François, illus. 2008. (ENG.). 96p. (J). (gr. 3-7). 17.95 (978-0-8109-7240-7(9), Abrams Bks. for Young Readers) Abrams, Inc.

Jr. Graphic Ghost Stories. 2014. (Jr. Graphic Ghost Stories Ser.). 24p. (J). (gr. 3-6). 157.50 (978-1-4777-7092-4(5), PowerKids Pr.) Rosen Publishing Group, Inc., The.

Kallen, Stuart A. Crop Circles. 2010. (Mysterious & Unknown Ser.). 104p. (YA). (gr. 7-12). lib. bdg. 26.95 (978-1-60152-103-3(0)) ReferencePoint Pr., Inc.

—Spontaneous Human Combustion. 2009. (Mysterious Encounters Ser.). (ENG., Illus.). 48p. (J). (gr. 4-8). lib. bdg. 29.00 (978-0-7377-4413-2(8), LML02109-245414, Kidhaven) Cengage Gale.

Kallio, Jamie. Bigfoot. 2015. (Unsolved Mysteries Ser.). (ENG.). 24p. (J). (gr. 1-4). 28.50 (978-1-63407-071-3(2), 208905) Child's World, Inc., The.

Kaplan, Asli. What, Why & How? 2013. (ENG., Illus.). 96p. (J). (gr. 3-7). pap. 9.95 (978-1-59784-287-7(7)) Tughra Bks.

—What, Why, & How? 2013. (ENG., Illus.). 104p. (J). (gr. 3-7). pap. 9.95 (978-1-59784-279-2(6)) Tughra Bks.

Karst, Ken. Bigfoot. 2015. (Enduring Mysteries Ser.). (J). lib. bdg. 23.30 (978-0-606-36993-0(7)) Turtleback Bks.

Khan, Hena. How to Be a Know-It-All on Almost Any Subject You Can Think Of. 2004. (How to Survive Anything Club Ser.). (Illus.). 80p. (J). pap. (978-0-439-57907-0(4)) Scholastic, Inc.

Krieger, Emily. Just When You Thought You Knew What You Knew ... Cocotos, Tom Nick, illus. 2014. (Myths Busted Ser.). (ENG.). 208p. (J). (gr. 4-7). pap. 7.99 (978-1-4263-1478-0(7), National Geographic Children's Bks.) National Geographic Society.

—National Geographic Kids Myths Busted! 2: Just When You Thought You Knew What You Knew ... Cocotos, Tom Nick, illus. 2014. (Myths Busted Ser.). (ENG.). 208p. (J). (gr. 4-7). lib. bdg. 16.90 (978-1-4263-1479-7(5), National Geographic Children's Bks.) National Geographic Society.

—Real or Fake? 2: More Far-Out Fibs, Fishy Facts, & Phony Photos to Test for the Truth. 2017. (ENG., Illus.). 208p. (J). (gr. 3-7). pap. 7.99 (978-1-4263-2778-0(1), National Geographic Children's Bks.) National Geographic Society.

Krohn, Katherine. Encountering Bigfoot: Eyewitness Accounts, 1 vol. Byers, Michael, illus. 2014. (Eyewitness to the Unexplained Ser.). (ENG.). 32p. (gr. 3-4). 30.65 (978-1-4914-0243-6(1), Graphic Library) Capstone Press of Coughlan Cos.

Kuligowski, Stephanie. Unsolved! Mysterious Events, 1 vol. 2nd rev. ed. 2013. (Nonfiction Readers Ser.). (ENG., Illus.). 48p. (J). (gr. 4-4). pap. 29.96 (978-1-4807-1103-7(9)) Shell Educational Publishing.

—Unsolved! Mysterious Places, 1 vol. 2nd rev. ed. 2013. (Nonfiction Readers Ser.). (ENG., Illus.). 48p. (J). (gr. 4-4). pap. 29.96 (978-1-4807-1104-4(7)) Shell Educational Publishing.

Lake, G. G. Take Your (Equally Horrible) Pick! 2017. (Take Your (Equally Horrible) Pick! Ser.). (ENG.). 32p. (gr. 1-2). 106.60 (978-1-5157-4490-0(6), Blazers) Capstone Press of Coughlan Cos.

Lara, Jose Luis Trueba. Descubrelas Diez Maravillas. 2006.Tr. of Discovery...The Ten Wonders. (SPA.). (J). (gr. 4-5). 18.95 (978-970-29-1058-9(7), AT33272) Santillana, Editorial, S.A. de C.V. MEX. Dist: Santillana USA Publishing Co., Inc.

Lassieur, Allison. Unsolved Historical Mysteries. 2015. (Unsolved Mystery Files Ser.). (ENG., Illus.). 32p. (gr. 3-4). pap. 7.95 (978-1-4914-4340-8(5)) Capstone Press of Coughlan Cos.

Lemke, Donald. Guinness World Records: Super Humans! 2016. (J). lib. bdg. 24.50 (978-0-606-38193-2(7)) Turtleback Bks.

Leokum, Arkady, et al. Weird & Wacky Facts. 2007. (ENG., Illus.). 352p. (J). (gr. 2-7). pap. 6.95 (978-1-4027-4987-2(2)) Sterling Publishing Co., Inc.

Levete, Sarah. Science Fact or Fiction? You Decide! 2010. (ENG.). 32p. (J). pap. (978-0-7787-9916-0(6)); (Illus.). (978-0-7787-9895-8(X), 1325460) Crabtree Publishing Co.

Life Magazine Editors. Greatest Unsolved Mysteries of All Time: 50 Baffling Cases from the Files. 2009. (ENG., Illus.). 128p. (gr. 7-17). 29.95 (978-1-60320-081-3(9)) Time Inc. Bks.

Life Strange but True. 2009. (Time Inc. Home Entertainment Library-Bound Titles Ser.). (ENG.). 128p. (gr. 5-12). 39.93 (978-0-7613-4231-1(1), Twenty-First Century Bks.) Lerner Publishing Group.

little bee books, little bee. Listopia: Planet Earth. 2016. (ENG., Illus.). 208p. (J). (gr. 2-4). pap. 9.99 (978-1-4998-0279-5(X)) Little Bee Books Inc.

Lonely Planet Publications Staff. Lonely Planet Unfolding Journeys - Following the Great Wall, 1 vol. 2017. (Lonely Planet Kids Ser.). (ENG., Illus.). 16p. (J). pap. 17.99 (**978-1-78657-198-4(6)**, 5414) Lonely Planet Pubns.

Lorimer, Janet. Strange but True Book 2, 1 vol. unabr. ed. 2011. (Strange but True Ser.). (ENG.). 75p. (YA). (gr. 9-12). pap. 8.95 (978-1-61651-766-3(2)) Saddleback Educational Publishing, Inc.

—Strange but True Book 3, 1 vol. unabr. ed. 2011. (Strange but True Ser.). (ENG.). 76p. (YA). (gr. 9-12). pap. 8.95 (978-1-61651-767-0(0)) Saddleback Educational Publishing, Inc.

—Strange but True Book 4, 1 vol. unabr. ed. 2011. (Strange but True Ser.). (ENG.). 76p. (YA). (gr. 9-12). pap. 8.95 (978-1-61651-768-7(9)) Saddleback Educational Publishing, Inc.

Magsamen, Susan. The Classic Collection of Childhood Wonders: Favorite Adventures, Stories, Poems, & Songs for Making Lasting Memories. 2010. (ENG.). 160p. (J). (gr. -1-2). lib. bdg. 28.90 (978-1-4263-0726-3(8), National Geographic Children's Bks.) National Geographic Society.

Magsamen, Susan & National Geographic Kids Staff. The Classic Treasury of Childhood Wonders: Favorite Adventures, Stories, Poems, & Songs for Making Lasting Memories. 2010. (ENG., Illus.). 160p. (J). (gr. -1-2). 19.95 (978-1-4263-0715-7(2), National Geographic Children's Bks.) National Geographic Society.

Make & Learn. 2014. (Make & Learn Ser.). 32p. (J). (gr. 3-6). pap. 70.50 (978-1-4777-7230-0(8), PowerKids Pr.) Rosen Publishing Group, Inc., The.

Malara, Maria. Mysterious Places. 2007. (Steck-Vaughn BOLDPRINT Anthologies Ser.). (ENG., Illus.). 48p. (gr. 4-8).

pap. 16.90 *(978-1-4190-4022-1(7))* Houghton Mifflin Harcourt Publishing Co.

Marek, Hillary. The smart ass guide to ridiculous Questions. 2010. 139p. pap. 11.06 *(978-0-557-30904-7(2))* Lulu Pr., Inc.

Martin, Mary-Jane. Let Me Put It This Way. 2004. (Illus.). 32p. 11.95 *(978-0-9730583-1-4(5))* Lion & Mouse Tales, Inc. CAN. Dist: Hushion Hse. Publishing, Ltd.

Martin, Michael, et al. A Creature in the Lake. 2013. (Unexplained Mysteries Ser.). (ENG.). 24p. (gr. 1-2). lib. bdg. 101.28 *(978-1-62065-137-7(8)*, First Facts) Capstone Press of Coughlan Cos.

—Unexplained Mysteries. 2013. (Unexplained Mysteries Ser.). (ENG.). 24p. (gr. 1-2). pap. 27.80 *(978-1-4765-3664-4(3))*; pap. 55.60 *(978-1-4765-3665-1(1))*; lib. bdg. 101.28 *(978-1-4765-3662-0(7))*; lib. bdg. 202.56 *(978-1-4765-3663-7(5))*; pap. 166.80 *(978-1-62065-815-4(1))*; pap. 27.80 *(978-1-62065-814-7(3))* Capstone Press of Coughlan Cos. (First Facts).

Martin, Steve, et al. I Wish I Knew That. Pinder, Andrew, illus. 2017. (Buster Reference Ser.). (ENG.). 128p. (J). (gr. 3-7). pap. 8.99 ***(978-1-78055-466-2(4))*** O'Mara, Michael Bks., Ltd. GBR. Dist: Independent Pubs. Group.

Martin, Steve, et al. The Wacky & Wonderful World Through Numbers: Over 2,000 Figures & Facts. 2015. (ENG., Illus.). 128p. (J). (gr. 3-7). pap. 11.99 *(978-1-4380-0590-4(3))* Barron's Educational Series, Inc.

Marzolf, Julie. Gross Things about Your Pets. 2012. (That's Gross! Ser.). (Illus.). 24p. (J). (gr. 2-5). 22.60 *(978-1-4339-7119-8(4))*; pap. 8.15 *(978-1-4339-7120-4(8))* Stevens, Gareth Publishing LLLP. (Gareth Stevens Learning Library).

Masoff, Joy. Oh, Yuck! The Encyclopedia of Everything Nasty. (ENG., Illus.). 1p. (J). pap. 119.60 *(978-0-7611-2529-7(9)*, 22529) Workman Publishing Co., Inc.

Masters, Deborah. The Magical Wisdom of Kids. 2005. (Illus.). 108p. per. 18.95 *(978-0-9740465-1-8(5))* Global Truth Publishing.

Mattern, Joanne & Herndon, Ryan, compiled by. Guinness World Records: Extraordinary Records of Unusual Facts & Feats. 2005. (Illus.). 90p. (J). pap. *(978-0-439-79192-2(8))* Scholastic, Inc.

McDonald, Megan. Stink It Up! A Guide to the Gross, the Bad, & the Smelly. 2013. (Stink Ser.). lib. bdg. 16.00 *(978-0-606-32100-6(4)*, Turtleback) Turtleback Bks.

—Stink-O-Pedia. 2009. (Stink Ser.). lib. bdg. 16.00 *(978-0-606-06752-2(3)*, Turtleback) Turtleback Bks.

—Stink-O-Pedia: Volume 1 Super Stink-Y Stuff from A to Zzzz, 1 vol. Reynolds, Peter H., illus. 2012. (Stink Ser.: No. 2). (ENG.). 144p. (J). (gr. 2-5). 24.21 *(978-1-59961-195-2(3))* Spotlight.

—Stink-O-Pedia: Volume 2 More Stink-Y Stuff from A to Z, 1 vol. Reynolds, Peter H., illus. 2012. (Stink Ser.: No. 2). (ENG.). 144p. (J). (gr. 2-5). 24.21 *(978-1-59961-196-9(1))* Spotlight.

Meister, Cari. Totally Wacky Facts about Modern History. 2016. (Mind Benders Ser.). (ENG., Illus.). 112p. (gr. 1-3). lib. bdg. 23.32 *(978-1-4914-8386-2(5))* Capstone Press of Coughlan Cos.

—Wacky Facts about History. 2016. (Mind Benders Ser.). (ENG., Illus.). 240p. (gr. 1-3). pap. 7.95 *(978-1-4914-8391-6(1))* Capstone Press of Coughlan Cos.

Merrell, Patrick. iFlush - Plunging into Mystery Bathroom Reader for Kids Only! 2014. (ENG., Illus.). 96p. (J). (gr. 1-6). 12.95 *(978-1-62686-042-1(4)*, Portable Pr.) Readerlink Distribution Services, LLC.

—iFlush- Hunting for Heroes. 2014. (ENG., Illus.). 96p. (J). (gr. 1-6). 12.95 *(978-1-62686-041-4(6)*, Portable Pr.) Readerlink Distribution Services, LLC.

—iFlush Swimming in Science. 2013. (ENG., Illus.). 96p. (J). (gr. 1-6). 12.95 *(978-1-60710-783-5(X)*, Portable Pr.) Readerlink Distribution Services, LLC.

Millard, Anne. Misterios de las Piramides. (Coleccion Misterios De). (SPA., Illus.). 48p. (YA). (gr. 5-8). 19.95 *(978-84-348-5690-5(5)*, SM6076) SM Ediciones ESP. Dist: AIMS International Bks., Inc., Lectorum Pubns., Inc.

Miller, Reagan. Step Forward with Curiosity. 2016. (Step Forward! Ser.). (ENG., Illus.). 24p. (J). (gr. 2-5). *(978-0-7787-2782-8(3))* Crabtree Publishing Co.

Millman, Christian. Absolutely Crazy Knowledge: The World's Funniest Collection of Amazing Facts. 2015. (ENG., Illus.). 160p. (J). (gr. 3-6). pap. 10.99 *(978-0-7944-3341-3(3))* Reader's Digest Assn., Inc., The.

Mizielinska, Aleksandra & Mizielinski, Daniel. Under Water, under Earth. 2016. (ENG., Illus.). 112p. (J). (gr. 2-4). 35.00 *(978-0-7636-8922-3(X)*, Big Picture Press) Candlewick Pr.

Mommy Why? Collection: Stories that answer your kid's toughest Questions: Stories that answer your kid's toughest Questions. 2007. (Illus.). 277p. (J). pap. 17.99 *(978-0-7684-2507-9(7))* Destiny Image Pubs.

Morse, Jenifer Corr. Scholastic Book of World Records. 2008. (Scholastic Book of World Records Ser.). (Illus.). 304p. (J). (gr. 4-7). 17.65 *(978-0-7569-8839-5(X))* Perfection Learning Corp.

—Scholastic Book of World Records, 2008. 2007. (Illus.). 304p. (J). *(978-1-4287-5691-5(4)*, Scholastic Reference) Scholastic, Inc.

—Scholastic Book of World Records 2014. 2013. (ENG.). 320p. (J). (gr. 3-7). pap. 10.99 *(978-0-545-56262-1(7)*, Scholastic Paperbacks) Scholastic, Inc.

—Scholastic Book of World Records 2015. 2014. (ENG.). 320p. (J). (gr. 3-7). pap. 10.99 *(978-0-545-67950-3(8)*, Scholastic Paperbacks) Scholastic, Inc.

Murrie, Matthew & McHugh, Andrew R. The Book of What If...? Questions & Activities for Curious Minds. (ENG., Illus.). 240p. (J). (gr. 3-7). 2017. pap. 12.99 *(978-1-58270-528-6(3))* 2016. 17.99 *(978-1-58270-529-3(1))* Aladdin/Beyond Words.

Mystery Files Set, 6 vols., Set. Incl. Bigfoot Caught on Film: And Other Monster Sightings! Teitelbaum, Michael. 29.00 *(978-0-531-12078-1(3))*; Cities of the Dead: Finding Lost Civilizations. Rinaldo, Denise. 29.00 *(978-0-531-12079-8(1))*; Ghosts: And Real-Life Ghost Hunters. Teitelbaum, Michael. 29.00 *(978-0-531-12077-4(5))*; Mummies Unwrapped! The Science of Mummy-Making. Grace, N. B. 29.00 *(978-0-531-12076-7(7))*; UFO's: What Scientists Say May Shock You! Grace, N. B. 29.00 *(978-0-531-12074-3(0))*; 64p. (J). (gr. 9-12)., Watts, Franklin (24/7: Science Behind the Scenes Ser.). (Illus.). 2008. 174.00 *(978-0-531-12479-6(7))* Scholastic Library Publishing.

Nagelhout, Ryan. How Did Death Valley Get Its Name? 2016. (Q & a: Life's Mysteries Solved! Ser.). (Illus.). 32p. (J). (gr. 4-3). pap. 10.50 *(978-1-4824-4733-0(9))* Stevens, Gareth Publishing LLLP.

National Geographic. National Geographic Kids Quiz Whiz 2: 1,000 Super Fun Mind-Bending Totally Awesome Trivia Questions. 2013. (ENG.). 176p. (J). (gr. 3-7). lib. bdg. 18.90 *(978-1-4263-1357-8(8)*, National Geographic Children's Bks.) National Geographic Society.

—National Geographic Kids Weird but True! Ripped from the Headlines 2. 2015. lib. bdg. 24.50 *(978-0-606-36425-6(0))* Turtleback Bks.

—Ultimate Weird but True 2: 1,000 Wild & Wacky Facts & Photos! 2013. (ENG., Illus.). 192p. (J). (gr. 3-7). lib. bdg. 28.90 *(978-1-4263-1359-2(4)*, National Geographic Children's Bks.) National Geographic Society.

National Geographic Editors. 1001 Inventions & Awesome Facts from Muslim Civilization. 2012. (ENG., Illus.). 96p. (J). (gr. 3-7). 14.95 *(978-1-4263-1258-8(X)*, National Geographic Children's Bks.) National Geographic Society.

National Geographic Kids. Bet You Didn't Know: Fascinating, Far-Out, Fun-tastic Facts! 2017. (ENG.). 192p. (J). (gr. 3-7). lib. bdg. 29.90 ***(978-1-4263-2838-1(9)***, National Geographic Children's Bks.) National Geographic Society.

—National Geographic Kids Almanac 2018. 2017. lib. bdg. 26.95 ***(978-0-606-40080-0(X))*** Turtleback Bks.

National Geographic Kids. 1,800 Outrageous Facts, Set. 2015. (ENG., Illus.). 1248p. (J). (gr. 1-4). pap. 47.99 *(978-1-4263-2389-8(1)*, National Geographic Children's Bks.) National Geographic Society.

National Geographic Kids & DuMont, Brianna. Weird but True! Know-it-All - U. S. Presidents. 2017. (ENG., Illus.). 192p. (J). (gr. 3-7). pap. 12.99 ***(978-1-4263-2796-4(X)***, National Geographic Children's Bks.) National Geographic Society.

—Weird but True Know-It-All: U. S. Presidents. 2017. (ENG.). 192p. (J). (gr. 3-7). lib. bdg. 22.90 ***(978-1-4263-2797-1(8)***, National Geographic Children's Bks.) National Geographic Society.

National Geographic Kids Staff. Bet You Didn't Know: Fascinating, Far-Out, Fun-tastic Facts. 2017. (ENG., Illus.). 192p. (J). (gr. 3-7). 19.99 ***(978-1-4263-2837-4(0)***, National Geographic Children's Bks.) National Geographic Society.

—Boredom-Busting Fun Stuff. 2015. (ENG., Illus.). 352p. (J). (gr. 3-7). pap. 14.99 *(978-1-4263-2106-1(6)*, National Geographic Children's Bks.) National Geographic Society.

—By the Numbers: 230. 333 Cool Stats & Figures. 2015. (ENG., Illus.). 256p. (J). (gr. 3-7). pap. 9.99 *(978-1-4263-2072-9(8)*, National Geographic Children's Bks.) National Geographic Society.

—By the Numbers 2. 0. 2016. (ENG., Illus.). 256p. (J). (gr. 3-7). pap. 9.99 *(978-1-4263-2528-1(2)*, National Geographic Children's Bks.) National Geographic Society.

—National Geographic Kids Almanac 2013. 2012. (ENG., Illus.). 352p. (J). (gr. 3-7). 21.95 *(978-1-4263-0925-0(2)*, National Geographic Children's Bks.) National Geographic Society.

—National Geographic Kids Almanac 2018. 2017. (National Geographic Almanacs Ser.). (ENG., Illus.). 352p. (J). (gr. 3-7). pap. 14.99 *(978-1-4263-2772-8(2)*, National Geographic Children's Bks.) National Geographic Society.

—Ripped from the Headlines: Real-Life Stories You Have to Read to Believe. 2014. (Weird but True Ser.). (ENG., Illus.). 176p. (J). (gr. 3-7). pap. 12.99 *(978-1-4263-1514-5(7)*, National Geographic Children's Bks.) National Geographic Society.

—Ripped from the Headlines 2: Real-Life Stories You Have to Read to Believe. 2015. (Weird but True Ser.). (ENG., Illus.). 176p. (J). (gr. 3-7). pap. 12.99 *(978-1-4263-1909-9(6)*, National Geographic Children's Bks.) National Geographic Society.

—Ripped from the Headlines 3: Real-Life Stories You Have to Read to Believe. 2016. (Weird but True Ser.). (ENG., Illus.). 176p. (J). (gr. 3-7). pap. 12.99 *(978-1-4263-2421-5(9)*, National Geographic Children's Bks.) National Geographic Society.

—Weird but True!, 3 vols., Set. 2012. (Weird but True Ser.). (ENG., Illus.). 624p. (J). (gr. 1-4). pap. 23.95 *(978-1-4263-1194-9(X)*, National Geographic Children's Bks.) National Geographic Society.

—Weird but True! Set 2: 900 Outrageous Facts. collector's ed. 2014. (ENG.). 624p. (J). (gr. 1-4). pap. 23.99 *(978-1-4263-2011-8(6)*, National Geographic Children's Bks.) National Geographic Society.

—Weird but True! 2: 300 Outrageous Facts. Halling, Jonathan, illus. 2010. (ENG.). 208p. (J). (gr. 3-7). pap. 7.95 *(978-1-4263-0688-4(1)*, National Geographic Children's Bks.) National Geographic Society.

—Weird but True! 4: 300 Outrageous Facts. 2012. (Weird but True Ser.). (ENG., Illus.). 208p. (J). (gr. 3-7). pap. 7.95 *(978-1-4263-1020-1(X))*; lib. bdg. 16.90 *(978-1-4263-1021-8(8))* National Geographic Society. (National Geographic Children's Bks.).

—Weird but True! 5: 300 Outrageous Facts. 2013. (Weird but True Ser.). (ENG.). 208p. (J). (gr. 3-7). lib. bdg. 16.90 *(978-1-4263-1125-3(7))*; (Illus.). pap. 7.95 *(978-1-4263-1124-6(9))* National Geographic Society. (National Geographic Children's Bks.).

—Weird but True! 8. 2016. (Weird but True Ser.). (ENG., Illus.). 208p. (J). (gr. 3-7). pap. 7.99 *(978-1-4263-2559-5(2)*, National Geographic Children's Bks.) National Geographic Society.

—Weird but True Gross. 2016. (Weird but True Ser.). (ENG., Illus.). 208p. (J). (gr. 3-7). lib. bdg. 17.90 *(978-1-4263-2336-2(0)*, National Geographic Children's Bks.) National Geographic Society.

—125 Wacky Roadside Attractions: See All the Weird, Wonderful, & Downright Bizarre Landmarks from Around the World! 2016. (ENG., Illus.). 112p. (J). (gr. 3-7). pap. 12.99 *(978-1-4263-2407-9(3)*, National Geographic Children's Bks.) National Geographic Society.

—300 Outrageous Facts. (Weird but True Ser.). (ENG., Illus.). 208p. (J). (gr. 3-7). 2015. pap. 7.99 *(978-1-4263-2086-6(8))* 2014. pap. 7.99 *(978-1-4263-1490-2(6))* National Geographic Society. (National Geographic Children's Bks.).

—300 Slimy, Sticky, & Smelly Facts. 2016. (Weird but True Ser.). (ENG., Illus.). 208p. (J). (gr. 3-7). pap. 7.99 *(978-1-4263-2335-5(2)*, National Geographic Children's Bks.) National Geographic Society.

—1,000 Super Fun Mind-Bending Totally Awesome Trivia Questions. (Quiz Whiz Ser.). (ENG., 176p. (J). (gr. 3-7). 2015. Illus.). pap. 9.99 *(978-1-4263-2084-2(1))* 2015. (Illus.). pap. 9.99 *(978-1-4263-1907-5(X))* 2014. (Illus.). pap. 9.99 *(978-1-4263-1709-5(3))* 2014. pap. 9.99 *(978-1-4263-1484-1(1))* National Geographic Society. (National Geographic Children's Bks.).

—1,000 Wild & Wacky Facts & Photos! 2015. (Weird but True Ser.). (ENG., Illus.). 192p. (J). (gr. 3-7). 19.99 *(978-1-4263-2068-2(X)*, National Geographic Children's Bks.) National Geographic Society.

—5,000 Awesome Facts. 2012. (ENG., Illus.). 224p. (J). (gr. 3-7). 19.95 *(978-1-4263-1049-2(8)*, National Geographic Children's Bks.) National Geographic Society.

—5,000 Awesome Facts 3 (About Everything!) 2016. (ENG., Illus.). 224p. (J). (gr. 3-7). 19.99 *(978-1-4263-2452-9(9)*, National Geographic Children's Bks.) National Geographic Society.

—5,000 Awesome Facts (About Everything!) 2012. (ENG., Illus.). 224p. (J). (gr. 3-7). lib. bdg. 24.95 *(978-1-4263-1050-8(1)*, National Geographic Children's Bks.) National Geographic Society.

—5,000 Awesome Facts (about Everything!) 2. 2014. (ENG., Illus.). 224p. (J). (gr. 3-7). 19.99 *(978-1-4263-1695-1(X))*; lib. bdg. 24.90 *(978-1-4263-1696-8(8))* National Geographic Society. (National Geographic Children's Bks.).

National Geographic Kids Staff & Beer, Julie. Food: 300 Bite-Size Facts about Incredible Edibles. 2015. (Weird but True Ser.). (ENG., Illus.). 208p. (J). (gr. 3-7). pap. 7.99 *(978-1-4263-1871-9(5)*, National Geographic Children's Bks.) National Geographic Society.

—300 Bite-Size Facts about Incredible Edibles! 2015. (Weird but True Ser.). (ENG., Illus.). 208p. (J). (gr. 3-7). lib. bdg. 16.90 *(978-1-4263-1872-6(3)*, National Geographic Children's Bks.) National Geographic Society.

National Geographic Staff. National Geographic Kids Quiz Whiz 2: 1,000 Super Fun Mind-Bending Totally Awesome Trivia Questions. 2013. (ENG., Illus.). 176p. (J). (gr. 3-7). pap. 9.99 *(978-1-4263-1356-1(X)*, National Geographic Children's Bks.) National Geographic Society.

—National Geographic Kids Ultimate Weird but True 2: 1,000 Wild & Wacky Facts & Photos! 2013. (ENG., Illus.). 192p. (J). (gr. 3-7). 19.95 *(978-1-4263-1358-5(6)*, National Geographic Children's Bks.) National Geographic Society.

—Ultimate Weird but True: 1,000 Wild & Wacky Facts & Photos! 2011. (ENG., Illus.). 192p. (J). (gr. 3-7). 19.95 *(978-1-4263-0864-2(7)*, National Geographic Children's Bks.) National Geographic Society.

Off the Record! 2014. (Off the Record! Ser.). 328p. (YA). (gr. 7-12). 153.00 *(978-1-4777-7839-5(X))* Rosen Publishing Group, Inc., The.

Old Farmer's Almanac Staff. The Old Farmer's Almanac for Kids, Vol. 5. 2013. (ENG., Illus.). 192p. (J). pap. 9.95 *(978-1-57198-613-9(8))* Yankee Publishing, Inc.

—The Old Farmer's Almanac for Kids, Volume 6. 2015. (ENG., Illus.). 192p. (J). pap. 9.95 *(978-1-57198-683-2(9))* Yankee Publishing, Inc.

Old Farmer's Almanac Staff, ed. The Old Farmer's Almanac for Kids, 4 vols., Vol. 4. 2011. (ENG., Illus.). 192p. pap. 9.95 *(978-1-57198-554-5(9))* Yankee Publishing, Inc.

Oliver, Martin. Boys' Miscellany. Phillips, Mike, illus. 2013. 128p. (J). *(978-1-4351-5047-8(3))* Barnes & Noble, Inc.

O'Mara Books, Michael & Allan, Stewart. 5 Seconds of Summer: Test Your Super-Fan Status. 2014. (ENG.). 96p. (J). (gr. 3-10). pap. 6.99 *(978-1-4380-0614-7(4))* Barron's Educational Series, Inc.

Omoth, Tyler. Handbook to Stonehenge, the Bermuda Triangle, & Other Mysterious Locations. 2016. (Paranormal Handbooks Ser.). (ENG., Illus.). 32p. (gr. 3-4). lib. bdg. 27.99 *(978-1-5157-1310-4(5)*, Edge Bks.) Capstone Press of Coughlan Cos.

Orme, David. Don't Try This at Home. 2008. (Trailblazers Ser.). (ENG., Illus.). 36p. pap. *(978-1-84167-652-4(7))* Ransom Publishing Ltd.

Osborne, Mary Pope & Boyce, Natalie Pope. Magic Tree House Incredible Fact Book. Murdocca, Sal, illus. 2016. (Magic Tree House Ser.). (ENG.). 144p. (J). (gr. 2-5). 16.99 *(978-0-399-55117-8(4)*, Random Hse. Bks. for Young Readers) Random Hse. Children's Bks.

Otway, Helen & Arcturus Publishing Staff. 1001 Unbelievable Facts: Mind-Boggling, Impossible, Weird! 2012. (ENG., Illus.). 208p. (J). pap. 9.95 *(978-1-84193-783-0(5)*, 9781841937830) Arcturus Publishing GBR. Dist: Bookmasters Distribution.

Overdeck, Laura. The Truth Comes Out. Paillot, Jim, illus. 2015. (Bedtime Math Ser.). (ENG.). 96p. (J). (gr. -1-2). 15.99 *(978-1-250-04775-5(7)*, 9781250047755) Feiwel & Friends.

Owings, Lisa. Ghost Ships. 2015. (Unexplained Mysteries Ser.). (ENG., Illus.). 24p. (J). (gr. 3-7). lib. bdg. 25.95 *(978-1-62617-202-9(1)*, Epic Bks.) Bellwether Media.

Pace, Eugenia Ann. I Am Curious. 2011. 40p. pap. 21.99 *(978-1-4568-5557-4(3))* Xlibris Corp.

Packard, Mary. Ripley's Believe It or Not! Bizarre Collection. Franson, Leanne, illus. 2004. 361p. (J). pap. 3.99 *(978-0-681-02479-3(8))* Scholastic, Inc.

—Totally Gross. Franson, Leanne, illus. 2004. 85p. (J). *(978-0-439-71739-7(6))* Scholastic, Inc.

Packard, Mary, ed. Ripley's Believe It or Not! Awesome Collection. Franson, Leanne, illus. 361p. (J). pap. *(978-0-681-15435-3(7))* Scholastic, Inc.

Parks, Peggy J. The Great Barrier Reef. 2004. (WONDERS of the WORLD Ser.). (ENG., Illus.). 48p. (J). (gr. 4-7). 27.50 *(978-0-7377-2054-9(9))* Cengage Gale.

Payne, Jan, et al. Attila the Hun Was Killed by a Nosebleed: And Other Facts about History. 2016. (True or False? Ser.). (Illus.). 48p. (J). (gr. 3-3). pap. 11.70 *(978-0-7660-7724-9(1))* Enslow Pubs., Inc.

—It Can Rain Frogs & Fish: And Other Facts about Planet Earth. 2016. (True or False? Ser.). 48p. (J). (gr. 3-3). pap. 11.70 *(978-0-7660-7732-4(2))* Enslow Pubs., Inc.

Peabody, Erin. Bigfoot. Rivas, Victor, illus. 2017. (Behind the Legend Ser.: 2). (ENG.). 128p. (J). (gr. 3-7). pap. 9.99 ***(978-1-4998-0425-6(3))*** Little Bee Books Inc.

Pearson, Gracie. Bentley's Yard: Welcome Home! 2011. 40p. pap. 21.99 *(978-1-4628-2958-3(9))* Xlibris Corp.

Pelleschi, Andrea. Crop Circles, 1 vol. 2012. (Unsolved Mysteries (el) Ser.). (ENG.). 112p. (J). (gr. 6-12). lib. bdg. 35.64 *(978-1-61783-300-7(2)*, Essential Library) ABDO Publishing Co.

Perritano, John. Disgusting Stuff. 2012. (Disgusting Stuff Ser.). (ENG.). 48p. (gr. 3-4). lib. bdg. 127.96 *(978-1-4296-8225-1(6))* Capstone Press of Coughlan Cos.

—The Most Disgusting Animals on the Planet, 1 vol. 2012. (Disgusting Stuff Ser.). (ENG., Illus.). 48p. (gr. 3-4). lib. bdg. 31.99 *(978-1-4296-7535-2(7))* Capstone Press of Coughlan Cos.

—The Most Disgusting Foods on the Planet, 1 vol. 2012. (Disgusting Stuff Ser.). (ENG.). 48p. (gr. 3-4). lib. bdg. 31.99 *(978-1-4296-7534-5(9))* Capstone Press of Coughlan Cos.

—The Most Disgusting Places on the Planet, 1 vol. 2012. (Disgusting Stuff Ser.). (ENG.). 48p. (gr. 3-4). lib. bdg. 31.99 *(978-1-4296-7533-8(0))* Capstone Press of Coughlan Cos.

Peters, Elisa. Everyday Wonders. 2008. (J). (gr. -1-3). 127.50 *(978-1-4042-8021-2(9)*, Editorial Buenas Letras) Rosen Publishing Group, Inc., The.

Peterson, Megan Cooley & Rustad, Martha E. H. Encountering Chupacabra & Other Cryptids: Eyewitness Accounts, 1 vol. Stevens, Matt, illus. 2014. (Eyewitness to the Unexplained Ser.). (ENG.). 32p. (gr. 3-4). 30.65 *(978-1-4914-0242-9(3)*, Graphic Library) Capstone Press of Coughlan Cos.

Peterson, Megan Cooley, et al. Eyewitness to the Unexplained, 1 vol. 2014. (Eyewitness to the Unexplained Ser.). (ENG.). 32p. (gr. 3-4). 122.60 *(978-1-4914-0246-7(6)*, Graphic Library) Capstone Press of Coughlan Cos.

Pohlen, Jerome. Oddball Indiana: A Guide to 350 Really Strange Places. 2nd ed. 2017. (Oddball Ser.). (ENG., Illus.). 288p. pap. 16.99 ***(978-1-61373-849-8(8))*** Chicago Review Pr., Inc.

Polette, Nancy. What Is This Thing? 2007. (J). pap. 11.95 *(978-1-931334-95-2(1))* Pieces of Learning.

Polydoros, Lori. Top 10 UFO & Alien Mysteries, 1 vol. 2012. (Top 10 Unexplained Ser.). (ENG.). 32p. (gr. 1-2). 26.65 *(978-1-4296-7639-7(6)*, Blazers) Capstone Press of Coughlan Cos.

Polydoros, Lori, et al. Top 10 Unexplained. 2012. (Top 10 Unexplained Ser.). (ENG.). 32p. (gr. 1-2). lib. bdg. 133.25 *(978-1-4296-9138-3(7)*, Blazers) Capstone Press of Coughlan Cos.

Poussin, Nichol. Still Spins the Spider of Rennes-le-Chateau. l.t. ed. 2004.Tr. of L' arraignee tisse sa toile a Rennes-le-Chateaua. (Illus.). 347p. pap. *(978-0-9541527-1-0(9)*, http//www.keysofantiquity.com) DEK Publishing.

Powell, Marie. Unsolved! 2015. (ENG., Illus.). 32p. (J). *(978-0-7787-8073-1(2))* Crabtree Publishing Co.

Powell, Michael. Do My Ears Ever Stop Growing? And 70 Other Questions That Keep You Awake at Night. 2009. (Illus.). 158p. (J). *(978-1-4351-1200-1(8))* Metro Bks.

Powerkids Readers. 2013. (PowerKids Readers Ser.). 24p. (J). (gr. k-2). 949.20 *(978-1-4777-1155-2(4))*; pap. 346.50 *(978-1-4777-2680-8(2))*; pap. 2079.00 *(978-1-4777-2679-2(9))* Rosen Publishing Group, Inc., The. (PowerKids Pr.).

Price, Sean Stewart, et al. Unsolved Mystery Files. 2015. (Unsolved Mystery Files Ser.). (ENG.). 32p. (gr. 3-4). 111.96 *(978-1-4914-6665-0(0)*, Edge Bks.) Capstone Press of Coughlan Cos.

Purney, Dawn. Lost & Found, 1 vol. unabr. ed. 2012. (Astonishing Headlines Ser.). (ENG.). 92p. (YA). (gr. 9-12). 8.95 *(978-1-61651-922-3(3))* Saddleback Educational Publishing, Inc.

Raij, Emily. Spooked! 2015. (Spooked Ser.). (ENG.). 32p. (gr. 1-2). 106.60 *(978-1-4914-6656-8(1)*, Blazers) Capstone Press of Coughlan Cos.

Rauker, Lucy. Awesome Animal Trivia. 2013. (Ultimate Trivia Challenge Ser.). (Illus.). 32p. (J). (gr. 2-5). pap. 10.50 *(978-1-4339-8289-7(7))*; lib. bdg. 25.25 *(978-1-4339-8288-0(9))* Stevens, Gareth Publishing LLLP.

Raum, Elizabeth. Taj Mahal. 2015. (Illus.). 32p. (J). lib. bdg. 28.50 *(978-1-60753-470-9(3))* Amicus Publishing.

Redfern, Nick. The Most Mysterious Places on Earth. 2013. (Haunted: Ghosts & the Paranormal Ser.). 208p. (YA). (gr. 7-12). 37.25 *(978-1-4777-0681-7(X))* Rosen Publishing Group, Inc., The.

Remarkable Art. 2014. (Ripleys Believe It or Not! Dare to Look Ser.: 8). 36p. (J). (gr. 4-18). lib. bdg. 20.95 *(978-1-4222-3144-9(5))* Mason Crest.

Remarkable Feats. 2014. (Ripleys Believe It or Not! Download the Weird Ser.: 8). 36p. (J). (gr. 4-18). lib. bdg. 20.95 *(978-1-4222-3152-4(6))* Mason Crest.

Reynolds, Toby & Calver, Paul. Wonders of the World. 2016. (Visual Explorers Ser.). (ENG., Illus.). 32p. (J). (gr. 3-7). pap. 6.99 *(978-1-4380-0830-1(9))* Barron's Educational Series, Inc.

Rhatigan, Joe, et al. Trivia Goes Bananas: 711 Brain Bafflers That'll Stump Ya! 2013. (ENG.). 160p. (J). pap. 7.95 *(978-1-60433-342-8(1)*, Applesauce Pr.) Cider Mill Pr. Bk. Pubs., LLC.

—Wild & Wacky Trivia: 717 Brain Drainers That'll Stump Ya! 2013. (ENG.). 160p. (J). pap. 7.95 *(978-1-60433-339-8(1)*, Applesauce Pr.) Cider Mill Pr. Bk. Pubs., LLC.

Rice, Dona Herweck. Unsolved! History's Mysteries, 1 vol. 2nd rev. ed. 2013. (Nonfiction Readers Ser.). (ENG., Illus.). 48p. (J). (gr. 4-4). pap. 29.96 *(978-1-4807-1105-1(5))* Shell Educational Publishing.

—Unsolved! History's Mysteries, 1 vol. 2nd rev. ed. 2012. (TIME for KIDS(r) Nonfiction Readers Ser.). (ENG.). 48p. (J). (gr. 4-4). pap. 9.99 *(978-1-4333-4829-7(2))* Teacher Created Materials, Inc.

Richards, Jon & Simkins, Ed. Record-Breaking People. 2015. (Infographic Top 10s Ser.). (ENG., Illus.). 32p. (J). (gr. 4-6). pap. 7.99 *(978-1-4677-9382-7(5)*, Lerner Pubns.) Lerner Publishing Group.

Ripley Entertainment. Beyond Understanding. 2010. (Ripley's Believe It or Not Ser.). 36p. (YA). (gr. 3-18). lib. bdg. 19.95 *(978-1-4222-1531-9(8))* Mason Crest.

—Life in the Fast Lane. 2010. (Ripley's Believe It or Not Ser.). 36p. (YA). (gr. 3-18). lib. bdg. 19.95 *(978-1-4222-1538-8(5))* Mason Crest.

—Was That a Good Idea? 2010. (Ripley's Believe It or Not Ser.). 36p. (YA). (gr. 3-18). lib. bdg. 19.95 *(978-1-4222-1543-2(1))* Mason Crest.
—Wonders of Science. 2010. (Ripley's Believe It or Not Ser.). 36p. (YA). (gr. 3-18). lib. bdg. 19.95 *(978-1-4222-1545-6(8))* Mason Crest.
Ripley Entertainment Staff, contrib. by. Fun & Games. 2010. (Ripley's Believe It or Not Ser.). 36p. (YA). (gr. 3-18). lib. bdg. 19.95 *(978-1-4222-1534-0(2))* Mason Crest.
Ripley Publishing Staff & Mason Crest Publishers Staff, contrib. by. Extraordinary Feats. 2013. (Illus.). 34p. (J). *(978-1-4222-2769-5(3))* Mason Crest.
Ripley Publishing Staff & Ripley Entertainment, Inc Staff, contrib. by. Believe It! 2013. (Illus.). 36p. (J). pap. *(978-1-4222-2790-9(1))* Mason Crest.
—Beyond Reason. 2013. (Ripley's Believe It or Not! Enter If You Dare Ser.). (Illus.). 36p. (J). (gr. 4-18). pap. 9.95 *(978-1-4222-2791-6(X))* Mason Crest.
—Body Tales. 2013. (Illus.). 36p. (J). pap. *(978-1-4222-2792-3(8))* Mason Crest.
—Crazy World. 2013. (Illus.). 36p. (J). pap. *(978-1-4222-2793-0(6))* Mason Crest.
—Strange Stories. 2013. (Illus.). 36p. (J). pap. *(978-1-4222-2799-2(5))* Mason Crest.
—Wacky World. 2013. (Ripley's Believe It or Not! Enter If You Dare Ser.). (Illus.). 36p. (J). (gr. 4-18). pap. 9.95 *(978-1-4222-2802-9(9))* Mason Crest.
Ripley, Robert. Ripley's Believe It or Not! 2004. (Illus.). 256p. 25.95 *(978-1-893951-73-0(1))* Ripley Entertainment, Inc.
—Ripley's Believe It or Not! The Original Cartoons That Started It All! 2014. (ENG., Illus.). 328p. 39.99 *(978-1-61377-890-6(2)*, 9781613778906) Idea & Design Works, LLC.
Ripley Twists, 8 vols., Set. Incl. Extreme Earth. Twist, Clint. pap. 8.95 *(978-1-4222-2067-2(2)*, 1318258); Human Body. De la Bédoyère, Camilla. pap. 8.95 *(978-1-4222-2068-9(0))*; Mighty Machines. Graham, Ian. pap. 8.95 *(978-1-4222-2069-6(9)*, 1318260); (Illus.). 48p. (J). (gr. 3-18). 2009. 2011. Set pap. 71.60 *(978-1-4222-2065-8(6))*; Set lib. bdg. 159.60 *(978-1-4222-1827-3(9))* Mason Crest.
Ripley's. Burp! 2012. (Ripley's Shout Outs Ser.: 4). lib. bdg. 14.75 *(978-0-606-23898-4(0)*, Turtleback) Turtleback Bks.
Ripley's Believe It or Not! 2012. (Illus.). 144p. (J). *(978-0-545-38474-2(5))* Scholastic, Inc.
Ripley's Believe It or Not, 16 vols., Set. Incl. All Consuming. Ripley Entertainment. (YA). (gr. 3-18). lib. bdg. 19.95 *(978-1-4222-1536-4(9))*; Amazing Earth. Ripley Entertainment. (YA). (gr. 3-18). lib. bdg. 19.95 *(978-1-4222-1539-5(3))*; Animal Antics. Ripley Entertainment Staff, contrib. by. (YA). (gr. 3-18). lib. bdg. 19.95 *(978-1-4222-1535-7(0))*; Arts & Entertainment. Ripley's Entertainment Inc Staff, contrib. by. (J). (gr. 5-18). lib. bdg. 19.95 *(978-1-4222-1530-2(X))*; Beyond Belief. Ripley Entertainment. (YA). (gr. 3-18). lib. bdg. 19.95 *(978-1-4222-1537-1(7))*; Beyond Understanding. Ripley Entertainment. (YA). (gr. 3-18). lib. bdg. 19.95 *(978-1-4222-1531-9(8))*; Body & Mind. Ripley Entertainment Staff, contrib. by. (YA). (gr. 3-18). lib. bdg. 19.95 *(978-1-4222-1532-6(6))*; Extraordinary Animals. Ripley Entertainment Staff, contrib. by. (YA). (gr. 3-18). lib. bdg. 19.95 *(978-1-4222-1533-3(4))*; Fun & Games. Ripley Entertainment Staff, contrib. by. (YA). (gr. 3-18). lib. bdg. 19.95 *(978-1-4222-1534-0(2))*; Life in the Fast Lane. Ripley Entertainment. (YA). (gr. 3-18). lib. bdg. 19.95 *(978-1-4222-1538-8(5))*; Off the Wall. Ripley Entertainment. (YA). (gr. 3-18). lib. bdg. 19.95 *(978-1-4222-1542-5(3))*; Taking Life to Extremes. Ripley Entertainment. (YA). (gr. 3-18). lib. bdg. 19.95 *(978-1-4222-1540-1(7))*; Totally Obsessed. Ripley Entertainment. (YA). (gr. 3-18). lib. bdg. 19.95 *(978-1-4222-1541-8(5))*; Was That a Good Idea? Ripley Entertainment. (YA). (gr. 3-18). lib. bdg. 19.95 *(978-1-4222-1543-2(1))*; What Are You Like? Ripley Entertainment. (YA). (gr. 3-18). lib. bdg. 19.95 *(978-1-4222-1544-9(X))*; Wonders of Science. Ripley Entertainment. (YA). (gr. 3-18). lib. bdg. 19.95 *(978-1-4222-1545-6(8))*; 36p. 2010. 2010. 319.20 *(978-1-4222-1529-6(6))* Mason Crest.
Ripley's Believe It or Not Editors. Expect the Unexpected: Amazing Animals. 2010. (Ripley's Remarkable & Unexpected Ser.). 36p. (J). (gr. 3-18). lib. bdg. 19.95 *(978-1-4222-2015-3(X))* Mason Crest.
—Expect the Unexpected: Breaking Boundaries. (Ripley's Remarkable & Unexpected Ser.). 36p. (J). (gr. 3-18). 2010. lib. bdg. 19.95 *(978-1-4222-2016-0(8))* 2009. pap. 8.95 *(978-1-4222-2050-4(8))* Mason Crest.
—Expect the Unexpected: Impossible Feats. 2010. (Ripley's Remarkable & Unexpected Ser.). 36p. (J). (gr. 3-18). lib. bdg. 19.95 *(978-1-4222-2021-4(4))* Mason Crest.
—Expect the Unexpected: Larger than Life. 2010. (Ripley's Remarkable & Unexpected Ser.). 36p. (J). (gr. 3-18). lib. bdg. 19.95 *(978-1-4222-2023-8(0))* Mason Crest.
—Expect the Unexpected: Simply Unbelievable. (Ripley's Remarkable & Unexpected Ser.). 36p. (J). (gr. 3-18). 2010. lib. bdg. 19.95 *(978-1-4222-2026-9(5))* 2009. pap. 8.95 *(978-1-4222-2060-3(5))* Mason Crest.
—Expect the Unexpected: Strange World. 2010. (Ripley's Remarkable & Unexpected Ser.). 36p. (J). (gr. 3-18). lib. bdg. 19.95 *(978-1-4222-2027-6(3))* Mason Crest.
—Expect the Unexpected: The Final Reckoning. (Ripley's Remarkable & Unexpected Ser.). 36p. (J). (gr. 3-18). 2010. lib. bdg. 19.95 *(978-1-4222-2020-7(6))* 2009. pap. 8.95 *(978-1-4222-2054-2(0))* Mason Crest.
—Expect the Unexpected: Weird & Wonderful. (Ripley's Remarkable & Unexpected Ser.). 36p. (J). (gr. 3-18). 2010. lib. bdg. 19.95 *(978-1-4222-2029-0(X))* 2009. pap. 8.95 *(978-1-4222-2063-4(X))* Mason Crest.
—Fun Facts & Silly Stories, Bk. 1. 2012. (Fun Facts Ser.: 1). (ENG.). 224p. (J). pap. 8.99 *(978-1-60991-054-9(0))* Ripley Entertainment, Inc.
—The Remarkable Revealed: Curious Creations. 2009. (Ripley's Remarkable & Unexpected Ser.). 36p. (J). (gr. 3-18). pap. 8.95 *(978-1-4222-2051-1(6))* Mason Crest.
—The Remarkable Revealed: Extraordinary Endeavors. 2010. (Ripley's Remarkable & Unexpected Ser.). 36p. (J). (gr. 3-18). lib. bdg. 19.95 *(978-1-4222-2018-4(4))* Mason Crest.
—The Remarkable Revealed: Fantastic Feats. (Ripley's Remarkable & Unexpected Ser.). 36p. (J). (gr. 3-18). 2010. lib. bdg. 19.95 *(978-1-4222-2019-1(2))* 2009. pap. 8.95 *(978-1-4222-2053-5(2))* Mason Crest.
—The Remarkable Revealed: Life's Curiosities. (Ripley's Remarkable & Unexpected Ser.). 36p. (J). (gr. 3-18). 2010. lib. bdg. 19.95 *(978-1-4222-2024-5(9))* 2009. pap. 8.95 *(978-1-4222-2058-0(3))* Mason Crest.
—The Remarkable Revealed: Over the Top. 2010. (Ripley's Remarkable & Unexpected Ser.). 36p. (J). (gr. 3-18). lib. bdg. 19.95 *(978-1-4222-2025-2(7))* Mason Crest.
—The Remarkable Revealed: Weird World. (Ripley's Remarkable & Unexpected Ser.). 36p. (J). (gr. 3-18). 2010. lib. bdg. 19.95 *(978-1-4222-2030-6(3))* 2009. pap. 8.95 *(978-1-4222-2064-1(8))* Mason Crest.
—Ripley's Remarkable & Unexpected, 16 vols., Set. Incl. Expect the Unexpected: Breaking Boundaries. pap. 8.95 *(978-1-4222-2050-4(8))*; Expect the Unexpected: Simply Unbelievable. pap. 8.95 *(978-1-4222-2060-3(5))*; Expect the Unexpected: The Final Reckoning. pap. 8.95 *(978-1-4222-2054-2(0))*; Expect the Unexpected: Weird & Wonderful. pap. 8.95 *(978-1-4222-2063-4(X))*; Remarkable Revealed: Curious Creations. pap. 8.95 *(978-1-4222-2051-1(6))*; Remarkable Revealed: Fantastic Feats. pap. 8.95 *(978-1-4222-2053-5(2))*; Remarkable Revealed: Incredible Animals. pap. 8.95 *(978-1-4222-2056-6(7))*; Remarkable Revealed: Life's Curiosities. pap. 8.95 *(978-1-4222-2058-0(3))*; Remarkable Revealed: Unusual Tales. pap. 8.95 *(978-1-4222-2062-7(1))*; Remarkable Revealed: Weird World. pap. 8.95 *(978-1-4222-2064-1(8))*; 36p. (J). (gr. 3-18). 2009. 2011. Set pap. 143.20 *(978-1-4222-2048-1(6))*; Set lib. bdg. 319.20 *(978-1-4222-2014-6(1))* Mason Crest.
Ripley's Believe It or Not Editors & Ripley's Believe It Or Not! Staff. Brutal Beasts. 2013. (Twist Ser.: 9). (ENG.). 48p. (J). (gr. 1-4). 12.95 *(978-1-60991-084-6(2))* Ripley Entertainment, Inc.
—Ripley's Fun Facts & Silly Stories 2. 2013. (Fun Facts Ser.: 2). (ENG.). 224p. (J). (gr. 1-4). pap. 8.99 *(978-1-60991-082-2(6))* Ripley Entertainment, Inc.
—Ripley's Weirdities Slipcase 2. 2013. (Weirdities Ser.: 2). (ENG.). 192p. (J). 19.99 *(978-1-60991-095-2(8))* Ripley Entertainment, Inc.
—Sharks: And Other Scary Sea Creatures. 2013. (Twist Ser.: 10). (ENG.). 48p. (J). (gr. 1-4). 12.95 *(978-1-60991-083-9(4))* Ripley Entertainment, Inc.
Ripley's Believe It or Not Editors & Ripley's Believe It Or Not! Staff, compiled by. Weird - Ities!, Set. 2013. (Fun Facts Ser.). (ENG.). 448p. (J). 16.99 *(978-1-60991-089-1(3))* Ripley Entertainment, Inc.
Ripley's Believe It Or Not! Staff. Amazing People. 2013. (Ripley's Believe It or Not! Enter If You Dare Ser.: 8). 36p. (J). (gr. 4-18). 19.95 *(978-1-4222-2770-1(7))* Mason Crest.
—Awesome Feats. 2012. (Ripley's Disbelief & Shock Ser.). 36p. (J). (gr. 3-4). 19.95 *(978-1-4222-2562-2(3))* Mason Crest.
—Believe It! 2013. (Ripley's Believe It or Not! Strikingly True Ser.: 8). 36p. (J). (gr. 4-18). 19.95 *(978-1-4222-2773-2(1))* Mason Crest.
—Beyond Reason. 2013. (Ripley's Believe It or Not! Enter If You Dare Ser.: 8). 36p. (J). (gr. 4-18). 19.95 *(978-1-4222-2774-9(X))* Mason Crest.
—Body Tales. 2013. (Ripley's Believe It or Not! Strikingly True Ser.: 8). 36p. (J). (gr. 4-18). 19.95 *(978-1-4222-2775-6(8))* Mason Crest.
—Crazy World. 2013. (Ripley's Believe It or Not! Strikingly True Ser.: 8). 36p. (J). (gr. 4-18). 19.95 *(978-1-4222-2776-3(6))* Mason Crest.
—Curious Creatures. 2012. (Ripley's Disbelief & Shock Ser.). 36p. (J). (gr. 3-4). 19.95 *(978-1-4222-2565-3(8))* Mason Crest.
—Curious Exploits. 2012. (Ripley's Disbelief & Shock Ser.). 36p. (J). (gr. 3-4). 19.95 *(978-1-4222-2566-0(6))* Mason Crest.
—Eating Habits. 2012. (Ripley's Disbelief & Shock Ser.). 36p. (J). (gr. 3-4). 19.95 *(978-1-4222-2567-7(4))* Mason Crest.
—Eccentric Tales. 2013. (Ripley's Believe It or Not! Enter If You Dare Ser.: 8). 36p. (J). (gr. 4-18). 19.95 *(978-1-4222-2777-0(4))* Mason Crest.
—Extraordinary Feats. 2013. (Ripley's Believe It or Not! Enter If You Dare Ser.: 8). 36p. (J). (gr. 4-18). 19.95 *(978-1-4222-2779-4(0))* Mason Crest.
—Fun Animals. 2012. (Ripley's Disbelief & Shock Ser.). 36p. (J). (gr. 3-4). 19.95 *(978-1-4222-2569-1(0))* Mason Crest.
—Incredible Feats. 2012. (Ripley's Disbelief & Shock Ser.). 36p. (J). (gr. 3-4). 19.95 *(978-1-4222-2570-7(4))* Mason Crest.
—Incredibly Strange. 2013. (Ripley's Believe It or Not! Strikingly True Ser.: 8). (Illus.). 36p. (J). (gr. 4-18). 19.95 *(978-1-4222-2781-7(2))* Mason Crest.
—The Last Word. 2012. (Ripley's Disbelief & Shock Ser.). 36p. (J). (gr. 3-4). 19.95 *(978-1-4222-2571-4(2))* Mason Crest.
—Prepare to Be Shocked: Epic Endeavors. 2012. (Ripley's Disbelief & Shock Ser.). 36p. (J). (gr. 3-4). 19.95 *(978-1-4222-2568-4(2))* Mason Crest.
—Seeing Is Believing. 2012. (Ripley's Disbelief & Shock Ser.). 36p. (J). (gr. 3-4). 19.95 *(978-1-4222-2561-5(5))*; 19.95 *(978-1-4222-2564-6(X))*; 19.95 *(978-1-4222-2574-5(7))* Mason Crest.
—Strange but True. 2012. (Ripley's Disbelief & Shock Ser.). 36p. (J). (gr. 3-4). 19.95 *(978-1-4222-2573-8(9))* Mason Crest.
—Strange Stories. 2013. (Ripley's Believe It or Not! Strikingly True Ser.: 8). 36p. (J). (gr. 4-18). 19.95 *(978-1-4222-2782-4(0))* Mason Crest.
—Unbelievable Feats. 2013. (Ripley's Believe It or Not! Strikingly True Ser.: 8). 36p. (J). (gr. 4-18). 19.95 *(978-1-4222-2784-8(7))* Mason Crest.
—Wacky World. 2013. (Ripley's Believe It or Not! Enter If You Dare Ser.: 8). 36p. (J). (gr. 4-18). 19.95 *(978-1-4222-2785-5(5))* Mason Crest.
—World Wonders. 2012. (Ripley's Disbelief & Shock Ser.). 36p. (J). (gr. 3-4). 19.95 *(978-1-4222-2576-9(3))* Mason Crest.
Ripley's Believe It Or Not! Staff, compiled by. The Big One! 2014. (Fun Facts Ser.). (ENG., Illus.). 144p. (J). 18.95 *(978-1-60991-118-8(0))* Ripley Entertainment, Inc.
—Perfectly Peculiar! 2017. (Curio Ser.: 11). (ENG.). 384p. 17.99 *(978-1-60991-176-8(8))* Ripley Entertainment, Inc.
—Ripley's Believe It or Not! 2014. (Fun Facts Ser.: 3). (ENG.). 224p. (J). pap. 8.99 *(978-1-60991-116-4(4))* Ripley Entertainment, Inc.
Ripley's Believe It Or Not! Staff & Ripley's Believe It Or Not! Editors, compiled by. Odd Around the World! 2016. (Fun Facts Ser.: 3). (ENG.). 144p. (J). 18.95 *(978-1-60991-168-3(7))* Ripley Entertainment, Inc.
Ripley's Entertainment Inc Staff. Ripley's Believe It or Not! 2014. 2013. (ENG.). 144p. (J). (gr. 3-7). 16.99 *(978-0-545-56647-6(9))* Scholastic, Inc.
—Ripley's Believe It or Not! 2015. 2014. (ENG.). 144p. (J). (gr. 3-7). 16.99 *(978-0-545-68162-9(6))* Scholastic, Inc.
Ripley's Entertainment Inc Staff, contrib. by. Ripley's Believe It or Not 2016. 2015. (ENG.). 144p. (J). (gr. 3-7). 16.99 *(978-0-545-85279-1(X))* Scholastic, Inc.
Ripley's Inc. Staff. Ripley's Fun Facts & Silly Stories. 2012. lib. bdg. 19.65 *(978-0-606-26883-7(9)*, Turtleback) Turtleback Bks.
—Roar! Graziano, John, illus. 2012. (Ripley's Shout Outs Ser.: 1). (ENG.). 96p. (J). (gr. 2-5). pap. 4.99 *(978-0-545-38075-1(8))* Scholastic, Inc.
—Woof! Graziano, John, illus. 2012. (Ripley's Shout Outs Ser.: 3). (ENG.). 96p. (J). (gr. 2-5). pap. 4.99 *(978-0-545-38077-5(4))* Scholastic, Inc.
Roberts, Christa. Guinness World Records: Amazing Body Records! 100 Mind-Blowing Body Records from Around the World! 2016. (J). lib. bdg. 16.00 *(978-0-606-38192-5(9))* Turtleback Bks.
—Guinness World Records: Incredible Animals: Amazing Animals & Their Awesome Feats! 2016. (J). lib. bdg. 16.00 *(978-0-606-38191-8(0))* Turtleback Bks.
Rooney, Anne. Strange Places. 2010. (Amazing Mysteries Ser.). (YA). (gr. 3-6). 28.50 *(978-1-59920-366-9(9))* Black Rabbit Bks.
Rosen Publishing Staff. Conspiracies & Cover-Ups, 1 vol. 2015. (Conspiracies & Cover-Ups Ser.). (ENG.). 250p. (YA). 153.00 *(978-1-4777-8161-6(7)*, Rosen Young Adult) Rosen Publishing Group, Inc., The.
Ruzicka, Oldrich. How Things Are Made. Hetmerová, Alexandra, illus. 2016. (ENG.). 36p. (J). (gr. 1-5). 16.95 *(978-1-4549-2085-4(8))* Sterling Publishing Co., Inc.
Samuel, Nigel. The 10 Coolest Wonders of the Universe. 2008. (Illus.). (J). 14.99 *(978-1-55448-490-4(1))* Scholastic Library Publishing.
Scholastic & Ripley's Entertainment Inc., Ripley's. Ripley's Believe It or Not! Special Edition 2017. 2016. (ENG.). 144p. (J). (gr. 3-7). 16.99 *(978-1-338-11324-2(0))* Scholastic, Inc.
Scholastic, Inc. Staff. Deep Dive: A LEGO(r) Adventure in the Real World. 2016. (LEGO Nonfiction Ser.). (ENG., Illus.). 32p. (J). (gr. -1-3). pap. 4.99 *(978-0-545-94770-1(7))* Scholastic, Inc.
Scholastic, Inc. Staff, contrib. by. Best & Buzzworthy 2017: World Records, Trending Topics & Viral Moments. 2016. (ENG.). 320p. (J). (gr. 3-7). pap. 12.99 *(978-1-338-03912-2(1))* Scholastic, Inc.
Scholastic, Inc. Staff & Arlon, Penelope. The Ultimate Book of Randomly Awesome Facts. 2015. (ENG.). 144p. (J). (gr. 3-7). pap. 8.99 *(978-0-545-82626-6(8)*, Scholastic Nonfiction) Scholastic, Inc.
Scholastic, Inc. Staff & Ripley's Entertainment Inc Staff. Ripley's Believe It or Not! 2012. (ENG.). 144p. (J). (gr. 3-7). 16.99 *(978-0-545-43505-5(6))* Scholastic, Inc.
Schutte, Mary. Dover Demon. 2009. (Mysterious Encounters Ser.). (ENG., Illus.). 48p. (J). 29.00 *(978-0-7377-4570-2(3)*, Greenhaven Pr., Inc.) Cengage Gale.
Seeing Is Believing. 2012. (J). *(978-1-4222-2560-8(7))* Mason Crest.
Seeley, M. H. Freaky Stories about the Paranormal. 2016. (Freaky True Science Ser.). (Illus.). 32p. (J). (gr. 5-4). pap. 10.50 *(978-1-4824-4846-7(7))* Stevens, Gareth Publishing LLLP.
Seriously Weird! 2014. (Ripleys Believe It or Not! Dare to Look Ser.: 8). 36p. (J). (gr. 4-18). lib. bdg. 20.95 *(978-1-4222-3142-5(9))* Mason Crest.
Sharkawy, Azza. Question It! 2014. (ENG., Illus.). 24p. (J). *(978-0-7787-0759-2(8))* Crabtree Publishing Co.
Silván, Sergio Gómez, illus. J.K. Rowling's Wizarding World: A Pop-up Gallery of Curiosities. 2016. (J. K. Rowling's Wizarding World Ser.). (ENG.). 10p. (J). (gr. 3-7). 27.99 *(978-0-7636-9588-0(2))* Candlewick Pr.
Silverstein, Janna. Close Encounters with Aliens. 2009. (Unsolved Mysteries: the Secret Files Ser.). 48p. (gr. 5-8). 53.00 *(978-1-60854-693-0(4)*, Rosen Reference) Rosen Publishing Group, Inc., The.
Silverthorne, Sandy. Two Truths & a Tall Tale: A True or False Trivia Challenge for the Whole Family. 2017. (ENG.). 144p. (J). pap. 7.99 *(978-0-7369-6900-0(4))* Harvest Hse. Pubs.
Simon, Seymour. Strange Mysteries from Around the World. 2012. (Dover Children's Science Bks.). (ENG., Illus.). 64p. (J). (gr. 3-5). pap. 5.99 *(978-0-486-48471-6(8))* Dover Pubns., Inc.
Simonds, Lucy. Wonders of the World. 2007. (Trackers-Math Ser.). (gr. 2-5). pap. 5.00 *(978-1-59055-925-3(8))* Pacific Learning, Inc.
Smith, A. G. Wonders of the World Coloring Book. 2003. (Dover History Coloring Book Ser.). (ENG., Illus.). 32p. (gr. 3-8). pap. 3.99 *(978-0-486-43044-7(8))* Dover Pubns., Inc.
Solving Science Mysteries, 14 vols., Set. Incl. Why Do Airplanes Fly? Moore, Rob. lib. bdg. 22.60 *(978-1-61531-890-2(9))*; Why Do Balls Bounce? Moore, Rob. lib. bdg. 22.60 *(978-1-61531-889-6(5))*; Why Do Diamonds Sparkle? All about Earth's Resources. Bethune, Helen. lib. bdg. 22.60 *(978-1-61531-894-0(1))*; Why Do Glaciers Grind? Bethune, Helen. lib. bdg. 22.60 *(978-1-4488-0391-0(8))*; Why Do Monkeys Chatter? Bethune, Helen. lib. bdg. 22.60 *(978-1-4488-0394-1(2))*; Why Do Shadows Lengthen? Brasch, Nicolas. lib. bdg. 22.60 *(978-1-61531-891-9(7))*; Why Do Spiders Live in Webs? Brasch, Nicolas. lib. bdg. 22.60 *(978-1-4488-0397-2(7))*; Why Do Stars Twinkle? McMahon, Michael. lib. bdg. 22.60 *(978-1-61531-895-7(X))*; Why Does Electricity Flow? Moore, Rob. lib. bdg. 22.60 *(978-1-61531-893-3(3))*; Why Does Water Evaporate? Moore, Rob. lib. bdg. 22.60 *(978-1-61531-892-6(5))*; Why Is It So Loud? Brasch, Nicolas. lib. bdg. 22.60 *(978-1-61531-888-9(7))*; (YA). (gr. 3-6). (Illus.). 24p. 2010. Set lib. bdg. 297.50 *(978-1-61531-924-4(7)*, PowerKids Pr.) Rosen Publishing Group, Inc., The.
Southwell, David. Unsolved Political Mysteries. 2009. (Mysteries & Conspiracies Ser.). 80p. (gr. 10-10). 61.20 *(978-1-61514-747-2(0))* Rosen Publishing Group, Inc., The.
Southwell, David & Twist, Sean. Unsolved Political Mysteries. 2007. (Mysteries & Conspiracies Ser.). (Illus.). 80p. (YA). (gr. 9-12). lib. bdg. 33.25 *(978-1-4042-1083-7(0))* Rosen Publishing Group, Inc., The.
Spilsbury, Louise. Superstar Plants. 2014. (Nature's Got Talent Ser.). 32p. (J). (gr. k-5). lib. bdg. 26.25 *(978-1-4777-7072-6(0)*, PowerKids Pr.) Rosen Publishing Group, Inc., The.
Spirn, Michele Sobel. Mysterious People. 2006. (True Tales: A Chapter Book Ser.). (ENG., Illus.). 48p. (J). (gr. 2-4). per. 4.95 *(978-0-516-25454-8(5)*, Children's Pr.) Scholastic Library Publishing.
Steele, Philip. Wow! Surprising Facts about Pirates. Aspinall, Marc, illus. 2014. (ENG.). 32p. (J). (gr. k-3). 15.99 *(978-0-7534-7188-3(4)*, 9780753471883, Kingfisher) Roaring Brook Pr.
Sterling Children's, Sterling & Schader Lee, Susan. Secrets of Our Nation's Capital: Weird & Wonderful Facts about Washington, DC. 2016. (ENG., Illus.). 160p. (J). (gr. 1-3). 8.95 *(978-1-4549-2003-8(3))* Sterling Publishing Co., Inc.
Stewart, David. Amaze, 3 vols., Set. Franklin, Carolyn, illus. Incl. How a Seed Grows into a Sunflower. 27.00 *(978-0-531-20442-9(1))*; How a Tadpole Grows into a Frog. 27.00 *(978-0-531-20443-6(X))*; How Your Body Works: A Good Look Inside Your Insides. 27.00 *(978-0-531-20444-3(8))*; (Illus.). 32p. (J). (gr. k-3). 2008. Set lib. bdg. 189.00 *(978-0-531-20445-0(6)*, Children's Pr.) Scholastic Library Publishing.
Stewart, Melissa. Tell Me Why, Tell Me How - Group 2, 6 bks., Set. Incl. How Do Bats Fly in the Dark? lib. bdg. 29.93 *(978-0-7614-2924-1(7))*; How Do Bees Make Honey? lib. bdg. 29.93 *(978-0-7614-2923-4(9))*; How Do Chameleons Change Color? lib. bdg. 29.93 *(978-0-7614-2922-7(0))*; How Do Spiders Make Webs? lib. bdg. 29.93 *(978-0-7614-2920-3(4))*; Why Do We See Rainbows? lib. bdg. 29.93 *(978-0-7614-2919-7(0))*; Why Does the Moon Change Shape? (YA). lib. bdg. 29.93 *(978-0-7614-2921-0(2))*; (Illus.). 32p. (gr. 3-18). 2008. Set lib. bdg. 179.57 *(978-0-7614-2918-0(2)*, Benchmark Bks.) Marshall Cavendish Corp.
Stride, Lottie. Girls Miscellany: Fascinating Information Every Girl Should Know. Tambellini, Stefano, illus. 2013. 128p. (J). *(978-1-4351-5048-5(1))* Barnes & Noble, Inc.
Strother, Ruth. Smithsonian Everything You Need to Know: Grades 2-3. 2015. (Smithsonian Everything You Need to Know Ser.). (ENG., Illus.). 275p. (J). (gr. 1). 19.95 *(978-1-62686-311-8(3)*, Silver Dolphin Bks.) Readerlink Distribution Services, LLC.
—Smithsonian Everything You Need to Know: Grades 4-5. 2015. (Smithsonian Everything You Need to Know Ser.). (ENG., Illus.). 275p. (J). (gr. 4-5). 19.95 *(978-1-62686-312-5(1)*, Silver Dolphin Bks.) Readerlink Distribution Services, LLC.
—Smithsonian Everything You Need to Know: Grades K-1. 2015. (Smithsonian Everything You Need to Know Ser.). (ENG., Illus.). 275p. (J). (gr. k). 19.95 *(978-1-62686-310-1(5)*, Silver Dolphin Bks.) Readerlink Distribution Services, LLC.
Symons, Mitchell. Why Spacemen Can't Burp. 2014. (ENG., Illus.). 272p. (J). (gr. 2-4). pap. 9.99 *(978-1-84941-551-4(X)*, Red Fox) Random House Children's Books GBR. Dist: Independent Pubs. Group.
—Why Spacemen Can't Burp. 2013. (ENG., Illus.). 352p. (J). (gr. 1-4). 14.99 *(978-0-85753-097-4(6))* Transworld Publishers Ltd. GBR. Dist: Independent Pubs. Group.
Taylor, Kim. Demasiado Pequeno para Verlo. (Coleccion Mundos Secretos). (SPA.). (J). (gr. k-2). 4.95 *(978-84-263-2045-2(7))* Vives, Luis Editorial (Edelvives) ESP. Dist: Lectorum Pubns., Inc.
Taylor, Marianne. What If... Humans Were Like Animals? Moran, Paul, illus. 2012. 128p. 7.99 *(978-1-78055-042-8(1)*, Buster Bks.) O'Mara, Michael Bks., Ltd. GBR. Dist: Littlehampton Bk Services, Ltd.
Terrell, Brandon. 12 Frightening Tales of Alien Encounters. 2017. (Scary & Spooky Ser.). (ENG., Illus.). 32p. (J). (gr. 3-6). 21.95 *(978-1-63235-293-4(1))* Pr. Room Editions LLC.
—12 Unsolved Mysteries. 2017. (Scary & Spooky Ser.). (ENG.). 32p. (J). (gr. 3-6). 21.95 *(978-1-63235-298-9(2))* Pr. Room Editions LLC.
That's Incredible! 2014. (Ripleys Believe It or Not! Dare to Look Ser.: 8). 36p. (J). (gr. 4-18). lib. bdg. 20.95 *(978-1-4222-3145-6(3))* Mason Crest.
That's Weird! 36p. (J). 2014. (Ripleys Believe It or Not! Download the Weird Ser.: 8). (gr. 4-18). lib. bdg. 20.95 *(978-1-4222-3153-1(4))* 2012. (Illus.). *(978-1-4222-3147-0(X))* Mason Crest.
Thomas, Isabel. Brilliant Birds, 1 vol. 2012. (Extreme Animals Ser.). (ENG.). 32p. (gr. 1-3). pap. 8.29 *(978-1-4109-4684-3(3))*; lib. bdg. 29.99 *(978-1-4109-4678-2(9))* Heinemann-Raintree. (Read Me!).
—Crazy Creepy Crawlies, 1 vol. 2012. (Extreme Animals Ser.). (ENG.). 32p. (gr. 1-3). pap. 8.29 *(978-1-4109-4685-0(1))*; lib. bdg. 29.99 *(978-1-4109-4679-9(7))* Heinemann-Raintree. (Read Me!).
—Marvelous Mammals, 1 vol. 2012. (Extreme Animals Ser.). (ENG.). 32p. (gr. 1-3). pap. 8.29 *(978-1-4109-4687-4(8)*, Read Me!) Heinemann-Raintree.
—Remarkable Reptiles, 1 vol. 2012. (Extreme Animals Ser.). (ENG.). 32p. (gr. 1-3). pap. 8.29 *(978-1-4109-4688-1(6))*; lib. bdg. 29.99 *(978-1-4109-4682-9(7))* Heinemann-Raintree. (Read Me!).
Thomas Nelson. Guess Where. 2015. (ENG.). 40p. (J). (gr. -1-k). pap. *(978-1-78393-593-2(6))* Make Believe Ideas.
Ticktock Media, Ltd. Staff. Undead: Zombies, Vampires, Werewolves. 2008. (ENG.). 96p. (J). (gr. 4-7). pap. 9.95 *(978-1-84696-797-9(X)*, TickTock Books) Octopus Publishing Group GBR. Dist: Independent Pubs. Group.
TK & Little Bee Books Staff. Crazy, Totally Awesome Facts. 2016. (ENG., Illus.). 224p. (J). (gr. 3-7). 14.99 *(978-1-4998-0211-5(0))* Little Bee Books Inc.
Torres, John & Healey, Tim. The World's Weirdest News Stories. 2016. (Making Headlines Ser.). 160p. (J). lib. bdg. 39.93 *(978-0-7660-8377-6(2))* Enslow Pubs., Inc.

Totally Bizarre. 2014. (Ripleys Believe It or Not! Download the Weird Ser.: 8). 36p. (J). (gr. 4-18). lib. bdg. 20.95 *(978-1-4222-3154-8(2))* Mason Crest.
Totally Fun Facts. 2008. (Best Friends Club Ser.). 96p. *(978-1-4075-1613-4(2))* Parragon, Inc.
Townsend, John. Gone Missing. 2010. (Amazing Mysteries Ser.). (YA). (gr. 3-6). 28.50 *(978-1-59920-364-5(2))* Black Rabbit Bks.
True or False? 2016. (True or False? Ser.). 48p. (gr. 3-3). pap. 46.80 *(978-0-7660-7990-8(2))*; lib. bdg. 111.72 *(978-0-7660-7497-2(8))* Enslow Pubs., Inc.
Turner, Tracey. World of the Weird. 2009. (ENG., Illus.). 144p. (J). (gr. 4-12). 14.95 *(978-1-55407-481-5(9)*, 9781554074815) Firefly Bks., Ltd.
U. S. National Geographic Society Staff. Ultimate Weird but True: 1,000 Wild & Wacky Facts & Photos! 2011. (ENG., Illus.). 192p. (J). (gr. 3-7). lib. bdg. 28.90 *(978-1-4263-0895-6(7)*, National Geographic Children's Bks.) National Geographic Society.
—Weird but True! 3: 300 Outrageous Facts. 2011. (ENG., Illus.). 208p. (J). (gr. 1-4). pap. 7.95 *(978-1-4263-0766-9(7)*, National Geographic Children's Bks.) National Geographic Society.
—Weird but True: Stupid Criminals: 100 Brainless Baddies Busted, Plus Wacky Facts. Cocotos, Tom Nick, illus. 2012. (ENG.). 176p. (J). (gr. 3-7). pap. 7.95 *(978-1-4263-0861-1(2)*, National Geographic Children's Bks.) National Geographic Society.
U. S. National Geographic Society Staff & National Geographic Kids Staff. 300 Outrageous Facts. Halling, Jonathan, illus. 2009. (ENG.). 208p. (J). (gr. 3-7). pap. 7.95 *(978-1-4263-0594-8(X)*, National Geographic Children's Bks.) National Geographic Society.
Unbelievable Bodies. (J). 2014. (Ripleys Believe It or Not! Dare to Look Ser.: 8). 36p. (gr. 4-18). lib. bdg. 20.95 *(978-1-4222-3146-3(1))* 2013. (Illus.). 35p. *(978-1-4222-3138-8(0))* Mason Crest.
Unbelievable Feats. 2013. 36p. (J). pap. *(978-1-4222-2801-2(0))* Mason Crest.
Unbelievable Stories. 2014. (Ripleys Believe It or Not! Download the Weird Ser.: 8). 36p. (J). (gr. 4-18). lib. bdg. 20.95 *(978-1-4222-3155-5(0))* Mason Crest.
Unglick, Richard. Journey Around the World. 2016. (Playmobil Ser.). (ENG., Illus.). 64p. (J). (gr. 1-7). 19.95 *(978-1-63322-079-9(6)*, Walter Foster Jr) Quarto Publishing Group USA.
Unter der Stadt. (GER.). *(978-3-411-09241-3(6))* Bibliographisches Institut & F. A. Brockhaus AG DEU. Dist: i. b. d., Ltd.
Unusual Histories. 2011. (Unusual Histories Ser.). (ENG.). 48p. (gr. 3-4). lib. bdg. 95.97 *(978-1-4296-5492-0(9))* Capstone Press of Coughlan Cos.
Van Vleet, Carmella. Seven Wonders of the World: Discover Amazing Monuments to Civilization with 20 Projects. Rizvi, Farah, illus. 2011. (Build It Yourself Ser.). (ENG.). 128p. (J). (gr. 3-7). 21.95 *(978-1-934670-82-8(0))*; pap. 15.95 *(978-1-936313-73-0(1))* Open City Bks.
Walden, Libby. In Focus. 2016. (360 Degrees Ser.). (ENG.). 28p. (J). (gr. 3-6). 22.99 *(978-1-944530-02-0(9)*, 360 Degrees) Tiger Tales.
Walker, Kathryn. Mysteries of the Ancients. 2009. (Unsolved! Ser.). (ENG., Illus.). 32p. (J). (gr. 3-5). pap. *(978-0-7787-4160-2(5))*; (gr. 4-6). lib. bdg. *(978-0-7787-4147-3(8))* Crabtree Publishing Co.
—Mysteries of the Cosmic Joker. 2009. (Unsolved! Ser.). (ENG., Illus.). 32p. (J). (gr. 3-5). pap. *(978-0-7787-4161-9(3))*; (gr. 4-6). *(978-0-7787-4148-0(6))* Crabtree Publishing Co.
Waxman, Laura Hamilton. Exploring Black Holes. 2011. (Searchlight Books Whats Amazing about Space Ser.). (ENG., Illus.). (gr. 3-5). pap. 51.01 *(978-0-7613-8413-7(8))* Lerner Publishing Group.
Weakland, Mark Andrew & Collins, Terry Lee. Scooby Doo Unmasks the Truth Behind Mummies. 2016. (Illus.). 24p. (J). *(978-1-4062-8897-1(7))* Capstone Press of Coughlan Cos.
—Scooby Doo Unmasks the Truth Behind Vampires. 2016. (Illus.). 24p. (J). *(978-1-4062-8895-7(0))* Capstone Press of Coughlan Cos.
—Scooby Doo Unmasks the Truth Behind Werewolves. 2016. (Illus.). 24p. (J). *(978-1-4062-8896-4(9))* Capstone Press of Coughlan Cos.
Webster, Christine. K2. 2008. (Natural Wonders Ser.). 32p. (J). (gr. 5-6). lib. bdg. 26.00 *(978-1-59036-938-8(6))*; (Illus.). pap. 9.95 *(978-1-59036-939-5(4))* Weigl Pubs., Inc.
Webster, Christy. Guinness World Records: Biggest & Smallest! 2016. (J). lib. bdg. 24.50 *(978-0-606-38195-6(3))* Turtleback Bks.
Weird-Ities! 2013. (Illus.). (J). *(978-1-60991-023-5(0))*; *(978-1-60991-026-6(5))*; *(978-1-60991-020-4(6))*; *(978-1-60991-024-2(9))* Random Hse. (Random House Business Books).
West, Tracey & dePaola, Tomie. No Way ... Way! Are You My Dinner? Flowers, Luke, illus. 2015. (Smithsonian Ser.). (ENG.). 208p. (J). (gr. 3-7). bds. 9.99 *(978-0-448-48689-5(X)*, Grosset & Dunlap) Penguin Young Readers Group.
What I Know: Set 1. 2016. (What I Know Ser.). 00024p. (J). lib. bdg. 135.60 ***(978-1-4824-5537-3(4))*** Stevens, Gareth Publishing LLLP.
Williams, Brian. What about World Wonders. 2008. 40p. pap. *(978-1-84810-076-3(0))* Miles Kelly Publishing, Ltd.
—Wonders of the World: Biggest & Best. 2004. (Biggest & Best Ser.). (Illus.). 40p. (J). pap. 7.95 *(978-1-84236-066-8(3))* Miles Kelly Publishing, Ltd. GBR. Dist: Independent Pubs. Group.
—World Wonders. 2010. (What About... Ser.). (Illus.). 40p. (J). (gr. 6-8). lib. bdg. 19.95 *(978-1-4222-1567-8(9))* Mason Crest.
Wonders & Winners. (YA). (gr. 7). 48.95 *(978-0-673-72660-5(6)*, Scott Foresman) Addison Wesley Schl.
Woodruff, Paul. M. Monsters, Myths, & Mysteries: A Tangled Tour Maze Book. Woodruff, Paul. M, illus. 2005. (Illus.). 52p. (J). 8.95 *(978-0-9764327-0-8(6))* Woodruff, Paul.
Woods, Michael & Woods, Mary B. Seven Natural Wonders of Africa. 2009. (Seven Wonders Ser.). (ENG., Illus.). 80p. (gr. 5-8). lib. bdg. 33.26 *(978-0-8225-9071-2(9))* Lerner Publishing Group.
—Seven Wonders, 14 vols., Set. Incl. Seven Natural Wonders of Africa. 2009. lib. bdg. 33.26 *(978-0-8225-9071-2(9))*; Seven Natural Wonders of Asia & the Middle East. 2009. 33.26 *(978-0-8225-9073-6(5))*; Seven Natural Wonders of Australia & Oceania. 2009. 33.26 *(978-0-8225-9074-3(3))*; Seven Natural Wonders of Central & South America. (YA). 2009. lib. bdg. 33.26 *(978-0-8225-9070-5(0))*; Seven Natural Wonders of Europe. 2009. 33.26 *(978-0-8225-9072-9(7))*; Seven Natural Wonders of North America. 2009. lib. bdg. 33.26 *(978-0-8225-9069-9(7))*; Seven Natural Wonders of the Arctic, Antarctica, & the Oceans. 2009. 33.26 *(978-0-8225-9075-0(1))*; Seven Wonders of Ancient Africa. 2008. lib. bdg. 33.26 *(978-0-8225-7571-9(X))*; Seven Wonders of Ancient Asia. 2008. lib. bdg. 33.26 *(978-0-8225-7569-6(8))*; Seven Wonders of Ancient Central & South America. 2008. lib. bdg. 33.26 *(978-0-8225-7570-2(1))*; Seven Wonders of Ancient Greece. (J). 2008. lib. bdg. 33.26 *(978-0-8225-7574-0(4))*; Seven Wonders of Ancient North America. 2008. lib. bdg. 33.26 *(978-0-8225-7572-6(8))*; Seven Wonders of the Ancient Middle East. 2008. lib. bdg. 33.26 *(978-0-8225-7573-3(6))*; Seven Wonders of the Ancient World. 2008. lib. bdg. 33.26 *(978-0-8225-7568-9(X))*; (Illus.). 80p. (gr. 5-8). (Seven Wonders Ser.). (ENG.). 2008. Set lib. bdg. 931.28 *(978-0-8225-7567-2(1)*, Twenty-First Century Bks.) Lerner Publishing Group.
World Book, Inc. Staff. Learning Ladders, 10 vols., Set. 2007. 320p. (J). (gr. k-3). 139.00 *(978-0-7166-7725-3(3))* World Bk., Inc.
World Book, Inc Staff, contrib. by. The Bermuda Triangle & Other Mysteries of the Deep. 2015. (Illus.). 48p. (J). *(978-0-7166-2672-5(1))* World Bk., Inc.
—Wonders of the World. 2011. (J). *(978-0-7166-1794-5(3))* World Bk., Inc.
The World's Deadliest, 6 vols. 2010. (World's Deadliest Ser.). (ENG.). 32p. (gr. 1-2). lib. bdg. 133.25 *(978-1-4296-4418-1(4)*, Blazers) Capstone Press of Coughlan Cos.
The World's Deadliest [Capstone Sole Source]. 2010. (World's Deadliest Ser.). 32p. lib. bdg. 151.92 *(978-1-4296-5890-4(8)*, Blazers) Capstone Press of Coughlan Cos.
Yerdon, Joe. America's Oddest Foods. 2016. (Weird America Ser.). (ENG., Illus.). 32p. (J). (gr. 3-4). pap. 10.50 *(978-1-4824-4012-6(1))* Stevens, Gareth Publishing LLLP.
York, M. J. 12 Ancient Mysteries. 2017. (Scary & Spooky Ser.). (ENG., Illus.). 32p. (J). (gr. 3-6). 21.95 *(978-1-63235-291-0(5))* Pr. Room Editions LLC.
Zoehfeld, Kathleen Weidner. Ghost Mysteries: Unraveling the World's Most Mysterious Hauntings. Hale, Nathan, illus. 2009. (ENG.). 128p. (J). (gr. 4-8). pap. 5.99 *(978-1-4169-6448-3(7)*, Aladdin) Simon & Schuster Children's Publishing.
Zullo, Allan. Fact or Fake? Test Your Smarts! 2013. (Illus.). 207p. (J). pap. *(978-0-545-53551-9(4))* Scholastic, Inc.
100 Facts You Should Know. 2014. (100 Facts You Should Know Ser.). 48p. (J). (gr. 4-6). 191.70 *(978-1-4824-1182-9(2))*; pap. 84.30 *(978-1-4824-1547-6(X))* Stevens, Gareth Publishing LLLP.
100 Facts You Should Know: Set 2. 2015. (100 Facts You Should Know Ser.). (ENG.). 48p. (J). (gr. 4-5). 223.65 *(978-1-4824-2197-2(6))* Stevens, Gareth Publishing LLLP.
100 Facts You Should Know: Set 3. 2015. (100 Facts You Should Know Ser.). (ENG.). 48p. (J). (gr. 4-5). pap., pap., pap. 505.80 *(978-1-4824-3430-9(X))* Stevens, Gareth Publishing LLLP.
100 Facts You Should Know: Set 4. 2016. (100 Facts You Should Know Ser.). 48p. (gr. 5-4). pap. 84.30 *(978-1-4824-5331-7(2))*; lib. bdg. 191.70 *(978-1-4824-5032-3(1))* Stevens, Gareth Publishing LLLP.

CURRENCY
see Money

CURRENTS, ELECTRIC
see Electric Currents

CUSTER, ELIZABETH BACON, 1842-1933
Arruda, Suzanne Middendorf. The Girl He Left Behind: The Life & Times of Libbie Custer. 2004. (Avisson Young Adult Ser.). (Illus.). 136p. (J). pap. 19.95 *(978-1-888105-67-4(4))* Avisson Pr., Inc.

CUSTER, GEORGE A. (GEORGE ARMSTRONG), 1839-1876
Anderson, Paul C. George Armstrong Custer: The Indian Wars & the Battle of the Little Bighorn. 2009. (Library of American Lives & Times Ser.). 112p. (gr. 5-5). 69.20 *(978-1-60853-483-8(9))* Rosen Publishing Group, Inc., The.
Anderson, Paul Christopher. George Armstrong Custer: The Indian Wars & the Battle at the Little Bighorn. 2005. (Library of American Lives & Times). (Illus.). 112p. (J). (gr. 4-8). lib. bdg. 34.60 *(978-0-8239-6631-8(3))* Rosen Publishing Group, Inc., The.
Arruda, Suzanne Middendorf. The Girl He Left Behind: The Life & Times of Libbie Custer. 2004. (Avisson Young Adult Ser.). (Illus.). 136p. (J). pap. 19.95 *(978-1-888105-67-4(4))* Avisson Pr., Inc.
Dunn, Joeming W. Custer's Last Stand, 1 vol. Smith, Tim, illus. 2008. (Graphic History Ser.). (ENG.). 32p. 28.50 *(978-1-60270-181-6(4)*, Graphic Planet- Nonfiction) ABDO Publishing Co.
Fradin, Dennis Brindell. Custer's Last Stand. 2006. (Turning Points in U. S. History Ser.). (Illus.). 48p. (gr. 3-7). lib. bdg. 31.36 *(978-0-7614-2124-5(6)*, Benchmark Bks.) Marshall Cavendish Corp.
Green, Carl R. Custer's Stunning Defeat by American Indians at the Little Bighorn. 2006. (Wild History of the American West Ser.). (Illus.). 128p. (J). (gr. 5-9). lib. bdg. 34.60 *(978-1-59845-020-0(4)*, MyReportLinks.com Bks.) Enslow Pubs., Inc.
King, Zelda. The Battle of the Little Bighorn: Both Sides of the Story. 2009. (Real Life Readers Ser.). 32p. (gr. 5-6). pap. 10.00 *(978-1-4358-0197-4(0)*, Rosen Classroom) Rosen Publishing Group, Inc., The.
Link, Theodore. George Armstrong Custer. 2004. (Primary Sources of Famous People in American History Ser.). (ENG., Illus.). 32p. (gr. 4-8). pap. 10.00 *(978-0-8239-4182-7(5))* Rosen Publishing Group, Inc., The.
—George Armstrong Custer: General de la caballería Estadounidense. 2004. (Grandes personajes en la historia de los Estados Unidos Ser.). (SPA.). 32p. (gr. 3-6). pap. 10.00 *(978-0-8239-4228-2(7)*, Rosen Classroom) Rosen Publishing Group, Inc., The.
—George Armstrong Custer: General de la caballería estadounidense (George Armstrong Custer: General of the U. S. Cavalry) 2009. (Grandes personajes en la historia de los Estados Unidos (Famous People in American History) Ser.). (SPA.). 32p. (gr. 2-3). 47.90 *(978-1-61512-799-3(2)*, Editorial Buenas Letras) Rosen Publishing Group, Inc., The.
—George Armstrong Custer: General of the U. S. Cavalry. 2009. (Primary Sources of Famous People in American History Ser.).Tr. of George Armstrong Custer: General de la Caballería Estadounidense. 32p. (gr. 2-3). 47.90 *(978-1-60851-680-3(6))* Rosen Publishing Group, Inc., The.
—George Armstrong Custer: General of the U. S. Cavalry / General de la caballería Estadounidense. 2009. (Famous People in American History/Grandes personajes en la historia de los Estados Unidos Ser.). (ENG & SPA.). 32p. (gr. 2-3). 47.90 *(978-1-61512-545-6(0)*, Editorial Buenas Letras) Rosen Publishing Group, Inc., The.
Rice, Earle. The Life & Times of the Brothers Custer: Galloping to Glory. 2008. (Profiles in American History Ser.). (Illus.). 48p. (J). (gr. 4-8). lib. bdg. 29.95 *(978-1-58415-665-9(1))* Mitchell Lane Pubs., Inc.
Roxburgh, Ellis. Sitting Bull vs. George Armstrong Custer: The Battle of the Little Bighorn. 2016. (History's Greatest Rivals Ser.). (ENG., Illus.). 48p. (J). (gr. 6-8). pap. 14.05 *(978-1-4824-4235-9(3))* Stevens, Gareth Publishing LLLP.
Silate, Jennifer. The Last Stand: The Final Military Campaign of General George Armstrong Custer. 2009. (Great Moments in American History Ser.). 32p. (gr. 3-3). 47.90 *(978-1-61513-154-9(X))* Rosen Publishing Group, Inc., The.

CUSTOMS, SOCIAL
see Manners and Customs

CYBERSPACE
see also Computers
Gordon, Sherri Mabry. Using Technology. 2011. (Life—a How-To Guide Ser.). (Illus.). 128p. (J). lib. bdg. 33.27 *(978-0-7660-3441-9(0))*; (gr. 6-18). pap. 10.95 *(978-1-59845-311-9(4))* Enslow Pubs., Inc.
Linde, Barbara. Cyberspace Research. 2012. (Cyberspace Survival Guide Ser.). (Illus.). 32p. (J). (gr. 3-6). 26.60 *(978-1-4339-7216-4(6))*; pap. 10.50 *(978-1-4339-7217-1(4))* Stevens, Gareth Publishing LLLP. (Gareth Stevens Learning Library).
Steffens, Bradley. Real-World Stem: Securing Cyberspace. 2017. (Real-World Stem Ser.). (ENG.). 80p. (YA). (gr. 5-12). ***(978-1-68282-249-4(4))*** ReferencePoint Pr., Inc.
Weber, Sandra. The Internet. 2003. (Transforming Power of Technology Ser.). (Illus.). 112p. (C). (gr. 9-13). 30.00 *(978-0-7910-7449-7(8)*, Chelsea Hse.) Facts On File, Inc.

CYCLES, MOTOR
see Motorcycles

CYCLING
see Bicycles and Bicycling; Motorcycles

CYCLOPEDIAS
see Encyclopedias and Dictionaries

CYPRUS
Etingoff, Kim. Cyprus. 2007. (European Union Ser.). (Illus.). 88p. (YA). (gr. 5-18). lib. bdg. 21.95 *(978-1-4222-0041-4(8)*, 1247983) Mason Crest.
Etingoff, Kim & Indovino, Shaina Carmel. Cyprus. 2012. (J). *(978-1-4222-2236-2(5))*; *(978-1-4222-2262-1(4))*; pap. *(978-1-4222-2265-2(9))*; pap. *(978-1-4222-2267-6(5))* Mason Crest.
Spilling, Michael & Spilling, Jo-Ann. Cyprus. 2nd rev. ed. 2009. (Cultures of the World 19 Ser.). 144p. (gr. 6). 42.79 *(978-0-7614-4855-6(1))* Marshall Cavendish GBR. Dist: Marshall Cavendish Corp.

CYRANO DE BERGERAC, 1619-1655—DRAMA
David, Peter, et al. Cyrano de Bergerac: A Heroic Comedy in Five Acts. (Classics Illustrated Ser.). (Illus.). 52p. (YA). pap. 4.95 *(978-1-57209-019-4(7))* Classics International Entertainment, Inc.

CYRUS, THE GREAT, KING OF PERSIA, -530 B.C. OR 529 B.C.
Crompton, Samuel Willard. Cyrus the Great. 2008. (Ancient World Leaders Ser.). (Illus.). 112p. (gr. 6-12). 30.00 *(978-0-7910-9636-9(X)*, Chelsea Hse.) Facts On File, Inc.

CYTOLOGY
see Cells

CZECH REPUBLIC
Docalavich, Heather & Indovino, Shaina Carmel. The Czech Republic. 2012. (J). pap. *(978-1-4222-2268-3(3))* Mason Crest.
Milivojevic, JoAnn. Czech Republic. 2004. (Enchantment of the World Ser.). (ENG., Illus.). 144p. (YA). (gr. 5-9). 37.00 *(978-0-516-24255-2(5)*, Children's Pr.) Scholastic Library Publishing.

CZECH REPUBLIC—FICTION
Cosson, M. J. Sherlock Holmes & A Scandal in Bohemia. rev. ed. 2010. pap. 39.62 *(978-0-7613-6954-7(6))* Lerner Publishing Group.
Gruenbaum, Michael & Hasak-Lowy, Todd. Somewhere There Is Still a Sun. 2017. lib. bdg. 19.65 ***(978-0-606-40203-3(9))*** Turtleback Bks.
Ish-Kishor, Sulamith. A Boy of Old Prague. Shahn, Ben, illus. 2008. (Dover Children's Classics Ser.). (ENG.). 96p. (J). (gr. 4-6). pap. 3.99 *(978-0-486-46766-5(X))* Dover Pubns., Inc.
Luna, Chelsea. A Forest of Wolves. 2016. (ENG., Illus.). 202p. (J). pap. 15.00 *(978-1-60183-512-3(4))* Kensington Publishing Corp.
Seredy, Kate. Philomena. Seredy, Kate, illus. 2008. (Illus.). 93p. (J). pap. 11.95 *(978-1-932350-19-7(5))* Bethlehem Bks.
Seven, John. The Alchemist War, 1 vol. Phillips, Craig, illus. 2013. (Time-Tripping Faradays Ser.). (ENG.). 160p. (gr. 4-5). 9.95 *(978-1-62370-011-9(6))*; (YA). pap. 5.95 *(978-1-4342-6438-1(6))*; (gr. 4-5). lib. bdg. 26.65 *(978-1-4342-6028-4(3))* Stone Arch Bks.
Taylor, Laini. Daughter of Smoke & Bone. 2011. (ENG.). 432p. (YA). (gr. 10-17). 20.00 *(978-0-316-13402-6(3))* Little Brown & Co.
—Daughter of Smoke & Bone. 2012. (ENG.). (YA). (gr. 10-17). 448p. pap. 12.99 *(978-0-316-13399-9(X))*; 624p. pap. 28.99 *(978-0-316-22435-2(9))* Little, Brown Bks. for Young Readers.
—Daughter of Smoke & Bone. 2012. (Daughter of Smoke & Bone Ser.: 1). (YA). lib. bdg. 24.50 *(978-0-606-26704-5(2)*, Turtleback) Turtleback Bks.
—Days of Blood & Starlight. (ENG.). (YA). (gr. 10-17). 2014. 544p. pap. 12.99 *(978-0-316-13398-2(1))* 2012. (Illus.). 528p. 18.99 *(978-0-316-13397-5(3))* 2012. 688p. 39.99 *(978-0-316-22433-8(2))* Little, Brown Bks. for Young Readers.
Wasserman, Robin. The Book of Blood & Shadow. 2012. (ENG.). 448p. (YA). (gr. 7). 17.99 *(978-0-375-86876-4(3))*; lib. bdg. 20.99 *(978-0-375-96876-1(8))* Random Hse. Children's Bks. (Knopf Bks. for Young Readers).

CZECH REPUBLIC—HISTORY
Cottrell, Robert C. Czechoslovakia & the Velvet Revolution. Matray, James I., ed. 2005. (Arbitrary Borders Ser.). (Illus.). 112p. (C). (gr. 9-13). 35.00 *(978-0-7910-8255-3(5)*, Chelsea Hse.) Facts On File, Inc.
Docalavich, Heather & Indovino, Shaina C. The Czech Republic. Bruton, John, ed. 2012. (Major European Union Nations Ser.). 64p. (J). (gr. 7). 22.95 *(978-1-4222-2237-9(3))* Mason Crest.
Gordon, Nick. The Bone Chapel. 2013. (Scariest Places on Earth Ser.). (ENG., Illus.). 24p. (J). (gr. 3-7). lib. bdg. 25.95 *(978-1-60014-946-7(4)*, Torque Bks.) Bellwether Media.
Guillain, Charlotte. Czech Republic, 1 vol. 2011. (Countries Around the World Ser.). (ENG.). 48p. (gr. 3-6). pap. 9.95 *(978-1-4329-5225-9(0))*; 33.32 *(978-1-4329-5200-6(5))* Heinemann-Raintree. (NA-h).
Simmons, Walter. The Czech Republic. 2012. (Exploring Countries Ser.). (ENG., Illus.). 32p. (J). (gr. 3-7). lib. bdg. 26.95 *(978-1-60014-728-9(3)*, Blastoff! Readers) Bellwether Media.
Sioras, Efstathia & Spilling, Michael. Czech Republic. 2nd rev. ed. 2009. (Cultures of the World 17 Ser.). 144p. (gr. 6). lib. bdg. 42.79 *(978-0-7614-4476-3(9))* Marshall Cavendish Corp.
Sís, Peter. The Wall: Growing up Behind the Iron Curtain. Sís, Peter, illus. 2007. (ENG., Illus.). 56p. (J). (gr. 3-7). 19.99 *(978-0-374-34701-7(8)*, 9780374347017, Farrar, Straus & Giroux (BYR)) Farrar, Straus & Giroux.

CZECHS—UNITED STATES—FICTION
Myers, Walter Dean. Game. 2008. (ENG.). 224p. (YA). (gr. 8-18). 17.99 *(978-0-06-058294-4(4)*, HarperTeen) HarperCollins Pubs.

D

DACHSHUND
see Dachshunds

DACHSHUNDS
Beal, Abigail. I Love My Dachshund. 2011. (Top Dogs Ser.). 24p. (J). (ENG.). pap. 8.25 *(978-1-4488-2658-2(6))*; (Illus.). lib. bdg. 22.60 *(978-1-4488-2537-0(7))* Rosen Publishing Group, Inc., The. (PowerKids Pr.).
Bozzo, Linda. I Like Dachshunds! 2016. (Discover Dogs with the American Canine Association Ser.). (Illus.). 24p. (J). pap. 9.35 *(978-0-7660-8161-1(3))*; lib. bdg. 22.60 *(978-0-7660-8163-5(X))* Enslow Pubs., Inc.
Finne, Stephanie. Dachshunds, 1 vol. 2014. (Dogs Set 12 Ser.). (ENG.). 24p. (gr. 3-6). 25.65 *(978-1-62403-674-3(0))* ABDO Publishing Co.
George, Charles & George, Linda. Dachshund. 2010. (J). 26.00 *(978-0-531-23243-9(3))* Scholastic Library Publishing.
Gray, Susan H. Dachshunds. 2008. (Domestic Dogs Ser.). (ENG., Illus.). 32p. (J). (gr. 2-5). 28.50 *(978-1-59296-964-7(X)*, 200140) Child's World, Inc., The.
Gray, Susan Heinrichs. Dachshunds. 2016. (J). *(978-1-4896-4589-0(6))* Weigl Pubs., Inc.
Johnson, Jinny. Dachshund. 2014. (My Favorite Dogs Ser.). (Illus.). 24p. (gr. k-3). 28.50 *(978-1-62588-173-1(8))* Black Rabbit Bks.
—Daschund. 2015. (My Favorite Dogs Ser.). (ENG., Illus.). 24p. (J). pap. 8.95 *(978-1-62588-331-5(5))* RiverStream Publishing.
Landau, Elaine. Dachshunds Are the Best! 2010. (Best Dogs Ever Ser.). (ENG.). 32p. (gr. 2-4). lib. bdg. 25.26 *(978-1-58013-563-4(3)*, Lerner Pubns.) Lerner Publishing Group.
Lowe, Jennifer. Dachshund. 2017. (Dog Lover's Guides: Vol. 18). (ENG.). (YA). (gr. 7-12). 26.95 ***(978-1-4222-3855-4(5))*** Mason Crest.
Lunis, Natalie. Dachshund: The Hot Dogger. 2009. (Little Dogs Rock! Ser.). (Illus.). 32p. (YA). (gr. 2-5). lib. bdg. 25.27 *(978-1-59716-744-4(4))* Bearport Publishing Co., Inc.
Mansfield, Carol M. Jake & Jebadiah Visit the Veterinarian, 1 vol. 2010. 22p. pap. 24.95 *(978-1-4489-2548-3(7))* PublishAmerica, Inc.
Schweitzer, Karen. The Dachshund. 2010. (J). *(978-1-932904-59-8(X))* Eldorado Ink.

DAEDALUS (GREEK MYTHOLOGY)
Watton, Ross, illus. Too Close to the Sun: The Story of Daedalus & Icarus: A Greek Legend. 2004. (ENG.). 20p. (J). (gr. 3-3). pap. 6.47 net. *(978-0-7685-2121-4(1)*, Dominie Elementary) Pearson Schl.

DAFFY DUCK (FICTITIOUS CHARACTER)—FICTION
Granny Vanishes. 2008. (Looney Tunes 8*8 Ser.). 24p. pap. *(978-1-4075-2641-6(3))*; pap. *(978-1-4075-2631-7(6))* Parragon, Inc.
Jewel Robbery. 2008. (Looney Tunes 8*8 Ser.). 24p. pap. *(978-1-4075-2642-3(1))*; pap. *(978-1-4075-2632-4(4))* Parragon, Inc.

DAHL, ROALD, 1916-1990
Boothroyd, Jennifer. Roald Dahl. 2008. pap. 40.95 *(978-0-8225-9475-8(7))* Lerner Publishing Group.
—Roald Dahl: A Life of Imagination. 2008. (Pull Ahead Books-Biographies Ser.). (ENG., Illus.). 32p. (gr. k-3). lib.

bdg. 22.60 (978-0-8225-8825-2(0), Lerner Pubns.) Lerner Publishing Group.
Dahl, Roald. Boy - Tales of Childhood. 2009. (gr. 3-6). lib. bdg. 18.40 (978-0-613-63922-4(7), Turtleback) Turtleback Bks.
—Boy & Going Solo. Blake, Quentin, illus. 2010. (ENG.). 400p. (J). (gr. 3-7). 10.99 (978-0-14-241741-6(6), Puffin Books) Penguin Young Readers Group.
—D Is for Dahl: A Gloriumptious A-Z Guide to the World of Roald Dahl. Blake, Quentin, illus. 2007. (ENG.). 160p. (J). (gr. 3-7). 6.99 (978-0-14-240934-3(0), Puffin Books) Penguin Young Readers Group.
—More about Boy. Blake, Quentin, illus. 2009. (ENG.). 240p. (J). (gr. 5-7). pap. 15.99 (978-0-14-241498-9(0), Puffin Books) Penguin Young Readers Group.
—More about Boy: Roald Dahl's Tales from Childhood. Blake, Quentin, illus. 2009. (ENG.). 240p. (J). (gr. 5-9). 24.99 (978-0-374-35055-0(8), 9780374350550, Farrar, Straus & Giroux (BYR)) Farrar, Straus & Giroux.
Fischel, Emma. The Life of Roald Dahl: A Marvellous Adventure. 2016. (ENG., Illus.). 64p. (J). (gr. 1-4). pap. 7.99 (978-1-4451-5159-5(6), Franklin Watts) Hachette Children's Group GBR. Dist: Hachette Bk. Group.
Gelletly, LeeAnne. Gift of Imagination: The Story of Roald Dahl. 2006. (World Writers Ser.). (Illus.). 160p. (gr. 6-12). lib. bdg. 27.95 (978-1-59935-026-4(2)) Reynolds, Morgan Inc.
Guillain, Charlotte. Roald Dahl, 1 vol. 2012. (Author Biographies Ser.). (ENG.). 24p. (gr. 1-2). pap. 6.79 (978-1-4329-5968-5(9), Heinemann Read & Learn) Heinemann-Raintree.
Houle, Michelle M. Roald Dahl: Author of Charlie & the Chocolate Factory. 2006. (Authors Teens Love Ser.). (Illus.). 104p. (J). (gr. 7-12). lib. bdg. 33.27 (978-0-7660-2353-6(2)) Enslow Pubs., Inc.
Kelley, True. Who Was Roald Dahl? Marchesi, Stephen & Harrison, Nancy, illus. 2012. (Who Was? Ser.). (ENG.). 112p. (J). (gr. 3-7). pap. 5.99 (978-0-448-46146-5(3), Grosset & Dunlap) Penguin Young Readers Group.
—Who Was Roald Dahl? 2012. (Who Was... ? Ser.). lib. bdg. 16.00 (978-0-606-26650-5(X), Turtleback) Turtleback Bks.
Leaf, Christina. Roald Dahl. 2015. (Children's Storytellers Ser.). (ENG., Illus.). 24p. (J). (gr. 2-5). lib. bdg. 25.95 (978-1-62617-270-8(6), Blastoff! Readers) Bellwether Media.
Rosen, Michael. Fantastic Mr. Dahl. Blake, Quentin, illus. 2012. (ENG.). 176p. (J). (gr. 3-7). pap. 6.99 (978-0-14-132213-1(6), Puffin Books) Penguin Young Readers Group.
Shavick, Andrea. Roald Dahl. 2009. (True Lives Ser.). (ENG., Illus.). 32p. (J). pap. 6.99 (978-0-19-911961-5(9)) Oxford Univ. Pr., Inc.
Wheeler, Jill C. Roald Dahl, 1 vol. 2007. (Children's Authors Set 4 Ser.). (ENG., Illus.). 24p. (J). (gr. 2-5). 25.65 (978-1-59679-763-5(0)) ABDO Publishing Co.

DAIRIES
see Dairying

DAIRY CATTLE
see Cows

DAIRY PRODUCTS
see also Dairying
also names of dairy products, e.g. Milk

Bodden, Valerie. Dairy. 2015. (J). (978-1-60818-508-5(7), Creative Education) Creative Co., The.
—Healthy Plates: Dairy. 2015. (Healthy Plates Ser.). (ENG.). 24p. (J). (gr. 1-3). pap. 9.99 (978-1-62832-108-1(3), Creative Paperbacks) Creative Co., The.
Borgert-Spaniol, Megan. Dairy Group. 2012. (Eating Right with Myplate Ser.). (ENG., Illus.). 24p. (J). (gr. k-3). lib. bdg. 25.95 (978-1-60014-754-8(2), Blastoff! Readers) Bellwether Media.
Burstein, John. Delicious Dairy. 2009. (Slim Goodbody's Nutrition Edition Ser.). (ENG., Illus.). 24p. (J). (gr. k-3). pap. (978-0-7787-5056-7(6)); lib. bdg. (978-0-7787-5041-3(8)) Crabtree Publishing Co.
Clark, Katie. The Dairy Group. 2013. (Healthy Eating with Myplate Ser.). (ENG.). 24p. (J). (gr. 1-4). 28.50 (978-1-62323-602-1(9), 206404) Child's World, Inc., The.
Cleary, Brian P. Yogurt & Cheeses & Ice Cream That Pleases: What Is in the Milk Group? Goneau, Martin, illus. 2011. (Food Is CATegorical Ser.). (ENG.). 32p. (gr. k-3). pap. 7.95 (978-0-7613-6388-0(2)) Lerner Publishing Group.
Cleary, Brian P. & Goneau, Martin. Yogurt & Cheeses & Ice Cream That Pleases: What Is in the Milk Group? 2011. (Food Is CATegorical Ser.). pap. 45.32 (978-0-7613-8354-3(9), Millbrook Pr.) Lerner Publishing Group.
Cleary, Brian P. & Nelson, Jennifer K. Yogurt & Cheeses & Ice Cream That Pleases: What Is the Milk Group? Goneau, Martin, illus. 2010. (Food Is CATegorical Ser.). (ENG.). 32p. (gr. k-3). lib. bdg. 25.26 (978-1-58013-590-0(0)) Lerner Publishing Group.
Derkazarian, Susan. Dairy. (Rookie Read-About Health Ser.). (ENG., Illus.). 32p. (J). (gr. k-2). 2006. per. 5.95 (978-0-516-25925-3(3)) 2005. lib. bdg. 20.50 (978-0-516-23672-8(5)) Scholastic Library Publishing. (Children's Pr.).
Dickmann, Nancy. Dairy. 2012. (Healthy Eating with Myplate Ser.). (ENG.). 24p. (gr. -1-1). pap. 6.29 (978-1-4329-6984-4(6), Acorn) Heinemann-Raintree.
Dilkes, D. H. Milk & Dairy. 2011. (All about Good Foods We Eat Ser.). (Illus.). 24p. (J). (gr. -1-18). pap. 7.95 (978-1-59845-253-2(3), Enslow Elementary); (gr. k-3). lib. bdg. 22.60 (978-0-7660-3924-7(2)) Enslow Pubs., Inc.
Etingoff, Kim. Dairy Products. 2013. (Feeding the World Ser.: 8). (Illus.). 48p. (J). (gr. 4-18). 19.95 (978-1-4222-2743-5(X)) Mason Crest.
Green, Emily K. Milk, Yogurt, & Cheese. 2006. (Blastoff! Readers Ser.). (ENG., Illus.). 24p. (J). (gr. k-3). lib. bdg. 24.95 (978-1-60014-000-6(9), Blastoff! Readers) Bellwether Media.
Hanson-Harding, Brian. Dairy: From the Farm to Your Table. 2012. (Truth about the Food Supply Ser.). (ENG., Illus.). 48p. (J). (gr. 5-8). lib. bdg. 27.95 (978-1-4488-6800-1(9), Rosen Reference) Rosen Publishing Group, Inc., The.
Head, Honor. Dairy. 2006. (QEB What's for Lunch? Ser.). (Illus.). 32p. (YA). (gr. 1-4). lib. bdg. 19.95 (978-1-59566-197-5(2)) QEB Publishing Inc.
—Milk, Cheese, & Eggs. 2010. (J). 24.25 (978-1-59920-335-5(9)) Black Rabbit Bks.
Heos, Bridget. From Milk to Cheese. Coleman, Stephanie Fizer, illus. 2017. (Who Made My Lunch? Ser.). (ENG.). 24p. (gr. 1-4). 20.95 (978-1-68151-119-1(3)) Amicus Publishing.
—From Milk to Ice Cream. Coleman, Stephanie Fizer, illus. 2017. (Who Made My Lunch? Ser.). (ENG.). 24p. (gr. 1-4). 20.95 (978-1-68151-121-4(5)) Amicus Publishing.
Hewitt, Sally. Milk & Cheese. 2008. (Good for Me Ser.). (Illus.). 24p. (J). (gr. -1-3). lib. bdg. 22.60 (978-1-4042-4268-5(6), PowerKids Pr.) Rosen Publishing Group, Inc., The.
Kalz, Jill. Dairy Products. 2003. 24p. (J). lib. bdg. 21.35 (978-1-58340-297-9(7)) Black Rabbit Bks.
Lassieur, Allison. Dairy. 2015. (Illus.). 32p. (J). lib. bdg. 28.50 (978-1-60753-499-0(1)) Amicus Publishing.
Lee, Sally. The Delicious Dairy Group, 1 vol. Poling, Kyle, illus. 2011. (First Graphics: Myplate & Healthy Eating Ser.). (ENG.). 24p. (gr. 1-2). lib. bdg. 23.99 (978-1-4296-6092-1(9)); pap. 35.70 (978-1-4296-7165-1(3)) Capstone Press of Coughlan Cos.
Marsico, Katie. Your Healthy Plate - Dairy. 2012. (21st Century Basic Skills Library: Your Healthy Plate Ser.). (ENG., Illus.). 24p. (J). (gr. k-3). lib. bdg. 22.79 (978-1-61080-350-2(7), 201288) Cherry Lake Publishing.
—Your Healthy Plate: Dairy. 2012. (21st Century Basic Skills Library: Your Healthy Plate Ser.). (ENG.). 24p. (gr. k-3). pap. 12.79 (978-1-61080-398-4(1), 201333) Cherry Lake Publishing.
Mayo, Gretchen Will. Milk. 2004. (Weekly Reader Early Learning Library). (Illus.). 24p. (gr. 1-4). pap. 8.15 (978-0-8368-4074-2(7), Weekly Reader Leveled Readers) Stevens, Gareth Publishing LLLP.
Nelson, Robin. Dairy. 2003. (First Step Nonfiction - Food Groups Ser.). (ENG., Illus.). 24p. (gr. k-2). lib. bdg. 23.93 (978-0-8225-4632-0(9)) Lerner Publishing Group.
Nugent, Samantha. Dairy. 2015. (Let's Learn about Food Ser.). (ENG.). (J). lib. bdg. 27.13 (978-1-4896-3991-2(8), AV2 by Weigl) Weigl Pubs., Inc.
Rondeau, Amanda. Milk Is Magnificent, 1 vol. 2003. (What Should I Eat? Ser.). (ENG., Illus.). 24p. (J). (gr. k-3). lib. bdg. 24.21 (978-1-57765-837-5(X), SandCastle) ABDO Publishing Co.
Rosenberg, Pam. How Did That Get to My Table? Peanut Butter. 2009. (Community Connections: How Did That Get to My Table? Ser.). (ENG.). 24p. (gr. 2-5). lib. bdg. 25.64 (978-1-60279-469-6(3), 200267) Cherry Lake Publishing.
Schuh, Mari. Dairy on Myplate, 1 vol. 2012. (What's on Myplate? Ser.). (ENG., 24p. (gr. k-1). Illus.). pap. 7.29 (978-1-4296-9410-0(6)); pap. 41.70 (978-1-4296-9411-7(4)) Capstone Press of Coughlan Cos. (Pebble Plus).
Schuh, Mari C. Dairy on Myplate, 1 vol. 2012. (What's on Myplate? Ser.). (ENG., Illus.). 24p. (gr. k-1). lib. bdg. 26.65 (978-1-4296-8744-7(4), Pebble Plus) Capstone Press of Coughlan Cos.
Sertori, Trisha. Dairy Foods. 2008. (Body Fuel for Healthy Bodies Ser.). 32p. (gr. 4-18). lib. bdg. 18.56 (978-0-7614-3797-0(5), Benchmark Bks.) Marshall Cavendish Corp.
Squire, Ann O. Milk. 2017. (True Book(tm), a — Farm to Table Ser.). (ENG., Illus.). 48p. (J). lib. bdg. 31.00 (978-0-531-22933-0(5), Children's Pr.) Scholastic Library Publishing.
Tuminelly, Nancy. Let's Cook with Cheese! Delicious & Fun Cheese Dishes Kids Can Make, 1 vol. 2012. (Super Simple Recipes Ser.). (ENG.). 32p. (J). (gr. k-4). lib. bdg. 27.07 (978-1-61783-420-2(3), Super SandCastle) ABDO Publishing Co.
Wissolik, Richard David. Ice Cream Joe: The Valley Dairy Story — & America's Love Affair with Ice Cream. Greubel, Joseph E., ed. 2004. (Illus.). 208p. 29.95 (978-1-885851-18-5(9)) St. Vincent College Ctr. for Northern Appalachian Studies.

DAIRYING
see also Cattle; Cows; Dairy Products; Milk

Apps, Jerry. Casper Jaggi: Master Swiss Cheese Maker. 2008. (Badger Biographies Ser.). (ENG., Illus.). 96p. (J). (gr. 3-7). per. 12.95 (978-0-87020-392-3(4)) Wisconsin Historical Society.
Bernard, Jan. Ice Cream Before the Store. McGeehan, Dan, illus. 2012. (Before the Store Ser.). (ENG.). 32p. (J). (gr. 2-5). lib. bdg. 29.93 (978-1-60973-677-4(X), 201252) Child's World, Inc., The.
Bingham, Jane. Producing Dairy & Eggs, 1 vol. 2012. (Technology of Farming Ser.). (ENG.). 48p. (gr. 4-6). lib. bdg. 33.32 (978-1-4329-6406-1(2), Heinemann InfoSearch) Heinemann-Raintree.
Fandel, Jennifer. You Can Write an Amazing Journal. 2012. (You Can Write Ser.). (ENG.). 24p. (gr. 1-2). pap. 41.70 (978-1-4296-9319-6(3), First Facts) Capstone Press of Coughlan Cos.
Flatt, Lizann. Life in a Farming Community. 2009. (Learn about Rural Life Ser.). (ENG., Illus.). 32p. (J). (gr. 3-6). pap. (978-0-7787-5084-0(1)) Crabtree Publishing Co.
Gish, Melissa. A Dairy Farm. 2003. (Field Trips Ser.). 24p. (J). lib. bdg. 14.95 (978-1-58340-325-9(6)) Black Rabbit Bks.
Lassieur, Allison. Dairy. 2015. (Illus.). 32p. (J). lib. bdg. 28.50 (978-1-60753-499-0(1)) Amicus Publishing.
Linsley, Barbara. I Can Help on Farm. 2010. 14.95 (978-1-935122-19-7(3)) K&B Products.
Malam, John. Journey of a Glass of Milk, 1 vol. 2012. (Journey of A... Ser.). (ENG.). 32p. (gr. 1-3). pap. 8.29 (978-1-4329-6610-2(3)); lib. bdg. 27.32 (978-1-4329-6603-4(0)) Heinemann-Raintree. (Heinemann First Library).
Mayo, Gretchen Will. Milk. 2004. (Weekly Reader Early Learning Library). (Illus.). 24p. (gr. 1-4). pap. 8.15 (978-0-8368-4074-2(7), Weekly Reader Leveled Readers) Stevens, Gareth Publishing LLLP.
Murray, Julie. Grass to Milk, 1 vol. 2006. (Beginning to End Ser.). (ENG., Illus.). 24p. (gr. k-4). 25.65 (978-1-59679-837-3(8), Buddy Bks.) ABDO Publishing Co.
Pendergast, George. At the Dairy Farm. 2016. (Fun on the Farm Ser.). 00024p. (J). pap. 8.15 (978-1-4824-5516-8(1)) Stevens, Gareth Publishing LLLP.
Pohl, Kathleen. What Happens at a Dairy Farm? 2006. (Where People Work Ser.). (Illus.). 24p. (gr. -1-3). pap. 8.15 (978-0-8368-6893-7(5)); lib. bdg. 22.00 (978-0-8368-6886-9(2)) Stevens, Gareth Publishing LLLP. (Weekly Reader Leveled Readers).
—What Happens at a Dairy Farm? (¿Qué pasa en una granja Lechera?) 2006. (Where People Work/Dónde Trabaja la Gente? Ser.). (ENG & SPA., Illus.). 24p. (gr. -1-3). pap. 8.15 (978-0-8368-7394-8(7), Weekly Reader Leveled Readers) Stevens, Gareth Publishing LLLP.
—What Happens at a Dairy Farm?/¿Qué Pasa en Una Granja Lechera? 2006. (Where People Work/Dónde Trabaja la Gente? Ser.). (SPA & ENG., Illus.). 24p. (J). (gr. -1-3). lib. bdg. 22.00 (978-0-8368-7387-0(4), Weekly Reader Leveled Readers) Stevens, Gareth Publishing LLLP.
Taus-Bolstad, Stacy. From Grass to Milk. (ENG., Illus.). 24p. (gr. k-3). 2012. (Start to Finish, Second Series: Food Ser.: No. 2). pap. 6.95 (978-1-58013-966-3(3)) 2012. (Start to Finish, Second Series: Food Ser.: No. 2). lib. bdg. 23.93 (978-0-7613-9179-1(7), Lerner Pubns.) 2003. (Start to Finish Ser.). 19.93 (978-0-8225-4664-1(7), Lerner Pubns.) Lerner Publishing Group.

DAIRYING—FICTION

Arena, Felice & Kettle, Phil. On the Farm/By Felice Arena & Phil Kettle; Illustrated by Susy Boyer. Boyer, Susy, illus. 2004. (J). pap. (978-1-59336-363-5(X)) Mondo Publishing.
Berendes, Mary & Aesop. The Maid & the Milk Pail. Harrison, Nancy, illus. 2010. (Aesop's Fables Ser.). (ENG.). 24p. (J). (gr. k-3). 28.50 (978-1-60253-526-8(4), 200030) Child's World, Inc., The.
Schmidt, Gary D. First Boy. 2007. (ENG.). 224p. (YA). (gr. 5-9). per. 10.99 (978-0-312-37149-4(7), 9780312371494) Square Fish.

DALLAS (TEX.)

Boehm Jerome, Kate. Dallas, Tx: Cool Stuff Every Kid Should Know. 2010. (Arcadia Kids Ser.). (ENG., Illus.). 48p. (J). (gr. 3-6). pap. 9.99 (978-1-4396-0067-2(8)) Arcadia Publishing.
Carole Marsh. Dallas Coloring & Activity Book. 2004. (City Bks.). 24p. (gr. k-5). pap. 3.95 (978-0-635-02231-8(1)) Gallopade International.
Epstein, Brad M. Dallas Cowboys 101. 2010. (Illus.). 24p. (J). bds. (978-1-60730-108-0(3), 101 Bk.) Michaelson Entertainment.
Furstinger, Nancy. Dallas, 1 vol. 2005. (Cities Set 1 Ser.). (ENG., Illus.). 32p. (gr. k-6). 27.07 (978-1-59197-858-9(0), Checkerboard Library) ABDO Publishing Co.
Gamble, Adam & Jasper, Mark. Good Night Dallas/Fort Worth. Veno, Joe, illus. 2016. (Good Night Our World Ser.). (ENG.). 20p. (J). (— 1). bds. 9.95 (978-1-60219-224-9(3)) Good Night Bks.
Greenspan, Judy. Dallas. 2016. (Dropping in On Ser.). (ENG., Illus.). 32p. (gr. 2-4). 32.79 (978-1-68191-407-7(7)) Rourke Educational Media.

DALLAS COWBOYS (FOOTBALL TEAM)

Aretha, David. America's Team: The Dallas Cowboys. 2007. (Sensational Sports Teams Ser.). (Illus.). 128p. (J). (gr. 5-9). lib. bdg. 34.60 (978-1-59845-046-0(8), MyReportLinks.com Bks.) Enslow Pubs., Inc.
Burgess, Zack. Meet the Dallas Cowboys. 2016. (Big Picture Sports Ser.). (ENG., Illus.). 24p. (J). (gr. k-3). lib. bdg. 22.60 (978-1-59953-732-0(X)) Norwood Hse. Pr.
Caffrey, Scott. The Story of the Dallas Cowboys. (NFL Today Ser.). 48p. (gr. 5-17). 2011. (ENG.). (J). pap. 9.99 (978-0-89812-534-4(0), Creative Paperbacks) 2009. (YA). 22.95 (978-1-58341-753-9(2)) Creative Co., The.
Epstein, Brad M. Dallas Cowboys 101. 2010. (Illus.). 24p. (J). bds. (978-1-60730-108-0(3), 101 Bk.) Michaelson Entertainment.
Frisch, Aaron. Dallas Cowboys. 2011. (Super Bowl Champions Ser.). (J). (gr. 1-3). 24.25 (978-1-60818-016-5(6)) Creative Co., The.
—Dallas Cowboys. 2014. (Illus.). 24p. (J). (978-1-60818-374-6(2), Creative Education) Creative Co., The.
Gilbert, Sara. NFL Today: Dallas Cowboys. 2013. (NFL Today Ser.). (ENG.). 48p. (J). (gr. 4-7). pap. 12.00 (978-0-89812-853-6(6), Creative Paperbacks) Creative Co., The.
—The Story of the Dallas Cowboys. 2013. (Illus.). 48p. (J). 35.65 (978-1-60818-300-5(9), Creative Education) Creative Co., The.
Hawkes, Brian. The History of the Dallas Cowboys. 2004. (NFL Today Ser.). (Illus.). 32p. (YA). (gr. 5-9). 18.95 (978-1-58341-294-7(8)) Creative Co., The.
Heits, Rudolph T. DeMarcus Ware. (Superstars of Pro Football Ser.). 64p. (YA). (gr. 5-18). 2010. lib. bdg. 22.95 (978-1-4222-1665-1(9)) 2009. pap. 9.95 (978-1-4222-1985-0(2)) Mason Crest.
Leboutillier, Nate. Dallas Cowboys. 2005. (Super Bowl Champions Ser.). (Illus.). 24p. (J). (gr. 1-4). lib. bdg. 16.95 (978-1-58341-382-1(0), Creative Education) Creative Co., The.
Mack, Larry. The Dallas Cowboys Story. 2016. (NFL Teams Ser.). (ENG., Illus.). 32p. (J). (gr. 3-7). lib. bdg. 26.95 (978-1-62617-363-7(X), Torque Bks.) Bellwether Media.
Macnow, Glen. Deion Sanders: Hall of Fame Football Superstar. 2014. (Hall of Fame Sports Greats Ser.). 64p. (J). (gr. 4-9). pap. 9.95 (978-1-62285-046-4(7)) Enslow Pubs., Inc.
—Troy Aikman: Hall of Fame Football Superstar. (Hall of Fame Sports Greats Ser.). 64p. (J). (gr. 4-9). 2014. pap. 9.95 (978-1-62285-041-9(6)) 2013. 15.95 (978-1-62285-040-2(8)) Enslow Pubs., Inc.
MacRae, Sloan. The Dallas Cowboys. (Illus.). 24p. (J). 2010. pap. 8.25 (978-1-4358-3394-4(5)) 2009. lib. bdg. 22.60 (978-1-4042-8145-5(2)) Rosen Publishing Group, Inc., The. (PowerKids Pr.).
Monteverde, Matthew. Giants vs. Cowboys. 2014. (Sports Greatest Rivalries Ser.). 24p. (J). (gr. 2-5). lib. bdg. 22.60 (978-1-4777-2781-2(7), PowerKids Pr.) Rosen Publishing Group, Inc., The.
Roselius, J. Chris. Dallas Cowboys, 1 vol. 2010. (Inside the NFL Ser.). (ENG.). 48p. (YA). (gr. 3-6). lib. bdg. 32.79 (978-1-61714-009-9(0)) ABDO Publishing Co.
Sandler, Michael. Troy Aikman & the Dallas Cowboys. 2008. (Super Bowl Superstars Ser.). (Illus.). 24p. (J). (gr. k-3). lib. bdg. 22.61 (978-1-59716-737-6(1)) Bearport Publishing Co., Inc.
Stewart, Mark. The Dallas Cowboys. rev. ed. 2012. (Team Spirit Ser.). (ENG., Illus.). 48p. (J). (gr. 3-6). lib. bdg. 29.27 (978-1-59953-520-3(3)) Norwood Hse. Pr.
Walsh, Christopher J. Cowboys Triviology: Fascinating Facts from the Sidelines. 2011. (Triviology: Fascinating Facts Ser.). (ENG., Illus.). 128p. pap. 9.95 (978-1-60078-622-8(7)) Triumph Bks.
—Packers Triviology: Fascinating Facts from the Sidelines. 2011. (Triviology: Fascinating Facts Ser.). (ENG., Illus.). 128p. pap. 12.95 (978-1-60078-620-4(0)) Triumph Bks.
Wyner, Zach. Dallas Cowboys. (Illus.). 32p. (J). 2015. pap. (978-1-4896-0815-4(X)) 2014. (ENG., (gr. 4-7). lib. bdg. 28.55 (978-1-4896-0814-7(1), AV2 by Weigl) Weigl Pubs., Inc.
Zappa, Marcia. Dallas Cowboys, 1 vol. 2014. (NFL's Greatest Teams Ser.). (ENG.). 32p. (gr. 7-11). lib. bdg. 28.50 (978-1-62403-360-5(1), Big Buddy Bks.) ABDO Publishing Co.

DALTON, JOHN, 1766-1844

Kjelle, Marylou. John Dalton & the Atomic Theory. 2004. (Uncharted, Unexplored, & Unexplained Ser.). (Illus.). 48p. (J). (gr. 4-8). lib. bdg. 29.95 (978-1-58415-308-5(3)) Mitchell Lane Pubs., Inc.

DAMIEN, FATHER, 1840-1889

Williams, Laura E. Father Damien. Kofsky, Kristen, illus. 2009. (ENG.). 60p. (J). (gr. 4). pap. (978-1-59700-757-3(9)) Island Heritage Publishing.

DAMS

Aldridge, Rebecca. The Hoover Dam. 2009. (Building America Ser.). (Illus.). 120p. (gr. 5-8). 35.00 (978-1-60413-069-0(5), Chelsea Hse.) Facts On File, Inc.
DuTemple, Lesley A. The Hoover Dam. 2003. (Great Building Feats Ser.). (ENG., Illus.). 96p. (gr. 5-9). 27.93 (978-0-8225-4691-7(4)) Lerner Publishing Group.
Frost, Jayson. The Science of Dams. 2013. (InfoMax Readers Ser.). (ENG.). 24p. (J). (gr. 3-4). pap. 49.50 (978-1-4777-2614-3(4)); pap. 8.25 (978-1-4777-2613-6(6)) Rosen Publishing Group, Inc., The. (Rosen Classroom).
Goldish, Meish. The Hoover Dam. 2016. (American Places: from Vision to Reality Ser.). (ENG.). 32p. (J). (gr. 2-7). 19.95 (978-1-944102-45-6(0)) Bearport Publishing Co., Inc.
Halls, Kelly Milner. The Story of the Hoover Dam: A History Perspectives Book. 2014. (Perspectives Library). (ENG., Illus.). 32p. (J). (gr. 4-8). 28.50 (978-1-62431-668-5(9), 203236) Cherry Lake Publishing.
Hesse, Leah. How Do Dams Work? 2013. (Rosen Readers Ser.). (ENG.). 24p. (J). (gr. 3-4). pap. 49.50 (978-1-4777-2555-9(5)); pap. 8.25 (978-1-4777-2554-2(7)) Rosen Publishing Group, Inc., The. (Rosen Classroom).
Latham, Donna. Canals & Dams: Investigate Feats of Engineering with 25 Projects. Christensen, Andrew, illus. 2013. (Build It Yourself Ser.). (ENG.). 128p. (J). (gr. 3-7). 21.95 (978-1-61930-169-6(5)); pap. 16.95 (978-1-61930-165-8(2)) Open City Bks.
Loh-Hagan, Virginia. Dams. 2017. (21st Century Junior Library: Extraordinary Engineering Ser.). (ENG., Illus.). 24p. (J). (gr. 2-5). lib. bdg. 27.07 (978-1-63472-163-9(2), 209224) Cherry Lake Publishing.
Mattern, Joanne. Floods, Dams, & Levees. 2011. (ENG., Illus.). 48p. (J). (gr. 4-6). pap. 10.95 (978-1-61741-988-1(5)) Rourke Educational Media.
Miller, Heather. The Hoover Dam. 2014. (Great Idea Ser.). (ENG., Illus.). 48p. (J). (gr. 4-6). lib. bdg. 26.60 (978-1-59953-595-1(5)) Norwood Hse. Pr.
Mullins, Matt. How Did They Build That? Dam. 2009. (Community Connections: How Did They Build That? Ser.). (ENG.). 24p. (gr. 2-5). lib. bdg. 25.64 (978-1-60279-488-7(X), 200255) Cherry Lake Publishing.
Nagelhout, Ryan. Dams. 2016. (Science on Patrol Ser.). 00048p. (J). pap. 14.05 (978-1-4824-5988-3(4)) Stevens, Gareth Publishing LLLP.
—How Do Dams Work? 2016. (STEM Waterworks Ser.). 32p. (J). (gr. 5-5). pap. 11.75 (978-1-4994-1999-3(6), PowerKids Pr.) Rosen Publishing Group, Inc., The.
Parks, Peggy J. Aswan High Dam. (Building World Landmarks Ser.). (J). 2004. 26.19 (978-1-4103-0204-5(0)) 2003. (Illus.). 48p. 24.95 (978-1-56711-329-7(X)) Cengage Gale. (Blackbirch Pr., Inc.).
Pettiford, Rebecca. Dams. 2015. (Illus.). 24p. (J). lib. bdg. 25.65 (978-1-62031-213-1(1)) Jump! Inc.
Phillips, Cynthia & Priwer, Shana. Dams & Waterways. 2009. (ENG., Illus.). 112p. (C). (gr. 6-18). lib. bdg. 158.00 (978-0-7656-8122-5(6), Y181910) Routledge.
Sikkens, Crystal. A Dam Holds Back. 2017. 24p. (J). (978-0-7787-2905-1(2)) Crabtree Publishing Co.
Spilsbury, Louise. Dams & Hydropower. 2011. (Development or Destruction? Ser.). (ENG., Illus.). 48p. (J). (gr. 5-8). 29.25 (978-1-4488-6990-9(0)); pap. 11.75 (978-1-4488-6994-7(3)) Rosen Publishing Group, Inc., The. (Rosen Reference).
Stefoff, Rebecca. Building Dams. 2015. (Great Engineering Ser.). (ENG.). 32p. (J). (gr. 3-4). pap. 10.58 (978-1-5026-0594-8(5)) Cavendish Square Publishing.
Thomas, Mark. The Itaipu Dam: World's Biggest Dam. 2009. (Record-Breaking Structures Ser.). 24p. (gr. 1-2). 42.50 (978-1-60852-455-6(8), PowerKids Pr.) Rosen Publishing Group, Inc., The.
—La represa de Itaipú: La represa más grande del mundo (the Itaipu Dam: World's Biggest Dam) 2009. (Estructuras extraordinarias (Record-Breaking Structures) Ser.). (SPA.). 24p. (gr. 1-2). 42.50 (978-1-61512-313-1(X), Editorial Buenas Letras) Rosen Publishing Group, Inc., The.
Weil, Ann. The World's Most Amazing Dams, 1 vol. 2011. (Landmark Top Tens Ser.). (ENG.). 32p. (gr. 3-5). pap. 8.29 (978-1-4109-4255-5(4)); 30.65 (978-1-4109-4244-9(9)) Heinemann-Raintree. (Raintree Perspectives).

DAMS—FICTION

Alcorn, Steve. Everything in Its Path: A Novel about the St. Francis Dam Disaster. 2003. 164p. (YA). pap. 12.99 (978-0-9729777-0-8(8)) Theme Perks, Inc.
Bloxam, Frances. Beau Beaver Goes to Town. Sollers, Jim, illus. 2009. (ENG.). 32p. (J). (gr. -1-3). 16.95 (978-0-89272-792-6(6)) Down East Bks.
Collier, Kristen & Collier, Kevin. Natalie's Ark. 2009. 84p. pap. 8.95 (978-1-61633-007-1(4)) Guardian Angel Publishing, Inc.
Holloway, Jamie. Beaver Works On. 2015. (Rosen REAL Readers: STEM & STEAM Collection). (ENG.). 8p. pap. 5.46 (978-1-4994-9489-1(0), Rosen Classroom) Rosen Publishing Group, Inc., The.

Plourde, Lynn. Only Cows Allowed!, 1 vol. Sollers, Jim & Reed, Rebecca Harrison, illus. 2011. (ENG.). 32p. (gr. -1-3). 16.95 *(978-0-89272-790-2(X))* Down East Bks.
Walsh, Ellen Stoll. Dot & Jabber & the Mystery of the Missing Stream. 2016. (Green Light Readers Level 2 Ser.). (ENG., Illus.). 32p. (J). (gr. -1-3). 12.99 *(978-0-544-79166-4(5)*, HMH Books For Young Readers) Houghton Mifflin Harcourt Publishing Co.

DANA GIRLS (FICTITIOUS CHARACTERS)—FICTION

Gallego García, Laura. LA LLAMADA DE LOS MUERTOS. 2004. (Ciclo el Valle de Los Lobos the Valley of the Wolves Cycle Ser.). (SPA.). 240p. (YA). 10.99 *(978-84-348-9439-6(4))* SM Ediciones ESP. Dist: Lectorum Pubns., Inc.

DANCE

see also Ballet; Folk Dancing

Abissi, Katherine Alexandra. I Love to Dance! 2013. 20p. pap. 13.77 *(978-1-4669-8383-0(3))* Trafford Publishing.
African Dance. 2nd rev. ed. 2010. (World of Dance Ser.). (Illus.). 136p. (C). (gr. 9-18). 35.00 *(978-1-60413-477-3(1)*, Chelsea Hse.) Facts On File, Inc.
Afzal, Uz. Dance to the Beat. 2005. (Big Cat Ser.). (gr. k-2). pap. 6.50 *(978-1-60457-058-8(X))* Pacific Learning, Inc.
Ancona, George. Boys Dancing: From School Gym to Theater Stage. Ancona, George, illus. 2017. (ENG., Illus.). 48p. (J). (gr. k-3). 16.99 *(978-0-7636-8202-6(0))* Candlewick Pr.
—Capoeira: Game! Dance! Martial Art! 2007. (ENG., Illus.). 48p. (J). (gr. 2-7). 18.95 *(978-1-58430-268-1(2))* Lee & Low Bks., Inc.
—Olé Flamenco! Ancona, George, photos by. 2010. (ENG., Illus.). 48p. (J). (gr. 2-6). 19.95 *(978-1-60060-361-7(0))* Lee & Low Bks., Inc.
—Olé Flamenco. 2016. (ENG.). (J). pap. 11.95 *(978-1-62014-313-1(5))* Lee & Low Bks., Inc.
Bailey, Diane. History of Dance, 1 vol. 2014. (Essential Library of Cultural History Ser.). (ENG., Illus.). 112p. (J). (gr. 6-12). lib. bdg. 35.64 *(978-1-62403-552-4(3)*, 1383004, Essential Library) ABDO Publishing Co.
Benzwie, Teresa. Numbers on the Move. 2011. (ENG., Illus.). 32p. (J). pap. 16.95 *(978-1-4399-0342-1(5))* Temple Univ. Pr.
Berton, Judy & Guimond, Rick. Do a Dance Picture Book. 2006. (Illus.). (J). spiral bd. 8.95 *(978-0-9761051-1-4(X))* Kidrich Corp.
Broadbent, Paul. Dance Fever. 2007. (Trackers-Math Ser.). (gr. 2-5). pap. 5.00 *(978-1-59055-930-7(4))* Pacific Learning, Inc.
Brown, Tracy. Staging & Choreography. 2012. (Glee Club Ser.). (ENG., Illus.). 64p. (J). (gr. 7-12). 31.95 *(978-1-4488-6874-2(2))*; pap. 12.95 *(978-1-4488-6879-7(3))* Rosen Publishing Group, Inc., The.
Carr, Aaron. Break Dance. 2014. (Bailemos Ser.). (SPA., Illus.). 24p. (J). (gr. -1-3). lib. bdg. 27.13 *(978-1-4896-2135-1(0)*, AV2 by Weigl) Weigl Pubs., Inc.
Clay, Kathryn. Bailando Jazz. Translation Services Staff & Translations.com Staff, trs. from ENG. 2010. (Baila, Baila, Baila/Dance, Dance, Dance Ser.).Tr. of Jazz Dancing. (SPA, ENG & MUL.). 24p. (gr. k-1). lib. bdg. 26.65 *(978-1-4296-5352-7(3))* Capstone Press of Coughlan Cos.
—Bailando Tap. Translation Services Staff & Translations.com Staff, trs. 2010. (Baila, Baila, Baila/Dance, Dance, Dance Ser.).Tr. of Tap Dancing. (MUL & SPA.). 24p. (gr. k-1). lib. bdg. 26.65 *(978-1-4296-5353-4(1))* Capstone Press of Coughlan Cos.
—Dance, Dance, Dance, 4 vols., Set. Incl. Ballet Dancing. (Illus.). lib. bdg. 26.65 *(978-1-4296-4002-2(2)*, 1308539); Tap Dancing. lib. bdg. 26.65 *(978-1-4296-4005-3(7))*; (gr. k-1). (Dance, Dance, Dance Ser.). (ENG.). 24p. 2010. Set lib. bdg. 53.30 *(978-1-4296-4415-0(X)*, Pebble Plus) Capstone Press of Coughlan Cos.
—Tap Dancing, 1 vol. 2010. (Dance, Dance, Dance Ser.). (ENG.). 24p. (gr. k-1). lib. bdg. 26.65 *(978-1-4296-4005-3(7)*, Pebble Plus) Capstone Press of Coughlan Cos.
Coachman, Mary Kaye. Dance Team. (Team Spirit! Ser.). 64p. 2009. (gr. 6-6). 53.00 *(978-1-60853-267-4(4))* 2006. (Illus.). (J). (gr. 3-7). lib. bdg. 31.95 *(978-1-4042-0731-8(7))* Rosen Publishing Group, Inc., The.
Collins, Pat Lowery. I Am a Dancer. Graham, Mark, illus. 2008. (Millbrook Picture Books Ser.). 30p. (J). (gr. 3-7). 22.60 *(978-0-8225-6369-3(X)*, Millbrook Pr.) Lerner Publishing Group.
Connie's Dance: Individual Title Six-Packs. (gr. 1-2). 25.00 *(978-0-7635-9143-4(2))* Rigby Education.
Crabtree, Marc. Meet My Neighbor, the Hip-Hop Dancer. 2012. (ENG., Illus.). 24p. (J). *(978-0-7787-4558-7(9))*; pap. *(978-0-7787-4563-1(5))* Crabtree Publishing Co.
Craig Quijada, Balinda. Dance for Fun! [Bridge Learning]. 2009. (For Fun!: Sports Ser.). 48p. (gr. 3-5). pap. 8.95 *(978-0-7565-4346-4(0)*, For Fun!) Compass Point Bks.
Cutcher, Jenai. Feel the Beat! Dancing in Music Videos. 2004. (Curtain Call Library of Dance Ser.). (Illus.). 48p. (YA). (gr. 5-8). lib. bdg. 29.25 *(978-0-8239-4558-0(8)*, Rosen Reference) Rosen Publishing Group, Inc., The.
—Gotta Dance! The Rhythms of Jazz & Tap. (Curtain Call Library of Dance Ser.). 48p. (gr. 5-8). 2009. 53.00 *(978-1-60853-421-0(9))* 2004. (Illus.). (J). lib. bdg. 29.25 *(978-0-8239-4554-2(5))* Rosen Publishing Group, Inc., The. (Rosen Reference).
Dance, Dance, Dance [Capstone Sole Source]. 2010. (Dance, Dance, Dance Ser.). 24p. lib. bdg. 95.96 *(978-1-4296-5849-2(5)*, Pebble Plus) Capstone Press of Coughlan Cos.
Dombey, Elizabeth. Beautiful Ballerinas. McNicholas, Shelagh, illus. 2014. (Penguin Core Concepts Ser.). (ENG.). 32p. (J). (gr. -1-k). 7.99 *(978-0-448-47791-6(2))*; 3.99 *(978-0-448-46714-6(3))* Penguin Young Readers Group. (Grosset & Dunlap).
Dorling Kindersley Publishing Staff. Dance. 2012. (ENG.). 144p. (J). (gr. 4-7). 19.99 *(978-0-7566-9797-6(2)*, DK Children) Dorling Kindersley Publishing, Inc.
Dorling Kindersley Publishing Staff & Grau, Andre. Dance. 2005. (DK Eyewitness Bks.). (ENG., Illus.). 72p. (J). (gr. 3-7). 16.99 *(978-0-7566-1065-4(6)*, 1241897, DK Children) Dorling Kindersley Publishing, Inc.
Dowd, Olympia. A Young Dancer's Apprenticeship. 2003. (Illus.). 128p. (J). (gr. 7-18). pap. 14.95 *(978-0-7613-1898-9(4)*, Twenty-First Century Bks.) Lerner Publishing Group.
Draper, Penny. Breaking Big, 1 vol. 2016. (Orca Limelights Ser.). (ENG.). 144p. (J). (gr. 6-9). pap. 9.95 *(978-1-4598-0923-9(8))* Orca Bk. Pubs. USA.
Dvorak, Antonin. Dances for Solo Piano. Buechner, Sara Davis, ed. 2013. (ENG.). 208p. pap. 19.95 *(978-0-486-49730-3(5))* Dover Pubns., Inc.
Edom, Helen & Katrak, N. Starting Ballet - Internet Linked. 2005. 32p. (J). pap. 4.99 *(978-0-7945-0673-5(9)*, Usborne) EDC Publishing.
European Dance: Ireland, Poland, Spain, & Greece. 2nd rev. ed. 2010. (World of Dance Ser.). (Illus.). 128p. (C). (gr. 9-18). 35.00 *(978-1-60413-480-3(1)*, Chelsea Hse.) Facts On File, Inc.
Feldman, Jane. We Love Ballet! 2004. (Pictureback Ser.). (ENG., Illus.). 24p. (J). (gr. -1-2). pap. 3.99 *(978-0-375-82831-7(1)*, Random Hse. Bks. for Young Readers) Random Hse. Children's Bks.
Fretland VanVoorst, Jenny. Dance. 2016. (Artist's Studio Ser.). 24p. (J). (gr. k-2). lib. bdg. 25.65 *(978-1-62031-281-0(6)*, Bullfrog Bks.) Jump! Inc.
Gagne, Tammy. African Dance Trends. 2014. (Illus.). 48p. (J). (gr. 4-8). 29.95 *(978-1-61228-557-3(0))* Mitchell Lane Pubs., Inc.
Garofoli, Wendy. Hip-Hop Dancing, 4 vols., Set. Incl. Vol. 3. Popping, Locking, & Everything in Between. lib. bdg. 31.99 *(978-1-4296-5486-9(4))*; Vol. 4. Dancing with a Crew Vol. 4. lib. bdg. 31.99 *(978-1-4296-5487-6(2))*; (gr. 3-4). (Hip-Hop Dancing Ser.). (ENG.). 48p. 2010. Set lib. bdg. 95.97 *(978-1-4296-5488-3(0))* Capstone Press of Coughlan Cos.
Gaskill, Rachel. Agnes de Mille. 2009. (Library of American Choreographers Ser.). 48p. (gr. 5-8). 53.00 *(978-1-60853-454-8(5)*, Rosen Reference) Rosen Publishing Group, Inc., The.
Gauch, Patricia Lee & GAUCH, PATRICIA LEE. Tanya entre Bastidores. Ichikawa, Satomi, illus. 2004.Tr. of Tanya & the Magic Wardrobe. (SPA.). (J). 16.99 *(978-84-8488-083-7(4))* Serres, Ediciones, S. L. ESP. Dist: Lectorum Pubns., Inc.
Gogerly, Liz. Street Dance. 2011. (On the Radar: Dance Ser.). (ENG., Illus.). 32p. (gr. 4-8). lib. bdg. 26.60 *(978-0-7613-7761-0(1))* Lerner Publishing Group.
Goggerly, Liz. Capoeira: Fusing Dance & Martial Arts. 2011. (On the Radar: Dance Ser.). (ENG., Illus.). 32p. (gr. 4-8). lib. bdg. 26.60 *(978-0-7613-7766-5(2))* Lerner Publishing Group.
Grayson, Robert. Dancing with the Stars. 2010. (Major Competitive Reality Shows Ser.). 48p. (YA). (gr. 7-18). pap. 7.95 *(978-1-4222-1936-2(4))* Mason Crest.
Guipre, Jewel Moreland. Dance with Me. 2012. 32p. 24.95 *(978-1-4560-6044-2(9))* America Star Bks.
Hamilton, Sue L. Rock. 2011. (Xtreme Dance Ser.). (Illus.). 32p. (gr. 3-9). 27.07 *(978-1-61714-733-3(8)*, A&D Xtreme) ABDO Publishing Co.
—Xtreme Dance, 6 vols., Set. Incl. Ballroom. 27.07 *(978-1-61714-729-6(X))*; Country & Western. 27.07 *(978-1-61714-730-2(3))*; Hip-Hop. 27.07 *(978-1-61714-731-9(1))*; Latin. 27.07 *(978-1-61714-732-6(X))*; Rock. 27.07 *(978-1-61714-733-3(8))*; Swing. 27.07 *(978-1-61714-734-0(6))*; (gr. 3-9). (Xtreme Dance Ser.). (Illus.). 32p. 2011. 162.42 *(978-1-61714-728-9(1)*, A&D Xtreme) ABDO Publishing Co.
Hamilton, Trenton, ed. The History of Western Dance. 2015. (Britannica Guide to the Visual & Performing Arts Ser.). (ENG., Illus.). 128p. (YA). 45.00 *(978-1-68048-079-5(0)*, Britannica Educational Publishing) Rosen Publishing Group, Inc., The.
Haney, Johannah. Capoeira. 2011. (Martial Arts in Action 2 Ser.). 48p. (gr. 6). lib. bdg. 29.93 *(978-0-7614-4932-4(9))* Marshall Cavendish Corp.
Hanley, Elizabeth A., ed. & intro. World of Dance. Hanley, Elizabeth A., intro. (Illus.). (gr. 9-13). lib. bdg. *(978-0-7910-8042-9(0)*, Chelsea Hse.) Facts On File, Inc.
Hapka, Cathy, pseud. Dancing. 2006. (Illus.). (J). *(978-1-57151-775-3(8))* Playhouse Publishing.
Heneghan, Judith. Dance: Where to Go - What to Wear - Tips from Top Dancers! 2016. (ENG., Illus.). 32p. (J). (gr. 4-6). pap. 11.99 *(978-0-7502-9456-0(6)*, Wayland) Hachette Children's Group GBR. Dist: Hachette Bk. Group.
James, Sara. Step Aerobics & Aerobic Dance. Hart, Diane H., ed. 2014. (Integrated Life of Fitness Ser.). 64p. (J). (gr. 7-18). pap. 11.95 *(978-1-4222-3202-6(6))*; 23.95 *(978-1-4222-3164-7(X))* Mason Crest.
Jones, Jen. Top Dance Tips. 2017. (Top Sports Tips Ser.). (ENG., Illus.). 32p. (gr. 3-4). lib. bdg. 27.99 *(978-1-5157-4724-6(7)*, Snap Bks.) Capstone Press of Coughlan Cos.
Joosten, Michael. Dance & Choreography. 2009. (J). 77.70 *(978-1-4358-5537-3(X))*; (ENG.). 64p. (YA). pap. 12.95 *(978-1-4358-5536-6(1))*; (ENG., Illus.). 64p. (J). lib. bdg. 31.95 *(978-1-4358-5261-7(3))* Rosen Publishing Group, Inc., The.
Kalman, Bobbie. Hip-Hop Dancers. 2010. (My World Ser.). (ENG., Illus.). 16p. (J). (gr. k-2). *(978-0-7787-9431-8(8))*; pap. *(978-0-7787-9475-2(X))* Crabtree Publishing Co.
Keeler, Patricia A. & Leitão, Júlio T. Drumbeat in Our Feet. 2014. (ENG., Illus.). 32p. (J). pap. 8.95 *(978-1-62014-079-6(9))* Lee & Low Bks., Inc.
—Drumbeat in Our Feet, 1 vol. Keeler, Patricia A., illus. 2012. (ENG., Illus.). 32p. (J). (gr. 1-6). lib. bdg. 16.95 *(978-1-58430-264-3(X))* Lee & Low Bks., Inc.
Kenney, Karen Latchana. Cool School Dance: Fun Ideas & Activities to Build School Spirit, 1 vol. 2011. (Cool School Spirit Ser.). (ENG., Illus.). 32p. (J). (gr. 3-6). 28.50 *(978-1-61714-667-1(6)*, Checkerboard Library) ABDO Publishing Co.
Kjelle, Marylou. Line Dances Around the World. 2014. 48p. (gr. 4-8). 29.95 *(978-1-61228-556-6(2))* Mitchell Lane Pubs., Inc.
—Trends in Hip-Hop Dance. 2014. 48p. (gr. 4-8). 29.95 *(978-1-61228-555-9(4))* Mitchell Lane Pubs., Inc.
Kupesic, Rajka, illus. & retold by. The White Ballets. Kupesic, Rajka, retold by. 2011. (ENG.). 42p. (J). (gr. k-12). 19.95 *(978-0-88776-923-8(3)*, Tundra Bks.) Tundra Bks. CAN. Dist: Penguin Random Hse. LLC.
Labrecque, Ellen. Impressive Dance Moves, 1 vol. 2013. (Try This at Home! Ser.). (ENG.). 32p. (gr. 1-2). pap. 8.29 *(978-1-4109-5011-6(5))*; lib. bdg. 29.99 *(978-1-4109-5004-8(2))* Heinemann-Raintree. (Read Me!).
Latin & Caribbean Dance. 2010. (World of Dance Ser.). (Illus.). 128p. (C). (gr. 9-18). 35.00 *(978-1-60413-481-0(X)*, Chelsea Hse.) Facts On File, Inc.
Learn to Dance. 2008. 96p. *(978-1-4075-1141-2(6))* Parragon, Inc.
The Library of American Choreographers, 8 bks., Set. 2006. (Illus.). (J). lib. bdg. 191.60 *(978-1-4042-0618-2(3))* Rosen Publishing Group, Inc., The.
Litchman, Kristin E., ed. Let's Dance! Dances for Children from America's Melting Pot, Dance Program for Pre-School & Elementary School Children. rev. ed. 2005. (Illus.). 260p. (J). 90.00 *(978-1-890034-19-1(3)*, Medley Pubns.) Medley.
Marsico, Katie. Choreographer. 2011. (21st Century Skills Library: Cool Arts Careers Ser.). (ENG.). 32p. (gr. 4-8). lib. bdg. 28.50 *(978-1-61080-136-2(9)*, 201150) Cherry Lake Publishing.
Mason, Jane B. & Stephens, Sarah Hines. Gymboree Dance Play. rev. ed. 2007. (ENG., Illus.). 36p. (J). (gr. -1-2). bds. *(978-1-55263-960-3(6))* Magma.
McAlpine, Margaret. Working in Music & Dance. 2005. (My Future Career Ser.). (Illus.). 64p. (gr. 3-7). lib. bdg. 27.00 *(978-0-8368-4777-2(6)*, Gareth Stevens Learning Library) Stevens, Gareth Publishing LLLP.
Modern Dance. 2nd rev. ed. 2010. (World of Dance Ser.). (Illus.). 120p. (C). (gr. 9-18). 35.00 *(978-1-60413-483-4(6)*, Chelsea Hse.) Facts On File, Inc.
Nelson, Robin. Dance Is Fun! 2013. (First Step Nonfiction - Sports Are Fun! Ser.). (ENG., Illus.). 24p. (gr. k-2). pap. 6.95 *(978-1-4677-1534-8(4))*; lib. bdg. 23.93 *(978-1-4677-1104-3(7)*, Lerner Pubns.) Lerner Publishing Group.
Palmer, Erin. School Dances, Yes or No. 2016. (Seeing Both Sides Ser.). (ENG.). 32p. (gr. 3-6). 32.79 *(978-1-68191-384-1(4))* Rourke Educational Media.
Peters, Craig. Techniques of Dance for Cheerleading. 2003. (Let's Go Team Ser.). (Illus.). 64p. (J). (gr. 5-18). lib. bdg. *(978-1-59084-531-8(5))* Mason Crest.
Popular Dance: From Ballroom to Hip-Hop. 2010. (World of Dance Ser.). (Illus.). 168p. (C). (gr. 9-18). 35.00 *(978-1-60413-484-1(4)*, Chelsea Hse.) Facts On File, Inc.
Powell, Jillian. Dance Just Like Me, 1 vol. Gulliver, Amanda, illus. 2013. (Start Reading Ser.). (ENG.). 24p. (gr. k-1). pap. 7.95 *(978-1-4765-3188-5(9))*; pap. 41.94 *(978-1-4765-3209-7(5))* Capstone Press of Coughlan Cos.
Rodriguez, Sonia & Browning, Kurt. T Is for Tutu: A Ballet Alphabet. Ong, Wilson, illus. 2011. (ENG.). 32p. (gr. k-5). 16.95 *(978-1-58536-312-4(X))* Sleeping Bear Pr.
Royston, Angela. Love to Dance. 2013. (Love to Dance Ser.). (ENG.). 32p. (gr. 1-3). pap. 31.96 *(978-1-4109-4929-5(X))*; lib. bdg. 119.96 *(978-1-4109-4924-0(9))* Heinemann-Raintree. (Read Me!).
—Tap, 1 vol. 2013. (Love to Dance Ser.). (ENG., Illus.). 32p. (gr. 1-3). 29.99 *(978-1-4109-4923-3(0))*; pap. 8.29 *(978-1-4109-4928-8(1))* Heinemann-Raintree. (Read Me!).
Schwaeber, Barbie Heit. Alphabet of Dance. Ward, Damian, illus. 2009. (Smithsonian Alphabet Books). (ENG.). 40p. (J). (gr. -1-k). 17.95 *(978-1-60727-110-9(9))* Soundprints.
—Alphabet of Dance. Wood, Damian, illus. 2009. (Smithsonian Alphabet Books). (ENG.). 40p. (J). (gr. -1-k). 9.95 *(978-1-60727-111-6(7))* Soundprints.
Seibert, Brian. George Balanchine. 2005. (Library of American Choreographers Ser.). (Illus.). 48p. (J). (gr. k-3). lib. bdg. 29.25 *(978-1-4042-0447-8(4))* Rosen Publishing Group, Inc., The.
Sleeping Bear Press. Little Dance. Benoit, Renné, illus. 2013. (ENG.). 20p. (J). (gr. -1-k). 8.99 *(978-1-58536-884-6(9)*, 202899) Sleeping Bear Pr.
Smith, Karen Lynn. Popular Dance: From Ballroom to Hip-Hop. 2010. (World of Dance Ser.). (Illus.). 168p. (gr. 6-12). pap. 10.95 *(978-1-60413-977-8(3)*, Checkmark Bks.) Facts On File, Inc.
Stemple, Heidi E. Y. & Yolen, Jane. Dance Stories. Cann, Helen, illus. 2010. (ENG.). 99p. (J). (gr. 3-18). 21.99 *(978-1-84686-219-9(1))* Barefoot Bks., Inc.
Sterling Publishing Co., Inc. My First Dance: Tap. 2016. (ENG., Illus.). 22p. (J). (— 1). bds. 6.95 *(978-1-4549-1874-5(8))* Sterling Publishing Co., Inc.
Stern, Leonard & Price, Roger. Dance Mania Mad Libs. 2009. (Mad Libs Ser.). (ENG.). 48p. (J). (gr. 3-7). 4.99 *(978-0-8431-3712-5(6)*, Mad Libs) Penguin Young Readers Group.
Storey, Rita. Irish Dancing: And Other National Dances. 2007. (Get Dancing Ser.). (Illus.). 32p. (J). lib. bdg. 28.50 *(978-1-59771-050-3(4))* Sea-To-Sea Pubns.
—Rock 'n' Roll: And Other Dance Crazes. 2007. (Get Dancing Ser.). (Illus.). 32p. (J). lib. bdg. 28.50 *(978-1-59771-051-0(2))* Sea-To-Sea Pubns.
—Street Jazz. 2006. (Get Dancing Ser.). (Illus.). 32p. (J). lib. bdg. 28.50 *(978-1-59771-049-7(0))* Sea-To-Sea Pubns.
Studio Mouse, creator. Let's Move: Nursery Rhymes for Moving & Learning. 2005. (Read-Aloud Book Ser.). (ENG., Illus.). 36p. (J). 7.95 *(978-1-59249-534-4(6)*, 1D204) Soundprints.
Swartz, Larry & Margolin, Indrani. The 10 Coolest Dance Crazes. 2008. 14.99 *(978-1-55448-523-9(1))* Scholastic Library Publishing.
Thomas, Isabel. Latin Dance. 2011. (On the Radar: Dance Ser.). (ENG., Illus.). 32p. (gr. 4-8). lib. bdg. 26.60 *(978-0-7613-7762-7(X))* Lerner Publishing Group.
Throp, Claire. Ice Dancing. 2017. (Figure Skating Ser.). (ENG.). 32p. (gr. 3-4). lib. bdg. 27.99 ***(978-1-5157-8185-1(2)***, Snap Bks.) Capstone Press of Coughlan Cos.
Tieck, Sarah. Dancing, 1 vol. 2013. (Move Your Body Ser.). (ENG.). 32p. (J). (gr. 2-5). 27.07 *(978-1-61783-561-2(7))* ABDO Publishing Co.
Torrington, Emma. Street Dance. 2012. (Master This! Ser.). (Illus.). 32p. (J). lib. bdg. 25.25 *(978-1-4488-5285-7(4)*, PowerKids Pr.) Rosen Publishing Group, Inc., The.
VanVoorst, Jenny Fretland. La Danza. 2016. (El Estudio del Artista (Artist's Studio)).Tr. of Dance. (SPA.). 24p. (J). (gr. k-2). lib. bdg. 25.65 *(978-1-62031-322-0(7)*, Bullfrog Bks.) Jump! Inc.
Veitch, Catherine. Bailar, 1 vol. 2010. (Deporte y Mi Cuerpo Ser.). (SPA.). 24p. (gr. k-2). 23.32 *(978-1-4329-4347-9(2))*; pap. 6.79 *(978-1-4329-4353-0(7))* Heinemann-Raintree.
What tap dancing's all about according to Dr. Jeni Legon, 1. 2007. (Illus.). 38p. (J). spiral bd. 25.00 *(978-0-9795696-0-9(5))* Haver, Nancy.
Williams, Ann-Marie. Learn to Speak Dance: A Guide to Creating, Performing & Promoting Your Moves. Kulak, Jeff & Owlkids Books Inc. Staff, illus. 2011. (Learn to Speak Ser.). (ENG.). 96p. (J). (gr. 4-7). pap. 14.95 *(978-1-926818-89-4(X))* Owlkids Bks. Inc. CAN. Dist: Publishers Group West (PGW).
Wilson, Iris. Boys Dance Too! 2009. 32p. pap. 16.95 *(978-1-4389-7684-6(4))* AuthorHouse.
Wood, Alix. You Can Be a Dancer, Vol. 1. 2014. (Let's Get Moving! Ser.). (Illus.). 32p. (J). (gr. 3-4). (ENG.). 26.60 *(978-1-4824-0271-1(8)*, 1368200); pap. 10.50 *(978-1-4824-0272-8(6)*, 1368200) Stevens, Gareth Publishing LLLP.
World of Dance, 8 vols., Set. 2010. (World of Dance Ser.). 1088p. (C). (gr. 9). 280.00 *(978-1-60413-944-0(7)*, Chelsea Hse.) Facts On File, Inc.

DANCE—FICTION

Aikins, Dave, illus. Bailando Al Rescate. 2005. (Dora la Exploradora Ser.). (SPA.). 24p. (J). pap. 3.99 *(978-1-4169-1504-1(4)*, Libros Para Ninos) Libros Para Ninos.
Alexander, Carol. Percy Mcgoo. 2012. 24p. pap. 15.99 *(978-1-4771-2359-1(8))* Xlibris Corp.
Alexander, Dorothy. Ce Ce & Her Shadow. 2012. 24p. pap. 15.99 *(978-1-4691-9090-7(7))* Xlibris Corp.
Andersen, Hans Christian. The Red Shoes. 2004. (Illus.). (J). (gr. 1-4). spiral bd. *(978-0-616-14558-6(6))* Canadian National Institute for the Blind/Institut National Canadien pour les Aveugles.
Anderson, Steven. Leap & Twirl. DeAnguelo Hout, Sarah, illus. 2012. 34p. (J). pap. 10.99 *(978-0-692-01667-1(8))* BalletMet Dance Centre.
Andreae, Giles. Giraffes Can't Dance. Parker-Rees, Guy, illus. (J). (gr. -1-3). 2012. (ENG.). 32p. bds. 6.99 *(978-0-545-39255-6(1)*, Cartwheel Bks.) 2008. (ENG.). 9.99 *(978-0-545-09738-3(X))* 2007. 24.95 incl. audio *(978-0-439-02733-5(0))* Scholastic, Inc.
—Giraffes Can't Dance. Parker-Rees, Guy, illus. unabr. ed. 2011. (J). (gr. -1-1). 29.95 *(978-0-439-02734-2(9))* Weston Woods Studios, Inc.
—Giraffes Can't Dance: Number Rumba. Parker-Rees, Guy, illus. 2014. (ENG.). 12p. (J). (gr. -1 — 1). bds. 7.99 *(978-0-545-63996-5(4)*, Cartwheel Bks.) Scholastic, Inc.
Andrews, Julie & Hamilton, Emma Walton. The Very Fairy Princess Takes the Stage. 2011. (Very Fairy Princess Ser.). (ENG., Illus.). 32p. (J). (gr. -1-3). 16.99 *(978-0-316-04052-5(5))* Little Brown & Co.
Anholt, Laurence. Degas & the Little Dancer. 2007. (Anholt's Artists Books for Children Ser.). (ENG., Illus.). 32p. (J). (gr. -1-3). pap. 9.99 *(978-0-7641-3852-2(9))* Barron's Educational Series, Inc.
Applegate, Katherine. Don't Tap-Dance on Your Teacher. Biggs, Brian, illus. 2009. (Roscoe Riley Rules Ser.: 5). (ENG.). 96p. (J). (gr. 1-5). pap. 4.99 *(978-0-06-114889-7(X))* HarperCollins Pubs.
—Don't Tap-Dance on Your Teacher. Biggs, Brian, illus. 2016. (Roscoe Riley Rules Ser.: 5). (ENG.). 112p. (J). (gr. 1-5). 14.75 *(978-0-606-39252-5(1))* Turtleback Bks.
—Don't Tap-Dance on Your Teacher. 2009. (Roscoe Riley Rules Ser.: 5). (J). lib. bdg. 14.75 *(978-0-606-05007-4(8)*, Turtleback) Turtleback Bks.
Aragón, Carla, et al. Dance of the Eggshells: Baile de los Cascarones. Saville, Kathy Dee, illus. 2010. (SPA & ENG.). 32p. (J). (gr. 1). 18.95 *(978-0-8263-4770-1(3))* Univ. of New Mexico Pr.
Asch, Frank. Moondance. Asch, Frank, illus. 2014. (Moonbear Ser.). (ENG., Illus.). 32p. (J). (gr. -1-3). 17.99 *(978-1-4424-6659-3(6)*, Aladdin) Simon & Schuster Children's Publishing.
Atwood, Megan. The Cursed Ballet. 2013. (Dario Quincy Academy of Dance Ser.: 3). (ENG.). 104p. (gr. 6-12). (J). lib. bdg. 27.93 *(978-1-4677-0932-3(8))*; (YA). pap. 7.95 *(978-1-4677-1485-3(2))* Lerner Publishing Group. (Darby Creek).
—Leaping at Shadows. 2013. (Dario Quincy Academy of Dance Ser.: 1). (ENG.). 112p. (YA). (gr. 6-12). pap. 7.95 *(978-1-4677-1483-9(6))*; lib. bdg. 27.93 *(978-1-4677-0930-9(1))* Lerner Publishing Group. (Darby Creek).
—Stolen Luck. 2013. (Dario Quincy Academy of Dance Ser.: 2). (ENG.). 112p. (gr. 6-12). (J). lib. bdg. 27.93 *(978-1-4677-0931-6(X))*; (YA). pap. 7.95 *(978-1-4677-1484-6(4))* Lerner Publishing Group. (Darby Creek).
—Twin Dangers. 2013. (Dario Quincy Academy of Dance Ser.: 4). (ENG.). 112p. (gr. 6-12). (J). lib. bdg. 27.93 *(978-1-4677-0933-0(6))*; (YA). pap. 7.95 *(978-1-4677-1486-0(0))* Lerner Publishing Group. (Darby Creek).
August, Elaine. Fira Gani: An Earthly Fable. 2012. 38p. 24.95 *(978-1-4626-9437-2(3))* America Star Bks.
Ball, Jeff. Son Who Returns. 2014. (ENG.). (YA). pap. 9.95 *(978-1-939053-04-6(8)*, 7th Generation) Book Publishing Co.
Bankole, Adekemi. The Rain Beat Dance. 2011. 32p. pap. 21.99 *(978-1-4568-7346-2(6))* Xlibris Corp.
Barber, Antonia. Dancing Shoes: Lucy's Next Step, Vol. 4. (Illus.). 96p. (J). 5.95 *(978-0-14-038685-1(8))* Penguin Bks., Ltd. GBR. Dist: Trafalgar Square Publishing.
—Dancing Shoes Friends & Rivals. (Illus.). 96p. (J). 5.95 *(978-0-14-038684-4(X))* Penguin Publishing Group.
Bardaus, Anna W. Dance, Dance, Baby! Grove, Christine, illus. 2013. (J). *(978-0-545-61899-1(1))* Scholastic, Inc.
Barden, Stephanie. Cinderella Smith. Goode, Diane, illus. (Cinderella Smith Ser.: 1). (ENG.). (J). (gr. 3-7). 2012. 176p. pap. 5.99 *(978-0-06-196425-1(5))* 2011. 160p. 16.99 *(978-0-06-196423-7(9))* HarperCollins Pubs.
Barton, Elizabeth & Shaw, Natalie. Olivia Leaps! Osterhold, Jared, illus. 2009. (Olivia TV Tie-In Ser.). (ENG.). 12p. (J). (gr. -1-1). bds. 6.99 *(978-1-4169-8572-3(7)*, Simon Spotlight) Simon Spotlight.
Batterson, Veronica Randolph. Billy's First Dance. 2010. (J). pap. 9.95 *(978-0-7414-5913-8(2))* Infinity Publishing.

C D

Bavati, Robyn. Pirouette. 2013. (ENG.). 312p. (YA). pap. 9.99 *(978-0-7387-3481-1(0),* Flux) North Star Editions.

Bedford, David. Daddy Does the Cha Cha Cha! Stevens-Marzo, Bridget, illus. 2010. (ENG.). 32p. (J). (gr. -1-k). pap. 8.99 *(978-1-921541-16-2(4))* Little Hare Bks. AUS. Dist: Independent Pubs. Group.

Beka. African Folk Fever. 2012. (Dance Class Graphic Novels Ser.). (ENG., Illus.). 48p. (J). 10.99 *(978-1-59707-363-9(6),* 9781597073639) Papercutz.

—A Funny Thing Happened on the Way to Paris..., No. 4. 2013. (Dance Class Graphic Novels Ser.). (ENG., Illus.). 48p. (J). (gr. 1-7). 10.99 *(978-1-59707-384-4(9),* 9781597073844) Papercutz.

—Romeo & Juliets. 2012. (Dance Class Graphic Novels Ser.). (ENG., Illus.). 48p. (J). 10.99 *(978-1-59707-317-2(2),* 9781597073172) Papercutz.

Bell, Cece. Sock Monkey Boogie-Woogie. Bell, Cece, illus. 2015. (ENG., Illus.). 32p. (J). (gr. -1-3). 14.00 *(978-0-7636-7758-9(2))* Candlewick Pr.

Bell, Krista & Smith, Craig. If the Shoe Fits. 2008. (Illus.). (Orig.). (J). 60p. (gr. -1-3). 14.95 *(978-1-58089-338-1(4));* (ENG., 64p. (gr. 4-7). pap. 5.95 *(978-1-58089-339-8(2))* Charlesbridge Publishing, Inc.

Benjamin, Brooks. My Seventh-Grade Life in Tights. 2016. (ENG.). 304p. (J). (gr. 4-7). 16.99 *(978-0-553-51250-2(1),* Delacorte Bks. for Young Readers) Random Hse. Children's Bks.

Bennett, Kelly. Dance Y'all, Dance. Murphy, Terri, illus. 2010. (ENG.). 32p. (J). (gr. k-2). 16.95 *(978-1-933979-65-6(8))* Bright Sky Pr.

Bentley, Sue. Dancing Days #5. Swan, Angela & Farley, Andrew, illus. 2014. (Magic Bunny Ser.: 5). (ENG.). 128p. (J). (gr. 1-3). 4.99 *(978-0-448-46793-1(3),* Grosset & Dunlap) Penguin Young Readers Group.

—Sparkling Steps #7, 7 vols. Farley, Andrew & Swan, Angela, illus. 2009. (Magic Kitten Ser.: 7). (ENG.). 128p. (J). (gr. 1-3). pap. 5.99 *(978-0-448-45063-6(1),* Grosset & Dunlap) Penguin Young Readers Group.

Bergman, Mara. Glitter Kitty. Monks, Lydia, illus. 2014. (ENG.). 32p. (J). 8.99 *(978-1-4711-2216-3(6),* Simon & Schuster Children's) Simon & Schuster, Ltd. GBR. Dist: Simon & Schuster, Inc.

Berk, Sheryl. Dance Divas - Showstopper. 2015. (Dance Divas Ser.). (ENG.). 144p. (YA). (gr. 3-6). 15.99 *(978-1-61963-575-3(5),* 9781619635753, Bloomsbury USA Childrens) Bloomsbury Publishing USA.

—Dance Divas - Showtime! 2013. (Dance Divas Ser.). (ENG.). 160p. (YA). (gr. 3-6). pap. 5.99 *(978-1-61963-181-6(4),* 9781619631816, Bloomsbury USA Childrens) Bloomsbury Publishing USA.

—Dance Divas - Step It Up. 2014. (Dance Divas Ser.). (ENG.). 152p. (YA). (gr. 3-6). 15.99 *(978-1-61963-582-1(8),* 9781619635821, Bloomsbury USA Childrens) Bloomsbury Publishing USA.

—Let's Rock! 2014. (Dance Divas Ser.). (ENG.). 168p. (YA). (gr. 3-6). 15.99 *(978-1-61963-224-0(1),* 9781619632240); pap. 5.99 *(978-1-61963-225-7(X),* 9781619632257) Bloomsbury Publishing USA. (Bloomsbury USA Childrens).

—On Pointe. 2014. (Dance Divas Ser.). (ENG.). 144p. (YA). (gr. 3-6). 15.99 *(978-1-61963-585-2(2),* 9781619635852, Bloomsbury USA Childrens) Bloomsbury Publishing USA.

—Showstopper. 2015. (Dance Divas Ser.). (ENG.). 144p. (YA). (gr. 3-6). pap. 5.99 *(978-1-61963-576-0(3),* 9781619635760, Bloomsbury USA Childrens) Bloomsbury Publishing USA.

—Showtime! 2013. (Dance Divas Ser.). (ENG.). 160p. (YA). (gr. 3-6). 15.99 *(978-1-61963-182-3(2),* 9781619631823, Bloomsbury USA Childrens) Bloomsbury Publishing USA.

—Step It Up. 2014. (Dance Divas Ser.). (ENG.). 152p. (YA). (gr. 3-6). pap. 5.99 *(978-1-61963-583-8(6),* 9781619635838, Bloomsbury USA Childrens) Bloomsbury Publishing USA.

—Two to Tango. 2014. (Dance Divas Ser.). (ENG.). 160p. (YA). (gr. 3-6). 15.99 *(978-1-61963-187-8(3),* 9781619631878); pap. 5.99 *(978-1-61963-188-5(1),* 9781619631885) Bloomsbury Publishing USA. (Bloomsbury USA Childrens).

Berton, Judy. City Dancin' Dancin' at Peppy's. Hernandez, Steven, illus. 2004. 36p. (J). per. 16.95 *(978-0-9761051-0-7(1))* Kidrich Corp.

Bessey, Lisa. Pretty Little Dot. 2008. 32p. per. 24.95 *(978-1-4241-8795-9(8))* America Star Bks.

Binkow, Howard. Howard B. Wigglebottom Listens to His Heart. Cornelison, Susan F., illus. 2nd ed. 2008. (ENG.). 32p. (J). 15.00 *(978-0-9715390-2-0(2))* We Do Listen Foundation.

Bird, Betsy. Giant Dance Party. Dorman, Brandon, illus. 2013. (ENG.). 32p. (J). (gr. k-3). 17.99 *(978-0-06-196083-3(7),* Greenwillow Bks.) HarperCollins Pubs.

Bissett, Josie. Boogie Monster. Atteberry, Kevan J., illus. 2011. 36p. (J). (gr. -1-3). 16.95 *(978-1-935414-10-0(0))* Compendium, Inc., Publishing & Communications.

Blevins, Wiley. Max Has a Fish. 2012. (Penguin Young Readers Level 1 Ser.). lib. bdg. 13.55 *(978-0-606-26640-6(2),* Turtleback) Turtleback Bks.

Blevins, Wiley & Bader, Bonnie. Max Finds an Egg. Clanton, Ben, illus. 2015. (Penguin Young Readers, Level 1 Ser.). (ENG.). 32p. (J). (gr. k-1). 3.99 *(978-0-448-47993-4(1),* Penguin Young Readers) Penguin Young Readers Group.

Bloom, Suzanne, illus. Bear Can Dance! 2015. (Goose & Bear Stories Ser.). (ENG.). 40p. (J). (-k). 16.95 *(978-1-62979-442-6(2))* Boyds Mills Pr.

Bloomberg, Sandi. Ava & the Magic Tutu. 2008. 40p. per. 13.95 *(978-1-59800-248-5(1))* Outskirts Pr., Inc.

Bluemle, Elizabeth. How Do You Wokka-Wokka? Cecil, Randy, illus. 2012. (ENG.). 32p. (J). (gr. -1-2). pap. 6.99 *(978-0-7636-6085-7(X))* Candlewick Pr.

Blundell, Judy. Strings Attached. (ENG.). 320p. (J). (gr. 7). 2012. pap. 9.99 *(978-0-545-22127-6(7),* Scholastic Paperbacks) 2011. 17.99 *(978-0-545-22126-9(9),* Scholastic Pr.) Scholastic, Inc.

Boll, Katherine. Dante the Dancing Goose. 2009. 20p. pap. 9.95 *(978-1-60844-278-2(0))* Dog Ear Publishing, LLC.

Boné, Thomas H., illus. The Teacher Who Would Not Retire Retires. 2017. (J). ***(978-0-9885295-7-1(2))*** Blue Marlin Pubns.

Bonwill, Ann. Naughty Toes. Murfin, Teresa, illus. 2011. (ENG.). 32p. 15.95 *(978-1-58925-103-8(2));* pap. 7.95 *(978-1-58925-430-5(9))* Tiger Tales.

Bound, Samantha-Ellen. Broadyway Baby. 2016. (Silver Shoes Ser.: 5). (ENG., Illus.). 144p. (J). (gr. 4-7). pap. 8.99 *(978-0-85798-903-1(0))* Random Hse. Australia AUS. Dist: Independent Pubs. Group.

—Dance till You Drop. 2015. (Silver Shoes Ser.: 4). (ENG.). 144p. (J). (gr. 4-7). pap. 8.99 *(978-0-85798-372-5(5))* Random Hse. Australia AUS. Dist: Independent Pubs. Group.

—Lights, Camera, Dance! 2016. (Silver Shoes Ser.: 6). (ENG., Illus.). 144p. (J). (gr. 4-7). pap. 8.99 *(978-0-85798-905-5(7))* Random Hse. Australia AUS. Dist: Independent Pubs. Group.

—Rhythm & Blues. 2016. (Silver Shoes Ser.: 7). (ENG., Illus.). 144p. (J). (gr. 4-7). pap. 8.99 *(978-0-85798-907-9(3))* Random Hse. Australia AUS. Dist: Independent Pubs. Group.

—Studio Showdown. 2016. (Silver Shoes Ser.: 8). (ENG., Illus.). 144p. (J). (gr. 1-7). pap. 8.99 *(978-0-85798-909-3(X))* Random Hse. Australia AUS. Dist: Independent Pubs. Group.

Boynton, Sandra. Barnyard Dance! (Lap Edition) 2011. (ENG., Illus.). 22p. (J). (gr. k — 1). bds. 11.95 *(978-0-7611-6616-0(5),* 16616) Workman Publishing Co., Inc.

Bozarth, Jan. Kerka's Book. Burden, Andrea, illus. 2010. (Fairy Godmother Academy Ser.: No. 2). (ENG.). 224p. (J). (gr. 3-7). pap. 6.99 *(978-0-375-85183-4(6),* Yearling) Random Hse. Children's Bks.

Braffet, Mary. Maile & the Huli Hula Chicken. Braffet, Holly, illus. 2010. 32p. (J). 12.95 *(978-1-56647-925-7(8))* Mutual Publishing LLC.

Branning, Debe. The Adventures of Chickolet Pigolet: The Bribe of Frankenbeans. Knold, Nijlon, illus. 2008. 48p. pap. 7.95 *(978-1-935137-40-5(9))* Guardian Angel Publishing, Inc.

Bruna, Dick. Miffy Dances. 2004. (Illus.). 24p. pap. 4.99 *(978-1-59226-010-2(1))* Big Tent Entertainment, Inc.

Bryant, Ann. Ballet Magic. 2007. (Ballerina Dreams Ser.). (Illus.). 322p. (J). (gr. 4-7). per. 7.99 *(978-0-7945-1740-3(4),* Usborne) EDC Publishing.

—The Christmas Nutcracker. 2006. (Ballerina Dreams Ser.). (Illus.). 181p. (J). (gr. 5). lib. bdg. 12.99 *(978-1-58086-919-5(X),* Usborne) EDC Publishing.

—Dancing Forever. 2006. (Ballerina Dreams Ser.). (Illus.). 105p. (J). (gr. 5). lib. bdg. 12.99 *(978-1-58086-920-1(3),* Usborne) EDC Publishing.

—Dancing Friends. 2007. (Ballerina Dreams Ser.). (Illus.). 326p. (J). (gr. 4-7). per. 7.99 *(978-0-7945-1741-0(2),* Usborne) EDC Publishing.

—Dancing Princess. 2006. (Ballerina Dreams Ser.). (Illus.). 103p. (J). (gr. 5). lib. bdg. 12.99 *(978-1-58086-921-8(1),* Usborne) EDC Publishing.

—Jasmine's Lucky Star. 2006. (Ballerina Dreams Ser.). (Illus.). 104p. (J). (gr. 5). lib. bdg. 12.99 *(978-1-58086-923-2(8),* Usborne) EDC Publishing.

—Jasmine's Lucky Star. Benton, Tim, illus. 2006. (Ballerina Dreams Ser.). 104p. (J). per. 4.99 *(978-0-7945-1295-8(X),* Usborne) EDC Publishing.

—Poppy's Secret Wish. Benton, Tim, illus. 2006. (Ballerina Dreams Ser.). 105p. (J). per. 4.99 *(978-0-7945-1294-1(1),* Usborne) EDC Publishing.

—Rose's Big Decision. 2006. (Ballerina Dreams Ser.). (Illus.). 103p. (J). (gr. 5). lib. bdg. 12.99 *(978-1-58086-925-6(4),* Usborne) EDC Publishing.

—Rose's Big Decision. Benton, Tim, illus. 2006. (Ballerina Dreams Ser.). 102p. (J). per. 4.99 *(978-0-7945-1296-5(8),* Usborne) EDC Publishing.

Buonanno, Graziella Pacini. Dancing on Grapes. Capaldi, Gina, illus. 2011. (ENG.). 32p. (J). (gr. k-3). 16.95 *(978-1-59078-833-2(8))* Boyds Mills Pr.

Burgard, Anna Marlis. Flying Feet: A Story of Irish Dance. Dees, Leighanne, illus. 2006. 31p. (J). (gr. 4-8). 16.00 *(978-1-4223-5255-7(2))* DIANE Publishing Co.

Bussell, Darcey. Christmas in Enchantia. 2010. (Magic Ballerina Ser.). (ENG., Illus.). 144p. (J). (gr. k-2). pap. 9.99 *(978-0-00-734800-8(2),* HarperCollins Children's Bks.) HarperCollins Pubs. Ltd. GBR. Dist: HarperCollins Pubs.

—Summer in Enchantia. 2009. (Magic Ballerina Ser.). (ENG., Illus.). 144p. (J). (gr. k-2). pap. 9.99 *(978-0-00-731721-9(2))* HarperCollins Pubs. Ltd. GBR. Dist: Independent Pubs. Group.

Butler, Dori Hillestad. Trading Places with Tank Talbott. 2003. (ENG.). 144p. (J). (gr. 3-7). 15.99 *(978-0-8075-1708-6(9))* Whitman, Albert & Co.

Cabot, Meg, et al. Prom Nights from Hell. 2010. (ENG.). 336p. (YA). (gr. 9). pap. 9.99 *(978-0-06-197600-1(8),* HarperTeen) HarperCollins Pubs.

Callahan, Sean. Shannon & the World's Tallest Leprechaun. Kemly, Kathleen, illus. 2008. (ENG.). 32p. (J). (gr. 2-3). lib. bdg. 15.95 *(978-0-8075-7326-6(4))* Whitman, Albert & Co.

Capucilli, Alyssa Satin. Katy Duck & the Tip-Top Tap Shoes. Cole, Henry, illus. 2013. (Katy Duck Ser.). (ENG.). 24p. (J). (gr. -1-1). 16.99 *(978-1-4424-5246-6(3));* pap. 3.99 *(978-1-4424-5245-9(5))* Simon Spotlight. (Simon Spotlight).

—Katy Duck, Center Stage. Cole, Henry, illus. 2008. (Katy Duck Ser.). (ENG.). 16p. (J). (gr. -1-k). bds. 7.99 *(978-1-4169-3338-0(7),* Little Simon) Little Simon.

—Katy Duck, Dance Star. Cole, Henry, illus. 2008. (Katy Duck Ser.). (ENG.). 16p. (J). (gr. -1-k). bds. 7.99 *(978-1-4169-3337-3(9),* Little Simon) Little Simon.

—Katy Duck, Dance Star/Katy Duck, Center Stage. Cole, Henry, illus. 2009. (Katy Duck Ser.). (ENG.). 24p. (J). (gr. -1-k). pap. 3.99 *(978-1-4169-8279-1(5),* Little Simon) Little Simon.

—Katy Duck Makes a Friend. Cole, Henry, illus. 2012. (Katy Duck Ser.). (ENG.). 24p. (J). (gr. -1-1). 16.99 *(978-1-4424-1977-3(6));* pap. 3.99 *(978-1-4424-1976-6(8))* Simon Spotlight. (Simon Spotlight).

—Starring Katy Duck. Cole, Henry, illus. 2011. (Katy Duck Ser.). (ENG.). 24p. (J). (gr. -1-1). pap. 3.99 *(978-1-4424-1974-2(1));* lib. bdg. 15.99 *(978-1-4424-1975-9(X))* Simon Spotlight. (Simon Spotlight).

Capucilli, Alyssa Satin & Cole, Henry. Katy Duck Is a Caterpillar. 2009. (Katy Duck Ser.). (ENG., Illus.). 32p. (J). (gr. -1-k). 14.99 *(978-1-4169-6061-4(9),* Little Simon) Little Simon.

Carlson, Nancy. Harriet's Recital. 2006. (Illus.). (J). 15.95 *(978-1-57505-898-6(7),* Carolrhoda Bks.) Lerner Publishing Group.

Carman, Debby. Cha Cha, the Dancing Dog. Carman, Debby, illus. 2007. (Illus.). 28p. (J). (gr. -1-1). 14.99 *(978-0-9777340-5-4(6))* Faux Paw Media Group.

Castor, Harriet. Dance Off. 2009. (Sleepover Club Ser.). (ENG.). 144p. (J). (gr. 2-6). pap. 6.99 *(978-0-00-726492-6(5))* HarperCollins Pubs. Ltd. GBR. Dist: Independent Pubs. Group.

Cecil, Carrie Gerlach & cecil, charli. Charli & Wilbur a Dancing Dog's Dream. 2012. 24p. pap. 7.99 *(978-0-615-62081-7(7))* Anachel Communications.

Charaipotra, Sona & Clayton, Dhonielle. Shiny Broken Pieces. 2017. 384p. (YA). (gr. 9). pap. 9.99 ***(978-0-06-234243-0(6),*** HarperTeen) HarperCollins Pubs.

Charaipotra, Sona & Clayton, Dhonielle. Tiny Pretty Things. 2015. (ENG.). 448p. (YA). (gr. 9). 17.99 *(978-0-06-234239-3(8),* HarperTeen) HarperCollins Pubs.

Ciminera, Siobhan & Testa, Maggie. Dancey Dance. Yoe! Studio Staff, illus. 2009. (Yo Gabba Gabba! Ser.). (ENG.). 32p. (J). (gr. -1-1). 4.99 *(978-1-4169-7100-9(9),* Simon Scribbles) Simon Scribbles.

—Meet OLIVIA. Childrens Books Staff & Rose, Drew, illus. 2009. (Olivia TV Tie-In Ser.). (ENG.). 32p. (J). (gr. -1-1). 4.99 *(978-1-4169-7188-7(2),* Simon Scribbles) Simon Scribbles.

Clarke, Jane. Dancing with the Dinosaurs. Wildish, Lee, illus. 2012. (ENG.). 32p. (J). (gr. -1-2). 12.95 *(978-1-936140-67-1(5))* Charlesbridge Publishing, Inc.

Clement, Rod. Olga the Brolga. Clement, Rod, illus. (Illus.). 32p. 2005. (ENG.). pap. *(978-0-207-19758-1(X))* 2004. *(978-0-207-19701-7(6))* HarperCollins Pubs. Australia.

Cofer, Judith Ortiz. ¡A Bailar! / Let's Dance! Rodriguez, Christina Ann, illus. 2011. (ENG & SPA.). (J). 16.95 *(978-1-55885-698-1(6),* Piñata Books) Arte Publico Pr.

Cohn, Diana. Crane Boy. 2015. (ENG., Illus.). 40p. (J). (gr. 2-5). 17.95 *(978-1-941026-16-8(8))* Cinco Puntos Pr.

Colbert, Brandy. Pointe. (ENG.). 352p. (YA). (gr. 9). 2015. pap. 9.99 *(978-0-14-751441-7(X),* Speak) 2014. 17.99 *(978-0-399-16034-9(5),* G.P. Putnam's Sons Books for Young Readers) Penguin Young Readers Group.

Conrad, Liz, illus. Skeleton Shake. 2008. (ENG.). 12p. (J). 6.95 *(978-1-58117-798-5(4),* Intervisual/Piggy Toes) Bendon, Inc.

Cook, Teri Ann. The Adventures of Mrs. Patsy's Farm: A Gift! Is a Gift! Is a Gift!, 1 vol. 2009. 24p. pap. 24.95 *(978-1-60749-549-9(X))* America Star Bks.

Copeland, Misty. Firebird. Myers, Christopher, illus. 2014. (ENG.). 40p. (J). (gr. k-3). 17.99 *(978-0-399-16615-0(7),* G.P. Putnam's Sons Books for Young Readers) Penguin Young Readers Group.

Craig, Lindsey. Dancing Feet! Brown, Marc, illus. 2010. (ENG.). 40p. (J). (gr. -1-2). 16.99 *(978-0-375-86181-9(5),* Knopf Bks. for Young Readers) Random Hse. Children's Bks.

Cronin, Doreen. Wiggle. Menchin, Scott, illus. 2005. (ENG.). 40p. (J). (gr. -1-3). 16.99 *(978-0-689-86375-2(6),* Atheneum Bks. for Young Readers) Simon & Schuster Children's Publishing.

Crosshill, Tom. The Cat King of Havana. 2016. 368p. (YA). (gr. 8). 17.99 *(978-0-06-242283-5(9),* Tegen, Katherine Bks) HarperCollins Pubs.

Crow, Kristyn. Zombelina: School Days. Idle, Molly, illus. (ENG.). (J). 2017. 40p. 16.99 *(978-1-61963-641-5(7),* 9781619636415) 2013. 32p. (gr. -1-3). 16.99 *(978-0-8027-2803-6(0),* 9780802728036) Bloomsbury Publishing USA. (Bloomsbury USA Childrens).

—Zombelina Dances the Nutcracker. Idle, Molly, illus. 2015. (ENG.). 40p. (J). (gr. -1-3). 16.99 *(978-1-61963-640-8(9),* 9781619636408, Bloomsbury USA Childrens) Bloomsbury Publishing USA.

Davis, Lois A. 5 Silly Elephants. 2013. 28p. pap. 24.95 *(978-1-63000-530-6(4))* America Star Bks.

Dawson, Jennifer. Silly Sally Sue. 2013. 24p. pap. 24.95 *(978-1-62709-938-7(7))* America Star Bks.

Dawson, Paola. A Dancing Dream. 2013. 38p. pap. 16.95 *(978-1-4497-8297-9(3),* WestBow Pr.) Author Solutions, Inc.

Defilippo, Lauren Frances. Dance with Me, Please. 2009. 24p. pap. 14.99 *(978-1-4490-0607-5(8))* AuthorHouse.

Denny, Elizabeth. Jenneli's Dance, 1 vol. Auchter, Chris, illus. 2008. (ENG.). 44p. pap. 12.95 *(978-1-894778-61-9(8))* Theytus Bks., Ltd. CAN. Dist: Univ. of Toronto Pr.

dePaola, Tomie. Oliver Button Is a Sissy. dePaola, Tomie, illus. 2017. (ENG., Illus.). 48p. (J). (gr. -1-3). 17.99 ***(978-1-4814-7757-4(9),*** Simon & Schuster Bks. For Young Readers) Simon & Schuster Bks. For Young Readers.

Depken, Kristen L. Pocoyo Dance (Pocoyo) Random House Staff, illus. 2012. (Pictureback(R) Ser.). (ENG.). 24p. (J). (gr. -1-2). pap. 3.99 *(978-0-307-98096-0(0),* Random Hse. Bks. for Young Readers) Random Hse. Children's Bks.

—We Love to Dance! 2015. (Dora the Explorer Step into Reading Ser.). lib. bdg. 14.75 *(978-0-606-36396-9(3))* Turtleback Bks.

—We Love to Dance! (Dora & Friends) Aikins, David, illus. 2015. (Step into Reading Ser.). (ENG.). 24p. (J). (gr. -1-1). 4.99 *(978-0-553-50857-4(1),* Random Hse. Bks. for Young Readers) Random Hse. Children's Bks.

DePrisco, Dorothea. Dinosaur Dance. 2006. (ENG.). 12p. 9.95 *(978-1-58117-480-9(2),* Intervisual/Piggy Toes) Bendon, Inc.

Derrick, Patricia & Sibbett, Joyce. Montgomery the Moose Can Shake His Caboose. Martinez, J-P Loppo, illus. 2007. 32p. (J). (gr. -1). 18.95 incl. audio compact disk *(978-1-933818-18-4(2))* Animalations.

deRubertis, Barbara. Dilly Dog's Dizzy Dancing. Alley, R. W., illus. 2010. (Animal Antics A to Z Ser.). 32p. (J). lib. bdg. 22.60 *(978-1-57565-307-5(9));* (ENG.). (gr. -1-3). pap. 7.95 *(978-1-57565-303-7(6))* Kane Press, Inc.

deRubertis, Barbara & DeRubertis, Barbara. Dilly Dog's Dizzy Dancing. Alley, R. W., illus. 2012. (Animal Antics A to Z Ser.). 32p. (J). (gr. 2 — 1). cd-rom 7.95 *(978-1-57565-397-6(4))* Kane Press, Inc.

Dixon, Heather. Entwined. (ENG.). 480p. (YA). (gr. 8). 2012. pap. 9.99 *(978-0-06-200104-7(3))* 2011. 17.99 *(978-0-06-200103-0(5))* HarperCollins Pubs. (Greenwillow Bks.).

Douglass Thom, Kara. Dancer Girl M. C's Story: One Step at a Time. Seatter, Pamela, illus. 2014. (Go! Go! Sports Girls Ser.). (ENG.). 32p. (J). (gr. k-2). pap. 4.99 *(978-1-940731-02-5(X))* Dream Big Toy Co.

Doyle, Bill. Trapped! The 2031 Journal of Otis Fitzmorgan. 6th ed. 2006. (ENG., Illus.). 144p. (J). (gr. 3-7). per. 16.99 *(978-0-316-05754-7(1))* Little, Brown Bks. for Young Readers.

Doyle, Bill H. Betrayed! The 1977 Journal of Zeke Moorie. 4th ed. 2006. (ENG., Illus.). 144p. (J). (gr. 3-7). per. 16.99 *(978-0-316-05741-7(X))* Little, Brown Bks. for Young Readers.

Draper, Sharon M. Panic. 2013. (ENG., Illus.). 272p. (YA). (gr. 9). 17.99 *(978-1-4424-0896-8(0),* Atheneum Bks. for Young Readers) Simon & Schuster Children's Publishing.

Driscoll, Laura. Dance to the Rescue. Aikins, Dave, illus. 2005. 24p. (J). lib. bdg. 9.00 *(978-1-4242-0981-1(1))* Fitzgerald Bks.

DuJardin, Rosamond. Senior Prom. 2003. (YA). pap. 12.95 *(978-1-930009-77-6(1),* 800-691-7779) Image Cascade Publishing.

Durango, Julia. Cha-Cha Chimps. Taylor, Eleanor, illus. 2010. (ENG.). 32p. (J). (gr. -1-3). 7.99 *(978-1-4169-9574-6(9),* Simon & Schuster Bks. For Young Readers) Simon & Schuster Bks. For Young Readers.

Dyess, Hal. The Night the Rabbits Dance: An Easter Story. 2011. 20p. pap. 10.00 *(978-1-4567-3613-2(2))* AuthorHouse.

Elliott, David. One Little Chicken: A Counting Book. Long, Ethan, illus. 2007. (ENG.). 24p. (J). (gr. -1-3). 16.95 *(978-0-8234-1983-8(5))* Holiday Hse., Inc.

Ellis, Debi. Just Dance. 2013. 28p. pap. 14.93 *(978-1-4669-8941-2(6))* Trafford Publishing.

Emery, Airin. Dance Divas: The Dance Series (Book #2) 2013. 128p. pap. *(978-1-927794-01-2(3))* Lechner Syndications.

—Tap In: The Dance Series (Book #3) 2013. 118p. pap. *(978-1-927794-02-9(1))* Lechner Syndications.

—Triple Threats: The Dance Series (Book #4) 2013. 108p. pap. *(978-1-927794-03-6(X))* Lechner Syndications.

Evans, D. D. Pixie Eden. 2011. 28p. pap. 12.03 *(978-1-4567-2732-1(X))* AuthorHouse.

Evans, Richard. The Dance. Linton, Jonathan, illus. 2014. (ENG.). 32p. (J). 16.99 *(978-1-4814-3112-5(9),* Simon & Schuster/Paula Wiseman Bks.) Simon & Schuster/Paula Wiseman Bks.

Falligant, Erin. Into the Spotlight. Studios, Arcana, illus. 2011. (ENG.). 120p. (YA). (gr. 3-18). pap. 8.95 *(978-1-59369-835-5(6))* American Girl Publishing, Inc.

Farley, Robin. Adventures of MIA. Ivanov, A. & Ivanov, O., illus. 2013. 158p. (J). *(978-1-4351-5061-4(9))* Barnes & Noble, Inc.

—Mia & the Big Sister Ballet. 2012. (Mia I Can Read Bks.). (J). lib. bdg. 13.55 *(978-0-606-26282-8(2),* Turtleback) Turtleback Bks.

—Mia & the Daisy Dance. Ivanov, Olga & Ivanov, Aleksey, illus. 2012. (My First I Can Read Ser.). (ENG.). 32p. (J). (gr. -1-3). 16.99 *(978-0-06-173306-2(7));* pap. 3.99 *(978-0-06-173305-5(9))* HarperCollins Pubs.

—Mia & the Dance for Two. Ivanov, Olga & Ivanov, Aleksey, illus. 2011. (My First I Can Read Ser.). (ENG.). 32p. (J). (gr. -1-3). 16.99 *(978-0-06-173304-8(0));* pap. 3.99 *(978-0-06-173303-1(2))* HarperCollins Pubs.

—Mia & the Girl with a Twirl. 2013. (Mia I Can Read Bks.). (J). lib. bdg. 13.55 *(978-0-606-31811-2(9),* Turtleback) Turtleback Bks.

—Mia & the Tiny Toe Shoes. 2012. (Mia I Can Read Bks.). (J). lib. bdg. 13.55 *(978-0-606-26863-9(4),* Turtleback) Turtleback Bks.

—Mia & the Too Big Tutu. Ivanov, Aleksey & Ivanov, Olga, illus. 2010. (My First I Can Read Ser.). (ENG.). 32p. (J). (gr. -1-3). 16.99 *(978-0-06-173302-4(4));* pap. 3.99 *(978-0-06-173301-7(6))* HarperCollins Pubs.

—Mia Dances Back to School! Ivanov, Olga & Ivanov, Aleksey, illus. 2013. (Mia Ser.). (ENG.). 24p. (J). (gr. -1-3). pap. 4.99 *(978-0-06-210014-6(9),* HarperFestival) HarperCollins Pubs.

—Mia Jazzes It Up! Ivanov, Olga & Ivanov, Aleksey, illus. 2013. (My First I Can Read Ser.). (ENG.). 32p. (J). (gr. -1-3). 16.99 *(978-0-06-208692-1(8));* pap. 3.99 *(978-0-06-208691-4(X))* HarperCollins Pubs.

—Mia Jazzes It Up! 2013. (Mia I Can Read Bks.). (J). lib. bdg. 13.55 *(978-0-606-32164-8(0),* Turtleback) Turtleback Bks.

—Mia Sets the Stage. Ivanov, Olga & Ivanov, Aleksey, illus. 2013. (My First I Can Read Ser.). (ENG.). 32p. (J). (gr. -1-3). pap. 3.99 *(978-0-06-208685-3(5))* HarperCollins Pubs.

—Time to Trick or Treat! Ivanov, Olga & Ivanov, Aleksey, illus. 2012. (Mia Ser.). (ENG.). 24p. (J). (gr. -1-3). pap. 4.99 *(978-0-06-210011-5(4),* HarperFestival) HarperCollins Pubs.

Feiffer, Jules. Rupert Can Dance. Feiffer, Jules, illus. 2014. (ENG., Illus.). 32p. (J). (gr. -1-1). 17.95 *(978-0-374-36363-5(3),* 9780374363635, Farrar, Straus & Giroux (BYR)) Farrar, Straus & Giroux.

Fitzgerald, Kevin. Dancing in the Moonlight. Fitzgerald, Anita, illus. 2005. (J). *(978-0-9765987-4-9(4))* Foundation, Pr. The.

Flint-Warren, Cathrine. To Dance with the Yellow Butterfly. 2007. 28p. per. 18.95 *(978-1-4327-0491-9(5))* Outskirts Pr., Inc.

Flor Ada, Alma. Celebra el Cinco de Mayo con un Jarabe Tapatío. Gomez, Marcela & Silva, David, illus. 2006. (Cuentos para Celebrar / Stories to Celebrate Ser.). 30p. (gr. k-6). per. 11.95 *(978-1-59820-118-5(2))* Ediciones Alfaguara ESP. Dist: Santillana USA Publishing Co., Inc.

—Celebra el Día De3 San Patricio con Samantha y Lola. Lavandeira, Sandra, illus. 2006. (Cuentos para Celebrar / Stories to Celebrate Ser.). (SPA.). 30p. (gr. k-6). per. 11.95 *(978-1-59820-117-8(4),* Alfaguara) Santillana USA Publishing Co., Inc.

Flor Ada, Alma & Campoy, F. Isabel. Celebrate St. Patrick's Day with Samantha & Lola. Hayes, Joe & Franco, Sharon, trs. 2006. (Stories to Celebrate Ser.). (Illus.). 30p. (gr. k-6). per. 11.95 *(978-1-59820-129-1(8),* Alfaguara) Santillana USA Publishing Co., Inc.

Fontes, Justine. Barbie in the Pink Shoes. 2013. (Book & Jewelry Ser.: 1). (ENG.). 24p. (J). (gr. -1-3). 10.99 *(978-0-7944-2785-6(5))* Reader's Digest Assn., Inc., The.

Fox, Paula. The Slave Dancer. unabr. ed. 2004. 152p. (J). (gr. 5-9). pap. 38.00 incl. audio *(978-0-8072-0458-0(7),* Listening Library) Random Hse. Audio Publishing Group.

Frank, Hannah. The Ballet Shoes. 2008. 44p. pap. 18.49 *(978-1-4389-1025-3(8))* AuthorHouse.

French, Jackie. Josephine Wants to Dance. Whatley, Bruce, illus. 2007. (ENG.). 32p. (J). (gr. -1-1). 17.95 *(978-0-8109-9431-7(3),* Abrams Bks. for Young Readers) Abrams, Inc.
—Josephine Wants to Dance. Whatley, Bruce, illus. 2006. 32p. *(978-0-207-20075-5(0))* HarperCollins Pubs. Australia.
Friedlander, Tim. The I Like Me Dance! Edwards, W M, illus. 2007. (Playdate Kids Musical Ser.). 27p. (J). (gr. -1-3). 14.95 incl. audio compact disk *(978-1-933721-07-1(3))* Playdate Kids Publishing.
Froman, Annabelle. Beezeur. 2013. 34p. pap. 9.95 *(978-0-9842053-1-8(4))* Breathless Vintage Enterprises.
Galjanic, Lisa. When Flowers Dance. Hope, Michelle, illus. 2007. (J). 9.95 *(978-1-933532-05-9(X))* LSG Pubns.
Gallagher, Diana G. Dance Trap: The Complicated Life of Claudia Cristina Cortez, 1 vol. Garvey, Brann, illus. 2007. (Claudia Cristina Cortez Ser.). (ENG.). 88p. (gr. 2-3). per. 6.10 *(978-1-59889-879-8(5),* Claudia Cristina Cortez) Stone Arch Bks.
Gambassi, Rod. The Boy Who Wanted to be a Dancer. Brownlee, Kelly Jackson, illus. 2007. 22p. (J). 23.95 *(978-1-889829-18-0(8))* Window Bks.
Gannon, Gretchen. Rince: The Fairytale of Irish Dance. 2012. (ENG.). 32p. (J). pap. 20.95 *(978-1-4327-8237-5(1));* pap. 12.95 *(978-1-4327-8235-1(5))* Outskirts Pr., Inc.
Garza, Shelly S. Dancing Danica. Weinstein, Holly, illus. 2013. 24p. (J). 12.99 net. *(978-1-61254-138-9(0))* Brown Books Publishing Group.
Gaulkin, Marianne Quigley. Playdance Studio. Baker, David, illus. 2011. 28p. pap. 24.95 *(978-1-4560-2163-4(X))* America Star Bks.
Gentry, Jennifer Mills. Maria Loves to Dance. 2011. 24p. pap. 24.95 *(978-1-4626-1869-9(3))* America Star Bks.
George, Jessica Day. Princess of the Midnight Ball. 2010. (Twelve Dancing Princesses Ser.). (ENG.). 304p. (YA). (gr. 7-9). pap. 9.99 *(978-1-59990-455-9(1),* 9781599904559, Bloomsbury USA Childrens) Bloomsbury Publishing USA.
Gerber, Carole. Jessica Mcbean, Tap Dance Queen. Barton, Patrice, illus. 2006. 144p. (J). 13.95 *(978-0-9718348-7-3(3))* Blooming Tree Pr.
—Jessica McBean, Tap Dance Queen. Barton, Patrice, illus. 2007. (ENG.). 144p. (J). (gr. 1-5). pap. 6.95 *(978-0-9718348-9-7(X))* Blooming Tree Pr.
Giff, Patricia Reilly. Fancy Feet. 77p. (J). (gr. 1-2). pap. 3.99 *(978-0-8072-1279-0(2),* Listening Library) Random Hse. Audio Publishing Group.
Goldberg, Whoopi. Sugar Plum to the Rescue! Roos, Maryn, illus. 2011. (ENG.). 160p. (J). (gr. 1-5). pap. 4.99 *(978-0-7868-5264-2(X),* Jump at the Sun) Hyperion Bks. for Children.
Golden Books Staff. Let's Dance! Fruchter, Jason, illus. 2005. (Paint Box Book Ser.). (ENG.). 32p. (J). (gr. -1-2). pap. 3.99 *(978-0-375-83478-3(8),* Golden Bks.) Random Hse. Children's Bks.
Golembe, Carla. The Story of Hula. 2004. (Illus.). 32p. (J). 16.95 incl. audio compact disk *(978-1-57306-185-8(9))* Bess Pr., Inc.
Grami, B. Help! I Have Rats in My Hair! 2011. 22p. (J). pap. 17.95 *(978-1-4327-5348-1(7))* Outskirts Pr., Inc.
Greaves, Margaret. Stories from the Ballet. Kopper, Lisa, tr. Kopper, Lisa, illus. 2003. 72p. (J). pap. *(978-0-7112-2162-8(6))* ReiseArt Buchhandlung GmbH.
Griffie, Sandra. The Snow Dancer. 2012. 28p. 24.95 *(978-1-4626-6777-2(5))* America Star Bks.
Guibert, Emmanuel. The Little Rats of the Opera. 2017. (Ariol Ser.: 10). (J). lib. bdg. 24.50 ***(978-0-606-39879-4(1))*** Turtleback Bks.
Guillain, Charlotte & Guillain, Adam. Cinderella & the Amazing Techno-Slippers. Moor, Becka, illus. 2016. (Fairy Tales Today Ser.). (ENG.). 24p. (gr. 1-2). 9.95 *(978-1-4795-8750-6(8))* Picture Window Bks.
Hanson, Warren. Bugtown Boogie. Johnson, Steve & Fancher, Lou, illus. 2008. 32p. (J). (gr. -1-3). 17.89 *(978-0-06-059938-6(3),* Geringer, Laura Book) HarperCollins Pubs.
Harris, Stephen. Ballroom Bonanza: A Hidden Pictures ABC Book. Rycroft, Nina, illus. 2010. (ENG.). 40p. (J). (gr. k-2). 16.95 *(978-0-8109-8842-2(9),* Abrams Bks. for Young Readers) Abrams, Inc.
Harris, Teresa E. American Girl: Girl of the Year 2017. 2017. (Girl of the Year 2017 Ser.: 2). (ENG.). 192p. (J). (gr. 3-7). pap. 9.99 *(978-1-338-13700-2(X))* Scholastic, Inc.
—Gabriela. 2016. (American Girl: Girl of the Year Ser.: 1). (ENG.). 208p. (J). (gr. 3-7). pap. 9.99 *(978-1-338-13698-2(4))* Scholastic, Inc.
Harrison, Emma. Toe the Line: A Rival High Novel. 2008. (YA). *(978-1-4114-0526-4(9),* Spark Publishing Group) Sterling Publishing Co., Inc.
Harrison, Lisi. Belle of the Brawl. 2010. (Alphas Ser.: 3). (ENG.). 240p. (YA). (gr. 7-17). pap. 9.99 *(978-0-316-03581-1(5),* Poppy) Little, Brown Bks. for Young Readers.
Harrison, Penny. Dance with Me. Jones, Gwynneth, illus. 2016. (ENG.). 32p. (J). (gr. -1-3). 17.99 *(978-1-925335-23-1(2),* EK Bks.) Exisle Publishing Pty Ltd. AUS. Dist: Hachette Bk. Group.
Harter, Debbie. Animal Boogie. Penner, Fred, illus. 2011. (ENG.). 32p. (J). (gr. -1-2). 9.99 *(978-1-84686-620-3(0))* Barefoot Bks., Inc.
Harvey, Alex. Dancing with the Star. 2013. (Spongebob Squarepants Step into Reading Ser.). lib. bdg. 13.55 *(978-0-606-23687-4(2),* Turtleback) Turtleback Bks.
Hayes, Joe. Dance, Nana, Dance (Baila, Nana, Baila) Trenard Sayago, Mauricio, illus. 2010. (ENG & SPA.). 128p. (J). (gr. 3-6). pap. 12.95 *(978-1-933693-61-3(4))* Cinco Puntos Pr.
HB Staff. The King Who Loved to Dance. 97th ed. 2003. (Signatures Ser.). (gr. 1-18). pap. 16.50 *(978-0-15-308161-3(9))* Harcourt Schl. Pubs.
Heidbreder, Robert. Drumheller Dinosaur Dance. Slavin, Bill et al, illus. 2006. (ENG.). 32p. (J). (gr. -1-2). pap. 7.95 *(978-1-55337-982-9(9))* Kids Can Pr., Ltd. CAN. Dist: Hachette Bk. Group.
Hinbest, Wendy. Frizzy Tizzy Dances. 2011. 20p. pap. 11.95 *(978-1-4583-5830-1(5))* Lulu Pr., Inc.
Hlad, Carole. Daisy's Dance Party: (from the Amanda's Cats Series) 2011. 24p. pap. 15.99 *(978-1-4628-8006-5(1))* Xlibris Corp.
Ho & Ho, Minfong. The Stone Goddess. 2006. (Reader's Workshop Ser.). (ENG., Illus.). 200p. (C). pap. 19.95 *(978-0-7362-3160-2(9))* CENGAGE Learning.
Hoffman, Mary. The Twelve Dancing Princesses. Clara, Miss, illus. 2013. (ENG.). 40p. (J). (gr. 1-5). 17.99 *(978-1-84686-966-2(8))* Barefoot Bks., Inc.
Hopkins, Jackie Mims. Three Armadillies Tuff, 1 vol. Brooks, S. G., illus. 2011. (ENG.). 32p. pap. 7.95 *(978-1-56145-598-0(9),* Peachtree Junior) Peachtree Pubs.
Home-Ingram, Gloria. Yonna Bonna the Purple Ballerin. 2012. 16p. pap. 12.68 *(978-1-4669-4169-4(3))* Trafford Publishing.
Howe, James. Brontorina. Cecil, Randy, illus. 2013. (ENG.). 32p. (J). (gr. -1-3). 6.99 *(978-0-7636-5323-1(3))* Candlewick Pr.
—Brontorina. 2013. lib. bdg. 17.20 *(978-0-606-31600-2(0),* Turtleback) Turtleback Bks.
Howell, Hayley L. Sammy's Two Left Feet: Groovin' with Mr. Smooth: Discovering How to Believe in Yourself. 2010. 32p. pap. 15.95 *(978-1-4520-5733-0(8))* AuthorHouse.
Howell, Heather. Emily's Ballet Recital. 2010. 32p. pap. 12.99 *(978-1-4490-8457-8(5))* AuthorHouse.
Howell, Jessica. Lilly Lu & the Pink Tutu. 2007. 29p. pap. 24.95 *(978-1-4241-8398-2(7))* America Star Bks.
Idle, Molly. Flora & the Chicks. 2017. (ENG., Illus.). 20p. (J). bds. 9.99 *(978-1-4521-4657-7(8))* Chronicle Bks. LLC.
—Flora & the Ostrich: An Opposites Book. 2017. (ENG., Illus.). 20p. (J). (gr. -1 — 1). bds. 9.99 *(978-1-4521-4658-4(6))* Chronicle Bks. LLC.
—Flora & the Peacocks. 2016. (ENG., Illus.). 40p. (J). (gr. -1-k). 17.99 *(978-1-4521-3816-9(8))* Chronicle Bks. LLC.
—Flora & the Penguin. 2014. (ENG., Illus.). 40p. (J). (gr. -1-k). 16.99 *(978-1-4521-2891-7(X))* Chronicle Bks. LLC.
Idle, Molly, illus. Flora & the Flamingo. 2013. (ENG.). 44p. (J). (gr. -1-1). 17.99 *(978-1-4521-1006-6(9))* Chronicle Bks. LLC.
Isadora, Rachel. Bea at Ballet. Isadora, Rachel, illus. (ENG., Illus.). 32p. (J). (gr. -1 — 1). 2014. bds. 7.99 *(978-0-399-16844-4(3))* 2012. 12.99 *(978-0-399-25409-3(9))* Penguin Young Readers Group. (Nancy Paulsen Books).
Janni, Rebecca. Jammy Dance, 1 vol. Dockray, Tracy, illus. 2012. (ENG.). 40p. (J). (gr. -1-1). 16.99 *(978-0-374-33680-6(6),* 9780374336806, Farrar, Straus & Giroux (BYR)) Farrar, Straus & Giroux.
Jennings, Sharon. Dancing on the Edge. Doherty, Catherine, illus. 2007. (HIP Edge Ser.). 112p. (YA). (gr. 7-18). pap. *(978-1-897039-27-4(1))* High Interest Publishing (HIP).
Joachimowski, Paula L. Swamp Band Lullaby. 2007. (J). per. 12.99 *(978-1-59879-211-9(3))* Lifevest Publishing, Inc.
Johnson, Craig. Dance & Donuts with Dad. 2012. 24p. pap. 17.99 *(978-1-4772-9173-3(3))* AuthorHouse.
Johnson, Stephen. Dance, Dance, Dance! 2016. (J). *(978-1-4169-9950-8(7))* Simon & Schuster Bks. For Young Readers.
Johnson, Tera. Berkeley's Barn Owl Dance. Howells, Tania, illus. 2008. (ENG.). 32p. (J). (gr. -1-2). 16.95 *(978-1-55453-263-6(9))* Kids Can Pr., Ltd. CAN. Dist: Hachette Bk. Group.
Jones, Christianne C. The Elf Boogie. Randall, Emma, illus. 2015. (Holiday Jingles Ser.). (ENG.). 20p. (gr. -1 — 1). bds. 5.99 *(978-1-4795-6493-4(1))* Picture Window Bks.
—The Reindeer Dance. Randall, Emma, illus. 2015. (Holiday Jingles Ser.). (ENG.). 20p. (gr. -1 — 1). bds. 5.99 *(978-1-4795-6496-5(6))* Picture Window Bks.
—The Snowman Shuffle. Randall, Emma, illus. 2015. (Holiday Jingles Ser.). (ENG.). 20p. (gr. -1 — 1). bds. 5.99 *(978-1-4795-6495-8(8))* Picture Window Bks.
Jones, James Lucas & Torres, J., eds. Yo Gabba Gabba: Comic Book Time. 2011. (Illus.). 128p. (J). 24.99 *(978-1-934964-49-1(2))* Oni Pr., Inc.
Jones, Janey Louise. Cloudberry Castle, 1 vol. 2010. (ENG., Illus.). 176p. (J). (gr. 2-5). 11.95 *(978-0-86315-765-3(3))* Floris Bks. GBR. Dist: SteinerBooks, Inc.
—Dancer the Wild Pony. Poh, Jennie, illus. 2016. (Superfairies Ser.). (ENG.). 56p. (gr. k-3). lib. bdg. 23.99 *(978-1-4795-8642-4(0))* Picture Window Bks.
Jones, Kari. Shimmy, 1 vol. 2015. (Orca Limelights Ser.). (ENG.). 144p. (J). (gr. 6-9). pap. 9.95 *(978-1-4598-0764-8(2))* Orca Bk. Pubs. USA.
Joyce, Melaine. Cinderella. 2009. (Fairydust Fairytales Ser.). (ENG.). 5p. (J). (gr. -1-k). bds. 6.95 *(978-1-84696-964-5(6),* TickTock Books) Octopus Publishing Group GBR. Dist: Independent Pubs. Group.
Kaldor, Connie. A Duck in New York City. Fil and Julie Staff, illus. 2005. (ENG.). 36p. (J). (gr. -1-2). 16.95 *(978-2-923163-02-4(8))* La Montagne Secrete CAN. Dist: Independent Pubs. Group.
Kantor, Melissa. Maybe One Day. 2014. (ENG.). 400p. (YA). (gr. 8). 17.99 *(978-0-06-227920-0(3),* HarperTeen) HarperCollins Pubs.
Katz, Karen. Nutcracker Twinkle Toes. 2010. (ENG.). 12p. (J). (gr. -1-k). bds. 8.99 *(978-0-448-45412-2(2),* Grosset & Dunlap) Penguin Young Readers Group.
Keene, Carolyn. Dance Off. Pamintuan, Macky, illus. 2011. (Nancy Drew & the Clue Crew Ser.: 30). (ENG.). 96p. (J). (gr. 1-4). pap. 5.99 *(978-1-4169-9459-6(9),* Aladdin) Simon & Schuster Children's Publishing.
Kent, Allegra. Ballerina Swan. McCully, Emily Arnold, illus. 2012. (ENG.). 32p. (J). (gr. -1-3). 16.95 *(978-0-8234-2373-6(5))* Holiday Hse., Inc.
—Ballerina Swan. McCully, Emily Arnold, illus. 2013. (ENG.). 32p. (J). (gr. -1-3). pap. 6.99 *(978-0-8234-2906-6(7))* Holiday Hse., Inc.
Kephart, Beth. House of Dance. 2010. (ENG.). 272p. (J). (gr. 8). pap. 10.99 *(978-0-06-142930-9(9))* 2008. 263p. (YA). (gr. 7-18). lib. bdg. 17.89 *(978-0-06-142929-3(5))* HarperCollins Pubs. (HarperTeen).
Kiefer, Janet Kennedy. Freckles. 2012. 40p. pap. *(978-1-77097-263-6(3))* FriesenPress.
Kilpatrick, Irene. Foofa's Happy Book. 2009. (Yo Gabba Gabba! Ser.). (ENG.). 12p. (J). (gr. -1-1). bds. 6.99 *(978-1-4169-7855-8(0),* Simon Spotlight) Simon Spotlight.
Kinerk, Robert. Clorinda. Kellogg, Steven, illus. 2007. (ENG.). 40p. (J). (gr. -1-3). 7.99 *(978-1-4169-3964-1(4),* Simon & Schuster/Paula Wiseman Bks.) Simon & Schuster/Paula Wiseman Bks.
Kirwan, Wednesday. Baby Loves to Boogie! Kirwan, Wednesday, illus. 2014. (ENG., Illus.). 30p. (J). (gr. -1 — 1). bds. 5.99 *(978-1-4814-0383-2(4),* Little Simon) Little Simon.
Knudson, Mike & Wilkinson, Steve. Dancing Dudes. Curtis, Stacy, illus. 2010. (Raymond & Graham Ser.). (ENG.). 144p. (J). (gr. 3-7). 6.99 *(978-0-14-241508-5(1),* Puffin Books) Penguin Young Readers Group.
Kodaka, Nao. Magical Dance. 2017. (ENG.). 192p. (J). Vol. 1. pap. 10.99 ***(978-1-4278-5677-7(X),*** 9781427856777) Vol. 2. pap. 10.99 ***(978-1-4278-5679-1(6),*** 9781427856791) TOKYOPOP, Inc.
Krakower, Harold. Sugarland: Sarah's Dance Recital. 2012. 36p. pap. 20.99 *(978-1-4772-6093-7(5))* AuthorHouse.
Krulik, Nancy. Dance Your Pants Off!, No. 9. Blecha, Aaron, illus. 2013. (George Brown, Class Clown Ser.: 9). (ENG.). 128p. (J). (gr. 2-4). pap. 5.99 *(978-0-448-45679-9(6),* Grosset & Dunlap) Penguin Young Readers Group.
—Dance Your Pants Off! 2013. (George Brown, Class Clown Ser.: 9). lib. bdg. 14.75 *(978-0-606-29802-5(9),* Turtleback) Turtleback Bks.
—Tip-Top Tappin' Mom!, 31 vols. John and Wendy Staff, illus. 2009. (Katie Kazoo, Switcheroo Ser.: 31). (ENG.). 80p. (J). (gr. 2-4). pap. 4.99 *(978-0-448-45041-4(0),* Grosset & Dunlap) Penguin Young Readers Group.
Lagonegro, Melissa. The Cookie Boogie (Disney Palace Pets: Whisker Haven Tales) RH Disney, illus. 2016. (Step into Reading Ser.). (ENG.). 24p. (J). (gr. -1-1). 4.99 *(978-0-7364-3623-6(5),* RH/Disney) Random Hse. Children's Bks.
Lamb. Bianca the Dancing Crocodile. Skon, Sandy, illus. 2008. 30p. pap. 24.95 *(978-1-60563-447-0(6))* America Star Bks.
Lancaster, Shannon E. Becky: The Budding Ballerina. 2008. 36p. pap. 15.99 *(978-1-4343-9860-4(9))* AuthorHouse.
Lasota, Mary. Kitty Piper, Angel Cat, Book 2: The Venusians Have Landed. 2010. 40p. pap. 18.46 *(978-1-4520-8823-5(3))* AuthorHouse.
Layne, Casey & Jordan, Cedar. The Back Alley Pupsters: Zac & Roxie for the Win. Fischer, Shan, illus. 2013. (ENG.). (J). (gr. -1-3). 14.95 *(978-1-62086-300-8(6))* Mascot Bks., Inc.
Leach, Sara. Warm Up, 1 vol. 2014. (Orca Limelights Ser.). (ENG.). 128p. (J). (gr. 6-9). pap. 9.95 *(978-1-4598-0428-9(7))* Orca Bk. Pubs. USA.
Lester, Helen & Munsinger, Lynn. Happy Birdday, Tacky! Lester, Helen & Munsinger, Lynn, illus. 2013. (Tacky the Penguin Ser.). (ENG., Illus.). 32p. (J). (gr. -1-3). 16.99 *(978-0-547-91228-8(5))* Houghton Mifflin Harcourt Publishing Co.
Let's Dance. 2003. (J). per. *(978-1-57657-875-9(5))* Paradise Pr., Inc.
Lickens, Alice V. Dance to the Boogaloo? 2014. (ENG., Illus.). 32p. (J). (gr. -1-k). pap. 9.99 *(978-1-84365-229-8(3),* Pavilion) Pavilion Bks. GBR. Dist: Independent Pubs. Group.
Lieberman, Leanne. Off Pointe, 1 vol. 2014. (Orca Limelights Ser.). (ENG.). 128p. (J). (gr. 6-9). pap. 9.95 *(978-1-4598-0280-3(2))* Orca Bk. Pubs. USA.
Lindner, Brooke. Dance with Brobee! (Yo Gabba Gabba! Ser.). (ENG.). 12p. (J). (gr. -1-1). 2012. bds. 5.99 *(978-1-4424-5445-3(8))* 2009. bds. 6.99 *(978-1-4169-7516-8(0))* Simon Spotlight. (Simon Spotlight).
Litwin, Eric. The Nuts: Sing & Dance in Your Polka Dot Pants. Magoon, Scott, illus. 2015. (ENG.). 32p. (J). (gr. -1-3). 18.00 *(978-0-316-32250-8(4))* Little Brown & Co.
Lord, Michelle & Hoshino, Felicia. Little Sap & Monsieur Rodin, 1 vol. 2006. (ENG., Illus.). 32p. (J). (gr. 1-5). 16.95 *(978-1-58430-248-3(8))* Lee & Low Bks., Inc.
Lorenz, Nancy. The Strength of Ballerinas. 2014. 249p. (YA). pap. 15.99 *(978-1-4621-1452-8(0))* Cedar Fort, Inc./CFI Distribution.
Love, Nicole M. Cool Cougar! Cool Cougar! Cool Cougar! & the Puma Dance. 2012. 24p. pap. 17.99 *(978-1-4685-7541-5(4))* AuthorHouse.
Lynn, Sarah. Tip-Tap Pop, 0 vols. Docampo, Valeria, illus. 2010. (ENG.). 32p. (J). (gr. -1-4). 17.99 *(978-0-7614-5712-1(7),* 9780761457121, Amazon Children's Publishing) Amazon Publishing.
Maccarone, Grace. A Day with Miss Lina's Ballerinas. Davenier, Christine, illus. 2014. (My Readers Ser.). (ENG.). 32p. (J). (gr. k-2). 15.99 *(978-1-250-04716-8(1),* 9781250047168) Square Fish.
—A Day with Miss Lina's Ballerinas. 2014. (My Readers: Level 1 Ser.). (J). lib. bdg. 13.55 *(978-0-606-35524-7(3))* Turtleback Bks.
MacKenzie, Jill. Spin the Sky. 2016. (ENG.). 352p. (YA). (gr. 6). 17.99 *(978-1-5107-0686-6(0),* Sky Pony Pr.) Skyhorse Publishing Co., Inc.
Macy, Tana. Tap Shoes & Horse Shoes. Gardiner, Nancy, illus. 2011. 50p. pap. 18.00 *(978-1-60976-086-1(7),* Eloquent Bks.) Strategic Book Publishing & Rights Agency (SBPRA).
Maddocks, Maria, illus. Two Little Ballerinas: A Girly Girl Book. 2009. (ENG.). 10p. (J). 9.95 *(978-1-58117-871-5(9),* Intervisual/Piggy Toes) Bendon, Inc.
Maddox, Jake. Dance Team Dilemma, 1 vol. Wood, Katie, illus. 2013. (Jake Maddox Girl Sports Stories Ser.). (ENG.). 72p. (gr. 2-3). pap. 5.95 *(978-1-4342-4201-3(3));* lib. bdg. 25.32 *(978-1-4342-4014-9(2))* Stone Arch Bks.
—Dancing Solo, 1 vol. Wood, Katie, illus. 2014. (Jake Maddox Girl Sports Stories Ser.). (ENG.). 72p. (gr. 2-3). 25.32 *(978-1-4342-4142-9(4))* Stone Arch Bks.
Magsamen, Sandra. You're Tutu Cute! 2014. (ENG., Illus.). 10p. (J). (gr. -1 — 1). bds. 7.99 *(978-0-316-25517-2(3))* Little, Brown Bks. for Young Readers.
Manushkin, Fran. Keep Dancing, Katie, 1 vol. 2014. (Katie Woo Ser.). (ENG.). 32p. (gr. k-2). 21.32 *(978-1-4795-5187-3(2))* Picture Window Bks.
Maresca, Beth Anne, illus. Megan Owlet. 2015. (ENG.). 32p. (J). (gr. -1-k). 16.99 *(978-1-63220-404-2(5),* Sky Pony Pr.) Skyhorse Publishing Co., Inc.
Marguerita, Ann. Fannie Annie & Her Little White Shoes. 2008. (Illus.). 68p. per. *(978-1-84748-259-4(7))* Athena Pr.
Martin, Bill & Sampson, Michael R. Spunky Little Monkey. Won, Brian, illus. 2017. (ENG.). 32p. (J). (gr. -1-k). 17.99 *(978-0-545-77643-1(0),* Scholastic Pr.) Scholastic, Inc.
Martin, Dawn L. Freeze Dance: A Story of the Dancing Cactus. 2011. 36p. pap. *(978-1-4269-8196-8(1))* Trafford Publishing (UK) Ltd.
Mastnak, Rosemary. Dancing with Grandma. Mastnak, Rosemary, illus. 2016. (ENG., Illus.). 32p. (J). (gr. -1-k). pap. 9.99 *(978-1-76012-618-6(7))* Little Hare Bks. AUS. Dist: Independent Pubs. Group.
May, Tessa. Bella Wishes. Rodriguez, Dave, illus. 2004. 35p. pap. 13.95 incl. audio compact disk *(978-0-9759325-0-6(0))* CarLou Interactive Media & Publishing.
McDaniel, Lurlene. Last Dance. 2006. (ENG.). 144p. (YA). (gr. 7-12). pap. 4.99 *(978-1-58196-031-0(X),* Darby Creek) Lerner Publishing Group.
McDonald, Abby. The Anti-Prom. 2011. (ENG., Illus.). 288p. (YA). (gr. 9-18). 16.99 *(978-0-7636-4956-2(2))* Candlewick Pr.
McKay, Kirsty. Ogres Do Disco. Judge, Chris, illus. 2016. (ENG.). 160p. (J). (gr. 2-4). 9.99 *(978-1-78344-296-6(4))* Andersen Pr. GBR. Dist: Independent Pubs. Group.
McLaren, Clemence. Dance for the Aina. 2003. 160p. 9.95 *(978-1-57306-151-3(4))* Bess Pr., Inc.
McMillan, Sue. The Star of the Show. Sapp, Karen, illus. 2014. (J). ***(978-0-545-81560-4(6))*** Scholastic, Inc.
McMullen, Nigel. Let's Dance, Grandma! McMullen, Nigel, illus. 2014. (ENG., Illus.). 32p. (J). (gr. -1-3). 16.99 *(978-0-06-050747-3(0))* HarperCollins Pubs.
Meadows, Daisy. Jade the Disco Fairy. 2009. (Rainbow Magic — the Dance Fairies Ser.). lib. bdg. 14.75 *(978-0-606-05380-8(8),* Turtleback) Turtleback Bks.
—Jessica the Jazz Fairy. 2009. (Rainbow Magic — the Dance Fairies Ser.). lib. bdg. 14.75 *(978-0-606-05439-3(1),* Turtleback) Turtleback Bks.
—Shannon the Ocean Fairy. 2009. (Rainbow Magic Ser.). (ENG.). 176p. (J). (gr. 2-5). 6.99 *(978-0-545-10576-7(5),* Scholastic Paperbacks) Scholastic, Inc.
—Vanessa the Choreography Fairy. 2013. (Rainbow Magic — the Superstar Fairies Ser.: 3). lib. bdg. 14.75 *(978-0-606-31515-9(2),* Turtleback) Turtleback Bks.
Meister, Cari. Flash Forward Fairy Tales: Cinderella in the City. 2014. (Scholastic Reader Level 2 Ser.). lib. bdg. 13.55 *(978-0-606-35820-0(X))* Turtleback Bks.
Meron, Renato Mas. Why Mangrove Roots Float. 2013. 20p. pap. 24.95 *(978-1-63000-427-9(8))* America Star Bks.
Meyer, Carolyn. Marie, Dancing. 2007. (ENG., Illus.). 272p. (YA). (gr. 7-18). pap. 15.95 *(978-0-15-205879-1(6))* Houghton Mifflin Harcourt Publishing Co.
Miller, Sibley. Heads Up, Horses! 2009. (Wind Dancers Ser.: 5). (ENG., Illus.). 80p. (J). (gr. 1-4). pap. 16.99 *(978-0-312-56220-5(9),* 9780312562205) Feiwel & Friends.
—Horses Her Way. Chang, Tara Larsen & Gershman, Jo, illus. 2009. (Wind Dancers Ser.: 6). (ENG.). 80p. (J). (gr. 1-4). pap. 16.99 *(978-0-312-56279-3(9),* 9780312562793) Feiwel & Friends.
Mills, Nancy Libbey. And Dance with the Orange Cow. Wells, Shan, illus. 2003. 32p. (J). pap. 7.95 *(978-1-893815-10-0(2));* per. 12.95 *(978-1-893815-09-4(9))* Pie in the Sky Publishing, LLC.
Mills, Timothy. The Mystery Kids: the Phantom Camper. 2010. 88p. pap. 14.95 *(978-0-557-55089-0(0))* Lulu Pr., Inc.
Mitton, Tony. Dinosaurumpus! Parker-Rees, Guy, illus. 2014. (ENG.). 30p. (J). (gr. -1-k). bds. 6.99 *(978-0-545-69480-3(9),* Cartwheel Bks.) Scholastic, Inc.
Mitton, Tony. Down by the Cool of the Pool (a StoryPlay Book) Parker-Rees, Guy, illus. 2017. (StoryPlay Ser.). (ENG.). 32p. (J). (gr. -1-k). 5.99 ***(978-1-338-15841-0(4),*** Cartwheel Bks.) Scholastic, Inc.
Montague, Gay & Wise, Erin. Peace Is a Bright Delight. 2008. 28p. pap. 13.99 *(978-1-4389-2153-2(5))* AuthorHouse.
Moses, Anne E. Gatos Musikos: A Secret Told by the Moon. 2013. (Illus.). 58p. 24.95 *(978-1-4575-2189-8(X))* Dog Ear Publishing, LLC.
Moss, Alexandra, pseud. Isabelle's Perfect Performance. 2005. (Royal Ballet School Diaries: 3). (ENG.). 144p. (J). (gr. 3-7). 5.99 *(978-0-448-43769-9(4),* Grosset & Dunlap) Penguin Young Readers Group.
Ms. Sue. Where Is Your Name? Ducy, George, illus. 2009. 24p. pap. 24.95 *(978-1-60672-711-9(7))* America Star Bks.
Mull, David Kenneth. His Date for the Dance was His Science Project. 2012. 80p. pap. 9.99 *(978-0-89824-371-0(8))* Royal Fireworks Publishing Co.
Nobisso, Josephine. The Numbers Dance: A Counting Comedy. Ziborova, Dasha, illus. 2005. (ENG.). 32p. (J). (gr. k-2). 16.95 *(978-0-940112-11-7(6));* pap. 8.95 *(978-0-940112-12-4(4))* Gingerbread Hse.
Noensie, Pamela & Lamore, Garretta. Tari: the Little Balinese Dancer. 2013. (ENG., Illus.). 32p. (J). (gr. k-3). 14.95 *(978-0-8048-4387-4(2))* Tuttle Publishing.
Numeroff, Laura Joffe & Evans, Nate. The Jellybeans & the Big Dance. Munsinger, Lynn, illus. 2008. (ENG.). 32p. (J). (gr. -1-1). 17.95 *(978-0-8109-9352-5(X),* Abrams Bks. for Young Readers) Abrams, Inc.
Ocean, Davy. Splash Dance. Blecha, Aaron, illus. 2015. (Shark School Ser.: 6). (ENG.). 128p. (J). (gr. 1-4). pap. 5.99 *(978-1-4814-0694-9(9),* Aladdin) Simon & Schuster Children's Publishing.
Olesen, Demetria Vassiliou. Lambyro. Forcada, Adiela & Giron, Elizabeth, illus. 2011. (ENG.). 32p. (J). 19.00 *(978-0-615-47664-3(3))* Elissian Publishing Co.
Ormerod, Jan. The Animal Bop Won't Stop! Gardiner, Lindsey, illus. 2011. (J). *(978-1-4380-8419-0(6))* Barron's Educational Series, Inc.
Ormerod, Jan & Gardiner, Lindsey. Doing the Animal Bop. 2005. (ENG., Illus.). 32p. (J). (gr. -1-k). pap. 11.99 *(978-0-7641-7899-3(7))* Barron's Educational Series, Inc.
Ortiz, Raquel M. & Ventura, Gabriela Baeza. Sofi & the Magic, Musical Mural. Dominguez, Maria, illus. 2015. (SPA & ENG.). (J). 17.95 *(978-1-55885-803-9(2),* Piñata Books) Arte Publico Pr.
Osborne, Robin. The Boy who Loved to Shim-sham Shimmy. 2004. (Illus.). 40p. (J). lib. bdg. 14.95 *(978-0-9762852-0-5(7))* Wooden Shoe Pr.
Oxenbury, Helen. La Clase de Baile (Dance Class) (SPA.). 16p. (J). 7.50 *(978-84-261-1947-6(6))* Juventud, Editorial ESP. Dist: AIMS International Bks., Inc.
Pace, Anne Marie. Vampirina Ballerina. Pham, LeUyen, illus. 2012. (Vampirina Ser.). (ENG.). 40p. (J). (gr. -1-k). 16.99 *(978-1-4231-5753-3(2))* Hyperion Pr.
—Vampirina Ballerina Hosts a Sleepover. Pham, LeUyen, illus. 2013. (Vampirina Ser.). (ENG.). 40p. (J). (gr. -1-k). 16.99 *(978-1-4231-7570-4(0))* Hyperion Pr.
Padian, Maria. Jersey Tomatoes Are the Best. 2012. (ENG.). 352p. (YA). (gr. 7). pap. 9.99 *(978-0-375-86563-3(2),* Ember) Random Hse. Children's Bks.

C
D

Parish, Herman. Amelia Bedelia Chapter Book #8: Amelia Bedelia Dances Off. Avril, Lynne, illus. 2015. (Amelia Bedelia Ser.). (ENG.). 160p. (J). (gr. 1-5). 15.99 *(978-0-06-233409-1(3)*, Greenwillow Bks.) HarperCollins Pubs.

—Amelia Bedelia Dances Off. 2015. (Amelia Bedelia Chapter Book Ser.: 8). (J). lib. bdg. 14.75 *(978-0-606-37635-8(6))* Turtleback Bks.

Parker, Emma. Dancing Class. 2010. (Illus.). pap. *(978-1-877561-05-4(3))* First Edition Ltd.

—Missy Hip Hoppo. 2010. (Illus.). 16p. pap. *(978-1-877561-56-6(8))* First Edition Ltd.

Parkinson, Kate. Grace. Parkinson, Kate, illus. 2015. (ENG., Illus.). 24p. (J). (gr. -1-3). 6.99 *(978-0-8234-3317-9(X))*; 14.95 *(978-0-8234-3207-3(6))* Holiday Hse., Inc.

Pavanello, Roberto. The Dancing Vampire. Zeni, Marco, tr. from ITA. Pisapia, Blasco & Brughera, Pamela, illus. 2012. (Echo & the Bat Pack Ser.). (ENG.). 128p. (gr. 2-3). 25.32 *(978-1-4342-3837-5(7)*, Echo & the Bat Pack) Stone Arch Bks.

Phipps, Alisha. Growing up with Allie: The Dance. 2005. 58p. pap. 16.95 *(978-1-4137-9713-8(X))* PublishAmerica, Inc.

Pichon, Liz. Everything's Amazing (Sort Of) Pichon, Liz, illus. 2015. (Tom Gates Ser.: 3). (ENG., Illus.). 416p. (J). (gr. 3-7). 12.99 *(978-0-7636-7473-1(7))* Candlewick Pr.

Pinkwater, Daniel M. Dancing Larry, 1 vol. Pinkwater, Jill, illus. 2006. (ENG.). 32p. (J). (gr. -1-3). 16.95 *(978-0-7614-5220-1(6))* Marshall Cavendish Corp.

Pirnot, Karen Hutchins. The Blue Penguin. Klanot, Makenna Karen, illus. 2008. 44p. pap. 14.95 *(978-1-934246-79-5(4))* Peppertree Pr., The.

Powell, Jillian. Hattie the Dancing Hippo. Dodson, Emma, illus. 2009. (Get Ready (Windmill Books) Ser.). 32p. (J). (gr. k-2). lib. bdg. 22.60 *(978-1-60754-264-3(1))* Windmill Bks.

—Hattie the Dancing Hippo. Dodson, Emma, illus. 2011. 32p. pap. *(978-1-84089-709-8(0))* Zero to Ten, Ltd.

Princess Aurora: A Special Day in Her Life. l.t. ed. 2005. (Illus.). 32p. (J). 5.95 *(978-0-9766640-0-0(3)*, 212-279-3492) Attitudes in Dressing, Inc.

Publications International Ltd. Staff, creator. Let's Dance!Vamos a Bailar! 2007. (Play-A-Sound Ser.). (J). 17.98 *(978-1-4127-9276-9(2))* Publications International, Ltd.

Pung, Alice & Masciullo, Lucia. Marly Walks on the Moon. 2016. (Our Australian Girl Ser.: 4). (ENG.). 144p. (J). (gr. 3-7). 12.99 *(978-0-14-330852-2(1))* Penguin Books Australia AUS. Dist: Independent Pubs. Group.

Quay, Emma. Scarlett, Starlet. 2017. 32p. 17.99 *(978-0-7333-3158-9(0))* ABC Bks. AUS. Dist: HarperCollins Pubs.

Rae, Angela. The Choices Witch Make Us. 2008. 113p. pap. 15.95 *(978-1-4357-4287-1(7))* Lulu Pr., Inc.

Ralls, Ken. Henrietta Hippo Learns to Dance. McQuitty, LaVonia Corbin, illus. 2nd ed. 2013. 24p. (J). 15.00 *(978-0-9884125-3-8(5))* Scribe's Closet Pubns., The.

Random House Disney Staff. Dancing Cinderella/Belle of the Ball. Random House Disney Staff, illus. 2009. (Pictureback(R) Ser.). (ENG., Illus.). 32p. (J). (gr. -1-2). pap. 4.99 *(978-0-7364-2560-5(8)*, RH/Disney) Random Hse. Children's Bks.

Random House Staff. Dancing with the Star (SpongeBob SquarePants) Random House Staff, illus. 2013. (Step into Reading Ser.). (ENG., Illus.). 32p. (J). (gr. -1-1). pap. 3.99 *(978-0-449-81438-3(6)*, Random Hse. Bks. for Young Readers) Random Hse. Children's Bks.

Ray, Mary Lyn. Deer Dancer. Stringer, Lauren, illus. 2014. (ENG.). 40p. (J). (gr. -1-3). 17.99 *(978-1-4424-3421-9(X)*, Beach Lane Bks.) Beach Lane Bks.

Redbank, Tennant. Pumpkin: Cinderella's Dancing Pup (Disney Princess: Palace Pets) RH Disney Staff et al, illus. 2015. (Disney Chapters Ser.). (ENG.). 64p. (J). (gr. 1-4). 5.99 *(978-0-7364-3423-2(2)*, RH/Disney) Random Hse. Children's Bks.

Reiner, Angela. You Can't Dance in Those Pants. 2008. 28p. pap. 18.65 *(978-1-4363-6798-1(0))* Xlibris Corp.

Rey, H. A. Curious George Dance Party CGTV Reader. 2013. (Curious George Ser.). (ENG., Illus.). 24p. (J). (gr. -1-3). 12.99 *(978-0-547-96819-3(1))* Houghton Mifflin Harcourt Publishing Co.

—Dance Party. 2013. (Curious George Ser.). (ENG., Illus.). 24p. (J). (gr. -1-3). pap. 3.99 *(978-0-547-96820-9(5))* Houghton Mifflin Harcourt Publishing Co.

—Jorge el Curioso el Baile. 2013. (Curious George Ser.). (SPA & ENG., Illus.). 24p. (J). (gr. -1-3). pap. 3.99 *(978-0-547-96822-3(1))* Houghton Mifflin Harcourt Publishing Co.

Rippin, Sally. The Bad Butterfly. Fukuoka, Aki, illus. 2012. 44p. (J). *(978-1-61067-132-3(5))* Kane Miller.

—The Copycat Kid: Billie B. Brown. Fukuoka, Aki, illus. 2016. (ENG.). 48p. (J). pap. 4.99 *(978-1-61067-389-1(1))* Kane Miller.

Robins, Eleanor. The Secret Admirer Mystery, 1 vol. unabr. ed. 2011. (Carter High Mysteries Ser.). (ENG.). 48p. (YA). (gr. 9-12). 7.95 *(978-1-61651-567-6(8))* Saddleback Educational Publishing, Inc.

Rochester, Andre, illus. The Sunflower & Rose. 2010. (ENG.). 36p. (J). 22.95 *(978-0-9817291-1-4(8))* Metaphors 4 Life.

Rodda, Emily. The Flower Fairies. Vitale, Raoul, illus. 2003. (Fairy Realm Ser.). 128p. (J). 8.99 *(978-0-06-009586-4(5))* HarperCollins Pubs.

Rottenberg, David Ira & Rottenberg, David Ira. Gwendolyn Goes Hollywood. Anderson, Lesley, illus. 2011. 40p. (J). 16.99 *(978-0-910291-11-8(X))* Cedar Crest Bks.

Rovetch, L. Bob. Frog Went A-Dancing. Berry, Holly, illus. 2006. (J). *(978-1-58987-008-6(5))* Kindermusik International.

Rubin, Sarah. Someday Dancer. 2012. (J). *(978-0-545-39379-9(5))* Scholastic, Inc.

Ruiz-Flores, Lupe. Lupita's First Dance / el Primer Baile de Lupita. Baeza Ventura, Gabriela, tr. Utomo, Gabhor, illus. 2013. (SPA.). 32p. (J). 17.95 *(978-1-55885-772-8(9)*, Piñata Books) Arte Publico Pr.

Ruiz-Flores, Lupe & Rosales-Yeomans, Natalia. Let's Salsa. Rosales-Yeomans, Natalia, tr. Casilla, Robert, illus. 2013.Tr. of Bailemos Salsa. (SPA & ENG.). 32p. (J). 17.95 *(978-1-55885-762-9(1)*, Piñata Books) Arte Publico Pr.

Ryder, Joanne. Dance by the Light of the Moon. Francis, Guy, illus. 2006. (ENG.). 40p. (J). (gr. -1-1). 15.99 *(978-0-7868-1820-4(4))* Hyperion Pr.

Rylant, Cynthia. Mr. Putter & Tabby Dance the Dance. 2013. (Mr. Putter & Tabby Ser.). lib. bdg. 16.00 *(978-0-606-32338-3(4)*, Turtleback) Turtleback Bks.

Rylant, Cynthia & Howard, Arthur. Mr. Putter & Tabby Dance the Dance. Howard, Arthur, illus. 2013. (Mr. Putter & Tabby Ser.). (ENG., Illus.). 40p. (J). (gr. 1-4). pap. 5.99 *(978-0-544-10496-9(X))* Houghton Mifflin Harcourt Publishing Co.

Sanders, Rob. Ruby Rose, Big Bravos. Ohi, Debbie Ridpath, illus. 2017. 40p. (J). (gr. -1-3). 15.99 ***(978-0-06-223571-8(0))*** HarperCollins Pubs.

Sargent, Dave, et al. Tattoos of Honor Vol. 17: (Osage) Be Gentle & Giving, 20 vols. Lenoir, Jane, illus. l.t. ed. 2004. (Story Keeper Ser.: Vol. 17). 42p. (J). pap. 10.95 *(978-1-56763-936-0(4))*; lib. bdg. 23.60 *(978-1-56763-935-3(6))* Ozark Publishing.

Sarn, Amélie & Trouillot, Virgile. The Audition. 2009. (Groove High Ser.). (Illus.). 112p. (YA). (gr. 5-8). 31.95 *(978-1-60754-203-2(X)*, 1293913); pap. 15.25 *(978-1-60754-204-9(8)*, 1293913) Windmill Bks.

—A Day of Surprises. 2009. (Groove High Ser.). (Illus.). 112p. (YA). (gr. 5-8). 31.95 *(978-1-60754-209-4(9)*, 1293912); pap. 15.25 *(978-1-60754-210-0(2)*, 1293912) Windmill Bks.

—Looking for Trouble. 2009. (Groove High Ser.). (Illus.). 112p. (YA). (gr. 5-8). 31.95 *(978-1-60754-206-3(4)*, 1293914); pap. 15.25 *(978-1-60754-207-0(2)*, 1293914) Windmill Bks.

—Love Is in the Air. Ducrest, Olivier, illus. 2009. (Groove High Ser.). 112p. (YA). (gr. 5-8). 31.95 *(978-1-60754-212-4(9)*, 1293915); pap. 15.25 *(978-1-60754-213-1(7)*, 1293915) Windmill Bks.

Sauer, Tammi. Chicken Dance. Santat, Dan, illus. 2015. (ENG.). 40p. (J). (gr. -1-2). pap. 6.95 *(978-1-4549-1477-8(7))* Sterling Publishing Co., Inc.

Schaefer, Elizabeth. Ballet Lesson. 2014. (Peppa Pig 8X8 Ser.). lib. bdg. 13.55 *(978-0-606-35866-8(8))* Turtleback Bks.

Scheffrin-Falk, Gladys. Another Celebrated Dancing Bear. Garrison, Barbara, illus. (J). 2007. 32p. (gr. -1-3). 18.95 *(978-1-930900-35-6(X))* 20th ed. 2011. 28p. 18.95 *(978-1-930900-50-9(3))* Purple Hse. Pr.

Schofield-Morrison, Connie. I Got the Rhythm. Morrison, Frank, illus. 2014. (ENG.). 32p. (J). (gr. -1-1). 16.99 *(978-1-61963-178-6(4)*, 9781619631786, Bloomsbury USA Childrens) Bloomsbury Publishing USA.

Schreiber, Ellen. Dance with a Vampire. 2009. (Vampire Kisses Ser.: 4). (ENG.). 208p. (YA). (gr. 8). pap. 8.99 *(978-0-06-177898-8(2)*, Tegen, Katherine Bks) HarperCollins Pubs.

Schulz. Permetti Questo Ballo Charl. pap. 19.95 *(978-88-451-8058-3(1))* Fabbri Editori - RCS Libri ITA. Dist: Distribooks, Inc.

Schwab, Victoria. Last Wishes. 2014. (Everyday Angel Ser.: 3). (ENG.). 208p. (J). (gr. 3-7). pap. 6.99 *(978-0-545-52848-1(8)*, Scholastic Paperbacks) Scholastic, Inc.

Schwartz, Fletcher. Willim was a Dancer. 2003. 60p. per. 12.95 *(978-1-932344-48-6(9))* Thornton Publishing, Inc.

Shaw, Natalie. OLIVIA Dances for Joy. Spaziante, Patrick, illus. 2012. (Olivia TV Tie-In Ser.). (ENG.). 24p. (J). (gr. -1-1). 16.99 *(978-1-4424-5257-2(9)*, Simon Spotlight) Simon Spotlight.

Shields, Carol Diggory. Saturday Night at the Dinosaur Stomp. 2008. (gr. k-3). 17.20 *(978-0-613-74752-3(6)*, Turtleback) Turtleback Bks.

Sia, Cress. The Bamboo Dance. Butler, Lisa, illus. 2011. (ENG.). 32p. (J). (gr. -1-3). 12.99 *(978-0-615-48984-1(2))* Hartlyn Kids Media, LLC.

Siegel, Siena Cherson. To Dance: A Ballerina's Graphic Novel. Siegel, Mark, illus. 2006. (ENG.). 64p. (J). (gr. 3-9). 19.99 *(978-0-689-86747-7(6)*, Atheneum/Richard Jackson Bks.); pap. 10.99 *(978-1-4169-2687-0(9)*, Atheneum Bks. for Young Readers) Simon & Schuster Children's Publishing.

Sif, Birgitta. Frances Dean Who Loved to Dance & Dance. Sif, Birgitta, illus. 2014. (ENG., Illus.). 32p. (J). (gr. -1-3). 15.99 *(978-0-7636-7306-2(4))* Candlewick Pr.

Silver Dolphin en Español Staff, creator. El Baile de las Princesas. 2005. (Disney Princess Ser.). (SPA., Illus.). 16p. (J). (gr. -1-7). *(978-970-718-288-2(1)*, Silver Dolphin en Español) Advanced Marketing, S. de R. L. de C. V.

Silves, Kate. Jamie the Giraffe Learns to Dance. 2013. 20p. pap. 13.77 *(978-1-4669-7305-3(6))* Trafford Publishing.

Simon, Chaman. Dance Team. 2013. (Surviving Southside Ser.). (ENG.). 104p. (YA). (gr. 6-12). pap. 7.95 *(978-1-4677-0707-7(4)*, Darby Creek); lib. bdg. 27.93 *(978-1-4677-0313-0(3))* Lerner Publishing Group.

Simon, Francesca. Higgledy Piggledy the Hen Who Loved to Dance. Moseng, Elisabeth, illus. 2016. (ENG.). 32p. (J). 17.99 *(978-0-00-813946-9(6)*, HarperCollins Children's Bks.) HarperCollins Pubs. Ltd. GBR. Dist: HarperCollins Pubs.

Sinclair, Gardine. Keira at Stageschool. 2013. 186p. (J). pap. *(978-1-78299-387-2(8))* FeedARead.com.

—Stageschool by the Sea. 2013. 176p. (J). pap. *(978-1-78299-389-6(4))* FeedARead.com.

Singer, Marilyn. Tallulah's Solo. Boiger, Alexandra, illus. 2012. (Tallulah Ser.). (ENG.). 40p. (J). (gr. -1-3). 16.99 *(978-0-547-33004-4(9))* Houghton Mifflin Harcourt Publishing Co.

—Tallulah's Tap Shoes. Boiger, Alexandra, illus. 2015. (ENG.). 48p. (J). (gr. -1-3). 16.99 *(978-0-544-23687-5(4))* Houghton Mifflin Harcourt Publishing Co.

—Tallulah's Tutu. Boiger, Alexandra, illus. 2011. (ENG.). 40p. (J). (gr. -1-3). 16.99 *(978-0-547-17353-5(9))* Houghton Mifflin Harcourt Publishing Co.

Smith, Alex T. Claude in the Spotlight, 1 vol. Smith, Alex T., illus. 2015. (Claude Ser.). (ENG., Illus.). 96p. (J). (gr. 1-3). 12.95 *(978-1-56145-895-0(3))* Peachtree Pubs.

Snyder, Betsy E., illus. I Can Dance. 2015. (ENG.). 14p. (J). (gr. -1 — 1). bds. 8.99 *(978-1-4521-2929-7(0))* Chronicle Bks. LLC.

SoftPlay Staff, contrib. by. Dora's Happy Dance. 2007. 8p. 12.98 *(978-1-59292-229-1(5))* SoftPlay, Inc.

Spalding, Andrea. Dance Baby Dance, 1 vol. 2009. (ENG.). 24p. (J). (gr. -1 — 1). bds. 9.95 *(978-1-55469-079-4(X))* Orca Bk. Pubs. USA.

Speer, Beth. LuLa. 2010. 24p. pap. 13.99 *(978-1-4520-1549-1(X))* AuthorHouse.

Spinelli, Eileen. Boy, Can He Dance! Yalowitz, Paul, illus. 2012. (ENG.). 32p. (J). (gr. -1-3). 16.99 *(978-1-4424-7441-3(6)*, Simon & Schuster Bks. For Young Readers) Simon & Schuster Bks. For Young Readers.

Squillace, Elisa, illus. Down in the Jungle. 2005. (Classic Books with Holes Board Book Ser.). (ENG.). 14p. (J). (gr. -1-1). bds. *(978-1-904550-61-7(4))* Child's Play International Ltd.

Stanton, Elizabeth Rose. Peddles. Stanton, Elizabeth Rose, illus. 2016. (ENG., Illus.). 40p. (J). (gr. -1-3). 17.99 *(978-1-4814-1691-7(X)*, Simon & Schuster Bks. For Young Readers) Simon & Schuster Bks. For Young Readers.

Step up 2: the Streets. 2008. 160p. pap. 4.99 *(978-1-4231-1319-5(5))* Disney Pr.

Stevenson, James. Flying Feet: A Mud Flat Story. Stevenson, James, illus. 2004. (Illus.). 48p. (J). 15.99 *(978-0-06-051975-9(4))* HarperCollins Pubs.

Stihler, Cherie B. Polar Polka: Counting Polar Bears in Alaska. Brooks, Erik, illus. 2008. (Paws IV Ser.). (ENG.). 32p. (J). (gr. -1-2). pap. 10.95 *(978-1-57061-520-7(9)*, Little Bigfoot) Sasquatch Bks.

Stout, Shawn K. Ballerina Weather Girl. Martini, Angela, illus. 2013. (Not-So-Ordinary Girl Ser.: 1). (ENG.). 192p. (J). (gr. 1-5). pap. 5.99 *(978-1-4424-7401-7(7)*, Aladdin) Simon & Schuster Children's Publishing.

—Ballerina Weather Girl. Martini, Angela, illus. 2013. (Not-So-Ordinary Girl Ser.: 1). (ENG.). 192p. (J). (gr. 1-5). 15.99 *(978-1-4424-7402-4(5)*, Simon & Schuster/Paula Wiseman Bks.) Simon & Schuster/Paula Wiseman Bks.

Strathy, Glen C. Dancing on the Inside. 2013. 236p. pap. 15.95 *(978-1-938908-28-6(7)*, iUniverse Star) iUniverse, Inc.

Swedeen, Staci. The Rumor Report, the Big Jump. 2011. (Readers' & Writers' Genre Workshop Ser.). (YA). pap. *(978-1-4509-3013-0(1))* Benchmark Education Co.

Taddonio, Lea. Book 1: First Dance. 2016. (Head over Heels Ser.). (ENG.). (J). (gr. 2-8). lib. bdg. 28.50 ***(978-1-62402-192-3(1))*** ABDO Publishing Co.

Taylor, Chloe. Lights, Camera, Fashion! Zhang, Nancy, illus. 2013. (Sew Zoey Ser.: 3). (ENG.). 176p. (J). (gr. 3-7). 15.99 *(978-1-4424-8980-6(4))*; pap. 5.99 *(978-1-4424-8979-0(0))* Simon Spotlight. (Simon Spotlight).

Taylor, Je'. The Animal Dance. 2009. 32p. pap. 14.49 *(978-1-4490-2626-4(5))* AuthorHouse.

Teague, Mark. The Sky Is Falling! 2015. (ENG., Illus.). 32p. (J). (gr. -1-k). 16.99 *(978-0-545-63217-1(X))* Scholastic, Inc.

Terada, Junzo. Animal Friends: Barnyard Jamboree! 2017. (ENG., Illus.). 10p. (J). bds. 9.99 *(978-1-4521-5189-2(X))* Chronicle Bks. LLC.

Thaler, Mike. The Spring Dance from the Black Lagoon. Lee, Jared, illus. 2009. 62p. (J). *(978-0-545-07223-6(9))* Scholastic, Inc.

—The Spring Dance from the Black Lagoon, 1 vol. Lee, Jared, illus. 2012. (Black Lagoon Adventures Ser.: No. 2). (ENG.). 64p. (J). (gr. 2-5). 24.21 *(978-1-59961-963-7(6))* Spotlight.

Thomas, Peggy. Snow Dance, 1 vol. Facklam, Paul, illus. 2008. (ENG.). 32p. (J). (gr. 1-3). 16.99 *(978-1-58980-478-4(3))* Pelican Publishing Co., Inc.

Thompson, Carol. Dance. Thompson, Carol, illus. 2017. (Amazing Me! Ser.: 4). (ENG., Illus.). 12p. (J). (gr. k-k). bds. ***(978-1-84643-959-9(0))*** Child's Play International Ltd.

Todd, Traci N. Wiggle, Waggle, Loop-De-Loo! Barner, Bob, illus. 2006. (J). *(978-1-58987-009-3(3))* Kindermusik International.

Turner, J. Hale. I Love to Sing & Dance. 2005. 41p. (J). pap. 12.00 *(978-1-4116-3270-7(2))* Lulu Pr., Inc.

Valentino, Carla. When Can We Run, Play & Dance Again? An Enchanting Story about Family, Learning & Imagination. 2011. 32p. (gr. 2-4). pap. 17.95 *(978-1-4567-5495-2(5))* AuthorHouse.

van Diepen, Allison. Raven. 2010. (ENG.). 304p. (YA). (gr. 9). pap. 8.99 *(978-1-4169-7468-0(7)*, Simon Pulse) Simon Pulse.

Vanasse, Deb. Lucy's Dance. 2011. (ENG., Illus.). 29p. 16.95 *(978-1-60223-127-6(3))*; 32p. pap. 10.95 *(978-1-60223-126-9(5))* Univ. of Alaska Pr.

Veit, Kimberly Michelle. To Be Thirteen. 2006. 57p. pap. 16.95 *(978-1-4241-1392-7(X))* PublishAmerica, Inc.

Venditti, Stacey Marie. Stashi the Rainbow Star: Her Journey Home. Provenzano, Jeannine, illus. 2008. 52p. pap. 24.95 *(978-1-60474-786-7(2))* America Star Bks.

Venkatraman, Padma. A Time to Dance. (ENG.). (YA). (gr. 7). 2015. 336p. pap. 9.99 *(978-0-14-751440-0(1)*, Speak) 2014. 320p. 17.99 *(978-0-399-25710-0(1)*, Nancy Paulsen Books) Penguin Young Readers Group.

Wahl, Jan. Bear Dance. Felix, Monique, illus. 2008. (ENG.). 32p. (J). (gr. k-17). 19.95 *(978-1-56846-199-1(2)*, Creative Editions) Creative Co., The.

Walker, Anna. I Love to Dance. Walker, Anna, illus. 2011. (ENG., Illus.). 32p. (J). (gr. -1-1). 9.99 *(978-1-4169-8323-1(6)*, Simon & Schuster Bks. For Young Readers) Simon & Schuster Bks. For Young Readers.

Walker, Susan Eileen. Secret of the Dance. 2006. (ENG.). 232p. (J). (gr. -1-12). per. 15.00 *(978-0-9766805-4-3(8))* Keene Publishing.

Warren, Dotti M. Dreama Lynn & the Magic Tu Tu. 2008. 16p. pap. 9.49 *(978-1-4389-2983-5(8))* AuthorHouse.

Watson Dubisch, Carolyn. The Horribles. 2010. 73p. pap. 16.96 *(978-0-557-35938-7(4))* Lulu Pr., Inc.

Webb, Sarah. Ask Amy Green: Dancing Daze. 2013. (Ask Amy Green Ser.: 5). (ENG.). 256p. (J). (gr. 5). 16.99 *(978-0-7636-5583-9(X))* Candlewick Pr.

Weeks, Kermit. The Spirit of Lindy. Premise Entertainment, illus. 2011. (J). 19.95 *(978-0-9790267-1-3(7))* KWIP, Inc.

Welch, Teri. My New Dance. 2011. 20p. 10.99 *(978-1-4567-1514-4(3))* AuthorHouse.

Wheeler, Lisa. Dino-Dancing. Gott, Barry, illus. 2017. (ENG.). 32p. (J). (gr. k-3). lib. bdg. 17.99 ***(978-1-5124-0316-9(4)***, Carolrhoda Bks.) Lerner Publishing Group.

Whittemore, Jo. Confidentially Yours #4: the Secret Talent. 2016. (Confidentially Yours Ser.: 4). 320p. (J). (gr. 3-7). pap. 6.99 *(978-0-06-235899-8(5))* HarperCollins Pubs.

Wigden, Susan. I Want to Learn to Dance. Franzese, Nora Tapp, illus. 2012. 36p. pap. 11.99 *(978-1-60820-725-1(0))* MLR Pr., LLC.

Willems, Mo. Elephants Cannot Dance! 2012. (Elephant & Piggie Bks.). (CHI & ENG.). (J). pap. ***(978-986-189-325-9(3))*** Grimm Cultural Ent., Co., Ltd.

—Elephants Cannot Dance! Willems, Mo, illus. 2009. (Elephant & Piggie Book Ser.). (ENG., Illus.). 64p. (J). (gr. -1-k). 9.99 *(978-1-4231-1410-9(8))* Hyperion Pr.

—Elephants Cannot Dance! 2011. (ENG & KOR.). (J). ***(978-89-7184-930-9(4))*** Pu-Reun-Sup Publishing Co., Ltd.

Williams-Garcia, Rita. P. S. Be Eleven. 2013. 288p. (J). (gr. 3-7). lib. bdg. 17.89 *(978-0-06-193863-4(7)*, Amistad) HarperCollins Pubs.

Wilson, Anna. The Parent Problem. 2016. (ENG., Illus.). 240p. (J). (gr. 4-6). 9.99 ***(978-1-5098-0131-2(6))*** Pan Macmillan GBR. Dist: Independent Pubs. Group.

Wilson, Karma. Hilda Must Be Dancing. Watts, Suzanne, illus. 2008. (ENG.). 32p. (J). (gr. -1-3). 7.99 *(978-1-4169-5083-7(4)*, McElderry, Margaret K. Bks.) McElderry, Margaret K. Bks.

Wing, Natasha. The Night Before My Dance Recital. Wummer, Amy, illus. 2015. (Night Before Ser.). lib. bdg. 14.75 *(978-0-606-37543-6(0))* Turtleback Bks.

Wing, Natasha & dePaola, Tomie. The Night Before My Dance Recital. Wummer, Amy, illus. 2015. (Night Before Ser.). (ENG.). 32p. (J). (-k). bds. 4.99 *(978-0-448-48845-5(0)*, Grosset & Dunlap) Penguin Young Readers Group.

Winslade, Jayn E. Emily & Jen Dance for Deeron. 2010. 352p. pap. *(978-1-907211-48-5(9))* Grosvenor Hse. Publishing Ltd.

Winthrop, Elizabeth & Winthrop. Dancing Granny, 1 vol. Murdocca, Sal, illus. 2003. (ENG.). 32p. (J). 16.95 *(978-0-7614-5141-9(2))* Marshall Cavendish Corp.

Wissman, Celeste Farris. When I Teach My Monkey How to Dance. 2012. 24p. pap. 17.99 *(978-1-4772-6035-7(8))* AuthorHouse.

Witte, Anna. El Fandango de Lola. Archer, Micha, illus. 2011. (SPA.). 32p. (J). (gr. k-5). 9.99 *(978-1-84686-359-2(7))* Barefoot Bks., Inc.

—Lola's Fandango. Masse, Josée & Archer, Micha, illus. 2011. (ENG.). 48p. (J). 16.99 *(978-1-84686-174-1(8))* Barefoot Bks., Inc.

Written By Tori Velle; Illustrated By Al. Tia Tot Rules! Aguila, Alicia del, illus. 2011. 44p. pap. 24.95 *(978-1-4241-7833-9(9))* America Star Bks.

Zapf, Marlena. Underpants Dance. Avril, Lynne, illus. 2014. (ENG.). 40p. (J). (gr. -1-k). 16.99 *(978-0-8037-3539-2(1)*, Dial Bks) Penguin Young Readers Group.

DANCE—VOCATIONAL GUIDANCE

Cutcher, Jenai. Feel the Beat! Dancing in Music Videos. (Curtain Call Library of Dance Ser.). 48p. (gr. 5-8). 2009. 53.00 *(978-1-60853-420-3(0))* 2004. (Illus.). (YA). lib. bdg. 29.25 *(978-0-8239-4558-0(8))* Rosen Publishing Group, Inc., The. (Rosen Reference).

Derezinski, Amelia. Star Turns: Dancing on Broadway. 2009. (Curtain Call Library of Dance Ser.). 48p. (gr. 5-8). 53.00 *(978-1-60853-422-7(7)*, Rosen Reference) Rosen Publishing Group, Inc., The.

Derezinzki, Amelia. Star Turns: Dancing on Broadway. 2004. (Curtain Call Library of Dance Ser.). (Illus.). 48p. (J). (gr. 5-8). lib. bdg. 29.25 *(978-0-8239-4557-3(X)*, Rosen Reference) Rosen Publishing Group, Inc., The.

Reeves, Diane Lindsey. Career Ideas for Kids Who Like Music & Dance. 2nd rev. ed. 2007. (Career Ideas for Kids Ser.). 208p. (gr. 4-9). pap. 16.95 *(978-0-8160-6538-7(1)*, Checkmark Bks.) Facts On File, Inc.

van der Linde, Laurel. So, You Want to Be a Dancer? The Ultimate Guide to Exploring the Dance Industry. 2015. (Be What You Want Ser.). (ENG., Illus.). 208p. (J). (gr. 3-7). pap. 11.99 *(978-1-58270-450-0(3))* Aladdin/Beyond Words.

DANCERS

Adelman, Heidi. Beautiful Ballerinas. 2016. (Illus.). 32p. (J). *(978-1-4896-4775-7(9))* Weigl Pubs., Inc.

Allman, Barbara & Haas, Shelly O. Dance of the Swan: A Story about Anna Pavlova. 2006. (Creative Minds Biographies Ser.). (Illus.). 64p. (gr. 4-8). lib. bdg. 22.60 *(978-1-57505-463-6(9))* Lerner Publishing Group.

Ancona, George. Olé Flamenco! Ancona, George, photos by. 2010. (ENG., Illus.). 48p. (J). (gr. 2-6). 19.95 *(978-1-60060-361-7(0))* Lee & Low Bks., Inc.

Barasch, Lynne. Knockin' on Wood: Starring Peg Leg Bates. 2004. (ENG., Illus.). 32p. (J). 16.95 *(978-1-58430-170-7(8))* Lee & Low Bks., Inc.

Bernstein, Richard. A Girl Named Faithful Plum: The True Story of a Dancer from China & How She Achieved Her Dream. 2012. (ENG.). 288p. (J). (gr. 5-9). 7.99 *(978-0-375-87158-0(6)*, Yearling) Random Hse. Children's Bks.

Cady, Jennifer. Jose Limon. 2005. (Library of American Choreographers Ser.). (Illus.). 48p. (J). (gr. k-3). lib. bdg. 29.25 *(978-1-4042-0449-2(0))* Rosen Publishing Group, Inc., The.

Calkhoven, Laurie. Misty Copeland. Dong, Monique, illus. 2016. (You Should Meet Ser.). (ENG.). 48p. (J). (gr. 1-3). pap. 3.99 *(978-1-4814-7043-8(4)*, Simon Spotlight) Simon Spotlight.

Celichowska, Renata. Seven Statements of Survival: Conversations with Dance Professionals. 2008. (Contemporary Discourse on Movement & Dance Ser.). (ENG., Illus.). 192p. (gr. 9-12). pap. 12.95 *(978-1-4042-9720-3(0))* Rosen Publishing Group, Inc., The.

Clibbon, Meg. My Beautiful Ballet Pack. Clibbon, Lucy, illus. 2008. (Imagine You're A ... Ser.). (ENG.). 32p. (J). 15.99 *(978-1-84089-485-1(7))* Meg and Lucy Bks. GBR. Dist: Independent Pubs. Group.

Collins, Pat Lowery. I Am a Dancer. Graham, Mark, illus. 2008. (Millbrook Picture Books Ser.). 30p. (J). (gr. 3-7). 22.60 *(978-0-8225-6369-3(X)*, Millbrook Pr.) Lerner Publishing Group.

Cruz, Barbara C. Alvin Ailey: Celebrating African-American Culture in Dance. 2004. (African-American Biographies Ser.). (Illus.). 112p. (J). lib. bdg. 26.60 *(978-0-7660-2293-5(5))* Enslow Pubs., Inc.

Cunningham, Meghan Engsberg. Bill Bojangles Robinson. 2016. (Artists of the Harlem Renaissance Ser.). (ENG.). 128p. (YA). (gr. 9-9). lib. bdg. 45.64 *(978-1-5026-1073-7(6))* Cavendish Square Publishing.

Cunxin, Li. Mao's Last Dancer. movie tie-in ed. 2010. (ENG.). 528p. (gr. 12). 17.00 *(978-0-425-24030-4(4)*, Berkley) Penguin Publishing Group.

De Mille, Agnes. Dance to the Piper. 2015. (ENG., Illus.). 368p. pap. 17.95 *(978-1-59017-908-6(0)*, NYRB Classics) New York Review of Bks., Inc., The.

Delmar, Pete. Zoe Saldana. 2016. (Hollywood Action Heroes Ser.). (ENG., Illus.). 32p. (gr. 3-4). lib. bdg. 27.99 *(978-1-5157-0962-6(0),* Edge Bks.) Capstone Press of Coughlan Cos.

Deprince, Michaela & DePrince, Elaine. Ballerina Dreams: From Orphan to Dancer. Morrison, Frank, illus. 2014. (Step into Reading Ser.). (ENG.). 48p. (J). (gr. 2-4). 3.99 *(978-0-385-75515-3(5),* Random Hse. Bks. for Young Readers) Random Hse. Children's Bks.

—Taking Flight: From War Orphan to Star Ballerina. 2014. (ENG.). 256p. (YA). (gr. 7). 16.99 *(978-0-385-75511-5(2));* lib. bdg. 19.99 *(978-0-385-75512-2(0))* Random Hse. Children's Bks. (Knopf Bks. for Young Readers).

Derezinski, Amelia. Twyla Tharp. (Library of American Choreographers Ser.). 48p. 2009. (gr. 5-8). 53.00 *(978-1-60853-461-6(8),* Rosen Reference) 2006. (ENG., Illus.). (gr. 5-8). pap. 11.75 *(978-1-4042-0646-5(9))* 2005. (Illus.). (J). (gr. k-3). lib. bdg. 29.25 *(978-1-4042-0451-5(2))* Rosen Publishing Group, Inc., The.

Dublin, Anne. Dynamic Women Dancers, 1 vol. 2009. (Women's Hall of Fame Ser.). (ENG., Illus.). 120p. (J). (gr. 4-8). pap. 10.95 *(978-1-897187-56-2(4))* Second Story Pr. CAN. Dist: Orca Bk. Pubs. USA.

Dunn, Mary R. I Want to Be a Ballet Dancer. 2009. (Dream Jobs Ser.). 24p. (gr. 2-3). 42.50 *(978-1-61512-202-8(8),* PowerKids Pr.); (Illus.). (YA). lib. bdg. 22.60 *(978-1-4042-4469-6(7))* Rosen Publishing Group, Inc., The.

Dyro, Janniche, illus. Forever Dancing. 32p. (J). (gr. 4-18). 16.00 *(978-0-9675413-8-9(7))* Libros, Encouraging Cultural Literacy.

Fandel, Jennifer. Rudolf Nureyev. 2005. (Extraordinary Artists Ser.). (Illus.). 48p. (J). (gr. 5-9). lib. bdg. 21.95 *(978-1-58341-380-7(4),* Creative Education) Creative Co., The.

Feinstein, Stephen. Savion Glover. 2008. (African-American Heroes Ser.). (Illus.). 24p. (J). (gr. 1-3). lib. bdg. 22.60 *(978-0-7660-2897-5(6),* Enslow Elementary) Enslow Pubs., Inc.

Flor Ada, Alma & Campoy, F. Isabel, contrib. by. Pasos. (Literature Collection of Puertas Al Sol Ser.).Tr. of Steps. (SPA.). 32p. (J). (gr. k-6). pap. 13.95 *(978-1-59437-704-4(9))* Santillana USA Publishing Co., Inc.

Gitenstein, Judy. Alvin Ailey. (Library of American Choreographers Ser.). 48p. 2009. (gr. 5-8). 53.00 *(978-1-60853-455-5(3),* Rosen Reference) 2006. (ENG., Illus.). (gr. 5-8). pap. 11.75 *(978-1-4042-0639-7(6))* 2005. (Illus.). (J). (gr. k-3). lib. bdg. 29.25 *(978-1-4042-0445-4(8))* Rosen Publishing Group, Inc., The.

Gourley, Catherine. Who Is Maria Tallchief? Taylor, Val Paul, illus. 2003. (Who Was... ? Ser.). 103p. 15.00 *(978-0-7569-1592-6(9))* Perfection Learning Corp.

Hasday, Judy L. Agnes de Mille. 2003. (Women in the Arts Ser.). (Illus.). 112p. (gr. 6-12). 30.00 *(978-0-7910-7457-2(9),* Chelsea Hse.) Facts On File, Inc.

Herweck, Diana. A Day in the Life of a Ballet Dancer, 1 vol. 2nd rev. ed. 2011. (Nonfiction Readers Ser.). (ENG.). 28p. (J). (gr. 3-3). pap. 8.99 *(978-1-4333-3650-8(2))* Teacher Created Materials, Inc.

Herweck, Dona. A Day in the Life of a Ballet Dancer, 1 vol. 2nd rev. ed. 2014. (TIME for KIDS(r) Nonfiction Readers Ser.). (ENG., Illus.). 28p. (J). (gr. 3-3). pap. 25.96 *(978-1-4807-1065-8(2))* Shell Educational Publishing.

I Want to be a Ballerina. 2008. (Magnetic Board Books Ser.). 7p. bds. *(978-1-4075-1414-7(8))* Parragon, Inc.

I'm Going to be the Best Ballerina Ever! 2008. (I'm Going to be Storybooks... Ser.). 32p. *(978-1-4075-1706-3(6))* Parragon, Inc.

Isbell, Hannah. Misty Copeland: Ballerina. 2016. (Junior Biographies Ser.). 24p. (J). pap. 9.35 *(978-0-7660-8177-2(X))* Enslow Pubs., Inc.

Kessel, Kristin. Martha Graham. (Library of American Choreographers Ser.). 48p. 2009. (gr. 5-8). 53.00 *(978-1-60853-460-9(X),* Rosen Reference) 2006. (ENG., Illus.). (gr. 5-8). pap. 11.75 *(978-1-4042-0644-1(2))* 2005. (Illus.). (J). lib. bdg. 29.25 *(978-1-4042-0450-8(4))* Rosen Publishing Group, Inc., The.

Mitchell, Missy. Ballet: Pointe by Pointe. 2009. (Curtain Call Library of Dance Ser.). 48p. (gr. 5-8). 53.00 *(978-1-60853-418-0(9),* Rosen Reference) Rosen Publishing Group, Inc., The.

O'Connor, Barbara. Barefoot Dancer: The Story of Isadora Duncan. 2003. (Illus.). 96p. (J). pap. 8.95 *(978-0-87614-911-9(5),* Carolrhoda Bks.) Lerner Publishing Group.

—Katherine Dunham: Pioneer of Black Dance. 2005. (Trailblazers Biographies Ser.). (Illus.). 112p. (gr. 5-9). 27.93 *(978-1-57505-353-0(5))* Lerner Publishing Group.

Orgill, Roxane. Footwork: The Story of Fred & Adele Astaire. Jorisch, Stéphane, illus. 2013. (Candlewick Biographies Ser.). (ENG.). 48p. (J). (gr. 3-7). pap. 4.99 *(978-0-7636-6215-8(1))* Candlewick Pr.

—Footwork: The Story of Fred & Adele Astaire. Jorisch, Stéphane, illus. 2013. (Candlewick Biographies Ser.). (ENG.). 48p. (J). (gr. 3-7). 14.99 *(978-0-7636-6460-2(X))* Candlewick Pr.

Paskevska, Anna. Ballet Beyond Tradition. 2004. (ENG., Illus.). 200p. 37.95 *(978-0-415-97018-1(0))* Routledge.

Powell, Patricia Hruby. Josephine: The Dazzling Life of Josephine Baker. Robinson, Christian, illus. 2014. (ENG.). 104p. (J). (gr. 2-5). 17.99 *(978-1-4521-0314-3(3))* Chronicle Bks. LLC.

Regan, Lisa. Ballet Dancer. 2012. (Stage School Ser.). (ENG., Illus.). 32p. (J). (gr. 3-6). 25.25 *(978-1-4488-8091-1(2));* pap. 10.00 *(978-1-4488-8150-5(1))* Windmill Bks.

Reich, Susanna. José! Born to Dance: The Story of Jose Limon. Colón, Raúl, illus. 2005. (ENG.). 32p. (J). (gr. k-3). 17.99 *(978-0-689-86576-3(7),* Simon & Schuster/Paula Wiseman Bks.) Simon & Schuster/Paula Wiseman Bks.

Royston, Angela. Diary of a Ballerina. 2013. (Diary of A... Ser.). (ENG., Illus.). 32p. (gr. 1-3). 27.32 *(978-1-4329-7579-1(X));* pap. 8.95 *(978-1-4329-7586-9(2))* Heinemann-Raintree. (Heinemann First Library).

Schroeder, Alan & Wagner, Heather Lehr. Josephine Baker: Entertainer. 2006. (Black Americans of Achievement Ser.). (Illus.). 119p. (YA). (gr. 7-12). lib. bdg. 35.00 *(978-0-7910-9212-5(7))* Facts On File, Inc.

Seibert, Brian. George Balanchine. (Library of American Choreographers Ser.). 48p. (gr. 5-8). 2009. 53.00 *(978-1-60853-457-9(X))* 2006. (ENG., Illus.). pap. 11.75 *(978-1-4042-0641-0(8))* Rosen Publishing Group, Inc., The. (Rosen Reference).

—Jerome Robbins. (Library of American Choreographers Ser.). 48p. (gr. 5-8). 2009. 53.00 *(978-1-60853-458-6(8),* Rosen Reference) 2006. (ENG.). pap. 11.75 *(978-1-4042-0642-7(6))* Rosen Publishing Group, Inc., The.

Shahan, Sherry. Willie Covan Loved to Dance. Van Wright, Cornelius & Ha, Ying-Hwa, trs. Van Wright, Cornelius & Ha, Ying-Hwa, illus. 2004. (J). 15.95 *(978-1-59034-445-3(6));* pap. *(978-1-59034-580-1(0))* Mondo Publishing.

Siempre Bailando. (SPA.). (J). *(978-0-9675413-9-6(5))* Libros, Encouraging Cultural Literacy.

Snyder, Laurel. Swan: The Life & Dance of Anna Pavlova. Morstad, Julie, illus. 2015. (ENG.). 52p. (J). (gr. 1-4). 17.99 *(978-1-4521-1890-1(6))* Chronicle Bks. LLC.

Staley, Erin. Misty Copeland: Principal Ballerina. 2017. (Influential Lives Ser.). 128p. (J). (gr. 7-8). lib. bdg. 37.27 ***(978-0-7660-8509-1(0))*** Enslow Pubs., Inc.

Terp, Gail. Misty Copeland. 2017. (Women Who Rock Ser.). (ENG.). 32p. (gr. 3-7). 31.35 ***(978-1-68072-065-5(1))*** Black Rabbit Bks.

Tonatiuh, Duncan. Danza! Amalia Hernández & Mexico's Folkloric Ballet. 2017. (ENG., Illus.). 32p. (J). (gr. 1-5). 18.95 ***(978-1-4197-2532-6(7),*** Abrams Bks. for Young Readers) Abrams, Inc.

Trenton, Trisha. Trisha Trenton: Dance Diva Dance! 2007. mass mkt. 39.95 *(978-0-9727410-0-2(3))* TEG Publishing.

Ziegler, Maddie. The Maddie Diaries: A Memoir. 2017. (ENG., Illus.). 240p. 21.99 *(978-1-5011-5066-1(9),* Gallery Bks.) Gallery Bks.

DANCERS—FICTION

Anonymous. Confessions of a Backup Dancer. 2004. (ENG.). 272p. (YA). (gr. 9). pap. 12.99 *(978-0-689-87075-0(2),* Simon Pulse) Simon Pulse.

Beka. A Funny Thing Happened on the Way to Paris..., No. 4. 2013. (Dance Class Graphic Novels Ser.). (ENG., Illus.). 48p. (J). (gr. 1-7). 10.99 *(978-1-59707-384-4(9),* 9781597073844) Papercutz.

—Romeo & Juliets. 2012. (Dance Class Graphic Novels Ser.). (ENG., Illus.). 48p. (J). 10.99 *(978-1-59707-317-2(2),* 9781597073172) Papercutz.

Bloomberg, Sandi. Ava & the Magic Tutu. 2008. 40p. per. 13.95 *(978-1-59800-248-5(1))* Outskirts Pr., Inc.

Bound, Samantha-Ellen. Lights, Camera, Dance! 2016. (Silver Shoes Ser.: 6). (ENG., Illus.). 144p. (J). (gr. 4-7). pap. 8.99 *(978-0-85798-905-5(7))* Random Hse. Australia AUS. Dist: Independent Pubs. Group.

Brandeis, Madeline. The Little Spanish Dancer. 2005. reprint ed. pap. 22.95 *(978-1-4191-4096-9(5))* Kessinger Publishing, LLC.

Burgess, Melvyn & Pearson Education Staff. Billy Elliot: 'A Writer of the Hightest Quality with Exceptional Powers of Insight' 2nd ed. 2008. (ENG., Illus.). 64p. pap. 11.99 *(978-1-4058-8176-0(3))* Pearson Education.

Bussell, Darcey. Delphie & the Glass Slippers, 4. 2008. (Magic Ballerina Ser.: 4). (ENG., Illus.). 96p. (J). (gr. k-2). pap. 6.99 *(978-0-00-728617-1(1),* HarperCollins Children's Bks.) HarperCollins Pubs. Ltd. GBR. Dist: HarperCollins Pubs.

—Delphie & the Masked Ball, 3. 2008. (Magic Ballerina Ser.: 3). (ENG., Illus.). 96p. (J). (gr. k-2). pap. 6.99 *(978-0-00-728610-2(4),* HarperCollins Children's Bks.) HarperCollins Pubs. Ltd. GBR. Dist: HarperCollins Pubs.

Caines-Floyd, Eydi. The Story of Wanton Desire. 2009. 64p. (J). pap. 26.49 *(978-1-4389-3156-2(5))* AuthorHouse.

Cayen, Alise. Patty Pom-Poms. 2009. 36p. pap. 16.50 *(978-1-60693-685-6(9),* Strategic Bk. Publishing) Strategic Book Publishing & Rights Agency (SBPRA).

Clibbon, Meg. Starry Ballerinas. Clibbon, Lucy, illus. 2011. (My World Of Ser.). (ENG.). 32p. (J). (gr. k-2). pap. 8.99 *(978-1-84089-593-3(4))* Meg and Lucy Bks. GBR. Dist: Independent Pubs. Group.

Dancing Dilemma. 2005. 46p. (J). 3.99 *(978-0-9763213-1-6(9))* OHC Group LLC.

DePalma, Johnny & Crabapple, Molly. Once upon a Christmas Tree - A Holiday Fairy Tale. 2007. 88p. pap. 10.50 *(978-0-615-15448-0(4))* Umbrelly Bks.

Dillon, Leo & Dillon, Diane. Rap a Tap Tap: Here's Bojangles - Think of That! 2005. (J). 28.95 incl. audio compact disk *(978-1-59519-369-8(3))* Live Oak Media.

Douglass Thom, Kara. Dancer Girl M. C's Story: One Step at a Time. Seatter, Pamela, illus. 2014. (Go! Go! Sports Girls Ser.). (ENG.). 32p. (J). (gr. k-2). pap. 4.99 *(978-1-940731-02-5(X))* Dream Big Toy Co.

Ehrlich, Amy. The Girl Who Wanted to Dance. Walsh, Rebecca, illus. 2009. (ENG.). 40p. (J). (gr. 1-4). 17.99 *(978-0-7636-1345-7(2))* Candlewick Pr.

Espluga, Maria. I Am a Ballerina. 2009. (I Am A... (Alphabet Soup) Ser.). (Illus.). 24p. (J). (gr. k-1). pap. 8.15 *(978-1-60754-252-0(8));* lib. bdg. 22.60 *(978-1-60754-251-3(X))* Windmill Bks.

—I, Ballerina: Yo, Bailarina. 2009. (ENG & SPA.). 28p. (J). 13.95 *(978-1-931398-55-8(0))* Me+Mi Publishing.

Farley, Robin. Mia Sets the Stage. 2013. (Mia I Can Read Bks.). (J). lib. bdg. 13.55 *(978-0-606-27160-8(0),* Turtleback) Turtleback Bks.

Fay, Nicole. Brittney & Beario Become Ballerinas. 2009. 16p. pap. 9.50 *(978-1-4389-1058-1(4))* AuthorHouse.

Fox, Paula. The Slave Dancer. unabr. ed. 2004. 152p. (J). (gr. 5-9). pap. 38.00 incl. audio *(978-0-8072-0458-0(7),* Listening Library) Random Hse. Audio Publishing Group.

Gamble, Adam & Jasper, Mark. Good Night Dancers. Blackmore, Katherine, illus. 2017. (Good Night Our World Ser.). (ENG.). 20p. (J). (gr. -1 — 1). bds. 9.95 *(978-1-60219-427-4(0))* Good Night Bks.

Gibson, Catherine. Through Sophie's Eyes. 2009. (Illus.). 32p. (J). 15.95 *(978-0-578-00980-3(3))* For Children With Love Pubns.

Gorzelanczyk, Melissa. Arrows. 2016. (ENG.). 240p. (YA). (gr. 9). 17.99 *(978-0-553-51044-7(4),* Delacorte Pr.) Random Hse. Children's Bks.

Gough, Erin. Get It Together, Delilah! 2017. (ENG., Illus.). 336p. (YA). 16.99 *(978-1-4521-5187-8(3))* Chronicle Bks. LLC.

Graham, Sabrina Depina. Breanna & Amber: Help Each Other Achieve Their Dreams (Christian Version) 2012. 92p. 19.99 *(978-1-4691-6411-3(6));* pap. 12.99 *(978-1-4691-6410-6(8))* Xlibris Corp.

Greenberg, Doris & Shandley, Pandré. The Legend of L'Esprit: Dance Legacy Series. 2011. 272p. pap. 15.95 *(978-1-4634-1800-7(0))* AuthorHouse.

Grindley, Sally & Dorling Kindersley Publishing Staff. Little Ballerina, Level 2. 2013. (DK Readers Ser.). (ENG.). 32p. (J). (gr. 1-3). pap. 3.99 *(978-1-4654-0942-3(4),* DK Children) Dorling Kindersley Publishing, Inc.

Hegarty, Pat. If I Were a... Ballerina. Pope, Liz & Pope, Kate, illus. 2008. (If I Were A Ser.). 10p. (J). (gr. -1-k). bds. 6.95 *(978-1-58925-834-1(7))* Tiger Tales.

Hicks, Holly Floyd. Ella's Birthday Wish. 2010. 108p. 20.95 *(978-1-4502-0932-8(7))* iUniverse, Inc.

Hicks, Holly Floyd, ed. Ella's Birthday Wish. 2010. 108p. pap. 10.95 *(978-1-4502-0933-5(5))* iUniverse, Inc.

Higginson, Sheila Sweeny. Leilani's Luau. Disney Storybook Artists Staff, illus. 2014. (ENG.). 32p. (J). (gr. -1-k). pap. 4.99 *(978-1-4231-9417-0(9))* Disney Pr.

Keene, Carolyn. The Red Slippers. 2015. (Nancy Drew Diaries: 11). (ENG., Illus.). 192p. (J). (gr. 3-7). pap. 6.99 *(978-1-4814-3813-1(1),* Aladdin) Simon & Schuster Children's Publishing.

Lieberman, Leanne. Off Pointe, 1 vol. 2014. (Orca Limelights Ser.). (ENG.). 128p. (J). (gr. 6-9). pap. 9.95 *(978-1-4598-0280-3(2))* Orca Bk. Pubs. USA.

Lowell, Susan. Josefina Javelina: A Hairy Tale. MacPherson, Bruce, illus. 2005. (ENG.). 32p. (J). (gr. -1-3). 15.95 *(978-0-87358-790-7(1))* Cooper Square Publishing Llc.

Marsh, Charis. I Forgot to Tell You: Ballet School Confidential (Large Print 16pt) 2013. 284p. pap. *(978-1-4596-6320-6(9))* ReadHowYouWant.com, Ltd.

—You're So Sweet: Ballet School Confidential (Large Print 16pt) 2013. 292p. pap. *(978-1-4596-6408-1(6))* ReadHowYouWant.com, Ltd.

Marshall, James. Swine Lake. 2004. (Illus.). (J). (gr. k-5). spiral bd. *(978-0-616-01712-8(X))* Canadian National Institute for the Blind/Institut National Canadien pour les Aveugles.

Maybarduk, Linda. James the Dancing Dog. Johnson, Gillian, illus. 2004. (ENG.). 24p. (J). (gr. -1-2). 15.95 *(978-0-88776-619-0(6),* Tundra Bks.) Tundra Bks. CAN. Dist: Penguin Random Hse. LLC.

Mayhew, James. Ella Bella Ballerina & Cinderella. 2009. (Ella Bella Ballerina Ser.). (ENG.). 32p. (J). (gr. -1-3). 14.99 *(978-0-7641-6268-8(3))* Barron's Educational Series, Inc.

—Ella Bella Ballerina & Swan Lake. 2011. (Ella Bella Ballerina Ser.). 32p. (J). (gr. -1-3). 14.99 *(978-0-7641-6407-1(4))* Barron's Educational Series, Inc.

—Ella Bella Ballerina & the Midsummer Night's Dream. 2015. (Ella Bella Ballerina Ser.). (ENG., Illus.). 32p. (J). (gr. -1-3). 14.99 *(978-0-7641-6797-3(9))* Barron's Educational Series, Inc.

—Nutcracker. 2012. (Ella Bella Ballerina Ser.). (ENG., Illus.). 32p. (J). (gr. 1-3). 14.99 *(978-0-7641-6581-8(X))* Barron's Educational Series, Inc.

—The Sleeping Beauty. 2008. (Ella Bella Ballerina Ser.). (ENG., Illus.). 32p. (J). (gr. -1-3). 14.99 *(978-0-7641-6118-6(0))* Barron's Educational Series, Inc.

McClintock, Barbara. Emma & Julia Love Ballet. 2016. (ENG., Illus.). 32p. (J). (gr. -1-3). 17.99 *(978-0-439-89401-2(8),* Scholastic Pr.) Scholastic, Inc.

Miller, Sibley & Lenhard, Elizabeth. Horses' Night Out. Chang, Tara Larsen & Gershman, Jo, illus. 2008. (Wind Dancers Ser.: 4). (ENG.). 80p. (J). (gr. 1-4). pap. 16.99 *(978-0-312-38283-4(9),* 9780312382834) Feiwel & Friends.

M.J.Higgy. The Bombay Bear. 2012. (Illus.). 16p. pap. 18.30 *(978-1-4685-8193-5(7))* AuthorHouse.

Myers, Walter Dean. Juba! (Illus.). 208p. (YA). (gr. 8). 2016. pap. 9.99 *(978-0-06-211273-6(2))* 2015. (ENG., 17.99 *(978-0-06-211271-2(6),* HarperTeen) HarperCollins Pubs.

Rautenberg, Karen Rita. Ballerina Detective & the Missing Jeweled Tiara. 2009. (ENG.). 198p. (J). (gr. 5-8). pap. *(978-1-933255-47-7(1))* DNA Pr.

Reicherter, Daryn. The Cambodian Dancer: Sophany & the Cambodian Dance. Penh, Bophal, tr. Hale, Christy, illus. 2015. (ENG.). 32p. (J). (gr. k-3). 14.95 *(978-0-8048-4516-8(6))* Tuttle Publishing.

Rippin, Sally. The Bad Butterfly: Billie B. Brown. Fukuoka, Aki, illus. 2013. (ENG.). 48p. (J). pap. 4.99 *(978-1-61067-095-1(7))* Kane Miller.

Sam, Amélie & Trouillot, Virgile. The Argument. 2009. (Groove High Ser.). (Illus.). 112p. (YA). (gr. 5-8). 31.95 *(978-1-60754-538-5(1));* pap. 15.25 *(978-1-60754-539-2(X))* Windmill Bks.

—Everyone on Stage. 2009. (Groove High Ser.). (Illus.). 112p. (YA). (gr. 5-8). 31.95 *(978-1-60754-529-3(2));* pap. 15.25 *(978-1-60754-530-9(6))* Windmill Bks.

—The New Girl. 2009. (Groove High Ser.). (Illus.). 112p. (YA). (gr. 5-8). 31.95 *(978-1-60754-536-1(5));* pap. 15.25 *(978-1-60754-535-4(7))* Windmill Bks.

Sobat, Gail Sidonie. Chance to Dance for You. 2011. (ENG.). 176p. pap. 14.95 *(978-1-926531-11-3(6),* Great Plains Teen Fiction) Great Plains Pubns. CAN. Dist: Publishers Group Canada.

Starwolf. The Dance of the Fire Fairies: Book 1-Just Beginning. 2013. 140p. pap. 47.39 *(978-1-4907-1009-9(4))* Trafford Publishing.

—Tiny Dancer. 2012. 36p. pap. 15.49 *(978-1-4669-5247-8(4))* Trafford Publishing.

Suma, Nova Ren. The Walls Around Us. (ENG.). 336p. (YA). (gr. 9-12). 2016. pap. 9.95 *(978-1-61620-590-4(3))* 2015. 17.95 *(978-1-61620-372-6(2))* Algonquin Bks. of Chapel Hill.

—The Walls Around Us. 2016. lib. bdg. 20.80 *(978-0-606-37957-1(6))* Turtleback Bks.

Webster, Christy. I Can Be a Ballerina. Random House Staff & Riley, Kellee, illus. 2011. (Step into Reading Ser.). (ENG.). 32p. (J). (gr. -1-1). pap. 3.99 *(978-0-375-86839-9(9),* Random Hse. Bks. for Young Readers) Random Hse. Children's Bks.

Williams, Nicole. Clash. 2012. (Crash Ser.: 2). (ENG.). 288p. (YA). (gr. 11). pap. 9.99 *(978-0-06-226715-3(9))* HarperCollins Pubs.

—Crash. 2012. (Crash Ser.: 1). (ENG.). 384p. (YA). (gr. 11). pap. 9.99 *(978-0-06-226714-6(0))* HarperCollins Pubs.

—Crush. 2013. (Crash Ser.: 3). (ENG.). 400p. (YA). (gr. 11). pap. 9.99 *(978-0-06-226717-7(5))* HarperCollins Pubs.

Winter, Jonah. Jazz Age Josephine: Dancer, Singer- Who's That, Who? Why That's Miss Josephine Baker, to You! Priceman, Marjorie, illus. 2012. (ENG.). 40p. (J). (gr. -1-3). 16.99 *(978-1-4169-6123-9(2),* Atheneum Bks. for Young Readers) Simon & Schuster Children's Publishing.

Winthrop, Elizabeth. Dumpy la Rue. Lewin, Betsy, illus. rev. ed. 2004. (ENG.). 40p. (J). (gr. -1-3). reprint ed. pap. 8.99 *(978-0-8050-7535-9(6),* 9780805075359, Holt, Henry & Co. Bks. For Young Readers) Holt, Henry & Co.

DANDELIONS

Dandelion. 2003. 38.95 *(978-0-8136-4127-0(6));* 36.95 *(978-0-8136-9262-3(8))* Modern Curriculum Pr.

Johnson, Jinny. Dandelion. Rosewarne, Graham, illus. 2010. (J). 28.50 *(978-1-59920-351-5(0))* Black Rabbit Bks.

Long, Olivia. The Dandelion Queen. Long, Olivia, illus. Date not set. (Our Precious Planet Ser.). (Illus.). 32p. (J). (gr. -1-4). 9.95 *(978-1-880042-08-3(8),* SL12461) Shelf-Life Bks.

Moore, Phillip. How Many Parts Do Dandelions Have? 2014. (Little Books of Answers: Level B Ser.). (Illus.). 16p. (gr. k-2). pap. 7.95 *(978-1-927136-18-8(0))* Three Crows Media NZL. Dist: RiverStream Publishing.

Nelson, Robin. Dandelions. 2009. pap. 34.95 *(978-0-7613-4116-1(1));* (ENG.). 24p. 23.93 *(978-0-7613-4069-0(6),* Lerner Pubns.) Lerner Publishing Group.

Posada, Mia. Dandelions: Stars in the Grass. Posada, Mia, illus. 2003. (Picture Bks.). (Illus.). 32p. (J). (gr. -1-3). 15.95 *(978-1-57505-383-7(7))* Lerner Publishing Group.

Weiss, Ellen. From Seed to Dandelion. 2007. (Scholastic News Nonfiction Readers Ser.). (ENG., Illus.). 24p. (J). (gr. 1-2). 22.00 *(978-0-531-18539-1(7));* pap. 6.95 *(978-0-531-18792-0(6))* Scholastic Library Publishing.

DANIEL (BIBLICAL FIGURE)

Burgdorf, Larry. Daniel & the Lions. 2010. (Arch Bks.). (Illus.). 16p. (J). (gr. k-4). pap. 2.49 *(978-0-7586-1857-3(3))* Concordia Publishing Hse.

Carlson, Amie. Daniel in the Lions' Den. 2015. (Bouncy Bible Buddies Ser.). (ENG.). 10p. (J). bds. 7.99 *(978-1-4964-1091-7(2))* Tyndale Hse. Pubs.

Dalmatian Press Staff, ed. Daniel in the Lion's Den. 2004. (ENG., Illus.). 24p. (J). 2.99 *(978-1-4037-0965-3(3),* Spirit Pr.) Bendon, Inc.

Daniel in the Lion's Den. Date not set. (J). stu. ed., act. bk. ed. 1.49 *(978-0-88271-233-8(0),* 1749) Regina Pr., Malhame & Co.

David, Juliet. Daniel & the Lions' Den, 1 vol. Denham, Gemma, illus. 2009. (Candle Playbook Ser.). 18p. (J). bds. 7.99 *(978-0-8254-7385-2(3),* Candle Bks.) Lion Hudson PLC GBR. Dist: Kregel Pubns.

Donaher, D F. & Bibleco. Daniel & the Lions. 2004. (Illus.). (J). bds. *(978-0-9746058-2-1(4),* Biblemania) Bibleco, Inc.

Fogle, Robin. Daniel & the Lions' Den Coloring Book. 2007. (Illus.). 16p. (J). pap. 1.89 *(978-1-59317-191-9(9))* Warner Pr., Inc.

Holder, Jennifer. Daniel & His Faithful Friends. Julien, Terry, illus. 2014. (Faith That Sticks Bks.). (ENG.). 27p. (J). pap. 3.99 *(978-1-4143-9827-3(1))* Tyndale Hse. Pubs.

Johnson, Alice W. Believe & You're There: When Daniel Was Delivered, Vol. 10. 2010. (Illus.). 96p. (J). pap. 6.99 *(978-1-60641-817-8(3))* Deseret Bk. Co.

Murdock, Hy. Daniel. (Bible Stories Ser.: No. S846-6). (Illus.). (J). (gr. -1-2). pap. 3.95 *(978-0-7214-5069-8(5),* Dutton Juvenile) Penguin Publishing Group.

Overstreet, Edward. From the Lion's Mouth: A Story of Daniel the Prophet. 2011. 144p. 40.95 *(978-1-258-07872-0(4))* Literary Licensing, LLC.

Paden, Cheryl A. Daniel. 2007. (Money at its Best: Millionaires of the Old Testament Ser.). 112p. (YA). (gr. 7-18). pap. 14.95 *(978-1-4222-0842-7(7))* Mason Crest.

—The Life of Daniel. 2009. (Money at its Best: Millionaires of the Old Testament Ser.). 112p. (YA). (gr. 7-12). 24.95 *(978-1-4222-0467-2(7))* Mason Crest.

Petach, Heidi. Daniel & the Lions. Dickson, Bill, illus. 2013. (Happy Day Ser.). (ENG.). 16p. (J). pap. 2.49 *(978-1-4143-9298-1(2))* Tyndale Hse. Pubs.

Pulley, Kelly & Zondervan Staff. Daniel y los Leones, 1 vol. Pulley, Kelly, illus. 2009. (I Can Read! / the Beginner's Bible / ¡Yo Sé Leer! Ser.).Tr. of Daniel & the Lions. (SPA & ENG., Illus.). 32p. (J). pap. 3.99 *(978-0-310-71891-8(0))* Zonderkidz.

Rabbit. Daniel in the Lion's Den. 2005. (J). 10.95 *(978-0-689-80239-3(0),* Simon & Schuster Bks. For Young Readers) Simon & Schuster Bks. For Young Readers.

Schmidt, Troy. The Lion & Daniel. Jones, Cory, illus. 2015. (Their Side of the Story Ser.). (ENG.). 32p. (J). (gr. -1-3). pap. 3.99 *(978-1-4336-8721-1(6),* B&H Kids) B&H Publishing Group.

Stories about Daniel. (Old Testament Pict-O-Graph Ser.). (J). 10.99 *(978-0-7847-1040-1(6))* Standard Publishing.

Zondervan Staff. Daniel & the Lions, 1 vol. Pulley, Kelly, illus. 2008. (I Can Read! / the Beginner's Bible Ser.). (ENG.). 32p. (J). (gr. -1-1). pap. 3.99 *(978-0-310-71551-1(2))* Zonderkidz.

—Daniel God's Faithful Follower, 1 vol. Jones, Dennis, illus. 2010. (I Can Read! / Dennis Jones Ser.). (ENG.). 32p. (J). (gr. -1-2). pap. 3.99 *(978-0-310-71834-5(1))* Zonderkidz.

DANTE ALIGHIERI, 1265-1321

Davenport, John C. Dante: Poet, Author & Proud Florentine. 2005. (Makers of the Middle Ages & Renaissance Ser.). (Illus.). 136p. (J). (gr. 5-8). lib. bdg. 32.95 *(978-0-7910-8634-6(8),* Chelsea Hse.) Facts On File, Inc.

DARE, VIRGINIA, 1587—FICTION

Haddix, Margaret Peterson. Sabotaged. (Missing Ser.: 3). (ENG.). (J). (gr. 3-7). 2011. 400p. pap. 8.99 *(978-1-4169-5425-5(2))* 2010. 384p. 17.99 *(978-1-4169-5424-8(4))* Simon & Schuster Bks. For Young Readers. (Simon & Schuster Bks. For Young Readers).

DARK AGES

see Middle Ages

DARWIN, CHARLES, 1809-1882

Adamson, Heather. Charles Darwin & the Theory of Evolution, 1 vol. Purcell, Gordon & Milgrom, Al, illus. 2007. (Inventions & Discovery Ser.). (ENG.). 32p. (gr. 3-4). 30.65 *(978-1-4296-0145-0(0),* Graphic Library) Capstone Press of Coughlan Cos.

C
D

Anderson, Margaret J. Charles Darwin: Genius of a Revolutionary Theory. 2015. (Genius Scientists & Their Genius Ideas Ser.). 96p. (J). (gr. 5-12). 27.94 (978-0-7660-6545-1(6)); pap. 10.95 (978-0-7660-6546-8(4)) Enslow Pubs., Inc.

Anderson, Margaret Jean. Charles Darwin: Naturalist. rev. ed. 2008. (Great Minds of Science Ser.). (Illus.). 128p. (J). (gr. 5-18). lib. bdg. 33.27 (978-0-7660-2794-7(5)) Enslow Pubs., Inc.

Ashby, Ruth. Young Charles Darwin & the Voyage of the Beagle. 1 vol. Duranceau, Suzanne, illus. 2009. (ENG.). 128p. (J). (gr. 2-5). 12.95 (978-1-56145-478-5(8), Peachtree Junior) Peachtree Pubs.

Barnham, Kay. Charles Darwin: Father of Evolution. 2016. (History VIPs Ser.). (ENG., Illus.). 32p. (J). (gr. 4-6). 17.99 (978-0-7502-8849-1(3), Wayland) Hachette Children's Group GBR. Dist: Hachette Bk. Group.

Bortz, Fred. Charles Darwin & the Theory of Evolution by Natural Selection. 2013. (Revolutionary Discoveries of Scientific Pioneers Ser.). (Illus.). 80p. (J). (gr. 7-12). 33.25 (978-1-4777-1802-5(8)) Rosen Publishing Group, Inc., The.

Bowler, Peter J. An Interview with Charles Darwin. 2014. (Meet the Masters Ser.). 112p. (YA). (gr. 9-12). lib. bdg. 42.79 (978-1-62712-909-1(X)) Cavendish Square Publishing.

Byrne, Eugene. Darwin: A Graphic Biography. Gurr, Simon, illus. 2013. (ENG.). 100p. (J). (gr. 7). pap. 9.95 (978-1-58834-352-9(9), Smithsonian Bks.) Smithsonian Institution Scholarly Pr.

Claybourne, Anna. Who Discovered Natural Selection? 2010. (Breakthroughs in Science & Technology Ser.). 48p. lib. bdg. 32.80 (978-1-84837-682-3(0)) Arcturus Publishing GBR. Dist: Black Rabbit Bks.

Colson, Mary. Charles Darwin & Alfred Russel Wallace. 2014. (Dynamic Duos of Science Ser.). 48p. (YA). (gr. 5-8). pap. 84.30 (978-1-4824-1280-2(2)) Stevens, Gareth Publishing LLLP.

Cook, Diane. Charles Darwin: British Naturalist. (Illus.). 32p. (J). 2013. (People of Importance Ser.: 21). (gr. 4-18). 19.95 (978-1-4222-2844-9(4)) 2004. (Great Names Ser.). (gr. 3-18). lib. bdg. 19.95 (978-1-59084-145-7(X)) Mason Crest.

Crump, Marty. The Mystery of Darwin's Frog. Jenkins, Steve & Rodriguez, Edel, illus. 2013. (ENG.). 40p. (J). (gr. 2-5). 16.95 (978-1-59078-864-6(8)) Boyds Mills Pr.

Gibbons, Alan. Charles Darwin. 2008. (Illus.). 64p. (J). (978-0-7534-1729-4(4), Kingfisher) Roaring Brook Pr.

Granström, Brita. What Mr Darwin Saw. Manning, Mick, illus. 2014. (ENG.). 48p. (J). (gr. 1-4). pap. 9.95 (978-1-84780-107-4(2), Frances Lincoln) Quarto Publishing Group UK GBR. Dist: Hachette Bk. Group.

Green, John. Charles Darwin. 2009. (Dover History Coloring Book Ser.). (ENG.). 32p. (J). (gr. 3-8). pap. 3.99 (978-0-486-47282-9(5)) Dover Pubns., Inc.

Heiligman, Deborah. Charles & Emma: The Darwins' Leap of Faith. 2009. (ENG.). 272p. (YA). (gr. 8-12). 18.95 (978-0-8050-8721-5(4), 9780805087215, Holt, Henry & Co. Bks. For Young Readers) Holt, Henry & Co.

—Charles & Emma: The Darwins' Leap of Faith. 2011. (ENG., Illus.). 296p. (YA). (gr. 8-12). pap. 10.99 (978-0-312-66104-5(5), 9780312661045) Square Fish.

Herbert, David. Charles Darwin's Religious Journey. 2010. (978-1-894400-34-3(8)) Joshua Pr., Inc.

Hopkinson, Deborah. Who Was Charles Darwin? Harrison, Nancy, illus. 2005. (Who Was? Ser.). (ENG.). 112p. (J). (gr. 3-7). pap. 5.99 (978-0-448-43764-4(3), Grosset & Dunlap) Penguin Young Readers Group.

Howell, Izzi. Charles Darwin's Voyages of Discovery. 2016. (Why Do We Remember? Ser.). (ENG., Illus.). 32p. (J). (gr. 1-3). 17.99 (978-1-4451-4853-3(6), Franklin Watts) Hachette Children's Group GBR. Dist: Hachette Bk. Group.

Hunter, Nick. Charles Darwin, 1 vol. 2014. (Science Biographies Ser.). (ENG.). 32p. (gr. 2-4). pap. 8.95 (978-1-4109-6602-5(X), Raintree Perspectives) Heinemann-Raintree.

Johnson, Sylvia A. Shaking the Foundation: Charles Darwin & the Theory of Evolution. 2013. (ENG.). 88p. (gr. 6-12). lib. bdg. 33.27 (978-0-7613-5486-4(7), Twenty-First Century Bks.) Lerner Publishing Group.

King, David C. & Dorling Kindersley Publishing Staff. Charles Darwin: A Photographic Story of a Life. 2006. (DK Biography Ser.). (ENG., Illus.). 128p. (J). (gr. 5-12). per. 6.99 (978-0-7566-2554-2(8), DK Children) Dorling Kindersley Publishing, Inc.

Krull, Kathleen. Charles Darwin. Kulikov, Boris, illus. (Giants of Science Ser.). (ENG.). 144p. (J). (gr. 3-7). 2015. 7.99 (978-0-14-751463-9(0), Puffin Books) 2010. 15.99 (978-0-670-06335-2(5), Viking Books for Young Readers) Penguin Young Readers Group.

Lasky, Kathryn. One Beetle Too Many: The Extraordinary Adventures of Charles Darwin. Trueman, Matthew, illus. 2014. (Candlewick Biographies Ser.). (ENG.). 48p. (J). (gr. 2-5). 14.99 (978-0-7636-6842-6(7)) Candlewick Pr.

Lawson, Kristan. Darwin & Evolution for Kids: His Life & Ideas with 21 Activities. 2003. (For Kids Ser.). (ENG., Illus.). 160p. (J). (gr. 4). pap. 16.95 (978-1-55652-502-5(8)) Chicago Review Pr., Inc.

Lin, Yoming S. Charles Darwin & Evolution. 2012. (Eureka! Ser.). (Illus.). 24p. (YA). (gr. 3-6). lib. bdg. 22.60 (978-1-4488-5031-0(2)) Rosen Publishing Group, Inc., The.

Luongo, Charlotte. Evolution. 2009. (Big Ideas in Science Ser.). (Illus.). 48p. (gr. 5-8). 31.36 (978-0-7614-4393-3(2)) Marshall Cavendish Corp.

MacDonald, Fiona. Inside the Beagle with Charles Darwin. Bergin, Mark, illus. 2005. (ENG.). 48p. (J). (gr. 3-6). 19.95 (978-1-59270-041-7(1)) Enchanted Lion Bks., LLC.

Novelli, Luca. Darwin & the True Story of the Dinosaurs. 2017. (Flashes of Genius Ser.). (ENG.). 128p. (J). (gr. 3). pap. 9.99 **(978-1-61373-873-3(0))** Chicago Review Pr., Inc.

O'Riordan, Aileen & Triggs, Pat. Following in Darwin's Footsteps. 2010. (ENG., Illus.). 40p. pap. 9.00 (978-1-84246-420-5(5)) Kew Publishing GBR. Dist: Chicago Distribution Ctr.

Ridley, Sarah. Charles Darwin. 2017. (Super Scientists Ser.). (ENG., Illus.). 24p. (J). (gr. 1-3). pap. 9.99 **(978-1-4451-5355-1(6)**, Franklin Watts) Hachette Children's Group GBR. Dist: Hachette Bk. Group.

Schanzer, Rosalyn & Darwin, Charles. What Darwin Saw: The Journey That Changed the World. 2009. (ENG., Illus.). 48p. (J). (gr. 5). lib. bdg. 26.90 (978-1-4263-0397-5(1)); 17.95 (978-1-4263-0396-8(3)) National Geographic Society. (National Geographic Children's Bks.).

Sís, Peter. The Tree of Life: Charles Darwin. Sis, Peter, illus. 2003. (ENG., Illus.). 44p. (J). (gr. k-3). 21.99 (978-0-374-45628-3(3), 9780374456283, Farrar, Straus & Giroux (BYR)) Farrar, Straus & Giroux.

—The Tree of Life: Charles Darwin. (Illus.). 22.95 (978-0-88899-564-3(4)) Groundwood Bks. CAN. Dist: Publishers Group West (PGW).

Thermes, Jennifer. Charles Darwin's Around-The-World Adventure. 2016. (ENG., Illus.). 48p. (J). (gr. k-2). 18.95 (978-1-4197-2120-5(8), Abrams Bks. for Young Readers) Abrams, Inc.

Weaver, Anne H. The Voyage of the Beetle: A Journey Around the World with Charles Darwin & the Search for the Solution to the Mystery of Mysteries, As Narrated by Rosie, an Articulate Beetle. Lawrence, George, illus. 2007. (ENG.). 80p. (J). (gr. 5-8). 19.95 (978-0-8263-4304-8(X)) Univ. of New Mexico Pr.

Webster, Stephen. Charles Darwin. 2016. (History Makers Ser.). (ENG., Illus.). 144p. (J). (gr. 9-9). 45.64 (978-1-5026-1916-7(4)) Cavendish Square Publishing.

Whiting, Jim. Charles Darwin & the Origin of the Species. 2005. (Uncharted, Unexplored, & Unexplained Ser.). (Illus.). 48p. (J). (gr. 3-8). lib. bdg. 29.95 (978-1-58415-364-1(4)) Mitchell Lane Pubs., Inc.

Winston, Robert M. L. Evolution Revolution. 2016. (Illus.). 96p. (J). (978-1-4844-8141-7(0)) Dorling Kindersley Publishing, Inc.

DARWIN, CHARLES, 1809-1882—FICTION

Balliett, Blue. The Danger Box. 2012. (ENG.). 320p. (J). (gr. 3-7). pap. 7.99 (978-0-439-85210-4(2), Scholastic Paperbacks) Scholastic, Inc.

Johnson, Vargie. Charles Darwin, the Discoverer: What Made Them Famous? 2006. (Illus.). 152p. (J). per. 15.00 (978-1-931195-91-1(9)) KiwE Publishing, Ltd.

Meyer, Carolyn. The True Adventures of Charley Darwin. 2011. (ENG., Illus.). 336p. (YA). (gr. 7). pap. 9.99 (978-0-547-41564-2(8)) Houghton Mifflin Harcourt Publishing Co.

Weaver, Anne H. The Voyage of the Beetle: A Journey Around the World with Charles Darwin & the Search for the Solution to the Mystery of Mysteries, As Narrated by Rosie, an Articulate Beetle. Lawrence, George, tr. Lawrence, George, illus. 2004. (Roman Mysteries Ser.). 80p. (J). (gr. 5-8). lib. bdg. 26.90 (978-0-7613-2923-7(4), Millbrook Pr.) Lerner Publishing Group.

DARWINISM

see Evolution

DATA PROCESSING

see Information Storage and Retrieval Systems

DATA STORAGE AND RETRIEVAL SYSTEMS

see Information Storage and Retrieval Systems

DATE ETIQUETTE

see Dating (Social Customs)

DATING (SOCIAL CUSTOMS)

see also Love; Marriage

Bailey, Lorilyn. The Original Dating Questionnaire for Teens: A Great Way to Get to Know Each Other. (Illus.). 128p. (Orig.). (YA). (gr. 7-12). pap. (978-0-9641239-7-7(5)) Lormax Communications.

Baish, Vanessa. Dating. 2007. (FAQ: Teen Life Ser.). (Illus.). 64p. (YA). (gr. 7-12). lib. bdg. 31.95 (978-1-4042-1969-4(2)) Rosen Publishing Group, Inc., The.

—Frequently Asked Questions about Dating. 2009. (FAQ: Teen Life Ser.). 64p. (gr. 5-6). 58.50 (978-1-61512-573-9(6)) Rosen Publishing Group, Inc., The.

Beisswenger, Iffer & Eldred, Margaret. The Way We See Things: Middle Schoolers Look at Themselves & Issues They Face Everyday. Krusi, Carolynne, ed. 2004. 96p. pap. 14.95 (978-0-9759264-0-6(3)) Anemone Publishing.

Bosworth, Lo. The Lo-Down. 2011. (ENG.). 256p. (YA). (gr. 9-18). pap. 9.99 (978-1-4424-1200-2(3), Simon & Schuster Bks. For Young Readers) Simon & Schuster Bks. For Young Readers.

Busby, Cylin. First Kiss (Then Tell) A Collection of True Lip-Locked Moments. 2008. (ENG., Illus.). 224p. (YA). (gr. 7). pap. 8.95 (978-1-59990-241-8(9), 9781599902418, Bloomsbury USA Childrens) Bloomsbury Publishing USA.

Chastain, Zachary. From the Parlor to the Altar: Romance & Marriage in The 1800s. 2009. (Daily Life in America in the 1800s Ser.). 64p. (YA). (gr. 7-18). pap. 9.95 (978-1-4222-1852-5(X)); lib. bdg. 22.95 (978-1-4222-1779-5(5)) Mason Crest.

Clark, Chap. Next Time I Fall in Love: How to Handle Sex, Intimacy, & Feelings in Dating Relationships. 2004. 144p. pap. 20.00 (978-1-59244-684-1(1), Wipf and Stock) Wipf & Stock Pubs.

Cobb, Carlene. Coping with an Abusive Relationship. 2005. (Coping Ser.). (Illus.). 192p. (YA). (gr. 7-12). lib. bdg. 34.60 (978-0-8239-2822-4(5)) Rosen Publishing Group, Inc., The.

Collins, Sophie. How to Love a Werewolf. 2010. (ENG., Illus.). 128p. (gr. -1-17). 12.50 (978-1-84601-368-3(2), Spruce) Octopus Publishing Group GBR. Dist: Hachette Bk. Group.

Culp, Jennifer. Dating Etiquette & Sexual Respect. 2016. (Etiquette Rules! Ser.). 00048p. (J). (gr. 6-6). pap. 11.75 (978-1-4994-6492-4(4)) Rosen Publishing Group, Inc., The.

Dzuver, Leo, et al. How to Get a Girlfriend. 2014. (Illus.). 31p. (J). pap. (978-0-545-80577-3(5)) Scholastic, Inc.

Eastham, Chad. The Truth about Breaking Up, Making Up, & Moving On, 1 vol. 2013. (ENG.). 240p. pap. 14.99 (978-1-4003-2115-5(8)) Nelson, Thomas Inc.

—The Truth about Guys: One Guy Reveals What Every Girl Should Know, 1 vol. ed. 2006. (ENG., Illus.). 240p. (gr. 8-13). pap. 12.99 (978-1-4003-0968-9(9)) Nelson, Thomas Inc.

Evert, J. Pure Love. 2004. pap. 1.33 (978-1-888992-13-7(1)) Catholic Answers, Inc.

The FrogBuster Dating Diary: The Perfect Dating Companion. 2004. 169p. (YA). spiral bd. (978-0-9703102-1-7(8)) Intralife Systems Publishing.

Garcia, David. Don't Awaken Love Before the Time: Why Young People Lose When They Date. 2003. (YA). pap. 7.99 (978-1-889893-99-0(4), Ambassador-Emerald, International) Emerald Hse. Group, Inc.

Gerdes, Louise, ed. Teen Dating. 2013. (Opposing Viewpoints Ser.). (ENG., Illus.). 240p. (gr. 10-12). pap. 29.45 (978-0-7377-6345-4(0)); lib. bdg. 42.95 (978-0-7377-6344-7(2)) Cengage Gale. (Greenhaven Pr., Inc.).

Gray, T. L. Keezy's 10 Awesome Rules for Teenaged Dating! 2011. (ENG., Illus.). 95p. pap. 12.00 (978-0-9834332-4-8(0)) Vabella Publishing.

Gunton, Sharon. Date & Acquaintance Rape. 2008. (Social Issues Firsthand Ser.). (ENG., Illus.). 107p. (YA). (gr. 10-12). lib. bdg. 33.75 (978-0-7377-4250-3(X), LML02109-243162, Greenhaven Pr., Inc.) Cengage Gale.

Haugen, David M. Interracial Relationships. 2006. (At Issue Ser.). (ENG.). 128p. (gr. 10-12). 39.40 (978-0-7377-2390-8(4)); 98p. (YA). (gr. 8-12). 24.45 (978-0-7377-2391-5(2), Greenhaven Pr., Inc.) Cengage Gale.

Hentges, Katie. Your First Boyfriend. 2012. (Relationships 101 Ser.). (ENG., Illus.). 48p. (J). (gr. 5-8). 27.95 (978-1-4488-6829-2(7)); pap. 11.75 (978-1-4488-6833-9(5)) Rosen Publishing Group, Inc., The. (Rosen Reference).

Heos, Bridget. Your First Girlfriend. 2012. (Relationships 101 Ser.). (ENG., Illus.). 48p. (J). (gr. 5-8). pap. 11.75 (978-1-4488-6836-0(X)); lib. bdg. 27.95 (978-1-4488-6830-8(0)) Rosen Publishing Group, Inc., The.

Hopkins, Cathy. The Mates, Dates Guide to Life, Love, & Looking Luscious. 2005. (Mates, Dates Ser.). (ENG., Illus.). 256p. (YA). (gr. 7). pap. 7.99 (978-1-4169-0279-9(1), Simon Pulse) Simon Pulse.

Kaplan, Arie. Dating & Relationships: Navigating the Social Scene. 2011. (Young Man's Guide to Contemporary Issues Ser.). (ENG.). 104p. (YA). (gr. 9-12). lib. bdg. 34.60 (978-1-4488-5523-0(3)) Rosen Publishing Group, Inc., The.

Landau, Elaine. Date Violence. 2005. (Life Balance Ser.). (ENG., Illus.). 80p. (J). (gr. 5-8). pap. 6.95 (978-0-531-16613-0(9), Watts, Franklin) Scholastic Library Publishing.

Levy, Barrie. In Love & in Danger: A Teen's Guide to Breaking Free of Abusive Relationships. 3rd rev. ed. 2006. (ENG., Illus.). 144p. (Orig.). per. 13.00 (978-1-58005-187-3(1)) Seal Pr.

Mayo, Jeanne. Uncensored: Dating, Friendship, & Sex. 2007. (Illus.). 237p. (YA). (gr. 7-12). per. 14.99 (978-1-57794-821-6(1)) Harrison House Pubs.

Miles, Lisa & Chown, Xanna Eve. How to Survive Dating. 2013. (Girl Talk Ser.). 48p. (J). (gr. 5-8). pap. 70.50 (978-1-4777-0719-7(0), Rosen Reference); (ENG., Illus.). pap. 11.75 (978-1-4777-0718-0(2), Rosen Classroom); (ENG., Illus.). lib. bdg. 29.25 (978-1-4777-0705-0(0), Rosen Reference) Rosen Publishing Group, Inc., The.

Rose, Lyman Hinckley. Pure & Chased. 2004. ix, 86p. pap. 7.95 (978-1-55517-774-4(3)) Cedar Fort, Inc./CFI Distribution.

Ross, Michael, et al. Dating, Relating, Waiting: God's Word on Purity. 2015. (ENG., Illus.). 192p. (YA). pap. 7.99 (978-1-63058-369-9(3), GoTandem) Barbour Publishing, Inc.

Scherer, Lauri S. Dating. Gale, ed. 2014. (Issues That Concern You Ser.). (ENG., Illus.). 144p. (gr. 7-10). lib. bdg. 42.00 (978-0-7377-6288-4(8), Greenhaven Pr., Inc.) Cengage Gale.

Smiler, Andrew M. Dating & Sex: A Guide for the 21st Century Teen Boy. 2015. 288p. (J). pap. (978-1-4338-2045-8(5), Magination Pr.) American Psychological Assn.

Stanley, Barb. What Catholics Teens Should Know When Dating Turns Violent. Larkin, Jean K., ed. 2004. (What Catholic Teens Should Know Ser.). (Illus.). 8p. (YA). 7.95 (978-0-89837-239-7(9), 441210) Pflaum Publishing Group.

Stewart, Ed & McDowell, Josh. Finding True Love. 2008. (Project 17:17 Ser.). (ENG.). 64p. (J). pap. 4.99 (978-1-84550-356-7(2), d5fc11fa-99e7-4d6c-b4b5-7793875dbf44) Christian Focus Pubns. GBR. Dist: Bookmasters Distribution.

Sundquist, Josh. We Should Hang Out Sometime: Embarrassingly, a True Story. 2016. (ENG.). 352p. (YA). (gr. 7-17). pap. 10.99 (978-0-316-25100-6(3)) Little, Brown Bks. for Young Readers.

Taylor, Paula. Run Farrah Run: Detecting, Ditching & Dealing with Dating Dopes. von Seeburg, Kate, ed. Foster, Frank, illus. 2004. 128p. (YA). pap. 12.95 (978-0-9749173-0-6(3)) Tea Party Pr.

Tomories, K. G. Someone Special for You to Know. 2010. 28p. pap. 13.99 (978-1-4389-9651-6(9)) AuthorHouse.

Vranich, Belisa & Eagleson, Holly. Boys Lie: How Not to Get Played. 2010. (ENG.). 264p. (YA). (gr. 13-18). pap. 12.95 (978-0-7573-1364-6(7), HCI Teens) Health Communications, Inc.

Wilkins, Jessica. Date Rape. 2010. (Straight Talk about... Ser.). (ENG.). 48p. (J). (gr. 7-10). pap. (978-0-7787-2135-2(3)); lib. bdg. (978-0-7787-2128-4(0)) Crabtree Publishing Co.

DATING (SOCIAL CUSTOMS)—FICTION

Abbott, Hailey. Forbidden Boy. 2008. (ENG.). 256p. (YA). (gr. 9-18). pap. 8.99 (978-0-06-125382-9(0), HarperTeen) HarperCollins Pubs.

—Getting Lost with Boys. 2006. (ENG.). 240p. (YA). (gr. 9). pap. 8.99 (978-0-06-082432-7(8), HarperTeen) HarperCollins Pubs.

—Next Summer. 2005. (Summer Boys Ser.: 2). (ENG.). 240p. (J). (gr. 7-12). pap. 9.99 (978-0-439-75540-5(9)) Scholastic, Inc.

—The Other Boy. 2008. (ENG.). 272p. (YA). (gr. 9-18). pap. 8.99 (978-0-06-125383-6(9), HarperTeen) HarperCollins Pubs.

—The Secrets of Boys. 2006. (ENG.). 272p. (YA). (gr. 9). pap. 8.99 (978-0-06-082433-4(6), HarperTeen) HarperCollins Pubs.

—Waking up to Boys. 2007. (ENG.). 256p. (YA). (gr. 9). pap. 8.99 (978-0-06-082435-8(2), HarperTeen) HarperCollins Pubs.

Adrian, Susan. Tunnel Vision: A Novel. 2015. (ENG.). 320p. (YA). (gr. 8-12). 18.99 (978-1-250-04792-2(7), 9781250047922, St. Martin's Griffin) St. Martin's Pr.

Aguirre, Ann. The Queen of Bright & Shiny Things. 2015. (ENG.). 336p. (YA). (gr. 7). 17.99 (978-1-250-04750-2(1), 9781250047502) Feiwel & Friends.

Aitken, Amber. Perfect Match, Vol. 4. 2011. (Cupid Company Ser.). (ENG.). 240p. (J). (gr. 4-6). pap. 9.99 (978-0-00-736263-9(3)) HarperCollins Pubs. Ltd. GBR. Dist: Independent Pubs. Group.

Akins, Karen. Twist. 2015. (ENG.). 336p. (YA). (gr. 7-12). 18.99 (978-1-250-03100-6(1), 9781250031006, St. Martin's Griffin) St. Martin's Pr.

Allen, Rachael. The Revenge Playbook. 2015. (ENG.). 368p. (YA). (gr. 8). pap. 9.99 (978-0-06-228136-4(4), HarperTeen) HarperCollins Pubs.

—17 First Kisses. 2014. (ENG.). 352p. (YA). (gr. 8). pap. 9.99 (978-0-06-228134-0(8), HarperTeen) HarperCollins Pubs.

Alpine, Rachele. A Void the Size of the World. 2017. (ENG., Illus.). 368p. (YA). (gr. 9). 17.99 **(978-1-4814-8571-5(7)**, Simon Pulse) Simon Pulse.

Anderson, Annette Latva. Alone into Darkness: Was It Fate or an Error in Judgment? 2013. (ENG.). 46p. (J). pap. 9.95 (978-1-4787-1208-4(2)) Outskirts Pr., Inc.

Anderson, Lily. The Only Thing Worse Than Me Is You. 2016. (ENG.). 352p. (YA). 18.99 (978-1-250-07909-1(8), 9781250079091, St. Martin's Griffin) St. Martin's Pr.

Appelt, Kathi. Kissing Tennessee: It's Night for & Love if You Dare. 2004. (ENG., Illus.). 132p. (YA). (gr. 7-12). reprint ed. pap. 7.99 (978-0-15-205127-3(9)) Houghton Mifflin Harcourt Publishing Co.

Applegate, Katherine & Grant, Michael. Claire Gets Caught & What Zoey Saw. 2015. (Islanders Ser.: 3). (ENG.). 464p. (YA). (gr. 8). pap. 9.99 (978-0-06-234080-1(8), HarperTeen) HarperCollins Pubs.

—The Islanders Vol. 2: Nina Won't Tell & Ben's in Love. 2015. (Islanders Ser.: 2). (ENG.). 464p. (YA). (gr. 8). pap. 9.99 (978-0-06-234078-8(6), HarperTeen) HarperCollins Pubs.

Armentrout, Jennifer L. Don't Look Back. 2014. (Novel Ser.: 1). (ENG.). 384p. (YA). (gr. 9-17). 16.99 (978-1-4231-7512-4(3)) Hyperion Bks. for Children.

Arnold, Elana K. Infandous. 2017. (ENG.). 200p. (gr. 8-12). 9.99 (978-1-5124-4146-8(5), Carolrhoda Bks.) Lerner Publishing Group.

Arnold, Elana K. What Girls Are Made Of. 2017. (ENG.). 208p. (YA). (gr. 8-12). 18.99 (978-1-5124-1024-2(1)); 9.99 **(978-1-5124-3437-8(X)**, Carolrhoda Lab™); 38.65 **(978-1-5124-2694-6(6)**, Carolrhoda Lab™); 38.65 **(978-1-5124-3438-5(8)**, Carolrhoda Lab™) Lerner Publishing Group.

Ashton, Victoria. Juicy Secrets. 2006. (Confessions of a Teen Nanny Ser.). 208p. (J). lib. bdg. 16.89 (978-0-06-077526-1(2)); (ENG.). (YA). (gr. 9-12). 15.99 (978-0-06-073181-6(8)) HarperCollins Pubs. (HarperTeen).

—Rich Girls. 2006. (Confessions of a Teen Nanny Ser.). (ENG.). 224p. (YA). (gr. 9-12). 15.99 (978-0-06-073179-3(6)) HarperCollins Pubs.

Baccellia, Kim. No More Goddesses. 2013. (ENG.). 252p. (YA). (gr. 3-7). pap. 14.99 (978-1-61271-012-9(3), Zumaya Thresholds) Zumaya Pubns. LLC.

Baer, Marianna. The Inconceivable Life of Quinn. 2017. (ENG.). 384p. (YA). 18.95 (978-1-4197-2302-5(2), Amulet Bks.) Abrams, Inc.

Baker, E. D. The Perfect Match. 2015. (Fairy-Tale Matchmaker Ser.). (ENG.). 288p. (YA). (gr. 3-6). 16.99 (978-1-61963-588-3(7), 9781619635883, Bloomsbury USA Childrens) Bloomsbury Publishing USA.

—The Truest Heart. 2016. (Fairy-Tale Matchmaker Ser.). (ENG.). 272p. (J). 16.99 (978-1-61963-849-5(5), 9781619638495, Bloomsbury USA Childrens) Bloomsbury Publishing USA.

Banash, Jennifer. The Elite. 2008. (ENG.). 256p. (YA). (gr. 9-18). 9.99 (978-0-425-22157-0(1), Berkley) Penguin Publishing Group.

—In Too Deep. 2009. (ENG.). 256p. (YA). (gr. 9-18). 9.99 (978-0-425-22353-6(1), Berkley) Penguin Publishing Group.

—Simply Irresistible. 2009. (ENG.). 256p. (YA). (gr. 9-18). 9.99 (978-0-425-22783-1(9), Berkley) Penguin Publishing Group.

Bankes, Liz. Undeniable. 2015. (ENG.). 256p. (YA). (gr. 9). 17.99 (978-0-8027-3623-9(8), 9780802736239, Bloomsbury USA Childrens) Bloomsbury Publishing USA.

Banks, Piper. Geek Abroad, 2 vols. 2008. (Geek High Ser.: 2). (ENG.). 256p. (YA). (gr. 9-18). 9.99 (978-0-451-22393-7(4), Berkley) Penguin Publishing Group.

—Geek High. 2007. (Geek High Ser.: 1). (ENG.). 256p. (YA). (gr. 9-18). 9.99 (978-0-451-22225-1(3), Berkley) Penguin Publishing Group.

—Summer of the Geek. 2010. (Geek High Ser.: 3). (ENG.). 256p. (YA). (gr. 5-18). 9.99 (978-0-451-22984-7(3), Berkley) Penguin Publishing Group.

Baratz-Logsted, Lauren. Red Girl, Blue Boy: An If Only Novel. 2015. (If Only... Ser.). (ENG.). 304p. (YA). (gr. 7). pap. 9.99 (978-1-61963-685-9(9), 9781619636859, Bloomsbury USA Childrens) Bloomsbury Publishing USA.

Barnholdt, Lauren. From This Moment. 2015. (Moment of Truth Ser.: 3). (ENG.). 272p. (YA). (gr. 8). pap. 9.99 (978-0-06-232143-5(9), HarperTeen) HarperCollins Pubs.

—Ghost of a Chance. 2014. (Girl Meets Ghost Ser.: 3). (ENG., Illus.). 240p. (J). (gr. 4-9). 15.99 (978-1-4424-4248-1(4), Aladdin) Simon & Schuster Children's Publishing.

—Girl Meets Ghost. 2013. (Girl Meets Ghost Ser.: 1). (ENG.). 240p. (J). (gr. 4-9). pap. 7.99 (978-1-4424-2146-2(0), Aladdin) Simon & Schuster Children's Publishing.

—Heat of the Moment. 2015. (Moment of Truth Ser.: 1). (ENG.). 304p. (YA). (gr. 8). pap. 9.99 (978-0-06-232139-8(0), HarperTeen) HarperCollins Pubs.

—One Moment in Time. 2015. (Moment of Truth Ser.: 2). (ENG.). 304p. (YA). (gr. 8). pap. 9.99 (978-0-06-232141-1(2), HarperTeen) HarperCollins Pubs.

—One Night That Changes Everything. (ENG., (YA). (gr. 9). 2011. Illus.). 272p. pap. 9.99 (978-1-4424-0367-3(5)) 2010. 256p. 16.99 (978-1-4169-9479-4(3)) Simon Pulse. (Simon Pulse).

—The Thing about the Truth. (ENG.). (YA). (gr. 9). 2013. 320p. pap. 9.99 (978-1-4424-3461-5(9)) 2012. 304p. 16.99 (978-1-4424-3460-8(0)) Simon Pulse. (Simon Pulse).

—Through to You. 2014. (ENG., Illus.). 288p. (YA). (gr. 9). 17.99 (978-1-4424-3463-9(5), Simon Pulse) Simon Pulse.

—Two-Way Street. 2013. (ENG., Illus.). 320p. (YA). (gr. 9). 17.99 (978-1-4424-8952-3(9), Simon Pulse) Simon Pulse.

Baskin, Nora Raleigh. The Summer Before Boys. (ENG.). 208p. (J). (gr. 4-7). 2012. pap. 6.99 (978-1-4169-8674-4(X)) 2011. 16.99 (978-1-4169-8673-7(1)) Simon & Schuster Bks. For Young Readers. (Simon & Schuster Bks. For Young Readers).

Bass, Alexis. Love & Other Theories. 2014. (ENG.). 384p. (YA). (gr. 9). 17.99 *(978-0-06-227532-5(1)*, HarperTeen) HarperCollins Pubs.
—What's Broken Between Us. 2015. (ENG.). 304p. (YA). (gr. 9). 17.99 *(978-0-06-227535-6(6)*, HarperTeen) HarperCollins Pubs.
Bateson, Catherine. Magenta Mcphee. 2010. (ENG.). 176p. (J). (gr. 3-7). pap. 16.95 *(978-0-8234-2253-1(4))* Holiday Hse., Inc.
Bauman, Beth Ann. Rosie & Skate. 2011. (ENG.). 224p. (YA). (gr. 9). pap. 8.99 *(978-0-385-73736-4(X)*, Ember) Random Hse. Children's Bks.
Belasen, Amy & Osborn, Jacob. Jenny Green's Killer Junior Year. 2008. (ENG.). 304p. (YA). (gr. 9-18). pap. 14.99 *(978-1-4169-6792-7(3)*, Simon Pulse) Simon Pulse.
Bennett, Cindy C. Geek Girl. 2011. 280p. (J). pap. 15.99 *(978-1-59955-925-4(0))* Bonneville B.V. NLD. Dist: Cedar Fort, Inc./CFI Distribution.
Bennett, Jenn. Alex, Approximately. 2017. (ENG., Illus.). 400p. (YA). (gr. 9). 17.99 *(978-1-4814-7877-9(X)*, Simon Pulse) Simon Pulse.
Benway, Robin. Audrey, Wait! l.t. ed. 2009. 435p. (YA). 23.95 *(978-1-4104-1422-9(1))* Thorndike Pr.
Billingsley, ReShonda Tate. Friends 'Til the End. 2009. (Good Girlz Ser.: 6). (ENG., Illus.). 208p. pap. 11.00 *(978-1-4165-5877-4(2)*, Gallery Bks.) Gallery Bks.
Birchall, Katy. Team Awkward. 2017. (It Girl Ser.: 2). (ENG., Illus.). 304p. (YA). (gr. 4-8). 16.99 *(978-1-4814-6365-2(9)*, Simon & Schuster/Paula Wiseman Bks.) Simon & Schuster/Paula Wiseman Bks.
Birdsall, Jeanne. The Penderwicks on Gardam Street. 2011. (Playaway Children Ser.). (J). (gr. 3-6). 44.99 *(978-1-61707-435-6(7))* Findaway World, LLC.
—The Penderwicks on Gardam Street. (Penderwicks Ser.). (ENG.). (J). (gr. 3-7). 2010. 336p. 7.99 *(978-0-440-42203-7(5)*, Yearling) 2008. 320p. 16.99 *(978-0-375-84090-6(7)*, Knopf Bks. for Young Readers) Random Hse. Children's Bks.
—The Penderwicks on Gardam Street. 2010. (Penderwicks Ser.: 2). lib. bdg. 18.40 *(978-0-606-14418-6(8)*, Turtleback) Turtleback Bks.
Birthday Vicious. 2014. (Ashley Project Ser.: 3). (ENG., Illus.). 304p. (J). (gr. 4-8). pap. 7.99 *(978-1-4424-9038-3(1)*, Aladdin) Simon & Schuster Children's Publishing.
Blackstone, Matt. Sorry You're Lost. 2014. (ENG.). 320p. (J). (gr. 5-9). 15.99 *(978-0-374-38065-6(1)*, 9780374380656, Farrar, Straus & Giroux (BYR)) Farrar, Straus & Giroux.
Block, Francesca Lia. Teen Spirit. 2014. (ENG.). 240p. (YA). (gr. 9). 17.99 *(978-0-06-200809-1(9)*, HarperTeen) HarperCollins Pubs.
Bloom, Ira. Hearts & Other Body Parts. 2017. (ENG.). 352p. (J). (gr. 9). 17.99 *(978-1-338-03073-0(6)*, Scholastic Pr.) Scholastic, Inc.
Bloom, M. Beth. Don't Ever Change. 2015. (ENG.). 368p. (YA). (gr. 9). 17.99 *(978-0-06-203688-9(2)*, HarperTeen) HarperCollins Pubs.
Bloom, Steve. The Stand-In. 2016. (ENG.). 360p. (YA). (gr. 8-12). 18.99 *(978-1-5124-1023-5(3))*; 38.65 *(978-1-5124-1121-8(3)*, Carolrhoda Lab™) Lerner Publishing Group.
Blount, Patty. TMI. 2013. (ENG.). 336p. (YA). (gr. 7-12). pap. 9.99 *(978-1-4022-7340-7(1)*, 9781402273407) Sourcebooks, Inc.
Bonin, Liane. Pretty on the Outside: Fame Unlimited. 2007. 288p. (YA). pap. 9.99 *(978-0-451-22122-3(2)*, N A L Trade) Penguin Publishing Group.
Boudreau, Helene. Real Mermaids Don't Need High Heels. 2013. (ENG.). 240p. (J). (gr. 4-8). pap. 6.99 *(978-1-4022-6458-0(5)*, Sourcebooks Jabberwocky) Sourcebooks, Inc.
Bradley, Alex. 24 Girls in 7 Days. 2006. (ENG.). 272p. (YA). (gr. 7-18). reprint ed. 6.99 *(978-0-14-240543-7(4)*, Speak) Penguin Young Readers Group.
Brahmachari, Sita. Jasmine Skies. 2014. (ENG.). 336p. (J). (gr. 3-7). 16.99 *(978-0-8075-3782-4(9))* Whitman, Albert & Co.
Brandes, Wendy L. Nina's Not Boy Crazy! (She Just Likes Boys) Lorenzet, Eleonora, illus. 2016. (Summer Camp Ser.). (ENG.). 96p. (gr. 4-6). lib. bdg. 24.65 *(978-1-4965-2601-4(5))* Stone Arch Bks.
Brewer, Heather. The Cemetery Boys. 2015. (ENG.). 288p. (YA). (gr. 8). 17.99 *(978-0-06-230788-0(6)*, HarperTeen) HarperCollins Pubs.
—The Cemetery Boys. 2016. 304p. (YA). (gr. 8). pap. 9.99 *(978-0-06-230789-7(4)*, HarperTeen) HarperCollins Pubs.
—The Cemetery Boys. 2016. (YA). lib. bdg. 20.85 *(978-0-606-38741-5(2))* Turtleback Bks.
Brian, Kate, pseud. Beautiful Disaster. 2009. (Privilege Ser.: No. 2). (ENG.). 288p. (YA). (gr. 9-18). pap. 9.99 *(978-1-4169-6760-6(5)*, Simon & Schuster Bks. For Young Readers) Simon & Schuster Bks. For Young Readers.
—Fake Boyfriend. 2009. (ENG.). 288p. (YA). (gr. 9). pap. 8.99 *(978-1-4169-1368-9(8)*, Simon & Schuster Bks. For Young Readers) Simon & Schuster Bks. For Young Readers.
—Inner Circle. 2007. (Private Ser.: No. 5). (ENG.). 224p. (YA). (gr. 9-12). pap. 9.99 *(978-1-4169-5041-7(9)*, Simon & Schuster Bks. For Young Readers) Simon & Schuster Bks. For Young Readers.
—Invitation Only. 2006. (Private Ser.: No. 2). (ENG.). 272p. (YA). (gr. 9-18). pap. 9.99 *(978-1-4169-1874-5(4)*, Simon & Schuster Bks. For Young Readers) Simon & Schuster Bks. For Young Readers.
—Last Christmas: The Private Prequel. 2008. (Private Ser.). (ENG.). 272p. (YA). (gr. 9-18). 16.99 *(978-1-4169-1369-6(6)*, Simon & Schuster Bks. For Young Readers) Simon & Schuster Bks. For Young Readers.
—Legacy. 2008. (Private Ser.: No. 6). (ENG.). 256p. (YA). (gr. 9). pap. 9.99 *(978-1-4169-5042-4(7)*, Simon & Schuster Bks. For Young Readers) Simon & Schuster Bks. For Young Readers.
—Paradise Lost. 2009. (Private Ser.: 9). (ENG.). 256p. (YA). (gr. 9-18). pap. 9.99 *(978-1-4169-5884-0(3)*, Simon & Schuster Bks. For Young Readers) Simon & Schuster Bks. For Young Readers.
—Pure Sin. 2010. (Privilege Ser.: Bk. 5). (ENG.). 208p. (YA). (gr. 9-18). pap. 9.99 *(978-1-4424-0786-2(7)*, Simon & Schuster Bks. For Young Readers) Simon & Schuster Bks. For Young Readers.
—Revelation. 2008. (Private Ser.: No. 8). (ENG.). 288p. (YA). (gr. 9-18). pap. 11.99 *(978-1-4169-5883-3(5)*, Simon & Schuster Bks. For Young Readers) Simon & Schuster Bks. For Young Readers.
—The V Club. 2004. (ENG., Illus.). 288p. (YA). (gr. 9). 14.95 *(978-0-689-86764-4(6)*, Simon & Schuster Bks. For Young Readers) Simon & Schuster Bks. For Young Readers.
—The Virginity Club. 2008. (ENG.). 304p. (YA). (gr. 9). pap. 8.99 *(978-1-4169-5370-8(1)*, Simon & Schuster Bks. For Young Readers) Simon & Schuster Bks. For Young Readers.
Brody, Jessica. A Week of Mondays. 2016. (ENG.). 464p. (YA). 17.99 *(978-0-374-38270-4(0)*, 9780374382704, Farrar, Straus & Giroux (BYR)) Farrar, Straus & Giroux.
Brown, Jennifer. Thousand Words. 2014. (YA). lib. bdg. 20.85 *(978-0-606-35311-3(9))* Turtleback Bks.
Brown, Teri. Read My Lips. 2008. (ENG.). 256p. (YA). (gr. 9-12). pap. 8.99 *(978-1-4169-5868-0(1)*, Simon Pulse) Simon Pulse.
Brunner, Kym. Flip the Bird. 2016. (ENG.). 368p. (YA). (gr. 7). 17.99 *(978-0-544-80085-4(0)*, HMH Books For Young Readers) Houghton Mifflin Harcourt Publishing Co.
Bryan, Sabrina & DeVillers, Julia. Princess of Gossip. 2008. (ENG.). 384p. pap. 23.99 *(978-1-4165-7065-3(9)*, MTV Bks.) MTV Books.
Bryant, Annie. Crush Alert. 2008. (Beacon Street Girls Ser.: 14). (ENG.). 288p. (J). (gr. 4-8). pap. 8.99 *(978-1-4169-6437-7(1)*, Aladdin) Simon & Schuster Children's Publishing.
—Letters from the Heart. 2008. (Beacon Street Girls Ser.: 3). (ENG., Illus.). 256p. (J). (gr. 4-8). pap. 6.99 *(978-1-4169-6426-1(6)*, Aladdin) Simon & Schuster Children's Publishing.
Buckle, J. A. Half My Facebook Friends Are Ferrets, 1 vol. 2014. (ENG.). 224p. (gr. 9-12). 16.95 *(978-1-63079-000-4(1))* Switch Pr.
Burd, Nick. The Vast Fields of Ordinary. 2009. (ENG.). 320p. (YA). (gr. 9-18). 16.99 *(978-0-8037-3340-4(2)*, Dial Bks) Penguin Young Readers Group.
Burkhart, Jessica. Take the Reins. 2009. (Canterwood Crest Ser.: 1). (ENG.). 256p. (J). (gr. 4-8). pap. 7.99 *(978-1-4169-5840-6(1)*, Aladdin) Simon & Schuster Children's Publishing.
Burnham, Niki. Sticky Fingers. 2005. (ENG.). 288p. (YA). (gr. 9-18). pap. 7.99 *(978-0-689-87649-3(1)*, Simon Pulse) Simon Pulse.
Burrell, Carol klio. Secret Diary. Neel, Julien, illus. 2012. (Lou! Ser.: 1). (ENG.). 48p. (J). (gr. 6-9). lib. bdg. 27.93 *(978-0-7613-8776-3(5)*, Graphic Universe™) Lerner Publishing Group.
—Summertime Blues. Neel, Julien, illus. 2012. (Lou! Ser.: 2). (ENG.). 48p. (J). (gr. 6-9). lib. bdg. 27.93 *(978-0-7613-8777-0(3)*, Graphic Universe™) Lerner Publishing Group.
Byars, Betsy. The Cybil War. l.t. ed. 2003. (LRS Large Print Heritage Ser.). 122p. (J). lib. bdg. 27.95 *(978-1-58118-111-1(6))* LRS.
Byler, Linda. The Little Amish Matchmaker: A Christmas Romance. 2012. (ENG.). 187p. 14.95 *(978-1-56148-776-9(7)*, Good Bks.) Skyhorse Publishing Co., Inc.
Cabot, Meg. In Waiting. 2008. (Princess Diaries: 4). (ENG.). 256p. (YA). (gr. 8). pap. 9.99 *(978-0-06-154364-7(0)*, HarperTeen) HarperCollins Pubs.
—Pants on Fire. (YA). 2008. (ENG.). 288p. (gr. 8). pap. 9.99 *(978-0-06-088017-0(1))* 2007. (ENG.). 272p. (gr. 7-10). 16.99 *(978-0-06-088015-6(5))* 2007. 260p. (gr. 7-10). lib. bdg. 17.89 *(978-0-06-088016-3(3))* HarperCollins Pubs. (HarperTeen).
—Princess in Waiting. 2003. (YA). (Princess Diaries: Vol. 4). (gr. 7-18). pap. 6.99 *(978-0-06-054065-4(6))*; Vol. IV. (Princess Diaries: 4). (ENG., Illus.). 240p. (gr. 8-18). 17.99 *(978-0-06-009607-6(1)*, HarperTeen) HarperCollins Pubs.
Cagan, Kayla. Piper Perish. 2017. (ENG., Illus.). 416p. (YA). 17.99 *(978-1-4521-5583-8(6))* Chronicle Bks. LLC.
Calame, Don. Swim the Fly. (ENG., Illus.). 352p. (YA). (gr. 9). 2010. pap. 7.99 *(978-0-7636-4776-6(4))* 2009. 16.99 *(978-0-7636-4157-3(X))* Candlewick Pr.
Caletti, Deb. Stay. (ENG.). (YA). (gr. 7). 2012. 336p. pap. 9.99 *(978-1-4424-0374-1(8))* 2011. 320p. 16.99 *(978-1-4424-0373-4(X))* Simon Pulse. (Simon Pulse).
Calloway, Cassidy. Confessions of a First Daughter. 2009. (ENG.). 224p. (YA). (gr. 8-18). pap. 9.99 *(978-0-06-172439-8(4)*, HarperTeen) HarperCollins Pubs.
—Secrets of a First Daughter. 2010. (ENG.). 208p. (YA). (gr. 8-18). pap. 8.99 *(978-0-06-172442-8(4)*, HarperTeen) HarperCollins Pubs.
Cann, Kate. Consumed. (ENG.). 336p. (J). (gr. 9). 2012. pap. 9.99 *(978-0-545-26387-0(5))* 2011. 16.99 *(978-0-545-26388-7(3))* Scholastic, Inc.
—Mediterranean Holiday: Or, How I Moved to a Tiny Island & Found the Love of My Life. 2007. (ENG.). 416p. (YA). (gr. 9-12). pap. 5.99 *(978-0-06-115216-0(1)*, HarperTeen) HarperCollins Pubs.
—Possessed. (ENG.). 336p. (J). (gr. 9-9). 2011. pap. 9.99 *(978-0-545-12813-1(7))* 2010. 16.99 *(978-0-545-12812-4(9))* Scholastic, Inc.
Carlson, Melody. Secret Admirer, 1 vol. 2016. (Faithgirlz / Girls of Harbor View Ser.). (ENG.). 272p. (J). pap. 9.99 *(978-0-310-75371-1(6))* Zonderkidz.
—Torch Red: Color Me Torn. 2004. (Truecolors Ser.: 3). (ENG.). 208p. (YA). pap. 14.99 *(978-1-57683-531-9(6)*, Th1nk Bks.) NavPress Publishing Group.
Carter, Ally. Cross My Heart & Hope to Spy. 2016. (Gallagher Girls Ser.: 2). (J). lib. bdg. 20.85 *(978-0-606-38296-0(8))* Turtleback Bks.
—Perfect Scoundrels. 2014. (Heist Society Novel Ser.). (ENG.). 336p. (YA). (gr. 7-12). pap. 9.99 *(978-1-4231-6681-8(7))* Hyperion Bks. for Children.
—Perfect Scoundrels. 2013. (Heist Society Novel Ser.). (ENG.). 336p. (YA). (gr. 7-17). 17.99 *(978-1-4231-6600-9(0))* Hyperion Pr.
Carter, Nikki & Elliott, Kevin. The Break-Up Diaries, Vol. 2. 2011. (ENG.). 288p. (YA). (gr. 9). pap. 9.95 *(978-0-7582-6888-4(2)*, K-Teen/Dafina) Kensington Publishing Corp.
Castellucci, Cecil. The Year of the Beasts. Powell, Nate, illus. 2012. (ENG.). 192p. (YA). (gr. 7-12). 16.99 *(978-1-59643-686-2(7)*, 9781596436862) Roaring Brook Pr.
—The Year of the Beasts. Powell, Nate, illus. 2014. (ENG.). 208p. (YA). (gr. 7-12). pap. 9.99 *(978-1-250-05076-2(6)*, 9781250050762) Square Fish.
Cerato, Mattia. Mom's New Friend. Cerato, Mattia, illus. 2014. (Family Snaps Ser.). (ENG., Illus.). 32p. (J). (gr. k-2). pap. 6.95 *(978-1-939656-61-2(3))* Red Chair Pr.
Certain Signals. 2014. (Gift Ser.). (ENG.). 112p. (YA). (gr. 6-12). lib. bdg. 27.93 *(978-1-4677-3511-7(6))* Lerner Publishing Group.
Chandler, Elizabeth. Summer in the City. 2006. (ENG.). 384p. (YA). (gr. 9). pap. 8.99 *(978-0-06-084734-0(4)*, HarperTeen) HarperCollins Pubs.
Chen, Justina. A Blind Spot for Boys. 2014. (ENG.). 336p. (YA). (gr. 7-17). 18.00 *(978-0-316-10253-7(9))* Little, Brown Bks. for Young Readers.
Cherry, Alison. For Real. 2016. (ENG.). 304p. (YA). (gr. 7). pap. 9.99 *(978-0-385-74296-2(7)*, Ember) Random Hse. Children's Bks.
Choyce, Lesley. Reacción, 1 vol. 2012. (Spanish Soundings Ser.). (SPA.). 112p. (YA). (gr. 8-12). pap. 9.95 *(978-1-4598-0308-4(6))* Orca Bk. Pubs. USA.
Clark, Bridie. Maybe Tonight? 2013. (Snap Decision Ser.: 1). (ENG.). 224p. (YA). (gr. 7). pap. 9.99 *(978-1-59643-816-3(9))* Roaring Brook Pr.
—You Only Live Once. 2014. (Snap Decision Ser.: 2). (ENG.). 224p. (YA). (gr. 7). pap. 9.99 *(978-1-59643-817-0(7)*, 9781596438170) Roaring Brook Pr.
Clark, Catherine. Banana Splitsville. 2008. (ENG.). 288p. (YA). (gr. 8). pap. 5.99 *(978-0-06-136715-1(X)*, HarperTeen) HarperCollins Pubs.
—Eleven Things I Promised. 2016. 304p. (YA). (gr. 8). pap. 9.99 *(978-0-06-226453-4(2)*, HarperTeen) HarperCollins Pubs.
—Frozen Rodeo. 2003. (ENG.). 304p. (J). (gr. 8-18). 15.99 *(978-0-06-009070-8(7))* HarperCollins Pubs.
—Love & Other Things I'm Bad At: Rocky Road Trip & Sundae My Prince Will Come. 2011. (ENG.). 592p. (YA). (gr. 9-18). pap. 9.99 *(978-0-06-177863-6(X)*, HarperTeen) HarperCollins Pubs.
—Picture Perfect. 2008. (ENG.). 352p. (YA). (gr. 9-18). pap. 5.99 *(978-0-06-137497-5(0)*, HarperTeen) HarperCollins Pubs.
—So Inn Love. 2007. (ENG.). 336p. (YA). (gr. 9-12). pap. 5.99 *(978-0-06-113904-8(1)*, HarperTeen) HarperCollins Pubs.
Cody, Paul. Love Is Both Wave & Particle. 2017. (ENG.). 320p. (YA). 17.99 *(978-1-62672-688-8(4)*, 9781626726888) Roaring Brook Pr.
Cofer, Judith Ortiz. An Island Like You: Stories of the Barrio. 2009. 243p. 17.00 *(978-1-60686-446-3(7))* Perfection Learning Corp.
Coffey, Jan. Tropical Kiss. 2005. (ENG.). 352p. (J). (gr. 9-18). pap. 5.99 *(978-0-06-076003-8(6)*, HarperTeen) HarperCollins Pubs.
Cohn, Rachel. Kill All Happies. 2017. (ENG.). 288p. (YA). (gr. 9-17). 17.99 *(978-1-4231-5722-9(2))* Hyperion Pr.
Cohn, Rachel & Levithan, David. Naomi & Ely's No Kiss List. 2008. (ENG.). 256p. (YA). (gr. 9). pap. 9.99 *(978-0-375-84441-6(4)*, Ember) Random Hse. Children's Bks.
Colasanti, Susane. All I Need. 2014. (ENG.). 240p. (YA). (gr. 7). pap. 9.99 *(978-0-14-242676-0(8)*, Speak) Penguin Young Readers Group.
—Now & Forever. 2014. (ENG.). 272p. (YA). (gr. 7). 17.99 *(978-0-670-01424-8(9)*, Viking Books for Young Readers) Penguin Young Readers Group.
—Take Me There. 2009. (ENG.). 320p. (YA). (gr. 7-18). 9.99 *(978-0-14-241435-4(2)*, Speak) Penguin Young Readers Group.
—Waiting for You. 2010. (ENG.). 336p. (YA). (gr. 7-18). 9.99 *(978-0-14-241575-7(8)*, Speak) Penguin Young Readers Group.
Colbert, Brandy. Little & Lion. 2017. (ENG.). 336p. (YA). (gr. 9-17). 17.99 ***(978-0-316-34900-0(3))*** Little, Brown Bks. for Young Readers.
Complete Nothing. 2014. (True Love Ser.: 2). (ENG., Illus.). 336p. (YA). (gr. 7). pap. 9.99 *(978-1-4424-7720-9(2)*, Simon & Schuster Bks. For Young Readers) Simon & Schuster Bks. For Young Readers.
Condie, Ally. Being Sixteen. 2010. (YA). *(978-1-60641-233-6(7))* Deseret Bk. Co.
—First Day. 2007. 304p. (YA). pap. 15.95 *(978-1-59038-775-7(9))* Deseret Bk. Co.
—Yearbook. 2006. 208p. (YA). pap. 14.95 *(978-1-59038-690-3(6))* Deseret Bk. Co.
Conrad, Lauren. The Fame Game. 2012. (YA). (Fame Game Ser.: 1). (ENG.). 336p. (gr. 9). pap. 10.99 *(978-0-06-207519-2(5))*; 313p. 12.99 *(978-0-06-209271-7(5))* HarperCollins Pubs.
—Infamous. 2013. 277p. (J). 12.00 *(978-0-06-224756-8(5))* HarperCollins Pubs.
—Starstruck. (YA). 2013. (Fame Game Ser.: 2). (ENG.). 320p. (gr. 9). pap. 10.99 *(978-0-06-207982-4(4))* 2012. (Fame Game Ser.: 2). (ENG.). 304p. (gr. 9). 18.99 *(978-0-06-207980-0(8))* 2012. 352p. pap. *(978-0-06-220964-1(7))* HarperCollins Pubs.
Converse, P. J. Subway Girl. 2011. (ENG.). 224p. (YA). (gr. 9-18). 16.99 *(978-0-06-157514-3(3)*, HarperTeen) HarperCollins Pubs.
Cook, Eileen. The Education of Hailey Kendrick. 2011. (ENG.). (YA). (gr. 9). 288p. pap. 9.99 *(978-1-4424-1326-9(3))*; 272p. 16.99 *(978-1-4424-1325-2(5))* Simon Pulse. (Simon Pulse).
—Year of Mistaken Discoveries. 2014. (ENG., Illus.). 272p. (YA). (gr. 9). 17.99 *(978-1-4424-4022-7(8)*, Simon Pulse) Simon Pulse.
Cooner, Donna. Worthy. 2017. (ENG.). 288p. (J). (gr. 7). 17.99 *(978-0-545-90393-6(9))* Scholastic, Inc.
Cotugno, Katie. 99 Days. (YA). (gr. 8). 2016. 400p. pap. 9.99 *(978-0-06-221639-7(2))* 2015. (ENG.). 384p. 17.99 *(978-0-06-221638-0(4))* HarperCollins Pubs.
Cozzo, Karole. How to Keep Rolling after a Fall. 2016. (ENG.). 272p. (YA). pap. 9.99 *(978-1-250-07928-2(4)*, 9781250079282) Feiwel & Friends.
—How to Say I Love You Out Loud. 2015. (ENG.). 240p. (YA). (gr. 7). pap. 9.99 *(978-1-250-06359-5(0))* Feiwel & Friends.
—The Truth about Happily Ever After. 2017. (ENG.). 320p. (YA). 17.99 *(978-1-250-12797-6(1)*, 9781250127976) Feiwel & Friends.
Croall, Marie P. My Boyfriend Is a Monster - Under His Spell. Park, Hyeondo, illus. 2011. (My Boyfriend Is a Monster Ser.: 4). (ENG.). 128p. (YA). (gr. 7-12). pap. 9.95 *(978-0-7613-7076-5(5)*, Graphic Universe™) Lerner Publishing Group.
—Under His Spell, 4 vols., No. 4. Park, Hyeondo, illus. 2011. (My Boyfriend Is a Monster Ser.: 4). (ENG.). 128p. (YA). (gr. 7-12). 29.27 *(978-0-7613-5602-8(9))* Lerner Publishing Group.
Cummins, Maria S. The Lamplighter. 2011. 308p. pap. 16.99 *(978-1-61203-228-3(1))* Bottom of the Hill Publishing.
Cumyn, Alan. Hot Pterodactyl Boyfriend. 2016. (ENG., Illus.). 416p. (YA). (gr. 9). 17.99 *(978-1-4814-3980-0(4)*, Atheneum/Caitlyn Dlouhy Books) Simon & Schuster Children's Publishing.
—Tilt. 2013. 260p. pap. *(978-1-4596-6448-7(5))* ReadHowYouWant.com, Ltd.
Czukas, Liz. Ask Again Later. 2014. (ENG.). 336p. (YA). (gr. 8). pap. 9.99 *(978-0-06-227239-3(X)*, HarperTeen) HarperCollins Pubs.
Dalton, Michelle. Fifteenth Summer. 2013. (ENG.). 272p. (YA). (gr. 7). 17.99 *(978-1-4424-7267-9(7))*; (Illus.). pap. 10.99 *(978-1-4424-7266-2(9))* Simon Pulse. (Simon Pulse).
—Pulled Under. 2014. (Sixteenth Summer Ser.). (ENG., Illus.). 288p. (YA). (gr. 7). pap. 9.99 *(978-1-4814-0700-7(7)*, Simon Pulse) Simon Pulse.
—Sixteenth Summer. 2011. (Sixteenth Summer Ser.). (ENG.). 304p. (YA). (gr. 7-18). pap. 9.99 *(978-1-4424-2344-2(7)*, Simon Pulse) Simon Pulse.
Darrows, Eva. The Awesome. 2015. (ENG.). 352p. (YA). (gr. 10). pap. 9.99 *(978-1-78108-324-6(X)*, Ravenstone) Rebellion GBR. Dist: Simon & Schuster, Inc.
Davis, Cynthia. Drink the Rain. 2007. (Illus.). 256p. (YA). per. 12.95 *(978-0-9712163-1-0(2))* Greenroom Bks.
Day, Susie. My Invisible Boyfriend. 2010. (ENG.). 288p. (J). (gr. 7-18). 16.99 *(978-0-545-07354-7(5)*, Scholastic Pr.) Scholastic, Inc.
De la Cruz, Melissa. The Au Pairs. (Au Pairs Ser.: 1). (ENG.). (YA). 2004. 304p. 14.95 *(978-0-689-87066-8(3))* 2005. 320p. reprint ed. pap. 9.99 *(978-0-689-87319-5(0))* Simon & Schuster Bks. For Young Readers. (Simon & Schuster Bks. For Young Readers).
—Crazy Hot. (Beach Lane Ser.: 4). (ENG., (YA). (gr. 9). 2013. Illus.). 288p. pap. 9.99 *(978-1-4424-7412-3(2))* 2008. 320p. pap. 9.99 *(978-1-4169-4808-7(2))* Simon & Schuster Bks. For Young Readers. (Simon & Schuster Bks. For Young Readers).
—Sun-Kissed. 2006. (Au Pairs Ser.: 3). (ENG.). 320p. (YA). (gr. 9-18). 15.95 *(978-1-4169-1746-5(2)*, Simon & Schuster Bks. For Young Readers) Simon & Schuster Bks. For Young Readers.
Demetrios, Heather. Bad Romance. 2017. (ENG.). 368p. (YA). 17.99 *(978-1-62779-772-6(6)*, 9781627797726, Holt, Henry & Co. Bks. For Young Readers) Holt, Henry & Co.
Deriso, C. H. Elisabeth & the Unwanted Advice. 2016. (Babysitter Chronicles Ser.). (ENG., Illus.). 160p. (gr. 4-7). lib. bdg. 26.65 *(978-1-4965-2757-8(7))* Stone Arch Bks.
Deriso, Christine Hurley. Elisabeth & the Unwanted Advice. 2016. (Babysitter Chronicles Ser.). (ENG., Illus.). 160p. (gr. 4-7). pap. 6.95 *(978-1-4914-8864-5(6))* Stone Arch Bks.
Derting, Kimberly. Body Finder. 2010. (Body Finder Ser.: 1). (ENG.). 336p. (YA). (gr. 9-18). 17.99 *(978-0-06-177981-7(4))* HarperCollins Pubs.
Desir, C. Fault Line. 2013. (ENG.). 240p. (YA). (gr. 10). 16.99 *(978-1-4424-6072-0(5)*, Simon Pulse) Simon Pulse.
Dessen, Sarah. Along for the Ride. (ENG.). (YA). (gr. 7-18). 2011. 432p. pap. 10.99 *(978-0-14-241556-6(1)*, Speak) 2009. 416p. 19.99 *(978-0-670-01194-0(0)*, Viking Books for Young Readers) Penguin Young Readers Group.
—Along for the Ride. 2011. lib. bdg. 20.85 *(978-0-606-15360-7(8)*, Turtleback) Turtleback Bks.
—The Moon & More. 2013. (ENG.). 384p. (J). (gr. 7). 19.99 *(978-0-670-78560-5(1)*, Viking Books for Young Readers) Penguin Young Readers Group.
—Once & for All. 2017. (ENG.). 368p. (YA). (gr. 7). 19.99 *(978-0-425-29033-0(6)*, Viking Books for Young Readers) Penguin Young Readers Group.
—Saint Anything. (ENG.). (YA). (gr. 7). 2016. 448p. pap. 10.99 *(978-0-14-751603-9(X)*, Speak) 2015. 432p. 19.99 *(978-0-451-47470-4(8)*, Viking Books for Young Readers) Penguin Young Readers Group.
—Saint Anything. 2016. lib. bdg. 22.10 *(978-0-606-38833-7(8))* Turtleback Bks.
Destiny, A. & Helms, Rhonda. Never Too Late. 2015. (Flirt Ser.). (ENG., Illus.). 224p. (YA). (gr. 7). pap. 9.99 *(978-1-4814-5188-8(X)*, Simon Pulse) Simon Pulse.
—Sparks in Scotland. 2015. (Flirt Ser.). (ENG.). 224p. (YA). (gr. 7). pap. 9.99 *(978-1-4814-2121-8(2)*, Simon Pulse) Simon Pulse.
Disney Book Group Staff. Pining Away. 2014. (Gravity Falls Ser.: 1). (J). lib. bdg. 14.75 *(978-0-606-35287-1(2))* Turtleback Bks.
Doktorski, Jennifer Salvato. Famous Last Words. 2013. (ENG.). 288p. (YA). (gr. 7). 17.99 *(978-0-8050-9367-4(2)*, 9780805093674, Holt, Henry & Co. Bks. For Young Readers) Holt, Henry & Co.
—The Summer after You & Me. 2015. (ENG.). 304p. (YA). (gr. 8-12). pap. 10.99 *(978-1-4926-1903-1(5))* Sourcebooks, Inc.
Dougherty, Meghan. Woe of Jade Doe. Birnbach, Alece, illus. 2015. (Dorothy's Derby Chronicles Ser.: 2). (ENG.). 288p. (J). (gr. 4-7). pap. 6.99 *(978-1-4926-0147-0(0)*, Sourcebooks Jabberwocky) Sourcebooks, Inc.
Downing, Erin. Drive Me Crazy. 2009. (Romantic Comedies Ser.). (ENG.). 240p. (YA). (gr. 7-18). mass mkt. 6.99 *(978-1-4169-7484-0(9)*, Simon Pulse) Simon Pulse.
Downing, Erin. Moon Shadow. 2017. (ENG., Illus.). 256p. (J). (gr. 3-7). 17.99 ***(978-1-4814-7521-1(5)***, Aladdin) Simon & Schuster Children's Publishing.
Doyle, Marissa. Betraying Season. 2010. (ENG.). 336p. (YA). (gr. 9-13). pap. 19.99 *(978-0-312-62916-8(8)*, 9780312629168) Square Fish.
Duff, Hilary. True: An Elixir Novel. (Elixir Ser.). (ENG., 304p. (YA). (gr. 7). 2014. Illus.). pap. 9.99 *(978-1-4424-0858-6(8))* 2013. 17.99 *(978-1-4424-0857-9(X))* Simon & Schuster Bks.

For Young Readers. (Simon & Schuster Bks. For Young Readers).

Duncan, Lois. Debutante Hill. 2013. (ENG., Illus.). 200p. (gr. 6). pap. 12.95 (978-1-939601-00-1(2)) Ig Publishing, Inc.

Dyer, Jonah Lisa & Dyer, Stephen. The Season. 2016. (ENG.). 352p. (YA). (gr. 9). 17.99 (978-0-451-47634-0(4), Viking Books for Young Readers) Penguin Young Readers Group.

Easton, Kelly. To Be Mona. (ENG.). 224p. (YA). (gr. 7). 2009. pap. 7.99 (978-1-4169-0055-9(1)) 2008. 16.99 (978-1-4169-0054-2(3)) McElderry, Margaret K. Bks. (McElderry, Margaret K. Bks.).

Echols, Jennifer. Biggest Flirts. 2014. (Superlatives Ser.). (ENG., Illus.). 336p. (YA). (gr. 9). pap. 9.99 (978-1-4424-7445-1(9), Simon Pulse) Simon Pulse.

—Most Likely to Succeed. 2015. (Superlatives Ser.). (ENG., Illus.). 352p. (YA). (gr. 9). 17.99 (978-1-4424-7452-9(1), Simon Pulse) Simon Pulse.

—The One That I Want. 2012. (ENG.). 288p. (YA). (gr. 7). pap. 9.99 (978-1-4424-5236-7(6), Simon Pulse) Simon Pulse.

—Perfect Couple. 2015. (Superlatives Ser.). (ENG., Illus.). 336p. (YA). (gr. 9). pap. 10.99 (978-1-4424-7448-2(3), Simon Pulse) Simon Pulse.

Eglington, Tara. How to Keep a Boy from Kissing You. 2016. (ENG.). 320p. (YA). 18.99 (978-1-250-04953-7(9), 9781250049537) St. Martin's Pr.

Eland, Lindsay. Scones & Sensibility. 2010. (ENG.). 320p. (J). (gr. 4-7). 6.99 (978-1-60684-158-7(0), Carolrhoda Bks.) Lerner Publishing Group.

Elkeles, Simone. Better Than Perfect. 2014. (Wild Cards Ser.). (ENG.). 352p. (YA). (gr. 9). pap. 9.99 (978-0-8027-3725-0(0), 9780802737250, Bloomsbury USA Childrens) Bloomsbury Publishing USA.

—Perfect Chemistry. 2015. (Perfect Chemistry Novel Ser.). (ENG.). 384p. (YA). (gr. 9). pap. 9.99 (978-1-61963-701-6(4), 9781619637016, Bloomsbury USA Childrens) Bloomsbury Publishing USA.

Ellen, Tom & Ivison, Lucy. A Totally Awkward Love Story. 2016. (ENG.). 320p. (YA). (gr. 9). 17.99 (978-0-553-53732-1(6), Delacorte Pr.) Random Hse. Children's Bks.

Elmendorf, Dana. South of Sunshine. 2017. (ENG.). 256p. (YA). (gr. 8-12). pap. 9.99 **(978-0-8075-7571-0(2))** Whitman, Albert & Co.

Emerson, Kevin. Exile. (Exile Ser.: 1). (ENG.). (YA). (gr. 9). 2015. 336p. pap. 9.99 (978-0-06-213396-0(9)) 2014. 320p. 17.99 (978-0-06-213395-3(0)) HarperCollins Pubs. (Tegen, Katherine Bks).

Emery, Anne. Dinny Gordon, Freshman. 2004. (J). per. 9.95 (978-1-930009-97-4(6)) Image Cascade Publishing.

—Dinny Gordon Sophomore. 2004. (J). per. 9.95 (978-1-930009-98-1(4)) Image Cascade Publishing.

—Senior Year. Krush, Beth, illus. 2006. (YA). per. 11.95 (978-1-59511-005-3(4)) Image Cascade Publishing.

Emond, Stephen. Bright Lights, Dark Nights. 2015. (ENG., Illus.). 384p. (YA). (gr. 7). 17.99 (978-1-62672-206-4(4)) Roaring Brook Pr.

—Happyface. 2011. (ENG., Illus.). 336p. (YA). (gr. 7-17). pap. 10.99 (978-0-316-04099-0(1)) Little, Brown Bks. for Young Readers.

—Winter Town. 2012. (ENG., Illus.). 352p. (YA). (gr. 7-17). pap. 10.99 (978-0-316-13331-9(0)) Little, Brown Bks. for Young Readers.

Eulberg, Elizabeth. Better off Friends. 2014. (ENG.). 288p. (J). (gr. 7). 17.99 (978-0-545-55145-8(5)) Scholastic, Inc.

—Just Another Girl. 2017. (ENG.). 256p. (J). (gr. 7). 17.99 (978-0-545-95628-4(5)) Scholastic, Inc.

—The Lonely Hearts Club. (ENG.). 304p. (J). 2011. (gr. 3-7). pap. 8.99 (978-0-545-14032-4(3)) 2010. (gr. 9-12). 17.99 (978-0-545-14031-7(5)) Scholastic, Inc.

—Take a Bow. 2012. (ENG.). 288p. (J). (gr. 7). 17.99 (978-0-545-33474-7(8)); 280p. (YA). pap. (978-0-545-43982-4(5)) Scholastic, Inc.

—We Can Work It Out. 2015. (ENG.). 320p. (J). (gr. 7). 17.99 (978-0-545-65461-6(0)) Scholastic, Inc.

Fallenstein, J. Graffiti. 2017. (Midnight Ser.). (ENG.). 88p. (YA). (gr. 6-12). 26.65 (978-1-5124-2767-7(5)); 12.99 **(978-1-5124-3489-7(2)**, Darby Creek); 39.99 **(978-1-5124-3488-0(4)**, Darby Creek); 39.99 **(978-1-5124-2787-5(X)**, Darby Creek) Lerner Publishing Group.

Fallenstein, J. The Witching Hour. 2017. (Midnight Ser.). (ENG.). 96p. (YA). (gr. 6-12). 26.65 (978-1-5124-2771-4(3)); 12.99 **(978-1-5124-3498-9(1)**, Darby Creek); 39.99 **(978-1-5124-2791-2(8)**, Darby Creek); 39.99 **(978-1-5124-3497-2(3)**, Darby Creek) Lerner Publishing Group.

Fantaskey, Beth. Jessica's Guide to Dating on the Dark Side. 2010. (ENG., Illus.). 384p. (YA). (gr. 9-18). pap. 8.99 (978-0-547-25940-6(9)) Houghton Mifflin Harcourt Publishing Co.

Farrant, Natasha. The Secret Diary of Lydia Bennet. 2016. (ENG.). 336p. (YA). (gr. 7). 17.99 (978-0-545-94031-3(1), Chicken Hse., The) Scholastic, Inc.

Farrar, Josh. A Song for Bijou. 2013. (ENG.). 304p. (YA). (gr. 5-8). 16.99 (978-0-8027-3394-8(8), 9780802733948, Bloomsbury USA Childrens) Bloomsbury Publishing USA.

Fault Line. 2014. (ENG., Illus.). 256p. (YA). (gr. 10). pap. 11.99 (978-1-4424-6073-7(3), Simon Pulse) Simon Pulse.

Federle, Tim. The Great American Whatever. (ENG.). (YA). (gr. 9). 2017. 304p. pap. 10.99 (978-1-4814-0410-5(5)) 2016. (Illus.). 288p. E-Book (978-1-4814-0411-2(3)) 2016. (Illus.). 288p. 17.99 (978-1-4814-0409-9(1)) Simon & Schuster Bks. For Young Readers. (Simon & Schuster Bks. For Young Readers).

Feinstein, John. Rush for the Gold: Mystery at the Olympics. 2013. (Sports Beat Ser.). (ENG.). 336p. (J). (gr. 5). pap. 7.99 (978-0-375-87168-9(3), Yearling) Random Hse. Children's Bks.

Finnegan, Amy. Not in the Script. 2014. (If Only... Ser.). (ENG.). 392p. (YA). (gr. 7). 17.99 (978-1-61963-397-1(3), 9781619633971, Bloomsbury USA Childrens) Bloomsbury Publishing USA.

Fison, Julie. The Call of the Wild. 2015. (ENG.). 288p. (J). pap. (978-1-61067-388-4(3)) Kane Miller.

Fitzpatrick, Becca. The Complete Hush, Hush Saga: Hush, Hush; Crescendo; Silence; Finale. 2012. (Hush, Hush Saga Ser.: Bks. 1-4). (ENG.). 1744p. (YA). (gr. 9). 74.99 (978-1-4424-7372-0(X), Simon & Schuster Bks. For Young Readers) Simon & Schuster Bks. For Young Readers.

—Crescendo. 2011. (Hush, Hush Saga: Bk. 2). (SPA.). 408p. (YA). pap. 20.95 (978-84-666-4639-0(6)) Ediciones B ESP. Dist: Spanish Pubs., LLC.

—Crescendo. (Hush, Hush Saga Ser.: Bk. 2). (ENG.). (YA). (gr. 9). 2012. 464p. pap. 12.99 (978-1-4169-8944-8(7)) 2010. 432p. 18.99 (978-1-4169-8943-1(9)) Simon & Schuster Bks. For Young Readers. (Simon & Schuster Bks. For Young Readers).

—Finale. (Hush, Hush Saga Ser.). (ENG., (YA). (gr. 9). 2013. Illus.). 480p. pap. 12.99 (978-1-4424-2668-9(3)) 2012. 464p. 19.99 (978-1-4424-2667-2(5)) Simon & Schuster Bks. For Young Readers. (Simon & Schuster Bks. For Young Readers).

—Hush, Hush. (SPA.). 368p. 2010. (Hush, Hush Saga: Bk. 1). (YA). pap. 20.95 (978-84-666-4417-4(2)) pap. 13.95 (978-84-9872-932-0(7)) Ediciones B ESP. Dist: Spanish Pubs., LLC.

—Hush, Hush, 3 vols. Ruiz, Derek, ed. 2012. (Hush, Hush Saga: Bk. 1). (Illus.). 120p. (YA). 19.95 (978-0-9836131-1-4(7)) Sea Lion Bks.

—Hush, Hush. (Hush, Hush Saga Ser.: Bk. 1). (ENG.). (YA). (gr. 9-18). 2010. 432p. pap. 11.99 (978-1-4169-8942-4(0)) 2009. 400p. 21.99 (978-1-4169-8941-7(2)) Simon & Schuster Bks. For Young Readers. (Simon & Schuster Bks. For Young Readers).

Fitzpatrick, Huntley. What I Thought Was True. 2014. (ENG.). 416p. (YA). (gr. 9). 17.99 (978-0-8037-3909-3(5), Dial Bks) Penguin Young Readers Group.

Flack, Sophie. Bunheads. 2012. (ENG.). 320p. (YA). (gr. 7-17). pap. 10.99 (978-0-316-12654-0(3), Poppy) Little, Brown Bks. for Young Readers.

Flinn, Alex. Breathing Underwater. unabr. ed. 2004. (Young Adult Cassette Librariestm Ser.). 272p. (J). (gr. 7-18). pap. 36.00 incl. audio (978-0-8072-0992-9(9), S YA 346 SP, Listening Library) Random Hse. Audio Publishing Group.

Fontes, Justine. Deadly Drive. 2013. (Surviving Southside Ser.). (ENG.). 104p. (YA). (gr. 6-12). pap. 7.95 (978-1-4677-0704-6(X)); lib. bdg. 27.93 (978-1-4677-0310-9(9)) Lerner Publishing Group.

Fredericks, Mariah. Head Games. 2006. (ENG., Illus.). 272p. (YA). (gr. 7). pap. 6.99 (978-1-4169-1335-1(1), Atheneum Bks. for Young Readers) Simon & Schuster Children's Publishing.

Freeman, Martha. 1,000 Reasons Never to Kiss a Boy. 2007. (ENG.). 240p. (YA). (gr. 7-18). 16.95 (978-0-8234-2044-5(2)) Holiday Hse., Inc.

Freeman, Shannon. High School High, 1 vol. 2013. (Port City High Ser.). (ENG.). 199p. (YA). (gr. 9-12). pap. 9.95 (978-1-62250-037-6(7)) Saddleback Educational Publishing, Inc.

—Taken, 1 vol. 2013. (Port City High Ser.). (ENG.). 199p. (YA). (gr. 9-12). pap. 9.95 (978-1-62250-038-3(5)) Saddleback Educational Publishing, Inc.

—Traumatized. 2014. (Port City High Ser.: 7). (YA). lib. bdg. 20.80 (978-0-606-36619-9(9)) Turtleback Bks.

French, Gillian. Grit. 2017. 304p. (YA). (gr. 9). 17.99 (978-0-06-264255-4(3), HarperTeen) HarperCollins Pubs.

Freymann-Weyr, Garret. After the Moment. 2010. (ENG.). 336p. (YA). (gr. 9). pap. 7.99 (978-0-547-33168-3(1)) Houghton Mifflin Harcourt Publishing Co.

Friedman, Laurie. Can You Say Catastrophe? 2014. (Mostly Miserable Life of April Sinclair Ser.: 1). (ENG.). 160p. (J). (gr. 5-9). pap. 5.95 (978-1-4677-0941-5(7), Darby Creek) 2013. 151p. pap. 17.95 (978-1-4677-1620-8(0)) 2013. (Mostly Miserable Life of April Sinclair Ser.: 1). (ENG.). 160p. (J). (gr. 5-9). 17.95 (978-1-4677-0925-5(5), Darby Creek) Lerner Publishing Group.

—Life, Loss, & Lemonade. Shaloshvili, Natasha, illus. 2017. (Mostly Miserable Life of April Sinclair Ser.: 8). (ENG.). 168p. (gr. 5-9). (J). 17.95 (978-1-4677-8591-4(1)); 35.99 **(978-1-5124-2699-1(7))** Lerner Publishing Group. (Darby Creek).

—Mallory McDonald, Super Snoop. Kalis, Jennifer, illus. (Mallory Ser.: 18). (ENG.). 152p. (J). (gr. 2-5). 2013. pap. 5.95 (978-1-4677-0929-3(8), Darby Creek) 2012. 15.95 (978-0-7613-6073-5(5)) Lerner Publishing Group.

—Not What I Expected. Shaloshvili, Natasha, illus. 2015. (Mostly Miserable Life of April Sinclair Ser.: 5). (ENG.). 176p. (J). (gr. 5-9). 17.99 (978-1-4677-8829-8(5), Darby Creek) Lerner Publishing Group.

—Oh Boy, Mallory. Kalis, Jennifer, illus. (Mallory Ser.: 17). (ENG.). 160p. (J). (gr. 2-5). 2013. pap. 5.95 (978-1-4677-0863-0(1)) 2012. 15.95 (978-0-7613-6072-8(7), Darby Creek) Lerner Publishing Group.

—Too Good to Be True. 2014. (Mostly Miserable Life of April Sinclair Ser.: 2). (ENG., Illus.). 168p. (J). (gr. 5-9). 17.95 (978-1-4677-0926-2(3), Darby Creek) Lerner Publishing Group.

—Too Much Drama. Shaloshvili, Natasha, illus. 2016. (Mostly Miserable Life of April Sinclair Ser.: 6). (ENG.). 184p. (gr. 5-9). (J). 17.95 (978-1-4677-8589-1(X)); 35.99 (978-1-4677-9570-8(4)) Lerner Publishing Group. (Darby Creek).

—Truth & Kisses. 2015. (ENG.). 168p. (J). (gr. 5-9). pap. 5.95 (978-1-4677-0943-9(3), Darby Creek) Lerner Publishing Group.

Friedman, Laurie B. Love or Something Like It. 2015. (J). 5.99 (978-1-4677-7790-2(0)); (Mostly Miserable Life of April Sinclair Ser.: 4). (ENG.). 184p. (gr. 5-9). 17.95 (978-1-4677-0928-6(X)) Lerner Publishing Group.

—Not What I Expected. Shaloshvili, Natasha, illus. 2015. (ENG.). 176p. (J). (gr. 5-9). 17.95 (978-1-4677-8588-4(1)) Lerner Publishing Group.

—Truth & Kisses. 2014. (Mostly Miserable Life of April Sinclair Ser.: 3). (ENG.). 168p. (J). (gr. 5-9). 17.95 (978-1-4677-0927-9(1)) Lerner Publishing Group.

Friend, Natasha. For Keeps. 2011. (ENG.). 272p. (YA). (gr. 7-18). 7.99 (978-0-14-241846-8(3), Speak) Penguin Young Readers Group.

—My Life in Black & White. 2012. (ENG.). 304p. (YA). (gr. 7-18). pap. 8.99 (978-0-670-78494-3(X), Viking Books for Young Readers) Penguin Young Readers Group.

Frost, Helen. When My Sister Started Kissing. 2017. (ENG.). 208p. (J). 16.99 (978-0-374-30303-7(7), 9780374303037, Farrar, Straus & Giroux (BYR)) Farrar, Straus & Giroux.

Frost, Melissa. The Dating Tutor. 2013. 98p. pap. (978-1-77130-562-4(2)) Evernight Publishing.

Fujishima, Kosuke. Oh My Goddess!, Vol. 34. Fujishima, Kosuke, illus. 2010. (ENG., Illus.). 144p. pap. 10.99 (978-1-59582-448-6(0)) Dark Horse Comics.

Gaiewski, Maria Louise. Only by Chance, 1 vol. 2010. 246p. pap. 24.95 (978-1-4489-5342-4(1)) America Star Bks.

Gale, Emily. Girl Out Loud. 2012. (YA). (978-0-545-30439-9(3)); (ENG.). 288p. (J). (gr. 7-7). 17.99 (978-0-545-30438-2(5)) Scholastic, Inc. (Chicken Hse., The).

Gallagher, Diana G. Haunted Love, 1 vol. (Claudia & Monica: Freshman Girls Ser.). (ENG.). 144p. (gr. 3-6). 2013. 9.95 (978-1-4342-6286-8(3)) 2012. lib. bdg. 26.65 (978-1-4342-3277-9(8)) Stone Arch Bks. (Claudia & Monica: Freshman Girls).

—Homecoming, 1 vol. 2012. (Claudia & Monica: Freshman Girls Ser.). (ENG.). 144p. (gr. 3-6). lib. bdg. 26.65 (978-1-4342-3276-2(X), Claudia & Monica: Freshman Girls) Stone Arch Bks.

—Monica & the Sweetest Song, 1 vol. 2011. (Monica Ser.). (ENG.). 88p. (gr. 2-3). lib. bdg. 26.65 (978-1-4342-2556-6(9)) Stone Arch Bks.

—New Firsts, 1 vol. 2012. (Claudia & Monica: Freshman Girls Ser.). (ENG.). 144p. (gr. 3-6). lib. bdg. 26.65 (978-1-4342-3275-5(1), Claudia & Monica: Freshman Girls) Stone Arch Bks.

—Tested, 1 vol. 2012. (Claudia & Monica: Freshman Girls Ser.). (ENG.). 144p. (gr. 3-6). lib. bdg. 26.65 (978-1-4342-3278-6(6), Claudia & Monica: Freshman Girls) Stone Arch Bks.

Ganger, Candace. The Inevitable Collision of Birdie & Bash. 2017. (ENG.). 320p. (YA). 17.99 (978-1-250-11622-2(8), 9781250116222, St. Martin's Griffin) St. Martin's Pr.

Garfield, Leon. The Complete Bostock & Harris. 2014. (ENG.). 336p. (J). (gr. 3-7). 17.95 (978-1-59017-783-9(5), NYR Children's Collection) New York Review of Bks., Inc., The.

Garrett, Nicole. The Cupid Factor. 2007. 203p. pap. 14.50 (978-1-4357-0276-9(X)) Lulu Pr., Inc.

Garza, Xavier. Maximilian & the Bingo Rematch: A Lucha Libre Sequel. 2013. (Max's Lucha Libre Adventures Ser.). (ENG., Illus.). 208p. (J). (gr. 2-7). pap. 12.95 (978-1-935955-46-7(2)) Cinco Puntos Pr.

Garza, Xavier, illus. Maximilian & the Bingo Rematch: A Lucha Libre Sequel. 2013. (Max's Lucha Libre Adventures Ser.). (ENG.). 208p. (J). 19.95 (978-1-935955-59-7(4)) Cinco Puntos Pr.

George, McKelle. Speak Easy, Speak Love. 2017. 432p. (YA). (gr. 8). 17.99 **(978-0-06-256092-6(1)**, Greenwillow Bks.) HarperCollins Pubs.

Geragotelis, Brittany. The Witch Is Back. 2014. (Life's a Witch Ser.). (ENG., Illus.). 352p. (YA). (gr. 9). 17.99 (978-1-4424-6688-3(X), Simon & Schuster Bks. For Young Readers) Simon & Schuster Bks. For Young Readers.

—The Witch Is Back: A Life's a Witch Book. 2015. (Life's a Witch Ser.). (ENG., Illus.). 352p. (YA). (gr. 9). pap. 11.99 (978-1-4424-6691-3(X)) Simon & Schuster Children's Publishing.

Gerhardt, Jake. My Future Ex-Girlfriend. 2017. (ENG.). 240p. (J). (gr. 5). 16.99 (978-0-451-47541-1(0), Viking Books for Young Readers) Penguin Young Readers Group.

Ghost of a Chance. 2014. (Girl Meets Ghost Ser.: 3). (ENG., Illus.). 240p. (J). (gr. 4-9). pap. 7.99 (978-1-4424-2148-6(7), Aladdin) Simon & Schuster Children's Publishing.

Glines, Abbi. Bad for You. 2015. (Sea Breeze Ser.). (ENG., Illus.). 320p. (YA). (gr. 11). pap. 11.99 (978-1-4814-2074-7(7), Simon Pulse) Simon Pulse.

—Breathe. 2013. (Sea Breeze Ser.). (ENG., Illus.). 352p. (YA). (gr. 11). 17.99 (978-1-4424-8870-0(0)); pap. 9.99 (978-1-4424-8869-4(7)) Simon Pulse. (Simon Pulse).

—Breathe. 2011. 166p. (gr. 8-12). pap. 9.99 (978-1-61798-004-6(8)) Wild Child Publishing.

—Just for Now. 2013. (Sea Breeze Ser.). (ENG., Illus.). 336p. (YA). (gr. 11). 17.99 (978-1-4424-8861-8(1)); pap. 9.99 (978-1-4424-8860-1(3)) Simon Pulse. (Simon Pulse).

—Misbehaving. 2014. (Sea Breeze Ser.). (ENG., Illus.). 352p. (YA). (gr. 11). 17.99 (978-1-4814-0674-1(4)); pap. 11.99 (978-1-4814-0673-4(6)) Simon Pulse. (Simon Pulse).

—The Vincent Boys. 2012. (ENG.). 288p. (YA). (gr. 11). 17.99 (978-1-4424-8526-6(4)); pap. 9.99 (978-1-4424-8525-9(6)) Simon Pulse. (Simon Pulse).

—The Vincent Boys Collection Set: The Vincent Boys & the Vincent Brothers. 2013. (ENG., Illus.). 592p. (YA). (gr. 11). pap. 19.99 (978-1-4424-9862-4(5), Simon Pulse) Simon Pulse.

—The Vincent Brothers. Frost, Michael, photos by. 2012. (ENG., Illus.). 304p. (YA). (gr. 11). 17.99 (978-1-4424-8529-7(9)); pap. 9.99 (978-1-4424-8528-0(0)) Simon Pulse. (Simon Pulse).

—While It Lasts. 2013. (Sea Breeze Ser.). (ENG., Illus.). 304p. (YA). (gr. 11). 18.99 (978-1-4424-8867-0(0)); pap. 9.99 (978-1-4424-8866-3(2)) Simon Pulse. (Simon Pulse).

Gloster, Dean. Dessert First. 2016. (ENG.). 304p. (YA). 17.99 (978-1-4405-9454-0(6), Simon Pulse) Simon Pulse.

Gold, Maya. Spellbinding. 2013. (ENG.). 272p. (J). (gr. 7). pap. 8.99 (978-0-545-43380-8(0)) Scholastic, Inc.

Goldberg, Whoopi. Terrible Terrel. Roos, Maryn, illus. 2010. (ENG.). 160p. (J). (gr. 1-17). pap. 4.99 (978-0-7868-5263-5(1), Jump at the Sun) Hyperion Bks. for Children.

Goo, Maurene. I Believe in a Thing Called Love. 2017. (ENG.). 336p. (YA). 17.99 (978-0-374-30404-1(1), 9780374304041, Farrar, Straus & Giroux (BYR)) Farrar, Straus & Giroux.

Goodman, Katie & Kisiel, Soren. The Night Our Parents Went Out. 2015. (ENG., Illus.). 32p. (J). (gr. -1-2). 16.95 (978-1-57687-747-0(7), powerHouse Bks.) powerHouse Cultural Entertainment, Inc.

Goslee, S. J. Whatever. 2016. (ENG.). 272p. (YA). 17.99 (978-1-62672-399-3(0), 9781626723993) Roaring Brook Pr.

Gottfred, B. T. The Nerdy & the Dirty. 2016. (ENG.). 304p. (YA). 17.99 (978-1-62779-850-1(1), 9781627798501, Holt, Henry & Co. Bks. For Young Readers) Holt, Henry & Co.

Gow, Kailin. Loving Summer. 2012. 250p. (-18). pap. 9.99 (978-1-59748-044-4(4), The Edge) Sparklesoup LLC.

—The Stoker Sisters. 2010. 266p. (YA). pap. (978-1-59748-947-8(6)) Sparklesoup LLC.

Gownley, Jimmy. When the Past Is a Present. Gownley, Jimmy, illus. 2011. (Amelia Rules! Ser.). (ENG., Illus.). 176p. (J). (gr. 2-7). 19.99 (978-1-4424-4541-3(6), Atheneum Bks. for Young Readers) Simon & Schuster Children's Publishing.

Grace, Amanda. No One Needs to Know. 2014. (ENG.). 240p. (YA). pap. 9.99 (978-0-7387-3625-9(2), Flux) North Star Editions.

Green, John. Will Grayson, Will Grayson. 2011. lib. bdg. 22.10 (978-0-606-15358-4(6), Turtleback) Turtleback Bks.

Green, John & Levithan, David. Will Grayson, Will Grayson. 2015. (SPA.). 336p. (YA). (gr. 7). pap. 12.95 (978-1-101-91070-2(4), Vintage Espanol) Knopf Doubleday Publishing Group.

—Will Grayson, Will Grayson. (ENG., (YA). (gr. 9-18). 2011. Illus.). 352p. 10.99 (978-0-14-241847-5(1), Speak) 2010. 320p. 17.99 (978-0-525-42158-0(0), Dutton Books for Young Readers) Penguin Young Readers Group.

Green, John, et al. Let It Snow: Three Holiday Romances. (ENG.). 368p. (YA). (gr. 7). 2014. mass mkt. 7.99 (978-0-14-751501-8(7)) 2008. pap. 10.99 (978-0-14-241214-5(7)) Penguin Young Readers Group. (Speak).

Greene, Vivi. Sing. 2016. 288p. (YA). (gr. 8). 17.99 (978-0-06-245983-1(X), HarperTeen) HarperCollins Pubs.

Greenwald, Lisa. Epic Kale: And Other Cleanses for a Broken Heart. 2017. (YA). pap. **(978-0-399-55641-8(9))** Random Hse., Inc.

—Kale, My Ex, & Other Things to Toss in a Blender. 2017. (ENG.). 272p. (YA). (gr. 7). 17.99 **(978-0-399-55638-8(9)**, Random Hse. Bks. for Young Readers) Random Hse. Children's Bks.

Greenwald, Lisa. Pink & Green Is the New Black: Pink & Green Book Three. (Pink & Green Ser.). (ENG.). 280p. (J). (gr. 3-7). 2015. pap. 7.95 (978-1-4197-1679-9(4)) 2014. 16.95 (978-1-4197-1225-8(X)) Abrams, Inc. (Amulet Bks.).

Greenwald, Tommy. Charlie Joe Jackson's Guide to Planet Girl. Coovert, J. P., illus. 2015. (Charlie Joe Jackson Ser.: 5). (ENG.). 208p. (J). (gr. 4-7). 13.99 (978-1-59643-841-5(X), 9781596438415) Roaring Brook Pr.

—Pete Milano's Guide to Being a Movie Star. Roher, Rebecca, illus. 2016. (ENG.). 256p. (J). 13.99 (978-1-62672-167-8(X), 9781626721678) Roaring Brook Pr.

Gregorio, I. W. None of the Above. 2015. (ENG.). 352p. (YA). (gr. 9). 17.99 (978-0-06-233531-9(6)) HarperCollins Pubs.

Guarente, Gabe. Satan's Prep: A Graphic Novel. 2014. (ENG., Illus.). 112p. (J). (gr. 6). 17.95 (978-1-62873-592-5(9), Sky Pony Pr.) Skyhorse Publishing Co., Inc.

Gurevich, Margaret. Runway Rundown. Hagel, Brooke, illus. 2015. (Chloe by Design Ser.). (ENG.). 96p. (gr. 5-8). 25.32 (978-1-4965-0506-4(9)) Stone Arch Bks.

Gurtler, Janet. Rachel's Secret. Wood, Katie, illus. 2015. (Mermaid Kingdom Ser.). (ENG.). 96p. (gr. 3-5). 23.99 (978-1-4342-9694-8(6)) Stone Arch Bks.

—Rachel's Worry. Wood, Katie, illus. 2016. (Mermaid Kingdom Ser.). (ENG.). 96p. (gr. 3-5). 23.99 (978-1-4965-2607-6(4)) Stone Arch Bks.

—The Truth about Us. 2015. (ENG.). 320p. (YA). (gr. 8-12). pap. 9.99 (978-1-4022-7800-6(4), 9781402278006) Sourcebooks, Inc.

Halahmy, Miriam. Behind Closed Doors. 2017. (ENG.). 208p. (J). (gr. 9). 16.95 (978-0-8234-3641-5(1)) Holiday Hse., Inc.

Han, Jenny. P.S. I Still Love You. 2015. (ENG., Illus.). 352p. (YA). (gr. 7). 17.99 (978-1-4424-2673-3(X)); (To All the Boys I've Loved Before Ser.: 2). E-Book (978-1-4424-2675-7(6)) Simon & Schuster Bks. For Young Readers. (Simon & Schuster Bks. For Young Readers).

—P.S. I Still Love You. 2017. (To All the Boys I've Loved Before Ser.: 2). (ENG.). 352p. (YA). (gr. 7). pap. 10.99 (978-1-4424-2674-0(8)) Simon & Schuster Children's Publishing.

—To All the Boys I've Loved Before. (ENG., Illus.). (YA). (gr. 7-10). 2016. 384p. pap. 10.99 (978-1-4424-2671-9(3)) 2014. 368p. 17.99 (978-1-4424-2670-2(5)) 2017. 1056p. 53.99 (978-1-4814-9536-3(4)) Simon & Schuster Bks. For Young Readers. (Simon & Schuster Bks. For Young Readers).

—To All the Boys I've Loved Before. 2016. lib. bdg. 22.10 (978-0-606-38270-0(4)) Turtleback Bks.

Handler, Daniel. Why We Broke Up. Kalman, Maira, illus. 2011. (ENG.). 368p. (YA). (gr. 10-17). 20.00 (978-0-316-12725-7(6)) Little, Brown Bks. for Young Readers.

Hapka, Catherine, pseud. Something Borrowed. 2008. (Romantic Comedies Ser.). (ENG.). 272p. (YA). (gr. 7-18). mass mkt. 6.99 (978-1-4169-5441-5(4), Simon Pulse) Simon Pulse.

Hapka, Catherine, pseud & Echols, Jennifer. Winter's Kiss: The Ex Games - The Twelve Dates of Christmas. 2012. (ENG.). 496p. (YA). (gr. 7). pap. 9.99 (978-1-4424-5040-0(1), Simon Pulse) Simon Pulse.

Harrington, K. A. Forget Me. 2014. (ENG.). 288p. (YA). (gr. 7). 17.99 (978-0-399-16529-0(0), G.P. Putnam's Sons Books for Young Readers) Penguin Young Readers Group.

Harrison, Emma. Escaping Perfect. 2016. (ENG., Illus.). 336p. (YA). (gr. 9). 17.99 (978-1-4814-4212-1(0), Simon Pulse) Simon Pulse.

—Finding What's Real. 2017. (ENG., Illus.). 304p. (YA). (gr. 9). 17.99 (978-1-4814-4215-2(5), Simon Pulse) Simon Pulse.

Harrison, Lisi. P. S. I Loathe You. 2009. (Clique Ser.: 10). (ENG.). 224p. (gr. 7-17). pap. 9.99 (978-0-316-00681-1(5), Poppy) Little, Brown Bks. for Young Readers.

—Sealed with a Diss. 2008. (Clique Novels Ser.). 248p. 20.00 (978-1-60686-345-9(2)) Perfection Learning Corp.

—These Boots Are Made for Stalking. 12th ed. 2010. (Clique Ser.: 12). (ENG.). 256p. (YA). (gr. 7-17). pap. 9.99 (978-0-316-00683-5(1), Poppy) Little, Brown Bks. for Young Readers.

Hartinger, Brent. Three Truths & a Lie. 2016. (ENG., Illus.). 272p. (YA). (gr. 9). 17.99 (978-1-4814-4960-1(5), Simon Pulse) Simon Pulse.

Harvey-Fitzhenry, Alyxandra. Broken, 1 vol. 2010. (ENG., Illus.). 176p. (YA). (gr. 7-12). pap. 12.95 (978-1-896580-41-8(6)) Tradewind Bks. CAN. Dist: Orca Bk. Pubs. USA.

Hasak-Lowy, Todd. Me Being Me Is Exactly As Insane As You Being You. 2015. (ENG., Illus.). 656p. (YA). (gr. 9). 17.99 (978-1-4424-9573-9(1), Simon Pulse) Simon Pulse.

Hautman, Pete. The Big Crunch. 2011. (ENG.). 288p. (J). (gr. 7-8). 17.99 (978-0-545-24075-8(1), Scholastic Pr.) Scholastic, Inc.

—What Boys Really Want. 2012. (ENG.). 304p. (J). (gr. 7). 17.99 *(978-0-545-11315-1(6)*, Scholastic Pr.) Scholastic, Inc.
Hawthorne, Rachel. The Boyfriend League. 2007. (ENG.). 336p. (YA). (gr. 9-12). pap. 8.99 *(978-0-06-113837-9(1)*, HarperTeen) HarperCollins Pubs.
—Dark of the Moon. 2009. (Dark Guardian Ser.: 3). (ENG.). 272p. (YA). (gr. 9-18). pap. 9.99 *(978-0-06-170957-9(3)*, HarperTeen) HarperCollins Pubs.
—Labor of Love. 2008. (ENG.). 320p. (YA). (gr. 9-18). pap. 5.99 *(978-0-06-136384-9(7)*, HarperTeen) HarperCollins Pubs.
—Moonlight. 2009. (Dark Guardian Ser.: No. 1). (ENG.). 272p. (YA). (gr. 9-18). pap. 8.99 *(978-0-06-170955-5(7)*, HarperTeen) HarperCollins Pubs.
—Snowed In. 2007. (ENG.). 272p. (YA). (gr. 9-18). pap. 5.99 *(978-0-06-113836-2(3)*, HarperTeen) HarperCollins Pubs.
—Suite Dreams. 2008. (ENG.). 288p. (YA). (gr. 9-18). pap. 5.99 *(978-0-06-168806-5(1)*, HarperTeen) HarperCollins Pubs.
—Thrill Ride. 2006. (ENG.). 320p. (YA). (gr. 9). pap. 5.99 *(978-0-06-083954-3(6)*, HarperTeen) HarperCollins Pubs.
Heidicker, Christian McKay. Cure for the Common Universe. 2016. (ENG., Illus.). 320p. (YA). (gr. 9). 19.99 *(978-1-4814-5027-0(1)*, Simon & Schuster Bks. For Young Readers) Simon & Schuster Bks. For Young Readers.
Heldring, Thatcher. The Football Girl. 2017. (YA). ***(978-0-375-99026-7(7)***, Delacorte Pr) Random House Publishing Group.
Helgeson, Kat. Say No to the Bro. 2017. (ENG., Illus.). 272p. (YA). (gr. 9). 17.99 ***(978-1-4814-7193-0(7)***, Simon & Schuster Bks. For Young Readers) Simon & Schuster Bks. For Young Readers.
Helms, Rhonda. Promposal. 2015. (ENG., Illus.). 224p. (YA). (gr. 7). pap. 9.99 *(978-1-4814-2231-4(6)*, Simon Pulse) Simon Pulse.
Heltzel, Anne. Charlie, Presumed Dead. (ENG.). 272p. (YA). (gr. 9). 2016. pap. 8.99 *(978-0-544-66869-0(3))* 2015. 17.99 *(978-0-544-38849-9(6))* Houghton Mifflin Harcourt Publishing Co. (HMH Books For Young Readers).
Hepler, Heather. Frosted Kisses. 2015. (ENG.). 272p. (J). (gr. 7). 17.99 *(978-0-545-79055-0(7))* Scholastic, Inc.
Hickey, Caroline. Isabelle's Boyfriend. 2009. (ENG.). 192p. (J). (gr. 6-9). pap. 18.99 *(978-0-312-60273-4(1)*, 9780312602734) Square Fish.
Hildebrand, Jens & Ridge, Sally. Cyberstalker. 2013. 242p. pap. *(978-3-929892-45-1(6))* Hildebrand, Jutta Warped Tomato Publishing.
Hogan, Mary. Pretty Face. (ENG.). 224p. (J). 2009. pap. 8.99 *(978-0-06-084113-3(3))* 2008. (gr. 9-18). 16.99 *(978-0-06-084111-9(7))* HarperCollins Pubs. (HarperTeen).
Hopkins, Cathy. Besties: Mates, Dates, & Sleepover Secrets; Mates, Dates, & Sole Survivors; Mates, Dates, & Mad Mistakes. 2009. (Mates, Dates Ser.). (ENG.). 576p. (YA). (gr. 7). pap. 8.99 *(978-1-4169-7837-4(2)*, Simon Pulse) Simon Pulse.
—Friend Me: Mates, Dates, & Inflatable Bras; Mates, Dates, & Cosmic Kisses; Mates, Dates, & Designer Divas. 2009. (Mates, Dates Ser.). (ENG.). 528p. (YA). (gr. 7). pap. 8.99 *(978-1-4169-7836-7(4)*, Simon Pulse) Simon Pulse.
—Love Lottery. 2012. (Truth or Dare Ser.). (ENG.). 208p. (YA). (gr. 7). pap. 11.99 *(978-1-4424-7176-4(X)*, Simon Pulse) Simon Pulse.
—Mates, Dates, & Great Escapes. 2011. (Mates, Dates Ser.). (ENG.). 224p. (YA). (gr. 7). pap. 10.99 *(978-1-4424-3080-8(X)*, Simon Pulse) Simon Pulse.
—Mates, Dates, & Inflatable Bras. 2011. (Mates, Dates Ser.). (ENG.). 176p. (YA). (gr. 7). pap. 9.99 *(978-1-4424-3113-3(X)*, Simon Pulse) Simon Pulse.
—Teen Queens & Has-Beens. 2010. (Truth or Dare Ser.). (ENG.). 192p. (YA). (gr. 7). pap. 9.99 *(978-1-4424-1416-7(2)*, Simon Pulse) Simon Pulse.
Hopkins, Ellen. Rumble. 2016. (ENG., Illus.). 576p. (YA). (gr. 9). pap. 12.99 *(978-1-4424-8285-2(0)*, McElderry, Margaret K. Bks.) McElderry, Margaret K. Bks.
—Tilt. (ENG., (YA). (gr. 9). 2014. Illus.). 624p. pap. 12.99 *(978-1-4169-8331-6(7))* 2012. 608p. 18.99 *(978-1-4169-8330-9(9))* McElderry, Margaret K. Bks. (McElderry, Margaret K. Bks.).
Houck, Colleen. Tiger's Destiny. 2015. (Tiger's Curse Ser.: Bk. 4). (ENG.). 464p. (J). (gr. 7). pap. 9.95 *(978-1-4549-0356-7(2))* Sterling Publishing Co., Inc.
—Tiger's Quest. (Tiger's Curse Ser.: Bk. 2). (ENG.). (J). (gr. 7). 2013. 512p. pap. 9.95 *(978-1-4549-0358-1(9))* 2011. 496p. 17.95 *(978-1-4027-8404-0(X))* Sterling Publishing Co., Inc.
—Tiger's Voyage. (Tiger's Curse Ser.: Bk. 3). (ENG.). (J). (gr. 7). 2014. 568p. pap. 9.95 *(978-1-4549-0357-4(0))*Bk. 3. 2011. 560p. 17.95 *(978-1-4027-8405-7(8))* Sterling Publishing Co., Inc.
Howland, Leila. Nantucket Blue. 2014. (Nantucket Blue Ser.). (ENG.). 320p. (YA). (gr. 9-17). pap. 8.99 *(978-1-4231-6139-4(4))* Hyperion Bks. for Children.
—Nantucket Red. 2014. (Nantucket Blue Ser.). (ENG.). 288p. (YA). (gr. 9-17). 16.99 *(978-1-4231-6095-3(9))* Hyperion Bks. for Children.
Huang, Charlotte. For the Record. (ENG.). 320p. (YA). (gr. 7). 2016. pap. 9.99 *(978-0-553-51185-7(8)*, Ember) 2015. 17.99 *(978-0-553-51182-6(3)*, Delacorte Pr.) Random Hse. Children's Bks.
Hubbard, Amanda & Hubbard, Mandy. Everything but the Truth. 2015. (If Only... Ser.). (ENG.). 288p. (YA). (gr. 7). 17.99 *(978-1-61963-659-0(X)*, 9781619636590, Bloomsbury USA Childrens) Bloomsbury Publishing USA.
Hubbard, Mandy. Fool Me Twice. 2014. (If Only... Ser.). (ENG.). 272p. (YA). (gr. 7). 17.99 *(978-1-61963-229-5(2)*, 9781619632295, Bloomsbury USA Childrens) Bloomsbury Publishing USA.
—Fool Me Twice: An If Only Novel. 2014. (If Only... Ser.). (ENG.). 272p. (YA). (gr. 7). pap. 9.99 *(978-1-61963-230-1(6)*, 9781619632301, Bloomsbury USA Childrens) Bloomsbury Publishing USA.
—You Wish. 2010. (ENG.). 304p. (YA). (gr. 7-18). pap. 8.99 *(978-1-59514-292-4(4)*, Razorbill) Penguin Young Readers Group.
Hutchinson, Shaun David. Deathday Letter. 2010. (ENG.). 256p. (YA). (gr. 9-18). pap. 9.99 *(978-1-4169-9608-8(7)*, Simon Pulse) Simon Pulse.
—Fml. 2013. (ENG.). 304p. (YA). (gr. 9). pap. 9.99 *(978-1-4424-3287-1(X))*; (Illus.). 17.99 *(978-1-4424-8318-7(0))* Simon Pulse. (Simon Pulse).
In a World Just Right. 2015. (ENG., Illus.). 432p. (YA). (gr. 7). 18.99 *(978-1-4814-1660-3(X))* Simon & Schuster Children's Publishing.
Ius, Dawn. Anne & Henry. Watcher, Jill, illus. 2015. (ENG.). 304p. (YA). (gr. 9). 18.99 *(978-1-4814-3941-1(3)*, Simon Pulse) Simon Pulse.
Jabaley, Jennifer. Crush Control. 2011. (ENG.). 336p. (YA). (gr. 7-18). 9.99 *(978-1-59514-424-9(2)*, Razorbill) Penguin Young Readers Group.
Jacobs, Evan. Screaming Quietly. 2013. (Gravel Road Ser.). (YA). lib. bdg. 20.80 *(978-0-606-32029-0(6)*, Turtleback) Turtleback Bks.
Jahn-Clough, Lisa. Me, Penelope. 2009. (ENG.). 208p. (YA). (gr. 9). pap. 12.99 *(978-0-547-07632-4(0))* Houghton Mifflin Harcourt Publishing Co.
Jimenez, Joe. Bloodline. 2016. (ENG.). 128p. (YA). (gr. 8-12). pap. 11.95 *(978-1-55885-826-2(8)*, Piñata Books) Arte Publico Pr.
Johansson, J. R. The Row. O'Malley, Janine, ed. 2016. (ENG.). 352p. (YA). 17.99 *(978-0-374-30025-8(9)*, 9780374300258, Farrar, Straus & Giroux (BYR)) Farrar, Straus & Giroux.
Johnson, Maureen. Scarlett Fever. (ENG.). 352p. (J). (gr. 7-7). 2011. pap. 9.99 *(978-0-545-09633-1(2))* 2010. 16.99 *(978-0-439-89928-4(1))* Scholastic, Inc.
Johnson, Shawn. The Flip Side. 2016. (ENG., Illus.). 320p. (YA). (gr. 7). 17.99 *(978-1-4814-6021-7(8)*, Simon & Schuster Bks. For Young Readers) Simon & Schuster Bks. For Young Readers.
Jones, Jen. Faith & the Dance Drama, No. 5. Adams, Liz, illus. 2012. (Team Cheer Ser.: No. 5). (ENG.). 112p. (gr. 4-4). lib. bdg. 25.32 *(978-1-4342-4033-0(9))* Stone Arch Bks.
—Faith & the Dance Drama: #5, 1 vol. 2013. (Team Cheer Ser.). (ENG.). 112p. (gr. 4-4). pap. 7.19 *(978-1-4342-4263-1(3)*, Team Cheer) Stone Arch Bks.
Jones, Patrick. Guarding Secrets. 2015. (J). 9.99 *(978-1-4677-7694-3(7))*; (ENG.). 96p. (gr. 6-12). lib. bdg. 27.99 *(978-1-4677-5801-7(9))* Lerner Publishing Group.
Jones, Rena. A Dinner Date for Dilly. Nielson, Ginger, illus. 2012. 28p. pap. 14.99 *(978-0-9852661-2-7(0))* 4RV Publishing, LLC.
Jordan, Dream. Bad Boy. 2012. (ENG.). 208p. (YA). (gr. 6-11). pap. 17.99 *(978-0-312-54997-8(0)*, 9780312549978, St. Martin's Griffin) St. Martin's Pr.
Jordan, Sophie. Firelight. (Firelight Ser.: 1). (ENG.). (YA). (gr. 8). 2011. 352p. pap. 9.99 *(978-0-06-193509-1(3))* 2010. 336p. 16.99 *(978-0-06-193508-4(5))* HarperCollins Pubs.
Joseph, Danielle. Pure Red. 2011. (ENG.). 240p. (YA). pap. 9.95 *(978-0-7387-2743-1(1)*, Flux) North Star Editions.
Juby, Susan. Alice MacLeod, Realist at Last. 2005. 320p. (J). (ENG.). 15.99 *(978-0-06-051549-2(X))*; lib. bdg. 16.89 *(978-0-06-051550-8(3))* HarperCollins Pubs. (HarperTeen).
Karre, Elizabeth. All You Are. 2014. (Gift Ser.). 120p. (YA). (gr. 6-12). (ENG.). pap. 7.95 *(978-1-4677-4477-5(8))*; lib. bdg. 27.93 *(978-1-4677-3510-0(8))* Lerner Publishing Group. (Darby Creek).
—Certain Signals. 2014. (Gift Ser.). (ENG.). 112p. (YA). (gr. 6-12). pap. 7.95 *(978-1-4677-4479-9(4)*, Darby Creek) Lerner Publishing Group.
Katcher, Brian. Almost Perfect. 2010. (ENG.). 368p. (YA). (gr. 9). pap. 9.99 *(978-0-385-73665-7(7)*, Delacorte Bks. for Young Readers) Random Hse. Children's Bks.
—Playing with Matches. 2009. (ENG.). 304p. (YA). (gr. 9). mass mkt. 8.99 *(978-0-385-73545-2(6)*, Laurel Leaf) Random Hse. Children's Bks.
Katschke, Judy. The Facts about Flirting. 2003. (Two of a Kind Ser.: Vol. 27). (Illus.). 112p. mass mkt. 4.99 *(978-0-06-009323-5(4)*, Harper Entertainment) HarperCollins Pubs.
Kendall, Grace, ed. I See Reality: Twelve Short Stories about Real Life. 2016. (ENG.). 304p. (YA). 17.99 *(978-0-374-30258-0(8)*, 9780374302580, Farrar, Straus & Giroux (BYR)) Farrar, Straus & Giroux.
Kenley, Holli. Another Way: A Novel. 2015. 155p. (YA). pap. *(978-1-61599-259-1(6))* Loving Healing Pr., Inc.
Kenneally, Miranda. Breathe, Annie, Breathe. (Hundred Oaks Ser.: Bk. 5). (ENG.). (YA). (gr. 8-12). 2015. 336p. pap. 9.99 *(978-1-4926-0866-0(1)*, 9781492608660) 2014. 320p. 16.99 *(978-1-4022-8479-3(9)*, 9781402284793) Sourcebooks, Inc.
—Things I Can't Forget. 2013. (Hundred Oaks Ser.: Bk. 3). (ENG.). 320p. (YA). (gr. 7-12). pap. 9.99 *(978-1-4022-7190-8(5)*, 9781402271908) Sourcebooks, Inc.
Keplinger, Kody. The DUFF: Designated Ugly Fat Friend. (ENG.). (YA). (gr. 10-17). 2011. 304p. pap., pap. 10.99 *(978-0-316-08424-6(7))* 2015. 320p. pap. 10.00 *(978-0-316-38180-2(2))* Little, Brown Bks. for Young Readers. (Poppy).
—Lying Out Loud: A Companion to the DUFF. 2015. (ENG.). 288p. (J). (gr. 9). 17.99 *(978-0-545-83109-3(1))* Scholastic, Inc.
—Lying Out Loud: a Companion to the DUFF. 2016. (ENG.). 304p. (J). (gr. 9). pap. 9.99 *(978-0-545-83110-9(5)*, Scholastic Paperbacks) Scholastic, Inc.
—Shut Out. 2012. (ENG.). 288p. (YA). (gr. 10-17). pap. 10.99 *(978-0-316-17555-5(2)*, Poppy) Little, Brown Bks. for Young Readers.
Kerns, Ann. I Date Dead People. Gorman, Mike & Görrissen, Janina, illus. 2012. (My Boyfriend Is a Monster Ser.: 5). (ENG.). 128p. (YA). (gr. 7-12). pap. 9.95 *(978-0-7613-8549-3(5)*, Graphic Universe™) Lerner Publishing Group.
—I Date Dead People. Görrissen, Janina, illus. 2012. (My Boyfriend Is a Monster Ser.: 5). (ENG.). 128p. (YA). (gr. 7-12). lib. bdg. 29.27 *(978-0-7613-6007-0(7))* Lerner Publishing Group.
Kerr, M. E., pseud. If I Love You, Am I Trapped Forever?, 0 vols. 2011. (ENG.). 192p. (J). (gr. 7-9). pap. 9.99 *(978-0-7614-5839-5(5)*, 9780761458395, Amazon Children's Publishing) Amazon Publishing.
Killian, Beth. Everything She Wants. 2006. (310 Ser.). (ENG.). 240p. (gr. 8-12). pap. 15.99 *(978-1-4165-2168-6(2)*, MTV Bks.) MTV Books.
Kinard, Kami. The Boy Prediction: Notes & Observations of Tabitha Reddy. 2014. (ENG., Illus.). 272p. (J). (gr. 3-7). 12.99 *(978-0-545-57586-7(9)*, Scholastic Pr.) Scholastic, Inc.
—The Boy Project. 2016. (ENG.). 256p. (J). (gr. 4-7). pap. 6.99 *(978-0-545-34516-3(2)*, Scholastic Paperbacks) Scholastic, Inc.
King, A. S. Reality Boy. 2014. (ENG.). 400p. (YA). (gr. 10-17). pap. 10.00 *(978-0-316-22271-6(2))* Little, Brown Bks. for Young Readers.
Klein, Jen. Shuffle, Repeat. (ENG.). (YA). (gr. 7). 2017. 352p. pap. 9.99 ***(978-0-553-50985-4(3)***, Ember) 2016. 336p. 17.99 *(978-0-553-50982-3(9)*, Random Hse. Bks. for Young Readers) Random Hse. Children's Bks.
—Summer Unscripted. 2017. (ENG.). 320p. (YA). (gr. 7). 17.99 ***(978-1-5247-0004-1(5)***, Random Hse. Bks. for Young Readers) Random Hse. Children's Bks.
Koertge, Ron. Now Playing: Stoner & Spaz II. 2011. (ENG., Illus.). 224p. (YA). (gr. 9-18). 16.99 *(978-0-7636-5081-0(1))* Candlewick Pr.
Korman, Susan. Overexposed. 2013. (Surviving Southside Ser.). (ENG.). 104p. (YA). (gr. 6-12). lib. bdg. 27.93 *(978-1-4677-0312-3(5))* Lerner Publishing Group.
Korman, Susan J. Overexposed. 2013. (Surviving Southside Ser.). (ENG.). 104p. (YA). (gr. 6-12). pap. 7.95 *(978-1-4677-0706-0(6)*, Darby Creek) Lerner Publishing Group.
Kottaras, E. Katherine. The Best Possible Answer. 2016. (ENG.). 272p. (YA). 18.99 *(978-1-250-07281-8(6)*, 9781250072818, St. Martin's Griffin) St. Martin's Pr.
Kropp, Paul. Home Run. 2006. (ENG.). 208p. (J). (gr. 7). pap. 11.95 *(978-0-385-66148-5(7)*, Doubleday Canada) Penguin Random House Canada Young Readers CAN. Dist: Penguin Random Hse. LLC.
—Running the Bases: Definitely Not a Book about Baseball. 2008. (ENG.). 208p. (J). (gr. 7). mass mkt. 7.99 *(978-0-7704-2975-1(0)*, Seal Bks.) Penguin Random House Canada Young Readers CAN. Dist: Penguin Random Hse. LLC.
Krulik, Nancy. Puppy Love. 2011. (Romantic Comedies Ser.). (ENG.). 224p. (YA). (gr. 7). pap. 12.99 *(978-1-4424-3079-2(6)*, Simon Pulse) Simon Pulse.
Kunze, Lauren & Onur, Rina. The Ivy. (Ivy Ser.: 1). (ENG.). (YA). (gr. 9). 2011. 336p. pap. 8.99 *(978-0-06-196046-8(2))* 2010. 320p. 16.99 *(978-0-06-196045-1(4))* HarperCollins Pubs. (Greenwillow Bks.).
—Rivals. 2012. (Ivy Ser.: 3). (ENG.). 384p. (YA). (gr. 9). 16.99 *(978-0-06-196049-9(7)*, Greenwillow Bks.) HarperCollins Pubs.
—Scandal. 2013. (Ivy Ser.: 4). (ENG.). 336p. (YA). (gr. 9). 17.99 *(978-0-06-196051-2(9)*, Greenwillow Bks.) HarperCollins Pubs.
—Secrets. 2011. (Ivy Ser.: 2). (ENG.). 320p. (YA). (gr. 9-18). 16.99 *(978-0-06-196047-5(0)*, Greenwillow Bks.) HarperCollins Pubs.
Laban, Elizabeth. The Tragedy Paper. (ENG.). 320p. (YA). (gr. 7). 2014. pap. 9.99 *(978-0-307-93048-4(3)*, Ember) 2013. (Illus.). 17.99 *(978-0-375-87040-8(7)*, Knopf Bks. for Young Readers) Random Hse. Children's Bks.
Landon, Kristen. Life in the Pit. 2008. (ENG., Illus.). 248p. (YA). (gr. 5-13). pap. 8.95 *(978-1-933831-08-4(1))* Blooming Tree Pr.
Lantz, Francess L. Current Affairs. 2004. (Luna Bay Ser.: No. 9). 176p. mass mkt. 4.99 *(978-0-06-059521-0(3)*, Harper Entertainment) HarperCollins Pubs.
Lauren, Christina. The House. 2015. (ENG., Illus.). 384p. (YA). (gr. 9). 18.99 *(978-1-4814-1371-8(6))* Simon & Schuster Children's Publishing.
Lazebnik, Claire. Epic Fail. 2011. (ENG.). 304p. (YA). (gr. 8-18). pap. 9.99 *(978-0-06-192126-1(2)*, HarperTeen) HarperCollins Pubs.
—The Last Best Kiss. 2014. (ENG.). 384p. (YA). (gr. 8). pap. 9.99 *(978-0-06-225228-9(3)*, HarperTeen) HarperCollins Pubs.
—Things I Should Have Known. 2017. (ENG.). 320p. (YA). (gr. 7). 17.99 *(978-0-544-82969-5(7)*, HMH Books For Young Readers) Houghton Mifflin Harcourt Publishing Co.
Leavitt, Lindsey. The Chapel Wars. 2014. (ENG.). 304p. (YA). (gr. 7). 17.99 *(978-1-59990-788-8(7)*, 9781599907888, Bloomsbury USA Childrens) Bloomsbury Publishing USA.
—Going Vintage. 2013. (ENG.). 320p. (YA). (gr. 7-12). 16.99 *(978-1-59990-787-1(9)*, 9781599907871, Bloomsbury USA Childrens) Bloomsbury Publishing USA.
Leblanc, Louise. Sophie Est en Orbite. Gay, Marie-Louise, tr. 2003. (Premier Roman Ser.). (FRE., Illus.). 64p. (J). (gr. 1-4). pap. *(978-2-89021-670-9(5))* Diffusion du livre Mirabel (DLM).
Lee, Darrien. 16 Going on 21. 2008. (ENG., Illus.). 288p. (YA). (gr. 9). 9.95 *(978-1-933967-71-4(4)*, Urban Renaissance) Kensington Publishing Corp.
Leigh, Britt. Ten Commandments for Kissing Gloria Jean. 2014. (ENG.). (YA). pap. 9.95 *(978-0-8198-7491-7(4))* Pauline Bks. & Media.
Lenzi, Danielle E. My Search for Prince Charming's Normal Brother. 2011. 136p. pap. 25.70 *(978-1-4634-0446-8(8))*; (gr. 10-12). 33.70 *(978-1-4634-0445-1(X))* AuthorHouse.
Leveen, Tom. Manicpixiedreamgirl. 2014. (ENG.). 256p. (YA). (gr. 9). pap. 8.99 *(978-0-375-87021-7(0)*, Ember) Random Hse. Children's Bks.
—Shackled: The Truth Doesn't Always Set You Free. 2015. (ENG., Illus.). 224p. (YA). (gr. 9). 17.99 *(978-1-4814-2249-9(9)*, Simon Pulse) Simon Pulse.
—Zero. 2013. (ENG.). 320p. (YA). (gr. 9). pap. 9.99 *(978-0-375-87337-9(6)*, Ember) Random Hse. Children's Bks.
Levithan, David. Hold Me Closer: The Tiny Cooper Story. 2015. (ENG.). 208p. (YA). (gr. 9). 17.99 *(978-0-525-42884-8(4)*, Dutton Books for Young Readers) Penguin Young Readers Group.
—Hold Me Closer: The Tiny Cooper Story. 2016. lib. bdg. 22.10 *(978-0-606-38390-5(5))* Turtleback Bks.
—21 Proms. 2015. lib. bdg. 20.85 *(978-0-606-36327-3(0))* Turtleback Bks.
Levy, Joanne. Small Medium at Large. 2012. (ENG.). 208p. (YA). (gr. 3-12). 15.99 *(978-1-59990-836-6(0)*, 9781599908366, Bloomsbury USA Childrens) Bloomsbury Publishing USA.
Levy, Marianne. Katie Cox Goes Viral. 2017. (ENG.). 368p. (J). (gr. 5-9). pap. 7.99 *(978-1-4926-4250-3(9)*, 9781492642503, Sourcebooks Jabberwocky) Sourcebooks, Inc.
Lindstrom, Eric. Not If I See You First. 2015. (ENG.). 320p. (YA). (gr. 10-17). 18.00 *(978-0-316-25985-9(3))* Little Brown & Co.
Lo, Catherine. How It Ends. 2016. (ENG.). 304p. (YA). (gr. 9). 17.99 *(978-0-544-54006-4(9)*, HMH Books For Young Readers) Houghton Mifflin Harcourt Publishing Co.
Lockhart, E. The Boy Book: A Study of Habits & Behaviors, Plus Techniques for Taming Them. 2008. (Ruby Oliver Quartet Ser.). (ENG.). 224p. (YA). (gr. 7). pap. 8.99 *(978-0-385-73209-3(0)*, Delacorte Pr.) Random Hse. Children's Bks.
—The Boyfriend List: 15 Guys, 11 Shrink Appointments, 4 Ceramic Frogs & Me, Ruby Oliver. 2006. (Ruby Oliver Quartet Ser.). (ENG.). 256p. (YA). (gr. 7-12). reprint ed. pap. 9.99 *(978-0-385-73207-9(4)*, Ember) Random Hse. Children's Bks.
—Real Live Boyfriends: Yes. Boyfriends, Plural. If My Life Weren't Complicated, I Wouldn't Be Ruby Oliver. 2011. (Ruby Oliver Quartet Ser.). (ENG.). 240p. (J). (gr. 7). pap. 8.99 *(978-0-385-73429-5(8)*, Ember) Random Hse. Children's Bks.
—The Treasure Map of Boys: Noel, Jackson, Finn, Hutch, Gideon - And Me, Ruby Oliver. 2010. (Ruby Oliver Quartet Ser.). (ENG.). 256p. (J). (gr. 7). pap. 8.99 *(978-0-385-73427-1(1)*, Delacorte Pr.) Random Hse. Children's Bks.
Logsted, Greg. Something Happened. 2008. (ENG.). 208p. (YA). (gr. 7-9). pap. 8.99 *(978-1-4169-5078-3(8)*, Simon Pulse) Simon Pulse.
Long, Hayley. Lottie Biggs Is Not Tragic. 2014. (ENG.). 272p. (YA). (gr. 7). pap. 10.99 *(978-1-4472-6555-9(6))* Pan Macmillan GBR. Dist: Independent Pubs. Group.
Lubar, David. Character, Driven: A Novel. 2017. (ENG.). 304p. (YA). pap. 9.99 *(978-0-7653-7694-7(6)*, 9780765376947, Tor Teen) Doherty, Tom Assocs., LLC.
—Sophomores & Other Oxymorons. 2015. (ENG.). 432p. (YA). (gr. 7). 17.99 *(978-0-525-42970-8(0)*, Dutton Books for Young Readers) Penguin Young Readers Group.
Luper, Eric. Seth Baumgartner's Love Manifesto. 2010. (ENG.). 304p. (YA). (gr. 8-18). 16.99 *(978-0-06-182753-2(3))* HarperCollins Pubs.
Lynch, Chris. Little Blue Lies. 2014. (ENG.). 224p. (YA). (gr. 7). 17.99 *(978-1-4424-4008-1(2)*, Simon & Schuster Bks. For Young Readers) Simon & Schuster Bks. For Young Readers.
Lyons, Stefanie. Dating Down. 2015. (ENG., Illus.). 312p. (YA). pap. 9.99 *(978-0-7387-4337-0(2)*, Flux) North Star Editions.
Maciel, Amanda. Lucky Girl. 2017. 320p. (YA). (gr. 9). 17.99 *(978-0-06-230533-6(6))* HarperCollins Pubs.
Madigan, L. K. Flash Burnout. 2010. (ENG.). 336p. (YA). (gr. 9). pap. 7.99 *(978-0-547-40493-6(X))* Houghton Mifflin Harcourt Publishing Co.
Mahmoodian, Maryam. Muslim Teens In: Pitfalls & Pranks. 2008. (YA). per. 10.95 *(978-0-9793577-3-2(X))* Muslim Writers Publishing.
Maizel, Rebecca. Between Us & the Moon. 2015. (ENG.). 384p. (YA). (gr. 9). 17.99 *(978-0-06-232761-1(5))* HarperCollins Pubs.
—A Season for Fireflies. 2016. 256p. (YA). (gr. 9). 17.99 *(978-0-06-232764-2(X)*, HarperTeen) HarperCollins Pubs.
Maness, Rowan. Bombshell. 2017. (ENG., Illus.). 320p. (YA). (gr. 9). 18.99 ***(978-1-4814-4164-3(7)***, Simon Pulse) Simon Pulse.
Mansbach, Adam & Zweibel, Alan. Benjamin Franklin: Huge Pain in My... 2015. (Benjamin Franklin Ser.). (ENG., Illus.). 208p. (J). (gr. 5-9). 12.99 *(978-1-4847-1304-4(4))* Hyperion Bks. for Children.
Mansbach, Adam & Zwiebel, Alan. Benjamin Franklin: You've Got Mail. 2017. (Benjamin Franklin Ser.). (ENG.). 224p. (J). (gr. 5-9). 12.99 *(978-1-4847-1305-1(2))* Hyperion Bks. for Children.
Marciniak, Christine. Honestly, Ali! 2014. (YA). *(978-1-61271-249-9(5))* Zumaya Pubns. LLC.
Marino, Peter. Magic & Misery. 2009. (ENG.). 272p. (YA). (gr. 9-18). 17.95 *(978-0-8234-2133-6(3))* Holiday Hse., Inc.
Marrone, Amanda. Revealers. 2008. (ENG.). 288p. (YA). (gr. 9-18). pap. 8.99 *(978-1-4169-5874-1(6)*, Simon Pulse) Simon Pulse.
—Uninvited. 2007. (ENG.). 224p. (YA). (gr. 9-12). pap. 8.99 *(978-1-4169-3978-8(4)*, Simon Pulse) Simon Pulse.
Martin, Ann M. The Summer Before. 2010. (Baby-Sitters Club Ser.). (ENG.). 224p. (J). (gr. 3-7). 16.99 *(978-0-545-16093-3(6))* Scholastic, Inc.
Mata, Julie. Kate Walden Directs: Bride of Slug Man. 2015. (ENG., Illus.). 288p. (J). (gr. 3-7). 16.99 *(978-1-4231-9460-6(8))* Disney Pr.
Matas, Carol. Far. 2008. (Freak Ser.). (ENG.). 152p. (J). (gr. 5-18). pap. *(978-1-55470-094-3(9))* Me to We.
Matson, Morgan. Since You've Been Gone. 2015. (ENG., Illus.). 480p. (YA). (gr. 7). pap. 9.99 *(978-1-4424-3501-8(1)*, Simon & Schuster Bks. For Young Readers) Simon & Schuster Bks. For Young Readers.
Matson, Stacey. A Year in the Life of a Complete & Total Genius. 2015. (Arthur Bean Stories Ser.: 0). (ENG.). 272p. (J). (gr. 3-7). 15.99 *(978-1-4926-2074-7(2)*, 9781492620747, Sourcebooks Jabberwocky) Sourcebooks, Inc.
Matthews, Owen. How to Win at High School. 2015. (ENG.). 496p. (YA). (gr. 9). 17.99 *(978-0-06-233686-6(X)*, HarperTeen) HarperCollins Pubs.
Mayhall, Robin. He Loves Me, He Loves Me Not. Cella, Kristen & Tiede, Dirk, illus. 2013. (My Boyfriend Is a Monster Ser.: 7). (ENG.). 128p. (YA). (gr. 7-12). lib. bdg. 29.27 *(978-0-7613-6005-6(0)*, Graphic Universe™) Lerner Publishing Group.
—He Loves Me, He Loves Me Not. Cella, Kristen et al, illus. 2013. (My Boyfriend Is a Monster Ser.: 7). (ENG.). 128p. (YA). (gr. 7-12). pap. 9.95 *(978-0-7613-8548-6(7)*, Graphic Universe™) Lerner Publishing Group.
McBride, Kristina. A Million Times Goodnight. 2016. (ENG.). 304p. (YA). (gr. 8). 17.99 *(978-1-5107-0401-5(9)*, Sky Pony Pr.) Skyhorse Publishing Co., Inc.
—One Moment. 2017. (ENG.). 272p. (YA). (gr. 8). pap. 9.99 *(978-1-5107-1455-7(3)*, Sky Pony Pr.) Skyhorse Publishing Co., Inc.

McCafferty, Megan. The (Totally Not) Guaranteed Guide to Stressing, Obsessing & Second-Guessing. 2015. (Jessica Darling's It List Ser.: 3). (ENG.). 224p. (J). (gr. 3-7). 17.00 (978-0-316-33324-5(7)) Little Brown & Co.

McCahan, Erin. I Now Pronounce You Someone Else. 2010. (ENG.). 272p. (J). (gr. 7-18). 16.99 (978-0-545-08818-3(6), Levine, Arthur A. Bks.) Scholastic, Inc.

McCahan, Erin. The Lake Effect. 2017. (ENG.). 400p. (YA). (gr. 7). 17.99 **(978-0-8037-4052-5(2),** Dial Bks) Penguin Young Readers Group.

McClintock, Norah. Change of Heart. 2013. (Robyn Hunter Mysteries Ser.: 7). (ENG.). 224p. (YA). (gr. 6-12). pap. 8.95 (978-1-4677-0701-5(5)); lib. bdg. 27.93 (978-0-7613-8317-8(4)) Lerner Publishing Group.

—Down, 1 vol. 2007. (Orca Soundings Ser.). (ENG.). 128p. (YA). (gr. 8-12). pap. 9.95 (978-1-55143-766-8(X)) Orca Bk. Pubs. USA.

—Nowhere to Turn. 2012. (Robyn Hunter Mysteries Ser.: 6). (ENG.). 240p. (YA). (gr. 6-12). pap. 8.95 (978-0-7613-9398-6(6), Darby Creek); lib. bdg. 27.93 (978-0-7613-8316-1(6)) Lerner Publishing Group.

McClymer, Kelly. Getting to Third Date. 2006. (Romantic Comedies Ser.). (ENG., Illus.). 304p. (YA). (gr. 9-18). mass mkt. 6.99 (978-1-4169-1479-2(X), Simon Pulse) Simon Pulse.

McDonald, Abby. Jane Austen Goes to Hollywood. (ENG.). 336p. (YA). (gr. 9). 2015. pap. 8.99 (978-0-7636-7669-8(1)) 2013. 17.99 (978-0-7636-5508-2(2)) Candlewick Pr.

McDonald, Megan. Cloudy with a Chance of Boys. 2011. (Sisters Club Ser.: 3). (ENG., Illus.). 272p. (J). (gr. 3-7). 15.99 (978-0-7636-4615-8(6)) Candlewick Pr.

Mcgill, Leslie. Gearhead. 2015. (Cap Central Ser.: 4). (YA). lib. bdg. 20.80 (978-0-606-36839-1(6)) Turtleback Bks.

McGovern, Kate. Rules for 50/50 Chances: If You could Find Out How it All Ends, Would You? 2015. (ENG.). 352p. (YA). (gr. 7). 17.99 (978-0-374-30158-3(1), 9780374301583, Farrar, Straus & Giroux (BYR)) Farrar, Straus & Giroux.

McLaughlin, Emma & Kraus, Nicola. The Real Real. 2009. (ENG.). 336p. (YA). (gr. 9). pap. 9.99 (978-0-06-172042-0(9)) HarperCollins Pubs.

McNamee, Graham. Defender. 2016. (ENG.). 240p. (YA). (gr. 9). 17.99 (978-0-553-49895-0(9), Lamb, Wendy Bks.) Random Hse. Children's Bks.

McNeil, Gretchen. I'm Not Your Manic Pixie Dream Girl. 2016. 352p. (YA). (gr. 8). 17.99 (978-0-06-240911-9(5)) HarperCollins Pubs.

McVoy, Terra Elan. Being Friends with Boys. (ENG.). (YA). (gr. 9). 2013. Illus.). 384p. pap. 10.99 (978-1-4424-2160-8(6)) 2012. 368p. 16.99 (978-1-4424-2159-2(2)) Simon Pulse. (Simon Pulse).

—Pure. (ENG.). (YA). 2010. 352p. (gr. 7). pap. 9.99 (978-1-4169-6748-4(6)) 2009. 336p. (gr. 9-18). 16.99 (978-1-4169-7872-5(0)) Simon Pulse. (Simon Pulse).

—The Summer of Firsts & Lasts. (ENG.). (YA). (gr. 9). 2012. 448p. pap. 9.99 (978-1-4424-0214-0(8)) 2011. 432p. 16.99 (978-1-4424-0213-3(X)) Simon Pulse. (Simon Pulse).

Meacham, Margaret. A Fairy's Guide to Understanding Humans. 2007. (ENG.). 160p. (J). (gr. 5-18). 16.95 (978-0-8234-2078-0(7)) Holiday Hse., Inc.

Mead, Richelle. The Golden Lily. (Bloodlines Ser.: 2). (ENG.). (YA). (gr. 7). 2013. 448p. pap. 10.99 (978-1-59514-602-1(4)) 2012. 432p. 18.99 (978-1-59514-318-1(1)) Penguin Young Readers Group. (Razorbill).

Meaney, Flynn. The Boy Recession. 2012. (ENG.). 256p. (YA). (gr. 10-17). 17.99 (978-0-316-10213-1(X), Poppy) Little, Brown Bks. for Young Readers.

Mellom, Robin. Ditched: A Love Story. 2013. (ENG.). 288p. (YA). (gr. 7-17). pap. 8.99 (978-1-4231-4351-2(5)) Disney Pr.

Menon, Sandhya. When Dimple Met Rishi. 2017. (ENG., Illus.). 384p. (YA). (gr. 7). 17.99 **(978-1-4814-7868-7(0),** Simon Pulse) Simon Pulse.

Mesrobian, Carrie. Just a Girl. 2017. 304p. (YA). (gr. 9). 17.99 (978-0-06-234991-0(0)) HarperCollins Pubs.

Metz, Melinda. Bri's Big Crush. 2016. (Babysitter Chronicles Ser.). (ENG.). 160p. (gr. 4-7). lib. bdg. 26.65 (978-1-4965-2756-1(9), 1400591) Stone Arch Bks.

Meyerhoff, Jenny. Playing Cupid. 2016. 246p. (J). **(978-0-545-86780-1(0))** Scholastic, Inc.

Michaels, Robbie. Caught. 2016. (ENG., Illus.). (J). 24.99 **(978-1-63477-950-0(9),** Harmony Ink Pr.) Dreamspinner Pr.

Michels, Anna. 26 Kisses. 2016. (ENG., Illus.). 304p. (YA). (gr. 9). 17.99 (978-1-4814-5246-5(0), Simon Pulse) Simon Pulse.

Milanes, Janelle. The Victoria in My Head. 2017. (ENG., Illus.). 400p. (YA). (gr. 7). 17.99 **(978-1-4814-8089-5(8),** Simon Pulse) Simon Pulse.

Mills, Emma. First & Then. 2015. (ENG.). 272p. (YA). (gr. 9-12). 17.99 (978-1-62779-235-6(X), 9781627792356, Holt, Henry & Co. Bks. For Young Readers) Holt, Henry & Co.

—This Adventure Ends. 2016. (ENG.). 320p. (YA). 17.99 (978-1-62779-935-5(4), 9781627799355, Holt, Henry & Co. Bks. For Young Readers) Holt, Henry & Co.

Mills, Wendy. Positively Beautiful. (ENG.). 368p. (YA). 2016. pap. 9.99 (978-1-68119-025-9(7), 9781681190259) 2015. (gr. 9). 17.99 (978-1-61963-341-4(8), 9781619633414) Bloomsbury Publishing USA. (Bloomsbury USA Childrens).

Minter, J. The Insiders. 2004. (Insiders Ser.). (ENG.). 288p. (YA). (gr. 9-18). pap. 8.95 (978-1-58234-895-7(2), 9781582348957, Bloomsbury USA Childrens) Bloomsbury Publishing USA.

Mlynowski, Sarah. Gimme a Call. 2011. (ENG.). 320p. (YA). (gr. 7). pap. 9.99 (978-0-385-73589-6(8), Ember) Random Hse. Children's Bks.

—I See London, I See France. 2017. 384p. (YA). (gr. 9). 17.99 **(978-0-06-239707-2(9),** HarperTeen) HarperCollins Pubs.

Mlynowski, Sarah. Parties & Potions. 2010. (Magic in Manhattan Ser.: No. 4). (ENG., Illus.). 368p. (YA). (gr. 7). pap. 10.99 (978-0-385-73646-6(0), Ember) Random Hse. Children's Bks.

Moffitt, Debra. Best Kept Secret. 2011. (Pink Locker Society Novels Ser.: 2). (ENG.). 128p. (J). (gr. 3-7). pap. 16.99 (978-0-312-64503-8(1), 9780312645038, St. Martin's Griffin) St. Martin's Pr.

Monninger, Joseph. Whippoorwill. (ENG.). 288p. (YA). (gr. 7). 2016. pap. 9.99 (978-0-544-81356-4(1)) 2015. 17.99 (978-0-544-53123-9(X)) Houghton Mifflin Harcourt Publishing Co. (HMH Books For Young Readers).

Monroe, Ella. Truth or Dare. 2013. (Capital Girls Ser.: 3). (ENG.). 304p. (YA). (gr. 8). pap. 20.99 (978-0-312-62304-3(6), 9780312623043, St. Martin's Griffin) St. Martin's Pr.

Moore, Stephanie. Better Than Picture Perfect. 2014. (Sharp Sisters Ser.: 2). (ENG.). 160p. (YA). (gr. 6-12). pap. 7.95 (978-1-4677-4486-7(7), Darby Creek) Lerner Publishing Group.

Moore, Stephanie Perry. Back That Thing. 2015. (Illus.). 103p. (YA). 9.99 (978-1-4677-7892-3(3)) Lerner Publishing Group.

—Better Than Picture Perfect. 2014. (Sharp Sisters Ser.: 2). (ENG.). 160p. (YA). (gr. 6-12). lib. bdg. 27.93 (978-1-4677-3725-8(9)) Lerner Publishing Group.

—Give It Up. 2015. (YA). 9.99 (978-1-4677-7886-2(9)); (Swoop List Ser.: 1). (ENG., Illus.). 128p. (gr. 6-12). lib. bdg. 27.99 (978-1-4677-5804-8(3)) Lerner Publishing Group.

—On Your Knees. 2015. (Swoop List Ser.: 2). (ENG., Illus.). 128p. (YA). (gr. 6-12). lib. bdg. 27.99 (978-1-4677-5805-5(1)) Lerner Publishing Group.

—Sit on Top. 2015. (Swoop List Ser.: 4). (ENG., Illus.). 112p. (YA). (gr. 6-12). pap. 9.99 (978-1-4677-6052-2(8)) Lerner Publishing Group.

Moore, Stephanie Perry & Moore, Stephanie. The Way We Roll. 2009. (ENG., Illus.). 224p. (YA). (gr. 9). 9.95 (978-0-7582-3443-8(0), K-Teen/Dafina) Kensington Publishing Corp.

Morgan, Melissa J. Sunrise. 2009. (Summer Confidential Ser.: 1). (ENG.). 240p. (J). (gr. 5-6). pap. 7.99 (978-0-448-44988-3(9), Grosset & Dunlap) Penguin Young Readers Group.

Morrill, Lauren. Meant to Be. (ENG.). 304p. (YA). (gr. 7). 2014. pap. 9.99 (978-0-385-74178-1(2), Ember) 2012. 17.99 (978-0-385-74177-4(4), Delacorte Pr.) 2012. E-Book (978-0-375-98711-3(8), Delacorte Pr.) Random Hse. Children's Bks.

Moss, Ronald. The Wizard Next Door. 2009. 198p. pap. 14.95 (978-1-60911-077-2(3), Eloquent Bks.) Strategic Book Publishing & Rights Agency (SBPRA).

Murdock, Catherine Gilbert. Front & Center. 2011. (ENG.). 288p. (YA). (gr. 7). pap. 8.99 (978-0-547-40305-2(4)) Houghton Mifflin Harcourt Publishing Co.

Murphy, Julie. Dumplin. (YA). (gr. 8). 2017. 400p. pap. 9.99 (978-0-06-232719-2(4)) 2015. (ENG.). 384p. 17.99 (978-0-06-232718-5(6)) HarperCollins Pubs.

—Dumplin. 2017. (YA). lib. bdg. 20.85 **(978-0-606-39647-9(0))** Turtleback Bks.

Myracle, Lauren. The Infinite Moment of Us. (ENG.). 336p. (YA). (gr. 9-17). 2014. pap. 8.95 (978-1-4197-1358-3(2)) 2013. 18.95 (978-1-4197-0793-3(0)) Abrams, Inc. (Amulet Bks.).

Naylor, Phyllis Reynolds. Alice in Rapture, Sort Of. 2011. (Alice Ser.: 2). (ENG.). 208p. (J). (gr. 5-9). pap. 6.99 (978-1-4424-2362-6(5), Atheneum Bks. for Young Readers) Simon & Schuster Children's Publishing.

—Incredibly Alice. (Alice Ser.: 23). (ENG.). (YA). (gr. 9). 2012. Illus.). 304p. pap. 8.99 (978-1-4169-7556-4(X)) 2011. 288p. 16.99 (978-1-4169-7553-3(5)) Simon & Schuster Children's Publishing. (Atheneum Bks. for Young Readers).

—You & Me & the Space in Between: Alice in Charge; Incredibly Alice; Alice on Board. 2013. (Alice Ser.). (ENG., Illus.). 880p. (YA). (gr. 9). pap. 10.99 (978-1-4424-8664-5(3), Atheneum Bks. for Young Readers) Simon & Schuster Children's Publishing.

Neel, Julien. Down in the Dumps. Neel, Julien, illus. 2012. (Lou! Ser.: 3). (ENG., Illus.). 48p. (J). (gr. 6-9). pap. 8.95 (978-0-8225-9165-8(0), Graphic Universe™) Lerner Publishing Group.

—The Perfect Summer. Neel, Julien, illus. 2012. (Lou! Ser.: 4). (ENG., Illus.). 48p. (J). (gr. 6-9). pap. 8.95 (978-0-8225-9169-6(3), Graphic Universe™) Lerner Publishing Group.

—Secret Diary. Neel, Julien, illus. 2012. (Lou! Ser.). (Illus.). 48p. (J). (gr. 4-8). pap. 51.02 (978-0-7613-9285-9(8)); (ENG., (gr. 6-9). pap. 8.95 (978-0-7613-8868-5(0)) Lerner Publishing Group. (Graphic Universe™).

—Summertime Blues. Neel, Julien, illus. 2012. (Lou! Ser.). (Illus.). 48p. (J). (gr. 4-8). pap. 51.02 (978-0-7613-9286-6(6)); (ENG., (gr. 6-9). pap. 8.95 (978-0-7613-8869-2(9)) Lerner Publishing Group. (Graphic Universe™).

Neel, Julien & Burrell, Carol klio. Down in the Dumps. Neel, Julien, illus. 2012. (Lou! Ser.: 3). (ENG., Illus.). 48p. (J). (gr. 6-9). lib. bdg. 27.93 (978-0-7613-8779-4(X), Graphic Universe™) Lerner Publishing Group.

—The Perfect Summer. Neel, Julien, illus. 2012. (Lou! Ser.: 4). (ENG., Illus.). 48p. (J). (gr. 6-9). lib. bdg. 27.93 (978-0-7613-8780-0(3), Graphic Universe™) Lerner Publishing Group.

Nelson, Blake. Boy. 2017. (ENG., Illus.). 368p. (YA). (gr. 9). 18.99 **(978-1-4814-8813-6(9),** Simon Pulse) Simon Pulse.

Nelson, Blake. Destroy All Cars. 2011. (ENG.). 224p. (J). (gr. 9-10). pap. 9.99 (978-0-545-10475-3(0), Scholastic Paperbacks) Scholastic, Inc.

Nguyen, Jenn P. & Nguyen, Phuong Anh. The Way to Game the Walk of Shame. 2016. (ENG.). 336p. (YA). pap. 9.99 (978-1-250-08407-1(5), 9781250084071) Feiwel & Friends.

Nichols, Travis. Matthew Meets the Man. 2012. (ENG., Illus.). 176p. (YA). (gr. 6-9). 24.99 (978-1-59643-545-2(3), 9781596435452) Roaring Brook Pr.

No Place to Fall. 2014. (ENG.). 368p. (YA). (gr. 9). 17.99 (978-0-06-227099-3(0)) HarperCollins Pubs.

Novak, Ali. My Life with the Walter Boys. 2014. (ENG.). 368p. (YA). (gr. 7-12). pap. 10.99 (978-1-4022-9786-1(6), 9781402297861) Sourcebooks, Inc.

Ockler, Sarah. The Summer of Chasing Mermaids. 2015. (ENG., Illus.). 416p. (YA). (gr. 9). 17.99 (978-1-4814-0127-2(0), Simon Pulse) Simon Pulse.

O'Connell, Jenny. The Book of Luke. 2007. (ENG.). 304p. pap. 11.00 (978-1-4165-2040-5(6), MTV Bks.) MTV Books.

—Local Girls: An Island Summer Novel. 2008. (ENG.). 320p. pap. 19.99 (978-1-4165-6335-8(0)) Pocket Books.

—Plan B. 2006. (ENG.). 288p. pap. 18.99 (978-1-4165-2033-7(3), MTV Bks.) MTV Books.

O'Connell, Tyne. A Royal Mess. 2011. (Calypso Chronicles Ser.). (ENG.). 512p. (YA). pap. 9.99 (978-1-59990-888-5(3), 9781599908885, Bloomsbury USA Childrens) Bloomsbury Publishing USA.

O'Connor, Jane. Fancy Nancy: Nancy Clancy Seeks a Fortune. Glasser, Robin Preiss & Bracken, Carolyn, illus. 2016. (Nancy Clancy Ser.: 7). 144p. (J). (gr. 1-5). 9.99 (978-0-06-226969-0(0)) HarperCollins Pubs.

—Nancy Clancy, Secret Admirer. Glasser, Robin Preiss, illus. 2013. (Nancy Clancy Ser.: 2). (ENG.). 144p. (J). (gr. 1-5). pap. 4.99 (978-0-06-208420-0(8)) HarperCollins Pubs.

—Nancy Clancy, Secret Admirer. 2013. (Nancy Clancy Ser.: 2). (J). lib. bdg. 14.75 (978-0-606-35045-7(4), Turtleback) Turtleback Bks.

—Nancy Clancy's Tres Charming, 3 vols., Set. Glasser, Robin Preiss, illus. 2013. (Fancy Nancy Ser.). (ENG.). 384p. (J). (gr. 1-5). 24.99 (978-0-06-227793-0(6)) HarperCollins Pubs.

—Secret Admirer, 3 vols. Glasser, Robin Preiss, illus. 2013. (Fancy Nancy Ser.: Bk. 2). (ENG.). 128p. (J). (gr. 1-5). 9.99 (978-0-06-208295-4(7)) HarperCollins Pubs.

Ohlin, Nancy. Always, Forever. 2014. (ENG., Illus.). 320p. (YA). (gr. 9). pap. 9.99 (978-1-4424-6487-2(9), Simon Pulse) Simon Pulse.

—Thorn Abbey. 2013. (ENG.). 304p. (YA). (gr. 9). 16.99 (978-1-4424-6486-5(0), Simon Pulse) Simon Pulse.

Olin, Sean. Reckless Hearts. 2015. (Wicked Games Ser.: 2). (ENG.). 336p. (YA). (gr. 9). 17.99 (978-0-06-219241-7(8), Tegen, Katherine Bks) HarperCollins Pubs.

Olsen, Nora. Swans & Klons. 2013. (ENG.). 192p. (gr. 7). pap. 11.95 (978-1-60282-874-2(1)) Bold Strokes Bks.

Omololu, C. J. The Third Twin. 2015. (ENG.). 336p. (YA). (gr. 7). 20.99 (978-0-375-99171-4(9), Delacorte Pr.) Random Hse. Children's Bks.

Ostow, Micol. Gettin' Lucky. 2007. (Romantic Comedies Ser.). (ENG.). 256p. (YA). (gr. 9-9). mass mkt. 6.99 (978-1-4169-3536-0(3), Simon Pulse) Simon Pulse.

Palmer, Robin. Little Miss Red. 2010. (ENG.). 320p. (YA). (gr. 7-18). 9.99 (978-0-14-241123-0(X), Speak) Penguin Young Readers Group.

Parkinson, Will. Wet Paint. 2016. (ENG., Illus.). (J). 24.99 **(978-1-63477-993-7(2),** Harmony Ink Pr.) Dreamspinner Pr.

Patrick, Cat. Forgotten. 2012. (ENG.). 320p. (J). (gr. 7-17). pap. 8.99 (978-0-316-09460-3(9)) Little, Brown Bks. for Young Readers.

—The Originals. (ENG.). (YA). (gr. 7-17). 2014. 320p. pap. 10.00 (978-0-316-21945-7(2)) 2013. 304p. 18.00 (978-0-316-21943-3(6)) Little, Brown Bks. for Young Readers.

Patrick, Cat & Young, Suzanne. Just Like Fate. (ENG., Illus.). (YA). (gr. 9). 2014. 336p. pap. 9.99 (978-1-4424-7272-3(3)) 2013. 304p. 16.99 (978-1-4424-7271-6(5)) Simon Pulse. (Simon Pulse).

Paul, Marcy Beller. Underneath Everything. Davis, Bill, illus. 2015. (ENG.). 304p. (YA). (gr. 9). 17.99 (978-0-06-232721-5(6)) HarperCollins Pubs.

Paulsen, Gary. Crush: The Theory, Practice & Destructive Properties of Love. (ENG.). 144p. (J). (gr. 4-7). 2013. pap. 6.99 (978-0-385-74231-3(2), Yearling) 2012. 12.99 (978-0-385-74230-6(4), Lamb, Wendy Bks.) Random Hse. Children's Bks.

Payne, K. E. Another 365 Days. 2013. (ENG.). 264p. (J). (gr. 7). pap. 11.95 (978-1-60282-775-2(3)) Bold Strokes Bks.

—365 Days. 2011. (ENG.). 280p. (J). (gr. 7). pap. 13.95 (978-1-60282-540-6(8)) Bold Strokes Bks.

Pellicioli, Anna. Where You End. 2015. (ENG.). 312p. (YA). pap. 9.99 (978-0-7387-4403-2(4), Flux) North Star Editions.

Perez, Marlene. The Comeback. 2009. (ENG.). 208p. (J). (gr. 7). pap. 8.99 (978-0-545-08807-7(0)) Scholastic, Inc.

Perkins, Stephanie. Lola & the Boy Next Door. (ENG.). (YA). (gr. 9). 2013. 368p. pap. 10.99 (978-0-14-242201-4(0), Speak) 2011. 352p. 16.99 (978-0-525-42328-7(1), Dutton Books for Young Readers) Penguin Young Readers Group.

—Summer Days & Summer Nights: Twelve Love Stories. 2017. (ENG.). 400p. (YA). pap. 10.99 (978-1-250-07913-8(6), 9781250079138, St. Martin's Griffin) St. Martin's Pr.

Perry, Jolene. The Summer I Found You. 2014. (ENG.). 256p. (YA). (gr. 8-12). 16.99 (978-0-8075-8369-2(3)) Whitman, Albert & Co.

Peterfreund, Diana. Ascendant. (ENG.). (YA). (gr. 9). 2012. 416p. pap. 8.99 (978-0-06-149005-7(9)) 2010. 400p. 17.99 (978-0-06-149002-6(4)) HarperCollins Pubs. (HarperTeen).

—Rampant. 2010. (ENG.). 432p. (YA). (gr. 9). pap. 8.99 (978-0-06-149004-0(0), HarperTeen) HarperCollins Pubs.

Petroff, Shani. The Good, the Bad, & the Ugly Dress. McKenney, J. David, illus. 2010. (Bedeviled Ser.: 2). (ENG.). 240p. (J). (gr. 5-7). pap. 6.99 (978-0-448-45112-1(3), Grosset & Dunlap) Penguin Young Readers Group.

Philips, Fleur. Crumble. 2013. 168p. (YA). pap. 8.99 (978-0-9889299-0-6(2)) Philips, Fleur.

Philips, Liz. Perfect Ten. 2017. (ENG.). 352p. (YA). (gr. 9). 17.99 (978-0-425-28811-5(0), Viking Books for Young Readers) Penguin Young Readers Group.

Phillips, Rebecca. Faking Perfect. 2015. (ENG.). 272p. (J). (gr. 9). pap. 9.95 (978-1-61773-880-7(8)) Kensington Publishing Corp.

Phillips, Rebecca. These Things I've Done. 2017. 352p. (YA). (gr. 9). 17.99 **(978-0-06-257090-1(0),** HarperTeen) HarperCollins Pubs.

Polacco, Patricia. Someone for Mr. Sussman. Polacco, Patricia, illus. 2008. (ENG., Illus.). 40p. (J). (gr. 1-3). 17.99 (978-0-399-25075-0(1), Philomel Bks.) Penguin Young Readers Group.

Polisner, Gae. The Summer of Letting Go. (ENG.). (YA). (gr. 7-10). 2015. 336p. pap. 9.95 (978-1-61620-480-8(X)) 2014. 320p. 16.95 (978-1-61620-256-9(4), 73256) Algonquin Bks. of Chapel Hill.

Portes, Andrea. Anatomy of a Misfit. 2014. (ENG.). 336p. (YA). (gr. 9). 17.99 (978-0-06-231364-5(9), HarperTeen) HarperCollins Pubs.

Poulsen, David A. Blind Date. 2nd rev. ed. 2008. (Lawrence High Yearbook Ser.). (ENG.). 96p. (J). (gr. 2-7). pap. (978-1-55263-933-7(9)) Me to We.

Preble, Joy. Finding Paris. 2015. (ENG.). 272p. (YA). (gr. 9). 17.99 (978-0-06-232130-5(7)) HarperCollins Pubs.

Prinz, Yvonne. All You Get Is Me. 2010. (ENG.). 288p. (YA). (gr. 9-18). 16.99 (978-0-06-171580-8(8)) HarperCollins Pubs.

Puppy Love. 2014. (Flirt Ser.). (ENG., Illus.). 240p. (YA). (gr. 7). pap. 10.99 (978-1-4424-8412-2(8), Simon Pulse) Simon Pulse.

Quintero, Sofia. Show & Prove. 2015. (ENG.). 352p. (YA). (gr. 7). 17.99 (978-0-375-84707-3(3), Knopf Bks. for Young Readers) Random Hse. Children's Bks.

Reed, Jaime. Fading Amber. 2012. (ENG., Illus.). 304p. (YA). (gr. 9). pap. 9.95 (978-0-7582-6926-3(9), K-Teen/Dafina) Kensington Publishing Corp.

Reeves, Dia. Slice of Cherry. 2011. (ENG.). (YA). (gr. 9). 528p. pap. 9.99 (978-1-4169-8621-8(9)); 512p. 16.99 (978-1-4169-8620-1(0)) Simon Pulse. (Simon Pulse).

Reinhardt, Dana. Tell Us Something True. 2016. (ENG.). 208p. (YA). (gr. 9). lib. bdg. 20.99 (978-0-375-99066-3(6), Lamb, Wendy Bks.) Random Hse. Children's Bks.

Reisfeld, Randi. CC (Cape Cod) 2012. (Summer Share Ser.). (ENG.). 304p. (YA). (gr. 9). pap. 14.99 (978-1-4169-0036-8(5), Simon Pulse) Simon Pulse.

—No Strings Attached: CC (Cape Cod); Partiers Preferred. 2013. (ENG., Illus.). 624p. (YA). (gr. 9). pap. 9.99 (978-1-4424-5978-6(6), Simon Pulse) Simon Pulse.

—Partiers Preferred. 2007. (Summer Share Ser.). (ENG.). 288p. (YA). (gr. 9-12). pap. 13.99 (978-1-4169-0037-5(3), Simon Pulse) Simon Pulse.

Rennison, Louise. Are These My Basoomas I See Before Me? Final Confessions of Georgia Nicolson. 2010. (Confessions of Georgia Nicolson Ser.: 10). (ENG.). 336p. (YA). (gr. 8-9). pap. 8.99 (978-0-06-145937-5(2), HarperTeen) HarperCollins Pubs.

—Dancing in My Nuddy-Pants. 2006. (Confessions of Georgia Nicolson Ser.: 4). (ENG.). 240p. (YA). (gr. 8). reprint ed. pap. 8.99 (978-0-06-009748-6(5), HarperTeen) HarperCollins Pubs.

—Love Is a Many Trousered Thing. 2008. (Confessions of Georgia Nicolson Ser.: 8). (ENG.). 304p. (YA). (gr. 8). pap. 9.99 (978-0-06-085389-1(1), HarperTeen) HarperCollins Pubs.

—On the Bright Side, I'm Now the Girlfriend of a Sex God: Further Confessions of Georgia Nicolson. (Confessions of Georgia Nicolson Ser.: 2). (ENG.). 2006. 272p. (YA). (gr. 8). pap. 8.99 (978-0-06-447226-5(4), HarperTeen) 2003. 256p. (J). pap. 6.99 (978-0-06-052185-1(6)) HarperCollins Pubs.

—Stop in the Name of Pants! (Confessions of Georgia Nicolson Ser.: 9). (YA). 2009. (ENG.). 336p. (gr. 8). pap. 9.99 (978-0-06-145934-4(8)) 2008. 256p. (gr. 7-18). 16.99 (978-0-06-145932-0(1)) 2008. 320p. (gr. 7-18). lib. bdg. 17.89 (978-0-06-145933-7(X)) HarperCollins Pubs. (HarperTeen).

—Stop in the Name of Pants!, 6 vols. 2010. (Confessions of Georgia Nicolson Ser.: 9). (YA). 85.75 (978-1-4407-7775-2(6)); 82.75 (978-1-4407-7777-6(2)); 1.25 (978-1-4407-7779-0(9)); 172.75 (978-1-4407-7772-1(1)); 67.75 (978-1-4407-7773-8(X)); 70.75 (978-1-4407-7771-4(3)) Recorded Bks., Inc.

—Then He Ate My Boy Entrancers: More Mad, Marvy Confessions of Georgia Nicolson. (Confessions of Georgia Nicolson Ser.: 6). 2006. (ENG.). 336p. (YA). (gr. 8-12). pap. 9.99 (978-0-06-058939-4(6)) 2005. 320p. (J). lib. bdg. 16.89 (978-0-06-058938-7(8)) HarperCollins Pubs. (HarperTeen).

Reyes, M. G. Vindicated. 2017. (Emancipated Ser.: 3). 352p. (YA). (gr. 9). 17.99 (978-0-06-228901-8(2), Tegen, Katherine Bks) HarperCollins Pubs.

Robar, Serena. Giving up the V. 2009. (ENG.). 272p. (YA). (gr. 9-18). pap. 8.99 (978-1-4169-7558-8(6), Simon Pulse) Simon Pulse.

Robins, Eleanor. Don't Get Caught, 1 vol. unabr. ed. 2011. (Choices Ser.). (ENG.). 52p. (YA). (gr. 9-12). 7.95 (978-1-61651-592-8(9)) Saddleback Educational Publishing, Inc.

—It Is Not a Date, 1 vol. unabr. ed. 2011. (Carter High Chronicles Ser.). (ENG.). 51p. (YA). (gr. 9-12). pap. 7.95 (978-1-61651-309-2(8)) Saddleback Educational Publishing, Inc.

—One Date Too Many. (Carter High Chronicles (High-Interest Readers) Ser.). 2004. (Illus.). 48p. (J). per. 3.95 (978-1-56254-689-2(9), SP6899) 2011. (ENG.). 50p. (YA). (gr. 9-12). pap. 7.95 (978-1-61651-310-8(1)) Saddleback Educational Publishing, Inc.

—Someone to Count, 1 vol. unabr. ed. 2011. (Carter High Senior Year Ser.). (ENG.). 50p. (YA). (gr. 9-12). pap. 7.95 (978-1-61651-328-3(4)) Saddleback Educational Publishing, Inc.

Robinson, A. M. Vampire Crush. 2010. (ENG.). 416p. (YA). (gr. 8-18). pap. 8.99 (978-0-06-198971-1(1), HarperTeen) HarperCollins Pubs.

Röder, Marlene. In the River Darkness. 2014. (Illus.). 224p. (YA). (gr. 9-12). pap. 10.95 (978-1-62324-011-0(5)) Enslow Pubs., Inc.

Rosenberg, Madelyn & Crockett, Mary. Dream Boy. 2014. (ENG.). 336p. (YA). (gr. 7-12). pap. 9.99 (978-1-4022-9583-6(9), 9781402295836) Sourcebooks, Inc.

Rosenfield, Kat. Amelia Anne Is Dead & Gone. 2013. (ENG.). 288p. (YA). (gr. 9). pap. 8.99 (978-0-14-242610-4(5), Speak) Penguin Young Readers Group.

Rosin, Lindsey. Cherry. 2016. (ENG., Illus.). 400p. (YA). (gr. 9). 17.99 (978-1-4814-5908-2(2), Simon Pulse) Simon Pulse.

Rostoker-Gruber, Karen & Isaacs, Ronald H. Farmer Kobi's Hanukkah Match. Decker, C. B., illus. 2015. (J). (978-1-68115-501-2(X)); pap. (978-0-87441-924-5(7)) Behrman Hse., Inc.

Rottman, S. L. Head above Water, 1 vol. 2003. (ENG.). 192p. (YA). (gr. 7-18). pap. 6.95 (978-1-56145-238-5(6), Q21186) Peachtree Pubs.

Ruby, Laura. Play Me. 2009. (ENG.). 336p. (YA). (gr. 9). pap. 9.99 (978-0-06-124329-5(9), HarperTeen) HarperCollins Pubs.

Ruditis, P. J. Love, Hollywood Style. 2013. (Romantic Comedies Ser.). (ENG., Illus.). 272p. (YA). (gr. 7). pap. 13.99 (978-1-4814-1539-2(5), Simon Pulse) Simon Pulse.

Ruditis, Paul. Rainbow Party. 2005. (ENG.). 256p. (YA). (gr. 9-18). pap. 12.95 (978-1-4169-0235-5(X), Simon Pulse) Simon Pulse.

Rumble. 2014. (ENG., Illus.). 560p. (YA). (gr. 9). 19.99 (978-1-4424-8284-5(2), McElderry, Margaret K. Bks.) McElderry, Margaret K. Bks.

Rushton, Rosie. How Could You Do This to Me, Mum? 2005. 224p. (J). pap. 5.99 (978-0-7868-5187-4(2)) Hyperion Bks. for Children.

—Where Do We Go from Here? 2005. 224p. (J). pap. 5.99 (978-0-7868-5189-8(9)) Hyperion Bks. for Children.

Russell, Rachel Renée. Tales from a Not-So-Happy Heartbreaker. 2013. (Dork Diaries: 6). lib. bdg. 25.75 *(978-0-606-32424-3(0),* Turtleback) Turtleback Bks.
Ryan, Jeanne. Charisma. 2015. (ENG.). 384p. (YA). (gr. 7). 17.99 *(978-0-8037-3966-6(4),* Dial Bks) Penguin Young Readers Group.
Ryan, Patrick. Gemini Bites. 2011. (ENG.). 240p. (J). (gr. 7-8). 17.99 *(978-0-545-22128-3(5),* Scholastic Pr.) Scholastic, Inc.
Saeed, Aisha & Airgood, Ellen. Written in the Stars. 2015. (ENG.). 304p. (YA). (gr. 9). 17.99 *(978-0-399-17170-3(3),* Nancy Paulsen Books) Penguin Young Readers Group.
Saft, Lauren. Those Girls. 2016. (ENG.). 336p. (YA). (gr. 10-17). pap. 9.99 *(978-0-316-26016-9(9),* Poppy) Little, Brown Bks. for Young Readers.
Sales, Leila. Past Perfect. 2012. (ENG.). 336p. (YA). (gr. 9). pap. 10.99 *(978-1-4424-0683-4(6),* Simon Pulse) Simon Pulse.
Salter, Helen. Does Snogging Count as Exercise? 2011. (ENG.). 256p. (YA). (gr. 7). pap. 12.99 *(978-1-4424-3111-9(3),* Simon Pulse) Simon Pulse.
Salter, Sydney. My Big Nose & Other Natural Disasters. 2009. (ENG., Illus.). 352p. (J). (gr. 7-18). pap. 19.95 *(978-0-15-206643-7(8))* Houghton Mifflin Harcourt Publishing Co.
—Swoon at Your Own Risk. 2010. (ENG., Illus.). 360p. (YA). (gr. 7-18). pap. 15.95 *(978-0-15-206649-9(7))* Houghton Mifflin Harcourt Publishing Co.
Sanchez, Alex. Boyfriends with Girlfriends. (ENG.). 224p. (YA). (gr. 7). 2012. pap. 10.99 *(978-1-4169-3775-3(7))* 2011. 16.99 *(978-1-4169-3773-9(0))* Simon & Schuster Bks. For Young Readers. (Simon & Schuster Bks. For Young Readers).
Sandberg, Winter. Private Display of Affection. 2016. (ENG., Illus.). (YA). (gr. 8-12). 24.99 ***(978-1-63533-065-6(3),*** Harmony Ink Pr.) Dreamspinner Pr.
Santopolo, Jill. Summer Love. 2014. (Follow Your Heart Ser.: 1). (ENG.). 224p. (YA). (gr. 7). pap. 9.99 *(978-0-14-751092-1(9),* Speak) Penguin Young Readers Group.
Sappenfield, Heather. The View from Who I Was. 2015. (ENG.). 336p. (YA). pap. 11.99 *(978-0-7387-4174-1(4),* Flux) North Star Editions.
S.C.A.M. 170p. (J). pap. *(978-1-4114-0441-0(6),* SparkNotes) Barnes & Noble, Inc.
Scheerger, Sarah Lynn. The Opposite of Love. 2014. (ENG.). 272p. (YA). (gr. 8-12). 16.99 *(978-0-8075-6132-4(0))* Whitman, Albert & Co.
Schneider, Erin L. Summer of Sloane. (ENG.). 304p. (YA). (gr. 9-17). 2017. pap. 9.99 *(978-1-4847-2670-9(7))* 2016. (Illus.). 17.99 *(978-1-4847-2525-2(5))* Hyperion Bks. for Children.
Schraff, Anne. If You Really Loved Me, 1 vol. unabr. ed. 2010. (Urban Underground Ser.). (ENG.). 181p. (YA). (gr. 9-12). pap. 9.95 *(978-1-61651-003-9(X))* Saddleback Educational Publishing, Inc.
—If You Were Mine, 1 vol. 2013. (Urban Underground Ser.). (ENG.). 195p. (YA). (gr. 9-12). pap. 9.95 *(978-1-62250-041-3(5))* Saddleback Educational Publishing, Inc.
—The Stranger, 1 vol. unabr. ed. 2011. (Urban Underground Ser.). (ENG.). 200p. (YA). (gr. 9-12). pap. 9.95 *(978-1-61651-266-8(0))* Saddleback Educational Publishing, Inc.
Schraff, Anne E. If You Were Mine. 2013. (Urban Underground — Harriet Tubman High School Ser.). (YA). lib. bdg. 20.80 *(978-0-606-31581-4(0),* Turtleback) Turtleback Bks.
—Misjudged. 2014. (Urban Underground — Cesar Chavez High School Ser.). (YA). lib. bdg. 20.80 *(978-0-606-35589-6(8))* Turtleback Bks.
—The One for Me. 2013. (Urban Underground — Harriet Tubman High School Ser.). lib. bdg. 20.80 *(978-0-606-31582-1(9),* Turtleback) Turtleback Bks.
Schreiber, Ellen. Love Bites. 2011. (Vampire Kisses Ser.: 7). (ENG.). 208p. (YA). (gr. 8). pap. 8.99 *(978-0-06-168944-4(0),* Tegen, Katherine Bks) HarperCollins Pubs.
—Magic of the Moonlight. (Full Moon Ser.: 2). (ENG.). (YA). (gr. 8). 2012. 256p. pap. 9.99 *(978-0-06-198656-7(9))* 2011. 240p. 17.99 *(978-0-06-198657-4(7))* HarperCollins Pubs. (Tegen, Katherine Bks).
—Once in a Full Moon. 2011. (Full Moon Ser.: 1). (ENG.). 320p. (YA). (gr. 8). pap. 8.99 *(978-0-06-198652-9(6),* Tegen, Katherine Bks) HarperCollins Pubs.
Schroeder, Lisa. Falling for You. 2013. (ENG., (YA). (gr. 9). Illus.). 384p. pap. 9.99 *(978-1-4424-4400-3(2));* 368p. 16.99 *(978-1-4424-4399-0(5))* Simon Pulse. (Simon Pulse).
Scott, Elizabeth. Bloom. 2007. (ENG.). 240p. (YA). (gr. 7-12). pap. 8.99 *(978-1-4169-2683-2(6),* Simon Pulse) Simon Pulse.
—Perfect You. 2008. (ENG.). 304p. (YA). (gr. 9-12). pap. 9.99 *(978-1-4169-5355-5(8),* Simon Pulse) Simon Pulse.
—The Unwritten Rule. (ENG.). (YA). (gr. 9). 2011. 240p. pap. 9.99 *(978-1-4169-7892-3(5))* 2010. 224p. 16.99 *(978-1-4169-7891-6(7))* Simon Pulse. (Simon Pulse).
Scott, Kieran. Geek Magnet. 2009. (ENG.). 320p. (YA). (gr. 7-18). 8.99 *(978-0-14-241417-0(4),* Speak) Penguin Young Readers Group.
—He's So Not Worth It. (He's So/She's So Trilogy Ser.). (ENG.). (YA). (gr. 7). 2012. 384p. pap. 9.99 *(978-1-4169-9954-6(X))* 2011. 368p. 17.99 *(978-1-4169-9953-9(1))* Simon & Schuster Bks. For Young Readers. (Simon & Schuster Bks. For Young Readers).
—Only Everything. 2014. (True Love Ser.: 1). (ENG., Illus.). 352p. (YA). (gr. 7). pap. 9.99 *(978-1-4424-7716-2(4),* Simon & Schuster Bks. For Young Readers) Simon & Schuster Bks. For Young Readers.
—Something True. 2015. (True Love Ser.: 3). (ENG., Illus.). 288p. (YA). (gr. 7). pap. 9.99 *(978-1-4424-7723-0(7))* Simon & Schuster Children's Publishing.
—This Is So Not Happening. (He's So/She's So Trilogy Ser.). (ENG., 320p. (YA). (gr. 7). 2013. Illus.). pap. 9.99 *(978-1-4169-9956-0(6))* 2012. 16.99 *(978-1-4169-9955-3(8))* Simon & Schuster Bks. For Young Readers. (Simon & Schuster Bks. For Young Readers).
Scott, Mindi. Live Through This. 2012. (ENG.). 304p. (YA). (gr. 9). 17.99 *(978-1-4424-4059-3(7));* pap. 9.99 *(978-1-4424-4060-9(0))* Simon Pulse. (Simon Pulse).
Sedgwick, Chantele. Love, Lucas. 2015. (ENG.). 280p. (J). (gr. 6). 16.99 *(978-1-63220-417-2(7),* Sky Pony Pr.) Skyhorse Publishing Co., Inc.
Seles, Monica. Love Match. 2014. (Academy Ser.). (ENG.). 224p. (YA). (gr. 7). pap. 9.99 *(978-1-59990-902-8(2),* 9781599909028, Bloomsbury USA Childrens) Bloomsbury Publishing USA.
Seles, Monica & LaRosa, James. Game On. 2013. (Academy Ser.). (ENG.). 256p. (YA). (gr. 7). 17.99 *(978-1-59990-976-9(6),* 9781599909769); pap. 9.99 *(978-1-59990-901-1(4),* 9781599909011) Bloomsbury Publishing USA. (Bloomsbury USA Childrens).
Selzer, Adam. I Kissed a Zombie, & I Liked It. 2010. (ENG.). 192p. (YA). (gr. 7-18). pap. 7.99 *(978-0-385-73503-2(0),* Delacorte Bks. for Young Readers) Random Hse. Children's Bks.
Serle, Rebecca. The Edge of Falling. 2014. (ENG., Illus.). 304p. (YA). (gr. 9). 17.99 *(978-1-4424-3316-8(7),* Simon Pulse) Simon Pulse.
—Famous in Love. 2014. (ENG.). 336p. (YA). (gr. 7-17). 18.00 *(978-0-316-36632-8(3),* Poppy) Little, Brown Bks. for Young Readers.
—Truly Madly Famously. 2015. (Famous in Love Ser.: 2). (ENG.). 320p. (YA). (gr. 7-17). 18.00 *(978-0-316-36640-3(4),* Poppy) Little, Brown Bks. for Young Readers.
—When You Were Mine. (ENG., (YA). (gr. 9). 2013. Illus.). 368p. pap. 9.99 *(978-1-4424-3314-4(0))* 2012. 352p. 16.99 *(978-1-4424-3313-7(2))* Simon Pulse. (Simon Pulse).
Sharif, Medeia. Bestest. Ramadan. Ever. 2011. (ENG.). 312p. (YA). pap. 9.95 *(978-0-7387-2323-5(1),* Flux) North Star Editions.
Shaw Wolf, Jennifer. Dead Girls Don't Lie. 2013. 336p. pap. 17.99 *(978-0-8027-3450-1(2))* Walker & Co.
Sheldon, Dyan. My Worst Best Friend. 2010. (ENG., Illus.). 304p. (YA). (gr. 7-18). 15.99 *(978-0-7636-4555-7(9))* Candlewick Pr.
Silvera, Adam. More Happy Than Not. (ENG.). (YA). (gr. 9). 2016. 336p. pap. 10.99 *(978-1-61695-677-6(1))* 2015. 304p. 18.99 *(978-1-61695-560-1(0))* Soho Pr., Inc. (Soho Teen).
Simon, Coco. Alexis & the Perfect Recipe. 2013. (Cupcake Diaries: 4). (ENG., Illus.). 160p. (J). (gr. 3-7). 15.99 *(978-1-4424-7493-2(9),* Simon Spotlight) Simon Spotlight.
Simone, Ni-Ni & London, Kelli. The Break-Up Diaries. 2011. (ENG.). 272p. (YA). (gr. 9-18). 9.95 *(978-0-7582-6316-2(3),* K-Teen/Dafina) Kensington Publishing Corp.
Sise, Katie. The Boyfriend App. 2013. (ENG.). 320p. (YA). (gr. 8). 17.99 *(978-0-06-219526-5(3))* HarperCollins Pubs.
Slater, Calvin. Lovers & Haters. 2014. (Coleman High Ser.: 1). (ENG., Illus.). 304p. (YA). (gr. 13). pap. 9.95 *(978-1-61773-132-7(3),* K-Teen) Kensington Publishing Corp.
Smith, Andrew. 100 Sideways Miles. 2014. (ENG., Illus.). 288p. (YA). (gr. 9). 17.99 *(978-1-4424-4495-9(9),* Simon & Schuster Bks. For Young Readers) Simon & Schuster Bks. For Young Readers.
Smith, Jennifer E. Hello, Goodbye, & Everything in Between. 2015. (ENG.). 256p. (YA). (gr. 7-17). 18.00 *(978-0-316-33442-6(1))* Little Brown & Co.
Smith, Robert F. Bitten: A Romantic Comedy. 2008. (YA). pap. *(978-1-59038-904-1(2))* Deseret Bk. Co.
Smith, Sarah. The Other Side of Dark. (ENG., 320p. (YA). (gr. 7). 2011. Illus.). pap. 11.99 *(978-1-4424-0281-2(4))* 2010. 16.99 *(978-1-4424-0280-5(6))* Simon & Schuster Children's Publishing. (Atheneum Bks. for Young Readers).
Snadowsky, Daria. Anatomy of a Boyfriend. 2008. (ENG.). 272p. (YA). (gr. 9). pap. 8.99 *(978-0-440-23944-4(3),* Ember) Random Hse. Children's Bks.
Sones, Sonya. What My Girlfriend Doesn't Know. 2013. (ENG., Illus.). 320p. (YA). (gr. 7). pap. 9.99 *(978-1-4424-9384-1(4),* Simon & Schuster Bks. For Young Readers) Simon & Schuster Bks. For Young Readers.
—What My Mother Doesn't Know. 2004. 259p. (gr. 7-12). 19.00 *(978-0-7569-4268-7(3))* Perfection Learning Corp.
—What My Mother Doesn't Know. 2013. (ENG., Illus.). 288p. (YA). (gr. 7). pap. 11.99 *(978-1-4424-9385-8(2),* Simon & Schuster Bks. For Young Readers) Simon & Schuster Bks. For Young Readers.
Spalding, Amy. Kissing Ted Callahan (and Other Guys) 2016. (ENG.). 336p. (YA). (gr. 10-17). pap. 9.99 *(978-0-316-37153-7(X),* Poppy) Little, Brown Bks. for Young Readers.
—Kissing Ted Callahan (and Other Guys) 2015. (ENG.). 320p. (YA). (gr. 10-17). 18.00 *(978-0-316-37152-0(1))* Sports Illustrated For Kids.
—The New Guy (and Other Senior Year Distractions) 2016. (ENG.). 320p. (YA). (gr. 7-17). 17.99 *(978-0-316-38278-6(7),* Poppy) Little, Brown Bks. for Young Readers.
Spangler, Brie. Beast. 2016. (ENG.). 336p. (YA). (gr. 7). 17.99 *(978-1-101-93716-7(5),* Knopf Bks. for Young Readers) Random Hse. Children's Bks.
Sparks, Megan. Boot Camp Blues, 1 vol. 2014. (Roller Girls Ser.). (ENG.). 256p. (gr. 8-10). 12.95 *(978-1-62370-057-7(4))* Capstone Young Readers of Coughlan Cos.
—In a Jam, 1 vol. 2014. (Roller Girls Ser.). (ENG.). 256p. (gr. 8-10). 12.95 *(978-1-62370-058-4(2))* Capstone Young Readers of Coughlan Cos.
Spencer, Katherine. More Than Friends: A Saving Grace Novel. 2008. (Saving Grace Ser.). (ENG., Illus.). 224p. (YA). (gr. 7-12). pap. 14.95 *(978-0-15-205746-6(3))* Houghton Mifflin Harcourt Publishing Co.
Spooner, M. Entrapment. 2010. (ENG.). 320p. (YA). (gr. 8). pap. 8.99 *(978-1-4424-0366-6(7),* McElderry, Margaret K. Bks.) McElderry, Margaret K. Bks.
—Entr@pment: A High School Comedy in Chat. 2009. (ENG.). 320p. (YA). (gr. 8-18). 16.99 *(978-1-4169-5889-5(4),* McElderry, Margaret K. Bks.) McElderry, Margaret K. Bks.
Spring, Melanie. Practice Makes Perfect. 2014. (Varsity Novel Ser.: 3). (ENG.). 192p. (YA). (gr. 7-17). pap. 10.00 *(978-0-316-22733-9(1),* Poppy) Little, Brown Bks. for Young Readers.
Springer, Kristina. The Espressologist. 2011. (ENG.). 208p. (YA). (gr. 7-12). pap. 15.99 *(978-0-312-65923-3(7))* Square Fish.
Stahl, Mary Louise. Louie. 2003. 122p. (YA). 20.95 *(978-0-595-74889-1(9));* pap. 10.95 *(978-0-595-28750-5(6))* iUniverse, Inc.
Stampler, Ann Redisch. Where It Began. 2013. (ENG.). 384p. (YA). (gr. 9). pap. 9.99 *(978-1-4424-2322-0(6),* Simon Pulse) Simon Pulse.
Stampler, Laura. Little Black Dresses, Little White Lies. 2016. (ENG., Illus.). 352p. (YA). (gr. 9). 17.99 *(978-1-4814-5989-1(9),* Simon Pulse) Simon Pulse.
Standiford, Natalie. Breaking up Is Really, Really Hard to Do. 2005. (ENG.). 224p. (YA). (gr. 7-17). pap. 18.99 *(978-0-316-11041-9(8))* Little, Brown Bks. for Young Readers.
—The Dating Game, No. 1. 2005. (ENG.). 224p. (YA). (gr. 7-17). pap. 18.99 *(978-0-316-11040-2(X))* Little, Brown Bks. for Young Readers.
—Parallel Parking. 6th ed. 2006. (ENG., Illus.). 224p. (YA). (gr. 7-17). pap. 18.99 *(978-0-316-11531-5(2))* Little, Brown Bks. for Young Readers.
—Speed Dating. 5th ed. 2006. (ENG.). 224p. (J). (gr. 8-12). per. 18.99 *(978-0-316-11530-8(4))* Little, Brown Bks. for Young Readers.
Staniszewski, Anna. The Dirt Diary. 2014. (Dirt Diary Ser.: 1). (ENG.). 256p. (J). (gr. 5-9). pap. 6.99 *(978-1-4022-8636-0(8),* 9781402286360, Sourcebooks Jabberwocky) Sourcebooks, Inc.
—The Gossip File. 2015. (Dirt Diary Ser.: 3). (ENG.). 224p. (J). (gr. 5-9). pap. 6.99 *(978-1-4926-0463-1(1),* 9781492604631, Sourcebooks Jabberwocky) Sourcebooks, Inc.
—Once upon a Cruise: a Wish Novel. 2016. (ENG.). 256p. (J). (gr. 3-7). pap. 6.99 *(978-0-545-87986-6(8),* Scholastic Paperbacks) Scholastic, Inc.
—The Prank List. 2014. (Dirt Diary Ser.: 2). (ENG.). 256p. (J). (gr. 5-9). pap. 6.99 *(978-1-4022-8639-1(2),* 9781402286391, Sourcebooks Jabberwocky) Sourcebooks, Inc.
Stanton, Andy. Sterling & the Canary. 2012. (Stoke Books Titles Ser.). 64p. (J). (gr. 5-8). pap. 7.95 *(978-1-78112-030-9(7));* lib. bdg. 22.60 *(978-1-78112-029-3(3))* Stoke Bks.
Stanton, Angie. Rock & a Hard Place. 2013. (Jamieson Brothers Ser.: 1). (ENG.). 304p. (YA). (gr. 9). pap. 9.99 *(978-0-06-227254-6(3),* HarperTeen) HarperCollins Pubs.
Stapleton, Rhonda. Flirting with Disaster. 2010. (ENG.). 256p. (YA). (gr. 7-18). pap. 9.99 *(978-1-4169-7465-9(2),* Simon Pulse) Simon Pulse.
—Pucker Up. 2010. (ENG.). 272p. (YA). (gr. 7-18). pap. 9.99 *(978-1-4169-7466-6(0),* Simon Pulse) Simon Pulse.
Stephens, Nia. Boy Shopping. 2007. (ENG., Illus.). 224p. (YA). (gr. 8-12). 9.95 *(978-0-7582-1929-9(6),* K-Teen/Dafina) Kensington Publishing Corp.
Stewart, Kiera. How to Break a Heart. (ENG., Illus.). (J). (gr. 5-9). 2016. 304p. pap. 7.99 *(978-1-4231-8531-4(5))* 2015. 316p. 16.99 *(978-1-4231-7181-2(0))* Hyperion Bks. for Children.
Stine, R. L. The Dead Boyfriend. 2016. 288p. (YA). pap. ***(978-1-250-11199-9(4),*** Dunne, Thomas Bks.) St. Martin's Pr.
—Party Poopers. Park, Trip, illus. (Rotten School Ser.: Bk. 9). 4.99 *(978-0-06-078826-1(7))* HarperCollins Pubs.
—Party Poopers, 1 vol. Park, Trip, illus. 2011. (Rotten School Ser.: No. 9). (ENG.). 128p. (gr. 2-5). 24.21 *(978-1-59961-833-3(8))* Spotlight.
—The Teacher from Heck. Park, Trip, illus. 2009. (Rotten School Ser.: No. 8). 128p. (J). pap. 4.99 *(978-0-06-078823-0(2),* Harper Trophy) HarperCollins Pubs.
Stokes, Paula. The Art of Lainey. 2014. (Art of Lainey Ser.). (ENG.). 384p. (YA). (gr. 9). pap. 9.99 *(978-0-06-223842-9(6),* HarperTeen) HarperCollins Pubs.
—Liars, Inc. 2015. (ENG.). 368p. (YA). (gr. 8). 17.99 *(978-0-06-232328-6(8),* HarperTeen) HarperCollins Pubs.
Stolarz, Laurie Faria. Deadly Little Lessons. 2013. (Touch Novel Ser.). (ENG., Illus.). 346p. (YA). (gr. 7-12). pap. 8.99 *(978-1-4231-3498-5(2))* Hyperion Pr.
Stone, Danika. Internet Famous. 2017. (ENG.). 336p. (YA). pap. 10.99 *(978-1-250-11437-2(3),* 9781250114372) Feiwel & Friends.
Stratton, Allan. Leslie's Journal. rev. ed. 2008. (ENG.). 200p. (YA). (gr. 8-12). 21.95 *(978-1-55451-149-5(6),* 9781554511495) Annick Pr., Ltd. CAN. Dist: Publishers Group West (PGW).
Strohm, Stephanie Kate. It's Not Me, It's You. (ENG.). 288p. (gr. 7). 2017. (J). pap. 9.99 ***(978-1-338-16066-6(4))*** 2016. (YA). 17.99 *(978-0-545-95258-3(1))* Scholastic, Inc.
Summers, Tamara. Never Bite a Boy on the First Date. 2009. (ENG.). 288p. (YA). (gr. 9-18). pap. 5.99 *(978-0-06-172154-0(9),* HarperTeen) HarperCollins Pubs.
Sutton, Michelle. It's Not about Me. 2012. (Second Glances Ser.). (ENG.). 252p. pap. 12.99 *(978-0-9838836-9-2(6))* Sword of the Spirit Publishing.
Tahmaseb, Charity & Vance, Darcy. The Geek Girl's Guide to Cheerleading. 2009. (ENG.). 352p. (YA). (gr. 9-18). pap. 8.99 *(978-1-4169-7834-3(8),* Simon Pulse) Simon Pulse.
Tashjian, Janet. Fault Line. 2006. (ENG.). 256p. (YA). (gr. 9-12). reprint ed. pap. 10.99 *(978-0-8050-8063-6(5),* 9780805080636, Holt, Henry & Co. Bks. For Young Readers) Holt, Henry & Co.
—For What It's Worth. 2012. (ENG.). 288p. (YA). (gr. 7-12). 16.99 *(978-0-8050-9365-0(6),* 9780805093650, Holt, Henry & Co. Bks. For Young Readers) Holt, Henry & Co.
Taylor, Michelle M. What's Happily Ever after, Anyway? 2004. (Illus.). 178p. (YA). (gr. 9-12). per. 10.95 *(978-0-9746481-3-2(2))* Brown Barn Bks.
Tharp, Tim. The Spectacular Now. (ENG.). 304p. (YA). (gr. 9). 2010. pap. 8.99 *(978-0-375-86502-2(0),* Knopf Bks. for Young Readers) 2013. pap. 9.99 *(978-0-385-75430-9(2),* Ember) Random Hse. Children's Bks.
—The Spectacular Now. 2010. lib. bdg. 19.65 *(978-0-606-14947-1(3),* Turtleback) Turtleback Bks.
Thorpe, Kiki, adapted by. Broken Hearts. 2003. (Lizzie Mcguire Ser.). (Illus.). 138p. (J). 12.65 *(978-0-7569-2718-9(8))* Perfection Learning Corp.
Tibensky, Arlaina. And Then Things Fall Apart. 2011. (ENG.). 272p. (YA). (gr. 9). pap. 9.99 *(978-1-4424-1323-8(9),* Simon Pulse) Simon Pulse.
To Be Perfectly Honest: A Novel Based on an Untrue Story. 2014. (ENG., Illus.). 496p. (YA). (gr. 7). pap. 11.99 *(978-0-689-87605-9(X),* Simon & Schuster Bks. For Young Readers) Simon & Schuster Bks. For Young Readers.
Tolan, Stephanie S. & Tolan, R. J. Applewhites Coast to Coast. 2017. 320p. (J). (gr. 3-7). 16.99 ***(978-0-06-213320-5(9))*** HarperCollins Pubs.
Toten, Teresa. The Unlikely Hero of Room 13B. 2015. (ENG.). 304p. (YA). (gr. 7). 17.99 *(978-0-553-50786-7(9),* Delacorte Pr.) Random Hse. Children's Bks.
Tracy, Kristen. Hung Up. 2014. (ENG., Illus.). 288p. (YA). (gr. 9). 17.99 *(978-1-4424-6075-1(X),* Simon Pulse) Simon Pulse.
—Project (un)Popular Book #2: Totally Crushed. 2017. (Project (un)Popular Ser.: 2). (ENG.). 224p. (J). (gr. 5). 16.99 ***(978-0-553-51052-2(5),*** Delacorte Bks. for Young Readers) Random Hse. Children's Bks.
—Totally Crushed. 2017. 211p. (J). ***(978-0-553-51053-9(3),*** Delacorte Pr) Random House Publishing Group.
Trigiani, Adriana. Viola in Reel Life. (Viola Ser.: 1). (ENG.). (YA). (gr. 8). 2011. 304p. pap. 8.99 *(978-0-06-145104-1(5))* 2009. 288p. 17.99 *(978-0-06-145102-7(9))* HarperCollins Pubs. (HarperTeen).
—Viola in the Spotlight. 2012. (Viola Ser.: 2). (ENG.). 288p. (YA). (gr. 8). pap. 8.99 *(978-0-06-145107-2(X),* HarperTeen) HarperCollins Pubs.
Tullson, Diane. Foolproof, 1 vol. 2015. (Orca Soundings Ser.). (ENG.). 120p. (YA). (gr. 8-12). pap. 9.95 *(978-1-4598-1034-1(1))* Orca Bk. Pubs. USA.
Vail, Rachel. If We Kiss. 2005. (If We Kiss Ser.: Bk. 1). (ENG.). 272p. (J). 15.99 *(978-0-06-056914-3(X))* HarperCollins Pubs.
—Kiss Me Again. 2012. (If We Kiss Ser.: 2). (ENG.). 256p. (YA). (gr. 8). 17.99 *(978-0-06-194717-9(2),* HarperTeen) HarperCollins Pubs.
—Well, That Was Awkward. 2017. (ENG.). 320p. (J). (gr. 5). 16.99 *(978-0-670-01308-1(0),* Viking Books for Young Readers) Penguin Young Readers Group.
Van Ark, Katie. The Boy Next Door. 2015. (ENG.). 368p. (YA). (gr. 7). pap. 9.99 *(978-1-250-06146-1(6))* Feiwel & Friends.
Van Tol, Alex. Oracle, 1 vol. 2012. (Orca Currents Ser.). (ENG.). 128p. (J). (gr. 5-9). pap. 9.95 *(978-1-4598-0132-5(6));* lib. bdg. 16.95 *(978-1-4598-0133-2(4))* Orca Bk. Pubs. USA.
Vance, Talia. Silver. 2012. (Bandia Novel Ser.: 1). (ENG.). 384p. (YA). pap. 9.99 *(978-0-7387-3303-6(2),* Flux) North Star Editions.
Vandereyken, Leen. Loulou in Love. 2008. (Girls Only Ser.). (ENG.). 155p. (YA). (gr. 4-18). 16.95 *(978-1-60537-025-5(8))* Clavis Publishing.
Verdi, Jessica. What You Left Behind. 2015. (ENG.). 368p. (YA). (gr. 8-12). pap. 9.99 *(978-1-4926-0874-5(2))* Sourcebooks, Inc.
Veronique, Catel. Bluesy Lucy - the Existential Chronicles of a Thirtysomething. 2013. (Bluesy Lucy - the Existential Chronicles of a Thirtysomething Ser.). (ENG., Illus.). 120p. 24.95 *(978-1-59465-048-2(9),* 9781594650482) Humanoids, Inc.
Voorhees, Coert. In Too Deep. 2014. (ENG.). 336p. (YA). (gr. 7-12). pap. 8.99 *(978-1-4231-4473-1(2))* Hyperion Bks. for Children.
Wakeham, Kate. Pride & Prejudice, 1 vol. Tempest, Annabel, illus. 2017. (ENG.). 30p. (J). 12.99 ***(978-1-4236-4783-6(1))*** Gibbs Smith, Publisher.
Walker, Kristin. A Match Made in High School. 2010. (ENG.). 288p. (YA). (gr. 7-18). 9.99 *(978-1-59514-257-3(6),* Razorbill) Penguin Young Readers Group.
Walker, Melissa. Small Town Sinners. (ENG.). (YA). (gr. 9-12). 2013. 304p. pap. 9.99 *(978-1-59990-982-0(0),* 9781599909820) 2011. 288p. 16.99 *(978-1-59990-527-3(2),* 9781599905273) Bloomsbury Publishing USA. (Bloomsbury USA Childrens).
Walton, Julia. Words on Bathroom Walls. 2017. (ENG.). 304p. (YA). (gr. 7). 17.99 ***(978-0-399-55088-1(7));*** lib. bdg. 20.99 ***(978-0-399-55089-8(5))*** Random Hse. Children's Bks. (Random Hse. Bks. for Young Readers).
Wang, Holman & Wang, Jack. Jane Austen's Pride & Prejudice. 2016. (ENG., Illus.). 24p. (J). (gr. -1 — 1). bds. 9.95 *(978-1-4521-5244-8(6))* Chronicle Bks. LLC.
Wang, Jack, et al. Jane Austen's Emma. 2016. (ENG., Illus.). 24p. (J). (gr. -1 — 1). bds. 9.95 *(978-1-4521-5255-4(1))* Chronicle Bks. LLC.
Wasserman, Robin. Envy. 2006. (Seven Deadly Sins Ser.: 2). (ENG.). 256p. (YA). (gr. 9-12). pap. 9.99 *(978-0-689-87783-4(8),* Simon Pulse) Simon Pulse.
—Greed. 2007. (Seven Deadly Sins Ser.: 7). (ENG.). 256p. (YA). (gr. 9). pap. 8.99 *(978-1-4169-0720-6(3),* Simon Pulse) Simon Pulse.
Watson, Renée. This Side of Home. 2015. (ENG.). 336p. (YA). (gr. 7). 17.99 *(978-1-59990-668-3(6),* 9781599906683, Bloomsbury USA Childrens) Bloomsbury Publishing USA.
Watt, Erin. Broken Prince. 2016. (Royals Ser.: 2). (ENG.). 370p. (gr. 7-12). pap. 14.99 *(978-1-68230-503-4(1),* EverAfter Romance) Diversion Publishing Corp.
Watt, Erin & Frederick, Jen. Paper Princess. 2016. (Royals Ser.: 1). (ENG., Illus.). 370p. pap. 14.99 *(978-1-68230-456-3(6),* EverAfter Romance) Diversion Publishing Corp.
Webb, Sarah. Ask Amy Green: Boy Trouble. 2010. (Ask Amy Green Ser.: 1). (ENG., Illus.). 288p. (YA). (gr. 7-18). 16.99 *(978-0-7636-5006-3(4))* Candlewick Pr.
—Ask Amy Green: Love & Other Drama-Ramas! 2012. (Ask Amy Green Ser.: 4). (ENG., Illus.). 224p. (YA). (gr. 7). 15.99 *(978-0-7636-5582-2(1))* Candlewick Pr.
—Boy Trouble. 2011. (Ask Amy Green Ser.: 1). (ENG., Illus.). 288p. (YA). (gr. 7). 6.99 *(978-0-7636-5063-6(3))* Candlewick Pr.
—Summer Secrets. (Ask Amy Green Ser.: 2). (ENG., Illus.). 288p. (YA). (gr. 7). 2012. pap. 6.99 *(978-0-7636-5705-5(0))* 2011. 16.99 *(978-0-7636-5071-1(4))* Candlewick Pr.
Weetman, Nova. A Hot Cold Summer: Choose Your Own Ever After. 2016. (ENG.). 256p. (J). pap. 5.99 *(978-1-61067-354-9(9))* Kane Miller.
Weingarten, Lynn. The Book of Love. 2013. (ENG.). 272p. (YA). (gr. 8). 17.99 *(978-0-06-192620-4(5),* HarperTeen) HarperCollins Pubs.
—The Secret Sisterhood of Heartbreakers. (ENG.). (YA). (gr. 8). 2013. 368p. pap. 9.99 *(978-0-06-192619-8(1))* 2011. 352p. 17.99 *(978-0-06-192618-1(3))* HarperCollins Pubs. (HarperTeen).
Wells, Pamela. The Crushes. 2009. (ENG.). 352p. (J). (gr. 7). pap. 8.99 *(978-0-439-92560-0(6))* Scholastic, Inc.
West, Kasie. By Your Side. 2017. 352p. (YA). (gr. 8). pap. 9.99 *(978-0-06-245586-4(9),* HarperTeen) HarperCollins Pubs.

—The Distance Between Us. 2013. (ENG.). 320p. (YA). (gr. 8). pap. 9.99 *(978-0-06-223565-7(6),* HarperTeen) HarperCollins Pubs.
—On the Fence. 2014. (ENG.). 304p. (YA). (gr. 8). pap. 9.99 *(978-0-06-223567-1(2),* HarperTeen) HarperCollins Pubs.
—P. S. I Like You. 2016. (ENG.). 336p. (YA). (gr. 7). 17.99 *(978-0-545-85097-1(5))* Scholastic, Inc.
Wettersten, Laura. My Faire Lady. 2014. (ENG., Illus.). 352p. (YA). (gr. 7). 17.99 *(978-1-4424-8933-2(2),* Simon & Schuster Bks. For Young Readers) Simon & Schuster Bks. For Young Readers.
Weyland, Jack. As Always, Dave. 2008. 320p. (YA). pap. 15.95 *(978-1-59038-849-5(6))* Deseret Bk. Co.
Whipple, Natalie. House of Ivy & Sorrow. 2014. (ENG.). 368p. (YA). (gr. 8). pap. 9.99 *(978-0-06-212018-2(2),* HarperTeen) HarperCollins Pubs.
Whitaker, Alecia. The Queen of Kentucky. 2013. (ENG.). 384p. (YA). (gr. 7-17). pap. 8.99 *(978-0-316-12494-2(X),* Poppy) Little, Brown Bks. for Young Readers.
—The Road to You. 2015. (Wildflower Ser.: 2). (ENG.). 352p. (YA). (gr. 7-17). 18.00 *(978-0-316-25140-2(2))* Sports Illustrated For Kids.
—The Way Back Home. 2016. (Wildflower Ser.: 3). (ENG.). 336p. (YA). (gr. 7-17). 17.99 *(978-0-316-25144-0(5),* Poppy) Little, Brown Bks. for Young Readers.
Whitney, Gary & Whitney, Molly. Thistle Downe. 2016. (ENG., Illus.). 128p. (J). 22.95 *(978-1-942945-14-7(0),* 9781942945147) Bright Sky Pr.
Whitten, A. J. The Cellar. 2011. (ENG.). 288p. (YA). (gr. 7-18). pap. 16.99 *(978-0-547-23253-9(5))* Houghton Mifflin Harcourt Publishing Co.
Whyman, Matt. The Savages. (ENG.). 288p. (gr. 8-14). 2015. pap. 9.99 *(978-1-4683-1071-9(2),* 461071) 2014. 16.99 *(978-1-4683-0856-3(4),* 460856) Overlook Pr., The.
Willard, Eliza, et al. Love Is in the Air. 2004. (ENG.). 128p. *(978-0-00-718094-3(2))* HarperCollins Pubs. Australia.
Willey, Margaret. Beetle Boy. 2014. (ENG.). 208p. (YA). (gr. 8-12). 17.95 *(978-1-4677-2639-9(7),* Carolrhoda Bks.) Lerner Publishing Group.
Williams, Carol Lynch. Signed, Skye Harper. 2014. (ENG., Illus.). 304p. (YA). (gr. 7). 17.99 *(978-1-4814-0032-9(0),* Simon & Schuster/Paula Wiseman Bks.) Simon & Schuster/Paula Wiseman Bks.
Winfrey, Kerry. Love & Other Alien Experiences. 2017. (ENG.). 272p. (YA). pap. 10.99 *(978-1-250-11952-0(9),* 9781250119520) Feiwel & Friends.
Wolf, Jennifer Shaw. Dead Girls Don't Lie. 2014. (ENG.). 368p. (YA). (gr. 9). pap. 9.99 *(978-0-8027-3753-3(6),* 9780802737533, Bloomsbury USA Childrens) Bloomsbury Publishing USA.
Wolitzer, Meg. Belzhar. (ENG.). 272p. (YA). (gr. 9). 2015. 10.99 *(978-0-14-242629-6(6),* Speak) 2014. 17.99 *(978-0-525-42305-8(2),* Dutton Books for Young Readers) Penguin Young Readers Group.
Wood, Fiona. Cloudwish. 2016. (ENG.). 320p. (YA). (gr. 7-17). 17.99 *(978-0-316-24212-7(8),* Poppy) Little, Brown Bks. for Young Readers.
Wood, Nathaniel. Play Me Backwards. 2014. (ENG., Illus.). 288p. (YA). (gr. 9). 18.99 *(978-1-4814-0102-9(5),* Simon & Schuster Bks. For Young Readers) Simon & Schuster Bks. For Young Readers.
Woodson, Jacqueline. If You Come Softly & Behind You. 2010. (ENG.). 352p. (YA). (gr. 7-18). 8.99 *(978-0-14-241918-2(4),* Puffin Books) Penguin Young Readers Group.
Wunsch, Emma. The Movie Version. 2016. (ENG.). 368p. (YA). (gr. 9-17). 18.95 *(978-1-4197-1900-4(9),* Amulet Bks.) Abrams, Inc.
Young, Suzanne. So Many Boys. 2010. (Naughty List Ser.: No. 2). (ENG.). 256p. (YA). (gr. 7-18). 9.99 *(978-1-59514-267-2(3),* Razorbill) Penguin Young Readers Group.
Zarr, Sara & Altebrando, Tara. Roomies. 2013. (ENG.). 288p. (YA). (gr. 7-17). 18.00 *(978-0-316-21749-1(2))* Little, Brown Bks. for Young Readers.
Zindel, Paul & Zindel, Paul. My Darling, My Hamburger. 2005. (ENG.). 176p. (YA). (gr. 8-18). pap. 8.99 *(978-0-06-075736-6(1),* HarperTeen) HarperCollins Pubs.

DAVID, KING OF ISRAEL

B&H Kids Editorial Staff. David. Conger, Holli, illus. 2016. (Little Words Matter(tm) Ser.). (ENG.). 24p. (J). (gr. -1 — 1). bds. 8.99 *(978-1-4336-8651-1(1),* B&H Kids) B&H Publishing Group.
Dalmatian Press Staff. David & Goliath. 2004. (ENG., Illus.). 24p. (J). 2.99 *(978-1-4037-0971-4(8),* Spirit Pr.) Bendon, Inc.
David. (Divertidas Historias Biblicas para Ninos Ser.). (SPA.). (J). 3.49 *(978-0-7899-0598-7(1),* 496645) Editorial Unilit.
David & Goliath. Date not set. (J). act. bk. ed. 1.49 *(978-0-88271-235-2(7),* 1751) Regina Pr., Malhame & Co.
David & Goliath: A Bible Story to Color. (Illus.). 16p. (J). pap. 1.50 *(978-0-87162-825-1(2),* E6018) Warner Pr., Inc.
David & Goliath Bible Sticker Book. 2003. (Illus.). 16p. (J). 2.98 *(978-1-4054-1554-5(1))* Parragon, Inc.
David C. Cook Publishing Company Staff. David Giant Fighter. 2008. (Pencil Fun Bks). 16p. (J). pap. 9.90 *(978-1-4347-6825-4(2))* Cook, David C.
Dickson, Bill, illus. David & Goliath. 2013. (Happy Day Ser.). (ENG.). 16p. (J). pap. 2.49 *(978-1-4143-9324-7(5))* Tyndale Hse. Pubs.
Dietrich, Julie. David & His Friend, Jonathan. Ramsey, Marcy, illus. 2005. (Arch Bks.). (ENG.). 16p. (J). 1.99 *(978-0-7586-0723-2(7))* Concordia Publishing Hse.
Edwards, Josh. Pull-Out David & Goliath, 1 vol. Embleton Hall, Chris, illus. 2014. (ENG.). 10p. (J). bds. 11.99 *(978-1-85985-997-1(6),* Candle Bks.) Lion Hudson PLC GBR. Dist: Kregel Pubns.
Frank, Penny. David & Goliath. Morris, Tony, illus. 2nd rev. ed. (ENG.). 24p. pap. 2.99 *(978-0-7459-4111-0(7),* Lion Books) Lion Hudson PLC GBR. Dist: Trafalgar Square Publishing.
Gamblin, Rose Tooley. King David. 2009. (SPA & ENG., Illus.). 31p. (J). 2.99 *(978-0-8127-0480-8(0))* Autumn Hse. Publishing Co.
Hansen, Janis. David & His Giant Battle, 5 vols. Francisco, Wendy, illus. 2003. (Bible Adventure Club Ser.). 36p. wbk. ed. 19.99 incl. audio, cd-rom *(978-1-58134-321-2(3))* Crossway.
Johnson, Alice W. Believe & You're There: When David Slew Goliath, Vol. 9. 2010. (Illus.). 96p. (J). pap. 6.99 *(978-1-60641-816-1(5))* Deseret Bk. Co.
Kovacs, Victoria. David/Esther Flip-Over Book. Krome, Mike, illus. 2015. (Little Bible Heroes(tm) Ser.). (ENG.). 32p. (J). (gr. k-2). pap. 3.99 *(978-1-4336-8713-6(5),* B&H Kids) B&H Publishing Group.
Lashbrook, Marilyn. I May Be Little. Britt, Stephanie McFetridge, illus. 2012. 32p. (J). pap. 8.00 *(978-1-935014-41-6(2))* Hutchings, John Pubs.
MacKenzie, Carine. David the Fugitive: True Friendship. 2009. (Bible Alive Ser.). (ENG., Illus.). 24p. (J). 3.99 *(978-1-84550-487-8(9),* cf0ac043-f2de-40dc-874b-d61d7396ad4f) Christian Focus Pubns. GBR. Dist: Bookmasters Distribution.
—David the Shepherd: A Man of Courage. 2009. (Bible Alive Ser.). (ENG., Illus.). 24p. (J). 3.99 *(978-1-84550-486-1(0),* 9781845504861) Christian Focus Pubns. GBR. Dist: Bookmasters Distribution.
—David the Soldier: True Friendship. 2009. (Bible Alive Ser.). (ENG., Illus.). 24p. (J). 3.99 *(978-1-84550-488-5(7),* 0b6e8c69-ec57-4af6-b61a-5c82981c8691) Christian Focus Pubns. GBR. Dist: Bookmasters Distribution.
MacLean, Ruth. The Shepherd King: A Puzzle Book about David. rev. ed. 2009. (Puzzle Ser.). (ENG., Illus.). 24p. (J). 4.99 *(978-1-84550-498-4(4),* c4a1705c-30c9-4390-96f6-fa425d40387e) Christian Focus Pubns. GBR. Dist: Bookmasters Distribution.
Murdock, Hy. David. (Bible Stories Ser.: No. S846-5). (Illus.). (J). (gr. -1-2). pap. 3.95 *(978-0-7214-5068-1(7),* Dutton Juvenile) Penguin Publishing Group.
Perry, Marilyn. The Adventures of David: The Story of a Shepherd Who Became King, 4 bklts. 2003. (ENG., Illus.). 208p. (J). (gr. 10-10). pap., pap. 69.95 *(978-1-55145-483-2(1))* Wood Lake Publishing, Inc. CAN. Dist: Westminster John Knox Pr.
Pingry, Patricia A. David & Goliath: A Story about Trusting in God: Based on 1 Samuel 17:1/50. Munger, Nancy, illus. 2005. (Children of the Bible Ser.). (ENG.). 23p. (J). bds. 6.95 *(978-0-8249-6570-9(1),* Ideal Pubns.) Worthy Publishing.
—The Story of David. Pulley, Kelly, illus. 2012. (J). *(978-0-8249-1886-6(X),* Ideal Pubns.) Worthy Publishing.
Powell Smith, Brendan. David & Goliath: The Brick Bible for Kids. 2013. (ENG., Illus.). 32p. (J). (gr. -1-1). 12.95 *(978-1-62087-982-5(4),* 620982, Sky Pony Pr.) Skyhorse Publishing Co., Inc.
Pulley, Kelly & Zondervan Staff. David & the Giant (David y el Gigante), 1 vol. Pulley, Kelly, illus. 2009. (I Can Read! / the Beginner's Bible / ¡Yo Sé Leer! Ser.). (SPA & ENG., Illus.). 32p. (J). pap. 3.99 *(978-0-310-71890-1(2))* Zonderkidz.
Sanders, Nancy I. King David, 1 vol. 2014. (Get to Know Ser.). (ENG.). 128p. (J). pap. 7.99 *(978-0-310-74475-7(X))* Zonderkidz.
Simon, Mary Manz. David & Goliath: Read & Learn the Bible. 2005. (ENG., Illus.). 24p. (J). pap. 2.99 *(978-1-4037-1161-8(5),* Spirit Pr.) Bendon, Inc.
Smart Kids Publishing Staff. David & Goliath: A Story about Courage. Sharp, Chris, illus. 2006. (I Can Read the Bible Ser.). (ENG.). 12p. (J). (gr. -1-3). 14.95 *(978-0-8249-6659-1(7),* Ideal Pubns.) Worthy Publishing.
Smith, Martina. The Story of King David: A Spark Bible Story. Grosshauser, Peter, illus. 2016. (Spark Bible Stories Ser.). (ENG.). 32p. (J). (gr. -1-2). 12.99 *(978-1-5064-0226-0(7),* Sparkhouse Family) Augsburg Fortress, Pubs.
Taylor, Zachary. David. (Money at its Best: Millionaires of the Old Testament Ser.). 112p. (YA). (gr. 7-12). 2009. 24.95 *(978-1-4222-0468-9(5))* 2007. pap. 14.95 *(978-1-4222-0843-4(5))* Mason Crest.
van Rijswijk, Cor. David & Goliath. Visser, Rino, illus. 2003. 43p. (J). *(978-1-894666-23-7(2))* Inheritance Pubns.
Youngs, C. R. David: Prince of Israel. 2004. 203p. (YA). mass mkt. 9.95 *(978-0-9760451-0-6(9))* Youngs, C. R.
Zondervan Staff. David & God's Giant Victory: Biblical Values, 1 vol. Jones, Dennis, illus. 2010. (I Can Read! / Dennis Jones Ser.). (ENG.). 32p. (J). (gr. -1-2). pap. 3.99 *(978-0-310-71879-6(1))* Zonderkidz.
—David & the Giant, 1 vol. Pulley, Kelly, illus. 2008. (I Can Read! / the Beginner's Bible Ser.). (ENG.). 32p. (J). (gr. -1-1). pap. 3.99 *(978-0-310-71550-4(4))* Zonderkidz.

DAVID, KING OF ISRAEL—FICTION

Booth, Bradley. Shepherd Warrior. 2007. 127p. (J). *(978-0-8163-2161-2(2))* Pacific Pr. Pubns.
Bowman, Crystal. Little David's Brave Day, 1 vol. Hartung, Susan Kathleen & Endersly, Frank, illus. 2010. (I Can Read! / Little David Ser.). (ENG.). 32p. (J). pap. 3.99 *(978-0-310-71709-6(4))* Zonderkidz.
Hardman, Christy. Against the Giant. 2008. 267p. (gr. 3-7). pap. 16.99 *(978-1-59955-117-3(9))* Cedar Fort, Inc./CFI Distribution.
Martin, Rachael Lynn. McKenzie Drew: Adventures with David. 2008. 56p. pap. 16.95 *(978-1-60610-389-0(X))* America Star Bks.
Page, Nick & Page, Claire. David & Goliath. Loy, Nikki, illus. 2006. (Read with Me (Make Believe Ideas) Ser.). 31p. (J). (gr. k-2). *(978-1-84610-173-1(5))* Make Believe Ideas.

DAVIS, JEFFERSON, 1808-1889

Aretha, David A. Jefferson Davis. 2009. (Leaders of the Civil War Era Ser.). (Illus.). 144p. (gr. 6-12). 35.00 *(978-1-60413-297-1(3),* Chelsea Hse.) Facts On File, Inc.
Burch, Joann J. Jefferson Davis: Soldier & President of the Confederacy. 2015. (Legendary American Biographies Ser.). 96p. (J). (gr. 6-12). 27.94 *(978-0-7660-6465-2(4));* pap. 10.95 *(978-0-7660-6466-9(2))* Enslow Pubs., Inc.
Hale, Sarah Elder, ed. Jefferson Davis & the Confederacy. 2005. (ENG., Illus.). 48p. (J). (gr. 3-9). 17.95 *(978-0-8126-7908-3(3))* Cobblestone Publishing Co.
Marsh, Carole. Jefferson Davis, Civil War Hero. 2004. 12p. (gr. k-4). 2.95 *(978-0-635-02366-7(0))* Gallopade International.
Miller, Reagan & Arthur, Martin. Great Leaders of the Civil War. 2011. (ENG.). 48p. (J). pap. *(978-0-7787-5359-9(X));* lib. bdg. *(978-0-7787-5342-1(5))* Crabtree Publishing Co.
Roxburgh, Ellis. Abraham Lincoln vs. Jefferson Davis: Presidents of a Divided Nation. 2016. (History's Greatest Rivals Ser.). (ENG., Illus.). 48p. (J). (gr. 6-8). pap. 14.05 *(978-1-4824-4219-9(1))* Stevens, Gareth Publishing LLLP.

DAY—FICTION

Alter, Anna. Francine's Day. Alter, Anna, illus. 2003. (Illus.). 32p. (J). lib. bdg. 16.89 *(978-0-06-623937-8(0))* HarperCollins Pubs.
Anderson, Sara. Noisy City Day (2015 Board Book) Anderson, Sara, illus. 2015. (ENG., Illus.). 12p. (J). (gr. -1-1). bds. 10.95 *(978-1-943459-00-1(2))* Sara Anderson Children's Bks.
Andreasen, Dan. Saturday with Daddy. Andreasen, Dan, illus. (ENG., Illus.). (J). 2017. 26p. bds. 7.99 *(978-1-250-11265-1(6),* 9781250112651) 2013. 24p. (gr. -1-2). 12.99 *(978-0-8050-8687-4(0),* 9780805086874) Holt, Henry & Co. (Holt, Henry & Co. Bks. For Young Readers).
Annmarie & Emma Chiarenza. The Yippee Day. 2011. 24p. pap. 15.99 *(978-1-4628-7217-6(4))* Xlibris Corp.
Ashman, Linda. Just Another Morning. Muñoz, Claudio, illus. 2004. (ENG.). 32p. (J). (gr. -1-3). 15.99 *(978-0-06-029053-5(6))* HarperCollins Pubs.
Awdry, Wilbert V. Blue Train, Green Train. Stubbs, Tommy, illus. 2006. (Bright & Early Books(R) Ser.). (ENG.). 36p. (J). (gr. k-k). 8.99 *(978-0-375-83463-9(X),* Random Hse. Bks. for Young Readers) Random Hse. Children's Bks.
Awdry, Wilbert V. & Awdry, W. Blue Train, Green Train. Stubbs, Tommy, illus. 2007. (Bright & Early Board Books(TM) Ser.). (ENG.). 24p. (J). (— 1). bds. 4.99 *(978-0-375-83984-9(4),* Random Hse. Bks. for Young Readers) Random Hse. Children's Bks.
Bakos, Lisa M. Wrong Side of the Bed. Raff, Anna, illus. 2016. (ENG.). 40p. (J). (-k). 16.99 *(978-0-399-16572-6(X),* G.P. Putnam's Sons Books for Young Readers) Penguin Young Readers Group.
Barchers, Suzanne I. Pete Has Fast Feet, 1 vol. 2011. (Targeted Phonics Ser.). (ENG., Illus.). 16p. (J). (gr. k-2). pap. 5.99 *(978-1-4333-2915-9(8))* Teacher Created Materials, Inc.
Barchers, Suzanne I. & Teacher Created Materials Staff. Big Day for Kate, 1 vol. 2011. (Targeted Phonics Ser.). (ENG., Illus.). 16p. (J). (gr. k-2). pap. 5.99 *(978-1-4333-2908-1(5))* Teacher Created Materials, Inc.
Berger, Carin. A Perfect Day. Berger, Carin, illus. 2012. (ENG., Illus.). 40p. (J). (gr. -1-3). 16.99 *(978-0-06-201580-8(X),* Greenwillow Bks.) HarperCollins Pubs.
Bernardo, Anilu. Un Dia con Mis Tias: A Day with My Aunts. Rodriguez, Christina, illus. 2006. (ENG & SPA.). 32p. (J). (gr. -1-2). 16.95 *(978-1-55885-374-4(X),* Piñata Books) Arte Publico Pr.
Braun, Sebastien. I Love My Daddy. Braun, Sebastien, illus. 2004. (ENG., Illus.). 32p. (J). (gr. -1-2). 12.99 *(978-0-06-054311-2(6))* HarperCollins Pubs.
Calmenson, Stephanie. Ollie's School Day. Carter, Abby, illus. 2012. (ENG.). 24p. (J). 15.95 *(978-0-8234-2377-4(8))* Holiday Hse., Inc.
Capucilli, Alyssa Satin. My Dad & Me. Mitchell, Susan, illus. 2009. (ENG.). 16p. (J). (gr. -1-1). 7.99 *(978-1-4169-5828-4(2),* Little Simon) Little Simon.
Carluccio, Maria. The Sounds Around Town. Carluccio, Maria, illus. 2010. (ENG., Illus.). 13p. (J). 14.99 *(978-1-84686-362-2(7))* Barefoot Bks., Inc.
—The Sounds Around Town. 2008. (ENG., Illus.). 24p. (J). (gr. -1-k). 16.99 *(978-1-905236-28-2(X))* Barefoot Bks., Inc.
Carluccio, Maria, illus. The Sounds Around Town. 2011. (ENG.). 24p. (J). (gr. -1-3). pap. 7.99 *(978-1-84686-430-8(5))* Barefoot Bks., Inc.
Carter, Anne Laurel. Night Boy, 1 vol. Pelletier, Ninon, illus. 2012. (ENG.). 32p. (J). (gr. -1-3). 19.95 *(978-1-55469-402-0(7))* Orca Bk. Pubs. USA.
Charlip, Remy. A Perfect Day. 2007. (Illus.). 40p. (J). (gr. -1). lib. bdg. 17.89 *(978-0-06-051973-5(8))* HarperCollins Pubs.
Chast, Roz. Around the Clock. Chast, Roz, illus. 2015. (ENG., Illus.). 32p. (J). (gr. -1-3). 18.99 *(978-1-4169-8476-4(3),* Atheneum Bks. for Young Readers) Simon & Schuster Children's Publishing.
Colors All Day. (J). 26.20 *(978-0-8136-8399-7(8));* (gr. -1-3). 59.50 *(978-0-8136-7918-1(4))* Modern Curriculum Pr.
Coop, Kay. Gertrude's Moving Day. 2003. (Illus.). 42p. (J). per. *(978-1-931456-70-8(4));* 2nd ed. 48p. per. *(978-1-932077-61-2(8))* Athena Pr.
Cousins, Lucy. Maisy's First Clock. Cousins, Lucy, illus. 2011. (Maisy Ser.). (ENG., Illus.). 16p. (J). (gr. k-k). bds. 14.99 *(978-0-7636-5095-7(1))* Candlewick Pr.
De Regniers, Beatrice Schenk. What Did You Put in Your Pocket? Date not set. 32p. (J). (gr. -1-1). pap. 5.95 *(978-0-06-443700-4(0))* HarperCollins Pubs.
Dewdney, Anna. Llama Llama Wakey-Wake. 2012. (Llama Llama Ser.). (ENG.). 14p. (J). (— 1). bds. 5.99 *(978-0-670-01326-5(9),* Viking Books for Young Readers) Penguin Young Readers Group.
DiCicco, Sue. Funny Bunnies: Morning, Noon, & Night. 2015. (Illus.). 32p. (J). *(978-1-4844-4595-2(3))* Scholastic, Inc.
Dicicco, Sue. Scholastic Reader Level 1: Funny Bunnies: Morning, Noon, & Night. 2014. (Scholastic Reader Level 1 Ser.). (ENG.). 32p. (J). (gr. -1-1). pap. 3.99 *(978-0-545-67631-1(2))* Scholastic, Inc.
Duburke, Randy. Little Mister. 2006. (ENG., Illus.). 22p. (J). (gr. -1-7). bds. 6.95 *(978-0-8118-4954-8(6))* Chronicle Bks. LLC.
Ficocelli, Elizabeth. Kid Tea, 0 vols. Dibley, Glin, illus. 2013. (ENG.). 36p. (J). (gr. -1-k). pap. 9.99 *(978-1-4778-4738-1(3),* 9781477847381, Amazon Children's Publishing) Amazon Publishing.
Finch, Donna. Amanda the Panda, 1 vol. Bolund, Inna, illus. 2009. (ENG.). 27p. pap. 24.95 *(978-1-61546-797-6(1))* America Star Bks.
Fisher, Doris & Sneed, Dani. My Even Day, 1 vol., Vol. 2. Lee, Karen, illus. 2007. (Basic Math Numbers Ser.). (ENG.). 32p. (J). (gr. -1-3). 15.95 *(978-0-9777423-3-2(4))* Arbordale Publishing.
Franco, Betsy & Franco-Feeney, Betsy. Birdsongs. Jenkins, Steve, illus. 2007. (ENG.). 40p. (J). (gr. -1-3). 17.99 *(978-0-689-87777-3(3),* McElderry, Margaret K. Bks.) McElderry, Margaret K. Bks.
François, Marie B. My busy day / Jounen m trè Chaje. 2004. (ENG & CRP.). (J). 12.50 *(978-1-58432-241-2(1))* Educa Vision Inc.
Freedman, Claire. My Precious Little Bear. Scott, Gavin, illus. 2011. (ENG.). 20p. (J). (gr. k — 1). bds. 8.99 *(978-0-545-27432-6(X),* Cartwheel Bks.) Scholastic, Inc.
Gale, Emily. Just Josie & the Perfect Day. Byrne, Mike, illus. 2010. (Picture Books Ser.). 25p. (J). (gr. -1-1). *(978-1-4075-9506-1(7))* Parragon, Inc.
Garza, R. Baby Blue Egg's Big Adventure. 2008. 16p. pap. 24.95 *(978-1-60441-880-4(X))* America Star Bks.
HB Staff. Today Is Monday. 97th ed. 2003. (Signatures Ser.). (gr. 1-18). pap. 16.50 *(978-0-15-308169-9(4))* Harcourt Schl. Pubs.
Heo, Yumi, illus. Sun & Moon Have a Tea Party. 2016. (J). *(978-0-385-39033-0(5),* Schwartz & Wade Bks.) Random Hse. Children's Bks.
Hill, Susan. Ruby's Perfect Day. Moore, Margie, illus. 2006. (I Can Read Bks.). 32p. (J). (gr. -1-3). 15.99 *(978-0-06-008982-5(2))* HarperCollins Pubs.
—Ruby's Perfect Day, 1 vol. Moore, Margie, illus. 2010. (I Can Read! / Ruby Raccoon Ser.). (ENG.). 32p. (J). pap. 3.99 *(978-0-310-72024-9(9))* Zonderkidz.
Himmelman, John. Chickens to the Rescue. Himmelman, John, illus. 2006. (Barnyard Rescue Ser.). (ENG., Illus.). 32p. (J). (gr. -1-3). 17.99 *(978-0-8050-7951-7(3),* 9780805079517, Holt, Henry & Co. Bks. For Young Readers) Holt, Henry & Co.
Hodgson, Karen J. Hugh's Blue Day. Collins, Ross, illus. 2010. (ENG.). 32p. (J). (gr. -1-k). pap. 9.99 *(978-1-907432-00-2(0))* Hogs Back Bks. GBR. Dist: Independent Pubs. Group.
Hopgood, Tim. Wow! Said the Owl. Hopgood, Tim, illus. 2009. (ENG., Illus.). 32p. (J). (gr. -1-k). 16.99 *(978-0-374-38518-7(1),* 9780374385187, Farrar, Straus & Giroux (BYR)) Farrar, Straus & Giroux.
I Can Say- My Day. 2005. (J). bds. *(978-1-4194-0034-6(7))* Paradise Pr., Inc.
Jeffers, Dawn. Beautiful Moon. Leick, Bonnie, illus. 2009. (ENG.). 32p. (J). (gr. -1-3). 16.95 *(978-1-934960-05-9(5),* Raven Tree Pr.,Csi) Continental Sales, Inc.
Jocelyn, Marthe. A Day with Nellie. Jocelyn, Marthe, illus. 2008. (ENG., Illus.). 16p. (J). (gr. k-k). bds. 7.95 *(978-0-88776-869-9(5),* Tundra Bks.) Tundra Bks. CAN. Dist: Penguin Random Hse. LLC.
Johnson, Angela. Lottie Paris Lives Here. Fischer, Scott M., illus. 2011. (ENG.). 32p. (J). (gr. k-4). 16.99 *(978-0-689-87377-5(8),* Simon & Schuster Bks. For Young Readers) Simon & Schuster Bks. For Young Readers.
Jordan, Deloris. Did I Tell You I Love You Today? Evans, Shane W., illus. 2004. (ENG.). 32p. (J). (gr. -1-3). 18.99 *(978-0-689-85271-8(1),* Simon & Schuster/Paula Wiseman Bks.) Simon & Schuster/Paula Wiseman Bks.
Kavanagh, Peter. I Love My Mama. Chapman, Jane, tr. Chapman, Jane, illus. 2003. 32p. (J). 12.95 *(978-1-85430-806-1(8),* Simon & Schuster Bks. For Young Readers) Simon & Schuster Bks. For Young Readers.
Kondrchek, Jamie. My Favorite Time of Day (Mi Hora Preferida del Dia) Vega, Eida de la, tr. from ENG. Rasemas, Joe, illus. 2009. (Day in the Life Ser.). (SPA & ENG.). 32p. (J). (gr. -1-1). lib. bdg. 25.70 *(978-1-58415-837-0(9))* Mitchell Lane Pubs., Inc.
Kupchella, Rick. Tell Me What We Did Today. Hanson, Warren, illus. (ENG.). 32p. (J). 15.95 *(978-0-9726504-0-3(7))* TRISTAN Publishing, Inc.
Levine, Arthur A. Monday Is One Day. Hector, Julian, illus. 2015. (ENG.). 32p. (J). (gr. -1-k). 6.99 *(978-0-439-78925-7(7))* Scholastic, Inc.
Lizzie Doodle's Beary Special Day. 2003. (J). 7.95 *(978-0-9713174-8-2(8))* Boyds Collection Ltd., The.
Lottie Paris Lives Here. 2014. (Classic Board Bks.). (ENG., Illus.). 34p. (J). (gr. -1-k). bds. 7.99 *(978-1-4814-0966-7(2),* Little Simon) Little Simon.
MacRae, Tom. When I Woke up I Was a Hippopotamus. Collins, Ross, illus. 2011. (Andersen Press Picture Books Ser.). (J). 16.95 *(978-0-7613-8099-3(X))* Andersen Pr. GBR. Dist: Lerner Publishing Group.
Marshall, Judy. Morning. Annelli, Nikki, illus. l.t. ed. 2005. 21p. (J). per. 9.99 *(978-1-59879-050-4(1))* Lifevest Publishing, Inc.
Mayer, Mercer. Mercer Mayer's Little Critter's Series, 2 bks. (Illus.). (J). (gr. k-1). lib. bdg. 27.90 *(978-1-56674-943-5(3))* Forest Hse. Publishing Co., Inc.
McKay, Sindy. We Both Read-My Day (Picture Book) Johnson, Meredith, illus. 2007. (We Both Read Ser.). 44p. (J). (gr. -1-2). lib. bdg. 14.95 *(978-1-60115-005-9(9))* Treasure Bay, Inc.
McKee, David. Elmer's Day. McKee, David, illus. 2014. (Elmer Ser.). (ENG., Illus.). 16p. (J). (-k). 8.99 *(978-0-86264-496-3(8))* Andersen Pr. GBR. Dist: Independent Pubs. Group.
—Elmer's Day. Mo'Allim, Nur M., tr. 2004. (Elmer Ser.). (ENG & SOM., Illus.). 14p. (J). (gr. -1). bds. 8.95 *(978-1-84059-400-3(4))* Milet Publishing.
Menge, Dawn & Rhoades, Heath. Queen Vernita Meets Sir HeathyBean the Astronomer. 2010. 33p. (J). pap. 19.95 *(978-1-4327-3120-5(3))* Outskirts Pr., Inc.
Meyers, Susan. This Is the Way a Baby Rides. Nakata, Hiroe, illus. 2005. (ENG.). 32p. (J). (gr. -1-1). 15.95 *(978-0-8109-5763-3(9),* Abrams Bks. for Young Readers) Abrams, Inc.
Miller, Jules, illus. When Night Became Day. 2015. (ENG.). 32p. (J). (gr. -1-k). 16.95 *(978-1-62914-632-4(3),* Sky Pony Pr.) Skyhorse Publishing Co., Inc.
Montardre, Hélène. Night & Day. 2003. (Illus.). 8p. (J). bds. 7.95 *(978-1-58728-481-6(2),* Two-Can Publishing) T&N Children's Publishing.
Newman, Lesléa. A Kiss on the Keppie, 0 vols. Blackmore, Katherine & Wiltse, Kris, illus. 2012. (ENG.). 24p. (J). (gr. -1-2). 12.99 *(978-0-7614-6241-5(4),* 9780761462415, Amazon Children's Publishing) Amazon Publishing.
Patterson, Lagene E. What a Peculiar Day. 2009. 16p. pap. 8.49 *(978-1-4490-1859-7(9))* AuthorHouse.
Rainey, L. E. Sad Sam, Glad Sam. 2006. (Illus.). 32p. (J). 16.95 *(978-0-9785521-0-7(5))* Shoetree Publishers, Inc.
Reynolds, Peter H. My Very Big Little World. Reynolds, Peter H., illus. 2006. (ENG., Illus.). 40p. (J). (gr. -1-3). 17.99 *(978-0-689-87621-9(1),* Atheneum Bks. for Young Readers) Simon & Schuster Children's Publishing.
Ringo, Mary Lou. That's Not Fair. 2012. 28p. pap. 24.95 *(978-1-4626-5153-5(4))* America Star Bks.
Ritchie, Alison. Me & My Dad! Edgson, Alison, illus. 2007. (J). pap. *(978-0-545-02064-0(6))* Scholastic, Inc.
Rosenthal, Amy Krouse. One of Those Days. Doughty, Rebecca, illus. 2006. (ENG.). 32p. (J). (gr. -1-3). 15.99 *(978-0-399-24365-3(8),* G.P. Putnam's Sons Books for Young Readers) Penguin Young Readers Group.

—Yes Day! Lichtenheld, Tom, illus. 2009. (ENG.). 40p. (J). (gr. -1-3). 14.99 *(978-0-06-115259-7(5))* HarperCollins Pubs.

Rothberg, Kimmy. Saturdays with Daddy. 2010. 20p. 11.95 *(978-0-557-50036-9(2))* Lulu Pr., Inc.

Ryder, Joanne & Ryder. My Mother's Voice. Catalanotto, Peter, illus. 2006. (ENG.). 32p. (J). (gr. -1-3). 16.99 *(978-0-06-029509-7(0))* HarperCollins Pubs.

Rylant, Cynthia. All in a Day. McClure, Nikki, illus. (ENG.). (J). 2017. 30p. bds. 8.95 *(978-1-4197-2612-5(9),* Abrams Appleseed) 2009. 32p. (gr. -1-k). 18.95 *(978-0-8109-8321-2(4),* Abrams Bks. for Young Readers) Abrams, Inc.

Scholastic, Inc. Staff, contrib. by. A Day in Heartlake City. 2013. (LEGO Friends Ser.). (ENG.). 16p. (J). (gr. 1-3). 6.99 *(978-0-545-51757-7(5))* Scholastic, Inc.

Schwartz, Amy. A Glorious Day. Schwartz, Amy, illus. 2010. (ENG., Illus.). 32p. (J). (gr. -1-k). 16.99 *(978-1-4424-2190-5(8),* Atheneum Bks. for Young Readers) Simon & Schuster Children's Publishing.

Shannon, David. Oops! A Diaper David Book. Shannon, David, illus. 2005. (Oops! Ser.). (ENG., Illus.). 12p. (J). (gr. -1-k). bds. 6.99 *(978-0-439-68882-6(5),* Blue Sky Pr., The) Scholastic, Inc.

Simon, Mary Manz. God Made the Sun. Walkley, Lizzie, illus. 2016. (J). *(978-0-8249-1980-1(7),* Ideal Pubns.) Worthy Publishing.

Slate, Joseph. Miss Bindergarten Has a Wild Day in Kindergarten. Wolff, Ashley, illus. 2006. (ENG.). 40p. (J). (gr. -1-k). reprint ed. pap. 6.99 *(978-0-14-240709-7(7),* Puffin Books) Penguin Young Readers Group.

A Story of Faith: Mary Ann's Book — My Bestest Day. 2006. (J). 19.95 *(978-0-9787761-0-7(0))* Mountain Ministries.

Sukhram-Harris, Karen. Saturdays with Mom. 2012. 16p. pap. 15.99 *(978-1-4772-7852-9(4))* AuthorHouse.

Tawa, Renee. Tink's Magical Day. 2011. (Illus.). (J). *(978-1-4508-1707-3(6))* Publications International, Ltd.

Tiger Tales Staff, creator. My Busy Day. 2014. (My First Jumbo Tab Bks.). (ENG., Illus.). 12p. (J). (gr. -1-k). bds. 8.99 *(978-1-58925-590-6(9))* Tiger Tales.

Tompert, Ann. Harry's Hats. Elizalde, Marcelo, illus. 2004. (Rookie Readers Ser.). 31p. (J). 19.50 *(978-0-516-23613-1(X),* Children's Pr.) Scholastic Library Publishing.

Underwood, Deborah. The Loud Book! Liwska, Renata, illus. 2011. (ENG.). 32p. (J). (gr. -1-3). 12.99 *(978-0-547-39008-6(4))* Houghton Mifflin Harcourt Publishing Co.

—The Quiet Book. Liwska, Renata, illus. (ENG.). 32p. (J). 2016. (gr. -1-3). pap. 6.99 *(978-0-544-80904-8(1),* HMH Books For Young Readers) 2013. (— 1). bds. 8.99 *(978-0-544-05667-1(1))* 2010. (gr. -1-3). 12.95 *(978-0-547-21567-9(3))* Houghton Mifflin Harcourt Publishing Co.

—The Quiet Book. 2016. lib. bdg. 17.20 *(978-0-606-38900-6(8))* Turtleback Bks.

Van Fleet, Matthew. Monday the Bullfrog. Van Fleet, Matthew, illus. 2010. (ENG., Illus.). 20p. (J). (gr. -1). 24.99 *(978-1-4424-0958-3(4),* Simon & Schuster/Paula Wiseman Bks.) Simon & Schuster/Paula Wiseman Bks.

Waite, Lance. A Day with My Dad. Pentangelo, Manuela, illus. 2008. 24p. (J). (gr. -1-3). 17.99 *(978-1-60131-015-6(3),* Parents Publishing Group) Big Tent Bks.

Ward, Cindy. Cookie's Week. dePaola, Tomie, illus. 2015. 32p. pap. 7.00 *(978-1-61003-528-6(3))* Center for the Collaborative Classroom.

Yee, Wong Herbert. Summer Days & Nights. Yee, Wong Herbert, illus. 2012. (ENG., Illus.). 32p. (J). (gr. -1-1). 16.99 *(978-0-8050-9078-9(9),* 9780805090789, Holt, Henry & Co. Bks. For Young Readers) Holt, Henry & Co.

Zimmerman, Kwanza A. What Day Is It? 2008. 16p. per. 24.95 *(978-1-4241-9954-9(9))* America Star Bks.

DAYS

see Birthdays; Fasts and Feasts; Holidays

DEAD SEA SCROLLS

Burnham, Brad. Qumran Caves: Hiding Place for the Dead Sea Scrolls. (Famous Caves of the World Ser.). 24p. 2009. (gr. 3-4). 42.50 *(978-1-61512-499-2(3))* 2003. (Illus.). (J). lib. bdg. 22.60 *(978-0-8239-6259-4(8))* Rosen Publishing Group, Inc., The. (PowerKids Pr.).

DEAF

Adams, Colleen. The Courage of Helen Keller. 2009. (Reading Room Collection 2 Ser.). 24p. (gr. 3-4). 42.50 *(978-1-60851-992-7(9),* PowerKids Pr.) Rosen Publishing Group, Inc., The.

Adler, David A. Helen Keller. Wallner, John, illus. 2006. (ENG.). 32p. (J). (gr. -1-3). 4.95 *(978-0-8234-2042-1(6))* Holiday Hse., Inc.

Barry, Holly M. Helen Keller's Best Friend Belle. Thermes, Jennifer, illus. 2013. (ENG.). 32p. (J). (gr. -1-3). 16.99 *(978-0-8075-3198-3(7))* Whitman, Albert & Co.

Basinger, Carol. Everything You Need to Know about Deafness. 2005. (Need to Know Library). (Illus.). 64p. (J). (gr. 7-12). lib. bdg. 31.95 *(978-0-8239-3165-1(X),* NTDEAF) Rosen Publishing Group, Inc., The.

Bates, Martine G. Heather Whitestone: Inspirational Miss America. 2007. (Illus.). 104p. (J). pap. *(978-1-59421-029-7(2))* Seacoast Publishing, Inc.

Bell, Cece. El Deafo. Lasky, David, illus. 2014. (ENG.). 248p. (J). (gr. 3-7). 21.95 *(978-1-4197-1020-9(6));* pap. 10.95 *(978-1-4197-1217-3(9))* Abrams, Inc. (Amulet Bks.).

—El Deafo. 2014. (J). lib. bdg. 22.05 *(978-0-606-36148-4(0))* Turtleback Bks.

Brearley, Sue. Talk to Me. (Illus.). 26p. (J). (gr. 1-4). *(978-0-7136-3192-0(9),* A&C Black) Bloomsbury Publishing Plc.

De Silva-Nijkamp, Tineke. Samaya: The Deaf Baby Elephant. Maters, Ingrid, illus. 2005. 33p. (J). *(978-955-599-438-5(2))* Sarvodaya Bk. Publishing Services.

Devillier, Christy. Helen Keller, 1 vol. 2004. (First Biographies Set Iv Ser.). (ENG., Illus.). 32p. (gr. k-4). 27.07 *(978-1-59197-514-4(X),* Buddy Bks.) ABDO Publishing Co.

DiGugno, Josh. I Heard That! 2017. (Text Connections Guided Close Reading Ser.). (J). (gr. 1). *(978-1-4900-1829-4(8))* Benchmark Education Co.

Fetty, Margaret. Helen Keller: Break down the Walls! 2006. (Defining Moments Ser.). (Illus.). 32p. (J). (gr. 2-5). lib. bdg. 25.27 *(978-1-59716-271-5(X))* Bearport Publishing Co., Inc.

Kelley, Walter P. The "I Love You" Story. McGregor, Tony L., illus. 2004. (J). *(978-0-9729569-4-9(8))* BuTo, Ltd. Co.

Kent, Deborah. What Is It Like to Be Deaf? 2012. (Overcoming Barriers Ser.). (Illus.). 48p. (J). (gr. 3-4). pap. 8.95 *(978-1-4644-0154-1(3),* Enslow Elementary) Enslow Pubs., Inc.

—What Is Sign Language? 2012. (Overcoming Barriers Ser.). 48p. (J). (gr. 3-4). (Illus.). pap. 8.95 *(978-1-4644-0156-5(X));* 25.27 *(978-0-7660-3771-7(1))* Enslow Pubs., Inc. (Enslow Elementary).

Koestler-Grack, Rachel A. Helen Keller. 2nd rev. ed. 2009. (Women of Achievement Ser.). (Illus.). 144p. (gr. 6-12). 35.00 *(978-1-60413-502-2(6),* Chelsea Hse.) Facts On File, Inc.

Levene, Anna. My Friend Is Deaf. 2003. (Illus.). (J). (gr. 3-5). lib. bdg. 16.95 *(978-1-932333-27-5(4))* Chrysalis Education.

Libal, Autumn. Deaf & Hard of Hearing. Albers, Lisa et al, eds. 2014. (Living with a Special Need Ser.: 16). 128p. (J). (gr. 7-18). 25.95 *(978-1-4222-3033-6(3))* Mason Crest.

—The Ocean Inside: Youth Who Are Deaf & Hard of Hearing. (Youth with Special Needs Ser.). (Illus.). (YA). 2004. 128p. 24.95 *(978-1-59084-729-9(6))* 2003. 127p. (gr. -1). pap. 14.95 *(978-1-4222-0427-6(8))* Mason Crest.

Mattern, Joanne. Helen Keller. 2015. (Rookie Biographies(r) Ser.). (ENG., Illus.). 32p. (J). pap. 5.95 *(978-0-531-20995-0(4))* Scholastic Library Publishing.

Parker, Vic. I Know Someone with a Hearing Impairment, 1 vol. 2011. (Understanding Health Issues Ser.). (ENG.). 32p. (gr. 1-3). 27.32 *(978-1-4329-4560-2(2),* Heinemann First Library) Heinemann-Raintree.

Rappaport, Doreen. Helen's Big World: The Life of Helen Keller. Tavares, Matt, illus. 2012. (Big Words Ser.). (ENG.). 48p. (J). (gr. 1-3). 17.99 *(978-0-7868-0890-8(X))* Hyperion Pr.

Schaefer, Lola M. Algunos Niños Son Sordos. 2010. (Comprendiendo Las Diferencias/Understanding Differences Ser.).Tr. of Some Kids Are Deaf. (MUL, SPA & ENG.). 24p. (gr. k-1). lib. bdg. 21.99 *(978-1-4296-4591-1(1))* Capstone Press of Coughlan Cos.

—Some Kids Are Deaf, 1 vol. 2007. (Understanding Differences Ser.). (ENG., Illus.). 24p. (gr. k-1). 21.99 *(978-1-4296-0811-4(0),* Pebble Bks.) Capstone Press of Coughlan Cos.

—Some Kids Are Deaf. Saunders-Smith, Gail, ed. rev. ed. 2008. (Understanding Differences Ser.). (ENG., Illus.). 24p. (gr. k-1). pap. 6.29 *(978-1-4296-1775-8(6),* Pebble Bks.) Capstone Press of Coughlan Cos.

—Some Kids Use Wheelchairs, 1 vol. 2007. (Understanding Differences Ser.). (ENG., Illus.). 24p. (gr. k-1). 21.99 *(978-1-4296-0812-1(9),* Pebble Bks.) Capstone Press of Coughlan Cos.

Scholastic Book Editors. Sign Language: My First 100 Words. Nelson, Michiyo, illus. 2008. 32p. (gr. -1-3). 17.00 *(978-0-7569-8911-8(6))* Perfection Learning Corp.

Stewart, Sheila & Flath, Camden. Listening with Your Eyes: Kids Who Are Deaf & Hard of Hearing. 2010. (Kids with Special Needs Ser.). 48p. (YA). (gr. 5-18). lib. bdg. 19.95 *(978-1-4222-1717-7(5))* Mason Crest.

Sutcliffe, Jane. Helen Keller. Verstraete, Elaine, illus. 2003. (On My Own Biographies Ser.). 48p. (J). (gr. 1-3). 6.95 *(978-0-87614-903-4(4),* Carolrhoda Bks.) Lerner Publishing Group.

Venezia, Mike. Alexander Graham Bell: Setting the Tone for Communication. Venezia, Mike, illus. 2008. (Getting to Know the World's Greatest Inventors & Scientists Ser.). (ENG., Illus.). 32p. (J). (gr. 2-5). 28.00 *(978-0-531-14976-8(5))* Scholastic Library Publishing.

Wyckoff, Edwin Brit & Library. Sign Language Man: Thomas H. Gallaudet & His Incredible Work. 2010. (Genius at Work! Great Inventor Biographies Ser.). (Illus.). 32p. (J). (gr. 2-5). lib. bdg. 23.94 *(978-0-7660-3447-1(X))* Enslow Pubs., Inc.

DEAF—EDUCATION

Bodkin, Odds. Doing, Doing, Doing. 2003. (Illus.). 14p. spiral bd. *(978-0-9657170-6-9(2))* Perkins Schl. for the Blind.

Kent, Deborah. What Is It Like to Be Deaf? 2012. (Overcoming Barriers Ser.). 48p. (J). (gr. 3-4). 25.27 *(978-0-7660-3769-4(X),* Enslow Elementary) Enslow Pubs., Inc.

Schneider, Elaine Ernst. Taking Hearing Impairment to School. Schader, Karen, ed. Dineen, Tom, illus. 2004. (Special Kids in School Ser.: Fifteenth). (J). per. 11.95 *(978-1-891383-23-6(X),* 70015) JayJo Bks., LLC.

DEAF—FICTION

Beamish, Diane. Amy's Silent World. 2006. 24p. 10.25 *(978-1-4116-5759-5(4))* Lulu Pr., Inc.

Berk, Josh. The Dark Days of Hamburger Halpin. 2011. (ENG.). 258p. (YA). (gr. 7). pap. 8.99 *(978-0-375-84625-0(5),* Ember) Random Hse. Children's Bks.

Bodkin, Odds. Perkins Goes Out. 2003. (Illus.). 22p. spiral bd. *(978-0-9657170-7-6(0))* Perkins Schl. for the Blind.

Brown, Teri. Read My Lips. 2008. (ENG.). 256p. (YA). (gr. 9-12). pap. 8.99 *(978-1-4169-5868-0(1),* Simon Pulse) Simon Pulse.

Bundy, Tamara. Walking with Miss Millie. 2017. (ENG.). 240p. (J). (gr. 5). 16.99 ***(978-0-399-54456-9(9),*** Nancy Paulsen Books) Penguin Young Readers Group.

Carey, Keelin, et al. The Smart Princess: And Other Deaf Tales, 1 vol. Halligan, Kelly C. et al, illus. 2007. (ENG.). 148p. (J). (gr. 3-7). per. 9.95 *(978-1-896764-90-0(8))* Second Story Pr. CAN. Dist: Orca Bk. Pubs. USA.

Carillo, Christina. Life Can Be A Smile. 2010. 30p. pap. 21.99 *(978-1-4500-2848-6(9))* Xlibris Corp.

Colledge, Anne. Falling into Fear. 2004. 92p. per. *(978-1-904529-12-5(7),* Back to Front) Solidus.

Dussling, Susanna. Sunny & her Cochlear Implants. 2010. 36p. pap. 16.95 *(978-1-4520-1636-8(4))* AuthorHouse.

Entinger, Chad. A Deaf Boy Meets Jesus. Schofield-Farmer, Twila, illus. 2011. 42p. (J). 10.00 *(978-1-59799-082-0(5))* Deaf Missions.

Ferris, Jean. Of Sound Mind. 2004. (ENG.). 224p. (YA). (gr. 7). reprint ed. pap. 10.99 *(978-0-374-45584-2(8),* 9780374455842, Farrar, Straus & Giroux (BYR)) Farrar, Straus & Giroux.

—Of Sound Mind. 2004. 215p. (YA). (gr. 7). 14.60 *(978-0-7569-2970-1(9))* Perfection Learning Corp.

Fudge, Benjamin. Enrique Speaks with His Hands. Edmonson, Tim, illus. 2008. (ENG.). 32p. (J). (gr. -1-3). 16.95 *(978-0-9800649-3-3(7))* Hilton Publishing Co.

Gibson, Catherine. Through Sophie's Eyes. 2009. (Illus.). 32p. (J). 15.95 *(978-0-578-00980-3(3))* For Children With Love Pubns.

Greene, Janice & Thomas, Terri. Read My Lips, 1 vol. unabr. ed. 2010. (Q Reads Ser.). (ENG.). 32p. (YA). (gr. 9-12). pap. 6.95 *(978-1-61651-216-3(4))* Saddleback Educational Publishing, Inc.

Grovet, Heather. A Friend for Zipper. 2008. (J). pap. 5.97 *(978-0-8163-2226-8(0))* Pacific Pr. Publishing Assn.

Honderich, Lou. Ricki. 2013. 170p. pap. 10.99 *(978-0-9856906-6-3(6))* Mockingbird Lane Pr.

Hubler, Marsha. Summer Camp Adventure, 1 vol. 2009. (Keystone Stables Ser.). (ENG.). 128p. (J). pap. 7.99 *(978-0-310-71795-9(7))* Zonderkidz.

Hughes, Jack. Dachy's Deaf. 2014. (Dinosaur Friends Ser.). (Illus.). 32p. (J). (gr. k-3). lib. bdg. 26.25 *(978-1-4777-9222-3(8))* Windmill Bks.

Imagination Stage Teacher's Study Guide: The Garden Wall. 2005. (J). pap. 3.95 *(978-0-9723729-2-3(X))* Imagination Stage, Inc.

John, Antony. Five Flavors of Dumb. 2011. (ENG.). 368p. (YA). (gr. 7-18). 8.99 *(978-0-14-241943-4(5),* Speak) Penguin Young Readers Group.

John, Louise. I Can Hear!, 1 vol. Elkerton, Andy, illus. 2013. (Start Reading Ser.). (ENG.). 24p. (gr. k-1). pap. 7.95 *(978-1-4765-3199-1(4));* pap. 41.94 *(978-1-4765-3219-6(2))* Capstone Press of Coughlan Cos.

Jordan, Sherryl. The Raging Quiet. l.t. ed. 2005. 416p. 22.95 *(978-0-7862-7313-3(5),* Large Print Pr.) Thorndike Pr.

Kent, Rose. Rocky Road. 2012. (ENG.). 304p. (J). (gr. 3-7). 7.99 *(978-0-375-86345-5(1),* Yearling) Random Hse. Children's Bks.

Kingsley, Linda Kurtz. Bringing up Sophie. Kingsley, Linda Kurtz, illus. 2010. (Illus.). 32p. (J). lib. bdg. 15.95 *(978-0-944727-25-6(5),* Turtle Bks.) Jason & Nordic Pubs.

—Bringing up Sophie. 2009. (Illus.). 32p. (J). pap. 9.95 *(978-0-944727-24-9(7),* Turtle Bks.) Jason & Nordic Pubs.

—Signs of Jays. Kingsley, Linda Kurtz, illus. 2008. (Illus.). 32p. (J). (ENG.). lib. bdg. 15.95 *(978-0-944727-23-2(9));* pap. 9.95 *(978-0-944727-22-5(0))* Jason & Nordic Pubs. (Turtle Bks.).

Kroupa, Robert J. Just Like You. 2011. (J). *(978-0-9825503-4-2(0))* IGI Pr.

Kupfer, Wendy. Let's Hear It for Almigal. Lyon, Tammie, illus. 2012. (ENG.). 32p. (J). (gr. k-2). 16.99 *(978-0-9838294-0-9(3))* Handfinger Pr.

Laughton, Geoff. At the Lake. 2016. (ENG., Illus.). (J). 24.99 ***(978-1-63477-937-1(1),*** Harmony Ink Pr.) Dreamspinner Pr.

Look, Lenore. Ruby Lu, Empress of Everything. Wilsdorf, Anne, illus. 2007. 164p. (gr. 1-5). 16.00 *(978-0-7569-8113-6(1))* Perfection Learning Corp.

—Ruby Lu, Empress of Everything. Wilsdorf, Anne, illus. (ENG.). 176p. (J). (gr. 1-5). 2007. pap. 5.99 *(978-1-4169-5003-5(6))* 2006. 16.99 *(978-0-689-86460-5(4))* Simon & Schuster Children's Publishing. (Atheneum Bks. for Young Readers).

Lytton, Deborah. Silence. 2015. (ENG.). 320p. (YA). (gr. 7). 17.99 *(978-1-60907-945-1(0),* Shadow Mountain) Shadow Mountain Publishing.

Matlin, Marlee. Deaf Child Crossing. 2004. (ENG., Illus.). 208p. (J). (gr. 3-7). pap. 7.99 *(978-0-689-86696-8(8),* Simon & Schuster Bks. For Young Readers) Simon & Schuster Bks. For Young Readers.

Matlin, Marlee & Cooney, Doug. Nobody's Perfect. 2006. (ENG., Illus.). 240p. (J). (gr. 3-7). 15.95 *(978-0-689-86986-0(X),* Simon & Schuster Bks. For Young Readers) Simon & Schuster Bks. For Young Readers.

Mayfield, Jamie. A Broken Kind of Life. 2016. (ENG., Illus.). (YA). (gr. 9-12). 24.99 ***(978-1-63477-926-5(6),*** Harmony Ink Pr.) Dreamspinner Pr.

Mcelfresh, Lynn. Strong Deaf. 2012. 130p. 18.95 *(978-1-60898-126-7(6));* pap. 9.95 *(978-1-60898-127-4(4))* namelos llc.

Mead, Richelle. Soundless. l.t. ed. 2016. (ENG.). 352p. 25.99 *(978-1-4104-8817-6(9))* Cengage Gale.

—Soundless. 2015. (ENG.). 272p. (YA). (gr. 7-10). 19.99 *(978-1-59514-763-9(2),* Razorbill) Penguin Publishing Group.

Mead, Richelle & Loftin, Nikki. Soundless. 2016. (ENG.). 288p. (YA). (gr. 7). 10.99 *(978-1-59514-764-6(0),* Razorbill) Penguin Young Readers Group.

Meredith, Susan Markowitz. A New Friend. 2011. (Early Connections Ser.). (J). *(978-1-61672-568-6(0))* Benchmark Education Co.

Miller, Sarah. Miss Spitfire: Reaching Helen Keller. (ENG.). (J). (gr. 5-7). 2010. 256p. pap. 7.99 *(978-1-4424-0851-7(0))* 2007. 240p. 17.99 *(978-1-4169-2542-2(2))* Simon & Schuster Children's Publishing. (Atheneum Bks. for Young Readers).

Moore-Mallinos, Jennifer. I Am Deaf. Fabrega, Marta, illus. 2009. (Live & Learn Ser.). (ENG.). 36p. (J). (gr. -1-2). pap. 7.99 *(978-0-7641-4179-9(1))* Barron's Educational Series, Inc.

Moskowitz, Hannah. Invincible Summer. 2011. (ENG.). 288p. (YA). (gr. 9-18). pap. 9.99 *(978-1-4424-0751-0(4),* Simon Pulse) Simon Pulse.

Nanette. Buddy & Muddy: The Twin Brown Skunks. 2004. (J). 12.95 *(978-0-9741269-5-1(0))* St. Bernard Publishing, LLC.

New Mexico School for the Deaf Staff, 2nd Grade. Too Many Hands??? l.t. ed. 2004. (Illus.). 32p. (J). 16.95 *(978-1-929115-10-5(5))* Azro Pr., Inc.

Nijssen, Elfi. Laurie. van Lindehuizen, Eline, illus. 2010. (ENG & DUT.). 24p. (J). (gr. -1-k). 16.95 *(978-1-60537-072-9(X))* Cobblestone Publishing Co.

Piper, Deb. From A — to Zulinski. 2008. (J). pap. *(978-0-88092-713-0(5));* lib. bdg. *(978-0-88092-712-3(7))* Royal Fireworks Publishing Co.

Roth, Judith L. & Rothshank, Brooke, illus. Julia's Words. 2008. (J). (gr. -1-3). pap. 12.99 *(978-0-8361-9417-3(9))* Herald Pr.

Salom, Susie. Kyle Finds Her Way. 2016. (ENG.). 256p. (J). (gr. 4-7). 16.99 *(978-0-545-85266-1(8),* Levine, Arthur A. Bks.) Scholastic, Inc.

Schrocke, Kathrin. Freak City. Tammi Reichel, tr. 2014. (Illus.). 224p. (YA). (gr. 9-12). pap. 10.95 *(978-1-62324-006-6(9))* Enslow Pubs., Inc.

—Freak City. Reichel, Tammi, tr. from GER. 2014. 224p. (YA). 18.95 *(978-1-62324-005-9(0))* Enslow Pubs., Inc.

Selznick, Brian. Wonderstruck. Selznick, Brian, illus. 2011. (ENG., Illus.). 640p. (J). (gr. 4-7). 29.99 *(978-0-545-02789-2(6),* Scholastic Pr.); 300.00 *(978-0-545-38985-3(2))* Scholastic, Inc.

Smith, D. James. The Boys of San Joaquin. 2006. (ENG.). 240p. (J). (gr. 3-7). pap. 11.99 *(978-1-4169-1619-2(9),* Atheneum Bks. for Young Readers) Simon & Schuster Children's Publishing.

—It Was September When We Ran Away the First Time. 2012. (ENG.). 240p. (J). (gr. 3-7). pap. 11.99 *(978-1-4169-3810-1(9),* Atheneum Bks. for Young Readers) Simon & Schuster Children's Publishing.

—Probably the World's Best Story about a Dog & the Girl Who Loved Me. 2011. (ENG.). 256p. (J). pap. 5.99 *(978-1-4169-9652-1(4),* Atheneum Bks. for Young Readers) Simon & Schuster Children's Publishing.

—Probably the World's Best Story about a Dog & The Girl Who Loved Me. 2010. (ENG.). 240p. (J). (gr. 4-7). pap. 11.99 *(978-1-4424-2194-3(0),* Atheneum Bks. for Young Readers) Simon & Schuster Children's Publishing.

Stinson, June. Milton Hears a Train. 2012. 32p. pap. 24.95 *(978-1-4626-8192-1(1))* America Star Bks.

Süskind, Patrick. DIE TAUBE. (GER.). pap. 15.95 *(978-3-257-21846-6(X))* Diogenes Verlag AG CHE. Dist: Distribooks, Inc.

Uhlberg, Myron. Dad, Jackie, & Me, 1 vol. Bootman, Colin, illus. (ENG.). 32p. (J). 2010. pap. 8.95 *(978-1-56145-531-7(8))* 2005. 16.95 *(978-1-56145-329-0(3))* Peachtree Pubs.

—The Printer, 1 vol. Sørensen, Henri, illus. 2009. (ENG.). 32p. (J). (gr. -1-3). pap. 8.95 *(978-1-56145-483-9(4))* Peachtree Pubs.

—The Printer, 1 vol. Sorensen, Henri, tr. Sorensen, Henri, illus. 2003. (ENG.). 32p. (J). (gr. k-3). 16.95 *(978-1-56145-221-7(1))* Peachtree Pubs.

Uhlberg, Myron & Papoulas, Ted. The Sound of All Things, 1 vol. 2016. (ENG.). 36p. (J). (gr. 1-5). 17.95 *(978-1-56145-833-2(3))* Peachtree Pubs.

Woodson, Jacqueline. Feathers. (ENG.). (J). (gr. 5-18). 2010. 160p. 8.99 *(978-0-14-241550-4(2),* Speak) 2007. 128p. 16.99 *(978-0-399-23989-2(8),* G.P. Putnam's Sons Books for Young Readers) Penguin Young Readers Group.

DEATH

see also Right to Die

Agnew, Kate, ed. Life & Death: A Collection of Classic Poetry & Prose. 2004. (ENG.). 208p. (YA). (gr. 7). per. 8.95 *(978-1-84046-567-9(0),* Wizard Books) Icon Bks., Ltd. GBR. Dist: Publishers Group Canada.

Alvarez, Julia. Where Do They Go? Field, Sabra, illus. 2016. (ENG.). 24p. (J). (gr. -1-2). 16.95 *(978-1-60980-670-5(0),* Triangle Square) Seven Stories Pr.

Amos, Janine. Death. 2009. (Changes Ser.). (Illus.). 32p. (J). (gr. k-2). 22.60 *(978-1-60754-478-4(4));* (gr. 2-5). pap. 10.55 *(978-1-60754-479-1(2))* Windmill Bks.

Answers to a Child's Questions about Death. 2005. (J). 3.99 *(978-1-882951-25-3(5))* Guideline Pubns. Co.

Barr, J. Bennett. Saying Goodbye. 2009. 20p. pap. 10.49 *(978-1-4490-0000-4(2))* AuthorHouse.

Berry, Joy. Good Answers to Tough Questions about Death. 2009. (ENG.). 52p. (J). (gr. k-7). pap. 7.95 *(978-1-60577-506-7(1))* Berry, Joy Enterprises.

Biskup, Agnieszka & Enz, Tammy. Science Behind Batman. Vecchio, Luciano, illus. 2016. (Science Behind Batman Ser.). (ENG.). 24p. (gr. 1-2). pap. 27.80 *(978-1-5157-2065-2(9),* DC Super Heroes) Stone Arch Bks.

Blackwood, Gary L. Unsolved History, 4 bks., Set. Incl. Debatable Deaths. 80p. (gr. 6). lib. bdg. 23.95 *(978-0-7614-1888-7(1));* Enigmatic Events. 80p. (gr. 6-7). lib. bdg. 23.95 *(978-0-7614-1889-4(X));* Legends or Lies. 72p. lib. bdg. *(978-0-7614-1891-7(1));* Perplexing People. 80p. (gr. 6-7). lib. bdg. 23.95 *(978-0-7614-1890-0(3));* (Illus.). 2005. *(978-0-7614-1892-4(X),* Benchmark Bks.) Marshall Cavendish Corp.

Blackwood, Gary L. & Shannon, Terry Miller. Debatable Deaths. 2009. (Benchmark Rockets: History's Mysteries Ser.). 32p. (gr. 3). 28.50 *(978-0-7614-4355-1(X))* Marshall Cavendish Corp.

Boritzer, Etan. What Is Death? Forrest, Nancy, illus. 2004. (What Is? Ser.). 40p. (J). (gr. k-5). pap. 6.95 *(978-0-9637597-5-7(2))* Lane, Veronica Bks.

Bow, James. Dealing with Loss. 2015. (ENG., Illus.). 48p. (J). *(978-0-7787-2201-4(5))* Crabtree Publishing Co.

Bragg, Georgia. How They Croaked: The Awful Ends of the Awfully Famous. O'Malley, Kevin, illus. 2012. (ENG.). 192p. (J). (gr. 5-14). pap. 9.99 *(978-0-8027-2794-7(8),* 9780802727947, Bloomsbury USA Childrens) Bloomsbury Publishing USA.

Bragg, Georgia & O'Malley, Kevin. How They Croaked: The Awful Ends of the Awfully Famous. 2012. (J). lib. bdg. 20.85 *(978-0-606-26137-1(0),* Turtleback) Turtleback Bks.

Britain, Lory. My Grandma Died: Child's Story about Death & Loss. Deach, Carol, illus. 2003. (ENG.). 32p. (J). (gr. -1-3). pap. 7.95 *(978-1-884734-26-7(X))* Parenting Pr., Inc.

Brown, Don. America Is under Attack: September 11, 2001: the Day the Towers Fell. 2014. (Actual Times Ser.: 4). (ENG., Illus.). 64p. (J). (gr. 1-5). pap. 9.99 *(978-1-250-04415-0(4),* 9781250044150) Square Fish.

Carter-Reed, Lorye. Grandpa Isn't Coming Anymore: A Child's Look at Death. 2010. 24p. 12.99 *(978-1-4520-6271-6(4))* AuthorHouse.

Casterline, L. C. & Packard, Mary. Beyond the Grave: Ripley's Believe It or Not! 2005. (Illus.). 62p. (J). *(978-1-884270-29-1(8))* Ripley Entertainment, Inc.

Coerr, Eleanor. Sadako & the Thousand Paper Cranes. Himler, Ronald, illus. 2004. (Puffin Modern Classics Ser.). (ENG.). 80p. (J). (gr. 3-7). pap. 6.99 *(978-0-14-240113-2(7),* Puffin Books) Penguin Young Readers Group.

Coping with the Loss of a Loved One: An Inspiring New Book about Appreciating Human Life & Death. 2003. 60p. per. 10.00 net. *(978-0-9620180-3-9(1))* Black, Clinton L.

Crosetto, Alice & Garcha, Rajinder. Death, Loss, & Grief in Literature for Youth: A Selective Annotated Bibliography for

K-12. 2012. (Literature for Youth Ser.). (ENG.). 266p. (gr. 17). 95.00 (978-0-8108-8560-8(3)) Scarecrow Pr., Inc.

Cunningham, Alan Blain, compiled by. Goodbye My Good Friend: Memories of Lost Animal Companions & Loved Ones. 2007. (ENG., Illus.). 112p. per. 15.95 (978-0-9777072-2-5(9)) Agreka Bks., LLC.

Dennison, Amy, et al, as told by. Our Dad Died: The True Story of Three Kids Whose Lives Changed. 2004. (Illus.). 112p. (J). pap. 9.95 (978-1-57542-135-3(6)) Free Spirit Publishing, Inc.

Diamond, Kathryn. The Day I Almost Drowned: A Child's near-Death Experience. 2009. 84p. pap. 11.00 (978-0-557-06946-0(7)) Lulu Pr., Inc.

Digging up the Dead. 2014. (Digging up the Dead Ser.). 32p. (J). (gr. 4-6). pap. 63.00 (978-1-4824-1559-9(3)) Stevens, Gareth Publishing LLLP.

Edwards, Dianna. Meet Patou. 2006. (J). pap. 29.95 (978-0-9767756-0-7(3)) Patou Bks., LLC.

—My Journal & Drawings. 2004. (J). spiral bd. (978-0-9767756-4-5(6)) Patou Bks., LLC.

—Why Can't Everything Just Stay the Same? Book Three. 2004. (J). (978-0-9767756-3-8(8)) Patou Bks., LLC.

Edwards, Nicola. A Pet. 2003. (Saying Goodbye to Ser.). (Illus.). 32p. (J). (gr. -1-2). lib. bdg. 16.95 (978-1-932333-19-0(3)) Chrysalis Education.

Enz, Tammy & Biskup, Agnieszka. Science Behind Batman. Vecchio, Luciano, illus. 2016. (Science Behind Batman Ser.). (ENG.). 24p. (gr. 1-2). 101.28 (978-1-5157-2062-1(4), DC Super Heroes) Stone Arch Bks.

Fitchett, Jilda, 4th. Aunt Molly's Transition — Seeing Death in A New Light. 2006. (Illus.). 91p. (J). per. 15.95 (978-0-9773244-0-8(0)) Light Line.

Gay, Kathlyn. Death & Dying A-Z: By Kathlyn Gay. 2004. (Greenhaven Encyclopedias Ser.). (J). 74.95 (978-0-7377-1495-1(6), Greenhaven Pr., Inc.) Cengage Gale.

Giddens, Sandra. Coping with Grieving & Loss. 2009. (Coping Ser.). 192p. (gr. 7-12). 63.90 (978-1-61511-999-8(X)) Rosen Publishing Group, Inc., The.

Gifford, Clive. Killer History: A Gruesome & Grisly Trip Through the Past. 2013. (ENG.). 144p. (YA). (gr. 4-6). 9.99 (978-1-62145-029-0(5)) Reader's Digest Assn., Inc., The.

—Killer History: A Gruesome & Grisly Trip Through the Past. 2012. 143p. (J). (978-1-62145-031-3(7)) Reader's Digest Assn., Ltd.

Gootman, Marilyn E. When a Friend Dies: A Book for Teens about Grieving & Healing. Espeland, Pamela, ed. 2004. 120p. (YA). (gr. 6-18). pap. 9.95 (978-0-915793-66-2(0), FS209) Free Spirit Publishing, Inc.

Grebin, Margaret. Baseball Forever! A Boy's Book on Grief, Loss, & Healing. 2004. (J). per. 10.95 (978-1-59094-076-1(8)) Jawbone Publishing Corp.

Grippo, Daniel. When Mom or Dad Dies: A Book of Comfort for Kids. Alley, R. W., illus. 2008. (J). pap. 7.95 (978-0-87029-415-0(6)) Abbey Pr.

Grollman, Earl A. Talking about Death: A Dialogue Between Parent & Child. 4th ed. 2011. (ENG., Illus.). 128p. pap. 20.00 (978-0-8070-2361-7(2)) Beacon Pr.

Havens, Sarita. My Grandma Is an Angel Now. Perunko, Linda, illus. 2008. 12p. pap. 24.95 (978-1-60672-350-0(2)) America Star Bks.

Higginbotham, Anastasia, illus. Death Is Stupid. 2016. (Ordinary Terrible Things Ser.). (ENG.). 66p. (J). (gr. -1-3). pap. 16.95 (978-1-55861-925-8(9)) Feminist Pr. at The City Univ. of New York.

Holford, Karen. I Miss Grandpa: A Story to Help Your Child Understand Death — & Eternal Life. 2004. (Illus.). 32p. (J). 4.97 (978-0-8163-2030-1(6)) Pacific Pr. Publishing Assn.

House, Catherine. Where Did Grandad Go? Ayres, Honor, illus. 2007. (J). 9.95 (978-0-8198-8312-4(3)) Pauline Bks. & Media.

Innes, Shona & Agocs, Irisz. Life Is Like the Wind. 2014. (Big Hug Ser.). (ENG.). 32p. (J). (gr. -1-2). 10.99 (978-0-7641-6747-8(2)) Barron's Educational Series, Inc.

Jackson, Aariane R. Can You Hear Me Smiling? A Child Grieves a Sister. 2004. (New Child & Family Press Titles Ser.). (Illus.). 40p. (J). pap. 9.95 (978-0-87868-835-7(8), 8358, Child & Family Pr.) Child Welfare League of America, Inc.

Jackson, Deb. Creamy Goes to Heaven. 2013. 48p. pap. 17.45 (978-1-4497-8762-2(2), WestBow Pr.) Author Solutions, Inc.

Jay, Caroline. Seeds of Hope Bereavement & Loss Activity Book: Helping Children & Young People Cope with Change Through Nature. Dale, Unity-Joy, illus. 2014. (ENG.). 84p. pap. 22.95 (978-1-84905-546-8(7), 5067) Kingsley, Jessica Pubs. GBR. Dist: Macmillan Distribution Ltd.

Jay, Caroline & Thomas, Jenni. What Does Dead Mean? A Book for Young Children to Help Explain Death & Dying. Dale, Unity-Joy, illus. 2012. (ENG.). 32p. 15.95 (978-1-84905-355-6(3), 3269) Kingsley, Jessica Pubs. GBR. Dist: Macmillan Distribution Ltd.

Kane, Darlene. Missing Hannah: Based on a True Story of Sudden Infant Death. 2006. 60p. pap. 26.49 (978-1-4259-0136-3(0)) AuthorHouse.

Kidde, Rita & Wilson, Antoine. Mourning a Death in the Family. 01 vols., 1. 2016. (Family Issues & You Ser.). (ENG.). 48p. (J). pap. 11.75 (978-1-4994-3689-1(0), Rosen Central) Rosen Publishing Group, Inc., The.

Kwalwasser, Eugene I. Beyond the Tears: Helping Jewish Kids Cope with Death. 2006. 110p. (J). (gr. 4-7). pap. 12.95 (978-1-932687-33-0(5), Pitspopany Pr.) Simcha Media Group.

Langwith, Jacqueline. Death & Dying. 2008. (Introducing Issues with Opposing Viewpoints Ser.). (ENG., Illus.). 144p. (gr. 10-12). 42.00 (978-0-7377-3974-9(6), Greenhaven Pr., Inc.) Cengage Gale.

LaVelle, Steven. Just Passing Through: A Grown-Up Book for Kids. 2003. (Illus.). 32p. (Orig.). (gr. k-3). 6.95 (978-0-87516-402-1(1), Devorss Pubns.) DeVorss & Co.

Lawrence, Sandra. Murder & Mayhem. 2016. (Hideous History Ser.). (ENG., Illus.). 64p. (J). (gr. 5-9). 11.99 (978-1-4998-0082-1(7)) Little Bee Books Inc.

Liss-Levinson, Nechama & Baskette, Molly Phinney. Remembering My Grandparent: A Kid's Own Grief Workbook in the Christian Tradition. 2006. (ENG., Illus.). 48p. (gr. 2-8). wbk. ed. 30.99 (978-1-59473-212-6(4), 9781594732126, Skylight Paths Publishing) LongHill Partners, Inc.

—Remembering My Pet: A Kid's Own Spiritual Workbook for When a Pet Dies. 2007. (ENG., Illus.). 48p. (gr. 3-7). wbk. ed. 30.99 (978-1-59473-221-8(3), 9781594732218, Skylight Paths Publishing) LongHill Partners, Inc.

Loewen, Nancy. Saying Good-Bye to Uncle Joe: What to Expect When Someone You Love Dies, 1 vol. Lyles, Christopher, illus. 2011. (Life's Challenges Ser.). (ENG.). 24p. (gr. 2-3). lib. bdg. 25.99 (978-1-4048-6677-5(9)) Picture Window Bks.

Machajewski, Sarah. Death Rituals. 2014. (Digging up the Dead Ser.). 32p. (J). (gr. 4-6). pap. 63.00 (978-1-4824-1228-4(4)) Stevens, Gareth Publishing LLLP.

Marsh, Dilleen, tr. & illus. What Happens When People Die? Marsh, Dilleen, illus. 2003. (J). 12.95 (978-1-57008-954-1(X)) Deseret Bk. Co.

McAuslan, Fiona & Nicholson, Peter. Resolving Bereavement. 2011. (Resolving Ser.). (ENG., Illus.). 88p. (J). pap. 8.95 (978-1-84730-254-0(8)) Veritas Pubns. IRL. Dist: Dufour Editions, Inc.

Morrison, Kevin. God's Garden: A story about What Happens When We Die. Bachoc, Patricia, illus. 2009. 32p. (J). pap. 9.95 (978-0-8091-6741-8(7), Ambassador Bks.) Paulist Pr.

Mundy, Michaelene. What Happens When Someone Dies? A Child's Guide to Death & Funerals. 2009. (Illus.). 32p. (J). pap. 7.95 (978-0-87029-424-2(5)) Abbey Pr.

Nagelhout, Ryan. Preserving the Dead. 2014. (Digging up the Dead Ser.). 32p. (J). (gr. 4-6). pap. 63.00 (978-1-4824-1234-5(9)) Stevens, Gareth Publishing LLLP.

Naik, Anita. Coping with Loss: The Life Changes Handbook. 2009. (Really Useful Handbooks Ser.). (ENG.). 48p. (J). (gr. 5-11). pap. (978-0-7787-4404-7(3)) Crabtree Publishing Co.

Nystrom, Carolyn. Will I Live Forever? Shilliam, Jo-Anne, illus. 2006. 32p. (J). (gr. -1-3). 11.99 (978-0-8254-7306-7(3), Candle Bks.) Lion Hudson PLC GBR. Dist: Kregel Pubns.

Owen, Ruth. Zombies & Other Walking Dead. 2013. (Not near Normal: the Paranormal Ser.). 32p. (J). (gr. 3-8). lib. bdg. 26.60 (978-1-61772-721-4(0)) Bearport Publishing Co., Inc.

Parks, Peggy J. Sudden Infant Death Syndrome. 2009. (Diseases & Disorders Ser.). (ENG., Illus.). 128p. (YA). (gr. 7-10). lib. bdg. 34.95 (978-1-4205-0202-2(6), LML02109-246867, Lucent Bks.) Cengage Gale.

Payne, Anna. Extra Sepcial: For When Someone You Love Dies. 2009. (ENG.). 32p. (J). pap. (978-1-85345-501-8(6)) Crusade for World Revival.

Phillips, Tracy A. Losing Someone You Love: Dealing with Death & Dying. 2009. (Issues in Focus Today Ser.). (Illus.). 104p. (J). (gr. 6-12). lib. bdg. 33.27 (978-0-7660-3067-1(9)) Enslow Pubs., Inc.

Piper, Don & Murphey, Cecil. 90 Minutes in Heaven: My True Story, 1 vol. 2009. (ENG.). 160p. (J). pap. 9.99 (978-0-8007-3399-5(1)) Revell.

Rajczak, Kristen. Famous Graveyards. 2014. (Digging up the Dead Ser.). (Illus.). 32p. (J). (gr. 4-6). pap. 63.00 (978-1-4824-1232-1(2)) Stevens, Gareth Publishing LLLP.

Roberts, Jillian. What Happens When a Loved One Dies? Our First Talk about Death, 1 vol. Revell, Cindy, illus. 2016. (Just Enough Ser.). (ENG.). 32p. (J). (gr. k-1). 19.95 (978-1-4598-0945-1(9)) Orca Bk. Pubs. USA.

Robinson, Timothy. What Happens When People Die? Reprint. 2009. 32p. 10.95 (978-1-60641-114-8(4)) Deseret Bk. Co.

Roza, Greg. Ossuaries & Charnel Houses. 2014. (Digging up the Dead Ser.). 32p. (J). (gr. 4-6). pap. 63.00 (978-1-4824-1233-8(0)) Stevens, Gareth Publishing LLLP.

Ruiz, Ruth Ann. Coping with the Death of a Brother or Sister. 2009. (Coping Ser.). 192p. (gr. 7-12). 63.90 (978-1-61512-015-4(7)) Rosen Publishing Group, Inc., The.

Ruiz, Ruth Anne. Coping with the Death of a Brother or Sister. 2005. (Coping Ser.). (Illus.). 192p. (YA). (gr. 7-12). lib. bdg. 34.60 (978-0-8239-2851-4(9)) Rosen Publishing Group, Inc., The.

Ryan, Victoria. When Your Pet Dies: A Healing Handbook for Kids. Ryan, Victoria & Alley, R. W., illus. 2003. (Elf-Help Books for Kids). 32p. (J). per. 7.95 (978-0-87029-376-4(1)) Abbey Pr.

Sanders, Bruce. Death & Dying. 2007. (Illus.). 32p. (J). 28.50 (978-1-59604-087-8(4)) Black Rabbit Bks.

Schleifer, Jay. Todo lo que necesitas saber sobre Cuando alguien a quien conoces ha mureto (Everything You Need to Know When Someone You Know Has Been Killed) 2009. (Todo lo que necesitas (the Need to Know Library) Ser.). (SPA.). 64p. (gr. 6-6). 58.50 (978-1-60854-406-6(0), Editorial Buenas Letras) Rosen Publishing Group, Inc., The.

Schmidt, Rebecca C. The Weird Things That Happen When Someone You Love Dies: A Book of Lists. 2015. (Illus.). 61p. (J). (978-1-935864-71-4(8)) Oncology Nursing Society.

Smith, B. Good Night Jonathan - Good Morning Laura. 2008. 300p. pap. (978-1-84747-425-4(X)) Chipmunkapublishing.

Solway, Andrew. Human Body: Investigating an Unexplained Death. Stayte, James, illus. 2013. (Anatomy of an Investigation Ser.). (ENG.). 56p. (gr. 7-8). 34.65 (978-1-4329-7604-0(4)); pap. 9.95 (978-1-4329-7610-1(9)) Heinemann-Raintree.

Stalfelt, Pernilla. The Death Book. 2003. (Illus.). (J). (gr. 3-18). 15.95 (978-0-88899-482-0(6)) Groundwood Bks. CAN. Dist: Publishers Group West (PGW).

Stewart, Sheila. A Place Called Dead. (Kids Have Troubles Too Ser.). (Illus.). 48p. (YA). (gr. 5-18). 2010. lib. bdg. 19.95 (978-1-4222-1701-6(9)) 2009. pap. 7.95 (978-1-4222-1914-0(3)) Mason Crest.

Stolle, Rachel Jeanette Hall. Why Do Our Loved Ones Die, Aunt Lou? 2011. 36p. pap. 24.95 (978-1-4626-0324-4(6)) America Star Bks.

Stone, Adam. Near-Death Experiences. 2010. (Unexplained Ser.). (ENG., Illus.). 24p. (J). (gr. 3-7). lib. bdg. 25.95 (978-1-60014-503-2(5), Torque Bks.) Bellwether Media.

Taylor, Richard Dean. Gonna Sing My Song. 2011. 338p. pap. 14.95 (978-0-9815221-5-9(7)) American Trek Bks.

Throp, Claire. The Horrors of the Bubonic Plague. 2017. (Deadly History Ser.). (ENG.). 48p. (gr. 3-4). lib. bdg. 33.32 **(978-1-4846-4167-5(1)**, Heinemann InfoSearch) Heinemann-Raintree.

Turner, Tracey. Dreadful Fates: What a Shocking Way to Go! Kindberg, Sally, illus. 2011. (ENG.). 112p. (J). (gr. 3-7). 14.95 (978-1-55453-644-3(8)) Kids Can Pr., Ltd. CAN. Dist: Hachette Bk. Group.

Wezeman, Phyllis Vos, et al. Wipe the Tears: 30 Children's Sermons on Death. 2005. (New Brown Bag Ser.). (Illus.). 96p. 10.00 (978-0-8298-1520-7(1)) Pilgrim Pr., The/United Church Pr.

Worth, Richard. Elisabeth Kubler-Ross: Encountering Death & Dying. 2004. (Women in Medicine Ser.). (Illus.). 112p. (gr. 6-12). 30.00 (978-0-7910-8027-6(7), Chelsea Hse.) Facts On File, Inc.

Yarbrough, Tammy. What Happens When Someone Dies? 2008. 24p. pap. 13.99 (978-1-4343-9667-9(3)) AuthorHouse.

Zagdanski, Doris. What's Dead Mean? How to Help Children Cope with Death. 2005. (Illus.). 32p. pap. 11.95 (978-0-85572-316-3(5)) Warwick Publishing CAN. Dist: Two Rivers Distribution.

Zucker, Bonnie. Something Very Sad Happened: A Toddler's Guide to Understanding Death. Fleming, Kim, illus. 2016. 32p. (J). 14.95 (978-1-4338-2266-7(0), Magination Pr.) American Psychological Assn.

DEATH—FICTION

A. L. O. E. The Triumph over Midian. 2006. 344p. per. 23.99 (978-1-4255-3466-0(X)) Michigan Publishing.

Abedí, Isabel. Farewell, Grandpa Elephant: What Happens When a Loved One Dies? Cordes, Miriam, illus. 2012. (ENG.). 28p. (J). (gr. -1-k). 16.95 (978-1-61608-655-8(6), 608655, Sky Pony Pr.) Skyhorse Publishing Co., Inc.

Abraham, Michelle Shapiro. Where Is Grandpa Dennis? Fried, Janice, illus. 2009. (J). (978-0-8074-1083-7(7)) URJ Pr.

Alexander, William. Ghoulish Song. 2013. (ENG., Illus.). 176p. (J). (gr. 3-7). 16.99 (978-1-4424-2729-7(9), McElderry, Margaret K. Bks.) McElderry, Margaret K. Bks.

Allgeyer, Amy. Dig Too Deep. (ENG.). 272p. (YA). (gr. 8-12). 2017. pap. 9.99 **(978-0-8075-1581-5(7))** 2016. 16.99 (978-0-8075-1580-8(9)) Whitman, Albert & Co.

Almond, David. Slog's Dad. McKean, Dave, illus. 2011. (ENG.). 64p. (J). (gr. 5-18). 15.99 (978-0-7636-4940-1(6)) Candlewick Pr.

Alsaid, Adi. North of Happy. 2017. (ENG.). 304p. 18.99 (978-0-373-21228-6(3), Harlequin Teen) Harlequin Enterprises, Ltd. CAN. Dist: HarperCollins Pubs.

Anderson, Jodi Lynn. My Diary from the Edge of the World. 2015. (ENG., Illus.). 432p. (J). (gr. 3-7). 16.99 (978-1-4424-8387-3(3), Aladdin) Simon & Schuster Children's Publishing.

—My Diary from the Edge of the World. 2017. (ENG., Illus.). 448p. (J). (gr. 3-7). pap. 7.99 (978-1-4424-8388-0(1), Simon & Schuster/Paula Wiseman Bks.) Simon & Schuster/Paula Wiseman Bks.

Anderson, Laurie Halse. Catalyst. 2003. (ENG.). 256p. (YA). (gr. 7-18). pap. 8.99 (978-0-14-240001-2(7), Speak) Penguin Young Readers Group.

—Frio, Vol. 1. 2010.Tr. of Wintergirls. (SPA.). 240p. (YA). pap. 19.95 (978-84-9918-137-0(6)) Roca Editorial ESP. Dist: Spanish Pubs., LLC.

—Wintergirls. 2009. 11.04 (978-0-7848-3717-7(1), Everbind) Marco Bk. Co.

—Wintergirls. (ENG.). (YA). (gr. 7-18). 2010. 304p. 10.99 (978-0-14-241557-3(X), Speak) 2009. 288p. 17.99 (978-0-670-01110-0(X), Viking Books for Young Readers) Penguin Young Readers Group.

—Wintergirls. 2009. 278p. 20.00 (978-1-60686-532-3(3)) Perfection Learning Corp.

—Wintergirls. 2010. lib. bdg. 22.10 (978-0-606-15195-5(8), Turtleback) Turtleback Bks.

Angell, Judie. Ronnie & Rosey. 223p. (YA). (gr. 7-18). pap. 3.95 (978-0-8072-1377-3(2), Listening Library) Random Hse. Audio Publishing Group.

Anhalt, Ariela. Freefall. 2011. (ENG.). 252p. (YA). (gr. 9). pap. 14.99 (978-0-547-55216-3(5)) Houghton Mifflin Harcourt Publishing Co.

Appelhans, Lenore. Level 2 Bk. 1: There Has to Be More to the Afterlife Than This. 2013. (Memory Chronicles Ser.: 1). (ENG.). 288p. (YA). (gr. 7). 17.99 (978-1-4424-4185-9(2), Simon & Schuster Bks. For Young Readers) Simon & Schuster Bks. For Young Readers.

—Memory of After. 2013. (Memory Chronicles Ser.: 1). (ENG.). 304p. (YA). (gr. 7). pap. 9.99 (978-1-4424-4186-6(0), Simon & Schuster Bks. For Young Readers) Simon & Schuster Bks. For Young Readers.

Applegate, Anne. The Last Academy. 2013. (ENG.). 320p. (J). (gr. 7). 17.99 (978-0-545-50204-7(7)) Scholastic, Inc.

Archer, Jennifer. The Shadow Girl. 2013. (ENG.). 336p. (YA). (gr. 8). pap. 9.99 (978-0-06-183460-8(2), HarperTeen) HarperCollins Pubs.

Arcos, Carrie. There Will Come a Time. 2014. (ENG., Illus.). 320p. (YA). (gr. 9). 17.99 (978-1-4424-9585-2(5), Simon Pulse) Simon Pulse.

Arenella, Betsy Bottino. Isabelle's Dream: A Story & Activity Book for a Child's Grief Journey. Henderson, Dana, illus. 2007. 64p. (gr. -1-3). per. 7.95 (978-0-9675532-9-0(6)) Quality of Life Publishing Co.

Arnold, David. Kids of Appetite. (ENG.). (YA). (gr. 9). 2017. 368p. pap. 10.99 **(978-0-14-751366-3(9)**, Speak) 2016. 352p. 18.99 (978-0-451-47078-2(8), Viking Books for Young Readers) Penguin Young Readers Group.

—Kids of Appetite. 2017. lib. bdg. 22.10 **(978-0-606-40491-4(0))** Turtleback Bks.

Arntson, Steven. The Wrap-Up List. 2014. (ENG.). 240p. (YA). (gr. 7). pap. 8.99 (978-0-544-23264-8(X), HMH Books For Young Readers) Houghton Mifflin Harcourt Publishing Co.

Auseon, Andrew. Jo-Jo & the Fiendish Lot. 2009. 473p. (YA). lib. bdg. 18.89 (978-0-06-113924-6(6), HarperTeen) HarperCollins Pubs.

Authords, D. K. Being Alone. 2013. 120p. pap. 19.95 (978-1-63000-114-8(7)) America Star Bks.

Avery, Lara. The Memory Book. 2016. (ENG.). 368p. (YA). (gr. 10-17). 17.99 (978-0-316-28374-8(6), Poppy) Little, Brown Bks. for Young Readers.

—The Memory Book. 2017. (YA). lib. bdg. 20.85 **(978-0-606-39907-4(0))** Turtleback Bks.

Ayarbe, Heidi. Freeze Frame. 2010. (ENG.). 400p. (YA). (gr. 8). pap. 8.99 (978-0-06-135175-4(X), HarperTeen) HarperCollins Pubs.

Bahr, Mary. If Nathan Were Here. Jerome, Karen A., illus. 2004. 32p. (J). (gr. 1-7). 16.00 (978-0-8028-5187-1(8)) Eerdmans, William B. Publishing Co.

Baker, Chandler. This Is Not the End. 2017. (ENG.). 384p. (YA). (gr. 9-17). 17.99 **(978-1-4847-5024-7(1))** Hyperion Bks. for Children.

Balla, Trace. Shine: A Story about Saying Goodbye. Balla, Trace, illus. 2016. (ENG., Illus.). 24p. (J). (gr. -1-1). 15.99 (978-1-74331-634-4(8)) Allen & Unwin AUS. Dist: Independent Pubs. Group.

Ballantyne, R. M. The Young Trawler. 2011. 250p. 27.95 (978-1-4638-9496-2(1)) Rodgers, Alan Bks.

Banerjee, Anjali. Looking for Bapu. 2008. (ENG.). 176p. (J). (gr. 3-7). 6.50 (978-0-553-49425-9(2), Yearling) Random Hse. Children's Bks.

Banting, Celia. I only said I couldn't Cope. 2006. (Illus.). 240p. (YA). per. 14.99 (978-0-9786648-2-4(5)) Wighita Pr.

Barbarite, Lynn. Kitty Heaven's in the Sky! 2004. (J). 8.95 (978-0-9791362-1-4(0)) Tony Tales.

Barnes, David-Matthew. Mesmerized. 2010. (ENG.). 264p. (J). (gr. 7). pap. 13.95 (978-1-60282-191-0(7)) Bold Strokes Bks.

Bassett, Kate. Words & Their Meanings. 2014. (ENG.). 360p. (YA). pap. 11.99 (978-0-7387-4029-4(2), Flux) North Star Editions.

Bast, Michael. Death's Academy. 2014. (J). pap. 14.99 (978-1-4621-1380-4(X), Horizon Pubs.) Cedar Fort, Inc./CFI Distribution.

Bateman, Teresa. Keeper of Soles. Yayo & Yayo, illus. 2006. (ENG.). 32p. (J). (gr. -1-3). 17.95 (978-0-8234-1734-6(4)) Holiday Hse., Inc.

Bayerl, Katie. A Psalm for Lost Girls. 2017. (ENG.). 368p. (YA). (gr. 7). 17.99 (978-0-399-54525-2(5), G.P. Putnam's Sons Books for Young Readers) Penguin Young Readers Group.

Bayne, Nancy. Great-Grandpa's Chair: A Story about Living & Dying, Shared Between A Great-Grandpa & His 10-year-old Grandson! Graber, Vickie, illus. Lt. ed. 2005. 22p. (J). per. 9.99 (978-1-59879-046-7(3)) Lifevest Publishing, Inc.

Beaty, Andrea. Secrets of the Cicada Summer. (ENG.). 176p. (gr. 3-7). 2010. (YA). pap. 6.95 (978-0-8109-8419-6(9)) 2008. (J). 16.95 (978-0-8109-9472-0(0)) Abrams, Inc. (Amulet Bks.).

Bell, Lisa M. E. I Talked to Mom. 2013. 104p. pap. 9.99 (978-1-60820-873-9(7)) MLR Pr., LLC.

Bernal, Estela. Can You See Me Now? 2014. (ENG.). (YA). pap. 10.95 (978-1-55885-783-4(4), Piñata Books) Arte Publico Pr.

Bertrand, Diane Gonzales. El Momento de Trino. Sanmiguel, Rosario, tr. from ENG. 2006. (SPA.). 181p. (J). (gr. 3-7). per. 9.95 (978-1-55885-473-4(8), Piñata Books) Arte Publico Pr.

Bick, Ilsa J. Monsters. 2013. (Ashes Trilogy Ser.: Bk. 3). (ENG.). 688p. (J). (gr. 9). 18.99 (978-1-60684-177-8(7), Carolrhoda Lab™) Lerner Publishing Group.

Bird, Faye. My Second Life. 2016. (ENG.). 272p. (YA). 17.99 (978-0-374-34886-1(3), 9780374348861, Farrar, Straus & Giroux (BYR)) Farrar, Straus & Giroux.

Blacker, Terence. Boy2Girl. 2007. (ENG.). 304p. (YA). (gr. 7-10). per. 12.99 (978-0-312-37146-3(2), 9780312371463) Square Fish.

Block, Francesca Lia. Pretty Dead. (ENG.). (YA). (gr. 9). 2010. 224p. pap. 8.99 (978-0-06-154787-4(5)) 2009. 208p. 16.99 (978-0-06-154785-0(9)) HarperCollins Pubs. (HarperTeen).

Blume, Judy. Tiger Eyes. 2014. (ENG., Illus.). 256p. (YA). (gr. 7). pap. 10.99 (978-1-4814-1387-9(2), Atheneum Bks. for Young Readers) Simon & Schuster Children's Publishing.

Booraem, Ellen. Texting the Underworld. 2013. (ENG.). 320p. (J). (gr. 5). 16.99 (978-0-8037-3704-4(1), Dial Bks) Penguin Young Readers Group.

Boscarelli, Bonnie & Dani. The Garden of Weeden: Hector the Hedgehog. 2009. 40p. pap. 16.99 (978-1-4490-0606-8(X)) AuthorHouse.

Bostic, Megan. Never Eighteen. 2012. (ENG.). 208p. (YA). (gr. 7). pap. 8.99 (978-0-547-55076-3(6)) Houghton Mifflin Harcourt Publishing Co.

Boyd, David. Closer to Hamlet. 2003. 120p. (YA). (gr. 6-9). pap. (978-0-921156-93-2(6)) Rubicon Publishing, Inc.

Brewis, Alan. Boris Returns A Hero! 2008. 72p. pap. 12.50 (978-1-4357-4377-9(6)) Lulu Pr., Inc.

Bridgeman, A. M. A Place Called Heaven. 2013. 28p. pap. 16.95 (978-1-4525-6546-0(5)) Balboa Pr.

Brockenbrough, Martha. Devine Intervention. 2012. (YA). pap. (978-0-545-38214-4(9)); (ENG.). 304p. (J). (gr. 7-7). 17.99 (978-0-545-38213-7(0)) Scholastic, Inc. (Levine, Arthur A. Bks.).

Bronstein, Arlene. How Did Nonnie Get to Heaven? Torres, Diana, illus. 2013. (J). 48p. 19.95 (978-1-60131-158-0(3)); 54p. pap. 13.95 (978-1-60131-159-7(1)) Big Tent Bks. (Castlebridge Bks.).

Brooks, Kevin. Martyn Pig. 2003. 230p. (J). (gr. 5-9). 15.65 (978-0-7569-7217-2(5)) Perfection Learning Corp.

Brown, Margaret Wise. The Dead Bird. Date not set. 32p. (J). pap. 5.99 (978-0-06-443668-7(3)); lib. bdg. 16.89 (978-0-06-028932-4(5)) HarperCollins Pubs.

—The Dead Bird. Robinson, Christian, illus. 2016. 32p. (J). (gr. -1-3). 17.99 (978-0-06-028931-7(7)) HarperCollins Pubs.

Bunting, Eve. Rudi's Pond. Himler, Ronald, illus. 2004. (ENG.). 32p. (J). (gr. -1-3). pap. 6.99 (978-0-618-48604-5(6)) Houghton Mifflin Harcourt Publishing Co.

—A Sudden Silence. 2007. (ENG., Illus.). 144p. (YA). (gr. 7-12). pap. 7.99 (978-0-15-205868-5(0)) Houghton Mifflin Harcourt Publishing Co.

Burgess, Melvin. The Hit. 2014. (ENG.). 304p. (J). (gr. 9). 17.99 (978-0-545-55699-6(6), Chicken Hse., The) Scholastic, Inc.

Burleigh, Robert. Good-Bye, Sheepie. 0 vols. Catalanotto, Peter, illus. 2010. (ENG.). 32p. (J). (gr. -1-k). 16.99 (978-0-7614-5598-1(1), 9780761455981, Amazon Children's Publishing) Amazon Publishing.

Burtenshaw, Jenna. Shadowcry. 2012. (Secrets of Wintercraft Ser.: 1). (ENG.). 336p. (YA). (gr. 8). pap. 8.99 (978-0-06-202643-9(7), Greenwillow Bks.) HarperCollins Pubs.

Byars, Betsy. A Blossom Promise. Haley, Amanda, illus. 4th ed. 2008. (Blossom Family Book Ser.: Bk. 4). (ENG.). 192p. (J). (gr. 4-7). pap. 6.95 (978-0-8234-2147-3(3)) Holiday Hse., Inc.

—A Blossom Promise. (Blossom Family Ser.: Bk. 4). 145p. (J). (gr. 4-6). pap. 4.50 *(978-0-8072-1444-2(2),* Listening Library) Random Hse. Audio Publishing Group.

Cabot, Meg. Awaken. 2013. (ENG.). 336p. (J). (gr. 9). 17.99 *(978-0-545-28412-7(0))* Scholastic, Inc.

—Twilight. 2005. (Mediator Ser.: No. 6). (ENG.). 256p. (J). 15.99 *(978-0-06-072467-2(6))* HarperCollins Pubs.

Caletti, Deb. The Last Forever. 2014. (ENG., Illus.). 336p. (YA). (gr. 7-7). 17.99 *(978-1-4424-5000-4(2),* Simon Pulse) Simon Pulse.

Call, Brian D., tr. & illus. Sarah's Cloud. Call, Brian D., illus. 2003. (J). 15.95 *(978-1-57008-955-8(8))* Deseret Bk. Co.

Camacho, Hector, Jr. & Warburton, Dustin. Macho Dad. Monroe, Daniel, illus. 2014. (ENG.). (J). 19.99 *(978-0-9960374-3-3(8))* Dragonbrush Arts.

Candelario, Margo. Looking to the Clouds for Daddy. Craft, Jerry, illus. 2009. (J). *(978-0-9820221-7-7(4))* Hunter, Karen Media.

Cantor, Jillian. The Life of Glass. 2010. (ENG.). 352p. (YA). (gr. 8-18). 16.99 *(978-0-06-168651-1(4),* HarperTeen) HarperCollins Pubs.

Carey, Janet Lee. Wenny Has Wings. 2004. (ENG.). 240p. (J). (gr. 3-7). reprint ed. pap. 11.99 *(978-0-689-86759-0(X),* Atheneum Bks. for Young Readers) Simon & Schuster Children's Publishing.

Carlson, Melody. Beyond Reach. 2007. (Secret Life of Samantha Mcgregor Ser.: No. 2). (ENG.). 256p. (J). (gr. 7-12). per. 14.99 *(978-1-59052-693-4(7),* Multnomah) Doubleday Religious Publishing Group, The.

Carmichael, Clay. Brother, Brother. 2013. (ENG.). 320p. (YA). (gr. 7). 17.99 *(978-1-59643-743-2(X))* Roaring Brook Pr.

Carnevale, Michael. The Hotel Coolidge. 2007. 91p. pap. 10.95 *(978-0-7414-3752-5(X))* Infinity Publishing.

Casella, Jody. Thin Space. 2013. (ENG.). 256p. (YA). (gr. 7). 16.99 *(978-1-58270-435-7(X));* pap. 10.99 *(978-1-58270-392-3(2))* Simon Pulse. (Simon Pulse).

Castellucci, Cecil. Grandma's Gloves. Denos, Julia, illus. 2010. (ENG.). 32p. (J). (gr. k-3). 15.99 *(978-0-7636-3168-0(X))* Candlewick Pr.

Catchpool, Michael. Grandpa's Boat. Williams, Sophy, illus. 2008. (ENG.). 32p. (J). (gr. k-k). 21.95 *(978-1-84270-690-9(X))* Andersen Pr. GBR. Dist: Independent Pubs. Group.

Chalifour, Francis. Le Fils du Pendu. 2006. (FRE.). 168p. (J). (gr. 7). per. 7.95 *(978-0-88776-795-1(8),* Livres Toundra) Tundra Bks. CAN. Dist: Penguin Random Hse. LLC.

Chandler, Elizabeth. Everafter. (Kissed by an Angel Ser.). (ENG., 272p. (YA). (gr. 9). 2014. Illus.). pap. 11.99 *(978-1-4424-0919-4(3))* 2013. 16.99 *(978-1-4424-0918-7(5))* Simon Pulse. (Simon Pulse).

—Evercrossed. (Kissed by an Angel Ser.). (ENG.). (YA). (gr. 7). 2012. 304p. pap. 9.99 *(978-1-4424-0915-6(0))* 2011. 288p. 16.99 *(978-1-4424-0914-9(2))* Simon Pulse. (Simon Pulse).

—Kissed by an Angel: Evercrossed; Everlasting; Everafter. 2014. (Kissed by an Angel Ser.). (ENG., Illus.). 912p. (YA). (gr. 9). pap. 29.99 *(978-1-4424-9494-7(8),* Simon Pulse) Simon Pulse.

—No Time to Die - The Deep End of Fear No. 2. 2010. (Dark Secrets Ser.: 2). (ENG.). 624p. (YA). (gr. 7). pap. 9.99 *(978-1-4169-9462-6(9),* Simon Pulse) Simon Pulse.

Chappell, Aimee. Good Bye Grandpa. 2013. 28p. pap. 9.21 *(978-1-4669-9463-8(0))* Trafford Publishing.

Chasing Before. 2014. (Memory Chronicles Ser.: 2). (ENG., Illus.). 368p. (YA). (gr. 7). 19.99 *(978-1-4424-4188-0(7),* Simon & Schuster Bks. For Young Readers) Simon & Schuster Bks. For Young Readers.

Chimenti, Maureen. The Day My Pet Went to Heaven. 2008. 44p. pap. 17.99 *(978-1-4389-3271-2(5))* AuthorHouse.

Church, Alfred J. Three Greek Children. 2008. (Illus.). 160p. pap. 9.95 *(978-1-59915-081-9(6))* Yesterday's Classics.

Clark, Andy S. Heavenly Magic: The Unforgettable Journey of Cassidy, the Valiant. 2013. 64p. pap. 23.95 *(978-1-4497-9874-1(8),* WestBow Pr.) Author Solutions, Inc.

Clark, Sandra. My Tears Count Too. 2009. 84p. pap. 28.99 *(978-1-4389-8357-8(3))* AuthorHouse.

Clements, Andrew. Things Hoped For. 2008. (ENG.). 176p. (J). (gr. 5-18). 7.99 *(978-0-14-241073-8(X),* Puffin Books) Penguin Young Readers Group.

—Things Hoped For. 2008. 167p. (gr. 5-9). 17.00 *(978-0-7569-8933-0(7))* Perfection Learning Corp.

—Things Hoped For. l.t. ed. 2008. (Thorndike Literacy Bridge Ser.). 207p. 23.95 *(978-1-4104-0500-5(1))* Thorndike Pr.

Clifford, Leah. A Touch Morbid. 2012. (Touch Mortal Trilogy Ser.: 2). (ENG.). 304p. (YA). (gr. 9). 16.99 *(978-0-06-200502-1(2),* Greenwillow Bks.) HarperCollins Pubs.

—A Touch Mortal. 2011. (Touch Mortal Trilogy Ser.: 1). (ENG.). 432p. (YA). (gr. 8-18). 17.99 *(978-0-06-200499-4(9),* Greenwillow Bks.) HarperCollins Pubs.

Cochran, Bill. The Forever Dog. Andreasen, Dan, illus. 2007. (ENG.). 32p. (J). (gr. -1-3). 16.99 *(978-0-06-053939-9(9))* HarperCollins Pubs.

—The Forever Dog. 2007. (J). (gr. -1-2). 27.95 incl. audio *(978-0-8045-6955-2(X));* 29.95 incl. audio compact disk *(978-0-8045-4177-0(9))* Spoken Arts, Inc.

Cohen, Miriam. Jim's Dog Muffins, 1 vol. Himler, Ronald, illus. 2008. 32p. (J). (ENG.). 15.95 *(978-1-59572-099-3(5));* (gr. -1-3). pap. 5.95 *(978-1-59572-100-6(2))* Star Bright Bks., Inc.

Coker, Lauren. The Phantom's Lullaby: A Novel. 2008. 332p. pap. 19.95 *(978-0-595-47695-4(9))* iUniverse, Inc.

Colin, Thompson. How to Live Forever. 2008. 32p. 16.99 *(978-0-681-49757-3(2),* State Street Pr.) Borders Pr.

Coman, Carolyn. Many Stones. 2009. (ENG.). 160p. (YA). pap. 12.95 *(978-1-59078-782-3(X),* Front Street) Boyds Mills Pr.

—Many Stones. 2011. 14.12 *(978-0-7848-3598-2(5),* Everbind) Marco Bk. Co.

Courtney, Suzanne Gene. Dear Diary: My Brother Died Today. 2013. 32p. pap. 14.95 *(978-1-62857-013-7(X),* Strategic Bk. Publishing) Strategic Book Publishing & Rights Agency (SBPRA).

Covey, Sean. Goob & His Grandpa. Curtis, Stacy, illus. 2013. (7 Habits of Happy Kids Ser.: 7). (ENG.). 32p. (J). (gr. -1-1). 7.99 *(978-1-4424-7653-0(2),* Simon & Schuster Bks. For Young Readers) Simon & Schuster Bks. For Young Readers.

Cox, Suzy. The Dead Girls Detective Agency. 2012. (ENG.). 368p. (YA). (gr. 9). pap. 9.99 *(978-0-06-202064-2(1),* HarperTeen) HarperCollins Pubs.

Crayon, Paula. An Angel in My Pocket. 2010. 44p. (J). pap. 17.99 *(978-1-4490-9921-3(1))* AuthorHouse.

Creech, Sharon. Absolutely Normal Chaos. 2012. (Walk Two Moons Ser.: 2). (ENG.). 256p. (J). (gr. 4-18). pap. 7.99 *(978-0-06-440632-1(6))* HarperCollins Pubs.

—Walk Two Moons. (Walk Two Moons Ser.: 1). (J). (gr. 3-7). 2011. 288p. pap. 7.99 *(978-0-06-440517-1(6))* 2003. 304p. pap. 7.99 *(978-0-06-056013-3(4),* HarperTeen) HarperCollins Pubs.

—Walk Two Moons. 280p. (J). (gr. 4-6). pap. 4.95 *(978-0-8072-1509-8(0),* Listening Library) Random Hse. Audio Publishing Group.

—Walk Two Moons. (J). 2011. (gr. 5-8). lib. bdg. 18.40 *(978-0-613-00204-2(0))* 2003. (gr. 7-12). 18.40 *(978-0-613-81971-8(3))* Turtleback Bks. (Turtleback).

Croall, Marie P. Marwe: Into the Land of the Dead - An East African Folktale. Lago, Ray & Hamilton, Craig, illus. 2008. (Graphic Myths & Legends Ser.). (ENG.). 48p. (gr. 4-8). 27.93 *(978-0-8225-7134-6(X),* Graphic Universe™) Lerner Publishing Group.

Crow, Matthew. The Brilliant Light of Amber Sunrise. 2015. (ENG., Illus.). 304p. (YA). (gr. 9). 17.99 *(978-1-4814-1873-7(4),* Simon Pulse) Simon Pulse.

Crowley, James. The Magic Hour. 2003. (Illus.). 280p. (J). pap. 17.95 *(978-1-55517-713-3(1),* 77131) Cedar Fort, Inc./CFI Distribution.

Crutcher, Chris. The Sledding Hill. 2006. (ENG.). 256p. (YA). (gr. 8-12). pap. 9.99 *(978-0-06-050245-4(2),* Greenwillow Bks.) HarperCollins Pubs.

Cummings, Lindsay. The Death Code. (Murder Complex Ser.: 2). 512p. (YA). (gr. 9). 2016. pap. 9.99 *(978-0-06-222004-2(7))* 2015. (ENG.). 17.99 *(978-0-06-222003-5(9))* HarperCollins Pubs. (Greenwillow Bks.).

Cummings, Priscilla. Red Kayak. 2006. (ENG.). 224p. (J). (gr. 5-18). 7.99 *(978-0-14-240573-4(6),* Puffin Books) Penguin Young Readers Group.

Curtis, Jessica Lynn. Papa's New Home. Harmon, Steve, illus. 2012. (ENG.). 40p. (J). *(978-0-931674-64-8(6),* Waldman House Pr.) TRISTAN Publishing, Inc.

Cypess, Leah. Nightspell. 2011. (ENG.). 336p. (YA). (gr. 8-18). 16.99 *(978-0-06-195702-4(X),* Greenwillow Bks.) HarperCollins Pubs.

Daley, James Ryan. Jesus Jackson. 2014. (ENG.). 278p. (YA). pap. 10.95 *(978-1-929345-06-9(2))* Poisoned Pen Pr.

Damaged. 2014. (ENG., Illus.). 384p. (YA). (gr. 8). 17.99 *(978-1-4424-5699-0(X),* Simon Pulse) Simon Pulse.

Damico, Gina. Croak. 2012. (ENG.). 320p. (YA). (gr. 7). pap. 8.99 *(978-0-547-60832-7(2))* Houghton Mifflin Harcourt Publishing Co.

—Croak. 2012. (Croak Ser.: 1). lib. bdg. 19.65 *(978-0-606-24776-4(9),* Turtleback) Turtleback Bks.

—Rogue. 2013. (ENG.). 336p. (YA). (gr. 7). pap. 8.99 *(978-0-544-10884-4(1))* Houghton Mifflin Harcourt Publishing Co.

—Scorch. 2012. (Croak Ser.: 2). lib. bdg. 19.65 *(978-0-606-26627-7(5),* Turtleback) Turtleback Bks.

Danesh, H. B. The Mysterious Case of the Iws: A Story to Help Children Cope with Death. Breton, Katia, illus. 2012. 48p. pap. *(978-0-9782845-9-6(3))* International Education for Peace Institute (Canada).

Davies, Benji. Grandad's Island. Davies, Benji, illus. 2016. (ENG., Illus.). 32p. (J). (gr. -1-3). 16.99 *(978-0-7636-9005-2(8))* Candlewick Pr.

Davies, Katie. The Great Hamster Massacre. Shaw, Hannah, illus. 2011. (Great Critter Capers Ser.). (ENG.). 208p. (J). (gr. 3-7). 12.99 *(978-1-4424-2062-5(6),* Beach Lane Bks.) Beach Lane Bks.

Davis, Bryan. Beyond the Gateway (Reapers Trilogy V2) 2015. (ENG.). 384p. (YA). pap. 12.99 *(978-0-9898122-4-5(3))* Scrub Jay Journeys.

de Gramont, Nina. Meet Me at the River. (ENG., Illus.). 384p. (YA). (gr. 9). 2014. pap. 11.99 *(978-1-4169-8016-2(4),* Atheneum Bks. for Young Readers) 2013. 17.99 *(978-1-4169-8014-8(8))* Simon & Schuster Children's Publishing.

De Kockere, Geert & Dom, An. Dragon Fire. Van Hemeldonck, Tineke, illus. 2015. (ENG.). 32p. (J). (gr. -1-k). 16.99 *(978-1-63220-599-5(8),* Sky Pony Pr.) Skyhorse Publishing Co., Inc.

De Palma, Toni. The Devil's Triangle. 2013. 216p. pap. 14.99 *(978-1-939173-03-4(5))* Crescent Moon Pr.

Deaver, Julie Reece & Deaver, Julie. Say Goodnight, Gracie. 20th anniv. ed. 2009. (Charlotte Zolotow Bk.). (ENG.). 224p. (YA). (gr. 8-18). pap. 8.99 *(978-0-06-447007-0(5),* HarperTeen) HarperCollins Pubs.

Deem, James M. 3 NBs of Julian Drew. 2004. (ENG.). 208p. (YA). (gr. 7-18). pap. 13.95 *(978-0-618-43907-2(2))* Houghton Mifflin Harcourt Publishing Co.

Dekker, James C. Impact, 1 vol. 2009. (Orca Soundings Ser.). (ENG.). 112p. (YA). (gr. 8-12). 16.95 *(978-1-55143-997-6(2));* pap. 9.95 *(978-1-55143-995-2(6))* Orca Bk. Pubs. USA.

Delacre, Lulu. Alicia Afterimage. 2008. (ENG.). 144p. (YA). (gr. 7-18). 19.95 *(978-1-60060-242-9(8))* Lee & Low Bks., Inc.

Dellaira, Ava. Love Letters to the Dead. 2014. (ENG.). 336p. (YA). (gr. 7). 17.99 *(978-0-374-34667-6(4),* 9780374346676, Farrar, Straus & Giroux (BYR)) Farrar, Straus & Giroux.

Demas, Corinne. Saying Goodbye to Lulu. Hoyt, Ard, illus. 2009. (ENG.). 32p. (J). (gr. -1-3). pap. 7.99 *(978-0-316-04749-4(X))* Little, Brown Bks. for Young Readers.

Dennard, Susan. Something Strange & Deadly. 2012. (Something Strange & Deadly Trilogy Ser.: 1). (ENG.). 400p. (YA). (gr. 9). 17.99 *(978-0-06-208326-5(0),* HarperTeen) HarperCollins Pubs.

dePaola, Tomie. Nana Upstairs & Nana Downstairs. unabr. ed. 2006. (J). (gr. k-3). pap. 17.95 incl. audio *(978-0-8045-6943-9(6));* pap. 19.95 incl. audio compact disk *(978-0-8045-4157-2(4))* Spoken Arts, Inc.

Deriso, Christine Hurley. Then I Met My Sister. 2011. (ENG.). 288p. (YA). (gr. 7-18). pap. 9.95 *(978-0-7387-2581-9(1),* Flux) North Star Editions.

Dessen, Sarah. The Truth about Forever. 2006. (ENG.). 400p. (YA). (gr. 7-18). reprint ed. 10.99 *(978-0-14-240625-0(2),* Speak) Penguin Young Readers Group.

—The Truth about Forever. 2007. 374p. (gr. 7-12). 20.00 *(978-0-7569-8275-1(8))* Perfection Learning Corp.

—The Truth about Forever. (YA). 2006. 1.25 *(978-1-4193-2647-9(3))* 2005. 127.75 *(978-1-4193-3880-9(3))* 2005. 107.75 *(978-1-4193-2650-9(3))* Recorded Bks., Inc.

Diaz, Luis. The Dream. 2010. 166p. pap. 12.98 *(978-0-557-09653-4(7))* Lulu Pr., Inc.

DiSunno, Rebecca, et al. Jeremy Goes to Camp Good Grief. l.t. ed. 2004. (Illus.). 48p. (J). per. 14.95 *(978-0-9754932-0-5(5))* East End Hospice, Inc.

Dixon, Heather. Entwined. (ENG.). 480p. (YA). (gr. 8). 2012. pap. 9.99 *(978-0-06-200104-7(3))* 2011. 17.99 *(978-0-06-200103-0(5))* HarperCollins Pubs. (Greenwillow Bks.).

Doggy Heaven's in the Sky! 2004. (J). 4.95 *(978-0-9791362-0-7(2))* Tony Tales.

Donley, Jan. The Side Door. 2010. (ENG.). 288p. (J). (gr. 9). pap. 14.95 *(978-1-935226-12-3(6))* Spinsters Ink Bks.

Donnelly, Jennifer. These Shallow Graves. (ENG.). (YA). (gr. 7). 2016. 512p. pap. 10.99 *(978-0-385-73766-1(1),* Ember) 2015. 496p. lib. bdg. 22.99 *(978-0-385-90679-1(X),* Delacorte Pr.) 2015. (Illus.). 496p. 19.99 *(978-0-385-73765-4(3),* Delacorte Pr.) Random Hse. Children's Bks.

—These Shallow Graves. 2016. (ENG.). 496p. (YA). (gr. 7). 22.10 *(978-0-606-39341-6(2))* Turtleback Bks.

Dooley, Sarah. Free Verse. 2017. lib. bdg. 19.65 ***(978-0-606-39788-9(4))*** Turtleback Bks.

Douglas, Eileen. Rachel & the Upside down Heart. 2006. (J). per. 14.95 *(978-0-9790041-0-0(1))* Dancing Magic Heart Bk.

Doyle, Roddy. A Greyhound of a Girl. 2013. (ENG.). 224p. (YA). (gr. 3-7). pap. 7.95 *(978-1-4197-0798-8(1),* Amulet Bks.) Abrams, Inc.

Draper, Sharon M. The Battle of Jericho. 2003. (Jericho Trilogy Ser.). (ENG., Illus.). 304p. (YA). (gr. 7). 19.99 *(978-0-689-84232-0(5),* Atheneum Bks. for Young Readers) Simon & Schuster Children's Publishing.

—The Battle of Jericho. 2005. (Jericho Trilogy Ser.). (ENG., Illus.). 352p. (YA). (gr. 7). mass mkt. 7.99 *(978-0-689-84233-7(3),* Simon Pulse) Simon Pulse.

—Tears of a Tiger. 2014. (Hazelwood High Trilogy Ser. 1 Ser.). (ENG.). 192p. (YA). (gr. 12-12). 12.24 *(978-1-63245-075-3(5))* Lectorum Pubns., Inc.

—Tears of a Tiger. 2007. (Hazelwood High Trilogy: Bk. 1). 45p. ring bd. 54.95 *(978-1-60843-737-5(X))* Prestwick Hse., Inc.

—Tears of a Tiger. 2013. (Hazelwood High Trilogy Ser.: 1). (ENG., Illus.). 192p. (J). (gr. 7). pap. 9.99 *(978-1-4424-8913-4(8),* Atheneum Bks. for Young Readers) Simon & Schuster Children's Publishing.

—Tears of a Tiger. l.t. ed. 2006. (Hazelwood High Trilogy: Bk. 1). 207p. (YA). (gr. 8-12). per. 10.95 *(978-0-7862-8361-3(0))* Thorndike Pr.

—Tears of a Tiger. 2013. (Hazelwood High Trilogy Ser.: 1). lib. bdg. 20.85 *(978-0-606-32332-1(5),* Turtleback) Turtleback Bks.

Dubosarsky, Ursula. The Golden Day. 2013. (ENG.). 160p. (YA). (gr. 7). 15.99 *(978-0-7636-6399-5(9))* Candlewick Pr.

Dunbar, Helene. What Remains. 2015. (ENG.). 264p. (YA). pap. 9.99 *(978-0-7387-4430-8(1),* Flux) North Star Editions.

Ebeling, Vicki. The Winners Group. 2007. (J). per. 7.95 *(978-0-9779768-0-5(7))* Ebeling, Vicki.

Echols, Jennifer. Going Too Far. 2009. (ENG.). 256p. pap. 16.99 *(978-1-4165-7173-5(6),* MTV Bks.) MTV Books.

Edwards, Michelle. Stinky Stern Forever. 2007. (Jackson Friends Bks.). (Illus.). 49p. (gr. 1-4). 15.95 *(978-0-7569-8198-3(0))* Perfection Learning Corp.

—Stinky Stern Forever: A Jackson Friends Book. 2007. (Jackson Friends Ser.). (ENG., Illus.). 56p. (J). (gr. 1-4). pap. 6.95 *(978-0-15-206101-2(0))* Houghton Mifflin Harcourt Publishing Co.

Eenie Meanie Me & the Very Sad Day. 2005. (J). *(978-0-9772878-0-2(7))* Bishop, Susan Lynn.

Elliott, Kate, pseud. Court of Fives. 2016. (YA). lib. bdg. 22.10 ***(978-0-606-39996-8(8))*** Turtleback Bks.

Elliott, Zetta & Strickland, Shadra. Bird, 1 vol. 2008. (ENG., Illus.). 48p. (J). (gr. 3-7). 19.95 *(978-1-60060-241-2(X))* Lee & Low Bks., Inc.

Elliott, Zetta & Terasaki, Stanley Todd. Bird. Shinjo, Shelly, illus. 2016. (ENG.). 32p. (J). (gr. 2-5). pap. 9.95 ***(978-1-62014-350-6(X))*** Lee & Low Bks., Inc.

Ellsworth, Loretta. The Shrouding Woman. 2007. (ENG., Illus.). 160p. (YA). (gr. 4-9). pap. 17.99 *(978-0-8050-8185-5(2),* 9780805081855, Holt, Henry & Co. Bks. For Young Readers) Holt, Henry & Co.

Elston, Ashley. This Is Our Story. 2016. (ENG.). 320p. (YA). (gr. 7-12). 17.99 *(978-1-4847-3089-8(5))* Hyperion Bks. for Children.

Enderle, Dotti. Hidden, 1 vol. Gentry, T. Kyle, illus. 2007. (ENG.). 104p. (J). (gr. 3-7). per. 8.95 *(978-1-58980-481-4(3))* Pelican Publishing Co., Inc.

Ephron, Delia. Frannie in Pieces. Beckerman, Chad, illus. 2007. 374p. (YA). (gr. 7-12). lib. bdg. 17.89 *(978-0-06-074717-5(X),* HarperTeen) HarperCollins Pubs.

Erlbruch, Wolf. Duck, Death & the Tulip. Erlbruch, Wolf, illus. 2011. (ENG., Illus.). 38p. (J). 17.95 *(978-1-877579-02-8(5))* Gecko Pr. NZL. Dist: Lerner Publishing Group.

Erlbruch, Wolf & Chidgey, Catherine. Duck, Death & the Tulip. Erlbruch, Wolf, illus. 2016. (ENG., Illus.). 38p. (gr. 4-12). 16.99 *(978-1-877467-14-1(6))* Gecko Pr. NZL. Dist: Lerner Publishing Group.

Erskine, Kathryn. Mockingbird. (ENG.). (J). (gr. 5-18). 2011. 256p. 7.99 *(978-0-14-241775-1(0),* Puffin Books) 2010. 240p. 16.99 *(978-0-399-25264-8(9),* Philomel Bks.) Penguin Young Readers Group.

—Mockingbird. (J). 2012. 1.25 *(978-1-4407-4671-0(0))* 2010. 72.75 *(978-1-4407-4667-3(2))* 2010. 74.75 *(978-1-4407-4665-9(6))* 2010. 210.75 *(978-1-4407-4662-8(1))* 2010. (SPA.). 62.75 *(978-1-4407-4663-5(X))* 2010. 64.75 *(978-1-4407-4661-1(3))* Recorded Bks., Inc.

—Mockingbird. 2011. lib. bdg. 18.40 *(978-0-606-15356-0(X),* Turtleback) Turtleback Bks.

Esparra, Lydia. Heaven Is All Around You. Esparra, Veronica, illus. 2012. 28p. pap. 12.95 *(978-1-61244-071-2(1))* Halo Publishing International.

Espinosa, Albert. El Mundo Azul: Ama Tu Caos. 2015. (SPA.). 222p. (J). (gr. 7). pap. 14.00 *(978-1-101-91253-9(7),* Vintage Espanol) Knopf Doubleday Publishing Group.

Evans, Alfreda. The Little Boy in Blue. 2009. 24p. pap. *(978-1-55452-399-3(0),* Guardian Bks.) Essence Publishing.

Evans, Alfreda Lockett. The Little Boy in Blue. 2009. 24p. pap. *(978-1-55452-402-0(4))* Essence Publishing.

Faircloth, M. L. When Will I See Aunt Carole? Ray, Michael, illus. 2012. (J). 26p. 19.95 *(978-1-61863-326-2(0));* 28p. pap. 9.99 *(978-1-61863-324-8(4))* Bookstand Publishing.

Fallon, Kevin A. Rest in Peas: What Does that Mean? 2005. per. 12.95 *(978-1-59196-943-3(3))* Instant Pub.

Fehler, Gene. Never Blame the Umpire, 1 vol. 2010. (ENG.). 192p. (J). (gr. 4-7). 12.99 *(978-0-310-71941-0(0))* Zonderkidz.

Ficklin, Sherry D. Losing Logan. 2014. (ENG.). 304p. (J). (gr. 10-12). pap. 9.95 *(978-1-940534-41-1(0))* Clean Teen Publishing.

Firestone, Carrie. The Loose Ends List. (ENG.). (YA). (gr. 9-17). 2017. 368p. pap. 9.99 *(978-0-316-38283-0(3))* 2016. 352p. 17.99 *(978-0-316-38282-3(5))* Little, Brown Bks. for Young Readers.

Fitzer, Robin. Summer Stories. 2008. 45p. pap. 24.95 *(978-1-60563-742-6(4))* America Star Bks.

Fletcher, Ralph. Flying Solo. 2008. (ENG.). 144p. (J). (gr. 5-7). pap. 7.99 *(978-0-547-07652-2(5))* Houghton Mifflin Harcourt Publishing Co.

Foreman, Michael. Evie & the Man Who Helped God. 2003. (ENG., Illus.). 32p. (J). 18.00 *(978-1-84270-219-2(X))* Andersen Pr. GBR. Dist: Independent Pubs. Group.

Forman, Gayle. If I Stay. 2011. (If I Stay Ser.: BK.1). (YA). 10.36 *(978-0-7848-3573-9(X),* Everbind) Marco Bk. Co.

—If I Stay. movie tie-in ed. 2014. (If I Stay Ser.: BK.1). (ENG.). 304p. (YA). (gr. 9). pap. 10.99 *(978-0-14-751453-0(3))* Penguin Publishing Group.

—If I Stay. (If I Stay Ser.: BK.1). (ENG.). (YA). (gr. 9-18). 2010. 320p. 10.99 *(978-0-14-241543-6(X),* Speak) 2009. 208p. 17.99 *(978-0-525-42103-0(3),* Dutton Books for Young Readers) 2014. 304p. 17.99 *(978-0-451-47464-3(3),* Viking Books for Young Readers) Penguin Young Readers Group.

—If I Stay. 2010. (If I Stay Ser.: BK.1). (ENG.). 262p. (YA). (gr. 9-12). 18.45 *(978-1-60686-742-6(3))* Perfection Learning Corp.

—If I Stay. l.t. ed. 2014. (If I Stay Ser.: BK.1). (ENG.). (YA). 482p. 23.99 *(978-1-4104-7543-5(3));* 480p. pap. 12.99 *(978-1-59413-814-0(1),* Large Print Pr.) Thorndike Pr.

Frank, E. R. Wrecked. (ENG., (YA). 2015. Illus.). 336p. (gr. 9). pap. 10.99 *(978-1-4814-5137-6(5))* 2007. 256p. (gr. 7-12). pap. 9.99 *(978-0-689-87384-3(0))* Simon & Schuster Children's Publishing. (Atheneum Bks. for Young Readers).

Franklin, Emily. Last Night at the Circle Cinema. 2015. (ENG.). 200p. (YA). (gr. 8-12). 18.99 *(978-1-4677-7489-5(8))* Lerner Publishing Group.

Freitas, Donna. The Survival Kit. 2011. (ENG.). 368p. (YA). (gr. 7-12). 17.99 *(978-0-374-39917-7(4),* Farrar, Straus & Giroux (BYR)) Farrar, Straus & Giroux.

Friend, Natasha. Perfect. 2004. (ENG.). 232p. (J). pap. 7.95 *(978-1-57131-651-6(5))* Milkweed Editions.

Frink-Hunter, Chene I. Grandma Died & Mommy Really, Really Cried: Death - Dying. Robertson, Michael, illus. (J). (gr. -1-6). *(978-0-9654185-1-5(0))* Hunter Pubns.

Furniss, Clare. The Year of the Rat. 2015. (ENG.). 304p. (YA). (gr. 7). pap. 10.99 *(978-1-4814-2100-3(X),* McElderry, Margaret K. Bks.) McElderry, Margaret K. Bks.

Gardner, Faith. Perdita. 2015. (ENG.). 224p. (YA). 17.99 *(978-1-4405-8811-2(2),* Simon Pulse) Simon Pulse.

Garrick, Lainie. Losing Papou: One Child's Journey Towards Understanding & Accepting Death. Mandarino, Gene, illus. l.t. ed. 2003. 32p. (J). *(978-0-9765725-0-3(8))* printONDEMANDpublisher.com.

Garsee, Jeannine. The Unquiet. 2012. (ENG.). 400p. (YA). (gr. 9). 16.99 *(978-1-59990-723-9(2),* 9781599907239, Bloomsbury USA Childrens) Bloomsbury Publishing USA.

Garvey, Amy. Cold Kiss. 2012. (Cold Kiss Ser.: 1). (ENG.). 336p. (YA). (gr. 8). pap. 8.99 *(978-0-06-199623-8(8),* HarperTeen) HarperCollins Pubs.

Ghent, Natale. Book of Living & Dying. 2006. (ENG.). 288p. (J). mass mkt. 6.99 *(978-0-00-639350-4(0),* Harper Trophy) HarperCollins Pubs.

Gibbs, Anna. The Mystery of the Healing Waters. 2005. 55p. pap. 10.00 *(978-1-4134-4533-6(0))* Xlibris Corp.

Glowatsky, Phyllis. The Light of Stars. Stringer, Karen, illus. 2003. 32p. (J). 19.95 *(978-1-931650-18-2(7))* Coastal Publishing Carolina, Inc.

Gogolewski, Kathe, illus. Tato. 2008. (J). *(978-0-9800064-2-1(2))* Red Engine Pr.

Going, K. L. The Garden of Eve. 2009. (ENG., Illus.). 240p. (J). (gr. 2-5). pap. 14.95 *(978-0-15-206614-7(4))* Houghton Mifflin Harcourt Publishing Co.

Goldman, Judy. Uncle Monarch & the Day of the Dead. Moreno, Rene King, illus. 2008. (ENG.). 32p. (J). (gr. 2-4). 16.95 *(978-1-59078-425-9(1))* Boyds Mills Pr.

Gonyea, Maria. Princess Maria. 2013. 28p. pap. 13.95 *(978-1-4525-8189-7(4),* Balboa Pr.) Author Solutions, Inc.

Graff, Lisa. Umbrella Summer. 2011. (ENG.). 240p. (J). (gr. 3-7). pap. 6.99 *(978-0-06-143189-0(3))* HarperCollins Pubs.

Grandma Is Now A Butterfly. 2005. (Illus.). 24p. (J). 8.00 *(978-0-9767077-0-7(5))* Carson, Tracy.

Gratton, Tessa. Blood Magic. 2011. (YA). pap. *(978-0-375-86486-5(5))* Random Hse. Children's Bks.

Gray, Keith. Ostrich Boys. 2011. (ENG.). 304p. (YA). (gr. 7). pap. 9.99 *(978-0-375-85844-4(X),* Random Hse. Bks. for Young Readers) Random Hse. Children's Bks.

Gray, Michael Loyd. King Biscuit. 2013. (J). pap. *(978-1-938237-04-1(8))* Tempest Bk. Shop.

Green, John. Looking for Alaska. 2014. (ENG.). 256p. (YA). (gr. 12-12). 14.24 *(978-1-63245-185-9(9))* Lectorum Pubns., Inc.

—Looking for Alaska. 2009. 11.04 *(978-0-7848-1838-1(X),* Everbind) Marco Bk. Co.

—Looking for Alaska. 2014. *(978-0-525-42728-5(7),* Dutton Adult) 2006. 20.00 *(978-0-7569-6726-0(0))* Penguin Publishing Group.

C
D

—Looking for Alaska. (ENG.). (YA). 2006. 256p. (gr. 9-18). pap. 10.99 *(978-0-14-240251-1(6)*, Speak) 2005. 160p. (gr. 8-12). 18.99 *(978-0-525-47506-4(0)*, Dutton Books for Young Readers) 10th anniv. ed. 2015. 368p. (gr. 9). 19.99 *(978-0-525-42802-2(X)*, Dutton Books for Young Readers) Penguin Young Readers Group.

—Looking for Alaska. l.t. ed. 2016. (ENG.). pap. 13.99 *(978-1-59413-982-6(2)*, Large Print Pr.) Thorndike Pr.

—Looking for Alaska. 2006. 221p. (gr. 7-12). lib. bdg. 20.85 *(978-1-4177-2915-9(5)*, Turtleback) Turtleback Bks.

Greene, Constance C. Beat the Turtle Drum. 128p. (J). (gr. 4-6). pap. 3.99 *(978-0-8072-1411-4(6)*, Listening Library) Random Hse. Audio Publishing Group.

Gregory, Nan. Wild Girl & Gran. 2004. (Illus.). (J). (gr. k-3). spiral bd. *(978-0-616-11112-3(6))* Canadian National Institute for the Blind/Institut National Canadien pour les Aveugles.

Griffin, Adele. Tighter. (ENG.). (YA). (gr. 7). 2012. 240p. pap. 8.99 *(978-0-375-85933-5(0)*, Ember) 2011. 224p. 16.99 *(978-0-375-86645-6(0)*, Knopf Bks. for Young Readers) Random Hse. Children's Bks.

—Where I Want to Be. 2007. (ENG.). 176p. (YA). (gr. 7-18). 7.99 *(978-0-14-240948-0(0)*, Speak) Penguin Young Readers Group.

Hall, S.C. Turns of Fortune & Other Tales. 2007. (ENG.). 116p. per. *(978-1-4065-1586-2(8))* Dodo Pr.

Halse Anderson, Laure. FRÍO. 2015. (SPA.). 240p. (YA). pap. 18.95 *(978-84-9918-925-3(3))* Roca Editorial ESP. Dist: Spanish Pubs., LLC.

Halse Anderson, Laurie. FRÍO. (SPA.). (YA). pap. 13.95 *(978-84-92833-70-2(X))* Roca Bolsillo ESP. Dist: Spanish Pubs., LLC.

Hannon, Rose. Finding Agate: An Epic Story of a Poodle's Heart & His Will to Survive. 2010. 268p. pap. 16.99 *(978-1-4490-8986-3(0))* AuthorHouse.

Harris, Mary. Freckles from Heaven. Harris, Brandy, illus. 2007. 28p. per. 24.95 *(978-1-4241-8647-1(1))* America Star Bks.

Harrison, Kim, pseud. Early to Death, Early to Rise. 2011. (Madison Avery Ser.: 2). (ENG., Illus.). 256p. (YA). (gr. 9). pap. 8.99 *(978-0-06-144169-1(4))* HarperCollins Pubs.

—Once Dead, Twice Shy. (Madison Avery Ser.: 1). 2010. (ENG.). 256p. (YA). (gr. 8). pap. 8.99 *(978-0-06-144168-4(6))* 2009. 240p. (J). lib. bdg. 17.89 *(978-0-06-171820-5(3)*, HarperTeen) 2009. 240p. (J). (gr. 9-18). 16.99 *(978-0-06-171816-8(5)*, HarperTeen) HarperCollins Pubs.

—Something Deadly This Way Comes. 2011. (Madison Avery Ser.: 3). (ENG.). 256p. (YA). (gr. 9-18). 16.99 *(978-0-06-171819-9(X))* HarperCollins Pubs.

Härtling, Peter. La Abuela. Mizsenko, Ingrid, illus. 2003. (SPA.). 103p. (J). (gr. 5-8). pap. 9.95 *(978-968-19-0730-3(2))* Santillana USA Publishing Co., Inc.

Harvey, Jacqueline. The Sound of the Sea. Crossett, Warren, illus. 2005. 32p. (J). *(978-0-7344-0742-9(4)*, Lothian Children's Bks.) Hachette Australia.

Haydu, Corey Ann. The Careful Undressing of Love. 2017. (ENG.). 288p. (YA). (gr. 9). 17.99 *(978-0-399-18673-8(5)*, Dutton Books for Young Readers) Penguin Young Readers Group.

Hayes, Daniel. Flyers. 2013. (ENG.). 208p. (YA). (gr. 7). pap. 10.99 *(978-1-4424-8881-6(6)*, Simon & Schuster Bks. For Young Readers) Simon & Schuster Bks. For Young Readers.

Hayes, Geoffrey. How to Say Goodbye. Hayes, Geoffrey, illus. 2016. (Benny & Penny Ser.). (ENG., Illus.). 32p. (J). (gr. -1-3). 12.95 *(978-1-935179-99-3(3))* TOON Books / RAW Junior, LLC.

Haynes, India K. Sweet Shana. 2007. (ENG.). 56p. per. 27.99 *(978-1-4134-1175-1(4))* Xlibris Corp.

Held, Kristen. Holding Court. 2016. (ENG.). 352p. (YA). pap. 9.99 *(978-1-63375-227-6(5)*, 9781633752276) Entangled Publishing, LLC.

Hemery, Kathleen Maresh. Sunflower Promise. Bordelois, Augusto, illus. 2005. (J). *(978-1-56123-188-1(6))* Centering Corp.

Henkes, Kevin. Sun & Spoon. 2007. (ENG.). 144p. (J). (gr. 3-7). pap. 8.99 *(978-0-06-128875-3(6)*, Greenwillow Bks.) HarperCollins Pubs.

Hereford, L. F. Gerry the Grape. Skardarasy, Doreen L., illus. 2005. (J). pap. *(978-0-9728969-9-3(6))* Acorn Publishing.

Hermes, Patricia. You Shouldn't Have to Say Goodbye: It's Hard Losing the Person You Love The Most. 2008. (ENG.). 128p. (J). (gr. 4-7). pap. 8.99 *(978-1-4022-1325-0(5)*, Sourcebooks Jabberwocky) Sourcebooks, Inc.

Hernandez, David. No More Us for You. 2009. (YA). 281p. lib. bdg. 17.89 *(978-0-06-117334-9(7))*; (ENG.). 288p. (gr. 9-18). 16.99 *(978-0-06-117333-2(9))* HarperCollins Pubs. (HarperTeen).

Hesse, Karen. Phoenix Rising. 2009. (ENG.). 208p. (J). (gr. 6-11). pap. 9.99 *(978-0-312-53562-9(7)*, 9780312535629) Square Fish.

Hest, Amy. My Old Pal, Oscar. Bates, Amy June, illus. 2016. (ENG.). 32p. (J). (gr. k-2). 16.95 *(978-1-4197-1901-1(7))* Abrams, Inc.

—Remembering Mrs. Rossi. Maione, Heather, illus. 2007. (ENG.). 192p. (J). (gr. 3-7). 14.99 *(978-0-7636-2163-6(3))* Candlewick Pr.

—Remembering Mrs. Rossi. Maione, Heather, illus. 2010. (ENG.). 192p. (J). (gr. 3-7). 6.99 *(978-0-7636-4089-7(1))* Candlewick Pr.

Hester, John C. Three Days in Hell. 2003. (J). 7.95 *(978-1-59196-311-0(7))* Instant Pub.

Higgins, F. E. The Bone Magician. 2011. (ENG.). 304p. (J). (gr. 5-9). pap. 10.99 *(978-0-312-65944-8(X)*, 9780312659448) Square Fish.

High, Linda Oatman. That Selfie Girl. 2016. (Gravel Road Ser.). (YA). lib. bdg. 22.05 *(978-0-606-37404-0(3))* Turtleback Bks.

Hinton, Paul Richard. Rammy, 1 vol. 2009. 177p. pap. 24.95 *(978-1-4489-2641-1(6))* America Star Bks.

Hobbs, Valerie. Defiance. 2009. (ENG.). 144p. (J). (gr. 5-8). pap. 8.99 *(978-0-312-53581-0(3)*, 9780312535810) Square Fish.

Hogan, Edward. The Messengers. 2015. (ENG.). 224p. (YA). (gr. 9). 16.99 *(978-0-7636-7112-9(6))* Candlewick Pr.

Holczer, Tracy. The Secret Hum of a Daisy. 2014. (ENG.). 320p. (J). (gr. 5). 16.99 *(978-0-399-16393-7(X)*, G.P. Putnam's Sons Books for Young Readers) Penguin Young Readers Group.

Hole, Stian. Anna's Heaven. 2014. (ENG., Illus.). 42p. (J). 17.00 *(978-0-8028-5441-4(9)*, Eerdmans Bks For Young Readers) Eerdmans, William B. Publishing Co.

Holt, Kimberly Willis. Keeper of the Night. 2011. (ENG.). 336p. (YA). (gr. 7-12). pap. 14.99 *(978-0-312-66103-8(7)*, 9780312661038) Square Fish.

Hooper, Mary. Newes from the Dead. 2010. (ENG., Illus.). 272p. (YA). (gr. 9-13). pap. 16.99 *(978-0-312-60864-4(0)*, 9780312608644) Square Fish.

Hosie, Donna. The Devil's Banshee. 2016. (ENG.). 336p. (YA). 17.95 *(978-0-8234-3650-7(0))* Holiday Hse., Inc.

—The Devil's Dreamcatcher. (ENG.). (YA). (gr. 10). 2016. 272p. pap. 7.99 *(978-0-8234-3693-4(4))* 2015. 288p. 16.95 *(978-0-8234-3390-2(0))* Holiday Hse., Inc.

—The Devil's Intern. 2014. (ENG.). 288p. (YA). (gr. 10-12). 16.95 *(978-0-8234-3195-3(9))* Holiday Hse., Inc.

Howard, Ellen. Murphy & Kate. Graham, Mark, illus. 2007. (ENG.). 32p. (J). (gr. -1-2). 13.99 *(978-1-4169-6157-4(7)*, Simon & Schuster/Paula Wiseman Bks.) Simon & Schuster/Paula Wiseman Bks.

Howells, Amanda. The Summer of Skinny Dipping. 2010. (ENG.). 304p. (YA). (gr. 7-12). pap. 9.99 *(978-1-4022-3862-8(2)*, Sourcebooks Jabberwocky) Sourcebooks, Inc.

Hubbard, Jenny. Paper Covers Rock. 2012. (ENG.). 192p. (YA). (gr. 9). pap. 7.99 *(978-0-385-74056-2(5)*, Ember) Random Hse. Children's Bks.

Hubler, Marsha. On the Victory Trail, 1 vol. rev. ed. 2009. (Keystone Stables Ser.). (ENG.). 144p. (J). pap. 7.99 *(978-0-310-71793-5(0))* Zonderkidz.

Hudicourt, Caroline. A Mango for Grandpa. Sainsilus, Ismer, illus. 2007. 32p. (J). (ARA & ENG.). pap. 14.95 *(978-1-60195-085-7(3))*; (POL.). pap. 14.95 *(978-1-60195-093-2(4))* International Step by Step Assn.

Hughes, Shirley. Alfie & the Birthday Surprise. Hughes, Shirley, illus. 2009. (Alfie Ser.). (ENG., Illus.). 32p. (J). (gr. -1-k). pap. 12.99 *(978-1-86230-787-2(3)*, Red Fox) Random House Children's Books GBR. Dist: Independent Pubs. Group.

Huntley, Amy. The Everafter. 2010. (ENG.). 272p. (YA). (gr. 8). pap. 9.99 *(978-0-06-177681-6(5))* HarperCollins Pubs.

Hurley, Tonya. Ghostgirl. 2010. (Ghostgirl Ser.: 1). (ENG.). 336p. (YA). (gr. 7-17). pap. 9.99 *(978-0-316-03635-1(8))* Little, Brown Bks. for Young Readers.

—Ghostgirl. Frieyro, Alicia, tr. Impey, Allison & Phillips, Craig, illus. 2009. (SPA.). 1200p. (YA). (gr. 8-12). pap. 19.99 *(978-607-11-0185-3(9)*, Alfaguara Juvenil) Santillana USA Publishing Co., Inc.

—Homecoming. 2010. (Ghostgirl Ser.: 2). (ENG.). 304p. (YA). (gr. 7-17). pap. 10.00 *(978-0-316-08943-2(5))* Little, Brown Bks. for Young Readers.

—Lovesick. 2011. (Ghostgirl Ser.: 3). (ENG.). 320p. (YA). (gr. 7-17). pap., pap. 9.99 *(978-0-316-13316-6(7))* Little, Brown Bks. for Young Readers.

Hurwin, Davida Wills. A Time for Dancing. 2009. (ENG.). 272p. (YA). (gr. 7-17). pap. 10.00 *(978-0-316-03634-4(X))* Little Brown & Co.

Jaden, Denise. Losing Faith. 2010. (ENG.). 400p. (YA). (gr. 9-18). pap. 9.99 *(978-1-4169-9609-5(5)*, Simon Pulse) Simon Pulse.

Jaques-Plester, Carol. Grandma Goes to Heaven. 2007. pap. 17.00 *(978-0-8059-8887-1(4))* Dorrance Publishing Co., Inc.

Jaskwhich, Cynthia Sheperd. Mema Says Good-Bye. Mazibuko, Luthando, illus. 2010. (J). *(978-0-87743-710-9(6))* Baha'i Publishing Trust, U.S.

Jayne, Hannah. The Dare. 2014. (ENG.). 288p. (YA). (gr. 7-12). pap. 9.99 *(978-1-4022-9457-0(3)*, 9781402294570) Sourcebooks, Inc.

Jean, Emiko. We'll Never Be Apart. 2015. (ENG.). 288p. (YA). (gr. 9). 17.99 *(978-0-544-48200-5(X)*, HMH Books For Young Readers) Houghton Mifflin Harcourt Publishing Co.

Jensen, Michael & King, David Powers. Woven. 2015. (ENG., Illus.). 352p. (J). (gr. 7). 18.99 *(978-0-545-68572-6(9)*, Scholastic Pr.) Scholastic, Inc.

Jensen, Michael R. & King, David Powers. Woven. 2015. (Illus.). 344p. (J). *(978-0-545-83117-8(2)*, Scholastic Pr.) Scholastic, Inc.

Jepson, Gill. Out of Time: The Secret of the Swan. 2011. (ENG.). 144p. pap. *(978-1-84876-612-9(2))* Troubador Publishing Ltd.

Johnson, Angela. A Certain October. (ENG.). 176p. (YA). (gr. 9). 2013. pap. 9.99 *(978-0-689-87065-1(5))* 2012. 16.99 *(978-0-689-86505-3(8))* Simon & Schuster Bks. For Young Readers. (Simon & Schuster Bks. For Young Readers).

Jones, Darynda. Death & the Girl He Loves. 2013. (Darklight Ser.: 3). (ENG.). 272p. (YA). (gr. 8-12). pap. 9.99 *(978-0-312-62522-1(7)*, 9780312625221, St. Martin's Griffin) St. Martin's Pr.

Jones, F. Thomas. Backstep Forward. 2011. 184p. 24.59 *(978-1-4520-8441-1(6))*; pap. 14.03 *(978-1-4520-8440-4(8))* AuthorHouse.

Joyce, Rita. Wandawillie. 2005. (J). lib. bdg. 17.95 *(978-1-59094-095-2(4))* Jawbone Publishing Corp.

Kade, Stacey. For This Life Only. 2016. (ENG., Illus.). 320p. (YA). (gr. 9). 17.99 *(978-1-4814-3248-1(6)*, Simon & Schuster Bks. For Young Readers) Simon & Schuster Bks. For Young Readers.

Kadohata, Cynthia. Kira-Kira. (ENG., Illus.). (J). (gr. 5-9). 2004. 256p. 17.99 *(978-0-689-85639-6(3))* 2006. 272p. reprint ed. pap. 7.99 *(978-0-689-85640-2(7))* Simon & Schuster Children's Publishing. (Atheneum Bks. for Young Readers).

Kain, Jamie. The Good Sister. 2015. (ENG.). 304p. (YA). (gr. 9-12). pap. 9.99 *(978-1-250-04774-8(9)*, 9781250047748, St. Martin's Griffin) St. Martin's Pr.

Kaplan, Debbie. Grandpa Went Away. 2011. (J). pap. *(978-1-57043-342-9(9))* Eckankar.

Kats, Jewel. Jenny & Her Dog Both Fight Cancer: A Tale of Chemotherapy & Caring. 2015. (J). pap. *(978-1-61599-279-9(0))* Loving Healing Pr., Inc.

Keeling, Annie E. Andrew Golding A Tale of the Great Plague. 2004. reprint ed. pap. 15.95 *(978-1-4191-0694-1(5))*; pap. 1.99 *(978-1-4192-0694-8(X))* Kessinger Publishing, LLC.

Kelly, Tom. Finn's Going. 2007. 278p. (YA). (gr. 8-12). 16.99 *(978-0-06-121453-0(1)*, Greenwillow Bks.) HarperCollins Pubs.

Kerz, Anna. The Mealworm Diaries, 1 vol. 2009. (ENG.). 160p. (J). (gr. 4-7). pap. 9.95 *(978-1-55143-982-2(4))* Orca Bk. Pubs. USA.

Keyser, Amber J. The Way Back from Broken. 2015. (ENG.). 216p. (YA). (gr. 6-12). 18.99 *(978-1-4677-8817-5(1)*, Carolrhoda Lab™); 18.99 *(978-1-4677-7590-8(8))* Lerner Publishing Group.

King, A. S. Please Ignore Vera Dietz. 2012. (ENG.). 336p. (YA). (gr. 9). pap. 9.99 *(978-0-375-86564-0(0)*, Ember) Random Hse. Children's Bks.

Kittredge, Caitlin. The Mirrored Shard: the Iron Codex Book Three. 2013. (Iron Codex Ser.). (ENG.). 304p. (YA). (gr. 7). 17.99 *(978-0-385-73833-0(1)*, Delacorte Bks. for Young Readers) Random Hse. Children's Bks.

Klause, Annette Curtis. The Silver Kiss. 2007. (ENG.). 224p. (YA). (gr. 7). pap. 8.99 *(978-0-385-73422-6(0)*, Delacorte Bks. for Young Readers) Random Hse. Children's Bks.

Kloepfer, John. Sludgment Day. Wolfhard, Steve, illus. 2012. (Zombie Chasers Ser.: 3). (ENG.). 224p. (J). (gr. 3-7). 16.99 *(978-0-06-185310-4(0))* HarperCollins Pubs.

Kolie & the Funeral. 2005. (J). 3.99 *(978-1-882951-40-6(9))* Guideline Pubns. Co.

Kranz, Jonathan David. Our Brothers at the Bottom of the Bottom of the Sea. 2015. (ENG.). 240p. (YA). (gr. 9-12). 17.99 *(978-1-62779-050-5(0)*, Holt, Henry & Co. Bks. For Young Readers) Holt, Henry & Co.

Kraus, Daniel. The Death & Life of Zebulon Finch Vol. 1: At the Edge of Empire. 2015. (Zebulon Finch Ser.: 1). (ENG., Illus.). 656p. (YA). (gr. 9). 21.99 *(978-1-4814-1139-4(X)*, Simon & Schuster Bks. For Young Readers) Simon & Schuster Bks. For Young Readers.

Kwaymullina, Ambelin. The Foretelling of Georgie Spider: The Tribe Book 3. 2017. (Tribe Ser.). (ENG.). 448p. (J). (gr. 7). 17.99 *(978-0-7636-9210-0(7))* Candlewick Pr.

LaFevers, Robin. Dark Triumph. (His Fair Assassin Ser.: 2). (ENG.). 400p. (YA). (gr. 9). 2014. pap. 9.99 *(978-0-544-22720-0(4)*, HMH Books For Young Readers) 2013. 17.99 *(978-0-547-62838-7(2))* Houghton Mifflin Harcourt Publishing Co.

—Dark Triumph, 10 vols. 2013. (His Fair Assassin Ser.: 2). (YA). *(978-1-4640-2397-2(2))* Recorded Bks., Inc.

—Grave Mercy. (His Fair Assassin Ser.: 1). (ENG., Illus.). (YA). (gr. 9). 2013. 576p. pap. 9.99 *(978-0-544-02249-2(1))* 2012. 560p. 17.99 *(978-0-547-62834-9(X))* Houghton Mifflin Harcourt Publishing Co.

—Grave Mercy, 10 vols. 2012. (His Fair Assassin Trilogy: Bk. 1). (YA). 132.75 *(978-1-4640-2388-0(3))*; 130.75 *(978-1-4640-2390-3(5))*; 287.75 *(978-1-4640-2386-6(7))*; 130.75 *(978-1-4640-2387-3(5))* Recorded Bks., Inc.

—Mortal Heart. 2014. (His Fair Assassin Ser.: 3). (ENG.). 464p. (YA). (gr. 9). 17.99 *(978-0-547-62840-0(4)*, HMH Books For Young Readers) Houghton Mifflin Harcourt Publishing Co.

Landau, Jeff. Saying Goodbye to Sophie. 2006. (Illus.). 48p. (J). per. 9.95 *(978-0-9728389-2-4(9))* InnerRESOURCES Pubns.

Larsen, Elisabeth Helland. Life & I: A Story about Death. Schneider, Marine, illus. 2016. (ENG.). 48p. (J). (gr. -1-3). 19.95 ***(978-3-89955-771-8(9))*** Die Gestalten Verlag DEU. Dist: Penguin Random Hse. LLC.

Larson, K. D. That Place. 2005. (Illus.). 32p. (J). *(978-0-615-12555-8(7))* Monkeytoes Pr.

Laughter in the Wind. 2004. (Illus.). (J). 17.95 *(978-0-9753417-0-4(7))* Cheerful Cherub.

Laurie, Victoria. When. 2016. (ENG.). 336p. (YA). (gr. 7-12). pap. 9.99 *(978-1-4847-0149-2(6))* Hyperion Bks. for Children.

—When. 2015. (ENG.). 336p. (YA). (gr. 7-12). 17.99 *(978-1-4847-0008-2(2))* Hyperion Pr.

—When. 2016. (YA). lib. bdg. 20.85 ***(978-0-606-39883-1(X))*** Turtleback Bks.

Leaver, Trisha. The Secrets We Keep. 2015. (ENG.). 304p. (YA). (gr. 7). 17.99 *(978-0-374-30046-3(1)*, Farrar, Straus & Giroux (BYR)) Farrar, Straus & Giroux.

Leavitt, Martine. Keturah & Lord Death. (ENG.). (YA). 2012. 224p. (gr. 9-12). pap. 9.95 *(978-1-59078-949-0(0))* 2006. 216p. (gr. 7-7). 16.95 *(978-1-932425-29-1(2)*, Front Street) Boyds Mills Pr.

Lee, Carol & Bell, Donna. Saying Goodbye to Hare: A Story about Death & Dying to Be Used with Children. Ages 5-9. 2013. (ENG., Illus.). 24p. pap. 6.95 *(978-1-85741-138-6(2))* Southgate Pubs. GBR. Dist: Parkwest Pubns., Inc.

Leibovici, Danielle. With You Always. Gabrielov, Julia, illus. l.t. ed. 2012. (ENG.). 62p. pap. 14.95 *(978-1-4565-2627-6(8))* CreateSpace Independent Publishing Platform.

Leigh, Kyra. Reaper. 2017. (ENG., Illus.). 256p. (YA). (gr. 7). 18.99 ***(978-1-4814-7196-1(1)***, Simon & Schuster/Paula Wiseman Bks.) Simon & Schuster/Paula Wiseman Bks.

Lemieux, Jean. Toby's Very Important Question. Casson, Sophia, illus. 2004. 61p. (J). lib. bdg. 12.00 *(978-1-4242-1246-0(4))* Fitzgerald Bks.

—Toby's Very Important Question, 1 vol. Cummins, Sarah, tr. from FRE. Casson, Sophie & Brochard, Philippe, illus. 2004. (Formac First Novels Ser.: 51). (ENG.). 64p. (J). (gr. 1-5). 4.95 *(978-0-88780-636-0(8)*, 9780887806360) Formac Publishing Co., Ltd. CAN. Dist: Casemate Pubs. & Bk. Distributors, LLC.

—Toby's Very Important Question. Cummins, Sarah, tr. from FRE. Casson, Sophie, illus. 2004. (Formac First Novels Ser.: 51). (ENG.). 64p. (J). (gr. 1-5). 14.95 *(978-0-88780-637-7(6)*, 9780887806377) Formac Publishing Co., Ltd. CAN. Dist: Casemate Pubs. & Bk. Distributors, LLC.

L'Engle, Madeleine. A Ring of Endless Light. 2006. (Austin Family Ser.: No. 5). 21.75 *(978-0-8446-7285-4(8))* Smith, Peter Pub., Inc.

—A Ring of Endless Light Bk. 4. 2008. (Austin Family Ser.: 4). (ENG.). 352p. (J). (gr. 6-12). pap. 8.99 *(978-0-312-37935-3(8)*, 9780312379353) Square Fish.

Levithan, David. Marly's Ghost. Selznick, Brian, illus. 2007. (ENG.). 208p. (YA). (gr. 7-18). 7.99 *(978-0-14-240912-1(X)*, Speak) Penguin Young Readers Group.

Lim, Rebecca. Exile (Mercy, Book 2) 2016. (Mercy Ser.: 2). (ENG.). 304p. (J). pap. 9.99 *(978-0-00-816904-6(7)*, HarperCollins Children's Bks.) HarperCollins Pubs. Ltd. GBR. Dist: HarperCollins Pubs.

Logsted, Greg. Something Happened. 2008. (ENG.). 208p. (YA). (gr. 7-9). pap. 8.99 *(978-1-4169-5078-3(8)*, Simon Pulse) Simon Pulse.

Londner, Renee. Stones for Grandpa. Avilés Junco, Martha, illus. 2013. 24p. (J). (gr. k-3). lib. bdg. 17.95 *(978-0-7613-7495-4(7)*, Kar-Ben Publishing) Lerner Publishing Group.

—Stones for Grandpa. Aviles, Martha, illus. 2013. (ENG.). 24p. (J). (gr. k-3). pap. 7.95 *(978-0-7613-7496-1(5)*, Kar-Ben Publishing) Lerner Publishing Group.

The Lonely. 2014. (ENG.). 288p. (YA). pap. 9.99 *(978-0-7387-4133-8(7)*, Flux) North Star Editions.

Longo, Jennifer. Six Feet over It. 2014. (ENG.). 352p. (YA). (gr. 7). 17.99 *(978-0-449-81871-8(3)*, Random Hse. Bks. for Young Readers) Random Hse. Children's Bks.

Look, Lenore. Alvin Ho: Allergic to Dead Bodies, Funerals, & Other Fatal Circumstances. Pham, LeUyen, illus. 2012. (Alvin Ho Ser.). (ENG.). 208p. (J). (gr. 1-4). 6.99 *(978-0-307-97695-6(5)*, Yearling) Random Hse. Children's Bks.

Loth, Sebastian. Remembering Crystal. 2010. (ENG., Illus.). 64p. (J). (gr. -1-3). 14.95 *(978-0-7358-2300-6(6))* North-South Bks., Inc.

Luenn, Nancy. A Gift for Abuelita/Un Regalo para Abuelita: Celebrating the Day of the Dead/En Celebration del Dia de los Muertos. Chapman, Robert, illus. 2004.Tr. of Un Regalo para Abuelita: En Celebration del Dia de los Muertos. (ENG, SPA & MUL.). 32p. (J). (gr. k-3). 15.95 *(978-0-87358-688-7(3))* Cooper Square Publishing Llc.

Lunde, Stein Erik. My Father's Arms Are a Boat. Dickson, Kari, tr. from NOR. Torseter, Øyvind, illus. 2013. (ENG.). 40p. (J). (gr. -1). 15.95 *(978-1-59270-124-7(8))* Enchanted Lion Bks., LLC.

Lupica, Mike. Hero. (ENG.). 304p. (J). (gr. 5-18). 2011. 7.99 *(978-0-14-241960-1(5)*, Puffin Books) 2010. 17.99 *(978-0-399-25283-9(5)*, Philomel Bks.) Penguin Young Readers Group.

—Hero. 2011. lib. bdg. 18.40 *(978-0-606-23142-8(0)*, Turtleback) Turtleback Bks.

—Last Man Out. (ENG.). (J). (gr. 5). 2017. 272p. 8.99 ***(978-0-14-751491-2(6)***, Puffin Books) 2016. 256p. 17.99 *(978-0-399-17279-3(3)*, Philomel Bks.) Penguin Young Readers Group.

Lynch, Chris. Angry Young Man. 2011. (ENG., Illus.). 176p. (YA). (gr. 7-18). 16.99 *(978-0-689-84790-5(4)*, Simon & Schuster Bks. For Young Readers) Simon & Schuster Bks. For Young Readers.

—Freewill. 2014. (ENG., Illus.). 160p. (YA). (gr. 7). 17.99 *(978-1-4424-8270-8(2)*, Simon & Schuster Bks. For Young Readers) Simon & Schuster Bks. For Young Readers.

—Hothouse. 2010. (ENG.). 208p. (YA). (gr. 8-18). 16.99 *(978-0-06-167379-5(X)*, HarperTeen) HarperCollins Pubs.

—Pieces. 2013. (ENG., (YA). (gr. 7). Illus.). 192p. pap. 9.99 *(978-1-4424-5441-5(5))*; 176p. 16.99 *(978-1-4169-2703-7(4))* Simon & Schuster Bks. For Young Readers. (Simon & Schuster Bks. For Young Readers).

MacDonald, Annie. Poppo's Very Best Trick. 2010. 32p. pap. 17.95 *(978-1-4520-1808-9(1))* AuthorHouse.

MacDonald, George. Malcolm. 2008. 232p. 29.95 *(978-1-60664-853-7(5))*; pap. 15.95 *(978-1-60664-099-9(2))* Aegypan.

MacHale, D. J. The Black. 2012. (Morpheus Road Ser.: 2). (ENG.). 432p. (J). (gr. 5-9). pap. 9.99 *(978-1-4169-6520-6(3)*, Aladdin) Simon & Schuster Children's Publishing.

—The Blood. (Morpheus Road Ser.: 3). (ENG.). 384p. (J). (gr. 5-9). 2013. pap. 8.99 *(978-1-4169-6521-3(1))* 2012. 17.99 *(978-1-4169-6518-3(1))* Simon & Schuster Children's Publishing. (Aladdin).

—The Light. 2010. (Morpheus Road Ser.: 1). (ENG.). 352p. (J). (gr. 5-9). pap. 9.99 *(978-1-4169-6519-0(X)*, Aladdin) Simon & Schuster Children's Publishing.

—The Light. 2010. (Morpheus Road Ser.: 1). (ENG.). 352p. (J). (gr. 5-18). 17.99 *(978-1-4169-6516-9(5)*, Simon & Schuster/Paula Wiseman Bks.) Simon & Schuster/Paula Wiseman Bks.

MacLachlan, Patricia. Edward's Eyes. 2009. (ENG.). 128p. (J). (gr. 3-7). pap. 7.99 *(978-1-4169-2744-0(1)*, Atheneum Bks. for Young Readers) Simon & Schuster Children's Publishing.

—Edward's Eyes. l.t. ed. 2008. (Literacy Bridge Middle Reader Ser.). 139p. (J). (gr. 3-7). 23.95 *(978-1-4104-0436-7(6))* Thorndike Pr.

Maddern, Eric & Williamson, Duncan. Death in a Nut. Hess, Paul, illus. 2005. (ENG.). 32p. (J). *(978-1-84507-081-6(X))* ReiseArt Buchhandlung GmbH.

Magoon, Kekla. How It Went Down. 2014. (ENG.). 336p. (YA). (gr. 9-12). 18.99 *(978-0-8050-9869-3(0)*, 9780805098693, Holt, Henry & Co. Bks. For Young Readers) Holt, Henry & Co.

—How It Went Down. Barcellona, Christine, ed. 2015. (ENG.). 352p. (YA). (gr. 9). pap. 9.99 *(978-1-250-06823-1(1)*, 9781250068231) Square Fish.

—How It Went Down. 2015. (YA). lib. bdg. 20.85 *(978-0-606-37593-1(7))* Turtleback Bks.

Mangum, Kay Lynn. A Love Like Lilly. 2006. 336p. (YA). pap. 15.95 *(978-1-59038-580-7(2))* Deseret Bk. Co.

Mansfield, Katherine. The Garden Party. l.t. ed. 2006. pap. *(978-1-84702-354-4(1))* Echo Library.

Mansur, Motesem. The Terry Tornado Story: The Wake-up Call. 2004. 25p. pap. 24.95 *(978-1-4137-2133-1(8))* PublishAmerica, Inc.

Manushkin, Fran. Goodbye to Goldie, 1 vol. Lyon, Tammie, illus. 2009. (Katie Woo Ser.). (ENG.). 32p. (J). (gr. k-2). 21.32 *(978-1-4048-5495-6(9))* Picture Window Bks.

Manushkin, Fran & Lyon, Tammie. Adiós a Goldie. Lyon, Tammie, illus. 2012. (Katie Woo en Español Ser.). (SPA., Illus.). 32p. (gr. k-2). pap. 6.95 *(978-1-4048-7676-7(6))*; lib. bdg. 21.32 *(978-1-4048-7524-1(7))* Picture Window Bks.

Marciano, John Bemelmans. The Nine Lives of Alexander Baddenfield. Blackall, Sophie, illus. 2013. (ENG.). 144p. (J). (gr. 5). 16.99 *(978-0-670-01406-4(0)*, Viking Books for Young Readers) Penguin Young Readers Group.

Martinez, Claudia Guadalupe. The Smell of Old Lady Perfume. 2008. (ENG., Illus.). 248p. (J). (gr. 4-9). 15.95 *(978-1-933693-18-7(5))* Cinco Puntos Pr.

Martínez, Claudia Guadalupe. Smell of Old Lady Perfume. 2011. (ENG., Illus.). 256p. (J). (gr. 4-10). pap. 7.95 *(978-1-933693-88-0(6))* Cinco Puntos Pr.

Mass, Wendy. A Mango-Shaped Space. 2005. (ENG.). 240p. (YA). (gr. 3-7). per. 8.99 *(978-0-316-05825-4(4))* Little, Brown Bks. for Young Readers.

Massachusetts Sabbath School Society Staff. Winnie Malone Written for the Mass S S Society, & Approved by the Committee of Publication. 2006. 144p. per. 18.99 (978-1-4255-1163-0(5)) Michigan Publishing.

Matson, Morgan. Amy & Roger's Epic Detour. (ENG.). (YA). (gr. 7). 2011. 384p. pap. 10.99 (978-1-4169-9066-6(6)) 2010. 352p. 19.99 (978-1-4169-9065-9(8)) Simon & Schuster Bks. For Young Readers. (Simon & Schuster Bks. For Young Readers).

McBride, Kristina. One Moment. 2017. (ENG.). 272p. (YA). (gr. 8). pap. 9.99 (978-1-5107-1455-7(3), Sky Pony Pr.) Skyhorse Publishing Co., Inc.

McBride, Lish. Hold Me Closer, Necromancer. 2010. (Necromancer Ser.: 1). (ENG.). 352p. (YA). (gr. 9-13). 16.99 (978-0-8050-9098-7(3), 9780805090987, Holt, Henry & Co. Bks. For Young Readers) Holt, Henry & Co.

McDaniel, Lurlene. Briana's Gift. 2008. (ENG.). 176p. (YA). (gr. 7-12). mass mkt. 6.50 (978-0-440-23869-0(2), Laurel Leaf) Random Hse. Children's Bks.

—The End of Forever. 2013. (ENG.). 320p. (YA). (gr. 7). pap. 8.99 (978-0-385-74380-8(7), Ember) Random Hse. Children's Bks.

—Heart to Heart. 2012. (ENG.). 224p. (YA). (gr. 7). pap. 8.99 (978-0-440-24017-4(4), Ember) Random Hse. Children's Bks.

—I Want to Live. 2003. (Dawn Rochelle Ser.: No. 2). (ENG., Illus.). 128p. (YA). (gr. 7-12). reprint ed. pap. 4.99 (978-1-58196-004-4(2)) Lerner Publishing Group.

—Kathleen's Story. 2006. (Angels in Pink Ser.). (ENG.). 256p. (YA). (gr. 7-12). mass mkt. 6.99 (978-0-440-23865-2(X), Laurel Leaf) Random Hse. Children's Bks.

—Keep Me in Your Heart: Three Novels. 2010. (ENG.). 624p. (YA). (gr. 7). pap. 10.99 (978-0-385-73982-5(6), Ember) Random Hse. Children's Bks.

—Mother, Please Don't Die. 2005. (ENG.). 128p. (Orig.). (YA). (gr. 7-12). per. 4.99 (978-1-58196-028-0(X), Darby Creek) Lerner Publishing Group.

—Six Months to Live. 2003. (Dawn Rochelle Ser.: No. 1). (ENG., Illus.). 144p. (YA). (gr. 7-12). reprint ed. pap. 4.99 (978-1-58196-003-7(4)) Lerner Publishing Group.

—Why Did She Have to Die? 2004. (ENG.). 128p. (YA). (gr. 7-12). per. 4.99 (978-1-58196-029-7(8), Darby Creek) Lerner Publishing Group.

McDonald, Joyce. Swallowing Stones. 2012. (ENG.). 256p. (YA). (gr. 7). pap. 9.99 (978-0-307-97609-3(2), Ember) Random Hse. Children's Bks.

McEntire, K. D. Never. 2013. (Lightbringer Ser.). (ENG.). 311p. (J). (gr. 7). 17.99 (978-1-61614-771-6(7)) Prometheus Bks., Pubs.

—Reaper. 2012. (ENG.). 342p. (YA). (gr. 7). 16.95 (978-1-61614-632-0(X)) Prometheus Bks., Pubs.

Mcghee, Alison. All Rivers Flow to the Sea. 2005. (ENG.). 176p. (YA). (gr. 9-12). 15.99 (978-0-7636-2591-7(4)) Candlewick Pr.

—Julia Gillian (and the Dream of the Dog) Kozjan, Drazen, illus. (Julia Gillian Ser.). (ENG.). 336p. (J). (gr. 3-7). 2011. pap. 6.99 (978-0-545-03353-4(5)) 2010. 16.99 (978-0-545-03351-0(9)) Scholastic, Inc. (Scholastic Pr.).

McGhee, Holly M. Matylda, Bright & Tender. 2017. (ENG.). 224p. (J). (gr. 3-7). 16.99 (978-0-7636-8951-3(3)) Candlewick Pr.

McMillion, Gloria. Whirlwinds Whirl Around. 2007. 136p. per. 11.95 (978-0-595-42248-7(9)) iUniverse, Inc.

McNish, Cliff. Breathe: A Ghost Story. (Exceptional Reading & Language Arts Titles for Intermediate Grades Ser.). (ENG.). 264p. (J). (gr. 4-8). 2009. pap. 6.95 (978-0-7613-4962-4(6), First Avenue Editions) 2006. lib. bdg. 15.95 (978-0-8225-6443-0(2), Carolrhoda Bks.) Lerner Publishing Group.

Means, J. P. Tales from Mean County Morgue. 2011. (ENG.). 82p. pap. 10.95 (978-1-4327-7856-9(0)) Outskirts Pr., Inc.

Mendes, Valerie. Lost & Found. 2004. (ENG.). 256p. (J). per. 8.99 (978-0-689-86049-2(8)) Simon & Schuster, Ltd. GBR. Dist: Simon & Schuster, Inc.

Meng, Cece. Always Remember. Jago, Alison, illus. 2016. (ENG.). 32p. (J). (gr. -1-2). 17.99 (978-0-399-16809-3(5), Philomel Bks.) Penguin Young Readers Group.

Messer, Celeste M. Forever & Always. Hoeffner, Deb, illus. 2004. 82-92p. 4.95 (978-0-9710145-0-3(7)) AshleyAlan Enterprises.

Michaels, Rune. Genesis Alpha. 2007. (ENG., Illus.). 208p. (YA). (gr. 7-12). 16.99 (978-1-4169-1886-8(8), Atheneum Bks. for Young Readers) Simon & Schuster Children's Publishing.

Mickelson, Marcia. The Huaca. 2013. (J). pap. 16.99 (978-1-4621-1190-9(4), Horizon Pubs.) Cedar Fort, Inc./CFI Distribution.

Miller, Mary Beth. Aimee. 2004. (ENG., Illus.). 288p. (YA). (gr. 7-18). 8.99 (978-0-14-240025-8(4), Speak) Penguin Young Readers Group.

Mills, Joyce C. Gentle Willow: A Story for Children about Dying. Pillo, Cary, illus. 2nd ed. 2003. 32p. (J). 14.95 (978-1-59147-071-7(4)); pap. 9.95 (978-1-59147-072-4(2)) American Psychological Assn. (Magination Pr.).

Mills, Tricia. Heartbreak River. 2009. (YA). (978-1-59514-220-7(7), Razorbill) Penguin Publishing Group.

Milton, Cathlene. The Wonders of Billy Sniggles: Billy Sniggles & the Dead Fish. 2013. 18p. pap. 9.99 (978-1-62509-780-4(8)) Salem Author Services.

Miracles, Max & Brigitte, Smadja. Los Milagros de Max. Rubio, Gabriela, illus. (SPA.). 84p. (J). (978-84-392-8700-1(3)) Gaviota Ediciones ESP. Dist: Lectorum Pubns., Inc.

Mitchard, Jacquelyn. All We Know of Heaven. 2008. (ENG.). 320p. (YA). (gr. 8-18). 16.99 (978-0-06-134578-4(4), HarperTeen) HarperCollins Pubs.

Monk, Isabell. Blackberry Stew. Porter, Janice Lee, illus. 2005. 32p. (J). (gr. -1 — 1). lib. bdg. 15.95 (978-1-57505-605-0(4)) Lerner Publishing Group.

Montoya, Louis R. Camilla. 2007. (J). pap. 8.00 (978-0-8059-7424-9(5)) Dorrance Publishing Co., Inc.

Moreton, Clara. Frank & Fanny: A Rural Story. 2007. (ENG.). 66p. per. 16.99 (978-1-4346-2717-9(9)); per. 18.99 (978-1-4346-2723-0(3)) Creative Media Partners, LLC.

Morgan, Amanda K. Secrets, Lies, & Scandals. (ENG.). (YA). (gr. 9). 2017. 368p. pap. 10.99 (978-1-4814-4955-7(9)) 2016. (Illus.). 352p. 17.99 (978-1-4814-4954-0(0)) Simon Pulse. (Simon Pulse).

Moundlic, Charlotte. The Scar. Tallec, Olivier, illus. 2011. (ENG.). 32p. (J). (gr. k-4). 14.99 (978-0-7636-5341-5(1)) Candlewick Pr.

Murphy, Barbara & Murphy, Barbara Beasley. Life! How I Love You! Baca, Elena, illus. 2004. (ENG.). 136p. (J). 9.95 (978-0-89013-468-9(5)) Museum of New Mexico Pr.

Murphy, Sally. Pearl Verses the World. Potter, Heather, illus. 2011. (ENG.). 80p. (J). (gr. 3-7). 14.99 (978-0-7636-4821-3(3)) Candlewick Pr.

Myers, Kate Kae. The Vanishing Game. (ENG.). (YA). (gr. 7). 2014. 384p. pap. 9.99 (978-1-61963-127-4(X), 9781619631274) 2012. 368p. 17.99 (978-1-59990-694-2(5), 9781599906942) Bloomsbury Publishing USA. (Bloomsbury USA Childrens).

Nadol, Jen. The Mark. (ENG.). (YA). (gr. 9-12). 2011. 256p. pap. 8.99 (978-1-59990-660-7(0), 9781599906607) 2010. 240p. 16.99 (978-1-59990-431-3(4), 9781599904313) Bloomsbury Publishing USA. (Bloomsbury USA Childrens).

Naphot, John A. God Culture for Kids: Why Do People Die. 2015. (ENG., Illus.). 32p. (J). pap. 8.99 (978-1-63047-264-1(6)) Morgan James Publishing.

Neal, Bethany. My Last Kiss. 2014. (ENG.). 368p. (YA). (gr. 7). 17.99 (978-0-374-35128-1(7), Farrar, Straus & Giroux (BYR)) Farrar, Straus & Giroux.

Nelson, Jandy. I'll Give You the Sun. 2015. (CHI.). 384p. (YA). (gr. 9). pap. (978-986-359-180-1(7)) Ecus Publishing Hse.

—I'll Give You the Sun. 2014. (ENG.). 384p. (YA). (gr. 9). 17.99 (978-0-8037-3496-8(4), Dial Bks) Penguin Publishing Group.

—I'll Give You the Sun. 2015. (ENG.). 400p. (YA). (gr. 9-12). pap. 10.99 (978-0-14-242576-3(1), Speak) Penguin Young Readers Group.

—I'll Give You the Sun. 2015. (ENG.). 400p. (YA). (gr. 9). 21.30 (978-1-68065-512-4(4)) Perfection Learning Corp.

—I'll Give You the Sun. 2015. lib. bdg. 22.10 (978-0-606-37572-6(4)) Turtleback Bks.

—The Sky Is Everywhere. (ENG.). (YA). (gr. 9-18). 2011. 320p. 9.99 (978-0-14-241780-5(7), Speak) 2010. 288p. 17.99 (978-0-8037-3495-1(6), Dial Bks) Penguin Young Readers Group.

—The Sky Is Everywhere. 2011. (ENG., Illus.). 275p. (gr. 9-12). 19.00 (978-1-61383-223-3(0)) Perfection Learning Corp.

Neri, Greg. Surf Mules. 2104. (ENG.). 288p. (YA). pap. (978-1-4677-4238-2(4)) Lerner Publishing Group.

Noël, Alyson. Blue Moon. 2009. (Immortals Ser.: 2). (ENG.). 304p. (YA). (gr. 7-12). pap. 11.99 (978-0-312-53276-5(8), 9780312532765, St. Martin's Griffin) St. Martin's Pr.

—Blue Moon. 2009. (Immortals Ser.: 2). (YA). lib. bdg. 20.85 (978-0-606-07221-2(7), Turtleback) Turtleback Bks.

—Blue Moon: The Immortals. 2013. (Immortals Ser.: 2). (ENG.). 304p. (YA). (gr. 7-12). mass mkt. 9.99 (978-1-250-04684-0(X), 9781250046840, St. Martin's Paperbacks) St. Martin's Pr.

—Desafío: Quinto Libro de la Serie de Los Inmortales. 2012. (Vintage Espanol Ser.). (SPA.). 336p. (YA). (gr. 7). pap. 10.95 (978-0-307-95147-2(2), Vintage Espanol) Knopf Doubleday Publishing Group.

—Luna Azul. 2010. (Vintage Espanol Ser.).Tr. of Blue Moon. (SPA.). 368p. (YA). (gr. 7). pap. 13.95 (978-0-307-74116-5(8), Vintage Espanol) Knopf Doubleday Publishing Group.

—Night Star. 2013. (Immortals Ser.: 5). (ENG.). 320p. (YA). (gr. 7-12). mass mkt. 9.99 (978-1-250-04688-8(2), 9781250046888, St. Martin's Paperbacks) St. Martin's Pr.

—Radiance. unabr. ed. 2011. (ENG.). 208p. pap. (978-0-330-52691-3(X), Macmillan Children's Bks.) Pan Macmillan.

—Radiance. 2011. pap. (978-0-545-34095-3(0)) Scholastic, Inc.

—Radiance. 2010. (Riley Bloom Book Ser.: 1). (ENG.). 192p. (J). (gr. 4-7). pap. 8.99 (978-0-312-62917-5(6), 9780312629175) Square Fish.

—Radiance. 2010. (Riley Bloom Ser.: 1). (J). lib. bdg. 19.65 (978-0-606-15131-3(1), Turtleback) Turtleback Bks.

—Whisper. 2012. (Riley Bloom Ser.: 4). (J). lib. bdg. 19.65 (978-0-606-23786-4(0), Turtleback) Turtleback Bks.

Nolt, Debbie. Love for Lyndon. 2011. (Illus.). 62p. (J). (gr. 3-6). 3.40 (978-0-7399-2430-3(3)) Rod & Staff Pubs., Inc.

Nora, David, Jr. Happy Balloon to You. 2005. 9.00 (978-0-8059-9870-2(5)) Dorrance Publishing Co., Inc.

Norris-Gooding, S. M. The Legend of Kerloup. 2011. 340p. (gr. -1). pap. 23.03 (978-1-4343-5229-3(3)) AuthorHouse.

Northrop, Michael. Book of the Dead. 2015. (TombQuest Ser.: Bk. 1). (J). 197p. (978-1-76015-315-1(X)); 208p. pap. (978-1-74362-924-6(9)) Scholastic, Inc.

—The Final Kingdom. 2016. (TombQuest Ser.: 5). (ENG.). 192p. (J). (gr. 3-7). 16.99 (978-0-545-87111-2(5)); 12.99 (978-0-545-72342-8(6)) Scholastic, Inc. (Scholastic Pr.).

—The Stone Warriors. 2015. (TombQuest Ser.: 4). (ENG.). 192p. (J). (gr. 3-7). 12.99 (978-0-545-72341-1(8), Scholastic Pr.) Scholastic, Inc.

Oakes, Colleen. Blood of Wonderland. 2017. (Queen of Hearts Ser.: 2). (YA). (gr. 8). 352p. pap. 9.99 **(978-0-06-240977-5(8))**; 336p. 17.99 (978-0-06-240976-8(X)) HarperCollins Pubs. (HarperTeen).

Oates, Joyce Carol. After the Wreck, I Picked Myself Up, Spread My Wings, & Flew Away. 2006. (YA). (gr. 9-12). 304p. 16.99 (978-0-06-073525-8(2)); 292p. lib. bdg. 17.89 (978-0-06-073526-5(0)) HarperCollins Pubs. (HarperTeen).

Ockun, Lisa C. Sammy the Tin Man. 2012. 32p. pap. 19.99 (978-1-4685-4328-5(8)) AuthorHouse.

Oliver, Lauren. Before I Fall. (ENG.). (YA). (gr. 9). 2016. 544p. pap. 10.99 (978-0-06-172681-1(8)) 2010. 480p. 17.99 (978-0-06-172680-4(X)) HarperCollins Pubs.

—Before I Fall. 2010. 368p. pap. (978-0-340-98090-3(7), Hodder Paperbacks) Hodder & Stoughton.

—Before I Fall. 2016. (YA). lib. bdg. 22.10 (978-0-606-23576-1(0), Turtleback) Turtleback Bks.

—Before I Fall Movie Tie-In Edition. 2017. 496p. (YA). (gr. 9). pap. 10.99 (978-0-06-265632-2(5)) HarperCollins Pubs.

—Liesl & Po. Acedera, Kei, illus. 2011. (ENG.). 320p. (J). (gr. 3-7). 16.99 (978-0-06-201451-1(X)) HarperCollins Pubs.

Oliviero, Jamie. Som See & the Magic Elephant. Kelly, Jo'Anne, illus. 2005. 27p. (J). (gr. -1-2). reprint ed. 17.00 (978-0-7567-8929-9(X)) DIANE Publishing Co.

Ormsbee, Kathryn. Lucky Few. (ENG., Illus.). (YA). (gr. 9). 2017. 400p. pap. 10.99 (978-1-4814-5529-9(X)) 2016. 384p. 17.99 (978-1-4814-5528-2(1)) Simon & Schuster Bks. For Young Readers. (Simon & Schuster Bks. For Young Readers).

Osborn, Kelly. The Green Knight. 2006. 64p. pap. 19.95 (978-1-4241-1741-3(0)) America Star Bks.

Ostrovski, Emil. Away We Go. 2016. 272p. (YA). (gr. 9). 17.99 (978-0-06-223855-9(8), Greenwillow Bks.) HarperCollins Pubs.

Paratore, Coleen Murtagh. The Funeral Director's Son. 2008. (Funeral Director's Son Ser.). (ENG.). 144p. (J). (gr. 3-7). 15.99 (978-1-4169-3594-0(0), Simon & Schuster Bks. For Young Readers) Simon & Schuster Bks. For Young Readers.

Park, Barbara. Mick Harte Was Here. 88p. (J). (gr. 4-6). pap. 4.99 (978-0-8072-1502-9(3), Listening Library) Random Hse. Audio Publishing Group.

Park, Barbara, ed. Mick Harte Was Here. unabr. ed. 2004. (Middle Grade Cassette Librariestm Ser.). 88p. (J). (gr. 3-7). pap. 29.00 incl. audio (978-0-8072-7797-3(5), S YA 922 SP, Listening Library) Random Hse. Audio Publishing Group.

Parrish, Jim. Dog Gone. 2012. 24p. pap. 17.99 (978-1-4685-6036-7(0)) AuthorHouse.

Pascuzzo, Margaret I. Anton Loses a Friend. Bicking, Judith, illus. 2009. 20p. pap. 12.00 (978-1-4269-0650-3(1)) Trafford Publishing.

Paterson, Katherine. Bridge to Terabithia. Diamond, Donna, illus. (ENG.). (J). (gr. 3-7). 2017. 192p. 16.99 (978-0-690-01359-7(0)) 2008. 208p. pap. 6.99 (978-0-06-073401-5(9), HarperTeen) 2006. 208p. pap. 6.99 (978-0-06-125370-6(7), HarperFestival) 2006. 176p. pap. 6.99 (978-0-06-122728-8(5), HarperFestival) HarperCollins Pubs.

—Bridge to Terabithia. Diamond, Donna, illus. l.t. ed. 2007. (Literacy Bridge Middle Reader Ser.). 187p. (J). (gr. 4-7). 23.95 (978-0-7862-9620-0(8)) Thorndike Pr.

—Bridge to Terabithia. Diamond, Donna, illus. 2017. (Trophy Bk.). (ENG.). 192p. (J). (gr. 3-7). reprint ed. pap. 7.99 (978-0-06-440184-5(7)) HarperCollins Pubs.

Patrick, Cat. Revived. 2013. (ENG.). 368p. (YA). (gr. 7-17). pap. 10.99 (978-0-316-09463-4(3)) Little, Brown Bks. for Young Readers.

Patterson, James & Paetro, Maxine. Confessions of a Murder Suspect. 2014. (Confessions Ser.: 1). (ENG.). 352p. (gr. 7-17). mass mkt. 8.00 (978-1-4555-4774-6(3), Jimmy Patterson) 2013. (ENG.). 400p. (J). (gr. 7-17). pap. 10.00 (978-0-316-20700-3(4), Jimmy Patterson) 2012. (Confessions Ser.: 1). (ENG.). 384p. (YA). (gr. 7-17). 19.99 (978-0-316-20698-3(9), Jimmy Patterson) 2012. 372p. (J). 11.99 (978-0-316-22641-7(6)) 2012. (Confessions Ser.: 1). (ENG.). 400p. (YA). (gr. 7-17). 31.99 (978-0-316-22418-5(9), Jimmy Patterson) Little Brown & Co.

—Confessions of a Murder Suspect. 2013. (Confessions Ser.: 1). lib. bdg. 20.85 (978-0-606-32278-2(7), Turtleback) Turtleback Bks.

Payne, C. C. Lula Bell on Geekdom, Freakdom, & the Challenges of Bad Hair, 0 vols. 2012. (ENG.). 276p. (J). (gr. 3-7). 16.99 (978-0-7614-6225-5(2), 9780761462255, Amazon Children's Publishing) Amazon Publishing.

Penn, Audrey. Chester Raccoon & the Acorn Full of Memories. Gibson, Barbara L., illus. 2009. (Kissing Hand Ser.). (ENG.). 32p. (J). (gr. -1-3). 16.95 (978-1-933718-29-3(3)) Tanglewood Pr.

Penney, Mary. Eleven & Holding. 2016. 256p. (J). (gr. 3-7). 16.99 (978-0-06-240547-0(0)) HarperCollins Pubs.

Pennypacker, Sara. Summer of the Gypsy Moths. (ENG.). 288p. (J). (gr. 3-7). 2013. pap. 6.99 (978-0-06-196422-0(0)) 2012. 15.99 (978-0-06-196420-6(4)) HarperCollins Pubs.

Pérez, Alfredo. Sueno de Novela. (SPA.). (J). 8.95 (978-958-04-6870-7(2)) Norma S.A. COL. Dist: Distribuidora Norma, Inc.

Perry, Sarah. Clara's Road. 2005. 64p. (J). per. (978-1-55306-945-4(5), Epic Pr.) Essence Publishing.

Peterson, Lois. The Wrong Bus, 1 vol. Meissner, Amy, illus. 2012. (Orca Echoes Ser.). (ENG.). 64p. (J). (gr. 2-3). pap. 6.95 (978-1-55469-869-1(3)) Orca Bk. Pubs. USA.

Pickard, W. Raymond. When an Angel Cries: (but I Don't Want to Be an Angel) 2006. 67p. pap. 16.95 (978-1-4241-0243-3(X)) PublishAmerica, Inc.

Pike, Christopher, pseud. The Midnight Club. 2012. (ENG.). 224p. (YA). (gr. 11). pap. 10.99 (978-1-4424-6054-6(7), Simon Pulse) Simon Pulse.

Pincus, Donna & Kaplow, Julie. Samantha Jane's Missing Smile: A Story about Coping with the Loss of a Parent. Speigel, Beth, illus. 2007. 32p. (J). (gr. -1-3). 14.95 (978-1-59147-808-9(1)); per. 9.95 (978-1-59147-809-6(X)) American Psychological Assn. (Magination Pr.).

Pitkethly, Maggie. Graeme Goes Home. Farmer, Suzanne, illus. 2008. 32p. pap. 12.00 (978-0-9791402-8-0(5)) Stewart, R. J. Bks.

Pittar, Gill. Milly, Molly & Jimmy's Seeds (book W/dolls) 2006. 28p. pap. (978-1-86972-091-9(1)) Milly Molly Bks.

Pixley, Marcella. Without Tess. 2014. (ENG.). 304p. (YA). (gr. 7-12). pap. 9.99 (978-1-250-04435-8(9), 9781250044358) Square Fish.

Poe, Edgar Allen. Edgar Allan Poe's Tales of Death & Dementia. Grimly, Gris, illus. 2009. (ENG.). 144p. (J). (gr. 6-9). 19.99 (978-1-4169-5025-7(7), Atheneum Bks. for Young Readers) Simon & Schuster Children's Publishing.

Polisner, Gae. The Pull of Gravity. 2013. (ENG.). 224p. (YA). (gr. 7). pap. 10.99 (978-1-250-01933-2(8), 9781250019332) Square Fish.

—The Summer of Letting Go. (ENG.). (YA). (gr. 7-10). 2015. 336p. pap. 9.95 (978-1-61620-480-8(X)) 2014. 320p. 16.95 (978-1-61620-256-9(4), 73256) Algonquin Bks. of Chapel Hill.

Portnoy, Mindy Avra. ¿Adónde Van Las Personas Cuando Mueren? Translations.com Staff, tr. from ENG. Haas, Shelly O., illus. 2008. (SPA & ENG.). 24p. (J). (gr. k-3). 15.95 (978-0-7613-3905-2(1)) Lerner Publishing Group.

—Where Do People Go When They Die? Haas, Shelly O., illus. 2004. (Carolrhoda Picture Books Ser.). 24p. (J). (gr. -1-3). 15.95 (978-1-58013-081-3(X), Kar-Ben Publishing) Lerner Publishing Group.

Powell, Dimity. The Fix-It Man. Johnston, Nicky, illus. 2017. (ENG.). 32p. (J). (gr. -1-3). 17.99 (978-1-925335-34-7(8), EK Bks.) Exisle Publishing Pty Ltd. AUS. Dist: Hachette Bk. Group.

Price, Reynolds. A Perfect Friend. 2013. (ENG.). (J). pap. 4.99 (978-0-689-83148-5(X), Simon & Schuster/Paula Wiseman Bks.) Simon & Schuster/Paula Wiseman Bks.

Priest, Cherie. I Am Princess X. Ciesemier, Kali, illus. 2015. (ENG.). 256p. (YA). (gr. 7). 18.99 (978-0-545-62085-7(6), Levine, Arthur A. Bks.) Scholastic, Inc.

Prose, Francine. Bullyville. (YA). 2008. (ENG.). 272p. (gr. 8). pap. 9.99 (978-0-06-057499-4(2)) 2007. 260p. (gr. 7-12). 16.99 (978-0-06-057497-0(6)) 2007. 260p. (gr. 7-12). lib. bdg. 17.89 (978-0-06-057498-7(4)) HarperCollins Pubs. (HarperTeen).

—Bullyville. 2011. 10.36 (978-0-7848-3625-5(6), Everbind) Marco Bk. Co.

Qualey, Marsha. Thin Ice. 2007. (YA). (978-0-9793444-0-4(9)) Quercus Pr.

Rabbett, Martin. Forever Buster: What a Name! What a Dog, We Exclaim! Burns, Donna, illus. 2007. (J). 13.95 (978-0-9794649-0-4(0)) Hula Moon Pr.

Randall, Thomas. The Waking: Dreams of the Dead. 2nd ed. 2010. (ENG., Illus.). 304p. (YA). (gr. 7-18). pap. 8.99 (978-1-59990-585-3(X), 9781599905853, Bloomsbury USA Childrens) Bloomsbury Publishing USA.

Ray, Delia. Here Lies Linc. (ENG.). 320p. (J). (gr. 3-7). 2012. 7.99 (978-0-375-86538-1(1), Yearling) 2011. 16.99 (978-0-375-86757-6(0), Knopf Bks. for Young Readers) Random Hse. Children's Bks.

Reagan, Jean & Pollema-Cahill, Phyllis. Always My Brother, 1 vol. 2009. (ENG., Illus.). 32p. (gr. 2-6). 16.95 (978-0-88448-313-7(4), 884313) Tilbury Hse. Pubs.

Reeves, Dia. Bleeding Violet. 2010. (ENG.). 480p. (YA). (gr. 9). pap. 20.99 (978-1-4169-8619-5(7), Simon Pulse) Simon Pulse.

Regenold, Theresa. Not Your Average Princess: A Real-Life Fairy Tale. 2005. 117p. pap. 19.95 (978-1-4137-9308-6(8)) PublishAmerica, Inc.

Revell, Mike. Stormwalker. 2016. (ENG.). 304p. (J). (gr. 5-9). 16.99 (978-1-68144-493-2(3)) Quercus NA.

Ringtved, Glenn. Cry, Heart, but Never Break. Moulthrop, Robert, tr. from DAN. Pardi, Charlotte, illus. 2016. (ENG.). 32p. (J). (gr. -1-3). 16.95 (978-1-59270-187-2(6)) Enchanted Lion Bks., LLC.

Roberts, Willo Davis. The One Left Behind. 2007. (ENG., Illus.). 144p. (J). (gr. 3-7). pap. 7.99 (978-0-689-85083-7(2), Aladdin) Simon & Schuster Children's Publishing.

Rodrigues, Carmen. 34 Pieces of You. (ENG.). (YA). (gr. 9). 2013. 352p. pap. 9.99 (978-1-4424-3907-8(6)) 2012. 336p. 16.99 (978-1-4424-3906-1(8)) Simon Pulse. (Simon Pulse).

Rogers, Leeann. Ms Tulper Is Her Name. 2011. 28p. pap. 16.95 (978-1-4626-2718-9(8)) America Star Bks.

Rohmann, Eric. Bone Dog. Rohmann, Eric, illus. 2011. (ENG., Illus.). 32p. (J). (gr. -1-3). 16.99 (978-1-59643-150-8(4), 9781596431508) Roaring Brook Pr.

Rollins, Ellie. Zip. 2013. (ENG.). 336p. (J). (gr. 3-7). pap. 7.99 (978-1-59514-571-0(0), Razorbill) Penguin Young Readers Group.

Rosen, Michael. Michael Rosen's Sad Book. Blake, Quentin, illus. 2005. (ENG.). 32p. (J). (gr. k-12). 16.99 (978-0-7636-2597-9(3)) Candlewick Pr.

Rosen, Michael & Quarto Generic Staff. Lovely Old Roly. Lamont, Priscilla, illus. 2004. (ENG.). 32p. (J). (gr. -1-2). pap. 7.95 (978-1-84507-144-8(1), Frances Lincoln) Quarto Publishing Group UK GBR. Dist: Hachette Bk. Group.

Rothenberg, Jess. The Catastrophic History of You & Me. 2013. (ENG.). 400p. (YA). (gr. 7). pap. 9.99 (978-0-14-242390-5(4), Speak) Penguin Young Readers Group.

Rought, A. E. Broken. 2013. (ENG.). 320p. (J). (gr. 9). pap. 9.99 (978-1-908844-31-6(0), Strange Chemistry) Watkins Media Limited GBR. Dist: Penguin Random Hse. LLC.

Roussin, Simon. Forever Young: the Boy Who Couldn't Die: A TOON Graphic. 2016. (ENG., Illus.). 48p. (J). (978-1-943145-10-2(5)) TOON Books / RAW Junior, LLC.

Rubin, Lance. Denton Little's Deathdate. 2015. (ENG.). 352p. (YA). (gr. 9). 17.99 (978-0-553-49696-3(4), Knopf Bks. for Young Readers) Random Hse. Children's Bks.

Rupp, Rebecca. After Eli. (ENG.). 256p. (J). (gr. 4-7). 2015. pap. 8.99 (978-0-7636-7674-2(8)) 2012. (Illus.). 15.99 (978-0-7636-5810-6(3)) Candlewick Pr.

Ryan, Amy Kathleen. Zen & Xander Undone. 2011. (ENG.). 228p. (YA). (gr. 9). pap. 13.99 (978-0-547-55030-5(8)) Houghton Mifflin Harcourt Publishing Co.

Ryan, Carrie. Daughter of Deep Silence. 2015. (ENG.). 384p. (YA). (gr. 9). 17.99 (978-0-525-42650-9(7), Dutton Books for Young Readers) Penguin Young Readers Group.

Ryan, Darlene. Five Minutes More, 1 vol. 2009. (ENG.). 224p. (YA). (gr. 7-12). pap. 12.95 (978-1-55469-006-0(4)) Orca Bk. Pubs. USA.

Ryan, P E. Saints of Augustine. 2007. 308p. (YA). (gr. 7-18). 16.99 (978-0-06-085810-0(9)); lib. bdg. 17.89 (978-0-06-085811-7(7)) HarperCollins Pubs. (HarperTeen).

Rylant, Cynthia. Missing May. unabr. ed. 2004. 89p. (J). (gr. 5-9). pap. 29.00 incl. audio (978-0-8072-8701-9(6), YA240SP, Listening Library) Random Hse. Audio Publishing Group.

—Missing May. 2004. (ENG.). 112p. (J). (gr. 3-7). pap. 5.99 (978-0-439-61383-5(3), Scholastic Paperbacks) Scholastic, Inc.

Sabatini, Kimberly. Touching the Surface. 2012. (ENG.). 352p. (YA). (gr. 9). 16.99 (978-1-4424-4002-9(3), Simon Pulse) Simon Pulse.

Sáenz, Benjamin Alire. The Inexplicable Logic of My Life. 2017. (ENG.). 464p. (gr. 7). 17.99 (978-0-544-58650-5(6)) Houghton Mifflin Harcourt Publishing Co.

Salisbury, Melinda. The Sin Eater's Daughter. 2015. (ENG.). 320p. (J). (gr. 9). 17.99 (978-0-545-81062-3(0), Scholastic Pr.) Scholastic, Inc.

Sample, Jewel. Flying Hugs & Kisses Activity Book. Kiplinger Pandy, Lori, illus. 2007. 68p. (J). (gr. -1-3). per. 13.99 (978-1-59879-377-2(2)) Lifevest Publishing, Inc.

Sanna, Francesca. The Journey. Sanna, Francesca, illus. 2016. (ENG., Illus.). 48p. (J). (gr. -1-2). 17.95 (978-1-909263-99-4(0)) Flying Eye Bks. GBR. Dist: Consortium Bk. Sales & Distribution.

Savage, Kim. Beautiful Broken Girls. 2017. (ENG.). 336p. (YA). 17.99 (978-0-374-30059-3(3), 9780374300593, Farrar, Straus & Giroux (BYR)) Farrar, Straus & Giroux.

Scanlon, Cara. Where Did Grandma Go? Mattes-Ruggiero, Lynn, illus. 2008. (J). (978-1-930596-85-6(5)) Amherst Pr.

—Where Did Grandpa Go? Mattes-Ruggiero, Lynn, illus. 2008. (J). (978-1-930596-86-3(3)) Amherst Pr.

Schmitt, Sarah. It's a Wonderful Death. 2015. (ENG.). 320p. (J). (gr. 6). 17.99 (978-1-63450-173-6(X), Sky Pony Pr.) Skyhorse Publishing Co., Inc.

Scholastic, Inc. Staff & Northrop, Michael. Book of the Dead. 2015. (TombQuest Ser.: 1). (ENG.). 208p. (J). (gr. 3-7). 12.99 (978-0-545-72338-1(8)) Scholastic, Inc.

Schroeder, Lisa. I Heart You, You Haunt Me. 2008. (ENG.). 240p. (YA). (gr. 9). pap. 10.99 (978-1-4169-5520-7(8), Simon Pulse) Simon Pulse.

Schutz, Samantha. You Are Not Here. 2010. (ENG.). 304p. (J). (gr. 9-18). 17.99 (978-0-545-16911-0(9), PUSH) Scholastic, Inc.

Schwiebert, Pat. We Were Gonna Have a Baby, but We Had an Angel Instead. Bills, Taylor, illus. 2004. 24p. pap. 7.95 (978-0-9724241-1-0(3), 717) Grief Watch.

Scott, Elizabeth. Love You Hate You Miss You. (ENG.). (YA). (gr. 8). 2010. 304p. pap. 8.99 (978-0-06-112285-9(8)) 2009. 288p. 16.99 (978-0-06-112283-5(1)) HarperCollins Pubs. (HarperTeen).

Scrimger, Richard. Me & Death: An Afterlife Adventure. 2010. (ENG.). 192p. (YA). (gr. 5). pap. 12.95 (978-0-88776-796-8(6), Tundra Bks.) Tundra Bks. CAN. Dist: Penguin Random Hse. LLC.

Seamon, Hollis. Somebody up There Hates You: A Novel. 2013. (ENG.). 256p. (YA). (gr. 8-12). 16.95 (978-1-61620-260-6(2), 73260) Algonquin Bks. of Chapel Hill.

Selzer, Adam. Just Kill Me. 2016. (ENG., Illus.). 336p. (YA). (gr. 9). 17.99 (978-1-4814-3494-2(2), Simon & Schuster Bks. For Young Readers) Simon & Schuster Bks. For Young Readers.

Serle, Rebecca. The Edge of Falling. 2014. (ENG., Illus.). 304p. (YA). (gr. 9). 17.99 (978-1-4424-3316-8(7), Simon Pulse) Simon Pulse.

Shaw, Susan. One of the Survivors. (ENG.). 208p. (J). (gr. 5-9). 2011. pap. 6.99 (978-1-4169-6389-9(8)) 2009. 15.99 (978-1-4169-6129-1(1)) McElderry, Margaret K. Bks. (McElderry, Margaret K. Bks.).

Sheinmel, Courtney. Positively. 2010. (ENG.). 240p. (J). (gr. 4-9). pap. 6.99 (978-1-4424-0622-3(4), Simon & Schuster Bks. For Young Readers) Simon & Schuster Bks. For Young Readers.

Shelton, Dave. Thirteen Chairs. (ENG.). 256p. (J). (gr. 7). 2016. pap. 9.99 (978-1-338-03248-2(8)) 2015. (Illus.). 17.99 (978-0-545-81665-6(3)) Scholastic, Inc.

Shepard, Sara. Never Have I Ever. (Lying Game Ser.: 2). (ENG.). (YA). (gr. 9). 2012. 336p. pap. 9.99 (978-0-06-186973-0(2)) 2011. 320p. 16.99 (978-0-06-186972-3(4)) HarperCollins Pubs. (HarperTeen).

Shepherd, Megan. The Secret Horses of Briar Hill. 2016. (ENG., Illus.). 240p. (J). (gr. 5). 16.99 (978-1-101-93975-8(3), Delacorte Bks. for Young Readers) Random Hse. Children's Bks.

Sherrard, Valerie. Kate. 2003. (ENG.). 200p. (YA). pap. 8.99 (978-1-55002-476-0(0)) Dundurn CAN. Dist: Ingram Publisher Services.

Shewver, Margaret. Without a Trace & Other Stories. 2005. 91p. (YA). (gr. 6-12). pap. 17.95 (978-0-936389-59-2(1)) Tudor Pubs., Inc.

Shireman, Abbie. The Fish Tank. 2012. 20p. pap. 17.99 (978-1-4772-8173-4(8)) AuthorHouse.

Shriver, Maria. What's Heaven? 2004. (Illus.). (J). (gr. k-3). spiral bd. (978-0-616-03056-1(8)) Canadian National Institute for the Blind/Institut National Canadien pour les Aveugles.

Shusterman, Neal. Antsy Does Time. 2010. (ENG.). 256p. (J). (gr. 5-18). pap. 6.99 (978-0-14-241487-3(5), Puffin Books) Penguin Young Readers Group.

—Chasing Forgiveness. 2015. (ENG., Illus.). 240p. (YA). (gr. 7). pap. 9.99 (978-1-4814-2991-7(4)) Simon & Schuster Children's Publishing.

—Everfound. 2012. (Skinjacker Trilogy Ser.: 3). (ENG.). 528p. (YA). (gr. 7). pap. 11.99 (978-1-4169-9050-5(X), Simon & Schuster Bks. For Young Readers) Simon & Schuster Bks. For Young Readers.

—Everlost. (Skinjacker Trilogy Ser.: 1). (ENG.). (YA). (gr. 7). 2009. 336p. pap. 11.99 (978-1-4169-9749-8(0)) 2006. 320p. 19.99 (978-0-689-87237-2(2)) Simon & Schuster Bks. For Young Readers. (Simon & Schuster Bks. For Young Readers).

—Everlost. rev. l.t. ed. 2007. (Skinjacker Trilogy: Bk. 1). 413p. (YA). (gr. 8-12). 22.95 (978-0-7862-9365-0(9)) Thorndike Pr.

—Everwild. 2009. (Skinjacker Trilogy Ser.: 2). (ENG., Illus.). 432p. (YA). (gr. 7-18). 18.99 (978-1-4169-5863-5(0), Simon & Schuster Bks. For Young Readers) Simon & Schuster Bks. For Young Readers.

—Scythe. 2016. (Arc of a Scythe Ser.: 1). (ENG., Illus.). 448p. (YA). (gr. 7). 18.99 (978-1-4424-7242-6(1), Simon & Schuster Bks. For Young Readers) Simon & Schuster Bks. For Young Readers.

Signor Sr., S. Ernest. The Book of Ruth. 2013. 52p. pap. 20.99 (978-1-4525-7311-3(5)) Balboa Pr.

Silberberg, Alan. Milo: Sticky Notes & Brain Freeze. Silberberg, Alan, illus. (ENG., Illus.). 288p. (J). (gr. 4-8). 2011. pap. 7.99 (978-1-4169-9431-2(9)) 2010. 15.99 (978-1-4169-9430-5(0)) Simon & Schuster Children's Publishing. (Aladdin).

Silvera, Adam. They Both Die at the End. 2017. 384p. (YA). (gr. 9). 17.99 (978-0-06-245779-0(9)) HarperCollins Pubs.

Singleton, Linda Joy. Dead Girl in Love. 2009. (Dead Girl Ser.: 3). (ENG.). 288p. (YA). pap. 9.95 (978-0-7387-1407-3(0), B06XZ9TSKM, Flux) North Star Editions.

—Dead Girl Walking. 2008. (Dead Girl Ser.: 1). (ENG.). 312p. (YA). (gr. 8-18). pap. 9.95 (978-0-7387-1405-9(4), Flux) North Star Editions.

Sinykin, Sheri. Giving up the Ghost, 1 vol. 2011. (ENG.). 240p. (YA). pap. 7.95 (978-1-56145-572-0(5)) Peachtree Pubs.

Skofield, James. Bear & Bird. Thermes, Jennifer, illus. 2014. (ENG.). 40p. (J). (gr. 1-3). 15.99 (978-1-58536-835-8(0), 203012) Sleeping Bear Pr.

Smelcer, John. The Great Death. 2009. (ENG.). 176p. (YA). (gr. 5-9). 17.99 (978-0-8050-8100-8(3), 9780805081008, Holt, Henry & Co. Bks. For Young Readers) Holt, Henry & Co.

Smith, Andrew. The Alex Crow. 2015. (ENG.). 336p. (YA). (gr. 9). 18.99 (978-0-525-42653-0(1), Dutton Books for Young Readers) Penguin Young Readers Group.

—The Alex Crow. 2016. lib. bdg. 22.10 (978-0-606-38854-2(0)) Turtleback Bks.

—Ghost Medicine. 2010. (ENG.). 384p. (YA). (gr. 8-13). pap. 18.99 (978-0-312-62912-0(5)) Square Fish.

Smith, Lane. Return to Augie Hobble. 2015. (ENG., Illus.). 288p. (J). (gr. 3-7). 16.99 (978-1-62672-054-1(1), 9781626720541) Roaring Brook Pr.

—Return to Augie Hobble. 2017. (J). lib. bdg. 18.40 (978-0-606-38550-3(9)) Turtleback Bks.

Smith, Tamara Ellis. Another Kind of Hurricane. 2015. (ENG.). 336p. (J). (gr. 4-7). 19.99 (978-0-553-51194-9(7)); 16.99 (978-0-553-51193-2(9)) Random Hse. Children's Bks. (Schwartz & Wade Bks.).

Smith, Walter. Grandad's Ashes. 2007. (ENG., Illus.). 32p. (gr. -1-3). 15.95 (978-1-84310-517-6(9), 4937) Kingsley, Jessica Pubs. GBR. Dist: Macmillan Distribution Ltd.

Sneve, Virginia Driving Hawk & Sneve, Virginia. Lana's Lakota Moons. 2007. (ENG., Illus.). 127p. (gr. 3-7). pap. 14.95 (978-0-8032-6028-3(8), Bison Bks.) Univ. of Nebraska Pr.

Snow, Carol. Switch. 2009. (ENG.). 240p. (YA). (gr. 8). pap. 8.99 (978-0-06-145210-9(6), HarperTeen) HarperCollins Pubs.

Spencer, Katherine. Saving Grace. 2007. (Saving Grace Ser.). (ENG., Illus.). 256p. (YA). (gr. 7-12). pap. 15.95 (978-0-15-206096-1(0)) Houghton Mifflin Harcourt Publishing Co.

Spillebeen, Geert. Kipling's Choice. Edelstein, Terese, tr. 2007. (ENG.). 160p. (YA). (gr. 7-9). pap. 12.95 (978-0-618-80035-3(2)) Houghton Mifflin Harcourt Publishing Co.

—Kipling's Choice. Edelstein, Terese, tr. 2007. 147p. (YA). (gr. 7-9). 15.65 (978-0-7569-8061-0(5)) Perfection Learning Corp.

Stalick, Garyanna. Cocoa's Collar, 1 vol. Goodwin, Wendy, illus. 2010. 36p. pap. 24.95 (978-1-4489-1888-1(X)) America Star Bks.

Standiford, Natalie. How to Say Goodbye in Robot. 2009. (ENG.). 288p. (J). (gr. 7-18). 17.99 (978-0-545-10708-2(3), Scholastic Pr.) Scholastic, Inc.

Staniszewski, Anna. Finders Reapers. 2016. (Switched at First Kiss Ser.: 2). (ENG.). 272p. (J). (gr. 5-8). pap. 7.99 (978-1-4926-1549-1(8), Sourcebooks Jabberwocky) Sourcebooks, Inc.

—I'm with Cupid. 2015. (Switched at First Kiss Ser.: 1). (ENG.). 240p. (J). (gr. 5-8). pap. 7.99 (978-1-4926-1546-0(3), 9781492615460, Sourcebooks Jabberwocky) Sourcebooks, Inc.

—Match Me If You Can. 2017. (Switched at First Kiss Ser.: 3). (ENG.). 240p. (J). (gr. 5-8). pap. 7.99 (978-1-4926-1552-1(8), 9781492615521, Sourcebooks Jabberwocky) Sourcebooks, Inc.

Steele, James M. Sadie Listens: An Inward Journey. l.t. ed. 2003. (Inward Journey Ser.: Vol. 1). (Illus.). iv, 48p. 17.95 (978-0-9716811-3-2(9)) Steele Studios.

Stevenson, Sarah Jamila. The Truth Against the World. 2014. (ENG.). 360p. (YA). pap. 9.99 (978-0-7387-4058-4(6), Flux) North Star Editions.

Stever, Susan. When Fairies Die. 2010. 28p. pap. 13.99 (978-1-4520-0912-4(0)) AuthorHouse.

Steveson, Nanci Turner. Georgia Rules. 2017. 272p. (J). (gr. 3-7). 16.99 (978-0-06-237457-8(5)) HarperCollins Pubs.

Stinson, Kathy. What Happened to Ivy, 1 vol. 2012. (ENG.). 256p. (YA). (gr. 6-9). pap. 11.95 (978-1-926920-81-8(3)) Second Story Pr. CAN. Dist: Orca Bk. Pubs. USA.

Stork, Francisco X. Irises. 2012. (YA). pap. (978-0-545-15136-8(8)); (ENG.). 304p. (J). (gr. 9). 17.99 (978-0-545-15135-1(X)) Scholastic, Inc. (Levine, Arthur A. Bks.).

Strange, Jason. Basement of the Undead, 1 vol. Parks, Phil, illus. 2011. (Jason Strange Ser.). (ENG.). 72p. (gr. 2-3). pap. 6.25 (978-1-4342-3433-9(9)); lib. bdg. 25.32 (978-1-4342-3234-2(4)) Stone Arch Bks.

Suzhen, Fang. Grandma Lives in a Perfume Village. Danowski, Sonja, illus. 2015. (ENG.). 48p. (J). 19.95 (978-0-7358-4216-8(7)) North-South Bks., Inc.

Tate, Nikki. Fallout, 1 vol. 2011. (Orca Soundings Ser.). (ENG.). 128p. (YA). (gr. 8-12). lib. bdg. 16.95 (978-1-55469-976-6(2)) Orca Bk. Pubs. USA.

Terrell, Brandon. Limbo's Diner. 2015. (Tartan House Ser.). (ENG., Illus.). 96p. (J). (gr. 5-12). (978-1-63235-164-7(1), 12-Story Library) Pr. Room Editions LLC.

Thiel, Annie. Chloe Loses Her Pet. Edwards, W M, illus. 2007. (Playdate Kids: Let's Be Friends! Ser.). 26p. (J). per. 6.95 (978-1-933721-21-7(9)) Playdate Kids Publishing.

Thiel Annie. The Playdate Kids Chloe Loses Her Pet. 2007. 32p. 12.95 (978-1-933721-00-2(6)) Playdate Kids Publishing.

Thong, Roseanne Greenfield. The Wishing Tree. McLennan, Connie, illus. 2004. (Wishing Tree Ser.). 32p. (J). (gr. -1-3). 16.95 (978-1-885008-26-8(0), Shen's Bks.) Lee & Low Bks., Inc.

Thottam, Meena, adapted by. Death, Where are You? 2006. (J). 3.95 (978-0-9776917-5-3(6), Curcumin Bks.) Davlaw Press.

Tinsley, Helen. Me & My Grandma: A Story for Children about AIDS. 2012.Tr. of 32. (Illus.). 34p. (J). pap. 14.95 (978-1-937622-21-3(5), Nefu Bks.) Africana Homestead Legacy Pubs., Inc.

Toon, Paige. The Accidental Life of Jessie Jefferson. 2016. (Jessie Jefferson Novels Ser.: 1). (ENG.). 336p. (J). pap. 9.99 (978-1-4711-4582-7(4), Simon & Schuster Children's) Simon & Schuster, Ltd. GBR. Dist: Simon & Schuster, Inc.

Town, Nathan. Ned Stapleton & the Wrath of the Death Gods. 2006. 174p. (YA). (978-0-9781040-0-9(5)) Emerald City Storytellers.

Trembath, Don. Rooster, 1 vol. 2005. (ENG.). 208p. (YA). (gr. 8-12). per. 15.00 (978-1-55143-261-8(7)) Orca Bk. Pubs. USA.

Tullson, Diane. Riley Park, 1 vol. 2009. (Orca Soundings Ser.). (ENG.). 128p. (YA). (gr. 8-12). pap. 9.95 (978-1-55469-123-4(0)) Orca Bk. Pubs. USA.

Turk, et al. 7 Days to Die. 2007. (Clifton Ser.: 3). (ENG., Illus.). 48p. (J). (gr. 4-7). per. 9.99 (978-1-905460-08-3(2)) CineBook GBR. Dist: National Bk. Network.

Turner, Amber McRee. Circa Now. 2014. (ENG., Illus.). 288p. (J). (gr. 3-7). 16.99 (978-1-4231-7639-8(1)) Hyperion Bks. for Children.

Urban, Linda. The Center of Everything. (ENG.). 208p. (J). (gr. 5-7). 2015. pap. 7.99 (978-0-544-34069-5(8), HMH Books For Young Readers) 2013. 15.99 (978-0-547-76348-4(4)) Houghton Mifflin Harcourt Publishing Co.

Valdes, Alisa. The Temptation. 2012. (ENG.). 320p. (YA). (gr. 9). pap. 8.99 (978-0-06-202420-6(5), HarperTeen) HarperCollins Pubs.

Valentine, Jenny. Me, the Missing, & the Dead. 2010. 224p. (YA). (gr. 9). pap. 8.99 (978-0-06-085070-8(1), HarperTeen) HarperCollins Pubs.

Van Draanen, Wendelin. Sammy Keyes & the Cold Hard Cash. 2010. (Sammy Keyes Ser.: Bk. 12). (ENG.). 320p. (J). (gr. 5-7). 8.99 (978-0-440-42113-9(6), Yearling) Random Hse. Children's Bks.

Van Tol, Alex. Redline, 1 vol. 2011. (Orca Soundings Ser.). (ENG.). (YA). (gr. 8-12). 136p. pap. 9.95 (978-1-55469-893-6(6)); 128p. lib. bdg. 16.95 (978-1-55469-894-3(4)) Orca Bk. Pubs. USA.

Verday, Jessica. The Hidden. (ENG.). 400p. (YA). (gr. 9). 2012. pap. 12.99 (978-1-4169-7898-5(4)) 2011. 17.99 (978-1-4169-7897-8(6)) Simon Pulse. (Simon Pulse).

Verne, Jules. The English at the North Pole. 2009. 160p. 24.95 (978-1-60664-684-7(2)); pap. 13.95 (978-1-60664-313-6(4)) Rodgers, Alan Bks.

Villareal, Ray. On the Other Side of the Bridge. 2014. (ENG.). 227p. (J). pap. 11.95 (978-1-55885-802-2(4), Piñata Books) Arte Publico Pr.

Volponi, Paul. Homestretch. 2009. (ENG.). 160p. (YA). (gr. 7-18). 16.99 (978-1-4169-3987-0(3), Atheneum Bks. for Young Readers) Simon & Schuster Children's Publishing.

—Rooftop. 2007. (ENG.). 224p. (YA). (gr. 7-18). 6.99 (978-0-14-240844-5(1), Puffin Books) Penguin Young Readers Group.

—Rooftop. 2007. 199p. 17.00 (978-0-7569-7958-4(7)) Perfection Learning Corp.

Walde, Christine. The Candy Darlings. 2006. (ENG.). 310p. (YA). (gr. 9-12). per. 18.95 (978-0-618-58969-2(4)) Houghton Mifflin Harcourt Publishing Co.

Wall, Pauline & Smith, Shelley. What the Mouse Saw: An Easter Story. 2013. 20p. pap. 16.82 (978-1-4669-3503-7(0)) Trafford Publishing.

Wallace, Bill. No Dogs Allowed! 2004. (ENG.). 214p. (J). (gr. 4-6). tchr. ed. 16.95 (978-0-8234-1818-3(9)) Holiday Hse., Inc.

Wallach, Diana Rodriguez. Proof of Lies. 2017. (Anastasia Phoenix Ser.). (ENG.). 400p. (YA). pap. 9.99 (978-1-63375-608-3(4), 9781633756083) Entangled Publishing, LLC.

Wallach, Tommy & Smith, Ali. Thanks for the Trouble. 2016. (ENG., Illus.). 288p. (YA). (gr. 9). 17.99 (978-1-4814-1880-5(7), Simon & Schuster Bks. For Young Readers) Simon & Schuster Bks. For Young Readers.

Walsh, Barbara. Sammy in the Sky. Wyeth, Jamie, illus. 2011. (ENG.). 32p. (J). (gr. -1-3). 16.99 (978-0-7636-4927-2(9)) Candlewick Pr.

Walton, K. M. Ultimatum. 2017. (ENG.). 320p. (YA). (gr. 7-12). 17.99 (978-1-4926-3507-9(3), 9781492635079) Sourcebooks, Inc.

Ward, Rachel. The Chaos. 2011. (Numbers Ser.: 2). (ENG.). 352p. (J). (gr. 9-9). 17.99 (978-0-545-24269-1(X), Chicken Hse., The) Scholastic, Inc.

—Infinity: 2012. (Numbers Ser.: 3). (ENG.). 256p. (J). (gr. 9-9). 17.99 (978-0-545-35092-1(1), Chicken Hse., The) Scholastic, Inc.

—Numbers. 2010. (Numbers Ser.: 1). (ENG.). 336p. (J). (gr. 7-12). 17.99 (978-0-545-14299-1(7), Chicken Hse., The) Scholastic, Inc.

Warwillow, Lucas D. Marick's Cross, 1 vol. 2010. 48p. pap. 16.95 (978-1-61546-563-7(4)) America Star Bks.

Wasserman, Robin. The Waking Dark. 2013. (ENG.). 464p. (YA). (gr. 9). 17.99 (978-0-375-86877-1(1), Knopf Bks. for Young Readers) Random Hse. Children's Bks.

Watt, Cliff. Jenny Brown & the Search for Eusebio's Star. 2008. 77p. pap. 19.95 (978-1-60672-169-8(0)) America Star Bks.

Weingarten, Lynn. Suicide Notes from Beautiful Girls. (ENG., Illus.). 336p. (YA). (gr. 9). 2016. pap. 10.99 (978-1-4814-1858-4(0)) 2015. 17.99 (978-1-4814-1853-9(X)) Simon Pulse. (Simon Pulse).

—Suicide Notes from Beautiful Girls. 2016. (ENG.). (YA). (gr. 9). lib. bdg. 22.10 **(978-0-606-39882-4(1))** Turtleback Bks.

Welford, Ross. Time Traveling with a Hamster. 2016. (ENG.). 432p. (J). (gr. 3-7). 16.99 (978-0-399-55149-9(2), Schwartz & Wade Bks.) Random Hse. Children's Bks.

Welsh, Phoebe. Wonder What Do First Day Heaven. 2006. 70p. pap. 16.95 (978-0-9769618-1-9(4)) Less is More Publishing, LLC.

West, Carly Anne. The Murmurings. (ENG., 384p. (YA). (gr. 9). 2014. Illus.). pap. 11.99 (978-1-4424-4180-4(1)) 2013. 16.99 (978-1-4424-4179-8(8)) Simon Pulse. (Simon Pulse).

Westerfeld, Scott. Afterworlds. 2014. (ENG., Illus.). 608p. (YA). (gr. 9). 19.99 (978-1-4814-2234-5(0), Simon Pulse) Simon Pulse.

Whaley, John Corey. Noggin. (ENG., Illus.). (YA). (gr. 9). 2015. 368p. pap. 12.99 (978-1-4424-5873-4(9)) 2014. 352p. 18.99 (978-1-4424-5872-7(0)) Simon & Schuster Children's Publishing. (Atheneum Bks. for Young Readers).

Whelan, Gloria. A Time to Keep Silent. 2004. 144p. (J). pap. 8.00 (978-0-8028-5255-7(6)) Eerdmans, William B. Publishing Co.

When Aunt Mattie Got Her Wings. 2014. (ENG., Illus.). 32p. (J). (gr. -1-3). 17.99 (978-1-4814-1044-1(X), Beach Lane Bks.) Beach Lane Bks.

Whitcomb, Laura. The Fetch. 2010. (ENG.). 384p. (YA). (gr. 7). pap. 20.99 (978-0-547-41163-7(4)) Houghton Mifflin Harcourt Publishing Co.

Wild, Margaret. Old Pig. Brooks, Ron, illus. 2017. (ENG.). 32p. (J). (gr. -1-1). 17.99 **(978-1-76029-389-5(X))** Allen & Unwin AUS. Dist: Independent Pubs. Group.

Wiles, Deborah. The Aurora County All-Stars. (ENG., Illus.). 256p. (J). 2009. (gr. 2-5). pap. 7.99 (978-0-15-206626-0(8)) 2007. (gr. 5-7). 16.00 (978-0-15-206068-8(5)) Houghton Mifflin Harcourt Publishing Co.

—Each Little Bird That Sings. 2006. (ENG., Illus.). 288p. (J). (gr. 2-5). reprint ed. pap. 7.99 (978-0-15-205657-5(2)) Houghton Mifflin Harcourt Publishing Co.

—Love, Ruby Lavender. 2005. (ENG., Illus.). 240p. (J). (gr. 2-5). reprint ed. pap. 7.99 (978-0-15-205478-6(2)) Houghton Mifflin Harcourt Publishing Co.

—Love, Ruby Lavender. 2004. 216p. (J). (gr. 3-7). pap. 36.00 incl. audio (978-0-8072-2096-2(5), Listening Library) Random Hse. Audio Publishing Group.

Williams, Erika. Through the Shattered Glass, 1 vol. 2010. 62p. pap. 19.95 (978-1-4489-5149-9(6)) America Star Bks.

Williams-Garcia, Rita. Clayton Byrd Goes Underground. Morrison, Frank, illus. 2017. 176p. (J). (gr. 3-7). 16.99 (978-0-06-221591-8(4)); (ENG.). E-Book (978-0-06-221594-9(9)) HarperCollins Pubs. (Amistad).

Williams, Lori Aurelia. Broken China. 2006. (ENG., Illus.). 272p. (YA). (gr. 7-12). reprint ed. mass mkt. 7.99 (978-1-4169-1618-5(0), Simon Pulse) Simon Pulse.

Willie's Reflection: A Story of Grief, Hope & Healing. 2008. (Illus.). 32p. (J). 15.95 (978-0-9799021-0-9(X)) Aspire Publishing.

Wilson, Wayne L. Kate, the Ghost Dog: Coping with the Death of a Pet. Soud, illus. 2009. 48p. (J). (gr. 3-8). 14.95 (978-1-4338-0554-7(5)); pap. 9.95 (978-1-4338-0555-4(3)) American Psychological Assn. (Magination Pr.).

Wittlinger, Ellen. Blind Faith. 2007. (ENG.). 304p. (YA). (gr. 7-12). pap. 9.99 (978-1-4169-4906-0(2), Simon & Schuster Bks. For Young Readers) Simon & Schuster Bks. For Young Readers.

Wood, Debra. Just A Little Child. Blake, Joshua Aaron, illus. l.t. ed. 2006. 33p. (J). per. 12.95 (978-1-59879-087-0(0)) Lifevest Publishing, Inc.

Wood, Douglas. Aunt Mary's Rose. Shed, Greg & Pham, LeUyen, illus. 2010. (ENG.). 32p. (J). (gr. -1-3). 16.99 (978-0-7636-1090-6(9)) Candlewick Pr.

—Grandad's Prayers of the Earth. Lynch, P. J., illus. 2009. 32p. pap. 6.99 (978-0-7636-1865-0(9)); (ENG.). (J). (gr. 1-4). pap. 7.99 (978-0-7636-4675-2(X)) Candlewick Pr.

—Grandad's Prayers of the Earth. Lynch, P. J., illus. 2004. 28p. (J). (gr. k-4). reprint ed. 17.00 (978-0-7567-7101-0(3)) DIANE Publishing Co.

Woodson, Jacqueline. Behind You. 2010. (ENG.). 176p. (YA). (gr. 7-18). 7.99 (978-0-14-241554-2(5), Puffin Books) Penguin Young Readers Group.

—Behind You. 2010. lib. bdg. 18.40 (978-0-606-14598-5(2), Turtleback) Turtleback Bks.

—If You Come Softly & Behind You. 2010. (ENG.). 352p. (YA). (gr. 7-18). 8.99 (978-0-14-241918-2(4), Puffin Books) Penguin Young Readers Group.

Wung-Sung, Jesper. The Last Execution. Van R, Lin, tr. from DAN. 2016. (ENG., Illus.). 144p. (YA). (gr. 9). 17.99 (978-1-4814-2965-8(5), Atheneum/Caitlyn Dlouhy Books) Simon & Schuster Children's Publishing.

Yabroff, Jennie. If You Were Here. 2017. (ENG.). 272p. (YA). 17.99 (978-1-5072-0002-5(1), Simon Pulse) Simon Pulse.

Yates, Alexander. The Winter Place. 2015. (ENG., Illus.). 448p. (YA). (gr. 9). 17.99 (978-1-4814-1981-9(1)) Simon & Schuster Children's Publishing.

York, Kelley & Altwood, Rowan. Other Breakable Things. 2017. (ENG.). 306p. (YA). pap. 9.99 (978-1-63375-594-9(0), 9781633755949) Entangled Publishing, LLC.

Young, Suzanne. The Epidemic. 2016. (Program Ser.: 4). (ENG., Illus.). 384p. (YA). (gr. 9). 17.99 (978-1-4814-4470-5(0), Simon Pulse) Simon Pulse.

—Hotel for the Lost. 2016. (ENG., Illus.). 304p. (YA). (gr. 9). pap. 10.99 (978-1-4814-2301-4(0), Simon Pulse) Simon Pulse.

—Hotel Ruby. 2015. (ENG., Illus.). 288p. (YA). (gr. 9). 17.99 (978-1-4814-2300-7(2), Simon Pulse) Simon Pulse.

—The Remedy. 2015. (Program Ser.: 3). (ENG., Illus.). 416p. (YA). (gr. 9). 17.99 (978-1-4814-3765-3(8), Simon Pulse) Simon Pulse.

Young, Tonya. Here's to the Nights. 2011. 190p. pap. 19.99 (978-1-4628-8707-1(4)) Xlibris Corp.

Yovanoff, Brenna. The Replacement. 2011. (ENG.). 368p. (YA). (gr. 7-18). 8.99 (978-1-59514-381-5(5), Razorbill) Penguin Young Readers Group.

Zaugg, Sandra L. Secret of the Yellow Van: A Book about Dealing with Loss. 2008. (J). pap. 8.99 (978-0-8163-2246-6(5)) Pacific Pr. Publishing Assn.

Zevin, Gabrielle. Elsewhere. 2007. 288p. (gr. 7). 20.00 (978-0-7569-8191-4(3)) Perfection Learning Corp.

—Elsewhere. 2007. (ENG.). 304p. (YA). (gr. 7). per. 9.99 (978-0-312-36746-6(5), 9780312367466) Square Fish.

Zimmerman, George G. Dougie & the Dane: Chelsea the Great Dane. 2004. (Illus.). 36p. 21.99 (978-1-4134-4139-0(4)) Xlibris Corp.

Zorka, Shawna. Carter Goes to a Funeral, 1 vol. Reyes, Arlene, illus. 2009. 47p. pap. 24.95 (978-1-60836-785-6(1)) America Star Bks.

Zorn, Claire. Protected. 2017. (ENG.). 288p. (YA). (gr. 6-12). 17.99 **(978-1-4926-5213-7(X))** Sourcebooks, Inc.

Zusak, Markus. The Book Thief. 2014. (ENG.). 576p. (YA). 17.24 (978-1-63245-052-4(6)) Lectorum Pubns., Inc.

—The Book Thief. 2009. 12.64 (978-0-7848-1941-8(6), Everbind) Marco Bk. Co.

—The Book Thief. 2008. 552p. (gr. 7-12). 23.00 (978-0-7569-8440-3(8)) Perfection Learning Corp.

—The Book Thief. (ENG., Illus.). (YA). (gr. 7). 2016. 592p. lib. bdg. 22.99 (978-0-399-55652-4(4)) 2007. 592p. pap. 12.99 (978-0-375-84220-7(9)) 2013. 576p. pap. 12.99 (978-0-385-75472-9(8)) 2016. 592p. 19.99 (978-1-101-93418-0(2)) Random Hse. Children's Bks. (Knopf Bks. for Young Readers).

—The Book Thief. l.t. ed. 2006. (ENG.). 552p. 23.99 (978-1-4104-6806-2(2)); 757p. (YA). (gr. 7-12). 24.95 (978-0-7862-9021-5(8)) Thorndike Pr.

—The Book Thief. 2008. (ENG., Illus.). 560p. pap. (978-0-552-77389-8(1), Black Swan) Transworld Publishers Ltd.

—The Book Thief. 2007. 552p. lib. bdg. 24.50 (978-1-4177-9738-7(X)) 2013. lib. bdg. 24.50 (978-0-606-34656-6(2)) Turtleback Bks. (Turtleback).

—La Ladrona de Libros. 2010. (Vintage Espanol Ser.).Tr. of Book Thief. (SPA.). 544p. (YA). (gr. 7). pap. 12.99 *(978-0-307-47573-2(5),* Vintage Espanol) Knopf Doubleday Publishing Group.

DEATH, MERCY

see Euthanasia

DEATH PENALTY

see Capital Punishment

DEATH VALLEY (CALIF. AND NEV.)

Besel, Jennifer M. The Hottest Places on Earth. 2010. (Extreme Planet Ser.). (ENG.). 24p. (gr. 1-2). lib. bdg. 25.32 *(978-1-4296-3964-4(4),* First Facts) Capstone Press of Coughlan Cos.

Cooper, Jason. Death Valley. Date not set. (Natural Wonders Discovery Library). 24p. (J). (gr. k-4). lib. bdg. 10.95 *(978-0-86625-015-3(8))* Rourke Educational Media.

Frisch, Nate. Death Valley National Park. 2013. (Illus.). 48p. (J). 35.65 *(978-1-60818-194-0(4),* Creative Education) Creative Co., The.

Gilbert, Sara. Death Valley. 2016. (Illus.). 22p. (J). *(978-1-60818-630-3(X),* Creative Education) Creative Co., The.

Guzman, Sienna. Visiting Death Valley: Represent & Interpret Data. 2014. (Rosen Common Core Math Readers Ser.). (ENG.). 24p. (J). (gr. 3-4). pap. 8.25 *(978-1-4777-4909-8(8),* Rosen Classroom) Rosen Publishing Group, Inc., The.

Hamilton, John. Death Valley National Park. 2008. (National Parks Set II Ser.). 32p. (gr. 4-9). 27.07 *(978-1-60453-091-9(X),* Abdo & Daughters) ABDO Publishing Co.

Rice, William. El Desierto Del Valle de la Muerte. 2017. (TIME for Kids en Español - Level 3 Ser.). (SPA.). 32p. (gr. 3-3). lib. bdg. 31.99 ***(978-1-5157-5179-3(1))*** Time for Kids Inc AUS. Dist: Capstone Pub.

Rice, William B. Death Valley Desert, 1 vol. 2nd rev. ed. 2012. (Nonfiction Readers Ser.). (ENG.). 32p. (J). (gr. 3-3). pap. 8.99 *(978-1-4333-3672-0(3))* Teacher Created Materials, Inc.

Robson, Gary D. Who Pooped in the Park? Scat & Tracks for Kids. Rath, Robert, illus. 2008. 48p. (J). (gr. 3-7). pap. 9.95 *(978-1-56037-403-9(9))* Farcountry Pr.

Vail, Grace. Death Valley. 2014. (Scariest Places on Earth Ser.). 24p. (J). (gr. 2-5). 22.60 *(978-1-4824-1146-1(6))* Stevens, Gareth Publishing LLLP.

DEBATES AND DEBATING

see also Parliamentary Practice

ABDO Publishing Company Staff. Essential Viewpoints, 1, Set. 2007. (Essential Viewpoints Set 1 Ser.: 8). (ENG.). (J). (gr. 6-12). lib. bdg. 285.12 *(978-1-59928-856-7(7),* Essential Library) ABDO Publishing Co.

Athans, Sandra K. & Parente, Robin W. Tips & Tricks for Evaluating an Argument & Its Claims. 2014. (Common Core Readiness Guide to Reading Ser.). 80p. (YA). (gr. 5-8). 32.95 *(978-1-4777-7559-2(5))* Rosen Publishing Group, Inc., The.

Burgett, Cindy. Policy Debate. (National Forensic League Library of Public Speaking & Debate Ser.). 48p. (gr. 5-5). 2009. 53.00 *(978-1-60854-048-8(0),* Rosen Reference) 2007. (Illus.). (J). lib. bdg. 29.25 *(978-1-4042-1024-0(5))* Rosen Publishing Group, Inc., The.

Duffy, Claire. The Australian Schoolkids' Guide to Debating & Public Speaking. 2015. (ENG., Illus.). 192p. pap. 26.99 *(978-1-74223-423-6(2),* UNSW Press) NewSouth Publishing AUS. Dist: Independent Pubs. Group.

Gottfried Hollander, Barbara. Participating in Plays, Skits, & Debates with Cool New Digital Tools. 2013. (Way Beyond PowerPoint: Making 21st Century Presentations Ser.). 48p. (J). (gr. 5-8). 29.95 *(978-1-4777-1838-4(9));* pap. 11.75 *(978-1-4777-1849-0(4))* Rosen Publishing Group, Inc., The. (Rosen Reference).

Great Historic Debates & Speeches, 6 Bks, Set. 2004. (J). 175.50 *(978-1-4042-0350-1(8))* Rosen Publishing Group, Inc., The.

Open for Debate Group 3, 5 bks., Set. Incl. Affirmative Action. Kowalski, Kathiann M. lib. bdg. 42.79 *(978-0-7614-2300-3(1));* Arab-Israeli Conflict. Worth, Richard. lib. bdg. 42.79 *(978-0-7614-2295-2(1));* Marriage. Stefoff, Rebecca. lib. bdg. 42.79 *(978-0-7614-2299-0(4));* Media Bias. Streissguth, Thomas. lib. bdg. 42.79 *(978-0-7614-2296-9(X));* Racial Profiling. Kops, Deborah. lib. bdg. 42.79 *(978-0-7614-2298-3(6));* (Illus.). 128p. (gr. 7-7). (Open for Debate 3 Ser.). 2006. Set lib. bdg. 213.93 *(978-0-7614-2294-5(3),* Benchmark Bks.) Marshall Cavendish Corp.

Orr, Tamra B. Extraordinary Debates. 2006. (F.W. Prep Ser.). (ENG., Illus.). 128p. (YA). (gr. 8-13). pap. 9.95 *(978-0-531-13905-9(0))* Scholastic Library Publishing.

Participating in Plays, Skits, & Debates with Cool New Digital Tools. 2013. (Way Beyond PowerPoint: Making 21st Century Presentations Ser.). 48p. (J). (gr. 5-8). pap. 70.50 *(978-1-4777-1850-6(8),* Rosen Reference) Rosen Publishing Group, Inc., The.

Raum, Elizabeth, et al. Let's Think About, 1 vol. 2014. (Let's Think About Ser.). (ENG.). 48p. (gr. 3-6). 133.28 *(978-1-4846-0294-2(3),* Heinemann InfoSearch) Heinemann-Raintree.

Rowell, Rebecca. Perspectives Flip Books: Issues. 2015. (Perspectives Flip Books: Issues Ser.). (ENG.). 64p. (gr. 5-6). lib. bdg. 135.96 *(978-0-7565-5062-2(9),* CPB Grades 4-8) Compass Point Bks.

Roy, Jennifer Rozines & Haney, Johannah. Sharpen Your Debate & Speech Writing Skills. 2011. (Sharpen Your Writing Skills Ser.). (Illus.). 64p. (J). (gr. 6-18). pap. 8.95 *(978-1-59845-341-6(6));* lib. bdg. 29.27 *(978-0-7660-3904-9(8))* Enslow Pubs., Inc.

Stearman, Kaye, et al. Ethical Debates. 2007. (J). 159.00 *(978-1-4042-1106-3(3),* Rosen Reference) Rosen Publishing Group, Inc., The.

Touchstones Discussion Project, prod. Touchpebbles Volume A - Student's Guide, Vol. A. 2003. 76p. per. 17.95 *(978-1-878461-65-0(6))* Touchstones Discussion Project.

—Touchpebbles Volume A - Teacher's Guide, Vol. A. 2003. 234p. tchr. ed., per. 34.95 *(978-1-878461-64-3(8))* Touchstones Discussion Project.

—Touchpebbles Volume B - Teacher's Guide, Vol. B. 2003. per., instr.'s gde. ed. 34.95 *(978-1-878461-66-7(4))* Touchstones Discussion Project.

Walker, Kevin. Learning a Second Language, Yes or No. 2016. (Seeing Both Sides Ser.). (ENG.). 32p. (gr. 3-6). 32.79 *(978-1-68191-386-5(0))* Rourke Educational Media.

Wolfson, Jonathan. The Great Debate! Freedom to Communicate! A Handbook for Policy Debate. 2003. 144p. per. 25.00 *(978-0-9746398-1-9(8))* LightningBolt Pr.

DEBORAH (BIBLICAL JUDGE)

Rottmann, Erik. Deborah Saves the Day. Marchesi, Stephen, illus. 2008. (Arch Bks.). 16p. (J). (gr. k-4). pap. 1.99 *(978-0-7586-1457-5(8))* Concordia Publishing Hse.

DEBS, EUGENE V. (EUGENE VICTOR), 1855-1926

Carey, Charles W. Eugene V. Debs: Outspoken Labor Leader & Socialist. 2003. (Historical American Biographies Ser.). (Illus.). 128p. (J). lib. bdg. 26.60 *(978-0-7660-1979-9(9))* Enslow Pubs., Inc.

DEBTS, PUBLIC

Fisanick, Christina. Debt. Greenhaven Press Editors, ed. 2013. (Introducing Issues with Opposing Viewpoints Ser.). (ENG., Illus.). 144p. (gr. 7-10). 42.00 *(978-0-7377-5673-9(X))* Cengage Gale.

Furgang, Kathy & Furgang, Adam. Understanding Budget Deficits & the National Debt. 2011. (Real World Economics Ser.). (ENG.). 80p. (YA). (gr. 7-12). lib. bdg. 33.25 *(978-1-4488-5570-4(5))* Rosen Publishing Group, Inc., The.

Lynette, Rachel. What to Do When Your Family Is in Debt. 2010. (Let's Work It Out Ser.). 24p. (J). (ENG.). pap. 8.25 *(978-1-4358-9770-0(6),* PowerKids Pr.); (Illus.). (gr. 2-5). lib. bdg. 22.60 *(978-1-4358-9341-2(7))* Rosen Publishing Group, Inc., The.

DEBUSSY, CLAUDE, 1862-1918

Babin, Pierre. Debussy, 1 vol. Voake, Charlotte, illus. 2012. (First Discovery Music Ser.). (ENG.). 28p. (J). (gr. 2-6). 19.99 *(978-1-85103-321-8(1))* Moonlight Publishing, Ltd. GBR. Dist: Independent Pubs. Group.

DECALOGUE

see Ten Commandments

DECATHLON

Page, Jason. Decathlon, High Jump, & Other Field Events. 2008. (Olympic Sports Ser.). (ENG., Illus.). 32p. (J). (gr. 3-7). pap. *(978-0-7787-4031-5(5))* Crabtree Publishing Co.

DECIMAL SYSTEM

Adler, David A. Place Value. Miller, Edward, illus. (ENG.). 32p. (J). (gr. k-3). 2017. 7.99 *(978-0-8234-3770-2(1))* 2016. 17.95 *(978-0-8234-3550-0(4))* Holiday Hse., Inc.

Aihara, Masaaki & Sarris, Eno, eds. Grade 4 Decimals & Fractions: Kumon Math Workbooks. 2008. (J). per. 7.95 *(978-1-933241-58-6(6))* Kumon Publishing North America, Inc.

—Grade 5 Decimals & Fractions: Kumon Math Workbooks. 2008. (J). per. 7.95 *(978-1-933241-59-3(4))* Kumon Publishing North America, Inc.

Cleary, Brian P. Do You Know Dewey? Exploring the Dewey Decimal System. Lew-Vriethoff, Joanne, illus. 2012. (Millbrook Picture Bks). (ENG.). 32p. (J). (gr. 2-5). lib. bdg. 22.60 *(978-0-7613-6676-8(8),* Millbrook Pr.) Lerner Publishing Group.

Collins Easy Learning, Collins Easy. Fractions & Decimals Bumper Book Ages 7-9. 2017. (Collins Easy Learning KS2 Ser.). (ENG.). 64p. (J). (gr. 2-4). pap. 9.99 ***(978-0-00-821243-8(0))*** HarperCollins Pubs. Ltd. GBR. Dist: Independent Pubs. Group.

Day, Amelia. Olivia's Ocean Adventure. 2013. (Core Math Skills: Numbers & Operations in Base 10 Ser.). 24p. (J). (gr. 1-2). 22.60 *(978-1-4777-2222-0(X),* Rosen Classroom) Rosen Publishing Group, Inc., The.

—Olivia's Ocean Adventure: Understand Place Value. 2013. (Rosen Math Readers Ser.). (ENG.). 24p. (J). (gr. 1-2). pap. 8.25 *(978-1-4777-2037-0(5));* pap. 49.50 *(978-1-4777-2038-7(3))* Rosen Publishing Group, Inc., The. (Rosen Classroom).

Findlay, Diane. Digging into Dewey. 2005. (Illus.). 126p. (J). pap. 16.95 *(978-1-932146-18-9(0),* Upstart Bks.) Highsmith Inc.

Kleist, Nick. Super Sports Numbers: Understand Place Value. 2014. (Math Masters: Number & Operations in Base Ten Ser.). 24p. (J). (gr. 2-3). 23.60 *(978-1-4777-6401-5(1));* (ENG.). pap. 8.25 *(978-1-4777-4666-0(8))* Rosen Publishing Group, Inc., The. (Rosen Classroom).

Kompelien, Tracy. Can You Count More Than Before?, 1 vol. 2007. (Math Made Fun Ser.). (ENG., Illus.). 24p. (J). (gr. k-3). lib. bdg. 24.21 *(978-1-59928-511-5(8),* SandCastle) ABDO Publishing Co.

New Decimal Dog. 2004. (J). *(978-1-59242-144-2(X))* Delta Education, LLC.

O'Donnell, Kerri. A Trip Around the World: Using Expanded Notation to Represent Numbers. (PowerMath Ser.). 24p. 2009. (gr. 3-4). pap. 8.25 *(978-0-8239-8871-6(6))* 2009. (gr. 3-4). 45.00 *(978-1-60851-377-2(7))* 2004. (J). lib. bdg. 22.50 *(978-0-8239-8966-9(6))* Rosen Publishing Group, Inc., The. (PowerKids Pr.).

Piddock, Claire. Decimals. 2010. (My Path to Math Ser.). (ENG., Illus.). 24p. (J). (gr. k-3). *(978-0-7787-6781-7(7),* 1317362); pap. *(978-0-7787-6790-9(6),* 1317362) Crabtree Publishing Co.

Steck-Vaughn Staff. Focus on Math Level F: Decimals. 2005. pap. 2.99 *(978-1-4190-0284-7(8))* Harcourt Schl. Pubs.

—Focus on Math Level F 10-pack: Decimals. 2005. pap. 29.95 *(978-1-4190-0308-0(9))* Harcourt Schl. Pubs.

—Top Line Math: Decimals. 2005. pap. 5.49 *(978-1-4190-0367-7(4));* pap., tchr. ed. 5.95 *(978-1-4190-0377-6(1))* Harcourt Schl. Pubs.

Wells, Robert E. Can You Count to a Googol? 2012. (J). *(978-1-61913-144-6(7))* Weigl Pubs., Inc.

Zuravicky, Orli. When There Were Dinosaurs: Using Expanded Notation to Represent Numbers in the Millions. (PowerMath Ser.). 32p. 2009. (ENG., Illus.). (gr. 4-5). pap. 10.00 *(978-0-8239-8901-0(1))* 2009. (gr. 4-5). 47.90 *(978-1-60851-404-5(8))* 2004. (Illus.). (J). lib. bdg. 25.25 *(978-0-8239-8988-1(7))* Rosen Publishing Group, Inc., The. (PowerKids Pr.).

DECISION MAKING

Adams, Phillip G. Decisions, Decisions, Decisions. 2004. 160p. per. 12.95 *(978-0-9762723-0-4(X))* Rhizoo Publishing.

Anderson, W. M. Talking about Making Good Choices. 2010. (Healthy Living Ser.). (Illus.). 32p. (J). (gr. 3-6). lib. bdg. 26.00 *(978-1-4339-3660-9(7))* Stevens, Gareth Publishing LLLP.

Baptiste, Tracey & Banas, Sharon L. Being a Leader & Making Decisions. 2009. (Character Education Ser.). (Illus.). 136p. (gr. 6-12). 35.00 *(978-1-60413-125-3(X),* Chelsea Hse.) Facts On File, Inc.

Barrett, Selby. The Diva Code Diary. 2007. 152p. pap. 19.48 *(978-0-615-15832-7(3))* Pick Me Up N Go Publishing Co.

Brezina, Corona. Great Decision-Making Skills. (Work Readiness Ser.). 64p. 2009. (gr. 6-6). 58.50 *(978-1-60854-823-1(6))* 2008. (Illus.). (J). (gr. 3-7). lib. bdg. 31.95 *(978-1-4042-1422-4(4))* Rosen Publishing Group, Inc., The.

Burstein, John. I Said No! Refusal Skills. 2009. (Slim Goodbody's Life Skills 101 Ser.). (ENG., Illus.). 32p. (J). (gr. 3-6). pap. *(978-0-7787-4805-2(7),* 1302928); lib. bdg. *(978-0-7787-4789-5(1),* 1302928) Crabtree Publishing Co.

—What Should I Do? Making Good Decisions. 2009. (Slim Goodbody's Life Skills 101 Ser.). (ENG., Illus.). 32p. (J). (gr. 3-6). pap. *(978-0-7787-4807-6(3),* 1302929); lib. bdg. *(978-0-7787-4791-8(3),* 1302929) Crabtree Publishing Co.

Cavell-Clarke, Steffi. Making Good Choices. 2017. (Illus.). 24p. (J). ***(978-0-7787-3262-4(2))*** Crabtree Publishing Co.

Covey, Stephen R. & Covey, Sean. The 6 Most Important Decisions You'll Ever Make: A Guide for Teens. 2006. (ENG., Illus.). 336p. (gr. 8-18). pap. 16.99 *(978-0-7432-6504-1(1),* Touchstone) Touchstone.

Ennis, Pat. Becoming a Young Woman Who Pleases God: A Teen's Guide to Discovering Her Biblical Potential. 2009. (Illus.). 160p. pap. 14.99 *(978-1-59669-240-4(5))* New Hope Pubs.

Free Spirit Publishing. What If? In a Jar: Questions & Dilemmas to Get Kids Thinking about Choices. 2017. (In a Jar(r) Ser.). (ENG.). (J). (gr. 3-6). 9.99 ***(978-1-63198-202-6(8))*** Free Spirit Publishing, Inc.

Harris, Michelle & Beer, Julie. This or That 4: Even More Wacky Choices to Reveal the Hidden You. 2016. (ENG., Illus.). 176p. (J). (gr. 3-7). pap. 12.99 *(978-1-4263-2345-4(X),* National Geographic Children's Bks.) National Geographic Society.

Hirschfeld, Leila & Hirschfeld, Tom. You Decide, Ben Franklin! Weber, Lisa K., illus. 2016. (J). pap. *(978-0-553-50952-6(7),* Salamander Bks.) Pavilion Bks.

Holt, Rinehart and Winston Staff. Decisions for Health Blue: Decision-Making. 4th ed. Date not set. pap., wbk. ed. 7.20 *(978-0-03-068356-5(4))* Holt McDougal.

Hugel, Bob. I Did It Without Thinking: True Stories about Impulsive Decisions That Changed Lives. 2008. (Scholastic Choices Ser.). (ENG.). 112p. (J). pap. 8.95 *(978-0-531-20526-6(6),* Watts, Franklin); (Illus.). (gr. 3-7). 27.00 *(978-0-531-13868-7(2),* Children's Pr.) Scholastic Library Publishing.

Human Relations Media, prod. Clued in! on Saying No. 2005. (ENG.). 32p. (J). pap. 4.95 *(978-1-55548-051-6(9),* 675) Human Relations Media.

Jackson, Sharinese. Choices. 2008. 44p. pap. 12.99 *(978-0-9815162-4-0(6))* Second Time Media & Communications.

—Choices: Upper Elementary. Nyamor, Eric, illus. 2010. 112p. pap. 12.95 *(978-0-9840660-3-2(9))* Second Time Media & Communications.

Kopp, Megan. Above & Beyond with Critical Thinking & Problem Solving. 2016. (Fueling Your Future! Going above & Beyond in the 21st Cent Ser.). (ENG.). 48p. (J). (gr. 5-8). *(978-0-7787-2842-9(0))* Crabtree Publishing Co.

Machen Pritchard, M. Ann. Phil the Pill & Friends: Making Positive Choices. Machen Pritchard, M. Ann, illus. 2005. (Illus.). 75p. (J). per. 11.99 *(978-0-9772210-0-4(8),* Phil the Pill & Friends) MAMP Creations.

Matlock, Mark. Wisdom On... Friends, Dating, & Relationships, 1 vol. 2008. (Wisdom Ser.). (ENG.). 144p. (YA). (gr. 7-14). pap. 9.99 *(978-0-310-27927-3(5))* Zondervan.

—Wisdom On... Making Good Decisions, 1 vol. 2008. (Invert Ser.). (ENG.). 144p. (YA). (gr. 7-14). pap. 9.99 *(978-0-310-27926-6(7))* Zondervan.

McCumbee, Stephie. The Garden in My Mind: Growing Through Positive Choices. Griffin, Lisa M., illus. 2014. (ENG.). 40p. (J). pap. 12.95 *(978-1-934490-54-9(7))* Boys Town Pr.

—The Garden in My Mind Activity Guide: Lessons for Social Skill & Common Core Development. Griffin, Lisa M., illus. 2014. (ENG.). 48p. pap. 20.95 *(978-1-934490-55-6(5))* Boys Town Pr.

Miller, Connie Colwell. You Can Control Your Voice: Loud or Quiet? Victoria Assanelli, illus. 2017. (Making Good Choices Ser.). (ENG.). 24p. (J). (gr. 1-4). 20.95 ***(978-1-68151-167-2(3),*** Amicus Illustrated) Amicus Publishing.

—You Can Handle Conflict: Hands or Words? Victoria Assanelli, illus. 2017. (Making Good Choices Ser.). (ENG.). 24p. (J). (gr. 1-4). 20.95 ***(978-1-68151-162-7(2),*** Amicus Illustrated) Amicus Publishing.

—You Can Stay in Control: Wild or Calm? Victoria Assanelli, illus. 2017. (Making Good Choices Ser.). (ENG.). 24p. (J). (gr. 1-4). 20.95 ***(978-1-68151-165-8(7),*** Amicus Illustrated) Amicus Publishing.

—You're Angry: Throw a Fit or Talk It Out? Victoria Assanelli, illus. 2017. (Making Good Choices Ser.). (ENG.). 24p. (J). (gr. 1-4). 20.95 ***(978-1-68151-164-1(9),*** Amicus Illustrated) Amicus Publishing.

—You're in Trouble: Fib or Truth? Victoria Assanelli, illus. 2017. (Making Good Choices Ser.). (ENG.). 24p. (J). (gr. 1-4). 20.95 ***(978-1-68151-163-4(0),*** Amicus Illustrated) Amicus Publishing.

Miller, Tiwana Mutch. Positive Outweighs Negative. 2007. (J). per. 10.00 *(978-0-9788937-1-2(9))* Amani Publishing, LLC.

Moore, Carol-Lynne. Movement & Making Decision: The Body-Mind Connection in the Workplace. 2009. (Contemporary Discourse on Movement & Dance Ser.). 144p. (gr. 9-9). 43.90 *(978-1-61511-922-6(1),* Dance & Movement Pr.) Rosen Publishing Group, Inc., The.

Parker, Vic. Making Choices. 2016. (Exploring Citizenship Ser.). (ENG.). 32p. pap. 8.29 *(978-1-4846-4000-5(4),* Heinemann First Library) Heinemann-Raintree.

—Tomar Decisiones, 1 vol. 2010. (Explorar el Civismo Ser.). (SPA & ENG.). 32p. (gr. 1-3). 27.32 *(978-1-4329-4464-3(9));* pap. 8.29 *(978-1-4329-4472-8(X))* Heinemann-Raintree.

Paxen Learning Staff. Decisions. 2007. (YA). pap. 52.50 *(978-1-934350-13-3(3))* Paxen Publishing LLC.

Raatma, Lucia. Making Smart Choices. 2013. (True Book(tm), a — Guides to Life Ser.). (ENG., Illus.). 48p. (J). lib. bdg. 31.00 *(978-0-531-25524-7(7));* pap. 6.95 *(978-0-531-23924-7(1))* Scholastic Library Publishing.

Rissman, Rebecca. Should Theo Say Thank You? Being Respectful, 1 vol. 2013. (What Would You Do? Ser.). (ENG.). 24p. (gr. -1-1). pap. 6.29 *(978-1-4329-7246-2(4));* lib. bdg. 22.65 *(978-1-4329-7240-0(5))* Heinemann-Raintree. (Acorn).

Rowe, Brooke. What Color Is Your Aura? 2016. (Best Quiz Ever Ser.). (ENG.). 32p. (J). (gr. 4-8). 29.93 *(978-1-63471-106-7(8),* 208535, 45th Parallel Press) Cherry Lake Publishing.

Schwartz, Heather E. Freedom Riders: A Primary Source Exploration of the Struggle for Racial Justice, 1 vol. 2014. (We Shall Overcome Ser.). (ENG.). 32p. (gr. 3-4). pap. 7.95 *(978-1-4914-0231-3(8))* Capstone Press of Coughlan Cos.

—Make Good Choices: Your Guide to Making Healthy Decisions. 2011. (Healthy Me Ser.). (ENG.). 32p. (gr. 3-4). pap. 47.70 *(978-1-4296-7296-2(X));* lib. bdg. 27.99 *(978-1-4296-6546-9(7))* Capstone Press of Coughlan Cos. (Snap Bks.).

Straight Talk About Sex, Gender & Media. (YA). (gr. 6-8). 69.95 *(978-1-55942-198-0(3),* 9240V9) Witcher Productions.

Welbourn, Shannon. Step Forward with Responsible Decision-Making. 2016. (Step Forward! Ser.). (ENG., Illus.). 24p. (J). (gr. 2-5). *(978-0-7787-2769-9(6))* Crabtree Publishing Co.

You Choose: Set 2. 2017. (You Choose Ser.). 32p. (gr. 2-2). pap. 42.08 ***(978-0-7660-8899-3(5));*** lib. bdg. 101.08 ***(978-0-7660-8076-8(5))*** Enslow Pubs., Inc.

DECLARATION OF INDEPENDENCE

see United States—Declaration of Independence

DECORATION, INTERIOR

see Interior Decoration

DECORATION AND ORNAMENT

see also Art, Decorative; Design; Design, Decorative; Enamel and Enameling; Flower Arrangement; Furniture; Gems; Illustration of Books; Interior Decoration; Jewelry; Leatherwork; Lettering; Metal-Work; Mosaics; Pottery; Sculpture; Tapestry; Wood-Carving

Adler, Jonathan. Patterns. 2014. (J). *(978-1-4197-1224-1(1))* Abrams, Inc.

Beak, Nick Huckleberry. How to Bend Balloons. 2013. (ENG., Illus.). 64p. (J). (gr. 3-7). 9.99 *(978-1-84322-864-6(5),* Armadillo) Anness Publishing GBR. Dist: National Bk. Network.

Braden, Linda. Mason Jar Crafts for Kids: More Than 25 Cool, Crafty Projects to Make for Your Friends, Your Family, & Yourself! 2015. (ENG., Illus.). 160p. (J). (gr. 1). pap. 14.99 *(978-1-63220-413-4(4),* Sky Pony Pr.) Skyhorse Publishing Co., Inc.

Felix, Rebecca. Mini Decorating. 2017. (Mini Makers Ser.). (ENG.). 32p. (J). (gr. 2-5). 12.99 ***(978-1-5124-3834-5(0),*** Lerner Pubns.); 39.99 ***(978-1-5124-3833-8(2),*** Lerner Pubns.); 39.99 ***(978-1-5124-2810-0(8),*** Lerner Pubns.); (Illus.). 26.65 *(978-1-5124-2632-8(6))* Lerner Publishing Group.

Fields, Stella. Decorating Projects for a Lazy Crafternoon. 2016. (Lazy Crafternoon Ser.). (ENG.). 32p. (gr. 3-4). lib. bdg. 27.99 *(978-1-5157-1435-4(7),* Snap Bks.) Capstone Press of Coughlan Cos.

—Party Planning for a Lazy Crafternoon. 2016. (Lazy Crafternoon Ser.). (ENG.). 32p. (gr. 3-4). lib. bdg. 27.99 *(978-1-5157-1437-8(3),* Snap Bks.) Capstone Press of Coughlan Cos.

Fontichiaro, Kristin. Hacking Fashion: T- Shirts. 2015. (21st Century Skills Innovation Library: Makers As Innovators Ser.). (ENG.). 32p. (J). (gr. 4-8). 29.93 *(978-1-63188-871-7(4),* 206064) Cherry Lake Publishing.

Hill, Isabel. Urban Animals of Washington, D. C. Hill, Isabel, photos by. 2013. (ENG., Illus.). (J). 17.99 *(978-1-59572-658-2(6))* Star Bright Bks., Inc.

Hill, Isabel T. Urban Animals, 1 vol. Hill, Isabel T., photos by. 2009. (ENG., Illus.). 32p. (J). (gr. 2-7). 17.95 *(978-1-59572-209-6(2));* pap. 7.95 *(978-1-59572-210-2(6))* Star Bright Bks., Inc.

Kachidurian, Debbie, et al. Bring on the Bling! Bracelets, Anklets, & Rings for All Occasions. 2016. (Accessorize Yourself! Ser.). (ENG., Illus.). 48p. (gr. 4-5). lib. bdg. 34.65 *(978-1-4914-8231-5(1))* Capstone Press of Coughlan Cos.

Kachidurian, Debbie Prestine, et al. Bring on the Bling! Bracelets, Anklets, & Rings for All Occasions. 2017. (Illus.). 47p. (J). pap. *(978-1-4914-8621-4(X))* Capstone Press of Coughlan Cos.

Lim, Annalees. Decorative Card Crafts, 01 vols., 1. 2016. (10-Minute Crafts Ser.). (ENG., Illus.). 24p. (J). pap. 10.60 *(978-1-5081-9081-3(X),* 1397684, Windmill Bks.) Rosen Publishing Group, Inc., The.

—Printing Crafts, Vol. 1. 2014. (Craft Attack! Ser.). 32p. (J). (gr. 3-5). 26.60 *(978-1-4824-0215-5(7));* pap. 10.50 *(978-1-4824-3300-5(1))* Stevens, Gareth Publishing LLLP.

McGee, Randel. Paper Crafts for Mardi Gras. 2011. (Paper Craft Fun for Holidays Ser.). (Illus.). 48p. (J). (gr. 2-5). lib. bdg. 25.27 *(978-0-7660-3724-3(X))* Enslow Pubs., Inc.

Moore Niver, Heather. Cool Careers Without College for People Who Can Build Things. 2013. (New Cool Careers Without College Ser.). (Illus.). 144p. (J). (gr. 7-12). 35.95 *(978-1-4777-1824-7(9))* Rosen Publishing Group, Inc., The.

Nail Art. 2008. (ENG.). 26p. 16.95 *(978-1-59174-595-2(0),* Klutz Certified) Klutz.

Noble, Marty. Decorative Tile Designs. 2006. (Dover Design Coloring Bks.). (ENG., Illus.). 32p. (gr. 3-8). 3.99 *(978-0-486-45195-4(X))* Dover Pubns., Inc.

Obrochta, Dale. Faces, Faces, Balloon Faces. 2003. (Illus.). 32p. (YA). *(978-0-9728793-0-9(7))* DEO Consulting, Inc.

Peterson, Megan Cooley & Rustad, Martha E. H. Kid Style: Cool Clothes for You!, 1 vol. 2014. (Make It Mine Ser.). (ENG.). 24p. (gr. k-1). lib. bdg. 26.65 *(978-1-4765-3971-3(5),* Pebble Plus) Capstone Press of Coughlan Cos.

C
D

—Kid Style: Rockin' Bedrooms for You!, 1 vol. 2014. (Make It Mine Ser.). (ENG.). 24p. (gr. k-1). lib. bdg. 26.65 *(978-1-4765-3970-6(7)*, Pebble Plus) Capstone Press of Coughlan Cos.

—Kid Style: Sweet Shoes for You!, 1 vol. 2014. (Make It Mine Ser.). (ENG.). 24p. (gr. k-1). lib. bdg. 26.65 *(978-1-4765-3968-3(5)*, Pebble Plus) Capstone Press of Coughlan Cos.

Rau, Dana Meachen. Decorating Eggs. 2012. (How-To Library). (ENG.). 32p. (gr. 3-6). 28.50 *(978-1-61080-474-5(0)*, 202084); pap. 14.21 *(978-1-61080-648-0(4)*, 202258) Cherry Lake Publishing.

—Having Fun with Hair Feathering. Petelinsek, Kathleen, illus. 2015. (How-To Library). (ENG.). 32p. (J). (gr. 3-6). 29.93 *(978-1-63362-371-2(8)*, 206904) Cherry Lake Publishing.

Rogers, Kirsteen & Everall, Nayera. Patterns Coloring Book. 2011. (Coloring Books Ser.). 26p. (J). pap. 5.99 *(978-0-7945-2967-3(4)*, Usborne) EDC Publishing.

Sieplinga, Drew. Paint Your Own Piggy Bank. 2007. (Illus.). 32p. (J). *(978-0-545-02112-8(X))* Scholastic, Inc.

Spilsbury, Richard. Decorated Pottery. 2009. (Stories in Art Ser.). (Illus.). 30p. (J). lib. bdg. 26.50 *(978-1-4042-4437-5(9)*, PowerKids Pr.) Rosen Publishing Group, Inc., The.

Trueit, Trudi Strain. Birthday Crafts. Gallagher-Cole, Mernie, illus. 2016. (Holiday Crafts Ser.). (ENG.). 24p. (J). (gr. k-3). 28.50 *(978-1-5038-0815-7(7)*, 210651) Child's World, Inc., The.

Trusty, Brad & Trusty, Cindy. The Kids' Guide to Balloon Twisting, 1 vol. 2010. (Kids' Guides). (ENG.). 32p. (gr. 3-4). lib. bdg. 27.99 *(978-1-4296-5444-9(9)*, Edge Bks.) Capstone Press of Coughlan Cos.

DECORATION ART

see Art, Decorative

DECORATIVE ARTS

see Art, Decorative; Art Industries and Trade; Decoration and Ornament; Design, Decorative; Interior Decoration

DEDUCTION LOGIC

see Logic

DEEP DIVING

see also Scuba Diving; Skin Diving

Arroyo, Sheri, et al. How Deep Sea Divers Use Math. 2009. (Math in the Real World Ser.). 32p. (gr. 4-6). 28.00 *(978-1-60413-611-1(1)*, Chelsea Clubhouse) Facts On File, Inc.

Cerullo, Mary M. Searching for Great White Sharks: A Shark Diver's Quest for Mr. Big, 1 vol. Rotman, Jeffrey L., photos by. 2014. (Shark Expedition Ser.). (ENG., Illus.). 40p. (gr. 5-7). lib. bdg. 31.99 *(978-0-7565-4884-1(5))* Compass Point Bks.

—Seeking Giant Sharks: A Shark Diver's Quest for Whale Sharks, Basking Sharks, & Manta Rays, 1 vol. Rotman, Jeffrey L., illus. Rotman, Jeffrey L., photos by. 2014. (Shark Expedition Ser.). (ENG.). 40p. (gr. 5-7). lib. bdg. 31.99 *(978-0-7565-4885-8(3))* Compass Point Bks.

—Sharks of the Deep: A Shark Photographer's Search for Sharks at the Bottom of the Sea, 1 vol. Rotman, Jeffrey L., illus. Rotman, Jeffrey L., photos by. 2014. (Shark Expedition Ser.). (ENG.). 40p. (gr. 5-7). lib. bdg. 31.99 *(978-0-7565-4886-5(1))* Compass Point Bks.

Chapman, Simon. Under the Sea. Chapman, Simon, illus. 2005. (Illus.). 112p. (J). lib. bdg. 20.00 *(978-1-4242-0631-5(6))* Fitzgerald Bks.

Marsh, Nigel. Exploring Shipwrecks. 2016. (ENG., Illus.). 48p. (J). (gr. 3-4). 14.99 *(978-1-921580-17-8(8))* New Holland Pubs. Pty. Ltd. AUS. Dist: Midpoint Trade Bks., Inc.

Matsen, Bradford. An Extreme Dive under the Antarctic Ice. 2003. (Incredible Deep-Sea Adventures Ser.). (Illus.). 48p. (J). lib. bdg. 25.27 *(978-0-7660-2190-7(4))* Enslow Pubs., Inc.

Pratt, Mary K. Exploring under the Sea, 1 vol. 2014. (Story of Exploration Ser.). (ENG.). 144p. (J). (gr. 6-12). lib. bdg. 37.07 *(978-1-62403-254-7(0)*, Essential Library) ABDO Publishing Co.

Westerskov, Kim, photos by. Diving in Antarctica. 2004. (Illus.). 32p. (J). *(978-0-7685-2384-3(2))* Dominie Pr., Inc.

DEEP-SEA TECHNOLOGY

see Oceanography

DEER

see also Reindeer

Barlow, Helen. Easy Read with Grandma Read: Book 1, Stage 3. 2009. (Illus.). 48p. pap. *(978-1-84748-507-6(3))* Athena Pr.

Beer, Amy-Jane. Deer. 2008. (Nature's Children Ser.). (Illus.). 52p. (J). *(978-0-7172-6253-3(7))* Grolier, Ltd.

Berger, Melvin & Berger, Gilda. Deer. 2010. (Illus.). 16p. (J). pap. *(978-0-545-24436-7(6))* Scholastic, Inc.

Bowman, Chris. White-Tailed Deer. 2015. (North American Animals Ser.). (ENG., Illus.). 24p. (J). (gr. k-3). lib. bdg. 25.95 *(978-1-62617-195-4(5)*, Blastoff! Readers) Bellwether Media.

Catt, Thessaly. Migrating with the Caribou. 2011. (Animal Journeys Ser.). (Illus.). 24p. (YA). (gr. 1-4). 22.60 *(978-1-4488-2541-7(5))* Rosen Publishing Group, Inc., The.

Chandler, Matt. Deer Hunting for Kids, 1 vol. 2012. (Into the Great Outdoors Ser.). (ENG., Illus.). 32p. (gr. 3-4). lib. bdg. 27.99 *(978-1-4296-8425-5(9)*, Edge Bks.) Capstone Press of Coughlan Cos.

Chandler, Matthew Allan. Deer Hunting for Kids, 1 vol. 2012. (Into the Great Outdoors Ser.). (ENG., Illus.). 32p. (gr. 3-4). pap. 7.95 *(978-1-4296-9267-0(7)*, Edge Bks.) Capstone Press of Coughlan Cos.

DiLorenzo, Michael A. Bows, Does & Bucks! An Introduction to Archery Deer Hunting. Julich, Jenniffer, illus. 2010. 88p. (J). 19.95 *(978-0-9777210-2-3(7))* Running Moose Publications.

Doudna, Kelly. It's a Baby White-Tailed Deer!, 1 vol. 2008. (Baby Mammals Ser.). (ENG., Illus.). 24p. (J). (gr. k-3). lib. bdg. 24.21 *(978-1-60453-033-9(2))* ABDO Publishing Co.

Fields, Shep. Deer & Fawns. 2017. (Animal Family Ser.). 24p. (gr. k-k). pap. 8.15 ***(978-1-4824-6373-6(3))*** Stevens, Gareth Publishing LLLP.

Galvin, Laura Gates. Fawn & Her Family. 2011. (Baby Animals (Soundprints) Ser.). (ENG., Illus.). 16p. (J). (gr. -1-k). 6.95 *(978-1-60727-283-0(0))* Soundprints.

George, Jean Craighead. Autumn Moon. 2003. (J). (gr. 3-7). 20.75 *(978-0-8446-7241-0(6))* Smith, Peter Pub., Inc.

Gilbert, Sara. Ice Age Mega Beasts: Stag-Moose. 2017. (Ice Age Mega Beasts Ser.). (ENG., Illus.). 24p. (J). (gr. 1-3). pap. 8.99 ***(978-1-62832-378-8(7)***, Creative Paperbacks) Creative Co., The.

Gilbert, Sara. Stag-Moose. 2017. (Illus.). 24p. (J). *(978-1-60818-770-6(5)*, Creative Education) Creative Co., The.

Graubart, Norman D. How to Track a Deer, 1 vol. 2015. (ENG., Illus.). 24p. (J). lib. bdg. 23.60 *(978-1-4777-5415-3(6)*, Windmill Bks.) Rosen Publishing Group, Inc., The.

Kalman, Bobbie. Baby Deer. 2008. (It's Fun to Learn about Baby Animals Ser.). (ENG., Illus.). 24p. (J). (gr. 3-7). pap. *(978-0-7787-3971-5(6))* Crabtree Publishing Co.

Kawa, Katie. Fawns. 2011. (Cute & Cuddly: Baby Animals Ser.). (Illus.). 24p. (gr. k-2). (J). pap. 8.15 *(978-1-4339-5544-0(X))*; (J). lib. bdg. 22.60 *(978-1-4339-5542-6(3))*; 69.20 *(978-1-4339-6896-9(7))* Stevens, Gareth Publishing LLLP.

Lake, G. G. White-Tailed Deer. 2016. (Woodland Wildlife Ser.). (ENG., Illus.). 24p. (gr. k-1). lib. bdg. 26.65 *(978-1-5157-0819-3(5)*, Pebble Plus) Capstone Press of Coughlan Cos.

Leach, Michael. Deer. 2009. (Animal Neighbors Ser.). 32p. (gr. k-5). pap. 10.60 *(978-1-4042-4573-0(1)*, Rosen Classroom); (Illus.). (J). lib. bdg. 25.25 *(978-1-4358-4996-9(5)*, PowerKids Pr.) Rosen Publishing Group, Inc., The.

Macken, JoAnn Early. Deer. 2nd rev. ed. 2009. (Animals That Live in the Forest Ser.). (ENG.). 24p. (J). (gr. -1-3). pap. 8.15 *(978-1-4339-2479-8(X))*; lib. bdg. 22.60 *(978-1-4339-2403-3(X))* Stevens, Gareth Publishing LLLP.

—Deer: Venados. 2nd rev. ed. 2009. (Animals That Live in the Forest/Animales del bosque Ser.). (ENG & SPA.). 24p. (J). (gr. -1-3). pap. 8.15 *(978-1-4339-2486-6(2))*; lib. bdg. 22.60 *(978-1-4339-2435-4(8))* Stevens, Gareth Publishing LLLP. (Weekly Reader Leveled Readers).

MacRae, Sloan. Deer Hunting. 2010. (Open Season Ser.). (ENG.). 32p. (J). pap. 10.00 *(978-1-4488-1381-0(6))*; lib. bdg. 25.25 *(978-1-4488-0710-9(7))* Rosen Publishing Group, Inc., The. (PowerKids Pr.).

Magby, Meryl. White-Tailed Deer. 2013. 24p. (J). (gr. k-5). 22.60 *(978-1-4777-0792-0(1))*; pap. 8.25 *(978-1-4777-0956-6(8))*; pap. 49.50 *(978-1-4777-0957-3(6))* Rosen Publishing Group, Inc., The. (PowerKids Pr.).

Mara, Wil. Deer. 2014. 32p. 28.50 *(978-1-62712-304-4(0))* Cavendish Square Publishing.

—Deer. 2008. (Animals Animals Ser.). (Illus.). 48p. (gr. 3-18). lib. bdg. 29.93 *(978-0-7614-2926-5(3)*, Benchmark Bks.) Marshall Cavendish Corp.

Marsico, Katie. White-Tailed Deer. 2014. (Nature's Children Ser.). (ENG.). 48p. (J). lib. bdg. 28.00 *(978-0-531-21230-1(0))* Scholastic Library Publishing.

McGill, Jordan. Deer. 2011. (J). 27.13 *(978-1-61690-936-9(6))* Weigl Pubs., Inc.

—Venados. 2012. (SPA.). (J). *(978-1-61913-193-4(5))* Weigl Pubs., Inc.

Migrating with the Caribou. 2011. (Animal Journeys Ser.). (Illus.). 24p. (J). pap. 8.25 *(978-1-4488-2666-7(7)*, PowerKids Pr.) Rosen Publishing Group, Inc., The.

Murray, Julie. Deer, 1 vol. 2005. (Animal Kingdom Set Ii Ser.). (ENG., Illus.). 24p. (gr. k-4). 25.65 *(978-1-59197-312-6(0)*, Buddy Bks.) ABDO Publishing Co.

Nelson, Robin. Deer. 2009. pap. 34.95 *(978-0-7613-4103-1(X))*; (ENG.). 24p. 23.93 *(978-0-7613-4067-6(X)*, Lerner Pubns.) Lerner Publishing Group.

O'Brien, Bridget. Deer. Keimig, Candice & LaViolette, Renee, illus. 2014. (Magic Readers Ser.). (ENG.). 24p. (J). (gr. 5-9). 24.21 *(978-1-62402-063-6(1))* ABDO Publishing Co.

—Deer Eat & Grow. Keimig, Candice & LaViolette, Renee, illus. 2014. (Magic Readers Ser.). (ENG.). 24p. (J). (gr. 5-9). 24.21 *(978-1-62402-064-3(X))* ABDO Publishing Co.

—Deer in the Woods. Keimig, Candice & LaViolette, Renee, illus. 2014. (Magic Readers Ser.). (ENG.). 24p. (J). (gr. 5-9). 24.21 *(978-1-62402-065-0(8))* ABDO Publishing Co.

Olson, Bethany. Baby Deer. 2013. (Super Cute! Ser.). (ENG., Illus.). 24p. (J). (gr. k-3). lib. bdg. 25.95 *(978-1-60014-925-2(1)*, Blastoff! Readers) Bellwether Media.

Open Court Staff. We Feed Deer. (J). pap. *(978-0-8126-1002-4(4)*, 61002) Open Court Publishing Co.

Patent, Dorothy Hinshaw. White-Tailed Deer. 2005. (Early Bird Nature Bks.). (J). 25.26 *(978-0-8225-3052-7(X)*, Lerner Pubns.) Lerner Publishing Group.

Pound, Blake. Deer Hunting. 2012. (Outdoor Adventures Ser.). (ENG., Illus.). 24p. (J). (gr. 3-8). lib. bdg. 25.95 *(978-1-60014-796-8(8)*, Pilot Bks.) Bellwether Media.

Raatma, Lucia. How Do We Live Together? Deer. 2010. (Community Connections: How Do We Live Together? Ser.). (ENG.). 24p. (gr. 2-5). lib. bdg. 25.64 *(978-1-60279-618-8(1)*, 200326) Cherry Lake Publishing.

Robertson, Charmaine. Deer Eat Buds & Leaves. 2016. (Rosen REAL Readers: STEM & STEAM Collection). 8p. (gr. 1-k). pap. 5.46 *(978-1-5081-2389-7(6)*, Rosen Classroom) Rosen Publishing Group, Inc., The.

Stefoff, Rebecca. Deer. 2007. (Animalways Ser.). (Illus.). 104p. (gr. 6-7). lib. bdg. 24.95 *(978-0-7614-2534-2(9)*, Benchmark Bks.) Marshall Cavendish Corp.

Webster, Christine. Deer. (J). 2012. 12.95 *(978-1-61913-263-4(X))* 2012. 27.13 *(978-1-61913-066-1(1))* 2007. (Illus.). 24p. (gr. -1-3). pap. 8.95 *(978-1-59036-676-9(X))* 2007. (Illus.). 24p. (gr. -1-3). lib. bdg. 24.45 *(978-1-59036-675-2(1))* Weigl Pubs., Inc.

Wendorff, Anne. Fawns. 2009. (Watch Animals Grow Ser.). (ENG., Illus.). 24p. (J). (gr. k-3). lib. bdg. 25.95 *(978-1-60014-240-6(0))* Bellwether Media.

—Fawns. 2009. (Blastoff! Readers Ser.). (ENG., Illus.). 24p. (J). (gr. k-3). 20.00 *(978-0-531-21628-6(4)*, Children's Pr.) Scholastic Library Publishing.

Wilsdon, Christina. White-Tailed Deer. 2006. (Illus.). 45p. (J). *(978-1-59939-073-4(6)*, Reader's Digest Young Families, Inc.) Studio Fun International.

Wilson, Christina & Wilsdon, Christina. Deer. 2009. (Amazing Animals Ser.). (ENG.). 48p. (J). (gr. 2-6). pap. 10.50 *(978-1-4339-2119-3(7)*, Gareth Stevens Learning Library); (YA). (gr. 3-6). lib. bdg. 28.00 *(978-0-8368-9115-7(5))* Stevens, Gareth Publishing LLLP.

Zobel, Derek. Deer. 2010. (Backyard Wildlife Ser.). (ENG., Illus.). 24p. (J). (gr. k-3). lib. bdg. 25.95 *(978-1-60014-440-0(3)*, Blastoff! Readers) Bellwether Media.

DEER—FICTION

Adams, Fernie. The Antelope Was a Beautiful Woman. 2012. 32p. pap. 19.99 *(978-1-4772-7401-9(4))* AuthorHouse.

Akkari, Hélène. Saving Kanki the Antelope. 2010. 20p. 11.49 *(978-1-4520-9156-3(0))* AuthorHouse.

Atlas, Lilly. Journey to the Deep Woods. 2008. 36p. pap. 16.99 *(978-1-4389-2596-7(4))* AuthorHouse.

Bailey, Carla R. A. Inner Beauty. 2013. 24p. pap. *(978-1-4602-1535-7(4))* FriesenPress.

Ballard, Lisa. A Moose for Mackenzie. Doucette, Constance, illus. 2008. 32p. pap. 24.95 *(978-1-60610-123-0(4))* America Star Bks.

Bambi: A Little Spring Shower. unabr. ed. Date not set. (My First Read Along Ser.). (Illus.). 18p. (J). 7.99 incl. audio *(978-1-55723-749-1(2))* Walt Disney Records.

Bartlett, Susan & Wrenn, Luanne. Opening Day, 1 vol. 2007. (ENG., Illus.). 32p. (gr. 1-4). 16.95 *(978-0-88448-288-8(X)*, 884288) Tilbury Hse. Pubs.

Blair's Deer. (Early Intervention Levels Ser.). 31.86 *(978-0-7362-0624-2(8))* CENGAGE Learning.

Brooks, Dawn Marie. Cat-Ice. 2004. 175p. pap. 13.95 *(978-0-7414-2240-8(9))* Infinity Publishing.

Bunce, Margaret. Adventures with Nature: A Story about Olivia & Her Little Dog, Jake. 2011. 24p. pap. 12.95 *(978-1-4567-2497-9(5))* AuthorHouse.

Burgess, Thornton W. The Adventures of Lightfoot the Deer. 2008. 108p. (gr. -1-3). 22.95 *(978-1-60664-951-0(5))*; 104p. per. 9.95 *(978-1-60312-501-7(9))* Aegypan.

—The Adventures of Lightfoot the Deer. (J). 19.95 *(978-0-8488-0393-3(0))* Amereon Ltd.

—The Adventures of Lightfoot the Deer. 2011. 108p. 23.95 *(978-1-4638-9556-3(9))* Rodgers, Alan Bks.

Burns, Joanne. Don't Fear Little Deer. 2005. 23p. (J). 9.99 *(978-1-4116-4798-5(X))* Lulu Pr., Inc.

Carpenter, Angie. Digewi Deer: The Tale of a Blind Deer. Berner Coble, Lynn, ed. 2013. 82p. (J). pap. 8.99 *(978-0-9846724-3-1(5))* Paws and Claws Publishing, LLC.

Chaffee, Allen. The Adventures of Fleet Foot & Her Fawns. 2007. 132p. 24.95 *(978-1-4344-9285-2(0))*; per. 14.95 *(978-1-4344-9284-5(2))* Wildside Pr., LLC.

Coates, Sue. Rusty: The Lame Reindeer. 2012. (Illus.). 12p. pap. 18.30 *(978-1-4772-3502-7(7))* AuthorHouse.

Collins, Pat Lowery. The Deer Watch. Slonim, David, illus. 2013. (ENG.). 32p. (J). (gr. -1-2). 15.99 *(978-0-7636-4890-9(6))* Candlewick Pr.

Davis, Izzy. The Croaks at Roaring River, 1 vol. 2009. 40p. pap. 24.95 *(978-1-60813-245-4(5))* America Star Bks.

The Deer & the Crocodile: Individual Title Six-Packs. (Literatura 2000 Ser.). (gr. 1-2). 28.00 *(978-0-7635-0130-3(1))* Rigby Education.

The Deer Report. 2005. (The Fawn Chapter Ser.). (J). 7.67 *(978-1-58453-311-5(0))* Pioneer Valley Bks.

Deshmukh, Manisha. Chinu's Day Out. 2008. 24p. pap. 11.49 *(978-1-4389-0601-0(3))* AuthorHouse.

Dharma Publishing Staff. The Spade Sage: The Story about Finding Happiness. 2nd ed. 2013. (ENG.). 36p. (gr. -1-7). pap. 8.95 *(978-0-89800-522-6(1))* Dharma Publishing.

Doerr, Bonnie J. Kenzie's Key. Aberle, Xylena Apotheloz, illus. 2003. 211p. (J). 16.95 *(978-0-9619155-6-8(0))* Laurel & Herbert, Inc.

Erickson, Mary Ellen. What Happened to the Deer? Peanut Butter Club Mysteries. 2007. 182p. (J). 23.95 *(978-0-595-68396-3(7))*; per. 13.95 *(978-0-595-42799-4(5))* iUniverse, Inc.

Fitzgerald, J. Rupert, the Sturdy Oak Tree: Who thought he was a little better than the other Trees. 2010. 16p. (J). pap. 14.95 *(978-1-4327-5734-2(2))* Outskirts Pr., Inc.

Fleury, Barbara. The Runaway Deer. 2008. (Illus.). 36p. (J). pap. 8.95 *(978-0-9728155-9-8(7))* CONVERPAGE.

Gigliotti, Sallie B. I'm Sorry, Said Denny. 2009. 20p. pap. 10.99 *(978-1-4343-9999-1(0))* AuthorHouse.

Gilchrist, J. Into the Land of Nede. 2010. 108p. (gr. 4-6). 20.95 *(978-1-4502-5433-5(0))*; pap. 10.95 *(978-1-4502-5432-8(2))* iUniverse, Inc.

Gilleland, Linda. I Love You, Baby Deer. Irish, Leigh Ann, illus. 2012. 56p. 19.99 *(978-1-61254-025-2(2))* Brown Books Publishing Group.

Gillingham, Sara. In My Forest. Siminovich, Lorena, illus. 2010. (ENG.). 12p. (J). (gr. -1 — 1). bds. 8.99 *(978-0-8118-7566-0(0))* Chronicle Bks. LLC.

Gilroy, Caroline. Redolf. 2012. 48p. pap. 19.99 *(978-1-62419-072-8(3))* Salem Author Services.

Gordon, Gus. Herman & Rosie. Gordon, Gus, illus. 2013. (ENG., Illus.). 32p. (J). (gr. 2-5). 17.99 *(978-1-59643-856-9(8)*, 9781596438569) Roaring Brook Pr.

Griffin, C. R. Runt & the Two Roses. 2011. 24p. pap. 15.99 *(978-1-4628-4589-7(4))* Xlibris Corp.

Harrison, Paula. Secret Promise. 2013. (Rescue Princesses Ser.: 1). lib. bdg. 14.75 *(978-0-606-31986-7(7)*, Turtleback) Turtleback Bks.

Hodson, Ann. Ben the Deer. 2009. (Illus.). 44p. pap. 16.99 *(978-1-4389-7965-6(7))* AuthorHouse.

Hughes, Mónica. Little Mouse Deer & the Crocodile. Moricuchi, Mique, illus. 2004. 24p. (J). lib. bdg. 23.65 *(978-1-59646-684-5(7))* Dingles & Co.

—More Little Mouse Deer Tales. Clemenston, John, illus. 2005. 24p. (J). lib. bdg. 23.65 *(978-1-59646-730-9(4))* Dingles & Co.

Jones, Janey Louise. Farrah the Shy Fawn. Poh, Jennie, illus. 2016. (Superfairies Ser.). (ENG.). 56p. (gr. k-3). lib. bdg. 23.99 *(978-1-5158-0432-1(1))* Picture Window Bks.

Joyce, Rita. Deer of the Dawn. 2004. (Illus.). 40p. (J). per. 8.95 *(978-1-59094-067-9(9)*, Jawbreakers for Kids) Jawbone Publishing Corp.

Kalar, Bonnie. Kirk & the Deer. Spreen, Kathe, illus. Date not set. 12p. (J). (gr. -1-2). pap. *(978-1-891619-43-4(8))* Corona Pr.

Keyes, Shirley. Diffee, the White Deer. 2003. (J). *(978-0-9747755-0-0(9))* Wilkes Publishing Co., Inc.

Kleven, Elisa. The Dancing Deer & the Foolish Hunter. 2013. 34p. 16.99 *(978-1-62352-040-3(1))*; pap. 9.99 *(978-1-62352-038-0(X))* IntoPrint Publishing LLC.

LaBounty, David. Eye of the Deer. 2004. (J). pap. 4.95 *(978-0-9745900-1-1(0)*, Castle Builder Pr.) Blue Cubicle Pr., LLC.

Leibenkop, T. The Sovereign of the Northern Winds. 2009. 30p. pap. 13.50 *(978-1-60693-847-8(9)*, Eloquent Bks.) Strategic Book Publishing & Rights Agency (SBPRA).

Marie, Barbara. Snowy & Felix Find Christmas. 2009. 24p. pap. 11.49 *(978-1-4389-7392-0(6))* AuthorHouse.

May, Karen. Shy Saelig. 2011. (Illus.). 22p. pap. *(978-1-908147-80-6(6))* YouWriteOn.

Mayfield, Helen, illus. The Enchanted Deer. 77p. (Orig.). (J). (gr. 6-18). pap. 4.00 *(978-1-884993-03-9(6))* Koldarana Pubns.

McCaffrey- Fassler, Ruth. A Safe Place. 2012. 28p. (-18). pap. 19.99 *(978-1-4772-8109-3(6))* AuthorHouse.

McGee. Logger's Return: The Continuing Adventures of our White-Tailed Deer Friend. 2011. 24p. pap. 24.95 *(978-1-4560-4230-1(0))* PublishAmerica, Inc.

McLisky, Marie. Kancil the Mouse Deer. 2017. (ENG.). 31p. (J). pap. 13.95 ***(978-1-78554-253-4(2)***, deae15c5-5838-4e02-b48b-54e9f8d82a01) Austin, Stan AUS. Dist: Bookmasters Distribution.

McWade, Michael. The Reindeer Chronicles: The Green Scarf. 2012. 32p. pap. 17.25 *(978-1-4669-5159-4(1))* Trafford Publishing.

Moffitt, Sara. Merlin & the Frog Meet Chatly & Noble. 2011. 25p. (J). pap. 18.95 *(978-1-4327-5921-6(3))* Outskirts Pr., Inc.

Moss, Patricia Crocker. Dillie & the Baby Deer. 2011. (J). 44p. 27.99 *(978-1-4568-4999-3(9))*; 48p. pap. 17.49 *(978-1-4568-4998-6(0))* Xlibris Corp.

Opal, Paola. Dotty. 2010. (Simply Small Ser.). (ENG., Illus.). 24p. (J). (gr. -1 — 1). bds. 7.95 *(978-1-897476-54-3(X))* Simply Read Bks. CAN. Dist: Ingram Publisher Services.

Paulsen, Gary. Tracker. 2007. (ENG.). 96p. (J). (gr. 5-9). pap. 6.99 *(978-1-4169-3940-5(7)*, Simon & Schuster Bks. For Young Readers) Simon & Schuster Bks. For Young Readers.

Rawlings, Marjorie Kinnan. The Yearling. Wyeth, N. C., illus. 2013. (Scribner Classics Ser.). (ENG.). 416p. (J). (gr. 5-9). 29.99 *(978-1-4424-8209-8(5)*, Atheneum Bks. for Young Readers) Simon & Schuster Children's Publishing.

Ray, Mary Lyn. Deer Dancer. Stringer, Lauren, illus. 2014. (ENG.). 40p. (J). (gr. -1-3). 17.99 *(978-1-4424-3421-9(X)*, Beach Lane Bks.) Beach Lane Bks.

Reich, J. J. Snort, Wheeze, Rattle & Grunt. Hillmann, Joe & Cox, Chad, illus. 2006. (J). 8.99 *(978-0-9762971-1-6(6))* Outdoor Originals LLC.

—Snort, Wheeze, Rattle & Grunt: Kampp Tales Outdoor Adventures. Johnathan, Kuehl, illus. 2006. 64p. (J). *(978-0-9762971-2-3(4))* Outdoor Originals LLC.

RH Disney Staff. Bambi. (FRE.). (J). (gr. 3-8). 13.95 *(978-0-7859-0613-1(4)*, S26622) French & European Pubns., Inc.

—Bambi. unabr. ed. (Read-Along Ser.). (J). 7.99 incl. audio *(978-1-55723-008-9(0))* Walt Disney Records.

Richter, Jeff, photos by. White Deer: Ghost of the Forest. 2007. (Illus.). 96p. pap. 19.95 *(978-0-9741883-1-7(X))* Nature's Pr.

Robertson, Charmaine. The Deer Feast. 2016. (Rosen REAL Readers: STEM & STEAM Collection). 8p. (gr. 1-k). pap. 5.46 *(978-1-5081-2604-1(6)*, Rosen Classroom) Rosen Publishing Group, Inc., The.

Salten, Felix. Bambi: A Life in the Woods. Chambers, Whittaker, tr. Fancher, Lou & Johnson, Steve, illus. 2014. (Scribner Classics Ser.). (ENG.). 192p. (J). (gr. 5). 29.99 *(978-1-4424-9345-2(3)*, Atheneum Bks. for Young Readers) Simon & Schuster Children's Publishing.

—Bambi: A Life in the Woods. Cowdrey, Richard, illus. 2013. (Bambi's Classic Animal Tales Ser.). (ENG.). 272p. (J). (gr. 3-7). 16.99 *(978-1-4424-6746-0(0)*, Aladdin) Simon & Schuster Children's Publishing.

—Bambi: A Life in the Woods. Cowdrey, Richard & Johnson, Steve, illus. 2013. (Bambi's Classic Animal Tales Ser.). (ENG.). 272p. (J). (gr. 3-7). pap. 6.99 *(978-1-4424-6745-3(2)*, Aladdin) Simon & Schuster Children's Publishing.

—Bambi - Life in the Woods. (J). 20.95 *(978-0-8488-1467-0(3))* Amereon Ltd.

—Bambi's First Day. van Frankenhuyzen, Gijsbert, illus. 2008. (ENG.). 32p. (J). (gr. k-6). 15.95 *(978-1-58536-422-0(3))* Sleeping Bear Pr.

Sams, Carl R., II & Stoick, Jean, photos by. Lost in the Woods: A Photographic Fantasy. 2004. (ENG., Illus.). 48p. (J). 19.95 *(978-0-9671748-8-4(0))* Sams, II, Carl R. Photography, Inc.

Sargent, Dave & Sargent, Pat. Dawn the Deer: Family & Friends, 56 vols., Vol. 8. Huff, Jeane, illus. 2nd rev. ed. 2003. (Animal Pride Ser.: Vol. 8). 42p. (J). lib. bdg. 20.95 *(978-1-56763-773-1(6))* Ozark Publishing.

Scruggs, Stephanie. Deer Can't Dance. 2009. 36p. pap. 15.95 *(978-1-4490-4535-7(9))* AuthorHouse.

Shanghai Animation Studio Staff & Tang, Sanmu. A Deer of Nine Colors. Lee, Yawtsong, tr. from CHI. 2010. (Favorite Children's Ser.). (ENG., Illus.). 32p. (J). (gr. -1-3). pap. 5.95 *(978-1-60220-976-3(6))* BetterLink Pr., Inc.

Shepard, Aaron. The Adventures of Mouse Deer. Gamble, Kim, illus. 2005. 48p. (J). (gr. -1-4). pap. 10.00 *(978-0-938497-32-5(4)*, Skyhook Pr.) Shepard Pubns.

Singhose, Rose. Granny's GIGGLES BOOK SIX. 2010. 34p. pap. 16.95 *(978-0-557-61003-7(6))* Lulu Pr., Inc.

Smith, Ivy. Roxie & the Deer. 2011. (Illus.). 32p. (J). 19.95 *(978-0-9635757-7-7(5))*; (ENG.). pap. 11.99 *(978-0-9635757-8-4(3))* Red Tail Publishing.

Smith, Lisa. Makini, the Impala with a Crooked Horn. 2011. 24p. pap. 24.95 *(978-1-4626-2608-3(4))* America Star Bks.

Soros, Barbara. Tenzin's Deer. Mayer, Danuta, illus. (ENG.). 32p. (J). (gr. 2-4). 2007. pap. 7.99 *(978-1-84686-130-7(6))* 2005. 16.99 *(978-1-905236-57-2(3))* Barefoot Bks., Inc.

—Tenzin's Deer: A Tibetan Tale. Mayer, Danuta, illus. 2003. 32p. (J). (gr. 2-5). 16.99 *(978-1-84148-811-0(9))* Barefoot Bks., Inc.

Springett, Martin. Kate & Pippin: An Unlikely Love Story. Springett, Isobel, photos by. 2012. (My Readers Ser.). (ENG., Illus.). 32p. (J). (gr. -1-3). 16.99 *(978-0-8050-9487-9(3)*, 9780805094879, Holt, Henry & Co. Bks. For Young Readers) Holt, Henry & Co.

Stauffacher, Sue. Animal Rescue Team: Hide & Seek. Lamont, Priscilla, illus. 2011. (Animal Rescue Team Ser.). (ENG.). 160p. (J). (gr. 3-7). 5.99 *(978-0-375-85133-9(X)*, Yearling) Random Hse. Children's Bks.

Storie Tree Inc, Staff. A Pocket Pearl of Light: Twinkle & Shinmet Come Home. l.t. ed. 2003. (Illus.). 27p. pap. 6.00 *(978-0-9679014-9-7(9))* Storie Tree, Inc., The.

Talbot, Amy. Deer & His Dear Friends: A Tale from India. 2006. (J). pap. *(978-1-4108-6173-3(2))* Benchmark Education Co.

Tenbeth, Kate. Burly & Grum & the Secret City. Jones, Rob, illus. 2012. 108p. pap. *(978-0-9572119-5-7(3))* Magic Toy Bks.

Tennant Iain Staff. Alby's Letters to Henry: Written from Isle of Mull. Smith, William, illus. 2007. (ENG.). 176p. (J). pap. 15.99 *(978-1-903071-14-4(3))* Bene Factum Publishing, Ltd. GBR. Dist: Independent Pubs. Group.

Wade, Mary H. Swift Fawn the Little Foundling. Betts, Louis, illus. 2005. reprint ed. pap. 15.95 *(978-1-4179-1811-9(X))* Kessinger Publishing, LLC.

Waguespack, Michael. The Deer Hunting Book. 2013. 104p. pap. 7.95 *(978-0-9754624-6-1(6))* Country Kid Publishing LLC.

Walker, Lane. Legend of the Ghost Buck. 2014. (ENG.). 135p. (YA). (gr. 7-13). pap. 9.99 *(978-1-58169-517-5(9)*, Evergreen Pr.) Genesis Communications, Inc.

Wallace, Robert E. The Adventures of Ichi, the Baby Deer Bk. 1: The Rescue. Wallace, Robert E., photos by. 2004. (Adventures of Ichi the Baby Deer Ser.: Bk. 1). (Illus.). (J). lib. bdg. 16.95 *(978-0-9755678-0-7(2))* Cirrus Publishing, LLC.

Wilson, Karen Collett. Autumn Rescue. Zerga, Susan A., photos by. 2004. (Deer Tales Ser.). (Illus.). (J). (gr. k-6). 15.95 *(978-0-9722570-1-5(2))* Snowbound Bks.

Wilson, Pip & Long, Ian. Blob Feelings Ball. 2017. (Blobs Ser.). (ENG.). 2p. (C). pap. 20.95 ***(978-0-86388-893-9(3)***, Y329884) Routledge.

Winslade, Jayn E. Emily & Jen Dance for Deeron. 2010. 352p. pap. *(978-1-907211-48-5(9))* Grosvenor Hse. Publishing Ltd.

Wolfe, Susan Markle. The Deer from Ponchatoula, 1 vol. Welch, Gracie, illus. 2009. 24p. pap. 24.95 *(978-1-60813-519-6(5))* America Star Bks.

Yamanushi, Toshiko. The Deer King. Tani, Toshihiko, illus. 2014. (J). 8.95 *(978-1-935523-70-3(8))* World Tribune Pr.

Zoehfeld, Kathleen Weidner. Fawn at Woodland Way. Snyder, Joel, illus. 2011. (Smithsonian's Backyard Ser.). (ENG.). 32p. (J). (gr. -1-3). 19.95 *(978-1-60727-637-1(2))* Soundprints.

DEERE, JOHN, 1804-1886

Maurer, Tracy Nelson. John Deere, That's Who! Zeltner, Tim, illus. 2017. (ENG.). 40p. (J). 17.99 *(978-1-62779-129-8(9)*, 9781627791298, Holt, Henry & Co. Bks. For Young Readers) Holt, Henry & Co.

Sutcliffe, Jane. John Deere. 2006. (History Maker Biographies Ser.). (Illus.). 48p. (J). (gr. 3-7). lib. bdg. 26.60 *(978-0-8225-6579-6(X)*, Lerner Pubns.) Lerner Publishing Group.

DEGAS, EDGAR, 1834-1917

Cernak, Linda. Edgar Degas. Morrow, J. T., illus. 2014. (World's Greatest Artists Ser.). (ENG.). 24p. (J). (gr. 2-5). 28.50 *(978-1-62687-349-0(6)*, 207189) Child's World, Inc., The.

Friedman, Samantha & Pieropan, Cristina. What Degas Saw. 2016. (ENG., Illus.). 40p. (J). (gr. k-2). 19.95 *(978-1-63345-004-2(X))* Museum of Modern Art.

Mattern, Joanne. Edgar Degas, 1 vol. 2005. (Great Artists Set 1 Ser.). (ENG., Illus.). 32p. (gr. k-6). 27.07 *(978-1-59197-843-5(2)*, Checkerboard Library) ABDO Publishing Co.

Merberg, Julie & Bober, Suzanne. Dancing with Degas. 2003. (Mini Masters Ser.: MINI). (ENG., Illus.). 22p. (J). (gr. -1-7). bds. 6.99 *(978-0-8118-4047-7(6))* Chronicle Bks. LLC.

Mis, Melody S. Edgar Degas. (Meet the Artist Ser.). 24p. (gr. 2-3). 2009. 42.50 *(978-1-61514-628-4(8)*, PowerKids Pr.) 2007. (Illus.). (YA). lib. bdg. 22.60 *(978-1-4042-3839-8(5))* Rosen Publishing Group, Inc., The.

Rubin, Susan Goldman. Degas & the Dance: The Painter & the Petits Rats, Perfecting Their Art. 2005. (Illus.). 31p. (J). (gr. 4-8). reprint ed. 18.00 *(978-0-7567-9291-6(6))* DIANE Publishing Co.

Spence, David. The Impressionists: Monet, Cezanne, Renoir, Degas. 2010. (ENG.). 128p. (J). (gr. 4-7). pap. 12.95 *(978-1-84696-217-2(X)*, TickTock Books) Octopus Publishing Group GBR. Dist: Independent Pubs. Group.

Vaughan, Carolyn. Invitation to Ballet: A Celebration of Dance & Degas. Isadora, Rachel, illus. 2012. (ENG.). 32p. (J). (gr. 1-4). 16.95 *(978-1-4197-0260-0(2)*, Abrams Bks. for Young Readers) Abrams, Inc.

Venezia, Mike. Edgar Degas. Venezia, Mike, illus. rev. ed. 2016. (Getting to Know the World's Greatest Artists Ser.). (ENG., Illus.). 40p. (J). pap. 7.95 *(978-0-531-22087-0(7)*, Children's Pr.) Scholastic Library Publishing.

Wood, Alix. Edgar Degas, 1 vol. 2015. (ENG., Illus.). 32p. (J). lib. bdg. 26.25 *(978-1-4777-5409-2(1)*, Windmill Bks.) Rosen Publishing Group, Inc., The.

DEGREES OF LATITUDE AND LONGITUDE

see Geodesy

DELACROIX, EUGENE, 1798-1863

Paredes, Julio. Eugène Delacroix. 2005. (SPA.). 132p. (YA). *(978-958-30-1358-4(7))* Panamericana Editorial.

Venezia, Mike. Eugene Delacroix. Venezia, Mike, illus. 2003. (Getting to Know World Artists Ser.). (ENG., Illus.). 32p. (J). 28.00 *(978-0-516-22576-0(6)*, Children's Pr.) Scholastic Library Publishing.

—Eugène Delacroix. Venezia, Mike, illus. 2003. (Getting to Know the World's Greatest Artists Ser.). (ENG., Illus.). 32p. (J). pap. 6.95 *(978-0-516-26976-4(3)*, Children's Pr.) Scholastic Library Publishing.

DELAWARE

Bennett, Kelly & Vargus, Nanci Reginelli. Delaware. 2004. (Rookie Read-About Geography Ser.). (J). 20.50 *(978-0-516-22752-8(1)*, Children's Pr.) Scholastic Library Publishing.

Brown, Dottie. Delaware. 2012. (J). lib. bdg. 25.26 *(978-0-7613-4526-8(4)*, Lerner Pubns.) Lerner Publishing Group.

Brown, Jonatha A. Delaware. 2006. (Portraits of the States Ser.). 32p. (gr. 2-6). pap. 10.50 *(978-0-8368-4715-4(6))*; (Illus.). lib. bdg. 26.00 *(978-0-8368-4698-0(2))* Stevens, Gareth Publishing LLLP. (Gareth Stevens Learning Library).

Brown, Vanessa. Delaware. (Bilingual Library of the United States of America Ser.). (ENG & SPA.). 32p. 2009. (gr. 2-2). 47.90 *(978-1-60853-350-3(6)*, Editorial Buenas Letras) 2005. (Illus.). (J). (gr. 3-6). lib. bdg. 25.25 *(978-1-4042-3073-6(4))* Rosen Publishing Group, Inc., The.

Crane, Carol. F Is for First State: A Delaware Alphabet. Traynor, Elizabeth, illus. 2005. (State Ser.). (ENG.). 40p. (J). (gr. -1-3). 17.95 *(978-1-58536-154-0(2))* Sleeping Bear Pr.

Crenson, Victoria. Horseshoe Crabs & Shorebirds: The Story of a Foodweb, 0 vols. Cannon, Annie, illus. unabr. ed. 2009. (ENG.). 42p. (J). (gr. 3-5). pap. 9.99 *(978-0-7614-5552-3(3)*, 9780761455523, Amazon Children's Publishing) Amazon Publishing.

Fontes, Justine & Fontes, Ron. Delaware, the First State. 2003. (World Almanac Library of the States). (Illus.). 48p. (gr. 4-9). pap. 14.05 *(978-0-8368-5319-3(9)*, Gareth Stevens Learning Library) Stevens, Gareth Publishing LLLP.

Gelletly, LeeAnne. The Mid-Atlantic States: Delaware, Maryland, & Washington, D. C. 2015. (Let's Explore the States Ser.). (Illus.). 64p. (J). (gr. 5). 23.95 *(978-1-4222-3327-6(8))* Mason Crest.

King, David C. Delaware. 2004. (It's My State! Ser.). (Illus.). 79p. (J). (gr. 3-7). lib. bdg. 27.07 *(978-0-7614-1826-9(1)*, Benchmark Bks.) Marshall Cavendish Corp.

Marsh, Carole. Delaware Current Events Projects: 30 Cool, Activities, Crafts, Experiments & More for Kids to Do to Learn about Your State! 2003. (Delaware Experience Ser.). 32p. (gr. k-8). pap. 5.95 *(978-0-635-02027-7(0)*, Marsh, Carole Bks.) Gallopade International.

—Delaware Geography Projects: 30 Cool, Activities, Crafts, Experiments & More for Kids to Do to Learn about Your State! 2003. (Delaware Experience Ser.). 32p. (gr. k-5). pap. 5.95 *(978-0-635-01827-4(6)*, Marsh, Carole Bks.) Gallopade International.

—Delaware Government Projects: 30 Cool, Activities, Crafts, Experiments & More for Kids to Do to Learn about Your State! 2003. (Delaware Experience Ser.). 32p. (gr. k-5). pap. 5.95 *(978-0-635-01927-1(2)*, Marsh, Carole Bks.) Gallopade International.

—Delaware People Projects: 30 Cool, Activities, Crafts, Experiments & More for Kids to Do to Learn about Your State! 2003. (Delaware Experience Ser.). 32p. (gr. k-5). pap. 5.95 *(978-0-635-01977-6(9)*, Marsh, Carole Bks.) Gallopade International.

—Delaware Symbols & Facts Projects: 30 Cool, Activities, Crafts, Experiments & More for Kids to Do to Learn about Your State! 2003. (Delaware Experience Ser.). 32p. (gr. k-5). pap. 5.95 *(978-0-635-01877-9(2)*, Marsh, Carole Bks.) Gallopade International.

Murray, Julie. Delaware, 1 vol. 2006. (Buddy Book Ser.). (ENG., Illus.). 32p. (gr. k-4). 27.07 *(978-1-59197-667-7(7)*, Buddy Bks.) ABDO Publishing Co.

Ollhoff, Jim. Delaware, 1 vol. 2009. (United States Ser.). (ENG., Illus.). 48p. (YA). (gr. 2-5). 27.07 *(978-1-60453-643-0(8))* ABDO Publishing Co.

Quasha, Jennifer. How to Draw Delaware's Sights & Symbols. 2009. (Kid's Guide to Drawing America Ser.). 32p. (gr. k-k). 50.50 *(978-1-61511-052-0(6)*, PowerKids Pr.) Rosen Publishing Group, Inc., The.

Reiter, Chris. Delaware: A MyReportLinks.com Book. 2003. (States Ser.). (Illus.). 48p. (J). (gr. 4-10). lib. bdg. 25.26 *(978-0-7660-5019-8(X)*, MyReportLinks.com Bks.) Enslow Pubs., Inc.

Schnobrich, Emily. Delaware. 2013. (Exploring the States Ser.). (ENG., Illus.). 32p. (gr. 3-7). lib. bdg. 26.95 *(978-1-62617-007-0(X)*, Blastoff! Readers) Bellwether Media.

Wimmer, Teresa. Delaware. 2008. (This Land Called America Ser.). 32p. (YA). (gr. 3-6). 22.95 *(978-1-58341-633-4(1))* Creative Co., The.

Wolny, Philip. Delaware: Past & Present. 2010. (United States: Past & Present Ser.). (ENG., Illus.). 48p. (J). pap. 11.75 *(978-1-4358-8502-8(3))*; lib. bdg. 29.25 *(978-1-4358-3526-9(3))* Rosen Publishing Group, Inc., The. (Rosen Reference).

DELAWARE—FICTION

Blair, Margaret Whitman. The Sand Castle: Blockade Running & the Battle of Fort Fisher. 2005. (White Mane Kids Ser.: 17). (Illus.). 187p. (J). (gr. 4-7). per. 8.95 *(978-1-57249-346-9(1)*, White Mane Kids) White Mane Publishing Co., Inc.

Combs, Sarah. The Light Fantastic. 2016. (ENG.). 320p. (J). (gr. 7). 17.99 *(978-0-7636-7851-7(1))* Candlewick Pr.

Jacobs, Lily. The Littlest Bunny in Delaware: An Easter Adventure. Dunn, Robert, illus. 2015. (ENG.). 32p. (J). (-3). 9.99 *(978-1-4926-1063-2(1)*, Sourcebooks Jabberwocky) Sourcebooks, Inc.

James, Eric. Santa's Sleigh Is on Its Way to Delaware: A Christmas Adventure. Dunn, Robert, illus. 2016. (ENG.). 32p. (J). (-2). 12.99 *(978-1-4926-4326-5(2)*, 9781492643265, Sourcebooks Jabberwocky) Sourcebooks, Inc.

Larsen, Elizabeth. Buster Hardings: Buster Makes New Friends. 2008. 104p. pap. 19.95 *(978-1-60563-951-2(6))* America Star Bks.

—A Party for Buster & Haylee! 2011. 34p. pap. 16.95 *(978-1-4560-6954-4(3))* America Star Bks.

Noble, Trinka Hakes. The Legend of the Cape May Diamond. Lewis, E. B., illus. rev. ed. 2007. (Legend (Sleeping Bear) Ser.). (ENG.). 40p. (J). (gr. 3-7). 17.95 *(978-1-58536-279-0(4))* Sleeping Bear Pr.

Schumacher, Julie. The Unbearable Book Club for Unsinkable Girls. 2013. (ENG.). 240p. (YA). (gr. 7). pap. 8.99 *(978-0-375-85127-8(5)*, Ember) Random Hse. Children's Bks.

Silvano, Wendi. Love Is All Around Delaware. Czernichowska, Joanna, illus. 2016. (ENG.). 32p. (J). (-6). 12.99 *(978-1-4926-2916-0(2)*, Sourcebooks Jabberwocky) Sourcebooks, Inc.

Smallman, Steve. Santa Is Coming to Delaware. Dunn, Robert, illus. 2013. (ENG.). 32p. (J). (-3). 9.99 *(978-1-4022-9508-9(1)*, Sourcebooks Jabberwocky) Sourcebooks, Inc.

Waldron, Douglas E. Cody Sackett of Montana: Tales of Adventure. 2008. 188p. per. 24.95 *(978-1-4241-9781-1(3))* America Star Bks.

DELAWARE—HISTORY

Barth, Linda J. Bridgetender's Boy. Lorenzetti, Doreen, illus. 2004. *(978-0-930973-35-3(6))*; pap. *(978-0-930973-34-6(8))* Moore, Hugh Historical Park & Museums, Inc. (Canal History & Technology Pr.).

Dillard, Sheri. What's Great about Delaware? 2015. (ENG., Illus.). 32p. (J). (gr. 2-5). 26.65 *(978-1-4677-3874-3(3))* Lerner Publishing Group.

Doherty, Craig A. & Doherty, Katherine M. Delaware. 2005. (Thirteen Colonies Ser.). (Illus.). 144p. (gr. 5-8). 35.00 *(978-0-8160-5414-5(2))* Facts On File, Inc.

Downey, Tika. Delaware: The First State. 2010. (Our Amazing States Ser.). (Illus.). 24p. (J). pap. 8.25 *(978-1-4358-9808-0(7))*; lib. bdg. 22.60 *(978-1-4358-9356-6(5))* Rosen Publishing Group, Inc., The. (PowerKids Pr.).

Durrie, Karen. Delaware: The First State. 2012. (J). *(978-1-61913-335-8(0))*; pap. *(978-1-61913-336-5(9))* Weigl Pubs., Inc.

Fontes, Justine & Fontes, Ron. Delaware: The First State. 2003. (World Almanac Library of the States). (Illus.). 48p. (gr. 4-9). lib. bdg. 31.00 *(978-0-8368-5148-9(X)*, Gareth Stevens Learning Library) Stevens, Gareth Publishing LLLP.

Gamble, Adam & Jasper, Mark. Good Night Delaware. Jasper, Mark, illus. 2012. (Good Night Our World Ser.). (ENG., Illus.). 20p. (J). (gr. k — 1). bds. 9.95 *(978-1-60219-066-5(6))* Good Night Bks.

Heinrichs, Ann. Delaware (Revised Edition) 2014. (America the Beautiful, Third Ser. (Revised Edition) Ser.). (ENG.). 144p. (J). lib. bdg. 40.00 *(978-0-531-28277-9(5))* Scholastic Library Publishing.

Hoffecker, Carol E. Delaware: The First State. 2nd rev. ed. 2005. (Illus.). 215p. (YA). (gr. 6-9). pap. *(978-0-9705804-0-5(1))* Middle Atlantic Pr.

Hossell, Karen & U. S. National Geographic Society Staff. Delaware, 1638-1776. 2006. (National Geographic Voices from ColonialAmerica Ser.). (ENG., Illus.). 112p. (J). (gr. 5-9). 21.95 *(978-0-7922-6408-8(8))*; lib. bdg. 32.90 *(978-0-7922-6864-2(4))* National Geographic Society. (National Geographic Children's Bks.).

King, David C. & Fitzgerald, Brian. Delaware. 2nd rev. ed. 2010. (It's My State! Ser.). 80p. (gr. 3-18). lib. bdg. 31.36 *(978-1-60870-048-6(8))* Marshall Cavendish Corp.

King, David C., et al. Delaware. 2015. (J). lib. bdg. *(978-1-62712-487-4(X))*; (ENG., Illus.). 80p. (gr. 4-4). lib. bdg. 34.21 *(978-1-5026-0009-7(9))* Cavendish Square Publishing.

Kirchner, Jason. Delaware. 2016. (States Ser.). (ENG., Illus.). 32p. (gr. 3-4). lib. bdg. 27.32 *(978-1-5157-0394-5(0))* Next Page Pr., The.

Marsh, Carole. Delaware History Projects: 30 Cool, Activities, Crafts, Experiments & More for Kids to Do to Learn about Your State! 2003. (Delaware Experience Ser.). 32p. (gr. k-5). pap. 5.95 *(978-0-635-01777-2(6)*, Marsh, Carole Bks.) Gallopade International.

—Exploring Delaware Through Project-Based Learning. 2016. (Delaware Experience Ser.). (ENG.). (J). pap. 9.99 *(978-0-635-12332-9(0))* Gallopade International.

McManus, Lori. Exploring the Delaware Colony. 2016. (Exploring the 13 Colonies Ser.). (ENG., Illus.). 48p. (gr. 3-4). lib. bdg. 31.99 *(978-1-5157-2239-7(2))* Capstone Press of Coughlan Cos.

Miller, Amy. Delaware. 2009. (From Sea to Shining Sea, Second Ser.). (ENG.). 80p. (J). pap. 7.95 *(978-0-531-21127-4(4)*, Children's Pr.) Scholastic Library Publishing.

Miller, Jake. The Colony of Delaware: A Primary Source History. (Primary Source Library of the Thirteen Colonies & the Lost Colony Ser.). 24p. (gr. 3-4). 2009. 42.50 *(978-1-60854-135-5(5))* 2006. (Illus.). (J). lib. bdg. 22.60 *(978-1-4042-3033-0(5))* Rosen Publishing Group, Inc., The. (PowerKids Pr.).

Raymond, Aaron. A Primary Source History of the Colony of Delaware. (Primary Sources of the Thirteen Colonies & the Lost Colony Ser.). 64p. 2009. (gr. 5-8). 58.50 *(978-1-60851-877-7(9))* 2006. (Illus.). (YA). (gr. 4-7). lib. bdg. 31.95 *(978-1-4042-0425-6(3))* 2006. (ENG., Illus.). (gr. 4-8). per. 12.95 *(978-1-4042-0670-0(1))* Rosen Publishing Group, Inc., The.

Schuman, Michael & Brill, Marlene Targ. Delaware. 2nd rev. ed. 2008. (Celebrate the States Ser.). 144p. (gr. 6-18). lib. bdg. 42.79 *(978-0-7614-3399-6(6)*, Benchmark Bks.) Marshall Cavendish Corp.

Winans, Jay D. Delaware. 2011. (Guide to American States Ser.). (Illus.). 48p. (YA). (gr. 3-6). 29.99 *(978-1-61690-780-8(0))*; (J). 29.99 *(978-1-61690-455-5(0))* Weigl Pubs., Inc.

—Delaware: The First State. 2016. (J). *(978-1-5105-0668-8(3))* SmartBook Media, Inc.

—Delaware: The First State. 2016. (J). *(978-1-4896-4836-5(4))* Weigl Pubs., Inc.

DELHI (INDIA)

Rowe, Percy & Coster, Patience. Delhi. 2004. (Great Cities of the World Ser.). (Illus.). 48p. (gr. 5-12). lib. bdg. 31.00 *(978-0-8368-5037-6(8)*, Gareth Stevens Secondary Library) Stevens, Gareth Publishing LLLP.

DELINQUENCY, JUVENILE

see Juvenile Delinquency

DELINQUENTS

see Criminals; Juvenile Delinquency

DELTORA (IMAGINARY PLACE)—FICTION

Rodda, Emily. City of the Rats. 2012. (Deltora Quest Ser.). (ENG.). 160p. (J). (gr. 3-7). pap. 5.99 *(978-0-545-46022-4(0))* Scholastic, Inc.

—Deltora Quest #2: the Lake of Tears. 2012. (Deltora Quest Ser.). (ENG.). 160p. (J). (gr. 3-7). pap. 5.99 *(978-0-545-46021-7(2))* Scholastic, Inc.

—Deltora Quest 4. Niwano, Makoto, illus. 2012. (Deltora Quest Ser.). (ENG.). 208p. (gr. 8-12). pap. 10.99 *(978-1-935429-31-9(0))* Kodansha America, Inc.

—Deltora Quest 5. 2012. (Deltora Quest Ser.). (ENG., Illus.). 208p. (gr. 8-12). pap. 10.99 *(978-1-61262-011-4(6))* Kodansha America, Inc.

—Deltora Quest 6. 2012. (Deltora Quest Ser.). (ENG., Illus.). 200p. (gr. 8-12). pap. 10.99 *(978-1-61262-012-1(4))* Kodansha America, Inc.

—Deltora Quest #6: the Maze of the Beast. 2012. (Deltora Quest Ser.). (ENG.). 160p. (J). (gr. 3-7). pap. 5.99 *(978-0-545-46026-2(3))* Scholastic, Inc.

—Deltora Quest 7. 2012. (Deltora Quest Ser.). (ENG., Illus.). 200p. (gr. 8-12). pap. 10.99 *(978-1-61262-013-8(2))* Kodansha America, Inc.

—Deltora Quest #7: the Valley of the Lost. 2012. (Deltora Quest Ser.). (ENG.). 160p. (J). (gr. 3-7). pap. 5.99 *(978-0-545-46027-9(1))* Scholastic, Inc.

—Deltora Quest 8. 2012. (Deltora Quest Ser.). (ENG., Illus.). 200p. (gr. 8-12). pap. 10.99 *(978-1-61262-014-5(0))* Kodansha America, Inc.

—Deltora Quest 9. 2012. (Deltora Quest Ser.). (ENG., Illus.). 200p. (gr. 8-12). pap. 10.99 *(978-1-61262-015-2(9))* Kodansha America, Inc.

—Return to Del. 2012. (Deltora Quest Ser.). (ENG.). 160p. (J). (gr. 3-7). pap. 5.99 *(978-0-545-46028-6(X))* Scholastic, Inc.

DELUSIONS

see Superstition; Witchcraft

DEMILLE, AGNES, 1908-1993

Gaskill, Rachel. Agnes de Mille. 2006. (Library of American Choreographers). (ENG., Illus.). 48p. (gr. 5-8). pap. 11.75 *(978-1-4042-0645-8(0))* Rosen Publishing Group, Inc., The.

—Agnes Demille. 2005. (Library of American Choreographers Ser.). (Illus.). 48p. (J). (gr. k-3). lib. bdg. 29.25 *(978-1-4042-0444-7(X))* Rosen Publishing Group, Inc., The.

DEMOCRACY

see also Aristocracy (Social Class); Equality; Liberty; Socialism; Suffrage

Anderson, Nancy. Citizens Vote in a Democracy. 2016. (Rosen REAL Readers: Social Studies Nonfiction / Fiction: Family, Community, & the World Ser.). 12p. (gr. 1-k). pap. 6.33 *(978-1-5081-2350-7(0)*, Rosen Classroom) Rosen Publishing Group, Inc., The.

Aung San Suu Kyi. 2014. (Making a Difference: Leaders Who Are Changing the World Ser.). 48p. (J). (gr. 5-8). 25.85 *(978-1-62275-430-4(1))* Rosen Publishing Group, Inc., The.

Bailey, Diane. Democracy. Colton, Timothy J., ed. 2012. (Major Forms of World Government Ser.). (Illus.). 64p. (J). (gr. 5). 22.95 *(978-1-4222-2137-2(7))* Mason Crest.

Boothroyd, Jennifer. What Is a Democracy? 2015. (ENG., Illus.). 24p. (J). (gr. k-2). 23.99 *(978-1-4677-8574-7(1))* Lerner Publishing Group.

Building America's Democracy. (J). (gr. k-5). 119.70 *(978-0-8239-7260-9(7))* Rosen Publishing Group, Inc., The.

Burling, Alexis. Aung San Suu Kyi: Burmese Politician & Activist for Democracy. 2017. (J). pap. ***(978-1-5383-8069-7(2))*** Rosen Publishing Group, Inc., The.

Burns, Jann. Can Democracy Succeed in the Middle East? Einfeld, Jann, ed. 2006. (At Issue Ser.). (ENG., Illus.). 128p. (gr. 10-12). 39.40 *(978-0-7377-3393-8(4))* Cengage Gale.

Connolly, Sean. Democracy. 2012. (Systems of Government Ser.). (Illus.). 48p. (gr. 6-12). lib. bdg. 37.10 *(978-1-59920-803-9(2))* Black Rabbit Bks.

Covert, Kim. Ancient Greece: Birthplace of Democracy, 1 vol. 2011. (Great Civilizations Ser.). (ENG.). 32p. (gr. 3-4). pap. 8.10 *(978-1-4296-7237-5(4))*; pap. 47.70 *(978-1-4296-7238-2(2))*; lib. bdg. 27.32 *(978-1-4296-6831-6(8))* Capstone Press of Coughlan Cos. (Fact Finders).

Documents of American Democracy. 2016. (Documents of American Democracy Ser.). 32p. (gr. 5-5). 157.50 *(978-1-4994-1985-6(6))*; pap. 60.00 *(978-1-5081-5258-3(6))* Rosen Publishing Group, Inc., The. (PowerKids Pr.).

Fandel, Jennifer & Fitzpatrick, Anne. Democracy. 2017. (Odysseys in Government Ser.). (ENG., Illus.). 80p. (J). (gr. 7-11). pap. 14.99 *(978-1-62832-320-7(5)*, Creative Paperbacks) Creative Co., The.

Friedman, Lauri S. Democracy. 2008. (Writing the Critical Essay Ser.). (ENG., Illus.). 120p. (YA). (gr. 7-12). lib. bdg. 31.80 *(978-0-7377-4036-3(1)*, LML02109-240004, Greenhaven Pr., Inc.) Cengage Gale.

Friedman, Mark. The Democratic Process. 2012. (Cornerstones of Freedom, Third Ser.). (ENG., Illus.). 64p. (J). pap. 8.95 *(978-0-531-28155-0(8))*; (gr. 4-6). lib. bdg. 30.00 *(978-0-531-23055-8(4))* Scholastic Library Publishing. (Children's Pr.).

Grodin, Elissa. D Is for Democracy: A Citizen's Alphabet. Juhasz, Victor, illus. 2006. (ENG.). 40p. (J). (gr. 1-4). per. 7.95 *(978-1-58536-328-5(6)*, 203807) Sleeping Bear Pr.

Hanson, Anders. Land of the Free: The Kids' Book of Freedom, 1 vol. 2014. (What We Stand For Ser.). (ENG.). 24p. (gr. 5-10). lib. bdg. 25.65 *(978-1-62403-295-0(8)*, Super SandCastle) ABDO Publishing Co.

Hardyman, Robyn. What Is a Democracy?, Vol. 1. 2014. (Understanding Political Systems Ser.). 48p. (YA). (gr. 6-8). 31.95 *(978-1-4824-0306-0(4))*; pap. 14.05 *(978-1-4824-0307-7(2))* Stevens, Gareth Publishing LLLP.

Haugen, David M. Democracy. 2012. (Opposing Viewpoints Ser.). (ENG., Illus.). 224p. (gr. 10-12). lib. bdg. 48.80 *(978-0-7377-5717-0(5))* Cengage Gale.

Haugen, David M., ed. Democracy. 2012. (Opposing Viewpoints Ser.). (ENG., Illus.). 240p. (J). (gr. 10-12). pap. 29.45 *(978-0-7377-5718-7(3)*, Greenhaven Pr., Inc.) Cengage Gale.

Landmarks of Democracy: American Institutions. 2017. (Landmarks of Democracy: American Institutions Ser.). 24p. (gr. 7-8). 118.00 ***(978-1-5081-6109-7(7))***; pap. 41.25 ***(978-1-5081-6110-3(0))*** Rosen Publishing Group, Inc., The. (PowerKids Pr.).

Lansford, Tom. Democracy. 2007. (Political Systems of the World Ser.). (Illus.). 143p. (J). (gr. 4-7). lib. bdg. 42.79 *(978-0-7614-2629-5(9)*, Benchmark Bks.) Marshall Cavendish Corp.

Leavitt, Amie Jane. Who Really Created Democracy?, 1 vol. (Race for History Ser.). (ENG., 32p. (gr. 3-4). 2011. Illus.). pap. 8.10 *(978-1-4296-6246-8(8))* 2011. pap. 47.70 *(978-1-4296-6414-1(2))* 2010. lib. bdg. 27.32 *(978-1-4296-3343-7(3))* Capstone Press of Coughlan Cos. (Fact Finders).

Lowery, Zoe, ed. Democracy. 2014. (Political & Economic Systems Ser.). 312p. (YA). (gr. 9-12). 45.00 *(978-1-62275-356-7(9))* Rosen Publishing Group, Inc., The.

Mara, Wil. Democracy at Work. 2016. (21st Century Skills Library: a Citizen's Guide Ser.). (ENG., Illus.). 32p. (J). (gr. 4-7). 29.93 *(978-1-63471-065-7(7)*, 208339) Cherry Lake Publishing.

Mason, Helen. Be an Active Citizen at Your School. 2016. (Citizenship in Action Ser.). (ENG.). 24p. (J). (gr. 1-4).

C D

(978-0-7787-2600-5(2)); pap. *(978-0-7787-2606-7(1))* Crabtree Publishing Co.

McGraw-Hill Education Staff. United States Government: Democracy in Action, Spanish Reading Essentials & Study Guide: Student Workbook. 2nd ed. 2005. (Government in the U. S. Ser.). (SPA., Illus.). 309p. (gr. 9-12). stu. ed., per., wbk. ed. 17.96 *(978-0-07-865920-1(5)*, 0078659205) McGraw-Hill Higher Education.

Miller, Debra A. Developing Nations. 2012. (Current Controversies Ser.). (ENG.). 224p. (gr. 10-12). pap. 32.00 *(978-0-7377-5615-9(2)*, Greenhaven Pr., Inc.); lib. bdg. 46.40 *(978-0-7377-5614-2(4))* Cengage Gale.

Miller, Reagan. What Is a Democracy? Crabtree Publishing Staff, ed. 2012. (Forms of Government Ser.: No. 1). (ENG.). 48p. (J). (gr. 5-8). pap. *(978-0-7787-5323-0(9))* Crabtree Publishing Co.

Miller, Reagan & Sue, Bright-Moore. What Is a Democracy? 2012. (Forms of Government Ser.). (ENG.). 48p. (J). (gr. 5-9). *(978-0-7787-5316-2(6))* Crabtree Publishing Co.

Ogden, Charlie. Government & Democracy. 2017. (Illus.). 32p. (J). ***(978-0-7787-3266-2(5))*** Crabtree Publishing Co.

O'Keefe, Sherry. Aung San Suu Kyi. 2012. (Champion of Freedom Ser.). (J). (gr. 7-12). 28.95 *(978-1-59935-168-1(4))* Reynolds, Morgan Inc.

Pegis, Jessica. Why Does Democracy Matter? 2016. (Citizenship in Action Ser.). (ENG.). 24p. (J). (gr. 1-4). *(978-0-7787-2597-8(9))* Crabtree Publishing Co.

Pratt, Mary K. Parliaments, 1 vol. 2011. (Exploring World Governments Ser.). (ENG., Illus.). 160p. (J). (gr. 9-12). lib. bdg. 37.07 *(978-1-61714-793-7(1)*, Essential Library) ABDO Publishing Co.

Rees, Peter. Liberty: Blessing or Burden? 2007. (Shockwave: the Human Experience Ser.). (ENG., Illus.). 36p. (J). (gr. 3-5). 25.00 *(978-0-531-17760-0(2)*, Children's Pr.) Scholastic Library Publishing.

Rose, Simon. Aung San Suu Kyi. 2011. (J). (gr. 4-6). pap. 12.95 *(978-1-61690-834-8(3)*, AV2 by Weigl); (Illus.). 24p. (YA). (gr. 3-6). 27.13 *(978-1-61690-833-1(5))* Weigl Pubs., Inc.

Stites, Bill. Democracy: A Primary Source Analysis. (Primary Sources of Political Systems Ser.). 64p. (gr. 5-8). 2009. 58.50 *(978-1-60851-836-4(1))* 2003. (Illus.). (YA). lib. bdg. 31.95 *(978-0-8239-4518-4(9))* Rosen Publishing Group, Inc., The.

Sullivan, Erin Ash. Math in a Democracy & Matemáticas en una Democracia: 6 English, 6 Spanish Adaptations. 2011. (ENG & SPA.). (J). 97.00 net. *(978-1-4108-5715-6(8))* Benchmark Education Co.

Thomas, William David. ¿Qué Es una Constitución? 2008. (Mi gobierno de Estados Unidos (My American Government) Ser.). (SPA., Illus.). 32p. (gr. 3-7). pap. 10.50 *(978-0-8368-8878-2(2)*, Gareth Stevens Learning Library) Stevens, Gareth Publishing LLLP.

—¿Qué Es Una Constitución? 2008. (Mi gobierno de Estados Unidos (My American Government) Ser.). (SPA.). 32p. (gr. 3-7). lib. bdg. 26.00 *(978-0-8368-8873-7(1)*, Gareth Stevens Learning Library) Stevens, Gareth Publishing LLLP.

—What Is a Constitution? 2008. (My American Government Ser.). 32p. (gr. 3-7). pap. 10.50 *(978-0-8368-8868-3(5))*; (Illus.). lib. bdg. 26.00 *(978-0-8368-8863-8(4))* Stevens, Gareth Publishing LLLP. (Gareth Stevens Learning Library).

Travis, Cathy. Constitution Translated for Kids. 3rd ed. 2008. (ENG.). 112p. (J). (gr. 5-17). pap. 11.95 *(978-0-9814534-1-5(4))* Ovation Bks.

—Constitution Translated for Kids / la Constitución traducida para Niños. 2008. (SPA & ENG., Illus.). 176p. (J). (gr. 3-7). pap. 12.95 *(978-0-9814534-2-2(2))* Ovation Bks.

Woolf, Alex. Democracy. 2005. (Systems of Government Ser.). (Illus.). 48p. (gr. 6-12). lib. bdg. 31.00 *(978-0-8368-5883-9(2)*, Gareth Stevens Secondary Library) Stevens, Gareth Publishing LLLP.

DEMOCRATIC PARTY (U.S.)

Bertatsky, Noah. The Democratic Party. Greenhaven Press Staff, ed. 2015. (Opposing Viewpoints Ser.). (ENG., Illus.). 224p. (gr. 10-12). pap. 33.80 *(978-0-7377-7253-1(0)*, Greenhaven Pr., Inc.) Cengage Gale.

Landau, Elaine. Friendly Foes: A Look at Political Parties. 2003. (How Government Works). (ENG., Illus.). 56p. (gr. 4-8). lib. bdg. 25.26 *(978-0-8225-1349-0(8))* Lerner Publishing Group.

Porterfield, Jason. Problems & Progress in American Politics: The Growth of the Democratic Party in the Late 1800s. 2009. (America's Industrial Society in the 19th Century Ser.). 32p. (gr. 4-4). 47.90 *(978-1-61511-339-2(8))* Rosen Publishing Group, Inc., The.

Roberts, Russell. A History of the Democratic Party. 2012. 48p. (J). (gr. 3-6). lib. bdg. 29.95 *(978-1-61228-259-6(8))* Mitchell Lane Pubs., Inc.

Ziff, John. The Modern Democratic Party. 2016. 64p. (J). *(978-1-61900-091-9(1))* Eldorado Ink.

Zilber, Jeremy. Why Mommy Is a Democrat. Firsova, Yuliya, illus. 2005. 28p. (J). pap. 8.00 *(978-0-9786688-0-8(4))* Zilber, Jeremy.

DEMONOLOGY

Coddington, Andrew. Demons. 2016. (Creatures of Fantasy Ser.). 64p. (J). (gr. 6-6). 34.21 *(978-1-5026-1860-3(5))* Cavendish Square Publishing.

Ganeri, Anita. Demons & Ghouls. West, David, illus. 2010. (Dark Side Ser.). 32p. (J). pap. 10.50 *(978-1-4488-1564-7(9))*; lib. bdg. 26.50 *(978-1-61531-896-4(8))* Rosen Publishing Group, Inc., The. (PowerKids Pr.).

Gregson, Susan R. Investigating Demons, Possessions, & Exorcisms, 1 vol. 2010. (Unexplained Phenomena Ser.). (ENG.). 48p. (gr. 3-4). lib. bdg. 31.99 *(978-1-4296-4815-8(5))* Capstone Press of Coughlan Cos.

Osborne, Rick & Strauss, Ed. Angels & Demons, 1 vol. 2004. (2:52 Ser.). (ENG., Illus.). 112p. (J). pap. 7.99 *(978-0-310-70775-2(7))* Zonderkidz.

DEMONOLOGY—FICTION

Agresti, Aimee. Illuminate: A Gilded Wings Novel, Book One. 2013. (ENG.). 544p. (YA). (gr. 7). pap. 9.99 *(978-0-544-02222-5(X))* Houghton Mifflin Harcourt Publishing Co.

—Infatuate: A Gilded Wings Novel, Book Two. 2013. (ENG.). 416p. (YA). (gr. 7). 17.99 *(978-0-547-62615-4(0))* Houghton Mifflin Harcourt Publishing Co.

Alexander, R. C. Unfamiliar Magic. 2011. (ENG.). 368p. (J). (gr. 3-7). pap. 8.99 *(978-0-375-85855-0(5)*, Yearling) Random Hse. Children's Bks.

Arroyo, Raymond. The Lost Staff of Wonders. 2017. (Will Wilder Ser.). (ENG.). 352p. (J). (gr. 3-7). 16.99 *(978-0-553-53967-7(1)*, Crown Books For Young Readers) Random Hse. Children's Bks.

Aryal, Aimee. Hello, Demon Deacon! Cooper, Blair, illus. 2004. 24p. (J). 19.95 *(978-1-932888-14-0(4))* Mascot Bks., Inc.

Barnes, Jennifer Lynn. Every Other Day. 2013. (ENG.). 352p. (J). (gr. 7). pap. 9.99 *(978-1-60684-415-1(6)*, Carolrhoda Lab™) Lerner Publishing Group.

Barrowman, John & Barrowman, Carole E. Nephilim. 2017. (Orion Chronicles Ser.: 2). (ENG.). 320p. (YA). (gr. 7). 16.99 ***(978-1-78185-641-3(9))*** Head of Zeus GBR. Dist: Independent Pubs. Group.

The Beautiful & the Damned. 2014. (ENG., Illus.). 288p. (YA). (gr. 7). pap. 11.99 *(978-1-4424-8836-6(0)*, Simon Pulse) Simon Pulse.

Black, Yelena. Dance of Shadows. 2013. (Dance of Shadows Ser.). (ENG., Illus.). 384p. (YA). (gr. 7-12). 17.99 *(978-1-59990-940-0(5)*, 9781599909400, Bloomsbury USA Childrens) Bloomsbury Publishing USA.

Bracken, Alexandra. The Dreadful Tale of Prosper Redding. 2017. (Prosper Redding Ser.). (ENG.). 368p. (J). (gr. 3-7). 16.99 ***(978-1-4847-7817-3(0))*** Hyperion Bks. for Children.

Braswell, Liz. The Fallen. movie tie-in ed. 2011. (Nine Lives of Chloe King Ser.: 1). (ENG.). 256p. (YA). (gr. 9). pap. 8.99 *(978-1-4424-4134-7(8)*, Simon Pulse) Simon Pulse.

Brennan, Sarah Rees. The Demon's Covenant. (Demon's Lexicon Trilogy Ser.: 2). (ENG., Illus.). (YA). (gr. 9). 2011. 464p. pap. 12.99 *(978-1-4169-6382-0(0))* 2010. 448p. 17.99 *(978-1-4169-6381-3(2))* McElderry, Margaret K. Bks. (McElderry, Margaret K. Bks.).

—The Demon's Lexicon. (Demon's Lexicon Trilogy Ser.: 1). (ENG., Illus.). (YA). (gr. 9). 2010. 352p. pap. 12.99 *(978-1-4169-6380-6(4))* 2009. 336p. 18.99 *(978-1-4169-6379-0(0))* McElderry, Margaret K. Bks. (McElderry, Margaret K. Bks.).

—The Demon's Surrender. 2012. (Demon's Lexicon Trilogy Ser.: 3). (ENG., Illus.). 400p. (YA). (gr. 9). pap. 9.99 *(978-1-4169-6384-4(7)*, McElderry, Margaret K. Bks.) McElderry, Margaret K. Bks.

Brothers, Marilee. Moon Rise. 2009. (YA). pap. 14.95 *(978-0-9821756-9-9(8)*, Bell Bridge Bks.) BelleBks., Inc.

—Shadow Moon. 2011. 230p. (YA). pap. *(978-1-61194-058-9(3))* BelleBks., Inc.

Buckingham, Royce. Demonkeeper. 2007. 216p. (J). *(978-1-4287-4608-4(0))* Penguin Publishing Group.

Catanese, P. W. Down in Flames. 2017. (Donny's Inferno Ser.: 2). (ENG., Illus.). 336p. (J). (gr. 3-7). 16.99 *(978-1-4814-3803-2(4)*, Simon & Schuster/Paula Wiseman Bks.) Simon & Schuster/Paula Wiseman Bks.

Chadda, Sarwat. The City of Death. 2013. (J). pap. *(978-0-545-38519-0(9))*; (ENG.). 336p. (gr. 4-7). 16.99 *(978-0-545-38518-3(0)*, Levine, Arthur A. Bks.) Scholastic, Inc.

—The Savage Fortress. 2012. (ENG.). 304p. (J). (gr. 4-7). 16.99 *(978-0-545-38516-9(4)*, Levine, Arthur A. Bks.) Scholastic, Inc.

Chandler, Elizabeth. Everafter. (Kissed by an Angel Ser.). (ENG., 272p. (YA). (gr. 9). 2014. Illus.). pap. 11.99 *(978-1-4424-0919-4(3))* 2013. 16.99 *(978-1-4424-0918-7(5))* Simon Pulse. (Simon Pulse).

—Evercrossed. (Kissed by an Angel Ser.). (ENG.). (YA). (gr. 7). 2012. 304p. pap. 9.99 *(978-1-4424-0915-6(0))* 2011. 288p. 16.99 *(978-1-4424-0914-9(2))* Simon Pulse. (Simon Pulse).

Clare, Cassandra. City of Ashes. 2008. (Mortal Instruments Ser.: Bk. 2). (YA). (gr. 9). 64.99 *(978-1-60640-964-0(6))* Findaway World, LLC.

—City of Ashes. 2008. (Mortal Instruments Ser.: 2). (ENG.). 464p. (YA). (gr. 9-12). 24.99 *(978-1-4169-1429-7(3)*, McElderry, Margaret K. Bks.) McElderry, Margaret K. Bks.

—City of Bones. (Mortal Instruments Ser.: Bk. 1). (ENG., Illus.). (YA). (gr. 9). 2015. 544p. pap. 13.99 *(978-1-4814-5592-3(3))* 2007. 496p. 21.99 *(978-1-4169-1428-0(5))* 2015. 544p. pap. 13.99 *(978-1-4814-7030-8(2))* McElderry, Margaret K. Bks. (McElderry, Margaret K. Bks.).

—City of Bones. 2008. (Mortal Instruments Ser.: Bk. 1). 485p. (gr. 9-12). 23.00 *(978-0-60686-361-9(4))* Perfection Learning Corp.

—City of Bones, 12 vols. 2007. (Mortal Instruments Ser.: 1). (YA). 131.75 *(978-1-4281-5454-4(X))*; 120.75 *(978-1-4281-5450-6(7))*; 1.25 *(978-1-4281-5445-2(0))*; 286.75 *(978-1-4281-5449-0(3))*; 122.75 *(978-1-4281-5448-3(5))*; 133.75 *(978-1-4281-5452-0(3))* Recorded Bks., Inc.

—City of Bones. 2013. (The Mortal Instruments Ser.: Bk. 1). pap. *(978-1-4424-9308-3(2))* Simon & Schuster, Inc.

—City of Bones. l.t. ed. 2008. (Mortal Instruments Ser.: 1). 629p. (YA). 31.95 *(978-1-4104-0958-4(9))* Thorndike Pr.

—City of Bones. 2015. (Mortal Instruments Ser.: Bk. 1). 544p. (YA). lib. bdg. 25.75 *(978-0-606-37731-7(X))* Turtleback Bks.

—City of Fallen Angels. 2011. (Mortal Instruments Ser.: 4). (ENG.). 432p. (YA). (gr. 9-18). 24.99 *(978-1-4424-0354-3(3)*, McElderry, Margaret K. Bks.) McElderry, Margaret K. Bks.

—City of Fallen Angels, 11 vols. (Mortal Instruments Ser.: 4). (YA). 2012. 133.75 *(978-1-4618-0638-7(0))* 2011. 135.75 *(978-1-4618-0637-0(2))* 2011. 1.25 *(978-1-4640-2483-2(9))* 2011. 317.75 *(978-1-4618-0642-4(9))* 2011. 133.75 *(978-1-4618-0641-7(0))* Recorded Bks., Inc.

—City of Glass. (Mortal Instruments Ser.: Bk. 3). (ENG., (YA). (gr. 9). 2015. Illus.). 592p. pap. 13.99 *(978-1-4814-5598-5(2))* 2009. 560p. 24.99 *(978-1-4169-1430-3(7))* McElderry, Margaret K. Bks. (McElderry, Margaret K. Bks.).

—City of Glass. 2010. 23.00 *(978-1-60686-827-0(6))* Perfection Learning Corp.

—City of Glass. 2009. pap. *(978-1-4424-9308-7(9))* Simon & Schuster.

—City of Glass. 2015. (Mortal Instruments Ser.: Bk. 3). 592p. (YA). lib. bdg. 25.75 *(978-0-606-37733-1(6))* Turtleback Bks.

—City of Heavenly Fire. 2014. (Mortal Instruments Ser.: No. 6). (ENG., Illus.). 752p. (YA). (gr. 9). 24.99 *(978-1-4424-1689-5(0)*, McElderry, Margaret K. Bks.) McElderry, Margaret K. Bks.

—City of Lost Souls. (Mortal Instruments Ser.: Bk. 5). (ENG., (YA). (gr. 9). 2015. Illus.). 592p. pap. 13.99 *(978-1-4814-5600-5(8))* 2012. 544p. 21.99 *(978-1-4424-1686-4(6))* McElderry, Margaret K. Bks. (McElderry, Margaret K. Bks.).

—City of Lost Souls, 16 vols. 2012. (Mortal Instruments Ser.: Bk. 5). (YA). 135.75 *(978-1-4640-3948-5(8))*; 317.75 *(978-1-4640-3949-2(6))*; 133.75 *(978-1-4640-3951-5(8))*; 133.75 *(978-1-4640-3952-2(6))* Recorded Bks., Inc.

—City of Lost Souls. 2015. (Mortal Instruments Ser.: Bk. 5). 592p. (YA). lib. bdg. 25.75 *(978-0-606-37736-2(0))* Turtleback Bks.

—City of Lost Souls. 2012. 512p. pap. *(978-1-4063-3760-0(9))* Walker Bks., Ltd.

—Clockwork Angel. (Infernal Devices Ser.: Bk. 1). (ENG., Illus.). (YA). (gr. 9). 2015. 544p. pap. 13.99 *(978-1-4814-5602-9(4))* 2010. 496p. 24.99 *(978-1-4169-7586-1(1))* McElderry, Margaret K. Bks. (McElderry, Margaret K. Bks.).

—Clockwork Angel. 2012. (Infernal Devices Ser.: 1). (ENG.). 240p. (gr. 8-17). pap. 13.00 *(978-0-316-20098-1(0)*, Yen Pr.) Orbit.

—Clockwork Angel. 2015. (Infernal Devices Ser.: Bk. 1). 544p. (YA). lib. bdg. 25.75 *(978-0-606-37737-9(9))* 2012. (Infernal Devices Graphic Novel Ser.: 1). lib. bdg. 24.55 *(978-0-606-32257-7(4)*, Turtleback) Turtleback Bks.

—Clockwork Prince. (Infernal Devices Ser.: Bk. 2). (YA). 2015. (ENG., Illus.). 560p. (gr. 9). pap. 13.99 *(978-1-4814-5601-2(6))* 2011. (ENG., Illus.). 528p. (gr. 9-18). 24.99 *(978-1-4169-7588-5(8))* 2011. 502p. *(978-1-4424-5174-2(2))* McElderry, Margaret K. Bks. (McElderry, Margaret K. Bks.).

—Clockwork Prince. 2013. (Infernal Devices Ser.: 2). (ENG., Illus.). 256p. (gr. 8-17). pap. 13.00 *(978-0-316-20096-7(4)*, Yen Pr.) Orbit.

—Clockwork Prince. 2015. (Infernal Devices Ser.: Bk. 2). 560p. (YA). lib. bdg. 25.75 *(978-0-606-37895-6(2))* 2013. (Infernal Devices Graphic Novel Ser.: 2). lib. bdg. 24.55 *(978-0-606-32258-4(2)*, Turtleback) Turtleback Bks.

—Clockwork Princess. 2013. (YA). (Infernal Devices Ser.: 3). (ENG., Illus.). 592p. (gr. 9). 24.99 *(978-1-4169-7590-8(X))*; 570p. *(978-1-4424-8541-9(8))* McElderry, Margaret K. Bks. (McElderry, Margaret K. Bks.).

—The Infernal Devices: Clockwork Angel; Clockwork Prince; Clockwork Princess. 2013. (Infernal Devices Ser.: Bks. 1-3). (ENG.). 1520p. (YA). (gr. 9). 74.99 *(978-1-4424-8372-9(5)*, McElderry, Margaret K. Bks.) McElderry, Margaret K. Bks.

—Lady Midnight. 2016. (Dark Artifices Ser.: 1). (ENG., Illus.). 720p. (YA). (gr. 9-12). 24.99 *(978-1-4424-6835-1(1)*, McElderry, Margaret K. Bks.) McElderry, Margaret K. Bks.

—Lady Midnight. 2017. lib. bdg. 26.95 ***(978-0-606-40535-5(6))*** Turtleback Bks.

Clare, Cassandra. The Mortal Instruments: City of Bones; City of Ashes; City of Glass; City of Fallen Angels; City of Lost Souls; City of Heavenly Fire. 2014. (Mortal Instruments Ser.). (ENG., Illus.). 3248p. (YA). (gr. 9). 137.99 *(978-1-4814-4296-1(1)*, McElderry, Margaret K. Bks.) McElderry, Margaret K. Bks.

Clare, Cassandra & Lewis, Joshua. The Shadowhunter's Codex. 2013. (Mortal Instruments Ser.). (ENG., Illus.). 288p. (YA). (gr. 9). 24.99 *(978-1-4424-1692-5(0))*; 49.99 *(978-1-4424-9682-8(7))* McElderry, Margaret K. Bks. (McElderry, Margaret K. Bks.).

Clare, Cassandra, et al. The Bane Chronicles. Clare, Cassandra, ed. 2014. (Bane Chronicles Ser.). (ENG., Illus.). 528p. (YA). (gr. 9). 22.99 *(978-1-4424-9599-9(5)*, McElderry, Margaret K. Bks.) McElderry, Margaret K. Bks.

Clement-Moore, Rosemary. Hell Week. 2009. (Maggie Quinn: Girl vs Evil Ser.). (ENG.). 336p. (YA). (gr. 9). pap. 9.99 *(978-0-385-73415-8(8)*, Delacorte Bks. for Young Readers) Random Hse. Children's Bks.

—Prom Dates from Hell. 2008. (Maggie Quinn: Girl vs Evil Ser.). (ENG.). 320p. (YA). (gr. 9). pap. 8.99 *(978-0-385-73413-4(1)*, Delacorte Bks. for Young Readers) Random Hse. Children's Bks.

Clifford, Leah. A Touch Menacing. 2013. (Touch Mortal Trilogy Ser.: 3). (ENG.). 320p. (YA). (gr. 9). 17.99 *(978-0-06-200505-2(7)*, Greenwillow Bks.) HarperCollins Pubs.

—A Touch Morbid. 2012. (Touch Mortal Trilogy Ser.: 2). (ENG.). 304p. (YA). (gr. 9). 16.99 *(978-0-06-200502-1(2)*, Greenwillow Bks.) HarperCollins Pubs.

—A Touch Mortal. 2011. (Touch Mortal Trilogy Ser.: 1). (ENG.). 432p. (YA). (gr. 8-18). 17.99 *(978-0-06-200499-4(9)*, Greenwillow Bks.) HarperCollins Pubs.

Cluess, Jessica. A Poison Dark & Drowning (Kingdom on Fire, Book Two) 2017. (Kingdom on Fire Ser.: 2). (ENG.). 432p. (YA). (gr. 7). 17.99 ***(978-0-553-53594-5(3)***, Random Hse. Bks. for Young Readers) Random Hse. Children's Bks.

Cohen, Marina. The Doll's Eye. 2017. (ENG.). 208p. (J). 16.99 *(978-1-62672-204-0(8)*, 9781626722040) Roaring Brook Pr.

Colfer, Eoin. Artemis Fowl & the Atlantis Complex. 2012. (ENG.). 384p. (J). (gr. 5-9). pap. 8.99 *(978-1-4231-2972-1(5))* Hyperion Pr.

—The Atlantis Complex. 2010. (Artemis Fowl Ser.: 7). (ENG.). 368p. (J). (gr. 5-9). 17.99 *(978-1-4231-2819-9(2))* Hyperion Pr.

—The Atlantis Complex. 2012. (Artemis Fowl Ser.: 7). (J). lib. bdg. 19.65 *(978-0-606-23614-0(7)*, Turtleback) Turtleback Bks.

—The Lost Colony. rev. ed. 2009. (Artemis Fowl Ser.). (ENG.). 432p. (J). (gr. 5-9). pap. 8.99 *(978-1-4231-2494-8(4))* Hyperion Pr.

Connolly, John. The Gates. 2009. (ENG.). 304p. 24.00 *(978-1-4391-7263-6(3)*, Beyond Words/Atria Bks.) Atria Bks.

Connolly, Tina. Seriously Wicked. 2016. (YA). lib. bdg. 20.85 *(978-0-606-38783-5(8))* Turtleback Bks.

Creagh, Kelly. Oblivion. 2015. (ENG.). 448p. (YA). (gr. 7). 18.99 *(978-1-4424-3627-5(1))* Simon & Schuster Children's Publishing.

Dawson, Delilah S. Servants of the Storm. 2014. (ENG., Illus.). 384p. (YA). (gr. 9). 17.99 *(978-1-4424-8378-1(4)*, Simon Pulse) Simon Pulse.

Desrochers, Lisa. Original Sin. 2011. (Personal Demons Ser.: 2). (ENG.). 400p. (YA). (gr. 9-18). pap. 25.99 *(978-0-7653-2809-0(7)*, 9780765328090, Tor Teen) Doherty, Tom Assocs., LLC.

Drago, Ty. The Undertakers: The Rise of the Corpses. 2011. (ENG.). 480p. (J). (gr. 5-8). 13.99 *(978-1-4022-4785-9(0)*, 9781402247859, Sourcebooks Jabberwocky) Sourcebooks, Inc.

Elliott, Jenny. Save Me. 2015. (ENG.). 336p. (YA). (gr. 7-12). pap. 9.99 *(978-1-250-06147-8(4)*, 9781250061478) Feiwel & Friends.

Fawkes, Ray. The Better House Trap, Vol. 3. 2012. (ENG., Illus.). 72p. (J). pap. 7.99 *(978-1-934964-76-7(X)*, 9781934964767) Oni Pr., Inc.

—Possessions Volume 2: The Ghost Table GN. 2011. (ENG., Illus.). 88p. (J). pap. 5.99 *(978-1-934964-61-3(1)*, 9781934964613) Oni Pr., Inc.

Frenette, Bethany. Dark Star. 2013. (Dark Star Ser.). (ENG.). 384p. (YA). (gr. 7-12). pap. 9.99 *(978-1-4231-4853-1(3))* Hyperion Pr.

Frost, Heather. Guardians. 2013. (Seers - Trilogy Ser.: Vol. 3). (ENG.). 424p. (J). (gr. 8-12). pap. 17.99 *(978-1-4621-1035-3(5)*, Sweetwater Bks.) Cedar Fort, Inc./CFI Distribution.

Garcia, Kami. Unbreakable. (Legion Ser.: 1). (ENG.). (YA). (gr. 7-17). 2014. 336p. pap. 10.00 *(978-0-316-21018-8(8))* 2013. 320p. 18.00 *(978-0-316-21017-1(X))* Little, Brown Bks. for Young Readers.

Gibbons, Alan. Renegade. 2010. (ENG., Illus.). 336p. (YA). (gr. 7-17). 8.99 *(978-1-4440-0079-5(9)*, Orion Children's Bks.) Hachette Children's Group GBR. Dist: Hachette Bk. Group.

—Scared to Death. 2010. (ENG., Illus.). 352p. (J). (gr. 4-6). pap. 8.99 *(978-1-4440-0143-3(4)*, Orion Children's Bks.) Hachette Children's Group GBR. Dist: Hachette Bk. Group.

Gier, Kerstin. Dream a Little Dream. Bell, Anthea, tr. from GER. 2015. (Silver Trilogy Ser.: 1). (ENG.). 336p. (YA). (gr. 7). 17.99 *(978-1-62779-027-7(6)*, 9781627790277, Holt, Henry & Co. Bks. For Young Readers) Holt, Henry & Co.

—Just Dreaming. Bell, Anthea, tr. from GER. 2017. (Silver Trilogy Ser.). (ENG.). 368p. (YA). 18.99 *(978-1-62779-080-2(2)*, 9781627790802, Holt, Henry & Co. Bks. For Young Readers) Holt, Henry & Co.

Goodman, Alison. The Dark Days Pact. 2017. (Lady Helen Novel Ser.: 2). (ENG.). 496p. (YA). (gr. 9). 18.99 *(978-0-670-78548-3(2)*, Viking Books for Young Readers) Penguin Young Readers Group.

Graves, Annie. The Demon Babysitter. McElhinney, Glenn, illus. 2015. (Nightmare Club Ser.: 7). (ENG.). 64p. (J). (gr. 2-5). pap. 6.99 *(978-1-4677-6041-6(2)*, Darby Creek); lib. bdg. 25.32 *(978-1-4677-4355-6(0))* Lerner Publishing Group.

Gustafson, Scott. Eddie: The Lost Youth of Edgar Allan Poe. Gustafson, Scott, illus. (ENG., Illus.). 208p. (J). (gr. 3-7). 2012. pap. 6.99 *(978-1-4169-9765-8(2))* 2011. 15.99 *(978-1-4169-9764-1(4))* Simon & Schuster Bks. For Young Readers. (Simon & Schuster Bks. For Young Readers).

Hawkins, Rachel. Demonglass. 2012. (ENG.). 384p. (YA). (gr. 6-17). pap. 8.99 *(978-1-4231-2844-1(3))* Hyperion Pr.

—Spell Bound (a Hex Hall Novel) 2013. (ENG.). 352p. (YA). (gr. 7-17). pap. 9.99 *(978-1-4231-2140-4(6))* Hyperion Pr.

Hayes, Gwen. Dreaming Awake. 2012. (ENG.). 332p. (YA). (gr. 7-18). 9.99 *(978-0-451-23554-1(1)*, Berkley) Penguin Publishing Group.

—Falling Under. 2011. (ENG.). 336p. (YA). (gr. 7-18). 9.99 *(978-0-451-23268-7(2)*, Berkley) Penguin Publishing Group.

Higgins, Wendy. Sweet Evil. 2012. (Sweet Evil Ser.: 1). (ENG.). 464p. (YA). (gr. 8). pap. 9.99 *(978-0-06-208561-0(1)*, HarperTeen) HarperCollins Pubs.

—Sweet Peril. 2013. (Sweet Evil Ser.: 2). (ENG.). 384p. (YA). (gr. 8). pap. 9.99 *(978-0-06-226594-4(6)*, HarperTeen) HarperCollins Pubs.

—Sweet Reckoning. 2014. (Sweet Evil Ser.: 3). (ENG.). 400p. (YA). (gr. 8). pap. 9.99 *(978-0-06-226597-5(0)*, HarperTeen) HarperCollins Pubs.

—Sweet Temptation. 2015. (Sweet Evil Ser.: 4). (ENG.). 512p. (YA). (gr. 8). pap. 9.99 *(978-0-06-238142-2(3)*, HarperTeen) HarperCollins Pubs.

Hulme-Cross, Benjamin. The House of Memories. Evergreen, Nelson, illus. 2015. (Dark Hunter Ser.). (ENG.). 64p. (J). (gr. 4-8). pap. 4.99 *(978-1-4677-8085-8(5))* Lerner Publishing Group.

Jasper, Rick & Reece, Richard. The Late Bus. 2011. (Night Fall Ser.). (ENG.). 112p. (YA). (gr. 6-12). pap. 7.95 *(978-0-7613-7812-9(X))*; lib. bdg. 27.93 *(978-0-7613-7745-0(X))* Lerner Publishing Group.

Johnson, Maureen. Devilish. 2013. (ENG.). 304p. (YA). (gr. 7). pap. 9.99 *(978-0-14-750855-3(X)*, Speak) Penguin Young Readers Group.

Jones, Kimberly K. The Genie Scheme. 2009. (ENG.). 192p. (J). (gr. 3-7). 15.99 *(978-1-4169-5554-2(2)*, McElderry, Margaret K. Bks.) McElderry, Margaret K. Bks.

Jones, Willie. Demonology. 2004. 110p. (YA). per. *(978-1-932496-13-0(0))* Penman Publishing, Inc.

Keeble, Helen. No Angel. 2013. (ENG.). 384p. (YA). (gr. 8). pap. 9.99 *(978-0-06-208227-5(2)*, HarperTeen) HarperCollins Pubs.

Kelly, Margo. Unlocked. 2016. (ENG.). 304p. (YA). 17.99 *(978-1-4405-9359-8(0)*, Simon Pulse) Simon Pulse.

Khulekani, Magubane. Angels Salvation. 2007. 96p. pap. *(978-1-86900-865-9(0))* UmSinsi Pr. ZAF. Dist: Michigan State Univ. Pr.

Kinde, Christa. The Hidden Deep, 1 vol. 2013. (Threshold Ser.). (ENG.). 272p. (J). 14.99 *(978-0-310-72489-6(9))* Zonderkidz.

Kurtagich, Dawn. The Dead House. 2015. (ENG., Illus.). 432p. (J). (gr. 10-17). 18.00 *(978-0-316-29868-1(9))* Little, Brown Bks. for Young Readers.

Lancett, Peter. The Shadow in the Dark, 1 vol. unabr. ed. 2010. (Dark Man Ser.). (ENG.). 34p. (YA). (gr. 9-12). pap. 7.95 *(978-1-61651-021-3(8))* Saddleback Educational Publishing, Inc.

Lewis, Richard. The Demon Queen. 2012. (ENG.). 240p. (YA). (gr. 7). pap. 11.99 *(978-1-4169-3590-2(8)*, Simon & Schuster Bks. For Young Readers) Simon & Schuster Bks. For Young Readers.

Lloyd-Jones, Emily. The Hearts We Sold. 2017. (ENG.). 400p. (YA). (gr. 10-17). 17.99 ***(978-0-316-31459-6(5))*** Little Brown & Co.

Lovegrove, James. The Lord of Fire (Five Lords of Pain Book 5) 2013. (Five Lords of Pain Ser.: 5). (ENG.). 96p. (YA). (gr.

8-12). pap. 7.95 *(978-1-78112-262-4(8))* Lerner Publishing Group.
—The Lord of Tears (Five Lords of Pain Book 3) 2013. (Five Lords of Pain Ser.: 3). (ENG.). 96p. (YA). (gr. 8-12). pap. 7.95 *(978-1-78112-256-3(3))* Lerner Publishing Group.
—The Lord of the Mountain (Five Lords of Pain Book 1) 2013. (Five Lords of Pain Ser.: 1). (ENG.). 96p. (YA). (gr. 8-12). pap. 7.95 *(978-1-78112-250-1(4))* Lerner Publishing Group.
—The Lord of the Typhoon (Five Lords of Pain Book 4) 2013. (Five Lords of Pain Ser.: 4). (ENG.). 96p. (YA). (gr. 8-12). pap. 7.95 *(978-1-78112-259-4(8))* Lerner Publishing Group.
—The Lord of the Void (Five Lords of Pain Book 2) 2013. (Five Lords of Pain Ser.: 2). (ENG.). 96p. (YA). (gr. 8-12). pap. 7.95 *(978-1-78112-253-2(9))* Lerner Publishing Group.
Lynn, Erin. Speed Demon. 2008. (ENG.). 192p. (YA). (gr. 9-18). 9.99 *(978-0-425-22366-6(3)*, Berkley) Penguin Publishing Group.
MacHale, D. J. Pendragon: The Merchant of Death; The Lost City of Fear; The Never War; The Reality Bug; Black Water. 2013. (Pendragon Ser.). (ENG., Illus.). 1968p. (J). (gr. 5-9). pap. 49.99 *(978-1-4424-9926-3(5)*, Simon & Schuster/Paula Wiseman Bks.) Simon & Schuster/Paula Wiseman Bks.
Mahoney, Karen. The Stone Demon. 2013. (Iron Witch Ser.: 3). (ENG.). 336p. (YA). pap. 9.99 *(978-0-7387-3340-1(7)*, Flux) North Star Editions.
Marks, Rachel A. Darkness Fair, 0 vols. 2016. (Dark Cycle Ser.: 2). (ENG.). 324p. (YA). (gr. 8-13). pap. 9.99 *(978-1-5039-5029-0(8)*, 9781503950290, Skyscape) Amazon Publishing.
Marr, Melissa. Untamed City - Carnival of Secrets. 2015. (Untamed City Ser.). (ENG.). 368p. (YA). (gr. 8). pap. 9.99 *(978-0-06-235494-5(9))* HarperCollins Pubs.
Mason-Black, Jennifer. Devil & the Bluebird. 2016. (ENG.). 336p. (J). (gr. 8-17). 17.95 *(978-1-4197-2000-0(7)*, Amulet Bks.) Abrams, Inc.
Matharu, Taran. The Battlemage. 2017. (Summoner Trilogy Ser.: bk.3). (ENG., Illus.). 384p. (YA). 18.99 ***(978-1-250-07632-8(3)***, 9781250076328) Feiwel & Friends.
—The Inquisition. 2016. (Summoner Trilogy: Bk. 2). (ENG.). 368p. (YA). (gr. 7). 17.99 *(978-1-250-07631-1(5)*, 9781250076311) Feiwel & Friends.
—The Inquisition. 2017. (Summoner Trilogy Ser.: Bk. 2). (ENG.). 384p. (YA). pap. 10.99 *(978-1-250-11521-8(3)*, 9781250115218) Square Fish.
—The Inquisition. 2017. (Summoner Ser.: 2). (YA). lib. bdg. 22.10 ***(978-0-606-39945-6(3))*** Turtleback Bks.
Matharu, Taran. The Novice. 2015. (Summoner Trilogy: Bk. 1). (ENG.). 384p. (YA). (gr. 7). 18.99 *(978-1-250-06712-8(X)*, 9781250067128) Feiwel & Friends.
—The Novice. Barcellona, Christine, ed. 2016. (Summoner Trilogy Ser.: Bk. 1). (ENG.). 384p. (YA). pap. 10.99 *(978-1-250-08005-9(3)*, 9781250080059) Square Fish.
—The Novice. 2016. (Summoner Trilogy: Bk. 1). (ENG.). (YA). (gr. 7-12). lib. bdg. 22.10 ***(978-0-606-39884-8(8))*** Turtleback Bks.
Mathews, Temple. The New Kid. 2010. (New Kid Ser.). (ENG.). 288p. (J). (gr. 6-11). pap. 9.99 *(978-1-935618-27-0(X))* BenBella Bks.
—The Sword of Armageddon. 2010. ix, 291p. *(978-1-935618-17-1(2))* BenBella Bks.
McGann, Erika. The Demon Notebook. 2014. (Demon Notebook Ser.: 1). (ENG.). 288p. (J). (gr. 3-6). pap. 6.99 *(978-1-4022-9538-6(3)*, 9781402295386, Sourcebooks Jabberwocky) Sourcebooks, Inc.
McNeil, Gretchen. Possess. (ENG.). (YA). (gr. 8). 2012. 400p. pap. 9.99 *(978-0-06-206072-3(4))* 2011. 384p. 17.99 *(978-0-06-206071-6(6))* HarperCollins Pubs.
Milford, Kate. The Boneshaker. Offermann, Andrea, illus. 2011. (ENG.). 384p. (J). (gr. 5-7). pap. 7.99 *(978-0-547-55004-6(9))* Houghton Mifflin Harcourt Publishing Co.
—The Broken Lands. Offermann, Andrea, illus. 2012. (ENG.). 464p. (YA). (gr. 7). 16.99 *(978-0-547-73966-3(4))* Houghton Mifflin Harcourt Publishing Co.
Mills, Samuel. The Demon Slayer. 2009. 192p. (YA). pap. 15.00 *(978-0-88010-701-3(4))* SteinerBooks, Inc.
Mitchell, Todd. The Secret to Lying. (ENG., Illus.). 336p. (YA). (gr. 9). 2011. pap. 7.99 *(978-0-7636-5620-1(8))* 2010. 17.99 *(978-0-7636-4084-2(0))* Candlewick Pr.
Molinari, Laurice E. Pillars of Fire, 1 vol. 2016. (Ether Novel Ser.). (ENG.). 368p. (J). pap. 8.99 *(978-0-310-73562-5(9))* Zonderkidz.
Molinari, Laurice Elehwany. Pillars of Fire, 1 vol. 2015. (Ether Novel Ser.). (ENG.). 368p. (J). 16.99 *(978-0-310-73556-4(4))* Zonderkidz.
Mosley, Walter. When the Thrill Is Gone, 3 vols. 2012. (Leonid McGill Mystery Ser.: Bk. 3). (ENG.). 384p. (gr. 12). 16.00 *(978-0-451-23565-7(7)*, Berkley) Penguin Publishing Group.
Myers, Bill. Invisible Terror Collection, 1 vol., Vol. 2. 2011. (Forbidden Doors Ser.). (ENG.). 368p. (YA). pap. 12.99 *(978-0-310-72904-4(1))* Zondervan.
Neff, Henry H. The Fiend & the Forge. 2011. (Tapestry Ser.). (ENG., Illus.). 560p. (J). (gr. 3-7). 7.99 *(978-0-375-83899-6(6)*, Yearling) Random Hse. Children's Bks.
—The Maelstrom: Book Four of the Tapestry. Neff, Henry H., illus. 2013. (Tapestry Ser.). (ENG., Illus.). 480p. (J). (gr. 3-7). 7.99 *(978-0-375-87148-1(9)*, Yearling) Random Hse. Children's Bks.
—The Second Siege. 2010. (Tapestry Ser.). (ENG., Illus.). 512p. (J). (gr. 3-7). 7.99 *(978-0-375-83897-2(X)*, Yearling) Random Hse. Children's Bks.
Neill, Chloe. Charmfall. 2012. (Dark Elite Ser.: 3). (ENG.). 288p. (YA). (gr. 9). 9.99 *(978-0-451-23080-5(9)*, Berkley) Penguin Publishing Group.
Oh, Ellen. Warrior. 2015. (Prophecy Ser.: 2). (ENG.). 352p. (YA). (gr. 8). pap. 9.99 *(978-0-06-209113-0(1)*, HarperTeen) HarperCollins Pubs.
Oliver, Jana. The Demon Trapper's Daughter. 2011. (Demon Trappers Ser.: 1). (ENG.). 368p. (YA). (gr. 7-18). pap. 9.99 *(978-0-312-61478-2(0)*, 9780312614782, St. Martin's Griffin) St. Martin's Pr.
—Forgiven. 2012. (Demon Trappers Ser.: 3). (ENG.). 368p. (YA). (gr. 7). pap. 9.99 *(978-0-312-61480-5(2)*, 9780312614805, St. Martin's Griffin) St. Martin's Pr.
Pashley, Hilton. Gabriel's Clock. 2014. (ENG.). 304p. (J). (gr. 5-7). 16.99 *(978-0-544-30176-4(5)*, HMH Books For Young Readers) Houghton Mifflin Harcourt Publishing Co.
Paver, Michelle. Ghost Hunter. Taylor, Geoff, illus. 2010. (Chronicles of Ancient Darkness Ser.: 6). 304p. (J). (gr. 5-18). 16.99 *(978-0-06-072840-3(X)*, Tegen, Katherine Bks) HarperCollins Pubs.
—Soul Eater. Taylor, Geoff, illus. 2008. (Chronicles of Ancient Darkness Ser.: 3). 352p. (J). (gr. 5). pap. 6.99 *(978-0-06-072833-5(7)*, Tegen, Katherine Bks) HarperCollins Pubs.
—Wolf Brother. Taylor, Geoff, illus. 2006. (Chronicles of Ancient Darkness Ser.: 1). 320p. (J). (gr. 5-9). reprint ed. per. 6.99 *(978-0-06-072827-4(2)*, Tegen, Katherine Bks) HarperCollins Pubs.
—Wolf Brother, 6 vols. 2005. (Chronicles of Ancient Darkness Ser.: 1). (J). 89.75 *(978-1-4193-3811-3(0))*; 91.75 *(978-1-4193-3809-0(9))*; 76.75 *(978-1-4193-2628-8(7))*; 73.75 *(978-1-4193-2630-1(9))* Recorded Bks., Inc.
Pearce, Jackson. As You Wish. 2009. (ENG.). 304p. (YA). (gr. 8-18). 16.99 *(978-0-06-166152-5(X)*, HarperTeen) HarperCollins Pubs.
Richardson, E. E. Black Bones. 2012. (Stoke Books Titles Ser.). (ENG.). 80p. (YA). (gr. 8-12). pap. 6.95 *(978-1-78112-100-9(1))*; lib. bdg. 22.60 *(978-1-78112-101-6(X))* Lerner Publishing Group.
Richardson, Sharde. Watched. 2011. (ENG.). 290p. (YA). pap. 12.99 *(978-0-9831498-0-4(1))* Jolt.
Romney, J. P. The Monster on the Road Is Me. 2016. (ENG.). 336p. (YA). 17.99 *(978-0-374-31654-9(6)*, 9780374316549, Farrar, Straus & Giroux (BYR)) Farrar, Straus & Giroux.
Rossi, Veronica. Riders. (ENG.). (YA). 2017. (Riders Ser.: 1). 384p. pap. 9.99 *(978-0-7653-8255-9(5)*, 9780765382559) 2016. 368p. 17.99 *(978-0-7653-8254-2(7)*, 9780765382542) Doherty, Tom Assocs., LLC. (Tor Teen).
Rubens, Michael. Emily & the Spellstone. 2017. (ENG.). 288p. (J). (gr. 5-7). 16.99 *(978-0-544-79086-5(3))* Houghton Mifflin Harcourt Publishing Co.
Shan, Darren, pseud. Bec. 2008. (ENG.). 256p. (YA). (gr. 10-17). pap. 10.00 *(978-0-316-01390-1(0))* Little, Brown Bks. for Young Readers.
—Blood Beast. 2008. (ENG.). 224p. (YA). (gr. 10-17). pap. 8.99 *(978-0-316-00378-0(6))* Little, Brown Bks. for Young Readers.
—Dark Calling. 2010. (ENG.). 224p. (YA). (gr. 10-17). pap. 10.00 *(978-0-316-04872-9(0))* Little, Brown Bks. for Young Readers.
—Death's Shadow. 2009. (ENG.). 240p. (YA). (gr. 10-17). pap. 10.00 *(978-0-316-00382-7(4))* Little Brown & Co.
—Demon Apocalypse. 2009. (ENG.). 208p. (YA). (gr. 10-17). pap. 9.99 *(978-0-316-00380-3(8))* Little, Brown Bks. for Young Readers.
—Demon Thief. 2007. (ENG.). 256p. (YA). (gr. 10-17). per. 10.00 *(978-0-316-01238-6(6))* Little, Brown Bks. for Young Readers.
—Lord Loss. 2005. (Demonata Ser.: Bk. 1). (Illus.). 272p. *(978-0-00-719321-9(1))* HarperCollins Pubs. Australia.
—Lord Loss. 2006. (ENG.). 240p. (J). (gr. 10-17). per. 10.99 *(978-0-316-01233-1(5))* Little, Brown Bks. for Young Readers.
—Lord Loss. 2006. (Demonata Ser.: 1). (J). 22.10 *(978-1-4177-8308-3(7)*, Turtleback) Turtleback Bks.
—Slawter. 2007. (ENG.). 240p. (J). (gr. 10-17). pap. 10.99 *(978-0-316-01388-8(9))* Little, Brown Bks. for Young Readers.
Shouoto, Aya. He's My Only Vampire, Vol. 4. 2015. (He's My Only Vampire Ser.: 4). (ENG., Illus.). 160p. (gr. 11-17). pap. 13.00 *(978-0-316-26168-5(8)*, Yen Pr.) Orbit.
Skovron, Jon. Misfit. 2011. (ENG.). 384p. (YA). (gr. 9-17). 16.95 *(978-1-4197-0021-7(9)*, Amulet Bks.) Abrams, Inc.
Slater, Adam. The Shadowing - Hunted. 2011. (ENG.). 208p. (gr. 7). 16.99 *(978-1-60684-261-4(7)*, Carolrhoda Lab™) Lerner Publishing Group.
—The Shadowing #2: Skinned. 2012. (ENG.). 256p. (J). (gr. 7-7). 16.99 *(978-1-60684-262-1(5)*, Carolrhoda Lab™) Lerner Publishing Group.
Smith, Alexander Gordon. Hellfighters. 2016. (Devil's Engine Ser.: 2). (ENG.). 320p. (YA). 18.99 *(978-0-374-30172-9(7)*, 9780374301729, Farrar, Straus & Giroux (BYR)) Farrar, Straus & Giroux.
—Hellraisers. 2015. (Devil's Engine Ser.: 1). (ENG.). 352p. (YA). (gr. 7). 17.99 *(978-0-374-30169-9(7)*, 9780374301699, Farrar, Straus & Giroux (BYR)) Farrar, Straus & Giroux.
Smith, Jada. Touched by an Angel. 2009. 76p. pap. 13.95 *(978-1-4251-8552-7(5))* Trafford Publishing.
Smith, L. J. The Temptation, Vol. 6. 2013. (Secret Circle Ser.: 6). (ENG.). 288p. (YA). (gr. 8). 17.99 *(978-0-06-213047-1(1)*, HarperTeen) HarperCollins Pubs.
Smith, Ronald L. Hoodoo. 2015. (ENG.). 224p. (J). (gr. 5-7). 16.99 *(978-0-544-44525-3(2)*, Clarion Bks.) Houghton Mifflin Harcourt Trade & Reference Pubs.
—Hoodoo. 2017. (ENG.). (J). (gr. 5-7). lib. bdg. 18.40 ***(978-0-606-39820-6(1))*** Turtleback Bks.
Stewart, Martin. Riverkeep. (ENG.). 416p. (YA). (gr. 7). 2017. pap. 10.99 ***(978-1-101-99831-1(8)***, Speak) 2016. (Illus.). 17.99 *(978-1-101-99829-8(6)*, Viking Books for Young Readers) Penguin Young Readers Group.
Tanabe, Yellow. Kekkaishi, Vol. 22. Tanabe, Yellow, illus. 2010. (ENG., Illus.). 192p. pap. 9.99 *(978-1-4215-3069-7(4))* Viz Media.
—Kekkaishi, Vol. 23. Tanabe, Yellow, illus. 2010. (ENG., Illus.). 192p. pap. 9.99 *(978-1-4215-3200-4(X))* Viz Media.
Taylor, Laini. Daughter of Smoke & Bone. 2011. (ENG.). 432p. (YA). (gr. 10-17). 20.00 *(978-0-316-13402-6(3))* Little Brown & Co.
—Daughter of Smoke & Bone. 2012. (ENG.). (YA). (gr. 10-17). 448p. pap. 12.99 *(978-0-316-13399-9(X))*; 624p. pap. 28.99 *(978-0-316-22435-2(9))* Little, Brown Bks. for Young Readers.
—Daughter of Smoke & Bone. 2012. (Daughter of Smoke & Bone Ser.: 1). (YA). lib. bdg. 24.50 *(978-0-606-26704-5(2)*, Turtleback) Turtleback Bks.
—Days of Blood & Starlight. (ENG.). (YA). (gr. 10-17). 2014. 544p. pap. 12.99 *(978-0-316-13398-2(1))* 2012. (Illus.). 528p. 18.99 *(978-0-316-13397-5(3))* 2012. 688p. 39.99 *(978-0-316-22433-8(2))* Little, Brown Bks. for Young Readers.
Thomson, Celia & Braswell, Liz. The Nine Lives of Chloe King: The Fallen; the Stolen; the Chosen. 2011. (Nine Lives of Chloe King Ser.). (ENG.). 784p. (YA). (gr. 9). pap. 13.99 *(978-1-4424-3570-4(4)*, Simon Pulse) Simon Pulse.
Toffler-Corrie, Laura. My Totally Awkward Supernatural Crush. 2013. (ENG.). 352p. (J). (gr. 7). 17.99 *(978-1-59643-733-3(2))* Roaring Brook Pr.
Varley, Dax. The Crow. Proctor, Jon, illus. 2016. (ENG.). 48p. (J). lib. bdg. *(978-1-62402-160-2(3))* Magic Wagon.
—Graveyard Dirt. Proctor, Jon, illus. 2016. (ENG.). 48p. (J). lib. bdg. *(978-1-62402-158-9(1))* Magic Wagon.
—Hideout. Proctor, Jon, illus. 2016. (ENG.). 48p. (J). lib. bdg. 28.50 *(978-1-62402-157-2(3))* Magic Wagon.
—The Locket. Proctor, Jon, illus. 2016. (ENG.). 48p. (J). lib. bdg. *(978-1-62402-159-6(X))* Magic Wagon.
Velasquez, Crystal. The Circle of Lies. 2016. (Hunters of Chaos Ser.: 2). (ENG., Illus.). 240p. (J). (gr. 3-7). 16.99 *(978-1-4814-2455-4(6)*, Aladdin) Simon & Schuster Children's Publishing.
—Hunters of Chaos. 2016. (Hunters of Chaos Ser.: 1). (ENG., Illus.). 288p. (J). (gr. 3-7). pap. 6.99 *(978-1-4814-2453-0(X)*, Aladdin) Simon & Schuster Children's Publishing.
Verday, Jessica. The Beautiful & the Damned. 2013. (ENG., Illus.). 272p. (YA). (gr. 7). 17.99 *(978-1-4424-8835-9(2)*, Simon Pulse) Simon Pulse.
Walsh, Pat. The Crowfield Demon. (J). 2013. 360p. *(978-0-545-37350-0(6))* 2012. (ENG.). 368p. (gr. 3-7). 16.99 *(978-0-545-31769-6(X)*, Chicken Hse., The) Scholastic, Inc.
Walters, Ednah. Awakened: Book One of the Guardian Legacy. 2010. 272p. (YA). pap. 12.99 *(978-1-61706-038-0(0))* Pill Hill Pr.
Webb, Mack H., Jr. Danny & the Detention Demons. Espinola, Nicole & Nealon, Eve, illus. l.t. ed. 2007. 52p. (J). per. 15.95 *(978-0-9779576-2-0(4))* Pilinut Pr., Inc.
West, Temple. Velvet. 2015. (ENG.). 416p. (YA). (gr. 8). pap. 9.99 *(978-1-250-05708-2(6)*, 9781250057082) Feiwel & Friends.
Whelan, Daniel. The Box of Demons. 2016. (ENG.). 256p. (YA). (gr. 7). pap. 10.99 *(978-1-4472-7373-8(7))* Pan Macmillan GBR. Dist: Independent Pubs. Group.
Yancey, Rick. Alfred Kropp: the Seal of Solomon. 2015. (Alfred Kropp Ser.). (ENG.). 352p. (YA). (gr. 7). pap. 9.99 *(978-1-61963-917-1(3)*, 9781619639171, Bloomsbury USA Childrens) Bloomsbury Publishing USA.
Yovanoff, Brenna. The Space Between. 2012. (ENG., Illus.). 384p. (YA). (gr. 9). pap. 8.99 *(978-1-59514-483-6(8)*, Razorbill) Penguin Young Readers Group.
Zafón, Carlos Ruiz. The Midnight Palace. 2012. (ENG.). 320p. (YA). (gr. 7-17). pap. 10.00 *(978-0-316-04474-5(1))* Little, Brown Bks. for Young Readers.

DENMARK

Docalavich, Heather. Denmark. 2007. (European Union Ser.). (Illus.). 88p. (YA). (gr. 3-7). lib. bdg. 21.95 *(978-1-4222-0043-8(4))* Mason Crest.
Weigand, John D. Wonderful, Wonderful Copenhagen! a Kid's Guide to Copenhagen, Denmark. Dyan, Penelope, photos by. 2011. (Illus.). 34p. pap. 11.95 *(978-1-935630-62-3(8))* Bellissima Publishing, LLC.
Zobel, Derek. Denmark. 2011. (Illus.). 32p. (J). lib. bdg. *(978-0-531-20952-3(0))*; (ENG., (gr. 3-7). lib. bdg. 26.95 *(978-1-60014-573-5(6)*, Blastoff! Readers) Bellwether Media.

DENMARK—FICTION

Andersen, Hans Christian. Andersen's Fairy Tales. 2005. pap. *(978-1-905432-22-6(4))* Dodo Pr.
—The Ice-Maiden & Other Tales. Fuller, Fanny, tr. 2007. 128p. per. 10.95 *(978-1-60312-043-2(2))* Aegypan.
—Tales of Hans Christian Andersen. Stewart, Joel, illus. 2010. (Candlewick Illustrated Classics Ser.). (ENG.). 208p. (J). (gr. 3-7). pap. 12.99 *(978-0-7636-4892-3(2))* Candlewick Pr.
Andersen, Hans Christian & Tatar, Maria. Hans Christian Andersen. Allen, Julie K., tr. from DAN. 2007. (ENG., Illus.). 496p. 39.95 *(978-0-393-06081-2(0)*, 6081) Norton, W. W. & Co., Inc.
Burglon, Nora. Sticks Across the Chimney: A Story of Denmark. 2005. (Illus.). 224p. (J). per. 11.95 *(978-1-892857-13-2(8))* Whole Spirit Pr.
Christensen, Gerda. Troll Peter Discovers the Bog-Woman's Secret & Other Stories. 2010. 40p. pap. 18.27 *(978-1-4251-8822-1(2))* Trafford Publishing.
Elvgren, Jennifer. The Whispering Town. Santomauro, Fabio, illus. 2014. (Holocaust Ser.). (ENG.). 32p. (J). (gr. 2-5). 17.95 *(978-1-4677-1194-4(2))*; 7.95 *(978-1-4677-1195-1(0))* Lerner Publishing Group.
Frisch, Wilhelmine. The Storks of Lillegaard. Jauss, Anne Marie, illus. 2011. 230p. 46.95 *(978-1-258-08105-8(9))* Literary Licensing, LLC.
Houts, Michelle. Winterfrost. 2016. (ENG.). 272p. (J). (gr. 3-7). pap. 7.99 *(978-0-7636-9101-1(1))* Candlewick Pr.
Jensen, Marie-Louise. Between Two Seas. 2009. pap. 1.00 *(978-1-4074-4422-2(0))* Recorded Bks., Inc.
Lois, Lowry. Compte les Etoiles. pap. 16.95 *(978-2-211-03436-4(5))* Archimède Editions FRA. Dist: Distribooks, Inc.
—Number the Stars. (ENG.). 160p. (J). (gr. 5-7). 2011. pap. 7.99 *(978-0-547-57709-8(5))* 25th anniv. ed. 2014. 17.99 *(978-0-544-34000-8(0)*, HMH Books For Young Readers) Houghton Mifflin Harcourt Publishing Co.
—Number the Stars. 2004. 144p. (J). (gr. 5-9). pap. 29.00 incl. audio *(978-1-4000-8637-5(X)*, Listening Library) Random Hse. Audio Publishing Group.
Marsden, John. Hamlet. 2009. (ENG., Illus.). 240p. (YA). (gr. 9-18). 16.99 *(978-0-7636-4451-2(X))* Candlewick Pr.
Matas, Carol. Code Name Kris. 2007. (ENG.). 164p. (J). (gr. 3-7). pap. 12.95 *(978-1-4169-6162-8(3)*, Aladdin) Simon & Schuster Children's Publishing.
—Lisa's War. 2007. (ENG.). 128p. (J). (gr. 3-7). pap. 11.95 *(978-1-4169-6163-5(1)*, Aladdin) Simon & Schuster Children's Publishing.
Nannestad, Katrina. When Mischief Came to Town. 2016. (ENG.). 192p. (J). (gr. 5-7). 16.99 *(978-0-544-53432-2(8)*, HMH Books For Young Readers) Houghton Mifflin Harcourt Publishing Co.
Peebles, Joseph. European Smack Down. 2005. (Illus.). (YA). pap. 19.95 *(978-0-9644758-5-4(5))* Peebco Publishing Hse., The.
Ray, Michelle. Falling for Hamlet. 2012. (ENG.). 368p. (YA). (gr. 10-17). pap. 17.99 *(978-0-316-10161-5(3)*, Poppy) Little, Brown Bks. for Young Readers.
Rayner, Keith. Torvig's Gift. 2006. 208p. pap. 19.95 *(978-1-4241-1518-1(3))* America Star Bks.
Shakespeare, William & Appignanesi, Richard. Hamlet. Vieceli, Emma, illus. 2007. (ENG.). 204p. (J). (gr. 2-8). pap. 12.95 *(978-0-8109-9324-2(4)*, Abrams Bks. for Young Readers) Abrams, Inc.
Soup, Cuthbert. Another Whole Nother Story. Timmins, Jeffrey Stewart, illus. 2010. (Whole Nother Story Ser.). (ENG.). 304p. (YA). (gr. 3-6). 16.99 *(978-1-59990-436-8(5)*, 9781599904368, Bloomsbury USA Childrens) Bloomsbury Publishing USA.
Stuchner, Joan Betty. A Time to Be Brave. Nugent, Cynthia, illus. 2014. (Stepping Stone Book(TM) Ser.). (ENG.). 112p. (J). (gr. 2-5). 4.99 *(978-0-385-39205-1(2)*, Random Hse. Bks. for Young Readers) Random Hse. Children's Bks.
Wung-Sung, Jesper. The Last Execution. Van R, Lin, tr. from DAN. 2016. (ENG., Illus.). 144p. (YA). (gr. 9). 17.99 *(978-1-4814-2965-8(5)*, Atheneum/Caitlyn Dlouhy Books) Simon & Schuster Children's Publishing.

DENMARK—HISTORY

Byers, Ann. Rescuing the Danish Jews: A Heroic Story from the Holocaust. 2011. (Holocaust Through Primary Sources Ser.). (Illus.). 128p. (J). (gr. 6-18). pap. 10.95 *(978-1-59845-343-0(2))*; (gr. 9-12). lib. bdg. 33.27 *(978-0-7660-3321-4(X))* Enslow Pubs., Inc.
Docalavich, Heather & Indovino, Shaina C. Denmark. Bruton, John, ed. 2012. (Major European Union Nations Ser.). 64p. (J). (gr. 7). 22.95 *(978-1-4222-2238-6(1))* Mason Crest.
Gifford, Clive. Denmark. 2017. (Unpacked Ser.). (ENG., Illus.). 32p. (J). (gr. 4-6). pap. 12.99 ***(978-0-7502-9162-0(1)***, Wayland) Hachette Children's Group GBR. Dist: Hachette Bk. Group.
Hoose, Phillip. The Boys Who Challenged Hitler: Knud Pedersen & the Churchill Club. 2015. (ENG., Illus.). 208p. (YA). (gr. 7-12). 19.99 *(978-0-374-30022-7(4)*, 9780374300227, Farrar, Straus & Giroux (BYR)) Farrar, Straus & Giroux.
Hopkinson, Deborah. Courage & Defiance: Stories of Spies, Saboteurs, & Survivors in World War II Denmark. (ENG.). 352p. (J). (gr. 3-7). 2016. pap. 6.99 *(978-0-545-59221-5(6))* 2015. (Illus.). 17.99 *(978-0-545-59220-8(8)*, Scholastic Pr.) Scholastic, Inc.
Levine, Ellen. Darkness over Denmark: The Danish Resistance & the Rescue of the Jews. 2005. (ENG., Illus.). 178p. (YA). (gr. 7-18). pap. 14.95 *(978-0-8234-1755-1(7))* Holiday Hse., Inc.
McKenna, Amy, ed. Denmark, Finland, & Sweden. 2013. (Britannica Guide to Countries of the European Union Ser.). (ENG., Illus.). 256p. (YA). (gr. 9-12). lib. bdg. 53.00 *(978-1-61530-969-6(1))* Rosen Publishing Group, Inc., The.
Pateman, Robert & Sullivan, Laura L. Denmark. 2016. (Cultures of the World (r) Ser.). (Illus.). 144p. (J). (gr. 5-5). 47.07 *(978-1-5026-1697-5(1))* Cavendish Square Publishing.
Stein, R. Conrad. Denmark. 2017. (Enchantment of the World(tm) Ser.). (ENG., Illus.). 144p. (J). lib. bdg. 40.00 *(978-0-531-22083-2(4)*, Children's Pr.) Scholastic Library Publishing.
Streissguth, Thomas. Denmark in Pictures. 2010. (Visual Geography Series, Second Ser.). (ENG.). 80p. (gr. 5-12). lib. bdg. 31.93 *(978-0-7613-4625-8(2))* Lerner Publishing Group.
Zobel, Derek. Denmark. 2011. (Illus.). 32p. (J). lib. bdg. *(978-0-531-20952-3(0))* Bellwether Media.

DENOMINATIONS, RELIGIOUS

see Sects

DENTAL ASSISTANTS

Byers, Ann. Careers in Dentistry. 2017. (J). ***(978-1-5383-8150-2(8))*** Rosen Publishing Group, Inc., The.
Hunsaker, Jennifer. Dental Hygienists. 2017. (Careers in Healthcare Ser.: Vol. 13). (ENG.). (YA). (gr. 7-12). 23.95 ***(978-1-4222-3797-7(4))*** Mason Crest.

DENTISTRY

see also Teeth

Allsop, Marcus. Nos gustan nuestros dientes / we like our Teeth. 2011th alt. ed. 2012. (We Like Toi Ser.). (ENG.). 32p. pap. 10.95 *(978-1-935826-09-5(3))* Kalindi Pr.
—We Like Our Teeth. 2011th alt. ed. 2012. (We Like To Ser.). (ENG.). 32p. pap. 9.95 *(978-1-935826-06-4(9))* Kalindi Pr.
Alpert. Attack of the Sugar Bugs. 2009. 40p. pap. 17.99 *(978-1-4389-7417-0(5))* AuthorHouse.
Arnold, Quinn M. Dentists. 2017. (J). ***(978-1-60818-872-7(8)***, Creative Education) Creative Co., The.
—Seedlings: Dentists. 2017. (Seedlings Ser.). (ENG.). 24p. (J). (gr. -1-1). pap. 7.99 ***(978-1-62832-487-7(2)***, Creative Paperbacks) Creative Co., The.
Bellamy, Adam. This Is My Dentist. 2016. (All about My World Ser.). (Illus.). 24p. (J). pap. 9.35 *(978-0-7660-8094-2(3))* Enslow Pubs., Inc.
Bernard, Jan. Toothpaste. 2016. (J). *(978-1-4896-4547-0(0))* Weigl Pubs., Inc.
Byers, Ann. A Career As a Dental Hygienist. 2012. (Essential Careers Ser.). (ENG., Illus.). 80p. (YA). (gr. 7-12). lib. bdg. 33.25 *(978-1-4488-8235-9(4))* Rosen Publishing Group, Inc., The.
Campbell, Fran. A Trip to the Dentist. 2008. (Real Readers - Upper Emergent Ser.). (ENG., Illus.). 12p. (gr. 1-2). pap. 5.90 *(978-0-8239-8201-1(7))* Rosen Publishing Group, Inc., The.
Capici, Gaetano. What Do They Do? Dentists. 2010. (Community Connections: What Do They Do? Ser.). (ENG.). 24p. (gr. 2-5). lib. bdg. 25.64 *(978-1-60279-806-9(0)*, 200502) Cherry Lake Publishing.
Civardi, Anne. Going to the Dentist. 2010. (First Experiences Ser.). 16p. (J). pap. 4.99 *(978-0-7945-2592-7(X)*, Usborne) EDC Publishing.
Cobb, Vicki. Your Body Battles a Cavity. Harris, Andrew, illus. Kunkel, Dennis, photos by. 2009. (Body Battles Ser.). (ENG.). 32p. (gr. 2-5). 25.26 *(978-0-8225-7469-9(1))* Lerner Publishing Group.
Crabtree, Marc. Meet My Neighbor, the Dentist. 2014. 24p. pap. 7.00 *(978-1-61003-355-8(8))* Center for the Collaborative Classroom.
Dember-Paige, Judith. Smile Wide Look Inside. 2005. (Illus.). 16p. (J). (gr. k-5). 15.00 *(978-0-9754008-0-7(0))* ABCDE

C D

Academic Bks. for Children's Development Through Education.

Gorman, Jacqueline Laks. Dentists. 2010. (People in My Community Ser.). (ENG.). 24p. (J). (gr. k-3). pap. 8.15 *(978-1-4339-3801-6(4))*; lib. bdg. 22.60 *(978-1-4339-3800-9(6))* Stevens, Gareth Publishing LLLP.

Guillain, Charlotte. Visiting the Dentist, 1 vol. 2011. (Growing Up Ser.). (ENG.). 24p. (gr. k-2). 23.32 *(978-1-4329-4804-7(0)*, Heinemann Read & Learn) Heinemann-Raintree.

Harcourt School Publishers Staff. Your Health Reader: The Dentist. 3rd ed. 2003. (Illus.). (gr. -1). pap. 9.40 *(978-0-15-338775-3(0))* Harcourt Schl. Pubs.

Harvey, Joanna & Crabtree, Marc. Meet My Neighbor, the Dentist. 2010. (ENG., Illus.). 24p. (J). pap. *(978-0-7787-4583-9(X))*; lib. bdg. *(978-0-7787-4573-0(2))* Crabtree Publishing Co.

Hengel, Katherine. Mouths Are for Smiling: The Sense of Taste, 1 vol. 2012. (All about Your Senses Ser.). (ENG.). 24p. (J). (gr. k-3). lib. bdg. 24.21 *(978-1-61783-199-7(9)*, SandCastle) ABDO Publishing Co.

Heos, Bridget. Let's Meet a Dentist. Poling, Kyle, illus. 2013. (Cloverleaf Books — Community Helpers Ser.). (ENG.). 24p. (gr. k-2). pap. 6.95 *(978-1-4677-0800-5(3))*; lib. bdg. 23.93 *(978-0-7613-9029-9(4))* Lerner Publishing Group. (Millbrook Pr.).

Herrington, Lisa M. I Have a Cavity. 2015. (Rookie Read-About(tm) Health Ser.). (ENG., Illus.). 32p. (J). lib. bdg. 25.00 *(978-0-531-21038-3(3))* Scholastic Library Publishing.

Hewitt, Sally. First Experiences: Going to the Dentist. 2004. (Illus.). 24p. (J). lib. bdg. 15.95 *(978-1-59566-011-4(9))* QEB Publishing Inc.

—Going to the Dentist. 2015. (ENG.). 24p. (gr. -1-2). 23.99 *(978-1-939581-83-9(4))* QEB Publishing Inc.

Hudson, Arthur K. The Lonesome Gnome. Whittemore, Constance, illus. 2011. 28p. pap. 35.95 *(978-1-258-09570-3(X))* Literary Licensing, LLC.

Hutmacher, Kimberly M. Your Senses at the Dentist's Office. 2011. (Out & about with Your Senses Ser.). (ENG.). 24p. (gr. k-1). lib. bdg. 26.65 *(978-1-4296-6664-0(1)*, Pebble Plus) Capstone Press of Coughlan Cos.

Kawa, Katie. My First Trip to the Dentist. Livingston, Jessica, illus. 2012. (My First Adventures Ser.). (ENG.). 24p. (J). (gr. k-2). pap. 8.15 *(978-1-4339-6243-1(8))*; lib. bdg. 22.60 *(978-1-4339-6241-7(1))* Stevens, Gareth Publishing LLLP.

—My First Trip to the Dentist: Mi Primera Visita Al Dentista. Livingston, Jessica, illus. 2012. (My First Adventures / Mis primeras aventuras Ser.). (ENG & SPA.). 24p. (J). (gr. k-2). lib. bdg. 22.60 *(978-1-4339-6627-9(1))* Stevens, Gareth Publishing LLLP.

Keller, Laurie. Open Wide: Tooth School Inside. Keller, Laurie, illus. rev. ed. 2003. (ENG., Illus.). 40p. (J). (gr. k-3). pap. 7.99 *(978-0-8050-7268-6(3)*, 9780805072686) Square Fish.

—Open Wide: Tooth School Inside. Keller, Laurie, illus. unabr. ed. 2006. (Illus.). (J). (gr. k-5). 18.95 *(978-0-439-84920-3(9)*, WPCD650); 29.95 *(978-0-439-84918-0(7)*, WHCD650) Weston Woods Studios, Inc.

Kenan, Tessa. Hooray for Dentists! 2017. (Bumba Books (tm) — Hooray for Community Helpers! Ser.). (ENG.). 24p. (J). (gr. -1-1). 25.32 ***(978-1-5124-3351-7(9))*** Lerner Publishing Group.

Klingel, Cynthia & Noyed, Robert B. Mouth. 2010. (Let's Read about Our Bodies Ser.). (Illus.). 24p. (gr. k-3). pap. 8.15 *(978-1-4339-3369-1(1))*; (J). lib. bdg. 22.00 *(978-1-4339-3368-4(3))* Stevens, Gareth Publishing LLLP.

—Mouth / la Boca. 2010. (Let's Read about Our Bodies / Hablemos del cuerpo humano Ser.). (SPA., Illus.). 24p. (gr. k-3). pap. 8.15 *(978-1-4339-3745-3(X))* Stevens, Gareth Publishing LLLP.

—Mouth/la Boca. 2010. (Let's Read about Our Bodies / Hablemos del cuerpo humano Ser.). (SPA., Illus.). 24p. (J). (gr. k-3). lib. bdg. 22.00 *(978-1-4339-3744-6(1))* Stevens, Gareth Publishing LLLP.

Klug, Kirsten. Healthy Smiles! 2011. (Illus.). 12p. (J). pap. 6.50 *(978-0-9798173-6-6(6))* Bamboo River Pr.

Lee, David. My Visit to the Dentist. 2016. (Community Helpers Ser.). 00024p. (J). (gr. 1-1). pap. 8.25 *(978-1-4994-2704-2(2)*, PowerKids Pr.) Rosen Publishing Group, Inc., The.

Libal, Autumn & Hovius, Christopher. Taking Care of Your Smile: A Teen's Guide to Dental Care. 2006. (Science of Health Ser.). (Illus.). 128p. (YA). lib. bdg. 24.95 *(978-1-59084-846-3(2))* Mason Crest.

Liebman, Daniel. I Want to Be a Dentist. 2016. (I Want to Be Ser.). (ENG., Illus.). 24p. (J). (gr. -1-2). pap. 3.99 *(978-1-77085-785-8(0)*, 9781770857858) Firefly Bks., Ltd.

Liebman, Daniel & Mlawer, Teresa. Quiero Ser Dentista. 2016. (Quiero Ser). (SPA., Illus.). 24p. (J). (gr. -1-2). pap. 6.99 *(978-1-77085-863-3(6)*, 9781770858633) Firefly Bks., Ltd.

Macdonald, Fiona. You Wouldn't Want to Live Without Dentists! Antram, David, illus. 2015. (You Wouldn't Want to Live Without... Ser.). (ENG.). 40p. (J). pap. 9.95 *(978-0-531-21410-7(9)*, Watts, Franklin) Scholastic Library Publishing.

Marsico, Katie. Visit the Dentist! 2015. (21st Century Junior Library: Your Healthy Body Ser.). (ENG., Illus.). 24p. (J). (gr. 2-5). 27.07 *(978-1-63188-986-8(9)*, 205856) Cherry Lake Publishing.

Miller, Heather. What Does a Dentist Do? 2006. (What Does a Community Helper Do? Ser.). (Illus.). 24p. (J). (gr. 1-3). lib. bdg. 22.60 *(978-0-7660-2323-9(0)*, Enslow Elementary) Enslow Pubs., Inc.

Minden, Cecilia & Armantrout, Linda M. Dentists. 2014. (People in Our Community Ser.). (ENG.). 24p. (J). (gr. k-3). 27.07 *(978-1-62687-011-6(X)*, 206801) Child's World, Inc., The.

Mortensen, Lori. Going to the Dentist, 1 vol. Thompson, Jeffrey, illus. 2010. (First Graphics: My Community Ser.). (ENG.). 24p. (gr. 1-2). 23.99 *(978-1-4296-4507-2(5))*; pap. 35.70 *(978-1-4296-5611-5(5))* Capstone Press of Coughlan Cos.

Murray, Aaron R. Dentists Help Us. 2012. (All about Community Helpers Ser.). 24p. (J). (gr. -1-1). 22.60 *(978-0-7660-4043-4(7))* Enslow Pubs., Inc.

Open Wide: Individual Title Six-Packs. (gr. k-1). 23.00 *(978-0-7635-8835-9(0))* Rigby Education.

QEB Start Reading Together National Book Stores Edition: First Experiences: Going to the Dentist. 2006. (J). per. *(978-1-59566-260-6(X))* QEB Publishing Inc.

Ready, Dee. Dentists Help, 1 vol. 2013. (Our Community Helpers Ser.). (ENG.). 24p. (gr. k-1). pap. 6.29 *(978-1-62065-841-3(0))*; pap. 35.70 *(978-1-62065-842-0(9))*; lib. bdg. 21.99 *(978-1-62065-081-3(9))* Capstone Press of Coughlan Cos. (Pebble Bks.).

Royston, Angela. Why Do I Brush My Teeth? 2012. (My Body Ser.). (ENG., Illus.). 24p. (gr. k-4). pap. 7.95 *(978-1-926853-99-4(7))* Saunders Bk. Co. CAN. Dist: RiverStream Publishing.

Rustad, Martha E. H. I Care for My Teeth. 2017. (Healthy Me Ser.). (ENG., Illus.). 24p. (gr. k-1). lib. bdg. 21.99 *(978-1-5157-3985-2(6))* Capstone Press of Coughlan Cos.

Salzmann, Mary Elizabeth. Brush Your Teeth! Healthy Dental Habits, 1 vol. 2014. (Healthy Habits Ser.). (ENG.). 24p. (J). (gr. -1-3). 24.21 *(978-1-62403-528-9(0))* ABDO Publishing Co.

—Dentist's Tools, 1 vol. 2011. (Professional Tools Ser.). (ENG., Illus.). 24p. (J). (gr. 3-5). lib. bdg. 25.65 *(978-1-61613-578-2(6)*, Super SandCastle) ABDO Publishing Co.

Scholastic, Inc. Staff, contrib. by. If I Were a Dentist. 2015. (Rookie Toddler(tm) Ser.). (ENG., Illus.). 12p. (J). bds. 6.95 *(978-0-531-21265-3(3)*, Children's Pr.) Scholastic Library Publishing.

Schuh, Mari C. Antojitos para Dientes Sanos. 2010. (Dientes Sanos/Healthy Teeth Ser.).Tr. of Snacks for Healthy Teeth. (MUL, ENG & SPA.). 24p. (gr. k-1). lib. bdg. 26.65 *(978-1-4296-4599-7(7))* Capstone Press of Coughlan Cos.

—At the Dentist, 1 vol. Saunders-Smith, Gail, ed. 2008. (Healthy Teeth Ser.). (ENG., Illus.). 24p. (gr. k-1). pap. 7.29 *(978-1-4296-1788-8(8)*, Pebble Plus) Capstone Press of Coughlan Cos.

Smith, Michael & Aguiler, Manny. A Smile: B una Sonrisa. Aguiler, Manny, illus. 2015. (SPA & ENG., Illus.). 36p. (J). *(978-0-9913454-5-8(2))* East West Discovery Pr.

Smith, Penny & Dorling Kindersley Publishing Staff. A Trip to the Dentist Level 1. 2006. (DK Readers Ser.). (ENG., Illus.). 32p. (J). (gr. k-2). pap. 3.99 *(978-0-7566-1914-5(9)*, DK Children) Dorling Kindersley Publishing, Inc.

The Tooth Chicken. (J). 8.40 *(978-0-934510-24-0(5)*, W013) American Dental Assn.

Tourville, Amanda Doering. Whose Gadgets Are These?, 1 vol. 2011. (Community Helper Mysteries Ser.). (ENG.). 24p. (gr. k-1). lib. bdg. 26.65 *(978-1-4296-6082-2(1)*, Pebble Plus) Capstone Press of Coughlan Cos.

Vittorini, Candace & Boyer-Quick, Sara. Joey Goes to the Dentist. 2007. (ENG., Illus.). 32p. 19.95 *(978-1-84310-854-2(2)*, 5287) Kingsley, Jessica Pubs. GBR. Dist: Macmillan Distribution Ltd.

Weston Woods Staff, creator. Open Wide- Tooth School Inside. 2011. 38.75 *(978-0-439-84913-5(6))* Weston Woods Studios, Inc.

Winchester, Elizabeth Siris & Siris-Winchester, Elizabeth. The Right Bite: Dentists As Detectives. 2007. (24/7: Science Behind the Scenes Ser.). (ENG., Illus.). 64p. (YA). (gr. 9-12). 29.00 *(978-0-531-12062-0(7)*, Watts, Franklin) Scholastic Library Publishing.

DENTISTRY—FICTION

Adkins, Patricia. Jeremy & the Crocodile Dentist. 2013. 24p. pap. 10.99 *(978-1-4908-0883-3(3)*, WestBow Pr.) Author Solutions, Inc.

Alpert, Sherri. Cassandra Gets Her Smile Back: Teaching Children to Care for Their Teeth. Seroya, Tea, illus. 2010. (Let's Talk Ser.). (ENG.). 48p. (J). (gr. -1-4). pap. 8.95 *(978-0-88282-314-0(0))* New Horizon Pr. Pubs., Inc.

Bancks, Tristan. Noob, Amateur Dentist. Gorissen, Dean, illus. 2015. (Legends in Their Own Lunchbox Ser.). (ENG.). 56p. (gr. 2-3). pap. 7.99 *(978-1-4966-0253-4(6)*, Legends in Their Own Lunchbox) Capstone Classroom.

Barber, Tom & Chapman, Lynne. Open Wide! 2004. (Illus.). 32p. 14.95 *(978-1-84458-241-9(8))* Avalon Publishing Group.

Barrett, Nana. A Terrible Case of the Collywobbles! 2008. 16p. pap. 24.95 *(978-1-4241-9603-6(5))* America Star Bks.

Benenfeld, Rikki. I Go to the Dentist. Rosenfeld, Dina & Leverton, Yossi, eds. Bennenfeld, Rikki, illus. 2011. (Toddler Experience Ser.). (ENG.). 32p. (J). 10.95 *(978-1-929628-60-5(9))* Hachai Publishing.

Bowe, Clara Brown. Tubba Toothpaste. 2010. 24p. pap. 15.99 *(978-1-4535-0449-9(4))* Xlibris Corp.

Civardi, Anne. Going to the Dentist. 2009. (First Experiences Sticker Bks). 18p. (J). pap. 6.99 *(978-0-7945-2429-6(X)*, Usborne) EDC Publishing.

—Going to the Dentist. Bates, Michelle, ed. Cartwright, Stephen, illus. rev. ed. 2005. (First Experiences Ser.). 16p. (J). (gr. -1). per. 4.95 *(978-0-7945-1007-7(8)*, Usborne) EDC Publishing.

Dale, Jay. Jo & Jess Go to the Dentist, 1 vol. Chapman, Katriona, illus. 2012. (Wonder Words Ser.). (ENG.). 32p. (gr. k-2). pap. 5.99 *(978-1-4296-8912-0(9)*, Engage Literacy) Capstone Press of Coughlan Cos.

The Dentist, 2 Packs. (Chiquilibros Ser.). (gr. -1-1). 12.00 *(978-0-7635-8545-7(9))* Rigby Education.

Deslauriers, Anne. La Fee Dentiste. Begin, Jean-Guy, illus. 2004. (Collection des 6 Ans). (FRE.). 64p. (J). 7.95 *(978-2-922565-99-7(8))* Editions de la Paix CAN. Dist: World of Reading, Ltd.

Dusablon, David. The Dentist, 1 vol. Spoerl, Amber, illus. 2009. 11p. pap. 24.95 *(978-1-60836-186-1(1))* America Star Bks.

Finnegan, Evelyn M. My Little Friend Goes to the Dentist. Houghton, Diane R., illus. 2006. 32p. (J). (gr. -1-3). reprint ed. pap. 7.00 *(978-1-4223-5404-9(0))* DIANE Publishing Co.

George, Mindy Lee. Sugar Bugs. 2013. (Illus.). 32p. pap. *(978-0-9878208-3-9(4))* Catching Rainbows.

Greig, Allison. Stacey's Adventures. 2006. (Illus.). 64p. pap. *(978-1-84401-035-6(X))* Athena Pr.

Griffiths, Andy. Killer Koalas from Outer Space & Lots of Other Very Bad Stuff That Will Make Your Brain Explode! Denton, Terry, illus. 2012. (ENG.). 192p. (J). (gr. 3-7). pap. 7.99 *(978-1-250-01017-9(9)*, 9781250010179) Square Fish.

Gutman, Dan. Funny Boy Meets the Dumbbell Dentist from Deimos (with Dangerous Dental Decay) Dietz, Mike, illus. 2012. (Funny Boy Ser.). (ENG.). 120p. (J). (gr. 2-5). pap. 6.99 *(978-1-4532-7070-7(1))* Open Road Integrated Media, Inc.

Hood, Karen Jean Matsko. Adventures of My Dentist & the Tooth Fairy: Activity & Coloring Book, bk. 2. Whispering Pine Press International, Inc. Staff, ed. Artistic Book and Web Design, illus. 2013. (ENG & JPN.). 174p. (J). pap. 19.95 *(978-1-59649-535-7(9))* Whispering Pine Pr. International, Inc.

—My Dentist & the Tooth Fairy: Activity & Coloring Book, bk. 10. Whispering Pine Press International, Inc. Staff, ed. 2013. (Hood Activity & Coloring Book Ser.). (ENG., Illus.). 160p. (J). pap. 19.95 *(978-1-59210-596-0(3))* Whispering Pine Pr. International, Inc.

Klein, Adria F. Max Goes to the Dentist. Gallagher-Cole, Mernie, illus. 2007. (Read-It! Readers: the Life of Max Ser.). (ENG.). 24p. (gr. -1-2). per. 3.95 *(978-1-4048-3061-5(8)*, Easy Readers) Picture Window Bks.

—Max Va Al Dentista, 1 vol. Lozano, Clara, tr. Gallagher-Cole, Mernie, illus. 2007. (Read-It! Readers en Español: la Vida de Max Ser.). (SPA.). 24p. (gr. -1-3). per. 3.95 *(978-1-4048-3039-4(1)*, Easy Readers) Picture Window Bks.

Mahadeo Rdh, Elizabeth. Teddy Visits the Dentist. Barth, Alexandra, illus. 2012. 40p. pap. *(978-0-9569438-0-4(2))* Mahadeo Movement, The.

Maloney, Peter & Zekauskas, Felicia. Lose That Tooth! 2005. (Illus.). 32p. (J). *(978-0-439-67639-7(8))* Scholastic, Inc.

Martin, C. L. Ducky Goes to the Dentist. 2013. 16p. pap. 24.95 *(978-1-62709-742-0(2))* America Star Bks.

McCarroll, Barbara. Tongue Turning Tales for the Classroom. Godfrey, Arthur Dwayne, illus. 2008. 36p. pap. 24.95 *(978-1-60703-254-0(6))* America Star Bks.

Meister, Cari. Snorp: The City Monster. Messner, Dennis, illus. 2009. (Monster Friends Ser.). (ENG.). 32p. (gr. 2-3). 22.65 *(978-1-4342-1632-8(2))* Stone Arch Bks.

—Three Claws the Mountain Monster. Messner, Dennis, illus. 2009. (Monster Friends Ser.). (ENG.). 32p. (gr. 2-3). 22.65 *(978-1-4342-1633-5(0))* Stone Arch Bks.

Nathanson, Laura. El Problema de los Miercoles. (SPA.). 160p. (YA). (gr. 5-8). *(978-84-279-3181-7(6)*, NG3677) Noguer y Caralt Editores, S. A. ESP. Dist: Lectorum Pubns., Inc.

Rey, H. A. & Margaret. Curious George Visits the Dentist. 2014. (Curious George Ser.). (ENG., Illus.). 24p. (J). (gr. -1-3). 13.99 *(978-0-544-14611-2(5)*, HMH Books For Young Readers) Houghton Mifflin Harcourt Publishing Co.

Roberts, Tony. Turquie the Turkey. 2011. 28p. pap. 15.99 *(978-1-4568-5969-5(2))* Xlibris Corp.

Romero, Alfonso Suárez. Maraca. Alvarado, Dalia & Pacheco, Luis Gabriel, illus. rev. ed. 2006. (Castillo de la Lectura Verde Ser.). (SPA & ENG.). 120p. (J). (gr. 2-4). pap. 7.95 *(978-970-20-0128-7(5))* Castillo, Ediciones, S. A. de C. V. MEX. Dist: Macmillan.

Sateren, Shelley Swanson. Max & Zoe at the Dentist, 1 vol. Sullivan, Mary, illus. (Max & Zoe Ser.). (ENG.). 32p. (gr. k-2). 2013. pap. 5.19 *(978-1-4048-8057-3(7))* 2011. lib. bdg. 21.32 *(978-1-4048-6206-7(4))* Picture Window Bks. (Max & Zoe).

Scholastic, Inc. Staff. Dentist Trip. 2015. (Peppa Pig 8X8 Ser.). (ENG.). 24p. (J). (gr. -1-k). lib. bdg. 14.75 *(978-0-606-38113-0(9))* Turtleback Bks.

Snyder, Judi. Emily's First Visit to the Dentist. 2013. 24p. pap. 9.95 *(978-1-4575-2181-2(4))* Dog Ear Publishing, LLC.

Steig, William. Doctor de Soto. 2003. (Picture Books Collection). (SPA.). 32p. (J). (gr. k-3). 16.95 *(978-84-372-6616-9(5))* Altea, Ediciones, S.A. - Grupo Santillana ESP. Dist: Santillana USA Publishing Co., Inc.

—Doctor de Soto. 2004. (J). (gr. k-3). spiral bd. *(978-0-616-01784-5(7))*; spiral bd. *(978-0-616-01785-2(5))* Canadian National Institute for the Blind/Institut National Canadien pour les Aveugles.

—Doctor de Soto. 2010. (J). lib. bdg. 18.40 *(978-0-606-14606-7(7)*, Turtleback) Turtleback Bks.

Stockham, Jessica, illus. Visiting the Dentist. 2011. (First Time Ser.). (ENG.). 24p. (J). (gr. 2-2). pap. *(978-1-84643-335-1(5))* Child's Play International Ltd.

Stockland, Patricia M. Tiger Toothache, 1 vol. Haugen, Ryan, illus. 2008. (Safari Friends Ser.). (ENG.). 32p. (gr. -1-3). 28.50 *(978-1-60270-087-1(7)*, Looking Glass Library) ABDO Publishing Co.

Valentine, Nancy. I Heart My Dentist. 2012. 38p. pap. 16.95 *(978-1-105-58726-9(6))* Lulu Pr., Inc.

Wallace, Jazey. Smile Bright. Fraser, Sigmund, illus. 2012. 24p. pap. 11.50 *(978-1-61897-755-7(5)*, Strategic Bk. Publishing) Strategic Book Publishing & Rights Agency (SBPRA).

Watt, Fiona. Complete Book of First Experiences. rev. ed. 2011. (First Experiences Ser.). 144p. (J). ring bd. 19.99 *(978-0-7945-2948-2(8)*, Usborne) EDC Publishing.

Weston Woods Staff, creator. Doctor de Soto. 2011. (SPA.). 38.75 *(978-0-439-78365-1(8))*; 29.95 *(978-0-439-73624-4(2))* Weston Woods Studios, Inc.

—Doctor Desoto. 2004. (SPA.). (J). 18.95 *(978-0-7882-0950-5(7))* Weston Woods Studios, Inc.

Williams-Reyes, Inez. Kimani's Visit to the Dentist. 2003. per. 5.00 *(978-0-9669289-3-8(8))* Publish To Go Pubns.

Willson, Sarah. Behold, No Cavities! A Visit to the Dentist. Moore, Harry, illus. 2007. (SpongeBob SquarePants Ser.: 15). (ENG.). 24p. (J). (gr. -1-3). pap. 3.99 *(978-1-4169-3566-7(5)*, Simon Spotlight/Nickelodeon) Simon Spotlight/Nickelodeon.

Wurm, Kristine. Truman's Loose Tooth Chesworth, Michael D., illus. 2005. (ENG.). 32p. (J). (gr. -1-3). 16.95 *(978-0-9768513-0-1(X))* Spirited Publishing, LLC.

DENTISTRY—VOCATIONAL GUIDANCE

Byers, Ann. Careers in Dentistry. 2017. (J). ***(978-1-5383-8150-2(8))*** Rosen Publishing Group, Inc., The.

De Nijs, Erika. A Dentist's Job. 2015. (Community Workers Ser.). (ENG., Illus.). 24p. (J). (gr. 1-1). pap. 8.22 *(978-1-5026-0424-8(8))* Cavendish Square Publishing.

Nelson, Kristin L. Dentists. 2005. (Pull Ahead Books: Community Helpers Ser.). (ENG., Illus.). 32p. (gr. k-3). lib. bdg. 22.60 *(978-0-8225-1688-0(8))* Lerner Publishing Group.

DENVER (COLO.)

Baker, Gayle. Denver: A Boomtown History. 2004. (Illus.). 96p. per. 9.95 *(978-0-9710984-4-2(1))* HarborTown Histories.

Lorbiecki, Marybeth. Escaping Titanic: A Young Girl's True Story of Survival, 1 vol. Lorbiecki, Marybeth & Heinzen, Kory S., illus. 2012. (ENG.). 32p. (gr. 3-5). pap. 8.95 *(978-1-4048-7235-6(3))*; lib. bdg. 28.65 *(978-1-4048-7143-4(8))* Picture Window Bks.

Ogintz, Eileen. The Kid's Guide to Denver, Boulder & Colorado's Ski Country. 2014. (Kid's Guides Ser.). (ENG., Illus.). 168p. (J). pap. 12.95 *(978-1-4930-0643-4(6))* Globe Pequot Pr., The.

Staton, Hilarie. Dropping in on Denver. 2017. (Dropping in On Ser.). (ENG.). (J). (gr. 3-5). 32.80 ***(978-1-68342-173-3(6))*** Rourke Educational Media.

Turnbull, Stacy. Robert Speer: Denver's Building Mayor. 2011. (ENG & SPA., Illus.). 64p. (J). pap. 8.95 *(978-0-86541-120-3(4))* Filter Pr., LLC.

DENVER BRONCOS (FOOTBALL TEAM)

Burgess, Zack. Meet the Denver Broncos. 2016. (Big Picture Sports Ser.). (ENG., Illus.). 24p. (J). (gr. k-3). lib. bdg. 22.60 *(978-1-59953-753-5(2))* Norwood Hse. Pr.

Frisch, Aaron. Denver Broncos. 2011. (Super Bowl Champions Ser.). (J). (gr. 1-3). 24.25 *(978-1-60818-017-2(4))* Creative Co., The.

—Denver Broncos. 2014. (Illus.). 24p. (J). *(978-1-60818-375-3(0)*, Creative Education) Creative Co., The.

Frisch, Nate. NFL Today: Denver Broncos. 2013. (NFL Today Ser.). (ENG., Illus.). 48p. (J). (gr. 4-7). pap. 12.00 *(978-0-89812-854-3(4)*, Creative Paperbacks) Creative Co., The.

—The Story of the Denver Broncos. 2013. (Illus.). 48p. (J). 35.65 *(978-1-60818-301-2(7)*, Creative Education) Creative Co., The.

Howell, Brian. Denver Broncos, 1 vol. 2010. (Inside the NFL Ser.). (ENG.). 48p. (YA). (gr. 3-6). lib. bdg. 32.79 *(978-1-61714-010-5(4))* ABDO Publishing Co.

Leboutillier, Nate. Denver Broncos. 2005. (Super Bowl Champions Ser.). (Illus.). 24p. (J). (gr. 5-9). lib. bdg. 16.95 *(978-1-58341-383-8(9))* Creative Co., The.

Omoth, Tyler. The Story of the Denver Broncos. (NFL Today Ser.). 48p. (gr. 5-17). 2011. (ENG.). (J). pap. 9.99 *(978-0-89812-535-1(9)*, Creative Paperbacks) 2009. (YA). 22.95 *(978-1-58341-754-6(0))* Creative Co., The.

Schmalzbauer, Adam. The History of the Denver Broncos. 2004. (NFL Today Ser.). (Illus.). 32p. (YA). (gr. 5-9). 18.95 *(978-1-58341-295-4(6))* Creative Co., The.

Wyner, Zach. Denver Broncos. (Illus.). 32p. (J). 2015. *(978-1-4896-0821-5(4))* 2014. (ENG.). (gr. 4-7). lib. bdg. 28.55 *(978-1-4896-0818-5(4)*, AV2 by Weigl) Weigl Pubs., Inc.

Zappa, Marcia. Denver Broncos, 1 vol. 2014. (NFL's Greatest Teams Set 2 Ser.). (ENG.). 32p. (gr. 2-5). 28.50 *(978-1-62403-585-2(X))* ABDO Publishing Co.

DEOXYRIBONUCLEIC ACID

see DNA

DEPARTMENT STORES

see also Sales Personnel

Gilbert, Sara. Built for Success: the Story of Target. 2015. (Built for Success Ser.). (ENG.). 48p. (J). (gr. 5-8). pap. 12.00 *(978-0-89812-984-7(2)*, Creative Paperbacks) Creative Co., The.

—The Story of Target. 2014. (Illus.). 46p. (J). *(978-1-60818-397-5(1)*, Creative Education) Creative Co., The.

Green, Sara. Target. 2015. (Brands We Know Ser.). (ENG., Illus.). 24p. (J). (gr. 3-8). lib. bdg. 25.95 *(978-1-62617-289-0(7)*, Pilot Bks.) Bellwether Media.

Perritano, John. A Toy Store Summer: Finding Area. 2013. (IMath Ser.). 32p. (J). (gr. 3-4). lib. bdg. 22.60 *(978-1-59953-565-4(3))* Norwood Hse. Pr.

Robertson, Charmaine. We Buy What We Need at the Department Store. 2016. (Rosen REAL Readers: Social Studies Nonfiction / Fiction: Family, Community, & the World Ser.). 12p. (gr. 1-k). pap. 6.33 *(978-1-5081-2335-4(7)*, Rosen Classroom) Rosen Publishing Group, Inc., The.

DEPARTMENT STORES—FICTION

Aldis, Dorothy Keeley. We're Going to Town! Gehr, Mary, illus. 2011. 58p. 36.95 *(978-1-258-08388-5(4))* Literary Licensing, LLC.

Bond, Michael. Paddington & the Christmas Surprise. Alley, R. W., illus. 2015. (Paddington Ser.). (ENG.). 32p. (J). (gr. -1-3). 17.99 *(978-0-06-231842-8(X))* HarperCollins Pubs.

Bray, Darrell. I Remember Pop's General Store. 2013. 24p. pap. 24.95 *(978-1-63004-679-8(5))* America Star Bks.

Corey, Shana. Milly & the Macy's Parade. Helquist, Brett, illus. 2006. 38p. (J). (gr. 4-8). reprint ed. 17.00 *(978-1-4223-5174-1(2))* DIANE Publishing Co.

Freeman, Don. Corduroy. 2011. (Corduroy Ser.). (ENG.). 28p. (J). (gr. -1 — 1). bds. 11.99 *(978-0-670-01311-1(0)*, Viking Books for Young Readers) Penguin Young Readers Group.

Hope, Laura Lee. Bunny Brown & His Sister Sue Keeping S. 2006. 26.95 *(978-1-4218-2975-3(4))*; pap. 11.95 *(978-1-4218-3075-9(2))* 1st World Publishing, Inc.

Mayer, Mercer. Just Grandma, Grandpa, & Me. 2016. (Little Critter Ser.). lib. bdg. 16.00 *(978-0-606-38482-7(0))* Turtleback Bks.

Pratchett, Terry. The Bromeliad Trilogy: Truckers, Diggers, & Wings. 2003. 512p. (J). (gr. 5-18). 18.89 *(978-0-06-054855-1(X))*; 19.99 *(978-0-06-009493-5(1))* HarperCollins Pubs.

Sharmat, Marjorie Weinman & Sharmat, Mitchell. Nate the Great & the Big Sniff. Weston, Martha, illus. 2003. (Nate the Great Ser.: No. 23). (ENG.). 80p. (J). (gr. 1-4). pap. 5.99 *(978-0-440-41502-2(0)*, Yearling) Random Hse. Children's Bks.

—Nate the Great & the Big Sniff. Weston, Martha, illus. 2003. (Nate the Great Ser.). 47p. (gr. -1-3). lib. bdg. 16.00 *(978-0-613-63966-8(9)*, Turtleback) Turtleback Bks.

Vinopol, Corinne & Bednarczyk, Angela. ASL Tales & Games for Kids - Biscuit Blvd: Computer Software in American Sign Language. 2004. (J). cd-rom 34.95 *(978-0-9667589-9-3(4))* Institute for Disabilities Research & Training, Inc.

Wells, Helen. Cherry Ames, Department Store Nurse. 2007. (Cherry Ames Nurse Stories Ser.). 224p. (YA). (gr. 8-12). 14.95 *(978-0-8261-0415-1(0))* Springer Publishing Co., Inc.

DEPENDENT CHILDREN

see Child Welfare

DEPRESSION, MENTAL

Abblett, Mitch R. & Willard, Christopher. Mindfulness for Teen Depression: A Workbook for Improving Your Mood. 2016. (ENG.). 144p. (YA). (gr. 6-12). pap. 16.95 (978-1-62625-382-7(X)) New Harbinger Pubns.

Aboff, Marcie. Everyone Feels Sad Sometimes, 1 vol. Ward, Damian, illus. 2010. (Everyone Has Feelings Ser.). (ENG.). 24p. (gr. k-2). lib. bdg. 25.99 (978-1-4048-5755-1(9)) Picture Window Bks.

Adams, Jacqueline. Obsessive-Compulsive Disorder. 2007. (Diseases & Disorders Ser.). (ENG., Illus.). 128p. (gr. 7-12). lib. bdg. 39.90 (978-1-4205-0000-4(7)) Cengage Gale.

Ayer, Eleanor H. Everything You Need to Know about Depression. 2009. (Need to Know Library). 64p. (gr. 5-5). 58.50 (978-1-60854-064-8(2)) Rosen Publishing Group, Inc., The.

Balinson, Andrea. Depression, Anxiety, & Bipolar Disorders. 2017. (J). **(978-1-4222-3755-7(9))** Mason Crest.

Benziger, Katherine. Overcoming Depression: The Easy to Read Simple to Use Little Book You Can Use to Turn Your Life Around. 2005th ed. 2005. (Illus.). 59p. spiral bd., wbk. ed. 15.00 (978-1-880931-46-2(X)) KBA, LLC.

Bingham, Jane. Stress & Depression. 2008. (Emotional Health Issues Ser.). (Illus.). 48p. (YA). (gr. 7-12). lib. bdg. 31.00 (978-0-8368-9203-1(8)) Stevens, Gareth Publishing LLLP.

Borchard, Therese. What Does Depressed Mean? A Guidebook for Children with a Depressed Loved One. 2011. (ENG., Illus.). (J). pap. 7.95 (978-0-87029-469-3(5)) Abbey Pr.

Cartlidge, Cherese. Teens & Suicide. 2017. (Teen Mental Health Ser.). (ENG.). 80p. (J). (gr. 5-12). **(978-1-68282-131-2(5))** ReferencePoint Pr., Inc.

Chilman-Blair, Kim & Deloache, Shawn. Medikidz Explain Depression. 2010. (Superheroes on a Medical Mission Ser.). (Illus.). 40p. (YA). pap. 11.75 (978-1-4488-1837-2(0)); (gr. 5-8). lib. bdg. 29.25 (978-1-4358-9455-6(3)) Rosen Publishing Group, Inc., The. (Rosen Reference).

Clarke, Julie & Kirby-Payne, Ann. Understanding Weight & Depression. 2005. (Teen Eating Disorder Prevention Book Ser.). (Illus.). 192p. (J). (gr. 7-12). lib. bdg. 34.60 (978-0-8239-2994-8(9), E2WEDE) Rosen Publishing Group, Inc., The.

Cobain, Beverly. When Nothing Matters Anymore: A Survival Guide for Depressed Teens. 2007. (ENG., Illus.). 176p. (YA). (gr. 7-12). pap. 14.99 (978-1-57542-235-0(2)) Free Spirit Publishing, Inc.

de Sosa, Linda. I'm Not Crazy: A Workbook for Teens with Depression & Bipolar Disorder. 2010. 128p. pap. 13.95 (978-0-595-52118-0(5)) iUniverse, Inc.

Docalavich, Heather. Antidepressants & Psychology: Talk Therapy vs. Medication. (Antidepressants Ser.). (Illus.). 104p. (YA). (gr. 7-18). 2008. lib. bdg. 24.95 (978-1-4222-0096-4(5)) 2007. pap. 14.95 (978-1-4222-0405-4(7)) Mason Crest.

Esherick, Joan. Drug Therapy & Mood Disorders. (Encyclopedia of Psychiatric Drugs & Their Disorders Ser.). (Illus.). (YA). 2004. 128p. lib. bdg. 24.95 (978-1-59084-568-4(4)) 2003. 126p. (gr. 4-7). pap. 14.95 (978-1-4222-0392-7(1)) Mason Crest.

Ford, Jean. Coping with Moods. Bridgemohan, Carolyn & Forman, Sara, eds. 2013. (Young Adult's Guide to the Science of Health Ser.: 15). 128p. (J). (gr. 7-18). 24.95 (978-1-4222-2806-7(1)) Mason Crest.

Hamil, Sara. My Feeling Better Workbook: Help for Kids Who Are Sad & Depressed. 2008. (Instant Help Ser.). (ENG.). 136p. (J). (gr. k-5). pap. 16.95 (978-1-57224-612-6(X), Instant Help Books) New Harbinger Pubns.

Hunter, David. Antidepressants & Advertising: Marketing Happiness. 2007. (Antidepressants Ser.). (Illus.). 112p. (YA). pap. 14.95 (978-1-4222-0404-7(9)) Mason Crest.

—But Smoking Makes Me Happy: The Link Between Nicotine & Depression. 2009. (Tobacco: the Deadly Drug Ser.). (Illus.). 112p. (YA). (gr. 7-12). 26.95 (978-1-4222-0244-9(5)); (J). pap. 26.95 (978-1-4222-1335-3(8)) Mason Crest.

Jones, Lloyd. The Princess & the Fog: A Story for Children with Depression. Jones, Lloyd, illus. 2015. (ENG., Illus.). 48p. (J). 17.95 (978-1-84905-655-7(2), 7963) Kingsley, Jessica Pubs. GBR. Dist: Macmillan Distribution Ltd.

Landau, Jennifer. Bipolar Disorder. 2013. (Teen Mental Health Ser.). (Illus.). 48p. (J). (gr. 7-12). 29.95 (978-1-4777-1747-9(1)) Rosen Publishing Group, Inc., The.

Langwith, Jacqueline. Depression. 2008. (Perspectives on Diseases & Disorders Ser.). (ENG., Illus.). 168p. (YA). (gr. 10-12). lib. bdg. 38.95 (978-0-7377-4246-6(1), LML02109-243158, Greenhaven Pr., Inc.) Cengage Gale.

Leonard, Basia & Jovinelly, Joann. Bipolar Disorder. 2011. (Understanding Brain Diseases & Disorders Ser.). (ENG.). 64p. (YA). (gr. 7-12). lib. bdg. 31.95 (978-1-4488-5542-1(X)) Rosen Publishing Group, Inc., The.

Levin, Judith. Depression & Mood Disorders. (Teen Mental Health Ser.). 48p. 2009. (gr. 5-6). 53.00 (978-1-60853-295-7(X)) 2008. (Illus.). (YA). (gr. 7-12). lib. bdg. 29.25 (978-1-4042-1798-0(3)) Rosen Publishing Group, Inc., The.

Libal, Autumn. Drug Therapy & Postpartum Disorders. (Encyclopedia of Psychiatric Drugs & Their Disorders Ser.). (Illus.). (YA). 2004. 128p. lib. bdg. 24.95 (978-1-59084-570-7(6)) 2003. 124p. (gr. 4-7). pap. 14.95 (978-1-4222-0395-8(6)) Mason Crest.

Libal, Joyce. Antidepressants & Social Anxiety: A Pill for Shyness? 2007. (Antidepressants Ser.). (Illus.). 112p. (YA). (gr. 7). pap. 14.95 (978-1-4222-0406-1(5)) Mason Crest.

Lin, Yoming S. Defeating Depression, 01 vols., 1. 2016. (Effective Survival Strategies Ser.). (ENG., Illus.). 64p. (J). 32.95 (978-1-4994-6175-6(5), Rosen Young Adult) Rosen Publishing Group, Inc., The.

Lucas, Eileen. More Than the Blues? Understanding & Dealing with Depression. 2009. (Issues in Focus Today Ser.). (Illus.). 112p. (J). (gr. 6-18). lib. bdg. 33.27 (978-0-7660-3065-7(2)) Enslow Pubs., Inc.

Mackay, Jennifer. Bipolar Disorder. Abramovitz, Melissa, ed. 2012. (Diseases & Disorders Ser.). (ENG., Illus.). 128p. (gr. 7-10). lib. bdg. 39.90 (978-1-4205-0853-6(9), Lucent Bks.) Cengage Gale.

Marsico, Katie. Depression & Stress. 2013. 80p. (YA). (gr. 7-12). 34.21 (978-1-60870-851-2(9)); pap. 17.64 (978-1-62712-127-9(7)) Cavendish Square Publishing.

McIntosh, Kenneth. The History of Depression: the Mind-Body Connection. 2008. (Antidepressants Ser.). (Illus.). 120p. (YA). (gr. 8-12). pap. 14.95 (978-1-4222-0413-9(8)) Mason Crest.

McIntosh, Kenneth & Kleiman, Andrew. Natural Alternatives to Antidepressants: St. John's Wort, Kava Kava, & Others. 2007. (Antidepressants Ser.). (Illus.). 104p. (YA). (gr. -1). pap. 14.95 (978-1-4222-0414-6(6)) Mason Crest.

Meisel, Abigail. Depression & Bipolar Disorder: Examining Chemical Imbalances & Mood Disorders. 2014. (Diseases, Disorders, Symptoms Ser.). (Illus.). 96p. (gr. 9-12). (J). 27.94 (978-1-62293-060-9(6)); pap. 10.95 (978-1-62293-061-6(4)) Enslow Pubs., Inc.

—Investigating Depression & Bipolar Disorder: Real Facts for Real Lives. 2010. (Investigating Diseases Ser.). (Illus.). 160p. (YA). (gr. 9-12). 35.94 (978-0-7660-3340-5(6)) Enslow Pubs., Inc.

Miller, Debra A. Postpartum Depression. 2007. (Diseases & Disorders Ser.). (ENG., Illus.). 104p. (YA). (gr. 7-12). lib. bdg. 34.95 (978-1-4205-0001-1(5)) Cengage Gale.

Moragne, Wendy. Depression. 2011. (USA TODAY Health Reports: Diseases & Disorders Ser.). (ENG.). 128p. (gr. 6-12). 34.60 (978-0-7613-5882-4(X)) Lerner Publishing Group.

Owens, Michael & Gelman, Amy. I'm Depressed, Now What? 2011. (Teen Life 411 Ser.). (YA). (gr. 7-12). lib. bdg. 34.60 (978-1-4488-4656-6(0)) Rosen Publishing Group, Inc., The.

Parks, Peggy J. Teen Depression. 2012. (Diseases & Disorders Ser.). (ENG., Illus.). 128p. (gr. 7-10). lib. bdg. 39.90 (978-1-4205-0837-6(7), Lucent Bks.) Cengage Gale.

Parys, Sabrina. Everything You Need to Know about Stress & Depression. 2017. (Need to Know Library). 64p. (J). (gr. 12-11). 34.45 **(978-1-5081-7416-5(4))**; pap. 12.95 **(978-1-5081-7414-1(8))** Rosen Publishing Group, Inc., The. (Rosen Young Adult).

Peak, Lizabeth & Hardman, Lizabeth. Mood Disorders. 2008. (Diseases & Disorders Ser.). (ENG., Illus.). 128p. (gr. 7-10). lib. bdg. 39.90 (978-1-4205-0072-1(4), LML02109-242076, Lucent Bks.) Cengage Gale.

Poole, H. W. Bipolar Disorder, Vol. 13. Walters, Anne S., ed. 2015. (Mental Illnesses & Disorders: Awareness & Understanding Ser.). (Illus.). 48p. (J). (gr. 5). 20.95 (978-1-4222-3369-6(3)) Mason Crest.

—Depression, Vol. 13. Walters, Anne S., ed. 2015. (Mental Illnesses & Disorders: Awareness & Understanding Ser.). (Illus.). 48p. (J). (gr. 5). 20.95 (978-1-4222-3370-2(7)) Mason Crest.

Rauf, Don, et al. Are You Depressed? 2015. (Got Issues? Ser.). (ENG., Illus.). 128p. (J). (gr. 7-7). lib. bdg. 37.27 (978-0-7660-6981-7(8)) Enslow Pubs., Inc.

Reynolds, Shirley & Parkinson, Monika. Am I Depressed & What Can I Do about It? A CBT Self-Help Guide for Teenagers Experiencing Low Mood & Depression. 2015. (ENG., Illus.). 384p. (gr. 16-17). pap. 15.99 **(978-1-4721-1453-2(1)**, Constable) Little, Brown Book Group Ltd. GBR. Dist: Hachette Bk. Group.

Russell, Craig. Antidepressants & Side Effects: Managing the Risks. 2007. (Antidepressants Ser.). (Illus.). 112p. (YA). (gr. 8-12). pap. 14.95 (978-1-4222-0410-8(3)) Mason Crest.

Schwartz, Tina P. Depression: The Ultimate Teen. 2014. (It Happened to Me Ser.: 42). (ENG., Illus.). 196p. (J). (gr. 7-13). 45.00 (978-0-8108-8387-1(2)) Scarecrow Pr., Inc.

Silverstein, Alvin, et al. The Depression & Bipolar Disorder Update. 2008. (Disease Update Ser.). (Illus.). 128p. (J). (gr. k-5). lib. bdg. 33.27 (978-0-7660-2801-2(1)) Enslow Pubs., Inc.

Smith, Emily Wing. All Better Now: My Life As the Thank-God-She-got-hit-by-a-car Girl. 2016. (ENG., Illus.). 304p. (YA). (gr. 7). 17.99 (978-0-525-42624-0(8), Dutton Books for Young Readers) Penguin Young Readers Group.

Smith, Paula. Depression & Other Mood Disorders. 2013. 48p. (J). (978-0-7787-0831-5(4)); (Illus.). pap. (978-0-7787-0857-5(8)) Crabtree Publishing Co.

Thakkar, Vatsal. Depression & Bipolar Disorder. Collins, Christine, ed. 2006. (Psychological Disorders Ser.). (Illus.). 100p. (YA). (gr. 7-12). lib. bdg. 37.50 (978-0-7910-8542-4(2)) Facts On File, Inc.

Thomas, Peggy. Post-Traumatic Stress Disorder. 2007. (Diseases & Disorders Ser.). (ENG., Illus.). 104p. (YA). (gr. 7-12). lib. bdg. 34.95 (978-1-4205-0002-8(3)) Cengage Gale.

Walker, Maryalice. The Development of Antidepressants: The Chemistry of Depression. (Antidepressants Ser.). (Illus.). 112p. (YA). (gr. 7-18). 2008. lib. bdg. 24.95 (978-1-4222-0102-2(3)) 2007. pap. 14.95 (978-1-4222-0411-5(1)) Mason Crest.

Wilde, Jerry. Hot Stuff to Help Kids Cheer Up: The Depression & Self-Esteem Workbook. 2007. (ENG.). 80p. (J). (gr. 4-7). pap. 9.95 (978-1-4022-0926-0(6), Sourcebooks Jabberwocky) Sourcebooks, Inc.

Worth, Richard. Helping a Friend Who Is Depressed. 2016. (How Can I Help? Friends Helping Friends Ser.). 00064p. (J). (gr. 6-6). pap. 12.95 (978-1-4994-6440-5(1)) Rosen Publishing Group, Inc., The.

Zucker, Faye. Depression. 2004. (Life Balance Ser.). (ENG.). 80p. (YA). (gr. 5-8). pap. 6.95 (978-0-531-15578-3(1), Watts, Franklin) Scholastic Library Publishing.

DEPRESSION, MENTAL—FICTION

Believarexic, 1 vol. 2015. (ENG.). 464p. (YA). (gr. 8-11). 18.95 (978-1-56145-771-7(X)) Peachtree Pubs.

Blakemore, Megan Frazer. Good & Gone. 2017. 304p. (YA). (gr. 8). 17.99 **(978-0-06-234842-5(6)**, HarperTeen) HarperCollins Pubs.

Brewer, Zac. Madness. 2017. 304p. (YA). (gr. 9). 17.99 **(978-0-06-245785-1(3))** HarperCollins Pubs.

Caletti, Deb. Essential Maps for the Lost. 2016. (ENG., Illus.). 336p. (YA). (gr. 9). 17.99 (978-1-4814-1516-3(6), Simon Pulse) Simon Pulse.

Centre for Addiction and Mental Health Staff. Can I Catch It Like a Cold? Coping with a Parent's Depression. Weissmann, Joe, illus. 2009. (Coping Ser.). (ENG.). 32p. (J). (gr. k-3). 17.95 (978-0-88776-956-6(X), Tundra Bks.) Tundra Bks. CAN. Dist: Penguin Random Hse. LLC.

Chilman-Blair, Kim & Deloache, Shawn. Medikidz Explain Depression: What's up with James? 2010. (Illus.). 32p. (J). pap. (978-1-906935-10-8(6)) Medikidz Ltd.

Danneberg, Julie. Family Reminders. Shelley, John, illus. 2009. (ENG.). 112p. (J). (gr. 3-7). 14.95 (978-1-58089-320-6(1)) Charlesbridge Publishing, Inc.

Dellasega, Cheryl. Nugrl90, 0 vols. LaPierre, Karina, illus. 2007. (Bloggrls Ser.: 1). (ENG.). 192p. (YA). (gr. 7-11). pap. 9.99 (978-0-7614-5396-3(2), 9780761453963, Amazon Children's Publishing) Amazon Publishing.

Diggle, David Mark. Reggie: Learns to Roll with It. Preuss, Sarah Louise, illus. 2011. 24p. (J). pap. (978-0-9871658-3-1(6)) Diggle de Doo Productions Pty, Ltd.

Doyle, Roddy. Brilliant. Hughes, Emily, illus. 2015. (ENG.). 192p. (J). (gr. 3-7). 16.95 (978-1-4197-1479-5(1), Amulet Bks.) Abrams, Inc.

Dreyer, Ellen. The Glow Stone, 1 vol. 2006. (ENG.). 224p. (YA). (gr. 7-18). 15.95 (978-1-56145-370-2(6)) Peachtree Pubs.

Engelman, Stephanie. A Single Bead. 2016. 199p. (YA). pap. (978-0-8198-9054-2(5)) Pauline Bks. & Media.

Farrey, Brian. The Secret of Dreadwillow Carse. 2016. (ENG.). 256p. (J). (gr. 3-7). 16.95 (978-1-61620-505-8(9)) Algonquin Bks. of Chapel Hill.

Fernandez, Texanna. My Mighty Mother. 2010. 16p. pap. 9.00 (978-1-4490-5409-0(9)) AuthorHouse.

Foley, James. Danny & the Blue Cloud: Coping with Childhood Depression. Ng-Benitez, Shirley, illus. 2016. 32p. (J). (978-1-4338-2103-5(6), Magination Pr.) American Psychological Assn.

Goldhagen, Shari. 100 Days of Cake. (ENG.). 352p. (YA). (gr. 9). 2017. pap. 11.99 (978-1-4814-4857-4(9)) 2016. (Illus.). 17.99 (978-1-4814-4856-7(0), Atheneum Bks. for Young Readers) Simon & Schuster Children's Publishing.

Hemingway, Edith M. Road to Tater Hill. 2011. (ENG.). 224p. (J). (gr. 3-7). 7.99 (978-0-375-84544-4(5), Yearling) Random Hse. Children's Bks.

Hiranandani, Veera. The Whole Story of Half a Girl. 2013. (ENG.). 224p. (J). (gr. 4-7). 6.99 (978-0-375-87167-2(5), Yearling) Random Hse. Children's Bks.

Holmes, Sara Lewis. Letters from Rapunzel. 2007. 184p. (J). (gr. 3-7). lib. bdg. 16.89 (978-0-06-078074-6(6)) HarperCollins Pubs.

Hurwitz, Laura. Disappear Home. 2015. (ENG.). 256p. (J). (gr. 8-12). 16.99 (978-0-8075-2468-8(9)) Whitman, Albert & Co.

Huston, Donna. The Woe down Clown. 2006. (J). spiral bd. 19.95 (978-0-9771192-1-9(1)) Shayne Publishing.

Hutchinson, Shaun David. We Are the Ants. 2016. (ENG., Illus.). 464p. (YA). (gr. 9). 17.99 (978-1-4814-4963-2(X), Simon Pulse) Simon Pulse.

Jacobus, Ann. Romancing the Dark in the City of Light: A Novel. 2015. (ENG.). 288p. (YA). (gr. 7-12). 18.99 (978-1-250-06443-1(0), 9781250064431) St. Martin's Pr.

Johnson, J. J. Believarexic, 1 vol. 2017. (ENG.). 464p. (YA). (gr. 8-11). pap. 9.95 **(978-1-68263-007-5(2))** Peachtree Pubs.

Jones, Traci L. Silhouetted by the Blue. 2011. (ENG.). 208p. (J). (gr. 5-9). 16.99 (978-0-374-36914-9(3), 9780374369149, Farrar, Straus & Giroux (BYR)) Farrar, Straus & Giroux.

Kate, Lauren. Teardrop. 2013. 441p. (YA). (978-0-385-37491-0(7)); (978-0-385-38372-1(X)) Random House Publishing Group. (Delacorte Pr).

—Teardrop. (Teardrop Ser.). (ENG.). (YA). (gr. 7). 2014. 480p. pap. 10.99 (978-0-385-74266-5(5), Ember) 2013. 464p. 18.99 (978-0-385-74265-8(7), Delacorte Pr.) Random Hse. Children's Bks.

LaFleur, Suzanne. Love, Aubrey. 2011. (ENG.). 272p. (J). (gr. 3-7). pap. 7.99 (978-0-375-85159-9(3), Yearling) Random Hse. Children's Bks.

Legrand, Claire. Some Kind of Happiness. 2016. (ENG., Illus.). 384p. (J). (gr. 3-7). 17.99 (978-1-4424-6601-2(4), Simon & Schuster Bks. For Young Readers) Simon & Schuster Bks. For Young Readers.

Lewandowski, Lisa & Trost, Shannon. Darcy Daisy & the Firefly Festival: Learning about Bipolar Disorder & Community. Shaw-Peterson, Kimberly, illus. 2005. 32p. (J). (gr. -1-9). pap. 9.95 (978-0-9785075-2-7(5), Ferne Pr.) Nelson Publishing & Marketing.

Lord, Emery. When We Collided. (ENG.). (YA). 2017. 368p. pap. 9.99 (978-1-68119-203-1(9), 9781681192031) 2016. 352p. 17.99 (978-1-61963-845-7(2), 9781619638457) Bloomsbury Publishing USA. (Bloomsbury USA Childrens).

Marchetta, Melina. Saving Francesca. 2006. (ENG.). 258p. (YA). (gr. 7-12). reprint ed. per. 8.99 (978-0-375-82983-3(0), Knopf Bks. for Young Readers) Random Hse. Children's Bks.

Maynard, Joyce. The Cloud Chamber. 2006. (ENG.). 288p. (YA). (gr. 7-7). pap. 13.99 (978-1-4169-2699-3(2), Simon Pulse) Simon Pulse.

McNamara, Amy. Lovely, Dark & Deep. (ENG.). 352p. (YA). (gr. 9). 2013. pap. 10.99 (978-1-4424-3437-0(6)) 2012. 16.99 (978-1-4424-3435-6(X)) Simon & Schuster Bks. For Young Readers. (Simon & Schuster Bks. For Young Readers).

Messer, Celeste M. A Message from Teddy. Hoeffner, Deb, illus. 2004. 82-92p. 4.95 (978-0-9702171-5-8(3)) AshleyAlan Enterprises.

Ozmun, Lori. The Monster in Lulu's Head: The Tale of Two Spoons. 2013. 56p. pap. 31.99 (978-1-4797-6780-9(8)) Xlibris Corp.

Peters, Andrew Fusek & Peters, Polly. The Color Thief. Littlewood, Karin, illus. 2015. (ENG.). 24p. (J). (gr. -1-3). 16.99 (978-0-8075-1273-9(7)) Whitman, Albert & Co.

Peterson, Lois. Meeting Miss 405, 1 vol. 2008. (Orca Young Readers Ser.). (ENG.). 112p. (J). (gr. 3-6). pap. 7.95 (978-1-55469-015-2(3)) Orca Bk. Pubs. USA.

Prosek, James. The Day My Mother Left. Prosek, James, illus. 2009. (ENG., Illus.). 304p. (J). (gr. 4-7). pap. 7.99 (978-1-4169-0771-8(8), Simon & Schuster Bks. For Young Readers) Simon & Schuster Bks. For Young Readers.

Quick, Matthew. Sorta Like a Rock Star. 2011. (ENG.). 384p. (YA). (gr. 7-17). pap., pap. 10.99 (978-0-316-04353-3(2)) Little, Brown Bks. for Young Readers.

Rice, Luanne. The Beautiful Lost. 2017. (ENG.). 304p. (J). (gr. 7). 18.99 **(978-1-338-11107-1(8))** Scholastic, Inc.

Roskos, Evan. Dr. Bird's Advice for Sad Poets. 2013. (ENG.). 320p. (YA). (gr. 9). 17.99 (978-0-547-92853-1(X)) Houghton Mifflin Harcourt Publishing Co.

Sappenfield, Heather. The View from Who I Was. 2015. (ENG.). 336p. (YA). pap. 11.99 (978-0-7387-4174-1(4), Flux) North Star Editions.

Schumacher, Julie. Black Box. 2010. (ENG.). 176p. (YA). (gr. 7-18). pap. 7.99 (978-0-440-24064-8(6), Delacorte Bks. for Young Readers) Random Hse. Children's Bks.

Stevens, Liza. Not Today, Celeste! A Dog's Tale about Her Human's Depression. 2016. (ENG., Illus.). 36p. (J). 17.95 (978-1-78592-008-0(1), 8254) Kingsley, Jessica Pubs. GBR. Dist: Macmillan Distribution Ltd.

Stork, Francisco X. The Memory of Light. 2016. (Arthur a Levine Novel Bks.). (ENG.). 336p. (YA). (gr. 7). 17.99 (978-0-545-47432-0(9)) Scholastic, Inc.

Taylor, Whitney. Definitions of Indefinable Things. 2017. (ENG.). 336p. (YA). (gr. 9). 17.99 (978-0-544-80504-0(6), HMH Books For Young Readers) Houghton Mifflin Harcourt Publishing Co.

Tyrrell, Karen. Bailey Beats the Blah. Pocock, Aaron, illus. 2013. 34p. pap. (978-0-9872740-4-5(X)) Digital Future Press.

Vizzini, Ned. It's Kind of a Funny Story. 2007. (ENG.). 464p. (YA). (gr. 7-12). per. 9.99 (978-0-7868-5197-3(X)) Disney Publishing Worldwide.

—It's Kind of a Funny Story. 2011. 11.04 (978-0-7848-3383-4(4), Everbind) Marco Bk. Co.

—It's Kind of a Funny Story. 2007. (YA). lib. bdg. 20.85 (978-1-4178-1818-1(2), Turtleback) Turtleback Bks.

Wittlinger, Ellen. Blind Faith. 2007. (ENG.). 304p. (YA). (gr. 7-12). pap. 9.99 (978-1-4169-4906-0(2), Simon & Schuster Bks. For Young Readers) Simon & Schuster Bks. For Young Readers.

Young, Janet Ruth. The Opposite of Music. 2008. (ENG.). 352p. (YA). (gr. 7-12). pap. 15.99 (978-1-4169-5823-9(1), Atheneum Bks. for Young Readers) Simon & Schuster Children's Publishing.

Younge-Ullman, Danielle. Everything Beautiful Is Not Ruined. 2017. (ENG.). 368p. (YA). (gr. 9). 17.99 (978-0-425-28759-0(9), Viking Books for Young Readers) Penguin Young Readers Group.

DEPRESSIONS

Baxter, Roberta. The Great Depression. 2014. (Perspectives Library). (ENG., Illus.). 32p. (J). (gr. 4-8). pap. 14.21 (978-1-63137-663-4(2), 205256) Cherry Lake Publishing.

—The Great Depression: A History Perspectives Book. 2014. (Perspectives Library). (ENG., Illus.). 32p. (J). (gr. 4-8). 28.50 (978-1-63137-618-4(7), 205255) Cherry Lake Publishing.

Benchmark Education Co., LLC. The Roaring Twenties & the Great Depression. 2014. (PRIME Ser.). (J). (gr. 6-8). pap. (978-1-4509-9498-9(9)) Benchmark Education Co.

Benchmark Education Company. The Great Depression by the Numbers (Teacher Guide) 2004. (978-1-4108-2590-2(6)) Benchmark Education Co.

Brown, Don. The Great American Dust Bowl. 2017. (ENG., Illus.). 80p. (YA). (gr. 7). pap. 9.99 **(978-1-328-74087-8(0)**, HMH Books For Young Readers) Houghton Mifflin Harcourt Publishing Co.

—The Great American Dust Bowl. Brown, Don, illus. 2013. (ENG., Illus.). 80p. (YA). (gr. 7). 18.99 (978-0-547-81550-3(6)) Houghton Mifflin Harcourt Publishing Co.

Brown, Harriet & Witowski, Teri. Kit's World: A Girl's-Eye View of the Great Depression. Rane, Walter & Hood, Philip, illus. 2008. 30p. (YA). (gr. 3-18). 24.95 (978-1-59369-459-3(8)) American Girl Publishing, Inc.

Burg, David F. The Great Depression. 2nd rev. ed. 2005. (Eyewitness History Ser.). (Illus.). 464p. (C). (gr. 9). 80.00 (978-0-8160-5709-2(5)) Facts On File, Inc.

Burgan, Michael. The Great Depression: An Interactive History Adventure, 1 vol. (You Choose: Historical Eras Ser.). (ENG.). 112p. (gr. 3-4). 2011. pap. 6.95 (978-1-4296-6276-5(X)) 2011. pap. 41.70 (978-1-4296-6740-1(0)) 2010. 31.99 (978-1-4296-5480-7(5)) Capstone Press of Coughlan Cos. (You Choose Bks.).

Connell, Kate. Hoping for Rain: The Dust Bowl Adventures of Patty & Earl Buckler. 2004. (I Am American Ser.). (ENG., Illus.). 40p. (J). (gr. 3-7). pap. 6.99 (978-0-7922-6903-8(9), National Geographic Children's Bks.) National Geographic Society.

Connell, Kate & National Geographic Learning Staff. Dust Bowl Days. 2007. (Reading Expeditions Ser.). (ENG., Illus.). 40p. (J). pap. 19.95 (978-0-7922-4557-5(1)) CENGAGE Learning.

Crayton, Lisa A. & Porterfield, Jason. Economic Depression: What It Is & How It Works. 2016. (Economics in the 21st Century Ser.). (ENG.). 96p. (J). (gr. 8-8). 34.60 (978-0-7660-7195-7(2)) Enslow Pubs., Inc.

Crewe, Sabrina & Ingram, Scott. The Stock Market Crash of 1929. 2005. (Events That Shaped America Ser.). (Illus.). 32p. (gr. 3-6). lib. bdg. 26.00 (978-0-8368-3416-1(X), Gareth Stevens Learning Library) Stevens, Gareth Publishing LLLP.

Dugan, Christine. Between the Wars, 1 vol. 2007. (Primary Source Readers Ser.). (ENG.). 32p. (J). (gr. 5-5). pap. 8.99 (978-0-7439-0666-1(7)) Shell Educational Publishing.

Favreau, Marc. Crash: The Fall & Rise of America in the 1930s. 2017. (J). **(978-0-316-46489-5(9))** Little, Brown Bks. for Young Readers.

Freedman, Russell. Children of the Great Depression. 2010. (ENG., Illus.). 128p. (J). (gr. 5-7). pap. 10.99 (978-0-547-48035-0(0)) Houghton Mifflin Harcourt Publishing Co.

Fremon, David K. The Great Depression in United States History. 2014. (In United States History Ser.). 96p. (J). (gr. 5-12). 27.94 (978-0-7660-6087-6(X)); (Illus.). pap. 10.95 (978-0-7660-6088-3(8)) Enslow Pubs., Inc.

Gedney, Mona K. The Story of the Great Depression. 2005. (Monumental Milestones Ser.). (Illus.). 48p. (YA). (gr. 4-7). lib. bdg. 29.95 (978-1-58415-403-7(9)) Mitchell Lane Pubs., Inc.

George, Linda & George, Charles. The Great Depression. 2013. (Illus.). 96p. (J). lib. bdg. (978-1-60152-492-8(7)) ReferencePoint Pr., Inc.

Gitlin, Martin. The Great Depression & World War II: 1929-1945. 2007. (Presidents of the United States Ser.). (Illus.). 48p. (J). (gr. 4-7). lib. bdg. 29.05 (978-1-59036-749-0(9)); per. 10.95 (978-1-59036-750-6(2)) Weigl Pubs., Inc.

Gow, Mary. The Stock Market Crash Of 1929: Dawn of the Great Depression. 2003. (American Disasters Ser.). (Illus.).

48p. (J). lib. bdg. 23.93 *(978-0-7660-2111-2(4))* Enslow Pubs., Inc.

Grant, R. G. Why Did the Great Depression Happen? 2010. (Moments in History Ser.). (Illus.). 48p. (YA). (gr. 5-9). lib. bdg. 31.95 *(978-1-4339-4169-6(4))*; (gr. 6-8). pap. 14.05 *(978-1-4339-4170-2(8)*, Gareth Stevens Secondary Library) Stevens, Gareth Publishing LLLP.

Graves, Kerry A. School in the Great Depression. 2016. (It's Back to School ... Way Back! Ser.). (ENG., Illus.). 32p. (gr. 3-4). lib. bdg. 27.32 *(978-1-5157-2098-0(5)*, Fact Finders) Capstone Press of Coughlan Cos.

The Great Depression 1929-1938. 2010. (Discovering U. S. History Ser.). (Illus.). 136p. (gr. 5-8). 35.00 *(978-1-60413-357-8(0)*, Chelsea Hse.) Facts On File, Inc.

Gunderson, Cory. Great Depression, 1 vol. 2004. (American Moments Ser.). (ENG.). 48p. (gr. 4-8). 27.07 *(978-1-59197-286-0(8)*, Abdo & Daughters) ABDO Publishing Co.

Hamen, Susan E. The New Deal, 1 vol. 2010. (Essential Events Set 5 Ser.). (ENG.). 112p. (J). (gr. 6-12). lib. bdg. 35.64 *(978-1-61613-684-0(7))* ABDO Publishing Co.

Haugen, David M., et al. The Great Depression. 2010. (Perspectives on Modern World History Ser.). (Illus.). 224p. (YA). (gr. 10-12). 42.45 *(978-0-7377-4795-9(1)*, Greenhaven Pr., Inc.) Cengage Gale.

Hill, Jeff. The WPA — Putting America to Work. 2013. (Defining Moments Ser.). (ENG.). 264p. lib. bdg. 55.00 *(978-0-7808-1331-1(6))* Omnigraphics, Inc.

Hurt, Avery. The Great Depression. 2017. (J). ***(978-1-5026-2713-1(2))*** Cavendish Square Publishing.

Hyde, Natalie. Black Tuesday & the Great Depression. 2015. (Uncovering the Past: Analyzing Primary Sources Ser.). (ENG., Illus.). 48p. (J). (gr. 5-8). *(978-0-7787-1708-9(9))* Crabtree Publishing Co.

Ingram, Scott. The Stock Market Crash of 1929. 2004. (Landmark Events in American History Ser.). (Illus.). 48p. (gr. 5-12). pap. 14.05 *(978-0-8368-5425-1(X)*, Gareth Stevens Secondary Library) Stevens, Gareth Publishing LLLP.

Johnson, Robin. The Great Depression. 2013. (ENG., Illus.). 48p. (J). *(978-0-7787-1173-5(0))*; pap. *(978-0-7787-1186-5(2))* Crabtree Publishing Co.

Kupperberg, Paul. Critical Perspectives on the Great Depression. 2005. (Critical Anthologies of Nonfiction Writing Ser.). 176p. (YA). (gr. 7-12). lib. bdg. 37.95 *(978-1-4042-0061-6(4))* Rosen Publishing Group, Inc., The.

Kupperberg, Paul, ed. Critical Perspectives on the Great Depression. 2009. (Critical Anthologies of Nonfiction Writing Ser.). 176p. (gr. 8-8). 63.90 *(978-1-61512-081-9(5))* Rosen Publishing Group, Inc., The.

Langston-George, Rebecca. A Primary Source History of the Dust Bowl. 2015. (Primary Source History Ser.). (ENG., Illus.). 32p. (gr. 3-4). lib. bdg. 27.32 *(978-1-4914-1840-6(0))* Capstone Press of Coughlan Cos.

Malchik, Antonia E. The Great Depression by the Numbers: Set Of 6. 2010. (Navigators Ser.). (J). pap. 50.00 net. *(978-1-4108-2575-9(2))* Benchmark Education Co.

Malchik, E. The Great Depression by the Numbers & Los números de la Gran Depresión: 6 English, 6 Spanish Adaptations. 2011. (ENG & SPA.). (J). 101.00 net. *(978-1-4108-5730-9(1))* Benchmark Education Co.

Marrin, Albert. Years of Dust: The Story of the Dust Bowl. (ENG.). (J). (gr. 5). 2012. 144p. mass mkt. 9.99 *(978-0-14-242579-4(6)*, Puffin Books) 2009. (Illus.). 128p. 22.99 *(978-0-525-42077-4(0)*, Dutton Books for Young Readers) Penguin Young Readers Group.

Marriott, Emma. Did Anything Good Come Out of the Great Depression?, 01 vols., 1. 2016. (Innovation Through Adversity Ser.). (ENG.). 48p. (J). 30.25 *(978-1-5081-7072-3(X)*, Rosen Young Adult) Rosen Publishing Group, Inc., The.

McDaniel, Melissa. The Great Depression. 2012. (Cornerstones of Freedom, Third Ser.). (ENG., Illus.). 64p. (J). pap. 8.95 *(978-0-531-28156-7(6))*; (gr. 4-6). lib. bdg. 30.00 *(978-0-531-23056-5(2))* Scholastic Library Publishing.

McNeilly, Linden K. Perspectives on the Great Depression. 2018. (ENG.). 32p. (gr. 3-6). ***(978-1-63235-401-3(2)***, 12-Story Library) Pr. Room Editions LLC.

Mullenbach, Cheryl. The Great Depression for Kids: Hardship & Hope in 1930s America, with 21 Activities. 2015. (For Kids Ser.). (ENG., Illus.). 144p. (J). (gr. 4). pap. 16.95 *(978-1-61373-051-5(9))* Chicago Review Pr., Inc.

Nardo, Don. Migrant Mother: How a Photograph Defined the Great Depression, 1 vol. 2011. (Captured History Ser.). (ENG.). 64p. (gr. 5-7). lib. bdg. 34.65 *(978-0-7565-4397-6(5)*, CPB Grades 4-8) Compass Point Bks.

Parks, Peggy J. The Great Depression. 2003. (Daily Life Ser.). (Illus.). 48p. (J). 26.20 *(978-0-7377-1399-2(2)*, Greenhaven Pr., Inc.) Cengage Gale.

Pascal, Janet. What Was the Great Depression? 2015. (What Was... ? Ser.). lib. bdg. 16.00 *(978-0-606-37550-4(3))* Turtleback Bks.

Pascal, Janet & dePaola, Tomie. What Was the Great Depression? Putra, Dede, illus. 2015. (What Was? Ser.). (ENG.). 112p. (J). (gr. 3-7). 5.99 *(978-0-448-48427-3(7)*, Penguin Workshop) Penguin Young Readers Group.

Peterson, Sheryl. The Great Depression & World War II. 2011. (Explorer Library: Language Arts Explorer Ser.). (ENG.). 32p. (gr. 4-8). pap. 14.21 *(978-1-61080-287-1(X)*, 201210); lib. bdg. 28.50 *(978-1-61080-199-7(7)*, 201174) Cherry Lake Publishing.

Porterfield, Jason. How a Depression Works. 2009. (Real World Economics Ser.). (Illus.). 80p. (YA). (gr. 7-12). lib. bdg. 33.25 *(978-1-4358-5322-5(9))* Rosen Publishing Group, Inc., The.

—How A Depression Works (Real World Economics) l.t. ed. 2012. 142p. pap. *(978-1-4596-3376-6(8))* ReadHowYouWant.com, Ltd.

Reis, Ronald A. The Dust Bowl. 2008. (Great Historic Disasters Ser.). (Illus.). 128p. (gr. 5-8). lib. bdg. 35.00 *(978-0-7910-9737-3(4)*, Chelsea Hse.) Facts On File, Inc.

Rigby. When Day Turned to Night. 2014. (Rigby Literacy Ser.). (ENG.). 32p. (gr. 4-4). pap. 11.10 *(978-0-7578-2002-1(6))* Rigby Education.

Ruth, Amy. Growing up in the Great Depression, 1929 to 1941. 2003. (Our America Ser.). (Illus.). 64p. (J). (gr. 4-7). lib. bdg. 26.60 *(978-0-8225-0655-3(6))* Lerner Publishing Group.

Stanley, George Edward. The Great Depression & World War II (1929-1949) 2005. (Primary Source History of the United States Ser.). (Illus.). 48p. (gr. 5-12). pap. 14.05 *(978-0-8368-5838-9(7))*; lib. bdg. 31.00 *(978-0-8368-5829-7(6))* Stevens, Gareth Publishing LLLP. (Gareth Stevens Secondary Library).

Stein, R. Conrad. The New Deal: Pulling America Out of the Great Depression. 2006. (American Saga Ser.). (Illus.). 128p. (J). (gr. 5-9). lib. bdg. 33.27 *(978-0-7660-2570-7(5))* Enslow Pubs., Inc.

Taylor, B. J. Ella Mae & the Great Depression. 2013. 40p. pap. 19.57 *(978-1-4907-1016-7(7))* Trafford Publishing.

Vander Hook, Sue. The Dust Bowl, 1 vol. 2009. (Essential Events Set 3 Ser.). (ENG., Illus.). 112p. (J). (gr. 6-12). lib. bdg. 35.64 *(978-1-60453-512-9(1))* ABDO Publishing Co.

Winter, Jonah. Born & Bred in the Great Depression. Root, Kimberly Bulcken, illus. 2011. (ENG.). 40p. (J). (gr. k-4). 17.99 *(978-0-375-86197-0(1)*, Schwartz & Wade Bks.) Random Hse. Children's Bks.

World Book, Inc Staff, contrib. by. The Great Depression. 2010. (J). *(978-0-7166-1505-7(3))* World Bk., Inc.

Wright, John & Waugh, Steven. The USA, 1929-1980. 2005. (Illus.). 144p. pap. 38.50 *(978-0-340-88903-9(9)*, Hodder Education) Hodder Education Group GBR. Dist: Trans-Atlantic Pubns., Inc.

DEPRESSIONS—FICTION

Adler, David A. The Babe & I. Widener, Terry, illus. 2006. 28p. (gr. 1-4). 18.00 *(978-0-7569-6560-0(8))* Perfection Learning Corp.

Andrews, Sandy. Best Friends - the Depression Years. 2012. 218p. pap. 12.95 *(978-1-937912-87-1(6))* Cordon Pubns.

Ayres, Katherine. Macaroni Boy. 2004. (ENG.). 192p. (J). (gr. 3-7). per. 6.99 *(978-0-440-41884-9(4)*, Yearling) Random Hse. Children's Bks.

Banks, Sara Harrell. The Everlasting Now, 1 vol. 2010. (ENG.). 168p. (J). (gr. 3-7). 15.95 *(978-1-56145-525-6(3)*, Peachtree Junior) Peachtree Pubs.

Barnaby, Hannah. Wonder Show. (ENG., 288p. (YA). (gr. 7). 2013. Illus.). pap. 8.99 *(978-0-544-10483-9(8))* 2012. 16.99 *(978-0-547-59980-9(3))* Houghton Mifflin Harcourt Publishing Co.

Bayard, Louis. Lucky Strikes. 2016. (ENG., Illus.). 320p. (YA). 16.99 *(978-1-62779-390-2(9)*, 9781627793902, Holt, Henry & Co. Bks. For Young Readers) Holt, Henry & Co.

—Lucky Strikes. 2017. (YA). lib. bdg. 20.85 ***(978-0-606-39951-7(8))*** Turtleback Bks.

Birtha, Becky. Lucky Beans. Tadgell, Nicole, illus. 2010. (ENG.). 32p. (J). (gr. 2-3). 16.99 *(978-0-8075-4782-3(4))* Whitman, Albert & Co.

Blume, Lesley M. M. Tennyson. 2009. (ENG.). 240p. (J). (gr. 3-7). 7.99 *(978-0-440-24061-7(1)*, Yearling) Random Hse. Children's Bks.

Brookins, Cara. Doris Free. Barrow, Ann, illus. 2006. 127p. (J). pap. *(978-1-59336-333-8(8))* Mondo Publishing.

Cory, Kim Delmar. Tending Ben's Garden. 2009. (J). pap. *(978-0-88092-778-9(X))* Royal Fireworks Publishing Co.

Curtis, Christopher Paul. Bud, Not Buddy. unabr. ed. 2004. 256p. (J). (gr. 4-7). pap. 36.00 incl. audio *(978-0-8072-8210-6(3)*, LYA 140 S{, Listening Library) Random Hse. Audio Publishing Group.

—Bud, Not Buddy. 2004. (ENG., Illus.). 288p. (J). (gr. 3-7). mass mkt. 7.99 *(978-0-553-49410-5(4)*, Laurel Leaf) Random Hse. Children's Bks.

—The Mighty Miss Malone. (ENG.). 320p. (J). (gr. 4-7). 2013. pap. 7.99 *(978-0-440-42214-3(0)*, Yearling) 2012. 15.99 *(978-0-385-73491-2(3)*, Lamb, Wendy Bks.) Random Hse. Children's Bks.

—The Mighty Miss Malone. 2013. lib. bdg. 18.40 *(978-0-606-27007-6(8)*, Turtleback) Turtleback Bks.

Dagg, Carole Estby. Sweet Home Alaska. 2016. (ENG.). 304p. (J). (gr. 5). 16.99 *(978-0-399-17203-8(3)*, Nancy Paulsen Books) Penguin Young Readers Group.

Edwards, Judith. Invasion on the Mountain: The Adventures of Will Ryan & the Civilian Conservation Corps 1933. 2011. (ENG., Illus.). 90p. (J). (gr. 3-7). pap. 12.50 *(978-1-884592-55-3(4))* Images from the Past, Inc.

—Trouble on the Mountain: The Adventures of Will Ryan & the Civilian Conservation Corps, 1934-35. 2012. (ENG., Illus.). 118p. (J). (gr. 3-7). pap. 12.50 *(978-1-884592-60-7(0))* Images from the Past, Inc.

Elster, Jean Alicia. Who's Jim Hines? 2008. (Great Lakes Books Ser.). (ENG., Illus.). 146p. (J). pap. 14.99 *(978-0-8143-3402-7(4)*, 2162) Wayne State Univ. Pr.

Ernst, Kathleen. Midnight in Lonesome Hollow: A Kit Mystery. 2007. (American Girl Mysteries Ser.). (ENG., Illus.). 192p. (gr. 4-7). 10.95 *(978-1-59369-161-5(0)*, American Girl) American Girl Publishing, Inc.

—Midnight in Lonesome Hollow: A Kit Mystery. Tibbles, Jean-Paul, illus. 2007. (ENG.). 192p. (gr. 4-7). pap. 6.95 *(978-1-59369-160-8(2)*, American Girl) American Girl Publishing, Inc.

Giff, Patricia Reilly. R My Name Is Rachel. 2012. (ENG.). 176p. (J). (gr. 4-7). pap. 6.99 *(978-0-440-42176-4(4)*, Yearling) Random Hse. Children's Bks.

Golden, Laura. Every Day After. 2013. (ENG.). 224p. (J). (gr. 4-7). 15.99 *(978-0-385-74326-6(2)*, Delacorte Bks. for Young Readers) Random Hse. Children's Bks.

Guest, Jacqueline. Secret Signs, 1 vol. 2006. (Orca Young Readers Ser.). (ENG., Illus.). 144p. (J). (gr. 3-6). per. 7.95 *(978-1-55143-599-2(3))* Orca Bk. Pubs. USA.

Hale, Marian. The Truth about Sparrows. 2007. (ENG.). 288p. (YA). (gr. 7-12). per. 9.99 *(978-0-312-37133-3(0)*, 9780312371333) Square Fish.

Harper, Jo & Harper, Josephine. Finding Daddy: A Story of the Great Depression. Mazellan, Ron, illus. 2005. (ENG.). 48p. (J). (gr. k). 16.95 *(978-1-890515-31-7(0))* Turtle Bks.

Hart, Alison. Risky Chance. Sanderson, Ruth, illus. 2011. (Horse Diaries). (ENG.). 176p. (J). (gr. 3-7). pap. 7.99 *(978-0-375-86833-7(X)*, Random Hse. Bks. for Young Readers) Random Hse. Children's Bks.

Hendershot, Eric. At Season's End. 2012. pap. 13.99 *(978-1-59955-995-7(1))* Cedar Fort, Inc./CFI Distribution.

Hesse, Karen. Out of the Dust. 240p. (YA). (gr. 5-18). pap. 4.99 *(978-0-8072-1526-5(0)*, Listening Library) Random Hse. Audio Publishing Group.

—Out of the Dust. 2009. (gr. 5-8). 18.40 *(978-0-613-11953-5(3)*, Turtleback) Turtleback Bks.

Hoberman, Mary Ann. Strawberry Hill. 2010. (ENG., Illus.). 240p. (J). (gr. 3-7). pap. 7.99 *(978-0-316-04135-5(1))* Little, Brown Bks. for Young Readers.

Holm, Jennifer L. Full of Beans. 2016. (ENG.). 208p. (J). (gr. 3-7). 16.99 *(978-0-553-51036-2(3))*; lib. bdg. 19.99 *(978-0-553-51037-9(1))* Random Hse. Children's Bks. (Random Hse. Bks. for Young Readers).

—Turtle in Paradise. 2012. (CHI.). 187p. (J). (gr. 3-7). pap. *(978-7-221-10316-1(X))* Guizhou People's Publishing Hse.

—Turtle in Paradise. 2009. 9.14 *(978-7-7848-3781-8(3)*, Everbind) Marco Bk. Co.

—Turtle in Paradise. 2011. (ENG.). 224p. (J). (gr. 3-7). pap. 7.99 *(978-0-375-83690-9(X)*, Yearling) Random Hse. Children's Bks.

—Turtle in Paradise. 2011. lib. bdg. 18.40 *(978-0-606-23877-9(8)*, Turtleback) Turtleback Bks.

Ingold, Jeanette. Hitch. 2006. (ENG., Illus.). 288p. (YA). (gr. 7-12). pap. 7.99 *(978-0-15-205619-3(X))* Houghton Mifflin Harcourt Publishing Co.

Jennings, Patrick. Wish Riders. 2008. (ENG.). 288p. pap. 6.99 *(978-1-4231-0015-7(8))* Hyperion Pr.

Koss, Amy Goldman. The Not-So-Great Depression. 2010. (ENG.). 272p. (YA). (gr. 7-18). pap. 19.99 *(978-1-59643-613-8(1))* Roaring Brook Pr.

Laskas, Gretchen Moran. The Miner's Daughter. 2007. (ENG.). 256p. (YA). (gr. 7-12). 17.99 *(978-1-4169-1262-0(2)*, Simon & Schuster Bks. For Young Readers) Simon & Schuster Bks. For Young Readers.

Lasky, Kathryn. Christmas after All. 2012. (Dear America Ser.). (ENG.). 192p. (J). (gr. 3-7). 12.99 *(978-0-545-38177-2(0))* Scholastic, Inc.

Lincoln Collier, James. The Worst of Times. 2004. 142p. (J). lib. bdg. 16.92 *(978-1-4242-0766-4(5))* Fitzgerald Bks.

Mackall, Dandi Daley. Rudy Rides the Rails: A Depression Era Story. Ellison, Chris, illus. rev. ed. 2007. (Tales of Young Americans Ser.). (ENG.). 32p. (J). (gr. -1-3). 17.95 *(978-1-58536-286-8(7))* Sleeping Bear Pr.

Mackall, Dandi Daley & Kingsbury, Karen. The Gift of the Christmas Cookie: Sharing the True Meaning of Jesus' Birth, 1 vol. Chabrian, Deborah L., illus. 2008. (ENG.). 32p. (J). (gr. -1-2). 16.99 *(978-0-310-71328-9(5))* Zonderkidz.

Mangin, John F. Squirt Blossom Jubilation. 2006. pap. 13.00 *(978-0-8059-9885-6(3)*, RoseDog Bks.) Dorrance Publishing Co., Inc.

Mangum, Kay Lynn. A Love Like Lilly. 2006. 336p. (YA). pap. 15.95 *(978-1-59038-580-7(2))* Deseret Bk. Co.

Marsh, Carole. The Puzzle of the Indian Arrowhead. 2006. (Three Amigos Ser.). (Illus.). 54p. (J). (gr. 1-3). 14.95 *(978-0-635-06201-7(1))* Gallopade International.

Martin, Ann M. Better to Wish. 2013. (Family Tree Ser.). (ENG.). 240p. (J). (gr. 3-7). 16.99 *(978-0-545-35942-9(2)*, Scholastic Pr.) Scholastic, Inc.

—Family Tree Book One: Better to Wish. 2014. (Family Tree Ser.: 1). (ENG.). 240p. (J). (gr. 3-7). pap. 6.99 *(978-0-545-67518-5(9))* Scholastic, Inc.

McKissack, Patricia C. The All-I'll-Ever-Want Christmas Doll. Pinkney, Jerry, illus. 2007. (J). *(978-0-375-83615-2(2)*, Schwartz & Wade Bks.) Random Hse. Children's Bks.

—The All-I'll-Ever-Want Christmas Doll. Pinkney, Jerry, illus. 2007. (ENG.). 40p. (J). (gr. -1-3). 17.99 *(978-0-375-83759-3(0)*, Schwartz & Wade Bks.) Random Hse. Children's Bks.

Miller, William. Rent Party Jazz. Riley-Webb, Charlotte, illus. (ENG.). 32p. (J). 2013. (gr. 1-5). 16.95 *(978-1-58430-025-0(6))* 2011. pap. 9.95 *(978-1-60060-344-0(0))* Lee & Low Bks., Inc.

Moss, Marissa. Rose's Journal: The Story of a Girl in the Great Depression. 2003. (Young American Voices Ser.). (ENG., Illus.). 56p. (J). (gr. 2-5). pap. 7.99 *(978-0-15-204605-7(4))* Houghton Mifflin Harcourt Publishing Co.

—Rose's Journal: The Story of a Girl in the Great Depression. 2004. (Young American Voice Bks.). (Illus.). (J). (gr. 3-7). 17.00 *(978-0-7569-4230-4(6))* Perfection Learning Corp.

Osborne, Mary Pope. Blizzard of the Blue Moon. Murdocca, Sal, illus. 2007. (Magic Tree House Merlin Mission Ser.: 8). (ENG.). 144p. (J). (gr. 2-5). 5.99 *(978-0-375-83038-9(3)*, Random Hse. Bks. for Young Readers) Random Hse. Children's Bks.

Paul, Curtis Christopher. Bud, Not Buddy. 2014. (ENG.). 256p. (J). (gr. 12-12). 11.24 *(978-1-63245-063-0(1))* Lectorum Pubns., Inc.

Peck, Richard. A Long Way from Chicago. 2004. (Puffin Modern Classics Ser.). (ENG.). 160p. (J). (gr. 5-7). pap. 7.99 *(978-0-14-240110-1(2)*, Puffin Books) Penguin Young Readers Group.

—A Year down Yonder. unabr. ed. 2004. (Middle Grade Cassette Librariestm Ser.). 144p. (J). (gr. 5-9). pap. 29.00 incl. audio *(978-0-8072-0991-2(0)*, S YA 256 SP, Listening Library) Random Hse. Audio Publishing Group.

Peterson, J. D. R. & Reimer, Diana. Priscilla Bailey: A Story of the Great Depression. 2009. 196p. 24.95 *(978-1-4401-3929-1(6))*; pap. 14.95 *(978-1-4401-3927-7(X))* iUniverse, Inc.

Pfitsch, Patricia Curtis. Riding the Flume. 2004. (Aladdin Historical Fiction Ser.). 232p. (gr. 5-9). 15.00 *(978-0-7569-2938-1(5))* Perfection Learning Corp.

Platt, Randall Beth. Liberty's Christmas. 2012. (ENG.). 224p. (YA). (gr. 7-12). 19.95 *(978-0-89672-766-3(1))* Texas Tech Univ. Pr.

Rees, Gwyneth. My Mum's from Planet Pluto, 4. 3rd unabr. ed. 2008. (ENG.). 176p. (J). (gr. 4-6). pap. 9.99 *(978-0-330-43728-8(3))* Pan Macmillan GBR. Dist: Independent Pubs. Group.

Ryan, Pam Muñoz. Esperanza Rising. unabr. ed. 2004. (Middle Grade Cassette Librariestm Ser.). 272p. (J). (gr. 4-7). pap. 36.00 incl. audio *(978-0-8072-1726-9(3)*, S YA 281 SP, Listening Library) Random Hse. Audio Publishing Group.

Sanders, Scott Russell. Bad Man Ballad. 2004. (Library of Indiana Classics Ser.). (ENG.). 256p. reprint ed. pap. 14.95 *(978-0-253-21688-5(5)*, 0253216885) Indiana Univ. Pr.

Simons, Joseph. Under a Living Sky, 1 vol. 2005. (Orca Young Readers Ser.). (ENG., Illus.). 112p. (J). (gr. 3-6). per. 5.95 *(978-1-55143-355-4(9))* Orca Bk. Pubs. USA.

Taylor, Kim. Cissy Funk. Date not set. 224p. (YA). (gr. 5-18). mass mkt. 4.99 *(978-0-06-440880-6(9))* HarperCollins Pubs.

Taylor, Mildred D. Roll of Thunder, Hear My Cry. 2004. 276p. (gr. 4-8). reprint ed. pap. 10.00 *(978-0-7567-7955-9(3))* DIANE Publishing Co.

—Song of the Trees. Pinkney, Jerry, illus. 2003. (ENG.). 80p. (J). (gr. 5-7). 7.99 *(978-0-14-250075-0(5)*, Puffin Books) Penguin Young Readers Group.

Thrasher, Crystal. The Dark Didn't Catch Me. 2004. (Library of Indiana Classics Ser.). (ENG.). 192p. reprint ed. pap. 14.95 *(978-0-253-21685-4(0)*, 0253216850) Indiana Univ. Pr.

Tripp, Valerie. Kit's Surprise. Rane, Walter & McAliley, Susan, illus. 2004. (American Girls Collection: Bk. 3). (ENG.). 71p. (gr. 2-18). 12.95 *(978-1-58485-021-2(3))* American Girl Publishing, Inc.

Vanderpool, Clare. Moon over Manifest. (ENG.). (J). (gr. 3-7). 2011. 384p. 7.99 *(978-0-375-85829-1(6)*, Yearling) 2010. 368p. 16.99 *(978-0-385-73883-5(8)*, Delacorte Bks. for Young Readers) Random Hse. Children's Bks.

—Moon over Manifest. l.t. ed. 2011. (ENG.). 452p. 23.99 *(978-1-4104-3780-8(9))* Thorndike Pr.

—Moon over Manifest. 2011. lib. bdg. 18.40 *(978-0-606-23875-5(1)*, Turtleback) Turtleback Bks.

Whitby, Adele. Kay's Story 1934. 2015. (Secrets of the Manor Ser.: 6). (ENG., Illus.). 160p. (J). (gr. 3-7). pap. 6.99 *(978-1-4814-2755-5(5)*, Simon Spotlight) Simon Spotlight.

White, Joseph C. Forged in a Country Crucible. 2003. (Illus.). 278p. per. 19.95 *(978-0-9726095-1-7(2)*, FCC2003) Crossing Trails Pubns.

Whitmore, Arvella. The Bread Winner. 2004. (ENG.). 144p. (J). (gr. 5-7). pap. 6.99 *(978-0-618-49479-8(0))* Houghton Mifflin Harcourt Publishing Co.

Wiechman, Kathy Canon. Empty Places. 2016. (ENG., Illus.). 240p. (J). (gr. 3-7). 17.95 *(978-1-62979-451-8(1)*, Calkins Creek) Boyds Mills Pr.

Winthrop, Elizabeth. Franklin Delano Roosevelt: Letters from a Mill Town Girl. Winthrop, Elizabeth, illus. unabr. ed. 2003. (Illus.). (J). (gr. 4-7). 25.95 incl. audio *(978-1-59112-213-5(9))* Live Oak Media.

Wyatt, Leslie J. Poor Is Just a Starting Place. 2005. (ENG.). 192p. (J). (gr. 6-17). 16.95 *(978-0-8234-1884-8(7))* Holiday Hse., Inc.

Young, Judy. The Lucky Star. Ellison, Chris, illus. 2008. (Tales of Young Americans Ser.). (ENG.). 32p. (J). (gr. 3-7). 17.95 *(978-1-58536-348-3(0))* Sleeping Bear Pr.

DERMATOLOGY

see Skin—Diseases

DESERT ANIMALS

see also Camels

Allgor, Marie. Endangered Desert Animals. 2012. (Save Earth's Animals! Ser.). (ENG., Illus.). 24p. (J). (gr. k-5). 22.60 *(978-1-4488-7423-1(8))*; pap. 8.25 *(978-1-4488-7496-5(3))* Rosen Publishing Group, Inc., The. (PowerKids Pr.).

Anderson, Sheila. What Can Live in a Desert? 2010. (First Step Nonfiction - Animal Adaptations Ser.). (ENG.). 24p. (gr. k-2). pap. 6.95 *(978-0-7613-5674-5(6))*; (Illus.). lib. bdg. 23.93 *(978-0-7613-4570-1(1))* Lerner Publishing Group.

—What Can Live in the Desert? 2010. pap. 33.92 *(978-0-7613-6907-3(4))* Lerner Publishing Group.

Animals & Birds of the Desert. (Butterfly Bks.). (ARA., Illus.). 32p. (J). (gr. 4-8). 9.95 *(978-0-86685-398-9(7)*, LDL251) International Bk. Ctr., Inc.

Arnold, Caroline. A Day & Night in the Desert. Arnold, Caroline, illus. 2015. (Caroline Arnold's Habitats Ser.). (ENG., Illus.). 24p. (gr. 2-3). lib. bdg. 27.99 *(978-1-4795-6072-1(3))* Picture Window Bks.

Auch, Alison. Life in the Desert, 1 vol. 2011. (Habitats Around the World Ser.). (ENG.). 24p. (gr. k-1). pap. 7.29 *(978-1-4296-7150-7(5))*; pap. 41.70 *(978-1-4296-7154-5(8))*; lib. bdg. 26.65 *(978-1-4296-6817-0(2))* Capstone Press of Coughlan Cos. (Pebble Plus).

AZ Books Staff. Sounds of the Savanna & Desert. Migiz, Anna, ed. 2012. (Sounds Around Us Ser.). (ENG.). 16p. (J). (gr. 1-3). bds. 17.95 *(978-1-61889-031-3(X))* AZ Bks. LLC.

Bessesen, Brooke. Look Who Lives in the Desert. 2004. (Illus.). 48p. (J). 16.95 *(978-1-932082-09-8(3))* Arizona Highways.

Bochenski, Cristina. Wildlife of the Great Basin. 2013. (Rosen Readers Ser.). (ENG.). 24p. (J). (gr. 3-4). pap. 8.25 *(978-1-4777-2476-7(1))*; pap. 49.50 *(978-1-4777-2477-4(X))* Rosen Publishing Group, Inc., The. (Rosen Classroom).

Bradley, Timothy J. Danger in the Desert, 1 vol. 2nd rev. ed. 2013. (Nonfiction Readers Ser.). (ENG.). 64p. (J). (gr. 5-5). pap. 10.99 *(978-1-4333-4897-6(7))*; (Illus.). pap. 31.96 *(978-1-4333-7420-3(X))* Teacher Created Materials, Inc.

Bredeson, Carmen. Baby Animals of the Desert. 2012. (Nature's Baby Animals Ser.). (Illus.). 24p. (J). (gr. k-18). pap. 7.95 *(978-1-59845-404-8(8)*, Enslow Elementary) Enslow Pubs., Inc.

Callery, Sean. Life Cycles: Desert. 2013. (Lifecycles Ser.). (ENG., Illus.). 32p. (J). (gr. 2-5). 6.99 *(978-0-7534-7075-6(6)*, 9780753470756, Kingfisher) Roaring Brook Pr.

Clarke, Nadine. Get Bushwise: on Safari Desert, River, Bushveld: A Young Explorer's Guide. 2013. 192p. pap. 23.00 *(978-1-4317-0206-0(4))* Penguin Random House Grupo Editorial ESP. Dist: Casemate Pubs. & Bk. Distributors, LLC.

Davin, Rose. Meet Desert Animals. 2017. (Meet Desert Animals Ser.). (ENG.). 24p. (gr. k-1). 159.90 *(978-1-5157-4605-8(4)*, Pebble Plus) Capstone Press of Coughlan Cos.

Dayton, Connor. Desert Animals. 2009. (American Habitats Ser.). 24p. (gr. 2-5). (ENG., Illus.). (J). pap. 8.25 *(978-1-4358-3195-7(0)*, PowerKids Pr.); 42.50 *(978-1-61511-348-4(7)*, PowerKids Pr.); (YA). lib. bdg. 22.60 *(978-1-4358-2766-0(X))* Rosen Publishing Group, Inc., The.

de Lambilly-Bresson, Elisabeth. Animales del Desierto. 2007. (Animales Nos Cuentan Su Vida (Animal Show & Tell) Ser.). (SPA., Illus.). 16p. (gr. -1-3). lib. bdg. 19.00 *(978-0-8368-8214-8(8)*, Gareth Stevens Learning Library) Stevens, Gareth Publishing LLLP.

—Animals in the Desert. 2007. (Animal Show & Tell Ser.). (Illus.). 16p. (gr. -1-3). lib. bdg. 19.00 *(978-0-8368-8204-9(0)*, Gareth Stevens Learning Library) Stevens, Gareth Publishing LLLP.

Donald, Rhonda Lucas. Deep in the Desert, 1 vol. Neidigh, Sherry, illus. 2011. (ENG.). 32p. (J). (gr. -1-3). 16.95 *(978-1-60718-125-5(8))*; pap. 8.95 *(978-1-60718-135-4(5))* Arbordale Publishing.

Fleisher, Paul. Desert Food Webs in Action. 2013. (Searchlight Books What Is a Food Web Ser.). (ENG., Illus.). 40p. (gr. 3-5). (J). lib. bdg. 27.93 *(978-1-4677-1294-1(9)*, Lerner Pubns.); pap. 8.95 *(978-1-4677-1552-2(2))* Lerner Publishing Group.

Franchino, Vicky. Sahara Desert. 2016. (Community Connections: Getting to Know Our Planet Ser.). (ENG.). 24p. (J). (gr. 2-5). 27.07 *(978-1-63470-518-9(1)*, 207803) Cherry Lake Publishing.

Fredericks, Anthony D. Around One Cactus: Owls, Bats, & Leaping Rats, 1 vol. DiRubbio, Jennifer, tr. DiRubbio, Jennifer, illus. 2004. (Sharing Nature with Children Book Ser.). 32p. (J). (ENG.). 16.95 *(978-1-58469-051-1(8))*; pap. 7.95 *(978-1-58469-052-8(6))* Dawn Pubns.

—Desert Night Desert Day. Spengler, Kenneth J., illus. 2011. 32p. (J). 15.95 *(978-1-933855-70-7(3))* Rio Nuevo Pubs.

Gaarder-Juntti, Oona. What Lives in the Desert?, 1 vol. 2008. (Animal Habitats Ser.). (ENG., Illus.). 24p. (J). (gr. k-3). 25.65 *(978-1-60453-173-2(8))* ABDO Publishing Co.

Ganeri, Anita. Arabian Oryx, 8 vols. Incl. Fennec Fox. (Illus.). pap. 6.79 *(978-1-4329-4780-4(X))*; Gila Monster. (Illus.). pap. 6.79 *(978-1-4329-4781-1(8))*; Roadrunner. (Illus.). pap. 6.49 *(978-1-4329-4784-2(2))*; Scorpion. pap. 6.79 *(978-1-4329-4765-9(0))*; (gr. k-2). (Day in the Life: Desert Animals Ser.). (ENG.). 24p. 2011. Set pap. 20.37 *(978-1-4329-4786-6(9)*, Heinemann Read & Learn) Heinemann-Raintree.

—Exploring Deserts: A Benjamin Blog & His Inquisitive Dog Investigation, 1 vol. 2014. (Exploring Habitats with Benjamin Blog & His Inquisitive Dog Ser.). (ENG.). 32p. (gr. 1-3). lib. bdg. 29.99 *(978-1-4329-8778-7(X)*, NA-h) Heinemann-Raintree.

—Scorpion Set, 8 vols. Incl. Arabian Oryx. (Illus.). lib. bdg. 23.32 *(978-1-4329-4769-9(9))*; Meerkat. (Illus.). 23.32 *(978-1-4329-4773-6(7))*; Red Kangaroo. 23.32 *(978-1-4329-4774-3(5))*; Scorpion. (Illus.). 23.32 *(978-1-4329-4776-7(1))*; (gr. k-2). (Day in the Life: Desert Animals Ser.). (ENG.). Illus.). 24p. 2011. Set lib. bdg. 93.28 *(978-1-4329-4777-4(X)*, Heinemann Read & Learn) Heinemann-Raintree.

George, Jean Craighead. Summer Moon. 2003. (J). (gr. 3-7). 20.75 *(978-0-8446-7243-4(2))* Smith, Peter Pub., Inc.

Gordon, Sharon. Animales del Desierto. Victory Productions, Inc. Staff, tr. from ENG. 2008. (Animales Salvajes Ser.). (SPA.). 24p. (gr. k-1). lib. bdg. 15.95 *(978-0-7614-3427-6(5)*, Benchmark Bks.) Marshall Cavendish Corp.

—Desert Animals. 2008. (Animals in the Wild Ser.). 24p. (gr. k-1). lib. bdg. 15.95 *(978-0-7614-2898-5(4)*, Benchmark Bks.) Marshall Cavendish Corp.

Gray, Leon. Deserts. 2011. (Geography Wise Ser.). (Illus.). 32p. (YA). (gr. 2-5). lib. bdg. 26.50 *(978-1-4488-3280-4(2))* Rosen Publishing Group, Inc., The.

Gregoire, Maryellen. Life in a Desert. 2012. (Wonder Readers Emergent Level Ser.). (ENG.). (gr. -1-1). 16p. pap. 35.94 *(978-1-4296-9204-5(9))*; 32p. pap. 5.99 *(978-1-4296-9194-9(8))* Capstone Press of Coughlan Cos. (Wonder Readers).

—La Vida en el Desierto (Life in a Desert) 2012. (Wonder Readers Spanish Emergent Ser.). (SPA.). 16p. (gr. -1-1). pap. 35.94 *(978-1-62065-567-2(5))* Capstone Press of Coughlan Cos.

HELMAN, Wolfe Jecan. C Is for Coyote: A Southwest Alphabet Book, Vol. 2017. (ENG., Illus.). 32p. (J). (gr. k-3). 7.95 *(978-1-63076-300-8(4))* Muddy Boots Pr.

Hine, Eileen, illus. Desert Opposites. 2005. (ENG.). 12p. (J). (gr. -1 — 1). bds. 5.95 *(978-0-87358-890-4(8))* Cooper Square Publishing Llc.

Hodge, Deborah. Desert Animals. Stephens, Pat, illus. 2008. (Who Lives Here? Ser.). (ENG.). 24p. (J). (gr. -1-2). 14.95 *(978-1-55453-047-2(4))*; pap. 5.95 *(978-1-55453-048-9(2))* Kids Can Pr., Ltd. CAN. Dist: Hachette Bk. Group.

Jango-Cohen, Judith. Desert Iguanas. (Pull Ahead Bks.). (Illus.). 32p. (gr. k-3). 2005. lib. bdg. 22.60 *(978-0-8225-3635-2(8))* 2003. (J). pap. 5.95 *(978-0-8225-3642-0(0))* Lerner Publishing Group.

Kalman, Bobbie. Baby Animals in Desert Habitats. 2011. (Habitats of Baby Animals Ser.). (ENG.). 24p. (J). (gr. k-3). *(978-0-7787-7725-0(1))*; pap. *(978-0-7787-7738-0(3))* Crabtree Publishing Co.

Kavanagh, James. My First Deserts Nature. Leung, Raymond, illus. 2011. (Nature Activity Book Ser.). (ENG.). 32p. (J). (gr. 2-4). act. bk. ed. 6.95 *(978-1-58355-587-3(0))* Western National Parks Assn.

—Southwest Desert Wildlife Nature. Leung, Raymond, illus. 2nd ed. 2011. (Nature Activity Book Ser.). (ENG.). 32p. (J). (gr. 4-7). act. bk. ed. 6.95 *(978-1-58355-585-9(4))* Western National Parks Assn.

Kopp, Megan. What Do You Find on a Saguaro Cactus? 2016. (ENG., Illus.). 24p. (J). *(978-0-7787-2265-6(1))* Crabtree Publishing Co.

Landstrom, Lee Ann & Shragg, Karen. Nature's Yucky! 2: The Desert Southwest. Rogge, Rachel, illus. 2007. (Nature's Yucky Ser.). 48p. (J). (gr. k-7). pap. 12.00 *(978-0-87842-529-7(2))* Mountain Pr. Publishing Co., Inc.

Lewis, J. Patrick. My Home in the Desert. 2017. (Rookie Poetry(tm) — Animal Homes Ser.). (ENG., Illus.). 24p. (J). lib. bdg. 25.00 *(978-0-531-22871-5(1)*, Children's Pr.) Scholastic Library Publishing.

Macgregor, Eloise. Roadrunner. 2015. (Desert Animals Searchin' for Shade Ser.). (ENG.). 24p. (J). (gr. -1-3). lib. bdg. 23.93 *(978-1-62724-533-3(2))* Bearport Publishing Co., Inc.

Macken, JoAnn Early. Animals That Live in the Desert;Animales del desierto Complete Series, 6 vols. 2nd rev. ed. 2009. (Animals That Live in the Desert/Animales del desierto Ser.). (ENG & SPA.). 24p. (J). (gr. 1-1). pap. 35.70 *(978-1-4339-2462-0(5)*, Weekly Reader Leveled Readers) Stevens, Gareth Publishing LLLP.

Mattern, Joanne. What Desert Animals Eat. 2006. (Nature's Food Chains Ser.). (Illus.). 24p. (gr. k-3). pap. 8.15 *(978-0-8368-6877-7(3))*; lib. bdg. 22.00 *(978-0-8368-6870-8(6))* Stevens, Gareth Publishing LLLP. (Weekly Reader Leveled Readers).

—What Desert Animals Eat (¿Qué comen los animales del Desierto?) 2006. (Nature's Food Chains/ Las cadenas alimentarias en la naturaleza Ser.). (SPA., Illus.). 24p. (gr. k-3). lib. bdg. 22.00 *(978-0-8368-7371-9(8)*, Weekly Reader Leveled Readers) Stevens, Gareth Publishing LLLP.

—What Desert Animals Eat/Que Comen los Animales Del Desierto? Qué Comen los Animales Del Desierto? 2006. (Nature's Food Chains/ Las cadenas alimentarias en la naturaleza Ser.). (ENG & SPA., Illus.). 24p. (gr. k-3). pap. 8.15 *(978-0-8368-7378-8(5)*, Weekly Reader Leveled Readers) Stevens, Gareth Publishing LLLP.

McCurry, Kristen. Desert Babies. 2003. (Animal Babies Ser.). (ENG., Illus.). 22p. (J). (gr. -1 — 1). bds. 6.95 *(978-1-55971-872-1(2))* Cooper Square Publishing Llc.

McKissack, Fredrick L. & McKissack, Lisa Beringer. Counting in the Desert. 2008. (Counting in the Biomes Ser.). (Illus.). 32p. (J). (gr. 3-7). lib. bdg. 23.94 *(978-0-7660-2988-0(3)*, Enslow Elementary) Enslow Pubs., Inc.

Miller, Mirella S. Desert Ecosystems. 2018. (ENG.). 32p. (gr. 3-6). ***(978-1-63235-454-9(3)***, 12-Story Library) Pr. Room Editions LLC.

Miller, Tori & Lynette, Rachel. Who Lives in the Dry, Hot Desert? 2010. (Exploring Habitats Ser.). (ENG.). 24p. (J). pap. 8.25 *(978-1-4488-1285-1(2))*; lib. bdg. 22.60 *(978-1-4488-0679-9(8))* Rosen Publishing Group, Inc., The. (PowerKids Pr.).

Murphy, Julie. Desert Animal Adaptations, 1 vol. 2011. (Amazing Animal Adaptations Ser.). (ENG.). 32p. (gr. 1-2). pap. 8.10 *(978-1-4296-7025-8(8))*; pap. 47.70 *(978-1-4296-7035-7(5))*; lib. bdg. 27.32 *(978-1-4296-6030-3(9))* Capstone Press of Coughlan Cos. (Aplus Bks.).

Murphy, Stuart J. Coyotes All Around. Björkman, Steve, illus. 2003. (MathStart 2 Ser.). (ENG.). 40p. (J). (gr. 1-18). pap. 5.99 *(978-0-06-051531-7(7))* HarperCollins Pubs.

—Coyotes All Around. Björkman, Steve, illus. 2003. (MathStart Level 2 Ser.). 32p. (J). (gr. -1-3). 16.00 *(978-0-613-68415-6(X)*, Turtleback) Turtleback Bks.

Newland, Sonya. Desert Animals. 2011. (Saving Wildlife Ser.). 32p. (YA). (gr. 3-6). lib. bdg. 28.50 *(978-1-59920-655-4(2))* Black Rabbit Bks.

Nicholson, Sue. Animal Babies in Deserts. 2006. (Animal Babies Ser.). (ENG., Illus.). 10p. (J). (gr. -1-k). bds. 6.99 *(978-0-7534-5942-3(6)*, 9780753459423, Kingfisher) Roaring Brook Pr.

NorthWord Books for Young Readers Editors, contrib. by. Desert Babies. 2005. (SPA.). (J). bds. 5.95 *(978-1-55971-907-0(9)*, NorthWord Bks. for Young Readers) T&N Children's Publishing.

Oliver, Narelle. Sand Swimmers: The Secret Life of Australia's Desert Wilderness. Oliver, Narelle, illus. 2015. (ENG., Illus.). 40p. (J). (gr. 2-5). 16.99 *(978-0-7636-6761-0(7))* Candlewick Pr.

Pattison, Darcy. Desert Baths, 1 vol. Rietz, Kathleen, illus. 2012. (SPA & ENG.). 32p. (J). (gr. -1-3). 17.95 *(978-1-60718-525-3(3))*; pap. 9.95 *(978-1-60718-534-5(2))* Arbordale Publishing.

—Las Duchas en el Desierto, 1 vol. Rietz, Kathleen, illus. 2012. (SPA & ENG.). 32p. (J). (gr. -1-3). 17.95 *(978-1-60718-676-2(4))* Arbordale Publishing.

Pettiford, Rebecca. Desert Food Chains. 2016. (Who Eats What?). 24p. (J). (gr. 2-5). lib. bdg. 25.65 *(978-1-62031-301-5(4)*, Pogo) Jump! Inc.

Phillips, Dee. Find It in the Desert. 2006. (Can You Find It? Ser.). (Illus.). 24p. (gr. k-3). lib. bdg. 23.00 *(978-0-8368-6300-0(3)*, Gareth Stevens Learning Library) Stevens, Gareth Publishing LLLP.

Pratt, Sabina Carlin. Range Land Animal Tales: Nature's School on the High Desert of Oregon. 2011. 56p. 36.95 *(978-1-258-08228-4(4))* Literary Licensing, LLC.

Profiri, Charline. Guess Who's in the Desert. Swan, Susan, illus. 2013. (J). *(978-1-933855-79-0(7))* Rio Nuevo Pubs.

Radley, Gail. Grasslands & Deserts. Sherlock, Jean, illus. (Vanishing from Ser.). 32p. 2005. (J). (gr. 6-12). lib. bdg. 22.60 *(978-1-57505-406-3(X))* 2003. (YA). (gr. 3-5). 6.95 *(978-1-57505-568-8(6)*, Carolrhoda Bks.) Lerner Publishing Group.

Rice, William. Animales Del Desierto en Peligro. 2016. (TIME for Kids en Español - Level 5 Ser.). (SPA.). 64p. (gr. 5-5). lib. bdg. 31.99 *(978-1-5157-2934-1(6))* Time for Kids Inc AUS. Dist: Capstone Pub.

Rice, William B. Endangered Animals of the Desert, 1 vol. 2nd rev. ed. 2013. (Nonfiction Readers Ser.). (ENG.). 64p. (J). (gr. 5-5). pap. 10.99 *(978-1-4333-4936-2(1))*; (Illus.). pap. 31.96 *(978-1-4333-7435-7(8))* Teacher Created Materials, Inc.

Rivera, Sheila. Desert. 2005. (Illus.). 24p. (J). pap. 5.95 *(978-0-8225-5373-1(2))*; (ENG., lib. bdg. 23.93 *(978-0-8225-2597-4(6)*, Lerner Pubns.) Lerner Publishing Group.

Rodríguez, Ana María. Gray Foxes, Rattlesnakes, & Other Mysterious Animals of the Extreme Deserts. 2012. (Extreme Animals in Extreme Environments Ser.). (Illus.). 48p. (J). (gr. 5-18). pap. 8.95 *(978-1-4644-0020-9(2))* Enslow Pubs., Inc.

—Gray Foxes, Rattlesnakes, & Other Mysterious Animals of the Extreme Deserts. 2012. (Extreme Animals in Extreme Environments Ser.). (Illus.). 48p. (J). (gr. 5-18). 25.27 *(978-0-7660-3697-0(9))* Enslow Pubs., Inc.

Royston, Angela. Desert Food Chains, 1 vol. 2014. (Food Chains & Webs Ser.). (ENG., Illus.). 32p. (gr. 1-3). 27.32 *(978-1-4846-0521-9(7)*, Heinemann First Library) Heinemann-Raintree.

Rustad, Martha E. H. Animal Camouflage in the Desert [Scholastic]. 2010. (Hidden in Nature Ser.). pap. 0.52 *(978-1-4296-5046-5(X)*, Pebble Plus) Capstone Press of Coughlan Cos.

Shaw, Daniel. Southwest Aquatic Habitats: On the Trail of Fish in a Desert. 2013. (Barbara Guth Worlds of Wonder Science Series for Young Readers Ser.). (ENG., Illus.). 112p. (J). 34.95 *(978-0-8263-5309-2(6))* Univ. of New Mexico Pr.

Shea, Betty. Animals of the Desert: Adapting to Survive. 2009. (Real Life Readers Ser.). 24p. (gr. 3-4). pap. 8.25 *(978-1-4358-0125-7(3)*, Rosen Classroom); 24p. (gr. 3-3). 42.50 *(978-1-61511-213-5(8)*, PowerKids Pr.); (J). lib. bdg. 22.60 *(978-1-4358-2970-1(0)*, PowerKids Pr.) Rosen Publishing Group, Inc., The.

Slade, Suzanne. What Eats What in a Desert Food Chain, 1 vol. Wertheim, Anne, illus. 2012. (Food Chains Ser.). (ENG.). 24p. (gr. 2-3). 25.99 *(978-1-4048-7386-5(4))*; pap. 8.95 *(978-1-4048-7690-3(1))* Picture Window Bks.

Snyder, Jane. Desert Animals. 2003. (Real Readers - Upper Emergent Ser.). (ENG., Illus.). 12p. (gr. 1-2). pap. 5.90 *(978-0-8239-6365-2(9))* Rosen Publishing Group, Inc., The.

Spilsbury, Richard & Spilsbury, Louise. At Home in the Desert, 01 vols., 1. 2016. (Home in the Biome Ser.). (ENG.). 32p. (J). pap. 10.00 *(978-1-5081-4560-8(1)*, PowerKids Pr.) Rosen Publishing Group, Inc., The.

Summers, Portia & Grady, Colin. The Desert Biome. 2016. (Zoom in on Biomes Ser.). 24p. (J). (gr. 2-2). pap. 9.35 *(978-0-7660-7758-4(6))* Enslow Pubs., Inc.

Underwood, Deborah. Hiding in Deserts, 1 vol. 2010. (Creature Camouflage Ser.). (ENG.). 32p. (gr. 1-3). 27.32 *(978-1-4329-4021-8(X))*; pap. 8.29 *(978-1-4329-4030-0(9))* Heinemann-Raintree. (Heinemann First Library).

West, David. Desert Animals. 2016. (Safari Sam's Wild Animals Ser.). 24p. (gr. k-3). 28.50 *(978-1-62588-070-3(7)*, Smart Apple Media) Black Rabbit Bks.

Wilkins, Mary-Jane. Deserts. 2017. (Fast Track: Who Lives Here? Ser.). (Illus.). 24p. (gr. k-3). 28.50 ***(978-1-78121-346-9(1))*** Brown Bear Bks.

World Book, Inc Staff, contrib. by. Deserts & Scrublands. 2012. (J). *(978-0-7166-0445-7(0))* World Bk., Inc.

Zubal, Lynn. Sonoran Desert Frog. Zubal, Lynn, illus. 2011. (ENG., Illus.). 22p. (J). pap. 16.95 *(978-1-59299-600-1(0))* Inkwater Pr.

DESERT PLANTS

Betanzos, Sue, illus. My New Backyard Garden. 2006.Tr. of Mi Nuevo Jardín del Traspatio. (SPA & ENG.). (J). *(978-0-9792253-0-7(2))* Tucson Botanical Gardens.

Bochenski, Cristina. Wildlife of the Great Basin. 2013. (Rosen Readers Ser.). (ENG.). 24p. (J). (gr. 3-4). pap. 8.25 *(978-1-4777-2476-7(1))*; pap. 49.50 *(978-1-4777-2477-4(X))* Rosen Publishing Group, Inc., The. (Rosen Classroom).

Bradley, Timothy J. Danger in the Desert, 1 vol. 2nd rev. ed. 2013. (Nonfiction Readers Ser.). (ENG.). 64p. (J). (gr. 5-5). pap. 10.99 *(978-1-4333-4897-6(7))* Teacher Created Materials, Inc.

Clarke, Nadine. Get Bushwise: on Safari Desert, River, Bushveld: A Young Explorer's Guide. 2013. 192p. pap. 23.00 *(978-1-4317-0206-0(4))* Penguin Random House Grupo Editorial ESP. Dist: Casemate Pubs. & Bk. Distributors, LLC.

Fleisher, Paul. Desert Food Webs in Action. 2013. (Searchlight Books What Is a Food Web Ser.). (ENG., Illus.). 40p. (gr. 3-5). (J). lib. bdg. 27.93 *(978-1-4677-1294-1(9)*, Lerner Pubns.); pap. 8.95 *(978-1-4677-1552-2(2))* Lerner Publishing Group.

Gray, Leon. Deserts. 2011. (Geography Wise Ser.). (Illus.). 32p. (YA). (gr. 2-5). lib. bdg. 26.50 *(978-1-4488-3280-4(2))* Rosen Publishing Group, Inc., The.

Gregoire, Maryellen. La Vida en el Desierto (Life in a Desert) 2012. (Wonder Readers Spanish Emergent Ser.). (SPA.). 16p. (gr. -1-1). pap. 35.94 *(978-1-62065-567-2(5))* Capstone Press of Coughlan Cos.

Kavanagh, James. My First Deserts Nature. Leung, Raymond, illus. 2011. (Nature Activity Book Ser.). (ENG.). 32p. (J). (gr. 2-4). act. bk. ed. 6.95 *(978-1-58355-587-3(0))* Western National Parks Assn.

King, Sally, illus. Desert Blooms. 2007. 39p. pap. 7.95 *(978-1-55566-405-3(9)*, Johnson Bks.) Bower Hse.

Latou, Pierre. Why Can Plants Grow in the Desert? 2014. (Little Books of Answers: Level e Ser.). (Illus.). 16p. (gr. k-2). pap. 7.95 *(978-1-927136-48-5(2))* Three Crows Media NZL. Dist: RiverStream Publishing.

Miller, Mirella S. Desert Ecosystems. 2018. (ENG.). 32p. (gr. 3-6). ***(978-1-63235-454-9(3)***, 12-Story Library) Pr. Room Editions LLC.

Phillips, Dee. Find It in the Desert. 2006. (Can You Find It? Ser.). (Illus.). 24p. (gr. k-3). lib. bdg. 23.00 *(978-0-8368-6300-0(3)*, Gareth Stevens Learning Library) Stevens, Gareth Publishing LLLP.

Plants & Flowers of Desert. (Butterfly Bks.). (ARA., Illus.). 32p. (J). (gr. 3-5). 8.95 *(978-0-86685-402-3(9)*, LDL252) International Bk. Ctr., Inc.

Rae, Rowena. Cacti. 2016. (Illus.). 24p. (J). *(978-1-5105-1405-8(8))* SmartBook Media, Inc.

Rivera, Sheila. Desert. 2005. (First Step Nonfiction - Habitats Ser.). (ENG., Illus.). 24p. (gr. k-2). lib. bdg. 23.93 *(978-0-8225-2597-4(6)*, Lerner Pubns.) Lerner Publishing Group.

Summers, Portia & Grady, Colin. The Desert Biome. 2016. (Zoom in on Biomes Ser.). 24p. (J). (gr. 2-2). pap. 9.35 *(978-0-7660-7758-4(6))* Enslow Pubs., Inc.

Yomtov, Nel. From African Plant to Vaccine Preservation. 2014. (21st Century Skills Innovation Library: Innovations from Nature Ser.). (ENG., Illus.). 32p. (J). (gr. 4-8). 28.50 *(978-1-62431-753-8(7)*, 203280); pap. 14.21 *(978-1-62431-759-0(6)*, 203281) Cherry Lake Publishing.

DESERTS

see also Desert Animals; Desert Plants

Adams, Alison. Deserts. 2011. (Early Connections Ser.). (J). *(978-1-61672-520-4(6))* Benchmark Education Co.

Allaby, Michael, et al. Deserts & Semideserts, 1 vol. 2nd ed. 2010. (Biomes Atlases Ser.). (ENG.). 64p. (gr. 6-9). 34.65 *(978-1-4329-4175-8(5))* Heinemann-Raintree.

Arnold, Quinn M. Deserts. (Seedlings Ser.). (Illus.). 24p. (J). (gr. k-2). 2017. (ENG.). pap. 7.99 *(978-1-62832-337-5(X)*, Creative Paperbacks) 2016. *(978-1-60818-741-6(1)*, Creative Education) Creative Co., The.

AZ Books Staff. In the Prairie & Desert. Efimova, Tatiana & Goncharik, Irina, eds. 2012. (Animal Sounds Ser.). (ENG.). 14p. (J). (gr. -1-k). bds. 7.95 *(978-1-61889-128-0(6))* AZ Bks. LLC.

Bailey, Gerry. Dry in the Desert. 2014. (ENG., Illus.). 32p. (J). *(978-0-7787-0429-4(7))* Crabtree Publishing Co.

Banting, Erinn. Deserts. (J). 2011. (gr. 5-8). pap. 13.95 *(978-1-61690-650-4(2)*, AV2 by Weigl) 2011. (Illus.). 32p. (gr. 2-5). 28.55 *(978-1-61690-644-3(8))* 2005. (Illus.). 32p. (gr. 4-6). lib. bdg. 26.00 *(978-1-59036-344-7(2))* Weigl Pubs., Inc.

Barnes, Julia. 101 Facts about Deserts. 2003. (One Hundred One Facts about Our World Ser.). (Illus.). 32p. (gr. 1-4). lib. bdg. 26.00 *(978-0-8368-3706-3(1)*, Gareth Stevens Learning Library) Stevens, Gareth Publishing LLLP.

Benchmark Education Company. Dry As a Desert (Teacher Guide) 2005. *(978-1-4108-4642-6(3))* Benchmark Education Co.

Benduhn, Tea. Living in Deserts. 2007. (Life on the Edge Ser.). 24p. (gr. 1-4). pap. 8.15 *(978-0-8368-8346-6(2))*; (Illus.). lib. bdg. 22.00 *(978-0-8368-8341-1(1))* Stevens, Gareth Publishing LLLP. (Weekly Reader Leveled Readers).

—La Vida en los Desiertos. 2007. (vida al limite (Spanish- Life on the Edge) Ser.). (SPA., Illus.). 24p. (gr. 1-4). pap. 8.15 *(978-0-8368-8356-5(X))*; lib. bdg. 22.00 *(978-0-8368-8351-0(9))* Stevens, Gareth Publishing LLLP. (Weekly Reader Leveled Readers).

Bennett, Paul. Desert Habitats. 2006. (Exploring Habitats Ser.). (Illus.). 36p. (gr. 3-7). lib. bdg. 26.00 *(978-0-8368-7253-8(3)*, Gareth Stevens Learning Library) Stevens, Gareth Publishing LLLP.

Benoit, Peter. Deserts. 2011. (True Bks.). 48p. (J). (gr. 3-5). 29.00 *(978-0-531-20555-6(X)*, Children's Pr.); (ENG.). pap. 6.95 *(978-0-531-28104-8(3))* Scholastic Library Publishing.

Bodden, Valerie. Deserts. 2006. (Our World Ser.). (Illus.). 24p. (J). (gr. -1-3). lib. bdg. 16.95 *(978-1-58341-461-3(4)*, Creative Education) Creative Co., The.

Bradley, Timothy. Peligro en el Desierto. 2016. (TIME for Kids en Español - Level 5 Ser.). (SPA.). 64p. (gr. 5-5). lib. bdg. 31.99 *(978-1-5157-2940-2(0))* Time for Kids Inc AUS. Dist: Capstone Pub.

Bradley, Timothy J. Danger in the Desert, 1 vol. 2nd rev. ed. 2013. (Nonfiction Readers Ser.). (ENG., Illus.). 64p. (J). (gr. 5-5). pap. 31.96 *(978-1-4333-7420-3(X))* Teacher Created Materials, Inc.

Brannon, Barbara. Discover Deserts. 2005. (J). pap. *(978-1-4108-5129-1(X))* Benchmark Education Co.

Brewer, Duncan. Deserts. (Illus.). 64p. (YA). (gr. 4-18). lib. bdg. 29.95 *(978-1-59389-128-2(8))* Chrysalis Education.

Brezina, Corona. Disappearing Forests: Deforestation, Desertification, & Drought. 2009. (Extreme Environmental Threats Ser.). 64p. (gr. 6-6). 58.50 *(978-1-61512-426-8(8))* Rosen Publishing Group, Inc., The.

Brooks, David. You Can Count in the Desert. Brooks, David, illus. 2005. (You Can Count Ser.). (ENG., Illus.). 24p. (J). (gr. -1 — 1). bds. 7.95 *(978-1-55971-910-0(9))* Cooper Square Publishing Llc.

Cefrey, Holly. Deserts. (Biomes Ser.). 24p. 2009. (gr. 2-3). 42.50 *(978-1-61511-591-4(9))* 2003. (Illus.). (J). lib. bdg. 22.60 *(978-0-8239-6456-7(6))* Rosen Publishing Group, Inc., The. (PowerKids Pr.).

Clarke, Ginjer L. & dePaola, Tomie. What's up in the Gobi Desert. 2016. (What's Up Ser.). (ENG., Illus.). 144p. (J). (gr. 3-7). bds. 8.99 *(978-0-448-48104-3(9)*, Grosset & Dunlap) Penguin Young Readers Group.

Claybourne, Anna. Deserts. 2004. (Geography Fact Files Ser.). (J). lib. bdg. 28.50 *(978-1-58340-425-6(2))* Black Rabbit Bks.

Cohen, Marina. Deserts Inside Out. 2014. (ENG.). 32p. (J). *(978-0-7787-0627-4(3))* Crabtree Publishing Co.

Cole, Melissa S. Desert. 2003. (Wild America Habitats Ser.). (Illus.). 24p. (J). 24.94 *(978-1-56711-799-8(6)*, Blackbirch Pr., Inc.) Cengage Gale.

Davies, Nicola. Deserts. 2017. (Discover Science Ser.). (ENG.). 56p. (J). pap. 7.99 *(978-0-7534-7333-7(X)*, 9780753473337, Kingfisher) Roaring Brook Pr.

Delano, Marfe Ferguson. Desierto. 2008. (Descubre la Naturaleza Ser.). (SPA., Illus.). 60p. (J). (gr. 4-7). 12.95 *(978-1-58087-128-0(3))* National Geographic Society.

Do You Really Want to Visit a Desert? 2015. (Do You Really Want to Visit... ? Ser.). (Illus.). 24p. (J). 27.10 *(978-1-60753-450-1(9))* Amicus Publishing.

Doeden, Matt. Can You Survive the Desert? An Interactive Survival Adventure, 1 vol. 2012. (You Choose: Survival Ser.). (ENG.). 112p. (gr. 3-4). pap. 6.95 *(978-1-4296-7995-4(6))*; 31.99 *(978-1-4296-7543-7(8))*; pap. 41.70 *(978-1-4296-8479-8(8))* Capstone Press of Coughlan Cos. (You Choose Bks.).

Dunphy, Madeleine. Here Is the Southwestern Desert. Coe, Anne, illus. 2006. (Web of Life Ser.). (ENG.). 32p. (J). (gr. -1-3). 16.95 *(978-0-9773795-7-6(4))*; pap. 9.95 *(978-0-9773795-6-9(6))* Web of Life Children's Bks.

Franklin, Yvonne. Los Desiertos, 1 vol. rev. ed. 2010. (Science Readers: a Closer Look Ser.). (SPA., Illus.). 32p. (J). (gr. 2-3). pap. 8.99 *(978-1-4333-2139-9(4))* Shell Educational Publishing.

Gaarder-Juntti, Oona. What Lives in the Desert?, 1 vol. 2008. (Animal Habitats Ser.). (ENG., Illus.). 24p. (J). (gr. k-3). 25.65 *(978-1-60453-173-2(8))* ABDO Publishing Co.

Gaff, Jackie. I Wonder Why the Sahara Is Cold at Night. 2014. 32p. pap. 7.00 *(978-1-61003-351-0(5))* Center for the Collaborative Classroom.

—I Wonder Why the Sahara Is Cold at Night. 2nd ed. 2012. (I Wonder Why Ser.). (ENG., Illus.). 32p. (J). (gr. k-3). 6.99 *(978-0-7534-6797-8(6)*, 9780753467978, Kingfisher) Roaring Brook Pr.

Ganeri, Anita. Esos Desesperantes Desiertos. (Coleccion Esa Horrible Geografía). (SPA.). (YA). (gr. 5-8). pap. *(978-84-272-2155-0(X)*, ML31292) Molino, Editorial ESP. Dist: Lectorum Pubns., Inc.

—Exploring Deserts: A Benjamin Blog & His Inquisitive Dog Investigation, 1 vol. 2014. (Exploring Habitats with Benjamin Blog & His Inquisitive Dog Ser.). (ENG.). 32p. (gr. 1-3). lib. bdg. 29.99 *(978-1-4329-8778-7(X)*, NA-h) Heinemann-Raintree.

Ganeri, Anita & Collins UK Staff. The Arabian Desert. 2016. (ENG.). 56p. (J). (gr. 4-5). pap. 9.95 *(978-0-00-816397-6(9))* HarperCollins Pubs. Ltd. GBR. Dist: Independent Pubs. Group.

Gardner, Robert. Desert Experiments: 11 Science Experiments in One Hour or Less. 2014. (Last Minute Science Projects with Biomes Ser.). (Illus.). 48p. (J). (gr. 5-12). 25.27 *(978-0-7660-5917-7(0))* Enslow Pubs., Inc.

Gilkerson, Patricia. My Adventure in the Desert. 2006. 44p. (J). 8.99 *(978-1-59092-278-1(6))* Blue Forge Pr.

Goldish, Meish. Lost in a Desert. 2015. (Illus.). 32p. (J). lib. bdg. *(978-1-62724-285-1(6))* Bearport Publishing Co., Inc.

Gordon, Sharon. At Home in the Desert. 2005. (Bookworms Ser.). (SPA., Illus.). 32p. (J). (gr. 3-7). lib. bdg. *(978-0-7614-1963-1(2)*, Benchmark Bks.) Marshall Cavendish Corp.

—At Home in the Desert/Mi Casa en el Desierto. 2006. (Bookworms Ser.). (ENG & SPA., Illus.). 32p. (gr. k-2). lib. bdg. 15.95 *(978-0-7614-2453-6(9))* Marshall Cavendish Corp.

C D

—Mi Casa en el Desierto. 2006. (Bookworms Ser.). (SPA & ENG., Illus.). 32p. (gr. k-2). lib. bdg. 15.95 (978-0-7614-2373-7(7)) Marshall Cavendish Corp.

Gowan, Barbara. D Is for Desert: A World Deserts Alphabet. 2012. (ENG., Illus.). 32p. (J). (gr. 1-5). 16.95 (978-1-58536-501-2(7)) Sleeping Bear Pr.

Grant, Donald. The Desert. Grant, Donald, illus. 2012. (ENG., Illus.). 34p. (J). (gr. k-3). pap. 11.99 (978-1-85103-299-0(1)) Moonlight Publishing, Ltd. GBR. Dist: Independent Pubs. Group.

Green, Jen. Deserts & Polar Regions Around the World. 2009. (Geography Now! Ser.). (ENG., Illus.). 32p. (J). (gr. 4-6). pap. 10.00 (978-1-4358-2960-2(3), PowerKids Pr.); (YA). (gr. 3-6). lib. bdg. 26.50 (978-1-4358-2874-2(7)) Rosen Publishing Group, Inc., The.

—Life in the Desert. 2010. (Nature in Focus Ser.). (Illus.). 32p. (gr. 2-5). (J). pap. 10.50 (978-1-4339-3421-6(3), Gareth Stevens Learning Library); (YA). lib. bdg. 26.00 (978-1-4339-3420-9(5), 1309291) Stevens, Gareth Publishing LLLP.

Greenberger, Robert. Deserts: The Living Landscape. 2009. (Biomes of the World Ser.). 48p. (gr. 5-8). (ENG., Illus.). (J). pap. 11.75 (978-1-4358-5431-4(4)); 53.00 (978-1-61511-602-7(8), Rosen Reference); (YA). lib. bdg. 29.25 (978-1-4358-5005-7(X)) Rosen Publishing Group, Inc., The.

Gritzner, Charles F. Deserts. 2007. (Geography of Extreme Environments Ser.). (Illus.). 100p. (YA). (gr. 7-12). lib. bdg. 30.00 (978-0-7910-9234-7(8)) Facts On File, Inc.

Group/McGraw-Hill, Wright. Life in the Deserts, 6 vols. (Book2WebTM Ser.). (gr. 4-8). 36.50 (978-0-322-04436-4(7)) Wright Group/McGraw-Hill.

Harris, Nathaniel. Atlas of the World's Deserts. 2003. (ENG., Illus.). 192p. (C). (gr. 6-18). 195.00 (978-1-57958-310-1(5), RT19225) Routledge.

Harvey, Gill. True Desert Adventures. Woodcock, John, illus. 2004. (True Adventure Stories Ser.). 144p. (J). pap. 4.95 (978-0-7945-0381-9(0), Usborne) EDC Publishing.

Hinds, Kathryn. The Countryside. 2008. (Life in the Medieval Muslim World Ser.). 96p. (J). (gr. 6-18). lib. bdg. 34.21 (978-0-7614-3091-9(1), Benchmark Bks.) Marshall Cavendish Corp.

Holland, Gini. I Live in the Desert. 2004. (Weekly Reader Early Learning Library). (Illus.). 24p. (gr. k-3). pap. 8.15 (978-0-8368-4087-2(9)); lib. bdg. 22.00 (978-0-8368-4080-3(1)) Stevens, Gareth Publishing LLLP. (Weekly Reader Leveled Readers).

—I Live in the Desert/Vivo en el Desierto. Coffey, Colleen & Carrillo, Consuelo, trs. 2004. (Weekly Reader Early Learning Library). (ENG & SPA., Illus.). 24p. (gr. k-3). pap. 8.15 (978-0-8368-4135-0(2)); lib. bdg. 22.00 (978-0-8368-4128-2(X)) Stevens, Gareth Publishing LLLP. (Weekly Reader Leveled Readers).

Howard, Fran. Deserts, 1 vol. 2006. (Habitats Ser.). (ENG., Illus.). 32p. (J). (gr. -1-3). lib. bdg. 27.07 (978-1-59679-776-5(2), Buddy Bks.) ABDO Publishing Co.

Hunter, Nick. Deserts: An Explorer Travel Guide, 1 vol. HL Studios Staff, illus. 2013. (Explorer Travel Guides). (ENG.). 48p. (gr. 3-6). 29.99 (978-1-4109-5429-9(3)); pap. 8.95 (978-1-4109-5436-7(6)) Heinemann-Raintree. (NA-r).

Hyde, Natalie. Desert Extremes. 2008. (Extreme Nature Ser.). (ENG., Illus.). 32p. (J). (gr. 2-3). pap. (978-0-7787-4517-4(1)); lib. bdg. (978-0-7787-4500-6(7)) Crabtree Publishing Co.

Jenson-Elliott, Cindy. Desert Communities Past & Present, 1 vol. 2014. (Who Lived Here? Ser.). (ENG.). 24p. (gr. 1-2). pap. 7.95 (978-1-4765-5141-8(3)); lib. bdg. 25.32 (978-1-4765-4059-7(4)) Capstone Press of Coughlan Cos. (First Facts).

Johansson, Philip. The Dry Desert: A Web of Life. 2004. (World of Biomes Ser.). (Illus.). 48p. (J). (gr. 3-4). lib. bdg. 25.27 (978-0-7660-2200-3(5)) Enslow Pubs., Inc.

Johnson, Robin. Sonoran Desert Research Journal. 2017. (Illus.). 32p. (J). **(978-0-7787-3491-8(9))**; pap. **(978-0-7787-3497-0(8))** Crabtree Publishing Co.

Kalman, Bobbie. Where on Earth Are Deserts? 2014. (ENG., Illus.). 32p. (J). (978-0-7787-0499-7(8)) Crabtree Publishing Co.

Kalman, Bobbie & MacAulay, Kelley. Cadenas Alimentarias del Desierto. 2006. (Cadenas Alimentarias Ser.). (SPA., Illus.). 32p. (J). (gr. 3-7). pap. (978-0-7787-8546-0(7)) Crabtree Publishing Co.

—Desert Food Chains. 2004. (Food Chains Ser.). (ENG., Illus.). 32p. (J). pap. (978-0-7787-1990-8(1)) Crabtree Publishing Co.

King, Zelda. Examining Desert Habitats. 2009. (Graphic Organizers: Habitats Ser.). 24p. (gr. 2-4). (Illus.). (J). pap. 8.25 (978-1-4358-3125-4(X), 1291756); 42.50 (978-1-61513-091-7(8)); (J). lib. bdg. 22.60 (978-1-4358-2721-9(X)) Rosen Publishing Group, Inc., The. (PowerKids Pr.).

Krebbs, Karen. Desert Life of the Southwest Activity Book. Juliano, Phil, illus. 2017. (Color & Learn Ser.). (ENG.). 64p. (gr. 1-3). pap. 6.95 (978-1-59193-655-8(1)) Adventure Pubns.

Kumar, Monica & Kumar, Asha. The Great Desert Adventure. 2008. (HIN & ENG., Illus.). 32p. (J). (978-0-9797191-1-0(9)) MeeraMasi, Inc.

Labrecque, Ellen. Living in a Desert. 2015. (Places We Live Ser.). (ENG., Illus.). 32p. (gr. 1-3). 27.32 (978-1-4846-0802-9(X), Heinemann First Library) Heinemann-Raintree.

LaPlante, Walter. There's a Desert in My Backyard! 2016. (Backyard Biomes Ser.). 00024p. (J). pap. 8.15 (978-1-4824-5555-7(2)) Stevens, Gareth Publishing LLLP.

Lawrence, Katherine. Life in the Desert. 2009. (Life in Extreme Environments Ser.). 64p. (gr. 5-8). 53.00 (978-1-61514-271-2(1), Rosen Reference) Rosen Publishing Group, Inc., The.

Lawrence, Katherine Drobot. Life in the Desert. 2004. (Life in Extreme Environments Ser.). (Illus.). 64p. (gr. 5-8). lib. bdg. 31.95 (978-0-8239-3985-5(5), Rosen Reference) Rosen Publishing Group, Inc., The.

Life Cycles, Vol. 2. 2005. (Animals, Animals, Animals Ser.). (YA). (gr. k-3). 267.30 (978-0-7368-4208-2(X), Pebble Bks.) Capstone Press of Coughlan Cos.

Lonely Planet Publications Staff. Lonely Planet Let's Explore... Desert, 1 vol. 2017. (Lonely Planet Kids Ser.). (ENG., Illus.). 60p. (J). pap. 9.99 (978-1-78657-314-8(8), 5400) Lonely Planet Pubns.

Looye, Juliette, text. I Live in the Desert. 2004. (Illus.). 16p. (J). pap. (978-0-7367-1934-6(2)) Zaner-Bloser, Inc.

Lynch, Wayne. Sonoran Desert. 2009. (ENG.). 64p. (J). (gr. 3-7). 16.95 (978-1-58979-389-7(7)) Taylor Trade Publishing.

Lynch, Wayne, photos by. Sonoran Desert. 2008. (Illus.). (J). (978-1-55971-984-1(2)); pap. (978-1-55971-985-8(0)) T&N Children's Publishing. (NorthWord Bks. for Young Readers).

MacAulay, Kelley & Kalman, Bobbie. A Desert Habitat. 2006. (Introducing Habitats Ser.). (ENG., Illus.). 32p. (J). (gr. -1-3). pap. (978-0-7787-2978-5(8)); lib. bdg. (978-0-7787-2950-1(8)) Crabtree Publishing Co.

—Un Habitat de Desierto. 2007. (Libro de Bobbie Kalman Ser.). (SPA & ENG., Illus.). 32p. (J). (gr. 1-2). lib. bdg. (978-0-7787-8326-8(X)); (gr. k-3). pap. (978-0-7787-8350-3(2)) Crabtree Publishing Co.

Macken, JoAnn Early. Deserts. 2006. (Where on Earth? World Geography Ser.). (Illus.). 24p. (gr. 1-4). pap. 8.15 (978-0-8368-6400-7(X)); lib. bdg. 22.00 (978-0-8368-6393-2(3)) Stevens, Gareth Publishing LLLP. (Weekly Reader Leveled Readers).

Markovics, Joyce L. Patterns in the Desert. 2014. (Math Blast!: Seeing Patterns All Around Ser.). (ENG.). 32p. (J). (gr. -1-3). lib. bdg. 26.60 (978-1-62724-337-7(2)) Bearport Publishing Co., Inc.

Max And Steven Oscherwitz. Gilbert's Adventure. 2008. 56p. pap. 27.99 (978-1-4257-4577-6(6)) Xlibris Corp.

McKissack, Fredrick L. & McKissack, Lisa Beringer. Counting in the Desert. 2008. (Counting in the Biomes Ser.). (Illus.). 32p. (J). (gr. 3-7). lib. bdg. 23.94 (978-0-7660-2988-0(3), Enslow Elementary) Enslow Pubs., Inc.

McNeil, Niki, et al. Desert Habitats. 2007. (In the Hands of a Child: Custom Designed Project Pack Ser.). (Illus.). 110p. spiral bd. 22.50 (978-1-60308-083-5(X)) In the Hands of a Child.

Meachen Rau, Dana. Deserts. 2007. (Wonders of Nature Ser.). (SPA & ENG.). 32p. (gr. 1-2). lib. bdg. 15.95 (978-0-7614-2667-7(1), Benchmark Bks.) Marshall Cavendish Corp.

—Deserts/Los Desiertos. 2007. (Wonders of Nature/Maravillas de la Naturaleza Ser.). (SPA & ENG., Illus.). 32p. (gr. 1-2). lib. bdg. 15.95 (978-0-7614-2830-5(5), Benchmark Bks.) Marshall Cavendish Corp.

—Los Desiertos. 2007. (Maravillas de la Naturaleza Ser.). (SPA & ENG., Illus.). 32p. (gr. 1-2). lib. bdg. 15.95 (978-0-7614-2806-0(2), Benchmark Bks.) Marshall Cavendish Corp.

Morrison, Ian A. Deserts of the World. 2009. (Our Planet Ser.). (YA). (gr. 3-6). lib. bdg. 25.25 (978-1-4358-2815-5(1)) Rosen Publishing Group, Inc., The.

Murray, Aaron R. Counting in the Desert 1-2-3. 2012. (All about Counting in the Biomes Ser.). 24p. (J). (gr. -1-1). 22.60 (978-0-7660-4051-9(8)); (Illus.). pap. 7.95 (978-1-4644-0061-2(X)) Enslow Pubs., Inc.

Nester, Tony. Desert Survival Tips, Tricks, & Skills. 2003. per. 10.95 (978-0-9713811-1-7(9)) Diamond Creek Publishing.

Owen, Ruth. Desert Survival Guide. 2010. (ENG., Illus.). 32p. (J). pap. (978-0-7787-7554-6(2)); lib. bdg. (978-0-7787-7532-4(1)) Crabtree Publishing Co.

Parish, Patrick. Survive on a Desert Island. 2016. (Survival Zone Ser.). (ENG., Illus.). 24p. (J). (gr. 3-7). 25.95 (978-1-62617-448-1(2), Torque Bks.) Bellwether Media.

Pledger, Maurice, illus. Sounds of the Wild: Safari. 2015. (Pledger Sounds Ser.). (ENG.). 16p. (J). (gr. k). 18.95 (978-1-62686-420-7(9), Silver Dolphin Bks.) Readerlink Distribution Services, LLC.

Publishers, Wayland & Newland, Sonya. Trekking the Sahara Desert. 2016. (Travelling Wild Ser.). (ENG., Illus.). 32p. (J). (gr. 4-6). 17.99 (978-0-7502-8584-1(2), Wayland) Hachette Children's Group GBR. Dist: Hachette Bk. Group.

Pyers, Greg. Biodiversity of Deserts. 2010. (Biodiversity Ser.). 32p. (gr. 4-18). 28.50 (978-1-60870-071-4(2)) Marshall Cavendish Corp.

Rabe, Tish. Why Oh Why Are Deserts Dry? All about Deserts. Ruiz, Aristides & Mathieu, Joe, illus. 2011. (Cat in the Hat's Learning Library). (ENG.). 48p. (J). (gr. -1-3). 9.99 (978-0-375-85868-0(7), Random Hse. Bks. for Young Readers) Random Hse. Children's Bks.

Rau, Dana Meachen. In the Desert. 2007. (J). pap. 6.99 (978-0-7614-3307-1(4)) Marshall Cavendish Corp.

Rice, Bill. Survival! Desert, 1 vol. 2nd rev. ed. 2013. (Nonfiction Readers Ser.). (ENG., Illus.). 48p. (J). (gr. 4-4). pap. 29.96 (978-1-4807-1094-8(6)) Shell Educational Publishing.

Rice, Howard. Step into the Desert, 1 vol. 2nd rev. ed. 2013. (Nonfiction Readers Ser.). (ENG., Illus.). 28p. (J). (gr. 2-2). pap. 23.96 (978-1-4807-1050-4(4)) Shell Educational Publishing.

—Step into the Desert, 1 vol. 2nd rev. ed. 2011. (Nonfiction Readers Ser.). (ENG.). 28p. (J). (gr. 2-2). pap. 6.99 (978-1-4333-3629-4(4)) Teacher Created Materials, Inc.

Rice, William. ¡Supervivencia! Desierto. 2017. (TIME for Kids en Español - Level 4 Ser.). (SPA., Illus.). 48p. (gr. 4-4). lib. bdg. 31.99 (978-1-5157-5123-6(6)) Time for Kids Inc AUS. Dist: Capstone Pub.

Rice, William & Franklin, Yvonne. Deserts, 1 vol. 2009. (Science Readers: a Closer Look Ser.). (ENG.). 32p. (J). (gr. 3-3). pap. 8.99 (978-1-4333-0315-9(9)) Teacher Created Materials, Inc.

Rice, William B. Death Valley Desert, 1 vol. 2nd rev. ed. 2014. (TIME for KIDS(r) Nonfiction Readers Ser.). (ENG., Illus.). 32p. (J). (gr. 3-3). pap. 25.96 (978-1-4807-1081-8(4)) Shell Educational Publishing.

—Survival! Desert, 1 vol. 2nd rev. ed. 2012. (Nonfiction Readers Ser.). (ENG., Illus.). 48p. (J). (gr. 4-4). pap. 9.99 (978-1-4333-4818-1(7)) Teacher Created Materials, Inc.

Rissman, Rebecca. Living & Nonliving in the Desert, 1 vol. 2013. (Is It Living or Nonliving? Ser.). (ENG.). 24p. (gr. k-2). 23.32 (978-1-4109-5380-3(7)); pap. 6.95 (978-1-4109-5387-2(4)) Heinemann-Raintree.

Rivera, Sheila. Desert. 2005. (First Step Nonfiction - Habitats Ser.). (ENG., Illus.). 24p. (gr. k-2). lib. bdg. 23.93 (978-0-8225-2597-4(6), Lerner Pubns.) Lerner Publishing Group.

Rodríguez, Ana María. Gray Foxes, Rattlesnakes, & Other Mysterious Animals of the Extreme Deserts. 2012. (Extreme Animals in Extreme Environments Ser.). (Illus.). 48p. (J). (gr. 5-18). pap. 8.95 (978-1-4644-0020-9(2)) Enslow Pubs., Inc.

—Gray Foxes, Rattlesnakes, & Other Mysterious Animals of the Extreme Deserts. 2012. (Extreme Animals in Extreme Environments Ser.). (Illus.). 48p. (J). (gr. 5-18). 25.27 (978-0-7660-3697-0(9)) Enslow Pubs., Inc.

Romero, Libby. Dry as a Desert. 2005. (J). pap. (978-1-4108-4594-8(X)) Benchmark Education Co.

Roumanis, Alexis. Deserts. 2014. (Illus.). 24p. (978-1-4896-3002-5(3)) Weigl Pubs., Inc.

Sandler, Michael. Deserts: Surviving in the Sahara. 2005. (X-treme Places Ser.). (Illus.). 32p. (J). (gr. 2-5). lib. bdg. 25.27 (978-1-59716-085-8(7)) Bearport Publishing Co., Inc.

Schomp, Virginia. 24 Hours in the Desert. 2013. 48p. (J). (gr. 4-8). 29.93 (978-1-60870-893-2(4)); pap. 12.93 (978-1-62712-066-1(1)) Cavendish Square Publishing.

Schuetz, Kari. Life in a Desert. 2016. (Biomes Alive! Ser.). (ENG., Illus.). 24p. (J). (gr. k-3). lib. bdg. 25.95 (978-1-62617-316-3(8), Blastoff! Readers) Bellwether Media.

Senker, Cath. Desert Climates. 2017. (Focus on Climate Zones Ser.). (ENG., Illus.). 48p. (gr. 4-6). lib. bdg. 33.32 (978-1-4846-3781-4(X), Heinemann InfoSearch) Heinemann-Raintree.

Serafini, Frank. Looking Closely Across the Desert. Serafini, Frank, illus. 2008. (Looking Closely Ser.). (ENG., Illus.). 40p. (J). (gr. -1-2). 16.95 (978-1-55453-211-7(6)) Kids Can Pr., Ltd. CAN. Dist: Hachette Bk. Group.

Sill, Cathryn. About Habitats-Deserts, 1 vol. Sill, John, illus. 2007. (About Habitats Ser.). (ENG.). 48p. (J). (gr. k-3). 16.95 (978-1-56145-390-0(0)) Peachtree Pubs.

—About Habitats: Deserts. Sill, John, illus. 2012. (About Habitats Ser.). (ENG.). (J). (gr. 4-7). 16.95 (978-1-56145-641-3(1)) Peachtree Pubs.

Silverman, Buffy. Desert Food Chains, 1 vol. 2010. (Protecting Food Chains Ser.). (ENG.). 48p. (gr. 3-6). 33.32 (978-1-4329-3856-7(8)); pap. 9.95 (978-1-4329-3863-5(0)) Heinemann-Raintree. (Heinemann InfoSearch).

—Let's Visit the Desert. 2016. (Lightning Bolt Books (tm) — Biome Explorers Ser.). (ENG., Illus.). 32p. (J). (gr. 1-3). 26.65 (978-1-5124-1190-4(6)) Lerner Publishing Group.

Soffer, Ruth. BOOST North American Desert Life Coloring Book. 2013. (BOOST Educational Ser.). (ENG.). 48p. (J). (gr. 3-5). pap. 5.99 (978-0-486-49436-4(5)) Dover Pubns., Inc.

Soll, Karen. Hottest Places on the Planet. 2016. (Extreme Earth Ser.). (ENG., Illus.). 24p. (gr. k-1). lib. bdg. 26.65 (978-1-4914-8341-1(5), Pebble Plus) Capstone Press of Coughlan Cos.

Spilsbury, Louise. Surviving the Desert. 2016. (Sole Survivor Ser.). 48p. (gr. 5-4). pap. 14.05 (978-1-4824-5091-0(7)) Stevens, Gareth Publishing LLLP.

Spilsbury, Louise & Spilsbury, Richard. In the Desert. 2016. (Science on Patrol Ser.). 00048p. (J). pap. 14.05 **(978-1-4824-5976-0(0))** Stevens, Gareth Publishing LLLP.

Stone, Lynn M. Deserts. 2003. (Rourke Discovery Library). (Illus.). 24p. (J). 20.64 (978-1-58952-683-9(X)) Rourke Educational Media.

Tarbox, A. D. The Desert. 2007. (Nature's Bounty Ser.). (J). 22.95 (978-1-58341-597-9(1), Creative Education) Creative Co., The.

Taylor, Trace & Zorzi, Gina. This Is a Desert. (Power 100 - Ecosystems Ser.). 36p. 2011. pap. 45.32 (978-1-61541-236-5(0)) 2010. (ENG.). (J). pap. 5.99 (978-1-61541-219-8(0)) American Reading Co.

Tull, Mary. Deserts. 2007. (Reading Expeditions Ser.). (ENG., Illus.). 32p. (J). pap. 17.95 (978-0-7922-4565-0(2)) CENGAGE Learning.

Warhol, Tom. Desert. 2006. (Earth's Biomes Ser.). (Illus.). 80p. (gr. 6-7). lib. bdg. 34.21 (978-0-7614-2194-8(7), Benchmark Bks.) Marshall Cavendish Corp.

Weldon-Owe. Shifting Sands. 2003. (Rigby InfoQuest Ser.). (ENG.). 24p. (gr. 4-4). pap. 9.50 (978-0-7578-5718-8(3)) Rigby Education.

Wiewandt, Thomas A. Hidden Life of the Desert. 2nd ed. 2010. (J). (978-0-87842-555-6(1)) Mountain Pr. Publishing Co., Inc.

Wilkes, Angela. Wild Places: Combined Volume. 2009. (Explainers Ser.). 96p. (J). pap. 12.99 (978-0-7945-2499-9(0), Usborne) EDC Publishing.

Woods, Michael & Woods, Mary B. Seven Natural Wonders of Africa. 2009. (Seven Wonders Ser.). (ENG., Illus.). 80p. (gr. 5-8). lib. bdg. 33.26 (978-0-8225-9071-2(9)) Lerner Publishing Group.

World Book, Inc Staff, contrib. by. Mountains, Deserts, & Grasslands. 2008. 64p. (J). (978-0-7166-1403-6(0)) World Bk., Inc.

Zorzi, Gina & Sánchez, Lucía M. Desiertos: This Is a Desert. 2011. (2G Ecosistemas Ser.). (SPA.). 36p. (J). (gr. k-2). pap. 6.99 (978-1-61541-424-6(X)) American Reading Co.

Zorzi, Gina & Sanchez, Lucia M. Desiertos (This Is a Desert) 2011. (poder de 100 - Ecosistemas Ser.). (SPA.). 36p. pap. 45.32 (978-1-61541-425-3(8)) American Reading Co.

DESERTS—FICTION

Baylor, Byrd & Parnall, Peter. Desert Voices. 2014. 32p. pap. 8.00 (978-1-61003-343-5(4)) Center for the Collaborative Classroom.

Bordiglioni, Stephen & Bordiglioni, Stefano. Desert Adventure. Bertolucci, Federico, illus. 2009. (Dinodino's Dinosaur Adventures Ser.). 56p. (J). (gr. k-4). 27.95 (978-1-60754-714-3(7)); pap. 12.85 (978-1-60754-721-1(X)) Windmill Bks.

Brodien-Jones, Christine. The Scorpions of Zahir. Murphy, Kelly, illus. 2012. (ENG.). 384p. (J). (gr. 5). 17.99 (978-0-385-73933-7(8), Delacorte Bks. for Young Readers) Random Hse. Children's Bks.

Burchett, Jan & Vogler, Sara. Desert Danger, 1 vol. Le Feyer, Diane, illus. 2013. (Wild Rescue Ser.). (ENG.). 152p. (gr. 3-6). 9.95 (978-1-4342-4892-3(5)) Stone Arch Bks.

Campbell, Roy. Song of the Jackalope. Bosworth, David, illus. 2nd ed. 2006. 140p. (YA). pap. 12.95 (978-1-933538-04-4(X)) Bridgeway Bks.

Carrillo, P. S. Desert Passage. 2008. (ENG.). 192p. (YA). (gr. 6-18). pap. 10.95 (978-1-55885-517-5(3), Piñata Books) Arte Publico Pr.

Caselio-Atassi, Rosemarie. Camel's Tales: The Journey to Bethlehem. 2013. 86p. pap. 15.99 (978-1-4797-7565-1(7)) Xlibris Corp.

Chapman, Allan W. Mr Wugidgem & the Dark Journey. 2012. 40p. pap. 7.99 (978-0-9796780-3-5(X)) AC Writings.

Collins, Bert McLemore. Excitement at Double B Acres. 2009. 52p. pap. 22.49 (978-1-4389-8447-6(2)) AuthorHouse.

Davies, Stephen. Sophie & the Albino Camel. 2009. 1.00 (978-1-4074-4344-7(5)) Recorded Bks., Inc.

de los Santos, Marisa & Teague, David. Connect the Stars. 2015. (ENG.). 352p. (J). (gr. 3-7). 16.99 (978-0-06-227465-6(1)) HarperCollins Pubs.

Durst, Sarah Beth. Vessel. (ENG., Illus.). 432p. (YA). (gr. 7). 2013. pap. 9.99 (978-1-4424-2377-0(3)) 2012. 16.99 (978-1-4424-2376-3(5)) McElderry, Margaret K. Bks. (McElderry, Margaret K. Bks.).

Flanagan, John. Erak's Ransom, Bk. 7. (Ranger's Apprentice Ser.: 7). (ENG.). (J). (gr. 5-18). 2011. 416p. 8.99 (978-0-14-241525-2(1), Puffin Books) 2010. 384p. 18.99 (978-0-399-25205-1(3), Philomel Bks.) Penguin Young Readers Group.

Fredericks, Anthony D. I Am the Desert. Reisch, Jesse, illus. 2012. (J). (978-1-933855-73-8(8)) Rio Nuevo Pubs.

Gonzalez, Maya Christina. My Colors, My World. Gonzalez, Maya Christina, illus. 2013.Tr. of Mis Colores, Mi Mundo. (ENG & SPA., Illus.). 32p. (J). pap. 9.95 (978-0-89239-278-0(9), Children's Book Press) Lee & Low Bks., Inc.

Greenburg, J. C. In the Desert. Gerardi, Jan, illus. 2008. (Andrew Lost Ser.: 17). (ENG.). 96p. (J). (gr. 1-4). per. 3.99 (978-0-375-84667-0(0), Random Hse. Bks. for Young Readers) Random Hse. Children's Bks.

Hanson, Ed. Desert Ordeal. 2003. (Barclay Family Adventure Ser.: Bk. 3). (Illus.). 64p. (J). (gr. k-6). per. 3.95 (978-1-56254-552-9(3), SP 5523) Saddleback Educational Publishing, Inc.

Have You Seen a Javelina? Individual Title Six-Packs. (Literatura 2000 Ser.). (gr. 2-3). 33.00 (978-0-7635-0201-0(4)) Rigby Education.

Hiscock, Bruce. Coyote & Badger: Desert Hunters of the Southwest. 2003. (ENG., Illus.). 32p. (J). (gr. 2-4). 15.95 (978-1-56397-848-7(2)) Boyds Mills Pr.

Hodgson, Julie. Juno & the Half -Man. 2010. 42p. pap. 12.95 (978-1-4461-6589-8(2)) Lulu Pr., Inc.

Hodgson, Mona Gansberg. Desert Critter Friends Set, 12 vols. (Desert Critter Friends Ser.). (J). 54.99 (978-0-7586-0007-3(0)) Concordia Publishing Hse.

Howey, Paul M. Freckles: The Mystery of the Little White Dog in the Desert. Zabriskie, Judy Mehn, illus. 2003. 72p. (gr. 2-5). lib. bdg. 14.95 (978-0-9677292-1-3(1)) AZTexts Publishing, Inc.

Jackson, Barry E. Danny Diamondback. Jackson, Barry E., illus. 2008. (Illus.). 40p. (J). (gr. k-2). lib. bdg. 17.89 (978-0-06-113185-1(7)) HarperCollins Pubs.

Jensen, Jon. Adventures in the Desert. 2013. 32p. pap. 17.25 (978-1-4907-0918-5(5)) Trafford Publishing.

Johnson, Julia. Gift of the Sands. Stacey International Staff, ed. Styles, Emily, illus. 2004. (ENG.). 48p. 12.99 (978-1-900988-91-9(7), Stacey International) Stacey Publishing GBR. Dist: Casemate Pubs. & Bk. Distributors, LLC.

Johnston, Tony. Desert Song, 1 vol. Young, Ed, illus. 2010. (ENG.). 32p. (J). (gr. 3-4). pap. 7.99 (978-1-57805-171-7(1)) Sierra Club Bks. for Children.

Jones, Christianne C. How the Camel Got Its Hump, 1 vol. Rooney, Ronnie, illus. 2011. (My First Classic Story Ser.). (ENG.). 32p. (gr. k-3). 236-5(0) pap. 7.10 (978-1-4048-7358-2(9), My First Classic Story) Picture Window Bks.

Jones, Christianne C. & Kipling, Rudyard. How the Camel Got Its Hump, 1 vol. Rooney, Ronnie, illus. 2010. (My First Classic Story Ser.). (ENG.). 32p. (gr. k-3). lib. bdg. 22.65 (978-1-4048-6075-9(4), My First Classic Story) Picture Window Bks.

Marr, Melissa. Desert Tales. 2013. (Wicked Lovely Ser.). (ENG.). 272p. (YA). (gr. 8). pap. 9.99 (978-0-06-228756-4(7)) HarperCollins Pubs.

—Resolve. Xian Nu Studio, illus. 2011. (Wicked Lovely: Desert Tales Ser.: 3). (ENG.). 176p. (YA). (gr. 8-18). pap. 9.99 (978-0-06-149350-8(3)) HarperCollins Pubs.

Mason, Prue. Camel Rider. 2007. (ENG.). 208p. (J). (gr. 5-7). 15.95 (978-1-58089-314-5(7)) Charlesbridge Publishing, Inc.

—Camel Rider. 2011. 9.49 (978-0-7848-3618-7(3), Everbind) Marco Bk. Co.

Meadows, Daisy. Esme the Ice Cream Fairy. 2014. (Sugar & Spice Fairies Ser.: 2). (ENG.). 80p. (J). (gr. 2-5). pap. 4.99 (978-0-545-60532-8(6), Scholastic Paperbacks) Scholastic, Inc.

Morrison, Kevin. Frank Is a Chihuahua. De La Cruz, Erin Harris, illus. 2007. 32p. (J). (gr. 1-4). (978-1-929039-43-2(3)) Ambassador Bks., Inc.

Nix, Pamela. Tummel the Tumbleweed. Barnes, Trisha, ed. Paulson, Arlie & Nix, Pamela, illus. 2011. 26p. (J). pap. 7.99 (978-0-9815914-9-0(3)) River Canyon Pr.

Otis, James. Dick in the Desert. 2005. reprint ed. pap. 15.95 (978-1-4179-0335-1(X)) Kessinger Publishing, LLC.

O'Toole-Freel, Judy. Zigzag the Rocking Roadrunner. Freel, Mirle, illus. 2012. 40p. 24.95 (978-1-4626-9970-4(7)) America Star Bks.

Parpan, Justin, illus. Gwango's Lonesome Trail. 2006. 32p. (J). (gr. -1-3). 15.95 (978-1-60108-004-2(2)) Red Cygnet Pr.

Patron, Susan. Lucky Breaks. Phelan, Matt, illus. 2010. (ENG.). 208p. (J). (gr. 3-7). pap. 7.99 (978-1-4169-9772-6(5), Atheneum Bks. for Young Readers) Simon & Schuster Children's Publishing.

Peet, Mal & Graham, Elspeth. Mysterious Traveler. Lynch, P. J., illus. 2013. (ENG.). 48p. (J). (gr. k-3). 15.99 (978-0-7636-6232-5(1)) Candlewick Pr.

Phanton, Rick. Boston & the Bean. 2012. 112p. pap. 19.95 (978-1-4626-4809-2(6)) America Star Bks.

Radosevich, Tina. The Binky Story. 2013. 20p. pap. 17.99 (978-1-4817-0001-6(4)) AuthorHouse.

Roberts, Nick H. Tyler the Tumbleweed & His Family Adventure. 2013. 28p. pap. 13.55 (978-1-4669-7782-2(5)) Trafford Publishing.

Rossetti, Rinsai. The Girl with Borrowed Wings. 2012. (ENG.). 304p. (YA). (gr. 7). 17.99 (978-0-8037-3566-8(9), Dial Bks) Penguin Young Readers Group.

Sally Spencer. Juanita's Flowers. Phil Brannan & Sunni Brannan, illus. 2009. 32p. pap. 14.49 (978-1-4389-4841-6(7)) AuthorHouse.

Saunders, Harry M. Teenagers on an Adventure: Journey of Two Boys & a Girl. 2013. 168p. pap. 19.95 *(978-1-62709-466-5(0))* America Star Bks.
Skilton, Sarah. High & Dry. 2014. (ENG.). 272p. (YA). (gr. 9-17). 16.95 *(978-1-4197-0929-6(1)*, Amulet Bks.) Abrams, Inc.
Slade, Nicholas. Joon the Zsun & His Magical Spoon. 2009. (Illus.). 32p. pap. 12.99 *(978-1-4389-3496-9(3))* AuthorHouse.
Stein, David Ezra. Cowboy Ned & Andy. Stein, David Ezra, illus. (ENG., Illus.). 32p. (J). (gr. -1-1). 2011. 6.99 *(978-1-4424-3619-0(0))* 2006. 16.99 *(978-1-4169-0041-2(1))* Simon & Schuster/Paula Wiseman Bks. (Simon & Schuster/Paula Wiseman Bks.).
Steiner, Christina. The Sad Tree & Pronuba. 2013. (ENG.). 32p. (J). pap. 14.95 *(978-1-4327-9893-2(6))* Outskirts Pr., Inc.
Tibo, Gilles & Vaillancourt, François. El Senor Patapum. (Barril Sin Fondo Ser.). (SPA.). (J). (gr. 3-5). pap. *(978-968-6465-58-7(8))* Casa de Estudios de Literatura y Talleres Artisticos Amaquemecan A.C. MEX. Dist: Lectorum Pubns., Inc.
Tsinajinnie, Veronica. Johonaa'ei: Bringer of Dawn. Thomas, Peter A., tr. from NAV. Singer, Ryan, illus. 2007. (ENG & NAV.). 32p. (J). (gr. -1-3). 17.95 *(978-1-893354-54-8(7))* Salina Bookshelf Inc.
Turner, Tracey. Lost in the Desert of Dread. 2014. (ENG., Illus.). 128p. (J). *(978-0-7787-0725-7(3))* Crabtree Publishing Co.
Van Zant, Dawn. Bradford & the Journey to the Desert of Lop. 2005. (Illus.). 36p. (J). pap. 17.99 *(978-0-9761768-2-4(3))* Wild Heart Ranch, Inc.
Wallace, Sally. A Big Secret: A Nativity Story. 2009. 40p. pap. 16.99 *(978-1-4490-1660-9(X))* AuthorHouse.
Ward, Jennifer. The Seed & the Giant Saguaro. Rangner, Mike K., illus. 2003. (ENG.). 32p. (J). (gr. -1-3). 15.95 *(978-0-87358-845-4(2))* Cooper Square Publishing Llc.
—The Sunhat. Sisson, Stéphanie Roth, illus. 2013. (ENG.). (J). 15.95 *(978-1-933855-78-3(9)*, Rio Nuevo Pubs.) Rio Nuevo Pubs.
Whybrow, Ian. More Meerkat Madness. 2013. (Awesome Animals Ser.). (ENG., Illus.). 192p. (J). (gr. 2-6). pap. 6.99 *(978-1-4380-0305-4(6))* Barron's Educational Series, Inc.
Winderman, Jay B. Thunder on the Desert. Becker, LuAnne E. & Becker, Lisa E., illus. 2005. 152p. (J). (gr. 3-7). per. 13.95 *(978-0-9761623-1-5(8))* Pill Bug Pr.
—Thunder on the Reservation. Becker, LuAnne E., illus. 2007. 147p. (J). (gr. 3-7). per. 13.95 *(978-0-9761623-2-2(6))* Pill Bug Pr.

DESIGN

see also Costume Design
also subdivision Design under topical headings where the subdivision Design and Construction is not appropriate

Abraham, Chuck. Intricate Valentines: 45 Lovely Designs to Color. 2009. (ENG.). 96p. pap. 6.95 *(978-0-7624-3674-3(3))* Running Pr. Bk. Pubs.
Adamson, Thomas K. The Kids' Guide to Sports Design & Engineering, 1 vol. 2014. (SI Kids Guide Bks.). (ENG.). 48p. (gr. 4-9). lib. bdg. 31.99 *(978-1-4765-4155-6(8))* Capstone Press of Coughlan Cos.
Arato, Rona. Design It! The Ordinary Things You Use Every Day & the Not-So-Ordinary Ways They Came to Be. Newell, Claudia, illus. 2010. (ENG.). 72p. (J). (gr. 4-7). pap. 20.95 *(978-0-88776-846-0(6)*, Tundra Bks.) Tundra Bks. CAN. Dist: Penguin Random Hse. LLC.
Beech, Terry. Design, Graphics & Visual Communication for New Zealand Years 9 & 10. 2013. (ENG.). pap., stu. ed. *(978-1-107-61205-1(5))* Cambridge Univ. Pr.
Brommer, Gerald F. Illustrated Elements of Art & Principles of Design: Full Color Reproductions, Descriptions of Each Concept, Hands-On Activities. 2010. 72p. (J). spiral bd. 19.95 *(978-1-56290-665-8(8))* Crystal Productions.
Bryant, Jill & Second Story Press Staff. Dazzling Women Designers, 1 vol. 2010. (Women's Hall of Fame Ser.). (ENG., Illus.). 128p. (J). (gr. 3-5). pap. 10.95 *(978-1-897187-82-1(3))* Second Story Pr. CAN. Dist: Orca Bk. Pubs. USA.
Burton, Margie, et al. Looking for Patterns. 2011. (Early Connections Ser.). (J). *(978-1-61672-497-9(8))* Benchmark Education Co.
—What Comes Next? 2011. (Early Connections Ser.). (J). *(978-1-61672-546-4(X))* Benchmark Education Co.
Dakers, Diane. Calvin Klein: Fashion Design Superstar. 2010. (Crabtree Groundbreaker Biographies Ser.). (ENG., Illus.). 112p. (J). (gr. 5-8). lib. bdg. *(978-0-7787-2534-3(0))* Crabtree Publishing Co.
D'Cruz, Anna-Marie. Make Your Own Books. 2009. (Do It Yourself Projects! Ser.). lib. bdg. 25.25 *(978-1-4358-2855-1(0)*, PowerKids Pr.) Rosen Publishing Group, Inc., The.
De Long, Ron, et al. Dream-Makers Principles of Art & Design: Art & Design. De Long, Ron et al, eds. 2007. (Illus.). 104p. spiral bd. 9.99 *(978-0-86696-329-9(4))* Binney & Smith, Inc.
Design. 3rd rev. ed. 2010. (Careers in Focus Ser.). (Illus.). 192p. (gr. 6-12). 32.95 *(978-0-8160-8024-3(0)*, Ferguson Publishing Co.) Facts On File, Inc.
Design, Build, Experiment. 2015. (Design, Build, Experiment Ser.). (ENG.). 128p. (J). (gr. 7-7). 223.62 *(978-0-7660-6695-3(9))* Enslow Pubs., Inc.
Design It! 2017. (Design It! Ser.). 32p. (gr. 3-4). pap. 63.00 ***(978-1-5382-0830-4(X))***; lib. bdg. 159.60 ***(978-1-5382-0777-2(X))*** Stevens, Gareth Publishing LLLP.
Dunn, Mary R. Quiero Ser Diseñador de Modas. 2009. (Trabajos de Ensueño (Dream Jobs) Ser.).Tr. of I Want to Be a Fashion Designer. (SPA & ENG., Illus.). 24p. (J). (gr. 2-4). lib. bdg. 22.60 *(978-1-4042-8154-7(1)*, Editorial Buenas Letras) Rosen Publishing Group, Inc., The.
Enz, Tammy. Build Your Own Fort, Igloo, & Other Hangouts, 1 vol. Haus, Estudio, illus. 2010. (Build It Yourself Ser.). (ENG.). 32p. (gr. 3-4). lib. bdg. 27.99 *(978-1-4296-5436-4(8)*, Edge Bks.) Capstone Press of Coughlan Cos.
—Build Your Own Mini Golf Course, Lemonade Stand, & Other Things to Do, 1 vol. 2010. (Build It Yourself Ser.). (ENG.). 32p. (gr. 3-4). lib. bdg. 27.99 *(978-1-4296-5438-8(4)*, Edge Bks.) Capstone Press of Coughlan Cos.
Evans, Sian & Cymru, Addysg Cyfryngau. Gweithgareddau Dylunio a Thechnoleg CA1/2. 2005. *(978-1-902346-02-1(5))* Addysg Y Cyfryngau Cymru.
Fontichiaro, Kristin. Design Thinking. 2015. (21st Century Skills Innovation Library: Makers As Innovators Ser.). (ENG., Illus.). 32p. (J). (gr. 4-8). lib. bdg. 29.93 *(978-1-63188-870-0(6)*, 206060) Cherry Lake Publishing.
Fridell, Ron. Earth-Friendly Energy. 2009. pap. 58.95 *(978-0-7613-4692-0(9))* Lerner Publishing Group.
Gregory, Josh. From Thistle Burrs to... Velcro. 2012. (21st Century Skills Innovation Library: Innovations from Nature Ser.). (ENG.). 32p. (gr. 4-8). 28.50 *(978-1-61080-494-3(5)*, 202104); pap. 14.21 *(978-1-61080-668-8(9)*, 202278) Cherry Lake Publishing.
Hendler, Muncie. Infinite Designs Coloring Book. 2006. (Dover Design Coloring Bks.). (ENG., Illus.). 32p. (J). (gr. 3-8). 3.99 *(978-0-486-44892-3(4))* Dover Pubns., Inc.
Henry, Sandi. Making Amazing Art! 40 Activities Using the 7 Elements of Art Design. Cole, Sarah, illus. 2008. (ENG.). 128p. (J). (gr. 3-7). pap. 12.99 *(978-0-8249-6795-6(X)*, Ideal Pubns.) Worthy Publishing.
Jones, Tammy. What Has Stripes? 2009. (Sight Word Readers Set A Ser.). (J). 3.49 net. *(978-1-60719-151-3(2))* Newmark Learning LLC.
Kallen, Stuart A. Careers If You Like the Arts. 2016. (ENG.). 80p. (J). (gr. 5-12). lib. bdg. *(978-1-68282-008-7(4))* ReferencePoint Pr., Inc.
Klutz Editors. Paper Fashions. 2nd rev. ed. 2012. (ENG.). 60p. (J). (gr. 3-7). 21.99 *(978-0-545-44944-1(8))* Klutz.
LaCoste, Michael, ed. & frwd. Design Denied: The Dynamics of Withholding Good Design & its Ethical Implications: The Dynamics of Withholding Good Design & its Ethical ImplicationsThe Withholding of Good Design & its Ethical Implications LaCoste, Michael, frwd. 2005. (Illus.). 120p. per. 20.00 *(978-0-9753405-2-3(2))* Archeworks.
Magruder, Trula & American Girl Editors, eds. Design by Me Wings: Fancy Art & Fun Display Ideas! Ingham, Julie, illus. 2011. (ENG.). 32p. (J). spiral bd. 14.95 *(978-1-59369-897-3(6))* American Girl Publishing, Inc.
Mazurkiewicz, Jessica & Coloring Books Staff. Organic Designs Coloring Book. 2011. (Dover Coloring Bks.). (ENG., Illus.). 32p. (J). (gr. 2-5). pap. 3.99 *(978-0-486-47987-3(0))* Dover Pubns., Inc.
McVey, Randall, et al. Mesmerizing Mandalas. 2012. (Adult Coloring Ser.). (ENG., Illus.). 64p. (gr. 3). pap. 5.99 *(978-0-486-49961-1(8))* Dover Pubns., Inc.
Meredith, Susan Markowitz. Patterns at the Beach. 2011. (Early Connections Ser.). (J). *(978-1-61672-371-2(8))* Benchmark Education Co.
Newman, Heather. Creating Digital Brochures. Petelinsek, Kathleen, illus. 2013. (Explorer Library: Information Explorer Ser.). (ENG.). 32p. (J). (gr. 4-8). 28.50 *(978-1-62431-128-4(8)*, 202832); pap. 14.21 *(978-1-62431-260-1(8)*, 202834) Cherry Lake Publishing.
Nsrc. Science & Technology for Children Books: Motion & Design. 2004. (Illus.). 64p. (J). *(978-1-933008-03-5(2))* Smithsonian Science Education Ctr. (SSEC).
Oleck, Joan. Graphic Design & Desktop Publishing. 2010. (Digital & Information Literacy Ser.). (ENG.). 48p. (YA). pap. 11.75 *(978-1-4488-0593-8(7))*; lib. bdg. 29.25 *(978-1-4358-9425-9(1))* Rosen Publishing Group, Inc., The. (Rosen Reference).
Oscar de la Renta. 2010. (Great Hispanic Heritage Ser.). (Illus.). 128p. (gr. 6-12). 35.00 *(978-1-60413-733-0(9)*, Chelsea Hse.) Facts On File, Inc.
Owen, Ruth. Building Green Places: Careers in Planning, Designing, & Building. 2009. (Green-Collar Careers Ser.). (ENG., Illus.). 64p. (J). (gr. 5-8). pap. *(978-0-7787-4863-2(4))*; lib. bdg. *(978-0-7787-4852-6(9))* Crabtree Publishing Co.
Pease, Pamela. Design Dossier. (Design Dossiers Ser.). (ENG., Illus.). (J). (gr. 4). 2011. 96p. 24.00 *(978-0-9777905-1-7(7))* 2009. 78p. 24.00 *(978-0-9777905-0-0(9))* Paintbox Pr.
Pomaska, Anna. My First Geometric Designs Coloring Book. 2010. (Dover Coloring Bks.). (ENG., Illus.). 32p. (J). (gr. -1-2). pap. 3.99 *(978-0-486-47557-8(3))* Dover Pubns., Inc.
Rabbat, Suzy. Super Smart Information Strategies: Creating a Digital Portfolio. 2011. (Explorer Library: Information Explorer Ser.). (ENG.). 32p. (gr. 4-8). lib. bdg. 28.50 *(978-1-61080-121-8(0)*, 201128) Cherry Lake Publishing.
Science & Technology for Children Books, Motion & Design Set, 8 vols. 2004. (Illus.). 64p. (J). *(978-1-933008-15-8(6))* Smithsonian Science Education Ctr. (SSEC).
Sirota, Lyn A. Science Lab: Technological Design. 2011. (Explorer Library: Language Arts Explorer Ser.). (ENG.). 32p. (gr. 4-8). pap. 14.21 *(978-1-61080-297-0(7)*, 201219); lib. bdg. 28.50 *(978-1-61080-208-6(X)*, 201192) Cherry Lake Publishing.
Spilsbury, Richard. Hi-Tech Clothes, 1 vol. 2013. (Design & Engineering for STEM Ser.). (ENG., Illus.). 56p. (gr. 6-8). pap. 9.99 *(978-1-4329-7037-6(2)*, NA-h); lib. bdg. 34.65 *(978-1-4329-7032-1(1))* Heinemann-Raintree.
Spilsbury, Richard & Graham, Ian. Iconic Designs. 2015. (Iconic Designs Ser.). (ENG.). 48p. (gr. 4-6). lib. bdg. 133.28 *(978-1-4846-2620-7(6)*, Heinemann InfoSearch) Heinemann-Raintree.
Stegenga, Wil & Coloring Books for Adults. Geometric Whirlwind Coloring Book. 2010. (Dover Design Coloring Bks.). (ENG., Illus.). 32p. (J). (gr. 3-5). pap. 3.99 *(978-0-486-47391-8(0))* Dover Pubns., Inc.
Sterling Children's, Sterling. Curious Jane. 2017. (ENG., Illus.). 128p. (J). (gr. 1-6). pap. 16.95 *(978-1-4549-2235-3(4))* Sterling Publishing Co., Inc.
Sundance/Newbridge LLC Staff. Design It! Build It! 2007. (Early Science Ser.). (gr. k-3). 18.95 *(978-1-4007-6603-1(6))*; pap. 6.10 *(978-1-4007-6599-7(4))* Sundance/Newbridge Educational Publishing.
Swanson, Maggie. Sun, Moon & Stars Designs to Color. 2013. (ENG., Illus.). 32p. (gr. 3-8). pap. 3.99 *(978-0-486-49227-8(3))* Dover Pubns., Inc.
Veitch, Catherine. Changing Designs. 2015. (Collins Big Cat Ser.). (ENG.). 32p. (J). (gr. 2-2). pap. 7.95 *(978-0-00-759123-7(3))* HarperCollins Pubs. Ltd. GBR. Dist: Independent Pubs. Group.
Welsbacher, Anne. Earth-Friendly Design. 2009. pap. 58.95 *(978-0-7613-4693-7(7))* Lerner Publishing Group.
Wood, Alix. Interior Design. 2017. (Design It! Ser.). 32p. (gr. 3-4). pap. 63.00 ***(978-1-5382-0784-0(2))*** Stevens, Gareth Publishing LLLP.
Wooster, Patricia. Fashion Designer. 2011. (21st Century Skills Library: Cool Arts Careers Ser.). (ENG.). 32p. (gr. 4-8). lib. bdg. 28.50 *(978-1-61080-131-7(8)*, 201140) Cherry Lake Publishing.
Yes Magazine Editors. Fantastic Feats & Failures. Kurisu, Jane, illus. 2004. (ENG.). 52p. (J). (gr. 3-7). 9.95 *(978-1-55337-634-7(X))* Kids Can Pr., Ltd. CAN. Dist: Hachette Bk. Group.

DESIGN, DECORATIVE

see also Art, Decorative; Decoration and Ornament; Drawing; Lettering; Tapestry

Pease, Pamela. Design Dossier. 2011. (Design Dossiers Ser.). (ENG., Illus.). 96p. (J). (gr. 4-7). 24.00 *(978-0-9777905-4-8(1))* Paintbox Pr.

DESSERTS

Alexander, Heather. Easy Desserts from Around the World. 2011. (Easy Cookbooks for Kids Ser.). (Illus.). 48p. (J). lib. bdg. 25.27 *(978-0-7660-3765-6(7))*; (gr. 3-18). pap. 8.95 *(978-1-59845-270-9(3))* Enslow Pubs., Inc. (Enslow Elementary).
Beery, Barbara. Pink Princess Cookbook, 1 vol. Snortum, Marty, photos by. 2006. (ENG., Illus.). 64p. (J). (gr. -1-3). spiral bd. 14.99 *(978-1-4236-0173-9(4))* Gibbs Smith, Publisher.
Besel, Jen. Custom Confections, 1 vol. 2014. (Custom Confections Ser.). (ENG.). 48p. (gr. 4-5). 95.97 *(978-1-4914-0862-9(6))* Capstone Press of Coughlan Cos.
Besel, Jennifer M. Custom Confections: Delicious Desserts You Can Create & Enjoy, 1 vol. 2014. (Craft It Yourself Ser.). (ENG.). 112p. (gr. 3-4). pap. 12.95 *(978-1-62370-136-9(8))* Capstone Young Readers of Coughlan Cos.
—Sweet Tooth! No-Bake Desserts to Make & Devour, 1 vol. 2014. (Custom Confections Ser.). (ENG., Illus.). 48p. (gr. 4-5). lib. bdg. 31.99 *(978-1-4914-0860-5(X))* Capstone Press of Coughlan Cos.
Brash, Lorna. Professor Cook's Fruity Desserts. 2013. (Professor Cook's... Ser.). 32p. (J). lib. bdg. 23.94 *(978-0-7660-4302-2(9))*; (gr. 4-12). pap. 7.95 *(978-1-4644-0549-5(2))* Enslow Pubs., Inc.
Closer Look At Dessert. (J). (gr. 4-6). pap. 10.75 *(978-0-669-15885-4(2))* Houghton Mifflin Harcourt School Pubs.
Closer Look at Dessert. (J). (gr. 4-6). 75.00 *(978-0-669-15079-7(7))* Houghton Mifflin Harcourt School Pubs.
Cornell, Kari. Dandy Desserts. Cohen, Brie, photos by. 2013. (You're the Chef Ser.). (ENG., Illus.). 32p. (gr. 3-5). lib. bdg. 26.60 *(978-0-7613-6644-7(X)*, Millbrook Pr.) Lerner Publishing Group.
—Sweet Cookies & Bars. Cohen, Brie, photos by. 2013. (You're the Chef Ser.). (ENG., Illus.). 32p. (gr. 3-5). lib. bdg. 26.60 *(978-0-7613-6638-6(5)*, Millbrook Pr.) Lerner Publishing Group.
Davies, Monika. Art & Culture: Desserts Around the World: Comparing Fractions (Grade 3) 2017. (Mathematics Readers Ser.). (Illus.). 32p. (gr. 3-3). 8.99 ***(978-1-4807-5804-9(3))*** Teacher Created Materials, Inc.
Davis, Robin & Starr, Lara. Wookiee Pies, Clone Scones, & Other Galactic Goodies. 2012. (ENG., Illus.). 64p. (J). (gr. -1-17). 22.99 *(978-1-4521-0466-9(2))* Chronicle Bks. LLC.
Desserts from Three Generations. 2004. 128p. per. 25.00 *(978-0-9754003-0-2(4))* Ivy Fund, The.
Engfer, Lee. Desserts Around the World. 2nd rev. ed. 2003. (Easy Menu Ethnic Cookbooks 2nd Edition Ser.). (ENG., Illus.). 72p. (J). (gr. 5-12). 25.26 *(978-0-8225-4126-4(2))* Lerner Publishing Group.
—Desserts Around the World: Culturally Authentic Foods Including Low-Fat & Vegetarian Recipes. rev. ed. 2003. (Easy Menu Ethnic Cookbooks 2nd Edition Ser.). (ENG., Illus.). 72p. (J). (gr. 5-12). pap. 7.95 *(978-0-8225-4165-3(3))* Lerner Publishing Group.
Gilpin, Rebecca & Atkinson, Catherine. Yummy Little Cookbook. Taylor, Non et al, illus. rev. ed. 2007. (Children's Cooking Ser.). (ENG.). 96p. (J). (gr. -1-3). 7.99 *(978-0-7945-1655-0(6)*, Usborne) EDC Publishing.
Johnson, Kristi. Monkey Pudding & Other Dessert Recipes, 1 vol. 2008. (Fun Foods for Cool Cooks Ser.). (ENG., Illus.). 32p. (gr. 3-4). 27.99 *(978-1-4296-1337-8(8)*, Snap Bks.) Capstone Press of Coughlan Cos.
Kalman, Bobbie. Delicious Desserts. 2003. (Kid Power Ser.). (ENG., Illus.). 32p. (J). pap. *(978-0-7787-1276-3(1))*; (gr. 3). lib. bdg. *(978-0-7787-1254-1(0))* Crabtree Publishing Co.
Kuskowski, Alex. Cool Treats & Sweets, 1 vol. 2014. (Cool Home Cooking Ser.). (ENG.). 32p. (gr. 3-6). 28.50 *(978-1-62403-505-0(1))* ABDO Publishing Co.
—Super Simple Bar Cookies: Easy Cookie Recipes for Kids!, 1 vol. 2016. (Super Simple Cookies Ser.). (ENG., Illus.). 32p. (J). (gr. k-4). 27.07 *(978-1-62403-946-1(4))* ABDO Publishing Co.
—Super Simple No-Bake Cookies: Easy Cookie Recipes for Kids!, 1 vol. 2016. (Super Simple Cookies Ser.). (ENG., Illus.). 32p. (J). (gr. k-4). 27.07 *(978-1-62403-950-8(2))* ABDO Publishing Co.
Martineau, Susan & James, Hel. Sweets & Snacks. 2012. (Healthy Eating Ser.). (Illus.). 32p. (gr. 2-6). pap. 8.95 *(978-1-59920-246-4(8))* Black Rabbit Bks.
Owen, Ruth. Christmas Sweets & Treats. 2012. (Holiday Cooking for Kids! Ser.). (ENG., Illus.). 32p. (J). (gr. 3-6). 26.50 *(978-1-4488-8081-2(5))*; pap. 11.75 *(978-1-4488-8128-4(5))* Windmill Bks.
—Easter Sweets & Treats. 2012. (Holiday Cooking for Kids! Ser.). (ENG., Illus.). 32p. (J). (gr. 3-6). 26.50 *(978-1-4488-8084-3(X))*; pap. 11.75 *(978-1-4488-8131-4(5))* Windmill Bks.
—Halloween Sweets & Treats. 2012. (Holiday Cooking for Kids! Ser.). (ENG., Illus.). 32p. (J). (gr. 3-6). 26.50 *(978-1-4488-8079-9(3))*; pap. 11.75 *(978-1-4488-8126-0(9))* Windmill Bks.
—Valentine's Day Sweets & Treats. 2012. (Holiday Cooking for Kids! Ser.). (ENG., Illus.). 32p. (J). (gr. 3-6). 26.50 *(978-1-4488-8080-5(7))*; pap. 11.75 *(978-1-4488-8127-7(7))* Windmill Bks.
Publications International Ltd. Staff, ed. Jello Simply Stunning Holiday Desserts. 2008. spiral bd. 3.98 *(978-1-4127-2866-9(5))* Publications International, Ltd.
Rau, Dana Meachen. Dessert Designer. 2012. (Dessert Designer Ser.). (ENG.). 32p. (gr. 3-4). lib. bdg. 111.96 *(978-1-4296-9178-9(6)*, Snap Bks.) Capstone Press of Coughlan Cos.
Segarra, Mercedes. Tasty Desserts: Little Chef Recipes. 2013. (Little Chef Ser.). (Illus.). 36p. (J). lib. bdg. 23.94 *(978-0-7660-4261-2(8))*; pap. 7.95 *(978-1-4644-0465-8(8))* Enslow Pubs., Inc. (Enslow Elementary).
Tuminelly, Nancy. Super Simple Desserts: Easy No-Bake Recipes for Kids, 1 vol. 2010. (Super Simple Cooking Ser.). (ENG.). 32p. (gr. k-4). 27.07 *(978-1-61613-384-9(8)*, Super SandCastle) ABDO Publishing Co.
Vega, Ali. Cat Litter Cake & Other Horrifying Desserts. 2017. (Little Kitchen of Horrors Ser.). (ENG.). 32p. (J). (gr. 2-5). 12.99 ***(978-1-5124-3768-3(9)***, Lerner Pubns.); 39.99 ***(978-1-5124-3767-6(0)***, Lerner Pubns.); 39.99 ***(978-1-5124-2805-6(1)***, Lerner Pubns.); (Illus.). 26.65 *(978-1-5124-2574-1(5))* Lerner Publishing Group.
Wagner, Lisa. Cool Sweets & Treats to Eat: Easy Recipes for Kids to Cook, 1 vol. 2007. (Cool Cooking Ser.). (ENG., Illus.). 32p. (gr. 4-7). 28.50 *(978-1-59928-726-3(9)*, Checkerboard Library) ABDO Publishing Co.
Waldron, Melanie. Deserts, 1 vol. 2012. (Habitat Survival Ser.). (ENG.). 32p. (gr. 2-4). pap. 8.29 *(978-1-4109-4603-4(7))*; lib. bdg. 30.65 *(978-1-4109-4594-5(4))* Heinemann-Raintree. (Raintree Perspectives).
Walton, Ruth. Let's Bake a Cake. 2013. (Let's Find Out Ser.). (Illus.). 32p. (gr. k-5). 28.50 *(978-1-59771-386-3(4))* Sea-To-Sea Pubns.
Yolen, Jane. Fairy Tale Desserts: A Cookbook for Young Readers & Eaters. Béha, Philippe, illus. 2009. (Fairy Tale Cookbooks Ser.). 32p. (J). (gr. 2-5). 22.60 *(978-1-60754-583-5(7))*; pap. 10.55 *(978-1-60754-584-2(5))* Windmill Bks.

DETECTIVE AND MYSTERY STORIES

see Mystery and Detective Stories

DETECTIVES

see also Criminal Investigation; Police; Secret Service

Allman, Toney. The Homicide Detective. 2009. (Crime Scene Investigations Ser.). (ENG., Illus.). 128p. (YA). (gr. 7-12). 35.45 *(978-1-4205-0109-4(7))* Cengage Gale.
Arnone, Marilyn P. & Coatney, Sharon. Mac, Information Detective, in the Curious Kids... - Digging for Answers: A Storybook Approach to Introducing Research Skills, 2 vols. Stockley, Gerry, illus. 2006. 104p. (C). 35.00 *(978-1-59158-397-4(7)*, LU3977, Libraries Unlimited) ABC-CLIO, LLC.
Barber, Nicola, et al. Primary Source Detectives, 1 vol. 2014. (Primary Source Detectives Ser.). (ENG.). 64p. (gr. 7-8). lib. bdg. 215.94 *(978-1-4329-9608-6(8))* Heinemann-Raintree.
Beak, Nick Huckleberry. How to Be a Detective! Crack the Case with 25 Devious Disguises & Devices! 2014. (ENG., Illus.). 64p. (J). (gr. 3-7). 9.99 *(978-1-84322-890-5(4)*, Armadillo) Anness Publishing GBR. Dist: National Bk. Network.
Broadbent, Paul. Detective Work. 2007. (Trackers-Math Ser.). (gr. 2-5). pap. 5.00 *(978-1-59055-931-4(2))* Pacific Learning, Inc.
Clemens, Micki. The 10 Most Ingenious Fictional Detectives. 2007. (Illus.). (J). 14.99 *(978-1-55448-514-7(2))* Scholastic Library Publishing.
Croce, Nicholas. Detectives: Life of Investigating Crime. 2005. (Extreme Careers Ser.). (Illus.). 64p. (YA). (gr. 5-9). 31.95 *(978-0-8239-3796-7(8))* Rosen Publishing Group, Inc., The.
Herweck, Diana. En Escena: La Vida de un CSI. 2017. (TIME for Kids en Español - Level 4 Ser.). (SPA., Illus.). 48p. (gr. 4-4). lib. bdg. 31.99 *(978-1-5157-5130-4(9))* Time for Kids Inc AUS. Dist: Capstone Pub.
Klein, Hilary Dole. A Day with a Chef. 2007. (Reading Rocks! Ser.). (ENG., Illus.). 32p. (J). (gr. 2-5). 28.50 *(978-1-59296-857-2(0)*, 200738) Child's World, Inc., The.
Poole, Hazel. Spies & Detectives. 2008. (Factastic Journey Ser.). (Illus.). 32p. (J). (gr. k-7). pap. 8.95 *(978-1-59905-243-4(1))* Saddleback Educational Publishing, Inc.
Seiple, Samantha. Lincoln's Spymaster: Allan Pinkerton, America's First Private Eye. 2015. (Illus.). 211p. (J). ***(978-0-545-90821-4(3))*** Scholastic, Inc.
Seiple, Samantha. Lincoln's Spymaster: Allan Pinkerton, America's First Private Eye. 2015. (ENG., Illus.). 224p. (J). (gr. 5-9). 17.99 *(978-0-545-70897-5(4)*, Scholastic Pr.) Scholastic, Inc.
Zullo, Allan. Crime Scene Investigators. 2008. 149p. (J). pap. *(978-0-439-93406-0(0))* Scholastic, Inc.

DETECTIVES—FICTION

Adler, David A. The Mystery of the Stolen Corn Popper, 11 vols. Natti, Susanna, illus. 2004. (Cam Jansen Ser.: 11). (ENG.). 64p. (J). (gr. 2-5). 4.99 *(978-0-14-240178-1(1)*, Puffin Books) Penguin Young Readers Group.
Aguayo, Sal. The Tiny Detective. 2008. 48p. pap. 16.95 *(978-1-60703-859-7(5))* America Star Bks.
Allen, Betsy. The Mystery of the Ruby Queens: Connie Blair Mystery Series. 2011. 192p. 42.95 *(978-1-258-09539-0(4))* Literary Licensing, LLC.
—The Silver Secret: A Connie Blair Mystery. 2011. 184p. 42.95 *(978-1-258-09883-4(0))* Literary Licensing, LLC.
Anderson, Jane. Inspector Insector. 2005. (J). pap. *(978-1-4108-4196-4(0))* Benchmark Education Co.
Bailey, Linda. How Can a Brilliant Detective Shine in the Dark?, No. 6. 2003. (Stevie Diamond Mystery Ser.). (ENG.). 200p. (J). (gr. 13-18). 14.95 *(978-1-55074-896-3(3))* Kids Can Pr., Ltd. CAN. Dist: Hachette Bk. Group.
Bellino, Sarah. The Little Miss Detectives: Case Number 1. 2012. 32p. pap. 14.51 *(978-1-4669-6867-7(2))* Trafford Publishing.
Biedrzycki, David. Ace Lacewing: Bug Detective. Biedrzycki, David, illus. 2008. (ENG., Illus.). 40p. (J). (gr. k-4). pap. 8.95 *(978-1-57091-684-7(5))* Charlesbridge Publishing, Inc.
—Ace Lacewing, Bug Detective: Bad Bugs Are My Business. Biedrzycki, David, illus. 2009. (ENG., Illus.). 44p. (J). (gr. k-4). 16.95 *(978-1-57091-692-2(6))* Charlesbridge Publishing, Inc.

C
D

—Ace Lacewing, Bug Detective: The Big Swat. Biedrzycki, David, illus. 2010. (ENG., Illus.). 44p. (J). (gr. k-4). 16.95 *(978-1-57091-747-9(7))* Charlesbridge Publishing, Inc.

Bingham, Jane, retold by. Around the World in Eighty Days. 2004. (Young Reading Gift Books Ser.). 64p. (J). (gr. 2-18). 8.95 *(978-0-7945-0826-5(X)*, Usborne) EDC Publishing.

Blaisdell, Patty. The Haunted Shed, 1 vol. 2009. 32p. pap. 24.95 *(978-1-60836-674-3(X))* America Star Bks.

Blake-Garrett, Andrea. The Adventures of Izzy & Juju: Twin Detective Investigators (T. D. I.) 2012. 28p. pap. 19.99 *(978-1-4685-0683-9(8))* AuthorHouse.

Brooks, Kevin. Johnny Delgado: Private Detective. 2012. (Stoke Books Titles Ser.). (ENG.). 80p. (YA). (gr. 8-12). pap. 6.95 *(978-1-78112-115-3(X))*; lib. bdg. 22.60 *(978-1-78112-116-0(8))* Lerner Publishing Group.

Brooks, Walter R. Freddy & the Ignormus, 4 vols. 2003. (Freddy the Pig Ser.). (J). 57.75 *(978-0-7887-2996-6(9)*, 40878) Recorded Bks., Inc.

Buckeridge, Anthony. Jennings & Darbishire. 2008. (Jennings Ser.: 4). (ENG.). 210p. (J). (gr. -1-12). pap. 12.95 *(978-0-7551-0153-5(7))* House of Stratus, Inc. GBR. Dist: Gardners Bks. Ltd.

Byars, Betsy. Dead Letter. 2006. (Herculeah Jones Mystery Ser.). (ENG.). 160p. (J). (gr. 3-7). 5.99 *(978-0-14-240564-2(7)*, Puffin Books) Penguin Young Readers Group.

Chaisson, Samuel Jam. Larry & Joe's Detective Agency. 2005. pap. 26.50 *(978-1-4184-6878-1(9))* AuthorHouse.

Child, Lauren. Ruby Redfort Look into My Eyes. Child, Lauren, illus. 2013. (Ruby Redfort Ser.: 1). (ENG., Illus.). 400p. (J). (gr. 5-9). pap. 7.99 *(978-0-7636-6257-8(7))* Candlewick Pr.

—Ruby Redfort Take Your Last Breath. Child, Lauren, illus. 2013. (Ruby Redfort Ser.: 2). (ENG., Illus.). 432p. (J). (gr. 5-9). 16.99 *(978-0-7636-5468-9(X))* Candlewick Pr.

Clark, Joan. Penny Nichols & the Black Imp. 2012. 136p. pap. *(978-1-78139-156-3(4))* Benediction Classics.

—Penny Nichols & the Knob Hill Mystery. 2012. 124p. pap. *(978-1-78139-157-0(2))* Benediction Classics.

—Penny Nichols & the Mystery of the Lost Key. 2012. 124p. pap. *(978-1-78139-155-6(6))* Benediction Classics.

—Penny Nichols Finds a Clue. 2012. 128p. pap. *(978-1-78139-154-9(8))* Benediction Classics.

—Penny Nichols Omnibus - Finds a Clue, Mystery of the Lost Key, Black Imp, & Knob Hill Mystery. 2012. 484p. *(978-1-78139-158-7(0))* Benediction Classics.

Crowley, Ashley. Officer Panda - Fingerprint Detective. Crowley, Ashley, illus. 2015. (Officer Panda Ser.: 1). (ENG., Illus.). 32p. (J). (gr. -1-3). 17.99 *(978-0-06-236626-9(2))* HarperCollins Pubs.

—Officer Panda: Sky Detective. Crowley, Ashley, illus. 2016. (Officer Panda Ser.: 2). (Illus.). 32p. (J). (gr. -1-3). 17.99 *(978-0-06-236627-6(0))* HarperCollins Pubs.

The Detective Business. 2005. (Georgie Giraffe Chapter Ser.). (J). 7.67 *(978-1-932570-45-8(4))* Pioneer Valley Bks.

Dixon, Franklin W. & Walker, Jeff. Typhoon Island, Vol. 180. 2003. (Hardy Boys Ser.: 180). (ENG., Illus.). 160p. (J). (gr. 3-7). pap. 5.99 *(978-0-689-85884-0(1)*, Aladdin) Simon & Schuster Children's Publishing.

Doyle, Arthur Conan. The Hound of the Baskervilles. Harvey, Bob, illus. 2004. (Paperback Classics Ser.). 158p. (J). (gr. 5). lib. bdg. 12.95 *(978-1-58086-605-7(0))* EDC Publishing.

Doyle, Patrick H. T. Edgar Font's Hunt for a House to Haunt: Adventure One: the Castle Tower Lighthouse. 2006. (Illus.). 213p. (J). (gr. -1). per. 6.99 *(978-0-9786132-0-4(1))* Armadillo Bks.

Dunlop, Ed. Sherlock Jones: The Assassination Plot. 2004. 116p. (J). 8.99 *(978-1-59166-315-7(6))* BJU Pr.

Faber, Toni Tuso. The Poodle Tales: Book Six. Rudd, Benton, illus. 2013. 24p. 16.99 *(978-0-9892711-2-7(9))*; pap. 10.99 *(978-0-9892711-3-4(7))* Mindstir Media.

Falkner, Brian. Task Force. 2013. (Recon Team Angel Ser.). (ENG., Illus.). 288p. (YA). (gr. 7). 17.99 *(978-0-449-81299-0(5)*, Random Hse. Bks. for Young Readers) Random Hse. Children's Bks.

Fox, R. J. Stuart & His Incredibly Obnoxious Magical Book: Soccer, 1 vol. 2009. 86p. pap. 19.95 *(978-1-4489-9833-3(6))* America Star Bks.

Friesen, Ray. RQW, Vol. 3. 2003. (YA). 2.95 *(978-0-9728177-2-1(7))* Don't Eat Any Bugs Prodns.

Gaetz, Dayle Campbell. Barkerville Gold, 1 vol. 2004. (ENG.). 192p. (J). (gr. 3-7). pap. 6.95 *(978-1-55143-306-6(0))* Orca Bk. Pubs. USA.

Gegner, Rose G. Detective Rooster Rue. 2014. 32p. pap. 22.54 *(978-1-4828-9517-9(X))* Partridge Pub.

Gerber, Lisa Ann. Elaina's Sleuthing Days, 1 vol. 2009. 60p. pap. 16.95 *(978-1-60749-623-6(2))* PublishAmerica, Inc.

Gray, Kes. Daisy & the Trouble with Burglars. Sharratt, Nick & Parsons, Garry, illus. 2014. (Daisy Ser.: 8). (ENG.). 304p. (J). (gr. 2-4). pap. 11.99 *(978-1-84941-681-8(8)*, Red Fox) Random House Children's Books GBR. Dist: Independent Pubs. Group.

Greenberg, Carmel. Who Stole Pop Pop's Underwear? Jennings, Randy, illus. 2009. (ENG.). 46p. 16.99 *(978-0-615-20924-1(6)*, d1f87490-1e8c-4369-845e-33a85fc9fd96) Kicks and Giggles Today.

Gunderson, Jessica A. How to Keep a Secret for Detectives. 2008. 206p. pap. 15.50 *(978-0-557-01369-2(0))* Lulu Pr., Inc.

Haesche, Richard Paul, Sr. The Mystery of Dismal Swamp. 2007. 402p. (YA). 10.99 *(978-0-9798536-8-5(0))* Kreative X-Pressions Pubns.

—The Treasure of Pirates Cave. 2007. (ENG.). 378p. (YA). 11.99 *(978-0-9798536-7-8(2))* Kreative X-Pressions Pubns.

Hale, Bruce. Farewell, My Lunchbag. unabr. ed. 2004. (Chet Gecko Mystery Ser.: No. 3). 128p. (J). (gr. 3-6). pap. 17.00 incl. audio *(978-0-8072-1708-5(5)*, S FTR 273 SP, Listening Library) Random Hse. Audio Publishing Group.

Hartley, A. J. Steeplejack. 2016. (Steeplejack Ser.: 1). (ENG.). 336p. (YA). 17.99 *(978-0-7653-8342-6(X)*, 9780765383426, Tor Teen) Doherty, Tom Assocs., LLC.

Hillan, Pamela & Dyan, Penelope. The Mystery on Burgundy Street. 2013. 134p. pap. 8.95 *(978-1-61477-086-2(7))* Bellissima Publishing, LLC.

Hupf, Zetta & Hupf, Mitchellx. Detective Buddy & the Case of the Missing Football, 1 vol. Hupf, Zetta, illus. 2009. (Illus.). 23p. pap. 19.95 *(978-1-61582-312-3(3))* PublishAmerica, Inc.

Isaacson, Rick. The Magic Museum. 2013. 34p. pap. 19.95 *(978-0-9844938-4-5(0))* Lexingford Publishing.

Itoh, Shimpei. Hyper Dolls, Vol. 4. 2003. 218p. pap. 15.95 *(978-1-929090-44-0(7))* International Comics & Entertainment L.L.C.

Jennings, Sharon. Franklin the Detective. Gagnon, Celeste et al, illus. 2004. 32p. (J). lib. bdg. 15.38 *(978-1-4242-1171-5(9))* Fitzgerald Bks.

Keene, Carolyn. Mystery at Malachite Mansion. 2011. (Nancy Drew (All New) Girl Detective Ser.: 46). (ENG.). 144p. (J). (gr. 3-7). pap. 5.99 *(978-1-4424-2297-1(1)*, Aladdin) Simon & Schuster Children's Publishing.

—Pit of Vipers. 18th ed. 2006. (Nancy Drew (All New) Girl Detective Ser.: 18). (ENG.). 160p. (J). (gr. 3-7). pap. 5.99 *(978-1-4169-1180-7(4)*, Aladdin) Simon & Schuster Children's Publishing.

—Riverboat Ruse, Vol. 11. 11th ed. 2005. (Nancy Drew (All New) Girl Detective Ser.: 11). (ENG.). 160p. (J). (gr. 3-7). pap. 5.99 *(978-0-689-87335-5(2)*, Aladdin) Simon & Schuster Children's Publishing.

—Seeing Green: Book Three in the Eco Mystery Trilogy. 2010. (Nancy Drew (All New) Girl Detective Ser.: 41). (ENG.). 160p. (J). (gr. 3-7). pap. 6.99 *(978-1-4169-7845-9(3)*, Aladdin) Simon & Schuster Children's Publishing.

—Snowman Surprise. Casale, Paul, illus. Frost, Michael, photos by. 63rd ed. 2004. (Nancy Drew Notebooks Ser.: 63). (ENG.). 80p. (J). (gr. 1-4). pap. 4.99 *(978-0-689-87411-6(1)*, Aladdin) Simon & Schuster Children's Publishing.

—Without a Trace Set: A Race Against Time - False Notes - High Risk. 2004. (Nancy Drew (All New) Girl Detective Ser.). (ENG., Illus.). 640p. (J). (gr. 3-7). pap. 23.99 *(978-0-689-03691-0(4)*, Aladdin) Simon & Schuster Children's Publishing.

Klim, Christopher. Firecracker Jones Is on the Case. 2006. (Illus.). 116p. (J). lib. bdg. 19.95 *(978-1-933435-11-4(9))* Hopewell Pubns., LLC.

Krosoczka, Jarrett J. Platypus Police Squad: Never Say Narwhal. Krosoczka, Jarrett J., illus. 2016. (Platypus Police Squad Ser.: 4). (Illus.). 256p. (J). (gr. 3-7). 12.99 *(978-0-06-207170-5(X)*, Walden Pond Pr.) HarperCollins Pubs.

Kvasnosky, Laura McGee. The Big Picture. Kvasnosky, Laura McGee, illus. 2010. (Zelda & Ivy Ser.). (ENG., Illus.). 48p. (J). (gr. k-4). 14.99 *(978-0-7636-4180-1(4))* Candlewick Pr.

—Zelda & Ivy - The Big Picture. Kvasnosky, Laura McGee, illus. 2013. (Candlewick Sparks Ser.). (ENG., Illus.). 48p. (J). (gr. k-4). pap. 3.99 *(978-0-7636-6637-8(8))* Candlewick Pr.

Ladd, Debbie. Ethan the Ending Eater. Nakasone, Shaun, illus. 2008. 64p. (J). 17.95 *(978-0-9727615-2-9(7))* Deb on Air Bks.

Lance, John & Narvarro. Priscilla Holmes & the Case of the Glass Slipper. 2011. 24p. pap. 14.99 *(978-0-9826594-9-6(0))* 4RV Publishing, LLC.

Landon, Lucinda. Meg Mackintosh & the Stage Fright Secret: A Solve-It-Yourself Mystery. 2004. (Meg Mackintosh Mystery Ser.: 8). (ENG., Illus.). 48p. (J). (gr. 2-4). pap. 6.95 *(978-1-888695-07-6(2))* Secret Passage Pr.

—Meg Mackintosh Solves Seven American History Mysteries: A Solve-It-Yourself Mystery. 2008. (Meg Mackintosh Mystery Ser.: 9). (ENG.). 96p. (J). (gr. 2-4). pap. 8.95 *(978-1-888695-12-0(9))* Secret Passage Pr.

Lash, Batton, et al. The Scrapyard Detectives: Collected Cases. 2007. (Illus.). 102p. (J). (gr. 3-5). per. *(978-0-9797193-0-1(5))* Diversity Foundation, The.

Lement, Wendy. Keri Tarr - Cat Detective. Burrows, Jeffrey Scott, illus. 2004. (ENG.). 80p. (J). pap. 9.95 *(978-1-891369-52-0(0))* Breakaway Bks.

Levinthal, David. Who Pushed Humpty Dumpty? And Other Notorious Nursery Tale Mysteries. Nickle, John, illus. 2012. (ENG.). 40p. (J). (gr. -1-3). 17.99 *(978-0-375-84195-8(4))*; 20.99 *(978-0-375-94595-3(4))* Random Hse. Children's Bks. (Schwartz & Wade Bks.).

Low, A. J. Sherlock Sam & the Ghostly Moans in Fort Canning: Book Two. 2016. (Sherlock Sam Ser.: 2). (ENG.). 120p. (J). pap. 7.99 *(978-1-4494-7788-2(7))* Andrews McMeel Publishing.

—Sherlock Sam & the Missing Heirloom in Katong: Book One. 2016. (Sherlock Sam Ser.: 1). (ENG.). 112p. (J). pap. 7.99 *(978-1-4494-7789-9(5))* Andrews McMeel Publishing.

Marini, Enrico & Dufaux, Jean. Rapaces, Vol. 4. 2005. (SPA., Illus.). 56p. pap. 17.95 *(978-1-59497-107-5(2))* Public Square Bks.

McClintock, Norah. Tru Detective, 1 vol. Hughes, Steven, illus. 2015. (ENG.). 128p. (YA). (gr. 10-12). pap. 19.95 *(978-1-4598-0379-4(5))* Orca Bk. Pubs. USA.

McLaren, Meg. Pigeon P. I. 2017. (ENG., Illus.). 40p. (J). (gr. -1-3). 16.99 ***(978-1-328-71561-6(2)**, Clarion Bks.)* Houghton Mifflin Harcourt Trade & Reference Pubs.

Miller, Michael. Hilde und Günter Level Two Reader, 2 books. 2003. (GER., Illus.). 53p. 6.00 *(978-0-9743522-0-6(9)*, 0-9743522-0-9) Miller, Michael.

Monsell, Mary Elise. Mr Pin: The Chocolate Files. 2007. 68p. (gr. -1-3). per. 8.95 *(978-0-595-47318-2(0)*, Backinprint.com) iUniverse, Inc.

Neal, Terry L. The Find It Club. 2007. 80p. per. 19.95 *(978-1-4241-7490-4(2))* America Star Bks.

Obrist, Jurg. Case Closed?! 40 Mini-Mysteries for You to Solve. 2003. (Single Titles Ser.). 96p. (J). pap. 6.95 *(978-0-7613-1999-3(9))* Lerner Publishing Group.

Obrist, Jürg. Case Closed?! 40 Mini-Mysteries for You to Solve. 2003. (Mini-Mysteries for You to Solve Ser.). (ENG.). 96p. (gr. 4-6). 23.93 *(978-0-7613-2739-4(8)*, Millbrook Pr.) Lerner Publishing Group.

Obrist, Jurg. Complex Cases: Three Major Mysteries for You to Solve. 2006. (Illus.). (J). pap. 6.95 *(978-0-8225-5975-7(7)*, First Avenue Editions) Lerner Publishing Group.

Odgers, Darrel & Odgers, Sally. The Kitnapped Creature. 2008. (Illus.). 76p. (J). pap. *(978-0-545-03338-1(1))* Scholastic, Inc.

Odgers, Sally & Odgers, Darrel. The Buried Biscuits. Dawson, Janine, illus. 2008. (Jack Russell: Dog Detective Ser.: 7). 96p. (J). (gr. 1-6). pap. 4.99 *(978-1-933605-77-7(4))* Kane Miller.

—The Lying Postman. Dawson, Janine, illus. 2007. (Jack Russell: Dog Detective Ser.: 4). 96p. (J). pap. 4.99 *(978-1-933605-31-9(6)*, 05319) Kane Miller.

—The Mugged Pug. Dawson, Janine, illus. 2007. (Jack Russell: Dog Detective Ser.: 3). 96p. (J). pap. 4.99 *(978-1-933605-32-6(4)*, 05326) Kane Miller.

O'Dowd, Chris & Murphy, Nick V. The Fish Detective. 2016. (Moone Boy Ser.). (ENG., Illus.). 336p. (J). 14.99 *(978-1-250-05947-5(X)*, 9781250059475) Feiwel & Friends.

Osborne, William. Hitler's Secret. 2013. (Illus.). 333p. (YA). *(978-0-545-51533-7(5))*; (ENG.). 352p. (J). (gr. 7). 17.99 *(978-0-545-49646-9(2))* Scholastic, Inc. (Chicken Hse., The).

Petit, Karen. The Mystery of the Stolen Stallion. 2007. (Illus.). 246p. (J). per. 14.95 *(978-0-9794420-4-9(4))* Red Letter Pr.

Petrucha, Stefan & Kinney, Sarah. Nancy Drew: High School Musical Mystery II - "The Lost Verse" 2010. (Nancy Drew Graphic Novels: Girl Detective Ser.). (ENG., Illus.). 96p. (J). (gr. 3-7). pap. 8.99 *(978-1-59707-195-6(1)*, 9781597071956) Papercutz.

—Sleight of Dan. 14th ed. 2008. (Nancy Drew Graphic Novels: Girl Detective Ser.: 14). (ENG., Illus.). 112p. (J). (gr. 3-7). pap. 7.95 *(978-1-59707-107-9(2)*, 9781597071079) Papercutz.

—Vampire Slayer. Murase, Sho, illus. 2010. (Nancy Drew the New Case Files Ser.: 2). (ENG.). 64p. (J). (gr. 3-7). 10.99 *(978-1-59707-234-2(6)*, 9781597072342) Papercutz.

Poulsen, David A. The Hunk Machine. 2nd rev. ed. 2007. (Salt & Pepper Chronicles). (ENG.). 160p. (J). (gr. 4-7). 6.95 *(978-1-55263-723-4(9))* Leaf Storm Pr.

Robbins, Trina. The Night of the Living Dogs. Page, Tyler, illus. 2012. (Chicagoland Detective Agency Ser.: 3). (ENG.). 64p. (gr. 4-8). pap. 6.95 *(978-0-7613-5637-0(1)*, Graphic Universe™) Lerner Publishing Group.

Rosellini, Eleanor. Mystery of the Ancient Coins. 2003. (Illus.). 116p. 18.95 *(978-1-57860-122-6(3))* Clerisy Pr.

Rylant, Cynthia. The Case of the Climbing Cat. Karas, G. Brian, illus. 2003. (High-Rise Private Eyes Ser.: No. 2). (J). (gr. -1-3). 25.96 incl. audio *(978-1-59112-190-9(6))*; pap. 29.95 incl. audio *(978-1-59112-191-6(4))* Live Oak Media.

—The Case of the Missing Monkey. Karas, G. Brian, illus. 2003. (High-Rise Private Eyes Ser.: No. 1). (J). 25.95 incl. audio *(978-1-59112-194-7(9))*; pap. 29.95 incl. audio *(978-1-59112-195-4(7))* Live Oak Media.

—The Case of the Missing Monkey. Karas, G. Brian, illus. 2003. (High-Rise Private Eyes Ser.: 1). 46p. (J). (gr. 1-17). 13.55 *(978-0-613-44194-0(X)*, Turtleback) Turtleback Bks.

—The Case of the Puzzling Possum. Karas, G. Brian, illus. 2003. (High-Rise Private Eyes Ser.: No. 3). (J). (gr. -1-3). 25.95 incl. audio *(978-1-59112-198-5(1))*; (gr. k-3). pap. 29.95 incl. audio *(978-1-59112-199-2(X))* Live Oak Media.

Sadar, Albin. Hamster Holmes: A Mystery Comes Knocking. Fabbretti, Valerio, illus. 2015. (Hamster Holmes Ser.: 1). (ENG.). 32p. (J). (gr. k-2). 16.99 *(978-1-4814-2037-2(2)*, Simon Spotlight) Simon Spotlight.

—Hamster Holmes, Combing for Clues. Fabbretti, Valerio, illus. 2015. (Hamster Holmes Ser.: 2). (ENG.). 32p. (J). (gr. k-2). pap. 3.99 *(978-1-4814-2039-6(9)*, Simon Spotlight) Simon Spotlight.

—A Mystery Comes Knocking. Fabbretti, Valerio, illus. 2015. (Hamster Holmes Ser.: 1). (ENG.). 32p. (J). (gr. k-2). pap. 3.99 *(978-1-4814-2036-5(4)*, Simon Spotlight) Simon Spotlight.

Santopolo, Jill. The Nina, the Pinta, & the Vanishing Treasure. 2009. (Alec Flint Mystery Ser.: 1). (ENG.). 192p. (J). (gr. 2-5). pap. 6.99 *(978-0-439-90353-0(X)*, Scholastic Paperbacks) Scholastic, Inc.

Schaedler, Peggy. Dagger & Dash: The Scrimshaw Medallion. 2012. 156p. (gr. 4-6). 30.95 *(978-1-4582-0279-6(8))*; (J). pap. 12.99 *(978-1-4582-0277-2(1))* Author Solutions, Inc. (Abbott Pr.).

Scheunemann, Pam. Cat Tails, 1 vol. Chawla, Neena, illus. 2006. (Animal Tales Ser.). 24p. (J). (gr. k-3). (ENG.). lib. bdg. 24.21 *(978-1-59679-927-1(7)*, SandCastle); pap. 48.42 *(978-1-59679-928-8(5))* ABDO Publishing Co.

Scott, Maisie. Coloured Detectives. 2005. 38p. pap. *(978-1-84401-250-3(6))* Athena Pr.

Simwenyi, Robbinson Namasaka. The Young Detectives. 2012. 84p. pap. 17.95 *(978-1-4512-2168-8(1))* America Star Bks.

Small, VTaylor. Maggie the Shih Tzu Detective: Volume I: Faith. 2009. 54p. pap. 15.99 *(978-1-4500-0453-4(9))* Xlibris Corp.

Snell, Roy J. Triple Spies. 2008. 112p. (gr. -1-7). 22.95 *(978-1-60664-743-1(1))* Rodgers, Alan Bks.

Stilton, Geronimo. The Peculiar Pumpkin Thief. 2010. (Geronimo Stilton Ser.: 42). (ENG.). 128p. (J). (gr. 2-5). 7.99 *(978-0-545-10372-5(X)*, Scholastic Paperbacks) Scholastic, Inc.

—Singing Sensation. 2009. (Geronimo Stilton Ser.: 39). (ENG.). 128p. (J). (gr. 2-5). pap. 7.99 *(978-0-545-10368-8(1)*, Scholastic Paperbacks) Scholastic, Inc.

Styles, Walker. The Soccer Ball Monster Mystery. Whitehouse, Ben, illus. 2016. (Rider Woofson Ser.: 6). (ENG.). 128p. (J). (gr. k-4). pap. 5.99 *(978-1-4814-7110-7(4)*, Little Simon) Little Simon.

—Undercover in the Bow-Wow Club. Whitehouse, Ben, illus. 2016. (Rider Woofson Ser.: 3). (ENG.). 128p. (J). (gr. k-4). pap. 5.99 *(978-1-4814-6303-4(9)*, Little Simon) Little Simon.

Sutton, Margaret. The Black Cat's Clue, No. 23. Doane, Pelagie, illus. 2008. (Judy Bolton Mysteries Ser.). (ENG.). 224p. (J). (gr. 4-7). pap. 14.95 *(978-1-4290-9043-8(X))* Applewood Bks.

—The Clue in the Ruined Castle, No. 26. Doane, Pelagie, illus. 2008. (Judy Bolton Mysteries Ser.). (ENG.). 192p. (J). (gr. 4-7). pap. 14.95 *(978-1-4290-9046-9(4))* Applewood Bks.

—The Clue of the Stone Lantern, No. 21. Doane, Pelagie, illus. 2008. (Judy Bolton Mysteries Ser.). (ENG.). 224p. (J). (gr. 4-7). pap. 14.95 *(978-1-4290-9041-4(3))* Applewood Bks.

—The Haunted Attic, No. 2. Doane, Pelagie, illus. 2008. (Judy Bolton Mysteries Ser.). (ENG.). 240p. (J). (gr. 4-7). pap. 14.95 *(978-1-4290-9022-3(7))* Applewood Bks.

—The Haunted Fountain: A Judy Bolton Mystery. 2011. 192p. 42.95 *(978-1-258-10127-5(0))* Literary Licensing, LLC.

—The Hidden Clue, No. 35. Doane, Pelagie, illus. 2008. (Judy Bolton Mysteries Ser.). (ENG.). 184p. (J). (gr. 4-7). pap. 14.95 *(978-1-4290-9055-1(3))* Applewood Bks.

—The Invisible Chimes, No. 3. Doane, Pelagie, illus. 2008. (Judy Bolton Mysteries Ser.). (ENG.). 236p. (J). (gr. 4-7). pap. 14.95 *(978-1-4290-9023-0(5))* Applewood Bks.

—The Midnight Visitor, No. 12. 2008. (Judy Bolton Mysteries Ser.). (ENG.). 264p. (J). (gr. 4-7). pap. 14.95 *(978-1-4290-9032-2(4))* Applewood Bks.

—The Mystic Ball, No. 7. Doane, Pelagie, illus. 2008. (Judy Bolton Mysteries Ser.). (ENG.). 236p. (J). (gr. 4-7). pap. 14.95 *(978-1-4290-9027-8(8))* Applewood Bks.

—The Riddle of the Double Ring, No. 10. Doane, Pelagie, illus. 2008. (Judy Bolton Mysteries Ser.). (ENG.). 236p. (J). (gr. 4-7). pap. 14.95 *(978-1-4290-9030-8(8))* Applewood Bks.

—Seven Strange Clues, No. 4. Doane, Pelagie, illus. Sutton, Margaret, photos by. 2008. (Judy Bolton Mysteries Ser.). (ENG.). 236p. (J). (gr. 4-7). pap. 14.95 *(978-1-4290-9024-7(3))* Applewood Bks.

—The Trail of the Green Doll, No. 27. Doane, Pelagie, illus. 2008. (Judy Bolton Mysteries Ser.). (ENG.). 196p. (J). (gr. 4-7). pap. 14.95 *(978-1-4290-9047-6(2))* Applewood Bks.

Sylvester, Merrill. Ho-Ho Where Did All My Reindeer Go? The Chicken Leg Detective Service. 2011. 72p. pap. 19.95 *(978-1-4626-0794-5(2))* America Star Bks.

Tenbeth, Kate. Burty & Grum & the Birthday Surprise. Jones, Rob, illus. 2012. 108p. pap. *(978-0-9572119-9-5(6))* Magic Toy Bks.

Trembath, Don. Emville Confidential, 1 vol. 2007. (ENG.). 198p. (J). (gr. 4-8). per. 7.95 *(978-1-55143-671-5(X))* Orca Bk. Pubs. USA.

Wallace, Karen. Detective Derek. Blake, Beccy, illus. 2009. (Go! Readers Ser.). 48p. (J). (gr. 2-5). pap. 12.85 *(978-1-60754-276-6(5))*; lib. bdg. 29.25 *(978-1-60754-275-9(7))* Windmill Bks.

Wells, Helen. The Silver Ring Mystery: The Vicki Barr Flight Stewardess Series. 2011. 190p. 42.95 *(978-1-258-10005-6(3))* Literary Licensing, LLC.

Whybrow, Ian. Little Wolf, Forest Detective. Ross, Tony, illus. 2005. (Middle Grade Fiction Ser.). 112p. (J). (gr. 3-6). 14.95 *(978-1-57505-413-1(2))* Lerner Publishing Group.

Widmark, Martin. The Diamond Mystery, No. 1. Willis, Helena, illus. 2014. (Whodunit Detective Agency Ser.: 1). (ENG.). 80p. (J). (gr. 2-4). 5.99 *(978-0-448-48066-4(2)*, Grosset & Dunlap) Penguin Young Readers Group.

Wirt, Mildred A. Guilt of the Brass Thieves. 2011. 178p. pap. 9.99 *(978-1-935774-80-8(8))*, Resurrected Pr.) Intrepid Ink, LLC.

—Saboteurs on the River. 2011. 174p. pap. 12.99 *(978-1-935774-86-0(7)*, Resurrected Pr.) Intrepid Ink, LLC.

—Signal in the Dark. 2011. 170p. pap. 9.99 *(978-1-935774-82-2(4)*, Resurrected Pr.) Intrepid Ink, LLC.

—Voice from the Cave. 2011. 168p. pap. 9.99 *(978-1-935774-81-5(6)*, Resurrected Pr.) Intrepid Ink, LLC.

Wright, Elsie. Patty & Jo, Detectives. 2005. reprint ed. pap. 24.95 *(978-1-4179-9752-7(4))* Kessinger Publishing, LLC.

Yasuda, Anita. Dino Detectives. Harpster, Steve, illus. 2013. (Dino Detectives Ser.). (ENG.). 32p. (gr. 1-3). pap. 47.60 *(978-1-4342-6221-9(9))*; pap. 23.80 *(978-1-4342-6220-2(0))* Stone Arch Bks.

—Dino Detectives. Cameron, Craig, illus. 2013. (Dino Detectives Ser.). (ENG.). 32p. (gr. 1-3). lib. bdg. 90.60 *(978-1-4342-6058-1(5))* Stone Arch Bks.

—Dino Detectives. Harpster, Steve, illus. 2013. (Dino Detectives Ser.). (ENG.). 32p. (gr. 1-3). lib. bdg. 181.20 *(978-1-4342-6059-8(3))* Stone Arch Bks.

DETROIT (MICH.)

Knudsen, Anders. Antoine de la Mothe Cadillac: French Settlements at Detroit & Louisiana. 2006. (In the Footsteps of Explorers Ser.). (ENG., Illus.). 32p. (J). (gr. 3-9). lib. bdg. *(978-0-7787-2429-2(8))*; (gr. 4-7). pap. *(978-0-7787-2465-0(4))* Crabtree Publishing Co.

Robinson, Julia Marie. Race, Religion, & the Pulpit: Rev. Robert L. Bradby & the Making of Urban Detroit. 2015. (Great Lakes Books Ser.). (ENG., Illus.). 216p. 39.99 *(978-0-8143-3291-7(9)*, 3073) Wayne State Univ. Pr.

Shapiro, J. H. Magic Trash. Brantley-Newton, Vanessa, illus. 2015. (ENG.). 32p. (J). (gr. k-3). pap. 7.95 *(978-1-58089-386-2(4))* Charlesbridge Publishing, Inc.

DETROIT (MICH.)—FICTION

Clement, Ben & LoPatin, Norman. Stone's Throw Away. 2011. (Illus.). 74p. pap. 21.50 *(978-1-60976-477-7(3)*, Eloquent Bks.) Strategic Book Publishing & Rights Agency (SBPRA).

Elster, Jean Alicia. The Colored Car. 2013. (Great Lakes Books Ser.). (ENG.). 224p. (YA). pap. 14.99 *(978-0-8143-3606-9(X)*, 2988) Wayne State Univ. Pr.

Kelly, David A. The Tiger Troubles. Meyers, Mark, illus. 2015. (Ballpark Mysteries Ser.: 11). (ENG.). 112p. (J). (gr. 1-4). pap. 4.99 *(978-0-385-37878-9(5)*, Random Hse. Bks. for Young Readers) Random Hse. Children's Bks.

Lupica, Mike. The Batboy. 2011. (ENG.). 272p. (J). (gr. 5-18). 7.99 *(978-0-14-241782-9(3)*, Puffin Books) Penguin Young Readers Group.

—The Batboy. 2011. lib. bdg. 18.40 *(978-0-606-15352-2(7)*, Turtleback) Turtleback Bks.

Marsh, Carole. The Mystery at Motown. Friedlander, Randolyn, illus. 2011. (Carole Marsh Mysteries Ser.). 32p. pap. 7.99 *(978-0-635-07962-6(3)*, Marsh, Carole Mysteries) Gallopade International.

McClintock, Norah. From the Dead, 1 vol. 2014. (Seven Sequels Ser.). (ENG., Illus.). 288p. (J). (gr. 5-10). pap. 10.95 *(978-1-4598-0537-8(2))* Orca Bk. Pubs. USA.

Polacco, Patricia. Christmas Tapestry. 2008. (ENG.). 48p. (J). (gr. 1-4). pap. 7.99 *(978-0-14-241165-0(5)*, Puffin Books) Penguin Young Readers Group.

Portis, Nathanial. Things in Between. 2008. (ENG.). 208p. (YA). per. 9.99 *(978-0-9760372-0-0(3))* Quick Quest Pubns. LLC.

Scott, Victoria. Titans. 2016. (ENG.). 320p. (J). (gr. 7). 17.99 *(978-0-545-80601-5(1)*, Scholastic Pr.) Scholastic, Inc.

Sitomer, Alan Lawrence. Caged Warrior. 2014. (ENG., Illus.). 224p. (YA). (gr. 7-12). 16.99 *(978-1-4231-7124-9(1))* Disney Pr.

—Caged Warrior. 2015. (Caged Warrior Ser.). (ENG., Illus.). 240p. (YA). (gr. 7-12). pap. 8.99 *(978-1-4847-2280-0(9))* Hyperion Bks. for Children.

Slater, Calvin. Game On. 2015. 332p. (YA). *(978-1-4806-9396-8(0))* Kensington Publishing Corp.

—Hold Me Down. 2015. (Coleman High Ser.: 2). (ENG., Illus.). 328p. (J). (gr. 9). pap. 9.95 *(978-1-61773-134-1(X)*, Dafina) Kensington Publishing Corp.

Winston, Sherri. President of the Whole Sixth Grade. 2015. (ENG.). 320p. (J). (gr. 3-7). 17.00 *(978-0-316-37723-2(6))* Little Brown & Co.
—President of the Whole Sixth Grade. 2016. (President Ser.: 2). (ENG.). 336p. (J). (gr. 3-7). pap. 7.99 *(978-0-316-37724-9(4))* Little, Brown Bks. for Young Readers.

DETROIT LIONS (FOOTBALL TEAM)

Bodden, Valerie. The Big Time - Calvin Johson. 2014. (Big Time Ser.). (ENG., Illus.). 24p. (J). (gr. 1-3). pap. 9.99 *(978-1-62832-076-3(1)*, Creative Paperbacks) Creative Co., The.
Burgess, Zack. Meet the Detroit Lions. 2016. (Big Picture Sports Ser.). (ENG., Illus.). 24p. (J). (gr. k-3). lib. bdg. 22.60 *(978-1-59953-739-9(7))* Norwood Hse. Pr.
Frisch, Aaron. The History of the Detroit Lions. 2004. (NFL Today Ser.). (Illus.). 32p. (YA). (gr. 5-9). 18.95 *(978-1-58341-296-1(4))* Creative Co., The.
Frisch, Nate. NFL Today: Detroit Lions. 2013. (NFL Today Ser.). (ENG., Illus.). 48p. (J). (gr. 4-7). pap. 12.00 *(978-0-89812-855-0(2)*, Creative Paperbacks) Creative Co., The.
—The Story of the Detroit Lions. 2013. (Illus.). 48p. (J). 35.65 *(978-1-60818-302-9(5)*, Creative Education) Creative Co., The.
Hasday, Judy L. & Crompton, Samuel Willard. Barry Sanders. 2008. (Football Superstars Ser.). (Illus.). 120p. (J). (gr. 7-12). 30.00 *(978-0-7910-9667-3(X))* Facts On File, Inc.
Howell, Brian. Detroit Lions. 2015. (Insider's Guide to Pro Football Ser.). (ENG.). 32p. (J). (gr. k-3). 28.50 *(978-1-63407-008-9(9)*, 208843) Child's World, Inc., The.
LeBoutillier, Nate. The Story of the Detroit Lions. 2009. (NFL Today Ser.). 48p. (YA). (gr. 5-9). 22.95 *(978-1-58341-755-3(9))* Creative Co., The.
Morey, Allan. The Detroit Lions Story. 2016. (NFL Teams Ser.). (ENG., Illus.). 32p. (J). (gr. 3-7). lib. bdg. 26.95 *(978-1-62617-365-1(6)*, Torque Bks.) Bellwether Media.
Petersen, Justin. Detroit Lions. 2014. (Inside the NFL Ser.). (ENG., Illus.). 32p. (J). (gr. 4-7). lib. bdg. 28.55 *(978-1-4896-0822-2(2)*, AV2 by Weigl) Weigl Pubs., Inc.
Peterson, Justin. Detroit Lions. 2015. (Illus.). 32p. pap. *(978-1-4896-0823-9(0))* Weigl Pubs., Inc.
Savage, Jeff. Calvin Johnson. 2012. (Amazing Athletes Ser.). (ENG., Illus.). 32p. (gr. 2-5). pap. 7.95 *(978-1-4677-0285-0(4))*; lib. bdg. 25.26 *(978-1-4677-0278-2(1)*, Lerner Pubns.) Lerner Publishing Group.
Stewart, Mark. The Detroit Lions. rev. ed. 2012. (Team Spirit Ser.). (ENG.). 48p. (J). (gr. 3-6). lib. bdg. 29.27 *(978-1-59953-522-7(X))* Norwood Hse. Pr.
Tustison, Matt. Detroit Lions, 1 vol. 2010. (Inside the NFL Ser.). (ENG.). 48p. (YA). (gr. 3-6). lib. bdg. 32.79 *(978-1-61714-011-2(2))* ABDO Publishing Co.
Willis, Chris. Dutch Clark: The Life of an NFL Legend & the Birth of the Detroit Lions. 2012. (ENG., Illus.). 422p. 72.00 *(978-0-8108-8520-2(4))* Scarecrow Pr., Inc.

DETROIT TIGERS (BASEBALL TEAM)

Connery-Boyd, Peg. Detroit Tigers. 2016. (Hawk's Nest Activity Bks.: 0). (ENG.). 64p. (J). (gr. k-3). pap., act. bk. ed. 8.99 *(978-1-4926-3564-2(2))* Sourcebooks, Inc.
Gerstner, Joanne. Detroit Tigers, 1 vol. (Inside MLB Ser.). (ENG., 48p. (gr. 3-6). 2011. Illus.). (YA). lib. bdg. 32.79 *(978-1-61714-043-3(0))* 2014. lib. bdg. 32.79 *(978-1-62403-469-5(1)*, SportsZone) ABDO Publishing Co.
Gilbert, Sara. The Story of the Detroit Tigers. 2007. (Baseball, the Great American Game Ser.). (Illus.). 48p. (YA). (gr. 4-7). lib. bdg. 32.80 *(978-1-58341-487-3(8))* Creative Co., The.
LeBoutillier, Nate. The Story of the Detroit Tigers. 2011. (J). 35.65 *(978-1-60818-040-0(9)*, Creative Education) Creative Co., The.
Publications International Ltd. Staff. Yesterday & Today Detroit Tigers. 2009. 144p. 24.95 *(978-1-4127-7515-1(9))* Publications International, Ltd.
Stewart, Mark. The Detroit Tigers. 2012. (Team Spirit Ser.). 48p. (J). (gr. 3-6). lib. bdg. 29.27 *(978-1-59953-481-7(9))* Norwood Hse. Pr.

DEVELOPING COUNTRIES

DeCarlo, Jacqueline. Fair Trade & How It Works. 2011. (Contemporary Issues Ser.). (Illus.). 166 ndash; 308p. (YA). (gr. 9-12). 37.95 *(978-1-4488-1865-5(6))* Rosen Publishing Group, Inc., The.
Entwicklungslaender. (Duden Abiturhilfen Ser.). (GER.). (YA). (gr. 12-13). *(978-3-411-70752-2(6))* Bibliographisches Institut & F. A. Brockhaus AG DEU. Dist: International Bk. Import Service, Inc.
McCarney, Rosemary. Because I Am a Girl: I Can Change the World, 1 vol. 2014. (ENG., Illus.). 72p. (J). (gr. 6-8). pap. 16.95 *(978-1-927583-44-9(6))* Second Story Pr. CAN. Dist: Orca Bk. Pubs. USA.
—The Way to School, 1 vol. 2015. (ENG., Illus.). 32p. (J). (gr. 1-4). 18.95 *(978-1-927583-78-4(0))* Second Story Pr. CAN. Dist: Orca Bk. Pubs. USA.
Pruessen, Linda. Saving Eyesight: Adventures of Seva Around the World. 2015. (ENG., Illus.). 64p. (J). (gr. 4-8). 19.95 *(978-1-77085-616-5(1)*, 9781770856165); pap. 9.95 *(978-1-77085-615-8(3)*, 9781770856158) Firefly Bks., Ltd.
Suen, Anastasia. Doctors Without Borders. 2009. (Helping Organizations Ser.). 24p. (gr. 2-2). 42.50 *(978-1-61513-258-4(9)*, PowerKids Pr.) Rosen Publishing Group, Inc., The.
Tate, Nikki. Down to Earth: How Kids Help Feed the World, 1 vol. (Orca Footprints Ser.). (ENG., Illus.). 48p. (J). (gr. 3-7). 2017. pap. 12.95 *(978-1-4598-1412-7(6))* 2013. 19.95 *(978-1-4598-0423-4(6))* Orca Bk. Pubs. USA.
Torr, James D. Civil Rights. 2004. (Current Controversies Ser.). (ENG.). 200p. (YA). (gr. 7-12). pap. 27.50 *(978-0-7377-1177-6(9)*, Greenhaven Pr., Inc.) Cengage Gale.

DEVELOPMENT

see Embryology; Evolution; Growth

DEVELOPMENTAL READING

Seeger, Laura Vaccaro. First the Egg. 2011. (J). (gr. -1-1). 29.95 *(978-0-545-13454-5(4))* Weston Woods Studios, Inc.

DEVIL

Bible Visuals International Staff, compiled by. Satan & His Demons Vol. 08: New Testament. 2006. (Illus.). (J). pap. *(978-1-932381-38-2(4)*, 1008) Bible Visuals International, Inc.
Greiner, Ruth. Satan, the Enemy of God Vol. 2: New Testament Volume 2: Life of Christ Part 2. Neal, Sharon et al, eds. 2008. (ENG., Illus.). 36p. (J). pap. *(978-1-932381-22-1(8)*, 1002) Bible Visuals International, Inc.
Pallotta, Jerry. Wolverine vs. Tasmanian Devil. Bolster, Rob, illus. 2009. 32p. (J). pap. *(978-0-545-45189-5(2))* Scholastic, Inc.
Portman, Michael. Tasmanian Devils in Danger. 2011. (Animals at Risk Ser.). (Illus.). 24p. (J). (gr. 2-5). 22.60 *(978-1-4339-5806-9(6))*; pap. 8.15 *(978-1-4339-5808-3(2))* Stevens, Gareth Publishing LLLP. (Gareth Stevens Learning Library).
Robson, David. The Devil. 2007. (Mysterious Encounters Ser.). (ENG., Illus.). 48p. (J). (gr. 3-7). lib. bdg. 29.00 *(978-0-7377-3780-6(8)*, Kidhaven) Cengage Gale.
Turner, Tracey. Who's Who of Horrors: An A to Z of Loathsome Lives. 2005. (ENG., Illus.). 144p. (J). (gr. -1-12). pap. 8.99 *(978-0-340-90294-3(9))* Hodder & Stoughton GBR. Dist: Hachette Bk. Group.

DEVIL—FICTION

Aryal, Aimee. Hello Blue Devil! Cooper, Blair, illus. 2004. 22p. (J). 19.95 *(978-1-932888-26-3(8))* Mascot Bks., Inc.
Babbitt, Natalie. The Devil's Storybooks: 20 Delightfully Wicked Stories. Babbitt, Natalie, illus. 2012. (ENG., Illus.). 224p. (J). (gr. 3-7). pap. 15.99 *(978-0-312-64158-0(3)*, 9780312641580) Square Fish.
Connolly, John. The Gates. 2011. (Samuel Lord Ser.: 1). (ENG.). 320p. (J). (gr. 5-9). pap. 8.99 *(978-1-4424-2933-8(X)*, Simon & Schuster Bks. For Young Readers) Simon & Schuster Bks. For Young Readers.
Damico, Gina. Hellhole. (ENG.). (YA). (gr. 9). 2016. 384p. pap. 9.99 *(978-0-544-54117-7(0))* 2015. 368p. 17.99 *(978-0-544-30710-0(0))* Houghton Mifflin Harcourt Publishing Co. (HMH Books For Young Readers).
De Palma, Toni. The Devil's Triangle. 2013. 216p. pap. 14.99 *(978-1-939173-03-4(5))* Crescent Moon Pr.
Delaney, Joseph. Attack of the Fiend. Arrasmith, Patrick, illus. 2009. (Last Apprentice Ser.: 4). (ENG.). 576p. (YA). (gr. 8-18). pap. 9.99 *(978-0-06-089129-9(7)*, Greenwillow Bks.) HarperCollins Pubs.
—Fury of the Seventh Son, Bk. 13. Arrasmith, Patrick, illus. 2014. (Last Apprentice Ser.: 13). (ENG.). 480p. (YA). (gr. 8). 17.99 *(978-0-06-219231-8(0)*, Greenwillow Bks.) HarperCollins Pubs.
Dudek, V. A. Soldiers of Fate. 2009. 94p. pap. 15.99 *(978-1-4415-2702-8(8))* Xlibris Corp.
Falcone, L. M. & Wahl, Charis. The Devil, the Banshee & Me. 2006. (ENG.). 192p. (J). (gr. 4-7). 6.95 *(978-1-55337-895-2(4))* Kids Can Pr., Ltd. CAN. Dist: Hachette Bk. Group.
Gill, David Macinnis. Soul Enchilada. (ENG.). (YA). (gr. 9). 2010. 384p. pap. 8.99 *(978-0-06-167303-0(X))* 2009. 368p. 16.99 *(978-0-06-167301-6(3))* HarperCollins Pubs. (Greenwillow Bks.).
Goodman-Schneps, Oriana. The Seventh Chime. 2009. 52p. pap. 15.99 *(978-1-4415-2748-6(6))* Xlibris Corp.
Green, Jack. Dusty the Dust Devil. 2011. 70p. pap. 19.95 *(978-1-4560-8507-0(7))* America Star Bks.
Hazell, Carolyn. Pav the Plumber Saves the Day. 2011. 84p. (gr. 4-6). pap. 11.76 *(978-1-4567-8148-4(0))* AuthorHouse.
Jenkins, A. M. Repossessed. 2008. (ENG.). 240p. (YA). (gr. 8). pap. 9.99 *(978-0-06-083570-5(2)*, HarperTeen) HarperCollins Pubs.
Jubert, Herve. Devil's Tango. Bell, Anthea, tr. from FRE. 2006. (Devil's Dances Ser.). 376p. (YA). (gr. 7-12). lib. bdg. 17.89 *(978-0-06-077721-0(4))* HarperCollins Pubs.
Khulekani, Magubane. Angels Salvation. 2007. 96p. pap. *(978-1-86900-865-9(0))* UmSinsi Pr. ZAF. Dist: Michigan State Univ. Pr.
Lavelle, Mary T. The Watcher. 2012. (Illus.). 44p. pap. 24.40 *(978-1-4772-5064-8(6))* AuthorHouse.
Lethcoe, Jason. Der Geheimnisvolle Mr. Spines - Wings. Altmann, Scott, illus. 2009. (Mysterious Mr. Spines Ser.: 1). (ENG.). 256p. (J). (gr. 5-18). pap. 7.99 *(978-0-448-44653-0(7)*, Grosset & Dunlap) Penguin Young Readers Group.
Mori, Kotaro. Stray Little Devil. (Stray Little Devil Ser.). (ENG., Illus.). (YA). Vol. 1. 2006. 200p. pap. 9.95 *(978-1-59796-043-4(8))* Vol. 2. 2006. 200p. pap. 9.95 *(978-1-59796-044-1(6))* Vol. 3. 2006. 200p. pap. 9.95 *(978-1-59796-045-8(4))* Vol. 4. 2007. 208p. pap. 9.95 *(978-1-59796-046-5(2))* DrMaster Pubns. Inc.
Murphy, Shirley Rousseau & Murphy, Pat J. The Cat, the Devil, the Last Escape: A Novel. 2015. (ENG., Illus.). 320p. 24.99 *(978-0-06-226910-2(0)*, Morrow, William & Co.) HarperCollins Pubs.
Napoli, Donna Jo. The Wager. 2010. (ENG.). 272p. (YA). (gr. 7-12). 16.99 *(978-0-8050-8781-9(8)*, 9780805087819, Holt, Henry & Co. Bks. For Young Readers) Holt, Henry & Co.
Nicolle, Ethan. Kill the Devil. 2008. (ENG., Illus.). 120p. (YA). pap. 10.95 *(978-1-59362-099-8(3)*, 9781593620998) Slave Labor Bks.
Pabbaraju, S. Adventures of Andreux: Book One - Aranya. 2008. 176p. 23.95 *(978-1-4401-0075-8(6))* iUniverse, Inc.
Petroff, Shani. Careful What You Wish For. McKenney, J. David, illus. 2010. (Bedeviled Ser.: 3). (ENG.). 240p. (J). (gr. 3-7). pap. 6.99 *(978-0-448-45113-8(1)*, Grosset & Dunlap) Penguin Young Readers Group.
—Daddy's Little Angel, No. 1. McKenney, J. David, illus. 2009. (Bedeviled Ser.: 1). (ENG.). 240p. (J). (gr. 5-7). pap. 7.99 *(978-0-448-45111-4(5)*, Grosset & Dunlap) Penguin Young Readers Group.
—The Good, the Bad, & the Ugly Dress. McKenney, J. David, illus. 2010. (Bedeviled Ser.: 2). (ENG.). 240p. (J). (gr. 5-7). pap. 6.99 *(978-0-448-45112-1(3)*, Grosset & Dunlap) Penguin Young Readers Group.
Portal, Alex. The Applegates, 1 vol. 2009. 32p. pap. 24.95 *(978-1-60749-727-1(1))* America Star Bks.
Poteat, Bruce S. Evil Deception. 2013. 192p. (gr. 10-12). 30.95 *(978-1-4497-9565-8(X))*; pap. 13.95 *(978-1-4497-9570-2(6))* Author Solutions, Inc. (WestBow Pr.).
Rousseau, Paul. Lucifer, Mon Grand-Pere: Tome 2. Guenette, Genevieve, illus. 2004. (Mon Roman Ser.). (FRE.). 184p. (J). (gr. 2). pap. *(978-2-89021-703-4(5))* Diffusion du livre Mirabel (DLM).
Sauls, Debra A. Angel Quest. 2008. 84p. pap. 19.95 *(978-1-60703-890-0(0))* America Star Bks.
Simon, Francesca. Pablo Diablo y el Dinero. 2005. (Pablo Diablo Ser.). (SPA., Illus.). 96p. (J). (gr. 2-3). 8.95 *(978-84-348-9124-1(7))* SM Ediciones ESP. Dist: Iaconi, Mariuccia Bk. Imports.
—Pablo Diablo Y la Bomba Fetida. 2005. (Pablo Diablo Ser.).Tr. of Horrid Harry & the Stink Bomb. (SPA., Illus.). (J). (gr. 2-3). pap. 8.95 *(978-84-348-9683-3(4))* SM Ediciones ESP. Dist: Iaconi, Mariuccia Bk. Imports.
—Pablo Diablo Y la Cangura Fantasma. 2005. (Pablo Diablo Ser.).Tr. of Horrid Harry & the Kangaroo Ghost. (SPA., Illus.). (J). (gr. 2-3). pap. 8.95 *(978-84-348-9684-0(2))* SM Ediciones ESP. Dist: Iaconi, Mariuccia Bk. Imports.
—Pablo Diablo y la Maldicion de la Momia. 2005. (Pablo Diablo Ser.). (SPA., Illus.). 94p. (J). (gr. 2-3). 8.95 *(978-84-348-9072-5(0))* SM Ediciones ESP. Dist: Iaconi, Mariuccia Bk. Imports.
—Pablo Diablo Y Los Piojos. 2005. (Pablo Diablo Ser.).Tr. of Horrid Harry & the Lice. (SPA., Illus.). (J). (gr. 2-3). pap. 8.95 *(978-84-348-8673-5(1))* SM Ediciones ESP. Dist: Iaconi, Mariuccia Bk. Imports.
—La Venganza de Pablo Diablo. 2005. (Pablo Diablo Ser.). (SPA., Illus.). 94p. (J). (gr. 2-3). 8.95 *(978-84-348-9017-6(8))* SM Ediciones ESP. Dist: Iaconi, Mariuccia Bk. Imports.
Stine, R. L. Slappy New Year! 2010. (Goosebumps Horrorland Ser.: 18). (ENG.). 160p. (J). (gr. 3-7). pap. 6.99 *(978-0-545-16199-2(1)*, Scholastic Paperbacks) Scholastic, Inc.
Vail, Rachel. Gorgeous. (Avery Sisters Trilogy Ser.: 2). (ENG.). (YA). (gr. 8). 2010. 304p. pap. 9.99 *(978-0-06-089048-3(7))* 2009. 288p. 16.99 *(978-0-06-089046-9(0))* HarperCollins Pubs.
Von Chamisso, Adelbert. Peter Schlemihl. Bowring, John, tr. 2011. 98p. pap. 8.95 *(978-1-60664-434-8(3))* Rodgers, Alan Bks.
Wilde, Gloria. Lucifer: Good Angel Gone Bad. Bauer, John, illus. 2007. 36p. 14.95 *(978-1-57258-462-4(9)*, 945-6323) TEACH Services, Inc.
Wood, Nathaniel. Play Me Backwards. 2014. (ENG., Illus.). 288p. (YA). (gr. 9). 18.99 *(978-1-4814-0102-9(5)*, Simon & Schuster Bks. For Young Readers) Simon & Schuster Bks. For Young Readers.

DE VIL, CRUELLA (FICTITIOUS CHARACTER)—FICTION

Disney Read-Along. 101 Dalmatians (Live Action) 2008. (Read-Along Ser.). (ENG.). (J). pap. *(978-0-7634-0102-3(1))* Walt Disney Records.
Disney Staff. 101 Dalmatians. (FRE.). 96p. (J). (gr. k-5). pap. 9.95 *(978-0-7859-8847-2(5))* French & European Pubns., Inc.
Smith, Dodie. 101 Dalmatians. 2004. (Illus.). 192p. (J). (gr. 3-5). pap. 36.00 incl. audio *(978-0-8072-0791-8(8)*, LYA 345 SP, Listening Library) Random Hse. Audio Publishing Group.

DEVON (ENGLAND: COUNTY)—FICTION

Greenham, Caz. The Adventures of Eric Seagull. Homfray, Nick, illus. 2013. 40p. pap. *(978-1-78132-093-8(4))* SilverWood Bks.
Landman, Tanya. Hell & High Water. 2017. (ENG.). 320p. (J). (gr. 7). 17.99 *(978-0-7636-8875-2(4))* Candlewick Pr.

DEVOTION

see Worship

DEVOTIONAL CALENDARS

AIO Team. 90 Devotions for Kids. 2012. (Adventures in Odyssey Bks.). (ENG.). 256p. (J). pap. 14.99 *(978-1-58997-682-5(7))* Tyndale Hse. Pubs.
B&H Editorial Staff, ed. The Big Picture Interactive 52-Week Bible Story Devotional: Connecting Christ Throughout God's Story. McPherson, Heath, illus. 2016. (Big Picture Interactive / the Gospel Project Ser.). (ENG.). 224p. (J). (gr. 1-5). 16.99 *(978-1-4336-8644-3(9)*, B&H Kids) B&H Publishing Group.
B&H Kids Editorial Staff. Devotions below the Surface: 52 Weeks Submerged in God's Love. 2016. (ENG.). 224p. (J). (gr. k-5). 12.99 *(978-1-4336-9054-9(3)*, B&H Kids) B&H Publishing Group.
—Devotions off the Map: A 52-Week Devotional Journey. 2015. (ENG.). 224p. (J). (gr. 1-5). 12.99 *(978-1-4336-8728-0(3)*, B&H Kids) B&H Publishing Group.
—Knowing Jesus (Blue Cover) The Essential Teen 365 Devotional. 2016. (ENG., Illus.). 368p. (J). (gr. 7-12). 14.99 *(978-1-4336-4407-8(X)*, B&H Kids) B&H Publishing Group.
—Knowing Jesus (Rose Cover) The Essential Teen 365 Devotional. 2016. (ENG., Illus.). 368p. (J). (gr. 7-12). 14.99 *(978-1-4336-4406-1(1)*, B&H Kids) B&H Publishing Group.
B&H Kids Editorial Staff, ed. What It Means to Be a Christian: 100 Devotions for Boys. 2015. (ENG.). 208p. (J). (gr. 3-7). pap. 9.99 *(978-1-4336-8568-2(X)*, B&H Kids) B&H Publishing Group.
—What It Means to Be a Christian: 100 Devotions for Girls. 2015. (ENG.). 208p. (J). (gr. 3-7). pap. 9.99 *(978-1-4336-8569-9(8)*, B&H Kids) B&H Publishing Group.
Bostrom, Kathleen Long. What about Heaven? Kucharik, Elena, illus. 2012. (Little Blessings Ser.). (ENG.). 32p. (J). pap. 3.99 *(978-1-4143-7510-6(7))* Tyndale Hse. Pubs.
Bowman, Crystal. My Grandma & Me: Rhyming Devotions for You & Your Grandchild. Kirkland, Katherine, illus. 2012. (ENG.). 68p. (J). 14.99 *(978-1-4143-7170-2(5)*, Tyndale Kids) Tyndale Hse. Pubs.
Bowman, Crystal & McKinley, Teri. Our Daily Bread for Kids. (Our Daily Bread for Kids Ser.). (ENG.). 384p. 2016. (gr. -1-3). pap. 11.99 *(978-1-62707-656-2(5))* 2014. 16.99 *(978-1-62707-332-5(9))* Discovery Hse. Pubs.
Byrd, Sandra. The One Year Be-Tween You & God: Devotions for Girls. 2012. (ENG.). 384p. (J). lthr. 16.99 *(978-1-4143-6245-8(5))* Tyndale Hse. Pubs.
Canwell, Nancy. He's Got Your Back: A Daily Devotional for Juniors. 2014. (J). *(978-0-8280-2804-2(4))* Review & Herald Publishing Assn.
Chambers, Oswald. Jesus Wants All of Me: Based on the Classic Devotional My Utmost for His Highest. Smouse, Phil A., illus. ltd. ed. 2003. 384p. (J). pap. 4.99 *(978-1-58660-841-5(X))* Barbour Publishing, Inc.
Cowman, L. B. E. Streams in the Desert for Kids: 365 Devotions of God's Awesome Love, 1 vol. 2014. (ENG.). 384p. (J). pap. 12.99 *(978-0-310-74786-4(4))* Zonderkidz.
DeVries, Mike, et al. Acts: Face of the Fire. 2003. (No Limits Discipleship Ser.). (ENG.). 120p. (gr. 3-7). per. 12.99 *(978-0-8341-5006-5(9)*, 083-415-0069) Beacon Hill Pr. of Kansas City.
Fischer, Jean. The Bible Promise Book: Devotional & Bible Memory Plan for Kids. 2016. (ENG.). 256p. (J). pap. 7.99 *(978-1-63058-873-1(3)*, Barbour Bks.) Barbour Publishing, Inc.
Florea, Jesse, et al. The One Year Father-Daughter Devotions. 2012. (ENG.). 400p. (J). pap. 14.99 *(978-1-4143-6486-5(5))* Tyndale Hse. Pubs.
Gallagher, Maureen & Hiesberger, Jean Marie. Take Ten: Daily Bible Reflections for Teens. 2004. (ENG.). 384p. (YA). (gr. 6-12). pap. 13.95 *(978-0-88489-821-4(0))* St. Mary's Pr. of MN.
Graham, Billy. Hope for Each Day: 365 Devotions for Kids, 1 vol. 2017. (ENG.). 400p. (J). 15.99 *(978-0-7180-8617-6(1))* Nelson, Thomas Inc.
Hall, Hannah. God Bless Our Country, 1 vol. Whitlow, Steve, illus. 2016. (God Bless Book Ser.). (ENG.). 20p. (J). bds. 9.99 *(978-0-7180-4017-8(1))* Nelson, Thomas Inc.
Hascall, Glenn. It All Matters to Jesus Devotional for Boys: Bullies, Bikes, & Baseball... He Cares about It All! 2016. (ENG.). 264p. (J). pap. 5.99 *(978-1-63058-921-9(7)*, Barbour Bks.) Barbour Publishing, Inc.
Hill, Nancy S. The One Year Did You Know Devotions. 2008. (ENG.). 416p. (J). pap. 14.99 *(978-1-4143-1813-4(8)*, Tyndale Kids) Tyndale Hse. Pubs.
Hummel, Patti M., compiled by. This Is Now: A Girl-to-Girl Devotional for Teens. 2006. (ENG.). 384p. (gr. 7-12). pap. 15.99 *(978-1-59052-605-7(8)*, Multnomah) Doubleday Religious Publishing Group, The.
Kelch, Kalie. Grab Your Boarding Pass: A Daily Devotional for Juniors/Earliteens. 2013. (ENG.). 384p. (J). 16.99 *(978-0-8280-2747-2(1))* Review & Herald Publishing Assn.
Nappa, Jon & Gosselin, Suzanne Hadley. God's Got an Answer for That Devotional. 2015. (ENG.). 96p. (J). pap. 9.99 *(978-0-7369-6123-3(2))* Harvest Hse. Pubs.
Nolan, Allia Zobel. Whatever Is Lovely: A 90-Day Devotional Journal, 1 vol. 2016. (Faithgirlz Ser.). (ENG.). 320p. (J). 14.99 *(978-0-310-75410-7(0))* Zonderkidz.
Parker, Amy. Faith, Hope, Love Devotional (padded) 100 Devotions for Kids & Parents to Share. 2016. (Faith, Hope, Love Ser.). (ENG.). 224p. (J). (gr. -1-2). 14.99 *(978-1-4336-9030-3(6)*, B&H Kids) B&H Publishing Group.
Robertson, Korie & Howard, Chrys. Duck Commander Devotions for Kids, 1 vol. 2015. (ENG.). 224p. (J). 16.99 *(978-0-7180-2249-5(1))* Nelson, Thomas Inc.
Shirer, Priscilla. Unseen: the Prince Warriors 365 Devotional. 2016. (Prince Warriors Ser.). (ENG., Illus.). 384p. (J). (gr. 3-7). pap. 14.99 *(978-1-4336-9018-1(7)*, B&H Kids) B&H Publishing Group.
Shivers, Holly Hawkins. I Can Learn the Bible: The Joshua Code for Kids: 52 Scriptures Every Kid Should Know, 1 vol. 2014. (ENG.). 224p. (J). 14.99 *(978-0-529-10899-9(2))* Nelson, Thomas Inc.
Simmons, JoAnne. It All Matters to Jesus Devotional for Girls: Mean Girls, Manicures, & Mondays... He Cares about It All. 2016. (ENG.). 264p. (J). pap. 5.99 *(978-1-63058-933-2(0)*, Barbour Bks.) Barbour Publishing, Inc.
Stephens, Andrea. True Beauty. 2004. 209p. pap. 11.99 *(978-0-8307-3509-9(7)*, Regal Bks.) Gospel Light Pubns.
Thomas Nelson, Thomas. Brave Girls 365-Day Devotional, 1 vol. 2016. (ENG., Illus.). 416p. (J). 16.99 *(978-0-7180-8976-4(6))* Nelson, Thomas Inc.
Trotman, Phd Gloria, et al. Fun Time with Jesus. 2011. 162p. pap. 14.99 *(978-1-61379-718-1(4))* Salem Author Services.
Veggietales. Growing Day by Day for Boys. 2015. (ENG., Illus.). 384p. (J). (gr. 3-7). pap. 9.99 *(978-1-61795-518-1(3))* Worthy Publishing.
—Growing Day by Day for Girls. 2015. (VeggieTales Ser.). (ENG.). 384p. (J). (gr. 3-7). pap. 9.99 *(978-1-61795-517-4(5))* Worthy Publishing.
Walsh, Sheila. The Bible Is My Best Friend — Flip Book. 2015. (Bible Is My Best Friend Ser.). (ENG.). 368p. (J). (gr. -1-5). spiral bd. 9.99 *(978-1-4336-8815-7(8)*, B&H Kids) B&H Publishing Group.
Young, Sarah. Jesus Calling: 365 Devotions for Kids. 2010. (ENG.). 392p. 15.99 *(978-1-4003-1634-2(0))* Nelson, Thomas Inc.
—Jesus Calling - 365 Devotions for Kids, 1 vol. deluxe ed. 2013. (ENG.). 392p. (J). 19.99 *(978-1-4003-2306-7(1))* Nelson, Thomas Inc.
—Jesus Today Devotions for Kids, 1 vol. 2016. (ENG.). 368p. (J). 15.99 *(978-0-7180-3805-2(3))* Nelson, Thomas Inc.

DIABETES

Allman, Toney. Diabetes. 2008. (Genes & Disease Ser.). (Illus.). 136p. (YA). (gr. 7-12). 35.00 *(978-0-7910-9585-0(1))* Facts On File, Inc.
Ambrose, Marylou. Diabetes: Examining Insulin & Blood Sugar. 2014. (Diseases, Disorders, Symptoms Ser.). (Illus.). 96p. (gr. 9-12). (J). 27.94 *(978-1-62293-065-4(7))*; pap. 10.95 *(978-1-62293-066-1(5))* Enslow Pubs., Inc.
—Investigating Diabetes: Real Facts for Real Lives. 2010. (Investigating Diseases Ser.). (Illus.). 160p. (YA). (gr. 9-12). 35.94 *(978-0-7660-3338-2(4))* Enslow Pubs., Inc.
Apel, Melanie Ann. Everything You Need to Know about Diabetes. 2005. (Need to Know Library). (Illus.). 64p. (YA). (gr. 7-12). lib. bdg. 31.95 *(978-0-8239-3090-6(4)*, NTDIAB) Rosen Publishing Group, Inc., The.
Bellenir, Karen, ed. Diabetes Information for Teens. 2nd rev. ed. 2012. (Teen Health Ser.). 424p. lib. bdg. 69.00 *(978-0-7808-1218-5(2))* Omnigraphics, Inc.
Bertozzi, Nick, illus. Diabetes & Me: An Essential Guide for Kids & Parents. 2013. (ENG.). 176p. pap. 15.00 *(978-0-8090-3871-8(4)*, 9780809038718, Hill & Wang) Farrar, Straus & Giroux.
Brill, Marlene Targ. Diabetes. 2011. (USA TODAY Health Reports: Diseases & Disorders Ser.). (ENG., Illus.). 128p. (gr. 6-12). lib. bdg. 34.60 *(978-0-7613-6085-8(9))* Lerner Publishing Group.
—Diabetes. 2007. (Twenty-First Century Medical Library). (Illus.). 118p. (YA). (gr. 7-12). lib. bdg. 33.26 *(978-0-8225-6785-1(7))* Twenty First Century Bks.
Chilman-Blair, Kim & Taddeo, John. "What's up with Ella?" Medikidz Explain Diabetes. 2010. (Superheroes on a Medical Mission Ser.). (Illus.). 40p. (YA). (gr. 5-8). lib. bdg.

C
D

29.25 *(978-1-4358-3538-2(7),* Rosen Reference) Rosen Publishing Group, Inc., The.

Clark, Michael. Michael's Story Life with Type 1 Diabetes. 2017. (Text Connections Guided Close Reading Ser.). (J). (gr. 2). *(978-1-4900-1861-4(1))* Benchmark Education Co.

Ehrman, M. K. Living with Diabetes, 1 vol. 2012. (Living with Health Challenges Set 1 Ser.). (ENG.). 112p. (J). (gr. 6-12). lib. bdg. 35.64 *(978-1-61783-126-3(3),* Essential Library) ABDO Publishing Co.

Hood, Korey K. Type 1 Teens: A Guide to Managing Your Diabetes. Ishe, Bryan, illus. 2010. 112p. (YA). (gr. 7-18). pap. 14.95 *(978-1-4338-0788-6(2),* Magination Pr.) American Psychological Assn.

Jeffery, Lisa. The Isles of Langerhans, a Magical Kingdom, & Diabetes: A Story to Help Children Understand Diabetes & Develop the Courage to Live with It. 2012. 86p. (-18). pap. 26.99 *(978-1-4259-9198-2(X))* AuthorHouse.

Kelly, P. Coping with Diabetes. 2009. (Coping Ser.). 192p. (gr. 7-12). 63.90 *(978-1-61511-998-1(1))* Rosen Publishing Group, Inc., The.

Kelly, Pat. Coping with Diabetes. 2005. (Coping Ser.). (Illus.). 192p. (YA). (gr. 7-12). lib. bdg. 34.60 *(978-0-8239-3756-1(9))* Rosen Publishing Group, Inc., The.

Lang, Rocky. Lara Takes Charge: For Kids with Diabetes, Their Friends, & Siblings, 2 bks, Book 1. Huss, Sally, illus. 2nd ed. 2012. 28p. (J). 12.95 *(978-1-934980-05-7(6))* Cable Publishing.

Life with Diabetes, Lacie the Lizard's Adventure. 2004. (J). 11.95 *(978-0-9745997-0-0(0))* CrittersInc.

Loughrey, Anita. Explaining Diabetes. 2010. (J). 34.25 *(978-1-59920-314-0(6))* Black Rabbit Bks.

Mayo Clinic Staff, contrib. by. 20 Tasty Recipes for People with Diabetes. 2004. (Mayo Clinic on Health Ser.). (Illus.). 36,52p. (YA). (gr. 8-18). lib. bdg. 15.95 *(978-1-59084-247-8(2))* Mason Crest.

McAuliffe, Bill. Diabetes. 2011. (Living with Disease Ser.). (Illus.). 48p. (J). (gr. 5-8). lib. bdg. 34.25 *(978-1-60818-074-5(3),* 1331496, Creative Education) Creative Co., The.

Moran, Katherine J. Diabetes: The Ultimate Teen Guide. Merriman, Lisa P., illus. 2006. (It Happened to Me Ser.: 7). (ENG.). 192p. (gr. 8-12). per. 20.00 *(978-0-8108-5642-4(5))* Scarecrow Pr., Inc.

—Diabetes: The Ultimate Teen Guide. 2004. (It Happened to Me Ser.: 7). (ENG., Illus.). 208p. (gr. 9). 55.00 *(978-0-8108-4806-1(6))* Scarecrow Pr., Inc.

Morrill, Rania. How Many Carbs Is a Booger: Make Carb Counting Fun. 2006. (J). 15.00 *(978-1-4276-0140-7(2))* Aardvark Global Publishing.

Olson, Karen. Cooper Has Diabetes. Pritchett and Hull Associates, Inc., illus. 2003. (ENG.). 34p. (J). 9.95 *(978-0-939838-82-0(6))* Pritchett & Hull Assocs., Inc.

Paradis, Anne. Caillou, Emma's Extra Snacks: Living with Diabetes. Sévigny, Eric, illus. 2015. (Playtime Ser.). (ENG.). 24p. (J). (gr. -1-k). pap. 4.99 *(978-2-89718-205-2(9))* Caillouet, Gerry.

Parker, Katrina. Living with Diabetes. (Teen's Guides). 176p. (gr. 6-12). 2008. per. 14.95 *(978-0-8160-7563-8(8),* Checkmark Bks.) 2007. 34.95 *(978-0-8160-6346-8(X))* Facts On File, Inc.

Parker, Vic. I Know Someone with Diabetes, 1 vol. 2011. (Understanding Health Issues Ser.). (ENG.). 32p. (gr. 1-3). 27.32 *(978-1-4329-4557-2(2),* Heinemann First Library) Heinemann-Raintree.

Peterson, Amanda. What You Need to Know about Diabetes. 2015. (Focus on Health Ser.). (ENG., Illus.). 32p. (gr. 3-4). pap. 7.95 *(978-1-4914-4901-1(2))* Capstone Press of Coughlan Cos.

Pirner, Connie White. Even Little Kids Get Diabetes. Westcott, Nadine Bernard, illus. 2012. (J). *(978-1-61913-145-3(5))* Weigl Pubs., Inc.

Robbins, Lynette. How to Deal with Diabetes. 2009. (Kids' Health Ser.). (Illus.). 24p. (J). pap. 8.25 *(978-1-4358-3425-5(9),* PowerKids Pr.); (YA). (gr. 2-5). lib. bdg. 22.60 *(978-1-4042-8144-8(4))* Rosen Publishing Group, Inc., The.

Schuh, Mari C. Diabetes-Aware Diets, 1 vol. 2014. (Special Diets Ser.). (ENG.). 24p. (gr. k-1). lib. bdg. 26.65 *(978-1-4914-0592-5(9),* Pebble Plus) Capstone Press of Coughlan Cos.

Sherman, Rebecca. Diabetes & Other Endocrinological Disorders. 2017. (J). ***(978-1-4222-3756-4(7))*** Mason Crest.

Silverstein, Alvin, et al. The Diabetes Update. 2006. (Disease Update Ser.). (Illus.). 128p. (J). (gr. 5-9). lib. bdg. 33.27 *(978-0-7660-2483-0(0))* Enslow Pubs., Inc.

Silverstein, Virginia. Handy Health Guide to Diabetes. 2013. (Handy Health Guides). 48p. (J). (gr. 5-12). pap. 8.95 *(978-1-4644-0493-1(3))* Enslow Pubs., Inc.

Silverstein, Virginia & Nunn, Laura Silverstein. Handy Health Guide to Diabetes. 2013. (Handy Health Guides). 48p. (J). (gr. 5-18). lib. bdg. 25.27 *(978-0-7660-4275-9(8))* Enslow Pubs., Inc.

DIABETES—FICTION

Baglio, Ben M. Corgi in the Cupcakes. Baum, Ann, illus. 2008. 142p. (J). pap. *(978-0-439-02533-1(8))* Scholastic, Inc.

Bilderback Abel, Mary & Borg, Stan W. Maddy Patti & the Great Curiosity: Helping Children Understand Diabetes. Dey, Lorraine, illus. 2015. (Let's Talk Ser.). (ENG.). 48p. (J). (gr. k-5). 9.95 *(978-0-88282-490-1(2))* New Horizon Pr. Pubs., Inc.

Carr, Sheryl. Little Drop & the Healing Place. Harris, La Verne Abe, illus. 2006. (J). 10.00 *(978-0-9791383-0-0(2))* Reliant Energy.

Chamberlin, Kate. Charles & David. Wroth, Dean, illus. 2010. 32p. (J). pap. 9.95 *(978-0-944727-37-9(9));* lib. bdg. 15.95 *(978-0-944727-36-2(0))* Jason & Nordic Pubs. (Turtle Bks.).

Chilman-Blair, Kim & DeLoache, Shawn. MediKidz Explain Type 1 Diabetes: What's up with Ashleigh? 2nd ed. 2012. (Illus.). 32p. (J). pap. *(978-1-906935-87-0(4))* Medikidz Ltd.

Christopher, Matt. Shoot for the Hoop. 2010. (Matt Christopher Sports Library). 128p. (J). (gr. 4-6). lib. bdg. 26.60 *(978-1-59953-357-5(X))* Norwood Hse. Pr.

Cuccia, Ronni. Maria & the Monster. 2010. 16p. 10.99 *(978-1-4520-8966-9(3))* AuthorHouse.

Daly, Mariah. James Has Diabetes. 2009. 56p. pap. 21.99 *(978-1-4389-3188-3(3))* AuthorHouse.

DeLand, M. Maitland. The Great Katie Kate Discusses Diabetes. 2010. (Illus.). 32p. 14.95 *(978-1-60832-039-4(1),* Greenleaf Book Group Pr.) Greenleaf Book Group.

Fogarty, Laura. I Can Do Anything! 2008. 24p. pap. 24.95 *(978-1-60563-501-9(4))* America Star Bks.

Ganz-Schmitt, Sue. Even Superheroes Get Diabetes. Chambers-Goldberg, Micah, illus. 36p. 2011. (gr. -1-3). 22.95 *(978-1-59858-303-8(4))* 2007. (J). per. 15.95 *(978-1-59858-302-1(6))* Dog Ear Publishing, LLC.

Gow, Kailin. Loving Summer. 2012. 250p. (-18). pap. 9.99 *(978-1-59748-044-4(4),* The Edge) Sparklesoup LLC.

Grimes, Nikki. Halfway to Perfect: A Dyamonde Daniel Book, 4 vols. Christie, R. Gregory, illus. 2012. (Dyamonde Daniel Book Ser.: 4). (ENG.). 128p. (J). (gr. 2-4). 10.99 *(978-0-399-25178-8(2),* G.P. Putnam's Sons Books for Young Readers) Penguin Young Readers Group.

Hautman, Pete. Sweetblood. 2010. (ENG.). 208p. (YA). (gr. 7). pap. 8.99 *(978-1-4424-0755-8(7),* Simon & Schuster Bks. For Young Readers) Simon & Schuster Bks. For Young Readers.

Kleiman, Deanna. Jacob's Journey, Living with Type 1 Diabetes. Brieger, Ms. Kirsten, illus. 2012. 28p. pap. 9.95 *(978-0-615-60112-0(X))* TwinsBooks.

Lepp, Kristin. Libby Louanne & the Amazing Hospital Mystery. 2010. 79p. pap. 10.95 *(978-0-557-61519-3(4))* Lulu Pr., Inc.

Martin, Ann M. The Truth about Stacey. 2010. (Baby-Sitters Club Ser.: 3). (ENG.). 176p. (J). (gr. 3-7). 6.99 *(978-0-545-17477-0(5),* Scholastic Paperbacks) Scholastic, Inc.

—The Truth about Stacey. Telgemeier, Raina, illus. rev. ed. 2015. (Baby-Sitters Club Graphix Ser.: 2). (ENG.). 144p. (J). (gr. 3-7). 24.99 *(978-0-545-81388-4(3));* pap. 10.99 *(978-0-545-81389-1(1))* Scholastic, Inc. (Graphix).

—The Truth about Stacey. 2015. (Baby-Sitters Club Graphix Ser.: 2). lib. bdg. 22.10 *(978-0-606-37027-1(7))* 2010. (Baby-Sitters Club Ser.: 3). lib. bdg. 17.20 *(978-0-606-14789-7(6),* Turtleback) Turtleback Bks.

Martin, Rebecca. Eyes for My Heart. 2003. (Illus.). 269p. 10.20 *(978-0-7399-2308-5(0),* 2231) Rod & Staff Pubs., Inc.

Morris, Cathy. I'm a Perfectly Normal Kid Who Happens to Have Diabetes! Grunden, Kimberly, illus. 2007. 24p. per. 12.95 *(978-1-934246-85-6(9))* Peppertree Pr., The.

Nicholson, Lorna Schultz. Interference, 1 vol. 2004. (Lorimer Sports Stories Ser.: 68). (ENG.). 96p. (J). (gr. 4-8). 9.95 *(978-1-55028-822-3(9),* 9781550288223) Lorimer, James & Co., Ltd., Pubs. CAN. Dist: Casemate Pubs. & Bk. Distributors, LLC.

Perry, Jolene. The Summer I Found You. 2014. (ENG.). 256p. (YA). (gr. 8-12). 16.99 *(978-0-8075-8369-2(3))* Whitman, Albert & Co.

Rankine-Van Wassenhoven, Jacqueline. A Little Honey for Serge. 2009. 16p. pap. 9.00 *(978-1-4490-0810-9(0))* AuthorHouse.

Reynolds, Jason. Patina. 2017. (J). pap. ***(978-1-4814-5019-5(0))***; (Track Ser.: 2). (ENG., Illus.). 240p. (gr. 5). 16.99 ***(978-1-4814-5018-8(2),*** Atheneum/Caitlyn Dlouhy Books) Simon & Schuster Children's Publishing.

Roberts, Willo Davis. Sugar Isn't Everything. 2012. (ENG., Illus.). 190p. (J). (gr. 3-7). pap. 9.99 *(978-0-689-71225-8(1),* Simon & Schuster/Paula Wiseman Bks.) Simon & Schuster/Paula Wiseman Bks.

Ruiz-Flores, Lupe. Alicia's Fruity Drinks / Las Aguas Frescas de Alicia. Baeza Ventura, Gabriela, tr. from ENG. Lacámara, Laura, illus. 2012. (SPA & ENG.). (J). 17.95 *(978-1-55885-705-6(2),* Piñata Books) Arte Publico Pr.

Schultz Nicholson, Lorna. Interference, 1 vol. 2004. (Lorimer Sports Stories Ser.: 68). (ENG.). 96p. (J). (gr. 4-8). 16.95 *(978-1-55028-823-0(7),* 9781550288230) Lorimer, James & Co., Ltd., Pubs. CAN. Dist: Casemate Pubs. & Bk. Distributors, LLC.

Shorkey, Cde. Jake Gets Diabetes. 2009. 28p. pap. 15.49 *(978-1-4490-5317-8(3))* AuthorHouse.

Souliere, Lisa. Guess What? I Have Diabetes. 2008. 36p. pap. 14.95 *(978-1-60693-287-2(X),* Eloquent Bks.) Strategic Book Publishing & Rights Agency (SBPRA).

Steinberg, Howard. Jackie's Got Game! A Story about Diabetes. Chris, Healey, illus. 2005. (J). 9.99 *(978-0-9777463-0-9(5))* dLife - For Your Diabetes Life.

Thompson, Colleen. Claudine & Claudette a Bug Story. 2011. 12p. pap. 8.32 *(978-1-4634-2286-8(5))* AuthorHouse.

Tirado, Margot A. New Friends. 2012. 48p. (gr. 1-2). pap. 9.89 *(978-1-4669-0508-5(5))* Trafford Publishing.

Tirey, Rodney. Coppershoo Saves the Sarge's Saddle! Tirey, Rodney, illus. 2007. (Illus.). 32p. (J). 16.95 *(978-0-9789591-0-4(8))* MirthMarks Publishing.

Winborne, Mamie Pearl. Sweet Sugar I Got Your Back. 2012. 150p. pap. 13.95 *(978-0-615-58624-3(4))* Professional Publishing Hse. LLC.

DIAGRAMS, STATISTICAL

see Statistics—Graphic Methods

DIAMONDS

Edwards, Ron & Dickie, Lisa. Diamonds & Gemstones. 2004. (Rocks, Minerals, & Resources Ser.). (ENG., Illus.). 32p. (J). pap. *(978-0-7787-1446-0(2))* Crabtree Publishing Co.

Ethan, Eric. Diamonds. 2011. (Gems: Nature's Jewels Ser.). (Illus.). 24p. (gr. 2-5). 22.60 *(978-1-4339-4715-5(3));* pap. 8.15 *(978-1-4339-4716-2(1))* Stevens, Gareth Publishing LLLP. (Gareth Stevens Learning Library).

Petersen, Christine. Diamonds, 1 vol. 2013. (Earth's Treasures Ser.). (ENG.). 32p. (J). (gr. 3-6). lib. bdg. 27.07 *(978-1-61783-870-5(5),* Checkerboard Library) ABDO Publishing Co.

Ungaro, Ellen. Diamonds: Set Of 6. 2011. (Navigators Ser.). (J). pap. 48.00 net. *(978-1-4108-6235-8(6))* Benchmark Education Co.

—Diamonds: Text Pairs. 2008. (Bridges/Navigators Ser.). (J). (gr. 5). 81.00 *(978-1-4108-8412-1(0))* Benchmark Education Co.

DIANA, PRINCESS OF WALES, 1961-1997

Beauregarde, Constance & Antal, Lara. Princess Diana: Royal Activist & Fashion Icon. 2016. (Leading Women Ser.). (Illus.). 128p. (J). (gr. 7-7). 39.93 *(978-1-5026-1987-7(3))* Cavendish Square Publishing.

Gilchrist, Cherry & Pearson Education Staff. Princess Diana. 2nd ed. 2008. (ENG., Illus.). 56p. pap. 11.99 *(978-1-4058-8201-9(8))* Pearson Education.

Gormley, Beatrice. Diana, Princess of Wales: Young Royalty. 2005. 204p. (J). lib. bdg. 18.46 *(978-1-4242-1728-1(8))* Fitzgerald Bks.

—Diana, Princess of Wales: Young Royalty. 2005. (Childhood of World Figures Ser.). (ENG., Illus.). 192p. (J). (gr. 3-7). pap. 9.99 *(978-1-4169-0021-4(7),* Aladdin) Simon & Schuster Children's Publishing.

Labrecque, Ellen. Who Was Princess Diana? 2017. (Who Was... ? Ser.). lib. bdg. 16.00 ***(978-0-606-39782-7(5))*** Turtleback Bks.

Labrecque, Ellen & Harrison, Nancy. Who Was Princess Diana? Hoare, Jerry, illus. 2017. (Who Was? Ser.). (ENG.). 112p. (J). (gr. 3-7). 5.99 *(978-0-448-48855-4(8),* Grosset & Dunlap) Penguin Young Readers Group.

Mattern, Joanne & Dorling Kindersley Publishing Staff. Princess Diana. 2006. (DK Biography Ser.). (ENG., Illus.). 128p. (J). (gr. 5-12). pap. 6.99 *(978-0-7566-1614-4(X),* DK Children) Dorling Kindersley Publishing, Inc.

Owings, Lisa. Diana: The People's Princess, 1 vol. 2012. (Lives Cut Short Set 2 Ser.). (ENG.). 112p. (J). (gr. 6-12). lib. bdg. 35.64 *(978-1-61783-545-2(5),* Essential Library) ABDO Publishing Co.

Paprocki, Sherry Beck. Diana, Princess of Wales. 2nd rev. ed. 2009. (Women of Achievement Ser.). (Illus.). 144p. (gr. 6-12). 35.00 *(978-1-60413-463-6(1),* Chelsea Hse.) Facts On File, Inc.

Trussell-Cullen, Alan. Princess Diana. 2009. pap. 13.25 *(978-1-60559-068-4(1))* Hameray Publishing Group, Inc.

DIARIES

see Autobiographies

DIARIES—FICTION

Adlington, L. J. The Diary of Pelly D. 2008. 304p. (YA). (gr. 9). per. 9.99 *(978-0-06-076617-7(4),* Greenwillow Bks.) HarperCollins Pubs.

Alexie, Sherman. The Absolutely True Diary of a Part-Time Indian. Forney, Ellen, illus. (ENG.). (YA). (gr. 7-17). 2009. 288p. pap. 15.99 *(978-0-316-01369-7(2))* 2007. 240p. 20.00 *(978-0-316-01368-0(4))* Little, Brown Bks. for Young Readers.

—The Absolutely True Diary of a Part-Time Indian. 10th anniv. ed. 2017. (ENG., Illus.). 320p. (YA). (gr. 7-17). 20.99 *(978-0-316-50404-1(1))* Little, Brown Bks. for Young Readers.

—The Absolutely True Diary of a Part-Time Indian. 2011. 10.36 *(978-0-7848-3391-9(5))* 2009. 14.44 *(978-0-7848-3800-6(3))* Marco Bk. Co. (Everbind).

—The Absolutely True Diary of a Part-Time Indian. Forney, Ellen, illus. 2008. 230p. 25.00 *(978-1-60686-072-4(0))* Perfection Learning Corp.

—The Absolutely True Diary of a Part-Time Indian. 2008. (YA). 1.25 *(978-1-4281-8291-2(8));* 78.49 *(978-1-4361-0259-6(6));* 68.75 *(978-1-4281-8300-1(0));* 57.75 *(978-1-4281-8294-3(2));* 55.75 *(978-1-4281-8296-7(9));* 212.75 *(978-1-4281-8295-0(0));* 70.75 *(978-1-4281-8298-1(5))* Recorded Bks., Inc.

—The Absolutely True Diary of a Part-Time Indian. Forney, Ellen, illus. l.t. ed. 2008. (Thorndike Literacy Bridge Ser.). (ENG.). 302p. (YA). (gr. 7-12). 23.95 *(978-1-4104-0499-2(4))* Thorndike Pr.

—The Absolutely True Diary of a Part-Time Indian. 2009. (YA). lib. bdg. 28.15 *(978-0-606-07296-0(9),* Turtleback) Turtleback Bks.

Amato, Mary. The Naked Mole-Rat Letters. (ENG., Illus.). 208p. (J). 2007. (gr. 4-7). pap. 7.99 *(978-0-8234-2098-8(1))* 2005. 16.95 *(978-0-8234-1927-2(4))* Holiday Hse., Inc.

Anderson, Jodi Lynn. My Diary from the Edge of the World. 2015. (ENG., Illus.). 432p. (J). (gr. 3-7). 16.99 *(978-1-4424-8387-3(3),* Aladdin) Simon & Schuster Children's Publishing.

—My Diary from the Edge of the World. 2017. (ENG., Illus.). 448p. (J). (gr. 3-7). pap. 7.99 *(978-1-4424-8388-0(1),* Simon & Schuster/Paula Wiseman Bks.) Simon & Schuster/Paula Wiseman Bks.

Anholt, Laurence. Frida Kahlo. 2016. (ENG., Illus.). 32p. (J). 19.99 *(978-1-84780-666-6(X),* Frances Lincoln Children's Bks.) Quarto Publishing Group UK GBR. Dist: Littlehampton Bk Services, Ltd.

Anonymous. The Book of David. 2014. (ENG., Illus.). 288p. (YA). (gr. 9). pap. 9.99 *(978-1-4424-8985-1(5),* Simon Pulse) Simon Pulse.

—Go Ask Alice. 2006. (ENG.). 224p. (YA). (gr. 7). pap. 9.99 *(978-1-4169-1463-1(3),* Simon Pulse) Simon Pulse.

—Jay's Journal. Sparks, Beatrice, ed. 2012. (ENG.). 240p. (YA). (gr. 9). 17.99 *(978-1-4424-8094-0(7),* Simon Pulse) Simon Pulse.

—Letting Ana Go. 2013. (ENG.). 304p. (YA). (gr. 9). 17.99 *(978-1-4424-7223-5(5));* (Illus.). pap. 10.99 *(978-1-4424-7213-6(8))* Simon Pulse. (Simon Pulse).

Arcos, Carrie. There Will Come a Time. 2014. (ENG., Illus.). 320p. (YA). (gr. 9). 17.99 *(978-1-4424-9585-2(5),* Simon Pulse) Simon Pulse.

Bachelet, Gilles. Mrs. White Rabbit. 2017. (ENG., Illus.). 32p. (J). 17.00 ***(978-0-8028-5483-4(4),*** Eerdmans Bks For Young Readers) Eerdmans, William B. Publishing Co.

Balliett, Blue. The Danger Box. 2012. (ENG.). 320p. (J). (gr. 3-7). pap. 7.99 *(978-0-439-85210-4(2),* Scholastic Paperbacks) Scholastic, Inc.

Bancks, Tristan. Mac Slater Hunts the Cool. 2010. (Mac Slater Hunts the Cool Ser.). (ENG.). 224p. (J). (gr. 3-7). 15.99 *(978-1-4169-8574-7(3),* Simon & Schuster Bks. For Young Readers) Simon & Schuster Bks. For Young Readers.

Barnholdt, Lauren. One Night That Changes Everything. (ENG., (YA). (gr. 9). 2011. Illus.). 272p. pap. 9.99 *(978-1-4424-0367-3(5))* 2010. 256p. 16.99 *(978-1-4169-9479-4(3))* Simon Pulse. (Simon Pulse).

Barshaw, Ruth McNally. New Kid in School. Barshaw, Ruth McNally, illus. 2013. (Ellie Mcdoodle Diaries). (ENG., Illus.). 192p. (YA). (gr. 3-6). 12.99 *(978-1-61963-174-8(1),* 9781619631748, Bloomsbury USA Childrens) Bloomsbury Publishing USA.

Bateson, Catherine. The Boyfriend Rules of Good Behavior. 2006. (ENG.). 192p. (YA). (gr. 8-12). 16.95 *(978-0-8234-2026-1(4))* Holiday Hse., Inc.

Becker Holstein, Barbara. Secrets: Diary of a Gutsy Teen. 2015. (ENG.). 144p. (J). (gr. 2-7). 12.95 *(978-1-62914-626-3(9),* Sky Pony Pr.) Skyhorse Publishing Co., Inc.

—The Truth: Diary of a Gutsy Tween. 2014. (ENG.). 176p. (J). (gr. 2-7). 12.95 *(978-1-62873-611-3(9),* Sky Pony Pr.) Skyhorse Publishing Co., Inc.

Benton, Jim. It's Not My Fault I Know Everything. 2009. (Dear Dumb Diary Ser.: 8). lib. bdg. 17.20 *(978-0-606-00142-7(5),* Turtleback) Turtleback Bks.

—Let's Pretend This Never Happened. Benton, Jim, illus. 2004. (Dear Dumb Diary Ser.: 1). (ENG., Illus.). 128p. (J). (gr. 4-7). pap. 6.99 *(978-0-439-62904-1(7),* Scholastic Paperbacks) Scholastic, Inc.

—Let's Pretend This Never Happened. Benton, Jim, illus. 2004. (Dear Dumb Diary Ser.: 1). (Illus.). 95p. (gr. -1-2). 17.20 *(978-1-4176-3050-9(7),* Turtleback) Turtleback Bks.

—Me (Just Like You, Only Better) Benton, Jim, illus. 2011. (Dear Dumb Diary Ser.: 12). (ENG., Illus.). 160p. (J). (gr. 3-7). pap. 6.99 *(978-0-545-11616-9(3),* Scholastic Paperbacks) Scholastic, Inc.

—Nobody's Perfect. I'm As Close As It Gets. Benton, Jim, illus. 2013. (Dear Dumb Diary Year Two Ser.: 3). (ENG., Illus.). 144p. (J). (gr. 3-7). pap. 5.99 *(978-0-545-37764-5(1),* Scholastic Paperbacks) Scholastic, Inc.

—Nobody's Perfect. I'm As Close As It Gets. 2013. (Dear Dumb Diary: Year Two Ser.: 3). lib. bdg. 16.00 *(978-0-606-31535-7(7),* Turtleback) Turtleback Bks.

—Okay, So Maybe I Do Have Superpowers. Benton, Jim, illus. 2011. (Dear Dumb Diary Ser.: 11). (ENG., Illus.). 160p. (J). (gr. 3-7). pap. 6.99 *(978-0-545-11615-2(5),* Scholastic Paperbacks) Scholastic, Inc.

—The Problem with Here Is That It's Where I'm From. 2007. (Dear Dumb Diary Ser.: 6). (ENG., Illus.). 128p. (J). (gr. 3-7). 6.99 *(978-0-439-79622-4(9),* Scholastic Paperbacks) Scholastic, Inc.

—The Problem with Here Is That It's Where I'm From. 2007. (Dear Dumb Diary Ser.: 6). 17.20 *(978-1-4177-8231-4(5),* Turtleback) Turtleback Bks.

—The Super-Nice Are Super-Annoying. Benton, Jim, illus. 2012. (Dear Dumb Diary Year Two Ser.). (ENG., Illus.). 144p. (J). (gr. 3-7). pap. 5.99 *(978-0-545-37763-8(3),* Scholastic Paperbacks) Scholastic, Inc.

—The Super-Nice Are Super-Annoying. 2012. (Dear Dumb Diary: Year Two Ser.: 2). lib. bdg. 16.00 *(978-0-606-26188-3(5),* Turtleback) Turtleback Bks.

—That's What Friends Aren't For. 2010. (Dear Dumb Diary Ser.: 09). lib. bdg. 17.20 *(978-0-606-06876-5(7),* Turtleback) Turtleback Bks.

—You Can Bet on That. Benton, Jim, illus. 2014. (Dear Dumb Diary Year Two Ser.: 5). (ENG., Illus.). 160p. (J). (gr. 3-7). pap. 5.99 *(978-0-545-64257-6(4),* Scholastic Paperbacks) Scholastic, Inc.

Berrow, G. M. My Little Pony: Applejack & the Honest-To-Goodness Switcheroo. 2014. (ENG.). 160p. (J). (gr. 3-7). pap. 5.99 *(978-0-316-24825-9(8))* Little, Brown Bks. for Young Readers.

Bloor, Edward. Tangerine. (ENG.). 320p. (J). (gr. 5-7). 2007. 18.00 *(978-0-15-201246-5(X))* 2006. (Illus.). pap. 8.99 *(978-0-15-205780-0(3))* Houghton Mifflin Harcourt Publishing Co.

—Tangerine Spanish Edition. de la Vega, Pablo, tr. 2014. (ENG.). 384p. (J). (gr. 5-7). 16.99 *(978-0-544-33611-7(9),* HMH Books For Young Readers) Houghton Mifflin Harcourt Publishing Co.

Blume, Lesley M. M. The Wondrous Journals of Dr. Wendell Wellington Wiggins. Foote, David, illus. 2013. (ENG.). 256p. (J). (gr. 3-7). pap. 7.99 *(978-0-375-87218-1(3),* Knopf Bks. for Young Readers) Random Hse. Children's Bks.

Boelter, Ashaki. Diaries of the Doomed. Boelter, Ashaki, illus. 2004. (Illus.). 88p. (YA). per. 6.95 *(978-0-9721067-4-0(X),* Writing Wild & Crazy) Shakalot High Entertainment.

Bowen, Fred. Quarterback Season, 1 vol. 2011. (ENG.). 144p. (J). (gr. 2-7). pap. 5.95 *(978-1-56145-594-2(6),* Peachtree Junior) Peachtree Pubs.

Brahmachari, Sita. Mira in the Present Tense. (ENG.). 288p. (J). (gr. 3-7). 2015. pap. 9.99 *(978-0-8075-5151-6(1))* 2013. 16.99 *(978-0-8075-5149-3(X))* Whitman, Albert & Co.

Brighton, Catherine. My Napoleon. Brighton, Catherine, illus. 2005. (Illus.). 26p. (J). (gr. k-4). reprint ed. 17.00 *(978-0-7567-8931-2(1))* DIANE Publishing Co.

Brockway, Stephanie. Mystic Phyles: Beasts. Masiello, Ralph, illus. 2011. (ENG.). 144p. (J). (gr. 4-7). 15.95 *(978-1-57091-718-9(3))* Charlesbridge Publishing, Inc.

Brooks, Kevin. The Bunker Diary. 2015. (ENG.). 264p. (YA). (gr. 8-12). 17.99 *(978-1-4677-5420-0(X))* Lerner Publishing Group.

Brown, Marc. Arthur & the Lost Diary. 2005. (Arthur Chapter Bks.: Bk. 9). (Illus.). 55p. (J). lib. bdg. 15.00 *(978-1-59054-723-6(3))* Fitzgerald Bks.

Bruchac, Joseph. On This Long Journey, the Journal of Jesse Smoke, a Cherokee Boy, the Trail of Tears 1838. 2014. (My Name Is America Ser.). (ENG.). 208p. (J). (gr. 3-7). pap. 6.99 *(978-0-545-53086-6(5),* Scholastic Paperbacks) Scholastic, Inc.

Bryant, Jen. Pieces of Georgia. 2007. (ENG., Illus.). 176p. (J). (gr. 5-9). per. 6.99 *(978-0-440-42055-2(5),* Yearling) Random Hse. Children's Bks.

Buckeridge, Anthony. Jennings' Diary. 2008. (Jennings Ser.: 5). (ENG.). 192p. (J). (gr. -1-12). pap. 12.95 *(978-0-7551-0163-4(4))* House of Stratus, Inc. GBR. Dist: Gardners Bks. Ltd.

Buckle, J. A. Half My Facebook Friends Are Ferrets, 1 vol. 2014. (ENG.). 224p. (gr. 9-12). 16.95 *(978-1-63079-000-4(1))* Switch Pr.

Bushnell, Candace. The Carrie Diaries. (Carrie Diaries: 1). (ENG.). (YA). (gr. 9). 2011. 416p. pap. 9.99 *(978-0-06-172892-1(6))* 2010. 400p. 18.99 *(978-0-06-172891-4(8))* 2012. 416p. pap. 10.99 *(978-0-06-223684-5(9))* HarperCollins Pubs.

—Summer & the City. (Carrie Diaries: 2). (ENG.). 416p. (YA). (gr. 9). 2012. pap. 9.99 *(978-0-06-172900-3(0))* 2013. pap. 10.99 *(978-0-06-223686-9(5))* HarperCollins Pubs.

Cabot, Meg. Forever Princess, Vol. X. 2009. (Princess Diaries: 10). (ENG.). 416p. (YA). (gr. 8). pap. 9.99 *(978-0-06-123294-7(7),* HarperTeen) HarperCollins Pubs.

—In Waiting. 2008. (Princess Diaries: 4). (ENG.). 256p. (YA). (gr. 8). pap. 9.99 *(978-0-06-154364-7(0),* HarperTeen) HarperCollins Pubs.

—Journal d'une Princesse.Tr. of Princess Diaries. pap. 13.95 *(978-2-01-321853-5(2))* Hachette Groupe Livre FRA. Dist: Distribooks, Inc.

—Party Princess. (ENG., (YA). 2006. (Princess Diaries: Vol. 7). Illus.). 304p. (gr. 7-12). 16.99 *(978-0-06-072453-5(6))* Vol. VII. 2008. (Princess Diaries: 7). 320p. (gr. 8). pap. 9.99 *(978-0-06-154374-6(8)*, HarperTeen) HarperCollins Pubs.

—The Princess Diaries. 2008. (Princess Diaries: 1). (ENG.). 256p. (YA). (gr. 8). pap. 9.99 *(978-0-06-147993-9(4))*Vols. 1-3, Set. 2006. (Princess Diaries: Vol. I). (J). pap., pap. 19.99 *(978-0-06-115389-1(3))* HarperCollins Pubs. (HarperTeen).

—The Princess Diaries. 2008. 20.00 *(978-0-7569-8793-0(8))* Perfection Learning Corp.

—The Princess Diaries. unabr. ed. 2004. (Princess Diaries: Vol. I). 240p. (J). (gr. 7-18). pap. 38.00 incl. audio *(978-0-8072-0669-0(5)*, Listening Library) Random Hse. Audio Publishing Group.

—The Princess Diaries. 2008. (Princess Diaries: 1). (YA). lib. bdg. 20.85 *(978-1-4178-2328-4(3)*, Turtleback) Turtleback Bks.

—The Princess Diaries Box Set: The Princess Diaries; Princess in the Spotlight; Princess in Love. 2003. (Princess Diaries). 304p. (gr. 7-18). pap. 19.99 *(978-0-06-058745-1(8))* HarperCollins Pubs.

—Princess in Love, Vol. 3. 2008. (Princess Diaries: 3). (ENG.). 256p. (YA). (gr. 8-12). pap. 9.99 *(978-0-06-147995-3(0)*, HarperTeen) HarperCollins Pubs.

—Princess in Love. 2004. (Princess Diaries: Vol. 3). 288p. (J). (gr. 7-18). pap. 38.00 incl. audio *(978-0-8072-2284-3(4)*, Listening Library) Random Hse. Audio Publishing Group.

—Princess in Pink. (ENG.). 2008. (Princess Diaries: 5). 288p. (YA). (gr. 8). pap. 9.99 *(978-0-06-154363-0(2)*, HarperTeen) 2004. (Princess Diaries: Vol. 5). (Illus.). 272p. (J). (gr. 7-18). 15.99 *(978-0-06-009610-6(1))* HarperCollins Pubs.

—Princess in Pink. 2008. (Princess Diaries: 5). 256p. (YA). (gr. 7-12). 20.85 *(978-1-4178-2563-9(4)*, Turtleback) Turtleback Bks.

—Princess in the Spotlight. 2008. (Princess Diaries). 222p. (gr. 7-12). 19.00 *(978-0-7569-8794-7(6))* Perfection Learning Corp.

—Princess in the Spotlight, unabr. ed. 2004. (Princess Diaries: Vol. 2). 272p. (J). (gr. 7-18). pap. 38.00 incl. audio *(978-0-8072-1197-7(4)*, S YA 332 SP, Listening Library) Random Hse. Audio Publishing Group.

—Princess in the Spotlight Vol. 2. 2008. (Princess Diaries: 2). (ENG.). 256p. (YA). (gr. 8-12). pap. 9.99 *(978-0-06-147994-6(2)*, HarperTeen) HarperCollins Pubs.

—Princess in Training. (ENG., 2005. (Princess Diaries: Vol. 6). Illus.). 288p. (J). (gr. 7-18). 16.99 *(978-0-06-009613-7(6))* Vol. VI. 2008. (Princess Diaries: 6). 304p. (YA). (gr. 8). pap. 9.99 *(978-0-06-154365-4(9)*, HarperTeen) HarperCollins Pubs.

—Princess in Waiting. 2003. (YA). (Princess Diaries: Vol. 4). (gr. 7-18). pap. 6.99 *(978-0-06-054065-4(6))*; Vol. IV. (Princess Diaries: 4). (ENG., Illus.). 240p. (gr. 8-18). 17.99 *(978-0-06-009607-6(1)*, HarperTeen) HarperCollins Pubs.

—Princess Mia. (ENG.). 2008. (Princess Diaries: Vol. 9). 256p. (J). (gr. 7-18). 16.99 *(978-0-06-072461-0(7))* Vol. 9. 2009. (Princess Diaries: 9). 304p. (YA). (gr. 8). pap. 9.99 *(978-0-06-072463-4(3)*, HarperTeen) HarperCollins Pubs.

—Princess Mia. 2009. (Princess Diaries: 9). (YA). lib. bdg. 20.85 *(978-0-606-02178-4(7)*, Turtleback) Turtleback Bks.

—Princess on the Brink. 2007. (Princess Diaries: Vol. 8). (ENG.). 256p. (J). 16.99 *(978-0-06-072456-6(0))* HarperCollins Pubs.

—The Princess Present. 2004. (Princess Diaries: 6.5). (ENG.). 96p. (YA). (gr. 8-18). 12.99 *(978-0-06-075433-4(8)*, HarperTeen) HarperCollins Pubs.

—Project Princess. 2003. (Princess Diaries: 4.5). (ENG.). 64p. (YA). (gr. 8-18). pap. 6.99 *(978-0-06-057131-3(4)*, HarperTeen) HarperCollins Pubs.

—Valentine Princess. 2006. (Princess Diaries: 7.75). (ENG.). 96p. (YA). (gr. 8-12). 12.99 *(978-0-06-084718-0(2)*, HarperTeen) HarperCollins Pubs.

Cabot, Meg & Cabot, Frank. From the Notebooks of a Middle School Princess. 2015. (From the Notebooks of a Middle School Princess Ser.). (ENG., Illus.). 192p. (J). (gr. 3-7). 16.99 *(978-1-250-06602-2(6)*, 9781250066022) Feiwel & Friends.

Calonita, Jen. Battle of the Bands. 2016. (VIP Ser.: 2). (ENG., Illus.). 320p. (J). (gr. 3-7). 16.99 *(978-0-316-25977-4(2))* Little, Brown Bks. for Young Readers.

—VIP: Battle of the Bands. 2017. (VIP Ser.: 2). (ENG.). 320p. (J). (gr. 3-7). pap. 6.99 *(978-0-316-25978-1(0))* Little, Brown Bks. for Young Readers.

Campbell, L. A. Cartboy & the Time Capsule. 2013. (Cartboy Ser.: 1). (ENG., Illus.). 208p. (J). (gr. 3-7). 12.99 *(978-0-7653-3317-9(1)*, 9780765333179, Starscape) Doherty, Tom Assocs., LLC.

—Cartboy Goes to Camp. 2014. (Cartboy Ser.: 2). (ENG., Illus.). 224p. (J). (gr. 3-7). 12.99 *(978-0-7653-3327-8(9)*, 9780765333278, Starscape) Doherty, Tom Assocs., LLC.

Carlson, Melody. I Do! 2005. (Diary of a Teenage Girl Ser.: Bk. 9). (ENG.). 272p. (J). (gr. 7). pap. 14.99 *(978-1-59052-320-9(2)*, Multnomah) Doubleday Religious Publishing Group, The.

—It's a Green Thing. 2009. (Diary of a Teenage Girl Ser.: Bk. 15). (ENG.). 256p. pap. 14.99 *(978-1-60142-118-0(4)*, Multnomah) Doubleday Religious Publishing Group, The.

—Just Ask. 2005. (Diary of a Teenage Girl Ser.: Bk. 10). (ENG.). 256p. (J). (gr. 7-12). per. 14.99 *(978-1-59052-321-6(0)*, Multnomah Bks.) Crown Publishing Group.

—My Name Is Chloe. 2005. (Diary of a Teenage Girl: Bk. 5). 288p. (YA). mass mkt. 7.99 *(978-1-59052-736-8(4)*, Multnomah) Doubleday Religious Publishing Group, The.

—What Matters Most. 2009. (Diary of a Teenage Girl Ser.: Bk. 3). (ENG.). 256p. pap. 13.99 *(978-1-60142-119-7(2)*, Multnomah) Doubleday Religious Publishing Group, The.

Cary, Kate. Bloodline. 2006. (ENG.). 352p. (YA). (gr. 7-12). 9.99 *(978-1-59514-078-4(6)*, Razorbill) Penguin Young Readers Group.

—Reckoning. 2008. (ENG.). 320p. (YA). (gr. 7-18). pap. 9.99 *(978-1-59514-179-8(0)*, Razorbill) Penguin Young Readers Group.

Cavanaugh, Nancy J. This Journal Belongs to Ratchet. 2014. (ENG.). 320p. (J). (gr. 3-6). pap. 6.99 *(978-1-4926-0109-8(8)*, 9781492601098, Sourcebooks Jabberwocky) Sourcebooks, Inc.

Chan, Gillian. An Ocean Apart: The Gold Mountain Diary of Chin Mei-Ling. 2004. (Dear Canada Ser.). (ENG., Illus.). 224p. (J). *(978-0-7791-1353-8(5))* Scholastic Canada, Ltd.

Chastain, Emma. Confessions of a High School Disaster. 2017. (Chloe Snow's Diary Ser.). (ENG., Illus.). 352p. (YA). (gr. 7). 17.99 *(978-1-4814-8875-4(9)*, Simon Pulse) Simon Pulse.

Chbosky, Stephen. The Perks of Being a Wallflower. 2014. (ENG.). 224p. (gr. 7-12). 18.25 *(978-1-63245-042-5(9))* Lectorum Pubns., Inc.

—The Perks of Being a Wallflower. 2012. (ENG.). 224p. 21.00 *(978-1-4516-9620-2(5))*; pap. 14.99 *(978-1-4516-9619-6(1))* MTV Books. (MTV Bks.).

—The Perks of Being a Wallflower. 2009. 13.77 *(978-0-7848-1530-4(5)*, Everbind) Marco Bk. Co.

—The Perks of Being a Wallflower. 2008. (ENG.). 24.30 *(978-1-60686-308-4(8)*, Covercraft) Perfection Learning Corp.

—The Perks of Being a Wallflower. 2007. 1.25 *(978-1-4281-3271-9(6))* Recorded Bks., Inc.

Chibbaro, Julie. Deadly. Sovak, Jean-Marc Superville, illus. (ENG.). 304p. (YA). (gr. 7). 2012. pap. 10.99 *(978-0-689-85739-3(X))* 2011. 17.99 *(978-0-689-85738-6(1))* Simon & Schuster Children's Publishing. (Atheneum Bks. for Young Readers).

Child, Lauren, et al. Fi'n Hollol, Carys Blodyn. 2005. (WEL., Illus.). 192p. pap. *(978-1-85596-675-8(1))* Dref Wen.

Colfer, Chris. Adventures from the Land of Stories Boxed Set: The Mother Goose Diaries & Queen Red Riding Hood's Guide to Royalty. 2015. (Land of Stories Ser.). (ENG.). 256p. (J). (gr. 3-7). 22.00 *(978-0-316-26151-7(3))* Little, Brown Bks. for Young Readers.

—The Mother Goose Diaries. 2017. (ENG.). 128p. (J). (gr. 3-7). 10.99 *(978-0-316-38334-9(1))* Little Brown & Co.

—The Mother Goose Diaries. Dorman, Brandon et al, illus. 2015. 121p. (J). *(978-0-316-38332-5(5))* Little Brown & Co.

—Queen Red Riding Hood's Guide to Royalty. Dorman, Brandon, illus. 2015. 118p. (J). *(978-0-316-38339-4(2))* Little Brown & Co.

Collins, Sheila. Truffles' Diary: The Encore. 2007. (Illus.). 76p. pap. *(978-1-906358-13-6(3))* Apex Publishing Ltd., Essex.

Collins, Tim. Adventures of a Wimpy Superhero: Rise of the Loser. 2016. (ENG., Illus.). 224p. (J). (gr. 3-7). pap. 9.99 *(978-1-78243-438-2(0))* O'Mara, Michael Bks., Ltd. GBR. Dist: Independent Pubs. Group.

—Diary of Dorkius Maximus. Pinder, Andrew, illus. 2014. (Diary of Dorkius Maximus Ser.: 1). (ENG.). 192p. (J). (gr. 4-6). pap. 8.99 *(978-1-78055-027-5(8))* O'Mara, Michael Bks., Ltd. GBR. Dist: Independent Pubs. Group.

—Diary of Dorkius Maximus in Egypt. Pinder, Andrew, illus. 2014. (Diary of Dorkius Maximus Ser.: 2). (ENG.). 192p. (J). (gr. 4-6). pap. 8.99 *(978-1-78055-028-2(6))* O'Mara, Michael Bks., Ltd. GBR. Dist: Independent Pubs. Group.

—Diary of Dorkius Maximus in Pompeii. Pinder, Andrew, illus. 2015. (Diary of Dorkius Maximus Ser.: 3). (ENG.). 192p. (J). (gr. 4-6). pap. 10.99 *(978-1-78055-268-2(8))* O'Mara, Michael Bks., Ltd. GBR. Dist: Independent Pubs. Group.

—Notes from a Hairy-Not-Scary Werewolf. Pinder, Andrew, illus. 2013. (ENG.). 288p. (J). (gr. 5-9). 12.99 *(978-1-4424-8207-4(9)*, Aladdin) Simon & Schuster Children's Publishing.

—Notes from a Totally Lame Vampire: Because the Undead Have Feelings Too! Pinder, Andrew, illus. 2010. (ENG.). 336p. (J). (gr. 5-9). 12.99 *(978-1-4424-1183-8(X)*, Aladdin) Simon & Schuster Children's Publishing.

—Prince of Dorkness: More Notes from a Totally Lame Vampire. Pinder, Andrew, illus. 2011. (ENG.). 336p. (J). (gr. 5-9). 12.99 *(978-1-4424-3388-5(4)*, Aladdin) Simon & Schuster Children's Publishing.

Cooper, Michelle. A Brief History of Montmaray. 2011. (Montmaray Journals). (ENG.). 324p. (YA). (gr. 7). pap. 8.99 *(978-0-375-85154-4(2)*, Knopf Bks. for Young Readers) Random Hse. Children's Bks.

—The FitzOsbornes at War. 2013. (Montmaray Journals). (ENG.). 560p. (YA). (gr. 7). pap. 10.99 *(978-0-307-93058-3(0)*, Ember) Random Hse. Children's Bks.

—The FitzOsbornes in Exile. 2012. (Montmaray Journals). (ENG.). 464p. (YA). (gr. 7). pap. 10.99 *(978-0-375-85155-1(0)*, Ember) Random Hse. Children's Bks.

Costain, Meredith. I Heart Pets: The Ella Diaries. McDonald, Danielle, illus. 2017. 144p. (J). pap. 5.99 *(978-1-61067-522-2(3))* Kane Miller.

Courtney, Suzanne Gene. Dear Diary: My Brother Died Today. 2013. 32p. pap. 14.95 *(978-1-62857-013-7(X)*, Strategic Bk. Publishing) Strategic Book Publishing & Rights Agency (SBPRA).

Coville, Bruce. Cursed. 2016. (Enchanted Files Ser.: 1). lib. bdg. 17.20 *(978-0-606-38460-5(X))* Turtleback Bks.

—Diary of a Mad Brownie. 2015. (Enchanted Files Ser.). (ENG., Illus.). 256p. (J). (gr. 3-7). lib. bdg. 19.99 *(978-0-385-39248-8(6)*, Random Hse. Bks. for Young Readers) Random Hse. Children's Bks.

—Diary of a Runaway Griffin. Douglas, Allen, illus. 2016. (Enchanted Files Ser.: 2). (ENG.). 272p. (J). (gr. 3-7). 16.99 *(978-0-385-39255-6(9)*, Random Hse. Bks. for Young Readers) Random Hse. Children's Bks.

—Hatched. Kidby, Paul, illus. 2017. (Enchanted Files Ser.: 2). (ENG.). 288p. (J). (gr. 3-7). pap. 6.99 *(978-0-385-39258-7(3)*, Yearling) Random Hse. Children's Bks.

Crist-Evans, Craig. Moon over Tennessee: A Boy's Civil War Journal. Christensen, Bonnie, illus. 2003. (ENG.). 64p. (J). (gr. 5-7). pap. 8.95 *(978-0-618-31107-1(6))* Houghton Mifflin Harcourt Publishing Co.

Cronin, Doreen. Diary of a Fly. Bliss, Harry, illus. (ENG.). 40p. (J). (gr. -1-3). 2013. 9.99 *(978-0-06-223298-4(3))* 2007. 16.99 *(978-0-06-000156-8(9))* HarperCollins Pubs.

—Diary of a Fly. Bliss, Harry, illus. 2008. (J). (gr. -1-3). 28.95 incl. audio compact disk *(978-1-4301-0407-0(4))*; 25.95 incl. audio *(978-1-4301-0404-9(X))* Live Oak Media.

—Diary of a Spider. Bliss, Harry, illus. (ENG.). 40p. (J). (gr. -1-3). 2013. 9.99 *(978-0-06-223300-4(9))* 2005. 16.99 *(978-0-06-000153-7(4))* HarperCollins Pubs.

—Diary of a Spider. Bliss, Harry, illus. unabr. ed. 2006. (Picture Book Readalong Ser.). (J). (gr. -1-2). 28.95 incl. audio compact disk *(978-1-59519-486-2(X))* Live Oak Media.

—Diary of a Spider. Bliss, Harry, illus. unabr. ed. 2006. (J). (gr. -1-3). 29.95 *(978-0-439-90579-4(6))* Weston Woods Studios, Inc.

—Diary of a Worm. 2003. (Illus.). (J). 127.92 *(978-0-06-056900-6(X))*; 127.92 *(978-0-06-056901-3(8))* HarperCollins Pubs.

—Diary of a Worm. Bliss, Harry, illus. 2003. 40p. (J). (gr. -1-3). (ENG.). 16.99 *(978-0-06-000150-6(X))*; lib. bdg. 18.89 *(978-0-06-000151-3(8))* HarperCollins Pubs.

—Diary of a Worm. Bliss, Harry, illus. pap. 18.95 incl. audio compact disk *(978-1-59112-871-7(4))*; pap. incl. audio compact disk *(978-1-59112-873-1(0))*; pap. incl. audio *(978-1-59112-869-4(2))*; pap. 16.95 incl. audio *(978-1-59112-867-0(6))* Live Oak Media.

—Diary of a Worm. 2004. (Illus.). (J). 28.95 incl. audio compact disk *(978-1-59112-872-4(2))* Live Oak Media.

—Diary of a Worm. 2013. (Diary of a Worm: I Can Read Level 1 Ser.). (J). lib. bdg. 13.55 *(978-0-606-31819-8(4)*, Turtleback) Turtleback Bks.

—Diary of a Worm: Teacher's Pet. Bliss, Harry & Nez, John, illus. 2013. (I Can Read Level 1 Ser.). (ENG.). 32p. (J). (gr. -1-3). 16.99 *(978-0-06-208705-8(3))*; pap. 3.99 *(978-0-06-208704-1(5))* HarperCollins Pubs.

—Nat the Gnat. 2014. (Diary of a Worm: I Can Read Level 1 Ser.). (J). lib. bdg. 13.55 *(978-0-606-35494-3(8))* Turtleback Bks.

Crook, Mackenzie. Ragetti's Secret Diary. 2008. (ENG.). 96p. (J). 9.99 *(978-1-4231-0931-0(7))* Disney Pr.

Curtin, Judi. Eva & the Hidden Diary. Fox, Woody, illus. 2013. (ENG.). 240p. (J). pap. 13.95 *(978-1-84717-588-5(0))* O'Brien Pr., Ltd., The IRL. Dist: Dufour Editions, Inc.

Cushman, Karen. Catherine, Called Birdy. 2012. lib. bdg. 18.40 *(978-0-606-24712-2(2)*, Turtleback) Turtleback Bks.

Danticat, Edwidge. Behind the Mountains. 2004. (First Person Fiction Ser.). (ENG.). 192p. (J). (gr. 7-10). pap. 6.99 *(978-0-439-37300-5(X)*, Orchard Bks.) Scholastic, Inc.

Day, Jan. The World's Greatest Explorer, 1 vol. Mason, Janeen, illus. 2009. (ENG.). 32p. (J). (gr. k-3). 16.99 *(978-1-58980-603-0(4))* Pelican Publishing Co., Inc.

De la Cruz, Melissa. Double Eclipse. 2016. (Summer on East End Ser.). (ENG.). 336p. (YA). (gr. 7). 17.99 *(978-0-399-17356-1(0)*, G.P. Putnam's Sons Books for Young Readers) Penguin Young Readers Group.

Deem, James M. 3 NBs of Julian Drew. 2004. (ENG.). 208p. (YA). (gr. 7-18). pap. 13.95 *(978-0-618-43907-2(2))* Houghton Mifflin Harcourt Publishing Co.

DeFelice, Cynthia C. The Ghost of Fossil Glen. 2010. (Ghost Mysteries Ser.: 1). (ENG.). 192p. (J). (gr. 3-7). pap. 7.99 *(978-0-312-60213-0(8)*, 9780312602130) Square Fish.

Denenberg, Barry. A True Patriot: The Journal of William Thomas Emerson, a Revolutionary War Patriot. 2012. lib. bdg. 17.20 *(978-0-606-26736-6(0)*, Turtleback) Turtleback Bks.

—When Will This Cruel War Be Over? The Diary of Emma Simpson, Gordonsville, Virginia 1864. 2011. (Dear America Ser.). (ENG.). 176p. (J). (gr. 3-7). 12.99 *(978-0-545-27598-9(9))* Scholastic, Inc.

Dent, Grace & Dent, Grace. Diva Without a Cause. 2009. (ENG.). 240p. (YA). (gr. 10-17). pap. 18.99 *(978-0-316-03482-1(7)*, Poppy) Little, Brown Bks. for Young Readers.

Deriso, Christine Hurley. Then I Met My Sister. 2011. (ENG.). 288p. (YA). (gr. 7-18). pap. 9.95 *(978-0-7387-2581-9(1)*, Flux) North Star Editions.

DeVillers, Julia. How My Private Personal Journal Became a Bestseller. 2005. (ENG.). 224p. (J). (gr. 3-7). 6.99 *(978-0-14-240332-7(6)*, Puffin Books) Penguin Young Readers Group.

Dockray, Tracy. My Life Story. Dockray, Tracy, illus. 2003. (Illus.). 40p. (J). lib. bdg. 15.95 *(978-1-58717-218-2(6)*, SeaStar Bks.) Chronicle Bks. LLC.

Donnelly, Jennifer. Revolution. 2011. (ENG.). 512p. (YA). (gr. 9). pap. 9.99 *(978-0-385-73764-7(5)*, Ember) Random Hse. Children's Bks.

Doxey, Heidi. The Jane Journals at Pemberley Prep: Liam Darcy, I Loathe You. 2015. 215p. (YA). pap. 14.99 *(978-1-4621-1682-9(5))* Cedar Fort, Inc./CFI Distribution.

Durbin, William. Until the Last Spike: The Journal of Sean Sullivan, a Transcontinental Railroad Worker, Nebraska & Points West 1867. 2013. (My Name Is America Ser.). lib. bdg. 17.20 *(978-0-606-32342-0(2)*, Turtleback) Turtleback Bks.

Elliott, Rebecca. Baxter Is Missing - A Branches Book. Elliott, Rebecca, illus. 2017. (Owl Diaries: 6). (ENG., Illus.). 80p. (J). (gr. k-2). pap. 4.99 ***(978-1-338-04284-9(X))*** Scholastic, Inc.

—Eva & the New Owl. 2016. (Owl Diaries: 4). (ENG., Illus.). 80p. (J). (gr. k-2). pap. 4.99 *(978-0-545-82559-7(8))* Scholastic, Inc.

—Eva Sees a Ghost. 2015. (Owl Diaries: 2). (ENG., Illus.). 80p. (J). (gr. k-2). 15.99 *(978-0-545-78784-0(X))*; pap. 4.99 *(978-0-545-78783-3(1))* Scholastic, Inc.

—Eva's Treetop Festival, Bk. 1. Elliott, Rebecca, illus. 2015. (Owl Diaries: 1). (ENG., Illus.). 80p. (J). (gr. k-2). pap. 4.99 *(978-0-545-68362-3(9))* Scholastic, Inc.

Emond, Stephen. Happyface. 2011. (ENG., Illus.). 336p. (YA). (gr. 7-17). pap. 10.99 *(978-0-316-04099-0(1))* Little, Brown Bks. for Young Readers.

Everett Hale, Edward. Last of the Peterkins with Others of the. 2006. pap. *(978-1-4068-1087-5(8))* Echo Library.

Farrant, Natasha. After Iris. 2013. (ENG.). 272p. (J). (gr. 5). 16.99 *(978-0-8037-3982-6(6)*, Dial Bks) Penguin Young Readers Group.

Fergus, Maureen. Exploits of a Reluctant (but Extremely Goodlooking) Hero. 2007. (ENG.). 216p. (J). (gr. 5-9). 7.95 *(978-1-55453-025-0(3))* Kids Can Pr., Ltd. CAN. Dist: Hachette Bk. Group.

Flinn, Alex. Breathing Underwater. unabr. ed. 2004. (Young Adult Cassette Librariestm Ser.). 272p. (J). (gr. 7-18). pap. 36.00 incl. audio *(978-0-8072-0992-9(9)*, S YA 346 SP, Listening Library) Random Hse. Audio Publishing Group.

Flint, Garrison. Sanity in Search of Peter Alexander. 2003. 198p. (YA). per. 13.95 *(978-1-885631-73-2(1))* Hutchison, G.F. Pr.

French, Jackie. Christmas Wombat. Whatley, Bruce, illus. 2012. (ENG.). 32p. (J). (gr. -1-3). 16.99 *(978-0-547-86872-1(3))* Houghton Mifflin Harcourt Publishing Co.

—Diary of a Baby Wombat. Whatley, Bruce, illus. 2010. (ENG.). 32p. (J). (gr. -1-3). 16.99 *(978-0-547-43005-8(1))* Houghton Mifflin Harcourt Publishing Co.

—Diary of a Wombat. Whatley, Bruce, illus. 2007. 16p. (J). bds. *(978-0-7322-8662-0(X))* HarperCollins Pubs. Australia.

—Diary of a Wombat. Whatley, Bruce, illus. (ENG.). 32p. (J). (gr. -1-3). 2009. pap. 6.99 *(978-0-547-07669-0(X))* 2003. 16.99 *(978-0-618-38136-4(8))* Houghton Mifflin Harcourt Publishing Co.

Friedman, Laurie. Can You Say Catastrophe? 2014. (Mostly Miserable Life of April Sinclair Ser.: 1). (ENG.). 160p. (J). (gr. 5-9). pap. 5.95 *(978-1-4677-0941-5(7)*, Darby Creek) 2013. 151p. pap. 17.95 *(978-1-4677-1620-8(0))* Lerner Publishing Group.

—Heart to Heart with Mallory. 2008. pap. 34.95 *(978-0-8225-9439-0(0))* Lerner Publishing Group.

—Heart to Heart with Mallory. Pollak, Barbara, illus. (Mallory Ser.: 6). (ENG.). 160p. (J). (gr. 2-5). 2007. per. 5.95 *(978-0-8225-7133-9(1)*, First Avenue Editions) 2006. lib. bdg. 15.95 *(978-1-57505-932-7(0)*, Twenty-First Century Bks.) Lerner Publishing Group.

—Life, Loss, & Lemonade. Shaloshvili, Natasha, illus. 2017. (Mostly Miserable Life of April Sinclair Ser.: 8). (ENG.). 168p. (J). (gr. 5-9). 17.95 *(978-1-4677-8591-4(1)*, Darby Creek) Lerner Publishing Group.

—Not What I Expected. Shaloshvili, Natasha, illus. 2015. (Mostly Miserable Life of April Sinclair Ser.: 5). (ENG.). 176p. (J). (gr. 5-9). 17.99 *(978-1-4677-8829-8(5)*, Darby Creek) Lerner Publishing Group.

—Oh Boy, Mallory. Kalis, Jennifer, illus. (Mallory Ser.: 17). (ENG.). 160p. (J). (gr. 2-5). 2013. pap. 5.95 *(978-1-4677-0863-0(1))* 2012. 15.95 *(978-0-7613-6072-8(7)*, Darby Creek) Lerner Publishing Group.

—On the Road with Mallory. Kalis, Jennifer, illus. 2016. (Mallory Ser.: 25). (ENG.). 160p. (J). (gr. 2-5). 15.95 *(978-1-4677-5029-5(8)*, Darby Creek) Lerner Publishing Group.

—Red, White, & True Blue Mallory. Kalis, Jennifer, illus. (Mallory Ser.: 11). (ENG.). 184p. (J). (gr. 2-5). 2010. pap. 5.95 *(978-0-7613-3946-5(9))* 2009. 15.95 *(978-0-8225-8882-5(X))* Lerner Publishing Group. (Carolrhoda Bks.).

—Too Good to Be True. 2014. (Mostly Miserable Life of April Sinclair Ser.: 2). (ENG., Illus.). 168p. (J). (gr. 5-9). 17.95 *(978-1-4677-0926-2(3)*, Darby Creek) Lerner Publishing Group.

—Too Much Drama. Shaloshvili, Natasha, illus. 2016. (Mostly Miserable Life of April Sinclair Ser.: 6). (ENG.). 184p. (gr. 5-9). (J). 17.95 *(978-1-4677-8589-1(X))*; 35.99 *(978-1-4677-9570-8(4))* Lerner Publishing Group. (Darby Creek).

—Truth & Kisses. 2015. (ENG.). 168p. (J). (gr. 5-9). pap. 5.95 *(978-1-4677-0943-9(3)*, Darby Creek) Lerner Publishing Group.

—A Twist of Fate. Shaloshvili, Natasha, illus. (Mostly Miserable Life of April Sinclair Ser.: Vol. 7). (ENG.). 168p. (gr. 5-9). 2017. (J). pap. 5.95 ***(978-1-5124-5866-4(X))*** 2016. 35.99 *(978-1-5124-0899-7(9))* Lerner Publishing Group. (Darby Creek).

Friedman, Laurie B. Love or Something Like It. 2015. (J). 5.99 *(978-1-4677-7790-2(0))*; (Mostly Miserable Life of April Sinclair Ser.: 4). (ENG.). 184p. (gr. 5-9). 17.95 *(978-1-4677-0928-6(X))* Lerner Publishing Group.

—Not What I Expected. Shaloshvili, Natasha, illus. 2015. (ENG.). 176p. (J). (gr. 5-9). 17.95 *(978-1-4677-8588-4(1))* Lerner Publishing Group.

—Truth & Kisses. 2014. (Mostly Miserable Life of April Sinclair Ser.: 3). (ENG.). 168p. (J). (gr. 5-9). 17.95 *(978-1-4677-0927-9(1))* Lerner Publishing Group.

Gale, Eric Kahn. The Bully Book. 2013. (ENG.). 256p. (J). (gr. 3-7). pap. 6.99 *(978-0-06-212513-2(3))* HarperCollins Pubs.

Gibbs, Gretchen. The Book of Maggie Bradstreet. 2012. (Bradstreet Chronicles). (ENG.). 183p. (YA). pap. 9.99 *(978-0-9852948-0-9(9))* Glenmere Pr.

Goldblatt, Mark. Twerp. 2013. (ENG.). 288p. (J). (gr. 4-7). 16.99 *(978-0-375-97142-6(4)*, Random Hse. Bks. for Young Readers) Random Hse. Children's Bks.

Gray, Dianne & Gray, Dianne E. Holding up the Earth. 2006. (ENG.). 210p. (J). (gr. 5-7). pap. 12.95 *(978-0-618-73747-5(2))* Houghton Mifflin Harcourt Publishing Co.

Green, Jessica. Diary of a Would-Be Princess: The Journal of Jillian Jones, 5b. 2007. (Illus.). 236p. (J). (gr. 4-7). 15.95 *(978-1-58089-166-0(7))* Charlesbridge Publishing, Inc.

Gregory, Kristiana. Cannons at Dawn: The Second Diary of Abigail Jane Stewart, Valley Forge, Pennsylvania, 1779. 2011. (Dear America Ser.). (ENG.). 256p. (J). (gr. 5-9). 12.99 *(978-0-545-21319-6(3))* Scholastic, Inc.

—The Winter of Red Snow. 2010. (Dear America Ser.). (ENG.). 192p. (J). (gr. 3-7). 12.99 *(978-0-545-23802-1(1)*, Scholastic Pr.) Scholastic, Inc.

Grimes, Nikki. Chasing Freedom: The Life Journeys of Harriet Tubman & Susan B. Anthony, Inspired by Historical Facts. Wood, Michele, illus. 2015. (ENG.). 56p. (J). (gr. 2-5). 18.99 *(978-0-439-79338-4(6)*, Orchard Bks.) Scholastic, Inc.

Gutman, Dan. Race for the Sky: The Kitty Hawk Diaries of Johnny Moore. 2003. (ENG., Illus.). 192p. (J). (gr. 5-9). 19.99 *(978-0-689-84554-3(5)*, Simon & Schuster Bks. For Young Readers) Simon & Schuster Bks. For Young Readers.

Haddix, Margaret Peterson. Don't You Dare Read This, Mrs. Dunphrey. 2012. (ENG.). 128p. (YA). (gr. 7-7). pap. 9.99 *(978-1-4424-4315-0(4)*, Simon & Schuster Bks. For Young Readers) Simon & Schuster Bks. For Young Readers.

Hale, Kathleen. No One Else Can Have You. 2014. (Kippy Bushman Ser.). (ENG.). 384p. (YA). (gr. 9). 17.99 *(978-0-06-221119-4(6))* HarperCollins Pubs.

Harmer, Wendy. I Lost My Mobile at the Mall. 2011. (ENG.). 272p. (YA). (gr. 7-18). 10.99 *(978-1-935279-97-6(1))* Kane Miller.

Harper, Candy. Keep the Faith. 2014. (ENG.). 288p. (J). pap. 8.99 *(978-0-85707-825-4(9)*, Simon & Schuster Children's) Simon & Schuster, Ltd. GBR. Dist: Simon & Schuster, Inc.

C
D

Harper, Charise Mericle. Just Grace Walks the Dog. 2009. (Just Grace Ser.: 3). (ENG., Illus.). 176p. (J). (gr. 1-4). pap. 5.99 *(978-0-547-23753-4(7))* Houghton Mifflin Harcourt Publishing Co.

Hays, Anna Jane, et al, illus. Smarty Sara. 2008. (Step into Reading Ser.). (ENG.). 32p. (J). (gr. -1-1). pap. 3.99 *(978-0-375-83512-4(1),* Random Hse. Bks. for Young Readers) Random Hse. Children's Bks.

Henry, Marguerite. Benjamin West & His Cat Grimalkin. Dennis, Wesley, illus. 2014. (ENG.). 160p. (J). (gr. 3-7). pap. 7.99 *(978-1-4814-0394-8(X),* Aladdin) Simon & Schuster Children's Publishing.

Hesse, Karen. Stowaway. unabr. ed. 2004. 328p. (J). (gr. 5-9). pap. 48.00 incl. audio *(978-0-8072-8760-6(1),* LYA 259 SP, Listening Library) Random Hse. Audio Publishing Group.

Hoffman, Mary. Daughters of Time: An Anthology from the History Girls. Hoffman, Mary, ed. 2014. (ENG.). 352p. (J). (gr. 4-7). pap. 13.99 *(978-1-84877-169-7(X))* Bonnier Publishing GBR. Dist: Independent Pubs. Group.

Hogarth, Ainslie. The Boy Meets Girl Massacre (Annotated) 2015. (ENG.). 288p. (YA). pap. 11.99 *(978-0-7387-4472-8(7),* Flux) North Star Editions.

Horowitz, Lena. Dancing with Molly. 2016. (ENG.). 272p. (YA). (gr. 9). pap. 10.99 *(978-1-4814-1551-4(4),* Simon Pulse) Simon Pulse.

Howie, Betsy. Unscripted by Lainey McBride. Lowery, Mike, illus. 2012. 183p. (J). *(978-0-545-39705-6(7))* Scholastic, Inc.

Hulet, Debra. Independence Rock. 2011. 208p. pap. 13.99 *(978-1-59955-441-9(0),* Bonneville Bks.) Cedar Fort, Inc./CFI Distribution.

Inglis, Lucy. Crow Mountain. 2016. (ENG.). 368p. (YA). (gr. 9). 17.99 *(978-0-545-90407-0(2),* Chicken Hse., The) Scholastic, Inc.

Jocelyn, Marthe. Mable Riley: A Reliable Record of Humdrum, Peril, & Romance. 2007. 279p. (gr. 4-7). 17.00 *(978-0-7569-8183-9(2))* Perfection Learning Corp.

The Journey. 2003. 170p. (YA). per. 10.95 *(978-0-9713292-8-7(1))* Aim Higher Bks.

Juby, Susan. Miss Smithers. 2004. (Illus.). 336p. (J). 15.99 *(978-0-06-051546-1(5),* HarperTeen) HarperCollins Pubs.

Kath, Natalie. The Summer I Lost It, 1 vol. (Stone Arch Novels Ser.). (ENG.). 128p. (gr. 4-8). 2012. pap. 6.95 *(978-1-4342-4067-5(3))* 2011. lib. bdg. 26.65 *(978-1-4342-3316-5(2))* Stone Arch Bks. (Stone Arch Novels).

Kats, Jewel. Miss Popular Steals the Show: Girls in Wheelchairs Rule! Stenton, Murray, illus. 2014. 37p. (J). pap. 14.95 *(978-1-61599-236-2(7))* Loving Healing Pr., Inc.

Kaufman, Sue. Diary of a Mad Housewife: A Novel. 2005. (ENG.). 320p. pap. 17.00 *(978-1-56025-687-8(7))* Seal Pr.

Keene, Carolyn. Curse of the Arctic Star. 2013. (Nancy Drew Diaries: 1). (ENG.). 208p. (J). (gr. 3-7). 15.99 *(978-1-4424-6610-4(3),* Aladdin) Simon & Schuster Children's Publishing.

—The Ghost of Grey Fox Inn. 2016. (Nancy Drew Diaries: 13). (ENG., Illus.). 192p. (J). (gr. 3-7). 17.99 *(978-1-4814-6596-0(1),* Simon & Schuster/Paula Wiseman Bks.) Simon & Schuster/Paula Wiseman Bks.

—Nancy Drew Diaries: Curse of the Arctic Star; Strangers on a Train; Mystery of the Midnight Rider; Once upon a Thriller. 2013. (Nancy Drew Diaries). (ENG., Illus.). 768p. (J). (gr. 3-7). pap. 27.99 *(978-1-4424-8896-0(4),* Aladdin) Simon & Schuster Children's Publishing.

—Nancy Drew Diaries 3-Books-In-1! Curse of the Arctic Star; Strangers on a Train; Mystery of the Midnight Rider. 2016. (Nancy Drew Diaries). (ENG., Illus.). 592p. (J). (gr. 3-7). pap. 8.99 *(978-1-4814-8554-8(7),* Aladdin) Simon & Schuster Children's Publishing.

—Once upon a Thriller. 2013. (Nancy Drew Diaries: 4). (ENG., Illus.). 144p. (J). (gr. 3-7). 15.99 *(978-1-4424-6612-8(X));* pap. 6.99 *(978-1-4169-9074-1(7))* Simon & Schuster Children's Publishing. (Aladdin).

Kelley, Gretchen. Superheroes Don't Eat Veggie Burgers. 2016. (ENG.). 272p. (J). 16.99 *(978-1-62779-089-5(6),* 9781627790895, Holt, Henry & Co. Bks. For Young Readers) Holt, Henry & Co.

Kelly, Katy. Working Myself to Pieces & Bits. Ferguson, Peter, illus. 2008. (Lucy Rose Ser.). (ENG.). 208p. (J). (gr. 3-7). 6.99 *(978-0-440-42186-3(1),* Yearling) Random Hse. Children's Bks.

Kelsey, Annie. Pippa Morgan's Diary. Larsen, Kate, illus. 2015. (Pippa Morgan's Diary Ser.: 1). (ENG.). 160p. (J). (gr. 3-7). 12.99 *(978-1-4926-2328-1(8),* 9781492623281, Sourcebooks Jabberwocky) Sourcebooks, Inc.

Kimmel, Elizabeth Cody. Lily B. on the Brink of Cool. 2005. 245p. (J). (gr. 5-9). 14.65 *(978-0-7569-5653-0(6))* Perfection Learning Corp.

Kinney, Jeff. Cabin Fever. 2011. (Diary of a Wimpy Kid Ser.). (ENG., Illus.). 224p. (J). (gr. 3-7). 13.95 *(978-1-4197-0223-5(8),* Amulet Bks.) Abrams, Inc.

—Cabin Fever. 2011. (Diary of a Wimpy Kid Ser.: 6). (J). 1.25 *(978-1-4640-4524-0(0)); (978-1-4640-2149-7(X));* 44.75 *(978-1-4640-2151-0(1));* 44.75 *(978-1-4640-2152-7(X));* 46.75 *(978-1-4640-2148-0(1))* Recorded Bks., Inc.

—Cabin Fever. 2011. (Diary of a Wimpy Kid Ser.: 6). (J). lib. bdg. 25.70 *(978-0-606-23667-6(8),* Turtleback) Turtleback Bks.

—Carnet de Bord de Greg Heffley. Zimmerman, Natalie, tr. 2012. (Journal d'un Degonfle Ser.: Vol. 1). (FRE., Illus.). 223p. (J). (gr. 4-8). pap. *(978-2-02-101196-8(8))* Editions du Seuil.

—El Diario de Greg, un Renacuajo. Morán, Esteban, tr. 2008. (SPA.). 218p. (J). (gr. 3-6). 17.99 *(978-1-933032-52-8(9))* Lectorum Pubns., Inc.

—Diary of a Wimpy Kid. 2014. pap. *(978-1-4197-1499-3(6))* 2013. pap. *(978-1-4197-1176-3(8))* 2009. pap. *(978-0-8109-8888-0(7))* 2007. (Diary of a Wimpy Kid Ser.). (ENG., Illus.). 224p. (J). (gr. 2-8). 13.95 *(978-0-8109-9313-6(9))* 2007. pap. *(978-0-8109-8893-4(3))* 2007. pap. *(978-0-8109-8292-5(7))* 2007. (Diary of a Wimpy Kid Ser.: Bk. 1). 217p. pap. *(978-0-8109-9455-3(0))*Bk. 1-4. 2014. (ENG.). 896p. (J). (gr. 3-7). 56.00 *(978-1-4197-1669-0(7))* Abrams, Inc. (Amulet Bks.).

—Diary of a Wimpy Kid. (Diary of a Wimpy Kid Ser.). (CHI., Illus.). (J). 2009. (gr. 4-8). *(978-986-84847-4-0(X))* 2008. (gr. 3-7). ***(978-986-84847-0-2(7))*** DaskoviK, Izdatel'sko-torgovaja korporacija.

—Diary of a Wimpy Kid. 2013. (Diary of a Wimpy Kid Ser.: 16). (CHI.). (J). pap. 13.95 *(978-7-5405-7891-6(2))* Guangdong New Era Publishing Hse. CHN. Dist: Chinasprout, Inc.

—Diary of a Wimpy Kid. 2009. (Diary of a Wimpy Kid Ser.: Bk. 1). 1.00 *(978-1-4074-4434-5(4))* 2008. (Diary of a Wimpy Kid Ser.: 1). (J). 75.75 *(978-1-4361-3290-9(8))* 2008. (Diary of a Wimpy Kid Ser.: 1). (J). 44.75 *(978-1-4281-8196-0(2))* 2008. (Diary of a Wimpy Kid Ser.: 1). (J). 46.75 *(978-1-4281-8194-6(6))* 2008. (Diary of a Wimpy Kid Ser.: 1). (J). 1.25 *(978-1-4281-8191-5(1))* 2008. (Diary of a Wimpy Kid Ser.: 1). (J). 173.75 *(978-1-4281-8195-3(4))* 2008. (Diary of a Wimpy Kid Ser.: 1). (J). 44.75 *(978-1-4281-8200-4(4))* 2008. (Diary of a Wimpy Kid Ser.: 1). (J). 46.75 *(978-1-4281-8198-4(9))* Recorded Bks., Inc.

—Diary of a Wimpy Kid. 2007. (Diary of a Wimpy Kid Ser.: 1). (Illus.). 217p. (J). lib. bdg. 25.70 *(978-0-606-23662-1(7),* Turtleback) Turtleback Bks.

—Dog Days. 2009. (Diary of a Wimpy Kid Ser.: 4). (ENG., Illus.). 224p. (J). (gr. 3-7). 13.95 *(978-0-8109-8391-5(5),* Amulet Bks.) Abrams, Inc.

—Dog Days. (Diary of a Wimpy Kid Ser.: 4). (J). 2011. 75.75 *(978-1-4407-7756-1(X))* 2010. (SPA.). 181.75 *(978-1-4407-7748-6(9))* 2010. 54.75 *(978-1-4407-7747-9(0))* 2010. 46.75 *(978-1-4407-7751-6(9))* 2010. 44.75 *(978-1-4407-7753-0(5))* 2009. 52.75 *(978-1-4407-7749-3(7))* 2009. 1.25 *(978-1-4407-7755-4(1))* Recorded Bks., Inc.

—Dog Days. 2009. (Diary of a Wimpy Kid Ser.: 4). (J). lib. bdg. 25.70 *(978-0-606-23665-2(1),* Turtleback) Turtleback Bks.

—Double Down. 2016. (Diary of a Wimpy Kid Ser.: Bk. 11). (ENG., Illus.). 224p. (J). (gr. 3-7). 13.95 *(978-1-4197-2344-5(8));* E-Book 12.56 *(978-1-61312-992-0(0))* Abrams, Inc. (Amulet Bks.).

—Double Down. 2016. (Diary of a Wimpy Kid Ser.: 11). (J). lib. bdg. 25.70 *(978-0-606-38998-3(9))* Turtleback Bks.

—Hard Luck. 2013. (Diary of a Wimpy Kid Ser.: Bk. 8). (ENG., Illus.). 224p. (J). (gr. 3-7). 13.95 *(978-1-4197-1132-9(6),* Amulet Bks.) Abrams, Inc.

—Hard Luck. 2013. (Diary of a Wimpy Kid Ser.: 8). (J). lib. bdg. 25.70 *(978-0-606-32062-7(8),* Turtleback) Turtleback Bks.

—The Last Straw. 2009. (Diary of a Wimpy Kid Ser.). (Illus.). (J). (gr. 3-7). (ENG.). 224p. 13.95 *(978-0-8109-7068-7(6),* Amulet Bks.); 218p. pap. *(978-0-8109-7108-0(9))* Abrams, Inc.

—The Last Straw. 2009. (Diary of a Wimpy Kid Ser.: 3). (ENG.). 224p. (J). (gr. 4-6). pap. 17.95 *(978-1-4395-8262-6(9),* 0008062297, Paw Prints) Baker & Taylor, CATS.

—The Last Straw. 2009. (Diary of a Wimpy Kid Ser.: Bk. 3). (JPN., Illus.). 221p. (J). *(978-4-591-10910-6(0))* Poplar Publishing.

—The Last Straw. 2010. (Diary of a Wimpy Kid Ser.: 3). (J). 1.25 *(978-1-4407-2984-3(0))* 2010. (Diary of a Wimpy Kid Ser.: 3). (J). 46.75 *(978-1-4407-2976-8(X))* 2009. (Diary of a Wimpy Kid Ser.: 3). (J). 75.75 *(978-1-4407-2986-7(7))* 2009. (Diary of a Wimpy Kid Ser.: 3). (J). 44.75 *(978-1-4407-2982-9(4))* 2009. (Diary of a Wimpy Kid Ser.: 3). (J). 173.75 *(978-1-4407-2977-5(8))* 2009. (Diary of a Wimpy Kid Ser.: 3). (J). 45.75 *(978-1-4407-2980-5(8))* 2009. (Diary of a Wimpy Kid Ser.: 3). (J). 44.75 *(978-1-4407-2978-2(6))* 2009. (Diary of a Wimpy Kid Ser.: Bk. 3). 1.00 *(978-1-4416-1788-0(4))* Recorded Bks., Inc.

—The Last Straw. 2009. (Diary of a Wimpy Kid Ser.: 3). (Illus.). 217p. (J). lib. bdg. 25.70 *(978-0-606-23664-5(3),* Turtleback) Turtleback Bks.

—The Long Haul. Kinney, Jeff, illus. 2014. (Diary of a Wimpy Kid Ser.: Bk. 9). (ENG., Illus.). 224p. (J). (gr. 3-7). 13.95 *(978-1-4197-1189-3(X),* Amulet Bks.) Abrams, Inc.

—The Long Haul. (CHI.). (J). 2015. 368p. (gr. 4-8). pap. *(978-986-6104-59-6(1))* 2014. *(978-986-6104-52-7(4))* DaskoviK, Izdatel'sko-torgovaja korporacija.

—The Long Haul. 2014. (JPN.). 221p. (J). *(978-4-591-14196-0(9))* Poplar Publishing.

—The Long Haul. 2013. (Diary of a Wimpy Kid Ser.: 9). (J). 40.75 *(978-1-4906-4383-0(4));* 43.75 *(978-1-4906-4058-7(4))* Recorded Bks., Inc.

—The Long Haul. 2014. (Diary of a Wimpy Kid Ser.: 9). (J). lib. bdg. 25.70 *(978-0-606-36074-6(3))* Turtleback Bks.

—Old School. 2015. (Diary of a Wimpy Kid Ser.: Bk. 10). (ENG., Illus.). 224p. (J). (gr. 3-7). 13.95 *(978-1-4197-1701-7(4),* Amulet Bks.) Abrams, Inc.

—Old School. 2015. (Diary of a Wimpy Kid Ser.: 10). (J). lib. bdg. 25.70 *(978-0-606-37422-4(1))* Turtleback Bks.

—Rodrick Rules. 2008. (Diary of a Wimpy Kid Ser.). (Illus.). (J). (ENG.). 224p. (gr. 3-7). 13.95 *(978-0-8109-9473-7(9),* Amulet Bks.); 216p. pap. 4.99 *(978-0-8109-9552-9(2))* Abrams, Inc.

—Rodrick Rules. 2008. (Diary of a Wimpy Kid Ser.: Bk. 2). (JPN., Illus.). 220p. (J). *(978-4-591-10464-4(8))* Poplar Publishing.

—Rodrick Rules, 2 vols. (Diary of a Wimpy Kid Ser.: 2). (J). 2010. 173.75 *(978-1-4361-3864-2(7))* 2010. 75.75 *(978-1-4407-0420-8(1))* 2009. 1.25 *(978-1-4361-3860-4(4))* 2009. 46.75 *(978-1-4361-3863-5(9))* 2009. 44.75 *(978-1-4361-3865-9(5))* 2009. 44.75 *(978-1-4361-3869-7(8))* 2009. (gr. 4-8). 46.75 *(978-1-4361-3867-3(1))* Recorded Bks., Inc.

—Rodrick Rules. 2008. (Diary of a Wimpy Kid Ser.: 2). (J). lib. bdg. 25.70 *(978-0-606-23663-8(5),* Turtleback) Turtleback Bks.

—The Third Wheel. 2012. (ENG.). (J). (gr. 3-7). pap. 8.49 *(978-1-4197-0584-7(9));* (Illus.). 224p. 13.95 *(978-1-4197-0584-7(9),* Amulet Bks.) Abrams, Inc.

—The Third Wheel. 2012. (Diary of a Wimpy Kid Ser.: 7). (Illus.). 217p. (YA). lib. bdg. 25.70 *(978-0-606-26514-0(7),* Turtleback) Turtleback Bks.

—The Ugly Truth. 2010. (Diary of a Wimpy Kid Ser.). (ENG.). 224p. (J). (gr. 3-7). 13.95 *(978-0-8109-8491-2(1),* Amulet Bks.) Abrams, Inc.

—The Ugly Truth. 2010. (Diary of a Wimpy Kid Ser.: Bk. 5). (JPN., Illus.). 221p. (J). (gr. 4-7). *(978-4-591-12117-7(8))* Poplar Publishing.

—The Ugly Truth, 2 vols. 2010. (Diary of a Wimpy Kid Ser.: 5). (J). 44.75 *(978-1-4498-4534-6(7));* 46.75 *(978-1-4498-4532-2(0));* 173.75 *(978-1-4498-4530-8(4));* 44.75 *(978-1-4498-4531-5(2));* 1.25 *(978-1-4498-4535-3(5))* Recorded Bks., Inc.

—The Ugly Truth. 2010. (Diary of a Wimpy Kid Ser.: 5). (J). lib. bdg. 25.70 *(978-0-606-23666-9(X),* Turtleback) Turtleback Bks.

Kirby, Jessi. Golden. (ENG.). 288p. (YA). (gr. 7). 2014. pap. 9.99 *(978-1-4424-5218-3(8))* 2013. 16.99 *(978-1-4424-5216-9(1))* Simon & Schuster Bks. For Young Readers. (Simon & Schuster Bks. For Young Readers).

Koertge, Ronald. Shakespeare Bats Cleanup. 2006. 116p. (gr. 7-12). 16.00 *(978-0-7569-6571-6(3))* Perfection Learning Corp.

Kraus, Jeanne. Get Ready for Jetty! My Journal about Adhd & Me. 2012. (J). pap. 9.95 *(978-1-4338-1197-5(9));* (Illus.). 14.95 *(978-1-4338-1196-8(0))* American Psychological Assn. (Magination Pr.).

Kuipers, Alice. Lost for Words. 2010. 224p. (YA). (gr. 8-18). 16.99 *(978-0-06-142922-4(8),* HarperTeen) HarperCollins Pubs.

LaCour, Nina. Hold Still. 2010. (ENG.). 272p. (YA). (gr. 7-18). 10.99 *(978-0-14-241694-5(0),* Speak) Penguin Young Readers Group.

Larson, Kirby. The Fences Between Us: The Diary of Piper Davis. 2010. (Dear America Ser.). (J). (ENG.). 320p. (gr. 3-7). 12.99 *(978-0-545-22418-5(7));* (Illus.). 313p. pap. *(978-0-545-27094-6(4))* Scholastic, Inc.

Lasky, Kathryn. Christmas after All. 2012. (Dear America Ser.). (ENG.). 192p. (J). (gr. 3-7). 12.99 *(978-0-545-38177-2(0))* Scholastic, Inc.

—A Journey to the New World: The Diary of Remember Patience Whipple, Mayflower 1620. 2010. (Dear America Ser.). (ENG.). 192p. (J). (gr. 3-7). 12.99 *(978-0-545-23801-4(3),* Scholastic Pr.) Scholastic, Inc.

Leavitt, Lindsey & Mellom, Robin. The Pages Between Us. Dening, Abby, illus. 2016. (Pages Between Us Ser.: 1). 288p. (J). (gr. 3-7). 16.99 *(978-0-06-237771-5(X))* HarperCollins Pubs.

—The Pages Between Us: in the Spotlight. 2017. (Pages Between Us Ser.: 2). 336p. (J). (gr. 3-7). 16.99 *(978-0-06-237774-6(4))* HarperCollins Pubs.

Li, Judith L. Ellie's Log: Exploring the Forest Where the Great Tree Fell. Herring, M. L., illus. 2013. (ENG.). 112p. (J). (gr. 3-6). pap. 17.95 *(978-0-87071-696-6(4))* Oregon State Univ. Pr.

Lisa's Diary: Individual Title Six-Packs. (gr. k-1). 23.00 *(978-0-7635-9066-6(5))* Rigby Education.

Lloyd, Saci. The Carbon Diaries 2015. 2008. (ENG., Illus.). 384p. (YA). pap. *(978-0-340-97015-7(4),* Hodder Children's Books) Hachette Children's Group.

—The Carbon Diaries 2015. 2009. (ENG.). 384p. (YA). (gr. 9-18). 17.95 *(978-0-8234-2190-9(2))* Holiday Hse., Inc.

—The Carbon Diaries 2017. (ENG.). (YA). (gr. 6). 2011. 384p. pap. 8.95 *(978-0-8234-2390-3(5))* 2010. 352p. 17.95 *(978-0-8234-2260-9(7))* Holiday Hse., Inc.

Luper, Eric. Gumball's Summer Journal That He Definitely Finished All on His Own. Reed, Stephen, illus. 2015. (Amazing World of Gumball Ser.). (ENG.). 112p. (J). (gr. 3-7). 8.99 *(978-0-8431-8282-8(2),* Cartoon Network Books) Penguin Young Readers Group.

MacHale, D. J. Pendragon: The Merchant of Death; The Lost City of Fear; The Never War; The Reality Bug; Black Water. 2013. (Pendragon Ser.). (ENG., Illus.). 1968p. (J). (gr. 5-9). pap. 49.99 *(978-1-4424-9926-3(5),* Simon & Schuster/Paula Wiseman Bks.) Simon & Schuster/Paula Wiseman Bks.

—The Pilgrims of Rayne. 2008. (Pendragon Ser.: 8). (ENG.). 576p. (J). (gr. 5-9). pap. 9.99 *(978-1-4169-1417-4(X),* Aladdin) Simon & Schuster Children's Publishing.

—The Quillan Games. 2007. (Pendragon Ser.: 7). (ENG.). 512p. (J). (gr. 5-9). pap. 9.99 *(978-0-689-86913-6(4),* Aladdin) Simon & Schuster Children's Publishing.

—The Rivers of Zadaa. 2006. (Pendragon Ser.: Bk. 6). 405p. (gr. 5-9). 19.00 *(978-0-7569-7040-6(7))* Perfection Learning Corp.

—The Rivers of Zadaa. (Pendragon Ser.: 6). (ENG.). 416p. (J). (gr. 5-9). 2006. pap. 9.99 *(978-0-689-86912-9(6))* 2005. 19.99 *(978-1-4169-0710-7(6))* Simon & Schuster Children's Publishing. (Aladdin).

—The Soldiers of Halla. (Pendragon Ser.: 10). (ENG.). 608p. (J). (gr. 5-9). 2010. pap. 9.99 *(978-1-4169-1421-1(8))* 2009. 17.99 *(978-1-4169-1420-4(X))* Simon & Schuster Children's Publishing. (Aladdin).

Manushkin, Fran. Katie Woo's Big Idea Journal: A Place for Your Best Stories, Drawings, Doodles, & Plans, 1 vol. Lyon, Tammie, illus. 2014. (Katie Woo Ser.). (ENG.). 144p. (gr. k-2). 9.95 *(978-1-62370-166-6(X))* Capstone Young Readers of Coughlan Cos.

—What's in Your Heart, Katie? Writing in a Journal with Katie Woo, 1 vol. Lyon, Tammie, illus. 2013. (Katie Woo: Star Writer Ser.). (ENG.). 32p. (gr. k-2). pap. 6.95 *(978-1-4795-1922-4(7));* lib. bdg. 20.65 *(978-1-4048-8127-3(1))* Picture Window Bks.

Mattel. Monster High Diaries: Lagoona Blue & the Big Sea Scarecation. 2016. (Monster High Diaries: 3). (ENG.). 160p. (J). (gr. 3-7). 9.99 *(978-0-316-30080-3(2))* Little, Brown Bks. for Young Readers.

May, Eleanor. The Bay School Blogger. 2008. pap. 34.95 *(978-1-58013-772-0(5))* Kane Press, Inc.

May, Kyla. Coco: My Delicious Life. 2013. (Lotus Lane Ser.: 2). (ENG., Illus.). 96p. (J). (gr. 1-3). 15.99 *(978-0-545-49615-5(2));* pap. 4.99 *(978-0-545-44514-6(0))* Scholastic, Inc.

—Coco: My Delicious Life. 2013. (Lotus Lane Ser.: 2). lib. bdg. 14.75 *(978-0-606-31978-2(6),* Turtleback) Turtleback Bks.

—Kiki: My Stylish Life. 2013. (Lotus Lane Ser.: 1). (ENG.). 96p. (J). (gr. 1-3). pap. 4.99 *(978-0-545-44512-2(4))* Scholastic, Inc.

—Kiki Bk. 1: My Stylish Life. 2013. (Lotus Lane Ser.: 1). (ENG.). 96p. (J). (gr. 1-3). lib. bdg. 15.99 *(978-0-545-49613-1(6))* Scholastic, Inc.

—Lulu: My Glamorous Life. 2013. (Lotus Lane Ser.: 3). (ENG.). 96p. (J). (gr. 1-3). 15.99 *(978-0-545-49618-6(7));* pap. 4.99 *(978-0-545-44516-0(7));* E-Book *(978-0-545-49682-7(9))* Scholastic, Inc.

—Mika: My New Life. 2013. (Lotus Lane Ser.: 4). (ENG.). 96p. (J). (gr. 1-3). pap. 4.99 *(978-0-545-44519-1(1))* Scholastic, Inc.

—Mika: My New Life. 2013. (Lotus Lane Ser.: 4). lib. bdg. 14.75 *(978-0-606-32365-9(1),* Turtleback) Turtleback Bks.

—My Glamorous Life. 2013. (Lotus Lane Ser.: 3). lib. bdg. 14.75 *(978-0-606-32364-2(3),* Turtleback) Turtleback Bks.

Mazer, Anne. Everything New under the Sun. 2003. (Amazing Days of Abby Hayes Ser.: Bk. 10). (Illus.). 105p. (J). (gr. 4-7). 12.65 *(978-0-7569-3931-1(3))* Perfection Learning Corp.

—Good Things Come in Small Packages. 2003. (Amazing Days of Abby Hayes Ser.: Bk. 12). (Illus.). 101p. (J). (gr. 4-7). 12.65 *(978-0-7569-3935-9(6))* Perfection Learning Corp.

McKissack, Patricia C. A Picture of Freedom: The Diary of Clotee, a Slave Girl, Belmont Plantation, Virginia, 1859. 2011. (Dear America Ser.). (ENG.). 240p. (J). (gr. 3-7). 14.99 *(978-0-545-24253-0(3),* Scholastic Pr.) Scholastic, Inc.

McMullan, Kate. A Fine Start Bk. 3: Meg's Prairie Diary. 2003. (My America Ser.). (ENG.). 112p. (J). 12.95 *(978-0-439-37061-5(2))* Scholastic, Inc.

—For This Land Bk. 2: Meg's Prairie Diary. 2003. (My America Ser.). (ENG., Illus.). 112p. (J). 10.95 *(978-0-439-37059-2(0),* Scholastic Pr.) Scholastic, Inc.

McNamee, Graham. Acceleration. 2012. (ENG.). 240p. (YA). (gr. 7). pap. 9.99 *(978-0-307-97595-9(9),* Ember) Random Hse. Children's Bks.

Meaney, Roisin. Don't Even Think about It. 2006. (Journals). (ENG., Illus.). 192p. (J). pap. 12.95 *(978-0-86278-984-8(2))* O'Brien Pr., Ltd., The IRL. Dist: Dufour Editions, Inc.

Mechling, Lauren, et al. The Rise & Fall of a 10th Grade Social Climber. 2005. (ENG.). 304p. (YA). (gr. 7). pap. 16.99 *(978-0-618-55519-2(6))* Houghton Mifflin Harcourt Publishing Co.

Menzie, Morgan. Diary of an Anorexic Girl, 1 vol. 2003. (ENG.). 192p. pap. 12.99 *(978-0-8499-4405-5(8))* Nelson, Thomas Inc.

Messner, Kate. Spitfire. 2007. (J). *(978-1-59531-018-7(5))* North Country Bks., Inc.

Meyer, Carolyn. Victoria Rebels. (ENG., Illus.). 272p. (YA). (gr. 7). 2014. pap. 9.99 *(978-1-4169-8730-7(4))* 2013. 16.99 *(978-1-4169-8729-1(0))* Simon & Schuster/Paula Wiseman Bks. (Simon & Schuster/Paula Wiseman Bks.).

Moerbeek, Kees. Cinderella. 2011. (My Secret Scrapbook Diary Ser.). (ENG., Illus.). 10p. (J). *(978-1-84643-450-1(5))* Child's Play International Ltd.

—Jack's & the Beanstalk. 2011. (My Secret Scrapbook Diary Ser.). (ENG., Illus.). 10p. (J). *(978-1-84643-449-5(1))* Child's Play International Ltd.

—Little Red Riding Hood. 2011. (My Secret Scrapbook Diary Ser.). (ENG., Illus.). 10p. (J). *(978-1-84643-447-1(5))* Child's Play International Ltd.

—The Three Little Pigs. 2011. (My Secret Scrapbook Diary Ser.). (ENG., Illus.). 10p. (J). *(978-1-84643-448-8(3))* Child's Play International Ltd.

Monstrata, Nessi. Monster High Diaries: Clawdeen Wolf & the Freaky-Fabulous Fashion Show. 2016. (Monster High Diaries: 4). (ENG., Illus.). 160p. (J). (gr. 3-7). 9.99 *(978-0-316-30078-0(0))* Little, Brown Bks. for Young Readers.

—Monster High Diaries: Cleo & the Creeperific Mummy Makeover. 2016. (Monster High Diaries: 5). (ENG.). 160p. (J). (gr. 3-7). 9.99 *(978-0-316-26636-9(1))* Little, Brown Bks. for Young Readers.

—Monster High Diaries: Draculaura & the New Stepmomster. 2015. (Monster High Diaries: 1). (ENG.). 160p. (J). (gr. 3-7). 9.99 *(978-0-316-30084-1(5))* Little, Brown Bks. for Young Readers.

—Monster High Diaries: Frankie Stein & the New Ghoul in School. 2015. (Monster High Diaries: 2). (ENG., Illus.). 160p. (J). (gr. 3-7). 9.99 *(978-0-316-30094-0(2))* Little, Brown Bks. for Young Readers.

Montano, Josie. Chicken Pox. . . Yuck! 2005. (Illus.). 160p. pap. *(978-0-7344-0335-3(6),* Lothian Children's Bks.) Hachette Australia.

Montes, Juan Mari. Diario del Autobus a de la Linea 3. 2006. (SPA., Illus.). 96p. (J). *(978-84-667-5192-6(0))* Grupo Anaya, S.A.

Moonshower, Candie. The Legend of Zoey. 2007. (ENG.). 224p. (J). (gr. 3-7). 6.99 *(978-0-440-23924-6(9),* Yearling) Random Hse. Children's Bks.

Moss, Alexandra, pseud. Kate's Special Secret. 2005. (Royal Ballet School Diaries: 5). (ENG.). 144p. (J). (gr. 3-7). pap. 5.99 *(978-0-448-43771-2(6),* Grosset & Dunlap) Penguin Young Readers Group.

Moss, Marissa. Amelia Writes Again. Moss, Marissa, illus. (Amelia Ser.). (ENG., Illus.). (J). (gr. 2-5). 2012. 32p. pap. 6.99 *(978-1-4169-1285-9(1))* 2006. 40p. 12.99 *(978-1-4169-0904-0(4))* Simon & Schuster/Paula Wiseman Bks. (Simon & Schuster/Paula Wiseman Bks.).

—Amelia's 5th-Grade Notebook. Moss, Marissa, illus. 2006. (Amelia Ser.). (ENG., Illus.). (J). 5.99 *(978-1-4169-1292-7(4));* 40p. (gr. 2-5). 12.99 *(978-1-4169-0912-5(5))* Simon & Schuster/Paula Wiseman Bks. (Simon & Schuster/Paula Wiseman Bks.).

—Amelia's 6th-Grade Notebook. Moss, Marissa, illus. 2005. (Amelia Ser.). (ENG., Illus.). 80p. (J). (gr. 4-7). 12.99 *(978-0-689-87040-8(X),* Simon & Schuster/Paula Wiseman Bks.) Simon & Schuster/Paula Wiseman Bks.

—Amelia's Are-We-There-Yet Longest Ever Car Trip. Moss, Marissa, illus. (Amelia Ser.). (ENG., Illus.). 40p. (J). (gr. 2-5). 2012. pap. 6.99 *(978-1-4169-1287-3(8))* 2006. 10.99 *(978-1-4169-0906-4(0))* Simon & Schuster/Paula Wiseman Bks. (Simon & Schuster/Paula Wiseman Bks.).

—Amelia's Back-to-School Survival Guide: Vote 4 Amelia - Amelia's Guide to Babysitting. Moss, Marissa, illus. 2012. (Amelia Ser.). (ENG., Illus.). 160p. (J). (gr. 5-8). 12.99 *(978-1-4424-4349-5(9),* Simon & Schuster/Paula Wiseman Bks.) Simon & Schuster/Paula Wiseman Bks.

—Amelia's Boy Survival Guide. Moss, Marissa, illus. 2012. (Amelia Ser.). (ENG., Illus.). 80p. (J). (gr. 4-8). 9.99 *(978-1-4424-4084-5(8),* Simon & Schuster/Paula Wiseman Bks.) Simon & Schuster/Paula Wiseman Bks.

—Amelia's Family Ties. Moss, Marissa, illus. 2013. (Amelia Ser.). (ENG., Illus.). (J). 5.99 *(978-1-4169-1293-4(2),* Simon & Schuster/Paula Wiseman Bks.) Simon & Schuster/Paula Wiseman Bks.

—Amelia's Longest, Biggest, Most-Fights-Ever Family Reunion. Moss, Marissa, illus. 2006. (Amelia Ser.). (ENG., Illus.). 80p. (J). (gr. 4-7). 12.99 *(978-0-689-87447-5(2),* Simon & Schuster/Paula Wiseman Bks.) Simon & Schuster/Paula Wiseman Bks.

—Amelia's Middle-School Graduation Yearbook. 2015. (ENG., Illus.). 80p. (J). (gr. 4-8). 12.95 (978-1-939547-09-5(1)) Creston Bks.

—Amelia's Most Unforgettable Embarrassing Moments. Moss, Marissa, illus. 2005. (Amelia Ser.). (ENG., Illus.). 80p. (J). (gr. 4-7). 12.99 (978-0-689-87041-5(8), Simon & Schuster/Paula Wiseman Bks.) Simon & Schuster/Paula Wiseman Bks.

—Amelia's Notebook. Moss, Marissa, illus. 2006. (Amelia Ser.). (ENG., Illus.). (J). 5.99 (978-1-4169-1286-6(X)); 40p. (gr. 2-5). 12.99 (978-1-4169-0905-7(2)) Simon & Schuster/Paula Wiseman Bks. (Simon & Schuster/Paula Wiseman Bks.).

—Blood Diaries: Tales of a 6th-Grade Vampire. Moss, Marissa, illus. 2014. (ENG., Illus.). 136p. (J). (gr. 2-7). 13.00 (978-1-939547-05-7(9)) Creston Bks.

—Emma's Journal. 2004. (Young American Voice Bks.). (Illus.). (gr. 3-7). 17.00 (978-0-7569-4110-9(5)) Perfection Learning Corp.

—The Fake Friend! Moss, Marissa, illus. 2012. (Daphne's Diary of Daily Disasters Ser.). (ENG., Illus.). 96p. (J). (gr. 2-5). 9.99 (978-1-4424-4014-2(7)); pap. 5.99 (978-1-4424-4015-9(5)) Simon & Schuster/Paula Wiseman Bks. (Simon & Schuster/Paula Wiseman Bks.).

—Mira's Diary: California Dreaming. Moss, Marissa, illus. 2016. (ENG., Illus.). 190p. (J). (gr. 2-8). 12.99 (978-1-939547-22-4(9)) Creston Bks.

—The Name Game! Moss, Marissa, illus. 2011. (Daphne's Diary of Daily Disasters Ser.). (ENG., Illus.). 80p. (J). (gr. 2-5). pap. 5.99 (978-1-4424-1738-0(2)); lib. bdg. 9.99 (978-1-4424-2676-4(4)) Simon & Schuster/Paula Wiseman Bks. (Simon & Schuster/Paula Wiseman Bks.).

—Rose's Journal: The Story of a Girl in the Great Depression. 2003. (Young American Voices Ser.). (ENG., Illus.). 56p. (J). (gr. 2-5). pap. 7.99 (978-0-15-204605-7(4)) Houghton Mifflin Harcourt Publishing Co.

—Rose's Journal: The Story of a Girl in the Great Depression. 2004. (Young American Voice Bks.). (Illus.). (gr. 3-7). 17.00 (978-0-7569-4230-4(6)) Perfection Learning Corp.

—The Vampire Dare! Moss, Marissa, illus. 2011. (Daphne's Diary of Daily Disasters Ser.). (ENG., Illus.). 80p. (J). (gr. 2-5). pap. 5.99 (978-1-4424-1737-3(4)); lib. bdg. 9.99 (978-1-4424-2677-1(2)) Simon & Schuster/Paula Wiseman Bks. (Simon & Schuster/Paula Wiseman Bks.).

Moss, Marissa, illus. Mira's Diary: Bombs over London. 2014. (ENG.). 190p. (J). (gr. 2-8). 12.99 (978-1-939547-12-5(1)) Creston Bks.

Murdock, Catherine Gilbert. Heaven Is Paved with Oreos. (ENG.). 208p. (J). (gr. 5-7). 2015. pap. 6.99 (978-0-544-43932-0(5), HMH Books For Young Readers) 2013. 16.99 (978-0-547-62538-6(3)) Houghton Mifflin Harcourt Publishing Co.

Murphy, Jim. On Enemy Soil: The Journal of James Edmond Pease, a Civil War Union Soldier. 2012. (ENG.). 176p. (J). (gr. 3-7). pap. 6.99 (978-0-545-39887-9(8)) Scholastic, Inc.

Murtagh, Ciaran. Action Hero. Wesson, Tim, illus. 2017. (Fincredible Diary of Fin Spencer Ser.: 3). (ENG.). 224p. (J). (gr. 4-7). pap. 7.99 (978-1-84812-532-2(1)) Bonnier Publishing GBR. Dist: Independent Pubs. Group.

—The Fincredible Diary of Fin Spencer: Stuntboy. Wesson, Tim, illus. 2016. (Fincredible Diary of Fin Spencer Ser.: 1). (ENG.). 224p. (J). (gr. 4-7). pap. 7.99 (978-1-84812-434-9(1)) Bonnier Publishing GBR. Dist: Independent Pubs. Group.

Myers, Walter Dean. Down to the Last Out: The Journal of Biddy Owens, the Negro Leagues, Birmingham, Alabama, 1948. 2013. (ENG.). 144p. (J). (gr. 3-7). pap. 6.99 (978-0-545-53050-7(4), Scholastic Paperbacks) Scholastic, Inc.

Nielsen, Susin. The Reluctant Journal of Henry K. Larsen. 2014. (ENG., Illus.). 256p. (J). (gr. 5). pap. 8.99 (978-1-77049-654-5(8), Tundra Bks.) Tundra Bks. CAN. Dist: Penguin Random Hse. LLC.

Noël, Alyson. Forever Summer. 2011. (ENG.). 464p. (YA). (gr. 8-12). pap. 9.99 (978-0-312-60439-4(4), 9780312604394, St. Martin's Griffin) St. Martin's Pr.

Nolen, Jerdine. Eliza's Freedom Road: An Underground Railroad Diary. Strickland, Shadra, illus. 2011. (ENG.). 160p. (J). (gr. 3-7). 16.99 (978-1-4169-5814-7(2), Simon & Schuster/Paula Wiseman Bks.) Simon & Schuster/Paula Wiseman Bks.

Oceanak, Karla. Bogus: An Aldo Zelnick Comic Novel. Spanjer, Kendra, illus. 2016. (Aldo Zelnick Comic Novel Ser.: 2). (ENG.). 160p. (J). (gr. 3-7). pap. 8.95 (978-1-934649-66-4(X)) Bailiwick Pr.

—Cahoots. Spanjer, Kendra, illus. 2011. (Aldo Zelnick Comic Novel Ser.: 3). (ENG.). 151p. (J). (gr. 3-7). 12.95 (978-1-934649-08-4(2)) Bailiwick Pr.

—Glitch: An Aldo Zelnick Comic Novel. Spanjer, Kendra, illus. 2016. (Aldo Zelnick Comic Novel Ser.: 7). (ENG.). 160p. (J). (gr. 1-8). pap. 8.95 (978-1-934649-71-8(6)) Bailiwick Pr.

—Hotdogger: An Aldo Zelnick Comic Novel. Spanjer, Kendra, illus. 2016. (Aldo Zelnick Comic Novel Ser.: 8). (ENG.). 160p. (J). (gr. 1-8). pap. 8.95 (978-1-934649-72-5(4)) Bailiwick Pr.

—Ignoramus: An Aldo Zelnick Comic Novel. Spanjer, Kendra, illus. 2016. (Aldo Zelnick Comic Novel Ser.: 9). (ENG.). 160p. (J). (gr. 1-8). pap. 8.95 (978-1-934649-73-2(2)) Bailiwick Pr.

—Jackpot: An Aldo Zelnick Comic Novel. Spanjer, Kendra, illus. 2016. (Aldo Zelnick Comic Novel Ser.: 10). (ENG.). 160p. (J). (gr. 1-8). pap. 8.95 (978-1-934649-74-9(0)) Bailiwick Pr.

—Logjam. Spanjer, Kendra, illus. 2016. (Aldo Zelnick Comic Novel Ser.: 12). (ENG.). 160p. (gr. 1-8). 12.95 (978-1-934649-64-0(3)) Bailiwick Pr.

Oldfield, Jenny. When Scott Got Lost No. 2. (Illus.). (J). mass mkt. 8.99 (978-0-340-85073-2(6)) Macmillan Pubs., Ltd. GBR. Dist: Trafalgar Square Publishing.

Olsen, Mary-Kate & Olsen, Ashley. Calling All Boys. 2003. (ENG., Illus.). 112p. (978-0-00-714472-3(5), HarperCollins Children's Bks.) HarperCollins Pubs. Ltd.

—P. S Wish You Were Here. 2003. (ENG., Illus.). 112p. (978-0-00-714470-9(9), HarperCollins Children's Bks.) HarperCollins Pubs. Ltd.

—Surf, Sand & Secrets. 2004. (ENG., Illus.). 112p. (978-0-00-714459-4(8), HarperCollins Children's Bks.) HarperCollins Pubs. Ltd.

Oram, Hiawyn. My Unwilling Witch Gets a Makeover. Warburton, Sarah, illus. 2010. (Rumblewick's Diary Ser.: 4). (ENG.). 112p. (J). (gr. 1-4). 7.99 (978-0-316-03462-3(2)) Little, Brown Bks. for Young Readers.

Orme, Helen. Don't Even Think It. 2008. (Cutting Edge Ser.). (ENG.). 168p. pap. (978-1-84167-698-2(5)) Ransom Publishing Ltd.

Ortiz, Michael J. Swan Town: The Secret Journal of Susanna Shakespeare. 2006. (Illus.). 197p. (J). (gr. 5-9). 15.99 (978-0-06-058126-8(3)) HarperCollins Pubs.

Osborne, Mary Pope. My Secret War: The World War II Diary of Madeline Beck, Long Island, New York 1941. 2008. (Dear America Ser.). (J). (gr. 3-7). 39.95 incl. audio compact disk (978-1-4301-0359-2(0)) Live Oak Media.

—Standing in the Light: The Diary of Catharine Carey Logan, Delaware Valley, Pennsylvania, 1763. 2011. (Dear America Ser.). (ENG.). 176p. (J). (gr. 5-9). 12.99 (978-0-545-26687-1(4)) Scholastic, Inc.

Osborne, Mary Pope, et al. A Time to Dance: Virginia's Civil War Diary. 2003. (My America Ser.). (ENG.). 112p. (J). 12.95 (978-0-439-44341-8(5)) Scholastic, Inc.

Park, Barbara. Aloha-Ha-Ha! Brunkus, Denise, illus. (Junie B. Jones Ser.: 26). (ENG.). 128p. (J). (gr. 1-4). 2007. per. 4.99 (978-0-375-83404-2(4)) 2006. lib. bdg. 13.95 (978-0-375-93403-2(0)) Random Hse. Children's Bks. (Random Hse. Bks. for Young Readers).

—Junie B., First Grader - Aloha-Ha-Ha! Brunkus, Denise, illus. 2007. (Junie B. Jones Ser.). 119p. (gr. 1-4). 15.00 (978-0-7569-8085-6(2)) Perfection Learning Corp.

—Junie B. First Grader - Aloha-Ha-Ha! 2007. (Junie B. Jones Ser.: 26). lib. bdg. 14.75 (978-1-4177-8157-7(2), Turtleback) Turtleback Bks.

Patron, Susan. Behind the Masks: The Diary of Angeline Reddy - Bodie, California 1880. 2012. (Dear America Ser.). (ENG.). 304p. (J). (gr. 3-7). 12.99 (978-0-545-30437-5(7)) Scholastic, Inc.

Patterson, James & Papademetriou, Lisa. Homeroom Diaries. Keino, illus. 2014. (ENG.). 272p. (YA). (gr. 7-17). 18.00 (978-0-316-20762-1(4), Jimmy Patterson) Little Brown & Co.

Pérez, Amada Irma. Mi Diario de Aquí Hasta Allá. Gonzalez, Maya Christina, illus. 2013.Tr. of My Diary from Here to There. (ENG & SPA.). 32p. (J). (gr. k). pap. 9.95 (978-0-89239-230-8(4)) Lee & Low Bks., Inc.

Perrin, Randy, et al. Time Like a River. 2004. 144p. (gr. 5-18). 14.95 (978-1-57143-061-8(X)) RDR Bks.

Pfeffer, Susan Beth. Life As We Knew It. 2008. (Life As We Knew It Ser.: 1). (ENG., Illus.). 352p. (YA). (gr. 7-18). pap. 9.99 (978-0-15-206154-8(1)) Houghton Mifflin Harcourt Publishing Co.

—Life As We Knew It. Howard, Arthur, illus. 2006. (Life As We Knew It Ser.: 1). (ENG.). 352p. (YA). (gr. 7-12). 17.99 (978-0-15-205826-5(5)) Houghton Mifflin Harcourt Publishing Co.

—Life As We Knew It. 2008. (Last Survivors Ser.: 1). 347p. (gr. 7-12). lib. bdg. 19.65 (978-1-4178-1541-8(8), Turtleback) Turtleback Bks.

—The Life As We Knew It Collection. 2015. (Life As We Knew It Ser.). (ENG.). 1252p. (YA). (gr. 7). 29.99 (978-0-544-54263-1(0), HMH Books For Young Readers) Houghton Mifflin Harcourt Publishing Co.

—This World We Live In, Bk. 3. 2011. (Life As We Knew It Ser.: 3). (ENG.). 256p. (YA). (gr. 7). pap. 8.99 (978-0-547-55028-2(6)) Houghton Mifflin Harcourt Publishing Co.

Pike, Kenneth & Stewart, Isaac. Jacob's Journal of Doom: Confessions of an Almost-Deacon. 2012. (J). 14.99 (978-1-60907-016-8(X)) Deseret Bk. Co.

Platt, Richard. Castle Diary: The Journal of Tobias Burgess. Riddell, Chris, illus. 2003. (ENG.). 128p. (J). (gr. 4-7). 6.99 (978-0-7636-2164-3(1)) Candlewick Pr.

—Egyptian Diary: The Journal of Nakht. Parkins, David, illus. 2014. (ENG.). 128p. (J). (gr. 4-7). pap. 6.99 (978-0-7636-7054-2(5)) Candlewick Pr.

—Roman Diary: The Journal of Iliona, a Young Slave. Parkins, David, illus. 2014. (ENG.). 128p. (J). (gr. 4-7). pap. 6.99 (978-0-7636-7053-5(7)) Candlewick Pr.

Portis, Antoinette. Kindergarten Diary. Portis, Antoinette, illus. 2010. (Illus.). 32p. (J). (gr. -1-3). (ENG.). 12.99 (978-0-06-145691-6(8)); lib. bdg. 14.89 (978-0-06-145692-3(6)) HarperCollins Pubs.

Preller, James. The Fall. 2015. (ENG.). 208p. (J). (gr. 4-9). 16.99 (978-0-312-64301-0(2), 9780312643010) Feiwel & Friends.

Randall, Alice. The Diary of B. B. Bright, Possible Princess. 2012. (J). (978-1-61858-016-0(7)) Turner Publishing Co.

Randall, Alice & Williams, Caroline Randall. The Diary of B. B. Bright, Possible Princess. Strickland, Shadra, illus. 2012. (ENG.). 192p. (J). (gr. 2-6). 19.95 (978-1-61858-015-3(9)) Turner Publishing Co.

Rasheed, Leila. Doughnuts, Dreams & Drama Queens. 2013. (Fantastic Diary of Bathsheba Claric de Trop Ser.). 299p. (J). pap. 5.99 (978-0-7945-3030-3(3), Usborne) EDC Publishing.

Raymundo, Peter. Third Grade Mermaid. 2017. (ENG.). 208p. (J). (gr. 1-3). 12.99 (978-0-545-91816-9(2), Scholastic Pr.) Scholastic, Inc.

Rees, Celia. Witch Child. unabr. ed. 2004. (Young Adult Cassette Librariestm Ser.). 304p. (J). (gr. 5-9). pap. 40.00 incl. audio (978-0-8072-1198-4(2), S YA 343 SP, Listening Library) Random Hse. Audio Publishing Group.

Rempel, Leah. Hey, Hmong Girl, Whassup? The Journal of Choua Vang. 2004. (Illus.). v, 138p. (YA). pap. (978-0-9723721-5-2(6)) Hamline Univ. Pr.

Rennison, Louise. Angus, Thongs & Full-Frontal Snogging. 2006. (Confessions of Georgia Nicolson Ser.: 1). (ENG.). 272p. (YA). (gr. 8-18). pap. 9.99 (978-0-06-447227-2(2), HarperTeen) HarperCollins Pubs.

—Angus, Thongs & Full-Frontal Snogging. 2009. (Confessions of Georgia Nicolson Ser.: No. 1). 10.36 (978-0-7848-1994-4(7), Everbind) Marco Bk. Co.

—Angus, Thongs & Full-Frontal Snogging. (Confessions of Georgia Nicolson Ser.: 1). (J). 2008. 70.49 (978-1-4281-7895-3(3)) 2005. 1.25 (978-1-4193-4293-6(2)) 2004. 68.75 (978-1-4025-9087-0(3)) Recorded Bks., Inc.

—Are These My Basoomas I See Before Me? Final Confessions of Georgia Nicolson. 2010. (Confessions of Georgia Nicolson Ser.: 10). (ENG.). 336p. (YA). (gr. 8-9). pap. 8.99 (978-0-06-145937-5(2), HarperTeen) HarperCollins Pubs.

—Dancing in My Nuddy-Pants. 2006. (Confessions of Georgia Nicolson Ser.: 4). (ENG.). 240p. (YA). (gr. 8). reprint ed. pap. 8.99 (978-0-06-009748-6(5), HarperTeen) HarperCollins Pubs.

—Knocked Out by My Nunga-Nungas. 2006. (Confessions of Georgia Nicolson Ser.: No. 3). 183p. (gr. 7-12). 19.00 (978-0-7569-6729-1(5)) Perfection Learning Corp.

—Love Is a Many Trousered Thing. 2008. (Confessions of Georgia Nicolson Ser.: 8). (ENG.). 304p. (YA). (gr. 8). pap. 9.99 (978-0-06-085389-1(1), HarperTeen) HarperCollins Pubs.

—On the Bright Side, I'm Now the Girlfriend of a Sex God: Further Confessions of Georgia Nicolson. (Confessions of Georgia Nicolson Ser.: 2). (ENG.). 2006. 272p. (YA). (gr. 8). pap. 8.99 (978-0-06-447226-5(4), HarperTeen) 2003. 256p. (J). pap. 6.99 (978-0-06-052185-1(6)) HarperCollins Pubs.

—Startled by His Furry Shorts. (Confessions of Georgia Nicolson Ser.: 7). (YA). 2007. (ENG.). 304p. (gr. 8-12). pap. 9.99 (978-0-06-085386-0(7)) 2006. 288p. (gr. 7-12). 16.99 (978-0-06-085384-6(0)) 2006. 278p. (gr. 7-12). lib. bdg. 17.89 (978-0-06-085385-3(9)) HarperCollins Pubs. (HarperTeen).

—Stop in the Name of Pants! (Confessions of Georgia Nicolson Ser.: 9). (YA). 2009. (ENG.). 336p. (gr. 8). pap. 9.99 (978-0-06-145934-4(8)) 2008. 256p. (gr. 7-18). 16.99 (978-0-06-145932-0(1)) 2008. 320p. (gr. 7-18). lib. bdg. 17.89 (978-0-06-145933-7(X)) HarperCollins Pubs. (HarperTeen).

—Stop in the Name of Pants!, 6 vols. 2010. (Confessions of Georgia Nicolson Ser.: 9). (YA). 85.75 (978-1-4407-7775-2(6)); 82.75 (978-1-4407-7777-6(2)); 70.75 (978-1-4407-7771-4(3)); 1.25 (978-1-4407-7779-0(9)); 172.75 (978-1-4407-7772-1(1)); 67.75 (978-1-4407-7773-8(X)) Recorded Bks., Inc.

—Then He Ate My Boy Entrancers: More Mad, Marvy Confessions of Georgia Nicolson. (Confessions of Georgia Nicolson Ser.: 6). 2006. (ENG.). 336p. (YA). (gr. 8-12). pap. 9.99 (978-0-06-058939-4(6)) 2005. 320p. (J). lib. bdg. 16.89 (978-0-06-058938-7(8)) HarperCollins Pubs. (HarperTeen).

Rettig, Liz. My Desperate Love Diary. 2007. (ENG.). 314p. (YA). (gr. 9-12). 16.95 (978-0-8234-2033-9(7)) Holiday Hse., Inc.

Rigby Education Staff. Cat's Diary. (Sails Literacy Ser.). (Illus.). 16p. (gr. 2-3). 27.00 (978-0-7635-9937-9(9), 699379C99) Rigby Education.

Rinaldi, Ann. Sarah's Ground. (ENG.). 192p. (YA). 2012. (gr. 7). pap. 9.99 (978-1-4424-8107-7(2)) 2004. (Illus.). 15.95 (978-0-689-85924-3(4)) Simon & Schuster Bks. For Young Readers. (Simon & Schuster Bks. For Young Readers).

Riordan, Rick. The Demigod Diaries. 2012. (ENG.). 256p. (YA). (gr. 5-9). 12.99 (978-1-4231-6300-8(1)) Hyperion Pr.

Rix, Jamie. Tough Turkey. 2003. (ENG., Illus.). 240p. pap. (978-0-440-86479-0(8), Yearling) Random Hse. Children's Bks.

Rogers, Amy Keating. The Journal of the Two Sisters: The Official Chronicles of Celestia & Luna. 2014. (ENG., Illus.). 192p. (J). (gr. 3-17). 14.99 (978-0-316-28224-6(3)) Little, Brown Bks. for Young Readers.

Roop, Connie & Roop, Peter. Good-Bye for Today: The Diary of a Young Girl at Sea. Allen, Thomas B., illus. 2008. (ENG.). 48p. (J). (gr. 4-6). 11.99 (978-1-4169-7573-1(X), Simon & Schuster/Paula Wiseman Bks.) Simon & Schuster/Paula Wiseman Bks.

Rosen, Michael J. Sailing the Unknown: Around the World with Captain Cook. Pritelli, Maria Cristina, illus. 2012. (ENG.). 40p. (J). (gr. 1-3). 19.99 (978-1-56846-216-5(6), Creative Editions) Creative Co., The.

Russell, Rachel Renée. Dork Diaries, Set. Russell, Rachel Renée, illus. 2013. (Dork Diaries: Nos. 4-6). (ENG., Illus.). 1056p. (J). (gr. 4-8). 41.99 (978-1-4424-9859-4(5), Aladdin) Simon & Schuster Children's Publishing.

—Dork Diaries Set, Set. Russell, Rachel Renée, illus. 2011. (Dork Diaries: Nos. 1-3). (ENG., Illus.). 928p. (J). (gr. 4-8). 41.99 (978-1-4424-2662-7(4), Aladdin) Simon & Schuster Children's Publishing.

—How to Dork Your Diary. Russell, Rachel Renée, illus. 2011. (Dork Diaries: No. 3.5). (ENG., Illus.). 288p. (J). (gr. 4-8). 13.99 (978-1-4424-2233-9(5), Aladdin) Simon & Schuster Children's Publishing.

—Tales from a Not-So-Dorky Drama Queen, 3 vols. unabr. ed. 2015. (Dork Diaries: 8). (ENG.). 320p. (gr. 4-8). audio compact disk 14.99 (978-1-4423-7023-4(8)) Simon & Schuster Audio.

—Tales from a Not-So-Dorky Drama Queen. Russell, Rachel Renée, illus. 2015. (Dork Diaries: Bk. 9). (ENG., Illus.). 352p. (J). (gr. 4-8). 13.99 (978-1-4424-8769-7(0), Aladdin Paperbacks) Simon & Schuster Children's Publishing.

—Tales from a Not-So-Fabulous Life. Russell, Rachel Renée, illus. 2009. (Dork Diaries: 1). (ENG., Illus.). 304p. (J). (gr. 4-8). 13.99 (978-1-4169-8006-3(7), Aladdin) Simon & Schuster Children's Publishing.

—Tales from a Not-So-Fabulous Life. 2009. (Dork Diaries: 1). lib. bdg. 25.75 (978-0-606-32419-9(4), Turtleback) Turtleback Bks.

—Tales from a Not-So-Friendly Frenemy. Russell, Rachel Renée, illus. 2016. (Dork Diaries: 11). (ENG., Illus.). 288p. (J). (gr. 4-8). 13.99 (978-1-4814-7920-2(2), Aladdin) Simon & Schuster Children's Publishing.

—Tales from a Not-So-Glam TV Star. Russell, Rachel Renée, illus. 2014. (Dork Diaries: 7). (ENG., Illus.). 336p. (J). (gr. 4-8). 13.99 (978-1-4424-8767-3(4), Aladdin) Simon & Schuster Children's Publishing.

—Tales from a Not-So-Graceful Ice Princess. Russell, Rachel Renée, illus. 2012. (Dork Diaries: 4). (ENG., Illus.). 368p. (J). (gr. 4-8). 13.99 (978-1-4424-1192-0(9), Aladdin) Simon & Schuster Children's Publishing.

—Tales from a Not-So-Happy Heartbreaker. Russell, Rachel Renée, illus. 2013. (Dork Diaries: 6). (ENG., Illus.). 352p. (J). (gr. 4-8). 13.99 (978-1-4424-4963-3(2), Aladdin) Simon & Schuster Children's Publishing.

—Tales from a Not-So-Happy Heartbreaker. 2013. (Dork Diaries: 6). lib. bdg. 25.75 (978-0-606-32424-3(0), Turtleback) Turtleback Bks.

—Tales from a Not-So-Perfect Pet Sitter. Russell, Rachel Renée, illus. 2015. (Dork Diaries: 10). (ENG., Illus.). 320p. (J). (gr. 4-8). 13.99 (978-1-4814-5704-0(7), Aladdin) Simon & Schuster Children's Publishing.

—Tales from a Not-So-Popular Party Girl. Russell, Rachel Renée, illus. 2010. (Dork Diaries: 2). (ENG., Illus.). 288p. (J). (gr. 4-8). 13.99 (978-1-4169-8008-7(3), Aladdin) Simon & Schuster Children's Publishing.

—Tales from a Not-So-Popular Party Girl. 2010. (Dork Diaries: 2). lib. bdg. 25.75 (978-0-606-32420-5(8), Turtleback) Turtleback Bks.

—Tales from a Not-So-Smart Miss Know-It-All. Russell, Rachel Renée, illus. 2012. (Dork Diaries: 5). (ENG., Illus.). 368p. (J). (gr. 4-8). 13.99 (978-1-4424-4961-9(6), Aladdin) Simon & Schuster Children's Publishing.

—Tales from a Not-So-Talented Pop Star. Russell, Rachel Renée, illus. 2011. (Dork Diaries: 3). (ENG., Illus.). 336p. (J). (gr. 4-8). 13.99 (978-1-4424-1190-6(2), Aladdin) Simon & Schuster Children's Publishing.

Russell, Rachel Renée, et al. Tales from a Not-So-Popular Party Girl. 2010. (ENG.). pap. (978-1-4424-4042-5(2), Aladdin Paperbacks) Simon & Schuster Children's Publishing.

Sand-Eveland, Cyndi. Dear Toni. 2010. (ENG., Illus.). 136p. (J). (gr. 4-7). pap. 9.95 (978-1-77049-249-3(6), Tundra Bks.) Tundra Bks. CAN. Dist: Penguin Random Hse. LLC.

Schlitz, Laura Amy. The Hired Girl. 2015. (ENG., Illus.). 400p. (J). (gr. 7-10). 17.99 (978-0-7636-7818-0(X)) Candlewick Pr.

—The Hired Girl. 2018. lib. bdg. 22.10 **(978-0-606-40389-4(2))** Turtleback Bks.

Schumacher, Julie. The Book of One Hundred Truths. 2008. (Yearling Bks.). (ENG.). 192p. (J). (gr. 3-7). 6.99 (978-0-440-42085-9(7), Yearling) Random Hse. Children's Bks.

Segal, Zoe. Confessions of a Tenth-Grade Social Climber. 2005. 290p. (YA). (978-0-618-44981-1(7)) Houghton Mifflin Harcourt Publishing Co.

Shulman, Dee. My Totally Secret Diary - Reality TV Nightmare. 2012. (ENG., Illus.). 144p. (J). (gr. 2-4). pap. 10.99 (978-1-86230-424-6(6), Red Fox) Random House Children's Books GBR. Dist: Independent Pubs. Group.

—On Stage in America. 2012. (My Totally Secret Diary Ser.). (ENG., Illus.). 144p. (J). (gr. 2-4). pap. 12.99 (978-1-86230-423-9(8), Red Fox) Random House Children's Books GBR. Dist: Independent Pubs. Group.

—Polly Price's Totally Secret Diary: Mum in Love. 2012. (ENG., Illus.). 144p. (J). (gr. 2-4). pap. 8.99 (978-1-84941-542-2(0), Red Fox) Random House Children's Books GBR. Dist: Independent Pubs. Group.

Shute, Henry. Sequil or Things Whitch Aint Finished in The. 2007. 108p. per. 14.99 (978-0-9773040-3-5(5)) Wilder Pubns., Corp.

Smith Dinbergs, Holly. Diary Disaster. Stewart, Chantal, illus. 2005. (Girlz Rock! Ser.). (J). pap. (978-1-59336-700-8(7)) Mondo Publishing.

Smith, Eunice Geil. Treasure Hunt. 2006. 119p. (J). (gr. 3-7). per. 9.99 (978-0-8361-9332-9(6)) Herald Pr.

Sommerdorf, Norma. Red River Girl. 2006. (ENG., Illus.). 192p. (J). (gr. 3-7). 16.95 (978-0-8234-1903-6(7)) Holiday Hse., Inc.

Spady, Angie. Catie Conrad: Faith, Friendship & Fashion Disasters. Everidge, Channing, illus. 2014. (Desperate Diva Diaries Ser.). (ENG.). 304p. (gr. 3-7). 12.99 (978-1-4336-8460-9(8), B&H Kids) B&H Publishing Group.

—Catie Conrad: How to Become the Most (un)Popular Girl in Jr. High. Everidge, Channing, illus. 2015. (Desperate Diva Diaries Ser.). (ENG.). 304p. (gr. 3-7). pap. 8.99 (978-1-4336-8461-6(6), B&H Kids) B&H Publishing Group.

Spinelli, Jerry. Love, Stargirl. 2009. (ENG.). 288p. (YA). (gr. 7). pap. 9.99 (978-0-375-85644-0(7), Ember) Random Hse. Children's Bks.

Staniszewski, Anna. The Dirt Diary. 2014. (Dirt Diary Ser.: 1). (ENG.). 256p. (J). (gr. 5-9). pap. 6.99 (978-1-4022-8636-0(8), 9781402286360, Sourcebooks Jabberwocky) Sourcebooks, Inc.

Starmer, Aaron. The Storyteller. 2016. (Riverman Trilogy Ser.: 3). (ENG.). 336p. (J). 16.99 (978-0-374-36313-0(7), 9780374363130, Farrar, Straus & Giroux (BYR)) Farrar, Straus & Giroux.

Steer, Dugald A. The Dragon Diary, Vol. 2. Carrel, Douglas, illus. 2010. (Ologies Ser.: Vol. 2). (ENG.). 272p. (J). (gr. 4-7). pap. 7.99 (978-0-7636-4514-4(1)) Candlewick Pr.

Sternberg, Julie. Friendship Over, Bk. 1. Wright, Johanna, illus. 2015. (Top-Secret Diary of Celie Valentine Ser.). (ENG.). 160p. (J). (gr. 2-6). pap. 6.95 (978-1-62979-405-1(8)) Boyds Mills Pr.

—Secrets Out!, Bk. 2. Wright, Johanna, illus. 2015. (Top-Secret Diary of Celie Valentine Ser.). (ENG.). 176p. (J). (gr. 2-6). 15.95 (978-1-62091-777-0(7)) Boyds Mills Pr.

Stevens, Eric. Finn Reeder, Flu Fighter: How I Survived a Worldwide Pandemic, the School Bully, & the Craziest Game of Dodge Ball Ever. Fraser, Kay, illus. 2009. (Finn Reeder Ser.). (ENG.). 80p. (gr. 2-3). lib. bdg. 26.65 (978-1-4342-2450-7(3)) Capstone Digital.

—Flu Fighter: How I Survived a Worldwide Pandemic, the School Bully, & the Craziest Game of Dodge Ball Ever. Fraser, Kay, illus. 2010. (Finn Reeder Ser.). (ENG.). 80p. (gr. 3-4). 9.99 (978-1-4342-2562-7(3)) Capstone Digital.

Stevermer, Caroline & Wrede, Patricia C. The Grand Tour: Being a Revelation of Matters of High Confidentiality & Greatest Importance, Including Extracts from the Intimate Diary of a Noblewoman & the Sworn Testimony of a Lady of Quality. 2006. (ENG., Illus.). 480p. (YA). (gr. 7-12). pap. 21.95 (978-0-15-205556-1(8)) Houghton Mifflin Harcourt Publishing Co.

Stewart, Sarah. The Journey. Smalls, David, illus. pap. incl. audio compact disk (978-1-59112-556-3(1)); pap. incl. audio (978-0-87499-924-2(3)); pap. 18.95 incl. audio compact disk (978-1-59112-344-6(5)); pap. 16.95 incl. audio (978-0-87499-922-8(7)) Live Oak Media.

—The Journey. Small, David, illus. 2006. (ENG.). 40p. (J). (gr. k-4). reprint ed. pap. 8.99 (978-0-374-40010-1(5), 9780374400101) Square Fish.

Strawberry Shortcake Berry Loveable Diary. 2005. 7.95 (978-1-59487-083-5(7)) Artist Studios, Ltd.

Tashjian, Janet. Tru Confessions. 2007. (ENG., Illus.). 176p. (J). (gr. 4-7). per. 15.99 (978-0-312-37273-6(6), 9780312372736) Square Fish.

Taylor, Sean & Quarto Generic Staff. A Waste of Good Paper. 2013. (ENG., Illus.). 290p. (J). (gr. 6-9). pap. 8.99

(978-1-84780-268-2(0), Frances Lincoln) Quarto Publishing Group UK GBR. Dist: Hachette Bk. Group.

Thomas, Frances. Polly's Running Away Book. Gardner, Sally, illus. 2012. (ENG.). 96p. (J). (gr. 2-4). pap. 11.99 (978-1-4088-2515-0(5), 9781408825150, Bloomsbury USA Childrens) Bloomsbury Publishing USA.

Thomson, Melissa. Keena Ford & the Field Trip Mix-Up. 2010. (Keena Ford Ser.). (ENG.). 112p. (J). (gr. 1-3). 5.99 (978-0-14-241572-6(3), Puffin Books) Penguin Young Readers Group.

—Keena Ford & the Secret Journal Mix-Up. Morrison, Frank, illus. 2011. (Keena Ford Ser.). (ENG.). 128p. (J). (gr. 1-3). 5.99 (978-0-14-241937-3(0), Puffin Books) Penguin Young Readers Group.

Thorne, Bella. Autumn Falls. 2014. (ENG.). 224p. (YA). (gr. 7). lib. bdg. 21.99 (978-0-375-99161-5(1), Delacorte Pr.) Random Hse. Children's Bks.

Tibensky, Arlaina. And Then Things Fall Apart. 2011. (ENG.). 272p. (YA). (gr. 9). pap. 9.99 (978-1-4424-1323-8(9), Simon Pulse) Simon Pulse.

Tibo, Gilles & Bisaillon, Josée. My Diary: The Totally True Story of ME! 2011. (Illus.). 48p. (J). (gr. 3-7). pap. 12.95 (978-1-4338-0958-3(3), Magination Pr.) American Psychological Assn.

Ting, Renee. The Prince's Diary. Dulemba, Elizabeth O., illus. 2005. (Prince's Diary Ser.). 32p. (J). (gr. -1-3). 16.95 (978-1-885008-27-5(9), Shen's Bks.) Lee & Low Bks., Inc.

Trottier, Maxine. The Death of My Country: The Plains of Abraham Diary of Geneviève Aubuchon. 2005. (Dear Canada Ser.). (ENG., Illus.). 216p. (978-0-439-96762-4(7)) Scholastic Canada, Ltd.

Tyre, Lisa Lewis & Airgood, Ellen. Last in a Long Line of Rebels. 2015. (ENG.). 288p. (J). (gr. 5). 16.99 (978-0-399-16838-3(9), Nancy Paulsen Books) Penguin Young Readers Group.

Ure, Jean. The Flower Power Collection: Passion Flower, Shrinking Violet & Pumpkin Pie. 2011. (ENG., Illus.). 544p. (J). (gr. 4-7). pap. 16.99 (978-0-00-720155-6(9), HarperCollins Children's Bks.) HarperCollins Pubs. Ltd. GBR. Dist: HarperCollins Pubs.

van de Ruit, John. Spud. 2005. 300p. pap. (978-0-14-302484-2(1)) Penguin Publishing Group.

—Spud. 2008. (ENG.). 336p. (YA). (gr. 7-18). 9.99 (978-1-59514-187-3(1), Razorbill) Penguin Young Readers Group.

Van De Ruit, John. Spud - The Madness Continues. 2009. (ENG.). 352p. (YA). (gr. 7-18). 9.99 (978-1-59514-245-0(2), Razorbill) Penguin Young Readers Group.

Van Draanen, Wendelin. Runaway. 2012. (ENG.). 272p. (YA). (gr. 5). pap. 9.99 (978-0-307-97597-3(5), Ember) Random Hse. Children's Bks.

Verano, M. Diary of a Haunting. (Diary of a Haunting Ser.). (ENG., Illus.). (YA). (gr. 9). 2016. 336p. pap. 10.99 (978-1-4814-3068-5(8)) 2015. 320p. 17.99 (978-1-4814-3069-2(6)) Simon Pulse. (Simon Pulse).

—Possession. 2016. (Diary of a Haunting Ser.). (ENG., Illus.). 352p. (YA). (gr. 9). 17.99 (978-1-4814-6441-3(8), Simon Pulse) Simon Pulse.

Vernon, Ursula. Nurk: The Strange, Surprising Adventures of a (Somewhat) Brave Shrew. 2008. (ENG., Illus.). 144p. (J). (gr. 3-7). 16.00 (978-0-15-206375-7(7)) Houghton Mifflin Harcourt Publishing Co.

Wallace, Daniel. Star Wars Rebels - Ezra's Journal. Barthelmes, Andrew, illus. 2014. (ENG.). 96p. (J). (gr. k-3). 9.99 (978-0-7944-3268-3(9)) Reader's Digest Assn., Inc., The.

Weatherbee, Tabatha. Shasta, 1 vol. 2009. 216p. pap. 24.95 (978-1-60703-586-2(3)) PublishAmerica, Inc.

Wein, Elizabeth. Rose under Fire. 2014. (ENG.). 384p. (YA). (gr. 9-17). pap. 9.99 (978-1-4231-8469-0(6)) Disney Pr.

—Rose under Fire. 2013. (ENG.). 368p. (YA). (gr. 9-17). 17.99 (978-1-4231-8309-9(6)) Hyperion Pr.

Welch, Jenna Evans. Love & Gelato. (ENG., Illus.). 400p. (YA). (gr. 7). 2017. pap. 10.99 **(978-1-4814-3255-9(9))** 2016. 17.99 (978-1-4814-3254-2(0)) Simon Pulse. (Simon Pulse).

Wells, Tina. Mackenzie Blue. 2013. (Mackenzie Blue Ser.: 1). (ENG.). 224p. (J). (gr. 3-7). pap. 6.99 (978-0-06-158310-0(3)) HarperCollins Pubs.

—Mackenzie Blue. Segawa, Michael, illus. 2009. (Mackenzie Blue Ser.: 1). (ENG.). 224p. (J). (gr. 3-7). 12.99 (978-0-06-158308-7(1)) HarperCollins Pubs.

—The Secret Crush. 2013. (Mackenzie Blue Ser.: 2). (ENG.). 240p. (J). (gr. 3-7). pap. 6.99 (978-0-06-158313-1(8)) HarperCollins Pubs.

—The Secret Crush. Segawa, Michael, illus. 2009. (Mackenzie Blue Ser.: 2). (ENG.). 240p. (J). (gr. 3-7). 10.99 (978-0-06-158311-7(1)) HarperCollins Pubs.

Weston, Carol. Ava & Pip. (Ava & Pip Ser.: 1). (ENG.). 224p. (J). (gr. 5-7). 2015. pap. 6.99 (978-1-4926-0183-8(7)) 2014. 15.99 (978-1-4022-8870-8(0), 9781402288708) Sourcebooks, Inc. (Sourcebooks Jabberwocky).

Weyn, Suzanne. Dr. Frankenstein's Daughters. 2013. (ENG.). 256p. (J). (gr. 7). 17.99 (978-0-545-42533-9(6), Scholastic Pr.) Scholastic, Inc.

Whitby, Adele. Beth's Story 1914. 2014. (Secrets of the Manor Ser.: 1). (ENG., Illus.). 160p. (J). (gr. 3-7). 16.99 (978-1-4814-0632-1(9), Simon Spotlight) Simon Spotlight.

Willey, Margaret. Four Secrets. Hauser, Bill, illus. (ENG.). 288p. (YA). (gr. 7-12). 2014. pap. 9.95 (978-1-4677-1626-0(X), Carolrhoda Lab™) 2012. 17.95 (978-0-7613-8535-6(5)) Lerner Publishing Group.

Williams, Lori. Being Me. 2003. (Summit Books Ser.). 268p. (J). (gr. 3-6). lib. bdg. 13.95 (978-0-7569-1372-4(1)); pap. 6.95 (978-0-7891-6024-9(2)) Perfection Learning Corp.

Williams, Sarah DeFord. Palace Beautiful. 2011. (ENG.). 240p. (J). (gr. 5-18). 6.99 (978-0-14-241745-4(9), Puffin Books) Penguin Young Readers Group.

Witherow, Wendy. Bridget's Blog. Pulley, Kelly, illus. 2007. 95p. (J). pap. (978-1-934306-09-3(6)) Mission City Pr., Inc.

Wooters, Duane. The Unnamed Manuscript. 2003. 70p. (YA). pap. 8.95 (978-0-595-29612-5(2)) iUniverse, Inc.

Wright, Betty Ren. Crandalls' Castle. 2005. (ENG.). 184p. (YA). (gr. 4-6). tchr. ed. 17.95 (978-0-8234-1726-1(3)) Holiday Hse., Inc.

Yee, Lisa. Millicent Min, Girl Genius. 2004. 248p. (gr. 3-7). 17.00 (978-0-7569-3919-9(4)) Perfection Learning Corp.

—Millicent Min, Girl Genius. 2004. (Millicent Min Trilogy Ser.: 1). (ENG.). 256p. (J). (gr. 4-7). reprint ed. pap. 6.99 (978-0-439-42520-9(4), Levine, Arthur A. Bks.) Scholastic, Inc.

Young, Karen Romano. Doodlebug: A Novel in Doodles. 2012. (ENG., Illus.). 128p. (J). (gr. 3-7). pap. 7.99 (978-1-250-01020-9(9), 9781250010209) Square Fish.

—Stuck in the Middle (of Middle School) A Novel in Doodles. 2013. (ENG., Illus.). 112p. (J). (gr. 3-7). 12.99 (978-0-312-55596-2(2), 9780312555962) Feiwel & Friends.

Zehr, E. Paul. Project Superhero. Peam, Kris, illus. 2014. (ENG.). 224p. (J). (gr. 2-7). 13.95 (978-1-77041-180-7(1)) Purple Bear Bks., Inc.

Zenk, Molly. Hyperion Keats. 2013. 134p. pap. 5.49 (978-0-9895262-5-8(9)) Highland Pr.

DICKENS, CHARLES, 1812-1870

Bloom, Harold, ed. & intro. Charles Dickens. Bloom, Harold, intro. 2nd rev. annot. ed. 2006. (Bloom's Modern Critical Views Ser.). 284p. (C). (gr. 9). 45.00 (978-0-7910-8568-4(6), Chelsea Hse.) Facts On File, Inc.

Browne, Barber & Browne, Lee. Charles Dickens. (Illus.). 32p. (J). (978-0-237-51742-7(6)) Evans Brothers, Ltd.

Bryfonski, Dedria. Class Conflict in a Tale of Two Cities. Greenhaven Press Editors, ed. 2013. (Social Issues in Literature Ser.). (ENG., Illus.). 224p. (gr. 10-12). pap. 32.00 (978-0-7377-6975-3(0), Greenhaven Pr., Inc.) Cengage Gale.

—Class Conflict in Charles Dicken's a Tale of Two Cities. Greenhaven Press Editors, ed. 2013. (Social Issues in Literature Ser.). (ENG., Illus.). 224p. (gr. 10-12). lib. bdg. 46.40 (978-0-7377-6974-6(2), Greenhaven Pr., Inc.) Cengage Gale.

Caravantes, Peggy. Best of Times: The Story of Charles Dickens. 2005. (World Writers Ser.). (Illus.). 160p. (gr. 3-7). lib. bdg. 28.95 (978-1-931798-68-6(0)) Reynolds, Morgan Inc.

Collins, David R. Tales for Hard Times: A Story about Charles Dickens. Mataya, David, illus. 2007. (Creative Minds Biographies Ser.). (ENG.). 64p. (gr. 4-8). pap. 8.95 (978-0-8225-6992-3(2)) Lerner Publishing Group.

Kenyon, Karen Smith. Charles Dickens: A Biography. 2008. (J). lib. bdg. (978-0-8225-7532-0(9)) Twenty First Century Bks.

Lacey, Saskia. The Prehistoric Masters of Literature: Discover Literary History with a Prehistoric Twist! 2016. (Jurassic Classics Ser.). (ENG., Illus.). 40p. (J). (gr. 2-6). 14.95 (978-1-63322-098-0(2)) Quarto Publishing Group USA.

Orr, Tamra. Charles Dickens. 2006. (J). lib. bdg. (978-1-58415-456-3(X)) Mitchell Lane Pubs., Inc.

Pollack, Pamela D. & Belviso, Meg. Who Was Charles Dickens? Geyer, Mark Edward & Harrison, Nancy, illus. 2014. (Who Was? Ser.). (ENG.). 112p. (J). (gr. 3-7). pap. 5.99 (978-0-448-47967-5(2), Grosset & Dunlap) Penguin Young Readers Group.

—Who Was Charles Dickens? 2014. (Who Was... ? Ser.). (Illus.). 105p. (J). lib. bdg. 14.75 (978-0-606-36180-4(4)) Turtleback Bks.

Rosen, Michael. Dickens: His Work & His World. Ingpen, Robert R., illus. 2005. (ENG.). 96p. (YA). (gr. 7-11). 19.99 (978-0-7636-2752-2(6)) Candlewick Pr.

Saddleback Educational Publishing Staff, ed. Christmas Carol. 2011. (Timeless Classics Ser.). (ENG.). 48p. (YA). (gr. 9-12). pupil's gde. ed. 19.95 incl. cd-rom (978-1-61651-130-2(3)) Saddleback Educational Publishing, Inc.

—Great Expectations. 2011. (Timeless Classics Ser.). (ENG.). 48p. (YA). (gr. 9-12). pupil's gde. ed. 19.95 incl. cd-rom (978-1-61651-135-7(4)) Saddleback Educational Publishing, Inc.

—Oliver Twist. 2011. (Timeless Classics Ser.). (ENG.). 48p. (YA). (gr. 9-12). pupil's gde. ed. 19.95 incl. cd-rom (978-1-61651-145-6(1)) Saddleback Educational Publishing, Inc.

—Tale of Two Cities. 2011. (Timeless Classics Ser.). (ENG.). 48p. (YA). (gr. 9-12). tchr. ed. 19.95 incl. cd-rom (978-1-61651-152-4(4)) Saddleback Educational Publishing, Inc.

Shipton, Paul & Pearson Education Staff. Charles Dickens, Pack. 2007. (ENG., Illus.). 64p. pap. 17.32 incl. cd-rom (978-1-4058-5211-1(9)) Pearson Education.

Twist, Clint & Wells-Cole, Catherine. Charles Dickens: England's Most Captivating Storyteller. 2011. (ENG., Illus.). 32p. (J). (gr. 3-7). 19.99 (978-0-7636-5567-9(8), Templar) Candlewick Pr.

Warren, Andrea. Charles Dickens & the Street Children of London. (ENG., Illus.). 160p. (gr. 7). 2017. (J). pap. 9.99 (978-0-544-93260-9(9), HMH Books For Young Readers) 2011. (YA). 18.99 (978-0-547-39574-6(4)) Houghton Mifflin Harcourt Publishing Co.

DICKENS, CHARLES, 1812-1870—CHARACTERS

Sweetser, Kate Dickinson. Ten Boys from Dickens. 2004. reprint ed. pap. 21.95 (978-1-4191-5096-8(0)); pap. 1.99 (978-1-4192-5096-5(5)) Kessinger Publishing, LLC.

—Ten Girls from Dickens. Williams, George Alfred, illus. 2004. reprint ed. pap. 27.95 (978-1-4179-3165-1(5)) Kessinger Publishing, LLC.

—Ten Girls from Dickens. 2004. reprint ed. pap. 1.99 (978-1-4192-5098-9(1)) Kessinger Publishing, LLC.

DICKINSON, EMILY, 1830-1886

Berry, S. L. Voices in Poetry: Emily Dickinson. 2015. (Voices in Poetry Ser.). (ENG.). 48p. (J). (gr. 5-8). pap. 12.00 (978-1-62832-054-1(0), Creative Paperbacks) Creative Co., The.

Berry, S. L. & Dickinson, Emily. Emily Dickinson. 2014. (Illus.). 47p. (J). (978-1-60818-326-5(2), Creative Education) Creative Co., The.

Bloom, Harold, ed. Emily Dickinson. 2nd. ed. 2008. (Modern Critical Views Ser.). 231p. (C). (gr. 9-18). 45.00 (978-0-7910-9613-0(0), Chelsea Hse.) Facts On File, Inc.

Borus, Audrey. Reading & Interpreting the Works of Emily Dickinson. 2016. (Lit Crit Guides). (ENG., Illus.). 160p. (J). (gr. 8-8). lib. bdg. 39.93 (978-0-7660-7344-9(0)) Enslow Pubs., Inc.

Griskey, Michele. Emily Dickinson. 2007. (Poets & Playwrights Ser.). (Illus.). 112p. (J). (gr. 3-7). lib. bdg. 37.10 (978-1-58415-429-7(2)) Mitchell Lane Pubs., Inc.

Herstek, Amy Paulson. Emily Dickinson: Solitary & Celebrated Poet. 2003. (Historical American Biographies Ser.). (Illus.). 128p. (J). lib. bdg. 26.60 (978-0-7660-1977-5(2)) Enslow Pubs., Inc.

Hinds, Maurene. Emily Dickinson, 1 vol. 2013. (Great American Authors Ser.). (ENG.). 48p. (J). (gr. 3-6). lib. bdg. 32.79 (978-1-61783-716-6(4)) ABDO Publishing Co.

Meltzer, Milton. Emily Dickinson: A Biography. 2006. (Literary Greats Ser.). (ENG.). 128p. (gr. 7-12). lib. bdg. 33.26 (978-0-7613-2949-7(8), Millbrook Pr.) Lerner Publishing Group.

Priddy, Anna. Bloom's How to Write about Emily Dickinson. 2007. (Bloom's How to Write about Literature Ser.). 262p. (C). (gr. 9-18). 45.00 (978-0-7910-9492-1(8), Chelsea Hse.) Facts On File, Inc.

DICTATORS

Benchmark Education Company. Three Twentieth Century Dictators (Teacher Guide) 2004. (978-1-4108-2593-3(0)) Benchmark Education Co.

Cawthorne, Nigel. Notorious Tyrants. 2012. (Great People in History Ser.). (ENG., Illus.). 128p. (YA). (gr. 8-12). lib. bdg. 34.60 (978-1-4777-0406-6(X)) Rosen Publishing Group, Inc., The.

Childress, Diana. Omar Al-Bashir's Sudan. 2009. (Dictatorships Ser.). (ENG., Illus.). 160p. (J). (gr. 9-12). 38.60 (978-0-8225-9096-5(4), 1299570) Lerner Publishing Group.

Connolly, Sean. Dictatorship. 2012. (Systems of Government Ser.). (Illus.). 48p. (gr. 6-12). lib. bdg. 37.10 (978-1-59920-804-6(0)) Black Rabbit Bks.

Donovan, Sandra. Military/Dictators. 2013. (ShockZone (tm) — Villains Ser.). (ENG., Illus.). 32p. (gr. 5-8). lib. bdg. 26.60 (978-1-4677-0609-4(4), Lerner Pubns.) Lerner Publishing Group.

Donovan, Sandy. Lethal Leaders & Military Madmen. (ShockZone (tm) — Villains Ser.). (ENG., Illus.). 32p. (gr. 5-8). 2015. 21.32 (978-1-4677-6002-7(1), Lerner Digital) 2013. pap. 8.95 (978-1-4677-0896-8(8)) Lerner Publishing Group.

Dowswell, Paul. Dictatorship. 2005. (Systems of Government Ser.). (Illus.). 48p. (gr. 6-12). pap. 14.05 (978-0-8368-5889-1(1)); lib. bdg. 31.00 (978-0-8368-5884-6(0)) Stevens, Gareth Publishing LLLP. (Gareth Stevens Secondary Library).

Ellis, Catherine & Roberts, Jeremy. Adolf Hitler, 01 vols., 1. 2016. (Holocaust Ser.). (ENG., Illus.). 112p. (J). 35.60 (978-1-4994-6248-7(4), Rosen Young Adult) Rosen Publishing Group, Inc., The.

Giblin, James Cross. The Life & Death of Adolf Hitler. 2015. (ENG., Illus.). 256p. (J). (gr. 5-7). pap. 9.99 (978-0-544-45591-7(6), HMH Books For Young Readers) Houghton Mifflin Harcourt Publishing Co.

—The Life & Death of Adolf Hitler. 2015. lib. bdg. 20.85 (978-0-606-36830-8(2)) Turtleback Bks.

Harrison, Paul. Dastardly Dictators, Rulers & Other Loony Leaders. 2017. (Barmy Biogs Ser.). (ENG., Illus.). 96p. (J). (gr. 4-6). pap. 7.99 **(978-0-7502-8392-2(0)**, Wayland) Hachette Children's Group GBR. Dist: Hachette Bk. Group.

Hunter, Nick. What Is a Dictatorship?, Vol. 1. 2014. (Understanding Political Systems Ser.). 48p. (J). (gr. 6-8). 31.95 (978-1-4824-0310-7(2)); pap. 14.05 (978-1-4824-0311-4(0)) Stevens, Gareth Publishing LLLP.

Marcovitz, Hal. Dictatorships, 1 vol. 2011. (Exploring World Governments Ser.). (ENG., Illus.). 160p. (J). (gr. 9-12). lib. bdg. 37.07 (978-1-61714-791-3(5), Essential Library) ABDO Publishing Co.

McCarthy, Rose. Dictatorship: A Primary Source Analysis. 2009. (Primary Sources of Political Systems Ser.). 64p. (gr. 5-8). 58.50 (978-1-60851-837-1(X)) Rosen Publishing Group, Inc., The.

Miller, Reagan & Boyle, Sarah B. What is a Dictatorship? Crabtree Publishing Staff, ed. 2012. (Forms of Government Ser.: No. 2). (ENG.). 48p. (J). (gr. 5-8). pap. (978-0-7787-5324-7(7)) Crabtree Publishing Co.

O'Reilly, Bill. Hitler's Last Days: The Death of the Nazi Regime & the World's Most Notorious Dictator. 2015. (Illus.). 320p. (J). pap. (978-1-62779-455-8(7)); (ENG., (gr. 5-9). 19.99 (978-1-62779-396-4(8), 9781627793964, Holt, Henry & Co. Bks. For Young Readers) Holt, Henry & Co.

—Hitler's Last Days: The Death of the Nazi Regime & the World's Most Notorious Dictator. Barcellona, Christine, ed. 2017. (ENG.). 336p. (J). pap. 12.99 (978-1-250-08859-8(3), 9781250088598) Square Fish.

Rice, Dona. Chicas y Chicos Malos Del Mundo Antiguo. 2016. (TIME for Kids en Español - Level 5 Ser.). (SPA.). 64p. (gr. 5-5). lib. bdg. 31.99 (978-1-5157-2953-2(2)) Time for Kids Inc AUS. Dist: Capstone Pub.

Ruby, India. Three Twentieth Century Dictators: Set Of 6. 2011. (Navigators Ser.). (J). pap. 50.00 net. (978-1-4108-2578-0(7)) Benchmark Education Co.

—Three Twentieth Century Dictators & Tres dictadores del siglo XX: 6 English, 6 Spanish Adaptations. 2011. (ENG & SPA.). (J). 101.00 net. (978-1-4108-5739-2(5)) Benchmark Education Co.

Thomson Gale Staff & Hermsen, Sarah. Prejudice in the Modern World: Biographies. Hanes, Richard C. & Rudd, Kelly, eds. rev. ed. 2007. (Prejudice in the Modern World Reference Library). (ENG.). 288p. (YA). 106.00 (978-1-4144-0207-9(4), UXL) Cengage Gale.

Zahler, Kathy A. The Assads' Syria. 2009. (Dictatorships Ser.). (ENG.). 160p. (gr. 9-12). 38.60 (978-0-8225-9095-8(6)) Lerner Publishing Group.

DIET

see also Beverages; Cooking; Digestion; Food; Menus; Vegetarianism; Weight Control

Benduhn, Tea. Fruit: Fruta. 2007. (Find Out about Food/ Conoce la comida Ser.). (SPA & ENG.). 24p. (gr. k-3). pap. 8.15 (978-0-8368-8462-3(0), Weekly Reader Leveled Readers) Stevens, Gareth Publishing LLLP.

—Fruit/Fruta. 2007. (Find Out about Food/Conoce la Comida Ser.). (SPA & ENG., Illus.). 24p. (gr. k-3). lib. bdg. 22.00 (978-0-8368-8455-5(8), Weekly Reader Leveled Readers) Stevens, Gareth Publishing LLLP.

Boothroyd, Jennifer. Taste Something New! Giving Different Foods a Try. 2016. (Lightning Bolt Books — Healthy Eating Ser.). (ENG., Illus.). 32p. (J). (gr. 1-3). 26.65 (978-1-4677-9472-5(4), Lerner Pubns.) Lerner Publishing Group.

—What's on My Plate? Choosing from the Five Food Groups. 2016. (Lightning Bolt Books — Healthy Eating Ser.). (ENG., Illus.). 32p. (gr. 1-3). 39.99 (978-1-5124-1669-5(X), Lerner Digital); (J). (gr. 2-3). E-Book 39.99 (978-1-4677-9672-9(7), 9781467796729, Lerner Pubns.) Lerner Publishing Group.

Bullard, Lisa. My Food, Your Food. Schneider, Christine, illus. 2015. (Cloverleaf Books (tm) — Alike & Different Ser.). (ENG.). 24p. (gr. k-2). (J). lib. bdg. 23.99 (978-1-4677-4903-9(6)); pap. 6.99 (978-1-4677-6031-7(5)) Lerner Publishing Group. (Millbrook Pr.).

Burgan, Michael. Making Food Choices, 1 vol. 2011. (Ethics of Food Ser.). (ENG.). 56p. (gr. 6-6). pap. 10.95 (978-1-4329-6194-7(2)) Heinemann-Raintree.

Canino, Kate. Maintaining a Healthy Weight. 2010. (Healthy Habits Ser.). (Illus.). 64p. (YA). (gr. 5-8). pap. 12.95 (978-1-4488-0609-6(7)); lib. bdg. 31.95 (978-1-4358-9439-6(1)) Rosen Publishing Group, Inc., The. (Rosen Reference).

Cardenas, Ernesto A. I Will Grow Strong & Healthy! 2009. 19.95 (978-1-60698-008-8(4)); pap. 3.95 (978-1-60698-006-4(8)) Milo Educational Bks. & Resources.

Centore, Michael. Gluten. 2017. (J). **(978-1-4222-3739-7(7))** Mason Crest.

Cleary, Brian P. Oils (Just a Bit) to Keep Your Body Fit: What Are Oils? Goneau, Martin, illus. 2010. (Food Is CATegorical Ser.). (ENG.). 32p. (gr. k-3). lib. bdg. 25.26 (978-1-58013-592-4(7)) Lerner Publishing Group.

Crockett, Kyle A. Managing Your Weight with Nutrition. Borus, Joshua, ed. 2013. (Understanding Nutrition: a Gateway to Physical & Mental Health Ser.: 11). (Illus.). 48p. (J). (gr. 5-18). 19.95 (978-1-4222-2881-4(9)) Mason Crest.

—The Numbers: Calories, BMI, & Portion Sizes. Borus, Joshua, ed. 2013. (Understanding Nutrition: a Gateway to Physical & Mental Health Ser.: 11). (Illus.). 48p. (J). (gr. 5-18). 19.95 (978-1-4222-2883-8(5)) Mason Crest.

—Nutrition & Your Future. Borus, Joshua, ed. 2013. (Understanding Nutrition: a Gateway to Physical & Mental Health Ser.: 11). (Illus.). 48p. (J). (gr. 5-18). 19.95 (978-1-4222-2885-2(1)) Mason Crest.

Deal, Darlene. Play with Your Food & Learn How to Eat Right: Nutritional Book about Fruits & Vegetables. 2004. (ENG & SPA., Illus.). 22p. (J). (gr. 1-4). pap. 9.95 (978-0-9747299-0-9(6)) Deal, Darlene.

Edwards, Hazel & Alexander, Goldie. Talking about What You Eat. 2010. (Healthy Living Ser.). (Illus.). 32p. (YA). (gr. 3-6). lib. bdg. 26.00 (978-1-4339-3656-2(9)) Stevens, Gareth Publishing LLLP.

Elton, Sarah. Meatless? A Fresh Look at What You Eat. McLaughlin, Julie, illus. 2017. (ENG.). 48p. (J). (gr. 4-8). 16.95 (978-1-926818-43-6(1)) Owlkids Bks. Inc. CAN. Dist: Publishers Group West (PGW).

Etingoff, Kim. Building a Healthy Diet with the 5 Food Groups. Prock, Lisa Albers, ed. 2014. (On My Plate Ser.: 6). 48p. (J). (gr. 5-18). 20.95 (978-1-4222-3095-4(3)) Mason Crest.

—Decisions, Decisions: Vegetarianism, Breakfasts, & Beyond. Borus, Joshua, ed. 2013. (Understanding Nutrition: a Gateway to Physical & Mental Health Ser.: 11). (Illus.). 48p. (J). (gr. 5-18). 19.95 (978-1-4222-2875-3(4)) Mason Crest.

—Diet Myths: Sorting Through the Hype. Borus, Joshua, ed. 2013. (Understanding Nutrition: a Gateway to Physical & Mental Health Ser.: 11). (Illus.). 48p. (J). (gr. 5-18). 19.95 (978-1-4222-2876-0(2)) Mason Crest.

Food Friends: How to Make Friends Out of Food. 2016. (J). (978-0-87659-713-2(4)) Gryphon Hse., Inc.

Francis, Amy. Vegetarianism. 2015. (Current Controversies Ser.). (ENG.). 224p. (J). (gr. 10-12). 46.40 (978-0-7377-7227-2(1), Greenhaven Pr., Inc.) Cengage Gale.

Gifford, Clive. Food & Cooking in Ancient Egypt. 2010. (Cooking in World Cultures Ser.). (Illus.). 32p. (J). (ENG.). pap. 10.60 (978-1-61532-359-3(7)); (gr. 3-5). lib. bdg. 26.50 (978-1-61532-337-1(6)) Rosen Publishing Group, Inc., The. (PowerKids Pr.).

—Food & Cooking in Ancient Greece. 2010. (Cooking in World Cultures Ser.). (Illus.). 32p. (J). (ENG.). pap. 10.60 (978-1-61532-361-6(9)); (gr. 3-5). lib. bdg. 26.50 (978-1-61532-338-8(4)) Rosen Publishing Group, Inc., The. (PowerKids Pr.).

—Food & Cooking in Ancient Rome. 2010. (Cooking in World Cultures Ser.). (Illus.). 32p. (J). (ENG.). pap. 10.60 (978-1-61532-363-0(5)); (gr. 3-5). lib. bdg. 26.50 (978-1-61532-339-5(2)) Rosen Publishing Group, Inc., The. (PowerKids Pr.).

—Food & Cooking in Viking Times. 2010. (Cooking in World Cultures Ser.). (Illus.). 32p. (J). (ENG.). pap. 10.60 (978-1-61532-365-4(1)); (gr. 3-5). lib. bdg. 26.50 (978-1-61532-354-8(6)) Rosen Publishing Group, Inc., The. (PowerKids Pr.).

Having a Healthy Baby - Diet & Nutrition. 2004. (YA). pap. 4.00 net. (978-1-930996-57-1(8)) Planned Parenthood Federation of America, Inc.

Hunnicutt, Susan C., ed. Is the Western Diet Making the World Sick? 2012. (At Issue Ser.). (ENG.). 128p. (gr. 10-12). pap. 27.80 (978-0-7377-6192-4(X), Greenhaven Pr., Inc.) Cengage Gale.

Hunt, Charles. The Perfect Diet: The Ultimate Weight Solution for Every Body. 2004. (978-0-9630377-2-5(2)) Hunt Thompson Media.

Hunt, Jamie. The Truth about Diets: What's Right for You? (Kids & Obesity Ser.). 48p. (YA). 2010. lib. bdg. 19.95 (978-1-4222-1710-8(8)) 2009. pap. 7.95 (978-1-4222-1898-3(8)) Mason Crest.

Jones, Kadeem. Healthy Fractions: Develop Understanding of Fractions & Numbers. 2014. (Rosen Common Core Math Readers Ser.). (ENG., Illus.). 24p. (J). (gr. 3-4). pap. 8.25 (978-1-4777-4920-3(9), Rosen Classroom) Rosen Publishing Group, Inc., The.

Kallen, Stuart. Obesity. 2016. (Matters of Opinion Ser.). (ENG.). 64p. (J). (gr. 4-6). pap. 14.60 (978-1-60357-859-2(5)) Norwood Hse. Pr.

Kesselring, Susan. Make a Meal Plan: Smart Food Shopping, 1 vol. 2012. (Move & Get Healthy Ser.). (ENG.). 32p. (J). (gr. k-3). 28.50 (978-1-61641-863-2(X)) Magic Wagon.

Knighton, Kate. Why Shouldn't I Eat Junk Food? Larkum, Adam, illus. 2008. (Usborne Ser.). 48p. (J). (gr. 4-7). pap. 6.99 (978-0-7945-1953-7(9), Usborne) EDC Publishing.

KociendaGenevieve. SUSHI NATION LOW INTERMEDIATE BOOK WITH ONLINE ACCESS. 2014. (ENG., Illus.). 28p. (J). pap. 9.50 *(978-1-107-63147-2(5))* Cambridge Univ. Pr.

Leedy, Loreen. The Edible Pyramid: Good Eating Every Day. Leedy, Loreen, illus. rev. ed. 2007. (Reading Rainbow Bks.). (ENG., Illus.). 32p. (J). (gr. -1-3). 6.95 *(978-0-8234-2075-9(2))* Holiday Hse., Inc.

Lin, Grace & McKneally, Ranida T. Our Food. Zong, Grace, illus. 2016. (ENG.). 40p. (J). (gr. k-3). lib. bdg. 16.95 *(978-1-58089-590-3(5))* Charlesbridge Publishing, Inc.

Llewellyn, Claire. Estoy Sano? Aprender Sobre Alimentacion y Actividad Fisica. Gordon, Mike, illus. (SPA.). (J). (gr. k-2). pap. *(978-950-24-0945-0(0))* Albatros ARG. Dist: Lectorum Pubns., Inc.

Lluch, Alex A. Lose up to 10 Pounds in 2 Weeks. 2011. (ENG.). 220p. pap., pupil's gde. ed. 11.95 *(978-1-936061-40-2(6))*; 360p. pap. 16.95 *(978-1-936061-17-4(1))* WS Publishing.

Matthew, John. Foods of Italy. 2011. (Culture in the Kitchen Ser.). 24p. (J). (gr. 2-5). pap. 8.15 *(978-1-4339-5712-3(4))*; lib. bdg. 22.60 *(978-1-4339-5710-9(8))* Stevens, Gareth Publishing LLLP. (Gareth Stevens Learning Library).

Maze, Stephanie, ed. Healthy Foods from A to Z: Comida Sana de la a a la Z. Comet, Renee, photos by. 2012. (SPA & ENG., Illus.). 32p. (J). (gr. -1-k). 15.95 *(978-0-9834983-1-5(8))* Moonstone Pr., LLC.

Morado, Leah. What's on My Plate? Develop Understanding of Fractions & Numbers, 1 vol. 2015. (InfoMax Common Core Math Readers Ser.). (ENG.). 24p. (J). pap. 8.25 *(978-1-4777-4609-7(9))*, Rosen Classroom) Rosen Publishing Group, Inc., The.

Nardo, Don. Vegan Diets. Greenhaven Press Editors, ed. 2014. (Nutrition & Health Ser.). (ENG., Illus.). 128p. (gr. 7-10). lib. bdg. 35.70 *(978-1-4205-1151-2(3))*, Lucent Bks.) Cengage Gale.

Olson, Karen. Eat, Run & Live Healthy. Hamelin, Marie-Micheline, illus. 2nd rev. ed. 2009. (Caring for Me Ser.). (ENG.). 20p. (J). pap. 9.95 *(978-1-894778-50-3(2))* Theytus Bks., Ltd. CAN. Dist: Univ. of Toronto Pr.

Person, Naomi, et al. Sow What? Hooper, Hadley & Stryk, Suzanne, illus. 2009. 94p. (YA). pap. *(978-0-88441-735-4(2))* Girl Scouts of the USA.

Peters, Celeste A. Health. 2016. (J). ***(978-1-5105-2237-4(9))*** SmartBook Media, Inc.

Pollan, Michael. The Omnivore's Dilemma for Kids. 2015. lib. bdg. 20.85 *(978-0-606-37390-6(X))* Turtleback Bks.

Roberts, Jeremy. Drugs & Dieting. 2005. (Drug Abuse Prevention Library). (Illus.). 64p. (YA). (gr. 7-12). lib. bdg. 31.95 *(978-0-8239-3357-0(1))* Rosen Publishing Group, Inc., The.

—Drugs & Dieting. 2009. (Drug Abuse Prevention Library). 64p. (gr. 5-5). 58.50 *(978-1-60853-428-9(6))* Rosen Publishing Group, Inc., The.

Rodger, Ellen. Reducing Your Foodprint: Farming, Cooking, & Eating for a Healthy Planet. 2010. (ENG., Illus.). 32p. (J). pap. *(978-0-7787-2936-5(2))* Crabtree Publishing Co.

Schaefer, Adam. Alimentos Saludables, 1 vol. 2010. (Salud y el Estado Fisico Ser.).Tr. of Healthy Food. (SPA.). 32p. (gr. 1-3). 27.32 *(978-1-4329-4444-5(4))*; pap. 8.29 *(978-1-4329-4449-0(5))* Heinemann-Raintree.

Schuh, Mari. Special Diets, 1 vol. 2014. (Special Diets Ser.). (ENG.). 24p. (gr. k-1). 106.60 *(978-1-4914-0665-6(8)*, Pebble Plus) Capstone Press of Coughlan Cos.

Schuh, Mari C. Gluten-Free Diets, 1 vol. 2014. (Special Diets Ser.). (ENG.). 24p. (gr. k-1). lib. bdg. 26.65 *(978-1-4914-0589-5(9)*, Pebble Plus) Capstone Press of Coughlan Cos.

Senker, Cath. Healthy Eating. 2008. (Healthy Choices Ser.). (Illus.). 24p. (J). (gr. 3-7). lib. bdg. 22.60 *(978-1-4042-4303-3(8)*, PowerKids Pr.) Rosen Publishing Group, Inc., The.

Sheen, Barbara, ed. Foods of Israel. 2011. (Taste of Culture Ser.). (Illus.). 65p. (YA). (gr. 9-12). 30.45 *(978-0-7377-5882-5(1))* Cengage Gale.

Sieving Pelkki, Jane. Healthy Eating. 2016. (True Book(tm), A — Health Ser.). (ENG., Illus.). 48p. (J). lib. bdg. 31.00 *(978-0-531-22848-7(7)*, Children's Pr.) Scholastic Library Publishing.

Simons, Rae. Bigger Isn't Always Better: Choosing Your Portions. 2010. (Kids & Obesity Ser.). (Illus.). 48p. (YA). lib. bdg. 19.95 *(978-1-4222-1706-1(X))* Mason Crest.

Sjonger, Rebecca. How to Choose Foods Your Body Will Use. 2016. (ENG.). 24p. (J). *(978-0-7787-2350-9(X))* Crabtree Publishing Co.

Sly, Stacey. What Should I Eat? Gentry, Susana, photos by. 2010. (Illus.). 26p. pap. 12.95 *(978-1-60911-432-9(9)*, Eloquent Bks.) Strategic Book Publishing & Rights Agency (SBPRA).

Smallwood, Sally. We Are What We Eat! 2008. (Things I Eat Ser.). (ENG., Illus.). 24p. (J). (gr. -1-k). *(978-1-84089-523-0(3))* Zero to Ten, Ltd.

Sullivan, Laura. The Colonial Cook. 2015. (Colonial People Ser.). (ENG.). 48p. (J). (gr. 4-4). lib. bdg. 31.36 *(978-1-5026-0488-0(4))* Cavendish Square Publishing.

Turner, Keith. H Is for Healthy Diet: H Is for Hope Book Series, 1. 2007. (Illus.). 24p. (J). 8.00 *(978-0-9794377-1-7(7))* Turngroup Technologies, LLC.

Ventura, Marne. Nutrition Myths, Busted! 2017. (Science Myths, Busted! Ser.). (ENG., Illus.). 32p. (J). (gr. 3-6). 21.95 *(978-1-63235-304-7(0))* Pr. Room Editions LLC.

Wilcox, Christine. Teens, Nutrition, & Dieting. 2015. (ENG., Illus.). 80p. (J). lib. bdg. *(978-1-60152-834-6(5))* ReferencePoint Pr., Inc.

Williams, Kara. Diet Drugs. 2009. (Danger Zone: Dieting & Eating Disorders Ser.). 64p. (gr. 5-6). 55.90 *(978-1-61512-123-6(4))* Rosen Publishing Group, Inc., The.

Zahensky, Barbara. Diet Fads. 2009. (Danger Zone: Dieting & Eating Disorders Ser.). 64p. (gr. 5-6). 55.90 *(978-1-61512-124-3(2))* Rosen Publishing Group, Inc., The.

DIET IN DISEASE

Schuh, Mari C. Dairy-Free Diets, 1 vol. 2014. (Special Diets Ser.). (ENG.). 24p. (gr. k-1). lib. bdg. 26.65 *(978-1-4914-0590-1(2)*, Pebble Plus) Capstone Press of Coughlan Cos.

—Nut-Free Diets, 1 vol. 2014. (Special Diets Ser.). (ENG.). 24p. (gr. k-1). lib. bdg. 26.65 *(978-1-4914-0591-8(0)*, Pebble Plus) Capstone Press of Coughlan Cos.

Watkins, Christine. Can Diets Be Harmful? 2011. (At Issue Ser.). (ENG.). 128p. (gr. 10-12). pap. 27.80 *(978-0-7377-5557-2(1)*, Greenhaven Pr., Inc.) Cengage Gale.

Watkins, Christine, ed. Can Diets Be Harmful? 2011. (At Issue Ser.). 128p. (YA). (gr. 9-12). 34.45 *(978-0-7377-5556-5(3))* Cengage Gale.

DIETETICS

see Diet

DIETITIANS

Hunsaker, Jennifer. Dietitian Nutritionists. 2017. (Careers in Healthcare Ser.: Vol. 13). (ENG.). (YA). (gr. 7-12). 23.95 ***(978-1-4222-3798-4(2))*** Mason Crest.

DIGESTION

see also Diet; Food; Nutrition

Andrews, Barbara. Discover the Nervous & Digestive Systems. 2006. (J). pap. *(978-1-4108-6515-1(0))* Benchmark Education Co.

Arnold, Nick & Saules, Tony de. Esa Repugnante Digestion. Saules, Tony de, tr. 2003. (Coleccion Esa Horrible Cienca). (SPA., Illus.). 156p. (YA). pap. *(978-84-272-2057-7(X)*, ML4090) Molino, Editorial ESP. Dist: Lectorum Pubns., Inc.

Bailey, Jacqui. What Happens When You Eat? (gr. k-5). 2009. 32p. pap. 10.60 *(978-1-4358-2619-9(1)*, Rosen Classroom) 2008. (Illus.). 30p. (J). lib. bdg. 26.50 *(978-1-4042-4429-0(8)*, PowerKids Pr.) Rosen Publishing Group, Inc., The.

Barraclough, Sue & Lanz, Helen. Eat & Drink. 2012. (Healthy Habits Ser.). 24p. (gr. 1-3). lib. bdg. 24.25 *(978-1-59771-307-8(4))* Sea-To-Sea Pubns.

Bennett, Howard J. Max Archer, Kid Detective: The Case of the Recurring Stomachaches. Gerrell, Spike, illus. 2012. 48p. (J). 14.95 *(978-1-4338-1130-2(8))*; pap. 9.95 *(978-1-4338-1129-6(4))* American Psychological Assn. (Magination Pr.).

Brett, Flora. Your Digestive System Works! 2015. (Your Body Systems Ser.). (ENG.). 24p. (J). (gr. 1-2). lib. bdg. 25.32 *(978-1-4914-2064-5(2))* Capstone Press of Coughlan Cos.

Burstein, John. Dynamic Digestive System: How Does My Stomach Work? 2009. (Slim Goodbody's Body Buddies Ser.). (ENG., Illus.). 32p. (J). (gr. 3-5). pap. *(978-0-7787-4429-0(9))* Crabtree Publishing Co.

—The Dynamic Digestive System: How Does My Stomach Work? 2009. (Slim Goodbody's Body Buddies Ser.). (ENG., Illus.). 32p. (J). (gr. 3-5). lib. bdg. *(978-0-7787-4415-3(9))* Crabtree Publishing Co.

Canavan, Thomas. Fueling the Body: Digestion & Nutrition. 2015. (How Your Body Works). (ENG.). 32p. (J). (gr. 4-4). pap. 10.00 *(978-1-4994-1227-7(4)*, PowerKids Pr.) Rosen Publishing Group, Inc., The.

Cho, Shinta. The Gas We Pass: The Story of Farts. Stinchecum, Amanda M., tr. 2006. (ENG., Illus.). 28p. (J). (gr. -1-18). pap. 7.99 *(978-1-929132-15-7(8))* Kane Miller.

Cohen, Robert Z. The Stomach & Intestines in Your Body, 1 vol. 2015. (ENG.). 32p. (J). 23.45 *(978-1-62275-632-2(0)*, Britannica Educational Publishing) Rosen Publishing Group, Inc., The.

Conklin, Wendy. Digestion & Using Food. 2015. (Science Readers: Content & Literacy Ser.). (Illus.). 32p. (J). (gr. 5-5). pap. 8.99 *(978-1-4807-4717-3(3))* Teacher Created Materials, Inc.

Corcoran, Mary K. The Quest to Digest. Czekaj, Jef, illus. 2006. (ENG.). 32p. (J). (gr. 3-7). pap. 7.95 *(978-1-57091-665-6(9))* Charlesbridge Publishing, Inc.

Farndon, John. Stickmen's Guide to Your Gurgling Guts. Dean, Venitia, illus. 2017. (Stickmen's Guides to Your Awesome Body Ser.). (ENG.). 32p. (J). (gr. 3-6). 26.65 ***(978-1-5124-3212-1(1))*** Lerner Publishing Group.

Ferguson, Beth. Digestive System. 2003. (Kaleidoscope Ser.). (Illus.). 48p. (gr. 3-18). lib. bdg. 20.95 *(978-0-7614-1591-6(2)*, Benchmark Bks.) Marshall Cavendish Corp.

Goldsmith, Mike. In One End & Out the Other. Watson, Richard, illus. 2014. (Flip Flap Journeys Ser.). (ENG.). 14p. (J). (gr. k-2). 12.99 *(978-1-4052-6830-1(1))* Egmont Bks., Ltd. GBR. Dist: Independent Pubs. Group.

Gordon, Sharon. My Stomach. 2004. (Bookworms Ser.). (ENG & SPA., Illus.). 31p. (J). 21.36 *(978-0-7614-1782-8(6))* Marshall Cavendish Corp.

Gray, Susan H. The Digestive System. 2014. (Human Body Ser.). (ENG.). 24p. (J). (gr. 2-5). 28.50 *(978-1-62687-335-3(6)*, 207175) Child's World, Inc., The.

Green, Emily & Manolis, Kay. The Digestive System. 2009. (Body Systems Ser.). (ENG., Illus.). 24p. (J). (gr. 2-5). lib. bdg. 25.95 *(978-1-60014-243-7(5))* Bellwether Media.

Greenhaven Press Editors. Celiac Disease. 2012. (Perspectives on Diseases & Disorders Ser.). (ENG., Illus.). 144p. (J). (gr. 10-12). lib. bdg. 38.95 *(978-0-7377-5772-9(8)*, Greenhaven Pr., Inc.) Cengage Gale.

Guillain, Charlotte. Nuestros Estómagos, 1 vol. 2010. (Nuestros Cuerpos Ser.).Tr. of Our Stomachs. (SPA.). 24p. (gr. -1-1). 22.65 *(978-1-4329-4296-0(4))*; pap. 6.29 *(978-1-4329-4305-9(7))* Heinemann-Raintree. (Bellota).

—Our Stomachs, 1 vol. 2010. (Our Bodies Ser.). (ENG.). 24p. (gr. -1-1). 22.65 *(978-1-4329-3591-7(7))*; pap. 6.29 *(978-1-4329-3600-6(X))* Heinemann-Raintree. (Acorn).

Halvorson, Karin. Inside the Stomach, 1 vol. 2013. (Super Simple Your Body Ser.). (ENG.). 32p. (J). (gr. k-4). lib. bdg. 27.07 *(978-1-61783-614-5(1)*, Super SandCastle) ABDO Publishing Co.

Hartman, Eve & Meshbesher, Wendy. Digestion & Nutrition: What Happens to the Food We Eat?, 1 vol. 2014. (Show Me Science Ser.). (ENG., Illus.). 32p. (gr. 3-5). lib. bdg. 30.65 *(978-1-4329-8748-0(8)*, Raintree Perspectives) Heinemann-Raintree.

Hewitt, Sally. My Digestive System. 2012. (My Body Ser.). (ENG., Illus.). 24p. (gr. k-4). pap. 7.95 *(978-1-926853-97-0(0))* Saunders Bk. Co. CAN. Dist: RiverStream Publishing.

Hoffmann, Gretchen. Digestive System. 2008. (Amazing Human Body Ser.). 80p. (gr. 5-18). lib. bdg. 34.21 *(978-0-7614-3058-2(X)*, Benchmark Bks.) Marshall Cavendish Corp.

Houghton, Gillian. The Digestive System. 2007. (How Your Body Works). (ENG., Illus.). 24p. (gr. 3-5). pap. 7.05 *(978-1-4042-2179-6(4)*, PowerKids Pr.) Rosen Publishing Group, Inc., The.

—Guts: The Digestive System. 2006. (Body Works Ser.). (Illus.). 24p. (YA). (gr. 2-5). lib. bdg. 22.60 *(978-1-4042-3470-3(5))* Rosen Publishing Group, Inc., The.

Johnson, Rebecca L. Digestive System. 2005. (Illus.). 48p. (YA). pap. 8.95 *(978-0-8225-2519-6(4)*, Lerner Pubns.) Lerner Publishing Group.

—Your Digestive System. 2012. (Searchlight Books — How Does Your Body Work? Ser.). (ENG., Illus.). 40p. (gr. 3-5). pap. 8.95 *(978-1-58013-960-1(4))*; lib. bdg. 27.93 *(978-0-7613-7448-0(5)*, Lerner Pubns.) Lerner Publishing Group.

Jordan, Apple & Rau, Dana Meachen. My Stomach. 2nd ed. 2013. (Illus.). 24p. (J). (gr. 1-3). 21.36 *(978-1-60870-437-8(8))* Cavendish Square Publishing.

Kolpin, Molly. A Tour of Your Digestive System. Jones, Chris B., illus. 2012. (First Graphics: Body Systems Ser.). (ENG.). 24p. (gr. 1-2). pap. 35.70 *(978-1-4296-9325-7(8))* Capstone Press of Coughlan Cos.

Kolpin, Molly Erin. A Tour of Your Digestive System, 1 vol. Jones, Chris B., illus. 2012. (First Graphics: Body Systems Ser.). (ENG.). 24p. (gr. 1-2). pap. 6.29 *(978-1-4296-9324-0(X))* Capstone Press of Coughlan Cos.

Korb, Rena B. & Weinhaus, Anthony J. My Stomach, 1 vol. Simard, Remy, illus. 2010. (My Body Ser.). (ENG.). 32p. (J). (gr. k-3). 28.50 *(978-1-60270-810-5(X))* Magic Wagon.

Libra, Anna. Why Does My Stomach Ache? An Inside Look at the Digestive System. 2003. (J). pap. *(978-1-58417-068-6(9))* Lake Street Pubs.

Marsico, Katie. Digestion. 2016. (J). *(978-1-4896-5295-9(7))* Weigl Pubs., Inc.

—I Burp. 2015. (Tell Me Why Library). (ENG., Illus.). 24p. (J). (gr. 2-5). 27.07 *(978-1-63188-992-9(3)*, 205880) Cherry Lake Publishing.

—I Throw Up. 2014. (Tell Me Why Library). (ENG., Illus.). 24p. (J). (gr. 2-5). 25.64 *(978-1-63188-006-3(3)*, 205431) Cherry Lake Publishing.

—Step-by-Step Experiments with Taste & Digestion. Ostrom, Bob, illus. 2012. (Step-By-Step Experiments Ser.). (ENG.). 32p. (J). (gr. 1-4). lib. bdg. 29.93 *(978-1-60973-614-9(1)*, 201240) Child's World, Inc., The.

Meachen Rau, Dana. El Estomago: Que Hay Dentro de Mi? 2006. (Bookworms Ser.). (SPA & ENG., Illus.). 32p. (gr. 1-2). lib. bdg. 15.95 *(978-0-7614-2407-9(5))* Marshall Cavendish Corp.

—My Stomach/el Estomago. 2006. (Bookworms Ser.). (ENG & SPA., Illus.). 32p. (gr. 1-2). lib. bdg. 15.95 *(978-0-7614-2485-7(7))* Marshall Cavendish Corp.

Monroe, Judy. Coping with Ulcers, Heartburn & Stress-Related Stomach Disorders. 2005. (Coping Ser.). (Illus.). 192p. (YA). (gr. 7-12). lib. bdg. 34.60 *(978-0-8239-2971-9(X)*, COULCE) Rosen Publishing Group, Inc., The.

Nardo, Don. Eating Disorders. 2003. (Understanding Issues Ser.). (ENG., Illus.). 48p. (J). (gr. 3-5). 27.50 *(978-0-7377-1384-8(4)*, Kidhaven) Cengage Gale.

Nuestro Sistema Digestivo. (SPA.). 96p. (J). 10.00 *(978-84-342-1807-9(0))* Parramon Ediciones S.A. ESP. Dist: Distribuidora Norma, Inc.

Ollhoff, Jim. The Digestive System. 2012. (J). *(978-1-61783-253-6(7))* ABDO Publishing Co.

Orr, Tamra B. Super Cool Science Experiments: Digestion. 2009. (Explorer Library: Science Explorer Ser.). (ENG., Illus.). 32p. (gr. 4-8). lib. bdg. 28.50 *(978-1-60279-518-1(5)*, 200303) Cherry Lake Publishing.

Owen, Ruth. What Happens When I Eat? 2013. (My Body: Inside & Out! Ser.). 24p. (J). (gr. -1-3). lib. bdg. 23.93 *(978-1-909673-26-7(9))* Ruby Tuesday Books Limited GBR. Dist: Bearport Publishing Co., Inc.

Petrie, Kristin. The Digestive System, 1 vol. 2007. (Human Body Ser.). (ENG., Illus.). 32p. (gr. 4-7). 27.07 *(978-1-59679-710-9(X)*, Checkerboard Library) ABDO Publishing Co.

Prior, Jennifer. The Digestive System, 1 vol. 2nd rev. ed. 2013. (Nonfiction Readers Ser.). (ENG., Illus.). 32p. (J). (gr. 3-3). pap. 25.96 *(978-1-4807-1086-3(5))* Shell Educational Publishing.

—The Digestive System, 1 vol. 2nd rev. ed. 2012. (Nonfiction Readers Ser.). (ENG.). 32p. (J). (gr. 3-3). pap. 8.99 *(978-1-4333-3677-5(4))* Teacher Created Materials, Inc.

Prior, Jennifer. El Sistema Digestivo. 2017. (TIME for Kids en Español - Level 3 Ser.). (SPA.). 32p. (gr. 3-3). lib. bdg. 31.99 ***(978-1-5157-5184-7(8))*** Time for Kids Inc AUS. Dist: Capstone Pub.

Randolph, Joanne, ed. Taste & Digestion. 2017. (Amazing Human Body Ser.). 48p. (J). (gr. 6-6). pap. 11.70 ***(978-0-7660-8989-1(4))*** Enslow Pubs., Inc.

Rau, Dana Meachen. My Stomach. 2013. (Bookworms Fluent — My Body Ser.). 24p. (gr. 1-3). pap. 8.22 *(978-1-62712-037-1(8))* Cavendish Square Publishing.

—My Stomach. 2007. (J). pap. 6.99 *(978-0-7614-3359-0(7))* Marshall Cavendish Corp.

Simon, Seymour. Guts: Our Digestive System. 2005. (ENG., Illus.). 32p. (J). (gr. k-5). 17.99 *(978-0-06-054651-9(4))* HarperCollins Pubs.

Snedden, Robert. Understanding Food & Digestion. 2010. (Understanding the Human Body Ser.). (Illus.). 48p. (YA). (gr. 5-8). (ENG.). pap. 11.75 *(978-1-4358-9693-2(9))*; lib. bdg. 29.25 *(978-1-4358-9687-1(4))* Rosen Publishing Group, Inc., The. (Rosen Reference).

Sohn, Emily. A Journey Through the Digestive System with Max Axiom, Super Scientist, 1 vol. 2009. (Graphic Science Ser.). (ENG.). 32p. (gr. 3-4). pap. 8.10 *(978-1-4296-3452-6(9)*, Graphic Library) Capstone Press of Coughlan Cos.

Solway, Andrew. Food & Digestion. 2011. (Your Body Inside & Out Ser.). (Illus.). 32p. (J). (gr. 3-6). lib. bdg. 28.50 *(978-1-59771-264-4(7))* Sea-To-Sea Pubns.

Taylor-Butler, Christine. The Digestive System. 2008. (True Bks.). (ENG.). 48p. (J). pap. 6.95 *(978-0-531-20731-4(5))*; (Illus.). (gr. 3-7). 29.00 *(978-0-531-16857-8(3))* Scholastic Library Publishing. (Children's Pr.).

Thomas, Isabel. Why Do I Burp? Digestion & Diet, 1 vol. 2011. (Inside My Body Ser.). (ENG.). 32p. (gr. 3-5). 30.65 *(978-1-4109-4014-8(4)*, NA-r) Heinemann-Raintree.

Toriello, James. The Stomach: Learning How We Digest. 2009. (3-D Library of the Human Body Ser.). 48p. (gr. 5-8). 55.90 *(978-1-60853-326-8(3)*, Rosen Reference) Rosen Publishing Group, Inc., The.

Turnbull, Stephanie. Why Do We Eat? Haggerty, Tim, illus. 2006. (Usborne Beginners Ser.). 32p. (J). (gr. 4-7). lib. bdg. 12.99 *(978-1-58086-933-1(5)*, Usborne) EDC Publishing.

Waldron, Melanie. Your Digestive System: Understand It with Numbers, 1 vol. 2014. (Your Body by Numbers Ser.). (ENG.). 48p. (gr. 3-5). lib. bdg. 32.65 *(978-1-4109-5982-9(1))* Heinemann-Raintree.

Woolf, Alex. The Science of Poop & Farts. 2017. (Science of the Body Ser.). (ENG.). 32p. (J). pap. 9.95 ***(978-0-531-23237-8(9)***, Watts, Franklin) Scholastic Library Publishing.

—The Science of Poop & Farts: The Smelly Truth about Digestion. 2017. (Science of the Body Ser.). (ENG.). 32p. (J). lib. bdg. 29.00 ***(978-0-531-23142-5(9)***, Watts, Franklin) Scholastic Library Publishing.

Woolf, Alex. You Wouldn't Want to Live Without Poop! Antram, David, illus. 2016. (You Wouldn't Want to Live Without... Ser.). (ENG.). 32p. (J). lib. bdg. 29.00 *(978-0-531-21489-3(3))* Scholastic Library Publishing.

World Book, Inc Staff, contrib. by. The Digestive System/The Urinary System. 2006. (World Book's Human Body Works). (Illus.). 48p. (J). *(978-0-7166-4429-3(0))* World Bk., Inc.

DIGIMON (FICTITIOUS CHARACTERS)—FICTION

Hongo, Akiyoshi. Digimon, 5, 3. Sheh, Stephanie, tr. rev. ed. 2003. (Illus.). 164p. (gr. 2-18). pap. 9.99 *(978-1-59182-158-8(4))* TOKYOPOP, Inc.

—Digimon, 5 vols., Vol. 1. Yuen Wong Yu, illus. 2003. 164p. (gr. 2-18). pap. 9.99 *(978-1-59182-076-5(6))* TOKYOPOP, Inc.

—Digimon, 5 vols., Vol. 4. 4th rev. ed. 2003. (Illus.). 164p. (gr. 2-18). pap. 9.99 *(978-1-59182-159-5(2))* TOKYOPOP, Inc.

Hongo, Akiyoshi, creator. Digimon Tamers, Vol. 4. 4th rev. ed. 2004. (Juvenile Favorite Ser.). (Illus.). 200p. pap. 9.99 *(978-1-59182-824-2(4))* TOKYOPOP, Inc.

Yu, Yuen Wong. Digimon, 5 vols., Vol. 2. rev. ed. 2003. (Illus.). 164p. (gr. 2-18). pap. 9.99 *(978-1-59182-090-1(1))* TOKYOPOP, Inc.

DIMAGGIO, JOE, 1914-1999

Joltin' Joe DiMaggio. 2014. (ENG., Illus.). 48p. (J). (gr. -1-3). 17.99 *(978-1-4169-4080-7(4)*, Atheneum Bks. for Young Readers) Simon & Schuster Children's Publishing.

Rosenstock, Barb. The Streak: How Joe DiMaggio Became America's Hero. Widener, Terry, illus. 2014. (ENG.). 32p. (J). (gr. 3). 16.95 *(978-1-59078-992-6(X)*, Calkins Creek) Boyds Mills Pr.

Sakany, Lois. Joe DiMaggio. 2004. (Baseball Hall of Famers Ser.). (Illus.). 112p. (gr. 5-8). lib. bdg. 34.60 *(978-0-8239-3779-0(8)*, Rosen Reference) Rosen Publishing Group, Inc., The.

—Joe Dimaggio. 2009. (Baseball Hall of Famers Ser.). 112p. (gr. 5-8). 63.90 *(978-1-61511-510-5(2)*, Rosen Reference) Rosen Publishing Group, Inc., The.

Viola, Kevin. Joe Dimaggio. 2005. (Sports Heroes & Legends Ser.). (Illus.). 106p. (YA). (gr. 7-12). lib. bdg. 27.93 *(978-0-8225-3081-7(3))* Lerner Publishing Group.

DINOSAURS

Abbott, John A. Press-Out & Play Dino Park. 2013. (ENG.). 18p. (J). pap. 4.99 *(978-1-78235-566-3(9))* Make Believe Ideas GBR. Dist: Nelson, Thomas Inc.

Abbott, Simon, illus. Dinosaurs. 2011. (Learn to Draw Ser.). (ENG.). 24p. (J). (gr. k-2). pap. 6.95 *(978-1-84898-202-4(X)*, TickTock Books) Octopus Publishing Group GBR. Dist: Independent Pubs. Group.

ABDO Publishing Company Staff. Dinosaurs Set 4. 2007. (Dinosaurs Set 4 Ser.). 162.42 *(978-1-59928-693-8(9)*, Buddy Bks.) ABDO Publishing Co.

ABDO Publishing Company Staff & Lennie, Charles. Dinosaurs. 2014. (Dinosaurs Ser.: 6). (ENG.). 24p. (J). (gr. 4-8). lib. bdg. 171.00 *(978-1-62970-021-2(5))* ABDO Publishing Co.

Accord Publishing Staff. Dinosaurs: A Mini Animotion Book. 2011. (ENG.). 12p. (J). 9.99 *(978-1-4494-0172-6(4))* Andrews McMeel Publishing.

After the Dinosaurs: Level P, 6 vols. (Wonder Worldtm Ser.). 48p. 39.95 *(978-0-7802-7084-8(3))* Wright Group/McGraw-Hill.

The Age of Dinosaurs. 2004. (Sticker Timelines Ser.). (Illus.). 12p. (J). pap. *(978-1-84229-843-5(7))* Top That! Publishing PLC.

Albee, Sarah. The World of Dinosaurs. 2013. (Jigsaw Journey Ser.). (ENG., Illus.). 48p. (J). (gr. k). 15.95 *(978-1-60710-948-8(4)*, Silver Dolphin Bks.) Readerlink Distribution Services, LLC.

Alderson, Phil. Busy Kids Dinosaurs Magnetic Playbook. 2007. (Busy Kids Ser.). (Illus.). 10p. (J). (gr. -1-3). bds. *(978-1-84610-552-4(8))* Make Believe Ideas.

Aliki. Digging up Dinosaurs. 33p. (J). (gr. 1-3). pap. 4.95 *(978-0-8072-1339-1(X)*, Listening Library) Random Hse. Audio Publishing Group.

Allen, Judy. Flip the Flaps: Dinosaurs. Humphries, Tudor, illus. 2011. (Flip the Flaps Ser.). (ENG.). 32p. (J). (gr. -1-1). pap. 6.99 *(978-0-7534-6496-0(9)*, 9780753464960, Kingfisher) Roaring Brook Pr.

Allosaurus: The Strange Lizard. 2009. (Graphic Dinosaurs Ser.). (ENG., Illus.). 32p. (J). 50.50 *(978-1-61531-878-0(X)*, PowerKids Pr.) Rosen Publishing Group, Inc., The.

Allyn, Daisy. Triceratops. 2015. (Look at Dinosaurs Ser.). (ENG.). 24p. (J). (gr. 1-2). 22.60 *(978-1-4824-1830-9(4))* Stevens, Gareth Publishing LLLP.

—Tyrannosaurus Rex. 2015. (Look at Dinosaurs Ser.). (ENG.). 24p. (J). (gr. 1-2). 22.60 *(978-1-4824-1834-7(7))* Stevens, Gareth Publishing LLLP.

American Museum of Natural History & Lach, Will. I Am NOT a Dinosaur! Lambert, Jonny, illus. 2016. (ENG.). 40p. (J). (gr. -1-2). 14.95 *(978-1-4549-1491-4(2))* Sterling Publishing Co., Inc.

American Museum of Natural History Staff. ABC Dinosaurs. Hartman, Scott, illus. 2011. (AMNH ABC Board Bks.). (ENG.). 18p. (J). (gr. -1-k). bds. 7.95 *(978-1-4027-7715-8(9))* Sterling Publishing Co., Inc.

—1-2-3 Dinosaurs Bite: A Prehistoric Counting Book. 2012. (ENG., Illus.). 18p. (J). (gr. -1-2). bds. 6.95 *(978-1-4027-7722-6(1)*, 1350121) Sterling Publishing Co., Inc.

Amery, Heather. Dinosaurs. (Up Close Ser.). 24p. (gr. 3-3). 2009. 47.90 *(978-1-60854-695-4(0))* 2007. (Illus.). (J). lib.

bdg. 25.25 (978-1-4042-3759-9(3)) Rosen Publishing Group, Inc., The. (PowerKids Pr.).

Amiot, Romain. Dinosaurs. Méhée, Loïc, illus. 2017. (ENG.). 32p. (J). 12.99 **(978-1-4413-2474-0(7),** 993b8c32-b56d-4ab5-a26e-28e02dfd336c) Peter Pauper Pr. Inc.

Andrews McMeel Publishing Staff. Dinosaurs. 2014. (ENG., Illus.). 12p. (J). bds. 5.99 (978-1-4494-6056-3(9)) Andrews McMeel Publishing.

—Go Fun! Dinosaur Doodle Book. 2015. (Go Fun! Ser.: 5). (ENG.). 88p. (J). pap. 10.99 (978-1-4494-6806-4(3)) Andrews McMeel Publishing.

Ankylosaurus: The Armored Dinosaur. 2009. (Graphic Dinosaurs Ser.). (ENG., Illus.). 32p. (J). 50.50 (978-1-61531-880-3(1), PowerKids Pr.) Rosen Publishing Group, Inc., The.

Appleby, Alex. Dinosaurs at School. 2013. (Dinosaur School Ser.). 24p. (J). (gr. k-1). pap. 48.90 (978-1-4339-9043-4(1)); (Illus.). pap. 8.15 (978-1-4339-9042-7(3)); (ENG., Illus.). lib. bdg. 22.60 (978-1-4339-9041-0(5)) Stevens, Gareth Publishing LLLP.

—Dinosaurs at the Zoo. 2013. (Dinosaur School Ser.). 24p. (J). (gr. k-1). pap. 8.15 (978-1-4339-9046-5(6)); pap. 48.90 (978-1-4339-9047-2(4)); (ENG., Illus.). lib. bdg. 22.60 (978-1-4339-9045-8(8)) Stevens, Gareth Publishing LLLP.

—Dinosaur's Five Senses. 2013. (Dinosaur School Ser.). 24p. (J). (gr. k-1). pap. 8.15 (978-1-4339-9050-2(4)); pap. 48.90 (978-1-4339-9051-9(2)); (ENG., Illus.). lib. bdg. 22.60 (978-1-4339-9049-6(0)) Stevens, Gareth Publishing LLLP.

—Dinosaurs Help Out. 2013. (Dinosaur School Ser.). 24p. (J). (gr. k-1). pap. 48.90 (978-1-4339-9055-7(5)); pap. 8.15 (978-1-4339-9054-0(7)); (ENG., Illus.). lib. bdg. 22.60 (978-1-4339-9053-3(9)) Stevens, Gareth Publishing LLLP.

—Dinosaurs on the Farm. 2013. (Dinosaur School Ser.). 24p. (J). (gr. k-1). pap. 48.90 (978-1-4339-9059-5(8)); pap. 8.15 (978-1-4339-9058-8(X)); (ENG., Illus.). lib. bdg. 22.60 (978-1-4339-9057-1(1)) Stevens, Gareth Publishing LLLP.

—Dinosaurs on the Go. 2013. (Dinosaur School Ser.). 24p. (J). (gr. k-1). pap. 48.90 (978-1-4339-9063-2(6)); pap. 8.15 (978-1-4339-9062-5(8)); (ENG., Illus.). lib. bdg. 22.60 (978-1-4339-9061-8(X)) Stevens, Gareth Publishing LLLP.

Applesauce Press Staff. Armored Dinosaurs. 2017. (ENG.). 64p. (J). 12.95 (978-1-60433-600-9(5), Applesauce Pr.) Cider Mill Pr. Bk. Pubs., LLC.

Applesauce Press Staff & Switek, Brian. The T-Rex Handbook. Csotonyi, Julius, illus. 2016. (ENG.). 64p. (J). 12.95 (978-1-60433-603-0(X), Applesauce Pr.) Cider Mill Pr. Bk. Pubs., LLC.

Arcturus Publishing Staff. The Dangerous Book of Dinosaurs. 2015. (ENG., Illus.). 128p. pap. 9.95 (978-1-78404-196-0(3), 9781784041960) Arcturus Publishing GBR. Dist: Bookmasters Distribution.

Arcturus Publishing Staff. Lots to Spot: Dinosaurs. 2017. (ENG., Illus.). 48p. (J). (gr. k-5). 9.99 **(978-1-78428-475-6(0),** 9781784284756) Arcturus Publishing GBR. Dist: Bookmasters Distribution.

Arlon, Penelope. Dinosaurs. 2012. (Scholastic Discover More Ser.). (ENG.). 80p. (J). (gr. -1-3). 12.99 (978-0-545-36572-7(4), Scholastic Reference) Scholastic, Inc.

Arlon, Penelope & Gordon-Harris, Tory. Dinosaurs. 2012. (J). lib. bdg. (978-0-531-22955-2(6)) Scholastic, Inc.

Arnold, Tedd. Dinosaurs. Arnold, Tedd, illus. 2014. (Fly Guy Presents Ser.). (ENG., Illus.). 32p. (J). (gr. k-2). pap. 3.99 (978-0-545-63159-4(9), Scholastic Reference) Scholastic, Inc.

—Dinosaurs. 2014. (Fly Guy Presents Ser.). lib. bdg. 13.55 (978-0-606-35194-2(9)) Turtleback Bks.

—Hombre Mosca Presenta/ Fly Man Presents: Dinosaurios/ Dinosaurs. 2016. (Fly Guy Presents Ser.). (ENG & SPA.). 32p. (J). (gr. k-2). 13.55 (978-0-606-39158-0(4)) Turtleback Bks.

Ashby, Ruth. My Favorite Dinosaurs. Sibbick, John, illus. 2005. 32p. (J). (gr. 1-3). 16.95 (978-0-689-03921-8(2)) ibooks, Inc.

Ashby, Ruth. My Favorite Dinosaurs. 2016. (ENG., Illus.). (J). (gr. k-3). 27.95 **(978-1-59687-517-3(8),** ipicturebooks) ibooks, Inc.

Austin, D. & Borgstedt, John. Dinosaurs A 2 Z: The Age of the Dinosaurs. 2011. 104p. (gr. -1). pap. 20.00 (978-1-4567-5949-0(3)) AuthorHouse.

AZ Books Staff. Living Book of Dinosaurs. Latushko, Julia, ed. 2012. (Our Amazing World Ser.). (ENG.). 12p. (J). (gr. 1-3). bds. 19.95 (978-1-61889-025-2(5)) AZ Bks. LLC.

—Meeting Dinosaurs. Vasilkova, Elena, ed. 2012. (Wild Theater Ser.). (ENG.). 8p. (J). (gr. -1-3). bds. 17.95 (978-1-61889-019-1(0)) AZ Bks. LLC.

—Sounds of Dinosaurs. Yaroshevich, Angelica, ed. 2012. (Sounds Around Us Ser.). (ENG.). 16p. (J). (gr. 1-3). bds. 17.95 (978-1-61889-027-6(1)) AZ Bks. LLC.

—Visiting Dinosaurs. Vol, Vera, ed. 2012. (Lively Pictures Ser.). (ENG.). 10p. (J). (gr. -1-k). bds. 9.95 (978-1-61889-181-5(2)) AZ Bks. LLC.

Baby's Very First Slide & See Dinosaurs. 2017. (Baby's Very First Slide & See BDs Ser.). (ENG.). (J). bds. 14.99 **(978-0-7945-3924-5(6),** Usborne) EDC Publishing.

Bacchin, Matteo, illus. A Jurassic Mystery: Archaeopteryx. 2008. (Dinosaurs: Ser.). (ENG.). 64p. (J). (gr. 3-7). 15.95 (978-0-7892-0979-5(9), Abbeville Kids) Abbeville Pr., Inc.

Bacchin, Matteo & Signore, Marco. The Journey: Plateosaurus. Shore, Marguerite, tr. from ITA. 2008. (Dinosaurs: Ser.). (ENG., Illus.). 61p. (J). (gr. 4-12). 18.95 (978-0-7892-1015-9(0), Abbeville Kids) Abbeville Pr., Inc.

—A Jurassic Mystery: Archaeopteryx. Shore, Marguerite, tr. from ITA. 2008. (Dinosaurs: Ser.). (ENG., Illus.). 61p. (J). (gr. 4-6). 18.95 (978-0-7892-1016-6(9), Abbeville Kids) Abbeville Pr., Inc.

Bailer, Darice. Dinomite! All about Dinisaurs. 2006. (Illus.). 32p. (J). (978-0-439-83862-7(2)) Scholastic, Inc.

Bailey, Gerry. Ankylosaurus. Chesterman, Adrian, illus. 2011. (Smithsonian Prehistoric Zone Ser.). (ENG.). 32p. (J). (gr. k-3). (978-0-7787-1797-3(6)); pap. (978-0-7787-1810-9(7)) Crabtree Publishing Co.

—Parasaurolophus. McIntosh, Gabe, illus. 2011. (Smithsonian Prehistoric Zone Ser.). (ENG.). 32p. (J). (gr. k-3). (978-0-7787-1799-7(2)); pap. (978-0-7787-1812-3(3)) Crabtree Publishing Co.

—Pterandon. Carr, Karen, illus. 2011. (Smithsonian Prehistoric Zone Ser.). (ENG.). 32p. (J). (gr. k-3). (978-0-7787-1800-0(X)); pap. (978-0-7787-1813-0(1)) Crabtree Publishing Co.

—Spinosaurus. Scalf, Chris & McIntosh, Gabe, illus. 2011. (Smithsonian Prehistoric Zone Ser.). (ENG.). 32p. (J). (gr. k-3). (978-0-7787-1802-4(6)); pap. (978-0-7787-1815-4(8)) Crabtree Publishing Co.

—Stegosaurus. Carr, Karen, illus. 2011. (Smithsonian Prehistoric Zone Ser.). (ENG.). 32p. (J). (gr. k-3). (978-0-7787-1803-1(4)) Crabtree Publishing Co.

—Triceratops. Carr, Karen, illus. 2011. (Smithsonian Prehistoric Zone Ser.). (ENG.). 32p. (J). (gr. k-3). lib. bdg. (978-0-7787-1804-8(2)); pap. (978-0-7787-1817-8(4)) Crabtree Publishing Co.

—Tyrannosaurus Rex. Carr, Karen, illus. 2011. (Smithsonian Prehistoric Zone Ser.). (ENG.). 32p. (J). (gr. k-3). (978-0-7787-1806-2(9)); pap. (978-0-7787-1819-2(0)) Crabtree Publishing Co.

—Velociraptor. Carr, Karen, illus. 2011. (Smithsonian Prehistoric Zone Ser.). (ENG.). 32p. (J). (gr. k-3). (978-0-7787-1807-9(7)); pap. (978-0-7787-1820-8(4)) Crabtree Publishing Co.

Bailey, Gerry & Reaveley, Trevor. Apatosaurus. 2011. (Smithsonian Prehistoric Zone Ser.). (ENG., Illus.). 32p. (J). (gr. k-3). (978-0-7787-1798-0(4)); pap. (978-0-7787-1811-6(5)) Crabtree Publishing Co.

Bailey, Jacqui. Monster Bones: The Story of a Dinosaur Fossil, 1 vol. Lilly, Matthew, illus. 2004. (Science Works). (ENG.). 32p. (gr. 3-6). 27.99 (978-1-4048-0565-1(6)) Picture Window Bks.

Baker, Robert. Complete Guides Dinosaurs. 2012. (ENG., Illus.). 144p. (978-1-4351-4405-7(8)) Barnes & Noble, Inc.

Bakker, Robert T. Dinosaurs! Rey, Luis V., illus. 2005. (Pictureback(R) Ser.). (ENG.). 24p. (J). (gr. -1-2). pap. 3.99 (978-0-375-83141-6(X), Random Hse. Bks. for Young Readers) Random Hse. Children's Bks.

—Raptor Pack. Skrepnick, Michael, illus. 2003. (Step into Reading Ser.). (ENG.). 48p. (J). (gr. 2-4). pap. 3.99 (978-0-375-82303-9(4), Random Hse. Bks. for Young Readers) Random Hse. Children's Bks.

Ball, Jacqueline A. Extreme Animals: Dinosaurs. 2015. (Extreme Animals Ser.). (ENG., Illus.). 48p. (J). (gr. 3). 17.95 (978-1-62686-383-5(0), Silver Dolphin Bks.) Readerlink Distribution Services, LLC.

Ball, Sara. Flip-O-Storic. Ball, Sara, illus. 2011. (ENG., Illus.). 11p. (J). (gr. -1-k). bds. 15.95 (978-0-7892-1099-9(1), Abbeville Kids) Abbeville Pr., Inc.

Balloon Dinosaurs. 2004. (Formula Fun Ser.). (Illus.). 48p. (J). pap. (978-1-84229-876-3(3)) Top That! Publishing PLC.

Barner, Bob. Dinosaur Bones. Barner, Bob, illus. unabr. ed. 2006. (Illus.). (J). (gr. -1-2). 29.95 (978-0-439-90580-0(X)) Weston Woods Studios, Inc.

—Dinosaurs! Matching Game. 2009. (ENG.). 72p. (J). (gr. -1-17). bds. 14.99 (978-0-8118-6980-5(6)) Chronicle Bks. LLC.

Barney's Super Dee Dooper Treasury. 2005. (Illus.). (J). (978-0-681-27945-2(1)) Scholastic, Inc.

Barrett, Paul M. Stegosaurus. 2017. (ENG.). 48p. 12.95 **(978-0-565-09388-4(6))** Natural History Museum Pubns. GBR. Dist: Independent Pubs. Group.

Basher, Simon & Green, Dan. Dinosaurs: The Bare Bones! Basher, Simon, illus. 2012. (Basher Basics Ser.). (ENG., Illus.). 64p. (J). (gr. 3-7). 12.99 (978-0-7534-6823-4(9), 9780753468234); pap. 7.99 (978-0-7534-6824-1(7), 9780753468241) Roaring Brook Pr. (Kingfisher).

Beaumont, Steve. Drawing Diplodocus & Other Plant-Eating Dinosaurs. 2010. (Drawing Dinosaurs Ser.). (Illus.). 32p. (J). pap. 11.75 (978-1-4488-0424-5(8)); (gr. 2-5). lib. bdg. 26.50 (978-1-61531-902-2(6)) Rosen Publishing Group, Inc., The.

—Drawing Giganotosaurus & Other Giant Dinosaurs. 2010. (Drawing Dinosaurs Ser.). (Illus.). 32p. (J). pap. 11.75 (978-1-4488-0430-6(2)); (gr. 2-5). lib. bdg. 26.50 (978-1-61531-905-3(0)) Rosen Publishing Group, Inc., The.

—Drawing Plesiosaurus & Other Ocean Dinosaurs. 2010. (Drawing Dinosaurs Ser.). (Illus.). 32p. (J). pap. 11.75 (978-1-4488-0426-9(4)); (gr. 2-5). lib. bdg. 26.50 (978-1-61531-903-9(4)) Rosen Publishing Group, Inc., The.

—Drawing Pteranodon & Other Flying Reptiles. 2010. (Drawing Dinosaurs Ser.). (Illus.). 32p. (J). pap. 11.75 (978-1-4488-0428-3(0)); (gr. 2-5). lib. bdg. 26.50 (978-1-61531-904-6(2)) Rosen Publishing Group, Inc., The.

—Drawing T. Rex & Other Meat-Eating Dinosaurs. 2010. (Drawing Dinosaurs Ser.). (Illus.). 32p. (J). pap. 11.75 (978-1-4488-0434-4(5)); (gr. 2-5). lib. bdg. 26.50 (978-1-61531-907-7(7)) Rosen Publishing Group, Inc., The.

—Drawing Triceratops & Other Armored Dinosaurs. 2010. (Drawing Dinosaurs Ser.). (Illus.). 32p. (J). pap. 11.75 (978-1-4488-0432-0(9)); (gr. 2-5). lib. bdg. 26.50 (978-1-61531-906-0(9)) Rosen Publishing Group, Inc., The.

Becker, Ann. Dinosaurs. 2009. (Illus.). 24p. (J). pap. 7.95 (978-1-60694-834-7(2)) Rourke Educational Media.

Benchmark Education Company. Dinosaurs (Teacher Guide) 2005. (978-1-4108-4662-4(8)) Benchmark Education Co.

Bennett, Leonie. Amazing Dinosaur Facts. 2007. (I Love Reading Ser.). (Illus.). 24p. (J). (gr. -1-2). lib. bdg. 19.96 (978-1-59716-546-4(8)) Bearport Publishing Co., Inc.

—Dinosaur Babies. 2007. (I Love Reading Ser.). (Illus.). 24p. (J). (gr. -1-2). lib. bdg. 19.96 (978-1-59716-544-0(1)) Bearport Publishing Co., Inc.

—Dinosaur Fossils. 2007. (I Love Reading Ser.). (Illus.). 24p. (J). (gr. -1-2). lib. bdg. 19.96 (978-1-59716-555-6(7)) Bearport Publishing Co., Inc.

—Dinosaur Hunting. 2007. (I Love Reading Ser.). (Illus.). 24p. (J). (gr. -1-2). lib. bdg. 19.96 (978-1-59716-554-9(9)) Bearport Publishing Co., Inc.

Bentley, Dawn & Studio Mouse Staff. Dinosaurs & More! Carr, Karent, illus. rev. ed. 2006. (ENG.). 60p. (J). 12.95 (978-1-59069-487-9(2)) Soundprints.

Benton, M. J. The Great Book of Dinosaurs. 2004. (Illus.). 128p. (YA). (978-1-904516-08-8(4), Pavilion Children's Books) Pavilion Bks.

Benton, Michael. The Awesome Book of Duckbills & Boneheads. Paiva, Johannah Gilman, ed. Field, James, illus. 2014. (ENG.). 32p. (J). (gr. 3-7). 7.99 (978-1-4867-0343-2(7)) Flowerpot Children's Pr. Inc. CAN. Dist: Cardinal Pubs. Group.

—The Awesome Book of Flesh-Eaters. Paiva, Johannah Gilman, ed. Field, James, illus. 2014. (ENG.). 32p. (gr. 3-7). 7.99 (978-1-4867-0341-8(0)) Flowerpot Children's Pr. Inc. CAN. Dist: Cardinal Pubs. Group.

—Flying Monsters. (Illus.). 32p. (YA). (gr. 3-18). lib. bdg. 27.10 (978-1-932333-61-9(4)) Chrysalis Education.

—The Kingfisher Dinosaur Encyclopedia: One Encylopedia, a World of Prehistoric Knowledge. 2017. (Kingfisher Encyclopedias Ser.). (ENG.). 160p. (J). pap. 13.99 (978-0-7534-7354-2(2), 9780753473542, Kingfisher) Roaring Brook Pr.

—Mighty Giants. (Illus.). 32p. (YA). (gr. 3-18). lib. bdg. 27.10 (978-1-932333-58-9(4)) Chrysalis Education.

Bergin, Mark. Dinosaurs. 2011. (It's Fun to Draw Ser.). (ENG., Illus.). 32p. (J). (gr. k-3). lib. bdg. 26.50 (978-1-61533-349-3(5)) Windmill Bks.

Berkowitz, Jacob. Jurassic Poop: What Dinosaurs (and Others) Left Behind. Mack, Steve, illus. 2006. (ENG.). 40p. (J). (gr. 3-7). 6.95 (978-1-55337-867-9(9)); 14.95 (978-1-55337-860-0(1)) Kids Can Pr., Ltd. CAN. Dist: Hachette Bk. Group.

Bertch, David P. & Bertch, Barbara A. The Dynamic Dinosaur of Faith's History Vol. I: From Christ to 1000 AD. Martin, Terry & Martin, Dyna, eds. Hopper, Billy, illus. (Roots of the Past Ser.: Bk. 1). 150p. (J). (gr. 6). stu. ed. 9.95 (978-0-9634472-4-1(6)) Good Works Pr.

Bicknell, Joanna & Pountney, Beth. Bedtime Buddy: Roarasaurus Loves Buddies. 2005. (Illus.). 8p. (J). (gr. -1-k). (978-1-84610-017-8(8)) Make Believe Ideas.

—Bedtime Buddy: Snugglesaurus Loves Cuddles. 2005. (Illus.). 8p. (J). (gr. -1-k). (978-1-84610-018-5(6)) Make Believe Ideas.

Birch, Robin. Bird-footed Dinosaurs. 2nd rev. ed. 2008. (Dinosaur World Ser.). 32p. (J). (gr. 2-4). 23.00 (978-1-60413-405-6(4)) Facts On File, Inc.

—Bony-skinned Dinosaurs. 2nd rev. ed. 2008. (Dinosaur World Ser.). 32p. (J). (gr. 2-4). 23.00 (978-1-60413-404-9(6)) Facts On File, Inc.

—Hard-headed Dinosaurs. 2nd rev. ed. 2008. (Dinosaur World Ser.). 32p. (J). (gr. 2-4). 23.00 (978-1-60413-403-2(8)) Facts On File, Inc.

—Long-necked Dinosaurs. 2nd rev. ed. 2008. (Dinosaur World Ser.). 32p. (J). (gr. 2-4). 23.00 (978-1-60413-406-3(2)) Facts On File, Inc.

—Meat-eating Dinosaurs. 2nd rev. ed. 2008. (Dinosaur World Ser.). 32p. (J). (gr. 2-4). 23.00 (978-1-60413-407-0(0)) Facts On File, Inc.

—Relatives of Dinosaurs. 2nd rev. ed. 2008. (Dinosaur World Ser.). 32p. (J). (gr. 2-4). 23.00 (978-1-60413-408-7(9)) Facts On File, Inc.

Blackwell, Archie. Secrets of the Dinosaur World: Jurassic Giants & Other Prehistoric Creatures. 2014. (ENG., Illus.). 80p. (J). (gr. 3). pap. 16.95 (978-1-78097-285-5(7)) Carlton Bks., Ltd. GBR. Dist: Sterling Publishing Co., Inc.

Bloomsbury. World of Dinosaurs. 2016. (ENG., Illus.). 12p. (J). bds. 8.99 (978-1-61963-827-3(4), 9781619638273, Bloomsbury Activity Bks.) Bloomsbury Publishing USA.

Boatner, Kay. National Geographic Kids Funny Fill-In: My Medieval Adventure. 2014. (ENG.). 48p. (J). (gr. 3-7). pap. 4.99 (978-1-4263-1684-5(4), National Geographic Children's Bks.) National Geographic Society.

Bohn, Kendall, creator. Prehistoric Adventure: A Kaleidoscopia Coloring Book. 2005. (Illus.). 56p. pap. 8.95 (978-0-929636-37-5(6)) Syren Bk. Co.

Bolte, Mari. Triceratops: Three-Horned Giant. Dove, Jason, illus. 2012. (First Graphics: Dinosaurs Ser.). (ENG.). 24p. (gr. 1-2). pap. 35.70 (978-1-4296-8365-4(1)); lib. bdg. 23.99 (978-1-4296-7601-4(9)) Capstone Press of Coughlan Cos.

Bonner, Hannah. Dining with Dinosaurs: A Tasty Guide to Mesozoic Munching. 2016. (ENG., Illus.). 48p. (J). (gr. 2-5). 18.99 (978-1-4263-2339-3(5), National Geographic Children's Bks.) National Geographic Society.

Boughton, Samantha. Dino Island Adventure Coloring Book. 2014. (ENG., Illus.). 48p. (J). (gr. k). pap. 4.99 (978-0-486-49155-4(2)) Dover Pubns., Inc.

Bowman, Donna H. Did Dinosaurs Eat People? And Other Questions Kids Have about Dinosaurs, 1 vol. Dumortier, Marjorie, illus. 2009. (Kids' Questions Ser.). (ENG.). 24p. (gr. 1-2). lib. bdg. 26.65 (978-1-4048-5527-4(0)) Picture Window Bks.

Brachiosaurus: The Long-Limbed Dinosaur. 2009. (Graphic Dinosaurs Ser.). (ENG., Illus.). 32p. (J). 50.50 (978-1-61531-879-7(8), PowerKids Pr.) Rosen Publishing Group, Inc., The.

Brannon, Barbara. Discover Dinosaurs. 2005. (J). pap. (978-1-4108-5120-8(6)) Benchmark Education Co.

Brecke, Nicole & Stockland, Patricia M. Dinosaurs & Other Prehistoric Creatures You Can Draw. Brecke, Nicole, illus. 2010. (Ready, Set, Draw! Ser.). (ENG., Illus.). 32p. (gr. 2-4). lib. bdg. 25.26 (978-0-7613-4169-7(2), Millbrook Pr.) Lerner Publishing Group.

Brett, Anna. Mr Bean's Disastrous DIY Doodle Book. 2015. (ENG.). 80p. (J). (gr. 2-6). pap. 9.99 (978-1-78312-138-0(6)) Carlton Bks., Ltd. GBR. Dist: Independent Pubs. Group.

Brett-Surman, Michael K. & Holtz, Thomas R. Jurassic World Dinosaur Field Guide (Jurassic World) Walters, Robert, illus. 2015. (ENG.). 160p. (J). (gr. 3-7). pap. 12.99 (978-0-553-53685-0(0), Random Hse. Bks. for Young Readers) Random Hse. Children's Bks.

Bright, Michael. Make & Move: T Rex. 2016. (Make & Move Ser.). (ENG., Illus.). 28p. (J). (gr. k). 19.95 (978-1-62686-491-7(8), Silver Dolphin Bks.) Readerlink Distribution Services, LLC.

Brimax Publishing, creator. My Little Book of Dinosaurs. 2008. (My Little Book of... (Brimax Publishing) Ser.). (Illus.). 24p. (J). (gr. -1-k). bds. (978-1-84656-019-4(5)) Brimax Books Ltd.

Brochu, Christopher & McHenry, Colin. Dinosaurs. 2007. (Illus.). 256p. 14.98 (978-1-74089-577-4(0)) Fog City Pr.

Brochu, Christopher A., et al. Dinosaurs. Brett-Surman, Michael K., ed. 2003. (Guides). (Illus.). 256-288p. pap. (978-1-877019-12-8(7)) Fog City Pr.

Brookes, Olicia. Predators. 2012. (Dinosaur Files Ser.). (ENG.). 32p. (J). (gr. 1-5). pap. 10.00 (978-1-61533-520-6(X)); lib. bdg. 25.25 (978-1-61533-516-9(1)) Windmill Bks.

Brookes, Olivia. The Age of Giants. 2012. (Dinosaur Files Ser.). (ENG., Illus.). 32p. (J). (gr. 1-5). pap. 10.00 (978-1-61533-524-4(2)); lib. bdg. 25.25 (978-1-61533-518-3(8)) Windmill Bks.

—A Dinosaur. 2009. (Ask Ser.). (Illus.). 32p. (J). lib. bdg. 26.50 (978-1-4358-2513-0(6), PowerKids Pr.) Rosen Publishing Group, Inc., The.

—Plant-Eaters. 2012. (Dinosaur Files Ser.). (ENG., Illus.). 32p. (J). (gr. 1-5). pap. 10.00 (978-1-61533-522-0(6)); lib. bdg. 25.25 (978-1-61533-517-6(X)) Windmill Bks.

—The Rise of the Reptiles. 2012. (Dinosaur Files Ser.). (ENG.). 32p. (J). (gr. 1-5). pap. 10.00 (978-1-61533-526-8(9)); lib. bdg. 25.25 (978-1-61533-519-0(6)) Windmill Bks.

Brooklyn, Isabella. If You Were Raised by a Dinosaur. Levesque, Haude, illus. 2013. (ENG.). 80p. (J). (gr. 2-5). pap. 9.95 (978-1-62354-015-9(1)) Charlesbridge Publishing, Inc.

Brooks, Felicity. Dinosarios. Litchfield, Jo, illus. 2004. (Titles in Spanish Ser.). (SPA.). 10p. (J). 4.95 (978-0-7460-6111-4(0), Usborne) EDC Publishing.

Brooks, Susie. A Day in the Life of T. Rex. Woodward, Jonathan, illus. 2016. (Reading Ladder Ser.). (ENG.). 32p. (J). (gr. 1-3). pap. 7.99 (978-1-4052-8040-2(9)) Egmont Bks., Ltd. GBR. Dist: Independent Pubs. Group.

Brooks, Susie. A Day in the Life of Triceratops. Woodward, Jonathan, illus. 2016. (Reading Ladder Ser.). (ENG.). 32p. (J). (gr. 1-4). pap. 6.99 **(978-1-4052-8042-6(5))** Egmont Bks., Ltd. GBR. Dist: Independent Pubs. Group.

Brown, Charlotte Lewis & Brown, Charlotte L. The Day the Dinosaurs Died. Wilson, Phil, illus. 2007. (I Can Read Level 2 Ser.). (ENG.). 48p. (J). (gr. -1-3). pap. 3.99 (978-0-06-000530-6(0)) HarperCollins Pubs.

Brusatte, Steve. Day of the Dinosaurs. Chester, Daniel, illus. 2016. (ENG.). 80p. (J). 22.99 (978-1-84780-821-9(2), Wide Eyed Editions) Quarto Publishing Group UK GBR. Dist: Littlehampton Bk Services, Ltd.

—Walking with Dinosaurs Encyclopedia. 2013. (Walking with Dinosaurs Ser.). (ENG.). 96p. (J). (gr. 3-7). 12.99 (978-0-06-223278-6(9), HarperFestival) HarperCollins Pubs.

Brusha, Joe. Dinosaurs & Prehistoric Predators. Dehart, Andy, ed. 2011. (ENG., Illus.). 120p. (gr. 4-9). pap. 9.99 (978-0-9827507-4-2(9), 9780982750742) Zenescope Entertainment.

Bryant-Mole, Karen. Dot-to-Dot Dinosaurs. 2005. 24p. (J). pap. 3.99 (978-0-7945-0491-5(4), Usborne) EDC Publishing.

Bugler, Matt. My First Encylopedia of Dinosaurs: A First Encyclopedia with Supersize Pictures. 2016. (ENG.). 24p. pap. 7.99 (978-1-86147-820-7(8), Armadillo) Anness Publishing GBR. Dist: National Bk. Network.

Bulletpoints Dinosaurs up Close. 2005. (Illus.). (J). per. 4.99 (978-1-933581-02-6(6)) Byeway Bks.

Burgin, Norma. Children's Dinosaur Encyclopedia. 2010. (Illus.). 224p. (978-1-4351-3680-9(2)) Barnes & Noble, Inc.

Butz, Steve. The Bone Race: A Quest for Dinosaur Fossils. 2007. (ENG.). 248p. (YA). (gr. 7). pap. (978-1-933255-30-9(7)) DNA Pr.

Cain, Marie Mowery. After the Dinosaurs. 2013. (Big Books, Blue Ser.). (ENG & SPA., Illus.). 16p. pap. 33.00 (978-1-59246-011-3(9)) Big Books, by George!

Campbell, Rod. Dinosaurs. Campbell, Rod, illus. 2015. (Dear Zoo & Friends Ser.). (ENG., Illus.). 14p. (J). (gr. -1 — 1). bds. 6.99 (978-1-4814-4985-4(0), Little Simon) Little Simon.

Candlewick Press Staff. Dinosaurs: a 3D Pocket Guide. KJA Artists Staff, illus. 2013. (Panorama Pops Ser.). (ENG.). 30p. (J). (gr. -1-2). 8.99 (978-0-7636-6235-6(6)) Candlewick Pr.

Capstone Press. Dinosaur Wars, 1 vol. 2010. (Dinosaur Wars Ser.). (ENG.). 32p. lib. bdg. 159.90 (978-1-4296-5930-7(0), Edge Bks.) Capstone Press of Coughlan Cos.

Carlton Books. Dinosaur Hunter's Handbook. 2016. (ENG., Illus.). 144p. (J). (gr. 2). pap. 16.95 (978-1-78312-113-7(0)) Carlton Kids GBR. Dist: Sterling Publishing Co., Inc.

Carlton Books & Rowlands, Caroline. Jurassic World: Where Dinosaurs Come to Life. 2015. (iExplore Ser.). (ENG., Illus.). 32p. (J). (gr. 3). 12.95 (978-1-78312-156-4(4)) Carlton Kids GBR. Dist: Sterling Publishing Co., Inc.

The Carnivorous Dinosaurs. 2005. (Life of the Past Ser.). (ENG., Illus.). 392p. 49.95 (978-0-253-34539-4(1), 0253345391) Indiana Univ. Pr.

Carpenter, Elizabeth. DinoMazes: The Colossal Fossil Book - 31 Poster-Size Prehistoric Fossil Nazes. 2011. (ENG., Illus.). 41p. (J). (gr. 3-12). pap. 11.95 (978-0-7611-6575-0(4), 16575) Workman Publishing Co., Inc.

Carr, Aaron. Ankylosaurus. 2016. (J). **(978-1-5105-1909-1(2))** SmartBook Media, Inc.

—Apatosaurus. 2016. (J). **(978-1-5105-1911-4(4))** SmartBook Media, Inc.

—Deinonychus. 2016. (J). **(978-1-5105-1913-8(0))** SmartBook Media, Inc.

—Pteranodon. 2016. (J). **(978-1-5105-1915-2(7))** SmartBook Media, Inc.

—Pterodactyl. 2016. (J). **(978-1-5105-1917-6(3))** SmartBook Media, Inc.

—Spinosaurus. 2016. (J). **(978-1-5105-1919-0(X))** SmartBook Media, Inc.

—Stegosaurus. 2016. (J). **(978-1-5105-1921-3(1))** SmartBook Media, Inc.

—Tiranosaurio Rex. 2014. (Descubriendo Dinosaurios Ser.). (SPA., Illus.). 24p. (J). (gr. -1-3). lib. bdg. 27.13 (978-1-4896-2069-9(9), AV2 by Weigl) Weigl Pubs., Inc.

—Triceratops. 2016. (J). **(978-1-5105-1923-7(8))** SmartBook Media, Inc.

—Tyrannosaurus Rex. 2016. (J). **(978-1-5105-1925-1(4))** SmartBook Media, Inc.

—Velociraptor. 2016. (J). **(978-1-5105-1927-5(0))** SmartBook Media, Inc.

Chaikin, Andrew. When Dinosaurs Walked. Wynne, Patricia, illus. 2004. (Treasure Tree Ser.). 32p. (J). (978-0-7166-1607-8(6)) World Bk., Inc.

Channing, Margot. Dinosaurs & Other Prehistoric Creatures. 2015. (Inside Eye Ser.). 32p. (gr. 3-6). 31.35 (978-1-906370-76-3(1)) Book Hse. GBR. Dist: Black Rabbit Bks.

Chevat, Richie. Magnetic Learning: Dinosaurs. 2015. (Magnetic Learning Ser.). (ENG., Illus.). 56p. (J). (gr. -1). 19.95 (978-1-62686-332-3(6), Silver Dolphin Bks.) Readerlink Distribution Services, LLC.

Chimal, Carlos. Mas Alla de los Dinosaurios. 2008. (SPA., Illus.). 40p. (J). (gr. 4-8). pap. 13.95 (978-970-29-0983-5(X))

Altea, Ediciones, S.A. - Grupo Santillana ESP. Dist: Two Rivers Distribution.

Chin, Karen & Holmes, Thom. Dino Dung: The Scoop on Fossil Feces. Carr, Karen, illus. 2005. (Step into Reading Ser.). 48p. (J). (gr. 2-5). 11.65 (978-0-7569-5163-4(1)) Perfection Learning Corp.

Chorkung, illus. Dinosaurs. 2017. (First Explorers Ser.). (ENG.). 10p. (J). (— 1). bds. 8.95 **(978-1-4549-2655-9(4))** Sterling Publishing Co., Inc.

Christiansen, Per. Prehistoric Beasts. 2008. (Nature's Monsters Ser.). (Illus.). 32p. (YA). (gr. 3-6). lib. bdg. 26.00 (978-0-8368-9217-8(8)) Stevens, Gareth Publishing LLLP.

Ciencin, Scott. Dino Defenses. 2006. (Illus.). 32p. (J). pap. (978-0-439-83871-9(1)) Scholastic, Inc.

Ciencin, Scott & Carrano, Matthew T. Growing up Dino. 2006. (Illus.). 32p. (J). pap. (978-0-439-83874-0(6)) Scholastic, Inc.

Clay, Kathryn. Stegosaurus: Armored Defender, 1 vol. Dove, Jason, illus. 2012. (First Graphics: Dinosaurs Ser.). (ENG.). 24p. (gr. 1-2). lib. bdg. 23.99 (978-1-4296-7604-5(3)) Capstone Press of Coughlan Cos.

—Stegosaurus: Armored Defender. Dove, Jason, illus. 2012. (First Graphics: Dinosaurs Ser.). (ENG.). 24p. (gr. 1-2). pap. 35.70 (978-1-4296-8364-7(3)) Capstone Press of Coughlan Cos.

Clay, Kathryn & Vonne, Mira. Ankylosaurus & Other Armored Dinosaurs: The Need-To-Know Facts. Hughes, Jon, illus. 2016. (Dinosaur Fact Dig Ser.). (ENG.). 32p. (gr. 1-2). lib. bdg. 27.32 (978-1-4914-9646-6(0), Aplus Bks.) Capstone Press of Coughlan Cos.

—Stegosaurus & Other Plated Dinosaurs: The Need-To-Know Facts. Hughes, Jon, illus. 2016. (Dinosaur Fact Dig Ser.). (ENG.). 32p. (gr. 1-2). lib. bdg. 27.32 (978-1-4914-9648-0(7), Aplus Bks.) Capstone Press of Coughlan Cos.

—Triceratops & Other Horned Dinosaurs: The Need-To-Know Facts. Hughes, Jon, illus. 2016. (Dinosaur Fact Dig Ser.). (ENG.). 32p. (gr. 1-2). lib. bdg. 27.32 (978-1-4914-9649-7(5), Aplus Bks.) Capstone Press of Coughlan Cos.

Clay, Kathryn, et al. First Graphics: Dinosaurs. Dove, Jason, illus. 2012. (First Graphics: Dinosaurs Ser.). (ENG.). 24p. (gr. 1-2). pap. 142.80 (978-1-4296-8369-2(4)); lib. bdg. 71.97 (978-1-4296-8143-8(8)) Capstone Press of Coughlan Cos.

Claybourne, Anna. Dinosaurs. Burnie, David, illus. 2016. (Scanorama Ser.). (ENG.). 32p. (J). (gr. 1). 18.99 (978-1-62686-630-0(9), Silver Dolphin Bks.) Readerlink Distribution Services, LLC.

Clemson, Wendy & Clemson, David. Digging for Dinosaurs. 2007. (Math Adventures Ser.). (Illus.). 32p. (gr. 1-4). pap. 10.50 (978-0-8368-8137-0(0)); lib. bdg. 26.00 (978-0-8368-7838-7(8)) Stevens, Gareth Publishing LLLP. (Gareth Stevens Learning Library).

Clissold, Caroline. Dinosaur. 2007. (Trackers-Math Ser.). (gr. 2-5). pap. 5.00 (978-1-59055-914-7(2)) Pacific Learning, Inc.

Close, Edward. Dinosaur Hunters. 2013. (Discovery Education: Discoveries & Inventions Ser.). 32p. (J). (gr. 3-6). pap. 60.00 (978-1-4777-1499-7(5), PowerKids Pr.) Rosen Publishing Group, Inc., The.

Cole, Joanna. Dinosaurs. 2014. (Magic School Bus Presents Ser.). lib. bdg. 17.20 (978-0-606-36329-7(7)) Turtleback Bks.

Cole, Joanna & Jackson, Tom. Magic School Bus Presents: Dinosaurs: A Nonfiction Companion to the Original Magic School Bus Series. Degen, Bruce & Bracken, Carolyn, illus. 2014. (Magic School Bus Presents Ser.). (ENG.). 32p. (J). (gr. 1-3). pap. 6.99 (978-0-545-68583-2(4), Scholastic Paperbacks) Scholastic, Inc.

Collins. Collins Fascinating Facts - Dinosaurs. rev. ed. 2016. (Collins Fascinating Facts Ser.). (ENG., Illus.). 72p. (J). (gr. 1-3). pap. 10.99 (978-0-00-816928-2(4)) HarperCollins Pubs. Ltd. GBR. Dist: Independent Pubs. Group.

Color All About: A Giant Coloring Book about Dinosaurs: Dinosaurs. 2004. (SPA & ENG., Illus.). 36p. (J). (978-1-59949-001-4(3)) Food Marketing Consultants, Inc.

Colson, Rob. Dinosaur Bones: And What They Tell Us. 2016. (ENG., Illus.). 96p. (J). (gr. 5-12). 19.95 (978-1-77085-717-9(6), 9781770857179); pap. 12.95 (978-1-77085-694-3(3), 9781770856943) Firefly Bks., Ltd.

Conklin, Tom. Soar! All about Pterosaurs. 2006. (Illus.). 32p. (J). pap. (978-0-439-83872-6(X)) Scholastic, Inc.

Conley, Erin, ed. Dinomite. 2006. (Spinner Bks.). (ENG., Illus.). 160p. (J). (gr. -1-3). pap. 7.95 (978-1-57528-948-9(2)) Univ. Games.

Cooley Peterson, Megan. Tyrannosaurus Rex & Its Relatives: The Need-To-Know Facts. Hughes, Jon, illus. 2016. (Dinosaur Fact Dig Ser.). (ENG.). 32p. (gr. 1-2). lib. bdg. 27.32 (978-1-4914-9650-3(9), Aplus Bks.) Capstone Press of Coughlan Cos.

Cooper, John. Dinosaurs. 2016. (Wise Up Ser.). 32p. (gr. 2-6). 31.35 (978-1-62588-339-1(0), Smart Apple Media) Black Rabbit Bks.

—Dinosaurs. 2006. (Illus.). 24p. (YA). (gr. 1-18). lib. bdg. 22.80 (978-1-931983-58-7(5)) Chrysalis Education.

Cooper, John A. Dinosaurs. 2003. (Knowledge Masters Ser.). (Illus.). 32p. (YA). pap. incl. cd-rom (978-1-903954-08-9(8), Pavilion Children's Books) Pavilion Bks.

Corporate Contibutor Staff. Dinosaur Alphabet. 2012. (ENG.). 24p. (J). (978-0-7787-7453-2(8)) Crabtree Publishing Co.

Corporate Contibutor Staff & West, David. Dinosaur Alphabet. 2012. (ENG.). 24p. (J). pap. (978-0-7787-7458-7(9)) Crabtree Publishing Co.

—Dinosaur Colors. 2012. (ENG.). 24p. (J). (978-0-7787-7454-9(6)); pap. (978-0-7787-7459-4(7)) Crabtree Publishing Co.

—Dinosaur Numbers. 2012. (ENG.). 24p. (J). (978-0-7787-7455-6(4)); pap. (978-0-7787-7460-0(0)) Crabtree Publishing Co.

—Dinosaur Shapes. 2012. (ENG.). 24p. (J). (978-0-7787-7456-3(2)); pap. (978-0-7787-7461-7(9)) Crabtree Publishing Co.

Cosneau, Olivia. In the Age of Dinosaurs: My Nature Sticker Activity Book. 2016. (ENG., Illus.). 24p. (J). (gr. k-3). pap. 7.99 (978-1-61689-469-6(5)) Princeton Architectural Pr.

Cosson, M. J. Troodon. 2006. (North American Dinosaurs Ser.). (Illus.). 24p. (J). (gr. -1-k). lib. bdg. 27.07 (978-1-60044-254-4(4)) Rourke Educational Media.

Coupe, Robert. Dinosaur Hunters. 2013. (Discovery Education: Discoveries & Inventions Ser.). (ENG., Illus.). 32p. (J). (gr. 3-6). pap. 10.00 (978-1-4777-1498-0(7)); lib. bdg. 25.25 (978-1-4777-1328-0(X)) Rosen Publishing Group, Inc., The. (PowerKids Pr.).

Couzens, Dominic & Nurney, David. Color Yourself Smart: Dinosaurs. 2013. (Color Yourself Smart Ser.). (ENG., Illus.). 128p. 19.95 (978-1-60710-573-2(X), Thunder Bay Pr.) Readerlink Distribution Services, LLC.

Creese, Sarah. Dinosaurs: I-Explore Reader. 2013. (ENG.). 32p. (J). pap. 4.99 (978-1-78235-156-6(6)) Make Believe Ideas GBR. Dist: Nelson, Thomas Inc.

—Mad about Triceratops T-Rex & Other Dinosaurs. 2009. (Mad About Ser.). (ENG., Illus.). 24p. (J). (gr. -1-3). pap. 3.99 (978-1-84879-005-6(8)) Make Believe Ideas GBR. Dist: Nelson, Thomas Inc.

Crosbie, Duncan. A Cool Kid's Field Guide to Dinosaurs. Field, James, illus. 2009. (Cool Kid's Field Guide Ser.). 26p. (J). (gr. 1-3). spiral bd. 6.99 (978-0-8416-7145-4(1)) Hammond World Atlas Corp.

Crumpton, Nick. Triassic Terrors. Lenkiewicz, Isaac, illus. 2013. (ENG.). 32p. (J). (gr. k). pap. 13.95 (978-1-909263-05-5(2)) Flying Eye Bks. GBR. Dist: Consortium Bk. Sales & Distribution.

Cunningham, Mark. Meet Ankylosaurus. 2014. (Age of Dinosaurs Ser.). 32p. (J). (gr. 3-5). lib. bdg. 28.50 (978-1-62712-785-1(2)) Cavendish Square Publishing.

—Meet Iguanodon. 2014. (Age of Dinosaurs Ser.). 32p. (J). (gr. 3-5). lib. bdg. 28.50 (978-1-62712-788-2(7)) Cavendish Square Publishing.

Dakota, Heather. Jurassic Survival Guide. 2014. (Illus.). 96p. (J). (978-0-545-80815-6(4)) Scholastic, Inc.

Dale, Jay. Dinosaurs, 1 vol. Vanzet, Gaston, illus. 2012. (Engage Literacy Blue Ser.). (ENG.). 32p. (gr. k-2). pap. 5.99 (978-1-4296-8974-8(9), Engage Literacy) Capstone Press of Coughlan Cos.

Dalla Vecchia, Fabio Marco. Iguanodon. Calvetti, Leonello & Massini, Luca, illus. 2007. (Dinosaur Profiles Ser.). (ENG.). 32p. (J). (gr. 3-7). lib. bdg. 25.65 (978-1-4103-0736-1(0), Blackbirch Pr., Inc.) Cengage Gale.

Danger! Dinosaurs. 2015. (Danger! Dinosaurs Ser.). (ENG.). 32p. (J). (gr. 4-5). 159.60 (978-1-4824-2557-4(2)); pap., pap., pap. 63.00 (978-1-4824-3449-1(0)); pap., pap., pap. 378.00 (978-1-4824-3448-4(2)) Stevens, Gareth Publishing LLLP.

Davidson, Susanna, et al. The Usborne Internet-Linked World Atlas of Dinosaurs. Rey, Luis V., illus. 2003. 144p. (J). (978-0-439-81840-7(0)) Scholastic, Inc.

Davidson, Susannah. Dinosaur Sticker Atlas. Turnbull, Stephanie, ed. 2004. (Sticker Atlas Ser.). (Illus.). 24p. (J). pap. 8.95 (978-0-7945-0668-1(2), Usborne) EDC Publishing.

—World Atlas of Dinosaurs: Internet-Linked. 2004. 144p. (J). lib. bdg. 30.95 (978-1-58086-635-4(2), Usborne) EDC Publishing.

Davis, Kenneth C. Don't Know Much about Dinosaurs. Date not set. 48p. (J). (gr. 1-4). pap. 5.99 (978-0-06-446233-4(1)) HarperCollins Pubs.

—Don't Know Much about Dinosaurs. Martin, Pedro, illus. 2004. (Picture Bks.: No. 7). 48p. (J). 15.99 (978-0-06-028619-4(9)) HarperCollins Pubs.

Davis, Lee. DK Readers L2: Dinosaur Dinners. 2015. (DK Readers Ser.). (ENG., Illus.). 48p. (J). (gr. 1-3). pap. 3.99 (978-1-4654-3492-0(5), DK Children) Dorling Kindersley Publishing, Inc.

De la Bédoyère, Camilla. Why Why Why Did Dinosaurs Lay Eggs? 2008. (Why Why Why Ser.). (Illus.). 32p. (J). (gr. -1-3). pap. (978-1-84810-001-5(9)) Miles Kelly Publishing, Ltd.

—Why Why Why... Were Dinosaurs Scaly? 2010. (Why Why Why Ser.). 32p. (J). (gr. 1-3). lib. bdg. 18.95 (978-1-4222-1574-6(1)) Mason Crest.

Degen, Bruce, illus. The Time of the Dinosaurs. (Magic School Bus Ser.). (FRE.). (J). (gr. 1-4). pap. 6.99 (978-0-590-24641-5(0)) Scholastic, Inc.

Design Eye Publishing Staff, et al. Amazing Automata — Dinosaurs! 2013. (Dover Origami Papercraft Ser.). (ENG.). 24p. (J). (gr. 5). 14.99 (978-0-486-49981-9(2)) Dover Pubns., Inc.

DeVillier, Christy. Corythosaurus. 2004. (Dinosaurs Set Iii Ser.). 32p. (gr. k-4). 27.07 (978-1-59197-537-3(9), Buddy Bks.) ABDO Publishing Co.

—Deinonychus. 2004. (Dinosaurs Set Iii Ser.). 32p. (gr. k-4). 27.07 (978-1-59197-538-0(7), Buddy Bks.) ABDO Publishing Co.

—Spinosaurus. 2004. (Dinosaurs Set Iii Ser.). 32p. (gr. k-4). 27.07 (978-1-59197-539-7(5), Buddy Bks.) ABDO Publishing Co.

Devillier, Christy. Styracosaurus. 2004. (Dinosaurs Set Iii Ser.). 32p. (gr. k-4). 27.07 (978-1-59197-540-3(9), Buddy Bks.) ABDO Publishing Co.

DeVillier, Christy. Troodon. 2004. (Dinosaurs Set Iii Ser.). 32p. (gr. k-4). 27.07 (978-1-59197-541-0(7), Buddy Bks.) ABDO Publishing Co.

Devillier, Christy & ABDO Publishing Company Staff. Dinosaurs Set 3, 6 vols. 2004. (Dinosaurs Set 3 Ser.). (J). (gr. k-4). 108.28 (978-1-59197-535-9(2), Buddy Bks.) ABDO Publishing Co.

Dinoclub: Deinonychus.Tr. of Dinosaur Book. (SPA.). (J). 5.98 (978-970-607-992-3(0)) Larousse, Ediciones, S. A. de C. V. MEX. Dist: Continental Bk. Co., Inc.

Dinoclub: Stegasaurus.Tr. of Stegasaurus Dino Book. (SPA.). (J). 5.98 (978-970-607-991-6(2)) Larousse, Ediciones, S. A. de C. V. MEX. Dist: Continental Bk. Co., Inc.

Dinosaur Alphabet Dinosaur Alphabet. bds. (978-1-58394-099-0(5)) North Atlantic Bks.

Dinosaur Balloons. 2004. (Whizz Kits Ser.). (Illus.). 48p. (J). (978-1-84229-961-6(1)) Top That! Publishing PLC.

The Dinosaur Boogie. (Sails Literacy Ser.). 24p. (gr. 2-3). 8.00 (978-0-7635-7035-4(4)) Rigby Education.

Dinosaur Coloring Book. (Illus.). (J). Bk. 1. pap. 1.99 (978-1-59340-008-8(X))Bk. 2. pap. 1.99 (978-1-59340-009-5(8)) Grandreams Bks., Inc.

Dinosaur Construction Kit: Tyrannosaurus Rex. (J). (gr. 4-6). 10.75 (978-0-669-15886-1(0)); 75.00 (978-0-669-15077-3(0)) Houghton Mifflin Harcourt School Pubs.

Dinosaur Discovery. 2011. (History Detectives Ser.). (ENG.). 32p. (J). (gr. 4-7). spiral bd. 9.95 (978-1-84898-189-8(9), TickTock Books) Octopus Publishing Group GBR. Dist: Independent Pubs. Group.

Dinosaur Discovery: Individual Title, 6 packs. (Story Steps Ser.). (gr. k-2). 32.00 (978-0-7635-9829-7(1)) Rigby Education.

Dinosaur Fact Dig: The Need-To-Know Facts. 2016. (Dinosaur Fact Dig Ser.). (ENG.). 32p. (gr. 1-2). 163.92 (978-1-4914-9652-7(5), Aplus Bks.) Capstone Press of Coughlan Cos.

The dinosaur Fan: Individual Title, 6 packs. (gr. 1-2). 25.00 (978-0-7635-9129-8(7)) Rigby Education.

Dinosaur Wars, 1 vol. 2010. (Dinosaur Wars Ser.). 32p. (ENG.). (gr. 3-4). lib. bdg. 111.96 (978-1-4296-4759-5(0)); lib. bdg. 106.60 (978-1-4296-5850-8(9)); (ENG.). (gr. 3-4). lib. bdg. 83.97 (978-1-4296-4422-8(2)) Capstone Press of Coughlan Cos. (Edge Bks.).

Dinosaur World, 12 vols. 2005. (Dinosaur World Ser.). (ENG., Illus.). 24p. (gr. k-3). 207.92 (978-1-4048-0991-8(0)) Picture Window Bks.

Dinosaur World Set, 6-Volumes. 2008. (Dinosaur World Ser.). (gr. 2-4). 138.00 (978-1-60413-431-5(3), Chelsea Clubhouse) Facts On File, Inc.

Dinosaurios. (Coleccion Adventuras con la Ciencia).Tr. of Dinosaurs. (SPA.). (J). (gr. 3-5). pap. (978-950-24-0522-3(6), AL5080) Albatros ARG. Dist: Lectorum Pubns., Inc.

Dinosaurios. 2003. (Megabites Ser.).Tr. of Dinosaurs. (SPA., Illus.). (J). pap. 8.95 (978-0-9715256-9-6(2)) Planeta Publishing Corp.

Dinosaurios. 2005. (Collection Abre Tus Ojos, Collection Eye Openers Ser.).Tr. of Dinosaurs. (SPA.). (J). (gr. k-2). 6.95 (978-950-11-0963-4(1)) Sigmar ARG. Dist: Iaconi, Mariuccia Bk. Imports.

Los Dinosaurios: Big Book Packages. 2003. 64.95 (978-0-673-58597-4(2)) Celebration Pr.

Dinosaurios con plumas (Feathered Dinosaurs) 2006. (J). pap. 6.95 (978-0-8225-6641-0(9), Ediciones Lerner) Lerner Publishing Group.

Los dinosaurios más inteligentes (the Smartest Dinosaurs) 2006. (J). pap. 6.95 (978-0-8225-6636-6(2), Ediciones Lerner) Lerner Publishing Group.

Los dinosaurios más mortíferos (the Deadliest Dinosaurs) 2006. (J). pap. 6.95 (978-0-8225-6639-7(7), Ediciones Lerner) Lerner Publishing Group.

Los dinosaurios más rápidos (the Fastest Dinosaurs) 2006. (J). pap. 6.95 (978-0-8225-6640-3(0), Ediciones Lerner) Lerner Publishing Group.

Dinosaurios y animales prehistoricos/Dinosaurs & Prehistoric Animals [Becker's]. 2010. (Dinosaurios y animales prehistoricos/Dinosaurs & Prehistoric Animals Ser.). 89.80 (978-1-4296-5776-1(6)) Capstone Digital.

Dinosaurios y animales prehistoricos/Dinosaurs & Prehistoric Animals [Becker's]. 2010. (Dinosaurios y animales prehistoricos/Dinosaurs & Prehistoric Animals Ser.). 24p. pap. 27.80 (978-1-4296-5775-4(8), Pebble Plus Bilingue/Bilingual) Capstone Press of Coughlan Cos.

Dinosaur/Libro De Dinosaurios Con Actividades. 2006. 64p. (J). pap., act. bk. ed. (978-0-9762071-9-1(2), 371-009) Big City Publishing.

Dinosaurs. (Color & Learn Ser.). (J). 36p. (gr. 1-5). pap. (978-1-882210-04-6(2)); 42p. (gr. 4-8). pap. (978-1-882210-51-0(4)) Action Publishing, Inc.

Dinosaurs. (Illus.). 24p. (J). 1.99 (978-1-59445-055-6(2)) Dogs in Hats Children's Publishing Co.

Dinosaurs. 2017. (Young Beginners Ser.). (ENG.). (J). 4.99 **(978-0-7945-3801-9(0)**, Usborne) EDC Publishing.

Dinosaurs. 2003. (Little Guides). (Illus.). 320p. pap. 8.95 (978-1-877019-53-1(4)); 256-288p. (978-1-876778-63-7(6)) Fog City Pr.

Dinosaurs. 2009. (FACT ATLAS Ser.). 72p. (J). (gr. 3-7). pap. 13.99 (978-0-8437-1882-9(X)) Hammond World Atlas Corp.

Dinosaurs. 2004. 24p. (J). pap. 1.99 (978-0-9821692-1-6(3)) International Graphic Group.

Dinosaurs. (Illus.). (J). (gr. -1-6). pap. 2.95 (978-0-565-01078-2(6)) Natural History Museum Pubns. GBR. Dist: Parkwest Pubns., Inc.

Dinosaurs. 2003. (J). per. (978-1-884907-32-6(6)); per. (978-1-884907-33-3(4)) Paradise Pr., Inc.

Dinosaurs. (Question & Answers of the Natural World Ser.). Date not set. 32p. 4.98 (978-0-7525-4332-1(6)) Date not set. (Illus.). 12p. (J). 3.98 (978-1-4054-0497-6(3)) Date not set. (Illus.). 40p. (J). 3.98 (978-1-4054-0173-9(7)) 2007. 8p. pap. (978-1-4075-0360-8(X)) Parragon, Inc.

Dinosaurs: Amazing Animal Discovery Books. 2009. (Amazing Animal Discovery Bks.). (ENG.). 12p. (J). (gr. -1). 5.95 (978-1-58117-848-7(4), Intervisual/Piggy Toes) Bendon, Inc.

Dinosaurs & Monsters. Date not set. (Illus.). 64p. (J). 2.98 (978-1-4054-0448-8(5)) Parragon, Inc.

Dinosaurs & Prehistoric Animals [Becker's]. 2010. (Dinosaurs & Prehistoric Animals Ser.). 24p. pap. 27.80 (978-1-4296-5774-7(X), Pebble Plus) Capstone Press of Coughlan Cos.

Dinosaurs & the Bible. 2003. (BUL.). (YA). 0.75 (978-1-893345-11-9(4)) Answers in Genesis Ministries.

Dinosaurs Dominate: Jurassic Life. 2013. (Awesome Ancient Animals Ser.). (Illus.). 32p. (J). (gr. 2-6). (978-1-84898-628-2(9), TickTock Books) Octopus Publishing Group.

Dinosaurs (Gr. PreK-5) 2003. (J). (978-1-58232-019-9(5)) ECS Learning Systems, Inc.

Dinosaurs Great & Small: A Supplement to Childcraft, the How & Why Library. 2015. (Illus.). 159p. (J). (978-0-7166-0634-5(8)) World Bk.-Childcraft International.

Dinosaurs, Level 2. 2016. (Ladybird Readers Ser.). (ENG.). 48p. (J). pap. 9.99 (978-0-241-25447-9(7)) Penguin Bks., Ltd. GBR. Dist: Independent Pubs. Group.

Dinosaurs Picture Puzzle Book. 2017. (Picture Puzzle Bks.). (ENG.). (J). bds. 14.99 **(978-0-7945-4005-0(8)**, Usborne) EDC Publishing.

DinoZone. 2016. (Dinozone Ser.). 00032p. (J). (gr. 2-3). 109.00 (978-1-4994-8143-3(8), Windmill Bks.) Rosen Publishing Group, Inc., The.

Disiena, Laura Lyn & Eliot, Hannah. Dinosaurs Live On! 2015. (Did You Know? Ser.). lib. bdg. 17.20 (978-0-606-36294-8(0)) Turtleback Bks.

DiSiena, Laura Lyn & Eliot, Hannah. Dinosaurs Live On! And Other Fun Facts. Spurgeon, Aaron, illus. 2015. (Did You Know? Ser.). (ENG.). 32p. (J). (gr. -1-3). pap. 6.99 (978-1-4814-2424-0(6), Little Simon) Little Simon.

Dixon, Dougal. The Big Book of Dinosaur Questions & Answers. Ticktock Media, Ltd. Staff, ed. 2010. (ENG.). 80p. (J). (gr. 2-4). pap. 12.95 (978-1-84898-352-6(2), TickTock Books) Octopus Publishing Group GBR. Dist: Independent Pubs. Group.

—Everything You Need to Know about Dinosaurs. 2016. (Everything You Need to Know Ser.). (ENG.). 160p. (J). pap. 12.99 (978-0-7534-7309-2(7), 9780753473092, Kingfisher) Roaring Brook Pr.

—My First Book of Dinosaurs. 2004. (Illus.). 48p. (J). 9.95 (978-1-86007-267-3(4), TickTock Books) Octopus Publishing Group GBR. Dist: Independent Pubs. Group.

Dixon, Dougal. My Little Book of Dinosaurs. 2014. (Illus.). 64p. (J). **(978-1-4351-5527-5(0))** Barnes & Noble, Inc.

Dixon, Dougal & Picture Window Books Staff. Tyrannosaurus & Other Dinosaurs of North America, 1 vol. Weston, Steve & Field, James, illus. 2007. (Dinosaur Find Ser.). (ENG.). 24p. (gr. k-3). lib. bdg. 26.65 (978-1-4048-2265-8(8)) Picture Window Bks.

Dixon, Douglas. Discovering Dinosaurs: An Exciting Guide to Prehistoric Creatures. 2014. (ENG., Illus.). 96p. (J). (gr. -1 — 1). pap. 7.99 (978-1-84322-770-0(3), Armadillo) Anness Publishing GBR. Dist: National Bk. Network.

Dodson, Peter & Library Association Staff. Diplodocus up Close: Long-Necked Dinosaur. Marshall, Todd & Bindon, John, illus. 2010. (Zoom in on Dinosaurs! Ser.). 24p. (J). (gr. k-3). 22.60 (978-0-7660-3333-7(3)) Enslow Pubs., Inc.

—Stegosaurus up Close: Plated Dinosaur. Marshall, Todd et al, illus. 2010. (Zoom in on Dinosaurs! Ser.). 24p. (J). (gr. k-3). 22.60 (978-0-7660-3334-4(1)) Enslow Pubs., Inc.

—Triceratops up Close: Horned Dinosaur. Marshall, Todd & Fields, Laura, illus. 2010. (Zoom in on Dinosaurs! Ser.). 24p. (J). (gr. k-3). 22.60 (978-0-7660-3335-1(X)) Enslow Pubs., Inc.

—Tyrannosaurus Rex up Close: Meat-Eating Dinosaur. Marshall, Todd et al, illus. 2010. (Zoom in on Dinosaurs! Ser.). 24p. (J). (gr. k-3). 22.60 (978-0-7660-3336-8(8)) Enslow Pubs., Inc.

—Velociraptor up Close: Swift Dinosaur. Fields, Laura & Walters, Bob, illus. 2010. (Zoom in on Dinosaurs! Ser.). 24p. (J). (gr. k-3). 22.60 (978-0-7660-3337-5(6)) Enslow Pubs., Inc.

Donald, Rhonda Lucas. Dino Tracks, 1 vol. Morrison, Cathy, illus. 2013. (ENG.). 32p. (J). (gr. 1-4). pap. 9.95 (978-1-60718-631-1(4)) Arbordale Publishing.

—Dino Treasures, 1 vol. Morrison, Cathy, illus. 2015. (ENG.). 32p. (J). (gr. 1-4). 17.95 (978-1-62855-450-2(9)) Arbordale Publishing.

¿Donde Fueron los Dinosaurios? (Coleccion Primeros Pasos en la Ciencia). (SPA., Illus.). (J). (gr. 1-3). pap. (978-950-724-217-5(1), LMA8220) Lumen ARG. Dist: Lectorum Pubns., Inc.

Dorling Kindersley Publishing Staff. Amazing Giant Dinosaurs. 2012. (Amazing Giant Ser.). (ENG., Illus.). 14p. (J). (gr. k-4). 19.99 (978-0-7566-9308-4(X), DK Children) Dorling Kindersley Publishing, Inc.

—The Big Book of Dinosaurs. 2015. (ENG., Illus.). 32p. (J). (gr. k-3). 14.99 (978-1-4654-4377-9(0), DK Children) Dorling Kindersley Publishing, Inc.

—Dinosaur. (ENG., Illus.). (J). (-k). 2017. 12p. bds. 9.99 (978-1-4654-5956-5(1), DK Children) 2016. 36p. bds. (978-0-241-23758-8(0)) Dorling Kindersley Publishing, Inc.

—Dinosaur! 2014. (ENG., Illus.). 208p. (J). (gr. 3-7). 24.99 (978-1-4654-2047-3(9), DK Children) Dorling Kindersley Publishing, Inc.

—Dinosaurs. (DK Find Out! Ser.). (ENG., (J). 2016. Illus.). 64p. (gr. 1-4). pap. 10.99 (978-1-4654-5429-4(2)) 2015. (Illus.). 14p. (gr. -1 — 1). bds. 9.99 (978-1-4654-3626-9(X)) 2014. 96p. (gr. 2-4). pap. 12.99 (978-1-4654-1656-8(0)) 2013. 304p. (gr. 2-5). pap. 19.99 (978-1-4654-1233-1(6)) 2013. (Illus.). 56p. (gr. k-4). 10.99 (978-1-4654-0905-8(X)) 2012. 12p. (gr. -1-k). bds. 6.99 (978-0-7566-9288-9(1)) Dorling Kindersley Publishing, Inc. (DK Children).

—Dinosaurs & Other Prehistoric Life. 2013. (Ultimate Sticker Collections). (ENG.). 96p. (J). (gr. 1-4). pap. 12.99 (978-1-4654-0886-0(X), DK Children) Dorling Kindersley Publishing, Inc.

—Dinosaurs Eye to Eye. (Illus.). 32p. (J). (978-1-57755-674-9(7)) Flying Frog Publishing, Inc.

—First Dinosaur Encyclopedia. 2016. (ENG., Illus.). 136p. (J). (gr. 2-5). 16.99 (978-1-4654-4346-5(0), 1405878, DK Children) Dorling Kindersley Publishing, Inc.

—Follow the Trail: Baby Dinosaurs. 2017. (Follow the Trail Ser.). (ENG., Illus.). 14p. (J). (— 1). bds. 9.99 (978-1-4654-5669-4(4), DK Children) Dorling Kindersley Publishing, Inc.

—The Good Dinosaur. 2015. (ENG.). 64p. (J). (gr. k-4). 12.99 (978-1-4654-1568-4(8), DK Children) Dorling Kindersley Publishing, Inc.

—My First Dinosaur. 2016. (ENG., Illus.). 36p. (J). (— 1). bds. 5.99 (978-1-4654-4491-2(2), DK Children) Dorling Kindersley Publishing, Inc.

—Pocket Genius: Dinosaurs. 2016. (Pocket Genius Ser.). (ENG., Illus.). 160p. (J). (gr. 3-7). pap. 4.99 (978-1-4654-4561-2(7), DK Children) Dorling Kindersley Publishing, Inc.

—Roar! Roar! Baby Dinosaur. 2016. (ENG., Illus.). 12p. (J). (— 1). bds. 14.99 (978-1-4654-5390-7(3), DK Children) Dorling Kindersley Publishing, Inc.

—Sticker Encyclopedia - Dinosaurs. 2009. (ENG.). 96p. (J). (gr. 1-4). pap. 12.99 (978-0-7566-5232-6(4), DK Children) Dorling Kindersley Publishing, Inc.

—Ultimate Dinosaurs. 2013. (ENG.). 128p. (J). (gr. 3-7). 16.99 (978-1-4654-0587-6(9), DK Children) Dorling Kindersley Publishing, Inc.

—Ultimate Sticker Book: Dinosaurs. 2016. (ENG.). 32p. (J). (gr. k-4). pap. 6.99 (978-1-4654-4718-0(0), DK Children) Dorling Kindersley Publishing, Inc.

—Utterly Amazing Dinosaur. 2016. (ENG., Illus.). 32p. (J). (gr. 1-4). 19.99 (978-1-4654-5366-2(0), DK Children) Dorling Kindersley Publishing, Inc.

—Visual Encyclopedia of Dinosaurs. 2005. (ENG., Illus.). 400p. (J). (gr. 5-12). pap. 14.99 (978-0-7566-0858-3(9), DK Children) Dorling Kindersley Publishing, Inc.

Dorling Kindersley Publishing Staff, ed. Dangerous Dinosaurs. 2004. (Ultimate Sticker Bks.). (ENG.). 16p. (J). (gr. k-3). pap.

6.99 *(978-0-7566-0565-0(2),* DK Children) Dorling Kindersley Publishing, Inc.

Dorling Kindersley Publishing Staff & Chambers, Catherine. Dinosaur Hunters: A Big Dig Adventure! 2014. (DK Adventures Ser.). (ENG.). 128p. (J). (gr. 3-7). pap. 5.99 *(978-1-4654-2833-2(X),* DK Children) Dorling Kindersley Publishing, Inc.

Dorling Kindersley Publishing Staff & Chambers, Catherine E. DK Adventures: Dinosaur Hunters: Dinosaur Hunters. 2014. (DK Adventures Ser.). (ENG.). 128p. (J). (gr. 3-7). 16.99 *(978-1-4654-2831-8(3),* DK Children) Dorling Kindersley Publishing, Inc.

Douglas, Jozua. Dinosaurs. van Rheenen, Barbara, illus. 2012. (Want to Know Ser.). (ENG.). 30p. (J). (gr. -1-2). 16.95 *(978-1-60537-136-8(X))* Cobblestone Publishing Co.

Dover. Dinosaurs Activities Dover Chunky Book. 2009. (Dover Little Activity Bks.). (ENG., Illus.). 320p. (J). (gr. -1-5). pap. 6.99 *(978-0-486-47426-7(7))* Dover Pubns., Inc.

Dover Staff & Printworks KMG Staff. Dinosaurs Field Guide. 2013. (ENG.). 48p. (J). (gr. 3-8). pap. 5.99 *(978-0-486-49156-1(0))* Dover Pubns., Inc.

Drehsen, Britta. Flip-O-Saurus. Ball, Sara, illus. 2010. (ENG.). 22p. (J). (gr. -1-k). bds. 15.95 *(978-0-7892-1061-6(4),* Abbeville Kids) Abbeville Pr., Inc.

Duhaime, Darla. Iguanas. 2017. (Reptiles! Ser.). (ENG.). (J). (gr. k-1). 28.51 ***(978-1-68342-158-0(2))*** Rourke Educational Media.

Duhig, Lee. Draw Dinosaurs! 2006. (Illus.). 64p. (J). pap. *(978-1-59412-158-6(3))* Mud Puddle, Inc.

Dunn, Mary. My Adventure on a Dinosaur Dig. 2006. 44p. (J). 8.99 *(978-1-59092-281-1(6))* Blue Forge Pr.

Eason, Sarah. Dinosaurs: Discover the Awesome Lost World of the Dinosaur. Field, James, illus. 2014. (ENG.). 64p. (J). (gr. -1-4). 14.99 *(978-1-86147-364-6(8),* Armadillo) Anness Publishing GBR. Dist: National Bk. Network.

Editors of Kingfisher. Deadly Dinosaurs. 2016. (It's All About... Ser.). (ENG., Illus.). 32p. (J). pap. 5.99 *(978-0-7534-7261-3(9),* 9780753472613, Kingfisher) Roaring Brook Pr.

—Monster Dinosaurs: Come Face to Face with These Prehistoric Giants. 2016. (Fast Facts Ser.). (ENG., Illus.). 32p. (J). pap. 6.99 *(978-0-7534-7245-3(7),* 9780753472453, Kingfisher) Roaring Brook Pr.

Editors of TIME For Kids Magazine. Dinosaurs 3D: An Incredible Journey Through Time. 2013. (ENG., Illus.). 80p. (J). (gr. 3-17). 19.95 *(978-1-61893-044-6(3))* Time Inc. Bks.

Edwards, Amelia. Name That Dinosaur. Jirankova-Limbrick, Martina, illus. 2009. (ENG.). 40p. (J). (gr. -1-3). 17.99 *(978-0-7636-3473-5(5))* Candlewick Pr.

Elora, Grace. Dinosaur Fossils. 2009. (Real Life Readers Ser.). 16p. (gr. 2-3). pap. 7.05 *(978-1-4358-0059-5(1),* Rosen Classroom) Rosen Publishing Group, Inc., The.

Encyclopaedia Britannica, Inc. Staff, compiled by. Britannica Illustrated Science Library: Reptiles & Dinosaurs. 16 vols. 2008. (Illus.). (J). 29.95 *(978-1-59339-395-3(4))* Encyclopaedia Britannica, Inc.

Encyclopaedia Britannica Staff, creator. Reptiles & Dinosaurs. 2011. (Britannica Illustrated Science Library Ser.). (J). 37.44 *(978-1-61535-464-1(6))* Encyclopaedia Britannica, Inc.

Encyclopedia of Dinosaurs. (Children's Reference Ser.). 224p. *(978-1-4054-9923-1(0))* Parragon, Inc.

Equipo Staff & DOWLAND, MELANIE. Mi Primer Libro de Dinosaurios. (SPA.). 16p. 12.95 *(978-84-272-1736-2(6))* Molino, Editorial ESP. Dist: Distribooks, Inc.

Esbaum, Jill & National Geographic Kids Staff. Dinosaurs: A Prehistoric Adventure! Tempesta, Franco, illus. 2016. (ENG.). 128p. (J). (gr. -1-3). pap. 9.99 *(978-1-4263-2460-4(X),* National Geographic Children's Bks.) National Geographic Society.

Everything You Need to Know about Dinosaurs. 2014. (Everything You Need to Know Ser.). (ENG.). 80p. (J). (gr. 2-5). 15.99 *(978-1-4654-1575-2(0),* DK Children) Dorling Kindersley Publishing, Inc.

Fearn, Katrina, illus. & des. First Dot-To-Dot Dinosaurs. Fearn, Katrina, des. 2013. (First Dot-To-Dot Ser.). 16p. (J). pap. 5.99 *(978-0-7945-3341-0(8),* Usborne) EDC Publishing.

—First Dot-To-Dot Pirates. Fearn, Katrina, des. 2013. (First Dot-To-Dot Ser.). 16p. (J). pap. 5.99 *(978-0-7945-3393-9(0),* Usborne) EDC Publishing.

Feldman, Thea. Kingfisher Readers L1: Tyrannosaurus. 2014. (Kingfisher Readers Ser.). (ENG., Illus.). 32p. (J). (gr. k-3). pap. 3.99 *(978-0-7534-7137-1(X),* 9780753471371, Kingfisher) Roaring Brook Pr.

Field, James & Weston, Steve, illus. Iguanodon & Other Leaf-Eating Dinosaurs, 1 vol. 2009. (Dinosaur Find Ser.). (ENG.). 24p. (gr. k-3). 26.65 *(978-1-4048-5174-0(7))* Picture Window Bks.

Fiesta de Dinosaurios, 6 Pks. (Chiquilibros Ser.). (SPA.). (gr. k-1). 23.00 *(978-0-7635-8786-4(9))* Rigby Education.

First Dinosaur. Date not set. (Illus.). (J). bds. 9.98 *(978-0-7525-9893-2(7))* Parragon, Inc.

First Discovery Staff, et al. Dinosaurs. Galeron, Henri, illus. 2006. (ENG.). 36p. (J). (gr. k-3). pap. 11.99 *(978-1-85103-150-4(2))* Moonlight Publishing, Ltd. GBR. Dist: Independent Pubs. Group.

Firth, Rachel. Dinosaurs. 2004. (Discovery Program Ser.). (SPA., Illus.). 64p. (J). (gr. 2-18). lib. bdg. 16.99 *(978-1-58086-354-4(X))* EDC Publishing.

—Dinosaurs - Internet Linked. rev. ed. 2008. (Discovery Nature Ser.). 64p. (J). 8.99 *(978-0-7945-2245-2(9),* Usborne) EDC Publishing.

Fisher, Diana & Shelly, Jeff, illus. All about Dinosaurs & Reptiles. 2010. (All about Drawing Ser.). 80p. (J). 34.25 *(978-1-936309-07-8(6))* Quarto Publishing Group USA.

Flowerpot Press, creator. Dinosaurs Coloring Book. 2013. (Sockheadz Ser.). (ENG., Illus.). 72p. (J). (gr. -1-3). 4.99 *(978-1-77093-544-0(4))* Flowerpot Pr.

Foran, Jill. Dinosaurs. 2004. (Prehistoric Life Ser.). (J). pap. 9.95 *(978-1-59036-171-9(7));* (Illus.). 32p. lib. bdg. 26.00 *(978-1-59036-110-8(5))* Weigl Pubs., Inc.

Franceschelli, Christopher. Dinoblock. Peskimo, illus. 2015. (Alphablock Ser.). (ENG.). 96p. (J). (gr. -1 — 1). bds. 16.95 *(978-1-4197-1674-4(3),* Abrams Appleseed) Abrams, Inc.

Francis, Suzanne. Extreme Dinos. 2006. (Illus.). 32p. (J). pap. *(978-0-439-83873-3(8))* Scholastic, Inc.

—Prehistoric Hunters. 2006. (Illus.). 32p. (J). *(978-0-439-83863-4(0))* Scholastic, Inc.

Franklin, Carolyn. Scary Dinosaurs. 2010. (Top 10 Worst Ser.). (Illus.). 32p. (J). (gr. 3-6). (ENG.). pap. 10.50 *(978-1-4339-4074-3(4));* lib. bdg. 26.60 *(978-1-4339-4073-6(6))* Stevens, Gareth Publishing LLLP. (Gareth Stevens Learning Library).

Freed, Kira. Living Dinosaurs. 2017. (Text Connections Guided Close Reading Ser.). (J). (gr. 2). *(978-1-4900-1843-0(3))* Benchmark Education Co.

French, Vivian. T. Rex: Read & Wonder. Bartlett, Alison, illus. 2006. (Read & Wonder Ser.). (ENG.). 32p. (J). (gr. -1-3). reprint ed. pap. 6.99 *(978-0-7636-3177-2(9))* Candlewick Pr.

Frith, Alex. Big Book of Dinosaurs Internet Referenced. Fiorin, Fabiano, illus. 2010. (Big Bks.). 16p. (J). bds. 13.99 *(978-0-7945-2770-9(1),* Usborne) EDC Publishing.

—See Inside the World of Dinosaurs. Scott, Peter, illus. 2007. 16p. (J). bds. 13.99 *(978-0-7945-1436-5(7),* Usborne) EDC Publishing.

Gabriele, Joseph. The First Days of the Dinosaurs: Text Edition. Hurst, Margaret, illus. 32p. (Orig.). (J). (gr. 1-3). pap. 1.95 *(978-0-911211-55-9(1))* Penny Lane Pubns., Inc.

Galeron, Henri, et al. My First Encyclopedia of Dinosaurs. 2013. (My First Discoveries Ser.). (ENG., Illus.). 76p. (J). (gr. -1-2). spiral bd. 14.99 *(978-1-85103-424-6(2))* Moonlight Publishing, Ltd. GBR. Dist: Independent Pubs. Group.

Gallina, Jill, et al. Dino Soaring! A Prehistoric Musical Adventure for Cross-Curricular Fun in the Classroom. 2012. (ENG.). 64p. pap. 24.99 incl. audio compact disk *(978-1-4584-2532-4(0),* 1458425320) Shawnee Pr., Inc.

Galvin, Laura Gates. First Look at Dinosaurs. Pindroh, Paula, illus. 2011. (First Look At... (Soundprints) Ser.). (ENG.). 16p. 6.95 *(978-1-60727-285-4(7))* Soundprints.

Gamble, Adam & Jasper, Mark. Good Night Dinosaur. Kelly, Cooper, illus. 2013. (Good Night Our World Ser.). (ENG.). 28p. (J). (— 1). bds. 9.95 *(978-1-60219-078-8(X))* Good Night Bks.

Ganeri, Anita & West, David. Dinosaurs. 2012. (Illus.). 31p. (J). 70.50 *(978-1-4488-5241-3(2));* pap. 11.75 *(978-1-4488-5240-6(4));* lib. bdg. 26.50 *(978-1-4488-5201-7(3))* Rosen Publishing Group, Inc., The. (PowerKids Pr.).

Gee & Rey. Dinosaurios Guia de Campo. 2003. (SPA.). 144p. *(978-84-7556-268-1(X),* 1500) Oceano Difusion Editorial, S. A.

George, Joshua. Dinosaurs. Myer, Ed, illus. 2016. (Sticker History Ser.). (ENG.). 38p. (J). (gr. k-6). pap. 8.99 *(978-1-78445-859-1(7))* Top That! Publishing PLC GBR. Dist: Independent Pubs. Group.

George, Thomas. Diplodocus. 2015. (Look at Dinosaurs Ser.). (ENG.). 24p. (J). (gr. 1-2). pap. 8.15 *(978-1-4824-1822-4(3))* Stevens, Gareth Publishing LLLP.

Gibbons, Gail. Dinosaur Discoveries. (ENG., Illus.). 32p. (J). (gr. 1-4). 2006. 6.95 *(978-0-8234-2030-8(2))* 2005. 17.95 *(978-0-8234-1971-5(1))* Holiday Hse., Inc.

—Dinosaurs. 34p. (J). (gr. -1-2). pap. 6.95 *(978-0-8072-1271-4(7),* Listening Library) Random Hse. Audio Publishing Group.

—Dinosaurs! Gibbons, Gail, illus. 2009. (ENG., Illus.). 32p. (J). (gr. -1-1). pap. 7.99 *(978-0-8234-2197-8(X))* Holiday Hse., Inc.

—Dinosaurs! 2008. (ENG., Illus.). 32p. (J). (gr. -1-1). 17.95 *(978-0-8234-2143-5(0))* Holiday Hse., Inc.

Gibbons, Tony & Snedden, Robert. Dinosaur Atlas. 2003. (J). bds. 5.98 *(978-0-7525-8919-0(9))* Parragon, Inc.

Gibson, Brylee. Dinosaur Discoveries. 2007. (Connectors Ser.). (gr. 2-5). pap. *(978-1-877453-13-7(7))* Global Education Systems Ltd.

Gigantes voladores de la época de los dinosaurios (Flying Giants of Dinosaur Time) 2006. (J). pap. 6.95 *(978-0-8225-6637-3(0),* Ediciones Lerner) Lerner Publishing Group.

Gilbert, Sara. Apatosaurus. (Age of Dinosaurs Ser.). 48p. (gr. 4-7). 2011. (ENG.). (J). pap. 9.99 *(978-0-89812-539-9(1),* Creative Education) 2010. (YA). 23.95 *(978-1-58341-974-8(8))* Creative Co., The.

—Triceratops. (Age of Dinosaurs Ser.). 48p. (gr. 4-7). 2011. (ENG.). (J). pap. 9.99 *(978-0-89812-542-9(1),* Creative Education) 2010. (YA). 23.95 *(978-1-58341-977-9(2))* Creative Co., The.

—Tyrannosaurus Rex. (Age of Dinosaurs Ser.). (gr. 4-7). 2011. (ENG.). 48p. (J). pap. 9.99 *(978-0-89812-543-6(X),* Creative Education) 2010. (YA). 23.95 *(978-1-58341-978-6(0))* Creative Co., The.

Giulieri, Anne. My Dinosaurs, 1 vol. Meldrum, Ned, photos by. 2012. (Engage Literacy Red Ser.). (ENG., Illus.). 32p. (gr. k-2). pap. 5.99 *(978-1-4296-8938-0(2),* Engage Literacy) Capstone Press of Coughlan Cos.

Glut, Donald F., tr. Discover Dinosaurs. 2005. (Discover Ser.). (Illus.). 48p. (J). 7.98 *(978-0-7853-6109-1(X),* 3073307) Publications International, Ltd.

Goecke, Michael P. Baryonyx, 1 vol. 2007. (Dinosaurs Ser.). (ENG., Illus.). 32p. (gr. -1-3). 27.07 *(978-1-59928-694-5(7),* Buddy Bks.) ABDO Publishing Co.

—Camarasaurus, 1 vol. 2007. (Dinosaurs Ser.). (ENG., Illus.). 32p. (gr. -1-3). 27.07 *(978-1-59928-695-2(5),* Buddy Bks.) ABDO Publishing Co.

—Compsognathus, 1 vol. 2007. (Dinosaurs Ser.). (ENG., Illus.). 32p. (gr. -1-3). 27.07 *(978-1-59928-696-9(3),* Buddy Bks.) ABDO Publishing Co.

—Giganotosaurus, 1 vol. 2007. (Dinosaurs Ser.). (ENG., Illus.). 32p. (gr. 2). 27.07 *(978-1-59928-697-6(1),* Buddy Bks.) ABDO Publishing Co.

—Oviraptor, 1 vol. 2007. (Dinosaurs Ser.). (ENG., Illus.). 32p. (gr. -1-3). 27.07 *(978-1-59928-698-3(X),* Buddy Bks.) ABDO Publishing Co.

—Pachycephalosaurus, 1 vol. 2007. (Dinosaurs Ser.). (ENG.). 32p. (gr. -1-3). 27.07 *(978-1-59928-699-0(8),* Buddy Bks.) ABDO Publishing Co.

Goldsmith, Mike. Digging for Dinosaurs. Daubney, Kate, illus. 2015. (I Explore Ser.). (ENG.). 12p. (J). (gr. -1-k). bds. 6.95 *(978-1-4549-1501-0(3))* Sterling Publishing Co., Inc.

—Dinosaurs. Abbott, Simon, illus. 2011. (Flip Flap Science Ser.). (ENG.). 10p. (J). (gr. -1-k). 9.95 *(978-1-84898-365-6(4),* TickTock Books) Octopus Publishing Group GBR. Dist: Independent Pubs. Group.

Grack, Rachel. 10 Fascinating Facts about Dinosaurs. 2017. (Rookie Star — Fact Finder Ser.). (ENG., Illus.). 32p. (J). lib. bdg. 25.00 *(978-0-531-22260-7(8),* Children's Pr.) Scholastic Library Publishing.

Graham, Ian. The Science of Prehistoric Giants: Dinosaurs That Used Size & Armor for Defense. 2017. (Science of Dinosaurs Ser.). (ENG.). 32p. (J). lib. bdg. 29.00 ***(978-0-531-25833-0(5),*** Watts, Franklin) Scholastic Library Publishing.

Graham-Kennedy, Elaine. Dinosaurs: Where Did They Come from & Where Did They Go? 2006. (Illus.). 80p. (J). 15.99 *(978-0-8163-2155-1(8))* Pacific Pr. Publishing Assn.

Grambo, Rebecca L. Digging Canadian Dinosaurs, 1 vol. Bonder, Dianna, illus. 2004. (ENG.). 64p. (J). (gr. 2-6). pap. *(978-1-55285-395-5(0))* Whitecap Bks., Ltd.

Grant, Donald & Delafosse, Claude. Dinosaurs at Large. Grant, Donald, illus. 2013. (ENG., Illus.). 36p. (J). (gr. -1-k). 14.99 *(978-1-85103-415-4(3))* Moonlight Publishing, Ltd. GBR. Dist: Independent Pubs. Group.

—Let's Look at Dinosaurs. Grant, Donald, illus. 2012. (ENG., Illus.). 38p. (J). (gr. k-3). pap. 11.99 *(978-1-85103-280-8(0))* Moonlight Publishing, Ltd. GBR. Dist: Independent Pubs. Group.

Gray, Susan H. Allosaurus. 2015. (Exploring Dinosaurs Ser.). (ENG.). 32p. (J). (gr. 1-4). 27.07 *(978-1-63143-975-9(8),* 208810) Child's World, Inc., The.

—Ankylosaurus. 2015. (Exploring Dinosaurs Ser.). (ENG.). 32p. (J). (gr. 1-4). 27.07 *(978-1-63143-976-6(6),* 208811) Child's World, Inc., The.

—Apatosaurus. 2015. (Exploring Dinosaurs Ser.). (ENG.). 32p. (J). (gr. 1-4). 27.07 *(978-1-63143-977-3(4),* 208812) Child's World, Inc., The.

—Compsognathus. 2015. (Exploring Dinosaurs Ser.). (ENG.). 32p. (J). (gr. 1-4). 27.07 *(978-1-63143-978-0(2),* 208813) Child's World, Inc., The.

—Dinosaur Armor. 2007. (Scholastic News Nonfiction Readers Ser.). (ENG., Illus.). 24p. (J). (gr. 1-2). 22.00 *(978-0-531-17481-4(6))* Scholastic Library Publishing.

—Dinosaur Dig! 2007. (Scholastic News Nonfiction Readers Ser.). (ENG., Illus.). 24p. (J). (gr. 1-2). 22.00 *(978-0-531-17482-1(4))* Scholastic Library Publishing.

—Dinosaur Eggs. 2007. (Scholastic News Nonfiction Readers Ser.). (ENG., Illus.). 24p. (J). (gr. 1-2). 22.00 *(978-0-531-17483-8(2))* Scholastic Library Publishing.

—Dinosaur Teeth. 2007. (Scholastic News Nonfiction Readers Ser.). (ENG., Illus.). 24p. (J). (gr. 1-2). 22.00 *(978-0-531-17484-5(0))* Scholastic Library Publishing.

—Dinosaur Tracks. 2007. (Scholastic News Nonfiction Readers Ser.). (ENG., Illus.). 24p. (J). (gr. 1-2). 22.00 *(978-0-531-17485-2(9))* Scholastic Library Publishing.

—Iguanodon. 2015. (Exploring Dinosaurs Ser.). (ENG.). 32p. (J). (gr. 1-4). 27.07 *(978-1-63143-979-7(0),* 208814) Child's World, Inc., The.

—Maiasaura. 2015. (Exploring Dinosaurs Ser.). (ENG.). 32p. (J). (gr. 1-4). 27.07 *(978-1-63143-980-3(4),* 208815) Child's World, Inc., The.

—Oviraptor. 2015. (Exploring Dinosaurs Ser.). (ENG.). 32p. (J). (gr. 1-4). 27.07 *(978-1-63143-981-0(2),* 208816) Child's World, Inc., The.

—Spinosaurus. 2015. (Exploring Dinosaurs Ser.). (ENG.). 32p. (J). (gr. 1-4). 27.07 *(978-1-63143-982-7(0),* 208817) Child's World, Inc., The.

—Stegosaurus. 2015. (Exploring Dinosaurs Ser.). (ENG.). 32p. (J). (gr. 1-4). 27.07 *(978-1-63143-983-4(9),* 208818) Child's World, Inc., The.

—Triceratops. 2015. (Exploring Dinosaurs Ser.). (ENG.). 32p. (J). (gr. 1-4). 27.07 *(978-1-63143-984-1(7),* 208819) Child's World, Inc., The.

—Tyrannosaurus Rex. 2015. (Exploring Dinosaurs Ser.). (ENG.). 32p. (J). (gr. 1-4). 27.07 *(978-1-63143-985-8(5),* 208820) Child's World, Inc., The.

—Velociraptor. 2015. (Exploring Dinosaurs Ser.). (ENG.). 32p. (J). (gr. 1-4). 27.07 *(978-1-63143-986-5(3),* 208821) Child's World, Inc., The.

Greenwell, Jessica. Dinosaurs. Scott, Peter, illus. 2010. (Lift & Look Board Bks.). 12p. (J). bds. 9.99 *(978-0-7945-2585-9(7),* Usborne) EDC Publishing.

Gregory, Josh. Brachiosaurus. 2015. (21st Century Junior Library: Dinosaurs & Prehistoric Creatures Ser.). (ENG., Illus.). 24p. (J). (gr. 2-5). lib. bdg. 27.07 *(978-1-63362-381-1(5),* 206944) Cherry Lake Publishing.

—Coelophysis. 2015. (21st Century Junior Library: Dinosaurs & Prehistoric Creatures Ser.). (ENG., Illus.). 24p. (J). (gr. 2-5). lib. bdg. 27.07 *(978-1-63362-382-8(3),* 206948) Cherry Lake Publishing.

—Diplodocus. 2013. (21st Century Junior Library: Dinosaurs Ser.). (ENG., Illus.). 24p. (J). (gr. 2-5). pap. 12.79 *(978-1-62431-297-7(7),* 202982); lib. bdg. 25.64 *(978-1-62431-165-9(2),* 202980) Cherry Lake Publishing.

—If You Were a Kid Discovering Dinosaurs. 2017. (If You Were a Kid Ser.). (ENG.). 32p. (J). pap. 7.95 ***(978-0-531-23948-3(9));*** lib. bdg. 26.00 ***(978-0-531-23747-2(8))*** Scholastic Library Publishing. (Children's Pr.).

—Plateosaurus. 2015. (21st Century Junior Library: Dinosaurs & Prehistoric Creatures Ser.). (ENG., Illus.). 24p. (J). (gr. 2-5). lib. bdg. 27.07 *(978-1-63362-384-2(X),* 206956) Cherry Lake Publishing.

—Spinosaurus. 2013. (21st Century Junior Library: Dinosaurs Ser.). (ENG., Illus.). 24p. (J). (gr. 2-5). 3rd ed. lib. bdg. 25.64 *(978-1-62431-164-2(4),* 202976) 4th ed. pap. 12.79 *(978-1-62431-296-0(9),* 202978) Cherry Lake Publishing.

Group/McGraw-Hill, Wright. I Dig Dinosaurs: Level K, 6 vols., Vol. 2. (First Explorers Ser.). 24p. (gr. 1-2). 34.95 *(978-0-7699-1460-2(8))* Shortland Pubns. (U. S. A.) Inc.

—Set 2: Los Dinosaurios, 6 vols., Vol. 2. (First Explorers. Primeros Exploradores Nonfiction Sets Ser.). (SPA.). (gr. 1-2). 34.95 *(978-0-7699-1484-8(5))* Shortland Pubns. (U. S. A.) Inc.

Guiberson, Brenda Z. Feathered Dinosaurs. Low, William & Cobalt Illustrations Studio Staff, illus. 2016. (ENG.). 40p. (J). 17.99 *(978-0-8050-9828-0(3),* 9780805098280, Holt, Henry & Co. Bks. For Young Readers) Holt, Henry & Co.

—The Greatest Dinosaur Ever. Spirin, Gennady, illus. 2013. (ENG.). 32p. (J). (gr. -1-3). 17.99 *(978-0-8050-9625-5(6),* 9780805096255, Holt, Henry & Co. Bks. For Young Readers) Holt, Henry & Co.

Gurney, Stella. The Prehistoric Times. Hodson, Matthew & Parker, Neave, illus. 2017. (ENG.). 32p. (J). (gr. k-3). pap. 8.99 ***(978-1-84780-921-6(9),*** Frances Lincoln Children's Bks.) Quarto Publishing Group UK GBR. Dist: Hachette Bk. Group.

Habiger, Geoff. Dinosaur Learning Activity Book. Habiger, Geoff & Gower, Jim, illus. 2005. 80p. (J). per. 7.95 *(978-1-932926-96-5(8))* Artemesia Publishing, LLC.

Hadrosaurus: The Duck-Billed Dinosaur. 2009. (Graphic Dinosaurs Ser.). (ENG., Illus.). 32p. (J). 50.50 *(978-1-61531-881-0(X),* PowerKids Pr.) Rosen Publishing Group, Inc., The.

Halls, Kelly Milner. Dinosaur Mummies: Beyond Bare-Bone Fossils. 2007. (J). pap. 8.95 *(978-1-58196-034-1(4),* Darby Creek) Lerner Publishing Group.

—Dinosaur Mummies: Beyond Bare-Bone Fossils. Spears, Rick, illus. 2003. (Junior Library Guild Selection Ser.). 48p. (J). (gr. 4-18). 17.95 *(978-1-58196-000-6(X),* Darby Creek) Lerner Publishing Group.

—Dinosaurs. Cosgrove, Lee, illus. 2015. (Lie Detector Ser.). (ENG.). 32p. (gr. k-3). pap. 5.95 *(978-1-4795-8514-4(9))* Picture Window Bks.

Ham, Ken. Dinosaurs for Kids. 2009. 64p. (YA). 14.99 *(978-0-89051-555-6(7))* Master Bks.

Hammer, Sheila. Tyrannosaurus Rex: Mighty Meat-Eater. Dove, Jason, illus. 2012. (First Graphics: Dinosaurs Ser.). (ENG.). 24p. (gr. 1-2). pap. 35.70 *(978-1-4296-8366-1(X))* Capstone Press of Coughlan Cos.

Hammerslough, J. Fandex Family Guide: Dinosaurs. (ENG., Illus.). 119.40 *(978-0-7611-3621-7(5),* 23621) Workman Publishing Co., Inc.

Hammerslough, Jane. Dinosaurs. 2004. (ENG., Illus.). 50p. (J). (gr. 4-12). 10.95 *(978-0-7611-2976-9(6),* 12976) Workman Publishing Co., Inc.

Hanrahan, Brendan. Great Day Trips in the Connecticut Valley of the Dinosaurs. 2004. (Road to Discovery Guides Ser.). (Illus.). 256p. pap. *(978-0-9630181-1-3(6),* A Road to Discovery Series Guide) Perry Heights Pr.

Hanson, Anders & Mann, Elissa. Biggest, Baddest Book of Dinosaurs, 1 vol. 2012. (Biggest, Baddest Books for Boys Ser.). (ENG.). 24p. (J). (gr. k-4). 25.65 *(978-1-61783-406-6(8))* ABDO Publishing Co.

Harimann, Sierra. All in the Family. 2009. (I Can Read Level 2 Ser.). (ENG.). 32p. (J). (gr. k-3). pap. 3.99 *(978-0-06-168977-2(7))* HarperCollins Pubs.

—Ice Age: Dawn of the Dinosaurs - Momma Mix-Up. 2009. (I Can Read Level 2 Ser.). (ENG.). 32p. (J). (gr. k-3). pap. 3.99 *(978-0-06-168978-9(5))* HarperCollins Pubs.

Harris, Nicholas, text. Dinosaurs. 2006. (Illus.). 23p. (J). *(978-0-7607-8154-8(0))* backpackbook.

Harris, Nicolas. Dinosaurs Through Time. Dennis, Peter, illus. 2009. (Fast Forward Ser.). 32p. (YA). (gr. 2-5). lib. bdg. 25.25 *(978-1-4358-2802-5(X))* Rosen Publishing Group, Inc., The.

Harrison, Paul. T. Rex. (Up Close Ser.). 24p. (gr. 3-3). 2009. 47.90 *(978-1-60854-706-7(X))* 2008. (Illus.). (J). lib. bdg. 25.25 *(978-1-4042-4225-8(2))* Rosen Publishing Group, Inc., The. (PowerKids Pr.).

Harrison, Paul & Arcturus Publishing Staff. The Amazing Book of 3D Thrillers: Fantastic Eye-Popping Experiences. 2012. (ENG., Illus.). 96p. (J). pap. 9.95 *(978-1-84837-876-6(9),* 9781848378766) Arcturus Publishing GBR. Dist: Bookmasters Distribution.

Harrub, Brad. God Made Dinosaurs. 2006. (ENG., Illus.). (J). (gr. -1-3). 3.00 *(978-0-932859-71-6(2))* Apologetics Pr., Inc.

Havercroft, Elizabeth. A Year in the World of Dinosaurs. 2008. (Time Goes By Ser.). (ENG.). (gr. k-2). pap. 39.62 *(978-0-7613-4714-9(3));* (Illus.). 24p. lib. bdg. 22.60 *(978-1-58013-548-1(X))* Lerner Publishing Group.

Hawcock, David. Dinosaurs! Pop-Up Paper Designs. Hawcock, David, illus. 2015. (ENG., Illus.). 16p. (J). (gr. -1-k). 14.99 *(978-1-85707-804-6(7))* Tango Bks. GBR. Dist: Independent Pubs. Group.

Haywood, R. Los Dinosaurios. 2004. (Great Searches Ser.).Tr. of Great Dinosaur Search. (SPA., Illus.). 32p. (J). (gr. -1-18). pap. 8.95 *(978-0-7460-4500-8(X));* lib. bdg. 16.95 *(978-1-58086-339-1(6))* EDC Publishing.

Head, Heno. God Made Dinosaurs. Fletcher, Rusty, illus. 2013. (Happy Day Ser.). (ENG.). 16p. (J). pap. 2.49 *(978-1-4143-9296-7(6))* Tyndale Hse. Pubs.

Heywood, Grand-Mere Geny. Proto: Que faire quand un dinosaure nait dans votre Jardin? Connors, Mary, illus. 2010. 56p. pap. 23.99 *(978-1-4490-5786-2(1))* AuthorHouse.

Heywood, Rosie. The Great Dinosaur Search. Wingate, Philippa, ed. Galante, Studio & Firenze, Inklink, illus. rev. ed. 2005. (Great Searches - New Format Ser.). 32p. (J). (gr. -1). pap. 7.99 *(978-0-7945-1046-6(9),* Usborne) EDC Publishing.

Hinkler Books Staff. Dinosaurs. Kiely, Rob, illus. rev. ed. 2006. (ENG.). 6p. (J). (gr. 2-5). 9.95 *(978-1-74157-725-9(X))* Hinkler Bks. Pty. Ltd. AUS. Dist: Penton Overseas, Inc.

Hixson, Bryce. Get Your Poop in a Group. Hixson, Bryce, illus. 2003. (Illus.). (J). per. 9.95 *(978-1-931801-01-0(0))* Loose In The Lab.

Hodge, Susie. Dinosaurs. 2010. (Let's Draw Ser.). (ENG., Illus.). 32p. (gr. 3-5). pap. 10.55 *(978-1-61533-267-0(7))* Windmill Bks.

—Dinosaurs. Roberts, Steve, illus. 2010. (Let's Draw Ser.). (ENG.). 32p. (gr. 3-5). 22.60 *(978-1-61533-264-9(2))* Windmill Bks.

—How to Draw Dinosaurs. Roberts, Steve, illus. 2008. (How to Draw Ser.). 47p. (J). (gr. 4-7). *(978-1-84810-006-0(X))* Miles Kelly Publishing, Ltd.

Hoena, Blake. National Geographic Kids Everything Dinosaurs: Chomp on Tons of Earthshaking Facts & Fun. 2014. (National Geographic Kids Everything Ser.). (ENG., Illus.). 64p. (J). (gr. 3-7). pap. 12.99 *(978-1-4263-1496-4(5),* National Geographic Children's Bks.) National Geographic Society.

Hoff, Syd. Syd Hoff's Dinosaur Stories & More. 2015. (ENG., Illus.). 160p. (J). (gr. 2-4). pap. 14.99 *(978-0-486-80024-0(5))* Dover Pubns., Inc.

Holmes & Thom. Dawn of the Dinosaur Age: The Triassic Period. 2008. (Prehistoric Earth Ser.). (Illus.). 192p. (YA). (gr. 9-12). 35.00 *(978-0-8160-5959-1(4))* Facts On File, Inc.

—Time of the Giants: The Mid-Late Jurassic Periods. 2008. (Prehistoric Earth Ser.). (Illus.). 159p. (YA). (gr. 9-12). 35.00 *(978-0-8160-5960-7(8))* Facts On File, Inc.

Holmes, Thom. Last of the Dinosaurs: The Late Cretaceous Period. 2008. (Prehistoric Earth Ser.). (Illus.). 240p. (YA). (gr. 9-12). 35.00 *(978-0-8160-5962-1(4))* Facts On File, Inc.

—Paleontologists: Searching for Dinosaur Bones. 2015. (Extreme Science Careers Ser.). (ENG., Illus.). 128p. (J). (gr. 7-7). 37.27 *(978-0-7660-6964-0(8))* Enslow Pubs., Inc.

—The Prehistoric Earth Set, 10-Volumes. 2008. (Prehistoric Earth Ser.). (C). (gr. 9-18). 350.00 *(978-0-8160-7841-7(6),* Chelsea Hse.) Facts On File, Inc.

Holmes, Thom & Holmes, Laurie. Baby Dinosaurs: Eggs, Nests, & Recent Discoveries. Skrepnick, Michael William, illus. 2003. (Dinosaur Library). 104p. (J). (gr. 6-12). lib. bdg. 26.60 *(978-0-7660-2074-0(6))* Enslow Pubs., Inc.

—Great Dinosaur Expeditions & Discoveries: Adventures with the Fossil Hunters. Skrepnick, Michael William, illus. 2003. (Dinosaur Library). 112p. (J). lib. bdg. 26.60 *(978-0-7660-2078-8(9))* Enslow Pubs., Inc.

Holtz, Thomas R., Jr. Digging for Brachiosaurus: A Discovery Timeline. 2015. (Dinosaur Discovery Timelines Ser.). (ENG.). 32p. (gr. 4-5). lib. bdg. 27.99 *(978-1-4914-2123-9(1))* Capstone Press of Coughlan Cos.

—Digging for Stegosaurus: A Discovery Timeline. 2015. (Dinosaur Discovery Timelines Ser.). (ENG., Illus.). 32p. (gr. 4-5). pap. 7.95 *(978-1-4914-2365-3(X))* Capstone Press of Coughlan Cos.

—Digging for Triceratops: A Discovery Timeline. 2015. (Dinosaur Discovery Timelines Ser.). (ENG., Illus.). 32p. (gr. 4-5). pap. 7.95 *(978-1-4914-2367-7(6))* Capstone Press of Coughlan Cos.

—Digging for Tyrannosaurus Rex: A Discovery Timeline. 2015. (Dinosaur Discovery Timelines Ser.). (ENG.). 32p. (gr. 4-5). lib. bdg. 27.99 *(978-1-4914-2125-3(8))* Capstone Press of Coughlan Cos.

—Dinosaur Discovery Timelines. 2015. (Dinosaur Discovery Timelines Ser.). (ENG.). 32p. (gr. 4-5). lib. bdg. 111.96 *(978-1-4914-2605-0(5))* Capstone Press of Coughlan Cos.

Holtz, Thomas R. Dinosaurs: The Most Complete, Up-to-Date Encyclopedia for Dinosaur Lovers of All Ages. Rey, Luis V., illus. 2007. (ENG.). 432p. (J). (gr. 3-7). 39.99 *(978-0-375-82419-7(7),* Random Hse. Bks. for Young Readers) Random Hse. Children's Bks.

Holtz, Thomas R. & Random House Staff. T. Rex: Hunter or Scavenger? Skrepnick, Michael, illus. 2015. (Step into Reading Ser.). (ENG.). 48p. (J). (gr. 2-4). pap. 3.99 *(978-0-375-81297-2(0),* Random Hse. Bks. for Young Readers) Random Hse. Children's Bks.

Horner, Jack. Digging up Dinosaurs. Rath, Robert & Wilson, Phil, illus. 2007. 49p. (J). (gr. 3-7). pap. 14.95 *(978-1-56037-396-4(2))* Farcountry Pr.

Hughes, Catherine D. National Geographic Little Kids First Big Book of Dinosaurs. Tempesta, Franco, illus. 2011. (ENG.). 128p. (J). (gr. -1-3). lib. bdg. 21.90 *(978-1-4263-0847-5(7),* National Geographic Children's Bks.) National Geographic Society.

Hughes, Jon. What Happened to Dinosaurs? Hughes, Jon, illus. 2007. (Collins Big Cat Ser.). (ENG., Illus.). 32p. (J). (gr. 2-4). pap. 8.99 *(978-0-00-723084-6(2))* HarperCollins Pubs. Ltd. GBR. Dist: Independent Pubs. Group.

Hughes, Mónica. Fighting Dinosaurs. 2007. (I Love Reading Ser.). (Illus.). 24p. (J). (gr. -1-2). lib. bdg. 19.96 *(978-1-59716-545-7(X))* Bearport Publishing Co., Inc.

—Really Big Dinosaurs & Other Giants. 2007. (I Love Reading Ser.). (Illus.). 24p. (J). (gr. -1-2). lib. bdg. 19.96 *(978-1-59716-543-3(3))* Bearport Publishing Co., Inc.

Hutton, Simon. Brilliant Billy's Big Book of Dinosaurs. Glicksman, Caroline, illus. 2008. (ENG.). 80p. (J). (gr. 2-4). pap. 8.95 *(978-1-84270-569-8(5))* Andersen Pr. GBR. Dist: Independent Pubs. Group.

Hyde, Natalie. Dinosaur Fossils. 2013. (ENG., Illus.). 32p. (J). *(978-0-7787-1262-6(1));* pap. *(978-0-7787-1266-4(4))* Crabtree Publishing Co.

Ikids Staff. Soft Shapes: Dinosaurs (Baby's First Book + Puzzle) Ski, Jenn, illus. 2010. (ENG.). 8p. (J). (gr. -1 — 1). 10.99 *(978-1-60169-043-2(6))* Innovative Kids.

Institute for Creation Research Staff. Guide to Dinosaurs. 2015. (ENG.). 120p. (J). 16.99 *(978-0-7369-6667-2(6))* Harvest Hse. Pubs.

Jackson, Tom. Dangerous Dinosaurs. 2010. (Dangerous Animals Ser.). (ENG.). 32p. (J). (gr. 2-6). pap. 10.50 *(978-1-4339-4038-5(8),* Gareth Stevens Learning Library); (YA). (gr. 3-6). lib. bdg. 26.60 *(978-1-4339-4037-8(X))* Stevens, Gareth Publishing LLLP.

—The Magnificent Book of Dinosaurs & Other Prehistoric Creatures. Farkas, Rudolf, illus. 2017. (ENG.). 80p. (J). (gr. 2). 18.99 *(978-1-62686-743-7(7),* Silver Dolphin Bks.) Readerlink Distribution Services, LLC.

Jeffrey, Gary. Elasmosaurus: The Long-Necked Swimmer. Riley, Terry, illus. 2008. (Graphic Dinosaurs Ser.). (ENG.). 32p. (J). 50.50 *(978-1-61532-138-4(1),* PowerKids Pr.); (gr. 2-5). lib. bdg. 26.50 *(978-1-4358-2505-5(5))* Rosen Publishing Group, Inc., The.

—Stegosaurus: The Plated Dinosaur. Field, James, illus. (Graphic Dinosaurs Ser.). (ENG.). 32p. 2009. (gr. 2-5). pap. 12.30 *(978-1-4042-7713-7(7),* PowerKids Pr.) 2008. (J). 50.50 *(978-1-61532-136-0(5),* PowerKids Pr.) 2008. (J). (gr. 2-5). lib. bdg. 26.50 *(978-1-4358-2503-1(9))* Rosen Publishing Group, Inc., The.

Jeffries, Joyce. Dinosaur Birthday Party. 2014. (Dinosaur School Ser.). 24p. (J). (gr. -1-1). 22.60 *(978-1-4824-0741-9(8))* Stevens, Gareth Publishing LLLP.

—Dinosaur Holidays. 2014. (Dinosaur School Ser.). 24p. (J). (gr. -1-1). pap. 8.15 *(978-1-4824-0737-2(X))* Stevens, Gareth Publishing LLLP.

—Dinosaur School: Set 4. 2014. (Dinosaur School Ser.). 24p. (J). (gr. -1-1). 135.60 *(978-1-4824-0766-2(3))* Stevens, Gareth Publishing LLLP.

—Dinosaur School: Sets 1-4. 2014. (Dinosaur School Ser.). 24p. (J). (gr. -1-1). 542.40 *(978-1-4824-1173-7(3))* Stevens, Gareth Publishing LLLP.

—Dinosaurs in the Fall. 2014. (Dinosaur School Ser.). 24p. (J). (gr. -1-1). 22.60 *(978-1-4824-0710-5(8))* Stevens, Gareth Publishing LLLP.

—Dinosaurs in the Spring. 2014. (Dinosaur School Ser.). 24p. (J). (gr. -1-1). pap. 8.15 *(978-1-4824-0622-1(5))* Stevens, Gareth Publishing LLLP.

—Dinosaurs in the Summer. 2014. (Dinosaur School Ser.). 24p. (J). (gr. -1-1). 22.60 *(978-1-4824-0714-3(0))* Stevens, Gareth Publishing LLLP.

—Dinosaurs in the Winter. 2014. (Dinosaur School Ser.). 24p. (J). (gr. -1-1). 22.60 *(978-1-4824-0717-4(5))* Stevens, Gareth Publishing LLLP.

Jenkins, Steve. Prehistoric Actual Size. 2005. (ENG., Illus.). 36p. (J). (gr. 2-5). 17.99 *(978-0-618-53578-1(0))* Houghton Mifflin Harcourt Publishing Co.

Jennings, Ken. Dinosaurs. Lowery, Mike, illus. 2016. (Ken Jennings' Junior Genius Guides). (ENG.). 160p. (J). (gr. 3-5). pap. 7.99 *(978-1-4814-2955-9(8),* Little Simon) Little Simon.

Jeunesse, Gallimard, et al. Dinosaurs. Prunier, James & Galeron, Henri, illus. 2007. (First Discovery Book Ser.). (ENG.). 24p. (J). (gr. -1-k). pap. 5.99 *(978-0-439-91089-7(7))* Scholastic, Inc.

Jewitt, Kathryn & Dogi, Fiametta. 3D Theater: Dinosaurs. 2012. (3D Theater Ser.). (ENG., Illus.). 20p. (J). (gr. -1-3). 19.99 *(978-0-7534-6890-6(5),* 9780753468906, Kingfisher) Roaring Brook Pr.

Johnson, Jinny. Armored Dinosaurs. 2014. (Discovering Dinosaurs Ser.). (Illus.). 24p. (gr. 3-6). 28.50 *(978-1-62588-012-3(X))* Black Rabbit Bks.

—Armored Dinosaurs. 2015. (Discovering Dinosaurs Ser.). (ENG., Illus.). 24p. (J). pap. 8.95 *(978-1-77092-160-3(5))* RiverStream Publishing.

—Brachiosaurus & Other Dinosaur Giants. Rosewarne, Graham, illus. 2009. (Dinosaurs Alive! Ser.). 32p. (J). (gr. 4-7). pap. 7.95 *(978-1-59920-182-5(8))* Black Rabbit Bks.

—The Children's Dinosaur Encyclopedia. 2004. (Illus.). 96p. (J). *(978-0-681-02672-8(3))* Marshall Editions.

—Clash of the Dinos: Watch Dinosaurs Do Battle! 2014. (ENG., Illus.). 64p. (J). (gr. 3-6). pap. 9.95 *(978-1-77085-458-1(4),* 9781770854581) Firefly Bks., Ltd.

—Dino Wars: Discover the Deadliest Dinosaurs, Bloodiest Battles, & Super Survival Strategies of the Prehistoric World. 2005. (ENG., Illus.). 144p. (J). (gr. 1-7). 19.95 *(978-0-8109-5798-5(1),* Abrams Bks. for Young Readers) Abrams, Inc.

—Dinosaur Giants. 2014. (Discovering Dinosaurs Ser.). (Illus.). 24p. (gr. 3-6). 28.50 *(978-1-62588-013-0(8))* Black Rabbit Bks.

—Dinosaur Giants. 2015. (Discovering Dinosaurs Ser.). (ENG., Illus.). 24p. (J). pap. 8.95 *(978-1-77092-161-0(3))* RiverStream Publishing.

—Iguanodon & Other Plant-Eating Dinosaurs. Rosewarne, Graham, illus. (Dinosaurs Alive! Ser.). 32p. (J). (gr. 4-7). 2009. pap. 7.95 *(978-1-59920-184-9(4))* 2007. lib. bdg. 28.50 *(978-1-59920-067-5(8))* Black Rabbit Bks.

—Mighty Killers. 2014. (Discovering Dinosaurs Ser.). (Illus.). 24p. (gr. 3-6). 28.50 *(978-1-62588-015-4(4))* Black Rabbit Bks.

—Mighty Killers. 2015. (Discovering Dinosaurs Ser.). (ENG., Illus.). 24p. (J). pap. 8.95 *(978-1-77092-163-4(X))* RiverStream Publishing.

—Peaceful Plant Eaters. 2014. (Discovering Dinosaurs Ser.). (Illus.). 24p. (gr. 3-6). 28.50 *(978-1-62588-016-1(2))* Black Rabbit Bks.

—Peaceful Plant-Eaters. 2015. (Discovering Dinosaurs Ser.). (ENG., Illus.). 24p. (J). pap. 8.95 *(978-1-77092-164-1(8))* RiverStream Publishing.

—Speedy Dinosaurs. 2014. (Discovering Dinosaurs Ser.). (Illus.). 24p. (gr. 3-6). 28.50 *(978-1-62588-017-8(0))* Black Rabbit Bks.

—Speedy Hunters. 2015. (Discovering Dinosaurs Ser.). (ENG., Illus.). 24p. (J). pap. 8.95 *(978-1-77092-165-8(6))* RiverStream Publishing.

—Triceratops & Other Horned & Armored Dinosaurs. Rosewarne, Graham, illus. 2009. (Dinosaurs Alive! Ser.). 32p. (J). (gr. 4-7). pap. 7.95 *(978-1-59920-181-8(X))* Black Rabbit Bks.

—Triceratops & Other Horned & Armored Dinosaurs. Rosewarne, Graham, illus. 2007. (Dinosaurs Alive! Ser.). 32p. (J). (gr. -1-3). lib. bdg. 28.50 *(978-1-59920-064-4(3))* Black Rabbit Bks.

—Tyrannosaurus & Other Mighty Hunters. Rosewarne, Graham, illus. 2009. (Dinosaurs Alive! Ser.). 32p. (J). (gr. 4-7). pap. 7.95 *(978-1-59920-180-1(1))* Black Rabbit Bks.

—Velociraptor & Other Speedy Killers. Rosewarne, Graham, illus. (Dinosaurs Alive! Ser.). 32p. (J). (gr. 4-7). 2009. pap. 7.95 *(978-1-59920-183-2(6))* 2007. lib. bdg. 28.50 *(978-1-59920-066-8(X))* Black Rabbit Bks.

Johnson, Rebecca L., et al. Paul Sereno: Digging for Dinosaurs. 2007. (Reading Expeditions Ser.). (ENG., Illus.). 32p. (J). pap. 17.95 *(978-0-7922-8887-9(4))* CENGAGE Learning.

Josephs, Ben. Where Dinosaurs Walked, 6, Set. 2003. (Phonics Readers 1-36 Ser.). (ENG.). 8p. (gr. k-1). pap. 29.70 *(978-0-7368-3206-9(8),* Phonics Readers) Capstone Press of Coughlan Cos.

Judge, Lita. Born to Be Giants: How Baby Dinosaurs Grew to Rule the World. Judge, Lita, illus. 2010. (ENG., Illus.). 48p. (J). (gr. 1-4). 17.99 *(978-1-59643-443-1(0),* 9781596434431) Roaring Brook Pr.

—How Big Were Dinosaurs? Judge, Lita, illus. 2013. (ENG., Illus.). 40p. (J). (gr. 1-4). 18.99 *(978-1-59643-719-7(7),* 9781596437197) Roaring Brook Pr.

Kalman, Bobbie. What Are Dinosaurs? 2010. (My World Ser.). (ENG.). 24p. (J). (gr. k-3). *(978-0-7787-9514-8(4));* pap. *(978-0-7787-9539-1(X))* Crabtree Publishing Co.

Kanner, Robert. What Has a Pointed Head & Eats Lizards? Daff, Russ, illus. 2008. (J). *(978-1-59646-832-0(7))* Dingles & Co.

—What Has Armor & a Tail Club? Daff, Russ, illus. 2008. (J). *(978-1-59646-828-3(9))* Dingles & Co.

—What Weighs 70,000 Pounds & Swallows Stones? Daff, Russ, illus. 2008. (J). *(978-1-59646-840-5(8))* Dingles & Co.

Kavanagh, James. Dinosaurs Nature Activity Book. Leung, Raymond, illus. 2nd ed. 2011. (Nature Activity Book Ser.). (ENG.). 32p. (J). (gr. 4-7). 6.95 *(978-1-58355-578-1(1))* Western National Parks Assn.

Keiran, Monique. Pachyrhinosaurus: The Mystery of the Horned Dinosaur, 1 vol. 2006. (ENG., Illus.). 56p. (J). (gr. 4-7). 9.95 *(978-1-894974-03-5(4))* Heritage Hse. CAN. Dist: Orca Bk. Pubs. USA.

Kelly, Harold G. How the Dinosaurs Disappeared. (Reading Room Collection 1 Ser.). 16p. 2009. (gr. 2-3). 37.50 *(978-1-60851-945-3(7))* 2006. (Illus.). (J). (gr. 3-7). lib. bdg. 17.25 *(978-1-4042-3340-9(7))* Rosen Publishing Group, Inc., The. (PowerKids Pr.).

Kelsey-Livin, Barbara. The Mighty Beasts. 2011. 36p. pap. 24.95 *(978-1-4626-2249-8(6))* America Star Bks.

Kerley, Barbara. The Dinosaurs of Waterhouse Hawkins: An Illuminating History of Mr. Warehouse Hawkins, Artist & Lecturer. Selznick, Brian, illus. 2011. (J). (gr. 2-5). 29.95 *(978-0-545-19697-0(3));* 18.95 *(978-0-545-19703-8(1))* Weston Woods Studios, Inc.

Khan, Sarah. Dinosuar Quiz Cards. 2012. (Activity Cards Ser.). 50p. (J). 9.99 *(978-0-7945-3262-8(4),* Usborne) EDC Publishing.

Kim, F. S. Dig Deep! Looking for Dinosaurs. 2006. (Illus.). 32p. (J). pap. *(978-0-439-83877-1(0))* Scholastic, Inc.

Knight, Sheryn. Meet Diplodocus. 2014. (Age of Dinosaurs Ser.). 32p. (J). (gr. 3-5). lib. bdg. 28.50 *(978-1-62712-782-0(8))* Cavendish Square Publishing.

—Meet Scipionyx. 2014. (Age of Dinosaurs Ser.). 32p. (J). (gr. 3-5). lib. bdg. 28.50 *(978-1-62712-791-2(7))* Cavendish Square Publishing.

Kolpin, Molly. Velociraptor: Clawed Hunter, 1 vol. Dove, Jason, illus. 2012. (First Graphics: Dinosaurs Ser.). (ENG.). 24p. (gr. 1-2). lib. bdg. 23.99 *(978-1-4296-7603-8(5))* Capstone Press of Coughlan Cos.

—Velociraptor: Clawed Hunter. Dove, Jason, illus. 2012. (First Graphics: Dinosaurs Ser.). (ENG.). 24p. (gr. 1-2). pap. 35.70 *(978-1-4296-8367-8(8))* Capstone Press of Coughlan Cos.

Korb, Rena. Discovering Giganotosaurus, 1 vol. Dawson, Ted, illus. 2008. (Dinosaur Digs Ser.). (ENG.). 32p. (gr. -1-5). 28.50 *(978-1-60270-106-9(7),* Looking Glass Library- Nonfiction) Magic Wagon.

—Discovering Ichthyosaurs, 1 vol. Dawson, Ted, illus. 2008. (Dinosaur Digs Ser.). (ENG.). 32p. (gr. -1-5). 28.50 *(978-1-60270-107-6(5),* Looking Glass Library- Nonfiction) Magic Wagon.

Korb, Rena B. Discovering Brachiosaurus, 1 vol. Dawson, Ted, illus. 2008. (Dinosaur Digs Ser.). (ENG.). 32p. (gr. -1-4). 28.50 *(978-1-60270-105-2(9),* Looking Glass Library- Nonfiction) Magic Wagon.

—Discovering Tyrannosaurus Rex, 1 vol. Dawson, Ted, illus. 2008. (Dinosaur Digs Ser.). (ENG.). 32p. (gr. -1-4). 28.50 *(978-1-60270-109-0(1),* Looking Glass Library- Nonfiction) Magic Wagon.

—Discovering Velociraptor, 1 vol. Dawson, Ted, illus. 2008. (Dinosaur Digs Ser.). (ENG.). 32p. (gr. -1-4). 28.50 *(978-1-60270-110-6(5),* Looking Glass Library- Nonfiction) Magic Wagon.

Korpella, Bob. Dinosaur Dictionary for Kids: The Everything Guide for Kids Who Love Dinosaurs. 2016. (ENG., Illus.). 200p. (J). (gr. 4-7). 13.95 *(978-1-61821-513-0(2))* Prufrock Pr.

Kosara, Tori. Big Dinosaurs. 2011. 28p. pap. *(978-0-545-37956-4(3))* Scholastic, Inc.

Kranking, Kathy. Gone! Dino Extinction. 2006. (Illus.). 32p. (J). pap. *(978-0-439-83878-8(9))* Scholastic, Inc.

Kranz, Peter M. Dinosaurs of the District of Columbia. 2003. (Illus.). vii, 31p. per. 14.95 *(978-0-9748618-0-7(4))* Dinosaur Fund.

Kricher, John C. Dinosaurs. Morrison, Gordon, illus. 2nd ed. 2013. (Peterson Field Guide Color-In Bks.). (ENG.). 64p. (J). 8.95 *(978-0-544-03255-2(1))* Houghton Mifflin Harcourt Publishing Co.

Krieger, Emily. National Geographic Kids Funny Fill-In: My Dinosaur Adventure. Sipple, Dan, illus. 2014. (ENG.). 48p. (J). (gr. 3-7). pap. 4.99 *(978-1-4263-1481-0(7),* National Geographic Children's Bks.) National Geographic Society.

Kudlinski, Kathleen V. Boy, Were We Wrong about Dinosaurs! Schindler, S. D., illus. (ENG.). 32p. (J). (gr. 1-3). 2008. pap. 6.99 *(978-0-14-241193-3(0),* Puffin Books) 2005. 16.99 *(978-0-525-46978-0(8),* Dutton Books for Young Readers) Penguin Young Readers Group.

Kurtz, Jane. Mister Bones: Dinosaur Hunter. Haverfield, Mary, illus. 2004. (Ready-To-Reads Ser.). (ENG.). 32p. (J). (gr. -1-1). pap. 3.99 *(978-0-689-85960-1(0),* Simon Spotlight) Simon Spotlight.

Lagonegro, Melissa & Wooster, Devin Ann. Big Dinosaur, Little Dinosaur. Random House Disney Staff, illus. 2016. (Step into Reading Ser.). (ENG.). 24p. (J). (gr. -1-1). 4.99 *(978-0-7364-3247-4(7),* RH/Disney) Random Hse. Children's Bks.

Lambert, David. Dinosaur. 2014. (DK Eyewitness Bks.). (ENG.). 72p. (J). (gr. 3-7). pap. 9.99 *(978-1-4654-2266-8(8),* DK Children) Dorling Kindersley Publishing, Inc.

Lambert, Nat. How to Draw Dinosaurs & Other Cool Stuff! Green, Barry, illus. 2015. (404 Things to Draw Ser.). (ENG.). 192p. (J). (gr. k). pap. 12.99 *(978-1-78445-274-2(2))* Top That! Publishing PLC GBR. Dist: Independent Pubs. Group.

Landau, Elaine. Tyrannosaurus Rex. Landau, Elaine, illus. rev. ed. 2007. (True Bks.). (ENG., Illus.). 48p. (J). (gr. 3-5). pap. 6.95 *(978-0-531-15472-4(6),* Children's Pr.) Scholastic Library Publishing.

—Velociraptor. Landau, Elaine, illus. rev. ed. 2007. (True Bks.). (ENG., Illus.). 48p. (J). (gr. 3-5). pap. 6.95 *(978-0-531-15473-1(4),* Children's Pr.) Scholastic Library Publishing.

Larousse Mexico Staff, ed. De Los Dinosaurios. 2008. (ENG & SPA., Illus.). 160p. 19.95 *(978-970-22-1507-3(2))* Larousse, Ediciones, S. A. de C. V. MEX. Dist: Houghton Mifflin Harcourt Publishing Co.

Lawson, Jim. Jim Lawson's Dinosaurs Coloring Book. 2016. (ENG.). 32p. (J). (gr. 2-5). pap. 3.99 *(978-0-486-80503-0(4))* Dover Pubns., Inc.

Leblanc, Catherine. How to Demolish Dinosaurs. Garrigue, Roland, illus. 2013. (ENG.). 32p. (J). (gr. -1). 14.99 *(978-1-60887-191-9(6))* Insight Editions.

Lee, Brian, illus. The World of Dinosaurs. 2005. (J). *(978-0-7607-6569-2(3))* backpackbook.

Lee, Cory. Velociraptor. 2015. (Look at Dinosaurs Ser.). (ENG.). 24p. (J). (gr. 1-2). 22.60 *(978-1-4824-1838-5(X))* Stevens, Gareth Publishing LLLP.

Lee, Sally. Allosaurus. 2015. (Little Paleontologist Ser.). (ENG.). 32p. (gr. 1-3). lib. bdg. 27.99 *(978-1-4914-2127-7(4))* Capstone Press of Coughlan Cos.

—Ankylosaurus, 1 vol. 2014. (Little Paleontologist Ser.). (ENG.). 32p. (gr. 1-3). lib. bdg. 27.99 *(978-1-4914-0808-7(1))* Capstone Press of Coughlan Cos.

—Apatosaurus. 2015. (Little Paleontologist Ser.). (ENG.). 32p. (gr. 1-3). lib. bdg. 27.99 *(978-1-4914-2128-4(2))* Capstone Press of Coughlan Cos.

—Diplodocus, 1 vol. 2014. (Little Paleontologist Ser.). (ENG.). 32p. (gr. 1-3). lib. bdg. 27.99 *(978-1-4914-0809-4(X))* Capstone Press of Coughlan Cos.

—Iguanodon. 2015. (Little Paleontologist Ser.). (ENG.). 32p. (gr. 1-3). lib. bdg. 27.99 *(978-1-4914-2129-1(0))* Capstone Press of Coughlan Cos.

—Little Paleontologist. 2015. (Little Paleontologist Ser.). (ENG.). 32p. (gr. 1-3). lib. bdg. 111.96 *(978-1-4914-2617-3(9))* Capstone Press of Coughlan Cos.

—Megalosaurus. 2015. (Little Paleontologist Ser.). (ENG.). 32p. (gr. 1-3). lib. bdg. 27.99 *(978-1-4914-2130-7(4))* Capstone Press of Coughlan Cos.

Leigh, Susannah. Puzzle Dinosaurs. Tyler, Jenny, ed. Haw, Brenda, illus. 2007. (Young Puzzles Ser.). 32p. (J). pap. 6.99 *(978-0-7945-1778-6(1),* Usborne) EDC Publishing.

Lennie, Charles. Apatosaurus, 1 vol. 2014. (Dinosaurs Ser.). (ENG.). 24p. (J). (gr. 4-8). lib. bdg. 28.50 *(978-1-62970-022-9(3))* ABDO Publishing Co.

—Pteranadon, 1 vol. 2014. (Dinosaurs Ser.). (ENG.). 24p. (J). (gr. 4-8). lib. bdg. 28.50 *(978-1-62970-023-6(1))* ABDO Publishing Co.

—Stegosaurus, 1 vol. 2014. (Dinosaurs Ser.). (ENG.). 24p. (J). (gr. 4-8). lib. bdg. 28.50 *(978-1-62970-024-3(X))* ABDO Publishing Co.

—Triceratops, 1 vol. 2014. (Dinosaurs Ser.). (ENG.). 24p. (J). (gr. 4-8). lib. bdg. 28.50 *(978-1-62970-025-0(8))* ABDO Publishing Co.

—Tyrannosaurus Rex, 1 vol. 2014. (Dinosaurs Ser.). (ENG.). 24p. (J). (gr. 4-8). lib. bdg. 28.50 *(978-1-62970-026-7(6))* ABDO Publishing Co.

—Velociraptor, 1 vol. 2014. (Dinosaurs Ser.). (ENG.). 24p. (J). (gr. 4-8). lib. bdg. 28.50 *(978-1-62970-027-4(4))* ABDO Publishing Co.

—Velociraptor. 2015. (Dinosaurios Ser.). (SPA., Illus.). 24p. (gr. k-1). pap. 7.95 *(978-1-4966-0439-2(3))* Capstone Classroom.

Lennie, Charles, et al. Apatosaurus. 2015. (Dinosaurios Ser.). (SPA., Illus.). 24p. (gr. k-1). pap. 7.95 *(978-1-4966-0429-3(6))* Capstone Classroom.

—Pteranodon. 2015. (Dinosaurios Ser.). (SPA., Illus.). 24p. (gr. k-1). pap. 7.95 *(978-1-4966-0431-6(8))* Capstone Classroom.

—Stegosaurus. 2015. (Dinosaurios Ser.). (SPA., Illus.). 24p. (gr. k-1). pap. 7.95 *(978-1-4966-0433-0(4))* Capstone Classroom.

—Tiranosaurio Rex. 2015. (Dinosaurios Ser.). (SPA., Illus.). 24p. (gr. k-1). pap. 7.95 *(978-1-4966-0435-4(0))* Capstone Classroom.

—Velociraptor. 2015. (Dinosaurios Ser.). (SPA., Illus.). 24p. (gr. k-1). pap. 7.95 *(978-1-4966-0437-8(7))* Capstone Classroom.

Lessem, Don. Armored Dinosaurs. Bindon, John, illus. 2004. (Meet the Dinosaurs Ser.). 32p. (gr. 2-5). (J). per. 6.95 *(978-0-8225-2570-7(4));* (ENG.). lib. bdg. 23.93 *(978-0-8225-1374-2(9))* Lerner Publishing Group.

—Carnivoros Gigantes. Bindon, John, illus. 2005.Tr. of Giant Meat-Eating Dinosaurs. (SPA.). 32p. (J). (gr. 2-4). pap. 6.95 *(978-0-8225-2963-7(7))* Lerner Publishing Group.

—Carnivoros Gigantes. Translations.com Staff, tr. from ENG. Bindon, John, illus. 2005. (Conoce A Los Dinosaurios (Meet the Dinosaurs) Ser.).Tr. of Giant Meat-Eating Dinosaurs. (SPA.). 32p. (gr. 2-4). lib. bdg. 23.93 *(978-0-8225-2962-0(9))* Lerner Publishing Group.

—The Deadliest Dinosaurs. Bindon, John, illus. (Meet the Dinosaurs Ser.). 32p. (gr. 2-4). 2005. (ENG.). lib. bdg. 23.93 *(978-0-8225-1421-3(4))* 2004. (J). per. 6.95 *(978-0-8225-2619-3(0))* Lerner Publishing Group.

—Dinosaurios Acorazados. Bindon, John, illus. 2005. (Meet the Dinosaurs Ser.).Tr. of Armored Dinosaurs. (SPA.). 32p. (J). (gr. 2-4). per. 6.95 *(978-0-8225-2958-3(0))* Lerner Publishing Group.

—Dinosaurios Acorazados. Translations.com Staff, tr. Bindon, John, illus. 2005. (Conoce A Los Dinosaurios (Meet the Dinosaurs) Ser.).Tr. of Armored Dinosaurs. (SPA.). 32p. (gr. 2-4). lib. bdg. 23.93 *(978-0-8225-2949-1(1))* Lerner Publishing Group.

—Dinosaurios Con Plumas. Translations.com Staff, tr. from ENG. Bindon, John, illus. 2006. (Conoce A Los Dinosaurios (Meet the Dinosaurs) Ser.).Tr. of Feathered Dinosaurs. (SPA.). 32p. (gr. 2-4). lib. bdg. 23.93 *(978-0-8225-6242-9(1))* Lerner Publishing Group.

—Dinosaurios Cornudos. Bindon, John, illus. 2005. (Meet the Dinosaurs Ser.).Tr. of Horned Dinosaurs. (SPA.). 32p. (J). (gr. 2-4). per. 6.95 *(978-0-8225-2967-5(X));* (gr. 3-7). lib. bdg. 23.93 *(978-0-8225-2966-8(1),* Ediciones Lerner) Lerner Publishing Group.

—Los Dinosaurios Mas Mortiferos. Bindon, John, illus. 2006. (Conoce A los Dinosaurios Ser.). 32p. (J). (gr. 3-7). lib. bdg. 23.93 *(978-0-8225-6240-5(5),* Ediciones Lerner) Lerner Publishing Group.

—Los Dinosaurios Mas Pequenos. Bindon, John, illus. 2005. (Meet the Dinosaurs Ser.).Tr. of Smallest Dinosaurs. (SPA.). 32p. (J). (gr. 2-4). per. 6.95 *(978-0-8225-2969-9(6))* Lerner Publishing Group.

—Los Dinosaurios Mas Rapidos. Translations.com Staff, tr. from ENG. Bindon, John, illus. 2006. (Conoce A Los Dinosaurios (Meet the Dinosaurs) Ser.). (SPA.). 32p. (gr. 2-4). lib. bdg. 23.93 *(978-0-8225-6241-2(3))* Lerner Publishing Group.

—Dinosaurios Pico de Pato. Bindon, John, illus. 2005. (Meet the Dinosaurs Ser.).Tr. of Duck-Billed Dinosaurs. (SPA.). 32p. (J). (gr. 2-4). per. 6.95 *(978-0-8225-2961-3(0))* Lerner Publishing Group.

—Dinosaurios Pico de Pato. Translations.com Staff, tr. Bindon, John, illus. 2005. (Conoce A Los Dinosaurios (Meet the Dinosaurs) Ser.).Tr. of Duck-Billed Dinosaurs. (SPA.). 32p. (gr. 2-4). lib. bdg. 23.93 *(978-0-8225-2959-0(9))* Lerner Publishing Group.

—Dinosaurs. 2005. (Time for Learning Ser.). (Illus.). 96p. 12.98 *(978-0-7853-8504-2(5),* 7190500) Publications International, Ltd.

—Duck-Billed Dinosaurs. Bindon, John, illus. (Meet the Dinosaurs Ser.). 32p. (J). 2005. (gr. 2-5). per. 6.95 *(978-0-8225-2571-4(2))* 2004. (gr. 3-7). lib. bdg. 23.93 *(978-0-8225-1369-8(2))* Lerner Publishing Group.

C D

—The Fastest Dinosaurs. Bindon, John, illus. 2005. 32p. (gr. 2-4). (J). pap. 6.95 (978-0-8225-2620-9(4)); (ENG.). lib. bdg. 23.93 (978-0-8225-1422-0(2)) Lerner Publishing Group.

—Feathered Dinosaurs. 2005. (Meet the Dinosaurs Ser.). (Illus.). 32p. (J). (gr. 3-7). lib. bdg. 23.93 (978-0-8225-1423-7(0)) Lerner Publishing Group.

—Feathered Dinosaurs. Bindon, John, illus. 2005. 32p. (J). (gr. 2-4). pap. 6.95 (978-0-8225-2621-6(2)) Lerner Publishing Group.

—Giant Meat-Eating Dinosaurs. Bindon, John, illus. 2004. (Meet the Dinosaurs Ser.). (J). 32p. (gr. 4-7). lib. bdg. 23.93 (978-0-8225-3925-4(X)); pap. 7.95 (978-0-8225-5326-7(0), Lerner Pubns.) Lerner Publishing Group.

—Giant Plant-Eating Dinosaurs. Bindon, John, illus. 2004. (Meet the Dinosaurs Ser.). 32p. (J). (gr. 3-7). lib. bdg. 23.93 (978-0-8225-1371-1(4)) Lerner Publishing Group.

—Gigantes Marinos de la Época de los Dinosaurios. Translations.com Staff, tr. from ENG. Bindon, John, illus. 2006. (Conoce A Los Dinosaurios (Meet the Dinosaurs) Ser.). (SPA.). 32p. (gr. 2-4). lib. bdg. 23.93 (978-0-8225-6244-3(8)) Lerner Publishing Group.

—Gigantes Voladores de la Epoca de los Dinosaurios. Translations.com Staff, tr. from ENG. Bindon, John, illus. 2006. (Conoce A Los Dinosaurios (Meet the Dinosaurs) Ser.).Tr. of Flying Giants of Dinosaur Time. (SPA.). 32p. (gr. 2-4). lib. bdg. 23.93 (978-0-8225-6243-6(X)) Lerner Publishing Group.

—Herbivoros Gigantes. Bindon, John, illus. 2005. (Meet the Dinosaurs Ser.).Tr. of Giant Plant-Eating Dinosaurs. (SPA.). 32p. (J). (gr. 2-4). per. 6.95 (978-0-8225-2965-1(3)) Lerner Publishing Group.

—Herbívoros Gigantes. Translations.com Staff, tr. Bindon, John, illus. 2005. (Conoce A Los Dinosaurios (Meet the Dinosaurs) Ser.). (SPA.). 32p. (gr. 2-4). lib. bdg. 23.93 (978-0-8225-2964-4(5)) Lerner Publishing Group.

—Horned Dinosaurs. Bindon, John, illus. (Meet the Dinosaurs Ser.). 32p. (gr. 2-5). 2005. (J). per. 6.95 (978-0-8225-2574-5(7)) 2004. (ENG.). lib. bdg. 23.93 (978-0-8225-1370-4(6)) Lerner Publishing Group.

—Los Dinosaurios Más Inteligentes. Translations.com Staff, tr. from ENG. Bindon, John, illus. 2006. (Conoce A Los Dinosaurios (Meet the Dinosaurs) Ser.). (SPA.). 32p. (gr. 2-4). lib. bdg. 23.93 (978-0-8225-6245-0(6)) Lerner Publishing Group.

—Los Dinosaurios Más Pequeños. Translations.com Staff, tr. Bindon, John, illus. 2005. (Conoce A Los Dinosaurios (Meet the Dinosaurs) Ser.).Tr. of Smallest Dinosaurs. (SPA.). 32p. (gr. 2-4). lib. bdg. 23.93 (978-0-8225-2968-2(8)) Lerner Publishing Group.

—National Geographic Kids Ultimate Dinopedia: The Most Complete Dinosaur Reference Ever. Tempesta, Franco, illus. 2010. (ENG.). 272p. (J). (gr. 2-5). 24.95 (978-1-4263-0164-3(2)); lib. bdg. 34.90 (978-1-4263-0165-0(0)) National Geographic Society. (National Geographic Children's Bks.).

—The Smallest Dinosaurs. Bindon, John, illus. 2004. (Meet the Dinosaurs Ser.). 32p. (J). (gr. -1-3). lib. bdg. 23.93 (978-0-8225-1372-8(2)); (gr. 2-5). per. 6.95 (978-0-8225-2575-2(5)) Lerner Publishing Group.

—The Smartest Dinosaurs. Bindon, John, illus. (Meet the Dinosaurs Ser.). 32p. (gr. 2-4). 2005. (ENG.). lib. bdg. 23.93 (978-0-8225-1373-5(0)) 2004. (J). pap. 6.95 (978-0-8225-2618-6(2)) Lerner Publishing Group.

Levy, Barbara Soloff. Dinosaurs Dot-to-Dot. 2006. (Dover Children's Activity Bks.). (ENG., Illus.). 32p. (J). (gr. -1-2). pap. 3.99 (978-0-486-45320-0(0)) Dover Pubns., Inc.

Lewis, Brenda Ralph. Meat-Eating Dinosaurs. 2006. (Nature's Monsters Ser.). (Illus.). 32p. (gr. 2-6). lib. bdg. 26.00 (978-0-8368-6843-2(9), Gareth Stevens Learning Library) Stevens, Gareth Publishing LLLP.

—Plant-Eating Dinosaurs. 2006. (Nature's Monsters Ser.). (Illus.). 32p. (gr. 2-6). lib. bdg. 26.00 (978-0-8368-6844-9(7), Gareth Stevens Learning Library) Stevens, Gareth Publishing LLLP.

—Small & Deadly Dinosaurs. 2006. (Nature's Monsters Ser.). (Illus.). 32p. (gr. 2-6). lib. bdg. 26.00 (978-0-8368-6846-3(3), Gareth Stevens Learning Library) Stevens, Gareth Publishing LLLP.

Li, Maggie. Dinosaur Detective. 2017. (ENG., Illus.). 32p. (J). (gr. k-3). 13.99 **(978-1-84365-307-3(9)**, Pavilion) Pavilion Bks. GBR. Dist: Independent Pubs. Group.

Lietha, Dan, et al, illus. Dinosaur Pak & Stak. 2007. (J). 10.99 (978-0-89051-486-3(0)) Master Bks.

Lindeen, Carol K. Velociraptor [Scholastic]. Hughes, Jon, illus. 2009. (Dinosaurs & Prehistoric Animals Ser.). 24p. (gr. k-1). pap. 1.00 (978-1-4296-4247-7(5), Pebble Plus) Capstone Press of Coughlan Cos.

Litchfield, J. & Brooks, F. Dinosaurs. 2004. (Illus.). 10p. (J). 4.95 (978-0-7945-0590-5(2)) EDC Publishing.

Little & Large Sticker Activity Dinosaurs. 2008. 24p. pap. (978-1-84810-058-9(2)) Miles Kelly Publishing, Ltd.

Little Children's Dinosaur Activity Book. 2017. (Activity Books for Little Children Ser.). (ENG.). (J). pap. 9.99 **(978-0-7945-3796-8(0)**, Usborne) EDC Publishing.

Litton, Jonathan. Noisy Dinosaurs. 2015. (My First Ser.). (ENG.). 12p. (J). (gr. -1-3). bds. 12.99 (978-1-58925-207-3(1)) Tiger Tales.

Living with the Dinosaurs. 2016. (Living with the Dinosaurs Ser.). 00024p. (J). pap. 48.90 **(978-1-4824-5834-3(9))** Stevens, Gareth Publishing LLLP.

Ljung, Kiki. Build A... T-Rex. 2017. (Build A... Ser.). (ENG.). 12p. (J). (gr. k-3). bds. 12.99 **(978-1-84780-923-0(5)**, Frances Lincoln Children's Bks.) Quarto Publishing Group UK GBR. Dist: Hachette Bk. Group.

Lonely Planet Publications Staff. How to Be a Dinosaur Hunter, 1 vol. 2013. (Lonely Planet Kids Ser.). (ENG., Illus.). 160p. (J). 17.99 (978-1-74321-908-9(3), 4620) Lonely Planet Pubns.

Long, John. Dinosaurs. 2007. (Insiders Ser.). (ENG., Illus.). 64p. (J). (gr. 3-7). 17.99 (978-1-4169-3857-6(5), Simon & Schuster Bks. For Young Readers) Simon & Schuster Bks. For Young Readers.

Long, John, ed. Dinosaurs. 2007. (Little Guides). (Illus.). 320p. pap. 7.98 (978-1-74089-347-3(6)) Fog City Pr.

Long, Olivia. There's a Dinosaur in My Bathtub! Long, Olivia, illus. Date not set. (World of Dinosaurs Ser.). (Illus.). 32p. (J). (gr. -1-4). (978-1-880042-11-3(8)) Shelf-Life Bks.

A Look at Dinosaurs. 2015. (Look at Dinosaurs Ser.). (ENG.). 24p. (J). (gr. 1-2). 135.60 (978-1-4824-1633-6(6)) Stevens, Gareth Publishing LLLP.

Lorini, Andrea. Diplodocus. 2015. (Mini Dinosaurs Ser.). (ENG., Illus.). 10p. (J). (gr. -1-k). bds. 6.99 (978-0-7641-6804-8(5)) Barron's Educational Series, Inc.

—Stegosaurus. 2015. (Mini Dinosaurs Ser.). (ENG., Illus.). 10p. (J). (gr. -1-k). bds. 6.99 (978-0-7641-6805-5(3)) Barron's Educational Series, Inc.

—T-Rex. 2015. (Mini Dinosaurs Ser.). (ENG., Illus.). 10p. (J). (gr. -1-k). bds. 6.99 (978-0-7641-6807-9(X)) Barron's Educational Series, Inc.

—Triceratops. 2015. (Mini Dinosaurs Ser.). (ENG., Illus.). 10p. (J). (gr. -1-k). bds. 6.99 (978-0-7641-6806-2(1)) Barron's Educational Series, Inc.

Loxton, Daniel. Ankylosaur Attack. Loxton, Daniel & Smith, Jim W. W., illus. 2011. (Tales of Prehistoric Life Ser.). (ENG.). 32p. (J). (gr. -1-2). 16.95 (978-1-55453-631-3(6)) Kids Can Pr., Ltd. CAN. Dist: Hachette Bk. Group.

—Pterosaur Trouble. Loxton, Daniel & Smith, Jim W. W., illus. 2013. (Tales of Prehistoric Life Ser.). (ENG.). 32p. (J). (gr. -1-2). 16.95 (978-1-55453-632-0(4)) Kids Can Pr., Ltd. CAN. Dist: Hachette Bk. Group.

Lunis, Natalie. Pet-Sized Dinos. 2008. (Dino Times Trivia Ser.). (Illus.). 24p. (J). (gr. k-3). lib. bdg. 21.28 (978-1-59716-710-9(X)) Bearport Publishing Co., Inc.

—A T. Rex Named Sue: Sue Hendrickson's Huge Discovery. 2006. (Fossil Hunters Ser.). (Illus.). 32p. (YA). (gr. 2-5). lib. bdg. 25.27 (978-1-59716-259-3(0)) Bearport Publishing Co., Inc.

—The Tiny Titanosaurs: Luis Chiappe's Dinosaur Nests. 2007. (Fossil Hunters Ser.). (Illus.). 32p. (YA). (gr. 2-5). lib. bdg. 25.27 (978-1-59716-373-6(2)) Bearport Publishing Co., Inc.

Lunis, Natalie & Sereno, Paul C. Supercroc: Paul Sereno's Dinosaur Eater. 2006. (Fossil Hunters Ser.). (Illus.). 32p. (YA). (gr. 2-5). lib. bdg. 25.27 (978-1-59716-255-5(8)) Bearport Publishing Co., Inc.

Lunis, Natalie & White, Nancy. Savage Slashers. 2008. (Dino Times Trivia Ser.). (Illus.). 24p. (J). (gr. k-3). lib. bdg. 21.28 (978-1-59716-709-3(6), 1284322) Bearport Publishing Co., Inc.

Maccarone, Grace & Lo, Erika. Dinosaurs: 4 Favorite Stories! 2007. (Scholastic Reader Level 1 Ser.). (ENG.). 144p. (J). (gr. -1-3). 6.99 (978-0-439-93251-6(3)) Scholastic, Inc.

MacDonald, Suse. Dino Shapes. MacDonald, Suse, illus. 2014. (ENG., Illus.). 20p. (J). (gr. -1-2). bds. 7.99 (978-1-4814-0093-0(2), Little Simon) Little Simon.

Machell, Dawn, illus. Super Sticker Activity: Dinos. 2016. (ENG.). 32p. (J). (gr. -1). 5.99 (978-1-62686-649-2(X), Silver Dolphin Bks.) Readerlink Distribution Services, LLC.

MacLeod, Elizabeth. Monster Fliers: From the Time of the Dinosaurs. Bindon, John, illus. 2010. (ENG.). 32p. (J). (gr. k-4). 16.95 (978-1-55453-199-8(3)) Kids Can Pr., Ltd. CAN. Dist: Hachette Bk. Group.

Malam, John. Dinosaur Ultimate Sticker Book. 2004. (J). 5.99 (978-0-7566-0402-8(8)) Dorling Kindersley Publishing, Inc.

Malam, John & Parker, Steve. Encyclopedia of Dinosaurs: And Other Prehistoric Creatures. 2003. (Illus.). 256p. (J). 12.98 (978-1-4054-0944-5(4)) Parragon, Inc.

Malam, John, et al. Children's Dinosaur Encyclopedia. 2010. (Illus.). 256p. (978-1-4075-8780-6(3)) Barnes & Noble, Inc.

—Dinosaur Atlas. Hughes, Jon, illus. 2006. (ENG.). 96p. (J). (gr. 5-12). 21.99 (978-0-7566-2235-0(2), DK Children) Dorling Kindersley Publishing, Inc.

Malm, John, et al. Atlas de Dinosaurios: Dinosaur Atlas. 2007. (Illus.). 96p. (J). (978-970-718-509-8(0), Silver Dolphin en Español) Advanced Marketing, S. de R. L. de C. V.

Manning, Mick & Granström, Brita. Dino-Dinners. 2007. (ENG., Illus.). 32p. (J). (gr. 3-7). 16.95 (978-0-8234-2089-6(2)) Holiday Hse., Inc.

—Dino-Dinners. Manning, Mick & Granström, Brita, illus. 2015. (ENG., Illus.). 32p. (J). (gr. -1-1). pap. 9.99 (978-1-84780-665-9(1), Frances Lincoln) Quarto Publishing Group UK GBR. Dist: Hachette Bk. Group.

Mara, Wil. Apatosaurus. 2012. (Rookie Read-About(tm) Dinosaurs Ser.). (ENG., Illus.). 32p. (J). lib. bdg. 25.00 (978-0-531-20865-6(6)); pap. 5.95 (978-0-531-20934-9(2)) Scholastic Library Publishing. (Children's Pr.).

—Oviraptor. 2012. (Rookie Read-About(tm) Dinosaurs Ser.). (ENG., Illus.). 32p. (J). lib. bdg. 25.00 (978-0-531-20863-2(X), Children's Pr.) Scholastic Library Publishing.

—Oviraptors. 2012. (Rookie Read-about Ser.). (ENG., Illus.). 32p. (J). pap. 5.95 (978-0-531-20932-5(6), Children's Pr.) Scholastic Library Publishing.

—Stegosaurus. 2012. (Rookie Read-About(tm) Dinosaurs Ser.). (ENG., Illus.). 32p. (J). lib. bdg. 25.00 (978-0-531-20860-1(5)); pap. 5.95 (978-0-531-20929-5(6)) Scholastic Library Publishing. (Children's Pr.).

—Triceratops. 2012. (Rookie Read-About(tm) Dinosaurs Ser.). (ENG., Illus.). 32p. (J). lib. bdg. 25.00 (978-0-531-20862-5(1)); pap. 5.95 (978-0-531-20931-8(8)) Scholastic Library Publishing. (Children's Pr.).

—Tyrannosaurus Rex. 2012. (Rookie Read-About(tm) Dinosaurs Ser.). (ENG., Illus.). 32p. (J). lib. bdg. 25.00 (978-0-531-20861-8(3)); pap. 5.95 (978-0-531-20930-1(X)) Scholastic Library Publishing. (Children's Pr.).

—Velociraptors. 2012. (Rookie Read-About(tm) Dinosaurs Ser.). (ENG., Illus.). 32p. (J). lib. bdg. 25.00 (978-0-531-20864-9(8)); pap. 5.95 (978-0-531-20933-2(4)) Scholastic Library Publishing. (Children's Pr.).

Markle, Sandra. Outside & Inside Dinosaurs. 2003. (ENG., Illus.). 40p. (J). (gr. k-4). 9.99 (978-0-689-85778-2(0), Aladdin) Simon & Schuster Children's Publishing.

Martin, Justin McCory. Dinosaurs. Gunson, Dave, illus. 2008. 32p. (978-0-545-08456-7(3)) Scholastic, Inc.

Marven, Nigel, told to. Prehistoric Park. 2007. (Illus.). 48p. (J). pap. 6.99 (978-0-696-23691-4(5)) Meredith Bks.

Marzollo, Jean & Wick, Walter. I Spy a Dinosaur's Eye. 2003. (I Spy — Scholastic Readers Level 1 Ser.). (gr. -1-2). lib. bdg. 13.55 (978-0-613-72243-8(4), Turtleback) Turtleback Bks.

Masiello, Ralph. Ralph Masiello's Dinosaur Drawing Book. Masiello, Ralph, illus. 2005. (ENG., Illus.). 48p. (J). (gr. k-3). per. 7.95 (978-1-57091-528-4(8)) Charlesbridge Publishing, Inc.

Mason, Conrad. Dinosaurs IR. 2010. (First Reading Level 2 Ser.). 48p. (J). 6.99 (978-0-7945-2730-3(2), Usborne) EDC Publishing.

Mattern, Joanne. Allosaurus. Mangiat, Jeffrey, illus. 2009. (Let's Read about Dinosaurs Ser.). 24p. (J). (gr. -1-3). lib. bdg. 22.00 (978-0-8368-9414-1(6), Weekly Reader Leveled Readers) Stevens, Gareth Publishing LLLP.

—Allosaurus. Magniat, Jeffrey, illus. 2009. (Let's Read about Dinosaurs Ser.). 24p. (gr. -1-3). pap. 8.15 (978-0-8368-9418-9(9), Weekly Reader Leveled Readers) Stevens, Gareth Publishing LLLP.

—Allosaurus; Alosaurio. 2009. (Let's Read about Dinosaurs;Conozcamos a los dinosaurios Ser.). (SPA & ENG.). 24p. (J). (gr. -1-3). pap. 8.15 (978-0-8368-9426-4(X)); lib. bdg. 22.00 (978-0-8368-9422-6(7)) Stevens, Gareth Publishing LLLP. (Weekly Reader Leveled Readers).

—Ankylosaurus. Mangiat, Jeffrey, illus. 2009. (Let's Read about Dinosaurs Ser.). 24p. (J). (gr. -1-3). lib. bdg. 22.00 (978-0-8368-9415-8(4), Weekly Reader Leveled Readers) Stevens, Gareth Publishing LLLP.

—Ankylosaurus. Magniat, Jeffrey, illus. 2009. (Let's Read about Dinosaurs Ser.). 24p. (gr. -1-3). pap. 8.15 (978-0-8368-9419-6(7), Weekly Reader Leveled Readers) Stevens, Gareth Publishing LLLP.

—Ankylosaurus; Anquilosaurio. 2009. (Let's Read about Dinosaurs;Conozcamos a los dinosaurios Ser.). (SPA.). 24p. (J). (gr. -1-3). pap. 8.15 (978-0-8368-9427-1(8)); lib. bdg. 22.00 (978-0-8368-9423-3(5)) Stevens, Gareth Publishing LLLP. (Weekly Reader Leveled Readers).

—Apatosaurus. Magniat, Jeffrey, illus. 2007. (Let's Read about Dinosaurs Ser.). 24p. (gr. k-3). pap. 8.15 (978-0-8368-7702-1(0)); lib. bdg. 22.00 (978-0-8368-7695-6(4)) Stevens, Gareth Publishing LLLP. (Weekly Reader Leveled Readers).

—Apatosaurus/Apatosaurio. Magniat, Jeffrey, illus. 2007. (Let's Read about Dinosaurs/ Conozcamos a los dinosaurios Ser.). (ENG & SPA.). 24p. (gr. k-3). lib. bdg. 22.00 (978-0-8368-8018-2(8), Weekly Reader Leveled Readers) Stevens, Gareth Publishing LLLP.

—Dinosaur Claws & Crests. 2005. (Prehistoric Creatures Ser.). (Illus.). 24p. (gr. 2-6). pap. 8.15 (978-0-8368-4903-5(5)); lib. bdg. 22.00 (978-0-8368-4896-0(9)) Stevens, Gareth Publishing LLLP. (Weekly Reader Leveled Readers).

—Dinosaur Skeletons & Skulls. 2005. (Prehistoric Creatures Ser.). (Illus.). 24p. (gr. 2-6). pap. 8.15 (978-0-8368-4904-2(3)); lib. bdg. 22.00 (978-0-8368-4897-7(7)) Stevens, Gareth Publishing LLLP. (Weekly Reader Leveled Readers).

—Dinosaur Spikes & Necks. 2005. (Prehistoric Creatures Ser.). (Illus.). 24p. (gr. 2-6). pap. 8.15 (978-0-8368-4905-9(1)); lib. bdg. 22.00 (978-0-8368-4898-4(5)) Stevens, Gareth Publishing LLLP. (Weekly Reader Leveled Readers).

—Dinosaur Tails & Armor. 2005. (Prehistoric Creatures Ser.). (Illus.). 24p. (gr. 2-6). pap. 8.15 (978-0-8368-4906-6(X)); lib. bdg. 22.00 (978-0-8368-4899-1(3)) Stevens, Gareth Publishing LLLP. (Weekly Reader Leveled Readers).

—Dinosaur Teeth & Beaks. 2005. (Prehistoric Creatures Ser.). (Illus.). 24p. (gr. 2-6). pap. 8.15 (978-0-8368-4907-3(8)); lib. bdg. 22.00 (978-0-8368-4900-4(0)) Stevens, Gareth Publishing LLLP. (Weekly Reader Leveled Readers).

—Dinosaur Wings & Fins. 2005. (Prehistoric Creatures Ser.). (Illus.). 24p. (gr. 2-6). pap. 8.15 (978-0-8368-4908-0(6)); lib. bdg. 22.00 (978-0-8368-4901-1(9)) Stevens, Gareth Publishing LLLP. (Weekly Reader Leveled Readers).

—Dinosaurios: Alas y Aletas. 2005. (Seres prehistoricos (Prehistoric Creatures- Spanish edition) Ser.). (SPA., Illus.). 24p. (gr. 2-6). lib. bdg. 22.00 (978-0-8368-6013-9(6), Weekly Reader Leveled Readers) Stevens, Gareth Publishing LLLP.

—Dinosaurios: Colas y Corazas. 2005. (Seres prehistoricos (Prehistoric Creatures- Spanish edition) Ser.). (SPA.). 24p. (gr. 2-6). lib. bdg. 22.00 (978-0-8368-6014-6(4), Weekly Reader Leveled Readers) Stevens, Gareth Publishing LLLP.

—Dinosaurios: Espinas Oseas y Cuellos. 2005. (Seres prehistoricos (Prehistoric Creatures- Spanish edition) Ser.). (SPA., Illus.). 24p. (gr. 2-6). lib. bdg. 22.00 (978-0-8368-6016-0(0), Weekly Reader Leveled Readers) Stevens, Gareth Publishing LLLP.

—Dinosaurios: Garras y Crestas. 2005. (Seres prehistoricos (Prehistoric Creatures- Spanish edition) Ser.). (ENG & SPA., Illus.). 24p. (gr. 2-6). lib. bdg. 22.00 (978-0-8368-6018-4(7), Weekly Reader Leveled Readers) Stevens, Gareth Publishing LLLP.

—Dinosaurios, Dientes y Picos. 2005. (Seres prehistoricos (Prehistoric Creatures- Spanish edition) Ser.). (ENG & SPA.). 24p. (gr. 2-6). lib. bdg. 22.00 (978-0-8368-6015-3(2), Weekly Reader Leveled Readers) Stevens, Gareth Publishing LLLP.

—Diplodocus. Magniat, Jeffrey, illus. 2009. (Let's Read about Dinosaurs Ser.). 24p. (gr. -1-3). (J). lib. bdg. 22.00 (978-0-8368-9416-5(2)); pap. 8.15 (978-0-8368-9420-2(0)) Stevens, Gareth Publishing LLLP. (Weekly Reader Leveled Readers).

—Diplodocus; Diplodocus. 2009. (Let's Read about Dinosaurs;Conozcamos a los dinosaurios Ser.). (SPA & ENG.). 24p. (J). (gr. -1-3). pap. 8.15 (978-0-8368-9428-8(6)); lib. bdg. 22.00 (978-0-8368-9424-0(3)) Stevens, Gareth Publishing LLLP. (Weekly Reader Leveled Readers).

—Giganotosaurus. Magniat, Jeffrey, illus. 2007. (Let's Read about Dinosaurs Ser.). 24p. (gr. k-3). pap. 8.15 (978-0-8368-7703-8(9), Weekly Reader Leveled Readers) Stevens, Gareth Publishing LLLP.

—Giganotosaurus/Gigantosaurio. Magniat, Jeffrey, illus. 2007. (Let's Read about Dinosaurs/ Conozcamos a los dinosaurios Ser.). (ENG & SPA.). 24p. (J). (gr. k-3). lib. bdg. 22.00 (978-0-8368-8019-9(6), Weekly Reader Leveled Readers) Stevens, Gareth Publishing LLLP.

—Oviraptor. Magniat, Jeffrey, illus. 2009. (Let's Read about Dinosaurs Ser.). 24p. (gr. -1-3). (J). lib. bdg. 22.00 (978-0-8368-9417-2(0)); pap. 8.15 (978-0-8368-9421-9(9)) Stevens, Gareth Publishing LLLP. (Weekly Reader Leveled Readers).

—Oviraptor; Oviraptor. 2009. (Let's Read about Dinosaurs;Conozcamos a los dinosaurios Ser.). (SPA.). 24p. (J). (gr. -1-3). pap. 8.15 (978-0-8368-9429-5(4)); lib. bdg. 22.00 (978-0-8368-9425-7(1)) Stevens, Gareth Publishing LLLP. (Weekly Reader Leveled Readers).

—Stegosaurus. 2007. (Let's Read about Dinosaurs Ser.). (Illus.). 24p. (gr. k-3). pap. 8.15 (978-0-8368-7704-5(7), Weekly Reader Leveled Readers) Stevens, Gareth Publishing LLLP.

—Stegosaurus. Magniat, Jeffrey, illus. 2007. (Let's Read about Dinosaurs Ser.). 24p. (gr. k-3). lib. bdg. 22.00 (978-0-8368-7697-0(0), Weekly Reader Leveled Readers) Stevens, Gareth Publishing LLLP.

—Stegosaurus (Estegosaurio) 2007. (Let's Read about Dinosaurs/ Conozcamos a los dinosaurios Ser.). (ENG & SPA.). 24p. (gr. k-3). pap. 8.15 (978-0-8368-8027-4(7), Weekly Reader Leveled Readers) Stevens, Gareth Publishing LLLP.

—Stegosaurus/Estegosaurio. Magniat, Jeffrey, illus. 2007. (Let's Read about Dinosaurs/ Conozcamos a los dinosaurios Ser.). (ENG & SPA.). 24p. (gr. k-3). lib. bdg. 22.00 (978-0-8368-8020-5(X), Weekly Reader Leveled Readers) Stevens, Gareth Publishing LLLP.

—Triceratops. Magniat, Jeffrey, illus. 2007. (Let's Read about Dinosaurs Ser.). 24p. (gr. k-3). pap. 8.15 (978-0-8368-7705-2(5)); lib. bdg. 22.00 (978-0-8368-7698-7(9)) Stevens, Gareth Publishing LLLP. (Weekly Reader Leveled Readers).

—Triceratops/Triceratops. Magniat, Jeffrey, illus. 2007. (Let's Read about Dinosaurs/ Conozcamos a los dinosaurios Ser.). (ENG & SPA.). 24p. (gr. k-3). lib. bdg. 22.00 (978-0-8368-8021-2(8), Weekly Reader Leveled Readers) Stevens, Gareth Publishing LLLP.

—Tyrannosaurus Rex. 2007. (Let's Read about Dinosaurs/ Conozcamos a los dinosaurios Ser.). (ENG & SPA., Illus.). 24p. (J). (gr. k-3). pap. 8.15 (978-0-8368-8029-8(3), Weekly Reader Leveled Readers) Stevens, Gareth Publishing LLLP.

—Tyrannosaurus Rex. Magniat, Jeffrey, illus. 2007. (Let's Read about Dinosaurs Ser.). 24p. (gr. k-3). pap. 8.15 (978-0-8368-7706-9(3), Weekly Reader Leveled Readers) Stevens, Gareth Publishing LLLP.

—Tyrannosaurus Rex/Tiranosaurio Rex. Magniat, Jeffrey, illus. 2007. (Let's Read about Dinosaurs/ Conozcamos a los dinosaurios Ser.). (ENG & SPA.). 24p. (J). (gr. k-3). lib. bdg. 22.00 (978-0-8368-8022-9(6), Weekly Reader Leveled Readers) Stevens, Gareth Publishing LLLP.

—Velociraptor. 2007. (Let's Read about Dinosaurs/ Conozcamos a los dinosaurios Ser.). (ENG & SPA.). 24p. (gr. k-3). pap. 8.15 (978-0-8368-8030-4(7), Weekly Reader Leveled Readers) Stevens, Gareth Publishing LLLP.

—Velociraptor. Magniat, Jeffrey, illus. 2007. (Let's Read about Dinosaurs Ser.). 24p. (gr. k-3). pap. 8.15 (978-0-8368-7707-6(1), Weekly Reader Leveled Readers) Stevens, Gareth Publishing LLLP.

—Velociraptor/Velociraptor. Magniat, Jeffrey, illus. 2007. (Let's Read about Dinosaurs/ Conozcamos a los dinosaurios Ser.). (ENG & SPA.). 24p. (gr. k-3). lib. bdg. 22.00 (978-0-8368-8023-6(4), Weekly Reader Leveled Readers) Stevens, Gareth Publishing LLLP.

Matthews, Rupert. Dinosaurs. 2010. (Ripley Twists Ser.). (J). 48p. (gr. 3-18). lib. bdg. 19.95 (978-1-4222-1828-0(7)); (Illus.). 40p. (gr. 6-8). lib. bdg. 19.95 (978-1-4222-1558-6(X)) Mason Crest.

—Fun Kits Let's Learn Dinosaurs. 2008. (978-1-84666-593-6(0)) Top That! Publishing PLC.

—Know How Know Why Dinosaurs. Head-Weston, Alex et al, illus. 2004. (Know How Know Why Ser.). 48p. (J). (gr. 3-7). pap. (978-1-84510-031-5(X)) Top That! Publishing PLC.

—World's Biggest Dinosaurs, 1 vol. 2012. (Extreme Dinosaurs Ser.). (ENG.). 32p. (gr. 1-2). pap. 8.29 (978-1-4109-4529-7(4)); lib. bdg. 29.99 (978-1-4109-4522-8(7)) Heinemann-Raintree. (Read Me!).

—World's Dumbest Dinosaurs, 1 vol. 2012. (Extreme Dinosaurs Ser.). (ENG.). 32p. (gr. 1-2). lib. bdg. 29.99 (978-1-4109-4523-5(5), Read Me!) Heinemann-Raintree.

—World's Fastest Dinosaurs, 1 vol. 2012. (Extreme Dinosaurs Ser.). (ENG.). 32p. (gr. 1-2). lib. bdg. 29.99 (978-1-4109-4524-2(3), Read Me!) Heinemann-Raintree.

—World's Weirdest Dinosaurs, 1 vol. 2012. (Extreme Dinosaurs Ser.). (ENG.). 32p. (gr. 1-2). lib. bdg. 29.99 (978-1-4109-4527-3(8), Read Me!) Heinemann-Raintree.

May, Paul. Dinosaurs. 2009. (Wild Reads Ser.). (ENG., Illus.). 32p. (YA). (gr. k). pap. 4.95 (978-0-19-911927-1(9)) Oxford Univ. Pr., Inc.

Mayes, Susan. The Usborne Book of Dinosaurs. Rey, Luis & Trotter, Stuart, illus. rev. ed. 2005. 32p. (J). pap., pap. 6.95 (978-0-7945-0849-4(9), Usborne) EDC Publishing.

McCurry, Kristen. How to Draw Incredible Dinosaurs. Calle, Juan, illus. 2012. (Smithsonian Drawing Bks.). (ENG.). 64p. (gr. 3-4). pap. 41.70 (978-1-4296-9451-3(3)) Capstone Press of Coughlan Cos.

McElligott, Matthew. Mad Scientist Academy: the Dinosaur Disaster. 2015. (Mad Scientist Academy Ser.: 1). (ENG., Illus.). 40p. (J). (gr. k-3). 17.99 (978-0-553-52374-4(0), Crown Books For Young Readers) Random Hse. Children's Bks.

McKay, Sindy. We Both Read Bilingual Edition-About Dinosaurs/Acerca de Los Dinosaurios. Walters, Robert, illus. 2011. (SPA.). 44p. (J). pap. 4.99 (978-1-60115-050-9(4)) Treasure Bay, Inc.

McMullan, Kate. Dinosaur Hunters. Jones, John R., illus. 2005. (Step into Reading Ser.: No. 5). (ENG.). 48p. (J). (gr. 2-4). per. 3.99 (978-0-375-82450-0(2), Random Hse. Bks. for Young Readers) Random Hse. Children's Bks.

Media, Cont. Dinosaurs. 2008. (ENG.). 96p. 17.99 (978-1-931703-03-1(5)); (Illus.). 48p. (YA). 12.99 (978-1-931703-18-5(3)) Creative Publishing Consultants.

Meet Plateosaurus. 2014. (Age of Dinosaurs Ser.). 32p. (J). (gr. 3-5). lib. bdg. 28.50 (978-1-62712-797-4(6)) Cavendish Square Publishing.

Mehing, Carl. Before the Dinosaurs. 2009. (Discovering Dinosaurs Ser.). (Illus.). 48p. (YA). (gr. 2-6). pap. 12.85 (978-1-60754-780-8(5)); (gr. 4-7). 29.25 (978-1-60754-772-3(4)) Windmill Bks.

—Giant Meat-Eating Dinosaurs. 2009. (Discovering Dinosaurs Ser.). (Illus.). 48p. (YA). (gr. 2-6). pap. 12.85 (978-1-60754-785-3(6)); (gr. 4-7). 29.25 (978-1-60754-777-8(5)) Windmill Bks.

—Small & Deadly Dinosaurs. 2009. (Discovering Dinosaurs Ser.). (Illus.). 48p. (YA). (gr. 2-6). pap. 12.85 (978-1-60754-784-6(8)); (gr. 4-7). 29.25 (978-1-60754-776-1(7)) Windmill Bks.

Mehling, Carl. Armored Dinosaurs. 2009. (Discovering Dinosaurs Ser.). (Illus.). 48p. (YA). (gr. 4-7). 29.25 *(978-1-60754-774-7(0))* Windmill Bks.

—Giant Plant-Eating Dinosaurs. 2009. (Discovering Dinosaurs Ser.). (Illus.). 48p. (YA). (gr. 4-7). 29.25 *(978-1-60754-778-5(3))* Windmill Bks.

—Horned, Spiked, & Crested Dinosaurs. 2009. (Discovering Dinosaurs Ser.). (Illus.). 48p. (YA). (gr. 4-7). 29.25 *(978-1-60754-775-4(9))* Windmill Bks.

Mehling, Carl, ed. Armored Dinosaurs. Mehling, Carl, . 2009. (Discovering Dinosaurs Ser.). (Illus.). 48p. (YA). (gr. 2-6). pap. 12.85 *(978-1-60754-782-2(1))* Windmill Bks.

—Giant Plant-Eating Dinosaurs. Mehling, Carl, . 2010. (Discovering Dinosaurs Ser.). (Illus.). 48p. (YA). (gr. 2-6). pap. 12.85 *(978-1-60754-786-0(4))* Windmill Bks.

—Horned, Spiked, & Crested Dinosaurs. Mehling, Carl, . 2009. (Discovering Dinosaurs Ser.). (Illus.). 48p. (YA). (gr. 2-6). pap. 12.85 *(978-1-60754-783-9(X))* Windmill Bks.

Mehling, Randi. Great Extinctions of the Past. 2007. (Scientific American Ser.). (Illus.). 72p. (YA). (gr. 5-9). lib. bdg. 30.00 *(978-0-7910-9049-7(3))* Facts On File, Inc.

Mertz, Leslie. Dinosaurs: Walk in the Footsteps of the World's Largest Lizards. 2015. (Fact Atlas Ser.). (ENG., Illus.). 72p. (J). (gr. 2-7). 14.99 *(978-1-63220-436-3(3)*, Sky Pony Pr.) Skyhorse Publishing Co., Inc.

Milbourne, Anna. Dinosaur. 2005. (First Discovery Ser.). 24p. (J). 9.95 *(978-0-7945-0906-4(1)*, Usborne) EDC Publishing.

Miles, Lisa. Origami Dinosaurs. 2013. (Amazing Origami Ser.). 32p. (J). (gr. 2-5). pap. 10.50 *(978-1-4339-9649-8(9))*; pap. 63.00 *(978-1-4339-9650-4(2))*; (ENG., Illus.). lib. bdg. 26.60 *(978-1-4339-9648-1(0))* Stevens, Gareth Publishing LLLP.

Miles, Liz. Dino Safari: Go Wild on a Prehistoric Adventure! 2012. (ENG., Illus.). 128p. (J). pap. 9.95 *(978-1-84858-542-3(X))* Arcturus Publishing GBR. Dist: Bookmasters Distribution.

—Dinosaur Defenders. 2015. (Danger! Dinosaurs Ser.). (ENG.). 32p. (J). (gr. 4-5). pap. 10.50 *(978-1-4824-3025-7(8))* Stevens, Gareth Publishing LLLP.

—Dinosaur Record Breakers. 2015. (Danger! Dinosaurs Ser.). (ENG.). 32p. (J). (gr. 4-5). pap. 10.50 *(978-1-4824-3029-5(0))* Stevens, Gareth Publishing LLLP.

—Dinosaurs & the Prehistoric World. 2015. (Danger! Dinosaurs Ser.). (ENG., Illus.). 32p. (J). (gr. 4-5). pap. 10.50 *(978-1-4824-3033-2(9))* Stevens, Gareth Publishing LLLP.

—Flying Monsters. 2015. (Danger! Dinosaurs Ser.). (ENG.). 32p. (J). (gr. 4-5). pap. 10.50 *(978-1-4824-3037-0(1))* Stevens, Gareth Publishing LLLP.

—Giant Dinosaurs. 2013. (Illus.). 32p. (J). *(978-1-84858-568-3(3))* Arcturus Pubs., Inc.

—Killer Dinosaurs. 2015. (Danger! Dinosaurs Ser.). (ENG.). 32p. (J). (gr. 4-5). pap. 10.50 *(978-1-4824-3041-7(X))* Stevens, Gareth Publishing LLLP.

Miller, Austin. Let's Look at the Dinosaurs: Set Of 6. 2010. (Early Connections Ser.). (J). pap. 37.00 net. *(978-1-4108-1074-8(7))* Benchmark Education Co.

Miller, Bryan. Dinosaur Fun: With Letters. 2008. (Illus.). 24p. (J). (gr. -1). bds. 11.99 *(978-0-89051-488-7(7))* Master Bks.

Miller, Henley. Meet Giganotosaurus. 2014. (Age of Dinosaurs Ser.). 32p. (J). (gr. 3-5). lib. bdg. 28.50 *(978-1-62712-800-1(X))* Cavendish Square Publishing.

Mini Dinosaurs: Brontosaurus. (Mini Dinosaurs Ser.). 10p. (J). 4.95 *(978-1-58117-289-8(3)*, Intervisual/Piggy Toes) Bendon, Inc.

Mini Dinosaurs: Stegosaurus. (Mini Dinosaurs Ser.). 10p. (J). 4.95 *(978-1-58117-290-4(7)*, Intervisual/Piggy Toes) Bendon, Inc.

Mini Dinosaurs: Triceratops. (Mini Dinosaurs Ser.). 10p. (J). 4.95 *(978-1-58117-291-1(5)*, Intervisual/Piggy Toes) Bendon, Inc.

Mini Dinosaurs: Tyrannosaurus. (Mini Dinosaurs Ser.). 10p. (J). 4.95 *(978-1-58117-292-8(3)*, Intervisual/Piggy Toes) Bendon, Inc.

Mitchell, Chris. Do Dinosaurs Make Good Pets? 2016. (Dr Dino's Learnatorium Ser.). (ENG., Illus.). 192p. (J). (gr. 4-7). pap. 8.99 *(978-1-78418-652-4(X))* Blake, John Publishing, Ltd. GBR. Dist: Independent Pubs. Group.

Modern Publishing Staff. Fisher-Price Spike the Ultra Dinosaur. 2009. (Giant Coloring & Activity Bks.). 96p. (J). (gr. -1). pap. 2.99 *(978-0-7666-3491-6(4))* Modern Publishing.

Moore Niver, Heather. Salamanders Lived with the Dinosaurs! 2016. (Living with the Dinosaurs Ser.). 00024p. (J). pap. 8.15 ***(978-1-4824-5661-5(3))*** Stevens, Gareth Publishing LLLP.

Morris, Ting & Morris, Neil. Dinosaurs. Levy, Ruth & Cowne, Joanne, illus. 2006. (Sticky Fingers Ser.). 32p. (J). lib. bdg. 28.50 *(978-1-59771-029-9(6))* Sea-To-Sea Pubns.

Most, Bernard. Dinosaur Questions. 2008. (Illus.). (J). pap. *(978-0-15-206475-4(3)*, Red Wagon Bks.) Harcourt Children's Bks.

—How Big Were the Dinosaurs? 2008. (Illus.). (J). pap. *(978-0-15-206469-3(9)*, Red Wagon Bks.) Harcourt Children's Bks.

Mugford, Simon. My Big Dinosaur World. Francis, John, illus. 2008. 60p. (J). *(978-1-84332-594-9(2)*, Priddy Bks.) St. Martin's Pr.

Munro, Roxie. Inside-Outside Dinosaurs, 0 vols. 2009. (ENG.). 40p. (J). (gr. k-6). 17.99 *(978-0-7614-5624-7(4)*, 9780761456247, Amazon Children's Publishing) Amazon Publishing.

Murray, Helen. Awesome Adventures. 2013. (DK Readers Ser.). (ENG.). 32p. (J). (gr. 1-3). pap. 3.99 *(978-1-4654-1695-7(1)*, DK Children) Dorling Kindersley Publishing, Inc.

Musgrave, Ruth. Funny Fill-In - My Pets Adventure. 2014. (ENG.). 48p. (J). (gr. 3-7). pap. 4.99 *(978-1-4263-1683-8(6)*, National Geographic Children's Bks.) National Geographic Society.

Myers, Tim. If You Give a T-Rex a Bone, 1 vol. Hovemann, Anisa Claire, illus. 2007. (Sharing Nature with Children Book Ser.). 32p. (J). (gr. -1-5). (ENG.). 8.95 *(978-1-58469-098-6(4))*; 16.95 *(978-1-58469-097-9(6))* Dawn Pubns.

Naish, Darren. Build the T. Rex. Bernstein, Galia & Ruffle, Mark, illus. 2013. (Build It Ser.). (ENG.). 32p. (J). (gr. k). 19.95 *(978-1-60710-415-5(6)*, Silver Dolphin Bks.) Readerlink Distribution Services, LLC.

—Jurassic Record Breakers. 2015. (ENG., Illus.). 48p. (J). (gr. 3). pap. 7.95 *(978-1-78312-118-2(1))* Carlton Kids GBR. Dist: Sterling Publishing Co., Inc.

Naish, Darren, contrib. by. IDinosaur. 2014. (IExplore Ser.). (ENG., Illus.). 32p. (J). (gr. 3). 12.95 *(978-1-78312-079-6(7))* Carlton Bks., Ltd. GBR. Dist: Sterling Publishing Co., Inc.

Nardo, Don. Deadliest Dinosaurs. 2016. (ENG.). 80p. (J). (gr. 5-12). lib. bdg. *(978-1-68282-048-3(3))* ReferencePoint Pr., Inc.

Nash, Dylan M. Dinosaurs. Barnard, Bryn, illus. 2007. (ENG.). 24p. (J). (gr. 1-18). 19.95 *(978-1-58117-580-6(9)*, Intervisual/Piggy Toes) Bendon, Inc.

National Geographic Editors & Esbaum, Jill. Angry Birds Playground - Dinosaurs. Tempesta, Franco, illus. 2013. (ENG.). 128p. (J). (gr. -1-3). lib. bdg. 21.90 *(978-1-4263-1325-7(X)*, National Geographic Children's Bks.) National Geographic Society.

National Geographic Kids Staff. Dino Records: The Most Amazing Prehistoric Creatures to Ever Walk the Earth! 2017. (ENG.). 208p. (J). (gr. 3-7). pap. 14.99 *(978-1-4263-2794-0(3)*, National Geographic Children's Bks.) National Geographic Society.

National Geographic Kids Staff & Esbaum, Jill. Dinosaurs: A Prehistoric Adventure! Tempesta, Franco, illus. 2013. (ENG.). 128p. (J). (gr. -1-3). 14.95 *(978-1-4263-1324-0(1)*, National Geographic Children's Bks.) National Geographic Society.

National System Of Public Lands, et al. Jurassic Explorer: Cleveland-Lloyd Dinosaur Quarry. 2012. 20p. pap. *(978-1-78266-042-2(9))* Bks. Express Publishing.

Newton, Robyn & Barber, Nicola, eds. Dinosaurs: Uncover the Prehistoric World! Horas, Elena, tr. 2013. (ENG., Illus.). 217p. 12.99 *(978-1-4723-2364-4(5))* Parragon, Inc.

Nichols, V. The Incredible Dionsaur. M. J. Studios Staff, illus. 128p. (J). (gr. k-6). pap., act. bk. ed. 2.95 *(978-1-879424-64-7(9))* Nickel Pr.

Nishida, Masaki. Drawing Manga Dinosaurs. 2007. (How to Draw Manga Ser.: Vol. 4). (Illus.). 24p. (J). (gr. -1-3). lib. bdg. 25.25 *(978-1-4042-3845-9(X))* Rosen Publishing Group, Inc., The.

Norman, D. Dinosaurs Sticker & Puzzle Kid Kit (Bag) 2007. (Kid Kits Ser.). 24p. (J). pap. 14.99 *(978-1-60130-054-6(9))* EDC Publishing.

Norman, David. Dinosaurs Sticker Book. Clarke, Phillip, ed. rev. ed. 2006. (Usborne Sticker Bks.). (Illus.). 23p. (J). pap. 8.99 *(978-0-7945-1323-8(9)*, Usborne) EDC Publishing.

Norman, Kim & American Museum of Natural History Staff. Dinosaurs: And Other Prehistoric Animals. Csotonyi, Julius & Marshall, Todd, illus. 2012. (Storytime Stickers Ser.). (ENG.). 16p. (J). (gr. k-2). pap. 5.95 *(978-1-4027-7349-5(8))* Sterling Publishing Co., Inc.

Nunn, Daniel. All about Dinosaurs, 1 vol. 2014. (All about Dinosaurs Ser.). (ENG.). 24p. (gr. -1-1). 135.90 *(978-1-4846-0209-6(9)*, Acorn) Heinemann-Raintree.

—Brachiosaurus, 1 vol. 2014. (All about Dinosaurs Ser.). (ENG., Illus.). 24p. (gr. -1-1). pap. 5.99 *(978-1-4846-0210-2(2)*, Acorn) Heinemann-Raintree.

—Diplodocus, 1 vol. 2014. (All about Dinosaurs Ser.). (ENG., Illus.). 24p. (gr. -1-1). pap. 5.99 *(978-1-4846-0211-9(0)*, Acorn) Heinemann-Raintree.

—Triceratops, 1 vol. 2014. (All about Dinosaurs Ser.). (ENG., Illus.). 24p. (gr. -1-1). pap. 5.99 *(978-1-4846-0213-3(7)*, Acorn) Heinemann-Raintree.

—Tyrannosaurus Rex, 1 vol. 2014. (All about Dinosaurs Ser.). (ENG., Illus.). 24p. (gr. -1-1). pap. 5.99 *(978-1-4846-0214-0(5)*, Acorn) Heinemann-Raintree.

—Velociraptor, 1 vol. 2014. (All about Dinosaurs Ser.). (ENG., Illus.). 24p. (gr. -1-1). 22.65 *(978-1-4846-0208-9(0)*, Acorn) Heinemann-Raintree.

Oburkova, Eva. Toby's Travels Through Time: Puzzle Adventures in Dinosaur Days. Oburkova, Eva, illus. 2007. (Toby's Travels Through Time: Puzzle Adventures in Dinosaur Days Ser.). (Illus.). 32p. (gr. k-3). lib. bdg. 28.00 *(978-0-8368-7497-6(8)*, Gareth Stevens Learning Library) Stevens, Gareth Publishing LLLP.

O'Donnell, Kerri. Aves: Dinosaurios de nuestros dias (Birds: Modern-Day Dinosaurs) 2009. (Reading Room Collection: Spanish Ser.). (SPA.). 24p. (gr. 3-4). 42.50 *(978-1-60854-176-8(2)*, Editorial Buenas Letras) Rosen Publishing Group, Inc., The.

—Birds: Modern-Day Dinosaurs. (Reading Room Collection 2 Ser.). 24p. (gr. 3-4). 2009. 42.50 *(978-1-60851-960-6(0)*, PowerKids Pr.) 2003. (ENG.). 43.95 *(978-0-8239-8732-0(9))* Rosen Publishing Group, Inc., The.

O'Hearn, Michael. Allosaurus vs. Brachiosaurus: Might Against Height. Renne, Philip K., illus. 2010. (Dinosaur Wars Ser.). (ENG.). 32p. (gr. 3-4). lib. bdg. 27.99 *(978-1-4296-3935-4(0)*, Edge Bks.) Capstone Press of Coughlan Cos.

—Deinonychus vs. Styracosaurus: When Claws & Spikes Collide, 1 vol. Renne, Philip K., illus. 2010. (Dinosaur Wars Ser.). (ENG.). 32p. (gr. 3-4). lib. bdg. 27.99 *(978-1-4296-4757-1(4)*, Edge Bks.) Capstone Press of Coughlan Cos.

—Triceratops vs. Stegosaurus: When Horns & Plates Collide. Renne, Philip K., illus. 2010. (Dinosaur Wars Ser.). (ENG.). 32p. (gr. 3-4). lib. bdg. 27.99 *(978-1-4296-3938-5(5)*, Edge Bks.) Capstone Press of Coughlan Cos.

—Tyrannosaurus Rex vs. Velociraptor: Power Against Speed. Renne, Philip K., illus. 2010. (Dinosaur Wars Ser.). (ENG.). 32p. (gr. 3-4). lib. bdg. 27.99 *(978-1-4296-3937-8(7)*, Edge Bks.) Capstone Press of Coughlan Cos.

Oldland, Nicholas. Dinosaur Countdown. Oldland, Nicholas, illus. 2012. (ENG., Illus.). 24p. (J). (gr. -1-1). 15.95 *(978-1-55453-834-8(3))* Kids Can Pr., Ltd. CAN. Dist: Hachette Bk. Group.

Olien, Rebecca. How Do We Know about Dinosaurs? A Fossil Mystery, 1 vol. McDee, Katie, illus. 2011. (First Graphics: Science Mysteries Ser.). (ENG.). 24p. (gr. 1-2). pap. 6.29 *(978-1-4296-7173-6(4))*; pap. 35.70 *(978-1-4296-7177-4(7))* Capstone Press of Coughlan Cos.

Oliver, Martin. Esos Extintos Dinosaurios. Postgate, Daniel, tr. Postgate, Daniel, illus. 2003. (Coleccion Esa Gran Cultura).Tr. of Dead Dinosaurs. (SPA.). 134p. (YA). 7.96 *(978-84-272-2137-6(1))* Molino, Editorial ESP. Dist: Lectorum Pubns., Inc.

Orme, David. Dinosaur! 2007. (Trailblazers Ser.). (ENG., Illus.). 36p. pap. *(978-1-84167-426-1(5))* Ransom Publishing Ltd.

—Dinosaurs! 2009. (Fact to Fiction Grafx Ser.). (Illus.). 36p. (J). pap. 6.95 *(978-1-7891-7900-5(8))* Perfection Learning Corp.

Osborne, Will & Osborne, Mary Pope. Dinosaurs: A Nonfiction Companion to Dinosaurs Before Dark. Murdocca, Sal, illus. 2004. (Magic Tree House Research Guides: No. 1). 119p. 16.00 *(978-0-7569-2209-2(7))* Perfection Learning Corp.

Page, Nick. Touch & Feel Noisy Dinosaurs. 2007. (Touch & Feel Ser.). (Illus.). 12p. (gr. -1). per., bds. *(978-1-84610-444-2(0))* Make Believe Ideas.

Pallotta, Jerry. Tyrannosaurus Rex vs. Velociraptor. Bolster, Robert, illus. 2016. (Who Would Win? Ser.). (ENG.). 32p. (J). (gr. 1-3). pap. 3.99 *(978-0-545-17573-9(9))* Scholastic, Inc.

Palmer, Douglas. Firefly Encyclopedia of Dinosaurs & Prehistoric Animals. 2014. (ENG., Illus.). 256p. (J). (gr. 4-7). pap. 19.95 *(978-1-77085-460-4(6)*, 9781770854604) Firefly Bks., Ltd.

Parker, Steve. Age of the Dinosaur. 2014. (ENG., Illus.). 48p. (J). (gr. 2-4). 7.99 *(978-0-565-09329-7(0))* Natural History Museum Pubns. GBR. Dist: Independent Pubs. Group.

—Did Dinosaurs Lay Eggs? And Other Questions & Answers about Prehistoric Reptiles. Rosewarne, Graham, illus. 2016. (ENG.). 32p. 7.99 *(978-1-86147-481-0(4)*, Armadillo) Anness Publishing GBR. Dist: National Bk. Network.

—Project Dinosaur: Bursting with Facts & Activities For 7-10. 2016. (ENG., Illus.). (J). bds. ***(978-1-78209-823-2(2))*** Miles Kelly Publishing, Ltd.

—T-Rex. 2010. (Mosaic of Magical Information Ser.). (Illus.). 48p. (YA). (gr. 3-18). 19.95 *(978-1-4222-1991-1(7))* Mason Crest.

—10 Things You Should Know about Dinosaurs. Gallagher, Belinda & Borton, Paula, eds. Bozer, Chris, illus. 2004. (10 Things You Should Know Ser.). 24p. (J). 6.99 *(978-1-84236-120-7(1))* Miles Kelly Publishing, Ltd. GBR. Dist: Independent Pubs. Group.

Parker, Steve & Dewan, Ted. Inside Dinosaurs & Other Prehistoric Creatures. (ENG., Illus.). 48p. (J). 18.95 *(978-0-590-74839-1(4))* Scholastic, Inc.

Parker, Steve & Flegg, Jim. Dinosaurs: Great Little Fact Books. 2003. (Great Little Fact Books Ser.). (Illus.). 40p. (J). pap. 7.95 *(978-1-84236-110-8(4))* Miles Kelly Publishing, Ltd. GBR. Dist: Independent Pubs. Group.

Paul, Gregory. The Early Cretaceous Volume 1: Notes, Drawings, & Observations from Prehistory. Alonso, Juan, illus. 2017. (Ancient Earth Journal Ser.). (ENG.). (J). (gr. 3-8). lib. bdg. 31.99 ***(978-1-942875-30-7(4)***, Walter Foster Jr) Quarto Publishing Group USA.

—The Early Cretaceous Volume 2: Notes, Drawings, & Observations from Prehistory. Alonso, Juan, illus. 2017. (Ancient Earth Journal Ser.). (ENG.). (J). (gr. 3-8). lib. bdg. 31.99 ***(978-1-942875-31-4(2)***, Walter Foster Jr) Quarto Publishing Group USA.

—The Early Jurassic Vol. 1: Notes, Drawings, & Observations from Prehistory. Alonso, Juan, illus. 2017. (Ancient Earth Journal Ser.). (ENG.). (J). (gr. 3-8). lib. bdg. 31.99 ***(978-1-942875-32-1(0)***, Walter Foster Jr) Quarto Publishing Group USA.

—The Early Jurassic Vol. 2: Notes, Drawings, & Observations from Prehistory. Alonso, Juan, illus. 2017. (Ancient Earth Journal Ser.). (ENG.). (J). (gr. 3-8). lib. bdg. 31.99 ***(978-1-942875-33-8(9)***, Walter Foster Jr) Quarto Publishing Group USA.

Pearcey, Alice. Usborne Dinosaur Stencil Book. Kushii, Tetsuo, illus. 2006. 14p. (J). (gr. -1-3). bds. 12.99 *(978-0-7945-1138-8(4)*, Usborne) EDC Publishing.

Pearcey, Alice, ed. Dinosaur Jigsaw Atlas. Bird, Glen, illus. 2004. 20p. (J). 14.95 *(978-0-7945-0913-2(4)*, Usborne) EDC Publishing.

Peers, Judi. Brontosaurus Brunch: A Smorgasbord of Dinosaur Delights. Coles, Mary, illus. 3rd ed. 2011. *(978-0-9810964-2-1(5))* Praise Publishing.

Penguin Books Staff, ed. Dinosaurs. (Learners Ser.). (Illus.). 48p. (J). 3.50 *(978-0-7214-1701-1(9)*, Dutton Juvenile) Penguin Publishing Group.

Penner, Lucille Recht. Dinosaur Babies. Barrett, Peter, illus. 2015. 32p. pap. 5.00 *(978-1-61003-602-3(6))* Center for the Collaborative Classroom.

Perez, Jessica. Who's Hiding Inside? Dinosaurs. Lensch, Chris, illus. 2005. (Who's Hiding Inside Ser.). 12p. (J). bds. 7.95 *(978-1-58117-246-1(X)*, Intervisual/Piggy Toes) Bendon, Inc.

Perritano, John & Hoena, Blake. Everything Dinosaurs: Chomp on Tons of Earthshaking Facts & Fun. 2014. (National Geographic Kids Everything Ser.). (ENG., Illus.). 64p. (J). (gr. 3-7). lib. bdg. 21.90 *(978-1-4263-1497-1(3)*, National Geographic Children's Bks.) National Geographic Society.

Peter Pauper Press Staff. Scratch & Sketch Dino Dudes: An Art Activity Book for Fossil Hunters of All Ages. 2005. (Activity Journal Ser.). 60p. 14.99 *(978-1-59359-973-7(0))* Peter Pauper Pr. Inc.

Peterson, Judy Monroe. Fossil Finders: Paleontologists. 2009. (Extreme Scientists Ser.). 24p. (gr. 2-3). 42.50 *(978-1-61512-452-7(7)*, PowerKids Pr.); (Illus.). (YA). lib. bdg. 22.60 *(978-1-4042-4524-2(3))* Rosen Publishing Group, Inc., The.

Peterson, Megan Cooley. Allosaurus & Its Relatives: The Need-To-Know Facts. Hughes, Jon, illus. 2016. (Dinosaur Fact Dig Ser.). (ENG.). 32p. (gr. 1-2). lib. bdg. 27.32 *(978-1-5157-2697-5(5))* Capstone Press of Coughlan Cos.

Peterson, Megan Cooley. Dinosaurs. 2017. (Rank It! Ser.). (ENG., Illus.). 32p. (J). (gr. 3-7). 31.35 ***(978-1-68072-060-0(0)***, Bolt) Black Rabbit Bks.

Peterson, Megan Cooley, et al. Dinosaur Fact Dig. 2016. (Dinosaur Fact Dig Ser.). (ENG.). 32p. (gr. 1-2). 273.20 *(978-1-5157-2715-6(7)*, Aplus Bks.) Capstone Press of Coughlan Cos.

Peterson, Sheryl. Pterodactyl. 2010. (Age of Dinosaurs Ser.). (YA). (gr. 4-7). 23.95 *(978-1-58341-975-5(6))* Creative Co., The.

—Stegosaurus. (Age of Dinosaurs Ser.). (gr. 4-7). 2011. (ENG.). 48p. (J). pap. 9.99 *(978-0-89812-541-2(3)*, Creative Education) 2010. (YA). 23.95 *(978-1-58341-976-2(4))* Creative Co., The.

—Velociraptor. (Age of Dinosaurs Ser.). 48p. (gr. 4-7). 2011. (ENG.). (J). pap. 9.99 *(978-0-89812-544-3(8)*, Creative Education) 2010. (Illus.). (YA). 23.95 *(978-1-58341-979-3(9))* Creative Co., The.

Phillips, Dee. I Want to Know about Dinosaurs. 2012. (I Want to Know about (New Forest Press) Ser.). (ENG., Illus.). 32p. (gr. 2-5). lib. bdg. 28.50 *(978-1-84898-527-8(4))* Black Rabbit Bks.

Pimentel, Annette Bay. Do You Really Want to Meet a Pterosaur? Fabbri, Daniele, illus. 2017. (Do You Really Want to Meet a Dinosaur? Ser.). (ENG.). 24p. (gr. 1-4). 20.95 ***(978-1-68151-113-9(4))*** Amicus Publishing.

—Do You Really Want to Meet a Stegosaurus? Fabbri, Daniele, illus. 2017. (Do You Really Want to Meet a Dinosaur? Ser.). (ENG.). 24p. (gr. 1-4). 20.95 ***(978-1-68151-114-6(2))*** Amicus Publishing.

—Do You Really Want to Meet Apatosaurus? Fabbri, Daniele, illus. 2017. (Do You Really Want to Meet a Dinosaur? Ser.). (ENG.). 24p. (gr. 1-4). 20.95 ***(978-1-68151-112-2(6))*** Amicus Publishing.

—Do You Really Want to Meet Triceratops? Fabbri, Daniele, illus. 2017. (Do You Really Want to Meet a Dinosaur? Ser.). (ENG.). 24p. (gr. 1-4). 20.95 ***(978-1-68151-115-3(0))*** Amicus Publishing.

—Do You Really Want to Meet Tyrannosaurus Rex? Fabbri, Daniele, illus. 2017. (Do You Really Want to Meet a Dinosaur? Ser.). (ENG.). 24p. (gr. 1-4). 20.95 ***(978-1-68151-116-0(9))*** Amicus Publishing.

—Do You Really Want to Meet Velociraptor? Fabbri, Daniele, illus. 2017. (Do You Really Want to Meet a Dinosaur? Ser.). (ENG.). 24p. (gr. 1-4). 20.95 ***(978-1-68151-117-7(7))*** Amicus Publishing.

Pledger, Maurice, illus. Dinosaurs & Bugs. 2014. (ENG.). 120p. (J). (gr. -1). act. bk. ed. 12.95 *(978-1-62686-106-0(4)*, Silver Dolphin Bks.) Readerlink Distribution Services, LLC.

Plumridge, Marianne. If Dinosaurs Lived in My Town. Eggleton, Bob, illus. 2013. (ENG.). 56p. (J). (gr. -1-3). 16.95 *(978-1-62636-176-8(2)*, 263176, Sky Pony Pr.) Skyhorse Publishing Co., Inc.

Podesto, Martine. Dinosaurs. 2008. (My Science Notebook Ser.). (Illus.). 104p. (YA). (gr. 5-9). lib. bdg. 31.00 *(978-0-8368-9213-0(5))* Stevens, Gareth Publishing LLLP.

Pomaska, Anna. BOOST Dinosaurs Coloring Book. 2013. (BOOST Educational Ser.). (ENG.). 32p. (J). (gr. 1-2). pap. 4.99 *(978-0-486-49415-9(2))* Dover Pubns., Inc.

—Dinosaurs. 2005. (Dover Coloring Bks.). (ENG., Illus.). 32p. (J). (gr. -1-2). 3.99 *(978-0-486-44701-8(4))* Dover Pubns., Inc.

Pop-Up Dinosaurs. 2017. (Pop-Up Bks.). (ENG.). (J). 14.99 ***(978-0-7945-3862-0(2)***, Usborne) EDC Publishing.

Prap, Lila. Dinosaurs!? 2015. (ENG., Illus.). 40p. (J). pap. 8.95 *(978-0-7358-4022-5(9))* North-South Bks., Inc.

Prehistoric Record Breakers, 6 Packs. (Discovery World Ser.). 24p. (gr. 1-2). 33.00 *(978-0-7635-8477-1(0))* Rigby Education.

Priddy Books Staff & Priddy, Roger. Dinosaur A-Z: For Kids Who Really Love Dinosaurs! l.t. rev. ed. 2004. (Smart Kids Ser.). (ENG., Illus.). 32p. (J). (gr. -1-2). bds. 9.99 *(978-0-312-49254-0(5)*, 9780312492540, Priddy Bks.) St. Martin's Pr.

Priddy, Roger. Dino Bites. 2015. (Fact Bites Ser.). (ENG.). 62p. (J). (gr. k-3). pap. 12.99 *(978-0-312-51847-9(1)*, 9780312518479, Priddy Bks.) St. Martin's Pr.

—Dinosaur. 2012. (ENG., Illus.). 36p. (J). (gr. -1-1). pap., act. bk. ed. 4.99 *(978-0-312-51329-0(1)*, 9780312513290, Priddy Bks.) St. Martin's Pr.

—Dinosaurs. 2012. (ENG., Illus.). 10p. (J). (gr. -1-k). 9.99 *(978-0-312-51511-9(1)*, 9780312515119, Priddy Bks.) St. Martin's Pr.

—My Big Dinosaur Book. 2011. (ENG.). (J). (gr. -1-k). bds. 8.99 *(978-0-312-51306-1(2)*, 9780312513061, Priddy Bks.) St. Martin's Pr.

Pringle, Laurence. Billions of Years, Amazing Changes: The Story of Evolution. Jenkins, Steve, illus. 2011. (ENG.). 112p. (J). (gr. 3). 17.95 *(978-1-59078-723-6(4))* Boyds Mills Pr.

Prokos, Anna. No Bones about It: Discovering Dinosaurs. Kendall, Gideon, illus. 2017. (Imagine That! Ser.). (ENG.). 32p. (J). (gr. 2-4). lib. bdg. 26.65 *(978-1-63440-150-0(6))*; 39.99 ***(978-1-63440-162-3(X))*** Red Chair Pr.

Prunier, James. Dinosaurs. Galeron, Henri, illus. 2012. (My First Discoveries Ser.: 3). (ENG.). 36p. (J). (gr. -1-k). 12.99 *(978-1-85103-379-9(3))* Moonlight Publishing, Ltd. GBR. Dist: Independent Pubs. Group.

Pryor, Kimberley Jane. Ankylosaurus. 2011. (Discovering Dinosaurs Ser.). 32p. (gr. 1). 28.50 *(978-1-60870-535-1(8))* Marshall Cavendish Corp.

—Muttaburrasaurus. 2011. (Discovering Dinosaurs Ser.). 32p. (gr. 1). 28.50 *(978-1-60870-537-5(4))* Marshall Cavendish Corp.

—Protoceratops. 2011. (Discovering Dinosaurs Ser.). 32p. (gr. 1). 28.50 *(978-1-60870-538-2(2))* Marshall Cavendish Corp.

—Tyrannosaurus Rex. 2011. (Discovering Dinosaurs Ser.). 32p. (gr. 1). 28.50 *(978-1-60870-539-9(0))* Marshall Cavendish Corp.

—Velociraptor. 2011. (Discovering Dinosaurs Ser.). 32p. (gr. 1). 28.50 *(978-1-60870-540-5(4))* Marshall Cavendish Corp.

Publications International Ltd. Staff, ed. Look & Find - My First Look & Find Barney. 2011. 18p. (J). bds. 3.75 net. *(978-1-4508-1892-6(7)*, 1450818927) Publications International, Ltd.

Punter, Russell. Stories of Dinosaurs. Decker, Cynthia, illus. 2006. (Young Reading Series 1 Ser.). 48p. (J). (gr. 2-5). per. 5.99 *(978-0-7945-1363-4(8)*, Usborne) EDC Publishing.

Raatma, Lucia. Allosaurus. 2012. (21st Century Junior Library: Dinosaurs Ser.). (ENG.). 24p. (gr. 2-5). 25.64 *(978-1-61080-466-0(X)*, 202076); pap. 12.79 *(978-1-61080-640-4(9)*, 202250) Cherry Lake Publishing.

—Ankylosaurus. 2012. (21st Century Junior Library: Dinosaurs Ser.). (ENG.). 24p. (gr. 2-5). 25.64 *(978-1-61080-461-5(9)*, 202071); pap. 12.79 *(978-1-61080-635-0(2)*, 202245) Cherry Lake Publishing.

—Apatosaurus. 2012. (21st Century Junior Library: Dinosaurs Ser.). (ENG.). 24p. (gr. 2-5). 25.64 *(978-1-61080-463-9(5)*, 202073); pap. 12.79 *(978-1-61080-637-4(9)*, 202247) Cherry Lake Publishing.

—Iguanodon. 2012. (21st Century Junior Library: Dinosaurs Ser.). (ENG.). 24p. (gr. 2-5). 25.64 *(978-1-61080-464-6(3)*, 202074); pap. 12.79 *(978-1-61080-638-1(7)*, 202248) Cherry Lake Publishing.

—Stegosaurus. 2012. (21st Century Junior Library: Dinosaurs Ser.). (ENG.). 24p. (gr. 2-5). 5th ed. 25.64

C
D

(978-1-61080-465-3(1), 202075) 6th ed. pap. 12.79 *(978-1-61080-639-8(5)*, 202249) Cherry Lake Publishing.

—Tyrannosaurus Rex. 2012. (21st Century Junior Library: Dinosaurs Ser.). (ENG.). 24p. (gr. 2-5). 9th ed. 25.64 *(978-1-61080-460-8(0)*, 202070) 10th ed. pap. 12.79 *(978-1-61080-634-3(4)*, 202244) Cherry Lake Publishing.

—Velociraptor. 2012. (21st Century Junior Library: Dinosaurs Ser.). (ENG.). 24p. (gr. 2-5). 11th ed. 25.64 *(978-1-61080-467-7(8)*, 202077) 12th ed. pap. 12.79 *(978-1-61080-641-1(7)*, 202251) Cherry Lake Publishing.

Rake, Matthew. Dinosaurs Rule. Minister, Peter, illus. 2015. (Prehistoric Field Guides). (ENG.). 32p. (J). (gr. 3-6). 26.65 *(978-1-4677-6349-3(7)*, Lerner Pubns.) Lerner Publishing Group.

—The Last Days of the Dinosaurs. Minister, Peter, illus. 2015. (Prehistoric Field Guides). (ENG.). 32p. (J). (gr. 3-6). lib. bdg. 26.65 *(978-1-4677-6350-9(0))* Lerner Publishing Group.

Rake, Matthew. Prehistoric Predators. Mendez, Simon, illus. 2017. (If Extinct Beasts Came to Life Ser.). (ENG.). 32p. (J). (gr. 3-6). 26.65 *(978-1-5124-0633-7(3))*; 7.99 ***(978-1-5124-3615-0(1))***; 39.99 ***(978-1-5124-3614-3(3))***; 39.99 ***(978-1-5124-0907-9(3))*** Lerner Publishing Group.

Rancourt, Heather & Gauches, Claudia. The Fossibles-Bursting from Extinction to Distinction. 2nd rev. ed. 2007. (Illus.). 151p. (J). per. 8.95 *(978-0-9702654-5-6(X))* 360 Marketing, LLC.

Random House Staff & Carbone, Courtney. Danger - Dinosaurs! Random House Staff, illus. 2015. (Step into Reading Ser.). (ENG., Illus.). 32p. (J). (gr. -1-1). 4.99 *(978-0-553-53687-4(7))*; lib. bdg. 12.99 *(978-0-553-53688-1(5))* Random Hse. Children's Bks. (Random Hse. Bks. for Young Readers).

Random House Staff & Holtz, Thomas R. T. Rex: Hunter or Scavenger? (Jurassic World) Random House Staff, illus. 2015. (Step into Reading Ser.). (ENG., Illus.). 48p. (J). (gr. 2-4). lib. bdg. 12.99 *(978-1-101-93409-8(3)*, Random Hse. Bks. for Young Readers) Random Hse. Children's Bks.

Raum, Elizabeth. Taipans. 2015. (Poisonous Animals Ser.). (ENG., Illus.). 32p. (J). (gr. 2-4). 19.95 *(978-1-60753-791-5(5))* Amicus Publishing.

Raymond, Jayne. Meet Deinonychus. 2014. (Age of Dinosaurs Ser.). 32p. (J). (gr. 3-5). lib. bdg. 28.50 *(978-1-62712-794-3(1))* Cavendish Square Publishing.

—Meet Velociraptor. 2014. (Age of Dinosaurs Ser.). 32p. (J). (gr. 3-5). lib. bdg. 28.50 *(978-1-62712-779-0(8))* Cavendish Square Publishing.

Reasoner, Charles. Fan-Tab-U-Lus: Dinosaurs. Devaney, Adam, illus. 2011. (Fan-Tab-U-Lus Bks.). (ENG.). 12p. (J). (gr. -1). bds. 9.99 *(978-1-935498-58-2(4))* Just For Kids Pr., LLC.

Red Bird Press Staff. Dinosaurs. 2004. (Mission Xtreme 3D Ser.). 18p. (J). pap. 5.95 *(978-1-902626-61-1(3))* Red Bird Publishing GBR. Dist: Weatherhill, Inc.

—Secret Spex Dinosaurs. 2004. (Secret Picture Search Ser.). 18p. (J). pap. 5.95 *(978-1-902626-65-9(6))* Red Bird Publishing GBR. Dist: Weatherhill, Inc.

Redmond, Shirley Raye & Redmond, Shirley Raye. The Dog That Dug for Dinosaurs. Sullivan, Simon, illus. 2004. (Ready-To-Reads Ser.). (ENG.). 32p. (J). (gr. 1-3). pap. 3.99 *(978-0-689-85708-9(X)*, Simon Spotlight) Simon Spotlight.

Reed, M. K. Dinosaurs: Fossils & Feathers. Flood, Joe, illus. 2016. 117p. (J). ***(978-1-4844-7999-5(8)***, First Second Bks.) Roaring Brook Pr.

Reed, M. K. Science Comics: Dinosaurs. Flood, Joe, illus. 2016. (Science Comics Ser.). (ENG.). 128p. (J). pap. 12.99 *(978-1-62672-143-2(2)*, 9781626721432, First Second Bks.) Roaring Brook Pr.

Reinhart, Matthew & Sabuda, Robert. Encyclopedia Prehistorica Dinosaurs. Reinhart, Matthew & Sabuda, Robert, illus. 2005. (Encyclopedia Prehistorica Ser.: 1). (ENG., Illus.). 12p. (J). (gr. k-4). 34.99 *(978-0-7636-2228-2(1))* Candlewick Pr.

Rhonda Lucas Donald, Rhonda Lucas. Dino Tracks, 1 vol. Morrison, Cathy, illus. 2013. (ENG.). 32p. (J). (gr. 1-4). 17.95 *(978-1-60718-619-9(5))* Arbordale Publishing.

Richardson, Hazel. Dinosaurs & Prehistoric Life. 2003. (Smithsonian Handbooks Ser.). (ENG., Illus.). 224p. pap. 22.00 *(978-0-7894-9361-3(6)*, DK) Dorling Kindersley Publishing, Inc.

Richmond, Dee & Colella, Cheryl. The Dino Abc. 2009. (Illus.). 56p. pap. 21.99 *(978-1-4389-9960-9(7))* AuthorHouse.

Rieger, Linda. Dinosaur Party. Bianchi, John, illus. 2007. 20p. (J). *(978-0-9779427-2-5(4))* Pathways into Science.

Riehecky, Janet. Carnotaurus & Other Odd Meat-Eaters: The Need-To-Know Facts. Hughes, Jon, illus. 2016. (Dinosaur Fact Dig Ser.). (ENG.). 32p. (gr. 1-2). lib. bdg. 27.32 *(978-1-5157-2695-1(9))* Capstone Press of Coughlan Cos.

—Iguanodon & Other Bird-Footed Dinosaurs: The Need-To-Know Facts. Hughes, Jon, illus. 2016. (Dinosaur Fact Dig Ser.). (ENG.). 32p. (gr. 1-2). lib. bdg. 27.32 *(978-1-5157-2696-8(7))* Capstone Press of Coughlan Cos.

—Megalodon [Scholastic]. 2009. (Dinosaurs & Prehistoric Animals Ser.). 24p. (gr. k-1). pap. 1.00 *(978-1-4296-4246-0(7)*, Pebble Plus) Capstone Press of Coughlan Cos.

—Show Me Dinosaurs: My First Picture Encyclopedia, 1 vol. 2013. (My First Picture Encyclopedias Ser.). (ENG.). 32p. (gr. 1-2). pap. 8.10 *(978-1-4765-3789-4(5)*, Aplus Bks.); (Illus.). 7.95 *(978-1-62065-916-8(6))*; lib. bdg. 27.32 *(978-1-62065-057-8(6))* Capstone Press of Coughlan Cos.

—Triceratops, 1 vol. 2014. (Little Paleontologist Ser.). (ENG.). 32p. (gr. 1-3). lib. bdg. 27.99 *(978-1-4914-0811-7(1))* Capstone Press of Coughlan Cos.

—Velociraptor, 1 vol. 2014. (Little Paleontologist Ser.). (ENG.). 32p. (gr. 1-3). lib. bdg. 27.99 *(978-1-4914-0813-1(8))* Capstone Press of Coughlan Cos.

Rigby Education Staff. Discovery World Red Prehistoric. (Discovery World Ser.). (Illus.). 12p. (gr. 1-2). 31.00 *(978-0-7635-2705-1(X))* Rigby Education.

Riggs, Kate. Apatosaurus. 2012. (J). 25.65 *(978-1-60818-116-2(2)*, Creative Education) Creative Co., The.

—Pterodactyls. 2012. (When Dinosaurs Lived Ser.). (ENG., Illus.). 24p. (J). (gr. 1-3). pap. 7.99 *(978-0-89812-731-7(9)*, Creative Paperbacks) Creative Co., The.

—Stegosaurus. 2012. (J). 25.65 *(978-1-60818-118-6(9)*, Creative Education) Creative Co., The.

—Triceratops. 2012. (J). 25.65 *(978-1-60818-119-3(7)*, Creative Education) Creative Co., The.

—Tyrannosaurus Rex. 2012. (J). 25.65 *(978-1-60818-120-9(0)*, Creative Education) Creative Co., The.

—Velociraptor. (J). 2015. pap. *(978-1-62832-213-2(6)*, Creative Paperbacks) 2012. 25.65 *(978-1-60818-121-6(9)*, Creative Education) Creative Co., The.

—When Dinosaurs Lived - Velociraptor. 2012. (When Dinosaurs Lived Ser.). (ENG., Illus.). 24p. (J). (gr. 1-3). pap. 7.99 *(978-0-89812-735-5(1)*, Creative Paperbacks) Creative Co., The.

—When Dinosaurs Lived: Apatosaurus. 2012. (When Dinosaurs Lived Ser.). (ENG., Illus.). 24p. (J). (gr. 1-3). pap. 7.99 *(978-0-89812-730-0(0)*, Creative Paperbacks) Creative Co., The.

—When Dinosaurs Lived: Stegosaurus. 2012. (When Dinosaurs Lived Ser.). (ENG., Illus.). 24p. (J). (gr. 1-3). pap. 6.99 *(978-0-89812-732-4(7)*, Creative Paperbacks) Creative Co., The.

—When Dinosaurs Lived: Triceratops. 2012. (When Dinosaurs Lived Ser.). (ENG., Illus.). 24p. (J). (gr. 1-3). pap. 6.99 *(978-0-89812-733-1(5)*, Creative Paperbacks) Creative Co., The.

Rigo, L., illus. Little Dinosaur. 2014. (Mini Look at Me Bks.). (ENG.). 10p. (J). (gr. -1 — 1). bds. 4.99 *(978-0-7641-6730-0(8))* Barron's Educational Series, Inc.

Ring, Susan. Dinosaurs. Kendall, Gideon, illus. 2008. (ENG.). 10p. (J). (gr. -1-1). 15.99 *(978-1-58476-730-5(8))* Innovative Kids.

Ringstad, Arnold. Dinosaur Myths, Busted! 2017. (Science Myths, Busted! Ser.). (ENG., Illus.). 32p. (J). (gr. 3-6). 21.95 *(978-1-63235-301-6(6))* Pr. Room Editions LLC.

Ripley, Esther. The Big Dinosaur Dig. 2003. (DK Readers Ser.). (Illus.). 48p. (J). (gr. -1-3). 11.65 *(978-0-7569-3355-5(2))* Perfection Learning Corp.

—Big Dinosaur Dig, Level 3. 2009. (DK Readers Ser.). (ENG.). 48p. (J). (gr. 2-4). 3.99 *(978-0-7566-5595-2(1)*, DK Children) Dorling Kindersley Publishing, Inc.

Rissman, Rebecca. Brachiosaurus & Other Big Long-Necked Dinosaurs: The Need-To-Know Facts. Hughes, Jon, illus. 2016. (Dinosaur Fact Dig Ser.). (ENG.). 32p. (gr. 1-2). lib. bdg. 27.32 *(978-1-4914-9647-3(9)*, Aplus Bks.) Capstone Press of Coughlan Cos.

—Edmontosaurus & Other Duck-Billed Dinosaurs: The Need-to-Know Facts. Hughes, Jon, illus. 2016. (Dinosaur Fact Dig Ser.). (ENG.). 32p. (gr. 1-2). lib. bdg. 27.32 *(978-1-5157-2698-2(3))* Capstone Press of Coughlan Cos.

—Velociraptor & Other Raptors: The Need-To-Know Facts. Hughes, Jon, illus. 2016. (Dinosaur Fact Dig Ser.). (ENG.). 32p. (gr. 1-2). lib. bdg. 27.32 *(978-1-4914-9651-0(7)*, Aplus Bks.) Capstone Press of Coughlan Cos.

Rober, Harold. Iguanodon. 2017. (Bumba Books (tm) — Dinosaurs & Prehistoric Beasts Ser.). (ENG.). 24p. (J). (gr. -1-1). 12.99 ***(978-1-5124-3711-9(5))***; 38.65 ***(978-1-5124-3710-2(7))***; 38.65 ***(978-1-5124-2737-0(3))*** Lerner Publishing Group. (Lerner Pubns.).

—Pterodactyl. 2017. (Bumba Books (tm) — Dinosaurs & Prehistoric Beasts Ser.). (ENG.). 24p. (J). (gr. -1-1). 12.99 ***(978-1-5124-3714-0(X))***; 38.65 ***(978-1-5124-2734-9(9))***; 38.65 ***(978-1-5124-3713-3(1))*** Lerner Publishing Group. (Lerner Pubns.).

—Triceratops. 2017. (Bumba Books (tm) — Dinosaurs & Prehistoric Beasts Ser.). (ENG.). 24p. (J). (gr. -1-1). 12.99 ***(978-1-5124-3720-1(4))***; 38.65 ***(978-1-5124-2736-3(5))***; 38.65 ***(978-1-5124-3719-5(0))*** Lerner Publishing Group. (Lerner Pubns.).

—Velociraptor. 2017. (Bumba Books (tm) — Dinosaurs & Prehistoric Beasts Ser.). (ENG.). 24p. (J). (gr. -1-1). 12.99 ***(978-1-5124-3723-2(9))***; 38.65 ***(978-1-5124-2735-6(7))***; 38.65 ***(978-1-5124-3722-5(0))*** Lerner Publishing Group. (Lerner Pubns.).

Rober, Harold T. Iguanodon. 2017. (Bumba Books (tm) — Dinosaurs & Prehistoric Beasts Ser.). (ENG., Illus.). 24p. (J). (gr. -1-1). 25.32 *(978-1-5124-2643-4(1))* Lerner Publishing Group.

—El Pterodáctilo. 2017. (Bumba Books (tm) en Español — Dinosaurios y Bestias Prehistóricas (Dinosaurs & Prehistoric Beasts) Ser.). (SPA.). 24p. (J). (gr. -1-1). 25.32 ***(978-1-5124-4114-7(7))*** Lerner Publishing Group.

—Pterodactyl. 2017. (Bumba Books (tm) — Dinosaurs & Prehistoric Beasts Ser.). (ENG., Illus.). 24p. (J). (gr. -1-1). 25.32 *(978-1-5124-2639-7(3))* Lerner Publishing Group.

—Triceratops. 2017. (Bumba Books (tm) — Dinosaurs & Prehistoric Beasts Ser.). (ENG., Illus.). 24p. (J). (gr. -1-1). 25.32 *(978-1-5124-2642-7(3))* Lerner Publishing Group.

—El Tricératops. 2017. (Bumba Books (tm) en Español — Dinosaurios y Bestias Prehistóricas (Dinosaurs & Prehistoric Beasts) Ser.). (SPA.). 24p. (J). (gr. -1-1). 25.32 ***(978-1-5124-4116-1(3))*** Lerner Publishing Group.

—Velociraptor. 2017. (Bumba Books (tm) — Dinosaurs & Prehistoric Beasts Ser.). (ENG.). 24p. (J). (gr. -1-1). 25.32 *(978-1-5124-2641-0(5))* Lerner Publishing Group.

Rober, Harold T. El Velociraptor. 2017. (Bumba Books (tm) en Español — Dinosaurios y Bestias Prehistóricas (Dinosaurs & Prehistoric Beasts) Ser.). (SPA.). 24p. (J). (gr. -1-1). 25.32 ***(978-1-5124-4115-4(5))*** Lerner Publishing Group.

Roberts, Russell. Where Did All the Dinosaurs Go? 2005. (Natural Disasters Ser.). (Illus.). 32p. (J). (gr. 1-4). lib. bdg. 25.70 *(978-1-58415-420-4(9))* Mitchell Lane Pubs., Inc.

Rockwood, Leigh. Allosaurus. 2012. (Illus.). 24p. (J). 49.50 *(978-1-4488-5095-2(9))*; pap. 8.25 *(978-1-4488-5094-5(0))*; lib. bdg. 22.60 *(978-1-4488-4972-7(1))* Rosen Publishing Group, Inc., The. (PowerKids Pr.).

—Ankylosaurus. 2012. (Illus.). 24p. (J). 49.50 *(978-1-4488-5085-3(1))*; pap. 8.25 *(978-1-4488-5084-6(3))*; lib. bdg. 22.60 *(978-1-4488-4967-3(5))* Rosen Publishing Group, Inc., The. (PowerKids Pr.).

—Brachiosaurus. 2012. (J). 49.50 *(978-1-4488-5093-8(2))*; pap. 8.25 *(978-1-4488-5092-1(4))*; (Illus.). 24p. lib. bdg. 22.60 *(978-1-4488-4971-0(3)*, 1329087) Rosen Publishing Group, Inc., The. (PowerKids Pr.).

—Diplodocus. 2012. (Illus.). 24p. (J). 49.50 *(978-1-4488-5083-9(5))*; pap. 8.25 *(978-1-4488-5082-2(7))*; lib. bdg. 22.60 *(978-1-4488-4966-6(7))* Rosen Publishing Group, Inc., The. (PowerKids Pr.).

—Hadrosaurus. 2012. (Illus.). 24p. (J). 49.50 *(978-1-4488-5097-6(5))*; pap. 8.25 *(978-1-4488-5096-9(7))*; lib. bdg. 22.60 *(978-1-4488-4973-4(X))* Rosen Publishing Group, Inc., The. (PowerKids Pr.).

—Iguanodon. 2012. (Illus.). 24p. (J). 49.50 *(978-1-4488-5099-0(1))*; pap. 8.25 *(978-1-4488-5098-3(3))*; lib. bdg. 22.60 *(978-1-4488-4974-1(8))* Rosen Publishing Group, Inc., The. (PowerKids Pr.).

—Stegosaurus. 2012. (Illus.). 24p. (J). 49.50 *(978-1-4488-5077-8(0))*; pap. 8.25 *(978-1-4488-5076-1(2))*; lib. bdg. 22.60 *(978-1-4488-4963-5(2))* Rosen Publishing Group, Inc., The. (PowerKids Pr.).

—T. Rex. 2012. (Illus.). 24p. (J). 49.50 *(978-1-4488-5079-2(7))*; pap. 8.25 *(978-1-4488-5078-5(9))*; lib. bdg. 22.60 *(978-1-4488-4964-2(0))* Rosen Publishing Group, Inc., The. (PowerKids Pr.).

—Triceratops. 2012. (Illus.). 24p. (J). 49.50 *(978-1-4488-5089-1(4))*; pap. 8.25 *(978-1-4488-5088-4(6))*; lib. bdg. 22.60 *(978-1-4488-4969-7(1))* Rosen Publishing Group, Inc., The. (PowerKids Pr.).

—Velociraptor. 2012. (J). 49.50 *(978-1-4488-5087-7(8))*; pap. 8.25 *(978-1-4488-5086-0(X))*; (Illus.). 24p. lib. bdg. 22.60 *(978-1-4488-4968-0(3)*, 1329112) Rosen Publishing Group, Inc., The. (PowerKids Pr.).

Roderick, Stacey. Dinosaurs from Head to Tail. Kwanchai, Moriya, illus. 2015. (Head to Tail Ser.). (ENG.). 36p. (J). (gr. -1-2). 16.95 *(978-1-77138-044-7(6))* Kids Can Pr., Ltd. CAN. Dist: Hachette Bk. Group.

Rodhe, Paul. Kids Meet the Dinosaurs. 2013. (Kids Meet Ser.: 1). (ENG.). 90p. (J). 15.95 *(978-1-60433-307-7(3)*, Applesauce Pr.) Cider Mill Pr. Bk. Pubs., LLC.

Rodhe, Paul & Beatrice, Paul. Kids Meet the Dinosaurs. 2009. (ENG., Illus.). 100p. (J). (gr. -1). pap. 12.95 *(978-1-60433-029-8(5)*, Applesauce Pr.) Cider Mill Pr. Bk. Pubs., LLC.

Romero, Libby. Dinosaurs. 2005. (J). pap. *(978-1-4108-4614-3(8))* Benchmark Education Co.

Rooney, Anne. Dinosaurs. 2003. (Wicked Wallets Ser.). (Illus.). 96p. (YA). pap. *(978-1-84347-037-3(3)*, Pavilion Children's Books) Pavilion Bks.

—Layer by Layer: Discovering Dinosaurs. Carpenter, Suzanne, illus. 2016. (Layer by Layer Ser.). (ENG.). 32p. (J). (gr. k). 19.99 *(978-1-62686-752-9(6)*, Silver Dolphin Bks.) Readerlink Distribution Services, LLC.

Rosewarne, Graham, illus. My First Dinosaur Book. 2015. (ENG.). 48p. bds. 9.99 *(978-1-86147-424-7(5)*, Armadillo) Anness Publishing GBR. Dist: National Bk. Network.

Rothrock, Megan H. The LEGO Adventure Book Vol. 2: Spaceships, Pirates, Dragons & More! 2013. (ENG., Illus.). 196p. (gr. 5). 24.95 *(978-1-59327-512-9(9)*, 9781593275129) No Starch Pr., Inc.

Rugg, Michael & Kieffer, Steve. Dinosaur Coloring Book. 2005. (Illus.). 24p. (J). pap. 4.95 *(978-0-88839-593-1(0))* Hancock Hse. Pubs.

Rupert, Matthews. Visual Factfinder Dinosaurs & Prehistoric Life. 2008. 512p. pap. *(978-1-84810-078-7(7))* Miles Kelly Publishing, Ltd.

—What about Dinosaurs. 2008. 400p. pap. *(978-1-84810-067-1(1))* Miles Kelly Publishing, Ltd.

Sabatino, Chris. Dinosaur Doodles, 1 vol. 2012. (ENG., Illus.). 272p. (J). pap. 9.99 *(978-1-4236-3084-5(X))* Gibbs Smith, Publisher.

Sabatino, Michael. T. Rex vs. Crocodile. 2015. (Bizarre Beast Battles Ser.). (ENG., Illus.). 24p. (J). (gr. 2-3). lib. bdg. 22.60 *(978-1-4824-2802-5(4))* Stevens, Gareth Publishing LLLP.

Sattler, Jennifer. Who's Hatching? 2017. (ENG.). 26p. (J). (gr. -1-k). bds. 7.99 ***(978-1-4380-5004-1(6))*** Barron's Educational Series, Inc.

Savery, Annabel. Dinosaurs. 2012. (It's Amazing Ser.). (Illus.). 32p. (gr. 3-6). lib. bdg. 31.35 *(978-1-59920-687-5(0))* Black Rabbit Bks.

Saviola, Ava. Dinosaur ABCs. 2012. (Dinosaur School Ser.). (Illus.). 24p. (J). (gr. -1-1). pap. 8.15 *(978-1-4339-7136-5(4))*; lib. bdg. 22.60 *(978-1-4339-7135-8(6))* Stevens, Gareth Publishing LLLP.

—Dinosaur Colors. 2012. (Dinosaur School Ser.). (Illus.). 24p. (J). (gr. -1-1). pap. 8.15 *(978-1-4339-7140-2(2))*; lib. bdg. 22.60 *(978-1-4339-7139-6(9))* Stevens, Gareth Publishing LLLP.

—Dinosaur Opposites. 2012. (Dinosaur School Ser.). (Illus.). 24p. (J). (gr. -1-1). pap. 8.15 *(978-1-4339-7144-0(5))*; lib. bdg. 22.60 *(978-1-4339-7143-3(7))* Stevens, Gareth Publishing LLLP.

—Dinosaur Shapes. 2012. (Dinosaur School Ser.). (Illus.). 24p. (J). (gr. -1-1). pap. 8.15 *(978-1-4339-7148-8(8))*; lib. bdg. 22.60 *(978-1-4339-7147-1(X))* Stevens, Gareth Publishing LLLP.

—Dinosaurs Count! 2012. (Dinosaur School Ser.). (Illus.). 24p. (J). (gr. -1-1). pap. 8.15 *(978-1-4339-7152-5(6))*; lib. bdg. 22.60 *(978-1-4339-7151-8(8))* Stevens, Gareth Publishing LLLP.

—Dinosaur's First Words. 2012. (Dinosaur School Ser.). (Illus.). 24p. (J). (gr. -1-1). pap. 8.15 *(978-1-4339-7156-3(9))*; lib. bdg. 22.60 *(978-1-4339-7155-6(0))* Stevens, Gareth Publishing LLLP.

Schatz, Dennis. Al Descubierto T Rex. 2003. (Al Descubierto Ser.). 16p. (J). bds. *(978-970-718-121-2(4)*, Silver Dolphin en Español) Advanced Marketing, S. de R. L. de C. V.

—Explore a T. Rex. Bonadonna, Davide & Keitzmueller, Christian, illus. 2016. (Explore Ser.). (ENG.). 16p. (J). (gr. 2). 21.95 *(978-1-62686-395-8(4)*, Silver Dolphin Bks.) Readerlink Distribution Services, LLC.

—King of the Dinosaurs. 2005. (Illus.). 32p. (J). pap. *(978-0-439-77757-5(7))* Scholastic, Inc.

Scholastic, Inc. Staff. Dino Safari: A LEGO(r) Adventure in the Real World. 2016. (LEGO Nonfiction Ser.). (ENG.). 32p. (J). (gr. -1-3). pap. 4.99 *(978-0-545-94766-4(9))* Scholastic, Inc.

—Dinos. 2016. (Scholastic Early Learners Ser.). (ENG.). 14p. (J). (gr. -1 — 1). bds. 6.99 *(978-0-545-90337-0(8))* Scholastic, Inc.

Scholastic, Inc. Staff, contrib. by. Dinosaurs. 2014. (Scholastic Discover More Ser.). (ENG.). 16p. (J). (gr. 2-5). 6.99 *(978-0-545-63627-8(2)*, Scholastic Reference) Scholastic, Inc.

Scholastic Library Publishing. Rookie Read-about(r) Dinosaurs. 2012. (Rookie Read-about Ser.). (J). 138.00 *(978-0-531-26720-2(2)*, Children's Pr.) Scholastic Library Publishing.

Schomp, Virginia. Ceratosaurus: And Other Horned Meat-Eaters. 2005. (Prehistoric World Ser.). (Illus.). 31p. (J). (gr. 3-7). lib. bdg. *(978-0-7614-2009-5(6)*, Benchmark Bks.) Marshall Cavendish Corp.

—Iguanodon: And Other Spiky-Thumbed Plant-Eaters. 2005. (Prehistoric World Ser.). (Illus.). 32p. (gr. 4-7). lib. bdg. 20.95 *(978-0-7614-2005-7(3)*, Benchmark Bks.) Marshall Cavendish Corp.

—Ornithomimus: And Other Speedy Ostrich Dinosaurs. 2005. (Prehistoric World Ser.). (Illus.). 31p. (J). (gr. 3-7). lib. bdg. *(978-0-7614-2006-4(1)*, Benchmark Bks.) Marshall Cavendish Corp.

—Plateosaurus: And Other Early Long-Necked Plant-Eaters. 2005. (Prehistoric World Ser.). (Illus.). 32p. (gr. 4-7). lib. bdg. 20.95 *(978-0-7614-2008-8(8)*, Benchmark Bks.) Marshall Cavendish Corp.

—Stegosaurus: And Other Plate-Backed Plant-Eaters. 2003. (Prehistoric World Ser.). (Illus.). 32p. (gr. 4-18). lib. bdg. 20.95 *(978-0-7614-1544-2(0)*, Benchmark Bks.) Marshall Cavendish Corp.

—Therizinosaurus: And Other Colossal-Clawed Plant-Eaters. 2005. (Prehistoric World Ser.). (Illus.). 32p. (gr. 4-7). lib. bdg. 20.95 *(978-0-7614-2007-1(X)*, Benchmark Bks.) Marshall Cavendish Corp.

Schuette, Sarah L. A Dinosaur Cookbook: Simple Recipes for Kids, 1 vol. 2012. (First Cookbooks Ser.). (ENG.). 24p. (gr. 1-2). lib. bdg. 25.32 *(978-1-4296-7621-2(3)*, First Facts) Capstone Press of Coughlan Cos.

Schwaeber, Barbie Heit. Alphabet of Dinosaurs. Buchs, Thomas et al, illus. 2011. (Alphabet Bks.). (ENG.). 40p. (J). (gr. -1-3). 17.95 *(978-1-60727-671-5(2))*; 9.95 *(978-1-60727-444-5(2))* Soundprints.

—Alphabet of Dinosaurs. Buchs, Thomas, illus. (ENG.). 40p. 2009. 9.95 *(978-1-59249-993-9(7))* 2007. (J). (gr. -1-2). 15.95 *(978-1-59249-724-9(1))* Soundprints.

Schwartz, Betty Ann & Seresin, Lynn. My Dinosaurs! A Read & Play Book. Bendall-Brunello, John, illus. 2014. (ENG.). 10p. (J). (gr. -1-k). bds. 7.99 *(978-0-545-69076-8(5)*, Cartwheel Bks.) Scholastic, Inc.

Scott, Peter David, illus. Dinosaur. 2006. 31p. (J). *(978-0-7607-7524-0(9))* backpackbooks.

Seah, Elliott. Elliott's Guide to Dinosaurs. 2016. (ENG., Illus.). 48p. (J). (gr. 1-5). 16.95 *(978-1-77164-237-8(8))* Greystone Books Ltd. CAN. Dist: Publishers Group West (PGW).

Searl, Duncan. The Maiasaura Nests: Jack Horner's Dinosaur Eggs. 2006. (Fossil Hunters Ser.). (Illus.). 32p. (YA). (gr. 2-5). lib. bdg. 25.27 *(978-1-59716-257-9(4))* Bearport Publishing Co., Inc.

Sereno, Paul C. & Lunis, Natalie. Supercroc: Paul Sereno's Dinosaur Eater. 2016. (Fossil Hunters Ser.). (ENG.). 32p. (J). (gr. 2-7). pap. 8.95 *(978-1-944998-74-5(8))* Bearport Publishing Co., Inc.

Shaw, Gina. Dinosaurs in a Box. 2014. (ENG.). 48p. (J). (gr. k-2). 9.99 *(978-0-545-68176-6(6)*, Scholastic Nonfiction) Scholastic, Inc.

Shaw-Russell, Susan. A Day with the Dinosaurs Sticker Activity Book. 2011. (Dover Little Activity Books Stickers Ser.). (ENG., Illus.). 4p. (J). (gr. k-3). 1.99 *(978-0-486-47236-2(1))* Dover Pubns., Inc.

Shealy, Dennis. My Little Golden Book about Dinosaurs. Laberis, Steph, illus. 2017. (Little Golden Book Ser.). (ENG.). 24p. (J). (-k). 4.99 ***(978-0-385-37861-1(0)***, Golden Bks.) Random Hse. Children's Bks.

Shelly, Jeff. Draw & Color Dinosaurs: Step-by-Step Instructions for 27 Prehistoric Creatures. Cerato, Mattia, illus. 2004. (Learn to Draw Ser.). (ENG.). 40p. (J). (gr. 1-3). per. 4.95 *(978-1-56010-817-7(7)*, 1560108177) Quarto Publishing Group USA.

Shofner, Melissa Raé. Gareth's Guide to Unearthing a Dinosaur. 2017. (Gareth Guides to an Extraordinary Life Ser.). 32p. (J). (gr. 4-5). pap. 63.00 ***(978-1-5382-0339-2(1))***; lib. bdg. 26.60 ***(978-1-5382-0360-6(X))*** Stevens, Gareth Publishing LLLP.

Shone, Rob. Allosaurus: The Strange Lizard. Riley, Terry, illus. 2009. (Graphic Dinosaurs Ser.). (ENG.). 32p. (J). pap. 12.30 *(978-1-4358-8592-9(9))*; (gr. 2-5). 26.50 *(978-1-4358-8588-2(0))* Rosen Publishing Group, Inc., The. (PowerKids Pr.).

—Archaeopteryx: The First Bird. 2012. (Illus.). 32p. (J). 73.80 *(978-1-4488-5247-5(1))*; pap. 12.30 *(978-1-4488-5246-8(3))*; lib. bdg. 26.50 *(978-1-4488-5204-8(8))* Rosen Publishing Group, Inc., The. (PowerKids Pr.).

—Brachiosaurus: The Long-Limbed Dinosaur. Riley, Terry, illus. 2009. (Graphic Dinosaurs Ser.). (ENG.). 32p. (J). pap. 12.30 *(978-1-4358-8600-1(3))*; (gr. 2-5). 26.50 *(978-1-4358-8589-9(9))* Rosen Publishing Group, Inc., The. (PowerKids Pr.).

—Diplodocus: The Whip-Tailed Dinosaur. Field, James, illus. 2008. (Graphic Dinosaurs Ser.). (ENG.). 32p. (J). 50.50 *(978-1-61532-137-7(3)*, PowerKids Pr.); (gr. 2-5). lib. bdg. 26.50 *(978-1-4358-2504-8(7))* Rosen Publishing Group, Inc., The.

—Giganotosaurus: The Giant Southern Lizard. Riley, Terry, illus. (Graphic Dinosaurs Ser.). (ENG.). 32p. 2009. (gr. 2-5). pap. 12.30 *(978-1-4042-7712-0(9)*, PowerKids Pr.) 2008. (J). 50.50 *(978-1-61532-135-3(7)*, PowerKids Pr.) 2008. (J). (gr. 2-5). lib. bdg. 26.50 *(978-1-4358-2502-4(0))* Rosen Publishing Group, Inc., The.

—Hadrosaurus: The Duck-Billed Dinosaur. Riley, Terry, illus. 2009. (Graphic Dinosaurs Ser.). (ENG.). 32p. (J). pap. 12.30 *(978-1-4358-8598-1(8))*; (gr. 2-5). 26.50 *(978-1-4358-8591-2(0))* Rosen Publishing Group, Inc., The. (PowerKids Pr.).

—Oviraptor: The Egg Thief. 2012. (Illus.). 32p. (J). 73.80 *(978-1-4488-5256-7(0))*; pap. 12.30 *(978-1-4488-5255-0(2))*; lib. bdg. 26.50 *(978-1-4488-5207-9(2))* Rosen Publishing Group, Inc., The. (PowerKids Pr.).

—Pachycephalosaurus: The Thick Headed Lizard. 2012. (Illus.). 32p. (J). 73.80 *(978-1-4488-5254-3(4))*; pap. 12.30 *(978-1-4488-5253-6(6))*; lib. bdg. 26.50 *(978-1-4488-5252-9(8))* Rosen Publishing Group, Inc., The. (PowerKids Pr.).

—Triceratops: The Three Horned Dinosaur. (Graphic Dinosaurs Ser.). (ENG.). 32p. 2009. (J). (gr. 4-4). 50.50 *(978-1-61512-914-0(6))* 2008. (Illus.). (gr. 2-5). pap. 12.30

(978-1-4042-9626-8(3)) Rosen Publishing Group, Inc., The. (PowerKids Pr.).

—Triceratops: The Three Horned Dinosaur. Riley, Terry & Ball, Geoff, illus. 2007. (Graphic Dinosaurs Ser.). (ENG.). 32p. (J). (gr. 2-5). lib. bdg. 26.50 *(978-1-4042-3896-1(4))* Rosen Publishing Group, Inc., The.

—Tyrannosaurus: The Tyrant Lizard. (Graphic Dinosaurs Ser.). (ENG.). 32p. 2009. (J). (gr. 4-4). 50.50 *(978-1-61512-917-1(0))* 2008. (Illus.). (gr. 2-5). pap. 12.30 *(978-1-4042-9627-5(1)*, 1270754) Rosen Publishing Group, Inc., The. (PowerKids Pr.).

—Tyrannosaurus: The Tyrant Lizard. Field, James, illus. 2007. (Graphic Dinosaurs Ser.). (ENG.). 32p. (J). (gr. 2-5). lib. bdg. 26.50 *(978-1-4042-3897-8(2))* Rosen Publishing Group, Inc., The.

Shone, Rob & Field, James, illus. Diplodocus: The Whip-Tailed Dinosaur. 2009. (Graphic Dinosaurs Ser.). (ENG.). 32p. (gr. 2-5). pap. 12.30 *(978-1-4042-7714-4(5))* Rosen Publishing Group, Inc., The.

Shore, Marguerite, tr. from ITA. The Journey: Plateosaurus. Bacchin, Matteo, illus. 2008. (Dinosaurs: Ser.: Vol. 1). (ENG.). 63p. (J). (gr. 3-6). 15.95 *(978-0-7892-0978-8(0)*, Abbeville Kids) Abbeville Pr., Inc.

Shulman, Mark. Dinosaurs Then & Wow! Ostrom, Bob, illus. 2005. (Storytime Stickers Ser.). (ENG.). 16p. (J). (gr. k-2). pap. 5.95 *(978-1-4027-1805-2(5))* Sterling Publishing Co., Inc.

Siamon, Sharon. Dinosaurs! Battle of the Bones. 2007. (DK Readers Ser.). (ENG., Illus.). 48p. (J). (gr. 3-7). per. 3.99 *(978-0-7566-3139-0(4)*, DK Children) Dorling Kindersley Publishing, Inc.

Sibbick, John. My Favorite Dinosaurs. 2012. (ENG., Illus.). 32p. (J). (gr. -1-3). pap. 5.95 *(978-1-59687-400-8(7)*, Milk & Cookies) ibooks, Inc.

Siegel, Elizabeth. Dinosaurs. 2007. (Steck-Vaughn BOLDPRINT Anthologies Ser.). (ENG., Illus.). 48p. (gr. 4-6). pap. 16.90 *(978-1-4190-4019-1(7))* Houghton Mifflin Harcourt Publishing Co.

Signore, Marco. Giant vs. Giant: Argentinosaurus & Giganotosaurus. Bacchin, Matteo, illus. 2010. (Dinosaurs: Ser.). (ENG.). 64p. (J). (gr. 3). 15.95 *(978-0-7892-1013-5(4)*, Abbeville Kids) Abbeville Pr., Inc.

—T. Rex & the Great Extinction. Bacchin, Matteo, illus. 2010. (Dinosaurs: Ser.). (ENG.). 64p. (J). (gr. 3). 15.95 *(978-0-7892-1014-2(2)*, Abbeville Kids) Abbeville Pr., Inc.

Silverman, Buffy. Can You Tell a Brachiosaurus from an Apatosaurus? 2013. (Lightning Bolt Books (tm) — Dinosaur Look-Alikes Ser.). (ENG.). 32p. (gr. k-2). lib. bdg. 26.60 *(978-1-4677-1360-3(0)*, Lerner Pubns.); (Illus.). pap. 7.95 *(978-1-4677-1540-9(9))* Lerner Publishing Group.

—Can You Tell a Giganotosaurus from a Spinosaurus? 2013. (Lightning Bolt Books (tm) — Dinosaur Look-Alikes Ser.). (ENG., Illus.). 32p. (gr. k-2). pap. 7.95 *(978-1-4677-1541-6(7))*; lib. bdg. 26.60 *(978-1-4677-1358-0(9)*, Lerner Pubns.) Lerner Publishing Group.

—Can You Tell a Stegosaurus from an Ankylosaurus? 2013. (Lightning Bolt Books (tm) — Dinosaur Look-Alikes Ser.). (ENG., Illus.). 32p. (gr. k-2). pap. 7.95 *(978-1-4677-1542-3(5))*; lib. bdg. 26.60 *(978-1-4677-1359-7(7)*, Lerner Pubns.) Lerner Publishing Group.

—Can You Tell a Triceratops from a Protoceratops? 2013. (Lightning Bolt Books (tm) — Dinosaur Look-Alikes Ser.). (ENG., Illus.). 32p. (gr. k-2). pap. 7.95 *(978-1-4677-1543-0(3))*; lib. bdg. 26.60 *(978-1-4677-1357-3(0)*, Lerner Pubns.) Lerner Publishing Group.

—Can You Tell a Tyrannosaurus from an Allosaurus? 2013. (Lightning Bolt Books (tm) — Dinosaur Look-Alikes Ser.). (ENG., Illus.). 32p. (gr. k-2). pap. 7.95 *(978-1-4677-1544-7(1))*; lib. bdg. 26.60 *(978-1-4677-1355-9(4)*, Lerner Pubns.) Lerner Publishing Group.

—Can You Tell a Velociraptor from a Deinonychus? 2013. (Lightning Bolt Books (tm) — Dinosaur Look-Alikes Ser.). (ENG., Illus.). 32p. (gr. k-2). pap. 7.95 *(978-1-4677-1545-4(X))*; lib. bdg. 26.60 *(978-1-4677-1356-6(2)*, Lerner Pubns.) Lerner Publishing Group.

Skrepnick, Michael W. Sinosauropteryx: Mysterious Feathered Dinosaur. 2005. (I Like Dinosaurs! Ser.). (Illus.). 24p. (J). (gr. 1-3). lib. bdg. 22.60 *(978-0-7660-2623-0(X)*, Enslow Elementary) Enslow Pubs., Inc.

Skrepnick, Michael William. Diplodocus — Gigantic Long-Necked Dinosaur. Skrepnick, Michael William, illus. 2005. (I Like Dinosaurs! Ser.). (Illus.). 24p. (J). lib. bdg. 22.60 *(978-0-7660-2622-3(1)*, Enslow Elementary) Enslow Pubs., Inc.

—Triceratops — Mighty Three-Horned Dinosaur. Skrepnick, Michael William, illus. 2005. (I Like Dinosaurs! Ser.). (Illus.). 24p. (J). lib. bdg. 22.60 *(978-0-7660-2620-9(5)*, Enslow Elementary) Enslow Pubs., Inc.

—Tyrannosaurus Rex — Fierce King of the Dinosaurs. Skrepnick, Michael William, illus. 2005. (I Like Dinosaurs! Ser.). (Illus.). 24p. (J). lib. bdg. 22.60 *(978-0-7660-2621-6(3)*, Enslow Elementary) Enslow Pubs., Inc.

Slade, Suzanne. What Do You Know about Fossils? 2008. (20 Questions: Science Ser.). (Illus.). 24p. (YA). (gr. 2-5). lib. bdg. 22.60 *(978-1-4042-4197-8(3))* Rosen Publishing Group, Inc., The.

Sloan, Christopher. How Dinosaurs Took Flight: The Fossils, the Science, What We Think We Know, & Mysteries yet Unsolved. 2005. (ENG., Illus.). 64p. (J). (gr. 5-9). 17.95 *(978-0-7922-7298-4(6))*; lib. bdg. 27.90 *(978-0-7922-7404-9(0))* National Geographic Society. (National Geographic Children's Bks.).

—Tracking Tyrannosaurs: Meet T. Rex's Fascinating Family, from Tiny Terrors to Feathered Giants. Lida, Xing & Yi, Liu, illus. 2013. (ENG.). 48p. (J). (gr. 3-7). 18.95 *(978-1-4263-1374-5(8))*; lib. bdg. 27.90 *(978-1-4263-1375-2(6))* National Geographic Society. (National Geographic Children's Bks.).

Small World Creations. Chalkboard Dinosaurs. 2016. (Chalkboard Bks.). (ENG.). 10p. (J). (gr. -1-2). bds. 7.99 *(978-0-7641-6870-3(3))* Barron's Educational Series, Inc.

SMARTLAB Creative Team. Mega 3D Puzzle Play Dinosaurs. 2010. 3p. mass mkt. 19.99 *(978-1-60380-092-1(1))* becker&mayer! books.

Smith, A. G. Glow-in-the-Dark Dinosaurs Stickers. 2006. (Dover Little Activity Books Stickers Ser.). (ENG., Illus.). 2p. (J). (gr. 1-4). 1.99 *(978-0-486-44997-5(1))* Dover Pubns., Inc.

Smith, Alastair & Tatchell, Judy. Dinosaurs. 2004. (Jumbo Lift-the-Flap Learners Ser.). (Illus.). 16p. (J). (gr. 1-18). 11.99 *(978-0-7945-0418-2(3)*, Usborne) EDC Publishing.

—Dinosaurs. Scott, Peter David, illus. 2005. (J). *(978-0-439-68903-8(1))* Scholastic, Inc.

Smithee, Allan. Dinosaurs. 2003. (Interfact Ser.). (SPA & ENG., Illus.). 48p. (J). (gr. 3-6). pap. 14.95 incl. cd-rom *(978-1-58728-343-7(3))* Cooper Square Publishing Llc.

Smithsonian Institution, ed. Dinosaurs & More! Write-with-Me Alphabet. 2009. (ENG.). 28p. 15.99 *(978-1-59069-826-6(6))* Studio Mouse LLC.

Snellenberger, Earl & Snellenberger, Bonita. The Wonders of God's World Dinosaur Activity Book. Snellenberger, Earl & Snellenberger, Bonita, illus. 2008. (Illus.). 128p. (J). (gr. -1). per. 8.99 *(978-0-89051-515-0(8))* Master Bks.

Snow, Alan. How Dinosaurs Really Work! Snow, Alan, illus. 2013. (ENG., Illus.). 32p. (J). (gr. -1-3). 17.99 *(978-1-4424-8294-4(X)*, Atheneum Bks. for Young Readers) Simon & Schuster Children's Publishing.

Sovak, Jan. Dinosaurs! Coloring Book. 2009. (Dover Nature Coloring Book Ser.). (ENG., Illus.). 32p. (J). (gr. 1-5). pap. 3.99 *(978-0-486-46987-4(5))* Dover Pubns., Inc.

—Dinosaurs of the Cretaceous Era. 2009. (Dover Nature Coloring Book Ser.). (ENG., Illus.). 32p. (J). (gr. 2-5). pap. 3.99 *(978-0-486-47264-5(7))* Dover Pubns., Inc.

—Dinosaurs of the Jurassic Era. 2009. (Dover Nature Coloring Book Ser.). (ENG., Illus.). 32p. (J). (gr. 2-5). pap. 3.99 *(978-0-486-46997-3(2))* Dover Pubns., Inc.

—Dinosaurs of the Triassic Era. 2010. (Dover Nature Coloring Book Ser.). (ENG., Illus.). 32p. (J). (gr. 2-5). pap. 3.99 *(978-0-486-47265-2(5))* Dover Pubns., Inc.

—Dinosaurs Stained Glass Coloring Book. 2005. (Dover Nature Stained Glass Coloring Book Ser.). (ENG., Illus.). 16p. (J). (gr. 1-5). pap. 7.99 *(978-0-486-44668-4(9))* Dover Pubns., Inc.

—3-D Coloring Book — Dinosaurs. 2011. (Dover 3-D Coloring Book Ser.). (ENG., Illus.). 32p. (J). (gr. 3-5). pap. 5.99 *(978-0-486-48162-3(X))* Dover Pubns., Inc.

Spizzirri, Linda, ed. Counting & Coloring Dinosaurs. (Illus.). 32p. (J). (gr. 1-8). pap. 4.98 incl. audio *(978-0-86545-044-8(7))* Spizzirri Pr., Inc.

—Dinosaurs. Kohn, Arnie, illus. 32p. (J). (gr. 1-8). pap. 4.98 incl. audio *(978-0-86545-019-6(6))* Spizzirri Pr., Inc.

Stansbie, Stephanie. Dinosaurs: A Busy Sticker Activity Book. Nowowiejska, Kasia, illus. 2016. (Little Snappers Ser.). (ENG.). 96p. (J). (gr. -1-1). 9.99 *(978-1-58925-319-3(1))* Tiger Tales.

Staunton, Joseph. Meat-Eating Dinosaurs. 2010. (Discover the Dinosaurs Ser.). 32p. (J). (gr. 2-5). 28.50 *(978-1-60753-109-8(7))* Amicus Publishing.

—Plant-Eating Dinosaurs. 2010. (Discover the Dinosaurs Ser.). 32p. (J). (gr. 2-5). 28.50 *(978-1-60753-110-4(0))* Amicus Publishing.

Staunton, Joseph & Flinthart, Dirk. Meat Eating Dinosaurs. Rey, Luis, illus. 2011. (Inside Crime Ser.). 48p. (YA). (gr. 5-9). 34.25 *(978-1-59920-395-9(2))* Black Rabbit Bks.

Sterling Publishing Co., Inc. Staff. Dinosaur Sticker Book. 2008. (ENG., Illus.). 14p. (J). (gr. -1-1). pap. 4.95 *(978-1-4027-5625-2(9))* Sterling Publishing Co., Inc.

Sterling Publishing Company Staff. Pocket Factfiles: Dinosaurs. 2004. (Illus.). 256p. (J). 4.98 *(978-1-4027-1849-6(7))* Sterling Publishing Co., Inc.

Stewart, David. Dinosaurs. Hewetson, Nick, illus. 2013. (World of Wonder Ser.). (ENG.). 32p. (gr. 1-3). lib. bdg. 31.35 *(978-1-908973-98-6(6))* Book Hse. GBR. Dist: Black Rabbit Bks.

—Dinosaurs. Hewetson, Nick, illus. 2008. (World of Wonder Ser.). (ENG.). 32p. (J). (gr. 1-4). 29.00 *(978-0-531-20450-4(2)*, Children's Pr.) Scholastic Library Publishing.

Stewart, Melissa. Why Does T. Rex Have Such Short Arms? And Other Questions about... Dinosaurs. Csotonyi, Julius, illus. 2014. (Good Question! Ser.). (ENG.). (J). (gr. 1). 40p. 12.95 *(978-1-4549-0678-0(2))*; 32p. pap. 5.95 *(978-1-4549-0679-7(0))* Sterling Publishing Co., Inc.

Stille, Darlene R. Hadrosaurus. 2006. (North American Dinosaurs Ser.). (Illus.). 24p. (J). (gr. -1-k). lib. bdg. 27.07 *(978-1-60044-252-0(8))* Rourke Educational Media.

Stine, Megan. What Was the Age of the Dinosaurs? Copeland, Gregory, illus. 2017. (What Was? Ser.). (ENG.). 112p. (J). (gr. 3-7). 5.99 *(978-0-451-53264-0(3)*, Penguin Workshop); lib. bdg. 15.99 *(978-0-451-53266-4(X)*, Grosset & Dunlap) Penguin Young Readers Group.

—What Was the Age of the Dinosaurs? 2017. (What Was... ? Ser.). lib. bdg. 16.00 ***(978-0-606-39774-2(4))*** Turtleback Bks.

Storey, Rita. Dinosaurs. 2013. (Have Fun with Arts & Crafts Ser.). 32p. (gr. 4-7). 31.35 *(978-1-59920-897-8(0))* Black Rabbit Bks.

Stout, William. New Dinosaur Discoveries A-Z. 2009. (ENG.). 64p. 14.95 *(978-1-933665-23-2(7))* Flesk Pubns.

Strauss, Bob. A Field Guide to Dinosaurs of North America: And Prehistoric Megafauna. 2015. (ENG., Illus.). 224p. (YA). (gr. 8-17). pap. 22.95 *(978-1-4930-0925-1(7))* Globe Pequot Pr., The.

Suen, Anastasia. Tyrannasaurus Rex. 2006. (North American Dinosaurs Ser.). (Illus.). 24p. (J). (gr. -1-k). lib. bdg. 27.07 *(978-1-60044-255-1(2))* Rourke Educational Media.

—Tyrannosaurus. 2007. (ENG., Illus.). 24p. (gr. 2-5). 28.50 *(978-1-60472-121-8(9))* Rourke Educational Media.

Sundance/Newbridge LLC Staff. The World of Dinosaurs. 2007. (Early Science Ser.). (gr. k-3). 18.95 *(978-1-4007-6495-2(5))*; pap. 6.10 *(978-1-4007-6491-4(2))* Sundance/Newbridge Educational Publishing.

T-Rex Is King: Cretaceous Life. 2013. (Awesome Ancient Animals Ser.). (ENG.). 32p. (J). (gr. 2-4). *(978-1-84898-625-1(4)*, TickTock Books) Octopus Publishing Group.

Tai, Elise See. Write & Draw Dinosaurs. 2014. (Wipe-Clean Stencil Bks.). (ENG., Illus.). 24p. (J). (gr. -1-1). bds. 9.99 *(978-0-7641-6710-2(3))* Barron's Educational Series, Inc.

Taplin, Sam. Dinosaurs. Lamb, Stacey, illus. 2011. (First Sticker Books Ser.). 16p. (J). pap. 6.99 *(978-0-7945-2994-9(1)*, Usborne) EDC Publishing.

—First Encyclopedia of Dinosaurs - Internet Linked. Hancock, David, illus. 2004. (First Encyclopedias Ser.). (ENG.). 64p. (J). (gr. 3-18). pap. 9.99 *(978-0-7945-0696-4(8)*, Usborne) EDC Publishing.

—First Encyclopedia of Dinosaurs II. rev. ed. 2011. (First Encyclopedias Ser.). 64p. (J). pap. 9.99 *(978-0-7945-3047-1(8)*, Usborne) EDC Publishing.

—First Picture Dinosaurs. Van Wyk, Hanri, illus. 2007. (First Picture Board Bks). 12p. (J). bds. 11.99 *(978-0-7945-1752-6(8)*, Usborne) EDC Publishing.

—Little Encyclopedia of Dinosaurs. 2005. (Illus.). 64p. (J). (gr. -1-3). 6.95 *(978-0-7945-1087-9(6)*, Usborne) EDC Publishing.

—This Is My Dinosaur. 2009. (Noisy Touchy-Feely Board Bks). (Illus.). 10p. (J). bds. 16.99 *(978-0-7945-2366-4(8)*, Usborne) EDC Publishing.

Temperley, Howard. In The Days of the Dinosaurs. Kline, Michael P., illus. 2008. (ENG.). 64p. (J). pap. 9.95 *(978-0-8249-6759-8(3)*, Ideal Pubns.) Worthy Publishing.

Tennant, Jon. Excavate! Dinosaurs. 2014. (ENG.). 82p. (J). (gr. 3-8). pap. 12.95 *(978-1-61212-520-6(4)*, 622520) Storey Publishing, LLC.

Teora, creator. Dinosaurs. 2007. (My First Sticker Encyclopedia Ser.). (Illus.). 18p. (J). (gr. -1-3). pap. 5.95 *(978-1-59496-143-4(3))* Teora USA LLC.

Theodorou, Rod. I Wonder Why - Triceratops Had Horns: And Other Questions about Dinosaurs. 2011. (I Wonder Why Ser.). (ENG., Illus.). 32p. (J). (gr. k-3). pap. 6.99 *(978-0-7534-6523-3(X)*, 9780753465233, Kingfisher) Roaring Brook Pr.

Theresa, Nina. Allosaurus. 2015. (Look at Dinosaurs Ser.). (ENG.). 24p. (J). (gr. 1-2). 22.60 *(978-1-4824-1818-7(5))* Stevens, Gareth Publishing LLLP.

Thimmesh, Catherine. Scaly Spotted Feathered Frilled: How Do We Know What Dinosaurs Really Looked Like? 2013. (ENG., Illus.). 64p. (J). (gr. 5-7). 17.99 *(978-0-547-99134-4(7))* Houghton Mifflin Harcourt Publishing Co.

Thomas, Brian. Stegosaurus. 2015. (Look at Dinosaurs Ser.). (ENG.). 24p. (J). (gr. 1-2). 22.60 *(978-1-4824-1826-2(6))* Stevens, Gareth Publishing LLLP.

Thomas Nelson. Daring Dinosaur Alphabet. 2016. (ENG.). 14p. (gr. -1). bds. *(978-1-78598-466-2(7))* Make Believe Ideas.

Thomson, Sarah L. Extreme Dinosaurs! Q & A. 2007. (Illus.). 48p. (J). (gr. k-4). 17.99 *(978-0-06-089971-4(9))* HarperCollins Pubs.

Thomson, Sarah L. & Plant, Andrew. Plesiosaur. 2017. (ENG., Illus.). 32p. (J). (gr. 1-4). lib. bdg. 12.99 *(978-1-58089-542-2(5))* Charlesbridge Publishing, Inc.

Throp, Claire. Fantasy Science Field Trips, 1 vol. 2014. (Fantasy Science Field Trips Ser.). (ENG.). 32p. (gr. 1-3). lib. bdg. 119.96 *(978-1-4109-6201-0(6)*, Read Me!) Heinemann-Raintree.

—A Weekend with Dinosaurs: Fantasy Science Field Trips, 1 vol. 2014. (Fantasy Science Field Trips Ser.). (ENG., Illus.). 32p. (gr. 1-3). pap. 8.95 *(978-1-4109-6203-4(2))*; lib. bdg. 29.99 *(978-1-4109-6198-3(2))* Heinemann-Raintree. (Read Me!).

Ticktock Media, Ltd. Staff. Amazing Dinosaurs. 2009. (Dinosaur Shape Bks.). (ENG.). 10p. (J). (gr. -1-k). bds. 5.95 *(978-1-84696-832-7(1)*, TickTock Books) Octopus Publishing Group GBR. Dist: Independent Pubs. Group.

—Friendly Dinosaurs. 2009. (Dinosaur Shape Bks.). (ENG.). 10p. (J). (gr. -1-k). bds. 5.95 *(978-1-84696-833-4(X)*, TickTock Books) Octopus Publishing Group GBR. Dist: Independent Pubs. Group.

—Hungry Dinosaurs. 2009. (Dinosaur Shape Bks.). (ENG.). 10p. (J). (gr. -1-k). bds. 5.95 *(978-1-84696-834-1(8)*, TickTock Books) Octopus Publishing Group GBR. Dist: Independent Pubs. Group.

—Scary Dinosaurs. 2009. (Dinosaur Shape Bks.). (ENG.). 10p. (J). (gr. -1-k). bds. 5.95 *(978-1-84696-835-8(6)*, TickTock Books) Octopus Publishing Group GBR. Dist: Independent Pubs. Group.

tictock Media, Ltd. The Ultimate Guide to Dinosaurs. 2009. (ENG.). 128p. (J). (gr. 4-7). pap. 12.95 *(978-1-84696-988-1(3)*, TickTock Books) Octopus Publishing Group GBR. Dist: Independent Pubs. Group.

Toms, Kate. Dinosaur Tails. 2006. (Illus.). 12p. (gr. -1-k). per., bds. *(978-1-84610-097-0(6))* Make Believe Ideas.

Top That Publishing Staff, ed. Dinosaurs. 2004. (Stickertastic Ser.). (Illus.). 24p. (J). pap. *(978-1-84510-116-9(2))* Top That! Publishing PLC.

—Lets Learn Dinosaurs. 2004. (Fun Kits Ser.). (Illus.). 48p. (J). *(978-1-84510-245-6(2))* Top That! Publishing PLC.

Toufexis, George. History's Mysteries! Dinosaurs: Activity Book. 2012. (Dover Children's Activity Bks.). (ENG.). 48p. (J). (gr. 3-8). pap. 4.99 *(978-0-486-48698-7(2))* Dover Pubns., Inc.

Trexler, David. Dinosaur Bone Doctor. 2017. (Text Connections Guided Close Reading Ser.). (J). (gr. 2). *(978-1-4900-1845-4(X))* Benchmark Education Co.

Troupe, Thomas Kingsley. I Want to Be a Brachiosaurus. Tejido, Jomike, illus. 2016. (I Want to Be... Ser.). (ENG.). 24p. (gr. k-3). lib. bdg. 26.65 *(978-1-4795-8770-4(2))* Picture Window Bks.

—I Want to Be a Triceratops. 2016. (I Want to Be... Ser.). (ENG., Illus.). 24p. (gr. k-3). lib. bdg. 26.65 *(978-1-4795-8768-1(0))* Picture Window Bks.

—I Want to Be a Tyrannosaurus Rex. 2016. (I Want to Be... Ser.). (ENG., Illus.). 24p. (gr. k-3). lib. bdg. 26.65 *(978-1-4795-8767-4(2))* Picture Window Bks.

—I Want to Be a Velociraptor. Tejido, Jomike, illus. 2016. (I Want to Be... Ser.). (ENG.). 24p. (gr. k-3). lib. bdg. 26.65 *(978-1-4795-8769-8(9))* Picture Window Bks.

Turnbull, S. Dino Kit (Box) rev. ed. 2008. (Kid Kits Ser.). 32p. (J). 19.99 *(978-1-60130-109-3(X)*, Usborne) EDC Publishing.

Turnbull, Stephanie. Los Dinosaurios Con Cuatro Puzzles Sencillos. Scott, Peter, illus. 2004. (Titles in Spanish Ser.). (SPA.). 6p. (J). 8.95 *(978-0-7460-6109-1(9)*, Usborne) EDC Publishing.

—Dinosaurs. Wray, Zoe & Kushii, Tetsuo, illus. 2006. (Beginners Nature: Level 2 Ser.). 32p. (J). (gr. 1-3). 4.99 *(978-0-7945-1334-4(4)*, Usborne) EDC Publishing.

—Dinosaurs. Kushii, Tetsuo, illus. 2006. (Usborne Beginners Ser.). 32p. (J). (gr. 2). lib. bdg. 12.99 *(978-1-58086-929-4(7)*, Usborne) EDC Publishing.

—Dinosaurs. 2004. (Beginners Ser.). 32p. (J). (gr. 1-18). lib. bdg. 12.95 *(978-1-58086-606-4(9)*, Usborne) EDC Publishing.

Turner, Alan H. Dinosaurios. 2007. (Libro y Modelos 3-D Ser.). (Illus.). 24p. (J). (gr. -1-3). *(978-970-718-507-4(4)*, Silver Dolphin en Español) Advanced Marketing, S. de R. L. de C. V.

Twist, Clint & Fitzgibbon, Monty. Tyrannosaur. Wallis, Diz & Nicholls, Emma, illus. 2008. (Amazing Wonders Collection: 1). (ENG.). 16p. (J). (gr. 1-4). 19.99 *(978-0-7636-3550-3(2))* Candlewick Pr.

U. S. National Geographic Society Staff. The Dinosaur Museum: An Unforgettable, Interactive Virtual Tour Through Dinosaur History. Quigley, Sebastian, illus. 2008. (ENG.). 24p. (J). (gr. 1-4). 19.95 *(978-1-4263-0335-7(1)*, National Geographic Children's Bks.) National Geographic Society.

U. S. National Geographic Society Staff, et al. Bizarre Dinosaurs: Some Very Strange Creatures & Why We Think They Got That Way. U. S. National Geographic Society Staff, illus. 2008. (ENG., Illus.). 32p. (J). (gr. 3-7). 16.95 *(978-1-4263-0330-2(0))*; (gr. 5). lib. bdg. 25.90 *(978-1-4263-0331-9(9))* National Geographic Society. (National Geographic Children's Bks.).

Unwin, Mike. Where Did Dinosaurs Go? Evans, Cheryl, ed. Goffe, Toni, illus. 2006. (Usborne Starting Point Science Ser.). 24p. (J). (gr. 2). lib. bdg. 12.99 *(978-1-58086-937-9(8)*, Usborne) EDC Publishing.

—Where Did Dinosaurs Go? Robinson, Andrew et al, illus. 2006. (Usborne Starting Point Science Ser.). 24p. (J). (gr. 1-4). pap. 4.99 *(978-0-7945-1410-5(3)*, Usborne) EDC Publishing.

Upgrade kit dsm-3 Dinos&fossils. (J). 2004. *(978-1-59242-528-0(3))* 2003. *(978-1-59242-411-5(2))* Delta Education, LLC.

Usborne Books Staff, creator. Dinosaur Excavation Kid Kit. 2006. (Kid Kits Ser.). (Illus.). 32p. (J). (gr. 1). 18.99 *(978-1-58086-977-5(7))* EDC Publishing.

—100 Dinosaurs to Spot. 2008. (Spotter's Cards Ser.). (Illus.). 52p. (J). 9.99 *(978-0-7945-1965-0(2)*, Usborne) EDC Publishing.

Uttridge, Sarah. Dinosaurs Around the World. 2014. (Animals Around the World Ser.). (Illus.). 32p. (gr. 2-5). 31.35 *(978-1-62588-192-2(4))* Black Rabbit Bks.

Van Buskirk, Steve. Dinosaurs. Van Buskirk, Steve, illus. 2007. (Dinosaurs Pop-up Bks.). (Illus.). (J). (gr. -1-3). 4.99 *(978-1-59340-379-9(8))* Grandreams Bks., Inc.

Walker, Niki & Kalman, Bobbie. Les Dinosaurs. Mondor, Lyne, tr. from ENG. 2005. (Petit Monde Vivant Ser.). (FRE., Illus.). 32p. (J). pap. 9.95 *(978-2-89579-050-1(7))* Bayard Canada Livres CAN. Dist: Crabtree Publishing Co.

—¿Qué Es un Dinosaurio? 2006. (Libro de Bobbie Kalman Ser.). (ENG & SPA., Illus.). 32p. (J). (gr. 3-7). pap. *(978-0-7787-8810-2(5))*; lib. bdg. *(978-0-7787-8764-8(8))* Crabtree Publishing Co.

Walker, Sally M. The Search for Antarctic Dinosaurs. 2009. pap. 40.95 *(978-0-7613-4822-1(0))* 2008. 48p. (J). pap. 6.95 *(978-0-8225-6752-3(0)*, First Avenue Editions) Lerner Publishing Group.

—The Search for Antarctic Dinosaurs. Bindon, John, illus. 2007. (On My Own Science Ser.). (ENG.). 48p. (gr. 2-4). lib. bdg. 25.26 *(978-0-8225-6749-3(0)*, Millbrook Pr.) Lerner Publishing Group.

Walt & Wells. Este No Es Mi Dinosaurio. 2004. (Touchy-Feely Board Bks.).Tr. of This Is Not My Dinosaur. (SPA., Illus.). 12p. (J). (gr. -1-18). 7.99 *(978-0-7460-5079-8(8))* EDC Publishing.

Walter Foster Creative Team. Dinosaurs: Interactive Fun with Reusable Stickers, Fold-Out Play Scene, & Punch-out, Stand-up Figures! Cerato, Mattia, illus. 2015. (Sticker, Punch-Out, & Play! Ser.). (ENG.). 12p. (J). (gr. -1-1). pap. 6.99 *(978-1-63322-000-3(1))* Quarto Publishing Group USA.

Walters, Robert, et al. Discovering Dinosaurs. 2014. (ENG., Illus.). 144p. (J). 19.95 *(978-1-60433-496-8(7)*, Applesauce Pr.) Cider Mill Pr. Bk. Pubs., LLC.

Watt, Fiona. Baby Dinosaur Cloth Bk. Wells, Rachel, illus. 2006. 10p. (J). 10.99 *(978-0-7945-1429-7(4)*, Usborne) EDC Publishing.

—Big Dinosaur Sticker Book. 2013. (Sticker Activity Bks). 34p. (J). pap. 8.99 *(978-0-7945-3373-1(6)*, Usborne) EDC Publishing.

—Dibujos Paso A Paso Dinosaurios. Figg, Non et al, illus. 2007. (Titles in Spanish Ser.). 31p. (J). 8.99 *(978-0-7460-8373-4(4)*, Usborne) EDC Publishing.

—Dinosaur Fun. Lovell, Katie, illus. 2009. (Preschool Activities Ser.). 24p. (J). (gr. -1). spiral bd. 12.99 *(978-0-7945-2133-2(9)*, Usborne) EDC Publishing.

—How to Draw Dinosaurs. Figg, Non et al, illus. 2005. (Usborne Activities Ser.). 31p. (J). (gr. -1-3). pap. 8.95 *(978-0-7945-1056-5(6)*, Usborne) EDC Publishing.

Weber, Belinda. I Wonder Why Dinosaurs Ruled Sticker Activity Book. 2013. (I Wonder Why Ser.). (ENG., Illus.). 24p. (J). (gr. k-3). 6.99 *(978-0-7534-6806-7(9)*, 9780753468067, Kingfisher) Roaring Brook Pr.

Wegwerth, A. L. Stegosaurus, 1 vol. 2014. (Little Paleontologist Ser.). (ENG.). 32p. (gr. 1-3). lib. bdg. 27.99 *(978-1-4914-0812-4(X))* Capstone Press of Coughlan Cos.

—Tyrannosaurus Rex, 1 vol. 2014. (Little Paleontologist Ser.). (ENG.). 32p. (gr. 1-3). lib. bdg. 27.99 *(978-1-4914-0810-0(3))* Capstone Press of Coughlan Cos.

Wells, Roth. The Big Book of Dinosaurs. 2010. 32p. 14.49 *(978-1-4520-3282-5(3))* AuthorHouse.

Wenzel, Gregory. The Feathered Dinosaurs of China. Wenzel, Gregory, illus. 2004. (ENG., Illus.). 32p. (J). (gr. 1-4). pap. 7.95 *(978-1-57091-562-8(8))* Charlesbridge Publishing, Inc.

West, David. Allosaurus & Other Dinosaurs & Reptiles from the Upper Jurassic. 2012. (Dinosaurs! Ser.). (ENG., Illus.). 32p. (J). (gr. 3-6). 26.60 *(978-1-4339-6704-7(9))*; pap. 10.50 *(978-1-4339-6705-4(7))* Stevens, Gareth Publishing LLLP. (Gareth Stevens Learning Library).

—Ankylosaurus: The Armored Dinosaur. West, David & Spender, Nik, illus. 2009. (Graphic Dinosaurs Ser.). (ENG.).

32p. (J). pap. 12.30 *(978-1-4358-8596-7(1))*; (gr. 2-5). 26.50 *(978-1-4358-8590-5(2))* Rosen Publishing Group, Inc., The. (PowerKids Pr.).
—Ankylosaurus & Other Armored & Plated Herbivores. 2010. (Dinosaurs Ser.). (Illus.). 32p. (J). (gr. 3-6). (ENG.). pap. 10.50 *(978-1-4339-4231-0(3))*; lib. bdg. 26.60 *(978-1-4339-4230-3(5))* Stevens, Gareth Publishing LLLP. (Gareth Stevens Learning Library).
—Armored Dinosaurs, 01 vols., 1. 2016. (Prehistoric Animals Ser.). (ENG., Illus.). 24p. (J). pap. 8.25 *(978-1-5081-9014-1(3)*, Windmill Bks.) Rosen Publishing Group, Inc., The.
—Brachiosaurus & Other Long-Necked Herbivores. 2010. (Dinosaurs Ser.). (Illus.). 32p. (J). (gr. 3-6). (ENG.). pap. 10.50 *(978-1-4339-4222-8(4))*; lib. bdg. 26.60 *(978-1-4339-4221-1(6))* Stevens, Gareth Publishing LLLP. (Gareth Stevens Learning Library).
—Cetiosaurus & Other Dinosaurs & Reptiles from the Middle Jurassic. 2012. (Dinosaurs! Ser.). (ENG., Illus.). 32p. (J). (gr. 3-6). 26.60 *(978-1-4339-6707-8(3))*; pap. 10.50 *(978-1-4339-6709-2(X))* Stevens, Gareth Publishing LLLP. (Gareth Stevens Learning Library).
—Coelophysis & Other Dinosaurs & Reptiles from the Upper Triassic. West, David, illus. 2012. (Dinosaurs! Ser.). (ENG., Illus.). 32p. (J). (gr. 3-6). pap. 10.50 *(978-1-4339-6713-9(8))*; lib. bdg. 26.60 *(978-1-4339-6711-5(1))* Stevens, Gareth Publishing LLLP. (Gareth Stevens Learning Library).
—Dinosaurs of the Lower Cretaceous: 25 Dinosaurs from 144 — 127 Million Years Ago. 2016. (Firefly Dinosaur Ser.). (ENG., Illus.). 32p. (J). (gr. 3-6). pap. 6.95 *(978-1-77085-831-2(8)*, 9781770858312) Firefly Bks., Ltd.
—Dinosaurs of the Middle Cretaceous: 25 Dinosaurs from 126 — 89 Million Years Ago. 2016. (Firefly Dinosaur Ser.). (ENG., Illus.). 32p. (J). (gr. 3-6). pap. 6.95 *(978-1-77085-833-6(4)*, 9781770858336) Firefly Bks., Ltd.
—Dinosaurs of the Middle Jurassic: 25 Dinosaurs from 175 — 165 Million Years Ago. 2016. (Firefly Dinosaur Ser.). (ENG., Illus.). 32p. (J). (gr. 3-6). pap. 6.95 *(978-1-77085-835-0(0)*, 9781770858350) Firefly Bks., Ltd.
—Dinosaurs of the Upper Cretaceous: 25 Dinosaurs from 89 — 65 Million Years Ago. 2016. (Firefly Dinosaur Ser.). (ENG., Illus.). 32p. (J). (gr. 3-6). pap. 6.95 *(978-1-77085-837-4(7)*, 9781770858374) Firefly Bks., Ltd.
—Dinosaurs of the Upper Jurassic: 25 Dinosaurs from 164 — 145 Million Years Ago. 2016. (Firefly Dinosaur Ser.). (ENG., Illus.). 32p. (J). (gr. 3-6). pap. 6.95 *(978-1-77085-839-8(3)*, 9781770858398) Firefly Bks., Ltd.
—Dinosaurs of the Upper Triassic & the Lower Jurassic: 25 Dinosaurs from 227 — 175 Million Years Ago. 2016. (Firefly Dinosaur Ser.). (ENG., Illus.). 32p. (J). (gr. 3-6). pap. 6.95 *(978-1-77085-841-1(5)*, 9781770858411) Firefly Bks., Ltd.
—Dinosaurs on My Street. 2013. (ENG., Illus.). 64p. (J). (gr. -1-3). 19.95 *(978-1-77085-220-4(4)*, 9781770852204); pap. 6.95 *(978-1-77085-221-1(2)*, 9781770852211) Firefly Bks., Ltd.
—Duck-Billed Dinosaurs, 01 vols., 1. 2016. (Prehistoric Animals Ser.). (ENG.). 24p. (J). pap. 8.25 *(978-1-5081-9018-9(6)*, Windmill Bks.) Rosen Publishing Group, Inc., The.
—Frilled Dinosaurs, 01 vols., 1. 2016. (Prehistoric Animals Ser.). (ENG., Illus.). 24p. (J). pap. 8.25 *(978-1-5081-9022-6(4)*, Windmill Bks.) Rosen Publishing Group, Inc., The.
—Giant Meat-Eating Dinosaurs, 01 vols., 1. 2016. (Prehistoric Animals Ser.). (ENG., Illus.). 24p. (J). pap. 8.25 *(978-1-5081-9026-4(7)*, Windmill Bks.) Rosen Publishing Group, Inc., The.
—Iguanodon. 2012. (Illus.). 32p. (J). 73.80 *(978-1-4488-5249-9(8))*; pap. 12.30 *(978-1-4488-5248-2(X))*; lib. bdg. 26.50 *(978-1-4488-5205-5(6))* Rosen Publishing Group, Inc., The. (PowerKids Pr.).
—Lesothosaurus & Other Dinosaurs & Reptiles from the Lower Jurassic. West, David, illus. 2012. (Dinosaurs! Ser.). (ENG., Illus.). 32p. (J). (gr. 3-6). pap. 10.50 *(978-1-4339-6717-7(0))*; lib. bdg. 26.60 *(978-1-4339-6715-3(4))* Stevens, Gareth Publishing LLLP. (Gareth Stevens Learning Library).
—Long-Necked Dinosaurs, 01 vols., 1. 2016. (Prehistoric Animals Ser.). (ENG., Illus.). 24p. (J). pap. 8.25 *(978-1-5081-9030-1(5)*, Windmill Bks.) Rosen Publishing Group, Inc., The.
—Parasaurolophus & Other Duck-Billed & Beaked Herbivores. 2010. (Dinosaurs Ser.). (Illus.). 32p. (J). (gr. 3-6). (ENG.). pap. 10.50 *(978-1-4339-4228-0(3))*; lib. bdg. 26.60 *(978-1-4339-4227-3(5))* Stevens, Gareth Publishing LLLP. (Gareth Stevens Learning Library).
—Prehistoric Flying Reptiles, 01 vols., 1. 2016. (Prehistoric Animals Ser.). (ENG., Illus.). 24p. (J). pap. 8.25 *(978-1-5081-9037-0(2)*, Windmill Bks.) Rosen Publishing Group, Inc., The.
—Pteranodon: Giant of the Sky. (Graphic Dinosaurs Ser.). (ENG.). 32p. 2009. (J). (gr. 4-4). 50.50 *(978-1-61512-909-6(X))* 2008. (Illus.). (gr. 2-5). pap. 12.30 *(978-1-4042-9625-1(5))* Rosen Publishing Group, Inc., The. (PowerKids Pr.).
—Sharp-Clawed Dinosaurs, 01 vols., 1. 2016. (Prehistoric Animals Ser.). (ENG., Illus.). 24p. (J). pap. 8.25 *(978-1-5081-9049-3(6)*, 1397682, Windmill Bks.) Rosen Publishing Group, Inc., The.
—Spinosaurus. 2012. (Illus.). 32p. (J). 73.80 *(978-1-4488-5245-1(5))*; pap. 12.30 *(978-1-4488-5244-4(7))*; lib. bdg. 26.50 *(978-1-4488-5203-1(X))* Rosen Publishing Group, Inc., The. (PowerKids Pr.).
—Spinosaurus & Other Dinosaurs & Reptiles from the Upper Cretaceous. 2012. (Dinosaurs! Ser.). (ENG., Illus.). 32p. (J). (gr. 3-6). 26.60 *(978-1-4339-6719-1(7))*; pap. 10.50 *(978-1-4339-6721-4(9))* Stevens, Gareth Publishing LLLP. (Gareth Stevens Learning Library).
—Triceratops & Other Horned Herbivores. 2010. (Dinosaurs Ser.). (Illus.). 32p. (J). (gr. 3-6). pap. 10.50 *(978-1-4339-4234-1(8))*; lib. bdg. 26.60 *(978-1-4339-4233-4(X))* Stevens, Gareth Publishing LLLP. (Gareth Stevens Learning Library).
—Tyrannosaurus Rex & Other Giant Carnivores. 2010. (Dinosaurs Ser.). (Illus.). 32p. (J). (gr. 3-6). (ENG.). pap. 10.50 *(978-1-4339-4237-2(2))*; lib. bdg. 26.60 *(978-1-4339-4236-5(4))* Stevens, Gareth Publishing LLLP. (Gareth Stevens Learning Library).
—Utahraptor & Other Dinosaurs & Reptiles from the Lower Cretaceous. 2012. (Dinosaurs! Ser.). (ENG., Illus.). 32p. (J). (gr. 3-6). 26.60 *(978-1-4339-6723-8(5))*; pap. 10.50 *(978-1-4339-6725-2(1))* Stevens, Gareth Publishing LLLP. (Gareth Stevens Learning Library).
—Velociraptor: The Speedy Thief. 2009. (Graphic Dinosaurs Ser.). (ENG.). 32p. (J). (gr. 4-4). 50.50 *(978-1-61512-920-1(0)*, PowerKids Pr.) Rosen Publishing Group, Inc., The.
—Velociraptor: The Speedy Thief. Field, James, illus. 2007. (Graphic Dinosaurs Ser.). (ENG.). 32p. (J). (gr. 2-5). lib. bdg. 26.50 *(978-1-4042-3898-5(0))* Rosen Publishing Group, Inc., The.
—Velociraptor & Other Raptors & Small Carnivores. 2010. (Dinosaurs Ser.). (Illus.). 32p. (J). (gr. 3-6). pap. 10.50 *(978-1-4339-4225-9(9))*; lib. bdg. 26.60 *(978-1-4339-4224-2(0))* Stevens, Gareth Publishing LLLP. (Gareth Stevens Learning Library).
Weston, Steve & Field, James, illus. Mahakala & Other Insect-Eating Dinosaurs, 1 vol. 2009. (Dinosaur Find Ser.). (ENG.). 24p. (J). (gr. k-3). lib. bdg. 26.65 *(978-1-4048-5177-1(1))* Picture Window Bks.
—Masiakasaurus & Other Fish-Eating Dinosaurs, 1 vol. 2009. (Dinosaur Find Ser.). (ENG.). 24p. (J). (gr. k-3). 26.65 *(978-1-4048-5171-9(2))* Picture Window Bks.
—Saurophaganax & Other Meat-Eating Dinosaurs, 1 vol. 2009. (Dinosaur Find Ser.). (ENG.). 24p. (J). (gr. k-3). lib. bdg. 26.65 *(978-1-4048-5180-1(1))* Picture Window Bks.
Wexo, John Bonnett. Dinosaurs. rev. ed. 2003. (Illus.). 24p. (J). (gr. 1-7). 10.95 *(978-1-932396-02-7(0)*, Zoo Bks.) Wildlife Education, Ltd.
Whales & Dolphins. 2014. (Animal Q & A Ser.). (Illus.). 24p. (J). (gr. k-3). lib. bdg. 23.60 *(978-1-4777-9202-5(3))* Windmill Bks.
Whelon, Chuck. Dinoscenes. 2009. (Dover Coloring Bks.). (ENG., Illus.). 32p. (J). (gr. -1-5). pap. 3.99 *(978-0-486-47263-8(9))* Dover Pubns., Inc.
—FLIP OUTS — Dinosaurs: Color Your Own Cartoon! 2015. (ENG., Illus.). 64p. (J). (gr. k-3). pap. 1.99 *(978-0-486-79486-0(5))* Dover Pubns., Inc.
—What to Doodle? Dinosaurs! 2010. (Dover Doodle Bks.). (ENG., Illus.). 64p. (J). (gr. 2-5). pap. 5.99 *(978-0-486-47514-1(X))* Dover Pubns., Inc.
Whelon, Chuck & Dinosaurs. Dinosaur Rampage Activity Book. 2012. (Dover Children's Activity Bks.). (ENG.). 48p. (J). (gr. 3-5). pap. 4.99 *(978-0-486-48099-2(2))* Dover Pubns., Inc.
White, Nancy. Giant-O-Saurs. 2008. (Dino Times Trivia Ser.). (Illus.). 24p. (J). (gr. k-3). lib. bdg. 21.28 *(978-1-59716-711-6(8)*, 1284320) Bearport Publishing Co., Inc.
Whitfield, Philip. Scholastic's Children's Guide to Dinosaurs. (Illus.). 96p. (J). pap. 21.95 *(978-0-590-24329-2(2))* Scholastic, Inc.
Wick, Walter. Dinosaurs. Wick, Walter, photos by. 2006. (Can You See What I See? Ser.). (ENG., Illus.). 16p. (J). (gr. k — 1). bds. 5.99 *(978-0-439-83297-7(7)*, Cartwheel Bks.) Scholastic, Inc.
Wilkes, Angela. The Big Book of Dinosaurs. (Illus.). 32p. (J). pap. 16.95 *(978-0-590-24371-1(3))* Scholastic, Inc.
William H. Sadlier Staff. Discovering Dinosaurs, Vol. 2. 2005. (Fluent Library). (gr. 1-3). 29.34 *(978-0-8215-8966-3(0))* Sadlier, William H. Inc.
Williams, Judith. The Discovery & Mystery of a Dinosaur Named Jane. 2007. (Prime (Elementary) Ser.). (Illus.). 48p. (J). (gr. 4-7). lib. bdg. 25.27 *(978-0-7660-2730-5(9))*; per. 8.95 *(978-0-7660-2709-1(0))* Enslow Pubs., Inc.
Wingate, Philippa. Dinosaurs. 2004. (Usborne Spotter's Guides). (Illus.). (J). (gr. -1-18). 64p. lib. bdg. 13.95 *(978-1-58086-311-7(6))*; (ENG., 1p. pap. 5.95 *(978-0-7460-4068-3(7))* EDC Publishing.
Winner, Cherie. Little Book of Dinosaurs. Chesterman, Al, illus. 2005. (Little Bks.). (ENG.). 24p. (J). (gr. -1-2). pap. 5.95 *(978-1-58728-516-5(9))* Cooper Square Publishing Llc.
—The Little Book of Dinosaurs. 2005. (Little Bks.). (ENG., Illus.). 24p. (J). (gr. -1-2). 9.95 *(978-1-58728-484-7(7))* Cooper Square Publishing Llc.
Wittmann, Kelly. The Bone Wars: The Race to Dig up Dinosaurs. 2017. (Great Race: Fight to the Finish Ser.). 48p. (gr. 4-5). pap. 84.30 ***(978-1-5382-0803-8(2))*** Stevens, Gareth Publishing LLLP.
Wood, Alix. Dinosaurs on the Map. 2014. (Fun with Map Skills Ser.). (Illus.). 32p. (J). (gr. 3-6). lib. bdg. 26.25 *(978-1-4777-6960-7(9)*, PowerKids Pr.) Rosen Publishing Group, Inc., The.
Wood, Hannah, illus. Dino Pop-up Faces: A Let's Pretend Pop-up Book. 2007. (ENG.). 12p. (J). (gr. -1-3). 14.95 *(978-1-58117-596-7(5)*, Intervisual/Piggy Toes) Bendon, Inc.
Woolf, Alex & Graham, Ian. The Science of Prehistoric Giants. 2017. (Science of Dinosaurs Ser.). (ENG.). 32p. (J). pap. 9.95 ***(978-0-531-26903-9(5)***, Watts, Franklin) Scholastic Library Publishing.
Woolley, Katie. Meat-Eating Dinosaurs. 2016. (Dinozone Ser.). 00032p. (J). (gr. 2-3). pap. 10.00 *(978-1-4994-8166-2(7)*, Windmill Bks.) Rosen Publishing Group, Inc., The.
—Plant-Eating Dinosaurs. 2016. (Dinozone Ser.). 00032p. (J). (gr. 2-3). pap. 10.00 *(978-1-4994-8170-9(5)*, Windmill Bks.) Rosen Publishing Group, Inc., The.
—The Story of the Dinosaurs. 2016. (Dinozone Ser.). 00032p. (J). (gr. 2-3). pap. 10.00 *(978-1-4994-8173-0(X)*, Windmill Bks.) Rosen Publishing Group, Inc., The.
—Tyrannosaurus Rex. 2016. (Dinozone Ser.). 00032p. (J). (gr. 2-3). pap. 10.00 *(978-1-4994-8176-1(4)*, Windmill Bks.) Rosen Publishing Group, Inc., The.
World Book, Inc Staff, contrib. by. Armored & Duckbilled Dinosaurs: The Ornithischians. 2012. (J). *(978-0-7166-0367-2(5))* World Bk., Inc.
—Armored Dinosaurs! The Ornithischians. 2013. (Illus.). 48p. (J). *(978-0-7166-0366-5(7))* World Bk., Inc.
—Giant Dinosaurs: The Sauropods. 2012. (J). *(978-0-7166-0370-2(5))* World Bk., Inc.
—Revealing the Secrets of Dinosaurs. 2015. (Illus.). 48p. (J). *(978-0-7166-2673-2(X))* World Bk., Inc.
—World of Dinosaurs. 2007. (J). *(978-0-7166-7734-5(2))* World Bk., Inc.
Wormell, Chris. Wings, Horns, & Claws: A Dinosaur Book of Epic Proportions. 2007. (Illus.). 64p. 18.95 *(978-0-7624-3213-4(6)*, Running Pr.) Running Pr. Bk. Pubs.
Worms, Penny. Dinosaurs. 2012. (My First Creativity Bks.). (ENG.). 66p. (J). (gr. -1-2). pap. 9.99 *(978-1-4380-0178-4(9))* Barron's Educational Series, Inc.
—Dinosaurs. 2016. (ENG., Illus.). 24p. (J). (gr. 1). pap. 11.95 *(978-1-78312-109-0(2))* Carlton Kids GBR. Dist: Sterling Publishing Co., Inc.
—Dinosaurs: Over 1000 Reusable Stickers! 2014. (Little Hands Creative Sticker Play Ser.). (ENG.). 64p. (J). (gr. -1-2). pap. 9.99 *(978-1-4380-0395-5(1))* Barron's Educational Series, Inc.
Wrecks, Billy. Dino Hybrid. Random House, illus. 2016. (Pictureback(R) Ser.). (ENG.). 24p. (J). (gr. -1-2). 5.99 *(978-0-399-55342-4(8)*, Random Hse. Bks. for Young Readers) Random Hse. Children's Bks.
Wright, Shannon. Dinosaurs & Monsters Coloring Book. 2013. (ENG.). 38p. 13.00 *(978-1-62884-683-6(6)*, Baby Professor (Education Kids)) Speedy Publishing LLC.
Wynne, Patricia J. Easy Dinosaur Mazes. 2006. (Dover Children's Activity Bks.). (ENG., Illus.). 48p. (J). (gr. -1-3). per. 4.99 *(978-0-486-45363-7(4))* Dover Pubns., Inc.
Wynne, Patricia J. & Whelon, Chuck. 3-D Mazes — Dinosaurs. 2012. (Dover 3-D Mazes Ser.). (ENG.). 32p. (J). (gr. 1-6). 5.99 *(978-0-486-49015-1(7))* Dover Pubns., Inc.
Yelagalawadi, Jyoti. Laugh with Dinosaurs. Nagaraju, Harsha, illus. 2004. 32p. (J). 14.99 *(978-0-9725901-1-2(0))* Lekha Pubs., LLC.
Yoon, Salina. Dinosaur Discovery. 2017. (Lift-The-Flap Adventures Ser.). (ENG., Illus.). 14p. (J). (gr. -1-2). bds. 8.95 *(978-1-4549-2087-8(4))* Sterling Publishing Co., Inc.
You Can Name 100 Dino Dis. 2003. (J). 53.70 *(978-0-590-69063-8(9))* Scholastic, Inc.
Zeiger, Jennifer. Compsognathus. 2012. (21st Century Junior Library: Dinosaurs Ser.). (ENG.). 24p. (gr. 2-5). 25.64 *(978-1-61080-462-2(7)*, 202072); pap. 12.79 *(978-1-61080-636-7(0)*, 202246) Cherry Lake Publishing.
—Maiasaura. 2013. (21st Century Junior Library: Dinosaurs Ser.). (ENG., Illus.). 24p. (J). (gr. 2-5). 25.64 *(978-1-62431-163-5(6)*, 202972); pap. 12.79 *(978-1-62431-295-3(0)*, 202974) Cherry Lake Publishing.
—Oviraptor. 2013. (21st Century Junior Library: Dinosaurs Ser.). (ENG., Illus.). 24p. (J). (gr. 2-5). lib. bdg. 25.64 *(978-1-62431-162-8(8)*, 202968); 2nd ed. pap. 12.79 *(978-1-62431-294-6(2)*, 202970) Cherry Lake Publishing.
—Pterosaur. 2015. (21st Century Junior Library: Dinosaurs & Prehistoric Creatures Ser.). (ENG., Illus.). 24p. (J). (gr. 2-5). lib. bdg. 27.07 *(978-1-63362-385-9(8)*, 206960) Cherry Lake Publishing.
—Triceratops. 2013. (21st Century Junior Library: Dinosaurs Ser.). (ENG., Illus.). 24p. (J). (gr. 2-5). pap. 12.79 *(978-1-62431-293-9(4)*, 202966); 7th ed. lib. bdg. 25.64 *(978-1-62431-161-1(X)*, 202964) Cherry Lake Publishing.
Zermeno, Rebeca M. Dinosaurios.Tr. of Dinosaurs. (SPA.). (J). 6.98 *(978-970-643-266-7(3))* Selector, S.A. de C.V. MEX. Dist: AIMS International Bks., Inc.
Zimmerman, Howard. Armored & Dangerous. 2008. (Dino Times Trivia Ser.). (Illus.). 24p. (J). (gr. k-3). lib. bdg. 21.28 *(978-1-59716-712-3(6)*, 1284319) Bearport Publishing Co., Inc.
Zocchi, Judith Mazzeo. What Has Three Horns & a Sharp Beak? Daff, Russ, illus. 2008. (J). *(978-1-59646-820-7(3))* Dingles & Co.
Zoehfeld, Kathleen Weidner. Did Dinosaurs Have Feathers? Washburn, Lucia, illus. (Let's-Read-and-Find-Out Science Ser.). 40p. (J). (gr. k-4). 2004. (ENG.). 15.99 *(978-0-06-029026-9(9))* 2004. lib. bdg. 16.89 *(978-0-06-029027-6(7))* 2003. (ENG.). pap. 5.99 *(978-0-06-445218-2(2))* HarperCollins Pubs.
—Dinosaur Tracks. Washburn, Lucia, illus. 2007. (Let's-Read-And-Find-Out Science 2 Ser.). (ENG.). 40p. (J). (gr. k-4). pap. 6.99 *(978-0-06-445217-5(4))* HarperCollins Pubs.
—Dinosaurs. 2011. (Readers Ser.). (ENG., Illus.). 32p. (J). (gr. -1-1). lib. bdg. 13.90 *(978-1-4263-0776-8(4)*, National Geographic Children's Bks.) National Geographic Society.
—Dinosaurs (1 Hardcover/1 CD) 2016. (National Geographic Readers: Pre-Reader Ser.). (ENG.). (J). *(978-1-4301-2110-7(6))* Live Oak Media.
—Dinosaurs (1 Paperback/1 CD) 2016. (National Geographic Readers: Pre-Reader Ser.). (ENG.). (J). pap. *(978-1-4301-2109-1(2))* Live Oak Media.
—Finding the First T. Rex. Nelson, Jim, illus. 2014. (Totally True Adventures Ser.). (ENG.). 112p. (J). (gr. 2-5). 4.99 *(978-0-375-84662-5(X)*, Random Hse. Bks. for Young Readers) Random Hse. Children's Bks.
—Where Did Dinosaurs Come From? Date not set. 40p. (J). lib. bdg. 16.89 *(978-0-06-029023-8(4))* HarperCollins Pubs.
—Where Did Dinosaurs Come From? Washburn, Lucia, illus. 2010. (Let's-Read-And-Find-Out Science 2 Ser.). (ENG.). 40p. (J). (gr. k-4). pap. 5.99 *(978-0-06-445216-8(6))* HarperCollins Pubs.
Zoehfeld, Kathleen Weidner & U. S. National Geographic Society Staff. Dinosaurs. 2011. (Readers Ser.). (ENG., Illus.). 32p. (J). (gr. -1-1). pap. 3.99 *(978-1-4263-0775-1(6)*, National Geographic Children's Bks.) National Geographic Society.
Zuravicky, Orli. When There Were Dinosaurs: Using Expanded Notation to Represent Numbers in the Millions. (PowerMath Ser.). 32p. 2009. (ENG., Illus.). (gr. 4-5). pap. 10.00 *(978-0-8239-8901-0(1))* 2009. (gr. 4-5). 47.90 *(978-1-60851-404-5(8))* 2004. (Illus.). (J). lib. bdg. 25.25 *(978-0-8239-8988-1(7))* Rosen Publishing Group, Inc., The. (PowerKids Pr.).

DINOSAURS—FICTION

Acopiado, Ginger. The Dinosaurs Went Marching On. Crenshaw, Derek, illus. 2007. 24p. (J). pap. 4.95 *(978-0-9729093-1-0(1))* Tike Time, Inc.
Adamson, Ged, illus. I Want to Grow. 2017. (ENG.). 32p. (J). (gr. -1-3). 16.95 *(978-1-62979-585-0(2))* Boyds Mills Pr.
Addabbo, Carole. Dina the Deaf Dinosaur. Valentine, illus. 2005. 32p. (J). pap. 19.95 *(978-1-889262-92-5(7))* Hannacroix Creek Bks., Inc.
Adler, David A. Bones & the Dinosaur Mystery. Newman, Barbara Johansen, illus. 2005. (Jeffrey Bones Mystery Ser.: No. 4). 32p. (J). *(978-0-670-05970-6(6)*, Viking Adult) Penguin Publishing Group.
—Bones & the Dinosaur Mystery, No. 4. Newman, Barbara Johansen, illus. 2009. (Bones Ser.: 4). (ENG.). 32p. (J). (gr. 1-3). mass mkt. 3.99 *(978-0-14-241341-8(0)*, Penguin Young Readers) Penguin Young Readers Group.
Agnew, Kate. Dinosaur Disasters. Jones, Anna, illus. (Reading Ladder Ser.). (ENG.). 48p. (J). (gr. k-2). 2016. 7.99 *(978-1-4052-8228-4(2))* 2010. pap. 5.99 *(978-1-4052-4778-8(9))* Egmont Bks., Ltd. GBR. Dist: Independent Pubs. Group.
Alphin, Elaine Marie. Dinosaur Hunter. Bolognese, Don, illus. 2003. (I Can Read Bks.). (J). 48p. 15.99 *(978-0-06-028303-2(3))*; 64p. (gr. 2-3). 16.89 *(978-0-06-028304-9(1))* HarperCollins Pubs.
—Dinosaur Hunter. Bolognese, Don, illus. 2004. (I Can Read Bks.). 48p. (gr. 2-4). 14.00 *(978-0-7569-3241-1(6))* Perfection Learning Corp.
Anderson, Carolyn. No Counting Sheep, 1 vol. 2010. 34p. 24.95 *(978-1-4489-9078-8(5))* PublishAmerica, Inc.
Anderson, Jon A. My T-Rex. 2010. 108p. 23.99 *(978-1-4520-0496-9(X))*; pap. 14.99 *(978-1-4520-0495-2(1))* AuthorHouse.
Andreae, Giles. Captain Flinn & the Pirate Dinosaurs. Ayto, Russell, illus. 2005. (Captain Flinn & the Pirate Dinosaurs Ser.). (ENG.). 32p. (J). (gr. -1-1). 17.99 *(978-1-4169-0713-8(0)*, McElderry, Margaret K. Bks.) McElderry, Margaret K. Bks.
—Missing Treasure! Ayto, Russell, illus. 2008. (Captain Flinn & the Pirate Dinosaurs Ser.). (ENG.). 32p. (J). (gr. -1-3). 17.99 *(978-1-4169-6745-3(1)*, McElderry, Margaret K. Bks.) McElderry, Margaret K. Bks.
—The Pop-Up Dinosaurs Galore! Wojtowycz, David, illus. 2008. 14p. (J). (gr. 4-7). 15.95 *(978-1-58925-837-2(1))* Tiger Tales.
Andrew, Carol B. Counting Dinosaurs: An Interactive Book to Learn about Numbers. 2005. (Illus.). (J). *(978-1-933577-02-9(9))* Learning Wood, LLC.
Anholt, Laurence. Stone Girl Bone Girl: The Story of Mary Anning. Moxley, Sheila, illus. 2006. (ENG.). 32p. (J). (gr. k-3). pap. 8.99 *(978-1-84507-700-6(8)*, Frances Lincoln Children's Bks.) Quarto Publishing Group UK GBR. Dist: Hachette Bk. Group.
Aureliani, Franco. Dino-Mike! Aureliani, Franco, illus. 2015. (Dino-Mike! Ser.). (ENG., Illus.). 128p. (gr. 1-3). lib. bdg. 101.28 *(978-1-4965-0311-4(2)*, Dino-Mike!) Stone Arch Bks.
—Dino-Mike & the Jurassic Portal. Aureliani, Franco, illus. 2015. (Dino-Mike! Ser.). (ENG., Illus.). 128p. (gr. 1-3). lib. bdg. 25.32 *(978-1-4342-9630-6(X))* Stone Arch Bks.
—Dino-Mike & the Museum Mayhem. Aureliani, Franco, illus. 2015. (Dino-Mike! Ser.). (ENG., Illus.). 128p. (gr. 1-3). lib. bdg. 25.32 *(978-1-4342-9628-3(8)*, Dino-Mike!) Stone Arch Bks.
—Dino-Mike & the T. Rex Attack. Aureliani, Franco, illus. 2015. (Dino-Mike! Ser.). (ENG., Illus.). 128p. (gr. 1-3). lib. bdg. 25.32 *(978-1-4342-9627-6(X))* Stone Arch Bks.
—Dino-Mike & the Underwater Dinosaurs. Aureliani, Franco, illus. 2015. (Dino-Mike! Ser.). (ENG., Illus.). 128p. (gr. 1-3). lib. bdg. 25.32 *(978-1-4342-9629-0(6))* Stone Arch Bks.
Aureliani, Franco, illus. Dino-Mike & the Museum Mayhem. 2015. (J). lib. bdg. *(978-1-4062-9391-3(1))* Stone Arch Bks.
Awdry, W. Dinos & Discoveries / Emily Saves the World. 2015. (Thomas & Friends 8X8 Ser.). lib. bdg. 14.75 *(978-0-606-36403-4(X))* Turtleback Bks.
Baby Stegosaurus. 2007. (Little Dinosaur Chapter Ser.). (J). per. 7.67 *(978-1-932570-66-3(7))* Pioneer Valley Bks.
Baker, Lavayne L. The Return of the Black Dinosaur. 2009. 28p. pap. 12.49 *(978-1-4490-1723-1(1))* AuthorHouse.
Barad-Cutler, Alexis. Walking with Dinosaurs: Friends Stick Together. 2013. (I Can Read Level 2 Ser.). (ENG., Illus.). 32p. (J). (gr. -1-3). 16.99 *(978-0-06-223286-1(X))*; pap. 3.99 *(978-0-06-223285-4(1))* HarperCollins Pubs.
Bardhan-Quallen, Sudipta. Tyrannosaurus Wrecks! OHora, Zachariah, illus. 2014. (ENG.). 32p. (J). (gr. k-2). 14.95 *(978-1-4197-1035-3(4)*, Abrams Bks. for Young Readers) Abrams, Inc.
Bardoe, Cheryl. The Ugly Duckling Dinosaur: A Prehistoric Tale. Kennedy, Doug & Kennedy, Roy D., illus. 2011. (ENG.). 32p. (J). (gr. -1-3). 16.95 *(978-0-8109-9739-4(8)*, Abrams Bks. for Young Readers) Abrams, Inc.
Bateman, Teresa. Hunting the Daddyosaurus. Huang, Benrei, illus. 2004. 29p. (J). (gr. k-4). reprint ed. 16.00 *(978-0-7567-7796-8(8))* DIANE Publishing Co.
Bateson, Maggie. Dinosaur Safari. Forshaw, Louise, illus. 2014. (ENG.). 10p. (J). 14.99 *(978-1-4711-2121-0(6)*, Simon & Schuster Children's) Simon & Schuster, Ltd. GBR. Dist: Simon & Schuster, Inc.
BeachHouse Publishing. If You Were a Dinosaur in Hawaii. Braffet, Holly, illus. 2010. 22p. (J). (gr. -1-1). bds. 7.95 *(978-1-933067-39-1(X))* Beachhouse Publishing, LLC.
Bean, Raymond. Saving Money (and the World from Killer Dinos!), 1 vol. Vimislik, Matthew, illus. 2014. (Benji Franklin: Kid Zillionaire Ser.). (ENG.). 88p. (gr. 2-3). 22.65 *(978-1-4342-6417-6(3))* Stone Arch Bks.
Beaumont, Karen. Dini Dinosaur. Roode, Daniel, illus. 2012. (ENG.). 32p. (J). (gr. -1-k). 14.99 *(978-0-06-207299-3(4)*, Greenwillow Bks.) HarperCollins Pubs.
Bell, Philip. Jack & Boo's Dinosaur Island. Bell, Eleanor, illus. 2013. 32p. pap. *(978-0-9562980-3-4(6))* Beachy Bks.
Bennett, Chris. Robots & Dinosaurs. 2012. (ENG.). 127p. (J). pap. 16.99 *(978-1-926780-26-9(4))* Key Publishing Hse., Inc., The CAN. Dist: Bookmasters Distribution.
Bentley, Dawn. A Busy Day for Stegosaurus. Carr, Karen, illus. 2005. (ENG.). 36p. (J). (gr. -1-2). 9.95 *(978-1-59249-156-8(1)*, PS2451) Soundprints.
—A Busy Day for Stegosaurus. Carr, Karen, tr. Carr, Karen, illus. 2005. (Smithsonian's Prehistoric Pals Ser.). (ENG.). 36p. (J). (gr. -1-2). 2.95 *(978-1-59249-155-1(3)*, S2451) Soundprints.
—A Busy Day for Stegosaurus. Carr, Karen, illus. 2004. (Smithsonian's Prehistoric Pals Ser.). (ENG.). 36p. (J). (gr. -1-2). 8.95 *(978-1-59249-210-7(X)*, SD2401); 14.95 *(978-1-59249-153-7(7)*, H2401); pap. 6.95 *(978-1-59249-154-4(5)*, S2401) Soundprints.
—It's Tyrannosaurus Rex! Carr, Karen, tr. Carr, Karen, illus. 2005. (Smithsonian's Prehistoric Pals Ser.). (ENG.). 36p. (J).

(gr. -1-2). 14.95 *(978-1-59249-157-5(X)*, H2400); pap. 6.95 *(978-1-59249-158-2(8)*, S2400) Soundprints.

—It's Tyrannosaurus Rex! Carr, Karen, illus. (Smithsonian's Prehistoric Pals Ser.). (ENG.). 36p. (J). (gr. -1-2). 2004. 8.95 *(978-1-59249-212-1(6)*, SD2400) 2003. 9.95 *(978-1-59249-160-5(X)*, PS2450) Soundprints.

—It's Tyrannosaurus Rex! 2003. (Smithsonian's Prehistoric Pals Ser.). (ENG., Illus.). 36p. (J). (gr. 2-2). 2.95 *(978-1-59249-159-9(6)*, S2450) Soundprints.

—Lead the Way, Velociraptor! Carr, Karen, illus. 2004. (Read & Discover (Soundprints) Ser.). (ENG.). 32p. (J). (gr. -1-3). pap. 3.95 *(978-1-59249-304-3(1)*, S2031) Soundprints.

—Parasaurolophus Escapes. McIntosh, Gabe, illus. 2006. (Smithsonian's Prehistoric Pals Ser.). (ENG.). 36p. (J). 2.95 *(978-1-59249-645-7(8))*; (gr. -1-3). pap. 6.95 *(978-1-59249-643-3(1))* Soundprints.

—Pteranodon Soars. Carr, Karen, illus. 2005. (Smithsonian's Prehistoric Pals Ser.). (ENG.). 36p. (J). (gr. -1-2). 8.95 *(978-1-59249-371-5(8)*, SD2405); 9.95 *(978-1-59249-373-9(4)*, PS2455); 14.95 *(978-1-59249-369-2(6)*, H2405); 2.95 *(978-1-59249-372-2(6)*, S2455); pap. 6.95 *(978-1-59249-370-8(X)*, S2405) Soundprints.

—Snack Time, Tyrannosaurus Rex! Carr, Karen, illus. 2004. (ENG.). 32p. (J). (gr. -1-3). pap. 3.95 *(978-1-59249-302-9(5)*, S2033) Soundprints.

—Surprise, Stegosaurus! Carr, Karen, illus. 2004. (ENG.). 32p. (J). (gr. -1-3). pap. 3.95 *(978-1-59249-305-0(X)*, S2032) Soundprints.

—Triceratops Gets Lost. Carr, Karen, illus. (Smithsonian's Prehistoric Pals Ser.). (J). 2009. 21.95 incl. audio compact disk *(978-1-59249-544-3(3))* 2005. (ENG.). 36p. (gr. -1-2). 8.95 *(978-1-59249-216-9(9)*, SD2403) Soundprints.

—Triceratops Gets Lost. Carr, Karen, tr. Carr, Karen, illus. 2005. (Smithsonian's Prehistoric Pals Ser.). (ENG.). 36p. (J). (gr. -1-2). 2.95 *(978-1-59249-167-4(7)*, S2453) Soundprints.

—Triceratops Gets Lost. Carr, Karen, illus. 2004. (Smithsonian's Prehistoric Pals Ser.). (ENG.). 36p. (J). (gr. -1-2). pap. 6.95 *(978-1-59249-166-7(9)*, S2403) Soundprints.

—Velociraptor: Small & Speedy. Carr, Karen, tr. Carr, Karen, illus. 2005. (Smithsonian's Prehistoric Pals Ser.). (ENG.). 36p. (J). (gr. -1-2). 14.95 *(978-1-59249-161-2(8)*, H2402); 2.95 *(978-1-59249-163-6(4)*, S2452) Soundprints.

—Velociraptor: Small & Speedy. Carr, Karen, illus. 2004. (Smithsonian's Prehistoric Pals Ser.). (ENG.). 36p. (J). (gr. -1-2). pap. 6.95 *(978-1-59249-162-9(6)*, S2402) Soundprints.

—Velociraptor - Small & Speedy. Carr, Karen, illus. 2004. (Smithsonian's Prehistoric Pals Ser.). (ENG.). 36p. (J). (gr. -1-2). 8.95 *(978-1-59249-214-5(2)*, SD2402) Soundprints.

—Watch Out, Triceratops! Carr, Karen, illus. 2004. (Read & Discover (Soundprints) Ser.). (ENG.). 32p. (J). (gr. -1-3). pap. 3.95 *(978-1-59249-303-6(3)*, S2030) Soundprints.

Bentley, Dawn & Studio Mouse Staff. Triceratops. Carr, Karen, illus. 2008. (ENG.). 24p. (J). (gr. 3-7). 4.99 *(978-1-59069-622-4(0))* Studio Mouse LLC.

—Tyrannosaurus Rex. Carr, Karen, illus. 2008. (ENG.). 24p. (J). (gr. 3-7). 4.99 *(978-1-59069-621-7(2))* Studio Mouse LLC.

Benton, Jim. Where Did All the Dinos Go? Benton, Jim, illus. 2016. (ENG., Illus.). 18p. (J). (— 1). bds. 7.99 *(978-0-545-64789-2(4)*, Cartwheel Bks.) Scholastic, Inc.

Berenstain, Jan & Berenstain, Mike. The Berenstain Bears' Dinosaur Dig. Berenstain, Jan & Berenstain, Mike, illus. 2012. (Berenstain Bears Ser.). (ENG., Illus.). 24p. (J). (gr. -1-3). pap. 3.99 *(978-0-06-207548-2(9)*, HarperFestival) HarperCollins Pubs.

—The Berenstain Bears' Dinosaur Dig. 2012. (Berenstain Bears Ser.). (J). lib. bdg. 13.55 *(978-0-606-26290-3(3)*, Turtleback) Turtleback Bks.

Biro, Val. Gumdrop & the Dinosaur. 2015. (ENG., Illus.). 32p. (J). pap. 9.99 *(978-1-78270-048-7(X))* Award Pubns. Ltd. GBR. Dist: Parkwest Pubns., Inc.

Björkman, Steve. Dinosaurs Don't, Dinosaurs Do. Björkman, Steve, illus. 2012. (I Like to Read(r) Ser.). (ENG., Illus.). 24p. (J). (gr. -1-2). pap. 6.99 *(978-0-8234-2640-9(8))* Holiday Hse., Inc.

Blackstone, Stella. I Dreamt I Was a Dinosaur. Beaton, Clare, illus. (ENG.). (J). (gr. -1-k). 2006. 24p. bds. 7.99 *(978-1-84686-015-7(6))* 2005. 32p. 15.99 *(978-1-84148-238-5(2))* Barefoot Bks., Inc.

Blackstone, Stella & Beaton, Clare. I Dreamt I Was a Dinosaur. Beaton, Clare, illus. 2011. (ENG., Illus.). 32p. (J). (gr. -1-k). pap. 7.99 *(978-1-84686-025-6(3))* Barefoot Bks., Inc.

Blasing, George. Uno and the Raptor Pack: The Journey Begins! Ramirez, Alberto, illus. 2007. (J). 4.95 *(978-0-9797304-1-2(4))* Raining Popcorn Media.

—Dinosaur George Prehistoric Safari: Raptor Island. Ramirez, Alberto, illus. 2007. (J). 4.95 *(978-0-9797304-2-9(2))* Raining Popcorn Media.

Blasing, George & Blasing, George. The Prehistoric Adventures of Dinosaur George: Jurassic Tigers. Smith, David, illus. 2007. 16p. (J). 4.95 *(978-0-9797304-0-5(6))* Raining Popcorn Media.

Bloomberg, Sandi. Michael & the Magic Dinosaur. Collier, Kevin, illus. 2012. 30p. pap. 13.95 *(978-1-61244-066-8(5))* Halo Publishing International.

Bloomsbury. Lift-The-Flap Friends: Dinosaurs. 2016. (ENG.). 14p. (J). bds. 9.99 *(978-1-68119-099-0(0)*, 9781681190990, Bloomsbury Activity Bks.) Bloomsbury Publishing USA.

Bodkin, Odds. Little Proto's T-Rex Adventure: A Musical Dinosaur Story. (Odds Bodkin Musical Story Collection). (J). 9.95 incl. audio *(978-1-882412-27-3(3)*, Odds Bodkin Storytelling Library, The) Rivertree Productions, Inc.

Book Company Staff. Are You a Dinosaur? 2003. (Novelty Bks.). (J). 12.95 *(978-1-74047-319-4(1))* Book Co. Publishing Pty, Ltd., The AUS. Dist: Penton Overseas, Inc.

—Dinosaurs. 2005. (Lift & Learn Ser.). (Illus.). 8p. (J). bds. 10.95 *(978-1-74047-619-5(0))* Book Co. Publishing Pty, Ltd., The AUS. Dist: Penton Overseas, Inc.

Bordiglioni, Stephen & Bordiglioni, Stefano. Desert Adventure. Bertolucci, Federico, illus. 2009. (Dinodino's Dinosaur Adventures Ser.). 56p. (J). (gr. k-4). 27.95 *(978-1-60754-714-3(7))*; pap. 12.85 *(978-1-60754-721-1(X))* Windmill Bks.

—Earthquake! Bertolucci, Federico, illus. 2009. (Dinodino's Dinosaur Adventures Ser.). 56p. (J). (gr. k-4). 27.95 *(978-1-60754-713-6(9))*; pap. 12.85 *(978-1-60754-719-8(8))* Windmill Bks.

—Volcano! Bertolucci, Federico, illus. 2009. (Dinodino's Dinosaur Adventures Ser.). 56p. (J). (gr. k-4). 27.95 *(978-1-60754-712-9(0))*; pap. 12.85 *(978-1-60754-717-4(1))* Windmill Bks.

Bower, Kevin. Fly Rex Fly. 2012. (Illus.). 24p. pap. 15.99 *(978-1-4771-4210-3(X))* Xlibris Corp.

Boyd, Charles O'Halloran. Mountains of the North. 2009. 172p. pap. 13.95 *(978-1-4401-4228-4(9))* iUniverse, Inc.

Boynton, Sandra. Dinosaur Dance! Boynton, Sandra, illus. 2016. (ENG., Illus.). 16p. (J). (gr. -1-k). bds. 5.99 *(978-1-4814-8099-4(5)*, Little Simon) Little Simon.

Bradbury, Ray. Dinosaur Tales. 2003. (Illus.). 144p. pap. 14.95 *(978-0-7434-5897-9(4))* ibooks, Inc.

Bradley, Timothy J. Time Jump, Bk. 3. 2014. (Sci Hi Ser.). (ENG.). 232p. (J). (gr. 3-6). lib. bdg. 26.96 *(978-1-4807-4217-8(1))* Teacher Created Materials, Inc.

Bradman, Tony. Dilly the Dinosaur: 30th Anniversary Edition. Hellard, Susan, illus. 2nd ed. 2016. (ENG.). 64p. (J). (gr. 1-4). pap. 7.99 ***(978-1-4052-8466-0(8))*** Egmont Bks., Ltd. GBR. Dist: Independent Pubs. Group.

Brezenoff, Steve. Dinosaur That Disappeared. 2013. (Field Trip Mysteries Ser.). (ENG.). 88p. (gr. 2-3). pap. 35.70 *(978-1-4342-6233-2(2))* Stone Arch Bks.

—The Dinosaur That Disappeared, 1 vol. Calo, Marcos, illus. 2013. (Field Trip Mysteries Ser.). (ENG.). 88p. (gr. 2-3). pap. 6.10 *(978-1-4342-6213-4(8))*; lib. bdg. 25.32 *(978-1-4342-5980-6(3))* Stone Arch Bks.

Brezenoff, Steven. The Case of the Haunted History Museum. Weber, Lisa K., illus. 2015. (Museum Mysteries Ser.). (ENG.). 128p. (gr. 2-3). lib. bdg. 26.65 *(978-1-4342-9687-0(3))* Stone Arch Bks.

—The Case of the Missing Mom. Weber, Lisa K., illus. 2016. (Museum Mysteries Ser.). (ENG.). 128p. (gr. 2-3). 26.65 *(978-1-4965-2517-8(5))* Stone Arch Bks.

Brian, Janeen. I'm a Dirty Dinosaur. James, Ann, illus. 2014. (ENG.). 22p. (J). 11.99 *(978-1-61067-296-2(8))* Kane Miller.

Bright, J. E. Walking with Dinosaurs: Patchi's Big Adventure. 2013. (Walking with Dinosaurs Ser.). (ENG.). 24p. (J). (gr. -1-3). pap. 4.99 *(978-0-06-223275-5(4)*, HarperFestival) HarperCollins Pubs.

—Walking with Dinosaurs: the Great Migration. 2013. (Walking with Dinosaurs Ser.). (ENG.). 24p. (J). (gr. -1-3). pap. 4.99 *(978-0-06-223273-1(8)*, HarperFestival) HarperCollins Pubs.

Broach, Elise. When Dinosaurs Came with Everything. Small, David, illus. 2007. (ENG.). 40p. (J). (gr. -1-3). 17.99 *(978-0-689-86922-8(3)*, Atheneum Bks. for Young Readers) Simon & Schuster Children's Publishing.

Brockenbrough, Martha. The Dinosaur Tooth Fairy. Sanchez, Israel, illus. 2013. (ENG.). 32p. (J). (gr. -1-3). 17.99 *(978-0-545-24466-4(8)*, Levine, Arthur A. Bks.) Scholastic, Inc.

Browne, Eileen. Mary Had a Dinosaur. Rivers, Ruth, illus. 2009. (Get Ready (Windmill Books) Ser.). 32p. (J). (gr. k-2). lib. bdg. 22.60 *(978-1-60754-262-9(5))* Windmill Bks.

Brownlow, Mike. Ten Little Dinosaurs. Rickerty, Simon, illus. 2016. (Ten Little Ser.). (ENG.). 32p. (J). (gr. -1-k). pap. ***(978-1-4083-3401-0(1)***, Orchard Bks.) Hachette Children's Group GBR. Dist: Hachette Bk. Group.

Brownlow, Mike, illus. Dinosaurs of Doom! 2011. (Time Pirates Ser.). (ENG.). 12p. (J). (gr. k-2). bds. 24.99 *(978-0-230-74179-9(7))* Macmillan Pubs., Ltd. GBR. Dist: Independent Pubs. Group.

Bryant, Ann. Dragons vs Dinos. 2014. (ENG., Illus.). 32p. (J). *(978-0-7787-1328-9(8))* Crabtree Publishing Co.

Bryant, Megan E. Alphasaurus. Powell, Luciana Navarro, illus. 2012. (ENG.). 20p. (J). (gr. -1 — 1). bds. 9.99 *(978-1-4521-0748-6(3))* Chronicle Bks. LLC.

—Colorasaurus. Powell, Luciana Navarro, illus. 2012. (ENG.). 20p. (J). (gr. -1 — 1). bds. 9.99 *(978-1-4521-0814-8(5))* Chronicle Bks. LLC.

—Countasaurus. Powell, Luciana Navarro, illus. 2012. (ENG.). 20p. (J). (gr. -1 — 1). bds. 9.99 *(978-1-4521-0747-9(5))* Chronicle Bks. LLC.

Burroughs, Edgar Rice. The Land That Time Forgot: Graphic Novel. Jones, K. L., illus. 2011. (Campfire Graphic Novels Ser.). (ENG.). 72p. (YA). (gr. 5-12). pap. 9.99 *(978-93-80028-38-5(5)*, Campfire) Steerforth Pr.

Burroughs, Scott, illus. Fossil Frenzy. 2014. (Hardy Boys: the Secret Files Ser.: 14). (ENG.). 96p. (J). (gr. 1-4). pap. 5.99 *(978-1-4424-9043-7(8)*, Aladdin) Simon & Schuster Children's Publishing.

Bush, Maureen. Feather Brain, 1 vol. 2008. (Orca Young Readers Ser.). (ENG.). 136p. (J). (gr. 3-6). pap. 7.95 *(978-1-55143-877-1(1))* Orca Bk. Pubs. USA.

Buzzeo, Toni. No T. Rex in the Library. Yoshikawa, Sachiko, illus. 2010. (ENG.). 32p. (J). (gr. -1-3). 17.99 *(978-1-4169-3927-6(X)*, McElderry, Margaret K. Bks.) McElderry, Margaret K. Bks.

Byrne, Lex. Ever Met the Hooferjackal? 2009. 32p. pap. 14.95 *(978-1-4490-4630-9(4))* AuthorHouse.

Byrne, Richard. The Really, Really, Really Big Dinosaur. 2012. (ENG.). 32p. (J). 16.99 *(978-1-58925-123-6(7))* Tiger Tales.

Caldwell, Daisy L. Sarah the Oh So Silly, but Shy Stegosaurus, 1 vol. 2009. 24p. pap. 24.95 *(978-1-61546-319-0(4))* America Star Bks.

Calmenson, Stephanie. No Honking Allowed. Ferrari, Antongionata, illus. 2017. (ENG.). 40p. (J). 16.95 ***(978-0-8234-3672-9(1))*** Holiday Hse., Inc.

Cammuso, Frank. The Misadventures of Salem Hyde: Dinosaur Dilemma. 2015. (Misadventures of Salem Hyde Ser.: 4). (ENG., Illus.). 96p. (J). (gr. 2-4). 14.95 *(978-1-4197-1534-1(8)*, Amulet Bks.) Abrams, Inc.

Carmine, Mary & Baynton, Martin. Daniel et Ses Dinosaures.Tr. of Daniel et Ses Dinosaures. (FRE., Illus.). (J). 13.99 *(978-0-590-74149-1(7))*; bds. 29.99 *(978-0-590-74124-8(1))* Scholastic, Inc.

Carrick, Carol. Patrick's Dinosaurs. Carrick, Donald, illus. 2006. (Read along Book & CD Ser.). (ENG.). 32p. (J). (gr. -1-3). audio compact disk 10.99 *(978-0-618-73275-3(6))* Houghton Mifflin Harcourt Publishing Co.

Castor, H. The Dinosaurs Next Door. 2004. (Young Reading Ser.). (ENG., Illus.). 48p. (J). (gr. 2-18). pap. 5.95 *(978-0-7945-0251-5(2)*, Usborne) EDC Publishing.

Catlow, Nikalas & Wesson, Tim. Robots vs. Gorillas in the Desert. Catlow, Nikalas & Wesson, Tim, illus. 2011. (Mega Mash-Up Ser.). (ENG., Illus.). 96p. (J). (gr. 2-5). pap. 6.99 *(978-0-7636-5873-1(1)*, Nosy Crow) Candlewick Pr.

—Romans vs. Dinosaurs on Mars. Catlow, Nikalas & Wesson, Tim, illus. 2011. (Mega Mash-Up Ser.). (ENG., Illus.). 96p. (J). (gr. 2-5). pap. 6.99 *(978-0-7636-5872-4(3)*, Nosy Crow) Candlewick Pr.

Choldenko, Gennifer. Dad & the Dinosaur. Santat, Dan, illus. 2017. (ENG.). 40p. (J). (gr. k-3). 17.99 *(978-0-399-24353-0(4)*, G.P. Putnam's Sons Books for Young Readers) Penguin Young Readers Group.

Church, Caroline Jayne. I Love My Dinosaur. 2015. (Love Meez Ser.: 2). (ENG., Illus.). 10p. (J). (gr. -1 — 1). bds. 7.99 *(978-0-545-83592-3(5)*, Cartwheel Bks.) Scholastic, Inc.

Clanton, Ben. Rex Wrecks It! Clanton, Ben, illus. 2017. (ENG., Illus.). 32p. (J). (-k). bds. 7.99 *(978-0-7636-9308-4(1))* Candlewick Pr.

Clarke, Jane. Dancing with the Dinosaurs. Wildish, Lee, illus. 2012. (ENG.). 32p. (J). (gr. -1-2). 12.95 *(978-1-936140-67-1(5))* Charlesbridge Publishing, Inc.

—How to Bathe Your Little Dino. Birkett, Georgie, illus. 2017. 16p. (J). bds. 8.99 *(978-1-61067-495-9(2))* Kane Miller.

Climo, Liz. Rory the Dinosaur: Me & My Dad. 2015. (Illus.). (J). (ENG.). 40p. (gr. -1-3). 17.00 *(978-0-316-27728-0(2))*; 48p. pap. *(978-0-316-26391-7(5))* Little Brown & Co.

—Rory the Dinosaur Wants a Pet. 2016. (ENG., Illus.). 40p. (J). (gr. -1-3). 16.99 *(978-0-316-27729-7(0))* Little Brown & Co.

Cohen, Melissa. PuzzlePal Books: Dear Dinosaur. Magnayon, Megan Coy, illus. 2013. (PuzzlePal Bks.). (ENG.). 10p. (J). (gr. -1). bds. 14.95 *(978-1-60710-699-9(X)*, Silver Dolphin Bks.) Readerlink Distribution Services, LLC.

Cole, Steve. Z. Rex. (ENG.). 256p. (J). (gr. 5-18). 2010. 8.99 *(978-0-14-241712-6(2)*, Puffin Books) 2009. 16.99 *(978-0-399-25253-2(3)*, Philomel Bks.) Penguin Young Readers Group.

Collins, Diana Sue. Elfin, the Elf. 2011. 44p. pap. 24.95 *(978-1-4560-8493-6(3))* America Star Bks.

Cook, Gerri. Where the Buffalo Jump. Yu, Chao & Wang, Jue, illus. 2003. (Dinosaur Soup Ser.). 120p. (YA). (gr. 3-5). pap. 9.95 *(978-1-895836-95-0(6))* River Bks. CAN. Dist: Fitzhenry & Whiteside, Ltd.

Cordone Warner, Debra. I Almost Found Some Dinosaur Bones! 2010. 56p. pap. 24.99 *(978-0-557-59624-9(6))* Lulu Pr., Inc.

Coster, Simon. My Dinosaur Is More Awesome! 2015. (ENG., Illus.). 48p. (J). (gr. -1-k). 16.99 *(978-1-63220-416-5(9)*, Sky Pony Pr.) Skyhorse Publishing Co., Inc.

Cowley, Joy, contrib. by. Dinosaur Morning. 2004. (Story Basket Ser.: Vol. 5). 8 or 16p. (gr. k-2). pap. 31.50 *(978-0-322-01923-2(0))* Wright Group/McGraw-Hill.

Crisp, Dan & Linn, Susie. Dinosaurs: Sticker Book Fun for Little Ones! 2017. (My First Sticker Book Ser.). (ENG.). 36p. (J). (gr. -1-k). pap. 8.99 *(978-1-78700-060-5(5))* Top That! Publishing PLC GBR. Dist: Independent Pubs. Group.

Crowson, Andrew. Flip Flap Prehistoric. Crowson, Andrew, illus. 2003. (Illus.). 12p. (J). pap. *(978-1-85602-474-7(1)*, Pavilion Children's Books) Pavilion Bks.

Crowther, Robert. Robert Crowther's Pop-Up Dinosaur ABC. Crowther, Robert, illus. 2015. (ENG., Illus.). 10p. (J). (gr. -1-3). 19.99 *(978-0-7636-7296-6(3))* Candlewick Pr.

Cua, Marcus Loo. How the Hungry T-Rex Got Fixed. 2012. 24p. pap. 28.03 *(978-1-4653-9643-3(8))* Xlibris Corp.

Cucko, D. Kirsten. If Dinosaurs Were Around Today. 2009. 20p. pap. 12.49 *(978-1-4490-2643-1(5))* AuthorHouse.

Cumyn, Alan. Hot Pterodactyl Boyfriend. 2016. (ENG., Illus.). 416p. (YA). (gr. 9). 17.99 *(978-1-4814-3980-0(4)*, Atheneum/Caitlyn Dlouhy Books) Simon & Schuster Children's Publishing.

Cunningham, Kay. Bucky: The Adventures of the Dinosaur Cowboy. Wilson, Mary Ann, illus. 2004. 32p. (J). 18.99 *(978-1-57860-173-8(8))* Clerisy Pr.

Dabrio-Martinez, Mutzai. The Day the Dinosaurs Came to St. Andrew. 2013. 112p. pap. 10.95 *(978-1-4759-6077-8(8))* iUniverse, Inc.

Dahl, Michael. Dino Death-Trap. Vecchio, Luciano, illus. 2016. (Batman Tales of the Batcave Ser.). (ENG.). 40p. (gr. 1-3). lib. bdg. 24.65 *(978-1-4965-4015-7(8)*, DC Super Heroes) Stone Arch Bks.

—Little Dinos Don't Bite, 1 vol. Record, Adam, illus. 2013. (Little Dinos Ser.). (ENG.). 20p. (gr. -1-k). bds. 7.99 *(978-1-4048-7536-4(0))* Picture Window Bks.

—Little Dinos Don't Hit, 1 vol. Record, Adam, illus. 2013. (Little Dinos Ser.). (ENG.). 20p. (gr. -1-k). bds. 7.99 *(978-1-4048-7533-3(6))* Picture Window Bks.

—Little Dinos Don't Push, 1 vol. Record, Adam, illus. 2013. (Little Dinos Ser.). (ENG.). 20p. (gr. -1-k). bds. 7.99 *(978-1-4048-7534-0(4))* Picture Window Bks.

—Little Dinos Don't Yell, 1 vol. Record, Adam, illus. 2013. (Little Dinos Ser.). (ENG.). 20p. (gr. -1-k). bds. 7.99 *(978-1-4048-7912-6(9))* Picture Window Bks.

—Thesaurus Rex. Kendall, Bradford, illus. 2016. 40p. (J). *(978-1-4747-1057-2(3))* Stone Arch Bks.

Daisy Dinosaur's Opposites. 2015. (Illus.). (J). *(978-1-58865-881-4(3))* Kidsbooks, LLC.

Dale, Jay. Baby Dinosaur Can Play, 1 vol. East, Jacqueline, illus. 2012. (Engage Literacy Red Ser.). (ENG.). 32p. (gr. k-2). pap. 5.99 *(978-1-4296-8936-6(6)*, Engage Literacy) Capstone Press of Coughlan Cos.

—Baby Dinosaur Is Hiding, 1 vol. East, Jacqueline, illus. 2012. (Engage Literacy Yellow Ser.). (ENG.). 32p. (gr. k-2). pap. 5.99 *(978-1-4296-8952-6(8)*, Engage Literacy) Capstone Press of Coughlan Cos.

—Baby Dinosaur Is Lost, 1 vol. East, Jacqueline, illus. 2012. (Engage Literacy Blue Ser.). (ENG.). 32p. (gr. k-2). pap. 5.99 *(978-1-4296-8972-4(2)*, Engage Literacy) Capstone Press of Coughlan Cos.

Dale, Penny. Dinosaur Dig! Dale, Penny, illus. 2012. (ENG., Illus.). 14p. (J). (gr. k-k). bds. 6.99 *(978-0-7636-6270-7(4)*, Nosy Crow) Candlewick Pr.

—Dinosaur Pirates! Dale, Penny, illus. 2017. (ENG., Illus.). 32p. (J). (-k). 15.99 *(978-0-7636-9330-5(8)*, Nosy Crow) Candlewick Pr.

—Dinosaur Rescue! Dale, Penny, illus. 2016. (ENG., Illus.). 24p. (J). (-k). bds. 6.99 *(978-0-7636-8000-8(1)*, Nosy Crow) Candlewick Pr.

—Dinosaur Rocket! Dale, Penny, illus. 2015. (ENG., Illus.). 32p. (J). (-k). 15.99 *(978-0-7636-7999-6(2)*, Nosy Crow) Candlewick Pr.

—Dinosaur Zoom! Dale, Penny, illus. (ENG., Illus.). (J). (-k). 2014. 24p. bds. 6.99 *(978-0-7636-7394-9(3))* 2013. 32p. 15.99 *(978-0-7636-6448-0(0))* Candlewick Pr. (Nosy Crow).

—Dinosaurs on the Go! Dale, Penny, illus. 2016. (ENG., Illus.). (J). (-k). bds. 19.99 *(978-0-7636-8936-0(X)*, Nosy Crow) Candlewick Pr.

Dare, Will. How to Catch a Dino Thief. 2017. (Dino Riders Ser.: 4). (ENG.). 128p. (J). (gr. 2-5). pap. 5.99 ***(978-1-4926-3623-6(1)***, Sourcebooks Jabberwocky) Sourcebooks, Inc.

—How to Rope a Giganotosaurus. 2017. (Dino Riders Ser.: 2). lib. bdg. 16.00 ***(978-0-606-40352-8(3))*** Turtleback Bks.

—How to Tame a Triceratops. 2017. (Dino Riders Ser.: 1). lib. bdg. 16.00 ***(978-0-606-40351-1(5))*** Turtleback Bks.

de Las Casas, Dianne. Dinosaur Mardi Gras, 1 vol. Gentry, Marita, illus. 2011. (ENG.). 32p. (J). (gr. k-3). 16.99 *(978-1-58980-966-6(1))* Pelican Publishing Co., Inc.

Dean, James. Cavecat Pete. Dean, James, illus. 2015. (Pete the Cat Ser.). (ENG., Illus.). 24p. (J). (gr. -1-3). pap. 4.99 *(978-0-06-219863-1(7)*, HarperFestival) HarperCollins Pubs.

dePaola, Tomie. Little Grunt & the Big Egg: A Prehistoric Fairy Tale. dePaola, Tomie, illus. 2008. (ENG., Illus.). 32p. (J). (gr. -1-3). pap. 6.99 *(978-0-14-241143-8(4)*, Puffin Books) Penguin Young Readers Group.

—Little Grunt & the Big Egg: A Prehistoric Fairy Tale. 2007. 27.95 incl. audio *(978-0-8045-6944-6(4))*; 29.95 incl. audio compact disk *(978-0-8045-4158-9(2))* Spoken Arts, Inc.

DePrisco, Dorothea. Dinosaur Dance. 2006. (ENG.). 12p. 9.95 *(978-1-58117-480-9(2)*, Intervisual/Piggy Toes) Bendon, Inc.

Derrick, David G., Jr. Play with Your Food. 2014. (ENG., Illus.). 36p. (J). (gr. -1-3). 15.95 *(978-1-59702-102-9(4))* Immedium.

DiCicco, Sue & Mawhinney, Art, illus. Diego y los Dinosaurios. 2008. (Go, Diego, Go! Ser.). Orig. Title: Diego's Great Dinosaur Rescue. (SPA & ENG.). 24p. (J). (gr. -1-2). pap. 3.99 *(978-1-4169-5871-0(1)*, Libros Para Ninos) Libros Para Ninos.

—Diego's Great Dinosaur Rescue. 2008. (Go, Diego, Go! Ser.). (ENG.). 24p. (J). (gr. -1-2). pap. 3.99 *(978-1-4169-5867-3(3)*, Simon Spotlight/Nickelodeon) Simon Spotlight/Nickelodeon.

Dino Detective. Date not set. 9.95 *(978-0-89868-271-7(1))*; pap. 3.95 *(978-0-89868-272-4(X))* ARO Publishing Co.

The Dinosaur Dance: Take-Home Book. 2005. (Emergent Library: Vol. 2). (YA). (gr. -1-1). 12.60 *(978-0-8215-7257-3(1))* Sadlier, William H. Inc.

Dinosaur Friends. 2014. (Dinosaur Friends Ser.). 32p. (J). (gr. k-3). 105.00 *(978-1-4777-9112-7(4))* Windmill Bks.

Dinosaur Girl: Individual Title, 6 packs. (Action Packs Ser.). 120p. (gr. 3-5). 44.00 *(978-0-7635-8394-1(4))* Rigby Education.

A Dinosaur Goes to Church. 2013. (ENG., Illus.). 32p. (J). 14.99 *(978-1-62108-423-5(X))* Covenant Communications, Inc.

Dinosaur Party: Individual Title, 6 packs. (Chiquilibros Ser.). (gr. k-1). 23.00 *(978-0-7635-0432-8(7))* Rigby Education.

Dinosaur School: Set 5. 2016. (Dinosaur School Ser.). 24p. (gr. k-k). pap. 48.90 *(978-1-4824-5337-9(1))*; lib. bdg. 135.60 *(978-1-4824-4517-6(4))* Stevens, Gareth Publishing LLLP.

Dinosaur Tales. (My Animal Library). (Illus.). 10p. (J). bds. *(978-2-7643-0104-3(9))* Phidal Publishing, Inc./Editions Phidal, Inc.

Dipucchio, Kelly. Dinosnores. Goembel, Ponder, illus. 2005. 32p. (J). (gr. -1 — 1). 17.99 *(978-0-06-051577-5(5))*; lib. bdg. 16.89 *(978-0-06-051578-2(3))* HarperCollins Pubs.

Disney Book Group Staff. The Good Dinosaur. Disney Storybook Artists Staff, illus. 2015. (ENG.). 44p. (J). (gr. 1-3). 17.99 *(978-1-4231-8752-3(0))* Disney Pr.

Dolby, Karen. The Incredible Dinosaur Expedition. Haw, Brenda, illus. 2004. (Puzzle Adventures Ser.). 48p. (J). pap. 4.95 *(978-0-7945-0022-1(6)*, Usborne) EDC Publishing.

Donnie Dinosaur's Tobacco Trouble. (J). 29.50 *(978-1-56230-276-4(0))* Syndistar, Inc.

Doodler, Todd H. Rawr! Doodler, Todd H., illus. 2013. (ENG., Illus.). 40p. (J). (gr. -1-k). 12.99 *(978-0-545-51118-6(6)*, Scholastic Pr.) Scholastic, Inc.

—Super Rawr! Doodler, Todd H., illus. 2016. (ENG., Illus.). 40p. (J). (gr. -1-k). 12.99 *(978-0-545-79969-0(4)*, Scholastic Pr.) Scholastic, Inc.

Dotlich, Rebecca Kai. Digger the Dinosaur. Gynux, illus. 2013. (My First I Can Read Ser.). (ENG.). 24p. (J). (gr. -1-3). 16.99 *(978-0-06-222222-0(8))*; pap. 3.99 *(978-0-06-222221-3(X))* HarperCollins Pubs.

—Digger the Dinosaur. 2013. (Digger the Dinosaur I Can Read Ser.). (J). lib. bdg. 13.55 *(978-0-606-31828-0(3)*, Turtleback) Turtleback Bks.

—Digger the Dinosaur & the Cake Mistake. Gynux, illus. 2013. (My First I Can Read Ser.). (ENG.). 24p. (J). (gr. -1-3). 16.99 *(978-0-06-222224-4(4))*; pap. 3.99 *(978-0-06-222223-7(6))* HarperCollins Pubs.

Draper, Sharon M. Stars & Sparks on Stage. Watson, Jesse Joshua, illus. 2007. (Ziggy & the Black Dinosaurs Ser.: 6). (ENG.). 160p. (J). pap. 4.99 *(978-1-4169-0001-6(2)*, Simon & Schuster/Paula Wiseman Bks.) Simon & Schuster/Paula Wiseman Bks.

DreamWorks. Dinotrux: Team Dinotrux! 2016. (ENG., Illus.). 32p. (J). (gr. -1-3). 12.99 *(978-0-316-26074-9(6))* Little, Brown Bks. for Young Readers.

Duddle, Jonny. Gigantosaurus. Duddle, Jonny, illus. 2014. (ENG., Illus.). 32p. (J). (gr. -1-2). 16.99 *(978-0-7636-7131-0(2)*, Templar) Candlewick Pr.

Duey, Kathleen. Rex. Epstein, Eugene, illus. Gould, Robert, photos by. 2003. (Time Soldiers Ser.: Bk. 1). (ENG.). 48p. (J). (gr. k-2). pap. 7.95 *(978-1-929945-20-7(5))* Big Guy Bks., Inc.

—Rex. Epstein, Eugene, illus. 2006. (Time Soldiers Ser.: Bk. 1). 96p. (J). (gr. -1-7). lib. bdg. 24.21 *(978-1-59961-227-0(5))* Spotlight.

—Rex 2. Epstein, Eugene, illus. Gould, Robert, photos by. 2003. (Time Soldiers Ser.: Bk. 2). (ENG.). 48p. (J). (gr. k-2). pap. 8.95 *(978-1-929945-27-6(2))* Big Guy Bks., Inc.

—Rex2. Epstein, Eugene, illus. Gould, Robert, photos by. 2007. (Time Soldiers Ser.). (ENG.). 96p. (gr. -1-7). 24.21 *(978-1-59961-228-7(3))* Spotlight.

C D

Duey, Kathleen & Gould, Robert. Rex 2. Epstein, Eugene, illus. Gould, Robert, photos by. 2003. (Soldados de Tiempo Libro: Vol. 2). (SPA & ENG.). 48p. (J). (gr. k-4). pap. 8.95 (978-1-929945-36-8(1)) Big Guy Bks., Inc.

—Rex2. Epstein, Eugene, illus. Gould, Robert, photos by. 2003. (Time Soldiers Ser.). 48p. (J). (gr. 4-7). 17.10 (978-0-7569-3472-9(9)) Perfection Learning Corp.

Durst, Sarah Beth. Roar & Sparkles Go to School. Whitehouse, Ben, illus. 2017. (ENG.). 40p. (J). (gr. -1-1). 16.99 **(978-0-7624-5986-5(7)**, Running Pr.) Running Pr. Bk. Pubs.

Dyan, Penelope. The Hatchling, the Story of Stegi Stegosaurus. Dyan, Penelope, illus. 2010. (Illus.). 42p. pap. 11.95 (978-1-935630-08-1(3)) Bellissima Publishing, LLC.

Echeverri, Catalina. There's a Dinosaur in My Bathtub. 2014. (ENG., Illus.). 32p. (J). (gr. -1-k). 21.00 (978-1-4088-3938-6(5), 9781408839386, Bloomsbury USA Childrens) Bloomsbury Publishing USA.

Edwards, Pamela Duncan. Dinosaur Sleepover. Allwright, Deborah, illus. 2013. (J). (978-1-4351-4923-6(8)) Barnes & Noble, Inc.

Edwards, Wallace. The Extinct Files: My Science Project. Edwards, Wallace, illus. (ENG., Illus.). 32p. (J). (gr. k-3). 2009. 8.95 (978-1-55453-386-2(4)) 2006. 17.95 (978-1-55337-971-3(3)) Kids Can Pr., Ltd. CAN. Dist: Hachette Bk. Group.

Egbert, Corey. If Dinosaurs Could Talk for Me. 2017. (ENG.). (J). 14.99 **(978-1-4621-1971-4(9)**, Sweetwater Bks.) Cedar Fort, Inc./CFI Distribution.

Elefritz, Erin. My Pet Dinosaur. Rolf, Heidi, illus. 2012. 24p. pap. 11.95 (978-1-61244-117-7(3)) Halo Publishing International.

Englehart, Steve. Jurassic Park: Aftershocks!: Vol. 5, 1 vol. 2013. (Jurassic Park Ser.). (ENG.). 32p. (J). (gr. 4-8). lib. bdg. 24.21 (978-1-61479-187-4(2)) Spotlight.

—Jurassic Park: Animals vs. Gods!: Vol. 9, 1 vol. 2013. (Jurassic Park Ser.). (ENG.). 32p. (J). (gr. 4-8). lib. bdg. 24.21 (978-1-61479-191-1(0)) Spotlight.

—Jurassic Park: Animals vs. Man!: Vol. 8, 1 vol. 2013. (Jurassic Park Ser.). (ENG.). 32p. (J). (gr. 4-8). lib. bdg. 24.21 (978-1-61479-190-4(2)) Spotlight.

—Jurassic Park: Dark Cargo!: Vol. 6, 1 vol. 2013. (Jurassic Park Ser.). (ENG.). 32p. (J). (gr. 4-8). lib. bdg. 24.21 (978-1-61479-188-1(0)) Spotlight.

—Jurassic Park: Gods vs. Men!: Vol. 10, 1 vol. 2013. (Jurassic Park Ser.). (ENG.). 32p. (J). (gr. 4-8). lib. bdg. 24.21 (978-1-61479-192-8(9)) Spotlight.

—Jurassic Park: Raptors Attack!: Vol. 7, 1 vol. 2013. (Jurassic Park Ser.). (ENG.). 32p. (J). (gr. 4-8). lib. bdg. 24.21 (978-1-61479-189-8(9)) Spotlight.

Eone, illus. George's New Dinosaur. 2017. (Peppa Pig Ser.). (ENG.). 24p. (J). (gr. -1-k). 3.99 **(978-1-338-13976-1(2))** Scholastic, Inc.

Esbaum, Jill. If a T. Rex Crashes Your Birthday Party. Tolstikova, Daria & Tolstikova, Dasha, illus. 2016. (ENG.). 40p. (J). (gr. -1-2). 14.95 (978-1-4549-1550-8(1)) Sterling Publishing Co., Inc.

Esola, Mike. Diary of a Dinosaur: The Attack of Benny. 2013. (ENG.). 154p. pap. 10.95 (978-1-4787-1363-0(1)) Outskirts Pr., Inc.

Evans, Dustin, illus. Dinosaur Drama, 1 vol. 2013. (Mystical Pencil Ser.). (ENG.). 32p. (J). (gr. 3-6). 28.50 (978-1-61641-927-1(X)) Magic Wagon.

Evans, Nate & Brown, Stephanie Gwyn. Bang! Boom! Roar! A Busy Crew of Dinosaurs. Santoro, Christopher, illus. 2012. (ENG.). 40p. (J). (gr. -1-2). 15.99 (978-0-06-087960-0(2)) HarperCollins Pubs.

—Dinosaur ABC. Santoro, Christopher, illus. 2011. (J). lib. bdg. 16.89 (978-0-06-087962-4(9)) HarperCollins Pubs.

Everett, Reese. Monster in the Mangroves. 2015. (ENG.). 48p. (gr. k-3). 27.07 (978-1-63430-377-4(6)) Rourke Educational Media.

Everson, Chance. Beginnings Vol. 2: Tales of the Mandrasaurs, Volume the Second. Geary, Steve, illus. 2004. cd-rom 9.95 (978-0-9760303-1-7(4)) R.A.R.E. TALES.

—Discoveries: Tales of the Mandrasaurs, Volume the Third. Geary, Steve, illus. 2004. cd-rom 9.95 (978-0-9760303-2-4(2)) R.A.R.E. TALES.

—Forever & a Day Vol. 1: Tales of the Mandrasaurs, Volume the First. Geary, Steve, illus. 2004. cd-rom 9.95 (978-0-9760303-0-0(6)) R.A.R.E. TALES.

—Verlin's Magical Blunder: Tales of the Mandrasaurs, Volume the Seventh. Geary, Steve, illus. 2004. cd-rom 9.95 (978-0-9760303-6-2(5)) R.A.R.E. TALES.

Failla, Marco & Bustos, Natacha, illus. Moon Girl & Devil Dinosaur Vol. 2: Cosmic Cooties. 2017. (ENG.). 136p. (J). (gr. 4-17). pap. 17.99 (978-1-302-90208-7(3)) Marvel Worldwide, Inc.

Fairgray, Richard & Jones, Terry, illus. My Grandpa Is a Dinosaur. 2016. (ENG.). 32p. (J). (gr. -1-k). 16.99 (978-1-63450-632-8(4), Sky Pony Pr.) Skyhorse Publishing Co., Inc.

Falcone, David A. The Adventures of Miss Aiden in Dinoland. 2011. 28p. pap. 15.99 (978-1-4568-4015-0(0)) Xlibris Corp.

Falk, Nick & Flowers, Tony. Tyrannosaurus in the Veggie Patch: Saurus Street 1 (Large Print 16pt) 2013. 102p. pap. (978-1-4596-5771-7(3)) ReadHowYouWant.com, Ltd.

Falkner, Brian. Battlesaurus: Rampage at Waterloo. 2016. (Battlesaurus Ser.: 2). (ENG.). 352p. (YA). 17.99 (978-0-374-30077-7(1), 9780374300777, Farrar, Straus & Giroux (BYR)) Farrar, Straus & Giroux.

Fawcett, Jack & Rimes, Raleigh. Dinosaurology. 2013. (Ologies Ser.). (ENG.). 30p. (J). (gr. 3-7). 21.99 (978-0-7636-6739-9(0)) Candlewick Pr.

Fehrenbach, Heather. Go to Sleep Dinosaurs. 2011. 36p. pap. 15.99 (978-1-4567-6302-2(4)) AuthorHouse.

Finch, Susan M. Dino Manners: Some Prehistoric Lessons Featuring Our Friends from the Cretaceous Period. Seda, Alison, illus. 2009. 32p. pap. 16.50 (978-1-4490-5102-0(2)) AuthorHouse.

Fine, Karen. Veggiesaurus Lex. 2009. 24p. pap. 12.99 (978-1-4490-0290-9(0)) AuthorHouse.

Fisch, Sholly & Ottolini, Horacio. Dinosaur Round-Up, 1 vol. Brizuela, Dario & Staton, Joe, illus. 2017. (DC Super Friends Ser.). (ENG.). 32p. (gr. 1-2). lib. bdg. 22.60 (978-1-4342-4542-7(X)) Stone Arch Bks.

Fladd, Jane. 1-2-3 Jump! 2009. 32p. pap. 12.99 (978-1-4389-3272-9(3)) AuthorHouse.

Fletcher, Tom & Poynter, Dougie. The Dinosaur That Pooped a Planet! Parsons, Garry, illus. 2017. (Dinosaur That Ser.). (ENG.). 32p. (J). (gr. -1-3). 15.99 **(978-1-4814-9866-1(5)**, Aladdin) Simon & Schuster Children's Publishing.

Foreman, Niki. Deadly Dinosaurs. 2014. (DK Readers Ser.). (ENG.). 32p. (J). (gr. k-4). 14.99 (978-1-4654-1603-2(X)); pap. 3.99 (978-1-4654-1720-6(6)) Dorling Kindersley Publishing, Inc. (DK Children).

Foster, John. Dinosaur Rap. Harter, Debbie, illus. 2016. (ENG.). 32p. (J). (gr. -1-1). 16.99 (978-1-78285-301-5(4)) Barefoot Bks., Inc.

Franco, Franco. Dino-Mike! Franco, Franco, illus. 2015. (Dino-Mike! Ser.). (ENG., Illus.). 128p. (gr. 1-3). pap. 23.80 (978-1-4965-2233-7(8), Dino-Mike!) Stone Arch Bks.

—Dino-Mike & Dinosaur Doomsday. Franco, Franco & Garcia, Eduardo, illus. 2016. (Dino-Mike! Ser.). (ENG.). 128p. (gr. 1-3). lib. bdg. 25.32 (978-1-4965-2491-1(8), Dino-Mike!) Stone Arch Bks.

—Dino-Mike & the Lunar Showdown. Franco, Franco & Garcia, Eduardo, illus. 2016. (Dino-Mike! Ser.). (ENG.). 128p. (gr. 1-3). lib. bdg. 25.32 (978-1-4965-2492-8(6), Dino-Mike!) Stone Arch Bks.

Franco, Franco & Garcia, Eduardo. Dino-Mike & the Dinosaur Cove. Franco, Franco, illus. 2016. (Dino-Mike! Ser.). (ENG., Illus.). 128p. (gr. 1-3). lib. bdg. 25.32 (978-1-4965-2490-4(X), Dino-Mike!) Stone Arch Bks.

—Dino-Mike & the Living Fossils. Franco, Franco, illus. 2016. (Dino-Mike! Ser.). (ENG., Illus.). 128p. (gr. 1-3). lib. bdg. 25.32 (978-1-4965-2489-8(6), Dino-Mike!) Stone Arch Bks.

Franks, Melissa. Warped! An Adventure Through Time Bk. 1: A What-a-saur? 2008. 96p. pap. 19.95 (978-1-60703-636-4(3)) America Star Bks.

Fredericks, Eleanor. The Adventures of Tyler the Dinosaur, 1 vol. Fredericks, Rob, illus. 2009. 31p. pap. 24.95 (978-1-61546-233-9(3)) America Star Bks.

Freedman, Claire. Aliens Love Dinopants. Cort, Ben, illus. 2016. (Underpants Bks.). (ENG.). 32p. (J). (gr. -1-2). 17.99 (978-1-4814-6736-0(0), Aladdin) Simon & Schuster Children's Publishing.

—Dinosaurs Love Underpants. Cort, Ben, illus. 2009. (Underpants Bks.). (ENG.). 32p. (J). (gr. -1-2). 16.99 (978-1-4169-8938-7(2), Aladdin) Simon & Schuster Children's Publishing.

French, Cindy. A Loud Roar. 2012. 24p. pap. 11.50 (978-1-61897-626-0(5), Strategic Bk. Publishing) Strategic Book Publishing & Rights Agency (SBPRA).

French, Jackie. Dinosaurs Love Cheese. Rycroft, Nina, illus. 2017. 32p. pap. 6.99 (978-1-4607-5080-3(2)) HarperCollins Pubs. Australia AUS. Dist: HarperCollins Pubs.

—My Dog the Dinosaur. King, Stephen Michael, illus. 2006. (Wacky Families Ser.). (ENG.). 112p. (978-0-207-19941-7(8)) HarperCollins Pubs. Australia.

Friedman, Stanley. I, Dinosaur. 2010. 166p. pap. 11.95 (978-1-935118-91-6(9)) Bellissima Publishing, LLC.

Froeb, Lori & Scollon, Bill. Disney*Pixar the Good Dinosaur - Plush Pal. 2015. (ENG.). 16p. (J). (gr. -1-k). bds. 14.99 (978-0-7944-3104-4(6), Reader's Digest Children's Bks.) Studio Fun International.

Froeb, Lori C. Disney*Pixar the Good Dinosaur. 2015. (ENG.). 12p. (J). (gr. -1-k). 12.99 (978-0-7944-3509-7(2), Reader's Digest Children's Bks.) Studio Fun International.

Funk, Josh. Pirasaurs! Slack, Michael H., illus. 2016. (ENG.). 40p. (J). (gr. -1-k). 14.99 (978-0-545-75049-3(0), Orchard Bks.) Scholastic, Inc.

Gall, Chris. Dinotrux Dig the Beach. 2015. (Dinotrux Ser.: 3). (ENG., Illus.). 32p. (J). (gr. -1-3). 17.00 (978-0-316-37553-5(5)) Little Brown & Co.

—Dinotrux Go to School. 2014. (Passport to Reading Level 1 Ser.). (ENG., Illus.). 32p. (J). (gr. -1-3). 3.99 (978-0-316-40061-9(0)) Little, Brown Bks. for Young Readers.

Galvin, Laura Gates. Ankylosaurus Fights Back. Chesterman, Adrian, illus. 2007. (Smithsonian's Prehistoric Pals Ser.). (ENG.). 36p. (J). 8.95 (978-1-59249-681-5(4)); (J). 14.95 (978-1-59249-679-2(2)); (J). pap. 6.95 (978-1-59249-680-8(6)); (J). (gr. -1-3). 2.95 (978-1-59249-682-2(2)); 9.95 (978-1-59249-683-9(0)) Soundprints.

—Iguanodon's Escape. 36p. (J). 2011. (ENG.). 8.95 (978-1-60727-167-3(2)) 2011. (ENG.). pap. 2.95 (978-1-60727-165-9(6)) 2010. (gr. -1-3). 17.95 (978-1-60727-166-6(4)) 2010. (ENG.). (gr. -1-3). pap. 6.95 (978-1-60727-164-2(8)) Soundprints.

Gardner, Sara. Emma & the Dinosaur. 2013. 26p. pap. 16.99 (978-1-4525-8441-6(9), Balboa Pr.) Author Solutions, Inc.

Garland, Michael. Miss Smith Reads Again! 2006. (Illus.). (J). (978-1-4156-8098-8(1), Dutton Juvenile) Penguin Publishing Group.

—Miss Smith Reads Again! Garland, Michael, illus. 2008. (ENG., Illus.). 32p. (J). (gr. -1-2). pap. 6.99 (978-0-14-241140-7(X), Puffin Books) Penguin Young Readers Group.

Garland, Sally. Tig & Tog's Dinosaur Discovery. 2015. (ENG., Illus.). 32p. (J). (gr. -1-3). 16.99 (978-1-4998-0155-2(6)) Little Bee Books Inc.

George, Kallie. Duck, Duck, Dinosaur. Vidal, Oriol, illus. 2016. 40p. (J). (gr. -1-3). 17.99 (978-0-06-235308-5(X)) HarperCollins Pubs.

—Duck, Duck, Dinosaur: Bubble Blast. Vidal, Oriol, illus. 2017. (My First I Can Read Ser.). 32p. (J). (gr. -1-3). pap. 3.99 (978-0-06-235311-5(X)) HarperCollins Pubs.

George, Kallie. Duck, Duck, Dinosaur: Perfect Pumpkin. Vidal, Oriol, illus. 2017. (My First I Can Read Ser.). 32p. (J). (gr. -1-3). 16.99 **(978-0-06-235315-3(2))**; pap. 3.99 **(978-0-06-235314-6(4))** HarperCollins Pubs.

Geraghty, Paul. Dinosaur in Danger. 2005. (Illus.). 40p. (J). pap. (978-0-09-943865-6(8), Red Fox) Random House Children's Books.

Gerwitz, Felice. Literature No. 2: Dinosaur Quest at Diamond Peak. 2003. (Truth Seeker's Mystery Ser.: 2). (YA). stu. ed., per. 6.50 (978-1-931941-05-1(X)) Media Angels, Inc.

Gerwitz, Felice & Gerwitz, Christina. Dinosaur Quest at Diamond Peak, 3, Vol. 2. 2nd rev. ed. 2007. (Truth Seeker's Mystery Ser.). 208p. (YA). per. 8.99 (978-1-931941-11-2(4)) Media Angels, Inc.

Gilley, Mel. Sam & the Sad Dinosaur. 2011. 28p. pap. 13.59 (978-1-4567-6751-8(8)) AuthorHouse.

Gilman, Grace. Dixie & the School Trip. 2012. (Dixie: I Can Read Ser.). (J). lib. bdg. 13.55 (978-0-606-26284-2(9), Turtleback) Turtleback Bks.

Glass, Calliope. Walking with Dinosaurs Handbook. 2013. (Walking with Dinosaurs Ser.). (ENG.). 112p. (J). (gr. 3-7). 9.99 (978-0-06-223288-5(6), HarperFestival) HarperCollins Pubs.

Glennon, Michelle. Duncan the Circus Dinosaur. Glennon, Michelle, illus. 2008. (Illus.). 21p. (J). 16.95 (978-0-9796625-5-3(9)) GDG Publishing.

Golant, Galina & Grant, Lisa. Play Checkers with Me. Golant, Evgenia, illus. 2003. 32p. (J). pap. 6.95 (978-1-932133-01-1(1)) Writers' Collective, The.

Golden Books. Dinosaur Dig! (Bubble Guppies) Jackson, Mike, illus. 2013. (Paint Box Book Ser.). (ENG.). 48p. (J). (gr. -1-2). pap. 3.99 (978-0-307-98166-0(5), Golden Bks.) Random Hse. Children's Bks.

—Thomas & the Dinosaur (Thomas & Friends) Lapadula, Thomas, illus. 2015. (Little Golden Book Ser.). (ENG.). 24p. (J). (-k). 4.99 (978-0-553-49681-9(6), Golden Bks.) Random Hse. Children's Bks.

—Who's Hatching? (Dinosaur Train) Fruchter, Jason, illus. 2013. (Holographic Sticker Book Ser.). (ENG.). 48p. (J). (gr. -1-2). pap. 3.99 (978-0-307-98102-8(9), Golden Bks.) Random Hse. Children's Bks.

Golden Books Staff. Find the Dinosaurs! (Team Umizoomi) Riley, Kellee et al, illus. 2012. (Little Golden Book Ser.). (ENG.). 24p. (J). (gr. -1-k). 4.99 (978-0-307-92995-2(7), Golden Bks.) Random Hse. Children's Bks.

—Triceratops for Lunch. Meurer, Caleb, illus. 2010. (Little Golden Book Ser.). (ENG.). 24p. (J). (gr. -1-2). 4.99 (978-0-375-86151-2(3), Golden Bks.) Random Hse. Children's Bks.

Gould, Robert. Dinosaurs. 2005. (Big Stuff Ser.: 7). (ENG., Illus.). 16p. (J). bds. 7.95 (978-1-929945-58-0(2)) Big Guy Bks., Inc.

Gould, Robert & Duey, Kathleen. Time Soldiers. 2005. 384p. pap. 16.95 (978-1-929945-60-3(4)) Big Guy Bks., Inc.

—Time Soldiers - Rex. Epstein, Eugene, illus. Gould, Robert, photos by. 2005. (Time Soldiers Ser.: Bk. 1). (ENG.). 96p. (J). (gr. k-2). per. 5.95 (978-1-929945-53-5(1)); per. 5.95 (978-1-929945-54-2(X)) Big Guy Bks., Inc.

Gould, Sloane. Dinosaurs Have Manners: Digital Citizenship. 2017. (Computer Science for the Real World Ser.). 8p. (gr. 5-6). pap. 6.20 **(978-1-5383-5080-5(7)**, Rosen Classroom) Rosen Publishing Group, Inc., The.

Graf, Mike & Kaske, Anne. Dinosaur Canyon. Weston, Steve, illus. 2005. 40p. pap. 8.53 (978-0-7578-9858-7(0)) Houghton Mifflin Harcourt Supplemental Pubs.

Grambling, Lois G. Can I Bring My Pterodactyl to School, Ms. Johnson? Love, Judy, illus. 2006. (Prehistoric Pets Ser.). (ENG.). 32p. (J). (gr. k-3). 7.95 (978-1-58089-141-7(1)) Charlesbridge Publishing, Inc.

—Here Comes T. Rex Cottontail. Davis, Jack E., illus. 2010. (ENG.). 32p. (J). (gr. -1-1). pap. 6.99 (978-0-06-053134-8(7), Tegen, Katherine Bks) HarperCollins Pubs.

—T. Rex & the Mother's Day Hug. Davis, Jack E., illus. 2011. (ENG.). 32p. (J). (gr. -1-1). pap. 6.99 (978-0-06-053128-7(2), Tegen, Katherine Bks) HarperCollins Pubs.

—T. Rex Trick-or-Treats. Davis, Jack E., illus. 32p. (J). 2008. (ENG.). (gr. -1-3). pap. 6.99 (978-0-06-050254-6(1)) 2005. 12.99 (978-0-06-050252-2(5)) HarperCollins Pubs. (Tegen, Katherine Bks).

Grandad's Dinosaur: Level M, 6 vols. 128p. (gr. 2-3). 49.95 (978-0-7699-0984-4(1)) Shortland Pubns. (U. S. A.) Inc.

Grandma Geny Heywood, Geny Heywood & Grandma Geny Heywood. Proto: What do you do when a dinosaur is born in your Garden? 2009. 48p. pap. 19.49 (978-1-4490-0993-9(X)) AuthorHouse.

The Great Dinosaur Hunt, 6 vols. (Woodland Mysteriestm Ser.). 133p. (gr. 3-7). 42.50 (978-0-7802-7929-2(8)) Wright Group/McGraw-Hill.

Green, Margaret. Dinotrux: It Takes Teamwork! 2016. (ENG., Illus.). 24p. (J). (gr. -1-3). pap. 4.99 (978-0-316-26077-0(0)) Little, Brown Bks. for Young Readers.

—Dinotrux: Meet Garby! 2016. (ENG., Illus.). 32p. (J). (gr. -1-3). pap. 3.99 (978-0-316-26083-1(5)) Little, Brown Bks. for Young Readers.

—Ty Finds a New Home. 2017. (Dinotrux 8X8 Ser.). (J). lib. bdg. 14.75 (978-0-606-39190-0(8)) Turtleback Bks.

Greenburg, J. C. With the Dinosaurs. Gerardi, Jan, illus. 2005. (Andrew Lost Ser.: 11). (ENG.). 96p. (J). (gr. 1-4). 3.99 (978-0-375-82951-2(2), Random Hse. Bks. for Young Readers) Random Hse. Children's Bks.

Greene, Kristy. How Penguins Lost Their Flight. 2012. 20p. pap. 24.95 (978-1-4626-7697-2(9)) America Star Bks.

Greenfield, Howard. Dinosaur Pet. Bowers, Tim, illus. 2012. (ENG.). 28p. (J). (gr. -1-3). 17.95 (978-1-936140-36-7(5)) Charlesbridge Publishing, Inc.

Griffin, Adele. Oona Finds an Egg. Wu, Mike, illus. 2016. (Oodlethunks Ser.: Bk. 1). (ENG.). 160p. (J). (gr. 3-7). 12.99 (978-0-545-73279-6(4), Scholastic Pr.) Scholastic, Inc.

—Steg-O-Normous. Wu, Mike, illus. 2016. (Oodlethunks Ser.: Bk. 2). (ENG.). 160p. (J). (gr. 3-7). 12.99 (978-0-545-73284-0(0), Scholastic Pr.) Scholastic, Inc.

Grimaldi. My Amazing Dinosaur. Burrell, Carol klio, tr. from FRE. Bannister, illus. 2014. (Tib & Tumtum Ser.: 2). (ENG.). 48p. (J). (gr. 2-5). lib. bdg. 26.60 (978-1-4677-1298-9(1), Graphic Universe™) Lerner Publishing Group.

—Welcome to the Tribe! Bannister, illus. 2013. (Tib & Tumtum Ser.: 1). (ENG.). 48p. (J). (gr. 2-5). pap. 6.95 (978-1-4677-1522-5(0)); lib. bdg. 26.60 (978-1-4677-1297-2(3)) Lerner Publishing Group. (Graphic Universe™).

Grimaldi, Flora. My Amazing Dinosaur. Burrell, Carol klio, tr. Bannister, illus. 2014. (Tib & Tumtum Ser.: 2). (ENG.). 48p. (J). (gr. 2-5). pap. 7.95 (978-1-4677-2181-3(6), Graphic Universe™) Lerner Publishing Group.

Grosso, Salvatore. The Butterfly & the Dinosaur: A true story of fiction Inspired by a Beautiful Butterfly. 2010. 32p. pap. 16.99 (978-1-4490-6603-1(8)) AuthorHouse.

Guettier, Bénédicte. Dinosaur Dinners. 2011. (Funny Faces Ser.). (Illus.). 14p. bds. (978-1-84089-677-0(9)) Zero to Ten, Ltd.

—Dinosaurs. Guettier, Bénédicte, illus. 2005. (ENG., Illus.). 14p. (J). (gr. -1-k). 11.95 (978-1-929132-86-7(7)) Kane Miller.

Gurney, James. Dinotopia: Journey to Chandara. 2016. (ENG., Illus.). 160p. pap. 19.99 (978-1-4494-7984-8(7)) Andrews McMeel Publishing.

—Dinotopia: The World Beneath. Gurney, James, illus. 2003. (Dinotopia Ser.). (ENG., Illus.). 160p. (J). pap. 19.99 (978-0-06-053065-5(0)) HarperCollins Pubs.

—Dinotopia: The World Beneath. 20th anniv. ed. 2012. (Calla Editions Ser.). (ENG., Illus.). 192p. (gr. 3). 30.00 (978-1-60660-033-7(8)) Dover Pubns., Inc.

—Dinotopia - First Flight. 20th anniv. ed. 2014. (ENG., Illus.). 112p. (gr. 5). 25.00 (978-1-60660-057-3(5)) Dover Pubns., Inc.

—Dinotopia, Journey to Chandara. 2017. (Calla Editions Ser.). (ENG., Illus.). 192p. 35.00 (978-1-60660-100-6(8)) Dover Pubns., Inc.

Gurney, James & Gurney, James. A Land Apart from Time. Gurney, James & Gurney, James, illus. 2003. (Dinotopia Ser.). (ENG., Illus.). 160p. (J). (gr. 3-7). pap. 21.99 (978-0-06-053064-8(2)) HarperCollins Pubs.

Gurney, John Steven. Dinosaur Train. Date not set. 32p. (J). (gr. -1-1). pap. 5.99 (978-0-06-443738-7(8)) HarperCollins Pubs.

Gutman, Dan. Rappy Goes to School. Bowers, Tim, illus. 2016. 40p. (J). (gr. -1-3). 17.99 (978-0-06-229181-3(5)) HarperCollins Pubs.

—Rappy the Raptor. Bowers, Tim, illus. 2015. (ENG.). 40p. (J). (gr. -1-3). 17.99 (978-0-06-229180-6(7)) HarperCollins Pubs.

Guttier, Benedicte. Dinosaur Dinners - Welsh Edition. 2011. (Funny Faces Ser.). (WEL., Illus.). 14p. bds. (978-1-84089-685-5(X)) Zero to Ten, Ltd.

Haesche, Richard Paul, Sr. My Pet Dinosaur. 2007. (ENG.). 60p. (J). 6.99 (978-0-9800552-0-7(2)) Kreative X-Pressions Pubns.

Hale, Bruce. Danny & the Dinosaur & the New Puppy. 2015. (I Can Read! Level 1 Ser.). (J). lib. bdg. 13.55 (978-0-606-37608-2(9)) Turtleback Bks.

Halpern, Shari. Dinosaur Parade. Halpern, Shari, illus. 2014. (ENG., Illus.). 32p. (J). (gr. -1-k). 16.99 (978-0-8050-9242-4(0), 9780805092424, Holt, Henry & Co. Bks. For Young Readers) Holt, Henry & Co.

Ham, Ken. What Really Happened to the Dinosaurs? 2004. 48p. pap. 0.75 (978-1-893345-22-5(X)) Answers in Genesis Ministries.

Ham, Ken & Ham, Mally. D Is for Dinosaur Coloring Book. 2016. (Illus.). 32p. (J). pap. 4.99 **(978-1-68344-015-4(3))** Master Bks.

Hansen, Dustin. Microsaurs: Adventure Awaits. Hansen, Dustin, illus. 2017. (Microsaurs Ser.: 1). (ENG., Illus.). 224p. (J). 13.99 (978-1-250-09021-8(0), 9781250090218) Feiwel & Friends.

—Microsaurs: Tiny-Raptor Pack Attack. Hansen, Dustin, illus. 2017. (Microsaurs Ser.: 2). (ENG., Illus.). 240p. (J). 13.99 (978-1-250-09025-6(3), 9781250090256) Feiwel & Friends.

Hapka, Catherine, pseud. Walking with Dinosaurs: the Winter Ground. 2013. (I Can Read Level 2 Ser.). (ENG., Illus.). 32p. (J). (gr. -1-3). 16.99 (978-0-06-223284-7(3)) HarperCollins Pubs.

Hapka, Catherine, pseud, et al. Dinosaur Discovery. Hines, Anna Grossnickle, illus. 2006. (Curious George Ser.). (ENG.). 24p. (J). (gr. -1-3). audio compact disk 10.99 (978-0-618-68945-3(1)) Houghton Mifflin Harcourt Publishing Co.

Harper, E. T. & Taylor, Dan. Dylan's Amazing Dinosaur: the Stegosaurus: With Pull-Out, Pop-Up Dinosaur Inside! 2015. (Dylan's Amazing Dinosaurs Ser.). (ENG., Illus.). 32p. (J). (gr. -1-2). pap. 7.99 (978-1-4380-0644-4(6)) Barron's Educational Series, Inc.

—Dylan's Amazing Dinosaur: the Tyrannosaurus Rex: With Pull-Out, Pop-Up Dinosaur Inside! 2015. (Dylan's Amazing Dinosaurs Ser.). (ENG.). 32p. (J). (gr. -1-2). pap. 7.99 (978-1-4380-0643-7(8)) Barron's Educational Series, Inc.

Harris, Jim. Dinosaur's Night Before Christmas, 1 vol. Harris, Jim, illus. 2010. (Night Before Christmas Ser.). (ENG., Illus.). 40p. (J). (gr. k-3). 16.99 (978-1-58980-850-8(9)) Pelican Publishing Co., Inc.

Harvey, Damien. Dinosaur Rock. Ward, Matt, illus. 2005. (Collins Big Cat Ser.). (ENG.). 56p. (J). (gr. -1-k). pap. 5.99 (978-0-00-718540-5(5)) HarperCollins Pubs. Ltd. GBR. Dist: Independent Pubs. Group.

Havercroft, Elizabeth. A Year in the World of Dinosaurs. 2009. (Time Goes By Ser.). (ENG.). 24p. (gr. k-3). pap. 6.95 (978-1-58013-802-4(0), First Avenue Editions) Lerner Publishing Group.

Hay DeSimone, Corkey. Dinosaur Explore Activity & Coloring Book: Dinosaurs designed for their littlest Fans. Hay DeSimone, Corkey, illus. 2006. (Illus.). (J). 4.95 (978-0-9777394-0-0(6)) Gentle Giraffe Pr.

Hayes, Felix. George & the Dinosaur. Heap, Sue, illus. 2015. (ENG.). 40p. (J). (gr. -1-2). 16.99 (978-1-4998-0077-7(0)) Little Bee Books Inc.

Hayes, Kimberly Wasserman. Princesses & Dinosaurs. 2011. (Illus.). 28p. pap. 14.09 (978-1-4567-8823-0(X)) AuthorHouse.

Heidbreder, Robert. Drumheller Dinosaur Dance. Slavin, Bill et al, illus. 2006. (ENG.). 32p. (J). (gr. -1-2). pap. 7.95 (978-1-55337-982-9(9)) Kids Can Pr., Ltd. CAN. Dist: Hachette Bk. Group.

Henry, LaTosha. Dino Treasure Hunt, 1 vol. Friesen, Wayne, illus. 2010. 16p. 24.95 (978-1-4489-3966-4(6)) PublishAmerica, Inc.

Herbert Hilligan's Prehistoric Adventure Curriculum Guide. 2004. ring bd. 24.95 (978-0-9743335-5-7(7)) Imaginative Publishing, Ltd.

Herman, Gail. Time for School, Little Dinosaur. Fleming, Michael, illus. 2017. (Step into Reading Ser.). (ENG.). 32p. (J). (gr. -1-1). pap. 3.99 **(978-0-399-55645-6(1))**; lib. bdg. 12.99 **(978-0-399-55646-3(X))** Random Hse. Children's Bks. (Random Hse. Bks. for Young Readers).

Herz, Henry L. Cap'n Rex & His Clever Crew. Schipper, Benjamin, illus. 2017. (ENG.). 32p. (J). (gr. k). 16.95 **(978-1-4549-2088-5(2))** Sterling Publishing Co., Inc.

Heywood, Grandma Geny. Tirano: Another Dinosaur Is Born! 2010. 48p. pap. 19.49 (978-1-4490-9541-3(0)) AuthorHouse.

Heywood, La Abuelita Geny. Proto: ¿Qué hacer cuando un dinosaurio nace en tu Jardín? 2010. 52p. pap. 22.49 *(978-1-4490-5628-5(8))* AuthorHouse.

Higgins, Nadia. Walk the Plank, Plankton, 1 vol. Holder, Jimmy, illus. 2008. (Barnacle Barb & Her Pirate Crew Ser.). (ENG.). 32p. (gr. -1-3). 28.50 *(978-1-60270-094-9(X)*, Looking Glass Library) ABDO Publishing Co.

Hines, Anna Grossnickle. I Am a Tyrannosaurus. Hines, Anna Grossnickle, illus. 2011. (ENG., Illus.). 40p. (J). (gr. -1-2). 12.99 *(978-1-58246-413-8(8)*, Tricycle Pr.) Random Hse. Children's Bks.

Hoff, Syd. Danny & the Dinosaur. Hoff, Syd, illus. (I Can Read Level 1 Ser.). (Illus.). (J). 2017. 72p. (gr. -1-3). 9.99 ***(978-0-06-257277-6(8))*** 50th anniv. ed. 2008. (ENG., 64p. (gr. -1-3). pap. 3.99 *(978-0-06-444002-8(8))*Set. 50th anniv. ed. 2008. (gr. k-3). pap. 11.99 *(978-0-06-143083-1(8))* HarperCollins Pubs.

—Danny & the Dinosaur. 2017. (Danny & the Dinosaur — I Can Read Ser.). lib. bdg. 13.55 ***(978-0-606-40063-3(X))*** Turtleback Bks.

—Danny & the Dinosaur - Too Tall. Hoff, Syd, illus. 2015. (I Can Read Level 1 Ser.). (ENG., Illus.). 32p. (J). (gr. -1-3). pap. 3.99 *(978-0-06-228155-5(0))* HarperCollins Pubs.

—Danny & the Dinosaur: a Very Dino Christmas. Hoff, Syd & Cutting, David, illus. 2017. 24p. (J). (gr. -1-3). pap. 6.99 ***(978-0-06-241046-7(6)***, HarperFestival) HarperCollins Pubs.

—Danny & the Dinosaur & the Big Storm. Hoff, Syd, illus. 2017. (Illus.). 24p. (J). (gr. -1-3). pap. 4.99 *(978-0-06-241045-0(8)*, HarperFestival) HarperCollins Pubs.

—Danny & the Dinosaur & the Girl Next Door. Hoff, Syd, illus. 2017. (I Can Read Level 1 Ser.). (Illus.). 32p. (J). (gr. -1-3). pap. 3.99 *(978-0-06-228158-6(5))* HarperCollins Pubs.

—Danny & the Dinosaur & the New Puppy. Hoff, Syd, illus. 2015. (I Can Read Level 1 Ser.). (ENG., Illus.). 32p. (J). (gr. -1-3). pap. 3.99 *(978-0-06-228152-4(6))* HarperCollins Pubs.

—Danny & the Dinosaur: Big Reading Collection. Hoff, Syd, illus. 2017. (I Can Read Level 1 Ser.). (Illus.). 190p. (J). (gr. -1-3). pap. 16.99 ***(978-0-06-241047-4(4))*** HarperCollins Pubs.

—Danny & the Dinosaur: First Valentine's Day. Hoff, Syd, illus. 2016. (Illus.). 24p. (J). (gr. -1-3). pap. 6.99 *(978-0-06-241044-3(X)*, HarperFestival) HarperCollins Pubs.

—Danny & the Dinosaur: Happy Halloween. Hoff, Syd, illus. 2016. (Illus.). 24p. (J). (gr. -1-3). pap. 6.99 *(978-0-06-241043-6(1)*, HarperFestival) HarperCollins Pubs.

—Danny & the Dinosaur: School Days. Hoff, Syd, illus. 2017. (I Can Read Level 1 Ser.). (Illus.). 32p. (J). (gr. -1-3). pap. 3.99 *(978-0-06-228161-6(5))* HarperCollins Pubs.

—The Danny & the Dinosaur Storybook Collection. Hoff, Syd, illus. 2016. (I Can Read Level 1 Ser.). (Illus.). 192p. (J). (gr. -1-3). 11.99 *(978-0-06-247070-6(1))* HarperCollins Pubs.

Hofsess, William. My Very First Dinosaur. 2012. 28p. pap. 15.99 *(978-1-4691-6057-3(9))* Xlibris Corp.

Hogan, Ellis. Tyrannosaurus Rex In: I've Got to Start Changing My Ways. 2012. 28p. pap. 16.09 *(978-1-4669-6685-7(8))* Trafford Publishing.

Holcomb, Sue A. & Holcomb, J. Paul. Tex R Masaur: Down in the Dump. Holcomb, Sue A., illus. (Tex R Masaur, Dinodillo Bks.). (Illus.). 32p. (Orig.). (J). (gr. k-3). pap. 3.95 *(978-0-9636122-2-9(0))* Post Oak Hill.

Holliday, Susan. The Time Street Gang & the Rag & Bone Boy. l.t. ed. 2007. 132p. pap. *(978-1-905665-64-8(4))* Pollinger In Print.

Holsey, Alvin I. Dinosaur Haunt. 2008. 188p. pap. 13.95 *(978-1-60693-282-7(9)*, Eloquent Bks.) Strategic Book Publishing & Rights Agency (SBPRA).

Hood, Susan. Just Say Boo! Henry, Jed, illus. 2012. (ENG.). 32p. (J). (gr. -1-3). 12.99 *(978-0-06-201029-2(8))* HarperCollins Pubs.

Hopper, Ada. Don't Disturb the Dinosaurs. Ricks, Sam, illus. 2016. (DATA Set Ser.: 2). (ENG.). 128p. (J). (gr. k-4). pap. 5.99 *(978-1-4814-5731-6(4)*, Little Simon) Little Simon.

How to clean a Dinosaur: Individual Title Six-Packs. (gr. 1-2). 25.00 *(978-0-7635-9136-6(X))* Rigby Education.

Howe, James. Brontorina. Cecil, Randy, illus. 2013. (ENG.). 32p. (J). (gr. -1-3). 6.99 *(978-0-7636-5323-1(3))* Candlewick Pr.

—Brontorina. 2013. lib. bdg. 17.20 *(978-0-606-31600-2(0)*, Turtleback) Turtleback Bks.

Hughes, Jack. Dachy's Deaf. 2014. (Dinosaur Friends Ser.). (Illus.). 32p. (J). (gr. k-3). lib. bdg. 26.25 *(978-1-4777-9222-3(8))* Windmill Bks.

—Emmy's Eczema. 2014. (Dinosaur Friends Ser.). (Illus.). 32p. (J). (gr. k-3). lib. bdg. 26.25 *(978-1-4777-9234-6(1))* Windmill Bks.

—Rex's Specs. 2014. (Dinosaur Friends Ser.). (Illus.). 32p. (J). (gr. k-3). lib. bdg. 26.25 *(978-1-4777-9226-1(0))* Windmill Bks.

—Steggie's Stutter. 2014. (Dinosaur Friends Ser.). (Illus.). 32p. (J). (gr. k-3). lib. bdg. 26.25 *(978-1-4777-9230-8(9))* Windmill Bks.

Hund, Thomas. Toby T-Rex: Lightning Strikes. 2012. 46p. pap. 21.99 *(978-1-4685-5305-5(4))* AuthorHouse.

Hunt, Debbie Colleen. The Dinosaur Who Loved to Bake & Eat Cakes. Hunt, Craig J. S., illus. 2012. 32p. 24.95 *(978-1-4626-3213-8(0))* America Star Bks.

Hunt, Elizabeth Singer. The Escape of the Deadly Dinosaur - USA. Williamson, Brian, illus. 2007. (Secret Agent Jack Stalwart Ser.: 1). (ENG.). 128p. (J). (gr. 1-4). per. 5.99 *(978-1-60286-004-9(1)*, Weinstein Bks.) Perseus Bks. Group.

Idle, Molly. Camp Rex. Idle, Molly, illus. 2014. (ENG., Illus.). 40p. (J). (gr. -1-k). 16.99 *(978-0-670-78573-5(3)*, Viking Books for Young Readers) Penguin Young Readers Group.

—Sea Rex. Idle, Molly, illus. 2015. (ENG., Illus.). 34p. (J). (-k). 16.99 *(978-0-670-78574-2(1)*, Viking Books for Young Readers) Penguin Young Readers Group.

—Tea Rex. 2013. (ENG., Illus.). 36p. (J). (gr. -1-k). 16.99 *(978-0-670-01430-9(3)*, Viking Books for Young Readers) Penguin Young Readers Group.

Islam, Shireen. Dinosaurs: The Final Chapter. 2012. (ENG.). pap. 50.00 *(978-1-4675-3890-9(6))* Independent Pub.

James, Hollis. Jurassic Bark! (PAW Patrol) Petrossi, Fabrizio, illus. 2017. (Little Golden Book Ser.). (ENG.). 24p. (J). (-k). 4.99 *(978-0-399-55880-1(2)*, Golden Bks.) Random Hse. Children's Bks.

James, Simon. Rex. James, Simon, illus. 2016. (ENG., Illus.). 40p. (J). (-k). 16.99 *(978-0-7636-7294-2(7))* Candlewick Pr.

Jennewein, Lenore. Chick-O-Saurus Rex. Jennewein, Daniel, illus. 2013. (ENG.). 32p. (J). (gr. -1-3). 16.99 *(978-1-4424-5186-5(6)*, Simon & Schuster Bks. For Young Readers) Simon & Schuster Bks. For Young Readers.

Jones, Gareth P. The Dinosaurs Are Having a Party! Parsons, Garry, illus. 2015. (J). 17.32 *(978-1-4677-6317-2(9))* Lerner Publishing Group.

Joseph, Doug. The Last Bye: Book Three of the Millennial Teleport Trilogy. 2011. (ENG.). 194p. pap. 9.95 *(978-1-4680-1209-5(6))* CreateSpace Independent Publishing Platform.

Joyce, William. Dinosaur Bob & His Adventures with the Family Lazardo. Joyce, William, illus. 2017. (World of William Joyce Ser.). (ENG., Illus.). 48p. (J). (gr. -1-3). 17.99 *(978-1-4814-8947-8(X)*, Atheneum/Caitlyn Dlouhy Books) Simon & Schuster Children's Publishing.

Jules. Bubble's World. 2009. (Dinosaur Days Ser.: Bk. 3). 36p. (J). pap. 15.49 *(978-1-4389-6782-0(9))* AuthorHouse.

Kaufman, Suzanne. Confiscated! Kaufman, Suzanne, illus. 2017. (Illus.). 32p. (J). (gr. -1-3). 17.99 ***(978-0-06-241086-3(5))*** HarperCollins Pubs.

Kelly, Deborah. Dinosaur Disco. Parton, Daron, illus. 2016. (ENG.). 32p. (J). (gr. -1-k). 16.99 *(978-0-85798-136-3(6))* Random Hse. Australia AUS. Dist: Independent Pubs. Group.

Kempshall, Paddy. The Lost Dinosaur. Chatterton, Chris, illus. 2017. (Pete's Magic Pants Ser.: 1). (ENG.). 32p. (J). (gr. -1-k). pap. 9.99 ***(978-1-4052-7913-0(3))*** Egmont Bks., Ltd. GBR. Dist: Independent Pubs. Group.

Kientz, Chris & Hockensmith, Steve. Claws & Effect. Nielsen, Lee, illus. 2016. (Secret Smithsonian Adventures Ser.: 2). (ENG.). 64p. (gr. 4-7). pap. 10.95 *(978-1-58834-567-7(X)*, Smithsonian Bks.) Smithsonian Institution Scholarly Pr.

Kimball, Angela. Of All the Silly Things. 2011. 52p. (gr. -1 — 1). pap. 25.49 *(978-1-4567-2259-3(X))* AuthorHouse.

Kimura, Yasuko. You Look Yummy! 2015. (Tyrannosaurus Ser.). (ENG.). 40p. (J). (gr. k-2). 16.99 *(978-1-940842-06-6(9))* Museyon.

King-smith, Dick. Dinosaur Trouble. Bruel, Nick, illus. 2012. (ENG.). 128p. (J). (gr. 2-5). pap. 16.99 *(978-1-59643-935-1(1)*, 9781596439351) Roaring Brook Pr.

Kirkman, Robert. Super Dinosaur. (ENG., Illus.). Vol. 1. 2011. 128p. (J). pap. 9.99 *(978-1-60706-420-6(0)*, 9781607064206) Vol. 2. 2012. 112p. pap. 12.99 *(978-1-60706-568-5(1)*, 9781607065685) Vol. 3. 2013. 112p. pap. 12.99 *(978-1-60706-667-5(X)*, 9781607066675) Image Comics.

Klio Burrell, Carol. Welcome to the Tribe!, 1. 2013. 48p. pap. 26.60 *(978-1-4677-1656-7(1))* Lerner Publishing Group.

Knapman, Timothy. Dinosaurs Don't Have Bedtimes! Dyson, Nikki, illus. 2016. (ENG.). 32p. (J). (gr. -1-2). 15.99 *(978-0-7636-8927-8(0))* Candlewick Pr.

Koenig, Faydra. Two Homes for Daniel. 2013. 30p. pap. 10.95 *(978-0-9891471-1-8(8))* Alpine River Pr.

Kolar, Bob. Stomp, Stomp! A Dino Romp. 2014. (ENG., Illus.). 34p. (J). (gr. -1-2). 14.95 *(978-0-7358-4169-7(1))* North-South Bks., Inc.

Krensky, Stephen. Dinosaurs in Disguise. Munsinger, Lynn, illus. 2016. (ENG.). 32p. (J). (gr. -1-3). 17.99 *(978-0-544-47271-6(3)*, HMH Books For Young Readers) Houghton Mifflin Harcourt Publishing Co.

Kroll, Steven. The Tyrannosaurus Game, 0 vols. Schindler, S. D., illus. 2010. (ENG.). 32p. (J). (gr. -1-3). 17.99 *(978-0-7614-5603-2(1)*, 9780761456032, Amazon Children's Publishing) Amazon Publishing.

Kubler, Annie. Dinosaur Diner. 2008. (Finger Puppet Bks.). (ENG., Illus.). 24p. (J). (gr. -1-1). *(978-1-84643-183-8(2))* Child's Play International Ltd.

Kulka, Joe. Vacation's Over! Return of the Dinosaurs. Kulka, Joe, illus. 2010. (Carolrhoda Picture Bks.). (ENG., Illus.). 32p. (J). (gr. k-3). lib. bdg. 17.95 *(978-0-7613-5212-9(0))* Lerner Publishing Group.

Kurokawa, Mitsuhiro. Dinosaur Valley. 2006. (ENG., Illus.). 56p. (J). (gr. -1-7). 16.95 *(978-0-8118-5231-9(8))* Chronicle Bks. LLC.

Kurtz, Jane. Mister Bones Dinosaur Hunter. Haverfield, Mary, illus. 2005. (Ready-to-Read Ser.). 32p. (J). lib. bdg. 15.00 *(978-1-59054-929-2(5))* Fitzgerald Bks.

La Fon-Cox, Angelique. A Tale of Kooshla & Saboo: The Great Dinosaur Discovery. 2010. 36p. 15.49 *(978-1-4490-8913-9(5))* AuthorHouse.

LaBrant, Kenneth R. Uncle Kenny's Crazy Bedtime Stories. 2008. 73p. pap. 19.95 *(978-1-60563-602-3(9))* America Star Bks.

Lambert, Teres. Mommy, Do You Love Me? 2008. 20p. pap. 24.95 *(978-1-60441-911-5(3))* America Star Bks.

Lampman, Evelyn Sibley. The Shy Stegosaurus of Cricket Creek. Buel, Hubert, illus. 2007. 218p. (J). (gr. 4-7). per. 12.00 *(978-1-930900-37-0(6))* Purple Hse. Pr.

Latimer, Alex. Never Follow a Dinosaur, 1 vol. Latimer, Alex, illus. 2016. (ENG., Illus.). 32p. (J). (gr. -1-3). 16.95 *(978-1-56145-704-5(3))* Peachtree Pubs.

Lawler, Janet. The Prehistoric Games, 1 vol. Davey, Martin, illus. 2016. (ENG.). 32p. (J). (gr. k-8). 16.99 *(978-1-4556-2138-5(2))* Pelican Publishing Co., Inc.

Lawson, Jim & Dooney, Michael. Paleo: Tales of the Late Cretaceous. 2003. (Illus.). 172p. (YA). reprint ed. pap. 12.95 *(978-0-9661985-3-9(0)*, Empty Sky) Zeromayo Studios, LLP.

LeapFrog Staff. T. Rex's Mighty Roar. 2008. (J). 13.99 *(978-1-59319-928-9(7))* LeapFrog Enterprises, Inc.

—T. Rex's Mighty Roar: Une belle journee pour Rugir. 2008. (J). 20.79 *(978-1-59319-943-2(0))* LeapFrog Enterprises, Inc.

Leighton, Davis L. & Strickland, Karen L. The Three Little Dinosaurs. 2010. (Illus.). 16p. (J). pap. 13.95 *(978-1-4327-5064-0(X))* Outskirts Pr., Inc.

Lemke, Amy J. Dinosaurs for Breakfast, 1 vol. Bradley, Jessica, illus. 2013. (Comics Land Ser.). (ENG.). 32p. (gr. k-2). 7.95 *(978-1-4342-4270-9(6))*; lib. bdg. 25.32 *(978-1-4342-4029-3(0))* Stone Arch Bks.

Lenz Mulligan Rights and Co. Staff & Chronicle Books Staff. Little Dino. 2008. (Little Finger Puppet Board Bks.: FING). (ENG., Illus.). 12p. (J). (gr. -1 — 1). bds. 6.99 *(978-0-8118-6353-7(0))* Chronicle Bks. LLC.

Leung, Erika. The Dinosaur Hunt. 2010. 28p. pap. 12.99 *(978-1-4490-9584-0(4))* AuthorHouse.

Lewis, Kevin. Dinosaur, Dinosaur. Kirk, Daniel, illus. 2006. (J). *(978-0-439-78228-9(7)*, Orchard Bks.) Scholastic, Inc.

Lewisson, Helene. Hem: The Duckbill Dinosaur. 2003. (J). pap. *(978-1-885275-41-7(2))* Howie, C.J. Co.

Lidberg, Micah, illus. Rise & Fall. 2012. (ENG.). 20p. (gr. k). 16.00 *(978-1-907704-30-7(2))* Nobrow Ltd. GBR. Dist: Consortium Bk. Sales & Distribution.

Lilly, Stephanie. The Amazing Adventures of Ethan-Tyrannosaurus-Rex: The Escape from Raptor Forest. 2009. 28p. pap. 15.30 *(978-1-4490-1105-5(5))* AuthorHouse.

Lippman, Peter & Gikow, Louise. The Land of Dinosaurs. 2012. (ENG., Illus.). 11p. 10.95 *(978-0-7611-6598-9(3)*, 16598) Workman Publishing Co., Inc.

Little Dinosaur Chapter Books. 2007. (J). per. *(978-1-932570-65-6(9))* Pioneer Valley Bks.

Little Dinosaur Runs Away. 2007. (Little Dinosaur Chapter Ser.). (J). per. 7.67 *(978-1-932570-67-0(5))* Pioneer Valley Bks.

Little Dinosaur's Skateboard. 2005. (Georgie Giraffe Set 1 Ser.). (J). 7.33 *(978-1-932570-42-7(X))* Pioneer Valley Bks.

Litton, Jonathan. Dino. Galloway, Fhiona, illus. 2016. (My Little World Ser.). (ENG.). 24p. (J). (gr. -1-k). mass mkt. 3.99 *(978-1-58925-485-5(6))* Tiger Tales.

Litwin, Eric. Ice Cream & Dinosaurs. Lichtenheld, Tom, illus. 2016. (Groovy Joe Ser.: 1). (ENG.). 40p. (J). (gr. -1-k). 17.99 *(978-0-545-88378-8(4)*, Orchard Bks.) Scholastic, Inc.

Liu, Julia. Gus, the Dinosaur Bus. Lynn, Bei, illus. 2013. (ENG.). 32p. (J). (gr. -1-3). 12.99 *(978-0-547-90573-0(4))* Houghton Mifflin Harcourt Publishing Co.

Lodge, Jo. Stomp! Little Dinosaur. 2013. (Push, Pull, Pop! Bks.). (ENG., Illus.). 10p. (J). (gr. -1 — 1). 6.99 *(978-0-7641-6632-7(8))* Barron's Educational Series, Inc.

Lomp, Stephan. Mamasaurus. 2016. (ENG., Illus.). 40p. (J). (gr. -1-k). 16.99 *(978-1-4521-4424-5(9))* Chronicle Bks. LLC.

—Papasaurus. 2017. (ENG., Illus.). 40p. (J). 16.99 *(978-1-4521-4425-2(7))* Chronicle Bks. LLC.

Lubar, David. Dinosaur Disaster. Loveridge, Matt, illus. 2013. (Looniverse Ser.: 3). (ENG.). 96p. (J). (gr. 1-3). 15.99 *(978-0-545-49605-6(5))*; pap. 4.99 *(978-0-545-49606-3(3))* Scholastic, Inc.

—Dinosaur Disaster. 2013. (Looniverse Ser.: 3). lib. bdg. 14.75 *(978-0-606-32367-3(8)*, Turtleback) Turtleback Bks.

Lucas, Gareth, illus. Dinos on Deck! 2017. (Gareth Lucas Noisy Bks.). (ENG.). 12p. (J). (gr. -1). bds. 14.99 *(978-1-62686-938-7(3)*, Silver Dolphin Bks.) Readerlink Distribution Services, LLC.

Lucas, Sally. Dancing Dinos at the Beach. Lucas, Margeaux, illus. 2010. (Step into Reading Ser.). (ENG.). 32p. (J). (gr. -1-1). pap. 3.99 *(978-0-375-85640-2(4)*, Random Hse. Bks. for Young Readers) Random Hse. Children's Bks.

—Dancing Dinos at the Beach. 2010. (Step into Reading Level 1 Ser.). lib. bdg. 13.55 *(978-0-606-14653-1(9)*, Turtleback) Turtleback Bks.

Lucas, Sally & Lucas, Margeaux. Dancing Dinos Go to School. 2006. (Step into Reading Ser.: Vol. 1). (ENG., Illus.). 32p. (J). (gr. -1-1). pap. 4.99 *(978-0-375-83241-3(6)*, Random Hse. Bks. for Young Readers) Random Hse. Children's Bks.

Lund, Deb. All Aboard the Dinotrain. Fine, Howard, illus. (ENG.). (J). (gr. -1 — 1). 2011. 30p. bds. 7.99 *(978-0-547-55415-0(X))* 2009. 40p. pap. 7.99 *(978-0-547-24825-7(3))* Houghton Mifflin Harcourt Publishing Co.

—Dinosailors. Fine, Howard, illus. 2008. (ENG.). 36p. (J). (gr. -1-3). pap. 6.99 *(978-0-15-206124-1(X))* Houghton Mifflin Harcourt Publishing Co.

—Dinosoaring. Fine, Howard, illus. 2012. (ENG.). 40p. (J). (gr. -1-3). 16.99 *(978-0-15-206016-9(2))* Houghton Mifflin Harcourt Publishing Co.

Lyons, Kelly Starling. One More Dino on the Floor. Flowers, Luke, illus. 2016. (ENG.). 32p. (J). (gr. -1-3). 16.99 *(978-0-8075-1598-3(1))* Whitman, Albert & Co.

MacHado, Ana Maria. Un Deseo Loco. (Torre de Papel Ser.). (SPA.). (YA). (gr. 6-18). 8.95 *(978-958-04-4529-6(X)*, NR30565) Norma S.A. COL. Dist: Distribuidora Norma, Inc., Lectorum Pubns., Inc.

Macht, Heather. You May Just Be a Dinosaur, 1 vol. Gillard, Jason, illus. 2015. (ENG.). 32p. (J). (gr. k-3). 16.99 *(978-1-4556-2040-1(8))* Pelican Publishing Co., Inc.

Magsamen, Sandra. I Love You, Snugglesaurus! 2014. (ENG., Illus.). 10p. (J). (gr. -1 — 1). bds. 7.99 *(978-0-316-25518-9(1))* Little, Brown Bks. for Young Readers.

Maier, Gary B. Key Masters: The Tyrannosaur Rebellion. 2013. 124p. pap. 11.50 *(978-1-62516-403-2(3)*, Strategic Bk. Publishing) Strategic Book Publishing & Rights Agency (SBPRA).

Mandell, B. B. Samanthasaurus Rex. Kaufman, Suzanne, illus. 2016. 32p. (J). (gr. -1-3). 17.99 *(978-0-06-234873-9(6))* HarperCollins Pubs.

Marsh, Carole. The Mystery of the Missing Dinosaurs. 2009. (Real Kids, Real Places Ser.). 146p. (J). 18.99 *(978-0-635-06995-5(4)*, Marsh, Carole Mysteries) Gallopade International.

—The Mystery of the Missing Dinosaurs (Hardcover) 2003. 160p. (gr. 2-8). 14.95 *(978-0-635-01662-1(1))* Gallopade International.

Marsoli, Lisa Ann. Dinosaurs are Big Babies. Smitherton, Jeb, illus. 2005. (J). bds. 14.99 *(978-0-9767325-0-1(5))* Toy Quest.

Martin, Kevin. Chomper the Stomper. 2012. 28p. pap. 11.00 *(978-0-578-10705-9(8))* Martin, Kevin.

Martin, Laura. The Ark Plan. DesChamps, Eric, illus. 2017. (Edge of Extinction Ser.: 1). 384p. (J). (gr. 3-7). pap. 6.99 *(978-0-06-241623-0(5))* HarperCollins Pubs.

—The Ark Plan. DesChamps, Eric, illus. 2017. (Edge of Extinction Ser.: 1). (J). (gr. 3-7). lib. bdg. 17.20 ***(978-0-606-40046-6(X))*** Turtleback Bks.

Marvel Comics Staff & Kirby, Jack, texts. Devil Dinosaur. 2014. (ENG., Illus.). 184p. (J). (gr. 4-17). pap. 24.99 *(978-0-7851-9037-0(6))* Marvel Worldwide, Inc.

Marzollo, Jean. I Spy a Dinosaur's Eye. Wick, Walter, illus. 2003. (Scholastic Reader Level 1 Ser.). (ENG.). 32p. (J). (gr. -1-3). pap. 3.99 *(978-0-439-52471-1(7)*, Cartwheel Bks.) Scholastic, Inc.

Matsuoka, Tatsuhide. When I Was a Dinosaur. 2017. (ENG., Illus.). 40p. (J). (gr. -1-3). 16.95 ***(978-1-927018-88-0(9))*** Simply Read Bks. CAN. Dist: Ingram Publisher Services.

Mattern, Joanne. Dino Disaster! Spaziante, Patrick & Giles, Mike, illus. 2005. (Adventures of Jimmy Neutron Ser.: 9). 24p. (J). lib. bdg. 15.00 *(978-1-59054-782-3(9))* Fitzgerald Bks.

Mawhinney, Art, illus. Dora & Diego Help the Dinosaur. 2011. (Dora & Diego Ser.). (ENG.). 24p. (J). pap. 3.99 *(978-1-4424-1400-6(6)*, Simon Spotlight/Nickelodeon) Simon Spotlight/Nickelodeon.

Mayer, Mercer. Little Critter Fall Storybook Collection. Mayer, Mercer, illus. 2015. (Little Critter Ser.). (ENG., Illus.). 192p. (J). (gr. -1-3). 11.99 *(978-0-06-238032-6(X))* HarperCollins Pubs.

—Too Many Dinosaurs. Mayer, Mercer, illus. 2012. (ENG., Illus.). 40p. (J). (gr. -1-2). pap. 6.99 *(978-0-8234-2543-3(6))* Holiday Hse., Inc.

Mayhew, James. Katie & the Dinosaurs. Mayhew, James, illus. 2014. (ENG., Illus.). 32p. (J). (gr. -1-k). 9.99 *(978-1-4083-3191-0(8))* Hodder & Stoughton GBR. Dist: Hachette Bk. Group.

McAnulty, Stacy. Dear Santasaurus. Kaminsky, Jef, illus. 2013. (ENG.). 32p. (J). (gr. k-3). 15.95 *(978-1-59078-876-9(1))* Boyds Mills Pr.

—It's Not a Dinosaur! Boldt, Mike, illus. 2016. (Dino Files Ser.: 3). (ENG.). 128p. (J). (gr. 2-5). 9.99 *(978-0-553-52197-9(7)*, Random Hse. Bks. for Young Readers) Random Hse. Children's Bks.

—A Mysterious Egg. Boldt, Mike, illus. (Dino Files Ser.: 1). (ENG.). 128p. (J). (gr. 2-5). 2017. 4.99 ***(978-1-5247-0150-5(5))*** 2016. 9.99 *(978-0-553-52191-7(8))* Random Hse. Children's Bks. (Random Hse. Bks. for Young Readers).

—Too Big to Hide. Boldt, Mike, illus. (Dino Files Ser.: 2). (ENG.). 128p. (J). (gr. 2-5). 2017. 4.99 ***(978-1-5247-0151-2(3))*** 2016. 9.99 *(978-0-553-52194-8(2))* Random Hse. Children's Bks. (Random Hse. Bks. for Young Readers).

McCabe, Jane. The Remarkable Story of the Very First Flower: And How She Changed the World. 2010. 56p. pap. 24.99 *(978-1-4490-8361-8(7))* AuthorHouse.

McCarty, Peter. T Is for Terrible. McCarty, Peter, illus. 2008. (ENG., Illus.). 32p. (J). (gr. -1-1). pap. 7.99 *(978-0-312-38423-4(8)*, 9780312384234) Square Fish.

McClatchy, Lisa & Thompson, Kay. Eloise & the Dinosaurs. Lyon, Tammie Speer & Lyon, Tammie, illus. 2007. (Eloise Ser.). (ENG.). 32p. (J). (gr. -1-1). pap. 3.99 *(978-0-689-87453-6(7)*, Simon Spotlight) Simon Spotlight.

McCurry, Meryl. Monto. 2009. 28p. pap. 13.99 *(978-1-4490-1403-2(8))* AuthorHouse.

McKay, Sindy. We Both Read-about Dinosaurs. Walters, Robert, illus. 2004. (We Both Read Ser.). 44p. (J). (gr. 1-2). 9.95 *(978-1-891327-53-7(4))* Treasure Bay, Inc.

—We Both Read-About Dinosaurs. Walters, Robert, illus. 2004. (We Both Read Ser.). 44p. (J). (gr. 1-2). pap. 4.99 *(978-1-891327-54-4(2))* Treasure Bay, Inc.

McKenzie, Heath. I Wanna Be a Great Big Dinosaur. 2016. (ENG.). 48p. (J). (-4). 16.99 *(978-1-4926-3299-3(6)*, 9781492632993, Sourcebooks Jabberwocky) Sourcebooks, Inc.

McMahon, Jean. Rex Finally Finds a Friend. 2005. (J). pap. 8.00 *(978-0-8059-6909-2(8))* Dorrance Publishing Co., Inc.

McMullan, Kate. I'm Bad! McMullan, Jim, illus. 2008. (ENG.). 40p. (J). (gr. -1-3). 16.99 *(978-0-06-122971-8(7))* HarperCollins Pubs.

—I'm Big! McMullan, Jim, illus. 2010. (ENG.). 40p. (J). (gr. -1-3). 16.99 *(978-0-06-122974-9(1))* HarperCollins Pubs.

Middleton, Julie. Are the Dinosaurs Dead, Dad?, 1 vol. Ayto, Russell, illus. 2013. (ENG.). 32p. (J). (gr. -1-3). pap. 16.95 *(978-1-56145-690-1(X))* Peachtree Pubs.

Milbourne, Anna. How Big Was a Dinosaur? 2011. (Picture Books Ser.). 24p. (J). ring bd. 10.99 *(978-0-7945-3002-0(8)*, Usborne) EDC Publishing.

Milbourne, Anna & Field, Mandy. The Dinosaur. 2004. (Illus.). *(978-0-439-78724-6(6))* Scholastic, Inc.

Miller, Austin. Sam Is Special. 2011. (Early Connections Ser.). (J). *(978-1-61672-597-6(4))* Benchmark Education Co.

—Sam Is Special: Set Of 6. 2011. (Early Connections Ser.). (J). pap. 37.00 net. *(978-1-4108-1358-9(4))* Benchmark Education Co.

Miller, Mona. Call of the Wild! Golden Books Staff & Fruchter, Jason, illus. 2011. (Color Plus Chunky Crayons Ser.). (ENG.). 48p. (J). (gr. -1-2). pap. 3.99 *(978-0-375-86158-1(0)*, Golden Bks.) Random Hse. Children's Bks.

—Hey, Buddy! Fruchter, Jason, illus. 2010. (Super Coloring Book Ser.). (ENG.). 96p. (J). (gr. -1-2). pap. 3.99 *(978-0-375-86155-0(6)*, Golden Bks.) Random Hse. Children's Bks.

Miller, Tim. Dinosaur Dump: What Happened to the Dinosaurs Is Grosser Than You Think... Stanton, Matt, illus. 2017. 32p. 17.99 *(978-0-7333-3463-4(6))* ABC Bks. AUS. Dist: HarperCollins Pubs.

Milton, Elizabeth. D-Structs Rescue. 2016. (Dinotrux 8X8 Ser.). (J). lib. bdg. 13.55 *(978-0-606-39188-7(6))* Turtleback Bks.

—Dinotrux: d-Structs Rescue. 2016. (ENG., Illus.). 24p. (J). (gr. -1-3). pap. 3.99 *(978-0-316-26087-9(8))* Little, Brown Bks. for Young Readers.

Miranda, Edward. The Truth about Dragons & Dinosaurs. Cassetta, Andrea, illus. 2007. 32p. per. 10.95 *(978-1-934246-22-1(0))* Peppertree Pr., The.

Mitchell, Colleen. A Dinosaur under My Bed. Daly, Karen Anne, illus. 2013. 24p. (J). pap. 7.49 *(978-0-9853600-2-3(X))* Thistlewood Publishing.

Mitton, Tony. Dinosaurumpus! Parker-Rees, Guy, illus. (ENG.). (J). (gr. -1-k). 2014. 30p. bds. 6.99 *(978-0-545-69480-3(9)*, Cartwheel Bks.) 2003. 32p. 16.99 *(978-0-439-39514-4(3)*, Orchard Bks.) Scholastic, Inc.

—Dinosaurumpus! (a StoryPlay Book) Parker-Rees, Guy, illus. 2016. (ENG.). 40p. (J). (gr. -1-k). 5.99 *(978-1-338-11536-9(7)*, Cartwheel Bks.) Scholastic, Inc.

—The Somethingosaur. Ayto, Russell, illus. 2014. (ENG.). 32p. (J). 17.99 *(978-0-00-758395-9(8)*, HarperCollins Children's Bks.) HarperCollins Pubs. Ltd. GBR. Dist: HarperCollins Pubs.

C
D

Miyanishi, Tatsuya. You Are My Best Friend. 2016. (Tyrannosaurus Ser.). (ENG.). 40p. (J). (gr. k-2). 16.99 *(978-1-940842-10-3(7))* Museyon.

Moncure, Jane Belk. A Wish-For Dinosaur: A Just-for-Fun Book. Regan, Dana, illus. 2013. (Magic Castle Readers Ser.). (ENG.). 32p. (J). (gr. -1-2). 25.64 *(978-1-62323-576-5(6)*, 206308) Child's World, Inc., The.

Moor-Doucette, Saba. Dinosaurs & Donuts. Noon, Connie & Zraick, Robert, illus. 2013. 28p. pap. 10.95 *(978-0-578-13447-5(0))* Gratitude Works.

Morgan, Michelle. Colorsaurus. 2009. 32p. pap. 18.00 *(978-0-557-06120-4(2))* Lulu Pr., Inc.

—Colorsaurus ABC. 2009. 32p. pap. 18.00 *(978-0-557-07782-3(6))* Lulu Pr., Inc.

Moses, Brian. Anna Angrysaurus. 2014. (Dinosaurs Have Feelings Ser.). (ENG.). 32p. (J). (gr. -1-1). pap. 6.99 *(978-1-4380-0404-4(4))* Barron's Educational Series, Inc.

—Jayden Jealousaurus. 2014. (Dinosaurs Have Feelings Ser.). (ENG.). 32p. (J). (gr. -1-1). pap. 6.99 *(978-1-4380-0402-0(8))* Barron's Educational Series, Inc.

—Samuel Scaredosaurus. 2014. (Dinosaurs Have Feelings Ser.). (ENG.). 32p. (J). (gr. -1-1). pap. 6.99 *(978-1-4380-0403-7(6))* Barron's Educational Series, Inc.

—Sophie Shyosaurus. 2014. (Dinosaurs Have Feelings Ser.). (ENG.). 32p. (J). (gr. -1-1). pap. 6.99 *(978-1-4380-0406-8(0))* Barron's Educational Series, Inc.

—William Worrydactyl. 2014. (Dinosaurs Have Feelings Ser.). (ENG.). 32p. (J). (gr. -1-1). pap. 6.99 *(978-1-4380-0405-1(2))* Barron's Educational Series, Inc.

Most, Bernard. ABC T-Rex. 2004. (ENG., Illus.). 40p. (J). (gr. -1-3). pap. 7.99 *(978-0-15-205028-3(0))* Houghton Mifflin Harcourt Publishing Co.

—Catch Me If You Can! (¡A Que No Me Alcanzas!) Flor Ada, Alma & Campoy, F. Isabel, trs. from ENG. 2007. (Green Light Readers Level 2 Ser.). (SPA & ENG., Illus.). 28p. (J). (gr. -1-3). pap. 3.95 *(978-0-15-205967-5(9))* Houghton Mifflin Harcourt Publishing Co.

Moynihan, Dan. Hiding Dinosaurs. 2015. (I Like to Read(r) Ser.). (ENG., Illus.). 24p. (J). (gr. -1-3). 14.95 *(978-0-8234-3196-0(7))* Holiday Hse., Inc.

Muecke, Anne & Moore, Clement C. The Dinosaurs' Night Before Christmas. Hale, Nathan, illus. 2008. (ENG.). 36p. (J). (gr. -1-3). 18.99 *(978-0-8118-6322-3(0))* Chronicle Bks. LLC.

Munoz, Mercedes C. Nalu the Dinosaur. 2010. (Illus.). 26p. (J). pap. 11.95 *(978-1-4327-5498-3(X))* Outskirts Pr., Inc.

Murphy, Hugh. T-Rex Trying. 2013. (ENG., Illus.). 128p. (gr. 12). 13.00 *(978-0-452-29902-3(0)*, Plume) Penguin Publishing Group.

Musco, Rance. The Hunt: Adventures of Austin & Rance. 2010. 28p. pap. 14.95 *(978-1-4490-5838-8(8))* AuthorHouse.

My Day with the Dinosaurs. 2004. (J). ring bd. 3.25 *(978-0-9762740-2-5(7)*, Flat Kids) Smart Smiles Co., The.

Nancee Jean. The Boomerang Babies Club. 2012. 36p. pap. 13.95 *(978-1-4525-5243-9(6))* Balboa Pr.

Nash, David. A Pete & Charley Adventure: The Sheri. 2005. 131p. pap. 24.95 *(978-1-4137-9449-6(1))* PublishAmerica, Inc.

Neubecker, Robert. Linus the Vegetarian T. Rex. Neubecker, Robert, illus. 2013. (ENG., Illus.). 40p. (J). (gr. -1-3). 16.99 *(978-1-4169-8512-9(3)*, Beach Lane Bks.) Beach Lane Bks.

Neusner, Dena Wallenstein. Colors of Spring. McKee, Darren, illus. 2003. (Barney Ser.). (ENG.). 32p. (J). pap., act. bk. ed. 3.99 *(978-1-58668-305-4(5))* Scholastic, Inc.

Nickel, Scott. T. Rex vs Robo-Dog 3000. Corts, Enrique, illus. 2008. (Graphic Sparks Ser.). (ENG.). 40p. (gr. 1-3). pap. 5.95 *(978-1-4342-0857-6(5)*, Graphic Sparks) Stone Arch Bks.

North, Ryan. Dinosaur Comics. North, Ryan, illus. 2005. (Illus.). 112p. 14.99 *(978-0-7560-0518-4(3))* Teacher's Discovery.

Nosy Crow Staff. Bizzy Bear: Dinosaur Safari. Davies, Benji, illus. 2015. (Bizzy Bear Ser.). (ENG.). 8p. (J). (— 1). bds. 6.99 *(978-0-7636-8170-8(9)*, Nosy Crow) Candlewick Pr.

Nussbaum, Ben. Is Apatosaurus Okay? Reaveley, Trevor, illus. 2005. (Smithsonian's Prehistoric Pals Ser.). (ENG.). (J). (gr. -1-2). 32p. 9.95 *(978-1-59249-510-8(9)*, PS2458); 36p. pap. 2.95 *(978-1-59249-509-2(5)*, S2458) Soundprints.

—Is Apatosaurus Okay? Reavely, Trevor, illus. 2005. (ENG.). 36p. (J). (gr. -1-2). 8.95 *(978-1-59249-508-5(7)*, SD2408); 14.95 *(978-1-59249-506-1(0)*, H2408); pap. 6.95 *(978-1-59249-507-8(9)*, S2408) Soundprints.

—Spinosaurus in the Storm. Scalf, Christopher & McIntosh, Gabe, illus. 2005. (Smithsonian's Prehistoric Pals Ser.). (ENG.). 36p. (J). (gr. 2-2). 14.95 *(978-1-59249-458-3(7)*, H2407) Soundprints.

—Spinosaurus in the Storm. Scalf, Christopher, illus. 2005. (Smithsonian's Prehistoric Pals Ser.). (ENG.). 36p. (J). (gr. -1 — 1). pap. 6.95 *(978-1-59249-459-0(5)*, S2407) Soundprints.

Nussbaum, Ben & McIntosh, G. B. Spinosaurus in the Storm. Scalf, Chris, illus. 2005. (Smithsonian's Prehistoric Pals Ser.). (ENG.). 36p. (J). (gr. -1-2). 2.95 *(978-1-59249-461-3(7)*, S2457) Soundprints.

Nye, Barry. Hannah & the Magic Blanket - Land of the Dinosaurs. 2009. 40p. pap. 18.50 *(978-0-557-03682-0(8))* Lulu Pr., Inc.

Oakes, Cory Putman. Dinosaur Boy. 2015. (Dinosaur Boy Ser.: 1). (ENG.). 224p. (J). (gr. 3-7). 12.99 *(978-1-4926-0537-9(9)*, 9781492605379, Sourcebooks Jabberwocky) Sourcebooks, Inc.

—Dinosaur Boy. 2016. (Dinosaur Boy Ser.: 1). lib. bdg. 18.40 *(978-0-606-38280-9(1))* Turtleback Bks.

—Dinosaur Boy Saves Mars. 2016. (Dinosaur Boy Ser.: 2). (ENG., Illus.). 224p. (J). (gr. 3-7). 12.99 *(978-1-4926-0540-9(9)*, 9781492605409, Sourcebooks Jabberwocky) Sourcebooks, Inc.

—Dinosaur Boy Saves Mars. 2016. (Dinosaur Boy Ser.: 2). (ENG.). 224p. (J). (gr. 3-7). 18.40 *(978-0-606-39306-5(4))* Turtleback Bks.

Obiols, Anna. Stegosaurus: the Friendliest Dinosaur. Subi, illus. 2012. (Dinosaur Bks.). (ENG.). 36p. (J). (gr. -1-1). pap. 6.99 *(978-1-4380-0107-4(X))* Barron's Educational Series, Inc.

—Triceratops: the Strongest Dinosaur. Subi, illus. 2012. (Dinosaur Bks.). (ENG.). 36p. (J). (gr. -1-1). pap. 6.99 *(978-1-4380-0108-1(8))* Barron's Educational Series, Inc.

O'Connor, George. If I Had a Triceratops. O'Connor, George, illus. 2015. (ENG., Illus.). 32p. (J). (gr. -1-2). 15.99 *(978-0-7636-6013-0(2))* Candlewick Pr.

Odgers, Sally. Where Did the Dinosaurs Go?, 1 vol. 2013. (Fiction Readers Ser.). (ENG., Illus.). 24p. (J). (gr. 2-2). pap. 6.99 *(978-1-4333-5528-8(0))* Shell Educational Publishing.

Olfet, Omid. In the Dark: Parts 3 And 4. 2009. 74p. pap. 8.95 *(978-1-4401-5811-7(8))* iUniverse, Inc.

Oliver, Butterworth. Enormous Egg. 2009. 188p. pap. 6.99 *(978-0-316-10602-3(X))* Little, Brown Bks. for Young Readers.

O'Malley, Kevin. Captain Raptor & the Moon Mystery. O'Brien, Patrick, illus. 2005. (Captain Raptor Ser.). (ENG.). 32p. (J). (gr. k-5). 17.99 *(978-0-8027-8935-8(8)*, 9780802789358, Bloomsbury USA Childrens) Bloomsbury Publishing USA.

O'Malley, Kevin & O'Brien, Patrick. Captain Raptor & the Space Pirates. O'Brien, Patrick, illus. 2007. (Captain Raptor Ser.). (ENG., Illus.). 32p. (J). (gr. k-3). 16.95 *(978-0-8027-9571-7(4)*, 9780802795717) Walker & Co.

Oppel, Kenneth. Every Hidden Thing. 2016. (ENG., Illus.). 368p. (YA). (gr. 9). 17.99 *(978-1-4814-6416-1(7)*, Simon & Schuster Bks. For Young Readers) Simon & Schuster Bks. For Young Readers.

Orshoski, Paul. We Both Read-My Sitter Is a T-Rex! (Level 1-2) Ebbeler, Jeffrey, illus. 2011. (ENG.). 44p. (J). 9.95 *(978-1-60115-253-4(1))*; pap. 4.99 *(978-1-60115-254-1(X))* Treasure Bay, Inc.

O'Ryan, Ray. The Prehistoric Planet. Jack, Colin, illus. 2013. (Galaxy Zack Ser.: 3). (ENG.). 128p. (J). (gr. k-4). 16.99 *(978-1-4424-6716-3(9))*; pap. 5.99 *(978-1-4424-6715-6(0))* Little Simon. (Little Simon).

—The Prehistoric Planet. 2013. (Galaxy Zack Ser.: 3). lib. bdg. 16.00 *(978-0-606-32461-8(5)*, Turtleback) Turtleback Bks.

Osborne, Mary Pope. Dinosaurios Al Atardecer. 2004. (Casa del Arbol Ser.: 1). (SPA.). (J). pap. 5.99 *(978-1-930332-49-2(1))* Lectorum Pubns., Inc.

—Dinosaurios al Atardecer. 2003. (Magic Tree House Ser.: 1). (SPA.). (gr. 3-6). lib. bdg. 16.00 *(978-0-613-64486-0(7)*, Turtleback) Turtleback Bks.

—Dinosaurs Before Dark. unabr. ed. 2004. (Magic Tree House Ser.: No. 1). 68p. (J). (gr. k-5). pap. 17.00 incl. audio *(978-0-8072-0330-9(0)*, FTR208SP, Listening Library) Random Hse. Audio Publishing Group.

—Dinosaurs Before Dark. Murdocca, Sal, illus. 20th anniv. ed. 2012. (Magic Tree House Ser.: 1). (ENG.). 96p. (J). (gr. k-3). 14.99 *(978-0-375-86988-4(3)*, Random Hse. Bks. for Young Readers) Random Hse. Children's Bks.

Osorio, Rick. The Great Adventure of Sally Rock & the Cretaceous Chicken. 2006. 65p. pap. 16.95 *(978-1-4241-0971-5(X))* PublishAmerica, Inc.

Ost, Nina. The Gingerbread Man & the Dinosaurs. 2011. 24p. (gr. -1). pap. 11.49 *(978-1-4567-4902-6(1))* AuthorHouse.

Owen, John Bailey. #Prehistoric: Follow the Dinosaurs. 2015. (ENG., Illus.). 128p. (J). (gr. 3-7). 9.99 *(978-0-545-82341-8(2))* Scholastic, Inc.

Palatini, Margie. Gorgonzola: A Very Stinkysaurus. Bowers, Tim, illus. 2008. (ENG.). 32p. (J). (gr. -1-2). 17.99 *(978-0-06-073897-6(9)*, Tegen, Katherine Bks) HarperCollins Pubs.

PaleoJoe. The Disappearance of Dinosaur Sue. Caszatt-Allen, Wendy, illus. 2006. (PaleoJoe's Dinosaur Detective Club Ser.: 1). (ENG.). 144p. (J). (gr. 2-5). pap. 8.95 *(978-1-934133-03-3(5)*, Mackinac Island Press, Inc.) Charlesbridge Publishing, Inc.

PaleoJoe & Caszatt-Allen, Wendy. Raptor's Revenge. 2007. (ENG.). 184p. (J). (gr. 2-5). pap. 8.95 *(978-1-934133-37-8(X)*, Mackinac Island Press, Inc.) Charlesbridge Publishing, Inc.

—Stolen Stegasaurus. 2006. (PaleoJoe's Dinosaur Detective Club Ser.: 2). (ENG., Illus.). 160p. (J). (gr. 2-5). pap. 8.95 *(978-1-934133-04-0(3)*, Mackinac Island Press, Inc.) Charlesbridge Publishing, Inc.

Pallotta, Jerry. Dinosaur Christmas. McWilliam, Howard, illus. (J). (gr. k-2). 2013. (ENG.). 32p. 12.99 *(978-0-545-43360-0(6))* 2011. *(978-0-545-24963-8(5))* Scholastic, Inc.

Parpan, Justin, illus. Gwango's Lonesome Trail. 2006. 32p. (J). (gr. -1-3). 15.95 *(978-1-60108-004-2(2))* Red Cygnet Pr.

Paul, Ruth. Stomp! 2013. pap. *(978-0-545-52940-2(9))* Scholastic, Inc.

Paul, Ruth & Lombana, J. P. Stomp! la Marcha! 2013. (SPA & ENG., Illus.). *(978-0-545-52795-8(3))* Scholastic, Inc.

Penado, Martha. Eggstinkt. 2008. 32p. pap. 24.95 *(978-1-60610-906-9(5))* America Star Bks.

Penner, Stephen. Professor Barrister's Dinosaur Mysteries #1: The Case of the Truncated Troodon. Penner, Stephen, illus. 2010. (Illus.). 44p. pap. 19.25 *(978-1-60888-005-8(2))* Nimble Bks. LLC.

—Professor Barrister's Dinosaur Mysteries #2: The Case of the Armored Allosaurus. 2010. 54p. pap. 19.60 *(978-1-60888-018-8(4))* Nimble Bks. LLC.

—Professor Barrister's Dinosaur Mysteries #4: The Case of the Colorful Caudipteryx. Penner, Stephen, illus. 2011. (Illus.). 62p. pap. 14.99 *(978-1-60888-111-6(3))* Nimble Bks. LLC.

Pett, Mark. Lizard from the Park. Pett, Mark, illus. 2015. (ENG., Illus.). 40p. (J). (gr. -1-3). 17.99 *(978-1-4424-8321-7(0)*, Simon & Schuster Bks. For Young Readers) Simon & Schuster Bks. For Young Readers.

Pez, Alberto. Mimosaurio! Cubillas, Roberto, illus. (SPA.). (J). 8.95 *(978-958-04-6035-0(3))* Norma S.A. COL. Dist: Distribuidora Norma, Inc.

Phelps, Donna & Phelps, Cameron. Cameron & the Dinosaur Heroes. 2011. 128p. 21.23 *(978-1-4567-2476-4(2))*; pap. 10.68 *(978-1-4389-6353-2(X))* AuthorHouse.

Piggy Toes Press, creator. Dinosaurs: Guess the Dinosaur. 2011. (Crayola (Piggy Toes Press) Ser.). (Illus.). 6p. (J). (gr. -1-3). 5.95 *(978-1-61524-287-0(2)*, Intervisual/Piggy Toes) Bendon, Inc.

Pigott, Kat. Green Dinosaur Pancakes, 1 vol. Sibley, Mason, illus. 2016. (ENG.). 32p. (J). (gr. k-3). 16.99 *(978-1-4556-2177-4(3))* Pelican Publishing Co., Inc.

Pike, Christopher, pseud. The Deadly Past. 2016. (Spooksville Ser.: 11). (ENG., Illus.). 128p. (J). (gr. 3-7). pap. 6.99 *(978-1-4814-1089-2(X)*, Aladdin) Simon & Schuster Children's Publishing.

Pilger, Seamus. Fartasaurus Rex. Gilpin, Stephen, illus. 2015. (Fart Squad Ser.: 2). (ENG.). 112p. (J). (gr. 1-5). 15.99 *(978-0-06-236632-0(7))*; pap. 4.99 *(978-0-06-229047-2(9))* HarperCollins Pubs.

Pilkey, Dav. Las Aventuras de Uuk y Gluk, Cavernícolas del Futuro y Maestros de Kung Fu. Pilkey, Dav, illus. 2011. (Captain Underpants Ser.). (SPA., Illus.). 176p. (J). (gr. 2-5). pap. 5.99 *(978-0-545-27916-1(X)*, Scholastic en Espanol) Scholastic, Inc.

—Ricky Ricotta's Mighty Robot vs. the Jurassic Jackrabbits from Jupiter. Santat, Dan, illus. 2014. (Ricky Ricotta Ser.: 5). (ENG.). 128p. (J). (gr. -1-3). pap. 5.99 *(978-0-545-63013-9(4))* Scholastic, Inc.

Pledger, Maurice. Dinosaur World. 2013. (Pledger Sticker Book Ser.). (ENG., Illus.). 80p. (J). (gr. -1). pap. 10.95 *(978-1-60710-819-1(4)*, Silver Dolphin Bks.) Readerlink Distribution Services, LLC.

Plumeri, Arnaud. Dinosaurs: In the Beginning... 2014. (Dinosaurs Graphic Novels Ser.). (ENG., Illus.). 64p. (J). (gr. 3-9). 10.99 *(978-1-59707-490-2(X)*, 9781597074902) Papercutz.

Pope, Jerald. Madeleine Claire & the Dinosaur. 2006. (Illus.). (J). 16.00 *(978-0-9700125-6-2(X))* Brave Ulysses Bks.

Pope, Psborne. Vallee des Dinosaurs. pap. 15.95 *(978-2-7470-0496-1(1))* Bayard Editions FRA. Dist: Distribooks, Inc.

Posner-Sanchez, Andrea. Dino-Might Tales. Random House Disney Staff, illus. 2016. (Friendship Box Ser.). (ENG.). 48p. (J). (gr. -1 — 1). bds. 10.99 *(978-0-7364-3224-5(8)*, RH/Disney) Random Hse. Children's Bks.

—Dinosaurs A to Z. Golden Books Staff et al, illus. 2011. (Padded Board Book Ser.). (ENG.). 28p. (J). (gr. -1 — 1). bds. 11.99 *(978-0-375-87143-6(8)*, Random Hse. Bks. for Young Readers) Random Hse. Children's Bks.

Prasadam-Halls, Smriti. T. Veg: The Story of a Carrot-Crunching Dinosaur. Manolessou, Katherina, illus. 2017. (ENG.). 32p. (J). (gr. -1-3). 16.95 *(978-1-4197-2494-7(0)*, Abrams Bks. for Young Readers) Abrams, Inc.

Preston-Gannon, Frann. Dinosaur Farm. 2014. (ENG., Illus.). 32p. (J). (gr. -1 — 1). 14.95 *(978-1-4549-1132-6(8))* Sterling Publishing Co., Inc.

Publications International Ltd. Staff, ed. Barney: Let's Play Together. 2011. 10p. (J). bds. 8.98 *(978-1-4508-0859-0(X))* Publications International, Ltd.

—Barney & Friends Book Box & Plush. 2011. 8p. (J). 14.98 *(978-1-4508-0854-5(9))* Publications International, Ltd.

—Dinosaur Train All Aboard! 2011. 10p. (J). bds. 10.98 *(978-1-4508-1140-8(X))* Publications International, Ltd.

Punter, Russell. The Dinosaur Who Lost His Roar. Elkerton, Andy, illus. 2007. (Usborne First Reading: Level 3 Ser.). 48p. (J). 8.99 *(978-0-7945-1547-8(9)*, Usborne) EDC Publishing.

—Stories of Dinosaurs. Decker, Cynthia, illus. 2006. (Usborne Young Reading: Series One Ser.). 48p. (J). (gr. 2). lib. bdg. 13.99 *(978-1-58086-940-9(8)*, Usborne) EDC Publishing.

Quisenberry, Stacey. Dinosaur George Pre-hysterical Adventures: What Color Were Dinosaurs? Browning, Suzan, illus. 2007. (J). 3.95 *(978-0-9797304-3-6(0))* Raining Popcorn Media.

Rader, Mark. Dinosaur. Sanborn, Casey, illus. 2008. (J). *(978-1-4127-9359-9(9))* Publications International, Ltd.

Rand, Johnathan. American Chillers #23 Wicked Velociraptors of West Virginia. 2008. 208p. (J). pap. 5.99 *(978-1-893699-94-6(3))* AudioCraft Publishing, Inc.

Random House & Shealy, Dennis R. The Park Is Open. Random House, illus. 2015. (Pictureback(R) Ser.). (ENG., Illus.). 16p. (J). (gr. -1-2). 4.99 *(978-0-553-53692-8(3)*, Random Hse. Bks. for Young Readers) Random Hse. Children's Bks.

Random House Disney Staff. A Dino Named Arlo/a Boy Named Spot, 2 bks. in 1. Random House Disney Staff, illus. 2015. (Pictureback(R) Ser.). (ENG., Illus.). 24p. (J). (gr. -1-2). 4.99 *(978-0-7364-3083-8(0)*, RH/Disney) Random Hse. Children's Bks.

—The Good Dinosaur Big Golden Book (Disney/Pixar the Good Dinosaur) Random House Disney Staff, illus. 2015. (Big Golden Book Ser.). (ENG., Illus.). 64p. (J). (gr. -1-2). 9.99 *(978-0-7364-3082-1(2)*, Golden/Disney) Random Hse. Children's Bks.

—Hello, Arlo. Random House Disney Staff, illus. 2016. (Tabbed Board Book Ser.). (ENG., Illus.). 16p. (J). (gr. -1 — 1). bds. 7.99 *(978-0-7364-3467-6(4)*, RH/Disney) Random Hse. Children's Bks.

Random House Disney Staff & Amerikaner, Susan. Crash, Boom, Roar! Random House Disney Staff & Disney Storybook Art Team, illus. 2015. (Step into Reading Ser.). (ENG.). 24p. (J). (gr. -1-1). 4.99 *(978-0-7364-3367-9(8)*, Random Hse. Bks. for Young Readers) Random Hse. Children's Bks.

Raney, Ken. It's Probably Good Dinosaurs Are Extinct. 2011. (ENG.). 32p. (J). (gr. -1-3). pap. 16.99 *(978-1-4424-5230-5(7)*, Simon & Schuster Bks. For Young Readers) Simon & Schuster Bks. For Young Readers.

Rauchwerger, Diane Levin. Dinosaur Goes to Israel. Wolff, Jason, illus. 2012. (Israel Ser.). (ENG.). 24p. (J). (gr. -1-1). pap. 7.95 *(978-0-7613-5134-4(5))*; lib. bdg. 16.95 *(978-0-7613-5133-7(7))* Lerner Publishing Group. (Kar-Ben Publishing).

—Dinosaur on Hanukkah. Wolff, Jason, illus. 2005. (ENG.). 24p. (J). (gr. -1-1). 15.95 *(978-1-58013-145-2(X))*; per. 7.95 *(978-1-58013-143-8(3))* Lerner Publishing Group. (Kar-Ben Publishing).

—Dinosaur on Passover. Wolff, Jason, illus. 2006. (ENG.). 24p. (J). (gr. -1-1). 15.95 *(978-1-58013-156-8(5))*; pap. 7.95 *(978-1-58013-161-2(1))* Lerner Publishing Group. (Kar-Ben Publishing).

Rauchwerger, Diane Levin & Levin, Diane. Dinosaur on Shabbat. Wolff, Jason, illus. 2006. (ENG.). 24p. (J). (gr. -1-1). lib. bdg. 15.95 *(978-1-58013-159-9(X)*, Kar-Ben Publishing) Lerner Publishing Group.

Reasoner, Charles. Dinosaur Babies. Devaney, Adam, illus. 2009. (Baby Animal Board Bks.). 12p. (J). (gr. -1-k). bds. 7.99 *(978-1-934650-49-3(8))* Just For Kids Pr., LLC.

—Dinosaurs. 2009. (Learning Tab Board Bks.). (Illus.). 10p. (J). (gr. -1-k). bds. 9.99 *(978-1-934650-77-6(3))* Just For Kids Pr., LLC.

—Dinosaurs. Doherty, Paula, illus. 2009. (Little Big Flap Bks.). 10p. (J). (gr. -1-k). 9.99 *(978-1-934650-24-0(2))* Just For Kids Pr., LLC.

Rechlin, Ted. ComicQuest TIME TRAVEL TROUBLE. 2013. (Dover Children's Activity Bks.). (ENG.). 48p. (J). (gr. 3-8). pap. 4.99 *(978-0-486-49949-9(9))* Dover Pubns., Inc.

Rees, Douglas. Tyrannosaurus Rex vs. Edna, the Very First Chicken. Henry, Jed, illus. 2017. (ENG.). 40p. (J). 17.99 ***(978-1-62779-510-4(3)***, 9781627795104, Holt, Henry & Co. Bks. For Young Readers) Holt, Henry & Co.

Reid, James. Dinosaur House, 1 vol. rev. ed. 2013. (Fiction Readers Ser.). (ENG., Illus.). 12p. (J). (gr. 1-1). pap. 4.99 *(978-1-4333-5459-5(4))*; pap. 12.96 *(978-1-4807-1138-9(1))* Shell Educational Publishing.

Reid, Julia. Could You Own a Dinosaur? 2008. 44p. pap. 24.95 *(978-1-60563-375-6(5))* America Star Bks.

Rey and others, Rey and. The Great Big Dinosaur Treasury. 2014. (ENG., Illus.). 272p. (J). (gr. -1-3). 18.99 *(978-0-544-32525-8(7)*, HMH Books For Young Readers) Houghton Mifflin Harcourt Publishing Co.

Rey, H. A. Curious George Museum Mystery (CGTV 8x8) 2017. (Curious George Ser.). (ENG., Illus.). 24p. (J). (gr. -1-3). 12.99 *(978-0-544-85992-0(8)*, HMH Books For Young Readers) Houghton Mifflin Harcourt Publishing Co.

RH Disney Staff. The Good Dinosaur Junior Novelization (Disney/Pixar the Good Dinosaur) RH Disney Staff, illus. 2015. (Junior Novel Ser.). (ENG., Illus.). 128p. (J). (gr. 4-7). 5.99 *(978-0-7364-3140-8(3)*, RH/Disney) Random Hse. Children's Bks.

—The Good Dinosaur Little Golden Book (Disney/Pixar the Good Dinosaur) RH Disney Staff, illus. 2015. (Little Golden Book Ser.). (ENG., Illus.). 24p. (J). (-k). 4.99 *(978-0-7364-3080-7(6)*, Golden/Disney) Random Hse. Children's Bks.

RH Disney Staff, et al. The Journey Home, Vol. 2. RH Disney Staff & Disney Storybook Art Team, illus. 2015. (Step into Reading Ser.). (ENG.). 24p. (J). (gr. -1-1). lib. bdg. 12.99 *(978-0-7364-8146-5(X)*, RH/Disney) Random Hse. Children's Bks.

Richler, Mordecai. Jacob Two-Two & the Dinosaur. Eyolfson, Norman, illus. 2004. (Jacob Two-Two Ser.). (ENG.). 96p. (J). (gr. 3-7). pap. 6.95 *(978-0-88776-712-8(5))* Tundra Bks. CAN. Dist: Random Hse., Inc.

—Jacob Two-Two & the Dinosaur. Petricic, Dusan, illus. 2009. (Jacob Two-Two Ser.). (ENG.). 104p. (J). (gr. 4-7). 10.95 *(978-0-88776-926-9(8))* Tundra Bks. CAN. Dist: Random Hse., Inc.

Richter, Dana, adapted by. Disney Dinosaur Play-a-sound. 15.98 *(978-0-7853-4190-1(0))* Publications International, Ltd.

Rigo, L., illus. Little Dinosaur. 2010. (Look at Me Bks.). (ENG.). 10p. (J). (gr. -1-k). bds. 8.99 *(978-0-7641-6356-2(6))* Barron's Educational Series, Inc.

Roberts, Daniel. Boy & Dinosaur. 2010. 86p. pap. 8.99 *(978-0-557-28024-7(9))* Lulu Pr., Inc.

—Harrison & His Dinosaur Robot & the Purple Spotted Sea Monster. 2012. 36p. pap. 20.99 *(978-1-4772-6979-4(7))* AuthorHouse.

Robinson, Donnell. Where's My L D ? 2008. 24p. pap. 12.95 *(978-1-4327-1825-1(8))* Outskirts Pr., Inc.

Rodenberg, Charlotte Vivian. Bronto, Friend of Ceratops. Rodenberg, Charlotte Vivian, illus. 2013. (ENG., Illus.). 32p. (J). 14.99 *(978-0-9844422-9-4(4))* Craigmore Creations.

Rossacci, Jacob. Dinosaurs Live Together. 2003. (J). 8.95 *(978-1-932205-14-5(4))* Word Association Pubs.

Rouse, Betty Munn. The Adventures of the Phillyfab Family. 2011. 68p. pap. 12.95 *(978-1-4567-3005-5(3))* AuthorHouse.

Roy, Ron. The Talking T. Rex. Gurney, John Steven, illus. 2003. (to Z Mysteries Ser.: 20). (gr. 3-6). lib. bdg. 14.75 *(978-0-613-85127-5(7)*, Turtleback) Turtleback Bks.

Sale, Carolyn. How to Read a Dinosaur & Other Museum Tales. Dubinsky, Lon, ed. 2004. (Illus.). 96p. *(978-1-895766-27-1(3)*, Pacific Educational Pr.) Univ. of British Columbia Pr.

Salmon, Michael. Dinosaur. 2006. (Illus.). 32p. (J). *(978-1-74178-213-4(9))* Bonnier Publishing Australia.

Sanders, Addie Meyer. I Don't Want to Go. Lt. ed. 2012. 43p. (J). pap. *(978-1-4596-3449-7(7))* ReadHowYouWant.com, Ltd.

Sauer, Drake & Sauer, Katheryn. Betsy the Brachiosaurus. 2012. 32p. pap. *(978-1-105-68969-7(7))* Lulu.com.

Sayres, Brianna Caplan. Tiara Saurus Rex. Boldt, Mike, illus. 2015. (ENG.). 32p. (J). (gr. -1-1). 16.99 *(978-1-61963-263-9(2)*, 9781619632639, Bloomsbury USA Childrens) Bloomsbury Publishing USA.

Schachner, Judy. Skippyjon Jones & the Big Bones. 2007. (Skippyjon Jones Ser.). (ENG.). 40p. (J). (gr. -1-k). 17.99 *(978-0-525-47884-3(1)*, Dutton Books for Young Readers) Penguin Young Readers Group.

Schmidt, Bryan Thomas. Abraham Lincoln Dinosaur Hunter. 2013. 80p. pap. 5.99 *(978-1-61941-054-1(0))* Delabarre Publishing.

Schneider, John Lee. Extinction: Dragons of Earth: A Novel. 2005. 173p. (YA). pap. *(978-1-890109-79-0(7)*, Cross Time) Crossquarter Publishing Group.

Schnetzler, Pattie. Ten Little Dinosaurs. Harris, Jim, illus. 2013. (ENG.). 26p. (J). 12.99 *(978-1-4494-4160-9(2))* Andrews McMeel Publishing.

—Ten Little Dinosaurs. Harris, Jim, illus. 2015. (ENG.). 24p. (J). bds. 9.99 *(978-1-4494-6491-2(2))* Andrews McMeel Publishing.

Schultz, Aronka. A Dinosaur on the Loose. 2010. 32p. pap. 12.99 *(978-1-4520-4400-2(7))* AuthorHouse.

Sciarra, John. Shoestrings-Paradox. 2006. (Illus.). 128p. (J). per. 14.95 *(978-0-9769555-1-6(2))* Wild Animal Publishing.

Scollon, Bill. Disney*Pixar the Good Dinosaur Movie Theater Storybook & Movie Projector. 2015. (Movie Theater Ser.: 13). (ENG.). 32p. (J). (gr. -1-1). 19.99 *(978-0-7944-3137-2(2)*, Reader's Digest Children's Bks.) Studio Fun International.

Sharfe, Elaine. There's a Dinosaur in My Room. Share, Brian, illus. 2005. 20p. (J). pap. 7.95 *(978-1-894601-05-4(X))* Chestnut Publishing Group CAN. Dist: Hushion Hse. Publishing, Ltd.

Sharkey, Niamh. Santasaurus. Sharkey, Niamh, illus. (ENG., Illus.). 32p. (J). (gr. -1-2). 2008. pap. 3.99 *(978-0-7636-3890-0(0))* 2005. 15.99 *(978-0-7636-2671-6(6))* Candlewick Pr.

Sharp, Anne, illus. Pop-up Dinosaur Danger! 2007. (ENG.). 10p. 28.95 *(978-1-4050-5332-7(1)*, Macmillan) Pan Macmillan GBR. Dist: Trans-Atlantic Pubns., Inc.

Shea, Bob. Dinosaur vs. Bedtime. Shea, Bob, illus. (Dinosaur vs. Book Ser.). (ENG., Illus.). (J). (gr. -1-k). 2011. 30p. bds. 6.99 *(978-1-4231-3788-7(4))* 2008. 40p. 16.99 *(978-1-4231-1335-5(7))* Hyperion Pr.

—Dinosaur vs. Mommy. Shea, Bob, illus. 2015. (Dinosaur vs. Book Ser.). (ENG., Illus.). 40p. (J). (gr. -1-k). 16.99 *(978-1-4231-6086-1(X))* Hyperion Bks. for Children.

—Dinosaur vs. Mommy Board Book. Shea, Bob, illus. 2017. (Dinosaur vs. Book Ser.). (ENG., Illus.). 32p. (J). (gr. -1-k). bds. 7.99 *(978-1-4231-6315-2(X))* Hyperion Bks. for Children.

—Dinosaur vs. Santa. Shea, Bob, illus. 2014. (Dinosaur vs. Book Ser.). (ENG., Illus.). 30p. (J). (gr. -1-k). bds. 7.99 *(978-1-4231-6824-9(0))* Hyperion Bks. for Children.

—Dinosaur vs. School. Shea, Bob, illus. (Dinosaur vs. Book Ser.). (ENG., Illus.). (J). (gr. -1-k). 2016. 32p. bds. 7.99 *(978-1-4231-6094-6(0))* 2014. 40p. 16.99 *(978-1-4231-6087-8(8))* Hyperion Bks. for Children.

—Dinosaur vs. the Library. Shea, Bob, illus. 2011. (ENG., Illus.). 40p. (J). (gr. -1-1). 16.99 *(978-1-4231-3338-4(2))* Hyperion Pr.

—Dinosaur vs. the Potty. Shea, Bob, illus. 2012. (ENG., Illus.). 30p. (J). (gr. -1-1). bds. 6.99 *(978-1-4231-5179-1(8))* Hyperion Pr.

—Kid Sheriff & the Terrible Toads. Smith, Lane, illus. 2014. (ENG.). 32p. (J). (gr. -1-3). 17.99 *(978-1-59643-975-7(0)*, 9781596439757) Roaring Brook Pr.

Shealy, Dennis. I'm a T. Rex! Biggs, Brian, illus. 2010. (Little Golden Book Ser.). (ENG.). 24p. (J). (gr. -1-2). 4.99 *(978-0-375-85806-2(7)*, Golden Bks.) Random Hse. Children's Bks.

Sher, Edie & Scollon, Bill. The Journey Home, No. 2. RH Disney Staff & Disney Storybook Art Team, illus. 2015. (Step into Reading Ser.). (ENG.). 24p. (J). (gr. -1-1). 4.99 *(978-0-7364-3093-7(8)*, RH/Disney) Random Hse. Children's Bks.

Sherry, Kevin. Monsters on the Run. 2015. (Yeti Files Ser.: 2). (ENG., Illus.). 128p. (J). (gr. 2-5). 8.99 *(978-0-545-55619-4(8)*, Scholastic Pr.) Scholastic, Inc.

Shields, Carol Diggory. Saturday Night at the Dinosaur Stomp. Nash, Scott, illus. 2008. (ENG.). 32p. (J). (gr. -1-3). pap. 6.99 *(978-0-7636-3887-0(0))* Candlewick Pr.

—Saturday Night at the Dinosaur Stomp. 2008. (gr. k-3). 17.20 *(978-0-613-74752-3(6)*, Turtleback) Turtleback Bks.

Shields, Kathleen J. Hamilton Troll Meets Dinosaurs. Klug, Leigh A. & Bryant, Carol W., illus. 6th ed. 2013. 36p. 14.00 *(978-0-9882745-5-6(8))* Erin Go Bragh Publishing.

Shioya, Hitoshi. Dinosaur Hour, Vol. 1. 2009. (ENG.). 200p. (J). pap. 7.99 *(978-1-4215-2648-5(4))* Viz Media.

Sibbick, John. My Favorite Dinosaurs. 2005. (ENG., Illus.). 32p. (J). (gr. -1-3). 16.95 *(978-1-59687-180-9(6))* IBks., Inc.

Sierra, Judy. Suppose You Meet a Dinosaur: A First Book of Manners. 2016. lib. bdg. 18.40 *(978-0-606-38459-9(6))* Turtleback Bks.

—Suppose You Meet a Dinosaur: a First Book of Manners. Bowers, Tim, illus. 2016. (ENG.). 40p. (J). (gr. -1-2). 7.99 *(978-1-101-93250-6(3)*, Dragonfly Bks.) Random Hse. Children's Bks.

Signore, Marco. Growing up in the Cretaceous: Scipionyx. Bacchin, Matteo, illus. 2009. (Dinosaurs: Ser.). (ENG.). 64p. (J). (gr. 3-9). 15.95 *(978-0-7892-1012-8(6)*, Abbeville Kids) Abbeville Pr., Inc.

—The Hunting Pack: Allosaurus. Bacchin, Matteo, illus. 2009. (Dinosaurs: Ser.). (ENG.). 64p. (J). (gr. 4-9). 15.95 *(978-0-7892-1011-1(8)*, Abbeville Kids) Abbeville Pr., Inc.

Silva, Sadie. Different Kinds of Communities: Putting Data in Order. 2017. (Computer Science for the Real World Ser.). 16p. (gr. 7-8). pap. 7.95 ***(978-1-5383-5198-7(6)***, Rosen Classroom) Rosen Publishing Group, Inc., The.

Silver Dolphin en Español Editors. Un Dia con los Dinosaurios. 2006. (Magnets on the Move Ser.). (Illus.). 8p. (J). (gr. -1). bds. *(978-970-718-369-8(1)*, Silver Dolphin en Español) Advanced Marketing, S. de R. L. de C. V.

—Dinosaurios. 2005. (Mezcla y Diviertete Ser.). (SPA., Illus.). 5p. (J). *(978-970-718-292-9(X)*, Silver Dolphin en Español) Advanced Marketing, S. de R. L. de C. V.

Silverthorne, Judith. Dinosaur Blackout, 1 vol. 2008. (Dinosaur Adventure Ser.). (ENG.). 240p. (J). (gr. 4-7). 8.95 *(978-1-55050-375-3(8))* Coteau Bks. CAN. Dist: Orca Bk. Pubs. USA.

—Dinosaur Breakout, 1 vol. 2004. (Dinosaur Adventure Ser.). (ENG.). 208p. (J). (gr. 4-7). pap. 6.95 *(978-1-55050-294-7(8))* Coteau Bks. CAN. Dist: Orca Bk. Pubs. USA.

—Dinosaur Stakeout, 1 vol. 2003. (Dinosaur Adventure Ser.). (ENG.). 192p. (J). (gr. 4-7). per. 7.95 *(978-1-55050-344-9(8))* Coteau Bks. CAN. Dist: Orca Bk. Pubs. USA.

Silverthorne, Judith & Coteau Books Staff. Dinosaur Hideout, 1 vol. 2006. (Dinosaur Adventure Ser.). (ENG.). 220p. (J). (gr. 4-7). pap. 6.95 *(978-1-55050-226-8(3))* Coteau Bks. CAN. Dist: Orca Bk. Pubs. USA.

Simonson, Walter & Englehart, Steve. Jurassic Park. 2013. (Jurassic Park Ser.: 10). 32p. (J). (gr. 4-8). lib. bdg. 242.10 *(978-1-61479-182-9(1))* Spotlight.

Sís, Peter. Dinosaur! Sís, Peter, illus. 2005. (ENG., Illus.). 28p. (J). (gr. -1-1). bds. 7.99 *(978-0-06-075967-4(4)*, Greenwillow Bks.) HarperCollins Pubs.

Skofield, James. Detective Dinosaur Undercover. Alley, R. W., illus. 2010. (I Can Read Level 2 Ser.). (ENG.). 48p. (J). (gr. -1-3). 16.99 *(978-0-06-623878-4(1))*; pap. 3.99 *(978-0-06-444319-7(1))* HarperCollins Pubs.

Skvarch, Angela & Skvarch, Jeffrey. Dinosaurs in Space. 2004. 48p. (J). per. 9.95 *(978-1-932560-35-0(1))* Aeon Publishing Inc.

Skwara, Maike Lena. Diogo the Little Dinosaur. Barr, Bailey, illus. 2013. 28p. (J). *(978-0-89985-475-5(3))* R. H. Publishing.

Slack, Michael. Shorty & Clem. Slack, Michael, illus. 2017. (Illus.). 40p. (J). (gr. -1-3). 17.99 *(978-0-06-242158-6(1))* HarperCollins Pubs.

Smith, Greg Leitich. Borrowed Time. 2015. (ENG., Illus.). 192p. (J). (gr. 5-7). 16.99 *(978-0-544-23711-7(0))* Houghton Mifflin Harcourt Publishing Co.

—Chronal Engine. Henry, Blake, illus. 2013. (ENG.). 192p. (J). (gr. 5-7). pap. 6.99 *(978-0-544-02277-5(7))* Houghton Mifflin Harcourt Publishing Co.

Smith, Michael. Thomas the T. Rex: The Journey of a Young Dinosaur to Los Angeles. Roski, Gayle Garner, illus. 2011. (J). *(978-0-9832278-4-7(5))*; 44p. (gr. 3-5). 19.95 *(978-0-9821675-3-3(9))* East West Discovery Pr.

Smith, Michael & Roski, Gayle Garner. Thomas the T. Rex: The Journey of a Young Dinosaur to Los Angeles. Roski, Gayle Garner, illus. 2011. (SPA & ENG., Illus.). (J). *(978-0-9832278-2-3(9))* East West Discovery Pr.

Smith, Nerissia. Prince de'Mario's Adventure, 1 vol. Dartes, Staci, illus. 2009. 29p. pap. 24.95 *(978-1-61582-972-9(5))* America Star Bks.

Soderberg, Erin. Dinosaur Dig, 1 vol. 2013. (Scooby-Doo! Picture Clue Bks.). (ENG.). 24p. (J). (gr. -1-1). lib. bdg. 24.21 *(978-1-61479-037-2(X)*, Essential Library) ABDO Publishing Co.

Sollinger, Emily. Dare to Repair! 2016. (Dinotrux 8X8 Ser.). (J). lib. bdg. 13.55 *(978-0-606-38318-9(2))* Turtleback Bks.

—Dinotrux: Dare to Repair! 2016. (ENG., Illus.). 24p. (J). (gr. -1-3). pap. 3.99 *(978-0-316-26082-4(7))* Little, Brown Bks. for Young Readers.

—Dinotrux: Dinotrux to the Rescue! 2016. (Passport to Reading Level 1 Ser.). (ENG., Illus.). 32p. (J). (gr. -1-3). pap. 3.99 *(978-0-316-26078-7(9))* Little, Brown Bks. for Young Readers.

—Dinotrux: Just Hatched! 2016. (ENG., Illus.). 10p. (J). (gr. -1 — 1). bds. 6.99 *(978-0-316-26080-0(0))* Little, Brown Bks. for Young Readers.

—Dinotrux to the Rescue! 2016. (Dinotrux Passport Reading Level 1 Ser.). (J). lib. bdg. 13.55 *(978-0-606-38320-2(4))* Turtleback Bks.

Sperring, Mark. Dino-Baby. Lloyd, Sam, illus. 2013. (ENG.). 32p. (J). (gr. -1-1). 14.99 *(978-1-61963-151-9(2)*, 9781619631519); lib. bdg. 15.89 *(978-1-61963-152-6(0)*, 9781619631526) Bloomsbury Publishing USA. (Bloomsbury USA Childrens).

—Dino-Daddy. Lloyd, Sam, illus. 2015. (ENG.). 32p. (J). (gr. -1-1). 18.99 *(978-1-4088-4969-9(0)*, 9781408849699, Bloomsbury USA Childrens) Bloomsbury Publishing USA.

Staniszewski, Anna. Dogosaurus Rex. Hawkes, Kevin, illus. 2017. (ENG.). 40p. (J). 17.99 *(978-0-8050-9706-1(6)*, 9780805097061, Holt, Henry & Co. Bks. For Young Readers) Holt, Henry & Co.

Stapley, Giles. Plinktus, the Little Pink Dinosaur. 2010. 84p. pap. 23.50 *(978-1-60911-796-2(4)*, Eloquent Bks.) Strategic Book Publishing & Rights Agency (SBPRA).

Stark, Barbara. Blue Dinosaur's Friends. l.t. ed. 2006. (Illus.). 24p. (J). E-Book 9.95 incl. cd-rom *(978-1-933090-20-7(0))* Guardian Angel Publishing, Inc.

Stein, David Ezra. Dinosaur Kisses. Stein, David Ezra, illus. (ENG., Illus.). (J). (-k). 2014. 34p. bds. 6.99 *(978-0-7636-7389-5(7))* 2013. 32p. 15.99 *(978-0-7636-6104-5(X))* Candlewick Pr.

Steinberg, Laya. Thesaurus Rex. Harter, Debbie, illus. (ENG.). 24p. (J). 2005. (gr. -1-2). pap. 6.99 *(978-1-84148-180-7(7))* 2003. 15.99 *(978-1-84148-042-8(8))* Barefoot Bks., Inc.

—Thesaurus Rex Finds a Friend. Harter, Debbie, illus. 2006. (J). *(978-1-905236-48-0(4))* Barefoot Bks., Inc.

Stevens, Jane. Walking with Dinosaurs: A Reusable Sticker Book. 2013. (Walking with Dinosaurs Ser.). (ENG.). 12p. (J). (gr. -1-3). pap. 6.99 *(978-0-06-223280-9(0)*, HarperFestival) HarperCollins Pubs.

Stilton, Geronimo. Dinosaurs in Action. Cooper-McGuinness, Nanette, tr. from ITA. 2011. (Geronimo Stilton Graphic Novels Ser.). (ENG., Illus.). 56p. (J). (gr. 2-6). 9.99 *(978-1-59707-239-7(7)*, 9781597072397) Papercutz.

—Journey Through Time. 2014. (Geronimo Stilton Special Edition Ser.). (ENG.). 320p. (J). (gr. 2-5). 14.99 *(978-0-545-55623-1(6)*, Scholastic Paperbacks) Scholastic, Inc.

—Valley of the Giant Skeletons. 2008. (Illus.). 111p. (J). lib. bdg. 15.38 *(978-1-4242-4303-7(3))* Fitzgerald Bks.

—Valley of the Giant Skeletons. 2008. (Geronimo Stilton Ser.). (Illus.). 110p. (gr. 2-5). 17.00 *(978-0-7569-8805-0(5))* Perfection Learning Corp.

—Valley of the Giant Skeletons. 2008. (Geronimo Stilton Ser.: 32). (ENG., Illus.). 128p. (J). (gr. 2-5). pap. 7.99 *(978-0-545-02132-6(4)*, Scholastic Paperbacks) Scholastic, Inc.

—Valley of the Giant Skeletons. 2008. (Geronimo Stilton Ser.: 32). lib. bdg. 18.40 *(978-1-4364-2713-5(4))* Turtleback Bks.

Stimson, Joan. The Dinosaur Next Door. 2009. (ENG., Illus.). 24p. (J). pap. *(978-0-7787-3904-3(X))*; lib. bdg. *(978-0-7787-3873-2(6))* Crabtree Publishing Co.

Stockton, Frank Richard. A Jolly Fellowship. 2008. 168p. 26.95 *(978-1-60664-873-5(X))*; pap. 13.95 *(978-1-60664-120-0(4))* Aegypan.

Stone, Jamie, ed. Danny Dino Ventures Out. 2013. (Pop-Up: Play & Listen Ser.). (ENG., Illus.). 10p. (J). (gr. -1-k). bds. 16.95 *(978-1-61889-034-4(4))* AZ Bks. LLC.

Storm, Zed. Will Solvit & the T-Rex Terror. 2010. (Will Solvit Ser.: Bk. 1). (Illus.). 128p. (J). (gr. 1-7). pap. *(978-1-4075-8982-4(2))* Parragon, Inc.

Strathie, Chae. Dear Dinosaur: With Real Letters to Read! O'Byrne, Nicola, illus. 2017. (ENG.). 28p. (J). (gr. -1-3). 11.99 ***(978-0-7641-6898-7(3))*** Barron's Educational Series, Inc.

Strong, Jeremy. Dinosaur Pox. Sharratt, Nick, illus. (ENG.). 128p. (J). 7.95 *(978-0-14-038979-1(2))* Penguin Bks., Ltd. GBR. Dist: Trafalgar Square Publishing.

Suen, Anastasia. Dino Hunt: A Robot & Rico Story. Laughead, Mike, illus. 2010. (Robot & Rico Ser.). (ENG.). 32p. (gr. 1-2). pap. 6.25 *(978-1-4342-2300-5(0))* Stone Arch Bks.

—We're Going on a Dinosaur Dig. Myer, Ed, illus. 2012. (ENG.). 24p. (gr. k-1). pap. 8.95 *(978-1-61810-299-7(0))* Rourke Educational Media.

Suhay, Lisa. Haddy the Doorstopasaurus: North America's First Dinosaur. 2003. 160p. 5.95 *(978-0-9679227-8-2(X)*, 329-006) Franklin Mason Pr.

Surgal, Jon. Have You Seen My Dinosaur? Mathieu, Joe, illus. 2010. (Beginner Books(R) Ser.). (ENG.). 48p. (J). (gr. -1-1). 9.99 *(978-0-375-85639-6(0)*, Random Hse. Bks. for Young Readers) Random Hse. Children's Bks.

Surplice, Holly. About a Bear. Surplice, Holly, illus. 2012. (ENG., Illus.). 32p. (J). *(978-1-58925-112-0(1))* Tiger Tales.

Suzuki, Mamoru. You Belong to Me. 2016. (ENG.). 32p. (J). (gr. -1-k). 12.99 *(978-1-940842-12-7(3))* Museyon.

Tagel, Peggy, illus. Dinosaurs. 2003. (Squishy Shapes Ser.). 10p. (J). 12.95 *(978-1-57145-740-0(2)*, Silver Dolphin Bks.) Readerlink Distribution Services, LLC.

Tanksley, David. Michael Waylon & His Dinosaur Crew. 2012. 24p. pap. 24.95 *(978-1-62709-763-5(5))* America Star Bks.

Taylor, Dereen. Journey to the World of the Dinosaurs: Peek Inside the Pop-Up Windows! Kavanagh, Peter, illus. 2014. (ENG.). 12p. (J). (gr. 2-7). 16.99 *(978-1-86147-319-6(2)*, Armadillo) Anness Publishing GBR. Dist: National Bk. Network.

Teacher Created Resources Staff & Collins, Susan. A Guide for Using Time Soldiers in the Classroom. 2009. (ENG.). 48p. pap. 9.99 *(978-1-4206-2003-0(7))* Teacher Created Resources, Inc.

Tengan, G. Shay. Marching Dinosaur Parade. 2012. (Illus.). 60p. 17.99 *(978-0-9883478-0-9(6))* Tengan, G. Shay Service Group.

Tennapel, Doug. Tommysaurus Rex. 2013. lib. bdg. 22.10 *(978-0-606-31965-2(4)*, Turtleback) Turtleback Bks.

Thaler, Mike. The School Bus Driver from the Black Lagoon, 1 vol. Lee, Jared, illus. 2012. (Black Lagoon Set 2 Ser.: No. 2). (ENG.). 32p. (J). (gr. 1-4). lib. bdg. 24.21 *(978-1-59961-957-6(1))* Spotlight.

Thomas, Rob. Boom! Boom! Boom! There's a Dinosaur in My Room! 2013. 26p. pap. 9.99 *(978-0-9910560-1-9(9))* Lincoln Bks.

Thomson, Ruth. Dinosaur's Day. 2009. (DK Readers Ser.). (ENG.). 32p. (J). (gr. k-2). 3.99 *(978-0-7566-5585-3(4)*, DK Children) Dorling Kindersley Publishing, Inc.

Thorold, Jade Melissa. The Dirty Dinosaur. 2010. 28p. pap. 15.99 *(978-1-4500-6483-5(3))* Xlibris Corp.

Thorsen, Jody & Gates, Jeremy S. The Boy Who Cried Dinosaur. 2012. 24p. pap. 15.99 *(978-1-4771-0990-8(0))* Xlibris Corp.

Ticktock Media, Ltd. Staff. Dinosaurs. 2009. (Animal Fun Touch & Feel Ser.). (ENG.). 10p. (J). (gr. -1-k). bds. 4.95 *(978-1-84696-829-7(1)*, TickTock Books) Octopus Publishing Group GBR. Dist: Independent Pubs. Group.

Tillworth, Mary. Zeg & the Egg. Foley, Niki, illus. 2016. 18p. (J). ***(978-1-4806-9878-9(4))*** Random Hse., Inc.

Time Soldiers Book: Rex. 2003. tchr. ed. *(978-1-929945-30-6(2))* Big Guy Bks., Inc.

Time Soldiers Book Vol. 2: Rex 2. 2003. tchr. ed. *(978-1-929945-31-3(0))* Big Guy Bks., Inc.

Tinyrannosaurus & the Bigfootosaurus. 2015. (ENG., Illus.). 24p. (J). (gr. -1-3). 19.99 *(978-1-85733-735-8(2))*; 7.99 *(978-1-85733-734-1(4))* Lerner Publishing Group.

Todd, John S. The Goodfellow Boys & the Talking Dinosaur. 2004. (Illus.). 32p. (gr. 3-5). 10.95 *(978-1-57197-190-6(4))* Pentland Pr., Inc.

Torres, Daniel. Tom Tu Gran Amigo: Juega al Fútbol, Vol. 5. 2005. (SPA., Illus.). 32p. 17.95 *(978-1-59497-120-4(X))* Public Square Bks.

—Tom Tu Gran Amigo Vol. 6: Descubre el Carnaval. 2005. (SPA., Illus.). 32p. 17.95 *(978-1-59497-121-1(8))* Public Square Bks.

—Tom Tu Gran Amigo en Paris, Vol. 4. 2005. (Tom Ser.). (SPA., Illus.). 32p. (J). (gr. -1-4). 19.95 *(978-1-59497-119-8(6))* Public Square Bks.

Toufexis, George. MONSTER MASH-Up — Dinosaurs Face Destruction. 2012. (Dover Coloring Bks.). (ENG.). 48p. (J). (gr. 3-8). pap. 4.99 *(978-0-486-48950-6(7))* Dover Pubns., Inc.

Trigg, Michael J. Greanwold & the Mystery Cave: Greanwold & the Minosaurs Story Books. 2013. 148p. pap. 12.97 *(978-1-61897-466-2(1)*, Strategic Bk. Publishing) Strategic Book Publishing & Rights Agency (SBPRA).

Trotter, Bob. Up the Wooden Hill: Bedtime Stories for Little Ones. Edgar, Barrie, illus. 2011. 98p. pap. 17.99 *(978-1-60976-139-4(1)*, Eloquent Bks.) Strategic Book Publishing & Rights Agency (SBPRA).

Tuma, Refe & Tuma, Susan. What the Dinosaurs Did at School. 2017. (What the Dinosaurs Did Ser.: 2). (ENG., Illus.). 40p. (J). (gr. -1-3). 17.99 ***(978-0-316-55289-9(5))*** Little, Brown Bks. for Young Readers.

Tuma, Refe & Tuma, Susan. What the Dinosaurs Did Last Night: A Very Messy Adventure. 2015. (What the Dinosaurs Did Ser.: 1). (ENG., Illus.). 40p. (J). (gr. -1-1). 17.00 *(978-0-316-33562-1(2))* Little Brown & Co.

Viorst, Judith. Lulu & the Brontosaurus. Smith, Lane, illus. (ENG.). 128p. (J). (gr. 1-5). 2012. pap. 7.99 *(978-1-4169-9962-1(0))* 2010. 17.99 *(978-1-4169-9961-4(2))* Simon & Schuster Children's Publishing. (Atheneum Bks. for Young Readers).

—Lulu & the Brontosaurus. 2012. (Lulu Ser.: 1). lib. bdg. 18.40 *(978-0-606-23676-8(7)*, Turtleback) Turtleback Bks.

Waddell, Martin. The Super Hungry Dinosaur. Lord, Leonie, illus. 2009. (ENG.). 32p. (J). (gr. -1-k). 17.99 *(978-0-8037-3446-3(8)*, Dial Bks) Penguin Young Readers Group.

—The Super Swooper Dinosaur. Lord, Leonie, illus. 2013. (J). *(978-1-4351-5000-3(7))* Barnes & Noble, Inc.

Wahl, Jan. I Met a Dinosaur. Sheban, Chris, illus. 2015. (ENG.). 32p. (J). (gr. 1-3). 17.99 *(978-1-56846-233-2(6)*, Creative Editions) Creative Co., The.

Waite, Judy. Digging for Dinosaurs. Parsons, Garry, illus. 2003. (Flying Foxes Ser.). (ENG.). 48p. (J). lib. bdg. *(978-0-7787-1483-5(7))* Crabtree Publishing Co.

Walsh, Joanna & Abbot, Judi. I Love Dad. 2016. (ENG., Illus.). 32p. (J). (gr. -1-3). 17.99 *(978-1-4814-6266-2(0)*, Simon & Schuster/Paula Wiseman Bks.) Simon & Schuster/Paula Wiseman Bks.

Warner, Gertrude Chandler, creator. The Mystery of the Stolen Dinosaur Bones. 2015. (Boxcar Children Mysteries Ser.: 139). (ENG., Illus.). 128p. (J). (gr. 1-5). 15.99 *(978-0-8075-5608-5(4))* Whitman, Albert & Co.

Watt, F. & Wells, R. That's Not My Dinosaur... It's Body Is Too Squashy. 2004. (Touchy-Feely Board Bks.). (SPA & ENG., Illus.). 1p. (J). (gr. -1-18). bds. 7.95 *(978-0-7945-0129-7(X)*, Usborne) EDC Publishing.

Watt, Fiona. That's Not My Dragon. rev. ed. 2011. (Touchy-Feely Board Bks). 10p. (J). ring bd. 8.99 *(978-0-7945-3092-1(3)*, Usborne) EDC Publishing.

Watterson, Michelle. My Pet Dinosaur. 2012. 24p. pap. 28.03 *(978-1-4771-4496-1(X))* Xlibris Corp.

Webster, Wendy. Magicus Perfecticum. 2009. (Illus.). 60p. pap. 11.49 *(978-1-4490-0765-2(1))* AuthorHouse.

Wehrmeijer, Annelien. Jacob & Rex. van de Liejgraaf, Deborah, illus. 2014. (My Best Friend & Me Ser.). (ENG.). 10p. (J). (gr. -1 — 1). bds. 7.99 *(978-0-7641-6663-1(8))* Barron's Educational Series, Inc.

Weinberg, Steven. Rex Finds an Egg! Egg! Egg! Weinberg, Steven, illus. 2015. (ENG., Illus.). 40p. (J). (gr. -1-3). 17.99 *(978-1-4814-0308-5(7)*, McElderry, Margaret K. Bks.) McElderry, Margaret K. Bks.

Wells, Mark & Wells, Meagan. Tommy's Lost Tooth. Wells, Mark, illus. 2011. (Illus.). 28p. pap. 11.99 *(978-1-61170-020-6(5))* Robertson Publishing.

Wesolick, Trenton. Why the Life of a Dinosaur Is Hard. 2013. 24p. pap. 14.95 *(978-1-4669-8233-8(0))* Trafford Publishing.

Weston Woods Staff, creator. How Do Dinosaurs Eat Their Food? 2011. 38.75 *(978-0-439-02740-3(3))*; 18.95 *(978-0-439-02748-9(9))* Weston Woods Studios, Inc.

—How Do Dinosaurs Get Well Soon? 2011. 29.95 *(978-0-439-76689-0(3))*; 38.75 *(978-0-439-84622-6(6))*; 18.95 *(978-0-439-84621-9(8))* Weston Woods Studios, Inc.

—How Do Dinosaurs Go to School? 2011. 38.75 *(978-0-545-19712-0(0))* Weston Woods Studios, Inc.

—T Is for Terrible. 2011. 38.75 *(978-0-545-11793-7(3))*; 18.95 *(978-0-545-11791-3(7))* Weston Woods Studios, Inc.

Wheeler, Lisa. Dino-Baseball. Gott, Barry, illus. 2010. (ENG.). 32p. (J). (gr. k-3). lib. bdg. 16.95 *(978-0-7613-4429-2(2)*, Carolrhoda Bks.) Lerner Publishing Group.

—Dino-Basketball. Gott, Barry, illus. 2011. (Carolrhoda Picture Bks.). (ENG.). 32p. (J). (gr. k-3). 16.95 *(978-0-7613-6393-4(9))* Lerner Publishing Group.

—Dino-Boarding. Gott, Barry, illus. 2014. (ENG.). 32p. (J). (gr. k-3). lib. bdg. 16.95 *(978-1-4677-0213-3(7)*, Carolrhoda Bks.) Lerner Publishing Group.

—Dino-Dancing. Gott, Barry, illus. 2017. (ENG.). 32p. (J). (gr. k-3). lib. bdg. 17.99 ***(978-1-5124-0316-9(4)***, Carolrhoda Bks.) Lerner Publishing Group.

—Dino-Football. Gott, Barry, illus. 2012. (Carolrhoda Picture Bks.). (ENG.). 32p. (J). (gr. k-3). lib. bdg. 16.95 *(978-0-7613-6394-1(7))* Lerner Publishing Group.

—Dino-Hockey. Gott, Barry, illus. 2007. (Carolrhoda Picture Bks.). (ENG.). 32p. (J). (gr. k-3). 16.95 *(978-0-8225-6191-0(3)*, Carolrhoda Bks.) Lerner Publishing Group.

—Dino-Racing. Gott, Barry, illus. 2016. (ENG.). 32p. (gr. k-3). (J). lib. bdg. 17.99 *(978-1-5124-0314-5(8))*; 35.99 *(978-1-5124-0886-7(7))* Lerner Publishing Group. (Carolrhoda Bks.).

—Dino-Soccer. Gott, Barry, illus. 2009. (Carolrhoda Picture Bks.). (ENG.). 32p. (J). (gr. k-3). 16.95 *(978-0-8225-9028-6(X))* Lerner Publishing Group.

—Dino-Swimming. Gott, Barry, illus. 2015. (ENG.). 32p. (J). (gr. k-3). 17.32 *(978-1-4677-8809-0(0))*; lib. bdg. 16.99 *(978-1-4677-0214-0(5))* Lerner Publishing Group. (Carolrhoda Bks.).

—Dino-Wrestling. Gott, Barry, illus. 2013. (ENG.). 32p. (J). (gr. k-3). 16.95 *(978-1-4677-0212-6(9)*, Carolrhoda Bks.) Lerner Publishing Group.

Whitmore, Andrew. Beast of the Jungle. 2007. 96p. (YA). pap. *(978-1-4207-0728-1(0))* Sundance/Newbridge Educational Publishing.

Whybrow, Ian. Harry & the Bucketful of Dinosaurs. Reynolds, Adrian, illus. 2010. (Harry & the Dinosaurs Ser.). (ENG.). 32p. (J). (gr. -1-2). pap. 7.99 *(978-0-375-85119-3(4)*, Dragonfly Bks.) Random Hse. Children's Bks.

—Harry & the Dinosaurs - The Flying Save! 2011. (Harry & the Dinosaurs Ser.). (ENG., Illus.). 128p. (J). (gr. 2-4). pap. 9.99 *(978-0-14-133281-9(6))* Penguin Bks., Ltd. GBR. Dist: Independent Pubs. Group.

—Harry & the Dinosaurs Go to School. Reynolds, Adrian, illus. 2015. (ENG.). 32p. (J). (gr. -1-2). 7.99 *(978-0-553-53400-9(9)*, Dragonfly Bks.) Random Hse. Children's Bks.

Whybrow, Ian, et al. Owain A'r Cloc. 2005. (WEL., Illus.). 20p. 6.99 *(978-1-84323-366-4(5))* Gomer Pr. GBR. Dist: Gomer Pr.

Wilhelm, Hans. Tyrone the Double Dirty Rotten Cheater. (FRE.). (J). pap. 6.99 *(978-0-590-74141-5(1))* Scholastic, Inc.

Wilkins, James Francis. The Queen & Mr Brown: A Day for Dinosaurs. 2015. (ENG., Illus.). 48p. (J). (gr. k-2). pap. 11.99 *(978-0-565-09354-9(1))* Natural History Museum Pubns. GBR. Dist: Independent Pubs. Group.

Willems, Mo. Edwina, the Dinosaur Who Didn't Know She Was Extinct. Willems, Mo, illus. 2006. (ENG., Illus.). 40p. (J). (gr. -1-k). 17.99 *(978-0-7868-3748-9(9))* Hyperion Pr.

—Goldilocks & the Three Dinosaurs. Willems, Mo, illus. 2012. (ENG., Illus.). 40p. (J). (gr. -1-2). 17.99 *(978-0-06-210418-2(7))* HarperCollins Pubs.

William H. Sadlier Staff. The Dinosaur Dance. 2005. (Emergent Library: Vol. 2). (gr. -1-1). 24.00 net. *(978-0-8215-8927-4(X))* Sadlier, William H. Inc.

Williams, Bonnie. Meet Teddy Rex! Gordon, John, illus. 2012. (Dino School Ser.). (ENG.). 24p. (J). (gr. -1-1). 15.99 *(978-1-4424-4996-1(9))*; pap. 3.99 *(978-1-4424-4995-4(0))* Simon Spotlight. (Simon Spotlight).

—Pete Can Fly! Gordon, John, illus. 2014. (Dino School Ser.). (ENG.). 24p. (J). (gr. -1-1). pap. 3.99 *(978-1-4814-0465-5(2)*, Simon Spotlight) Simon Spotlight.

Williams, Bonnie. Say Cheese, Teddy Rex! Gordon, John, illus. 2016. (Dino School Ser.). (J). (ENG.). 24p. (gr. -1-1). pap. 3.99 *(978-1-4814-6609-7(7))*; ***(978-1-5182-1896-5(2))*** Simon Spotlight. (Simon Spotlight).

Williams, Rozanne Lanczak. Writing Dino-Mite Poems. Adnet, Bernard, illus. 2006. (Learn to Write Ser.). 8p. (J). (gr. k-2). pap. 3.49 *(978-1-59198-285-2(5)*, 6179) Creative Teaching Pr., Inc.

Williams, Tracee, ed. Dinosaurs Write-with-Me Alphabet. 2011. (Write-with-Me Ser.). (ENG., Illus.). 10p. (J). 15.99 *(978-1-59069-922-5(X))* Studio Mouse LLC.

Willis, Jeanne. I'M Sure I Saw a Dinosaur. Reynolds, Adrian, illus. 2011. (Andersen Press Picture Books Ser.). 16.95 *(978-0-7613-8093-1(0))* Andersen Pr. GBR. Dist: Lerner Publishing Group.

Wilson, John. Bones, 1 vol. 2014. (Orca Currents Ser.). (ENG.). 128p. (J). (gr. 5-9). pap. 9.95 *(978-1-4598-0698-6(0))* Orca Bk. Pubs. USA.

C
D

Wishinsky, Frieda. Danger, Dinosaurs! Griffiths, Dean & Owlkids Books Inc. Staff, illus. 2007. (Canadian Flyer Adventures Ser.: 2). (ENG.). 96p. (J). (gr. 1-4). pap. 9.95 *(978-1-897066-82-9(1),* Owlkids) Owlkids Bks. Inc. CAN. Dist: Publishers Group West (PGW).

—Halifax Explodes! Lewis-MacDougall, Patricia Ann & Owlkids Books Inc. Staff, illus. 2011. (Canadian Flyer Adventures Ser.: 17). (ENG.). 96p. (J). (gr. 1-4). pap. 7.95 *(978-1-926818-98-6(9),* Maple Tree Pr.) Owlkids Bks. Inc. CAN. Dist: Publishers Group West (PGW).

Wood, Carol. Grandma Carol's Book of Stories in Rhyme. 2009. (Illus.). 48p. pap. 19.49 *(978-1-4389-5413-4(1))* AuthorHouse.

Woodson, Marion. Dinosaur Fever. 2008. (ENG.). 160p. (J). (gr. 4). pap. 11.99 *(978-1-55002-690-0(9),* Sandcastle Bks.) Dundurn CAN. Dist: Ingram Publisher Services.

Wooster, Devin Ann. Big Dinosaur, Little Dinosaur. 2016. (Step into Reading Level 1 Ser.). lib. bdg. 14.75 *(978-0-606-38479-7(0))* Turtleback Bks.

Wrate, Richard. Din-o-mite in Aarons Closet. 2009. 28p. (J). 14.99 *(978-0-615-19210-9(6))* Show n' Tell Publishing.

Wrecks, Billy & Shealy, Dennis. T. Rex Trouble! Random House Staff et al, illus. 2011. (Step into Reading Ser.). (ENG.). 32p. (J). (gr. -1-1). pap. 3.99 *(978-0-375-86777-4(5),* Random Hse. Bks. for Young Readers) Random Hse. Children's Bks.

Wyman, Dorothy. Kaysell the Dragon Pup. 2011. 28p. pap. 13.54 *(978-1-4269-4802-2(6))* Trafford Publishing.

Yasuda, Anita. The Beach Bandit, 1 vol. Harpster, Steve, illus. 2013. (Dino Detectives Ser.). (ENG.). 32p. (gr. 1-2). pap. 5.95 *(978-1-4342-4830-5(5));* lib. bdg. 22.65 *(978-1-4342-4154-2(8))* Stone Arch Bks.

—The Crazy Clues, 1 vol. Harpster, Steve, illus. 2013. (Dino Detectives Ser.). (ENG.). 32p. (gr. 1-2). lib. bdg. 22.65 *(978-1-4342-5971-4(4))* Stone Arch Bks.

—Crazy Clues. Harpster, Steve, illus. 2013. (Dino Detectives Ser.). (ENG.). 32p. (gr. 1-2). pap. 5.95 *(978-1-4342-6200-4(6))* Stone Arch Bks.

—Ghost Sounds, 1 vol. Harpster, Steve, illus. 2013. (Dino Detectives Ser.). (ENG.). 32p. (gr. 1-2). pap. 5.95 *(978-1-4342-4831-2(3));* lib. bdg. 22.65 *(978-1-4342-4152-8(1))* Stone Arch Bks.

—The Haunted House, 1 vol. Harpster, Steve, illus. 2013. (Dino Detectives Ser.). (ENG.). 32p. (gr. 1-2). lib. bdg. 22.65 *(978-1-4342-5970-7(6))* Stone Arch Bks.

—Haunted House. Harpster, Steve, illus. 2013. (Dino Detectives Ser.). (ENG.). 32p. (gr. 1-2). pap. 5.95 *(978-1-4342-6199-1(9))* Stone Arch Bks.

—The Missing Trumpet, 1 vol. Harpster, Steve, illus. 2013. (Dino Detectives Ser.). (ENG.). 32p. (gr. 1-2). pap. 5.95 *(978-1-4342-4832-9(1));* lib. bdg. 22.65 *(978-1-4342-4155-9(6))* Stone Arch Bks.

—The Mystery Coins, 1 vol. Harpster, Steve, illus. 2013. (Dino Detectives Ser.). (ENG.). 32p. (gr. 1-2). lib. bdg. 22.65 *(978-1-4342-5972-1(2))* Stone Arch Bks.

—Mystery Coins. Harpster, Steve, illus. 2013. (Dino Detectives Ser.). (ENG.). 32p. (gr. 1-2). pap. 5.95 *(978-1-4342-6201-1(4))* Stone Arch Bks.

—The Slime Attack, 1 vol. Harpster, Steve, illus. 2013. (Dino Detectives Ser.). (ENG.). 32p. (gr. 1-2). pap. 5.95 *(978-1-4342-4833-6(X));* lib. bdg. 22.65 *(978-1-4342-4153-5(X))* Stone Arch Bks.

—The Surprise Prize, 1 vol. Harpster, Steve, illus. 2013. (Dino Detectives Ser.). (ENG.). 32p. (gr. 1-2). lib. bdg. 22.65 *(978-1-4342-5969-1(2))* Stone Arch Bks.

—Surprise Prize. Harpster, Steve, illus. 2013. (Dino Detectives Ser.). (ENG.). 32p. (gr. 1-2). pap. 5.95 *(978-1-4342-6198-4(0))* Stone Arch Bks.

Yasuda, Anita & Harpster, Steve. The Crazy Clues. 2013. (Dino Detectives Ser.). (ENG.). 32p. (gr. 1-2). pap. 29.70 *(978-1-4342-6226-4(X))* Stone Arch Bks.

—The Haunted House. 2013. (Dino Detectives Ser.). (ENG.). 32p. (gr. 1-2). pap. 29.70 *(978-1-4342-6227-1(8))* Stone Arch Bks.

—The Mystery Coins. 2013. (Dino Detectives Ser.). (ENG.). 32p. (gr. 1-2). pap. 29.70 *(978-1-4342-6228-8(6))* Stone Arch Bks.

—The Surprise Prize. 2013. (Dino Detectives Ser.). (ENG.). 32p. (gr. 1-2). pap. 29.70 *(978-1-4342-6229-5(4))* Stone Arch Bks.

Yolen, Jane. ¿Cómo Aprenden los Colores los Dinosaurios? Teague, Mark, illus. 2006. (How Do Dinosaurs... Ser.).Tr. of How Do Dinosaurs Learn Their Colors? (SPA.). 12p. (J). (gr. -1-k). bds. 6.99 *(978-0-439-87192-1(1),* Scholastic en Espanol) Scholastic, Inc.

—¿Cómo Comen los Dinosaurios? Teague, Mark, illus. 2006. (How Do Dinosaurs... Ser.). (SPA.). 40p. (J). (gr. -1-k). pap. 6.99 *(978-0-439-76404-9(1),* Scholastic en Espanol) Scholastic, Inc.

—Como Dicen Estoy Enojado los Dinosaurios? Teague, Mark, illus. 2014. (SPA.). 40p. (J). (gr. -1-k). pap. 6.99 *(978-0-545-62780-1(X),* Scholastic en Espanol) Scholastic, Inc.

—How Do Dinosaurs Choose Their Pets? Teague, Mark, illus. 2016. (ENG.). 40p. (J). (gr. -1-k). 16.99 *(978-1-338-03278-9(X),* Blue Sky Pr., The) Scholastic, Inc.

—How Do Dinosaurs Clean Their Rooms? Teague, Mark, illus. 2004. (How Do Dinosaurs... Ser.). (ENG.). 12p. (J). (gr. -1-k). bds. 6.99 *(978-0-439-64950-6(1),* Blue Sky Pr., The) Scholastic, Inc.

—How Do Dinosaurs Count to Ten? Teague, Mark, illus. 2004. (How Do Dinosaurs... Ser.). (ENG.). 12p. (J). (gr. -1-k). bds. 6.99 *(978-0-439-64949-0(8),* Blue Sky Pr., The) Scholastic, Inc.

—How Do Dinosaurs Eat Cookies? Teague, Mark, illus. 2012. (How Do Dinosaurs... Ser.). (ENG.). 14p. (J). (gr. -1-k). bds. 7.99 *(978-0-545-38253-3(X),* Cartwheel Bks.) Scholastic, Inc.

—How Do Dinosaurs Eat Their Food? Teague, Mark, illus. 2005. (How Do Dinosaurs... ? Ser.). (ENG.). 40p. (J). (gr. -1-k). 16.99 *(978-0-439-24102-1(2),* Blue Sky Pr., The) Scholastic, Inc.

—How Do Dinosaurs Get Well Soon? Teague, Mark, illus. 2003. (How Do Dinosaurs... Ser.). (ENG.). 40p. (J). (gr. -1-3). 16.99 *(978-0-439-24100-7(6),* Blue Sky Pr., The) Scholastic, Inc.

—How Do Dinosaurs Go to School? Teague, Mark, illus. 2007. (How Do Dinosaurs... Ser.). (ENG.). 40p. (J). (gr. -1-k). 16.99 *(978-0-439-02081-7(6))* Scholastic, Inc.

—How Do Dinosaurs Go to School? Teague, Mark, illus. 2011. (J). (gr. -1-3). 18.95 *(978-0-545-19707-6(4));* 29.95 *(978-0-545-19700-7(7))* Weston Woods Studios, Inc.

—How Do Dinosaurs Go to Sleep? Teague, Mark, illus. 2016. (How Do Dinosaurs... ? Ser.). (ENG.). 12p. (J). (— 1). bds. 6.99 *(978-0-545-94120-4(2),* Blue Sky Pr., The) Scholastic, Inc.

—How Do Dinosaurs Laugh Out Loud? Teague, Mark, illus. 2010. (How Do Dinosaurs... Ser.). (ENG.). 16p. (J). (gr. -1-k). bds. 7.99 *(978-0-545-23652-2(5),* Cartwheel Bks.) Scholastic, Inc.

—How Do Dinosaurs Learn Their Colors? Teague, Mark, illus. 2006. (How Do Dinosaurs... Ser.). (ENG.). 12p. (J). (gr. -1-k). bds. 6.99 *(978-0-439-85653-9(1),* Blue Sky Pr., The) Scholastic, Inc.

—How Do Dinosaurs Love Their Cats? Teague, Mark, illus. 2010. (How Do Dinosaurs... ? Ser.). (ENG.). 6p. (J). (gr. -1-k). bds. 6.99 *(978-0-545-15354-6(9))* Scholastic, Inc.

—How Do Dinosaurs Love Their Dogs? Teague, Mark, illus. 2010. (How Do Dinosaurs... ? Ser.). (ENG.). 6p. (J). (gr. -1-k). bds. 6.99 *(978-0-545-15352-2(2))* Scholastic, Inc.

—How Do Dinosaurs Play with Their Friends? Teague, Mark, illus. 2006. (How Do Dinosaurs... Ser.). (ENG.). 12p. (J). (gr. -1-k). bds. 6.99 *(978-0-439-85654-6(X),* Blue Sky Pr., The) Scholastic, Inc.

—How Do Dinosaurs Say Good Night? Teague, Mark, illus. 2008. (How Do Dinosaurs... Ser.). (ENG.). (J). (gr. -1-3). 9.99 *(978-0-545-09319-4(8))* Scholastic, Inc.

—How Do Dinosaurs Say Good Night? Teague, Mark, illus. 2004. (J). (gr. -1-3). 29.95 *(978-1-55592-138-5(8))* Weston Woods Studios, Inc.

—How Do Dinosaurs Say Happy Birthday? Teague, Mark, illus. 2011. (How Do Dinosaurs... Ser.). (ENG.). 12p. (J). (gr. -1-k). bds. 6.99 *(978-0-545-15353-9(0),* Blue Sky Pr., The) Scholastic, Inc.

—How Do Dinosaurs Say Happy Chanukah? Teague, Mark, illus. 2012. (How Do Dinosaurs... ? Ser.). (ENG.). 40p. (J). (— 1). 16.99 *(978-0-545-41677-1(9),* Blue Sky Pr., The) Scholastic, Inc.

—How Do Dinosaurs Say I Love You? Teague, Mark, illus. 2009. (How Do Dinosaurs... ? Ser.). (ENG.). 40p. (J). (gr. k — 1). 16.99 *(978-0-545-14314-1(4),* Blue Sky Pr., The) Scholastic, Inc.

—How Do Dinosaurs Say I'm Mad? Teague, Mark, illus. 2013. (How Do Dinosaurs... ? Ser.). (ENG.). 40p. (J). (gr. -1-k). 16.99 *(978-0-545-14315-8(2),* Blue Sky Pr., The) Scholastic, Inc.

—How Do Dinosaurs Say Merry Christmas? Teague, Mark, illus. 2012. (How Do Dinosaurs... ? Ser.). (ENG.). 40p. (J). (gr. -1-k). 16.99 *(978-0-545-41678-8(7),* Blue Sky Pr., The) Scholastic, Inc.

—How Do Dinosaurs Stay Friends? Teague, Mark, illus. 2016. (ENG.). 40p. (J). (gr. -1-k). 16.99 *(978-0-545-82934-2(8),* Exhibit A) Scholastic, Inc.

—How Do Dinosaurs Stay Safe? Teague, Mark, illus. 2015. (ENG.). 40p. (J). (gr. -1-k). 16.99 *(978-0-439-24104-5(9),* Blue Sky Pr., The) Scholastic, Inc.

—How Do Dinosaurs Write Their ABC's with Chalk? Teague, Mark, illus. 2016. (How Do Dinosaurs... ? Ser.). (ENG.). 16p. (J). (gr. -1-k). bds. 10.99 *(978-0-545-89052-6(7),* Blue Sky Pr., The) Scholastic, Inc.

Yolen, Jane, narrated by. How Do Dinosaurs Eat Their Food? 2011. (J). (gr. -1-2). 29.95 *(978-0-439-02746-5(2))* Weston Woods Studios, Inc.

Yolen, Jane & Scholastic, Inc. Staff. How Do Dinosaurs Say Good Night? 2010. (How Do Dinosaurs... Ser.). (ENG.). (J). (gr. -1-3). pap. 12.99 incl. audio compact disk *(978-0-545-25416-8(7))* Scholastic, Inc.

York, John Randall. King Bronty in the Days of the Dinosaurs. 2012. 48p. pap. 9.95 *(978-1-60076-332-8(4))* StoneGarden.net Publishing.

Young, Jessica. Digging for Dinos. Burks, James, illus. 2016. (Haggis & Tank Unleashed Ser.: 2). (ENG.). 80p. (J). (gr. k-2). 15.99 *(978-0-545-81889-6(3))* Scholastic, Inc.

Zaionz, Ruth. Morris the Friendly Dinosaur. 2010. 24p. pap. 12.99 *(978-1-4490-6981-0(9))* AuthorHouse.

DINOSAURS—POETRY

Andreae, Giles. Dinosaurs Galore! Wojtowycz, David, illus. (ENG.). 32p. (J). 2006. (gr. -1-3). pap. 7.95 *(978-1-58925-399-5(X))* 2005. 16.95 *(978-1-58925-044-4(3))* Tiger Tales.

Beall, Pamela Conn & Nipp, Susan Hagen. Wee Sing Dinosaurs, 1 vol. 2006. (Wee Sing Ser.). (ENG., Illus.). 64p. (J). (gr. -1-2). 10.99 *(978-0-8431-2097-4(5),* Price Stern Sloan) Penguin Young Readers Group.

Cunningham, Steven C. Dinosaur Name Poems/Poemas de Nombres de Dinosaurios. Gorospe, Myriam, tr. Populon, Valeska M., illus. 2009. (SPA.). 70p. (J). pap. 12.95 *(978-0-9721241-6-4(0))* Three Conditions Pr.

Hopkins, Lee Bennett. Dizzy Dinosaurs: Silly Dino Poems. Gott, Barry, illus. 2011. (I Can Read Level 2 Ser.). (ENG.). 48p. (J). (gr. k-3). 16.99 *(978-0-06-135839-5(8));* pap. 3.99 *(978-0-06-135841-8(X))* HarperCollins Pubs.

Scholastic, Inc. Staff & Cannon, Nick. Neon Aliens Ate My Homework: And Other Poems. Cannon, Nick et al, illus. 2015. (ENG.). 144p. (J). (gr. 2-5). 14.99 *(978-0-545-72281-0(0))* Scholastic, Inc.

Temperley, Howard. In the Days of Dinosaurs: A Rhyming Romp Through Dino History. Kline, Michael P., illus. 2004. (J). pap. 9.95 *(978-1-885593-81-8(3),* Ideal Pubns.) Worthy Publishing.

DIPHTHERIA

Blake, Kevin. Balto's Story. 2014. (Dog Heroes Ser.). (ENG.). 32p. (J). (gr. 2-7). lib. bdg. 25.27 *(978-1-62724-286-8(4))* Bearport Publishing Co., Inc.

Margulies, Philip. Diphtheria. 2004. (Epidemics Ser.). (Illus.). 64p. (YA). (gr. 7-12). lib. bdg. 31.95 *(978-1-4042-0253-5(6))* Rosen Publishing Group, Inc., The.

Margulies, Phillip. Diptheria. 2009. (Epidemics Ser.). 64p. (gr. 5-5). 58.50 *(978-1-61512-280-6(X))* Rosen Publishing Group, Inc., The.

McCarthy, Meghan. The Incredible Life of Balto. 2011. (ENG., Illus.). 40p. (J). (gr. -1-2). 16.99 *(978-0-375-84460-7(0),* Knopf Bks. for Young Readers) Random Hse. Children's Bks.

Miller, Debbie S. & Van Zyle, Jon. The Great Serum Race: Blazing the Iditarod Trail. Van Zyle, Jon, illus. 2006. (ENG., Illus.). 40p. (J). (gr. 2-7). pap. 9.99 *(978-0-8027-7723-2(6),* 9780802777232, Bloomsbury USA Childrens) Bloomsbury Publishing USA.

DIPLOMACY

see also Diplomats

Gale Editors, ed. Worldmark Conflict & Diplomacy: 2 Volume Set, 2 vols. 2014. (Worldmark Conflict & Diplomacy Ser.). (ENG.). 1000p. 329.00 *(978-1-57302-726-7(X))* Cengage Gale.

Johnson, Cynthia. Worldmark Conflict & Diplomacy. 2014. (J). *(978-1-57302-727-4(8))* Cengage Gale.

DIPLOMATIC AND CONSULAR SERVICE—FICTION

Hale, Shannon. River Secrets. 2006. (Books of Bayern Ser.). (ENG., Illus.). 304p. (YA). (gr. 7-12). 18.99 *(978-1-58234-901-5(0),* 9781582349015, Bloomsbury USA Childrens) Bloomsbury Publishing USA.

DIPLOMATS

Barile, Mary Collins. J. Milton Turner; an American Hero. Guest, Peggy, illus. 2013. 52p. 24.95 *(978-0-9889643-0-3(9))* MathisJones Communications, LLC.

Byman, Jeremy. Madam Secretary: The Story of Madeleine Albright. rev. exp. ed. 2004. (Notable Americans Ser.). (Illus.). 128p. (YA). (gr. 6-12). 23.95 *(978-1-931798-34-1(6))* Reynolds, Morgan Inc.

Friedman, Lita. Mary Robinson: Fighter for Human Rights. 2004. (Avisson Young Adult Ser.). (Illus.). 142p. (YA). pap. 19.95 *(978-1-888105-65-0(8))* Avisson Pr., Inc.

Idzikowski, Lisa. Raoul Wallenberg: Rescuer of Hungarian Jews During the Holocaust. 2017. (J). ***(978-1-5383-8118-2(4));*** pap. ***(978-1-5383-8117-5(6))*** Rosen Publishing Group, Inc., The.

McArthur, Debra. Raoul Wallenberg: Rescuing Thousands from the Nazis' Grasp. 2005. (Holocaust Heroes & Nazi Criminals Ser.). (Illus.). 160p. (J). (gr. 6-12). lib. bdg. 27.93 *(978-0-7660-2530-1(6))* Enslow Pubs., Inc.

Mochizuki, Ken. Pasajea la Libertad. 2004. (SPA., Illus.). (J). (gr. k-4). spiral bd. *(978-0-616-03091-2(6))* Canadian National Institute for the Blind/Institut National Canadien pour les Aveugles.

—Passage to Freedom: The Sugihara Story. 2005. 19.45 *(978-0-7569-4773-6(1))* Perfection Learning Corp.

Mochizuki, Ken & Lee, Dom. Passage to Freedom: The Sugihara Story. 2010. (Rise & Shine Ser.). (ENG., Illus.). 32p. (C). pap. 14.95 *(978-1-58430-157-8(0))* National Geographic School Publishing, Inc.

Simon, Emma & Streissguth, Thomas. Raoul Wallenberg, 01 vols., 1. 2016. (Holocaust Ser.). (ENG., Illus.). 112p. (J). 35.60 *(978-1-4994-6242-5(5),* Rosen Young Adult) Rosen Publishing Group, Inc., The.

Watson, Marilyn Myrick. Raul Castro: Arizona's First Hispanic Governor. 2007. (J). *(978-0-9790826-6-5(8));* *(978-0-9790826-5-8(X))* Acacia Publishing, Inc.

DIPSOMANIA

see Alcoholism

DIPTERA

see Flies; Mosquitoes

DIRECTION, SENSE OF

see Orientation

DIRIGIBLE BALLOONS

see Airships

DISABLED PEOPLE

see People with Disabilities

DISARMAMENT

see also Peace; Security, International

Cahill, Bryon. Freedom from Fear. 2013. (Four Freedoms Ser.). (ENG., Illus.). 32p. (J). (gr. 3-6). pap. 8.95 *(978-1-937529-86-4(X));* lib. bdg. 19.95 net. *(978-1-937529-94-9(0))* Red Chair Pr.

Curley, Robert, ed. Weapons of Mass Destruction. 2011. (Britannica Guide to War Ser.). (ENG.). 160p. (YA). (gr. 10-12). lib. bdg. 35.25 *(978-1-61530-687-9(0))* Rosen Publishing Group, Inc., The.

Egan, Tracie. Weapons of Mass Destruction & North Korea. 2009. (Library of Weapons of Mass Destruction Ser.). 64p. (gr. 5-5). 58.50 *(978-1-60853-961-1(X))* Rosen Publishing Group, Inc., The.

Mason, Jennifer. The Nuclear Arms Race. 2017. (Great Race: Fight to the Finish Ser.). 48p. (gr. 4-5). pap. 84.30 ***(978-1-5382-0806-9(7))*** Stevens, Gareth Publishing LLLP.

Moe, Barbara. The Search for Weapons of Mass Destruction in Iraq. 2009. (Library of Weapons of Mass Destruction Ser.). 64p. (gr. 5-5). 58.50 *(978-1-60853-958-1(X))* Rosen Publishing Group, Inc., The.

Morris, Joseph. Nuclear Proliferation. 2009. (What If We Do Nothing? Ser.). 48p. (YA). (gr. 4-7). lib. bdg. 31.00 *(978-1-4339-1983-1(4))* Stevens, Gareth Publishing LLLP.

Olson, Steven P. The International Atomic Energy Agency. 2009. (Library of Weapons of Mass Destruction Ser.). 64p. (gr. 5-5). 58.50 *(978-1-60853-957-4(1))* Rosen Publishing Group, Inc., The.

Orr, Tamra. Iran & Nuclear Weapons. 2009. (Understanding Iran Ser.). (Illus.). 80p. (YA). (gr. 7-12). lib. bdg. 33.25 *(978-1-4358-5281-5(8))* Rosen Publishing Group, Inc., The.

Spalding, Frank. Nuclear Annihilation. 2010. (Doomsday Scenarios: Separating Fact from Fiction Ser.). 64p. (YA). (ENG.). pap. 12.95 *(978-1-4358-8522-6(8),* Rosen Reference); (gr. 5-8). E-Book 58.50 *(978-1-4488-1208-0(9));* (Illus.). (gr. 5-8). lib. bdg. 31.95 *(978-1-4358-3560-3(3),* Rosen Reference) Rosen Publishing Group, Inc., The.

DISASTERS

see also Accidents; Aircraft Accidents; Fires; Natural Disasters; Shipwrecks

ABDO Publishing Company. History's Greatest Disasters: Set Of 8. 2013. (History's Greatest Disasters Ser.: 8). 48p. (gr. 3-6). lib. bdg. 262.32 *(978-1-61783-953-5(1))* ABDO Publishing Co.

American Disasters, 29 bks., Set. Incl. Challenger Disaster: Tragic Space Flight. Bredeson, Carmen. (J). 1999. lib. bdg. 25.27 *(978-0-7660-1222-6(0));* Exxon Valdez: Tragic Oil Spill. Sherrow, Victoria. (J). 1998. lib. bdg. 25.27 *(978-0-7660-1058-1(9));* Fire in Oakland, California: Billion-Dollar Blaze. Bredeson, Carmen. (J). 1999. lib. bdg. 25.27 *(978-0-7660-1220-2(4));* Hurricane Andrew: Nature's Rage. Sherrow, Victoria. (YA). 1998. lib. bdg. 23.93 *(978-0-7660-1057-4(0));* L. A. Riots: Rage in the City of Angels. Cole, Michael D. (YA). 1999. lib. bdg. 23.93 *(978-0-7660-1219-6(0));* Love Canal: Toxic Waste Tragedy. Sherrow, Victoria. (J). 2001. lib. bdg. 23.93 *(978-0-7660-1553-1(X));* Mighty Midwest Flood: Raging Rivers. Bredeson, Carmen. (YA). 1999. lib. bdg. 23.93 *(978-0-7660-1221-9(2));* Mount St. Helens Volcano: Violent Eruption. Bredeson, Carmen. (YA). 2001. lib. bdg. 23.93 *(978-0-7660-1552-4(1));* Oklahoma City Bombing: Terror in the Heartland. Sherrow, Victoria. (YA). 1998. lib. bdg. 23.93 *(978-0-7660-1061-1(9));* Plains Outbreak Tornadoes: Killer Twisters. Sherrow, Victoria. (YA). 1998. lib. bdg. 23.93 *(978-0-7660-1059-8(7));* Polio Epidemic: Crippling Virus Outbreak. Sherrow, Victoria. (YA). 2001. lib. bdg. 23.93 *(978-0-7660-1555-5(6));* San Francisco Earthquake, 1989: Death & Destruction. Sherrow, Victoria. (YA). 1998. lib. bdg. 23.93 *(978-0-7660-1060-4(0));* Siege at Waco: Deadly Inferno. Cole, Michael D. (J). 1999. lib. bdg. 25.27 *(978-0-7660-1218-9(2));* Titanic: Disaster at Sea. Cole, Michael D. (YA). 2001. lib. bdg. 23.93 *(978-0-7660-1557-9(2));* TWA Flight 800: Explosion in Midair. Cole, Michael D. (YA). 1999. lib. bdg. 23.93 *(978-0-7660-1217-2(4));* World Trade Center Bombing: Terror in the Towers. Sherrow, Victoria. (YA). 1998. lib. bdg. 23.93 *(978-0-7660-1056-7(2));* 48p. (gr. 4-10). (Illus.). Set lib. bdg. 549.55 *(978-0-7660-1190-8(9))* Enslow Pubs., Inc.

Bardswich, Miriam & Reevely, Lorna. Catastrophe! 2007. (Steck-Vaughn BOLDPRINT Anthologies Ser.). (ENG., Illus.). 48p. (gr. 9-12). pap. 16.90 *(978-1-4190-4032-0(4))* Houghton Mifflin Harcourt Publishing Co.

Bearce, Stephanie. Twisted True Tales from Science: Disaster Discoveries. 2017. (Twisted True Tales from Science Ser.: 0). (ENG.). 125p. (J). (gr. 4-7). pap. 8.95 *(978-1-61821-574-1(4))* Prufrock Pr.

Benoit, Peter. A True Book: Disasters, 5 vols., Set. Incl. BP Oil Spill. lib. bdg. 29.00 *(978-0-531-20630-0(0));* Exxon Valdez Oil Spill. 29.00 *(978-0-531-20629-4(7));* Hindenburg Disaster. lib. bdg. 31.00 *(978-0-531-20626-3(2));* Krakatau Eruption. 29.00 *(978-0-531-20628-7(9));* Titanic Disaster. 29.00 *(978-0-531-20627-0(0));* 48p. (J). (gr. 3-5). 2011. Set lib. bdg. 290.00 *(978-0-531-26750-9(4),* Children's Pr.) Scholastic Library Publishing.

Berry, Joy. Good Answers to Tough Questions about Disasters. 2009. (ENG.). 52p. (J). (gr. k-7). pap. 7.95 *(978-1-60577-505-0(3))* Berry, Joy Enterprises.

—Good Answers to Tough Questions Disasters. Bartholomew, illus. 2010. (Good Answers to Tough Questions Ser.). (ENG.). 48p. (J). (gr. k-7). pap. 7.99 *(978-1-60577-510-4(X))* Berry, Joy Enterprises.

Blackwood, Gary L. Enigmatic Events. 2005. (Unsolved History Ser.). (Illus.). 80p. (gr. 6-7). lib. bdg. 23.95 *(978-0-7614-1889-4(X),* Benchmark Bks.) Marshall Cavendish Corp.

Blackwood, Gary L. & Follett, Katherine. Enigmatic Events. 2009. (Benchmark Rockets: History's Mysteries Ser.). 32p. (gr. 3). 28.50 *(978-0-7614-4358-2(4))* Marshall Cavendish GBR. Dist: Marshall Cavendish Corp.

Blohm, Craig E. Catastrophic Events of The 2000s. 2013. (YA). lib. bdg. *(978-1-60152-522-2(2))* ReferencePoint Pr., Inc.

Brook, Henry. True Sea Stories. 2005. (True Adventure Stories Ser.). (Illus.). 154p. (J). (gr. 5). lib. bdg. 12.95 *(978-1-58086-693-4(X))* EDC Publishing.

Brown, Don. Drowned City: Hurricane Katrina & New Orleans. 2017. (ENG., Illus.). 96p. (J). (gr. 7). pap. 9.99 *(978-0-544-58617-8(4),* HMH Books For Young Readers) Houghton Mifflin Harcourt Publishing Co.

Burgan, Michael. Total Devastation: The Story of Hurricane Katrina. 2016. (Tangled History Ser.). (ENG., Illus.). 112p. (gr. 3-4). lib. bdg. 31.99 *(978-1-4914-8452-4(7))* Capstone Press of Coughlan Cos.

Butts, Ed. SOS - Stories of Survival: True Tales of Disaster, Tragedy, & Courage. 2007. (ENG., Illus.). 128p. (J). (gr. 5-18). pap. 14.95 *(978-0-88776-786-9(9),* Tundra Bks.) Tundra Bks. CAN. Dist: Penguin Random Hse. LLC.

Calamities: Events That Touched the World. (Critical Reading Ser.). (YA). (gr. 6-12). pap. *(978-0-8092-1111-1(4))* Jamestown.

Capstone Press. Disasters. 2010. (Disasters Ser.). (ENG.). 32p. lib. bdg. 122.60 *(978-1-4296-5898-0(3))* Capstone Press of Coughlan Cos.

Chandler, Matt. Dangerous Times: History's Most Troubled Eras. 2013. (Dangerous History Ser.). (ENG.). 32p. (gr. 3-4). 27.99 *(978-1-4765-0126-0(2),* Edge Bks.) Capstone Press of Coughlan Cos.

Chiang, Mona. Oil Spill: Disaster in the Gulf. 2010. (Illus.). 32p. (J). pap. *(978-0-545-31128-1(4))* Scholastic, Inc.

Colson, Mary. The Environment, 1 vol. 2010. (From Fail to Win! Learning from Bad Ideas Ser.). (ENG., Illus.). 56p. (gr. 5-8). 34.65 *(978-1-4109-3912-8(X),* Raintree Freestyle) Heinemann-Raintree.

Cruise, Robin. The Nuclear Disaster at Chernobyl. Taylor, Marjorie, illus. rev. ed. 2003. (Take Ten Ser.). 46p. (J). (gr. 4-18). pap. 4.95 *(978-1-58659-022-2(7))* Artesian Pr.

Currie, Stephen. Escapes from Man-Made Disasters. 2003. (Great Escapes Ser.). (ENG., Illus.). 112p. (J). pap. 30.85 *(978-1-59018-277-2(4))* Cengage Gale.

Destination Disaster: Individual Title Six-Packs. (Action Packs Ser.). 104p. (gr. 3-5). 44.00 *(978-0-7635-3300-7(9))* Rigby Education.

Disasters. (Disasters Ser.). (ENG.). 48p. (gr. 3-4). 2011. pap. 20.90 *(978-1-4296-7359-4(1))* 2011. pap. 477.60 *(978-1-4296-7360-0(5))* 2011. lib. bdg. 223.93 *(978-1-4296-6599-5(8))* 2011. pap. 119.40 *(978-1-4296-6446-2(0))* 2010. lib. bdg. 159.95 *(978-1-4296-5496-8(1))* 2010. lib. bdg. 127.96 *(978-1-4296-4798-4(1))* Capstone Press of Coughlan Cos.

Dodd, Emily. Tsunamis. 2017. (ENG., Illus.). 32p. (J). pap. 7.99 ***(978-0-00-820873-8(5))*** HarperCollins Pubs. Ltd. GBR. Dist: Independent Pubs. Group.

Doomed! 2015. (Doomed! Ser.). (ENG.). 32p. (J). (gr. 4-5). 159.60 *(978-1-4824-2553-6(X));* pap., pap., pap. 378.00 *(978-1-4824-3456-9(3))* Stevens, Gareth Publishing LLLP.

Dougherty, Terri & Leavitt, Amie Jane. Disasters. 2011. (Disasters Ser.). (ENG.). 48p. (gr. 3-4). lib. bdg. 63.98 *(978-1-4296-6598-8(X))* Capstone Press of Coughlan Cos.

Duke, Shirley. Environmental Disasters. 2011. (ENG., Illus.). 48p. (gr. 4-6). pap. 10.95 *(978-1-61741-986-7(9))* Rourke Educational Media.

Eaton, Gale & Hoose, Phillip. A History of Civilization in 50 Disasters, 1 vol. 2015. (History In 50 Ser.: 0). (ENG., Illus.). 240p. (gr. 6-12). 24.95 *(978-0-88448-383-0(5),* 884383) Tilbury Hse. Pubs.

Faust, Daniel R. After Earth: Living on a Different Planet. (Jr. Graphic Environmental Dangers Ser.). (ENG., Illus.). 24p. (gr. 3-8). 2009. pap. 10.60 *(978-1-4042-4596-9(0),* PowerKids Pr.) 2008. (J). lib. bdg. 25.25 *(978-1-4042-4229-6(5))* Rosen Publishing Group, Inc., The.

Fradin, Dennis Brindell & Fradin, Judith Bloom. Hurricane Katrina. 2009. (Turning Points in U. S. History Ser.). 48p. (gr. 3-6). 31.36 *(978-0-7614-4261-5(8))* Marshall Cavendish Corp.

Gaetan-Beltran, Daniel. The Titanic. 2015. (Perspectives on Modern World History Ser.). (ENG., Illus.). 224p. (J). (gr. 10-12). 47.80 *(978-0-7377-7310-1(3),* Greenhaven Pr., Inc.) Cengage Gale.

Greeley, August. Fallout: Nuclear Disasters in Our World. 2009. (Man-Made Disasters Ser.). 24p. (gr. 3-3). 42.50 *(978-1-61514-348-1(3),* PowerKids Pr.) Rosen Publishing Group, Inc., The.

Greene, Janice. Strange but True, 1 vol., Bk. 5. unabr. ed. 2011. (Strange but True Ser.). (ENG.). 75p. (YA). (gr. 9-12). pap. 8.95 *(978-1-61651-769-4(7))* Saddleback Educational Publishing, Inc.

—Strange but True Book 1, 1 vol. unabr. ed. 2011. (Strange but True Ser.). (ENG.). 76p. (YA). (gr. 9-12). pap. 8.95 *(978-1-61651-765-6(4))* Saddleback Educational Publishing, Inc.

Guiberson, Brenda Z. Disasters: Natural & Man-Made Catastrophes Through the Centuries. Guiberson, Brenda Z., illus. 2014. (ENG., Illus.). 256p. (J). (gr. 5-9). pap. 12.99 *(978-1-250-05066-3(9),* 9781250050663) Square Fish.

Hanel, Rachael. Can You Survive an Earthquake? An Interactive Survival Adventure, 1 vol. 2013. (You Choose: Survival Ser.). (ENG.). 112p. (gr. 3-4). pap. 6.95 *(978-1-62065-709-6(0));* lib. bdg. 31.99 *(978-1-4296-9979-2(5))* Capstone Press of Coughlan Cos. (You Choose Bks.).

Hawkins, John. Air Disasters. 2011. (Catastrophe! Ser.). (ENG., Illus.). 48p. (J). (gr. 5-9). lib. bdg. 29.25 *(978-1-4488-6006-7(0))* Rosen Publishing Group, Inc., The.

Henningfeld, Diane Andrews. Disasters. Greenhaven Press Editors & Gale Editors, eds. 2014. (Global Viewpoints Ser.). (ENG., Illus.). 224p. (gr. 7-12). lib. bdg. 46.20 *(978-0-7377-6262-4(4),* Greenhaven Pr., Inc.) Cengage Gale.

—Disasters. Greenaven Press Staff & Gale Editors, eds. 2014. (Global Viewpoints Ser.). (ENG., Illus.). 224p. (gr. 7-12). pap. 31.70 *(978-0-7377-6438-3(4),* Greenhaven Pr., Inc.) Cengage Gale.

Higgins, Nadia. It's a Tsunami!, 1 vol. Ward, Damian, illus. 2010. (Weather Watchers Ser.). (ENG.). 32p. (J). (gr. k-3). 28.50 *(978-1-60270-731-3(6))* Magic Wagon.

Hoena, B. A. Can You Survive an Alien Invasion? An Interactive Doomsday Adventure. Fisher-Johnson, Paul, illus. 2015. (You Choose: Doomsday Ser.). (ENG.). 112p. (gr. 3-4). lib. bdg. 31.99 *(978-1-4914-5853-2(4),* You Choose Bks.) Capstone Press of Coughlan Cos.

Hoena, Blake & Doeden, Matt. You Choose: Doomsday. Nathan, James, illus. 2015. (You Choose: Doomsday Ser.). (ENG.). 112p. (gr. 3-4). 127.96 *(978-1-4914-6968-2(4),* You Choose Bks.) Capstone Press of Coughlan Cos.

Hollingsworth, Tamara. Catástrofes Que Marcaron la Historia. 2016. (TIME for Kids en Español - Level 5 Ser.). (SPA.). 64p. (gr. 5-5). lib. bdg. 31.99 *(978-1-5157-2928-0(1))* Time for Kids Inc AUS. Dist: Capstone Pub.

—Unforgettable Catastrophes, 1 vol. 2nd rev. ed. 2013. (Nonfiction Readers Ser.). (ENG.). 64p. (J). (gr. 5-5). pap. 10.99 *(978-1-4333-4946-1(9));* (Illus.). pap. 31.96 *(978-1-4333-7445-6(5))* Teacher Created Materials, Inc.

Hoose, Phillip & Eaton, Gale. A History in Civilization in 50 Disasters. 2015. (History In 50 Ser.: 0). (ENG., Illus.). 240p. (gr. 6-12). pap. 16.95 *(978-0-88448-489-9(0),* 884489) Tilbury Hse. Pubs.

Hunter, Nick. Disaster Relief, 1 vol. 2012. (Heroic Jobs Ser.). (ENG.). 32p. (gr. 1-2). pap. 8.29 *(978-1-4109-4365-1(8));* lib. bdg. 29.99 *(978-1-4109-4358-3(5))* Heinemann-Raintree. (Read Me!).

Ingram, Scott. The Chernobyl Nuclear Disaster. 2005. (Environmental Disasters Ser.). (Illus.). 112p. (J). (gr. 6-12). 35.00 *(978-0-8160-5755-9(9))* Facts On File, Inc.

Kissock, Heather, ed. Disasters. 2011. 48p. (gr. 5-8). *(978-1-77071-674-2(2));* pap. *(978-1-77071-677-3(7))* Weigl Educational Pubs. Ltd.

Koontz, Robin. What Was Hurricane Katrina? 2015. (What Was...? Ser.). lib. bdg. 16.00 *(978-0-606-36762-2(4))* Turtleback Bks.

Koontz, Robin & dePaola, Tomie. What Was Hurricane Katrina? Hinderliter, John & McVeigh, Kevin, illus. 2015. (What Was? Ser.). (ENG.). 112p. (J). (gr. 3-7). 5.99 *(978-0-448-48662-8(8),* Penguin Workshop) Penguin Young Readers Group.

La Bella, Laura. Not Enough to Drink: Pollution, Drought, & Tainted Water Supplies. 2009. (Extreme Environmental Threats Ser.). 64p. (gr. 6-6). 58.50 *(978-1-61512-432-9(2))* Rosen Publishing Group, Inc., The.

Lerner, K. Lee, et al. U-X-L Doomed: The Science Behind Disasters. 2015. (J). *(978-1-4103-1777-3(3))* Cengage Gale.

Lorimer, Janet. Strange but True Book 2, 1 vol. unabr. ed. 2011. (Strange but True Ser.). (ENG.). 75p. (YA). (gr. 9-12). pap. 8.95 *(978-1-61651-766-3(2))* Saddleback Educational Publishing, Inc.

—Strange but True Book 3, 1 vol. unabr. ed. 2011. (Strange but True Ser.). (ENG.). 76p. (YA). (gr. 9-12). pap. 8.95 *(978-1-61651-767-0(0))* Saddleback Educational Publishing, Inc.

—Strange but True Book 4, 1 vol. unabr. ed. 2011. (Strange but True Ser.). (ENG.). 76p. (YA). (gr. 9-12). pap. 8.95 *(978-1-61651-768-7(9))* Saddleback Educational Publishing, Inc.

Lusted, Marcia Amidon. The Jamestown Colony Disaster: A Cause-And-Effect Investigation. 2016. (Cause-And-Effect Disasters Ser.). (ENG., Illus.). 40p. (J). (gr. 4-6). lib. bdg. 30.65 *(978-1-5124-1116-4(7));* 46.65 *(978-1-5124-1127-0(2),* Lerner Pubns.) Lerner Publishing Group.

Machajewski, Sarah. Ravaged Landscapes. 2017. (Unnatural Disasters Ser.). 32p. (J). (gr. 4-5). pap. 10.50 ***(978-1-5382-0520-4(3))*** Stevens, Gareth Publishing LLLP.

Markovics, Joyce. Tsunami. 2014. (It's a Disaster! Ser.). 24p. (J). (gr. -1-3). lib. bdg. 23.93 *(978-1-62724-130-4(2))* Bearport Publishing Co., Inc.

Markovics, Joyce L. Tsunami. 2014. (Pedacitos Primeros Lectores: Que Desastre! Ser.). (SPA., Illus.). 24p. (J). (gr. -1-2). lib. bdg. 23.93 *(978-1-62724-248-6(1))* Bearport Publishing Co., Inc.

Marrin, Albert. Flesh & Blood So Cheap. 2015. lib. bdg. 28.15 *(978-0-606-36418-8(8))* Turtleback Bks.

McAuley, Kelly & Kalman, Bobbie. Living in Shelters. 2009. (Disaster Alert! Ser.). (ENG., Illus.). 32p. (J). (gr. 2-9). pap. *(978-0-7787-1620-4(1));* (gr. 3-7). lib. bdg. *(978-0-7787-1588-7(4))* Crabtree Publishing Co.

—Preparing for Disasters. 2009. (Disaster Alert! Ser.). (ENG., Illus.). 32p. (J). (gr. 2-9). pap. *(978-0-7787-1621-1(X));* (gr. 3-7). lib. bdg. *(978-0-7787-1589-4(2))* Crabtree Publishing Co.

McDaniel, Melissa. Disaster Search Dogs. 2005. (Dog Heroes Ser.). (Illus.). 32p. (J). (gr. 2-5). lib. bdg. 25.27 *(978-1-59716-012-4(1))* Bearport Publishing Co., Inc.

Merrick, Patrick. Droughts. 2015. (Forces of Nature Ser.). (ENG.). 24p. (J). (gr. 2-5). 27.07 *(978-1-63143-763-2(1),* 208603) Child's World, Inc., The.

Nature's Ultimate Disasters. 2016. (Nature's Ultimate Disasters Ser.). 00032p. (J). (gr. 3-4). pap. 60.00 *(978-1-4994-3161-2(9),* PowerKids Pr.) Rosen Publishing Group, Inc., The.

Nelson, John. Collision Course: Asteroids & Earth. 2008. (Jr. Graphic Environmental Dangers Ser.). (ENG.). 24p. (J). 47.90 *(978-1-61532-098-1(9),* PowerKids Pr.) Rosen Publishing Group, Inc., The.

—Trayectoria de Choque: Los Asteroides y la Tierra. 2009. (Historietas Juveniles: Peligros Del Medioambiente (Jr. Graphic Environmental Dangers) Ser.). (SPA., Illus.). 24p. (gr. 3-6). (YA). lib. bdg. 25.25 *(978-1-4358-8477-9(9));* pap. 10.60 *(978-1-4358-8478-6(7))* Rosen Publishing Group, Inc., The.

Peacock, L. A. The Truth (and Myths) about Disasters. Davis, Jon, illus. 2014. 96p. (J). pap. *(978-0-545-70565-3(7))* Scholastic, Inc.

Perritano, John. The Most Disgusting Places on the Planet, 1 vol. 2012. (Disgusting Stuff Ser.). (ENG.). 48p. (gr. 3-4). lib. bdg. 31.99 *(978-1-4296-7533-8(0))* Capstone Press of Coughlan Cos.

Poole, Hilary W. Catastrophes. 2017. (J). ***(978-1-4222-3721-2(4))*** Mason Crest.

Pratt, Mary K. Hurricane Katrina & the Flooding of New Orleans: A Cause-And-Effect Investigation. 2016. (Cause-And-Effect Disasters Ser.). (ENG., Illus.). 40p. (J). (gr. 4-6). lib. bdg. 30.65 *(978-1-5124-1117-1(5))* Lerner Publishing Group.

Prentzas, G. S. Lost at Sea. 2015. (Illus.). 32p. (J). lib. bdg. *(978-1-62724-290-5(2))* Bearport Publishing Co., Inc.

Publishers, Chelsea House, creator. Great Historic Disasters Set, 12-Volumes. 2008. (Great Historic Disasters Ser.). (gr. 5-8). 420.00 *(978-0-7910-9891-2(5),* Chelsea Hse.) Facts On File, Inc.

Putnam, Jeff. Tsunami! Deadly Wall of Water. 2016. (High Five Reading - Blue Ser.). (ENG.). 48p. (gr. 3-4). pap. 9.39 *(978-1-5157-4432-0(9),* High Five Reading (RBL)) Capstone Press of Coughlan Cos.

Richardson, Gillian. Kaboom! Explosions of All Kinds. 2009. (ENG., Illus.). 88p. (J). (gr. 6-12). 22.95 *(978-1-55451-204-1(2),* 9781554512041); 2nd ed. pap. 12.95 *(978-1-55451-203-4(4),* 9781554512034) Annick Pr., Ltd. CAN. Dist: Publishers Group West (PGW).

Rooney, Anne. Responding to Emergencies, 1 vol. 2012. (Charities in Action Ser.). (ENG.). 64p. (gr. 6-10). pap. 10.95 *(978-1-4329-6395-8(3));* lib. bdg. 35.99 *(978-1-4329-6388-0(0))* Heinemann-Raintree.

Roza, Greg. Disaster Relief Workers. 2007. (Extreme Careers Ser.). (Illus.). 64p. (J). (gr. 3-7). lib. bdg. 31.95 *(978-1-4042-0943-5(3))* Rosen Publishing Group, Inc., The.

Sandler, Martin W. America's Great Disasters. Sandler, Martin W., illus. 2003. (Illus.). 96p. (J). (gr. 3-18). 17.99 *(978-0-06-029107-5(9))* HarperCollins Pubs.

Sandler, Michael. Catastrophic Storms: Text Pairs. 2008. (Bridges/Navigators Ser.). (J). (gr. 5). 94.00 *(978-1-4108-8409-1(0))* Benchmark Education Co.

Scher, Linda. The Texas City Disaster. 2007. (Code Red Ser.). (Illus.). 32p. (YA). (gr. 2-5). lib. bdg. 25.27 *(978-1-59716-363-7(5))* Bearport Publishing Co., Inc.

Schuh, Mari C. Tsunamis. 2016. (Earth in Action Ser.). (ENG.). 24p. pap. 6.95 *(978-1-5157-6221-8(1),* Pebble Plus) Capstone Press of Coughlan Cos.

Sherman, Jill. The Irish Potato Famine: A Cause-And-Effect Investigation. 2016. (Cause-And-Effect Disasters Ser.). (ENG., Illus.). 40p. (J). (gr. 4-6). lib. bdg. 30.65 *(978-1-5124-1119-5(1))* Lerner Publishing Group.

Smith, Brendan Powell. Noah's Ark: The Brick Bible for Kids. 2012. (ENG., Illus.). 32p. (J). (gr. -1-k). 12.95 *(978-1-61608-737-1(4),* 608737, Sky Pony Pr.) Skyhorse Publishing Co., Inc.

Spalding, Frank. Catastrophic Climate Change & Global Warming. 2010. (Doomsday Scenarios: Separating Fact from Fiction Ser.). 64p. (YA). (gr. 5-8). E-Book 58.50 *(978-1-4488-1204-2(6))* Rosen Publishing Group, Inc., The.

Stefoff, Rebecca. Forensics & Modern Disasters. 2010. (Forensic Science Investigated 2 Ser.). (Illus.). 80p. (J). (gr. 5). lib. bdg. 34.21 *(978-0-7614-4144-1(1))* Marshall Cavendish Corp.

Suen, Anastasia. La Cruz Roja (the Red Cross) 2009. (Organizaciones de ayuda (Helping Organizations) Ser.). (SPA.). 24p. (gr. 2-2). 42.50 *(978-1-60851-146-4(4),* Editorial Buenas Letras) Rosen Publishing Group, Inc., The.

Survivor Stories, 6 bks., Set. Incl. Earthquake: True Stories of Survival. Roza, Greg. 2006. lib. bdg. 29.25 *(978-1-4042-0997-8(2),* 1267007); Hurricane: True Stories of Survival. Wolny, Philip. 2006. lib. bdg. 29.25 *(978-1-4042-0998-5(0),* 1267008); Plane Crash: True Stories of Survival. Spalding, Frank. 2006. lib. bdg. 29.25 *(978-1-4042-0999-2(9),* 1267009); Shipwreck: True Stories of Survival. Porterfield, Jason. 2006. lib. bdg. 29.25 *(978-1-4042-1000-4(8));* Terrorist Attack: True Stories of Survival. Silate, Jennifer. 2007. lib. bdg. 29.25 *(978-1-4042-1001-1(6));* Tsunamis: True Stories of Survival. Sommers, Michael A. 2006. lib. bdg. 29.25 *(978-1-4042-1002-8(4));* (Illus.). 48p. (YA). (gr. 5-9). 2007. Set lib. bdg. 159.00 *(978-1-4042-0938-1(7))* Rosen Publishing Group, Inc., The.

Tarshis, Lauren. Nature Attacks! 2015. (Illus.). (J). (I Survived True Stories Ser.: 2). (ENG.). 176p. (gr. 2-5). 12.99 *(978-0-545-85231-9(5),* Scholastic Paperbacks); 157p. *(978-0-545-90802-3(7),* Scholastic Pr.) Scholastic, Inc.

A True Book-Disasters. 2011. (True Book-Disasters Ser.). 140.00 *(978-0-531-27249-7(4),* Children's Pr.) Scholastic Library Publishing.

Unnatural Disasters. 2017. (Unnatural Disasters Ser.). 32p. (gr. 4-5). pap. 63.00 ***(978-1-5382-0492-4(4));*** lib. bdg. 159.60 ***(978-1-5382-0478-8(9))*** Stevens, Gareth Publishing LLLP.

Weil, Ann. Ecological Disasters, 1 vol. unabr. ed. 2012. (Disasters Ser.). (ENG.). 92p. (YA). (gr. 9-12). 8.95 *(978-1-61651-930-8(4))* Saddleback Educational Publishing, Inc.

—Fire Disasters, 1 vol. unabr. ed. 2012. (Disasters Ser.). (ENG.). 92p. (YA). (gr. 9-12). 8.95 *(978-1-61651-931-5(2))* Saddleback Educational Publishing, Inc.

West, David & Parker, Steve. Ecological Disasters. 2011. (ENG., Illus.). 32p. (J). pap. *(978-0-7787-7578-2(X));* lib. bdg. *(978-0-7787-7573-7(9))* Crabtree Publishing Co.

—Human-Made Disasters. 2011. (ENG., Illus.). 32p. (J). pap. *(978-0-7787-7580-5(1));* lib. bdg. *(978-0-7787-7575-1(5))* Crabtree Publishing Co.

Wimmer, Teresa. Environmental Protection Agency. (Agents of Government Ser.). 48p. (J). 2016. (ENG.). (gr. 5-9). pap. 12.00 *(978-1-62832-145-6(8),* Creative Paperbacks) 2015. (Illus.). *(978-1-60818-544-3(3),* Creative Education) Creative Co., The.

Wood, Alix. Disasters on the Map. 2014. (Fun with Map Skills Ser.). (Illus.). 32p. (J). (gr. 3-6). lib. bdg. 26.25 *(978-1-4777-6976-8(5),* PowerKids Pr.) Rosen Publishing Group, Inc., The.

Woods, Michael & Woods, Mary B. Environmental Disasters. 2008. (Disasters up Close Ser.). (ENG., Illus.). 64p. (gr. 4-8). lib. bdg. 27.93 *(978-0-8225-6774-5(1),* Lerner Pubns.) Lerner Publishing Group.

Yomtov, Nel. The Children's Blizzard Of 1888: A Cause-And-Effect Investigation. 2016. (Cause-And-Effect Disasters Ser.). (ENG., Illus.). 40p. (J). (gr. 4-6). lib. bdg. 30.65 *(978-1-5124-1118-8(3))* Lerner Publishing Group.

Zullo, Allan. Heroes of Hurricane Katrina. 2015. xii, 180p. (J). *(978-1-4806-8729-5(4))* Scholastic, Inc.

DISASTERS—FICTION

Boelter, Ashaki. Diaries of the Doomed 2: Fate of the Fatal. 2007. (Illus.). 114p. (J). per. 11.95 *(978-0-9796219-0-1(9),* Writing Wild & Crazy) Shakalot High Entertainment.

Bustard, Anne. Anywhere but Paradise. 2015. (ENG.). 288p. (gr. 5). 16.99 *(978-1-60684-585-1(3),* Carolrhoda Bks.) Lerner Publishing Group.

Calford, Farley. The Complete Disaster, Rhonda's Birthday Party. 2009. 86p. pap. 9.95 *(978-1-60860-210-0(9),* Eloquent Bks.) Strategic Book Publishing & Rights Agency (SBPRA).

Calvani, Mayra. Humberto, the Bookworm Hamster. Grady, Kit, illus. 2009. 20p. pap. 10.95 *(978-1-935137-92-4(1))* Guardian Angel Publishing, Inc.

Falkner, Brian. The Tomorrow Code. 2009. (ENG.). 368p. (YA). (gr. 7). pap. 9.99 *(978-0-375-84365-5(5),* Ember) Random Hse. Children's Bks.

Graphman, Wm. Matthew. Chel & Riley Adventures: The K9 Kidnapping Adventure. 2011. 80p. (gr. 4-6). pap. 9.99 *(978-1-4567-9574-0(0))* AuthorHouse.

Hanson, Ed. Disaster in Oceania. 2005. (Barclay Family Adventures 2 Ser.). 64p. (J). per. 3.95 *(978-1-56254-801-8(8),* SP8018) Saddleback Educational Publishing, Inc.

Hargreaves, Roger. Little Miss Whoops. 2008. (Mr. Men & Little Miss Ser.). (ENG.). 32p. (J). (gr. -1-2). mass mkt. 4.99 *(978-0-8431-3350-9(3),* Price Stern Sloan) Penguin Young Readers Group.

Harlow, Joan Hiatt. Joshua's Song. 2003. (ENG., Illus.). 160p. (J). (gr. 3-6). pap. 7.99 *(978-0-689-85542-9(7),* McElderry, Margaret K. Bks.) McElderry, Margaret K. Bks.

Hart, Alison. Emma's River, 1 vol. Bachem, Paul, illus. 2010. (ENG.). 160p. (J). (gr. 2-5). 12.95 *(978-1-56145-524-9(5),* Peachtree Junior) Peachtree Pubs.

Kennedy, Marlane. Blizzard Night. 2014. (Disaster Strikes Ser.: 3). lib. bdg. 14.75 *(978-0-606-36355-6(6))* Turtleback Bks.

Lavin, Christine & Franco-Feeney, Betsy. Hole in the Bottom of the Sea. McHugh, Patricia & Feeney, Kathryn, eds. Franco-Feeney, Betsy, illus. 2012. (ENG., Illus.). 32p. (J). 18.95 incl. audio compact disk *(978-0-9726487-8-3(X))* Puddle Jump Pr., Ltd.

Murphy, Jennifer. The Storm. 2013. 26p. 24.95 *(978-1-63004-419-0(9))* America Star Bks.

Pineno. It Doesn't Grow on Trees. 2009. 56p. pap. 10.49 *(978-1-4389-2678-0(2))* AuthorHouse.

Ratcliffe, Linda. Lindylou Starts a Fire. 2012. 32p. pap. 8.99 *(978-1-62419-875-5(9))* Salem Author Services.

Reece, William James. The Great Hippo Migration. 2007. 92p. per. 19.95 *(978-1-4241-9770-5(8))* America Star Bks.

Reinke, Beth Bence. Carla's Cloud Catastrophe. Nielson, Ginger, illus. 2011. 28p. pap. 14.99 *(978-0-9828346-0-2(8))* 4RV Publishing, LLC.

Renner, Ed. When A Glass Breaks. 2010. 94p. pap. 15.99 *(978-1-4500-3760-0(7))* Xlibris Corp.

Rhodes, Jewell Parker. Ninth Ward. 2012. (J). lib. bdg. 18.40 *(978-0-606-26158-6(3),* Turtleback) Turtleback Bks.

Seuling, Barbara. Robert & the Happy Endings. Brewer, Paul, illus. 2007. (Robert Bks.). (ENG.). 160p. (J). (gr. 1-4). 16.95 *(978-0-8126-2748-0(2))* Cricket Bks.

Stewart, Emma. The Adventures of Fillmore the Gerbil. 2008. 24p. pap. 13.50 *(978-1-60693-033-5(8),* Eloquent Bks.) Strategic Book Publishing & Rights Agency (SBPRA).

Tennapel, Doug. Cardboard. 2012. (ENG., Illus.). 288p. (J). (gr. 4-7). 24.99 *(978-0-545-41872-0(0));* pap. 12.99 *(978-0-545-41873-7(9))* Scholastic, Inc. (Graphix).

Tomasi-Dubois, Mary. Danger in the Jeweled City: A Matt & Heather Thriller. 2007. 188p. (YA). per. 15.95 *(978-0-9798633-5-6(X))* Robertson Publishing.

Treggiari, Jo. Ashes, Ashes. (ENG.). 352p. (J). (gr. 7). 2013. pap. 9.99 *(978-0-545-25564-6(3),* Scholastic Paperbacks) 2011. 17.99 *(978-0-545-25563-9(5),* Scholastic Pr.) Scholastic, Inc.

Trenchard, Robert. The Famous Frog Fiasco. 2008. 265p. (J). pap. 13.99 *(978-0-615-20974-6(2))* Soxwings Publishing.

Vosailagi, Jo, illus. Pentapus. 2006. 120p. per. 12.56 *(978-1-4120-9272-2(8))* Trafford Publishing.

White, Andrea. Radiant Girl. 2008. (J). *(978-1-933979-35-9(6))* Bright Sky Pr.

Winbolt-Lewis, Martin. Owliviah. Cressey, Roger, illus. 2013. 56p. (J). pap. *(978-1-78222-075-6(5))* Paragon Publishing, Rothersthorpe.

Wodarski, Bo. Caveboy Bob & the Hole of Doom. 2008. 24p. per. 24.95 *(978-1-4241-8563-4(3))* America Star Bks.

DISCIPLINE OF CHILDREN

see Child Rearing

DISCOVERERS

see Discoveries in Geography; Explorers

DISCOVERIES IN GEOGRAPHY

see also America—Discovery and Exploration; Antarctica; Arctic Regions; Explorers; Northwest Passage; Scientific Expeditions; Voyages and Travels

also names of countries with the subdivision description and travel, e.g. United States—Description and Travel

ABDO Publishing Company Staff. Story of Exploration. 2014. (Story of Exploration Ser.: 6). (ENG.). 144p. (J). (gr. 6-12). lib. bdg. 222.42 *(978-1-62403-248-6(6),* Essential Library) ABDO Publishing Co.

Adams, Simon. Encyclopedia of Great Explorers: Discover the World in the Footsteps of Famous Explorers. 2012. (Illus.). 224p. (J). *(978-1-4351-4350-0(7))* Barnes & Noble, Inc.

—Exploration & Discovery: A History of Remarkable Journeys & the People Who Made Them. 2016. (ENG., Illus.). 64p. (J). (gr. -1-12). 12.99 *(978-1-86147-764-4(3),* Armadillo) Anness Publishing GBR. Dist: National Bk. Network.

Age of Exploration DBA. 2003. spiral bd. 16.95 *(978-1-56004-169-6(2))* Social Studies Schl. Service.

Amazing Academy Assort. 2009. (J). *(978-1-84879-339-2(1))* Make Believe Ideas.

Aronson, Marc, et al. The World Made New: Why the Age of Exploration Happened & How It Changed the World. 2007. (Timelines of American History Ser.). (ENG., Illus.). 64p. (J). (gr. 5-9). 17.95 *(978-0-7922-6454-5(1));* lib. bdg. 27.90 *(978-0-7922-6978-6(0))* National Geographic Society. (National Geographic Children's Bks.).

Berne, Emma Carlson. Did Christopher Columbus Really Discover America? And Other Question about the New World. 2015. (Good Question! Ser.). (ENG., Illus.). 32p. (J). (gr. 2). pap. 5.95 *(978-1-4549-1259-0(6))* Sterling Publishing Co., Inc.

—Did Christopher Columbus Really Discover America? And Other Questions about the New World. 2015. (Good Question! Ser.). (ENG., Illus.). 40p. (J). (gr. 2). 12.95 *(978-1-4549-1258-3(8))* Sterling Publishing Co., Inc.

Bingham, Jane. Adventurers. 2011. (20th Century Lives Ser.). (ENG.). 32p. (YA). (gr. 3-6). lib. bdg. 26.50 *(978-1-4488-3291-0(8))* Rosen Publishing Group, Inc., The.

Bone, Emily. See Inside Exploration & Discovery IR. 2015. (See Inside Board Bks.). (ENG.). 16p. (J). (gr. k-5). 14.99 *(978-0-7945-3499-8(6),* Usborne) EDC Publishing.

Bowman, John S. Exploration in the World of the Ancients, Revised Edition. 2nd rev. ed. 2009. (Discovery & Exploration Ser.). (Illus.). 112p. (gr. 5-8). 35.00 *(978-1-60413-191-8(8),* Chelsea Hse.) Facts On File, Inc.

Britannica, creator. World Exploration from Ancient Times. 2011. (Learn & Explore Ser.). (Illus.). 106p. (YA). (gr. 7). 37.44 *(978-1-61535-454-2(9))* Encyclopaedia Britannica, Inc.

Calvert, Patricia. Vasco Da Gama: So Strong a Spirit. 2004. (Great Explorations Ser.). (Illus.). 80p. (gr. 6). 22.95 *(978-0-7614-1611-1(0),* Benchmark Bks.) Marshall Cavendish Corp.

Clarke, Penny. The Story of Explorers & Exploration. 2013. (Illus.). 64p. (J). *(978-1-4351-5031-7(7))* Barnes & Noble, Inc.

Collins. Collins Fascinating Facts - Explorers. 2016. (Collins Fascinating Facts Ser.). (ENG., Illus.). 72p. (J). (gr. 1-3). pap. 10.99 *(978-0-00-816926-8(8))* HarperCollins Pubs. Ltd. GBR. Dist: Independent Pubs. Group.

Curley, Robert, contrib. by. Explorers of the Renaissance. 2012. (Renaissance Ser.). (ENG.). 168p. (gr. 9-12). (J). lib. bdg. 38.75 *(978-1-61530-879-8(2));* (Illus.). (YA). 77.50 *(978-1-61530-885-9(7))* Rosen Publishing Group, Inc., The.

Currie, Stephen & National Geographic Learning Staff. Travels to Distant Lands, 1000-1400. 2007. (Nonfiction Reading & Writing Workshops Ser.). (ENG., Illus.). 32p. (J). pap. 17.95 *(978-0-7922-4542-1(3))* CENGAGE Learning.

Dawson, Patricia A. First Peoples of the Americas & the European Age of Exploration. 2015. (Exploring the Ancient & Medieval Worlds Ser.). (ENG., Illus.). 160p. (J). (gr. 8-8). lib. bdg. 45.64 *(978-1-5026-0685-3(2))* Cavendish Square Publishing.

Dowling, Lucy. Why Why Why... Do People Want to Explore? 2010. (Why Why Why Ser.). (Illus.). 32p. (J). (gr. 1-3). lib. bdg. 18.95 *(978-1-4222-1584-5(9))* Mason Crest.

Draper, Allison Stark. Vasco da Gama: The Portuguese Quest for a Sea Route from Europe to India. rev. ed. (Library of Explorers & Explorationtm Ser.). (Illus.). 112p. (YA). (gr. 5-8). lib. bdg. 31.95 *(978-1-4042-0637-3(X),* Rosen Reference) Rosen Publishing Group, Inc., The.

Elliott, Lynne. Exploration in the Renaissance. 2009. (Renaissance World Ser.). (ENG., Illus.). 32p. (J). (gr. 5-8). pap. *(978-0-7787-4613-3(5));* lib. bdg. *(978-0-7787-4593-8(7))* Crabtree Publishing Co.

Exploration & Discovery. (J). tchr. ed. 41.95 *(978-0-382-40667-6(2))* Cobblestone Publishing Co.

Exploration & Discovery. 2004. (Sticker Timelines Ser.). (Illus.). 12p. (J). pap. *(978-1-84229-845-9(3))* Top That! Publishing PLC.

Ganeri, Anita. The Top Ten Explorers That Changed the World. 2009. (J). 60.00 *(978-1-4358-9169-2(4),* PowerKids Pr.); (ENG.). 32p. (J). pap. 10.00 *(978-1-4358-9168-5(6),*

C D

PowerKids Pr.); (ENG., Illus.). 32p. (YA). (gr. 3-6). 26.50 *(978-1-4358-9167-8(8))* Rosen Publishing Group, Inc., The.

George, Lynn. What Do You Know about the Age of Exploration? (20 Questions: History Ser.). 24p. (gr. 2-3). 2009. 42.50 *(978-1-60854-956-6(9)*, PowerKids Pr.) 2008. (Illus.). (J). lib. bdg. 22.60 *(978-1-4042-4190-9(6))* Rosen Publishing Group, Inc., The.

Grant, Kevin Patrick. Exploration in the Age of Empire, 1750-1953, Revised Edition. 2nd rev. ed. 2009. (Discovery & Exploration Ser.). (Illus.). 120p. (gr. 5-8). 35.00 *(978-1-60413-189-5(6)*, Chelsea Hse.) Facts On File, Inc.

Great Explorations Group 4, 6 bks., Set. Incl. Christopher Columbus: To the New World. Collier, James Lincoln. 80p. (J). (gr. 3-7). lib. bdg. 32.79 *(978-0-7614-2221-1(8))*; David Livingstone: Deep in the Heart of Africa. Otfinoski, Steven. 79p. (J). (gr. 3-7). lib. bdg. 32.79 *(978-0-7614-2226-6(9))*; Edmund Hillary: First to the Top. Elish, Dan. 80p. (J). (gr. 3-7). lib. bdg. 32.79 *(978-0-7614-2224-2(2))*; Henry Hudson: In Search of the Northwest Passage. Otfinoski, Steven. 80p. (J). (gr. 3-7). lib. bdg. 32.79 *(978-0-7614-2225-9(0))*; Kit Carson: He Led the Way. Calvert, Patricia. 80p. (gr. 6-7). lib. bdg. 22.95 *(978-0-7614-2223-5(4))*; Richard Francis Burton: Explorer, Scholar, Spy. Young, Serinity. 80p. (gr. 6-7). lib. bdg. 22.95 *(978-0-7614-2222-8(6))*; (Illus.). 2006. 2007. Set lib. bdg. 196.71 *(978-0-7614-2219-8(6)*, Benchmark Bks.) Marshall Cavendish Corp.

Greenwood, Rosie. I Wonder Why Columbus Crossed the Ocean: And Other Questions about Explorers. 2013. (I Wonder Why Ser.). (ENG., Illus.). 32p. (J). (gr. k-3). 15.99 *(978-0-7534-6967-5(7)*, 9780753469675, Kingfisher) Roaring Brook Pr.

Harmon, Daniel E. Explorers of the South Pacific. 2004. (Exploration & Discovery Ser.). (Illus.). 64p. (YA). (gr. 5-18). lib. bdg. 19.95 *(978-1-59084-057-3(7))* Mason Crest.

Harris, Laurie Lanzen, ed. Biography for Beginners: World Explorers. 2003. (Illus.). 598p. (J). (gr. 3-6). lib. bdg. 55.00 *(978-1-931360-20-3(0))* Favorable Impressions.

Heckschler, Melissa & Shulman, Mark. The Explorer's Gazette: Amazing Stories of 30 Real-Life Journeys. 2004. (Illus.). (J). pap. *(978-0-439-67653-3(3))* Scholastic, Inc.

Henry Stanley & the Quest for the Source of the Nile. 2014. (ENG.). 176p. (J). (gr. 3-7). pap. 13.95 *(978-1-59077-348-2(9))* Evans, M. & Co., Inc.

Howell, Izzi. An Intrepid History of Explorers. 2017. (Blast Through the Past Ser.). (ENG., Illus.). 32p. (J). (gr. 2-4). 16.99 ***(978-1-4451-4931-8(1)***, Franklin Watts) Hachette Children's Group GBR. Dist: Hachette Bk. Group.

Hulick, Kathryn. Bad Days in Exploration. 2017. (Whoops! a History of Bad Days Ser.). (ENG., Illus.). 48p. (gr. 5-8). lib. bdg. 33.32 *(978-1-4109-8561-3(X))* Heinemann-Raintree.

Kerley, Barbara. The World Is Waiting for You. 2013. (Barbara Kerley Photo Inspirations Ser.). (ENG., Illus.). 48p. (J). (gr. -1-3). lib. bdg. 26.90 *(978-1-4263-1115-4(X)*, National Geographic Children's Bks.) National Geographic Society.

Kerley, Barbara & National Geographic Kids Staff. The World Is Waiting for You. 2013. (Barbara Kerley Photo Inspirations Ser.). (ENG., Illus.). 48p. (J). (gr. -1-3). 17.95 *(978-1-4263-1114-7(1)*, National Geographic Children's Bks.) National Geographic Society.

Kespert, Deborah. Explore! The Most Dangerous Journeys of All Time. 2016. (ENG., Illus.). 96p. (J). (gr. 4-6). pap. 13.95 *(978-0-500-29230-3(2)*, 529230) Thames & Hudson.

Kling, Andrew A., ed. Age of Exploration. 2013. (World History Ser.). (ENG., Illus.). 128p. (J). (gr. 7-10). lib. bdg. 34.95 *(978-1-4205-0930-4(6)*, Lucent Bks.) Cengage Gale.

Koestler-Grack, Rachel A. Ferdinand Magellan. 2009. (Great Explorers Ser.). (Illus.). 112p. (gr. 6-12). 30.00 *(978-1-60413-422-3(4)*, Chelsea Hse.) Facts On File, Inc.

—Vasco Da Gama & the Sea Route to India. Goetzmann, William H., ed. 2005. (Explorers of New Lands Ser.). (Illus.). 168p. (gr. 5-8). lib. bdg. 30.00 *(978-0-7910-8611-7(9))* Facts On File, Inc.

Krull, Kathleen. Lives of the Explorers: Discoveries, Disasters (and What the Neighbors Thought) Hewitt, Kathryn, illus. 2014. (ENG.). 96p. (J). (gr. 5-7). 20.99 *(978-0-15-205910-1(5)*, HMH Books For Young Readers) Houghton Mifflin Harcourt Publishing Co.

Landau, Jennifer. Vasco Da Gama. 2016. (Spotlight on Explorers & Colonization Ser.). 48p. (J). (gr. 6-6). pap. 11.75 *(978-1-4777-8825-7(5))* Rosen Publishing Group, Inc., The.

Malam, John. Extreme Exploration. 2009. (Difficult & Dangerous Ser.). (Illus.). 32p. (J). (gr. 4-7). pap. *(978-1-897563-24-3(8))* Saunders Bk. Co.

Miles, Justin. Ultimate Explorer Guide for Kids. 2015. (ENG., Illus.). 96p. (J). (gr. 5-8). pap. 9.95 *(978-1-77085-618-9(8)*, 9781770856189) Firefly Bks., Ltd.

Mooney, Carla. Explorers of the New World: Discover the Golden Age of Exploration with 22 Projects. Casteel, Tom, illus. 2011. (Build It Yourself Ser.). (ENG.). 128p. (J). (gr. 3-7). 21.95 *(978-1-936313-44-0(8))*; pap. 15.95 *(978-1-936313-43-3(X))* Open City Bks.

Napoli, Tony. Vasco Da Gama: Discovering the Sea Route to India. 2010. (Great Explorers of the World Ser.). (Illus.). 112p. (J). (gr. 7-12). 33.27 *(978-1-59845-127-6(8))* Enslow Pubs., Inc.

Orme, David. Great Journeys. 2009. (Fact to Fiction Grafx Ser.). (Illus.). 36p. (J). pap. 6.95 *(978-0-7891-7898-5(2))* Perfection Learning Corp.

Petrie, Kristin. Vasco Da Gama, 1 vol. 2004. (Explorers Set 1 Ser.). (ENG., Illus.). 32p. (gr. k-6). 27.07 *(978-1-59197-603-5(0)*, Checkerboard Library) ABDO Publishing Co.

Pletcher, Kenneth, ed. Explorers in the 20th & 21st Centuries. 2013. (Britannica Guide to Explorers & Adventurers Ser.). 232p. (YA). (gr. 9-12). 35.25 *(978-1-62275-022-1(5))* Rosen Publishing Group, Inc., The.

Putnam, Jeff. Explorers of the Land. 2004. (Trio Bks). (Illus.). 90p. (gr. 4-6). pap. 5.00 *(978-0-7367-1797-7(8))* Zaner-Bloser, Inc.

Ross, Stewart. Into the Unknown: How Great Explorers Found Their Way by Land, Sea, & Air. Biesty, Stephen, illus. (ENG.). 96p. (J). (gr. 3-7). 2014. pap. 9.99 *(978-0-7636-6992-8(X))* 2011. 19.99 *(978-0-7636-4948-7(1))* Candlewick Pr.

Schwartz, Heather E. Early Explorers. 2016. (Primary Source Readers Ser.). (Illus.). 32p. (J). (gr. 4-5). pap. 8.99 *(978-1-4938-3073-2(2))* Teacher Created Materials, Inc.

Steele, Philip. Explorers. 2016. (Epic! Ser.). (ENG., Illus.). 32p. (J). (gr. 4-6). pap. 11.99 *(978-0-7502-9733-2(6)*, Wayland) Hachette Children's Group GBR. Dist: Hachette Bk. Group.

Swanson, Jennifer. Bartolomeu Dias: First European Sailor to Reach the Indian Ocean. 2017. (Spotlight on Explorers & Colonization Ser.). 48p. (gr. 10-11). pap. 11.75 ***(978-1-5081-7495-0(4)***, Rosen Young Adult) Rosen Publishing Group, Inc., The.

Synge, M. B. The Discovery of New Worlds, Book II of the Story of the World. 2007. 224p. 21.99 *(978-1-60206-621-2(3))*; per. 14.99 *(978-1-60206-620-5(5))* Cosimo, Inc.

Teacher Created Resources Staff. Travel Through - China: Come on a Journey of Discovery. 2008. (Travel Through Ser.). (ENG., Illus.). 32p. (gr. 4-7). pap. 7.99 *(978-1-4206-8280-9(6))* Teacher Created Resources, Inc.

—Travel Through - Spain: Come on a Journey of Discovery. 2008. (Qeb Travel Through Ser.). (ENG., Illus.). 32p. (gr. 4-7). pap. 7.99 *(978-1-4206-8286-1(5))* Teacher Created Resources, Inc.

Turner, Tracey. Hard As Nails Travelers & Explorers. 2015. (Hard As Nails in History Ser.). (ENG., Illus.). 64p. (J). (gr. 3-6). *(978-0-7787-1521-4(3))* Crabtree Publishing Co.

Van Loon, Hendrik Willem. A Short History of Discovery: From the Earliest Times to the Founding of Colonies in the American Continent. 2007. 132p. per. 16.99 *(978-1-59605-799-9(8))* Cosimo, Inc.

Vietze, Andrew. Zheng He: China's Greatest Navigator. 2017. (Spotlight on Explorers & Colonization Ser.). 48p. (gr. 10-11). pap. 11.75 ***(978-1-5081-7507-0(1)***, Rosen Young Adult) Rosen Publishing Group, Inc., The.

West, David. Ten of the Best Adventures in New Worlds. 2015. (Ten of the Best: Stories of Exploration & Adventure Ser.). (ENG., Illus.). 24p. (J). (gr. 3-6). *(978-0-7787-1835-2(2))* Crabtree Publishing Co.

World Book, Inc Staff, contrib. by. Voyages of Exploration. 2011. (J). *(978-0-7166-1793-8(5))* World Bk., Inc.

Worth, Richard. Vasco da Gama. 2009. (Great Explorers Ser.). (Illus.). 104p. (gr. 6-12). 30.00 *(978-1-60413-423-0(2)*, Chelsea Hse.) Facts On File, Inc.

Young, Ian. Amazing Journeys: Following in History's Footsteps. 2003. (High Five Reading - Green Ser.). (ENG., Illus.). 48p. (gr. 3-4). per. 9.00 *(978-0-7368-2831-4(1)*, High Five Reading (RBL)) Capstone Press of Coughlan Cos.

DISCOVERIES IN GEOGRAPHY—FICTION

Brown, Carl & Brown, Kay. The Little Star. 2006. 123p. (J). pap. 15.99 *(978-1-4120-9079-7(2))* Trafford Publishing.

Lancaster, Susan. Hell's Gate. 2004. 200p. pap. *(978-0-9730350-2-5(1))* Snosrap Publishing.

DISCOVERIES IN SCIENCE

Astronomy Now!, 9 vols., Set. Incl. Look at Earth. Dunn, Mary R. (J). (gr. 3-7). lib. bdg. 21.25 *(978-1-4042-3827-5(1)*, PowerKids Pr.); Look at Jupiter. Slade, Suzanne. (J). (gr. 2-5). lib. bdg. 22.60 *(978-1-4042-3829-9(8))*; Look at Mars. Dunn, Mary R. (YA). (gr. 2-5). lib. bdg. 21.25 *(978-1-4042-3828-2(X))*; Look at Mercury. Dunn, Mary R. (YA). (gr. 2-5). lib. bdg. 22.60 *(978-1-4042-3825-1(5))*; Look at Neptune. Slade, Suzanne. (YA). (gr. 2-5). lib. bdg. 22.60 *(978-1-4042-3832-9(8))*; Look at Pluto & Other Dwarf Planets. Kaspar, Anna. (YA). (gr. 2-5). lib. bdg. 22.60 *(978-1-4042-3824-4(7))*; Look at Saturn. Slade, Suzanne. (J). (gr. 2-5). lib. bdg. 22.60 *(978-1-4042-3830-5(1))*; Look at Uranus. Slade, Suzanne. (J). (gr. 2-5). lib. bdg. 22.60 *(978-1-4042-3831-2(X))*; Look at Venus. Dunn, Mary R. (YA). (gr. 2-5). lib. bdg. 22.60 *(978-1-4042-3826-8(3))*; (Illus.). 24p. 2007. 2007. Set lib. bdg. 191.25 *(978-1-4042-3863-3(8))* Rosen Publishing Group, Inc., The.

Berger, Melvin & Berger, Gilda. Did It Take Creativity to Find Relativity, Albert Einstein? Dorman, Brandon, illus. 2007. (Scholastic Science Supergiants Ser.). (ENG.). 48p. (J). (gr. 2-5). pap. 4.99 *(978-0-439-83384-4(1)*, Scholastic Nonfiction) Scholastic, Inc.

Bow, James. Impossible Science. 2012. (ENG.). 32p. (J). *(978-0-7787-8009-0(0))*; pap. *(978-0-7787-8014-4(7))* Crabtree Publishing Co.

Bryson, Bill. A Really Short History of Nearly Everything. 2009. (ENG., Illus.). 176p. (J). (gr. 3-7). 19.99 *(978-0-385-73810-1(2)*, Delacorte Bks. for Young Readers) Random Hse. Children's Bks.

Carlton Books UK. Science Museum Kids Handbook. 2013. (ENG.). 40p. (J). (gr. 2-5). pap. 10.99 *(978-1-78097-346-3(2))* Carlton Bks., Ltd. GBR. Dist: Independent Pubs. Group.

Claybourne, Anna. Who Discovered Natural Selection? 2010. (Breakthroughs in Science & Technology Ser.). 48p. lib. bdg. 32.80 *(978-1-84837-682-3(0))* Arcturus Publishing GBR. Dist: Black Rabbit Bks.

Connolly, Sean. The Book of Potentially Catastrophic Science: 50 Experiments for Daring Young Scientists. 2010. (Irresponsible Science Ser.). (ENG., Illus.). 306p. (J). (gr. 3-9). 14.95 *(978-0-7611-5687-1(9)*, 15687) Workman Publishing Co., Inc.

Culp, Jennifer. Ancient Chinese Technology. 2016. (Spotlight on the Rise & Fall of Ancient Civilizations Ser.). 48p. (J). (gr. 6-6). pap. 11.75 *(978-1-4777-8897-4(2))* Rosen Publishing Group, Inc., The.

De la Bédoyère, Camilla. The Discovery of DNA. 2005. (Milestones in Modern Science Ser.). (Illus.). 48p. (gr. 6-12). lib. bdg. 31.00 *(978-0-8368-5851-8(4)*, Gareth Stevens Secondary Library) Stevens, Gareth Publishing LLLP.

Dynamic Duos of Science. 2014. (Dynamic Duos of Science Ser.). 48p. (YA). (gr. 5-8). 191.70 *(978-1-4824-1183-6(0))* Stevens, Gareth Publishing LLLP.

Eamer, Claire. Before the World Was Ready: Stories of Daring Genius in Science. Boothroyd, Sa, illus. 2013. (ENG.). 128p. (J). (gr. 4-7). pap. 14.95 *(978-1-55451-535-6(1)*, 9781554515356) Annick Pr., Ltd. CAN. Dist: Publishers Group West (PGW).

Eboch, M. M. The 12 Biggest Breakthroughs in Medicine. 2014. (ENG., Illus.). 32p. (J). *(978-1-63235-015-2(7))* Pr. Room Editions LLC.

Eureka!, 6 bks., Set. Incl. I've Discovered Electricity! Norlander, Britt. lib. bdg. 28.50 *(978-0-7614-3195-4(0))*; I've Discovered Energy! Plummer, Todd. lib. bdg. 28.50 *(978-0-7614-3202-9(7))*; I've Discovered Force! Plummer, Todd. lib. bdg. 28.50 *(978-0-7614-3204-3(3))*; I've Discovered Heat! Brent, Lynnette R. lib. bdg. 28.50 *(978-0-7614-3196-1(9))*; I've Discovered Light. Brent, Lynnette R. lib. bdg. 28.50 *(978-0-7614-3198-5(5))*; I've Discovered Sound. Barchers, Suzanne I. lib. bdg. 28.50 *(978-0-7614-3207-4(8))*; 32p. (gr. 4-18). (Eureka! Ser.). 2008. Set lib. bdg. 171.00 *(978-0-7614-3193-0(4)*, Benchmark Bks.) Marshall Cavendish Corp.

Gibson, Brylee. Dinosaur Discoveries. 2007. (Connectors Ser.). (gr. 2-5). pap. *(978-1-877453-13-7(7))* Global Education Systems Ltd.

Goldsmith, Mike. Eureka! The Most Amazing Scientific Discoveries of All Time. 2014. (ENG., Illus.). 96p. (J). (gr. 4-7). 19.95 *(978-0-500-65025-7(X)*, 565025) Thames & Hudson.

Goldsmith, Mike & Gifford, Clive. Eureka: The Most Amazing Scientific Discoveries of All Time. 2016. (ENG., Illus.). 96p. (J). (gr. 4-6). pap. 13.95 *(978-0-500-29227-3(2)*, 529227) Thames & Hudson.

Great Discoveries in Science. 2016. (Great Discoveries in Science Ser.). 128p. (gr. 9-9). lib. bdg. 365.12 *(978-1-5026-2001-9(4))* Cavendish Square Publishing.

Inventions & Discoveries. (Action Bks.). 64p. (J). (gr. 3-7). pap. *(978-1-882210-68-8(9))* Action Publishing, Inc.

Inventions & Discoveries, 12 vols., Set. 2009. (J). (gr. 4-6). lib. bdg. 239.00 *(978-0-7166-0380-1(2))* World Bk., Inc.

Jane Gardner. Black Achievement in Science: Chemistry, Vol. 10. Pouson, Mel, ed. 2016. (Black Achievement in Science Ser.: Vol. 10). (ENG., Illus.). 64p. (J). (gr. 7-12). 23.95 *(978-1-4222-3556-0(4))* Mason Crest.

Jango-Cohen, Judith. Ben Franklin's Big Shock. Lepp, Kevin, illus. 2006. (On My Own Science Ser.). 48p. (J). (gr. k-3). per. 5.95 *(978-0-8225-6450-8(5)*, First Avenue Editions) Lerner Publishing Group.

Jankowski, Connie. Pioneers of Light & Sound, 1 vol. 2007. (Science Readers Ser.). (ENG.). 32p. (J). (gr. 3-3). pap. 8.99 *(978-0-7439-0580-0(6))* Shell Educational Publishing.

Jarrow, Gail. Red Madness: How a Medical Mystery Changed What We Eat. 2014. (ENG., Illus.). 192p. (J). (gr. 5). 17.95 *(978-1-59078-732-8(3)*, Calkins Creek) Boyds Mills Pr.

Johnson, Rose. Discoveries in Earth & Space Science That Changed the World, 1 vol. 2015. (ENG.). 48p. (YA). 30.25 *(978-1-4777-8609-3(0)*, Rosen Reference) Rosen Publishing Group, Inc., The.

—Discoveries in Life Science That Changed the World, 1 vol. 2015. (ENG.). 48p. (YA). 30.25 *(978-1-4777-8607-9(4)*, Rosen Reference) Rosen Publishing Group, Inc., The.

—Discoveries in Medicine That Changed the World, 1 vol. 2015. (ENG.). 48p. (YA). 30.25 *(978-1-4777-8611-6(2)*, Rosen Reference) Rosen Publishing Group, Inc., The.

—Discoveries in Physics That Changed the World, 1 vol. 2015. (ENG.). 48p. (J). 30.25 *(978-1-4777-8603-1(1)*, Rosen Reference) Rosen Publishing Group, Inc., The.

Keranen, Rachel. Evolution. 2016. (Great Discoveries in Science Ser.). (Illus.). 128p. (J). (gr. 9-9). 45.64 *(978-1-5026-1951-8(2))* Cavendish Square Publishing.

Levy, Janey. Freaky Stories about Plants. 2016. (Freaky True Science Ser.). 32p. (J). (gr. 5-4). pap. 10.50 *(978-1-4824-4831-3(9))* Stevens, Gareth Publishing LLLP.

Machajewski, Sarah. Freaky Science Discoveries. 2015. (Freaky True Science Ser.). (ENG., Illus.). 32p. (J). (gr. 4-5). pap. 10.50 *(978-1-4824-2952-7(7))* Stevens, Gareth Publishing LLLP.

Mattern, Joanne. X-Ray Machines. 2015. (Rookie Read-About(tm) Science: How Things Work Ser.). (ENG., Illus.). 32p. (J). lib. bdg. 25.00 *(978-0-531-21371-1(4)*, Children's Pr.) Scholastic Library Publishing.

McCully, Emily Arnold. Caroline's Comets: A True Story. 2017. (ENG.). 40p. (J). (gr. -1-3). 16.95 *(978-0-8234-3664-4(0))* Holiday Hse., Inc.

Nardo, Don. The Scientific Revolution. 2011. (World History Ser.). (ENG., Illus.). 128p. (J). (gr. 7-10). lib. bdg. 39.90 *(978-1-4205-0613-6(7)*, Lucent Bks.) Cengage Gale.

Norlander, Britt. I've Discovered Electricity! 2008. (Eureka! Ser.). 32p. (gr. 4-18). lib. bdg. 28.50 *(978-0-7614-3195-4(0)*, Benchmark Bks.) Marshall Cavendish Corp.

Oachs, Emily Rose. The 12 Most Influential Scientific Discoveries of All Time. 2018. (ENG.). 32p. (gr. 3-6). 31.35 ***(978-1-63235-413-6(6)***, 12-Story Library) Pr. Room Editions LLC.

Oliver, Claire. Mind-Boggling Science. 2008. (Factastic Journey Ser.). (Illus.). 32p. (J). (gr. k-7). pap. 8.95 *(978-1-59905-242-7(3))* Saddleback Educational Publishing, Inc.

Oxlade, Chris. The Top Ten Scientific Discoveries That Changed the World. 2009. (J). 60.00 *(978-1-4358-9172-2(4)*, PowerKids Pr.); (ENG.). 32p. (J). pap. 10.00 *(978-1-4358-9171-5(6)*, PowerKids Pr.); (ENG., Illus.). 32p. (YA). (gr. 3-6). 26.50 *(978-1-4358-9170-8(8))* Rosen Publishing Group, Inc., The.

Pobst, Sandy. Scientific Discovery in the Renaissance: Set Of 6. 2010. (Navigators Ser.). (J). pap. 50.00 net. *(978-1-4108-6267-9(4))* Benchmark Education Co.

Rooney, Anne. Alan Turing & His Binary Computer Code. 2012. (Miracle Makers Ser.). (ENG., Illus.). 48p. (YA). (gr. 5-8). 27.95 *(978-1-4488-6037-1(7)*, Rosen Reference) Rosen Publishing Group, Inc., The.

—Albert Einstein & His Theory of Relativity. 2012. (Miracle Makers Ser.). (ENG.). 48p. (YA). (gr. 5-8). 27.95 *(978-1-4488-6038-8(5)*, Rosen Reference) Rosen Publishing Group, Inc., The.

—Alexander Fleming & the Discovery of Penicillin. 2012. (Miracle Makers Ser.). (ENG., Illus.). 48p. (YA). (gr. 5-8). 27.95 *(978-1-4488-6035-7(0)*, Rosen Reference) Rosen Publishing Group, Inc., The.

—James Watson & Francis Crick & the Discovery of Dna. 2012. (Miracle Makers Ser.). (ENG., Illus.). 48p. (YA). (gr. 5-8). 27.95 *(978-1-4488-6036-4(9)*, Rosen Reference) Rosen Publishing Group, Inc., The.

—Jonas Salk & the First Polio Vaccine. 2012. (Miracle Makers Ser.). (ENG.). 48p. (YA). (gr. 5-8). 27.95 *(978-1-4488-6034-0(2)*, Rosen Reference) Rosen Publishing Group, Inc., The.

Ryles, Briony & Hall, Derek. The Early 20th Century. 2010. (CC: Technology Through the Ages Ser.). 112p. (gr. 6-12). 42.80 *(978-1-933834-87-0(0))* Brown Bear Bks.

—The Modern World. 2010. (CC: Technology Through the Ages Ser.). 112p. (gr. 6-12). 42.80 *(978-1-933834-88-7(9))* Brown Bear Bks.

—Prehistory & the Classical Period. 2010. (CC: Technology Through the Ages Ser.). 112p. (gr. 6-12). 42.80 *(978-1-933834-83-2(8))* Brown Bear Bks.

Samuels, Charlie. The Age of the Atom (1900-1946) 2010. (Science Highlights: A Gareth Stevens Timeline Ser.). (ENG.). 48p. (J). (gr. 6-8). pap. 14.05 *(978-1-4339-4152-8(X))*; lib. bdg. 31.95 *(978-1-4339-4151-1(1))* Stevens, Gareth Publishing LLLP. (Gareth Stevens Secondary Library).

—The Digital Age (1947-Present Day) 2010. (Science Highlights: A Gareth Stevens Timeline Ser.). (ENG.). 48p. (J). (gr. 6-8). pap. 14.05 *(978-1-4339-4155-9(4)*, Gareth Stevens Secondary Library) Stevens, Gareth Publishing LLLP.

Schutten, Jan Paul. The Mystery of Life: How Nothing Became Everything. Watkinson, Laura, tr. from DUT. Rieder, Floor, illus. 2015. (ENG.). 240p. (YA). (gr. 5-9). 15.99 *(978-1-58270-525-5(9)*, Simon & Schuster/Paula Wiseman Bks.) Simon & Schuster/Paula Wiseman Bks.

Steele, Philip. Marie Curie: The Woman Who Changed the Course of Science. 2008. (National Geographic World History Biographies Ser.). (ENG., Illus.). 64p. (J). (gr. 3-7). pap. 7.99 *(978-1-4263-0249-7(5)*, National Geographic Children's Bks.) National Geographic Society.

Sturm, Jeanne. Inventors & Discoveries. 2011. (ENG., Illus.). 48p. (gr. 4-6). pap. 10.95 *(978-1-61741-987-4(7))* Rourke Educational Media.

Wood, Susan. Vaccine Innovators Pearl Kendrick & Grace Eldering. 2016. (STEM Trailblazer Bios Ser.). (ENG., Illus.). 32p. (J). (gr. 2-5). 26.65 *(978-1-5124-0790-7(9))* Lerner Publishing Group.

World Book, Inc Staff, contrib. by. Industry & Manufacturing. 2009. (J). *(978-0-7166-0389-4(6))* World Bk., Inc.

Young-Brown, Fiona. Nuclear Fusion & Fission. 2016. (Great Discoveries in Science Ser.). (Illus.). 128p. (J). (gr. 9-9). 45.64 *(978-1-5026-1949-5(0))* Cavendish Square Publishing.

Zuchora-Walske, Christine. Key Discoveries in Earth & Space Science. 2015. (Science Discovery Timelines Ser.). (ENG., Illus.). 48p. (J). (gr. 6-8). pap. 8.99 *(978-1-4677-6157-4(5))*; lib. bdg. 30.65 *(978-1-4677-5787-4(X))* Lerner Publishing Group. (Lerner Pubns.).

—Key Discoveries in Life Science. 2015. (Science Discovery Timelines Ser.). (ENG., Illus.). 48p. (gr. 6-8). (J). lib. bdg. 30.65 *(978-1-4677-5786-7(1)*, Lerner Pubns.); pap. 8.99 *(978-1-4677-6159-8(1))* Lerner Publishing Group.

DISCOVERIES, MARITIME

see Discoveries in Geography

DISCRIMINATION

Here are entered general works on social discrimination based on race, religion, sex, social minority status, or other factors.

see also Civil Rights; Minorities; Toleration

Blumenthal, Karen. Let Me Play: The Story of Title IX - The Law That Changed the Future of Girls in America. 2005. (ENG., Illus.). 160p. (J). (gr. 3-7). 22.99 *(978-0-689-85957-1(0)*, Atheneum Bks. for Young Readers) Simon & Schuster Children's Publishing.

Cockcroft, James D. Latinos in Beisbol. 2004. (Illus.). 207p. (J). (gr. 4-9). reprint ed. pap. 10.00 *(978-0-7567-7347-2(4))* DIANE Publishing Co.

Coy, John. Game Changer: John McLendon & the Secret Game. DuBurke, Randy, illus. 2015. (ENG.). 32p. (J). (gr. 2-5). 9.99 *(978-1-4677-9056-7(7)*, Carolrhoda Bks.); 17.99 *(978-1-4677-8810-6(4)*, Carolrhoda Bks.); 17.99 *(978-1-4677-9055-0(9)*, Carolrhoda Bks.); 17.99 *(978-1-4677-2604-7(4))* Lerner Publishing Group.

Davidson, Tish. Prejudice. 2003. (Life Balance Ser.). (ENG., Illus.). 80p. (J). 20.50 *(978-0-531-12252-5(2)*, Watts, Franklin) Scholastic Library Publishing.

Esherick, Joan. Guaranteed Rights: The Legislation That Protects Youths with Special Needs. 2003. (Youth with Special Needs Ser.). (Illus.). 127p. (YA). (gr. 7). pap. 14.95 *(978-1-4222-0423-8(5))* Mason Crest.

Friedman, Lauri S. Discrimination. 2009. (Writing the Critical Essay: an Opposing Viewpoints Guide Ser.). (ENG., Illus.). 128p. (YA). (gr. 7-12). lib. bdg. 33.75 *(978-0-7377-4403-3(0)*, LML02109-245404, Greenhaven Pr., Inc.) Cengage Gale.

Friedman, Lauri S. & Des Chenes, Elizabeth, eds. Discrimination. 2007. (Issues That Concern You Ser.). (ENG., Illus.). 144p. (YA). (gr. 7-12). lib. bdg. 36.95 *(978-0-7377-3813-1(8)*, LML02109-234553) Cengage Gale.

Gay, Kathlyn. Bigotry & Intolerance: The Ultimate Teen Guide. 2013. (It Happened to Me Ser.: 35). (ENG., Illus.). 182p. 55.00 *(978-0-8108-8360-4(0))* Scarecrow Pr., Inc.

Gold, Susan Dudley. Americans with Disabilities ACT. 2010. (Landmark Legislation Ser.). 128p. (YA). (gr. 7-12). 39.93 *(978-1-60870-039-4(9))* Marshall Cavendish Corp.

Gordon, Sherri Mabry. Confronting Class Discrimination. 2017. (J). pap. ***(978-1-5383-8168-7(0))*** Rosen Publishing Group, Inc., The.

Hanson, Anders. Everyone Is Equal: The Kids' Book of Tolerance, 1 vol. 2014. (What We Stand For Ser.). (ENG.). 24p. (gr. 5-10). lib. bdg. 25.65 *(978-1-62403-293-6(1)*, Super SandCastle) ABDO Publishing Co.

Harrison, Geoffrey C. & Scott, Thomas F. The Fight for Freedom. Stewart, Mark & Kennedy, Mike, eds. 2014. (Great Debates Ser.). (ENG.). 48p. (J). (gr. 5-8). lib. bdg. 29.27 *(978-1-59953-588-3(2))* Norwood Hse. Pr.

Haugen, David M. Discrimination. Greenhaven Press Editors, ed. 2014. (Teen Rights & Freedoms Ser.). (ENG., Illus.). 176p. (gr. 10-12). lib. bdg. 42.00 *(978-0-7377-6996-8(3)*, Greenhaven Pr., Inc.) Cengage Gale.

Hunt, Jamie. Homophobia: From Social Stigma to Hate Crimes. 2009. (Gallup's Guide to Modern Gay, Lesbian, & Transgender Lifestyle Ser.). 64p. (YA). (gr. 7-18). pap. 9.95 *(978-1-4222-1871-6(6))*; lib. bdg. 22.95 *(978-1-4222-1752-8(3))* Mason Crest.

Lynette, Rachel. How to Deal with Discrimination. 2009. (Let's Work It Out Ser.). (Illus.). 24p. (J). (gr. 2-5). lib. bdg. 22.60 *(978-1-4042-4518-1(9))* Rosen Publishing Group, Inc., The.

MacDonald, Fiona. Equal Opportunities. (World Issues Ser.). (Illus.). 57p. (J). lib. bdg. 28.50 *(978-1-931983-30-3(5))* Chrysalis Education.

Merino, Noël. Gender. 2010. (Issues on Trial Ser.). (ENG.). 240p. 42.15 *(978-0-7377-4948-9(2)*, Greenhaven Pr., Inc.) Cengage Gale.

—Sex Discrimination. 2010. (Issues on Trial Ser.). (Illus.). 240p. 42.15 *(978-0-7377-4740-9(4)*, Greenhaven Pr., Inc.) Cengage Gale.

Mooney, Carla. Confronting Discrimination Against Immigrants. 2017. (J). pap. **(978-1-5383-8164-9(8)**, Rosen Young Adult) Rosen Publishing Group, Inc., The.

Nichols, Susan. Confronting Ableism. 2017. (J). pap. **(978-1-5383-8160-1(5))** Rosen Publishing Group, Inc., The.

Palmer, Bill. Gallup Guides for Youth Facing Persistent Prejudice. 2012. (Gallup Guides for Youth Facing Persistent Prejudice Ser.). 64p. (J). (gr. 7-8). 22.95 *(978-1-4222-2466-3(X))* Mason Crest.

Sanna, Ellyn. Gallup Guides for Youth Facing Persistent Prejudice Muslims. 2012. (Gallup Guides for Youth Facing Persistent Prejudice Ser.). 64p. (J). (gr. 7-8). 22.95 *(978-1-4222-2468-7(6))* Mason Crest.

—People with Mental & Physical Challenges. 2012. (Gallup Guides for Youth Facing Persistent Prejudice Ser.). 64p. (J). (gr. 7-8). 22.95 *(978-1-4222-2470-0(8))* Mason Crest.

Solomon, Steven. Homophobia: Deal with It & Turn Prejudice into Pride. 1 vol. Johnson, Nick, illus. 2013. (Lorimer Deal with It Ser.). (ENG.). 32p. (J). (gr. 4-6). 24.95 *(978-1-4594-0441-0(6)*, 9781459404410); pap. 12.95 *(978-1-4594-0442-7(4)*, 9781459404427) Lorimer, James & Co., Ltd., Pubs. CAN. Dist: Casemate Pubs. & Bk. Distributors, LLC.

DISCRIMINATION—FICTION

Dempsey, Kristy. A Dance Like Starlight: One Ballerina's Dream. Cooper, Floyd, illus. 2014. (ENG.). 32p. (J). (gr. k-3). 16.99 *(978-0-399-25284-6(3)*, Philomel Bks.) Penguin Young Readers Group.

Gurtler, Janet. Cora's Decision. Wood, Katie, illus. 2015. (Mermaid Kingdom Ser.). (ENG.). 96p. (gr. 3-5). 23.99 *(978-1-4342-9695-5(4))* Stone Arch Bks.

Gutman, Dan. Satch & Me. 2009. (Baseball Card Adventures Ser.). (J). lib. bdg. 16.00 *(978-0-606-00023-9(2)*, Turtleback) Turtleback Bks.

Horowitz, Jeanine. Toady Toad's Move. 2006. (Illus.). 32p. (J). lib. bdg. 17.95 *(978-1-934190-03-6(9))* Ocean Front Bk. Publishing, Inc.

Karas, Phyllis. The Hate Crime. 2004. 190p. (YA). pap. 13.95 *(978-0-595-33138-3(6)*, Authors Choice Pr.) iUniverse, Inc.

Kochan, Vera. What If Your Best Friend Were Blue?, 0 vols. Garófoli, Viviana, illus. 2011. (ENG.). 24p. (J). (gr. -1-2). 12.99 *(978-0-7614-5897-5(2)*, 9780761458975, Amazon Children's Publishing) Amazon Publishing.

Maddox, Jake. Snowboard Duel. 1 vol. Tiffany, Sean, illus. 2007. (Jake Maddox Sports Stories Ser.). (ENG.). 72p. (gr. 2-3). pap. 5.95 *(978-1-59889-895-8(7))* Stone Arch Bks.

Meyer, Susan Lynn. New Shoes. Velasquez, Eric, illus. (ENG.). 32p. (J). 2016. 7.99 *(978-0-8234-3573-9(3))* 2015. (gr. 1-4). 16.95 *(978-0-8234-2528-0(2))* Holiday Hse., Inc.

Myers, Walter Dean. The Glory Field. 2008. (ENG.). 400p. (J). (gr. 7). pap. 9.99 *(978-0-545-05575-8(X)*, Scholastic Paperbacks) Scholastic, Inc.

Shepherd, Donna J. Dotty's Topsy Tale. Collier, Kevin Scott, illus. 2009. 16p. pap. 9.95 *(978-1-935137-55-9(7))* Guardian Angel Publishing, Inc.

Tunis, John Roberts. Keystone Kids. 2006. (Odyssey/Harcourt Young Classic Ser.). 239p. (J). (gr. 3). 13.65 *(978-0-7569-7102-1(0))* Perfection Learning Corp.

Wittenstein, Barry & Ladd, London. Waiting for Pumpsie. 2017. (ENG., Illus.). 32p. (J). (gr. k-3). lib. bdg. 16.99 *(978-1-58089-545-3(X))* Charlesbridge Publishing, Inc.

DISCRIMINATION IN EDUCATION

see also Segregation in Education

Anderson, Sonya, et al. eds. Facing Racism in Education. 3rd ed. 2005. (Harvard Educational Review Ser.: No. 39). (Illus.). 324p. (YA). pap. 29.95 *(978-0-916690-42-7(3)*, Harvard Educational Review Reprint Series) Harvard Education Publishing Group (HEPG).

Cushman, Clare, et al. Black, White, & Brown: The Landmark School Desegregation Case in Retrospect. 00 vols. rev. ed. 2004. (ENG., Illus.). 258p. (YA). (gr. 9-18). 65.00 *(978-1-56802-911-5(X))* CQ Pr.

Goodman, Susan E. The First Step: How One Girl Put Segregation on Trial. Lewis, E. B., illus. 2016. (J). *(978-0-8027-3741-0(2))* Bloomsbury Pr.

—The First Step: How One Girl Put Segregation on Trial. Lewis, E. B., illus. 2016. (ENG.). 40p. (J). 17.99 *(978-0-8027-3739-7(0)*, 9780802737397, Bloomsbury USA Childrens) Bloomsbury Publishing USA.

Hinton, KaaVonia. Desegregating America's Schools. 2009. (Monumental Milestones Ser.). 48p. (YA). (gr. 4-7). lib. bdg. 29.95 *(978-1-58415-737-3(2))* Mitchell Lane Pubs., Inc.

Klein, Rebecca T. Your Legal Rights in School. 1 vol. 2015. (ENG., Illus.). 64p. (J). 33.25 *(978-1-4777-8048-0(3)*, Rosen Reference) Rosen Publishing Group, Inc., The.

Kowalski, Kathiann M. Affirmative Action. 2006. (Open for Debate Ser.). (Illus.). 128p. (gr. 7-7). lib. bdg. 42.79 *(978-0-7614-2300-3(1)*, Benchmark Bks.) Marshall Cavendish Corp.

Lüsted, Marcia Amidon. The Little Rock Desegregation Crisis. 2017. (J). pap. **(978-1-5383-8041-3(2))** Rosen Publishing Group, Inc., The.

McNeese, Tim. Regents of the University of California V. Bakke: American Education & Affirmative Action. 2007. (Great Supreme Court Decisions Ser.). (Illus.). 152p. (YA). (gr. 5-9). lib. bdg. 32.95 *(978-0-7910-9260-6(7))* Facts On File, Inc.

Morrison, Toni. Remember: The Journey to School Integration. 2004. (ENG., Illus.). 80p. (J). (gr. -1-3). tchr. ed. 19.99 *(978-0-618-39740-2(X))* Houghton Mifflin Harcourt Publishing Co.

Telgen, Diane. Brown V. Board of Education. 2005. (Defining Moments Ser.). (Illus.). 256p. (gr. 7-12). 55.00 *(978-0-7808-0775-4(8))* Omnigraphics, Inc.

DISCRIMINATION IN EMPLOYMENT

Berlatsky, Noah. Working Women. 2015. (Opposing Viewpoints Ser.). (ENG.). 224p. (J). (gr. 10-12). 48.80 *(978-0-7377-7302-6(2)*, Greenhaven Pr., Inc.) Cengage Gale.

Henneberg, Susan, ed. Gender Politics. 2017. (At Issue Ser.). 128p. (YA). (gr. 10-12). pap. 27.80 **(978-1-5345-0041-9(3))**; lib. bdg. 39.40 **(978-1-5345-0014-3(6))** Greenhaven Publishing LLC. (Greenhaven Publishing).

Kowalski, Kathiann M. Affirmative Action. 2006. (Open for Debate Ser.). (Illus.). 128p. (gr. 7-10). lib. bdg. 42.79 *(978-0-7614-2300-3(1)*, Benchmark Bks.) Marshall Cavendish Corp.

Meyer, Susan. Affirmative Action. 2017. (J). pap. **(978-1-5383-8011-6(0))** Rosen Publishing Group, Inc., The.

DISCUSSION

see Debates and Debating

DISEASE (PATHOLOGY)

see Pathology

DISEASE GERMS

see Bacteriology

DISEASES

see also Sick

see also names of diseases and groups of diseases; and subjects with the subdivision Diseases

Abramovitz, Melissa. Copd. 2015. (Diseases & Disorders Ser.). (ENG.). 128p. (gr. 7-10). 39.90 *(978-1-4205-1239-7(0)*, Lucent Bks.) Cengage Gale.

—Parkinson's Disease. 2005. (Diseases & Disorders Ser.). (ENG., Illus.). 112p. (YA). (gr. 7-10). lib. bdg. 32.45 *(978-1-59018-300-7(2)*, Lucent Bks.) Cengage Gale.

—West Nile Virus. 2003. (Diseases & Disorders Ser.). (ENG., Illus.). 96p. (J). 33.45 *(978-1-59018-343-4(6)*, Lucent Bks.) Cengage Gale.

Alcamo, I. Edward, ed. Deadly Diseases & Epidemics. (Illus.). (gr. 9-13). pap. 47.80 *(978-0-7910-8398-7(5))*; lib. bdg. 467.10 *(978-0-7910-8326-0(8))* Facts On File, Inc. (Chelsea Hse.).

Alcamol, I. Edward, ed. Deadly Diseases & Epidemics. (Illus.). (J). 155.70 *(978-0-7910-7301-8(7)*, Chelsea Hse.) Facts On File, Inc.

Allman, Toney. The Importance of Germ Theory. 2015. (ENG., Illus.). 80p. (YA). lib. bdg. *(978-1-60152-890-2(6))* ReferencePoint Pr., Inc.

—Radiation Sickness. 2013. (Diseases & Disorders Ser.). (ENG., Illus.). 128p. (gr. 7-10). lib. bdg. 39.90 *(978-1-4205-0900-7(4)*, Lucent Bks.) Cengage Gale.

—Tuberculosis. 2006. (Diseases & Disorders Ser.). (ENG., Illus.). 128p. (J). (gr. 7-12). lib. bdg. 39.90 *(978-1-59018-968-9(X))* Cengage Gale.

Amos, Angela. Can I Tell You about Multiple Sclerosis? A Guide for Friends, Family & Professionals. Wiltshire, Sophie, illus. 2016. (Can I Tell You About...? Ser.). (ENG.). 48p. pap. 13.95 *(978-1-78592-146-9(0)*, 8721) Kingsley, Jessica Pubs. GBR. Dist: Macmillan Distribution Ltd.

Apel, Melanie Ann. Let's Talk about When You Have to Have Your Appendix Out. 2009. (Let's Talk Library). 24p. (gr. 2-3). 42.50 *(978-1-60853-448-7(0)*, PowerKids Pr.) Rosen Publishing Group, Inc., The.

Apte, Sunita. Michael J. Fox: I Can Make a Difference! 2006. (Defining Moments Ser.). (Illus.). 32p. (J). (gr. 2-5). lib. bdg. 25.27 *(978-1-59716-269-2(8))* Bearport Publishing Co., Inc.

Aronin, Miriam. Tuberculosis: The White Plague! 2010. (Nightmare Plagues Ser.). 32p. (YA). (gr. 4-9). lib. bdg. 25.27 *(978-1-936088-06-5(1))* Bearport Publishing Co., Inc.

Aronson, Virginia. Everything You Need to Know about Hepatitis. 2005. (Need to Know Library). (Illus.). 64p. (YA). (gr. 7-12). lib. bdg. 31.95 *(978-0-8239-3100-2(5)*, NTHEPA) Rosen Publishing Group, Inc., The.

Bailey, Diane. The Plague. 2010. (Epidemics & Society Ser.). (ENG.). 80p. (YA). lib. bdg. 33.25 *(978-1-4358-9435-8(9))* Rosen Publishing Group, Inc., The.

Benchmark Education Company. Fighting Disease (Teacher Guide) 2005. *(978-1-4108-4657-0(1))* Benchmark Education Co.

Berger, Melvin. Germs Make Me Sick! Hafner, Marylin, illus. 2015. (Let's-Read-And-Find-Out Science 2 Ser.). (ENG.). 32p. (J). (gr. -1-3). pap. 6.99 *(978-0-06-238187-3(3))* HarperCollins Pubs.

Berlatsky, Noah. The H1N1 Flu. 2010. (At Issue Ser.). (ENG.). 128p. (gr. 10-12). 39.40 *(978-0-7377-5089-8(8))*; pap. 27.80 *(978-0-7377-5090-4(1))* Cengage Gale. (Greenhaven Pr., Inc.).

Berry, Joy. Illness. 2009. (ENG.). 40p. (J). (gr. k — 1). bds. 7.95 *(978-1-60577-012-3(4))* Berry, Joy Enterprises.

Bjorklund, Ruth. Food-Borne Illnesses. 2005. (Health Alert Ser.). (Illus.). 64p. (YA). (gr. 4-7). lib. bdg. 32.79 *(978-0-7614-1917-4(9))* Marshall Cavendish Corp.

Bohland, Mark. Mystery Disease. 2003. pap. 12.95 *(978-1-883055-56-1(3))* Dandy Lion Pubns.

—Mystery Disease. 2005. (ENG.). 88p. (gr. 5-8). pap. 19.95 *(978-1-59363-110-9(3))* Prufrock Pr.

Brannon, Barbara. Discover Disease. 2005. (J). pap. *(978-1-4108-5137-6(0))* Benchmark Education Co.

Brill, Marlene Targ. Multiple Sclerosis. 2007. (Health Alert Ser.). (Illus.). 64p. (J). lib. bdg. 32.79 *(978-0-7614-2699-8(X)*, Benchmark Bks.) Marshall Cavendish Corp.

Brownlee, Christen. Beware of (Prairie) Dog! A Pet Swap Goes Viral. 2011. (J). pap. *(978-0-545-32805-0(5))* Scholastic, Inc.

Brunelle, Lynn & Gave, Marc. Viruses. 2003. (Discovery Channel School Science Ser.). (Illus.). 32p. (gr. 4-8). lib. bdg. 26.00 *(978-0-8368-3375-1(9)*, Gareth Stevens Learning Library) Stevens, Gareth Publishing LLLP.

Bueche, Shelley. The Ebola Virus. 2003. (Parasites Ser.). (ENG., Illus.). 32p. (J). 27.80 *(978-0-7377-1780-8(7)*, Greenhaven Pr., Inc.) Cengage Gale.

Bunch, Bryan H. & Tesar, Jenny E. Diseases, 8 vols., Set. 3rd ed. 2006. (YA). (gr. 6-18). 349.00 *(978-0-7172-6205-2(7)*, Grolier) Scholastic Library Publishing.

Burcaw, Shane. Laughing at My Nightmare. 2016. (YA). lib. bdg. 20.85 *(978-0-606-38222-9(4))* Turtleback Bks.

Burnett, Betty & Gevertz, Rob. Coping with Multiple Sclerosis. 2005. (Coping Ser.). (Illus.). 192p. (YA). (gr. 7-12). lib. bdg. 34.60 *(978-0-8239-3204-7(4))* Rosen Publishing Group, Inc., The.

Butler, Dori Hillestad. My Grandpa Had a Stroke. Wong, Nicole, illus. 2007. 31p. (J). (gr. 3-7). 14.95 *(978-1-59147-806-5(5))*; per. 9.95 *(978-1-59147-807-2(3))* American Psychological Assn. (Magination Pr.).

Chakraborty, Tirtha. Dengue Fever & Other Hemorrhagic Viruses. 2008. (Deadly Diseases & Epidemics Ser.). 102p. (C). (gr. 9). 34.95 *(978-0-7910-8506-6(6)*, Chelsea Hse.) Facts On File, Inc.

Chilman-Blair, Kim & Taddeo, John. Medikidz Explain Swine Flu: What's up with Jasmine? 2009. (Illus.). 32p. (J). pap. *(978-1-906935-33-7(5))* Medikidz Ltd.

Claybourne, Anna. Sick at Sea? Cure It or Cut It Off! 2010. (ENG.). 32p. (J). pap. *(978-0-7787-9922-1(0))* Crabtree Publishing Co.

—100 Deadliest Things on the Planet. 2012. (100 Most Ser.). lib. bdg. 18.40 *(978-0-606-26744-1(1)*, Turtleback) Turtleback Bks.

Cobb, Allan B. Frequently Asked Questions about Migraines & Headaches. 2008. (FAQ: Teen Life Ser.). (Illus.). 64p. (YA). (gr. 7-12). lib. bdg. 31.95 *(978-1-4042-1814-7(9))* Rosen Publishing Group, Inc., The.

Cobb, Vicki. Your Body Battles A Cold. 2009. pap. 40.95 *(978-0-7613-4619-7(8))* Lerner Publishing Group.

—Your Body Battles a Cold. Harris, Andrew, illus. Kunkel, Dennis, photos by. 2009. (Body Battles Ser.). (ENG.). 32p. (gr. 2-5). lib. bdg. 25.26 *(978-0-8225-6813-1(6))* Lerner Publishing Group.

—Your Body Battles A Stomachache. 2009. pap. 40.95 *(978-0-7613-4621-0(X))* Lerner Publishing Group.

—Your Body Battles a Stomachache. Harris, Andrew, illus. Kunkel, Dennis, photos by. 2009. (Body Battles Ser.). (ENG.). 32p. (gr. 2-5). lib. bdg. 25.26 *(978-0-8225-7166-7(8))* Lerner Publishing Group.

—Your Body Battles an Earache. 2009. pap. 40.95 *(978-0-7613-4618-0(X))* Lerner Publishing Group.

—Your Body Battles an Earache. Harris, Andrew, illus. Kunkel, Dennis, photos by. 2009. (Body Battles Ser.). (ENG.). 32p. (gr. 2-5). 25.26 *(978-0-8225-6812-4(8))* Lerner Publishing Group.

Contemporary Diseases & Disorders. 2015. (Contemporary Diseases & Disorders Ser.). (ENG.). 128p. (J). (gr. 7-7). 298.16 *(978-0-7660-6701-1(7))* Enslow Pubs., Inc.

Craig, Lizabeth. Parasitic Diseases. 2015. (Diseases & Disorders Ser.). (ENG., Illus.). 128p. (J). (gr. 7-10). 39.90 *(978-1-4205-1245-8(5)*, Lucent Bks.) Cengage Gale.

Deadliest Diseases of All Time. 2015. (Deadliest Diseases of All Time Ser.). (ENG.). 64p. (J). (gr. 7-7). 205.26 *(978-1-5026-0290-9(3))* Cavendish Square Publishing.

Deadly Diseases & Epidemics. 2011. (Deadly Diseases & Epidemics Ser.). (C). (gr. 9). 1712.55 *(978-0-7910-9985-8(7)*, Chelsea Hse.) Facts On File, Inc.

Dickmann, Nancy. What You Need to Know about Pink Eye. 2016. (Focus on Health Ser.). (ENG., Illus.). 32p. (gr. 3-4). lib. bdg. 27.32 *(978-1-4914-8241-4(9))* Capstone Press of Coughlan Cos.

DiConsiglio, John. Bad Breath: A Deadly Fungus Becomes Airborne. 2011. (J). pap. *(978-0-545-32811-1(X))* Scholastic, Inc.

—Mad Cow! Tracking down Killer Cattle. 2011. (J). pap. *(978-0-545-32808-1(X))* Scholastic, Inc.

Doak, Robin. Genetic Disorders: Set Of 6. 2011. (Navigators Ser.). (J). pap. 50.00 net. *(978-1-4108-6239-6(9))* Benchmark Education Co.

—Genetic Disorders: Text Pairs. 2008. (Bridges/Navigators Ser.). (J). (gr. 6). 94.00 *(978-1-4108-8437-4(6))* Benchmark Education Co.

Donaldson, Olivia. Influenza. 2015. (Deadliest Diseases of All Time Ser.). (ENG.). 64p. (J). (gr. 7-7). 34.21 *(978-1-5026-0092-9(7))* Cavendish Square Publishing.

Donovan, Sandy. Hawk & Drool: Gross Stuff in Your Mouth. Slack, Michael H., illus. 2009. (Gross Body Science Ser.). (ENG.). 48p. (gr. 3-5). lib. bdg. 29.27 *(978-0-8225-8966-2(4))* Lerner Publishing Group.

—Rumble & Spew: Gross Stuff in Your Stomach & Intestines. Slack, Michael H., illus. 2009. (Gross Body Science Ser.). (ENG.). 48p. (gr. 3-5). lib. bdg. 29.27 *(978-0-8225-8899-3(4))* Lerner Publishing Group.

Engdahl, Sylvia. Chronic Fatigue Syndrome. 2011. (Perspectives on Diseases & Disorders Ser.). (ENG., Illus.). 144p. (gr. 10-12). 44.30 *(978-0-7377-5773-6(6))* Cengage Gale.

—Meningitis. 2010. (Perspectives on Diseases & Disorders Ser.). (Illus.). 144p. (YA). 38.95 *(978-0-7377-4790-4(0)*, Greenhaven Pr., Inc.) Cengage Gale.

Epidemic! Series, 5 Bks, Set. 2004. (J). 149.64 *(978-0-7614-1632-6(3))* Marshall Cavendish Corp.

Epidemics: Deadly Diseases Throughout History, 6 bks. 2005. (YA). (gr. 7-12). Set 4. lib. bdg. 159.00 *(978-1-4042-0375-4(3))*Sets 1-4. lib. bdg. 598.50 *(978-1-4042-0502-4(0))* Rosen Publishing Group, Inc., The.

Evans, Michael. The Adventures of Medical Man: Kids' Illnesses & Injuries Explained. Williams, Gareth, illus. 2010. (ENG.). 72p. (J). (gr. 3-5). 21.95 *(978-1-55451-263-8(8)*, 9781554512638); pap. 12.95 *(978-1-55451-262-1(X)*, 9781554512621) Annick Pr., Ltd. CAN. Dist: Publishers Group West (PGW).

Farndon, John. Tiny Killers: When Bacteria & Viruses Attack. Dean, Venitia, illus. 2017. (Sickening History of Medicine Ser.). (ENG.). 32p. (J). (gr. 3-6). 26.65 *(978-1-5124-1558-2(8))*; 19.99 **(978-1-5124-3642-6(9))**; 30.65 **(978-1-5124-2710-3(1))**; 30.65 **(978-1-5124-3641-9(0))** Lerner Publishing Group.

Fredericks, Carrie. Parkinson's Disease. 2009. (Perspectives on Diseases & Disorders Ser.). (ENG., Illus.). 144p. (gr. 10-12). lib. bdg. 44.30 *(978-0-7377-4382-1(4)*, LML02109-245387, Greenhaven Pr., Inc.) Cengage Gale.

Freedman, Jeri. Hepatitis B. 2009. (Library of Sexual Health Ser.). 64p. (gr. 6-6). 58.50 *(978-1-60853-846-1(X))* Rosen Publishing Group, Inc., The.

Frender, Sam & Schiffmiller, Robin. Brotherly Feelings: Me, My Emotions, & My Brother with Asperger's Syndrome. Dittrich, Dennis, illus. 2007. (ENG.). 64p. (gr. 3-7). per. 15.95 *(978-1-84310-850-4(X)*, 2617) Kingsley, Jessica Pubs. GBR. Dist: Macmillan Distribution Ltd.

Friedlander, Mark P. Outbreak: Disease Detectives at Work. 2nd enl. rev. ed. (Discovery! Ser.). 2005. (Illus.). 120p. (gr. 5-12). 27.93 *(978-0-8225-0948-6(2))* 2009. (ENG.). 128p. (gr. 6-12). 31.93 *(978-0-8225-9039-2(5))* Lerner Publishing Group.

Frith, Sherry. Sticky Icky Booger Bugs. 2013. 32p. pap. 16.99 *(978-1-4808-0083-0(X))* Archway Publishing.

Gagne, Tammy. Battling Against Drug-Resistant Bacteria. 2017. (Science Frontiers Ser.). (ENG., Illus.). 32p. (J). (gr. 3-6). 21.95 *(978-1-63235-373-3(3))* Pr. Room Editions LLC.

Gallagher, Aileen. Hepatitis. 2009. (Epidemics Ser.). 64p. (gr. 5-5). 58.50 *(978-1-61512-283-7(4))* Rosen Publishing Group, Inc., The.

Genes & Disease Set, 10-Volumes. 2009. (Genes & Disease Ser.). (C). (gr. 9-18). 350.00 *(978-0-7910-9921-6(0)*, Chelsea Hse.) Facts On File, Inc.

Gibson, Brylee. Disease Detectives. 2007. (Connectors Ser.). (gr. 2-5). pap. *(978-1-877453-23-6(4))* Global Education Systems Ltd.

Giddens, Sandra. Everything You Need to Know about Crohn's Disease & Ulcerative Colitis. 2009. (Need to Know Library). 64p. (gr. 5-5). 58.50 *(978-1-60854-061-7(8))* Rosen Publishing Group, Inc., The.

—Suicide. 2006. (Coping in a Changing World Ser.). 112p. (YA). (gr. 7-12). lib. bdg. 34.60 *(978-1-4042-0952-7(2))* Rosen Publishing Group, Inc., The.

Giddens, Sandra & Giddens, Owen. Everything You Need to Know about Crohn's Disease & Colitis. 2005. (Need to Know Library). (Illus.). 64p. (YA). lib. bdg. 31.95 *(978-0-8239-3996-1(0))* Rosen Publishing Group, Inc., The.

Giddings, Sharon, et al. Cystic Fibrosis. 2009. (Genes & Disease Ser.). (Illus.). 128p. (YA). (gr. 7-12). 35.00 *(978-0-7910-9694-9(7))* Facts On File, Inc.

Goldsmith, Connie. The Ebola Epidemic: The Fight, the Future. 2016. (Nonfiction - Young Adult Ser.). (ENG., Illus.). 112p. (gr. 7-12). (J). 35.99 *(978-1-4677-9244-8(6))*; (YA). 53.32 *(978-1-4677-9577-7(1))* Lerner Publishing Group. (Twenty-First Century Bks.).

—Influenza. 2010. (USA TODAY Health Reports: Diseases & Disorders Ser.). (ENG.). 128p. (gr. 6-12). lib. bdg. 34.60 *(978-0-7613-5881-7(1))* Lerner Publishing Group.

—Meningitis. 2007. (Twenty-First Century Medical Library). (Illus.). 128p. (YA). (gr. 7-12). lib. bdg. 30.60 *(978-0-8225-7034-9(3))* Twenty First Century Bks.

Goldstein, Margaret J. Everything You Need to Know about Multiple Sclerosis. 2005. (Need to Know Library). (Illus.). 64p. (YA). (gr. 7-12). 31.95 *(978-0-8239-3292-4(3)*, NTMUSC) Rosen Publishing Group, Inc., The.

Gologan, Trena. Butterflies to Remember. 2009. 37p. pap. 26.60 *(978-0-557-07358-0(8))* Lulu Pr., Inc.

Goodbody, Slim. Staying Well. McGinnis, Ben, illus. Pinchbeck, Chris, photos by. 2007. (Slim Goodbody's Good Health Guides Ser.). 32p. (J). (gr. 2-6). lib. bdg. 26.00 *(978-0-8368-7744-1(6)*, Gareth Stevens Learning Library) Stevens, Gareth Publishing LLLP.

Gordon, Sharon. Pinkeye. 2003. (Rookie Read-About Health Ser.). (ENG., Illus.). 32p. (J). (-2). 20.50 *(978-0-516-22583-8(9)*, Children's Pr.) Scholastic Library Publishing.

Gosman, Gillian. I Have a Cold. 2012. (Get Well Soon! Ser.). (ENG., Illus.). 24p. (J). (gr. 1-3). lib. bdg. 22.60 *(978-1-4488-7408-8(4)*, PowerKids Pr.) Rosen Publishing Group, Inc., The.

Gray, Susan H. Disease Control. 2008. (21st Century Skills Innovation Library: Innovation in Medicine Ser.). (ENG., Illus.). 32p. (gr. 4-8). lib. bdg. 28.50 *(978-1-60279-228-9(3)*, 200159) Cherry Lake Publishing.

Grayson-Jones, Timothy. Cholera. 2015. (J). lib. bdg. *(978-1-62713-381-4(X))*; (ENG., Illus.). 64p. (gr. 7-7). 34.21 *(978-1-5026-0090-5(0))* Cavendish Square Publishing.

Greenhaven Press Editors, ed. Fibromyaligia. 2011. (Diseases & Disorders Ser.). (Illus.). 128p. (YA). (gr. 9-12). 34.95 *(978-1-4205-0673-0(0))* Cengage Gale.

Hall, Kirk. Carson & His Shaky Paws Grampa. Paolini, Alison, illus. 2011. 24p. (J). pap. 15.95 *(978-1-61314-009-3(6))*; lib. bdg. 19.95 *(978-1-936076-91-8(8))* Innovo Publishing, LLC.

Hall, Linley Erin. Doomsday Scenarios: Separating Fact from Fiction: Killer Viruses. 2010. (Doomsday Scenarios: Separating Fact from Fiction Ser.). (ENG.). 64p. (YA). pap. 12.95 *(978-1-4358-8524-0(4)*, Rosen Reference) Rosen Publishing Group, Inc., The.

—Killer Viruses. 2010. (Doomsday Scenarios: Separating Fact from Fiction Ser.). (Illus.). 64p. (YA). (gr. 5-8). lib. bdg. 31.95 *(978-1-4358-3561-0(1)*, Rosen Reference) Rosen Publishing Group, Inc., The.

Harris, Michael C. Unusual Diseases. 2010. (Cool Science Ser.). 48p. (J). (gr. 3-6). 28.50 *(978-0-7614-1913-6(6)*...

Hawkins, Carole. Asthma, Cystic Fibrosis, & Other Respiratory Disorders. 2017. (J). **(978-1-4222-3750-2(8))** Mason Crest.

Hawkins, Trisha. Everything You Need to Know about Measles & Rubella. 2005. (Need to Know Library). (Illus.). 64p. (YA). (gr. 7-12). 31.95 *(978-0-8239-3322-8(9))* Rosen Publishing Group, Inc., The.

Health Alert Series, 6 Bks, Set. 2004. (J). 171.00 *(978-0-7614-1797-2(4))* Marshall Cavendish Corp.

Herbst, Judith. Germ Theory. 2007. (Great Ideas of Science Ser.). (Illus.). 80p. (YA). (gr. 9-12). lib. bdg. 27.93 *(978-0-8225-2909-5(2))* Twenty First Century Bks.

Herrington, Lisa M. I Have a Cold. 2015. (Rookie Read-About(tm) Health Ser.). (ENG., Illus.). 32p. (J). lib. bdg. 25.00 *(978-0-531-21012-3(X))* Scholastic Library Publishing.

Hicks, Terry Allan. The Common Cold. 2006. (Health Alert Ser.). (Illus.). 64p. (J). (gr. 3-7). lib. bdg. 32.79 *(978-0-7614-1913-6(6)*, Benchmark Bks.) Marshall Cavendish Corp.

Hill, Eric M. Deliverance from Demons & Diseases: Freedom from Incurable Diseases & Persistent Problems 2004. 256p. per. 12.99 net. *(978-0-9673189-1-2(2))* SunHill Pubs.

Hoffman, Gretchen. Osteoporosis. 2007. (Health Alert Ser.). (Illus.). 64p. (YA). (gr. 4-7). lib. bdg. 32.79 *(978-0-7614-2702-5(3))* Marshall Cavendish Corp.

Hoffmann, Gretchen. Mononucleosis. 2006. (Health Alert Ser.). (Illus.). 64p. (J). (gr. 3-7). lib. bdg. 32.79 *(978-0-7614-1915-0(2)*, Benchmark Bks.) Marshall Cavendish Corp.

Holt, Rinehart and Winston Staff. Decisions for Health Blue, Chptr. 18: Noninfectious Diseases. 4th ed. 2004. pap. 11.20 *(978-0-03-068053-3(0))* Holt McDougal.

—Decisions for Health Red Chptr. 15: Noninfectious Diseases. 4th ed. 2004. pap. 11.20 *(978-0-03-068042-7(5))* Holt McDougal.

—A Lifetime of Health Chptr. 13: Prevention of Diseases. 4th ed. Date not set. pap. 11.20 *(978-0-03-068106-6(5))* Holt McDougal.

—A Lifetime of Health Chptr. 14: Lifestyle Diseases. 4th ed. Date not set. pap. 11.20 *(978-0-03-068107-3(3))* Holt McDougal.

—A Lifetime of Health Chptr. 15: Other Diseases. 4th ed. Date not set. pap. 11.20 *(978-0-03-068108-0(1))* Holt McDougal.

Hsu, Lewis. Hope & Destiny Jr: The Adolescent's Guide to Sickle Cell Diseases. 2013. (ENG.). pap. 19.95 *(978-0-9764443-1-2(3))* Hilton Publishing Co.

Huebner, Dawn. What to Do When Your Brain Gets Stuck: A Kid's Guide to Overcoming Ocd. Matthews, Bonnie, illus. 2007. 95p. (J). (gr. 3-7). per. 15.95 *(978-1-59147-805-8(7),* Magination Pr.) American Psychological Assn.

Jerome, Kate Boehm & National Geographic Learning Staff. Fighting Disease. 2007. (Rise & Shine Ser.). (ENG., Illus.). 32p. (J). pap. 17.95 *(978-0-7922-8865-7(3))* CENGAGE Learning.

Johanson, Paula. Muscular Dystrophy. 2009. (Genetic & Developmental Diseases & Disorders Ser.). 64p. (gr. 4-6). 58.50 *(978-1-61512-659-0(7))* Rosen Publishing Group, Inc., The.

Jones, Molly. Muscular Dystrophy & Other Neuromuscular Disorders. 2017. (J). ***(978-1-4222-3758-8(3))*** Mason Crest.

Kelly, Evelyn B. & Wilson, Claire. Influenza & Bird Flu: Examining the Flu. 2014. (Diseases, Disorders, Symptoms Ser.). (Illus.). 96p. (gr. 9-12). pap. 10.95 *(978-1-62293-076-0(2))* Enslow Pubs., Inc.

Kelly, Evelyn B., et al. Investigating Tuberculosis & Superbugs: Real Facts for Real Lives. 2010. (Investigating Diseases Ser.). 160p. (YA). (gr. 9-12). 35.94 *(978-0-7660-3343-6(0))* Enslow Pubs., Inc.

—Tuberculosis & Superbugs: Examining TB & Bacterial Infections. 2014. (Diseases, Disorders, Symptoms Ser.). (Illus.). 96p. (J). (gr. 9-12). 27.94 *(978-1-62293-085-2(1))* Enslow Pubs., Inc.

Keyser, Amber J. Anatomy of a Pandemic. 2011. (Disasters Ser.). (ENG.). 48p. (gr. 3-4). pap. 59.70 *(978-1-4296-6444-8(4))* Capstone Press of Coughlan Cos.

Klosterman, Lorrie. Rabies. 2007. (Health Alert Ser.). (Illus.). 64p. (YA). (gr. 8-12). lib. bdg. 32.79 *(978-0-7614-2704-9(X),* Benchmark Bks.) Marshall Cavendish Corp.

Knowles, Johanna. Huntington's Disease. 2006. (Genetic Diseases & Disorders Ser.). (Illus.). 64p. (YA). (gr. 5-9). lib. bdg. 31.95 *(978-1-4042-0694-6(9))* Rosen Publishing Group, Inc., The.

Kupperberg, Paul. How Do We Know the Nature of Disease. (Great Scientific Questions & the Scientists Who Answered Them Ser.). 112p. (gr. 7-12). 2009. 63.90 *(978-1-61513-200-3(7))* 2005. (Illus.). (J). lib. bdg. 34.60 *(978-1-4042-0075-3(4))* Rosen Publishing Group, Inc., The.

La Bella, Laura. Blood Pressure Basics. 2010. (Healthy Habits Ser.). (Illus.). 64p. (YA). (gr. 5-8). pap. 12.95 *(978-1-4488-0611-9(9));* lib. bdg. 31.95 *(978-1-4358-9441-9(3))* Rosen Publishing Group, Inc., The. (Rosen Reference).

Landau, Elaine. Pink Eye. 2009. (Head-to Toe Health 2 Ser.). 32p. (gr. 2). 28.50 *(978-0-7614-3504-4(2))* Marshall Cavendish Corp.

Landau, Jennifer. Endometriosis. 2015. (Your Sexual Health Ser.). (ENG., Illus.). 64p. (J). (gr. 6-7). 32.95 *(978-1-4994-6074-2(0),* Rosen Young Adult) Rosen Publishing Group, Inc., The.

Langwith, Jacqueline. Hepatitis. 2009. (Perspectives on Diseases & Disorders Ser.). (ENG., Illus.). 144p. (gr. 10-12). 44.30 *(978-0-7377-4553-5(3),* Greenhaven Pr., Inc.) Cengage Gale.

Langwith, Jacqueline, ed. Hpv. 2013. (Perspectives on Diseases & Disorders Ser.). (ENG., Illus.). 144p. (gr. 10-12). lib. bdg. 38.95 *(978-0-7377-6355-3(8),* Greenhaven Pr., Inc.) Cengage Gale.

Larson, Elaine Marie. The Chameleon Kid: Controlling Meltdown Before He Controls You. 2008. (ENG.). 41p. (J). 17.95 *(978-1-934575-22-2(4))* Autism Asperger Publishing Co.

Lawrence, David M. Huntington's Disease. 2009. (Genes & Disease Ser.). (Illus.). 128p. (C). (gr. 9-18). 35.00 *(978-0-7910-9586-7(X),* Chelsea Hse.) Facts On File, Inc.

Lee, Justin. Everything You Need to Know about Cystic Fibrosis. 2009. (Need to Know Library). 64p. (gr. 5-5). 58.50 *(978-1-60854-063-1(4))* Rosen Publishing Group, Inc., The.

Leech, Bonnie Coulter. Polygons. 2006. (Exploring Shapes Ser.: Vol. 3). (Illus.). 24p. (J). (gr. 3-7). lib. bdg. 22.60 *(978-1-4042-3497-0(7))* Rosen Publishing Group, Inc., The.

—Quadrilaterals. 2006. (Exploring Shapes Ser.: Vol. 3). (Illus.). 24p. (J). (gr. 3-7). lib. bdg. 22.60 *(978-1-4042-3496-3(9))* Rosen Publishing Group, Inc., The.

Leuenroth, Stephanie. Hantavirus Pulmonary Syndrome. 2006. (Deadly Diseases & Epidemics Ser.). (Illus.). 112p. (C). (gr. 9-12). 34.95 *(978-0-7910-8676-6(3),* Chelsea Hse.) Facts On File, Inc.

Levy, Janey. Alopecia Areata. 2009. (Genetic Diseases & Disorders Ser.). 64p. (gr. 6-6). 58.50 *(978-1-61512-662-0(7))* Rosen Publishing Group, Inc., The.

Libal, Autumn. Chained: Youth with Chronic Illness. 2004. (Youth with Special Needs Ser.). (Illus.). 128p. (YA). lib. bdg. 24.95 *(978-1-59084-735-0(0))* Mason Crest.

Libal, Joyce. Drug Therapy for Mental Disorders Caused by a Medical Condition. 2004. (Encyclopedia of Psychiatric Drugs & Their Disorders Ser.). (Illus.). 128p. (YA). lib. bdg. 24.95 *(978-1-59084-567-7(6))* Mason Crest.

Lucent Books, ed. Meningitis. 2014. (Diseases & Disorders Ser.). (ENG.). 128p. (gr. 7-10). lib. bdg. 39.90 *(978-1-4205-1221-2(8),* Lucent Bks.) Cengage Gale.

Magee, Elaine. Tell Me What to Eat If I Have Irritable Bowel Syndrome. 2008. (Tell Me What to Eat Ser.). 144p. (J). lib. bdg. 35.95 *(978-1-4042-1836-9(X))* Rosen Publishing Group, Inc., The.

Margulies, Philip. Creutzfeldt-Jakob Disease. 2004. (Epidemics Ser.). (Illus.). 64p. (YA). (gr. 7-12). lib. bdg. 31.95 *(978-0-8239-4199-5(X))* Rosen Publishing Group, Inc., The.

—Everything You Need to Know about Rheumatic Fever. (Need to Know Library). 64p. 2009. (gr. 5-5). 58.50 *(978-1-60854-084-6(7))* 2005. (Illus.). (YA). lib. bdg. 31.95 *(978-0-8239-4509-2(X))* Rosen Publishing Group, Inc., The.

Massari, Francesca. Everything You Need to Know about Cancer. 2005. (Need to Know Library). (Illus.). 64p. (YA). (gr. 7-12). lib. bdg. 31.95 *(978-0-8239-3164-4(1),* NTCANC) Rosen Publishing Group, Inc., The.

McGrody, Ellen. Coping with Gender Dysphoria. 2017. (Coping Ser.). 112p. (gr. 12-12). 37.10 ***(978-1-5081-7391-5(5),*** Rosen Young Adult) Rosen Publishing Group, Inc., The.

McPartland, Randall. E. Coli. 2015. (Deadliest Diseases of All Time Ser.). (ENG., Illus.). 64p. (J). (gr. 8-8). 34.21 *(978-1-5026-0644-0(5))* Cavendish Square Publishing.

—Tay-Sachs Disease. 2016. (Genetic Conditions Ser.). (ENG., Illus.). 64p. (J). (gr. 8-8). 34.21 *(978-1-5026-0946-5(0))* Cavendish Square Publishing.

Meningitis. 2nd rev. ed. 2010. (Deadly Diseases & Epidemics Ser.). (Illus.). 120p. (C). (gr. 9-18). 34.95 *(978-1-60413-241-0(8),* Chelsea Hse.) Facts On File, Inc.

Miller, Petra. Ebola. 2015. (Deadliest Diseases of All Time Ser.). (ENG., Illus.). 64p. (J). (gr. 8-8). 34.21 *(978-1-5026-0652-5(6))* Cavendish Square Publishing.

—Hepatitis. 2015. (Deadliest Diseases of All Time Ser.). (ENG., Illus.). 64p. (J). (gr. 8-8). 34.21 *(978-1-5026-0650-1(X))* Cavendish Square Publishing.

Minden, Cecilia. Keep It Clean: Achoo! 2010. (21st Century Basic Skills Library: Keep It Clean Ser.). (ENG.). 24p. (gr. k-3). lib. bdg. 22.79 *(978-1-60279-856-4(7),* 200578) Cherry Lake Publishing.

—Keep It Clean: Get Well Soon. 2010. (21st Century Basic Skills Library: Keep It Clean Ser.). (ENG.). 24p. (gr. k-3). lib. bdg. 22.79 *(978-1-60279-858-8(3),* 200582) Cherry Lake Publishing.

Moe, Barbara. Everything You Need to Know about Migraines & Other Headaches. 2005. (Need to Know Library). (Illus.). 64p. (YA). (gr. 7-12). lib. bdg. 31.95 *(978-0-8239-3291-7(5),* NTMIHE) Rosen Publishing Group, Inc., The.

Moehn, Heather. Everything You Need to Know When Someone You Know Has Leukemia. 2005. (Need to Know Library). (Illus.). 64p. (YA). (gr. 7-12). lib. bdg. 31.95 *(978-0-8239-3121-7(8),* NTLEUK) Rosen Publishing Group, Inc., The.

Monroe Peterson, Judy. Sickle Cell Anemia. 2009. (Genetic & Developmental Diseases & Disorders Ser.). 64p. (gr. 4-6). 58.50 *(978-1-61512-660-6(0))* Rosen Publishing Group, Inc., The.

Moran, Katherine J. Diabetes: The Ultimate Teen Guide. 2004. (It Happened to Me Ser.: 7). (ENG., Illus.). 208p. (gr. 9). 55.00 *(978-0-8108-4806-1(6))* Scarecrow Pr., Inc.

Naff, Clayton Farris, ed. Multiple Sclerosis. 2009. (Perspectives on Diseases & Disorders Ser.). (ENG., Illus.). 144p. (gr. 10-12). lib. bdg. 44.30 *(978-0-7377-4381-4(6),* LML02109-245386, Greenhaven Pr., Inc.) Cengage Gale.

—Muscular Dystrophy. 2011. (Perspectives on Diseases & Disorders Ser.). (ENG., Illus.). 144p. (gr. 10-12). 44.30 *(978-0-7377-5780-4(9))* Cengage Gale.

Naish, Sarah & Jefferies, Rosie. William Wobbly & the Very Bad Day: A Story about When Feelings Become Too Big. Farrell, Amy, illus. 2016. (Therapeutic Parenting Bks.). (ENG.). 32p. (J). pap. 14.95 *(978-1-78592-151-3(7),* 8678) Kingsley, Jessica Pubs. GBR. Dist: Macmillan Distribution Ltd.

Nardo, Don. Malnutrition. 2007. (Diseases & Disorders Ser.). (ENG., Illus.). 104p. (YA). (gr. 7-12). lib. bdg. 34.95 *(978-1-59018-677-0(X),* LML02109-221242) Cengage Gale.

—Teens & Gender Dysphoria. 2017. (ENG.). 80p. (J). (gr. 5-12). *(978-1-68282-124-4(2))* ReferencePoint Pr., Inc.

Newman, Patricia. Ebola: Fears & Facts. 2015. (ENG., Illus.). 48p. (gr. 4-8). 31.99 *(978-1-4677-9259-2(4),* Millbrook Pr.) Lerner Publishing Group.

O'Donnell, Judith A., et al. Pelvic Inflammatory Disease. Alcamo, I. Edward, ed. 2007. (Deadly Diseases & Epidemics Ser.). (Illus.). 112p. (YA). (gr. 9-12). lib. bdg. 34.95 *(978-0-7910-8507-3(4))* Facts On File, Inc.

Ollhoff, Jim. Smallpox, 1 vol. 2009. (History of Germs Ser.). (ENG., Illus.). 32p. (YA). (gr. 5-9). 27.07 *(978-1-60453-501-3(6))* ABDO Publishing Co.

Parks, Peggy J. Genetic Disorders. 2010. (Compact Research Ser.). 96p. (YA). (gr. 7-12). lib. bdg. 26.95 *(978-1-60152-096-8(4))* ReferencePoint Pr., Inc.

—Hpv. 2014. (Compact Research: Diseases & Disorders). (ENG., Illus.). 96p. (J). lib. bdg. 28.95 *(978-1-60152-690-8(3))* ReferencePoint Pr., Inc.

—Influenza. 2010. (Compact Research Ser.). (YA). (gr. 7-12). lib. bdg. 26.95 *(978-1-60152-118-7(9))* ReferencePoint Pr., Inc.

Parsons, Michelle Hyde. Fighting Disease. 2005. (J). pap. *(978-1-4108-4609-9(1))* Benchmark Education Co.

Payment, Simone. Michael J. Fox: Parkinson's Disease Research Advocate (Celebrity Activists) l.t. ed. 2012. 188p. pap. *(978-1-4596-3346-9(6))* ReadHowYouWant.com, Ltd.

Peters, Stephanie. Smallpox in the New World. 2003. (J). 32.79 *(978-0-7614-1637-1(4),* Benchmark Bks.) Marshall Cavendish Corp.

—The 1918 Influenza Pandemic. 2003. (Illus.). ix, 69p. (J). 29.93 *(978-0-7614-1636-4(6),* Benchmark Bks.) Marshall Cavendish Corp.

Porter, C. Coping with Crohn's Disease & Ulcerative Colitis. 2009. (Coping Ser.). 196p. (gr. 7-12). 63.90 *(978-1-61511-996-7(5))* Rosen Publishing Group, Inc., The.

Potter, Christina. Coping with Crohn's Disease & Ulcerative Colitis. 2005. (Coping Ser.). 192p. (YA). (gr. 7-12). lib. bdg. 34.60 *(978-0-8239-3962-6(6))* Rosen Publishing Group, Inc., The.

Powell, Jillian. Sore Throat. 2008. (Feeling Sick? Ser.). (Illus.). 23p. (J). (gr. 1-4). lib. bdg. 27.10 *(978-1-84234-473-6(0))* Cherrytree Pubns., Inc.

Ramen, Fred. Influenza. 2009. (Epidemics Ser.). 64p. (gr. 5-5). 58.50 *(978-1-61512-286-8(9))* Rosen Publishing Group, Inc., The.

—Sleeping Sickness & Other Parasitic Tropical Diseases. 2009. (Epidemics Ser.). 64p. (gr. 5-5). 58.50 *(978-1-61512-301-8(6))* Rosen Publishing Group, Inc., The.

—Tuberculosis. 2009. (Epidemics Ser.). 64p. (gr. 5-5). 58.50 *(978-1-61512-304-9(0))* Rosen Publishing Group, Inc., The.

Ray, Kurt. Typhoid Fever. 2009. (Epidemics Ser.). 64p. (gr. 5-5). 58.50 *(978-1-61512-305-6(9))* Rosen Publishing Group, Inc., The.

Reeves, Barbara. Grandpa's Crooked Smile: A Story of Stroke Survival. Sinclair, Peter, illus. 2007. (J). *(978-1-4276-2013-2(X))* Aardvark Global Publishing.

Reingold, Adam. Smallpox: Is It Over? 2010. (Nightmare Plagues Ser.). 32p. (YA). (gr. 4-9). lib. bdg. 25.27 *(978-1-936088-02-7(9))* Bearport Publishing Co., Inc.

Ridgway, Tom. Smallpox. 2009. (Epidemics Ser.). 64p. (gr. 5-5). 58.50 *(978-1-61512-302-5(4))* Rosen Publishing Group, Inc., The.

Rissman, Rebecca. Should Bella Go to Bed? Staying Healthy, 1 vol. 2013. (What Would You Do? Ser.). (ENG., Illus.). 24p. (gr. -1-1). pap. 6.29 *(978-1-4329-7256-1(1));* lib. bdg. 22.65 *(978-1-4329-7255-4(3))* Heinemann-Raintree. (Acorn).

Robertson, David Alexander. Scars. Henderson, Scott B., illus. 2010. (7 Generations Ser.: 2). (ENG.). 32p. (YA). pap. *(978-1-55379-228-4(9),* 4ae83eb9-baca-4c13-a381-ea5771ba95b7, HighWater Pr.) Portage & Main Pr.

Rogers, Kara, ed. The Endocrine System. 2011. (Human Body Ser.). (ENG.). 176 ndash; 288p. (YA). (gr. 9-12). lib. bdg. 38.75 *(978-1-61530-675-6(7))* Rosen Publishing Group, Inc., The.

Rosaler, Maxine. Botulism. (Epidemics Ser.). 64p. 2009. (gr. 5-5). 58.50 *(978-1-61512-274-5(5))* 2004. (Illus.). (YA). (gr. 7-12). lib. bdg. 31.95 *(978-0-8239-4197-1(3))* Rosen Publishing Group, Inc., The.

—Cystic Fibrosis. 2009. (Genetic Diseases & Disorders Ser.). 64p. (gr. 6-6). 58.50 *(978-1-61512-663-7(5))* Rosen Publishing Group, Inc., The.

—Listeriosis. 2004. (Epidemics Ser.). (Illus.). 64p. (gr. 5-8). lib. bdg. 31.95 *(978-0-8239-4202-2(3))* Rosen Publishing Group, Inc., The.

Ruffin, Frances E. Polycystic Ovary Syndrome. 2011. (Girls' Health Ser.). (YA). (gr. 5-9). lib. bdg. 29.25 *(978-1-4488-4576-7(9))* Rosen Publishing Group, Inc., The.

Saulmon, Greg. Genital Herpes. 2006. (Library of Sexual Health Ser.). (Illus.). 64p. (YA). (gr. 7-12). lib. bdg. 31.95 *(978-1-4042-0907-7(7))* Rosen Publishing Group, Inc., The.

Sheen, Barbara. Cerebral Palsy. 2003. (Diseases & Disorders Ser.). (ENG., Illus.). 96p. (J). 33.45 *(978-1-59018-038-9(0),* Lucent Bks.) Cengage Gale.

Sherman, Rebecca. Allergies & Other Immune System Disorders. 2017. (J). ***(978-1-4222-3749-6(4))*** Mason Crest.

—Crohn's Disease & Other Digestive Disorders. 2017. (J). ***(978-1-4222-3754-0(0))*** Mason Crest.

Shmaefsky, Brian R. Toxic Shock Syndrome. 2nd rev. ed. 2010. (Deadly Diseases & Epidemics Ser.). 128p. (C). (gr. 9). 34.95 *(978-1-60413-243-4(4),* Chelsea Hse.) Facts On File, Inc.

Silverstein, Alvin. Diseases & People, 40 bks., Set. (Illus.). (YA). (gr. 6-12). lib. bdg. 838.00 *(978-0-89490-571-1(6))* Enslow Pubs., Inc.

Silverstein, Alvin, et al. The Flu & Pneumonia Update. 2006. (Disease Update Ser.). (Illus.). 104p. (J). (gr. 4-7). lib. bdg. 33.27 *(978-0-7660-2480-9(6))* Enslow Pubs., Inc.

—Handy Health Guide to Headaches. 2014. (Illus.). 48p. (J). *(978-0-7660-5889-7(1))* Enslow Pubs., Inc.

—Scoliosis. 2003. (My Health Ser.). (ENG.). 48p. (J). (gr. 3-5). pap. 6.95 *(978-0-531-16639-0(2),* Watts, Franklin) Scholastic Library Publishing.

—The Tuberculosis Update. 2006. (Disease Update Ser.). (Illus.). 112p. (J). (gr. 5-9). lib. bdg. 33.27 *(978-0-7660-2481-6(4))* Enslow Pubs., Inc.

Silverstein, Virginia. Handy Health Guide to Headaches. 2013. (Handy Health Guides). 48p. (J). (gr. 5-12). pap. 8.95 *(978-1-4644-0497-9(6))* Enslow Pubs., Inc.

—Handy Health Guide to Sore Throats. 2013. (Handy Health Guides). 48p. (J). (gr. 5-12). pap. 8.95 *(978-1-4644-0501-3(8))* Enslow Pubs., Inc.

Silverstein, Virginia & Nunn, Laura Silverstein. Handy Health Guide to Colds & Flu. 2013. (Handy Health Guides). 48p. (J). (gr. 5-18). lib. bdg. 25.27 *(978-0-7660-4274-2(X))* Enslow Pubs., Inc.

—Handy Health Guide to Headaches. 2013. (Handy Health Guides). 48p. (J). lib. bdg. 25.27 *(978-0-7660-4277-3(4))* Enslow Pubs., Inc.

—Handy Health Guide to Sore Throats. 2013. (Handy Health Guides). 48p. (J). lib. bdg. 25.27 *(978-0-7660-4279-7(0))* Enslow Pubs., Inc.

Smith, Jennifer Crown. Dad's Falling Apart: Keeping It Together When a Family Member Has Multiple Sclerosis. Williams, Ron, illus. 2003. 32p. (J). per. 14.95 *(978-0-929173-36-8(8))* Health Press NA Incorporated.

Smith, Tara C. Streptococcus (Group B) Alcamo, I. Edward, ed. 2007. (Deadly Diseases & Epidemics Ser.). (Illus.). 112p. (YA). (gr. 9-12). lib. bdg. 34.95 *(978-0-7910-9243-9(7))* Facts On File, Inc.

Somervill, Barbara A. Graphing Health & Disease, 1 vol. 2010. (Real World Data Ser.). (ENG., Illus.). 32p. (gr. 3-5). lib. bdg. 29.99 *(978-1-4329-2619-9(5),* NA-h) Heinemann-Raintree.

Spilsbury, Richard. Health & Disease: Investigating a TB Outbreak, 1 vol. 2013. (Anatomy of an Investigation Ser.). (ENG.). 56p. (gr. 7-8). 34.65 *(978-1-4329-7603-3(6));* pap. 9.95 *(978-1-4329-7609-5(5))* Heinemann-Raintree.

Squire, Ann O. Flu. 2016. (True Book(tm), A — Health Ser.). (ENG., Illus.). 48p. (J). lib. bdg. 31.00 *(978-0-531-22846-3(0),* Children's Pr.) Scholastic Library Publishing.

—Lyme Disease. 2016. (True Book(tm), A — Health Ser.). (ENG., Illus.). 48p. (J). lib. bdg. 31.00 *(978-0-531-22841-8(X),* Children's Pr.) Scholastic Library Publishing.

Stanley, Debbie. Coping with Vision Disorders. 2005. (Coping Ser.). (Illus.). 192p. (YA). (gr. 7-12). lib. bdg. 34.60 *(978-0-8239-3198-9(6))* Rosen Publishing Group, Inc., The.

Stewart, Gail B. Fetal Alcohol Syndrome. 2012. (Diseases & Disorders Ser.). (ENG.). 128p. (gr. 7-10). lib. bdg. 39.90 *(978-1-4205-0695-2(1),* Lucent Bks.) Cengage Gale.

Teen's Guides, 5 vols., Set. Incl. Living with Anxiety Disorders. Miller, Allen R. 208p. 34.95 *(978-0-8160-6344-4(3));* Living with Cancer. Dreyer, ZoAnn. (Illus.). 192p. 34.95 *(978-0-8160-6484-7(9));* Living with Depression. Miller, Allen R. 208p. 34.95 *(978-0-8160-6345-1(1));* Living with Diabetes. Parker, Katrina. 176p. 34.95 *(978-0-8160-6346-8(X));* Teen's Guide to Living with Asthma. Berger, William E. 192p. 34.95 *(978-0-8160-6483-0(0));* (gr. 6-12). (Teen's Guides). 2007. 174.75 o.p. *(978-0-8160-7437-2(2))* Facts On File, Inc.

Tiny Battlefields. 2014. (Tiny Battlefields Ser.). 48p. (YA). (gr. 6-8). 191.70 *(978-1-4824-1185-0(7));* pap. 84.30 *(978-1-4824-1586-5(0))* Stevens, Gareth Publishing LLLP.

UXL Encyclopedia of Diseases & Disorders, 5 vols., Vol. 5. rev. ed. 2009. (ENG.). 458.00 *(978-1-4144-3065-2(5),* UXL) Cengage Gale.

Viegas, Jennifer. Parasites. 2009. (Germs: the Library of Disease-Causing Organisms Ser.). 48p. (gr. 5-5). 53.00 *(978-1-61512-717-7(8))* Rosen Publishing Group, Inc., The.

Walker, Richard. KFK Epidemics & Plagues. 2007. (Kingfisher Knowledge Ser.). 8.95 *(978-0-7534-6181-5(1),* Kingfisher) Roaring Brook Pr.

Washington-Gattis, Ishia L. Meet Camden: Living with Sickle Cell Anemia. 2010. 36p. 18.99 *(978-1-4490-8616-9(0))* AuthorHouse.

Watson, Stephanie. Endometriosis. 2006. (Library of Sexual Health Ser.). (Illus.). 64p. (YA). (gr. 7-12). lib. bdg. 31.95 *(978-1-4042-0904-6(2))* Rosen Publishing Group, Inc., The.

Way, Steve. Fighting Disease. 2011. (Planet SOS Ser.). (Illus.). 48p. (J). (gr. 3-6). pap. 14.05 *(978-1-4339-4971-5(7));* lib. bdg. 31.95 *(978-1-4339-4970-8(9))* Stevens, Gareth Publishing LLLP. (Gareth Stevens Learning Library).

Weitzman, Elizabeth. Let's Talk about When Someone You Love Has Alzheimer's Disease. 2006. (Let's Talk Library). (Illus.). 24p. (J). (gr. k-5). lib. bdg. 22.60 *(978-0-8239-6813-8(8),* PowerKids Pr.) Rosen Publishing Group, Inc., The.

Willett, Edward. Disease-Hunting Scientist: Careers Hunting Deadly Diseases. 2009. (Wild Science Careers Ser.). (Illus.). 112p. (J). (gr. 5-18). lib. bdg. 33.27 *(978-0-7660-3052-7(0))* Enslow Pubs., Inc.

—Ebola Virus. 2003. (Diseases & People Ser.). (Illus.). 112p. (J). lib. bdg. 26.60 *(978-0-7660-1595-1(5))* Enslow Pubs., Inc.

—What You Can Do about Ebola. 2015. (Contemporary Diseases & Disorders Ser.). (ENG.). 128p. (J). (gr. 7-7). lib. bdg. 37.27 *(978-0-7660-7036-3(0))* Enslow Pubs., Inc.

Winkler, Peter, et al. Keeping Fit. 2006. (Nonfiction Reading & Writing Workshops Ser.). (ENG., Illus.). 32p. (J). pap. 17.95 *(978-0-7922-8863-3(7))* CENGAGE Learning.

Winnick, Judd. Pedro & Me. 2011. 14.10 *(978-0-7848-3537-1(3),* Everbind) Marco Bk. Co.

Winters, Adam. Everything You Need to Know about Lupus. 2005. (Need to Know Library). (Illus.). 64p. (YA). (gr. 7-12). lib. bdg. 31.95 *(978-0-8239-3288-7(5),* NTLUPU) Rosen Publishing Group, Inc., The.

Wouk, Henry. Tuberculosis. 2009. (Health Alert 6 Ser.). 64p. (gr. 4). 32.79 *(978-0-7614-3979-0(X))* Marshall Cavendish GBR. Dist: Marshall Cavendish Corp.

Zimmerman, Barb. Buttons on my Head. 2010. 24p. pap. 12.99 *(978-1-4389-7244-2(X))* AuthorHouse.

DISEASES, COMMUNICABLE

see Communicable Diseases

DISEASES—FICTION

Abdullah, Patricia Noor. Saving Daddy. Cabri, Alexandra, illus. 2006. 32p. (J). (gr. 2-5). 17.95 *(978-1-933193-16-8(6))* EECI, Inc.

Adams, Clint. Angst Ist Nicht Alles. 2008. (YA). pap. *(978-0-9768375-5-8(2))* Credo Italia.

Albers, Megan & Albers, Christine. The Attack of Mr. Crohn's. Albers, Randy, ed. Jennenga, John, illus. 2008. 71p. (YA). pap. 8.00 *(978-0-615-19666-4(7))* Albers, Christine.

Allen, Lynn Marie. Asperger's? God Bless You! 2004. 31p. pap. 24.95 *(978-1-4137-3435-5(9))* America Star Bks.

Arrington, Gladys. Dallas: On Book One: JoJo KIDS. Arrington, Chiquila, illus. 2006. 49p. pap. 16.95 *(978-1-4241-1162-6(5))* PublishAmerica, Inc.

Ashkenas, Bruce. Sick Street. 2011. 102p. pap. 9.95 *(978-1-257-04901-1(1))* Lulu Pr., Inc.

Blume, Judy. Deenie. 2014. (ENG., Illus.). 208p. (J). (gr. 5-9). pap. 7.99 *(978-1-4814-1036-6(9),* Atheneum Bks. for Young Readers) Simon & Schuster Children's Publishing.

Boyce, Frank Cottrell. The Astounding Broccoli Boy. 2015. 384p. (J). (gr. 3-7). 16.99 *(978-0-06-240017-8(7),* Walden Pond Pr.) HarperCollins Pubs.

Brambles, Lindsay. Becoming Darkness. 2015. (ENG.). 496p. 17.95 *(978-1-63079-017-2(6))* Switch Pr.

Brix-Maffei, Angela & Brix-Maffei, John. The Christmas Dinosaur. 2008. 48p. pap. 22.49 *(978-1-4389-0499-3(1))* AuthorHouse.

Bykowski, Christy. Gluten-Free Me Beckman Goes to School. Thompson, Chad, illus. 2013. 24p. pap. 11.95 *(978-1-61244-228-0(5))* Halo Publishing International.

Chilman-Blair, Kim & DeLoache, Shawn. Medikidz Explain Childhood Glaucoma: What's up with Scott? 2012. (Illus.). 32p. (J). pap. *(978-1-906935-67-2(X))* Medikidz Ltd.

—Medikidz Explain Malaria: What's up with Ken? 2011. (Illus.). 32p. (J). pap. *(978-1-906935-19-1(X))* Medikidz Ltd.

—Medikidz Explain Parkinson's Disease: What's up with Alys' Grandad? 2013. (Illus.). 32p. (J). pap. *(978-1-906935-80-1(7))* Medikidz Ltd.

—MediKidz Explain Severe Asthma: What's up with Tim? 2012. (Illus.). 32p. (J). pap. *(978-1-906935-76-4(9))* Medikidz Ltd.

—Medikidz Explain Slipped Hip: What's up with Jacob? 2nd ed. 2012. (Illus.). 32p. (J). pap. *(978-1-906935-14-6(9))* Medikidz Ltd.

—Medikidz Explain Ulcerative Colitis: What's up with Sarah? 2013. (Illus.). 32p. (J). pap. *(978-1-906935-85-6(8))* Medikidz Ltd.

Chilman-Blair, Kim & Hersov, Kate. Medikidz Explain Haemophilia: What's up with Louis? Deloache, Shawn, illus. 2011. 32p. (J). pap. *(978-1-906935-29-0(7))* Medikidz Ltd.

—Medikidz Explain Inflammatory Bowel Disease: What's up with Adam? Deloache, Shawn, illus. 2011. 32p. (J). pap. *(978-1-906935-65-8(3))* Medikidz Ltd.

Chilman-Blair, Kim & Kipiniak, Chris. Medikidz Explain Hepatitis A: What's up with George? 2011. (Illus.). 32p. (J). pap. *(978-1-906935-72-6(6))* Medikidz Ltd.

—Medikidz Explain Kidney Transplants: What's up with Jonah? 2012. (Illus.). 32p. (J). pap. *(978-1-906935-69-6(6))* Medikidz Ltd.

—Medikidz Explain Seasonal Flu: What's up with Tom? 2011. (Illus.). 32p. (J). pap. *(978-1-906935-44-3(0))* Medikidz Ltd.

Chilman-Blair, Kim & Lee, Tony. MediKidz Explain HIV: What's up with Jason? 2012. (Illus.). 32p. (J). pap. *(978-1-906935-88-7(2))* Medikidz Ltd.

Chilman-Blair, Kim & Rimmer, Ian. Medikidz Explain Eczema: What's up with Kenzie? 2013. (Illus.). 24p. (J). pap. *(978-1-906935-12-2(2))* Medikidz Ltd.

—Medikidz Explain Multiple Sclerosis: What's up with Ryan's Mum? 2012. (Illus.). 32p. (J). pap. *(978-1-906935-78-8(5))* Medikidz Ltd.

Chilman-Blair, Kim, et al. Medikidz Explain Living with ADHD. Copter, Steve, illus. 2014. 16p. (J). pap. *(978-1-906935-84-9(X))* Medikidz Ltd.

Chow, Michelle Nel. To Be a Nut or Not! 2013. 20p. pap. *(978-0-9919142-1-0(X))* Allergygator Publishing.

The Contagious Colors of Mumpley Middle School. 2014. (ENG., Illus.). 288p. (J). (gr. 2-5). pap. 8.99 *(978-1-4424-7830-5(6),* Atheneum Bks. for Young Readers) Simon & Schuster Children's Publishing.

Cooner, Donna. Skinny. 2012. (ENG.). 272p. (J). (gr. 7). 17.99 *(978-0-545-42763-0(0))* Scholastic, Inc.

Cooney, Caroline B. Code Orange. 2007. 200p. (gr. 7-12). 17.00 *(978-0-7569-8210-2(3))* Perfection Learning Corp.

—Code Orange. 2007. (ENG.). 224p. (YA). (gr. 7-12). mass mkt. 6.99 *(978-0-385-73260-4(0),* Laurel Leaf) Random Hse. Children's Bks.

—Code Orange. 2007. lib. bdg. 17.20 *(978-1-4177-7788-4(5),* Turtleback) Turtleback Bks.

Cooper, Abby. Sticks & Stones. 2016. (ENG.). 288p. (J). 16.99 *(978-0-374-30287-0(1),* 9780374302870, Farrar, Straus & Giroux (BYR)) Farrar, Straus & Giroux.

Corn, Tori. Dixie Wants an Allergy. Cote, Nancy, illus. 2014. (ENG.). 32p. (J). (gr. -1-k). 16.95 *(978-1-62087-991-7(3),* Sky Pony Pr.) Skyhorse Publishing Co., Inc.

Cottrell, Kim. Jimmy Has the Bugaloo Zoo Flu. 2009. 32p. pap. 12.99 *(978-1-4389-5209-3(0))* AuthorHouse.

Cummings, K. M. I Hate Medicine! 2007. 24p. per. 10.95 *(978-1-4327-1382-9(5))* Outskirts Pr., Inc.

Dames-Johnson, Angela. What's Gerald Done Now? Supermarket Fun. 2009. 24p. pap. 24.95 *(978-1-60749-474-4(4))* America Star Bks.

Dashner, James. The Fever Code. 2016. (Maze Runner Ser.). (ENG.). 384p. (YA). (gr. 7). 18.99 *(978-0-553-51309-7(5));* lib. bdg. 21.99 *(978-0-553-51310-3(9))* Random Hse. Children's Bks. (Delacorte Pr.).

—The Kill Order. 2012. (Maze Runner Ser.: 4). (ENG.). 368p. (YA). (gr. 7). 18.99 *(978-0-385-74288-7(6),* Delacorte Pr.) Random Hse. Children's Bks.

De la Peña, Matt. The Hunted. 2015. (ENG.). 384p. (YA). (gr. 9). lib. bdg. 20.99 *(978-0-375-98992-6(7),* Delacorte Pr.) Random Hse. Children's Bks.

—The Living. (ENG.). (YA). (gr. 9). 2015. 336p. pap. 9.99 *(978-0-385-74121-7(9),* Ember) 2013. 320p. lib. bdg. 20.99 *(978-0-375-98991-9(9),* Delacorte Pr.) Random Hse. Children's Bks.

Demetris, Jean. Grandma's Box of Memories: Helping Grandma to Remember. Demetris, Alex, illus. 2014. (ENG.). 32p. 17.95 *(978-1-84905-993-0(4),* 2767) Kingsley, Jessica Pubs. GBR. Dist: Macmillan Distribution Ltd.

Denman, K. L. Me, Myself & Ike, 1 vol. 2009. (ENG.). 208p. (YA). (gr. 7-12). pap. 12.95 *(978-1-55469-086-2(2))* Orca Bk. Pubs. USA.

DeSio, Delores. Annie's Journey Through the Golden Door, 1 vol. 2009. 114p. pap. 19.95 *(978-1-4489-8470-1(X))* America Star Bks.

DeWitt, Fowler. The Contagious Colors of Mumpley Middle School. Montalvo, Rodolfo, illus. 2013. (ENG.). 272p. (J). (gr. 2-5). 16.99 *(978-1-4424-7829-9(2),* Atheneum Bks. for Young Readers) Simon & Schuster Children's Publishing.

Diggle, David Mark. George & Toby: Won't Have A Baaa of Bed Wetting. Diggle, Daniel James, illus. 2011. 24p. (J). pap. *(978-0-9871657-5-6(5))* Diggle de Doo Productions Pty, Ltd.

Duncan, Alexandra. Blight. 2017. 400p. (YA). (gr. 8). 17.99 *(978-0-06-239699-0(4),* Greenwillow Bks.) HarperCollins Pubs.

Edwards, W M, illus. Booger Boogie. 2007. (Playdate Kids Musical Ser.). 27p. (J). (gr. -1-3). 14.95 incl. audio compact disk *(978-1-933721-13-2(8))* Playdate Kids Publishing.

Egan, Kate & Cole, Joanna. The Magic School Bus Fights Germs. Bracken, Carolyn, illus. 2008. pap. *(978-0-545-03465-4(5),* Scholastic, Inc.) Scholastic, Inc.

Etlinger, Rebecca. To Be Me. 2005. pap. *(978-0-87424-452-6(8))* Western Psychological Services.

Evans, Richard. Rise of the Elgen. 2012. (Michael Vey Ser.: 2). (ENG., Illus.). 352p. (YA). (gr. 7). 17.99 *(978-1-4424-5414-9(8),* Simon Pulse/Mercury Ink) Simon Pulse/Mercury Ink.

Falls, Kat. Inhuman. 2015. (ENG.). 384p. (J). (gr. 7). pap. 9.99 *(978-0-545-37101-8(5),* Scholastic Pr.) Scholastic, Inc.

Foulks, Denine. Jimmy Pfeiffer Dragonmeyer. 2013. 44p. pap. 9.00 *(978-1-937260-97-2(6))* Sleepytown Pr.

Gershman, Jenifer. Where Did Mommy's Superpowers Go? Helping Kids Understand a Parent's Serious Illness. 2011. (ENG., Illus.). 36p. (J). pap. 16.95 *(978-0-9824461-9-5(5))* SDP Publishing.

Gilmore, Jennifer. We Were Never Here. 2016. 320p. (YA). (gr. 9). 17.99 *(978-0-06-239360-9(X),* HarperTeen) HarperCollins Pubs.

Gladen, Jennifer. Angel Donor. Bell, Samantha, illus. 2012. 24p. pap. 10.95 *(978-1-61633-274-7(3))* Guardian Angel Publishing, Inc.

Glewwe, Eleanor. Sparkers. 2014. (ENG.). 336p. (J). (gr. 5-8). 16.99 *(978-0-451-46876-5(7),* Viking Books for Young Readers) Penguin Young Readers Group.

Goepel, Meg. Farting Is Fun. 2010. 16p. pap. 9.99 *(978-1-4490-2346-1(0))* AuthorHouse.

Grab, Daphne. Alive & Well in Prague, New York. 2008. (Laura Geringer Bks.). 247p. (YA). (gr. 7-18). lib. bdg. 17.89 *(978-0-06-125671-4(4),* Geringer, Laura Book) HarperCollins Pubs.

Graham, Michael, illus. The Great Inhibinator. 2006. 44p. (J). *(978-0-9772977-0-2(5))* Bio Rx.

—I am Nate. 2007. 40p. (J). *(978-0-9772977-1-9(3))* Bio Rx.

Griffin, Michele. Picky, Picky Pete. 2010. (ENG.). 48p. (gr. -1). pap. 14.95 *(978-1-935567-21-9(7))* Sensory Resources.

Griffin, Sarah Maria. Spare & Found Parts. 2016. 416p. (YA). (gr. 9). 17.99 *(978-0-06-240888-4(7),* Greenwillow Bks.) HarperCollins Pubs.

Grindley, Sally. Hurricane Wills. 2007. (ENG.). 256p. (J). (gr. 4-7). pap. 8.95 *(978-0-7475-9095-8(8))* Bloomsbury Publishing Plc GBR. Dist: Independent Pubs. Group.

Haddix, Margaret Peterson. Because of Anya. 2004. (ENG.). 128p. (J). (gr. 3-7). reprint ed. pap. 6.99 *(978-0-689-86993-8(2),* Simon & Schuster Bks. For Young Readers) Simon & Schuster Bks. For Young Readers.

Hansen, Lynne. Reckless Revolution. 2007. (YA). *(978-1-4114-9672-9(8),* Spark Publishing Group) Sterling Publishing Co., Inc.

Hartpence, Craig. SHOTS Project (SuperHero's Operating Through Syringes) 2010. 83p. pap. 15.00 *(978-0-557-51803-6(2))* Lulu Pr., Inc.

Hatkoff, Craig & Hatkoff, Juliana Lee. Good-Bye Tonsils! Mets, Marilyn, illus. 2004. (ENG.). 32p. (J). (gr. k-3). pap. 6.99 *(978-0-14-240133-0(1),* Puffin Books) Penguin Young Readers Group.

Hawker, Kate "Ayasta". Faces of Our Children. 2009. 67p. pap. 26.60 *(978-0-557-09704-3(5))* Lulu Pr., Inc.

Hayatian, MaryAnn. The Flower Child. 2009. 32p. 20.00 *(978-0-557-06445-8(7))* Lulu Pr., Inc.

Heidi Heckelbeck Gets the Sniffles. 2014. (Heidi Heckelbeck Ser.: 12). (ENG., Illus.). 128p. (J). (gr. k-4). pap. 5.99 *(978-1-4814-1362-6(7),* Little Simon) Little Simon.

Hennessy, Mary L. Spring Breezes & Sneezes. 2012. 20p. pap. 17.99 *(978-1-4772-6042-5(0))* AuthorHouse.

Higginson, Sheila Sweeny. Chilly Catches a Cold. 2013. (Doc Mcstuffins 8X8 Ser.). (J). lib. bdg. 13.55 *(978-0-606-35109-6(4),* Turtleback) Turtleback Bks.

Higginson, Sheila Sweeny, et al. Chilly Catches a Cold. 2013. (Illus.). 24p. (J). *(978-1-4844-1108-7(0))* Disney Pr.

Hirsch, Jeff. Black River Falls. 2016. (ENG.). 336p. (YA). (gr. 7). 17.99 *(978-0-544-39099-7(7))* Houghton Mifflin Harcourt Publishing Co.

Hoopmann, Kathy. Blue Bottle Mystery - the Graphic Novel: An Asperger Adventure. 2015. (Asperger Adventures Ser.). (ENG., Illus.). 64p. (J). 18.95 *(978-1-84905-650-2(1),* 7952) Kingsley, Jessica Pubs. GBR. Dist: Macmillan Distribution Ltd.

Hopkinson, Deborah. The Great Trouble: A Mystery of London, the Blue Death, & a Boy Called Eel. 2013. (ENG.). 256p. (J). (gr. 5). 16.99 *(978-0-375-84818-6(5),* Knopf Bks. for Young Readers) Random Hse. Children's Bks.

Hostetter, Joyce Moyer. Blue. 2010. (Bakers Mountain Stories Ser.). (ENG.). 200p. (J). (gr. 6-9). pap. 7.95 *(978-1-59078-835-6(4),* Calkins Creek) Boyds Mills Pr.

Hultquist, A. A Day with Parkinson's. Lew-Vriethoff, Joanne, illus. 2016. (ENG.). 32p. (J). (gr. -1-3). 16.99 *(978-0-8075-5581-1(9))* Whitman, Albert & Co.

Hunter, Erin. The Blazing Star. 2014. (Warriors Ser.: Bk. 4). (ENG., Illus.). 320p. (J). 16.99 *(978-0-06-206358-8(8))* HarperCollins Pubs.

I'm Not Afraid of Needles. 2004. (J). 4.99 *(978-0-9776144-0-0(9))* Kidstalk, LLC.

James, Brian. Treasure Trouble. Zivoin, Jennifer, illus. 2008. (Pirate School Ser.: 5). (ENG.). 64p. (J). (gr. 1-3). pap. 3.99 *(978-0-448-44782-7(7),* Grosset & Dunlap) Penguin Young Readers Group.

Johnson, Jo. Grandpa Seashells. 2017. (ENG., Illus.). 32p. (C). pap. 6.95 ***(978-0-86388-997-4(2)***, Y328929) Routledge.

—My Mum Bakes Awesome Cakes! 2017. (ENG.). 28p. (C). pap. 6.95 ***(978-0-86388-998-1(0)***, Y328889) Routledge.

Johnson, Maerryane. I Am Still the Same Aubrey! 2013. 24p. pap. 24.95 *(978-1-4626-9878-3(6))* America Star Bks.

Kagawa, Julie. The Immortal Rules. 2013. (Blood of Eden Ser.: 1). lib. bdg. 20.85 *(978-0-606-26947-6(9),* Turtleback) Turtleback Bks.

Kerns, Kristen. Tommy Fakes the Flu. Barrett, Casey, illus. 2013. 24p. pap. 8.99 *(978-1-938768-28-6(0))* Gypsy Pubns.

Kessler, Jackie Morse. Loss. 2012. (Riders of the Apocalypse Ser.: 3). (ENG.). 272p. (YA). (gr. 7). pap. 8.99 *(978-0-547-71215-4(4))* Houghton Mifflin Harcourt Publishing Co.

—Loss. 2012. (Riders of the Apocalypse Ser.: 3). lib. bdg. 19.65 *(978-0-606-24742-9(4),* Turtleback) Turtleback Bks.

Ketchen, Susan. Made That Way. 2010. (ENG.). 160p. (J). pap. 12.95 *(978-0-88982-270-2(0))* Oolichan Bks. CAN. Dist: Univ. of Toronto Pr.

Keyser, Amber J. Pointe, Claw. 2017. (Fiction — Young Adult Ser.). (ENG.). 288p. (YA). (gr. 8-12). 9.99 ***(978-1-5124-3431-6(0))***; 38.65 ***(978-1-5124-0895-9(6))***; 38.65 ***(978-1-5124-3432-3(9))*** Lerner Publishing Group. (Carolrhoda Lab™).

—Pointe, Claw. Burrell, Carol klio, tr. 2017. (ENG.). 288p. (YA). (gr. 8-12). 18.99 *(978-1-4677-7591-5(6))* Lerner Publishing Group.

Khoury, Jessica. Kalahari. 2015. (ENG.). 368p. (YA). (gr. 7). 17.99 *(978-1-59514-765-3(9),* Razorbill) Penguin Young Readers Group.

Kim, Susan & Klavan, Laurence. Guardians. 2016. (Wasteland Ser.: 3). 432p. (YA). (gr. 9). pap. 9.99 *(978-0-06-211858-5(7),* HarperTeen) HarperCollins Pubs.

—Wasteland. 2013. (Wasteland Ser.: 1). (ENG.). 336p. (YA). (gr. 9). 17.99 *(978-0-06-211851-6(X),* HarperTeen) HarperCollins Pubs.

Kizer, Amber. A Matter of Days. 2016. (ENG.). 288p. (YA). (gr. 7). pap. 9.99 *(978-0-385-73974-0(5),* Ember) Random Hse. Children's Bks.

Koertge, Ronald. Shakespeare Bats Cleanup. 2006. (ENG.). 128p. (YA). (gr. 7-12). reprint ed. per. 6.99 *(978-0-7636-2939-7(1))* Candlewick Pr.

Konopka, Annie. The Tale of A Parkie Princess. 2008. 20p. 12.50 *(978-0-615-18598-9(3))* Konopka, Ann Marie.

Krall, Dan. Sick Simon. Krall, Dan, illus. 2015. (ENG., Illus.). 48p. (J). (gr. -1-3). 17.99 *(978-1-4424-9097-0(7),* Simon & Schuster Bks. For Young Readers) Simon & Schuster Bks. For Young Readers.

Kranowitz, Carol. The Goodenoughs Get in Sync: Five Different Ways SPD Can Affect You & Me! 2010. (ENG., Illus.). 96p. (gr. 3). pap. 14.95 *(978-1-935567-16-5(0))* Sensory Resources.

Kroupa, Robert J. Just Like You. 2011. (J). *(978-0-9825503-4-2(0))* IGI Pr.

Krulik, Nancy. Super Burp!, No. 1. Blecha, Aaron, illus. 2010. (George Brown, Class Clown Ser.: 1). (ENG.). 128p. (J). (gr. 2-4). pap. 5.99 *(978-0-448-45367-5(3),* Grosset & Dunlap) Penguin Young Readers Group.

—Trouble Magnet. Blecha, Aaron, illus. 2010. (George Brown, Class Clown Ser.: 2). (ENG.). 128p. (J). (gr. 2-4). pap. 5.99 *(978-0-448-45368-2(1),* Grosset & Dunlap) Penguin Young Readers Group.

—World's Worst Wedgie. Blecha, Aaron, illus. 2010. (George Brown, Class Clown Ser.: 3). (ENG.). 128p. (J). (gr. 2-4). pap. 5.99 *(978-0-448-45369-9(X),* Grosset & Dunlap) Penguin Young Readers Group.

Laban, Elizabeth. The Tragedy Paper. 2013. (ENG., Illus.). 320p. (YA). (gr. 7). 17.99 *(978-0-375-87040-8(7),* Knopf Bks. for Young Readers) Random Hse. Children's Bks.

Lafantasie, Shilo. House of Love. 2012. 32p. pap. 24.95 *(978-1-4560-9404-1(1))* America Star Bks.

Lane, Bryan. Stepbrothers. 2010. 16p. 9.00 *(978-1-4520-1305-3(5))* AuthorHouse.

Lasky, Kathryn. Chasing Orion. 2010. (ENG., Illus.). 368p. (J). (gr. 5-18). 17.99 *(978-0-7636-3982-2(6))* Candlewick Pr.

Leigh, Britt. Ten Commandments for Kissing Gloria Jean. 2014. (ENG.). (YA). pap. 9.95 *(978-0-8198-7491-7(4))* Pauline Bks. & Media.

Lesynski, Loris. Boy Soup. Martchenko, Michael, illus. 2nd ed. 2008. (ENG.). 32p. (J). (gr. -1-2). 18.95 *(978-1-55451-143-3(7),* 9781554511433); pap. 6.95 *(978-1-55451-142-6(9),* 9781554511426) Annick Pr., Ltd. CAN. Dist: Publishers Group West (PGW).

Liu, Carol & Caldarone, Marybeth Sidoti. Arlene on the Scene. 2010. 206p. (J). (gr. 3-5). pap. 7.95 *(978-1-934572-54-2(3))* Emerald Bk. Co.

Loveless, Ryan. Ethan. 2016. (ENG., Illus.). (YA). pap. 14.99 ***(978-1-63477-416-1(7)***, Harmony Ink Pr.) Dreamspinner Pr.

Low-Dumond, Sabrina. Weakling Willie, 1 vol. 2010. 26p. 24.95 *(978-1-4512-1509-0(6))* PublishAmerica, Inc.

Lowell, Jax Peters. No More Cupcakes & Tummy Aches. 2004. (Illus.). 38p. (J). 22.99 *(978-1-4134-6255-5(3))* Xlibris Corp.

Lucier, Makiia. A Death-Struck Year. 2014. (ENG.). 288p. (J). (gr. 7-12). 17.99 *(978-0-544-16450-5(4),* HMH Books For Young Readers) Houghton Mifflin Harcourt Publishing Co.

Lyon, George Ella. The Pirate of Kindergarten. Avril, Lynne, illus. 2010. (ENG.). 40p. (J). (gr. -1-3). 17.99 *(978-1-4169-5024-0(9),* Atheneum/Richard Jackson Bks.) Simon & Schuster Children's Publishing.

Mahony, Mary. Harry Scores A Hat Trick, Pawns, Pucks, & Scoliosis: The Sequel to Stand Tall, Harry. Pasternack, Susan, ed. Larkin, Catherine, illus. 2003. 130p. (YA). (gr. 5-8). per. 14.95 *(978-0-9658879-3-9(6))* Redding Pr.

Malley, Gemma. The Legacy. 2011. (Declaration Ser.). (ENG.). 272p. (YA). (gr. 7-18). 17.99 *(978-1-59990-567-9(1),* 9781599905679, Bloomsbury USA Childrens) Bloomsbury Publishing USA.

Maria Muirhead. Smoking = Problems: Flora-Lee's Journal. 2010. 56p. pap. 8.95 *(978-1-4502-0645-7(X))* iUniverse, Inc.

Marien, Donna. Waiting at the Bay: A Young Woman's Reflections on Journeys in the Sea of Life. 2003. 108p. (YA). pap. 10.95 *(978-0-595-26304-2(6),* Writers Club Pr.) iUniverse, Inc.

Marsh, Carole. The Puzzle of the Indian Arrowhead. 2006. (Three Amigos Ser.). (Illus.). 54p. (J). (gr. 1-3). 14.95 *(978-0-635-06201-7(1))* Gallopade International.

May, Cynthia. Ryan's Vitiligo. Nelson, Shannon, illus. 2003. (J). pap. 8.95 *(978-0-615-12578-7(6))* May, Cynthia D.

McCafferty, Megan. Bumped. (Bumped Ser.: 1). (ENG.). (YA). (gr. 9). 2012. 352p. pap. 9.99 *(978-0-06-196275-2(9))* 2011. 336p. 16.99 *(978-0-06-196274-5(0))* HarperCollins Pubs.

McClellan, Rachel. Escape to Eden. 2016. (ENG.). 295p. (YA). pap. 17.99 *(978-1-4621-1777-2(5),* Sweetwater Bks.) Cedar Fort, Inc./CFI Distribution.

McDonald, Megan. Triple Pet Trouble. Madrid, Erwin, illus. 2015. (Judy Moody Ser.: 6). (ENG.). 64p. (J). (gr. -1-1). 12.99 *(978-0-7636-7443-4(5))* Candlewick Pr.

McKain, W. J. Morris Hollett - & St Vernon's Ward for Strange & Unusual Diseases. 2013. 140p. pap. *(978-1-78148-193-6(8))* Grosvenor Hse. Publishing Ltd.

Melmed, Raun & Sexton, Annette. Marvin's Monster Diary: ADHD Attacks! (and I Win, Big Time) 2016. (ENG., Illus.). 106p. (J). pap. 12.94 *(978-1-942934-10-3(6))* Familius LLC.

Miles, Talaythea L. Fly, My Lupus Butterfly, Fly. 2012. 24p. pap. 14.93 *(978-1-4669-1504-6(8))* Trafford Publishing.

Minks, Joshua. Humania & the Legend of Commander Pancreator. 2010. 44p. pap. 20.00 *(978-1-4490-3333-0(4))* AuthorHouse.

Mith with an Itch. 2008. (Illus.). 34p. (J). 10.95 *(978-0-9800259-0-3(7))* Dream Weaver Ministries, Inc.

Muirhead, Maria. My Asthma Book. 2007. 72p. (J). (gr. 1-2). per. 11.95 *(978-0-595-42925-7(4))* iUniverse, Inc.

Myklusch, Matt. The End of Infinity. 2013. (Jack Blank Adventure Ser.: 3). (ENG., Illus.). 416p. (J). (gr. 3-7). pap. 8.99 *(978-1-4169-9568-5(4),* Aladdin) Simon & Schuster Children's Publishing.

—Jack Blank & the Imagine Nation. 2010. (Jack Blank Adventure Ser.: Bk. 1). (ENG., Illus.). 480p. (J). (gr. 3-7). 16.99 *(978-1-4169-9561-6(7),* Aladdin) Simon & Schuster Children's Publishing.

Nana, Auntie. I Can't Go to School Today. 2012. pap. 12.95 *(978-0-7414-8105-4(7))* Infinity Publishing.

—I Can't Go to School Today with CD. 2012. pap. 16.95 *(978-0-7414-7756-9(4))* Infinity Publishing.

Napoli, Donna Jo. Skin, 0 vols. 2013. (ENG.). 352p. (YA). (gr. 9-12). pap. 9.99 *(978-1-4778-1690-5(9),* 9781477816905, Amazon Children's Publishing) Amazon Publishing.

Ní Mhurchú, Caitriona & Feeney, Tatyana. An Run Mor. 2007. (Sraith Sos Ser.: 14). (ENG, GLE & IRI., Illus.). 64p. (J). pap. 9.95 *(978-1-84717-016-3(1))* O'Brien Pr., Ltd., The IRL. Dist: Dufour Editions, Inc.

Niner, Holly L. Mr. Worry: A Story about OCD. Swearingen, Greg, illus. 2003. (ENG.). 32p. (J). (gr. 2-3). 16.99 *(978-0-8075-5182-0(1))* Whitman, Albert & Co.

Niven, Jennifer. Holding up the Universe. 2016. (ENG.). 400p. (YA). (gr. 9). 17.99 *(978-0-385-75592-4(9));* lib. bdg. 20.99 *(978-0-385-75593-1(7))* Random Hse. Children's Bks. (Knopf Bks. for Young Readers).

Ormond, Jennifer. DJ's Allergies. Walstead, Curt, illus. 2011. 16p. (gr. -1-k). bds. 8.95 *(978-0-9792010-1-1(2))* Ormond, Jennifer.

Ostrovski, Emil. Away We Go. 2016. 272p. (YA). (gr. 9). 17.99 *(978-0-06-223855-9(8),* Greenwillow Bks.) HarperCollins Pubs.

Pagel, Beth. What's Wrong with Grandma? 2008. 32p. pap. 11.96 *(978-0-557-00302-0(4))* Lulu Pr., Inc.

Paquette, Ammi-Joan. Paradox. 2014. (ENG.). 240p. (YA). (gr. 7). pap. 9.99 *(978-0-375-87163-4(2),* Ember) Random Hse. Children's Bks.

Parker, Emma. Sooty the Stink Bomb. 2010. (Illus.). pap. *(978-1-877561-15-3(0))* First Edition Ltd.

Price, M. J. The Skin I'm In. 2013. 32p. pap. 24.95 *(978-1-63000-967-0(9))* America Star Bks.

Price, Robin. Threadneedle 01. McGrory, Paul, illus. 2016. (ENG.). 32p. (J). pap. *(978-1-906132-86-6(0))* Mogzilla.

Pyatt, Mary. Jack Has Moves. 2012. (ENG.). 22p. (J). pap. 10.95 *(978-1-4327-9495-8(7))* Outskirts Pr., Inc.

Racek, Jennifer. Cadberry's Letters. 2008. 33p. 13.90 *(978-1-4357-0566-1(1))* Lulu Pr., Inc.

Reichs, Kathy. Virals. 2014. lthr. 79.00 *(978-1-62715-582-3(1))* Leatherbound Bestsellers.

—Virals. (Virals Ser.: 1). (ENG.). (J). (gr. 5-18). 2011. 480p. 10.99 *(978-1-59514-426-3(9),* Puffin Books) 2010. 464p. 17.99 *(978-1-59514-342-6(4),* Razorbill) Penguin Young Readers Group.

—Virals. 2011. 20.00 *(978-1-61383-226-4(5))* Perfection Learning Corp.

Reichs, Kathy & Reichs, Brendan. Terminal. 2015. (Virals Ser.: 5). (ENG.). 432p. (J). (gr. 5). 17.99 *(978-1-59514-528-4(1),* G.P. Putnam's Sons Books for Young Readers) Penguin Young Readers Group.

—Virals. 2011. (Virals Ser.: 1). lib. bdg. 20.85 *(978-0-606-23069-8(6),* Turtleback) Turtleback Bks.

—Virals Short Stories Omnibus. 2016. (Virals Ser.). (ENG.). 304p. (J). (gr. 5). 9.99 *(978-0-14-751920-7(9),* Puffin Books) Penguin Young Readers Group.

reid, r. m. Our Little Blessing: A Story about Sickle Cell Disease. 2008. (Illus.). 24p. (J). 16.00 *(978-0-8059-7192-7(0))* Dorrance Publishing Co., Inc.

Robinson, Melissa. Special in Every Way. 2013. 24p. pap. 14.95 *(978-1-4669-8611-4(5))* Trafford Publishing.

Sachar, Louis. Fuzzy Mud. 2015. (KOR.). 228p. (J). (gr. 5). pap. *(978-89-364-5671-9(7))* Chang-jag and Bipyeong Co.

—Fuzzy Mud. 2015. (CHI.). 240p. (J). pap. *(978-986-211-551-0(3))* Hsaio Lu Publishing Co., Ltd.

—Fuzzy Mud. (ENG.). (J). (gr. 5). 2017. 208p. 7.99 *(978-0-385-37022-6(9),* Yearling) 2015. (Illus.). 192p. 16.99 *(978-0-385-74378-5(5),* Delacorte Bks. for Young Readers) 2015. (Illus.). 192p. lib. bdg. 19.99 *(978-0-375-99129-5(8),* Delacorte Bks. for Young Readers) Random Hse. Children's Bks.

—Fuzzy Mud. 2017. lib. bdg. 18.40 ***(978-0-606-39871-8(6))*** Turtleback Bks.

Sandler, Karen. Awakening. 2013. (ENG.). 400p. (YA). 18.95 *(978-1-60060-982-4(1),* Tu Bks.) Lee & Low Bks., Inc.

Sasso, Emilie. Cystic Fibrosis & You. 2008. 23p. pap. 24.95 *(978-1-60672-405-7(3))* America Star Bks.

Schneider, Robyn. Extraordinary Means. 2015. (ENG.). 336p. (YA). (gr. 8). 17.99 *(978-0-06-221716-5(X),* Tegen, Katherine Bks) HarperCollins Pubs.

Shannon, David. Bugs in My Hair! Shannon, David, illus. 2013. (ENG., Illus.). 32p. (J). (gr. -1-3). 17.99 *(978-0-545-14313-4(6),* Blue Sky Pr., The) Scholastic, Inc.

Skurzynski, Gloria. Virtual War: The Virtual War Chronologs — Book 1. 2008. (ENG.). 188p. (YA). (gr. 7). pap. 10.99 *(978-1-4169-7577-9(2),* Simon Pulse) Simon Pulse.

Spergel, Heather. Free to Be Gluten Free! Martino, Anita, illus. 2013. (ENG.). 48p. (J). 19.99 *(978-1-938501-18-0(7))* Turn the Page Publishing.

Spinale, Wendy. Everland. 2016. (ENG.). 320p. (J). (gr. 7). 17.99 *(978-0-545-83694-4(8),* Scholastic Pr.) Scholastic, Inc.

Stevens, Eric. Flu Fighter: How I Survived a Worldwide Pandemic, the School Bully, & the Craziest Game of Dodge Ball Ever. Fraser, Kay, illus. 2010. (Finn Reeder Ser.). (ENG.). 80p. (gr. 3-4). 9.99 *(978-1-4342-2562-7(3))* Capstone Digital.

Teague, Patricia. Gilda the Gluten Free Mouse: A Story about Living Gloriously with Celiac Sprue Disease. 2013. 24p. pap. 10.95 *(978-1-4908-1276-2(8),* WestBow Pr.) Author Solutions, Inc.

Terry, Elliah. I Am Calliope June. 2017. (ENG.). 336p. (J). 16.99 *(978-1-250-09627-2(8),* 9781250096272) Feiwel & Friends.

Thomas, Lex. The Giant. 2016. (Quarantine Ser.: 4). (ENG.). 352p. (gr. 9-12). 17.99 *(978-1-5124-0103-5(X),* Carolrhoda Bks.) Lerner Publishing Group.

—The Loners. (Quarantine Ser.: No. 1). (ENG.). 416p. (gr. 9). 2013. (J). pap. 9.99 *(978-1-60684-438-0(5))* 2012. 17.99 *(978-1-60684-329-1(X))* Lerner Publishing Group. (Carolrhoda Lab™).

—Quarantine: The Saints Book 2. 2014. (Quarantine Ser.: No. 2). (ENG.). 400p. (J). (gr. 9). pap. 9.99 *(978-1-60684-540-0(3))* Lerner Publishing Group.

Thompson, Colleen. Claudine & Claudette: A Bug Story. 2010. 12p. 8.49 *(978-1-4520-7902-8(1))* AuthorHouse.

Thompson, Lisa. The Goldfish Boy. 2017. (ENG.). 320p. (J). (gr. 3-7). 16.99 *(978-1-338-05392-0(2),* Scholastic Pr.) Scholastic, Inc.

To Wait Is to Win. 2004. (J). *(978-0-9762904-7-6(2))* Layne Morgan Media, Inc.

Torday, Piers. The Last Wild. 2015. (Last Wild Ser.: 1). (ENG.). 352p. (J). (gr. 3-7). 8.99 *(978-0-14-750965-9(3),* Puffin Books) Penguin Young Readers Group.

Treggiari, Jo. Ashes, Ashes. 2013. (ENG.). 352p. (J). (gr. 7). pap. 9.99 *(978-0-545-25564-6(3),* Scholastic Paperbacks) Scholastic, Inc.

Tsao, Don. Anna Gets Her Vaccination. 2008. 24p. pap. 12.99 *(978-1-4389-2941-5(2))* AuthorHouse.

Ventresca, Yvonne. Pandemic. 2014. (ENG.). 352p. (J). (gr. 6-12). 16.95 *(978-1-62873-609-0(7),* Sky Pony Pr.) Skyhorse Publishing Co., Inc.

Vernick, Audrey & Scanlon, Liz Garton. Bob, Not Bob! Cordell, Matthew, illus. 2017. (ENG.). 40p. (J). (gr. -1-k). 17.99 *(978-1-4847-2302-9(3))* Disney Pr.

Voisin, Mandy Madson. Star of Deliverance. 2014. pap. 17.99 *(978-1-4621-1454-2(7))* Cedar Fort, Inc./CFI Distribution.

Weissman, Elissa Brent. The Short Seller. (ENG.). (J). (gr. 3-7). 2014. 272p. pap. 8.99 *(978-1-4424-5256-5(0))* 2013. (Illus.). 256p. 15.99 *(978-1-4424-5255-8(2))* Simon & Schuster Children's Publishing.

Wells, Dan. Partials. (ENG.). (YA). 2013. (Partials Sequence Ser.: 1). 528p. (gr. 9). pap. 9.99 *(978-0-06-207105-7(X))* 2012. (Partials Sequence Ser.: 1). 480p. (gr. 9). 17.99

(978-0-06-207104-0(1)) 2012. 496p. pap. 9.99 (978-0-06-213569-8(4)) HarperCollins Pubs.

Wethington, Julie & Wethington, Lang. Yes I Can! Have My Cake & Food Allergies Too. Wethington, Julie & Wethington, Lang, illus. 2012. (Illus.). (J). (978-0-9761444-1-0(7)) DragonWing Bks.

White, Nonie H. D. The Woodpecker Who Suffered from Headaches. White, Nonie H. D., illus. 2006. (Illus.). (J). pap. 14.95 (978-0-9786147-0-6(4)) Westside Studio.

Williams, Felisha. Allison's Rainbow. 2012. 28p. pap. 15.99 (978-1-4797-0969-4(7)) Xlibris Corp.

Yangas, Angela Marie. The Bugguzz: Let There Be Light. 2007. 19.99 (978-0-9801796-0-6(2)) Binx Bks.

Yep, Laurence. When the Circus Came to Town. Wang, Suling, illus. 2004. 112p. (J). (gr. 3-5). 13.65 (978-0-7569-2969-5(5)) Perfection Learning Corp.

Young, Candice June. My Name Is Wes & My Mema Has Ms. 2013. 24p. pap. 24.95 (978-1-4137-7777-2(5)) America Star Bks.

Zweig, Eric. Fever Season. 2009. (ENG.). 256p. (YA). (gr. 4-18). pap. 10.99 (978-1-55488-432-2(2), Dundurn Pr.) Dundurn CAN. Dist: Ingram Publisher Services.

DISEASES—HISTORY

Auden, Scott. Medical Mysteries: Science Researches Conditions from Bizarre to Deadly. 2008. (National Geographic Investigates Ser.). (ENG., Illus.). 64p. (J). (gr. 5). lib. bdg. 27.90 (978-1-4263-0261-9(4), National Geographic Children's Bks.) National Geographic Society.

Auden, Scott & National Geographic Kids Staff. Medical Mysteries: Science Researches Conditions from Bizarre to Deadly. 2008. (National Geographic Investigates Science Ser.). (ENG., Illus.). 64p. (J). (gr. 5). 17.95 (978-1-4263-0356-2(4), National Geographic Children's Bks.) National Geographic Society.

Cunningham, Kevin. Diseases in History Set, vols. 4, vol. 4. Incl. Flu. 176p. lib. bdg. 28.95 (978-1-59935-105-6(6)); HIV/AIDS. 144p. (gr. 9-18). lib. bdg. 28.95 (978-1-59935-104-9(8)); Malaria. 144p. (gr. 9-18). 28.95 (978-1-59935-103-2(X)); Plague. 144p. (gr. 9-18). lib. bdg. 28.95 (978-1-59935-102-5(1)); (YA). 2009. 2009. Set lib. bdg. 115.80 (978-1-59935-101-8(3)) Reynolds, Morgan Inc.

Jarrow, Gail. Red Madness: How a Medical Mystery Changed What We Eat. 2014. (ENG., Illus.). 192p. (J). (gr. 5). 17.95 (978-1-59078-732-8(3), Calkins Creek) Boyds Mills Pr.

Medical Files Set, 6 vols., Set. Incl. Belly-Busting Worm Invasions! Parasites That Love Your Insides! Tilden, Thomasine E. Lewis & Lewis-Tilden, Thomasine E. (gr. 9-12). 29.00 (978-0-531-12068-2(6)); Blood Suckers! Deadly Mosquito Bites. Diconsiglio, John. (gr. 9-12). 29.00 (978-0-531-12070-5(8)); Help! Whats Eating My Flesh? Runaway Staph & Strep Infections! Tilden, Thomasine E. Lewis & Lewis-Tilden, Thomasine E. (gr. 9-12). 29.00 (978-0-531-12073-6(2)); There's a Fungus among Us! True Stories of Killer Molds. Diconsiglio, John. (gr. 9-12). 29.00 (978-0-531-12071-2(6)); When Birds Get Flu & Cows Go Mad! How Safe Are We? Diconsiglio, John. (gr. 8-12). 29.00 (978-0-531-12069-9(4)); 64p. (J). (24/7: Science Behind the Scenes Ser.). (Illus.). 2007. 174.00 (978-0-531-12478-9(9), Watts, Franklin) Scholastic Library Publishing.

DISEASES, INFECTIONS

see Communicable Diseases

DISEASES, MENTAL

see Mental Illness; Psychology, Pathological

DISEASES AND PESTS

see Fungi; Insect Pests; Parasites

see names of individual pests (e.g. Locusts)

DISEASES OF ANIMALS

see Veterinary Medicine

DISEASES OF CHILDREN

see Children—Diseases

DISEASES OF THE BLOOD

see Blood—Diseases

DISHES

see Glassware; Porcelain; Pottery

DISHONESTY

see Honesty

DISNEY, WALT, 1901-1966

Allahverdi, Artin. My Good Friend Walt Disney. 2009. 68p. pap. 11.99 (978-1-4490-4627-9(4)) AuthorHouse.

Bodden, Valerie. The Story of Disney. 2011. (Built for Success Ser.). (ENG.). 48p. (J). (gr. 4-7). pap. 12.00 (978-0-89812-754-6(8), Creative Paperbacks) Creative Co., The.

—The Story of Disney. 2011. (ENG., Illus.). 48p. (J). (gr. 5-17). pap. (978-1-897563-01-4(9)) Saunders Bk. Co.

Brown, Jonatha A. Walt Disney. 2005. (People We Should Know Ser.). 24p. (gr. 1-4). (SPA.). pap. 8.15 (978-0-8368-4767-3(9)); (Illus.). pap. 8.15 (978-0-8368-4753-6(9)); (SPA., Illus.). lib. bdg. 22.00 (978-0-8368-4760-4(1)); (Illus.). lib. bdg. 22.00 (978-0-8368-4746-8(6)) Stevens, Gareth Publishing LLLP. (Weekly Reader Leveled Readers).

Busby, Barbara Sheen. Walt Disney. Greenhaven Press Editors, ed. 2014. (Eye on Art Ser.). (ENG., Illus.). 128p. (gr. 7-10). lib. bdg. 39.40 (978-1-4205-0898-7(9), Lucent Bks.) Cengage Gale.

Disney Book Group Staff & Scollon, Bill. Walt Disney: Drawn from Imagination. Disney Storybook Artists Staff, illus. 2014. (ENG.). 136p. (J). (gr. 3-7). pap. 14.99 (978-1-4231-9647-1(3)) Disney Pr.

Feinstein, Stephen. Read about Walt Disney. 2005. (I Like Biographies! Ser.). (Illus.). 24p. (J). (gr. 1-3). lib. bdg. 22.60 (978-0-7660-2595-0(0), Enslow Elementary) Enslow Pubs., Inc.

Ford, Carin T. Walt Disney: Meet the Cartoonist. 2003. (Meeting Famous People Ser.). (Illus.). 32p. (J). (gr. 1-4). lib. bdg. 23.94 (978-0-7660-1857-0(1)) Enslow Pubs., Inc.

Gitlin, Martin. Walt Disney: Entertainment Visionary, 1 vol. 2009. (Essential Lives Set 4 Ser.). (ENG., Illus.). 112p. (J). (gr. 6-12). lib. bdg. 35.64 (978-1-60453-700-0(0)) ABDO Publishing Co.

Green, Sara. Disney. (Disney Ser.). 24p. (J). (gr. 3-8). 2017. pap. 7.99 (**978-1-61891-247-3(X)**) 2015. (ENG., Illus.). lib. bdg. 25.95 (978-1-62617-205-0(6)) Bellwether Media. (Pilot Bks.).

Haldy, Emma E. Walt Disney. Bane, Jeff, illus. 2016. (My Early Library: My Itty-Bitty Bio Ser.). (ENG.). 24p. (J). (gr. k-1). 28.50 (978-1-63471-024-4(X), 208176) Cherry Lake Publishing.

Hansen, Grace. Walt Disney: Animator & Founder, 1 vol. 2014. (History Maker Biographies Ser.). (ENG.). 24p. (J). (gr. 2-4). lib. bdg. 28.50 (978-1-62970-706-8(6)) ABDO Publishing Co.

Josephson, Judith Pinkerton. Walt Disney: Genius of Entertainment. 2006. (People to Know Today Ser.). (Illus.). 128p. (J). (gr. 6). lib. bdg. 33.27 (978-0-7660-2624-7(8)) Enslow Pubs., Inc.

Kampff, Joseph. Walt Disney, 01 vols., 1. 2016. (Britannica Beginner Bios Ser.). (ENG., Illus.). 32p. (J). pap. 12.90 (978-1-5081-0059-1(4), Britannica Educational Publishing) Rosen Publishing Group, Inc., The.

Klimo, Kate. Walt Disney's Magic. Ivanov, O. & Ivanov, A., illus. 2017. (J). pap. (978-0-399-55534-3(X)) Random Hse., Inc.

Lenburg, Jeff. Walt Disney. 2011. (Legends of Animation Ser.). (Illus.). 142p. (gr. 6-12). 34.95 (978-1-60413-836-8(X), Chelsea Hse.) Facts On File, Inc.

Mattern, Joanne. Walt Disney. 2013. (Rookie Biographies(r) Ser.). (ENG.). 32p. (J). 23.00 (978-0-531-24740-2(6)); pap. 5.95 (978-0-531-24706-8(6)) Scholastic Library Publishing. (Children's Pr.).

Miller, Diane Disney & Miller, Diane D. Walt Disney: His Life in Pictures. 2009. (ENG.). 64p. (YA). (gr. 3-17). 14.95 (978-1-4231-2105-3(8)) Disney Pr.

Norwich, Grace. I Am #11: Walt Disney. 2014. (I Am Ser.: 11). (ENG.). 128p. (J). (gr. 2-5). pap. 5.99 (978-0-545-62918-8(7), Scholastic Paperbacks) Scholastic, Inc.

Orr, Tamra B. Walt Disney. 2013. (ENG.). 48p. (J). 29.00 (978-0-531-24780-8(5)) Scholastic Library Publishing.

—Walt Disney: The Man Behind the Magic. 2013. (ENG.). 48p. (J). pap. 6.95 (978-0-531-28466-7(2)) Scholastic Library Publishing.

Rice, Dona. 20th Century Superstar: Disney. 2017. (J). pap. (978-1-4938-3632-1(3)) Teacher Created Materials, Inc.

Richardson, Adele D. The Story of Disney. 2003. (Built for Success Ser.). (Illus.). 48p. (J). 19.95 (978-1-58340-291-7(8)) Black Rabbit Bks.

Saddleback Educational Publishing Staff, ed. Walt Disney, 1 vol. unabr. ed. 2008. (Graphic Biographies Ser.). (ENG., Illus.). 25p. (YA). (gr. 9-12). pap. 7.95 (978-1-59905-230-4(X)) Saddleback Educational Publishing, Inc.

Stewart, Whitney. Who Was Walt Disney? Harrison, Nancy, illus. 2009. (Who Was? Ser.). (ENG.). 112p. (J). (gr. 3-7). pap. 5.99 (978-0-448-45052-0(6), Grosset & Dunlap) Penguin Young Readers Group.

—Who Was Walt Disney? 2009. (Who Was... ? Ser.). lib. bdg. 16.00 (978-0-606-04160-7(5), Turtleback) Turtleback Bks.

Sutcliffe, Jane & Walt Disney Company Staff. Walt Disney. 2009. (History Maker Biographies Ser.). (gr. 3-6). 26.60 (978-1-58013-704-1(0), Lerner Pubns.) Lerner Publishing Group.

Tieck, Sarah. Walt Disney, 1 vol. 2010. (First Biographies Set 6 Ser.). (ENG., Illus.). 32p. (J). (gr. 1-4). 27.07 (978-1-60453-984-4(4)) ABDO Publishing Co.

Weakland, Mark. When Walt Disney Rode a Pig. Pino, Pablo, illus. 2017. (Leaders Doing Headstands Ser.). (ENG.). 32p. (gr. 2-3). lib. bdg. 27.99 (**978-1-5158-1576-1(5)**) Picture Window Bks.

DISPLACED PERSONS

see Refugees

DISPOSAL OF REFUSE

see Refuse and Refuse Disposal

DISRAELI, BENJAMIN, EARL OF BEACONSFIELD, 1804-1881

Lee, Stephen J. Gladstone & Disraeli. 2005. (Questions & Analysis in History Ser.). (ENG., Illus.). 208p. (C). 110.00 (978-0-415-32356-7(8), RU27027); per. 30.95 (978-0-415-32357-4(6)) Routledge.

DISSENTERS

Carr, Simonetta. John Owen. Abraxas, Matt, illus. 2010. (ENG.). 62p. (J). 18.00 (978-1-60178-088-1(5)) Reformation Heritage Bks.

DuMont, Brianna. Fantastic Fugitives: Criminals, Cutthroats, & Slaves Who Changed History (While on the Run!) Straker, Bethany, illus. 2016. (Changed History Ser.). (ENG.). 192p. (J). (gr. 3-7). 16.99 (978-1-63220-412-7(6), Sky Pony Pr.) Skyhorse Publishing Co., Inc.

Scandiffio, Laura. People Who Said No: Courage Against Oppression. 2nd ed. 2012. (ENG., Illus.). 172p. (J). (gr. 5-7). 24.95 (978-1-55451-383-3(9), 9781554513833); pap. 14.95 (978-1-55451-382-6(0), 9781554513826) Annick Pr., Ltd. CAN. Dist: Publishers Group West (PGW).

DISTRIBUTION (ECONOMICS)

see Commerce; Marketing

DISTRIBUTION OF WEALTH

see Economics

DIVERSITY, BIOLOGICAL

see Biodiversity

DIVIDENDS

see Stocks

DIVINATION

see also Astrology; Clairvoyance; Dreams; Fortune-Telling; Occultism; Superstition

Adcock, Will. Guia Practica Del I Ching. (SPA.). 64p. (J). 12.00 (978-84-342-3019-4(4)) Parramon Ediciones S.A. ESP. Dist: Distribuidora Norma, Inc.

Place, Robert M. Astrology & Divination. 2008. (Mysteries, Legends, & Unexplained Phenomena Ser.). (Illus.). 136p. (YA). (gr. 7-12). lib. bdg. 29.95 (978-0-7910-9385-6(9)) Facts On File, Inc.

DIVINE HEALING

see Christian Science

DIVING

Cerullo, Mary M. Journey to Shark Island: A Shark Photographer's Close Encounters, 1 vol. Rotman, Jeffrey L., illus. Rotman, Jeffrey L., photos by. 2014. (Shark Expedition Ser.). (ENG.). 40p. (gr. 5-7). lib. bdg. 31.99 (978-0-7565-4887-2(X)) Compass Point Bks.

Gifford, Clive. Swimming & Diving. 2011. (Olympic Sports Ser.). 32p. (YA). (gr. 4-7). 19.95 (978-1-60753-192-0(5)) Amicus Publishing.

—Swimming & Diving. 2011. (ENG., Illus.). 32p. (J). pap. 10.95 (978-1-77092-039-2(0)) Saunders Bk. Co. CAN. Dist: RiverStream Publishing.

Greathouse, Lisa. Escalar y Saltar, 1 vol. rev. ed. 2010. (Science Readers: a Closer Look Ser.). (SPA., Illus.). 32p. (J). (gr. 2-3). pap. 8.99 (978-1-4333-2147-4(5)) Shell Educational Publishing.

Hamilton, S. L. Diving. 2015. (Illus.). 32p. (J). 27.07 (978-1-62403-750-4(X), 1391380) ABDO Publishing Co.

Hoblin, Paul. Girls Play to Win Swimming & Diving. 2011. (Girls Play to Win Ser.). 64p. (J). (gr. 3-6). lib. bdg. 27.93 (978-1-59953-466-4(5)) Norwood Hse. Pr.

Kehm, Greg. Olympic Swimming & Diving. (Great Moments in Olympic History Ser.). 48p. (gr. 5-6). 2009. 53.00 (978-1-61513-162-4(0), Rosen Reference) 2007. (Illus.). (YA). lib. bdg. 29.25 (978-1-4042-0970-1(0)) Rosen Publishing Group, Inc., The.

Labrecque, Ellen. Cliff Diving. 2012. (Extreme Sports Ser.). (ENG., Illus.). 32p. (J). (gr. 2-5). lib. bdg. 28.50 (978-1-60973-178-6(6), 201123) Child's World, Inc., The.

Lanser, Amanda. The Science Behind Swimming, Diving, & Other Water Sports. 2016. (Illus.). 32p. (J). (978-1-4914-8169-1(2)) Capstone Press of Coughlan Cos.

Loh-Hagan, Virginia. Extreme Cliff Diving. 2016. (Nailed It! Ser.). (ENG., Illus.). 32p. (J). (gr. 4-8). 29.93 (978-1-63471-089-3(4), 208467, 45th Parallel Press) Cherry Lake Publishing.

Norman, Tony. Diving. 2006. (Action Sports Ser.). (Illus.). 32p. (gr. 3-6). lib. bdg. 26.00 (978-0-8368-6367-3(4), Gareth Stevens Learning Library) Stevens, Gareth Publishing LLLP.

Page, Jason. Swimming, Diving, & Other Water Sports. 2008. (Olympic Sports Ser.). (ENG., Illus.). 32p. (J). (gr. 3-7). pap. (978-0-7787-4036-0(6)); lib. bdg. (978-0-7787-4019-3(6)) Crabtree Publishing Co.

Peterson, Christine. The Science Behind Swimming, Diving, & Other Water Sports. 2016. (Science of the Summer Olympics Ser.). (ENG.). 32p. (gr. 3-4). pap. 7.95 (978-1-4914-8161-5(7), Edge Bks.) Capstone Press of Coughlan Cos.

Reichard, Susan E. Who on Earth Is Sylvia Earle? Undersea Explorer of the Ocean. 2009. (Scientists Saving the Earth Ser.). (Illus.). 112p. (J). (gr. 5-9). lib. bdg. 33.27 (978-1-59845-118-4(9)) Enslow Pubs., Inc.

Rosen, Karen. Great Moments in Olympic Swimming & Diving, 1 vol. 2014. (Great Moments in Olympic Sports Ser.). (ENG.). 64p. (J). (gr. 10-14). lib. bdg. 32.79 (978-1-62403-399-5(7), SportsZone) ABDO Publishing Co.

Thomas, Isabel. Animal Swimming & Diving. 2016. (Animalympics Ser.). (ENG., Illus.). 32p. (gr. 1-3). lib. bdg. 29.99 (978-1-4109-8092-2(8), Read Me!) Heinemann-Raintree.

Yoo, Paula. Sixteen Years in Sixteen Seconds: The Sammy Lee Story, 1 vol. Lee, Dom, illus. 2005. (ENG.). 32p. (J). (gr. 1-5). 16.95 (978-1-58430-247-6(X)) Lee & Low Bks., Inc.

DIVING—FICTION

Baxter, Nicola. Trouble under the Ocean: First Reading Books for 3-5 Year Olds. Ball, Geoff, illus. 2015. (ENG.). 24p. bds. 6.99 (978-1-86147-493-3(8), Armadillo) Anness Publishing GBR. Dist: National Bk. Network.

Brouwer, Sigmund. Absolute Pressure, 1 vol. 2009. (Orca Sports Ser.). (ENG.). 176p. (YA). (gr. 6-10). pap. 9.95 (978-1-55469-130-2(3)) Orca Bk. Pubs. USA.

Child, Lauren. Take Your Last Breath. Child, Lauren, illus. 2014. (Ruby Redfort Ser.: 2). (ENG., Illus.). 432p. (J). (gr. 5-9). pap. 7.99 (978-0-7636-6932-4(6)) Candlewick Pr.

Christopher, Matt. Dive Right In. 2005. (Sports Classics IV Ser.). 133p. (J). lib. bdg. 15.00 (978-1-59054-753-3(5)) Fitzgerald Bks.

Cornwall, Gaia. Jabari Jumps. Cornwall, Gaia, illus. 2017. (ENG., Illus.). 32p. (J). (gr. -1-3). 15.99 (978-0-7636-7838-8(4)) Candlewick Pr.

Cox, Buddy. Quicksilver Deep 2004. 401p. per. 19.95 (978-0-9709104-3-1(6)) Hickory Tales Publishing.

Dean, James, illus. Pete the Cat: Scuba-Cat. 2016. 31p. (J). (978-1-4844-7052-7(4)) Harper & Row Ltd.

Johnson, Julia. The Pearl Diver. Stacey International Staff, ed. Al-Fakhri, Patricia, illus. 2003. (ARA & ENG.). 240p. (J). (gr. 3-6). (978-1-900988-62-9(3), Stacey International) Stacey Publishing.

Lemke, Donald B. Diver Down, 1 vol. 2011. (Good vs Evil Ser.). (ENG.). 48p. (gr. 1-2). lib. bdg. 23.99 (978-1-4342-2092-9(3), Good vs Evil) Stone Arch Bks.

Rand, Johnathan. American Chillers #29 Oregon Oceanauts. 2010. 208p. (J). pap. 5.99 (978-1-893699-24-3(2)) AudioCraft Publishing, Inc.

Saddleback Educational Publishing Staff, ed. Dive, 1 vol. unabr. ed. 2011. (Heights Ser.). (ENG.). 50p. (gr. 5-8). pap. 7.95 (978-1-61651-282-8(2)) Saddleback Educational Publishing, Inc.

Scholastic, Inc. Staff & King, Trey. Deep Sea Treasure Dive. Hyland, Greg, illus. 2016. (Lego City Ser.). (ENG.). 24p. (J). (gr. 2-5). pap. 3.99 (978-0-545-90591-6(5)) Scholastic, Inc.

Spurlin, Barbara & Bernhardt, Michael J. Jellyfish on the Menu. 2011. (Illus.). 120p. (J). pap. (978-0-692-01277-2(X)) Kan sasana Printer.

Stephens, Ann Marie. Scuba Dog. Golden, Jess, illus. 2016. (ENG.). 40p. (J). (gr. -1-3). 17.99 (978-1-4998-0143-9(2)) Little Bee Books Inc.

Streib, Sally. Octopus Encounter. 2007. (Illus.). 126p. (J). 6.97 (978-0-8163-2210-7(4)) Pacific Pr. Publishing Assn.

DIVING, SKIN

see Skin Diving

DIVING, SUBMARINE

see Bathyscaphe; Deep Diving

DIVORCE

see also Marriage

Amos, Janine. Divorce. 2009. (Changes Ser.). (Illus.). 32p. (J). (gr. k-2). 22.60 (978-1-60754-481-4(4)); (gr. 2-5). pap. 10.55 (978-1-60754-482-1(2)) Windmill Bks.

Aydt, Rachel. Why Me? A Teen Guide to Divorce & Your Feelings. 2005. (Divorce Resource Library). (Illus.). 64p. (J). (gr. 7-12). lib. bdg. 31.95 (978-0-8239-3113-2(7), DIWHME) Rosen Publishing Group, Inc., The.

Bergin, Rory M. & Meyer, Jared. Frequently Asked Questions about Divorce. 2011. (FAQ: Teen Life Ser.). (J). lib. bdg. 31.95 (978-1-4488-4632-0(3)) Rosen Publishing Group, Inc., The.

Berry, Joy. Good Answers to Tough Questions about Divorce. 2009. (ENG.). 52p. (J). (gr. k-7). pap. 7.95 (978-1-60577-504-3(5)) Berry, Joy Enterprises.

—Good Answers to Tough Questions Divorce. Bartholomew, illus. 2010. (Good Answers to Tough Questions Ser.). (ENG.). 48p. (J). (gr. k-7). pap. 7.99 (978-1-60577-509-8(6)) Berry, Joy Enterprises.

Beyl, Charles, illus. My Parents Are Divorced Too: A Book for Kids by Kids. 2nd ed. 2006. 71p. (J). (gr. 3-7). 14.95 (978-1-59147-241-4(5)); per. 9.95 (978-1-59147-242-1(3)) American Psychological Assn. (Magination Pr.).

Bianchi, Anne. Understanding the Law: A Teen Guide to Family Court & Minors' Rights. 2005. (Divorce Resource Library). (Illus.). 64p. (YA). (gr. 7-12). lib. bdg. 31.95 (978-0-8239-3152-1(8), DIUNLA) Rosen Publishing Group, Inc., The.

Calhoun, Florence. No Easy Answers: A Teen Guide to Why Divorce Happens. 2005. (Divorce Resource Library). (Illus.). 64p. (YA). (gr. 7-12). lib. bdg. 31.95 (978-0-8239-3153-8(6), DINOEA) Rosen Publishing Group, Inc., The.

Callahan, Timothy & Bianchi, Anne. Divorce, Family Court, & Family Law. 2016. (Divorce & Your Family Ser.). 64p. (J). (gr. 7-7). lib. bdg. 34.45 (978-1-5081-7126-3(2)) Rosen Publishing Group, Inc., The.

Cassella, Lynn. When Parents Divorce. 2003. (YA). pap. 1.95 net. (978-0-7648-1061-9(8)) Liguori Pubns.

Crabtree Publishing Company Staff & Iorizzo, Carrie. Divorce & Blended Families. 2012. (ENG., Illus.). 48p. (J). (978-0-7787-2182-6(5)); pap. (978-0-7787-2189-5(2)) Crabtree Publishing Co.

The Divorce Resource Series, 6 bks. Incl. Finding Your Place: A Teen Guide to Life in a Blended Family. Leibowitz, Julie. (YA). lib. bdg. 31.95 (978-0-8239-3114-9(5), DIFIPL); Money Matters: A Teen Guide to the Economics of Divorce. Frisch, Carlienne A. (J). lib. bdg. 31.95 (978-0-8239-3151-4(X), DIMOMA); No Easy Answers: A Teen Guide to Why Divorce Happens. Calhoun, Florence. (YA). lib. bdg. 31.95 (978-0-8239-3153-8(6), DINOEA); Understanding the Law: A Teen Guide to Family Court & Minors' Rights. Bianchi, Anne. (YA). lib. bdg. 31.95 (978-0-8239-3152-1(8), DIUNLA); Why Me? A Teen Guide to Divorce & Your Feelings. Aydt, Rachel. (J). lib. bdg. 31.95 (978-0-8239-3113-2(7), DIWHME); 64p. (gr. 7-12). (Illus.). 2005. Set lib. bdg. 159.00 (978-0-8239-9050-4(8), DIVRES) Rosen Publishing Group, Inc., The.

Donahue, Mary R. & Thornburgh, Gail. What's My Job? Helping Children Navigate the Rough Waters of Separation & Divorce. 2010. 32p. pap. 12.99 (978-1-4490-4669-9(X)) AuthorHouse.

Dotterweich, Kass. What Catholic Teens Should Know about Divorce. Larkin, Jean, ed. 2003. (What Catholic Teens Should Know Ser.). (Illus.). 8p. (YA). 7.95 (978-0-89837-189-5(9), 440210) Pflaum Publishing Group.

Edwards, Nicola. Divorce. (Illus.). 32p. (YA). (gr. 1-18). lib. bdg. 27.10 (978-1-932335-05-3(3)) Chrysalis Education.

Espejo, Roman. Custody & Divorce. 2013. (Teen Rights & Freedoms Ser.). (ENG., Illus.). 176p. (gr. 10-12). lib. bdg. 42.00 (978-0-7377-6400-0(7), Greenhaven Pr., Inc.) Cengage Gale.

Frisch, Carlienne A. Money Matters: A Teen Guide to the Economics of Divorce. 2005. (Divorce Resource Library). (Illus.). 64p. (J). (gr. 7-12). lib. bdg. 31.95 (978-0-8239-3151-4(X), DIMOMA) Rosen Publishing Group, Inc., The.

Gay, Kathlyn. Divorce: The Ultimate Teen Guide. 2014. (It Happened to Me Ser.: 41). (ENG., Illus.). 220p. 45.00 (978-0-8108-9238-5(3)) Rowman & Littlefield Publishers, Inc.

Grollman, Earl A. Talking about Divorce & Separation: A Dialogue Between Parent & Child. Pitzer, Suzanne, illus. 2005. (J). (978-1-56123-155-3(X)) Centering Corp.

Hewitt, Sally. My Stepfamily. 2009. (J). 28.50 (978-1-59920-229-7(8)) Black Rabbit Bks.

Higginbotham, Anastasia. Divorce Is the Worst. 2015. (Ordinary Terrible Things Ser.). (ENG., Illus.). 64p. (J). (gr. -1-3). 16.95 (978-1-55861-880-0(5)) Feminist Pr. at The City Univ. of New York.

Higgins, Melissa. Weekends with Dad: What to Expect When Your Parents Divorce, 1 vol. Kirwan, Wednesday, illus. 2011. (Life's Challenges Ser.). (ENG.). 24p. (gr. 2-3). lib. bdg. 25.99 (978-1-4048-6678-2(7)) Picture Window Bks.

Hudson, David L., Jr. & Marzilli, Alan. Child Custody Issues. 2012. (Point/Counterpoint Ser.). (Illus.). 100p. (C). (gr. 9). 35.00 (978-1-60413-689-0(8), Chelsea Hse.) Facts On File, Inc.

Jones, Viola & Frisch, Carlienne. Divorce & Family Finances. 2016. (Divorce & Your Family Ser.). 64p. (J). (gr. 7-7). 34.45 (978-1-5081-7125-6(4)) Rosen Publishing Group, Inc., The.

Katie & Coco: A Color Book for Parents & Preschoolers about Divorce. 2004. (J). 5.00 (978-0-9767215-0-5(3)) Family Guidance & Outreach Ctr. of Lubbock.

Lenarki, Becky & Calhoun, Florence. Understanding Your Parents' Divorce. 2016. (Divorce & Your Family Ser.). 64p. (J). (gr. 7-7). 34.45 (978-1-5081-7127-0(0)) Rosen Publishing Group, Inc., The.

Levins, Sandra. Was It the Chocolate Pudding? A Story for Little Kids about Divorce. Langdo, Bryan, illus. 2005. 40p. (J). 14.95 (978-1-59147-308-4(X)); (gr. -1-3). per. 9.95 (978-1-59147-309-1(8)) American Psychological Assn. (Magination Pr.).

MacGregor, Cynthia. The Divorce Helpbook for Teens. 2004. (Rebuilding Books, for Divorce & Beyond). (ENG.). 144p. (YA). (gr. 10-12). pap. 15.95 (978-1-886230-57-6(9), Impact Pubs.) New Harbinger Pubns.

Manley, Claudia. Everything You Need to Know about Custody. 2009. (Need to Know Library). 64p. (gr. 5-5). 58.50 (978-1-60854-062-4(6)) Rosen Publishing Group, Inc., The.

Mastel, Julie. Jesus Was with Me All Along: A Book about Divorce. 2013. 20p. pap. 10.95 (978-1-4908-0162-9(6), WestBow Pr.) Author Solutions, Inc.

McDowell, Josh & Stewart, Ed. Divorce of Parents. 2009. (Project 17:17 Ser.). (ENG.). 64p. (J). mass mkt. 4.99 (978-1-84550-441-0(0), 9781845504410) Christian Focus Pubns. GBR. Dist: Bookmasters Distribution.

McKenna, Susan. Feelings Only I Know: Mom & Dad Are Getting Divorced. Johannes, Shelley, illus. 2007. 24p. (J). 14.95 *(978-0-9789965-0-5(X))* Wayfarer Pr., LLC.
—More Feelings Only I Know: Divorce & Fighting Are Hurting My Heart. Johannes, Shelley, illus. 2007. 24p. (J). 14.95 *(978-0-9789965-1-2(8))* Wayfarer Pr., LLC.
McLaughlin, Jerry & Krohn, Katherine E. Dealing with Your Parents' Divorce, 01 vols., 1. 2016. (Family Issues & You Ser.). (ENG.). 48p. (J). pap. 11.75 *(978-1-4994-3709-6(9),* Rosen Central) Rosen Publishing Group, Inc., The.
Menéndez-Aponte, Emily. My Family Is Changing: A Book about Divorce. Fitzgerald, Anne, illus. 2013. 32p. (J). pap. 7.95 *(978-0-87029-555-3(1))* Abbey Pr.
Moore-Malinos, Jennifer & Fabrega, Marta. When My Parents Forgot How to Be Friends. 2005. (Let's Talk about It! Ser.). (ENG., Illus.). 32p. (J). (gr. -1-3). pap. 7.99 *(978-0-7641-3172-1(9))* Barron's Educational Series, Inc.
Morrow, Paula. My Parents Are Divorcing. Now What?, 1 vol. 2015. (ENG.). 112p. (YA). 35.60 *(978-1-4777-7986-6(8),* Rosen Young Adult) Rosen Publishing Group, Inc., The.
Naik, Anita. Coping with Loss: The Life Changes Handbook. 2009. (Really Useful Handbooks Ser.). (ENG.). 48p. (J). (gr. 5-11). pap. *(978-0-7787-4404-7(3))* Crabtree Publishing Co.
Naik, Anita & Cronin, Ali. Coping with Loss: The Life Changes Handbook. 2009. (Really Useful Handbooks Ser.). (ENG.). 48p. (J). (gr. 5-11). lib. bdg. *(978-0-7787-4391-0(8))* Crabtree Publishing Co.
Peterman, Rosie L., et al. Divorce & Stepfamilies. 2012. (Teen Mental Health Ser.). (ENG., Illus.). 48p. (J). (gr. 7-12). lib. bdg. 27.95 *(978-1-4488-6893-3(9))* Rosen Publishing Group, Inc., The.
Powell, Jillian. My New Stepdad. 2012. (New Beginnings Ser.). (ENG., Illus.). 24p. (J). (gr. k-3). 21.25 *(978-1-4488-6635-9(9),* PowerKids Pr.) Rosen Publishing Group, Inc., The.
Prentzas, G. S. The Law & Your Family: Your Legal Rights, 1 vol. 2015. (ENG., Illus.). 64p. (J). 33.25 *(978-1-4777-8012-1(2),* Rosen Reference) Rosen Publishing Group, Inc., The.
Price, Elizabeth. Divorce & Teens: When a Family Splits Apart. 2004. (Teen Issues Ser.). (Illus.). 64p. (J). lib. bdg. 22.60 *(978-0-7660-1670-5(6))* Enslow Pubs., Inc.
Roberts, Jillian. Why Do Families Change? Our First Talk about Separation & Divorce, 1 vol. Revell, Cindy, illus. 2017. (Just Enough Ser.). (ENG.). 32p. (J). (gr. k-1). 19.95 *(978-1-4598-0951-2(3))* Orca Bk. Pubs. USA.
Sam & Sarge. 2004. (J). 5.00 *(978-0-9767215-1-2(1))* Family Guidance & Outreach Ctr. of Lubbock.
Stephens, Edna, et al. B. B. the Bear: Helps Kids with Divorce. 2008. (J). pap. 15.95 *(978-0-9798088-1-4(2))* EDCO Publishing, Inc.
Stern, Zoe & Stern, Evan. Divorce Is Not the End of the World: Zoe's & Evan's Coping Guide for Kids. 2nd rev. ed. 2008. (ENG., Illus.). 112p. (J). (gr. 3-7). pap. 9.99 *(978-1-58246-241-7(0),* Tricycle Pr.) Random Hse. Children's Bks.
Stewart, Sheila. I Live in Two Homes: Adjusting to Divorce & Remarriage. 2009. (Kids Have Troubles Too Ser.). 48p. (YA). (gr. 5-18). pap. 7.95 *(978-1-4222-1907-2(0))* Mason Crest.
Stewart, Sheila & Simons, Rae. I Live in Two Homes: Adjusting to Divorce & Remarriage. 2010. (Kids Have Troubles Too Ser.). 48p. (YA). (gr. 5-18). lib. bdg. 19.95 *(978-1-4222-1694-1(2))* Mason Crest.
Waddington, Emma. Why Don't We All Live Together Anymore? Big Issues for Little People after a Family Break-Up. Thomas, Louis & Thomas, Louis, illus. 2016. (Life & Soul Library). (ENG.). 32p. (J). (gr. -1-3). 12.99 ***(978-1-84780-867-7(0),*** Frances Lincoln Children's Bks.) Quarto Publishing Group UK GBR. Dist: Hachette Bk. Group.
Wilson, Mike. Divorce. 2008. (Opposing Viewpoints Ser.). (ENG., Illus.). (gr. 10-12). 224p. 48.80 *(978-0-7377-4204-6(6),* LML02109-243101); 200p. (YA). 29.45 *(978-0-7377-4205-3(4),* LML02109-243134) Cengage Gale. (Greenhaven Pr., Inc.).
WJW. Leroy & Cheryl's Adventure. 2013. 60p. pap. 10.30 *(978-1-4669-9368-6(5))* Trafford Publishing.
Wolfelt, Alan D. & Maloney, Raelynn. Healing after Divorce: 100 Practical Ideas for Kids. 2011. (Healing Your Grieving Heart Ser.). (ENG.). 128p. (J). (gr. 1-7). pap. 11.95 *(978-1-61722-138-5(4))* Companion Pr.
Young, Diana S. Daddy Doesn't Live with Me Anymore. 2010. 20p. pap. 10.83 *(978-1-4490-7550-7(9))* AuthorHouse.

DIVORCE—FICTION

Ali, S. K. Saints, Misfits, Monsters, & Mayhem. 2017. (ENG., Illus.). 336p. (YA). (gr. 9). 18.99 ***(978-1-4814-9924-8(6),*** Salaam Reads) Simon & Schuster Bks. For Young Readers.
Alsop, Bonnie. Sharing Me: Helping Young Children Deal with Divorce. McKay, Siobhan, illus. 2013. 24p. pap. 11.50 *(978-1-62212-232-5(1),* Strategic Bk. Publishing) Strategic Book Publishing & Rights Agency (SBPRA).
Alvarez, Julia. De Como la Tia Lola Aprendio a Ensenar. 2011. (Tia Lola Stories Ser.). (SPA & ENG.). 160p. (J). (gr. 3-7). 7.99 *(978-0-375-85793-5(1),* Yearling) Random Hse. Children's Bks.
—How Tia Lola Came to Visit Stay. 2004. 147p. (gr. 3-7). 17.00 *(978-0-7569-3641-9(1))* Perfection Learning Corp.
—How Tia Lola Learned to Teach. 2011. (Tia Lola Stories Ser.). (ENG., Illus.). 144p. (J). (gr. 3-7). pap. 7.99 *(978-0-375-85792-8(3),* Yearling) Random Hse. Children's Bks.
Anholt, Laurence. Two Nests. Coplestone, Jim, illus. 2013. (ENG.). 32p. (J). (gr. -1-1). 17.99 *(978-1-84780-323-8(7),* Frances Lincoln) Quarto Publishing Group UK GBR. Dist: Hachette Bk. Group.
Atkinson, Elizabeth. Lisa's Totally Unforgettable Winter. 2006. (ENG.). 56p. per. 16.95 *(978-1-4241-6249-9(1))* America Star Bks.
Baldwin, Quinn. Crossover. 2011. 168p. pap. 15.00 *(978-0-557-74844-0(5))* Lulu Pr., Inc.
Bartlett, Roberta. How I Met an Alien. 2011. 74p. pap. 19.95 *(978-1-4560-7818-8(6))* America Star Bks.
Baskin, Nora Raleigh. Subway Love. 2014. (ENG.). 224p. (YA). (gr. 9). 16.99 *(978-0-7636-6845-7(1))* Candlewick Pr.
Bateson, Catherine. Stranded in Boringsville. (ENG.). 144p. (J). (gr. 5-9). 2007. pap. 6.95 *(978-0-8234-2113-8(9))* 2005. 16.95 *(978-0-8234-1969-2(X))* Holiday Hse., Inc.
Bauer, Joan. Stand Tall. 2005. (ENG.). 192p. (YA). (gr. 7-5). pap. 8.99 *(978-0-14-240427-0(6),* Speak) Penguin Young Readers Group.
Bender, Randy L. Bunko's Journey. LaGrange, Tiffany, illus. 2008. 44p. pap. 13.95 *(978-0-9818683-2-5(0))* Peppertree Pr., The.
Benton, Jim. That's What Friends Aren't For. Benton, Jim, illus. 2010. (Dear Dumb Diary Ser.: 9). (ENG., Illus.). 144p. (J). (gr. 3-7). 6.99 *(978-0-545-11612-1(0),* Scholastic Paperbacks) Scholastic, Inc.
Beverly, Cleary. Dear Mr. Henshaw. 2014. (Cleary Reissue Ser.). (ENG.). 160p. (J). (gr. 7-12). 10.24 *(978-1-63245-195-8(6))* Lectorum Pubns., Inc.
Block, Francesca Lia. Pink Smog: Becoming Weetzie Bat. 2012. (Weetzie Bat Ser.: 6). (ENG.). 208p. (YA). (gr. 9). 17.99 *(978-0-06-156598-4(9),* HarperTeen) HarperCollins Pubs.
Blume, Judy. It's Not the End of the World. 174p. (YA). (gr. 5-18). pap. 4.50 *(978-0-8072-1365-0(9),* Listening Library) Random Hse. Audio Publishing Group.
—It's Not the End of the World. 2014. (ENG., Illus.). 240p. (J). (gr. 3-7). pap. 7.99 *(978-1-4814-1116-5(0),* Atheneum Bks. for Young Readers) Simon & Schuster Children's Publishing.
Blumenthal, Deborah. The Lifeguard. (ENG.). 288p. (YA). (gr. 8-12). 2013. 9.99 *(978-0-8075-4536-2(8))* 2012. 16.99 *(978-0-8075-4535-5(X))* Whitman, Albert & Co.
Boochever, Annie. Bristol Bay Summer. 2014. (ENG., Illus.). 258p. (J). (gr. 3-7). 28.99 *(978-1-941821-27-5(8));* pap. 12.99 *(978-0-88240-994-8(8))* Graphic Arts Ctr. Publishing Co. (Alaska Northwest Bks.).
Bowe, Julie. Big & Little Questions (According to Wren Jo Byrd) 2017. (ENG.). 240p. (J). (gr. 2-4). 16.99 *(978-0-8037-3693-1(2),* Kathy Dawson Books) Penguin Young Readers Group.
Brandes, Wendy L. Emily's Pranking Problem. Lorenzet, Eleonora, illus. 2016. (Summer Camp Ser.). (ENG.). 96p. (gr. 4-6). lib. bdg. 24.65 *(978-1-4965-2599-4(X))* Stone Arch Bks.
Brown Lcsw, Jennifer. Star Realizes She Is Not Alone. 2013. 28p. pap. 19.99 *(978-1-4772-7043-1(4))* AuthorHouse.
—Star's Unexpected News. 2011. 32p. pap. 13.49 *(978-1-4389-3567-6(6))* AuthorHouse.
Brown, Marc. Arthur & the 1,001 Dads, Bk. 28. Brown, Marc, illus. 2003. (ENG., Illus.). 64p. (J). (gr. 1-4). pap. 4.25 *(978-0-316-12280-1(7))* Little, Brown Bks. for Young Readers.
Bunting, Eve. My Mom's Wedding. Papp, Lisa, illus. 2006. (ENG.). 32p. (J). (gr. k-6). 16.95 *(978-1-58536-288-2(3))* Sleeping Bear Pr.
Burnell, Pamela H. The Light Keeper: An Epps Kids Mystery. 2008. 76p. pap. 19.95 *(978-1-60474-847-5(8))* America Star Bks.
Calabrese, Dianne. The Inspirational Guide, 1 vol. 2010. 24p. 24.95 *(978-1-4489-4844-4(4))* PublishAmerica, Inc.
Caletti, Deb. The Secret Life of Prince Charming. (ENG.). (YA). (gr. 7). 2010. 352p. pap. 11.99 *(978-1-4169-5941-0(6))* 2009. 336p. 16.99 *(978-1-4169-5940-3(8))* Simon Pulse. (Simon Pulse).
Cassidy, Cathy. Dizzy. 2005. (ENG.). 272p. (J). (gr. 3-7). 6.99 *(978-0-14-240474-4(8),* Puffin Books) Penguin Young Readers Group.
Christopher, Matt. Comeback Challenge. 2008. (New Matt Christopher Sports Library). 160p. (J). (gr. 4-6). lib. bdg. 26.60 *(978-1-59953-211-0(5))* Norwood Hse. Pr.
Clements, Andrew. Head of the Class: Frindle - The Landry News - The Janitor's Boy. Selznick, Brian, illus. 2007. (ENG.). 416p. (J). (gr. 3-7). pap. 20.99 *(978-1-4169-4974-9(7),* Atheneum Bks. for Young Readers) Simon & Schuster Children's Publishing.
—El Periodico Landry. Selznick, Brian, illus. 2004.Tr. of Landry News. (SPA.). (YA). pap. 9.99 *(978-84-241-7886-4(6))* Everest Editora ESP. Dist: Lectorum Pubns., Inc.
Cochran, Bill. My Parents Are Divorced My Elbows Have Nicknames & Other Fact. Björkman, Steve, illus. 2009. (ENG.). 32p. (J). (gr. -1-3). 17.99 *(978-0-06-053942-9(9))* HarperCollins Pubs.
Colasanti, Susane. So Much Closer. 2012. (ENG.). 272p. (YA). (gr. 7-18). pap. 8.99 *(978-0-14-242114-7(6),* Speak) Penguin Young Readers Group.
—Waiting for You. 2010. (ENG.). 336p. (YA). (gr. 7-18). 9.99 *(978-0-14-241575-7(8),* Speak) Penguin Young Readers Group.
Cook, Julia. The D Word: Divorce. Rodgers, Phillip W., illus. 2011. (ENG.). (J). (gr. 2-7). pap. 9.95 *(978-1-931636-76-6(1))* National Ctr. For Youth Issues.
Corriveau, Art. How I Got a Life & a Dog. 2012. (ENG.). 288p. (J). (gr. 3-7). pap. 7.95 *(978-1-4197-0015-6(4),* Amulet Bks.) Abrams, Inc.
—How I, Nicky Flynn, Finally Got a Life (And a Dog) 2010. (ENG.). 272p. (YA). (gr. 3-7). 16.95 *(978-0-8109-8298-7(6),* Amulet Bks.) Abrams, Inc.
Couloumbis, Audrey. Lexie. Denos, Julia, illus. 2012. (ENG.). 208p. (J). (gr. 3-7). pap. 6.99 *(978-0-375-85633-4(1),* Yearling) Random Hse. Children's Bks.
—Not Exactly a Love Story. 2014. (ENG.). 288p. (YA). (gr. 7). pap. 9.99 *(978-0-375-86606-7(X),* Ember) Random Hse. Children's Bks.
Cowing, Sue. Call Me Drog. 2014. (ENG.). 320p. (J). 13.99 *(978-0-00-757804-7(0))* HarperCollins Pubs. Ltd. GBR. Dist: Independent Pubs. Group.
—You Will Call Me Drog. 2011. (Exceptional Reading & Language Arts Titles for Intermediate Grades Ser.). (ENG.). 288p. (J). (gr. 4-7). 16.95 *(978-0-7613-6076-6(X),* Carolrhoda Bks.) Lerner Publishing Group.
Coy, John. Top of the Order. 2010. (4 For 4 Ser.: 1). (ENG.). 208p. (J). (gr. 3-7). pap. 8.99 *(978-0-312-61111-8(0),* 9780312611118) Square Fish.
Daly, Cathleen. Emily's Blue Period. Brown, Lisa, illus. 2014. (ENG.). 56p. (J). (gr. -1-2). 17.99 *(978-1-59643-469-1(4),* 9781596434691) Roaring Brook Pr.
Danziger, Paula. Amber Brown Goes Fourth. Ross, Tony, illus. 2007. (Amber Brown Ser.: No. 3). 101p. (gr. 2-5). 15.00 *(978-0-7569-8197-6(2))* Perfection Learning Corp.
—Amber Brown Goes Fourth. (Amber Brown Ser.: No. 3). 112p. (J). (gr. 3-6). pap. 3.99 *(978-0-8072-1291-2(1),* Listening Library) Random Hse. Audio Publishing Group.
—Amber Brown Goes Fourth. Ross, Tony, illus. 2007. (Amber Brown Ser.: 3). (ENG.). 128p. (J). (gr. 2-5). 5.99 *(978-0-14-240901-5(4),* Puffin Books) Penguin Young Readers Group.
—Amber Brown Is Feeling Blue. 2010. (Amber Brown Ser.: 7). (ENG.). 160p. (J). (gr. 2-5). 5.99 *(978-0-14-241686-0(X),* Puffin Books) Penguin Young Readers Group.
—Amber Brown Is Feeling Blue. 2004. (Amber Brown Ser.: No. 7). 131p. (J). (gr. 2-4). pap. 17.00 incl. audio *(978-0-8072-2063-4(9),* Listening Library) Random Hse. Audio Publishing Group.
—Amber Brown Is Feeling Blue. 2010. (Amber Brown Ser.: 7). (gr. 3-6). lib. bdg. 16.00 *(978-0-613-20096-7(9),* Turtleback) Turtleback Bks.
—Amber Brown Is Green with Envy. 2014. (Amber Brown Ser.: 9). (ENG., Illus.). 176p. (J). (gr. 2-5). pap. 5.99 *(978-0-14-242699-9(7),* Puffin Books) Penguin Young Readers Group.
—Amber Brown Is Green with Envy. Ross, Tony, illus. 2004. (Amber Brown Ser.: No. 9). 151p. (J). (gr. 2-5). 12.65 *(978-0-7569-2978-7(4))* Perfection Learning Corp.
—Amber Brown Sees Red. 2011. (Amber Brown Ser.: No. 6). 7.64 *(978-0-7848-3448-0(2),* Everbind) Marco Bk. Co.
—Amber Brown Sees Red. 2009. (Amber Brown Ser.: 6). (ENG.). 144p. (J). (gr. 2-5). 5.99 *(978-0-14-241261-9(9),* Puffin Books) Penguin Young Readers Group.
—Amber Brown Sees Red. (Amber Brown Ser.: No. 6). 116p. (J). (gr. 3-6). pap. 3.99 *(978-0-8072-1294-3(6),* Listening Library) Random Hse. Audio Publishing Group.
—Amber Brown Sees Red. 2009. (Amber Brown Ser.: 6). (gr. 3-6). lib. bdg. 16.00 *(978-0-613-09442-9(5),* Turtleback) Turtleback Bks.
—Amber Brown Wants Extra Credit. Ross, Tony, illus. 2008. (Amber Brown Ser.: 4). (ENG.). 144p. (J). (gr. 2-5). 5.99 *(978-0-14-241049-3(7),* Puffin Books) Penguin Young Readers Group.
—Amber Brown Wants Extra Credit. (Amber Brown Ser.: No. 4). 120p. (J). (gr. 3-6). pap. 3.99 *(978-0-8072-1292-9(X),* Listening Library) Random Hse. Audio Publishing Group.
—The Divorce Express. 2007. (ENG.). 208p. (J). (gr. 5-18). 8.99 *(978-0-14-240712-7(7),* Puffin Books) Penguin Young Readers Group.
—The Divorce Express. 160p. (J). pap. 3.99 *(978-0-8072-1376-6(4),* Listening Library) Random Hse. Audio Publishing Group.
—I, Amber Brown. Ross, Tony, illus. 2011. (Amber Brown Ser.: 8). (ENG.). 160p. (J). (gr. 2-5). 5.99 *(978-0-14-241965-6(6),* Puffin Books) Penguin Young Readers Group.
—I, Amber Brown. 2004. (Amber Brown Ser.: No. 8). 144p. (J). (gr. 2-4). pap. 17.00 incl. audio *(978-0-8072-2064-1(7),* Listening Library) Random Hse. Audio Publishing Group.
—You Can't Eat Your Chicken Pox, Amber Brown. Ross, Tony, illus. 2006. (Amber Brown Ser.: No. 2). 100p. (J). (gr. 2-5). 15.00 *(978-0-7569-6756-7(2))* Perfection Learning Corp.
—You Can't Eat Your Chicken Pox, Amber Brown. (Amber Brown Ser.: No. 2). 101p. (J). (gr. 3-6). pap. 3.50 *(978-0-8072-1290-5(3),* Listening Library) Random Hse. Audio Publishing Group.
—You Can't Eat Your Chicken Pox, Amber Brown. Ross, Tony, illus. 2006. (Amber Brown Ser.: 2). (ENG.). 128p. (J). (gr. 2-5). 5.99 *(978-0-14-240629-8(5),* Puffin Books) Penguin Young Readers Group.
Danziger, Paula & Mazer, Anne. Is Green with Envy. Ross, Tony, illus. 2004. (Amber Brown Ser.: 9). (ENG.). 160p. (J). (gr. 2-5). pap. 4.99 *(978-0-439-07171-0(2),* Scholastic Paperbacks) Scholastic, Inc.
Davidson, Barbara. Billys Most Difficult Choice. 2007. 49p. 16.95 *(978-1-4241-6153-9(3))* America Star Bks.
Del George, Dana. The Queen of Fire & the King of Ice. 2009. 24p. 12.50 *(978-0-578-00730-4(4))* Del George, Dana.
Dellasega, Cheryl. Nugrl90, 0 vols. LaPierre, Karina, illus. 2007. (Bloggrls Ser.: 1). (ENG.). 192p. (YA). (gr. 7-11). pap. 9.99 *(978-0-7614-5396-3(2),* 9780761453963, Amazon Children's Publishing) Amazon Publishing.
Dessen, Sarah. Along for the Ride. (ENG.). (YA). (gr. 7-18). 2011. 432p. pap. 10.99 *(978-0-14-241556-6(1),* Speak) 2009. 416p. 19.99 *(978-0-670-01194-0(0),* Viking Books for Young Readers) Penguin Young Readers Group.
—Along for the Ride. 2011. lib. bdg. 20.85 *(978-0-606-15360-7(8),* Turtleback) Turtleback Bks.
—What Happened to Goodbye. 2013. (ENG.). 432p. (YA). (gr. 7). pap. 9.99 *(978-0-14-242383-7(1),* Speak) Penguin Young Readers Group.
—What Happened to Goodbye. 2013. lib. bdg. 20.85 *(978-0-606-30864-9(4),* Turtleback) Turtleback Bks.
Deuker, Carl. Night Hoops. 2009. (ENG.). 224p. (YA). (gr. 7). pap. 8.99 *(978-0-547-24891-2(1))* Houghton Mifflin Harcourt Publishing Co.
—Night Hoops. 2009. 250p. (gr. 7-12). lib. bdg. 19.65 *(978-0-613-61919-6(6),* Turtleback) Turtleback Bks.
Doodle, Nanny. Divorced at Six. 2006. 158p. pap. 24.95 *(978-1-4241-3963-7(5))* PublishAmerica, Inc.
Dower, Laura. For Emme, Baked with Love. Lazuli, Lilly, illus. 2016. (Dessert Diaries). (ENG.). 160p. (gr. 4-5). pap. 5.95 *(978-1-4965-4142-0(1));* lib. bdg. 26.65 *(978-1-4965-3122-3(1))* Stone Arch Bks.
Dumble, Carol. R U My Friend? 2011. 20p. pap. 11.99 *(978-1-4567-1825-1(8))* AuthorHouse.
Dumont, Virginie, et al. Enredos de Familia. Boucher, Michel, illus. 2004. (Arbol de la Vida Ser.). (SPA.). 64p. (J). 13.99 *(978-84-8488-098-1(2))* Serres, Ediciones, S. L. ESP. Dist: Lectorum Pubns., Inc.
Emond, Stephen. Happyface. 2011. (ENG., Illus.). 336p. (YA). (gr. 7-17). pap. 10.99 *(978-0-316-04099-0(1))* Little, Brown Bks. for Young Readers.
Ernst, Kathleen. Highland Fling. 2006. (ENG.). 192p. (J). (gr. 3-8). 15.95 *(978-0-8126-2742-8(3))* Cricket Bks.
Falk, Jennifer & Morgan. A Heart Daddy for Chrissie. 2005. 43p. (J). pap. 16.00 *(978-1-4116-3585-2(X))* Lulu Pr., Inc.
Fass, Tara. Turtlebird's Double Dip Shuffle. Conn, Alexandra, illus. 2013. 18p. pap. 10.00 *(978-0-9838120-4-3(7))* Huqua Pr.
Feinstein, John. The Walk On. 2015. (Triple Threat Ser.). (ENG.). 384p. (J). (gr. 5). pap. 7.99 *(978-0-385-75349-4(7),* Yearling) Random Hse. Children's Bks.
—The Walk On. 2015. (Triple Threat Ser.: 1). lib. bdg. 18.40 *(978-0-606-37704-1(2))* Turtleback Bks.
Fitch, Sheree. One More Step, 1 vol. 2006. (Orca Soundings Ser.). (ENG.). 112p. (YA). (gr. 8-12). 14.95 *(978-1-55143-554-1(3))* Orca Bk. Pubs. USA.
Flesher, Brandon. Shattered Dreams in Light. 2014. (J). *(978-1-938237-10-2(2))* Skywater Publishing Co.
Flint, Shamini. Ten. 2009. (Illus.). 146p. pap. *(978-981-08-1597-4(2))* Sunbear Publishing.
—Ten: A Soccer Story. 2017. (ENG.). 176p. (J). (gr. 5-7). 16.99 *(978-0-544-85001-9(7),* Clarion Bks.) Houghton Mifflin Harcourt Trade & Reference Pubs.
Fox Mazer, Norma. Taking Terri Mueller. 2015. (ENG.). 224p. (J). (gr. 5). pap. 12.95 *(978-1-939601-38-4(X))* Ig Publishing, Inc.
Furraway, Bec. Sarah Meets a Bully. 2008. 36p. pap. 18.50 *(978-1-60693-214-8(4),* Eloquent Bks.) Strategic Book Publishing & Rights Agency (SBPRA).
Gallagher, Mary Collins. Ginny Morris & Dads New Girlfriend. Martin, Whitney, illus. 2006. (Ginny Morris Ser.). 63p. (J). (gr. 3-7). 14.95 *(978-1-59147-386-2(1));* per. 9.95 *(978-1-59147-387-9(X))* American Psychological Assn. (Magination Pr.).
—Nine Is Not an Even Number. Martin, Whitney, illus. 2005. 48p. (J). 14.95 *(978-1-59147-157-8(5));* pap. 9.95 *(978-1-59147-158-5(3))* American Psychological Assn. (Magination Pr.).
Gant, Gene. The Thunder in His Head [Library Edition]. 2012. 200p. (-18). pap. 14.99 *(978-1-62380-903-4(7),* Harmony Ink Pr.) Dreamspinner Pr.
Gary, Paulsen. Hatchet. 2014. (ENG.). 192p. (J). (gr. 3-3). 12.24 *(978-1-63245-105-7(0))* Lectorum Pubns., Inc.
Gasparro, Marie & Falletta, Bernadette. The Magnificent Hole. 2005. 13p. (J). 12.95 *(978-1-4116-5924-7(4))* Lulu Pr., Inc.
Gephart, Donna. Olivia Bean, Trivia Queen. (ENG.). 288p. (J). 2013. (gr. 4-7). 6.99 *(978-0-375-87261-7(2),* Yearling) 2012. (gr. 3-7). 16.99 *(978-0-385-74052-4(2),* Delacorte Bks. for Young Readers) Random Hse. Children's Bks.
Glaser, Linda. Alask. 2012. 28p. pap. 21.99 *(978-1-4797-3781-9(X))* Xlibris Corp.
Gownley, Jim. Amelia in Speak Softee to Me: #5, 1 vol. Gownley, Jim, illus. 2011. (Amelia Rules! Ser.). (ENG., Illus.). 36p. 24.21 *(978-1-59961-791-6(9))* Spotlight.
—Amelia vs. the Sneeze Barf: #1, 1 vol. Gownley, Jim, illus. 2011. (Amelia Rules! Ser.). (ENG., Illus.). 36p. 24.21 *(978-1-59961-787-9(0))* Spotlight.
Gownley, Jimmy. Superheroes. Gownley, Jimmy, illus. 2011. (Amelia Rules! Ser.). (ENG., Illus.). 176p. (J). (gr. 2-7). 19.99 *(978-1-4424-4540-6(8),* Atheneum Bks. for Young Readers) Simon & Schuster Children's Publishing.
—What Makes You Happy. Gownley, Jimmy, illus. 2009. (Amelia Rules! Ser.). (ENG., Illus.). 176p. (J). (gr. 2-7). pap. 12.99 *(978-1-4169-8605-8(7),* Atheneum Bks. for Young Readers) Simon & Schuster Children's Publishing.
Grabenstein, Chris. The Island of Dr. Libris. 2016. (ENG.). 272p. (J). (gr. 3-7). 7.99 *(978-0-385-38845-0(4),* Yearling) Random Hse. Children's Bks.
Graff, Lisa. Double Dog Dare. (ENG.). (J). (gr. 3-7). 2013. 320p. pap. 7.99 *(978-0-14-242412-4(9),* Puffin Books) 2012. 304p. 16.99 *(978-0-399-25516-8(8),* Philomel Bks.) Penguin Young Readers Group.
—The Great Treehouse War. 2017. (ENG.). 288p. (J). (gr. 3-7). 16.99 *(978-0-399-17500-8(8),* Philomel Bks.) Penguin Young Readers Group.
Grant, Katy. Hide & Seek, 1 vol. (ENG.). 240p. (J). 2012. pap. 7.95 *(978-1-56145-669-7(1))* 2010. (gr. 3-7). 15.95 *(978-1-56145-542-3(3))* Peachtree Pubs.
Green, Tim. Best of the Best. 2012. (Baseball Great Ser.: 3). (J). lib. bdg. 17.20 *(978-0-606-23590-7(6),* Turtleback) Turtleback Bks.
—Best of the Best: A Baseball Great Novel. 2011. (Playaway Children Ser.). (J). (gr. 5-8). 64.99 *(978-1-61707-137-9(4))* Findaway World, LLC.
—Best of the Best: A Baseball Great Novel. (Baseball Great Ser.: 3). (ENG.). (J). (gr. 3-7). 2012. 288p. pap. 7.99 *(978-0-06-168624-5(7))* 2011. 272p. 16.99 *(978-0-06-168622-1(0))* HarperCollins Pubs.
Harrington, Claudia. My Two Homes, 1 vol. Persico, Zoe, illus. 2016. (ENG.). 32p. (J). *(978-1-62402-109-1(3))* Magic Wagon.
Hasak-Lowy, Todd. Me Being Me Is Exactly As Insane As You Being You. 2015. (ENG., Illus.). 656p. (YA). (gr. 9). 17.99 *(978-1-4424-9573-9(1),* Simon Pulse) Simon Pulse.
Haven, Gayle Jeanine. Love from Both Houses, My Parents Love. 2012. 28p. pap. 19.99 *(978-1-4685-9810-0(4))* AuthorHouse.
Henkes, Kevin. Bird Lake Moon. (ENG.). 192p. (J). (gr. 3-7). 2010. pap. 5.99 *(978-0-06-147079-0(1))* 2008. 17.99 *(978-0-06-147076-9(7))* HarperCollins Pubs. (Greenwillow Bks.).
Higgins, M. G. Family Fix-It Plan. Taylor, Jo, illus. 2016. (Sibling Split Ser.). (ENG.). 112p. (gr. 2-3). lib. bdg. 25.32 *(978-1-4965-2590-1(6))* Stone Arch Bks.
—The Impossible Wish. Taylor, Jo, illus. 2016. (Sibling Split Ser.). (ENG.). 112p. (gr. 2-3). lib. bdg. 25.32 *(978-1-4965-2593-2(0))* Stone Arch Bks.
—Party of Nine. Taylor, Jo, illus. 2016. (Sibling Split Ser.). (ENG.). 112p. (gr. 2-3). lib. bdg. 25.32 *(978-1-4965-2592-5(2))* Stone Arch Bks.
—Trouble in the City. Taylor, Jo, illus. 2016. (Sibling Split Ser.). (ENG.). 112p. (gr. 2-3). lib. bdg. 25.32 *(978-1-4965-2591-8(4))* Stone Arch Bks.
Holmes, Elizabeth. The Normal Kid. 2012. (Exceptional Reading & Language Arts Titles for Intermediate Grades Ser.). (ENG.). 248p. (J). (gr. 4-9). 17.95 *(978-0-7613-8085-6(X),* Carolrhoda Bks.) Lerner Publishing Group.
Hubler, Marsha. Leading the Way, 1 vol. 2010. (Keystone Stables Ser.). (ENG.). 128p. (J). pap. 7.99 *(978-0-310-71796-6(5))* Zonderkidz.
The Island of Dr. Libris. 2015. (ENG.). 256p. (J). (gr. 3-7). 16.99 *(978-0-385-38844-3(6));* lib. bdg. 19.99 *(978-0-385-38846-7(2))* Random Hse. Children's Bks. (Random Hse. Bks. for Young Readers).
Jaskulka, Marie. The Lost Marble Notebook of Forgotten Girl & Random Boy. 2015. (ENG.). 272p. (J). (gr. 6). 16.99 *(978-1-63220-426-4(6),* Sky Pony Pr.) Skyhorse Publishing Co., Inc.

C
D

Johnson, Kristel. Even When We Are Apart. 2008. 20p. pap. 24.95 *(978-1-60610-435-4(7))* America Star Bks.
Joseph, Beverly L. Don't Forget about Me. Swope, Brenda, illus. 2011. 28p. pap. 24.95 *(978-1-4560-0972-4(9))* America Star Bks.
Judd-Leisten, Betty. Tell It for a Toll, Toll It for a Tale. 2005. 102p. per. 7.95 *(978-1-59824-057-3(9))* E-BookTime LLC.
Julia, Alvarez. How Tia Lola Came to Visit Stay. 2014. (Tia Lola Stories Ser.). (ENG.). 160p. (J). (gr. 3-7). 11.24 *(978-1-63245-289-4(8))* Lectorum Pubns., Inc.
Kaplan, Isabel. Hancock Park. 2010. (ENG.). 272p. (YA). (gr. 9). pap. 8.99 *(978-0-06-137370-1(2),* HarperTeen) HarperCollins Pubs.
Kennedy, Pamela. Two Homes for Tyler: A Story about Understanding Divorce. Wummer, Amy, illus. 2008. (ENG.). 32p. (J). (gr. -1). 8.99 *(978-0-8249-5582-3(X),* Ideal Pubns.) Worthy Publishing.
Kim, Cecil. Mommy & Daddy Love You. Ladecka, Anna, illus. 2014. (MySELF Bookshelf Ser.). (ENG.). 32p. (J). (gr. k-2). pap. 11.94 *(978-1-60357-691-8(6));* lib. bdg. 25.27 *(978-1-59953-656-9(0))* Norwood Hse. Pr.
Klassen, Kirsten L. Katelyn's Affection. 2004. (ENG.). 280p. pap. 11.99 *(978-0-8361-9281-0(8))* Herald Pr.
Klein, Adria F. Max Se Queda a Dormir, 1 vol. Robledo, Sol, tr. from ENG. Gallagher-Cole, Memie, illus. 2007. (Read-It! Readers en Español: la Vida de Max Ser.). (SPA.). 24p. (gr. -1-3). lib. bdg. 21.32 *(978-1-4048-3797-3(3),* Easy Readers) Picture Window Bks.
Klise, Kate. Homesick. 2014. (ENG.). 208p. (J). (gr. 5-9). pap. 7.99 *(978-1-250-06511-7(9),* 9781250065117) Square Fish.
Koenig, Faydra. Two Homes for Daniel. 2013. 30p. pap. 10.95 *(978-0-9891471-1-8(8))* Alpine River Pr.
Konen, Leah. The Romantics. 2016. (ENG.). 336p. (YA). (gr. 8-17). 18.95 *(978-1-4197-2193-9(3),* Amulet Bks.) Abrams, Inc.
Korman, Gordon. Pop. 272p. (YA). (gr. 8). 2011. pap. 9.99 *(978-0-06-174261-3(9))* 2009. 16.99 *(978-0-06-174228-6(7))* HarperCollins Pubs.
Kramer, Paul M. Divorce Stinks. 2012. (ENG & ABK.). 32p. 15.95 *(978-0-9819745-4-5(6))* Aloha Wellness Pubs.
Krensky, Stephen. Arthur & the 1,001 Dads. 2003. (Marc Brown Arthur Chapter Bks.). (Illus.). 57p. (J). (gr. 1-4). 11.90 *(978-0-7569-1600-8(3))* Perfection Learning Corp.
Krueger, Kathryn L. Road to Grandma's House. 2005. 128p. pap. 13.95 *(978-1-59800-366-6(6))* Outskirts Pr., Inc.
Krupic, Janice. Felicia's Family Divorces. 2004. 72p. *(978-0-9745219-0-9(6))* Children Concept Publishing.
Kuno, Dorothy. Micah. 2012. 124p. (-18). 29.99 *(978-1-4797-0546-7(2));* pap. 19.99 *(978-1-4797-0545-0(4))* Xlibris Corp.
LaFaye, A. The Year of the Sawdust Man. 2008. (ENG.). 224p. (J). (gr. 2-8). pap. 6.95 *(978-1-57131-679-0(5))* Milkweed Editions.
Laskin, Pamela L. Getting to Know You. 2003. (YA). 16.95 *(978-0-936389-92-9(3))* Tudor Pubs., Inc.
Lee, Thomas. The Battle at Otter Lake. 2007. 167p. pap. 24.95 *(978-1-60441-488-2(X))* America Star Bks.
Levine, Karen R. Daddy's Picture. Stasuyk, Max, illus. 2013. 24p. pap. 14.95 *(978-1-57258-794-6(6),* Aspect Bk.) TEACH Services, Inc.
Levins, Sandra. Do You Sing Twinkle? A Story about Remarriage & New Family. Langdo, Bryan, illus. 2009. 32p. (J). (gr. -1-3). 14.95 *(978-1-4338-0539-4(1));* pap. 9.95 *(978-1-4338-0551-6(0))* American Psychological Assn. (Magination Pr.).
Levy, Marianne. Katie Cox Goes Viral. 2017. (ENG.). 368p. (J). (gr. 5-9). pap. 7.99 *(978-1-4926-4250-3(9),* 9781492642503, Sourcebooks Jabberwocky) Sourcebooks, Inc.
Locklear, Morgan & Locklear, Jennifer. Exposure. 2014. (ENG.). 271p. pap. 19.99 *(978-1-62342-121-2(7))* Omnific Publishing.
Lubbe, Angela C. Don't Forget about Us. 2012. 16p. pap. 15.99 *(978-1-4685-9538-3(5))* AuthorHouse.
Maddox, Jake. Behind the Plate, 1 vol. Tiffany, Sean, illus. 2012. (Jake Maddox Sports Stories Ser.). (ENG.). 72p. (gr. 2-3). pap. 5.95 *(978-1-4342-4205-1(6));* lib. bdg. 25.32 *(978-1-4342-4010-1(X))* Stone Arch Bks.
—Power Play. 2016. (Jake Maddox JV Girls Ser.). (ENG.). 96p. (gr. 3-4). lib. bdg. 25.99 *(978-1-4965-3673-0(8))* Stone Arch Bks.
Maddox, Jake & Berne, Emma Carlson. Rebound Time, 1 vol. Wood, Katie, illus. 2013. (Jake Maddox Girl Sports Stories Ser.). (ENG.). 72p. (gr. 2-3). pap. 5.95 *(978-1-4342-4202-0(1));* lib. bdg. 25.32 *(978-1-4342-4013-2(4))* Stone Arch Bks.
Mancusi, Mari. Gamer Girl. 2010. (ENG.). 256p. (YA). (gr. 7-18). 7.99 *(978-0-14-241509-2(X),* Speak) Penguin Young Readers Group.
Marino, Peter. Dough Boy. 2005. (ENG.). 176p. (YA). (gr. 7-12). 17.95 *(978-0-8234-1873-2(1))* Holiday Hse., Inc.
Marovic, Mason A. Divorce & Me. 2009. 44p. pap. 21.99 *(978-1-4363-9171-9(7))* Xlibris Corp.
Martin, Ann M. Dawn on the Coast. (Baby-Sitters Club Ser.: No. 23). 10p. (J). (gr. 3-7). pap. 3.95 *(978-0-590-42007-5(0))* Scholastic, Inc.
Martinusen-Coloma, Cindy. Ruby Unscripted, 1 vol. 2009. (ENG.). 272p. (YA). (gr. 7-18). pap. 12.99 *(978-1-59554-356-1(2))* Nelson, Thomas Inc.
Masurel, Claire. Two Homes. Denton, Kady MacDonald, illus. 2003. (ENG.). 40p. (J). (gr. -1-2). 6.99 *(978-0-7636-1984-8(1))* Candlewick Pr.
—Two Homes. 2003. 17.20 *(978-0-613-69470-4(8),* Turtleback) Turtleback Bks.
Mazur, Cathy May. Pizza Heart. Tyler, Tim, illus. 2007. 20p. per. 24.95 *(978-1-4241-8747-8(8))* America Star Bks.
McDonald, Megan. Happy New Year, Julie, Bk. 3. McAliley, Susan & Hunt, Robert, illus. 2007. (American Girl Ser.). (ENG.). 88p. (J). (gr. 3-7). 12.95 *(978-1-59369-292-6(7))* American Girl Publishing, Inc.
McGriff, Shawna A. Princess Pink: Princess Pink Helps Zion, Melinda, & Jasmine Learn to Communicate about Their Parents' Divorces. 2010. 56p. pap. 24.00 *(978-1-4520-3941-1(0))* AuthorHouse.
McKissack, Patricia C. A Friendship for Today. 2008. 172p. (J). pap. *(978-0-545-06563-4(1))* Scholastic, Inc.
McNeal, Laura. Dark Water. 2011. (ENG.). 324p. (YA). (gr. 7). pap. 9.99 *(978-0-375-84330-3(2),* Ember) Random Hse. Children's Bks.
Meredith, Amberley. Bessie Bump Gets a New Family. Lee, Nikita, illus. 2010. 26p. pap. 13.95 *(978-1-60911-901-0(0),* Eloquent Bks.) Strategic Book Publishing & Rights Agency (SBPRA).
Morphew, Chris. The Man in the Shadows. 2017. (Phoenix Files Ser.: 1). (ENG.). 512p. (YA). (gr. 7). pap. 12.99 ***(978-1-76012-425-0(7))*** Hardie Grant Egmont Pty, Ltd. AUS. Dist: Independent Pubs. Group.
Morphew, Chris. The Phoenix Files, Arrival. 2013. 304p. (J). pap. 6.99 *(978-1-61067-091-3(4))* Kane Miller.
Moss, Marissa. Amelia's Family Ties. Moss, Marissa, illus. 2013. (Amelia Ser.). (ENG., Illus.). (J). 5.99 *(978-1-4169-1293-4(2),* Simon & Schuster/Paula Wiseman Bks.) Simon & Schuster/Paula Wiseman Bks.
Musili Whitesell, Marjorie. I Have Four Parents. 2009. (Illus.). 20p. pap. 10.95 *(978-1-60860-448-7(9),* Eloquent Bks.) Strategic Book Publishing & Rights Agency (SBPRA).
Myers, Lily. This Impossible Light. 2017. (ENG.). 352p. (YA). (gr. 7). 17.99 *(978-0-399-17372-1(2),* Philomel Bks.) Penguin Young Readers Group.
Nkemayang, Chelsea. Split Ville. 2012. (Illus.). 36p. pap. 22.88 *(978-1-4772-4177-6(9))* AuthorHouse.
Ockler, Sarah. Bittersweet. 2012. (ENG.). (YA). (gr. 9). 400p. pap. 9.99 *(978-1-4424-3036-5(2));* 384p. 16.99 *(978-1-4424-3035-8(4))* Simon Pulse. (Simon Pulse).
Orr, Wendy. Lost! - A Dog Called Bear. Boase, Susan, illus. 2011. (Rainbow Street Shelter Ser.: 1). (ENG.). 112p. (J). (gr. 2-5). pap. 5.99 *(978-0-8050-9381-0(8),* 9780805093810, Holt, Henry & Co. Bks. For Young Readers) Holt, Henry & Co.
Owens, L. L. If You Want My Advice- Tolson, Scott, illus. 2004. 25p. *(978-1-57021-030-3(6))* Comprehensive Health Education Foundation.
Paulsen, Gary. Hatchet. 2003. (ENG.). 160p. (J). mass mkt. 9.99 *(978-0-330-31045-1(3),* Pan) Pan Macmillan GBR. Dist: Trafalgar Square Publishing.
—Hatchet. 2006. (ENG.). 192p. (J). (gr. 5-9). pap. 7.99 *(978-1-4169-3647-3(5),* Simon & Schuster Bks. For Young Readers) Simon & Schuster Bks. For Young Readers.
—Hatchet. Willis, Drew, illus. 20th anniv. ed. 2007. (ENG.). 192p. (J). (gr. 5-9). 19.99 *(978-1-4169-2508-8(2),* Simon & Schuster Bks. For Young Readers) Simon & Schuster Bks. For Young Readers.
—Hatchet. 2006. (ENG., Illus.). 208p. (YA). (gr. 7-9). mass mkt. 7.99 *(978-1-4169-3646-6(7),* Simon Pulse) Simon Pulse.
—Hatchet. 2006. 18.40 *(978-1-4177-6883-7(5),* Turtleback) Turtleback Bks.
—Hatchet: With Related Readings. 2004. (EMC Masterpiece Series Access Editions). (J). 11.99 *(978-0-8219-2960-5(7))* EMC/Paradigm Publishing.
Pemikoff, Doug. So What If My Parents Got Divorced. 2009. 36p. 11.99 *(978-0-9816923-1-9(1))* Cochran, Russ Co., The.
Perry, Anne M. Just Like Always. Lyon, Tammie, illus. (Rookie Ready to Learn Ser.). (J). 2011. 40p. pap. 5.95 *(978-0-531-26675-5(3))* 2011. 40p. (gr. -1-k). lib. bdg. 23.00 *(978-0-531-26370-9(3))* 2005. (ENG.). 32p. (gr. 1-2). 19.50 *(978-0-516-25154-7(6))* Scholastic Library Publishing. (Children's Pr.).
Ploof, Douglas. Weekend at Dad's. 2012. 32p. pap. 24.95 *(978-1-4626-7597-5(2))* America Star Bks.
Portnoy, Mindy Avra. A Tale of Two Seders. Cis, Valeria, illus. 2010. (ENG.). 32p. (J). (gr. k-4). lib. bdg. 17.95 *(978-0-8225-9907-4(4));* pap. 7.95 *(978-0-8225-9931-9(7))* Lerner Publishing Group. (Kar-Ben Publishing).
Powell, Angela. Alicia's Blended Family. Gillen, Rosemarie, illus. 2013. 24p. pap. 9.99 *(978-1-61286-153-1(9))* Avid Readers Publishing Group.
Preller, James. Bystander. 2011. (ENG.). 256p. (YA). (gr. 5-9). pap. 8.99 *(978-0-312-54796-7(X),* 9780312547967) Square Fish.
Prosek, James. The Day My Mother Left. Prosek, James, illus. 2009. (ENG., Illus.). 304p. (J). (gr. 4-7). pap. 7.99 *(978-1-4169-0771-8(8),* Simon & Schuster Bks. For Young Readers) Simon & Schuster Bks. For Young Readers.
Reinhardt, Dana. How to Build a House. 2009. (ENG.). 240p. (YA). (gr. 9-11). pap. 8.99 *(978-0-375-84454-6(6),* Ember) Random Hse. Children's Bks.
—We Are the Goldens. 2015. (ENG.). 208p. (YA). (gr. 9). pap. 9.99 *(978-0-385-74258-0(4),* Ember) Random Hse. Children's Bks.
Ribay, Randy. An Infinite Number of Parallel Universes. 2015. (ENG.). 240p. (YA). 17.99 *(978-1-4405-8814-3(7),* Simon Pulse) Simon Pulse.
Richardson, Faith. Angel Walker. 2003. Orig. Title: The Sea, the Song & the Trumpetfish. (Illus.). 172p. (J). 19.95 *(978-0-9744989-2-8(0));* pap. 12.95 *(978-0-9744989-3-5(9))* Fox Song Bks.
Riley, Elliot. Sonya's Family. Bassani, Srimalie, illus. 2017. (All Kinds of Families Ser.). (ENG.). (J). (gr. k-1). 28.51 ***(978-1-68342-146-7(9))*** Rourke Educational Media.
Robe, Kim. Robbie's Trail Through Divorce. Gavet, Nathalie, illus. 2012. 40p. (-18). pap. 23.99 *(978-1-935831-11-2(9))* Robe Communications, Inc.
—Robbie's Trail Through Divorce - Activity Book. Gavet, Nathalie, illus. 2012. 28p. (-18). pap. 16.99 *(978-1-935831-12-9(7))* Robe Communications, Inc.
—Robbie's Trail Through Divorce - Adult Guide. Gavet, Nathalie, illus. 2012. 28p. (-18). pap. 16.99 *(978-1-935831-13-6(5))* Robe Communications, Inc.
Roth, Rhonda. The Most Important Thing. Grajczyk, Shane, illus. 2007. (ENG.). 32p. (J). (gr. -1-3). 16.95 *(978-0-9770141-0-1(X),* Crossing Guard Bks.) Crossing Guard Bks., LLC.
Rowland, Joanna & Weber, Penny. Always Mom, Forever Dad. 2014. (ENG., Illus.). 32p. (gr. -1-3). 16.95 *(978-0-88448-367-0(3),* 884367) Tilbury Hse. Pubs.
Royal, Randal. Spirit Mountain: Wounded-Fox. 2004. (YA). per. 10.00 *(978-0-9747918-1-4(4))* 153 Fish Publishing.
Ruby, Laura. Bad Apple. (ENG.). (YA). (gr. 8). 2011. 272p. pap. 8.99 *(978-0-06-124333-2(7))* 2009. 256p. 16.99 *(978-0-06-124330-1(2))* HarperCollins Pubs. (HarperTeen).
Santucci, Barbara. Loon Summer. Shine, Andrea, illus. 2004. 32p. (J). (gr. k-3). 16.00 *(978-0-8028-5182-6(7))* Eerdmans, William B. Publishing Co.
Schmitz, Tamara. Standing on My Own Two Feet: A Child's Affirmation of Love in the Midst of Divorce. Schmitz, Tamara, illus. 2008. (ENG., Illus.). 32p. (J). (gr. -1-2). 15.99 *(978-0-8431-3221-2(3),* Price Stern Sloan) Penguin Young Readers Group.
Scholastic, Inc. Staff & Grimes, Nikki. A Day with Daddy. Tadgell, Nicole, illus. 2004. (Just for You Ser.). (ENG.). 32p. pap. 3.99 *(978-0-439-56850-0(1),* Teaching Resources) Scholastic, Inc.
Schwartz, Kristi. Divorced Together: For teh Sake of the Children. 2009. (ENG.). 32p. pap. 11.95 *(978-1-933916-47-7(8),* Ferne Pr.) Nelson Publishing & Marketing.
Sewell, Kele. Beewee & Meager to the Rescue! the Underbed Entertainment Network. 2008. 28p. pap. 12.50 *(978-1-60693-326-8(4),* Eloquent Bks.) Strategic Book Publishing & Rights Agency (SBPRA).
Sheinmel, Courtney. The Kindness Club. 2016. (Kindness Club Ser.). (ENG.). 224p. (J). 15.99 *(978-1-68119-091-4(5),* 9781681190914, Bloomsbury USA Childrens) Bloomsbury Publishing USA.
Shoup, Barbara. Wish You Were Here. 2008. (ENG.). 336p. (YA). (gr. 7). pap. 9.95 *(978-0-7387-1355-7(4),* Flux) North Star Editions.
Shreeve, Elizabeth. Oliver at the Window. McDonald, Candice Hartsough, illus. 2009. (ENG.). 32p. (J). (gr. -1-1). 16.95 *(978-1-59078-548-5(7),* Front Street) Boyds Mills Pr.
Simner, Janni Lee. Secret of the Three Treasures. 2006. (ENG.). 160p. (YA). (gr. 8-12). 16.95 *(978-0-8234-1914-2(2))* Holiday Hse., Inc.
Simon, Leslie & Kelley, Trevor. Wish You Were Here: An Essential Guide to Your Favorite Music Scenes - From Punk to Indie & Everything in Between. Dobi, Rob, illus. 2009. (ENG.). 256p. pap. 14.99 *(978-0-06-157371-2(X))* HarperCollins Pubs.
Smith, Robert Kimmel. The Squeaky Wheel. 2008. 196p. (gr. 4-7). pap. 14.95 *(978-0-595-52203-3(3))* iUniverse, Inc.
Smith, Yeardley. I, Lorelei. 2009. 352p. (J). (gr. 3-7). lib. bdg. 17.89 *(978-0-06-149345-4(7),* Geringer, Laura Book) HarperCollins Pubs.
Spyropolous, Angelo. RV. 2005. pap. 12.99 *(978-1-894869-98-0(2),* PO 00128) Zumaya Pubns. LLC.
Staniszewski, Anna. Once upon a Cruise: a Wish Novel. 2016. (ENG.). 256p. (J). (gr. 3-7). pap. 6.99 *(978-0-545-87986-6(8),* Scholastic Paperbacks) Scholastic, Inc.
Stanley, Brenda. I Am Nuchu. 2010. 334p. (YA). (gr. 9-18). 16.95 *(978-1-934813-47-8(8))* Westside Bks.
Stanton, Karen. Monday, Wednesday, & Every Other Weekend. Stanton, Karen, illus. 2014. (ENG., Illus.). 40p. (J). (gr. -1-1). 16.99 *(978-1-250-03489-2(2),* 9781250034892) Feiwel & Friends.
Starcher, Michele. The Ornery Angel. 2005. 68p. per. 13.95 *(978-1-59858-039-6(6))* Dog Ear Publishing, LLC.
Stephens, Edna Cucksey, et al. You & Me Make Three. Drescher, Heather, illus. 2008. (Build-A-Bear Workshop Ser.). 32p. (J). (gr. -1-3). 0.00 *(978-0-9798088-0-7(4))* EDCO Publishing, Inc.
—You & Me Make Three & Accompanying Plush B. B. the Bear. Drescher, Heather, illus. 2008. 32p. (J). 35.00 *(978-0-9798088-2-1(0))* EDCO Publishing, Inc.
Still, Teresa B. Tessa Has Two Homes. 2009. 28p. pap. 14.99 *(978-1-4389-8202-1(X))* AuthorHouse.
Stinson, Kathy. Mom & Dad Don't Live Together Anymore. Oelofsen, Vian, illus. rev. ed. 2007. (ENG.). 24p. (J). (gr. -1-2). 19.95 *(978-1-55451-094-8(5),* 9781554510948) Annick Pr., Ltd. CAN. Dist: Publishers Group West (PGW).
—Mom & Dad Don't Live Together Anymore. Oelofsen, Vian, illus. 3rd rev. ed. 2007. (ENG.). 24p. (J). (gr. -1-2). pap. 6.95 *(978-1-55451-093-1(7),* 9781554510931) Annick Pr., Ltd. CAN. Dist: Publishers Group West (PGW).
—One Year Commencing. 2006. (ENG.). 152p. pap. 11.95 *(978-1-895449-65-5(0))* Thistledown Pr., Ltd. CAN. Dist: Univ. of Toronto Pr.
Stratton, Allan. Leslie's Journal. rev. ed. 2008. (ENG.). 200p. (YA). (gr. 8-12). 21.95 *(978-1-55451-149-5(6),* 9781554511495) Annick Pr., Ltd. CAN. Dist: Publishers Group West (PGW).
Suma, Nova Ren. Fade Out. 2012. (ENG.). 288p. (YA). (gr. 7). pap. 9.99 *(978-1-4169-7565-6(9),* Simon Pulse) Simon Pulse.
Tabak, Lawrence. In Real Life. 2014. (ENG.). 288p. (J). (gr. 7-12). 16.99 *(978-0-8048-4478-9(X))* Tuttle Publishing.
Taylor, Cora. Champlain & Cartier, 1 vol. 2004. (Ghost Voyages Ser.: No. 4). (ENG., Illus.). 128p. (J). (gr. 3-6). pap. 7.95 *(978-1-55050-374-6(X))* Coteau Bks. CAN. Dist: Orca Bk. Pubs. USA.
Taylor, Jeannie St. John & St. John Taylor, Jeannie. Out at Home: A Novel. 2004. 144p. (J). pap. 7.99 *(978-0-8254-3724-3(5))* Kregel Pubns.
Thiel, Annie. Cosmos' Mom & Dad Are Moving Apart. Edwards, William M. & Marjoribanks, Karen, illus. 2006. (Playdate Kids Ser.). 32p. (J). (gr. -1-3). 14.95 *(978-1-933721-04-0(9))* Playdate Kids Publishing.
Thiel Annie. The Playdate Kids Cosmos' Mom & Dad are Moving Apart 2ED 2007. 2007. 32p. 12.95 *(978-1-933721-31-6(6));* pap. 6.95 *(978-1-933721-27-9(8))* Playdate Kids Publishing.
Thomas, Rob. Rats Saw God. 2009. 9.00 *(978-0-7848-2881-6(4),* Everbind) Marco Bk. Co.
—Rats Saw God. 2010. (ENG.). 202p. 17.10 *(978-0-7569-8366-6(5))* Perfection Learning Corp.
—Rats Saw God. 2013. (ENG.). 224p. (YA). (gr. 7). 16.99 *(978-1-4424-5976-2(X));* (Illus.). pap. 10.99 *(978-1-4424-5738-6(4))* Simon & Schuster Bks. For Young Readers. (Simon & Schuster Bks. For Young Readers).
Thompson, Vinny. Vinny & Bud. 2009. 64p. pap. 11.99 *(978-1-4490-2557-9(X))* AuthorHouse.
Tolan, Stephanie S. Wishworks, Inc. Bates, Amy June, illus. 2011. (ENG.). 160p. (J). (gr. 2-5). pap. 5.99 *(978-0-545-03155-4(9),* Levine, Arthur A. Bks.) Scholastic, Inc.
Tregay, Sarah. Love & Leftovers. 2014. (ENG.). 464p. (YA). (gr. 8). pap. 9.99 *(978-0-06-202360-5(8),* Tegen, Katherine Bks) HarperCollins Pubs.
Triana, Gaby. Summer of Yesterday. 2014. (ENG., Illus.). 272p. (YA). (gr. 9). pap. 9.99 *(978-1-4814-0130-2(0),* Simon Pulse) Simon Pulse.
Tromly, Stephanie. Trouble Is a Friend of Mine. 2015. (ENG.). 336p. (YA). (gr. 7-12). 17.99 *(978-0-525-42840-4(2),* Kathy Dawson Books) Penguin Young Readers Group.
Urban, Linda. Weekends with Max & His Dad. Kath, Katie, illus. 2016. (ENG.). 160p. (J). (gr. 2-5). 16.99 *(978-0-544-59817-1(2),* HMH Books For Young Readers) Houghton Mifflin Harcourt Publishing Co.
Vernick, Audrey. Water Balloon. 2011. (ENG.). 320p. (J). (gr. 5-7). 16.99 *(978-0-547-59554-2(9),* Clarion Bks.) Houghton Mifflin Harcourt Trade & Reference Pubs.
Vivian, Siobhan. A Little Friendly Advice. 2015. (ENG.). 256p. (J). (gr. 7). pap. 9.99 *(978-0-545-75801-7(7),* PUSH) Scholastic, Inc.
Voigt, Cynthia. A Solitary Blue. 2012. (Tillerman Cycle Ser.: 3). (ENG., Illus.). 256p. (YA). (gr. 7). 18.99 *(978-1-4424-5062-2(2));* pap. 8.99 *(978-1-4424-2880-5(5))* Simon & Schuster Children's Publishing. (Atheneum Bks. for Young Readers).
—A Solitary Blue. Lt. ed. 2005. (Tillerman Cycle Ser.: Bk. 3). 359p. (J). pap. 10.95 *(978-0-7862-7912-8(5))* Thorndike Pr.
Wallace, Rich. Southpaw. 2006. 105p. (J). lib. bdg. 15.38 *(978-1-4242-2166-0(8))* Fitzgerald Bks.
—Southpaw. 6th ed. 2007. (Winning Season Ser.). (ENG.). 128p. (J). (gr. 3-7). 5.99 *(978-0-14-240785-1(2),* Puffin Books) Penguin Young Readers Group.
Walsh, Melanie. Living with Mom & Living with Dad. Walsh, Melanie, illus. 2012. (ENG., Illus.). 40p. (J). (gr. -1-2). 15.99 *(978-0-7636-5869-4(3))* Candlewick Pr.
Warner Press Staff. Divorce Comes to Our House. 2003. pap. *(978-1-59317-009-7(2))* Warner Pr., Inc.
Warner, Sally. Excellent Emma. Harper, Jamie, illus. 2010. (Emma Ser.). (ENG.). 144p. (J). (gr. 3-7). 6.99 *(978-0-14-241569-6(3),* Puffin Books) Penguin Young Readers Group.
Warner, Sally & Harper, Jamie. Excellent Emma. Harper, Jamie, illus. 2009. (Emma Ser.). (ENG., Illus.). 144p. (J). (gr. 3-7). 14.99 *(978-0-670-06310-9(X),* Viking Books for Young Readers) Penguin Young Readers Group.
Weber, Lori. Split, 1 vol. 2005. (Lorimer SideStreets Ser.). (ENG.). 152p. (YA). (gr. 9-12). 16.95 *(978-1-55028-879-7(2),* 9781550288797); 8.95 *(978-1-55028-878-0(4),* 9781550288780) Lorimer, James & Co., Ltd., Pubs. CAN. Dist: Casemate Pubs. & Bk. Distributors, LLC.
—Tattoo Heaven, 1 vol. 2005. (Lorimer SideStreets Ser.). (ENG.). 168p. (YA). (gr. 9-12). 16.95 *(978-1-55028-903-9(9),* 9781550289039); 9.95 *(978-1-55028-902-2(0),* 9781550289022) Lorimer, James & Co., Ltd., Pubs. CAN. Dist: Casemate Pubs. & Bk. Distributors, LLC.
West, Kasie. Pivot Point. 2013. (Pivot Point Ser.: Bk. 1). (ENG.). 352p. (YA). (gr. 8). 17.99 *(978-0-06-211737-3(8),* HarperTeen) HarperCollins Pubs.
Wilkins, LaTanya. The Adventures of Dedan & Dylan Jackson: The Second Day of School. 2010. 48p. pap. 13.99 *(978-1-4520-5963-1(2))* AuthorHouse.
Wilson, Jacqueline. Candyfloss. Sharratt, Nick, illus. 2008. (ENG.). 352p. (J). (gr. 4-7). pap. 9.99 *(978-0-312-38418-0(1),* 9780312384180) Square Fish.
Wright, Bill & Wright, Bil. When the Black Girl Sings. 2008. (ENG.). 272p. (YA). (gr. 7-12). 16.99 *(978-1-4169-3995-5(4),* Simon & Schuster Bks. For Young Readers) Simon & Schuster Bks. For Young Readers.
—When the Black Girl Sings. 2009. (ENG.). 272p. (YA). (gr. 7). mass mkt. 6.99 *(978-1-4169-4003-6(0),* Simon Pulse) Simon Pulse.
Zei, Alki. Tina's Web. Thornley, John, tr. from GRE. 2007. (ENG.). 300p. per. 18.95 *(978-0-9551566-1-8(0))* Aurora Metro Pubns. Ltd. GBR. Dist: Consortium Bk. Sales & Distribution.
Ziegler, Jennifer. Revenge of the Angels. 2015. (ENG.). 256p. (J). (gr. 3-7). 16.99 *(978-0-545-83899-3(1),* Scholastic Pr.) Scholastic, Inc.

DIXON, JOHNNY (FICTITIOUS CHARACTER)—FICTION

Bellairs, John. The Curse of the Blue Figurine (A Johnny Dixon Mystery: Book One) 2011. 150p. pap. 15.95 *(978-1-61756-324-9(2))* Open Road Integrated Media, Inc.
—The Eyes of the Killer Robot (A Johnny Dixon Mystery: Book Five) 2011. 126p. pap. 14.95 *(978-1-61756-340-9(4))* Open Road Integrated Media, Inc.
—The Mummy, the Will, & the Crypt (A Johnny Dixon Mystery: Book Two) 2011. 126p. pap. 14.95 *(978-1-61756-328-7(5))* Open Road Integrated Media, Inc.
—The Revenge of the Wizard's Ghost (A Johnny Dixon Mystery: Book Four) 2011. 108p. pap. 14.95 *(978-1-61756-336-2(6))* Open Road Integrated Media, Inc.
—The Secret of the Underground Room (A Johnny Dixon Mystery: Book Eight) 2011. 96p. pap. 14.95 *(978-1-61756-352-2(8))* Open Road Integrated Media, Inc.
—The Spell of the Sorcerer's Skull (A Johnny Dixon Mystery: Book Three) 2011. 124p. pap. 14.95 *(978-1-61756-332-4(3))* Open Road Integrated Media, Inc.

DNA

Anders, Mason. DNA, Genes, & Chromosomes. 2017. (Genetics Ser.). (ENG.). 32p. (gr. 3-4). lib. bdg. 27.32 ***(978-1-5157-7256-9(X))*** Capstone Press of Coughlan Cos.
Arbuthnott, Gill. What Makes You You? Mones, Marc, illus. 2016. (ENG.). 64p. (J). *(978-0-7787-2239-7(2))* Crabtree Publishing Co.
Bortz, Fred. The Double Helix Structure of Dna. 2013. (Revolutionary Discoveries of Scientific Pioneers Ser.). (Illus.). 80p. (J). (gr. 7-12). 33.25 *(978-1-4777-1809-4(5))* Rosen Publishing Group, Inc., The.
Building Blocks of Science: Understanding Cells & DNA Teacher's Guide (Firsthand Learning) 2007. ring bd. *(978-0-89278-338-0(9))* Carolina Biological Supply Co.
Building Blocks of Science: Understanding Cells & DNA Unit Kit (Firsthand Learning) 2007. ring bd. *(978-0-89278-433-2(4))* Carolina Biological Supply Co.
Claybourne, Anna. Introduction to Genes & DNA. 2004. (Genes & Dna Ser.). (ENG., Illus.). 64p. (J). pap. 11.95 *(978-0-7945-0444-1(2),* Usborne) EDC Publishing.
Conklin, Wendy. DNA. 2015. (Science Readers: Content & Literacy Ser.). (Illus.). 32p. (gr. 5-5). pap. 8.99 *(978-1-4807-4719-7(X))* Teacher Created Materials, Inc.

De la Bédoyère, Camilla. The Discovery of DNA. 2005. (Milestones in Modern Science Ser.). (Illus.). 48p. (gr. 6-12). lib. bdg. 31.00 *(978-0-8368-5851-8(4)*, Gareth Stevens Secondary Library) Stevens, Gareth Publishing LLLP.

Einspruch, Andrew. DNA Detectives. 2012. (Discovery Education: Technology Ser.). (ENG., Illus.). 32p. (J). (gr. 3-6). pap. 10.00 *(978-1-4488-7965-6(5))*; lib. bdg. 25.25 *(978-1-4488-7883-3(7))* Rosen Publishing Group, Inc., The. (PowerKids Pr.).

Hall, Linley Erin. DNA & RNA. 2010. (Understanding Genetics Ser.). (ENG.). 80p. (YA). lib. bdg. 33.25 *(978-1-4358-9532-4(0))* Rosen Publishing Group, Inc., The.

Hamilton, Janet. James Watson: Solving the Mystery of DNA. 2004. (Nobel Prize-Winning Scientists Ser.). (Illus.). 104p. (J). lib. bdg. 27.94 *(978-0-7660-2258-4(7))* Enslow Pubs., Inc.

Hamilton, Sue L. DNA Analysis: Forensic Fluids & Follicles, 1 vol. 2008. (Crime Scene Investigation Ser.). (ENG.). 32p. (gr. 4-8). 27.07 *(978-1-59928-987-8(3)*, Abdo & Daughters) ABDO Publishing Co.

Hartman, Eve & Meshbesher, Wendy. What Are the Issues with Genetic Technology?, 1 vol. 2012. (Sci-Hi: Science Issues Ser.). (ENG., Illus.). 48p. (gr. 4-4). pap. 9.95 *(978-1-4109-4471-9(9)*, Sci-Hi) Heinemann-Raintree.

Hirsch, Rebecca E. De-Extinction: The Science of Bringing Lost Species Back to Life. 2017. (Nonfiction — Young Adult Ser.). (ENG.). 120p. (gr. 8-12). (YA). 19.99 ***(978-1-5124-3902-1(9)***, Twenty-First Century Bks.); (YA). 53.32 ***(978-1-5124-3903-8(7)***, Twenty-First Century Bks.); (YA). 53.32 ***(978-1-5124-2848-3(5)***, Twenty-First Century Bks.); (Illus.). (J). lib. bdg. 35.99 *(978-1-4677-9490-9(2))* Lerner Publishing Group.

Holt, Rinehart and Winston Staff. Holt Science & Technology Chapter 6: Life Science: Genes & DNA. 5th ed. 2004. (Illus.). pap. 12.86 *(978-0-03-030186-5(6))* Holt McDougal.

Hunter, William. DNA Analysis. Noziglia, Carla Miller & Siegel, Jay A., eds. 2013. (Solving Crimes with Science: Forensics Ser.: 12). (Illus.). 112p. (J). (gr. 7-18). 22.95 *(978-1-4222-2864-7(9))* Mason Crest.

—DNA Analysis. 2007. (Forensics Ser.). (Illus.). 112p. (YA). (gr. 7-18). lib. bdg. 22.95 *(978-1-4222-0026-1(4))* Mason Crest.

Hyde, Natalie. DNA. 2009. (Let's Relate to Genetics Ser.). (ENG.). 48p. (J). (gr. 6-9). pap. *(978-0-7787-4965-3(7))* Crabtree Publishing Co.

Johnson, Rebecca L. Amazing DNA. Desrocher, Jack & Fairman, Jennifer, illus. 2007. (Microquests Ser.). (ENG.). 48p. (gr. 3-5). lib. bdg. 29.27 *(978-0-8225-7139-1(0)*, Millbrook Pr.) Lerner Publishing Group.

—Amazing Dna. 2008. pap. 52.95 *(978-0-8225-9380-5(7))* Lerner Publishing Group.

Keyser, Amber J., et al. Decoding Genes with Max Axiom, Super Scientist, 1 vol. 2010. (Graphic Science Ser.). (ENG.). 32p. (gr. 3-4). pap. 8.10 *(978-1-4296-4862-2(7))*; lib. bdg. 30.65 *(978-1-4296-3976-7(8))* Capstone Press of Coughlan Cos. (Graphic Library).

Kiesbye, Stefan, ed. DNA Databases. 2011. (At Issue Ser.). 128p. (J). pap. 24.45 *(978-0-7377-5891-7(0)*, Greenhaven Pr., Inc.); (gr. 9-12). 34.45 *(978-0-7377-5890-0(2))* Cengage Gale.

Kyi, Tanya Lloyd. DNA Detective. Crump, Lil, illus. 2015. (ENG.). 120p. (YA). (gr. 5-8). 24.95 *(978-1-55451-774-9(5)*, 9781554517749) Annick Pr., Ltd. CAN. Dist: Publishers Group West (PGW).

Latta, Sara L. DNA & Blood: Dead People Do Tell Tales. 2011. (True Forensic Crime Stories Ser.). (Illus.). 104p. (J). (gr. 7-12). lib. bdg. 33.27 *(978-0-7660-3667-3(7))* Enslow Pubs., Inc.

Litmanovich, Ellina & Latta, Sara L. Investigating DNA & Blood. 2017. (J). ***(978-0-7660-9184-9(8))*** Enslow Pubs., Inc.

Marzilli, Alan. DNA Evidence. 2004. (Point/Counterpoint Ser.). (Illus.). 112p. (C). (gr. 9-13). 35.00 *(978-0-7910-8092-4(7)*, Chelsea Hse.) Facts On File, Inc.

Meredith, Susan. Genes & Dna - Internet Linked. rev. ed. 2006. 64p. (J). pap. 11.99 *(978-0-7945-1562-1(2)*, Usborne) EDC Publishing.

Mooney, Carla. Genetics: Breaking the Code of Your DNA. Carbaugh, Samuel, illus. 2014. (Inquire & Investigate Ser.). (ENG.). 128p. (J). (gr. 6-10). 21.95 *(978-1-61930-208-2(X))*; pap. 16.95 *(978-1-61930-212-9(8))* Open City Bks.

Nardo, Don. DNA Evidence. 2007. (Crime Scene Investigations Ser.). (ENG., Illus.). 104p. (YA). (gr. 7-12). lib. bdg. 33.45 *(978-1-59018-951-1(5))* Cengage Gale.

Parks, Peggy J. DNA Evidence & Investigation. 2010. (Compact Research Ser.). 96p. (YA). (gr. 7-12). lib. bdg. 25.95 *(978-1-60152-102-6(2))* ReferencePoint Pr., Inc.

Phelan, Glen. Double Helix: The Quest to Uncover the Structure of DNA. 2006. (Science Quest Ser.). (ENG., Illus.). 64p. (J). (gr. 5-9). 17.95 *(978-0-7922-5541-3(0))*; lib. bdg. 25.90 *(978-0-7922-5542-0(9))* National Geographic Society. (National Geographic Children's Bks.).

Prokos, Anna. Guilty by a Hair! Real-Life DNA Matches! 2007. (24/7: Science Behind the Scenes Ser.). (ENG., Illus.). 64p. (J). (gr. 9-12). 29.00 *(978-0-531-11821-4(5)*, Watts, Franklin) Scholastic Library Publishing.

Rainis, Kenneth G. Blood & DNA Evidence: Crime-Solving Science Experiments. 2006. (Forensic Science Projects Ser.). (Illus.). 104p. (J). (gr. 3-7). lib. bdg. 33.27 *(978-0-7660-1958-4(6))* Enslow Pubs., Inc.

Rand, Casey. DNA & Heredity, 1 vol. 2010. (Investigating Cells Ser.). (ENG., Illus.). 48p. (gr. 3-6). 33.32 *(978-1-4329-3880-2(0)*, Heinemann InfoSearch) Heinemann-Raintree.

Rooney, Anne. James Watson & Francis Crick & the Discovery of Dna. 2012. (Miracle Makers Ser.). (ENG., Illus.). 48p. (YA). (gr. 5-8). 27.95 *(978-1-4488-6036-4(9)*, Rosen Reference) Rosen Publishing Group, Inc., The.

Sandvold, Lynnette Brent. Genetics. 2009. (Big Ideas in Science Ser.). 48p. (gr. 5). 31.36 *(978-0-7614-4396-4(7))* Marshall Cavendish Corp.

Schafer, Susan. DNA & Genes. 2009. (ENG., Illus.). 96p. (C). (gr. 6-18). lib. bdg. 158.00 *(978-0-7656-8135-5(8)*, Y181927) Routledge.

Shea, John M. DNA up Close. 2013. (Under the Microscope Ser.). 32p. (J). (gr. 4-6). pap. 11.70 *(978-1-4339-8343-6(5))*; pap. 70.20 *(978-1-4339-8344-3(3))*; lib. bdg. 26.60 *(978-1-4339-8342-9(7))* Stevens, Gareth Publishing LLLP.

Silverstein, Alvin, et al. DNA. 2008. (Science Concepts Ser.). (Illus.). 104p. (J). (gr. 5-9). lib. bdg. 31.93 *(978-0-8225-8654-8(1))* Twenty First Century Bks.

Yount, Lisa. Rosalind Franklin. 2011. (Trailblazers in Science & Technology Ser.). 152p. (gr. 6-12). 35.00 *(978-1-60413-660-9(X)*, Chelsea Hse.) Facts On File, Inc.

DOCTOR SEUSS, 1904-1991

see Seuss, Dr., 1904-1991

DOCTORS

see Physicians

DOCTRINAL THEOLOGY

see Theology

DOCTRINES

see Theology

DODGSON, CHARLES LUTWIDGE, 1832-1898

see Carroll, Lewis, 1832-1898

DODO

Green, Tamara. The Dodo: Extinct Species. Gibbons, Tony, illus. 2007. 24p. (J). reprint ed. 15.00 *(978-1-4223-6677-6(4))* DIANE Publishing Co.

Higgins, Melissa. Dodos. 2015. (Ice Age Animals Ser.). (ENG.). 24p. (gr. k-1). pap. 6.95 *(978-1-4914-2318-9(8)*, Pebble Plus) Capstone Press of Coughlan Cos.

DODO—FICTION

Hu, Jennifer. Dodo's Story: Journey in America. 2010. 40p. 16.99 *(978-1-4520-6095-8(9))* AuthorHouse.

Panda, Jake G. The Case of the Cursed Dodo. 2014. (Illus.). 173p. (J). pap. 8.99 *(978-0-9909391-1-5(1))* Woolley Family Studios.

Racine, Patrice. The Quest of the Last Dodo Bird. 2011. (Adventures of Cosmo the Dodo Bird Ser.). (ENG., Illus.). 112p. (J). (gr. 4-7). pap. 10.95 *(978-1-77049-241-7(0)*, Tundra Bks.) Tundra Bks. CAN. Dist: Penguin Random Hse. LLC.

Sattler, Jennifer. Uh-Oh, Dodo! Sattler, Jennifer, illus. 2013. (ENG., Illus.). 32p. (J). (gr. -1-k). 15.95 *(978-1-59078-929-2(6))* Boyds Mills Pr.

DOG

see Dogs

DOG GUIDES

see Guide Dogs

DOG SHOWS

Green, Jen. Inheritance of Traits: Why Is My Dog Bigger Than Your Dog?, 1 vol. 2014. (Show Me Science Ser.). (ENG.). 32p. (gr. 3-5). lib. bdg. 30.65 *(978-1-4329-8747-3(X)*, Raintree Perspectives) Heinemann-Raintree.

Grogan, John. Marley Steals the Show. Cowdrey, Richard & Lyon, Tammie, illus. 2010. (Marley Ser.). (ENG.). 24p. (J). (gr. -1-2). pap. 3.99 *(978-0-06-185377-7(1)*, HarperFestival) HarperCollins Pubs.

Grogan, John & Hill, Susan. Marley & the Runaway Pumpkin. Cowdrey, Richard & Halverson, Lydia, illus. 2010. (I Can Read Level 2 Ser.). (ENG.). 32p. (J). (gr. k-3). pap. 3.99 *(978-0-06-185389-0(5))* HarperCollins Pubs.

Rauen, Amy & Ayers, Amy. Measuring at the Dog Show. 2007. (Math in Our World Ser.). 24p. (gr. 1-2). pap. 8.15 *(978-0-8368-8483-8(3)*, Weekly Reader Leveled Readers) Stevens, Gareth Publishing LLLP.

—Measuring at the Dog Show. Walter, Lorin, photos by. 2007. (Math in Our World Ser.). (Illus.). 24p. (gr. 1-2). lib. bdg. 22.00 *(978-0-8368-8474-6(4)*, Weekly Reader Leveled Readers) Stevens, Gareth Publishing LLLP.

—Midiendo en la Exposicion de Perros. 2007. (Las matimaticas en nuestro mundo (Spanish- Math in Our World) Ser.). (SPA.). 24p. (gr. 1-2). pap. 8.15 *(978-0-8368-8501-9(5)*, Weekly Reader Leveled Readers) Stevens, Gareth Publishing LLLP.

DOGMATIC THEOLOGY

see Theology

DOGS

see also Beagle (Dog Breed); Chihuahua (Dog Breed); Collie; German Shepherd Dog; Guide Dogs; Police Dogs; Poodles

Abdo Publishing. Dogs Set 10, 1 vol. 2013. (Dogs Set 10 Ser.: 6). (ENG.). 24p. (J). (gr. 3-6). lib. bdg. 153.90 *(978-1-61783-587-2(0)*, Checkerboard Library) ABDO Publishing Co.

ABDO Publishing Company Staff. Dogs Set 9, 1 vol. 2012. (Dogs Set 9 Ser.: 6). (ENG., Illus.). 24p. 153.90 *(978-1-61714-987-0(X)*, Checkerboard Library) ABDO Publishing Co.

Abrams, Patricia. Noah & the Search Dogs. 2012. 20p. pap. 12.95 *(978-1-61493-031-0(7))* Peppertree Pr., The.

Adams, Michelle Medlock. Care for a Puppy. 2009. (How to Convince Your Parents You Can ... Ser.). 32p. (J). (gr. 1-4). 25.70 *(978-1-58415-802-8(6))* Mitchell Lane Pubs., Inc.

Adkins, Linda. The Dog Who Couldn't Wag His Tail: A True Story about a Stray Who Made a Difference. Dilworth, Kristopher & Rhodes, Sean C., eds. 2003. (J). 13.95 *(978-0-9718632-0-0(2))* Keep Me Company Publishing Co.

Alcott, Louisa May. Under the Lilacs. l.t. ed. 2005. 444p. pap. *(978-1-84637-059-5(0))* Echo Library.

Alderton, David. How to Look after Your Pet Dog: A Practical Guide to Caring for Your Pet, in Step-By-Step Photographs. 2013. (ENG., Illus.). 20p. 8.99 *(978-1-84322-839-4(4))* Anness Publishing GBR. Dist: National Bk. Network.

Algeo, Matthew. Abe & Fido: Lincoln's Love of Animals & the Touching Story of His Favorite Canine Companion. 2015. (ENG., Illus.). 176p. 22.95 *(978-1-55652-222-2(3))* Chicago Review Pr., Inc.

Allberti, Frances C. Finding Rover. Gremillion, Barry, illus. 2006. (J). per. *(978-0-9785937-1-1(5))* Open Pages Publishing.

Allen, Kathy. Labradoodle: A Cross Between a Labrador Retriever & a Poodle, 1 vol. 2012. (Designer Dogs Ser.). (ENG.). 32p. (gr. 3-4). lib. bdg. 27.99 *(978-1-4296-7666-3(3)*, Snap Bks.) Capstone Press of Coughlan Cos.

Anjou, Colette. Westie the Dog. Niles, Kim, illus. 2005. 28p. (J). (gr. -1-3). per. 15.95 *(978-0-9748933-6-5(6))* E & E Publishing.

Appleton-Smith, Laura. Dog Agility. White, Keinyo, illus. 2007. (ENG.). 19p. (J). pap. 8.95 *(978-1-60541-012-8(8)*, Books To Remember) Flyleaf Publishing.

Apte, Sunita. Combat-Wounded Dogs. 2009. (Dog Heroes Ser.). (Illus.). 32p. (YA). (gr. 2-5). lib. bdg. 25.27 *(978-1-59716-864-9(5))* Bearport Publishing Co., Inc.

—Pomeranian: Pom Pom Ado. 2009. (Little Dogs Rock! Ser.). (Illus.). 32p. (YA). (gr. 2-5). lib. bdg. 25.27 *(978-1-59716-745-1(2))* Bearport Publishing Co., Inc.

Aretha, David. When Dogs Smile. 2017. (Animal Emotions Ser.). 32p. (J). (gr. 3-3). lib. bdg. 25.27 ***(978-0-7660-8613-5(5))*** Enslow Pubs., Inc.

Aronin, Miriam. The Prairie Dog's Town: A Perfect Hideaway. 2009. (Spectacular Animal Towns Ser.). (Illus.). 32p. (J). (gr. 2-7). lib. bdg. 25.27 *(978-1-59716-870-0(X))* Bearport Publishing Co., Inc.

Artlist Collection Staff. The Dog from Arf! Arf! to Zzzzzz. Artlist Collection Staff, illus. 2007. (Artlist Collection: the Dog Ser.). (Illus.). 40p. (J). (gr. -1-3). 6.99 *(978-0-06-059859-4(X))* HarperCollins Pubs.

Ashton, Anna. Our New Puppy. 2006. (Illus.). 80p. pap. *(978-1-84401-164-3(X))* Athena Pr.

Augello, Barbara. Dogs. 2005. (Illus.). 32p. (J). *(978-0-439-78475-7(1))* Scholastic, Inc.

Austen, Amy. Look Out for the Dingo! 2015. (Surprisingly Scary! Ser.). (ENG., Illus.). 24p. (J). (gr. 2-3). pap. 8.25 *(978-1-4994-0878-2(1)*, PowerKids Pr.) Rosen Publishing Group, Inc., The.

Avi. The Good Dog. 2006. pap. 8.75 *(978-0-15-365188-5(1))* Harcourt Schl. Pubs.

Baillie, Marilyn. My Pet Puppy. Kurisu, Jane, illus. 2005. (ENG.). 32p. (J). (gr. k-3). 6.95 *(978-1-55337-651-4(X))* Kids Can Pr., Ltd. CAN. Dist: Hachette Bk. Group.

Baines, Becky. National Geographic Kids Everything Dogs: All the Canine Facts, Photos, & Fun You Can Get Your Paws On! 2012. (National Geographic Kids Everything Ser.). (ENG., Illus.). 64p. (J). (gr. 3-7). lib. bdg. 21.90 *(978-1-4263-1025-6(0)*, National Geographic Children's Bks.) National Geographic Society.

Baines, Becky & National Geographic Kids Staff. Everything Dogs: All the Canine Facts, Photos, & Fun You Can Get Your Paws On! 2012. (National Geographic Kids Everything Ser.). (ENG., Illus.). 64p. (J). (gr. 3-7). pap. 12.95 *(978-1-4263-1024-9(2)*, National Geographic Children's Bks.) National Geographic Society.

Baker, Joan. Beagle Tales. 2013. 16p. pap. 7.95 *(978-1-4908-0747-8(0)*, WestBow Pr.) Author Solutions, Inc.

—A Tale of Two Beagles. 2013. 16p. pap. 7.95 *(978-1-4908-1539-8(2)*, WestBow Pr.) Author Solutions, Inc.

Baldwin, Sage & Wolfe, Rita M. A Puppy's Life. 2007. (Illus.). 40p. (J). 18.95 *(978-0-9792439-9-8(8))* Maximus Publishing.

Barnes, Julia. Dogs at Work. 2006. (Animals at Work Ser.). (Illus.). 32p. (gr. 3-6). lib. bdg. 26.00 *(978-0-8368-6223-2(6)*, Gareth Stevens Learning Library) Stevens, Gareth Publishing LLLP.

—Pet Dogs. 2006. (Pet Pals Ser.). (Illus.). 32p. (gr. 2-6). lib. bdg. 26.00 *(978-0-8368-6777-0(7)*, Gareth Stevens Learning Library) Stevens, Gareth Publishing LLLP.

Barnes, Nico. Bulldogs, 1 vol. 2014. (Dogs Ser.). (ENG.). 24p. (J). (gr. 4-8). lib. bdg. 28.50 *(978-1-62970-029-8(0))* ABDO Publishing Co.

—El Golden Retriever, 1 vol. 2014. (Perros Ser.). (SPA., Illus.). 24p. (J). (gr. 4-8). lib. bdg. 28.50 *(978-1-62970-325-1(7)*, 1377543) ABDO Publishing Co.

—Golden Retrievers, 1 vol. 2014. (Dogs Ser.). (ENG.). 24p. (J). (gr. 4-8). lib. bdg. 28.50 *(978-1-62970-031-1(2))* ABDO Publishing Co.

—El Jack Russell Terrier, 1 vol. 2014. (Perros Ser.). (SPA., Illus.). 24p. (J). (gr. 4-8). lib. bdg. 28.50 *(978-1-62970-326-8(5)*, 1377544) ABDO Publishing Co.

—Jack Russell Terriers, 1 vol. 2014. (Dogs Ser.). (ENG.). 24p. (J). (gr. 4-8). lib. bdg. 28.50 *(978-1-62970-032-8(0))* ABDO Publishing Co.

—Labrador Retrievers, 1 vol. 2014. (Dogs Ser.). (ENG.). 24p. (J). (gr. 4-8). lib. bdg. 28.50 *(978-1-62970-033-5(9))* ABDO Publishing Co.

—Los Bulldogs, 1 vol. 2014. (Perros Ser.). (SPA., Illus.). 24p. (J). (gr. 4-8). lib. bdg. 28.50 *(978-1-62970-323-7(0)*, 1377541) ABDO Publishing Co.

—Pugs, 1 vol. 2014. (Dogs Ser.). (ENG.). 24p. (J). (gr. 4-8). lib. bdg. 28.50 *(978-1-62970-034-2(7))* ABDO Publishing Co.

Barry, Holly M. Helen Keller's Best Friend Belle. Thermes, Jennifer, illus. 2013. (ENG.). 32p. (J). (gr. -1-3). 16.99 *(978-0-8075-3198-3(7))* Whitman, Albert & Co.

Basner, Shannon. Mojo's Magical Ride: True Story of Courage, Transformation & Love; an Alaskan Dog Rescue Story. 2013. 40p. pap. 24.95 *(978-1-4626-6154-1(8))* America Star Bks.

Beal, Abigail. I Love My Golden Retriever. 2011. (Top Dogs Ser.). 24p. (J). (ENG.). pap. 8.25 *(978-1-4488-2656-8(X))*; (Illus.). lib. bdg. 22.60 *(978-1-4488-2536-3(9))* Rosen Publishing Group, Inc., The. (PowerKids Pr.).

—I Love My Pug. 2011. (Top Dogs Ser.). (Illus.). 24p. (J). (gr. k-5). lib. bdg. 22.60 *(978-1-4488-2539-4(3)*, PowerKids Pr.) Rosen Publishing Group, Inc., The.

—I Love My Yorkshire Terrier. 2011. (Top Dogs Ser.). 24p. (J). (ENG.). pap. 8.25 *(978-1-4488-2660-5(8))*; (Illus.). lib. bdg. 22.60 *(978-1-4488-2538-7(5))* Rosen Publishing Group, Inc., The. (PowerKids Pr.).

—Top Dogs, 6 vols., Set. Incl. I Love My Beagle. lib. bdg. 22.60 *(978-1-4488-2540-0(7))*; I Love My Dachshund. lib. bdg. 22.60 *(978-1-4488-2537-0(7))*; I Love My German Shepherd. lib. bdg. 22.60 *(978-1-4488-2535-6(0))*; I Love My Golden Retriever. lib. bdg. 22.60 *(978-1-4488-2536-3(9))*; I Love My Pug. lib. bdg. 22.60 *(978-1-4488-2539-4(3))*; I Love My Yorkshire Terrier. lib. bdg. 22.60 *(978-1-4488-2538-7(5))*; (J). (gr. k-5). (Top Dogs Ser.). (Illus.). 24p. 2011. Set lib. bdg. 127.50 *(978-1-4488-2779-4(5)*, PowerKids Pr.) Rosen Publishing Group, Inc., The.

Becker, John E. Frenemies for Life: Cheetahs & Anatolian Shepherd Dogs. 2010. 56p. (YA). (gr. 5-8). pap. 8.95 *(978-0-9841554-1-5(4))*; lib. bdg. 18.95 *(978-0-9841554-0-8(6))* Columbus Zoo & Aquarium, The.

Belyeu, Monti L. Hot Diggity Doggerels: Delightful Dittys about the Dog. 2010. 28p. pap. 12.95 *(978-1-4251-6973-2(2))* Trafford Publishing.

Berman, Ruth. My Pet Dog. Hustace, Billy, photos by. 2005. (All about Pets Ser.). (Illus.). 64p. (gr. 2-6). lib. bdg. 22.60 *(978-0-8225-2259-1(4))* Lerner Publishing Group.

BHB International Staff & Simons, Phillida Brooke. Jock of the Bushveld. 2016. (Illus.). 32p. pap. 12.00 *(978-0-86978-477-8(3))* Penguin Random House Grupo Editorial ESP. Dist: Casemate Pubs. & Bk. Distributors, LLC.

Biniok, Janice. 21st Century Security Dogs. 2012. (J). *(978-1-61900-000-1(8))*; pap. *(978-1-61900-001-8(6))* Eldorado Ink.

Birchall, Mark. Copy Cat. 2010. (Child's Play Library). (ENG., Illus.). 32p. (J). (gr. 1-2). *(978-1-84643-367-2(3))* Child's Play International Ltd.

Blake, Kevin. Rescue Dogs. 2015. (Dog Heroes Ser.). (ENG., Illus.). 32p. (J). (gr. 2-7). lib. bdg. 26.60 *(978-1-62724-861-7(7))* Bearport Publishing Co., Inc.

Bluemel Oldfield, Dawn. Dog. 2017. (See Them Grow Ser.). (ENG., Illus.). 24p. (J). (gr. -1-3). 17.95 ***(978-1-68402-043-0(3))*** Bearport Publishing Co., Inc.

Bly, Nicole. Liam Likes to Play. 2011. 48p. 25.99 *(978-1-4567-3387-2(7))* AuthorHouse.

Bodden, Valerie. Bulldogs. 2014. (J). 25.65 *(978-1-60818-361-6(0)*, Creative Education) Creative Co., The.

—Fetch!: Bulldogs. 2014. (Fetch! Ser.). (ENG., Illus.). 24p. (J). (gr. 1-3). pap. 7.99 *(978-0-89812-940-3(0)*, Creative Paperbacks) Creative Co., The.

—Fetch!: German Shepherds. 2014. (Fetch! Ser.). (ENG.). 24p. (J). (gr. 1-3). pap. 7.99 *(978-0-89812-941-0(9)*, Creative Paperbacks) Creative Co., The.

—Fetch!: Retrievers. 2014. (Fetch! Ser.). (ENG., Illus.). 24p. (J). (gr. 1-3). pap. 7.99 *(978-0-89812-943-4(5)*, Creative Paperbacks) Creative Co., The.

—Fetch!: Terriers. 2014. (Fetch! Ser.). (ENG., Illus.). 24p. (J). (gr. 1-3). pap. 7.99 *(978-0-89812-944-1(3)*, Creative Paperbacks) Creative Co., The.

—Retrievers. 2014. (J). 25.65 *(978-1-60818-364-7(5)*, Creative Education) Creative Co., The.

—Terriers. 2014. (Illus.). 24p. (J). 25.65 *(978-1-60818-365-4(3)*, Creative Education) Creative Co., The.

Bolan, Sandra. The Labrador Retriever. 2008. (Illus.). lib. bdg. 32.95 *(978-1-932904-23-9(9))* Eldorado Ink.

Boothroyd, Jennifer. Hero Law Enforcement Dogs. 2017. (Lightning Bolt Books (tm) — Hero Dogs Ser.). (ENG., Illus.). 32p. (J). (gr. 1-3). pap. 8.99 *(978-1-5124-3108-7(7))* Lerner Publishing Group.

Boothroyd, Jennifer. Hero Service Dogs. 2017. (Lightning Bolt Books (tm) — Hero Dogs Ser.). (ENG.). 32p. (J). (gr. 1-3). 7.99 ***(978-1-5124-3651-8(8)***, Lerner Pubns.); 39.99 ***(978-1-5124-2802-5(7)***, Lerner Pubns.); 39.99 ***(978-1-5124-3650-1(X)***, Lerner Pubns.); (Illus.). 26.65 *(978-1-5124-2541-3(9))* Lerner Publishing Group.

Bowman, Chris. German Shepherds. 2015. (Awesome Dogs Ser.). (ENG., Illus.). 24p. (J). (gr. k-3). lib. bdg. 25.95 *(978-1-62617-240-1(4)*, Blastoff! Readers) Bellwether Media.

—Golden Retrievers. 2015. (Awesome Dogs Ser.). (ENG., Illus.). 24p. (J). (gr. k-3). lib. bdg. 25.95 *(978-1-62617-241-8(2)*, Blastoff! Readers) Bellwether Media.

—Great Danes. 2016. (Awesome Dogs Ser.). (ENG., Illus.). 24p. (J). (gr. k-3). lib. bdg. 25.95 *(978-1-62617-306-4(0)*, Blastoff! Readers) Bellwether Media.

—Labrador Retrievers. 2015. (Awesome Dogs Ser.). (ENG., Illus.). 24p. (J). (gr. k-3). lib. bdg. 25.95 *(978-1-62617-242-5(0)*, Blastoff! Readers) Bellwether Media.

—Siberian Huskies. 2016. (Awesome Dogs Ser.). (ENG., Illus.). 24p. (J). (gr. k-3). lib. bdg. 25.95 *(978-1-62617-308-8(7)*, Blastoff! Readers) Bellwether Media.

Boynton, Sandra. Perritos: Un Libro para Contar y Ladrar. Boynton, Sandra, illus. 2004.Tr. of Doggies. (SPA., Illus.). 14p. (J). (gr. -1 — 1). bds. 5.99 *(978-0-689-86303-5(9)*, Libros Para Ninos) Libros Para Ninos.

Bozzo, Linda. I Like Airedale Terriers! 2017. (J). pap. ***(978-0-7660-9119-1(8))*** Enslow Pubs., Inc.

—I Like Akitas! 2017. (J). pap. ***(978-0-7660-9123-8(6))*** Enslow Pubs., Inc.

—I Like Australian Shepherds! 2017. (Discover Dogs with the American Canine Association Ser.). 24p. (J). (gr. 1-2). lib. bdg. 22.60 ***(978-0-7660-8634-0(8))*** Enslow Pubs., Inc.

—I Like Basset Hounds! 2017. (J). pap. ***(978-0-7660-9127-6(9))*** Enslow Pubs., Inc.

—I Like Beagles! 2012. (Discover Dogs with the American Canine Association Ser.). 24p. (J). (gr. k-3). 22.60 *(978-0-7660-3846-2(7)*, Enslow Elementary) Enslow Pubs., Inc.

—I Like Bernese Mountain Dogs! 2017. (Discover Dogs with the American Canine Association Ser.). 24p. (J). (gr. 1-2). lib. bdg. 22.60 ***(978-0-7660-8636-4(4))*** Enslow Pubs., Inc.

—I Like Boxers! 2017. (Discover Dogs with the American Canine Association Ser.). 24p. (J). (gr. 1-2). lib. bdg. 22.60 ***(978-0-7660-8638-8(0))*** Enslow Pubs., Inc.

—I Like Cocker Spaniels! 2017. (J). pap. ***(978-0-7660-9131-3(7))*** Enslow Pubs., Inc.

—I Like Collies! 2012. (Discover Dogs with the American Canine Association Ser.). 24p. (J). (gr. k-3). 22.60 *(978-0-7660-3847-9(5)*, Enslow Elementary) Enslow Pubs., Inc.

—I Like Dalmatians! 2016. (Discover Dogs with the American Canine Association Ser.). 24p. (J). pap. 9.35 *(978-0-7660-8153-6(2))* Enslow Pubs., Inc.

—I Like French Bulldogs! 2016. (Discover Dogs with the American Canine Association Ser.). (Illus.). 24p. (J). pap. 9.35 *(978-0-7660-8132-1(X))* Enslow Pubs., Inc.

—I Like German Shepherds! 2012. (Discover Dogs with the American Canine Association Ser.). 24p. (J). (gr. k-3). 22.60 *(978-0-7660-3849-3(1)*, Enslow Elementary) Enslow Pubs., Inc.

—I Like Greyhounds! 2017. (Discover Dogs with the American Canine Association Ser.). 24p. (J). (gr. 1-2). lib. bdg. 22.60 ***(978-0-7660-8640-1(2))*** Enslow Pubs., Inc.

—I Like Irish Wolfhounds! 2017. (Discover Dogs with the American Canine Association Ser.). 24p. (J). (gr. 1-2). lib. bdg. 22.60 ***(978-0-7660-8642-5(9))*** Enslow Pubs., Inc.

—I Like Jack Russell Terriers! 2017. (Discover Dogs with the American Canine Association Ser.). 24p. (J). (gr. 1-2). lib. bdg. 22.60 ***(978-0-7660-8644-9(5))*** Enslow Pubs., Inc.

—I Like Labradoodles! 2016. (Discover Dogs with the American Canine Association Ser.). 24p. (J). pap. 9.35 *(978-0-7660-8169-7(9))* Enslow Pubs., Inc.

—I Like Labrador Retrievers! 2012. (Discover Dogs with the American Canine Association Ser.). 24p. (J). (gr. k-3). (Illus.). pap. 7.95 *(978-1-4644-0120-6(9))*; 22.60 *(978-0-7660-3848-6(3))* Enslow Pubs., Inc. (Enslow Elementary).
—I Like Mixed-Breed Dogs! 2012. (Discover Dogs with the American Canine Association Ser.). 24p. (J). (gr. k-3). (Illus.). pap. 7.95 *(978-1-4644-0122-0(5))*; 22.60 *(978-0-7660-3845-5(9))* Enslow Pubs., Inc. (Enslow Elementary).
—I Like Newfoundlands! 2017. (J). pap. ***(978-0-7660-9135-1(X))*** Enslow Pubs., Inc.
—I Like Pit Bulls! 2016. (Discover Dogs with the American Canine Association Ser.). 24p. (J). pap. 9.35 *(978-0-7660-8157-4(5))* Enslow Pubs., Inc.
—I Like Poodles! 2012. (Discover Dogs with the American Canine Association Ser.). 24p. (J). (gr. k-3). 22.60 *(978-0-7660-3850-9(5)*, Enslow Elementary) Enslow Pubs., Inc.
—I Like Portuguese Water Dogs! 2017. (J). pap. ***(978-0-7660-9115-3(5))*** Enslow Pubs., Inc.
—I Like Yorkshire Terriers! 2016. (Discover Dogs with the American Canine Association Ser.). (Illus.). 24p. (J). pap. 9.35 *(978-0-7660-8165-9(6))* Enslow Pubs., Inc.
—Mi Primer Perro. 2008. (My First Pet Bilingual Library from the American Humane Association Ser.). Tr. of My First Dog. (ENG & SPA., Illus.). 32p. (J). (gr. 1-3). lib. bdg. 23.94 *(978-0-7660-3032-9(6))* Enslow Pubs., Inc.
—My First Dog. 2007. (My First Pet Library from the American Humane Association Ser.). (Illus.). 32p. (J). (gr. 1-2). lib. bdg. 23.94 *(978-0-7660-2754-1(6)*, Enslow Elementary) Enslow Pubs., Inc.
Bozzo, Linda & Library Association Staff. Search & Rescue Dog Heroes. 2010. (Amazing Working Dogs with American Humane Ser.). (Illus.). 48p. (J). (gr. 2-5). 25.27 *(978-0-7660-3201-9(9))* Enslow Pubs., Inc.
—Service Dog Heroes. 2010. (Amazing Working Dogs with American Humane Ser.). (Illus.). 48p. (J). (gr. 2-5). 25.27 *(978-0-7660-3199-9(3))* Enslow Pubs., Inc.
Braun, Eric. Simply Sound: Science Adventures with Jasper the Origami Bat, 1 vol. Christoph, Jamey, illus. 2014. (Origami Science Adventures Ser.). (ENG.). 24p. (gr. 3-4). lib. bdg. 27.32 *(978-1-4795-2187-6(6))* Picture Window Bks.
Britton, Ann. Labrador Retriever. 2017. 128p. (J). ***(978-1-4222-3858-5(X))*** Mason Crest.
Britton, Tamara L. Bull Terriers, 1 vol. 2013. (Dogs Set 10 Ser.). (ENG.). 24p. (J). (gr. 3-6). lib. bdg. 25.65 *(978-1-61783-589-6(7)*, Checkerboard Library) ABDO Publishing Co.
—French Bulldogs, 1 vol. 2013. (Dogs Set 10 Ser.). (ENG.). 24p. (J). (gr. 3-6). lib. bdg. 25.65 *(978-1-61783-590-2(0)*, Checkerboard Library) ABDO Publishing Co.
—Rottweilers, 1 vol. 2013. (Dogs Set 10 Ser.). (ENG.). 24p. (J). (gr. 3-6). lib. bdg. 25.65 *(978-1-61783-591-9(9)*, Checkerboard Library) ABDO Publishing Co.
Brooks. Come Back, Energy Man. Date not set. 224p. (J). 14.99 *(978-0-06-020670-3(5))*; 15.89 *(978-0-06-020671-0(3))* HarperCollins Pubs.
Brown, Domini. Australian Shepherds. 2016. (Awesome Dogs Ser.). (ENG., Illus.). 24p. (J). (gr. k-3). 25.95 *(978-1-62617-391-0(5)*, Blastoff! Readers) Bellwether Media.
—Pomeranians. 2016. (Awesome Dogs Ser.). (ENG., Illus.). 24p. (J). (gr. k-3). 25.95 *(978-1-62617-394-1(X)*, Blastoff! Readers) Bellwether Media.
Brown, Tricia. Patsy Ann of Alaska: The True Story of a Dog. Fowler, Jim, illus. 2011. (Paws IV Ser.). (ENG.). 32p. (J). (gr. -1-2). pap. 10.99 *(978-1-57061-697-6(3)*, Little Bigfoot) Sasquatch Bks.
Bruce, Relly. Meet Meekus: From the Meekus & Myron Collection (Book 1), 1 vol. 2010. 16p. pap. 24.95 *(978-1-4489-9174-7(9))* PublishAmerica, Inc.
Buckley, Carol. Tarra & Bella: The Elephant & Dog Who Became Best Friends. Buckley, Carol, photos by. 2009. (ENG., Illus.). 32p. (J). (gr. -1-k). 16.99 *(978-0-399-25443-7(9)*, G.P. Putnam's Sons Books for Young Readers) Penguin Young Readers Group.
Bugbird, Tim. Charm Books Kittens/Puppies Clip Strip. 2007. (Illus.). 64p. (J). (gr. -1-3). *(978-1-84610-702-3(4))* Make Believe Ideas.
—Charm Books Kittens/Puppies Pos Rack. 2007. (Illus.). 64p. (J). (gr. -1-3). *(978-1-84610-706-1(7))* Make Believe Ideas.
—Charm Books Puppies Poly Bag. 2007. (Illus.). 64p. (J). (gr. -1-3). *(978-1-84610-704-7(0))* Make Believe Ideas.
Burgan Cpdt-Ka, Kimberly. Poppy & Puppy Are Friends: A Child's First Introduction to Responsible Dog Ownership. 2012. 44p. pap. 21.99 *(978-1-4670-4145-4(9))* AuthorHouse.
Burke Battistini, Maryanne. Lacey's Story: A Little Tale That Wags. 2009. 72p. pap. 24.99 *(978-1-4389-8874-0(5))* AuthorHouse.
Burns, Matthew. Golden Retriever. 2017. (Dog Lover's Guides: Vol. 18). (ENG.). (YA). (gr. 7-12). 26.95 ***(978-1-4222-3857-8(1))*** Mason Crest.
Burris, Andrea & Schad, Anna. A Dog Lover's Alphabet Book. Burris, Andrea, illus. 2007. (ENG., Illus.). 32p. (J). (gr. k-2). 14.95 *(978-0-9743294-1-3(X))* A & D Bks.
Byerly, Robbie. Look at All the Dogs. 2016. (1G Science Ser.). (ENG., Illus.). 28p. (J). pap. 5.99 ***(978-1-63437-606-8(4))*** American Reading Co.
Camerena, Rebecca & Ganeri, Anita. My Dog Is a Hero. 2012. (ENG.). 96p. (J). (gr. 3-7). pap. 7.99 *(978-0-545-49595-0(4))* Scholastic, Inc.
Capstone Press. Working Dogs. 2010. (Working Dogs Ser.). (ENG.). 32p. lib. bdg. 143.94 *(978-1-4296-5902-4(5)*, Pebble Plus) Capstone Press of Coughlan Cos.
Carmichael, L. E. Fox Talk. Bronson, Jody, illus. 2013. 62p. *(978-0-9881638-5-0(3))* Ashby-BP Publishing.
Carney, Elizabeth. Cats vs. Dogs. 2011. (Readers Ser.). (ENG., Illus.). 48p. (J). (gr. 1-4). pap. 3.99 *(978-1-4263-0755-3(1))*; lib. bdg. 13.90 *(978-1-4263-0756-0(X))* National Geographic Society. (National Geographic Children's Bks.).
—Dog Finds Lost Dolphins! And More True Stories of Amazing Animal Heroes. 2012. (NGK Chapters Ser.). (ENG., Illus.). 112p. (J). (gr. 2-5). pap. 5.99 *(978-1-4263-1031-7(5))*; lib. bdg. 14.90 *(978-1-4263-1032-4(3))* National Geographic Society. (National Geographic Children's Bks.).
Carolina Canines for Service & Nowak, Pat. A Job for Arabella. Baumgardner, Mary Alice, illus. 2007. 56p. (J). per. *(978-0-9800070-0-8(3))* Carolina Canines for Service Inc.
Carr, Aaron. Dog. 2011. (J). *(978-1-61690-921-5(8))*; *(978-1-61690-567-5(0))* Weigl Pubs., Inc.
—Dogs. 2014. (J). *(978-1-4896-3204-3(2))* Weigl Pubs., Inc.
—El Perro. 2012. (SPA.). (J). *(978-1-61913-182-8(X))* Weigl Pubs., Inc.
Cartwright, Mary, told to. Little Book of Little Puppies. 2011. (Baby's Very First Ser.). 10p. (J). ring bd. 6.99 *(978-0-7945-2957-4(7)*, Usborne) EDC Publishing.
Cary, Bob. Born to Pull: The Glory of Sled Dogs. de Marcken, Gail, illus. 2009. (ENG.). 96p. pap. 12.95 *(978-0-8166-6773-4(X))* Univ. of Minnesota Pr.
Castaldo, Nancy F. Sniffer Dogs: How Dogs (and Their Noses) Save the World. 2014. (ENG., Illus.). 160p. (J). (gr. 5-7). 16.99 *(978-0-544-08893-1(X)*, HMH Books For Young Readers) Houghton Mifflin Harcourt Publishing Co.
Cats & Dogs (Gr. PreK-5) 2003. (J). *(978-1-58232-018-2(7))* ECS Learning Systems, Inc.
Chadwick, Anita. Rosebuds Puppies. 2012. 20p. pap. 13.77 *(978-1-4669-1632-6(X))* Trafford Publishing.
Cheehy, Debra/Ilene. I Like Dogs. Hilliard, Carol, illus. 2009. 52p. (J). 16.95 *(978-0-9820817-0-9(7))* Four Foot Pr. LLC.
Chimes, Lisa. My First Puppy. Burke, Tina, illus. 2016. (ENG.). 32p. (J). 10.99 *(978-1-61067-516-1(9))* Kane Miller.
Chin, Amanda. Pet's Playground: Playing Safe in a Dog-And-Cat World. Feldman, Luke, illus. 2009. 104p. (J). pap. 11.95 *(978-1-58326-115-6(X))* American Animal Hospital Assn. Pr.
Clapper, Nikki Bruno. Saint Bernards. 2016. (Big Dogs Ser.). (ENG., Illus.). 24p. (gr. k-1). lib. bdg. 26.65 *(978-1-4914-7977-3(9)*, 1399458, Pebble Plus) Capstone Press of Coughlan Cos.
Clarke, Phillip. Little Book of Dogs & Puppies: Internet-Linked. 2009. (Miniature Editions Ser.). 64p. (YA). (gr. 3-18). 6.99 *(978-0-7945-2300-8(5)*, Usborne) EDC Publishing.
Clay, Kathryn. Farm Dogs, 1 vol. 2012. (Farm Animals Ser.). (ENG., Illus.). 24p. (gr. k-1). lib. bdg. 26.65 *(978-1-4296-8651-8(0)*, Pebble Plus) Capstone Press of Coughlan Cos.
Clements, Andrew. Brave Norman. Beier, Ellen, illus. 2015. 32p. pap. 4.00 *(978-1-61003-600-9(X))* Center for the Collaborative Classroom.
Clever Coyote & other Wild Dogs: Level L, 6 vols. 128p. (gr. 2-3). 40.50 *(978-0-7699-1033-8(5))* Shortland Pubns. (U. S. A.) Inc.
Clutton-Brock, Juliet. Dog. 2014. (DK Eyewitness Bks.). (ENG.). 72p. (J). (gr. 3-7). pap. 9.99 *(978-1-4654-2051-0(7)*, DK Children) Dorling Kindersley Publishing, Inc.
Cohn, Riley, illus. Martin in the Narthex. 2011. (ENG.). 40p. (J). 14.95 *(978-0-940672-82-6(0))* Shearer Publishing.
Collard, Sneed B., III. Shep: Our Most Loyal Dog. Yardley, Joanna, illus. 2006. (ENG.). 32p. (J). (gr. k-6). 16.95 *(978-1-58536-259-2(X))* Sleeping Bear Pr.
Colson, Mary. The Truth about Dogs: What Dogs Do When You're Not Looking. 2017. (Pets Undercover! Ser.). (ENG., Illus.). 32p. (gr. 2-4). lib. bdg. 29.99 *(978-1-4109-8606-1(3)*, Read Me!) Heinemann-Raintree.
Connelly, Claire K. Moxie. Jacobs, Joyce M., illus. 2010. 84p. pap. 10.49 *(978-1-4520-7634-8(0))* AuthorHouse.
Coon, Kathy. Dog Intelligence Test: Kathy Coon's Dog Intelligence Test. rev. ed. 2003. Orig. Title: The Dog Intelligence Test. (Illus.). 88p. (J). pap. *(978-0-9741300-0-2(1))* Coon, Kathy.
Coren, Stanley. Why Do Dogs Have Wet Noses? 2008. (ENG., Illus.). 64p. (J). (gr. 3-7). pap. 9.95 *(978-1-55337-658-3(7))* Kids Can Pr., Ltd. CAN. Dist: Hachette Bk. Group.
Cotton, Jack. A Dog's Guide to Life: Lessons from "Moose" 2005. (Illus.). 32p. (J). *(978-1-59490-025-9(6))* Tide-Mark Pr., Ltd.
Crabtree, Marc & Kalman, Bobbie. Les Labradors. 2012. (FRE., Illus.). 32p. (J). pap. 9.95 *(978-2-89579-437-0(5))* Bayard Canada CAN. Dist: Crabtree Publishing Co.
Creese, Sarah. Mad about Perfect Puppies & Cute Kittens. 2009. (Mad About Ser.). (ENG., Illus.). 24p. (J). (gr. -1-3). pap. 3.99 *(978-1-84879-006-3(6))* Make Believe Ideas GBR. Dist: Nelson, Thomas Inc.
Crisp, Marty. Everything Dog: What Kids Really Want to Know about Dogs. 2003. (Kids Faqs Ser.). (ENG., Illus.). 64p. (J). (gr. 3-6). pap. 7.95 *(978-1-55971-854-7(4))* Cooper Square Publishing Llc.
Crosby, Jeff & Jackson, Shelley Ann. Little Lions, Bull Baiters & Hunting Hounds: A History of Dog Breeds. Crosby, Jeff & Jackson, Shelley Ann, illus. 2008. (ENG., Illus.). 72p. (J). (gr. k-12). 19.95 *(978-0-88776-815-6(6)*, Tundra Bks.) Tundra Bks. CAN. Dist: Penguin Random Hse. LLC.
Cummins, Judi, creator. Ginger & Snoops, 1. 2006. (Illus.). 22p. (J). per. *(978-0-9760377-0-5(X))* Cummins, Judi.
—Ginger the Wonder Beagle. 2005. (Illus.). 26p. (J). per. *(978-0-9760377-1-2(8))* Cummins, Judi.
Daronco, Mickey & Ohanesian, Diane. My Pet Pup: Set of 6. 2nd rev. ed. 2003. (BuildUp Ser.). (J). pap. 22.00 *(978-1-4108-0744-1(4))* Benchmark Education Co.
De la Bédoyère, Camilla. Dogs & Puppies. 2010. (Mosaic of Magical Information Ser.). 48p. (YA). (gr. 3-18). 19.95 *(978-1-4222-1988-1(7))* Mason Crest.
Dee, Joan. Bertie. 2012. (Illus.). 48p. pap. 9.60 *(978-1-909300-01-9(2))* Action Publishing Technology Ltd GBR. Dist: Printondemand-worldwide.com.
Dennis, Brian, et al. Nubs: The True Story of a Mutt, a Marine & a Miracle. 2009. (ENG., Illus.). 48p. (J). (gr. -1-3). 18.99 *(978-0-316-05318-1(X))* Little, Brown Bks. for Young Readers.
Designer Dogs: Set 2. 2014. (Designer Dogs Ser.). 32p. (J). (gr. k-5). 157.50 *(978-1-4777-7051-1(8)*, PowerKids Pr.) Rosen Publishing Group, Inc., The.
Designer Dogs: Sets 1-2. 2014. (Designer Dogs Ser.). 32p. (J). (gr. k-5). pap. 120.00 *(978-1-4777-7256-0(1))*; pap. 720.00 *(978-1-4777-7257-7(X))* Rosen Publishing Group, Inc., The. (PowerKids Pr.).
Detector Dog, 6 Pack. (Bookweb Ser.). 32p. (gr. 3-18). 34.00 *(978-0-7635-3953-5(8))* Rigby Education.
Dewin, Howard, told to. The Dog: Dogs Rule Cats Drool. 2007. (Artist Collection). (Illus.). 31p. pap. *(978-0-545-01196-9(5))* Scholastic, Inc.
—The Dog: Why Do Dogs Love to Sniff?: The Do's & Don'ts of the Dogs. 2007. (Illus.). 29p. (J). pap. *(978-0-439-02255-2(X))* Scholastic, Inc.
Dewin, Howie. Why Are Dogs' Noses Wet? And Other True Facts. 2006. (Artist Collection Ser.). (ENG., Illus.). 32p. (J). (gr. -1-3). pap. 3.99 *(978-0-439-92214-2(3))* Scholastic, Inc.
Dicker, Katie & Johnson, Jinny. Cavalier King Charles Spaniel. 2014. (My Favorite Dogs Ser.). 24p. (gr. k-3). 28.50 *(978-1-62588-176-2(2))* Black Rabbit Bks.
—Collie. 2014. (My Favorite Dogs Ser.). 24p. (gr. k-3). 28.50 *(978-1-62588-172-4(X))* Black Rabbit Bks.
—Doberman Pinscher. 2014. (My Favorite Dogs Ser.). 24p. (gr. k-3). 28.50 *(978-1-62588-174-8(6))* Black Rabbit Bks.
—Great Dane. 2014. (My Favorite Dogs Ser.). 24p. (gr. k-3). 28.50 *(978-1-62588-175-5(4))* Black Rabbit Bks.
—Miniature Schnauzer. 2014. (My Favorite Dogs Ser.). 24p. (gr. k-3). 28.50 *(978-1-62588-177-9(0))* Black Rabbit Bks.
—Rottweiler. 2014. (My Favorite Dogs Ser.). 24p. (gr. k-3). 28.50 *(978-1-62588-178-6(9))* Black Rabbit Bks.
—Siberian Husky. 2014. (My Favorite Dogs Ser.). 24p. (gr. k-3). 28.50 *(978-1-62588-179-3(7))* Black Rabbit Bks.
Dickmann, Nancy. A Dog's Life, 1 vol. 2010. (Watch It Grow Ser.). (ENG.). 24p. (gr. -1-1). 22.65 *(978-1-4329-4229-8(8))*; pap. 6.29 *(978-1-4329-4232-8(8))* Heinemann-Raintree. (Acorn).
—La Vida del Perro. 2011. (¡Mira Cómo Crece! Ser.). 24p. (gr. -1-1). (SPA & ENG.). 22.65 *(978-1-4329-5278-5(1))*; (ENG & SPA.). pap. 6.29 *(978-1-4329-5290-7(0))* Heinemann-Raintree. (Bellota).
Dike, Diane. Gracie Comes Home: The Adventures of Gracie & Diane. Grasso, Craig A. & Grasso, Samantha A., illus. 2007. (J). 14.95 *(978-1-932738-45-2(2))* Western Reflections Publishing Co.
Dilly Dog & the Party. 2004. (Play Pals Ser.). (Illus.). 12p. (J). bds. *(978-1-84229-642-4(6))* Top That! Publishing PLC.
Discover Dogs with the American Canine Association: Set 2. 2016. (Discover Dogs with the American Canine Association Ser.). 24p. (gr. 2-1). pap. 56.10 *(978-0-7660-7967-0(8))*; lib. bdg. 135.60 *(978-0-7660-7490-3(0))* Enslow Pubs., Inc.
Discover Dogs with the American Canine Association: Set 3. 2016. (Discover Dogs with the American Canine Association Ser.). 24p. (J). lib. bdg. 135.60 *(978-0-7660-8378-3(0))* Enslow Pubs., Inc.
Discover Dogs with the American Canine Association: Set 4. 2017. (Discover Dogs with the American Canine Association Ser.). 24p. (gr. 1-2). pap. 56.10 ***(978-0-7660-8895-5(2))***; lib. bdg. 135.60 ***(978-0-7660-8590-9(2))*** Enslow Pubs., Inc.
Dodd, Emma. Dog's Farmyard Friends. (Illus.). 140p. (J). bds. *(978-1-902272-43-6(9))* Tucker Slingsby, Ltd.
Dog Artist Collection Staff. The Dog from Arf! Arf! to Zzzzzz. Dog Artist Collection Staff, illus. 2004. (Illus.). 40p. (J). (ENG.). 14.99 *(978-0-06-059857-0(3))*; lib. bdg. 16.89 *(978-0-06-059858-7(1))* HarperCollins Pubs.
A Dog Book. 2007. 224p. *(978-1-4075-0585-5(8))* Parragon, Inc.
The Dog Family: Individual Title Six-Packs. (Story Steps Ser.). (gr. k-2). 32.00 *(978-0-7635-9835-8(6))* Rigby Education.
Dog Tales: True Stories about Amazing Dogs Set, 5-Volumes. 2007. (Dog Tales: True Stories about Amazing Dogs Ser.). 80p. (gr. 4-6). 140.00 *(978-0-7910-9685-7(8)*, Chelsea Clubhouse) Facts On File, Inc.
Dogs & Puppies. 2006. (Illus.). (J). cd-rom 9.99 *(978-0-9795190-0-0(4))* Color & Learn.
Dogs & Puppies Sticker Activity Book. (My Sticker Activity Ser.). (Illus.). 12p. (J). *(978-1-4054-1180-6(5))* Parragon, Inc.
Dorling Kindersley Publishing Staff. Baby Touch & Feel: Puppies. 2017. (Baby Touch & Feel Ser.). (ENG., Illus.). 14p. (J). (— 1). bds. 5.99 *(978-1-4654-5621-2(X)*, DK Children) Dorling Kindersley Publishing, Inc.
—Pocket Genius: Dogs. 2016. (Pocket Genius Ser.). (ENG., Illus.). 160p. (J). (gr. 3-7). pap. 4.99 *(978-1-4654-4585-8(4)*, DK Children) Dorling Kindersley Publishing, Inc.
—Pocket Genius: Dogs. 2014. (Pocket Genius Ser.). (ENG.). 160p. (J). (gr. 3-7). 7.99 *(978-1-4654-2014-5(2)*, DK Children) Dorling Kindersley Publishing, Inc.
—Puppies & Kittens. 2008. (Baby Touch & Feel Ser.). (ENG., Illus.). 14p. (J). (gr. -1 — 1). bds. 5.99 *(978-0-7566-3835-1(6)*, DK Children) Dorling Kindersley Publishing, Inc.
—Woof! Woof! 2013. (ENG., Illus.). 12p. (J). (gr. -1 — 1). bds. 9.99 *(978-1-4654-0929-4(7)*, DK Children) Dorling Kindersley Publishing, Inc.
Dorling Kindersley Publishing Staff, creator. Dog. 2005. (Ultimate Sticker Bks.). (ENG., Illus.). 16p. (J). (gr. k-3). pap. 6.99 *(978-0-7566-1457-7(0)*, DK Children) Dorling Kindersley Publishing, Inc.
—Puppy. 2005. (Ultimate Sticker Bks.). (ENG., Illus.). 16p. (J). (gr. k-3). pap. 6.99 *(978-0-7566-1458-4(9)*, DK Children) Dorling Kindersley Publishing, Inc.
Dorling Kindersley Publishing Staff & Buller, Laura. DK Readers L2: Amazing Dogs. 2016. (DK Readers Ser.). (ENG., Illus.). 48p. (J). (gr. k-2). 14.99 *(978-1-4654-4595-7(1))*; pap. 3.99 *(978-1-4654-4596-4(X))* Dorling Kindersley Publishing, Inc. (DK Children).
Dunn, Joeming & Dunn, Ben. Laika: The 1st Dog in Space, 1 vol. 2011. (Famous Firsts: Animals Making History Ser.). (ENG., Illus.). 32p. (YA). (gr. 3-6). 28.50 *(978-1-61641-641-6(6))* Magic Wagon.
Early, Sandy. Tell Tanner Tales: We're Adopted! 2012. (ENG.). 21p. (J). pap. 18.95 *(978-1-4327-9028-8(5))* Outskirts Pr., Inc.
Edison, Erin. Favorite Designer Dogs, 1 vol. 2014. (Favorite Designer Dogs Ser.). (ENG.). 24p. (gr. k-1). 159.90 *(978-1-4914-0662-5(3)*, Pebble Plus) Capstone Press of Coughlan Cos.
—You'll Love Chiweenies, 1 vol. 2014. (Favorite Designer Dogs Ser.). (ENG.). 24p. (gr. k-1). 26.65 *(978-1-4914-0567-3(8)*, Pebble Plus) Capstone Press of Coughlan Cos.
—You'll Love Puggles, 1 vol. 2014. (Favorite Designer Dogs Ser.). (ENG.). 24p. (gr. k-1). 26.65 *(978-1-4914-0572-7(4)*, Pebble Plus) Capstone Press of Coughlan Cos.
Eggleton, Jill. Davy D's Dog: 3-in-1 Package. Gibson, Dave, illus. (Sails Literacy Ser.). 24p. (gr. k-18). 57.00 *(978-0-7578-8615-7(9))* Rigby Education.
—Davy D's Dog: 6 Small Books. Gibson, Dave, illus. (Sails Literacy Ser.). 24p. (gr. k-18). 25.00 *(978-0-7578-7728-5(1))* Rigby Education.
—Davy D's Dog: Big Book Only. Gibson, Dave, illus. (Sails Literacy Ser.). 24p. (gr. k-18). 27.00 *(978-0-7578-6198-7(9))* Rigby Education.
Ekberg, Jodi & Lisman, Jaclyn. The Adventures of Cain & Frankie: The Husky Brothers - the Beginning. 2013. 24p. pap. 13.97 *(978-1-62212-529-6(0)*, Strategic Bk. Publishing) Strategic Book Publishing & Rights Agency (SBPRA).
Elora, Grace. Puppies. 2011. (Cute & Cuddly: Baby Animals Ser.). (Illus.). 24p. (gr. k-2). 69.20 *(978-1-4339-6153-3(9))*; (J). lib. bdg. 22.60 *(978-1-4339-4519-9(3))* Stevens, Gareth Publishing LLLP.
Endres, Hollie. Dogs. 2007. (Farm Animals Ser.). (ENG., Illus.). 24p. (J). (gr. k-3). lib. bdg. 25.95 *(978-1-60014-083-9(1))* Bellwether Media.
Entrekin, Allison Weiss. For the Love of Dogs: An A-to-Z Primer for Dog Lovers of All Ages. Anderson, Mark, illus. 2011. (For the Love Of... Ser.). (ENG.). 48p. 16.95 *(978-1-60078-371-5(6))* Triumph Bks.
Fact Atlas: Dogs. 2009. (FACT ATLAS Ser.). 72p. (J). 14.95 *(978-0-8437-1977-2(X))* Hammond World Atlas Corp.
Fahiner, Paul. Dog & Cat. Chambliss, Maxie, illus. 2004. (My First Reader Ser.). (ENG.). 32p. (J). (gr. k-1). pap. 3.95 *(978-0-516-24626-0(7)*, Children's Pr.) Scholastic Library Publishing.
Feldman, Thea. Stella: The Dog with the Big Heart. Danger, Chris, illus. 2015. (Hero Dog Ser.). (ENG.). 32p. (J). (gr. k-2). pap. 3.99 *(978-1-4814-2243-7(X))* Simon & Schuster Children's Publishing.
Fenton, Corinne. Bob the Railway Dog: The True Story of an Adventurous Dog. Mclean, Andrew, illus. 2016. (ENG.). 32p. (J). (gr. k-3). 16.99 *(978-0-7636-8097-8(4))* Candlewick Pr.
Fernandez, Amy. Puppies: A Guide to Caring for Your Puppy. Francais, Isabelle, photos by. 2006. (Complete Care Made Easy Ser.). (ENG., Illus.). 200p. (gr. 3-7). per. 9.95 *(978-1-931993-76-0(9))* i-5 Publishing LLC.
Fetty, Margaret. Miniature Schnauzer: Whiskers. 2010. (Little Dogs Rock! II Ser.). 32p. (YA). (gr. 2-5). lib. bdg. 25.27 *(978-1-936088-20-1(7))* Bearport Publishing Co., Inc.
—Seizure-Alert Dogs. 2009. (Dog Heroes Ser.). (Illus.). 32p. (YA). (gr. 2-5). lib. bdg. 25.27 *(978-1-59716-865-6(3))* Bearport Publishing Co., Inc.
—Yorkshire Terrier: Tiny but Tough. 2009. (Little Dogs Rock! Ser.). (Illus.). 32p. (YA). (gr. 2-5). lib. bdg. 25.27 *(978-1-59716-748-2(7))* Bearport Publishing Co., Inc.
Fiedler, Julie. Bulldogs. (Tough Dogs Ser.). 24p. (gr. 3-4). 2009. 42.50 *(978-1-60854-562-9(8))* 2006. (Illus.). (J). lib. bdg. 22.60 *(978-1-4042-3119-1(6))* Rosen Publishing Group, Inc., The. (PowerKids Pr.).
—Doberman Pinschers. 2006. (Tough Dogs Ser.). (Illus.). 24p. lib. bdg. 22.60 *(978-1-4042-3120-7(X)*, PowerKids Pr.) Rosen Publishing Group, Inc., The.
—Great Danes. (Tough Dogs Ser.). 24p. (gr. 3-4). 2009. 42.50 *(978-1-60854-565-0(2))* 2006. (Illus.). (J). lib. bdg. 22.60 *(978-1-4042-3122-1(6))* Rosen Publishing Group, Inc., The. (PowerKids Pr.).
—Pit Bulls. 2009. (Tough Dogs Ser.). 24p. (gr. 3-4). 42.50 *(978-1-60854-566-7(0)*, PowerKids Pr.) Rosen Publishing Group, Inc., The.
—Rottweilers. (Tough Dogs Ser.). 24p. (gr. 3-4). 2009. 42.50 *(978-1-60854-567-4(9))* 2006. (Illus.). (J). lib. bdg. 22.60 *(978-1-4042-3118-4(8))* Rosen Publishing Group, Inc., The. (PowerKids Pr.).
Fink, Jeri, et al. The Gizmo Tales: Working Dogs. 2004. (Illus.). (J). per. 14.94 *(978-0-9716567-3-4(8))* Book Web Publishing, Limited.
Finne, Stephanie. Golden Retrievers, 1 vol. 2014. (Dogs Set 12 Ser.). (ENG.). 24p. (gr. 3-6). 25.65 *(978-1-62403-675-0(9))* ABDO Publishing Co.
—Old English Sheepdogs, 1 vol. 2014. (Dogs Set 12 Ser.). (ENG.). 24p. (gr. 3-6). 25.65 *(978-1-62403-676-7(7))* ABDO Publishing Co.
—Yorkshire Terriers, 1 vol. 2014. (Dogs Set 12 Ser.). (ENG.). 24p. (gr. 3-6). 25.65 *(978-1-62403-677-4(5))* ABDO Publishing Co.
Fiorella, Christina. My Boy Kyle. 2010. 20p. 13.99 *(978-1-4520-6519-9(5))* AuthorHouse.
Fishman, Jon M. Hero Military Dogs. 2017. (Lightning Bolt Books (tm) — Hero Dogs Ser.). (ENG.). 32p. (J). (gr. 1-3). 7.99 ***(978-1-5124-3648-8(8)***, Lerner Pubns.); 39.99 ***(978-1-5124-2801-8(9)***, Lerner Pubns.); 39.99 ***(978-1-5124-3647-1(X)***, Lerner Pubns.); (Illus.). 26.65 *(978-1-5124-2543-7(5))* Lerner Publishing Group.
Fleischman, Carol. Nadine, My Funny & Trusty Guide Dog, 1 vol. Ford, Stephanie, illus. 2015. 32p. (J). 16.99 *(978-1-4556-1927-6(2))* Pelican Publishing Co., Inc.
Flowers, Pam. Big-Enough Anna. Farnsworth, Bill, illus. 2003. (ENG.). 32p. (J). (gr. -1-18). 15.95 *(978-0-88240-577-3(2))* Graphic Arts Ctr. Publishing Co.
—Big-Enough Anna. Farnsworth, Bill, tr. Farnsworth, Bill, illus. 2003. (ENG.). 32p. (J). pap. 10.99 *(978-0-88240-580-3(2))* Graphic Arts Ctr. Publishing Co.
—Douggie: The Playful Pup Who Became a Sled Dog Hero. Zyle, Jon Van, illus. 2008. (ENG.). 32p. (J). (gr. k-5). 15.95 *(978-0-88240-654-1(X)*, Alaska Northwest Bks.) Graphic Arts Ctr. Publishing Co.
—Douggie: The Playful Pup Who Became a Sled Dog Hero. Van Zyle, Jon, illus. 2008. (ENG.). 32p. (J). (gr. k-5). pap. 10.99 *(978-0-88240-655-8(8)*, Alaska Northwest Bks.) Graphic Arts Ctr. Publishing Co.
—Ordinary Dogs, Extraordinary Friendships: Stories of Loyalty, Courage, & Compassion. Baskin, Jason, illus. 2013. (ENG.). 144p. (YA). (gr. 5). 23.99 *(978-0-88240-978-8(6))*; pap. 12.99 *(978-0-88240-916-0(6))* Graphic Arts Ctr. Publishing Co. (Alaska Northwest Bks.).
Flowers, Pam & Farnsworth, Bill. Ellie's Long Walk: The True Story of Two Friends on the Appalachian Trail. 2012. (ENG., Illus.). 32p. (J). (gr. -1-3). pap. 11.99 *(978-0-88240-885-9(2)*, West Winds Pr.) Graphic Arts Ctr. Publishing Co.
Foran, Jill. Caring for Your Dog. 2005. (Caring for Your Pet Ser.). (Illus.). 32p. (J). (gr. 2-5). lib. bdg. 26.00 *(978-1-59036-033-0(8))* Weigl Pubs., Inc.
—Caring for Your Dog. Marshall, Diana & Nault, Jennifer, eds. 2003. (Caring for Your Pet Ser.). (Illus.). 32p. (J). pap. 9.95 *(978-1-59036-063-7(X))* Weigl Pubs., Inc.

—Dog. 2008. (My Pet Ser.). (Illus.). 32p. (J). (gr. 3-5). pap. 9.95 *(978-1-59036-903-6(3))*; lib. bdg. 26.00 *(978-1-59036-902-9(5))* Weigl Pubs., Inc.
Foster, Dara. Now You See It! Pupstyle Red Carpet Pups. Foster, Dara, photos by. 2013. (ENG., Illus.). 64p. (J). (gr. 2-5). pap. 5.99 *(978-0-545-53245-7(0))* Math Solutions.
Frances, Ethel & Miller, Marcia. Tales from a Tail Wagging Dog. Starr, Joyce, ed. 2013. 102p. pap. 12.70 *(978-0-9882394-1-8(8))* Dr. Joyce STARR Publishing.
Friesen-Wood, Judy. Aloha Cheerio. 2011. 24p. pap. 12.99 *(978-1-4634-3118-1(X))* AuthorHouse.
Frisch, Joy. Bulldogs. 2003. (Dog Breeds Ser.). 24p. (J). lib. bdg. 21.35 *(978-1-58340-316-7(7))* Black Rabbit Bks.
—Retrievers. 2003. (Dog Breeds Ser.). 24p. (J). lib. bdg. 21.35 *(978-1-58340-312-9(4))* Black Rabbit Bks.
Furfur, Christopher. How Should I Care for My Doggy? 2008. (Illus.). 64p. (J). 15.95 *(978-0-9742845-6-9(4))* Mystic Ridge Bks.
Furstinger, Nancy. Lhasa Apsos, 1 vol. 2006. (Dogs Set 6 Ser.). (ENG., Illus.). 24p. (J). (gr. 2-5). 25.65 *(978-1-59679-271-5(X))* ABDO Publishing Co.
—Maltese, 1 vol. 2006. (Dogs Set 6 Ser.). (ENG.). 24p. (J). (gr. 2-5). 25.65 *(978-1-59679-272-2(8))* ABDO Publishing Co.
—Mastiffs, 1 vol. 2006. (Dogs Set 6 Ser.). (ENG., Illus.). 24p. (J). (gr. 2-5). 25.65 *(978-1-59679-273-9(6))* ABDO Publishing Co.
—Miniature Schnauzers, 1 vol. 2006. (Dogs Set 6 Ser.). (ENG., Illus.). 24p. (J). (gr. 2-5). 25.65 *(978-1-59679-274-6(4))* ABDO Publishing Co.
—Paws of Courage: True Tales of Heroic Dogs That Protect & Serve. 2016. (ENG., Illus.). 160p. (J). (gr. 5). 12.99 *(978-1-4263-2377-5(8)*, National Geographic Children's Bks.) National Geographic Society.
—Pointers, 1 vol. 2006. (Dogs Set 6 Ser.). (ENG., Illus.). 24p. (J). (gr. 2-5). 25.65 *(978-1-59679-275-3(2))* ABDO Publishing Co.
Gabe: The Dog Who Sniffs Out Danger. 2014. (Hero Dog Ser.). (ENG., Illus.). 32p. (J). (gr. k-2). pap. 3.99 *(978-1-4814-2237-6(5)*, Simon Spotlight) Simon Spotlight.
Gagne, Tammy. Bulldogs, Poodles, Dalmatians, & Other Non-Sporting Dogs. 2016. (Dog Encyclopedias Ser.). (ENG., Illus.). 32p. (gr. 3-4). lib. bdg. 27.99 *(978-1-5157-0299-3(5))* Capstone Press of Coughlan Cos.
—Care for a Wolfdog. 2009. (How to Convince Your Parents You Can ... Ser.). 32p. (J). (gr. 1-4). 25.70 *(978-1-58415-796-0(8))* Mitchell Lane Pubs., Inc.
—Chihuahuas, Pomeranians, & Other Toy Dogs. 2016. (Dog Encyclopedias Ser.). (ENG., Illus.). 32p. (gr. 3-4). lib. bdg. 27.99 *(978-1-5157-0300-6(2))* Capstone Press of Coughlan Cos.
—Collies, Corgis, & Other Herding Dogs. 2016. (Dog Encyclopedias Ser.). (ENG., Illus.). 32p. (gr. 3-4). lib. bdg. 27.99 *(978-1-5157-0301-3(0))* Capstone Press of Coughlan Cos.
—Dog Care: Feeding Your Pup a Healthy Diet & Other Dog Care Tips, 1 vol. 2011. (Dog Ownership Ser.). (ENG.). 32p. (gr. 3-4). lib. bdg. 27.99 *(978-1-4296-6527-8(0)*, Edge Bks.) Capstone Press of Coughlan Cos.
—The Dog Encyclopedia for Kids. 2017. (ENG.). 208p. (gr. 3-4). pap. 14.95 *(978-1-62370-694-4(7))* Capstone Young Readers of Coughlan Cos.
—Dog Encyclopedias. 2016. (Dog Encyclopedias Ser.). (ENG.). 32p. (gr. 3-4). lib. bdg. 195.93 *(978-1-5157-0339-6(8)*, Edge Bks.) Capstone Press of Coughlan Cos.
—Foxhounds, Coonhounds, & Other Hound Breeds. 2016. (Dog Encyclopedias Ser.). (ENG., Illus.). 32p. (gr. 3-4). lib. bdg. 27.99 *(978-1-5157-0302-0(9))* Capstone Press of Coughlan Cos.
—Huskies, Mastiffs, & Other Working Dogs. 2016. (Dog Encyclopedias Ser.). (ENG., Illus.). 32p. (gr. 3-4). lib. bdg. 27.99 *(978-1-5157-0303-7(7))* Capstone Press of Coughlan Cos.
—Military Dogs, 1 vol. 2013. (Dogs on the Job Ser.). (ENG.). 32p. (gr. 3-4). 27.99 *(978-1-4765-0130-7(0)*, Edge Bks.) Capstone Press of Coughlan Cos.
—Pointers: Loyal Hunting Companions, 1 vol. 2013. (Hunting Dogs Ser.). (ENG., Illus.). 32p. (gr. 3-4). 7.95 *(978-1-62065-935-9(2))*; lib. bdg. 27.99 *(978-1-4296-9908-2(6))* Capstone Press of Coughlan Cos.
—Retrievers: Loyal Hunting Companions, 1 vol. 2013. (Hunting Dogs Ser.). (ENG.). 32p. (gr. 3-4). 7.95 *(978-1-62065-936-6(0))*; lib. bdg. 27.99 *(978-1-4296-9909-9(4))* Capstone Press of Coughlan Cos.
—Spaniels: Loyal Hunting Companions, 1 vol. 2013. (Hunting Dogs Ser.). (ENG., Illus.). 32p. (gr. 3-4). 7.95 *(978-1-62065-938-0(7))*; lib. bdg. 27.99 *(978-1-4296-9907-5(8))* Capstone Press of Coughlan Cos.
—Spaniels, Retrievers, & Other Sporting Dogs. 2016. (Dog Encyclopedias Ser.). (ENG., Illus.). 32p. (gr. 3-4). lib. bdg. 27.99 *(978-1-5157-0305-1(3))* Capstone Press of Coughlan Cos.
—West Highlands, Scotties, & Other Terriers. 2016. (Dog Encyclopedias Ser.). (ENG., Illus.). 32p. (gr. 3-4). lib. bdg. 27.99 *(978-1-5157-0304-4(5))* Capstone Press of Coughlan Cos.
Gagne, Tammy, et al. Hunting Dogs: Loyal Hunting Companions. 2013. (Hunting Dogs Ser.). (ENG.). 32p. (gr. 3-4). lib. bdg. 167.94 *(978-1-4296-9910-5(8)*, Edge Bks.) Capstone Press of Coughlan Cos.
Gaines, Ann. Kids Top 10 Pet Dogs. 2015. (American Humane Association Top 10 Pets for Kids Ser.). 48p. (J). (gr. 3-4). 25.27 *(978-0-7660-6635-9(5))* Enslow Pubs., Inc.
Gaines, Ann Graham. Kids Top 10 Pet Dogs. 2015. (American Humane Association Top 10 Pets for Kids Ser.). 48p. (J). (gr. 3-4). pap. 8.95 *(978-0-7660-6636-6(3)*, Enslow Elementary) Enslow Pubs., Inc.
—Top 10 Dogs for Kids. 2008. (Top Pets for Kids with American Humane Ser.). (Illus.). 48p. (J). (gr. 2-5). lib. bdg. 25.27 *(978-0-7660-3070-1(9))* Enslow Pubs., Inc.
Gallina, Danielle. Dear God, Are There Any Flies in Heaven? Foy, Denis, illus. 2013. (ENG.). (J). 15.98 *(978-1-62086-380-0(4))* Mascot Bks., Inc.
Ganeri, Anita. Ruff's Guide to Caring for Your Dog, 1 vol. Peterson, Rick, illus. 2013. (Pets' Guides). (ENG.). 32p. (gr. 1-3). pap. 8.29 *(978-1-4329-7138-0(7))*; lib. bdg. 27.32 *(978-1-4329-7131-1(X))* Heinemann-Raintree. (Heinemann First Library).
Gardeski, Christina Mia. Dogs: Questions & Answers. 2016. (Pet Questions & Answers Ser.). (ENG., Illus.). 24p. (gr. k-1). lib. bdg. 26.65 *(978-1-5157-0355-6(X)*, Pebble Plus) Capstone Press of Coughlan Cos.
Gardner, Jane P. African Wild Dogs. 2013. (Wild Canine Pups Ser.). 24p. (J). (gr. -1-3). lib. bdg. 21.32 *(978-1-61772-932-4(9))* Bearport Publishing Co., Inc.
George, Charles & George, Linda. Boxer. 2010. (J). 26.00 *(978-0-531-23240-8(9))* Scholastic Library Publishing.
—Labrador Retriever. 2010. (J). 26.00 *(978-0-531-23244-6(1))* Scholastic Library Publishing.
—Miniature Schnauzer. 2010. (J). 26.00 *(978-0-531-23245-3(X))* Scholastic Library Publishing.
—Shih Tzu. 2010. (J). 26.00 *(978-0-531-23246-0(8))* Scholastic Library Publishing.
George, Jean Craighead. How to Talk to Your Dog. Truesdell, Sue & Meisel, Paul, illus. 2003. (ENG.). 40p. (J). (gr. 1-4). pap. 6.99 *(978-0-06-000623-5(4))* HarperCollins Pubs.
Gerry, Lisa M. Puppy Love: True Stories of Doggie Devotion. 2015. (ENG., Illus.). 160p. (J). (gr. 5). 12.99 *(978-1-4263-1867-2(7)*, National Geographic Children's Bks.) National Geographic Society.
Gersten, Dan, creator. Ask Curtis: Dog-Sense Advice from Curtis the Dog, 1. 2005. (Illus.). 146p. per. *(978-0-9766846-0-2(8))* Dogwalk Pr.
Getting Lucky. 2003. (J). lib. bdg. 25.00 *(978-0-9747527-0-9(3))* Nicoll Creations.
Ghigna, Charles. A Parade of Puppies, 1 vol. Bridgeman, Kristi, illus. 2016. (ENG.). 26p. (J). (gr. -1-k). bds. 9.95 *(978-1-4598-0963-5(7))* Orca Bk. Pubs. USA.
Gilbert, H. K. Reporting for Duty: A Day at the White House. 2009. 50p. pap. 9.95 *(978-1-4401-5686-1(7))* iUniverse, Inc.
Gilkerson, Patricia. My Adventure with Dogs. 2009. (ENG.). 44p. (J). 8.99 *(978-1-59092-451-8(7))* Blue Forge Pr.
Gill, Shelley. Alaska's Dog Heroes: True Stories of Remarkable Canines. James, Robin, illus. 2014. (Paws IV Ser.). (ENG.). 32p. (J). (gr. 1-4). pap. 10.99 *(978-1-57061-909-0(3)*, Little Bigfoot) Sasquatch Bks.
—Gabe. Scheff, Marc, illus. 2016. (ENG.). 64p. (J). (gr. 3-7). lib. bdg. 12.95 *(978-1-57091-354-9(4))* Charlesbridge Publishing, Inc.
Gish, Melissa. Living Wild: Prairie Dogs. 2017. (Living Wild Ser.). (ENG.). 48p. (J). (gr. 5-7). pap. 12.00 ***(978-1-62832-436-5(8)***, Creative Paperbacks) Creative Co., The.
Glaser, Rebecca. Puppies Chase. 2017. (Amicus Ink Board Bks.). (ENG., Illus.). 14p. (J). (gr. -1 — 1). bds. 7.99 ***(978-1-68152-196-1(2))*** Amicus.
Glover, A. Libro de Pegatinas Perros. 2004. (Spotter's Guides Sticker Bks.).Tr. of Dogs Sticker Book. (SPA., Illus.). 24p. (J). (gr. 2-18). pap. 7.95 *(978-0-7460-3643-3(4))* EDC Publishing.
Glover, Harry. Dogs. 2004. (Spotter's Guides). 64p. (J). pap. 5.95 *(978-0-7945-0620-9(8))* EDC Publishing.
Goldish, Meish. Baghdad Pups. 2011. (Dog Heroes Ser.). (Illus.). 32p. (J). (gr. 2-5). lib. bdg. 25.27 *(978-1-61772-150-2(6)*, 1321528) Bearport Publishing Co., Inc.
—Brave Hearts. 2015. (Dog Heroes Ser.). (ENG., Illus.). 32p. (J). (gr. 2-7). lib. bdg. 26.60 *(978-1-62724-516-6(2))* Bearport Publishing Co., Inc.
—Disabled Dogs. 2013. (Dog Heroes Ser.). 32p. (J). (gr. 2-7). lib. bdg. 25.27 *(978-1-61772-697-2(4))* Bearport Publishing Co., Inc.
—Dogs. 2007. (Smart Animals! Ser.). (Illus.). 32p. (J). (gr. 2-5). lib. bdg. 25.27 *(978-1-59716-368-2(6))* Bearport Publishing Co., Inc.
—Ground Zero Dogs. 2012. (Dog Heroes Ser.). 32p. (J). (gr. 2-7). lib. bdg. 25.27 *(978-1-61772-576-0(5))* Bearport Publishing Co., Inc.
—Hollywood Dogs. 2007. (Dog Heroes Ser.). (Illus.). 32p. (J). (gr. 2-5). lib. bdg. 25.27 *(978-1-59716-404-7(6)*, 1265962) Bearport Publishing Co., Inc.
—K-9 Cops. 2016. (Police: Search & Rescue! Ser.). (ENG., Illus.). 32p. (J). (gr. 2-7). 19.95 *(978-1-943553-13-6(0))* Bearport Publishing Co., Inc.
—Pest-Sniffing Dogs. 2012. (Dog Heroes Ser.). 32p. (J). (gr. 2-7). lib. bdg. 25.27 *(978-1-61772-454-1(8))* Bearport Publishing Co., Inc.
—Prison Puppies. 2011. (Dog Heroes Ser.). 32p. (YA). (gr. 2-5). lib. bdg. 25.27 *(978-1-61772-151-9(4))* Bearport Publishing Co., Inc.
—R. E. A. D. Dogs. 2015. (Dog Heroes Ser.). (ENG.). 32p. (J). (gr. 2-7). lib. bdg. 26.60 *(978-1-62724-517-3(0))* Bearport Publishing Co., Inc.
—Rottweiler: Super Courageous. 2011. (Big Dogs Rule! Ser.). 32p. (YA). (gr. 2-5). lib. bdg. 25.27 *(978-1-61772-298-1(7))* Bearport Publishing Co., Inc.
—Science Dogs. 2013. (Dog Heroes Ser.). 32p. (J). (gr. 2-7). lib. bdg. 25.27 *(978-1-61772-887-7(X))* Bearport Publishing Co., Inc.
—Shelter Dogs. 2013. (Dog Heroes Ser.). 32p. (J). (gr. 2-7). lib. bdg. 25.27 *(978-1-61772-886-0(1))* Bearport Publishing Co., Inc.
—Skydiving Dogs. 2014. (Dog Heroes Ser.). 32p. (J). (gr. 2-7). lib. bdg. 25.27 *(978-1-62724-087-1(X))* Bearport Publishing Co., Inc.
—Toy Fox Terrier: America's Dog. 2010. (Little Dogs Rock! II Ser.). 32p. (YA). (gr. 2-5). lib. bdg. 25.27 *(978-1-936088-18-8(5))* Bearport Publishing Co., Inc.
—Toy Poodle: Oodles of Fun. 2009. (Little Dogs Rock! Ser.). (Illus.). 32p. (YA). (gr. 2-5). lib. bdg. 25.27 *(978-1-59716-746-8(0))* Bearport Publishing Co., Inc.
Goodbody, Slim & Burstein, John. Dogs. McGinnis, Ben, illus. 2008. (Slim Goodbody's Inside Guide to Pets Ser.). 32p. (gr. 2-6). lib. bdg. 26.00 *(978-0-8368-8955-0(X)*, Gareth Stevens Learning Library) Stevens, Gareth Publishing LLLP.
Gordon, Bob. Touch & Feel Noisy Puppy. 2006. (Touch & Feel Noisy Ser.). (Illus.). 10p. (gr. -1). per., bds. *(978-1-84610-285-1(5))* Make Believe Ideas.
Gorrell, Gena K. Working Like a Dog: The Story of Working Dogs Through History. 2003. (ENG., Illus.). 160p. (J). (gr. 5-18). pap. 16.95 *(978-0-88776-589-6(0)*, Tundra Bks.) Tundra Bks. CAN. Dist: Penguin Random Hse. LLC.
Graffito Books Staff & Helm, Zebedee. Dogs of the World: Ultimate Guide Books to Everything! Helm, Zebedee, illus. 2012. (ENG., Illus.). 32p. (J). (gr. k-2). 14.99 *(978-0-9560284-3-3(8))* Korero Books LLP GBR. Dist: Independent Pubs. Group.
Graubart, Norman D. Mi Perro / My Dog, 1 vol., 1. Green, Christina, ed. 2014. (¡Las Mascotas Son Geniales! / Pets Are Awesome! Ser.). (SPA & BYN.). 24p. (J). (gr. k-2). 23.60 *(978-1-4777-3301-1(9)*, PowerKids Pr.) Rosen Publishing Group, Inc., The.
—My Dog, 1 vol., 1. 2014. (Pets Are Awesome! Ser.). (ENG.). 24p. (J). (gr. k-2). 23.60 *(978-1-4777-2864-2(3)*, PowerKids Pr.) Rosen Publishing Group, Inc., The.
Gray, Susan H. Animals Helping to Detect Diseases. 2015. (ENG.). 48p. (J). pap. 6.95 *(978-0-531-21288-2(2)*, Orchard Bks.) Scholastic Library Publishing.
—Bulldogs. 2008. (Domestic Dogs Ser.). (ENG., Illus.). 32p. (J). (gr. 2-5). 28.50 *(978-1-59296-962-3(3)*, 200137) Child's World, Inc., The.
—Pomeranians. 2008. (Domestic Dogs Ser.). (ENG., Illus.). 32p. (J). (gr. 2-5). 28.50 *(978-1-59296-966-1(6)*, 200144) Child's World, Inc., The.
—Scottish Terriers. 2008. (Domestic Dogs Ser.). (ENG., Illus.). 32p. (J). (gr. 2-5). 28.50 *(978-1-59296-968-5(2)*, 200147) Child's World, Inc., The.
Gray, Susan Heinrichs. Basset Hounds. 2016. (J). *(978-1-4896-4579-1(9))* Weigl Pubs., Inc.
—Border Collies. 2016. (J). *(978-1-4896-4583-8(7))* Weigl Pubs., Inc.
—Bulldogs. 2016. (J). *(978-1-4896-4585-2(3))* Weigl Pubs., Inc.
—Cocker Spaniels. 2016. (J). *(978-1-4896-4587-6(X))* Weigl Pubs., Inc.
—Pomeranians. 2016. (J). *(978-1-4896-4593-7(4))* Weigl Pubs., Inc.
—Pugs. 2016. (J). *(978-1-4896-4595-1(0))* Weigl Pubs., Inc.
—Rottweilers. 2016. (J). *(978-1-4896-4597-5(7))* Weigl Pubs., Inc.
—Scottish Terriers. 2016. (J). *(978-1-4896-4599-9(3))* Weigl Pubs., Inc.
—Yorkshire Terriers. 2016. (J). *(978-1-4896-4601-9(9))* Weigl Pubs., Inc.
Gray, Susan Heinrichs & Gray, Susan H. Basset Hounds. 2007. (Domestic Dogs Ser.). (ENG., Illus.). 32p. (J). (gr. 2-5). 28.50 *(978-1-59296-771-1(X)*, 200134) Child's World, Inc., The.
—Cocker Spaniels. 2008. (Domestic Dogs Ser.). (ENG., Illus.). 32p. (J). (gr. 2-5). 28.50 *(978-1-59296-963-0(1)*, 200139) Child's World, Inc., The.
—Pugs. 2007. (Domestic Dogs Ser.). (ENG., Illus.). 32p. (J). (gr. 2-5). 28.50 *(978-1-59296-776-6(0)*, 200145) Child's World, Inc., The.
—Rottweilers. 2008. (Domestic Dogs Ser.). (ENG., Illus.). 32p. (J). (gr. 2-5). 28.50 *(978-1-59296-967-8(4)*, 200146) Child's World, Inc., The.
—Yorkshire Terriers. 2007. (Domestic Dogs Ser.). (ENG., Illus.). 32p. (J). (gr. 2-5). 28.50 *(978-1-59296-778-0(7)*, 200149) Child's World, Inc., The.
Gray, Susan Heinrichs & Koran, Maria. Golden Retrievers. 2016. (J). ***(978-1-4896-5605-6(7))*** Weigl Pubs., Inc.
—Labradors. 2016. (J). ***(978-1-4896-5611-7(1))*** Weigl Pubs., Inc.
—Shih Tzus. 2016. (J). ***(978-1-4896-5608-7(1))*** Weigl Pubs., Inc.
Green, Jen. Inheritance of Traits: Why Is My Dog Bigger Than Your Dog?, 1 vol. 2014. (Show Me Science Ser.). (ENG.). 32p. (gr. 3-5). lib. bdg. 30.65 *(978-1-4329-8747-3(X)*, Raintree Perspectives) Heinemann-Raintree.
Green, John. Dogs to Paint or Color. 2008. (Dover Art Coloring Book Ser.). (ENG., Illus.). 48p. (gr. 3-5). pap. 5.99 *(978-0-486-46541-8(1))* Dover Pubns., Inc.
Green, Sara. Basset Hounds. 2011. (Dog Breeds Ser.). (ENG., Illus.). 24p. (J). (gr. 2-5). lib. bdg. 25.95 *(978-1-60014-564-3(7)*, Blastoff! Readers) Bellwether Media.
—Bomb-Sniffing Dogs. 2013. (Dogs to the Rescue! Ser.). (ENG., Illus.). 24p. (J). (gr. 3-8). lib. bdg. 25.95 *(978-1-60014-954-2(5)*, Pilot Bks.) Bellwether Media.
—Border Collies. 2011. (Dog Breeds Ser.). (ENG., Illus.). 24p. (J). (gr. 2-5). lib. bdg. 25.95 *(978-1-60014-565-0(5)*, Blastoff! Readers) Bellwether Media.
—Boxers. 2008. (Dog Breeds Ser.). (ENG., Illus.). 24p. (J). (gr. 2-5). lib. bdg. 25.95 *(978-1-60014-219-2(2))* Bellwether Media.
—Bulldogs. 2010. (Dog Breeds Ser.). (ENG., Illus.). 24p. (J). (gr. 2-5). lib. bdg. 25.95 *(978-1-60014-297-0(4))* Bellwether Media.
—Chihuahuas. 2010. (Dog Breeds Ser.). (ENG., Illus.). 24p. (J). (gr. 2-5). lib. bdg. 25.95 *(978-1-60014-298-7(2))* Bellwether Media.
—Cocker Spaniels. 2010. (Dog Breeds Ser.). (ENG., Illus.). 24p. (J). (gr. 2-5). lib. bdg. 25.95 *(978-1-60014-457-8(8)*, Blastoff! Readers) Bellwether Media.
—Dachshunds. 2008. (Dog Breeds Ser.). (ENG., Illus.). 24p. (J). (gr. 2-5). lib. bdg. 25.95 *(978-1-60014-218-5(4))* Bellwether Media.
—Dalmatians. 2010. (Dog Breeds Ser.). (ENG., Illus.). 24p. (J). (gr. 2-5). lib. bdg. 25.95 *(978-1-60014-458-5(6))* Bellwether Media.
—Doberman Pinschers. 2010. (Dog Breeds Ser.). (ENG., Illus.). 24p. (J). (gr. 2-5). lib. bdg. 25.95 *(978-1-60014-459-2(4)*, Blastoff! Readers) Bellwether Media.
—Fire Dogs. 2013. (Dogs to the Rescue! Ser.). (ENG., Illus.). 24p. (J). (gr. 3-8). lib. bdg. 25.95 *(978-1-60014-953-5(7)*, Pilot Bks.) Bellwether Media.
—Military Dogs. 2013. (Dogs to the Rescue! Ser.). (ENG., Illus.). 24p. (J). (gr. 3-8). lib. bdg. 25.95 *(978-1-60014-956-6(1)*, Pilot Bks.) Bellwether Media.
—Pomeranians. 2011. (Dog Breeds Ser.). (ENG., Illus.). 24p. (J). (gr. 2-5). lib. bdg. 25.95 *(978-1-60014-567-4(1)*, Blastoff! Readers) Bellwether Media.
—Rottweilers. 2010. (Dog Breeds Ser.). (ENG., Illus.). 24p. (J). (gr. 2-5). lib. bdg. 25.95 *(978-1-60014-460-8(8)*, Blastoff! Readers) Bellwether Media.
—Service Dogs. 2013. (Dogs to the Rescue! Ser.). (ENG., Illus.). 24p. (J). (gr. 3-8). lib. bdg. 25.95 *(978-1-60014-958-0(8)*, Pilot Bks.) Bellwether Media.
—Snow Search Dogs. 2013. (Dogs to the Rescue! Ser.). (ENG., Illus.). 24p. (J). (gr. 3-8). lib. bdg. 25.95 *(978-1-60014-959-7(6)*, Pilot Bks.) Bellwether Media.
—Therapy Dogs. 2013. (Dogs to the Rescue! Ser.). (ENG., Illus.). 24p. (J). (gr. 3-8). lib. bdg. 25.95 *(978-1-60014-960-3(X)*, Pilot Bks.) Bellwether Media.
—Water Rescue Dogs. 2013. (Dogs to the Rescue! Ser.). (ENG., Illus.). 24p. (J). (gr. 3-8). lib. bdg. 25.95 *(978-1-60014-961-0(8)*, Pilot Bks.) Bellwether Media.
—West Highland White Terriers. 2010. (Dog Breeds Ser.). (ENG., Illus.). 24p. (J). (gr. 2-5). lib. bdg. 25.95 *(978-1-60014-300-7(8))* Bellwether Media.
—Wilderness Search Dogs. 2013. (Dogs to the Rescue! Ser.). (ENG., Illus.). 24p. (J). (gr. 3-8). lib. bdg. 25.95 *(978-1-60014-962-7(6)*, Pilot Bks.) Bellwether Media.
—Yorkshire Terriers. 2008. (Dog Breeds Ser.). (ENG., Illus.). 24p. (J). (gr. 2-5). lib. bdg. 25.95 *(978-1-60014-214-7(1))* Bellwether Media.
Greenberg, Daniel A. Wilderness Search Dogs. 2005. (Dog Heroes Ser.). (Illus.). 32p. (J). lib. bdg. 25.27 *(978-1-59716-019-3(9))* Bearport Publishing Co., Inc.
Gregory, Josh. Working Dogs. 2013. (Nature's Children Ser.). (ENG.). 48p. (J). 28.00 *(978-0-531-20984-4(9))*; pap. 6.95 *(978-0-531-24310-7(9))* Scholastic Library Publishing. (Children's Pr.).
Griner, Jack. Best Paw Forward. 2013. 24p. pap. 12.60 *(978-1-4669-9477-5(0))* Trafford Publishing.
Grogan, John. Marley: A Dog Like No Other. (J). 2008. (ENG., Illus.). 208p. (gr. 3-7). pap. 6.99 *(978-0-06-124035-5(4)*, Collins) 2007. (ENG., Illus.). 192p. (gr. 3-7). 16.99 *(978-0-06-124033-1(8))* 2008. 208p. pap. 6.99 *(978-0-06-168608-5(5)*, Harper Entertainment) HarperCollins Pubs.
—Sit, Marley, Sit! Cowdrey, Richard & Lyon, Tammie, illus. 2010. (Marley Ser.). (ENG.). 24p. (J). (gr. -1-2). pap. 3.99 *(978-0-06-185380-7(1)*, HarperFestival) HarperCollins Pubs.
Guillain, Charlotte. Dogs, 1 vol. 2013. (Animal Abilities Ser.). (ENG.). 32p. (gr. 2-4). 29.99 *(978-1-4109-5237-0(1))*; pap. 8.95 *(978-1-4109-5244-8(4))* Heinemann-Raintree. (Raintree Perspectives).
Gunderson, Megan M. Australian Shepherds, 1 vol. 2013. (Dogs Set 10 Ser.). (ENG.). 24p. (J). (gr. 3-6). lib. bdg. 25.65 *(978-1-61783-588-9(9)*, Checkerboard Library) ABDO Publishing Co.
—Scottish Deerhounds, 1 vol. 2013. (Dogs Set 10 Ser.). (ENG.). 24p. (J). (gr. 3-6). lib. bdg. 25.65 *(978-1-61783-592-6(7)*, Checkerboard Library) ABDO Publishing Co.
—Whippets, 1 vol. 2013. (Dogs Set 10 Ser.). (ENG.). 24p. (J). (gr. 3-6). lib. bdg. 25.65 *(978-1-61783-593-3(5)*, Checkerboard Library) ABDO Publishing Co.
Gunzi, Christiane. Let's Count Noisy Puppies. 2015. (ENG., Illus.). 10p. (J). 9.99 *(978-1-905503-18-6(0))* Award Pubns. Ltd. GBR. Dist: Parkwest Pubns., Inc.
Halls, Kelly Milner. Wild Dogs: Past & Present. 2005. (ENG., Illus.). 64p. (gr. 6-12). lib. bdg. 18.95 *(978-1-58196-027-3(1)*, Darby Creek) Lerner Publishing Group.
Hamilton, S. L. Dogs. 2013. (Xtreme Pets Ser.). (Illus.). 32p. (J). (gr. 3-9). lib. bdg. 27.07 *(978-1-61783-972-6(8)*, Abdo & Daughters) ABDO Publishing Co.
Hammer, Sheila. Chorkie: A Cross Between a Chihuahua & a Yorkshire Terrier, 1 vol. 2012. (Designer Dogs Ser.). (ENG., Illus.). 32p. (gr. 3-4). lib. bdg. 27.99 *(978-1-4296-7669-4(8)*, Snap Bks.) Capstone Press of Coughlan Cos.
Hammond, Charmaine. Toby, the Pet Therapy Dog, & His Hospital Friends. Prevac, Rose Anne, illus. 2011. (ENG.). 36p. (J). pap. 12.99 *(978-0-9836045-0-1(9)*, Kendahl Hse. Pr.) Youngs, Bettie Bks.
—Toby, the Pet Therapy Dog, Says Be a Buddy, Not a Bully. 2013. (ENG., Illus.). 34p. (J). pap. 12.99 *(978-0-9836045-4-9(1))* Youngs, Bettie Bks.
—Toby, the Pet Therapy Dog, Says Be a Buddy Not a Bully. Prevec, Rose Anne, illus. 2013. (ENG.). (J). pap. 12.95 *(978-0-9836045-5-6(X)*, Kendahl Hse. Pr.) Youngs, Bettie Bks.
Hansen, Jennifer. Lucy's Grade School Adventure. Marsden, Ken, illus. 2006. (J). *(978-0-9774822-7-6(8))* Crosam Pr.
Hanson, Anders. Bold Boxers, 1 vol. Doucet, Bob, illus. 2009. (Dog Daze Ser.). (ENG.). 24p. 25.65 *(978-1-60453-615-7(2)*, Super SandCastle) ABDO Publishing Co.
—Shaggy Shih Tzus, 1 vol. Doucet, Bob, illus. 2009. (Dog Daze Ser.). (ENG.). 24p. 25.65 *(978-1-60453-619-5(5)*, Super SandCastle) ABDO Publishing Co.
Harpan, Gaile. True Puppy Tails. 2010. 24p. pap. 12.95 *(978-1-936343-26-3(6))* Peppertree Pr., The.
Harries, Brigitte. Puppies: Keeping & Caring for Your Pet. 2013. (Keeping & Caring for Your Pet Ser.). 72p. (J). lib. bdg. 29.27 *(978-0-7660-4187-5(5))*; (gr. 6-12). pap. 8.95 *(978-1-4644-0305-7(8))* Enslow Pubs., Inc.
Hart, Anne. Dogs with Careers: Ten Happy-Ending Stories of Purpose & Passion. 2007. 348p. per. 19.95 *(978-0-595-47474-5(8)*, ASJA Pr.) iUniverse, Inc.
Hart, Joyce. Big Dogs. 2007. (Great Pets Ser.). (Illus.). 48p. (J). (gr. 2-4). lib. bdg. 29.93 *(978-0-7614-2707-0(4)*, Benchmark Bks.) Marshall Cavendish Corp.
—Small Dogs. 2008. (Great Pets Ser.). 48p. (YA). (gr. 3-18). lib. bdg. 29.93 *(978-0-7614-2995-1(6)*, Benchmark Bks.) Marshall Cavendish Corp.
Haskins, Lori. Sled Dogs. 2006. (Dog Heroes Ser.). (Illus.). 32p. (J). (gr. 2-5). lib. bdg. 25.27 *(978-1-59716-171-8(3)*, 1251393) Bearport Publishing Co., Inc.
Haworth, Dianne. Paddy the Wanderer. (Illus.). 2008. 240p. *(978-1-86950-712-1(6))* 2007. 176p. *(978-1-86950-625-4(1))* HarperCollins Pubs. Australia.
Haydel-Vicidomina, Lisa. Run Ru Run: A Story of the Thin, Pink-Chested Dog. 2011. 20p. pap. 24.95 *(978-1-4626-4324-0(8))* America Star Bks.
Heit Schwaeber, Barbie. Alphabet of Dogs. 2011. (ENG.). 40p. (J). 9.95 *(978-1-60727-198-7(2))* Soundprints.
Helbrough, Emma. Dogs. Donaera, Patrizia & Mayer, Uwe, illus. 2006. (Beginners Nature: Level 1 Ser.). 32p. (J). (gr. k-2). 4.99 *(978-0-7945-1395-5(6))*; (gr. 1). lib. bdg. 12.99 *(978-1-58086-943-0(2))* EDC Publishing. (Usborne).
Helms, Jo. Grizz's Story-A Greater Courage: A Dog's Journey. ltd. ed. 2003. 86p. 14.95 *(978-0-9745319-0-8(1))* Helms, Jo Publishing.

C
D

Heneghan, Judith. Love Your Dog. 2013. (Your Perfect Pet Ser.). (ENG., Illus.). 32p. (gr. k-5). 25.25 *(978-1-4777-0185-0(0))*; pap. 10.00 *(978-1-4777-0198-0(2))* Windmill Bks.

Hengel, Katherine. Brainy Brittanys, 1 vol. Doucet, Bob, illus. 2009. (Dog Daze Ser.). (ENG.). 24p. 25.65 *(978-1-60453-616-4(0)*, Super SandCastle) ABDO Publishing Co.

—Burly Bulldogs, 1 vol. Doucet, Bob, illus. 2010. (Super SandCastle Ser.). (ENG.). 24p. 25.65 *(978-1-61613-376-4(7)*, Super SandCastle) ABDO Publishing Co.

—Proud Portuguese Water Dogs, 1 vol. Doucet, Bob, illus. 2010. (Super SandCastle Ser.). (ENG.). 24p. 25.65 *(978-1-61613-380-1(5)*, Super SandCastle) ABDO Publishing Co.

Heos, Bridget. Do You Really Want a Dog? Longhi, Katya, illus. 2013. (Do You Really Want a Pet? Ser.). (ENG.). 24p. (gr. 1-4). 27.10 *(978-1-60753-204-0(2))* Amicus Publishing.

Hieronymus, Carol Fegley. Blackie & Her Kittens: A True Story. 2011. 28p. pap. 13.99 *(978-1-4567-4768-8(1))* AuthorHouse.

Hirschmann, Kris. Is a Paw a Foot? All about Measurement. 2006. (Artist Collection: the Dog Ser.). (ENG., Illus.). 32p. (J). (gr. -1-3). pap. 3.99 *(978-0-439-92213-5(5))* Scholastic, Inc.

Hoena, Blake. Bernese Mountain Dogs. 2016. (Big Dogs Ser.). (ENG., Illus.). 24p. (gr. k-1). lib. bdg. 26.65 *(978-1-4914-7982-7(5)*, Pebble Plus) Capstone Press of Coughlan Cos.

—Great Danes. 2016. (Big Dogs Ser.). (ENG., Illus.). 24p. (gr. k-1). lib. bdg. 26.65 *(978-1-4914-7978-0(7)*, Pebble Plus) Capstone Press of Coughlan Cos.

—Irish Wolfhounds. 2016. (Big Dogs Ser.). (ENG., Illus.). 24p. (gr. k-1). lib. bdg. 26.65 *(978-1-4914-7981-0(7)*, Pebble Plus) Capstone Press of Coughlan Cos.

—Mastiffs. 2016. (Big Dogs Ser.). (ENG., Illus.). 24p. (gr. k-1). lib. bdg. 26.65 *(978-1-4914-7979-7(5)*, Pebble Plus) Capstone Press of Coughlan Cos.

—Newfoundlands. 2016. (Big Dogs Ser.). (ENG., Illus.). 24p. (gr. k-1). lib. bdg. 26.65 *(978-1-4914-7980-3(9)*, Pebble Plus) Capstone Press of Coughlan Cos.

Hoena, Blake, et al. Big Dogs. 2016. (Big Dogs Ser.). (ENG.). 24p. (gr. k-1). 159.90 *(978-1-4914-8678-8(3)*, Pebble Plus) Capstone Press of Coughlan Cos.

Hoffman, Mary Ann. Guard Dogs. 2011. (Working Dogs Ser.). (Illus.). 24p. (J). (gr. 2-5). pap. 8.15 *(978-1-4339-4648-6(3)*, Gareth Stevens Learning Library); lib. bdg. 22.60 *(978-1-4339-4647-9(5))* Stevens, Gareth Publishing LLLP.

—Herding Dogs. 2011. (Working Dogs Ser.). (Illus.). 24p. (J). (gr. 2-5). pap. 8.15 *(978-1-4339-4656-1(4)*, Gareth Stevens Learning Library); lib. bdg. 22.60 *(978-1-4339-4655-4(6))* Stevens, Gareth Publishing LLLP.

Holzer, Angela. My Dog, Eddie. Funk, Debbie, illus. 2009. 36p. (J). lib. bdg. 8.99 *(978-0-9821563-5-3(9))* Good Sound Publishing.

Hosley, Maria. Dogs, 1 vol. 2007. (First Drawings Ser.). (ENG., Illus.). 24p. (gr. -1-3). 25.65 *(978-1-59679-803-8(3)*, Buddy Bks.) ABDO Publishing Co.

Houran, Lori Haskins. Pug: What a Mug! 2009. (Little Dogs Rock! Ser.). (Illus.). 32p. (J). (gr. 2-5). lib. bdg. 25.27 *(978-1-59716-750-5(9))* Bearport Publishing Co., Inc.

Houran, Lori Haskins. Sled Dogs. 2016. (Dog Heroes Ser.). (ENG.). 32p. (J). (gr. 2-7). pap. 8.95 ***(978-1-944998-53-0(5))*** Bearport Publishing Co., Inc.

Houston, Dick. Bulu: African Wonder Dog. 2011. (ENG.). 336p. (J). (gr. 3-7). 7.99 *(978-0-375-84724-0(3)*, Yearling) Random Hse. Children's Bks.

Howard, Denise. Jameela's Big Adventure. 2009. 84p. pap. 10.49 *(978-1-4490-5355-0(6))* AuthorHouse.

Hubbard, Ben. Caring for Dogs & Puppies. 2016. (Battersea Dogs & Cats Home Pet Care Guides). (ENG., Illus.). 64p. (J). (gr. 2-4). pap. 6.99 *(978-1-4451-2779-8(2)*, Franklin Watts) Hachette Children's Group GBR. Dist: Hachette Bk. Group.

—I Want a Dog. Chapman, Jason, illus. 2017. (Battersea Dogs & Cats Home Ser.). (ENG.). 32p. (J). (gr. k-2). 16.99 *(978-1-4451-5065-9(4)*, Franklin Watts) Hachette Children's Group GBR. Dist: Hachette Bk. Group.

Hutmacher, Kimberly M. I Want a Dog, 1 vol. 2012. (I Want a Pet Ser.). (ENG.). 24p. (gr. k-1). lib. bdg. 26.65 *(978-1-4296-7595-6(0)*, Pebble Plus) Capstone Press of Coughlan Cos.

Jackson, Emma. A Home for Dixie: The True Story of a Rescued Puppy. Carey, Bob, illus. 40p. (J). (gr. -1-3). 2010. (ENG.). pap. 6.99 *(978-0-06-144964-2(4)*, Collins) 2008. lib. bdg. 17.89 *(978-0-06-144963-5(6))* HarperCollins Pubs.

James, Michael. Yorkshire Terrier. 2017. (Dog Lover's Guides: Vol. 18). (ENG.). (YA). (gr. 7-12). 26.95 ***(978-1-4222-3862-2(8))*** Mason Crest.

Jeffrey, Laura S. Choosing a Dog: How to Choose & Care for a Dog. 2013. (American Humane Association Pet Care Ser.). 48p. (J). (gr. 3-18). lib. bdg. 25.27 *(978-0-7660-4080-9(1))*; pap. 8.95 *(978-1-4644-0215-9(9)*, Enslow Elementary) Enslow Pubs., Inc.

—Dogs: How to Choose & Care for a Dog. 2004. (American Humane Pet Care Library). (Illus.). 48p. (J). lib. bdg. 25.27 *(978-0-7660-2520-2(9))* Enslow Pubs., Inc.

Jenkins, Steve. Dogs & Cats. 2012. lib. bdg. 18.40 *(978-0-606-26606-2(2)*, Turtleback) Turtleback Bks.

Johnson, Bruce. We Both Read-about Dogs. 2009. (ENG., Illus.). 44p. (J). (gr. -1-3). 9.95 *(978-1-60115-237-4(X))* Treasure Bay, Inc.

—We Both Read-About Dogs. 2009. (ENG., Illus.). 44p. (J). pap. 4.99 *(978-1-60115-238-1(8))* Treasure Bay, Inc.

Johnson, Bruce & McKay, Sindy. We Both Read Bilingual Edition-About Dogs/Acerca de Los Perros. 2011. (ENG & SPA., Illus.). 44p. (J). pap. 4.99 *(978-1-60115-048-6(2))* Treasure Bay, Inc.

Johnson, Jinny. Boxer. 2013. (My Favorite Dogs Ser.). (Illus.). 24p. (gr. k-3). 28.50 *(978-1-59920-840-4(7))* Black Rabbit Bks.

—Bulldog. 2013. (My Favorite Dogs Ser.). (Illus.). 24p. (gr. k-3). 28.50 *(978-1-59920-841-1(5))* Black Rabbit Bks.

—Dogs & Puppies. 2009. (Get to Know Your Pet Ser.). (Illus.). 32p. (J). (gr. 4-7). pap. *(978-1-897563-29-8(9))* Saunders Bk. Co.

—Golden Retriever. 2013. (My Favorite Dogs Ser.). (Illus.). 24p. (gr. k-3). 28.50 *(978-1-59920-843-5(1))* Black Rabbit Bks.

—Labrador Retriever. 2013. (My Favorite Dogs Ser.). (Illus.). 24p. (gr. k-3). 28.50 *(978-1-59920-844-2(X))* Black Rabbit Bks.

—Puppy. 2014. (My New Pet Ser.). 24p. (gr. k-3). lib. bdg. 28.50 *(978-1-62588-027-7(8))* Black Rabbit Bks.

—Puppy. 2014. (My New Pet Ser.). (ENG., Illus.). 24p. (J). (gr. -1-3). pap. 8.95 *(978-1-77092-209-9(1))* Saunders Bk. Co. CAN. Dist: RiverStream Publishing.

—Yorkshire Terrier. 2013. (My Favorite Dogs Ser.). (Illus.). 24p. (gr. k-3). 28.50 *(978-1-59920-846-6(6))* Black Rabbit Bks.

Johnson, Julie. Rottweiler. 2017. (J). ***(978-1-4222-3848-6(2))*** Mason Crest.

Johnson, Lincoln. Hal the Hound: The Happiest Day Yet. 2011. 48p. (gr. -1). pap. 39.02 *(978-1-4269-8976-6(8))* Trafford Publishing.

Johnson, Sheri A. Cockapoo: A Cross Between a Cocker Spaniel & a Poodle, 1 vol. 2012. (Designer Dogs Ser.). (ENG.). 32p. (gr. 3-4). lib. bdg. 27.99 *(978-1-4296-7763-9(5)*, Snap Bks.) Capstone Press of Coughlan Cos.

Johnston, Tony. Desert Dog, 1 vol. Weatherford, Robert, illus. 2008. (ENG.). 32p. (J). (gr. 1-6). pap. 7.95 *(978-1-57805-133-5(9))* Sierra Club Bks. for Children.

Jojo. Landon Wants a Puppy. 2009. 68p. pap. 26.99 *(978-1-4389-4656-6(2))* AuthorHouse.

Jones, Charlotte Foltz. The King Who Barked. Yayo, illus. 2009. (ENG.). 40p. (J). (gr. 1-5). 16.95 *(978-0-8234-1925-8(8))* Holiday Hse., Inc.

Jordan, Apple. Guess Who Sniffs. 2nd rev. ed. 2011. (Bookworms 2nd Edition: Guess Who Ser.). 24p. (gr. k-2). 21.36 *(978-1-60870-430-9(0))* Marshall Cavendish GBR. Dist: Marshall Cavendish Corp.

Jordan, Apple, told to. The Dog: Best in Show. 2008. (Illus.). 32p. (J). *(978-0-545-01184-6(1))*; pap. *(978-0-545-10738-9(5))* Scholastic, Inc.

Joyner, Melinda Bramlett. Boogie Dog & Guine. 2011. 28p. pap. 15.99 *(978-1-4568-6765-2(2))* Xlibris Corp.

Julia Barnes. Puppies, Vol. 12. 2016. (Understanding & Caring for Your Pet Ser.: Vol. 12). (ENG., Illus.). 128p. (J). (gr. 5-8). 25.95 *(978-1-4222-3702-1(8))* Mason Crest.

Kaleta, Don. Puppy Scents: The Kids' Guide to Puppy Care. Habel, Helen, illus. 2010. (ENG.). 72p. (J). pap. 17.95 *(978-0-615-39881-5(2))* Kaleta Publishing, LLC.

Kalman, Bobbie. My Dog Likes Me. 2010. (My World Ser.). (ENG.). 16p. (J). (gr. k-3). *(978-0-7787-9499-8(7))*; pap. *(978-0-7787-9524-7(1))* Crabtree Publishing Co.

—Wild & Pet Puppies. 2008. (It's Fun to Learn about Baby Animals Ser.). (ENG., Illus.). 24p. (J). (gr. k-3). pap. *(978-0-7787-3976-0(7))*; (gr. 1-3). lib. bdg. *(978-0-7787-3957-9(0))* Crabtree Publishing Co.

Kalman, Bobbie & Sotzek, Hannelore. ¿Que Es un Perro? 2006. (Libro de Bobbie Kalman Ser.). (SPA., Illus.). 32p. (J). (gr. 3-7). lib. bdg. *(978-0-7787-8765-5(6))* Crabtree Publishing Co.

—¿Qué Es un Perro? 2006. (Libro de Bobbie Kalman Ser.). (SPA., Illus.). 32p. (J). (gr. 3-7). pap. *(978-0-7787-8811-9(3))* Crabtree Publishing Co.

Karwoski, Gail Langer. Search & Rescue Dogs, 1 vol. 2013. (Dogs on the Job Ser.). (ENG.). 32p. (gr. 3-4). 27.99 *(978-1-4765-0131-4(9)*, Edge Bks.) Capstone Press of Coughlan Cos.

—Terriers: Loyal Hunting Companions, 1 vol. 2013. (Hunting Dogs Ser.). (ENG.). 32p. (gr. 3-4). 7.95 *(978-1-62065-939-7(5))*; lib. bdg. 27.99 *(978-1-4296-9989-1(2))* Capstone Press of Coughlan Cos. (Edge Bks.).

Karwoski, Gail Langer, et al. Dogs on the Job. 2011. (Dogs on the Job Ser.). (ENG.). 32p. (gr. 3-4). lib. bdg. 111.96 *(978-1-62065-970-0(0)*, Edge Bks.) Capstone Press of Coughlan Cos.

Kast, Edie. Heroic Animals. 2005. (Illus.). 24p. (J). *(978-0-328-13606-3(9)*, Scott Foresman) Addison-Wesley Educational Pubs., Inc.

Katz, Jon. Lenore Finds a Friend: A True Story from Bedlam Farm. Katz, Jon, photos by. 2012. (My Readers Ser.). (ENG., Illus.). 32p. (J). (gr. -1-3). 15.99 *(978-0-8050-9220-2(X)*, 9780805092202, Holt, Henry & Co. Bks. For Young Readers) Holt, Henry & Co.

—Lenore Finds a Friend: A True Story from Bedlam Farm. Katz, Jon, photos by. 2014. (My Readers Ser.). (ENG., Illus.). 32p. (J). (gr. -1-3). 15.99 *(978-1-250-03432-8(9)*, 9781250034328) Square Fish.

—Meet the Dogs of Bedlam Farm. Katz, Jon, photos by. 2011. (ENG., Illus.). 32p. (J). (gr. -1-3). 17.99 *(978-0-8050-9219-6(6)*, 9780805092196, Holt, Henry & Co. Bks. For Young Readers) Holt, Henry & Co.

Kavanagh, James. The World of Wild Dogs. 2014. (Jeff Corwin's Explorer Ser.). (ENG., Illus.). 12p. 7.95 *(978-1-58355-851-5(9))* Western National Parks Assn.

Kavanaugh, Missy & Gurman, Sarah, texts. Puppies. 2009. (Illus.). 8p. (J). ***(978-1-4351-1783-9(2))*** Barnes & Noble, Inc.

Kawa, Katie. Lovable Dogs. 2011. (Pet Corner Ser.). 24p. (gr. k-2). (J). pap. 8.15 *(978-1-4339-5593-8(8))*; (J). lib. bdg. 22.60 *(978-1-4339-5591-4(1))*; (Illus.). 69.20 *(978-1-4339-6881-5(9))* Stevens, Gareth Publishing LLLP.

—Lovable Dogs: Perros Adorables. 2011. (Pet Corner / RincóN de Las Mascotas Ser.). (SPA & ENG., Illus.). 24p. (J). (gr. k-3). lib. bdg. 22.60 *(978-1-4339-5595-2(4))* Stevens, Gareth Publishing LLLP.

Keating, Laurel. Find Scruncheon & Touton 2: All Around Newfoundland, 1 vol. Keating, Nancy, illus. 2012. (ENG.). 32p. (J). (gr. k-3). pap. 10.95 *(978-1-897174-89-0(6)*, Tuckamore Bks) Creative Bk. Publishing CAN. Dist: Orca Bk. Pubs. USA.

—Search for Scruncheon & Touton, 1 vol. Keating, Nancy, illus. 2012. (ENG.). 32p. (J). (gr. -1-3). 10.95 *(978-1-897174-69-2(1)*, Tuckamore Bks) Creative Bk. Publishing CAN. Dist: Orca Bk. Pubs. USA.

Keenan, Margaret. Dogs. 2009. (Illus.). 160p. (YA). *(978-1-84406-129-7(9))* Taj Bks., Ltd.

Kenan, Tessa. I Love Dogs. 2016. (Bumba Books (tm) — Pets Are the Best Ser.). (ENG.). 24p. (J). (gr. -1-1). 25.32 *(978-1-5124-1414-1(X))* Lerner Publishing Group.

Kennedy, Edward M. My Senator & Me: A Dog's-Eye View of Washington, D. C. Small, David, illus. 2011. (J). (gr. 2-5). 29.95 *(978-0-545-04379-3(4))* Weston Woods Studios, Inc.

Kessler, Liz. Poppy the Pirate Dog. Phillips, Mike, illus. 2015. (Candlewick Sparks Ser.). (ENG.). 64p. (J). (gr. k-4). pap. 3.99 *(978-0-7636-7661-2(6))* Candlewick Pr.

Khu, Jannell. Dogs. 2009. (My World of Animals Ser.). 24p. (gr. 1-1). 37.50 *(978-1-61514-712-0(8)*, PowerKids Pr.) Rosen Publishing Group, Inc., The.

The Kids Guide to Pet Jokes, Rhymes & Riddles: For Kids Who Love Pets. 2006. (J). 7.95 *(978-0-9744749-3-9(2))* Crazy Pet Pr., The.

Kimmelman, Leslie. A Dog Named Honey. 2005. (IOpeners Ser.). (Illus.). 8p. (J). pap. 7.56 *(978-0-7652-5144-2(2))* Celebration Pr.

King, Vickie. Search Dogs & You, a Wilderness Safety Guide from American Search Dogs. 2009. 32p. pap. 13.00 *(978-1-60860-105-9(6)*, Strategic Bk. Publishing) Strategic Book Publishing & Rights Agency (SBPRA).

Kip & Tip 6 Packs. KinderReaders Individual Title. (Kinderstarters Ser.). 8p. (gr. -1-1). 21.00 *(978-0-7635-8650-8(1))* Rigby Education.

Kirchmeier, Jenn-Ann, illus. The Tails of Brinkley the Berner: The Beginning. 2008. 32p. (J). 16.95 *(978-0-9793288-0-0(2))* Brinkley Bks., Inc.

Kishel, Ann-Marie. Dogs & Puppies. 2006. (First Step Nonfiction - Animal Families Ser.). (ENG., Illus.). 8p. (gr. -1-1). pap. 4.95 *(978-0-8225-5650-3(2)*, Lerner Pubns.) Lerner Publishing Group.

Klimo, Kate. Dog Diaries #8: Fala. Jessell, Tim, illus. 2016. (Dog Diaries). (ENG.). 160p. (J). (gr. 2-5). lib. bdg. 12.99 *(978-0-553-53491-7(2)*, Random Hse. Bks. for Young Readers) Random Hse. Children's Bks.

—Fala. Jessell, Tim, illus. 2016. (Dog Diaries). (ENG.). 160p. (J). (gr. 2-5). pap. 7.99 *(978-0-553-53490-0(4)*, Random Hse. Bks. for Young Readers) Random Hse. Children's Bks.

Koehler-Pentacoff, Elizabeth. John Muir & Stickeen: An Alaskan Adventure. Swanson, Karl W., illus. 2003. (Single Titles Ser.). 32p. (J). 14.95 *(978-0-7613-1997-9(2))* Lerner Publishing Group.

Koffman, Donna Carol & Segel, Lawrence. Kooper's Tale. Macbeth, Seth, illus. 2016. (ENG.). (J). (gr. 4-5). pap. ***(978-1-55483-998-8(X))*** Insomniac Pr.

Kolpin, Molly. Chiweenie: A Cross Between a Chihuahua & a Dachshund, 1 vol. 2012. (Designer Dogs Ser.). (ENG.). 32p. (gr. 3-4). lib. bdg. 27.99 *(978-1-4296-7667-0(1)*, Snap Bks.) Capstone Press of Coughlan Cos.

—Puggle: A Cross Between a Pug & a Beagle, 1 vol. 2012. (Designer Dogs Ser.). (ENG.). 32p. (gr. 3-4). lib. bdg. 27.99 *(978-1-4296-7665-6(5)*, Snap Bks.) Capstone Press of Coughlan Cos.

Kolpin, Molly, et al. Designer Dogs. 2012. (Designer Dogs Ser.). (ENG.). 32p. (gr. 3-4). lib. bdg. 167.94 *(978-1-4296-8216-9(7)*, Snap Bks.) Capstone Press of Coughlan Cos.

Konnecke, Ole. The Big Book of Words & Pictures. Konnecke, Ole, illus. 2017. (ENG., Illus.). 20p. (gr. -1-k). 14.99 *(978-1-77657-135-2(5))* Gecko Pr. NZL. Dist: Lerner Publishing Group.

Korotky, V. Yvonne. Abbey's Story. 2012. 52p. pap. 24.99 *(978-1-4772-7186-5(4))* AuthorHouse.

Krämer, Eva-Maria. Get to Know Dog Breeds: The 200 Most Popular Breeds. 2014. (Get to Know Cat, Dog, & Horse Breeds Ser.). 160p. (J). 33.27 *(978-0-7660-4258-2(8))* Enslow Pubs., Inc.

Krmer, Eva-Maria. Get to Know Dog Breeds: The 200 Most Popular Breeds. 2014. (Get to Know Cat, Dog, & Horse Breeds Ser.). 160p. (J). pap. 10.95 *(978-1-4644-0459-7(3))* Enslow Pubs., Inc.

Kunhardt, Katharine. Let's Count the Puppies. 2004. (Illus.). 32p. (J). (gr. -1-1). 13.89 *(978-0-06-054337-2(X))* HarperCollins Pubs.

Kuskowski, Alex. Puppies, 1 vol. 2013. (Baby Animals Set 1 Ser.). (ENG.). 24p. (J). (gr. k-3). lib. bdg. 24.21 *(978-1-61783-840-8(3)*, SandCastle) ABDO Publishing Co.

Laidlaw, Rob. No Shelter Here: Making the World a Kinder Place for Dogs. (ENG., Illus.). 64p. (J). (gr. 3-7). 2013. pap. 11.95 *(978-0-9869495-2-4(3))* 2012. 15.95 *(978-0-9869495-5-5(8))* Pajama Pr. CAN. Dist: Ingram Publisher Services.

Landau, Elaine. The Best Dogs Ever, 24 vols., Set. Incl. Beagles Are the Best! 2009. lib. bdg. 25.26 *(978-1-58013-559-7(5))*; Boston Terriers Are the Best! (Illus.). 2010. lib. bdg. 25.26 *(978-0-7613-5055-2(1))*; Boxers Are the Best! 2009. 25.26 *(978-1-58013-560-3(9))*; Bulldogs Are the Best! 2010. lib. bdg. 25.26 *(978-1-58013-566-5(8))*; Cocker Spaniels Are the Best! (Illus.). 2010. lib. bdg. 25.26 *(978-0-7613-5056-9(X))*; Dachshunds Are the Best! 2010. lib. bdg. 25.26 *(978-1-58013-563-4(3))*; Golden Retrievers Are the Best! 2010. lib. bdg. 25.26 *(978-1-58013-562-7(5))*; Great Danes Are the Best! 2011. lib. bdg. 25.26 *(978-0-7613-6079-7(4))*; Labrador Retrievers Are the Best! 2009. lib. bdg. 25.26 *(978-1-58013-556-6(0))*; Mastiffs Are the Best! 2011. lib. bdg. 25.26 *(978-0-7613-6083-4(2))*; Miniature Schnauzers Are the Best! 2010. lib. bdg. 25.26 *(978-1-58013-565-8(X))*; Newfoundlands Are the Best! (Illus.). 2011. lib. bdg. 25.26 *(978-0-7613-6082-7(4))*; Pit Bulls Are the Best! 2011. lib. bdg. 25.26 *(978-0-7613-6078-0(6))*; Pomeranians Are the Best! (Illus.). 2010. lib. bdg. 25.26 *(978-0-7613-5057-6(8))*; Poodles Are the Best! 2010. lib. bdg. 25.26 *(978-1-58013-561-0(7))*; Pugs Are the Best! (Illus.). 2010. lib. bdg. 25.26 *(978-0-7613-5058-3(6))*; Rottweilers Are the Best! (Illus.). 2010. lib. bdg. 25.26 *(978-0-7613-5059-0(4))*; Saint Bernards Are the Best! 2011. lib. bdg. 25.26 *(978-0-7613-6080-3(8))*; Shih Tzus Are the Best! (Illus.). 2010. lib. bdg. 25.26 *(978-1-58013-564-1(1))*; Yorkshire Terriers Are the Best! 2009. lib. bdg. 25.26 *(978-1-58013-557-3(9))*; 32p. (gr. 2-4)., Lerner Pubns. (Best Dogs Ever Ser.). (ENG.). 2009. Set lib. bdg. 606.24 *(978-1-58013-555-9(2))* Lerner Publishing Group.

—Boston Terriers Are the Best! 2010. (Best Dogs Ever Ser.). (ENG., Illus.). 32p. (gr. 2-4). lib. bdg. 25.26 *(978-0-7613-5055-2(1)*, Lerner Pubns.) Lerner Publishing Group.

—Boxers Are the Best! 2009. (Best Dogs Ever Ser.). (ENG.). 32p. (gr. 2-4). 25.26 *(978-1-58013-560-3(9)*, Lerner Pubns.) Lerner Publishing Group.

—Bulldogs Are the Best! 2010. (Best Dogs Ever Ser.). (ENG.). 32p. (gr. 2-4). lib. bdg. 25.26 *(978-1-58013-566-5(8)*, Lerner Pubns.) Lerner Publishing Group.

—Cocker Spaniels Are the Best! 2010. (Best Dogs Ever Ser.). (ENG., Illus.). 32p. (gr. 2-4). lib. bdg. 25.26 *(978-0-7613-5056-9(X)*, Lerner Pubns.) Lerner Publishing Group.

—Golden Retrievers Are the Best! 2010. (Best Dogs Ever Ser.). (ENG.). 32p. (gr. 2-4). lib. bdg. 25.26 *(978-1-58013-562-7(5)*, Lerner Pubns.) Lerner Publishing Group.

—Great Danes Are the Best! 2011. (Best Dogs Ever Ser.). (ENG.). 32p. (gr. 2-4). lib. bdg. 25.26 *(978-0-7613-6079-7(4)*, Lerner Pubns.) Lerner Publishing Group.

—Labrador Retrievers Are the Best! 2009. (Best Dogs Ever Ser.). (ENG.). 32p. (gr. 2-4). lib. bdg. 25.26 *(978-1-58013-556-6(0)*, Lerner Pubns.) Lerner Publishing Group.

—Mastiffs Are the Best! 2011. (Best Dogs Ever Ser.). (ENG.). 32p. (gr. 2-4). lib. bdg. 25.26 *(978-0-7613-6083-4(2)*, Lerner Pubns.) Lerner Publishing Group.

—Miniature Schnauzers Are the Best! 2010. (Best Dogs Ever Ser.). (ENG.). 32p. (gr. 2-4). lib. bdg. 25.26 *(978-1-58013-565-8(X)*, Lerner Pubns.) Lerner Publishing Group.

—Newfoundlands Are the Best! 2011. (Best Dogs Ever Ser.). (ENG., Illus.). 32p. (gr. 2-4). lib. bdg. 25.26 *(978-0-7613-6082-7(4)*, Lerner Pubns.) Lerner Publishing Group.

—Pit Bulls Are the Best! 2011. (Best Dogs Ever Ser.). (ENG.). 32p. (gr. 2-4). lib. bdg. 25.26 *(978-0-7613-6078-0(6)*, Lerner Pubns.) Lerner Publishing Group.

—Pomeranians Are the Best! 2010. (Best Dogs Ever Ser.). (ENG., Illus.). 32p. (gr. 2-4). lib. bdg. 25.26 *(978-0-7613-5057-6(8)*, Lerner Pubns.) Lerner Publishing Group.

—Pugs Are the Best! 2010. (Best Dogs Ever Ser.). (ENG., Illus.). 32p. (gr. 2-4). lib. bdg. 25.26 *(978-0-7613-5058-3(6)*, Lerner Pubns.) Lerner Publishing Group.

—Rottweilers Are the Best! 2010. (Best Dogs Ever Ser.). (ENG., Illus.). 32p. (gr. 2-4). lib. bdg. 25.26 *(978-0-7613-5059-0(4)*, Lerner Pubns.) Lerner Publishing Group.

—Saint Bernards Are the Best! 2011. (Best Dogs Ever Ser.). (ENG.). 32p. (gr. 2-4). lib. bdg. 25.26 *(978-0-7613-6080-3(8)*, Lerner Pubns.) Lerner Publishing Group.

—Shih Tzus Are the Best! 2010. (Best Dogs Ever Ser.). (ENG., Illus.). 32p. (gr. 2-4). lib. bdg. 25.26 *(978-1-58013-564-1(1)*, Lerner Pubns.) Lerner Publishing Group.

—Yorkshire Terriers Are the Best! 2009. (Best Dogs Ever Ser.). (ENG.). 32p. (gr. 2-4). lib. bdg. 25.26 *(978-1-58013-557-3(9)*, Lerner Pubns.) Lerner Publishing Group.

Laroyster, Angela. Puppy. (See How They Grow Ser.). (Illus.). 21p. (J). 10.95 *(978-0-590-73805-7(4))* Scholastic, Inc.

Larson, Kirby & Nethery, Mary. Two Bobbies. Cassels, Jean, illus. 2015. 36p. pap. 8.00 *(978-1-61003-411-1(2))* Center for the Collaborative Classroom.

—Two Bobbies: A True Story of Hurricane Katrina, Friendship, & Survival. Cassels, Jean, illus. 2008. (ENG.). 32p. (J). (gr. k-3). 16.99 *(978-0-8027-9754-4(7)*, 9780802797544, Bloomsbury USA Childrens) Bloomsbury Publishing USA.

Latham, Donna. Fire Dogs. 2005. (Dog Heroes Ser.). (Illus.). 32p. (J). lib. bdg. 25.27 *(978-1-59716-141-1(1))* Bearport Publishing Co., Inc.

Lauber, Patricia. The True-or-False Book of Dogs. Schanzer, Rosalyn, illus. 2003. (ENG.). 32p. (J). 15.99 *(978-0-06-029767-1(0))* HarperCollins Pubs.

Laughlin, Kara L. Seizure-Alert Dogs. 2014. (Service Dogs Ser.). (ENG.). 24p. (J). (gr. 1-4). 27.07 *(978-1-62687-312-4(7)*, 208268) Child's World, Inc., The.

—Therapy Dogs. 2014. (Service Dogs Ser.). (ENG.). 24p. (J). (gr. 1-4). 27.07 *(978-1-62687-313-1(5)*, 207153) Child's World, Inc., The.

Lawrence, Donna. The Miracle of Susie the Puppy That Changed the Law. Coble, Lynn Bemer, ed. Cappoen, Jennifer Tipton, illus. 2012. 54p. 24.95 *(978-0-9846724-2-4(7))* Paws and Claws Publishing, LLC.

Lawrence-Loughlin, Amy. For the Love of Gus: A True Rescue to Riches Tale. 2012. 36p. pap. 15.49 *(978-1-4669-5371-0(3))* Trafford Publishing.

Leaf, Christina. Boston Terriers. 2017. (Awesome Dogs Ser.). (ENG., Illus.). 24p. (J). (gr. k-3). lib. bdg. 25.95 *(978-1-62617-557-0(8)*, Blastoff! Readers) Bellwether Media.

—Shetland Sheepdogs. 2017. (Awesome Dogs Ser.). (ENG.). 24p. (J). (gr. k-3). lib. bdg. 25.95 *(978-1-62617-559-4(4)*, Blastoff! Readers) Bellwether Media.

Leduc-Lenmark, MaryAlice. Meet Mister Muttley. Speas, Joann, illus. 2004. 25p. (J). 16.95 *(978-0-9760733-0-7(7))* Heartstrings Publishing.

Leigh, Sharon. Tiramisu: My Little Lamb. 2013. (ENG., Illus.). 16p. (J). (gr. -1-3). pap. 12.95 *(978-0-938467-64-9(6))* Headline Bks., Inc.

Leighton, Christina. Doberman Pinschers. 2016. (Awesome Dogs Ser.). (ENG., Illus.). 24p. (J). (gr. k-3). 25.95 *(978-1-62617-392-7(3)*, Blastoff! Readers) Bellwether Media.

—Pembroke Welsh Corgis. 2016. (Awesome Dogs Ser.). (ENG., Illus.). 24p. (J). (gr. k-3). 25.95 *(978-1-62617-393-4(1)*, Blastoff! Readers) Bellwether Media.

Lendroth, Susan. Calico Dorsey: Mail Dog of the Mining Camps. Gustavson, Adam, illus. 2010. (ENG.). 32p. (J). (gr. -1-2). 16.99 *(978-1-58246-318-6(2)*, Tricycle Pr.) Random Hse. Children's Bks.

Lentini, Joe. Mickey the Monster: He's Just Misunderstood. 2011. 24p. pap. 11.32 *(978-1-4634-3924-8(5))* AuthorHouse.

Leonard, Dion. Finding Gobi: The True Story of One Little Dog's Big Journey. 2017. (ENG.). 208p. (J). pap. 14.99 ***(978-0-7180-7531-6(5))*** Nelson, Thomas Inc.

Levine, Becky D. Hounds: Loyal Hunting Companions, 1 vol. 2013. (Hunting Dogs Ser.). (ENG.). 32p. (gr. 3-4). 7.95 *(978-1-62065-934-2(4))*; lib. bdg. 27.99 *(978-1-4296-9990-7(6))* Capstone Press of Coughlan Cos. (Edge Bks.).

Levine, Becky D., et al. Hunting Dogs: Loyal Hunting Companions. 2013. (Hunting Dogs Ser.). (ENG.). 32p. (gr.

3-4). 47.70 *(978-1-62065-940-3(9),* Edge Bks.) Capstone Press of Coughlan Cos.

Levy, Debbie & Panza, Rosana. Dozer's Run: A True Story of a Dog & His Race. Opie, David, illus. 2014. (ENG.). 32p. (J). (gr. 1-4). 16.99 *(978-1-58536-896-9(2),* 203665) Sleeping Bear Pr.

Lindeen, Mary. It's a Dog's Life, 1 vol. 2011. (Wonder Readers: Social Studies). (ENG.). (gr. -1-2). 20p. lib. bdg. 22.65 *(978-1-4296-8640-2(5));* 16p. pap. 35.94 *(978-1-4296-8098-1(9));* 32p. pap. 5.99 *(978-1-4296-7946-6(8))* Capstone Press of Coughlan Cos. (Wonder Readers).

Lockwood, Robert. Siberian Husky. 2017. (Dog Lover's Guides: Vol. 18). (ENG.). (YA). (gr. 7-12). 26.95 ***(978-1-4222-3948-3(9))*** Mason Crest.

Lodien, Jennie, des. A Doggie Diary: The story of our Dog. 2003. (Illus.). 48p. (YA). ring bd. 16.95 *(978-0-9746341-7-3(4))* Chin & A Pr.

—Life on a Leash: My Dog's Story. 2003. (Illus.). 48p. (YA). ring bd. 16.95 *(978-0-9746341-6-6(6))* Chin & A Pr.

Loewen, Nancy. Dalmatians. 2003. (Dog Breeds Ser.). 24p. (J). lib. bdg. 21.35 *(978-1-58340-317-4(5))* Black Rabbit Bks.

Long, David. War School for Dogs: Band 16/Sapphire. 2017. (ENG., Illus.). 56p. (J). pap. 8.99 ***(978-0-00-820891-2(3))*** HarperCollins Pubs. Ltd. GBR. Dist: Independent Pubs. Group.

Lorenzo, Rose, et al. A Dog's Life. 2007. (Windows on Literacy Ser.). (ENG., Illus.). 8p. (J). pap. 9.95 *(978-0-7922-8480-2(1))* National Geographic School Publishing, Inc.

Lubka, S. Ruth. Pupniks: The Story of Two Space Dogs, 1 vol. 2003. (ENG., Illus.). 32p. (J). (gr. k-3). 16.95 *(978-0-7614-5137-2(4))* Marshall Cavendish Corp.

Luginbuhl, Susan. Puppies from Heaven. 2007. 196p. per. 12.95 *(978-1-59526-817-4(0),* Llumina Pr.) Aeon Publishing Inc.

Lunis, Natalie. Greyhound: Canine Blur! 2010. (Blink of an Eye: Superfast Animals Ser.). 24p. (J). (gr. k-3). lib. bdg. 22.61 *(978-1-936087-90-7(1))* Bearport Publishing Co., Inc.

—Jack Russell Terrier: Bundle of Energy. 2009. (Little Dogs Rock! Ser.). (Illus.). 32p. (YA). (gr. 2-5). lib. bdg. 25.27 *(978-1-59716-747-5(9))* Bearport Publishing Co., Inc.

—Lifeguard Dogs. 2014. (Dog Heroes Ser.). (Illus.). 32p. (J). (gr. 2-7). lib. bdg. 25.27 *(978-1-62724-088-8(8))* Bearport Publishing Co., Inc.

Lynch, Annabelle. Dogs & Puppies. 2017. (Animals & Their Babies Ser.). (Illus.). 24p. (gr. k-3). 28.50 ***(978-1-62588-416-9(8),*** Smart Apple Media) Black Rabbit Bks.

MacAulay, Kelley & Kalman, Bobbie. Los Cocker Spaniel. 2007. (Cuidado de las Mascotas Ser.). (SPA., Illus.). 32p. (J). (gr. 3-7). lib. bdg. *(978-0-7787-8458-6(4))* Crabtree Publishing Co.

—Los Cocker Spaniel. Crabtree, Marc, photos by. rev. ed. 2007. (Cuidado de las Mascotas Ser.). (SPA., Illus.). 32p. (J). (gr. 1-5). pap. *(978-0-7787-8480-7(0))* Crabtree Publishing Co.

—Cocker Spaniels. Crabtree, Marc, photos by. 2006. (Pet Care Ser.). (ENG., Illus.). 32p. (J). (gr. -1-3). pap. *(978-0-7787-1792-8(5),* 1259503); lib. bdg. *(978-0-7787-1760-7(7),* 1259503) Crabtree Publishing Co.

—Los Dálmatas. Crabtree, Marc, photos by. rev. ed. 2007. (Cuidado de las Mascotas Ser.). (SPA., Illus.). 32p. (J). (gr. 1-5). pap. *(978-0-7787-8481-4(9))* Crabtree Publishing Co.

—Dalmatians. Crabtree, Marc, photos by. 2006. (Pet Care Ser.). (ENG., Illus.). 32p. (J). (gr. -1-3). pap. *(978-0-7787-1793-5(3),* 1259504); lib. bdg. *(978-0-7787-1761-4(5),* 1259504) Crabtree Publishing Co.

—Labrador Retrievers. 2006. (Pet Care Ser.). (ENG., Illus.). 32p. (J). (gr. -1-4). pap. *(978-0-7787-1794-2(1))* Crabtree Publishing Co.

—Labrador Retrievers. Crabtree, Marc, photos by. 2006. (Pet Care Ser.). (ENG., Illus.). 32p. (J). (gr. -1-4). lib. bdg. *(978-0-7787-1762-1(3))* Crabtree Publishing Co.

—Los Dálmatas: Un Libro de Bobbie Kalman. 2007. (Cuidado de las Mascotas Ser.). (SPA., Illus.). 32p. (J). (gr. 3-7). lib. bdg. *(978-0-7787-8459-3(2))* Crabtree Publishing Co.

—Los Perros Labrador. 2007. (Cuidado de las Mascotas Ser.). (SPA & ENG., Illus.). 32p. (J). (gr. -1-4). lib. bdg. *(978-0-7787-8460-9(6))* Crabtree Publishing Co.

—Los Perros Labrador. Crabtree, Marc, photos by. rev. ed. 2007. (Cuidado de las Mascotas Ser.). (SPA & ENG., Illus.). 32p. (J). (gr. -1-4). pap. *(978-0-7787-8482-1(7))* Crabtree Publishing Co.

Macken, JoAnn Early. Puppies. 2003. (Weekly Reader Early Learning Library). (Illus.). 24p. (gr. k-3). pap. 8.15 *(978-0-8368-3848-0(3),* Weekly Reader Leveled Readers) Stevens, Gareth Publishing LLLP.

MacKenzie, Edie. Golden Retrievers. 2010. (J). *(978-0-7641-4492-9(8))* Barron's Educational Series, Inc.

MacKey, Esther L. Meet Mickey. 2012. 28p. pap. 7.95 *(978-1-937260-18-7(6))* Sleepytown Pr.

Mair, Cole. Dogs from Head to Tail. 2016. (Animals from Head to Tail Ser.). (Illus.). 24p. (J). (gr. k-k). lib. bdg. 22.60 *(978-1-4824-4537-4(9))* Stevens, Gareth Publishing LLLP.

Makowski, Robin Lee, illus. Dogs. 2004. (J). *(978-1-59203-088-0(2))* Learning Challenge, Inc.

Mara, Wil. What Should I Do? If I See a Stray Animal. 2011. (Community Connections: What Should I Do? Ser.). (ENG., Illus.). 24p. (J). (gr. 2-5). lib. bdg. 25.64 *(978-1-61080-050-1(8),* 1330905) Cherry Lake Publishing.

Marie, Christian. Little Dogs. 2006. (Born to Be Wild Ser.). (Illus.). 24p. (J). (gr. k-3). lib. bdg. 23.00 *(978-0-8368-6164-8(7),* Gareth Stevens Learning Library) Stevens, Gareth Publishing LLLP.

Markle, Sandra. Tasmanian Devils. 2005. (Animal Scavengers Ser.). (ENG., Illus.). 40p. (gr. 3-6). lib. bdg. 26.26 *(978-0-8225-3199-9(2),* Lerner Pubns.) Lerner Publishing Group.

Markovics, Joyce. French Bulldog: The Frenchie. 2010. (Little Dogs Rock! II Ser.). 32p. (YA). (gr. 2-5). lib. bdg. 25.27 *(978-1-936088-21-8(5))* Bearport Publishing Co., Inc.

—Papillon: Monsieur Butterfly. 2010. (Little Dogs Rock! II Ser.). 32p. (YA). (gr. 2-5). lib. bdg. 25.27 *(978-1-936088-17-1(7))* Bearport Publishing Co., Inc.

—Sled Dogs. 2014. (Bow Wow! Dog Helpers Ser.). 24p. (J). (gr. -1-3). lib. bdg. 23.93 *(978-1-62724-123-6(X))* Bearport Publishing Co., Inc.

—Therapy Dogs. 2014. (Bow Wow! Dog Helpers Ser.). 24p. (J). (gr. -1-3). lib. bdg. 23.93 *(978-1-62724-119-9(1))* Bearport Publishing Co., Inc.

Markovics, Joyce L. Shih Tzu: Lion Dog. 2010. (Little Dogs Rock! II Ser.). 32p. (YA). (gr. 2-5). lib. bdg. 25.27 *(978-1-936088-19-5(3))* Bearport Publishing Co., Inc.

Martin, Claudia. Helpers. 2010. (Working Animals Ser.). 64p. (gr. 5-18). lib. bdg. 28.50 *(978-1-60870-163-6(8))* Marshall Cavendish Corp.

Martin, Matthew. The Adventure & Life -n- Times of Cleatus. 2011. 40p. pap. 19.95 *(978-1-4567-3167-0(X))* AuthorHouse.

—Cleatus goes Drag Racing. 2011. 44p. pap. 19.95 *(978-1-4567-4316-1(3))* AuthorHouse.

Mason, Adrienne. Lost & Found. Cupples, Pat, illus. 2008. (Kids Can Read Ser.). (ENG.). 32p. (J). (gr. 1-2). 14.95 *(978-1-55453-251-3(5));* pap. 3.95 *(978-1-55453-252-0(3))* Kids Can Pr., Ltd. CAN. Dist: Hachette Bk. Group.

Mason, Paul. Dogs. Elsom, Clare, illus. 2013. (Animal Family Albums Ser.). (ENG.). 32p. (gr. 2-4). pap. 8.29 *(978-1-4109-4941-7(9));* 30.65 *(978-1-4109-4936-3(2))* Heinemann-Raintree. (Raintree Perspectives).

Massey, Wayland. Casper, the Friendly Service Dog. Massey, Ed, photos by. 2011. (Illus.). 28p. pap. 14.95 *(978-1-936343-73-7(8))* Peppertree Pr., The.

Mataya, Marybeth. Are You My Dog?, 1 vol. Williams, Matthew, illus. 2008. (Are You My Pet? Ser.). (ENG.). 32p. (J). (gr. 1-4). 28.50 *(978-1-60270-243-1(8))* Magic Wagon.

Mathea, Heidi. Cocker Spaniels, 1 vol. 2011. (Dogs Set 1 *2011 Ser.). (ENG.). 24p. (J). (gr. 2-5). 25.65 *(978-1-61613-404-4(6))* ABDO Publishing Co.

—Dalmatians, 1 vol. 2011. (Dogs Set 1 *2011 Ser.). (ENG.). 24p. 25.65 *(978-1-61613-405-1(4),* Checkerboard Library) ABDO Publishing Co.

—German Shepherds, 1 vol. 2011. (Dogs Set 1 *2011 Ser.). (ENG.). 24p. 25.65 *(978-1-61613-406-8(2),* Checkerboard Library) ABDO Publishing Co.

—Labrador Retrievers, 1 vol. 2011. (Dogs Set 1 *2011 Ser.). (ENG.). 24p. 25.65 *(978-1-61613-407-5(0),* Checkerboard Library) ABDO Publishing Co.

Mattern, Joanne. Border Collies, 1 vol. 2012. (Dogs Set 9 Ser.). (ENG., Illus.). 24p. (J). (gr. 2-5). 25.65 *(978-1-61714-989-4(6))* ABDO Publishing Co.

—Irish Red & White Setters, 1 vol. 2012. (Dogs Set 9 Ser.). (ENG., Illus.). 24p. (J). (gr. 2-5). 25.65 *(978-1-61714-991-7(8))* ABDO Publishing Co.

—True Tales of Courageous Dogs. 2007. 95p. (J). pap. *(978-0-439-02713-7(6))* Scholastic, Inc.

McCarthy, Meghan. The Incredible Life of Balto. 2011. (ENG., Illus.). 40p. (J). (gr. -1-2). 16.99 *(978-0-375-84460-7(0),* Knopf Bks. for Young Readers) Random Hse. Children's Bks.

McConnell, J. Bradfield. What a Blind Dog Sees. 2012. (ENG.). 23p. (J). pap. 12.95 *(978-1-4327-9797-3(2))* Outskirts Pr., Inc.

McCreary, Candace. Meki & the Three Cockers. 2012. (ENG.). 24p. (J). pap. 12.95 *(978-1-4787-1952-6(4))* Outskirts Pr., Inc.

McDaniel, Catherine A. My First Pet. 2009. 40p. pap. 16.99 *(978-1-4490-4502-9(2))* AuthorHouse.

McDaniel, Melissa. Disaster Search Dogs. 2005. (Dog Heroes Ser.). (Illus.). 32p. (J). (gr. 2-5). lib. bdg. 25.27 *(978-1-59716-012-4(1))* Bearport Publishing Co., Inc.

McDonnell, Patrick. The Mutts Diaries. 2014. (Mutts Kids Ser.: 1). (ENG., Illus.). 224p. (J). pap. 9.99 *(978-1-4494-5870-6(X))* Andrews McMeel Publishing.

McGrath Avery, Pat. Famous Dogs & a Cat. 2013. 94p. pap. 7.99 *(978-1-937958-34-3(5))* Red Engine Pr.

—15 Dogs & a Cat Speak Out: Interviews by Luke the Detective Dog. 2012. 119p. pap. 6.99 *(978-1-937958-11-4(6))* Red Engine Pr.

McKinnon, Elaine. Dingoes. 2016. (Wild Canines Ser.). 24p. (J). (gr. 3-3). pap. 8.25 *(978-1-4994-2019-7(6),* PowerKids Pr.) Rosen Publishing Group, Inc., The.

—Pets at the Vet. 2016. (Community Helpers Ser.). 00024p. (J). (gr. 1-1). pap. 8.25 *(978-1-4994-2706-6(9),* PowerKids Pr.) Rosen Publishing Group, Inc., The.

McNeil, Niki, et al. HOCPP1029 the Iditarod. 2004. spiral bd. 15.50 *(978-1-60308-029-3(5))* In the Hands of a Child.

Meinking, Mary. Dingoes. 2013. (Wild Canine Pups Ser.). 24p. (J). (gr. -1-3). lib. bdg. 21.32 *(978-1-61772-930-0(2))* Bearport Publishing Co., Inc.

Meister, Cari. Dogs. 2014. (Illus.). 24p. (J). lib. bdg. 25.65 *(978-1-62031-122-6(4),* Bullfrog Bks.) Jump! Inc.

Meyer, Karl. Dog Heroes: A Poster Book. 2008. (ENG., Illus.). 64p. (J). (gr. 2-8). pap. 9.95 *(978-1-60342-116-4(5),* 62116) Storey Publishing, LLC.

Meyer, Susan. Hunting Dogs: Different Breeds & Special Purposes. 2012. (Hunting: Pursuing Wild Game! Ser.). (ENG., Illus.). 64p. (J). (gr. 5-8). pap. 12.95 *(978-1-4488-8281-6(8));* lib. bdg. 31.95 *(978-1-4488-8276-2(1))* Rosen Publishing Group, Inc., The. (Rosen Reference).

Mi. Mi's Pets. 2012. 20p. pap. 13.77 *(978-1-4669-4019-2(0))* Trafford Publishing.

Mi Perro, 6 Packs. (Literatura 2000 Ser.). (SPA.). (gr. -1-1). 28.00 *(978-0-7635-1197-5(8))* Rigby Education.

Miller, Connie Colwell. Search & Rescue Dogs. 2013. (Animals with Jobs Ser.). (ENG.). 32p. (gr. 1-4). 28.50 *(978-1-60753-380-1(4))* Amicus Publishing.

Miller, Dave. Dogs, Frogs, & Hogs. 2006. (ENG., Illus.). (J). 3.00 *(978-0-932859-88-4(7))* Apologetics Pr., Inc.

Miller, Marie-Therese. Distinguished Dogs. 2007. (Dog Tales: True Stories about Amazing Dogs Ser.). (Illus.). 80p. (gr. 4-6). lib. bdg. 28.00 *(978-0-7910-9039-8(6),* Chelsea Hse.) Facts On File, Inc.

—Hunting & Herding Dogs. 2007. (Dog Tales: True Stories about Amazing Dogs Ser.). (Illus.). 80p. (gr. 4-6). lib. bdg. 28.00 *(978-0-7910-9038-1(8),* Chelsea Hse.) Facts On File, Inc.

—Search & Rescue Dogs. 2007. (Dog Tales: True Stories about Amazing Dogs Ser.). 80p. (gr. 4-6). 28.00 *(978-0-7910-9037-4(X),* Chelsea Hse.) Facts On File, Inc.

Miller, Mirella S. Search & Rescue Dogs on the Job. 2017. (Helping Dogs Ser.). (ENG.). 24p. (J). (gr. 2-5). lib. bdg. 27.07 *(978-1-5038-1615-2(X),* 211174) Child's World, Inc., The.

Miller, Sophia. Aussie's Adventures. Heath, illus. 2nd rev. ed. 2016. (ENG.). (J). (gr. -1-4). 9.99 *(978-1-945033-07-0(X),* Atlas Publishing) Atlas Publishing LLC.

Minden, Cecilia. Farm Animals: Dogs. 2009. (21st Century Junior Library: Farm Animals Ser.). (ENG., Illus.). 24p. (gr. 2-4). lib. bdg. 25.64 *(978-1-60279-547-1(9),* 200272) Cherry Lake Publishing.

—Puppies Grow up to Be Dogs. 2010. (21st Century Basic Skills Library: Animals Grow Up Ser.). (ENG.). 24p. (gr. k-3). lib. bdg. 22.79 *(978-1-60279-851-9(6),* 200568) Cherry Lake Publishing.

Miniature Dogs, 1 vol. 2014. (Mini Animal Marvels Ser.). (ENG., Illus.). 24p. (J). (gr. -1-3). 24.21 *(978-1-62403-065-9(3))* ABDO Publishing Co.

Mitchell, Michael D. The Cinnamon Von Strudel Story: The Little Dachshund Who Tried to Become A City Mascot. 2007. 56p. per. 18.95 *(978-1-4327-0804-7(X))* Outskirts Pr., Inc.

Morey, Allan. Boston Terriers. 2016. (Tiny Dogs Ser.). (ENG., Illus.). 24p. (gr. k-1). lib. bdg. 26.65 *(978-1-5157-1963-2(4),* Pebble Plus) Capstone Press of Coughlan Cos.

—Hunting Dogs on the Job. 2017. (Helping Dogs Ser.). (ENG.). 24p. (J). (gr. 2-5). lib. bdg. 27.07 *(978-1-5038-1612-1(5),* 211171) Child's World, Inc., The.

—Papillons. 2016. (Tiny Dogs Ser.). (ENG., Illus.). 24p. (gr. k-1). lib. bdg. 26.65 *(978-1-5157-1965-6(0),* Pebble Plus) Capstone Press of Coughlan Cos.

—Shih Tzus. 2016. (Tiny Dogs Ser.). (ENG.). 24p. (gr. k-1). lib. bdg. 26.65 *(978-1-5157-1964-9(2),* Pebble Plus) Capstone Press of Coughlan Cos.

—Sled Dogs on the Job. 2017. (Helping Dogs Ser.). (ENG.). 24p. (J). (gr. 2-5). lib. bdg. 27.07 *(978-1-5038-1617-6(6),* 211176) Child's World, Inc., The.

—Tiny Dogs. 2016. (Tiny Dogs Ser.). (ENG.). 24p. (gr. k-1). 159.90 *(978-1-5157-1988-5(X),* Pebble Plus) Capstone Press of Coughlan Cos.

Morgan, Lynne. Crackers. 2007. (Illus.). 60p. per. 9.99 *(978-0-9795935-0-5(6),* Eloquent Bks.) Strategic Book Publishing & Rights Agency (SBPRA).

Morgan, Sally. Dogs. 2012. (Pets Plus Ser.). (Illus.). 32p. (gr. 3-6). lib. bdg. 31.35 *(978-1-59920-699-8(4))* Black Rabbit Bks.

Morn, September. The Golden Retriever. 2008. (Illus.). lib. bdg. 32.95 *(978-1-932904-22-2(0))* Eldorado Ink.

Morris, Mary Ann. My Sunshine-A Mind of Her Own: Lessons My Dog Taught Me. 2011. 38p. pap. 16.95 *(978-1-4560-7762-4(7))* America Star Bks.

Muir, John. Stickeen. Buell, Carl Dennis, illus. Date not set. 94p. (J). 16.95 *(978-0-8488-2803-5(8))* Amereon Ltd.

Murdoch, J. D. The African Wild Dog. 2009. (Library of Wolves & Wild Dogs Ser.). 24p. (gr. 3-3). 42.50 *(978-1-60853-967-3(9),* PowerKids Pr.) Rosen Publishing Group, Inc., The.

Murphy, Claire Rudolf & Haigh, Jane G. Gold Rush Dogs. 2012. (Illus.). 120p. pap. 16.95 *(978-0-9627530-6-0(8))* Hillside Pr.

Murphy, Frank. George Washington & the General's Dog. Walz, Richard, illus. 2015. 48p. pap. 5.00 *(978-1-61003-605-4(0))* Center for the Collaborative Classroom.

—George Washington & the General's Dog. 2003. (J). 1.25 *(978-1-4025-4103-2(1))* Recorded Bks., Inc.

Murray, Julie. Airedale Terrier, 1 vol. 2003. (Dogs Set 5 Ser.). (ENG., Illus.). 24p. (J). (gr. 2-5). 25.65 *(978-1-57765-919-8(8))* ABDO Publishing Co.

—Beagles, 1 vol. 2003. (Animal Kingdom Ser.). (ENG.). 24p. (J). (gr. 1-4). 25.65 *(978-1-57765-643-2(1))* ABDO Publishing Co.

—Bloodhound, 1 vol. 2003. (Dogs Set 5 Ser.). (ENG., Illus.). 24p. (J). (gr. 2-5). 25.65 *(978-1-57765-920-4(1))* ABDO Publishing Co.

—Cocker Spaniels, 1 vol. 2005. (Animal Kingdom Set Ii Ser.). (ENG., Illus.). 24p. (gr. k-4). 25.65 *(978-1-59197-307-2(4),* Buddy Bks.) ABDO Publishing Co.

—Dalmatians, 1 vol. 2003. (Buddy Book Ser.). (ENG.). 24p. (J). (gr. 1-4). 25.65 *(978-1-57765-642-5(3))* ABDO Publishing Co.

—Dogs, 1 vol. 2015. (ENG., Illus.). 24p. (J). 27.07 *(978-1-62970-900-0(X),* 1391170) ABDO Publishing Co.

—Golden Retrievers, 1 vol. 2005. (Animal Kingdom Set Ii Ser.). (ENG.). 24p. (gr. k-4). 25.65 *(978-1-59197-316-4(3),* Buddy Bks.) ABDO Publishing Co.

—Great Dane, 1 vol. 2003. (Dogs Set 5 Ser.). (ENG., Illus.). 24p. (gr. k-6). 25.65 *(978-1-57765-923-5(6),* Checkerboard Library) ABDO Publishing Co.

—Jack Russell Terriers, 1 vol. 2005. (Animal Kingdom Set Ii Ser.). (ENG., Illus.). 24p. (gr. k-4). 25.65 *(978-1-59197-321-8(X),* Buddy Bks.) ABDO Publishing Co.

—Labrador Retrievers, 1 vol. 2005. (Animal Kingdom Set Ii Ser.). (ENG., Illus.). 24p. (gr. k-4). 25.65 *(978-1-59197-324-9(4),* Buddy Bks.) ABDO Publishing Co.

—Mutts, 1 vol. 2003. (Animal Kingdom Ser.). (ENG.). 24p. (gr. k-4). 25.65 *(978-1-57765-641-8(5),* Buddy Bks.) ABDO Publishing Co.

—Search-and-Rescue Animals, 1 vol. 2009. (Going to Work:Animal Edition Ser.). (ENG., Illus.). 32p. (J). (gr. 2-5). 27.07 *(978-1-60453-563-1(6))* ABDO Publishing Co.

Murray, Julie & Kallen, Stuart A. Bichon Frise, 1 vol. 2003. (Dogs Set 5 Ser.). (ENG., Illus.). 24p. (J). (gr. 2-5). 25.65 *(978-1-57765-921-1(X))* ABDO Publishing Co.

—Brittany Spaniel, 1 vol. 2003. (Dogs Set 5 Ser.). (ENG., Illus.). 24p. (J). (gr. 2-5). 25.65 *(978-1-57765-922-8(8))* ABDO Publishing Co.

—Irish Setter, 1 vol. 2003. (Dogs Set 5 Ser.). (ENG., Illus.). 24p. (gr. k-6). 25.65 *(978-1-57765-924-2(4),* Checkerboard Library) ABDO Publishing Co.

Murray, Laura K. Retrievers. 2016. (Seedlings Ser.). 24p. (J). (gr. k-2). (ENG.). pap. 7.99 *(978-1-62832-249-1(7),* Creative Paperbacks); (Illus.). 28.50 *(978-1-60818-664-8(4),* Creative Education) Creative Co., The.

—Terriers. 2016. (Seedlings Ser.). 24p. (J). (gr. k-2). (ENG.). pap. 7.99 *(978-1-62832-251-4(9),* Creative Paperbacks); (Illus.). 28.50 *(978-1-60818-666-2(0),* Creative Education) Creative Co., The.

National Geographic Kids. National Geographic Kids Dogs Sticker Activity Book. 2017. (NG Sticker Activity Bks.). (ENG.). 56p. (J). (gr. -1-3). pap. 6.99 ***(978-1-4263-2801-5(X),*** National Geographic Children's Bks.) National Geographic Society.

National Geographic Kids & Donohue, Moira Rose. National Geographic Kids Chapters: Dog on a Bike. 2017. (NGK Chapters Ser.). (ENG., Illus.). 112p. (J). (gr. 2-5). pap. 5.99 *(978-1-4263-2705-6(6),* National Geographic Children's Bks.) National Geographic Society.

National Geographic Kids Staff. Dogs. 2014. (Look & Learn Ser.). (ENG.). 24p. (J). (-k). bds. 6.99 *(978-1-4263-1705-7(0),* National Geographic Children's Bks.) National Geographic Society.

—Jump, Pup! - National Geographic Kids. 2014. (ENG., Illus.). 24p. (J). pap. *(978-1-4263-1795-8(6))* National Geographic Society.

Nelson, Maria. Labrador Retrievers. 2011. (Great Big Dogs Ser.). (Illus.). 24p. (J). (gr. 2-5). pap. 8.15 *(978-1-4339-5784-0(1),* Gareth Stevens Learning Library); lib. bdg. 22.60 *(978-1-4339-5782-6(5))* Stevens, Gareth Publishing LLLP.

—Mastiffs. 2011. (Great Big Dogs Ser.). 24p. (J). (gr. 2-5). pap. 8.15 *(978-1-4339-5788-8(4),* Gareth Stevens Learning Library); lib. bdg. 22.60 *(978-1-4339-5786-4(8))* Stevens, Gareth Publishing LLLP.

—Saint Bernards. 2011. (Great Big Dogs Ser.). 24p. (J). (gr. 2-5). pap. 8.15 *(978-1-4339-5792-5(2),* Gareth Stevens Learning Library); lib. bdg. 22.60 *(978-1-4339-5790-1(6))* Stevens, Gareth Publishing LLLP.

Neuman, Susan B. National Geographic Readers: Jump Pup! 2014. (Readers Ser.). (ENG.). 24p. (J). (-k). pap. 3.99 *(978-1-4263-1508-4(2),* National Geographic Children's Bks.) National Geographic Society.

Niven, Felicia Lowenstein & Library Association Staff. Learning to Care for a Dog. 2010. (Beginning Pet Care with American Humane Ser.). 48p. (J). 25.27 *(978-0-7660-3190-6(X),* Enslow Elementary) Enslow Pubs., Inc.

Novesky, Amy. Mister & Lady Day: Billie Holiday & the Dog Who Loved Her. Brantley Newton, Vanessa, illus. 2017. (ENG.). 32p. (J). (gr. -1-3). 6.99 *(978-0-544-80905-5(X),* HMH Books For Young Readers) Houghton Mifflin Harcourt Publishing Co.

O'Brien, Renee McMullen. The Amazing Mocha & His Courageous Journey. O'Brien, Renee McMullen, illus. 2009. (Illus.). 28p. pap. 12.95 *(978-1-936051-60-1(5))* Peppertree Pr., The.

Oldfield, Dawn Bluemel. English Mastiff: The World's Heaviest Dog. 2013. (Even More SuperSized! Ser.). 24p. (J). (gr. k-3). lib. bdg. 23.93 *(978-1-61772-728-3(8))* Bearport Publishing Co., Inc.

—Newfoundland: Water Rescuer. 2011. (Big Dogs Rule! Ser.). 32p. (YA). (gr. 2-5). lib. bdg. 25.27 *(978-1-61772-296-7(0))* Bearport Publishing Co., Inc.

Orcutt, Cherie. A Beautiful Husky Needs a Home. Frongia, Daniela, illus. 2012. 32p. pap. 21.00 *(978-1-4685-7156-1(7))* AuthorHouse.

Ormiston, Rickey. My Dog Wiggles. 2010. 20p. 11.49 *(978-1-4490-9824-7(X))* AuthorHouse.

Osborne, Mary Pope & Boyce, Natalie Pope. Dog Heroes: A Nonfiction Companion to Magic Tree House No. 46 Dogs in the Dead of Night. Murdocca, Sal, illus. 2011. (Magic Tree House - Fact Tracker Ser.: 24). (ENG.). 128p. (J). (gr. 2-5). 6.99 *(978-0-375-86012-6(6),* Random Hse. Bks. for Young Readers) Random Hse. Children's Bks.

—Dogsledding & Extreme Sports: A Nonfiction Companion to Magic Tree House #54: Balto of the Blue Dawn. Molinari, Carlo, illus. 2016. (Magic Tree House - Fact Tracker Ser.: 34). (ENG.). 128p. (J). (gr. 2-5). 6.99 *(978-0-385-38644-9(3),* Random Hse. Bks. for Young Readers) Random Hse. Children's Bks.

O'Sullivan, Robyn. More Than Man's Best Friend: The Story of Working Dogs. 2006. (Science Chapters Ser.). (ENG., Illus.). 48p. (J). (gr. 1-4). lib. bdg. 17.90 *(978-0-7922-5940-4(8),* National Geographic Children's Bks.) National Geographic Society.

Otfinoski, Steven. Dogs. 2009. (Animals Animals 10 Ser.). 48p. (gr. 3). 29.93 *(978-0-7614-3970-7(6))* Marshall Cavendish GBR. Dist: Marshall Cavendish Corp.

Owen, Ruth. Cavachons. 2012. (Designer Dogs Ser.). (ENG., Illus.). 32p. (J). (gr. k-5). 25.25 *(978-1-4488-7854-3(3));* pap. 10.00 *(978-1-4488-7907-6(8))* Rosen Publishing Group, Inc., The. (PowerKids Pr.).

—Chugs. 2014. (Designer Dogs Ser.). (Illus.). 32p. (J). (gr. k-5). lib. bdg. 26.25 *(978-1-4777-7047-4(X),* PowerKids Pr.) Rosen Publishing Group, Inc., The.

—Cockapoos. 2012. (Designer Dogs Ser.). (ENG., Illus.). 32p. (J). (gr. k-5). 25.25 *(978-1-4488-7855-0(1));* pap. 10.00 *(978-1-4488-7908-3(6))* Rosen Publishing Group, Inc., The. (PowerKids Pr.).

—Goldadors. 2014. (Designer Dogs Ser.). (Illus.). 32p. (J). (gr. k-5). lib. bdg. 26.25 *(978-1-4777-7039-9(9),* PowerKids Pr.) Rosen Publishing Group, Inc., The.

—Labradoodles. 2012. (Designer Dogs Ser.). (ENG., Illus.). 32p. (J). (gr. k-5). lib. bdg. 25.25 *(978-1-4488-7857-4(8),* PowerKids Pr.) Rosen Publishing Group, Inc., The.

—Peekapoos. 2014. (Designer Dogs Ser.). (Illus.). 32p. (J). (gr. k-5). lib. bdg. 26.25 *(978-1-4777-7031-3(3),* PowerKids Pr.) Rosen Publishing Group, Inc., The.

—Puggles. 2012. (Designer Dogs Ser.). (ENG., Illus.). 32p. (J). (gr. k-5). pap. 10.00 *(978-1-4488-7911-3(6));* lib. bdg. 25.25 *(978-1-4488-7858-1(6))* Rosen Publishing Group, Inc., The. (PowerKids Pr.).

—Schnoodles. 2012. (Designer Dogs Ser.). (ENG., Illus.). 32p. (J). (gr. k-5). 25.25 *(978-1-4488-7859-8(4));* pap. 10.00 *(978-1-4488-7912-0(4))* Rosen Publishing Group, Inc., The. (PowerKids Pr.).

—Yochons. 2014. (Designer Dogs Ser.). (Illus.). 32p. (J). (gr. k-5). lib. bdg. 26.25 *(978-1-4777-7043-6(7),* PowerKids Pr.) Rosen Publishing Group, Inc., The.

—Yorkipoos. 2014. (Designer Dogs Ser.). (Illus.). 32p. (J). (gr. k-5). lib. bdg. 26.25 *(978-1-4777-7035-1(6),* PowerKids Pr.) Rosen Publishing Group, Inc., The.

—Your Dog's Superhero Skills. 2015. (It's a Fact Ser.). (ENG.). 32p. (J). (gr. 3-6). lib. bdg. 26.60 *(978-1-909673-86-1(2))* Bearport Publishing Co., Inc.

C D

Owings, Lisa. Wild Dog Attack. 2012. (Animal Attacks Ser.). (ENG., Illus.). 24p. (J). (gr. 3-7). lib. bdg. 25.95 *(978-1-60014-793-7(3)*, Torque Bks.) Bellwether Media.

Palika, Liz & Gagne, Tammy. Dog Ownership. 2011. (Dog Ownership Ser.). (ENG.). 32p. (gr. 3-4). lib. bdg. 55.98 *(978-1-4296-6529-2(7)*, Edge Bks.) Capstone Press of Coughlan Cos.

Palmer, Andrea. Cats & Dogs! 2017. (Animals in My World Ser.). 24p. (gr. 4-6). pap. 8.25 ***(978-1-5383-2189-8(0)***, PowerKids Pr.) Rosen Publishing Group, Inc., The.

Pata, Sharae & Linzy, Jan. Poodle (Standard) Champions, 1983-2003. 2004. (Illus.). 198p. spiral bd. 46.95 *(978-1-55893-154-1(6))* Camino E.E. & Bk. Co.

Patent, Dorothy Hinshaw. Dogs on Duty: Soldiers' Best Friends on the Battlefield & Beyond. 2014. (ENG., Illus.). 48p. (J). (gr. 2-4). pap. 8.99 *(978-0-8027-3650-5(5)*, 9780802736505, Bloomsbury USA Childrens) Bloomsbury Publishing USA.

Patent, Dorothy Hinshaw & Young, Jeffrey. Dog on Board: The True Story of Eclipse, the Bus-Riding Dog. Munoz, William, illus. 2016. (ENG.). 40p. (J). (gr. -1-3). 16.99 *(978-0-399-54988-5(9)*, Crown Books For Young Readers) Random Hse. Children's Bks.

Paulsen, Gary. Woodsong. unabr. ed. 2004. 132p. (J). (gr. 6-18). pap. 29.00 incl. audio *(978-0-8072-0460-3(9)*, Listening Library) Random Hse. Audio Publishing Group.

Peacock-Williams, Carol A. Adoption of Terry the Terrible Terrier. 2012. 20p. pap. 13.77 *(978-1-4669-6234-7(8))* Trafford Publishing.

Pearson, Claudia. This Way, Watson! A Map & Directions Primer, 1 vol. 2017. (ENG.). 32p. (J). 12.99 ***(978-1-4236-4765-2(3))*** Gibbs Smith, Publisher.

Perlow, Janet, illus. Show Dog. 2007. 40p. (J). pap. 14.95 incl. audio compact disk *(978-0-9795049-0-7(2))* Kidz Entertainment, Inc.

Perry, Phyllis Jean. Sherlock Hounds: Our Heroic Search & Rescue Dogs. 2006. (Illus.). 32p. (J). pap. *(978-1-59336-728-2(7))* Mondo Publishing.

Person, Stephen. Great Dane: Gentle Giant. 2011. (Big Dogs Rule! Ser.). 32p. (YA). (gr. 2-5). lib. bdg. 25.27 *(978-1-61772-297-4(9))* Bearport Publishing Co., Inc.

—Sled Dog: Powerful Miracle. 2011. (Built for Cold Ser.). 32p. (YA). (gr. 1-4). lib. bdg. 25.27 *(978-1-61772-134-2(4))*; (J). (gr. 4-5). lib. bdg., E-Book 49.22 *(978-1-61772-222-6(7))* Bearport Publishing Co., Inc.

Peters, Jean Norman. I Am Her Ears: A Story with Pictures of a Three Year Old Rescued Dog Who Leads a New Life As a Certified Hearing Dog. Archer, Mary Jane, illus. Archer, Mary Jane, photos by. 2004. 26p. (J). *(978-0-9749911-0-8(4)*, 1237614) Gizmo Pr.

Peterson, Megan Cooley & Rustad, Martha E. H. Show Me Dogs: My First Picture Encyclopedia, 1 vol. 2013. (My First Picture Encyclopedias Ser.). (ENG., Illus.). 32p. (gr. 1-2). 7.95 *(978-1-62065-927-4(1)*, Aplus Bks.) Capstone Press of Coughlan Cos.

Phillips, Dee. Prairie Dog's Hideaway. 2012. (Hole Truth! Underground Animal Life Ser.). 24p. (J). (gr. -1-3). lib. bdg. 23.93 *(978-1-61772-408-4(4))* Bearport Publishing Co., Inc.

Pickett, Robert & Pickett, Justine, illus. Dog. Pickett, Robert & Pickett, Justine, photos by. 2004. 32p. (J). lib. bdg. 27.10 *(978-1-58340-430-0(9))* Black Rabbit Bks.

Piers, Helen & Sutton, Kate. How to Look after Your Puppy. 2015. (Pet Cadet Ser.). (ENG.). 32p. (J). (gr. k-3). 9.99 *(978-1-84780-699-4(6)*, Wide Eyed Editions) Quarto Publishing Group UK GBR. Dist: Hachette Bk. Group.

Polinsky, Paige V. Australian Cattle Dogs, 1 vol. 2016. (ENG., Illus.). 24p. (J). 25.65 *(978-1-68078-174-8(X))* ABDO Publishing Co.

—Bluetick Coonhounds, 1 vol. 2016. (ENG., Illus.). 24p. (J). *(978-1-68078-175-5(8))* ABDO Publishing Co.

—Chinese Shar-Peis, 1 vol. 2016. (ENG., Illus.). 24p. (J). *(978-1-68078-176-2(6))* ABDO Publishing Co.

—Greater Swiss Mountain Dogs, 1 vol. 2016. (ENG., Illus.). 24p. (J). *(978-1-68078-177-9(4))* ABDO Publishing Co.

—Rat Terriers, 1 vol. 2016. (ENG., Illus.). 24p. (J). *(978-1-68078-178-6(2))* ABDO Publishing Co.

—Samoyeds, 1 vol. 2016. (ENG., Illus.). 24p. (J). *(978-1-68078-179-3(0))* ABDO Publishing Co.

Popular Dog Library. 2005. (Popular Dog Library). (gr. 6-12). 137.50 *(978-0-7910-9190-6(2)*, Chelsea Hse.) Facts On File, Inc.

Price, Pamela S. Cool Pet Treats: Easy Recipes for Kids to Bake, 1 vol. 2010. (Cool Baking Ser.). (ENG.). 32p. (gr. 3-6). 28.50 *(978-1-60453-777-2(9)*, Checkerboard Library) ABDO Publishing Co.

Priddy, Roger. Puppies. 2005. (ENG.). 12p. (J). 0.97 *(978-0-312-49609-8(5)*, Priddy Bks.) St. Martin's Pr.

Puchalski, Robin. Foo Foo the Shih Poo: My First Day Home. 2012. 20p. pap. 24.95 *(978-1-4626-6625-6(6))* America Star Bks.

Pudsey. Pudsey: A Pup Star's Story. 2013. (ENG., Illus.). 272p. (YA). (gr. 3-5). pap. 10.99 *(978-0-349-00165-4(0))* Little, Brown Book Group Ltd. GBR. Dist: Hachette Bk. Group.

Puppies. 2003. (Three Minute Tales Ser.). 32p. (J). 5.98 *(978-0-7525-8918-3(0))*; 7.95 *(978-0-7525-5538-6(3))* Parragon, Inc.

Puppy. 2004. (J). per. *(978-1-57657-397-6(4))* Paradise Pr., Inc.

Puppy. (Buggy Buddies Ser.). (Illus.). (J). (gr. -1). bds. *(978-1-56021-351-2(5)*, 202) W.J. Fantasy, Inc.

Pyne, Jane. Rosie's Story - an Alpaca's Tale. 2012. 24p. pap. *(978-1-908341-91-4(2))* Paragon Publishing, Rothersthorpe.

Quattlebaum, Mary. National Geographic Kids Chapters: Hero Dogs. 2017. (NGK Chapters Ser.). (ENG.). 112p. (J). (gr. 2-5). lib. bdg. 15.90 ***(978-1-4263-2820-6(6))***; (Illus.). pap. 5.99 ***(978-1-4263-2819-0(2))*** National Geographic Society. (National Geographic Children's Bks.).

Quigley, Karen. Everyone Loves Elwood. 2007. (Illus.). 42p. (YA). 15.00 *(978-0-9800449-1-0(X))* Quigley, Karen.

Quinton, Sasha. Rat-A-Tat: A Phonics Reader. 2009. (Illus.). pap. *(978-1-936199-04-4(1))* Book Shop, Ltd., The.

Raatma, Lucia. Animals Helping at Home. 2015. (ENG., Illus.). 48p. (J). pap. 6.95 *(978-0-531-21285-1(8)*, Orchard Bks.) Scholastic Library Publishing.

Rabe, Tish. If I Ran the Dog Show: All about Dogs. Ruiz, Aristides & Mathieu, Joe, illus. 2012. (Cat in the Hat's Learning Library). (ENG.). 48p. (J). (gr. k-3). 9.99 *(978-0-375-86682-1(5)*, Random Hse. Bks. for Young Readers) Random Hse. Children's Bks.

Raffaelli, Sean & Dreske, Erin. Dogs Don't Have Pockets. Konecny, John, illus. 2013. 24p. pap. 9.99 *(978-1-937165-55-0(8))* Orange Hat Publishing.

Raffin, Deborah. Mitzi's World: Seek & Discover More Than 150 Details in 15 Works of Folk Art. Scott, Jane Wooster, illus. 2009. (ENG.). 32p. (J). (gr. k-2). 18.95 *(978-0-8109-8004-4(5)*, Abrams Bks. for Young Readers) Abrams, Inc.

Rains, Deborah. Sebastian Rae. 2011. 20p. pap. 24.95 *(978-1-4489-4280-0(2))* America Star Bks.

Rajczak, Kristen. Great Danes. 2011. (Great Big Dogs Ser.). (Illus.). 24p. (J). (gr. 2-5). pap. 8.15 *(978-1-4339-5776-5(0)*, Gareth Stevens Learning Library); lib. bdg. 22.60 *(978-1-4339-5774-1(4))* Stevens, Gareth Publishing LLLP.

—Irish Wolfhounds. 2011. (Great Big Dogs Ser.). (Illus.). 24p. (J). (gr. 2-5). pap. 8.15 *(978-1-4339-5780-2(9)*, Gareth Stevens Learning Library); lib. bdg. 22.60 *(978-1-4339-5778-9(7))* Stevens, Gareth Publishing LLLP.

Random House. Team Colors (Paw Patrol) Random House, illus. 2015. (Board Book Ser.). (ENG., Illus.). 24p. (J). (— 1). bds. 6.99 *(978-0-553-49771-7(5)*, Random Hse. Bks. for Young Readers) Random Hse. Children's Bks.

Rau-Tobin, Joanna. Ted E. Bear the Labradoodle. Rau, Dinah M., illus. 2013. 32p. 19.95 *(978-1-59299-849-4(6))*; pap. 12.95 *(978-1-59299-850-0(X))* Inkwater Pr.

Raven, Margot Theis. Rags Hero Dog of WWI: A True Story. Brown, Petra, illus. 2014. (ENG.). 32p. (J). (gr. 2-5). 16.99 *(978-1-58536-258-5(1)*, 203672) Sleeping Bear Pr.

Rayner, Matthew & BVetMed MRCVS Staff. Dog. Burton, Jane & Greenaway, Frank, photos by. 2004. (I Am Your Pet Ser.). (Illus.). 32p. (gr. k-4). lib. bdg. 26.00 *(978-0-8368-4103-9(4)*, Gareth Stevens Learning Library) Stevens, Gareth Publishing LLLP.

Redmond, Shirley Raye & Redmond, Shirley Raye. The Dog That Dug for Dinosaurs. Sullivan, Simon, illus. 2004. (Ready-To-Reads Ser.). (ENG.). 32p. (J). (gr. 1-3). pap. 3.99 *(978-0-689-85708-9(X)*, Simon Spotlight) Simon Spotlight.

Reed, Kevin. The Dog's Guide to Surfing: Hanging Ten with Man's Best Friend. Crump, A. K., ed. 2005. (ENG., Illus.). 128p. (gr. 5-18). pap. *(978-0-9674898-7-2(3))* Temmen, Edition, Horst Temmen.

Rende, Thomas & Rende, Crystal. Novel Ideas 3 Great Dog Stories. 2007. (J). spiral bd. 12.99 *(978-0-9793576-3-3(2))* New Learning Publishing.

Richmond, Marianne R. Goodbye, Faithful Friend: Remembering Your Dog with Love. 2005. (ENG., Illus.). 40p. (YA). 7.95 *(978-0-9770000-1-2(X)*, Marianne Richmond Studios, Inc.) Sourcebooks, Inc.

Riggs, Kate. Bulldogs. 2016. (Seedlings Ser.). 24p. (J). (gr. k-2). (ENG.). pap. 7.99 *(978-1-62832-247-7(0)*, Creative Paperbacks); (Illus.). 28.50 *(978-1-60818-662-4(8)*, Creative Education) Creative Co., The.

Ring, Susan. Good Dog! 2005. (Yellow Umbrella Fluent Level Ser.). (ENG.). 16p. (gr. k-1). pap. 35.70 *(978-0-7368-5305-7(7)*, Yellow Umbrella Bks.) Capstone Press of Coughlan Cos.

Ritland, Mike, et al. Navy SEAL Dogs: My Tale of Training Canines for Combat. 2013. (ENG., Illus.). 208p. (YA). (gr. 7). 17.99 *(978-1-250-04182-1(1)*, 9781250041821, St. Martin's Griffin) St. Martin's Pr.

Ritthaler, Lynn. Pepper. 2012. 142p. (gr. -1). 23.99 *(978-1-4772-8009-6(X))*; pap. 14.95 *(978-1-4772-8010-2(3))* AuthorHouse.

Robb, Jackie & Stringle, Berny. The Story of Dog. Duncan, Karen & Stringle, Sam, illus. 2004. (Bang on the Door Ser.). 32p. (YA). pap. *(978-1-85602-315-3(X)*, Pavilion Children's Books) Pavilion Bks.

Roberts, Walter, Jr. Therapy Dogs, 1 vol. 2013. (Dogs on the Job Ser.). (ENG.). 32p. (gr. 3-4). 27.99 *(978-1-4765-0132-1(7)*, Edge Bks.) Capstone Press of Coughlan Cos.

Rockwood, Leigh. Dogs Are Smart! 2010. (Super Smart Animals Ser.). (Illus.). 24p. (J). pap. 8.25 *(978-1-4358-9836-3(2)*, PowerKids Pr.); (YA). (gr. 2-5). lib. bdg. 22.60 *(978-1-4358-9374-0(3))* Rosen Publishing Group, Inc., The.

Rome, Lori April. The Adventures of Salt & Soap at Grand Canyon. Bauerle, Tanja, illus. 2009. (ENG.). 32p. (gr. 2-4). pap. 9.95 *(978-1-934656-04-4(6))* Grand Canyon Assn.

Rondinone, Craig. Jeepers. Simonton, Tom, illus. 2005. (ENG.). 16p. (J). 5.75 *(978-1-57274-755-5(2)*, 2750, Bks. for Young Learners) Owen, Richard C. Pubs., Inc.

Roth, Susan L. & Trumbore, Cindy. Prairie Dog Song. Roth, Susan L., illus. 2016. (ENG., Illus.). 40p. (J). (gr. 1-7). 18.95 *(978-1-62014-245-5(7))* Lee & Low Bks., Inc.

Royston, Angela. Diary of a Dog Walker, 1 vol. 2013. (Diary of A... Ser.). (ENG.). 32p. (gr. 1-3). 27.32 *(978-1-4329-7581-4(1))*; pap. 8.95 *(978-1-4329-7588-3(9))* Heinemann-Raintree. (Heinemann First Library).

Rudolph, Ellen K. Willi Gets a History Lesson: In Virginia's Historic Triangle. Rudolph, Ellen K., photos by. 2007. (ENG., Illus.). 80p. pap. 24.00 *(978-0-9791348-0-7(3))* EKR Pubns.

Rudolph, Jessica. Labrador Retriever: Most Popular. 2011. (Big Dogs Rule! Ser.). 32p. (YA). (gr. 2-5). lib. bdg. 25.27 *(978-1-61772-300-1(2))* Bearport Publishing Co., Inc.

—Saint Bernard: Mountain Retriever. 2011. (Big Dogs Rule! Ser.). 32p. (YA). (gr. 2-5). lib. bdg. 25.27 *(978-1-61772-295-0(2))* Bearport Publishing Co., Inc.

—Search-And-Rescue Dogs. 2014. (Bow Wow! Dog Helpers Ser.). 24p. (J). (gr. -1-3). lib. bdg. 23.93 *(978-1-62724-122-9(1))* Bearport Publishing Co., Inc.

—Service Dogs. 2014. (Bow Wow! Dog Helpers Ser.). 24p. (J). (gr. -1-3). lib. bdg. 23.93 *(978-1-62724-121-2(3))* Bearport Publishing Co., Inc.

Ruffin, Frances E. Medical Detective Dogs. 2006. (Dog Heroes Ser.). (Illus.). 32p. (YA). (gr. 2-5). lib. bdg. 25.27 *(978-1-59716-251-7(5))* Bearport Publishing Co., Inc.

—Military Dogs. 2006. (Dog Heroes Ser.). (Illus.). 32p. (YA). (gr. 2-5). lib. bdg. 25.27 *(978-1-59716-273-9(6))* Bearport Publishing Co., Inc.

—Police Dogs. 2016. (Dog Heroes Ser.). (ENG.). 32p. (J). (gr. 2-7). pap. 8.95 *(978-1-944998-52-3(7))* Bearport Publishing Co., Inc.

—Water Rescue Dogs. 2005. (Dog Heroes Ser.). (Illus.). 32p. (J). (gr. 3-7). lib. bdg. 25.27 *(978-1-59716-142-8(X))* Bearport Publishing Co., Inc.

Ruffin, Frances E. & Melville, Wilma. Military Dogs. 2016. (Dog Heroes Ser.). (ENG.). 32p. (J). (gr. 2-7). pap. 8.95 *(978-1-944998-62-2(4))* Bearport Publishing Co., Inc.

Rustad, Martha E. H. Beagles. 2017. (Favorite Dog Breeds Ser.). (ENG.). 24p. (gr. 1-4). 20.95 *(978-1-68151-124-5(X))* Amicus Publishing.

—Boxers. 2017. (Favorite Dog Breeds Ser.). (ENG.). 24p. (gr. 1-4). 20.95 *(978-1-68151-125-2(8))* Amicus Publishing.

—Bulldogs. 2017. (Favorite Dog Breeds Ser.). (ENG.). 24p. (gr. 1-4). 20.95 *(978-1-68151-126-9(6))* Amicus Publishing.

—Dogs, 1 vol. 2014. (Little Scientist Ser.). (ENG.). 32p. (gr. 1-2). lib. bdg. 27.99 *(978-1-4914-0791-2(3))* Capstone Press of Coughlan Cos.

—Labrador Retrievers. 2017. (Favorite Dog Breeds Ser.). (ENG.). 24p. (J). (gr. 1-4). 20.95 ***(978-1-68151-128-3(2))*** Amicus Publishing.

—Poodles. 2017. (Favorite Dog Breeds Ser.). (ENG.). 24p. (gr. 1-4). 20.95 *(978-1-68151-129-0(0))* Amicus Publishing.

—Saint Bernards. 2017. (Favorite Dog Breeds Ser.). (ENG.). 24p. (gr. 1-4). 20.95 ***(978-1-68151-130-6(4))*** Amicus Publishing.

—Scottish Terriers. 2017. (Favorite Dog Breeds Ser.). (ENG.). 24p. (gr. 1-4). 20.95 ***(978-1-68151-131-3(2))*** Amicus Publishing.

Sadie: The Dog Who Finds the Evidence. 2014. (Hero Dog Ser.). (ENG., Illus.). 32p. (J). (gr. k-2). pap. 3.99 *(978-1-4814-2240-6(5)*, Simon Spotlight) Simon Spotlight.

Salzmann, Mary Elizabeth. Airedale to Zuchon: Dogs from A to Z, 1 vol. 2009. (Let's Learn A to Z Ser.). (ENG., Illus.). 32p. (J). (gr. -1-2). 27.07 *(978-1-60453-491-7(5))* ABDO Publishing Co.

—Dandy Dogs, 1 vol. 2007. (Perfect Pets Ser.). (ENG., Illus.). 24p. (J). (gr. k-3). lib. bdg. 24.21 *(978-1-59928-746-1(3)*, SandCastle) ABDO Publishing Co.

—Super Saint Bernards, 1 vol. Doucet, Bob, illus. 2010. (Super SandCastle Ser.). (ENG.). 24p. 25.65 *(978-1-61613-381-8(3)*, Super SandCastle) ABDO Publishing Co.

Sander, Sonia, told to. The Dog: New You for the New Year: The Dogs Share Their Health Secrets! 2007. (Illus.). 30p. *(978-0-545-01183-9(3))* Scholastic, Inc.

Saunders, Margaret Marshall. Beautiful Joe: Der Hund, der die Menschen verändert hat. 2007. 262p. pap. 23.55 *(978-1-4303-1348-9(X))* Lulu Pr., Inc.

Saunders-Smith, Gail. You'll Love Chorkies, 1 vol. 2014. (Favorite Designer Dogs Ser.). (ENG.). 24p. (gr. k-1). 26.65 *(978-1-4914-0568-0(6)*, Pebble Plus) Capstone Press of Coughlan Cos.

—You'll Love Cockapoos, 1 vol. 2014. (Favorite Designer Dogs Ser.). (ENG.). 24p. (gr. k-1). 26.65 *(978-1-4914-0569-7(4)*, Pebble Plus) Capstone Press of Coughlan Cos.

—You'll Love Labradoodles, 1 vol. 2014. (Favorite Designer Dogs Ser.). (ENG.). 24p. (gr. k-1). 26.65 *(978-1-4914-0570-3(8)*, Pebble Plus) Capstone Press of Coughlan Cos.

—You'll Love Morkies, 1 vol. 2014. (Favorite Designer Dogs Ser.). (ENG.). 24p. (gr. k-1). 26.65 *(978-1-4914-0571-0(6)*, Pebble Plus) Capstone Press of Coughlan Cos.

Schaefer, Peggy. More Stories of Dogs. 2005. (Illus.). 205p. 12.95 *(978-0-8249-4639-5(1)*, Ideal Pubns.) Worthy Publishing.

Scheunemann, Pam. Daring Dalmatians, 1 vol. Doucet, Bob, illus. 2010. (Super SandCastle Ser.). (ENG.). 24p. 25.65 *(978-1-61613-378-8(3)*, Super SandCastle) ABDO Publishing Co.

—Dogs Bark!, 1 vol. 2009. (Animal Sounds Set 1 Ser.). (ENG., Illus.). 24p. (J). (gr. k-3). lib. bdg. 24.21 *(978-1-60453-570-9(9)*, SandCastle) ABDO Publishing Co.

—Jumping Jack Russell Terriers, 1 vol. Doucet, Bob, illus. 2009. (Dog Daze Ser.). (ENG.). 24p. 25.65 *(978-1-60453-617-1(9)*, Super SandCastle) ABDO Publishing Co.

—Lovely Labrador Retrievers, 1 vol. Doucet, Bob, illus. 2009. (Dog Daze Ser.). (ENG.). 24p. 25.65 *(978-1-60453-618-8(7)*, Super SandCastle) ABDO Publishing Co.

—Perky Poodles, 1 vol. Doucet, Bob, illus. 2010. (Super SandCastle Ser.). (ENG.). 24p. 25.65 *(978-1-61613-379-5(1)*, Super SandCastle) ABDO Publishing Co.

Schindel, John. Busy Doggies. Sparks, Beverly, photos by. 2003. (Busy Book Ser.). (ENG., Illus.). 20p. (J). (— 1). bds. 6.99 *(978-1-58246-090-1(6)*, Knopf Bks. for Young Readers) Random Hse. Children's Bks.

Schott, Edward. The Dogs of King Park. 2012. 16p. pap. 12.68 *(978-1-4269-9463-0(X))* Trafford Publishing.

Schuetz, Kari. Baby Dogs. (Illus.). 24p. (J). 2014. *(978-0-531-22279-9(9))* 2013. (ENG., lib. bdg. 25.95 *(978-1-60014-926-9(X)*, Blastoff! Readers) Bellwether Media.

—Pugs. 2017. (Awesome Dogs Ser.). (ENG., Illus.). 24p. (J). (gr. k-3). lib. bdg. 25.95 *(978-1-62617-558-7(6)*, Blastoff! Readers) Bellwether Media.

—Shih Tzus. 2017. (Awesome Dogs Ser.). (ENG.). 24p. (J). (gr. k-3). lib. bdg. 25.95 *(978-1-62617-560-0(8)*, Blastoff! Readers) Bellwether Media.

Schuh, Mari. Beagles. 2015. (Awesome Dogs Ser.). (ENG., Illus.). 24p. (J). (gr. k-3). lib. bdg. 25.95 *(978-1-62617-237-1(4)*, Blastoff! Readers) Bellwether Media.

—Boxers. 2016. (Awesome Dogs Ser.). (ENG., Illus.). 24p. (J). (gr. k-3). lib. bdg. 25.95 *(978-1-62617-303-3(6)*, Blastoff! Readers) Bellwether Media.

—Bulldogs. 2016. (Awesome Dogs Ser.). (ENG., Illus.). 24p. (J). (gr. k-3). lib. bdg. 25.95 *(978-1-62617-304-0(4)*, Blastoff! Readers) Bellwether Media.

—Chihuahuas. 2016. (Awesome Dogs Ser.). (ENG., Illus.). 24p. (J). (gr. k-3). lib. bdg. 25.95 *(978-1-62617-305-7(2)*, Blastoff! Readers) Bellwether Media.

—Dachshunds. 2015. (Awesome Dogs Ser.). (ENG., Illus.). 24p. (J). (gr. k-3). lib. bdg. 25.95 *(978-1-62617-238-8(2)*, Blastoff! Readers) Bellwether Media.

—Dalmatians. 2017. (Awesome Dogs Ser.). (ENG.). 24p. (J). (gr. k-3). lib. bdg. 25.95 ***(978-1-62617-613-3(2)***, Blastoff! Readers) Bellwether Media.

—French Bulldogs. 2015. (Awesome Dogs Ser.). (ENG., Illus.). 24p. (J). (gr. k-3). lib. bdg. 25.95 *(978-1-62617-239-5(0)*, Blastoff! Readers) Bellwether Media.

—German Shepherds. 2008. (Dog Breeds Ser.). (ENG., Illus.). 24p. (J). (gr. 2-5). lib. bdg. 25.95 *(978-1-60014-215-4(X))* Bellwether Media.

—Golden Retrievers. 2008. (Dog Breeds Ser.). (ENG., Illus.). 24p. (J). (gr. 2-5). lib. bdg. 25.95 *(978-1-60014-216-1(8))* Bellwether Media.

—Labrador Retrievers. 2008. (Dog Breeds Ser.). (ENG., Illus.). 24p. (J). (gr. 2-5). lib. bdg. 25.95 *(978-1-60014-213-0(3))* Bellwether Media.

—Rottweilers. 2016. (Awesome Dogs Ser.). (ENG., Illus.). 24p. (J). (gr. k-3). lib. bdg. 25.95 *(978-1-62617-307-1(9)*, Blastoff! Readers) Bellwether Media.

—Yorkshire Terriers. 2015. (Awesome Dogs Ser.). (ENG., Illus.). 24p. (J). (gr. k-3). lib. bdg. 25.95 *(978-1-62617-244-9(7)*, Blastoff! Readers) Bellwether Media.

Schuh, Mari C. Assistance Dogs, 1 vol. 2010. (Working Dogs Ser.). (ENG.). 24p. (gr. k-1). 26.65 *(978-1-4296-4474-7(5)*, Pebble Plus) Capstone Press of Coughlan Cos.

—Search & Rescue Dogs, 1 vol. 2010. (Working Dogs Ser.). (ENG.). 24p. (gr. k-1). 26.65 *(978-1-4296-4473-0(7)*, Pebble Plus) Capstone Press of Coughlan Cos.

Schwartz, Heather E. Morkie: A Cross Between a Maltese & a Yorkshire Terrier, 1 vol. 2012. (Designer Dogs Ser.). (ENG.). 32p. (gr. 3-4). lib. bdg. 27.99 *(978-1-4296-7668-7(X)*, Snap Bks.) Capstone Press of Coughlan Cos.

Scollen, Chris. Busy Kids Kittens & Puppies Sb. 2008. (Busy Kids Ser.). (Illus.). 20p. (J). (gr. -1-3). 4.99 *(978-1-84610-632-3(X))* Make Believe Ideas GBR. Dist: Nelson, Thomas Inc.

Searl, Duncan. Cairn Terrier: Hero of Oz. 2010. (Little Dogs Rock! II Ser.). 32p. (YA). (gr. 2-5). lib. bdg. 25.27 *(978-1-936088-16-4(9))* Bearport Publishing Co., Inc.

Seibold, J. Otto. Quincy, the Hobby Photographer Vol. 1: Dogs. 2006. (ENG., Illus.). 68p. (J). 16.00 *(978-0-15-216331-0(X))* Harcourt Children's Bks.

Selbert, Kathryn. War Dogs. Selbert, Kathryn, illus. 2016. (ENG., Illus.). 48p. (J). (gr. 2-5). pap. 7.95 *(978-1-58089-415-9(1))* Charlesbridge Publishing, Inc.

Sexton, Colleen. The Life Cycle of a Dog. 2010. (Life Cycles Ser.). (ENG., Illus.). 24p. (J). (gr. k-3). lib. bdg. 25.95 *(978-1-60014-307-6(5)*, Blastoff! Readers) Bellwether Media.

—Puppies. 2008. (Watch Animals Grow Ser.). (ENG., Illus.). 24p. (J). (gr. k-3). lib. bdg. 25.95 *(978-1-60014-170-6(6))* Bellwether Media.

Shaggy Sheepdog & the Hairdresser's. 2004. (Play Pals Ser.). (Illus.). 12p. (J). bds. *(978-1-84229-648-6(5))* Top That! Publishing PLC.

Shahan, Sherry, photos by. Dashing Through the Snow: The Story of the Jr. Iditarod. 2nd ed. 2006. (Illus.). (J). pap. *(978-1-59336-714-5(7))* Mondo Publishing.

Shaw-Russell, Susan. Pampered Pooches Sticker Activity Book. 2012. (Dover Little Activity Books Stickers Ser.). (ENG.). 4p. (J). (gr. k-3). pap. 1.50 *(978-0-486-48940-7(X))* Dover Pubns., Inc.

Shene, Paula. Mandy - The Alpha Dog: The Chronicles of the K-9 Boys & Girls on Locus Street. Shene, Prescott, illus. 2009. 36p. pap. 24.95 *(978-1-60836-710-8(X))* America Star Bks.

Shores, Erika L. All about Boxers, 1 vol. 2012. (Dogs, Dogs, Dogs Ser.). (ENG., Illus.). 24p. (gr. k-1). lib. bdg. 26.65 *(978-1-4296-8723-2(1)*, Pebble Plus) Capstone Press of Coughlan Cos.

—All about Rottweilers, 1 vol. 2012. (Dogs, Dogs, Dogs Ser.). (ENG., Illus.). 24p. (gr. k-1). lib. bdg. 26.65 *(978-1-4296-8728-7(2)*, Pebble Plus) Capstone Press of Coughlan Cos.

—All about Yorkshire Terriers, 1 vol. 2012. (Dogs, Dogs, Dogs Ser.). (ENG., Illus.). 24p. (gr. k-1). lib. bdg. 26.65 *(978-1-4296-8729-4(0)*, Pebble Plus) Capstone Press of Coughlan Cos.

—Pet Dogs up Close. 2015. (Pets up Close Ser.). (ENG.). 24p. (gr. k-1). pap. 6.95 *(978-1-4914-7765-6(2)*, Pebble Plus) Capstone Press of Coughlan Cos.

Shores, Erika L. & Wittrock, Jeni. Dogs, Dogs, Dogs. 2012. (Dogs, Dogs, Dogs Ser.). (ENG.). 24p. (gr. k-1). lib. bdg. 213.20 *(978-1-4296-9167-3(0)*, Pebble Plus) Capstone Press of Coughlan Cos.

Silverman, Maida. Snow Search Dogs. 2005. (Dog Heroes Ser.). 32p. (J). lib. bdg. 25.27 *(978-1-59716-017-9(2))* Bearport Publishing Co., Inc.

Silverstein, Alvin, et al. Hairless Dogs: Cool Pets! 2012. (Far-Out & Unusual Pets Ser.). 48p. (J). (gr. 3-4). (Illus.). pap. 8.95 *(978-1-4644-0124-4(1))*; 25.27 *(978-0-7660-3879-0(3))* Enslow Pubs., Inc. (Enslow Elementary).

Simmonds, Jane. Cocker Spaniel. 2017. (Dog Lover's Guides: Vol. 18). (ENG.). (YA). (gr. 7-12). 26.95 ***(978-1-4222-3854-7(7))*** Mason Crest.

Simms, Rk. Me & My Dog, Petey. 2008. 32p. pap. 19.99 *(978-1-4363-2842-5(X))* Xlibris Corp.

Simon, Seymour. Dogs. Simon, Seymour, illus. 2009. (ENG., Illus.). 32p. (J). (gr. k-4). pap. 6.99 *(978-0-06-446255-6(2))* HarperCollins Pubs.

Sjonger, Rebecca & Kalman, Bobbie. Los Cachorros. Crabtree, Marc, photos by. 2006. (Cuidado de las Mascotas Ser.). (Illus.). 32p. (J). (gr. 3-7). (SPA.). pap. *(978-0-7787-8477-7(0))*; (ENG & SPA., lib. bdg. *(978-0-7787-8455-5(X))* Crabtree Publishing Co.

—Puppies. 2003. (Pet Care Ser.). (ENG., Illus.). 32p. (J). lib. bdg. *(978-0-7787-1751-5(8))* Crabtree Publishing Co.

Sjonger, Rebecca, et al. Les Chiots. 2010. (Petit Monde Vivant Ser.). (FRE., Illus.). 32p. (J). pap. 9.95 *(978-2-89579-326-7(3))* Bayard Canada Livres CAN. Dist: Crabtree Publishing Co.

Skiles, Janet & Coloring Books Staff. How to Care for Your Dog: A Color & Learn Guide for Kids. 2011. (Dover Children's Activity Bks.). (ENG., Illus.). 32p. (J). (gr. -1-2). pap. 3.99 *(978-0-486-48149-4(2))* Dover Pubns., Inc.

Slade, Suzanne. From Puppy to Dog: Following the Life Cycle, 1 vol. Yesh, Jeff, illus. 2008. (Amazing Science: Life Cycles Ser.). (ENG.). 24p. (gr. 1-4). 26.65 *(978-1-4048-4928-0(9)*, 1285104) Picture Window Bks.

—Why Do Dogs Drool? And Other Questions Kids Have about Dogs, 1 vol. Pillo, Cary, illus. 2010. (Kids' Questions Ser.).

(ENG.). 24p. (gr. 1-2). lib. bdg. 26.65 *(978-1-4048-5762-9(1))* Picture Window Bks.
Smith, Cynthia & Wishbone. Dogs Get Cancer Too: A True Story. 2010. 48p. 19.49 *(978-1-4490-4129-8(9))* AuthorHouse.
Soffer, Ruth. Dogs Stained Glass Coloring Book. 2010. (Dover Nature Stained Glass Coloring Book Ser.). (ENG., Illus.). 32p. (J). (gr. 2-5). pap. 6.99 *(978-0-486-47802-9(5))* Dover Pubns., Inc.
Solberg, Jessica L. First Dog: Unleashed in the Montana Capitol. Rath, Robert, illus. 2007. (J). 11.95 *(978-1-56037-419-0(5))* Farcountry Pr.
Sommer, Nathan. Cocker Spaniels. 2017. (Awesome Dogs Ser.). (ENG.). 24p. (J). (gr. k-3). 25.95 ***(978-1-62617-611-9(6))*** Bellwether Media.
—Newfoundlands. 2017. (Awesome Dogs Ser.). (ENG.). 24p. (J). (gr. k-3). lib. bdg. 25.95 ***(978-1-62617-614-0(0)***, Blastoff! Readers) Bellwether Media.
—Saint Bernards. 2017. (Awesome Dogs Ser.). (ENG.). 24p. (J). (gr. k-3). lib. bdg. 25.95 ***(978-1-62617-615-7(9)***, Blastoff! Readers) Bellwether Media.
Spizzirri, Linda. Dogs of the Wild: An Educational Coloring Book. (J). pap. 1.99 *(978-0-86545-216-9(4))* Spizzirri Pr., Inc.
Spooner, J. B. & Seaver, Richard. The Story of the Little Black Dog. Seeley, Terre Lamb, illus. 2011. (Little Black Dog Ser.). (ENG.). 32p. (J). (gr. -1-k). 16.95 *(978-1-61145-001-9(2)*, 611001, Arcade Publishing) Skyhorse Publishing Co., Inc.
Spooner, J. B. & Seeley, Terre Lamb. The Little Black Dog Has Puppies. Seeley, Terre Lamb, illus. 2011. (Little Black Dog Ser.). (ENG., Illus.). 32p. (J). (gr. -1-k). 16.95 *(978-1-61145-006-4(3)*, 611006, Arcade Publishing) Skyhorse Publishing Co., Inc.
Stamper, Judith Bauer. Eco Dogs. 2016. (Dog Heroes Ser.). (ENG.). 32p. (J). (gr. 2-7). pap. 8.95 *(978-1-944998-63-9(2))* Bearport Publishing Co., Inc.
Stanley, Sheryl. Hank Becomes a Hero. 2009. 40p. pap. 18.49 *(978-1-4389-6081-4(6))* AuthorHouse.
Starke, Katherine. Dogs & Puppies. Watt, Fiona, ed. rev. ed. 2004. (First Pets Ser.). 32p. (J). (gr. 1-18). pap. 5.99 *(978-0-7945-0790-9(5)*, Usborne) EDC Publishing.
Starke, Katherine & Watt, Fiona. Dogs & Puppies. Fox, Christyan, illus. 2004. 31p. (J). *(978-0-439-78715-4(7))* Scholastic, Inc.
Stevens, Kathryn. Dogs. 2015. (Pet Care Ser.). (ENG.). 24p. (J). (gr. -1-2). 25.64 *(978-1-63143-727-4(5)*, 208544) Child's World, Inc., The.
Steward, Martha. Darby's Story: The Life of an Adopted Dog. 2009. 36p. pap. 15.95 *(978-1-4490-2775-9(X))* AuthorHouse.
Stoltman, Joan. My First Dog. 2017. (Let's Get a Pet! Ser.). 24p. (gr. 1-2). pap. 8.15 ***(978-1-4824-6449-8(7))*** Stevens, Gareth Publishing LLLP.
Stone, Lynn. Cocker Spaniels. 2008. (Illus.). 24p. (J). lib. bdg. 27.07 *(978-1-60472-362-5(9))* Rourke Educational Media.
Stone, Lynn M. Basset Hounds. 2004. (Eye to Eye with Dogs Ser.). (Illus.). 24p. (gr. 2-5). lib. bdg. 27.07 *(978-1-59515-291-6(1))* Rourke Educational Media.
—Labradoodles. 2008. (Illus.). 24p. (J). lib. bdg. 27.07 *(978-1-60472-363-2(7))* Rourke Educational Media.
The Story of Shadow. 2006. (J). per. 12.00 *(978-0-9787695-0-5(3))* Scafe, Claire.
Strother, Ruth. W Is for Woof: A Dog Alphabet. Frankenhuyzen, Gijsbert van, illus. 2009. (ENG.). 40p. (J). (gr. k-6). pap. 7.95 *(978-1-58536-477-0(0))* Sleeping Bear Pr.
—W Is for Woof: A Dog Alphabet. van Frankenhuyzen, Gijsbert, illus. 2008. (ENG.). 40p. (J). (gr. k-6). 17.95 *(978-1-58536-343-8(X))* Sleeping Bear Pr.
Summers, Alex. Rescue & Shelter Dogs. 2015. (ENG.). 24p. (gr. 1-4). 28.50 *(978-1-63430-064-3(5))* Rourke Educational Media.
Swensen, C. Dogs. 2016. (In the Barnyard Ser.). (ENG.). 24p. (J). (gr. k-3). 27.07 *(978-1-5038-0826-3(2)*, 210670) Child's World, Inc., The.
Swinney, Nicola Jane. My Little Book of Dogs & Puppies. 2016. (Illus.). 64p. (J). ***(978-1-4351-6414-7(8))*** Barnes & Noble, Inc.
Tabler, Judith. Rat Terrier, 1 vol. 2011. (Breedlover's Guide(tm) Ser.). (ENG., Illus.). 144p. spiral bd. 14.95 *(978-0-7938-4179-0(8))* TFH Pubns., Inc.
Tagliaferro, Linda. Dogs & Their Puppies [Scholastic]. 2011. (Animal Offspring Ser.). 24p. pap. 0.50 *(978-1-4296-6293-2(X)*, Pebble Plus) Capstone Press of Coughlan Cos.
—Service Dogs. 2005. (Dog Heroes Ser.). (Illus.). 32p. (J). lib. bdg. 25.27 *(978-1-59716-016-2(4))* Bearport Publishing Co., Inc.
—Therapy Dogs. 2005. (Dog Heroes Ser.). (Illus.). 32p. (J). lib. bdg. 25.27 *(978-1-59716-018-6(0))* Bearport Publishing Co., Inc.
Tait, Leia. Pecorino. 2008. (Inspiring Animals Ser.). (Illus.). 24p. (J). (gr. 2-4). pap. 8.95 *(978-1-59036-859-6(2))*; lib. bdg. 24.45 *(978-1-59036-858-9(4))* Weigl Pubs., Inc.
Taylor, Trace. Dogs. 2010. pap. 39.62 *(978-1-61541-095-8(3))* American Reading Co.
Teagarden, Janine. A Dog Named Opposite. Kennedy, Kelly, illus. 2010. 16p. (J). *(978-0-545-24821-1(3))* Scholastic, Inc.
Tedesco, Leah/Hollis. Junior Showmanship How to get started in One of the Best Family Sports. 2007. (YA). 6.95 *(978-0-9792059-0-3(5))* JBT Publishing.
Teora, creator. Dogs. 2007. (My First Sticker Encyclopedia Ser.). (Illus.). 18p. (J). (gr. -1-3). pap. 5.95 *(978-1-59496-145-8(X))* Teora USA LLC.
Thomas, Isabel. Designer Dog Projects. 2015. (Pet Projects Ser.). (ENG., Illus.). 32p. (gr. 3-5). 27.99 *(978-1-4109-8066-3(9)*, Snap Bks.) Capstone Press of Coughlan Cos.
Thomas, Leanne & Schiebold, Olivia, illus. Puppylicious. 2010. 96p. (J). *(978-0-545-26020-6(5))* Scholastic, Inc.
Tiger Tales, ed. & compiled by. Puppies. Tiger Tales, compiled by. 2014. (My First Touch & Feel Ser.). (ENG.). 10p. (J). (gr. -1 — 1). bds. 8.99 *(978-1-58925-564-7(X))* Tiger Tales.
Top That Publishing Staff, ed. Puppies & Dogs. 2005. (Illus.). 24p. *(978-1-84510-540-2(0))* Top That! Publishing PLC.
Tough Dogs. (Illus.). (J). (gr. k-6). 112.50 *(978-1-4042-3297-6(4))* Rosen Publishing Group, Inc., The.
Tracqui, Valérie. Face-to-Face with the Dog: Loyal Companion. Laird, Lisa, tr. from FRE. Hubert, Marie-Luce & Klein, Jean-Louis, photos by. 2004. (Face-to-Face Ser.). (Illus.). 28p. (J). (gr. 2-4). 9.95 *(978-1-57091-452-2(4))* Charlesbridge Publishing, Inc.
Troup, Roxanne. Military Dogs on the Job. 2017. (Helping Dogs Ser.). (ENG.). 24p. (J). (gr. 2-5). lib. bdg. 27.07 *(978-1-5038-1613-8(3)*, 211172) Child's World, Inc., The.
Tuxworth, Nicola. Puppies. 2016. (ENG., Illus.). 20p. bds. 6.99 *(978-1-86147-631-9(0)*, Armadillo) Anness Publishing GBR. Dist: National Bk. Network.
Twine, Alice. Puppies. (Baby Animals Ser.). 24p. 2009. (gr. 1-1). 42.50 *(978-1-61511-495-5(5))* 2008. (Illus.). (J). (gr. 3-7). lib. bdg. 22.60 *(978-1-4042-4143-5(4))* Rosen Publishing Group, Inc., The. (PowerKids Pr.).
—Puppies/Cachorros. 2009. (Baby Animals/Animales bebé Ser.). (ENG & SPA.). 24p. (gr. 1-1). 42.50 *(978-1-61511-507-5(2)*, Editorial Buenas Letras) Rosen Publishing Group, Inc., The.
—Puppies/Cachorros. Obregon, Jose Maria, tr. from ENG. 2008. (Baby Animals / Animales Bebé Ser.). (Illus.). 24p. (J). (gr. -1-3). lib. bdg. 22.60 *(978-1-4042-7687-1(4)*, Editorial Buenas Letras) Rosen Publishing Group, Inc., The.
Unruh, Cindy. Sierra, the Black Lab Who Loved to Eat: (a True Story) Krehbiel, Angie, illus. 2012. 32p. pap. 24.95 *(978-1-4626-5537-3(8))* America Star Bks.
Urbigkit, Cat. Brave Dogs, Gentle Dogs: How They Guard Sheep. (ENG & SPA., Illus.). 32p. (J). 2009. (gr. 2-4). pap. 8.95 *(978-1-59078-674-1(2))* 2005. (gr. 1-7). 17.95 *(978-1-59078-317-7(4))* Boyds Mills Pr.
—The Guardian Team: On the Job with Rena & Roo. Urbigkit, Cat, photos by. 2011. (ENG., Illus.). 32p. (J). (gr. 2-5). 16.95 *(978-1-59078-770-0(6))* Boyds Mills Pr.
Van Steenwyk, Elizabeth. First Dog Fala, 1 vol. Montgomery, Michael G., illus. 2008. (ENG.). 32p. (J). (gr. k-3). 16.95 *(978-1-56145-411-2(7))* Peachtree Pubs.
Ventura, Marne. Service Dogs on the Job. 2017. (Helping Dogs Ser.). (ENG.). 24p. (J). (gr. 2-5). lib. bdg. 27.07 *(978-1-5038-1616-9(8)*, 211175) Child's World, Inc., The.
—Therapy Dogs on the Job. 2017. (Helping Dogs Ser.). (ENG.). 24p. (J). (gr. 2-5). lib. bdg. 27.07 *(978-1-5038-1618-3(4)*, 211177) Child's World, Inc., The.
Wales, Dirk. A Lucky Dog: Owney, U.S. Rail Mail Mascot. Kenna, Diane, illus. 2003. 32p. (J). 15.95 *(978-0-9632459-0-8(2))* Great Plains Pr.
Walker, Kathryn. See How Dogs Grow. 2009. (See How They Grow Ser.). (J). (gr. k-3). (ENG., Illus.). 24p. pap. 8.25 *(978-1-4358-2877-3(1))*; lib. bdg. 22.60 *(978-1-4358-2830-8(5))* Rosen Publishing Group, Inc., The. (PowerKids Pr.).
Walker, Robyn. Sergeant Gander: A Canadian Hero. 2009. (ENG., Illus.). 176p. (YA). (gr. 4-18). pap. 19.99 *(978-1-55488-463-6(2))* Dundurn CAN. Dist: Ingram Publisher Services.
Walter Foster Creative Team. Dogs & Puppies: Step-by-Step Insructions for 25 Different Breeds. Fisher, Diana, illus. 2011. (Learn to Draw Ser.). 32p. (J). (gr. 1-4). 28.50 *(978-1-936309-18-4(1))* Quarto Publishing Group USA.
Watson, Jennifer. French Bulldog. 2017. (Dog Lover's Guides: Vol. 18). (ENG.). (YA). (gr. 3-7). 26.95 ***(978-1-4222-3945-2(4))*** Mason Crest.
Watt, Fiona. Puppies. rev. ed. 2005. 10p. (J). 11.99 *(978-0-7945-0958-3(4)*, Usborne) EDC Publishing.
Watt, Fiona & Wells, Rachel. That's Not My Puppy... Its Coat Is Too Hairy. 2004. (Touchy-Feely Board Bks.). (SPA & ENG., Illus.). 10p. (J). (gr. -1-18). 8.99 *(978-0-7460-3778-2(3))* EDC Publishing.
Webb, Willyn. Baby, the Poodle Cow Dog. Theobald, Denise, illus. 2007. 32p. (J). 13.95 *(978-1-932738-40-7(1))* Western Reflections Publishing Co.
Webre, Mary M. Just a Little Hugo. 2012. 20p. pap. 17.99 *(978-1-4772-5641-1(5))* AuthorHouse.
Weil, Ann. Bomb-Sniffing Dogs. 2013. (Animals with Jobs Ser.). (ENG.). 32p. (gr. 1-4). 28.50 *(978-1-60753-378-8(2))* Amicus Publishing.
Wendorff, Anne. Pugs. 2010. (Dog Breeds Ser.). (ENG., Illus.). 24p. (J). (gr. 2-5). lib. bdg. 25.95 *(978-1-60014-301-4(6))* Bellwether Media.
—Saint Bernards. 2010. (Dog Breeds Ser.). (ENG., Illus.). 24p. (J). (gr. 2-5). lib. bdg. 25.95 *(978-1-60014-304-5(0))* Bellwether Media.
—Shetland Sheepdogs. 2010. (Dog Breeds Ser.). (ENG., Illus.). 24p. (J). (gr. 2-5). lib. bdg. 25.95 *(978-1-60014-302-1(4))* Bellwether Media.
—Siberian Huskies. 2010. (Dog Breeds Ser.). (ENG., Illus.). 24p. (J). (gr. 2-5). lib. bdg. 25.95 *(978-1-60014-303-8(2))* Bellwether Media.
Wheeler, Jill C. Bernese Mountain Dogs, 1 vol. 2010. (Dogs Set 8 Ser.). (ENG.). 24p. (J). (gr. 2-5). 25.65 *(978-1-60453-781-9(7))* ABDO Publishing Co.
—Cockapoos, 1 vol. 2008. (Dogs Set 7:Designer Dogs Ser.). (ENG., Illus.). 24p. (YA). (gr. 2-5). 25.65 *(978-1-59928-962-5(8))* ABDO Publishing Co.
—Labradoodles, 1 vol. 2008. (Dogs Set 7:Designer Dogs Ser.). (ENG., Illus.). 24p. (J). (gr. 2-5). 25.65 *(978-1-59928-964-9(4))* ABDO Publishing Co.
—Newfoundlands, 1 vol. 2010. (Dogs Set 8 Ser.). (ENG.). 24p. (J). (gr. 2-5). 25.65 *(978-1-60453-783-3(3))* ABDO Publishing Co.
—Portuguese Water Dogs, 1 vol. 2010. (Dogs Set 8 Ser.). (ENG.). 24p. (J). (gr. 2-5). 25.65 *(978-1-60453-784-0(1))* ABDO Publishing Co.
—Puggles, 1 vol. 2008. (Dogs Set 7:Designer Dogs Ser.). (ENG., Illus.). 24p. (J). (gr. 2-5). 25.65 *(978-1-59928-965-6(2))* ABDO Publishing Co.
—Schnoodles, 1 vol. 2008. (Dogs Set 7:Designer Dogs Ser.). (ENG., Illus.). 24p. (J). (gr. 2-5). 25.65 *(978-1-59928-966-3(0))* ABDO Publishing Co.
—Weimaraners, 1 vol. 2010. (Dogs Set 8 Ser.). (ENG.). 24p. (J). (gr. 2-5). 25.65 *(978-1-60453-785-7(X))* ABDO Publishing Co.
—Welsh Corgis, 1 vol. 2010. (Dogs Set 8 Ser.). (ENG.). 24p. (J). (gr. 2-5). 25.65 *(978-1-60453-786-4(8))* ABDO Publishing Co.
—Yorkie-Poos, 1 vol. 2008. (Dogs Set 7:Designer Dogs Ser.). (ENG., Illus.). 24p. (J). (gr. 2-5). 25.65 *(978-1-59928-967-0(9))* ABDO Publishing Co.
Where's the Dog?, 6 Pack. (gr. 1-2). 22.00 *(978-0-7635-9157-1(2))* Rigby Education.
White-Adams, Beverly & Adams, Rusty. The Adventures of Rusty: Rusty Goes to Virginia Vol. 1. 2011. 32p. pap. *(978-1-4269-8935-3(0))* Trafford Publishing (UK) Ltd.
White, Andrea & Mimi, Vance. Tummies on the Run. Shepperson, Rob, illus. 2012. 32p. pap. 11.95 *(978-1-60898-134-2(7))* namelos llc.
Wilcox, Charlotte. All about Dogs. (All about Dogs Ser.). (ENG.). 32p. 2016. lib. bdg. 111.96 *(978-1-5157-4029-2(3))* 2011. (gr. 3-4). 111.96 *(978-1-4296-7717-2(1))* Capstone Press of Coughlan Cos. (Edge Bks.).
—Chow Chows. 2011. (All about Dogs Ser.). (ENG.). 32p. (gr. 3-4). lib. bdg. 27.99 *(978-1-4296-7712-7(0)*, Edge Bks.) Capstone Press of Coughlan Cos.
—Greyhounds. 2011. (All about Dogs Ser.). (ENG.). 32p. (gr. 3-4). lib. bdg. 27.99 *(978-1-4296-7713-4(9)*, Edge Bks.) Capstone Press of Coughlan Cos.
—Newfoundlands. 2011. (All about Dogs Ser.). (ENG.). 32p. (gr. 3-4). lib. bdg. 27.99 *(978-1-4296-7714-1(7)*, Edge Bks.) Capstone Press of Coughlan Cos.
—Weimaraners. 2011. (All about Dogs Ser.). (ENG.). 32p. (gr. 3-4). lib. bdg. 27.99 *(978-1-4296-7715-8(5)*, Edge Bks.) Capstone Press of Coughlan Cos.
Williams, Christopher. One Incredible Dog! Lady. Friedman, Judith, illus. 2004. (ENG.). 32p. (J). (gr. -1-3). 15.95 *(978-0-9724853-3-3(3)*, 845-987-7750) Keene Publishing.
Williams, Ellen. Pug. 2017. (Dog Lover's Guides: Vol. 18). (ENG.). (YA). (gr. 7-12). 26.95 ***(978-1-4222-3947-6(0))*** Mason Crest.
Wilsdon, Christina. Dogs. (Amazing Animals Ser.). 48p. 2009. (gr. 2-6). pap. 10.50 *(978-1-4339-2012-7(3)*, Gareth Stevens Learning Library) 2008. (J). (gr. 3-6). lib. bdg. 28.00 *(978-0-8368-9095-2(7))* Stevens, Gareth Publishing LLLP.
—Dogs. 2007. (J). *(978-1-59939-135-9(X)*, Reader's Digest Young Families, Inc.) Studio Fun International.
Wilson, Jeanette. Miniature Schnauzer. 2017. (Dog Lover's Guides: Vol. 18). (ENG.). (J). (gr. 3-7). 26.95 ***(978-1-4222-3946-9(2))*** Mason Crest.
Winkelstein, Steven Paul. Brisko: A True Tale of Holocaust Survival. Juliano, Dana, illus. 2014. 104p. (J). *(978-0-9824498-6-8(0))* Mystic Waters Publishing.
The Wisdom of Zeus. 2005. (J). *(978-0-9765840-0-1(X))* Zeus Media LLC.
Wittrock, Jeni. All about Pit Bulls, 1 vol. 2012. (Dogs, Dogs, Dogs Ser.). (ENG., Illus.). 24p. (gr. k-1). lib. bdg. 26.65 *(978-1-4296-8726-3(6)*, Pebble Plus) Capstone Press of Coughlan Cos.
—Laika the Space Dog: First Hero in Outer Space, 1 vol. Toth, Shannon, illus. 2014. (Animal Heroes Ser.). (ENG.). 32p. (gr. k-2). 28.65 *(978-1-4795-5463-8(4))*; pap. 7.95 *(978-1-4795-5467-6(7))* Picture Window Bks.
Wittrock, Jeni, et al. Animal Heroes, 1 vol. 2014. (Animal Heroes Ser.). (ENG.). 32p. (gr. k-2). 114.60 *(978-1-4795-5555-0(X))* Picture Window Bks.
Wood, Alix. Miniature Dogs. 2016. (Mini Animals Ser.). 00032p. (J). (gr. 2-3). pap. 10.00 *(978-1-4994-8158-7(6)*, Windmill Bks.) Rosen Publishing Group, Inc., The.
Wood, Mandy. My First Puppy. 2013. (ENG.). 24p. (gr. 1-6). pap. 8.95 *(978-1-61448-531-5(3))* Morgan James Publishing.
Wood, Selina. Dog. 2008. (Owning a Pet Ser.). (Illus.). 32p. (YA). (gr. 2-5). lib. bdg. 28.50 *(978-1-59771-056-5(3))* Sea-To-Sea Pubns.
Working Dogs. 2010. (Working Dogs Ser.). (ENG.). 24p. (gr. k-1). lib. bdg. 79.95 *(978-1-4296-5690-0(5))*; lib. bdg. 79.95 *(978-1-4296-4489-1(3))* Capstone Press of Coughlan Cos. (Pebble Plus).
World Book, Inc Staff, contrib. by. Bulldogs & Other Nonsporting Dogs. 2009. (J). *(978-0-7166-1371-8(9))* World Bk., Inc.
—Dogs, from Woofs to Wags. 2008. (J). *(978-0-7166-0620-8(8))* World Bk., Inc.
—Golden Retrievers & Other Sporting Dogs. 2007. (World Book's Animals of the World Ser.). (Illus.). 64p. (J). *(978-0-7166-1328-2(X))* World Bk., Inc.
Wummel, Jeanette. Zendoodle Coloring: Playful Puppies: Furry Friends to Color & Display. 2017. (ENG., Illus.). 128p. pap. 13.99 *(978-1-250-14158-3(3)*, 9781250141583, St. Martin's Griffin) St. Martin's Pr.
Young, Jeff C. Leading the Pack: Dogsled Racing, 1 vol. 2011. (Adrenaline Adventure Ser.). (ENG., Illus.). 32p. (YA). (gr. 3-6). 27.07 *(978-1-61613-549-2(2))* ABDO Publishing Co.
Zeiger, Jennifer. Animals Helping after Disasters. 2015. (ENG.). 48p. (J). pap. 6.95 *(978-0-531-21286-8(6)*, Orchard Bks.) Scholastic Library Publishing.
Zobel, Derek. Caring for Your Dog. 2010. (Pet Care Library). (ENG., Illus.). 24p. (J). (gr. 2-5). lib. bdg. 25.95 *(978-1-60014-466-0(7)*, Blastoff! Readers) Bellwether Media.
Zuchora-Walske, Christine. Let's Look at Prairie Dogs. (Lightning Bolt Books (tm) — Animal Close-Ups Ser.). 32p. 2015. (ENG., Illus.). (J). (gr. 2-3). E-Book 39.99 *(978-1-5124-1056-3(X)*, 9781512410563, Lerner Pubns.) 2009. (J). (gr. k-2). lib. bdg. 25.26 *(978-0-7613-3891-8(8)*, Lerner Pubns.) 2009. (ENG., Illus.). (J). (gr. k-2). pap. 7.95 *(978-0-7613-5004-0(7))* Lerner Publishing Group.
—Setters: Loyal Hunting Companions, 1 vol. 2013. (Hunting Dogs Ser.). (ENG.). 32p. (gr. 3-4). 7.95 *(978-1-62065-937-3(9))*; lib. bdg. 27.99 *(978-1-4296-9906-8(X))* Capstone Press of Coughlan Cos. (Edge Bks.).

DOGS—FICTION

A Boy And His Dog & Bozak, Jon. Demo: The Story of the Junkyard Dog. 2007. 56p. (J). 19.99 *(978-0-9794769-1-4(7))* Adibooks.com.
AaronG, Driftin'. Claude Henry, the Iditarod Mouse: The Adventures Begin. 2007. 108p. (J). per. 9.95 *(978-0-595-44990-3(5))* iUniverse, Inc.
Abadzis, Nick. Laika. 2014. (YA). lib. bdg. 22.10 *(978-0-606-36130-9(8))* Turtleback Bks.
Abbott, Raymond. Rosie Finds A Home. 2004. 92p. pap. 19.95 *(978-1-4137-3680-9(7))* America Star Bks.
Abdo Publishing. Scooby-Doo Graphic Novels Set 3, 1 vol. 2013. (Scooby-Doo Graphic Novels Set 3 Ser.: 6). (ENG.). 24p. (J). (gr. 2-6). lib. bdg. 145.26 *(978-1-61479-048-8(5)*, Essential Library) ABDO Publishing Co.
—Scooby-Doo Mysteries Set 2, 1 vol. 2013. (Scooby-Doo Mysteries Set 2 Ser.: 6). (ENG.). 64p. (J). (gr. 3-6). lib. bdg. 145.26 *(978-1-61479-041-9(8)*, Essential Library) ABDO Publishing Co.
—Scooby-Doo! Picture Clue Books, 1 vol. 2013. (Scooby-Doo! Picture Clue Bks.: 6). (ENG.). 24p. (J). (gr. -1-1). lib. bdg. 145.26 *(978-1-61479-034-1(5))* ABDO Publishing Co.
About Town with Benny Be. 2005. (J). bds. 15.99 *(978-0-9774752-0-9(4))* Bentley, Trish.
Abramson, Jill & O'Connor, Jane. Holiday Helper. Melmon, Deborah, illus. 2014. (Penguin Young Readers, Level 2 Ser.). (ENG.). 32p. (J). (gr. 1-3). pap. 3.99 *(978-0-448-45677-5(X)*, Penguin Young Readers) Penguin Young Readers Group.
—Puppy Parade. Melmon, Deborah, illus. 2013. (Penguin Young Readers, Level 2 Ser.). (ENG.). 32p. (J). (gr. 1-2). 14.99 *(978-0-448-46574-6(4))*; pap. 3.99 *(978-0-448-45676-8(1))* Penguin Young Readers Group. (Penguin Young Readers).
—Puppy Parade. 2013. (Penguin Young Readers Level 2 Ser.). lib. bdg. 13.55 *(978-0-606-31707-8(4)*, Turtleback) Turtleback Bks.
Abu-Bakr, Sandra. Tales of Lovable Spike: Spike- on the Go! 2008. 72p. pap. 8.95 *(978-0-595-47326-7(1))* iUniverse, Inc.
Accord Publishing Staff. Oliver's First Christmas. Valiant, Kristi, illus. 2012. (ENG.). 14p. (J). (-k). bds. 5.99 *(978-1-4494-2245-5(4))* Andrews McMeel Publishing.
Achilles, Carole. Jocelyn's Theatre. Scoggins, Jocelyn, illus. 2011. 20p. pap. 24.95 *(978-1-4560-8333-5(3))* America Star Bks.
Ackelsberg, Amy. Puppy Love! Artful Doodlers Limited Staff, illus. 2014. (Strawberry Shortcake Ser.). (ENG.). 24p. (J). (gr. -1-k). 4.99 *(978-0-448-48150-0(2)*, Grosset & Dunlap) Penguin Young Readers Group.
Acosta, Margarita. The Girl on the Bench. 2013. 38p. pap. 15.95 *(978-1-62550-045-8(9)*, Llumina Pr.) Aeon Publishing Inc.
Adamowski, Rob. Bernice: Oh my gosh It's a Bear! 2011. (Illus.). 32p. (J). 16.99 *(978-0-9830423-1-0(4))* OctiRam Publishing Co.
Adams, Ben. Polly the Farm Puppy. Cameron, Craig, illus. 2013. (Googly Eyes Ser.). (ENG.). 12p. (J). (gr. -1-k). bds. 6.99 *(978-1-84322-319-1(8)*, Armadillo) Anness Publishing GBR. Dist: National Bk. Network.
Adams, Jean Ekman. When Dogs Dream. 2013. 32p. (J). 15.95 *(978-1-933855-84-4(3)*, Rio Nuevo Pubs.) Rio Nuevo Pubs.
Adams, Laurie Gifford. Finding Atticus. 2009. 208p. pap. 14.95 *(978-1-4401-3779-2(X))* iUniverse, Inc.
Adams, Paul Robert. Buntley's Wing Kit. Oliver, Liana, illus. 2012. 34p. pap. *(978-0-9871712-6-9(7))* Fastnet Bks.
Adams, Pauline Jacqueline. Valentine's Journey. 2012. 24p. pap. 15.99 *(978-1-4771-0984-7(6))* Xlibris Corp.
Adamson, Ged. Douglas, You Need Glasses! 2016. (ENG., Illus.). 40p. (J). (gr. -1-2). 16.99 *(978-0-553-52243-3(4)*, Schwartz & Wade Bks.) Random Hse. Children's Bks.
Adderson, Caroline. A Simple Case of Angels, 1 vol. 2014. (ENG.). 160p. (J). (gr. 2-6). 16.95 *(978-1-55498-428-2(9))* Groundwood Bks. CAN. Dist: Publishers Group West (PGW).
Adel, Deborah. Tiego's Love. 2008. 24p. per. 24.95 *(978-1-4241-9506-0(3))* America Star Bks.
Adler, David A. Bones & the Dog Gone Mystery, No. 2. Newman, Barbara Johansen, illus. 2008. (Bones Ser.: 2). (ENG.). 32p. (J). (gr. 1-3). mass mkt. 3.99 *(978-0-14-241043-1(8)*, Penguin Young Readers) Penguin Young Readers Group.
—Bones & the Dog Gone Mystery. Newman, Barbara Johansen, illus. 2008. (Puffin Easy-to-Read Ser.: Bk. 2). 32p. (gr. k-3). 14.00 *(978-0-7569-8916-3(7))* Perfection Learning Corp.
—Danny's Doodles: The Dog Biscuit Breakfast. 2015. (Danny's Doodles Ser.: 3). (ENG., Illus.). 144p. (J). (gr. 2-5). pap. 4.99 *(978-1-4926-1665-8(6)*, Sourcebooks Jabberwocky) Sourcebooks, Inc.
—The Mystery of the Television Dog, 4 vols. Natti, Susanna, illus. 2004. (Cam Jansen Ser.: 4). (ENG.). 64p. (J). (gr. 2-5). 4.99 *(978-0-14-240013-5(0)*, Puffin Books) Penguin Young Readers Group.
Aesop. The Dog & the Shadow. 2012. (J). *(978-1-61913-101-9(3))* Weigl Pubs., Inc.
Agee, Jon. It's Only Stanley. 2015. (J). 49.99 *(978-1-63379-786-4(4))*; 14.99 *(978-1-63379-787-1(2))* Dreamscape Media, LLC.
—It's Only Stanley. 2015. (ENG., Illus.). 32p. (J). (gr. k-3). 17.99 *(978-0-8037-3907-9(9)*, Dial Bks) Penguin Young Readers Group.
Aguila, Priscilla. As Different As Can Be. 2006. 48p. pap. 17.96 *(978-1-4116-5609-3(1))* Lulu Pr., Inc.
Aguillo, Don Ellis, illus. Boomer, the Missing Pomeranian. 2005. 34p. (J). pap. *(978-1-932864-45-8(8))* Masthof Pr.
Ahlberg, Jessica. Fairy Tales for Mr. Barker: A Peek-Through Story. Ahlberg, Jessica, illus. 2016. (ENG., Illus.). 32p. (J). (-k). 15.99 *(978-0-7636-8124-1(5))* Candlewick Pr.
Ahrens, Albrecht. Simply Out in the Woods: An Inspirational Children's Story. 2013. 232p. pap. *(978-1-4602-0688-1(6))* FriesenPress.
Aitchison, Jim & Sparks, Marilyn. Tin Pot Puppy. 2013. (Illus.). 76p. pap. 7.50 *(978-1-78035-579-5(3)*, Fastprint Publishing) Upfront Publishing Ltd. GBR. Dist: Printondemand-worldwide.com.
Akchurin, Sergo. Blackie & the Magic Stone. 2011. 16p. 12.99 *(978-1-4269-6337-7(8))* Trafford Publishing.
Albee, Sarah. Hello, Cat, Hello, Dog. Leigh, Tom, illus. 2006. (Step-By-Step Readers Ser.). (J). pap. *(978-1-59939-054-3(X)*, Reader's Digest Young Families, Inc.) Studio Fun International.
Albee, Sarah & Hood, Susan. Blue's Bad Dream. Chernichaw, Ian, illus. 2006. (Blue's Clues Ser.: 21). (ENG.). 24p. (J). (gr. -1-2). pap. 3.99 *(978-1-4169-1553-9(2)*, Simon Spotlight/Nickelodeon) Simon Spotlight/Nickelodeon.
Albuquerque, Blossom. Dashing Duke & His Dodgy Adventures. Flinn, Hannah, illus. 2011. 36p. pap. 13.95 *(978-1-60911-743-6(3)*, Strategic Bk. Publishing) Strategic Book Publishing & Rights Agency (SBPRA).
Alcott, Louisa May. Under the Lilacs. 2005. 28.95 *(978-1-4218-1487-2(0))*; 280p. pap. 13.95 *(978-1-4218-1587-9(7))* 1st World Publishing, Inc. (1st World Library - Literary Society).

—Under the Lilacs. 2012. (ENG., Illus.). 328p. (gr. 3-9). pap. 17.95 *(978-1-4290-9311-8(0))* Applewood Bks.

—Under the Lilacs. 2007. 228p. pap. 20.99 *(978-1-4346-3618-8(6))*; 248p. pap. 22.99 *(978-1-4346-3635-5(6))* Creative Media Partners, LLC.

—Under the Lilacs. 2005. pap. *(978-1-4065-0105-6(0))* Dodo Pr.

—Under the Lilacs. 2011. 226p. 26.95 *(978-1-4638-9588-4(7))*; (gr. 4-7). pap. 15.95 *(978-1-60664-504-8(8))* Rodgers, Alan Bks.

—Under the Lilacs. 2007. 296p. per. 13.45 *(978-1-59462-879-5(3)*, Book Jungle) Standard Pubns., Inc.

—Under the Lilacs. 2007. 316p. (gr. 4-7). 32.95 *(978-1-4344-8357-7(6))*; per. 19.95 *(978-1-4344-8356-0(8))* Wildside Pr., LLC.

Alderton, Sylvia. A Real Name for Puppy. McCartney, Michael David, illus. 2006. (J). *(978-1-930566-58-3(1)*, WestWind Pr.) Scott, D.& F. Publishing, Inc.

Aldrick, Shirley H. F. Gordon, the Great Gobbley Grasshopper. 2011. 32p. pap. 13.00 *(978-1-60976-643-6(1)*, Strategic Bk. Publishing) Strategic Book Publishing & Rights Agency (SBPRA).

Alen, Antonia. My Three Little Dogs. 2003. 32p. pap. 8.00 *(978-0-8059-5490-6(2))* Dorrance Publishing Co., Inc.

Alexander, Brooke. Little Mia's Big Heart. 2013. 72p. pap. *(978-1-4602-1670-5(9))* FriesenPress.

Alexander, Carol. Percy Mcgoo. 2012. 24p. pap. 15.99 *(978-1-4771-2359-1(8))* Xlibris Corp.

Alexander, Heather. Wallace & Grace & the Lost Puppy. Zarrin, Laura, illus. 2017. (Wallace & Grace Ser.). (ENG.). 80p. (J). 9.99 ***(978-1-68119-012-9(5)***, 9781681190129, Bloomsbury USA Childrens) Bloomsbury Publishing USA.

Alexander, Scott L. My Dog Named Whatever. 2007. 68p. per. 10.95 *(978-1-4327-1572-4(0))* Outskirts Pr., Inc.

Alfano, Vicki D. Pound Puppy to Fire Dog. 2011. 28p. (gr. 1-2). pap. 12.95 *(978-1-4567-5034-3(8))* AuthorHouse.

Alfaro, Manuel. Griego el Magnífico y la Gotita Verde Golosa Pegajos. Harrington, David, illus. 2007. (SPA.). 36p. per. 15.50 *(978-1-59858-337-3(9))* Dog Ear Publishing, LLC.

Alkire, Don. Mischief's Big Night Out. 2011. 24p. 11.50 *(978-1-4567-1334-8(5))* AuthorHouse.

Allbritton, Jan. Super Sweetie to the Rescue. 2008. 16p. pap. 10.95 *(978-1-4389-3803-5(9))* AuthorHouse.

Alligator Books Staff & Fabiny, Sarah. Pip Puppy Looks for Mom. Hughes, Cathy, illus. 2012. (Squeaky Board Bks.). (ENG.). 18p. (J). bds. 4.99 *(978-0-7641-6482-8(1))* Barron's Educational Series, Inc.

Allison, Teresa J. Bobble Stories: The Bobbleup Pup. Allison, Charles T., illus. 2013. 42p. pap. 12.99 *(978-0-9887612-2-3(X))* Tawnsy Publishing.

Altes, Marta. No! 2011. (Child's Play Library). (ENG., Illus.). 32p. (J). *(978-1-84643-417-4(3))* Child's Play International Ltd.

Alumenda, Stephen. Toko & the Lost Kittens. 2004. (Illus.). 24p. pap. *(978-9966-25-170-1(7))* Heinemann Kenya, Limited (East African Educational Publishers Ltd E.A.E.P.) KEN. Dist: Michigan State Univ. Pr.

Alvarez, Jennifer Lynn. The Pet Washer. 2nd ed. 2012. (ENG.). 171p. (J). (gr. 3-7). pap. 8.99 *(978-0-9848484-5-4(2))* Dreamcatcher Bks.

Amato, Mary. Dog Gone! Jenkins, Ward, illus. 2014. (ENG.). 128p. (J). (gr. 2-4). 14.99 *(978-1-60684-397-0(4))*; (Good Crooks Ser.: Bk. 2). 4.99 *(978-1-60684-510-3(1))* Lerner Publishing Group. (Darby Creek).

Amery, H. & Cartwright, S. Where's Rusty? 2004. (Treasury of Farmyard Tales Ser.). 10p. (J). 7.95 *(978-0-7945-0545-5(7))* EDC Publishing.

Amery, Heather. Rusty's Train Ride. Cartwright, Stephen, illus. rev. ed. 2007. (Farmyard Tales Readers Ser.). 16p. (J). (gr. -1-3). pap. 5.99 *(978-0-7945-0802-9(2)*, Usborne) EDC Publishing.

Ammirato, Lidia. Why Does the Dog Chase the Cat & the Cat Chase the Mouse? 2012. 24p. pap. 15.99 *(978-1-4771-0651-8(0))* Xlibris Corp.

Amundson, Susan. Free to Be Me: The Eskimo Way. Geiken, Brenda, illus. 2003. 56p. lib. bdg. 16.95 *(978-1-883477-65-3(4)*, Lone Oak Pr., Ltd.) Finney Co., Inc.

and Ellen Brenneman, John W. Lane. A Friend Indeed. 2009. 36p. pap. 16.90 *(978-0-557-11601-0(5))* Lulu Pr., Inc.

Anderson, Joan F. Buster B. Basset Hound, the Label Buster (Book & Music CD) Labeled as ADHD (Attention Deficit Hyperactive Dog) by the Sneaky Label Maker Buster B. Basset Hound Turns into a Hero, the Label Buster. 2004. (Illus.). (J). per. 15.00 *(978-0-9665545-5-7(8))* Block System, The.

Anderson, Laurie Halse. End of the Race, 12 vols. 2012. (Vet Volunteers Ser.: 12). (ENG.). 160p. (J). (gr. 3-7). 6.99 *(978-0-14-241228-2(7)*, Puffin Books) Penguin Young Readers Group.

—Fight for Life. 2007. (Vet Volunteers Ser.: 1). (ENG.). 160p. (J). (gr. 3-7). 6.99 *(978-0-14-240862-9(X)*, Puffin Books) Penguin Young Readers Group.

—Say Good-Bye, No. 5. 2008. (Vet Volunteers Ser.: 5). (ENG.). 160p. (J). (gr. 3-7). 7.99 *(978-0-14-241100-1(0)*, Puffin Books) Penguin Young Readers Group.

—Trapped. 2009. (Vet Volunteers Ser.: 8). (ENG.). 144p. (J). (gr. 3-7). 6.99 *(978-0-14-241223-7(6)*, Puffin Books) Penguin Young Readers Group.

Anderson, Michael, Jr. Blaze & the Lost Quarry. (J). (gr. 1-4). 22.75 *(978-0-8446-7001-0(4))* Smith, Peter Pub., Inc.

Anderson, Wayne R. Paula's Perilous Adventure. 2006. 48p. (YA). 12.95 *(978-0-9773478-0-3(X))*; 19.95 incl. DVD *(978-0-9773478-2-7(6))* IMAGECRAFTERS.

Andrews, Joan. A Best Friend for Thurston. 2010. 20p. 13.77 *(978-1-4269-2976-2(5))* Trafford Publishing.

Andrews McMeel Publishing Staff & Vasan, Gandee. Silly Dogs. 2009. (ENG.). 10p. (J). (gr. -1). bds. 7.99 *(978-0-7407-8113-1(8))* Andrews McMeel Publishing.

Andurlakis, Anna. Mickey the Mailman Dog. 2010. 24p. pap. 15.00 *(978-1-4490-9711-0(1))* AuthorHouse.

Angus, Sam. Soldier Dog. 2014. (ENG.). 272p. (J). (gr. 4-7). pap. 7.99 *(978-1-250-04417-4(0)*, 9781250044174) Square Fish.

Animal Friends Squeaky- Dog. 2005. (J). bds. *(978-1-4194-0093-3(2))* Paradise Pr., Inc.

Ann. We Call Him Puddles. 2007. 24p. per. 24.95 *(978-1-4241-8738-6(9))* America Star Bks.

Anthony, Wes. Binger & Stumpy the B D Dawg Series - Book. 2010. 534p. 35.95 *(978-1-60911-088-8(9)*, Eloquent Bks.) Strategic Book Publishing & Rights Agency (SBPRA).

Antle, Bhagavan. Suryia & Roscoe: The True Story of an Unlikely Friendship. Antle, Bhagavan & Bland, Barry, illus. 2011. (ENG.). 32p. (J). (gr. -1-3). 18.99 *(978-0-8050-9316-2(8)*, 9780805093162, Holt, Henry & Co. Bks. For Young Readers) Holt, Henry & Co.

Anyanwu, Francis Eze. The Awesome Dog: How the Dog Became Man's Best Friend. 2011. 73p. pap. 14.95 *(978-1-4327-5666-6(4))* Outskirts Pr., Inc.

Appello, Lisa K. Zuky's World. 2012. pap. 8.95 *(978-0-7414-7951-8(6))* Infinity Publishing.

Appelt, Kathi. Bubba & Beau, Best Friends. Howard, Arthur, illus. 2006. (Bubba & Beau Ser.). (ENG.). 32p. (J). (gr. -1-3). pap. 6.99 *(978-0-15-205580-6(0))* Houghton Mifflin Harcourt Publishing Co.

—Mogie: The Heart of the House. Rosenthal, Marc, illus. 2014. (ENG.). 40p. (J). (gr. -1-3). 17.99 *(978-1-4424-8054-4(8)*, Atheneum Bks. for Young Readers) Simon & Schuster Children's Publishing.

—The Underneath. Small, David, illus. 2010. (KOR.). 395p. (YA). pap. *(978-89-527-5767-8(X))* Sigongsa Co., Ltd.

—The Underneath. Small, David, illus. (ENG.). (J). (gr. 5-9). 2010. 336p. pap. 8.99 *(978-1-4169-5059-2(1))* 2008. 320p. 17.99 *(978-1-4169-5058-5(3))* Simon & Schuster Children's Publishing. (Atheneum Bks. for Young Readers).

—The Underneath. 2010. lib. bdg. 19.65 *(978-0-606-14504-6(4)*, Turtleback) Turtleback Bks.

Applegate, Katherine. Don't Swap Your Sweater for a Dog. Biggs, Brian, illus. (Roscoe Riley Rules Ser.: 3). (J). (gr. 1-5). 2016. 128p. pap. 4.99 *(978-0-06-239250-3(6))* 2008. (ENG.). 96p. 15.99 *(978-0-06-114886-6(5))* 2008. (ENG.). 96p. pap. 4.99 *(978-0-06-114885-9(7))* HarperCollins Pubs.

—Don't Swap Your Sweater for a Dog. 2016. (Roscoe Riley Rules Ser.: 3). (J). lib. bdg. 14.75 *(978-0-606-38736-1(6))* Turtleback Bks.

Appleman, Pamela J. Copper Becomes a Farm Dog. 2013. 26p. pap. 9.99 *(978-0-9913190-4-6(4))* Mindstir Media.

Archambault, John. Cat in the Tree. Cooper, Stephanie, illus. 2007. (J). *(978-1-58669-230-8(5))* Childcraft Education Corp.

Archer, Catharine. Doug the Pug: A Fine Working Dog. 2016. (Illus.). 64p. pap. *(978-1-910455-15-9(6))* Intersentia Ltd.

Arden, Lynne. Guess What Happened to Me, Auntie Kate! Marino, Natalie, illus. 2008. 52p. pap. 18.95 *(978-1-59858-733-3(1))* Dog Ear Publishing, LLC.

Ardizzone, Edward. Tim's Friend Towser. 2015. (Little Tim Ser.). (ENG., Illus.). 56p. (J). (gr. -1-2). 18.99 *(978-1-84780-631-4(7)*, Frances Lincoln) Quarto Publishing Group UK GBR. Dist: Hachette Bk. Group.

Arguello, Tito. A Dog in Love. 2005. 114p. (J). pap. 8.95 *(978-1-4116-2287-6(1))* Lulu Pr., Inc.

Armstrong, Cara. Moxie: The Dachshund of Fallingwater. 2010. (ENG.). 32p. (J). 19.95 *(978-1-933979-70-0(4)*, 10cb4a3a-e256-4798-b1d9-ce1ed88e1459) Bright Sky Pr.

Armstrong, William H. Sounder. l.t. ed. 2005. 111p. (YA). pap. 10.95 *(978-0-7862-7915-9(X))* Thorndike Pr.

Arnoff, Rebecca D. The Trouble with Tooth Fairies: The Adventures of Sam & Angela. 2013. 24p. 22.99 *(978-1-4582-1028-9(6))*; pap. 12.99 *(978-1-4582-1026-5(X))* Author Solutions, Inc. (Abbott Pr.).

Arnold, Elana K. Far from Fair. 2016. (ENG.). 240p. (J). (gr. 5-7). 16.99 *(978-0-544-60227-4(7)*, HMH Books For Young Readers) Houghton Mifflin Harcourt Publishing Co.

Arruzza, Rick. El Paseo de Sparky. Newton, Pilar, illus. 2003. (SPA.). 24p. mass mkt. 7.95 *(978-0-9744509-1-9(X))* Three Spots Productions.

—Sparky's Walk. Newton, Pilar, illus. 2003. 24p. (J). mass mkt. 7.95 *(978-0-9744509-0-2(1))* Three Spots Productions.

Arthur Hamilton & His Dog. 2004. reprint ed. pap. 15.95 *(978-1-4191-0774-0(7))*; pap. 1.99 *(978-1-4192-0774-7(1))* Kessinger Publishing, LLC.

Artz, D. M. Maggie & the Magic Sparkle Seed. 2007. 30p. 16.95 *(978-1-4357-0152-6(6))* Lulu Pr., Inc.

As Told by Milo: My Very Own Family. 2005. (J). 14.95 *(978-0-9772000-0-9(0))* Andrus, Ashley.

Asare, Meshack. Sosu's Call. Asare, Meshack, illus. 2006. (ENG., Illus.). 40p. (J). (gr. k-4). 11.99 *(978-1-929132-21-8(2))* Kane Miller.

Ashworth, Susan M. Jo-Jo Helps with the Housework. l.t. ed. 2003. (Illus.). 20p. (J). per. 8.95 *(978-1-932338-35-5(7))* Lifevest Publishing, Inc.

Asquith, Ros. Trixie Fights for Furry Rights. 2011. (ENG., Illus.). 208p. (J). (gr. 3-6). pap. 9.99 *(978-0-00-722359-6(5))* HarperCollins Pubs. Ltd. GBR. Dist: HarperCollins Pubs.

Atchison, David C. The Adventures of Black Bart: an Encounter with Regret. 2008. 84p. pap. 7.94 *(978-0-615-23723-7(1))* Black Bart Bks.

Atha, Shirley Swigart. Angel with a Wagging Tail. 2012. 24p. pap. 15.95 *(978-0-9787766-3-3(1))* CAI Publishing.

Athens, Sandra & Colarik, Kim. The Adventures of Foxy: The Lonely Lost Dog. 2009. 44p. pap. 18.50 *(978-1-4490-0506-1(3))* AuthorHouse.

Atkins, Laura. Sled Dog Dachshund. Phan, An, illus. 2016. (ENG.). 32p. (J). (gr. k-2). 14.99 *(978-0-9965454-3-3(3))* Minted Prose, LLC.

Atticus, C. J. Stranded in Space: The Stellar Life of Jpeg the Robot Dog. Domschke, Angelika, illus. 2013. 119p. (J). pap. 6.95 *(978-0-9887780-2-3(5))* Atticus, C. J.

Atwarie, Rossi. The Adventures of Fox Brown. Bachan, Krystal Ann, illus. 2011. 62p. pap. 19.00 *(978-1-60911-845-7(6)*, Eloquent Bks.) Strategic Book Publishing & Rights Agency (SBPRA).

Aubry, Cécile. Belle & Sebastien: The Child of the Montains. Norminton, Gregory, tr. from FRE. Stephens, Helen, illus. 2016. (ENG.). 200p. (J). 10.99 ***(978-1-84749-591-4(5)***, 9781847495914, Alma Classics) Bloomsbury Publishing USA.

Auch, Mary Jane. A Dog on His Own. (ENG., Illus.). 160p. (J). 2009. (gr. 3-7). pap. 7.95 *(978-0-8234-2243-2(7))* 2008. (gr. 4-7). 16.95 *(978-0-8234-2088-9(4))* Holiday Hse., Inc.

—I Was a Third Grade Bodyguard. Auch, Herm, illus. 2003. (ENG.). 73p. (J). (gr. 4-6). tchr. ed. 16.95 *(978-0-8234-1775-9(1))* Holiday Hse., Inc.

—I Was a Third Grade Spy. Auch, Herm, illus. 2004. 86p. (gr. 2-5). 16.00 *(978-0-7569-4138-3(5))* Perfection Learning Corp.

—I Was a Third Grade Spy. Auch, Herm, illus. 2003. (ENG.). 96p. (J). (gr. 3-7). 5.99 *(978-0-440-41871-9(2)*, Yearling) Random Hse. Children's Bks.

Auerbach, Annie. Scooby-Doo in the Coolsville Contraption Contest, 1 vol. 2016. (Scooby-Doo! Set 3 Ser.). (ENG., Illus.). 32p. (J). (gr. k-4). lib. bdg. 24.21 *(978-1-61479-409-7(X))* Spotlight.

—Scooby-Doo in the Mystery Mansion, 1 vol. 2016. (Scooby-Doo! Set 3 Ser.). (ENG., Illus.). 32p. (J). (gr. k-4). lib. bdg. 24.21 *(978-1-61479-411-0(1)*, 1401187) Spotlight.

Auntie Annie. Knute: Dreams of Africa. 2013. 32p. pap. 17.25 *(978-1-4669-7519-4(9))* Trafford Publishing.

—Knute: In the Magical Meadow. 2013. 32p. pap. 17.25 *(978-1-4669-9778-3(8))* Trafford Publishing.

—Knute: Meets Mike in the Magical Meadow. 2013. 28p. pap. 16.09 *(978-1-4669-9780-6(X))* Trafford Publishing.

Austin, Rikey. Chunky & the Bone: Alice's Bear Shop. 2012. 28p. pap. *(978-1-78092-152-5(7))* MX Publishing, Ltd.

Auty, Rob. A Hare's Tale 2 - the Golden Hare. Wood, Chaz, illus. 2013. 102p. pap. *(978-1-908098-90-0(2))* 2QT, Ltd. (Publishing).

Avelino, Kawehi. No Ka Ilio Moo. 2008. 36p. 14.95 *(978-0-87336-156-9(3))* Kamehameha Publishing.

Avery, Terry, illus. Who Will Save Mr Squeaky? 2004. 29p. (J). *(978-1-929115-11-2(3))* Azro Pr., Inc.

Avi. The Good Dog. 2003. 243p. (gr. 3-7). 17.00 *(978-0-7569-1389-2(6))* Perfection Learning Corp.

—The Good Dog. 2003. (ENG.). 256p. (J). (gr. 3-7). mass mkt. 7.99 *(978-0-689-83825-5(5)*, Atheneum Bks. for Young Readers) Simon & Schuster Children's Publishing.

Award, Anna & Aesop. The Lion & the Mouse with the Donkey & the Lapdog. Biro, Val, illus. 2014. (ENG.). 24p. (J). pap. 6.95 *(978-1-84135-953-3(X))* Award Pubns. Ltd. GBR. Dist: Parkwest Pubns., Inc.

Ayers, Sanda. Tommy Tractor Goes to the City, 1 vol. Young, Sue, illus. 2009. 29p. pap. 19.95 *(978-1-61582-054-2(X))* PublishAmerica, Inc.

Ayres, S. C. Finding the Perfect Fit. Steckler, Megan, illus. 2011. 28p. pap. 24.95 *(978-1-4560-0912-0(5))* America Star Bks.

AZ Books Staff. Who Is the Puppy Looking For? Gridina, Anna, ed. 2012. (Who Is There Ser.). (ENG.). 10p. (J). (-k). bds. 11.95 *(978-1-61889-038-2(7))* AZ Bks. LLC.

B. Lee Schmidt. My Name Is Buttonz. 2009. 20p. pap. 10.49 *(978-1-4389-6338-9(6))* AuthorHouse.

Babee says No. 2006. (YA). spiral bd. *(978-1-59872-479-0(7))* Instant Pub.

Babooram, Vima. Poco & His Missing Puppy. Babooram, Aasha, illus. 2012. 24p. pap. *(978-1-4602-0296-8(1))* FriesenPress.

Backues, E. Sharol. Stories of a Dragonfly Spy, a Dog Named Droop & a Little Calf That Wondered Why? 2011. 28p. pap. 21.99 *(978-1-4653-6343-5(2))* Xlibris Corp.

Baczynski, Jolanta & Baczynski, Olga. Freddie & Jet. 2013. 36p. pap. *(978-0-9918166-4-4(1))* Flower Pr.

Bader, Bonnie. Pup-Pup-Puppies. 2014. (Penguin Young Readers, Level 2 Ser.). (ENG.). 32p. (J). (gr. 1-3). pap. 3.99 *(978-0-448-47995-8(8)*, Penguin Young Readers) Penguin Young Readers Group.

Baglio, Ben M. Collie with a Card. Baum, Ann, illus. 2004. 136p. (J). pap. *(978-0-439-68760-7(8))* Scholastic, Inc.

—Come Back, Buddy! 2004. (Illus.). 118p. (J). pap. *(978-0-439-68883-3(3))* Scholastic, Inc.

—Corgi in the Cupcakes. Baum, Ann, illus. 2008. 142p. (J). pap. *(978-0-439-02533-1(8))* Scholastic, Inc.

—Dalmatian in the Daisies. Baum, Ann & Lasher, Mary Ann, illus. 2007. 154p. (J). *(978-0-439-87120-4(4))* Scholastic, Inc.

—Help Find Honey! 2006. (Pet Finders Club Ser.: Vol. 10). (Illus.). 157p. (J). *(978-0-439-87143-3(3))* Scholastic, Inc.

—Husky with a Heart. 2006. 139p. *(978-0-439-77523-6(X))* Scholastic, Inc.

—Vanishing Point. Ettlinger, Doris, illus. 2007. 158p. (J). pap. *(978-0-439-87145-7(X))* Scholastic, Inc.

Baglio, Ben M. & Daniels, Lucy. Labrador on the Lawn. Gregory, Jenny, illus. 2005. (Animal Ark Hauntings Ser.: No. 38). (ENG.). 144p. (J). (gr. 2-5). 3.99 *(978-0-439-68488-0(9))* Scholastic, Inc.

Bail, Mina Mauerstein. Max & Voltaire Getting to Know You. Choquette, Gabriel, illus. 2015. 66p. (J). pap. 16.95 *(978-1-59095-151-4(4))* TotalRecall Pubns.

Bailey, Frank. Brian - in the Jungle. Edmeades, Sue, illus. 2015. (ENG.). 22p. (J). (gr. 1-2). pap. 14.99 *(978-1-78455-026-4(4)*, 437212b2-56d8-4503-a3a5-04cb66349a07) Austin, Stan AUS. Dist: Bookmasters Distribution.

Bailey, Linda. Stanley at Sea. Slavin, Bill, illus. 2008. (ENG.). 32p. (J). (gr. -1-2). 16.95 *(978-1-55453-193-6(4))* Kids Can Pr., Ltd. CAN. Dist: Hachette Bk. Group.

—Stanley's Beauty Contest. Slavin, Bill, illus. 2009. (ENG.). 32p. (J). (gr. -1-2). 17.95 *(978-1-55453-318-3(X))* Kids Can Pr., Ltd. CAN. Dist: Hachette Bk. Group.

—Stanley's Party. Slavin, Bill, illus. 2004. (ENG.). 32p. (J). (gr. -1-2). pap. 8.99 *(978-1-55337-768-9(0))* Kids Can Pr., Ltd. CAN. Dist: Hachette Bk. Group.

—Stanleys Wild Ride. Slavin, Bill, illus. (ENG.). 32p. (J). (gr. -1-2). 2008. pap. 7.95 *(978-1-55453-254-4(X))* 2006. 16.95 *(978-1-55337-960-7(8))* Kids Can Pr., Ltd. CAN. Dist: Hachette Bk. Group.

Bailey, Lori Gayle. The Dog Who Loved Cucumbers. 2009. 24p. pap. 11.95 *(978-1-4490-2457-4(2))* AuthorHouse.

Bailey, Peter, illus. Jack & Rebel, the Police Dog. 2007. 183p. (J). (gr. 3-7). 15.99 *(978-0-06-088049-1(X))* HarperCollins Pubs.

Bailey, Vicki. Catland Adventures. 2009. 32p. pap. 9.96 *(978-0-557-06543-1(7))* Lulu Pr., Inc.

Bailey's Birthday - Evaluation Guide: Evaluation Guide. 2006. (J). *(978-1-55942-399-1(4))* Witcher Productions.

Baker, Barbara. Digby & Kate & the Beautiful Day. Winborn, Marsha, illus. 2004. (Puffin Easy-to-Read Ser.). 48p. (J). (gr. 1-4). 11.65 *(978-0-7569-2959-6(8))* Perfection Learning Corp.

Baker, Cristal. Popsicle Goes to Church. 2006. 2p. 9.83 *(978-1-4116-8288-7(2))* Lulu Pr., Inc.

Baker, Darryl. Kamik Joins the Pack, 1 vol. Leng, Qin, illus. 2016. (ENG.). 32p. (J). (gr. k-2). pap. 10.95 *(978-1-77227-125-6(X))* Inhabit Media Inc. CAN. Dist: Independent Pubs. Group.

Balaam, Lisa & Balaam, Steven. Abbey the Cavi in Miami Beach. 2006. 52p. (J). 19.95 *(978-1-4196-1004-2(X))* CreateSpace Independent Publishing Platform.

Balaam, Steven & Balaam, Lisa. Abbey the Cavi: And Friends. 2007. (Illus.). 102p. (J). per. 9.95 *(978-0-9785585-0-5(2))* Balaam Books LLC.

Balaban, Mariah. Scooby-Doo & the Scary Snowman, 1 vol. Duendes Del Sur Staff, illus. 2012. (Scooby-Doo! Set 2 Ser.: No. 2). (ENG.). 24p. (J). (gr. k-3). lib. bdg. 24.21 *(978-1-59961-869-2(9))* Spotlight.

—Scooby-Doo & the Thanksgiving Terror, 1 vol. Duendes Del Sur Staff, illus. 2012. (Scooby-Doo! Set 2 Ser.: No. 2). (ENG.). 24p. (J). (gr. k-3). lib. bdg. 24.21 *(978-1-59961-870-8(2))* Spotlight.

Balch, Glenn. White Ruff: Famous Dog Stories. Priest, Dick, illus. 2011. 240p. 46.95 *(978-1-258-09962-6(4))* Literary Licensing, LLC.

Baldwin, Laura. Harry Loves Greens. Marlette, Andy, illus. 2012. 30p. (J). pap. 10.00 *(978-1-61153-013-1(X))* Light Messages Publishing.

—Harry Loves Turnips (Not!) Marlette, Andy, illus. 2012. 30p. (J). pap. 10.00 *(978-1-61153-023-0(7))* Light Messages Publishing.

Ball, Duncan. Selby Santa. Stomann, Allan, illus. 2007. 192p. *(978-0-7322-8679-8(4))* HarperCollins Pubs. Australia.

—Selby Supersnoop. Stomann, Allan, illus. 2003. 176p. *(978-0-207-20005-2(X))* HarperCollins Pubs. Australia.

Ballantyne, R. M. The Dog Crusoe. 2006. (Illus.). pap. *(978-1-4065-0529-0(3))* Dodo Pr.

Ballantyne, Robert Michael. My Doggie & I. 2007. 120p. pap. 18.99 *(978-1-4346-3682-9(8))*; (ENG.). 130p. pap. 19.99 *(978-1-4346-3730-7(1))* Creative Media Partners, LLC.

Ballard Beath, Ernest, III & Ruark Gibb, Paula. A Golden's Retreat. 2007. (YA). *(978-0-9789936-0-3(8))* Patriot Publishing.

Balsamello, Melissa. Happy the Hotdog Dog. 2011. 24p. (gr. 1-2). pap. 15.00 *(978-1-4567-4861-6(0))* AuthorHouse.

—Happy's Adventure at Se: Starring... Happy the Hotdog Dog. 2011. 28p. pap. 15.00 *(978-1-4634-0821-3(8))* AuthorHouse.

Baltazar, Art. Starro & the Space Dolphins, 1 vol. Baltazar, Art, illus. 2012. (DC Super-Pets Ser.). (ENG., Illus.). 56p. (gr. 2-2). pap. 4.95 *(978-1-4048-7217-2(5))*; lib. bdg. 23.99 *(978-1-4048-6487-0(3))* Picture Window Bks. (DC Super-Pets).

Banim, Lisa. In the Doghouse. 2005. 124p. (J). lib. bdg. 16.92 *(978-1-4242-0685-8(5))* Fitzgerald Bks.

Banks, Kate & Sheldrake, Rupert. Boy's Best Friend. 2015. (ENG.). 224p. (J). (gr. 3-7). 15.99 *(978-0-374-38008-3(2)*, 9780374380083, Farrar, Straus & Giroux (BYR)) Farrar, Straus & Giroux.

Bansch, Helga. I Want a Dog! Bansch, Helga, illus. 2009. (ENG., Illus.). 32p. (J). (gr. -1-3). 17.95 *(978-0-7358-2255-9(7))* North-South Bks., Inc.

Barad, Alexis. Puppy Love. East, Jacqueline, illus. 2013. (J). *(978-0-545-47733-8(6))* Scholastic, Inc.

Barba, Theresa. How Talia Met Tanner. 2012. 40p. pap. 20.99 *(978-1-4772-1617-0(0))* AuthorHouse.

Barbie. Barbie Fall Movie Sliding Tab. 2015. (Barbie Movie Tie-In Ser.: 1). (ENG.). 12p. (J). (gr. -1-1). bds. 10.99 *(978-0-7944-3529-5(7))* Studio Fun International.

Barbie Loves Lacey/Adora a Lacey. 2014.Tr. of English/Spanish Book. (SPA., Illus.). 10p. (J). (gr. -1-k). bds. 8.99 *(978-0-7944-3208-9(5))* Studio Fun International.

Barbo, Maria S. Treasure Hunt, 1 vol. 2013. (Scooby-Doo! Picture Clue Bks.). (ENG.). 24p. (J). (gr. -1-1). lib. bdg. 24.21 *(978-1-61479-040-2(X)*, Essential Library) ABDO Publishing Co.

Barbo, Maria S. & Bridwell, Norman. Thanksgiving Parade. Artful Doodlers, illus. 2010. (J). *(978-0-545-25332-1(2))* Scholastic, Inc.

Barbo, Theresa Mitchell & Webster, W. Russell. The Daring Coast Guard Rescue of the Pendleton Crew. Marshall, Julia, illus. 2013. Orig. Title: The Daring Coast Guard Rescue of the Pendleton Crew. (ENG.). 128p. (J). (gr. 4-7). 14.99 *(978-1-62619-095-5(X)*, History Pr., The) Arcadia Publishing.

Barchers, Suzanne I. Rose & Bose, 1 vol. 2011. (Targeted Phonics Ser.). (ENG., Illus.). 16p. (J). (gr. k-2). pap. 5.99 *(978-1-4333-2913-5(1))* Teacher Created Materials, Inc.

—You Can Do It!, 1 vol. 2011. (Targeted Phonics Ser.). (ENG., Illus.). 16p. (J). (gr. k-2). pap. 5.99 *(978-1-4333-2424-6(5))* Teacher Created Materials, Inc.

Barclay, Eric. Counting Dogs. Barclay, Eric, illus. 2015. (ENG., Illus.). 16p. (J). (gr. -1-k). bds. 10.99 *(978-0-545-78392-7(5)*, Cartwheel Bks.) Scholastic, Inc.

Barger, Caroline. The Roundup. 2008. 12p. per. 24.95 *(978-1-4241-8845-1(8))* America Star Bks.

Barkley, Callie. Ellie the Flower Girl. Bishop, Tracy, illus. 2016. (Critter Club Ser.: 14). (ENG.). 128p. (J). (gr. k-4). pap. 5.99 *(978-1-4814-6718-6(2)*, Little Simon) Little Simon.

Barnard, Carolyn. Boom Boom's Tale, 1 vol. 2009. 22p. pap. 24.95 *(978-1-61582-055-9(8))* America Star Bks.

Barner, Bob. I Have a Garden. Barner, Bob, illus. 2014. (I Like to Read(r) Ser.). (ENG., Illus.). 24p. (J). (gr. -1-3). 6.99 *(978-0-8234-3056-7(1))* Holiday Hse., Inc.

Barnett, Penny. Matilda & Puppy's Beach Adventure. 2012. 24p. pap. 15.99 *(978-1-4797-1106-2(3))* Xlibris Corp.

Barreintez, Elsa. I'm Only Eight, by Reynaldo: I Survived Being Eight. 2010. 46p. pap. 14.95 *(978-1-4327-5489-1(0))* Outskirts Pr., Inc.

Barreto, Sonia. Onyx. Switzer, Bobbi, illus. 2008. 36p. pap. 13.95 *(978-1-4327-1787-2(1))* Outskirts Pr., Inc.

Barrett, Susanna. Isabella Goes to the City. 2011. 20p. pap. 11.99 *(978-1-4634-0203-7(1))* AuthorHouse.

Barriman, Lydia. The Runaway Puppy: A Mystery with Probability. Grutzik, Becky, illus. 2010. (Manga Math Mysteries Ser.: 8). (ENG.). 48p. (gr. 3-5). 29.27 *(978-0-7613-4910-5(3))* Lerner Publishing Group.

Barrow, Randi. Saving Zasha. 2013. (ENG.). 256p. (J). (gr. 3-7). pap. 6.99 *(978-0-545-20633-4(2)*, Scholastic Paperbacks) Scholastic, Inc.

Bartlett, Arthur C. Yankee Doodle: The Story of A Pioneer Boy & His Dog. Cue, Harold, illus. 2011. 322p. 50.95 *(978-1-258-06634-5(3))* Literary Licensing, LLC.

Bartoletti, Susan Campbell. Nobody's Diggier Than a Dog. Giacobbe, Beppe, illus. 2005. (ENG.). 40p. (gr. -1-17). 15.99 *(978-0-7868-1824-2(7))* Hyperion Pr.

Barton, Brittney B. Piper & Pickle: Smile. Young, Susan, illus. 2013. 68p. 18.99 *(978-0-9856336-0-8(3))* P2 Publishing.
BARWICK, Adam Mark. Three tales of Twaddle. 2009. 73p. pap. 12.50 *(978-1-4092-5181-1(0))* Lulu Pr., Inc.
Bashline, Trent. How Jake & Daisy Stopped Bullying at Dogwood Elementary. 2011. 32p. pap. 12.79 *(978-1-4634-2895-2(2))* AuthorHouse.
Baskin, Nora Raleigh. Runt. (ENG., Illus.). 208p. (J). (gr. 3-7). 2014. pap. 6.99 *(978-1-4424-5808-6(9))* 2013. 15.99 *(978-1-4424-5807-9(0))* Simon & Schuster Bks. For Young Readers. (Simon & Schuster Bks. For Young Readers).
Bassler, Joni. Chee Choo's Adventures, 1 vol. Leonard, Kaycee, illus. 2007. (ENG.). 33p. 24.95 *(978-1-4241-8773-7(7))* America Star Bks.
Bateman, Teresa. The Christmas Pups. Kanzler, John, illus. 2012. (J). *(978-1-61913-112-5(9))* Weigl Pubs., Inc.
—Fluffy: Scourge of the Sea. Chesworth, Michael, illus. 2006. (ENG.). 32p. (J). (gr. -1-2). pap. 7.95 *(978-1-58089-152-3(7))* Charlesbridge Publishing, Inc.
—Job Wanted. Sheban, Chris, illus. 2015. (ENG.). 32p. (J). (gr. k-3). 16.95 *(978-0-8234-3391-9(9))* Holiday Hse., Inc.
Bates, Amy, illus. My Puppy's First Year. 2007. (ENG.). 24p. (gr. k-3). pap. 12.99 *(978-0-8249-5571-7(4),* Ideal Pubns.) Worthy Publishing.
Batson, Susann. A Duck at the Dog Pound. 2007. (Illus.). 32p. (J). E-Book 5.00 incl. cd-rom *(978-1-933090-23-8(5))* Guardian Angel Publishing, Inc.
Battersea Dogs and Cats Home Staff & Red Fox Staff. Rusty's Story. 2010. (ENG., Illus.). 112p. (J). pap. 8.99 *(978-1-84941-124-0(7),* Red Fox) Random House Children's Books GBR. Dist: Independent Pubs. Group.
Battersea Dogs Home Staff & Red Fox Staff. Chester's Story. 2010. (ENG., Illus.). 128p. (J). pap. 8.99 *(978-1-84941-123-3(9),* Red Fox) Random House Children's Books GBR. Dist: Independent Pubs. Group.
Bauer, Linda. Fruits & Flowers & Footprints OH MY!!! 2007. (Illus.). 29p. (J). 13.99 *(978-0-9798146-0-0(X))* Bauer, Linda.
Bauer, Marion Dane. Little Cat's Luck. Bell, Jennifer A., illus. 2016. (ENG.). 224p. (J). (gr. 3-7). 17.99 *(978-1-4814-2488-2(2),* Simon & Schuster Bks. For Young Readers) Simon & Schuster Bks. For Young Readers.
—Little Dog, Lost. Bell, Jennifer A., illus. (ENG.). 208p. (J). (gr. 3-7). 2013. pap. 6.99 *(978-1-4424-3424-0(4))* 2012. 16.99 *(978-1-4424-3423-3(6))* Simon & Schuster Children's Publishing. (Atheneum Bks. for Young Readers).
Baugh, Ayana Sala. Loopiethotamus, the Chihuahua Who Thinks He Is a Hippopotamus: A Loopiethotamus Christmas. 2012. 32p. pap. 19.99 *(978-1-4685-8111-9(2))* AuthorHouse.
—Loopiethotamus, the Chihuahua Who Thinks He Is a Hippopotamus: His Life. 2011. 24p. pap. 16.99 *(978-1-4567-4002-3(4))* AuthorHouse.
Baum, Diane Ganzer & Olson, Dan. Dakota's Trail. 2011. 48p. pap. 11.99 *(978-1-61286-029-9(X))* Avid Readers Publishing Group.
Baum, Roger S. Toto of Oz & the Surprise Party. Seitzinger, Victoria, illus. 2004. (ENG.). 32p. (J). 13.95 *(978-1-57072-284-4(6),* 1233723) Overmountain Pr.
Bausley, Alicia. Tucker Goes to Heaven. 2006. 32p. pap. 13.95 *(978-1-59526-457-2(4))* Aeon Publishing Inc.
Baxter, Nicola. The Puppy Tales Collection: Twelve Silly Stories from Houndsville. Shuttleworth, Cathie, illus. 2014. (ENG.). 80p. (J). (gr. k-5). pap. 9.99 *(978-1-84322-935-3(8),* Armadillo) Anness Publishing GBR. Dist: National Bk. Network.
Baxter, Stephanie. The Adventures of Jack Brown & Friends. 2013. 72p. pap. 17.99 *(978-0-9890288-2-0(8))* Mindstir Media.
Be Kind, Be Friendly, Be Thankful: The Adventures of Brisky Bear & Trooper Dog. 2007. Orig. Title: Friends for Always. (J). pap. 7.95 incl. audio compact disk *(978-0-9795127-0-4(0))* Glory Be Collectibles.
Beall, Linda. Four PAWS & Lucky Little Duke Dog. 2013. 28p. pap. 9.99 *(978-1-62697-252-0(4))* Salem Author Services.
—Four Paws & Lucky Little Duke Dog. 2013. 28p. 20.99 *(978-1-62697-253-7(2))* Salem Author Services.
Beall, Linda R. We , Four Paws & Me at Yellowstone National Park. 2012. 40p. pap. 24.95 *(978-1-4626-8305-5(3))* America Star Bks.
Bean, Shelly. Rooty Toot Rambler: Finds a Home. 2003. (Illus.). 20p. (J). per. 5.95 *(978-0-9674915-4-7(1))* Day By Day Recovery Resources, LLC.
Beasley, Linda L. Meltdowns First Adventure. 2010. 28p. 16.95 *(978-1-4490-9725-7(1))* AuthorHouse.
—Meltdown's Next Adventure: The White House. 2012. 48p. pap. 21.99 *(978-1-4772-6070-8(6))* AuthorHouse.
Beaumont, Karen. Crybaby. Yelchin, Eugene, illus. 2015. (ENG.). 40p. (J). (gr. -1-1). 17.99 *(978-0-8050-8974-5(8),* 9780805089745, Holt, Henry & Co. Bks. For Young Readers) Holt, Henry & Co.
—Doggone Dogs! Catrow, David, illus. 2008. (ENG.). 40p. (J). (gr. -1-k). 16.99 *(978-0-8037-3157-8(4),* Dial Bks) Penguin Young Readers Group.
—Move over, Rover! Dyer, Jane, illus. (ENG.). 40p. (J). (gr. -1-3). 2016. 7.99 *(978-0-544-80900-0(9),* HMH Books For Young Readers) 2006. 16.99 *(978-0-15-201979-2(0))* Houghton Mifflin Harcourt Publishing Co.
Because of Winn Dixie. 2011. 9.14 *(978-0-7848-3659-0(0),* Everbind) Marco Bk. Co.
Bechtold, Lisze. Buster & Phoebe: The Great Bone Game. 2010. (ENG.). 48p. (J). pap. 5.95 *(978-0-618-58547-2(8))* Houghton Mifflin Harcourt Trade & Reference Pubs.
—Buster the Very Shy Dog. 2015. (Green Light Readers Level 3 Ser.). (ENG., Illus.). 32p. (J). (gr. 1-4). pap. 3.99 *(978-0-544-33606-3(2),* HMH Books For Young Readers) Houghton Mifflin Harcourt Publishing Co.
—Buster the Very Shy Dog & the Great Bone Game. 2016. (Green Light Readers Level 3 Ser.). (ENG., Illus.). 32p. (J). (gr. 1-4). 3.99 *(978-0-544-66846-1(4),* HMH Books For Young Readers) Houghton Mifflin Harcourt Publishing Co.
—Buster the Very Shy Dog Finds a Kitten. 2015. (Green Light Readers Level 3 Ser.). (ENG., Illus.). 32p. (J). (gr. 1-4). pap. 3.99 *(978-0-544-33605-6(4),* HMH Books For Young Readers) Houghton Mifflin Harcourt Publishing Co.
Beck, Andrea. Pierre le Poof!, 1 vol. Beck, Andrea, illus. 2009. (Pierre le Poof Ser.: 1). (ENG., Illus.). 32p. (J). (gr. -1-3). 19.95 *(978-1-55469-028-2(5))* Orca Bk. Pubs. USA.
—Pierre's Friends, 1 vol. Beck, Andrea, illus. 2010. (Pierre le Poof Ser.: 2). (ENG., Illus.). 32p. (J). (gr. -1-3). 19.95 *(978-1-55469-030-5(7))* Orca Bk. Pubs. USA.
Beck, Carolyn. Wellington's Rainy Day, 1 vol. Kerrigan, Brooke, illus. 2011. (ENG.). 32p. (J). (gr. -1-3). 19.95 *(978-1-55469-284-2(9))* Orca Bk. Pubs. USA.
Beck, Crystall. The Adventures of Carter & Vincent. 2012. 28p. pap. 9.95 *(978-1-4787-1662-4(2))* Outskirts Pr., Inc.
Becker, Helaine. Let Sleeping Dogs Lie, 1 vol. 2016. (Dirk Daring, Secret Agent Ser.: 2). (ENG., Illus.). 240p. (J). (gr. 3-6). pap. 9.95 *(978-1-4598-1038-9(4))* Orca Bk. Pubs. USA.
Becker, May R. Woodland Party. 2013. 10.95 *(978-0-7414-8170-2(7))* Infinity Publishing.
—Woodland Party - Color. 2013. pap. 19.95 *(978-0-7414-8171-9(5))* Infinity Publishing.
Bedford, David. Hound Dog. Williamson, Melanie, illus. 2006. (J). pap. 6.95 *(978-1-58925-397-1(3))* Tiger Tales.
Bedford, David & James, Ann. The Way I Love You. 2004. (Illus.). 24p. *(978-1-877003-49-3(2))* Little Hare Bks. AUS. Dist: HarperCollins Pubs. Australia.
—The Way I Love You Box Set. 2007. 24p. *(978-1-921049-95-8(2))* Little Hare Bks. AUS. Dist: HarperCollins Pubs. Australia.
Bee, William. Migloo's Day. Bee, William, illus. 2015. (ENG., Illus.). (J). (gr. -1-2). 14.99 *(978-0-7636-7374-1(9))* Candlewick Pr.
Beha, Eileen. Tango: The Tale of an Island Dog. 2010. (ENG.). 256p. (YA). (gr. 3-6). pap. 7.99 *(978-1-59990-485-6(3),* 9781599904856, Bloomsbury USA Childrens) Bloomsbury Publishing USA.
Behrens, Andy. The Fast & the Furriest. 2011. (ENG.). 256p. (J). (gr. 3-7). 7.99 *(978-0-375-85900-7(4),* Yearling) Random Hse. Children's Bks.
Beil, Karen Magnuson. Jack's House. Wohnoutka, Mike, illus. 2009. (ENG.). 32p. (J). (gr. -1-3). pap. 7.99 *(978-0-8234-2242-5(9))* Holiday Hse., Inc.
Belanger, Kathleen. Cooldog's Holiday Adventures. Baker, David, illus. 2012. 48p. 24.95 *(978-1-4626-3045-5(6))* America Star Bks.
—Cooldog's New Adventures. 2013. 78p. pap. 16.95 *(978-1-63004-207-3(2))* America Star Bks.
Bell, Anthea, ed. & tr. The Bremen Town Musicians. Bell, Anthea, tr. Lai, Hsin-Shih, illus. 2007. 32p. (J). (gr. -1-3). 17.95 *(978-0-88010-583-5(6),* Bell Pond Bks.) SteinerBooks, Inc.
Bell, Cece. Itty Bitty. Bell, Cece, illus. (ENG., Illus.). (J). (gr. -1-2). 2017. 24p. bds. 6.99 ***(978-0-7636-9313-8(8))*** 2009. 32p. 9.99 *(978-0-7636-3616-6(9))* Candlewick Pr.
Bell, Elvee. Wups. 2010. 16p. 8.49 *(978-1-4520-3071-5(5))* AuthorHouse.
Bell, Karen. Cookie's Victorian. 2010. 84p. pap. 31.95 *(978-1-4497-0558-9(8),* WestBow Pr.) Author Solutions, Inc.
Bell, Phillip. Kurt the Dog & His Friend Lisa the Cat. 2012. 20p. pap. 24.95 *(978-1-4626-8140-2(9))* America Star Bks.
Bella & Rosie Play Hide & Seek. 2003. (Bella & Rosie Set 1 Ser.). (J). 7.67 *(978-1-932570-11-3(X))* Pioneer Valley Bks.
Bella & Rosie Set 1. 2003. (J). *(978-1-932570-08-3(X))* Pioneer Valley Bks.
Bella & Rosie Set 2. 2004. (J). *(978-1-932570-15-1(2))* Pioneer Valley Bks.
Bella & Rosie, Set 3. 2006. (J). *(978-1-932570-59-5(4))* Pioneer Valley Bks.
Bella & Rosie Trick or Treat. 2004. (Bella & Rosie Set 2 Ser.). (J). 7.67 *(978-1-932570-17-5(9))* Pioneer Valley Bks.
Bella Is a Bad Dog. 2003. (Bella & Rosie Set 1 Ser.). (J). 7.67 *(978-1-932570-14-4(4))* Pioneer Valley Bks.
Bella's Birthday. 2003. (Bella & Rosie Set 1 Ser.). (J). 7.67 *(978-1-932570-09-0(8))* Pioneer Valley Bks.
Bellisario, Gina. Super Fluffy to the Rescue. Von Innerebner, Jessika, illus. 2016. (Ellie Ultra Ser.). (ENG.). 128p. (gr. 2-3). lib. bdg. 25.99 *(978-1-4965-3142-1(6))* Stone Arch Bks.
Bello, Rodolfo S. My Baby Doggie. 2012. 32p. pap. 24.95 *(978-1-4626-8683-4(4))* America Star Bks.
Belmudes, Bonnie. The Adventures of Gus & Gunther: How They Met. 2012. 44p. pap. 21.99 *(978-1-4772-5350-2(5))* AuthorHouse.
Belverio, Tom. Cindy Learns a Lesson. 2008. 25p. pap. 24.95 *(978-1-60672-496-5(7))* America Star Bks.
Bemelmans, Ludwig. Madeline's Rescue. 2004. (J). (gr. -1-2). spiral bd. *(978-0-616-11864-1(3))* Canadian National Institute for the Blind/Institut National Canadien pour les Aveugles.
—Madeline's Rescue, 1 vol. 2009. (Madeline Ser.). (ENG.). 15p. (J). (gr. -1-2). 9.99 *(978-0-14-241444-6(1),* Puffin Books) Penguin Young Readers Group.
Benchmark Education Co., LLC. Dog Hair EVERYWHERE! Big Book. 2014. (Shared Reading Foundations Ser.). (J). (gr. -1). *(978-1-4509-9442-2(3))* Benchmark Education Co.
Bender, Randy L. Bunko's Journey. LaGrange, Tiffany, illus. 2008. 44p. pap. 13.95 *(978-0-9818683-2-5(0))* Peppertree Pr., The.
Benedis-Grab, Daphne. Clementine for Christmas. 2015. (ENG.). 256p. (J). (gr. 3-7). 16.99 *(978-0-545-83951-8(3),* Scholastic Pr.) Scholastic, Inc.
Benjamin, A. H. Shamwood. 2006. 140p. pap. 24.95 *(978-1-4137-9193-8(X))* PublishAmerica, Inc.
Bennett, Jeffrey. Max Goes to the Moon: A Science Adventure with Max the Dog. Okamoto, Alan, illus. 2nd ed. 2012. (Science Adventures with Max the Dog Ser.). (ENG.). 32p. (J). (gr. 2-4). 15.00 *(978-1-937548-20-9(1))* Big Kid Science.
Bennett, Shirley. Missy - a Tail-Wagging Good Life. 2012. 32p. pap. 19.99 *(978-1-4685-9476-8(1))* AuthorHouse.
Benson, Cindy. Chloe & Hairy Go to School. 2012. 32p. pap. 12.99 *(978-0-9855202-9-8(9))* Kids At Heart Publishing, LLC.
Benson, Donna. Dog Gone Drama, the Cupcakes Club #2. 2008. 130p. (J). pap. 7.95 *(978-0-9799159-1-8(0))* Pink Lemonade, LLC.
Benson, Glenda. The Adventures of Pepe & Gracie: Trouble in the Park. 2012. 20p. pap. 13.77 *(978-1-4669-0840-6(8))* Trafford Publishing.
Benson, Linda. Finding Chance. Lane, Nancy, illus. 2006. 112p. (J). *(978-1-59336-696-4(5))* Mondo Publishing.
Bentley, Dawn. Jack: Lights, Camera, Action! (Pet Tales Ser.). (ENG., Illus.). 32p. (J). (gr. -1-2). 2006. 9.95 *(978-1-59249-504-7(4),* 1B041) 2005. 4.95 *(978-1-59249-502-3(8),* 1B039) 2005. pap. 2.95 *(978-1-59249-503-0(6),* 1B040) Soundprints.
Bentley, Sue. Classroom Princess. 2013. (Magic Puppy Ser.: 9). lib. bdg. 16.00 *(978-0-606-32122-8(5),* Turtleback) Turtleback Bks.
—Classroom Princess #9. Swan, Angela, illus. 2013. (Magic Puppy Ser.: 9). (ENG.). 128p. (J). (gr. 1-3). 5.99 *(978-0-448-46732-0(1),* Grosset & Dunlap) Penguin Young Readers Group.
—Cloud Capers, 3 vols. Swan, Angela & Farley, Andrew, illus. 2009. (Magic Puppy Ser.: 3). (ENG.). 128p. (J). (gr. 1-3). pap. 5.99 *(978-0-448-45046-9(1),* Grosset & Dunlap) Penguin Young Readers Group.
—Cloud Capers. 2009. (Magic Puppy Ser.: 3). lib. bdg. 14.75 *(978-0-606-06977-9(1),* Turtleback) Turtleback Bks.
—A Forest Charm. 2008. (ENG., Illus.). 128p. (J). pap. *(978-0-14-132380-0(9),* Puffin) Penguin Bks., Ltd.
—A Forest Charm, 6 vols. Farley, Andrew & Swan, Angela, illus. 2010. (Magic Puppy Ser.: 6). (ENG.). 128p. (J). (gr. 1-3). pap. 5.99 *(978-0-448-45065-0(8),* Grosset & Dunlap) Penguin Young Readers Group.
—Friendship Forever. 2013. (Magic Puppy Ser.: 10). lib. bdg. 14.75 *(978-0-606-32123-5(3),* Turtleback) Turtleback Bks.
—Friendship Forever #10. Swan, Angela, illus. 2013. (Magic Puppy Ser.: 10). (ENG.). 128p. (J). (gr. 1-3). 5.99 *(978-0-448-46733-7(X),* Grosset & Dunlap) Penguin Young Readers Group.
—Magic Puppy - A New Beginning. 2009. (Magic Puppy Ser.: 1). lib. bdg. 16.00 *(978-0-606-06017-2(0),* Turtleback) Turtleback Bks.
—Magic Puppy: Books 1-3. Swan, Angela & Farley, Andrew, illus. 2014. (Magic Puppy Ser.). (ENG.). 368p. (J). (gr. 1-3). 8.99 *(978-0-448-48460-0(9),* Grosset & Dunlap) Penguin Young Readers Group.
—Muddy Paws, No. 2. Swan, Angela & Farley, Andrew, illus. 2009. (Magic Puppy Ser.: 2). (ENG.). 128p. (J). (gr. 1-3). pap. 5.99 *(978-0-448-45045-2(3),* Grosset & Dunlap) Penguin Young Readers Group.
—Muddy Paws. 2009. (Magic Puppy Ser.: 2). lib. bdg. 14.75 *(978-0-606-06021-9(9),* Turtleback) Turtleback Bks.
—New Beginning, No. 1. Swan, Angela & Farley, Andrew, illus. 2009. (Magic Puppy Ser.: 1). (ENG.). 128p. (J). (gr. 1-3). pap. 5.99 *(978-0-448-45044-5(5),* Grosset & Dunlap) Penguin Young Readers Group.
—Party Dreams. 5th ed. 2008. (ENG., Illus.). 128p. (J). pap. *(978-0-14-132379-4(5),* Puffin) Penguin Bks., Ltd.
—Party Dreams, 5 vols. Farley, Andrew & Swan, Angela, illus. 2010. (Magic Puppy Ser.: 5). (ENG.). 128p. (J). (gr. 1-3). pap. 5.99 *(978-0-448-45064-3(X),* Grosset & Dunlap) Penguin Young Readers Group.
—The Perfect Secret. 2014. (Magic Puppy Ser.: 14). lib. bdg. 14.75 *(978-0-606-35686-2(X))* Turtleback Bks.
—The Perfect Secret #14. Swan, Angela & Farley, Andrew, illus. 2014. (Magic Puppy Ser.: 14). (ENG.). 128p. (J). (gr. 1-3). 5.99 *(978-0-448-46799-3(2),* Grosset & Dunlap) Penguin Young Readers Group.
—School of Mischief, 8 vols., No. 8. Farley, Andrew & Swan, Angela, illus. 2010. (Magic Puppy Ser.: 8). (ENG.). 128p. (J). (gr. 1-3). pap. 5.99 *(978-0-448-45067-4(4),* Grosset & Dunlap) Penguin Young Readers Group.
—Snowy Wishes. Swan, Angela, illus. 2013. (Magic Puppy Ser.). (ENG.). 128p. (J). (gr. 1-3). 5.99 *(978-0-448-46737-5(2),* Grosset & Dunlap) Penguin Young Readers Group.
—Snowy Wishes. 2013. (Magic Puppy Ser.). lib. bdg. 16.00 *(978-0-606-32124-2(1),* Turtleback) Turtleback Bks.
—Sparkling Skates. 2014. (Magic Puppy Ser.: 13). lib. bdg. 14.75 *(978-0-606-35685-5(1))* Turtleback Bks.
—Sparkling Skates #13. Swan, Angela & Farley, Andrew, illus. 2014. (Magic Puppy Ser.: 13). (ENG.). 128p. (J). (gr. 1-3). 4.99 *(978-0-448-46798-6(4),* Grosset & Dunlap) Penguin Young Readers Group.
—Spellbound at School. 2014. (Magic Puppy Ser.: 11). lib. bdg. 16.00 *(978-0-606-34140-0(4),* Turtleback) Turtleback Bks.
—Spellbound at School #11. Swan, Angela & Farley, Andrew, illus. 2014. (Magic Puppy Ser.: 11). (ENG.). 128p. (J). (gr. 1-3). 5.99 *(978-0-448-46790-0(9),* Grosset & Dunlap) Penguin Young Readers Group.
—Star of the Show, 4 vols. Swan, Angela & Farley, Andrew, illus. 2009. (Magic Puppy Ser.: 4). (ENG.). 128p. (J). (gr. 1-3). pap. 5.99 *(978-0-448-45047-6(X),* Grosset & Dunlap) Penguin Young Readers Group.
—Star of the Show. 2009. (Magic Puppy Ser.: 4). lib. bdg. 16.00 *(978-0-606-06978-6(X),* Turtleback) Turtleback Bks.
—Sunshine Shimmers. 2014. (Magic Puppy Ser.: 12). lib. bdg. 14.75 *(978-0-606-34141-7(2),* Turtleback) Turtleback Bks.
—Sunshine Shimmers #12. Swan, Angela & Farley, Andrew, illus. 2014. (Magic Puppy Ser.: 12). (ENG.). 128p. (J). (gr. 1-3). 5.99 *(978-0-448-46791-7(7),* Grosset & Dunlap) Penguin Young Readers Group.
—Twirling Tails, 7 vols. Farley, Andrew & Swan, Angela, illus. 2010. (Magic Puppy Ser.: 7). (ENG.). 128p. (J). (gr. 1-3). pap. 5.99 *(978-0-448-45066-7(6),* Grosset & Dunlap) Penguin Young Readers Group.
Bently, Peter. Train Is on Track. Conway, Louise, illus. 2015. (Busy Wheels Ser.). (ENG.). 24p. (J). (gr. -1-k). 14.95 *(978-1-60992-790-5(7))* QEB Publishing Inc.
Benton, Jim. Attack of the 50-Ft. Cupid. Benton, Jim, illus. 2004. (Franny K. Stein, Mad Scientist Ser.: 2). (ENG., Illus.). 112p. (J). (gr. 2-5). 16.99 *(978-0-689-86292-2(X),* Simon & Schuster Bks. For Young Readers) Simon & Schuster Bks. For Young Readers.
—Attack of the 50-Ft. Cupid, 1 vol. Benton, Jim, illus. 2011. (Franny K. Stein, Mad Scientist Ser.). (ENG., Illus.). 112p. (gr. 3-6). 24.21 *(978-1-59961-818-0(4))* Spotlight.
Beranek, Malinda. Rocky, the Country Squirrel. 2008. 12p. pap. 24.95 *(978-1-60563-018-2(7))* America Star Bks.
Berenstain, Jan, et al. My Favorite Dog Stories: Learning to Read Box Set. 2014. (I Can Read Level 1 Ser.). (ENG.). (J). (gr. -1-3). pap. 16.99 *(978-0-06-231331-7(2))* HarperCollins Pubs.
Berenstain, Stan & Berenstain, Jan. The Berenstain Bears' New Pup. Berenstain, Jan, illus. 2005. (I Can Read Level 1 Ser.). (ENG., Illus.). 32p. (J). (gr. k-3). pap. 3.99 *(978-0-06-058344-6(4))* HarperCollins Pubs.
Berman, Valerie & Berman, Neil. Bubba Goes to New York: Bubba Travel Series. 2009. 44p. pap. 16.99 *(978-1-4389-6860-5(4))* AuthorHouse.
Bern, Dave. Best Friends. 2006. 28p. pap. 9.95 *(978-1-4327-0036-2(7))* Outskirts Pr., Inc.
Berner, Rotraut Susanne. Hound & Hare, 1 vol. Tanaka, Shelley, tr. from GER. 2011. (ENG., Illus.). 80p. (J). (gr. k-4). 18.95 *(978-0-88899-987-0(9))* Groundwood Bks. CAN. Dist: Publishers Group West (PGW).
Berry, Lynne. Pig & Pug. Correll, Gemma, illus. 2015. (ENG.). 40p. (J). (gr. -1-3). 16.99 *(978-1-4814-2131-7(X),* Simon & Schuster Bks. For Young Readers) Simon & Schuster Bks. For Young Readers.
Berube, Kate. Hannah & Sugar. 2016. (ENG., Illus.). 32p. (J). (gr. k-2). 16.95 *(978-1-4197-1890-8(8),* Abrams Bks. for Young Readers) Abrams, Inc.
Bester, Maryanne. Three Friends & a Taxi. Bester, Shayle, illus. 2007. (Cool Nguni Ser.: 1). (ENG.). 24p. (J). (gr. k-2). 12.00 *(978-1-77009-265-5(X))* Jacana Media ZAF. Dist: Independent Pubs. Group.
Bethany: Adventures of the Mighty Mustard Seed. 2004. Orig. Title: Bethany in Beulah Land. (J). mass mkt. 12.95 *(978-0-9745440-0-7(0))* McKatib Pr.
Betts, Betty. Dylan's Adventure. 2005. 60p. pap. 11.95 *(978-1-4208-2293-9(4))* AuthorHouse.
Betts, Joan D. Bagley B. Butterfield: A Dog Book for People. 2011. 24p. pap. 16.99 *(978-1-4520-9280-5(X))* AuthorHouse.
Bevan, Clare. Freckle the Fairy Puppy. Johnson-Isaacs, Cally, illus. 2015. (Mimi's Magical Fairy Friends Ser.: 2). (ENG.). 32p. (J). (gr. -1-2). pap. 10.99 ***(978-1-4472-7700-2(7))*** Pan Macmillan GBR. Dist: Independent Pubs. Group.
Bevans, Donna. Don't Do That, Harry! The Puppy Story. 2010. 20p. 10.49 *(978-1-4490-2927-2(2))* AuthorHouse.
—Scooter & His Friends. 2012. 40p. pap. 16.99 *(978-1-4772-1288-2(4))* AuthorHouse.
Beverly, James. Seamus the Sheltie to the Rescue! 2011. 156p. pap. 14.95 *(978-1-933449-88-3(8))* Nightengale Pr.
Beyers, Kathryn. Babe's Vacation. 2012. 32p. pap. 17.49 *(978-1-4771-5671-1(2))* Xlibris Corp.
Bezek, Lyn. Ribbon the Border Collie: From Herder to Healer. 2008. (J). pap. 11.95 *(978-1-932738-51-3(7))* Western Reflections Publishing Co.
Big Red's Greatest Find. 2006. (J). per. *(978-0-9725286-5-8(2))* Sheppard Publishing.
Billy & Baxter at the Airport, 4 vols. 2005. (Illus.). 24p. (J). (gr. -1-7). 8.95 *(978-1-58087-100-6(3))* Stampley, C. D. Enterprises, Inc.
Bird, Benjamin. Scooby-Doo's 1-2-3 Mystery. 2015. (Scooby-Doo! Little Mysteries Ser.). (ENG., Illus.). 20p. (gr. -1 — 1). bds. 7.99 *(978-1-62370-177-2(5))* Capstone Press of Coughlan Cos.
—Scooby-Doo's ABC Mystery. 2015. (Scooby-Doo! Little Mysteries Ser.). (ENG., Illus.). 20p. (gr. -1 — 1). bds. 7.99 *(978-1-62370-175-8(9))* Capstone Press of Coughlan Cos.
—Scooby-Doo's Color Mystery. 2015. (Scooby-Doo! Little Mysteries Ser.). (ENG., Illus.). 20p. (gr. -1 — 1). bds. 7.99 *(978-1-62370-176-5(7))* Capstone Press of Coughlan Cos.
—Scooby-Doo's Shape Mystery. 2015. (Scooby-Doo! Little Mysteries Ser.). (ENG., Illus.). 20p. (gr. -1 — 1). bds. 7.99 *(978-1-62370-178-9(3))* Capstone Press of Coughlan Cos.
Bird, J. K. Shadow the Dog. 2010. 28p. 13.99 *(978-1-4520-3476-8(1))* AuthorHouse.
Bird, Janie. Freddy in the City: Memorable Monday. Treffeisen, Brian, photos by. 2nd rev. ed. 2005.Tr. of Freddy en la Ciudad un Lunes Memorble. (SPA., Illus.). 32p. (J). 10.95 *(978-1-59494-005-7(3))* CPCC Pr.
Birdsall, Jeanne. Lucky & Squash. Dyer, Jane, illus. 2012. (ENG.). 32p. (J). (gr. -1-2). 16.99 *(978-0-06-083150-9(2))* HarperCollins Pubs.
—The Penderwicks Paperback 4-Book Boxed Set, 4 vols. 2016. (ENG.). 270p. (J). (gr. 3-7). 31.96 *(978-1-101-93760-0(2),* Yearling) Random Hse. Children's Bks.
Birney, Betty G. Humphrey's Playful Puppy Problem. Burris, Priscilla, illus. 2014. (Humphrey's Tiny Tales Ser.: 2). (ENG.). 96p. (J). (gr. k-3). pap. 4.99 *(978-0-14-751484-4(3),* Puffin Books) Penguin Young Readers Group.
Birt, Michael. Kody the Conservation Pup: Helps Tori Cross the Road. Trammell, Brandon, illus. 2012. 58p. 27.95 *(978-0-578-11315-9(5));* pap. 19.95 *(978-0-578-11306-7(6))* Birt Hse. Publishing.
Bishop, Carol. The Chronicles of Rusty. 2013. 68p. pap. *(978-3-7103-0628-0(0))* united p.c. Verlag.
Bishop, Clive. Trophy Trouble. 2009. 74p. pap. 9.99 *(978-1-60860-547-7(7),* Strategic Bk. Publishing) Strategic Book Publishing & Rights Agency (SBPRA).
Bishop, Rose. Arielle's Pursuit. 2007. 100p. pap. 10.95 *(978-0-7414-3804-1(6))* Infinity Publishing.
Bistricean, Karen. The Adventures of Fergus & Lady: Home Sweet Home. Bistricean, Claudius, illus. 2006. (J). *(978-0-9786975-1-8(0))* Fergus & Lady Publishing.
—The Adventures of Fergus & Lady: The Beginning. Bistricean, Claudius, illus. 2006. (J). *(978-0-9786975-0-1(2))* Fergus & Lady Publishing.
Bittle Jr., Paul. Me too, Little Puppies, Me Too, 1 vol. 2010. 16p. pap. 24.95 *(978-1-61582-922-4(9))* PublishAmerica, Inc.
Bix, Daisy. At the Dog Park with Sam & Lucy. Hansen, Amelia, illus. 2006. (Sit! Stay! Read! Ser.). (ENG.). 24p. (J). (gr. k-2). 15.95 *(978-0-940719-00-2(2))* Gryphon Pr., The.
—Buddy Unchained. Hyatt, Joe, illus. 2006. (Sit! Stay! Read! Ser.). (ENG.). 24p. (J). (gr. k-2). 16.95 *(978-0-940719-01-9(0))* Gryphon Pr., The.
Bixley, Donovan. Dogfight. 2016. (Flying Furballs Ser.: 1). (ENG., Illus.). 112p. (J). (gr. 2-4). pap. 8.99 *(978-1-927262-53-5(4))* Upstart Pr. NZL. Dist: Independent Pubs. Group.
Bixley, Donovan. Hot Air. Bixley, Donovan, illus. 2017. (Flying Furballs Ser.: 2). (ENG., Illus.). 112p. (J). (gr. 2-4). pap. 8.99 ***(978-1-927262-54-2(2))*** Upstart Pr. NZL. Dist: Independent Pubs. Group.
Biz, Jen. A Letter to My Beagle. 2013. 24p. pap. 24.95 *(978-1-4626-9764-9(X))* America Star Bks.
Bjelkier Press. Hero Finds His Path. 2012. (Illus.). (J). 16.95 *(978-0-9828217-4-9(3))* Bjelkier Pr.
Blabey, Aaron. Pig the Pug. 2016. (ENG., Illus.). 32p. (J). (gr. -1-k). 14.99 *(978-1-338-11245-0(7),* Scholastic Pr.) Scholastic, Inc.

C
D

—Pig the Winner. 2017. (Pig the Pug Ser.). (ENG.). 32p. (J). (gr. -1-k). 14.99 (978-1-338-13638-8(0), Scholastic Pr.) Scholastic, Inc.

Blace, Maria. Lunie Balloonies. Swope, Brenda, illus. 2011. 24p. pap. 24.95 (978-1-4560-0947-2(8)) America Star Bks.

Black, Cary & Schott, Gretchen Victoria. French Quarter Tori & the Red Owl. Travis, Caroline, illus. 2012. 38p. pap. 12.95 (978-0-9754279-8-9(9)); pap. 14.95 (978-0-9754279-7-2(0)) Red Owl Pubns.

Black, Robyn Hood. Sir Mike. Murphy, David, illus. 2006. (Rookie Reader Skill Set Ser.). (ENG.). 32p. (J). (gr. k-2). per. 4.95 (978-0-516-25020-5(5), Children's Pr.) Scholastic Library Publishing.

Black, Simon. The Dog Child. Robledo, Honorio, illus. 2006. (ENG.). 32p. (J). (gr. -1-3). 17.95 (978-0-938317-42-5(3)) Cinco Puntos Pr.

Blackaby, Susan. Meg Sale a Pasear, 1 vol. Ruíz, Carlos, tr. from ENG. Holme, Sharon, illus. 2006. (Read-It! Readers en Español: Story Collection).Tr. of Meg Takes a Walk. (SPA.). 24p. (gr. -1-3). 21.32 (978-1-4048-1685-5(2), Easy Readers) Picture Window Bks.

Blackcrane, Gerelchimeg. Black Flame, 1 vol. Holmwood, Anna, tr. from CHI. 2013. (ENG.). 224p. (J). (gr. 5). 15.95 (978-1-55498-135-9(2)) Groundwood Bks. CAN. Dist: Publishers Group West (PGW).

Blackstone, Stella. Cleo & Caspar. Mockford, Caroline, illus. 2013. (ENG.). 24p. (J). 6.99 (978-1-78285-053-3(8)) Barefoot Bks., Inc.

—Cleo on the Move. Mockford, Caroline, illus. 2013. (ENG.). 24p. (J). (gr. -1-k). pap. 6.99 (978-1-78285-057-1(0)) Barefoot Bks., Inc.

—Una Isla Bajo el Sol. Ceccoli, Nicoletta, illus. 2003. (SPA.). 24p. (J). pap. 6.99 (978-1-84148-144-9(0)) Barefoot Bks., Inc.

Blackstone, Stella & Barefoot Books Staff. An Island in the Sun. Ceccoli, Nicoletta, illus. 2005. (ENG.). 24p. (J). pap. 6.99 (978-1-84148-079-4(7)) Barefoot Bks., Inc.

Blake, Bronwyn. Nick Riley's Ninth Life. 100p. (YA). pap. (978-0-7344-0333-9(X), Lothian Children's Bks.) Hachette Australia.

Blake, Robert J. Akiak. 2004. (Illus.). 28p. (gr. -1-3). 17.00 (978-0-7569-3207-7(6)) Perfection Learning Corp.

—Akiak: A Tale from the Iditarod. Blake, Robert J., illus. 2004. (ENG., Illus.). 40p. (J). (gr. k-3). reprint ed. pap. 7.99 (978-0-14-240185-9(4), Puffin Books) Penguin Young Readers Group.

—Painter & Ugly. Blake, Robert J., illus. 2011. (ENG., Illus.). 48p. (J). (gr. k-3). 16.99 (978-0-399-24323-3(2), Philomel Bks.) Penguin Young Readers Group.

—Victor & Hugo. Blake, Robert J., illus. 2017. (ENG., Illus.). 40p. (J). (gr. -1-2). 16.99 (978-0-399-24324-0(0), Philomel Bks.) Penguin Young Readers Group.

Blalock, Rachel. The dog & the Flea. 2005. 15p. 8.97 (978-1-4116-2784-0(9)) Lulu Pr., Inc.

Blanc, Katherine. No Dogs, Please! Blanc, Katherine, illus. 2013. (ENG., Illus.). (J). (gr. -1-3). 14.95 (978-1-62086-388-6(X)) Mascot Bks., Inc.

Blas, Larry. The Adventures of Island Stickman & His Dog Name Pearl. 2013. 28p. pap. 24.95 (978-1-4626-9943-8(X)) America Star Bks.

Blatchford, David. The Story of Mr Tomkins. 2012. (Illus.). 50p. pap. (978-1-908773-29-6(4)) Iponymous Publishing, Ltd.

Blaylock, Janet. Crissy LeeAnn's Life. 2008. 33p. pap. 13.50 (978-1-4357-5437-9(9)) Lulu Pr., Inc.

Blevins, Wiley. A New Friend. 2013. (Penguin Young Readers, Level 1 Ser.). (ENG.). 32p. (J). (gr. k-1). 14.99 (978-0-448-46572-2(8)); pap. 3.99 (978-0-448-46180-9(3)) Penguin Young Readers Group. (Penguin Young Readers).

—A New Friend. 2013. (Penguin Young Readers Level 1 Ser.). lib. bdg. 13.55 (978-0-606-31705-4(8), Turtleback) Turtleback Bks.

Bloch, Beth. My Oh My Sweet Potato Pie. Bloch, Beth, illus. 2005. (Illus.). 32p. (J). 16.00 (978-0-9771515-0-9(6)) Dream Creek Pr.

Bloker Cantrell, Jeannette, et al. The Summer of Joanie & Bobo. 2012. 72p. pap. 12.00 (978-1-4349-1759-1(2)) Dorrance Publishing Co., Inc.

Blom, Jen K. Possum Summer. Rayyan, Omar, illus. 2011. (ENG.). 256p. (J). (gr. 3-7). 17.95 (978-0-8234-2331-6(X)) Holiday Hse., Inc.

Bloncourt, Nelson. Fanny the Flying French Bulldog. Polyansky, Nikita, illus. 2014. (ENG.). 40p. 20.00 (978-0-9851696-3-3(X)) Glitterati, Inc.

Bloncourt, Nelson & Botero, Fernando. Botero: Paintings & Works on Paper. Polyansky, Nikita, illus. 2013. (ENG.). 252p. 125.00 (978-0-9881745-1-1(0)) Glitterati, Inc.

Bluemle, Elizabeth. Dogs on the Bed. Wilsdorf, Anne, illus. 2013. (ENG.). 32p. (J). (gr. -1-2). pap. 6.99 (978-0-7636-6736-8(6)) Candlewick Pr.

—My Father the Dog. Cecil, Randy, illus. (ENG.). 32p. (J). (gr. -1-3). 2008. pap. 6.99 (978-0-7636-3077-5(2)) 2006. 15.99 (978-0-7636-2222-0(2)) Candlewick Pr.

Blumenthal, Deborah. The Blue House Dog, 1 vol. Gustavson, Adam, illus. 2010. (ENG.). 32p. (J). (gr. -1-3). 15.95 (978-1-56145-537-9(7), Peachtree Junior) Peachtree Pubs.

Blyton, Enid. Children of Green Meadows. 2013. (ENG.). 240p. (J). pap. 9.99 (978-1-84135-645-7(X)) Award Pubns. Ltd. GBR. Dist: Parkwest Pubns., Inc.

Bobowicz, Pamela. 101 Dalmatians. 2015. (Step into Reading Level 1 Ser.). lib. bdg. 13.55 (978-0-606-36004-3(2)) Turtleback Bks.

—101 Dalmatians (Disney 101 Dalmatians) RH Disney Staff, illus. 2015. (Step into Reading Ser.). (ENG.). 32p. (J). (gr. -1-1). 3.99 (978-0-7364-3182-8(9), RH/Disney) Random Hse. Children's Bks.

Bocanegra, Haley. New Dog Food for Mozart. 2005. 14p. 9.76 (978-1-4116-3896-9(4)) Lulu Pr., Inc.

Bochynek, Halina. A Beagle's Tale. 2008. 152p. pap. 14.99 (978-1-4389-1960-7(3)) AuthorHouse.

Bodin, Britt. A Puppy Named Hope. 2012. (ENG.). (J). pap. 10.95 (978-1-4675-3207-5(X)) Independent Pub.

Boelts, Maribeth. Before You Were Mine. Walker, David, illus. 2007. (ENG.). 32p. (J). (gr. -1-3). 15.99 (978-0-399-24526-8(X), G.P. Putnam's Sons Books for Young Readers) Penguin Young Readers Group.

—Before You Were Mine. Walker, David, illus. 2008. (J). (gr. -1-3). 29.95 incl. audio compact disk (978-0-8045-4184-8(1)); 27.95 incl. audio (978-0-8045-6961-3(4)) Spoken Arts, Inc.

—Dogerella. Wu, Donald, illus. 2008. (Step into Reading Ser.). (ENG.). 48p. (J). (gr. k-3). pap. 3.99 (978-0-375-83393-9(5), Random Hse. Bks. for Young Readers) Random Hse. Children's Bks.

—The Fairy Dogmother. 2017. (Step into Reading Ser.). (ENG.). 48p. (J). (gr. k-3). 3.99 (978-1-101-93446-3(8), Random Hse. Bks. for Young Readers) Random Hse. Children's Bks.

—The PS Brothers. 2011. (ENG.). 144p. (J). (gr. 2-5). pap. 6.99 (978-0-547-57717-3(6)) Houghton Mifflin Harcourt Publishing Co.

—Pupunzel. 2016. (Step into Reading Ser.). (ENG., Illus.). 48p. (J). (gr. k-3). lib. bdg. 12.99 (978-1-101-93447-0(6), Random Hse. Bks. for Young Readers) Random Hse. Children's Bks.

Bogardus, Ray & Bogardus, Karin. Hannah the Magic Shelter Dog. Seltzer, Jerry, illus. 2005. 143p. (J). pap. 14.99 (978-1-932864-30-4(X)) Masthof Pr.

Bohmer, Kara Dale. Walking Sarah: First Day Out. 2013. 32p. (978-1-4602-0076-6(4)); pap. (978-1-4602-0077-3(2)) FriesenPress.

Bojunga, Lygia. Los Amigos. (SPA.). (J). 8.95 (978-958-04-6262-0(3)) Norma S.A. COL. Dist: Distribuidora Norma, Inc.

Bolam, Emily. Dog. 2003. (Chunky Pet Bks.). (ENG., Illus.). 14p. (J). bds. 5.99 (978-0-7641-5610-6(1)) Barron's Educational Series, Inc.

Boldi, Fiorina, illus. Pug in Boots. 2013. 42p. pap. 9.99 (978-0-9829132-6-0(5)) Left Paw Pr.

Boldt, Claudia. Odd Dog. 2012. (ENG., Illus.). 32p. (J). (gr. -1-1). 16.95 (978-0-7358-4068-3(7)) North-South Bks., Inc.

—Star Gazers, Skyscrapers & Extraordinary Sausages. Boldt, Claudia, illus. 2010. (Child's Play Library). (ENG., Illus.). 32p. (J). (gr. 1-2). pap. (978-1-84643-344-3(4)) Child's Play International Ltd.

Boles, Jim. Ivan the Invacar & the Cave. Cunningham, Bob, illus. 2013. 52p. pap. 19.95 (978-0-9858052-2-7(6)) People Ink Pr.

—Ivan the Invacar Helps Big Dog. Cunningham, Bob, illus. 2012. 56p. pap. 19.95 (978-0-9845983-5-9(9)) People Ink Pr.

Bolton, Nicola Joanne. Jasper. 2009. 58p. pap. 10.50 (978-1-4092-4609-1(4)) Lulu Pr., Inc.

Bombaci, James J. The Million Dollar Dog. 2010. 32p. pap. 14.99 (978-1-4490-4936-2(2)) AuthorHouse.

Bonar, Troy A. Safety = Caring. 2013. 28p. pap. 9.95 (978-1-4787-0745-5(3)) Outside the Box Publishing, LLC.

Bond, Roland. Harvey Plumstead & the Dinnertime Dog. 2012. (Illus.). 96p. (gr. 4-18). pap. 13.66 (978-1-4772-4317-6(8)) AuthorHouse.

Bonder, Dianna. Dogabet, 1 vol. Bonder, Dianna, illus. 2007. (ENG., Illus.). 32p. (J). (gr. -1-2). (978-1-55285-797-7(2), Walrus Bks.) Whitecap Bks., Ltd.

Bonk, John J. Subway Crush. Trissler, Rebecca Johns, ed. Kubic, Ginger, illus. (Adventures of Storydog Ser.). 75p. (J). pap. (978-0-9722690-1-8(0), 1001) Storydog, Inc.

Bonner, Gayle. Life on Peavine Creek: Sam's Story. Johnson, Brandon, illus. 2008. 33p. pap. 24.95 (978-1-60610-624-2(4)) America Star Bks.

Bonnett-Rampersaud, Louise. The Dyno-Mite Dog Show, 0 vols. McHeffey, Adam, illus. 2015. (Secret Knock Club Ser.: 0). (ENG.). 112p. (J). (gr. 1-4). pap. 9.99 (978-0-7614-6325-2(9), 9780761463252, Amazon Children's Publishing) Amazon Publishing.

Book, Jennie Hale. Baby Dog Beans Comes Home: A Paul & Beans Adventure. 2005. (J). per. 13.95 (978-0-9767514-2-7(9), 2000) Abbott Avenue Pr.

Booth, Martin. War Dog. 2012. (ENG.). 144p. (YA). (gr. 7). pap. 8.99 (978-1-4424-7297-6(9), McElderry, Margaret K. Bks.) McElderry, Margaret K. Bks.

Bourgeois, Paulette. Benjamin et Son Voisinage. 2004.Tr. of Franklin's Neighborhood. (FRE., Illus.). (J). (gr. -1-2). spiral bd. (978-0-616-01826-2(6)) Canadian National Institute for the Blind/Institut National Canadien pour les Aveugles.

Bova, Della L. The Adventures of Pono: A Puppy Dog's Tale. 2011. 24p. pap. 11.49 (978-1-4490-7354-1(9)) AuthorHouse.

Bove, Candace Scobie. Calypso: A Day in the Life of a Puppy. 2012. 24p. 24.95 (978-1-4626-4122-2(9)) America Star Bks.

Bowater, Alan. A Pig Called Pete Meets a Dog Called Doug. Pascoe, Pete, illus. 2009. (Pig Called Pete Ser.). 32p. (J). (gr. -1-2). 22.60 (978-1-60754-564-4(0)); pap. 10.55 (978-1-60754-565-1(9)) Windmill Bks.

Bowen, Anne. Scooter in the Outside. Carter, Abby, illus. 2012. (ENG.). 32p. (J). 16.95 (978-0-8234-2326-2(3)) Holiday Hse., Inc.

Bowen, Jessica Tiare. Park Avenue Pound Puppy. 2010. 32p. pap. 25.00 (978-0-557-48814-8(1)) Lulu Pr., Inc.

Bowles, B. R. Pauley the Pancake Boy. 2012. 24p. 24.95 (978-1-4626-6026-1(6)) America Star Bks.

Bowles, Paula. Messy Jesse. Bowles, Paula, illus. 2015. (ENG., Illus.). 32p. (J). 16.99 (978-1-58925-133-5(4)) Tiger Tales.

Bowman, Vicki. Julie Through the Looking Glass. 2005. 55p. pap. 16.95 (978-1-4137-4679-2(9)) America Star Bks.

Bowness, Kim. The Brave Engineers. 2007. (Illus.). 30p. (J). lib. bdg. 19.95 (978-1-933732-36-7(9)) Big Ransom Studio.

Boyd, Lizi. Inside Outside. Boyd, Lizi, illus. 2013. (ENG., Illus.). 40p. (J). (gr. -1-1). 15.99 (978-1-4521-0644-1(4)) Chronicle Bks. LLC.

Boyd, Sonya. I Have What It Takes. 2011. 28p. pap. 9.95 (978-1-4327-7975-7(3)) Outskirts Pr., Inc.

Boyden, Linda. Boy & Poi Poi Puppy. Boyden, Linda, illus. 2013. (Illus.). (J). (gr. -1-2). (ENG.). 50p. 17.95 (978-1-940834-00-9(7)); 40p. pap. 11.95 (978-0-9888568-2-0(4)) Rising Phoenix Pr.

Boyer, Cecile. Run, Dog! 2014. (ENG., Illus.). 48p. (J). (gr. -1-k). 16.99 (978-1-4521-2708-8(5)) Chronicle Bks. LLC.

Boyer, Cécile, illus. Woof Meow Tweet-Tweet. 2011. (ENG.). 48p. (J). (gr. -1). 15.95 (978-1-934734-60-5(8)) Seven Footer Pr.

Boyer, Mitch. Vivian the Dog Moves to the City. Boyer, Mitch, illus. 2017. (Illus.). 40p. (J). (gr. -1-3). 17.99 **(978-0-06-267327-5(0))** HarperCollins Pubs.

Boyes, Alison. What Charlotte Ate: The Story of a Naughty Dog Who Loved to Eat. Boyes, Faye, illus. 2012. 28p. (J). pap. (978-0-9808685-7-9(2)) Mono Unlimited.

Boylan, Bill & Boylan, Sue. Billy & the Mad Dog. 2016. (ENG., Illus.). (J). (gr. 3-6). pap. **(978-1-925515-27-5(3))** Vivid Publishing.

Boyle, Keri Claiborne. Teddy the Dog: Be Your Own Dog. Sneider, Jonathan, illus. 2016. (Teddy the Dog Ser.: 1). 32p. (J). (gr. -1-3). 17.99 (978-0-06-238283-2(7)) HarperCollins Pubs.

—Teddy the Dog: (Almost) Best in Show. Sneider, Jonathan, illus. 2017. (Teddy the Dog Ser.). 32p. (J). (gr. -1-3). 17.99 (978-0-06-238284-9(5)) HarperCollins Pubs.

Boynton, Sandra. Snuggle Puppy! 2003. (ENG., Illus.). 24p. (J). (gr. k — 1). bds. 6.95 (978-0-7611-3067-3(5), 13067) Workman Publishing Co., Inc.

Bozak, Jon. Demo: The Story of a Junkyard Dog. Bruns, Scott, illus. 2008. (ENG.). 56p. (J). (gr. 2-4). 16.95 (978-0-9816188-0-7(4)) Fifth Paw Pr.

Bracken, Beth. Henry Helps with the Dog, 1 vol. Busby, Ailie, illus. 2012. (Henry Helps Ser.). (ENG.). 24p. (gr. -1 — 1). pap. 5.95 (978-1-4048-7673-6(1), Henry Helps) Picture Window Bks.

Braddock, Pauline. The long way Home. 2010. 156p. pap. 9.17 (978-1-4452-9248-9(3)) Lulu Pr., Inc.

Bradford, Karleen. Ghost Wolf, 1 vol. Cormack, Allan & Drew-Brook, Deborah, illus. 2005. (Orca Echoes Ser.). (ENG.). 64p. (J). (gr. 2-3). per. 6.95 (978-1-55143-341-7(9)) Orca Bk. Pubs. USA.

Braeuner, Shellie. The Great Dog Wash. Neubecker, Robert, illus. 2009. (ENG.). 32p. (J). (gr. -1-1). 15.99 (978-1-4169-7116-0(5), Simon & Schuster Bks. For Young Readers) Simon & Schuster Bks. For Young Readers.

Branan, Nellie. Fritzi Finds a New Home. 2012. (ENG.). 31p. (J). pap. 13.95 (978-1-4327-9597-9(X)) Outskirts Pr., Inc.

Brandon, Anthony G. Moving Day. Yee, Wong Herbert, illus. 2005. (Green Light Readers Level 2 Ser.). (ENG.). 32p. (J). (gr. -1-3). pap. 3.95 (978-0-15-205652-0(1)) Houghton Mifflin Harcourt Publishing Co.

Brannen, Sarah S. Madame Martine. Brannen, Sarah S., illus. 2014. (ENG., Illus.). 32p. (J). (gr. -1-3). 16.99 (978-0-8075-4905-6(3)) Whitman, Albert & Co.

—Madame Martine Breaks the Rules. Brannen, Sarah S., illus. 2015. (ENG., Illus.). 32p. (J). (gr. -1-3). 16.99 (978-0-8075-4907-0(X)) Whitman, Albert & Co.

Brannen, Sarah S., illus. Madame Martine. 2015. 32p. (J). (978-1-4896-3864-9(4)) Weigl Pubs., Inc.

Bray, Sorcha. The Adventures of Powerpup & Wonderboy & the Case of the Wicked Chickens. 2010. 48p. pap. 19.75 (978-1-4490-7133-2(3)) AuthorHouse.

Brazina, Rhonda & Margolis, Ida R. Carrots for Charlie. 2012. 42p. pap. 9.95 (978-0-9851184-6-4(6)) Barringer Publishing.

Breathed, Berkeley. Flawed Dogs: The Novel: the Shocking Raid on Westminster. 2017. lib. bdg. 19.65 **(978-0-606-39787-2(6))** Turtleback Bks.

Bremmer, Patricia A. The Christmas Westie. 2007. 48p. (J). kivar 17.99 (978-0-9745884-5-2(8)) Windcall Publishing.

Brendler, Carol. The Pickwicks' Picnic: A Counting Adventure. Kurilla, Renée, illus. 2017. (ENG.). 40p. (J). (gr. -1-3). 16.99 **(978-0-544-83958-8(7)**, Clarion Bks.) Houghton Mifflin Harcourt Trade & Reference Pubs.

Brenner, Harriett A. Corky's Humane Tail Tale. Kelly, Julia, illus. 2006. 32p. (J). bds. 16.95 (978-0-9768667-0-1(6)) M & D Publishing, Inc.

Brenning, Juli. Maggi & Milo. Burris, Priscilla, illus. 2014. (ENG.). 32p. (J). (gr. -1-k). 16.99 (978-0-8037-3795-2(5), Dial Bks) Penguin Young Readers Group.

Brett, Jan. The First Dog. Brett, Jan, illus. 2015. (ENG., Illus.). 32p. (J). (gr. -1-k). 17.99 (978-0-399-17270-0(X), G.P. Putnam's Sons Books for Young Readers) Penguin Young Readers Group.

Brewer, Dottie A. Jessie's Walk. Naenix, Robin, illus. 2004. 20p. (J). 4.95 (978-0-9707945-7-4(6)) Billion $ Baby Pubns.

Brezinova, Ivona. To Have a Dog. Deisadze, Zaur, illus. 2007. (POL & ENG.). 32p. (J). pap. 12.95 (978-1-60195-106-9(X)) International Step by Step Assn.

Brianna, et al. The Adventures of Sam Spike. 2012. 50p. pap. 11.95 (978-0-9711774-0-6(6)) AnEx Pubns.

Bridwell, Norman. Clifford & the Halloween Parade. Bridwell, Norman, illus. 2004. (Scholastic Reader, Level 1 Ser.). (ENG., Illus.). 32p. (J). (gr. -1-3). 3.99 (978-0-439-09834-2(3)) Scholastic, Inc.

—Clifford at the Circus. 2011. (Be Big! Work Together Ser.). (ENG., Illus.). (gr. -1-3). 14.00 (978-1-60686-965-9(5)) Perfection Learning Corp.

—Clifford at the Circus. (Clifford, the Big Red Dog Ser.). (Illus.). (J). (gr. k-2). 6.95 (978-0-590-68639-6(9)) Scholastic, Inc.

—Clifford at the Circus. Bridwell, Norman, illus. 2010. (Clifford 8x8 Ser.). (ENG., Illus.). 32p. (J). (gr. -1-3). pap. 3.99 (978-0-545-21584-8(6), Cartwheel Bks.) Scholastic, Inc.

—Clifford Collection. Bridwell, Norman, illus. 2012. (ENG., Illus.). 192p. (J). (gr. -1-k). 12.99 (978-0-545-45013-3(6)) Scholastic, Inc.

—Clifford Goes to Dog School. Bridwell, Norman, illus. 2010. (Clifford 8x8 Ser.). (ENG., Illus.). 32p. (J). (gr. -1-3). pap. 3.99 (978-0-545-21577-0(3), Cartwheel Bks.) Scholastic, Inc.

—Clifford Goes to Dog School. 2010. (Clifford 8x8 Ser.). (gr. -1-2). lib. bdg. 13.55 (978-0-613-45580-0(0), Turtleback) Turtleback Bks.

—Clifford Makes the Team. Bridwell, Norman, illus. 2011. (Scholastic Reader Level 1 Ser.). (ENG., Illus.). 32p. (J). (gr. -1-2). pap. 3.99 (978-0-545-23141-1(8)) Scholastic, Inc.

—Clifford Sees America. 2012. (Scholastic Reader Level 1 Ser.). (ENG.). 32p. (J). (gr. -1-3). pap. 3.99 (978-0-545-23144-2(2), Cartwheel Bks.) Scholastic, Inc.

—Clifford Sees America. 2012. (Clifford: Scholastic Readers Level 1 Ser.). lib. bdg. 13.55 (978-0-606-23908-0(1), Turtleback) Turtleback Bks.

—Clifford Takes a Trip. Bridwell, Norman, illus. 2011. (Clifford Ser.). (ENG., Illus.). 32p. (J). (gr. -1-k). pap. 3.99 (978-0-545-21591-6(9), Cartwheel Bks.) Scholastic, Inc.

—Clifford Takes a Trip. 2007. (Clifford Ser.). (ENG.). (J). (gr. -1-3). 18.95 (978-0-545-00409-1(8)) Scholastic, Inc.

—Clifford Takes a Trip. Bridwell, Norman, illus. 2007. (Clifford, the Big Red Dog Ser.). (ENG., Illus.). (J). (gr. -1-3). 9.95 (978-0-545-00358-2(X)) Scholastic, Inc.

—Clifford the Big Red Dog. Bridwell, Norman, illus. 2010. (Clifford 8x8 Ser.). (ENG., Illus.). 32p. (J). (gr. -1-3). pap. 3.99 (978-0-545-21578-7(1), Cartwheel Bks.) Scholastic, Inc.

—Clifford the Big Red Dog. 2006. (Clifford Ser.). (ENG.). (J). (gr. -1-3). 18.95 (978-0-439-87593-6(5)) Scholastic, Inc.

—Clifford the Big Red Dog. 2010. (Clifford 8x8 Ser.). lib. bdg. 13.55 (978-0-88103-203-1(4), Turtleback) Turtleback Bks.

—Clifford the Firehouse Dog. Bridwell, Norman, illus. 2010. (Clifford 8x8 Ser.).Tr. of Clifford the Firehouse Dog. (ENG., Illus.). 32p. (J). (gr. -1-3). pap. 3.99 (978-0-545-21580-0(3), Cartwheel Bks.) Scholastic, Inc.

—Clifford the Small Red Puppy. 2007. (Clifford Ser.). (ENG.). (J). (gr. -1-3). 18.95 (978-0-439-02313-9(0)) Scholastic, Inc.

—Clifford y la Hora de Dormir. 2003. (Clifford Ser.).Tr. of Clifford's Bedtime. (SPA & ENG., Illus.). 7p. (J). (— 1). 4.99 (978-0-439-54568-6(4), Scholastic en Espanol) Scholastic, Inc.

—Clifford y la Hora del Bano. 2003. (Clifford Ser.).Tr. of Clifford's Bathtime. (SPA & ENG., Illus.). 16p. (J). (— 1). bds. 4.99 (978-0-439-54567-9(6), Scholastic en Espanol) Scholastic, Inc.

—Clifford y los Sondios de los Animales. 2003. (Clifford Ser.).Tr. of Clifford's Animal Sounds. (SPA & ENG.). 7p. (J). (— 1). bds. 4.99 (978-0-439-55109-0(9), Scholastic en Espanol) Scholastic, Inc.

—Clifford's Bedtime Story. Bridwell, Norman, illus. 2013. (Clifford Ser.). (ENG., Illus.). 20p. (J). (gr. -1-k). bds. 8.99 (978-0-545-49577-6(6)) Scholastic, Inc.

—Clifford's Birthday Party. Bridwell, Norman, illus. 50th anniv. ed. 2013. (Clifford Ser.). (ENG., Illus.). 32p. (J). (gr. -1-3). pap. 4.99 (978-0-545-47956-1(8)) Scholastic, Inc.

—Clifford's Class Trip. Bridwell, Norman, illus. 2011. (Scholastic Reader Level 1 Ser.). (ENG., Illus.). 32p. (J). (gr. -1-2). pap. 3.99 (978-0-545-22319-5(9), Cartwheel Bks.) Scholastic, Inc.

—Clifford's Day with Dad. Bridwell, Norman, illus. 2011. (Clifford 8x8 Ser.). (ENG., Illus.). 32p. (J). (gr. -1-k). pap. 3.99 (978-0-545-21593-0(5), Cartwheel Bks.) Scholastic, Inc.

—Clifford's Family. Bridwell, Norman, illus. 2010. (Clifford 8x8 Ser.). (ENG., Illus.). 32p. (J). (gr. -1-3). pap. 3.99 (978-0-545-21585-5(4), Cartwheel Bks.) Scholastic, Inc.

—Clifford's Field Day. 2012. (Scholastic Reader Level 1 Ser.). (ENG.). 32p. (J). (gr. -1-3). pap. 3.99 (978-0-545-22325-6(3), Cartwheel Bks.) Scholastic, Inc.

—Clifford's Field Day. 2012. (Clifford: Scholastic Readers Level 1 Ser.). lib. bdg. 13.55 (978-0-606-23907-3(3), Turtleback) Turtleback Bks.

—Clifford's First Christmas. (Clifford, the Big Red Dog Ser.). (FRE., Illus.). (J). (gr. k-2). pap. 5.99 (978-0-590-24374-2(8)) Scholastic, Inc.

—Clifford's First Christmas. Bridwell, Norman, illus. 2010. (Clifford Ser.). (ENG., Illus.). 20p. (J). (gr. k — 1). bds. 6.99 (978-0-545-21773-6(3), Cartwheel Bks.) Scholastic, Inc.

—Clifford's First Easter. Bridwell, Norman, illus. 2010. (Clifford Ser.). (ENG., Illus.). 14p. (J). (gr. k — 1). bds. 6.99 (978-0-545-20010-3(5), Cartwheel Bks.) Scholastic, Inc.

—Clifford's Good Deeds. Bridwell, Norman, illus. 2010. (Clifford 8x8 Ser.). (ENG., Illus.). 32p. (J). (gr. -1-3). pap. 3.99 (978-0-545-21579-4(X), Cartwheel Bks.) Scholastic, Inc.

—Clifford's Good Deeds. abr. ed. 2007. (Clifford Ser.). (ENG.). (J). (gr. -1-k). 18.95 (978-0-545-01779-4(3)); 9.95 (978-0-545-01483-0(2)) Scholastic, Inc.

—Clifford's Manners. 2011. (Clifford's Big Ideas Ser.). (ENG., Illus.). (gr. -1). 14.00 (978-1-60686-963-5(9)) Perfection Learning Corp.

—Clifford's Pals. unabr. ed. 2008. (Clifford, the Big Red Dog Ser.). (ENG.). (J). (gr. -1-3). 18.95 (978-0-545-05249-8(1)) Scholastic, Inc.

—Clifford's School Story Box. Bridwell, Norman, illus. 2015. (ENG., Illus.). (J). (gr. -1-k). 10.99 (978-0-545-83737-8(5)) Scholastic, Inc.

—Clifford's Sports Day. (Clifford, the Big Red Dog Ser.). (Illus.). 32p. (J). (gr. k-2). pap. 5.99 (978-0-590-16002-5(8)) Scholastic, Inc.

—Clifford's Tricks. (Clifford, the Big Red Dog Ser.). (FRE., Illus.). (J). (gr. k-2). pap. 5.99 (978-0-590-73954-2(9)) Scholastic, Inc.

—Halloween. Bridwell, Norman, illus. 2017. (Clifford Ser.). (ENG., Illus.). 48p. (J). (gr. -1-k). 8.99 **(978-1-338-18831-8(3))** Scholastic, Inc.

Bridwell, Norman. The Small Red Puppy. 2017. (Clifford Ser.). (ENG.). 48p. (J). (gr. -1-k). 8.99 (978-1-338-12424-8(2)) Scholastic, Inc.

Bridwell, Norman & Scholastic, Inc. Staff. Clifford the Big Red Dog. Bridwell, Norman, illus. unabr. ed. 2006. (Clifford Ser.). (ENG., Illus.). (J). (gr. -1-3). 9.99 (978-0-439-87587-5(0)) Scholastic, Inc.

Brie, Erin. Poor Max! 2012. 36p. pap. 15.00 (978-1-105-49285-3(0)) Lulu Pr., Inc.

Briggs, Raymond. The Snowman & the Snowdog. 2015. (Step into Reading Ser.). (ENG., Illus.). 32p. (J). (gr. -1-1). 12.99 (978-0-385-38735-4(0), Random Hse. Bks. for Young Readers) Random Hse. Children's Bks.

Brighton, Wendy. Bosley Beats the Burglars. 2005. (Illus.). pap. 11.45 (978-1-4208-6436-6(X)) AuthorHouse.

Brisland, Toni. DemiChat & the Lost Mummy. de los reyes Cruz, Cheryl, illus. 2013. 142p. (J). pap. 14.95 (978-1-60131-173-3(7)) Big Tent Bks.

Brisson, Pat. Sometimes We Were Brave. Brassard, France, illus. 2010. (ENG.). 32p. (J). (gr. k-2). 16.95 (978-1-59078-586-7(X)) Boyds Mills Pr.

Britland, Jan. The Adventures of Rodger Dodger Dog. Swaim, Michael, illus. 2009. 40p. pap. 15.95 (978-1-936051-23-6(0)) Peppertree Pr., The.

—The Adventures of Rodger Dodger Dog: A Christmas Story. Swaim, Michael, illus. 2009. 52p. pap. 18.95 (978-1-936051-48-9(6)) Peppertree Pr., The.

Broach, Elise. Wet Dog! Catrow, David, illus. 2007. (ENG.). 32p. (J). (gr. k-3). pap. 5.99 (978-0-14-240855-1(7), Puffin Books) Penguin Young Readers Group.

Broad, Michael. Hypno Hounds!, No. 3. Broad, Michael, illus. 2011. (Agent Amelia Ser.: 3). (ENG., Illus.). 144p. (J). (gr. 2-5). pap. 5.95 (978-0-7613-8062-7(0), Darby Creek); lib. bdg. 22.60 (978-0-7613-8058-0(2)) Lerner Publishing Group.

—#3 Hypno Hounds! 2011. (Agent Amelia Ser.). pap. 33.92 (978-0-7613-8343-7(3), Darby Creek) Lerner Publishing Group.

Broadhurst, Sherree. Bella's Adventures: Bella in the City. Broadhurst, Colin, illus. 2010. 38p. pap. 14.50 *(978-1-60976-179-0(0),* Eloquent Bks.) Strategic Book Publishing & Rights Agency (SBPRA).

—Bella's Adventures: Bella Rescues Gumleaf the Joey. 2010. 46p. pap. 16.50 *(978-1-60911-068-0(4),* Eloquent Bks.) Strategic Book Publishing & Rights Agency (SBPRA).

Brock, Robert E. Little Dott Finds a Home. 2009. 36p. 17.95 *(978-0-615-26492-9(1))* Corgi Tales Publishing.

Brodsky, Kathy. Just Sniffing Around. Bennett, Cameron, illus. 2009. (ENG.). 40p. 19.99 *(978-0-578-03620-5(7))* Helpingwords.

Brody, Leslie. The Bouncing Worry Ball & Mighty Mitt. 2012. 68p. pap. 15.50 *(978-1-105-48841-2(1))* Lulu Pr., Inc.

Bronstein, S. N. Private Eye Cats Book Two: The Case of the Kidnapped Dog. 2013. 116p. (gr. 4-6). 23.99 *(978-1-4817-2421-0(5));* pap. 14.95 *(978-1-4817-2422-7(3))* AuthorHouse.

Brooke, Samantha. Apple-Picking Day! Durk, Jim, illus. 2007. (Clifford's Puppy Days Ser.). (J). *(978-0-545-02841-7(8))* Scholastic, Inc.

Brooks, Tyrice M. Only the Truth Will Tell. 2012. 64p. pap. 17.95 *(978-1-62709-155-8(6))* America Star Bks.

Brophy, Ann. Novus 3 & Me: Six Short Stories about Friendship. 2010. 44p. pap. 18.49 *(978-1-4490-7132-5(5))* AuthorHouse.

Broughton, Theresa. Three Amazing Farm Animals. 2008. 12p. pap. 24.95 *(978-1-60474-545-0(2))* America Star Bks.

Brown, Alison. Eddie & Dog. 1 vol. 2014. (ENG.). 32p. (gr. -1-2). 14.95 *(978-1-62370-114-7(7))* Capstone Young Readers of Coughlan Cos.

Brown, Benjamin Thomas. The Best Dog. 2010. 16p. 8.49 *(978-1-4520-1010-6(2))* AuthorHouse.

Brown, Gladys M. Home Away from Home. 2005. 36p. pap. 6.95 *(978-1-4116-3026-0(2))* Lulu Pr., Inc.

Brown, Marc. Arthur & the Dog Show. 14th rev. ed. 2006. (ENG., Illus.). 24p. (J). (gr. -1-1). pap. 3.99 *(978-0-316-05774-5(6))* Little, Brown Bks. for Young Readers.

—Arthur's New Puppy. (Arthur Adventure Ser.). (J). (gr. k-3). 7.98 incl. audio NewSound, LLC.

—Arthur's Pet Business. Brown, Marc, illus. rev. ed. 2007. (ENG., Illus.). 32p. (J). (gr. -1-3). pap. 10.99 *(978-0-316-11863-7(X))* Little, Brown Bks. for Young Readers.

Brown, Margaret Wise. Mister Dog. Williams, Garth, illus. 2003. (Little Golden Book Ser.). (ENG.). 24p. (J). (gr. -1-2). 3.99 *(978-0-307-10336-9(6),* Golden Bks.) Random Hse. Children's Bks.

Brown, Margaret Wise. The Noisy Book Board Book. Weisgard, Leonard, illus. 2017. 36p. (J). (gr. -1 — 1). bds. 7.99 ***(978-0-06-248465-9(6),*** HarperFestival) HarperCollins Pubs.

Brown, Maureen E. Tanker's Adventures in Monterey. Brown, Michael D., illus. 2007. 24p. (J). 13.95 *(978-0-615-16200-3(2))* TankerToys.

Brown, Peter. Chowder. 2012. (Chowder Book Ser.). (ENG., Illus.). 32p. (J). (gr. -1-3). pap. 7.99 *(978-0-316-20088-2(3))* Little, Brown Bks. for Young Readers.

—Chowder. 2012. (J). lib. bdg. 18.40 *(978-0-606-26146-3(X),* Turtleback) Turtleback Bks.

Brown, Rosie L. Zach & Rob's Journey: The Lost Eggs. 2007. 24p. per. 24.95 *(978-1-4241-8401-9(0))* America Star Bks.

Brown, Ruth. Greyfriars Bobby. Brown, Ruth, illus. 2013. (ENG., Illus.). 32p. (J). (gr. -1-k). pap. 12.99 *(978-1-84939-632-5(9))* Andersen Pr. GBR. Dist: Independent Pubs. Group.

Brown, Sheila M. A Dog Named Ben & His Two Best Friends. 2011. 16p. (gr. 1-2). 9.95 *(978-1-4567-2478-8(9))* AuthorHouse.

Brown, Tricia. Bobbie the Wonder Dog: A True Story. Porter, Cary, illus. 2016. (ENG.). 32p. (J). 16.99 *(978-1-943328-36-9(6),* West Winds Pr.) Graphic Arts Ctr. Publishing Co.

—Musher's Night Before Christmas, 1 vol. Dubac, Debra, illus. 2011. (Night Before Christmas Ser.). (ENG.). 32p. (J). (gr. k-3). 16.99 *(978-1-58980-843-0(6))* Pelican Publishing Co., Inc.

Browne, Christopher. Marlo. Browne, Christopher, illus. 2017. (Illus.). 40p. (J). (gr. -1-3). 17.99 *(978-0-06-244113-3(2))* HarperCollins Pubs.

Brueggemann, Mindy. Who Is Lilly? Brueggemann, Mindy, photos by. 2013. (Illus.). 44p. pap. 9.95 *(978-0-9855676-1-3(9))* Dankworth Publishing.

Bruel, Nick. Bad Kitty School Daze. 2014. (Bad Kitty Chapter Bks.). (J). lib. bdg. 17.20 *(978-0-606-34010-6(6),* Turtleback) Turtleback Bks.

—Bad Kitty vs. Uncle Murray. Bruel, Nick, illus. 2011. (Bad Kitty Ser.). (ENG., Illus.). 176p. (J). (gr. 2-5). pap. 6.99 *(978-0-312-67483-0(X),* 9780312674830) Square Fish.

—Bad Kitty vs. Uncle Murray. 2011. (Bad Kitty Chapter Bks.). (J). lib. bdg. 17.20 *(978-0-606-23753-6(4),* Turtleback) Turtleback Bks.

—Bad Kitty vs. Uncle Murray: The Uproar at the Front Door. Bruel, Nick, illus. 2010. (Bad Kitty Ser.). (ENG., Illus.). 160p. (J). (gr. 2-5). 14.99 *(978-1-59643-596-4(8),* 9781596435964) Roaring Brook Pr.

—Does Not Like Dogs. 2 vols. 2015. (Bad Kitty Ser.). (ENG., Illus.). 24p. (J). (gr. -1-k). 4.99 *(978-1-62672-231-6(5),* 9781626722316) Square Fish.

—Poor Puppy & Bad Kitty. Bruel, Nick, illus. 2012. (Bad Kitty Ser.). (ENG., Illus.). 40p. (J). (gr. -1-3). 17.99 *(978-1-59643-844-6(4),* 9781596438446) Roaring Brook Pr.

—Puppy's Big Day. Bruel, Nick, illus. 2015. (Bad Kitty Ser.). (ENG., Illus.). 160p. (J). (gr. 2-5). 13.99 *(978-1-59643-976-4(9),* 9781596439764) Roaring Brook Pr.

—Puppy's Big Day. 2016. (Bad Kitty Chapter Bks.). (J). lib. bdg. 17.20 *(978-0-606-38431-5(6))* Turtleback Bks.

Bruno, Debra. Petey's Tale: A Story of Survival Inspired by Actual Events. 2010. 28p. pap. 12.49 *(978-1-4490-6597-3(X))* AuthorHouse.

Bruno's Birthday: Individual Title Six-Packs. (Literatura 2000 Ser.). (gr. 1-2). 28.00 *(978-0-7635-0086-3(0))* Rigby Education.

Brunson Vlasis, Caroline. Mooney Finds a Bed. 2009. 24p. pap. 12.99 *(978-1-4490-4246-2(5))* AuthorHouse.

Bruss, Deborah. Big Box for Ben, 1 vol. Bogacki, Tomek, illus. 2011. (ENG.). 16p. (J). (gr. -1-k). bds. 6.95 *(978-1-59572-265-2(3))* Star Bright Bks., Inc.

Bruton, Seth. I'm So Cute, You Can't Be Mad. Hicks, Kaylee, illus. 2012. 24p. pap. 13.97 *(978-1-61204-897-0(8),* Strategic Bk. Publishing) Strategic Book Publishing & Rights Agency (SBPRA).

Bruton, W., illus. The Dogs' Grand Dinner Party. 2011. (American Antiquarian Society Ser.). (ENG.). 16p. (gr. 1). 24.95 *(978-1-4290-9738-3(8))* Applewood Bks.

Bryan, Marcia. Dandy Lion: The Adventure Begins. 2006. (Illus.). 40p. (J). (gr. -1-5). 18.95 *(978-1-57736-376-7(0))* Providence Hse Pubs.

Bryan, Sean. The Juggling Pug. Murphy, Tom, illus. (ENG.). 32p. (J). 2014. (-k). 12.95 *(978-1-62873-596-3(1))* 2011. (gr. -1-k). 12.95 *(978-1-61608-329-8(6),* 608329) Skyhorse Publishing Co., Inc. (Sky Pony Pr.).

Bubble Guppies, Bubble. Bubble Guppies: Let's Play, Bubble Puppy! A PeekABoo Book. 2015. (ENG.). 10p. (J). (gr. -1-k). bds. 10.99 *(978-0-7944-3470-0(3),* Reader's Digest Children's Bks.) Studio Fun International.

BubbleGirl, Season. A Doggy Diary. 2006. 93p. (J). per. *(978-0-9775120-0-3(2))* Carpe Diem Publishing.

Buchwald, Claire. Are You Ready for Me? Hansen, Amelia, illus. (Sit! Stay! Read! Ser.). (ENG.). 24p. (J). (gr. k-1). 2009. pap. 7.95 *(978-0-940719-08-8(8))* 2007. 15.95 *(978-0-940719-04-0(5))* Gryphon Pr., The.

—Max Talks to Me. Ritz, Karen, illus. 2007. (Sit! Stay! Read! Ser.). (ENG.). 24p. (J). (gr. k-2). 16.95 *(978-0-940719-03-3(7))* Gryphon Pr., The.

Buckingham, Will. Lucy & the Rocket Dog. Arnaldo, Monica, illus. 2017. (ENG.). 160p. (J). (gr. 3-7). 16.99 ***(978-0-399-55432-2(7));*** lib. bdg. 19.99 ***(978-0-399-55433-9(5))*** Random Hse. Children's Bks. (Knopf Bks. for Young Readers).

Bucklaschuk, Angela. Movember with My Doggy. Gillen, Rosemarie, illus. 2013. 32p. pap. 11.95 *(978-1-61286-188-3(1))* Avid Readers Publishing Group.

Buehner, Caralyn. Dex: The Heart of a Hero. Buehner, Mark, illus. 2007. (ENG.). 32p. (J). (gr. -1-3). pap. 6.99 *(978-0-06-443845-2(7))* HarperCollins Pubs.

—Superdog: The Heart of a Hero. Buehner, Mark, illus. 2004. 32p. (J). (gr. -1-3). lib. bdg. 17.89 *(978-0-06-623621-6(5))* HarperCollins Pubs.

Buffalo, Tom And Tracey. Loganæs Big Night Out. 2008. 24p. pap. 11.99 *(978-1-4389-1893-8(3))* AuthorHouse.

Buffy: Individual Title Six-Packs. (Literatura 2000 Ser.). (gr. -1-1). 28.00 *(978-0-7635-0002-3(X))* Rigby Education.

Buffy's Tricks: Individual Title Six-Packs. (Literatura 2000 Ser.). (gr. 1-2). 28.00 *(978-0-7635-0087-0(9))* Rigby Education.

Bug, Patty Cat & the Woong: An I've Got Feelings! Feel Better Book. 2010. 48p. pap. 18.49 *(978-1-4520-5270-0(0))* AuthorHouse.

Buggs, Michael A. Tabard. Buggs, Michael A., illus. (Illus.). 64p. (Orig.). (J). (gr. 2-6). pap. 15.00 *(978-0-9657723-0-3(6))* Mogul Comics.

Bunce, Margaret. Adventures with Nature: A Story about Olivia & Her Little Dog, Jake. 2011. 24p. pap. 12.95 *(978-1-4567-2497-9(5))* AuthorHouse.

Bunting, Eve. I Love You, Too! Sweet, Melissa, illus. 2015. (ENG.). 24p. (J). (— 1). bds. 7.99 *(978-0-545-81390-7(5),* Cartwheel Bks.) Scholastic, Inc.

—My Dog Jack Is Fat, 0 vols. Rex, Michael, illus. 2011. (ENG.). 32p. (J). (gr. -1-3). 16.99 *(978-0-7614-5809-8(3),* 9780761458098, Amazon Children's Publishing) Amazon Publishing.

—Reggie. Burkett, D. Brent, illus. 2006. (ENG.). 112p. (J). (gr. 1-4). 16.95 *(978-0-8126-2746-6(6))* Cricket Bks.

Burchett, Loni. Bear & Katie in A Riverboat Ride, 4 vols., Vol. 4. 2006. (Illus.). 104p. (J). per. 12.95 *(978-0-9742815-3-7(0))* Black Lab Publishing LLC.

Burchett, Loni R. Bear & Katie in a Day with Friends, Vol. 3. l.t. ed. 2005. (Illus.). 68p. (J). per. 11.95 *(978-0-9742815-2-0(2),* bk003) Black Lab Publishing LLC.

Burchette, Ruby J. The Dog Went to School, 1 vol. 2010. 48p. pap. 16.95 *(978-1-4489-4962-5(9))* America Star Bks.

Burgess, Karin Whiting. It's Always a Good Day for Crabbing. 2005. (J). 16.95 *(978-0-9718303-4-9(7))* Flat Hammock Pr.

Burgess, Melvin. Lady: My Life as a Bitch. 2003. (Illus.). 272p. (J). pap. 6.99 *(978-0-06-054033-3(8))* HarperCollins Pubs.

Burgess, Thornton W. Bowser the Hound. 2007. 128p. (gr. 4-7). per. 10.95 *(978-0-60312-295-5(8));* 23.95 *(978-1-60312-713-4(5))* Aegypan.

—Bowser the Hound. (J). 19.95 *(978-0-8488-0391-9(4))* Amereon Ltd.

—Bowser the Hound. 2010. (Dover Children's Thrift Classics Ser.). (ENG., Illus.). 96p. (J). (gr. 3-8). pap. 4.00 *(978-0-486-42847-5(8))* Dover Pubns., Inc.

—Bowser the Hound. 2004. reprint ed. pap. 24.95 *(978-1-4179-2323-6(7))* Kessinger Publishing, LLC.

Burleigh, Liz. Matilda the Bassett Hound. 2008. 20p. per. 10.95 *(978-1-4327-1562-5(3))* Outskirts Pr., Inc.

Burleigh, Robert. Good-Bye, Sheepie, 0 vols. Catalanotto, Peter, illus. 2010. (ENG.). 32p. (J). (gr. -1-k). 16.99 *(978-0-7614-5598-1(1),* 9780761455981, Amazon Children's Publishing) Amazon Publishing.

Burlingham, Abi. Best Friends. Everitt-Stewart, Andy, illus. 2009. (Stories to Grow with Ser.). 24p. (J). (gr. -1-2). 22.60 *(978-1-60754-475-3(X));* pap. 8.15 *(978-1-60754-476-0(8))* Windmill Bks.

Burnford, Sheila. Bel Ria: Dog of War. 2006. (New York Review Children's Collection). (ENG.). 256p. (J). (gr. 4-7). 17.95 *(978-1-59017-211-7(6),* NYR Children's Collection) New York Review of Bks., Inc., The.

—The Incredible Journey. unabr. ed. 2004. 145p. (J). (gr. 5-9). pap. 29.00 incl. audio *(978-0-8072-8322-6(3),* YA162SP, Listening Library) Random Hse. Audio Publishing Group.

Burns, Catherine Lloyd. The Good, the Bad & the Beagle. 2014. (ENG.). 336p. (J). (gr. 5-7). 16.99 *(978-0-374-30039-5(9),* 9780374300395, Farrar, Straus & Giroux (BYR)) Farrar, Straus & Giroux.

Burns, Joanne. Frog's Dog Days. 2005. 30p. 9.99 *(978-1-4116-4829-6(3))* Lulu Pr., Inc.

Burris, Andrea. Tater & Tot. 2008. (Tater & Tot Ser.). (ENG.). 32p. (J). (gr. -1-k). 15.95 *(978-0-9743294-2-0(8))* A & D Bks.

Burroughs, Scott, illus. The Disappearing Dog. 2011. (Hardy Boys: the Secret Files Ser.: 7). (ENG.). 96p. (J). (gr. 1-4). pap. 4.99 *(978-1-4424-2314-5(5),* Aladdin) Simon & Schuster Children's Publishing.

Burton, Bria & burton, brain. Lance & Ringo Tails: The Wild Adventures of a Dog & a Cat As Told by Their Human. 2013. 134p. pap. 9.99 *(978-1-939181-45-9(3))* Soul Attitude Press.

Burton, Julie. The Miracle of the Missing Puppies. 2012. 40p. pap. 20.99 *(978-1-4772-3679-6(1))* AuthorHouse.

Bushell, Abby. Pc Rob Has a Very Important Job: Talking about Strangers. 2010. (Illus.). 20p. pap. 10.49 *(978-1-4490-6628-4(3))* AuthorHouse.

Butcher, Derek. Max the ed up Dog: Max & Matts Adventures. 2009. 56p. pap. 10.49 *(978-1-4389-6551-2(6))* AuthorHouse.

Butler, Debra Rae. BenjiB. 2008. 24p. pap. 24.95 *(978-1-60441-484-4(7))* America Star Bks.

Butler, Dori Hillestad. The Buddy Files Bk. 3: The Case of the Missing Family. Tugeau, Jeremy, illus. 2010. (Buddy Files Ser.: 3). (ENG.). 128p. (J). (gr. 1-5). 14.99 *(978-0-8075-0912-8(4))* Whitman, Albert & Co.

—The Buddy Files Bk. 4: The Case of the Fire Alarm. Tugeau, Jeremy, illus. 2011. (Buddy Files Ser.: 4). (ENG.). 144p. (J). (gr. 1-5). pap. 5.99 *(978-0-8075-0935-7(3))* Whitman, Albert & Co.

—The Case of the Library Monster. Tugeau, Jeremy, illus. 2012. (Buddy Files Ser.: 5). (J). lib. bdg. 16.00 *(978-0-606-23839-7(5),* Turtleback) Turtleback Bks.

—The Case of the Library Monster. Tugeau, Jeremy & Crisp, Dan, illus. 2012. (Buddy Files Ser.: 5). (ENG.). 128p. (J). (gr. 1-5). pap. 5.99 *(978-0-8075-0936-4(1))* Whitman, Albert & Co.

—The Case of the Lost Boy. Tugeau, Jeremy, illus. 2010. (Buddy Files Ser.: 1). (ENG.). 128p. (J). (gr. 1-5). 14.99 *(978-0-8075-0910-4(8));*Bk. 1. pap. 5.99 *(978-0-8075-0932-6(9))* Whitman, Albert & Co.

—The Case of the Missing Family, 1 vol., Bk. 3. Tugeau, Jeremy, illus. 2010. (Buddy Files Ser.: 3). (ENG.). 144p. (J). (gr. 1-5). pap. 5.99 *(978-0-8075-0934-0(5))* Whitman, Albert & Co.

—The Case of the Mixed-Up Mutts, Bk. 2. Tugeau, Jeremy, illus. 2010. (Buddy Files Ser.: 2). (ENG.). 128p. (J). (gr. 1-5). 14.99 *(978-0-8075-0911-1(6))* Whitman, Albert & Co.

—The Case of the Mixed-Up Mutts Bk. 2, 1 vol., Bk. 2. Tugeau, Jeremy, illus. 2010. (Buddy Files Ser.: 2). (ENG.). 128p. (J). (gr. 1-5). pap. 5.99 *(978-0-8075-0933-3(7))* Whitman, Albert & Co.

—The Case of the School Ghost. 2013. (Buddy Files Ser.: 6). lib. bdg. 16.00 *(978-0-606-31843-3(7),* Turtleback) Turtleback Bks.

—The Case of the School Ghost. Tugeau, Jeremy, illus. (Buddy Files Ser.: 6). (ENG.). (J). (gr. 1-5). 2012. 128p. 14.99 *(978-0-8075-0915-9(9))*Bk. 6. 2013. 144p. pap. 5.99 *(978-0-8075-0937-1(X))* Whitman, Albert & Co.

—King & Kayla & the Case of the Missing Dog Treats, 1 vol. Meyers, Nancy, illus. 2017. (King & Kayla Ser.). (ENG.). 48p. (J). (gr. 2-4). 14.95 *(978-1-56145-877-6(5))* Peachtree Pubs.

—King & Kayla & the Case of the Mysterious Mouse, 1 vol. Meyers, Nancy, illus. 2017. (King & Kayla Ser.). (ENG.). 48p. (J). (gr. 2-4). 14.95 ***(978-1-56145-879-0(1))*** Peachtree Pubs.

Butler, Dori Hillestad. King & Kayla & the Case of the Secret Code, 1 vol. Meyers, Nancy, illus. 2017. (King & Kayla Ser.). (ENG.). 48p. (J). (gr. 2-4). 14.95 *(978-1-56145-878-3(3))* Peachtree Pubs.

Butler, Dori Hillestad & dePaola, Tomie. The Ghost at the Fire Station, No. 6. Damant, Aurore, illus. 2015. (Haunted Library: 6). (ENG.). 128p. (J). (gr. 1-3). bds. 5.99 *(978-0-448-48334-4(3),* Grosset & Dunlap) Penguin Young Readers Group.

Butler, Kristi T. Rip's Secret Spot. Cepeda, Joe, illus. 2003. (Green Light Readers Level 1 Ser.). (ENG.). 24p. (J). (gr. -1-3). pap. 3.95 *(978-0-15-204849-5(9))* Houghton Mifflin Harcourt Publishing Co.

—Rip's Secret Spot. 2003. (Green Light Readers — Level 1 Ser.). (gr. k-3). 13.50 *(978-0-613-66374-8(8),* Turtleback) Turtleback Bks.

Butler, Nathalie. Ruby Red Sees Blue. 2017. (Learning with Stories Ser.). 24p. (gr. 4-6). pap. 8.25 ***(978-1-5081-6229-2(8),*** PowerKids Pr.) Rosen Publishing Group, Inc., The.

Butterfield, Moira. Muddypaws. Mendez, Simon, illus. (Picture Books Ser.). (J). 2010. (gr. -1-k). bds. *(978-1-4075-8757-8(9))* 2008. 32p. *(978-1-4075-1840-4(2))* Parragon, Inc.

Butterworth, Nick & Butterworth, Annette. Jake Again. (Illus.). 60p. (J). pap. 7.99 *(978-0-340-68728-4(2))* Hodder & Stoughton GBR. Dist: Trafalgar Square Publishing.

Byars, Betsy. Tornado. Ben-Ami, Doron, illus. 2004. (Trophy Chapter Bks.). (ENG.). 64p. (J). (gr. 1-5). pap. 4.99 *(978-0-06-442063-1(9))* HarperCollins Pubs.

—Tornado. 2004. (J). (gr. 3-6). lib. bdg. 14.75 *(978-0-613-01485-4(5),* Turtleback) Turtleback Bks.

—Wanted... Mud Blossom. Haley, Amanda, illus. 5th ed. 2008. (Blossom Family Book Ser.: Bk. 5). (ENG.). 192p. (J). (gr. 4-7). pap. 8.95 *(978-0-8234-2148-0(1))* Holiday Hse., Inc.

Byrd, Michael. The Adventures of Banter & Jafar: Spoiled Rotten, 1 vol. Bai, Jenny, illus. 2009. 36p. pap. 24.95 *(978-1-60836-131-1(4))* America Star Bks.

Byrne, Jennifer. Adopting Ahava. 2013. 44p. (J). pap. 9.99 *(978-0-9851067-3-7(5))* Dodi Pr.

Byrne, Mary. Only Children Hear Me: Jake Is a Friend You Can Talk To. 2007. 96p. (J). per. 10.95 *(978-0-595-44359-8(1))* iUniverse, Inc.

Byrne, Richard. This Book Is Out of Control! 2016. (ENG., Illus.). 32p. (J). 16.99 *(978-1-62779-933-1(8),* 9781627799331, Holt, Henry & Co. Bks. For Young Readers) Holt, Henry & Co.

—This Book Just Ate My Dog! Byrne, Richard, illus. 2014. (ENG., Illus.). 32p. (J). (gr. -1). 16.99 *(978-1-62779-071-0(3),* 9781627790710, Holt, Henry & Co. Bks. For Young Readers) Holt, Henry & Co.

C D Stampley Enterprises, creator. Billy & Baxter Learn to Build, 4 vols. 2005. (Illus.). 24p. (J). (gr. -1 — 1). 8.95 *(978-1-58087-099-3(6))* Stampley, C. D. Enterprises, Inc.

—Billy & Baxter on City Streets, 4 vols. 2005. (Illus.). 24p. (J). (gr. -1 — 1). 8.95 *(978-1-58087-101-3(1))* Stampley, C. D. Enterprises, Inc.

Cabla, Rhonda. Charlie's World. 2013. 16p. pap. 7.95 *(978-1-4624-0717-0(X),* Inspiring Voices) Author Solutions, Inc.

Cabral, Jeane. Bad Dog Ben. 2009. (Jeane Cabral Bks.). (Illus.). (J). bds. 12.99 *(978-1-934650-05-9(6))* Just For Kids Pr., LLC.

Caine, Paul. Jake's Journey. 2010. 68p. pap. 10.49 *(978-1-4520-0508-9(7))* AuthorHouse.

Cakes, Patty. God: When Will You Answer My Prayers. 2007. 56p. per. 17.95 *(978-1-59800-272-0(4))* Outskirts Pr., Inc.

Caldas, Iara. The Fisherman Collection: The Fishery. 2013. (ENG.). 35p. (J). pap. 13.95 *(978-1-4327-9406-4(X))* Outskirts Pr., Inc.

Caldwell, Bruce. Sidecar Scooter. Hawyard, Charlie O., illus. 2008. 32p. (J). pap. 9.95 *(978-0-9792612-9-9(5))* Blue Gate Bks.

Caletti, Deb. The Story of Us. (ENG.). 400p. (YA). (gr. 7). 2013. pap. 9.99 *(978-1-4424-2347-3(1))* 2012. 16.99 *(978-1-4424-2346-6(3))* Simon Pulse. (Simon Pulse).

The Call of the Wild Guide. 16.47 *(978-0-13-425968-0(8))* Prentice Hall PTR.

Callen, Sharon. Boris Keeps Fit, 1 vol. rev. ed. 2013. (Fiction Readers Ser.). (ENG., Illus.). 20p. (J). (gr. 1-1). pap. 15.96 *(978-1-4807-1148-8(9));* pap. 4.99 *(978-1-4333-5492-2(6))* Shell Educational Publishing.

—Boris the Bassett, 1 vol. rev. ed. 2013. (Fiction Readers Ser.). (ENG., Illus.). 12p. (J). (gr. 1-1). pap. 12.96 *(978-1-4807-1133-4(0));* pap. 4.99 *(978-1-4333-5454-0(3))* Shell Educational Publishing.

—Ms. Wilde & Oscar, 1 vol. rev. ed. 2013. (Fiction Readers Ser.). (ENG., Illus.). 32p. (J). (gr. 3-3). pap. 8.99 *(978-1-4333-5611-7(2))* Shell Educational Publishing.

—Ms. Wilde & Oscar. rev. ed. 2013. (Fiction Readers Ser.). (ENG., Illus.). 32p. (gr. 3-3). pap. 19.96 *(978-1-4807-1733-6(9))* Teacher Created Materials, Inc.

Calmenson, Stephanie. May I Pet Your Dog? The How-to Guide for Kids Meeting Dogs (and Dogs Meeting Kids) Ormerod, Jan, illus. 2007. (ENG.). 32p. (J). (gr. -1-3). 13.99 *(978-0-618-51034-4(6),* Clarion Bks.) Houghton Mifflin Harcourt Trade & Reference Pubs.

Calmenson, Stephanie & Cole, Joanna. Hot Diggity Dogs. Ross, Heather, illus. 2015. (Ready, Set, Dogs! Ser.: 2). (ENG.). 112p. (J). (gr. 1-4). 14.99 *(978-0-8050-9649-1(3),* 9780805096491, Holt, Henry & Co. Bks. For Young Readers) Holt, Henry & Co.

—No Dogs Allowed. Ross, Heather, illus. 2014. (Ready, Set, Dogs! Ser.: 1). (ENG.). 144p. (J). (gr. 1-4). pap. 5.99 *(978-1-250-04414-3(6),* 9781250044143) Square Fish.

—Teacher's Pets. Ross, Heather, illus. 2015. (Ready, Set, Dogs! Ser.: 2). (ENG.). 144p. (J). (gr. 1-4). pap. 5.99 *(978-1-250-05705-1(1),* 9781250057051) Square Fish.

Caloyeras, Jennifer. Strays: A Novel. 2015. (ENG.). 219p. (J). pap. 17.95 *(978-1-61822-037-0(3),* Ashland Creek Pr.) Byte Level Research.

Calucag, Angela. Little Freddy S Journey. 2012. 32p. pap. 17.99 *(978-1-62419-840-3(6))* Salem Author Services.

Calvani, Mayra. Chocalin! Pylypchuck, Anna, illus. 2009. 24p. pap. 10.95 *(978-1-935137-69-6(7))* Guardian Angel Publishing, Inc.

Calvani, Mayra & Pylypchuk, Anna. Crash! 2008. 24p. pap. 10.95 *(978-1-933090-54-2(5))* Guardian Angel Publishing, Inc.

Calvert, Patricia. Bigger. Minor, Wendell, illus. 2003. (ENG.). 144p. (J). (gr. 3-7). pap. 8.95 *(978-0-689-86003-4(X),* Simon & Schuster/Paula Wiseman Bks.) Simon & Schuster/Paula Wiseman Bks.

Cameron, Ann. Spunky Tells All. Castillo, Lauren, illus. 2011. (ENG.). 112p. (J). (gr. 3-6). 16.99 *(978-0-374-38000-7(7),* 9780374380007, Farrar, Straus & Giroux (BYR)) Farrar, Straus & Giroux.

Cameron, Jill. Miffy, the Crooked-Eyed Cat. 2009. 28p. pap. 12.99 *(978-1-60860-353-4(9),* Eloquent Bks.) Strategic Book Publishing & Rights Agency (SBPRA).

Cameron, W. Bruce. Bailey's Story: A Dog's Purpose Novel. 2016. (ENG., Illus.). 208p. (J). (gr. 3-7). 16.99 *(978-0-7653-8840-7(5),* 9780765388407, Starscape) Doherty, Tom Assocs., LLC.

—Ellie's Story: A Dog's Purpose Novel. 2015. (Dog's Purpose Ser.). (ENG., Illus.). 208p. (J). (gr. 3-7). 16.99 *(978-0-7653-7469-1(2),* 9780765374691, Starscape) Doherty, Tom Assocs., LLC.

Cameron, W. Bruce. Molly's Story: A Dog's Purpose Novel. 2017. (Dog's Purpose Ser.: bk.1). (ENG.). 208p. (J). 16.99 ***(978-0-7653-9493-4(6),*** 9780765394934, Starscape) Doherty, Tom Assocs., LLC.

Campbell, Howard. A Dog Named Pavlov: Un Perro Llamado Pavlov. McCloskey, Kevin, illus. 2010. 4p. (J). pap. *(978-0-9790350-4-3(X))* Star Fire.

Campbell, Lori. The Adventures of Tinkerbelle & Peanut. 2012. 36p. pap. 21.99 *(978-1-4771-4835-8(3))* Xlibris Corp.

Campbell, Mari. Maggiemoosetracks: Making Friends. Katsumoto, Sayaka, tr. Jennings, Randy, illus. 2013. 108p. pap. 21.99 *(978-0-9895205-6-0(0))* MaggieMooseTracks.

—Maggiemoosetracks: Making Friends. Jennings, Randy, illus. 2013. 84p. pap. 21.00 *(978-0-9895205-0-8(1))* MaggieMooseTracks.

—Maggiemoosetracks: Wolf Pack. Jennings, Randy, illus. 2013. 106p. pap. 21.00 *(978-0-9895205-5-3(2))* MaggieMooseTracks.

Campbell, Mari & Jennings, Randy. Maggiemoosetracks: Christmas Star. 2013. 106p. pap. 21.00 *(978-0-9895205-4-6(4))* MaggieMooseTracks.

Campbell, Todd M. Puppy Dog's New Friend. 2012. 24p. 24.95 *(978-1-4626-6127-5(0))* America Star Bks.

Campion, Lynn & Brown, Stoney. Tucker Tees Off. Waddell, Theodore, illus. 2015. (YA). 16.95 *(978-0-692-53082-5(7))* Riverbend Publishing.

Candlewick Press Staff. FETCH! with Ruff Ruffman: Doggie Duties. WGBH Educational Foundation Staff, illus. 2014. (Fetch! with Ruff Ruffman Ser.). (ENG.). 48p. (J). (gr. 1-4). pap. 4.99 *(978-0-7636-6815-0(X),* Candlewick Entertainment) Candlewick Pr.

Cannon, Janell. Dog for Sale. 2010. (Illus.). 48p. (J). (gr. k-3). 16.00 *(978-0-15-205424-3(3),* Houghton Mifflin Bks. for Children) Houghton Mifflin Harcourt Trade & Reference Pubs.

C
D

Cantrell, Caley. You're Bringing Me a Baby?! 2013. (Illus.). 40p. (J). 15.95 *(978-0-9859358-7-0(1)*, Belle Isle Bks.) Brandylane Pubs., Inc.

Cantu, Sarah. The Dogs that Follow their Detective Dreams. Adventure No. 1: Find a New Home. 2008. 48p. pap. 20.95 *(978-0-615-18600-9(9))* Cantu, Ricardo.

Capehart, Staci. Furry Tails: The Adventures of Mr. Mackie. 2009. 40p. pap. 16.99 *(978-1-4343-6974-1(9))* AuthorHouse.

Capozzi, Suzy & Finnegan, Delphine. Lady & the Tramp. Random House Disney Staff, illus. 2012. (Step into Reading Ser.). (ENG.). 32p. (J). (gr. -1-1). pap. 3.99 *(978-0-7364-3026-5(1)*, RH/Disney) Random Hse. Children's Bks.

Capucilli, Alyssa Satin. Biscuit. Schories, Pat, illus. (My First I Can Read Ser.). 32p. (J). (gr. -1-3). 2017. 9.99 *(978-0-06-257276-9(8))* 10th anniv. ed. 2006. (ENG.). 16.99 *(978-0-06-026197-9(8))* HarperCollins Pubs.

—Biscuit. Schories, Pat, illus. 2006. (Biscuit: My First I Can Read! Ser.). 26p. (J). (gr. -1-k). lib. bdg. 13.55 *(978-0-613-37688-4(9)*, Turtleback) Turtleback Bks.

—Biscuit: 5-Minute Biscuit Stories. Schories, Pat, illus. 2017. 192p. (J). (gr. -1-3). 12.99 *(978-0-06-256725-3(X))* HarperCollins Pubs.

—Biscuit & the Baby. Schories, Pat, illus. 2005. (My First I Can Read Ser.). (ENG.). 32p. (J). (gr. -1 — 1). 16.99 *(978-0-06-009459-1(1))* HarperCollins Pubs.

—Biscuit & the Little Pup. Schories, Pat, illus. 2007. (My First I Can Read Ser.). (ENG.). 32p. (J). (gr. -1 — 1). 16.99 *(978-0-06-074170-9(8))* HarperCollins Pubs.

—Biscuit & the Little Pup. Schories, Pat, illus. 2007. (Biscuit: My First I Can Read! Ser.). 29p. (J). (gr. -1-3). lib. bdg. 13.55 *(978-1-4178-1002-4(5)*, Turtleback) Turtleback Bks.

—Biscuit & the Lost Teddy Bear. Schories, Pat, illus. 2011. (My First I Can Read Ser.). (ENG.). 32p. (J). (gr. -1 — 1). 16.99 *(978-0-06-117751-4(2))*; pap. 3.99 *(978-0-06-117753-8(9))* HarperCollins Pubs.

—Biscuit Feeds the Pets. Schories, Pat, illus. 2016. (My First I Can Read Ser.). 32p. (J). (gr. -1-3). pap. 3.99 *(978-0-06-223696-8(2))* HarperCollins Pubs.

—Biscuit Flies a Kite. Schories, Pat, illus. 2017. (My First I Can Read Ser.). 32p. (J). (gr. -1-3). pap. 3.99 *(978-0-06-223700-2(4))* HarperCollins Pubs.

—Biscuit Gives a Gift. Schories, Pat, illus. 2004. (ENG.). 16p. (J). (gr. -1-3). bds. 4.99 *(978-0-06-009467-6(2)*, HarperFestival) HarperCollins Pubs.

—Biscuit Goes Camping. Schories, Pat, illus. 2015. (My First I Can Read Ser.). (ENG.). 32p. (J). (gr. -1-3). pap. 3.99 *(978-0-06-223693-7(8))* HarperCollins Pubs.

—Biscuit Goes to School. Schories, Pat, illus. 2003. (My First I Can Read Ser.). (ENG.). 32p. (J). (gr. -1-3). pap. 3.99 *(978-0-06-443616-8(0))* HarperCollins Pubs.

—Biscuit Goes to School. Schories, Pat, illus. 2003. (Biscuit: My First I Can Read! Ser.). 21p. (J). (gr. -1-3). lib. bdg. 13.55 *(978-0-613-66941-2(X)*, Turtleback) Turtleback Bks.

—Biscuit in the Garden. Schories, Pat, illus. 2013. (My First I Can Read Ser.). (ENG.). 32p. (J). (gr. -1-3). 16.99 *(978-0-06-193505-3(0))*; pap. 3.99 *(978-0-06-193504-6(2))* HarperCollins Pubs.

—Biscuit in the Garden. 2013. (Biscuit: My First I Can Read! Ser.). (J). lib. bdg. 13.55 *(978-0-606-27157-8(0)*, Turtleback) Turtleback Bks.

—Biscuit Is Thankful. Schories, Pat, illus. 2003. (Biscuit Ser.). (ENG.). 16p. (J). (gr. -1-1). bds. 4.99 *(978-0-694-01519-1(9)*, HarperFestival) HarperCollins Pubs.

—Biscuit Loves Father's Day. Schories, Pat & Young, Mary O'Keefe, illus. 2004. (ENG.). 20p. (J). (gr. -1-1). pap. 6.99 *(978-0-06-009463-8(X)*, HarperFestival) HarperCollins Pubs.

—Biscuit Loves Mother's Day. Schories, Pat & Young, Mary O'Keefe, illus. 2004. (ENG.). 20p. (J). (gr. -1-1). pap. 6.99 *(978-0-06-009462-1(1)*, HarperFestival) HarperCollins Pubs.

—Biscuit Loves the Library. Schories, Pat, illus. 2014. (My First I Can Read Ser.). (ENG.). 32p. (J). (gr. -1-3). 16.99 *(978-0-06-193507-7(7))*; pap. 3.99 *(978-0-06-193506-0(9))* HarperCollins Pubs.

—Biscuit Loves the Library. 2014. (Biscuit: My First I Can Read! Ser.). (J). lib. bdg. 13.55 *(978-0-606-35068-6(3)*, Turtleback) Turtleback Bks.

—Biscuit Meets the Class Pet. Schories, Pat, illus. 2009. (My First I Can Read Ser.). (ENG.). 32p. (J). (gr. -1-3). 16.99 *(978-0-06-117747-7(4))*; pap. 3.99 *(978-0-06-117749-1(0))* HarperCollins Pubs.

—Biscuit Meets the Class Pet. 2009. (Biscuit: My First I Can Read! Ser.). (J). lib. bdg. 13.55 *(978-0-606-06960-1(7)*, Turtleback) Turtleback Bks.

—Biscuit Phonics Fun. Schories, Pat, illus. 2008. (My First I Can Read Ser.). (ENG.). 100p. (J). (gr. -1 — 1). pap. 12.99 *(978-0-06-143204-0(0))* HarperCollins Pubs.

—Biscuit Plays Ball. Schories, Pat, illus. 2012. (My First I Can Read Ser.). (ENG.). 32p. (J). (gr. -1-2). 16.99 *(978-0-06-193503-9(4))*; pap. 3.99 *(978-0-06-193502-2(6))* HarperCollins Pubs.

—Biscuit Plays Ball. 2012. (Biscuit: My First I Can Read! Ser.). (J). lib. bdg. 13.55 *(978-0-606-23583-9(3)*, Turtleback) Turtleback Bks.

—Biscuit Storybook Collection. Schories, Pat, illus. 2004. (Biscuit Ser.). (ENG.). 192p. (J). (gr. -1-3). 11.99 *(978-0-06-075904-9(6)*, HarperFestival) HarperCollins Pubs.

—Biscuit Take-Along Storybook Set: Biscuit's Birthday; Meet Biscuit!; Biscuit's Show & Share Day; Mind Your Manners, Biscuit!; Biscuit Visits the Doctor. Schories, Pat, illus. 2017. (Biscuit Ser.). 120p. (J). (gr. -1-3). pap. 11.99 *(978-0-06-162516-9(7)*, HarperFestival) HarperCollins Pubs.

—Biscuit Takes a Walk. Schories, Pat, illus. 2009. (My First I Can Read Ser.). (ENG.). 32p. (J). (gr. -1 — 1). 16.99 *(978-0-06-117745-3(8))*; pap. 3.99 *(978-0-06-117746-0(6))* HarperCollins Pubs.

—Biscuit Visits the Big City. Schories, Pat, illus. (My First I Can Read Ser.). (ENG.). 32p. (J). (gr. -1 — 1). 2007. pap. 3.99 *(978-0-06-074166-2(X))* 2006. 16.99 *(978-0-06-074164-8(3))* HarperCollins Pubs.

—Biscuit Visits the Big City. Schories, Pat, illus. 2007. (Biscuit Ser.). 28p. (gr. -1-k). lib. bdg. 14.00 *(978-0-7569-8109-9(3))* Perfection Learning Corp.

—Biscuit Visits the Big City. 2007. (Biscuit: My First I Can Read! Ser.). (J). lib. bdg. 13.55 *(978-1-4178-1004-8(1)*, Turtleback) Turtleback Bks.

—Biscuit Wins a Prize. Schories, Pat, illus. (My First I Can Read Ser.). 32p. (J). (gr. -1-3). 2005. (ENG.). pap. 3.99 *(978-0-06-009458-4(3))* 2003. (ENG.). 16.99 *(978-0-06-009455-3(9))* 2003. lib. bdg. 17.89 *(978-0-06-009457-7(5))* HarperCollins Pubs.

—Biscuit's 123. Schories, Pat & Berlin, Rose Mary, illus. 2012. (Biscuit Ser.). (ENG.). 16p. (J). (gr. -1-1). pap. 6.99 *(978-0-06-162523-7(X)*, HarperFestival) HarperCollins Pubs.

—Biscuit's ABCs. Schories, Pat, illus. 2011. (Biscuit Ser.). (ENG.). 16p. (J). (gr. -1 — 1). pap. 6.99 *(978-0-06-162518-3(3)*, HarperFestival) HarperCollins Pubs.

—Biscuit's Big Friend. Schories, Pat, illus. 2003. (My First I Can Read Ser.). 32p. (J). (gr. -1 — 1). (ENG.). pap. 3.99 *(978-0-06-444288-6(8))*; (ENG.). 16.99 *(978-0-06-029167-9(2))*; lib. bdg. 17.89 *(978-0-06-029168-6(0))* HarperCollins Pubs.

—Biscuit's Christmas Eve. Schories, Pat, illus. 2007. (Biscuit Ser.). (ENG.). 20p. (J). (gr. -1-1). pap. 6.99 *(978-0-06-112836-3(8)*, HarperFestival) HarperCollins Pubs.

—Biscuit's Christmas Storybook Collection. Schories, Pat, illus. 2013. (ENG.). 192p. (J). (gr. -1-3). 11.99 *(978-0-06-228842-4(3)*, HarperFestival) HarperCollins Pubs.

—Biscuit's Day at the Farm. Schories, Pat, illus. 2007. (My First I Can Read Ser.). (ENG.). 32p. (J). (gr. -1 — 1). 16.99 *(978-0-06-074167-9(8))* HarperCollins Pubs.

—Biscuit's Day at the Farm. 2007. (Biscuit: My First I Can Read! Ser.). (J). lib. bdg. 13.55 *(978-1-4177-9810-0(6)*, Turtleback) Turtleback Bks.

—Biscuit's Earth Day Celebration. Wenzel, David T. & Schories, Pat, illus. 2010. (Biscuit Ser.). (ENG.). 24p. (J). (gr. -1-1). pap. 3.99 *(978-0-06-162514-5(0)*, HarperFestival) HarperCollins Pubs.

—Biscuit's First Beach Day. Schories, Pat, illus. 2010. (Biscuit Ser.). (ENG.). 24p. (J). (gr. -1-3). pap. 3.99 *(978-0-06-162515-2(9)*, HarperFestival) HarperCollins Pubs.

—Biscuit's First Trip. Berlin, Rose Mary & Schories, Pat, illus. 2010. (Biscuit Ser.). (ENG.). 24p. (J). (gr. -1-1). pap. 3.99 *(978-0-06-162524-4(8)*, HarperFestival) HarperCollins Pubs.

—Biscuit's First Trip. 2010. (Biscuit 8x8 Ser.). (J). lib. bdg. 13.55 *(978-0-606-10115-8(2)*, Turtleback) Turtleback Bks.

—Biscuit's Pet & Play Halloween. Andreasen, Dan & Schories, Pat, illus. 2007. (Biscuit Ser.). (ENG.). 12p. (J). (gr. -1-1). bds. 7.99 *(978-0-06-112833-2(3)*, HarperFestival) HarperCollins Pubs.

—Biscuit's Show & Share Day. Schories, Pat & Young, Mary O'Keefe, illus. 2007. (Biscuit Ser.). (ENG.). 24p. (J). (gr. -1-1). pap. 3.99 *(978-0-06-112832-5(5)*, HarperFestival) HarperCollins Pubs.

—Bizcocho Encuentra un Amigo, 1 vol. Pasternac, Susana, tr. Schories, Pat, illus. 2008. (My First I Can Read Ser.).Tr. of Biscuit Finds a Friend. (SPA.). 32p. (J). (gr. -1 — 1). pap. 4.99 *(978-0-06-143526-3(0))* HarperCollins Pubs.

—Katy Duck Makes a Friend. Cole, Henry, illus. 2012. (Katy Duck Ser.). (ENG.). 24p. (J). (gr. -1-1). 16.99 *(978-1-4424-1977-3(6))*; pap. 3.99 *(978-1-4424-1976-6(8))* Simon Spotlight. (Simon Spotlight).

—Meet Biscuit! Schories, Pat, illus. 2005. (Biscuit Ser.). (ENG.). 24p. (J). (gr. -1-1). pap. 3.99 *(978-0-06-057846-6(7)*, HarperFestival) HarperCollins Pubs.

—Mind Your Manners, Biscuit! Schories, Pat & Young, Mary O'Keefe, illus. 2007. (Biscuit Ser.). (ENG.). 24p. (J). (gr. -1-1). pap. 3.99 *(978-0-06-112835-6(X)*, HarperFestival) HarperCollins Pubs.

—Ralph & the Rocket Ship. Cole, Henry, illus. 2016. (Ready-To-Reads Ser.). (ENG.). 24p. (J). (gr. -1-1). pap. 3.99 *(978-1-4814-5866-5(3)*, Simon Spotlight) Simon Spotlight.

—Reading Is Fun with Biscuit: Biscuit; Biscuit Wants to Play; Biscuit Finds a Friend. Schories, Pat, illus. 2003. (My First I Can Read Ser.). (J). (gr. -1 — 1). pap. 11.99 *(978-0-06-058933-2(7))* HarperCollins Pubs.

—Tulip & Rex Write a Story. Massini, Sarah, illus. 2015. (ENG.). 32p. (J). (gr. -1-3). 17.99 *(978-0-06-209416-2(5))* HarperCollins Pubs.

—Tulip Loves Rex. Massini, Sarah, illus. 2013. (ENG.). 32p. (J). (gr. -1-3). 17.99 *(978-0-06-209413-1(0)*, Tegen, Katherine Bks) HarperCollins Pubs.

—Where Is Love, Biscuit? A Pet & Play Book. Berlin, Rose Mary & Schories, Pat, illus. 2009. (Biscuit Ser.). (ENG.). 12p. (J). (gr. -1 — 1). bds. 7.99 *(978-0-06-162521-3(3)*, HarperFestival) HarperCollins Pubs.

Carbone, Elisa & Lewis, E. B. Night Running. 2012. (ENG., Illus.). 40p. (J). (gr. k-3). pap. 7.99 *(978-0-553-11284-9(8)*, Dragonfly Bks.) Random Hse. Children's Bks.

Cardona, Nancy. Beethoven. Swope, Brenda, illus. 2011. 28p. pap. 24.95 *(978-1-4560-0961-8(3))* America Star Bks.

Carey, Cassandra L. The Adventures of Uncle Joe: Uncle Joe & His Bear. 2012. 30p. 24.95 *(978-1-4626-5563-2(7))* America Star Bks.

Carey-Costa, Denise. A Tale of Three Tails. Sjostrom, Nicole & Iseminger, Jonathon, illus. 2009. 81p. 10.99 *(978-1-4251-8492-6(8))* Trafford Publishing.

Carkhuff Jr., Sam. The Ranch Race. Crow, Katie, illus. 2012. 36p. 16.99 *(978-1-939054-03-6(6))*; pap. 11.99 *(978-1-939054-02-9(8))* Rowe Publishing and Design.

Carl And Betty Coggins. Mr Bowbow. 2009. 24p. pap. 12.99 *(978-1-4490-1010-2(5))* AuthorHouse.

Carlile-Grattopp, Kari & Grattopp, Matthew. When I Turned Five. 2009. 12p. pap. 24.95 *(978-1-60836-753-5(3))* America Star Bks.

Carlson, Nancy. Harriet & George's Christmas Treat. Carlson, Nancy, illus. 2005. (Picture Bks.). (Illus.). 32p. (J). (gr. k-2). 15.95 *(978-1-57505-506-0(6))* Lerner Publishing Group.

—Harriet & George's Christmas Treat. 2003. (ENG., Illus.). 32p. (J). (gr. k-2). pap. 9.95 *(978-1-57505-639-5(9))* Lerner Publishing Group.

—Harriet & the Roller Coaster. 20th anniv. ed. (Nancy Carlson's Neighborhood Ser.). (Illus.). 32p. (gr. k-2). 2005. 15.95 *(978-1-57505-053-9(6))* 2003. (ENG., (J). 6.95 *(978-1-57505-202-1(4))* Lerner Publishing Group.

—Harriet & Walt. rev. ed. 2004. (Carolrhoda Picture Books Ser.). (ENG., Illus.). 32p. (J). (gr. k-2). 15.95 *(978-1-57505-672-2(0))*; pap. 6.95 *(978-1-57505-723-1(9))* Lerner Publishing Group.

—Harriet's Halloween Candy. (Harriet Bks.). (Illus.). 32p. (gr. k-2). anniv. rev. ed. 2003. (ENG.). (J). per. 6.95 *(978-0-87614-926-3(3)*, Carolrhoda Bks.) 20th anniv. ed. 2005. 15.95 *(978-0-87614-913-3(1))* Lerner Publishing Group.

—Harriet's Recital. 2006. (Illus.). (J). 15.95 *(978-1-57505-898-6(7)*, Carolrhoda Bks.); (ENG., 32p. per. 9.95 *(978-1-57505-929-7(0)*, First Avenue Editions) Lerner Publishing Group.

—Poor Carl. Carlson, Nancy, illus. 2012. (Nancy Carlson Picture Bks). (Illus.). 32p. (J). (gr. k-2). 56.72 *(978-0-7613-9305-4(6))*; (ENG., 9.95 *(978-0-7613-8950-7(4))* Lerner Publishing Group. (Carolrhoda Bks.).

Carman, Debby. Cha Cha, the Dancing Dog. Carman, Debby, illus. 2007. (Illus.). 28p. (J). (gr. -1-1). 14.99 *(978-0-9777340-5-4(6))* Faux Paw Media Group.

—Chewdalootie, Doing My Duty. Carman, Debby, illus. 2007. (Illus.). 28p. (J). (gr. -1-1). 14.99 *(978-0-9777340-3-0(X))* Faux Paw Media Group.

Carmen & Thane Johnson. Dogs Don't Wear Underwear. Bianca & Annie West, illus. 2009. 20p. pap. 12.99 *(978-1-4389-4128-8(5))* AuthorHouse.

Carnesi, Mônica. Little Dog Lost: The True Story of a Brave Dog Named Baltic. Carnesi, Mônica, illus. 2012. (ENG., Illus.). 32p. (J). (gr. -1-k). 16.99 *(978-0-399-25666-0(0)*, Nancy Paulsen Books) Penguin Young Readers Group.

Carney, John & Carney, Veta. Teddy's Journey. 2009. 37p. pap. 15.98 *(978-0-557-15269-8(0))* Lulu Pr., Inc.

Carol, Darlene. A Puppy Called Runt: The Adventure Begins. 2008. 224p. pap. 12.95 *(978-1-935105-00-8(0))* Avid Readers Publishing Group.

Carol Muller-Funk. Proxmire & the Exodus of Prairieville. 2009. 400p. pap. 17.99 *(978-1-4389-4013-7(0))* AuthorHouse.

Caron, Eleonore. Gizmo & Ellen Mysteries: The Case of the Missing Boy. 2012. 24p. pap. 24.95 *(978-1-4626-6747-5(3))* America Star Bks.

Carr, Bernie. Jake & Miller's Big Adventure: A Prepper's Book for Kids. Wells, Aja & Mulford, Aja, illus. 2014. (ENG.). 32p. (J). (gr. -1). 15.95 *(978-1-61243-271-7(9))* Ulysses Pr.

Carr, Elias. Ava y el Picnic Raquitico. Garton, Michael, illus. 2016. (SPA.). (J). ***(978-1-5064-2095-0(8))*** Augsburg Fortress, Pubs.

—Rufus y Su Cola Enojada. Garton, Michael, illus. 2016. (SPA.). (J). ***(978-1-5064-2096-7(6))*** Augsburg Fortress, Pubs.

Carroll, Ruth & Carroll, Latrobe. Beanie & Tough Enough. 2015. (ENG., Illus.). 192p. (J). (gr. 3-6). pap. 14.99 *(978-0-486-80223-7(X))* Dover Pubns., Inc.

Carson Sr., Johnny. Little Dog. 2013. 28p. pap. 24.95 *(978-1-63000-014-1(0))* America Star Bks.

Carter, Keisha. Maloni's Shoes. 2013. 28p. pap. 9.95 *(978-1-4327-9958-8(4))* Outskirts Pr., Inc.

Carter, Pete. Our Dog Benji. Henderson, James, illus. 2017. (ENG.). 32p. (J). (gr. -1-3). 17.99 *(978-1-925335-33-0(X)*, EK Bks.) Exisle Publishing Pty Ltd. AUS. Dist: Hachette Bk. Group.

Cartwright, Ran. The Adventures of Billy Space Boy, 1 vol. 2010. 208p. pap. 24.95 *(978-1-4489-3901-5(1))* America Star Bks.

Cartwright, Stephen. Little Book of Train Stories. rev. ed. 2011. (Farmyard Tales Readers Ser.). 64p. (J). ring bd. 8.99 *(978-0-7945-3070-9(2)*, Usborne) EDC Publishing.

Cartwright, Stephen, illus. Find the Puppy. 2007. (Find-its Board Bks). 12p. (J). (gr. -1-k). bds. 6.99 *(978-0-7945-1802-8(8)*, Usborne) EDC Publishing.

Carville, Declan. A Day to Remember at the Giant's Causeway. Ellis, Brendan, illus. 29p. (J). (gr. 2-5). pap. 7.95 *(978-0-9538222-0-1(6))* Discovery Pubns. GBR. Dist: Irish Bks. & Media, Inc.

Casanova, Mary. Danger at Snow Hill. Rayyan, Omar, illus. 2006. (Dog Watch Ser.: 3). (ENG.). 128p. (J). (gr. 3-7). pap. 4.99 *(978-0-689-86812-2(X)*, Simon & Schuster/Paula Wiseman Bks.) Simon & Schuster/Paula Wiseman Bks.

—Dog-Napped! Rayyan, Omar, illus. 2006. (Dog Watch Ser.: 2). (ENG.). 144p. (J). (gr. 3-7). pap. 8.99 *(978-0-689-86811-5(1)*, Simon & Schuster/Paula Wiseman Bks.) Simon & Schuster/Paula Wiseman Bks.

—Extreme Stunt Dogs. Rayyan, Omar, illus. 2007. (Dog Watch Ser.: 5). (ENG.). 144p. (J). (gr. 3-7). pap. 4.99 *(978-1-4169-4782-0(5)*, Simon & Schuster/Paula Wiseman Bks.) Simon & Schuster/Paula Wiseman Bks.

—Some Cat! Hoyt, Ard, illus. 2012. (ENG.). 40p. (J). (gr. -1-k). 17.99 *(978-0-374-37123-4(7)*, 9780374371234, Farrar, Straus & Giroux (BYR)) Farrar, Straus & Giroux.

—Some Dog! Hoyt, Ard, illus. 2007. (ENG.). 40p. (J). (gr. -1-1). 17.99 *(978-0-374-37133-3(4)*, 9780374371333, Farrar, Straus & Giroux (BYR)) Farrar, Straus & Giroux.

—To Catch a Burglar. Rayyan, Omar, illus. 2007. (Dog Watch Ser.: 4). (ENG.). 144p. (J). (gr. 3-7). pap. 4.99 *(978-0-689-86813-9(8)*, Simon & Schuster/Paula Wiseman Bks.) Simon & Schuster/Paula Wiseman Bks.

—Trouble in Pembrook. Rayyan, Omar, illus. 2006. (Dog Watch Ser.: 1). (ENG.). 128p. (J). (gr. 3-7). pap. 5.99 *(978-0-689-86810-8(3)*, Simon & Schuster/Paula Wiseman Bks.) Simon & Schuster/Paula Wiseman Bks.

—The Turtle-Hatching Mystery. Rayyan, Omar, illus. 2008. (Dog Watch Ser.: 6). (ENG.). 144p. (J). (gr. 3-7). pap. 8.99 *(978-1-4169-4783-7(3)*, Simon & Schuster/Paula Wiseman Bks.) Simon & Schuster/Paula Wiseman Bks.

Case, Layne. Charlie. 2007. (Illus.). (J). pap. 12.00 *(978-0-9789546-9-7(6))* Back Channel Pr.

Case, Linda. Brigits Day of Fun. 2006. 28p. pap. 9.95 *(978-1-4327-0001-0(4))* Outskirts Pr., Inc.

Cason, Anjanette. Praise Puppy's Adventure in Praise. 2007. (J). *(978-0-9755234-7-6(3))* DOMINIONHOUSE Publishing & Design.

Casper, Gina R. Corky Beagle. 2011. 32p. pap. *(978-1-77067-348-9(2))* FriesenPress.

Cassidy, Anne. Wizard Woof, 1 vol. Remphry, Martin, illus. 2013. (Start Reading Ser.). (ENG.). 24p. (gr. k-1). pap. 7.95 *(978-1-4765-4147-1(7))* Capstone Press of Coughlan Cos.

Casteel, Seth. Puppy Pool Party! An Underwater Dogs Adventure. 2016. (ENG., Illus.). 40p. (J). (gr. -1-3). 16.99 *(978-0-316-37633-4(7))* Little Brown & Co.

Castelli, Jeanette. Los Gatos en la Luna/the Cats on the Moon. Santana, Andrea, illus. 2005. (Bilingual Collection). (SPA.). 51p. (J). (gr. k-2). *(978-958-30-1767-4(1))* Panamericana Editorial.

Castillo, Ina. Red the Super Wiener. 2008. 24p. pap. 24.95 *(978-1-60474-897-0(4))* America Star Bks.

Catalanotto, Peter. Daisy 1, 2, 3. Catalanotto, Peter, illus. 2003. (ENG., Illus.). 32p. (J). (gr. -1-1). 17.99 *(978-0-689-85457-6(9)*, Atheneum/Richard Jackson Bks.) Simon & Schuster Children's Publishing.

—Dylan's Day Out. Catalanotto, Peter, illus. 2006. (Illus.). pap. 7.99 *(978-0-9777720-0-1(4))* Southpaw Books LLC.

—Ivan the Terrier. Catalanotto, Peter, illus. 2007. (ENG., Illus.). 32p. (J). (gr. -1-3). 17.99 *(978-1-4169-1247-7(9)*, Atheneum/Richard Jackson Bks.) Simon & Schuster Children's Publishing.

Catrow, David. Best in Show. 2013. (Scholastic Reader Level 1 Ser.). lib. bdg. 13.55 *(978-0-606-31509-8(8)*, Turtleback) Turtleback Bks.

—Dinosaur Hunt. 2009. (J). *(978-0-545-11686-2(4)*, Orchard Bks.) Scholastic, Inc.

—Fun in the Sun. Catrow, David, illus. 2016. (ENG., Illus.). 32p. (J). 6.99 *(978-0-8234-3569-2(5))* Holiday Hse., Inc.

Cazet, Denys. Grandpa Spanielson's Chicken Pox Stories No. 1: The Octopus. Cazet, Denys, illus. 2005. (I Can Read Bks.). (Illus.). 48p. (J). (gr. -1-3). lib. bdg. 16.89 *(978-0-06-051089-3(7))* HarperCollins Pubs.

—The Octopus. Cazet, Denys, illus. 2008. (Grandpa Spanielson's Chicken Pox Stories Ser.). (Illus.). (J). (gr. -1-3). pap. 16.95 incl. audio *(978-1-4301-0455-1(4))*;Set. pap. 31.95 incl. audio compact disk *(978-1-4301-0460-5(0))*;Set. pap. 29.95 incl. audio *(978-1-4301-0457-5(0))* Live Oak Media.

—The Shrunken Head. 2007. (I Can Read Bks.: No. 3). (Illus.). 48p. (J). (gr. -1-3). lib. bdg. 16.89 *(978-0-06-073014-7(5))* HarperCollins Pubs.

—A Snout for Chocolate. 2006. (I Can Read Bks.). (Illus.). (J). (gr. -1-3). (ENG.). 48p. 15.99 *(978-0-06-051093-0(5))*; 47p. lib. bdg. 16.89 *(978-0-06-051094-7(3))* HarperCollins Pubs.

—A Snout for Chocolate. Cazet, Denys, illus. 2008. (Grandpa Spanielson's Chicken Pox Stories Ser.). (Illus.). (J). (gr. -1-3). pap. 16.95 incl. audio *(978-1-4301-0463-6(5))*;Set. pap. 31.95 incl. audio compact disk *(978-1-4301-0468-1(6))*;Set. pap. 29.95 incl. audio *(978-1-4301-0465-0(1))* Live Oak Media.

—A Snout for Chocolate. 2007. (I Can Read Bks.). (Illus.). 48p. (gr. -1-3). 15.00 *(978-0-7569-8056-6(9))* Perfection Learning Corp.

Cecil, Carrie Gerlach & cecil, charli. Charli & Wilbur a Dancing Dog's Dream. 2012. 24p. pap. 7.99 *(978-0-615-62081-7(7))* Anachel Communications.

Cento, Nucci. Maverick & Miss Murphy at Rascal's Rescue Ranch. 2009. 48p. pap. 12.50 *(978-1-60860-388-6(1)*, Eloquent Bks.) Strategic Book Publishing & Rights Agency (SBPRA).

Ceville, Laura. My Dog, Jack. 2013. 24p. pap. 8.99 *(978-1-938768-25-5(6))* Gypsy Pubns.

Chall, Marsha Wilson. One Pup's Up. Cole, Henry, illus. 2010. (ENG.). 32p. (J). (gr. -1 — 1). 16.99 *(978-1-4169-7960-9(3)*, McElderry, Margaret K. Bks.) McElderry, Margaret K. Bks.

—Pick a Pup. Henry, Jed, illus. 2011. (ENG.). 32p. (J). (gr. -1-k). 16.99 *(978-1-4169-7961-6(1)*, McElderry, Margaret K. Bks.) McElderry, Margaret K. Bks.

Chamberlin, Kathleen H. Marcy Mary: The Memoirs of a Dachshund American Princess. 2009. 200p. pap. 14.95 *(978-1-60844-092-4(3))* Dog Ear Publishing, LLC.

Chambers, Cindy. Beamer Learns the Signs of a Stroke & How to Help. 2013. 28p. pap. 14.95 *(978-1-4575-1725-9(6))* Dog Ear Publishing, LLC.

—Beamer Visits the Children's Rehabilitation Center: The Beamer Book Series. 2012. 32p. pap. 14.95 *(978-1-4575-1596-5(2))* Dog Ear Publishing, LLC.

Chambers, Cindy & Demme, Tina. Beamer Visits the Emergency Room. Huber, Jim, illus. 2012. 32p. pap. 14.95 *(978-1-4575-1289-6(0))* Dog Ear Publishing, LLC.

Chambers, Darci. My Name Is Dawson: The Fun Begins. 2010. 24p. 12.99 *(978-1-4490-5280-5(0))* AuthorHouse.

Chambers, Melinda. The Day the Snapdragons Snapped Back. Spiker, Sue Ann, illus. 2007. 32p. (J). 16.95 *(978-0-929915-72-2(0))* Headline Bks., Inc.

Chandler, Jean. The Adventures of Molly: Molly Visits the Farm. 2012. 28p. pap. 13.55 *(978-1-4669-1380-6(0))* Trafford Publishing.

—The Adventures of Molly: No Dogs Allowed. 2012. 48p. pap. 18.40 *(978-1-4669-1378-3(9))* Trafford Publishing.

Chandler, Jeff. The Fire Dog Champ. 2008. 28p. pap. 24.95 *(978-1-4241-8615-0(3))* America Star Bks.

Chao, Eileen. Go Away, Sam! 2004. (J). pap. 8.00 *(978-0-8059-6505-6(X))* Dorrance Publishing Co., Inc.

Chapman, Carlene. Jackson Goes to the Beach. 2010. 24p. pap. 11.95 *(978-1-4490-9768-4(5))* AuthorHouse.

Chapman, Nancy Kapp & Chapman, Nancy. Tripper's Travels: An International Scrapbook, 1 vol. Chapman, Lee, illus. 2005. (ENG.). 32p. (J). (gr. 1-5). 16.95 *(978-0-7614-5240-9(0))* Marshall Cavendish Corp.

Charles, Norma M. Fuzzy Wuzzy. 2005. (ENG., Illus.). 1p. (J). pap. 5.95 *(978-0-9730831-2-5(3))* Hodgepog Bks. CAN. Dist: Fitzhenry & Whiteside, Ltd.

Charles, Valerie. The Dancing Light. 2013. 118p. pap. *(978-1-84944-167-4(7))* UKUnpublished.

Charlesworth, Liza. Dog & Frog: An Animal Friends Reader. Smith, Ian, illus. 2015. 16p. (J). ***(978-0-545-85962-2(X))*** Scholastic, Inc.

Chase, Diana. Daisy Street. Bradley, Vanessa, illus. 2005. 128p. (Orig.). (J). pap. 13.50 *(978-1-920731-11-3(3))* Fremantle Pr. AUS. Dist: Independent Pubs. Group.

Chatterton, Martin. Can Dogs Fly? Fido's Book of Pop-up Transportation Surprises. 2005. (Illus.). 12p. (J). (gr. k-4). reprint ed. 10.00 *(978-0-7567-8838-4(2))* DIANE Publishing Co.

Chavez, Orlando. A Dog for Tommy. 2004. 112p. pap. 11.45 *(978-1-4140-2796-8(6))* AuthorHouse.

Cheng, Jack. See You in the Cosmos. 2017. (ENG.). 320p. (J). (gr. 5-9). 16.99 *(978-0-399-18637-0(9)*, Dial Bks) Penguin Young Readers Group.

Cherna. Patch's Country Quilt. Cherna, illus. 2013. (Illus.). 54p. 25.95 *(978-1-60571-188-1(8))*; 50p. pap. 17.95 *(978-1-60571-187-4(X))* Northshire Pr.

Chetkowski, Emily. Mabel Takes the Ferry, 1 vol. Peterson, Dawn, illus. 2nd ed. 2012. (ENG.). 32p. (J). pap. 12.95 *(978-1-934031-99-5(2)*,

0da48001-1b7b-4d70-849d-d13163dabbc6) Islandport Pr., Inc.
Chichester Clark, Emma. Love Is My Favorite Thing. Chichester Clark, Emma, illus. 2015. (ENG., Illus.). 32p. (J). (gr. -1-k). 16.99 *(978-0-399-17503-9(2),* Nancy Paulsen Books) Penguin Young Readers Group.
—Piper. Chichester Clark, Emma, illus. 2007. (Illus.). 32p. (J). (gr. k-3). 17.00 *(978-0-8028-5314-1(5),* Eerdmans Bks For Young Readers) Eerdmans, William B. Publishing Co.
—Plenty of Love to Go Around. Chichester Clark, Emma, illus. 2016. (ENG., Illus.). 32p. (J). (-k). 17.99 *(978-0-399-54666-2(9),* Nancy Paulsen Books) Penguin Young Readers Group.
Child, Jeremy. Puppy. Davies, Caroline, illus. 2013. (Rock & Rattle Bks.). (ENG.). 8p. (J). (gr. -1 — 1). bds. 3.99 *(978-0-7641-6592-4(5))* Barron's Educational Series, Inc.
Chin, Oliver. The Year of the Dog: Tales from the Chinese Zodiac. Alcorn, Miah, illus. 2006. (Tales from the Chinese Zodiac Ser.). (ENG.). 36p. (J). (gr. k-7). 15.95 *(978-1-59702-002-2(8))* Immedium.
Chisman, James Ph. D. Bullette & Jessic. 2011. 74p. 24.99 *(978-1-4628-8880-1(1));* pap. 15.99 *(978-1-4628-8881-8(X))* Xlibris Corp.
Choffel, Theodora L. A Coat for Ebony. 2007. (ENG.). 32p. pap. 16.00 *(978-1-4196-7719-9(5))* CreateSpace Independent Publishing Platform.
Choldenko, Gennifer. Notes from a Liar & Her Dog. 2003. (ENG.). 240p. (J). (gr. 3-7). pap. 7.99 *(978-0-14-250068-2(2),* Puffin Books) Penguin Young Readers Group.
—Notes from a Liar & Her Dog. 2004. 224p. (J). (gr. 4-7). pap. 38.00 incl. audio *(978-0-8072-2097-9(3),* Listening Library) Random Hse. Audio Publishing Group.
Chorao, Kay. Bad Boy, Good Boy. 2013. (ENG., Illus.). 32p. (J). (gr. k-2). 17.95 *(978-1-4197-0520-5(2),* Abrams Bks. for Young Readers) Abrams, Inc.
Christelow, Eileen. The Desperate Dog Writes Again. 2010. (ENG., Illus.). 40p. (J). (gr. -1-3). 16.99 *(978-0-547-24205-7(0))* Houghton Mifflin Harcourt Publishing Co.
—Letters from a Desperate Dog. 2006. (ENG., Illus.). 32p. (J). (gr. 1-4). 16.99 *(978-0-618-51003-0(6))* Houghton Mifflin Harcourt Publishing Co.
Christian, Cheryl. Where's the Puppy? (Haitian Creole/English), 1 vol. Dwight, Laura, photos by. 2005. (Photoflaps Ser.). (HAT & ENG., Illus.). 12p. (J). (gr. -1). 5.95 *(978-1-59572-029-0(4))* Star Bright Bks., Inc.
—Where's the Puppy? (Korean), 1 vol. Choi, Jin, tr. Dwight, Laura, photos by. 2004. (KOR & ENG., Illus.). 12p. (J). 5.95 *(978-1-932065-79-4(2))* Star Bright Bks., Inc.
—Where's the Puppy? (Russian/English), 1 vol. Dwight, Laura, photos by. 2005. (Photo Flap Bks.). (RUS & ENG., Illus.). 12p. (J). 5.95 *(978-1-932065-85-5(7))* Star Bright Bks., Inc.
—Where's the Puppy? (Simplified Mandarin), 1 vol. Dwight, Laura, photos by. 2004. (CHI & ENG., Illus.). 12p. (J). 5.95 *(978-1-932065-67-1(9))* Star Bright Bks., Inc.
—Where's the Puppy? (Traditional Cantonese) Dwight, Laura, photos by. 2004. (CHI., Illus.). 12p. (J). bds. 5.95 *(978-1-932065-61-9(X))* Star Bright Bks., Inc.
—Where's the Puppy? (Vietnamese) Dwight, Laura, photos by. 2004. (VIE., Illus.). 12p. (J). bds. 5.50 *(978-1-932065-73-2(3))* Star Bright Bks., Inc.
Christianson, Leslie Rose. Malinda Matters: Malinda's Birthday Surprise. 2010. 44p. pap. 16.99 *(978-1-4490-6915-5(0))* AuthorHouse.
Christopher, Matt. The Dog That Called the Pitch. Vasconcellos, Dan, illus. 2010. (Matt Christopher Sports Readers Ser.). 48p. (J). (gr. 1-3). lib. bdg. 23.93 *(978-1-59953-353-7(7))* Norwood Hse. Pr.
—The Dog That Called the Signals. Ogden, Bill, illus. 2010. (Matt Christopher Sports Readers Ser.). 48p. (J). (gr. 1-3). lib. bdg. 23.93 *(978-1-59953-349-0(9))* Norwood Hse. Pr.
—The Dog That Pitched a No-Hitter. 2013. (Passport to Reading Level 3 Ser.). (ENG., Illus.). 48p. (J). (gr. 1-4). 4.99 *(978-0-316-21848-1(0))* Little, Brown Bks. for Young Readers.
—The Dog That Pitched a No-Hitter. Vasconcellos, Dan, illus. 2010. (Matt Christopher Sports Readers Ser.). 48p. (J). (gr. 1-3). lib. bdg. 23.93 *(978-1-59953-351-3(0))* Norwood Hse. Pr.
—The Dog That Stole Football Plays. Vasconcellos, Daniel et al, illus. 2013. (Passport to Reading Level 3 Ser.). (ENG.). 32p. (J). (gr. 1-4). pap. 4.99 *(978-0-316-21849-8(9))* Little, Brown Bks. for Young Readers.
—The Dog That Stole the Football Plays. Ogden, Bill, illus. 2010. (Matt Christopher Sports Readers Ser.). 48p. (J). (gr. 1-3). lib. bdg. 23.93 *(978-1-59953-350-6(2))* Norwood Hse. Pr.
—You Lucky Dog. Vasconcellos, Daniel, illus. 8th ed. 2003. (ENG.). 64p. (J). (gr. 1-4). pap. 13.99 *(978-0-316-73805-7(0))* Little, Brown Bks. for Young Readers.
—You Lucky Dog. Vasconcellos, Daniel, illus. 2003. (Soccer Cats Ser.: Bk. 8). 49p. (J). (gr. 2-4). 12.65 *(978-0-7569-3907-6(0))* Perfection Learning Corp.
Chrystyn, Julie. Hachiko: The Story of a Loyal Akita & the Royal Dogs of Japan. 2009. 48p. pap. 7.95 *(978-1-59777-629-5(7))* Phoenix Bks., Inc.
Chung, Arree. Out. Chung, Arree, illus. 2017. (ENG., Illus.). 40p. (J). 17.99 *(978-1-62779-553-1(7),* 9781627795531, Holt, Henry & Co. Bks. For Young Readers) Holt, Henry & Co.
Church, Caroline Jayne. I Love My Puppy. Church, Caroline Jayne, illus. 2015. (Love Meez Ser.). (ENG., Illus.). 10p. (J). (gr. -1 — 1). bds. 7.99 *(978-0-545-83594-7(1),* Cartwheel Bks.) Scholastic, Inc.
—Ruff! And the Wonderfully Amazing Busy Day. Church, Caroline Jayne, illus. 2013. (ENG., Illus.). 32p. (J). (gr. k-3). 17.99 *(978-0-06-201498-6(6))* HarperCollins Pubs.
Ciardi, John. The Wish-Tree. Glanzman, Louis S., illus. 2015. (ENG.). 96p. (J). pap. 9.99 *(978-0-486-79618-5(3))* Dover Pubns., Inc.
Ciminera, Siobhan & Faulkner, Keith. A Yummy Mystery: A Scratch-and-Sniff Story. 2007. (Puppy Scooby-Doo Ser.). 16p. (J). pap. 5.99 *(978-0-448-44406-2(2),* Grosset & Dunlap) Penguin Publishing Group.
Cis, Daniel Z. Gino & His Trullo: An Abandoned Dog Who Walked into Paradise. 2012. 48p. (-18). pap. 18.95 *(978-1-62212-231-8(3),* Strategic Bk. Publishing) Strategic Book Publishing & Rights Agency (SBPRA).
Citra, Becky. Dog Days, 1 vol. 2003. (Orca Young Readers Ser.). (ENG., Illus.). 96p. (J). (gr. 3-6). pap. 4.99 *(978-1-55143-256-4(0))* Orca Bk. Pubs. USA.
Civardi, Anna. New Puppy Sticker Book. 2009. (First Experiences Sticker Book Ser.). 16p. (J). pap. 6.99 *(978-0-7945-2573-6(3),* Usborne) EDC Publishing.
Clamp, Janet. The Adventures of Lilly the Bloodhound & Her Friends: Lilly Gets a New Home & Family. 2013. 20p. pap. 17.99 *(978-1-4817-0057-3(X))* AuthorHouse.
Clampitt, Edward L. Team Dawg It's All about Respect. 2nd ed. 2012. (ENG., Illus.). 32p. (J). lib. bdg. 12.99 *(978-0-9749378-6-1(X))* Team Dawg Productions, Inc.
Clanchy, Kate. Our Cat Henry Comes to the Swings. Bird, Jemima, illus. 2007. 32p. (J). (gr. -1-1). 16.00 *(978-1-56148-563-5(2),* Good Bks.) Skyhorse Publishing Co., Inc.
Clancy, Charmaine. My Zombie Dog. 2012. 132p. pap. *(978-0-9872863-1-4(5))* Hot Doggy Digital Pr.
Clark Mancuso, Jackie. Hudson in Provence: A Paris-Chien Adventure. Clark Mancuso, Jackie, illus. l.t. ed. 2015. (Paris-Chien Adventure Ser.). (ENG., Illus.). 32p. (J). (gr. k-2). 17.95 *(978-0-9886058-4-8(8))* La Librairie Parisienne.
Clark, Rosalind. Bruce's Diary: It's a Geriatric Dog's Life. 2004. (Illus.). 160p. pap. *(978-1-84401-327-2(8))* Athena Pr.
Clark, Sherryl. Kim's Pet Scoop. McKenzie, Heath, illus. 2015. (J). pap. *(978-1-4966-0238-1(2))* Capstone Classroom.
Clarke, Angelique. Boomer Explores Annapolis, 1 vol. Hunt, Jim, illus. 2012. (ENG.). 32p. (J). 12.99 *(978-0-7643-4008-6(5),* 9780764340086) Schiffer Publishing, Ltd.
Clarke, Jane. Posy the Puppy. 2016. (Dr. KittyCat Ser.: 1). (ENG.). 96p. (J). (gr. 2-5). pap. 4.99 *(978-0-545-87333-8(9),* Scholastic Paperbacks) Scholastic, Inc.
Class, Albert. The infallible Dog. 2005. 44p. per. 21.99 *(978-1-4208-8994-9(X))* AuthorHouse.
Class 1-208. Pizza Place Ghost, 1 vol. 2013. (Scooby-Doo! Picture Clue Bks.). (ENG.). 24p. (J). (gr. -1-1). lib. bdg. 24.21 *(978-1-61479-038-9(8),* Essential Library) ABDO Publishing Co.
Claude on the Slopes, 1 vol. 2014. (Claude Ser.). (ENG., Illus.). 96p. (J). (gr. 1-3). 12.95 *(978-1-56145-805-9(8))* Peachtree Pubs.
Clayton, Emily. If my Parents Only Knew... 2011. (Illus.). 28p. (gr. -1). pap. 14.09 *(978-1-4567-7405-9(0))* AuthorHouse.
Cleary, Beverly. Henry & Ribsy. Darling, Louis et al, illus. 2014. (Henry Huggins Ser.: 3). (ENG.). 192p. (J). (gr. 3-7). 16.99 *(978-0-688-21382-4(0))* HarperCollins Pubs.
—The Henry & Ribsy Box Set: Henry Huggins, Henry & Ribsy, Ribsy. 2015. (Henry Huggins Ser.). (ENG.). 624p. (J). (gr. 3-7). pap. 18.99 *(978-0-06-236063-2(9))* HarperCollins Pubs.
—Henry Huggins. Darling, Louis et al, illus. 2014. (Henry Huggins Ser.: 1). (ENG.). 208p. (J). (gr. 3-7). 16.99 *(978-0-688-21385-5(5))* HarperCollins Pubs.
—Henry Huggins, 1 vol. Darling, Louis, illus. 2004. (Henry Huggins Ser.: 1). (SPA.). 160p. (J). (gr. 3-7). pap. 7.99 *(978-0-06-073600-2(3))* HarperCollins Pubs.
—Henry Huggins. Darling, Louis et al, illus. 50th anniv. ed. 2016. (Henry Huggins Ser.: 1). (ENG.). 208p. (J). (gr. 3-7). pap. 6.99 *(978-0-380-70912-0(0))* HarperCollins Pubs.
—Ribsy. Darling, Louis et al, illus. 2014. (Henry Huggins Ser.: 6). (ENG.). 240p. (J). (gr. 3-7). 16.99 *(978-0-688-21662-7(5));* pap. 7.99 *(978-0-380-70955-7(4))* HarperCollins Pubs.
Clegg, Maryanne & Bester, Maryanne. Why Dog Is Afraid of Storms. Bester, Shayle, illus. 2012. (ENG.). 32p. (J). (gr. -1-k). pap. 12.95 *(978-1-4314-0219-9(2))* Jacana Media ZAF. Dist: Independent Pubs. Group.
Clement, Gary. The Great Poochini. 2004. (J). (gr. 1-4). spiral bd. *(978-0-616-03027-1(4))* Canadian National Institute for the Blind/Institut National Canadien pour les Aveugles.
—The Great Poochini, 1 vol. 2010. (ENG., Illus.). 32p. (J). (gr. -1-2). pap. 7.95 *(978-0-88899-990-0(9))* Groundwood Bks. CAN. Dist: Publishers Group West (PGW).
Clerici, Lorenzo. The Dog Book: A Minibombo Book. Clerici, Lorenzo, illus. 2017. (Minibombo Ser.). (ENG., Illus.). 32p. (J). (-k). 9.99 *(978-0-7636-9487-6(8))* Candlewick Pr.
Clifton, Lutricia. Immortal Max. Sheban, Chris, illus. 2014. (ENG.). 192p. (J). (gr. 3-7). 16.95 *(978-0-8234-3041-3(3))* Holiday Hse., Inc.
Cline, H. R. Baxter's Backyard Adventures. 2009. 32p. pap. 13.99 *(978-1-4389-5939-9(7))* AuthorHouse.
Cobb, Debbie. Gracie's Big Adventure... with Augustine the Beaver. Ferchaud, Steve, illus. 2006. (J). per. 10.95 *(978-0-9787376-0-3(1))* Laurob Pr.
Cocca-Leffler, Maryann. Dog Wash Day. Cocca-Leffler, Maryann, illus. 2004. (All Aboard Picture Reader Ser.). (ENG., Illus.). 32p. (J). (gr. -1-k). mass mkt. 3.99 *(978-0-448-43370-7(2),* Grosset & Dunlap) Penguin Young Readers Group.
—A Vacation for Pooch. Cocca-Leffler, Maryann, illus. 2013. (ENG., Illus.). 32p. (J). (gr. -1-2). 16.99 *(978-0-8050-9106-9(8),* 9780805091069, Holt, Henry & Co. Bks. For Young Readers) Holt, Henry & Co.
Cochran, Bill. The Forever Dog. Andreasen, Dan, illus. 2007. (ENG.). 32p. (J). (gr. -1-3). 16.99 *(978-0-06-053939-9(9))* HarperCollins Pubs.
—The Forever Dog. 2007. (J). (gr. -1-2). 27.95 incl. audio *(978-0-8045-6955-2(X));* 29.95 incl. audio compact disk *(978-0-8045-4177-0(9))* Spoken Arts, Inc.
Cochrane, Ian. Shian & the Corryvreckan. 2013. (Illus.). 96p. pap. *(978-1-909465-09-1(7))* Cloister Hse. Pr., The.
Coe, Victoria J. Fenway & Hattie & the Evil Bunny Gang. 2017. (Fenway & Hattie Ser.). (ENG.). 192p. (J). (gr. 3-7). 16.99 *(978-1-101-99633-1(1),* G.P. Putnam's Sons Books for Young Readers) Penguin Young Readers Group.
Coffelt, Nancy. Fred Stays with Me! Tusa, Tricia, illus. 2011. (ENG.). 32p. (J). (gr. -1-3). pap. 7.99 *(978-0-316-07791-0(7))* Little, Brown Bks. for Young Readers.
—Pug in a Truck. 2006. (Illus.). (J). *(978-0-16-856319-7(3))* Houghton Mifflin Harcourt Publishing Co.
Coffey, Ethel. How Meg Changed Her Mind. Schweitzer-Johnson, Betty, illus. 2014. (ENG.). 32p. pap. 11.95 *(978-1-4525-8377-8(3),* Balboa Pr.) Author Solutions, Inc.
Coffin, Rebecca, et al. Binkie & the Firemen: A Lost Puppy Rescued in A Basement Fire Becomes the Firemen's Pet. 2011. 50p. 35.95 *(978-1-258-06785-4(4))* Literary Licensing, LLC.
Coffman, Jan. A Common Bond. 2008. 73p. pap. 19.95 *(978-1-60672-302-9(2))* America Star Bks.
Cofreros, Felipe. Sam's Wish. 2007. 28p. per. 21.99 *(978-1-4257-8486-7(0))* Xlibris Corp.
Cohen, Barbara S. Forever Friends. Hall, Dorothy Louise, illus. 2015. (ENG.). 100p. (J). reprint ed. pap. 9.95 *(978-1-931290-54-8(7))* Tallfellow Pr.
Cohen, Pamela. Ashie: Lost in a Hurricane, 1 vol. 2010. 40p. 24.95 *(978-1-4512-1169-6(4))* PublishAmerica, Inc.
Cohen, Pamela June. Ashie: Lost in the Hurricane. Lang, Allison, illus. 2008. 40p. pap. 24.95 *(978-1-60474-961-8(X))* America Star Bks.
Cohen, Sonia. Gigi. l.t. ed. 2005. (Illus.). 34p. (J). 14.95 *(978-0-615-12926-6(9))* Gigi Enterprises.
Cohn, Edith. Spirit's Key. 2014. (ENG.). 320p. (J). (gr. 4-7). 16.99 *(978-0-374-30011-1(9),* 9780374300111, Farrar, Straus & Giroux (BYR)) Farrar, Straus & Giroux.
Cole, Babette. El Libro de Etiqueta de Lady Lupina. 2003. (Babette Cole Ser.).Tr. of Lady Lupin's Book of Etiquett. (SPA.). (J). 18.95 *(978-84-233-3337-0(X))* Ediciones Destino ESP. Dist: Planeta Publishing Corp.
Cole, Barbara. Anna & Natalie, 1 vol. Himler, Ronald, illus. 2007. (ENG.). 32p. (J). 16.95 *(978-1-59572-105-1(3))* Star Bright Bks., Inc.
Cole, Barbara H. Anna & Natalie, 1 vol. Himler, Ronald, illus. 2010. (ENG.). 32p. (J). pap. 6.95 *(978-1-59572-211-9(4))* Star Bright Bks., Inc.
Cole, Dina. Maggie's Magic Unicorn. 2012. 28p. pap. 19.99 *(978-1-4685-7734-1(4))* AuthorHouse.
Cole-McCrea, Candace. The Seeing-Eye Dog: A Story of Brotherly Love. 2012. 28p. pap. 13.95 *(978-1-4624-0050-8(7),* Inspiring Voices) Author Solutions, Inc.
Coleman, Claudia. Yo Yo & the Great Flood. 2008. 100p. pap. 22.95 *(978-1-60145-606-9(9))* Booklocker.com, Inc.
Collard, Sneed B., III. Dog 4491. 2013. (Illus.). 256p. (J). 13.99 *(978-0-9844460-4-9(4))* Bucking Horse Bks.
Collard, Sneed B., 3rd. Dog 4491. 2013. (ENG., Illus.). 256p. (J). pap. 8.00 *(978-0-9844460-5-6(2))* Mountain Pr. Publishing Co., Inc.
Collard, Sneed B., III. Dog Sense, 1 vol. (ENG.). 192p. (J). (gr. 3-7). 2008. pap. 7.95 *(978-1-56145-460-0(5))* 2005. 14.95 *(978-1-56145-351-1(X))* Peachtree Pubs.
—The Governor's Dog Is Missing. 2011. (Slate Stephens Mysteries Ser.). 176p. (J). (gr. 4-6). 16.00 *(978-0-9844460-1-8(X))* Bucking Horse Bks.
Collins, Terry. High-Flying Sam. Date not set. (Rocket Power Ready-to-Read Ser.: Vol. 5). (J). pap. 3.50 *(978-0-689-86582-4(1),* Simon Spotlight/Nickelodeon) Simon Spotlight/Nickelodeon.
Colorado, Papa. Nui & Kiwi's Fantastic Adventures. 2011. 70p. pap. 19.95 *(978-1-4626-2806-3(0))* PublishAmerica, Inc.
Come Here Puppy. 2006. (Bella & Rosie Set 3 Ser.). (J). 7.67 *(978-1-932570-53-3(5))* Pioneer Valley Bks.
Comfort, Philip. Rescued Retriever. 2005. 129p. pap. 19.95 *(978-1-4137-6536-6(X))* America Star Bks.
Comfort, Ray. Scratch & Sniff. Hohnstadt, Cedric, illus. 2007. (Creation for Kids Ser.). 24p. (gr. -1-5). 14.99 *(978-0-88270-328-2(5))* Bridge-Logos, Inc.
Cone, Breanna. The Adventures of Pirate & Black Bart. 2006. 41p. pap. 8.25 *(978-1-4116-6494-4(9))* Lulu Pr., Inc.
Conford, Ellen. Annabel the Actress Starring in the Hound of the Barkervilles. Andriani, Renee W., illus. 2004. (Annabel the Actress Ser.). 83p. (gr. 2-5). 14.00 *(978-0-7569-2180-4(5))* Perfection Learning Corp.
—Annabel the Actress Starring in the Hound of the Barkervilles. Andriani, Renee W., illus. 2003. (ENG.). 96p. (J). (gr. 2-5). pap. 6.99 *(978-0-689-84791-2(2),* Simon & Schuster/Paula Wiseman Bks.) Simon & Schuster/Paula Wiseman Bks.
Conley, Cindy Taylor. For Little Louie Someday. 2013. 44p. pap. 24.95 *(978-1-63000-044-8(2))* America Star Bks.
Connellan, Sue. Special Treasure. 2009. 40p. pap. 18.49 *(978-1-4343-7644-2(3))* AuthorHouse.
Connelly, Peg. If the Forest Is Silent, Beware! 2007. 108p. pap. 19.95 *(978-1-60441-548-3(7))* America Star Bks.
Conner, Sharon Landsberg. The Magnetizing Princess: A children's story that uses some of the most powerful tools available, to get more of what you Want. 2007. 56p. per. 8.95 *(978-0-595-44229-4(3))* iUniverse, Inc.
Conroy, Kathy. Life Through a Dog's Eyes: The Adventures of Ralph. 2008. (ENG.). 44p. pap. 19.69 *(978-1-4343-8465-2(9))* AuthorHouse.
Cook, Andrew. Skipper & Tango: In Search for the Golden Egg. 2012. (Illus.). 28p. pap. 15.99 *(978-1-4771-0346-3(5))* Xlibris Corp.
Cook, Julia. I Want to Be the Only Dog! DuFalla, Anita, illus. 2015. (ENG.). 32p. (J). pap. 10.95 *(978-1-934490-86-0(5))* Boys Town Pr.
Cook, Sherry & Johnson, Terri. Nosey Nina, 26 vols. Kuhn, Jesse, illus. l.t. ed. 2006. (Quirkles — Exploring Phonics through Science Ser.: 14). 32p. (J). 7.99 *(978-1-933815-13-8(2),* Quirkles, The) Creative 3, LLC.
Coon, Kathyann. We Are Different. 2013. 16p. pap. 24.95 *(978-1-63004-413-8(X))* America Star Bks.
Cooper, Elisha. Homer. Cooper, Elisha, illus. 2012. (ENG., Illus.). 32p. (J). (gr. -1-3). 16.99 *(978-0-06-201248-7(7),* Greenwillow Bks.) HarperCollins Pubs.
Cooper, Ilene. Little Lucy. Kanzler, John, illus. 2011. (Step into Reading Ser.). (ENG.). 48p. (J). (gr. k-3). pap. 3.99 *(978-0-375-86760-6(0),* Random Hse. Bks. for Young Readers) Random Hse. Children's Bks.
—Look at Lucy! Merrell, David, illus. 2009. (Lucy Ser.: No. 3). (ENG.). 112p. (J). (gr. 1-4). 4.99 *(978-0-375-85558-0(0),* Random Hse. Bks. for Young Readers) Random Hse. Children's Bks.
—Lucy on the Ball. Merrell, David, illus. 2011. (Lucy Ser.). (ENG.). 112p. (J). (gr. 1-4). 4.99 *(978-0-375-85559-7(9),* Random Hse. Bks. for Young Readers) Random Hse. Children's Bks.
—Lucy's Holiday Surprise. Fitzgerald, Royce, illus. 2015. (Lucy Ser.: 7). (ENG.). 112p. (J). (gr. 1-4). 12.99 *(978-0-385-39131-3(5),* Random Hse. Bks. for Young Readers) Random Hse. Children's Bks.
—Lucy's Tricks & Treats. Merrell, David, illus. 2012. (Lucy Ser.). (ENG.). 112p. (J). (gr. 1-4). 4.99 *(978-0-375-86997-6(2),* Random Hse. Bks. for Young Readers) Random Hse. Children's Bks.
—Thanks to Lucy. Merrell, David, illus. 2013. (Lucy Ser.). (ENG.). 112p. (J). (gr. 1-4). 4.99 *(978-0-375-86998-3(0),* Random Hse. Bks. for Young Readers) Random Hse. Children's Bks.
Coover, Colleen & Tobin, Paul. Adventure Time: The Flip Side. 2014. lib. bdg. 33.05 *(978-0-606-36120-0(0))* Turtleback Bks.
Cope, Andrew. Captured! 2nd ed. 2006. (Spy Dog Ser.: 2). (ENG., Illus.). 176p. (J). (gr. 2-7). pap. 7.99 *(978-0-14-131885-1(6))* Penguin Bks., Ltd. GBR. Dist: Independent Pubs. Group.
—The Gunpowder Plot. 2017. (Spy Dog Ser.: 12). (ENG., Illus.). 176p. (J). (gr. 2-7). pap. 7.99 ***(978-0-14-136999-0(X))*** Penguin Bks., Ltd. GBR. Dist: Independent Pubs. Group.
—Rollercoaster! 7th ed. 2015. (Spy Dog Ser.). (ENG., Illus.). 160p. (J). (gr. 2-7). pap. 7.99 *(978-0-14-133882-8(2))* Penguin Bks., Ltd. GBR. Dist: Independent Pubs. Group.
—Safari. 3rd ed. 2016. (ENG., Illus.). 160p. (J). (gr. 2-7). pap. 7.99 *(978-0-14-135718-8(5))* Penguin Bks., Ltd. GBR. Dist: Independent Pubs. Group.
—Spy Dog. Wallace, Tig, ed. 2005. (Spy Dog Ser.: 1). (ENG., Illus.). 176p. (J). (gr. 2-7). pap. 7.99 *(978-0-14-131884-4(8))* Penguin Bks., Ltd. GBR. Dist: Independent Pubs. Group.
—Spy Dog & Captured!, 2 bks. in 1. 2014. (Spy Dog Ser.). (ENG., Illus.). 352p. (J). (gr. 2-7). 14.99 *(978-0-14-135097-4(0))* Penguin Bks., Ltd. GBR. Dist: Independent Pubs. Group.
—Spy Dog Unleashed. 3rd ed. 2007. (Spy Dog Ser.: 3). (ENG., Illus.). 160p. (J). (gr. 2-7). pap. 7.99 *(978-0-14-132123-3(7))* Penguin Bks., Ltd. GBR. Dist: Independent Pubs. Group.
—Storm Chaser. 10th ed. 2015. (Spy Dog Ser.: 11). (ENG., Illus.). 160p. (J). (gr. 2-7). pap. 7.99 *(978-0-14-135715-7(0))* Penguin Bks., Ltd. GBR. Dist: Independent Pubs. Group.
—Superbrain. 4th ed. 2008. (Spy Dog Ser.: 4). (ENG., Illus.). 160p. (J). (gr. 2-7). pap. 7.99 *(978-0-14-132244-5(6))* Penguin Bks., Ltd. GBR. Dist: Independent Pubs. Group.
—Teacher's Pet. 7th ed. 2011. (Spy Dog Ser.: 6). (ENG., Illus.). 160p. (J). (gr. 2-7). pap. 7.99 *(978-0-14-133620-6(X))* Penguin Bks., Ltd. GBR. Dist: Independent Pubs. Group.
—Training School. 6th ed. 2015. (Spy Pups Ser.: 6). (ENG., Illus.). 144p. (J). (gr. 2-7). pap. 7.99 *(978-0-14-133881-1(4))* Penguin Bks., Ltd. GBR. Dist: Independent Pubs. Group.
Coppel, Chris. Far from Burden Dell. 2005. 286p. (J). (gr. 6-16). per. 4.95 *(978-0-9746481-6-3(7))* Brown Barn Bks.
Cordell, Ryan & Cordell, Evie. Two Girls Want a Puppy. Lam, Maple, illus. 2015. (ENG.). 32p. (J). (gr. -1-3). 17.99 *(978-0-06-229261-2(7))* HarperCollins Pubs.
Corderoy, Tracey. Shifty Mcgifty & Slippery Sam. Lenton, Steven, illus. 2013. (ENG.). 32p. (J). (gr. -1-3). 14.99 *(978-0-7636-6838-9(9),* Nosy Crow) Candlewick Pr.
Cordone Warner, Debra. Henry's Daily Walk. 2010. 56p. pap. 24.99 *(978-0-557-60667-2(5))* Lulu Pr., Inc.
Corey's Web Unleashed. 2003. (J). *(978-0-9716567-8-9(9))* Book Web Publishing, Limited.
Coronado, Mark & Jackson, Dominic. Swamp Life. 2012. 16p. pap. 15.99 *(978-1-4772-1042-0(3))* AuthorHouse.
Corriveau, Art. How I Got a Life & a Dog. 2012. (ENG.). 288p. (J). (gr. 3-7). pap. 7.95 *(978-1-4197-0015-6(4),* Amulet Bks.) Abrams, Inc.
—How I, Nicky Flynn, Finally Got a Life (And a Dog) 2010. (ENG.). 272p. (YA). (gr. 3-7). 16.95 *(978-0-8109-8298-7(6),* Amulet Bks.) Abrams, Inc.
Costain, Meredith. Daddies Are Awesome. Lovsin, Polona, illus. (ENG.). (J). 2017. 28p. bds. 7.99 *(978-1-250-10720-6(2),* 9781250107206) 2016. 32p. 16.99 *(978-1-62779-452-7(2),* 9781627794527) Holt, Henry & Co. (Holt, Henry & Co. Bks. For Young Readers).
—Stella & the Pet Parade. McGowan, Shane, illus. 2015. (Legends in Their Own Lunchbox Ser.). (ENG.). 48p. (gr. 1-2). pap. 7.99 *(978-1-4966-0243-5(9),* Legends in Their Own Lunchbox) Capstone Classroom.
—Stella's Got Talent. McGowan, Shane, illus. 2015. (Legends in Their Own Lunchbox Ser.). (ENG.). 48p. (gr. 1-2). pap. 7.99 *(978-1-4966-0249-7(8),* Legends in Their Own Lunchbox) Capstone Classroom.
Coste, Marion. Wild Beach. Gray, Cissy, illus. 2005. 32p. (J). pap. 8.25 *(978-0-89317-062-2(3),* WW-623); lib. bdg. 17.95 *(978-0-89317-061-5(5),* WW-0615) Finney Co., Inc. (Windward Publishing).
Cotterill, Samantha. No More Bows. Cotterill, Samantha, illus. 2017. (Illus.). 40p. (J). (gr. -1-3). 17.99 *(978-0-06-240870-9(4))* HarperCollins Pubs.
Cottringer, Anne. Hot Dog. Walker, Katherine, illus. 2005. (ENG.). 24p. (J). lib. bdg. 23.65 *(978-1-59646-738-5(X))* Dingles & Co.
—Mary Is Scary. Gale, Cathy, illus. 2007. (Bloomsbury Paperbacks Ser.). (ENG.). 32p. (J). (gr. k-2). pap. 9.99 *(978-0-7475-7927-4(X))* Bloomsbury Publishing Plc GBR. Dist: Independent Pubs. Group.
Coulton, Mia. At Grandma Ruth's House. Coulton, Mia, photos by. 2008. (ENG., Illus.). pap. 5.35 *(978-1-933624-32-7(9))* Maryruth Bks., Inc.
—Danny Likes Red. Coulton, Mia, photos by. 2003. (ENG., Illus.). pap. 5.35 *(978-0-9720295-2-0(4))* Maryruth Bks., Inc.
—Danny Likes to Help. Coulton, Mia, photos by. 2005. (ENG., Illus.). pap. 5.35 *(978-0-9746475-9-3(4))* Maryruth Bks., Inc.
—Danny's Castle. Coulton, Mia, photos by. 2005. (ENG., Illus.). 16p. pap. 5.35 *(978-1-933624-00-6(0))* Maryruth Bks., Inc.
—Danny's Rocket. Coulton, Mia, photos by. 2009. (ENG., Illus.). pap. 5.35 *(978-1-933624-40-2(X))* Maryruth Bks., Inc.
—Danny's Special Tree. Coulton, Mia, photos by. 2008. (ENG., Illus.). pap. 6.95 *(978-1-933624-25-9(6))* Maryruth Bks., Inc.
—Danny's Window. Coulton, Mia, photos by. 2005. (ENG., Illus.). pap. 5.35 *(978-0-9746475-8-6(6))* Maryruth Bks., Inc.
—Five Danny Dogs. Coulton, Mia, photos by. 2005. (ENG., Illus.). pap. 5.35 *(978-1-933624-01-3(9))* Maryruth Bks., Inc.
—Get down Danny. Coulton, Mia, photos by. 2003. (ENG., Illus.). pap. 5.35 *(978-0-9720295-5-1(9))* Maryruth Bks., Inc.

—I Am Danny. Coulton, Mia, photos by. 2003. (ENG., Illus.). pap. 5.35 (978-0-9720295-7-5(5)) Maryruth Bks., Inc.

—Spy Danny. Coulton, Mia, photos by. 2006. (ENG., Illus.). pap. 5.35 (978-1-933624-03-7(5)) Maryruth Bks., Inc.

—Super Danny. Coulton, Mia, photos by. 2012. (ENG., Illus.). 13p. bds. 6.99 (978-1-933197-90-6(0)) Orange Frazer Pr.

Counce, Paula. A Journey Remembered. l.t. ed. 2004. (Illus.). 135p. (J). 19.95 (978-0-9762776-0-6(3)) Counce, Paula.

Cousins, C. J. Bailey & Friends Have a Party. 2012. 16p. pap. 15.99 (978-1-4772-7346-3(8)) AuthorHouse.

Cousins, Lucy. I'm the Best. Cousins, Lucy, illus. 2013. (ENG., Illus.). 32p. (J). (-k). 6.99 (978-0-7636-6348-3(4)) Candlewick Pr.

Coven, Wanda. Heidi Heckelbeck & the Magic Puppy. Burris, Priscilla, illus. 2017. (Heidi Heckelbeck Ser.: 20). (ENG.). 128p. (J). (gr. k-4). pap. 5.99 **(978-1-4814-9521-9(6)**, Little Simon) Little Simon.

—Heidi Heckelbeck & the Magic Puppy. 2017. (Heidi Heckelbeck Ser.: 20). lib. bdg. 16.00 **(978-0-606-40205-7(5))** Turtleback Bks.

Cowan, C. C. Amanda's Amazing Adventures: The Case of the Missing Pooch, 6 vols., Vol. 1. Rashid, Abdul, illus. 2009. 40p. pap. 14.95 (978-0-9677385-0-5(4)); 100p. pap. 14.95 (978-0-9677385-1-2(2)) CCP Publishing & Entertainment.

Cowen-Fletcher, Jane. Hello, Puppy! Cowen-Fletcher, Jane, illus. 2010. (ENG., Illus.). 32p. (J). (gr. -1-k). 12.99 (978-0-7636-4303-4(3)) Candlewick Pr.

—My New Puppy. Cowen-Fletcher, Jane, illus. 2013. (ENG., Illus.). 32p. (J). (-k). pap. 4.99 (978-0-7636-6225-7(9)) Candlewick Pr.

Cox, Denise L. Ginger Is Adopted, 1 vol. 2010. 26p. pap. 24.95 (978-1-61582-892-0(3)) PublishAmerica, Inc.

Cox, James. Earth Dogs Don't Speak. 2009. (Illus.). 112p. pap. 31.99 (978-1-4389-3990-2(6)) AuthorHouse.

Cox, Judy. Puppy Power. Björkman, Steve, illus. (ENG.). 96p. (J). 2009. (gr. 2-4). pap. 6.95 (978-0-8234-2210-4(0)) 2008. (gr. -1-3). 15.95 (978-0-8234-2073-5(6)) Holiday Hse., Inc.

Cox, Phil Roxbee & Cartwright, S. Rusty's Bone. 2004. (Farmyard Tales Touchy Feely Board Bks.). (ENG., Illus.). 1p. (J). bds. 7.95 (978-0-7945-0012-2(9), Usborne) EDC Publishing.

Cox, Sarah Webster. The Adventures of Willy & Tilly. 2013. 16p. pap. 12.99 (978-1-4669-7957-4(7)) Trafford Publishing.

Craighill, Lina. Buster Teases Emily. 2006. 16p. (J). 12.00 (978-1-4116-8404-1(4)) Lulu Pr., Inc.

Crane, Jordan. Keep Our Secrets. 2012. (ENG., Illus.). 32p. (J). (gr. -1-4). bds. 15.95 (978-1-936365-52-4(9)) McSweeney's Publishing.

Crane, Noelle L. The Clever Pug. Crane, Noelle L., illus. 2013. (Illus.). 66p. pap. 9.99 (978-0-9846119-8-0(3)) Pluriverse Publishing.

Crawford, John. Life in Honeysuckle Valley the Adventur. 2006. pap. 14.95 (978-1-4327-0104-8(5)) Outskirts Pr., Inc.

Crayon, Paula. Wrong Dog in the Right Bathroom. 2011. 40p. (gr. -1). pap. 18.50 (978-1-4567-6344-2(X)) AuthorHouse.

Creal, Nancy & Taylor, Ann Creal. Lydia Ann & Scraggles: The Adventures of a Girl & Her Dog. Taylor, Ann Creal, illus. 2013. (Illus.). 28p. (J). 12.00 (978-0-9800059-4-3(9)) Taylor, Ann.

Creel, Ann Howard. Nicki, Bk. 1. Ben-Ami, Doron, illus. 2007. (ENG.). 136p. (J). (gr. 4-7). pap. 6.95 (978-1-59369-259-9(5), Pleasant Co.) American Girl Publishing, Inc.

Crimi, Carolyn. Pugs in a Bug. Buscema, Stephanie, illus. 2012. (ENG.). 32p. (J). (gr. -1-k). 16.99 (978-0-8037-3320-6(8), Dial Bks) Penguin Young Readers Group.

—There Might Be Lobsters. Molk, Laurel, illus. 2017. (ENG.). 32p. (J). (gr. -1-2). 16.99 (978-0-7636-7542-4(3)) Candlewick Pr.

Crisanaz, Catherine M. The Best House for Molly. 2008. 36p. per. 24.95 (978-1-4241-9093-5(2)) America Star Bks.

Cronin, Doreen. The Chicken Squad. Cornell, Kevin, illus. 2014. 92p. (J). **(978-0-605-90609-9(2))** Simon & Schuster Children's Publishing.

—The Chicken Squad: The First Misadventure. Cornell, Kevin, illus. 2015. (Chicken Squad Ser.: 1). (ENG.). 112p. (J). (gr. 2-5). pap. 6.99 (978-1-4424-9677-4(0), Atheneum Bks. for Young Readers) Simon & Schuster Children's Publishing.

—The Legend of Diamond Lil. Cornell, Kevin, illus. 2012. 144p. (J). (gr. 1-5). (ENG.). 14.99 (978-0-06-177996-1(2)); lib. bdg. 15.89 (978-0-06-198578-2(3)) HarperCollins Pubs.

—Smick! Medina, Juana, illus. 2015. (ENG.). 34p. (J). (gr. -1-k). 16.99 (978-0-670-78578-0(4), Viking Books for Young Readers) Penguin Young Readers Group.

—The Trouble with Chickens. Cornell, Kevin, illus. (J). (gr. 1-5). 2012. (ENG.). 144p. pap. 5.99 (978-0-06-121534-6(1)) 2011. (ENG.). 128p. 14.99 (978-0-06-121532-2(5)) 2011. 128p. lib. bdg. 15.89 (978-0-06-121533-9(3)) HarperCollins Pubs.

Crow, Melinda Melton. My Two Dogs. Sassin, Eva, illus. 2013. (My Two Dogs Ser.). (ENG.). 32p. (gr. 1-3). lib. bdg. 90.60 (978-1-4342-6068-0(2)); lib. bdg. 181.20 (978-1-4342-6069-7(0)) Stone Arch Bks.

—Rocky & Daisy & the Birthday Party. Sassin, Eva, illus. 2013. (My Two Dogs Ser.). (ENG.). 32p. (gr. 1-3). pap. 29.70 (978-1-4342-6296-7(0)); (gr. 2-3). pap. 5.95 (978-1-4342-6205-9(7)); (gr. 2-3). lib. bdg. 22.65 (978-1-4342-6011-6(9)) Stone Arch Bks.

—Rocky & Daisy at the Park, 1 vol. Brownlow, Mike, illus. 2013. (My Two Dogs Ser.). (ENG.). 32p. (gr. 2-3). pap. 5.95 (978-1-4342-6118-2(2)); lib. bdg. 22.65 (978-1-4342-4163-4(7)) Stone Arch Bks.

—Rocky & Daisy Get Trained, 1 vol. Brownlow, Mike, illus. 2013. (My Two Dogs Ser.). (ENG.). 32p. (gr. 2-3). pap. 5.95 (978-1-4342-6116-8(6)); lib. bdg. 22.65 (978-1-4342-4161-0(0)) Stone Arch Bks.

—Rocky & Daisy Go Camping, 1 vol. Brownlow, Mike, illus. 2013. (My Two Dogs Ser.). (ENG.). 32p. (gr. 2-3). pap. 5.95 (978-1-4342-6117-5(4)); lib. bdg. 22.65 (978-1-4342-4162-7(9)) Stone Arch Bks.

—Rocky & Daisy Go Home, 1 vol. Brownlow, Mike, illus. 2013. (My Two Dogs Ser.). (ENG.). 32p. (gr. 2-3). pap. 5.95 (978-1-4342-6115-1(8)); lib. bdg. 22.65 (978-1-4342-4160-3(2)) Stone Arch Bks.

—Rocky & Daisy Go to the Vet. Sassin, Eva, illus. 2013. (My Two Dogs Ser.). (ENG.). 32p. (gr. 1-3). pap. 29.70 (978-1-4342-6297-4(9)); (gr. 2-3). pap. 5.95 (978-1-4342-6203-5(0)); (gr. 2-3). lib. bdg. 22.65 (978-1-4342-6009-3(7)) Stone Arch Bks.

—Rocky & Daisy Take a Vacation. Sassin, Eva, illus. 2013. (My Two Dogs Ser.). (ENG.). 32p. (gr. 1-3). pap. 29.70 (978-1-4342-6298-1(7)); (gr. 2-3). lib. bdg. 22.65 (978-1-4342-6008-6(9)) Stone Arch Bks.

—Rocky & Daisy Wash the Van. Sassin, Eva, illus. 2013. (My Two Dogs Ser.). (ENG.). 32p. (gr. 1-3). pap. 29.70 (978-1-4342-6299-8(5)); (gr. 2-3). pap. 5.95 (978-1-4342-6204-2(9)); (gr. 2-3). lib. bdg. 22.65 (978-1-4342-6010-9(0)) Stone Arch Bks.

Crow, Melinda Melton & Sassin, Eva. Rocky & Daisy Take a Vacation, 1 vol. 2013. (My Two Dogs Ser.). (ENG.). 32p. (gr. 2-3). pap. 5.95 (978-1-4342-6202-8(2)) Stone Arch Bks.

Crowder, Melanie. Parched. (ENG.). 160p. (J). (gr. 5-7). 2014. pap. 7.99 (978-0-544-33631-5(3), HMH Books For Young Readers) 2013. 15.99 (978-0-547-97651-8(8)) Houghton Mifflin Harcourt Publishing Co.

Crowe, Ellie & Fry, Juliet. HOKU the Stargazer: The Exciting Pirate Adventure! Petosa-Sigel, Kristi, illus. 2009. (ENG.). 28p. (J). (978-1-59700-601-9(7)) Island Heritage Publishing.

Crown Peak Publishing. Just Be You. Crown Peak Publishing, illus. 2008. (ENG., Illus.). 40p. (J). 19.95 (978-0-9645663-5-4(4)) Crown Peak Publishing.

Cruikshank, Beth & Johnston, Lynn. Farley & the Lost Bone. 2011. (ENG.). 32p. (J). 14.99 (978-1-4494-0306-5(9)) Andrews McMeel Publishing.

Crummel, Susan Stevens. City Dog, Country Dog, 0 vols. Donohue, Dorothy, illus. 2010. (ENG.). 42p. (J). (gr. k-4). pap. 9.99 (978-0-7614-5538-7(8), 9780761455387, Amazon Children's Publishing) Amazon Publishing.

—Sherlock Bones & the Missing Cheese, 0 vols. Donohue, Dorothy, illus. 2012. (ENG.). 40p. (J). (gr. k-3). 17.99 (978-0-7614-6186-9(8), 9780761461869, Amazon Children's Publishing) Amazon Publishing.

—Ten-Gallon Bart, 0 vols. Donohue, Dorothy, illus. 2010. (ENG.). 32p. (J). (gr. k-3). pap. 9.99 (978-0-7614-5719-0(4), 9780761457190, Amazon Children's Publishing) Amazon Publishing.

—Ten-Gallon Bart & the Wild West Show, 0 vols. 2013. (ENG.). 40p. (J). (gr. k-3). pap. 9.99 (978-1-4778-1671-4(2), 9781477816714, Amazon Children's Publishing) Amazon Publishing.

—Ten-Gallon Bart Beats the Heat, 0 vols. Donohue, Dorothy, illus. 2010. (ENG.). 40p. (J). (gr. k-3). 17.99 (978-0-7614-5634-6(1), 9780761456346, Amazon Children's Publishing) Amazon Publishing.

Crummel, Susan Stevens & Donohue, Dorothy. City Dog & Country Dog. Donohue, Dorothy, illus. unabr. ed. 2006. (Illus.). (J). (gr. k-3). 27.95 incl. audio (978-0-8045-6942-2(8), SAC6942) Spoken Arts, Inc.

Cruzan, Patricia. Molly's Mischievous Dog. 2004. pap. 15.50 (978-1-4120-1871-5(4)) Trafford Publishing.

—The Wonder in the Woods. Brewer, Kathaleen, illus. 2013. 250p. pap. 15.00 (978-0-9653543-7-0(7)) Clear Creek Pubs.

Cruzan, Patricia & Solly, Gloria, illus. Molly's Mischievous Dog. l.t. ed. 2004. 121p. (J). per. (978-0-9653543-3-2(4)) Clear Creek Pubs.

Cullen, Lynn. Little Scraggly Hair: A Dog on Noah's Ark. Rogers, Jacqueline, illus. 2003. (ENG.). 32p. (J). (gr. k-3). tchr. ed. 16.95 (978-0-8234-1772-8(7)) Holiday Hse., Inc.

Cumming, Hannah. The Red Boat. Cumming, Hannah, illus. 2012. (Child's Play Library). (ENG., Illus.). 32p. (J). (978-1-84643-493-8(9)) Child's Play International Ltd.

Cunningham, S. C. Ginormous Joe's Broken Bark. 2009. 48p. pap. 21.90 (978-1-4490-3116-9(1)) AuthorHouse.

Curtis, Christopher Paul. Mr. Chickee's Funny Money. 2007. (ENG.). 160p. (J). (gr. 3-7). 6.99 (978-0-440-22919-3(7), Yearling) Random Hse. Children's Bks.

—Mr. Chickee's Messy Mission. 2008. (ENG., Illus.). 240p. (J). (gr. 3-7). 6.99 (978-0-440-22922-3(7), Yearling) Random Hse. Children's Bks.

Curwood, James Oliver. Baree Son of Kazan. 2004. reprint ed. pap. 1.99 (978-1-4192-0891-1(8)); pap. 21.95 (978-1-4191-0891-4(3)) Kessinger Publishing, LLC.

Cusick, N. L. Tales from Grey Squirrel Manor #1 - a Tale of Two Squirrels. 2013. 24p. pap. (978-1-4602-0814-4(5)) FriesenPress.

Cussler, Clive. The Adventures of Hotsy Totsy. 2011. (ENG., Illus.). 176p. (J). (gr. 3-7). 6.99 (978-0-14-241873-4(0), Puffin Books) Penguin Young Readers Group.

Custard, P. T. Jules the Lighthouse Dog, 1. Greer, Ana, illus. 2006. (ENG.). 32p. (J). 12.95 (978-0-9785317-0-6(1)) Black Plum Bks.

—Kid Canine - Superhero! Custard, P. T. & Pearson, David, illus. 2008. 32p. (J). 13.95 (978-0-9785317-1-3(X)) Black Plum Bks.

Custureri, Mary C. Meet Happy Anderson. 2nd ed. 2013. 68p. pap. 15.95 (978-0-9887836-1-4(4)) Taylor and Seale Publishing, LLC.

Cuyler, Margery. Hooray for Reading Day! Howard, Arthur, illus. 2008. (Jessica Worries Ser.). (ENG.). 32p. (J). (gr. k-3). 17.99 (978-0-689-86188-8(5), Simon & Schuster Bks. For Young Readers) Simon & Schuster Bks. For Young Readers.

Cvetkovic, Judith. Mandy & Star's Sheep Ranch Getaway, 1 vol. 2010. 108p. pap. 19.95 (978-1-4489-5673-9(0)) America Star Bks.

Cvetkovic, Judith Lynn. Mandy's Lost Adventure. 2008. 48p. per. 24.95 (978-1-4241-9709-5(0)) PublishAmerica, Inc.

Cynthia, Rylant. Henry & Mudge. 2014. (Henry & Mudge Ser.). (ENG.). 40p. (J). (gr. 5-7). 8.24 (978-1-63245-231-3(6)) Lectorum Pubns., Inc.

Czekaj, Jef. Austin, Lost in America: A Geography Adventure. Czekaj, Jef, illus. 2015. (ENG., Illus.). 40p. (J). (gr. -1-3). 17.99 (978-0-06-228017-6(1)) HarperCollins Pubs.

—Dog Rules. Czekaj, Jef, illus. 2016. (Illus.). 32p. (J). (gr. -1-3). 17.99 (978-0-06-228018-3(X)) HarperCollins Pubs.

Daggett, Wade. Coco's New Friend. 2004. 35p. pap. 24.95 (978-1-4137-2001-3(3)) PublishAmerica, Inc.

Dahl, Michael. Me & My Dog. Persico, Zoe, illus. 2016. (Me & My Pet Ser.). (ENG.). 24p. (gr. 1-2). 6.95 (978-1-62370-793-4(5)) Capstone Young Readers of Coughlan Cos.

—Me & My Dog. Persico, Zoe, illus. 2016. (Me & My Pet Ser.). (ENG.). 24p. (gr. 1-2). lib. bdg. 22.65 (978-1-5158-0238-9(8), Fiction Picture Bks.) Picture Window Bks.

Dale, Jay. Carlos & the Puppies, 1 vol. Dybing, Michelle, illus. 2012. (Wonder Words Ser.). (ENG.). 32p. (gr. k-2). pap. 5.99 (978-1-4296-8902-1(1), Engage Literacy) Capstone Press of Coughlan Cos.

Dale, Jenny. Bubble & Squeak. Hellard, Susan, illus. 2005. 60p. (J). (978-0-439-79122-9(7)) Scholastic, Inc.

—Murphy's Mystery. Reid, Mick, illus. 2003. 110p. (J). (978-0-439-54364-4(9)) Scholastic, Inc.

—The Puppy Express. Reid, Mick, illus. 2003. 108p. (J). (978-0-439-45355-4(0)) Scholastic, Inc.

—Puppy Power. Reid, Mick, illus. 2003. 105p. (J). (978-0-439-45351-6(8)) Scholastic, Inc.

—Snowy the Surprise Puppy. Hellard, Susan, illus. 2005. 60p. (J). pap. (978-0-439-79124-3(3)) Scholastic, Inc.

—Top Dog! Reid, Mick, illus. 2003. 107p. (J). (978-0-439-54360-6(6)) Scholastic, Inc.

Daley-Prado, M. The Super Heroes Save Christmas! 2007. 24p. per. 24.95 (978-1-4241-9123-9(8)) America Star Bks.

Damschroder, Scott. Small Dog, Small Dog, Small, Small, Dog. Faust, Laurie, illus. 2004. 24p. (J). lib. bdg. 19.95 (978-0-9754728-2-8(8)) Big Ransom Studio.

Dando-Collins, Stephen. Caesar the War Dog - Operation Black Shark. 2016. (Caesar the War Dog Ser.: 5). (ENG.). 288p. (J). (gr. 4-6). pap. 11.99 (978-0-85798-863-8(8)) Random Hse. Australia AUS. Dist: Independent Pubs. Group.

Daniel, Beverly. The Adventures of Madilyn Millicent Middleton-Mew. Daniel, Cindy, ed. Daniel, Beverly, illus. 2013. (Illus.). 64p. pap. 8.95 (978-0-9789429-6-0(5)) Batelier Publishing.

Daniels, Kristine. Floyd & the Irresistible Cookie. 2009. 32p. pap. 18.00 (978-1-60844-276-8(4)) Dog Ear Publishing, LLC.

—Floyd & the Mysterious Night Time Noise. 2011. (Illus.). 34p. pap. 18.00 (978-1-4575-0141-8(4)) Dog Ear Publishing, LLC.

Dannenbring, Cheryl. My Puppy Gave to Me, 1 vol. Kremsner, Cynthia, illus. 2014. (ENG.). 32p. (J). (gr. k-3). 16.99 (978-1-4556-1943-6(4)) Pelican Publishing Co., Inc.

Danner, Pamela. Andre' Angel in a Poodle Suit. Neuburger, Jenny, illus. 2003. 32p. (J). per. (978-0-9728429-0-7(X), 4290X) Poodle Suit Publishing.

Darding, Kathy Meismer. Through Mitzy's Eyes: A Dog's Tale. 2012. 126p. 19.95 (978-1-4626-7420-6(8)); pap. 19.95 (978-1-4626-8138-9(7)) America Star Bks.

Darling, Nina. Pet Shop Talk: A Grooming for Max, 1 vol. 2009. 27p. pap. 24.95 (978-1-60813-646-9(9)) America Star Bks.

Darrington, Rebecca. Doodletoot- a Happy Little Basset Hound Dog. 2012. 24p. pap. 17.99 (978-1-61996-337-5(X)) Salem Author Services.

Dauer, Marty. Harvey's Woods: the Royal Adventures. LaRiccia, Mike, illus. 2007. 52p. per. 16.95 (978-1-4241-7924-4(6)) America Star Bks.

D'Aulaire, Ingri & D'Aulaire, Edgar Parin. Foxie, the Singing Dog. 2008. (ENG., Illus.). 48p. (J). (gr. -1-2). 14.95 (978-1-59017-264-3(7), NYR Children's Collection) New York Review of Bks., Inc., The.

—Too Big. 2008. (New York Review Children's Collection). (ENG., Illus.). 40p. (J). (gr. k-k). 14.95 (978-1-59017-291-9(4), NYR Children's Collection) New York Review of Bks., Inc., The.

Dave, Safety. Safety Dave & Daisy Ride the Bus. 2011. 16p. 8.95 (978-1-4520-7218-0(3)) AuthorHouse.

Davey, Owen. Laika: Astronaut Dog. Davey, Owen, illus. 2013. (ENG., Illus.). 32p. (J). (gr. k-3). 15.99 (978-0-7636-6822-8(2), Templar) Candlewick Pr.

David, Erica. Mr. Peabody & Sherman Big Golden Book (Mr. Peabody & Sherman) Laguna, Fabio & Spaziante, Patrick, illus. 2014. (Big Golden Book Ser.). (ENG.). 48p. (J). (gr. k-4). 9.99 (978-0-385-37142-1(X), Golden Bks.) Random Hse. Children's Bks.

—Mr. Peabody & Sherman Junior Novelization (Mr. Peabody & Sherman) Random House, illus. 2014. (Junior Novel Ser.). (ENG.). 128p. (J). (gr. 2-5). 5.99 (978-0-385-37141-4(1), Random Hse. Bks. for Young Readers) Random Hse. Children's Bks.

David, Erica, adapted by. Hotel for Dogs. movie tie-in novel ed. 2008. (Hotel for Dogs Ser.). (ENG., Illus.). 128p. (J). pap. 5.99 (978-1-4169-7183-2(1), Simon Spotlight) Simon Spotlight.

Davidson, Margaret. Five True Dog Stories. (FRE.). (J). pap. 4.99 (978-0-590-73687-9(6)) Scholastic, Inc.

Davidson, Susanna. That's Not My Puppy. 2009. (Touchy-Feely Board Bks). 10p. (J). bds. 8.99 (978-0-7945-2511-8(3), Usborne) EDC Publishing.

Davies, Becky. Three Little Pugs & the Big Bad Cat. Attia, Caron, illus. 2017. (ENG.). 32p. (J). (gr. -1-2). 16.99 **(978-1-68010-043-3(2))** Tiger Tales.

Davies, Katie. The Great Dog Disaster. Shaw, Hannah, illus. 2013. (Great Critter Capers Ser.). (ENG.). 208p. (J). (gr. 3-7). 12.99 (978-1-4424-4517-8(3), Beach Lane Bks.) Beach Lane Bks.

Davis, Anne. No Dogs Allowed!, No. 1. Davis, Anne, illus. 2011. (ENG., Illus.). 32p. (J). (gr. -1-3). 16.99 (978-0-06-075353-5(6)) HarperCollins Pubs.

Davis, Beth. Sago, A Very Special Service Dog: N/a. Schilling, Deborah, illus. 2011.Tr. of N/a. 28p. (J). 15.00 (978-0-9822974-9-0(1)); lib. bdg. 24.00 (978-0-9822974-8-3(3)) Rolemommy.

Davis, Cathy Mackey. Lucky el Perro de la Estación de Bomberos, 1 vol. rev. ed. 2007. (Building Fluency Through Reader's Theater Ser.). (SPA.). 20p. (J). (gr. 1-2). pap. 6.99 (978-1-4333-0016-5(8)) Teacher Created Materials, Inc.

Davis, Christine. For Every Dog an Angel. 2nd ed. 2004. (Illus.). 32p. (J). 9.95 (978-0-9659225-2-4(9)) Lighthearted Pr., Inc.

—The Shelter Dog. Davis, Christine, illus. 2008. (Illus.). 32p. (J). (gr. -1-3). 11.95 (978-0-9659225-4-8(5)) Lighthearted Pr., Inc.

Davis, David. Rock 'n' Roll Dogs, 1 vol. Galey, Chuck, illus. 2006. (ENG.). 32p. (J). (gr. k-3). 16.99 (978-1-58980-349-7(3)) Pelican Publishing Co., Inc.

Davis, Dayna. All White Dogs Love Mud. Osker, Denise, illus. 14p. (J). (gr. 1-5). pap. (978-0-9660350-1-8(1)) Suzalooz Pr.

Davis, Donna. Martha May Finds a Home. 2008. 24p. per. 24.95 (978-1-4241-8833-8(4)) America Star Bks.

Davis, Eleanor. Flop to the Top! TOON Level 3. Weing, Drew, illus. 2015. (ENG.). 40p. (J). (gr. k). 12.95 (978-1-935179-89-4(6)) TOON Books / RAW Junior, LLC.

Davis, Jacky. I Love You, Bingo. 2015. (Penguin Young Readers Level 2 Ser.). lib. bdg. 13.55 (978-0-606-37578-8(3)) Turtleback Bks.

Davis, Jacky & Soman, David. Ladybug Girl & Bingo. Soman, David, illus. 2012. (Ladybug Girl Ser.). (ENG., Illus.). 40p. (J). (gr. -1-k). 16.99 (978-0-8037-3582-8(0), Dial Bks) Penguin Young Readers Group.

—Ladybug Girl Feels Happy. Soman, David, illus. 2012. (Ladybug Girl Ser.). (ENG., Illus.). 12p. (J). (gr. -1 — 1). bds. 5.99 (978-0-8037-3890-4(0), Dial Bks) Penguin Young Readers Group.

Davis, Lydia & Ollivant, Alfred. Alfred Ollivant's Bob, Son of Battle: The Last Gray Dog of Kenmuir. Kirmse, Marguerite, illus. 2014. (ENG.). 320p. (J). (gr. 3-7). 17.95 (978-1-59017-729-7(0), NYR Children's Collection) New York Review of Bks., Inc., The.

Davis, Melissa. Remy's First Day of School. Kalpart, illus. 2013. 20p. pap. 10.95 (978-1-62212-480-0(4), Strategic Bk. Publishing) Strategic Book Publishing & Rights Agency (SBPRA).

Davis, Tim, illus. The Case of the Purple Diamonds. 2011. 88p. pap. 9.95 (978-1-934606-07-0(3)) TAG Publishing, LLC.

Dawkins, Rotha J. Treats & Tales. 2012. 196p. 24.77 (978-1-4669-5918-7(5)); pap. 14.77 (978-1-4669-5919-4(3)) Trafford Publishing.

Dawson, Brianóg Brady. Pageboy Danny. Connor, Michael, illus. 2006. (Pandas Ser.: 34). (ENG.). 64p. (J). pap. 9.95 (978-0-86278-950-3(8)) O'Brien Pr., Ltd., The IRL. Dist: Dufour Editions, Inc.

Dawson, Piper. The Adventures of Fenway & Becc. 2012. 76p. pap. 8.95 (978-1-4502-8646-6(1)) iUniverse, Inc.

Day, Alexandra. Carl & the Baby Duck. 2011. (My Readers Ser.). (ENG., Illus.). 32p. (J). (gr. -1-1). pap. 4.99 (978-0-312-62485-9(9), 9780312624859) Square Fish.

—Carl & the Kitten. 2011. (My Readers Ser.). (ENG., Illus.). 32p. (J). (gr. -1-1). pap. 4.99 (978-0-312-68197-5(6), 9780312681975) Square Fish.

—Carl & the Puppies. Day, Alexandra, illus. 2011. (My Readers Ser.). (ENG., Illus.). 32p. (J). (gr. -1-1). pap. 3.99 (978-0-312-62483-5(2), 9780312624835) Square Fish.

—Carl & the Sick Puppy. 2012. (My Readers Ser.). (ENG., Illus.). 32p. (J). (gr. -1-1). 15.99 (978-1-250-00152-8(8), 9781250001528); pap. 4.99 (978-1-250-00153-5(6), 9781250001535) Square Fish.

—Carl & the Sick Puppy. 2012. (My Readers: Level 1 Ser.). (J). lib. bdg. 13.55 (978-0-606-26121-0(4), Turtleback) Turtleback Bks.

—Carl at the Dog Show, 1 vol. Day, Alexandra, illus. 2012. (Carl Ser.). (ENG., Illus.). 40p. (J). (gr. -1-1). 15.99 (978-0-374-31083-7(1), 9780374310837, Farrar, Straus & Giroux (BYR)) Farrar, Straus & Giroux.

—Carl's Christmas. 2014. (Carl Ser.). (J). lib. bdg. 18.40 (978-0-606-36127-9(8)) Turtleback Bks.

—Carl's Halloween. Day, Alexandra, illus. 2015. (Carl Ser.). (ENG., Illus.). 32p. (J). (gr. -1-2). 14.99 (978-0-374-31082-0(3), 9780374310820, Farrar, Straus & Giroux (BYR)) Farrar, Straus & Giroux.

—Carl's Snowy Afternoon. Day, Alexandra, illus. 2009. (Carl Ser.). (ENG., Illus.). 32p. (J). (gr. -1-1). 13.99 (978-0-374-31086-8(6), 9780374310868, Farrar, Straus & Giroux (BYR)) Farrar, Straus & Giroux.

—Carl's Summer Vacation. Day, Alexandra, illus. 2008. (Carl Ser.). (ENG., Illus.). 32p. (J). (gr. -1-1). 15.99 (978-0-374-31085-1(8), 9780374310851, Farrar, Straus & Giroux (BYR)) Farrar, Straus & Giroux.

—The Fairy Dogfather. Day, Alexandra, illus. 2012. (ENG., Illus.). 32p. (J). 8.95 (978-1-59583-455-3(9), Green Tiger Pr.) Laughing Elephant.

Day, Ed D. Why Dogs Bark: & Other Tall Tales. Scott, Sarah C., illus. 2006. 50p. (J). per. 12.95 (978-1-933002-20-0(4)) PublishingWorks.

Day, Karen. A Million Miles from Boston. 2012. (ENG.). 224p. (J). (gr. 3-7). pap. 6.99 (978-0-375-85974-8(8), Yearling) Random Hse. Children's Bks.

Day, Kathleen. The Sweet Song of Rainbow Bird. 2012. 32p. pap. 14.75 (978-1-4669-3555-6(3)) Trafford Publishing.

Day, Sunnie. Sunnie & Her Peeps. 2011. 46p. pap. 16.95 (978-1-4626-4092-8(3)) America Star Bks.

Day, Tracy. The Silver Lining: Book the First of the Kadnohkka Grey Series. 2007. 96p. per. 11.95 (978-1-59858-440-0(5)) Dog Ear Publishing, LLC.

De Fonté, Desiree. Zach: A Story of Obedience. 2012. 36p. pap. 24.95 (978-1-4626-5114-6(3)) America Star Bks.

de Lint, Charles. Dingo. 2008. (ENG.). 224p. (YA). (gr. 7-18). 11.99 (978-0-14-240816-2(6), Firebird) Penguin Young Readers Group.

de Monfreid, Dorothée. Shhh! I'm Sleeping. de Monfreid, Dorothée, illus. 2016. (ENG., Illus.). 24p. (gr. -1-1). 12.99 (978-1-927271-95-7(9)) Gecko Pr. NZL. Dist: Lerner Publishing Group.

Dean, Sara. The Puppy Who Found a Boy, 1 vol. Hacker, Randy, illus. 2009. 13p. pap. 24.95 (978-1-61546-278-0(3)) America Star Bks.

DeArville, J. It's Kambri Time! 2007. 28p. per. 9.95 (978-1-4327-0812-2(0)) Outskirts Pr., Inc.

DeBear, Kirsten. Toby & Tutter Therapy Dogs. Dwight, Laura, photos by. 2012. (ENG., Illus.). 32p. (J). 17.95 (978-0-9847812-0-1(X)) Toby & Tutter Publishing.

Debra's Dog: 6 Small Books. (gr. k-3). 24.00 (978-0-7635-6229-8(7)) Rigby Education.

Deeley, Patrick. Mo Mhadra Beoga. Fagan, Martin, illus. 2005. (Sraith Sos Ser.: 12). (IRI, ENG & GLE.). 64p. (J). pap. 9.95 (978-0-86278-942-8(7)) O'Brien Pr., Ltd., The IRL. Dist: Dufour Editions, Inc.

DeFelice, Cynthia. The Ghost of Cutler Creek. 2011. (Ghost Mysteries Ser.: 3). (ENG.). 208p. (J). (gr. 3-7). pap. 9.99 (978-0-312-62967-0(2), 9780312629670) Square Fish.

—Wild Life. 2013. (ENG.). 208p. (J). (gr. 3-7). pap. 7.99 (978-1-250-03407-6(8), 9781250034076) Square Fish.

DeFelice, Cynthia C. The Ghost of Cutler Creek. 2006. (Ghost Mysteries Ser.). 181p. (J). (gr. 3-7). 13.60 (978-0-7569-8185-3(9)) Perfection Learning Corp.

Degen, Bruce. I Gotta Draw. Degen, Bruce, illus. 2012. (ENG., Illus.). 40p. (J). (gr. k-4). 16.99 *(978-0-06-028417-6(X))* HarperCollins Pubs.

Dehghanpisheh, Corine. Buddy's Dream. Dehghanpisheh, Corine, illus. 2013. (Illus.). 34p. pap. 12.95 *(978-0-9851930-4-1(2))* Dehghanpisheh, Corine.

Delduce, Karen Blanchard. Poodles in the Park: A Poodle Party. 2009. 20p. 10.49 *(978-1-4490-3724-6(0))* AuthorHouse.

De'Leon, Lunden. Oops Loops. 2006. 28p. pap. 9.95 *(978-1-4327-0114-7(2))* Outskirts Pr., Inc.

Demarest, Jeannie. My Best Friend Troubles. 2009. 28p. pap. 21.99 *(978-1-4415-3236-7(6))* Xlibris Corp.

Demas, Corinne. Here Comes Trouble! Jones, Noah, illus. 2013. (J). *(978-0-545-55449-7(7)*, Scholastic Pr.) Scholastic, Inc.

—Saying Goodbye to Lulu. Hoyt, Ard, illus. 2009. (ENG.). 32p. (J). (gr. -1-3). pap. 7.99 *(978-0-316-04749-4(X))* Little, Brown Bks. for Young Readers.

Dembar Greene, Jacqueline. Speak up, Tommy! Melmon, Deborah, illus. 2012. (Kar-Ben Favorites Ser.). (ENG.). 32p. (J). (gr. -1-3). 7.95 *(978-0-7613-7498-5(1)*, Kar-Ben Publishing) Lerner Publishing Group.

Dembinski, Chris. Maxi the Taxi. 2011. 28p. pap. 24.95 *(978-1-4512-8509-3(4))* America Star Bks.

Deming, Lynette. Day in Matthews Shoes. 2006. 28p. pap. 9.95 *(978-1-4327-0100-0(2))* Outskirts Pr., Inc.

Denega, Danielle. Graduation Day. Johnson, Jay, illus. 2007. (J). pap. *(978-0-439-90900-6(7))* Scholastic, Inc.

Denega, Danielle & Bridwell, Norman. Pumpkin Patch Puppy. 2006. (Illus.). 26p. (J). pap. *(978-0-439-87764-0(4))* Scholastic, Inc.

DePalma, Mary Newell, illus. Bow-Wow Wiggle Waggle. 2012. (ENG.). 32p. (J). 14.00 *(978-0-8028-5408-7(7)*, Eerdmans Bks For Young Readers) Eerdmans, William B. Publishing Co.

dePaola, Tomie. Meet the Barkers: Morgan & Moffat Go to School. dePaola, Tomie, illus. 2003. (Barker Twins Ser.). (ENG., Illus.). 32p. (J). (gr. -1-3). 6.99 *(978-0-14-250083-5(6)*, Puffin Books) Penguin Young Readers Group.

—Meet the Barkers: Morgan & Moffat Go to School. 2005. (J). (gr. k-3). pap. 17.95 incl. audio *(978-0-8045-6934-7(7)*, SAC6934) Spoken Arts, Inc.

Depken, Kristen L. Chase's Space Case. 2016. (Step into Reading Level 1 Ser.). lib. bdg. 14.75 *(978-0-606-38480-3(4))* Turtleback Bks.

—Chase's Space Case (Paw Patrol) Jackson, Mike, illus. 2016. (Step into Reading Ser.). (ENG.). 24p. (J). (gr. -1-1). 4.99 *(978-0-553-53886-1(1)*, Random Hse. Bks. for Young Readers) Random Hse. Children's Bks.

—Pit Crew Pups. Jackson, Mike, illus. 2015. (Step into Reading Ser.). (ENG.). 24p. (J). (gr. -1-1). 4.99 *(978-0-553-50853-6(9)*, Random Hse. Bks. for Young Readers) Random Hse. Children's Bks.

—The Poky Little Puppy. 2015. (Step into Reading Level 1 Ser.). lib. bdg. 13.55 *(978-0-606-36407-2(2))* Turtleback Bks.

—Rubble to the Rescue! (Paw Patrol) Jackson, Mike, illus. 2015. (Step into Reading Ser.). (ENG.). 24p. (J). (gr. -1-1). 4.99 *(978-0-553-52290-7(6)*, Random Hse. Bks. for Young Readers) Random Hse. Children's Bks.

—Rubble's Big Wish (PAW Patrol) Moore, Harry, illus. 2017. (Step into Reading Ser.). (ENG.). 24p. (J). (gr. -1-1). pap. 4.99 *(978-0-399-55884-9(5)*, Random Hse. Bks. for Young Readers) Random Hse. Children's Bks.

DePrisco, Dorothea. Willie & Buster Take the Train. Ansley, Frank, illus. 2003. (Stories to Share Ser.). 10p. (J). 10.95 *(978-1-58117-183-9(8)*, Intervisual/Piggy Toes) Bendon, Inc.

Depucci, Diana M. Lady, 1 vol. Stutz, Chris, illus. 2009. 25p. pap. 24.95 *(978-1-61546-677-1(0))* America Star Bks.

Derksen, Barbara Ann. Alexis Learns to Trust: Shih-Tzu Puppy Adventures. 2007. (J). 9.99 *(978-1-59872-845-3(8))* Instant Pub.

Derrick, Patricia. Dody the Dog Has a Rainbow. Martinez, J-P Loppo, illus. 2007. 32p. 18.95 incl. audio compact disk *(978-1-933818-10-8(7))* Animalations.

deRubertis, Barbara. Dilly Dog's Dizzy Dancing. Alley, R. W., illus. 2010. (Animal Antics A to Z Ser.). 32p. (J). lib. bdg. 22.60 *(978-1-57565-307-5(9))*; (ENG.). (gr. -1-3). pap. 7.95 *(978-1-57565-303-7(6))* Kane Press, Inc.

deRubertis, Barbara & DeRubertis, Barbara. Dilly Dog's Dizzy Dancing. Alley, R. W., illus. 2012. (Animal Antics A to Z Ser.). 32p. (J). (gr. 2 — 1). cd-rom 7.95 *(978-1-57565-397-6(4))* Kane Press, Inc.

Desrosiers, Sylvie. Hocus Pocus. Simard, Rémy, illus. 2011. (Hocus Pocus Ser.). (ENG.). 32p. (J). (gr. -1-2). 16.95 *(978-1-55453-577-4(8))* Kids Can Pr., Ltd. CAN. Dist: Hachette Bk. Group.

DeStefano, Anthony. The Puppy That No One Wanted. Cowdrey, Richard, illus. 2015. (ENG.). 32p. 14.99 *(978-1-61636-928-6(0)*, Servant Bks.) Franciscan Media.

Deutsch, Stacia & Cohon, Rhody. Lucky Phoo. 2013. 182p. pap. *(978-1-927792-28-5(2))* Imajin Bks.

Dewdney, Anna. Grumpy Gloria. Dewdney, Anna, illus. 2006. (ENG., Illus.). 28p. (J). (gr. -1-k). 16.99 *(978-0-670-06123-5(9)*, Viking Books for Young Readers) Penguin Young Readers Group.

Dewin, Howard. Lab to the Rescue! 2009. (Illus.). 77p. (J). *(978-0-545-10484-5(X))* Scholastic, Inc.

—A Star Is Born. 2009. (Illus.). 77p. pap. *(978-0-545-11541-4(8))* Scholastic, Inc.

Di-Nsteins, The Albert. No Reading Allowed. 2012. 32p. pap. *(978-1-77093-477-1(4))* Flowerpot Children's Pr. Inc.

Un Dia de Perros!, 6 packs. (Chiquilibros Ser.). (SPA.). (gr. k-1). 23.00 *(978-0-7635-8602-7(1))* Rigby Education.

Diane Lair, Lair & Lair, Diane. Miss Muggles: The Comical Dog. 2010. 28p. pap. 16.09 *(978-1-4269-2844-4(0))* Trafford Publishing.

DiCamillo, Kate. Because of Winn-Dixie. braille ed. 2003. (J). (gr. 2). spiral bd. *(978-0-616-15263-8(9))* Canadian National Institute for the Blind/Institut National Canadien pour les Aveugles.

—Because of Winn-Dixie. aut. ed. (Because of Winn-Dixie Ser.). (ENG., Illus.). 192p. (J). 2010. (gr. 4-7). 15.99 *(978-0-7636-5007-0(2))* 2010. (gr. 4-7). 50.00 *(978-0-7636-5185-5(0))* 2004. (gr. 3-7). mass mkt. 6.99 *(978-0-7636-2558-0(2))* Candlewick Pr.

—Because of Winn-Dixie. unabr. ed. 2004. 192p. (J). (gr. 4-7). pap. 29.00 incl. audio *(978-0-8072-0707-9(1)*, Listening Library) Random Hse. Audio Publishing Group.

—Il Cane Piú Brutto del Mondo. pap. 22.95 *(978-88-04-50721-5(7))* Mondadori ITA. Dist: Distribooks, Inc.

—Gracias a Winn-Dixie. 2010.Tr. of Because of Winn-Dixie. (SPA.). 152p. (gr. 4-6). pap. 12.99 *(978-84-279-3265-4(0))* Noguer y Caralt Editores, S. A. ESP. Dist: Lectorum Pubns., Inc.

Dickinson, Peter. Chuck & Danielle. 115p. (J). (gr. 3-5). pap. 3.99 *(978-0-8072-1504-3(X)*, Listening Library) Random Hse. Audio Publishing Group.

Diehl, Jean Heilprin. Loon Chase, 1 vol. Freeman, Kathryn S., illus. 2006. (ENG.). 32p. (J). (gr. 1-5). 15.95 *(978-0-9764943-8-6(8))* Arbordale Publishing.

Dig: KinderReaders Individual Title Six-Packs. (Kinderstarters Ser.). 8p. (gr. -1-1). 21.00 *(978-0-7635-8659-1(5))* Rigby Education.

Dillingham, Mike. Rivers Book Two: Through the Eyes of a Blind Sled Dog. 2003. (YA). pap. 13.95 *(978-1-59433-004-9(2))* Publication Consultants.

Dipucchio, Kelly. Antoinette. Robinson, Christian, illus. 2017. (Gaston & Friends Ser.). (ENG.). 40p. (J). (gr. -1-3). 17.99 *(978-1-4814-5783-5(7))* Simon & Schuster Children's Publishing.

—Dog Days of School. Biggs, Brian, illus. 2014. (ENG.). 40p. (J). (gr. 1-3). 16.99 *(978-0-7868-5493-6(6))* Hyperion Bks. for Children.

—Dog Days of School. 2017. (J). lib. bdg. 16.00 ***(978-0-606-39971-5(2))*** Turtleback Bks.

—Dog Days of School [8x8 with Stickers]. Biggs, Brian, illus. 2017. (ENG.). 40p. (J). (gr. -1-k). pap. 5.99 ***(978-1-368-00297-4(8))*** Hyperion Bks. for Children.

—Gaston. Robinson, Christian, illus. 2014. (Gaston & Friends Ser.). (ENG.). 40p. (J). (gr. -1-3). 17.99 *(978-1-4424-5102-5(5)*, Atheneum Bks. for Young Readers) Simon & Schuster Children's Publishing.

—Gastón. 2016. (SPA.). 32p. (J). (gr. k-2). 23.99 ***(978-607-96900-0-7(4))*** Editorial Leetra MEX. Dist: Lectorum Pubns., Inc.

Dipucchio, Kelly. Gaston. Robinson, Christian, illus. 2017. (Gaston & Friends Ser.). (ENG.). 80p. (J). (gr. -1-3). 35.99 *(978-1-5344-0002-3(8)*, Atheneum Bks. for Young Readers) Simon & Schuster Children's Publishing.

Dirst, Tracy. The Adventures of Pixie & Pete: They Meet. 2011. 16p. 9.50 *(978-1-4567-1077-4(X))* AuthorHouse.

Disney Book Group. Puppy Dog Pals Design-A-Dog. Disney Storybook Art Team & Premise Entertainment Staff, illus. 2017. (ENG.). 24p. (J). (gr. -1-k). pap. 4.99 ***(978-1-368-00418-3(0))*** Disney Pr.

—Puppy Dog Pals Hawaii Pug-O. Disney Storybook Art Team & Premise Entertainment Staff, illus. 2017. (ENG.). 24p. (J). (gr. -1-k). pap. 5.99 ***(978-1-368-00419-0(9))*** Disney Pr.

Disney Book Group Staff. Sheriff Callie's Wild West Toby Braves the Bully. Disney Storybook Art Team, illus. 2015. (ENG.). 16p. (J). (gr. -1-k). pap. 6.99 *(978-1-4847-1562-8(4))* Disney Pr.

Disney Press Editors. Peaches Pie, Take a Bath! 2015. (World of Reading Ser.). (J). lib. bdg. 13.55 *(978-0-606-36900-8(7))* Turtleback Bks.

Disney Read-Along. 101 Dalmatians (Live Action) 2008. (Read-Along Ser.). (ENG.). (J). pap. *(978-0-7634-0102-3(1))* Walt Disney Records.

Disney Staff. 101 Dalmatians. (FRE.). 96p. (J). (gr. k-5). pap. 9.95 *(978-0-7859-8847-2(5))* French & European Pubns., Inc.

Ditchfield, Lily K. & Zielski, Juile A. The Witches That Saved the Dogs. 2009. 26p. pap. 12.95 *(978-1-60264-494-6(2))* Virtualbookworm.com Publishing, Inc.

Dixon, Ronald. The Adventures of Nip & Dip, on a Dog Named Duffy. 2010. 28p. 13.99 *(978-1-4490-7533-0(9))* AuthorHouse.

Dmaples. Big Dog, Little Puppy. 2012. 28p. pap. 19.99 *(978-1-4685-6064-0(6))* AuthorHouse.

Dodd, Emma. Dog's Colorful Day: A Messy Story about Colors & Counting. Dodd, Emma, illus. 2003. (ENG., Illus.). 32p. (J). (gr. k-k). 6.99 *(978-0-14-250019-4(4)*, Puffin Books) Penguin Young Readers Group.

Dodd, Emma. On the Farm. 2017. (ENG., Illus.). 12p. (J). (gr. -1-12). bds. 9.99 ***(978-1-86147-838-2(0)***, Armadillo) Anness Publishing GBR. Dist: National Bk. Network.

Dodd, Emma, illus. Dog's ABC: An Alphabet Adventure! 2016. (ENG.). 14p. bds. 14.99 *(978-1-86147-699-9(X)*, Armadillo) Anness Publishing GBR. Dist: National Bk. Network.

—Tick Tock Dog: A Tell the Time Book - with a Special Movable Clock! 2016. (ENG.). 12p. (J). (gr. -1-12). bds. 14.99 *(978-1-86147-718-7(X)*, Armadillo) Anness Publishing GBR. Dist: National Bk. Network.

Dodd, Lynley. Hairy Maclary's Caterwaul Caper. Dodd, Lynley, illus. 2009. (Hairy Maclary & Friends Ser.). (ENG., Illus.). 32p. (J). (gr. -1-2). pap. 6.99 *(978-1-58246-307-0(7)*, Tricycle Pr.) Random Hse. Children's Bks.

—Schnitzel Von Krumm, Dogs Never Climb Trees. 2004. (Gold Star First Readers Ser.). (Illus.). 32p. (gr. -1-3). lib. bdg. 23.00 *(978-0-8368-4092-6(5)*, Gareth Stevens Learning Library) Stevens, Gareth Publishing LLLP.

Doder, Joshua. A Dog Called Grk. 2008. (Grk Bks.). (ENG.). 272p. (J). (gr. 3-7). 6.99 *(978-0-440-42147-4(0)*, Yearling) Random Hse. Children's Bks.

—Grk: Operation Tortoise. 2009. 219p. (J). pap. *(978-0-440-42152-8(7)*, Delacorte Pr) Random House Publishing Group.

—Grk Takes Revenge. 2010. (J). *(978-0-385-90655-5(2))*; *(978-0-385-73723-4(8))* Random House Publishing Group. (Delacorte Pr).

A Dog Day! Individual Title Six-Packs. (Chiquilibros Ser.). (gr. k-1). 23.00 *(978-0-7635-0419-9(X))* Rigby Education.

Doggie Daze. (Illus.). 12p. (J). bds. *(978-2-7643-0126-5(X))* Phidal Publishing, Inc./Editions Phidal, Inc.

A Doggone Good Story. 2006. (J). *(978-0-9779606-0-6(9))* Isaacs, John.

Doggy Heaven's in the Sky! 2004. (J). 4.95 *(978-0-9791362-0-7(2))* Tony Tales.

Dolheguy, Heather. Meg & Mr Biggs - the Magic Cat. 2008. 64p. 32.78 *(978-1-4092-2382-5(5))* Lulu Pr., Inc.

Dominguez, Angela. Santiago Stays. 2013. (ENG., Illus.). 32p. (J). (gr. -1-k). 13.95 *(978-1-4197-0821-3(X)*, Abrams Appleseed) Abrams, Inc.

Donaldson, Julia. Wrong Kind of Bark. Parsons, Garry, illus. 2004. (Red Bananas Ser.). (ENG.). 48p. (J). (gr. k-2). pap. 5.99 *(978-1-4052-1062-1(1))* Egmont Bks., Ltd. GBR. Dist: Independent Pubs. Group.

Donovan, Dawn. Nosey Rosie. 2011. 28p. pap. 14.00 *(978-1-4634-1542-6(7))* AuthorHouse.

Don't Worry: Individual Title Six-Packs. (Literatura 2000 Ser.). (gr. 2-3). 33.00 *(978-0-7635-0167-9(0))* Rigby Education.

Doreen Norberg. The Soldier's Dog. 2010. 24p. pap. 15.99 *(978-1-4535-0898-5(8))* Xlibris Corp.

Dormer, Frank W. Click! Dormer, Frank W., illus. 2016. (ENG., Illus.). 38p. (J). (-k). 17.99 *(978-0-451-47644-9(1)*, Viking Books for Young Readers) Penguin Young Readers Group.

Doty, Jean Slaughter. Gabriel. 2012. (ENG.). 144p. (YA). (gr. 7). pap. 8.99 *(978-1-4424-8609-6(0)*, Simon & Schuster Bks. For Young Readers) Simon & Schuster Bks. For Young Readers.

Doudna, Kelly. Doggie Pants, 1 vol. Haberstroh, Anne, illus. 2006. (Animal Tales Ser.). 24p. (J). (gr. k-3). (ENG.). lib. bdg. 24.21 *(978-1-59679-931-8(5)*, SandCastle); pap. 48.42 *(978-1-59679-932-5(3))* ABDO Publishing Co.

Douglas, Rich. The Secret of the Dogs. 2008. (ENG.). 266p. pap. 12.50 *(978-1-4196-8783-9(2))* CreateSpace Independent Publishing Platform.

Dowell, Frances O'Roark. Blasts Off! McDaniels, Preston, illus. 2011. (From the Highly Scientific Notebooks of Phineas L. MacGuire Ser.). (ENG.). 224p. (J). (gr. 3-7). pap. 7.99 *(978-1-4424-2204-9(1)*, Atheneum Bks. for Young Readers) Simon & Schuster Children's Publishing.

—Trouble the Water. (ENG.). (J). (gr. 4-8). 2017. 304p. pap. 7.99 *(978-1-4814-2464-6(5))* 2016. (Illus.). 288p. 16.99 *(978-1-4814-2463-9(7))* Simon & Schuster Children's Publishing.

Dower, Laura. Sunny & the Secret Passage. 2013. (Palace Puppies Ser.: 4). (J). lib. bdg. 14.75 *(978-0-606-35108-9(6)*, Turtleback) Turtleback Bks.

Downie, David. David & Jacko. Tatsi, Andreanna, tr. Seroya, Tea, illus. 2012. 52p. pap. *(978-1-922159-24-3(7))*; pap. *(978-1-922159-15-1(8))* Blue Peg Publishing.

—David & Jacko. Ivanova, Kalina, tr. Seroya, Tea, illus. 2012. 52p. pap. *(978-1-922159-01-4(8))* Blue Peg Publishing.

—David & Jacko. Seroya, Tea, illus. 2012. 52p. pap. *(978-1-922159-99-1(9))* Blue Peg Publishing.

Doyle, Arthur Conan. Le Chien des Baskerville.Tr. of Hound of the Baskervilles. (FRE.). pap. 16.95 *(978-2-07-051346-8(7))* Gallimard, Editions FRA. Dist: Distribooks, Inc.

—The Hound of the Baskervilles. Harvey, Bob, illus. 2004. (Paperback Classics Ser.). 158p. (J). (gr. 5). lib. bdg. 12.95 *(978-1-58086-605-7(0))* EDC Publishing.

Doyle, Roddy. Brilliant. Hughes, Emily, illus. 2015. (ENG.). 192p. (J). (gr. 3-7). 16.95 *(978-1-4197-1479-5(1)*, Amulet Bks.) Abrams, Inc.

Draeger, Manuela. In the Time of the Blue Ball. Evenson, Brian, tr. 2011. 134p. pap. 16.00 *(978-0-9844693-3-8(8))* Dorothy, a publishing project.

Dragonheart, Jesse C. Y. When I Grow Up. 2008. 28p. per. 24.95 *(978-1-4241-8737-9(0))* America Star Bks.

Drake, R. C. Let's Find a Toy for Moo Moo the Mutdog. 2011. 24p. pap. 24.95 *(978-1-4560-0881-9(1))* America Star Bks.

Draper, Melissa J. Holly the Christmas Collie. Kravanek, J. Elise, illus. 2004. 63p. (J). *(978-0-9741081-3-1(8))* Acres Publishing.

Drogo, Susette. Five Blessings. Lukas, Mary, illus. 2008. 24p. (J). pap. 15.00 *(978-0-9800611-8-5(0))* Orr Bks.

Drummond, Ree. Charlie & the Christmas Kitty. deGroat, Diane, illus. 2012. (Charlie the Ranch Dog Ser.). (ENG.). 40p. (J). (gr. -1-3). 17.99 *(978-0-06-199657-3(2))* HarperCollins Pubs.

—Charlie & the New Baby. deGroat, Diane, illus. 2014. (Charlie the Ranch Dog Ser.). (ENG.). 40p. (J). (gr. -1-3). 17.99 *(978-0-06-229750-1(3))* HarperCollins Pubs.

—Charlie Goes to School. deGroat, Diane, illus. 2013. (Charlie the Ranch Dog Ser.). (ENG.). 40p. (J). (gr. -1-3). 17.99 *(978-0-06-221920-6(0))* HarperCollins Pubs.

—Charlie Goes to the Doctor. 2014. (I Can Read! Level 1 Ser.). (J). lib. bdg. 13.55 *(978-0-606-35492-9(1))* Turtleback Bks.

—Charlie Plays Ball. deGroat, Diane, illus. 2015. (Charlie the Ranch Dog Ser.). (ENG.). 40p. (J). (gr. -1-3). 17.99 *(978-0-06-229752-5(X))* HarperCollins Pubs.

—Charlie the Ranch Dog. deGroat, Diane, illus. 2011. (Charlie the Ranch Dog Ser.). (ENG.). 40p. (J). (gr. -1-3). 17.99 *(978-0-06-199655-9(6))* HarperCollins Pubs.

—Charlie the Ranch Dog. 2013. (I Can Read! Level 1 Ser.). (J). lib. bdg. 13.55 *(978-0-606-31822-8(4)*, Turtleback) Turtleback Bks.

—Charlie the Ranch Dog: Charlie Goes to the Doctor. deGroat, Diane, illus. 2014. (I Can Read Level 1 Ser.). (ENG.). 32p. (J). (gr. -1-3). pap. 3.99 *(978-0-06-221917-6(0))* HarperCollins Pubs.

—Charlie the Ranch Dog: Charlie's New Friend. deGroat, Diane, illus. 2014. (I Can Read Level 1 Ser.). (ENG.). 32p. (J). (gr. -1-3). 16.99 *(978-0-06-221915-2(4))*; pap. 3.99 *(978-0-06-221914-5(6))* HarperCollins Pubs.

—Charlie the Ranch Dog: Charlie's Snow Day. deGroat, Diane, illus. 2013. (I Can Read Level 1 Ser.). (ENG.). 32p. (J). (gr. -1-3). 16.99 *(978-0-06-221912-1(X))*; pap. 3.99 *(978-0-06-221911-4(1))* HarperCollins Pubs.

—Charlie the Ranch Dog: Rock Star. deGroat, Diane, illus. 2015. (I Can Read Level 1 Ser.). (ENG.). 32p. (J). (gr. -1-3). pap. 3.99 *(978-0-06-234777-0(2))* HarperCollins Pubs.

—Charlie the Ranch Dog: Stuck in the Mud. deGroat, Diane & Whipple, Rick, illus. 2015. (I Can Read Level 1 Ser.). (ENG.). 32p. (J). (gr. -1-3). 16.99 *(978-0-06-234775-6(6))*; pap. 3.99 *(978-0-06-234774-9(8))* HarperCollins Pubs.

—Charlie the Ranch Dog: Where's the Bacon? deGroat, Diane, illus. 2013. (I Can Read Level 1 Ser.). (ENG.). 32p. (J). (gr. -1-3). 16.99 *(978-0-06-221909-1(X))*; pap. 3.99 *(978-0-06-221908-4(1))* HarperCollins Pubs.

—Charlie's New Friend. 2014. (I Can Read! Level 1 Ser.). (J). lib. bdg. 13.55 *(978-0-606-35041-9(1)*, Turtleback) Turtleback Bks.

—Charlie's Snow Day. 2013. (I Can Read! Level 1 Ser.). (J). lib. bdg. 13.55 *(978-0-606-32161-7(6)*, Turtleback) Turtleback Bks.

Drummond, Sarah, illus. Raven & the Red Ball. 2013. (ENG.). 28p. (J). 9.95 *(978-0-7649-6609-5(X))* Pomegranate Communications, Inc.

Duckers, John. The Amazing Adventures of the Silly Six. 2013. (Illus.). 188p. pap. *(978-1-78148-626-9(3))* Grosvenor Hse. Publishing Ltd.

Dudek, Mike. The Fairytale of the Morley Dog. 2007. (Illus.). 40p. (YA). spiral bd. 2.49 *(978-0-9740380-1-8(6))* Dudek, Mike.

Duerr, Doug. The Adventures of Jazz & Elliott: Danielle goes to the Magical Land of Roop-E-Doo. 2010. 29p. (J). pap. 17.95 *(978-1-4327-5405-1(X))* Outskirts Pr., Inc.

Duff, Ms. Michelle Ann. Five Cats, One Dog, a Motorcycle & a Lady in a Hot Pink Jacket. 2012. 146p. pap. *(978-0-9685706-7-8(4))* Mad8 Publishing.

Duffett-Smith, James. Stella & Steve Travel Through Space! Straker, Bethany, illus. 2014. (ENG.). 32p. (J). (gr. -1-k). 14.95 *(978-1-62873-815-5(4)*, Sky Pony Pr.) Skyhorse Publishing Co., Inc.

Duffey, Betsy. Boy in the Doghouse. 2011. (ENG.). 96p. (J). (gr. 4-6). pap. 6.99 *(978-1-4424-5226-8(9)*, Simon & Schuster Bks. For Young Readers) Simon & Schuster Bks. For Young Readers.

Duffy, Jacqueline Ann. Dillon the Dog Finds His Family. 2008. 24p. pap. 24.95 *(978-1-60563-331-2(3))* America Star Bks.

Dumin, Jennifer. Wolfie & Freddie: the New Puppy. 2006. (ENG.). 44p. per. 22.65 *(978-1-4257-0680-7(0))* Xlibris Corp.

Duncan, Al. Rescue Dog. Panse, Sonal, illus. 2005. (J). per. 10.00 *(978-0-9754298-6-0(8)*, Ithaca Pr.) Authors & Artists Publishers of New York, Inc.

Duncan, Brenda. Reese - the Dog Who Almost Ruined Christmas. 2012. 24p. pap. 17.99 *(978-1-4772-6105-7(2))* AuthorHouse.

Duncan, Lois. Hotel for Dogs. 2008. (ENG.). 192p. (J). (gr. 3-7). 6.99 *(978-0-545-10792-1(X))*; (Illus.). 16.99 *(978-0-545-10923-9(X))* Scholastic, Inc. (Scholastic Paperbacks).

Dungy, Tony & Dungy, Lauren. Ruby's New Home. Newton, Vanessa Brantley, illus. 2011. (Tony & Lauren Dungy Ready-To-Reads Ser.). (ENG.). 32p. (J). (gr. k-2). pap. 3.99 *(978-1-4169-9784-9(9))*; lib. bdg. 15.99 *(978-1-4424-2948-2(8))* Simon Spotlight. (Simon Spotlight).

Dunkle, Clare B. The Walls Have Eyes. 2009. (ENG.). 240p. (YA). (gr. 7). 16.99 *(978-1-4169-5379-1(5)*, Atheneum Bks. for Young Readers) Simon & Schuster Children's Publishing.

Dunn-Dern, Lisa. Dr. Duncan Dog on Duty! Yomtob, Andrea, illus. 2007. (J). (gr. -1-3). per. 16.99 *(978-1-933156-20-0(1)*, Visikid Bks.) GSVQ Publishing.

Dunn, Phoebe & Dunn, Judy. The Little Puppy. 2015. (ENG., Illus.). 14p. (J). (— 1). bds. 6.99 *(978-0-553-51139-0(4)*, Random Hse. Bks. for Young Readers) Random Hse. Children's Bks.

Dwyer, Joe & Levison, Doug. Daniel - the Miracle Beagle: A Story for Young Readers. 2012. 34p. pap. 14.95 *(978-1-4575-1381-7(1))* Dog Ear Publishing, LLC.

Dyan, Penelope. Gabriela's Dogs — -Because Happiness Really Is a Warm Puppy! Dyan, Penelope, illus. 2008. (Illus.). 44p. pap. 11.95 *(978-1-935118-37-4(4))* Bellissima Publishing, LLC.

—Mikey & Me & the Fly — -the Continuing Story of a Girl & Her Dog. Dyan, Penelope, illus. 2010. (Illus.). 50p. pap. 14.95 *(978-1-935118-94-7(3))* Bellissima Publishing, LLC.

—Mikey & Me & the Frogs — -the Continuing Story of a Girl & Her Dog. Dyan, Penelope, illus. 2010. (Illus.). 50p. pap. 14.95 *(978-1-935118-93-0(5))* Bellissima Publishing, LLC.

—Mikey & Me & the Spider — -the Continuing Story of a Girl & Her Dog. Dyan, Penelope, illus. 2010. (Illus.). 50p. pap. 14.95 *(978-1-935118-95-4(1))* Bellissima Publishing, LLC.

—Mikey & Me & the Valentines — -the Continuing Story of a Girl & Her Dog. Dyan, Penelope, illus. 2010. (Illus.). 50p. pap. 14.95 *(978-1-935118-96-1(X))* Bellissima Publishing, LLC.

D'yans, Masha. Razzle-Dazzle Ruby. D'yans, Masha, illus. 2011. (ENG., Illus.). 20p. (J). (— 1). bds. 17.99 *(978-0-545-22500-7(0))* Scholastic, Inc.

Dzidrums, Christine. Timmy Adopts a Girl Dog. Lopez, Lyle & Dzidrums, Joseph, illus. 2012. 48p. pap. 6.99 *(978-1-938438-03-5(5))* Creative Media Publishing.

Eagle, Rita. Sniffy the Beagle. Rasmussen, Gerry, illus. 2007. (ENG.). 44p. per. 13.95 *(978-1-59800-537-0(5))* Outskirts Pr., Inc.

Earhart, Kristin. Puppy Powers #2: Wag, You're It! 2014. (Puppy Powers Ser.: 2). (ENG., Illus.). 96p. (J). (gr. 2-5). pap. 4.99 *(978-0-545-61760-4(X)*, Scholastic Paperbacks) Scholastic, Inc.

—Puppy Powers #3: Take a Bow-Wow. 2014. (Puppy Powers Ser.: 3). (ENG.). 96p. (J). (gr. 2-5). pap. 4.99 *(978-0-545-61761-1(8)*, Scholastic Paperbacks) Scholastic, Inc.

—Puppy Powers #4: Hide & Go Fetch. 2014. (Puppy Powers Ser.: 4). (ENG.). 96p. (J). (gr. 2-5). pap. 4.99 *(978-0-545-61762-8(6)*, Scholastic Paperbacks) Scholastic, Inc.

Eastman, P. D. Big Dog ... Little Dog: A Bedtime Story. 2006. (Bright & Early Board Books(TM) Ser.). (ENG., Illus.). 24p. (J). (— 1). bds. 4.99 *(978-0-375-87539-7(5))*, Random Hse. Bks. for Young Readers) Random Hse. Children's Bks.

—Go, Dog. Go! Eastman, P. D., illus. 2008. (ENG., Illus.). 64p. pap. *(978-0-00-722546-0(6))* HarperCollins Pubs. Ltd.

—Go, Dog. Go! 2015. (Big Bright & Early Board Book Ser.). (ENG., Illus.). 24p. (J). (gr. -1-2). bds. 6.99 *(978-0-553-52109-2(8)*, Random Hse. Bks. for Young Readers) Random Hse. Children's Bks.

—Ve, Perro, Ve! Perdomo, Adolfo Perez, tr. 2003. (Bright & Early Board Books(TM) Ser.).Tr. of Go, Dog, Go! (SPA & ENG., Illus.). 24p. (J). (— 1). bds. 4.99 *(978-0-375-82361-9(1)*, Random House Para Ninos) Random Hse. Children's Bks.

Eastman, P. D. & Eastman, Tony. Big Dog... Little Dog. Eastman, P. D. & Eastman, Tony, illus. 2003. (Beginner Books(R) Ser.). (ENG., Illus.). 48p. (J). (gr. -1-2). 9.99 *(978-0-375-82297-1(6)*, Random Hse. Bks. for Young Readers) Random Hse. Children's Bks.

C D

Eastman, P. D. & Frith, Michael. The Little Red Box of Bright & Early Board Books. 2014. (Bright & Early Board Books(TM) Ser.). (ENG., Illus.). 24p. (J). (— 1). bds. 19.96 (978-0-385-39207-5(9), Random Hse. Bks. for Young Readers) Random Hse. Children's Bks.

Eastman, Peter. Fred & Ted Go Camping. 2005. (Beginner Books(R) Ser.). (ENG., Illus.). 48p. (J). (gr. -1-2). 9.99 (978-0-375-82965-9(2), Random Hse. Bks. for Young Readers) Random Hse. Children's Bks.

—Fred & Ted's Road Trip. 2011. (Beginner Books(R) Ser.). (ENG., Illus.). 48p. (J). (gr. -1-2). 9.99 (978-0-375-86764-4(3), Random Hse. Bks. for Young Readers) Random Hse. Children's Bks.

Edgar, Amy. The Muddy Puppy (Scholastic Reader, Level 2: Pet Charms #1) Tejido, Jomike, illus. 2017. (Scholastic Reader, Level 2 Ser.: 1). (ENG.). 32p. (J). (gr. k-2). pap. 5.99 (978-1-338-04589-5(X)) Scholastic, Inc.

Edgin, Brenda. Little Winston & his Big Adventures in Natchez: Down in the Bayou. 2011. 16p. 12.95 (978-1-4567-4421-2(6)) AuthorHouse.

Edmonds, Lin. Patric the Pony & the Flash of Lightning. 2009. 34p. pap. 13.99 (978-1-4389-6302-0(5)) AuthorHouse.

—Patric the Pony & the Race for Freedom. 2011. 32p. pap. 15.50 (978-1-4670-3662-7(5)) AuthorHouse.

Edward, J. P. Bobby & Buddy Friends for Life. Hose, Ryan, illus. 2011. 16p. pap. 24.95 (978-1-4560-7520-0(9)) America Star Bks.

Edwards, Karl Newsom. I Got a New Friend. 2017. (ENG., Illus.). 32p. (J). (gr. -1-3). 16.99 (978-0-399-55700-2(8), Knopf Bks. for Young Readers) Random Hse. Children's Bks.

Edwards, Nicholas. The Adventures of Santa Paws. 2010. (Santa Paws Ser.). (ENG.). 336p. (J). (gr. 3-7). pap. 7.99 (978-0-545-22551-9(5), Scholastic Paperbacks) Scholastic, Inc.

—Dog Whisperer: Storm Warning. 2011. (Dog Whisperer Ser.: 2). (ENG.). 224p. (J). (gr. 3-7). pap. 9.99 (978-0-312-37095-4(4), 9780312370954) Square Fish.

—Dog Whisperer: the Ghost. 2012. (Dog Whisperer Ser.: 3). (ENG.). 224p. (J). (gr. 3-7). pap. 9.99 (978-0-312-37096-1(2), 9780312370961) Square Fish.

Edwards, Nicholas & White, Ellen Emerson. The Rescue. 2009. (Dog Whisperer Ser.: 1). (ENG.). 224p. (J). (gr. 3-7). pap. 9.99 (978-0-312-36768-8(6), 9780312367688) Square Fish.

Edwards, S. Neil. My Dog, Digger. 2006. 122p. pap. 19.95 (978-1-4241-0514-4(5)) America Star Bks.

Eggleton, Jill. Big Red Comes to Stay. Cammell, Sandra, illus. 2004. (Rigby Sails Early Ser.). (ENG.). 16p. (gr. 1-2). pap. 6.95 (978-0-7578-9303-2(1)) Houghton Mifflin Harcourt Publishing Co.

Ehlert, Lois. RRRalph. Ehlert, Lois, illus. 2011. (ENG., Illus.). 40p. (J). (gr. -1-1). 17.99 (978-1-4424-1305-4(0), Beach Lane Bks.) Beach Lane Bks.

Ehrenhaft, Daniel. The Last Dog on Earth. 2004. (ENG.). 240p. (J). (gr. 3-7). pap. 6.99 (978-0-440-41950-1(6), Yearling) Random Hse. Children's Bks.

Eitner-England, Lita. Bullmina the Courageous Bulldog to the Rescue. 2010. 588p. 33.99 (978-1-4490-8225-3(4)); pap. 15.00 (978-1-4490-8224-6(6)) AuthorHouse.

Elchgar, Yasmin. Noonoo the Doctor. 2013. 20p. pap. 13.77 (978-1-4907-1037-2(X)) Trafford Publishing.

Elden, Roxanna. Rudy's New Human. Seehafer, Ginger, illus. 2016. (ENG.). 32p. (J). (gr. -1-k). 16.99 (978-1-63450-189-7(6), Sky Pony Pr.) Skyhorse Publishing Co., Inc.

Eley, Kitt. Cindy Lou. 2013. 24p. pap. 24.95 (978-1-4626-9367-2(9)) America Star Bks.

Elizabeth, Julie & Elizabeth, Annelise. Take Care of Our Friend, Baby Dog. 2012. 24p. pap. 13.95 (978-1-61493-115-7(1)) Peppertree Pr., The.

Elliott, Emilia. Patricia. 2007. 64p. per. (978-1-4065-2466-6(2)) Dodo Pr.

Elliott, Rebecca. Dalmatian in a Digger. 2017. (Fiction Picture Bks.). (ENG.). 32p. (gr. k-2). lib. bdg. 27.99 (978-1-5158-0684-4(7), Fiction Picture Bks.) Picture Window Bks.

Ellis, Dianne. Rusty Rumble & His Smelly Socks. 2012. 36p. pap. 32.70 (978-1-4691-9914-6(9)) Xlibris Corp.

—Rusty Rumble's Day at the Beach. 2012. 40p. pap. 32.70 (978-1-4797-0360-9(5)) Xlibris Corp.

Ellis, Jesse. My Pal Willie: Willie Gets a Home. 2013. 24p. pap. 24.95 (978-1-63000-876-5(1)) America Star Bks.

Ellis, Rolant. Cyfres Cled: Castell Marwolaeth Boenus AC Erchyll. 2005. (WEL., Illus.). 75p. pap. (978-0-86243-377-2(0)) Y Lolfa.

Ellsberry, Sharon. The Spaniel Family Goes to the State Fair. Espinosa, Chris, illus. 2004. 24p. (J). 9.00 (978-0-9724637-2-0(0)) Sky Rocket Pr.

Eman, Leisa M. Pugsley's Imagination. 2007. 52p. per. 8.95 (978-0-595-44247-8(1)) iUniverse, Inc.

Emerson, Scott. The Case of the Cat with the Missing Ear: From the Notebooks of Edward R. Smithfield, D. V. M. Mullett, Viv, illus. 2011. (Adventures of Samuel Blackthorne Ser.: 1). (ENG.). 240p. (J). (gr. 3-7). pap. 11.99 (978-0-689-87615-8(7), Simon & Schuster Bks. For Young Readers) Simon & Schuster Bks. For Young Readers.

Emily Breaks Free - Evaluation Guide. 2006. (J). (978-1-55942-404-2(4)) Witcher Productions.

Engel, Natalie. Marely & Me - Meet Marley. 2008. (I Can Read Level 1 Ser.). (ENG.). 32p. (J). (gr. k-3). pap. 3.99 (978-0-06-170439-0(3)) HarperCollins Pubs.

Engle, Dawn A. Ella's Golden Heart Goes to Camp. 2011. 40p. pap. 14.95 (978-1-60911-392-6(6), Eloquent Bks.) Strategic Book Publishing & Rights Agency (SBPRA).

Engle, Dawn D. Ella's Golden Hearts. 2009. 40p. pap. 14.75 (978-1-60860-218-6(4), Strategic Bk. Publishing) Strategic Book Publishing & Rights Agency (SBPRA).

Engle, Margarita. Mountain Dog. Ivanov, Aleksey & Ivanov, Olga, illus. 2013. (ENG.). 224p. (J). (gr. 3-7). 17.99 (978-0-8050-9516-6(0), 9780805095166, Holt, Henry & Co. Bks. For Young Readers) Holt, Henry & Co.

—Mountain Dog. Ivanov, Aleksey & Ivanov, Olga, illus. 2014. (ENG.). 240p. (J). (gr. 3-7). pap. 7.99 (978-1-250-04424-2(3), 9781250044242) Square Fish.

—When You Wander: A Search-and-Rescue Dog Story. Morgan, Mary, illus. 2013. (ENG.). 32p. (J). (gr. -1-3). 16.99 (978-0-8050-9312-4(5), 9780805093124, Holt, Henry & Co. Bks. For Young Readers) Holt, Henry & Co.

Englert, June Scott. My Story by Jake, 1 vol. 2010. 48p. pap. 16.95 (978-1-4489-5308-0(1)) America Star Bks.

English, Karen. Dog Days. Freeman, Laura, illus. 2014. (Carver Chronicles Ser.). (ENG.). 128p. (J). (gr. 1-4). pap. 5.99 (978-0-544-33912-5(6), HMH Books For Young Readers) Houghton Mifflin Harcourt Publishing Co.

Erickson, Carol. Not a Used Dog, at All. 2009. 32p. pap. 14.49 (978-1-4389-5204-8(X)) AuthorHouse.

Erickson, John R. The Big Question. Holmes, Gerald L., illus. 2012. 128p. (J). pap. (978-1-59188-160-5(9)) Maverick Bks.

—The Big Question. Holmes, Gerald L., illus. 2012. (Hank the Cowdog Ser.: Vol. 60). (ENG.). 128p. (J). (gr. 3-6). 15.99 (978-1-59188-260-2(5)) Maverick Bks., Inc.

—The Case of the Black-Hooded Hangmans. Holmes, Gerald L., illus. 2011. (Hank the Cowdog Ser.). (ENG.). 113p. (J). (gr. 3-6). pap. 5.99 (978-1-59188-124-7(2)) Maverick Bks., Inc.

—The Case of the Blazing Sky. Holmes, Gerald L., illus. 2011. (Hank the Cowdog Ser.). (ENG.). 129p. (J). (gr. 3-6). pap. 5.99 (978-1-59188-151-3(X)) Maverick Bks., Inc.

—The Case of the Booby-Trapped Pickup. Holmes, Gerald L., illus. 2011. (Hank the Cowdog Ser.). (ENG.). 129p. (J). (gr. 3-6). pap. 5.99 (978-1-59188-149-0(8)) Maverick Bks., Inc.

—The Case of the Burrowing Robot. Holmes, Gerald L., illus. 2011. (Hank the Cowdog Ser.). (ENG.). 125p. (J). (gr. 3-6). pap. 5.99 (978-1-59188-142-1(0)) Maverick Bks., Inc.

—The Case of the Car-Barkaholic Dog. Holmes, Gerald L., illus. 2011. (Hank the Cowdog Ser.). (ENG.). 115p. (J). (gr. 3-6). pap. 5.99 (978-1-59188-117-9(X)) Maverick Bks., Inc.

—The Case of the Coyote Invasion. Holmes, Gerald L., illus. 2011. (Hank the Cowdog Ser.: No. 56). (ENG.). 132p. (J). (gr. 3-6). pap. 5.99 (978-1-59188-156-8(0)) Maverick Bks., Inc.

—The Case of the Deadly Ha-Ha Game. Holmes, Gerald L., illus. 2011. (Hank the Cowdog Ser.). (ENG.). 128p. (J). (gr. 3-6). pap. 5.99 (978-1-59188-137-7(4)) Maverick Bks., Inc.

—The Case of the Dinosaur Birds. Holmes, Gerald L., illus. 2011. (Hank the Cowdog Ser.). (ENG.). 125p. (J). (gr. 3-6). pap. 5.99 (978-1-59188-154-4(4)) Maverick Bks., Inc.

—The Case of the Double Bumblebee Sting. Holmes, Gerald L., illus. 2011. (Hank the Cowdog Ser.: No. 22). (ENG.). 114p. (J). (gr. 3-6). pap. 5.99 (978-1-59188-122-3(6)) Maverick Bks., Inc.

—The Case of the Falling Sky. Holmes, Gerald L., illus. 2011. (Hank the Cowdog Ser.: No. 45). (ENG.). 129p. (J). (gr. 3-6). pap. 5.99 (978-1-59188-145-2(5)) Maverick Bks., Inc.

—The Case of the Fiddle-Playing Fox. Holmes, Gerald L., illus. 2011. (Hank the Cowdog Ser.: No. 12). (ENG.). 118p. (J). (gr. 3-6). pap. 5.99 (978-1-59188-112-4(9)) Maverick Bks., Inc.

—The Case of the Halloween Ghost. Holmes, Gerald L., illus. 2011. (Hank the Cowdog Ser.). (ENG.). 123p. (J). (gr. 3-6). pap. 5.99 (978-1-59188-109-4(9)) Maverick Bks., Inc.

—The Case of the Haystack Kitties. Holmes, Gerald L., illus. 2011. (Hank the Cowdog Ser.). (ENG.). 123p. (J). (gr. 3-6). pap. 5.99 (978-1-59188-130-8(7)) Maverick Bks., Inc.

—The Case of the Hooking Bull. Holmes, Gerald L., illus. 2011. (Hank the Cowdog Ser.). (ENG.). 119p. (J). (gr. 3-6). pap. 5.99 (978-1-59188-118-6(8)) Maverick Bks., Inc.

—The Case of the Kidnapped Collie. Holmes, Gerald L., illus. 2011. (Hank the Cowdog Ser.). (ENG.). 113p. (J). (gr. 3-6). pap. 5.99 (978-1-59188-126-1(9)) Maverick Bks., Inc.

—The Case of the Measled Cowboy. Holmes, Gerald L., illus. 2011. (Hank the Cowdog Ser.: No. 33). (ENG.). 126p. (J). (gr. 3-6). pap. 5.99 (978-1-59188-133-9(1)) Maverick Bks., Inc.

—The Case of the Midnight Rustler. Holmes, Gerald L., illus. 2011. (Hank the Cowdog Ser.: No. 19). (ENG.). 113p. (J). (gr. 3-6). pap. 5.99 (978-1-59188-119-3(6)) Maverick Bks., Inc.

—The Case of the Missing Bird Dog. Holmes, Gerald L., illus. 2011. (Hank the Cowdog Ser.: No. 40). (ENG.). 126p. (J). (gr. 3-6). pap. 5.99 (978-1-59188-140-7(4)) Maverick Bks., Inc.

—The Case of the Missing Cat. Holmes, Gerald L., illus. 2011. (Hank the Cowdog Ser.: No. 15). (ENG.). 114p. (J). (gr. 3-6). pap. 5.99 (978-1-59188-115-5(3)) Maverick Bks., Inc.

—The Case of the Monkey Burglar. Holmes, Gerald L., illus. 2011. (Hank the Cowdog Ser.: No. 48). (ENG.). 129p. (J). (gr. 3-6). pap. 5.99 (978-1-59188-148-3(X)) Maverick Bks., Inc.

—The Case of the Mysterious Voice. Holmes, Gerald L., illus. 2012. (Hank the Cowdog (Quality) Ser.: Vol. 58). (ENG.). 123p. (J). (gr. 3-6). pap. 5.99 (978-1-59188-158-2(7)) Maverick Bks., Inc.

—The Case of the Night-Stalking Bone Monster. Holmes, Gerald L., illus. 2011. (Hank the Cowdog Ser.). (ENG.). 115p. (J). (gr. 3-6). pap. 5.99 (978-1-59188-127-8(7)) Maverick Bks., Inc.

—The Case of the One-Eyed Killer Stud Horse. Holmes, Gerald L., illus. 2011. (Hank the Cowdog Ser.: No. 8). (ENG.). 120p. (J). (gr. 3-6). pap. 5.99 (978-1-59188-108-7(0)) Maverick Bks., Inc.

—The Case of the Perfect Dog. Holmes, Gerald L., illus. 2012. 127p. (J). (978-1-59188-259-6(1)) Maverick Bks.

—The Case of the Perfect Dog. Holmes, Gerald L., illus. 2012. (Hank the Cowdog (Quality) Ser.). (ENG.). 127p. (J). (gr. 3-6). pap. 5.99 (978-1-59188-159-9(5)) Maverick Bks., Inc.

—The Case of the Raging Rottweiler. Holmes, Gerald L., illus. 2011. (Hank the Cowdog Ser.). (ENG.). 131p. (J). (gr. 3-6). pap. 5.99 (978-1-59188-136-0(6)) Maverick Bks., Inc.

—The Case of the Saddle House Robbery. Holmes, Gerald L., illus. 2011. (Hank the Cowdog Ser.: No. 35). (ENG.). 125p. (J). (gr. 3-6). pap. 5.99 (978-1-59188-135-3(8)) Maverick Bks., Inc.

—The Case of the Secret Weapon. Holmes, Gerald L., illus. 2011. (Hank the Cowdog Ser.). (ENG.). 125p. (J). (gr. 3-6). pap. 5.99 (978-1-59188-155-1(2)) Maverick Bks., Inc.

—The Case of the Shipwrecked Tree. Holmes, Gerald L., illus. 2011. (Hank the Cowdog Ser.: No. 41). (ENG.). 119p. (J). (gr. 3-6). pap. 5.99 (978-1-59188-141-4(2)) Maverick Bks., Inc.

—The Case of the Swirling Killer Tornado. Holmes, Gerald L., illus. 2011. (Hank the Cowdog Ser.). (ENG.). 112p. (J). (gr. 3-6). pap. 5.99 (978-1-59188-125-4(0)) Maverick Bks., Inc.

—The Case of the Tender Cheeping Chickies. Holmes, Gerald L., illus. 2011. (Hank the Cowdog Ser.). (ENG.). 129p. (J). (gr. 3-6). pap. 5.99 (978-1-59188-147-6(1)) Maverick Bks., Inc.

—The Case of the Three Rings. Holmes, Gerald L., illus. 2014. 124p. (J). pap. (978-1-59188-164-3(1)) Maverick Bks., Inc.

—The Case of the Tricky Trap. Holmes, Gerald L., illus. 2011. (Hank the Cowdog Ser.). (ENG.). 126p. (J). (gr. 3-6). pap. 5.99 (978-1-59188-146-9(3)) Maverick Bks., Inc.

—The Case of the Twisted Kitty. Holmes, Gerald L., illus. 2004. (Hank the Cowdog Ser.: No. 43). 131p. (J). lib. bdg. 17.00 (978-1-4242-1600-0(1)) Fitzgerald Bks.

—The Case of the Twisted Kitty. Holmes, Gerald L., illus. 2011. (Hank the Cowdog Ser.). (ENG.). 131p. (J). (gr. 3-6). pap. 5.99 (978-1-59188-143-8(9)) Maverick Bks., Inc.

—The Case of the Vampire Cat. Holmes, Gerald L., illus. 2011. (Hank the Cowdog Ser.). (ENG.). 115p. (J). (gr. 3-6). pap. 5.99 (978-1-59188-121-6(8)) Maverick Bks., Inc.

—The Case of the Vampire Vacuum Sweeper. Holmes, Gerald L., illus. 2011. (Hank the Cowdog Ser.). (ENG.). 119p. (J). (gr. 3-6). pap. 5.99 (978-1-59188-129-2(3)) Maverick Bks., Inc.

—The Case of the Vanishing Fishhook. Holmes, Gerald L., illus. 2011. (Hank the Cowdog Ser.: No. 31). (ENG.). 124p. (J). (gr. 3-6). pap. 5.99 (978-1-59188-131-5(5)) Maverick Bks., Inc.

—The Curse of the Incredible Priceless Corncob. Holmes, Gerald L., illus. 2011. (Hank the Cowdog Ser.: No. 7). (ENG.). 127p. (J). (gr. 3-6). pap. 5.99 (978-1-59188-107-0(2)) Maverick Bks., Inc.

—The Disappearance of Drover. Holmes, Gerald L., illus. 2011. (Hank the Cowdog Ser.). (ENG.). 122p. (J). (gr. 3-6). pap. 5.99 (978-1-59188-157-5(9)) Maverick Bks., Inc.

—Drover's Secret Life. Holmes, Gerald L., illus. 2011. (Hank the Cowdog Ser.). (ENG.). 118p. (J). (gr. 3-6). pap. 5.99 (978-1-59188-153-7(6)) Maverick Bks., Inc.

—The Dungeon of Doom. Holmes, Gerald L., illus. 2004. (Hank the Cowdog Ser.: No. 44). 122p. (J). lib. bdg. 17.00 (978-1-4242-1601-7(X)) Fitzgerald Bks.

—The Dungeon of Doom. Holmes, Gerald L., illus. 2011. (Hank the Cowdog Ser.). (ENG.). 122p. (J). (gr. 3-6). pap. 5.99 (978-1-59188-144-5(7)) Maverick Bks., Inc.

—Every Dog Has His Day. Holmes, Gerald L., illus. 2011. (Hank the Cowdog Ser.). (ENG.). 118p. (J). (gr. 3-6). pap. 5.99 (978-1-59188-110-0(2)) Maverick Bks., Inc.

—Faded Love. Holmes, Gerald L., illus. 2011. (Hank the Cowdog Ser.: No. 5). (ENG.). 125p. (J). (gr. 3-6). pap. 5.99 (978-1-59188-105-6(6)) Maverick Bks., Inc.

—The Fling. Holmes, Gerald L., illus. 2011. (Hank the Cowdog Ser.). (ENG.). 126p. (J). (gr. 3-6). pap. 5.99 (978-1-59188-138-4(2)) Maverick Bks., Inc.

—The Garbage Monster from Outer Space. Holmes, Gerald L., illus. 2011. (Hank the Cowdog Ser.). (ENG.). 126p. (J). (gr. 3-6). pap. 5.99 (978-1-59188-132-2(3)) Maverick Bks., Inc.

—The Ghost of Rabbits Past. Holmes, Gerald L., illus. 2013. 128p. (J). pap. (978-1-59188-162-9(5)) Maverick Bks., Inc.

—Hank Cowdog 50. Holmes, Gerald L., illus. 2007. 256p. 16.99 (978-0-670-62249-8(4), Viking Adult) Penguin Publishing Group.

—Hank the Cowdog & Monkey Business. Holmes, Gerald L., illus. 2011. (Hank the Cowdog Ser.). (ENG.). 110p. (J). (gr. 3-6). pap. 5.99 (978-1-59188-114-8(5)) Maverick Bks., Inc.

—It's a Dog's Life. Holmes, Gerald L., illus. (Hank the Cowdog Ser.: No. 3). (J). 100p. (gr. 2-5). 9.95 (978-0-916941-04-8(3)); 2011. (ENG.). 127p. (gr. 3-6). pap. 5.99 (978-1-59188-103-2(X)) Maverick Bks., Inc.

—Let Sleeping Dogs Lie. Holmes, Gerald L., illus. 2011. (Hank the Cowdog Ser.: No. 6). (ENG.). 129p. (J). (gr. 3-6). pap. 5.99 (978-1-59188-106-3(4)) Maverick Bks., Inc.

—Lost in the Blinded Blizzard. Holmes, Gerald L., illus. 2011. (Hank the Cowdog Ser.). (ENG.). 115p. (J). (gr. 3-6). pap. 5.99 (978-1-59188-116-2(1)) Maverick Bks., Inc.

—Lost in the Dark Unchanted Forest. Holmes, Gerald L., illus. 2011. (Hank the Cowdog Ser.). (ENG.). 124p. (J). (gr. 3-6). pap. 5.99 (978-1-59188-111-7(0)) Maverick Bks., Inc.

—Moonlight Madness. Holmes, Gerald L., illus. 2011. (Hank the Cowdog Ser.: No. 23). (ENG.). 114p. (J). (gr. 3-6). pap. 5.99 (978-1-59188-123-0(4)) Maverick Bks., Inc.

—The Mopwater Files. Holmes, Gerald L., illus. 2011. (Hank the Cowdog Ser.). (ENG.). 111p. (J). (gr. 3-6). pap. 5.99 (978-1-59188-128-5(5)) Maverick Bks., Inc.

—Murder in the Middle Pasture. Holmes, Gerald L., illus. 2011. (Hank the Cowdog Ser.). (ENG.). 120p. (J). (gr. 3-6). pap. 5.99 (978-1-59188-104-9(8)) Maverick Bks., Inc.

—The Original Adventures of Hank the Cowdog. Holmes, Gerald L., illus. (ENG.). 127p. (J). (gr. 3-6). 2012. (Hank the Cowdog Ser.: Vol. 1). 15.99 (978-1-59188-201-5(X)) 2011. (Hank the Cowdog Ser.: No. 1). pap. 5.99 (978-1-59188-101-8(3)) Maverick Bks., Inc.

—The Phantom in the Mirror. Holmes, Gerald L., illus. 2011. (Hank the Cowdog Ser.: No. 20). (ENG.). 114p. (J). (gr. 3-6). pap. 5.99 (978-1-59188-120-9(X)) Maverick Bks., Inc.

—The Quest for the Great White Quail. Holmes, Gerald L., illus. 2011. (Hank the Cowdog Ser.). (ENG.). 123p. (J). (gr. 3-6). pap. 5.99 (978-1-59188-152-0(8)) Maverick Bks., Inc.

—The Return of the Charlie Monsters. Holmes, Gerald L., illus. 2014. 128p. (J). pap. (978-1-59188-163-6(3)) Maverick Bks., Inc.

—The Secret Laundry Monster Files. Holmes, Gerald L., illus. 2011. (Hank the Cowdog Ser.). (ENG.). 128p. (J). (gr. 3-6). pap. 5.99 (978-1-59188-139-1(0)) Maverick Bks., Inc.

—Slim's Good-Bye. Holmes, Gerald L., illus. 2011. (Hank the Cowdog Ser.). (ENG.). 132p. (J). (gr. 3-6). pap. 5.99 (978-1-59188-134-6(X)) Maverick Bks., Inc.

—The Wounded Buzzard on Christmas Eve. Holmes, Gerald L., illus. 2011. (Hank the Cowdog Ser.: No. 13). (ENG.). 112p. (J). (gr. 3-6). pap. 5.99 (978-1-59188-113-1(7)) Maverick Bks., Inc.

Erickson, John R. & Holmes, Gerald L., illus. The Case of the Prowling Bear. 2013. 126p. (J). (978-1-59188-261-9(3)); pap. (978-1-59188-161-2(7)) Maverick Bks.

Erickson, Mary Ellen. Snowstorm. 2005. (J). (978-0-9765453-3-0(0)) Dr. Mary's Bks.

Erlandson, Nick. Duncan & the Bone Tree, 1 vol. 2009. 40p. pap. 24.95 (978-1-60813-864-7(X)) America Star Bks.

Escher, Jill. The Boneyville Dogs - Scuba Dogs. 2011. 24p. 12.79 (978-1-4567-1908-1(4)) AuthorHouse.

Esparza-Vela, Mary. Lucky's Lick. Prouix, Denis, illus. 2013. 16p. pap. 9.95 (978-1-61633-406-2(1)) Guardian Angel Publishing, Inc.

Estefan, Gloria & Garland, Michael. Noelle's Treasure Tale: A New Magically Mysterious Adventure. 2006. (SPA & ENG., Illus.). 32p. (gr. -1-3). 17.95 (978-0-06-112614-7(4), Rayo) HarperCollins Pubs.

Estep, Lorena. Puddles on the Floor. Thayne, Tamira Ci, illus. 2008. 24p. 15.95 (978-0-615-21952-3(7)) Who Chains You.

Estergren, Fred B. Tale of a Dog Called Sunshine, 1 vol. 2009. 201p. pap. 24.95 (978-1-4489-2575-9(4)) America Star Bks.

Eubank, Patricia Reeder. The Leprechaun's Big Pot of Gold. Eubank, Patricia Reeder, illus. 2012. (Illus.). 20p. (J). bds. 6.99 (978-0-8249-1877-4(0), Ideal Pubns.) Worthy Publishing.

—Seaman's Journal. 2010. 40p. (J). pap. 9.99 (978-0-8249-5619-6(2), Ideal Pubns.) Worthy Publishing.

Evans, Betty A. The World's Greatest Possum Trainer. 2011. 52p. (gr. 4-6). pap. 9.99 (978-1-4567-6409-8(8)) AuthorHouse.

Evans, Cathy. Halo & the Rainbows. 2013. 36p. pap. 16.95 (978-1-4624-0704-0(8), Inspiring Voices) Author Solutions, Inc.

Evans, Dan C. The High Peaks Paradigm Shift: A Canine Agent Teabo Adventure, 1 vol. 2010. 362p. pap. 29.95 (978-1-61582-712-1(9)) America Star Bks.

Everett, Anita. Abc Adventures Continued: D e F G. 2012. 44p. pap. 21.99 (978-1-4691-7797-7(8)) Xlibris Corp.

Evert, Lori. The Brave Little Puppy. Breiehagen, Per, illus. 2016. (ENG.). 28p. (J). (-k). bds. 8.99 (978-0-399-54945-8(5), Random Hse. Bks. for Young Readers) Random Hse. Children's Bks.

Exelby, Kathy. My Dog Harpo: The Biggest Kid I Know. Wall Darby, Colleen, illus. 2007. (J). per. 20.00 (978-1-932583-39-7(4)) digital@batesjackson llc.

Faber, Jules. Dog Stories. 2017. (ENG.). 208p. (J). (gr. 1-4). 12.99 **(978-0-14-378097-7(2))** Random Hse. Australia AUS. Dist: Independent Pubs. Group.

Faber, Toni Tuso. The Poodle Tales: Book Eight. Rudd, Benton, illus. 2013. 24p. 16.99 (978-0-9897168-0-2(5)); pap. 10.99 (978-0-9897168-1-9(3)) Mindstir Media.

—The Poodle Tales: Book Five. Rudd, Benton, illus. 2013. 24p. 16.99 (978-0-9892711-0-3(2)); pap. 10.99 (978-0-9892711-1-0(0)) Mindstir Media.

—The Poodle Tales: Book Four. Rudd, Benton, illus. 2013. 24p. 16.99 (978-0-9890288-9-9(5)); pap. 10.99 (978-0-9890288-8-2(7)) Mindstir Media.

—The Poodle Tales: Book Nine. Rudd, Benton, illus. 2013. 24p. 16.99 (978-0-9897168-2-6(1)) Mindstir Media.

—The Poodle Tales: Book Seven. Rudd, Benton, illus. 2013. 26p. 16.99 (978-0-9894748-6-3(0)); pap. 10.99 (978-0-9894748-7-0(9)) Mindstir Media.

—The Poodle Tales: Book Six. Rudd, Benton, illus. 2013. 24p. 16.99 (978-0-9892711-2-7(9)); pap. 10.99 (978-0-9892711-3-4(7)) Mindstir Media.

—The Poodle Tales: Book Ten. Rudd, Benton, illus. 2013. 24p. 16.99 (978-0-9910324-1-9(1)) Mindstir Media.

—The Poodle Tales: Book Twelve. Rudd, Benton, illus. 2013. 24p. pap. 10.99 (978-0-9913190-8-4(7)) Mindstir Media.

Fair, Sherry. The Best Parade Day: Spatz. Rutland, Jarrett, illus. 2006. (Spatz Ser.). 40p. (J). (gr. -1-5). 18.95 (978-1-57736-375-0(2)) Providence Hse Pubs.

Fair, Sherry W. The Scratching Sound: Spatz. Rutland, Jarrett, illus. 2005. 28p. (J). (gr. -1-7). 16.98 (978-1-57736-348-4(5)) Providence Hse Pubs.

Faith, Susan. Purple Puppy. Offner, Naomi, illus. 2005. 32p. (J). 19.95 (978-0-9707793-0-4(5)) Purple People, Inc.

Falkner, Brian. Northwood, 1 vol. Bixley, Donovan, illus. 2014. (ENG.). 272p. (gr. 3-3). 27.93 (978-1-4342-8667-3(3)) Stone Arch Bks.

—Northwood, 1 vol. 2013. (ENG.). 32p. (J). pap. (978-1-4342-8666-6(5)) Stone Arch Bks.

Faller, Regis. The Adventures of Polo. Faller, Regis, illus. 2006. (Adventures of Polo Ser.). (ENG., Illus.). 80p. (J). (gr. -1-3). 19.99 (978-1-59643-160-7(1), 9781596431607) Roaring Brook Pr.

Falletta, Bernadette & Gasparro, Marie. Reflections of the Dog That Learned English. 2005. 16p. (J). 14.95 (978-1-4116-6524-8(4)) Lulu Pr., Inc.

Famularo, Joe. Taco/Fatso: The Story of a Fat Dog, Too Fat to Fly. 2013. 32p. pap. 17.25 (978-1-4669-4926-3(0)) Trafford Publishing.

Fann, Linsey. Puppy Love. Abdulai, David, ed. Fann, Linsey, illus. Date not set. (Illus.). 32p. (J). (gr. 4-6). pap. 19.95 (978-0-9647012-6-7(X), Dawn of a New Day Pubns., The) Konkori International.

Fanny, Nanny. The New Girl in Town: A Children's Book. Fanny, Nanny, illus. 2013. (Illus.). 32p. pap. 12.99 (978-1-62516-179-6(4), Strategic Bk. Publishing) Strategic Book Publishing & Rights Agency (SBPRA).

Farb, Carolyn. Lucas Comes to America. 2011. 34p. (J). 14.99 (978-1-4567-4541-7(7)) AuthorHouse.

Faris, Stephanie. Piper Morgan to the Rescue. Fleming, Lucy, illus. 2016. (Piper Morgan Ser.: 3). (ENG.). 112p. (J). (gr. 1-4). pap. 5.99 (978-1-4814-5714-9(4), Aladdin) Simon & Schuster Children's Publishing.

Farkas, Steven E. Annie Pooh, Princess Pup: How Annie Pooh was lost, was found, & became Princess Pup. 2011. 24p. (gr. 2-4). pap. 15.99 (978-1-4670-3321-3(9)) AuthorHouse.

Farris, Judy. Mr Boo Bear. Farris, Michael, illus. 2009. 24p. pap. 15.49 (978-1-4389-4553-8(1)) AuthorHouse.

Fath, Teresa. The Train Track Trolley & the Bell Dogs. 2009. 32p. pap. 21.99 (978-1-4415-4350-9(3)) Xlibris Corp.

Fauske, Tore. Sid. 2009. (Illus.). 104p. pap. 10.99 (978-1-4389-6533-8(8)) AuthorHouse.

Faust, Laurie, illus. A New Home for Honey. 2006. (Adventures of Honey Ser.). (J). pap. 9.95 (978-0-9789227-0-2(0)) Weeping Willow Publishing.

Fay, Nancy Cartnick. I Wanted a Puppy - Not Fish! 2012. 24p. pap. 15.99 (978-1-4691-7535-5(5)) Xlibris Corp.

Faye. Jazzy Shoes. l.t. ed. 2006. (ENG., Illus.). 28p. per. 9.95 (978-1-4327-0176-5(2)) Outskirts Pr., Inc.

Faye Morningstar. Little Dream Athe: The Sand Prince. 2012. 20p. pap. 17.99 (978-1-4772-9540-3(2)) AuthorHouse.

Feaster, Raven Joye Raye. Merrileggs of Macon County. 2011. 72p. (gr. -1). pap. 10.75 *(978-1-4567-6971-0(5))* AuthorHouse.
Fedorovich, Debbie. The Adventures of Sheila the Therapy Dog. 2007. 36p. per. 13.95 *(978-1-4327-0198-7(3))* Outskirts Pr., Inc.
Feiffer, Jules. Bark, George. 2004. (J). (gr. -1-k). spiral bd. *(978-0-616-01637-4(9))*; spiral bd. *(978-0-616-01638-1(7))* Canadian National Institute for the Blind/Institut National Canadien pour les Aveugles.
Feiffer, Kate. Henry the Dog with No Tail. Feiffer, Jules, illus. 2007. (ENG.). 32p. (J). (gr. -1-3). 18.99 *(978-1-4169-1614-7(8)*, Simon & Schuster/Paula Wiseman Bks.) Simon & Schuster/Paula Wiseman Bks.
—The Problem with the Puddles. Tusa, Tricia, illus. (ENG.). 208p. (J). (gr. 3-7). 2011. pap. 7.99 *(978-1-4424-2101-1(0))* 2009. 16.99 *(978-1-4169-4961-9(5))* Simon & Schuster/Paula Wiseman Bks. (Simon & Schuster/Paula Wiseman Bks.).
—Which Puppy? Feiffer, Kate & Feiffer, Jules, illus. 2009. (ENG.). 32p. (J). (gr. -1-3). 16.99 *(978-1-4169-9147-2(6)*, Simon & Schuster/Paula Wiseman Bks.) Simon & Schuster/Paula Wiseman Bks.
Feldman, Thea. Adventure in the Park. Ward, April, illus. 2006. 20p. (J). *(978-0-696-23234-3(0))* Meredith Bks.
—ASPCA Pet Rescue Club - Too Big to Run. 2015. (ENG.). 128p. (J). (gr. 1-3). lib. bdg. 16.99 *(978-0-7944-3513-4(0)*, Reader's Digest Children's Bks.) Studio Fun International.
—Backyard Pirates. Conger, Holli, illus. 2007. (Magnix Imagination Activity Bks.). 6p. bds. 5.99 *(978-1-932915-40-2(0))* Sandvik Innovations, LLC.
Felton, Jerilyn E. The Master's Companion: A Christian Midrash. 2007. (Illus.). 134p. 16.75 *(978-0-88489-936-5(5))* St. Mary's Pr. of MN.
Fenton, Karen B. It's Raining Outside & I'm Gonna Be Bored! Roth, Stacy Schulstrom, illus. 2006. (J). lib. bdg. 16.82 *(978-0-9778196-4-5(7))* Harbour Arts, LLC.
Fergus, Maureen. Buddy & Earl, 1 vol. Sookocheff, Carey, illus. 2015. (Buddy & Earl Ser.: 1). (ENG.). 32p. (J). (gr. -1-2). 16.95 *(978-1-55498-712-2(1))* Groundwood Bks. CAN. Dist: Publishers Group West (PGW).
—Buddy & Earl & the Great Big Baby, 1 vol. Sookocheff, Carey, illus. 2016. (Buddy & Earl Ser.). (ENG.). 32p. (J). (gr. -1-2). 16.95 *(978-1-55498-716-0(4))* Groundwood Bks. CAN. Dist: Publishers Group West (PGW).
—Buddy & Earl Go Exploring, 1 vol. Sookocheff, Carey, illus. 2016. (Buddy & Earl Ser.: 2). (ENG.). 32p. (J). (gr. k-2). 16.95 *(978-1-55498-714-6(8))* Groundwood Bks. CAN. Dist: Publishers Group West (PGW).
Ferraro, Maureen. Sugar & Els: The Mystery. 2011. 28p. pap. 15.99 *(978-1-4628-5347-2(1))* Xlibris Corp.
Ferreira, Ann Devine & Bailey. Hi I'm Bailey & I'm Getting A New Special Family. 2011. 32p. 17.95 *(978-1-4269-5303-3(8))* Trafford Publishing.
Ferry, Beth. Land Shark. Mantle, Ben, illus. 2015. (ENG.). 36p. (J). (gr. -1-k). 16.99 *(978-1-4521-2458-2(2))* Chronicle Bks. LLC.
Fichthorn, Ashley. Big E, Meet Zeke, Your New Brother. Moise, Nahomie, illus. 2011. 36p. pap. 24.95 *(978-1-4560-6941-4(1))* America Star Bks.
Fickling, Phillip. Fillmore & Geary Take Off! Shulman, Mark, illus. 2003. 40p. (J). lib. bdg. *(978-1-58717-258-8(5)*, SeaStar Bks.) Chronicle Bks. LLC.
Fidler, Kathleen. Flash the Sheepdog. 3rd rev. ed. (ENG., Illus.). 176p. 12.00 *(978-0-86315-581-9(2))* Floris Bks. GBR. Dist: SteinerBooks, Inc.
Fields, Bryan W. Lunchbox & the Aliens. Atteberry, Kevan, illus. 2009. (Froonga Ser.). (ENG.). 208p. (J). (gr. 4-7). pap. 11.99 *(978-0-312-56115-4(6)*, 9780312561154) Square Fish.
Figley, Marty Rhodes. Emily & Carlo. Stock, Catherine, illus. 2012. (ENG.). 32p. (J). (gr. k-3). 15.95 *(978-1-58089-274-2(4))* Charlesbridge Publishing, Inc.
Filippello, Michael. In a Place Called Barrontippeny. 2008. 24p. pap. 24.95 *(978-1-60813-295-9(1))* America Star Bks.
Finch, Kate. Calling All Pets! 2013. (Pet Hotel Ser.: 1). lib. bdg. 14.75 *(978-0-606-31984-3(0)*, Turtleback) Turtleback Bks.
—Pet Hotel #1: Calling All Pets! Gurney, John Steven & Jessell, Tim, illus. 2013. (Pet Hotel Ser.: 1). (ENG.). 96p. (J). (gr. 2-5). pap. 4.99 *(978-0-545-50180-4(6)*, Scholastic Paperbacks) Scholastic, Inc.
Fine, Anne. Ruggles. Brown, Ruth, illus. 2011. (ENG.). 32p. (J). (gr. k-k). pap. 8.99 *(978-1-84939-206-8(4))* Andersen Pr. GBR. Dist: Independent Pubs. Group.
Finnegan, Delphine. Lady & the Tramp. 2012. (Step into Reading Level 2 Ser.). lib. bdg. 13.55 *(978-0-606-26794-6(8)*, Turtleback) Turtleback Bks.
Finney, Jefferson. Clever Dog. Hopper, Pegge, illus. 2007. 32p. (J). pap. 15.95 *(978-1-56647-845-8(6))* Mutual Publishing LLC.
Finney, Kathryn, illus. Little Louie. 2014. (ENG.). 32p. (J). (gr. -1-k). 16.95 *(978-1-62914-615-7(3)*, Sky Pony Pr.) Skyhorse Publishing Co., Inc.
Finney, Patricia. I, Jack. Bailey, Peter, illus. 2004. 192p. (J). 15.99 *(978-0-06-052207-0(0))*; lib. bdg. 16.89 *(978-0-06-052208-7(9))* HarperCollins Pubs.
—Jack & Rebel, the Police Dog. 2007. (Illus.). 183p. (J). (gr. 3-7). lib. bdg. 16.89 *(978-0-06-088050-7(3))* HarperCollins Pubs.
Fisch, Sarah. The Little Flower Seed. Roper, Robert, illus. 2007. (J). pap. *(978-0-439-90899-3(X))* Scholastic, Inc.
Fisch, Sarah & Bridwell, Norman. Backpack Puppy. Durk, Jim, illus. 2005. (J). pap. *(978-0-439-73379-3(0))* Scholastic, Inc.
—The Little Blue Easter Egg. Goldberg, Barry, illus. 2006. (Clifford's Puppy Days Ser.). 23p. (J). *(978-0-439-81617-5(3))* Scholastic, Inc.
—Lots of Love. Johnson, Jay B., illus. 2008. (J). *(978-0-545-02843-1(4))* Scholastic, Inc.
Fisch, Sholly. Scooby-Doo in Fangs, but No Fangs!, 1 vol. 2013. (Scooby-Doo Graphic Novels Set 3 Ser.). (ENG.). 24p. (J). (gr. 2-6). lib. bdg. 24.21 *(978-1-61479-051-8(5)*, Essential Library) ABDO Publishing Co.
Fischer, Ellen. Latke, the Lucky Dog. Beeke, Tiphanie, illus. 2014. 24p. (J). (gr. -1-2). 17.95 *(978-0-7613-9038-1(3)*, Kar-Ben Publishing) Lerner Publishing Group.
Fischer, P. J. Grandma & Her Chocolate Labrador. 2014. (ENG.). 36p. (J). (gr. k-2). 14.99 *(978-0-9905721-8-3(8))* Minted Prose, LLC.
Fisher, C. R. The Adventures of Sam Fisher: It's Ruff to Be A Puppy. 2008. 64p. pap. 19.49 *(978-1-4389-2040-5(7))* AuthorHouse.
Fisher, David & Fisher, David Dayan. Puppy School. 2010. 77p. (J). pap. 5.50 *(978-0-578-06095-8(7))* Sunnyfields Publishing.
Fisher, Doris & Sneed, Dani. One Odd Day, 1 vol. Lee, Karen, illus. 2006. (Basic Math Numbers Ser.). (ENG.). 32p. (J). (gr. -1-3). 15.95 *(978-0-9768823-3-6(7))* Arbordale Publishing.
Fisher, Karianne M. A Pup Named Moose. 2011. 20p. pap. 24.95 *(978-1-4512-3373-5(6))* America Star Bks.
Fisher, Sandy, illus. The Adventures of CJ & Angel; the Scary Helicopter Ride. 2008. 24p. (J). *(978-0-9779072-1-2(X))* Creative Life Publishing.
Fitzgerald, Laurie. My Dog Wears Shoes & Her Name Is Maggie Mae. 2006. 32p. 17.95 *(978-1-887542-30-2(2))* Seven Locks Pr.
Fitzgerald, Mary. Samson's Best Friend. 2012. (ENG.). 32p. (J). 22.95 *(978-1-4327-9039-4(0))* Outskirts Pr., Inc.
Five Little Dogs. 2004. (Bella & Rosie Set 2 Ser.). (J). 7.67 *(978-1-932570-19-9(5))* Pioneer Valley Bks.
Five O'Clock Dog: Firestorm Trail. 5 vols. 2005. (J). pap. 9.95 *(978-0-9767887-0-6(5))* Five O'clock Dog.
Fleck, Denise. Don't Judge a Book by Its Cover. Chin, Lili, illus. 2013. 24p. pap. 14.99 *(978-1-4575-1758-7(2))* Dog Ear Publishing, LLC.
Fleischer, Barbara R. The Adventures of Scooby, Charlie, & Fluffy. 2011. 64p. pap. 28.95 *(978-1-4567-2496-2(7))* AuthorHouse.
Fleischman, Sid. Jim Ugly. Smith, Jos. A., illus. 2003. (ENG.). 144p. (J). (gr. 3-7). pap. 6.99 *(978-0-06-052121-9(X)*, Greenwillow Bks.) HarperCollins Pubs.
Fleming, Bryn. Jasper & Willie: Wildfire. 2015. (Range Riders Ser.). (ENG.). 130p. (J). 28.99 *(978-1-941821-92-3(8))*; pap. 9.99 *(978-1-941821-71-8(5))* Graphic Arts Ctr. Publishing Co. (West Winds Pr.).
Fleming, Denise. Buster Goes to Cowboy Camp. Fleming, Denise, illus. 2008. (ENG., Illus.). 40p. (J). (gr. -1-2). 16.95 *(978-0-8050-7892-3(4)*, 9780805078923, Holt, Henry & Co. Bks. For Young Readers) Holt, Henry & Co.
—Maggie & Michael Get Dressed. Fleming, Denise, illus. 2016. (ENG., Illus.). 40p. (J). 17.99 *(978-0-8050-8794-9(X)*, 9780805087949, Holt, Henry & Co. Bks. For Young Readers) Holt, Henry & Co.
Flemming, Denise. Buster. 2007. (J). (gr. k-3). 27.95 incl. audio *(978-0-8045-6959-0(2))*; 29.95 incl. audio compact disk *(978-0-8045-4182-4(5))* Spoken Arts, Inc.
Flesher, Vivienne. Alfred's Nose. Flesher, Vivienne, illus. 2008. (Illus.). 32p. (J). (gr. -1-2). lib. bdg. 17.89 *(978-0-06-084314-4(4))* HarperCollins Pubs.
Fletcher, Ashlee. My Dog, My Cat. 2012. (ENG., Illus.). 16p. (J). (gr. k — 1). bds. 7.99 *(978-1-933718-81-1(1))* Tanglewood Pr.
—My Dog, My Cat. Fletcher, Ashlee, illus. 2011. (ENG., Illus.). 32p. (J). (gr. -1-3). 13.95 *(978-1-933718-22-4(6))* Tanglewood Pr.
Fliess, Sue. Puppy Princess. Salerno, Steven, illus. 2016. (Little Golden Book Ser.). (ENG.). 24p. (J). (-k). 4.99 *(978-0-553-51209-0(9)*, Golden Bks.) Random Hse. Children's Bks.
Flint-Warren, Cathrine. To Dance with the Yellow Butterfly. 2007. 28p. per. 18.95 *(978-1-4327-0491-9(5))* Outskirts Pr., Inc.
Flo & Wendell Explore. 2014. (ENG.). 32p. (J). (gr. -1-k). 17.99 *(978-0-8037-3930-7(3)*, Dial Bks) Penguin Young Readers Group.
Flor Ada, Alma. Celebrate Fourth of July with Champ, the Scamp. Mazali, Gustavo, illus. 2006. (Cuentos para Celebrar / Stories to Celebrate Ser.). 30p. (gr. k-6). per. 11.95 *(978-1-59820-131-4(X))* Santillana USA Publishing Co., Inc.
Florence, Leigh Anne. The Adoption. Asher, James, illus. 2003. (Woody: the Kentucky Wiener Ser.). 32p. (J). (gr. -1-3). per. 12.95 *(978-0-9741417-0-1(4))* HotDiggetyDog Pr.
—Dog House Divided. 2012. (ENG.). (J). pap. 12.95 *(978-1-4675-3545-8(1))* Independent Pub.
—Welcomes a Dad, Vol. 2. Asher, James, illus. 2004. (Woody: the Kentucky Wiener Ser.). 32p. (J). (gr. -1-3). per. 12.95 *(978-0-9741417-1-8(2))* HotDiggetyDog Pr.
Florence, Tyler. Tyler Makes a Birthday Cake! Frazier, Craig, illus. 2014. (ENG.). 40p. (J). (gr. -1-3). 17.99 *(978-0-06-204760-1(4))* HarperCollins Pubs.
—Tyler Makes Spaghetti! Frazier, Craig, illus. 2013. (ENG.). 40p. (J). (gr. -1-3). 17.99 *(978-0-06-204756-4(6))* HarperCollins Pubs.
Flowers, Fran. Rosita: The Journey Home. 2012. 108p. (gr. 4-6). 28.95 *(978-1-4497-3505-0(3))*; pap. 11.95 *(978-1-4497-3503-6(7))* Author Solutions, Inc. (WestBow Pr.).
Flowers, Pam. Sojo: Memoir of a Reluctant Sled Dog. Farnsworth, Bill, illus. 2016. (ENG.). 120p. (J). pap. 12.99 *(978-1-943328-53-6(6)*, Alaska Northwest Bks.) Graphic Arts Ctr. Publishing Co.
—Sojo: Memoirs of a Reluctant Sled Dog. Farnsworth, Bill, illus. 2016. (ENG.). 120p. (J). 23.99 *(978-1-943328-55-0(2)*, Alaska Northwest Bks.) Graphic Arts Ctr. Publishing Co.
The Flying Pig & the Daredevil Dog: Individual Title Six-Packs. (Action Packs Ser.). 104p. (gr. 3-5). 44.00 *(978-0-7635-2985-7(0))* Rigby Education.
Fogliano, Julie. Old Dog Baby Baby. Raschka, Chris, illus. 2016. (ENG.). 32p. (J). 17.99 *(978-1-59643-853-8(3)*, 9781596438538) Roaring Brook Pr.
Folgueira, Rodrigo. Bob the Dog. Bernatene, Poly, illus. 2014. (J). *(978-1-4351-5774-3(5))* Barnes & Noble, Inc.
Forbush, Kyle. Balto: The Dog Hero. Forbush, Lisa, illus. 2004. (J). pap. 14.95 *(978-1-57833-267-0(2))* Todd Communications.
Ford, Bernette G. Princess Puppy. Williams, Sam, illus. 2013. (J). *(978-0-545-53967-8(6)*, Cartwheel Bks.) Scholastic, Inc.
Ford, Laura. Buster Brown & Tige in Misfit Heroes. 2004. (Illus.). 320p. 19.95 *(978-1-881554-28-8(7))* Skyward Publishing Co.
Foreman, Jack. Say Hello. Foreman, Michael, illus. 2012. (ENG.). 40p. (J). (gr. -1-2). pap. 6.99 *(978-0-7636-6087-1(6))* Candlewick Pr.
Foreman, Jack & Foreman, Michael. Say Hello. 2015. 40p. pap. 7.00 *(978-1-61003-409-8(0))* Center for the Collaborative Classroom.
Foreman, Michael. Cat & Dog. Foreman, Michael, illus. 2014. (ENG., Illus.). 32p. (J). (gr. -1-3). 16.95 *(978-1-4677-5124-7(3))* Lerner Publishing Group.
—Oh! If Only... Foreman, Michael, illus. 2013. (Illus.). 32p. (gr. -1-3). 16.95 *(978-1-4677-1213-2(2))* Andersen Pr. GBR. Dist: Lerner Publishing Group.
Forton-Barnes, Therese. Zaki & Venus. 2007. 13.95 *(978-1-59526-388-9(8))* Aeon Publishing Inc.
Fox & the Hound. (Read-Along Ser.). (J). 7.99 incl. audio *(978-1-55723-019-5(6))* Walt Disney Records.
Fox, Diane. The Cat, the Dog, Little Red, the Exploding Eggs, the Wolf, & Grandma. Fox, Christyan, illus. 2014. (ENG.). 32p. (J). (gr. -1-3). 16.99 *(978-0-545-69481-0(7)*, Scholastic Pr.) Scholastic, Inc.
Fox, Mem. Nellie Belle. Austin, Mike, illus. 2015. (ENG.). 32p. (J). (gr. -1-3). 17.99 *(978-1-4169-9005-5(4)*, Beach Lane Bks.) Beach Lane Bks.
Fox, Paula. Gus Cara de Piedra.Tr. of Stone-Faced Boy. (SPA.). 128p. (J). (gr. 3-5). *(978-84-279-3450-4(5)*, NG4694) Noguer y Caralt Editores, S. A. ESP. Dist: Lectorum Pubns., Inc.
Franciosi, Pete. Dusty Wants A Kitty. 2011. 23p. 14.95 *(978-1-4327-7596-4(0))* Outskirts Pr., Inc.
Francis, Pauline, retold by. Call of the Wild. 2010. (Essential Classics - Adventure Ser.). (Illus.). 56p. pap. *(978-0-237-54081-4(9))* Evans Brothers, Ltd.
—White Fang. 2010. (Essential Classics - Adventure Ser.). (Illus.). 48p. pap. *(978-0-237-54101-9(7))* Evans Brothers, Ltd.
Francis, Pauline & London, Jack. White Fang. 2003. (Fast Track Classics Ser.). (Illus.). 48p. (YA). pap. *(978-0-237-52532-3(1))* Evans Brothers, Ltd.
Frank, Vincent. The Six Pack. 2010. 48p. (J). pap. 18.99 *(978-1-4490-9471-3(6))* AuthorHouse.
Franks, Kevin. Scurvy Dogs. Franks, Kevin, illus. 2017. (ENG., Illus.). 96p. (J). pap. 5.99 *(978-1-61067-459-1(6))* Kane Miller.
Franks, T. S. ZZ Dogs. d'Obrin, Felix, illus. 2003. (J). 15.99 *(978-0-9722304-0-7(8)*, 5000, ZZ Dogs Pr.) That's Life Publishing, Inc.
Frasier, Debra. Spike: Ugliest Dog in the Universe. Frasier, Debra, illus. 2013. (ENG., Illus.). 40p. (J). (gr. -1-3). 16.99 *(978-1-4424-1452-5(9)*, Beach Lane Bks.) Beach Lane Bks.
Frazee, Marla. Boot & Shoe. Frazee, Marla, illus. 2012. (ENG., Illus.). 40p. (J). (gr. -1-3). 17.99 *(978-1-4424-2247-6(5)*, Beach Lane Bks.) Beach Lane Bks.
Freedman, Bill. Boy Who Wanted to Marry His Dog. 2011. 50p. (J). pap. 14.99 *(978-1-926780-10-8(8))* Key Publishing Hse., Inc., The CAN. Dist: Bookmasters Distribution.
Freeman, Martha. The Case of the Diamond Dog Collar. 2nd ed. (First Kids Mystery Ser.: 2). (ENG., 144p. (J). 2012. Illus.). (gr. 3-5). pap. 6.99 *(978-0-8234-2642-3(4))* 2011. 16.95 *(978-0-8234-2337-8(9))* Holiday Hse., Inc.
—The Case of the Missing Dinosaur Egg. Dibley, Glin, illus. 2014. (First Kids Mystery Ser.: 5). (ENG.). 115p. (J). (gr. 3-7). pap. 6.99 *(978-0-8234-3061-1(8))* Holiday Hse., Inc.
—The Case of the Missing Dinosaur Egg. 2013. (First Kids Mystery Ser.: 5). (ENG.). 144p. (J). (gr. 3-7). 16.95 *(978-0-8234-2523-5(1))* Holiday Hse., Inc.
—The Case of the Rock 'N' Roll Dog. 2010. (First Kids Mystery Ser.: 1). (ENG., Illus.). 128p. (J). (gr. 1-5). 16.95 *(978-0-8234-2267-8(4))* Holiday Hse., Inc.
—The Case of the Rock 'n' Roll Dog. 2012. (First Kids Mystery Ser.: 1). (ENG.). 128p. (J). (gr. 3-5). pap. 6.99 *(978-0-8234-2549-5(5))* Holiday Hse., Inc.
—The Case of the Ruby Slippers. (First Kids Mystery Ser.: 3). (ENG.). 128p. (J). 2013. pap. 6.99 *(978-0-8234-2764-2(1))* 2012. 16.95 *(978-0-8234-2409-2(X))* Holiday Hse., Inc.
—Mrs. Wow Never Wanted a Cow. Salerno, Steven, illus. 2006. (Beginner Books(R) Ser.). (ENG.). 48p. (J). (gr. -1-2). 9.99 *(978-0-375-83418-9(4)*, Random Hse. Bks. for Young Readers) Random Hse. Children's Bks.
—Strudel's Forever Home. 2016. (ENG.). 192p. (J). 16.95 *(978-0-8234-3534-0(2))* Holiday Hse., Inc.
Freitag, Fred. On Hills & Meadows by the River. 2013. 28p. pap. 24.95 *(978-1-63000-584-9(3))* America Star Bks.
French, Jackie. One Big Wacky Family. 2008. (Illus.). 464p. pap. *(978-0-7322-8745-0(6))* HarperCollins Pubs. Australia.
—Pete the Sheep. Whatley, Bruce, illus. 2008. 30p. (J). bds. *(978-0-7322-8794-8(4))* HarperCollins Pubs. Australia.
French, Sarah. Summer Friends. 2011. (ENG., Illus.). 32p. (J). 17.95 *(978-0-9827146-5-2(3))* Vineyard Stories.
Freyou, Lerin. The Adventures of Piston the Puppy: A Journey Through the Alphabet as Piston Discovers the World Around Him. 2009. 31p. 15.80 *(978-0-557-12597-5(9))* Lulu Pr., Inc.
Frick, Lisa. "Evie" the Little Jack Russell with Brown Around Her Eyes. 2009. 64p. pap. 31.99 *(978-1-4415-2911-4(X))* Xlibris Corp.
Friedman, Joe. The Secret Dog. Archbold, Tim, illus. 2016. (ENG.). 208p. (J). (gr. 2-4). pap. *(978-1-78027-287-0(1))* Birlinn, Ltd.
Friedman, Laurie. Mallory vs. Max. Schmitz, Tamara, illus. (Mallory Ser.: 3). (ENG.). 160p. (J). (gr. 2-5). 2006. per. 5.95 *(978-1-57505-863-4(4)*, First Avenue Editions) 2005. 15.95 *(978-1-57505-795-8(6))* Lerner Publishing Group.
—Mallory's Guide to Boys, Brothers, Dads, & Dogs. Kalis, Jennifer, illus. (Mallory Ser.). 160p. (J). (gr. 2-5). 2012. pap. 33.92 *(978-0-7613-9206-4(8)*, Darby Creek) 2012. (ENG.). pap. 5.95 *(978-0-7613-5250-1(3)*, Darby Creek) 2011. (ENG.). 15.95 *(978-0-8225-8886-3(2)*, Carolrhoda Bks.) Lerner Publishing Group.
Fritz, Jean & Clute, Tom. Champion Dog, Prince Tom. 10.00 *(978-0-89064-070-8(X))* National Assn. for Visually Handicapped.
Fritz, Kevin. The Newf & the Dane. 2003. 108p. (J). pap. 9.95 *(978-0-595-27050-7(6)*, Writers Club Pr.) iUniverse, Inc.
Fritz, Laura. Poodle on a Noodle. 2013. (ENG.). 28p. (J). pap. 9.99 *(978-1-936815-88-3(5))* Yawn's Bks. & More, Inc.
Froeb, Lori. I Am Daisy. Lemay, Violet, illus. 2015. (ENG.). 32p. (J). (gr. 1-3). pap. 3.99 *(978-0-7944-3311-6(1)*, Reader's Digest Children's Bks.) Studio Fun International.
—I Am Picasso. Melman, Debra, illus. 2015. (Rescue Readers Ser.: 4). (ENG.). 32p. (J). (gr. 1-2). lib. bdg. 16.99 *(978-0-7944-3505-9(7))* Reader's Digest Assn., Inc., The.
Froeb, Lori C. ASPCA Rescue Readers - I Am Picasso! Melman, Debra, illus. 2015. (Rescue Readers Ser.). (ENG.). 32p. (J). (gr. k-2). pap. 3.99 *(978-0-7944-3514-1(9)*, Reader's Digest Children's Bks.) Studio Fun International.
—I Am McKinley, Level 2. Sakamoto, Miki, illus. 2015. (Rescue Readers Ser.: 1). (ENG.). 32p. (J). (gr. 1-2). pap. 3.99 *(978-0-7944-3310-9(3)*, Reader's Digest Children's Bks.) Studio Fun International.
Frohmuth, Shawn. The Wiblet. 2005. 200p. (YA). pap. 12.95 *(978-0-595-36956-0(1))* iUniverse, Inc.
Frost, Helen. Diamond Willow. 2011. (ENG.). 144p. (J). (gr. 5-9). pap. 7.99 *(978-0-312-60383-0(5)*, 9780312603830) Square Fish.
Frueh, Pamela. Who Loves Pugs? 2007. 24p. 10.95 *(978-1-4303-2286-3(1))* Lulu Pr., Inc.
Fucile, Tony. Poor Louie. Fucile, Tony, illus. 2017. (ENG., Illus.). 40p. (J). (gr. -1-2). 16.99 *(978-0-7636-5828-1(6))* Candlewick Pr.
Fujii, Jocelyn. Pono the Dog That Dreams. Burns, Donna, illus. 2008. (ENG.). 40p. (YA). 14.95 *(978-0-9794649-2-8(7))* Hula Moon Pr.
Fun in the Snow. 2003. (Bella & Rosie Set 1 Ser.). (J). 7.67 *(978-1-932570-13-7(6))* Pioneer Valley Bks.
Funk, Bev. Wool E. Woola. 2006. spiral bd. 9.45 *(978-0-9789092-0-8(8))* Moonbow Pr., LLc.
Funk, Michele Housholder. The Adventures of Pete & Max: And the Lost Sock. 2011. (Illus.). 36p. pap. 16.86 *(978-1-4567-3724-5(4))* AuthorHouse.
Funke, Cornelia. Emma & the Blue Genie. Latsch, Oliver, tr. from GER. Meyer, Kerstin, illus. 2014. (ENG.). 96p. (J). (gr. 2-5). 9.99 *(978-0-385-37540-5(9)*, Random Hse. Bks. for Young Readers) Random Hse. Children's Bks.
Fussell, Sandy. Sad, the Dog. Suwannakit, Tull, illus. 2015. (ENG.). 32p. (J). (gr. -1-2). 15.99 *(978-0-7636-7826-5(0))* Candlewick Pr.
Fyne, Olga M. You Can't Teach an Old Dog New Tricks Because. 2010. (Illus.). 26p. pap. 9.99 *(978-1-935105-66-4(3))* Avid Readers Publishing Group.
G., Judi. Mercury the Mitzvah Dog. 2011. 24p. pap. *(978-1-4269-7579-0(1))* Trafford Publishing (UK) Ltd.
Gaetz, Dayle Campbell. Sea Dog. Meissner, Amy, illus. 2006. 62p. (J). lib. bdg. 20.00 *(978-1-4242-1249-1(9))* Fitzgerald Bks.
—Sea Dog, 1 vol. Meissner, Amy, illus. 2006. (Orca Echoes Ser.). (ENG.). 64p. (J). (gr. 2-3). per. 6.95 *(978-1-55143-406-3(7))* Orca Bk. Pubs. USA.
Gág, Wanda. Nothing at All. 2004. (Fesler-Lampert Minnesota Heritage Ser.). (ENG., Illus.). 32p. 14.95 *(978-0-8166-4418-6(7))* Univ. of Minnesota Pr.
Galbraith, Kathryn O. Sparky & Tidbit. Kelley, Gerald, illus. 2015. (Ready-To-Reads Ser.). (ENG.). 40p. (J). (gr. 1-3). pap. 3.99 *(978-1-4814-0424-2(5)*, Simon Spotlight) Simon Spotlight.
Gale, Eric Kahn. The Wizard's Dog. 2017. (ENG., Illus.). 288p. (J). (gr. 3-7). 16.99 *(978-0-553-53736-9(9)*, Crown Books For Young Readers) Random Hse. Children's Bks.
Gale, Paul. Lisek's Great Adventure. 2012. 28p. pap. 16.09 *(978-1-4669-4509-8(5))* Trafford Publishing.
Gall, Chris. Dog vs. Cat. 2014. (ENG., Illus.). 32p. (J). (gr. -1-3). 17.99 *(978-0-316-23801-4(5))* Little, Brown Bks. for Young Readers.
Gallagher, Diana G. The Doggone Dog, 1 vol. Juarez, Adriana & Puglisi, Adriana, illus. 2013. (Pet Friends Forever Ser.). (ENG.). 88p. (gr. 1-3). pap. 5.95 *(978-1-4795-1865-4(4))*; lib. bdg. 25.32 *(978-1-4048-7502-9(6))* Picture Window Bks.
—The Great Kitten Challenge, 1 vol. Juarez, Adriana & Puglisi, Adriana, illus. 2013. (Pet Friends Forever Ser.). (ENG.). 88p. (gr. 1-3). pap. 5.95 *(978-1-4795-1864-7(6))*; lib. bdg. 25.32 *(978-1-4048-7501-2(8))* Picture Window Bks.
—Problem Pup, 1 vol. Puglisi, Adriana, illus. 2014. (Pet Friends Forever Ser.). (ENG.). 88p. (gr. 1-3). 25.32 *(978-1-4795-2176-0(0))* Picture Window Bks.
Galland, Nicole. Stepdog. 2015. lib. bdg. 26.95 *(978-0-606-36944-2(9))* Turtleback Bks.
Gallion, Sue Lowell. Pug & Pig Trick-or-Treat. Wan, Joyce, illus. 2017. (Pug & Pig Ser.). (ENG.). 40p. (J). (gr. -1-3). 17.99 ***(978-1-4814-4977-9(X)***, Beach Lane Bks.) Beach Lane Bks.
Gallion, Sue Lowell. Pug Meets Pig. Wan, Joyce, illus. 2016. (Pug & Pig Ser.). (ENG.). 40p. (J). (gr. -1-3). 17.99 *(978-1-4814-2066-2(6)*, Beach Lane Bks.) Beach Lane Bks.
El Gallo, la Zorra, y el Perro. (Coleccion Fabulas y Cuentos Populares). (SPA.). (J). (gr. 2-4). *(978-84-246-1559-8(X)*, GL0414) La Galera, S.A. Editorial ESP. Dist: Lectorum Pubns., Inc.
Gallo, Tina. OLIVIA & the Puppy Wedding. Spaziante, Patrick, illus. 2012. (Olivia TV Tie-In Ser.). (ENG.). 24p. (J). (gr. -1-2). pap. 3.99 *(978-1-4424-5315-9(X)*, Simon Spotlight) Simon Spotlight.
Galvin, Laura Gates & Odierno, Lisa. Puppy Explores. 2008. (ENG.). 16p. (J). (gr. -1-k). 13.95 *(978-1-59249-864-2(7))*; 6.95 *(978-1-59249-863-5(9))* Soundprints.
Gamble, Rev. Vivian T. I Think All the Time.... Ummm. 2012. 28p. pap. 9.95 *(978-1-4787-1359-3(3))* Outskirts Pr., Inc.
—Just to Be Myself. 2012. 28p. pap. 9.95 *(978-1-4787-1358-6(5))* Outskirts Pr., Inc.
Gamble, Shanae. God's Dogs go to Heaven: Christian myths & Fables. 2011. 28p. pap. 15.99 *(978-1-4520-5424-7(X))* AuthorHouse.
Gandolfi, Claudine. The Night Before Dog-Mas. Anagost, Karen, illus. 2007. (Petite Plush Kit Ser.). 64p. (J). (gr. -1-3). 9.95 *(978-1-59359-883-9(1))* Peter Pauper Pr. Inc.
Ganges, Montse. Cooper, Flying Dog. Urberuaga, Emilio, illus. 2009. (Cooper Ser.). 24p. (J). (gr. -1-3). 22.60 *(978-1-60754-239-1(0))*; pap. 8.15 *(978-1-60754-240-7(4))* Windmill Bks.
—Cooper, King of Cushion Island. Urberuaga, Emilio, illus. 2009. (Cooper Ser.). 24p. (J). (gr. -1-3). pap. 8.15 *(978-1-60754-243-8(9))* Windmill Bks.
—Fly Hunter. Urberuaga, Emilio, illus. 2009. (Cooper Ser.). 24p. (J). (gr. -1-3). pap. 8.15 *(978-1-60754-237-7(4))*; lib. bdg. 22.60 *(978-1-60754-236-0(6))* Windmill Bks.
—King of Cushion Island. Urberuaga, Emilio, illus. 2009. (Cooper Ser.). 24p. (J). (gr. -1-3). lib. bdg. 22.60 *(978-1-60754-242-1(0))* Windmill Bks.
—Meet Cooper. Urberuaga, Emilio, illus. 2009. (Cooper Ser.). 24p. (J). (gr. -1-3). pap. 8.15 *(978-1-60754-234-6(X))* Windmill Bks.

C
D

Ganges, Montse & Urberuaga, Emilio. Meet Cooper. 2009. (Cooper Ser.). (Illus.). 24p. (J). (gr. -1-3). lib. bdg. 22.60 (978-1-60754-233-9(1)) Windmill Bks.

Ganny, Charlee. Chihuawolf: A Tail of Mystery & Horror. Slater, Nicola, illus. 2011. (ENG.). 144p. (J). (gr. 4-6). pap. 6.99 (978-1-4022-5940-1(9), Sourcebooks Jabberwocky) Sourcebooks, Inc.

Ganzer, Diane. Patrick the Wayward Setter: A Christmas Miracle. 2005. 60p. pap. 16.95 (978-1-4137-8351-3(1)) PublishAmerica, Inc.

Garbowska, Agata, et al. Gandy & Parker Escape the Zoo: An Illustrated Adventure. Garbowska, Agata, illus. 2013. (Illus.). 97p. pap. (978-1-897472-82-8(X)) Golden Meteorite Pr.].

Garces Iii, Joseph Louis. Garrett the Firefighter. Abercrombie, Bethaney, illus. 2008. 24p. pap. 12.99 (978-1-59858-716-6(1)) Dog Ear Publishing, LLC.

—Tyler the Cowpoke. 2012. 24p. 19.99 (978-1-4575-1724-2(8)); pap. 10.99 (978-1-4575-1609-2(8)) Dog Ear Publishing, LLC.

Garcia, Alaycia. Roxy & Chopper Visit the Animal Shelter. Carter, Kelly, illus. 2011. 44p. pap. 24.95 (978-1-4560-7336-7(2)) America Star Bks.

García, Cristina. The Dog Who Loved the Moon. Serra, Sebastia, illus. 2011. (ENG.). 32p. (J). (gr. -1-3). 16.99 (978-1-4424-3089-1(3), Atheneum Bks. for Young Readers) Simon & Schuster Children's Publishing.

Garcia-Webb, Peter. Aeron. 2008. 32p. E-Book 15.99 (978-0-9924756-9-7(4), Philomel) Penguin Publishing Group.

Gardiner, C. Pirate Betty of Wigan. 2013. 12p. pap. 10.60 (978-1-291-30672-9(2)) Lulu Pr., Inc.

Gardiner, John Reynolds. Stone Fox. Sewall, Marcia, illus. 25th anniv. ed. 2005. (ENG.). 96p. (J). (gr. 2-6). 16.99 (978-0-690-03983-2(2)) HarperCollins Pubs.

—Stone Fox. Sewall, Marcia & Hargreaves, Greg, illus. 30th anniv. ed. 2010. (Trophy Bk.). (ENG.). 96p. (J). (gr. 2-6). pap. 6.99 (978-0-06-440132-6(4)) HarperCollins Pubs.

—Stone Fox. 48p. (J). pap. 4.50 (978-0-8072-1267-7(9), Listening Library) Random Hse. Audio Publishing Group.

Gardiner, John Reynolds & Gardiner, J. Stone Fox. 2010. (J). (gr. 3-6). 17.20 (978-0-8085-6651-9(2), Turtleback) Turtleback Bks.

Garis, Howard R. The Curlytops & Their Pets. 2009. 120p. 22.95 (978-1-60664-609-0(5)); pap. 10.95 (978-1-60664-341-9(X)) Rodgers, Alan Bks.

—Dick Hamilton's Airship. 2008. 160p. pap. 13.95 (978-1-60664-155-2(7)) Aegypan.

Garland, Michael. Lost Dog. 2015. (I Like to Read(r) Ser.). (ENG., Illus.). 24p. (J). (gr. -1-3). 14.95 (978-0-8234-3429-9(X)) Holiday Hse., Inc.

Garn, Laura Aimee. Bella Basset Ballerina. Sokolova, Valerie, illus. 2006. 32p. (J). (gr. -1-3). 15.95 (978-0-9759378-0-8(4)) Pretty Please Pr., Inc.

Garr, Hillary. Dino the Dog & His Day in the Country. Kirton, Pamela T., illus. Date not set. 15.95 (978-0-9637143-3-6(3)) Amicus Pr.

Garza, Armando N. Itty Bitty Saves the Day. 2007. (Illus.). 22p. (J). (gr. -1-3). 21.99 (978-1-59879-482-3(5)); per. 12.99 (978-1-59879-330-7(6)) Lifevest Publishing, Inc.

Gates Ed D., James Terry. Georgie's Saturday Quest. 2013. 134p. pap. 9.95 (978-0-9894749-0-0(9)) Archer's Pr.

Gaudet, M. K. Marley & Me: Marley to the Rescue! 2008. (I Can Read Level 1 Ser.). (ENG.). 32p. (J). (gr. k-3). pap. 3.99 (978-0-06-170437-6(7)) HarperCollins Pubs.

—Marley to the Rescue! 2008. (Marley: I Can Read! Ser.). (Illus.). 32p. (J). (gr. -1-3). lib. bdg. 13.55 (978-1-4178-2918-7(4), Turtleback) Turtleback Bks.

Gavin, Rohan. Knightley & Son - K-9. 2015. (Knightley & Son Ser.: 2). (ENG., Illus.). 304p. (YA). (gr. 4-6). 16.99 (978-1-61963-494-7(5), 9781619634947, Bloomsbury USA Childrens) Bloomsbury Publishing USA.

Gay, Marie-Louise. Buenas Noches Samuel. 2004.Tr. of Good Night Sam. (SPA.). (J). (gr. k-18). pap. 7.99 (978-980-257-296-0(9)) Ekare, Ediciones VEN. Dist: Lectorum Pubns., Inc.

Gayatri Stein, Mari. Puddle Moon. 2010. (ENG., Illus.). 32p. 17.95 (978-0-9793840-0-4(1), Riverwood Bks.) White Cloud Pr.

Gee, Lulu. Dolly's Wonderful New Life. 2009. (Illus.). 96p. pap. 31.99 (978-1-4389-4433-3(0)) AuthorHouse.

Gellock, Ed. The Top Dog Lives Indoors & My Neighbors Live Outside. 2013. 32p. pap. 24.95 (978-1-63000-511-5(8)) America Star Bks.

Gelsey, James. Scooby-Doo! & the Carnival Creeper, 1 vol. 2013. (Scooby-Doo Mysteries Set 2 Ser.). (ENG.). 64p. (J). (gr. 3-6). lib. bdg. 24.21 (978-1-61479-042-6(6)) ABDO Publishing Co.

—Scooby-Doo! & the Frankenstein Monster, 1 vol. 2013. (Scooby-Doo Mysteries Set 2 Ser.). (ENG.). 64p. (J). (gr. 3-6). lib. bdg. 24.21 (978-1-61479-043-3(4)) ABDO Publishing Co.

—Scooby-Doo! & the Groovy Ghost, 1 vol. 2013. (Scooby-Doo Mysteries Set 2 Ser.). (ENG.). 64p. (J). (gr. 3-6). lib. bdg. 24.21 (978-1-61479-044-0(2)) ABDO Publishing Co.

—Scooby-Doo! & the Gruesome Goblin, 1 vol. 2013. (Scooby-Doo Mysteries Set 2 Ser.). (ENG.). 64p. (J). (gr. 3-6). lib. bdg. 24.21 (978-1-61479-045-7(0)) ABDO Publishing Co.

—Scooby-Doo! & the Howling Wolfman, 1 vol. 2013. (Scooby-Doo Mysteries Set 2 Ser.). (ENG.). 64p. (J). (gr. 3-6). lib. bdg. 24.21 (978-1-61479-046-4(9)) ABDO Publishing Co.

—Scooby-Doo! & the Spooky Strikeout, 1 vol. 2013. (Scooby-Doo Mysteries Set 2 Ser.). (ENG.). 64p. (J). (gr. 3-6). lib. bdg. 24.21 (978-1-61479-047-1(7)) ABDO Publishing Co.

Gelsey, James & Duendes Del Sur Staff. Scooby-Doo & the Karate Caper, 1 vol. 2011. (Scooby-Doo Mysteries Ser.). (ENG., Illus.). 64p. (J). (gr. 3-6). 24.21 (978-1-59961-891-3(5)) Spotlight.

—Scooby-Doo & the Runaway Robot, 1 vol. 2011. (Scooby-Doo Mysteries Ser.). (ENG., Illus.). 64p. (J). (gr. 3-6). 24.21 (978-1-59961-892-0(3)) Spotlight.

—Scooby-Doo & the Vampire's Revenge, 1 vol. 2011. (Scooby-Doo Mysteries Ser.). (ENG., Illus.). 64p. (J). (gr. 3-6). 24.21 (978-1-59961-894-4(X)) Spotlight.

—Scooby-Doo & the Witch Doctor, 1 vol. 2011. (Scooby-Doo Mysteries Ser.). (ENG., Illus.). 64p. (J). (gr. 3-6). 24.21 (978-1-59961-895-1(8)) Spotlight.

—Scooby-Doo & the Zombie's Treasure, 1 vol. 2011. (Scooby-Doo Mysteries Ser.). (ENG., Illus.). 64p. (J). (gr. 3-6). 24.21 (978-1-59961-896-8(6)) Spotlight.

Gemeinhart, Dan. The Honest Truth. 2015. (ENG.). 240p. (J). (gr. 3-7). 16.99 (978-0-545-66573-5(6), Scholastic Pr.) Scholastic, Inc.

—The Honest Truth. 2015. (ENG.). 240p. (J). (gr. 3-7). lib. bdg. 17.20 (978-0-606-38060-7(4)) Turtleback Bks.

George, Lindsay Barrett. Maggie's Ball. George, Lindsay Barrett, illus. 2010. (ENG., Illus.). 32p. (J). (gr. -1-k). 16.99 (978-0-06-172166-3(2), Greenwillow Bks.) HarperCollins Pubs.

—That Pup! George, Lindsay Barrett, illus. 2011. (ENG., Illus.). 32p. (J). (gr. -1-k). 16.99 (978-0-06-200413-0(1), Greenwillow Bks.) HarperCollins Pubs.

George, Olivia. The Bravest Girls in the World. DuBurke, Randy, illus. 2004. 32p. (J). lib. bdg. 15.00 (978-1-4242-0241-6(8)) Fitzgerald Bks.

Gerber, Lisa Ann. Elaina's Sleuthing Days, 1 vol. 2009. 60p. pap. 16.95 (978-1-60749-623-6(2)) PublishAmerica, Inc.

Geremia, Denise. The Pouty Puppy. 2013. 24p. (978-0-9918658-0-2(4)) Polished Publishing Group.

Gerheim, Su. Bayocor Adventures, the Secret Cave. 2012. 92p. pap. 10.95 (978-1-61493-034-1(1)) Peppertree Pr., The.

Gerlach-Babb nee Maines, Mary & Gerlach, Susan. Best Christmas Gift. 2007. (ENG.). 52p. per. 16.95 (978-1-4241-6389-2(7)) America Star Bks.

Gershel, Yolande. Alice. 2007. 32p. (J). pap. 15.00 (978-0-8059-7613-7(2)) Dorrance Publishing Co., Inc.

Geyer, Kim. Go to Sleep, Monty! Geyer, Kim, illus. 2015. (ENG., Illus.). 32p. (J). (gr. -1-3). 17.99 (978-1-4677-9311-7(6)) Lerner Publishing Group.

Giambroni, Shannon. Tugger in the Country. 2013. 24p. pap. 12.56 (978-1-4669-8668-8(9)) Trafford Publishing.

Giancamilli, Vanessa. Patches Finds a Home. Hatala, Dan, illus. 2006. (Pet Tales Ser.). (ENG.). 32p. (J). (gr. -1-3). 4.95 (978-1-59249-639-6(3)); pap. 2.95 (978-1-59249-640-2(7)) Soundprints.

Gianferrari, Maria. Hello Goodbye Dog. Barton, Patrice, illus. 2017. (ENG.). 40p. (J). 16.99 (978-1-62672-177-7(7), 9781626721777) Roaring Brook Pr.

—Officer Katz & Houndini: A Tale of Two Tails. Chatzikonstantinou, Danny, illus. 2016. (ENG.). 32p. (J). (gr. -1-2). 17.99 (978-1-4814-2265-9(0), Aladdin) Simon & Schuster Children's Publishing.

—The School Show. Heder, Thyra, illus. 2015. (Penny & Jelly Ser.). (ENG.). 32p. (J). (gr. -1-3). 16.99 (978-0-544-23014-9(0), HMH Books For Young Readers) Houghton Mifflin Harcourt Publishing Co.

—Slumber under the Stars. Heder, Thyra, illus. 2016. (Penny & Jelly Ser.). (ENG.). 32p. (J). (gr. -1-3). 16.99 (978-0-544-28005-2(9), HMH Books For Young Readers) Houghton Mifflin Harcourt Publishing Co.

Gibson, Sonya. My Dog, Trinity. 2012. 20p. pap. 24.95 (978-1-4626-8102-0(6)) America Star Bks.

Gibson, Steve. Sparky the Firehouse Dog, 1 vol. Weishampel, Winifred Ann, illus. 2009. 20p. pap. 24.95 (978-1-60836-254-7(X)) America Star Bks.

Gidwitz, Adam. The Inquisitor's Tale: Or, the Three Magical Children & Their Holy Dog. Aly, Hatem, illus. 2016. (ENG.). 384p. (J). (gr. 5). 17.99 (978-0-525-42616-5(7), Dutton Books for Young Readers) Penguin Young Readers Group.

Giff, Patricia Reilly. Fiercely & Friends: the Sneaky Snow Fox. Palmisciano, Diane, illus. 2012. (Fiercely & Friends Ser.). (ENG.). 40p. (J). (gr. k-2). 16.99 (978-0-545-43378-5(9), Orchard Bks.) Scholastic, Inc.

—The Garden Monster. Palmisciano, Diane, illus. (Fiercely & Friends Ser.). (J). (gr. k-2). 2014. (ENG.). 40p. 16.99 (978-0-545-43379-2(7)) 2013. (978-0-545-24460-2(9)) Scholastic, Inc. (Orchard Bks.).

Giff, Patricia Reilly. Jubilee. (ENG.). 160p. (J). (gr. 3-7). 2017. 6.99 **(978-0-385-74489-8(7)**, Yearling) 2016. 16.99 (978-0-385-74486-7(2), Lamb, Wendy Bks.) Random Hse. Children's Bks.

A Gift to Share. 2005. (J). 17.00 (978-0-9721457-1-8(0)) Silent Moon Bks.

Gigi, Jessy. The Sky Ride of Jimmy & Friends. 2011. 20p. pap. 24.95 (978-1-4626-2723-3(4)) America Star Bks.

Giglio, Judy. The Tapping Tale. Cepeda, Joe, illus. 2003. (Green Light Readers Level 1 Ser.). (ENG.). 24p. (J). (gr. -1-3). pap. 3.95 (978-0-15-204852-5(9)) Houghton Mifflin Harcourt Publishing Co.

Gilbert, Melissa. Daisy & Josephine. Kuo, Julia, illus. 2014. (ENG.). 32p. (J). (gr. -1-3). 17.99 (978-1-4424-4578-9(5), Simon & Schuster/Paula Wiseman Bks.) Simon & Schuster/Paula Wiseman Bks.

Gilbery, Barbara. Abby Helps Make It Happen. 2011. (Illus.). 20p. pap. 10.19 (978-1-4567-7286-4(4)) AuthorHouse.

Giles, Doris. Foursome. 2009. 24p. pap. 13.49 (978-1-4389-1203-5(X)) AuthorHouse.

Giles, Polly. Have You Ever Been Afraid of Animals? 2012. 28p. pap. 15.99 (978-1-4691-2517-6(X)) Xlibris Corp.

Giles, S. A. A Home for All: How a Little Black Puppy Gets a Name. 2007. 23.00 (978-0-8059-8864-2(5)) Dorrance Publishing Co., Inc.

—A Home for All: How a Little Puppy Finds a Home. 2006. 20.00 (978-0-8059-9076-8(3)) Dorrance Publishing Co., Inc.

Giles, Susan. Lola & Luigi. 2011. 32p. pap. 14.39 (978-1-4567-0063-8(4)) AuthorHouse.

Gilks, Tina M. My Dog Mo. 2011. 32p. pap. 17.25 (978-1-4269-4931-9(6)) Trafford Publishing.

Gill, Shelley. Kiana's Iditarod. Cartwright, Shannon, illus. 2008. (Paws IV Ser.). (ENG.). 32p. (J). (gr. -1-3). pap. 10.99 (978-1-57061-589-4(6), Little Bigfoot) Sasquatch Bks.

Gilman, Grace. Dixie. McConnell, Sarah, illus. 2011. (I Can Read Level 1 Ser.). (ENG.). 32p. (J). (gr. -1-3). 16.99 (978-0-06-171914-1(5)); pap. 3.99 (978-0-06-171913-4(7)) HarperCollins Pubs.

—Dixie & the Best Day Ever. Rogers, Jacqueline, illus. 2014. (I Can Read Level 1 Ser.). (ENG.). 32p. (J). (gr. -1-3). pap. 3.99 (978-0-06-208659-4(6)) HarperCollins Pubs.

—Dixie & the Class Treat. Rogers, Jacqueline, illus. 2012. (I Can Read Level 1 Ser.). (ENG.). 32p. (J). (gr. -1-3). 16.99 (978-0-06-208606-8(5)); pap. 3.99 (978-0-06-208605-1(7)) HarperCollins Pubs.

—Dixie & the Good Deeds. McConnell, Sarah, illus. 2013. (I Can Read Level 1 Ser.). (ENG.). 32p. (J). (gr. -1-3). 16.99 (978-0-06-208657-0(X)); pap. 3.99 (978-0-06-208643-3(X)) HarperCollins Pubs.

—Dixie & the School Trip. McConnell, Sarah, illus. 2012. (I Can Read Level 1 Ser.). (ENG.). 32p. (J). (gr. -1-3). 16.99 (978-0-06-208609-9(X)); pap. 3.99 (978-0-06-208608-2(1)) HarperCollins Pubs.

—Dixie & the School Trip. 2012. (Dixie: I Can Read Ser.). (J). lib. bdg. 13.55 (978-0-606-26284-2(9), Turtleback) Turtleback Bks.

—Dixie Loves School Pet Day. McConnell, Sarah, illus. 2011. (I Can Read Level 1 Ser.). (ENG.). 32p. (J). (gr. -1-3). 16.99 (978-0-06-171912-7(9)); pap. 3.99 (978-0-06-171911-0(0)) HarperCollins Pubs.

—Dixie Wins the Race. Rogers, Jacqueline, illus. 2012. (I Can Read Level 1 Ser.). (ENG.). 32p. (J). (gr. -1-3). 16.99 (978-0-06-208618-1(9)); pap. 3.99 (978-0-06-208614-3(6)) HarperCollins Pubs.

—Dixie Wins the Race. 2012. (Dixie: I Can Read Ser.). (J). lib. bdg. 13.55 (978-0-606-26851-6(0), Turtleback) Turtleback Bks.

Gilman, Jan Levinson. Murphy's Three Homes: A Story for Children in Foster Care. O'Malley, Kathy, illus. 2008. 32p. (J). (gr. -1-2). 14.95 (978-1-4338-0384-0(4)); pap. 9.95 (978-1-4338-0385-7(2)) American Psychological Assn. (Magination Pr.).

Gipson, Fred. Old Yeller. Date not set. 192p. (J). 20.95 (978-0-8488-2273-6(0)) Amereon Ltd.

—Old Yeller. 2003. (Trophy Bk.). (ENG.). 192p. (J). (gr. 5-18). pap. 6.99 (978-0-06-440382-5(3)) HarperCollins Pubs.

—Old Yeller. 2009. (Perennial Classics Ser.). 132p. (gr. 4-7). 20.85 (978-0-613-85744-4(5), Turtleback) Turtleback Bks.

Gipson, Fred & Polson, Steven. Old Yeller. 2009. (Perennial Classics Ser.). (ENG., Illus.). 144p. (gr. 4-7). pap. 12.99 (978-0-06-093547-4(2), Harper Perennial) HarperCollins Pubs.

Gissing, Kathleen. Buddy & the Poi Puppy. Swiatoviak, Jeri, illus. 2012. 24p. pap. 24.95 (978-1-4626-8089-4(5)) America Star Bks.

Gizmo Gets His Wish. 2005. (J). pap. (978-0-9716567-5-8(4)) Book Web Publishing, Limited.

The Gizmo Tales: Hero Dogs. 2005. (YA). pap. 14.94 (978-0-9716567-6-5(2)) Book Web Publishing, Limited.

Glass, Timothy. Sleepytown Beagles Penny's 4th of July. Mikle, Toby, illus. 2006. 24p. (J). per. 15.95 (978-1-888461-10-7(1)); 16.95 (978-1-888461-11-4(X)) Islewest Publishing.

Glazer, Maryann. The Adventures of Teddy Bark-Lee: Teddy Comes Home. 2009. 28p. pap. 13.99 (978-1-4389-4569-9(8)) AuthorHouse.

Glenn, Kenny. The First Race for Luvable Me. 2010. 28p. pap. 14.95 (978-1-60844-494-6(5)) Dog Ear Publishing, LLC.

Glessner, Gordon. Water Wars, Secrets Revealed. 2012. 24p. 12.00 (978-0-9859603-0-8(2)) Laughing Rhino Bks.

Glymph, Rikimah. Are You My Friend? 2006. (Illus.). 32p. (J). lib. bdg. 17.95 (978-1-934190-00-5(4)) Ocean Front Bk. Publishing, Inc.

Gnoske, Alexandra. Loui Saves the Earth. 2010. 16p. 9.49 (978-1-4520-0034-3(4)) AuthorHouse.

Goertzen, Glenda. City Dogs, 1 vol. Hudecki, Peter, illus. 2007. (ENG.). 133p. (J). (gr. 4-7). pap. (978-1-55455-005-0(X)) Fitzhenry & Whiteside, Ltd.

—The Prairie Dogs, 1 vol. Béha, Philippe, illus. 2004. (ENG.). 164p. pap. (978-1-55005-113-1(X)) Fitzhenry & Whiteside, Ltd.

Going, K. L. Dog in Charge. Santat, Dan, illus. 2012. (ENG.). 40p. (J). (gr. -1-k). 16.99 (978-0-8037-3479-1(4), Dial Bks) Penguin Young Readers Group.

Gold, Willa. Stella & Tulip: A Home for Us. 2010. (ENG.). 36p. (J). (gr. k-2). 17.99 (978-0-930773-95-3(0)) Black Heron Pr.

Goldberg, Nancy Solomon. I Am Moxxy Dog! 2010. 40p. 16.99 (978-1-4520-5387-5(1)) AuthorHouse.

Golden Books. Barbie: My Book of Puppies (Barbie) 2017. (Little Golden Book Ser.). (ENG., Illus.). 24p. (J). (-k). 4.99 **(978-1-5247-1508-3(5)**, Golden Bks.) Random Hse. Children's Bks.

—The Big Book of Paw Patrol (Paw Patrol) Golden Books, illus. 2014. (Big Golden Book Ser.). (ENG., Illus.). 32p. (J). (gr. -1-2). 9.99 (978-0-553-51276-2(5), Golden Bks.) Random Hse. Children's Bks.

—Howl for Halloween! (PAW Patrol) Golden Books & Lovett, Nate, illus. 2016. (Big Golden Book Ser.). (ENG.). 32p. (J). (gr. -1-2). 9.99 (978-0-399-55873-3(X), Golden Bks.) Random Hse. Children's Bks.

—Marshall to the Rescue! (Paw Patrol) Golden Books & Jackson, Mike, illus. 2016. (Big Golden Book Ser.). (ENG.). 32p. (J). (gr. -1-2). 9.99 (978-1-101-93847-8(1), Golden Bks.) Random Hse. Children's Bks.

—PAW Patrol Awesome Sticker Collection (PAW Patrol) Golden Books, illus. 2017. (4 Color Plus 1,000 Stickers Ser.). (ENG., Illus.). 64p. (J). (gr. -1-2). pap. 12.99 **(978-1-5247-1682-0(0)**, Golden Bks.) Random Hse. Children's Bks.

—The Poky Little Puppy's Playtime. DiCicco, Sue, illus. 2017. (Tabbed Board Book Ser.). (ENG.). 16p. (J). (— 1). bds. 8.99 **(978-0-399-55289-2(8)**, Golden Bks.) Random Hse. Children's Bks.

—Puppy Birthday to You! (Paw Patrol) Petrossi, Fabrizio, illus. 2015. (Little Golden Book Ser.). (ENG.). 24p. (J). (-k). 4.99 (978-0-553-52277-8(9), Golden Bks.) Random Hse. Children's Bks.

—Puppy Love! (Bubble Guppies) Golden Books, illus. 2012. (Full-Color Activity Book with Stickers Ser.). (ENG., Illus.). 32p. (J). (gr. -1-2). pap. 3.99 (978-0-307-98197-4(5), Golden Bks.) Random Hse. Children's Bks.

—The Pups Save Christmas! (Paw Patrol) Moore, Harry, illus. 2015. (Big Golden Book Ser.). (ENG.). 48p. (J). (gr. -1-2). 9.99 (978-0-553-52391-1(0), Golden Bks.) Random Hse. Children's Bks.

—The Pups Save Friendship Day! (PAW Patrol) Jackson, Mike, illus. 2016. (Big Golden Book Ser.). (ENG.). 32p. (J). (gr. -1-2). 9.99 (978-1-5247-1388-1(0), Golden Bks.) Random Hse. Children's Bks.

Golden Books Staff. All Fired up! (Paw Patrol) Lovett, Nate, illus. 2016. (Hologramatic Sticker Book Ser.). (ENG.). 64p. (J). (gr. -1-2). pap. 4.99 (978-1-101-93167-7(1), Golden Bks.) Random Hse. Children's Bks.

—All Paws on Deck! (Paw Patrol) Golden Books Staff & Lovett, Nate, illus. 2014. (Deluxe Paint Box Book Ser.). (ENG.). 128p. (J). (gr. -1-2). pap. 7.99 (978-0-385-38446-9(7), Golden Bks.) Random Hse. Children's Bks.

—It's Time for Bubble Puppy! Unten, Eren Blanquet, illus. 2012. (Little Golden Book Ser.). (ENG.). 24p. (J). (gr. -1-k). 4.99 (978-0-307-93028-6(9), Golden Bks.) Random Hse. Children's Bks.

—The Itty-Bitty Kitty Rescue (Paw Patrol) Golden Books Staff & Petrossi, Fabrizio, illus. 2014. (Little Golden Book Ser.). (ENG.). 24p. (J). (-k). 4.99 (978-0-553-50884-0(9), Golden Bks.) Random Hse. Children's Bks.

—Pirate Pups! (Paw Patrol) Petrossi, Fabrizio, illus. 2016. (Little Golden Book Ser.). (ENG.). 24p. (J). (gr. -1-k). 4.99 (978-0-553-53888-5(8), Golden Bks.) Random Hse. Children's Bks.

Goldish, Meish. Mystery at the Mall. Andrae, Tom, illus. 2017. (Hound Town Chronicles Ser.). (ENG.). 32p. (J). (gr. 2-6). 19.95 **(978-1-62724-870-9(6))** Bearport Publishing Co., Inc.

Goldman, Marcia, photos by. Lola & Tattletale Zeke. 2015. (Lola Ser.). (ENG., Illus.). 32p. (J). (gr. -1-3). 16.95 (978-1-939547-16-3(4)) Creston Bks.

—Lola Goes to the Doctor. 2014. (Lola Ser.). (ENG., Illus.). 32p. (J). (gr. -1-3). 16.95 (978-1-939547-11-8(3)) Creston Bks.

Goldsmith, Connie. Dogs at War: Military Canine Heroes. 2017. (Nonfiction — Young Adult Ser.). (ENG.). 104p. (YA). (gr. 8-12). 19.99 **(978-1-5124-3905-2(3))**; 53.32 **(978-1-5124-3906-9(1))**; 53.32 **(978-1-5124-2852-0(3))** Lerner Publishing Group. (Twenty-First Century Bks.).

Goniwicha, William. Spike a Relli: A Week at the Lake. 2009. 28p. pap. 13.99 (978-1-4389-2902-6(1)) AuthorHouse.

—Spike a Relli: The Mini Doberman. 2009. 28p. pap. 13.99 (978-1-4389-5678-7(9)) AuthorHouse.

Gonzalez, Owner Lucy. Puppy Trapped in Cyberspace! 2010. 57p. pap. 15.29 (978-0-557-44662-9(7)) Lulu Pr., Inc.

Good Dog... Not So Good Dog. 2007. (J). (978-0-9793568-1-0(4)) Merlin, Debbi.

The Good-for-Nothing Dog, 6 vols., Vol. 2. (Woodland Mysteriestm Ser.). 133p. (gr. 3-7). 42.50 (978-0-7802-7936-0(0)) Wright Group/McGraw-Hill.

Good, Yvonne & Good, Sr. Bubble Gum & Polka Dot. 2009. 96p. pap. 13.95 (978-1-4389-6640-3(7)) AuthorHouse.

Goodall, Liam. Puppy Minding. 2016. (ENG., Illus.). 26p. (J). pap. 28.22 **(978-1-5245-1883-7(2))** Xlibris Corp.

Goode, Diane. Thanksgiving Is Here! Goode, Diane, illus. 2005. (ENG., Illus.). 32p. (J). (gr. -1-3). pap. 6.99 (978-0-06-051590-4(2)) HarperCollins Pubs.

Goodhart, Pippa. Rescued by a Dog Called Flow. Lewis, Anthony, illus. 2006. 121p. (J). (gr. 4-7). pap. 6.95 (978-1-903015-47-6(2)) Barn Owl Bks, London GBR. Dist: Independent Pubs. Group.

Goodman, Jill. Mustang, the Little Dog Who Was Afraid to Go to School. 2004. (Illus.). (J). pap. (978-1-889636-63-4(0)) Youthlight, Inc.

Goodman, Peggy. Ritzi's Bath. Bunker, Thomas, illus. 2012. 28p. 24.95 (978-1-4560-4138-0(X)) America Star Bks.

Goodrich, Carter. Mister Bud Wears the Cone. Goodrich, Carter, illus. 2014. (ENG., Illus.). 48p. (J). (gr. -1-3). 16.99 (978-1-4424-8088-9(2), Simon & Schuster Bks. For Young Readers) Simon & Schuster Bks. For Young Readers.

—Say Hello to Zorro! Goodrich, Carter, illus. 2011. (ENG., Illus.). 48p. (J). (gr. -1-3). 15.99 (978-1-4169-3893-4(1), Simon & Schuster Bks. For Young Readers) Simon & Schuster Bks. For Young Readers.

—Zorro Gets an Outfit. Goodrich, Carter, illus. 2012. (ENG., Illus.). 48p. (J). (gr. -1-3). 15.99 (978-1-4424-3535-3(6), Simon & Schuster Bks. For Young Readers) Simon & Schuster Bks. For Young Readers.

Gordon, Domenica More. Archie. 2012. (ENG., Illus.). 48p. (J). (gr. -1-1). 17.99 (978-1-59990-936-3(7), 9781599909363, Bloomsbury USA Childrens) Bloomsbury Publishing USA.

—Archie Loves Skipping. Gordon, Domenica More, illus. 2015. (ENG., Illus.). 32p. (J). (gr. -1-1). 17.99 (978-1-4088-2930-1(4), 9781408829301, Bloomsbury USA Childrens) Bloomsbury Publishing USA.

—Archie's Vacation. 2014. (ENG., Illus.). 32p. (J). (gr. -1-1). 17.99 (978-1-61963-190-8(3), 9781619631908, Bloomsbury USA Childrens) Bloomsbury Publishing USA.

Gordon, Judy Ann. Grammie's Magical Garden: Beyond the Gate. 2012. 68p. pap. 28.99 (978-1-4772-7973-1(3)) AuthorHouse.

Gormley, Greg. Dog in Boots. Angaramo, Roberta, illus. 2011. (ENG.). 32p. (J). (gr. -1-1). 17.95 (978-0-8234-2347-7(6)) Holiday Hse., Inc.

Goss, Anthony & Blair, Janet. The Golden Dog Bone. 2012. 50p. 24.95 (978-1-4626-5929-6(2)) America Star Bks.

Gossett, Robert A. The Legend of Jake, the Salty Dog. Yarbrough, Mark, illus. 2007. (J). 8.95 (978-0-9793560-0-1(8)) Salty Dog, Inc., The.

Gosule, Bette & Longmire, Lynda. Sneakers Hangs Out. Dewitt, Kenny, illus. 2012. 26p. (J). 14.95 (978-1-60131-129-0(X), Castlebridge Bks.) Big Tent Bks.

Gotsch, Connie. Belle's Star. Cogan, John, illus. 2009. 134p. (J). pap. 8.99 (978-1-932926-01-9(1), Kinkajou Pr.) Artemesia Publishing, LLC.

—Belle's Trial. Cogan, John, illus. 2010. (ENG & ABK.). 150p. (J). pap. 8.99 (978-1-932926-12-5(7), Kinkajou Pr.) Artemesia Publishing, LLC.

Gottesfeld, Jeff. World's Ugliest Dog. 2015. (Red Rhino Ser.). (J). lib. bdg. 18.40 (978-0-606-37208-4(3)) Turtleback Bks.

Gould, Lorraine. Warren the Watchdog. 2010. 48p. pap. 19.49 (978-1-4490-6845-5(6)) AuthorHouse.

Gould, Terry. The Adventures of Sir Sniffsalot & His Friends. Proulx, Denis, illus. 2007. 48p. (gr. -1-3). pap. 15.99 (978-0-9789057-3-6(3)) Huntington Ludlow Media Group.

Goulet, Willette. Gizmo's Day Out. 2013. 32p. pap. 19.99 (978-1-4343-7104-1(2)) AuthorHouse.

Gourley, Barbara. The Legacy of Tip: The Catahoula. 2012. 40p. pap. 20.95 (978-1-4772-6337-2(3)) AuthorHouse.

—The True Adventures of Tip the Catahoula-Leopard Cowdog. 2011. 28p. pap. 17.95 *(978-1-4634-2316-2(0))* AuthorHouse.
Grace, Kathleen. The Perfect Pug. 2011. 24p. pap. 24.95 *(978-1-4512-7557-5(9))* America Star Bks.
Graham, Bob. Benny: An Adventure Story. 2006. (J). (gr. k-3). pap. 17.95 incl. audio *(978-0-8045-6939-2(8))*; pap. 19.95 incl. audio compact disk *(978-0-8045-4138-1(8))* Spoken Arts, Inc.
—"Let's Get a Pup!" Said Kate. Graham, Bob, illus. 2003. (ENG., Illus.). 32p. (J). (gr. -1-2). pap. 6.99 *(978-0-7636-2193-3(5))* Candlewick Pr.
Graham, Cheryl. Stephanie's Shoes. 2010. 28p. pap. 9.95 *(978-1-4327-5944-5(2))* Outskirts Pr., Inc.
Graham, David. The Adventures of Inky - Escape from London. 2011. (Illus.). 98p. pap. *(978-1-908105-76-9(3))* Grosvenor Hse. Publishing Ltd.
Granata, Diana. Come & Meet Baci, 1 vol. 2008. (ENG.). 39p. 24.95 *(978-1-60474-463-7(4))* America Star Bks.
Grant, Carolyn E. Maggie's Neighborhood. 2009. 24p. pap. 11.99 *(978-1-4389-7230-5(X))* AuthorHouse.
Grant, Mark J. Lila: The Sign of the Elven Queen. 2013. (ENG.). 230p. (J). (gr. 3-7). 14.95 *(978-1-62086-357-2(X))* Mascot Bks., Inc.
Grant, Ron & Ovadia, Ron. First Dog of 1600 Pooch'Lvania Avenue: My First Year in Arf, Arf Office!! Garbot, Dave, illus. 2010. 34p. pap. 13.95 *(978-1-59858-995-5(4))* Dog Ear Publishing, LLC.
Graves, Keith. Puppy! 2016. (ENG., Illus.). 32p. (J). 16.99 *(978-1-62672-225-5(0)*, 9781626722255) Roaring Brook Pr.
Graves, Sue. Mop Top. McClelland, Maddy, illus. 2008. (Tadpoles Ser.). (ENG.). 24p. (J). (gr. -1-3). pap. *(978-0-7787-3888-6(4))*; lib. bdg. *(978-0-7787-3857-2(4))* Crabtree Publishing Co.
Graves, Susan Elaine. Rescued & Making New Friends. 2011. 50p. pap. 24.95 *(978-1-4560-6776-2(1))* America Star Bks.
Gravett, Emily. Dogs. 2009. (ENG., Illus.). 32p. 21.95 *(978-0-230-70422-0(0)*, Macmillan) Pan Macmillan GBR. Dist: Trans-Atlantic Pubns., Inc.
—Dogs. Gravett, Emily, illus. 2010. (ENG., Illus.). 32p. (J). (gr. -1-1). 15.99 *(978-1-4169-8703-1(7)*, Simon & Schuster Bks. For Young Readers) Simon & Schuster Bks. For Young Readers.
Gray, Kes & Gray, Claire. Dog on a Frog? Field, Jim, illus. 2017. (ENG.). 32p. (J). (gr. -1-k). 16.99 ***(978-1-338-11695-3(9)***, Scholastic Pr.) Scholastic, Inc.
Graybill, Guy, Jr. The Dogs of Saint George: The Dogs of St George, 1 vol. 2005. 101p. (YA). per. *(978-0-9747039-2-3(3))* Ironhorse Publishing Co.
Green, Babs Brumer, illus. Take Her Back: An Andy-Bear Tale. 2003. 19p. (J). pap. *(978-0-9753119-0-5(5))* ATU Golden Pubns.
Green, Jonathan, illus. Amadeus, the Leghorn Rooster. 2004. (J). 17.95 *(978-0-87844-174-7(3))* Sandlapper Publishing Co., Inc.
Green, Wendy. Helen & Nicky: A Story of a Special Great Dane & Her Wonderful Girl. 2012. 148p. pap. 13.99 *(978-1-60844-405-2(8))* Dog Ear Publishing, LLC.
Greenberg, Nicki. My Dog Dash. 2016. (ENG.). 32p. (J). (gr. -1-1). 19.99 ***(978-1-76011-067-3(1))*** Allen & Unwin AUS. Dist: Independent Pubs. Group.
Greene, Brenda. Dog Gone: Boomer's Story. Cheryl H. Hahn, illus. 2005. 127p. (YA). per. 8.99 *(978-0-9770279-0-3(2))* Three Willows Pr.
Greene, Daryl C. Benjamin's Dog Joseph: A Three Legged Hero. Akers-Bell, Mary, illus. 2003. 48p. (J). (gr. 2-4). pap. 9.95 *(978-0-9700827-4-9(6))*; lib. bdg. 17.95 *(978-0-9700827-5-6(4))* Densmore-Reid Pubns.
Greene, Jacqueline Dembar. Speak up, Tommy! Melmon, Deborah, illus. 2012. (Kar-Ben Favorites Ser.). (ENG.). 32p. (J). (gr. -1-3). lib. bdg. 17.95 *(978-0-7613-7497-8(3)*, Kar-Ben Publishing) Lerner Publishing Group.
Greene, Montrell. The Magic in Me Series #3: Believing in Me. 2011. 20p. pap. 13.95 *(978-1-4634-1943-1(0))* AuthorHouse.
Greene, Stephanie. Princess Posey & the Next-Door Dog, 3 vols. Sisson, Stéphanie Roth, illus. 2011. (Princess Posey, First Grader Ser.: 3). (ENG.). 96p. (J). (gr. k-3). 5.99 *(978-0-14-241939-7(7)*, Puffin Books); 12.99 *(978-0-399-25463-5(3)*, G.P. Putnam's Sons Books for Young Readers) Penguin Young Readers Group.
Greenlee, Don. This Countryboy Guardian Was Heaven Sent. 2007. (Illus.). 114p. (YA). per. 14.95 net. *(978-0-9795574-0-8(2))* Country Boy Publishing Co.
Greenwald, Lisa. Dog Beach Unleashed. 2015. (Seagate Summers Ser.). (ENG., Illus.). 240p. (YA). (gr. 5-9). 15.95 *(978-1-4197-1481-8(3)*, Amulet Bks.) Abrams, Inc.
—Welcome to Dog Beach. (Seagate Summers Ser.). (ENG.). (YA). (gr. 3-7). 2015. 288p. pap. 6.95 *(978-1-4197-1497-9(X))* 2014. 272p. 15.95 *(978-1-4197-1018-6(4))* Abrams, Inc. (Amulet Bks.).
Greenwald, Tom. My Dog Is Better Than Your Dog. Stower, Adam, illus. 2015. 198p. (J). pap. *(978-0-545-91669-1(0)*, Scholastic Pr.) Scholastic, Inc.
Greenwald, Tommy. It's a Doggy Dog World. Stower, Adam, illus. 2016. (Crimebiters Ser.: 2). (ENG.). 240p. (J). (gr. 3-7). 12.99 *(978-0-545-78397-2(6)*, Scholastic Pr.) Scholastic, Inc.
—My Dog Is Better Than Your Dog (Crimebiters! #1) Stower, Adam, illus. 2015. (Crimebiters Ser.: 1). (ENG.). 208p. (J). (gr. 3-7). 12.99 *(978-0-545-77332-4(6)*, Scholastic Pr.) Scholastic, Inc.
Greer, Tom C. Honey's Peanut Butter Adventure. Faust, Laurie A., illus. 2007. (Adventures of Honey Ser.). (J). per. 9.95 *(978-0-9789227-1-9(9))* Weeping Willow Publishing.
Gregg, John Hunter. Where Dogs Run. 2006. (YA). per. *(978-0-9790165-5-4(X))* 302 Publishing.
Gregory, Caroline. Puppy Stew. Suorsa, Michael, illus. 2009. (ENG.). 28p. (J). pap. 8.99 *(978-0-9772025-9-1(3))* Sortis Publishing.
Greiner, Linda. Sashi Adopts a Brother. Spicer, Morgan, illus. 2015. (ENG.). 40p. (J). 14.95 net. *(978-1-61254-856-2(3))* Brown Books Publishing Group.
—Sashi, the Scared Little Sheltie. Spicer, Morgan, illus. 2015. (ENG.). 32p. (J). 14.95 net. *(978-1-61254-214-0(X))* Brown Books Publishing Group.
Grew, David. The Wild Dog of Edmonton. Segner, Ellen, illus. 2011. 208p. 44.95 *(978-1-258-09902-2(0))* Literary Licensing, LLC.
Greyling, Emma. The Mystical Life of the Dog with Three Legs. 2010. 236p. pap. 14.49 *(978-1-4520-1925-3(8))* AuthorHouse.
Griebel, Roberta L. Joyful Noise! 2007. (ENG.). 56p. per. 16.95 *(978-1-4241-6037-2(5))* America Star Bks.
Griffin, Paul. When Friendship Followed Me Home. 2016. (ENG.). 256p. (J). (gr. 5-9). 16.99 *(978-0-8037-3816-4(1)*, Dial Bks) Penguin Young Readers Group.
Griffiths, Andy. Ed & Ted & Ted's Dog Fred. Denton, Terry, illus. 2014. (My Readers Ser.). (ENG.). 32p. (J). (gr. -1-1). 15.99 *(978-1-250-04447-1(2)*, 9781250044471) Square Fish.
—Ed & Ted & Ted's Dog Fred. 2014. (My Readers: Level 2 Ser.). (J). lib. bdg. 13.55 *(978-0-606-35525-4(1))* Turtleback Bks.
Griggs, Joyce. Imanis Good Deed. 2006. pap. 9.95 *(978-1-4327-0071-3(5))* Outskirts Pr., Inc.
Grimm, Kristi. Mommy, Tell Me a Story about a Car, 2nd Edition. Grimm, Dave, illus. 2nd ed. 2013. 32p. pap. 13.99 *(978-0-9855699-9-0(9))* Richer Life, LLC.
Grimmer, Constance Marie. Santa's Christmas Dogs: A Legend Begins... 2009. 28p. pap. 15.49 *(978-1-4490-5920-0(1))* AuthorHouse.
Grinnell, Suzanne. Where Is Beau? Peter, Joshua, illus. 2008. 24p. pap. 12.99 *(978-1-59858-612-1(2))* Dog Ear Publishing, LLC.
Grinstead, Krista. Frenchie & Friends: The Walk. 2010. 28p. pap. 13.50 *(978-1-4490-0678-5(7))* AuthorHouse.
Griver, Jeanette A. CURIO a Shetland Sheepdog & Friends: A Story of Change for Children of All Ages. 2005. (Illus.). 64p. (J). per. 6.95 *(978-0-929948-05-8(X))* Compsych Systems, Inc., Pubns. Div.
—CURIO a Shetland Sheepdog & her Pals: All ages Will enjoy the Tales of Friendship. 2007. (J). per. 8.50 *(978-0-929948-06-5(8))* Compsych Systems, Inc., Pubns. Div.
Grizzell, Whitney. HaleyBeth & Pink Rose Meet for the First Time. 2009. 24p. pap. 24.95 *(978-1-60749-403-4(5))* America Star Bks.
Grogan, John. Bad Dog, Marley! Cowdrey, Richard, illus. (ENG.). 40p. (J). (gr. -1-3). 2011. pap. 6.99 *(978-0-06-117116-1(6))* 2007. 17.99 *(978-0-06-117114-7(X))* HarperCollins Pubs.
—Bad Dog, Marley! Beloved Book & Plush Puppy. Cowdrey, Richard, illus. 2007. 40p. (J). (gr. -1-3). 24.99 *(978-0-06-143496-9(5))* HarperCollins Pubs.
—The Dog Who Ate My Homework. 2012. (Marley: I Can Read! Ser.). (J). lib. bdg. 13.55 *(978-0-606-26283-5(0)*, Turtleback) Turtleback Bks.
—The Dog Who Cried Woof. Cowdrey, Richard, illus. 2011. (I Can Read Level 2 Ser.). (ENG.). 32p. (J). (gr. k-3). pap. 3.99 *(978-0-06-198943-8(6))* HarperCollins Pubs.
—Farm Dog. Cowdrey, Richard, illus. 2011. (I Can Read Level 2 Ser.). (ENG.). 32p. (J). (gr. k-3). pap. 3.99 *(978-0-06-198937-7(1))* HarperCollins Pubs.
—Marley: Firehouse Dog. Cowdrey, Richard & Halverson, Lydia, illus. 2012. (I Can Read Level 2 Ser.). (ENG.). 32p. (J). (gr. -1-3). 16.99 *(978-0-06-207484-3(9))*; pap. 3.99 *(978-0-06-207483-6(0))* HarperCollins Pubs.
—Marley: The Dog Who Ate My Homework. Cowdrey, Richard & Whipple, Rick, illus. 2012. (I Can Read Level 2 Ser.). (ENG.). 32p. (J). (gr. k-3). pap. 3.99 *(978-0-06-207480-5(6))* HarperCollins Pubs.
—Marley - Not a Peep! Cowdrey, Richard & Whipple, Rick, illus. 2012. (I Can Read Level 2 Ser.). (ENG.). 32p. (J). (gr. k-3). pap. 3.99 *(978-0-06-207477-5(6))* HarperCollins Pubs.
—Marley & the Kittens. Cowdrey, Richard, illus. 2010. (Marley Ser.). 40p. (J). (gr. -1-3). (ENG.). 17.99 *(978-0-06-171486-3(0))*; lib. bdg. 18.89 *(978-0-06-171487-0(9))* HarperCollins Pubs.
—Marley Goes to School. Cowdrey, Richard, illus. (Marley Ser.). 40p. (J). (gr. -1-3). 2012. (ENG.). 9.99 *(978-0-06-211366-5(6))* 2009. (ENG.). 17.99 *(978-0-06-156151-1(7))* 2009. lib. bdg. 18.89 *(978-0-06-156152-8(5))* HarperCollins Pubs.
—Marley Learns a Lesson. Cowdrey, Richard, illus. 2013. (I Can Read Level 2 Ser.). (ENG.). 32p. (J). (gr. -1-3). 16.99 *(978-0-06-207487-4(3))* HarperCollins Pubs.
—Marley Looks for Love. Cowdrey, Richard, illus. 2010. (Marley Ser.). (ENG.). 16p. (J). (gr. -1-1). pap. 6.99 *(978-0-06-185590-0(1)*, HarperFestival) HarperCollins Pubs.
—Marley Storybook Treasury. Cowdrey, Richard, illus. 2012. (I Can Read Level 2 Ser.). (ENG.). 192p. (J). (gr. k-3). 11.99 *(978-0-06-212331-2(9))* HarperCollins Pubs.
—Marley's Big Adventure. 2009. (Marley: I Can Read! Ser.). (J). lib. bdg. 13.55 *(978-0-606-06942-7(9)*, Turtleback) Turtleback Bks.
—Messy Dog. Cowdrey, Richard, illus. 2011. (I Can Read Level 2 Ser.). (ENG.). 32p. (J). (gr. k-3). 16.99 *(978-0-06-198940-7(1))*; pap. 3.99 *(978-0-06-198939-1(8))* HarperCollins Pubs.
—Not a Peep! Cowdrey, Richard & Whipple, Rick, illus. 2012. (I Can Read Level 2 Ser.). (ENG.). 32p. (J). (gr. k-3). 16.99 *(978-0-06-207478-2(4))* HarperCollins Pubs.
—Not a Peep! 2012. (Marley: I Can Read! Ser.). (J). lib. bdg. 13.55 *(978-0-606-23569-3(8)*, Turtleback) Turtleback Bks.
—Snow Dog Marley. Cowdrey, Richard, illus. 2010. (I Can Read Level 2 Ser.). (ENG.). 32p. (J). (gr. k-3). 16.99 *(978-0-06-185393-7(3))*; pap. 3.99 *(978-0-06-185392-0(5))* HarperCollins Pubs.
—Thanks, Mom & Dad! Cowdrey, Richard, illus. 2011. (Marley Ser.). (ENG.). 24p. (J). (gr. -1-2). pap. 3.99 *(978-0-06-185381-4(X)*, HarperFestival) HarperCollins Pubs.
—A Thanksgiving to Remember. Cowdrey, Richard & Whipple, Rick, illus. 2011. (Marley Ser.). (ENG.). 16p. (J). (gr. -1-1). pap. 6.99 *(978-0-06-185591-7(X)*, HarperFestival) HarperCollins Pubs.
—Trick or Treat, Marley! Cowdrey, Richard, illus. (Marley Ser.). (ENG.). 40p. (J). (gr. -1-3). 2013. 9.99 *(978-0-06-211368-9(2))* 2011. 17.99 *(978-0-06-185755-3(6))* HarperCollins Pubs.
—A Very Marley Christmas. Cowdrey, Richard, illus. (Marley Ser.). (ENG.). 40p. (J). (gr. -1-3). 2014. 9.99 *(978-0-06-211367-2(4))* 2008. 17.99 *(978-0-06-137292-6(7))* HarperCollins Pubs.
—A Very Marley Christmas. Cowdrey, Richard, illus. (ENG.). 32p. pap. *(978-0-00-728723-9(2)*, HarperCollins Children's Bks.) HarperCollins Pubs. Ltd.
Grogan, John & Hill, Susan. Marley's Big Adventure. Cowdrey, Richard & Halverson, Lydia, illus. 2009. (I Can Read Book 2 Ser.). 32p. (J). (gr. -1-3). 16.99 *(978-0-06-185384-5(4))*; (ENG.). (gr. k-3). pap. 3.99 *(978-0-06-185383-8(6))* HarperCollins Pubs.
—Strike Three, Marley! Cowdrey, Richard & Beier, Ellen, illus. 2010. (I Can Read Level 2 Ser.). (ENG.). 32p. (J). (gr. k-3). pap. 3.99 *(978-0-06-185386-9(0))* HarperCollins Pubs.
Grooms, Molly. We Are Puppies. 2005. 40p. bds. *(978-90-5843-815-7(5))* YoYo Bks.
Gross, Scott. Scooby-Doo & the Aliens of Area 49, 1 vol. 2013. (Scooby-Doo Graphic Novels Set 3 Ser.). (ENG.). 24p. (J). (gr. 2-6). lib. bdg. 24.21 *(978-1-61479-049-5(3)*, Essential Library) ABDO Publishing Co.
Group/McGraw-Hill, Wright. Seiko the Watchdog: Level N, 6 vols. 128p. (gr. 3-6). 36.95 *(978-0-322-05883-5(X))* Wright Group/McGraw-Hill.
Grover, Jan Zita. A Home for Dakota. 2008. (Sit! Stay! Read! Ser.). (ENG., Illus.). 24p. (J). (gr. k-2). 16.95 *(978-0-940719-05-7(3))* Gryphon Pr., The.
Grover, Neha Lamba. Shaurya's Adventures. 2010. 43p. pap. 17.40 *(978-0-557-12636-1(3))* Lulu Pr., Inc.
Grovet, Heather Marie. Marvelous Mark & His No-Good Dog. 2003. (Review Kids Ser.). 128p. (J). pap. 7.99 *(978-0-8280-1734-3(4)*, 132-670) Review & Herald Publishing Assn.
Gruber, Daveda. More Tales of a Tiny Dog. 2009. 71p. pap. 32.50 *(978-1-4092-6657-0(5))* Lulu Pr., Inc.
—Tales of a Tiny Dog. 2010. 74p. pap. 29.50 *(978-0-557-43600-2(1))* Lulu Pr., Inc.
Gruelle, Johnny. Raggedy Ann & Rags. Palmer, Jan, illus. 2010. (Raggedy Ann Ser.). (ENG.). 40p. (J). (gr. -1-2). 19.99 *(978-1-4424-2198-1(3)*, Simon & Schuster Bks. For Young Readers) Simon & Schuster Bks. For Young Readers.
Gruffudd, Elena. Gelert. 2005. (WEL., Illus.). 36p. pap. *(978-0-86381-291-0(0))* Gwasg Carreg Gwalch.
Gudeon, Adam. Ping Wants to Play. Gudeon, Adam, illus. 2014. (I Like to Read(r) Ser.). (ENG., Illus.). 24p. (J). (gr. -1-3). 14.95 *(978-0-8234-2854-0(0))* Holiday Hse., Inc.
Gudeon, Adam & Gudeon, Adam. Ping Wants to Play. 2015. (I Like to Read(r) Ser.). (ENG.). 24p. (J). (gr. -1-3). 6.99 *(978-0-8234-3313-1(7))* Holiday Hse., Inc.
Guest, Elissa Haden. Bella's Rules. Halpin, Abigail, illus. 2013. (ENG.). 32p. (J). (gr. -1-k). 16.99 *(978-0-8037-3393-0(3)*, Dial Bks) Penguin Young Readers Group.
Guibert, Emmanuel. Top Dog. 2016. (Ariol Ser.: 7). (J). lib. bdg. 24.50 *(978-0-606-37581-8(3))* Turtleback Bks.
Guibert, Susan Mullen & O'Shaughnessy, Brendan. Clashmore Mike Comes Home. Pynaert, Andrea, illus. 2012. 24p. (J). 19.95 *(978-0-9859377-3-7(4))* Corby Books.
—Clashmore Mike_Dublin to Dome. Pynaert, Andrea, illus. 2012. 36p. (J). 19.95 *(978-0-9859377-1-3(8))* Corby Books.
Guillain, Charlotte. The Kitten Who Cried Dog, 1 vol. Beacon, Dawn, illus. 2013. (Animal Fairy Tales Ser.). (ENG.). 24p. (gr. -1-2). pap. 6.49 *(978-1-4109-5029-1(8))*; lib. bdg. 23.99 *(978-1-4109-5023-9(9))* Heinemann-Raintree. (NA-r).
Guillain, Charlotte & Aesop. The Kitten Who Cried Dog. Beacon, Dawn, illus. 2013. (Animal Fairy Tales Ser.). (ENG.). 24p. (gr. -1-2). 26.00 *(978-1-4109-5041-3(7)*, NA-r) Heinemann-Raintree.
Gulliksen, Anne. The Smartest Dog on the Planet. 2012. 32p. pap. 14.98 *(978-1-4575-0973-5(3))* Dog Ear Publishing, LLC.
Gumbo Goes Downtown - Evaluation Guide: Evaluation Guide. 2006. (J). *(978-1-55942-407-3(9))* Witcher Productions.
Gummelt, Donna & Melchiorre, Dondino. Cow Puppies. Wall, Randy Hugh, ed. Varela, Juan D., tr. Varela, Juan D., illus. 2006.Tr. of Cachorros Vaqueros. (SPA.). 32p. (J). 14.95 *(978-0-9764798-7-1(7))* Story Store Collection Publishing.
Gumnut, I. B. Mad Dogs. 2012. 24p. pap. 10.95 *(978-1-4525-0450-6(4))* Balboa Pr.
Gunning, P. M. The Adventures of Corrie & Trix. 2012. (Illus.). 36p. pap. 22.88 *(978-1-4772-1950-8(1))* AuthorHouse.
Gutierrez-Haley, Lisa. The New Pet: Adventures of Hayden & Jace. 2011. 20p. pap. 24.95 *(978-1-4626-1872-9(3))* America Star Bks.
Gutman, Anne. Gaspard & Lisa's Christmas Surprise. Hallensleben, Georg, illus. 2012. lib. bdg. 17.20 *(978-0-606-26782-3(4)*, Turtleback) Turtleback Bks.
—Lisa's Baby Sister. Hallensleben, Georg, illus. 2012. (ENG.). 32p. (J). (gr. k-3). pap. 6.99 *(978-0-449-81012-5(7)*, Dragonfly Bks.) Random Hse. Children's Bks.
Gutman, Dan. Miss Klute Is a Hoot! Paillot, Jim, illus. 2014. (My Weirder School Ser.: 11). 112p. (J). (gr. 1-5). 15.89 *(978-0-06-219845-7(9))*; (ENG.). pap. 4.99 *(978-0-06-219844-0(0))* HarperCollins Pubs.
—Miss Klute Is a Hoot! 2014. (My Weirder School Ser.: 11). (J). lib. bdg. 14.75 *(978-0-606-35503-2(0))* Turtleback Bks.
Guzman, Lila. Kichi in Jungle Jeopardy. Johnson, Regan, illus. (J). 2007. (ENG.). 135p. (gr. 2-7). pap. 8.95 *(978-0-9769417-2-9(4))* 2006. 144p. 13.95 *(978-0-9769417-1-2(6))* Blooming Tree Pr.
Habek, Wendy. Good Boy, Troy! 2009. 20p. (J). pap. 13.95 *(978-1-4327-3192-2(0))* Outskirts Pr., Inc.
Haddon, Mark. The Curious Incident of the Dog in the Night-Time. 2007. (ENG., Illus.). 320p. mass mkt. *(978-1-4000-2535-0(4)*, Seal Bks) Doubleday Canada, Ltd. CAN. Dist: Random Hse., Inc.
Haesche, Richard, Sr. A Dog Named Wishbone. 2007. 155p. (J). 6.75 *(978-0-9798536-2-3(1))* Kreative X-Pressions Pubns.
Haggerty, Robert. Bailey's Day. 2010. (Illus.). 45p. (J). pap. 17.95 *(978-1-4327-4550-9(6))* Outskirts Pr., Inc.
Haircuts for Bella & Rosie. 2004. (Bella & Rosie Set 2 Ser.). (J). 7.67 *(978-1-932570-18-2(7))* Pioneer Valley Bks.
Halbur, Donna. The Puppy & the Guppy. 2nd ed. 2005. (YA). per. 9.95 *(978-0-9603520-1-2(5))* Halbur Publishing.
Hale, Bruce. Danny & the Dinosaur & the New Puppy. 2015. (I Can Read! Level 1 Ser.). (J). lib. bdg. 13.55 *(978-0-606-37608-2(9))* Turtleback Bks.
Hale, Mary. Karly & Sheila's Walk. 2012. (ENG.). 23p. (J). pap. 11.95 *(978-1-4327-8647-2(4))* Outskirts Pr., Inc.
Haley, Annie. Rumpus & Bumpus: If we could do Anything... ... 2008. 32p. pap. 13.95 *(978-1-59858-803-3(6))* Dog Ear Publishing, LLC.
Hall, Adam Z. The Little Purple Puppy. 2013. 16p. pap. 15.99 *(978-1-4817-0179-2(7))* AuthorHouse.
Hall, Kirsten. The Jacket. Tolstikova, Dasha, illus. 2014. (ENG.). 48p. (J). (gr. -1-3). 17.95 *(978-1-59270-168-1(X))* Enchanted Lion Bks., LLC.
Hall, Natalie Susan. Andy Anole's Adventure, 1 vol. 2009. 26p. pap. 24.95 *(978-1-60813-350-5(8))* America Star Bks.
Hall, Terri L. & Babeaux, Denise L. The Story of Chester the Chow Chow. 2011. 48p. pap. 24.95 *(978-1-4560-3748-2(X))* America Star Bks.
Hall, William. Just Like Me: My Diggety Dog - Paws4Learning. 2013. 32p. pap. *(978-1-4602-1368-1(8))* FriesenPress.
Hallinan, P. K. Let's Be Helpful. Hallinan, P. K., illus. 2009. (ENG., Illus.). 24p. (J). (gr. -1-2). 8.99 *(978-0-8249-5611-0(7)*, Ideal Pubns.) Worthy Publishing.
Hallstrand, John & Sarah & Hawley, Karen. Zoey Helps the Mystery Dog Find a Home. 2011. 24p. pap. 11.99 *(978-1-4634-1094-0(8))* AuthorHouse.
Hamilton, Elizabeth L. Pandora Puppy's Caring Circle. 2004. (Character Critters Ser.: No. 5). (Illus.). 32p. (J). per. 5.95 *(978-0-9754629-0-4(3)*, Character-in-Action) Quiet Impact, Inc.
Hamilton, Eric E. Buddy the Bassett Hound Follows His Nose. 2013. 94p. pap. 17.95 *(978-1-4137-7764-2(3))* America Star Bks.
Hamilton, John. Dog Friday. 2010. (Illus.). 60p. pap. 21.99 *(978-1-4490-9468-3(6))* AuthorHouse.
Hamilton, Kersten. The Ire of Iron Claw. Hamilton, James, illus. (Gadgets & Gears Ser.: 2). (ENG.). (J). (gr. 2-5). 2016. 192p. pap. 6.99 *(978-0-544-66854-6(5)*, HMH Books For Young Readers) 2015. 176p. 16.99 *(978-0-544-22502-2(3))* Houghton Mifflin Harcourt Publishing Co.
—The Tick-Tock Man. Hamilton, James, illus. 2016. (Gadgets & Gears Ser.: 3). (ENG.). 144p. (J). (gr. 2-5). 16.99 *(978-0-544-43300-7(9))* Houghton Mifflin Harcourt Publishing Co.
Hamilton, Martha & Weiss, Mitch. Why Animals Never Got Fire: A Story of the Couer d'Alene Indians. MacDonald, Bruce, illus. 2005. (ENG.). 12p. (J). 5.75 *(978-1-57274-715-9(3)*, 2793, Bks. for Young Learners) Owen, Richard C. Pubs., Inc.
Hamilton, Pat. Peaches the Private Eye Poodle: The Missing Muffin Caper. 2008. 32p. pap. 13.50 *(978-1-60693-277-3(2)*, Eloquent Bks.) Strategic Book Publishing & Rights Agency (SBPRA).
Hamilton, Patricia D. Peaches the Private Eye Poodle: Finding Foster a Home. 2010. 36p. (gr. -1-3). pap. 13.50 *(978-1-60911-108-3(7)*, Eloquent Bks.) Strategic Book Publishing & Rights Agency (SBPRA).
—Peaches the Private Eye Poodle: Where Is Loosey Goosey? 2009. 32p. pap. 13.50 *(978-1-60860-063-2(7)*, Eloquent Bks.) Strategic Book Publishing & Rights Agency (SBPRA).
Hamilton, Tim. But! Hamilton, Tim, illus. 2014. (ENG., Illus.). 32p. (J). (gr. -1-2). 16.95 *(978-0-8234-3046-8(4))* Holiday Hse., Inc.
Hammel, Sara. The Underdogs. 2016. (ENG.). 320p. (J). 16.99 *(978-0-374-30161-3(1)*, 9780374301613, Farrar, Straus & Giroux (BYR)) Farrar, Straus & Giroux.
Hammond, Barbara, illus. The Duffy Chronicles. Hammond, Barbara, . 2007. 60p. pap. 11.99 *(978-0-9800675-4-5(5))* Mirror Publishing.
Hammond, Sandra. A Day with Duke. 2010. 28p. pap. 12.49 *(978-1-4520-0774-8(8))* AuthorHouse.
Hanna, H. Y. Curse of the Scarab (Big Honey Dog Mysteries #1) Curse of the Scarab. 2013. 258p. (J). pap. *(978-0-9923153-1-3(X))* Hanna, H.Y.
Hannam, John-Pierre M., Sr. Uncle Jake's Hat. 2009. 43p. pap. 20.00 *(978-0-557-02568-8(0))* Lulu Pr., Inc.
Hannigan, Katherine. Dirt + Water = Mud. Hannigan, Katherine, illus. 2016. (Illus.). 40p. (J). (gr. -1-3). 17.99 *(978-0-06-234517-2(6)*, Greenwillow Bks.) HarperCollins Pubs.
Hanning, Jacob. Mommy's Little Helper: That's Me. 2012. 28p. pap. 24.95 *(978-1-4626-5649-3(8))* America Star Bks.
Hannon, Rose. Finding Agate: An Epic Story of a Poodle's Heart & His Will to Survive. 2010. 268p. pap. 16.99 *(978-1-4490-8986-3(0))* AuthorHouse.
Hansen, Amelia, illus. It's Raining Pups & Dogs! 2013. (Sit! Stay! Read! Ser.). (ENG.). 24p. (J). (gr. k). 16.95 *(978-0-940719-16-3(9))* Gryphon Pr., The.
Hanson, Paige & Hanson, Jon. Harry Spotter: The Incontinent Puppy Sellers, Amy, illus. l.t. ed. 2005. 44p. (J). per. 20.00 *(978-0-9721146-1-5(0))* Monroe Educational Media.
Hao, K. T. Who Did This? Bernatene, Poly, illus. 2008. (ENG.). 32p. (J). (gr. -1). lib. bdg. 16.50 *(978-1-933327-33-4(2))* Purple Bear Bks., Inc.
—Who Did This? Bernatene, Poly, illus. 2008. (ENG.). 32p. (J). (gr. -1). 15.95 *(978-1-933327-32-7(4))* Purple Bear Bks., Inc.
Hapka, Catherine, pseud. Meet the Buddies! Lyon, Tammie, illus. 2013. (World of Reading Ser.). (ENG.). 32p. (J). (gr. 1-3). pap. 3.99 *(978-1-4231-6946-8(8))* Disney Pr.
—A New Home for Truman. Regan, Dana, illus. 2015. (Pet Rescue Club Ser.: 1). (ENG.). 128p. (J). (gr. 1-3). lib. bdg. 16.99 *(978-0-7944-3351-2(0))* Reader's Digest Assn., Inc., The.
—A New Home for Truman. Regan, Dana, illus. 2015. (Pet Rescue Club Ser.: 1). (ENG.). 128p. (J). (gr. 1-3). pap. 5.99 *(978-0-7944-3312-3(X))* Studio Fun International.
—Too Big to Run. 2015. (Pet Rescue Club Ser.: 4). (ENG.). 128p. (J). (gr. 1-3). pap. 5.99 *(978-0-7944-3453-3(3)*, Reader's Digest Children's Bks.) Studio Fun International.
Happel, Roberta L. Lynd. 2009. 16p. pap. 8.99 *(978-1-4389-4088-5(2))* AuthorHouse.
Hardy, Ralph. Argos: The Story of Odysseus As Told by His Loyal Dog. 2016. 400p. (J). (gr. 3-7). 16.99 *(978-0-06-239678-5(1))* HarperCollins Pubs.
Hargreaves, G. N. Douglas. 2011. (Illus.). (J). (gr. -1-3). pap. *(978-0-85757-145-8(1))* Egmont Bks., Ltd.
Harimann, Sierra. Diploma Day. 2011. (Illus.). 30p. (J). pap. *(978-0-545-28143-0(1))* Scholastic, Inc.
—Easter Egg Hunt. 2014. (Illus.). 30p. (J). pap. *(978-0-545-59212-3(7))* Scholastic, Inc.
—Puppies on Parade. 2014. (Illus.). 30p. (J). pap. *(978-0-545-59211-6(9))* Scholastic, Inc.
—Puppy Love. 2011. (Illus.). 30p. (J). pap. *(978-0-545-28142-3(3))* Scholastic, Inc.

—A Puppy Tale. 2013. (LEGO Friends Comic Readers Ser.: 1). lib. bdg. 13.55 *(978-0-606-31549-4(7)*, Turtleback) Turtleback Bks.

—Water Pups. 2013. (Illus.). 30p. (J). *(978-0-545-47235-7(0))* Scholastic, Inc.

Harlan. My Best Friend. 2011. 28p. pap. 9.95 *(978-1-4327-7164-5(7))* Outskirts Pr., Inc.

Harley, Stephen. The Christmastime Dog Rescue. 2013. 24p. pap. 10.95 *(978-1-4624-0774-3(9)*, Inspiring Voices) Author Solutions, Inc.

Harlow, Honey. Honey's Shoes. 2013. 28p. pap. 9.95 *(978-1-4327-9921-2(5))* Outskirts Pr., Inc.

Harlow, Joan Hiatt. Thunder from the Sea. (ENG., Illus.). (J). (gr. 3-7). 2005. 240p. pap. 6.99 *(978-0-689-86404-9(3))* 2004. 208p. 17.99 *(978-0-689-86403-2(5))* McElderry, Margaret K. Bks. (McElderry, Margaret K. Bks.).

Harmon, Douglas. Momma Whats a Stranger. 2011. 28p. pap. *(978-1-4269-7247-8(4))* Trafford Publishing (UK) Ltd.

Harms, Carol. What If? 2010. 20p. 10.49 *(978-1-4520-8463-3(7))* AuthorHouse.

Harner, Ron. Move It Milton! Surrey, Michael, illus. 2009. 36p. pap. 11.95 *(978-1-59858-738-8(2))* Dog Ear Publishing, LLC.

Harp, Susan. Evie Goes Clean & Green. Siau, Jon, illus. 2013. 24p. (J). lib. bdg. 14.95 *(978-1-938730-09-2(7))* M.T. Publishing Co., Inc.

—Retrieving with Evie. Siau, John, illus. 2007. (ENG.). 24p. (J). lib. bdg. 12.95 *(978-1-932439-67-0(6))* M.T. Publishing Co., Inc.

Harper, Aimee. Crystal. 2010. (Dream Dogs Ser.: Bk. 4). (ENG., Illus.). 112p. (J). (gr. -1-3). 5.99 *(978-0-00-732037-0(X))* HarperCollins Pubs. Ltd. GBR. Dist: Independent Pubs. Group.

—Dream Dogs - Nugget. 2010. (Dream Dogs Ser.: Bk. 3). (ENG., Illus.). 112p. (J). (gr. -1-3). 6.99 *(978-0-00-732036-3(1))* HarperCollins Pubs. Ltd. GBR. Dist: Independent Pubs. Group.

Harper, Charise Mericle. Just Grace Three Books in One! Just Grace, Still Just Grace, Just Grace Walks the Dog. 2016. (ENG.). 480p. (J). (gr. 1-4). 14.99 *(978-0-544-85453-6(5)*, HMH Books For Young Readers) Houghton Mifflin Harcourt Publishing Co.

—Just Grace Walks the Dog. 2009. (Just Grace Ser.: 3). (ENG., Illus.). 176p. (J). (gr. 1-4). pap. 5.99 *(978-0-547-23753-4(7))* Houghton Mifflin Harcourt Publishing Co.

Harper, Chris. The Dogges of Barkshire - the Charge of the Light Brigade. 2013. 42p. pap. *(978-1-78222-171-5(9))* Paragon Publishing, Rothersthorpe.

—The Dogges of Barkshire - the Grand Kennel. Harper, Chris, illus. 2013. (Illus.). 26p. (J). pap. *(978-1-78222-086-2(0))* Paragon Publishing, Rothersthorpe.

Harper, Dan. Sit, Truman! Moser, Barry & Moser, Cara, illus. 2004. (ENG.). 32p. (J). (gr. -1-3). reprint ed. pap. 6.99 *(978-0-15-205068-9(X))* Houghton Mifflin Harcourt Publishing Co.

Harper, Lee. Snow! Snow! Snow! Harper, Lee, illus. 2009. (ENG., Illus.). 40p. (J). (gr. -1-3). 14.99 *(978-1-4169-8454-2(2)*, Simon & Schuster/Paula Wiseman Bks.) Simon & Schuster/Paula Wiseman Bks.

Harper, Richard. Richie Gets a Dog: A Father & Son Book about Adopting Animals Shelter Dogs & Cats. 2012. 28p. pap. 24.95 *(978-1-4626-6549-5(7))* America Star Bks.

Harries, Tony. Zeegpaw & the Cat Cult. 2008. 304p. pap. 18.95 *(978-1-4357-0754-2(0))* Lulu Pr., Inc.

Harrington, Claudia. Book 1: Otis the Very Large Dog. 2016. (Hank the Pet Sitter Ser.). (ENG.). (gr. -1-3). lib. bdg. 27.07 ***(978-1-62402-187-9(5))*** ABDO Publishing Co.

Harrington, Linda. Holly's Backyard Adventures, 1 vol. 2010. 20p. pap. 24.95 *(978-1-4512-9277-0(5))* PublishAmerica, Inc.

Harris, Brooke. Where Has My Dog Gone? Harrington, David, illus. 2010. (Rising Readers Ser.). (J). 3.49 *(978-1-60719-693-8(X))* Newmark Learning LLC.

Harris, Dorothy Joan. Un Perro Muy Diferente. Rioja, Alberto Jimenez, tr. from ENG. LaFave, Kim, illus. 2006. (SPA.). 28p. (J). (gr. 5-6). pap. 7.99 *(978-1-933032-04-7(9))* Lectorum Pubns., Inc.

Harris, M. S. Ed Rebecca a. & Harris, M. S. Ed. Megan's Monster. Lee, Joe, illus. 2009. 28p. pap. 15.00 *(978-1-4490-2822-0(5))* AuthorHouse.

Harris, Marian. Ten Little Puppies. Harris, Jim, illus. 2009. (ENG.). 26p. (J). (gr. -1-3). 16.99 *(978-0-7407-8481-1(1))* Andrews McMeel Publishing.

Harris, Patricia. The Cat & the Dog. 2017. (Farmyard Tales Ser.). 24p. (gr. 4-6). pap. 8.25 ***(978-1-5383-2178-2(5)***, PowerKids Pr.) Rosen Publishing Group, Inc., The.

Harris, Trudy. Over, under, in, & Ouch! Haskamp, Steve, illus. 2003. (Silly Millies Level 2 Ser.). (ENG.). 32p. (gr. 1-3). lib. bdg. 21.27 *(978-0-7613-2912-1(9)*, Millbrook Pr.) Lerner Publishing Group.

Harrison, Cora. Two Mad Dogs. Myler, Terry, illus. 2003. (Chimps Ser.: 4). (ENG.). 64p. (J). pap. 10.95 *(978-1-901737-44-8(6))* Anvil Bks., Ltd. IRL. Dist: Dufour Editions, Inc.

—Wolf in the Midnight Forest. (ENG., Illus.). 240p. pap. 5.95 *(978-0-86327-882-2(5))* Wolfhound Pr. IRL. Dist: Interlink Publishing Group, Inc.

Harrison, Hannah E. Extraordinary Jane. 2014. (ENG.). 40p. (J). (gr. -1-k). 16.99 *(978-0-8037-3914-7(1)*, Dial Bks) Penguin Young Readers Group.

Harrison, Jack. Bozo the Criminal Dog. 2010. 56p. pap. 8.50 *(978-1-4461-2895-4(4))* Lulu Pr., Inc.

Harrison, Joanna & Briggs, Raymond. The Snowman & the Snowdog. 2014. (ENG., Illus.). 40p. (J). (gr. -1-2). 17.99 *(978-0-385-38714-9(8)*, Random Hse. Bks. for Young Readers) Random Hse. Children's Bks.

Harrison, Paula. The Silver Locket. 2014. (Rescue Princesses Ser.: 9). (ENG.). 128p. (J). (gr. 2-5). pap. 4.99 *(978-0-545-66162-1(5)*, Scholastic Paperbacks) Scholastic, Inc.

Harry How Books. Just Luke. l.t. ed. 2006. (ENG., Illus.). 28p. per. 9.95 *(978-1-4327-0178-9(9))* Outskirts Pr., Inc.

Hart, Alison. Darling, Mercy Dog of World War I, 1 vol. Montgomery, Michael G., illus. (Dog Chronicles Ser.: 5). (ENG.). (J). (gr. 2-5). 2017. 170p. pap. 7.95 *(978-1-56145-981-0(X))* 2013. 160p. 12.95 *(978-1-56145-705-2(1))* Peachtree Pubs.

—Finder, Coal Mine Dog, 1 vol. Montgomery, Michael G., illus. 2015. (Dog Chronicles Ser.). (ENG.). 185p. (J). (gr. 2-5). 12.95 *(978-1-56145-860-8(0))* Peachtree Pubs.

—Leo, Dog of the Sea, 1 vol. Montgomery, Michael G., illus. 2017. (Dog Chronicles Ser.: 5). (ENG.). 176p. (J). (gr. 2-5). 12.95 *(978-1-56145-964-3(X))* Peachtree Pubs.

Harvey, Natalie. Peppermint Pixie. Winfield, Amy, illus. 2013. 44p. pap. *(978-1-909202-10-8(X))* Little Acorns Publishing.

Harvey, Sarah N. Puppies on Board, 1 vol. Cowles, Rose, illus. 2005. (ENG.). 32p. (J). (gr. -1-3). 17.95 *(978-1-55143-390-5(7))* Orca Bk. Pubs. USA.

Harvey, Tom. Top Dog. 2011. 48p. pap. *(978-1-4269-7612-4(7))* Trafford Publishing (UK) Ltd.

Hasbro & O'Ryan, Ellie. Littlest Pet Shop - Terriers & Tiara Reunion: Starring Zoe Trent! 2015. (ENG.). 160p. (J). (gr. 3-7). pap. 5.99 *(978-0-316-30136-7(1))* Little, Brown Bks. for Young Readers.

Haskell, Rachael. The Biggest Little Hero. 2010. 29p. 15.50 *(978-0-615-21356-9(1))* Haskell, Rachael A.

Hatton, Jenny. Finding Aunt Joan. Rankin, Joan, illus. 2012. (Lucy Bks.). (ENG.). 32p. (J). (gr. k-2). pap. 6.95 *(978-1-77009-803-9(8))* Jacana Media ZAF. Dist: Independent Pubs. Group.

Haughton, Chris. Oh No, George! Haughton, Chris, illus. (ENG., Illus.). 32p. (J). 2015. (-k). bds. 7.99 *(978-0-7636-7652-0(7))* 2012. (gr. -1-k). 16.99 *(978-0-7636-5546-4(5))* Candlewick Pr.

Hauman, Carrie. Zoe the Magic Love Dog. 2003. (Illus.). 32p. (J). 16.00 *(978-0-9746333-8-1(0))* Alma Pr.

The Haunted House. 2007. (Choose Your Own Adventure Ser.). (Illus.). 80p. (J). (gr. 4-7). pap. 7.99 *(978-1-933390-51-2(4))* Chooseco LLC.

Hawe, Christine. The Dog That Peed on Mars. 2016. (ENG.). 34p. (J). pap. 8.95 *(978-1-78554-454-5(3)*, ed439c50-2322-4bfa-9df2-f6d05a805fc5) Austin, Stan AUS. Dist: Bookmasters Distribution.

Hawksley, Gerald. Good Puppy. Stanley, Mandy, illus. 2005. (J). *(978-1-890647-14-8(4))* TOMY International, Inc.

Hay, Sam. Hour of the Doomed Dog. 2016. (Undead Pets Ser.: 8). lib. bdg. 16.00 *(978-0-606-38839-9(7))* Turtleback Bks.

—Hour of the Doomed Dog #8. Cooper, Simon, illus. 2016. (Undead Pets Ser.: 8). (ENG.). 112p. (J). (gr. 1-3). 5.99 *(978-0-448-49004-5(8)*, Grosset & Dunlap) Penguin Young Readers Group.

—Night of the Howling Hound, No. 3. Cooper, Simon, illus. 2014. (Undead Pets Ser.: 3). (ENG.). 112p. (J). (gr. 1-3). 5.99 *(978-0-448-47797-8(1)*, Grosset & Dunlap) Penguin Young Readers Group.

—Night of the Howling Hound. 2014. (Undead Pets Ser.: 3). lib. bdg. 16.00 *(978-0-606-36219-1(3))* Turtleback Bks.

—Revenge of the Phantom Furball. Cooper, Simon, illus. 2014. (Undead Pets Ser.: 2). (ENG.). 112p. (J). (gr. 1-3). 5.99 *(978-0-448-47796-1(3)*, Grosset & Dunlap) Penguin Young Readers Group.

—That Dog! Oelofsen, Vian, illus. 2011. (My Phonics Readers: Level 2 Ser.). 24p. (J). (gr. -1-1). 24.25 *(978-1-84898-510-0(X))* Sea-To-Sea Pubns.

Hayes, Dale. Kc the Good Little Diggy Dog Who Does Naughty Things... Is Going Home. 2013. 32p. pap. *(978-1-4602-0428-3(X))* FriesenPress.

Hayes, Joe. The Coyote under the Table (El Coyote Debajo de la Mesa) Castro L., Antonio, illus. 2011. (ENG & SPA.). 144p. (J). (gr. 1-7). 19.95 *(978-1-935955-21-4(7))* Cinco Puntos Pr.

Hayes, Karel. Snowflake Comes to Stay. 2010. (ENG.). 32p. (J). (gr. -1-3). 16.95 *(978-0-89272-850-3(7))* Down East Bks.

Hayes, Kate. All about Poop. Garnsworthy, Marlo, ed. Vaughan, Brenna, illus. 2012. (ENG.). 38p. (J). pap. 14.95 *(978-0-9854248-0-0(X))* Pinwheel Bks.

Hayes, Malcolm. The Dreamcatchers. 2006. 282p. pap. 20.14 *(978-1-4120-8320-1(6))* Trafford Publishing.

Hays, Anna Jane. The Pup Speaks Up. Petrone, Valeria, illus. 2003. (Step into Reading Ser.). 32p. (gr. -1-1). 14.00 *(978-0-7569-1696-1(8))* Perfection Learning Corp.

—The Pup Speaks Up. Petrone, Valeria, illus. 2003. (Step into Reading Ser.). (ENG.). 32p. (J). (gr. -1-1). pap. 3.99 *(978-0-375-81232-3(6)*, Random Hse. Bks. for Young Readers) Random Hse. Children's Bks.

Hays, K. D. & Weidman, Meg. Toto's Tale. Martinez, April, illus. 2010. 248p. (J). pap. 14.99 *(978-1-936144-61-7(1)*, Zumaya Thresholds) Zumaya Pubns. LLC.

Hays, Patricia Quinn. First Dog. 2012. (ENG.). (J). 14.95 *(978-1-59982-273-0(3))*; pap. *(978-1-59982-274-7(1))* St. Mary's Pr. of MN.

Heald, Robin. Liberty Saves the Day! Elkerton, Andy, illus. 2017. (J). ***(978-0-87935-290-5(6))*** Colonial Williamsburg Foundation.

Heape, David. R. That's What Friends Do. l.t. ed. 2006. (ENG., Illus.). 28p. per. 9.95 *(978-1-4327-0177-2(0))* Outskirts Pr., Inc.

Hearne, Betsy. The Canine Connection: Stories about Dogs & People. 2007. (ENG.). 128p. (YA). (gr. 7). pap. 8.95 *(978-1-4169-6817-7(2)*, Simon Pulse) Simon Pulse.

Hearth, Liese. My Dog Burps. 2008. 14p. pap. 24.95 *(978-1-4241-9608-1(6))* America Star Bks.

Heckman, Dennise. Mountain Doggies. 2010. 36p. pap. 19.95 *(978-0-557-22048-9(3))* Lulu Pr., Inc.

Heede, Sylvia Vanden. What Dog Knows. Tolman, Marije, illus. 2016. 128p. (J). pap. 19.99 *(978-1-77657-037-9(5))* Gecko Pr. NZL. Dist: Lerner Publishing Group.

Hefferman, Danielle. Puppy Dog Tales. 2010. (Illus.). pap. *(978-0-9561590-5-2(2)*, Blue Cloud Pubns.) Black Leaf Publishing Group, The.

Heflick, LaMonte. The Story of Big Dog. 2004. (Illus.). 64p. pap. 3.99 *(978-1-56175-888-3(4))* Remedia Pubns.

Heiligman, Deborah. Cool Dog, School Dog, 0 vols. 2013. (ENG.). 32p. (J). (gr. -1-3). pap. 9.99 *(978-1-4778-1670-7(4)*, 9781477816707, Amazon Children's Publishing) Amazon Publishing.

—Fun Dog, Sun Dog, 0 vols. Bowers, Tim, illus. 2011. (ENG.). 34p. (J). (gr. -1-2). pap. 7.99 *(978-0-7614-5836-4(0)*, 9780761458364, Amazon Children's Publishing) Amazon Publishing.

—Snow Dog, Go Dog, 0 vols. Bowers, Tim, illus. 2013. (ENG.). 32p. (J). (gr. -1-2). 15.99 *(978-1-4778-1724-7(7)*, 9781477817247, Amazon Children's Publishing) Amazon Publishing.

Helakoski, Leslie. Doggone Feet! Helakoski, Leslie, illus. 2013. (ENG., Illus.). 40p. (J). (gr. -1-2). 16.95 *(978-1-59078-933-9(4))* Boyds Mills Pr.

Helemano, Butch. Sleeping Giant of Waimea. 2008. 25p. 9.95 *(978-0-9754567-1-2(7))* Kana'i Records.

Heller, Marcy. Loco Dog & the Dust Devil in the Railyard. Poes, Nancy, illus. 2007. 30p. (J). (gr. -1-7). 19.95 *(978-1-929115-17-4(2))* Azro Pr., Inc.

—Loco Dog in the Santa Fe Rail Yard, 1 vol. 2nd rev. ed. 2015. (Historical New Mexico for Children Ser.: Volume 1). (ENG., Illus.). 48p. pap. 16.95 *(978-0-9912516-1-2(X))* SCB Distributors.

Heller, Maryellen. My Big Sister's First Day of School. Soman, David, illus. 2009. (J). *(978-0-8037-3246-9(5)*, Dial) Penguin Publishing Group.

Hellmann-Hurpol, Odile. Devuelvanme Mi Perro. (Torre de Papel Ser.). (SPA., Illus.). (J). 7.95 *(978-958-04-5637-7(2))* Norma S.A. COL. Dist: Distribuidora Norma, Inc.

Help for Rosie. 2003. (Bella & Rosie Set 1 Ser.). (J). 7.67 *(978-1-932570-10-6(1))* Pioneer Valley Bks.

Helvey, Rebecca. Greta's Purpose. Helvey, Rebecca, illus. 2008. (Illus.). 68p. (J). pap. 14.95 *(978-0-9774754-7-6(6))* Spiritbuilding.

Henderson, Kathy. Dog Story. Granström, Brita, illus. (ENG.). 32p. (J). 2005. pap. 12.99 *(978-0-7475-7133-9(3))* 2004. 17.95 *(978-0-7475-5071-6(9))* Bloomsbury Publishing Plc GBR. Dist: Independent Pubs. Group.

Henderson, Sara. Howie Finds a Hug, 1 vol. Zenz, Aaron, illus. 2008. (I Can Read! / Howie Ser.). (ENG.). 32p. (J). (gr. -1-3). pap. 3.99 *(978-0-310-71607-5(1))* Zonderkidz.

—Howie's Tea Party, 1 vol. Zenz, Aaron, illus. 2008. (I Can Read! / Howie Ser.). (ENG.). 32p. (J). (gr. -1-3). pap. 3.99 *(978-0-310-71605-1(5))* Zonderkidz.

Henderson, Sara & Zenz, Aaron. Howie Wants to Play, 1 vol. Henderson, Sara & Zenz, Aaron, illus. 2009. (I Can Read! / Howie Series / ¡Yo Sé Leer! / Serie: Fido Ser.). (ENG., Illus.). 32p. (J). pap. 3.99 *(978-0-310-71875-8(9))* Zonderkidz.

Henity, Kristi. Kimi's Grand Adventures, Vol. 1. 2004. 55p. pap. 16.95 *(978-1-4137-2869-9(3))* America Star Bks.

Henkes, Kevin. Protecting Marie. 2007. (ENG.). 224p. (J). (gr. 3-7). pap. 6.99 *(978-0-06-128876-0(4)*, Greenwillow Bks.) HarperCollins Pubs.

Henne, R. J. & Wilson, Marlys. Harley Boogle & His Bulldog Buster, 1 vol. 2009. 77p. pap. 19.95 *(978-1-60672-955-7(1))* America Star Bks.

Henrikson, Jerilynn. Teddy, the Ghost Dog of Red Rocks. 2013. 72p. pap. 11.95 *(978-1-939054-23-4(0))* Rowe Publishing and Design.

Henry, Regene. The Barefoot Boys of Fayette. Stich, Carolyn R., illus. 2005. 180p. (J). (gr. 4-7). pap. 9.95 *(978-0-9749412-3-3(9))* EDCO Publishing, Inc.

Hensley, Terri Anne. The Silliest Bug & Insect Book Ever. Hall, Norris, illus. 2007. 28p. per. 6.99 *(978-0-9789057-7-4(6))* Huntington Ludlow Media Group.

Heos, Bridget. Queen Dog. O'Keeffe, Alejandro, illus. 2017. (ENG.). 40p. (J). (gr. -1-k). 16.99 *(978-1-4847-2852-9(1))* Disney Pr.

Hepworth, Emily. Stray Dog. 2009. 39p. pap. 9.81 *(978-0-557-21434-1(3))* Lulu Pr., Inc.

Herbert, Frances. Fran's Van & the Naughty Terrier. Herbert, Frances, illus. 2013. (Illus.). 32p. pap. *(978-1-78222-164-7(6))* Paragon Publishing, Rothersthorpe.

Herfurtner, Ralph. Niki y el Perrito. (Torre de Papel Ser.). (SPA., Illus.). (J). 7.95 *(978-958-04-5034-4(X))* Norma S.A. COL. Dist: Distribuidora Norma, Inc.

Herlong, M. H. Buddy. 2013. (ENG.). 320p. (J). (gr. 5). pap. 7.99 *(978-0-14-242544-2(3)*, Puffin Books) Penguin Young Readers Group.

Herman, Gail. Fall Fright. Duendes Del Sur Staff, illus. 2005. (Hello Reader! Ser.). 32p. (J). pap. *(978-0-439-78358-3(5))* Scholastic, Inc.

—New Dog in Town. Nez, John, illus. 2006. (Social Studies Connects). 32p. (J). (gr. -1-3). pap. 5.95 *(978-1-57565-165-1(3))* Kane Press, Inc.

—Scooby-Doo: A Scooby-Rific Reader. 2012. (Illus.). (J). *(978-1-4351-3986-2(0))* Scholastic, Inc.

—Scooby-Doo in the Lighthouse Mystery, 1 vol. 2016. (Scooby-Doo! Set 3 Ser.). (ENG., Illus.). 32p. (J). (gr. k-4). lib. bdg. 24.21 *(978-1-61479-410-3(3))* Spotlight.

Hernandez, Annette. Captain Holo's Journey through the Alphabet: An ABC Book. 2010. (Illus.). 30p. (J). pap. 19.95 *(978-1-4327-5261-3(8))* Outskirts Pr., Inc.

Hernandez, Regina. Jail Break Spells Double the Trouble: Jake the Beagle's Crazy Adventures. Woods, Carol, ed. 2003. (Jake the Beagle Crazy Adventure Ser.: 5). (Illus.). 90p. (J). pap. 5.99 *(978-0-9727771-8-6(0))* Regal Enterprises.

—Texas Roundup: Jake the Beagle's Crazy Adventures. Woods, Carol, ed. Fetherston, Catherine & Miller, Tom, illus. 2003. (Jake the Beagle Crazy Adventure Ser.: 2). 90p. (J). pap. 5.99 *(978-0-9727771-2-4(1))* Regal Enterprises.

Herr, Margaret J. Fritz, the Donut-Tailed Dog. 2013. 62p. pap. 17.95 *(978-1-63000-635-8(1))* America Star Bks.

Hesse, Karen. Sable. Sewall, Marcia, illus. 2010. (ENG.). 96p. (J). (gr. 2-5). pap. 7.99 *(978-0-312-37610-9(3)*, 9780312376109) Square Fish.

Hest, Amy. Charley's First Night. Oxenbury, Helen, illus. 2012. (ENG.). 32p. (J). (gr. -1-2). 15.99 *(978-0-7636-4055-2(7))* Candlewick Pr.

—The Dog Who Belonged to No One. Bates, Amy, illus. 2008. (ENG.). 32p. (J). (gr. k-2). 18.95 *(978-0-8109-9483-6(6)*, Abrams Bks. for Young Readers) Abrams, Inc.

—Letters to Leo. Denos, Julia, illus. 2012. (ENG.). 160p. (J). (gr. 3-7). 14.99 *(978-0-7636-3695-1(9))* Candlewick Pr.

—Letters to Leo. Denos, Julia, illus. 2014. (ENG.). 160p. (J). (gr. 3-7). pap. 6.99 *(978-0-7636-7165-5(7))* Candlewick Pr.

—My Old Pal, Oscar. Bates, Amy June, illus. 2016. (ENG.). 32p. (J). (gr. k-2). 16.95 *(978-1-4197-1901-1(7))* Abrams, Inc.

—The Reader, 0 vols. Castillo, Lauren, illus. 2012. (ENG.). 32p. (J). (gr. -1-1). 16.99 *(978-0-7614-6184-5(1)*, 9780761461845, Amazon Children's Publishing) Amazon Publishing.

Hicks, Kay. Dukes the Ginger Dog. 2010. 28p. pap. 15.99 *(978-1-4500-7938-9(5))* Xlibris Corp.

Hicks, Michael Christopher. Tales of Drake: The Tale of the Lost Dog. 2011. 40p. pap. 18.99 *(978-1-4634-1823-6(X))* AuthorHouse.

Higdon, Hal. Run, Dogs, Run! Summers, Dana, illus. 2003. 56p. (J). *(978-0-9636346-3-4(1))* Roadrunner Pr.

Higgins, Kitty. Mushing in Alaska. 2005. (J). pap. *(978-1-4108-4228-2(2))* Benchmark Education Co.

Higgins, Nadia. Avast, Ye Dog Thief!, 1 vol. Holder, Jimmy, illus. 2008. (Barnacle Barb & Her Pirate Crew Ser.). (ENG.). 32p. (gr. -1-3). 28.50 *(978-1-60270-089-5(3)*, Looking Glass Library) ABDO Publishing Co.

Higginson, Sheila Sweeny. Drip, Drop! the Rain Won't Stop! Your Turn, My Turn Reader. Yee, Josie, illus. 2010. (Playskool Ser.). (ENG.). 24p. (J). (gr. -1-k). pap. 3.99 *(978-1-4169-9046-8(1)*, Simon Spotlight) Simon Spotlight.

Highet, Alistair. Lucas. Delessert, Etienne, illus. 2011. (ENG.). 40p. (J). (gr. 4-17). pap. 8.95 *(978-0-89812-014-1(4)*, Creative Paperbacks) Creative Co., The.

Hilditch, Kevin M. Kevin & the Smiling Dog. 38p. 2011. pap. 19.99 *(978-1-257-01514-6(1))* 2010. pap. 9.99 *(978-0-557-56904-5(4))* Lulu Pr., Inc.

Hileman, Jane & Pitt, Marilyn. Home Alone. Bianchi, John, illus. 2011. (Power 50 - Potato Chip Bks). 12p. pap. 33.92 *(978-1-61541-408-6(8))* American Reading Co.

—I Love to Sleep. Bianchi, John, illus. 2009. (1G Potato Chip Bks.). (ENG.). 12p. (J). (gr. k-1). pap. 5.99 *(978-1-59301-797-2(9))* American Reading Co.

—I Want a Dog. Bianchi, John, illus. 2009. (1G Potato Chip Bks.). (ENG.). 12p. (J). (gr. k-1). pap. 5.99 *(978-1-59301-768-2(5))* American Reading Co.

—Let Me In. Bianchi, John, illus. 2011. (Power 50 - Potato Chip Bks). 12p. pap. 33.92 *(978-1-61541-169-6(0))* American Reading Co.

—Snow Dog. Bianchi, John, illus. (Power 50 - Potato Chip Bks). 12p. 2011. pap. 33.92 *(978-1-61541-298-3(0))* 2010. (ENG.). (J). pap. 5.99 *(978-1-61541-297-6(2))* American Reading Co.

—The Storm. Bianchi, John, illus. 2011. (Power 50 - Potato Chip Bks). 12p. pap. 33.92 *(978-1-61541-233-4(6))* American Reading Co.

—Time for a Bath. Bianchi, John, illus. 2009. (1G Potato Chip Bks.). (ENG.). 12p. (J). (gr. k-1). pap. 5.99 *(978-1-59301-772-9(3))* American Reading Co.

—You Can't Have It! Bianchi, John, illus. 2009. (1G Potato Chip Bks.). (ENG.). 12p. (J). (gr. k-1). pap. 5.99 *(978-1-59301-767-5(7))* American Reading Co.

Hill, Amye Rose. The Amazing Mr. Buddy. 10th ed. 2005. (Illus.). (J). 6.99 *(978-0-9769234-0-4(8))* Zany Angel Projects LLC.

Hill, Eric. Donde Esta Spot? (SPA.). pap. 10.95 *(978-950-07-1960-5(6))* Editorial Sudamericana S.A. ARG. Dist: Distribooks, Inc.

—First Christmas. Hill, Eric, illus. 2004. (Spot Ser.). (ENG., Illus.). 20p. (J). (gr. -1-k). 7.99 *(978-0-14-240202-3(8)*, Warne) Penguin Young Readers Group.

—Good Night, Spot. Hill, Eric, illus. 2004. (Spot Ser.). (ENG., Illus.). 16p. (J). (gr. -1 — 1). bds. 4.99 *(978-0-399-24319-6(4)*, Warne) Penguin Young Readers Group.

—Los Juguetes de Spot. (SPA.). pap. 4.95 *(978-950-07-1963-6(0))* Editorial Sudamericana S.A. ARG. Dist: Distribooks, Inc.

—Night-Night, Spot. 2012. (Spot Ser.). (ENG.). 24p. (J). (gr. -1-k). bds. 8.99 *(978-0-448-46456-5(X)*, Warne) Penguin Young Readers Group.

—Night-Night, Spot. Hill, Eric, illus. 2005. (Spot Ser.). (ENG., Illus.). 32p. (J). (gr. -1-k). pap. 3.99 *(978-0-448-43810-8(0)*, Warne) Penguin Young Readers Group.

—La Primera Navidad de Spot.Tr. of Spot's First Christmas. (SPA.). pap. 10.95 *(978-950-07-2016-8(7))* Editorial Sudamericana S.A. ARG. Dist: Distribooks, Inc.

—Puppy Love. Hill, Eric, illus. 2016. (Spot Ser.). (ENG., Illus.). 40p. (J). (gr. -1-k). 6.99 *(978-0-399-20935-2(2)*, Warne) Penguin Young Readers Group.

—Spot Bakes a Cake. Hill, Eric, illus. 2003. (ENG., Illus.). 22p. (J). (gr. -1-1). bds. 7.99 *(978-0-399-24013-3(6))* Penguin Publishing Group.

—Spot Bakes a Cake. Hill, Eric, illus. 2005. (Spot Ser.). (ENG., Illus.). 20p. (J). (gr. k — 1). 6.99 *(978-0-14-240329-7(6)*, Warne) Penguin Young Readers Group.

—Spot Can Count. 2009. (Spot (Chinese) Ser.). (CHI., Illus.). 22p. *(978-957-762-468-0(5))* Hsin Yi Pubns.

—Spot Can Count. Hill, Eric, illus. 2005. (ENG., Illus.). 22p. (J). (gr. -1-1). bds. 7.99 *(978-0-399-24361-5(5))* Penguin Publishing Group.

—Spot Can Count. Hill, Eric, illus. 2003. (Spot Ser.). (ENG., Illus.). 24p. (J). (gr. -1-k). 6.99 *(978-0-14-250121-4(2)*, Warne) Penguin Young Readers Group.

—Spot Goes Shopping. Hill, Eric, illus. 2014. (Spot Ser.). (ENG., Illus.). 12p. (J). (gr. -1-k). bds. 5.99 *(978-0-7232-8997-5(2)*, Warne) Penguin Young Readers Group.

—Spot Goes to School. Hill, Eric, illus. 2004. (Spot Ser.). (ENG., Illus.). 24p. (J). (gr. -1-k). 6.99 *(978-0-14-240167-5(6)*, Warne) Penguin Young Readers Group.

—Spot Goes to the Farm. Hill, Eric, illus. 2003. (Spot Ser.). (ENG., Illus.). 24p. (J). (gr. -1-k). 7.99 *(978-0-14-250123-8(9)*, Warne) Penguin Young Readers Group.

—Spot Goes to the Farm. 2003. (Spot Ser.). (gr. -1-2). lib. bdg. 18.40 *(978-0-613-86708-5(4)*, Turtleback) Turtleback Bks.

—Spot Goes to the Park. Hill, Eric, illus. 2005. (Spot Ser.). (ENG., Illus.). 24p. (J). (gr. -1 — 1). bds. 7.99 *(978-0-399-24363-9(1)*, Warne) Penguin Young Readers Group.

—Spot's Baby Sister. Hill, Eric, illus. 2004. (Spot Ser.). (ENG., Illus.). 24p. (J). (gr. -1-k). 7.99 *(978-0-14-240169-9(2)*, Warne) Penguin Young Readers Group.

—Spot's Birthday Party. Hill, Eric, illus. 2007. (Spot Ser.). (ENG., Illus.). 24p. (J). (gr. -1 — 1). bds. 7.99 *(978-0-399-24770-5(X)*, Warne) Penguin Young Readers Group.

—Spot's Christmas. Hill, Eric, illus. 2004. (Spot Ser.). (ENG., Illus.). 12p. (J). (gr. -1 — 1). bds. 5.99 *(978-0-399-24320-2(8)*, Warne) Penguin Young Readers Group.

—Spot's Favorite Things. Hill, Eric, illus. 2012. (Spot Ser.). (ENG., Illus.). 12p. (J). (gr. -1 — 1). bds. 8.99

(978-0-399-25758-2(6), Warne) Penguin Young Readers Group.

—Spot's First Walk. Hill, Eric, illus. (Spot Ser.). (ENG., Illus.). 24p. (J). (gr. -1 — 1). 2005. bds. 7.99 (978-0-399-24482-7(4)) 2004. 7.99 (978-0-14-240085-2(8)) Penguin Young Readers Group. (Warne).

—Spot's Halloween. Hill, Eric, illus. 2003. (Spot Ser.). (ENG., Illus.). 14p. (J). (gr. -1 — 1). bds. 5.99 (978-0-399-24185-7(X), Warne) Penguin Young Readers Group.

—Spot's Peekaboo. Hill, Eric, illus. 2015. (Spot Ser.). (ENG., Illus.). 12p. (J). (-k). bds. 9.99 (978-0-14-136170-3(0), Warne) Penguin Young Readers Group.

—Spot's Thanksgiving. Hill, Eric, illus. 2016. (Spot Ser.). (ENG., Illus.). 10p. (J). (gr. -1-k). bds. 6.99 (978-0-399-24186-4(8), Warne) Penguin Young Readers Group.

—Where's Spot? Hill, Eric, illus. 2003. (Spot Ser.). (Illus.). (J). (gr. -1 — 1). (SPA & ENG.). 12p. bds. 7.99 (978-0-399-24046-1(2), 53517281); (ENG., 24p. 7.99 (978-0-14-250126-9(3)) Penguin Young Readers Group. (Warne).

—Where's Spot? Hill, Eric, illus. 2007. (Spot Ser.). (ENG., Illus.). 18.00 (978-0-7569-7965-2(X)) Perfection Learning Corp.

—Where's Spot? 2003. (Spot Ser.). 18.40 (978-1-4176-3889-5(3), Turtleback) Turtleback Bks.

Hill, Eveline. Hugo & Oscar Go Travelling: Continuing the Adventures of Hugo & Oscar. 2012. (Illus.). 52p. pap. 27.45 (978-1-4772-2733-6(4)) AuthorHouse.

Hill, Janet. Miss Moon: Wise Words from a Dog Governess. 2016. (ENG., Illus.). 48p. (J). (gr. -1-3). 17.99 (978-1-101-91793-0(8), Tundra Bks.) Tundra Bks. CAN. Dist: Penguin Random Hse. LLC.

Hill, Janet Muirhead. Kendall's Storm. Leonhard, Herb, illus. 2011. (J). pap. 12.00 (978-0-9820893-0-9(9)) Raven Publishing Inc. of Montana.

Hill, Meggan. Nico & Lola: Kindness shared between a boy & a dog. 2009. 32p. (J). (978-0-615-23040-5(7)) Genuine Prints, LLC.

—Nico & Lola: Kindness Shared Between a Boy & a Dog. Graunke, Susan M., illus. 2010. (ENG.). 40p. (J). (gr. -1-3). 16.99 (978-0-06-199043-4(4)) HarperCollins Pubs.

Hill, Monica. Rin Tin Tin & the Lost Indian. Greene, Hamilton, illus. 2011. 28p. pap. 35.95 (978-1-258-00567-2(0)) Literary Licensing, LLC.

Hill, Ryan. J P Trouble. 2012. 32p. pap. 12.95 (978-1-886057-15-9(X)) Warren Publishing, Inc.

Hill, Susan. Lassie Come-Home: An Adaptation of Eric Knight's Classic Story. Ivanov, Aleksey & Olga, illus. 75th ed. 2015. (ENG.). 32p. (J). (gr. -1-3). 17.99 (978-1-62779-294-3(5), 9781627792943, Holt, Henry & Co. Bks. For Young Readers) Holt, Henry & Co.

Hillert, Margaret. Dear Dragon Gets a Pet. Pullan, Jack, illus. 2015. (BeginningtoRead Ser.). (ENG.). 32p. (J). (gr. k-2). lib. bdg. 22.60 (978-1-59953-706-1(0)) Norwood Hse. Pr.

—A House for Little Red. Chung, Chi, illus. 2016. (BeginningtoRead Ser.). (ENG.). 32p. (J). (gr. -1-2). 22.60 (978-1-59953-798-6(2)); pap. 11.94 (978-1-60357-939-1(7)) Norwood Hse. Pr.

Hills, Frederic F. & Hills, Tad. Rocket's 100th Day of School. 2014. (Rocket Ser.). (ENG.). 32p. (J). (gr. 1-4). pap. 3.99 (978-0-385-39097-2(1), Random Hse. Bks. for Young Readers) Random Hse. Children's Bks.

Hills, Jodi. Hope-So. Bjornson, Barbara, illus. 2004. (ENG.). 36p. (J). 16.95 (978-0-9726504-2-7(3)) TRISTAN Publishing, Inc.

Hills, Tad. Drop It, Rocket! 2014. (ENG., Illus.). 32p. (J). (gr. 1-4). 12.99 (978-0-385-37247-3(7), Schwartz & Wade Bks.) Random Hse. Children's Bks.

—How Rocket Learned to Read. Hills, Tad, illus. 2010. (ENG., Illus.). 40p. (J). (gr. -1-2). 17.99 (978-0-375-85899-4(7), Schwartz & Wade Bks.) Random Hse. Children's Bks.

—R Is for Rocket: an ABC Book. 2015. (ENG., Illus.). 32p. (J). (gr. -1-2). 17.99 (978-0-553-52228-0(0), Schwartz & Wade Bks.) Random Hse. Children's Bks.

—Rocket Writes a Story. Hills, Tad, illus. 2012. (ENG., Illus.). 40p. (J). (gr. -1-3). 17.99 (978-0-375-87086-6(5), Schwartz & Wade Bks.) Random Hse. Children's Bks.

—Rocket's Learning Box, 2 vols. Hills, Tad, illus. 2012. (ENG., Illus.). 40p. (J). (gr. -1-3). 35.98 (978-0-307-98235-3(1), Schwartz & Wade Bks.) Random Hse. Children's Bks.

—Rocket's Mighty Words. 2013. (ENG.). 22p. (J). (-k). bds. 10.99 (978-0-385-37233-6(7), Schwartz & Wade Bks.) Random Hse. Children's Bks.

Himmelman, John. Katie & the Puppy Next Door. Himmelman, John, illus. 2013. (ENG., Illus.). 32p. (J). (gr. -1-1). 16.99 (978-0-8050-9484-8(9), 9780805094848, Holt, Henry & Co. Bks. For Young Readers) Holt, Henry & Co.

—Katie Loves the Kittens. Himmelman, John, illus. 2008. (ENG., Illus.). 32p. (J). (gr. -1-3). 18.99 (978-0-8050-8682-9(X), 9780805086829, Holt, Henry & Co. Bks. For Young Readers) Holt, Henry & Co.

Hinds, Ruth McNaughton. Puppy & I. 2006. (J). per. 7.95 (978-0-9764232-2-5(7)) River City Pr.

Hites, Kati. Winnie & Waldorf. Hites, Kati, illus. 2015. (ENG., Illus.). 40p. (J). (gr. -1-3). 17.99 (978-0-06-231161-0(1)) HarperCollins Pubs.

—Winnie & Waldorf: Disobedience School. Hites, Kati, illus. 2016. (Illus.). 40p. (J). (gr. -1-3). 17.99 (978-0-06-231162-7(X)) HarperCollins Pubs.

Hobbs, Valerie. Maggie & Oliver or a Bone of One's Own. Thermes, Jennifer, illus. 2013. (ENG.). 208p. (J). (gr. 3-7). pap. 6.99 (978-1-250-01672-0(X), 9781250016720) Square Fish.

—Sheep. 2009. (ENG.). 144p. (J). (gr. 3-7). pap. 7.99 (978-0-312-56116-1(4), 9780312561161) Square Fish.

—Wolf. 2013. (ENG.). 128p. (J). (gr. 3-7). 15.99 (978-0-374-31575-7(2), 9780374315757, Farrar, Straus & Giroux (BYR)) Farrar, Straus & Giroux.

Hobbs, Will & Hobbs, William. Wild Man Island. 2003. (ENG.). 192p. (J). (gr. 5-18). pap. 5.99 (978-0-380-73310-1(2)) HarperCollins Pubs.

Hobbs, William. Down the Yukon. unabr. ed. 2004. (Middle Grade Cassette Librariestm Ser.). 208p. (J). (gr. 5-9). pap. 36.00 incl. audio (978-0-8072-0786-4(1), S YA 310 SP, Listening Library) Random Hse. Audio Publishing Group.

Hodder, Beth. The Ghost of Schafer Meadows. 2007. (J). per. 7.99 (978-0-9793963-0-4(1)) Grizzly Ridge Publishing.

—Stealing the Wild. 2010. 166p. (J). pap. 11.95 (978-0-9793963-1-1(X)) Grizzly Ridge Publishing.

Hodgson, Mona. The Princess Twins & the Puppy, 1 vol. Olson, Julie, illus. 2015. (I Can Read! / Princess Twins Ser.). (ENG.). 32p. (J). pap. 3.99 (978-0-310-75064-2(4)) Zonderkidz.

—The Princess Twins Play in the Garden, 1 vol. Olson, Julie, illus. 2015. (I Can Read! / Princess Twins Ser.). (ENG.). 32p. (J). pap. 3.99 (978-0-310-75050-5(4)) Zonderkidz.

Hodgson, Mona Gansberg. The Princess Twins & the Puppy, 1 vol. Hansen, Red, illus. 2011. (I Can Read! / Princess Twins Ser.). (ENG.). 32p. (J). pap. 3.99 (978-0-310-72709-5(X)) Zonderkidz.

Hodson, Ann & Mason, David. The Adventures of Kef, Dael & Emma. 2010. (Illus.). 84p. pap. 28.99 (978-1-4520-2138-6(4)) AuthorHouse.

Hoff, Syd. Danny & the Dinosaur & the New Puppy. Hoff, Syd, illus. 2015. (I Can Read Level 1 Ser.). (ENG., Illus.). 32p. (J). (gr. -1-3). pap. 3.99 (978-0-06-228152-4(6)) HarperCollins Pubs.

Hoffman, Don. A Very Special Snowflake. Dakins, Todd, illus. 2nd ed. 2016. (ENG.). 28p. (J). (gr. -1-k). pap. 3.99 (978-1-943154-01-2(5)) Peek-A-Boo Publishing.

Hoffmann, Catherine E. & Hoffmann, Dana Marie. Here Little Teacup! up! Up! O'Leary Brown, Erin, illus. 2005. 16p. (J). 6.95 (978-0-9753106-2-5(3)) Hoffmann Partnership, The.

Hofmeister, Nick. Adventures of Eli Deuce - SPECIAL EDITION - Fourth & Final Part Added. 2009. 360p. pap. 23.50 (978-0-557-12192-2(2)) Lulu Pr., Inc.

Hogan, Anne Harmon. The Three Amigos. 2011. 26p. pap. 14.95 (978-1-61434-276-2(8)) Booklocker.com, Inc.

Hogan Ii, Haywood. The Horse, the Dog, & the Bird. 2012. 24p. pap. 16.95 (978-1-4685-7633-7(X)) AuthorHouse.

Holder, Ramona V. Paco & Lexus Are Good Friends: Paco y Lexus son Buen Amigos. 2009. 24p. pap. 12.99 (978-1-4389-5778-4(5)) AuthorHouse.

Holdman, Shirley Terrill. The Adventures of Giggles & Owen: A True Story. Riecks Goss, Carol, illus. 2010. 26p. pap. 14.95 (978-1-60844-490-8(2)) Dog Ear Publishing, LLC.

Holmes, Stephanie. Grady Goes to Puppy School. 2011. 20p. (gr. 1-2). pap. 11.99 (978-1-4634-1000-1(X)) AuthorHouse.

Holt, Christopher. Dark Waters. 2013. (Last Dogs Ser.: 2). (J). lib. bdg. 18.40 (978-0-606-35308-3(9)) Turtleback Bks.

—Journey's End. 2014. (Last Dogs Ser.: 4). (J). lib. bdg. 18.40 (978-0-606-35944-3(3)) Turtleback Bks.

—The Last Dogs: The Vanishing. Call, Greg, illus. 2012. (Last Dogs Ser.: 1). (ENG.). 384p. (J). (gr. 3-7). 16.99 (978-0-316-20005-9(0)) Little, Brown Bks. for Young Readers.

—The Last Dogs - The Vanishing. 2013. (Last Dogs Ser.: 1). (J). lib. bdg. 18.45 (978-0-606-31744-3(9), Turtleback) Turtleback Bks.

—The Last Dogs: Dark Waters. Douglas, Allen, illus. 2013. (Last Dogs Ser.: 2). (ENG.). 352p. (J). (gr. 3-7). pap. 7.99 (978-0-316-20009-7(3)) Little, Brown Bks. for Young Readers.

—The Last Dogs: Journey's End. Douglas, Allen, illus. 2014. (Last Dogs Ser.: 4). (ENG.). 320p. (J). (gr. 3-7). 17.00 (978-0-316-20007-3(7)) Little, Brown Bks. for Young Readers.

—The Last Dogs: the Long Road. Douglas, Allen, illus. 2014. (Last Dogs Ser.: 3). (ENG.). 352p. (J). (gr. 3-7). pap. 7.99 (978-0-316-20016-5(6)) Little, Brown Bks. for Young Readers.

—The Long Road. 2014. (Last Dogs Ser.: 3). (J). lib. bdg. 18.40 (978-0-606-35309-0(7)) Turtleback Bks.

—The Vanishing. Call, Greg, illus. 2013. (Last Dogs Ser.: 1). (ENG.). 400p. (J). (gr. 3-7). pap. 8.99 (978-0-316-20004-2(2)) Little, Brown Bks. for Young Readers.

Holub, Joan. Shampoodle. Bowers, Tim, illus. 2009. (Step into Reading Ser.). (ENG.). 32p. (J). (gr. -1-1). pap. 3.99 (978-0-375-85576-4(9), Random Hse. Bks. for Young Readers) Random Hse. Children's Bks.

—Vampoodle. Bowers, Tim, illus. 2017. (Step into Reading Ser.). (ENG.). 32p. (J). (gr. -1-1). pap. 3.99 (978-1-101-93666-5(5), Random Hse. Bks. for Young Readers) Random Hse. Children's Bks.

Holzer, Julie. Maggie's Forever Home. 2012. 36p. pap. 18.41 (978-1-4669-1647-0(8)) Trafford Publishing.

Homework, 6 Packs. (gr. -1-2). 27.00 (978-0-7635-9453-4(9)) Rigby Education.

Hong, Seonna. Animus. 2015. (ENG., Illus.). 100p. (J). (gr. -1-7). pap. 25.00 (978-0-9729388-5-3(0)) Baby Tattoo Bks.

Hood, Susan. Pup & Hound. Hendry, Linda, illus. 2004. (Kids Can Read Ser.). (ENG.). 32p. (J). (gr. k-1). 3.95 (978-1-55337-673-6(0)); 14.95 (978-1-55337-572-2(6)) Kids Can Pr., Ltd. CAN. Dist: Hachette Bk. Group.

—Pup & Hound at Sea. Hendry, Linda, illus. 2006. (Kids Can Read Ser.). (ENG.). 32p. (J). (gr. k-1). 3.95 (978-1-55337-805-1(9)) Kids Can Pr., Ltd. CAN. Dist: Hachette Bk. Group.

—Pup & Hound Catch a Thief. Hendry, Linda, illus. 2007. (Kids Can Read Ser.). (ENG.). 32p. (J). (gr. k-1). 3.95 (978-1-55337-973-7(X)) Kids Can Pr., Ltd. CAN. Dist: Hachette Bk. Group.

—Pup & Hound Hatch an Egg. Hendry, Linda, illus. 2007. (Kids Can Read Ser.). (ENG.). 32p. (J). (gr. k-1). 3.95 (978-1-55337-975-1(6)) Kids Can Pr., Ltd. CAN. Dist: Hachette Bk. Group.

—Pup & Hound in Trouble. Hendry, Linda, illus. 2005. (Kids Can Read Ser.). (ENG.). 32p. (J). (gr. k-1). 3.95 (978-1-55337-677-4(3)) Kids Can Pr., Ltd. CAN. Dist: Hachette Bk. Group.

—Pup & Hound Lost & Found. Hendry, Linda, illus. 2006. (Kids Can Read Ser.). (ENG.). 32p. (J). (gr. k-1). 3.95 (978-1-55337-807-5(5)) Kids Can Pr., Ltd. CAN. Dist: Hachette Bk. Group.

—Pup & Hound Move In. Hendry, Linda, illus. 2004. (Kids Can Read Ser.). (ENG.). 32p. (J). (gr. k-1). 3.95 (978-1-55337-675-0(7)); 14.95 (978-1-55337-674-3(9)) Kids Can Pr., Ltd. CAN. Dist: Hachette Bk. Group.

—Pup & Hound Play Copycats. Hendry, Linda, illus. 2007. (Kids Can Read Ser.). (ENG.). 32p. (J). (gr. k-1). 3.95 (978-1-55453-145-5(4)) Kids Can Pr., Ltd. CAN. Dist: Hachette Bk. Group.

—Pup & Hound Scare a Ghost. Hendry, Linda, illus. 2007. (Kids Can Read Ser.). (ENG.). 32p. (J). (gr. k-1). 3.95 (978-1-55453-143-1(8)) Kids Can Pr., Ltd. CAN. Dist: Hachette Bk. Group.

—Pup & Hound Stay up Late. Hendry, Linda, illus. 2005. (Kids Can Read Ser.). (ENG.). 32p. (J). (gr. k-1). 3.95 (978-1-55337-679-8(X)); 14.95 (978-1-55337-678-1(1)) Kids Can Pr., Ltd. CAN. Dist: Hachette Bk. Group.

Hood, Susan & Hendry, Linda. Pup & Hound. Hendry, Linda, illus. 2012. (ENG., Illus.). 32p. (J). (gr. -1 — 1). bds. 7.95 (978-1-55453-818-8(1)) Kids Can Pr., Ltd. CAN. Dist: Hachette Bk. Group.

Hope, Laura Lee. Freddie & Flossie & Snap. Pyle, Chuck, illus. 2005. (Bobbsey Twins Ser.). (ENG.). 32p. (J). (gr. -1-k). pap. 13.99 (978-1-4169-0267-6(8), Simon Spotlight) Simon Spotlight.

—Freddie & Flossie & the Leaf Monster. Ruppert, Larry, illus. 2005. (Bobbsey Twins Ser.). (ENG.). 32p. (J). (gr. -1-k). pap. 13.99 (978-1-4169-0271-3(6), Simon Spotlight) Simon Spotlight.

—Freddie & Flossie at the Beach. Pyle, Chuck, illus. 2005. (Bobbsey Twins Ser.). (ENG.). 32p. (J). (gr. -1-k). pap. 13.99 (978-1-4169-0268-3(6), Simon Spotlight) Simon Spotlight.

Hopkins, Leslie. A World Apart. 2012. 20p. pap. 17.99 (978-1-4772-6783-7(2)) AuthorHouse.

Hopper, Celia. Blade & the Story of the Little Spotted Dog. 2006. (J). lib. bdg. (978-0-9779662-3-3(2)) Creative Bk. Pubs.

Hord, Colleen. Little Miss Midge. Poole, Helen, illus. 2012. (ENG.). 24p. (gr. 1-2). pap. 8.95 (978-1-61810-311-6(3)) Rourke Educational Media.

Horne, Jane & Page, Claire. I Really Like Puppies. 2010. (ENG., Illus.). 12p. (J). (gr. -1-k). bds. 9.99 (978-1-84610-963-8(9)) Make Believe Ideas GBR. Dist: Nelson, Thomas Inc.

Hornsey, Chris & Perkins, Gwyn. Why Do I Have to Eat off the Floor? (Illus.). 24p. 2006. pap. (978-1-921049-58-3(8)) 2005. (978-1-921049-02-6(2)) Little Hare Bks. AUS. Dist: HarperCollins Pubs. Australia.

Horse, Harry. The Last Castaways. Horse, Harry, illus. 2009. (ENG., Illus.). 128p. (J). (gr. 1-5). 12.95 (978-1-56145-439-6(7)) Peachtree Pubs.

—The Last Cowboys. Horse, Harry, illus. 2008. (ENG., Illus.). 128p. (J). (gr. 1-5). 12.95 (978-1-56145-451-8(6), Peachtree Junior) Peachtree Pubs.

—The Last Gold Diggers: Being as It Were, an Account of a Small Dog's Adventures, down Under. Horse, Harry, illus. 2008. (ENG., Illus.). 128p. (J). (gr. 1-5). 12.95 (978-1-56145-435-8(4)) Peachtree Pubs.

—The Last Polar Bears. Horse, Harry, illus. 2007. (ENG., Illus.). 128p. (J). (gr. 1-5). 12.95 (978-1-56145-379-5(X), Peachtree Junior) Peachtree Pubs.

Horvath, James. Build, Dogs, Build: A Tall Tail. Horvath, James, illus. 2013. (ENG., Illus.). 40p. (J). (gr. -1-3). 15.99 (978-0-06-218967-7(0)) HarperCollins Pubs.

—Dig, Dogs, Dig. Horvath, James, illus. 2016. (I Can Read Level 1 Ser.). (Illus.). 32p. (J). (gr. -1-3). pap. 3.99 (978-0-06-235702-1(6)) HarperCollins Pubs.

—Dig, Dogs, Dig: A Construction Tail. Horvath, James, illus. 2013. (ENG., Illus.). 40p. (J). (gr. -1-3). 15.99 (978-0-06-218964-6(6)) HarperCollins Pubs.

—Work, Dogs, Work: A Highway Tail. Horvath, James, illus. (I Can Read Level 1 Ser.). (Illus.). (J). (gr. -1-3). 2017. 32p. pap. 3.99 (978-0-06-235708-3(5)) 2014. (ENG., 40p. 15.99 (978-0-06-218970-7(0)) HarperCollins Pubs.

Houran, Lori Haskins. A Thousand Theos: Doubling. Pitz, M. H., illus. 2015. (ENG.). 32p. (gr. 1-3). (J). pap. 5.95 (978-1-57565-803-2(8)); 11.99 (978-1-57565-804-9(6)) Kane Press, Inc.

Howard, Arthur. My Dream Dog. Howard, Arthur, illus. 2016. (ENG., Illus.). 32p. (J). (gr. -1-3). 17.99 (978-1-4814-5838-2(8), Beach Lane Bks.) Beach Lane Bks.

Howard, Assuanta. Doggie Bets. Sandoz, Matt, illus. 2013. 32p. pap. 7.99 (978-1-934947-76-0(8)) Asta Publications, LLC.

Howard, Dave. Lady's Day to Play. Howard, Dave, illus. 2011. (ENG., Illus.). 32p. (J). (gr. -1-3). pap. 14.95 (978-0-938467-25-0(5)) Headline Bks., Inc.

Howard, Ellen. Murphy & Kate. Graham, Mark, illus. 2007. (ENG.). 32p. (J). (gr. -1-2). 13.99 (978-1-4169-6157-4(7), Simon & Schuster/Paula Wiseman Bks.) Simon & Schuster/Paula Wiseman Bks.

Howard, J. J. Sit, Stay, Love. 2016. (ENG.). 256p. (J). (gr. 4-7). pap. 6.99 (978-0-545-86157-1(8), Scholastic Paperbacks) Scholastic, Inc.

Howard, Lee. Scooby-Doo & the High Tech House of the Future, 1 vol. 2016. (Scooby-Doo Comic Readers Ser.). (ENG.). 32p. (J). (gr. k-3). lib. bdg. 24.21 (978-1-61479-452-3(9), Graphic Planet) Magic Wagon.

—Scooby-Doo & the Unnatural, 1 vol. 2016. (Scooby-Doo Comic Readers Ser.). (ENG.). 32p. (J). (gr. k-3). lib. bdg. 24.21 (978-1-61479-453-0(7), Graphic Planet) Magic Wagon.

—Scooby-Doo in Bake-Off Mayhem, 1 vol. 2016. (Scooby-Doo Leveled Readers Ser.). (ENG., Illus.). 32p. (J). (gr. k-4). lib. bdg. 24.21 (978-1-61479-418-9(9)) Spotlight.

—Scooby-Doo in Mummy Scares Best, 1 vol. 2016. (Scooby-Doo Comic Readers Ser.). (ENG.). 32p. (J). (gr. k-3). lib. bdg. 24.21 (978-1-61479-455-4(3), Graphic Planet) Magic Wagon.

—Scooby-Doo in There's No Creature Like Snow Creature, 1 vol. 2016. (Scooby-Doo Comic Readers Ser.). (ENG.). 32p. (J). (gr. k-3). lib. bdg. 24.21 (978-1-61479-456-1(1), Graphic Planet) Magic Wagon.

Howard, Victoria. The Adventures of Max: Max & His Friends Save the World. 2013. 68p. pap. 28.99 (978-1-4817-0732-9(9)) AuthorHouse.

—The Adventures of Max: The Bolognese Dog. 2012. 72p. pap. 28.99 (978-1-4772-6560-4(0)) AuthorHouse.

—The Adventures of Max & Molly: A Love Story about a Dog & a Horse. 2012. 52p. pap. 24.99 (978-1-4772-4866-9(8)) AuthorHouse.

Howe, Deborah & Howe, James. A Rabbit-Tale of Mystery. unabr. ed. 2004. (Bunnicula Ser.). 98p. (J). (gr. 3-7). pap. 29.00 incl. audio (978-0-8072-8204-5(9), YYA139SP, Listening Library) Random Hse. Audio Publishing Group.

Howe, James. Bud Barkin, Private Eye. Helquist, Brett, illus. (Tales from the House of Bunnicula Ser.: 5). (ENG.). (J). (gr. 2-5). 2004. 112p. pap. 5.99 (978-0-689-86989-1(4)) 2003. 96p. 13.99 (978-0-689-85632-7(6)) Simon & Schuster Children's Publishing. (Atheneum Bks. for Young Readers).

—Bunnicula Strikes Again! 2004. (Bunnicula Ser.). 116p. (J). (gr. 3-7). pap. 29.00 incl. audio (978-0-8072-8213-7(8), Listening Library) Random Hse. Audio Publishing Group.

—Bunnicula Strikes Again! Daniel, Alan, illus. 2007. (Bunnicula & Friends Ser.). (ENG.). 144p. (J). (gr. 3-7). pap. 6.99 (978-1-4169-3968-9(7), Atheneum Bks. for Young Readers) Simon & Schuster Children's Publishing.

—Hot Fudge. Mack, Jeff, illus. 2006. (Bunnicula & Friends Ser.). (gr. k-4). 14.00 (978-0-7569-7224-0(8)) Perfection Learning Corp.

—Hot Fudge. Mack, Jeff, tr. Mack, Jeff, illus. 2004. (Bunnicula & Friends Ser.: 2). (ENG.). 48p. (J). (gr. 1-3). 16.99 (978-0-689-85725-6(X), Atheneum Bks. for Young Readers) Simon & Schuster Children's Publishing.

—Hot Fudge. Mack, Jeff, illus. 2006. (Bunnicula & Friends Ser.: 2). (ENG.). 48p. (J). (gr. 1-3). pap. 3.99 (978-0-689-85750-8(0), Simon Spotlight) Simon Spotlight.

—Houndsley & Catina. Gay, Marie-Louise, illus. (ENG.). 40p. (J). (gr. k-4). 2013. (Candlewick Sparks Ser.). pap. 3.99 (978-0-7636-6638-5(6)) 2006. (Houndsley & Catina Ser.: 1). 15.99 (978-0-7636-2404-0(7)) Candlewick Pr.

—Houndsley & Catina. Gay, Marie-Louise, illus. 2007. 36p. (J). (gr. k-2). lib. bdg. 12.65 (978-0-7569-8141-9(7)) Perfection Learning Corp.

—Houndsley & Catina. 2013. (Candlewick Sparks Ser.). lib. bdg. 13.55 (978-0-606-31608-8(6), Turtleback) Turtleback Bks.

—Houndsley & Catina & the Birthday Surprise. Gay, Marie-Louise, illus. (ENG.). 48p. (J). (gr. k-4). 2013. (Candlewick Sparks Ser.). pap. 3.99 (978-0-7636-6639-2(4)) 2006. (Houndsley & Catina Ser.: 2). 15.99 (978-0-7636-2405-7(5)) Candlewick Pr.

—Houndsley & Catina & the Quiet Time. Gay, Marie-Louise, illus. (ENG.). 48p. (J). (gr. k-4). 2013. (Candlewick Sparks Ser.). pap. 3.99 (978-0-7636-6863-1(X)) 2008. (Houndsley & Catina Ser.: 3). 15.99 (978-0-7636-3384-4(4)) Candlewick Pr.

—Houndsley & Catina Plink & Plunk. Gay, Marie-Louise, illus. 2013. (Candlewick Sparks Ser.). (ENG.). 48p. (J). (gr. k-4). pap. 3.99 (978-0-7636-6640-8(8)) Candlewick Pr.

—Howie Monroe & the Doghouse of Doom. Helquist, Brett, illus. 2003. (Tales from the House of Bunnicula Ser.: 3). (ENG.). 112p. (J). (gr. 2-4). pap. 5.99 (978-0-689-83952-8(9), Atheneum Bks. for Young Readers) Simon & Schuster Children's Publishing.

—Howie Monroe & the Doghouse of Doom. 2004. (Tales from the House of Bunnicula Ser.). 85p. (J). (gr. 3-6). pap. 17.00 incl. audio (978-1-4000-8634-4(5), Listening Library) Random Hse. Audio Publishing Group.

—Howliday Inn. Munsinger, Lynn, illus. 2006. 195p. (gr. 3-7). 16.00 (978-0-7569-6807-6(0)) Perfection Learning Corp.

—Howliday Inn. Munsinger, Lynn, illus. 2nd ed. 2006. (Bunnicula & Friends Ser.). (ENG.). 224p. (J). (gr. 3-7). pap. 7.99 (978-1-4169-2815-7(4), Atheneum Bks. for Young Readers) Simon & Schuster Children's Publishing.

—Invasion of the Mind Swappers from Asteroid 6! 2004. (Tales from the House of Bunnicula Ser.). 112p. (J). (gr. 3-6). pap. 17.00 incl. audio (978-1-4000-8633-7(7), Listening Library) Random Hse. Audio Publishing Group.

—Invasion of the Mind Swappers from Asteroid 6! Helquist, Brett, illus. 2003. (Tales from the House of Bunnicula Ser.). 89p. (J). (gr. 2-5). 11.65 (978-0-7569-2814-8(1)) Perfection Learning Corp.

—Invasion of the Mind Swappers from Asteroid 6! Helquist, Brett, illus. 2003. (Tales from the House of Bunnicula Ser.: 2). (ENG.). 112p. (J). (gr. 2-5). pap. 5.99 (978-0-689-83950-4(2), Simon & Schuster/Paula Wiseman Bks.) Simon & Schuster/Paula Wiseman Bks.

—It Came from Beneath the Bed! Helquist, Brett, illus. 2003. (Tales from the House of Bunnicula Ser.: 1). (ENG.). 112p. (J). (gr. 2-4). pap. 6.99 (978-0-689-83948-1(0), Atheneum Bks. for Young Readers) Simon & Schuster Children's Publishing.

—It Came from Beneath the Bed! 2004. (Tales from the House of Bunnicula Ser.). 112p. (J). (gr. 3-6). pap. 17.00 incl. audio (978-1-4000-8632-0(9), Listening Library) Random Hse. Audio Publishing Group.

—Nighty-Nightmare. unabr. ed. 2004. (Bunnicula Ser.). 128p. (J). (gr. 3-7). pap. 29.00 incl. audio (978-0-8072-8397-4(5), YA201SP, Listening Library) Random Hse. Audio Publishing Group.

—Nighty-Nightmare. Morrill, Leslie, illus. 2007. (Bunnicula & Friends Ser.). (ENG.). 144p. (J). (gr. 3-7). pap. 6.99 (978-1-4169-3966-5(0), Atheneum Bks. for Young Readers) Simon & Schuster Children's Publishing.

—The Odorous Adventures of Stinky Dog. Helquist, Brett, illus. 2003. (Tales from the House of Bunnicula Ser.: 6). (ENG.). 112p. (J). (gr. 2-5). 13.99 (978-0-689-85633-4(4), Atheneum Bks. for Young Readers) Simon & Schuster Children's Publishing.

—The Odorous Adventures of Stinky Dog. Helquist, Brett, illus. 2004. (Tales from the House of Bunnicula Ser.: 6). (ENG.). 112p. (J). (gr. 2-5). pap. 4.99 (978-0-689-87412-3(X), Simon & Schuster/Paula Wiseman Bks.) Simon & Schuster/Paula Wiseman Bks.

—Plink & Plunk. Gay, Marie-Louise, illus. 2009. (Houndsley & Catina Ser.). (ENG.). 48p. (J). (gr. k-4). 15.99 (978-0-7636-3385-1(2)) Candlewick Pr.

—Rabbit-Cadabra! Mack, Jeff, illus. (Bunnicula & Friends Ser.: 4). (ENG.). 48p. (J). (gr. 1-3). 2007. pap. 3.99 (978-0-689-85752-2(7)) 2006. 16.99 (978-0-689-85727-0(6)) Simon Spotlight. (Simon Spotlight).

—Return to Howliday Inn. unabr. ed. 2004. (Bunnicula Ser.). 128p. (J). (gr. 3-7). pap. 29.00 incl. audio (978-0-8072-8416-2(5), YA192SP, Listening Library) Random Hse. Audio Publishing Group.

—Return to Howliday Inn. Daniel, Alan, illus. 2007. (Bunnicula & Friends Ser.). (ENG.). 192p. (J). (gr. 3-7). pap. 6.99 (978-1-4169-3967-2(9), Atheneum Bks. for Young Readers) Simon & Schuster Children's Publishing.

C
D

—Return to Howliday Inn. Daniel, Alan, illus. 2007. (Bunnicula Ser.: 5). (gr. 4-7). lib. bdg. 17.20 *(978-1-4177-9044-9(X),* Turtleback) Turtleback Bks.

—Scared Silly. Mack, Jeff, illus. 2006. (Bunnicula & Friends Ser.). 42p. (gr. 1-3). 14.00 *(978-0-7569-7225-7(6))* Perfection Learning Corp.

—Scared Silly. Mack, Jeff, illus. 2005. (Bunnicula & Friends Ser.: 3). (ENG.). 48p. (J). (gr. 1-3). 16.99 *(978-0-689-85726-3(8),* Atheneum Bks. for Young Readers) Simon & Schuster Children's Publishing.

—Scared Silly. Mack, Jeff, illus. 2006. (Bunnicula & Friends Ser.: 3). (ENG.). 48p. (J). (gr. 1-3). pap. 3.99 *(978-0-689-85751-5(9),* Simon Spotlight) Simon Spotlight.

—Screaming Mummies of the Pharaoh's Tomb II. Helquist, Brett, illus. (Tales from the House of Bunnicula Ser.: 4). (ENG.). 112p. (J). (gr. 2-5). 2004. pap. 6.99 *(978-0-689-83954-2(5))* 2003. 13.99 *(978-0-689-83953-5(7))* Simon & Schuster Children's Publishing. (Atheneum Bks. for Young Readers).

—The Vampire Bunny. Mack, Jeff, illus. 2005. (Bunnicula & Friends Ser.: 1). (ENG.). 48p. (J). (gr. 1-3). pap. 3.99 *(978-0-689-85749-2(7),* Simon Spotlight) Simon Spotlight.

Howe, Peter. Waggit Again. Rayyan, Omar, illus. (Waggit Ser.: 2). (ENG.). (J). (gr. 5). 2010. 320p. pap. 6.99 *(978-0-06-124266-3(7))* 2009. 304p. 16.99 *(978-0-06-124264-9(0))* HarperCollins Pubs.

—Waggit Forever. Rayyan, Omar, illus. (Waggit Ser.: 3). (ENG.). (J). (gr. 5). 2011. 288p. pap. 6.99 *(978-0-06-176516-2(3))* 2010. 272p. 16.99 *(978-0-06-176517-9(1))* HarperCollins Pubs.

—Waggit's Tale. Rayyan, Omar, illus. 2009. (Waggit Ser.: 1). (ENG.). 304p. (J). (gr. 5). pap. 6.99 *(978-0-06-124263-2(2))* HarperCollins Pubs.

Howell, Trisha Adelena. Addie, the Playful Pekingese. Hohn, David, illus. 2005. 128p. (YA). pap. 11.95 *(978-1-931210-27-0(6))* Howell Canyon Pr.

—The Poopy Pekinese. Marshall, Jamie, illus. 2005. 32p. (J). 15.95 *(978-1-931210-09-6(8))* Howell Canyon Pr.

—The Princess & the Pekinese. 2003. (Illus.). 32p. 15.95 *(978-1-931210-03-4(9))* Howell Canyon Pr.

Howey, Paul M. Freckles: The Mystery of the Little White Dog in the Desert. Zabriskie, Judy Mehn, illus. 2003. 72p. (gr. 2-5). lib. bdg. 14.95 *(978-0-9677292-1-3(1))* AZTexts Publishing, Inc.

Howland, Ashley. Obi the Super Puppy & the Mystery of the Red Mist. 2011. 88p. pap. 12.97 *(978-1-61204-278-7(3),* Strategic Bk. Publishing) Strategic Book Publishing & Rights Agency (SBPRA).

Huang, SuHua. A Faithful Reading Partner: A Story from a Hakka Village. 2012. 28p. pap. 19.99 *(978-1-4685-6267-5(3))* AuthorHouse.

Hubbard, Ben. My Very Own Puppy. Guile, Gill, illus. 2014. (ENG.). 12p. (gr. -1). *(978-1-78244-603-3(6))* Top That! Publishing PLC.

Hubbell, Patricia. Shaggy Dogs, Waggy Dogs, 0 vols. Wu, Donald, illus. 2011. (ENG.). 32p. (J). (gr. -1-3). 17.99 *(978-0-7614-5957-6(X),* 9780761459576, Amazon Children's Publishing) Amazon Publishing.

Huchel, Gerald D. She-Devil & the Pup. 2012. 32p. (-18). pap. 16.95 *(978-1-62709-156-5(4))* America Star Bks.

Hudgins, Larry. My Dog Spike, 1 vol. 2009. 55p. pap. 16.95 *(978-1-60836-421-3(6))* America Star Bks.

Hudspeth, Jodi. Unconditional Love. 2009. 80p. pap. 28.99 *(978-1-4343-6383-1(X))* AuthorHouse.

Hughes, Devon. Unnaturals: The Battle Begins. Richardson, Owen, illus. 2015. (Unnaturals Ser.: 1). (ENG.). 352p. (J). (gr. 3-7). 16.99 *(978-0-06-225754-3(4))* HarperCollins Pubs.

Hughes, Shirley. Dogger. Hughes, Shirley, illus. ltd. l.t. ed. 2010. (ENG., Illus.). 32p. (J). (gr. k-k). pap. 12.99 *(978-1-86230-805-3(5),* Red Fox) Random House Children's Books GBR. Dist: Independent Pubs. Group.

Hughes, Stephen B. The Adventures of Bruno a Dogg & Bowser T Houn' 2009. 80p. pap. 14.98 *(978-1-4389-8677-7(7))* AuthorHouse.

Hughes, Susan. Bailey. 2016. (Puppy Pals Ser.: 1). (ENG.). 112p. (J). (gr. 2-5). pap. 5.99 *(978-1-4926-3394-5(1),* 9781492633945, Sourcebooks Jabberwocky) Sourcebooks, Inc.

—Bijou. 2017. (Puppy Pals Ser.: 4). (ENG.). 112p. (J). (gr. 2-5). pap. 5.99 *(978-1-4926-3403-4(4),* 9781492634034, Sourcebooks Jabberwocky) Sourcebooks, Inc.

—Murphy. 2016. (Puppy Pals Ser.: 3). (ENG.). 128p. (J). (gr. 2-5). pap. 5.99 *(978-1-4926-3400-3(X),* 9781492634003, Sourcebooks Jabberwocky) Sourcebooks, Inc.

—Riley. 2016. (Puppy Pals Ser.: 2). (ENG.). 128p. (J). (gr. 2-5). pap. 5.99 *(978-1-4926-3397-6(6),* 9781492633976, Sourcebooks Jabberwocky) Sourcebooks, Inc.

Hughes, Vi. The Graveyard Hounds, 1 vol. Liest, Christina, illus. 2009. (ENG.). 168p. (J). (gr. 3-5). pap. 12.95 *(978-1-896580-49-4(1))* Tradewind Bks. CAN. Dist: Orca Bk. Pubs. USA.

Huiner, Jacque. Anna Ate. 2009. 36p. pap. 21.99 *(978-1-4389-1765-8(1))* AuthorHouse.

Huizenga, Nathaniel. Justice in Winter: Justice the Dog Series. 2009. 28p. pap. 13.99 *(978-1-4389-7361-6(6))* AuthorHouse.

Hulen, Laurie. Paw Prints. 2012. 44p. pap. 19.99 *(978-1-4772-8212-0(2))* AuthorHouse.

Hulst, W. G. van de & Hulst, Willem G. van de, illus. The Basket. 2014. (J). *(978-1-928136-04-0(4))* Inheritance Pubns.

—Footprints in the Snow. 2014. (J). *(978-1-928136-13-2(3))* Inheritance Pubns.

Huneck, Stephen. Sally at the Farm. 2014. (Sally Board Bks.). (ENG., Illus.). 20p. (J). (gr. -1 — 1). bds. 7.95 *(978-1-4197-1030-8(3),* Abrams Appleseed) Abrams, Inc.

—Sally Goes to Heaven. 2014. (ENG., Illus.). 48p. (J). (gr. k-2). 18.95 *(978-1-4197-0969-2(0),* Abrams Bks. for Young Readers) Abrams, Inc.

—Sally Goes to the Vet. Huneck, Stephen, illus. 2004. (ENG., Illus.). 32p. (J). (gr. -1-3). 19.95 *(978-0-8109-4813-6(3))* Abrams, Inc.

—Sally in the Forest. 2014. (Sally Board Bks.). (ENG., Illus.). 20p. (J). (gr. -1 — 1). bds. 7.95 *(978-1-4197-1226-5(8),* Abrams Appleseed) Abrams, Inc.

—Sally in the Sand. 2014. (Sally Board Bks.). (ENG., Illus.). 20p. (J). (gr. -1 — 1). bds. 7.95 *(978-1-4197-1029-2(X),* Abrams Appleseed) Abrams, Inc.

—Sally in the Snow. 2014. (Sally Board Bks.). (ENG., Illus.). 20p. (J). (gr. -1 — 1). bds. 7.95 *(978-1-4197-1227-2(6),* Abrams Appleseed) Abrams, Inc.

—Sally's Great Balloon Adventure. 2010. (ENG., Illus.). 32p. (J). (gr. 1-4). 16.95 *(978-0-8109-8331-1(1),* Abrams Bks. for Young Readers) Abrams, Inc.

—Sally's Snow Adventure. Huneck, Stephen, illus. 2006. (ENG., Illus.). 32p. (J). (gr. -1-3). 15.95 *(978-0-8109-7061-8(9))* Abrams, Inc.

Hunger, Chrissy. Kuna Caught a Tun. 2012. 36p. pap. 20.99 *(978-1-4772-6125-5(7))* AuthorHouse.

A Hungry Puppy. 2006. (Bella & Rosie Set 3 Ser.). (ENG.). (J). pap. 7.67 *(978-1-932570-54-0(3))* Pioneer Valley Bks.

Hunt, Bonnie. The Missing Chimp: A Grayson Twins Adventures, 1 vol. 2009. 100p. pap. 19.95 *(978-1-60813-481-6(4))* America Star Bks.

Hunt, James. I Have A New Puppy! Now What? 2007. 44p. 17.95 *(978-0-9764010-4-9(5))* Susy Dorn Productions, LLC.

Hunter, Erin. The Broken Path. 2014. (Survivors Ser.: 4). 320p. (J). (gr. 3-7). lib. bdg. 17.89 *(978-0-06-210269-0(9))* HarperCollins Pubs.

—A Dangerous Path. Richardson, Owen & Stevenson, Dave, illus. 2015. (Warriors: the Prophecies Begin Ser.: 5). (ENG.). 368p. (J). (gr. 3-7). pap. 7.99 *(978-0-06-236700-6(5))* HarperCollins Pubs.

—A Dangerous Path. Stevenson, Dave, illus. 2004. (Warriors: the Prophecies Begin Ser.: 5). (ENG.). 336p. (J). (gr. 3-7). 16.99 *(978-0-06-000006-6(6))* HarperCollins Pubs.

—A Dangerous Path. 2015. (Warriors Ser.: 5). (J). lib. bdg. 18.40 *(978-0-606-36498-0(6))* Turtleback Bks.

—Darkness Falls. (Survivors Ser.: 3). (J). (gr. 3-7). 2014. (ENG.). 320p. pap. 7.99 *(978-0-06-210266-9(4))* 2013. 304p. lib. bdg. 17.89 *(978-0-06-210265-2(6))* 2013. (ENG.). 304p. 16.99 *(978-0-06-210264-5(8))* HarperCollins Pubs.

—Darkness Falls. 2014. (Survivors Ser.: 3). (J). lib. bdg. 18.40 *(978-0-606-35496-7(4))* Turtleback Bks.

—Dead of Night. 2017. (Survivors Gathering Darkness Ser.: 2). (J). lib. bdg. 18.40 ***(978-0-606-39621-9(7))*** Turtleback Bks.

—The Empty City. (Survivors Ser.: 1). (J). (gr. 3-7). 2013. (ENG.). 304p. pap. 7.99 *(978-0-06-210258-4(3))* 2012. (ENG.). 288p. 16.99 *(978-0-06-210256-0(7))* 2012. 288p. lib. bdg. 17.89 *(978-0-06-210257-7(5))* HarperCollins Pubs.

—The Empty City. 2013. (Survivors Ser.: 1). (J). lib. bdg. 18.40 *(978-0-606-31803-7(8),* Turtleback) Turtleback Bks.

—The Empty City & a Hidden Enemy. 2014. (Survivors Ser.). (ENG.). 592p. (J). (gr. 3-7). pap. 7.99 *(978-0-06-232146-6(3))* HarperCollins Pubs.

—The Endless Lake. 2014. (Survivors Ser.: 5). 320p. (J). (gr. 3-7). (ENG.). 16.99 *(978-0-06-210272-0(9))*; lib. bdg. 17.89 *(978-0-06-210273-7(7))* HarperCollins Pubs.

—A Hidden Enemy. (Survivors Ser.: 2). (J). (gr. 3-7). 2014. (ENG.). 304p. pap. 7.99 *(978-0-06-210262-1(1))* 2013. 288p. lib. bdg. 17.89 *(978-0-06-210261-4(3))* 2013. (ENG.). 288p. 16.99 *(978-0-06-210260-7(5))* HarperCollins Pubs.

—A Hidden Enemy. 2014. (Survivors Ser.: 2). (J). lib. bdg. 18.40 *(978-0-606-35056-3(X),* Turtleback) Turtleback Bks.

—Storm of Dogs. 2015. (Survivors Ser.: 6). (J). (gr. 3-7). (ENG.). 304p. pap. 7.99 *(978-0-06-210278-2(8))*; (ENG.). 288p. 16.99 *(978-0-06-210276-8(1))*; 288p. lib. bdg. 17.89 *(978-0-06-210277-5(X))* HarperCollins Pubs.

—Storm of Dogs. 2015. (Survivors Ser.: 6). (J). lib. bdg. 18.40 *(978-0-606-37632-7(1))* Turtleback Bks.

—Survivors: the Gathering Darkness #1: a Pack Divided. Kubinyi, Laszlo & Green, Julia, illus. 2015. (Survivors: the Gathering Darkness Ser.: 1). (ENG.). 304p. (J). (gr. 3-7). 16.99 *(978-0-06-234333-8(5))* HarperCollins Pubs.

—Survivors: the Gathering Darkness #3: into the Shadows. Kubinyi, Laszlo & Green, Julia, illus. 2017. (Survivors: the Gathering Darkness Ser.: 3). (J). (gr. 3-7). 336p. pap. 7.99 ***(978-0-06-234343-7(2))***; 320p. 16.99 *(978-0-06-234341-3(6))* HarperCollins Pubs.

—Survivors: the Gathering Darkness #4: Red Moon Rising. Kubinyi, Laszlo & Green, Julia, illus. 2017. (Survivors: the Gathering Darkness Ser.: 4). 304p. (J). (gr. 3-7). 16.99 ***(978-0-06-234345-1(9))*** HarperCollins Pubs.

Hunter, Erin. Tales from the Packs. 2015. (Survivors Ser.). (ENG.). 320p. (J). (gr. 3-7). pap. 6.99 *(978-0-06-229154-7(8))* HarperCollins Pubs.

Hunter, Ian. Scaredy Jack. 2012. 36p. pap. 20.99 *(978-1-4685-8078-5(7))* AuthorHouse.

Hunter, John P. Red Thunder: Secrets, Spies, & Scoundrels at Yorktown. 2006. 234p. (YA). (gr. 6-8). 7.95 *(978-0-87935-231-8(0))* Colonial Williamsburg Foundation.

Hurd, Thacher & Hurd. Art Dog. Hurd, Thacher, illus. 2004. (ENG., Illus.). 32p. (J). (gr. -1-3). 18.99 *(978-0-06-024424-8(0))* HarperCollins Pubs.

Hurley, Jorey. Fetch. Hurley, Jorey, illus. 2015. (ENG., Illus.). 40p. (J). (gr. -1-2). 17.99 *(978-1-4424-8969-1(3),* Simon & Schuster Bks. For Young Readers) Simon & Schuster Bks. For Young Readers.

Hutton, Clare. Zombie Dog. 2012. (Rotten Apple Ser.: Vol. 2). (ENG.). 192p. (J). (gr. 3-7). pap. 5.99 *(978-0-545-39824-4(X),* Scholastic Paperbacks) Scholastic, Inc.

Hveem, Todd. The Adventures of Celtic. 2011. 36p. pap. 15.14 *(978-1-4567-0076-8(6))* AuthorHouse.

—The Adventures of Celtic: Road Trip. 2011. 44p. pap. 18.46 *(978-1-4634-4703-8(5))* AuthorHouse.

Hyde, Margaret. Mo Smells Blue: A Scentsational Journey. Giacomini, Amanda, illus. 3rd ed. 2010. (Mo's Nose Ser.). (ENG.). 24p. (J). (gr. k-k). 17.95 *(978-0-9816255-4-6(1))* Mo's Nose, LLC.

—Mo Smells Christmas: A Scentsational Journey. Giacomini, Amanda, illus. 4th ed. 2010. (Mo's Nose Ser.). (ENG.). 24p. (J). (gr. k-k). 17.95 *(978-0-9816255-6-0(8))* Mo's Nose, LLC.

—Mo Smells Green: A Scentsational Journey. Giacomini, Amanda, illus. 2009. (Mo's Nose Ser.). (ENG.). 16p. (J). (gr. k-k). 17.95 *(978-0-9816255-2-2(5))* Mo's Nose, LLC.

—Mo Smells Pink: A Scentsational Journey. Giacomini, Amanda, illus. 5th ed. 2011. (Mo's Nose Ser.). (ENG.). 24p. (J). (gr. k-k). 17.95 *(978-0-9816255-5-3(X))* Mo's Nose, LLC.

—Mo Smells the Ballpark. Chaudhary, Aman, illus. 2014. (ENG.). 24p. (J). (gr. -1-k). 14.95 *(978-1-62873-668-7(2),* Sky Pony Pr.) Skyhorse Publishing Co., Inc.

—Mo Smells the Holidays: A Scentsational Journey. Giacomini, Amanda, illus. 2009. (Mo's Nose Ser.). (ENG.). 24p. (J). (gr. k-k). 17.95 *(978-0-9816255-3-9(3))* Mo's Nose, LLC.

Hyde, Noreen. The Adventures of Miss Chief: Miss Chief Goes to School. Pushee, Marisa, illus. 2007. 28p. per. 9.95 *(978-1-59858-368-7(9))* Dog Ear Publishing, LLC.

I Am A Dog. 2008. (Illus.). 26p. 24.95 *(978-0-9801054-0-7(4))* Teahouse of Danger.

I Dream of Sleeping Dogs. 2006. (J). 24.95 *(978-0-9789633-0-9(X))* Village Monkey LLC, The.

I Only Like Dogs. 2013. (Illus.). 36p. pap. 9.99 *(978-1-941037-01-0(1))* Gordon Rocket.

Ianieri, Tom. Polar Pals. 2011. 28p. pap. 15.99 *(978-1-4628-5403-5(6))* Xlibris Corp.

Ibarrola, Begonia. Chusco the Stray Dog. Herranz, Yésica, ed. Souto, Jose, illus. 2013. (ENG.). 40p. (J). (gr. k-2). 13.95 *(978-84-95923-99-8(8))* Primera Persona ESP. Dist: Independent Pubs. Group.

Ibbotson, Eva. One Dog & His Boy. 2012. (ENG.). 288p. (J). (gr. 3-7). 16.99 *(978-0-545-35196-6(0),* Scholastic Pr.) Scholastic, Inc.

Illek, Nuala. The Chinese Sausage Dog, the Panicky Porcupine & Mrs Shoo an Animal Tale of Friendship in Chin. 2009. 50p. pap. 9.99 *(978-1-60860-781-5(X),* Eloquent Bks.) Strategic Book Publishing & Rights Agency (SBPRA).

ImageBooks Staff. Little Dog: Finger Puppet Book. 2014. (Little Finger Puppet Board Bks.). (ENG.). 12p. (J). (gr. -1 — 1). bds. 6.99 *(978-1-4521-2915-0(0))* Chronicle Bks. LLC.

Inches, Alison. My Visit with Periwinkle. Levy, David B., illus. 2003. (Blue's Clues Ser.). (ENG.). 24p. (J). pap. 3.99 *(978-0-689-85230-5(4),* Simon Spotlight/Nickelodeon) Simon Spotlight/Nickelodeon.

Ingle, Annie & Klimo, Kate. Dog Diaries #2: Buddy. Jessell, Tim, illus. 2013. (Dog Diaries). (ENG.). 160p. (J). (gr. 2-5). pap. 7.99 *(978-0-307-97904-9(0),* Random Hse. Bks. for Young Readers) Random Hse. Children's Bks.

Ingram, Jacquelyn. Dakota's Doggie Tale. 2009. 32p. pap. 14.99 *(978-1-4490-1327-1(9))* AuthorHouse.

Inkpen, Chloë & Inkpen, Mick. Hello Oscar! (Zoe & Beans Ser.). (ENG., Illus.). 32p. (J). (-k). 2013. pap. 9.99 *(978-1-4472-1026-9(3))* 2012. 17.99 *(978-0-230-76368-5(5))* Pan Macmillan GBR. Dist: Independent Pubs. Group.

—How Many Pets? 2015. (Zoe & Beans Ser.). (ENG., Illus.). 12p. (J). (— 1). bds. 9.99 *(978-0-230-76653-2(6))* Pan Macmillan GBR. Dist: Independent Pubs. Group.

—Look at Me! - Zoe & Beans. 2015. (Zoe & Beans Ser.). (ENG., Illus.). 12p. (J). (— 1). bds. 9.99 *(978-0-230-76654-9(4))* Pan Macmillan GBR. Dist: Independent Pubs. Group.

Inkpen, Mick. Beachmoles & Bellvine. MC, ed. 2006. (Blue Nose Island Ser.: Bk. 2). (Illus.). 34p. (J). (gr. -1). 13.95 *(978-1-84456-225-1(5))* Hodder & Stoughton GBR. Dist: Trafalgar Square Publishing.

—Beachmoles & Bellvine. 2004. (ENG., Illus.). 32p. (J). (gr. -1-k). 16.99 *(978-0-340-87865-1(7))* Hodder & Stoughton GBR. Dist: Hachette Bk. Group.

—I Will Love You Anyway. Inkpen, Chloe, illus. 2016. (ENG.). 32p. (J). (gr. -1-1). 17.99 *(978-1-4814-7099-5(X),* Aladdin) Simon & Schuster Children's Publishing.

—Kipper. (ENG & FRE., Illus.). 32p. (J). *(978-1-85430-330-1(9),* 93450); *(978-1-85430-333-2(3),* 93451) Little Tiger Pr. Group.

—Kipper's A to Z: An Alphabet Adventure. 2006. (Kipper Ser.). (Illus.). 54p. (gr. -1-2). 18.00 *(978-0-7569-6557-0(8))* Perfection Learning Corp.

—Kipper's Monster. 2008. (ENG., Illus.). 32p. (J). (gr. -1-12). pap. 10.99 *(978-0-340-93208-7(2))* Hodder & Stoughton GBR. Dist: Hachette Bk. Group.

—Kipper's Toybox. (Illus.). 25p. (J). (CHI, ENG, URD, VIE & FRE.). *(978-1-85430-350-9(3),* 93452); (ENG, FRE, URD, VIE & CHI., *(978-1-85430-351-6(1),* 93453) Little Tiger Pr. Group.

Innis-Weissenseder, Emma May. Silky: The Dog That Saved the Day. Sherrard, Laura, illus. 2008. (ENG.). 65p. pap. 9.00 *(978-1-894372-43-5(3))* DreamCatcher Publishing CAN. Dist: Univ. of Toronto Pr.

Ioan, Elwyn & Gruffudd, Garmon. Llywelyn a Gelert, No. 2. 2005. (WEL., Illus.). 16p. pap. *(978-0-86243-379-6(7))* Y Lolfa.

Ip, Ivy S. Clues at the Carnival, 1 vol. 2013. (Scooby-Doo! Picture Clue Bks.). (ENG.). 24p. (J). (gr. -1-1). lib. bdg. 24.21 *(978-1-61479-036-5(1),* Essential Library) ABDO Publishing Co.

Ipcar, Dahlov, illus. Black & White. 2015. (Dahlov Ipcar Collection). (ENG.). 40p. (J). (gr. -1-2). 17.95 *(978-1-909263-44-4(3))* Flying Eye Bks. GBR. Dist: Consortium Bk. Sales & Distribution.

Ippolito, Heidi. Bobo's New Home. 2009. 24p. pap. 11.50 *(978-1-60860-220-9(6),* Strategic Bk. Publishing) Strategic Book Publishing & Rights Agency (SBPRA).

Irwin, Gayle. Sage Learns to Share, 1 vol. Araujo, Katie, illus. 2009. 45p. pap. 24.95 *(978-1-60836-409-1(7))* America Star Bks.

Isaacs, John. A Doggone Good Story. 2009. 30p. pap. 16.50 *(978-1-60693-471-5(6),* Eloquent Bks.) Strategic Book Publishing & Rights Agency (SBPRA).

Isaacs, Latricia. Mason & Baylee Learn to Count. 2011. 16p. (gr. -1). pap. 8.32 *(978-1-4634-0442-0(5))* AuthorHouse.

Isaacs, Michael. The Fuzzy Escape Artists. Artigas, Alexandra, illus. 2006. 32p. (J). (gr. -1-7). 15.95 *(978-0-9742845-8-3(0))* Mystic Ridge Bks.

Isbell, Tessa J. Animal Adventures: Goosey & Beauty Take a Mystery Magic Carpet Ride to Jamaica. 2013. 48p. pap. 21.99 *(978-1-4669-7217-9(3))* Trafford Publishing.

Isom, Michelle. Human Dogs. 2012. 28p. (-18). pap. 16.09 *(978-1-4669-5842-5(1))* Trafford Publishing.

Itow, Rebecca Chiyoko & Anderson II, Norman E. A Boy, A Dog & Persnickety Log. 2007. 50p. pap. 24.50 *(978-0-615-14376-7(8))* R&N Productions.

It's Hard to Say Good-Bye: The Story of How the Only Hearts Club Was Formed. 2005. 40p. (J). 3.99 *(978-0-9763213-0-9(0))* OHC Group LLC.

J, Granny. Pinky Gets a New Puppy: Pinky Frink's Adventures. 2012. 38p. pap. 17.99 *(978-1-105-86479-7(0))* Lulu Pr., Inc.

Jack's Special Day. 2003. lib. bdg. 12.95 *(978-0-9741295-0-1(X))* Crowther, Debra.

Jackson, Debra Ann. Canines on Patrol. 2005. (J). pap. 8.00 *(978-0-8059-6896-5(2))* Dorrance Publishing Co., Inc.

Jackson, Ellen B. The Ballad of Booster Bogg. Carolan, Christine, illus. 2011. (J). *(978-1-934860-07-6(7))* Shenanigan Bks.

Jackson, Jocelyn. Ariel's Adventures: the Series: Ariel's New Home. 2010. 32p. pap. 13.95 *(978-1-4497-0383-7(6),* WestBow Pr.) Author Solutions, Inc.

Jackson, Mike. The Best Dog House Ever! 2013. (Step into Reading Level 1 Ser.). lib. bdg. 13.55 *(978-0-606-26981-0(9),* Turtleback) Turtleback Bks.

Jacobson, Jennifer Richard. Andy Shane Is Not in Love. Carter, Abby, illus. 2009. (Andy Shane Ser.: 4). (ENG.). 64p. (J). (gr. k-3). 4.99 *(978-0-7636-4403-1(X))* Candlewick Pr.

Jacobson, Ryan. Jack London's Call of the Wild - A Choose Your Path Book. 2011. (Can You Survive? Ser.). (ENG.). 160p. (J). (gr. 3-8). pap. 8.95 *(978-0-9774122-3-5(7))* Lake 7 Creative, LLC.

Jacques, Brian. The Angel's Command. Elliot, David & Schoenherr, Ian, illus. 2005. (ENG.). 384p. (J). (gr. 3-7). 7.99 *(978-0-14-240285-6(0),* Firebird) Penguin Young Readers Group.

—The Angel's Command. 2003. (Castaways of the Flying Dutchman Ser.: No. 2). 1.00 *(978-1-4175-5393-8(6))* Recorded Bks., Inc.

Jake D. The Puppy Child Smiles Again. 2009. 48p. pap. 18.50 *(978-1-4389-4311-4(3))* AuthorHouse.

Jakubowski, Michele. Big Dog Decisions, 1 vol. Montalto, Luisa, illus. 2014. (Sidney & Sydney Ser.). (ENG.). 128p. (gr. 1-3). 25.32 *(978-1-4795-5226-9(7))* Picture Window Bks.

—Poppy's Puppy. Waters, Erica-Jane, illus. 2015. (Perfectly Poppy Ser.). (ENG.). 32p. (gr. k-2). 22.65 *(978-1-4795-5799-8(4))* Picture Window Bks.

James, Hollis. Jurassic Bark! (PAW Patrol) Petrossi, Fabrizio, illus. 2017. (Little Golden Book Ser.). (ENG.). 24p. (J). (-k). 4.99 *(978-0-399-55880-1(2),* Golden Bks.) Random Hse. Children's Bks.

James L. Fuller. The Lost Coal Mine to Oz. 2009. 184p. pap. 16.60 *(978-1-4269-1829-2(1))* Trafford Publishing.

James, Laura. Captain Pug. Ceulemans, Eglantine, illus. 2017. (Adventures of Pug Ser.). (ENG.). 128p. (J). 16.99 *(978-1-68119-380-9(9),* 9781681193809, Bloomsbury USA Childrens) Bloomsbury Publishing USA.

James, Laura. Captain Pug: The Dog Who Sailed the Seas. 2017. (J). lib. bdg. 17.20 ***(978-0-606-40346-7(9))*** Turtleback Bks.

James, Scilla. Princess Phoebe - a Greyhound's Adventure. 2013. 118p. pap. *(978-0-9568148-4-5(0))* Swift Publishing.

Jameson, Pam. The Betty Book! The Life & Times of Betty. 2012. (ENG.). 33p. (J). pap. 12.95 *(978-1-4327-8915-2(5))* Outskirts Pr., Inc.

Jameson, Rosemary. Mortimer & Teasdale's Adventures. 2009. 44p. pap. 14.50 *(978-1-60693-441-8(4),* Eloquent Bks.) Strategic Book Publishing & Rights Agency (SBPRA).

Jane, Rebecca. Hamster Heroes to the Rescue: The Mystery of the Shadow in the Yard & Retirement. 2012. 84p. 19.95 *(978-1-4626-6862-5(3))* America Star Bks.

Jarvis. Lazy Dave. Jarvis, illus. 2015. (ENG., Illus.). 32p. (J). (gr. -1-3). 17.99 *(978-0-06-235598-0(8))* HarperCollins Pubs.

Jasheway, Leigh Anne. Bedtime Stories for Dogs. 2016. (ENG.). 96p. pap. 9.99 *(978-1-4494-7191-0(9))* Andrews McMeel Publishing.

Jax, T. L. Fraidy-Frieda's Light Show. Jax, T. L., illus. l.t. ed. 2004. (Illus.). 30p. (J). 9.95 *(978-0-9743890-2-8(1))* Flaxenfluff Pr., LLC.

Jay, Eli. Poppy & the Fat Puppy. 2013. (ENG.). 40p. (J). pap. 19.95 *(978-1-4787-0003-6(3))* Outskirts Pr., Inc.

Jazz. Gizmo & Scatz: A Tail of Friendship. 2012. (Illus.). 16p. pap. 17.55 *(978-1-4678-8267-5(4))* AuthorHouse.

Jean, April. A Little Dachshund's Tale. Cross, Kevin, illus. 2012. 36p. pap. 9.95 *(978-1-61897-367-2(3),* Strategic Bk. Publishing) Strategic Book Publishing & Rights Agency (SBPRA).

Jefferson, A. C. The Adventures of Lucy the Wiener Dog. 2012. 24p. pap. 17.99 *(978-1-4772-7214-5(3))* AuthorHouse.

Jenisch, Betty. Rennie. 2007. 9.00 *(978-0-8059-8947-2(1))* Dorrance Publishing Co., Inc.

Jenkins, Emily. A Greyhound, a Groundhog. Appelhans, Chris, illus. 2017. (ENG.). 32p. (J). (gr. -1-2). 17.99 *(978-0-553-49805-9(3))*; lib. bdg. 20.99 *(978-0-553-49806-6(1))* Random Hse. Children's Bks. (Schwartz & Wade Bks.).

—Skunkdog. Pratt, Pierre, illus. 2008. (ENG.). 32p. (J). (gr. -1-3). 16.95 *(978-0-374-37009-1(5),* 9780374370091, Farrar, Straus & Giroux (BYR)) Farrar, Straus & Giroux.

—That New Animal. Jenkins, Emily, illus. 2006. (Illus.). (J). (gr. -1-4). 29.95 *(978-0-439-84925-8(X),* WHCD687) Weston Woods Studios, Inc.

Jenkins, June M. All about Me: Tales for Tiny Tots. 2008. (Illus.). 52p. per. *(978-1-84748-222-8(8))* Athena Pr.

Jennicrai, Susanna. Button & Bow: Friends Forever. 2013. 28p. pap. 16.09 *(978-1-4669-8779-1(0))* Trafford Publishing.

Jennings, Linda. Duna y Dan. Chapman, Jane, illus. (SPA.). 28p. (J). (gr. k-1). *(978-84-8418-027-2(1),* ZZ4481) Zendrera Zariquiey, Editorial ESP. Dist: Lectorum Pubns., Inc.

Jennings, Patrick. Guinea Dog 3. 2017. (Guinea Dog Ser.: 3). (ENG.). 176p. (gr. 3-6). 6.99 *(978-1-5124-4147-5(3),* Darby Creek) Lerner Publishing Group.

Jennings, Richard W. Scribble. 2004. (ENG.). 160p. (YA). (gr. 5-9). tchr. ed. 15.00 *(978-0-618-43367-4(8))* Houghton Mifflin Harcourt Publishing Co.

Jennings, Sharon. C'mere, Boy! Spires, Ashley, illus. 2010. (ENG.). 32p. (J). (gr. -1-2). 16.95 *(978-1-55453-440-1(2))* Kids Can Pr., Ltd. CAN. Dist: Hachette Bk. Group.

Jensen, Ned. Sam: Set Of 6. 2010. (Early Connections Ser.). (J). 33.00 net. *(978-1-59000-722-8(0))* Benchmark Education Co.

Jerome, Louie. Peter & the Black Dog. 2009. 120p. 22.50 *(978-1-60693-737-2(5),* Strategic Bk. Publishing) Strategic Book Publishing & Rights Agency (SBPRA).

(Jerry) Deal, Gerald R. Famous Dog Chowski. 2013. 44p. pap. 20.72 *(978-1-4669-9707-3(9))* Trafford Publishing.

Jiang, Mingyan. Stella Doggy: Book One of Stella's Awesome Adventures. 2011. 88p. (gr. 4-6). 19.95 *(978-1-4620-4610-2(X))*; pap. 9.95 *(978-1-4620-4608-9(8))* iUniverse, Inc.

Jin, Chris & Trimmer, Christian. Simon's New Bed. Van der Paardt, Melissa, illus. 2015. (ENG.). 32p. (J). (gr. -1-3). 17.99 *(978-1-4814-3019-7(X))* Simon & Schuster Children's Publishing.

Jjdenson. Kitty Crunch & Doggy Chow. 2011. 32p. pap. 21.99 *(978-1-4500-7383-7(2))* Xlibris Corp.

Joe & Trish. The Adventures of Sasha, the Six-Fingered Cat. 2010. 36p. pap. 16.99 *(978-1-4520-8406-0(8))* AuthorHouse.

Johansen, Zdenka. When You Give of Yourself. 2006. 28p. pap. 9.95 *(978-1-4327-0059-1(6))* Outskirts Pr., Inc.

Johnsen, Erin L. The Adventures of the Big Dog & the Little Dog: They First Meet! Nishii, illus. 2013. 32p. pap. 24.95 *(978-1-4626-2346-4(8))* America Star Bks.

Johnson, Dwayne. My Angel. 2013. (Illus.). 12p. pap. 18.30 *(978-1-4817-8188-6(X))* AuthorHouse.

Johnson, Gillian. My Sister Gracie. 2005. (ENG., Illus.). 32p. (J). (gr. -1-k). pap. 7.95 *(978-0-88776-750-0(8)*, Tundra Bks.) Tundra Bks. CAN. Dist: Penguin Random Hse. LLC.

Johnson, James. Sidney Gets a House. 2011. 24p. pap. 24.95 *(978-1-4512-7918-4(3))* America Star Bks.

Johnson, Jeremy. Rallo's Goal. 2016. (What's Your Dream? Ser.). (ENG.). 96p. (gr. 3-4). lib. bdg. 25.32 *(978-1-4965-3444-6(1))* Capstone Press of Coughlan Cos.

Johnson, Judith Margaret. Feeling Great with Jasper State: Eat Your Green Things Every Day. Johnson, Patrick Henry, illus. 2011. 32p. 14.95 *(978-0-9820228-5-6(9))* Jasper State Brand, Inc.

Johnson, Linda. The Fortunate Puppy. 2012. 32p. pap. 16.99 *(978-1-4525-6424-1(8))* Balboa Pr.

Johnson, Lucille M. Titus the Magnificent: The Adventures of Titus. 2013. 32p. pap. 13.99 *(978-1-4624-0755-2(2)*, Inspiring Voices) Author Solutions, Inc.

Johnson-McCue, Joyce. Gizmo's Great Adventure. 2008. (Illus.). 32p. (J). pap. 8.00 *(978-0-8059-7550-5(0))* Dorrance Publishing Co., Inc.

Johnson, Michael E. Barley & Betsy: Journey #1 A cat & dog's great adventure to the Mall. Atchley, Kendra, illus. 2011. 36p. pap. 24.95 *(978-1-4560-4077-2(4))* America Star Bks.

Johnson, Mimi Evelyn. A Day in the Life of Div. 2011. 24p. pap. 15.99 *(978-1-4628-9649-3(9))* Xlibris Corp.

Johnson, Paul Brett. Fearless Jack. Johnson, Paul Brett, illus. 2007. (ENG., Illus.). 32p. (J). (gr. -1-3). 10.99 *(978-1-4169-6833-7(4)*, Simon & Schuster/Paula Wiseman Bks.) Simon & Schuster/Paula Wiseman Bks.

Johnson, Sandi. Black Ridge Mountain. Durant, Sybrina, ed. Sturgen, Bobbi, illus. 2014. (ENG.). 34p. (J). (gr. k-5). pap. 12.99 *(978-1-929063-66-6(0)*, 165) Moons & Stars Publishing For Children.

Johnson, Shane L., illus. OLIVIA & the Dog Wash. 2012. (Olivia TV Tie-In Ser.). (ENG.). 16p. (J). (gr. -1-1). pap. 5.99 *(978-1-4424-4638-0(2)*, Simon Spotlight) Simon Spotlight.

Johnston-Brown, A. M. The Chronicles of Pleasant Grove. 2006. (J). pap. 12.95 *(978-0-9760718-5-3(1))* Retriever Pr.

—The Chronicles of Pleasant Grove (Glossary of Terms) 2006. (J). pap. 1.95 *(978-0-9760718-6-0(X))* Retriever Pr.

Johnston, Gail. The Shaggy Pony & the Spotted Pup. 2010. 24p. 11.32 *(978-1-4520-9653-7(8))* AuthorHouse.

Johnston, Jan. Amélie the Most Amazing Butterfly: I Do So Love Being a Butterfly ... 2013. (Illus.). 24p. pap. 17.99 *(978-1-4817-8018-6(2))* AuthorHouse.

—Lisa Finds a Playful Tree Elf: No! I Am Not a Fairy! 2013. (Illus.). 24p. pap. 17.99 *(978-1-4817-8020-9(4))* AuthorHouse.

—Ruby - the Naughty Little Black Kitten: Hello! My Name Is Ruby ... 2013. (Illus.). 24p. pap. 17.99 *(978-1-4817-8023-0(9))* AuthorHouse.

Johnston, Tony. A Small Thing ... but Big. Hooper, Hadley, illus. 2016. (ENG.). 40p. (J). 17.99 *(978-1-62672-256-9(0)*, 9781626722569) Roaring Brook Pr.

Jones, Anita. My 15 Dogs: A 55-Year Journey of Love. 2007. 59p. pap. 7.96 *(978-1-4303-2592-5(5))* Lulu Pr., Inc.

Jones, Anthony S. Little Puppy Du. 2011. 38p. pap. 14.99 *(978-1-61379-501-9(7))* Salem Author Services.

Jones, Cheryl. Where Are My Shoes? 2011. 28p. pap. 9.95 *(978-1-4327-7157-7(4))* Outskirts Pr., Inc.

Jones, Cheryl & Joseph, Rahzheena. Jojo the Dappled Dachshund. Simmons, Ann, illus. 2013. 30p. pap. 15.95 *(978-1-4787-0560-4(4))* Outskirts Pr., Inc.

Jones, Dennis. Fruitiebears: Yorkies Birthday Today: Book 1. 2010. 36p. pap. 18.99 *(978-1-4520-7037-7(7))* AuthorHouse.

Jones, Diana Wynne. Dogsbody. 2012. (ENG.). 288p. (YA). (gr. 7-18). 9.99 *(978-0-14-242013-3(1)*, Firebird) Penguin Young Readers Group.

Jones, Elwynn. Frank's Frantic Friday. 2010. 40p. pap. 16.95 *(978-1-60911-750-4(6)*, Eloquent Bks.) Strategic Book Publishing & Rights Agency (SBPRA).

Jones, Jen. Dog Days for Delaney. Franco, Paula, illus. 2014. (Sleepover Girls Ser.). (ENG.). 128p. (gr. 3-5). 22.65 *(978-1-4342-9756-3(X))* Stone Arch Bks.

Jones, Lisa A. The Black Dog. 2008. 20p. pap. 24.95 *(978-1-60474-960-1(1))* America Star Bks.

Jones, Nancy. The Grandpaws. 2005. 57p. pap. 16.95 *(978-1-4137-4778-2(7))* America Star Bks.

Jones, Noah Z. The Three Little Pugs. 2015. (ENG., Illus.). 80p. (J). (gr. k-2). pap. 4.99 *(978-0-545-84857-2(1))* Scholastic, Inc.

Jones, V. M. & Tulloch, Scott. Echo & Hush. 2008. (Illus.). 32p. pap. *(978-1-86950-690-2(1))* HarperCollins Pubs. Australia.

Jones, Val. Who Wants Broccoli? Jones, Val, illus. 2015. (ENG., Illus.). 40p. (J). (gr. -1-3). 17.99 *(978-0-06-230351-6(1))* HarperCollins Pubs.

Jones, Yevad. The Sea Quill. 2010. 112p. pap. 14.95 *(978-1-4452-7066-1(8))* Lulu Pr., Inc.

Jordan, Daniel. Joni. 2012. 72p. pap. 19.95 *(978-1-4626-8246-1(4))* America Star Bks.

Jordan, Evora. Annie Love: A Hannah Gray Dog Story. 2003. (Hannah Gray Mysteries). (J). per. *(978-0-9725071-2-7(4))* EvoraBooks, LLC.

Jorden, Edwin W. Cookie Paws. Waywell, Valerie J., illus. 2nd ed. 2007. (ENG.). 32p. (J). (gr. -1-3). 9.95 *(978-0-9793483-0-3(7))* Gilded Dog Enterprises LLC.

—Cookie Paws/Spreadin' the Sweetness. Waywell, Valerie J., illus. 2008. 32p. (J). 12.95 *(978-0-9793483-1-0(5))* Gilded Dog Enterprises LLC.

Josephine Breglia. The Adventures of Poke Sa' Baar. 2012. 28p. pap. 24.95 *(978-1-4626-8820-3(9))* America Star Bks.

Joy, Angela. My Dog. Slater, Nicola, illus. 2005. 14p. (J). 12.95 *(978-1-58925-759-7(6))* Tiger Tales.

Joyce, B. Big Easy & His Quest for the Stars. 2007. 84p. per. 16.95 *(978-1-4241-0427-7(0))* PublishAmerica, Inc.

Joyce, Samantha & Joyce, Caroline. Fluffy's Story Part 1 Fluffy's Journey. Moore, Debra, illus. 2005. 48p. (J). 16.95 *(978-0-9770898-0-2(0))* Paw Print Publishing.

Joyce, Sandie May. Aunt Sandie Goes to School - the Comics. 2008. 55p. pap. 22.50 *(978-0-557-02295-3(9))* Lulu Pr., Inc.

Joyce, William. Rolie Polie Olie. Joyce, William, illus. 2017. (World of William Joyce Ser.). (ENG., Illus.). 48p. (J). (gr. -1-2). 17.99 ***(978-1-4814-8957-7(7)**, Atheneum Bks. for Young Readers)* Simon & Schuster Children's Publishing.

Judybee. Danny Strikes Out in Americ: A R. E. A. d Book. Kecskés, Anna, illus. 2013. 32p. pap. *(978-1-78092-335-2(X))* MX Publishing, Ltd.

Jukes, Carlisle E. The Rhino & the Rat: The Delightful Story of Coco & Max. 2009. 28p. pap. 13.25 *(978-1-4389-6751-6(9))* AuthorHouse.

Julian, Russell. Busy Dog. 2005. (Farm Board Book Ser.). (ENG., Illus.). 12p. (J). bds. 9.99 *(978-1-4052-1031-7(1))* Egmont Bks., Ltd. GBR. Dist: Trafalgar Square Publishing.

June-Bug. Sweetbread & Tattletale. 2012. 32p. 24.95 *(978-1-4626-6040-7(1))* America Star Bks.

Juscik, Andy. Tear Catchers. 2010. 36p. pap. 14.95 *(978-1-60911-488-6(4)*, Eloquent Bks.) Strategic Book Publishing & Rights Agency (SBPRA).

Jusino, Cindy M. Toodle's Big Race: Interactive for Children That Don't Like to Sit Still! Studio, Gau Family, illus. 2013. 44p. 20.00 *(978-0-9888003-2-8(2))* Sensational Pubns.

K. Elizabeth, Sterling. Austin's First Puppy. 2007. 48p. (J). pap. 10.95 *(978-0-7414-3263-6(3))* Infinity Publishing.

K/H (Pathways). Kindergarten Stepping Stones: Kindergarten the Bravest Dog Ever - The True Story of Balto Trade Book. rev. ed. 2010. (ENG.). 48p. pap. 9.00 *(978-0-7575-8646-0(5))* Kendall Hunt Publishing Co.

Kadilak, Kathy. Tommy Finds His Forever Home. 2009. 28p. pap. 12.49 *(978-1-4490-0177-3(7))* AuthorHouse.

Kadohata, Cynthia. Cracker! The Best Dog in Vietnam. (ENG.). 320p. (J). (gr. 5-9). 2008. pap. 8.99 *(978-1-4169-0638-4(X))* 2007. (Illus.). 18.99 *(978-1-4169-0637-7(1))* Simon & Schuster Children's Publishing. (Atheneum Bks. for Young Readers).

Kalman, Maira. Max Makes a Million. 2017. (ENG., Illus.). 48p. (J). (gr. k-3). 18.95 ***(978-1-68137-170-2(7)**, NYR Children's Collection)* New York Review of Bks., Inc., The.

—Smartypants: Pete in School. 2005. (J). 29.95 incl. audio compact disk *(978-0-8045-4105-3(1)*, SACD4105); 27.95 incl. audio *(978-0-8045-6929-3(0)*, SAC6929) Spoken Arts, Inc.

—What Pete Ate from A to Z. 2003. (ENG., Illus.). 48p. (J). (gr. -1-2). pap. 6.99 *(978-0-14-250159-7(X)*, Puffin Books) Penguin Young Readers Group.

Kalz, Jill. Tuckerbean on the Moon, 1 vol. Mahan, Benton, illus. 2009. (Read-It! Readers: Adventures of Tuckerbean Ser.). (ENG.). 24p. (gr. -1-3). 21.32 *(978-1-4048-5234-1(4)*, Easy Readers) Picture Window Bks.

Kaminski, Tom. Miss Olivia, the Little Red Poodle: Her First Big Adventure. Fallon, Lisa, illus. 2006. (J). pap. 16.00 *(978-0-8059-7253-5(6))* Dorrance Publishing Co., Inc.

Kamofonas, Mary Katherine. In the Doghouse. 2013. 24p. pap. *(978-1-77097-510-1(1))* FriesenPress.

Kann, Victoria. Puptastic! Kann, Victoria, illus. 2013. (I Can Read Level 1 Ser.). (ENG., Illus.). 32p. (J). (gr. -1-3). 16.99 *(978-0-06-218786-4(4))* HarperCollins Pubs.

—Puptastic! 2013. (Pinkalicious I Can Read Ser.). (J). lib. bdg. 13.55 *(978-0-606-31792-4(9)*, Turtleback) Turtleback Bks.

Kaplan, Kathy Walden. The Dog of Knots. 2005. 139p. (J). pap. 7.50 *(978-0-8028-5274-8(2))* Eerdmans, William B. Publishing Co.

Kasza, Keiko. The Dog Who Cried Wolf. Kasza, Keiko, illus. 2009. (ENG., Illus.). 32p. (J). (gr. -1-2). pap. 6.99 *(978-0-14-241305-0(4)*, Puffin Books) Penguin Young Readers Group.

Katey, Miss. Jelly Bean: A Puppy's Tale. 2005. (ENG., Illus.). 25p. (J). (gr. -1-3). per. 13.99 *(978-1-4134-8093-1(4))* Xlibris Corp.

Kathleen, Jo Ann. NATALIA, O' MIA, WHITE LACES & SHOES. l.t. ed. 2006. (ENG., Illus.). 28p. per. 9.95 *(978-1-4327-0314-1(5))* Outskirts Pr., Inc.

Katis, Michael. Cheech the Pup: With Illustrations by Sharyn Crownover. 2008. pap. 17.00 *(978-0-8059-7915-2(8))* Dorrance Publishing Co., Inc.

Kats, Jewel. Jenny & Her Dog Both Fight Cancer: A Tale of Chemotherapy & Caring. 2015. (J). pap. *(978-1-61599-279-9(0))* Loving Healing Pr., Inc.

Kats, Jewel. Prince Preemie: A Tale of a Tiny Puppy Who Arrives Early. Lenart, Claudia, illus. 2016. (J). pap. ***(978-1-61599-306-2(1))*** Loving Healing Pr., Inc.

Katz, Karen. Where Is Baby's Puppy? Katz, Karen, illus. 2011. (ENG., Illus.). 14p. (J). (gr. -1 — 1). bds. 6.99 *(978-1-4169-8684-3(7)*, Little Simon) Little Simon.

Katzwinkle, William, et al. Walter the Farting Dog Goes on a Cruise. Colman, Audrey, illus. 2008. (J). 13.99 *(978-1-59319-939-5(2))* LeapFrog Enterprises, Inc.

Kaupp, Rosemarie. The Amberella Tales: Amberella & Double Double Trouble. 2013. 144p. (gr. 2-4). 20.77 *(978-1-4669-9233-7(6))*; pap. 10.77 *(978-1-4669-9234-4(4))* Trafford Publishing.

—The Amberella Tales: Amberella in the City. 2012. 120p. (gr. 4-6). 22.33 *(978-1-4669-0594-8(8))*; pap. 12.33 *(978-1-4669-0595-5(6))* Trafford Publishing.

Kavanagh, Charlene Kate. Going Home: The Lost Story of Chief the Fire Dog. 2007. 116p. 20.95 *(978-0-595-88236-6(6))*; 112p. (gr. 10-12). per. 10.95 *(978-0-595-40946-4(6))* iUniverse, Inc.

Kawamura, Yayo. A Day with Pepe & Milli. Kawamura, Yayo, illus. 2017. (Pepe & Millie Ser.). (ENG., Illus.). 16p. (J). (gr. -1 — 1). bds. 9.99 ***(978-0-8075-6481-3(8))*** Whitman, Albert & Co.

Kearney, Meg. Trouper. Lewis, E. B., illus. 2013. (ENG.). 32p. (J). (gr. -1-3). 16.99 *(978-0-545-10041-0(0)*, Scholastic Pr.) Scholastic, Inc.

Keats, Ezra Jack. Kitten for a Day. 2008. (Illus.). lib. bdg. 17.00 *(978-0-7569-9008-4(4))* Perfection Learning Corp.

—Whistle for Willie. 2015. 32p. pap. 7.00 *(978-1-61003-537-8(2))* Center for the Collaborative Classroom.

Kebbi, Yann. Americanine: A Haute Dog in New York. 2015. (ENG., Illus.). 72p. (J). 19.95 *(978-1-59270-172-8(8))* Enchanted Lion Bks., LLC.

Keefe, Susan. Toby's Tails. 2012. 202p. pap. 14.00 *(978-1-61204-791-1(2)*, Strategic Bk. Publishing) Strategic Book Publishing & Rights Agency (SBPRA).

Keenan, Sheila. Dogs of War. Fox, Nathan, illus. 2013. (ENG.). 176p. (J). (gr. 3-7). pap. 12.99 *(978-0-545-12888-9(9)*, Graphix) Scholastic, Inc.

Keene, Carolyn. A Musical Mess. Pamintuan, Macky, illus. 2014. (Nancy Drew & the Clue Crew Ser.: 38). (ENG.). 96p. (J). (gr. 1-4). pap. 5.99 *(978-1-4424-9512-8(X)*, Aladdin) Simon & Schuster Children's Publishing.

Keener, A. E. My Name Is Charlie. 2010. 20p. pap. 11.00 *(978-1-4490-7576-7(2))* AuthorHouse.

Kees Csa, Cecile Marie. Patrick & Puppy Wuppy: Life in Grade Two. 2012. 20p. pap. 17.99 *(978-1-4772-1047-5(4))* AuthorHouse.

Kegereis, Carl. Tibby & His Friend's Big Secret. 2010. 96p. pap. 13.95 *(978-1-4327-4449-6(6))* Outskirts Pr., Inc.

Kehret, Peg. Bone Breath & the Vandals. 2008. (Frightmares Ser.: 2). (ENG.). 128p. (YA). (gr. 7). pap. 8.99 *(978-1-4169-8484-9(4)*, Simon & Schuster Bks. For Young Readers) Simon & Schuster Bks. For Young Readers.

—Ghost Dog Secrets. 2011. (ENG.). 192p. (J). (gr. 5-18). 6.99 *(978-0-14-241964-9(8)*, Puffin Books) Penguin Young Readers Group.

—Runaway Twin. 2011. (ENG.). 208p. (J). (gr. 5-18). 6.99 *(978-0-14-241849-9(8)*, Puffin Books) Penguin Young Readers Group.

Keil, James. Tiger & the Poachers. 2010. 54p. pap. 15.52 *(978-0-557-34105-4(1))* Lulu Pr., Inc.

Kelahan, Renee. Agua, the Mysterious Portuguese Water Dog. 2009. 108p. 20.95 *(978-1-4401-5443-0(0))*; pap. 10.95 *(978-1-4401-5442-3(2))* iUniverse, Inc.

Keller, Holly. Sophie's Window. Keller, Holly, illus. 2005. (Illus.). 32p. (J). 16.89 *(978-0-06-056283-0(8))* HarperCollins Pubs.

Kelley, Lisa. Nutty. 2010. 20p. 10.49 *(978-1-4520-0303-0(3))* AuthorHouse.

Kelley, Lynn. The First Boykin Spaniels: The Story of Dumpy & Singo. Gardiner, Lisa, illus. 2012. (Distributed for the Author Ser.). (ENG.). 31p. (Orig.). (J). per. 13.50 *(978-0-9761463-0-8(4))* Univ. of South Carolina Pr.

Kelley, True. The Dog Who Saved Santa. Kelley, True, illus. 2008. (ENG., Illus.). 32p. (J). (gr. -1-3). 16.95 *(978-0-8234-2120-6(1))* Holiday Hse., Inc.

Kellogg, Steven. Pinkerton, Behave! 2014. (ENG., Illus.). 32p. (J). (gr. -1-3). 17.99 *(978-0-8037-4130-0(8)*, Dial Bks) Penguin Young Readers Group.

Kelly, Irene. A Small Dog's Big Life: Around the World with Owney. 2005. (ENG., Illus.). 32p. (J). 16.95 *(978-0-8234-1863-3(4))* Holiday Hse., Inc.

Kelly, Sharon L. C. M. Coco's Vineyard Vacation: Double Fun on Martha's Vineyard. Galbraith, Alison L., illus. 2005. 40p. (J). 16.95 *(978-0-9766283-0-9(9))* Secret Garden Bookworks.

Kelman, Jennifer. Mrs Pinkelmeyer & Moopus Mcglinden Prance into New York City. 2011. 44p. pap. 15.99 *(978-1-4575-0497-6(9))* Dog Ear Publishing, LLC.

Kelsey, Stacy. Meet the Pro's with Sproket the Moto Dog, 1 vol. 2010. 38p. 24.95 *(978-1-4489-4785-0(5))* PublishAmerica, Inc.

—Sproket the Moto Dog, 1 vol. 2009. 40p. pap. 24.95 *(978-1-60749-899-5(5))* America Star Bks.

Kelso, Mary Jean. Andy & Spirit in Search & Rescue. Snider, Kc, illus. 2013. 28p. 19.95 *(978-1-61633-410-9(X))*; pap. 10.95 *(978-1-61633-408-6(8))* Guardian Angel Publishing, Inc.

Kemp, Anna. Dogs Don't Do Ballet. Ogilvie, Sara, illus. 2010. (ENG.). 32p. (J). (gr. -1-3). 17.99 *(978-1-4169-9839-6(X)*, Simon & Schuster Bks. For Young Readers) Simon & Schuster Bks. For Young Readers.

—Dogs Don't Do Ballet. Ogilvie, Sara, illus. 2010. (ENG.). 32p. pap. *(978-1-84738-474-4(9))* Simon & Schuster, Ltd.

Kenah, Katharine. Ferry Tail. Wong, Nicole, illus. 2014. (ENG.). 32p. (J). (gr. k-3). 16.99 *(978-1-58536-829-7(6)*, 203011) Sleeping Bear Pr.

Kendall, Gillian Murray. The Garden of Darkness. 2014. (ENG.). 336p. (YA). (gr. 6-12). pap. 9.99 *(978-1-78108-248-5(0)*, Ravenstone) Rebellion GBR. Dist: Simon & Schuster, Inc.

Kendall, Stan P. Samson Gets a Family. 2005. 22p. (J). 13.50 *(978-1-4116-5756-4(X))* Lulu Pr., Inc.

Kennedy, Anne Vittur. Ragweed's Farm Dog Handbook. Kennedy, Anne Vittur, illus. 2015. (ENG., Illus.). 32p. (J). (gr. -1-2). 15.99 *(978-0-7636-7417-5(6))* Candlewick Pr.

Kennedy Center Staff. Unleashed: The Lives of White House Pets. Hoyt, Ard, illus. 2011. (ENG.). 112p. (J). (gr. 2-5). pap. 5.99 *(978-1-4169-4862-9(7)*, Simon & Schuster Bks. For Young Readers) Simon & Schuster Bks. For Young Readers.

Kennedy, Marlane. The Dog Days of Charlotte Hayes. 2009. (ENG., Illus.). 240p. (J). (gr. 3-7). 15.99 *(978-0-06-145241-3(6)*, Greenwillow Bks.) HarperCollins Pubs.

Kenney, Cindy. Project Precious Paws, Bk. 3. 2009. 86p. (J). 9.95 *(978-0-9817159-5-7(8))*; pap. 5.99 *(978-0-9817159-4-0(X))* Precious Moments, Inc.

Kent, Derek Taylor. El Perro con Sombrero: A Bilingual Doggy Tale. Henry, Jed, illus. 2015. (ENG & SPA.). 40p. (J). (gr. -1-2). 17.99 *(978-0-8050-9989-8(1)*, 9780805099898, Holt, Henry & Co. Bks. For Young Readers) Holt, Henry & Co.

Keough, Kevin. Snoozy Dog: And Curly Cat Too! 2011. 24p. (gr. -1). pap. 12.98 *(978-1-4389-4794-5(1))* AuthorHouse.

Kerby, Johanna. Little Pink Pup. Kerby, Johanna, photos by. 2010. (ENG., Illus.). 32p. (J). (gr. -1-k). 16.99 *(978-0-399-25435-2(8)*, G.P. Putnam's Sons Books for Young Readers) Penguin Young Readers Group.

Kerby, Mona. Owney, the Mail-Pouch Pooch. Barasch, Lynne, illus. 2008. (ENG.). 40p. (J). (gr. k-3). 17.99 *(978-0-374-35685-9(8)*, 9780374356859, Farrar, Straus & Giroux (BYR)) Farrar, Straus & Giroux.

Kertell, Lynn Maslen. Buddy to the Rescue. Hendra, Sue, illus. 2012. (Scholastic Reader Level 1 Ser.). (ENG.). 32p. (J). (gr. -1-2). pap. 3.99 *(978-0-545-38273-1(4))* Scholastic, Inc.

—Buddy to the Rescue. 2012. (BOB Books: Scholastic Readers Level 1 Ser.: 6). lib. bdg. 13.55 *(978-0-606-26753-3(0)*, Turtleback) Turtleback Bks.

Kessler, Kathryn. Marvin Discovers Snow. 2010. 36p. (J). pap. 15.77 *(978-1-4520-0590-4(7))* AuthorHouse.

Kessler, Liz. Poppy the Pirate Dog. Phillips, Mike, illus. 2013. (ENG.). 64p. (J). (gr. k-3). 14.99 *(978-0-7636-6569-2(X))* Candlewick Pr.

—Poppy the Pirate Dog & the Missing Treasure. Phillips, Mike, illus. (Candlewick Sparks Ser.). (ENG.). 64p. (J). (gr. k-4). 2016. pap. 3.99 *(978-0-7636-8772-4(3))* 2015. 14.99 *(978-0-7636-7497-7(4))* Candlewick Pr.

—Poppy the Pirate Dog's New Shipmate. Phillips, Mike, illus. (Candlewick Sparks Ser.). (ENG.). 64p. (J). (gr. k-4). 2015. pap. 3.99 *(978-0-7636-8031-2(1))* 2014. 14.99 *(978-0-7636-6751-1(X))* Candlewick Pr.

Ketter-Brust, Sandra. Sir Guinness of Wildridge. 2006. 48p. pap. 16.95 *(978-1-4241-4626-0(7))* PublishAmerica, Inc.

Kibuishi, Kazu. Copper. 2010. lib. bdg. 24.50 *(978-0-606-14274-8(6)*, Turtleback) Turtleback Bks.

Kiick, Lisa. Bailey & Friends. Stouch, Ryan, illus. 2008. 40p. pap. 14.95 *(978-1-59858-743-2(9))* Dog Ear Publishing, LLC.

Kilgras, Heidi. Peanut. Reed, Mike, illus. 2003. (Step into Reading Ser.). (ENG.). 32p. (J). (gr. -1-1). pap. 3.99 *(978-0-375-80618-6(0)*, Random Hse. Bks. for Young Readers) Random Hse. Children's Bks.

Kilpatrick, Sheila. Anastasia's Rain. 2013. 1. (ENG.). 48p. (-4). pap. 9.95 *(978-1-61448-625-1(5))* Morgan James Publishing.

Kimmel, Elizabeth Cody. Legend of the Ghost Dog. (J). 2014. (ENG.). 208p. (gr. 3-7). pap. 6.99 *(978-0-545-39128-3(8))* 2012. (ENG.). 208p. (gr. 3-7). 16.99 *(978-0-545-39127-6(X))* 2012. 200p. pap. *(978-0-545-50705-9(7))* Scholastic, Inc. (Scholastic Pr.).

—Secret of the Mountain Dog. 2014. (ENG.). 208p. (J). (gr. 3-7). 16.99 *(978-0-545-60369-0(2)*, Scholastic Pr.) Scholastic, Inc.

Kimmelman, Leslie. In the Doghouse: An Emma & Bo Story. Kelley, True, illus. 2006. (Holiday House Reader Ser.: Level 2). (ENG.). 32p. (J). (gr. 5-8). 14.95 *(978-0-8234-1882-4(0))* Holiday Hse., Inc.

—The Shabbat Puppy, 0 vols. Zollars, Jaime, illus. 2012. (Shofar Ser.: 0). (ENG.). 32p. (J). (gr. -1-3). 17.99 *(978-0-7614-6145-6(0)*, 9780761461456, Amazon Children's Publishing) Amazon Publishing.

Kimpton, Paul & Kimpton, Ann Kaczkowski. Dog Tags: A Boy & His Bugle in America During WWII. 2012. (Adventures with Music Ser.: 2). (ENG.). 120p. (J). (gr. 4-7). pap. 8.95 *(978-1-57999-882-0(8))* G I A Pubns., Inc.

King, B. J. Through a Dog's Eye: A Dog's Tale. 2010. 40p. pap. 18.49 *(978-1-4490-4928-7(1))* AuthorHouse.

King-smith, Dick. Titus Rules! Eastwood, John, illus. 2004. (ENG.). 96p. (J). (gr. 1-4). reprint ed. 5.50 *(978-0-440-42000-2(8)*, Yearling) Random Hse. Children's Bks.

King-smith, Dick & Fox Busters Ltd. Staff. Smasher. Bernal, Richard, illus. 2006. (Stepping Stone Book(TM) Ser.). (ENG.). 80p. (J). (gr. 1-4). 3.99 *(978-0-679-88330-2(4)*, Random Hse. Bks. for Young Readers) Random Hse. Children's Bks.

King, Stephen Michael. Mutt Dog! King, Stephen Michael, illus. 2005. (Illus.). 32p. (J). *(978-1-86504-636-5(1))*; pap. *(978-1-86504-637-2(X))* Scholastic, Inc. (Scholastic Pr.).

King, Terrie. The Six-Toed Dog & the Big-Headed Puppy. 2008. 104p. pap. 19.95 *(978-1-60672-765-2(6))* America Star Bks.

Kingsley, Linda Kurtz. Bringing up Sophie. Kingsley, Linda Kurtz, illus. 2010. (Illus.). 32p. (J). lib. bdg. 15.95 *(978-0-944727-25-6(5)*, Turtle Bks.) Jason & Nordic Pubs.

—Bringing up Sophie. 2009. (Illus.). 32p. (J). pap. 9.95 *(978-0-944727-24-9(7)*, Turtle Bks.) Jason & Nordic Pubs.

Kinsella, Audrey. Dingle: The Helpful Ice Cream Cone Delivery Dog. 2010. 24p. 14.49 *(978-1-4490-8362-5(5))* AuthorHouse.

Kirk, Katie. Eli, No! 2011. (ENG., Illus.). 32p. (J). (gr. -1-k). 14.95 *(978-0-8109-8964-1(6)*, Abrams Bks. for Young Readers) Abrams, Inc.

Kirsch, Amanda. Honor Bound. 2013. pap. 11.95 *(978-1-59433-375-0(0))* Publication Consultants.

Kitchen, David. The Adventures of Chesed & Cadence. 2012. 28p. pap. 9.95 *(978-1-4787-1712-6(2))* Outskirts Pr., Inc.

—The Adventures of David & Freddie Boo. 2012. 28p. pap. 9.95 *(978-1-4327-6610-8(4))* Outskirts Pr., Inc.

Kjelgaard, Jim. Big Red. 2011. (ENG., Illus.). 254p. (J). pap. 8.95 *(978-0-8234-2391-0(3))* Holiday Hse., Inc.

Kjersgaard, Carly. Muffins' New Beginning. 2009. 20p. pap. 10.95 *(978-1-4389-8001-0(9))* AuthorHouse.

Klass, David. Firestorm. 2008. (Caretaker Trilogy Ser.: 1). (ENG.). 320p. (YA). (gr. 9-13). pap. 11.99 *(978-0-312-38018-2(6)*, 9780312380182) Square Fish.

—Firestorm. rev. l.t. ed. 2007. (Caretaker Trilogy: Bk. 1). 435p. (YA). (gr. 9). 23.95 *(978-0-7862-9364-3(0))* Thorndike Pr.

Klein, Adria F. Hank Hammer & the Puppy, 1 vol. Rowland, Andrew, illus. 2012. (Tool School Ser.). (ENG.). 32p. (gr. 1-3). pap. 6.25 *(978-1-4342-4233-4(1))*; lib. bdg. 22.65 *(978-1-4342-4020-0(7))* Stone Arch Bks.

Klimo, Kate. Barry. Jessell, Tim, illus. 2013. (Dog Diaries). (ENG.). 160p. (J). (gr. 2-5). pap. 7.99 *(978-0-449-81280-8(4)*, Random Hse. Bks. for Young Readers) Random Hse. Children's Bks.

—Barry. 2013. (Dog Diaries: 3). lib. bdg. 18.40 *(978-0-606-32455-7(0)*, Turtleback) Turtleback Bks.

—Buddy. 2013. (Dog Diaries: 2). lib. bdg. 18.40 *(978-0-606-27000-7(0)*, Turtleback) Turtleback Bks.

—Dash. 2014. (Dog Diaries: 5). lib. bdg. 18.40 *(978-0-606-36021-0(2))* Turtleback Bks.

—Dog Diaries No. 4: Togo. Jessell, Tim, illus. 2014. (Dog Diaries). (ENG.). 176p. (J). (gr. 2-5). pap. 7.99

C D

(978-0-385-37335-7(X), Random Hse. Bks. for Young Readers) Random Hse. Children's Bks.
—Dog Diaries #10: Rolf. Jessell, Tim, illus. 2017. (Dog Diaries). (ENG.). 160p. (J). (gr. 2-5). pap. 7.99 *(978-0-399-55128-4(X)*, Random Hse. Bks. for Young Readers) Random Hse. Children's Bks.
—Dog Diaries #5: Dash. Jessell, Tim, illus. 2014. (Dog Diaries). (ENG.). 160p. (J). (gr. 2-5). pap. 7.99 *(978-0-385-37338-8(4)*, Random Hse. Bks. for Young Readers) Random Hse. Children's Bks.
—Fala. 2016. (Dog Diaries: 8). lib. bdg. 18.40 *(978-0-606-38448-3(0))* Turtleback Bks.
—Ginger. 2013. (Dog Diaries: 1). lib. bdg. 18.40 *(978-0-606-27002-1(7)*, Turtleback) Turtleback Bks.
—Rolf. 2017. (Dog Diaries: 10). lib. bdg. 18.40 ***(978-0-606-40240-8(3))*** Turtleback Bks.
—Sparky. Jessell, Tim, illus. 2016. (Dog Diaries: 9). (ENG.). 160p. (J). (gr. 2-5). pap. 7.99 *(978-0-553-53493-1(9)*, Random Hse. Bks. for Young Readers) Random Hse. Children's Bks.
—Stubby. Jessell, Tim, illus. 2015. (Dog Diaries: 7). (ENG.). 160p. (J). (gr. 2-5). lib. bdg. 12.99 *(978-0-385-39244-0(3)*, Random Hse. Bks. for Young Readers) Random Hse. Children's Bks.
—Sweetie, No. 6. Jessell, Tim, illus. 2015. (Dog Diaries: 6). (ENG.). 160p. (J). (gr. 2-5). pap. 7.99 *(978-0-385-39240-2(0)*, Random Hse. Bks. for Young Readers) Random Hse. Children's Bks.
—Tiny Tim. Jessell, Tim, illus. 2017. (Dog Diaries: 11). (ENG.). 176p. (J). (gr. 2-5). pap. 7.99 ***(978-0-399-55131-4(X))***; lib. bdg. 12.99 ***(978-0-399-55132-1(8))*** Random Hse. Children's Bks. (Random Hse. Bks. for Young Readers).
—Togo. 2014. (Dog Diaries: 4). lib. bdg. 18.40 *(978-0-606-35568-1(5))* Turtleback Bks.
—Twinky the Dinky Dog. Fleming, Michael, illus. 2013. (Step into Reading Ser.). (ENG.). 48p. (J). (gr. k-3). pap. 3.99 *(978-0-307-97667-3(X)*, Random Hse. Bks. for Young Readers) Random Hse. Children's Bks.
Kline, Joel. Cookie's Colorful World. Borsch, Kim, illus. 2011. 32p. pap. 24.95 *(978-1-4560-7578-1(0))* America Star Bks.
Kline, Trish & Donev, Mary. Coming Home: KA Reader 8. 2007. (Illus.). 32p. (J). per. 20.00 *(978-1-934307-01-4(7))* Ghost Hunter Productions.
Klingel, Deanna K. Avery's Battlefield. 2011. (J). *(978-1-60682-171-8(7))* BJU Pr.
Klise, Kate. Stay: A Girl, a Dog, a Bucket List. Klise, M. Sarah, illus. 2017. (ENG.). 32p. (J). 17.99 *(978-1-250-10714-5(8)*, 9781250107145) Feiwel & Friends.
—Till Death Do Us Bark. Klise, M. Sarah, illus. 2012. (43 Old Cemetery Road Ser.: 3). (ENG.). 144p. (J). (gr. 2-5). pap. 6.99 *(978-0-547-85081-8(6))* Houghton Mifflin Harcourt Publishing Co.
—Till Death Do Us Bark. 2012. (43 Old Cemetery Road Ser.: 3). lib. bdg. 17.20 *(978-0-606-26543-0(0)*, Turtleback) Turtleback Bks.
Klise, Kate & Klise, M. Sarah. Till Death Do Us Bark. Klise, Kate & Klise, M. Sarah, illus. 2011. (43 Old Cemetery Road Ser.: 3). (ENG., Illus.). 144p. (J). (gr. 2-5). 16.99 *(978-0-547-40036-5(5))* Houghton Mifflin Harcourt Publishing Co.
Knapp, Jennifer F. A Walk with Ovid. 2003. (Illus.). 30p. (YA). per. 14.95 *(978-0-9742249-0-9(1))* JFK Online Studios, LLC.
Knapp, Susan. Bells Goes to the Fair. Whitehurst, John et al, illus. l.t. ed. 2003. 40p. (J). (gr. -1-3). 12.95 *(978-1-888223-34-7(0))* McMillen Publishing.
Kneff, Steff F. Emlyn & the Gremlin: Emlyn & the Gremlin Series. Spooner, Luke, illus. l.t. ed. 2014. 1. (ENG.). 52p. (gr. k-3). 26.95 *(978-1-62253-399-2(2))*; pap. 10.95 *(978-1-62253-398-5(4))* Evolved Publishing.
Knight, Eric. Lassie Come-Home. Kirmse, Marguerite, illus. rev. ed. 2003. (ENG.). 256p. (J). (gr. 3-7). 24.99 *(978-0-8050-7206-8(3)*, 9780805072068, Holt, Henry & Co. Bks. For Young Readers) Holt, Henry & Co.
—Lassie Come-Home. Kirmse, Marguerite, illus. 2007. (ENG.). 256p. (J). (gr. 3-7). per. 7.99 *(978-0-312-37131-9(4)*, 9780312371319) Square Fish.
Knight, Hilary. Eloise Throws a Party! Lyon, Tammie, illus. 2008. (Eloise Ser.). (ENG.). 32p. (J). (gr. -1-1). pap. 3.99 *(978-1-4169-6172-7(0)*, Simon Spotlight) Simon Spotlight.
Knights, Nancy. Gracie's Hill. Norie, Rooney, illus. 2007. 28p. per. 7.95 *(978-1-58275-192-4(7))* Black Forest Pr.
Knk Adventures. Ruth & Her Shepherd. 2012. 40p. pap. *(978-1-4602-0309-5(7))* FriesenPress.
Knoch, Frank. The Big Rescue: The Greenwood Forest Series, 1 vol. Meierhofer, Brian, illus. 2010. 32p. pap. 24.95 *(978-1-4489-6158-0(0))* PublishAmerica, Inc.
Knudsen, Michelle. Big Mean Mike. Magoon, Scott, illus. 2012. (ENG.). 40p. (J). (gr. -1-3). 15.99 *(978-0-7636-4990-6(2))* Candlewick Pr.
Ko, Sangmi. A Dog Wearing Shoes. 2015. (ENG., Illus.). 40p. (J). (gr. -1-3). 16.99 *(978-0-385-38396-7(7)*, Schwartz & Wade Bks.) Random Hse. Children's Bks.
Koch, Janet Marie. Hallie's Best Birthday. 2008. 48p. pap. 24.95 *(978-1-60610-812-3(3))* America Star Bks.
Koffsky, Ann D., illus. Kayla & Kugel. 2015. (J). *(978-0-87441-898-9(4))*; *(978-1-68115-502-9(8))* Behrman Hse., Inc.
—Kayla & Kugel's Almost-Perfect Passover. 2016. (J). *(978-1-68115-508-1(7))* Behrman Hse., Inc.
Koja, Kathe. Straydog. 2004. (ENG.). 128p. (YA). (gr. 7-18). reprint ed. 7.99 *(978-0-14-240071-5(8)*, Speak) Penguin Young Readers Group.
Konecny, Linda. Dave's First Christmas. 2011. 26p. pap. 9.99 *(978-1-61379-817-1(2))* Salem Author Services.
Korman, Gordon. Hideout. 2013. (Swindle Ser.: 5). (ENG.). (J). (gr. 3-7). 288p. pap. 6.99 *(978-0-545-44867-3(0)*, Scholastic Paperbacks); 256p. 16.99 *(978-0-545-44866-6(2)*, Scholastic Pr.) Scholastic, Inc.
—Hideout. 2013. (Swindle Ser.: 5). lib. bdg. 17.20 *(978-0-606-32405-2(4)*, Turtleback) Turtleback Bks.
—Showoff. 2012. (ENG.). 256p. (J). (gr. 3-7). pap. 6.99 *(978-0-545-32060-3(7)*, Scholastic Paperbacks); (Swindle Ser.: 4). 16.99 *(978-0-545-32059-7(3)*, Scholastic Pr.) Scholastic, Inc.
Korman, Justine. The Poky Little Puppy's First Christmas. Korman, Justine, illus. 2014. (Little Golden Board Book Ser.). (ENG., Illus.). 26p. (J). (-k). bds. 7.99 *(978-0-385-38473-5(4)*, Golden Bks.) Random Hse. Children's Bks.
—101 Dalmatians. Langley, Bill & Dias, Ron, illus. 2007. (Little Golden Book Ser.). (ENG.). 24p. (J). (gr. -1-2). 4.99 *(978-0-7364-2420-2(2)*, Golden/Disney) Random Hse. Children's Bks.
Korr, Mary. Winston the water Dog: Portuguese water dog tales book One. 2009. 40p. pap. 17.49 *(978-1-4415-8406-9(4))* Xlibris Corp.
Korte, Steve. The Cat Crime Club, 1 vol. Baltazar, Art, illus. 2012. (DC Super-Pets Ser.). (ENG.). 56p. (gr. 2-2). pap. 4.95 *(978-1-4048-7665-1(0))*; 23.99 *(978-1-4048-6493-1(8))* Picture Window Bks. (DC Super-Pets).
Kosara, Victoria. Graduation Party. Durk, Jim, illus. 2010. (J). pap. *(978-0-545-23400-9(X))* Scholastic, Inc.
Koster, Gloria. Mitzi's Mitzvah. Conger, Holli, illus. 2013. (ENG.). 12p. (J). (gr. -1 — 1). 5.95 *(978-1-4677-0695-7(7)*, Kar-Ben Publishing) Lerner Publishing Group.
Kotzwinkle, William & Murray, Glenn. Walter Canis Inflatus: Walter the Farting Dog, Latin-Language Edition. Dobbin, Rob, tr. from ENG. Colman, Audrey, illus. 2004.Tr. of Walter the Farting Dog. (LAT.). 32p. (J). (gr. k-4). 15.95 *(978-1-58394-110-2(X)*, Frog Ltd.) North Atlantic Bks.
—Walter el Perro Pedorrero. Bohorquez, Eduardo, tr. from ENG. Colman, Audrey, illus. 2004.Tr. of Walter the Farting Dog. (SPA.). 32p. (J). (gr. k-4). 15.95 *(978-1-58394-103-4(7)*, Frog Children's Bks.) North Atlantic Bks.
—Walter the Farting Dog: Trouble at the Yard Sale. Coleman, Audrey & Audrey, Colman, illus. 2006. (ENG.). 32p. (J). (gr. k-3). reprint ed. pap. 6.99 *(978-0-14-240626-7(0)*, Puffin Books) Penguin Young Readers Group.
Kotzwinkle, William, et al. Rough Weather Ahead for Walter the Farting Dog. Colman, Audrey, illus. 2007. (ENG.). 32p. (J). (gr. k-3). pap. 6.99 *(978-0-14-240845-2(X)*, Puffin Books) Penguin Young Readers Group.
—Walter the Farting Dog: Banned from the Beach. Coleman, Audrey, illus. 2009. (ENG.). 32p. (J). (gr. k-3). pap. 7.99 *(978-0-14-241394-4(1)*, Puffin Books) Penguin Young Readers Group.
—Walter the Farting Dog Goes on a Cruise. Coleman, Audrey, illus. (ENG.). 32p. (J). (gr. k-3). 2008. pap. 6.99 *(978-0-14-241142-1(6)*, Puffin Books) 2006. 16.99 *(978-0-525-47714-3(4)*, Dutton Books for Young Readers) Penguin Young Readers Group.
Koumjian, Gay Melanie. Mojo's Mojo. 2013. (ENG.). 23p. (J). pap. 12.95 *(978-1-4787-1623-5(1))* Outskirts Pr., Inc.
Kovacs, Deborah. Catie Copley. Williams, Jared T., illus. 2007. (ENG.). 32p. (J). (gr. -1-3). 17.95 *(978-1-56792-332-2(1))* Godine, David R. Pub.
—Catie Copley's Great Escape. Williams, Jared T., illus. 2009. (J). 17.95 *(978-1-56792-382-7(8))*; (ENG.). 32p. (gr. -1-3). 17.95 *(978-1-56792-379-7(8))* Godine, David R. Pub.
Kovanchak, Danielle. It's about Time. 2009. 44p. pap. 16.99 *(978-1-4389-7023-3(4))* AuthorHouse.
Kowalski, Eli. Kushka, the Dog Named Cat. 2010. (ENG.). (J). 14.95 *(978-0-9819861-4-2(5))* Sports Challenge Network.
Kramer, Alan. The Three Little Pigs Wise up & the Princess Prince & the Vegetables. 2011. (Navigators Ser.). (J). pap. *(978-1-61672-962-2(7))* Benchmark Education Co.
Kranowitz, Carol Stock. The Goodenoughs Get in Sync: A Story for Kids about the Tough Day When Filibuster Grabbed Darwin's Rabbit's Foot... Wylie, T. J., illus. 2004. 86p. (J). 14.95 *(978-1-931615-17-4(9)*, 978-1-931615-17-4) Sensory Resources.
Kravitz, Cathy. A Dog's Day. 2005. (J). 10.95 *(978-1-59858-025-9(6))*; per. 16.95 *(978-1-59858-009-9(4))* Dog Ear Publishing, LLC.
Kreple, Pat. 4 Dog Tales. 2012. (ENG.). pap. *(978-1-4675-5124-3(4))* Independent Pub.
Krinsky, Ed. Pip, Veronica & the Harmonica. Evans, Casey, illus. 2013. 32p. pap. 13.00 *(978-1-62516-945-7(0)*, Strategic Bk. Publishing) Strategic Book Publishing & Rights Agency (SBPRA).
Kristen, Judith. My Name Is Henley: My life & times as a rescued Dog. 2007. 150p. (J). per. 11.95 *(978-0-9800448-0-5(4))* Aquinas & Krone Publishing, LLC.
Kristiansen, Kate. Black Dog White Dog. 2004. (Illus.). 16p. (J). 13.99 *(978-0-9764175-0-7(2))* Winking Moon Pr.
Kroll, Steven. Pooch on the Loose: A Christmas Adventure, 0 vols. Garland, Michael, illus. 2013. (ENG.). 40p. (J). (gr. -1-3). pap. 9.99 *(978-0-7614-5443-4(8))*, 9780761454434, Two Lions) Amazon Publishing.
Kroll, Steven & Droll. Pooch on the Loose: A Christmas Adventure, 1 vol. Garland, Michael, illus. 2005. (ENG.). 32p. (J). (gr. -1-3). 14.95 *(978-0-7614-5239-3(7))* Marshall Cavendish Corp.
Kroll, Virginia. Selvakumar Knew Better. Li, Xiaojun, illus. 2009. (Selvakumar Knew Better Ser.). 32p. (J). (gr. -1-3). pap. 8.95 *(978-1-885008-36-7(8)*, Shen's Bks.) Lee & Low Bks., Inc.
Krone, Thelma Smith. Sadie. Snader, Gregory, illus. 2008. 6p. (J). pap. 7.95 *(978-1-934696-02-6(1)*, Shooting Star Edition) American Literary Pr.
Krueger, Kathryn L. Road to Grandma's House. 2005. 128p. pap. 13.95 *(978-1-59800-366-6(6))* Outskirts Pr., Inc.
Krulik, Nancy. Be Careful What You Sniff For, No. 1. Braun, Sebastien, illus. 2013. (Magic Bone Ser.: 1). (ENG.). 128p. (J). (gr. 1-3). pap. 5.99 *(978-0-448-46399-5(7)*, Grosset & Dunlap) Penguin Young Readers Group.
—Be Careful What You Sniff For. 2013. (Magic Bone Ser.: 1). lib. bdg. 16.00 *(978-0-606-31680-4(9)*, Turtleback) Turtleback Bks.
—Catch That Wave. Braun, Sebastien, illus. 2013. (Magic Bone Ser.: 2). (ENG.). 128p. (J). (gr. 1-3). pap. 5.99 *(978-0-448-46444-2(6)*, Grosset & Dunlap) Penguin Young Readers Group.
—Catch That Wave. 2013. (Magic Bone Ser.: 2). lib. bdg. 14.75 *(978-0-606-31681-1(7)*, Turtleback) Turtleback Bks.
—Doggone It! John and Wendy Staff, illus. 8th ed. 2006. (Katie Kazoo, Switcheroo Ser.: 8). (ENG.). 80p. (J). (gr. 2-4). pap. 4.99 *(978-0-448-43172-7(6)*, Grosset & Dunlap) Penguin Young Readers Group.
—Don't Mess with the Ninja Puppy!, No. 6. Braun, Sebastien, illus. 2014. (Magic Bone Ser.: 6). (ENG.). 128p. (J). (gr. 1-3). 5.99 *(978-0-448-48095-4(6)*, Grosset & Dunlap) Penguin Young Readers Group.
—Don't Mess with the Ninja Puppy! 2014. (Magic Bone Ser.: 6). lib. bdg. 14.75 *(978-0-606-36162-0(6))* Turtleback Bks.
—Follow That Furball. Braun, Sebastien, illus. 2013. (Magic Bone Ser.: 3). (ENG.). 128p. (J). (gr. 1-3). 5.99 *(978-0-448-46445-9(4)*, Grosset & Dunlap) Penguin Young Readers Group.
—Follow That Furball. 2013. (Magic Bone Ser.: 3). lib. bdg. 16.00 *(978-0-606-32127-3(6)*, Turtleback) Turtleback Bks.
—Go Fetch! Braun, Sebastien, illus. 2014. (Magic Bone Ser.: 5). (ENG.). 128p. (J). (gr. 1-3). 4.99 *(978-0-448-48094-7(8)*, Grosset & Dunlap) Penguin Young Readers Group.
—Go Fetch! 2014. (Magic Bone Ser.: 5). lib. bdg. 14.75 *(978-0-606-35701-2(7))* Turtleback Bks.
—Magic Bone: Two Tales, One Dog. Braun, Sebastien, illus. 2016. (Magic Bone Ser.: 12). (ENG.). 192p. (J). (gr. 1-3). 6.99 *(978-0-448-48877-6(9)*, Grosset & Dunlap) Penguin Young Readers Group.
—Never Box with a Kangaroo #11. Braun, Sebastien, illus. 2016. (Magic Bone Ser.: 11). (ENG.). 128p. (J). (gr. 1-3). 4.99 *(978-0-448-48876-9(0)*, Grosset & Dunlap) Penguin Young Readers Group.
—Nice Snowing You! Braun, Sebastien, illus. 2014. (Magic Bone Ser.: 4). (ENG.). 128p. (J). (gr. 1-3). 5.99 *(978-0-448-46446-6(2)*, Grosset & Dunlap) Penguin Young Readers Group.
—Nice Snowing You! 2014. (Magic Bone Ser.: 4). lib. bdg. 14.75 *(978-0-606-34145-5(5)*, Turtleback) Turtleback Bks.
—Puppy Love. 2011. (Romantic Comedies Ser.). (ENG.). 224p. (YA). (gr. 7). pap. 12.99 *(978-1-4424-3079-2(6)*, Simon Pulse) Simon Pulse.
—Super Special: Two Tales, One Dog. Braun, Sebastien, illus. 2016. (Magic Bone Ser.: Vol. 12). (ENG.). 192p. (J). (gr. 1-3). 17.20 *(978-0-606-39309-6(9))* Turtleback Bks.
Krulik, Nancy & dePaola, Tomie. Dogs Don't Have Webbed Feet. Braun, Sebastien, illus. 2015. (Magic Bone Ser.: 7). (ENG.). 128p. (J). (gr. 1-3). bds. 5.99 *(978-0-448-48096-1(4)*, Grosset & Dunlap) Penguin Young Readers Group.
—Pup Art #9. Braun, Sebastien, illus. 2015. (Magic Bone Ser.: 9). (ENG.). 128p. (J). (gr. 1-3). bds. 4.99 *(978-0-448-48749-6(7)*, Grosset & Dunlap) Penguin Young Readers Group.
—Rootin' Tootin' Cow Dog #8. Braun, Sebastien, illus. 2015. (Magic Bone Ser.: 8). (ENG.). 128p. (J). (gr. 1-3). bds. 4.99 *(978-0-448-48097-8(2)*, Grosset & Dunlap) Penguin Young Readers Group.
Krulik, Nancy E. Broadway Doggie. 2016. (Magic Bone Ser.: 10). lib. bdg. 14.75 *(978-0-606-38416-2(2))* Turtleback Bks.
—Dogs Don't Have Webbed Feet. 2015. (Magic Bone Ser.: 7). lib. bdg. 16.00 *(978-0-606-36585-7(0))* Turtleback Bks.
—Pup Art. 2015. (Magic Bone Ser.: 9). lib. bdg. 14.75 *(978-0-606-37546-7(5))* Turtleback Bks.
—Rootin' Tootin' Cow Dog. 2015. (Magic Bone Ser.: 8). lib. bdg. 14.75 *(978-0-606-36765-3(9))* Turtleback Bks.
Kruse, Anne. Takota's Dream. 2010. pap. 16.99 *(978-0-578-05291-5(1))* Sisterhaus Publishing.
Kshir, Donna M. & Potter, Sandra Dawn. The Three Little Golden Retrievers. 2010. 32p. pap. 14.50 *(978-0-557-30026-6(6))* Lulu Pr., Inc.
Kubik, Dorothy. The Adventures of Elbert & Leopoldina. James, Annie, illus. 2006. 104p. (J). per. 15.00 *(978-0-9790775-1-7(6))* Touchstone Communications.
Kulling, Monica. Merci Mister Dash! Melo, Esperanca, illus. 2011. (ENG.). 32p. (J). (gr. -1-2). 17.95 *(978-0-88776-964-1(0)*, Tundra Bks.) Tundra Bks. CAN. Dist: Penguin Random Hse. LLC.
Kumar, Navina Magesh. Haley's Wish. 2011. 28p. pap. 12.99 *(978-1-4567-6318-3(0))* AuthorHouse.
Kumin, Maxine. What Color Is Caesar? Friend, Alison, illus. 2010. (ENG.). 56p. (J). (gr. -1-k). 16.99 *(978-0-7636-3432-2(8))* Candlewick Pr.
Kunhardt, Dorothy. Pat the Bunny: First Books for Baby, 3 vols. 2015. (Touch-And-Feel Ser.). (ENG., Illus.). 20p. (J). (— 1). pap. 29.99 *(978-0-553-50838-3(5)*, Golden Bks.) Random Hse. Children's Bks.
Kupperberg, Paul. Scooby-Doo & the Night of the Undead!, 1 vol. 2013. (Scooby-Doo Graphic Novels Set 3 Ser.). (ENG.). 24p. (J). (gr. 2-6). lib. bdg. 24.21 *(978-1-61479-050-1(7)*, Essential Library) ABDO Publishing Co.
—Scooby-Doo in over the Boardwalk, 1 vol. 2013. (Scooby-Doo Graphic Novels Set 3 Ser.). (ENG., Illus.). 24p. (J). (gr. 2-6). lib. bdg. 24.21 *(978-1-61479-052-5(3)*, Essential Library) ABDO Publishing Co.
—Scooby-Doo in Read All about It!, 1 vol. 2013. (Scooby-Doo Graphic Novels Set 3 Ser.). (ENG.). 24p. (J). (gr. 2-6). lib. bdg. 24.21 *(978-1-61479-053-2(1)*, Essential Library) ABDO Publishing Co.
Kurtz, Chris. The Adventures of a South Pole Pig: A Novel of Snow & Courage. 2013. (ENG., Illus.). 288p. (J). (gr. 5-7). 16.99 *(978-0-547-63455-5(2))* Houghton Mifflin Harcourt Publishing Co.
—The Pup Who Cried Wolf. Francis, Guy, illus. 2010. (ENG.). 144p. (YA). (gr. 2-4). 15.99 *(978-1-59990-497-9(7)*, 9781599904979); pap. 5.99 *(978-1-59990-492-4(6)*, 9781599904924) Bloomsbury Publishing USA. (Bloomsbury USA Childrens).
Kusugak, Michael. The Littlest Sled Dog, 1 vol. Krykorka, Vladyana, illus. 2010. (ENG.). 32p. (J). (gr. -1-3). pap. 10.95 *(978-1-55469-174-6(5))* Orca Bk. Pubs. USA.
La Fontaine, Jean De. The Falcon & the Little Dog. 2004. reprint ed. pap. 15.95 *(978-1-4191-6181-0(4))* Kessinger Publishing, LLC.
La Rue, Coco. The Dog Rules. May, Kyla, illus. 2011. (ENG.). 128p. (J). (gr. 2-5). pap. 4.99 *(978-0-545-28261-1(6)*, Scholastic Paperbacks) Scholastic, Inc.
—A New Pig in Town. May, Kyla, illus. 2013. 127p. (J). pap. *(978-0-545-46607-3(5))* Scholastic, Inc.
Labatt, Mary. Lake Monster Mix-Up. Rioux, Jo-Anne, illus. 2009. (Sam & Friends Mystery Ser.). (ENG.). 96p. (J). (gr. 2-5). 7.95 *(978-1-55337-302-5(2))*; 16.95 *(978-1-55337-822-8(9))* Kids Can Pr., Ltd. CAN. Dist: Hachette Bk. Group.
—Mummy Mayhem. Rioux, Jo-Anne, illus. 2010. (Sam & Friends Mystery Ser.). (ENG.). 96p. (J). (gr. 2-5). 16.95 *(978-1-55453-470-8(4))*; pap. 7.95 *(978-1-55453-471-5(2))* Kids Can Pr., Ltd. CAN. Dist: Hachette Bk. Group.
—A Parade for Sam. Sarrazin, Marisol, illus. 2005. (Kids Can Read Ser.). (ENG.). 32p. (J). (gr. k-1). pap. 3.95 *(978-1-55337-788-7(5))* Kids Can Pr., Ltd. CAN. Dist: Hachette Bk. Group.
—A Puppy Is for Loving, 1 vol. Liwska, Renata, illus. 2007. (Orca Echoes Ser.). (ENG.). 64p. (J). (gr. 2-3). per. 6.95 *(978-1-55143-477-3(6))* Orca Bk. Pubs. USA.
—Sam at the Seaside. Sarrazin, Marisol, illus. 2006. (Kids Can Read Ser.). (ENG.). 32p. (J). (gr. k-1). pap. 4.95 *(978-1-55337-877-8(6))* Kids Can Pr., Ltd. CAN. Dist: Hachette Bk. Group.
—Sam Finds a Monster. Sarrazin, Marisol, illus. 2003. 32p. (J). pap. *(978-0-439-58742-6(5))* Scholastic, Inc.
—Sam Gets Lost. Sarrazin, Marisol, tr. Sarrazin, Marisol, illus. 2004. (Kids Can Read Ser.: Vol. 1). (ENG.). 32p. (J). (gr. k-1). 3.95 *(978-1-55337-563-0(7))* Kids Can Pr., Ltd. CAN. Dist: Hachette Bk. Group.
—Sam Goes Next Door. Sarrazin, Marisol, illus. 2006. (Kids Can Read Ser.). (ENG.). 32p. (J). (gr. k-1). 3.95 *(978-1-55337-879-2(2))* Kids Can Pr., Ltd. CAN. Dist: Hachette Bk. Group.
—Sam Goes to School. Sarrazin, Marisol, tr. Sarrazin, Marisol, illus. 2004. (Kids Can Read Ser.: Vol. 1). (ENG.). 32p. (J). (gr. k-1). 4.95 *(978-1-55337-565-4(3))* Kids Can Pr., Ltd. CAN. Dist: Hachette Bk. Group.
—Sam's Snowy Day. Sarrazin, Marisol, illus. 2005. (Kids Can Read Ser.). (ENG.). 32p. (J). (gr. k-1). pap. 3.95 *(978-1-55337-790-0(7))* Kids Can Pr., Ltd. CAN. Dist: Hachette Bk. Group.
—Witches' Brew. Rioux, Jo-Anne, illus. 2011. (Sam & Friends Mystery Ser.). (ENG.). 96p. (J). (gr. 2-5). 16.95 *(978-1-55453-472-2(0))*; pap. 7.95 *(978-1-55453-473-9(9))* Kids Can Pr., Ltd. CAN. Dist: Hachette Bk. Group.
Laberje, Reji. Max Explores the Beach. Fenech, Liza, illus. 2015. (Max Explores Ser.). (ENG.). 20p. (J). (— 1). bds. 9.95 *(978-1-62937-101-6(7))* Triumph Bks.
LaBree Stute, Lela. Freedom Pugs! 2010. 38p. pap. 19.99 *(978-0-557-42621-8(9))* Lulu Pr., Inc.
—My Name Is Ingah, I Am A Pug. 2010. 32p. pap. 19.99 *(978-0-557-44925-5(1))* Lulu Pr., Inc.
—Summer Pugs. 2010. 44p. pap. 19.99 *(978-0-557-41763-6(5))* Lulu Pr., Inc.
—The Sunnyset Pugs. 2010. 34p. pap. 19.99 *(978-0-557-41751-3(1))* Lulu Pr., Inc.
—The Sunshine Pugs. 2010. 54p. pap. 21.99 *(978-0-557-60601-6(2))* Lulu Pr., Inc.
—Three Pugs & a Trout. 2010. 42p. pap. 19.99 *(978-0-557-44673-5(2))* Lulu Pr., Inc.
—Three Pugs & One Vacation. 2010. 46p. pap. 24.99 *(978-0-557-50641-5(7))* Lulu Pr., Inc.
—Wonder Pugs. 2010. 36p. pap. 19.99 *(978-0-557-42611-9(1))* Lulu Pr., Inc.
Ladd, Debbie. Ethan the Ending Eater. Nakasone, Shaun, illus. 2008. 64p. (J). 17.95 *(978-0-9727615-2-9(7))* Deb on Air Bks.
Laddy, Lee & Lipson, Amy Kron. Rufus Rules! from Underdog to Top Dog - a Playful Journey of Acceptance. 2012. (ENG.). 42p. (J). pap. 20.95 *(978-1-4327-8172-9(3))* Outskirts Pr., Inc.
Laden, Nina. The Night I Followed the Dog. 2017. (ENG., Illus.). 40p. (J). 7.99 *(978-1-4521-6134-1(8))* Chronicle Bks. LLC.
Laganke, Traci Smith. The Way Home. 2012. 36p. pap. 21.99 *(978-1-4772-5688-6(1))* AuthorHouse.
Laietta, Luann. Tonka the Special Puppy. 2011. 24p. pap. 15.99 *(978-1-4628-5263-5(7))* Xlibris Corp.
Lake, Mary. Piccolo. Collier, Kevin Scott, illus. 2007. (J). (gr. -1-3). 25p. 14.99 *(978-1-59879-358-1(6))*; per. 10.99 *(978-1-59879-253-9(9))* Lifevest Publishing, Inc.
Lalla, C. R. Wiggles & Wags Tale: Coming Home. 2009. (Illus.). 24p. pap. 15.99 *(978-1-59858-789-0(7))* Dog Ear Publishing, LLC.
Lamb, Braden. Adventure Time. Paroline, Shelli, illus. 2014. (Adventure Time Ser.: 3). (ENG.). 128p. (J). (gr. 4). 34.99 *(978-1-60886-347-1(6))* Boom! Studios.
Lamb, Phillip C. Ace Canary & Dud Clutch. Lamb, Michael, illus. 2011. 40p. pap. 24.95 *(978-1-4626-0401-2(3))* America Star Bks.
Lambert, Noelle. Can I Play Too? 2009. (ENG., Illus.). 24p. (J). pap. 18.95 *(978-1-85390-944-3(0))* Veritas Pubns. IRL. Dist: Dufour Editions, Inc.
Laminack, Lester. Three Hens & a Peacock, 1 vol. Cole, Henry, illus. 2014. (ENG.). 32p. (J). (gr. -1-3). pap. 7.95 *(978-1-56145-726-7(4))* Peachtree Pubs.
Laminack, Lester L. Three Hens & a Peacock, 1 vol. Cole, Henry, illus. 2011. (ENG.). 32p. (J). (gr. -1-3). 15.95 *(978-1-56145-564-5(4))* Peachtree Pubs.
Lamuth, Nancy. Lucky & Me. Thomas, Richard A., illus. 2012. 20p. pap. 24.95 *(978-1-4626-0665-8(2))* America Star Bks.
Landau, Jeff. Saying Goodbye to Sophie. 2006. (Illus.). 48p. (J). per. 9.95 *(978-0-9728389-2-4(9))* InnerRESOURCES Pubns.
Landolf, Diane Wright. Hog & Dog. Harris, Jennifer Beck, illus. 2005. (Step into Reading Ser.: Vol. 1). (ENG.). 32p. (J). (gr. -1-1). per. 3.99 *(978-0-375-83165-2(7)*, Random Hse. Bks. for Young Readers) Random Hse. Children's Bks.
Lane, Nathan & Elliott, Devlin. Naughty Mabel Sees It All. Krall, Dan, illus. 2016. (Naughty Mabel Ser.). (ENG.). 48p. (J). (gr. -1-3). 17.99 *(978-1-4814-3024-1(6)*, Simon & Schuster Bks. For Young Readers) Simon & Schuster Bks. For Young Readers.
Lang, Andrew. The Violet Fairy Book. 2005. 404p. pap. 16.95 *(978-1-4218-0107-0(8)*, 1st World Library - Literary Society) 1st World Publishing, Inc.
Lang, Kathy. Spaced Out Gerbil. Cotton, Sue Lynn, illus. 2013. 20p. pap. 12.95 *(978-1-61493-190-4(9))* Peppertree Pr., The.
Lange, Willem. Favor Johnson: A Christmas Story. Dodson, Bert, illus. 2009. (ENG.). 32p. (J). (gr. 1-3). 16.95 *(978-1-59373-082-6(9))* Bunker Hill Publishing, Inc.
Langford, Jane. Hero. Vince, Dawn, illus. 2005. (ENG.). 24p. (J). lib. bdg. 23.65 *(978-1-59646-720-0(7))* Dingles & Co.
Lansdowne, Marcella. The Adventures of Patty & Annabel: Apache Lake & the Chakras. 2009. 28p. pap. 15.95 *(978-1-4389-1643-9(4))* AuthorHouse.
—The Adventures of Patty & Annabel: The Javelinas & Releasing the Cords. 2009. 28p. pap. 15.95 *(978-1-4389-1645-3(0))* AuthorHouse.
—The Adventures of Patty & Annabel: The Monsoon & the Auric Field. 2009. 28p. pap. 15.95 *(978-1-4389-4786-0(0))* AuthorHouse.

Lapidot, Gila. Shakel Shakelovitz Finds a Treasure. 2013. 40p. pap. (978-965-550-200-8(7)) Contento De Semrik.
LaRochelle, David. The Best Pet of All. Wakiyama, Hanako, illus. (ENG.). 32p. (J). (gr. -1-k). 2009. pap. 7.99 (978-0-14-241272-5(4), Puffin Books) 2004. 16.99 (978-0-525-47129-5(4), Dutton Books for Young Readers) Penguin Young Readers Group.
Larson, Kirby. Dash. 2014. (Dogs of World War II Ser.). (ENG.). 256p. (J). (gr. 3-7). 17.99 (978-0-545-41635-1(3), Scholastic Pr.) Scholastic, Inc.
—Duke. (Dogs of World War II Ser.). (ENG.). 240p. (J). (gr. 3-7). 2015. pap. 7.99 (978-0-545-41638-2(8), Scholastic Paperbacks) 2013. 16.99 (978-0-545-41637-5(X), Scholastic Pr.) Scholastic, Inc.
—Liberty. 2016. (Dogs of World War II Ser.). (ENG.). 240p. (J). (gr. 3-7). 16.99 (978-0-545-84071-2(6), Scholastic Pr.) Scholastic, Inc.
Larson, Kirby, et al. Lucky Dog: Twelve Tales of Rescued Dogs. 2014. (ENG.). 192p. (J). (gr. 3-7). 15.99 (978-0-545-55451-0(9), Scholastic Pr.) Scholastic, Inc.
Lartey, Ben. The Last Hero of Foreverland. 2012. 64p. pap. 24.99 (978-1-4685-8824-8(9)) AuthorHouse.
Larwick, Valerie. A Cat Named Frenchy Blue: Arrow Yellow Dog of the great Northwest. 2011. 60p. pap. 23.88 (978-1-4634-0868-8(4)) AuthorHouse.
Lashawn Graves, M. Ed. Listen & Embrace When Children Care. 2012. 28p. pap. 9.95 (978-1-4327-8895-7(7)) Outskirts Pr., Inc.
Lasky, Kathryn. Poodle & Hound. Vane, Mitch, illus. 2011. (ENG.). 48p. (J). (gr. k-3). pap. 6.95 (978-1-58089-323-7(6)) Charlesbridge Publishing, Inc.
Lasota, Mary. Kitty Piper, Angel Cat, Book: A tribute to Scooter. 2011. 32p. pap. 14.39 (978-1-4634-4750-2(7)) AuthorHouse.
Lassiter, Nancy. Proud Racer: Blind Faith. 2003. 48p. (YA). per. 12.00 (978-1-932496-07-9(6)) Penman Publishing, Inc.
Lastoka, Mariann. Pete & Patricia Prairie Dog & their Pack of Prairie Pups. Carpenter, Debra, illus. 2003. 40p. 6.50 (978-1-892860-05-7(8), 5) M R L, Inc.
Latimer, Àlex. Stay! a Top Dog Story, 1 vol. Latimer, Àlex, illus. 2015. (ENG., Illus.). 32p. (J). (gr. -1-3). 16.95 (978-1-56145-884-4(8)) Peachtree Pubs.
Latta, Leslie Jay. Patches' Day Out. 2011. 24p. pap. 24.95 (978-1-4626-3486-6(9)) PublishAmerica, Inc.
Lattak, Cheryl. Puppy Tales. Rimes, Nicole, illus. 2011. 28p. pap. 24.95 (978-1-4560-2720-9(4)) America Star Bks.
Laufer, Tiffany A. The Porch Dream. 2009. (Bellaboo & Friends Ser.). (Illus.). 32p. 15.99 (978-0-9820088-2-9(1)) Bellaboozle Books, Inc.
Lauture, Mireille B. Bobo, Chen Odasye A / Bobo, the Sneaky Dog: Mancy's Haitian Folktale Collection. Minckler, Kathleen L., illus. 2010. 28p. pap. 12.49 (978-1-4520-6173-3(4)) AuthorHouse.
Lauzon, Christi. Where's Owen Goin'? 2009. 40p. pap. 14.75 (978-1-60860-543-9(4), Eloquent Bks.) Strategic Book Publishing & Rights Agency (SBPRA).
Lavohn, Jodi. Sam's Adventure. 2011. 54p. pap. 16.95 (978-1-4560-7758-7(9)) America Star Bks.
Lawlor, Laurie. He Will Go Fearless. (ENG.). 224p. (J). (gr. 5-9). 2012. pap. 10.99 (978-0-689-86580-0(5)) 2006. 15.95 (978-0-689-86579-4(1)) Simon & Schuster Bks. For Young Readers. (Simon & Schuster Bks. For Young Readers).
Lawrence, Donna. Susie's Tale Hand with Paw We Changed the Law. Coble, Lynn Berner, ed. Cappoen, Jennifer Tipton, illus. 2012. 64p. 24.95 (978-0-9846724-1-7(9)) Paws and Claws Publishing, LLC.
Lawson, Barbara. An Ugly Black Bird, 1 vol. Lafarge, Kelly, illus. 2009. 35p. pap. 24.95 (978-1-61546-656-6(8)) America Star Bks.
Lawson, Rob, illus. Duke Finds a Home. 2006. (Duke's Tails Ser.). 32p. (J). (978-0-9779308-0-7(7)) Bush Brothers & Co.
Layne, Casey & Jordan, Cedar. The Back Alley Pupsters: Zac & Roxie for the Win. Fischer, Shan, illus. 2013. (ENG.). (J). (gr. -1-3). 14.95 (978-1-62086-300-8(6)) Mascot Bks., Inc.
Le Bec, Yann & Le Bec, Gwendal. Raymond. 2017. (ENG.). 32p. (J). (gr. -1-2). 16.99 (978-0-7636-8950-6(5)) Candlewick Pr.
Lean, Sarah. A Dog Called Homeless. 2012. (ENG.). 208p. (J). (gr. 3-7). 16.99 (978-0-06-212220-9(7), Tegen, Katherine Bks) HarperCollins Pubs.
—Hero. 2015. (ENG.). 208p. (J). (gr. 3-7). 16.99 (978-0-06-212238-4(X)) HarperCollins Pubs.
Leary, Vicki. Roberto el R?ípido: Rapid Robert. 2010. 25p. (J). pap. 14.95 (978-1-4327-5730-4(X)) Outskirts Pr., Inc.
Leavey, Peggy Dymond. Trouble at Turtle Narrows. 2008. (ENG.). 144p. (J). (gr. 4-18). pap. 9.95 (978-1-894917-71-1(5), Napoleon & Co.) Dundurn CAN. Dist: Ingram Publisher Services.
LeBaron, Cecilia. Sam & Val. 2007. (Illus.). 16p. (J). 5.95 (978-0-9798869-3-5(7)) Crush Publishing.
Ledeaux, Lola. If A Dog Could Blog. 2010. 28p. 12.49 (978-1-4520-7575-4(1)) AuthorHouse.
Ledray, Michael. Fifi Loves You! 2010. 40p. pap. 21.00 (978-0-557-27099-6(5)) Lulu Pr., Inc.
Lee, David. Duke the Dog. 2017. (Pet Tales! Ser.). 24p. (J). (gr. 4-6). 23.60 **(978-1-5081-5736-6(7)**, PowerKids Pr.) Rosen Publishing Group, Inc., The.
Lee, Gia. Hurricane Hound. Davis, Jason, illus. 2011. 40p. pap. 24.95 (978-1-4560-9743-1(1)) America Star Bks.
Lee, Jenny. Elvis & the Underdogs. Light, Kelly, illus. 2013. (Elvis & the Underdogs Ser.: 1). (ENG.). 304p. (J). (gr. 3-7). 16.99 (978-0-06-223554-1(0)) HarperCollins Pubs.
—Elvis & the Underdogs: Secrets, Secret Service, & Room Service. Light, Kelly, illus. (Elvis & the Underdogs Ser.: 2). (ENG.). 352p. (J). (gr. 3-7). 2015. pap. 6.99 (978-0-06-223557-2(5)) 2014. 16.99 (978-0-06-223556-5(7)) HarperCollins Pubs.
Lee, Mary R. Island Dog Books. 2009. 32p. (J). 20.99 (978-1-4363-0351-4(6)) Xlibris Corp.
Lee, Patty. Three Dogs & a Horse Named Blue. Lee, Jack, illus. 2009. 80p. pap. 10.49 (978-1-4389-9685-1(3)) AuthorHouse.
Lee, Quinlan B. Beach Day. Haefele, Steve, illus. 2006. (J). (978-0-439-81618-2(1)) Scholastic, Inc.
—Valentine Surprise. Haefele, Steve, illus. 2008. (Clifford the Big Red Dog Ser.). (J). (978-0-545-02845-5(0)) Scholastic, Inc.
Lee, Quinlan B. & Bridwell, Norman. Happy St. Patrick's Day, Clifford! Haefele, Steve, illus. 2010. (Clifford the Big Red Dog Ser.). (J). (978-0-545-23401-6(8)) Scholastic, Inc.
Lee, Sharon Alberta. Mickey of Las Vegas. 2009. 32p. (J). 31.99 (978-1-4363-4642-9(8)) Xlibris Corp.
Leech, Richard W. Adventures of Button Broken Tail, Bk. II. 2011. 249p. (J). 29.99 (978-1-4535-5219-3(7)); pap. 19.99 (978-1-4535-5218-6(9)) Xlibris Corp.
Leedy, Loreen. Mapping Penny's World. Leedy, Loreen, illus. rev. ed. 2003. (Penny Ser.). (ENG., Illus.). 32p. (J). (gr. k-3). pap. 7.99 (978-0-8050-7262-4(4), 9780805072624) Square Fish.
Leeth, Dawna. Pipa & the Puppy Parlor. 2007. (Illus.). 20p. (J). 9.99 (978-0-9799184-0-7(5)) Leeth, Dawna.
LeLeu, Lisa. Diggity the Dog Puppet Show Play Set. 2004. (Lisa Leleu Puppet Show Books Ser.). (J). 19.95 (978-0-9710537-2-4(3), LeLeu, Lisa Puppet Show Bks.) LeLeu, Lisa Studios! Inc.
LeMaistre, Gretchen, photos by. Boo ABC: A to Z with the World's Cutest Dog. 2013. (ENG., Illus.). 32p. (J). (gr. -1-1). 12.99 (978-1-4521-0919-0(2)) Chronicle Bks. LLC.
Lemke, Donald B. The Amazing Mini-Mutts, 1 vol. Baltazar, Art, illus. 2012. (DC Super-Pets Ser.). (ENG.). 56p. (gr. 2-2). pap. 4.95 (978-1-4048-7218-9(3)); lib. bdg. 23.99 (978-1-4048-6488-7(1)) Picture Window Bks. (DC Super-Pets).
Lemos, Lauren M. If I Could Have a Puppy. 2007. (Illus.). 52p. (J). pap. 9.95 (978-0-9798343-1-8(7)) Animal Crackers Publishing, LLC.
L'Engle, Madeleine. The Other Dog. Davenier, Christine, illus. 2003. 37p. (J). (gr. 2-5). reprint ed. 16.00 (978-0-7567-6970-3(1)) DIANE Publishing Co.
Lennard, Daric. My Name Is Berta. 2008. 48p. pap. 16.95 (978-1-60672-036-3(8)) America Star Bks.
Lennon, Margie. Snowball's Sheepdog Adventures: Summer. 2012. 24p. pap. 14.99 (978-1-4685-4655-2(4)) AuthorHouse.
Lensmire, Lynn E. Chaucer's Toy Box. 2011. (Illus.). 32p. pap. 13.49 (978-1-4520-8842-6(X)) AuthorHouse.
Lentini, Joe. Mickey the Monster's New Adventure: The Mysterious Fence. 2012. 28p. pap. 19.99 (978-1-4685-8510-0(X)) AuthorHouse.
Leonard, Debra R. The Lubby Lubby Story. 2011. 20p. pap. (978-1-4269-6265-3(7)) Trafford Publishing (UK) Ltd.
Leonard, Marcia. Trae la Pelota, Tito. Handelman, Dorothy, photos by. 2005.Tr. of Get the Ball, Slim. (Illus.). 32p. (J). (ENG & SPA.). (gr. -1-1). pap. 4.99 (978-0-8225-3293-4(X)); (SPA., (gr. 1-1). per. 5.95 (978-0-8225-3292-7(1), Ediciones Lerner) Lerner Publishing Group.
Leonard, Mary T. Three Best Friends. Russell, Terry, illus. 2004. 96p. (J). per. 12.00 (978-0-9740683-8-1(1)) Authors & Artists Publishers of New York, Inc.
Leslie, Lashawn. Thundermonsters. 2012. 16p. pap. 15.99 (978-1-4772-5422-6(6)) AuthorHouse.
Lettich, Sheldon, et al. Max: Best Friend, Hero, Marine. 2015. (ENG.). 256p. (J). (gr. 3-7). pap. 6.99 (978-0-06-242039-8(9)) HarperCollins Pubs.
Levering, Vicki. Postcards from the Pound. 2008. 48p. pap. 23.99 (978-1-4363-1406-0(2)) Xlibris Corp.
Levin, Betty. The Unmaking of Duncan Veerick. 2007. (ENG.). 212p. (J). (gr. 9-12). 16.95 (978-1-932425-96-3(9), Front Street) Boyds Mills Pr.
Levin, Jack E. & Levin, Norma R. My Dog Spot. Levin, Jack E. & Levin, Norma R., illus. 2016. (ENG., Illus.). 40p. (J). (gr. -1-3). 17.99 (978-1-4814-6907-4(X), Aladdin) Simon & Schuster Children's Publishing.
Levine, Anna. Jodie's Shabbat Surprise. Topaz, Ksenia, illus. 2015. (J). (gr. k-3). (ENG.). 32p. lib. bdg. 17.95 (978-1-4677-3465-3(9)); 6.99 (978-1-4677-6204-5(0)) Lerner Publishing Group. (Kar-Ben Publishing).
Levine, Rhoda. He Was There from the Day We Moved In. Gorey, Edward, illus. 2012. (ENG.). 32p. (J). (gr. -1-2). 14.95 (978-1-59017-515-6(8), NYR Children's Collection) New York Review of Bks., Inc., The.
Levy, Elizabeth. A Hare-Raising Tale. Gerstein, Mordicai, illus. unabr. ed. 2006. (First Chapter Bks.). (J). (gr. 2-4). pap. 20.95 incl. audio compact disk (978-1-59519-705-1(2)); pap. 17.95 incl. audio (978-1-59519-704-7(4)) Live Oak Media.
—The Mixed-Up Mask Mystery: A Fletcher Mystery. Gerstein, Mordicai, illus. unabr. ed. 2006. (First Chapter Bks.). (J). (gr. 2-4). pap. 20.95 incl. audio compact disk (978-1-59519-711-5(7)); pap. 17.95 incl. audio (978-1-59519-710-8(9)) Live Oak Media.
—The Principal's on the Roof. Gerstein, Mordicai, illus. 2005. 74p. (J). lib. bdg. 15.00 (978-1-59054-912-4(0)) Fitzgerald Bks.
—The Principal's on the Roof. Gerstein, Mordicai, illus. unabr. ed. 2006. (First Chapter Bks.). (J). (gr. 2-4). pap. 17.95 incl. audio (978-1-59519-698-9(6)); pap. 20.95 incl. audio compact disk (978-1-59519-699-6(4)) Live Oak Media.
Levy, Elizabeth & Brunkus, Denise. The Mystery of the Missing Dog. (Hello Reader! Ser.). (FRE., Illus.). (J). pap. 5.99 (978-0-590-16010-0(9)) Scholastic, Inc.
Levy, Elizabeth & Coville, Bruce. The Dragon of Doom. Gerstein, Mordicai & Coville, Katherine, illus. 2005. 71p. (J). lib. bdg. 15.00 (978-1-59054-903-2(1)) Fitzgerald Bks.
Levy, Viv. The Mysterious Disappearance at Bird Bridge: A Dog Detective Story. 2013. (ENG., Illus.). 156p. 24.00 (978-0-906362-75-4(X)) Gothic Image Pubns. GBR. Dist: SCB Distributors.
Lewis, Amey. Nipper of Drayton Hall. McElroy, Gerry, illus. 2015. (Young Palmetto Bks.). (ENG.). 40p. (J). (gr. 5-5). 19.95 (978-1-61117-625-4(5)) Univ. of South Carolina Pr.
Lewis, Elfyn. Scruff & Friends. 2012. (Illus.). 12p. pap. 18.30 (978-1-4772-1449-7(6)) AuthorHouse.
Lewis, Gill. Murphy & the Great Surf Rescue. Home, Sarah, illus. 2017. (Puppy Academy Ser.). (ENG.). 128p. (J). 16.99 (978-1-62779-800-6(5), 9781627798006, Holt, Henry & Co. Bks. For Young Readers) Holt, Henry & Co.
—Pip & the Paw of Friendship. Home, Sarah, illus. 2017. (Puppy Academy Ser.). (ENG.). 128p. (J). pap. 5.99 (978-1-250-09285-4(X), 9781250092854, Holt, Henry & Co. Bks. For Young Readers) Holt, Henry & Co.
—Scout & the Sausage Thief. Home, Sarah, illus. 2016. (Puppy Academy Ser.). (ENG.). 128p. (J). 16.99 (978-1-62779-794-8(7), 9781627797948, Holt, Henry & Co. Bks. For Young Readers) Holt, Henry & Co.
—Star on Stormy Mountain. Home, Sarah, illus. 2016. (Puppy Academy Ser.). (ENG.). 128p. (J). 16.99 (978-1-62779-796-2(3), 9781627797962, Holt, Henry & Co. Bks. For Young Readers) Holt, Henry & Co.
Lewis, J. Patrick & Zappitello, Beth. First Dog. Bowers, Tim, illus. 2009. (ENG.). 32p. (J). (gr. k-6). 15.95 (978-1-58536-467-1(3)) Sleeping Bear Pr.
Lewis, J. Patrick, et al. First Dog's White House Christmas. Bowers, Tim, illus. 2010. (ENG.). 32p. (J). (gr. 1-4). 15.95 (978-1-58536-503-6(3), 202197) Sleeping Bear Pr.
Lewis, Joan Lane. See with Me. Hough, Hannah Bliss, illus. 2011. 32p. pap. 24.95 (978-1-4626-2347-1(6)) America Star Bks.
Lewis, Kevin & Kirk, Daniel. My Truck Is Stuck! Kirk, Daniel, illus. 2006. (ENG., Illus.). 30p. (J). (gr. -1 — 1). bds. 7.99 (978-0-7868-3739-7(X)) Hyperion Pr.
Lewis, Larry. Laddie's Tales & Travels. 2005. 38p. pap. 24.95 (978-1-4137-3390-7(5)) PublishAmerica, Inc.
Lewis, Maria. Rescued: Benny's Story. 2005. 38p. (J). 10.23 (978-1-4116-6172-1(9)) Lulu Pr., Inc.
Lewis, Melinda. Bulls-Eye Bob & the Backyard Buddies. 2008. 68p. pap. 15.99 (978-1-4363-3109-8(9)) Xlibris Corp.
Lewis, Siân. Billy Jones Dog Star. Roberts, Maggy, tr. Roberts, Maggy, illus. 2003. (ENG.). 56p. pap. 11.95 (978-1-84323-169-1(7)) Beekman Bks., Inc.
Lewison, Wendy Cheyette. The Prince & the Potty. Motoyama, Keiko, illus. 2006. (ENG.). 40p. (J). (gr. -1-3). 16.99 (978-0-689-87808-4(7), Simon & Schuster Bks. For Young Readers) Simon & Schuster Bks. For Young Readers.
Liberts, Jennifer. Princesses & Puppies (Disney Princess) Legramandi, Francesco & Matta, Gabriella, illus. 2016. (Step into Reading Ser.). (ENG.). 24p. (J). (gr. -1-1). pap. 4.99 (978-0-7364-3660-1(X), RH/Disney) Random Hse. Children's Bks.
Lide, Emily. Zimbabwe. 2006. per. 11.95 (978-1-59094-120-1(9)) Jawbone Publishing Corp.
Lieberman Hackelberg, Lori. Shep & the Wounded Soldier. 2012. pap. 11.95 (978-0-7414-7353-0(4)) Infinity Publishing.
Liepelt, Juanita. Blue: The Luckiest Dog in the World. Kasy, Frank, illus. 2008. 48p. 19.95 (978-0-9791317-0-7(7), RealtyIsBooks) RealtyIsBooks.com, Inc.
Lifton, Betty Jean. Taka-Chan & I: A Dog's Journey to Japan by Runcible. Hosoe, Eikoh, photos by. 2012. (ENG., Illus.). 64p. (J). (gr. k-4). 16.95 (978-1-59017-502-6(6), NYR Children's Collection) New York Review of Bks., Inc., The.
Lilley, Andrew, Sr. The Story of Old Dog. 2005. (J). pap. 8.00 (978-0-8059-6744-9(3)) Dorrance Publishing Co., Inc.
Lincoln, Jacqueline Michelle. The Adventures of Sheila the Awesome (Aussie) Dog. 2005. (J). 7.95 (978-0-9748426-3-9(X), Accent Pubns.) Ajoyin Publishing, Inc.
Lincoln, Ray & Lincoln, Emma. Dog in a Box: The Story of Free vs. Crated Champ. 2012. 114p. (J). pap. 11.99 (978-0-9840538-6-5(7)) Awesome Bk. Publishing.
Lindeman, Craig. The Big Black Dog & the Big Blue Se. Shoop, Johanna, illus. 2009. 40p. pap. 15.95 (978-1-60844-047-4(8)) Dog Ear Publishing, LLC.
Linden, Dianne. Shimmerdogs, 1 vol. 2008. (ENG.). 176p. (J). pap. 10.95 (978-1-897235-37-9(2)) Thistledown Pr., Ltd. CAN. Dist: Univ. of Toronto Pr.
Linder, Karen A. Jack the Curly Black Dog: Goes to the Beach. 2010. 20p. 13.80 (978-1-4520-3434-8(6)) AuthorHouse.
Lindman. Flicka, Ricka, Dicka & the Little Dog. Lindman, illus. 2013. (Flicka, Ricka, Dicka Ser.). (ENG., Illus.). 32p. (J). (gr. k-3). 9.99 (978-0-8075-2509-8(X)) Whitman, Albert & Co.
Linseman, Daniel. Shroobear's First Swim: Book I of the Shroobear Short Stories. 2008. 36p. pap. 15.49 (978-1-4343-8252-8(4)) AuthorHouse.
Lionheart, Amelia. The Dolphin Heptad. 2009. 200p. (gr. 4-6). pap. 14.95 (978-1-4401-8028-6(8)) iUniverse, Inc.
Little, Jean. Forward, Shakespeare!, 1 vol. 2005. (Orca Young Readers Ser.). (ENG., Illus.). 112p. (J). (gr. 3-6). per. 5.95 (978-1-55143-339-4(7)) Orca Bk. Pubs. USA.
—I Know an Old Laddie. 2004. (Illus.). (J). (gr. k-3). spiral bd. (978-0-616-01703-6(0)) Canadian National Institute for the Blind/Institut National Canadien pour les Aveugles.
Little Puppy. 2003. (Goodnight Mr. Moon Ser.). (Illus.). (J). bds. 2.98 (978-0-7525-4742-8(9)) Parragon, Inc.
Litwin, Eric. Dance Party Countdown. Lichtenheld, Tom, illus. 2017. (Groovy Joe Ser.: 2). (ENG.). 40p. (J). (gr. -1-k). 17.99 **(978-0-545-88379-5(2)**, Orchard Bks.) Scholastic, Inc.
Litwin, Eric. Ice Cream & Dinosaurs. Lichtenheld, Tom, illus. 2016. (Groovy Joe Ser.: 1). (ENG.). 40p. (J). (gr. -1-k). 17.99 (978-0-545-88378-8(4), Orchard Bks.) Scholastic, Inc.
Lively, Deborah Dreher. Hateya Sam. 2009. 32p. pap. 13.75 (978-1-60860-029-8(7), Eloquent Bks.) Strategic Book Publishing & Rights Agency (SBPRA).
Livingston, R. E. Super Scamper & Jayden's Big Adventure. 2012. (Illus.). 16p. pap. 18.30 (978-1-4772-1775-7(4)) AuthorHouse.
Liz Collard. Jeremiah, the Schoolhouse Dog. 2009. 28p. pap. 12.79 (978-1-4269-0990-0(X)) Trafford Publishing.
Llewellyn, Claire. Bad Dog, Digby!, 1 vol. East, Jacqueline, illus. 2013. (Start Reading Ser.). (ENG.). 24p. (J). (gr. k-1). pap. 7.95 (978-1-4765-4085-6(3)) Capstone Press of Coughlan Cos.
Lloyd, Stacy K. A Girl & Her Dog. 2005. 32p. pap. 12.00 (978-1-4116-1359-1(7)) Lulu Pr., Inc.
Lobiondo, Christine. Red Rock Capers. 2007. 56p. per. 19.95 (978-1-4327-1039-2(7)) Outskirts Pr., Inc.
Lockhart, Barbara. Mosey's Field, 1 vol. Crow, Heather, illus. 2013. (ENG.). 32p. (J). 16.99 (978-0-7643-4388-9(2), 9780764343889) Schiffer Publishing, Ltd.
Lodge, Jo. Dig! Little Puppy. Lodge, Jo, illus. 2017. (Little Movers Ser.). (ENG., Illus.). 10p. (J). (gr. -1-k). bds. 9.99 **(978-1-5098-0668-3(7))** Pan Macmillan GBR. Dist: Independent Pubs. Group.
Logan, Wanda. Caesar, a Story about a Dog. 2005. (Illus.). 103p. (J). per. 13.95 (978-1-59405-055-8(4)) New Age World Publishing.
Loggins, Kenny. Moose N' Me. Nash, Joshua, illus. 2013. (ENG.). 32p. (J). (gr. -1-3). 14.95 (978-0-578-07552-5(0)) Charlesbridge Publishing, Inc.
Logue, Stephanie. Mango's Revenge. Murphy, Chris, illus. 2006. (J). pap. (978-1-59336-769-5(4)) Mondo Publishing.
Lois, Lowry. Stay! Keeper's Story. 2017. (ENG., Illus.). 204p. (J). (gr. 1-4). pap. 5.99 (978-0-544-81315-1(4), HMH Books For Young Readers) Houghton Mifflin Harcourt Publishing Co.
London, C. Alexander. Divided We Fall. 2014. (Dog Tags Ser.: 4). (ENG.). 192p. (J). (gr. 5-9). pap. 5.99 (978-0-545-47707-9(7), Scholastic Paperbacks) Scholastic, Inc.
—Prisoners of War. 2014. (Dog Tags Ser.: 3). (ENG.). 192p. (J). (gr. 5-9). pap. 5.99 (978-0-545-47706-2(9), Scholastic Paperbacks) Scholastic, Inc.
—Semper Fido. 2013. (Dog Tags Ser.: 1). (ENG.). 224p. (J). (gr. 5-9). pap. 5.99 (978-0-545-47704-8(2)) Scholastic, Inc.
London, Jack. The Call of the Wild. 2014. iv, 96p. (J). pap. (978-1-4677-4602-1(9), First Avenue Editions) Lerner Publishing Group.
—The Call of the Wild, 1 vol. VanArsdale, Anthony, illus. 2011. (Calico Illustrated Classics Ser.). (ENG.). 112p. (YA). (gr. 3-6). 27.07 (978-1-60270-742-9(1)) Magic Wagon.
—The Call of the Wild. Terrazzini, Daniela Jaglenka, illus. 2011. (Puffin Classics Ser.). (ENG.). 160p. (J). (gr. 5-7). 16.99 (978-0-14-133654-1(4), Puffin Books) Penguin Young Readers Group.
—The Call of the Wild. Moser, Barry, illus. 2011. (ENG.). 144p. (J). (gr. 4-9). pap. 8.99 (978-1-4424-3411-0(2), Simon & Schuster Bks. For Young Readers) Simon & Schuster Bks. For Young Readers.
—The Call of the Wild. 2003. (Aladdin Classics Ser.). (ENG.). 160p. (J). (gr. 4-7). mass mkt. 6.99 (978-0-689-85674-7(1), Aladdin) Simon & Schuster Children's Publishing.
—The Call of the Wild. Clift, Eva, tr. Clift, Eva, illus. 2003. (Values in Action Illustrated Classics Ser.). (J). (978-1-59203-047-7(5)) Learning Challenge, Inc.
—The Call of the Wild. Corvino, Lucy, illus. 2005. (Classic Starts(tm) Ser.). (ENG.). 160p. (J). (gr. 2-4). 6.95 (978-1-4027-1274-6(X)) Sterling Publishing Co., Inc.
—Call of the Wild. 2014. (Differentiated Timeless Classics Ser.). (ENG.). 80p. (YA). (gr. 9-12). 12.95 (978-1-62250-720-7(7)) Saddleback Educational Publishing, Inc.
—The Call of the Wild. Green, John, illus. abr. l.t. ed. 2011. (Dover Children's Thrift Classics Ser.). (ENG.). 64p. (J). (gr. 3-8). pap. 3.00 (978-0-486-40551-3(6)) Dover Pubns., Inc.
—The Call of the Wild: Prestwick House Literary Touchstone Edition. 2005. 100p. (YA). per. 3.99 (978-1-58049-584-4(2), PWH5842) Prestwick Hse., Inc.
—The Call of the Wild - Spotlight Edition. Grudzina, Douglas, ed. 2005. 100p. (YA). per. 5.95 (978-1-58049-552-3(4), PWH5524) Prestwick Hse., Inc.
—The Call of the Wild & White Fang. McKowen, Scott, illus. 2004. (Sterling Unabridged Classics Ser.). (ENG.). 312p. (J). (gr. 5). 9.95 (978-1-4027-1455-9(6)) Sterling Publishing Co., Inc.
—La Llamada de la Naturaleza. 2003. (Historias de Siempre Ser.).Tr. of Call of the Wild. (SPA., Illus.). 92p. (J). (gr. 5-8). pap. 10.95 (978-84-204-5731-4(0)) Santillana USA Publishing Co., Inc.
—Michael Brother of Jerry. 2006. 228p. per. 15.95 (978-1-59818-075-6(4)) Aegypan.
—White Fang. Guillope, Antoine, illus. 2013. (ENG.). 40p. (J). (gr. 2). 14.95 (978-2-7338-2145-9(8)) Auzou, Philippe Editions FRA. Dist: Consortium Bk. Sales & Distribution.
—White Fang. Andreasen, Dan, illus. 2006. (Classic Starts(tm) Ser.). (ENG.). 160p. (J). (gr. 2-4). 6.95 (978-1-4027-2500-5(0)) Sterling Publishing Co., Inc.
—White Fang, 1 vol. VanArsdale, Anthony, illus. 2011. (Calico Illustrated Classics Ser.: No. 3). (ENG.). 112p. (J). (gr. 3-6). 27.07 (978-1-61641-112-1(0)) Magic Wagon.
—White Fang: With a Discussion of Resilience. Walker, Karen, illus. 2003. (Values in Action Illustrated Classics Ser.). 191p. (J). (978-1-59203-038-5(6)) Learning Challenge, Inc.
—White Fang Study Guide. 2003. (Saddleback Classics Ser.). (Illus.). 48p. (J). (gr. 4-7). per. 17.95 (978-1-56254-536-9(1), SP5361) Saddleback Educational Publishing, Inc.
London, Jonathan. Froggy Gets a Doggy. Remkiewicz, Frank, illus. (Froggy Ser.). (ENG.). 32p. (J). (gr. -1-k). 2015. 6.99 (978-0-14-242230-4(4), Puffin Books) 2014. 16.99 (978-0-670-01428-6(1), Viking Books for Young Readers) Penguin Young Readers Group.
Long, Ethan. Pug. Long, Ethan, illus. 2016. (I Like to Read(r) Ser.). (ENG., Illus.). 24p. (J). 6.99 (978-0-8234-3688-0(8)); 14.95 (978-0-8234-3645-3(4)) Holiday Hse., Inc.
Long, Loren. Otis & the Puppy. Long, Loren, illus. (Otis Ser.: 3). (ENG., Illus.). (J). (gr. -1-k). 2014. 38p. bds. 8.99 (978-0-399-17196-3(7)) 2013. 40p. 17.99 (978-0-399-25469-7(2)) Penguin Young Readers Group. (Philomel Bks.).
Long, Olivia. The Boy & the Dog. Long, Olivia, illus. Date not set. (Pets & Their People Ser.). (Illus.). 32p. (J). (gr. k-5). (978-1-880042-07-6(X)) Shelf-Life Bks.
Look, Lenore. Ruby Lu, Star of the Show. Choi, Stef, illus. (ENG.). 144p. (J). (gr. 1-5). 2012. pap. 6.99 (978-1-4169-1776-2(4)) 2011. 15.99 (978-1-4169-1775-5(6)) Simon & Schuster Children's Publishing. (Atheneum Bks. for Young Readers).
Lopez, Joe. Solemates. 2013. 28p. pap. 9.95 (978-1-4787-2494-0(3)) Outskirts Pr., Inc.
Lopez, Patricia. A Dog Named Pom Pom & Friends. Lopez, Patricia, illus. l.t. ed. 2011. (ENG., Illus.). 34p. pap. 15.99 (978-1-4610-4886-2(9)) CreateSpace Independent Publishing Platform.
Lord, Cynthia. A Handful of Stars. (ENG.). 192p. (J). (gr. 3-7). 2017. pap. 6.99 **(978-0-545-70028-3(0))** 2015. 16.99 (978-0-545-70027-6(2)) Scholastic, Inc. (Scholastic Pr.).
—Happy Birthday Hamster. Anderson, Derek, illus. 2011. (ENG.). 40p. (J). (gr. -1-k). 18.99 (978-0-545-25522-6(8), Scholastic Pr.) Scholastic, Inc.
—Hot Rod Hamster. Anderson, Derek, illus. 2010. (ENG.). 40p. (J). (gr. -1-k). 18.99 (978-0-545-03530-9(9), Scholastic Pr.) Scholastic, Inc.
—Hot Rod Hamster & the Awesome ATV Adventure! Anderson, Derek, illus. 2015. (ENG.). 32p. (J). 16.99 (978-0-545-76734-7(2)); pap. 3.99 (978-0-545-62680-4(3)) Scholastic, Inc. (Scholastic Pr.).
—Hot Rod Hamster Meets His Match! Anderson, Derek, illus. 2016. (Scholastic Reader, Level 2 Ser.). (ENG.). 32p. (J). (gr. -1-2). pap. 3.99 (978-0-545-82591-7(1), Scholastic Pr.) Scholastic, Inc.

C
D

—Paloma. McGuire, Erin, illus. 2016. (Shelter Pet Squad Ser.: 3). (ENG.). 128p. (J). (gr. 2-5). pap. 5.99 *(978-0-545-63604-9(3))* Scholastic, Inc.

Lord, Grant. Tales of Rex Riley Aged 10 & a Bit, It's A Dog's Life. 2009. 141p. pap. 12.95 *(978-1-4092-4782-1(1))* Lulu Pr., Inc.

Lorentz, Dayna. The Pack. 2011. (Dogs of the Drowned City Ser.: No. 2). (ENG.). 240p. (J). (gr. 3-7). 16.99 *(978-0-545-27644-3(6)*, Scholastic Pr.) Scholastic, Inc.

Lost in the Woods. 2003. (Bella & Rosie Set 1 Ser.). (J). 7.67 *(978-1-932570-12-0(8))* Pioneer Valley Bks.

Lovascio, Jane. Casey & Bella Go to New York. Jasuna, Aija, illus. 2008. 24p. (J). 14.95 *(978-1-60131-007-1(2))* Big Tent Bks.

Lovett, Darrell. Hi, I'm Alex. l.t. ed. 2006. (ENG., Illus.). 28p. per. 9.95 *(978-1-4327-0195-6(9))* Outskirts Pr., Inc.

—My Dog Tony. l.t. ed. 2006. (ENG., Illus.). 28p. per. 9.95 *(978-1-4327-0187-1(8))* Outskirts Pr., Inc.

Lovett, Darrell F. Darrell's Lake Franklin. 2007. 13.00 *(978-0-8059-8807-9(6))* Dorrance Publishing Co., Inc.

Lowery, Rae. The Case of the Pack-Rat Park. 2008. 57p. pap. 19.95 *(978-1-60610-426-2(8))* America Star Bks.

Lowrey, Janette Sebring. The Poky Little Puppy. Tenggren, Gustaf, illus. 2011. (Little Golden Book Ser.). (ENG.). 24p. (J). (— 1). bds. 6.99 *(978-0-375-86129-1(7)*, Golden Bks.) Random Hse. Children's Bks.

—The Poky Little Puppy. Tenggren, Gustaf, illus. 2007. (Little Golden Book Ser.). (ENG.). 26p. (J). (gr. k — 1). bds. 4.99 *(978-0-375-83925-2(9)*, Golden Bks.) Random Hse. Children's Bks.

—The Poky Little Puppy. Tenggren, Gustaf, illus. deluxe ed. Date not set. 23p. (J). (gr. -1-2). reprint ed. *(978-1-929566-56-3(5))*; *(978-1-929566-50-1(6))* Cronies.

Lucia, Doriane. The Story of Lilly & Lou: Based on a True Story. DeVito, Anthony T., illus. 2008. 56p. (J). pap. *(978-0-9809995-4-9(5)*, CCB Publishing) CCB Publishing.

Luebke, Rose. Beagle Bailey Looks for a Job. 2011. 28p. pap. 15.99 *(978-1-4628-6937-4(8))* Xlibris Corp.

Lueck, Andrew M. Chicabee. 2006. (Illus.). 32p. (gr. -1-3). 16.95 *(978-0-9774547-0-9(3))* Lueck Studios.

Luke, Melinda. The Green Dog. Manning, Jane K., illus. 2006. (Science Solves It Ser.). 32p. (J). pap. 7.99 *(978-0-15-356581-6(0))* Houghton Mifflin Harcourt School Pubs.

—El Perro Verde; the Green Dog. 2008. pap. 34.95 *(978-1-58013-770-6(9))* Kane Press, Inc.

Lukesh, Jean A. My Favorite Dog & Cat Story: My Favorite Dog Story/My Favorite Cat Story. Lukesh, Ronald E., illus. 2013. 38p. (J). pap. 14.95 *(978-0-9888021-0-0(4))* Field Mouse Productions.

Lumley, Jemima. The Journey Home from Grandpa's. Fatus, Sophie, illus. 2010. (ENG.). 16p. (J). (gr. -1-3). pap. 5.99 *(978-1-84686-277-9(9))* Barefoot Bks., Inc.

Luthardt, Kevin. Larabee. 1 vol. Luthardt, Kevin, illus. 2009. (ENG., Illus.). 32p. (J). (gr. -1-1). pap. 7.95 *(978-1-56145-482-6(6))* Peachtree Pubs.

Luthardt, Kevin & Luthardt, Kevin. Larabee. 1 vol. 2004. (ENG., Illus.). 32p. (J). (gr. k-1). 15.95 *(978-1-56145-300-3(5))* Peachtree Pubs.

Lutz II, William. Seeking Mason. 2009. 212p. pap. 14.00 *(978-0-557-03737-7(9))* Lulu Pr., Inc.

Lydia Jane. Fifth Moon: The First Installment in the Gates Trilogy. 2007. 480p. 35.95 *(978-0-595-91408-1(X))*; per. 25.95 *(978-0-595-43671-2(4))* iUniverse, Inc.

Lyford, Joan. Daisybelle & Dash, a Bedtime Story. 2012. 24p. pap. 14.93 *(978-1-4669-1154-3(9))* Trafford Publishing.

Lynch, Chris. Cyberia. 2008. (Cyberia Ser.: 1). (ENG.). 160p. (J). (gr. 3-7). 16.99 *(978-0-545-02793-9(4)*, Scholastic Pr.) Scholastic, Inc.

—Monkey See, Monkey Don't. (Cyberia Ser.: 2). (ENG.). 144p. (J). (gr. 3-7). 2011. pap. 5.99 *(978-0-545-02797-7(7)*, Scholastic Paperbacks) 2009. 16.99 *(978-0-545-02794-6(2)*, Scholastic Pr.) Scholastic, Inc.

Lynch, Lauren Boehm. The Yellow Butterfly. DeBroeck, Sarah, illus. 2011. 28p. pap. 24.95 *(978-1-4560-0982-3(6))* America Star Bks.

Lynn, Diana & Arroyo, George. Dog's Scratch: Los Perritos Se Rascan. 2003. (SPA & ENG.). (J). 4.95 *(978-0-9745864-0-3(4))* Brookteam Corp.

Lynn, Diana & Arroyo, George, creators. Dogs Scratch: Les Chiens Se Grattent. l.t. ed. 2003. (FRE & ENG., Illus.). 6p. (J). 4.95 *(978-0-9745864-2-7(0)*, Shirt Tales) Brookteam Corp.

Lynn, Elizabeth B. Forget the Vet. Meyer, Ashley M., illus. 2012. 32p. 24.95 *(978-1-936688-21-0(2))* AKA:yoLa.

Lynn, Tammy. Happy Birthday Puppy: An I See Puppy Book. Stewart, Elaine, ed. Lynn, Tammy, illus. 2006. (Illus.). 12p. (J). bds. 6.99 *(978-0-9774277-0-3(6)*, 0-9774277-0-6) I See Puppy, LLP.

Lyon, Tammie. Olive & Snowflake, 0 vols. 2011. (ENG.). 32p. (J). (gr. -1-3). 16.99 *(978-0-7614-5955-2(3)*, 9780761459552, Amazon Children's Publishing) Amazon Publishing.

Lyons, Jayne. 100% Wolf. Rivas, Victor, illus. 2009. (ENG.). 256p. (J). (gr. 2-7). 16.99 *(978-1-4169-7474-1(1)*, Atheneum Bks. for Young Readers) Simon & Schuster Children's Publishing.

Lysiak, Hilde & Lysiak, Matthew. Hero Dog! Lew-Vriethoff, Joanne, illus. 2017. (Hilde Cracks the Case Ser.: 1). (ENG.). 96p. (J). (gr. 1-3). pap. 4.99 ***(978-1-338-14155-9(4))*** Scholastic, Inc.

Maccarone, Grace. The Cowboy. Müller, Hildegard, illus. 2015. (I Like to Read(r) Ser.). (ENG.). 24p. (J). (gr. -1-3). 14.95 *(978-0-8234-3202-8(5))* Holiday Hse., Inc.

MacDonald, Hugh. Morgan's Boat Ride, 1 vol. Bald, Anna, illus. 2014. (ENG.). 24p. (J). (gr. -1-3). pap. 12.95 *(978-1-894838-96-2(3))* Acorn Pr., The CAN. Dist: Orca Bk. Pubs. USA.

MacDonald, James. Levi, Adventures of a Police Dog. 2005. (Illus.). 96p. (J). 16.95 *(978-0-9716923-1-2(9))* Regency Hse., Ltd.

MacFarlane, John. Stormstruck! 2015. (ENG.). 160p. (J). (gr. 3-7). 16.95 *(978-0-8234-3394-0(3))* Holiday Hse., Inc.

MacHalek, Bj. The Adventures of a Noble Duchess: Duchess on Yard Patrol. 2012. 32p. pap. 17.37 *(978-1-4389-6886-5(8))* AuthorHouse.

MacHoka, Rebecca. The Dog Sisters: One Missing Sister. 2010. 36p. pap. 15.49 *(978-1-4490-8306-9(4))* AuthorHouse.

Mackall, Dandi Daley. Mad Dog. 2008. (Starlight Animal Rescue Ser.: 2). (ENG.). 224p. (J). (gr. 5-9). mass mkt. 5.99 *(978-1-4143-1269-9(5)*, Tyndale Kids) Tyndale Hse. Pubs.

MacKay, Lisa. Nick Finds a Home. 2009. 32p. pap. 12.99 *(978-1-4490-3245-6(1))* AuthorHouse.

MacKenzie, Buckley. PAW Patrol: Movie Theater Storybook & Movie Projector. 2016. (ENG.). 32p. (J). (gr. -1-1). 19.99 *(978-0-7944-3325-3(1)*, Reader's Digest Children's Bks.) Studio Fun International.

MacKenzie, Catherine. The Lonely Grey Dog at No. 6: Tammy & Jake Learn about Love & Loyalty. 2005. (Tales from Canterbury Place Ser.). (ENG., Illus.). 160p. (J). per. 6.99 *(978-1-84550-103-7(9)*, bb65d1c0-1fc5-4a1a-8cb0-8c01c9ccdb70) Christian Focus Pubns. GBR. Dist: Bookmasters Distribution.

MacLachlan, Patricia. Barkus. Boutavant, Marc, illus. 2017. (Barkus Ser.: 1). (ENG.). 56p. (J). (gr. 1-4). 14.99 *(978-1-4521-1182-7(0))* Chronicle Bks. LLC.

—Kindred Souls. (J). (gr. 1-5). 2013. (ENG.). 144p. pap. 5.99 *(978-0-06-052299-5(2))* 2012. (ENG.). 128p. 16.99 *(978-0-06-052297-1(6))* 2012. 128p. lib. bdg. 17.89 *(978-0-06-052298-8(4))* HarperCollins Pubs. (Tegen, Katherine Bks).

—The Truth of Me. (J). (gr. 1-5). 2015. (ENG.). 144p. pap. 5.99 *(978-0-06-199861-4(3))* 2013. (ENG.). 128p. 16.99 *(978-0-06-199859-1(1))* 2013. 128p. lib. bdg. 17.89 *(978-0-06-199860-7(5))* HarperCollins Pubs. (Tegen, Katherine Bks).

—Waiting for the Magic. Bates, Amy June, illus. (ENG.). (J). (gr. 3-7). 2012. 176p. pap. 6.99 *(978-1-4169-2746-4(8))* 2011. 160p. 16.99 *(978-1-4169-2745-7(X))* Simon & Schuster Children's Publishing. (Atheneum Bks. for Young Readers).

—White Fur Flying. (ENG., Illus.). (J). (gr. 2-6). 2014. 144p. pap. 7.99 *(978-1-4424-2172-1(X))* 2013. 128p. 15.99 *(978-1-4424-2171-4(1))* McElderry, Margaret K. Bks. (McElderry, Margaret K. Bks.).

MacLachlan, Patricia & Charest, Emily MacLachlan. I Didn't Do It. Schneider, Katy, illus. 2010. (ENG.). 32p. (J). (gr. -1-3). 16.99 *(978-0-06-135833-3(9))*, Tegen, Katherine Bks) HarperCollins Pubs.

Macmillan, Sue. Bouncy, Pouncy Puppy. Ward, Sarah, illus. 2014. (Cheery Chasers Ser.). (ENG.). 8p. (J). (gr. -1 — 1). bds. 4.99 *(978-0-7641-6698-3(0))* Barron's Educational Series, Inc.

—Happy, Hoppy Bunny. Ward, Sarah, illus. 2014. (Cheery Chasers Ser.). (ENG.). 8p. (J). (gr. -1 — 1). bds. 4.99 *(978-0-7641-6699-0(9))* Barron's Educational Series, Inc.

Macomber, Debbie & Carney, Mary Lou. The Yippy, Yappy Yorkie in the Green Doggy Sweater. Lambert, Sally Anne, illus. 2011. (ENG.). 32p. (J). (gr. -1-2). 16.99 *(978-0-06-165096-3(X))* HarperCollins Pubs.

MacVicar, Andrea. Tales of Zoftic. Morse, Patti, illus. 2007. 58p. (J). per. 16.95 *(978-0-9798395-0-4(5))* Inspiration Pr. Inc.

Maddox, Tony & Wen, Dref. Ffred Ar y Môr: Cyfres Ffred Ci'r Fferm. 2005. (WEL., Illus.). 32p. pap. *(978-1-85596-666-6(2))* Dref Wen.

Magnuson, Gregory. Crab & Will, a Tale of Shakespeare's Dog. 2012. 36p. pap. 19.95 *(978-1-105-95102-2(2))* Lulu Pr., Inc.

Magsamen, Sandra. I Ruff You (Made with Love) Magsamen, Sandra, illus. 2016. (ENG., Illus.). 12p. (J). (gr. -1-k). bds. 7.99 *(978-1-338-11082-1(9)*, Cartwheel Bks.) Scholastic, Inc.

Make Believe Ideas. Paulette the Pinkest Puppy. 2014. (ENG.). 32p. (J). 15.99 *(978-1-78235-975-3(3))* Make Believe Ideas GBR. Dist: Nelson, Thomas Inc.

—Paulette the Pinkest Puppy in the World. 2014. (ENG.). 32p. (J). pap. 6.99 *(978-1-78235-974-6(5))* Make Believe Ideas GBR. Dist: Nelson, Thomas Inc.

Maldonado, Helen. Big Dog & His Family. 2003. (J). pap. 8.00 *(978-0-8059-5812-6(6))* Dorrance Publishing Co., Inc.

Malnor, Carol L. Wild Ones: Observing City Critters. Morrison, Cathy, illus. 2016. 32p. (J). (gr. k-4). 16.95 *(978-1-58469-553-0(6))* Dawn Pubns.

Malpass, Suzanne M. A Lab's Tale. Morgan, Trish, illus. 2012. 38p. (J). 12.95 *(978-1-937406-68-4(7))* Mascot Bks., Inc.

Mancuso, Jackie Clark. Paris-Chien: Adventures of an Ex-Pat Dog. 2013. (ENG., Illus.). 32p. (J). (gr. k-2). 17.95 *(978-0-615-54542-4(4))* La Librairie Parisienne.

Mann, T. L. The Adventures of Magellan. 2009. 23p. (J). pap. 13.95 *(978-1-4327-3490-9(3))* Outskirts Pr., Inc.

Mannering, Rose. Boo's Beard. Straker, Bethany, illus. 2015. (ENG.). 32p. (J). (gr. -1-k). 16.99 *(978-1-63450-207-8(8)*, Sky Pony Pr.) Skyhorse Publishing Co., Inc.

Manning, Matthew K. The Mist. Lima, Rico & Bello, Thiago Dal, illus. 2016. (EOD Soldiers Ser.). (ENG.). 40p. (gr. 4-8). lib. bdg. 26.65 *(978-1-4965-3108-7(6))* Stone Arch Bks.

—The Mystery of the Mayhem Mansion. Neely, Scott, illus. 2016. (You Choose Stories: Scooby-Doo Ser.). (ENG.). 112p. (gr. 2-3). lib. bdg. 32.65 *(978-1-4965-2661-8(9)*, You Choose Bks.) Capstone Press of Coughlan Cos.

—Mystery of the Mist Monster. Neely, Scott, illus. 2016. (Scooby-Doo Comic Chapter Bks.). (ENG.). 88p. (gr. 3-7). pap. 5.95 *(978-1-4965-3590-0(1))* Capstone Press of Coughlan Cos.

—Secret of the Haunted Cave. Neely, Scott, illus. 2016. (Scooby-Doo Comic Chapter Bks.). (ENG.). 88p. (gr. 3-7). pap. 5.95 *(978-1-4965-3589-4(8))* Capstone Press of Coughlan Cos.

Mannone, Christine. Flowers for Pudding Street. Carolan, Christine, illus. 2009. (ENG.). 32p. (J). 15.95 *(978-1-934860-02-1(6))* Shenanigan Bks.

Manny the Tv Watching Dog. 2013. (Illus.). 32p. pap. 13.95 *(978-1-61160-908-0(9))* Whiskey Creek Restorations.

Manos, Helen. Samsara Dog. Vivas, Julie, illus. 2007. (ENG.). 40p. (J). (gr. 3-6). 10.99 *(978-1-933605-51-7(0))* Kane Miller.

Manus, Willard. A Dog Called Leka. 2007. (ENG.). 122p. pap. 7.99 *(978-0-9740551-3-8(1))* Smith, Viveca Publishing.

Manushkin, Fran. Goodbye to Goldie, 1 vol. Lyon, Tammie, illus. 2009. (Katie Woo Ser.). (ENG.). 32p. (gr. k-2). 21.32 *(978-1-4048-5495-6(9))* Picture Window Bks.

Manushkin, Fran & Lyon, Tammie. Adiós a Goldie. Lyon, Tammie, illus. 2012. (Katie Woo en Español Ser.). (SPA., Illus.). 32p. (gr. k-2). pap. 6.95 *(978-1-4048-7676-7(6))*; lib. bdg. 21.32 *(978-1-4048-7524-1(7))* Picture Window Bks.

Manwiller, S. A. The Adventures of Jack & Max: What Jack & Max Love. Manwiller, S. A., illus. 2013. (Illus.). 30p. 19.99 *(978-0-9838427-4-3(4))* SevenHorns Publishing.

Manzano, Sonia. No Dogs Allowed! Muth, Jon J., illus. 2005. (J). 29.95 incl. audio compact disk *(978-0-8045-4101-5(9)*, SACD4101); 27.95 incl. audio *(978-0-8045-6927-9(4)*, SAC6927) Spoken Arts, Inc.

Manzano, Sonia & Muth, Jon J. No Dogs Allowed! Muth, Jon J., illus. 2004. (ENG., Illus.). 32p. (J). (gr. -1-2). 17.99 *(978-0-689-83088-4(2)*, Atheneum Bks. for Young Readers) Simon & Schuster Children's Publishing.

Manzione, Lisa. Let's Visit Jerusalem! Adventures of Bella & Harry. Lucco, Kristine, illus. 2013. (Adventures of Bella & Harry Ser.: 10). (ENG.). 35p. (J). (gr. k-3). 16.95 *(978-1-937616-00-7(2))* Bella & Harry, LLC.

—Let's Visit London! Adventures of Bella & Harry. Lucco, Kristine, illus. 2011. (Adventures of Bella & Harry Ser.: 3). (ENG.). 35p. (J). (gr. k-3). 16.95 *(978-1-937616-03-8(7))* Bella & Harry, LLC.

Maple, Daphne. A Bone to Pick. Metayer, Annabelle, illus. 2017. (Roxbury Park Dog Club Ser.: 6). 208p. (J). (gr. 3-7). pap. 6.99 *(978-0-06-237102-7(9))* HarperCollins Pubs.

—Mission Impawsible. Metayer, Annabelle, illus. 2016. (Roxbury Park Dog Club Ser.: 1). 224p. (J). (gr. 3-7). pap. 6.99 *(978-0-06-232767-3(4))* HarperCollins Pubs.

—A New Leash on Life. Metayer, Annabelle, illus. 2017. (Roxbury Park Dog Club Ser.: 5). 224p. (J). (gr. 3-7). pap. 6.99 *(978-0-06-237100-3(2))* HarperCollins Pubs.

—Roxbury Park Dog Club #2: When the Going Gets Ruff. Metayer, Annabelle, illus. 2016. (Roxbury Park Dog Club Ser.: 2). 224p. (J). (gr. 3-7). pap. 6.99 *(978-0-06-232769-7(0))* HarperCollins Pubs.

—Top Dog. Metayer, Annabelle, illus. 2016. (Roxbury Park Dog Club Ser.: 3). 224p. (J). (gr. 3-7). pap. 6.99 *(978-0-06-232771-0(2))* HarperCollins Pubs.

Marchesani, Laura & Medina, Zenaides A., Jr. Pig & Pug. Jarvis, illus. 2015. (Penguin Young Readers, Level 2 Ser.). (ENG.). 32p. (J). (gr. 1-2). pap. 3.99 *(978-0-448-48342-9(4)*, Penguin Young Readers) Penguin Young Readers Group.

Marchese, Allison Marie. Patty's Best Friend. 2008. (Illus.). 16p. (J). 7.00 *(978-0-8059-7533-8(0))* Dorrance Publishing Co., Inc.

Marciano, John Bemelmans. Madeline & Her Dog. 2011. (Madeline Ser.). (ENG.). 32p. (J). (gr. 1-2). pap. 3.99 *(978-0-448-45438-2(6)*, Penguin Young Readers) Penguin Young Readers Group.

Margolis, Alysia. Sit! Stay! Sign! Miller, Paton, illus. 2007. 32p. (J). *(978-1-4257-5919-3(X))* Margolis, Marion.

Margolis, Leslie. Boys Are Dogs. (Annabelle Unleashed Ser.). (ENG.). (YA). (gr. 3-6). 2009. 224p. pap. 6.99 *(978-1-59990-381-1(4)*, 9781599903811) 2008. (Illus.). 208p. 15.99 *(978-1-59990-221-0(4)*, 9781599902210) Bloomsbury Publishing USA. (Bloomsbury USA Childrens).

—Girl's Best Friend. 2010. (Maggie Brooklyn Mystery Ser.). (ENG.). 272p. (YA). (gr. 3-6). 14.99 *(978-1-59990-525-9(6)*, 9781599905259, Bloomsbury USA Childrens) Bloomsbury Publishing USA.

—The Secrets at the Chocolate Mansion. 2013. (Maggie Brooklyn Mystery Ser.). (ENG.). 256p. (YA). (gr. 3-6). 16.99 *(978-1-61963-036-9(2)*, 9781619630369, Bloomsbury USA Childrens) Bloomsbury Publishing USA.

—Secrets at the Chocolate Mansion. 2014. (Maggie Brooklyn Mystery Ser.). (ENG.). 272p. (YA). (gr. 3-6). pap. 7.99 *(978-1-61963-493-0(7)*, 9781619634930, Bloomsbury USA Childrens) Bloomsbury Publishing USA.

—Vanishing Acts. (Maggie Brooklyn Mystery Ser.). (ENG.). (YA). (gr. 3-6). 2013. 256p. pap. 6.99 *(978-1-59990-981-3(2)*, 9781599909813) 2012. 240p. 15.99 *(978-1-59990-536-5(1)*, 9781599905365) Bloomsbury Publishing USA. (Bloomsbury USA Childrens).

Marie, Carissa. The Lonely Puppy. 2011. 20p. 12.95 *(978-1-4490-8264-2(5))* AuthorHouse.

Marino, Gianna. A Boy, a Ball, & a Dog. 2016. (ENG., Illus.). 40p. (J). 17.99 *(978-1-62672-287-3(0)*, 9781626722873) Roaring Brook Pr.

Markey, Neil. Woof! Spremulli, Pam, illus. 2011. (ENG.). 34p. (J). (gr. k-k). 14.00 *(978-1-935557-77-7(7))* Purple Bear Bks., Inc.

Marks, Nancy Freeman. Just As You Are: The Story of Leon & Sam. Buchheim, Su Jen, illus. 2003. 32p. (J). 15.00 *(978-0-9722430-1-8(1))* Wave Publishing.

Marks, William C. Lawrence the Laughing Cookie Jar. Taylor, Josephine, illus. 2003. 16.95 *(978-0-9715541-0-8(2))* MPC Pr. International.

Marlow, Herb. Sisters, Wild Dogs & Catfish Bait. Caffee, Julie, illus. 2005. 122p. (J). lib. bdg. 24.95 *(978-1-893595-45-3(5))*; per. 16.95 *(978-1-893595-48-4(X))* Four Seasons Bks., Inc.

Marquardt, Michelle. The Perfect Puppy. Murfield, Anna, illus. 2013. 24p. pap. 9.99 *(978-1-937165-65-9(5))* Orange Hat Publishing.

Marr, Ella J. The Adventures of Curtis & Grammy. 2006. 57p. pap. 16.95 *(978-1-4241-4743-4(3))* PublishAmerica, Inc.

Marrero, Rosa M. Nickolas Loves Toby. 2011. 28p. pap. 9.95 *(978-1-4327-7452-3(2))* Outskirts Pr., Inc.

Marsh, Carole. The Riddle of the Missing Puppies. 2006. (Criss Cross Applesauce Ser.). (Illus.). 54p. (J). (gr. 4-7). 14.95 *(978-0-635-06203-1(8))* Gallopade International.

Marsoli, Lisa Ann. Puppy Love. Durk, Jim, illus. 2003. pap. *(978-0-439-61116-9(4))* Scholastic, Inc.

Marsoli, Lisa Ann & Bridwell, Norman. The Snow Dog. Haefele, Steve, illus. 2004. (Big Red Reader Ser.). (J). pap. *(978-0-439-58559-0(7))* Scholastic, Inc.

Martelli, Dawn. Like Me. Wharton, Jennifer Heyd, illus. 2004. (J). *(978-1-893516-01-4(6))* Our Child Pr.

Martín Anguita, Carmen & Carmen, Martín Anguita. El Cumpleaños de Laika. Cortazar, Alicia Canas, illus. 2008. (SPA.). 32p. (J). 10.99 *(978-84-241-5803-3(2))* Everest Editora ESP. Dist: Lectorum Pubns., Inc.

Martin, Ann M. A Dog's Life: The Autobiography of a Stray. 2007. (ENG.). 192p. (J). (gr. 3-7). pap. 7.99 *(978-0-439-71700-7(0)*, Scholastic Paperbacks) Scholastic, Inc.

—Everything for a Dog. 2011. (ENG.). 240p. (J). (gr. 4-7). pap. 7.99 *(978-0-312-67484-7(8)*, 9780312674847) Square Fish.

—Rain Reign. 2014. (ENG.). 240p. (J). (gr. 4-7). 16.99 *(978-0-312-64300-3(4)*, 9780312643003) Feiwel & Friends.

Martin, Ann M., ed. Because of Shoe & Other Dog Stories. Ivanov, Aleksey & Ivanov, Olga, illus. 2012. (ENG.). 272p. (J). (gr. 3-7). 15.99 *(978-0-8050-9314-8(1)*, 9780805093148, Holt, Henry & Co. Bks. For Young Readers) Holt, Henry & Co.

—Because of Shoe & Other Dog Stories. Ivanov, Olga & Ivanov, Aleksey, illus. 2013. (ENG.). 288p. (J). (gr. 3-7). pap. 7.99 *(978-1-250-02728-3(4)*, 9781250027283) Square Fish.

Martin, Anne E. Flip Flops for Paige. 2007. (Illus.). 36p. (J). per. 14.99 *(978-1-59879-243-0(1))* Lifevest Publishing, Inc.

Martin-Fluet, Marie T. The Fairies' Century Celebration. 2011. 40p. pap. 18.62 *(978-1-4567-2477-1(0))* AuthorHouse.

Martin, Harvey. The Shaggy Dog Story Book. 2009. 108p. pap. 10.00 *(978-1-59858-932-0(6))* Dog Ear Publishing, LLC.

Martin, Kristina. Cozzi Dog Can't See. 2012. 40p. pap. 32.70 *(978-1-4771-3053-7(5))* Xlibris Corp.

Martin, Lisa. Holly the Deaf Dalmatian: Holly Gets A New Home. 2010. 20p. 13.99 *(978-1-4269-4531-1(0))* Trafford Publishing.

Martin, Lisa & Martin, Valerie. Anton & Cecil, Book 3: Cats Aloft. Murphy, Kelly, illus. 2016. (Anton & Cecil Ser.: 3). (ENG.). 272p. (J). (gr. 3-7). 16.95 *(978-1-61620-459-4(1))* Algonquin Bks. of Chapel Hill.

Martin, Mary. God Made Nuts. Derstine, Charlene, illus. 2012. 53p. (J). *(978-0-7399-2501-0(6))* Rod & Staff Pubs., Inc.

Martin, Matthew. Cleatus Goes Camping. 2011. 44p. pap. 19.95 *(978-1-4634-3646-9(7))* AuthorHouse.

Martin, Michelle Nicole. Princess & Missy's Magical Adventures: The Crystal Heart. 2010. 55p. pap. 10.95 *(978-1-4327-4954-5(4))* Outskirts Pr., Inc.

Martin, Rosemary. Rosie's Story. 2011. (ENG., Illus.). 32p. pap. *(978-1-84876-699-0(8))* Troubador Publishing Ltd.

Martinez, Maureen Cerminaro. Just Be Yourself! the Adventures of Ted the Pom-Poo. 2013. 36p. pap. 15.95 *(978-1-4787-2005-8(0))* Outskirts Pr., Inc.

Martins, Isabel Minhós. My Neighbor Is a Dog. Herring, John, tr. from POR. Matoso, Madalena, illus. 2013. (ENG.). 32p. (J). (gr. -1-4). 16.95 *(978-1-926973-68-5(2))* Owlkids Bks. Inc. CAN. Dist: Publishers Group West (PGW).

Marty the Dog Staff. I Am Found by Marty. 2004. (Illus.). 36p. (J). 3.99 *(978-0-9746587-7-3(4)*, Beacon Street Girls) B*tween Productions, Inc.

Mary Barr. The Ditch Dog the Hedge Cat. 2009. 108p. 20.95 *(978-1-4401-5560-4(7))*; pap. 10.95 *(978-1-4401-5558-1(5))* iUniverse, Inc.

Mason, Adrienne. Secret Spies. Cupples, Patricia & Cupples, Pat, illus. 2008. (Kids Can Read Ser.). (ENG.). 32p. (J). (gr. 1-2). 14.95 *(978-1-55453-276-6(0))*; pap. 3.95 *(978-1-55453-277-3(9))* Kids Can Pr., Ltd. CAN. Dist: Hachette Bk. Group.

Mason, Alexis. Just an Ordinary Little Dog: Barnaby's Story. Bunch, Paul, illus. 2010. (J). *(978-0-9755280-4-4(1))* Insight Technical Education.

Mason, Jane B. Super Hero Splash Down, 1 vol. Baltazar, Art, illus. 2011. (DC Super-Pets Ser.). (ENG.). 56p. (gr. 2-2). pap. 4.95 *(978-1-4048-6624-9(8))*; lib. bdg. 23.99 *(978-1-4048-6357-6(5))* Picture Window Bks. (DC Super-Pets).

Mason, Jane B. & Stephens, Sarah Hines. A Dog & His Girl Mysteries #3: Cry Woof. 2013. (ENG.). 208p. (J). (gr. 3-7). pap. 5.99 *(978-0-545-43626-7(5)*, Scholastic Paperbacks) Scholastic, Inc.

Masrud, Judy. Second Chance: A Tale of Two Puppies, 1 vol. Pool, Cathy, illus. 2006. 81p. (J). (gr. 1-7). per. 9.95 *(978-0-9774142-0-8(5)*, Birdseed Books for Kids) Birdseed Bks.

Massey, Craig. Twig the Collie. 2005. 172p. (J). *(978-1-56265-076-6(9))* Accelarated Christian Education, Inc.

Masters, Susan Rowan. Night Journey to Vicksburg. Killcoyne, Hope L., ed. Smith, Duane A., illus. 2003. (Adventures in America Ser.). 74p. (gr. 4). 14.95 *(978-1-893110-30-4(3))* Silver Moon Pr.

Masurel, Claire. A Cat & a Dog. Kolar, Bob, illus. 2003. (Cheshire Studio Book Ser.). (ENG.). 32p. (J). (gr. -1). 7.95 *(978-0-7358-1780-7(4))* North-South Bks., Inc.

Matthews Culp, Dawn. What's up Willie? the Birthday Puppy! 2008. (Illus.). 24p. (J). 28.95 *(978-0-615-22222-6(6))* Sprouting Peanut Pubs.

Maxwell, Andre L. & Maxwell, Amanda L. The Great Chicken Caper. Carter, Jill, illus. 2012. 34p. (-18). 18.00 *(978-0-9881811-1-3(8))* Maxwell, Andre.

Maybarduk, Linda. James the Dancing Dog. Johnson, Gillian, illus. 2004. (ENG.). 24p. (J). (gr. -1-2). 15.95 *(978-0-88776-619-0(6)*, Tundra Bks.) Tundra Bks. CAN. Dist: Penguin Random Hse. LLC.

Maycock, Dianne. Lucky's Mountain, 1 vol. 2007. (Orca Young Readers Ser.). (ENG.). 112p. (J). (gr. 3-8). per. 6.95 *(978-1-55143-682-1(5))* Orca Bk. Pubs. USA.

Mayer, Kirsten. Dude-It-Yourself Adventure Journal. Spaziante, Patrick, illus. 2012. (Adventure Time Ser.). (ENG.). 112p. (J). (gr. 2-5). 7.99 *(978-0-8431-7244-7(4)*, Price Stern Sloan) Penguin Young Readers Group.

Mayer, Linda & Mayer, Jason. Frankie: The World's Greatest Hot Dog. 2009. 24p. pap. 12.99 *(978-1-4389-4307-7(5))* AuthorHouse.

Mayer, Mercer. A Boy, a Dog, & a Frog. Mayer, Mercer, illus. 2003. (Boy, a Dog, & a Frog Ser.). (ENG., Illus.). 32p. (J). (gr. -1-k). 6.99 *(978-0-8037-2880-6(8)*, Dial Bks) Penguin Young Readers Group.

—Just Me & My Buddies. 2017. (Pictureback(R) Ser.). (ENG., Illus.). 48p. (J). (gr. -1-2). 5.99 *(978-0-399-55376-9(2)*, Random Hse. Bks. for Young Readers) Random Hse. Children's Bks.

—Just One More Pet. Mayer, Mercer, illus. 2013. (Little Critter Ser.). (ENG., Illus.). 24p. (J). (gr. -1-2). pap. 3.99 *(978-0-06-147807-9(5)*, HarperFestival) HarperCollins Pubs.

Mayer, Mercer & Mayer, Marianna. A Boy, a Dog, a Frog & a Friend. Mayer, Mercer & Mayer, Marianna, illus. 2003. (Boy, a Dog, & a Frog Ser.). (ENG., Illus.). 32p. (J). (gr. -1-k). 6.99 *(978-0-8037-2882-0(4)*, Dial Bks) Penguin Young Readers Group.

Maynard, Adam G. The Adventures of Dynamo Dog & the Case of the Missing Jewelery. 2010. 24p. 15.49 *(978-1-4490-9186-6(5))* AuthorHouse.

Mazzafro, Howard. No Room for George. 2011. (Illus.). 24p. (gr. -1). pap. 14.93 *(978-1-4269-6782-5(9))* Trafford Publishing.
Mbe na Nkita: The Tortoise & the Dog. 2008. (YOR & ENG., Illus.). 36p. 16.00 *(978-0-9801243-1-6(X))* Blazing Ideas Ltd.
McAnulty, Stacy. Excellent Ed. Sarcone-Roach, Julia, illus. 2016. (ENG.). 32p. (J). (gr. -1-3). 16.99 *(978-0-553-51023-2(1),* Knopf Bks. for Young Readers) Random Hse. Children's Bks.
McCann, Jesse L., et al. Bad Moon Rising, 1 vol. 2014. (Krypto the Superdog Ser.). (ENG., Illus.). 32p. (gr. 1-2). 22.60 *(978-1-4342-6475-6(0))* Stone Arch Bks.
—Crisis of Infinite Kryptos, 1 vol. 2014. (Krypto the Superdog Ser.). (ENG., Illus.). 32p. (gr. 1-2). 22.60 *(978-1-4342-6471-8(8))* Stone Arch Bks.
—Here Comes Krypto, 1 vol. 2014. (Krypto the Superdog Ser.). (ENG., Illus.). 32p. (gr. 1-2). 22.60 *(978-1-4342-4785-8(6))* Stone Arch Bks.
—Houndin' the Mail Carrier!, 1 vol. 2014. (Krypto the Superdog Ser.). (ENG., Illus.). 32p. (gr. 1-2). 22.60 *(978-1-4342-6472-5(6))* Stone Arch Bks.
—Krypto the Superdog, 1 vol. 2014. (Krypto the Superdog Ser.). (ENG., Illus.). 32p. (gr. 1-2). 113.00 *(978-1-4342-8934-6(6))* Stone Arch Bks.
—The Purr-Fect Crime, 1 vol. 2014. (Krypto the Superdog Ser.). (ENG., Illus.). 32p. (gr. 1-2). 22.60 *(978-1-4342-6474-9(2))* Stone Arch Bks.
—Three Naughty Doggies!, 1 vol. 2014. (Krypto the Superdog Ser.). (ENG., Illus.). 32p. (gr. 1-2). 22.60 *(978-1-4342-6473-2(4))* Stone Arch Bks.
McCann, Jesse Leon. Scooby-Doo & Museum Madness, 1 vol. Duendes Del Sur Staff, illus. 2012. (Scooby-Doo! Set 2 Ser.: No. 2). (ENG.). 24p. (J). (gr. k-3). lib. bdg. 24.21 *(978-1-59961-867-8(2))* Spotlight.
—Scooby-Doo & the Fishy Phantom, 1 vol. Duendes Del Sur Staff, illus. 2012. (Scooby-Doo! Set 2 Ser.: No. 2). (ENG.). 24p. (J). (gr. k-3). lib. bdg. 24.21 *(978-1-59961-866-1(4))* Spotlight.
McCardie, Amanda. Our Very Own Dog. Rubbino, Salvatore, illus. 2017. (ENG.). 32p. (J). (gr. -1-2). 15.99 *(978-0-7636-8948-3(3))* Candlewick Pr.
McCarty, Jerry. A Dog to Treasure. 2003. 130p. per. 14.95 *(978-1-59196-228-1(5))* Instant Pub.
McCarty, Peter. Fabian Escapes. McCarty, Peter, illus. rev. ed. 2007. (ENG., Illus.). 40p. (J). (gr. -1-1). 21.99 *(978-0-8050-7713-1(8),* 9780805077131, Holt, Henry & Co. Bks. For Young Readers) Holt, Henry & Co.
—Hondo & Fabian. McCarty, Peter, illus. 2007. (ENG., Illus.). 40p. (J). (gr. -1-1). per. 8.99 *(978-0-312-36747-3(3),* 9780312367473) Square Fish.
—Hondo & Fabian. unabr. ed. 2006. (Illus.). (J). (gr. -1-3). 29.95 *(978-0-439-84906-7(3),* WHCD688) Weston Woods Studios, Inc.
McClafferty, Lisa. Matilda Private Eye: The Case of the Missing Socks. Aines, Diane, illus. 2012. 34p. 29.95 *(978-1-4489-5049-2(X))* 2007. (ENG.). 31p. 24.95 *(978-1-4241-8637-2(4))* America Star Bks.
McClear, Preston. Frannie & Pickles. Dollak, Nicholas, illus. 2003. 48p. (J). (gr. k-5). 16.95 *(978-1-929084-13-5(7))* Malibu Bks. for Children.
McClintock, Norah. El Soplón, 1 vol. 2010. (Spanish Soundings Ser.).Tr. of Snitch. (SPA.). 112p. (YA). (gr. 8-12). pap. 9.95 *(978-1-55469-315-3(2))* Orca Bk. Pubs. USA.
McCloskey, John J. Warrior Ching. 2006. 179p. pap. 24.95 *(978-1-4241-2389-6(5))* PublishAmerica, Inc.
McCorkle, Barbara. Brutis' New Friend. 2005. (Illus.). 23p. (J). (gr. -1-3). per. 8.99 *(978-1-932338-60-7(8))* Lifevest Publishing, Inc.
McCranie, Stephen. Belly Flop! Book 3. McCranie, Stephen, illus. 3rd ed. 2012. (Mal & Chad Ser.: 3). (ENG., Illus.). 240p. (J). (gr. 3-7). pap. 9.99 *(978-0-399-25658-5(X),* Philomel Bks.) Penguin Young Readers Group.
—Food Fight!, 2 vols. McCranie, Stephen, illus. 2nd ed. 2012. (Mal & Chad Ser.: 2). (ENG., Illus.). 224p. (J). (gr. 3-7). 9.99 *(978-0-399-25657-8(1),* Philomel Bks.) Penguin Young Readers Group.
—Mal & Chad - The Biggest, Bestest Time Ever! McCranie, Stephen, illus. 2011. (Mal & Chad Ser.: 1). (ENG., Illus.). 224p. (J). (gr. 3-7). 9.99 *(978-0-399-25221-1(5),* Philomel Bks.) Penguin Young Readers Group.
Mccroary, Greg. Mia. 2008. (ENG., Illus.). 1p. (J). 6.95 *(978-1-74110-636-7(2))* New Holland Pubs. Pty, Ltd. AUS. Dist: Tuttle Publishing.
McCue, Lisa. Quiet Bunny & Noisy Puppy. (ENG., Illus.). (J). 2013. 30p. (gr. -1 — 1). bds. 7.95 *(978-1-4549-0860-9(2))* 2011. 32p. 14.95 *(978-1-4027-8559-7(3))* Sterling Publishing Co., Inc.
McCullough, Dicy. Tired of Being Different. 2012. 28p. pap. 15.99 *(978-1-4653-1076-7(2))* Xlibris Corp.
McCully, Emily Arnold. Strongheart: The World's First Movie Star Dog. McCully, Emily Arnold, illus. 2014. (ENG., Illus.). 40p. (J). (gr. -1-3). 17.99 *(978-0-8050-9448-0(2),* 9780805094480, Holt, Henry & Co. Bks. For Young Readers) Holt, Henry & Co.
McDonald, Diane O. The Adventures of Tweed. 2011. 52p. 24.99 *(978-1-4535-1701-7(4));* pap. 15.99 *(978-1-4535-1700-0(6))* Xlibris Corp.
McDonald, Megan. Girl Detective. Reynolds, Peter H., illus. (Judy Moody Ser.: 9). (ENG.). 192p. (J). (gr. 1-4). 2011. pap. 5.99 *(978-0-7636-4349-2(1))*Bk. 9. 2010. 15.99 *(978-0-7636-3450-6(6))* Candlewick Pr.
—Shoe Dog. Tillotson, Katherine, illus. 2014. (ENG.). 40p. (J). (gr. -1-2). 17.99 *(978-1-4169-7932-6(8),* Atheneum/Richard Jackson Bks.) Simon & Schuster Children's Publishing.
McDonnell, Patrick. The Gift of Nothing. (ENG., Illus.). 56p. (gr. -1-3). 2005. (J). 15.99 *(978-0-316-11488-2(X))* 2009. 19.99 *(978-0-316-05441-6(0))* Little, Brown Bks. for Young Readers.
—The Little Gift of Nothing. 2016. (ENG., Illus.). 30p. (J). (gr. -1 — 1). bds. 7.99 *(978-0-316-39473-4(4))* Little, Brown Bks. for Young Readers.
—The Mutts Autumn Diaries. 2016. (Mutts Kids Ser.: Vol. 3). (ENG., Illus.). (J). (gr. 4-6). 33.99 ***(978-1-4494-8500-9(6))*** Andrews McMeel Publishing.
—The Mutts Autumn Diaries. 2016. (Mutts for Kids Ser.). lib. bdg. 20.85 *(978-0-606-39181-8(9))* Turtleback Bks.
—The Mutts Diaries. 2016. (ENG., Illus.). 226p. (J). (gr. 3-7). 29.99 *(978-1-4494-7380-8(6))* Andrews McMeel Publishing.
—Wag! 2009. (ENG., Illus.). 40p. (J). (gr. -1-3). 17.00 *(978-0-316-04548-3(9))* Little, Brown Bks. for Young Readers.
McDougal-Littell Publishing Staff. Literature Connections English: Where the Red Fern Grows. 2004. (McDougal Littell Literature Connections Ser.). (ENG.). 328p. (gr. 7-7). 16.90 *(978-0-395-77528-8(0),* 2-80097) Great Source Education Group, Inc.
McFall, Jessica & McFall, Ernest. Unselfish Love. l.t. ed. 2006. (ENG., Illus.). 28p. per. 9.95 *(978-1-4327-0076-8(6))* Outskirts Pr., Inc.
McFarland, Lyn Rossiter. Widget. McFarland, Jim, illus. 2004. (J). (gr. -1-k). spiral bd. *(978-0-616-11122-2(3));* spiral bd. *(978-0-616-11121-5(5))* Canadian National Institute for the Blind/Institut National Canadien pour les Aveugles.
—Widget. McFarland, Jim, illus. 2006. (ENG.). 32p. (J). (gr. -1-1). per. 8.99 *(978-0-374-48386-9(8),* 9780374483869) Square Fish.
McFarlane, Sheryl. This is the Dog, 1 vol. Wysotski, Chrissie, illus. 2003. (ENG.). 32p. *(978-1-55041-551-3(4))* Fitzhenry & Whiteside, Ltd.
Mcghee, Alison. Always. Lemaître, Pascal, illus. 2009. (ENG.). 40p. (J). (gr. -1-3). 15.99 *(978-1-4169-7481-9(4),* Simon & Schuster/Paula Wiseman Bks.) Simon & Schuster/Paula Wiseman Bks.
—Julia Gillian - And the Art of Knowing. Kozjan, Drazen, illus. 2009. (Julia Gillian Ser.). (ENG.). 304p. (J). (gr. 3-7). 6.99 *(978-0-545-03349-7(7),* Scholastic Paperbacks) Scholastic, Inc.
—Julia Gillian (and the Dream of the Dog) Kozjan, Drazen, illus. (Julia Gillian Ser.). (ENG.). 336p. (J). (gr. 3-7). 2011. pap. 6.99 *(978-0-545-03353-4(5))* 2010. 16.99 *(978-0-545-03351-0(9))* Scholastic, Inc. (Scholastic Pr.).
McGhee, Allison. Julia Gillian 3. 2010. *(978-0-545-10467-8(X))* Scholastic, Inc.
McGougan, Kathy. Buddy Plays Ball. 2007. (J). pap. 5.00 *(978-0-9799980-4-1(2))* Buddy Bks. Publishing.
—Buddy's Christmas Joy. 2011. 20p. pap. 12.95 *(978-1-4634-3763-3(3))* AuthorHouse.
—Buddy's Toys. 2007. (J). pap. 5.00 *(978-0-9799980-2-7(6))* Buddy Bks. Publishing.
—Fixin' Buddy's Little Red Wagon. Hale, Sally, illus. 2009. 16p. pap. 9.95 *(978-1-4251-8975-4(X))* Trafford Publishing.
McGovern, Cammie. Chester & Gus. 2017. 272p. (J). (gr. 3-7). 16.99 *(978-0-06-233068-0(3))* HarperCollins Pubs.
McGrath, Maureen. Spunky's Special Friend. 2009. (Illus.). 24p. pap. 13.50 *(978-1-60693-735-8(9),* Eloquent Bks.) Strategic Book Publishing & Rights Agency (SBPRA).
McGuire Woods, Molly. Barbie & Her Sisters in a Puppy Chase. 2016. (Barbie Chapters Ser.). (ENG., Illus.). 64p. (J). (gr. 1-4). 5.99 *(978-0-399-55136-9(0),* Random Hse. Bks. for Young Readers) Random Hse. Children's Bks.
McGuirk, Leslie. Gobble, Gobble, Tucker! McGuirk, Leslie, illus. 2014. (ENG., Illus.). 32p. (J). (-k). bds. 7.99 *(978-0-7636-6887-7(7))* Candlewick Pr.
—Ho, Ho, Ho, Tucker! McGuirk, Leslie, illus. 2010. (Candlewick Storybook Animations Ser.). (ENG., Illus.). 32p. (J). (-k). 8.99 *(978-0-7636-5043-8(9))* Candlewick Pr.
—Lucky Tucker. 2008. 14.75 *(978-1-4178-1914-0(6),* Turtleback) Turtleback Bks.
—Tucker's Spooky Halloween. McGuirk, Leslie, illus. (Candlewick Storybook Animations Ser.). (ENG., Illus.). (J). 2011. 32p. (gr. k-k). 8.99 *(978-0-7636-5113-8(3))* 2007. 28p. (gr. -1-k). bds. 7.99 *(978-0-7636-3181-9(7))* Candlewick Pr.
—Tucker's Valentine. McGuirk, Leslie, illus. 2010. (ENG., Illus.). 28p. (J). (gr. -1-k). bds. 6.99 *(978-0-7636-4357-7(2))* Candlewick Pr.
McHenry, E. B. Poodlena. 2004. (Illus.). (J). *(978-1-58234-962-6(2))* Bloomsbury Publishing USA.
—Poodlena. McHenry, E. B., illus. 2004. (ENG., Illus.). 32p. (J). (gr. -1-3). 16.95 *(978-1-58234-824-7(3),* 9781582348247, Bloomsbury USA Childrens) Bloomsbury Publishing USA.
McHugh, Rosetta. Poodiky Oglethorpe. 2009. 20p. pap. 24.95 *(978-1-60749-086-9(2))* America Star Bks.
Mcinvale, Rebecca. Emmy the Bug-Gulping Dog. 2009. 16p. pap. 8.99 *(978-1-4389-9954-8(2))* AuthorHouse.
McKay, Hilary. Lulu & the Dog from the Sea. Lamont, Priscilla, illus. (Lulu Ser.: Book 2). (ENG.). 112p. (J). (gr. 1-5). 2014. pap. 4.99 *(978-0-8075-4821-9(9))* 2013. 13.99 *(978-0-8075-4820-2(0))* Whitman, Albert & Co.
McKay, Hilary & McKay, Hilary. El Perro Viernes. (Barco de Vapor). (SPA.). (YA). (gr. 5-8). pap. *(978-84-348-6214-2(X))* SM Ediciones.
McKay, Sindy. We Both Read-My Car Trip. Johnson, Meredith, illus. 2005. (We Both Read Ser.). 48p. (J). (gr. -1-2). lib. bdg. 7.99 *(978-1-891327-63-6(1));* per. 4.99 *(978-1-891327-64-3(X))* Treasure Bay, Inc.
Mckee, Jessica. Piddle Diddle Stuck in the Middle. 2010. 24p. (J). pap. *(978-0-9867017-0-2(X))* Little Black Dog Publishing.
McKibben, Marion A. Pearl the Rodeo Queen. 2006. 24p. (J). per. 12.00 *(978-1-59971-711-1(5))* Aardvark Global Publishing.
McKimmie, Chris. Me, Teddy. 2016. (ENG.). 32p. (J). (gr. -1-3). 19.99 *(978-1-76029-133-4(1))* Allen & Unwin AUS. Dist: Independent Pubs. Group.
McKissack, Patricia C. Tippy Lemmey. Keeter, Susan, illus. 2003. (Ready-For-Chapters Ser.). (ENG.). 64p. (J). (gr. 2-5). pap. 5.99 *(978-0-689-85019-6(0),* Simon & Schuster/Paula Wiseman Bks.) Simon & Schuster/Paula Wiseman Bks.
McKoin, Cathy Taylor. Little Pup Finds a Home! 2009. 28p. pap. 15.99 *(978-1-4415-3407-1(5))* Xlibris Corp.
McLean, Claire. Bo & the Ghosts of the White House Pets. 2012. 88p. pap. 17.95 *(978-1-4626-7416-9(X))* America Star Bks.
McMahon, Kim. My Dog, Buddy, 1 vol. 2010. 16p. pap. 24.95 *(978-1-4489-6624-0(8))* PublishAmerica, Inc.
McMillian, Gordon. Scout. 2012. (ENG., Illus.). 40p. (J). 14.95 *(978-1-58536-797-9(4))* Sleeping Bear Pr.
McMullan, Kate. Bulldog's Big Day. Lemaître, Pascal, illus. 2011. (J). *(978-0-545-17156-4(3),* Orchard Bks.) Scholastic, Inc.
—Knight for a Day, 1 vol. Basso, Bill, illus. 2007. (Dragon Slayers' Academy Ser.: No. 5). (ENG.). 109p. (gr. 2-5). 24.21 *(978-1-59961-377-2(8))* Spotlight.
McNamara, Margaret. The First Day of School. Gordon, Mike, illus. 2008. (Robin Hill School Ser.). (J). (gr. -1-3). pap. 16.95 *(978-1-4301-0604-3(2))* Live Oak Media.
—The First Day of School. Gordon, Mike, illus. 2005. (Robin Hill School Ser.). (ENG.). 32p. (J). (gr. -1-1). pap. 3.99 *(978-0-689-86914-3(2),* Simon Spotlight) Simon Spotlight.
McPhail, David. Bad Dog. 2014. (I Like to Read(r) Ser.). (ENG.). 24p. (J). (gr. -1-3). 14.95 *(978-0-8234-2852-6(4))* Holiday Hse., Inc.
—Boy, Bird, & Dog. McPhail, David, illus. (I Like to Read(r) Ser.). (ENG., Illus.). 24p. (J). (gr. -1-2). 2012. pap. 6.99 *(978-0-8234-2639-3(4))* 2011. 14.95 *(978-0-8234-2346-0(8))* Holiday Hse., Inc.
—Dot & Bob. 2008. (Green Light Readers Level 1 Ser.). (ENG., Illus.). 24p. (J). (gr. -1-1). pap. 3.95 *(978-0-15-206541-6(5))* Houghton Mifflin Harcourt Publishing Co.
—Sick Day. (I Like to Read(r) Ser.). (ENG.). 24p. (J). (gr. -1-3). 2013. pap. 6.99 *(978-0-8234-2910-3(5))* 2012. 14.95 *(978-0-8234-2424-5(3))* Holiday Hse., Inc.
—Weezer Changes the World. McPhail, David, illus. 2009. (ENG., Illus.). 40p. (J). (gr. -1-2). 15.99 *(978-1-4169-9000-0(3),* Beach Lane Bks.) Beach Lane Bks.
McPhail, David & McPhail, David. Bad Dog. 2015. (I Like to Read(r) Ser.). (ENG.). 24p. (J). (gr. -1-3). 6.99 *(978-0-8234-3298-1(X))* Holiday Hse., Inc.
McPherson, Dottie. Kizzi's Special Friends. 2003. (Illus.). (J). 14.95 *(978-0-9724979-0-9(0),* Advocate Hse.) A Cappela Publishing.
McRary, Janie. The Rock That Became a Friend. 2011. 24p. pap. 12.74 *(978-1-4634-3018-4(3))* AuthorHouse.
McSpadden, J. Walker. Famous Dogs in Fiction. 2005. reprint ed. pap. 31.95 *(978-1-4179-0414-3(3))* Kessinger Publishing, LLC.
McVeigh, Mark, et al. Clifford for President. LaPadula, Tom, illus. 2004. (Clifford's Big Red Reader Ser.). (ENG.). 32p. (J). (gr. -1-3). pap. 3.99 *(978-0-439-69391-2(8))* Scholastic, Inc.
McWatt, Irene. Pongo-Peter: The Life & Thoughts of an Extraordinary Mongrel. 2007. 168p. per. *(978-1-906210-00-7(4))* Grosvenor Hse. Publishing Ltd.
Me & Dog. 2014. (ENG., Illus.). 48p. (J). (gr. -1-3). 17.99 *(978-1-4424-9413-8(1),* Simon & Schuster Bks. For Young Readers) Simon & Schuster Bks. For Young Readers.
Meadows, Daisy. Evie Scruffypup's Big Surprise. 2016. (Magic Animal Friends Ser.: 1). (ENG., Illus.). 112p. (J). (gr. 2-5). pap. 4.99 *(978-0-545-94077-1(X),* Scholastic Paperbacks) Scholastic, Inc.
—Evie Scruffypup's Surprise. 2016. (Magic Animal Friends Ser.: 10). lib. bdg. 14.75 *(978-0-606-38800-9(1))* Turtleback Bks.
—Magic Animal Friends - Poppy Muddlepup's Daring Rescue. 2015. (Magic Animal Friends Ser.: 1). (ENG., Illus.). 176p. (J). (gr. 2-5). pap. 6.99 *(978-0-545-90750-7(0))* Scholastic, Inc.
Meadows, Michelle. Pilot Pups. Andreasen, Dan, illus. 2008. (ENG.). 32p. (J). (gr. -1-3). 17.99 *(978-1-4169-2484-5(1),* Simon & Schuster Bks. For Young Readers) Simon & Schuster Bks. For Young Readers.
—Traffic Pups. Andreasen, Dan, illus. 2011. (ENG.). 32p. (J). (gr. -1-3). 15.99 *(978-1-4169-2485-2(X),* Simon & Schuster Bks. For Young Readers) Simon & Schuster Bks. For Young Readers.
Meagher, Ed. D. Zach & His Dog: A Story of Bonding, Love, & Loss for Children & Adults to Share Together. 2009. 56p. pap. 23.99 *(978-1-4389-4228-5(1))* AuthorHouse.
Means, J. D. Millie & Honey: The Incredible, Instantaneous, Interplanetary Adventure - Volume Ii - Appleopolis. 2012. 112p. pap. 12.95 *(978-1-4575-1394-7(3))* Dog Ear Publishing, LLC.
Meckley, Phyllis. Free Puppies. 2008. 56p. pap. 12.95 *(978-1-4327-2947-9(0))* Outskirts Pr., Inc.
Meddaugh, Susan. Canine Comics: Six Daring Doggie Adventures. (Martha Speaks Ser.). (ENG., Illus.). 112p. (J). (gr. 1-4). 2014. pap. 5.99 *(978-0-544-22056-0(0),* HMH Books For Young Readers) 2013. 9.99 *(978-0-547-86784-7(0))* Houghton Mifflin Harcourt Publishing Co.
—Detective Dog. 2013. (Martha Speaks Ser.). (ENG., Illus.). 96p. (J). (gr. 1-4). pap. 5.99 *(978-0-547-77512-8(1))* Houghton Mifflin Harcourt Publishing Co.
—Farm Dog Martha (Martha, la Perra Pastora) 2016. (Martha Speaks Ser.). (ENG., Illus.). 24p. (J). (gr. -1-3). 3.99 *(978-0-544-64107-5(8),* HMH Books For Young Readers) Houghton Mifflin Harcourt Publishing Co.
—Fireworks for All. 2011. (Martha Speaks Ser.). (Illus.). 24p. (J). (gr. -1-3). (ENG.). pap. 3.99 *(978-0-547-42892-5(8));* (SPA & ENG., pap. 3.99 *(978-0-547-55620-8(9))* Houghton Mifflin Harcourt Publishing Co.
—Fireworks for All/Fuegos Artificiales para Todos. 2011. (Martha Speaks Ser.). (ENG., Illus.). 24p. (J). (gr. -1-3). 12.99 *(978-0-547-42897-0(9))* Houghton Mifflin Harcourt Publishing Co.
—Football Fumble. 2013. (Martha Speaks Ser.). (ENG., Illus.). 24p. (J). (gr. -1-3). pap. 3.99 *(978-0-544-08902-0(2))* Houghton Mifflin Harcourt Publishing Co.
—Funny Bone Jokes & Riddles. 2013. (Martha Speaks Ser.). (ENG., Illus.). 24p. (J). (gr. -1-3). pap. 3.99 *(978-0-547-86579-9(1))* Houghton Mifflin Harcourt Publishing Co.
—Haunted House. 2010. (Martha Speaks Ser.). (ENG., Illus.). 24p. (J). (gr. -1-3). pap. 3.99 *(978-0-547-21073-5(6))* Houghton Mifflin Harcourt Publishing Co.
—Martha & Skits. 2005. (Martha Speaks Ser.). (ENG., Illus.). 32p. (J). (gr. -1-3). pap. 6.99 *(978-0-618-60917-8(2))* Houghton Mifflin Harcourt Publishing Co.
—Martha & Skits Out West. 2011. (Martha Speaks Ser.). (ENG., Illus.). 96p. (J). (gr. 1-4). pap. 5.99 *(978-0-547-21074-2(4))* Houghton Mifflin Harcourt Publishing Co.
—Martha Bakes a Cake. 2012. (Martha Speaks Ser.). (ENG., Illus.). 24p. (J). (gr. -1-3). 12.99 *(978-0-547-68102-3(X));* pap. 3.99 *(978-0-547-68113-9(5))* Houghton Mifflin Harcourt Publishing Co.
—Martha Bakes a Cake (Martha Hornea un Pastel) 2012. (Martha Speaks Ser.). (ENG & SPA., Illus.). 24p. (J). (gr. -1-3). pap. 3.99 *(978-0-547-71896-5(9))* Houghton Mifflin Harcourt Publishing Co.
—Martha Camps Out. 2011. (Martha Speaks Ser.). (ENG., Illus.). 24p. (J). (gr. -1-3). 12.99 *(978-0-547-55618-5(7));* pap. 3.99 *(978-0-547-55619-2(5))* Houghton Mifflin Harcourt Publishing Co.
—Martha Camps Out (Martha Va de Campamento) 2011. (Martha Speaks Ser.). (ENG & SPA., Illus.). 24p. (J). (gr. -1-3). pap. 3.99 *(978-0-547-55795-3(7))* Houghton Mifflin Harcourt Publishing Co.
—Martha Go, Go, Goes Green! 2013. (Martha Speaks Ser.). (ENG., Illus.). 24p. (J). (gr. -1-3). pap. 3.99 *(978-0-547-97017-2(X))* Houghton Mifflin Harcourt Publishing Co.
—Martha Habla: Conoce a Martha/Martha Speaks: Meet Martha Bilingual Reader. 2015. (Martha Speaks Ser.). (SPA & ENG., Illus.). 24p. (J). (gr. -1-3). 12.99 *(978-0-544-43508-7(7),* HMH Books For Young Readers) Houghton Mifflin Harcourt Publishing Co.
—Martha Habla: Martha, la Perra Pastora/Martha Speaks: Farm Dog Martha (Bilingual Reader) 2016. (Martha Speaks Ser.). (ENG., Illus.). 24p. (J). (gr. -1-3). 12.99 *(978-0-544-64103-7(5),* HMH Books For Young Readers) Houghton Mifflin Harcourt Publishing Co.
—Martha on the Case. 2010. (Martha Speaks Ser.). (ENG., Illus.). 112p. (J). (gr. 1-4). pap. 5.99 *(978-0-547-21055-1(8))* Houghton Mifflin Harcourt Publishing Co.
—Martha Says It with Flowers. 2010. (Martha Speaks Ser.). (ENG., Illus.). 32p. (J). (gr. -1-3). 12.99 *(978-0-547-21058-2(2))* Houghton Mifflin Harcourt Publishing Co.
—Martha Speaks: Detective Dog (Chapter Book) 2013. (Martha Speaks Ser.). (ENG., Illus.). 96p. (J). (gr. 1-4). 14.99 *(978-0-547-86021-3(8))* Houghton Mifflin Harcourt Publishing Co.
—Martha Speaks: Football Fumble (Reader) 2013. (Martha Speaks Ser.). (ENG., Illus.). 24p. (J). (gr. -1-3). 12.99 *(978-0-544-08764-4(X))* Houghton Mifflin Harcourt Publishing Co.
—Martha Speaks: Funny Bone Jokes & Riddles. 2013. (Martha Speaks Ser.). (ENG., Illus.). 24p. (J). (gr. -1-3). 12.99 *(978-0-547-86577-5(5))* Houghton Mifflin Harcourt Publishing Co.
—Martha Speaks: Haunted House (Reader) 2010. (Martha Speaks Ser.). (ENG., Illus.). 24p. (J). (gr. -1-3). 12.99 *(978-0-547-39353-7(9))* Houghton Mifflin Harcourt Publishing Co.
—Martha Speaks: Martha Go, Go, Goes Green! (Reader) 2013. (Martha Speaks Ser.). (ENG., Illus.). 24p. (J). (gr. -1-3). 12.99 *(978-0-547-99547-2(4))* Houghton Mifflin Harcourt Publishing Co.
—Martha Speaks: Martha Stinks! (Reader) 2013. (Martha Speaks Ser.). (ENG., Illus.). 24p. (J). (gr. -1-3). 12.99 *(978-0-544-09662-2(2))* Houghton Mifflin Harcourt Publishing Co.
—Martha Speaks: Martha's Nose for News (chapter Book) 2013. (Martha Speaks Ser.). (ENG., Illus.). 96p. (J). (gr. 1-4). 14.99 *(978-0-544-13567-3(9))* Houghton Mifflin Harcourt Publishing Co.
—Martha Speaks: Meet Martha (Picture Reader) 2010. (Martha Speaks Ser.). (ENG., Illus.). 24p. (J). (gr. -1-3). 12.99 *(978-0-547-36904-4(2))* Houghton Mifflin Harcourt Publishing Co.
—Martha Speaks: Secret Agent Dog (Chapter Book) 2012. (Martha Speaks Ser.). (ENG., Illus.). 96p. (J). (gr. 1-4). pap. 5.99 *(978-0-547-57660-2(9))* Houghton Mifflin Harcourt Publishing Co.
—Martha Speaks: So You Want to Be a Dog? (Chapter Book) 2013. (Martha Speaks Ser.). (ENG., Illus.). 96p. (J). (gr. 1-4). 14.99 *(978-0-547-97483-5(3))* Houghton Mifflin Harcourt Publishing Co.
—Martha Speaks: Thanksgiving Reunion (Chapter Book) 2013. (Martha Speaks Ser.). (ENG., Illus.). 96p. (J). (gr. 1-4). 14.99 *(978-0-547-86580-5(5))* Houghton Mifflin Harcourt Publishing Co.
—Martha Stinks! 2013. (Martha Speaks Ser.). (ENG., Illus.). 24p. (J). (gr. -1-3). pap. 3.99 *(978-0-544-10012-1(3))* Houghton Mifflin Harcourt Publishing Co.
—Martha Walks the Dog. 2003. (Martha Speaks Ser.). (ENG., Illus.). 32p. (J). (gr. -1-3). pap. 6.99 *(978-0-618-38005-3(1))* Houghton Mifflin Harcourt Publishing Co.
—Meet Martha. 2010. (Martha Speaks Ser.). (ENG., Illus.). 24p. (J). (gr. -1-3). pap. 3.99 *(978-0-547-21079-7(5))* Houghton Mifflin Harcourt Publishing Co.
—Nose for News. 2013. (Martha Speaks Ser.). (ENG., Illus.). 96p. (J). (gr. 1-4). pap. 5.99 *(978-0-544-08572-5(8))* Houghton Mifflin Harcourt Publishing Co.
—Perfectly Martha. (Martha Speaks Ser.). (ENG., Illus.). 32p. (J). (gr. -1-3). 2008. pap. 6.99 *(978-0-547-13732-2(X))* 2004. tchr. ed. 15.00 *(978-0-618-37857-9(X))* Houghton Mifflin Harcourt Publishing Co.
—Perritos en Invierno. 2011. (Martha Speaks Ser.).Tr. of Winter's Tail. (SPA & ENG., Illus.). 24p. (J). (gr. -1-3). pap. 3.99 *(978-0-547-59560-3(3))* Houghton Mifflin Harcourt Publishing Co.
—Pool Party. 2011. (Martha Speaks Ser.). (ENG., Illus.). 24p. (J). (gr. -1-3). pap. 3.99 *(978-0-547-43882-5(6))* Houghton Mifflin Harcourt Publishing Co.
—Puppy Dog Tales Collection. 2015. (Martha Speaks Ser.). (ENG., Illus.). 304p. (J). (gr. 1-4). pap. 8.99 *(978-0-544-34117-3(1),* HMH Books For Young Readers) Houghton Mifflin Harcourt Publishing Co.
—A Pup's Tale. 2010. (Martha Speaks Ser.). (ENG., Illus.). 96p. (J). (gr. 1-4). pap. 5.99 *(978-0-547-21077-3(9))* Houghton Mifflin Harcourt Publishing Co.
—Purrfect Friends. 2012. (Martha Speaks Ser.). (ENG., Illus.). 24p. (J). (gr. -1-3). pap. 3.99 *(978-0-547-68123-8(2))* Houghton Mifflin Harcourt Publishing Co.
—Shelter Dog Blues. 2010. (Martha Speaks Ser.). (ENG., Illus.). 112p. (J). (gr. 1-4). pap. 5.99 *(978-0-547-21050-6(7))* Houghton Mifflin Harcourt Publishing Co.
—The Show Must Go On. 2012. (Martha Speaks Ser.). (ENG., Illus.). 96p. (J). (gr. 1-4). 14.99 *(978-0-547-69145-9(9));* pap. 5.99 *(978-0-547-69147-3(5))* Houghton Mifflin Harcourt Publishing Co.
—Sniffing for Clues Collection. 2015. (Martha Speaks Ser.). (ENG., Illus.). 304p. (J). (gr. 1-4). pap. 8.99 *(978-0-544-34118-0(X),* HMH Books For Young Readers) Houghton Mifflin Harcourt Publishing Co.

C
D

—So You Want to Be a Dog? 2013. (Martha Speaks Ser.). (ENG., Illus.). 96p. (J). (gr. 1-4). pap. 5.99 (978-0-547-97018-9(8)) Houghton Mifflin Harcourt Publishing Co.

—Space Dogs. 2012. (Martha Speaks Ser.). (ENG., Illus.). 96p. (J). (gr. 1-4). 14.99 (978-0-547-68119-1(4)); pap. 5.99 (978-0-547-68118-4(6)) Houghton Mifflin Harcourt Publishing Co.

—Summer Fun, 3 bks. in 1. 2013. (Martha Speaks Ser.). (ENG., Illus.). 72p. (J). (gr. -1-3). pap. 7.99 (978-0-547-97025-7(0)) Houghton Mifflin Harcourt Publishing Co.

—Teacher's Pet. 2014. (Martha Speaks Ser.). (ENG., Illus.). 96p. (J). (gr. 1-4). pap. 5.99 (978-0-544-22797-2(2), HMH Books For Young Readers) Houghton Mifflin Harcourt Publishing Co.

—Thanksgiving Reunion. 2013. (Martha Speaks Ser.). (ENG., Illus.). 96p. (J). (gr. 1-4). pap. 5.99 (978-0-547-86581-2(3)) Houghton Mifflin Harcourt Publishing Co.

—Toy Trouble. 2010. (Martha Speaks Ser.). (ENG., Illus.). 24p. (J). (gr. -1-3). pap. 3.99 (978-0-547-21078-0(7)) Houghton Mifflin Harcourt Publishing Co.

—White House Dog. 2011. (Martha Speaks Ser.). (ENG., Illus.). 96p. (J). (gr. 1-4). 14.99 (978-0-547-39359-9(8)); pap. 5.99 (978-0-547-21076-6(0)) Houghton Mifflin Harcourt Publishing Co.

—The Witches' Supermarket. 2014. (Martha Speaks Ser.). (ENG., Illus.). 32p. (J). (gr. -1-3). pap. 4.99 (978-0-544-32358-2(0), HMH Books For Young Readers) Houghton Mifflin Harcourt Publishing Co.

Meek, Nora. Sniffing for Democracy. 2004. (J). per. (978-0-9753852-0-3(8)) PM, INK.

Meek, S. P. Surfman: The Adventures of A Coast Guard Dog. 2011. 284p. 48.95 (978-1-258-08361-8(2)) Literary Licensing, LLC.

Meisel, Paul. See Me Dig. Meisel, Paul, illus. (I Like to Read(r) Ser.). (ENG., Illus.). 24p. (J). (gr. -1-3). 2014. 6.99 (978-0-8234-3057-4(X)) 2013. 14.95 (978-0-8234-2743-7(9)) Holiday Hse., Inc.

—See Me Run. Meisel, Paul, illus. (I Like to Read(r) Ser.). (ENG., Illus.). 24p. (J). (gr. -1-2). 2012. pap. 6.99 (978-0-8234-2638-6(6)) 2011. 14.95 (978-0-8234-2349-1(2)) Holiday Hse., Inc.

Meisel, Peter. Stinky Spike & the Royal Rescue. Meisel, Paul, illus. 2017. (ENG.). 80p. (J). 9.99 (978-1-61963-883-9(5), 9781619638839, Bloomsbury USA Childrens) Bloomsbury Publishing USA.

—Stinky Spike the Pirate Dog. Meisel, Paul, illus. 2017. (ENG.). 80p. (J). 9.99 (978-1-61963-778-8(2), 9781619637788, Bloomsbury USA Childrens) Bloomsbury Publishing USA.

Meister, Cari. Scholastic Reader Level 2: Flash Forward Fairy Tales: Snow White & the Seven Dogs. Waters, Erica-Jane, illus. 2014. (Scholastic Reader Level 2 Ser.). (ENG.). 32p. (J). (gr. 1-2). pap. 3.99 (978-0-545-56569-1(3)) Scholastic, Inc.

—Tiny Goes Back to School. Davis, Rich, illus. 2014. (Tiny Ser.). (ENG.). 32p. (J). (gr. k-1). pap. 3.99 (978-0-448-48134-0(0), Penguin Young Readers) Penguin Young Readers Group.

—Tiny Goes Camping. Davis, Rich, illus. 2007. (Tiny Ser.). (ENG.). 32p. (J). (gr. k-1). mass mkt. 3.99 (978-0-14-056741-0(0), Penguin Young Readers) Penguin Young Readers Group.

—Tiny Goes to the Movies. 2016. (Penguin Young Readers Level 2 Ser.). lib. bdg. 13.55 (978-0-606-38851-1(6)) Turtleback Bks.

—Tiny on the Farm. Davis, Rich, illus. 2008. (Tiny Ser.). (ENG.). 32p. (J). (gr. -1-1). 16.99 (978-0-670-06246-1(4), Viking Books for Young Readers) Penguin Young Readers Group.

—Tiny the Birthday Dog. Davis, Rich, illus. 2013. (Tiny Ser.). (ENG.). 32p. (J). (gr. k-1). 14.99 (978-0-670-01413-2(3)); pap. 3.99 (978-0-448-46478-7(0)) Penguin Young Readers Group. (Penguin Young Readers).

—Tiny the Birthday Dog. 2013. (Penguin Young Readers Level 1 Ser.). lib. bdg. 13.55 (978-0-606-31706-1(6), Turtleback) Turtleback Bks.

Melcher, Mary, illus. Puppies Count. 2010. (J). (978-1-58865-596-7(2)) Kidsbooks, LLC.

Melinda, Luke. El perro verde (the Green Dog) 2008. (SPA.). (J). pap. 5.95 (978-1-57565-264-1(1)) Kane Press, Inc.

Melton, Lexi. Max the Superdog. 2008. 96p. pap. 15.49 (978-1-4343-8868-1(9)) AuthorHouse.

Menchen, Antonio Martinez. Fosco. (SPA.). 104p. (YA). (gr. 5-8). (978-84-204-4101-6(5), AF1750) Ediciones Alfaguara ESP. Dist: Lectorum Pubns., Inc.

Menchin, Scott. Harry Goes to Dog School. Menchin, Scott, illus. 2012. (ENG., Illus.). 32p. (J). (gr. -1-3). 16.99 (978-0-06-195801-4(8)) HarperCollins Pubs.

Mendicino, Ellen, et al. Zuko the Zany Dog. 2013. 70p. pap. 9.99 (978-0-9890288-0-6(1)) Mindstir Media.

Mercaldo, David. Little Boy Boo: The Adventures of A Yorkshire Terrier Who Thought He Was a Boy. 2009. 112p. pap. 11.99 (978-1-61579-099-9(3)) Salem Author Services.

Merello, Gwyn. La Piccola Pooch. 2003. 135p. (J). pap. 13.95 (978-0-595-29260-8(7)) iUniverse, Inc.

Merrick, Sylvia Bach. Me & My Flea Steed, Clyde, at Home on Ralph. Cerda, Edward, illus. 2011. 24p. pap. 24.95 (978-1-60813-938-5(7)) America Star Bks.

Merritt, Michael. Tack & Mame Book. 2012. 48p. pap. 20.00 (978-1-105-80829-6(7)) Lulu Pr., Inc.

Meschenmoser, Sebastian. Pug Man's 3 Wishes. 2016. (ENG., Illus.). 48p. (J). (gr. -1-3). 16.95 (978-0-7358-4261-8(2)) North-South Bks., Inc.

Meshon, Aaron. The Best Days Are Dog Days. 2016. (ENG., Illus.). 40p. (J). (-k). 16.99 (978-0-525-42817-6(8), Dial Bks) Penguin Young Readers Group.

Messervy-Norman, J. Philos. 2007. 156p. pap. 16.50 (978-1-84753-927-4(0)) Lulu Pr., Inc.

Messner, Kate. Danger in Ancient Rome. McMorris, Kelley, illus. 2015. (Ranger in Time Ser.: 2). (ENG.). 160p. (J). (gr. 2-5). pap. 5.99 (978-0-545-63917-0(4), Scholastic Pr.) Scholastic, Inc.

—Escape from the Great Earthquake. McMorris, Kelley, illus. 2017. (Ranger in Time Ser.: 6). (ENG.). 160p. (J). (gr. 2-5). pap. 5.99 **(978-0-545-90983-9(X))** Scholastic, Inc.

—Land of Fire & Ice. McMorris, Kelley, illus. 2017. (Ranger in Time Ser.: 5). (ENG.). 160p. (J). (gr. 2-5). pap. 5.99 (978-0-545-90978-5(3)) Scholastic, Inc.

—Long Road to Freedom. McMorris, Kelley, illus. 2015. (Ranger in Time Ser.: 3). (ENG.). 160p. (J). (gr. 2-5). pap. 5.99 (978-0-545-63920-0(4)) Scholastic, Inc.

—Race to the South Pole. McMorris, Kelley, illus. 2016. (Ranger in Time Ser.: 4). (ENG.). 160p. (J). (gr. 2-5). pap. 5.99 (978-0-545-63925-5(5)) Scholastic, Inc.

—Rescue on the Oregon Trail. McMorris, Kelley, illus. 2015. (Ranger in Time Ser.: 1). (ENG.). 144p. (J). (gr. 2-5). pap. 5.99 (978-0-545-63914-9(X), Scholastic Pr.) Scholastic, Inc.

Metz, Teresa L. Friends for Phoebe. 2010. 43p. pap. 24.40 (978-0-557-16884-2(8)) Lulu Pr., Inc.

Meyer, Franklyn E. Me & Caleb. Smith, Lawrence Beall, illus. 2006. (J). kivar 16.95 (978-0-9789388-0-2(1)) Hester Publishing.

—Me & Caleb Again. Liese, Charles, illus. 2006. (J). kivar 16.95 (978-0-9789388-1-9(X)) Hester Publishing.

Meyer, Kathy. Daisy & Digger. 2007. 41p. 15.95 (978-1-4243-1507-9(7)) Independent Publisher Services.

Meyers, Terri. Shih Tzu Achoo!! 2009. 24p. pap. 12.99 (978-1-4389-5696-1(7)) AuthorHouse.

Michael-Angelo Goes to School. 2012. (Illus.). 34p. pap. 9.99 (978-1-937107-10-9(8)) Morning Joy Media.

Michaels, Joanna. Call Me Charly. Specht, Jessica, illus. 2012. 92p. pap. 10.95 (978-1-61493-102-7(X)) Peppertree Pr., The.

Michiko Florence, Debbi. Dorothy & Toto. Roe, Monika, illus. 2016. (Dorothy & Toto Ser.). (ENG.). 40p. (gr. k-2). 85.28 (978-1-4795-8714-8(1)) Capstone Press of Coughlan Cos.

—Little Dog Lost. Roe, Monika, illus. 2016. (Dorothy & Toto Ser.). (ENG.). 40p. (gr. k-2). lib. bdg. 21.32 (978-1-4795-8705-6(2)) Capstone Press of Coughlan Cos.

Middendorf, Gay. The Little Girl Who Lived on the Countertop. 2011. 20p. pap. 10.99 (978-1-4634-4708-3(6)) AuthorHouse.

Middleton, Sydney Elise. Green Dog & Red Cat. 2011. 12p. 8.79 (978-1-4567-2736-9(2)) AuthorHouse.

Mignerey, Mary Buhs. If Dogs Could Talk: & Dogs Can Talk Two. 2007. 56p. per. 16.95 (978-1-4241-7675-5(1)) America Star Bks.

Mikkelsen, Jon. Storm Shelter. Lueth, Nathan, illus. 2008. (We Are Heroes Ser.). (ENG.). 40p. (gr. 2-3). lib. bdg. 23.99 (978-1-4342-0787-6(0), Keystone Bks.) Stone Arch Bks.

Miles, Ellen. Bandit. 2012. (Puppy Place Ser.: 24). lib. bdg. 14.75 (978-0-606-23923-3(5), Turtleback) Turtleback Bks.

—Bear. 2009. (J). (Puppy Place Ser.: 14). (ENG.). 80p. (gr. 2-5). 4.99 (978-0-545-08348-5(6), Scholastic Paperbacks); 75p. (978-1-60744-366-7(X)) Scholastic, Inc.

—Bear. 2009. (Puppy Place Ser.: 14). lib. bdg. 14.75 (978-0-606-04427-1(2), Turtleback) Turtleback Bks.

—Bonita. 2016. 84p. (J). **(978-1-5182-1585-8(8))** Scholastic, Inc.

—Bonita. 2016. (Puppy Place Ser.: 42). (ENG.). 96p. (J). (gr. 2-5). 14.75 (978-0-606-39143-6(6)) Turtleback Bks.

—Bonita (the Puppy Place #42) 2016. (Puppy Place Ser.: 42). (ENG.). 96p. (J). (gr. 2-5). pap. 4.99 (978-0-545-85725-3(2), Scholastic Paperbacks) Scholastic, Inc.

—Boomer (the Puppy Place #37) 2015. (Puppy Place Ser.: 37). (ENG.). 96p. (J). (gr. 2-5). pap. 4.99 (978-0-545-72644-3(1), Scholastic Paperbacks) Scholastic, Inc.

—Bubbles & Boo. 2017. (Puppy Place Ser.: 44). lib. bdg. 14.75 **(978-0-606-39729-2(9))** Turtleback Bks.

—Bubbles & Boo (the Puppy Place #44) 2017. (Puppy Place Ser.: 44). (ENG.). 96p. (J). (gr. 2-5). pap. 4.99 (978-1-338-06900-6(4), Scholastic Paperbacks) Scholastic, Inc.

—Buddy. 2007. (Puppy Place Ser.: 5). (ENG., Illus.). 96p. (J). (gr. 2-5). pap. 4.99 (978-0-439-87410-6(6)) Scholastic, Inc.

—Champ. 2016. (Puppy Place Ser.: 43). (ENG.). 96p. (J). (gr. 2-5). pap. 4.99 (978-0-545-85727-7(9), Scholastic Paperbacks) Scholastic, Inc.

—Champ. 2016. (Puppy Place Ser.: 43). (ENG.). 96p. (J). (gr. 2-5). 14.75 (978-0-606-39138-2(X)) Turtleback Bks.

—Chewy & Chica. 2010. (J). 132p. pap. (978-0-545-22697-4(X)); (ENG.). 144p. (gr. 2-5). 5.99 (978-0-545-20024-0(5), Scholastic Paperbacks) Scholastic, Inc.

—Cocoa. 2012. (Puppy Place Ser.). (ENG.). 96p. (J). (gr. 2-5). pap. 4.99 (978-0-545-34835-5(8), Scholastic Paperbacks) Scholastic, Inc.

—Cocoa. 2012. (Puppy Place Ser.: 25). lib. bdg. 14.75 (978-0-606-26760-1(3), Turtleback) Turtleback Bks.

—Cooper. 2014. (Puppy Place Ser.: 35). lib. bdg. 14.75 (978-0-606-36060-9(3)) Turtleback Bks.

—Daisy. 2015. (Puppy Place Ser.: 38). lib. bdg. 14.75 (978-0-606-37778-2(6)) Turtleback Bks.

—Daisy (the Puppy Place #38) 2015. (Puppy Place Ser.: 38). (ENG.). 96p. (J). (gr. 2-5). pap. 4.99 (978-0-545-72645-0(X), Scholastic Paperbacks) Scholastic, Inc.

—Gizmo. 2014. (Puppy Place Ser.: 33). (ENG.). 96p. (J). (gr. 2-5). pap. 4.99 (978-0-545-60380-5(3), Scholastic Paperbacks) Scholastic, Inc.

—Goldie. 2006. (Puppy Place Ser.: 1). (ENG., Illus.). 80p. (J). (gr. 2-5). 4.99 (978-0-439-79379-7(3), Scholastic Paperbacks) Scholastic, Inc.

—Gus. 2015. (Puppy Place Ser.: 39). lib. bdg. 14.75 (978-0-606-37062-2(5)) Turtleback Bks.

—Honey. 2009. 75p. (J). (978-1-60744-367-4(8)) Scholastic, Inc.

—Liberty. 2014. (Puppy Place Ser.: 32). lib. bdg. 14.75 (978-0-606-35399-1(2)) Turtleback Bks.

—Lola. 2017. (Puppy Place Ser.: 45). lib. bdg. 14.75 **(978-0-606-40168-5(7))** Turtleback Bks.

—Lola (the Puppy Place #45) 2017. (Puppy Place Ser.: 45). (ENG.). 96p. (J). (gr. 2-5). pap. 4.99 **(978-1-338-06910-5(1)**, Scholastic Paperbacks) Scholastic, Inc.

—Lucky. 2010. (Puppy Place Ser.: 15). (ENG.). 96p. (J). (gr. 2-5). 4.99 (978-0-545-08347-8(8), Scholastic Paperbacks) Scholastic, Inc.

—Lucky. 2010. (Puppy Place Ser.: 15). lib. bdg. 14.75 (978-0-606-06868-0(6), Turtleback) Turtleback Bks.

—Maggie & Max. 2008. (Puppy Place Ser.: 10). (ENG.). 96p. (J). (gr. 2-5). 4.99 (978-0-545-03456-2(6), Scholastic Paperbacks) Scholastic, Inc.

—Mocha. 2013. (Puppy Place Ser.). (ENG.). 96p. (J). (gr. 2-5). pap. 4.99 (978-0-545-46240-2(1), Scholastic Paperbacks) Scholastic, Inc.

—Mocha. 2013. (Puppy Place Ser.: 29). lib. bdg. 14.75 (978-0-606-32384-0(8), Turtleback) Turtleback Bks.

—Molly. 2013. (Puppy Place Ser.: 31). lib. bdg. 14.75 (978-0-606-32385-7(6), Turtleback) Turtleback Bks.

—Nala. 2016. 89p. (J). **(978-1-4844-8019-9(8))** Scholastic, Inc.

—Nala. 2016. (Puppy Place Ser.: 41). 89p. (J). lib. bdg. 14.75 (978-0-606-38786-6(2)) Turtleback Bks.

—Nala (the Puppy Place #41) 2016. (Puppy Place Ser.: 41). (ENG.). 96p. (J). (gr. 2-5). pap. 4.99 (978-0-545-85723-9(6), Scholastic Paperbacks) Scholastic, Inc.

—Noodle. 2008. 88p. (J). (978-1-60744-364-3(3)) Scholastic, Inc.

—Oscar. 2013. (Puppy Place Ser.). (ENG.). 96p. (J). (gr. 2-5). pap. 4.99 (978-0-545-46241-9(X), Scholastic Paperbacks) Scholastic, Inc.

—Oscar. 2013. (Puppy Place Ser.: 30). lib. bdg. 14.75 (978-0-606-32003-0(2), Turtleback) Turtleback Bks.

—Patches. 2007. (Puppy Place Ser.: 8). (ENG.). 80p. (J). (gr. 2-5). 4.99 (978-0-439-87413-7(0), Scholastic Paperbacks) Scholastic, Inc.

—Pugsley. 2008. 81p. (J). (978-0-545-09948-6(X)) Scholastic, Inc.

—The Puppy Place #31: Molly. 2013. (Puppy Place Ser.). (ENG.). 96p. (J). (gr. 2-5). pap. 4.99 (978-0-545-46242-6(8), Scholastic Paperbacks) Scholastic, Inc.

—The Puppy Place #34: Zipper. 2014. (Puppy Place Ser.: 34). (ENG.). 96p. (J). (gr. 2-5). pap. 4.99 (978-0-545-60381-2(1), Scholastic Paperbacks) Scholastic, Inc.

—The Puppy Place #35: Cooper. 2014. (Puppy Place Ser.: 35). (ENG.). 96p. (J). (gr. 2-5). pap. 4.99 (978-0-545-60382-9(X), Scholastic Paperbacks) Scholastic, Inc.

—The Puppy Place #36: Stella. 2015. (Puppy Place Ser.: 36). (ENG.). 96p. (J). (gr. 2-5). pap. 4.99 (978-0-545-72643-6(3), Scholastic Pr.) Scholastic, Inc.

—The Puppy Place #39: Gus. 2015. (Puppy Place Ser.: 39). (ENG.). 96p. (J). (gr. 2-5). pap. 4.99 (978-0-545-72646-7(8), Scholastic Paperbacks) Scholastic, Inc.

—Rascal. 2007. (Puppy Place Ser.: 4). (ENG., Illus.). 80p. (J). (gr. 2-5). pap. 4.99 (978-0-439-79382-7(3), Scholastic Paperbacks) Scholastic, Inc.

—Rocky. 2012. (Puppy Place Ser.). (ENG.). 96p. (J). (gr. 2-5). 4.99 (978-0-545-34836-2(6), Scholastic Paperbacks) Scholastic, Inc.

—Rocky. 2012. (Puppy Place Ser.: 26). lib. bdg. 14.75 (978-0-606-26185-2(0), Turtleback) Turtleback Bks.

—Shadow. 2007. (Puppy Place Ser.: 3). (ENG.). 80p. (J). (gr. 2-5). 4.99 (978-0-439-79381-0(5)) Scholastic, Inc.

—Snowball. 2006. (Puppy Place Ser.: 2). (ENG., Illus.). 80p. (J). (gr. 2-5). 4.99 (978-0-439-79380-3(7), Scholastic Paperbacks) Scholastic, Inc.

—Stella. 2015. (Puppy Place Ser.: 36). lib. bdg. 14.75 (978-0-606-36350-1(5)) Turtleback Bks.

—Sugar, Gummi & Lollipop. 2016. (Puppy Place Ser.: 4). (ENG.). 96p. (J). (gr. 2-5). pap. 4.99 (978-0-545-85720-8(1), Scholastic Paperbacks) Scholastic, Inc.

—Sugar, Gummi, & Lollipop. 2016. 89p. (J). **(978-1-5182-0885-0(1))** Scholastic, Inc.

—Sugar, Gummi, & Lollipop. 2016. (Puppy Place Ser.: 40). (ENG.). 96p. (J). (gr. 2-5). lib. bdg. 14.75 (978-0-606-38079-9(5)) Turtleback Bks.

—Teddy. 2013. (Puppy Place Ser.). (ENG.). 96p. (J). (gr. 2-5). pap. 4.99 (978-0-545-46239-6(8), Scholastic Paperbacks) Scholastic, Inc.

—Teddy. 2013. (Puppy Place Ser.: 28). lib. bdg. 14.75 (978-0-606-31529-6(2), Turtleback) Turtleback Bks.

—Zipper. 2014. (Puppy Place Ser.: 34). lib. bdg. 14.75 (978-0-606-36059-3(X)) Turtleback Bks.

Milgrim, David. Moo Dog. Milgrim, David, illus. 2016. (Scholastic Reader, Level 1 Ser.). (ENG., Illus.). 32p. (J). (gr. -1-1). pap. 3.99 (978-0-545-82503-0(2)) Scholastic, Inc.

—My Friend Lucky. Milgrim, David, illus. 2017. (Ready-To-Reads Ser.). (ENG., Illus.). 32p. (J). (gr. -1-k). pap. 3.99 **(978-1-4814-8901-0(1)**, Simon Spotlight) Simon Spotlight.

Milgrim, David. My Friend Lucky: A Love Story. Milgrim, David, illus. 2010. (ENG., Illus.). 32p. (J). (gr. -1-2). 13.99 (978-1-4424-2937-6(2), Atheneum Bks. for Young Readers) Simon & Schuster Children's Publishing.

Militzer, Jill. Kizzy's Castle. 2005. 35p. 13.24 (978-1-4116-5538-6(9)) Lulu Pr., Inc.

Miller, Barbara Anne. The Adventures of Emily-Faith. 2012. (ENG.). pap. 10.95 (978-1-4675-1181-0(1)) Independent Pub.

Miller, Jay. Opal, Herby, & Squeaky. 2008. 44p. pap. 18.99 (978-1-4389-1808-2(9)) AuthorHouse.

Miller, Paula. One-Eyed Jack. Forrest, Chris, illus. (J). 2007. (ENG.). 133p. (gr. 2-7). pap. 8.95 (978-0-9769417-0-5(8)) 2006. 144p. 13.95 (978-0-9718348-8-0(1)) Blooming Tree Pr.

Miller, Scott. Prairie Whispers. 2006. 99p. pap. 16.95 (978-1-4241-4790-8(5)) PublishAmerica, Inc.

Miller, Sibley. A Horse's Best Friend. Chang, Tara Larsen & Gershman, Jo, illus. 2011. (Wind Dancers Ser.: 9). (ENG.). 80p. (J). (gr. 1-4). pap. 6.99 (978-0-312-60542-1(0), 9780312605421) Feiwel & Friends.

Mills, Claudia. Basketball Disasters. Francis, Guy, illus. 2013. (Mason Dixon Ser.). (ENG.). 176p. (J). (gr. 2-5). pap. 6.99 (978-0-375-87276-1(0), Yearling) Random Hse. Children's Bks.

—Pet Disasters. Francis, Guy, illus. 2012. (Mason Dixon Ser.). (ENG.). 176p. (J). (gr. 4-7). 6.99 (978-0-375-87274-7(4), Yearling) Random Hse. Children's Bks.

Mills, Enos A. Stories of Scotch. l.t. ed. 2006. (Illus.). 43p. pap. 9.50 (978-1-928878-36-0(9)) Temporal Mechanical Pr.

Minarik, Else Holmelund. Cat & Dog. Siebel, Fritz, illus. 2017. (My First I Can Read Ser.). 40p. (J). (gr. -1-3). 9.99 (978-0-06-265174-7(9)) HarperCollins Pubs.

—Cat & Dog. Langdo, Bryan, illus. 2005. (My First I Can Read Ser.). (ENG.). 32p. (J). (gr. -1 — 1). 16.99 (978-0-06-074247-8(X)) HarperCollins Pubs.

Miner, Audrey. Rebbie. 2006. pap. 10.00 (978-1-4257-2710-9(7)) Xlibris Corp.

Mini Cuentos: Hazanas de Baltazar, Pipo, el Perro Fiel.Tr. of Mini Faiy Tales: Pipo, the Loyal Dog. (SPA.). (J). (gr. k-4). 4.98 (978-970-607-622-9(0)) Larousse, Ediciones, S. A. de C. V. MEX. Dist: Continental Bk. Co., Inc.

Miracle, Joan. Tia's Shoes. 2013. 28p. pap. 9.95 (978-1-4787-2603-6(2)) Outskirts Pr., Inc.

Miranda, Edward. A Ribbon for Diego. Bohart, Lisa, illus. 2008. 28p. pap. 12.95 (978-0-9821654-5-4(5)) Peppertree Pr., The.

Miranda, Twyla T. The Beagles' Tale: A Longfeather Ponds Adventure, 1 vol. 2010. 82p. pap. 19.95 (978-1-4512-1547-2(9)) America Star Bks.

The Misadventures of Wags & Freckles. (J). 4.00 (978-1-56230-043-2(1)) Syndistar, Inc.

The Missing Puppy. 2006. (Bella & Rosie Set 3 Ser.). (J). 7.67 (978-1-932570-56-4(X)) Pioneer Valley Bks.

Mitchell, Derrick Lee & Howard, Assuanta. Miyah & Koala's First Day. Mitchell, Derrick Lee, illus. 2012. (Illus.). 30p. 18.00 (978-1-934947-69-2(5)) Asta Publications, LLC.

Mitchell, Gwendolyn. For the Love of Sapphire: The Promise. May, Sandy, illus. 2008. 27p. pap. 24.95 (978-1-60813-029-0(0)) America Star Bks.

Mitchell, Lee Ann. Milo the Mighty Protector. 2010. 32p. pap. 12.99 (978-1-4490-5447-2(1)) AuthorHouse.

Mitchell, Melanie, illus. Good Morning, Good Night! A Touch & Feel Bedtime Book. 2006. 12p. (J). (gr. -1-k). 12.95 (978-1-58117-461-8(6), Intervisual/Piggy Toes) Bendon, Inc.

Mitchell, Sharon Kay, VIII. What Great Thing Can Patches Do? l.t. ed. 2005. (Illus.). 40p. (J). 12.95 (978-0-9772222-0-9(9)) KOBZ.

Mitchell, Stan R. Oskar & Myer at the Lake. 2013. 24p. pap. 24.95 (978-1-63000-414-9(6)) America Star Bks.

—Oskar Wins the Race. 2013. 28p. pap. 24.95 (978-1-63000-407-1(3)) America Star Bks.

Mitchell, Taylor. Blue Bell. 2012. 28p. pap. 15.99 (978-1-4797-0292-3(7)) Xlibris Corp.

Mittendorf, Adam And Alex. Beth the Tracker. 2012. 40p. pap. 20.99 (978-1-4772-7021-9(3)) AuthorHouse.

Mo, Grandma. Liberty the Lion Hearted. 2011. 28p. pap. 15.99 (978-1-4628-6317-4(5)) Xlibris Corp.

Mobley, Cyn. A Very Airey Christmas. 2004. pap. 16.00 (978-0-9724136-0-2(X)) Greyhound Bks.

Modica, Cathy & Van Eyck, Laura. Niik & Bling: The Friendship Begins. Modica, Cathy, photos by. l.t. ed. 2005. (Illus.). 40p. (J). 19.95 (978-0-9762466-0-2(0)) Wholesome Puppy Tales.

Molloy, Sheila. Jack - King of the Dogs. Steed, Tobias, ed. Molloy, Michael, illus. 2004. (Jack Ser.: 1). (ENG.). 100p. (J). (gr. 4-7). pap. 9.99 (978-1-904872-30-6(1), Can of Worms Kids Pr.) Can of Worms Pr. GBR. Dist: Independent Pubs. Group.

Molski, Carol. Swimming Sal. DePalma, Mary Newell, illus. 2009. 36p. (J). (gr. -1-3). 17.00 (978-0-8028-5327-1(7), Eerdmans Bks For Young Readers) Eerdmans, William B. Publishing Co.

Moncure, Jane Belk. Mr. Doodle Had a Poodle: A Book about Fun Activities. Regan, Dana, illus. 2013. (Magic Castle Readers Ser.). (ENG.). 32p. (J). (gr. -1-2). 25.64 (978-1-62323-574-1(X), 206310) Child's World, Inc., The.

—Polka-Dot Puppy: A Just-for-Fun Book. Regan, Dana, illus. 2013. (Magic Castle Readers Ser.). (ENG.). 32p. (J). (gr. -1-2). 25.64 (978-1-62323-575-8(8), 206311) Child's World, Inc., The.

Monninger, Joseph. Whippoorwill. (ENG.). 288p. (YA). (gr. 7). 2016. pap. 9.99 (978-0-544-81356-4(1)) 2015. 17.99 (978-0-544-53123-9(X)) Houghton Mifflin Harcourt Publishing Co. (HMH Books For Young Readers).

Monroe, Chris, illus. Cookie, the Walker. 2013. (ENG.). 32p. (J). (gr. -1-2). lib. bdg. 16.95 (978-0-7613-5617-2(7), Carolrhoda Bks.) Lerner Publishing Group.

Montardre, Hélène. The Cat & the Dog. 2003. (Illus.). 8p. (J). bds. 7.95 (978-1-58728-483-0(9), Two-Can Publishing) T&N Children's Publishing.

Montgomery, R. A. Lost Dog! 2011. (Dragonlarks Ser.). (Illus.). 80p. (J). (gr. k-3). pap. 7.99 (978-1-933390-00-0(X)) Chooseco LLC.

—Return to Haunted House. 2010. (Illus.). 80p. (J). pap. 7.99 (978-1-933390-40-6(9)) Chooseco LLC.

Montparker, Carol. Polly & the Piano. 2004. (ENG., Illus.). 40p. pap. 19.95 (978-1-57467-093-6(X), 157467093X, Amadeus Press) Leonard, Hal Corp.

Moore, Ashley L. The Story of Princess K. 2012. 20p. pap. 24.95 (978-1-4626-6800-7(3)) America Star Bks.

Moore, Judith. Jessica the Furry Baroo. Brown, Karen, illus. 2007. 44p. per. 14.95 (978-1-59858-364-9(6)) Dog Ear Publishing, LLC.

Moore, Stephen. Skin & Bone. mass mkt. 8.99 (978-0-340-70455-4(1)) Hodder & Stoughton GBR. Dist: Trafalgar Square Publishing.

Moore, Suzi. Whoops! Ayto, Russell, illus. 2016. (ENG.). 32p. (J). (gr. -1-2). 16.99 (978-0-7636-8180-7(6), Templar) Candlewick Pr.

Moore, Thomas. Zoe & the Back Yard Boys: The Magic Garden Haunted House Adventure. 2012. 24p. pap. 17.99 (978-1-4772-9086-6(9)) AuthorHouse.

More Gordon, Domenica. Archie. More Gordon, Domenica, illus. 2012. (ENG., Illus.). 48p. (J). (gr. -1-1). 18.89 (978-1-59990-947-9(2), 9781599909479, Bloomsbury USA Childrens) Bloomsbury Publishing USA.

More Trouble. 2006. (Bella & Rosie Set 3 Ser.). (J). 7.67 (978-1-932570-58-8(6)) Pioneer Valley Bks.

Moree, Ronda. The Story of Squeaks: Princess Baby Meets Squeaks. 2011. 24p. pap. 12.74 (978-1-4567-5279-8(0)) AuthorHouse.

Morgan, Clay. The Boy Who Returned from the Sea. 2009. (ENG.). 256p. (J). (gr. 3-7). pap. 7.99 (978-0-14-241395-1(X), Puffin Books) Penguin Young Readers Group.

—The Boy Who Spoke Dog. 2005. (ENG.). 176p. (J). (gr. 3-7). 5.99 (978-0-14-240343-3(1), Puffin Books) Penguin Young Readers Group.

Morgan, Gloria. Dream Me Home. 2012. 294p. pap. 13.50 (978-1-84426-661-6(3), Fastprint Publishing) Upfront Publishing Ltd. GBR. Dist: Printondemand-worldwide.com.

Morgan, Kristy. The Adventures of Rocky & Skeeter: Rocky Goes to Jail. 2011. 52p. pap. 8.95 (978-1-4620-2219-9(7)) iUniverse, Inc.

Morgan, Margaret. Wuffy the Wonder Dog. Knight, Vanessa, illus. 2005. 60p. (J). per. 9.95 *(978-1-59594-034-6(0),* Wingspan Pr.) WingSpan Publishing.

Morgan-McCray, Sheila. Untied Shoes. 2008. 28p. pap. 9.95 *(978-1-4327-1093-4(1))* Outskirts Pr., Inc.

Morin, Kimberly. A Pup Is Born, 1 vol. 2010. 18p. 24.95 *(978-1-4489-5977-8(2))* PublishAmerica, Inc.

Morpurgo, Michael. Conker. Brown, Petra, illus. 2016. (Reading Ladder Ser.). (ENG.). 48p. (J). (gr. k-2). pap. 7.99 *(978-1-4052-8254-3(1))* Egmont Bks., Ltd. GBR. Dist: Independent Pubs. Group.

—It's a Dog's Life. Allibone, Judith & Benson, Patrick, illus. 2010. 32p. (J). *(978-1-4052-1336-3(1))* Egmont Bks., Ltd.

—Shadow. 2012. (ENG.). 192p. (J). (gr. 5-9). 16.99 *(978-0-312-60659-6(1),* 9780312606596) Feiwel & Friends.

—Shadow. 2014. (ENG.). 208p. (J). (gr. 5-9). pap. 6.99 *(978-1-250-03996-5(7),* 9781250039965) Square Fish.

Morris, Dawn. Concorde the Beautiful Flying Collie. 2012. 32p. pap. 21.99 *(978-1-4691-8098-4(7))* Xlibris Corp.

Morris, Garvin. Dump Dog. Morris, Garvin, illus. (Illus.). (J). 2008. 32p. pap. 6.95 *(978-1-60108-022-6(0))* 2007. 40p. (gr. -1-2). 15.95 *(978-1-60108-012-7(3))* Red Cygnet Pr.

Morris, Kyle. Watching the Puppy Grow. 2017. (Text Connections Guided Close Reading Ser.). (J). (gr. 1). *(978-1-4900-1805-8(0))* Benchmark Education Co.

Morris, Lolita. Mike & Me-Sh. 2012. 24p. pap. 14.93 *(978-1-4669-6169-2(4))* Trafford Publishing.

Morrison, Janet Love. Radar the Rescue Dog. 2013. 40p. pap. *(978-1-4602-2575-2(9))* FriesenPress.

Morrison, Kenny. Sevenlives & the Woof Pack. 2011. (Illus.). 104p. pap. 13.32 *(978-1-4567-8595-6(8))* AuthorHouse.

Morrison, Kevin. Frank Is a Chihuahua. De La Cruz, Erin Harris, illus. 2007. 32p. (J). (gr. 1-4). *(978-1-929039-43-2(3))* Ambassador Bks., Inc.

Morrison, Nancy. Tock the Clock, 1 vol. 2010. 38p. pap. 24.95 *(978-1-4489-2603-9(3))* PublishAmerica, Inc.

Mortensen, Carl. Flea & Gang & the Tube Dogs. Mortensen, Carl, illus. 2009. (Illus.). 16p. pap. 11.95 *(978-1-4251-8657-9(2))* Trafford Publishing.

Mortensen, Lori. Cowpoke Clyde & Dirty Dawg. Austin, Michael Allen, illus. 2013. (ENG.). 32p. (J). (gr. -1-3). 16.99 *(978-0-547-23993-4(9))* Houghton Mifflin Harcourt Publishing Co.

—Cowpoke Clyde Rides the Range. Austin, Michael Allen, illus. 2016. (ENG.). 32p. (J). (gr. -1-3). 16.99 *(978-0-544-37030-2(9))* Houghton Mifflin Harcourt Publishing Co.

Morton, E. D. Frasier: Help Me! I Just Do Not Understand! 2012. 28p. pap. 21.99 *(978-1-4691-5056-7(5))* Xlibris Corp.

Moscovich, Rotem, et al. Curious George Snowy Day. 2007. (Curious George Ser.). (ENG., Illus.). 24p. (J). (gr. -1-3). 3.99 *(978-0-618-80043-8(3))* Houghton Mifflin Harcourt Publishing Co.

Moses, Will. Raining Cats & Dogs: A Collection of Irresistible Idioms & Illustrations to Tickle the Funny Bones. Moses, Will, illus. 2008. (ENG., Illus.). 40p. (J). (gr. k-3). 17.99 *(978-0-399-24233-5(3),* Philomel Bks.) Penguin Young Readers Group.

Moss, Miriam. Wiley & Jasper. Bucker, Jutta, tr. Bucker, Jutta, illus. 2003. (J). 25p. pap. *(978-1-59336-061-0(4));* 32p. 15.95 *(978-1-59336-060-3(6))* Mondo Publishing.

Moss, Patricia Crocker. Dillie & the Baby Deer. 2011. (J). 44p. 27.99 *(978-1-4568-4999-3(9));* 48p. pap. 17.49 *(978-1-4568-4998-6(0))* Xlibris Corp.

Mowat, Farley. The Dog Who Wouldn't Be. (J). 21.95 *(978-0-89190-819-7(6))* Amereon Ltd.

Moyer, Anna B. Her Name Is Sophi. 2013. 28p. pap. 16.09 *(978-1-4669-7275-9(0))* Trafford Publishing.

Muir, Sally. Patch's Grand Dog Show. Osborne, Joanna, illus. 2016. (ENG.). 32p. (J). (gr. -1-1). 12.99 *(978-1-84365-298-4(6),* Pavilion) Pavilion Bks. GBR. Dist: Independent Pubs. Group.

Müller, Hildegard. The Cowboy. Müller, Hildegard, illus. 2015. (I Like to Read(r) Ser.). (ENG., Illus.). 24p. (J). (gr. -1-3). 6.99 *(978-0-8234-3316-2(1))* Holiday Hse., Inc.

Munsell, Jill. What a Day for a Parade. 2010. 48p. pap. 19.95 *(978-1-4389-9080-4(4))* AuthorHouse.

Murphy, Gold Rush Dog, 1 vol. 2014. (Dog Chronicles Ser.). (ENG., Illus.). 160p. (J). (gr. 2-5). 12.95 *(978-1-56145-769-4(8))* Peachtree Pubs.

Murphy, Nancy K. Rv Adventures by Sweetie, Miss Bell, Pierce & Sadie: By Sweetie Miss Bell, Pierce & Sad. 2011. 50p. pap. 15.99 *(978-1-4653-4158-7(7))* Xlibris Corp.

Murphy, Peg. I Can Do Anything. l.t. ed. 2006. (ENG., Illus.). 28p. per. 9.95 *(978-1-4327-0175-8(4))* Outskirts Pr., Inc.

Murray, Alison. Hickory Dickory Dog. Murray, Alison, illus. 2014. (ENG., Illus.). 32p. (J). (-k). 16.99 *(978-0-7636-6826-6(5))* Candlewick Pr.

—The House That Zack Built. Murray, Alison, illus. 2016. (ENG., Illus.). 32p. (J). (-k). 16.99 *(978-0-7636-7844-9(9))* Candlewick Pr.

—One Two That's My Shoe! Murray, Alison, illus. 2012. (ENG., Illus.). 32p. (J). (gr. -1-1). 16.99 *(978-1-4231-4329-1(9))* Hyperion Pr.

Murray, Pamela. Pirates of Texas. 2012. 28p. (-18). pap. 24.95 *(978-1-4626-9996-4(0))* America Star Bks.

Musacchia, Sofia Rose. A Dog's Tail Will Not Wag. 2009. 20p. pap. 12.50 *(978-1-4490-0745-4(7))* AuthorHouse.

Musick, Stacy. Waiting for Wings, Angel's Journey from Shelter Dog to Therapy Dog. Cotton, Sue Lynn, illus. 2012. 32p. 21.95 *(978-1-61493-055-6(4));* pap. 12.95 *(978-1-61493-054-9(6))* Peppertree Pr., The.

Mustaine Hettinger, Cynthia. Penelope, the Busy Hen. Ramsey, Jayne, illus. 2004. (Electra's Acres Ser.: Bk. 3). 32p. (J). per. 14.95 *(978-0-9746330-4-6(6))* Anton Berkshire Publishing.

Muszynski, Julie. Henley on Safari. 2012. (ENG., Illus.). 48p. (J). (gr. -1-12). 20.00 *(978-0-9832702-3-2(6))* Glitterati, Inc.

My Dog & Other Stories, 6 Packs. (Story Steps Ser.). (gr. k-2). 48.00 *(978-0-7635-9833-4(X))* Rigby Education.

My Dog Rusty, 6 Packs. (gr. -1-2). 27.00 *(978-0-7635-9464-0(4))* Rigby Education.

My Super-Spy Diary. 2014. (Eliza Boom Ser.: 2). (ENG., Illus.). 128p. (J). (gr. 1-4). pap. 5.99 *(978-1-4814-0652-9(3),* Aladdin) Simon & Schuster Children's Publishing.

My Two Dogs. 2013. (My Two Dogs Ser.). (ENG.). 32p. (gr. 1-3). pap. 23.80 *(978-1-4342-9042-7(5));* pap. 23.80 *(978-1-4342-6119-9(0))* Stone Arch Bks.

My Way Sally: Evaluation Guide. 2006. (J). *(978-1-55942-418-9(4))* Witcher Productions.

Mycek-Wodecki, Anna. The Bilingual Dog. Abt, Diana, tr. Mycek-Wodecki, Anna, illus. 2008. (Minutka Ser.). (SPA & ENG., Illus.). 48p. (J). (gr. -1-k). 9.95 *(978-1-84059-509-3(4))* Milet Publishing.

—The Bilingual Dog. 2007. (Minutka Ser.). (POL & ENG., Illus.). 48p. (J). (gr. -1-k). pap. 9.95 *(978-1-84059-504-8(3))* Milet Publishing.

—The Bilingual Dog/Iki Dilli Kopek. Erdogan, Fatih, tr. Mycek-Wodecki, Anna, illus. 2008. (Minutka Ser.). (TUR & ENG., Illus.). 48p. (J). (gr. -1-k). 9.95 *(978-1-84059-510-9(8))* Milet Publishing.

—Minutka: The Bilingual Dog & Friends. Mycek-Wodecki, Anna, illus. 2009. (Minutka Ser.). (Illus.). 48p. (J). (gr. k — 1). (POL & ENG.). 9.95 *(978-1-84059-523-9(X));* (SPA & ENG.). 9.95 *(978-1-84059-527-7(2))* Milet Publishing.

Myers, Nancy. Tad's Story. 2010. 95p. pap. 9.99 *(978-0-557-60737-2(X))* Lulu Pr., Inc.

Myers, Tim J. The Furry-Legged Teapot, 0 vols. 2013. (ENG.). 32p. (J). (gr. k-3). pap. 9.99 *(978-1-4778-1026-2(9),* 9781477810262, Amazon Children's Publishing) Amazon Publishing.

Myhan, Esther. A Boy & His Dog. 2012. 28p. pap. 19.99 *(978-1-4772-3720-5(8))* AuthorHouse.

The Mystery of the Missing Dog, 6 vols. (Woodland Mysteriestm Ser.). 133p. (gr. 3-7). 42.50 *(978-0-7802-7930-8(1))* Wright Group/McGraw-Hill.

Naas, Katy Newton. Missing Max. 2017. (ENG.). 36p. (J). pap. 8.99 *(978-1-68350-088-9(1))* Morgan James Publishing.

Nadja. Perro Azul. (SPA.). 40p. *(978-84-95150-30-1(1));* *(978-84-95150-40-0(9))* Corimbo, Editorial S.L.

A name for a Dog: Individual Title Six-Packs. (gr. 1-2). 25.00 *(978-0-7635-9127-4(0))* Rigby Education.

Nanette. Sunny the Orange Puppy. 2004. (Life on Granny's Farm Ser.). (J). 12.95 *(978-0-9741269-6-8(9))* St. Bernard Publishing, LLC.

Nanny & I Meet Odie. 2006. (J). lib. bdg. 18.99 *(978-0-9724394-1-1(2))* Sylables.

Nara, Yoshitomo. The Lonesome Puppy. 2008. (ENG., Illus.). 40p. (J). (gr. -1-17). 17.99 *(978-0-8118-5640-9(2))* Chronicle Bks. LLC.

Narr, Rachel. Fuzzy Wishey Dandelion. 2011. 36p. 16.99 *(978-1-4567-1963-0(7))* AuthorHouse.

Nash, Margaret. Dog's New Coat. 2011. (Tadpoles Ser.). (ENG., Illus.). 24p. (J). (gr. k-2). lib. bdg. *(978-0-7787-0576-5(5));* pap. *(978-0-7787-0587-1(0))* Crabtree Publishing Co.

Nason, Seldon E. The Adventures of Otis & Amigo, Book Two - the President's Request. 2016. (ENG., Illus.). 46p. (J). pap. 11.95 *(978-1-5069-0207-4(3))* First Edition Design eBook Publishing.

Naylor, Phyllis Reynolds. Shiloh. 144p. (J). (Shiloh Ser.: No. 1). (gr. 4-7). pap. 4.99 *(978-0-8072-8330-1(4));*No. 1. 2004. (gr. 3-7). pap. 29.00 incl. audio *(978-0-8072-8329-5(0),* YA164SP) Random Hse. Audio Publishing Group. (Listening Library).

—A Shiloh Christmas. 2015. (Shiloh Quartet Ser.). (ENG., Illus.). 256p. (J). (gr. 3-7). 17.99 *(978-1-4814-4151-3(5))* Simon & Schuster Children's Publishing.

—The Shiloh Collection: Shiloh; Saving Shiloh; Shiloh Season; Shiloh Christmas. 2016. (Shiloh Quartet Ser.: 6). (ENG., Illus.). 688p. (J). (gr. 3-7). pap. 31.99 *(978-1-4814-8677-4(2),* Atheneum/Caitlyn Dlouhy Books) Simon & Schuster Children's Publishing.

—Shiloh Season. unabr. ed. 2004. (Shiloh Ser.: No. 2). 120p. (J). (gr. 3-7). pap. 29.00 incl. audio *(978-0-8072-8707-1(5),* YA242SP, Listening Library) Random Hse. Audio Publishing Group.

Neal, Michael. Bonnie's Rescue: A Courageous Critters« Series Book. 2009. 56p. pap. 8.95 *(978-1-4401-1237-9(1))* iUniverse, Inc.

Neeck, Alessa. Bella Bunhead. 2013. 34p. pap. 9.99 *(978-0-9894402-0-2(6))* Bella & Bruno Bks.

Nefflen, Marjorie E. Bashful the Brown-Eyed Dog Gets a Home. 2013. 34p. 24.95 *(978-1-63004-199-1(8));* 36p. pap. 24.95 *(978-1-4626-9881-3(6))* America Star Bks.

Neftzger, Amy. All That the Dog Ever Wanted. 2005. (Illus.). 32p. (J). lib. bdg. 21.99 *(978-0-9746296-1-2(8),* FOG104) Fields of Gold Publishing, Inc.

Neighbors, Jolene. Nobody's Dog. 2010. 107p. pap. 14.95 *(978-1-4327-5957-5(4))* Outskirts Pr., Inc.

Neilson, G. E. F. Cosmic Aviators - Book 1 - Flight Edition. 2013. 288p. pap. *(978-0-9576132-5-6(3))* Buzzword Pr.

Neimark, Susie. The Adventures of Sunny & the Chocolate Dog: Sunny & the Chocolate Dog Go to the Beach. Hammerstrom, Kent, illus. 2003. per. *(978-0-9725945-1-6(5))* Sunny & The Chocolate Dog, LLC.

—The Adventures of Sunny & the Chocolate Dog: Sunny & the Chocolate Dog Go to the Doctor. Hammerstrom, Kent, illus. 2003. per. *(978-0-9725945-2-3(3))* Sunny & The Chocolate Dog, LLC.

—The Adventures of Sunny & the Chocolate Dog: Sunny Meets Her Baby Sister. Hammerstrom, Kent, illus. 2003. per. *(978-0-9725945-0-9(7))* Sunny & The Chocolate Dog, LLC.

Nelson, Gail M. & Nelson, Katie M. Go Eat, Pete. Nelson, Gail M., illus. 2013. (Illus.). 32p. pap. 9.99 *(978-1-936499-05-2(3))* Jewel Publishing LLC.

Nelson, Kathy Harvey. Ev: The Perfect Little Puppy. 2011. 36p. pap. *(978-1-4269-7292-8(X))* Trafford Publishing (UK) Ltd.

Nelson, Marilyn. Snook Alone. Ering, Timothy Basil, illus. (ENG.). 48p. (J). (gr. -1-3). 2012. pap. 7.99 *(978-0-7636-6120-5(1))* 2010. 16.99 *(978-0-7636-2667-9(8))* Candlewick Pr.

Nelson-Schmidt, Michelle. Dogs, Dogs! Nelson-Schmidt, Michelle, illus. 2011. (ENG., Illus.). 32p. (J). pap. 5.99 *(978-1-61067-041-8(8))* Kane Miller.

Nesbit, Edith. Pussy & Doggy Tales. 2011. 106p. 22.95 *(978-1-4638-9856-4(8));* pap. 9.95 *(978-1-4638-0127-4(0))* Rodgers, Alan Bks.

Nettrour, Nelani A. All about Krammer: Dogtails 2. Nettrour, Heather, illus. 2005. 100p. pap. 11.95 *(978-1-932657-30-2(4))* Third Millennium Pubns.

Nevels, Lourene. A Dog's Life. 2011. (Illus.). 52p. pap. 19.95 *(978-1-4575-0538-6(X))* Dog Ear Publishing, LLC.

Nevis, Lance. Animal Rain. Laible MBA, Steve William, ed. Piper, Tom, illus. 2012. 36p. pap. 10.99 *(978-0-9850142-7-8(X))* Kodel Group, LLC, The.

Newberry, Peggy. Margie & the Goat. 2010. 24p. pap. 15.99 *(978-1-4500-7475-9(8))* Xlibris Corp.

Newbery, Linda. A Dog Called Whatnot. 2006. (Red Bananas Ser.). (ENG., Illus.). 48p. (J). (gr. -1-3). *(978-0-7787-1094-3(7));* lib. bdg. *(978-0-7787-1078-3(5))* Crabtree Publishing Co.

—Whatnot Takes Charge. Ripper, Georgie, illus. 2006. (Red Bananas Ser.). (ENG.). 48p. (J). (gr. k-2). pap. 5.99 *(978-1-4052-1205-2(5))* Egmont Bks., Ltd. GBR. Dist: Independent Pubs. Group.

Newell, Jeff. Skimper-Scamper. Hranilovich, Barbara, illus. 2005. (Green Light Readers Level 2 Ser.). (J). (gr. k-2). 11.60 *(978-0-7569-5244-0(1))* Perfection Learning Corp.

Newland, Laura. Nicky Boy, I Love You. 2009. 24p. pap. 14.99 *(978-1-4389-2210-2(8))* AuthorHouse.

Newman, Lesléa. Dogs, Dogs, Dogs! Oller, Erika, illus. 2011. (ENG.). 30p. (J). (gr. -1-3). pap. 16.99 *(978-1-4424-5228-2(5),* Simon & Schuster Bks. For Young Readers) Simon & Schuster Bks. For Young Readers.

—Hachiko Waits. Kodaira, Machiyo, illus. 2008. (ENG.). 96p. (J). (gr. 3-5). pap. 7.99 *(978-0-312-55806-2(6),* 9780312558062) Square Fish.

Newton, June. The Kingdom of the Doberman. 2004. 120p. 23.45 *(978-1-4184-4992-6(X))* AuthorHouse.

Nez, John. One Smart Cookie. Nez, John, illus. 2006. (ENG., Illus.). 32p. (J). (gr. k-3). lib. bdg. 16.99 *(978-0-8075-6099-0(5))* Whitman, Albert & Co.

Nichols, Earline. Through the Eyes of Casey. 2012. 32p. pap. 21.99 *(978-1-4797-1403-2(8))* Xlibris Corp.

Nick, Papa. Never Ending Stories. 2011. 44p. pap. 24.95 *(978-1-4626-3792-8(2))* America Star Bks.

Nickel, Scott. Dognapped! Jimmy Sniffles. Harpster, Steve, illus. 2006. (Graphic Sparks Ser.). (ENG.). 40p. (gr. 1-3). per. 5.95 *(978-1-59889-226-0(6),* Graphic Sparks) Stone Arch Bks.

—Jimmy Sniffles Dognapped! 2007. (J). (gr. 3-5). 21.52 incl. audio compact disk *(978-1-4342-0379-3(4));* 31.92 incl. cd-rom *(978-1-4342-0372-4(7))* Stone Arch Bks.

—Monster Trouble. Fentz, Mike, illus. 2004. (Scholastic Reader Ser.). 22p. (J). pap. *(978-0-439-66977-1(4))* Scholastic, Inc.

Nickelodeon. PAW Patrol: Pawsome Teamwork. 2016. (ENG.). 12p. (J). (gr. -1-k). bds. 9.99 *(978-0-7944-3759-6(1))* Studio Fun International.

—PAW Patrol: the Night Before Christmas. 2016. (ENG.). 10p. (J). (gr. -1-k). bds. 8.99 *(978-0-7944-3800-5(8),* Reader's Digest Children's Bks.) Studio Fun International.

Nicklaus, Terry. Schweppe. 2012. 24p. pap. 15.99 *(978-1-4771-4565-4(6))* Xlibris Corp.

Nielsen, Jon. Laney Gets Her Ridge. 2011. 32p. pap. 17.99 *(978-1-4567-3618-7(3))* AuthorHouse.

Niles, Kim. Muggles' New Home. 2010. 27p. 16.95 *(978-0-578-06335-5(2))* KiniArt Publishing.

Nix, Garth. Frogkisser! 2017. (ENG.). 384p. (J). (gr. 7). 18.99 *(978-1-338-05208-4(X),* Scholastic Pr.) Scholastic, Inc.

Nixon, Tom, illus. Sled Dog Wisdom: Humorous & Heartwarming Tales from Alaska's Mushers. 2006. (ENG.). 64p. 4.95 *(978-0-9745014-5-1(X))* Epicenter Pr., Inc.

Nobel, Zack. The Twisted Teenage Mysteries. 2009. 48p. pap. 17.49 *(978-1-4389-1127-4(0))* AuthorHouse.

Nodset, Joan L. Go Away, Dog. Meisel, Paul, illus. 2003. (My First I Can Read Ser.). (ENG.). 32p. (J). (gr. -1-3). pap. 3.99 *(978-0-06-444231-2(4))* HarperCollins Pubs.

—Go Away, Dog. Meisel, Paul, illus. 2003. (My First I Can Read Ser.). 32p. (J). (gr. -1-k). lib. bdg. 13.55 *(978-0-613-13602-0(0),* Turtleback) Turtleback Bks.

Noel, Pamela. Same Ol' Moon: The little things of life & Love. 2010. 191p. pap. 13.95 *(978-1-4327-6132-5(3))* Outskirts Pr., Inc.

Nolan, Lucy. Bad to the Bone, 0 vols. Reed, Mike, illus. 2011. (Down Girl & Sit Ser.: 3). (ENG.). 64p. (J). (gr. 1-4). pap. 9.99 *(978-0-7614-5834-0(4),* 9780761458340, Amazon Children's Publishing) Amazon Publishing.

—Home on the Range, 0 vols. Reed, Mike, illus. 2010. (Down Girl & Sit Ser.: 4). (ENG.). 64p. (J). (gr. 1-4). 14.99 *(978-0-7614-5649-0(X),* 9780761456490, Amazon Children's Publishing) Amazon Publishing.

—On the Road, 0 vols. Reed, Mike, illus. unabr. ed. 2009. (Down Girl & Sit Ser.: 2). (ENG.). 68p. (J). (gr. 1-4). pap. 9.99 *(978-0-7614-5572-1(8),* 9780761455721, Amazon Children's Publishing) Amazon Publishing.

—Smarter Than Squirrels, 0 vols. Reed, Mike, illus. unabr. ed. 2009. (Down Girl & Sit Ser.: 1). (ENG.). 68p. (J). (gr. 1-4). pap. 9.99 *(978-0-7614-5571-4(X),* 9780761455714, Amazon Children's Publishing) Amazon Publishing.

Nolan, M. L. Hello Dollie. 2008. 32p. pap. 16.00 *(978-1-4389-2428-1(3))* AuthorHouse.

Nolan, Tina. Honey the Unwanted Puppy. Rentta, Sharon, illus. 2008. 96p. (J). (gr. 1-5). 3.99 *(978-1-58148-649-6(3),* Good Bks.) Skyhorse Publishing Co., Inc.

—The Unwanted Puppy. Chernyshova, Anna, illus. 2016. (Animal Rescue Center Ser.). (ENG.). 96p. (J). (gr. 1-3). pap. 4.99 *(978-1-58925-492-3(9))* Tiger Tales.

Nolen, Jerdine. Max & Jax Plant a Garden. Schmidt, Katen, illus. Date not set. (J). 14.00 *(978-0-15-201672-2(4),* Silver Whistle) Harcourt Children's Bks. CAN. Dist: Harcourt Trade Pubs.

Nordling, Lee. BirdCatDog. Bosch, Meritxell, illus. 2014. (J). lib. bdg. 25.32 *(978-1-4677-4522-2(7),* Graphic Universe™) Lerner Publishing Group.

—BirdCatDog. 2014. (ENG.). 32p. pap. 6.95 *(978-1-4677-4523-9(5))* Lerner Publishing Group.

Norfolk, Bobby & Norfolk, Sherry. Billy Brown & the Belly Button Beastie. Hoffmire, Baird, illus. 2007. (Buried Treasure Ser.). (ENG.). 32p. (J). (gr. -1-3). 16.95 *(978-0-87483-831-2(2))* August Hse. Pubs., Inc.

Norman, Kim. Puddle Pug. Yamaguchi, Keika, illus. 2014. (ENG.). 40p. (J). (gr. -1). 14.95 *(978-1-4549-0436-6(4))* Sterling Publishing Co., Inc.

Normandin, Jeri. Nicole's Adventures in Her Wheelchair. 2013. 20p. pap. 24.95 *(978-1-62709-683-6(3))* America Star Bks.

North, Ryan. Adventure Time, Vol. 2. Paroline, Shelli & Lamb, Braden, illus. 2013. (Adventure Time Ser.: 1). (ENG.). 128p. (J). (gr. 4). 34.99 *(978-1-60886-321-1(2))* Boom! Studios.

—Adventure Time Vol. 2. Paroline, Shelli & Lamb, Braden, illus. 2013. (Adventure Time Ser.). (ENG.). 112p. (J). (gr. 4). pap. 14.99 *(978-1-60886-323-5(9))* Boom! Studios.

—Adventure Time Vol. 3. Paroline, Shelli & Lamb, Braden, illus. 2013. (Adventure Time Ser.). (ENG.). 112p. (J). (gr. 4). pap. 14.99 *(978-1-60886-317-4(4))* Boom! Studios.

North, Ryan & Lamb, Branden. Adventure Time, Vol. 1. Paroline, Shelli, illus. 2012. (Adventure Time Ser.). (ENG.). 128p. (J). (gr. 4). pap. 14.99 *(978-1-60886-280-1(1))* Boom! Studios.

North, Sherry. Champ's Story: Dogs Get Cancer Too!, 1 vol. Rietz, Kathleen, illus. 2010. (ENG.). 32p. (J). (gr. -1-4). 16.95 *(978-1-60718-077-7(4));* pap. 8.95 *(978-1-60718-088-3(X))* Arbordale Publishing.

—La Historia de Campeona: ¡a Los Perros También les Da Cáncer!, 1 vol. Rietz, Kathleen, illus. 2010. (SPA & ENG.). 32p. (J). (gr. -1-4). 17.95 *(978-1-60718-681-6(0))* Arbordale Publishing.

Northrop, Michael. Rotten. 2013. (ENG.). 256p. (J). (gr. 7). 17.99 *(978-0-545-49587-5(3),* Scholastic Pr.) Scholastic, Inc.

Norton, Dr J. Renae & Norton, J. Renae. A Maji & Mongo Book. 2011. 28p. pap. 19.95 *(978-1-4634-3334-5(4))* AuthorHouse.

Noto, Nick & Noto, Larissa. The Adventures of Pyrgos: Volume 1. 2011. 36p. pap. 16.39 *(978-1-4634-5250-6(0))* AuthorHouse.

Noullet, Georgette. Bed Hog, 0 vols. Slonim, David, illus. 2011. (ENG.). 24p. (J). (gr. -1-3). 12.99 *(978-0-7614-5823-4(9),* 9780761458234, Amazon Children's Publishing) Amazon Publishing.

Novesky, Amy. Mister & Lady Day: Billie Holiday & the Dog Who Loved Her. Newton, Vanessa Brantley, illus. 2013. (ENG.). 32p. (J). (gr. -1-3). 16.99 *(978-0-15-205806-7(0))* Houghton Mifflin Harcourt Publishing Co.

Nuestro perro Sam 6 Packs. Individual Title. (Literatura 2000 Ser.). (SPA.). (gr. k-1). 28.00 *(978-0-7635-1025-1(4))* Rigby Education.

Nugent, Cynthia. Francesca & the Magic Bike. 2005. 4p. (J). pap., tchr. ed. *(978-1-55192-825-8(6))* Raincoast Bk. Distribution CAN. Dist: Publishers Group West (PGW).

—Fred & Pete at the Beach, 1 vol. 2009. (ENG., Illus.). 32p. (J). (gr. -1-3). 19.95 *(978-1-55469-126-5(5))* Orca Bk. Pubs. USA.

Numeroff, Laura Joffe. Happy Valentine's Day, Mouse! Bond, Felicia, illus. 2009. (If You Give... Ser.). (ENG.). 24p. (J). (gr. -1-3). bds. 6.99 *(978-0-06-180432-8(0))* HarperCollins Pubs.

—If You Give a Dog a Donut. Bond, Felicia, illus. 2011. (If You Give... Ser.). 32p. (J). (gr. -1-3). 17.89 *(978-0-06-026684-4(8));* (ENG.). 17.99 *(978-0-06-026683-7(X))* HarperCollins Pubs.

—What Puppies Do Best. Munsinger, Lynn, illus. 2011. (ENG.). 32p. (J). (gr. -1-2). 14.99 *(978-0-8118-6601-9(7))* Chronicle Bks. LLC.

Nuzum, K. A. The Leanin' Dog. (ENG.). 256p. (J). (gr. 3-7). 2010. pap. 6.99 *(978-0-06-113936-9(X))* 2008. 15.99 *(978-0-06-113934-5(3))* HarperCollins Pubs.

Nye, Julie & Nye, Julie. Scout: The Secret at les Cheneaux. 2007. (Illus.). 160p. (YA). per. *(978-0-9767762-1-5(9))* Fieldstone Hill Pr.

Nygaard, Orla & Lonvig, Asbjorn. Biggi Verdens Bedste Hund. 2013. 28p. pap. *(978-87-90608-11-8(9))* Nygaard & Lonvig, Denmark.

Nyikos, Stacy. Waggers. Anegon, Tamara, illus. 2014. (ENG.). 32p. (J). (gr. -1-k). 16.95 *(978-1-62914-629-4(3),* Sky Pony Pr.) Skyhorse Publishing Co., Inc.

Oakes, Krista Ralston. Jake the Puppy & Emma the Cat. Fuhriman, Raphael Scott, illus. 2012. 36p. (J). 19.99 *(978-0-9838321-2-6(9))* Higher Ground Pr.

O'Brien, Annemarie. Lara's Gift. 2014. (ENG.). 208p. (J). (gr. 5). 7.99 *(978-0-307-93175-7(7),* Yearling) Random Hse. Children's Bks.

O'Brien, Jack. The Return of Silver Chief. (J). 21.95 *(978-0-89190-398-7(4))* Amereon Ltd.

—Silver Chief's Revenge. Wiese, Kurt, illus. 2011. 222p. 44.95 *(978-1-258-09709-7(5))* Literary Licensing, LLC.

O'Connor, Barbara. How to Steal a Dog. 2009. (ENG.). 192p. (J). (gr. 3-7). pap. 6.99 *(978-0-312-56112-3(1),* 9780312561123) Square Fish.

—The Small Adventure of Popeye & Elvis. 2011. (ENG.). 176p. (J). (gr. 3-7). pap. 7.99 *(978-0-312-65932-5(6),* 9780312659325) Square Fish.

—Wish. 2016. (ENG.). 240p. (J). 16.99 *(978-0-374-30273-3(1),* 9780374302733, Farrar, Straus & Giroux (BYR)) Farrar, Straus & Giroux.

O'Connor, Jane. Fancy Nancy & the Posh Puppy. Glasser, Robin Preiss, illus. (Fancy Nancy Ser.). 32p. (J). (gr. -1-2). 2012. (ENG.). 9.99 *(978-0-06-221052-4(1))* 2007. (ENG.). 17.99 *(978-0-06-054213-9(6))* 2007. lib. bdg. 18.89 *(978-0-06-054215-3(2))* HarperCollins Pubs.

—Fancy Nancy & the Posh Puppy (Nancy la Elegante y la Perrita Popoff), 1 vol. Glasser, Robin Preiss, illus. 2011. (Fancy Nancy Ser.). (SPA & ENG.). 32p. (J). (gr. -1-3). 16.99 *(978-0-06-179961-7(0))* HarperCollins Pubs.

—Puppy Party. 2013. (Fancy Nancy Picture Bks.). (J). lib. bdg. 13.55 *(978-0-606-31788-7(0),* Turtleback) Turtleback Bks.

O'connor, Jane. Time for Puppy School. 2017. (Fancy Nancy - I Can Read! Ser.). lib. bdg. 13.55 ***(978-0-606-40059-6(1))*** Turtleback Bks.

O'Dea, Lori. Super Dog. Greenhead, Bill, illus. 2017. (Text Connections Guided Close Reading Ser.). (J). (gr. k). *(978-1-4900-1770-9(4))* Benchmark Education Co.

O'Dell, Scott. Black Star, Bright Dawn. 2008. (ENG., Illus.). 144p. (J). (gr. 5-7). pap. 6.99 *(978-0-547-05319-6(3))* Houghton Mifflin Harcourt Publishing Co.

Odgers, Darrel & Odgers, Sally. The Awful Pawful. Dawson, Janine, illus. 2007. (Jack Russell: Dog Detective Ser.: 5). 96p. (J). (gr. 1-6). pap. 4.99 *(978-1-933605-53-1(7))* Kane Miller.

—The Awful Pawful. 2006. (Illus.). 78p. (J). *(978-0-439-88021-3(1))* Scholastic, Inc.

—Cranky Paws. Dawson, Janine, illus. 2009. (Pet Vet Ser.: 1). 96p. (J). (gr. 2-6). pap. 4.99 *(978-1-935279-01-3(7))* Kane Miller.

C
D

—The Kitnapped Creature. Dawson, Janine, illus. 2008. (Jack Russell: Dog Detective Ser.: 8). 96p. (J). (gr. 2-6). pap. 4.99 *(978-1-933605-82-1(0))* Kane Miller.

—The Kitnapped Creature. 2008. (Illus.). 76p. (J). pap. *(978-0-545-03338-1(1))* Scholastic, Inc.

—The Lying Postman. 2005. (Illus.). 78p. (J). pap. *(978-0-439-88020-6(3))* Scholastic, Inc.

—The Mare's Tale. Dawson, Janine, illus. 2009. (Pet Vet Ser.: 2). 96p. (J). (gr. 2-6). pap. 4.99 *(978-1-935279-02-0(5))* Kane Miller.

—The Mugged Pug. Dawson, Janine, illus. 2007. 76p. (J). *(978-0-439-88018-3(1))* Scholastic, Inc.

—The Sausage Situation. Dawson, Janine, illus. 2007. (Jack Russell: Dog Detective Ser.: 6). 96p. (J). (gr. 1-6). pap. 4.99 *(978-1-933605-54-8(5))* Kane Miller.

—The Sausage Situation. 2006. (Jack Russell, Dog Detective Ser.: Bk. 6). (Illus.). 78p. (J). pap. *(978-0-439-92197-8(X))* Scholastic, Inc.

Odgers, Darrel & Sally. The Pup's Tale: Pet Vet Book 6. Dawson, Janine, illus. 2015. 96p. (J). pap. 4.99 *(978-1-61067-351-8(4))* Kane Miller.

Odgers, Sally & Odgers, Darrel. The Buried Biscuits. Dawson, Janine, illus. 2008. (Jack Russell: Dog Detective Ser.: 7). 96p. (J). (gr. 1-6). pap. 4.99 *(978-1-933605-77-7(4))* Kane Miller.

—Dog Den Mystery. Dawson, Janine, illus. 2006. (Jack Russell: Dog Detective Ser.: 1). 96p. (J). (gr. 1-5). pap. 4.99 *(978-1-933605-18-0(9))* Kane Miller.

—The Lying Postman. Dawson, Janine, illus. 2007. (Jack Russell: Dog Detective Ser.: 4). 96p. (J). pap. 4.99 *(978-1-933605-31-9(6))*, 05319) Kane Miller.

—The Mugged Pug. Dawson, Janine, illus. 2007. (Jack Russell: Dog Detective Ser.: 3). 96p. (J). pap. 4.99 *(978-1-933605-32-6(4))*, 05326) Kane Miller.

—The Phantom Mudder. Dawson, Janine, illus. 2006. (Jack Russell: Dog Detective Ser.: 2). 96p. (J). (gr. 1-5). pap. 4.99 *(978-1-933605-19-7(7))* Kane Miller.

O'Doherty, Orla. That's Odi! 2007. 36p. per. 21.32 *(978-1-4257-7793-7(7))* Xlibris Corp.

O'Donnel, Liam. Scout Hits the Trail. Huerta, Catherine, illus. (Pet Tales Ser.). (ENG.). 32p. (J). (gr. -1-3). 2008. 4.95 *(978-1-59249-740-9(3))* 2007. 9.95 *(978-1-59249-742-3(X))* Soundprints.

O'Donnell, Liam. Duncan: A Brave Rescue. Hynes, Robert, illus. 2004. (ENG.). 32p. (J). (gr. -1-2). 9.95 *(978-1-59249-317-3(3)*, 1B004) Soundprints.

—Ginger Leads the Way. Diefendorf, Cathy, illus. (Pet Tales Ser.). (ENG.). 32p. (J). (gr. -1-2). 2005. 2.95 *(978-1-59249-359-3(9)*, 1B024) 2005. 4.95 *(978-1-59249-358-6(0)*, 1B023) 2004. 9.95 *(978-1-59249-360-9(2)*, 1B025) Soundprints.

—Scout Hits the Trail. Huerta, Catherine, illus. 2007. (ENG.). 32p. (J). 2.95 *(978-1-59249-741-6(1))* Soundprints.

—Tracker on the Job. Hynes, Robert, illus. (Pet Tales Ser.). (ENG.). 32p. (J). (gr. -1-2). 2005. 2.95 *(978-1-59249-294-7(0)*, 1B009) 2004. 9.95 *(978-1-59249-318-0(1)*, 1B010) Soundprints.

—Tracker on the Job. Hynes, Robert, illus. 2004. (Pet Tales Ser.). (ENG.). 32p. (J). (gr. -1-2). 4.95 *(978-1-59249-293-0(2)*, 1B007) Soundprints.

—Winston in the City. (ENG., Illus.). 32p. (J). (gr. -1-2). 9.95 *(978-1-59249-449-1(8)*, 1B033) Soundprints.

—Winston in the City. Hatala, Dan, illus. 2005. (Pet Tales Ser.). (ENG.). 32p. (J). (gr. -1-2). pap. 2.95 *(978-1-59249-448-4(X)*, 1B032) Soundprints.

—Winston in the City. Hatala, Dan, illus. 2005. (Pet Tales Ser.). (ENG.). 32p. (J). (gr. -1 — 1). 4.95 *(978-1-59249-447-7(1)*, 1B031) Soundprints.

O'Donnell, Liam & O'Donnell, Laura. Duncan: A Brave Rescue. Hynes, Robert, illus. 2004. (Pet Tales Ser.). (ENG.). 32p. (J). (gr. -1-3). 4.95 *(978-1-59249-291-6(6)*, 1B001) Soundprints.

—Duncan: A Brave Rescue. Hynes, Robert, illus. 2005. (Pet Tales Ser.). (ENG.). 32p. (J). (gr. -1-2). 2.95 *(978-1-59249-292-3(4)*, 1B003) Soundprints.

Oehmichen, Ariel. Chosen Last. Du Pont, Brittany, illus. 2012. 28p. pap. 9.99 *(978-1-937165-26-0(4))* Orange Hat Publishing.

O'Hair, Margaret. My Pup, 0 vols. Lyon, Tammie, illus. 2010. (ENG.). 24p. (J). (gr. -1-2). bds. 7.99 *(978-0-7614-5644-5(9)*, 9780761456445, Amazon Children's Publishing) Amazon Publishing.

Ohanesian, Diane. The ABCs of Thanks & Please. Chamberlain, Margaret, illus. 2011. (J). *(978-0-545-37962-5(8))* Scholastic, Inc.

Oldfield, Jenny. Speckled & Sinbad. 2 bks. in 1. (Illus.). mass mkt. 11.99 *(978-0-340-70880-4(8))* Hodder & Stoughton GBR. Dist: Trafalgar Square Publishing.

Oldham, Lacy. A Dog Named Timmy, 1 vol. 2009. 52p. pap. 16.95 *(978-1-4489-1707-5(7))* PublishAmerica, Inc.

Oliveira, Luis. The DogMan 2. 2009. 60p. pap. 15.50 *(978-0-578-02385-4(7))* Desktop Prepress Services.

Oliveto, Michelle. My Dog the Faker. 2012. 24p. 24.95 *(978-1-4560-2194-8(X))* America Star Bks.

Olsen, S. R. When Dogs Dream. Showalter, Kristin, illus. 2013. 48p. pap. 13.95 *(978-0-9842560-2-0(4))* Sleepy Dog Publishing.

Olson, Regan. Penny Penelope & the Beep Factory. 2008. 36p. pap. 24.95 *(978-1-60441-169-0(4))* America Star Bks.

O'Malley, Kevin. The Perfect Dog. 2016. (ENG., Illus.). 40p. (J). (gr. -1-2). 17.99 *(978-1-101-93441-8(7)*, Crown Books For Young Readers) Random Hse. Children's Bks.

O'Neill, Catharine. Annie & Simon. O'Neill, Catharine, illus. 2008. (ENG., Illus.). 64p. (J). (gr. k-4). 15.99 *(978-0-7636-2688-4(0))* Candlewick Pr.

—Annie & Simon: The Sneeze & Other Stories. O'Neill, Catharine, illus. (Candlewick Sparks Ser.). (ENG., Illus.). 64p. (J). (gr. k-4). 2015. pap. 3.99 *(978-0-7636-7788-6(4))* 2013. 15.99 *(978-0-7636-4921-0(X))* Candlewick Pr.

—Annie & Simon: Banana Muffins & Other Stories. O'Neill, Catharine, illus. 2017. (ENG., Illus.). 64p. (J). (gr. k-3). 15.99 *(978-0-7636-7498-4(2))* Candlewick Pr.

Oneones. Happy Birthday Coco. Oneones, illus. 2006. (ENG., Illus.). 56p. (J). 9.99 *(978-1-933605-13-5(8))* Kane Miller.

Oneones (Firm) Staff, contrib. by. Happy Birthday Coco. 2006. (Illus.). (J). *(978-1-4287-0411-4(6))* Kane Miller.

Onley, Sandra. Halley the Sheepdog. 2011. (Illus.). 28p. pap. 12.50 *(978-1-61204-237-4(6)*, Strategic Bk. Publishing) Strategic Book Publishing & Rights Agency (SBPRA).

Onus, Katie. Island of the Wolves. 2012. 180p. pap. 11.99 *(978-0-9823271-7-3(X))* Adventure Bks. of Seattle.

Operation: Lost Puppy. 2003. (J). per. *(978-1-57657-825-4(9))* Paradise Pr., Inc.

Oplinger, Jon & Cooke, Elizabeth. The Wicked Small People of Whiskey Bridge. 2011. 156p. (gr. 4-6). 22.95 *(978-1-4620-4948-6(6))*; pap. 12.95 *(978-1-4620-4947-9(8))* iUniverse, Inc.

Oppel, Kenneth. The King's Taster. Johnson, Steve & Fancher, Lou, illus. 2009. 32p. (J). (gr. -1-1). (ENG.). 17.99 *(978-0-06-075372-6(2))*; lib. bdg. 18.89 *(978-0-06-075373-3(0))* HarperCollins Pubs.

Oram, Hiawyn. My Friend Fred. Reeve, Rosie, illus. 2012. (ENG.). 32p. (J). *(978-1-58925-105-2(9))* Tiger Tales.

Organ, Beryl E. Tiggy's World. 2010. 26p. pap. 15.99 *(978-1-4500-7915-0(6))* Xlibris Corp.

Ori, Anthony. Snow Makes a Snowman. 2008. 24p. pap. 24.95 *(978-1-60703-308-0(9))* America Star Bks.

Orietta, Susan. The Day Tyson Became a Hero. 2011. 24p. pap. 15.99 *(978-1-4628-6823-0(1))* Xlibris Corp.

Ormand, Kate & Louise, Kate. Pierre the French Bulldog Recycles. Straker, Bethany, illus. 2015. (ENG.). 32p. (J). (gr. -1-k). 14.99 *(978-1-63220-411-0(8)*, Sky Pony Pr.) Skyhorse Publishing Co., Inc.

Oroge, Sabinah. Oluwatofarati & Friends. 2013. 28p. pap. 9.95 *(978-1-4787-0520-8(5))* Outskirts Pr., Inc.

Orr, Wendy. Discovered! A Beagle Called Bella. Castelao, Patricia, illus. 2013. (Rainbow Street Shelter Ser.: 6). (ENG.). 128p. (J). (gr. 2-5). 15.99 *(978-0-8050-9505-0(5)*, 9780805095050, Holt, Henry & Co. Bks. For Young Readers) Holt, Henry & Co.

—Lost! - A Dog Called Bear. Boase, Susan, illus. 2011. (Rainbow Street Shelter Ser.: 1). (ENG.). 112p. (J). (gr. 2-5). pap. 5.99 *(978-0-8050-9381-0(8)*, 9780805093810, Holt, Henry & Co. Bks. For Young Readers) Holt, Henry & Co.

—Wanted! - A Guinea Pig Called Henry. Castelao, Patricia, illus. 2012. (Rainbow Street Shelter Ser.: 3). (ENG.). 128p. (J). (gr. 2-5). 15.99 *(978-0-8050-8933-2(0)*, 9780805089332, Holt, Henry & Co. Bks. For Young Readers) Holt, Henry & Co.

Orson, Claire M. My Name Is Misty: This Is My Book. 2012. 28p. pap. 19.99 *(978-1-4772-7323-4(9))* AuthorHouse.

O'Ryan, Ellie & Lewman, David. The Case of the Disappearing Dogs. 2012. (Club CSI Ser.: 3). (ENG.). 160p. (J). (gr. 3-7). 15.99 *(978-1-4424-4671-7(4))*; pap. 7.99 *(978-1-4424-3396-0(5))* Simon Spotlight. (Simon Spotlight).

Osborne, Joey N. Boxes, Boxes, Everywhere Boxes, 1 vol. 2009. 32p. pap. 24.95 *(978-1-60749-732-5(8))* America Star Bks.

Osborne, Mary Pope. Dogs in the Dead of Night. Murdocca, Sal, illus. 2013. (Magic Tree House (R) Merlin Mission Ser.: 18). (ENG.). 144p. (J). (gr. 2-5). 5.99 *(978-0-375-86796-5(1)*, Random Hse. Bks. for Young Readers) Random Hse. Children's Bks.

—Dogs in the Dead of Night. 2013. (Magic Tree House Merlin Missions Ser.: 18). lib. bdg. 16.00 *(978-0-606-31939-3(5)*, Turtleback) Turtleback Bks.

—The Mystery of the Enchanted Dog, 4 vols., Set. Murdocca, Sal, illus. 2009. (ENG.). 96p. (J). (gr. 1-4). 23.96 *(978-0-375-85811-6(3)*, Random Hse. Bks. for Young Readers) Random Hse. Children's Bks.

—Tigers at Twilight. unabr. ed. 2004. (Magic Tree House Ser.: No. 19). 72p. (J). (gr. k-3). pap. 17.00 incl. audio *(978-0-8072-0928-8(7)*, S FTR 251 SP, Listening Library) Random Hse. Audio Publishing Group.

Osborne, Mary Pope, et al. Tigres Al Anochecer. Murdocca, Sal, illus. 2008. (Casa del Arbol Ser.: 19).Tr. of Tigers at Twilight. (SPA.). (J). (gr. 2-4). pap. 5.99 *(978-1-933032-49-8(9))* Lectorum Pubns., Inc.

Osterhold, Jared, illus. OLIVIA & the Pet Project. 2015. (Olivia TV Tie-In Ser.). (ENG.). 24p. (J). (gr. -1-1). pap. 3.99 *(978-1-4814-2895-8(0)*, Simon Spotlight) Simon Spotlight.

Ostermann, Ruby. Willie Tucker & His Gramma: The Life of a Dog. l.t. ed. 2012. (Illus.). 30p. (J). pap. 16.95 *(978-1-937912-93-2(0))* Cordon Pubns.

Otitoloju/Blazing Ideas Ltd, Ololade/Adewunmi, retold by. Kunkuru Da Kare: The Tortoise & the Dog. 2008. (YOR & ENG., Illus.). 36p. 16.00 *(978-0-9801243-6-1(0))* Blazing Ideas Ltd.

Otto, Denise A. You Decide. 2012. 68p. pap. 12.95 *(978-1-4772-1247-9(7))* AuthorHouse.

Ouida. A Dog of Flanders. 2011. (Dover Children's Thrift Classics Ser.). (ENG., Illus.). 80p. (J). (gr. 3-8). reprint ed. pap. 4.00 *(978-0-486-27087-6(4))* Dover Pubns., Inc.

Our Dog Sam, 6 Pack. (Literatura 2000 Ser.). (gr. k-1). 28.00 *(978-0-7635-0036-8(4))* Rigby Education.

Owens, Bettina. Athena, Never A Bite. 2010. 32p. 18.99 *(978-1-4520-6381-2(8))* AuthorHouse.

Owens, Donna. NIBBLES: Volume 2, Nibbles Adventures. 2008. 38p. pap. 14.95 *(978-1-4357-4621-3(X))* Lulu Pr., Inc.

—NIBBLES:VOLUME 3, Nibbles enjoys the Holidays. 2008. 38p. pap. 14.95 *(978-1-4357-4715-9(1))* Lulu Pr., Inc.

—NIBBLES:Volume one, Nibbles finds a Home. 2008. 39p. pap. 14.96 *(978-1-4357-4410-3(1))* Lulu Pr., Inc.

Owens, Wanda. Sammie the Lil' Dog on the Porch. Hill, Shannon, illus. 2011. 20p. pap. 24.95 *(978-1-4560-5736-7(7))* America Star Bks.

Oz, Galia. Dog Trouble! 2017. (ENG.). 144p. (J). (gr. 3-7). 15.99 ***(978-0-399-55020-1(8)***, Crown Books For Young Readers) Random Hse. Children's Bks.

Paco Dog's When I Get Home from School! 2003. 3.99 *(978-0-915960-30-9(3))* Ebon Research Systems Publishing, LLC.

Padilla, Gerane & Sky. Penelope Potts & the Christmas Pup. 2009. 32p. pap. 16.49 *(978-1-4490-4781-8(5))* AuthorHouse.

Page, Gail. How to Be a Good Cat. 2011. (ENG., Illus.). 32p. (J). 16.99 *(978-1-59990-474-0(8)*, 9781599904740, Bloomsbury USA Childrens) Bloomsbury Publishing USA.

—How to Be a Good Cat. Page, Gail, illus. 2011. (ENG., Illus.). 32p. (J). (gr. -1-1). 17.89 *(978-1-59990-475-7(6)*, 9781599904757, Bloomsbury USA Childrens) Bloomsbury Publishing USA.

—How to Be a Good Dog. Page, Gail, illus. (ENG., Illus.). 32p. (J). (gr. -1-3). 2007. pap. 7.99 *(978-1-59990-151-0(X)*, 9781599901510) 2006. 15.95 *(978-1-58234-683-0(6)*, 9781582346830) Bloomsbury Publishing USA. (Bloomsbury USA Childrens).

Paley, Jane. Hooper Finds a Family: A Hurricane Katrina Dog's Survival Tale. 2011. (ENG.). 144p. (J). (gr. 3-7). 16.99 *(978-0-06-201103-9(0))* HarperCollins Pubs.

Pallotta, Jerry. Santa Pups. Terry, Will, illus. 2016. (ENG.). 32p. (J). (gr. -1-k). 6.99 *(978-0-545-48479-4(0))* Scholastic, Inc.

Palmer, Amy. In the Doghouse. 2004. (ENG.). 29p. 14.95 *(978-1-4137-3085-2(X))* PublishAmerica, Inc.

Palumbo, Mary Lou. Skippy the Dog in the Band. Mikle, Toby, illus. 2009. 48p. pap. 19.49 *(978-1-4389-9218-1(1))* AuthorHouse.

Pampered Pupz Secret Diary. (Bratz Secret Diary Ser.). 96p. *(978-1-4054-8744-3(5))* Parragon, Inc.

Pampered Pupz Sticker Scene. (Bratz Sticker Scene Books Ser.). 12p. pap. *(978-1-4054-8870-9(0))* Parragon, Inc.

The Paper Pup. 2004. 39p. pap. 24.95 *(978-1-4137-3012-8(4))* PublishAmerica, Inc.

Papp, Lisa. Madeline Finn & the Library Dog, 1 vol. Papp, Lisa, illus. 2016. (ENG., Illus.). 32p. (J). (gr. -1-3). 16.95 *(978-1-56145-910-0(0))* Peachtree Pubs.

Papp, Robert L., illus. The Dog-Gone Mystery. 2009. (Boxcar Children Mysteries Ser.: 119). (ENG.). 128p. (J). (gr. 1-5). pap. 5.99 *(978-0-8075-1657-7(0))*; lib. bdg. 14.99 *(978-0-8075-1658-4(9))* Whitman, Albert & Co.

Paquette, Ammi-Joan. Petey & Pru & the Hullabaloo. Ang, Joy, illus. 2013. (ENG.). 40p. (J). (gr. -1-3). 16.99 *(978-0-544-03888-2(6))* Houghton Mifflin Harcourt Publishing Co.

Parenteau, Shirley. Dolls of Hope. 2015. (ENG.). 336p. (J). (gr. 3-7). 16.99 *(978-0-7636-7752-7(3))* Candlewick Pr.

Parille, Anna. Teddy & His Magical Paw: A New Home for the Honeypies. 2010. 52p. pap. 22.99 *(978-1-4520-5711-8(7))* AuthorHouse.

Parish, Herman. Amelia Bedelia Chapter Book #2: Amelia Bedelia Unleashed (Special Edition) 2013. (ENG., Illus.). 160p. (J). *(978-0-06-227056-6(7)*, Collins Design) HarperCollins Pubs.

Parker, Amy. A Night Night Prayer, 1 vol. Pedler, Caroline, illus. 2014. (Night Night Ser.). (ENG.). 20p. (J). bds. 9.99 *(978-1-4003-2431-6(9))* Nelson, Thomas Inc.

Parker, Emma. Can Your Dog? 2010. (Illus.). pap. *(978-1-877547-96-6(4))* First Edition Ltd.

—The Naughty Puppy. 2010. (Illus.). pap. *(978-1-877547-89-8(1))* First Edition Ltd.

Parker, Jim. Howard the Flying Bloodhound. 2011. 28p. 13.59 *(978-1-4567-4106-8(3))* AuthorHouse.

Parker, Linda & Langdon, Katie. Austin & Charlie Adventures: Washington DC Adventure. 2007. 32p. (J). 14.95 *(978-0-9785473-1-8(4)*, Austin & Charlie Adventures) Paw Print Pubns.

Parker, Patty J. Little Puppy Saves the Day. 2012. 24p. (-18). pap. 17.32 *(978-1-4797-4186-1(8))* Xlibris Corp.

Parker, Vic, ed. The Dog in the Manger & Other Fables. 2014. (Aesop's Fables Ser.). 40p. (J). (gr. 2-5). pap. 84.95 *(978-1-4824-0817-1(1))* Stevens, Gareth Publishing LLLP.

Parr, Todd. Doggy Kisses 123. 2013. (ENG., Illus.). 24p. (J). (gr. -1 — 1). bds. 7.99 *(978-0-316-20737-9(3))* Little, Brown Bks. for Young Readers.

—Otto Goes to School. 2013. (Passport to Reading Level 1 Ser.). (J). lib. bdg. 14.75 *(978-0-606-31740-5(6)*, Turtleback) Turtleback Bks.

—Otto Goes to the Beach. 2014. (Passport to Reading Level 1 Ser.). (ENG., Illus.). 32p. (J). (gr. -1-1). 3.99 *(978-0-316-24602-6(6))* Little, Brown Bks. for Young Readers.

Parrish, Jim. Dog Gone. 2012. 24p. pap. 17.99 *(978-1-4685-6036-7(0))* AuthorHouse.

Parsons, Garry. Krong! Parsons, Garry, illus. 2006. (Illus.). 32p. (J). (gr. -1-3). 15.95 *(978-1-58925-061-1(3))* Tiger Tales.

Parvela, Timo. Bicycling to the Moon. Talvitie, Virpi, illus. 2016. (ENG.). 128p. (gr. k-5). 16.99 *(978-1-77657-031-7(6))*; 9.99 *(978-1-77657-078-2(2))*; 16.99 *(978-1-77657-080-5(4))*; 16.99 *(978-1-77657-091-1(X))* Gecko Pr. NZL. Dist: Lerner Publishing Group.

Paschkis, Julie, illus. The Great Smelly, Slobbery, Small-Tooth Dog: A Folktale from Great Britain. 2007. (ENG.). 32p. (J). (gr. -1-3). 16.95 *(978-0-87483-808-4(8))* August Hse. Pubs., Inc.

Passen, Lisa. Dweezil. 2016. (ENG., Illus.). 116p. (J). pap. 10.99 *(978-1-944770-24-2(0))* MLR Pr., LLC.

Patchett, Mary Elwyn. Ajax: Golden Dog of the Australian Bush. Tansley, Eric, illus. 2011. 172p. 42.95 *(978-1-258-01103-1(4))* Literary Licensing, LLC.

Patenaude, Jeremy, et al. Playful Puppy. 2014. (DK Readers Ser.). (ENG.). 32p. (J). (gr. k-4). pap. 3.99 *(978-1-4654-1999-6(3)*, DK Children) Dorling Kindersley Publishing, Inc.

Paterson, Katherine. El Clan de los Perros. 2003.Tr. of Field of the Dogs. (SPA.). 464p. (J). 7.95 *(978-84-279-3854-0(3))* Noguer y Caralt Editores, S. A. ESP. Dist: Lectorum Pubns., Inc.

Paticoff, Melanie. Sophie's Tales: Overcoming Obstacles. Vales, Chrissie, illus. 2012. 42p. 25.95 *(978-0-9851575-6-2(9))* Sophie's Tales, LLC.

Patricelli, Leslie. The Patterson Puppies & the Midnight Monster Party. Patricelli, Leslie, illus. 2010. (ENG., Illus.). 32p. (J). (gr. -1-k). 14.99 *(978-0-7636-3243-4(0))* Candlewick Pr.

—The Patterson Puppies & the Rainy Day. Patricelli, Leslie, illus. 2009. (ENG., Illus.). 40p. (J). (gr. -1-k). 14.99 *(978-0-7636-3242-7(2))* Candlewick Pr.

Patrick Book & Plush Dog. (J). *(978-1-58209-078-8(5))* Bks. Are Fun, Ltd.

Patterson, Eric. Fluffy, a Puppy with a Purpose. Mathis, Leslie, illus. 2013. 146p. pap. 6.99 *(978-1-61286-150-0(4))* Avid Readers Publishing Group.

Patterson, James & Tebbetts, Chris. Middle School: Dog's Best Friend. Tejido, Jomike, illus. 2016. (Middle School: Book 8 Ser.: 8). (ENG.). 256p. (J). (gr. 3-7). 13.99 *(978-0-316-34954-3(2)*, Jimmy Patterson) Little Brown & Co.

Patterson, Michael. The Adventures of Spot: Cody, Boozer & Aaliyah, 1 vol. 2010. 68p. pap. 19.95 *(978-1-4489-5517-6(3))* America Star Bks.

Pauba, Judy. A Tale of Two Dogs. 2006. (Illus.). 32p. (J). per. 5.95 *(978-0-9747994-1-4(6))* Julenda Enterprises.

Paul. Best Friends. 2012. 24p. pap. 17.99 *(978-1-4772-0755-0(4))* AuthorHouse.

Paul, J. D. The Little Lost Dog, 1 vol. 2010. 12p. pap. 24.95 *(978-1-4489-9251-5(6))* PublishAmerica, Inc.

Paul, Ruth. Bad Dog Flash. 2014. (ENG., Illus.). 32p. (J). (-2). 15.99 *(978-1-4926-0153-1(5)*, 9781492601531, Sourcebooks Jabberwocky) Sourcebooks, Inc.

—Go Home Flash. 2015. (ENG., Illus.). 32p. (J). (-2). 15.99 *(978-1-4926-1523-1(4)*, 9781492615231) Sourcebooks, Inc.

Paulhus, Jonathan. Chester, the Light Golden Retriever. 2013. 36p. pap. 24.95 *(978-1-63004-640-8(X))* America Star Bks.

Paulsen, Gary. Brian's Hunt. 2005. 103p. (YA). (gr. 4-8). reprint ed. 15.00 *(978-0-7567-9570-2(2))* DIANE Publishing Co.

—Brian's Hunt. 2012. (Hatchet Adventure Ser.). (ENG.). 144p. (YA). (gr. 5). pap. 9.99 *(978-0-307-92959-4(0)*, Ember) Random Hse. Children's Bks.

—Dogsong. 2007. (ENG.). 192p. (J). (gr. 5-9). pap. 7.99 *(978-1-4169-3962-7(8)*, Simon & Schuster Bks. For Young Readers) Simon & Schuster Bks. For Young Readers.

—Dogsong. 2007. (ENG.). 192p. (YA). (gr. 7). mass mkt. 7.99 *(978-1-4169-3919-1(9)*, Simon Pulse) Simon Pulse.

—Paintings from the Cave: Three Novellas. (ENG.). (YA). (gr. 7-7). 2012. 174p. pap. 8.99 *(978-0-553-49466-2(X)*, Ember) 2011. 176p. 15.99 *(978-0-385-74684-7(9)*, Lamb, Wendy Bks.) Random Hse. Children's Bks.

Paulsen, Gary & Paulsen, Jim. Field Trip. 2015. (ENG.). 128p. (J). (gr. 5). 12.99 *(978-0-553-49674-1(3)*, Lamb, Wendy Bks.) Random Hse. Children's Bks.

—Road Trip. 2014. (ENG.). 128p. (J). (gr. 5). pap. 6.99 *(978-0-307-93086-6(6)*, Yearling) Random Hse. Children's Bks.

PAW Patrol on the Roll! 2016. (Illus.). (J). ***(978-1-5182-2638-0(8))*** Random House Children's Books.

Paw Patrol, Paw. Paw Patrol: Pups Save the Day - A Slide Surprise Book. 2015. (Sliding Surprise Ser.: 4). (ENG.). 12p. (J). (gr. -1-k). bds. 10.99 *(978-0-7944-3558-5(0)*, Reader's Digest Children's Bks.) Studio Fun International.

Payne, Gaynell. I Go Exploring. Buffinet, Jacqueline, illus. 2012. 34p. 21.99 *(978-0-9884657-0-1(1))* DreamLand Mediaworks LLC.

Payne, Helen. Vacation Paws. Youngblood, Carol, illus. 2006. 50p. per. 10.00 *(978-0-9786276-6-9(0))* Mentzer Printing Ink.

Paytras, C. J. The Littlest Homeless Angel: Darby's Story. 2011. 28p. pap. 24.95 *(978-1-4560-6708-3(7))* America Star Bks.

Pea, M. J. The adventures of Benje & Sammy: Probably the naughtiest dogs in the World. 2011. (Illus.). 72p. (gr. -1). pap. 24.83 *(978-1-4567-7812-5(9))* AuthorHouse.

Pearce, Margaret. A Belinda Robinson Novel Book 2: Belinda & the Holidays It Rained. 2013. 78p. pap. *(978-1-922233-22-6(6))* Writers Exchange E-Publishing.

Pearson, Betty Jean. Learn with Ladee: A Service Dog. 2008. 30p. pap. 24.95 *(978-1-4241-9507-7(1))* America Star Bks.

Pease, J. L. Barnabas the Shaggedy, Raggedy Dog. 2005. (J). pap. 9.00 *(978-0-8059-6880-4(6))* Dorrance Publishing Co., Inc.

Pedersen, Kelly. Finding Love on Summer Hill. Pedersen, Kelly, illus. 2016. (ENG., Illus.). 38p. (J). pap. 9.95 *(978-1-63047-860-5(1))* Morgan James Publishing.

Pelton, Lisa. Logos & Adoption: Remi's Journey. 2012. 40p. pap. 14.95 *(978-1-4497-5378-8(7)*, WestBow Pr.) Author Solutions, Inc.

—Logos & Obedience: Listening to His Father's Voice. 2009. 32p. pap. 13.99 *(978-1-4389-5177-5(9))* AuthorHouse.

Pemberton, Bert. Three for Adventure. 2013. 70p. pap. *(978-1-910053-03-4(1))* Legend Pr.

Pen, Chenda. Dara Learns How to Ride a Bike! An Autism Story. 2010. 24p. pap. 14.99 *(978-1-4490-6943-8(6))* AuthorHouse.

Penberthy, Stephen. The Adventures of Bird Dog & Friends. 2009. 24p. pap. 10.99 *(978-1-4269-0977-1(2))* Trafford Publishing.

Penn, M. W. Square Bear Meets Round Hound: A Fairytale of Shapes. Firos, Daphne, illus. 2012. (ENG.). 38p. (J). pap. 11.95 *(978-0-9840425-8-6(X))* MathWord Pr., LLC.

Pepin, Rebecca. Bobby Dog & the Flying Frog. Fuller, Cari, illus. 2004. (J). (gr. 4-18). 16.99 *(978-0-9760684-0-2(0))*; pap. 11.99 *(978-0-9760684-1-9(9))* FullofPep Pubns.

Perkins, Lynne Rae. Frank & Lucky Get Schooled. Perkins, Lynne Rae, illus. 2016. (Illus.). 32p. (J). (gr. -1-3). 17.99 *(978-0-06-237345-8(5)*, Greenwillow Bks.) HarperCollins Pubs.

—Snow Music. Perkins, Lynne Rae, illus. 2003. (Illus.). 40p. (J). lib. bdg. 16.89 *(978-0-06-623958-3(3))* HarperCollins Pubs.

Perkins, Lynne Rae & Perkins, Lynne R. Snow Music. Perkins, Lynne Rae, illus. 2003. (ENG., Illus.). 40p. (J). (gr. -1-3). 16.99 *(978-0-06-623956-9(7)*, Greenwillow Bks.) HarperCollins Pubs.

Perl, Erica S. Aces Wild. (ENG.). 224p. (J). (gr. 3-7). 2015. 7.99 *(978-0-307-93173-3(0)*, Yearling) 2013. 15.99 *(978-0-307-93172-6(2)*, Knopf Bks. for Young Readers) Random Hse. Children's Bks.

—When Life Gives You O. J. (ENG.). 224p. (J). (gr. 3-7). 2013. 6.99 *(978-0-375-85902-1(0)*, Yearling) 2011. 15.99 *(978-0-375-85924-3(1)*, Knopf Bks. for Young Readers) Random Hse. Children's Bks.

Perry, Douglas M. Boomer Likes to Point. 2013. 32p. pap. 24.95 *(978-1-62709-377-4(X))* America Star Bks.

Perry, Pete. The Secret of Bedside Manor. 2009. (Illus.). 140p. pap. 36.49 *(978-1-4389-6668-7(7))* AuthorHouse.

Perry, Rex. Coco's Girls. Perry, Rex, illus. 2008. (ENG., Illus.). 36p. (YA). per. 12.95 *(978-0-9740212-1-8(0))* Cedar Grove Bks.

Perry, Tristan. Cinnamon Takes a Vacation: Furry Tails #2, 1 vol. 2009. 122p. pap. 19.95 *(978-1-60836-451-0(8))* America Star Bks.

—Furry Tails: The Adventures of Cinnamon Persimmon. 2006. (ENG.). 108p. per. 19.95 *(978-1-4241-4788-5(3))* PublishAmerica, Inc.

Peruski, Steven. My Friend & Teacher Sammie. 2006. (ENG., Illus.). (YA). 21.99 *(978-0-615-13428-4(9))* Compassion Pets Publishing.

Peschke, Marci. Cupcake Queen, 1 vol. Mourning, Tuesday, illus. 2013. (Kylie Jean Ser.). (ENG.). 112p. (gr. 2-3). 8.95

(978-1-4048-8102-0(6)); lib. bdg. 22.65 (978-1-4048-7580-7(8)) Picture Window Bks. (Kylie Jean).
Petersen, Jeffrey Lee. A Boy a Dog & a Creek. 2013. 102p. pap. (978-1-78299-794-8(6)) FeedARead.com.
Peterson, J. D. R. & Reimer, Diana. Priscilla Bailey: A Story of the Great Depression. 2009. 196p. 24.95 (978-1-4401-3929-1(6)); pap. 14.95 (978-1-4401-3927-7(X)) iUniverse, Inc.
Petit, Karen. The Mystery of the Screecher Creature: A Shandon's Ivy League Mystery. 2006. (J). per. 14.95 (978-1-59872-666-4(8)) Instant Pub.
—The Mystery of the Stolen Stallion. 2007. (Illus.). 246p. (J). per. 14.95 (978-0-9794420-4-9(4)) Red Letter Pr.
Pfister, Marcus. Snow Puppy. 2011. (ENG., Illus.). 32p. (J). (gr. -1-2). 17.95 (978-0-7358-4031-7(8)) North-South Bks., Inc.
Phanton, Richard G. Frankie. Baker, David, illus. 2012. 40p. 24.95 (978-1-4560-3509-9(6)) America Star Bks.
Phelps, Karen. The Grass Is Always Greener & Let Sleeping Dogs Lie: Two Original Fables. 2006. (J). pap. (978-1-4108-7155-8(X)) Benchmark Education Co.
Philipson, Sandra. Max's Rules. Campbell, Jenny, illus. 2004. (J). 9.95 (978-1-929821-10-5(7)) Chagrin River Publishing Co.
Philipson, Sandra J. Forever Home. Campbell, Jenny, illus. 2007. (ENG.). 89p. (J). (gr. 3-7). bds. 7.95 (978-1-59624-080-3(6)) Cleveland Clinic Pr.
—Ollie's Monsters & Other Stories. Campbell, Jenny, illus. 2010. 48p. (J). pap. 10.95 (978-1-929821-09-9(3)) Chagrin River Publishing Co.
Phillipps, J. C. Monkey Ono. 2013. (ENG., Illus.). 40p. (J). (gr. -1-k). 16.99 (978-0-670-78505-6(9)), Viking Books for Young Readers) Penguin Young Readers Group.
Phillips, Hope Ann. Buddy's Play Date Day... 2013. 26p. 24.95 (978-1-63000-574-0(6)) 2012. 28p. pap. 24.95 (978-1-4626-9936-0(7)) America Star Bks.
—Hoover's Day Out. 36p. 2013. 24.95 (978-1-4626-3509-2(1)) 2011. pap. 24.95 (978-1-4560-7493-7(8)) America Star Bks.
Phillips, Kelly. Macs the Wonder Dog. 2008. 21p. pap. 24.95 (978-1-4241-8937-3(3)) America Star Bks.
Phillips-Poovey, Lisa. Lucy Wants to Go to School. 2013. 32p. pap. 10.95 (978-1-936912-71-1(6)) Parsons Porch Bks.
Phillips, Ruby Ann. Pet Psychic. Isik, Semur, illus. 2015. (Krystal Ball Ser.). (ENG.). 112p. (gr. 2-3). lib. bdg. 25.32 (978-1-4795-5875-9(3)) Picture Window Bks.
Phillips, Vivian A. My Dog & His Bone. Date not set. (Illus.). (J). Vol. I. 15p. pap. (978-1-888413-03-8(4)) Vol. II. 14p. (978-1-888413-07-6(7)) Seasoning Quilting (Arts & Crafts).
Pichon, Liz. Bored Bill. Pichon, Liz, illus. 2006. (Illus.). 32p. (J). (gr. -1-3). 15.95 (978-1-58925-053-6(2)) Tiger Tales.
Pickell, Sammy. Doxie. Everett, J. H., illus. 2013. (ENG.). (J). 18.99 (978-0-9827972-3-5(0)) MMJ Foundation.
Pickering, Jimmy. Skelly & Femur. Pickering, Jimmy, illus. 2009. (ENG., Illus.). 32p. (J). (gr. -1-2). 12.99 (978-1-4169-7143-6(2), Simon & Schuster Bks. For Young Readers) Simon & Schuster Bks. For Young Readers.
—Skelly the Skeleton Girl. Pickering, Jimmy, illus. 2007. (ENG., Illus.). 32p. (J). (gr. -1-2). 14.99 (978-1-4169-1192-0(8), Simon & Schuster Bks. For Young Readers) Simon & Schuster Bks. For Young Readers.
Pickford, Sue. Bob & Rob. 2014. (ENG., Illus.). 32p. (J). (gr. -1-2). 17.99 (978-1-84780-343-6(1), Frances Lincoln) Quarto Publishing Group UK GBR. Dist: Hachette Bk. Group.
Picou, Lin. Do I Have To... Reese, Bob, illus. 2011. (ENG.). 24p. (J). (gr. 1-2). pap. 8.95 (978-1-61236-020-1(3)) Rourke Educational Media.
Pieniozek, Lillian & Family. Meet the Knucklepuppies. 2003. (J). 10.95 (978-0-9708959-4-3(1), Accent Pubns.) Ajoyin Publishing, Inc.
Pierce, Craig. A Greyhound's Tale: Running for Glory, Walking for Home. Santiago, Tony, illus. 2004. (J). per. 15.00 (978-0-9762564-0-3(1), American Dog) Ideate Prairie.
—A Labrador's Tale: An Eye for Heroism. Santiago, Tony, illus. 2006. 30p. (J). 15.00 (978-0-9762564-3-4(6), American Dog) Ideate Prairie.
—A Labrador's Tale 2: The Incredible Thank You Gift, 1. Santiago, Tony, illus. 2006. 34p. (J). 15.00 (978-0-9762564-1-4(4), 2500, American Dog) Ideate Prairie.
—Sit. Stay. Work. Play: All Dogs Have Their Day. Santiago, Tony, illus. 2008. 40p. (J). per. 5.95 (978-0-9762564-5-8(2)) Ideate Prairie.
Pierro, Rita. Dear God, Will You Give Me A Dog?, 1 vol. French, David, illus. 2009. 35p. pap. 19.95 (978-1-61582-589-9(4)) PublishAmerica, Inc.
—The Duck Who Couldn't Swim, 1 vol. French, David, illus. 2010. 26p. 24.95 (978-1-4489-6405-5(9)) PublishAmerica, Inc.
Pigram, John. My Dog Jack. 2009. 20p. pap. 14.64 (978-1-4269-2038-7(5)) Trafford Publishing.
Pilkey, Dav. Big Dog & Little Dog Getting in Trouble (Reader) 2015. (Green Light Readers Level 1 Ser.). (ENG., Illus.). 24p. (J). (gr. -1-3). pap. 3.99 (978-0-544-53095-9(0), HMH Books For Young Readers) Houghton Mifflin Harcourt Publishing Co.
—Big Dog & Little Dog Going for a Walk (Reader) 2015. (Green Light Readers Level 1 Ser.). (ENG., Illus.). 24p. (J). (gr. -1-3). pap. 3.99 (978-0-544-43071-6(9), HMH Books For Young Readers) Houghton Mifflin Harcourt Publishing Co.
—Big Dog & Little Dog Making a Mistake (reader) 2016. (Green Light Readers Level 1 Ser.). (ENG., Illus.). 24p. (J). (gr. -1-3). 12.99 (978-0-544-65114-2(6), HMH Books For Young Readers) Houghton Mifflin Harcourt Publishing Co.
—Big Dog & Little Dog (Reader) 2015. (Green Light Readers Level 1 Ser.). (ENG., Illus.). 24p. (J). (gr. -1-3). pap. 3.99 (978-0-544-43069-3(7), HMH Books For Young Readers) Houghton Mifflin Harcourt Publishing Co.
—Big Dog & Little Dog Wearing Sweaters (Reader) 2015. (Green Light Readers Level 1 Ser.). (ENG., Illus.). 24p. (J). (gr. -1-3). 12.99 (978-0-544-53097-3(7), HMH Books For Young Readers) Houghton Mifflin Harcourt Publishing Co.
—Dog Breath! The Horrible Trouble with Hally Tosis. 2004. (Scholastic Bookshelf Ser.). (Illus.). 32p. (gr. -1-3). 17.00 (978-0-7569-3189-6(4)) Perfection Learning Corp.
—Dog Breath! The Horrible Trouble with Hally Tosis. Pilkey, Dav, illus. 3rd ed. 2004. (Scholastic Bookshelf Ser.). (ENG., Illus.). 32p. (J). (gr. -1-3). pap. 6.99 (978-0-439-59839-2(7), Scholastic Paperbacks) Scholastic, Inc.
—Dog Man. Pilkey, Dav, illus. 2016. (Dog Man Ser.: 1). (ENG., Illus.). 240p. (J). (gr. 2). 9.99 (978-0-545-58160-8(5), Graphix) Scholastic, Inc.
—Dog Man Unleashed. 2016. (Dog Man Ser.: 2). (ENG., Illus.). 224p. (J). (gr. 2-7). 9.99 (978-0-545-93520-3(2), Graphix) Scholastic, Inc.
—Dog Man Unleashed. 2016. (Dog Man Ser.: 2). (ENG.). (J). (gr. 2). lib. bdg. 20.85 **(978-0-606-39709-4(4))**; 240p. 20.85 (978-0-606-39115-3(0)) Turtleback Bks.
—Dogzilla. Pilkey, Dav, illus. 2014. (Illus.). 32p. pap. 7.00 (978-1-61003-187-5(3)) Center for the Collaborative Classroom.
—Dogzilla. 2003. (ENG., Illus.). 32p. (J). (gr. -1-3). pap. 5.95 (978-0-15-204949-2(5)) Houghton Mifflin Harcourt Publishing Co.
—Dogzilla: Starring Flash, Rabies, Dwayne, & Introducing Leia as the Monster. 2003. 15.95 (978-0-613-71633-8(7), Turtleback) Turtleback Bks.
—The Hallo-Wiener. Pilkey, Dav, illus. 2014. (ENG., Illus.). 32p. (J). (gr. -1-k). bds. 6.99 (978-0-545-66136-2(6)) Scholastic, Inc.
—The Paperboy. 2015. 32p. pap. 7.00 (978-1-61003-556-9(9)) Center for the Collaborative Classroom.
Pilkey, Dav. A Tale of Two Kitties. 2017. (Dog Man Ser.: bk.3). (ENG., Illus.). 256p. (J). (gr. 2-5). 9.99 **(978-0-545-93521-0(0)**, Graphix) Scholastic, Inc.
—A Tale of Two Kitties. 2017. (Dog Man Ser.: 3). lib. bdg. 20.85 **(978-0-606-40547-8(X))** Turtleback Bks.
Pinfold, Levi. Black Dog. Pinfold, Levi, illus. 2012. (ENG., Illus.). 32p. (J). (gr. -1-3). 15.99 (978-0-7636-6097-0(3), Templar) Candlewick Pr.
Pingry, Patricia A. Dear Santa... Rasmussen, Wendy, illus. 2005. (ENG.). 24p. (J). (gr. -1-k). bds. 6.95 (978-0-8249-6618-8(X), Ideal Pubns.) Worthy Publishing.
Pinkwater, Daniel M. I Am the Dog. Davis, Jack E., illus. 2010. (ENG.). 32p. (J). (gr. -1-3). 16.99 (978-0-06-055505-4(X)) HarperCollins Pubs.
Pintozzi, Nick. Bentley & the Cactus Rustlers. Pintozzi, Nick & Pintozzi, Connie, illus. 2006. per. 11.00 (978-0-9749465-4-2(0)) BentDaiSha, LLC.
—Bentley & the Great Fire. Pintozzi, Nick et al, illus. 2004. 16.95 (978-0-9749465-2-8(4)) BentDaiSha, LLC.
Pippa's Pet Pest, 6 Packs. (gr. -1-2). 23.00 (978-0-7635-8794-9(X)) Rigby Education.
Pitt, Marilyn. Cat Walk. 2015. (1B Potato Chip Bks.). (ENG., Illus.). 16p. (J). pap. 5.99 (978-1-63437-055-4(4)) American Reading Co.
Pitt, Marilyn & Hileman, Jane. I Like My Stuff. Bianchi, John, illus. 2009. (1G Potato Chip Bks.). (ENG.). 12p. (J). (gr. k-1). pap. 5.99 (978-1-59301-769-9(3)) American Reading Co.
—My Babies. 2010. pap. 39.62 (978-1-61541-066-8(X)) American Reading Co.
—Where Is My Boy? Bianchi, John, illus. 2009. (1G Potato Chip Bks.). (ENG.). 12p. (J). (gr. k-1). pap. 5.99 (978-1-59301-766-8(9)) American Reading Co.
—Where Is That Dog? Bianchi, John, illus. 2009. (1G Potato Chip Bks.). (ENG.). 12p. (J). (gr. k-1). pap. 5.99 (978-1-59301-770-5(7)) American Reading Co.
Pitt, Marilyn & Sanchez, Lucia M. La Nevada: Snow Dog. Bianchi, John, illus. 2011. (poder de 50 - Libros papas fritas Ser.). (SPA.). 12p. pap. 33.92 (978-1-61541-439-0(8)) American Reading Co.
—Perro en Apuros: Let Me In. Bianchi, John, illus. 2011. (poder de 50 - Libros papas fritas Ser.). (SPA.). 12p. pap. 33.92 (978-1-61541-165-8(8)) American Reading Co.
Pitt, Marilyn & Sánchez, Lucía M. Solos en Casa. Bianchi, John, illus. 2011. (1G Libros Papas Fritas Ser.).Tr. of Home Alone. (SPA.). 12p. (J). (gr. k-1). pap. 6.99 (978-1-61541-409-3(6)) American Reading Co.
Pitt, Marilyn & Sanchez, Lucia M. La Tormenta: The Storm. Bianchi, John, illus. 2011. (poder de 50 - Libros papas fritas Ser.). (SPA.). 12p. pap. 33.92 (978-1-61541-441-3(X)) American Reading Co.
Pitt, Marilyn, et al. Perro en Apuros: Let Me In. Bianchi, John & Taylor, Trace, illus. 2010. (1G Our World Ser.). (ENG.). 24p. (J). pap. 5.99 (978-1-61541-170-2(4)) American Reading Co.
Pittman, Seth. Raggy's Island. 2010. 124p. pap. 9.95 (978-0-557-59557-0(6)) Lulu Pr., Inc.
Pitts, Constance. Chulita the Blind Cat. 2007. (Illus.). 48p. (J). (978-0-9652902-2-7(0)) Beevinwood, Inc.
Pizzoli, Greg. Number One Sam. Pizzoli, Greg, illus. 2014. (ENG., Illus.). 40p. (J). (gr. -1-k). 16.99 (978-1-4231-7111-9(X)) Hyperion Bks. for Children.
Plourde, Lynn. Maxi's Secrets: (or What You Can Learn from a Dog) (ENG.). 272p. (J). (gr. 5). 2017. 8.99 **(978-0-399-54568-9(9)**, Puffin Books) 2016. 16.99 (978-0-399-54567-2(0), Nancy Paulsen Books) Penguin Young Readers Group.
Pogo the Clown. Along Little Dogie: Harley's Great Adventures. Miller, Richard, illus. 2005. (J). 12.95 (978-0-9755253-3-6(6)) Chiliric Pubns.
Polan, Alex. Cracking the Magikarp Code. 2016. (Unofficial Adventures for Pokemon GO Players Ser.: 4). lib. bdg. 18.40 **(978-0-606-39656-1(X))** Turtleback Bks.
Polden, Kelly Carper. Puppy Tales: The Adventures of Adam the Australian Sheppard. 2007. (ENG.). 72p. pap. 11.99 (978-1-4196-7458-7(7)) CreateSpace Independent Publishing Platform.
Politi, Leo. Emmet. 2009. (ENG., Illus.). 32p. 16.95 (978-0-89236-992-8(2)) Oxford Univ. Pr., Inc.
Pollard, Tara. Season's Christmas Quest: The Dog's Story. 2012. 138p. (gr. 1-1). 21.95 (978-1-4759-4008-4(4)); pap. 11.95 (978-1-4759-4009-1(2)) iUniverse, Inc.
Poole, Cheryl J. A. Farmer & Me! Making Silage. 2012. (Illus.). 24p. pap. 19.82 (978-1-4772-2360-4(6)) AuthorHouse.
—Farmer & Me! Milking the Cows. 2012. (Illus.). 24p. (-18). pap. 19.82 (978-1-4772-3947-6(2)) AuthorHouse.
Pope, Mildred. But I Don't Wanna Take a Bath! A Mike & Tyke Series. 2011. 36p. (gr. -1). 15.95 (978-1-4567-3939-3(5)) AuthorHouse.
Poploff, Michelle. Where Triplets Go, Trouble Follows. Jamieson, Victoria, illus. 2015. (ENG.). 96p. (J). (gr. 2-6). 16.95 (978-0-8234-3289-9(0)) Holiday Hse., Inc.
Port, Cynthia. Kibble Talk. Port, Cynthia, illus. 2013. (Illus.). 214p. pap. 9.99 (978-0-9912278-0-8(8)) Port, Cynthia L.
Porter, Gary. Duffy: The Tale of a Terrier. 2011. (Illus.). 256p. (J). 22.95 (978-1-59298-369-8(3)) Beaver's Pond Pr., Inc.
Porter, Harry. Dylan's Tale. Hedrick, Mandy, illus. 2011. 52p. pap. 10.99 (978-0-9828346-1-9(6)) 4RV Publishing, LLC.
Porter, Pamela. The Crazy Man, 1 vol. 2006. (ENG.). 176p. (J). (gr. 3-7). pap. 8.95 (978-0-88899-695-4(0)) Groundwood Bks. CAN. Dist: Publishers Group West (PGW).
—The Crazy Man. 2013. 164p. pap. (978-1-4596-6446-3(9)) ReadHowYouWant.com, Ltd.
Posner-Sanchez, Andrea. Teacup to the Rescue! (Disney Princess: Palace Pets) RH Disney Staff & DiCicco, Sue, illus. 2015. (Little Golden Book Ser.). (ENG.). 24p. (J). (-k). 4.99 (978-0-7364-3364-8(3), Golden/Disney) Random Hse. Children's Bks.
Posner-Sanchez, Andrea, illus. Dog Days. 2016. 22p. (J). **(978-1-5182-3229-9(9))** Random Hse., Inc.
Post, Grace. Three Dogs Go Walking. Mogyorosi, Nicole, illus. 2009. 32p. pap. 24.95 (978-1-61546-147-9(7)) America Star Bks.
Postgate, Daniel. Love Stinks. 2012. (J). (978-1-61913-132-3(3)) Weigl Pubs., Inc.
Potter-Kotecki, Kerry. I'm a Doggie Detective. 2008. (J). pap. 10.00 (978-0-9792371-7-1(3), Moo Pr.) Keene Publishing.
Pounders, Louis. Frank, an Architect's Dog. 2015. (Illus.). 28p. (J). (gr. 1-12). bds. 15.00 (978-0-692-33113-2(1)) Pounders Publishing.
Powell, Christine. Bootsie's Underground Adventure. 2012. 28p. pap. 24.95 (978-1-4626-7449-7(6)) America Star Bks.
Powell, Jillian. Oh, Jet! 2011. (Tadpoles Ser.). (ENG., Illus.). 24p. (J). (gr. k-2). lib. bdg. (978-0-7787-0582-6(X)); pap. (978-0-7787-0593-2(5)) Crabtree Publishing Co.
Powell, Richard. Puppy's Tail. Davis, Carolina A., illus. 2003. (Animal Tails Ser.). 12p. (J). 3.95 (978-1-58925-674-3(3)) Tiger Tales.
Powell-Tuck, Maudie. The Messy Book. Smythe, Richard, illus. 2016. (ENG.). 32p. (J). (gr. -1-2). 16.99 (978-1-68010-037-2(8)) Tiger Tales.
Powers-Fish, Amy Rose. Buddy's Forever Home. l.t. ed. 2006. (Illus.). 41p. (J). (gr. -1-3). per. 11.99 (978-1-59879-192-1(3)) Lifevest Publishing, Inc.
Powers, Nelda Means & Terrell, Caitlyn. Puddle Puppy Goes to the Farm. 2012. 32p. pap. (978-1-77067-628-2(7)) FriesenPress.
Pranai. Daisy & Friends. 2013. (Illus.). 48p. (gr. 2-4). pap. 13.66 (978-1-4817-8270-8(3)) AuthorHouse.
Presnall, Judith Janda. Yukon: Sled Dog, 0 vols. Elliot, Mark, illus. 2013. (ENG.). 32p. (J). (gr. 1-8). 17.99 (978-1-4778-1731-5(X), 9781477817315, Amazon Children's Publishing) Amazon Publishing.
Press Out Sticker: Paulette the Pinkest Puppy in the World. 2015. (ENG.). 36p. (J). (gr. -1-7). pap. (978-1-78393-780-6(7)) Make Believe Ideas.
Preston-Gannon, Frann. Hot Dog, Cold Dog. 2014. (ENG., Illus.). 20p. (J). (gr. -1-2). bds. 12.95 (978-1-57687-679-4(9), powerHouse Bks.) powerHouse Cultural Entertainment, Inc.
Price, David. Sly the Fox & Advice from la Princessa Roja. 2008. (Illus.). 34p. (J). 14.95 (978-0-9779701-2-4(4)) Wishingstone Publishing.
Price, Justine. The Dreams of a Puppy. 2013. 28p. pap. 24.95 (978-1-63000-049-3(3)) America Star Bks.
Price, Margaret. Chillipop. 2009. 196p. pap. 18.95 (978-1-4490-0958-6(1)) AuthorHouse.
Price, Mathew. Cachorro. Goldman, Judy, tr. Kemp, Moira, illus. 2010. (SPA & ENG.). 10p. bds. 5.99 (978-1-935021-64-3(8)) Price, Mathew Ltd.
Price, Roger & Stern, Leonard, creators. Adventure Time Mad Libs. 2012. (Adventure Time Ser.). (ENG.). 48p. (J). (gr. 3-7). 4.99 (978-0-8431-7221-8(5), Mad Libs) Penguin Young Readers Group.
Price, Tom, illus. Champion Sleeper. 2008. 32p. (J). pap. 9.95 (978-0-9748226-1-7(2)) Murphy's Bone Publishing.
Priceman, Marjorie. How to Make a Cherry Pie & See the U. S. A. Priceman, Marjorie, illus. 2013. (ENG., Illus.). 40p. (J). (gr. k-3). 7.99 (978-0-385-75293-0(8), Dragonfly Bks.) Random Hse. Children's Bks.
Priddy, Roger. Happy Birthday: A Touch-and-Feel Book. 2014. (Little Friends Ser.). (ENG.). 10p. (J). (gr. -1 — 1). bds. 6.99 (978-0-312-51680-2(0), 9780312516802, Priddy Bks.) St. Martin's Pr.
—Little Friends: Big Adventure. 2015. (Little Friends Ser.). (ENG., Illus.). 12p. (J). (gr. -1 — 1). bds. 14.99 (978-0-312-51869-1(2), 9780312518691, Priddy Bks.) St. Martin's Pr.
—Puppy. 2015. (Animal Buddies Ser.). (ENG., Illus.). 8p. (J). (gr. -1 — 1). bds. 5.99 (978-0-312-51867-7(6), 9780312518677, Priddy Bks.) St. Martin's Pr.
Prince, Cheryl. Belle's Wild Journey. 2012. 24p. pap. 24.95 (978-1-4626-9794-6(1)) America Star Bks.
Prince-Stokes, Cathy. The Story of Peabo, 1 vol. Edsall, Steven, illus. 2009. 35p. pap. 24.95 (978-1-61582-732-9(3)) America Star Bks.
Pringle, Cindy & Pringle, Kirby. Happy Tails: Earl & Pearl on the Farm. l.t. ed. 2006. (ENG., Illus.). 32p. (J). (gr. k-2). (978-0-9777126-0-1(5)) Dogtown Artworks.
Prins, Piet. The Flying Phantom. 2006. (Illus.). 142p. (J). pap. (978-1-894666-45-9(3)) Inheritance Pubns.
—The Haunted Castle. 2006. (Illus.). 139p. (J). pap. (978-1-894666-44-2(5)) Inheritance Pubns.
—The Mystery of the Abandoned Mill. Kramer, Jaap, illus. 2006. 127p. (J). pap. (978-1-894666-48-0(8)) Inheritance Pubns.
—The Sailing Sleuths. Kramer, Jaap, illus. 2006. 137p. (J). pap. (978-1-894666-46-6(1)) Inheritance Pubns.
—Scout's Distant Journey. 2006. (Illus.). 141p. (J). pap. (978-1-894666-49-7(6)) Inheritance Pubns.
—The Search for Sheltie. Kramer, Jaap, illus. 2006. 137p. (J). pap. (978-1-894666-43-5(7)) Inheritance Pubns.
—The Treasure of Rodensteyn Castle. Kramer, Jaap, illus. 2006. 132p. (J). pap. (978-1-894666-47-3(X)) Inheritance Pubns.
Printers, Caxton. Rufus & Friends. 2012. (ENG.). pap. (978-1-4675-4752-9(2)); pap. (978-1-4675-4751-2(4)) Independent Pub.
Prisant, Guillermo Murray. Que Miedo! rev. ed. 2006. (Castillo del Terror Ser.). (SPA & ENG.). 112p. (J). (gr. 6-9). pap. 6.95 (978-970-20-0338-0(5)) Castillo, Ediciones, S. A. de C. V. MEX. Dist: Macmillan.
Pritchett, Andy. Stick! 2013. (ENG., Illus.). 32p. (J). (gr. -1-2). 15.99 (978-0-7636-6616-3(5)) Candlewick Pr.
Prochovnic, Dawn Babb. Silly Sue: Sign Language for Actions, 1 vol. Bauer, Stephanie, illus. 2009. (Story Time with Signs & Rhymes Ser.). (ENG.). 32p. (gr. -1-3). 28.50 (978-1-60270-672-9(7), Looking Glass Library) ABDO Publishing Co.
Proimos, James, Jr. Apocalypse Meow Meow. Proimos, James, Jr., illus. 2015. (ENG., Illus.). 224p. (J). (gr. 3-6). 13.99 (978-1-61963-472-5(4), 9781619634725, Bloomsbury USA Childrens) Bloomsbury Publishing USA.
Proimos, James, III & Proimos, James, Jr. Apocalypse Bow Wow. Proimos, James, III & Proimos, James, Jr., illus. (ENG., Illus.). 224p. (J). 2016. pap. 7.99 (978-1-68119-088-4(5), 9781681190884) 2015. (gr. 3-6). 13.99 (978-1-61963-442-8(2), 9781619634428) Bloomsbury Publishing USA. (Bloomsbury USA Childrens).
Prokopowicz, Linda. Rocky the Reading Dog. 2013. 26p. 14.99 (978-1-937165-59-8(0)); pap. 9.99 (978-1-937165-58-1(2)) Orange Hat Publishing.
Provensen, Alice. A Day in the Life of Murphy. Provensen, Alice, illus. unabr. rev. ed. 2005. (Illus.). (J). (gr. -1-2). 28.95 incl. audio compact disk (978-1-59519-538-8(6)) Live Oak Media.
—A Day in the Life of Murphy. Provensen, Alice, illus. 2003. (ENG., Illus.). 40p. (J). (gr. -1-3). 17.99 (978-0-689-84884-1(6), Simon & Schuster Bks. For Young Readers) Simon & Schuster Bks. For Young Readers.
—A Day in the Life of Murphy. Provensen, Alice, illus. 2006. (ENG., Illus.). 40p. (J). (gr. -1-3). reprint ed. 7.99 (978-1-4169-1800-4(0), Simon & Schuster/Paula Wiseman Bks.) Simon & Schuster/Paula Wiseman Bks.
—Murphy in the City. Provensen, Alice, illus. 2015. (ENG., Illus.). 40p. (J). (gr. -1-3). 17.99 (978-1-4424-1971-1(7), Simon & Schuster Bks. For Young Readers) Simon & Schuster Bks. For Young Readers.
Pryce, Sasha. Labby's Adventures. 2009. 52p. pap. 14.95 (978-1-4092-8020-0(9)) Lulu Pr., Inc.
Publications International Ltd. Staff, ed. Puppy Learning. 2007. (J). 4.00 (978-1-4127-6959-4(0)) Publications International, Ltd.
—10 Tiny Puppies: A Counting Book. 2010. (J). bds. 7.98 (978-1-60553-436-7(6)) Phoenix International Publications, Inc.
Pugiano-Martin, Carol & Bridwell, Norman. The Snow Champion. Haefele, Steve, illus. 2006. (Big Red Reader Ser.). (J). (978-0-439-80845-3(6)) Scholastic, Inc.
Pullen, Ken. Rescue Me. 2006. 137p. (J). per. 11.95 (978-1-60002-170-1(0), 4133) Mountain Valley Publishing, LLC.
Puppy Love. 2003. (J). per. (978-1-57657-890-2(9)) Paradise Pr., Inc.
Puppy Love. 2014. (Flirt Ser.). (ENG., Illus.). 240p. (YA). (gr. 7). pap. 10.99 (978-1-4424-8412-2(8), Simon Pulse) Simon Pulse.
Puppy Trouble. 2006. (Bella & Rosie Set 3 Ser.). (J). 7.67 (978-1-932570-57-1(8)) Pioneer Valley Bks.
Puppy's House. Date not set. (Illus.). (J). bds. 4.98 (978-1-4054-0787-8(5)) Parragon, Inc.
Pyatt, K. C. Rebekah As Her Journey Begins. 2008. 60p. pap. 9.95 (978-1-933912-00-4(6)) Westview Publishing Co., Inc.
—Rebekah on the Farm. 2012. 132p. 29.99 (978-1-4797-2188-7(3)); pap. 19.99 (978-1-4797-2187-0(5)) Xlibris Corp.
Pyron, Bobbie. The Dogs of Winter. 2014. (ENG.). 320p. (J). (gr. 5-9). pap. 7.99 (978-0-545-39931-9(9), Levine, Arthur A. Bks.) Scholastic, Inc.
—A Dog's Way Home. 2012. (ENG.). 336p. (J). (gr. 3-7). pap. 6.99 (978-0-06-198672-7(0), Tegen, Katherine Bks) HarperCollins Pubs.
—A Dog's Way Home. Jessell, Tim, illus. 2011. (ENG.). 336p. (J). (gr. 3-7). 16.99 (978-0-06-198674-1(7), Tegen, Katherine Bks) HarperCollins Pubs.
Quick, Matthew. Sorta Like a Rock Star. 2011. (ENG.). 384p. (YA). (gr. 7-17). pap., pap. 10.99 (978-0-316-04353-3(2)) Little, Brown Bks. for Young Readers.
Quinn, Spencer, pseud. ARF - A Bowser & Birdie Novel. 2016. (ENG.). 304p. (J). (gr. 3-7). 16.99 (978-0-545-64334-4(1), Scholastic Pr.) Scholastic, Inc.
—Bow Wow: a Bowser & Birdie Novel. 2017. (ENG.). 304p. (J). (gr. 3-7). 16.99 **(978-1-338-09134-2(4)**, Scholastic Pr.) Scholastic, Inc.
—Paw & Order: A Chet & Bernie Mystery. 2015. (Chet & Bernie Mystery Ser.: 7). (ENG.). 336p. pap. 16.00 (978-1-4767-0340-4(X)) Simon & Schuster, Inc.
—Woof. (Bowser & Birdie Mystery Ser.). (ENG.). 304p. (J). (gr. 3-7). 2016. pap. 7.99 (978-0-545-64332-0(5)) 2015. 16.99 (978-0-545-64331-3(7), Scholastic Pr.) Scholastic, Inc.
—Woof. 2016. lib. bdg. 18.40 (978-0-606-39011-8(1)) Turtleback Bks.
Rabbett, Martin. Forever Buster: What a Name! What a Dog, We Exclaim! Burns, Donna, illus. 2007. (J). 13.95 (978-0-9794649-0-4(0)) Hula Moon Pr.
Raden, Tammy. My Dog Blue. 2009. 24p. pap. 11.49 (978-1-4490-3228-9(1)) AuthorHouse.
—New Puppy. 2010. 24p. 11.49 (978-1-4520-0797-7(7)) AuthorHouse.
Radzinski, Kandy. What Dogs Want for Christmas. Radzinski, Kandy, illus. 2008. (ENG., Illus.). 32p. (J). (gr. k-6). 16.95 (978-1-58536-363-6(4)) Sleeping Bear Pr.
Raffa, Edwina & Rigsby, Annelle. Kidnapped in Key West. (Florida Historical Fiction for Youth Ser.). (ENG.). (J). 2012. 138p. pap. 9.95 (978-1-56164-537-4(0)) 2008. (Illus.). 127p. (gr. 3-7). 14.95 (978-1-56164-413-1(7)) Pineapple Pr., Inc.
Raglin, Tim. The Curse of Catunkhamun. 2007. (Illus.). (J). (978-0-9788969-0-4(4), Exhibit A) TR Bks.
Rahme, Linda. The Adventures of Judah, the Lion Dog. 2013. 40p. pap. 16.95 (978-1-4624-0759-0(5), Inspiring Voices) Author Solutions, Inc.
Rakusin, Sudie. Dear Calla Roo... Love, Savannah Blue No. 2: A Letter about Getting Sick & Feeling Better. Rakusin, Sudie, illus. 2003. (Illus.). 32p. (J). (gr. -1-4). 16.95 (978-0-9664805-3-5(8)) Winged Willow Pr.
Ramage, Rosalyn Rikel. The Windmill. 2013. 182p. (gr. 4-6). pap. 11.66 (978-1-4907-0909-3(6)) Trafford Publishing.

C
D

Rand, Emily. A Dog Day. 2015. (ENG., Illus.). 32p. (gr. -1 — 1). 18.95 (978-1-84976-290-8(2)) Tate Publishing, Ltd. GBR. Dist: Abrams, Inc.

Randall, MarilynMae. Wellington's Windows. McCarter, Zack, illus. 2003. 146p. (J). per. 15.00 (978-0-9713589-6-6(6)) Ubaviel's Gifts.

Randles, Slim & Montoya, Jerry, illus. Ol' Jimmy Dollar. 2015. 42p. (J). (978-1-936744-40-4(6)) LPD Pr.

Random House. Chase's Super Sniffer! Random House, illus. 2017. (Scratch-And-Sniff Book Ser.). (ENG., Illus.). 24p. (J). (gr. -1-2). 9.99 (978-0-399-55373-8(8), Random Hse. Bks. for Young Readers) Random Hse. Children's Bks.

—Gold Rush Pups! (PAW Patrol) MJ Illustrations, illus. 2017. (Pictureback(R) Ser.). (ENG.). 16p. (J). (gr. -1-2). pap. 5.99 **(978-1-5247-1684-4(7)**, Random Hse. Bks. for Young Readers) Random Hse. Children's Bks.

—High-Flying Skye (PAW Patrol) MJ Illustrations, illus. 2016. (Book & CD Ser.). (ENG.). 24p. (J). (gr. -1-2). pap. 6.99 (978-1-101-93686-3(X), Random Hse. Bks. for Young Readers) Random Hse. Children's Bks.

—Holiday Helpers! (PAW Patrol) Random House, illus. 2016. (Pictureback(R) Ser.). (ENG., Illus.). 24p. (J). (gr. -1-2). pap. 5.99 (978-0-399-55874-0(8), Random Hse. Bks. for Young Readers) Random Hse. Children's Bks.

—Lend a Helping Paw (PAW Patrol) Jackson, Mike, illus. 2016. (Touch-And-Feel Ser.). (ENG.). 10p. (J). (— 1). 12.99 (978-1-101-94027-3(1), Random Hse. Bks. for Young Readers) Random Hse. Children's Bks.

—Let's Find Adventure! (Paw Patrol) Jackson, Mike, illus. 2015. (Nifty Lift-And-Look Ser.). (ENG.). 12p. (J). (-k). bds. 5.99 (978-0-553-51027-0(4), Random Hse. Bks. for Young Readers) Random Hse. Children's Bks.

—The Little Red Rescue Box (PAW Patrol) Random House, illus. 2016. (ENG., Illus.). 96p. (J). (— 1). bds. 14.99 (978-0-399-55135-2(2), Random Hse. Bks. for Young Readers) Random Hse. Children's Bks.

—Meet the Pets. Random House, illus. 2016. (Step into Reading Ser.). (ENG., Illus.). 32p. (J). (gr. -1-2). 4.99 (978-0-399-55483-4(1), Random Hse. Bks. for Young Readers) Random Hse. Children's Bks.

—PAW Patrol Big Lift-And-Look Board Book (PAW Patrol) Moore, Harry, illus. 2017. (Big Lift-And-Look Book Ser.). (ENG.). 12p. (J). (— 1). bds. 11.99 **(978-1-5247-1722-3(3)**, Random Hse. Bks. for Young Readers) Random Hse. Children's Bks.

—PAW Patrol Deluxe Step into Reading (PAW Patrol) Random House, illus. 2016. (Step into Reading Ser.). (ENG., Illus.). 24p. (J). (gr. -1-1). pap. 4.99 (978-0-553-52288-4(4), Random Hse. Bks. for Young Readers) Random Hse. Children's Bks.

—PAW Patrol on the Roll! (PAW Patrol) Random House, illus. 2016. (Pictureback(R) Ser.). (ENG., Illus.). 16p. (J). (gr. -1-2). 4.99 (978-1-101-93867-6(6), Random Hse. Bks. for Young Readers) Random Hse. Children's Bks.

—Pawsome Puppy Adventures! Random House, illus. 2016. (Pictureback Favorites Ser.). (ENG., Illus.). 96p. (J). (gr. -1-2). 9.99 (978-1-5247-1438-3(0), Random Hse. Bks. for Young Readers) Random Hse. Children's Bks.

—Pup, Pup, & Away! (Paw Patrol) Moore, Harry, illus. 2015. (Pictureback(R) Ser.). (ENG.). 24p. (J). (gr. -1-2). 5.99 (978-0-553-50794-2(X), Random Hse. Bks. for Young Readers) Random Hse. Children's Bks.

—The Pups Save the Bunnies (Paw Patrol) Jackson, Mike, illus. 2016. (Pictureback(R) Ser.). (ENG.). 16p. (J). (gr. -1-1). 4.99 (978-1-101-93168-4(X), Random Hse. Bks. for Young Readers) Random Hse. Children's Bks.

—Pups to the Rescue! (Paw Patrol) Random House, illus. 2014. (Pictureback(R) Ser.). (ENG., Illus.). 16p. (J). (gr. -1-2). 3.99 (978-0-385-38444-5(0), Random Hse. Bks. for Young Readers) Random Hse. Children's Bks.

—Save the Kitten!/Buster's Big Day (Team Umizoomi) Ostrom, Bob, illus. 2014. (Pictureback(R) Ser.). (ENG.). 32p. (J). (gr. -1-2). 4.99 (978-0-385-37520-7(4), Random Hse. Bks. for Young Readers) Random Hse. Children's Bks.

—Shape Patrol! (Paw Patrol) MJ Illustrations, illus. 2016. (ENG.). 24p. (J). (— 1). bds. 6.99 (978-1-101-93695-5(9), Random Hse. Bks. for Young Readers) Random Hse. Children's Bks.

—The Spooky Cabin (PAW Patrol) Fruchter, Jason, illus. 2017. (Step into Reading Ser.). (ENG.). 24p. (J). (gr. -1-1). pap. 4.99 **(978-1-5247-1694-3(4))**; lib. bdg. 12.99 **(978-1-5247-1695-0(2))** Random Hse. Children's Bks. (Random Hse. Bks. for Young Readers).

Random House. Super Pup Heroes! (PAW Patrol) Random House, illus. 2016. (Tabbed Board Book Ser.). (ENG., Illus.). 16p. (J). (— 1). bds. 7.99 (978-0-399-55313-4(4), Random Hse. Bks. for Young Readers) Random Hse. Children's Bks.

Random House & Man-Kong, Mary. Meet the Pets. Random House, illus. 2016. (Step into Reading Ser.). (ENG., Illus.). 32p. (J). (gr. -1-2). 12.99 (978-0-399-55484-1(X), Random Hse. Bks. for Young Readers) Random Hse. Children's Bks.

Random House & Posner-Sanchez, Andrea. Dog Days. Random House, illus. 2016. (Step into Reading Level 2 Ser.). (ENG., Illus.). 24p. (J). (gr. -1-2). 14.75 (978-0-606-39356-0(0)) Turtleback Bks.

Random House Disney Staff. Go for the Gold! Random House Disney Staff & Petrossi, Fabrizio, illus. 2016. (Pictureback(R) Ser.). (ENG.). 16p. (J). (gr. -1-2). pap. 4.99 (978-0-399-55595-4(1), Random Hse. Bks. for Young Readers) Random Hse. Children's Bks.

Random House Disney Staff & Redbank, Tennant. Teacup: Belle's Star Pup (Disney Princess: Palace Pets) Legramandi, Francesco & Matta, Gabriella, illus. 2015. (Stepping Stone Book(TM) Ser.). (ENG.). 64p. (J). (gr. 1-4). 5.99 (978-0-7364-3345-7(7), RH/Disney) Random Hse. Children's Bks.

Random House Editors. Dora's Puppy, Perrito! 2013. lib. bdg. 13.55 (978-0-606-32218-8(3), Turtleback) Turtleback Bks.

Random House Editors. Mission PAW. 2017. (Step into Reading Level 2 Ser.). lib. bdg. 14.75 **(978-0-606-39862-6(7))** Turtleback Bks.

Random House Editors & RH Disney Staff. Aurora & the Helpful Dragon/Tiana & Her Furry Friend. Disney Storybook Artists Staff & Studio Iboix Staff, illus. 2011. (Pictureback(R) Ser.). (ENG.). 32p. (J). (gr. -1-2). pap. 4.99 (978-0-7364-2757-9(0), RH/Disney) Random Hse. Children's Bks.

Random House Staff. The Best Doghouse Ever! Random House Staff & Jackson, Mike, illus. 2013. (Step into Reading Ser.). (ENG.). 24p. (J). (gr. -1-1). pap. 3.99 (978-0-449-81388-1(6), Random Hse. Bks. for Young Readers) Random Hse. Children's Bks.

—Chase Is on the Case! (Paw Patrol) Random House Staff & Petrossi, Fabrizio, illus. 2014. (Step into Reading Ser.). (ENG.). 24p. (J). (gr. -1-1). 3.99 (978-0-385-38447-6(5), Random Hse. Bks. for Young Readers) Random Hse. Children's Bks.

—Dog Days (Team Umizoomi) Random House Staff & O'Connell, Lorraine, illus. 2013. (Step into Reading Ser.). (ENG.). 24p. (J). (gr. -1-1). pap. 3.99 (978-0-449-81436-9(X), Random Hse. Bks. for Young Readers) Random Hse. Children's Bks.

—Dora's Puppy, Perrito! (Dora the Explorer) Aikins, David, illus. 2013. (Step into Reading Ser.). (ENG.). 32p. (J). (gr. -1-1). 3.99 (978-0-449-81857-2(8), Random Hse. Bks. for Young Readers) Random Hse. Children's Bks.

—Team Numbers (Paw Patrol) Random House Staff, illus. 2016. (ENG., Illus.). 24p. (J). (gr. -1 — 1). bds. 6.99 (978-0-553-53885-4(3), Random Hse. Bks. for Young Readers) Random Hse. Children's Bks.

Random House Staff & Posner-Sanchez, Andrea. Dog Days. Random House Staff, illus. 2016. (Step into Reading Ser.). (ENG., Illus.). 24p. (J). (gr. -1-2). 4.99 (978-0-399-55497-1(1), Random Hse. Bks. for Young Readers) Random Hse. Children's Bks.

Rankin, Joan E. First Day. Rankin, Joan E., illus. 2007. (ENG., Illus.). 32p. (J). (gr. -1-2). 10.99 (978-1-4169-6848-1(2), Simon & Schuster/Paula Wiseman Bks.) Simon & Schuster/Paula Wiseman Bks.

Ransom, Jeanie Franz. There's a Cat in Our Class! A Tale about Getting Along. Langdo, Bryan, illus. 2016. 32p. (J). (978-1-4338-2262-9(8), Magination Pr.) American Psychological Assn.

Rapoport, Cindy. The Adventures of Poca & Flea Bert. 2008. 64p. pap. 19.95 (978-1-60672-901-4(2)) America Star Bks.

Raschka, Chris. A Ball for Daisy. Raschka, Chris, illus. (ENG., Illus.). (J). (gr. -1-2). 2015. 36p. bds. 8.99 (978-0-553-53723-9(7)) 2011. 32p. 17.99 (978-0-375-85861-1(X)) Random Hse. Children's Bks. (Schwartz & Wade Bks.).

—A Ball for Daisy. 2013. (CHI.). 48p. (J). (gr. -1-2). (978-7-5414-5730-2(2)) Yunnan Juvenile and Children's Bks. Pr.

—Daisy Gets Lost. Raschka, Chris, illus. 2013. (ENG., Illus.). 32p. (J). (gr. -1-2). 17.99 (978-0-449-81741-4(5), Schwartz & Wade Bks.) Random Hse. Children's Bks.

—Doggy Dog. Raschka, Chris, illus. 2014. (Thingy Things Ser.). (ENG., Illus.). 24p. (J). (gr. -1-k). 6.95 (978-1-4197-1203-6(9), Abrams Appleseed) Abrams, Inc.

—Hip Hop Dog. Radunsky, Vladimir, illus. 2010. (ENG.). 32p. (J). (gr. -1-3). 16.99 (978-0-06-123963-2(1)) HarperCollins Pubs.

Rawlings, Marjorie Kinnan. The Secret River. Dillon, Leo & Dillon, Diane, illus. 2011. (ENG.). 56p. (J). (gr. -1-3). 19.99 (978-1-4169-1179-1(0), Atheneum Bks. for Young Readers) Simon & Schuster Children's Publishing.

Rawls, Wilson. Where the Red Fern Grows. 249p. (YA). (gr. 5-18). pap. 5.99 (978-0-8072-1358-2(6)); pap. 5.99 (978-0-8072-1467-1(1)) Random Hse. Audio Publishing Group. (Listening Library).

—Where the Red Fern Grows. l.t. ed. 2005. 376p. pap. 10.95 (978-0-7862-7312-6(7), Large Print Pr.) Thorndike Pr.

Ray Charles Lockamy, Inez Eason. The Adventures of Tracks & Cookout. 2010. 40p. pap. (978-1-4269-2159-9(4)) Trafford Publishing (UK) Ltd.

Ray, Mary Lyn. Goodnight, Good Dog. Malone, Rebecca, illus. 2015. (ENG.). 32p. (J). (gr. -1-3). 16.99 (978-0-544-28612-2(X), HMH Books For Young Readers) Houghton Mifflin Harcourt Publishing Co.

—A Lucky Author Has a Dog. Henry, Steven, illus. 2015. (ENG.). 40p. (J). (gr. -1-3). 16.99 (978-0-545-51876-5(8)) Scholastic, Inc.

Rea, Loretta Vandivier. Eddie Builds a House: Go Home, Eddie. 2012. 36p. pap. 15.50 (978-1-4669-4101-4(4)) Trafford Publishing.

Reading Friends Staff. Puppies Single. (J). (978-0-8136-3766-2(X)) Modern Curriculum Pr.

Ream, Jacquie. Bully Dogs. 2009. (ENG., Illus.). 119p. (J). pap. 9.95 (978-1-935359-14-2(2)) Book Pubs. Network.

Reasoner, Charles, illus. Puppy Love. 2015. (J). (978-1-4795-5946-6(6)) Picture Window Bks.

Rebello, Kevin. Julia & Mckinley's Day at the Beach. 2009. 32p. pap. 12.99 (978-1-4389-7330-2(6)) AuthorHouse.

Red Fox Picture Books Staff & Transworld Publishing Staff. Better Play Times. 2006. (ENG., Illus.). 24p. (J). (gr. k-k). pap. 7.95 (978-1-86230-164-1(6), Red Fox) Random House Children's Books GBR. Dist: Independent Pubs. Group.

Redbank, Tennant. The Great Mountain Adventure. RH Disney et al, illus. 2016. (Disney Chapters Ser.). (ENG.). 64p. (J). (gr. 1-4). 5.99 (978-0-7364-3636-6(7), RH/Disney) Random Hse. Children's Bks.

—Pumpkin: Cinderella's Dancing Pup (Disney Princess: Palace Pets) RH Disney Staff et al, illus. 2015. (Disney Chapters Ser.). (ENG.). 64p. (J). (gr. 1-4). 5.99 (978-0-7364-3423-2(2), RH/Disney) Random Hse. Children's Bks.

—Teacup: Belle's Star Pup. 2015. (Disney Princess Palace Pets Ser.). lib. bdg. 16.00 (978-0-606-36391-4(2)) Turtleback Bks.

Redfern, Holly. The Adventures of Remmington the Dog: An Unexpected Friend. Burton, Claudia, illus. 2007. 28p. (gr. -1-3). per. 14.95 (978-1-59858-317-5(4)) Dog Ear Publishing, LLC.

Redmond, Pamela Woods. Elf Dog. LaFrance, Debbie, illus. 2005. 44p. (J). 15.95 (978-0-9760767-0-4(5)) Redmond, Pamela.

Reeve, Elizabeth. Sassy: the short stories of being a service Dog. 2010. 35p. pap. 17.00 (978-0-557-39319-0(1)) Lulu Pr., Inc.

Reeve, Philip. Pugs of the Frozen North. McIntyre, Sarah, illus. 2016. (Not-So-Impossible Tale Ser.). (ENG.). 224p. (J). (gr. 2-5). 12.99 (978-0-385-38796-5(2), Random Hse. Bks. for Young Readers) Random Hse. Children's Bks.

Regan, Marti. Lazy Daisy, the Love Dog. 2013. (Illus.). 40p. pap. 16.46 (978-1-4669-7789-1(2)) Trafford Publishing.

Reichs, Kathy & Reichs, Brendan. Code. 2013. (Virals Ser.: 3). lib. bdg. 19.65 (978-0-606-32140-2(3), Turtleback) Turtleback Bks.

—Terminal. 2015. (Virals Ser.: 5). (ENG.). 432p. (J). (gr. 5). 17.99 (978-1-59514-528-4(1), G.P. Putnam's Sons Books for Young Readers) Penguin Young Readers Group.

Reid, Christy. Simon the Guide Dog. Poole, Steven R., illus. 2012. 38p. 24.95 (978-1-4626-6052-0(5)) America Star Bks.

Reid, Jim, as told by. Schultze's Stories: Celebrating Friends Through a Puppy's Eyes. 2006. (ENG.). 144p. (J). per. 19.95 (978-0-86534-494-5(9)) Sunstone Pr.

Reisfeld, Randi & Gilmour, H. B. What the Dog Said. 2012. (ENG.). 256p. (YA). (gr. 4-14). 16.99 (978-1-59990-702-4(X), 9781599907024, Bloomsbury USA Childrens) Bloomsbury Publishing USA.

Resau, Laura. Estrella en el Bosque (Star in the Forest) 2016. (ENG & SPA.). 160p. (J). (gr. 2-5). 18.40 (978-0-606-39132-0(0)) Turtleback Bks.

—Star in the Forest. 2012. (ENG.). 160p. (J). (gr. 2-5). 6.99 (978-0-375-85410-1(X), Yearling) Random Hse. Children's Bks.

Rey. Attention aux Chiens. pap. 16.95 (978-2-09-250164-1(X)) Nathan, Fernand FRA. Dist: Distribooks, Inc.

Rey, H. A. & Rey, Margret. Curious George & the Puppies. 2007. (Curious George Ser.). (ENG., Illus.). 24p. (J). (gr. -1-3). audio compact disk 10.99 (978-0-618-80065-0(4)) Houghton Mifflin Harcourt Publishing Co.

—Dog Show. 2007. (Curious George Ser.). (ENG., Illus.). 24p. (J). (gr. -1-3). 3.99 (978-0-618-72397-3(8)) Houghton Mifflin Harcourt Publishing Co.

Reyes, Gabrielle. Winter Friends. 2013. (Illus.). 30p. (J). pap. (978-0-545-59210-9(0)) Scholastic, Inc.

Reyes, Sharon D. Frank, 1 vol. 2010. 48p. pap. 24.95 (978-1-4489-6114-6(9)) PublishAmerica, Inc.

Reynolds, Gardiner John. Stone Fox. 30th rev. ed. 2014. (Trophy Bk Ser.). (ENG.). 96p. (J). (gr. 7-12). 10.24 (978-1-63245-175-0(1)) Lectorum Pubns., Inc.

Reynolds, Lori. My Name Is Mac. Cardwell, Brett, illus. 2016. (ENG.). (J). **(978-1-925515-56-5(7))**; pap. **(978-1-925515-45-9(1))** Vivid Publishing.

Reynolds, Mignon C. Life as Bonkers. 2006. 137p. pap. 12.95 (978-1-4116-7357-1(3)) Lulu Pr., Inc.

RH Disney Staff. My Hero. RH Disney Staff, illus. 2008. (Step into Reading Ser.). (ENG., Illus.). 32p. (J). (gr. k-3). pap. 3.99 (978-0-375-84812-4(6), RH/Disney) Random Hse. Children's Bks.

Riad, Hala. Twinkie Has a New Home. 2011. 24p. pap. 14.93 (978-1-4269-7120-4(6)) Trafford Publishing.

Ribble, S. A Child's Book of Kitty-cat & Puppy-dog Tales. 2007. (Illus.). 72p. per. (978-1-84401-961-8(6)) Athena Pr.

Ricci, Christine. Puppy Takes a Bath. Mangano, Tom, illus. 2006. (Dora the Explorer Ser.: 10). (ENG.). 24p. (J). (gr. 3-7). pap. 3.99 (978-1-4169-1483-9(8), Simon Spotlight/Nickelodeon) Simon Spotlight/Nickelodeon.

Rice, Dona Herweck & Thompson, Chad. Old Mother Hubbard, 1 vol. 2009. (Early Childhood Themes Ser.). (ENG., Illus.). 16p. (J). (gr. -1-2). pap. 19.99 (978-1-4333-1478-0(9)) Shell Educational Publishing.

Richard Bellingham Edd. The Fables of Boris: Invitations to Meaningful Conversations. 2009. 280p. 27.95 (978-1-4401-6247-3(6)); pap. 17.95 (978-1-4401-6245-9(X)) iUniverse, Inc.

Richter, Cindy. Pete's Big Paws - Hardcover. Peters, Rob, illus. 2012. 32p. 15.99 (978-0-9849732-0-0(6)) Coast View Publishing.

Riddell, Chris. Goth Girl & the Wuthering Fright. 2017. (Goth Girl Ser.: 3). (ENG., Illus.). 224p. (J). (gr. 2-6). 14.99 (978-1-4472-7789-7(9)) Pan Macmillan GBR. Dist: Independent Pubs. Group.

Ridell, Chris. Ottoline va al colegio/ Ottolina Goes To School. 2008. (SPA.). 172p. (J). 13.95 (978-84-263-6833-1(6)) Vives, Luis Editorial (Edelvives) ESP. Dist: Baker & Taylor Bks.

—Ottoline y la gata amarilla/ Ottolina & the Yellow Cat. 2008. (SPA.). 172p. (J). 13.95 (978-84-263-6832-4(8)) Vives, Luis Editorial (Edelvives) ESP. Dist: Baker & Taylor Bks.

Ries, Lori. Aggie & Ben: Three Stories. Dormer, Frank W., illus. 2007. (ENG.). 48p. (J). (gr. -1-3). 5.95 (978-1-57091-649-6(7)) Charlesbridge Publishing, Inc.

—Aggie Gets Lost. Dormer, Frank W., illus. 2011. (ENG.). 48p. (J). (gr. -1-3). 12.95 (978-1-57091-633-5(0)) Charlesbridge Publishing, Inc.

—Aggie the Brave. Dormer, Frank W., illus. (ENG.). 48p. (J). (gr. -1-3). 2012. pap. 5.95 (978-1-57091-636-6(5)) 2010. 12.95 (978-1-57091-635-9(7)) Charlesbridge Publishing, Inc.

—Good Dog, Aggie. Dormer, Frank W., illus. (ENG.). 48p. (J). (gr. -1-3). 2012. pap. 5.95 (978-1-57091-646-5(2)) 2009. 12.95 (978-1-57091-645-8(4)) Charlesbridge Publishing, Inc.

Ries, Lori, et al. Tita y Ben: Tres Cuentos. Dormer, Frank W., illus. 2010. (SPA.). 48p. (J). (gr. -1-3). 13.95 (978-1-57091-934-3(8)); pap. 5.95 (978-1-57091-935-0(6)) Charlesbridge Publishing, Inc.

Rigby Education Staff. Dog's Diary. (Sails Literacy Ser.). (Illus.). 16p. (gr. 2-3). 27.00 (978-0-7635-9936-2(0), 699360C99) Rigby Education.

—The Happy House. (Sails Literacy Ser.). (Illus.). 16p. (gr. 1-2). 27.00 (978-0-7635-9908-9(5), 699085C99) Rigby Education.

Rigg, Jo. Rocky Dog. 2007. (Illus.). 10p. (J). (978-1-84332-474-4(1)) Priddy Bks.

Riggi, Samantha K. Wesley Reece: Fourth Grade Hero. 2011. 52p. (gr. 4-6). pap. 9.99 (978-1-4634-1640-9(7)) AuthorHouse.

Rigo, L., illus. Little Puppy. 2012. (Mini Look at Me Bks.). (ENG.). 10p. (J). bds. 4.99 (978-0-7641-6512-2(7)) Barron's Educational Series, Inc.

Riley, D. H. The Mysterians, 1 vol. 2009. 54p. pap. 16.95 (978-1-60836-374-2(0)) America Star Bks.

Ringo. Loss of a Friend. 2009. 24p. pap. 19.95 (978-1-4389-8680-7(7)) AuthorHouse.

Rippl, Terry. Tippy, Dog Gone Detective: From the Files of the World's Shortest Private Eye. 2012. 36p. pap. 12.99 (978-1-4575-1599-6(7)) Dog Ear Publishing, LLC.

Rissi, Anica Mrose. Anna, Banana, & the Big-Mouth Bet. Park, Meg, illus. 2016. (Anna, Banana Ser.: 3). (ENG.). 128p. (J). (gr. 1-5). pap. 5.99 (978-1-4814-1612-2(X), Simon & Schuster Bks. For Young Readers) Simon & Schuster Bks. For Young Readers.

—Anna, Banana, & the Friendship Split. Park, Meg, illus. 2015. (Anna, Banana Ser.: 1). (ENG.). 128p. (J). (gr. 1-5). 16.99 (978-1-4814-1605-4(7), Simon & Schuster Bks. For Young Readers) Simon & Schuster Bks. For Young Readers.

—Anna, Banana, & the Little Lost Kitten. Park, Meg, illus. 2017. (Anna, Banana Ser.: 5). (ENG.). 144p. (J). (gr. 1-5). 16.99 **(978-1-4814-8669-9(1)**, Simon & Schuster Bks. For Young Readers) Simon & Schuster Bks. For Young Readers.

—Anna, Banana, & the Monkey in the Middle. Park, Meg, illus. 2015. (Anna, Banana Ser.: 2). (ENG.). 128p. (J). (gr. 1-5). 15.99 (978-1-4814-1608-5(1), Simon & Schuster Bks. For Young Readers) Simon & Schuster Bks. For Young Readers.

—Anna, Banana, & the Puppy Parade. Park, Meg, illus. 2017. (Anna, Banana Ser.: 4). (ENG.). 144p. (J). (gr. 1-5). pap. 5.99 (978-1-4814-1615-3(4), Simon & Schuster Bks. For Young Readers) Simon & Schuster Bks. For Young Readers.

Rissman, Rebecca. A Dog's Day, 1 vol. 2014. (ENG.). 32p. (gr. 1-2). 26.65 (978-1-4109-6173-0(7), NA-r) Heinemann-Raintree.

Ritner, Amelia. The Puppy Who Wasn't. Leidemer, Adam, illus. 2012. 24p. 24.95 (978-1-4626-6221-0(8)) America Star Bks.

Ritz, C. Tiger's World: Growing Up. 2013. 72p. pap. (978-1-77097-596-5(9)) FriesenPress.

Rivera, Nicole. The Sweet Smell of Freedom (Max's Mini Coloring Book) 2011. (ENG.). 36p. pap. 7.99 (978-1-4610-7649-0(8)) CreateSpace Independent Publishing Platform.

Rivers-Moore, Debbie. Puppy. Larranaga, Ana Martin, illus. 2012. (Come Out & Play Bks.). (ENG.). 10p. (J). bds. 2.99 (978-0-7641-6521-4(6)) Barron's Educational Series, Inc.

Rivot, Jean Mahassel. The Secret of Pet Heaven. 2013. 46p. pap. 12.00 (978-0-9888901-0-7(0)) Night Sky, LLC.

Rizzo, Cynthia Marie. No No, Coco. 2008. 49p. pap. 16.95 (978-1-60563-819-5(6)) America Star Bks.

Rizzo, M. Anthony. Sir Bentley the Beginning. 2009. 36p. pap. 14.95 (978-1-60860-648-1(1), Strategic Bk. Publishing) Strategic Book Publishing & Rights Agency (SBPRA).

Rizzuto, Katherine. Poodles Don't Play Tennis. Murphy, Liz, illus. 2013. (ENG.). 32p. (J). 19.99 (978-1-938501-06-7(3)) Turn the Page Publishing.

Roane, E. M. Quincy's First Year. 2013. 56p. pap. 15.99 (978-1-4797-8075-4(8)) Xlibris Corp.

Roba, Jean. Bored Silly with Billy. 2010. (Billy & Buddy Ser.: 2). (ENG., Illus.). 48p. (J). (gr. 3-17). pap. 11.95 (978-1-84918-049-8(0)) CineBook GBR. Dist: National Bk. Network.

—It's a Dog's Life. 2013. (Billy & Buddy Ser.: 4). (ENG., Illus.). 48p. (J). (gr. 3-12). pap. 11.95 (978-1-84918-171-6(3)) CineBook GBR. Dist: National Bk. Network.

Robbins, Trina. The Bark in Space. Page, Tyler, illus. 2013. (Chicagoland Detective Agency Ser.: 5). (ENG.). 64p. (gr. 4-8). pap. 6.95 (978-1-4677-0725-1(2), Graphic Universe™) Lerner Publishing Group.

—The Big Flush. Page, Tyler, illus. 2012. (Chicagoland Detective Agency Ser.: 4). (ENG.). 64p. (gr. 4-8). pap. 6.95 (978-0-8225-9161-0(8)); lib. bdg. 29.27 (978-0-7613-8165-5(1)) Lerner Publishing Group. (Graphic Universe™).

—Night of the Living Dogs. Page, Tyler, illus. 2012. (Chicagoland Detective Agency Ser.). 64p. (J). (gr. 4-8). pap. 39.62 (978-0-7613-9313-9(7), Graphic Universe™); (ENG.). lib. bdg. 29.27 (978-0-7613-4616-6(3)) Lerner Publishing Group.

Roberts, Curt. The Story of Scruffy of Smithfield, Virginia. Traylor, Waverley, ed. Roberts, Curt & Traylor, Waverley, illus. l.t. ed. 2005. 14p. (J). (gr. k-6). pap. 3.95 (978-0-9715068-4-8(1)) Traylor, Waverley Publishing.

Roberts, Daniel. The Naughty Dog. 2010. 32p. 14.95 (978-1-4490-8344-1(7)) AuthorHouse.

Roberts, Phyllis. Teeny Tiny Star. 2007. (Illus.). 30p. (J). lib. bdg. 19.95 (978-1-933732-40-4(7)) Big Ransom Studio.

Roberts, Willo Davis. Rebel. 2005. 153p. (J). (gr. 3-7). 13.65 (978-0-7569-5076-7(7)) Perfection Learning Corp.

—Rebel. 2012. (ENG., Illus.). 160p. (J). (gr. 3-7). pap. 8.99 (978-0-689-85081-3(6), Aladdin) Simon & Schuster Children's Publishing.

Robertson, Neil. The Captain & the Infinite Watch Dog. 2015. (ENG., Illus.). 136p. (J). pap. (978-1-78222-437-2(8)) Paragon Publishing, Rothersthorpe.

Robertson, Susan, illus. Little Puppy. 2005. (Bedtime Babies Ser.). 8p. (J). (gr. -1). per., bds. 6.99 (978-1-57755-501-8(5)) Flying Frog Publishing, Inc.

Robinson, Hilary. Over the Moon. Abbott, Jane, illus. 2009. (Tadpoles Ser.). (ENG.). 24p. (J). (gr. k-2). pap. (978-0-7787-3899-2(X)); lib. bdg. (978-0-7787-3868-8(X)) Crabtree Publishing Co.

Robinson, Mary. Days of Terriers. 2008. 32p. pap. 13.50 (978-1-60693-481-4(3), Eloquent Bks.) Strategic Book Publishing & Rights Agency (SBPRA).

Robinson, Melissa. Cheena Comes to Americ. 2012. 34p. (-18). pap. 19.95 (978-1-105-97187-7(2)) Lulu Pr., Inc.

Robison, Peggy. Prince Cody Meets A Monster. Clay, Doris, illus. 2004. 40p. pap. 9.95 (978-0-9708395-7-2(X)) Legacy Publishing Services, Inc.

—Prince Cody Runs Ahead of the Hurricane. Clay, Doris, illus. 2005. 64p. per. 9.95 (978-0-9764982-7-8(8)) Legacy Publishing Services, Inc.

Rochelle, Maria. Jasmine at Work. Linsdell, Jo, illus. 2013. 34p. pap. 9.99 (978-0-9913342-1-6(3)) Draper Publishing.

Rock, Zack. Homer Henry Hudson's Curio Museum. 2014. (ENG., Illus.). 32p. (J). (gr. 1-3). 18.99 (978-1-56846-260-8(3), Creative Editions) Creative Co., The.

Rockitter, Leslie. Chester, the Water-Loving, Pool-Hopping, Salad-Eating, St Bernard Dog. 2006. 104p. (gr. 1-4). per. 7.95 (978-1-59858-175-1(9)) Dog Ear Publishing, LLC.

Roddy, Lee. Dooger, the Grasshopper Hound. 2008. (D. J. Dillon Adventure Ser.: No. 3). (J). 7.99 (978-0-88062-267-7(9)) Mott Media.

—The Ghost Dog of Stoney Ridge. 2008. (D. J. Dillon Adventure Ser.: No. 4). (J). 7.99 (978-0-88062-268-4(7)) Mott Media.

—The Hair-Pulling Bear Dog. 2008. (D. J. Dillon Adventure Ser.: No. 1). (J). 7.99 *(978-0-88062-265-3(2))* Mott Media.
—The Hermit of Mad River. 2008. (D. J. Dillon Adventure Ser.: No. 9). (J). 8.99 *(978-0-88062-273-8(3))* Mott Media.
—Mad Dog of Lobo Mountain. 2008. (D. J. Dillon Adventure Ser.: No. 5). (J). 7.99 *(978-0-88062-269-1(5))* Mott Media.
—Tracked by the Wolf Pack. 2006. (Ladd Family Adventure Ser.: Vol. 15). (J). 7.99 *(978-0-88062-264-6(4))* Mott Media.
Rodman, Mary Ann. Camp K-9, 1 vol. Hayashi, Nancy, illus. 2011. (ENG.). 32p. (J). (gr. -1-3). 15.95 *(978-1-56145-561-4(X))* Peachtree Pubs.
Rodriguez, Marisela. Violet's Shoes. 2012. 28p. pap. 9.95 *(978-1-4327-9616-7(X))* Outskirts Pr., Inc.
Roelofsen, Marjorie. Where Have All the Puppies Gone? A Sequel to SAM. 2010. 24p. pap. 14.00 *(978-1-4490-6211-8(3))* AuthorHouse.
Roesser, Griffin. Digger Makes a Friend. 2006. (Neighborhood Readers Ser.). (ENG.). 8p. (gr. -1-3). pap. 5.15 *(978-1-4042-5774-0(8),* Rosen Classroom) Rosen Publishing Group, Inc., The.
Rog&eacute. The French Fry King. Rog&eacute, illus. 2012. (ENG., Illus.). 32p. (J). (gr. -1-1). 17.95 *(978-1-77049-350-6(6),* Tundra Bks.) Tundra Bks. CAN. Dist: Penguin Random Hse. LLC.
Rogala, Judy. The Dog Days of Christmas. Stroede, Paul, illus. 2012. 32p. (J). 12.95 *(978-1-59598-219-3(1),* Goblin Fern Pr.) HenschelHAUS Publishing.
Roger, Moore & Ron, Kurtz. Arfie Plays Pirates. 2007. 40p. 17.95 *(978-0-9710343-5-8(4))* Photographs Naturally, Inc.
Rogers, Andy. The Puppy Brothers Adventures with Forest Friends - Children's Picture Book for Ages 3 To 8. 2013. 38p. pap. 10.00 *(978-1-63022-036-5(1))* Speedy Publishing LLC.
Rogers, Gregory. The Hero of Little Street. Rogers, Gregory, illus. 2012. (ENG., Illus.). 32p. (J). (gr. k-3). 17.99 *(978-1-59643-729-6(4),* 9781596437296) Roaring Brook Pr.
Rogers, Jewels. The Princess & the Puppy. 2010. 28p. pap. 16.99 *(978-1-4269-4177-1(3))* Trafford Publishing.
Rogers, Suzanne. Pawsitive Tails. 2012. 40p. pap. *(978-1-77067-927-6(8))* FriesenPress.
Rohmann, Eric. Bone Dog. Rohmann, Eric, illus. 2011. (ENG., Illus.). 32p. (J). (gr. -1-3). 16.99 *(978-1-59643-150-8(4),* 9781596431508) Roaring Brook Pr.
Roller, Ellen. Trading Places. Shea, Gary, illus. 2008. (J). pap. 11.95 *(978-0-9792645-0-4(2))* Edgewood Publishing, LLC.
Romer, Ruth. Los cuidadores de mascotas & Pet Care Kids. 2005. spiral bd. 76.00 *(978-1-4108-5795-8(6))* Benchmark Education Co.
Romero, Alfonso Suárez. Maraca. Alvarado, Dalia & Pacheco, Luis Gabriel, illus. rev. ed. 2006. (Castillo de la Lectura Verde Ser.). (SPA & ENG.). 120p. (J). (gr. 2-4). pap. 7.95 *(978-970-20-0128-7(5))* Castillo, Ediciones, S. A. de C. V. MEX. Dist: Macmillan.
Romero-Robinette, Joella. The Allie & Bailey Show: Meet Our Family. 2010. 32p. pap. 13.00 *(978-1-60911-368-1(3),* Eloquent Bks.) Strategic Book Publishing & Rights Agency (SBPRA).
Ronne, Susan. Webster the Spelling Dog. 2012. (ENG.). (J). pap. *(978-1-4675-1184-1(6))* Independent Pub.
Roop, Peter. Abe Lincoln's Dog. 2003. (Illus.). 14.95 *(978-0-59319-020-0(4))* LeapFrog Enterprises, Inc.
Rose, Andrea. A Home for Abby. 2011. 24p. pap. 12.79 *(978-1-4634-2121-2(4))* AuthorHouse.
Rose, D. M. A Tail of Friendship: The Psychiatrist Is In. 2012. 34p. 24.95 *(978-1-4626-5240-2(9))* America Star Bks.
Rose, Lisa. Shmulik Paints the Town. Echeverri, Catalina, illus. 2016. (ENG.). 32p. (J). (gr. -1-3). 17.99 *(978-1-4677-5239-8(8),* Kar-Ben Publishing) Lerner Publishing Group.
Rose, Sandra. Doggone Grief. 2008. 20p. pap. 24.95 *(978-1-60474-623-5(8))* America Star Bks.
Rosebrock, Katie. Tabitha & Dundee: A Story of Friendship. 2013. 16p. pap. 15.99 *(978-1-4817-1257-6(8))* AuthorHouse.
Rosemary Wells. McDuff & the Baby. Rusan Jeffers, illus. 2014. 28p. pap. 9.99 *(978-1-61003-384-8(1))* Center for the Collaborative Classroom.
Rosen, Lucy. ParaNorman: Meet the Ghosts. movie tie-in ed. 2012. (Passport to Reading Level 2 Ser.). (ENG., Illus.). 32p. (J). (gr. -1-3). pap. 3.99 *(978-0-316-20982-3(1))* Little, Brown Bks. for Young Readers.
Rosen, Michael. Snore! Langley, Jonathan, illus. 2003. (ENG.). 32p. (J). (gr. -1-k). pap. 10.99 *(978-0-00-716031-0(3),* HarperCollins Children's Bks.) HarperCollins Pubs. Ltd. GBR. Dist: HarperCollins Pubs.
Rosen, Michael J. The Tale of Rescue. Fellows, Stan, illus. 2015. (ENG.). 112p. (J). (gr. 5). 14.99 *(978-0-7636-7167-9(3))* Candlewick Pr.
Rosenberg, Madelyn. How to Behave at a Dog Show. Ross, Heather, illus. 2015. (ENG.). 32p. (J). (gr. -1-3). 17.99 *(978-0-06-227927-9(0))* HarperCollins Pubs.
Rosenthal, Cathy M. The Lucky Tale of Two Dogs. Warrick, Jessica, illus. 2012. 40p. (J). pap. 12.95 *(978-0-9853752-0-1(5))* Pet Pundit Publishing.
Rosie Is Cold. 2004. (Bella & Rosie Set 2 Ser.). (J). 7.67 *(978-1-932570-20-5(9))* Pioneer Valley Bks.
Ross, Dev. We Both Read-Frank & the Tiger. Reinhart, Larry, illus. 2012. 44p. (J). pap. 4.99 *(978-1-60115-260-2(4))* Treasure Bay, Inc.
Ross, Thea. Lucy Wants to Help. 2005. 16p. (J). bds. 3.99 *(978-1-59384-028-0(4))* Parklane Publishing.
Ross, Theodore J. Lucy Wants to Play. 2003. (Illus.). 16p. (J). 3.99 *(978-1-59384-029-7(2))* Parklane Publishing.
Roth, Silke. Creak, Thump, Bonk! 2007. (ENG.). 40p. (J). (gr. -1-3). 11.99 *(978-1-4169-6159-8(3),* Simon & Schuster/Paula Wiseman Bks.) Simon & Schuster/Paula Wiseman Bks.
Rovetch, L. Bob. And the Surprisingly Slobbery Attack of the Dog-Wash Doggies. Whamond, Dave, illus. 2007. (Hot Dog & Bob Ser.: HOTD). (ENG.). 96p. (J). (gr. 1-5). per. 4.95 *(978-0-8118-5746-8(8))* Chronicle Bks. LLC.
—Hot Dog & Bob: And the Particularly Pesky Attack of the Pencil People. Whamond, Dave, illus. 2006. (Hot Dog & Bob Ser.: HOTD). (ENG.). 96p. (J). (gr. 1-5). pap. 4.95 *(978-0-8118-5322-4(5))* Chronicle Bks. LLC.
Rowan, John & Rowan, Heather. Jake the Bombed Out Bomb Dog. 2010. 28p. pap. 14.50 *(978-1-4490-7162-2(7))* AuthorHouse.
Rowe, Jeannette. YoYo Goes Next Door. Rowe, Jeannette, illus. 2003. (Illus.). 16p. (J). 5.95 *(978-1-58925-368-1(X))* Tiger Tales.
—YoYo Goes to the Park. Rowe, Jeannette, illus. 2003. (Illus.). 12p. (J). pap. 5.95 *(978-1-58925-369-8(8))* Tiger Tales.
Rowe, W. W. The Wizard's Wayward Wand. 2010. (ENG.). 99p. (J). (gr. 3-7). pap. 12.95 *(978-0-9843754-0-0(6))* Sanctuary Publishing, Inc.
Rowen, Amy & Rowen, Tyla Marie. Waggin' Tails. 2003. 182p. 23.95 *(978-0-595-65740-7(0));* pap. 13.95 *(978-0-595-28171-8(0))* iUniverse, Inc.
—Waggin' Tales. 2003. 182p. (YA). 23.95 *(978-0-595-66087-2(8));* pap. 13.95 *(978-0-595-29955-3(5))* iUniverse, Inc.
Rowlinson, Joanne. Catching Boo. Brown, Mari, illus. 2008. 24p. (J). (gr. -1-3). *(978-0-9739962-2-7(6))* Wuehr, Tina.
Roxbee-Cox, Phil. Find the Puppy. Cartwright, Stephen, illus. rev. ed. 2004. (Treasury of Farmyard Tales Ser.). (ENG.). 1p. (J). bds. 3.99 *(978-0-7460-3824-6(0))* EDC Publishing.
Roy, Philip. Seas of South Africa. 2013. (ENG.). 250p. pap. 11.95 *(978-1-55380-247-1(0))* Ronsdale Pr. CAN. Dist: SPD-Small Pr. Distribution.
Roy, Ron. July Jitters. Gurney, John Steven, illus. 2012. (Calendar Mysteries Ser.: 7). (ENG.). 80p. (J). (gr. 1-4). 4.99 *(978-0-375-86882-5(8),* Random Hse. Bks. for Young Readers) Random Hse. Children's Bks.
—July Jitters. 2012. (Calendar Mysteries Ser.: 7). lib. bdg. 14.75 *(978-0-606-26402-0(7),* Turtleback) Turtleback Bks.
—White House White-Out. Gurney, John Steven, illus. 2008. (A to Z Mysteries Ser.: No. 3). 124p. (gr. 1-4). 15.00 *(978-0-7569-8799-2(7))* Perfection Learning Corp.
—White House White-Out. Gurney, John Steven, illus. 2008. (to Z Mysteries Ser.: 3). (ENG.). 144p. (J). (gr. 1-4). 5.99 *(978-0-375-84721-9(9),* Random Hse. Bks. for Young Readers) Random Hse. Children's Bks.
Roy, Ronald. Calendar Mysteries #12: December Dog. Gurney, John Steven, illus. 2014. (Calendar Mysteries Ser.: 12). (ENG.). 80p. (J). (gr. 1-4). 4.99 *(978-0-385-37168-1(3),* Random Hse. Bks. for Young Readers) Random Hse. Children's Bks.
—December Dog. 2014. (Calendar Mysteries Ser.: 12). lib. bdg. 14.75 *(978-0-606-36019-7(0))* Turtleback Bks.
Rozum, John. Scooby-Doo in Yankee Doodle Danger, 1 vol. 2013. (Scooby-Doo Graphic Novels Set 3 Ser.). (ENG.). 24p. (J). (gr. 2-6). lib. bdg. 24.21 *(978-1-61479-054-9(X),* Essential Library) ABDO Publishing Co.
Rubin, Diana. King Choco the Great. 2009. 45p. (J). pap. 10.95 *(978-1-4327-2972-1(1))* Outskirts Pr., Inc.
Rubino, Tony. Animal Farm. 2013. 24p. pap. 24.95 *(978-1-62709-615-7(9))* America Star Bks.
Rudge, Leila. A Perfect Place for Ted. Rudge, Leila, illus. 2014. (ENG., Illus.). 32p. (J). (gr. -1-2). 16.99 *(978-0-7636-6781-8(1))* Candlewick Pr.
Ruelle, Karen Gray. Bark Park, 1 vol. Ruelle, Karen Gray, illus. (ENG., Illus.). 32p. (J). (gr. -1-1). 2014. pap. 7.95 *(978-1-56145-773-1(6))* 2008. 15.95 *(978-1-56145-434-1(6))* Peachtree Pubs.
Rusch, Brian. The Bear Who Barked Like a Dog. 2011. 122p. pap. 12.50 *(978-1-60976-005-2(0),* Eloquent Bks.) Strategic Book Publishing & Rights Agency (SBPRA).
Rushing, John Alan. A. J. Puppy Learns to Swim. Fay, David, illus. 2009. 48p. (J). pap. *(978-0-9776958-9-8(1))* CyPress Pubns.
Russell, Ann. Little Truff & the Siamese Cat. Morris, Adrienne, ed. 2nd ed. 2013. 144p. pap. *(978-0-473-26077-4(8))* Bellbird Pubns.
Russell, Christopher. Dogboy. 2006. 272p. (J). (gr. 5). 15.99 *(978-0-06-084116-4(8),* Greenwillow Bks.) HarperCollins Pubs.
—Hunted. 2007. (J). (gr. 5-9). 254p. 15.99 *(978-0-06-084119-5(2));* 272p. lib. bdg. 16.89 *(978-0-06-084120-1(6),* Greenwillow Bks.) HarperCollins Pubs.
Russell, James. The Dragon Hunters. Choi, Link, illus. 2017. (Dragon Brothers Ser.: 1). (ENG.). 32p. (J). (-4). 16.99 *(978-1-4926-4861-1(2),* 9781492648611, Sourcebooks Jabberwocky) Sourcebooks, Inc.
Russell, James. The Dragon Riders. Choi, Link, illus. 2017. (Dragon Brothers Ser.: 3). (ENG.). 32p. (J). (-4). 16.99 ***(978-1-4926-4867-3(1)***, Sourcebooks Jabberwocky) Sourcebooks, Inc.
Russell, Peggy. Patsy Goes to a New Home: The Patsy Adventures Volume 1. Scott, Larry, illus. 2008. 16p. pap. 24.95 *(978-1-60703-799-6(8))* America Star Bks.
Rutley, Erika L. Adventures in Pup-A-Dupping. 2012. 36p. pap. 24.95 *(978-1-62709-710-9(4))* America Star Bks.
Ryherd, Saundra. The Adventures of Sparky, 1 vol. 2009. 48p. pap. 16.95 *(978-1-60813-516-5(0))* America Star Bks.
Rylant, Cynthia. Annie & Snowball & the Teacup Club. Stevenson, Suçie, illus. (Annie & Snowball Ser.: 3). (ENG.). 40p. (J). (gr. k-2). 2009. pap. 3.99 *(978-1-4169-1461-7(7))* 2008. 16.99 *(978-1-4169-0940-8(0))* Simon Spotlight. (Simon Spotlight).
—Annie & Snowball & the Thankful Friends. 2012. (Annie & Snowball Ready-To-Read Ser.). lib. bdg. 13.55 *(978-0-606-26917-9(7),* Turtleback) Turtleback Bks.
—The Eagle. McDaniels, Preston, illus. 2004. (Lighthouse Family Ser.: 3). (ENG.). 64p. (J). (gr. 1-5). 15.99 *(978-0-689-86243-4(1),* Simon & Schuster Bks. For Young Readers) Simon & Schuster Bks. For Young Readers.
—Henry & Mudge: The First Book. Stevenson, Suçie, illus. 2012. (Henry & Mudge Ser.). (ENG.). 280p. (J). (gr. k-2). pap. 15.96 *(978-1-4424-4952-7(7),* Simon Spotlight) Simon Spotlight.
—Henry & Mudge & a Very Merry Christmas. Stevenson, Suçie, illus. 2005. (Henry & Mudge Ser.). 40p. (gr. -1-3). 14.00 *(978-0-7569-5816-9(4))* Perfection Learning Corp.
—Henry & Mudge & a Very Merry Christmas. Stevenson, Suçie, illus. (Henry & Mudge Ser.: 25). (ENG.). 40p. (J). (gr. k-2). 2005. pap. 3.99 *(978-0-689-83448-6(9))* 2004. 16.99 *(978-0-689-81168-5(3))* Simon Spotlight. (Simon Spotlight).
—Henry & Mudge & Mrs. Hopper's House. Bracken, Carolyn, illus. 2004. (Ready-to-Read Ser.). 40p. (gr. k-2). 14.00 *(978-0-7569-2200-9(3))* Perfection Learning Corp.
—Henry & Mudge & Mrs. Hopper's House. Bracken, Carolyn, illus. (Henry & Mudge Ser.: 22). (ENG.). 40p. (J). (gr. k-2). 2004. pap. 3.99 *(978-0-689-83446-2(2))* 2003. 15.99 *(978-0-689-81153-1(5))* Simon Spotlight. (Simon Spotlight).
—Henry & Mudge & Mrs. Hopper's House. Bracken, Carolyn, illus. 2004. (Henry & Mudge Ready-To-Read Ser.: 22). 40p. (gr. k-2). lib. bdg. 13.55 *(978-0-613-90376-9(5),* Turtleback) Turtleback Bks.
—Henry & Mudge & the Big Sleepover. Stevenson, Suçie, illus. 2007. (Henry & Mudge Ser.). 40p. (gr. k-2). lib. bdg. 14.00 *(978-0-7569-8117-4(4))* Perfection Learning Corp.
—Henry & Mudge & the Big Sleepover. Stevenson, Suçie & Stevenson, Suçie, illus. 2006. (Henry & Mudge Ser.: 28). (ENG.). 40p. (J). (gr. k-2). 16.99 *(978-0-689-81171-5(3),* Simon Spotlight) Simon Spotlight.
—Henry & Mudge & the Big Sleepover, Bk. 28. Stevenson, Suçie, illus. 2007. (Henry & Mudge Ser.: 28). (ENG.). 40p. (J). (gr. k-2). pap. 3.99 *(978-0-689-83451-6(9),* Simon Spotlight) Simon Spotlight.
—Henry & Mudge & the Big Sleepover. Stevenson, Suçie, illus. 2007. (Henry & Mudge Ready-To-Read Ser.: 28). 40p. (gr. -1-3). lib. bdg. 13.55 *(978-1-4177-8140-9(8),* Turtleback) Turtleback Bks.
—Henry & Mudge & the Funny Lunch. Bracken, Carolyn, illus. 2005. (Henry & Mudge Ready-To-Read Ser.: 24). 40p. (gr. k-2). lib. bdg. 13.55 *(978-1-4176-7107-6(6),* Turtleback) Turtleback Bks.
—Henry & Mudge & the Great Grandpas. Stevenson, Suçie, illus. 2006. (Henry & Mudge Ser.). 40p. (gr. k-2). 14.00 *(978-0-7569-6793-2(7))* Perfection Learning Corp.
—Henry & Mudge & the Great Grandpas. Stevenson, Suçie, illus. 2006. (Henry & Mudge Ser.: 26). (ENG.). 40p. (J). (gr. k-2). pap. 3.99 *(978-0-689-83447-9(0),* Simon Spotlight) Simon Spotlight.
—Henry & Mudge & the Great Grandpas. Stevenson, Suçie & Stevenson, Suçie, illus. 2005. (Henry & Mudge Ser.: 26). (ENG.). 40p. (J). (gr. k-2). 15.99 *(978-0-689-81170-8(5),* Simon Spotlight) Simon Spotlight.
—Henry & Mudge & the Tall Tree House. Bracken, Carolyn, illus. 2003. (Henry & Mudge Ser.). (ENG.). 40p. (J). (gr. k-2). pap. 3.99 *(978-0-689-83445-5(4),* Simon Spotlight) Simon Spotlight.
—Henry & Mudge & the Tall Tree House. 2003. (Henry & Mudge Ready-To-Read Ser.: 21). (gr. k-3). lib. bdg. 13.55 *(978-0-613-90605-0(5),* Turtleback) Turtleback Bks.
—Henry & Mudge & the Tumbling Trip. Bracken, Carolyn, illus. 2006. (Henry & Mudge Ser.). 40p. (gr. k-3). 14.00 *(978-0-7569-6904-2(2))* Perfection Learning Corp.
—Henry & Mudge & the Tumbling Trip. Bracken, Carolyn, illus. (Henry & Mudge Ser.: 27). (ENG.). 40p. (J). (gr. k-2). 2006. pap. 3.99 *(978-0-689-83452-3(7))* 2005. 16.99 *(978-0-689-81180-7(2))* Simon Spotlight. (Simon Spotlight).
—Henry & Mudge & the Wild Goose Chase. Bracken, Carolyn, illus. 2004. (Henry & Mudge Ser.). 40p. (gr. k-2). 14.00 *(978-0-7569-3366-1(8))* Perfection Learning Corp.
—Henry & Mudge & the Wild Goose Chase. Bracken, Carolyn, illus. 2004. (Henry & Mudge Ready-To-Read Ser.: 26). 40p. (gr. k-2). lib. bdg. 13.55 *(978-1-4176-4340-0(4),* Turtleback) Turtleback Bks.
—Henry & Mudge Get the Cold Shivers. Stevenson, Suçie, illus. (Henry & Mudge Ser.). 9.95 *(978-1-59112-290-6(2))* Live Oak Media.
—Henry & Mudge Ready-To-Read Value Pack #2: Henry & Mudge & the Long Weekend; Henry & Mudge & the Bedtime Thumps; Henry & Mudge & the Big Sleepover; Henry & Mudge & the Funny Lunch; Henry & Mudge & the Great Grandpas; Henry & Mudge & the Tall Tree House. Stevenson, Suçie, illus. 2013. (Henry & Mudge Ser.). (ENG.). 240p. (J). (gr. k-2). pap. 15.96 *(978-1-4424-9441-1(7),* Simon Spotlight) Simon Spotlight.
—Mr. Putter & Tabby Dance the Dance. Howard, Arthur, illus. 2012. (Mr. Putter & Tabby Ser.: 21). (ENG.). 40p. (J). (gr. 1-4). 14.99 *(978-0-15-206415-0(X))* Houghton Mifflin Harcourt Publishing Co.
—Mr. Putter & Tabby Dance the Dance. 2013. (Mr. Putter & Tabby Ser.). lib. bdg. 16.00 *(978-0-606-32338-3(4),* Turtleback) Turtleback Bks.
—Mr. Putter & Tabby Hit the Slope. Howard, Arthur, illus. 2016. (Mr. Putter & Tabby Ser.). (ENG.). 40p. (J). (gr. 1-4). 14.99 *(978-0-15-206427-3(3),* HMH Books For Young Readers) Houghton Mifflin Harcourt Publishing Co.
—Mr. Putter & Tabby Ring the Bell. Howard, Arthur, illus. (Mr. Putter & Tabby Ser.). (ENG.). 44p. (J). (gr. 1-4). 2012. pap. 5.99 *(978-0-547-85075-7(1))* 2011. 14.99 *(978-0-15-205071-9(X))* Houghton Mifflin Harcourt Publishing Co.
—Mr. Putter & Tabby Ring the Bell. Howard, Arthur, illus. 2012. (Mr. Putter & Tabby Ser.). lib. bdg. 16.00 *(978-0-606-26614-7(3),* Turtleback) Turtleback Bks.
—Mr. Putter & Tabby Smell the Roses. Howard, Arthur, illus. (Mr. Putter & Tabby Ser.: 24). (ENG.). 40p. (J). (gr. 1-4). 2016. pap. 5.99 *(978-0-544-80907-9(6))* 2015. 14.99 *(978-0-15-206081-7(2))* Houghton Mifflin Harcourt Publishing Co. (HMH Books For Young Readers).
—Mr. Putter & Tabby Spin the Yarn. Howard, Arthur, illus. 2007. (Mr. Putter & Tabby Ser.). (ENG.). 44p. (J). (gr. 1-4). pap. 5.99 *(978-0-15-206095-4(2))* Houghton Mifflin Harcourt Publishing Co.
—Mr. Putter & Tabby Spin the Yarn. Howard, Arthur, illus. 2007. (Mr. Putter & Tabby Ser.). (gr. 1-4). lib. bdg. 16.00 *(978-0-7569-8062-7(3))* Perfection Learning Corp.
—Mr. Putter & Tabby Stir the Soup. Howard, Arthur, illus. 2004. (Mr. Putter & Tabby Ser.). (ENG.). 44p. (J). (gr. 1-4). pap. 5.99 *(978-0-15-205058-0(2))* Houghton Mifflin Harcourt Publishing Co.
—Mr. Putter & Tabby Stir the Soup. Howard, Arthur, illus. 2004. (Mr. Putter & Tabby Ser.). (gr. 1-4). 16.00 *(978-0-7569-3915-1(1))* Perfection Learning Corp.
—Mr. Putter & Tabby Turn the Page. Howard, Arthur, illus. (Mr. Putter & Tabby Ser.). (ENG.). 40p. (J). (gr. 1-4). 2015. pap. 5.99 *(978-0-544-58232-3(2))* 2014. 14.99 *(978-0-15-206063-3(4))* Houghton Mifflin Harcourt Publishing Co. (HMH Books For Young Readers).
—Mr. Putter & Tabby Turn the Page. 2015. (Mr. Putter & Tabby Ser.). lib. bdg. 16.00 *(978-0-606-37453-8(1))* Turtleback Bks.
—Mr. Putter & Tabby Walk the Dog. Howard, Arthur, illus. 2007. (Mr. Putter & Tabby Ser.). pap. 7.93 *(978-1-4189-5209-9(5))* Houghton Mifflin Harcourt Trade & Reference Pubs.
—The Old Woman Who Named Things. Brown, Kathryn, illus. 2015. 32p. pap. 7.00 *(978-1-61003-498-2(8))* Center for the Collaborative Classroom.
—The Old Woman Who Named Things. Brown, Kathryn, illus. 2004. (gr. -1-3). 17.00 *(978-0-7569-4204-5(7))* Perfection Learning Corp.
—Puppy Mudge Finds a Friend. Stevenson, Suçie, illus. (Puppy Mudge Ser.). (ENG.). 32p. (J). (gr. -1-k). 2005. pap. 3.99 *(978-1-4169-0369-7(0))* 2004. 16.99 *(978-0-689-83982-5(0))* Simon Spotlight. (Simon Spotlight).
—Puppy Mudge Has a Snack. Mones, Isidre, illus. 2005. (Puppy Mudge Ser.). (gr. -1-k). 14.00 *(978-0-7569-5764-3(8))* Perfection Learning Corp.
—Puppy Mudge Has a Snack. Mones, Isidre, illus. (Puppy Mudge Ser.). (ENG.). 32p. (J). (gr. -1-k). 2004. pap. 3.99 *(978-0-689-86995-2(9))* 2003. 16.99 *(978-0-689-83981-8(2))* Simon Spotlight. (Simon Spotlight).
—Puppy Mudge Loves His Blanket. Mones, Isidre, illus. (Puppy Mudge Ser.). (ENG.). 32p. (J). (gr. -1-k). 2005. pap. 3.99 *(978-1-4169-0336-9(4))* 2004. 16.99 *(978-0-689-83983-2(9))* Simon Spotlight. (Simon Spotlight).
—Puppy Mudge Wants to Play. Stevenson, Suçie, illus. (Puppy Mudge Ser.). (ENG.). 32p. (J). (gr. -1-k). 2006. pap. 3.99 *(978-1-4169-1556-0(7))* 2005. 16.99 *(978-0-689-83984-9(7))* Simon Spotlight. (Simon Spotlight).
—The Storm. McDaniels, Preston, illus. 2003. (Lighthouse Family Ser.: 1). (ENG.). 80p. (J). (gr. 1-5). pap. 5.99 *(978-0-689-84882-7(X),* Simon & Schuster Bks. For Young Readers) Simon & Schuster Bks. For Young Readers.
—We Love You, Rosie! Davick, Linda, illus. 2017. (ENG.). 48p. (J). (gr. -1-2). 17.99 *(978-1-4424-6511-4(5),* Beach Lane Bks.) Beach Lane Bks.
Rylant, Cynthia & Bracken, Carolyn. Henry & Mudge & the Funny Lunch. Bracken, Carolyn, illus. 2004. (Henry & Mudge Ser.: 24). (ENG., Illus.). 40p. (J). (gr. k-2). 16.99 *(978-0-689-81178-4(0),* Simon Spotlight) Simon Spotlight.
—Henry & Mudge & the Wild Goose Chase. 2004. (Henry & Mudge Ser.: 23). (ENG., Illus.). 40p. (J). (gr. k-2). pap. 3.99 *(978-0-689-83450-9(0),* Simon Spotlight) Simon Spotlight.
—Henry & Mudge & the Wild Goose Chase. Bracken, Carolyn, illus. 2003. (Henry & Mudge Ser.: 23). (ENG., Illus.). 40p. (J). (gr. k-2). 16.99 *(978-0-689-81172-2(1),* Simon Spotlight) Simon Spotlight.
Rylant, Cynthia & Howard, Arthur. Mr. Putter & Tabby Dance the Dance. Howard, Arthur, illus. 2013. (Mr. Putter & Tabby Ser.). (ENG., Illus.). 40p. (J). (gr. 1-4). pap. 5.99 *(978-0-544-10496-9(X))* Houghton Mifflin Harcourt Publishing Co.
Rylant, Cynthia & Mones, Isidre. Puppy Mudge Takes a Bath. Mones, Isidre, illus. 2004. (Puppy Mudge Ser.). (ENG., Illus.). 32p. (J). (gr. -1-k). pap. 3.99 *(978-0-689-86621-0(6),* Simon Spotlight) Simon Spotlight.
Rylant, Cynthia & National Geographic Learning Staff. Tulip Sees America. Desimini, Lisa, illus. 2010. (Rise & Shine Ser.). (ENG.). 32p. (C). (gr. -1-18). pap. 21.95 *(978-0-439-39978-4(5))* National Geographic School Publishing, Inc.
Ryshpan-Harris, Joanne. The Great Adventures of Bottom the Bassett Hound. Bouganim, Revital, illus. 2008. 60p. (J). pap. 5.95 *(978-1-4259-8558-5(0))* AuthorHouse.
Sabo, J. Train Wrecker. 2011. 28p. pap. 24.95 *(978-1-4626-4379-0(5))* America Star Bks.
Sabo-Western, Deborah. Peter Penny: Discovers the Gift. 2007. (ENG.). 46p. pap. 15.99 *(978-1-4196-8115-8(X))* CreateSpace Independent Publishing Platform.
Sackett, Frances. The Misadventures of the Magician's Dog. 2013. (ENG.). 192p. (J). (gr. 2-7). 16.95 *(978-0-8234-2869-4(9))* Holiday Hse., Inc.
The Sacrament Series. 2005. (J). *(978-0-9772007-0-2(1))* Layne Morgan Media, Inc.
Sáenz, Benjamin Alire. La Perrita Que le Encantaban las Tortillas. Garcia, Geronimo, illus. 2009. (Little Diego Book Ser.).Tr. of Dog Who Loved Tortillas. (SPA & ENG.). 40p. (J). (gr. 1-4). 17.95 *(978-1-933693-54-5(1))* Cinco Puntos Pr.
Sagar, Marie. Cuddly Sam. 2009. 24p. pap. 12.99 *(978-1-4389-9334-8(X))* AuthorHouse.
Sakowski, Nadeen. The Adventures of Bailey Wiggins. 2009. 70p. pap. 26.50 *(978-0-557-06610-0(7))* Lulu Pr., Inc.
Salamoff, Paul J. Bo Obama: The White House Tails. 2010. (ENG.). 40p. pap. 6.99 *(978-1-61623-925-1(5))* Bluewater Productions, Inc.
Salamon, Julie. Cat in the City. Weber, Jill, illus. 2014. (ENG.). 208p. (J). (gr. 3-7). 16.99 *(978-0-8037-4056-3(5),* Dial Bks) Penguin Young Readers Group.
—Mutt's Promise. Weber, Jill, illus. 2016. (ENG.). 256p. (J). (gr. 3-7). 16.99 *(978-0-525-42778-0(3),* Dial Bks) Penguin Young Readers Group.
Salas-Tristan, M. U. Rocky's ABC Book with His Friends: Photographic Bilingual. 2012. (ENG.). 32p. (J). pap. 29.95 *(978-1-4327-9381-4(0))* Outskirts Pr., Inc.
Salisbury, Graham. Calvin Coconut: Dog Heaven. Rogers, Jacqueline, illus. 2011. (Calvin Coconut Ser.). (ENG.). 160p. (J). (gr. 3-7). 6.99 *(978-0-375-84602-1(6),* Yearling) Random Hse. Children's Bks.
Salisbury, Linda G. Trouble in Contrary Woods: A Bailey Fish Adventure. Tomatore, Carol, illus. 2009. (J). 8.85 *(978-1-881539-46-9(6))* Tabby Hse. Bks.
Salmon, Casey. The Adventures of Mabel & Stinky: Mabel, Stinky, & the Terrified Toad. 2009. 44p. pap. 19.99 *(978-1-4389-7454-5(X))* AuthorHouse.
Salten, Felix. Djibi. Levin, Raya, tr. 2016. (Bambi's Classic Animal Tales Ser.). (ENG., Illus.). 192p. (J). (gr. 3-7). pap. 8.99 *(978-1-4424-8764-2(X),* Aladdin) Simon & Schuster Children's Publishing.
—The Hound of Florence. Paterson, Huntley, tr. from GER. 2014. (Bambi's Classic Animal Tales Ser.). (ENG., Illus.). 288p. (J). (gr. 3-7). pap. 6.99 *(978-1-4424-8748-2(8),* Aladdin) Simon & Schuster Children's Publishing.
—Renni the Rescuer. Kaufman, Kenneth C., tr. from GER. 2013. (Bambi's Classic Animal Tales Ser.). (ENG., Illus.). 384p. (J). (gr. 3-7). pap. 6.99 *(978-1-4424-8273-9(7),* Aladdin) Simon & Schuster Children's Publishing.
—Renni the Rescuer. Kaufman, Kenneth C., tr. from GER. 2013. (Bambi's Classic Animal Tales Ser.). (ENG., Illus.). 384p. (J). (gr. 3-7). 16.99 *(978-1-4424-8274-6(5),* Simon & Schuster/Paula Wiseman Bks.) Simon & Schuster/Paula Wiseman Bks.

Saltzberg, Barney. Arlo Needs Glasses. 2012. (ENG., Illus.). 24p. (gr. k-1). 17.95 *(978-0-7611-6879-9(6)*, 16879) Workman Publishing Co., Inc.
Salzman, Jeremiah. The Day of the Sandwich. Smith, Stephan, illus. 2010. (Very Small Adventures of Daisie Pup! Ser.). 48p. (J). pap. 8.99 *(978-0-9842632-8-8(4))* Scandora.
Sam the Dog. 2003. (Chunky Animal Shaped Boards Ser.). (J). 10p. bds. 9.95 *(978-0-7525-7856-9(1))*; (Illus.). bds. 1.98 *(978-0-7525-7777-7(8))* Parragon, Inc.
Sampson, Brent. Aidan's Shoes. Switzer, Bobbi, illus. 2006. (ENG.). 28p. per. 12.95 *(978-1-59800-684-1(3))* Outskirts Pr., Inc.
Sanchez, Helen. The Buddy Boys. 2008. 15p. pap. 24.95 *(978-1-60672-352-4(9))* America Star Bks.
Sanchez, Juanita L. Pancho the Green Parrot Lays an Egg, 1 vol. Ramirez, Samuel, illus. 2009. 24p. pap. 24.95 *(978-1-61546-150-9(7))* America Star Bks.
Sanchez, Priscilla. Champ the Boxing Boxer. 2011. 12p. pap. 8.32 *(978-1-4634-7423-2(7))* AuthorHouse.
Sander, Sonia. Big-Top Scooby-Doo! Movie Reader. 2012. (Scooby Doo Reader Ser.). lib. bdg. 13.55 *(978-0-606-26542-3(2)*, Turtleback) Turtleback Bks.
—Help Is on the Way! 2009. (Lego City Ser.). (ENG.). 32p. (J). (gr. -1-k). pap. 3.99 *(978-0-545-15068-2(X))* Scholastic, Inc.
—Help Is on the Way! 2009. (LEGO City Adventures Scholastic Readers Level 1 Ser.: 2). lib. bdg. 13.55 *(978-0-606-07119-2(9)*, Turtleback) Turtleback Bks.
—LEGO City Reader Collection: LEGO City Emergency. 2012. (Illus.). 127p. (J). *(978-1-4351-3985-5(2))* Scholastic, Inc.
—Scooby-Doo & the Chocolate Phantom, 1 vol. 2016. (Scooby-Doo Comic Readers Ser.). (ENG.). 32p. (J). (gr. k-3). lib. bdg. 24.21 *(978-1-61479-451-6(0)*, Graphic Planet) Magic Wagon.
—Scooby-Doo & the International Express. 2009. (Illus.). 32p. (J). pap. *(978-0-545-16283-8(1))* Scholastic, Inc.
—Scooby-Doo in Food Fight!, 1 vol. 2016. (Scooby-Doo Comic Readers Ser.). (ENG.). 32p. (J). (gr. k-3). lib. bdg. 24.21 *(978-1-61479-454-7(5)*, Graphic Planet) Magic Wagon.
—Scooby-Doo in Keepaway Camp, 1 vol. 2016. (Scooby-Doo! Set 3 Ser.). (ENG., Illus.). 32p. (J). (gr. k-3). lib. bdg. 24.21 *(978-1-61479-407-3(3)*, 1401183) Spotlight.
—Scooby-Doo in Raging River Adventure, 1 vol. 2016. (Scooby-Doo Leveled Readers Ser.). (ENG., Illus.). 32p. (J). (gr. k-4). lib. bdg. 24.21 *(978-1-61479-420-2(0))* Spotlight.
—Scooby-Doo in Shiver Me Timbers, 1 vol. 2016. (Scooby-Doo! Set 3 Ser.). (ENG., Illus.). 32p. (J). (gr. k-4). lib. bdg. 24.21 *(978-1-61479-408-0(1)*, 1401184) Spotlight.
—Scooby-Doo Steals the Dog Show, 1 vol. 2016. (Scooby-Doo Leveled Readers Ser.). (ENG., Illus.). 32p. (J). (gr. k-4). lib. bdg. 24.21 *(978-1-61479-421-9(9))* Spotlight.
—Witching Hour. 2009. (Scooby Reader 25 Ser.). (ENG., Illus.). 32p. (J). (gr. -1-3). pap. 3.99 *(978-0-545-16106-0(1))* Scholastic, Inc.
Sander, Sonia & Bridwell, Norman. Clifford Helps Santa. Cuddy, Robbin, illus. 2006. (Clifford the Big Red Dog Ser.). (J). pap. *(978-0-439-90456-8(0))* Scholastic, Inc.
Sands, Kathryn Ann. How Chili Willie Got His Name. 2013. 24p. pap. 17.99 *(978-1-4817-0641-4(1))* AuthorHouse.
Sanford, Joyce. Goldenlocks & Her 3 Homes. 2013. (ENG.). 34p. (J). 24.95 *(978-1-4787-0151-4(X))* Outskirts Pr., Inc.
Santiago, Tony, illus. A Greyhound's Tale: Running for Glory, Walking for Home. 2006. 40p. (J). 15.00 *(978-0-9762564-2-7(8))* Ideate Prairie.
Santillo, LuAnn. The Dog. Santillo, LuAnn, ed. 2003. (Half-Pint Kids Readers Ser.). (Illus.). 7p. (J). (gr. -1-1). pap. 1.00 *(978-1-59256-065-3(2))* Half-Pint Kids, Inc.
—Go West. Santillo, LuAnn, ed. 2003. (Half-Pint Kids Readers Ser.). (Illus.). 7p. (J). (gr. -1-1). pap. 1.00 *(978-1-59256-071-4(7))* Half-Pint Kids, Inc.
Santini, Philip. Harvey's Adventures. Chambers, Z., illus. 2011. 44p. pap. 24.95 *(978-1-4626-2078-4(7))* America Star Bks.
Santopolo, Jill. Purple Nails & Puppy Tails. 2014. (Sparkle Spa Ser.: 2). (ENG., Illus.). 128p. (J). (gr. 2-5). pap. 5.99 *(978-1-4424-7383-6(5)*, Aladdin) Simon & Schuster Children's Publishing.
—Sparkle Spa 4-Books-In-1! All That Glitters; Purple Nails & Puppy Tails; Makeover Magic; True Colors. 2016. (Sparkle Spa Ser.). (ENG., Illus.). 496p. (J). (gr. 2-5). 14.99 *(978-1-4814-7594-5(0)*, Aladdin) Simon & Schuster Children's Publishing.
Saphin, Wendy. Rosie's Box: A Box Full of Surprises. Saphin, Wendy, illus. 2012. (Illus.). 20p. pap. 10.95 *(978-1-62212-457-2(X)*, Strategic Bk. Publishing) Strategic Book Publishing & Rights Agency (SBPRA).
Sarcone-Roach, Julia. The Bear Ate Your Sandwich. 2015. (ENG., Illus.). 40p. (J). (gr. -1-2). 16.99 *(978-0-375-85860-4(1))*; lib. bdg. 19.99 *(978-0-375-95860-1(6))* Random Hse. Children's Bks. (Knopf Bks. for Young Readers).
Sargeant, Theresa. The Drainpipe Gang - the Adventures of Chris & Andy Smy. 2011. 112p. pap. *(978-1-907256-80-6(6))* Abela Publishing.
Sargent, Dave & Sargent, Pat. A Puppy for Bobby/un cachorro para Robertito, 10 vols. Robinson, Laura, illus. 2004. (Learn to Read Ser.: 10). (ENG & SPA.). 18p. (J). pap. 10.95 *(978-1-56763-982-7(8))* Ozark Publishing.
—Puppy for Bobby/un cachorro para Robertito, 10, 11. Robinson, Laura, illus. 2004. (Learn to Read Ser.: 10). (ENG & SPA.). 18p. (J). lib. bdg. 19.95 *(978-1-56763-981-0(X))* Ozark Publishing.
—Young Dawn: Friends Care! Woodword, Elaine, illus. 2005. (Young Animal Pride Ser.: 8). (J). 8. pap. 6.95 *(978-1-56763-878-3(3))* Vol. 8. lib. bdg. 20.95 *(978-1-56763-877-6(5))* Ozark Publishing.
—Young Sammy: I'm a Little Stinker!, Vol. 9. Woodword, Elaine, illus. 2005. (Young Animal Pride Ser.). 24p. (J). pap. 10.95 *(978-1-56763-880-6(5))* Ozark Publishing.
—Young White Thunder: I'm a Leader!, Vol. 6. Woodword, Elaine, illus. 2005. (Young Animal Pride Ser.). 24p. (J). pap. 10.95 *(978-1-56763-874-5(0))* Ozark Publishing.
Sargent, Dave, et al. A Puppy for Bobby, 10 vols. 2004. (Learn to Read Ser.: 10). (Illus.). 18p. (J). pap. 10.95 *(978-1-56763-818-9(X))*; lib. bdg. 20.95 *(978-1-56763-817-2(1))* Ozark Publishing.
—Young Chrissy: Mind Your Mama!, Vol. 7. 2005. (Young Animal Pride Ser.). (Illus.). 24p. (J). lib. bdg. 20.95 *(978-1-56763-875-2(9))* Ozark Publishing.
Sargent, Dave M., Jr. Vicious Vera, 9 vols. Huff, Jeane Lirley, illus. 2004. (Doggie Tails Ser.: 9). (J). pap. 10.95 *(978-1-56763-854-7(6))* Ozark Publishing.
Sargent, David M., Jr. Autumn's Emergency. Huff, Jeane Lirley, illus. 2003. (Doggie Tails Ser.). 32p. (J). pap. 10.95 *(978-1-56763-846-2(5))* Ozark Publishing.
—Buffy's Revenge. Huff, Jeane Lirley, illus. 2003. (Doggie Tails Ser.). 32p. (J). pap. 10.95 *(978-1-56763-844-8(9))*; lib. bdg. 20.95 *(978-1-56763-843-1(0))* Ozark Publishing.
Sargent, David M. Emma! Huff, Jeane, illus. 2004. (Doggie Tails Ser.). (J). *(978-1-56763-851-6(1))*; pap. *(978-1-56763-852-3(X))* Ozark Publishing.
Sargent, David M., Jr. Guard Dog Mary, 9 vols. Huff, Jeane Lirley, illus. 2003. (Doggie Tails Ser.). 32p. (J). pap. 10.95 *(978-1-56763-850-9(3))* Ozark Publishing.
—Portia's Prank, 9 vols. Huff, Jeane Lirley, illus. 2003. (Doggie Tails Ser.). 32p. (J). pap. 10.95 *(978-1-56763-848-6(1))*; lib. bdg. 20.95 *(978-1-56763-847-9(3))* Ozark Publishing.
Sargent, Pat. The Black Panther, 6 vols., Vol. 2. Lenoir, Jane, illus. 2003. (Barney the Bear Killer Ser.: Vol. 2). 137p. (J). pap. 10.95 *(978-1-56763-966-7(6))*; lib. bdg. 26.25 *(978-1-56763-965-0(8))* Ozark Publishing.
—The Bobcat, 8 vols., Vol. 5. Lenoir, Jane, illus. 2003. (Barney the Bear Killer Ser.: Vol. 5). 136p. (J). lib. bdg. 26.25 *(978-1-56763-971-1(2))* Ozark Publishing.
Sargent, Pat L. Jaguar #8 (PB), 6 vols. 2007. (Barney the Bear Killer Ser.: 8). (YA). pap. 9.95 *(978-1-59381-425-0(9))* Ozark Publishing.
Sarkan, Carole. And Candy Smiled. 2012. 32p. 24.95 *(978-1-4575-1359-6(5))*; pap. 14.95 *(978-1-4575-1210-0(6))* Dog Ear Publishing, LLC.
Sartorius, Evohn. Bobbie, His Family & Dog Bingo, 1 vol. 2009. 42p. pap. 24.95 *(978-1-61546-409-8(3))* America Star Bks.
Satchwell, Sm. Len Stories. 2012. (Illus.). 24p. pap. 19.82 *(978-1-4685-0478-1(9))* AuthorHouse.
Sateren, Shelley Swanson. Fearless Freddie. Melmon, Deborah, illus. 2015. (Adventures at Hound Hotel Ser.). (ENG.). 72p. (gr. 2-3). lib. bdg. 25.32 *(978-1-4795-5898-8(2)*, Adventures at Hound Hotel) Picture Window Bks.
—Growling Gracie. Melmon, Deborah, illus. 2015. (Adventures at Hound Hotel Ser.). (ENG.). 72p. (gr. 2-3). lib. bdg. 25.32 *(978-1-4795-5899-5(0)*, Adventures at Hound Hotel) Picture Window Bks.
—Homesick Herbie. Melmon, Deborah, illus. 2015. (Adventures at Hound Hotel Ser.). (ENG.). 72p. (gr. 2-3). lib. bdg. 25.32 *(978-1-4795-5897-1(4)*, Adventures at Hound Hotel) Picture Window Bks.
—Max & Zoe: the Science Fair, 1 vol. Sullivan, Mary, illus. 2013. (Max & Zoe Ser.). (ENG.). 32p. (gr. k-2). pap. 5.19 *(978-1-4795-2330-6(5)*, Max & Zoe) Picture Window Bks.
—Mudball Molly. Melmon, Deborah, illus. 2015. (Adventures at Hound Hotel Ser.). (ENG.). 72p. (gr. 2-3). lib. bdg. 25.32 *(978-1-4795-5900-8(8)*, Adventures at Hound Hotel) Picture Window Bks.
—The Science Fair. Sullivan, Mary, illus. 2013. (Max & Zoe Ser.). (ENG.). 32p. (gr. k-2). lib. bdg. 21.32 *(978-1-4048-7202-8(7)*, Max & Zoe) Picture Window Bks.
Sather, Connie. Sadie the Sled Dog? 2009. 44p. (J). pap. 13.95 *(978-1-4327-4164-8(0))* Outskirts Pr., Inc.
Satterly, Denise B. The Adventures of Icky & Weezy: Fall Has Arrived. 2011. 20p. (gr. -1 — 1). pap. 10.03 *(978-1-4520-2046-4(9))* AuthorHouse.
Sattler, Jennifer. Chick 'n' Pug. 2013. (ENG., Illus.). 30p. (J). (gr. -1-1). bds. 7.99 *(978-1-61963-078-9(8)*, 9781619630789, Bloomsbury USA Childrens) Bloomsbury Publishing USA.
—A Chick 'n' Pug Christmas. 2014. (ENG., Illus.). 32p. (J). (gr. -1-1). 16.99 *(978-1-59990-602-7(3)*, 9781599906027, Bloomsbury USA Childrens) Bloomsbury Publishing USA.
—Chick 'n' Pug Meet the Dude. (ENG., Illus.). (J). (gr. -1-1). 2014. 30p. bds. 7.99 *(978-1-61963-402-2(3)*, 9781619634022) 2013. 32p. 16.99 *(978-1-59990-600-3(7)*, 9781599906003) 2013. 32p. 17.89 *(978-1-59990-760-4(7)*, 9781599907604) Bloomsbury Publishing USA. (Bloomsbury USA Childrens).
—Chick 'n' Pug: the Love Pug. 2015. (ENG., Illus.). 32p. (J). (gr. -1-1). 16.99 *(978-1-61963-672-9(7)*, 9781619636729, Bloomsbury USA Childrens) Bloomsbury Publishing USA.
Sattler, Jennifer Gordon. Chick 'n' Pug. 2010. (ENG., Illus.). 32p. (J). (gr. -1-1). 14.99 *(978-1-59990-534-1(5)*, 9781599905341, Bloomsbury USA Childrens) Bloomsbury Publishing USA.
Sattler, Jennifer Gordon, illus. A Chick 'n' Pug Christmas. 2014. (J). *(978-1-61963-463-3(5))* Bloomsbury Pr.
Saumier, Chantelle. Vinnie! Star of the Show. 2013. 40p. *(978-1-4602-3098-5(1))*; pap. *(978-1-4602-1741-2(1))* FriesenPress.
—Vinnie! the Hurricane. 2013. 32p. *(978-1-4602-3097-8(3))*; pap. *(978-1-4602-1729-0(2))* FriesenPress.
Saunders, Maggie. The Adventures of Morgan & Malyk: The Lost Dog Mystery. 2012. 48p. (gr. 1-2). pap. 8.99 *(978-1-4582-0338-0(7)*, Abbott Pr.) Author Solutions, Inc.
Saunders, Margaret Marshall. Tilda Jane: A Rambunctious Orphan's Misadventures Finding a Home in the Early 1900s. 2008. (Fiction Treasures Ser.). (ENG.). 318p. pap. 16.95 *(978-0-88780-780-0(1)*, 9780887807800) Formac Publishing Co., Ltd. CAN. Dist: Casemate Pubs. & Bk. Distributors, LLC.
Saunders, Marshall. Beautiful Joe: An AutoBiography of a Dog. 2006. (ENG.). 244p. pap. 20.99 *(978-1-4264-4034-2(0))* 2007. 266p. pap. 23.99 *(978-1-4264-4093-9(6))* Creative Media Partners, LLC.
—Beautiful Joe a Dog's Own Story. 2006. 256p. pap. 18.45 *(978-1-59462-261-8(2)*, 297); pap. 18.45 *(978-1-59462-284-7(1)*, 320) Standard Pubns., Inc. (Book Jungle).
Saunders, Vivien. The Adventures of Annika. Muckle, Christine, illus. 2013. 42p. pap. *(978-1-909730-02-1(5))* Abbotsley Publishing.
Sazaklis, John. The Biggest Little Hero, 1 vol. Baltazar, Art, illus. 2012. (DC Super-Pets Ser.). (ENG.). 56p. (gr. 2-2). pap. 4.95 *(978-1-4048-7664-4(2))*; lib. bdg. 23.99 *(978-1-4048-6490-0(3))* Picture Window Bks. (DC Super-Pets).
—Candy Store Caper, 1 vol. Baltazar, Art, illus. 2012. (DC Super-Pets Ser.). (ENG.). 56p. (gr. 2-2). pap. 4.95 *(978-1-4048-7214-1(0))*; lib. bdg. 23.99 *(978-1-4048-6484-9(9))* Picture Window Bks. (DC Super-Pets).
—The Dangers of Dog Walking. Robinson, Lee, illus. 2016. (Billy Burger, Model Citizen Ser.). (ENG.). 96p. (gr. 2-3). lib. bdg. 22.65 *(978-1-4965-2587-1(6))* Stone Arch Bks.
—Swamp Thing vs the Zombie Pets, 1 vol. Baltazar, Art, illus. 2012. (DC Super-Pets Ser.). (ENG.). 56p. (gr. 2-2). pap. 4.95 *(978-1-4048-7667-5(7))*; lib. bdg. 23.99 *(978-1-4048-6491-7(1))* Picture Window Bks. (DC Super-Pets).
Scarry, Huck & Scarry, Richard. A Day at the Police Station. Scarry, Richard, illus. 2004. (Look-Look Ser.). (ENG., Illus.). 24p. (J). (gr. -1-2). pap. 4.99 *(978-0-375-82822-5(2)*, Golden Bks.) Random Hse. Children's Bks.
Schachner, Judy. Class Action. 2017. (Skippyjon Jones Ser.). lib. bdg. 19.65 ***(978-0-606-40104-3(0))*** Turtleback Bks.
—Color Crazy. Schachner, Judy, illus. 2007. (Skippyjon Jones Ser.). (ENG., Illus.). 12p. (J). (gr. -1 — 1). bds. 6.99 *(978-0-525-47782-2(9)*, Dutton Books for Young Readers) Penguin Young Readers Group.
—The Great Bean Caper. 2009. (Skippyjon Jones Ser.). (ENG.). 32p. (J). (gr. -1-k). mass mkt. 3.99 *(978-0-448-45167-1(0)*, Grosset & Dunlap) Penguin Young Readers Group.
—Skippyjon Jones. 2009. (Illus.). 32p. 17.00 *(978-1-60686-417-3(3))* Perfection Learning Corp.
—Skippyjon Jones & the Big Bones. 2007. (Skippyjon Jones Ser.). (ENG.). 40p. (J). (gr. -1-k). 17.99 *(978-0-525-47884-3(1)*, Dutton Books for Young Readers) Penguin Young Readers Group.
—Skippyjon Jones Cirque de Ole. 2012. (Skippyjon Jones Ser.). (ENG.). 32p. (J). (gr. -1-k). 17.99 *(978-0-8037-3782-2(3)*, Dial Bks) Penguin Young Readers Group.
—Skippyjon Jones, Class Action. (Skippyjon Jones Ser.). (ENG.). (J). 2017. (-k). pap. 8.99 ***(978-0-425-28892-4(7)***, Puffin Books) 2011. 32p. (gr. -1-k). 17.99 *(978-0-525-42228-0(5)*, Dutton Books for Young Readers) Penguin Young Readers Group.
—Skippyjon Jones in Mummy Trouble. 2008. (Skippyjon Jones Ser.). (ENG.). 32p. (J). (gr. -1-k). pap. 6.99 *(978-0-14-241211-4(2)*, Puffin Books) Penguin Young Readers Group.
—Skippyjon Jones in Mummy Trouble. Schachner, Judy, illus. 2006. (Skippyjon Jones Ser.). (ENG., Illus.). 32p. (J). (gr. -1-k). 17.99 *(978-0-525-47754-9(3)*, Dutton Books for Young Readers) Penguin Young Readers Group.
—Skippyjon Jones in Mummy Trouble. 2009. (Skippyjon Jones Ser.). 17.00 *(978-1-60686-418-0(1))* Perfection Learning Corp.
—Skippyjon Jones in the Doghouse. Schachner, Judy, illus. 2007. (Skippyjon Jones Ser.). (ENG., Illus.). 32p. (J). (gr. -1-k). pap. 6.99 *(978-0-14-240749-3(6)*, Puffin Books) Penguin Young Readers Group.
—Skippyjon Jones in the Doghouse. Wilhelm, James J., ed. Schachner, Judy, illus. 2005. (Skippyjon Jones Ser.). (ENG., Illus.). 32p. (J). (gr. -1-18). 16.99 *(978-0-525-47297-1(5)*, Dutton Books for Young Readers) Penguin Young Readers Group.
—Skippyjon Jones in the Doghouse. 2009. (Illus.). 32p. 17.00 *(978-1-60686-419-7(X))* Perfection Learning Corp.
—Skippyjon Jones, Lost in Spice. Schachner, Judy, illus. 2009. (Skippyjon Jones Ser.). (ENG., Illus.). 32p. (J). (gr. -1-k). 17.99 *(978-0-525-47965-9(1)*, Dutton Books for Young Readers) Penguin Young Readers Group.
—Skippyjon Jones, Lost in Spice. 2009. (Skippyjon Jones Ser.). (J). 37.75 *(978-1-4407-6558-2(8))*; 192.75 *(978-1-4407-6557-5(X))*; 1.25 *(978-1-4407-6563-6(4))* Recorded Bks., Inc.
—Skippyjon Jones Presto-Change-O. 2010. (Skippyjon Jones Ser.). (ENG.). 32p. (J). (gr. -1-k). 17.99 *(978-0-525-42358-4(3)*, Dutton Books for Young Readers) Penguin Young Readers Group.
—Skippyjon Jones Snow What. 2014. (Skippyjon Jones Ser.). (ENG., Illus.). 32p. (J). (gr. -1-k). 17.99 *(978-0-8037-3789-1(0)*, Dial Bks) Penguin Publishing Group.
Schaefer, Lola M. Mittens, Where Is Max? Hartung, Susan Kathleen, illus. 2011. (My First I Can Read Ser.). (ENG.). 32p. (J). (gr. -1 — 1). 16.99 *(978-0-06-170227-3(7))*; pap. 3.99 *(978-0-06-170226-6(9))* HarperCollins Pubs.
—What's That, Mittens? Hartung, Susan Kathleen, illus. 2009. (My First I Can Read Ser.). (ENG.). 32p. (J). (gr. -1 — 1). pap. 3.99 *(978-0-06-054664-9(6))* HarperCollins Pubs.
Scheffler, Axel, illus. Pip the Puppy. 2015. (Buggy Buddies Ser.). (ENG.). 12p. (J). (— 1). bds. 7.99 *(978-0-230-75617-5(4))* Pan Macmillan GBR. Dist: Independent Pubs. Group.
Scherer, Catherine W. Simon & Barklee in China, Book 1 - the Southeast. 2007. (Another Country Calling Ser.). (J). per. 15.00 *(978-0-9714502-6-4(9)*, Explorer Media) Simon & Barklee, Inc./ExplorerMedia.
Schettler, Amanda. The Adventures of Mike & Fanny: A Story about A Dog & A Goat. 2011. 50p. 35.95 *(978-1-258-08538-4(0))* Literary Licensing, LLC.
Scheunemann, Pam. Cat Tails, 1 vol. Chawla, Neena, illus. 2006. (Animal Tales Ser.). 24p. (J). (gr. k-3). (ENG.). lib. bdg. 24.21 *(978-1-59679-927-1(7)*, SandCastle); pap. 48.42 *(978-1-59679-928-8(5))* ABDO Publishing Co.
Schieber, Barry J. An Open Heart: A Story about Moritz. 2006. (Illus.). 32p. (J). 17.00 *(978-0-9721457-2-5(9))* Silent Moon Bks.
Schlosser, Bobbi. Pilgrim: A True Story. 2013. 34p. pap. 17.25 *(978-1-4669-8968-9(8))* Trafford Publishing.
Schmidt, Werner. Prisoners of the Witchaiks. 2005. 173p. pap. 12.50 *(978-1-4116-4728-2(9))* Lulu Pr., Inc.
Schoene, Kerstin & Gunetsreiner, Nina. Milo Is Not a Dog Today. 2015. (Illus.). 32p. (J). *(978-1-4896-3867-0(9))* Weigl Pubs., Inc.
—Milo Is Not a Dog Today. Schoene, Kerstin & Gunetsreiner, Nina, illus. 2014. (ENG., Illus.). 32p. (J). (gr. -1-3). 16.99 *(978-0-8075-4793-9(X))* Whitman, Albert & Co.
Scholastic, Inc. Staff. Dear Mrs. Larue. 2005. (ENG.). (J). pap. 550.00 *(978-0-439-70787-9(0)*, Sidekicks TM) Scholastic, Inc.
Scholastic, Inc. Staff, contrib. by. Let's Go to the Firehouse. 2015. (ENG.). 20p. (J). (gr. -1 — 1). pap. 12.99 *(978-0-545-76634-0(6)*, Cartwheel Bks.) Scholastic, Inc.
Scholastic, Inc. Staff & Duendes Del Sur Staff, contrib. by. Scooby-Doo! & the Mummy's Curse. 2005. (Illus.). 24p. (J). *(978-1-4156-3913-9(2))* Scholastic, Inc.
Scholastic, Inc. Staff & Hooks, Gwendolyn. The Mystery of the Missing Dog. Devard, Nancy, illus. 2004. (Just for You Ser.). (ENG.). 32p. (gr. k-3). pap. 3.99 *(978-0-439-56864-7(1)*, Teaching Resources) Scholastic, Inc.
Schombs, James. The Little Boy in a Dog Suit, 1 vol. Weidman, James, illus. 2010. 28p. pap. 24.95 *(978-1-61582-053-5(1))* PublishAmerica, Inc.
Schopp, Bernice Frances. The Legend of Moon-Goblin Town. 2012. 32p. pap. 21.99 *(978-1-4771-4475-6(7))* Xlibris Corp.
Schories, Pat. Breakfast for Jack. 2004. (Jacks Ser.). (ENG., Illus.). 32p. (J). 13.95 *(978-1-932425-16-1(0)*, Lemniscaat) Boyds Mills Pr.
—Jack & the Missing Piece. 2004. (Jacks Ser.). (ENG., Illus.). 32p. (J). 13.95 *(978-1-932425-17-8(9)*, Lemniscaat) Boyds Mills Pr.
—Jack & the Night Visitors. 2006. (Jack's Bks.). (ENG., Illus.). 32p. (J). (gr. -1-1). 14.95 *(978-1-932425-33-8(0)*, Lemniscaat) Boyds Mills Pr.
—Jack Wants a Snack. 2008. (Jacks Ser.). (ENG.). 32p. (J). (gr. -1-1). 13.95 *(978-1-59078-546-1(0)*, Front Street) Boyds Mills Pr.
—When Jack Goes Out. 2010. (Jacks Ser.). (ENG., Illus.). 32p. (J). (gr. -1-1). 14.95 *(978-1-59078-652-9(1)*, Front Street) Boyds Mills Pr.
Schories, Pat, illus. Biscuit Visits the Farm. 2012. (J). *(978-1-4351-4383-8(3)*, HarperFestival) HarperCollins Pubs.
—Biscuit's Fourth of July. 2005. (J). *(978-1-4156-0311-6(1)*, HarperFestival) HarperCollins Pubs.
—Biscuit's Graduation Day. 2005. (J). *(978-1-4155-9660-9(3)*, HarperFestival) HarperCollins Pubs.
—Jack Wants a Snack. 2015. (Jack Bks.). (ENG.). 32p. (J). (— 1). bds. 7.99 *(978-1-62979-406-8(6))* Boyds Mills Pr.
Schories, Pat & Capucilli, Alyssa Satin. Biscuit & the Little Pup. Schories, Pat, illus. 2007. (My First I Can Read Ser.). (ENG., Illus.). 32p. (J). (gr. -1 — 1). pap. 3.99 *(978-0-06-074172-3(4))* HarperCollins Pubs.
Schrader, Jessica R. Carrie's New Puppy. 2006. (J). pap. 17.50 *(978-0-9776440-6-3(5))* Working Title Publishing.
Schrader, Racheal. Doodlebugs: Trouble On Moss Farm. Schrader, Racheal, illus. 2008. (Illus.). 156p. (YA). per. 7.99 *(978-0-9815274-0-6(X))* Schrader, Racheal.
Schraff, Anne. When Sleeping Dogs Awaken (Mystery), 1 vol. 2017. (Pageturners Ser.). (ENG.). 76p. (YA). (gr. 9-12). 8.95 ***(978-1-68021-391-1(1))*** Saddleback Educational Publishing, Inc.
Schrenk, Kathleen. A Dog Steals Home, 1 vol. 2017. (ENG.). 128p. (J). (gr. 3-7). pap. 8.95 *(978-1-4556-2228-3(1))* Pelican Publishing Co., Inc.
Schroeder, Erin, illus. Oh no! it's the helpful hound... & the days of the Week. Schroeder, Erin, . 2006. (FRE, JPN, SPA & GER.). 27p. (J). per. 7.95 *(978-0-9779155-0-7(6))* Erinsillart.
Schroeder, Frauna. Elwood: A Dog with Heart. Carlson, Kim, illus. 2006. 32p. (J). per. 9.95 *(978-1-892076-20-5(9))* Dancing Moon Pr.
Schroeder, Lisa. Keys to the City. 2017. (ENG.). 240p. (J). (gr. 3-7). 16.99 ***(978-0-545-90738-5(1)***, Scholastic Pr.) Scholastic, Inc.
Schroeder, Lisa. Libby's Sweet Surprise. 2014. (Charmed Life Ser.: 3). lib. bdg. 16.00 *(978-0-606-35851-4(X))* Turtleback Bks.
Schubert, Dieter. The Umbrella Doodle Book. 2012. (ENG., Illus.). 48p. (J). (gr. -1). 7.95 *(978-1-935954-15-6(6)*, 9781935954156) Lemniscaat USA.
Schubert, Ingrid & Schubert, Dieter. The Umbrella. 2011. (ENG., Illus.). 40p. (J). (gr. -1). 16.95 *(978-1-935954-00-2(8)*, 9781935954002) Lemniscaat USA.
Schubert, Leda. Reading to Peanut. Haley, Amanda, illus. 2011. (ENG.). 32p. (J). 16.95 *(978-0-8234-2339-2(5))* Holiday Hse., Inc.
Schueler, M. A. Penny the Beach Westie Big Trouble for a Little Dog. 2009. 24p. pap. 16.50 *(978-1-60860-424-1(1)*, Eloquent Bks.) Strategic Book Publishing & Rights Agency (SBPRA).
Schuette, Leslie Elaine. The Adventures of Little Autumn. Walker, Bradley, illus. 2013. 24p. 24.95 *(978-1-63004-507-4(1))* America Star Bks.
—The Adventures of Little Autumn. Walker, Bradley, illus. 2013. 24p. pap. 24.95 *(978-1-4626-9778-6(X))* America Star Bks.
—Little Autumn's Adventure in the Smoky Mountains. 2013. 30p. 24.95 *(978-1-63004-952-2(2))*; 32p. pap. 24.95 *(978-1-4626-9924-7(3))* America Star Bks.
Schult, Sherry. The Adventures of Didi & Mr Taco. Banks, Sandra, illus. 2011. 16p. pap. 24.95 *(978-1-4560-8083-9(0))* America Star Bks.
Schultz, Caleb. Keela & Capone's Take That Dog Back! 2012. 24p. pap. 17.99 *(978-1-4772-3718-2(6))* AuthorHouse.
Schultze, Gwendolyn. The Dog That's Not a Poodle. Cameron, Ed, illus. 2011. 54p. (J). pap. 12.00 *(978-1-892076-97-7(7))* Dancing Moon Pr.
Schulz, Charles. Where Is Woodstock?, 1 vol. 2013. (Peanuts Picture Bks.). (ENG.). 24p. (J). (gr. -1-4). lib. bdg. 24.21 *(978-1-61479-033-4(7))* ABDO Publishing Co.
Schulz, Charles & Pastis, Stephan. Happiness Is a Warm Blanket, Charlie Brown! Scott, Bob, illus. 2011. (Peanuts Ser.). (ENG.). 96p. (gr. 3). pap. 9.99 *(978-1-60886-681-6(5))*; (J). 19.99 *(978-1-60886-682-3(3))* Boom! Studios.
Schulz, Charles M. It's the Easter Beagle, Charlie Brown, 1 vol. 2013. (Peanuts Picture Bks.). (ENG.). 48p. (J). (gr. -1-4). lib. bdg. 24.21 *(978-1-61479-031-0(0))* ABDO Publishing Co.
—It's the Easter Beagle, Charlie Brown. Scott, Vicki, illus. 2016. (Peanuts Ser.). (ENG.). 32p. (J). (gr. -1). 7.99 *(978-1-4814-6159-7(1)*, Simon Spotlight) Simon Spotlight.
—It's the Easter Beagle, Charlie Brown: with Sound & Music. 2013. (ENG., Illus.). 48p. (J). (gr. -1-17). 19.95 *(978-0-7624-4608-7(0)*, Running Pr. Kids) Running Pr. Bk. Pubs.
Schwartz, Amy. Oma & Bobo. 2013. (ENG., Illus.). 32p. (J). (gr. -1-3). 16.99 *(978-1-4814-2149-2(2)*, Atheneum Bks. for Young Readers) Simon & Schuster Children's Publishing.

Schwartz, Anna L. Okie the Wonder Dog. Dumm, Brian Caleb, illus. 2016. 62p. (J). pap. *(978-1-63293-111-5(7))* Sunstone Pr.

Schwartz, Betty & Seresin, Lynn. Puppies, Puppies, Everywhere! A Back-And-Forth Opposites Book. Powell, Luciana Navarro, illus. 2015. (J). *(978-1-62370-236-6(4))* Capstone Young Readers of Coughlan Cos.

Schwarz, Viviane. Is There a Dog in This Book? Schwarz, Viviane, illus. 2014. (ENG., Illus.). 32p. (J). (gr. -1-2). 16.99 *(978-0-7636-6991-1(1))* Candlewick Pr.

Schweitzer, C. V. The Making of an Angel. 2012. 48p. (-18). pap. 31.99 *(978-1-4797-3502-0(7))* Xlibris Corp.

Scimone, Diana. Adventures with Pawpaw: China. Wiedemer, Leah, illus. 2003. 32p. (J). 8.95 *(978-0-9729507-0-1(2))* Peapod Publishing, Inc.

Sclafani, Terry. The Thompson Twins Cruise Adventure. 2007. 84p. per. 10.95 *(978-1-4327-1542-7(9))* Outskirts Pr., Inc.

Scollon, Bill. The Pirate Pup. 2013. (Picture Viewer Ser.: 1). (ENG.). 24p. (J). (gr. -1-2). 12.99 *(978-0-7944-2592-0(5))* Reader's Digest Assn., Inc., The.

Scott, Gwen. The Dog That Wore Glasses. 2012. 20p. pap. 24.95 *(978-1-4626-8268-3(5))* America Star Bks.

Scott, Shirley A. The Adventures of Jack & Dobbie: Doggie Holidays. 2011. 40p. pap. 17.95 *(978-1-4567-3426-8(1))* AuthorHouse.

—The Adventures of Jack & Dobbie: Happy Tails. 2010. 32p. pap. 13.95 *(978-1-4490-9865-0(7))* AuthorHouse.

—The Adventures of Jack & Dobbie: The Beginning. 2009. 32p. pap. 13.95 *(978-1-4389-4840-9(9))* AuthorHouse.

—The Adventures of Jack & Dobbie: Traveling Buddies. 2012. 30p. pap. 18.99 *(978-1-4772-7851-2(6))* AuthorHouse.

Scott, Terrence. Bryce Coris Blessing. 2006. 28p. pap. 9.95 *(978-1-4327-0000-3(6))* Outskirts Pr., Inc.

Scullin, Sara. Tiki the Prima Donn. 2012. 28p. pap. 21.99 *(978-1-4797-1119-2(5))* Xlibris Corp.

Sebring Lowrey, Janette. Little Golden Book Poky Little Puppy Tales. Tenggren, Gustaf, illus. 2015. (Little Golden Book Favorites Ser.). (ENG.). 80p. (J). (-k). 7.99 *(978-0-553-51208-3(0),* Golden Bks.) Random Hse. Children's Bks.

Secret Agent Cat Purse: The Case of the Dog with Golden Wings. 2006. (J). *(978-0-9743359-3-3(2))* Murdock Publishing Co.

Sedrak, Asham. The Santa Claus Fox. 2011. 28p. pap. 13.59 *(978-1-4670-2484-6(8))* AuthorHouse.

Seeger, Laura Vaccaro. Dog & Bear: Tricks & Treats. Seeger, Laura Vaccaro, illus. 2014. (Dog & Bear Ser.). (ENG., Illus.). 32p. (J). (gr. -1-3). 14.99 *(978-1-59643-632-9(8),* 9781596436329) Roaring Brook Pr.

—Dog & Bear, Level 2: Two Friends, Three Stories. Seeger, Laura Vaccaro, illus. 2012. (My Readers Ser.). (ENG., Illus.). 32p. (J). (gr. k-2). pap. 3.99 *(978-0-312-54799-8(4),* 9780312547998) Square Fish.

—Dog Changes His Name. 2017. (Dog & Bear Ser.). (ENG., Illus.). 18p. (J). bds. 5.99 *(978-1-62672-498-3(9),* 9781626724983) Roaring Brook Pr.

—Two Friends, Three Stories. Seeger, Laura Vaccaro, illus. 2007. (Dog & Bear Ser.). (ENG., Illus.). 32p. (J). (gr. -1-3). 15.99 *(978-1-59643-053-2(2),* 9781596430532) Roaring Brook Pr.

Segvic-Boudreaux, Ivana. Desperately Seeking Talent: A Puppy's Journey. 2010. 108p. pap. 13.95 *(978-1-4327-6112-7(9))* Outskirts Pr., Inc.

Seidler, Tor. Gully's Travels. Cole, Brock, illus. 2008. (ENG.). 192p. (J). (gr. -1-3). 17.95 *(978-0-545-02506-5(0),* Di Capua, Michael) Scholastic, Inc.

Sekoto, Gerard. Short & Billy Boy: A Tale of Two Naughty Dogs. 2014. (ENG.). 40p. (J). (gr. k-2). pap. 13.95 *(978-1-4314-0606-7(6))* Jacana Media ZAF. Dist: Independent Pubs. Group.

Selfors, Suzanne. Smells Like Dog. 2011. (Smells Like Dog Ser.: 1). (ENG.). 384p. (J). (gr. 3-7). pap. 7.99 *(978-0-316-04397-7(4))* Little, Brown Bks. for Young Readers.

Seltzer, Eric. Doodle Dog. Seltzer, Eric, illus. 2005. (Doodle Dog Ser.). (ENG., Illus.). 32p. (J). (gr. -1-1). pap. 3.99 *(978-0-689-85910-6(4),* Simon Spotlight) Simon Spotlight.

—Granny Doodle Day. Seltzer, Eric, illus. 2006. (Doodle Dog Ser.). (ENG., Illus.). 32p. (J). (gr. -1-1). pap. 3.99 *(978-0-689-85911-3(2),* Simon & Schuster/Paula Wiseman Bks.) Simon & Schuster/Paula Wiseman Bks.

—The Long Dog. 2015. (Illus.). 32p. (J). *(978-1-4806-9084-4(8))* Scholastic, Inc.

—The Long Dog (Scholastic Reader, Level 1) 2015. (Scholastic Reader, Level 1 Ser.). (ENG., Illus.). 32p. (J). (gr. -1-1). pap. 3.99 *(978-0-545-74632-8(9))* Scholastic, Inc.

Seltzer, Eric & Hall, Kirsten. Dog on His Bus. Braun, Sebastien, illus. 2012. (Penguin Young Readers, Level 2 Ser.). (ENG.). 32p. (J). (gr. 1-2). pap. 3.99 *(978-0-448-45904-2(3),* Penguin Young Readers) Penguin Young Readers Group.

—Dog on His Bus. Braun, Sebastien, illus. 2012. (Penguin Young Readers Level 2 Ser.). lib. bdg. 13.55 *(978-0-606-25815-9(9),* Turtleback) Turtleback Bks.

Sendak, Maurice. Didola Pidola Pon! O la Vida Debe Ofrecer Algo Mas. (SPA.). 80p. (J). (gr. 2-4). *(978-84-204-3107-9(9))* Ediciones Alfaguara ESP. Dist: Lectorum Pubns., Inc.

Sepulveda, Sandra. The Adventures of Halo & Manny: Lost in the City. 2008. 176p. pap. 14.99 *(978-1-4389-0156-5(9))* AuthorHouse.

Servi Machlin, Edda. My Puppy Marrano. 2007. (YA). 19.95 *(978-1-878857-13-2(4))* Giro Pr.

Seton, Ernest Thompson. Rolf in the Woods: The Adventures of a Boy Scout with Indian Quonab & Little Dog Skookum. 2013. (ENG., Illus.). 400p. (J). (gr. 6-17). pap. 14.95 *(978-1-62087-386-1(9),* 620386) Skyhorse Publishing Co., Inc.

Sewell, Sue. Poppy the Three-Legged Puppy. 2013. 40p. 17.99 *(978-0-9898820-3-3(9))* Mindstir Media.

Sexton, Bethany. Big Dog, Little Dog, Fish. Briggs Johnson, Chloe, illus. 2015. (ENG.). 17.95 *(978-1-59298-862-4(8))* Beaver's Pond Pr., Inc.

S.H., Addan. Guardabosque Del Ano 3000: Canis Familiaris Evolucion. 2004. (SPA., Illus.). 340p. pap. *(978-1-84401-133-9(X))* Athena Pr.

Shadrick, Crystal Star. My Name Was Fear. Stone, Karen, ed. Marie, Berri, illus. 2013. 60p. pap. 12.95 *(978-1-935186-41-0(8))* Waldenhouse Pubs., Inc.

Shafer, Janet. Woof: The Story of a Girl & Her Dog. 2013. (Illus.). 30p. pap. 14.95 *(978-1-4575-2244-4(6))* Dog Ear Publishing, LLC.

Shafer, Patty. Annie the Texas Ranch Dog - Danger at Lost Maples. Retzlaff, Shay, illus. 2012. (ENG.). 96p. (J). pap. 9.95 *(978-1-61899-009-9(8),* Tadpole Pr. 4 Kids) Smooth Sailing Pr., LLC.

—Annie the Texas Ranch Dog - Injured Hero. Retzlaff, Shay, illus. 2012. 96p. (J). pap. 9.95 *(978-1-61899-008-2(X),* Tadpole Pr. 4 Kids) Smooth Sailing Pr., LLC.

—Annie the Texas Ranch Dog - New Life in Utopia. Retzlaff, Shay, illus. 2012. 96p. (J). pap. 9.95 *(978-1-61899-007-5(1),* Tadpole Pr. 4 Kids) Smooth Sailing Pr., LLC.

Shaffer, Jason. The Quick Brown Fox Jumps over the Lazy Dog. 2012. 36p. pap. 21.99 *(978-1-4771-3824-3(2))* Xlibris Corp.

Shaffert, Charles F. Googus to the Rescue. Stringer, Margaret, illus. l.t. ed. 2005. 31p. (J). per. 10.00 *(978-1-59879-043-6(9))* Lifevest Publishing, Inc.

Shamaley, Rochelle. Buddy Finds a Home. 2013. 28p. pap. 19.99 *(978-1-4817-0315-4(3))* AuthorHouse.

Shanker, Myrna Gelman. Lazar, the Good Deed Dog. Robinson, Linda, illus. 2010. (J). *(978-0-9829273-0-4(4))* IGI Pr.

Shankman, Ed. I Went to the Party in Kalamazoo. Frank, Dave, illus. 2013. (ENG.). 40p. pap. 12.95 *(978-1-938700-22-4(8),* Commonwealth Editions) Applewood Bks.

Shanks, Ronnie. Oh Where, Oh Where Is My Teddy Bear? 2004. 22p. pap. 24.95 *(978-1-4137-2693-0(3))* PublishAmerica, Inc.

Shannon, Carole. Melody's Surprise. 2011. 24p. pap. 15.99 *(978-1-4500-5484-3(6))* Xlibris Corp.

Shannon, David. Good Boy, Fergus! Shannon, David, illus. 2006. (ENG., Illus.). 40p. (J). (gr. -1-k). 17.99 *(978-0-439-49027-6(8),* Blue Sky Pr., The) Scholastic, Inc.

Shannon, George. Tippy-Toe Chick, Go! Dronzek, Laura, illus. 2003. (ENG.). 32p. (J). (gr. -1-3). 17.99 *(978-0-06-029823-4(5),* Greenwillow Bks.) HarperCollins Pubs.

Shannon-Riddle, Deidre. Peeka's Perseverance. 2011. 28p. pap. 24.95 *(978-1-4560-7583-5(7))* America Star Bks.

Sharmat, Marjorie Weinman. Nate the Great on the Owl Express. Sharmat, Mitchell & Weston, Martha, illus. 2004. (Nate the Great Ser.: No. 24). (ENG.). 80p. (J). (gr. 1-4). 5.99 *(978-0-440-41927-3(1),* Yearling) Random Hse. Children's Bks.

Sharmat, Marjorie Weinman & Sharmat, Mitchell. Nate the Great & the Big Sniff. Weston, Martha, illus. 2003. (Nate the Great Ser.: No. 23). (ENG.). 80p. (J). (gr. 1-4). pap. 5.99 *(978-0-440-41502-2(0),* Yearling) Random Hse. Children's Bks.

—Nate the Great & the Big Sniff. Weston, Martha, illus. 2003. (Nate the Great Ser.). 47p. (gr. -1-3). lib. bdg. 16.00 *(978-0-613-63966-8(9),* Turtleback) Turtleback Bks.

Shaw, Ellie. Together Again. 2012. 24p. pap. 24.95 *(978-1-4626-6427-6(X))* America Star Bks.

Shaw, Nancy. Sheep Go to Sleep. Apple, Margot, illus. 2015. (ENG.). 32p. (J). (gr. -1-3). 16.99 *(978-0-544-30989-0(8),* HMH Books For Young Readers) Houghton Mifflin Harcourt Publishing Co.

Shaw, Nancy E. Sheep Go to Sleep (board Book) Apple, Margot, illus. 2016. (Sheep in a Jeep Ser.). (ENG.). 30p. (J). (gr. -1-3). bds. 7.99 *(978-0-544-64053-5(5),* HMH Books For Young Readers) Houghton Mifflin Harcourt Publishing Co.

Shaw, Sandy. The Adventures of Dilly Dog: Dilly at the Lakes. 2017. (ENG., Illus.). 16p. (J). pap. 13.95 ***(978-1-78693-586-1(4),*** 5d695943-b94e-4707-ab27-a18a86393def) Austin, Stan AUS. Dist: Bookmasters Distribution.

Shaw, Stephanie. A Cookie for Santa. Robert, Bruno, illus. 2014. (ENG.). 32p. (J). (gr. 1-4). 15.99 *(978-1-58536-883-9(0),* 203675) Sleeping Bear Pr.

Shea, Therese. Un alboroto en el autobús (A Fuss on the Bus) 2007. (Lecturas del barrio (Neighborhood Readers) Ser.). (SPA.). 12p. 33.50 *(978-1-4042-7081-7(7),* Rosen Classroom) Rosen Publishing Group, Inc., The.

—Digger Has a Bath. 2006. (Neighborhood Readers Ser.). (ENG.). 12p. (gr. -1-3). pap. 5.90 *(978-1-4042-6467-0(1),* Rosen Classroom) Rosen Publishing Group, Inc., The.

—A Fuss on the Bus. (Neighborhood Readers Ser.). 12p. 2007. (SPA.). 33.50 *(978-1-4042-7080-0(9))* 2006. (ENG.). (gr. -1-3). pap. 5.90 *(978-1-4042-5744-3(6))* Rosen Publishing Group, Inc., The. (Rosen Classroom).

Sheckels, Astrid, illus. Nic & Nellie, 1 vol. 2013. (ENG.). 32p. (J). (gr. 1-4). 17.95 *(978-1-934031-52-0(6),* 9781934031520) Islandport Pr., Inc.

Sheinmel, Courtney. Stella Batts - Who's in Charge? Bell, Jennifer A., illus. 2013. (Stella Batts Ser.). (ENG.). 152p. (J). (gr. 1-3). 9.99 *(978-1-58536-849-5(0),* 202888) Sleeping Bear Pr.

Shephard, H. Ferebee. Jonathan & Roscoe. 2011. 24p. pap. 14.39 *(978-1-4634-4881-3(3))* AuthorHouse.

Sherlock, Patti. Letters from Wolfie. 2007. (ENG.). 240p. (J). (gr. 5-18). 7.99 *(978-0-14-240358-7(X),* Puffin Books) Penguin Young Readers Group.

Sherman, Caroline. A Dog's Life, 0 vols. Wu, Donald, illus. 2012. (ENG.). 24p. (J). (gr. -1-2). 12.99 *(978-0-7614-6200-2(7),* 9780761462002, Amazon Children's Publishing) Amazon Publishing.

Shivkumar, Suganthi Mahadevan. Every Dog Has His Day! 2016. (ENG.). 46p. (J). (gr. 4-6). 10.95 *(978-1-78554-946-5(4),* 5d07ae3b-b677-4afc-a359-000168d67c3a) Austin, Stan AUS. Dist: Bookmasters Distribution.

Shoemaker, Sharon. Sir Waltie of Shoe. Whiting, Sandra, illus. 2004. (J). per. 12.95 *(978-0-9759499-0-0(X))* Water Shoe Pr.

Shorkey, Cde. Jake Gets Diabetes. 2009. 28p. pap. 15.49 *(978-1-4490-5317-8(3))* AuthorHouse.

Shotz, Jennifer Li. Hero. 2016. (Hero Ser.: 1). 224p. (J). (gr. 3-7). 17.99 *(978-0-06-256041-4(7));* pap. 7.99 *(978-0-06-256039-1(5))* HarperCollins Pubs.

—Hero - Rescue Mission. 2017. (Hero Ser.: 3). 192p. (J). (gr. 3-7). pap. 7.99 ***(978-0-06-256045-2(X))*** HarperCollins Pubs.

—Hero: Hurricane Rescue. 2017. (Hero Ser.: 2). 192p. (J). (gr. 3-7). 12.99 ***(978-0-06-279139-9(7));*** pap. 7.99 *(978-0-06-256043-8(3))* HarperCollins Pubs.

—Hurricane Rescue. 2017. (Hero Ser.: 2). lib. bdg. 18.40 ***(978-0-606-40134-0(2))*** Turtleback Bks.

—Max: Best Friend. Hero. Marine. 2017. 256p. (J). (gr. 3-7). 12.99 ***(978-0-06-279138-2(9))*** HarperCollins Pubs.

Shuff, Lana Tanaka. Kira Helps A Friend. l.t. ed. 2007. (ENG., Illus.). 28p. (J). per. 9.95 *(978-1-4327-0810-8(4))* Outskirts Pr., Inc.

Shugars, Betty. Smokey the Tailess Dog. 2004. pap. 14.00 *(978-0-8059-6324-3(3))* Dorrance Publishing Co., Inc.

Shuler, Nancy. Nick the Basset Hound. 2013. 24p. pap. 8.99 *(978-1-938768-11-8(6))* Gypsy Pubns.

Shulman, Mark. Fillmore & Geary Take Off! The Adventures of a Robot Boy & a Boy Boy. Fickling, Phillip, illus. 2004. (ENG.). 40p. (J). (gr. -1-7). 14.95 *(978-1-58717-256-4(9),* SeaStar Bks.) Chronicle Bks. LLC.

Shultz, Charles M. & Katschke, Judy. Take a Hike, Snoopy, 1 vol. 2011. (Peanuts Ready-To-Reads Ser.). (ENG., Illus.). 32p. (gr. -1-2). lib. bdg. 24.21 *(978-1-59961-808-1(7))* Spotlight.

Shumate, Robert O. Snuffley. Sutherland, Nicholas, illus. 2008. 28p. pap. 24.95 *(978-1-60610-707-2(0))* America Star Bks.

Shyba, Jessica. Bathtime with Theo & Beau. 2016. (ENG., Illus.). 40p. (J). 16.99 *(978-1-250-05907-9(0),* 9781250059079) Feiwel & Friends.

—Naptime with Theo & Beau. 2015. (ENG., Illus.). 40p. (J). (gr. -1-k). 16.99 *(978-1-250-05906-2(2),* 9781250059062) Feiwel & Friends.

Sias, Ryan. Sniff! Sniff! 2015. (ENG., Illus.). 32p. (J). (gr. -1-2). 14.95 *(978-1-4197-1490-0(2))* Abrams, Inc.

Sievert, Jean & Cloninger, Shirley. Gabriel the Gordian Angel. 2009. 60p. pap. 21.99 *(978-1-4490-1254-0(X))* AuthorHouse.

Signer, Billie Touchstone. The Ozarks with a Dog Named Bo. 2011. 90p. pap. 19.95 *(978-1-4560-9739-4(3))* PublishAmerica, Inc.

Silver Dolphin en Español Editors. Todo Sobre los Perros: Libro Interactivo con Marioneta. 2006. (Baby Einstein Ser.). (Illus.). 8p. (J). (gr. -1). bds. *(978-970-718-402-2(7),* Silver Dolphin en Español) Advanced Marketing, S. de R. L. de C. V.

Simee. Giggles Feel Good, 1 vol. 2010. 18p. pap. 24.95 *(978-1-4489-4878-9(9))* PublishAmerica, Inc.

Simmons, Lynn. Bo & the Christmas Bandit, 1 vol. Lyne, Alison, illus. 2009. (Bo Ser.). (ENG.). 128p. (J). (gr. 3-6). pap. 8.95 *(978-1-58980-723-5(5))* Pelican Publishing Co., Inc.

—Bo & the Night Intruder, 1 vol. 2005. (Bo Ser.). (ENG., Illus.). 104p. (J). (gr. 3-6). pap. 8.95 *(978-1-58980-266-7(7))* Pelican Publishing Co., Inc.

Simmons, Lynn Sheffield. Bo & the Missing Dogs, 1 vol. Hampton, Lin, illus. 2003. (Bo Ser.). (ENG.). 128p. (J). (gr. 3-6). 8.95 *(978-1-58980-219-3(5))* Pelican Publishing Co., Inc.

—Bo & the Roaring Pines, 1 vol. Lyne, Alison Davis, illus. 2008. (Bo Ser.). (ENG.). 120p. (J). (gr. 3-6). pap. 8.95 *(978-1-58980-522-4(4))* Pelican Publishing Co., Inc.

—Bo, the Famous Retriever, 1 vol. Hampton, Lin, illus. 2003. (Bo Ser.). (ENG.). 128p. (J). (gr. 3-6). 10.95 *(978-1-58980-217-9(9))* Pelican Publishing Co., Inc.

Simon, Chaman. Sam the Dog: Guard the House, Sam!/Sam's Pet/Show-and-Tell Sam. 2006. (ENG., Illus.). 93p. (J). (gr. k-2). pap. 9.95 *(978-0-531-16922-3(7),* Children's Pr.) Scholastic Library Publishing.

Simon, Linda. Pug on Wheels. 2015. (Pug on Wheels Ser.). (ENG., Illus.). 48p. (J). (gr. -1-2). pap. 10.95 *(978-1-941437-94-0(X))* Heritage Builders, LLC.

Simon, Mary Manz. Puppy Makes Friends. Couri, Kathy & Clearwater, Linda, illus. 2006. (First Virtues for Toddlers Ser.). 20p. (J). 5.99 *(978-0-7847-1414-0(2),* 04066) Standard Publishing.

Simont, Marc. El Perro Vagabundo, 1 vol. Simont, Marc, illus. 2003.Tr. of Stray Dog. (SPA., Illus.). 32p. (J). (gr. -1-3). pap. 6.99 *(978-0-06-052274-2(7))* HarperCollins Pubs.

—El Perro Vagabundo, 4 bks. 2004. (Picture Book Readalong in Spanish Ser.).Tr. of Stray Dog. (J). (Illus.). pap. 37.95 incl. audio *(978-1-59112-937-0(0));* pap. 39.95 incl. audio compact disk *(978-1-59112-941-7(9))* Live Oak Media.

—The Stray Dog. Simont, Marc, illus. 2003. (ENG., Illus.). 32p. (J). (gr. -1-3). pap. 6.99 *(978-0-06-443669-4(1))* HarperCollins Pubs.

—The Stray Dog. Simont, Marc, illus. 2004. (Illus.). (gr. -1-3). 17.00 *(978-0-7569-1912-2(6))* Perfection Learning Corp.

Simpson, Albert. The Adventures of Billy, Ras, & Al. 2012. 24p. pap. 17.99 *(978-1-4772-1641-5(3))* AuthorHouse.

Sinclair, Nicholas, et al. The Cookie Story. Wall, Randy Hugh, ed. Varela, Juan D., tr. Varela, Juan D., illus. l.t. ed. 2005.Tr. of Cuent de Galletas. (SPA.). 33p. (J). 14.95 *(978-0-9764798-1-9(8))* Story Store Collection Publishing.

Singer, Marilyn. What Is Your Dog Doing? Habbley, Kathleen, illus. 2011. (ENG.). 32p. (J). (gr. -1-2). 12.99 *(978-1-4169-7931-9(X),* Atheneum Bks. for Young Readers) Simon & Schuster Children's Publishing.

Singleton, Linda Joy. A Cat Is Better. Martin, Jorge, illus. 2017. (ENG.). 32p. (J). (gr. -1-3). 16.99 *(978-1-4998-0278-8(1))* Little Bee Books Inc.

—Snow Dog, Sand Dog. Golden, Jess, illus. 2014. (ENG.). 32p. (J). (gr. -1-3). 16.99 *(978-0-8075-7536-9(4))* Whitman, Albert & Co.

Sirotich, Erica & Sirotich, Erica. Found Dogs. 2017. (ENG., Illus.). 32p. (J). (-k). 16.99 ***(978-0-399-18641-7(7),*** Dial Bks) Penguin Young Readers Group.

Sís, Peter. Madlenka's Dog, 1 vol. (ENG., Illus.). 32p. 19.95 *(978-0-88899-462-2(1))* Groundwood Bks. CAN. Dist: Publishers Group West (PGW).

Sisco, K. B. Jackpot's Tail. 2008. (ENG.). 32p. pap. 15.99 *(978-1-4196-4475-7(0))* CreateSpace Independent Publishing Platform.

Sitzenstock, Gabriele. Raising Puppy. 2006. (J). spiral bd. 12.95 *(978-1-59872-721-0(4))* Instant Pub.

Sivier, Janet. Charlotte & Jackson: The Butterfly. 2012. 28p. pap. 16.09 *(978-1-4669-4555-5(9))* Trafford Publishing.

—Charlotte & Jackson: The Strange Flowers. 2012. 16p. pap. 12.68 *(978-1-4669-3965-3(6))* Trafford Publishing.

Skafish, Brad. Outnumbered! the Bad Cats Learn about Numbers. 2011. 20p. pap. 12.95 *(978-1-61434-290-8(3))* Booklocker.com, Inc.

Skewes, John & Fox, Andrew. Larry Gets Lost in Washington, D. C. Skewes, John, illus. 2014. (Larry Gets Lost Ser.). (ENG., Illus.). 32p. (J). (gr. -1-2). 17.99 *(978-1-57061-899-4(2),* Little Bigfoot) Sasquatch Bks.

Skotnicki, Jill. Ham & Beans: Have You Seen the Color Green? 2010. 28p. pap. 12.49 *(978-1-4520-6452-9(0))* AuthorHouse.

Slater, Teddy, text. I Love Korky. 2008. (ENG., Illus.). 32p. (J). (gr. -1-k). 14.95 *(978-1-905417-81-0(0))* Boxer Bks., Ltd. GBR. Dist: Sterling Publishing Co., Inc.

Sleepy Pup: KinderConcepts Individual Title Six-Packs. (Kinderstarters Ser.). 8p. (gr. -1-1). 21.00 *(978-0-7635-8733-8(8))* Rigby Education.

Slegers, Liesbet. A Puppy for Kevin. Slegers, Liesbet, illus. 2013. (Kevin & Katie Ser.). (ENG., Illus.). 32p. (J). (— 1). 13.95 *(978-1-60537-144-3(0))* Cobblestone Publishing Co.

Slifka, Linda. Where's My Puppy? 2004. 32p. 14.95 *(978-1-932820-11-9(6))* Outland Communications, LLC.

Slonim, David. Patch. Slonim, David, illus. 2013. (ENG., Illus.). 32p. (J). (gr. k-2). 15.99 *(978-1-59643-643-5(3),* 9781596436435) Roaring Brook Pr.

Slusser, Janet S. Smokey & the Big Snow. 2003. (Illus.). 32p. (J). per. 15.95 *(978-0-9745171-0-0(0))* RiverCreek Bks., Inc.

Small, VTaylor. Maggie the Shih Tzu Detective: Volume I: Faith. 2009. 54p. pap. 15.99 *(978-1-4500-0453-4(9))* Xlibris Corp.

Smelser, Lynne M. Noodles & Goo: All over Baby. 2013. 34p. pap. 9.99 *(978-0-9789631-2-5(1))* Three Socks Publishing.

Smerek, Kim. What Is Zazu?, 1 bk. Smerek, Kim, illus. 2003. (Illus.). 24p. (J). bds. 7.95 *(978-0-9745116-0-3(9))* Sunshine Bks. for Children.

Smith, Alex T. Claude at the Beach, 1 vol. Smith, Alex T., illus. (Claude Ser.). (ENG., Illus.). 96p. (J). (gr. 1-3). 2016. pap. 7.95 *(978-1-56145-919-3(4))* 2014. 12.95 *(978-1-56145-703-8(5))* Peachtree Pubs.

—Claude at the Circus, 1 vol. Smith, Alex T., illus. 2013. (Claude Ser.). (ENG., Illus.). 96p. (J). (gr. 2-4). 12.95 *(978-1-56145-702-1(7))* Peachtree Pubs.

—Claude in the City, 1 vol. Smith, Alex T., illus. (Claude Ser.). (ENG., Illus.). 96p. (J). (gr. 2-4). 2015. pap. 7.95 *(978-1-56145-843-1(0))* 2013. 12.95 *(978-1-56145-697-0(7))* Peachtree Pubs.

—Claude in the Country, 1 vol. Smith, Alex T., illus. 2016. (Claude Ser.). (ENG., Illus.). 96p. (J). (gr. 1-3). 12.95 *(978-1-56145-918-6(6))* Peachtree Pubs.

—Claude in the Spotlight, 1 vol. Smith, Alex T., illus. 2015. (Claude Ser.). (ENG., Illus.). 96p. (J). (gr. 1-3). 12.95 *(978-1-56145-895-0(3))* Peachtree Pubs.

—Claude on the Slopes, 1 vol. Smith, Alex T., illus. 2016. (Claude Ser.). (ENG., Illus.). 96p. (J). (gr. 1-3). pap. 7.95 *(978-1-56145-923-0(2))* Peachtree Pubs.

Smith, Brooke. Mimi & Maty to the Rescue! Book 1: Roger the Rat Is on the Loose! Arnold, Alli, illus. 2014. (ENG.). 88p. (J). (gr. k-4). pap. 9.95 *(978-1-62914-619-5(6),* Sky Pony Pr.) Skyhorse Publishing Co., Inc.

—Mimi & Maty to the Rescue! Book 2: Sadie the Sheep Disappears Without a Peep! Arnold, Alli, illus. 2014. (ENG.). 96p. (J). (gr. 1-5). 14.95 *(978-1-62636-344-1(7),* Sky Pony Pr.) Skyhorse Publishing Co., Inc.

—Mimi & Maty to the Rescue! Book 3: C. C. the Parakeet Flies the Coop! Arnold, Alli, illus. 2014. (ENG.). 96p. (J). (gr. k-4). 14.95 *(978-1-62914-620-1(X),* Sky Pony Pr.) Skyhorse Publishing Co., Inc.

—Mimi & Maty to the Rescue! Bk. 1: Roger the Rat Is on the Loose! Arnold, Alli, illus. 2012. (ENG.). 88p. (J). (gr. 1-4). 14.95 *(978-1-62087-252-9(8),* 620252, Sky Pony Pr.) Skyhorse Publishing Co., Inc.

Smith, Chrysa. The Adventures of the Poodle Posse: [happy Tales 1 & 2]. Achilles, Pat, illus. 2007. 26p. (J). *(978-1-4243-3335-6(0))* Independent Publisher Services.

Smith, D. James. Probably the World's Best Story about a Dog & the Girl Who Loved Me. 2011. (ENG.). 256p. (J). pap. 5.99 *(978-1-4169-9652-1(4),* Atheneum Bks. for Young Readers) Simon & Schuster Children's Publishing.

—Probably the World's Best Story about a Dog & The Girl Who Loved Me. 2010. (ENG.). 240p. (J). (gr. 4-7). pap. 11.99 *(978-1-4424-2194-3(0),* Atheneum Bks. for Young Readers) Simon & Schuster Children's Publishing.

Smith, Dodie. 101 Dalmatians. 2003. (ENG., Illus.). 32p. (C). pap. 28.73 *(978-0-582-52979-3(4))* Pearson ESL.

—101 Dalmatians. 2004. (Illus.). 192p. (J). (gr. 3-5). pap. 36.00 incl. audio *(978-0-8072-0791-8(8),* LYA 345 SP, Listening Library) Random Hse. Audio Publishing Group.

Smith, Kathleen. A Puppy for the White House. Hansen, Laurie, illus. 2009. 32p. (J). 16.99 *(978-0-615-30165-5(7))* Lollipop Publishing, LLC.

Smith, Linda. The Inside Tree. Brown, Kathryn, illus. Date not set. 32p. (J). (gr. -1-3). 5.99 *(978-0-06-443542-0(3))* HarperCollins Pubs.

Smith-Mansell, Dana. The Smith Family's New Puppy: Helping Children Cope with a New Family Member. Voerg, Kathy, illus. 2008. (Let's Talk Ser.). (ENG.). 48p. (J). (gr. -1-4). pap. 8.95 *(978-0-88282-327-0(2))* New Horizon Pr. Pubs., Inc.

Smith, Peggy. The Champ: The Adventures of a Boy & His New Puppy. Told in One-syllable Words for the Barton Reading & Spelling System. 2003. (J). pap. 7.95 *(978-0-9744343-3-9(7),* SA-304) Bright Solutions for Dyslexia, LLC.

Smith, Roland. The Captain's Dog: My Journey with the Lewis & Clark Tribe. 2008. (ENG., Illus.). 304p. (J). (gr. 5-7). pap. 7.99 *(978-0-15-202696-7(7))* Houghton Mifflin Harcourt Publishing Co.

Smith, S. Hey Silly Cat! Dont Tease the Dog! 2010. (Illus.). 32p. (J). 17.99 *(978-0-9842632-9-5(2))* Scandora.

Smith, Sherrie. Not Another Dog. 2007. 61p. pap. 19.95 *(978-1-60441-434-9(0))* America Star Bks.

Smith, Sindy. Rosie the Rottweiler. Smith, Sindy, illus. 2012. (Illus.). 26p. 29.95 *(978-1-4626-9860-8(3))* America Star Bks.

—Rosie the Rottweiler. 2012. 28p. pap. 24.95 *(978-1-4626-8797-8(0))* America Star Bks.

Smithsonian Institution, ed. Oh Where, Oh Where Has My Little Dog Gone? 2009. (ENG.). 24p. 4.99 *(978-1-59069-822-8(3))* Studio Mouse LLC.

Smyth, Jimmy. The Leprechaun. Ozzy, illus. 2013. 32p. pap. *(978-0-9569314-1-2(3))* Smith, Jimmy.

—The Lost Fairy. 2013. 34p. pap. *(978-0-9569314-3-6(X))* Smith, Jimmy.

Snellenberger, Tracy. Tyler the Toddler Feeds the Cows. 2010. 28p. 13.99 *(978-1-4520-5169-7(0))* AuthorHouse.

C
D

Snelson, Doug. Who's Got the Face? 2007. (Illus.). 48p. (J). 16.95 (978-0-9777811-0-2(0)) Petalous Publishing, LLC.

Snicket, Lemony, pseud. 13 Words. Kalman, Maira, illus. (ENG.). 40p. (J). (gr. -1-3). 2014. pap. 6.99 (978-0-06-166467-0(7)) 2010. 16.99 (978-0-06-166465-6(0)) HarperCollins Pubs.

Snowman, Sally R. Sammy the Boston Lighthouse Dog. 2005. (J). (gr. 3-5). 15.00 (978-0-9674666-2-0(8)) Snowman Learning Center, The.

Snyder, Casey. Miss Fit the Dog & the Football Eating Tree. 2012. 28p. pap. 24.95 (978-1-4626-8635-3(4)) America Star Bks.

—Miss Fit the Dog Saves Christmas. 2013. 20p. pap. 24.95 (978-1-62709-358-3(3)) America Star Bks.

Snyder, Deanna Sytek. Lee the Pe. 2009. 24p. pap. 12.99 (978-1-4389-2405-2(4)) AuthorHouse.

Snyder, Maria V. Storm Watcher. 2013. 228p. (gr. 4-8). pap. 9.99 (978-1-61603-033-9(X)) Leap Bks.

Snyder, Sandy. New Orleans Dogs Allowed. 2008. 60p. pap. 19.95 (978-1-60672-781-2(8)) America Star Bks.

—There's Only One I in Charlie. Ferrenburg, Susie, illus. 2011. 48p. pap. 24.95 (978-1-4626-4086-7(9)) America Star Bks.

Snyder, Sharon J. Zeus Comes Home. 2012. 20p. pap. 24.95 (978-1-4626-5860-2(1)) America Star Bks.

Soderberg, Erin. Catnapped! 2016. (Puppy Pirates Ser.). (ENG., Illus.). 96p. (J). (gr. 1-4). lib. bdg. 12.99 (978-0-553-51174-1(2), Random Hse. Bks. for Young Readers) Random Hse. Children's Bks.

—Dinosaur Dig, 1 vol. 2013. (Scooby-Doo! Picture Clue Bks.). (ENG.). 24p. (J). (gr. -1-1). lib. bdg. 24.21 (978-1-61479-037-2(X), Essential Library) ABDO Publishing Co.

—Ghost Ship. 2016. (Puppy Pirates Ser.: 1). (ENG., Illus.). 128p. (J). (gr. 1-4). 5.99 (978-1-101-93773-0(4), Random Hse. Bks. for Young Readers) Random Hse. Children's Bks.

—Puppy Pirates #5: Search for the Sea Monster. 2016. (Puppy Pirates Ser.). (ENG., Illus.). 96p. (J). (gr. 1-4). 4.99 (978-1-101-93776-1(9), Random Hse. Bks. for Young Readers) Random Hse. Children's Bks.

—Puppy Pirates Super Special #2: Best in Class. 2017. (Puppy Pirates Ser.: 2). (ENG.). 128p. (J). (gr. 1-4). lib. bdg. 12.99 (978-1-5247-1329-4(5)); (Illus.). 5.99 (978-1-5247-1328-7(7)) Random Hse. Children's Bks. (Random Hse. Bks. for Young Readers).

Soderberg, Erin. Sea Sick. 2016. (Puppy Pirates Ser.). (ENG., Illus.). 96p. (J). (gr. 1-4). 4.99 (978-0-553-51176-5(9), Random Hse. Bks. for Young Readers) Random Hse. Children's Bks.

Soderberg, Erin & Wasserman, Robin. Stowaway! 2015. (Puppy Pirates Ser.: 1). (ENG., Illus.). 96p. (J). (gr. 1-4). pap. 4.99 (978-0-553-51167-3(X)); lib. bdg. 12.99 (978-0-553-51168-0(8)) Random Hse. Children's Bks. (Random Hse. Bks. for Young Readers).

Sokol, Ron. Retrieval. 2013. 56p. (978-1-4602-1490-9(0)); pap. (978-1-4602-1491-6(9)) FriesenPress.

Solberg, Jessica. First Dog: Unleashed in the Montana Capital. Rath, Robert, illus. 2007. 40p. (J). (gr. 2-4). 17.95 (978-1-56037-425-1(X)) Farcountry Pr.

Soling, Cevin. Boris the Dog. Kille, Steve, illus. 2015. (ENG.). 44p. 14.95 (978-0-9767771-6-8(9)) Spectacle Films, Inc.

Solomon, Michelle & Pereira, Lavinia. Too Big! Faust, Laurie A., illus. 2009. 24p. pap. 10.96 (978-1-4251-8949-5(0)) Trafford Publishing.

Sonberg, Caryn. Six Dogs & a Police Officer. Dorenkamp, Michelle, illus. 2006. 31p. pap. 8.40 (978-1-55501-776-7(2)) Ballard & Tighe Pubs.

Sonneborn, Scott. Attack of the Invisible Cats, 1 vol. Baltazar, Art, illus. 2011. (DC Super-Pets Ser.). (ENG.). 56p. (gr. 2-2). pap. 4.95 (978-1-4048-6847-2(X)); lib. bdg. 23.99 (978-1-4048-6481-8(4)) Picture Window Bks. (DC Super-Pets).

Soto, Gary. Chato Goes Cruisin' Guevara, Susan, illus. 2008. (Chato Ser.). (J). 25.95 incl. audio (978-1-59519-906-5(3)) Live Oak Media.

—Chato Goes Cruisin' Guevara, Susan, illus. 2007. (Chato Ser.). (J). (gr. -1-3). 14.65 (978-0-7569-8147-1(6)) Perfection Learning Corp.

Sowards, Penny. Naper & the Missing News Paper Caper. 2010. 28p. pap. 13.99 (978-1-4520-6808-4(9)) AuthorHouse.

Sowerby, Dale. The Adventures of Baggy & Paxton: Trouble in Dawlish Warren. 2010. (ENG., Illus.). 48p. pap. (978-1-84748-704-9(1)) Athena Pr.

Spafford-Fitz, Karen. Dog Walker, 1 vol. 2006. (Orca Currents Ser.). (ENG.). 136p. (J). (gr. 5-9). per. 9.95 (978-1-55143-522-0(5)) Orca Bk. Pubs. USA.

Spedding, Steven. Boriscat & the Quest for the Golden Carp. 2010. 136p. pap. 10.99 (978-1-4520-5759-0(1)) AuthorHouse.

Spence, Craig. Einstein Dog. Tucker, Diane, ed. 2009. (ENG., Illus.). 304p. (J). pap. 14.95 (978-1-897235-65-2(8)) Thistledown Pr., Ltd. CAN. Dist: Univ. of Toronto Pr.

Spencer, Frances Mcneil. Dee & the Dog: Home at Last. 2012. 90p. (gr. 4-6). pap. 13.95 (978-1-4772-6709-7(3)) AuthorHouse.

Spinelli, Eileen. Do You Have a Dog? Valério, Geraldo, illus. 2011. (ENG.). 26p. (J). 16.00 (978-0-8028-5387-5(0), Eerdmans Bks For Young Readers) Eerdmans, William B. Publishing Co.

Spinelli, Patti. Mackenzie & Emma Get a Puppy. 2004. (Illus.). (YA). (gr. k-18). lib. bdg. 11.95 (978-0-9742328-2-9(3)) Spinelli, Patti.

—Mackenzie & Emma Visit York Beach. Spinelli, Patti, illus. 2003. (Illus.). (J). (978-0-9742328-0-5(7)) Spinelli, Patti.

Spitz, Eleanor. Phoenix the Rising Star. 2013. 26p. pap. 11.95 (978-1-61244-223-5(4)) Halo Publishing International.

Springett, Martin. Kate & Pippin: An Unlikely Love Story. Springett, Isobel, photos by. 2012. (My Readers Ser.). (ENG., Illus.). 32p. (J). (gr. -1-3). 16.99 (978-0-8050-9487-9(3), 9780805094879, Holt, Henry & Co. Bks. For Young Readers) Holt, Henry & Co.

St. John, Laurence. Metatron: The Angel Has Risen. 2012. 102p. pap. (978-1-926997-64-3(6)) Imajin Bks.

St John, Patroca. Friska My Friend. 2007. (Illus.). 93p. pap. (978-1-84427-289-1(3)) Scripture Union.

Stacey, Tom. The First Dog to Be Somebody's Best Friend: A Likely Story in Two Bits & a Decide. Landels, Angela, illus. 2007. (ENG.). 46p. 15.95 (978-1-905299-34-8(6), Stacey International) Stacey Publishing GBR. Dist: Casemate Pubs. & Bk. Distributors, LLC.

Stainton, Sue. I Love Dogs. Truesdell, Sue, illus. 2010. (J). lib. bdg. 15.89 (978-0-06-117058-4(5)) HarperCollins Pubs.

—I Love Dogs! Truesdell, Sue & Staake, Bob, illus. 2014. (ENG.). 32p. (J). (gr. -1-3). 14.99 (978-0-06-117057-7(7)) HarperCollins Pubs.

Stalling-Patton, Deborah. Shypoodle: Getting to Know You. 2009. 40p. pap. 17.99 (978-1-4389-3899-8(3)) AuthorHouse.

Standifer, Charley. Butch the One-Of-a-Kind Dog. 2013. 32p. 25.99 (978-1-4582-1118-7(5), Abbott Pr.) Author Solutions, Inc.

star, celina. Paw Prints on the Road. 2008. 79p. pap. 9.96 (978-0-557-02420-9(X)) Lulu Pr., Inc.

Star, Eloney. Heavy Duty Trucker. 2007. 28p. (J). per. 7.99 (978-1-59879-287-4(3)) Lifevest Publishing, Inc.

Starks-Johnson, Annie. Doggie Day Care. 2009. 24p. pap. 11.49 (978-1-4389-7447-7(7)) AuthorHouse.

Starr, Barbara May. A Home for Finn: The Tail of an Alaska Rescue Dog, 1 vol. 2009. 23p. pap. 24.95 (978-1-60749-679-3(8)) America Star Bks.

Stauffacher, Sue. Animal Rescue Team: Hide & Seek. Lamont, Priscilla, illus. 2011. (Animal Rescue Team Ser.). (ENG.). 160p. (J). (gr. 3-7). 5.99 (978-0-375-85133-9(X), Yearling) Random Hse. Children's Bks.

Staunton, Ted. Morgan's Pet Plot, 1 vol. Slavin, Bill & Shannon, Ben, illus. 2003. (Formac First Novels Ser.: 24). (ENG.). 64p. (J). (gr. 1-5). 4.95 (978-0-88780-587-5(6), 9780887805875) Formac Publishing Co., Ltd. CAN. Dist: Casemate Pubs. & Bk. Distributors, LLC.

—Morgan's Pet Plot. Slavin, Bill, illus. 2003. (Formac First Novels Ser.: 24). (ENG.). 64p. (J). (gr. 1-5). 14.95 (978-0-88780-588-2(4), 9780887805882) Formac Publishing Co., Ltd. CAN. Dist: Casemate Pubs. & Bk. Distributors, LLC.

Stayer, Elizabeth. Get off My Corner!! 2012. 40p. pap. 16.99 (978-1-4772-1297-4(3)) AuthorHouse.

Stead, Vince. Rusty the Runaway Golden Retriever. 2007. 73p. 19.95 (978-1-4241-5739-6(0)) America Star Bks.

—Sammy, the Runaway Mastiff: Sammy Breaks Out of His Kennel. 2006. 102p. per. 8.95 (978-1-59824-314-7(4)) E-BookTime LLC.

Steedley-Tolan, Chopper. I'm Not Sick! Chopper's Tails of the Doctor. 2012. 32p. (-18). pap. 12.95 (978-1-4772-8618-0(7)) AuthorHouse.

—I've Been Picked! Chopper's Tail of Adoption. 2011. 32p. pap. 12.95 (978-1-4634-3554-7(1)) AuthorHouse.

Steel, Danielle. Pretty Minnie in Hollywood. Valiant, Kristi, illus. 2016. (ENG.). 32p. (J). (gr. -1-2). 17.99 (978-0-553-53755-0(5), Doubleday Bks. for Young Readers) Random Hse. Children's Bks.

—Pretty Minnie in Paris. Valiant, Kristi, illus. 2014. (ENG.). 32p. (J). (gr. -1-2). 17.99 (978-0-385-37000-4(8), Doubleday Bks. for Young Readers) Random Hse. Children's Bks.

Steele, Michael Anthony. The Case of the Fright Flight. Neely, Scott, illus. 2016. (You Choose Stories: Scooby-Doo Ser.). (ENG.). 112p. (gr. 2-3). lib. bdg. 32.65 (978-1-4965-2662-5(7), You Choose Bks.) Capstone Press of Coughlan Cos.

—Creepy Cowboy Caper. Jeralds, Scott, illus. 2017. (Scooby-Doo! Beginner Mysteries Ser.). (ENG.). 112p. (gr. 2-3). lib. bdg. 22.65 (978-1-4965-4768-2(3)) Capstone Press of Coughlan Cos.

—Monster Mutt Madness. Jeralds, Scott, illus. 2017. (Scooby-Doo! Beginner Mysteries Ser.). (ENG.). 112p. (gr. 2-3). lib. bdg. 22.65 (978-1-4965-4767-5(5)) Capstone Press of Coughlan Cos.

—Skeleton Crew Showdown. Jeralds, Scott, illus. 2017. (Scooby-Doo! Beginner Mysteries Ser.). (ENG.). 112p. (gr. 2-3). lib. bdg. 22.65 (978-1-4965-4769-9(1)) Capstone Press of Coughlan Cos.

—Vampire Zoo Hullabaloo. Jeralds, Scott, illus. 2017. (Scooby-Doo! Beginner Mysteries Ser.). (ENG.). 112p. (gr. 2-3). lib. bdg. 22.65 (978-1-4965-4770-5(5)) Capstone Press of Coughlan Cos.

Steig, William. Dominic. 146p. (J). (gr. 3-6). pap. 4.95 (978-0-8072-1512-8(0), Listening Library) Random Hse. Audio Publishing Group.

—Dominic. Steig, William, illus. 2007. (ENG., Illus.). 160p. (J). (gr. 3-7). per. 6.99 (978-0-312-37144-9(6), 9780312371449) Square Fish.

Stein, David Ezra. I'm My Own Dog. Stein, David Ezra, illus. 2014. (ENG., Illus.). 32p. (J). (gr. -1-3). 15.99 (978-0-7636-6139-7(2)) Candlewick Pr.

—I'm My Own Dog. 2014. 36.75 (978-1-4906-4378-6(8)); 38.75 (978-1-4906-4052-5(5)) Recorded Bks., Inc.

Stein, Garth. Enzo - Races in the Rain! Alley, R. W., illus. 2014. (ENG.). 40p. (J). (gr. -1-3). 17.99 (978-0-06-229533-0(0)) HarperCollins Pubs.

—Enzo & the Christmas Tree Hunt! Alley, R. W., illus. 2015. (ENG.). 40p. (J). (gr. -1-3). 17.99 (978-0-06-229532-3(2)) HarperCollins Pubs.

—Enzo & the Fourth of July Races. Alley, R. W., illus. 2017. 40p. (J). (gr. -1-3). 17.99 (978-0-06-238059-3(1)) HarperCollins Pubs.

—Enzo's Very Scary Halloween. Alley, R. W., illus. 2016. 40p. (J). (gr. -1-3). 17.99 (978-0-06-238061-6(3)) HarperCollins Pubs.

—Racing in the Rain: My Life as a Dog. 2011. (ENG., Illus.). 304p. (J). (gr. 3-7). 16.99 (978-0-06-201574-7(5)); pap. 6.99 (978-0-06-201576-1(1)) HarperCollins Pubs.

Steinkraus, Kyla. In the Doghouse. Myer, Ed, illus. 2012. (ENG.). 24p. (gr. 2-3). pap. 8.95 (978-1-61810-332-1(6)) Rourke Educational Media.

Steinsiek, Sabra Brown. The Tale of the Pronghorned Cantaloupe. Chilton, Noel Dora, illus. 2013. 48p. 24.95 (978-1-936744-11-4(2), Rio Grande Bks.) LPD Pr.

—The Tale of the Pronghorned Cantaloupe. Chilton, Noel, illus. 2009. (SPA & ENG.). 48p. (J). (gr. -1-3). pap. 17.95 (978-1-890689-85-8(8), Rio Grande Bks.) LPD Pr.

Stejskal, Susan. The Little Dog Who Did Big Things. 2006. (J). (978-0-615-13395-9(9)) Stejskal, Susan M.

Stelljes, Susan. Wonder Dog: The Story of Silverton Bobbie. 2005. (Illus.). 167p. (YA). pap. 14.95 (978-0-9761124-7-1(7)) For The Love of Dog Bks.

Stelten, Gene. A House for Wally & Me. Johnson, Chelsea, illus. 2009. 32p. (J). 13.95 (978-1-935130-13-0(7)) Grateful Steps.

Stephens, Ann Marie. Scuba Dog. Golden, Jess, illus. 2016. (ENG.). 40p. (J). (gr. -1-3). 17.99 (978-1-4998-0143-9(2)) Little Bee Books Inc.

Stephens, Kat. Where Did Gypsy Go? 2010. 32p. (gr. -1). 15.50 (978-1-4490-8008-2(1)) AuthorHouse.

Stephens, Sarah. Pooches of Power!, 1 vol. Baltazar, Art, illus. 2011. (DC Super-Pets Ser.). (ENG.). 56p. (gr. 2-2). pap. 4.95 (978-1-4048-6620-1(5)); lib. bdg. 23.99 (978-1-4048-6306-4(0)) Picture Window Bks. (DC Super-Pets).

Stephens, Sarah Hines. Backward Bowwow, 1 vol. Baltazar, Art, illus. 2011. (DC Super-Pets Ser.). (ENG.). 56p. (gr. 2-2). pap. 4.95 (978-1-4048-6845-8(3)); lib. bdg. 23.99 (978-1-4048-6480-1(6)) Picture Window Bks. (DC Super-Pets).

—Night of the Scaredy Crows, 1 vol. Baltazar, Art, illus. 2012. (DC Super-Pets Ser.). (ENG.). 56p. (gr. 2-2). pap. 4.95 (978-1-4048-7663-7(4)); lib. bdg. 23.99 (978-1-4048-6492-4(X)) Picture Window Bks. (DC Super-Pets).

—Superpowered Pony, 1 vol. Baltazar, Art, illus. 2011. (DC Super-Pets Ser.). (ENG.). 56p. (gr. 2-2). pap. 4.95 (978-1-4048-6846-5(1)); lib. bdg. 23.99 (978-1-4048-6479-5(2)) Picture Window Bks. (DC Super-Pets).

Sterling Children's, Sterling, ed. Sleepy Puppy. 2015. (ENG., Illus.). 22p. (J). (— 1). bds. 6.95 (978-1-4549-1465-5(3)) Sterling Publishing Co., Inc.

Stern, A. J. Doggy Day Care, 2 vols. Marts, Doreen Mulryan, illus. 2010. (Frankly, Frannie Ser.: 2). (ENG.). 128p. (J). (gr. 1-3). pap. 4.99 (978-0-448-45350-7(9), Grosset & Dunlap) Penguin Young Readers Group.

Sternberg, Demetria. Hey, What's Going on down There? 2005. 23p. pap. 24.95 (978-1-4137-3806-3(0)) PublishAmerica, Inc.

Sternberg, Julie. Puppy, Puppy, Puppy. Koehler, Fred, illus. 2017. (ENG.). 32p. (J). (-k). 16.95 (978-1-62979-466-2(X)) Boyds Mills Pr.

Steve Van Der Merwe. Policeman Bobby & Stinky. 2009. (Illus.). 24p. pap. 12.99 (978-1-4389-6935-0(X)) AuthorHouse.

Stevens, Beverly. This Dog Team Lives in the House. 2005. (Illus.). 32p. (J). pap. 9.95 (978-1-57833-317-2(2)) Todd Communications.

Stevens, Janet & Crummel, Susan Stevens. Find a Cow Now! Stevens, Janet, illus. 2012. (ENG., Illus.). 32p. (J). (gr. -1-3). 16.95 (978-0-8234-2218-0(6)) Holiday Hse., Inc.

—Help Me, Mr. Mutt! Expert Answers for Dogs with People Problems. 2008. (ENG., Illus.). 56p. (J). (gr. -1-3). 17.99 (978-0-15-204628-6(3)) Houghton Mifflin Harcourt Publishing Co.

—Help Me, Mr. Mutt! Expert Answers for Dogs with People Problems. 2010. (J). (gr. 1-4). 29.95 incl. audio compact disk (978-0-8045-4217-3(1)) Spoken Arts, Inc.

Stevens, Janet & Stevens Crummel, Susan. My Big Dog. Stevens, Janet, illus. 2009. (Golden Classic Ser.). (ENG., Illus.). 32p. (J). (gr. -1-2). pap. 7.99 (978-0-375-85103-2(8), Dragonfly Bks.) Random Hse. Children's Bks.

Stevenson, Richard. Alex Anklebone & Andy the Dog. Masi, P. J., illus. 2005. (ENG.). 32p. (J). (gr. -1-17). (978-1-896209-57-9(2)) Bayeux Arts, Inc.

Stevenson-Ringo, Angela. Keith's Shoes. 2009. 28p. pap. 9.95 (978-1-4327-2344-6(8)) Outskirts Pr., Inc.

—Where Are My Shoes? 2009. 28p. pap. 9.95 (978-1-4327-2343-9(X)) Outskirts Pr., Inc.

Stewart, H. E. The Patched Heart: A Gift of Friendship & Caring, 1 vol. 2010. (ENG., Illus.). 32p. (J). (gr. -1-3). 19.95 (978-0-9693852-5-7(0)) Tudor Hse. GBR. Dist: Orca Bk. Pubs. USA.

Stewart, Kiera. Fetching. 2012. (ENG.). 304p. (YA). (gr. 5-9). pap. 7.99 (978-1-4231-4245-4(4)) Hyperion Pr.

Stewart, Whitney. Marshall: A Nantucket Sea Rescue. Lyall, Dennis, illus. 2008. (ENG.). 32p. (J). (gr. -1-2). 2.95 (978-1-59249-856-7(6)); 6.95 (978-1-59249-855-0(8)); 10.95 (978-1-59249-857-4(4)) Soundprints.

—Marshall, the Sea Dog. 2010. (ENG.). 56p. (J). (gr. 4-7). 17.95 (978-1-60727-183-3(4)) Soundprints.

Stier, Catherine. Barnaby the Bedbug Detective. Sapp, Karen, illus. 2015. (Av2 Fiction Readalong 2016 Ser.). (ENG.). (J). (gr. k-3). lib. bdg. 34.28 (978-1-4896-3849-6(0), AV2 by Weigl) Weigl Pubs., Inc.

—Barnaby the Bedbug Detective. Sapp, Karen, illus. 2013. (ENG.). 32p. (J). (gr. -1-3). 16.99 (978-0-8075-0904-3(3)) Whitman, Albert & Co.

Stihler, Chérie B. Wiggle-Waggle Woof: Counting Sled Dogs in Alaska. Bania, Michael, illus. 2009. (Paws IV Ser.). (ENG.). 32p. (J). (gr. -1-2). pap. 10.99 (978-1-57061-559-7(4), Little Bigfoot) Sasquatch Bks.

Still, Cynthia W. Gypsy Travels the World. 2012. 48p. pap. 21.99 (978-1-4685-5839-5(0)) AuthorHouse.

Stine, R. L. Frankenstein's Dog. 2013. (Goosebumps Most Wanted Ser.: 4). (ENG.). 160p. (J). (gr. 3-7). pap. 6.99 (978-0-545-41801-0(1), Scholastic Paperbacks) Scholastic, Inc.

—Frankenstein's Dog. 2013. (Goosebumps Most Wanted Ser.: 4). 136p. (J). lib. bdg. 17.20 (978-0-606-32006-1(7), Turtleback) Turtleback Bks.

—The Great Smelling Bee, 1 vol. Park, Trip, illus. 2011. (Rotten School Ser.: No. 2). (ENG.). 128p. (gr. 2-5). 24.21 (978-1-59961-826-5(5)) Spotlight.

—The Werewolf of Fever Swamp. 2009. (Goosebumps Ser.: 11). lib. bdg. 17.20 (978-0-606-00241-7(3), Turtleback) Turtleback Bks.

Stinson, June. A Basset Named Fred. 2012. 28p. pap. 24.95 (978-1-4626-8190-7(5)) America Star Bks.

Stofko, Michael D. A Visit from the Zoo. 2011. 32p. pap. 12.77 (978-1-4567-2968-4(3)) AuthorHouse.

Storer, June. Kip, Brenda & Emong's Adventure. 2013. 164p. pap. (978-0-9923603-1-3(5)) BWM Bks.

Stormer, Kate. Casey's Unexpected Friend. Lowes, Tom, illus. l.t. ed. 2003. 38p. (J). 16.95 (978-0-9722099-7-7(2), CUF) Caseys World Bks.

Strachen, Iona. Adventures in a Red Tartan Duffle Coat. 2003. 62p. pap. (978-1-84401-090-5(2)) Athena Pr.

Stravinskas, Janice. Pam the Dog: A Hawaiian Adventure. 2009. 32p. pap. 13.00 (978-1-60860-692-4(9), Eloquent Bks.) Strategic Book Publishing & Rights Agency (SBPRA).

Strnad, George J. The Adventures of Colonel Bob B Beagle Us Army Canine Corp: The Adventures of Colonel Bob. 2004. 108p. 21.95 (978-1-4140-7832-8(3)) AuthorHouse.

Stroll with Mr. Emmett: A Walk Through Charleston. 2004. (J). lib. bdg. 15.95 (978-0-9759346-0-9(0)) Mr. Emmett Publishing.

Stroud-Peace, Glenda. Pearlie. Larkin, Paige A., illus. 2009. 48p. pap. 16.95 (978-1-60844-033-7(8)) Dog Ear Publishing, LLC.

Stroud, Scott. Baby Kong. Hunt, Jim, illus. 2006. (J). 8.95 (978-1-60131-001-9(3), Castlebridge Bks.) Big Tent Bks.

Strouse, Benjamin. Hey, Boy. Phelan, Jennifer, illus. 2014. (ENG.). 40p. (J). pap. 7.95 (978-1-4575-3341-9(3)) Dog Ear Publishing, LLC.

—Hey, Boy. Phelan, Jennifer, illus. 2017. (ENG.). 48p. (J). (gr. -1-3). 15.99 (978-1-4814-7101-5(5), McElderry, Margaret K. Bks.) McElderry, Margaret K. Bks.

Strouss, Jessica & Strouss, Stephen. There's a Dog at My Feet when I Eat. 2010. 36p. 15.49 (978-1-4269-4342-3(3)) Trafford Publishing.

Strykowski, Marcia. Call Me Amy. 2013. (ENG.). 176p. (J). (gr. 3-10). 24.95 (978-1-935462-76-7(8)); pap. 14.95 (978-1-935462-75-0(X)) Luminis Bks., Inc.

Stuchner, Joan Betty. Bagels Come Home, 1 vol. Whamond, Dave, illus. 2014. (Orca Echoes Ser.). (ENG.). 64p. (J). (gr. 2-3). pap. 6.95 (978-1-4598-0346-6(9)) Orca Bk. Pubs. USA.

—Bagels on Board, 1 vol. Whamond, Dave, illus. 2015. (Orca Echoes Ser.). (ENG.). 80p. (J). (gr. 2-3). pap. 6.95 (978-1-4598-0695-5(6)) Orca Bk. Pubs. USA.

—Bagels the Brave, 1 vol. Whamond, Dave, illus. 2015. (Orca Echoes Ser.). (ENG.). 64p. (J). (gr. 2-3). pap. 6.95 (978-1-4598-0493-7(7)) Orca Bk. Pubs. USA.

Studio Mouse Staff. Puppy Dog Tails. 2005. (Read-Aloud Board Book Ser.). (ENG., Illus.). 12p. (J). (gr. -1-3). bds. 12.95 (978-1-59249-474-3(9), 1D101) Soundprints.

Studley, Wanda Jean. Shorty Stories: A Story about a Dog & Her Famous Wheels. 2006. (J). pap. 9.00 (978-0-8059-7149-1(1)) Dorrance Publishing Co., Inc.

Stute, Lela LaBree. The New Guy, 1 vol. 2010. 30p. 24.95 (978-1-4489-9676-6(7)) PublishAmerica, Inc.

—When Pugs Fly! 2011. 36p. pap. 24.95 (978-1-4489-5484-1(3)) America Star Bks.

Stute, Lela Labree & Stute, Lela LaBree. Three Pugs & a Canadian Spy. 2011. 74p. pap. 26.90 (978-1-257-82229-4(2)) Lulu Pr., Inc.

Styles, Walker. The Big Bad Woof. Whitehouse, Ben, illus. 2017. (Rider Woofson Ser.: 8). (ENG.). 128p. (J). (gr. k-4). pap. 5.99 (978-1-4814-9188-4(1), Little Simon) Little Simon.

—The Case of the Missing Tiger's Eye. Whitehouse, Ben, illus. 2016. (Rider Woofson Ser.: 1). (ENG.). 128p. (J). (gr. k-4). 16.99 (978-1-4814-5738-5(1), Little Simon) Little Simon.

—Ghosts & Goblins & Ninja, Oh My! Whitehouse, Ben, illus. 2016. (Rider Woofson Ser.: 4). (ENG.). 128p. (J). (gr. k-4). pap. 5.99 (978-1-4814-6306-5(3), Little Simon) Little Simon.

—Labra-Cadabra-dor's Revenge. Whitehouse, Ben, illus. 2017. (Rider Woofson Ser.: 7). (ENG.). 128p. (J). (gr. k-4). 16.99 (978-1-4814-8593-7(8), Little Simon) Little Simon.

—Labra-Cadabra-Dor's Revenge. Whitehouse, Ben, illus. 2017. (Rider Woofson Ser.: 7). (ENG.). 128p. (J). (gr. k-4). pap. 5.99 (978-1-4814-8592-0(X), Little Simon) Little Simon.

—The Rival Detective. Whitehouse, Ben, illus. 2016. (Rider Woofson Ser.: 5). (ENG.). 128p. (J). (gr. k-4). pap. 5.99 (978-1-4814-7107-7(4), Little Simon) Little Simon.

—The Soccer Ball Monster Mystery. Whitehouse, Ben, illus. 2016. (Rider Woofson Ser.: 6). (ENG.). 128p. (J). (gr. k-4). pap. 5.99 (978-1-4814-7110-7(4), Little Simon) Little Simon.

—Something Smells Fishy. Whitehouse, Ben, illus. 2016. (Rider Woofson Ser.: 2). (ENG.). 128p. (J). (gr. k-4). 16.99 (978-1-4814-5742-2(X), Little Simon) Little Simon.

—Undercover in the Bow-Wow Club. Whitehouse, Ben, illus. 2016. (Rider Woofson Ser.: 3). (ENG.). 128p. (J). (gr. k-4). pap. 5.99 (978-1-4814-6303-4(9), Little Simon) Little Simon.

Sullivan, Dana. Ozzie & the Art Contest. Sullivan, Dana, illus. 2013. (ENG., Illus.). 15.99 (978-1-58536-820-4(2)) Sleeping Bear Pr.

Sullivan, Mary. Ball. (ENG., Illus.). (J). 2016. 32p. (— 1). bds. 12.99 (978-0-544-81901-6(2), HMH Books For Young Readers) 2015. 32p. (— 1). bds. 7.99 (978-0-544-31361-3(5), HMH Books For Young Readers) 2013. 40p. (gr. -1-3). lib. bdg. 12.99 (978-0-547-75936-4(3)) Houghton Mifflin Harcourt Publishing Co.

—Frankie. 2017. (ENG., Illus.). 40p. (J). (gr. -1-3). 12.99 (978-0-544-61113-9(6), HMH Books For Young Readers) Houghton Mifflin Harcourt Publishing Co.

Sullivan, Maureen. Custard & Mustard: Carlos in Coney Island. Josephs, Alison, illus. 2009. 32p. 17.95 (978-0-9820381-1-6(9)) MoJo InkWorks.

Sullivan, Maureen & Josephs, Alison. Ankle Soup: A Thanksgiving Story. Josephs, Alison, illus. 2008. (Illus.). 32p. 17.95 (978-0-9820381-0-9(0)) MoJo InkWorks.

Sulurayok, Matilda. Kamik's First Sled, 1 vol. Leng, Qin, illus. 2015. (ENG.). 32p. (J). (gr. k-2). 10.95 (978-1-77227-020-4(2)) Inhabit Media Inc. CAN. Dist: Independent Pubs. Group.

Sundberg, Peggy. Jazmine's Incredible Story. Wiles, Pat, illus. 2006. 32p. (J). 16.95 (978-0-9721057-5-0(1), Cowgirl Peg Bks.) Cowgirl Peg Enterprises.

Sundell, Joanne. Arctic Will. 2016. (ENG.). 326p. (YA). 25.95 (978-1-4328-3175-2(5), Five Star) Cengage Gale.

Sutherland, E. B. Tallie's in a Sea of Trouble. 2013. 44p. pap. 21.99 (978-1-4797-3988-2(X)) Xlibris Corp.

Sutton, Laurie S. The Curse of Atlantis. Neely, Scott, illus. 2015. (You Choose Stories: Scooby-Doo Ser.). (ENG.). 112p. (gr. 2-3). lib. bdg. 32.65 (978-1-4965-0477-7(1)) Stone Arch Bks.

—The Fright at Zombie Farm. Neely, Scott, illus. 2015. (You Choose Stories: Scooby-Doo Ser.). (ENG.). 112p. (gr. 2-3). lib. bdg. 32.65 (978-1-4342-9713-6(6), You Choose Bks.) Capstone Press of Coughlan Cos.

—The Ghost of the Bermuda Triangle, 1 vol. Neely, Scott, illus. 2014. (You Choose Stories: Scooby-Doo Ser.). (ENG.). 112p. (gr. 2-3). 32.65 (978-1-4342-9126-4(X), You Choose Bks.) Capstone Press of Coughlan Cos.

—The House on Spooky Street. Neely, Scott, illus. 2015. (You Choose Stories: Scooby-Doo Ser.). (ENG.). 112p. (gr. 2-3). lib. bdg. 32.65 (978-1-4342-9714-3(4), You Choose Bks.) Capstone Press of Coughlan Cos.

—Legend of the Gator Man. Neely, Scott, illus. 2016. (Scooby-Doo Comic Chapter Bks.). (ENG.). 88p. (gr. 3-7). pap. 5.95 (978-1-4965-3588-7(X)) Capstone Press of Coughlan Cos.

—The Mystery of the Aztec Tomb, 1 vol. Neely, Scott, illus. 2014. (You Choose Stories: Scooby-Doo Ser.). (ENG.). 112p. (gr. 2-3). 32.65 (978-1-4342-9127-1(8), You Choose Bks.) Capstone Press of Coughlan Cos.

—You Choose: Scooby-Doo. 2013. (You Choose Stories: Scooby Doo Ser.). (ENG.). 112p. pap. 166.80 (978-1-4342-9604-7(0)) Stone Arch Bks.

Swanson Sateren, Shelley. Adventures of Hound Hotel. Melmon, Deborah, illus. 2015. (Adventures at Hound Hotel Ser.). (ENG.). 72p. (gr. 2-3). 101.28 (978-1-4795-6291-6(2), Adventures at Hound Hotel) Picture Window Bks.

—Cool Crosby. Melmon, Deborah, illus. 2016. (Adventures at Hound Hotel Ser.). (ENG.). 72p. (gr. 2-3). lib. bdg. 25.32 (978-1-5158-0066-8(0), Adventures at Hound Hotel) Picture Window Bks.

—Drooling Dudley. Melmon, Deborah, illus. 2016. (Adventures at Hound Hotel Ser.). (ENG.). 72p. (gr. 2-3). lib. bdg. 25.32 (978-1-5158-0220-4(5), Adventures at Hound Hotel) Picture Window Bks.

—Mighty Murphy. Melmon, Deborah, illus. 2016. (Adventures at Hound Hotel Ser.). (ENG.). 72p. (gr. 2-3). lib. bdg. 25.32 (978-1-5158-0067-5(9), Adventures at Hound Hotel) Picture Window Bks.

—Stinky Stanley. Melmon, Deborah, illus. 2016. (Adventures at Hound Hotel Ser.). (ENG.). 72p. (gr. 2-3). lib. bdg. 25.32 (978-1-5158-0221-1(3), Adventures at Hound Hotel) Picture Window Bks.

Sweet, J. H. Foo & Friends Storybook. 2013. 290p. 26.94 (978-1-936660-04-9(0)) Sweet, Joanne.

Swenson, Jamie. Woof & Quack in Winter (reader) Sias, Ryan, illus. 2017. (Green Light Readers Level 1 Ser.). (ENG.). 32p. (J). (gr. -1-3). 12.99 **(978-0-544-95949-1(3)**, HMH Books For Young Readers) Houghton Mifflin Harcourt Publishing Co.

Swerling, Lisa & Lazar, Ralph. Dogs Going Places. 2004. 64p. 9.95 (978-1-84072-604-6(0)) M Q Pubns.

Swift, K. Marie. The Adventures of Jake & George: Jake Gets a New Brother. Paul, Kate, illus. 2010. 26p. pap. 11.75 (978-1-60693-863-8(0), Eloquent Bks.) Strategic Book Publishing & Rights Agency (SBPRA).

Swift, Thomas. Ted Tumble: So Cuddly. 2010. 28p. pap. 10.50 (978-1-60911-764-1(6), Eloquent Bks.) Strategic Book Publishing & Rights Agency (SBPRA).

Swindells, Robert. The Ghosts of Givenham Keep. 2015. (ENG., Illus.). 108p. (J). pap. 9.99 (978-1-78270-056-2(0)) Award Pubns. Ltd. GBR. Dist: Parkwest Pubns., Inc.

Swiney, Wendy D. Harvey's Very Favorite Place. 2009. 20p. pap. 12.99 (978-1-4389-6547-5(8)) AuthorHouse.

Sykes, Julie. Dora's Eggs. Chapman, Jane, illus. 2007. (Storytime Board Bks.). (J). (gr. -1-3). bds. 6.95 (978-1-58925-801-3(0)) Tiger Tales.

T. The Adventures of Sugar the Pup. Baker, David, illus. 2011. 36p. pap. 24.95 (978-1-4560-5724-4(3)) America Star Bks.

Taeckens, Geri. Walking along with My Dog. Carney, Deborah, illus. 2005. (J). 16.99 (978-0-9774546-0-0(6)) Accessibilities.

Taeschner, Jacquelin. Boss. 2005. pap. 32.50 (978-1-4208-7369-6(5)) AuthorHouse.

Takemori, Lianne K. The Four Dog Blues Band, or How Chester Boy, Dog in the Fog, & Diva Took the Big City by Storm. Dietrick, Robin C. & Klein, Bradley S., eds. 2010. (ENG., Illus.). 48p. 15.95 (978-1-887422-13-0(7)) Mississippi Museum of Art.

Talbott, Hudson. From Wolf to Woof. Talbott, Hudson, illus. 2016. (ENG., Illus.). 40p. (J). (gr. k-3). 16.99 (978-0-399-25404-8(8), Nancy Paulsen Books) Penguin Young Readers Group.

Tamez, Juliza. Trixie & Dixie: The Mystery of the Missing Cape. Almanza, Roberto, illus. 2013. (ENG.). (J). 12.95 (978-1-62086-426-5(6)) Mascot Bks., Inc.

Tanaka, Shinsuke, illus. Wings. 2006. (ENG.). 80p. (J). (gr. -1). 14.95 (978-1-933327-19-8(7)) Purple Bear Bks., Inc.

Tansil-Mitchell, Angela. Kimmie C Sunshine: When Mommy & Daddy Loses Their Jobs. 2011. 24p. pap. 13.79 (978-1-4567-5666-6(4)) AuthorHouse.

Taqi, Aliage Monique. Why Wait? I Want It Now! 2007. 36p. (YA). per. 18.95 (978-1-4327-0490-2(7)) Outskirts Pr., Inc.

Tarsy, Jean. Just Molly & Me & Nikki Make Three. LaGrange, Tiffany, illus. 2008. 36p. pap. 12.95 (978-0-9820479-6-5(7)) Peppertree Pr., The.

Tavadze, Olesya. Bursunsul & Paskualina. Ivanov, Evgueni, illus. 2007. (POL & ENG.). 32p. (J). pap. 16.95 (978-1-60195-095-6(0)) International Step by Step Assn.

Tavano, Joe. A Dachshund's Wish. Yu, Ji, illus. 2006. (ENG.). 80p. (J). (gr. 2-4). pap. 16.99 (978-0-9744287-1-0(X)) Minted Prose, LLC.

Taylor, Alastair. Mr. Blewitt's Nose. 2005. (J). (gr. k-3). 16.00 (978-0-618-58111-5(1)) Houghton Mifflin Harcourt Trade & Reference Pubs.

Taylor, G. P. The Tizzle Sisters & Erik. 2007. 188p. (978-1-905692-22-4(6)) Markosia Enterprises, Ltd.

Taylor, Lenette. Brutus the French Mastiff: The Case of the Missing Sock. 2012. 36p. 24.95 (978-1-4626-3677-8(2)) America Star Bks.

Taylor, Mark. Henry Explores the Jungle. Booth, Graham, illus. 2012. (ENG.). 48p. (J). (gr. -1-3). 18.95 (978-1-930900-56-1(2)) Purple Hse. Pr.

—Henry the Castaway. Booth, Graham, illus. 2010. 48p. (J). (gr. -1-3). 18.95 (978-1-930900-47-9(3)) Purple Hse. Pr.

Taylor, Pearl Fleming. Snowbird Weenie, 1 vol. 2009. 59p. pap. 16.95 (978-1-60836-745-0(2)) America Star Bks.

Taylor, R. W. The Curiosity of Sadie: A Collection of 35 Individual Stories about an Individual Little Girl & Her Puppy. 2011. 172p. (gr. 4-6). pap. 15.66 (978-1-4567-8202-3(9)) AuthorHouse.

Taylor, Richard B. Chispita Service Dog Extraordinaire: Volume 2. the Pack Trip. 2010. 52p. pap. 20.49 (978-1-4490-5326-0(2)) AuthorHouse.

—Chispita Service Dog Extraordinaire: Volume 3. Alaskan Cruise. 2010. 52p. pap. 20.49 (978-1-4490-5563-9(X)) AuthorHouse.

—Chispita Service Dog Extraordinaire: Volume 4. Alaskan Land Cruise. 2010. 68p. pap. 23.49 (978-1-4490-5613-1(X)) AuthorHouse.

—Chispita Service Dog Extraordinaire: Volume 5. Indian Country. 2010. 60p. pap. 21.99 (978-1-4490-5617-9(2)) AuthorHouse.

—Chispita Service Dog Extraordinaire Volume 1: Introduction. 2010. 44p. pap. 16.99 (978-1-4490-5540-0(0)) AuthorHouse.

Taylor, Sean. Don't Call Me Choochie Pooh! Hindley, Kate, illus. 2016. (ENG.). 32p. (J). (gr. -1-2). 16.99 (978-0-7636-8119-7(9)) Candlewick Pr.

Taylor, Trace. Dogtown #4. 2010. (Dogtown Comics Ser.). 24p. (J). pap. 6.95 (978-1-61541-140-5(2)) American Reading Co.

—Dogtown #5. 2010. (Dogtown Comics Ser.). 24p. (J). pap. 6.95 (978-1-61541-142-9(9)) American Reading Co.

—Dogtown #6. 2010. (Dogtown Comics Ser.). 24p. (J). pap. 6.95 (978-1-61541-144-3(5)) American Reading Co.

—Dogtown Diner. 2010. pap. 39.62 (978-1-61541-088-0(0)) American Reading Co.

—Dogtown Diner. Taylor, Trace, illus. 2010. (1G ARC Press Comics Ser.). (ENG., Illus.). 24p. (J). (gr. k-2). pap. 5.99 (978-1-61541-073-6(2)) American Reading Co.

—Dogtown's Got Talent. 2010. (Dogtown Comics Ser.). 24p. (J). pap. 6.95 (978-1-61541-136-8(4)); pap. 39.62 (978-1-61541-137-5(2)); (ENG.). 24p. (J). pap. 5.99 (978-1-61541-079-8(1)) American Reading Co.

—Flying over Dogtown. 2010. pap. 39.62 (978-1-61541-141-2(0)) American Reading Co.

—Hair Day in Dogtown. 2010. pap. 39.62 (978-1-61541-143-6(7)) American Reading Co.

—Happy Birthday Dogtown. 2010. pap. 39.62 (978-1-61541-139-9(9)) American Reading Co.

—Wedding Day in Dogtown. 2010. pap. 39.62 (978-1-61541-145-0(3)) American Reading Co.

—Who Took That Dog? Taylor, Trace, illus. 2008. (1B Graphic Novels Ser.). (ENG., Illus.). 32p. (J). (gr. k-2). pap. 5.99 (978-1-59301-757-6(X)) American Reading Co.

Taylor, Vernon T. Why Do Dogs Bark? 2012. 24p. pap. 24.95 (978-1-4626-5083-5(X)) America Star Bks.

Taylor, Yvonne. Hartlie: The Streak. Taylor, Yvonne, ed. (Hartlie: Vol. 1). (Illus.). 32p. (J). 10.99 (978-0-9709187-0-3(4)) Peaceable Productions.

Teague, Mark. Dear Mrs. LaRue: Letters from Obedience School. Teague, Mark, illus. 2003. (LaRue Bks.). (ENG., Illus.). 32p. (J). (gr. -1-3). 17.99 (978-0-439-20663-1(4), Scholastic Pr.) Scholastic, Inc.

—Detective LaRue: Letters from the Investigation. Teague, Mark, illus. 2004. (LaRue Bks.). (ENG., Illus.). 32p. (J). (gr. -1-3). 17.99 (978-0-439-45868-9(4), Scholastic Pr.) Scholastic, Inc.

Teague, Mark. Firehouse! Teague, Mark, illus. (StoryPlay Ser.). (ENG., Illus.). (J). (gr. -1-k). 2017. 40p. 5.99 **(978-1-338-18159-3(9))** 2013. 32p. bds. 6.99 (978-0-545-49215-7(7)) Scholastic, Inc. (Cartwheel Bks.).

Tennapel, Doug. Tommysaurus Rex. 2013. (ENG., Illus.). 144p. (J). (gr. 4-7). pap. 10.99 (978-0-545-48383-4(2), Graphix) Scholastic, Inc.

TenNapel, Doug. Tommysaurus Rex. 2013. (ENG., Illus.). 144p. (J). (gr. 3-7). 19.99 (978-0-545-48382-7(4), Graphix) Scholastic, Inc.

Terhaar, April. Through the Eyes of Snowball. 2010. 24p. (J). pap. 13.99 (978-1-4520-0748-9(9)) AuthorHouse.

Terhume, Albert Pays. Further Adventures of Lad. 2006. pap. (978-1-4068-1162-9(9)) Echo Library.

—His Dog. 2006. pap. (978-1-4068-1163-6(7)) Echo Library.

Terhune, Albert Payson. Buff, a Collie & Other Dog Stories. 2007. 348p. per. 18.95 (978-1-59462-809-2(2), Book Jungle) Standard Pubns., Inc.

—Grey Dawn. 2005. pap. 27.95 (978-1-885529-66-4(X)) Stevens Publishing.

—His Dog. 2013. 132p. pap. 12.95 (978-1-61895-105-2(X)) Bibliotech Pr.

—His Dog. 2010. 134p. pap. 14.95 (978-1-60444-088-1(0)) IndoEuropeanPublishing.com.

—Lad of Sunnybank. 2012. (ENG.). 336p. (J). (gr. 3). pap. 17.95 (978-1-4290-9317-0(X)) Applewood Bks.

—Lochinvar Luck. 2005. pap. 30.95 (978-1-885529-68-8(6)) Stevens Publishing.

Ternes, Caroline. Will You Be My Friend? The Prancer & Button Story. 2010. 20p. 14.99 (978-1-4490-7731-0(5)) AuthorHouse.

Terry, Anne. Honest Bob, the Dog, Has a Tea Party. 2013. 30p. pap. 9.83 (978-1-62884-761-1(1)) Speedy Publishing LLC.

Terry Anne. Honest Bob, the Dog, Plays Ball. 2013. 24p. pap. 9.52 (978-1-62884-441-2(8)) Speedy Publishing LLC.

—Honest Bob, the Dog, Tells the Truth. 2013. 26p. pap. 9.66 (978-1-63022-211-6(9)) Speedy Publishing LLC.

Tesler, Ellen. Maggie Adopts a Rescue Dog. 2013. 24p. pap. 17.99 (978-1-4817-0570-7(9)) AuthorHouse.

Tetrick, Chase. A Hot Dog Who Wanted to Play Basketball. 2009. 16p. pap. 12.50 (978-1-4490-2078-1(X)) AuthorHouse.

Texas Golden Retriever, Casanova & Jason, Daniel. I Can't Do That I Have Paws. 2005. (J). per. 9.99 (978-0-9659470-4-6(1)) 5 Star Stories, Inc.

Thames, Fiona. A Dog's Mad Dash for Home. 2008. 32p. pap. 24.95 (978-1-4241-8672-3(2)) America Star Bks.

Thayer, Jane. Part-Time Dog. Barasch, Lynne & McCue, Lisa, illus. 2004. (ENG.). 32p. (J). (gr. -1-3). 14.99 (978-0-06-029693-3(3)) HarperCollins Pubs.

—The Puppy Who Wanted a Boy. McCue, Lisa, illus. 2005. (ENG.). 32p. (J). (gr. -1-3). pap. 6.99 (978-0-06-052698-6(X)) HarperCollins Pubs.

Therriault - Bruder, Dovie G. Life on the Farm - Adventure with the Dogs: Story Ten. 2012. 36p. pap. 20.99 (978-1-4685-6347-4(5)) AuthorHouse.

Thiel, Annie. Chloe Loses Her Pet. Edwards, W M, illus. 2007. (Playdate Kids: Let's Be Friends! Ser.). 26p. (J). per. 6.95 (978-1-933721-21-7(9)) Playdate Kids Publishing.

Thiel Annie. The Playdate Kids Chloe Loses Her Pet. 2007. 32p. 12.95 (978-1-933721-00-2(6)) Playdate Kids Publishing.

Thiele, Colin. The Cave & the Glory of Galumph. (Illus.). 160p. pap. (978-0-7344-0413-8(1), Lothian Children's Bks.) Hachette Australia.

Thierry, Raphael. Green Butterfly. 2007. (Superdog Adventure Ser.). (ENG., Illus.). 24p. (J). (gr. -1-k). pap. 6.99 (978-1-84270-449-3(4)) Transworld Publishers Ltd. GBR. Dist: Independent Pubs. Group.

Thomas, Chandler Turner. Fundays Food Dilemm. 2011. 32p. pap. 24.95 (978-1-4626-0679-5(2)) America Star Bks.

—Fundays with the Crime Fighters for Justice. 2011. 36p. pap. 24.95 (978-1-4560-8419-6(4)) America Star Bks.

Thomas, Charlene. A Dog Named Munson Finds the Missing Game Ball. Repetto, Laurie, illus. 2012. 38p. (J). 14.95 (978-1-62086-054-0(6)) Mascot Bks., Inc.

Thomas, Christina L. Lizzie Thompson: My Dog Knows Kung Fu! 2013. 60p. (gr. 2-4). pap. 10.30 (978-1-4669-9997-8(7)) Trafford Publishing.

Thomas, Dagny. Courageous Hearts. 2007. 190p. pap. 11.98 (978-0-615-17087-9(0)) Thomastar Publishing.

Thomas, Jan. The Doghouse. 2008. (ENG., Illus.). 40p. (J). (gr. -1-k). 12.95 (978-0-15-206533-1(4)) Houghton Mifflin Harcourt Publishing Co.

Thomas, Lisa E. The Puppy. 20p. (J). (gr. 1-6). pap. (978-1-885091-03-1(6)); pap. (978-1-885091-02-4(8)) Eco-Busters.

Thomas, M. L. Brut Mccloud & His Friends. 2012. 44p. pap. 18.99 (978-1-4670-4259-8(5)) AuthorHouse.

Thomas Nelson. Playdate Pals Puppy Says Please. 2016. (ENG.). 24p. (J). (gr. -1-7). pap. (978-1-78598-480-8(2)) Make Believe Ideas.

Thomas, P. J. The Cloud & the Cat. 2012. 52p. pap. 24.95 (978-1-4626-7211-0(6)) America Star Bks.

Thomas, Patsy E. My Favorite Dog. 2011. 16p. (gr. 2-4). pap. 10.67 (978-1-4269-6258-5(4)) Trafford Publishing.

Thompson, Chad. Old Mother Hubbard, 1 vol. 2009. (Early Childhood Themes Ser.). (ENG., Illus.). 16p. (J). (gr. -1-2). pap. 6.99 (978-1-4333-1477-3(0)) Teacher Created Materials, Inc.

Thompson, Colin. Stanley. 2016. 32p. 17.99 (978-0-7333-3285-2(4)) ABC Bks. AUS. Dist: HarperCollins Pubs.

Thompson, Holly Sue. Molly, the Good Furry Friend. Thompson, Kristi June, illus. 2011. 36p. pap. 14.75 (978-1-60911-431-2(0), Eloquent Bks.) Strategic Book Publishing & Rights Agency (SBPRA).

—Molly's Muffins. 2009. 28p. pap. 14.50 (978-1-60860-479-1(9), Eloquent Bks.) Strategic Book Publishing & Rights Agency (SBPRA).

Thompson, Kate. I'm Just a Little Puppy. Green, Barry, illus. 2016. (Googley-Eye Bks.). (ENG.). 12p. (J). (gr. -1-k). bds. 7.99 (978-1-78445-862-1(7)) Top That! Publishing PLC GBR. Dist: Independent Pubs. Group.

Thompson, Laurie Ann. My Dog Is the Best. Schmid, Paul, illus. 2015. (ENG.). 40p. (J). (gr. -1-1). 17.99 (978-0-374-30051-7(8), 9780374300517, Farrar, Straus & Giroux (BYR)) Farrar, Straus & Giroux.

Thomson, Malcolm. Let's Go Nuts. 2012. (Illus.). 48p. pap. 24.40 (978-1-4772-3913-1(8)) AuthorHouse.

Thomson, Rachel Starr. Theodore Pharris Saves the Universe. 2013. 176p. pap. (978-1-927658-18-5(7)) Little Dozen Press.

Thorhauer, Laura L. Molly's Wings. 2011. 40p. pap. 21.99 (978-1-4568-4815-6(1)) Xlibris Corp.

Thornton, M. H. Kylee & Lexie: Mystery of the Gholdees. 2010. 64p. pap. 10.99 (978-1-4269-3713-2(X)) Trafford Publishing.

The Three Pups. (Lexile Levels Ser.). 47.88 (978-1-56334-092-5(5)) CENGAGE Learning.

Tiger Tales, ed. & compiled by. Stories for Boys. Tiger Tales, compiled by. 2015. (ENG.). 176p. (J). (gr. -1-3). 12.99 (978-1-58925-535-7(6)) Tiger Tales.

Tillworth, Mary. All-Star Pups! (Paw Patrol) Petrossi, Fabrizio, illus. 2016. (Little Golden Book Ser.). (ENG.). 24p. (J). (-k). 4.99 (978-1-101-93685-6(1), Golden Bks.) Random Hse. Children's Bks.

—King for a Day! (PAW Patrol) Jackson, Mike, illus. 2016. (Step into Reading Ser.). (ENG.). 24p. (J). (gr. -1-1). 4.99 (978-1-101-93684-9(3), Random Hse. Bks. for Young Readers) Random Hse. Children's Bks.

—Nickelodeon 5-Minute Stories Collection. Random House, illus. 2016. (5-Minute Story Collection). (ENG.). 160p. (J). (gr. -1-2). 12.99 (978-0-399-55314-1(2), Random Hse. Bks. for Young Readers) Random Hse. Children's Bks.

—The Puppy & the Ring (Bubble Guppies) Random House Staff & MJ Illustrations Staff, illus. 2014. (Pictureback Ser.). (ENG.). 24p. (J). (gr. -1-2). 3.99 (978-0-385-38408-7(4), Random Hse. Bks. for Young Readers) Random Hse. Children's Bks.

Tilson, Gina L. Patches: Adventures of a Country Cavalier. 2011. 48p. pap. 9.99 (978-1-4567-6386-2(5)) AuthorHouse.

Tireman, Loyd. Big Fat. Douglass, Ralph, illus. 2015. (Mesaland Ser.). (ENG.). 48p. (J). 12.95 (978-0-8263-5605-5(2)) Univ. of New Mexico Pr.

Tjernagel, Shirley. Obee & the Great Bank Heist. 2011. 28p. pap. 12.99 (978-1-4634-1913-4(9)) AuthorHouse.

Tobin, Richard K. Skating on Thick Ice. LeBlanc, Rebecca, ed. Chapman, Jesse, illus. 2013. 122p. (J). pap. 12.00 (978-1-929882-96-0(3)) Biographical Publishing Co.

Toft, Julie. Blot on the Landscape. 2010. (Illus.). 48p. pap. 10.49 (978-1-4490-6453-2(1)) AuthorHouse.

Tofte, Mavis. Doogie Dork & Marta. 2005. (Illus.). 64p. (J). per. 5.75 (978-0-9709906-4-8(2)) Creative Quill Publishing, Inc.

—Doogie Dork & the Storm. Tofte, Mavis, illus. 2006. (Illus.). 64p. (J). per. 6.75 (978-0-9709906-5-5(0)) Creative Quill Publishing, Inc.

Tokidoki. Tokidoki Cactus Pups. 2008. 5.99 (978-1-59396-993-6(7)) Diamond Bk. Distributors.

Tolan, Stephanie S. Wishworks, Inc. Bates, Amy June, illus. 2011. (ENG.). 160p. (J). (gr. 2-5). pap. 5.99 (978-0-545-03155-4(9), Levine, Arthur A. Bks.) Scholastic, Inc.

Tolbert-Klein, Wa-Landa. Paladin: A Different Type of Werewolf Story. 2011. 156p. pap. 11.95 (978-1-4327-6185-1(4)) Outskirts Pr., Inc.

Tolstoi, Leo & Riordan, James. The Lion & the Puppy: And Other Stories for Children. Riordan, James, tr. from RUS. Sievert, Claus, illus. 2012. (ENG.). 76p. (J). (gr. 4-7). 16.95 (978-1-61608-484-4(7), 608484, Sky Pony Pr.) Skyhorse Publishing Co., Inc.

Tomberg, Andrea. Teddie's Tales: A Very Busy Day. 2008. 32p. pap. 12.99 (978-1-4389-3319-1(3)) AuthorHouse.

Tompkins, Robyn Lee. Miss Molly's Adventure at the Beach: Another Great Adventure Brought to You by Miss Molly & Her Dog Reyburn, 10 vols. Kantz, Bill, illus. 2004. (J). per. (978-0-9741647-5-5(5)) NRG Pubns.

—Miss Molly's Adventure in the Park: Another Great Adventure Brought to You by Miss Molly & Her Dog Reyburn, 10 vols. Carson, Shawn K., illus. l.t. ed. 2005. (ENG.). 60p. (J). per. (978-0-9741647-6-2(3)) NRG Pubns.

Toms, Kate. Funny Faces Cloth Book Jogger Dog. 2006. (Funny Faces (Make Believe Ideas) Ser.). (Illus.). 4p. (gr. -1). (978-1-84610-289-9(8)) Make Believe Ideas.

Toms, Kate & Funny Faces Staff. Jogger Dog. 2007. (Funny Faces (Make Believe Ideas) Ser.). (Illus.). (gr. -1). (978-1-84610-268-4(5)) Make Believe Ideas.

Tooty. Patches in Winter. 2012. 32p. pap. 9.00 (978-1-4349-7288-0(7), RoseDog Bks.) Dorrance Publishing Co., Inc.

Torrey, Richard. My Dog, Bob. Torrey, Richard, illus. 2016. (ENG., Illus.). 32p. (J). (gr. -1-3). 6.99 (978-0-8234-3691-0(8)) Holiday Hse., Inc.

—My Dog, Bob. 2015. (ENG., Illus.). 32p. (J). (gr. -1-3). 16.95 (978-0-8234-3386-5(2)) Holiday Hse., Inc.

Torricelli, Dr Richard & Torricelli, Richard. A Tale of a Schnauzer. 2011. 44p. pap. 14.95 (978-1-936343-77-5(0)) Peppertree Pr., The.

Torseter, Øyvind & Steven, Kenneth. Why Dogs Have Wet Noses. 2015. (ENG., Illus.). 40p. (J). (gr. -1-3). 17.95 (978-1-59270-173-5(6)) Enchanted Lion Bks., LLC.

Touma, Patricia. Happy Times, Book: Ish & Mish Go to the Carnival. 2007. 56p. per. 9.95 (978-1-59899-093-5(4)) Long Dash Publishing.

Towne, C. Ross. Old Jack: The very smart Dog. 2011. 16p. 8.32 (978-1-4567-2178-7(X)) AuthorHouse.

Townsend, Michael. Cute & Cuter. 2013. (ENG., Illus.). 40p. (J). (gr. k-3). lib. bdg. 18.99 (978-0-375-95718-5(9), Knopf Bks. for Young Readers) Random Hse. Children's Bks.

Townsend, Peter. Shelly & Muffin's Big Lesson Learned. 2008. 11p. pap. 24.95 (978-1-60672-379-1(0)) America Star Bks.

Tracy, Roseann. Whose Toes Are Those? 2008. 24p. pap. 12.99 (978-1-4343-9291-6(0)) AuthorHouse.

Trafford, Adrienne. SPARK Cat & Dog Around the World Coloring Book. 2017. (Dover Coloring Bks.). (ENG.). 64p. (J). (gr. 1-4). pap. 5.99 (978-0-486-81433-9(5)) Dover Pubns., Inc.

Trapani, Iza. Oh Where, Oh Where Has My Little Dog Gone? Trapani, Iza, illus. 2008. (ENG., Illus.). 32p. (J). (gr. -1-k). pap. 7.99 (978-1-58089-005-2(9)) Charlesbridge Publishing, Inc.

Travis, Lucille. Timna. 2009. (ENG.). 168p. (J). (gr. 3-9). pap. 9.99 (978-0-8361-9484-5(5)) Herald Pr.

Trees, Annie Mae. The Mystery of the Big Bone. 2012. 24p. pap. 24.95 (978-1-4626-6104-6(1)) America Star Bks.

Treggiari, Jo. Ashes, Ashes. (ENG.). 352p. (J). (gr. 7). 2013. pap. 9.99 (978-0-545-25564-6(3), Scholastic Paperbacks) 2011. 17.99 (978-0-545-25563-9(5), Scholastic Pr.) Scholastic, Inc.

Trembath, Brent. Scruggy Puppies Book. 2012. (ENG.). pap. 10.00 (978-1-4675-2260-1(0)) Independent Pub.

Trimble, Marcia. Peppy's Shadow. Pellegrini, Will, illus. 2003. 32p. (J). (gr. -1-3). 15.95 (978-1-891577-70-3(0)); pap. 7.95 (978-1-891577-71-0(9)) Images Pr.

Trine, Greg. Attack of the Valley Girls. Montijo, Rhode, illus. 6th ed. 2008. (Melvin Beederman, Superhero Ser.: 6). (ENG.). 144p. (J). (gr. 2-5). pap. 8.99 (978-0-8050-8161-9(5), 9780805081619) Square Fish.

—Dinos Are Forever. Dormer, Frank W., illus. (Adventures of Jo Schmo Ser.: 1). (ENG.). 112p. (J). (gr. 1-4). 2014. pap. 5.99 (978-0-544-00325-5(X), HMH Books For Young Readers) 2012. 12.99 (978-0-547-76341-5(7)) Houghton Mifflin Harcourt Publishing Co.

—Pinkbeard's Revenge. Dormer, Frank W., illus. (Adventures of Jo Schmo Ser.: 4). (ENG.). 128p. (J). (gr. 1-4). 2015. pap. 5.99 (978-0-544-45601-3(7), HMH Books For Young Readers) 2013. 12.99 (978-0-547-80797-3(X)) Houghton Mifflin Harcourt Publishing Co.

—Shifty Business. Dormer, Frank W., illus. (Adventures of Jo Schmo Ser.: 3). (ENG.). 112p. (J). (gr. 1-4). 2014. pap. 5.99 (978-0-544-33911-8(8), HMH Books For Young Readers) 2013. 12.99 (978-0-547-80796-6(1)) Houghton Mifflin Harcourt Publishing Co.

—Wyatt Burp Rides Again. Dormer, Frank W., illus. 2014. (Adventures of Jo Schmo Ser.: 2). (ENG.). 112p. (J). (gr. 1-4). pap. 5.99 (978-0-544-01899-0(0), HMH Books For Young Readers) Houghton Mifflin Harcourt Publishing Co.

Tripp, Jenny. Pete & Fremont. Manders, John, illus. 2008. (ENG.). 192p. (J). (gr. 3-7). pap. 12.95 (978-0-15-206238-5(6)) Houghton Mifflin Harcourt Publishing Co.

Trissler, Rebecca Johns. Vinny's Secret. (Adventures of Storydog Ser.). 75p. (J). pap. (978-0-9722690-0-1(2), 1000) Storydog, Inc.

Trites, Judy. Charlie's Challenge. 2011. 24p. pap. 15.99 (978-1-4628-4568-2(1)) Xlibris Corp.

Trivette, Donna K. Ringo & Girl. 2011. 40p. pap. 24.95 (978-1-4626-1369-4(1)) America Star Bks.

Trotta-Gilbert, Susan. What Ever Happened to Puppy? 2009. 36p. pap. 16.75 (978-1-4490-4482-4(4)) AuthorHouse.

True, J. J. Billy Brite: Africa & Beyond. 2011. (Illus.). 112p. pap. 14.03 (978-1-4567-7281-9(3)) AuthorHouse.

Trueit, Trudi. Mom, There's a Dinosaur in Beeson's Lake. Paillot, Jim, illus. 2011. (Secrets of a Lab Rat Ser.). (ENG.). 160p. (J). (gr. 3-7). pap. 5.99 (978-1-4169-6112-3(7), Aladdin) Simon & Schuster Children's Publishing.

—Scab for Treasurer? Paillot, Jim, illus. 2011. (Secrets of a Lab Rat Ser.). (ENG.). 160p. (J). (gr. 3-7). pap. 5.99 (978-1-4169-6113-0(5), Aladdin) Simon & Schuster Children's Publishing.

—Scab for Treasurer? Paillot, Jim, illus. 2011. (Secrets of a Lab Rat Ser.). (ENG.). 160p. (J). (gr. 3-7). 15.99 (978-1-4169-7594-6(2), Simon & Schuster/Paula Wiseman Bks.) Simon & Schuster/Paula Wiseman Bks.

Trueit, Trudi Strain. Mom, There's a Dinosaur in Beeson's Lake. Paillot, Jim, illus. 2010. (Secrets of a Lab Rat Ser.). (ENG.). 160p. (J). (gr. 3-7). 14.99 (978-1-4169-7593-9(4), Simon & Schuster/Paula Wiseman Bks.) Simon & Schuster/Paula Wiseman Bks.

Trueman, Terry. Life Happens Next. 2012. (Stuck in Neutral Ser.: 3). (ENG.). 144p. (YA). (gr. 9). 17.99 *(978-0-06-202803-7(0),* HarperTeen) HarperCollins Pubs.
Trumbore, Cindy. Three Cheers for Liberty! Elkerton, Andy, illus. 2016. (J). pap. ***(978-0-87935-287-5(6))*** Colonial Williamsburg Foundation.
Tubb, Kristin O'Donnell. A Dog Like Daisy. 2017. 192p. (J). (gr. 3-7). 16.99 *(978-0-06-246324-1(1),* Tegen, Katherine Bks) HarperCollins Pubs.
Turchan, Monique. Mydoit. Turchan, Monique, illus. 2013. (Illus.). 24p. pap. 11.95 *(978-1-61244-144-3(0))* Halo Publishing International.
Turnbull, Betty. A Sergeant in the House. Senning, Susan, illus. 2013. 44p. (J). 19.95 *(978-1-61153-059-9(8))* Light Messages Publishing.
Turnbull, Betty J. A Sergeant in the House. Senning, Susan, illus. 2013. 44p. pap. 14.95 *(978-1-61153-060-5(1))* Light Messages Publishing.
Turner, Corey W. Little Benjamin, the Bugs, & the Holy Spirit. 2010. 40p. 16.99 *(978-1-4490-8498-1(2))* AuthorHouse.
Turner, Deborah & Mohler, Diana. How Willy Got His Wings: The Continuing Adventures of Wheely Willy. Ahrends, Susan, illus. 2003. (ENG.). 32p. 15.95 *(978-0-944875-88-9(2))* i-5 Publishing LLC.
Turner, Stephanie. Dirty the Dog & the King of Mud Puddles. 2008. 20p. pap. 12.50 *(978-1-60693-008-3(7),* Eloquent Bks.) Strategic Book Publishing & Rights Agency (SBPRA).
Tveite, William P. The Adventures of Maximillian P. Dogg - Rescue Dog: Max Finds a New Home. Steele, Gregory D., illus. 2012. (ENG.). 30p. (J). pap. 12.95 *(978-1-61863-289-0(2))* Bookstand Publishing.
Typaldos, Sylvia. Don't Call Me Lassie! The Fascinating Lives of Seven Family Dogs. 2003. Orig. Title: Family Dogs: an Animal Rights Novel about Dogs. 192p. (YA). per. 16.95 *(978-0-9729863-0-4(8))* Haven Harbor.
Tysseland, Elsie. Hershel the Dog. Fitch, Rik, illus. 2008. (ENG.). 32p. pap. 12.99 *(978-1-4389-2130-3(6))* AuthorHouse.
Ugly Pugsy: Individual Title Six-Packs. (Bookweb Ser.). 32p. (gr. 5-18). 34.00 *(978-0-7635-3779-1(9))* Rigby Education.
Uluadluak, Donald. Kamik: An Inuit Puppy Story, 1 vol. Leng, Qin, illus. 2013. (ENG.). 32p. (J). (gr. 1-3). 10.95 *(978-1-927095-11-9(5))* Inhabit Media Inc. CAN. Dist: Independent Pubs. Group.
Uncle Bob. Tobi the Little Puppy Dog. Arnold, Stephen, illus. 2006. (Uncle Bob Ser.). 12p. (J). pap. 3.95 *(978-1-930596-61-0(8))* Amherst Pr.
Underwood, Deborah. Here Comes Valentine Cat. Rueda, Claudia, illus. 2015. (ENG.). 88p. (J). (-k). 16.99 *(978-0-525-42915-9(8),* Dial Bks) Penguin Young Readers Group.
Underwood, Ralph Kim. His Dogness Finds a Blue Heart. Goldman, Garnet, illus. 2004. 32p. (J). 16.95 *(978-0-89587-304-0(4))* Blair, John F. Pub.
Unger, Pam. Fly, Greyhound Racer: A Special Dog's Tale. 2005. (Illus.). 60p. (YA). pap. 14.99 *(978-1-933570-38-9(5))* Aardvark Global Publishing.
Unglick, Richard. Sherlock Holmes: the Hound of the Baskervilles. 2016. (Playmobil Ser.). (ENG.). 96p. (J). (gr. 1-7). 19.95 *(978-1-63322-078-2(8),* Walter Foster Jr) Quarto Publishing Group USA.
Unknown, Unknown & Grosset and Dunlap Staff. Dick & Jane Fun Wherever We Are. 2004. (Dick & Jane Ser.). (ENG., Illus.). 144p. (J). (gr. -1-1). 8.99 *(978-0-448-43614-2(0),* Grosset & Dunlap) Penguin Young Readers Group.
Untermeyer, Louis. One & One & One. Jones, Robert, illus. 2016. (ENG.). 64p. (gr. k-3). pap. 9.99 *(978-0-486-81065-2(8))* Dover Pubns., Inc.
Urbanovic, Jackie. Sitting Duck. Urbanovic, Jackie, illus. 2010. (Illus.). 40p. (J). (gr. -1-2). (ENG.). 17.99 *(978-0-06-176583-4(X));* lib. bdg. 18.89 *(978-0-06-176584-1(8))* HarperCollins Pubs.
Urbigkit, Cat. Puppies, Puppies Everywhere! 2006. (ENG., Illus.). 24p. (J). (gr. -1-1). 12.95 *(978-1-59078-363-4(8))* Boyds Mills Pr.
Ure, Jean. Fortune Cookie. 2009. (ENG.). 192p. (J). (gr. 4-7). pap. 9.95 *(978-0-00-722462-3(1),* HarperCollins Children's Bks.) HarperCollins Pubs. Ltd. GBR. Dist: HarperCollins Pubs.
Urish, J. D. The Adventures of Rex Bolton Volume 1. 2010. 60p. pap. 9.98 *(978-0-578-03676-2(2))* Jentmedia.
Urmston, Kathleen. Sammy. Gedeon, Gloria, illus. 2005. (ENG.). 16p. (gr. k-1). pap. 7.95 *(978-1-57874-089-5(4),* Kaeden Bks.) Kaeden Corp.
—When Sammy Was a Puppy. Tomsi, Gary, illus. 2012. (ENG.). 12p. (gr. k-2). pap. 7.95 *(978-1-61181-242-8(9),* Kaeden Bks.) Kaeden Corp.
—When Sammy Was a Puppy (6 Pack) Tottisi, Gary, illus. 2012. (ENG.). 12p. (gr. k-2). pap. *(978-1-61181-243-5(7),* Kaeden Bks.) Kaeden Corp.
Vail, Rochelle Kelly. Critters: A Dog's Tale. 2007. 140p. per. 11.95 *(978-1-4327-0826-9(0))* Outskirts Pr., Inc.
Vajda, Joseph. The Great Orange. Kis, Gabor Norbert, illus. 2017. (ENG.). (gr. 1-4). ***(978-1-78222-499-0(8))*** Paragon Publishing, Rothersthorpe.
Valente, Shannon. The Puddle That Ate My Boot! 2009. 16p. pap. 10.79 *(978-1-4389-5325-0(9))* AuthorHouse.
Van Allsburg, Chris. The Sweetest Fig. 2014. 32p. pap. 9.00 *(978-1-61003-223-0(3))* Center for the Collaborative Classroom.
van de Vendel, Edward. The Dog That Nino Didn't Have. Van Hertbruggen, Anton, illus. 2015. (ENG.). 34p. (J). 17.00 *(978-0-8028-5451-3(6),* Eerdmans Bks For Young Readers) Eerdmans, William B. Publishing Co.
Van Der Merwe, Steve. Policeman Bobby. 2008. 68p. pap. 11.99 *(978-1-4389-1899-0(2))* AuthorHouse.
Van Draanen, Wendelin. Sammy Keyes & the Runaway Elf. 2008. (Sammy Keyes Ser.: Bk. 4). (J). 54.99 *(978-1-60640-644-1(2))* Findaway World, LLC.
Van Dusen, Chris. A Camping Spree with Mr. Magee. 2003. (Mr. Mcgee Ser.: MCGE). (ENG., Illus.). 36p. (J). (gr. -1-7). 15.99 *(978-0-8118-3603-6(7))* Chronicle Bks. LLC.
—Learning to Ski with Mr. Magee. 2010. (ENG., Illus.). 36p. (J). (gr. -1-3). 15.99 *(978-0-8118-7495-3(8))* Chronicle Bks. LLC.
Van Dusen, Ross, illus. Crocka Dog in the Evil Forest. 2015. (J). *(978-1-936744-54-1(6),* Rio Grande Bks.) LPD Pr.
—How Crocka Dog Came to Be. 2015. (J). *(978-1-936744-39-8(2))* LPD Pr.
Van Fleet, Matthew. Color Dog. Stanton, Brian, illus. Stanton, Brian, photos by. 2015. (ENG.). 22p. (J). (gr. -1-k). 19.99 *(978-1-4814-4986-1(9),* Simon & Schuster Bks. For Young Readers) Simon & Schuster Bks. For Young Readers.
—Dog. Stanton, Brian, photos by. 2007. (ENG., Illus.). 20p. (J). (gr. -1-2). 18.99 *(978-1-4169-4137-8(1),* Simon & Schuster/Paula Wiseman Bks.) Simon & Schuster/Paula Wiseman Bks.
Van Gorder, Vivian Ezeife. Master Kofi & Friskey the Dog. 2012. 20p. pap. 17.99 *(978-1-4772-6817-9(0))* AuthorHouse.
Van Patter, Bruce. Farley Found It! 2006. (ENG., Illus.). 32p. (J). (gr. -1-1). 17.95 *(978-1-59078-351-1(4))* Boyds Mills Pr.
van Reek, Wouter, creator. Coppernickel Goes Mondrian. 2012. (Artist Tribute Ser.). (ENG., Illus.). 40p. (J). (gr. -1-3). 15.95 *(978-1-59270-119-3(1))* Enchanted Lion Bks., LLC.
Vancil, Marybelle. Adventures with Macy & the Sneezy, Sneezy Dog: First Adventure: We Visit Indians. 2010. (Illus.). 43p. (J). pap. 23.95 *(978-1-4327-5038-1(0))* Outskirts Pr., Inc.
Vandalay, Martha. Pittsburgh a to Z. 2003. per. 6.95 *(978-1-932205-18-3(7))* Word Association Pubs.
Vande Velde, Vivian. Smart Dog. 2007. (ENG., Illus.). 160p. (J). (gr. 5-7). pap. 7.99 *(978-0-15-206172-2(X))* Houghton Mifflin Harcourt Publishing Co.
Vanden Heede, Sylvia. Wolf & Dog. Nagelkerke, Bill, tr. from DUT. Tolman, Marije, illus. 2013. (ENG.). 96p. *(978-1-877579-47-9(5))* Gecko Pr.
VanDerbilt, Deanna. The Dog with a Thousand Names. 2012. 20p. pap. 17.99 *(978-1-4772-7984-7(9))* AuthorHouse.
Vaneck Holub, Helen. Beloved Companion. 2011. 90p. pap. 16.95 *(978-1-257-63213-8(2))* Lulu Pr., Inc.
Vaniko, K. L. Why the Dog Chases the Cat & the Cat Chases the Mouse. 2006. 189p. 30.99 *(978-1-59926-863-7(9))* Xlibris Corp.
Varon, Sara. Robot Dreams. Varon, Sara, illus. 2007. (ENG., Illus.). 208p. (J). (gr. 3-7). pap. 17.99 *(978-1-59643-108-9(3),* 9781596431089, First Second Bks.) Roaring Brook Pr.
Vassallo, Rebecca. Listen to Luther. 2006. 24p. (J). 10.87 *(978-1-4116-8169-9(X))* Lulu Pr., Inc.
Vermazen, Eve. Dogtales: Sebastian & the Destiny Stone. 2012. 36p. pap. 32.70 *(978-1-4797-4032-1(2))* Xlibris Corp.
Verne, Jules. A Journey to the Interior of the Earth. 2006. 196p. per. 13.95 *(978-1-59818-461-7(X))* Aegypan.
Vernick, Audrey. Water Balloon. 2011. (ENG.). 320p. (J). (gr. 5-7). 16.99 *(978-0-547-59554-2(9),* Clarion Bks.) Houghton Mifflin Harcourt Trade & Reference Pubs.
Villa, Leesan. The Angel on Top of the Tree. 2011. 68p. pap. 31.99 *(978-1-4628-7837-6(7))* Xlibris Corp.
Villaloz, ChiChi & Etheridge, Katy. Do Dogs Dream? Villaloz, ChiChi & Etheridge, Katy, illus. 2003. (Illus.). 32p. (J). lib. bdg. 16.95 *(978-0-9722180-5-4(X))* Malamute Pr.
—Do Dogs Vote? Villaloz, ChiChi & Etheridge, Katy, illus. 2008. (Illus.). 32p. (J). lib. bdg. 24.95 *(978-0-9722180-0-9(9))* Malamute Pr.
Vine, Joshua M. Gnomey & Froggie. 2012. 46p. pap. 21.99 *(978-1-4772-7529-0(0))* AuthorHouse.
Vinopol, Corinne & Bednarczyk, Angela. ASL Tales & Games for Kids - Biscuit Blvd: Computer Software in American Sign Language. 2004. (J). cd-rom 34.95 *(978-0-9667589-9-3(4))* Institute for Disabilities Research & Training, Inc.
Viorst, Judith. Lulu Walks the Dogs. Smith, Lane, illus. (ENG.). (J). (gr. 1-5). 2014. 176p. pap. 7.99 *(978-1-4424-3580-3(1))* 2012. 160p. 16.99 *(978-1-4424-3579-7(8))* Simon & Schuster Children's Publishing. (Atheneum Bks. for Young Readers).
—Lulu Walks the Dogs. 2014. (Lulu Ser.: 2). lib. bdg. 18.40 *(978-0-606-35438-7(7))* Turtleback Bks.
Vischer, Frans. Fuddles & Puddles. Vischer, Frans, illus. 2016. (ENG., Illus.). 32p. (J). (gr. -1-3). 17.99 *(978-1-4814-3839-1(5),* Aladdin) Simon & Schuster Children's Publishing.
Viz Media Staff. Meet Mameshiba! 2011. (ENG.). 96p. (J). pap. 6.99 *(978-1-4215-3972-0(1))* Viz Media.
Voake, Steve. Daisy Dawson & the Big Freeze. Meserve, Jessica, illus. 2011. (Daisy Dawson Ser.). (ENG.). 96p. (J). (gr. 1-4). pap. 5.99 *(978-0-7636-5627-0(5))* Candlewick Pr.
—Daisy Dawson Is on Her Way! Meserve, Jessica, illus. 2009. (Daisy Dawson Ser.: 1). (ENG.). 112p. (J). (gr. 1-4). pap. 5.99 *(978-0-7636-4294-5(0))* Candlewick Pr.
Voigt, Cynthia. Angus & Sadie. Leigh, Tom, illus. (ENG.). 208p. (J). (gr. 3-7). 2008. pap. 6.99 *(978-0-06-074584-4(3))* 2005. 16.99 *(978-0-06-074582-0(7))* HarperCollins Pubs.
—The Rosie Stories. Smith, Cat Bowman, illus. 2003. (ENG.). 48p. (J). (gr. k-3). tchr. ed. 16.95 *(978-0-8234-1625-7(9))* Holiday Hse., Inc.
—Young Fredle. Yates, Louise, illus. 2011. (ENG.). 240p. (J). (gr. 3-7). 16.99 *(978-0-375-86457-5(1),* Knopf Bks. for Young Readers) Random Hse. Children's Bks.
Volker, Kerstin. Henry Builds a Tree House. 2003. (Funny Friends Lift-and-Learn Bks.). (Illus.). 14p. (J). 5.99 *(978-1-59384-023-5(3))* Parklane Publishing.
von Klan, Stella and Laurene. Beauty & the Boy. 2009. 32p. 16.98 *(978-0-578-00322-1(8))* von Klan, Laurene.
Waber, Bernard. Lyle, Lyle, Crocodile Storybook Treasury. 2012. (Lyle the Crocodile Ser.). (ENG., Illus.). 192p. (J). (gr. -1-3). 11.99 *(978-0-547-51618-9(5))* Houghton Mifflin Harcourt Publishing Co.
—Lyle Walks the Dogs. Waber, Paulis, illus. 2010. (ENG.). 24p. (J). (gr. -1-3). 17.99 *(978-0-547-22323-0(4))* Houghton Mifflin Harcourt Publishing Co.
Waddell, James M. Puppy Dog Tails. 2005. 217p. pap. 19.95 *(978-0-7414-2438-9(X))* Infinity Publishing.
Waddell, Martin. The Super Hungry Dinosaur. Lord, Leonie, illus. 2009. (ENG.). 32p. (J). (gr. -1-k). 17.99 *(978-0-8037-3446-3(6),* Dial Bks) Penguin Young Readers Group.
Wade, Joan. Zoey Finds a New Home. Swope, Brenda, illus. 2011. 28p. pap. 24.95 *(978-1-4560-0899-4(4))* PublishAmerica, Inc.
Wagner, Jenny. High Hopes on Sea. Rogers, Gregory, illus. 2005. (UQP Children's Fiction Ser.). 80p. (Orig.). (J). pap. *(978-0-7022-3525-2(3))* Univ. of Queensland Pr.
Wagner, Rachel A. Bogie the Boxer: Gardens. 2012. 24p. pap. 9.99 *(978-0-9685180-4-9(X))* Mindstir Media.
Wagstaff, Janiel. Stella Tells Her Story. 2015. (ENG.). pap. 7.95 *(978-1-63133-023-0(3))* Staff Development for Educators.
Wainwright, Debra. That Kind of Dog. 2009. (ENG., Illus.). 32p. (J). (gr. k-2). 16.95 *(978-0-9792035-4-1(6))* Pleasant St. Pr.
Waite, Judy. Digging for Dinosaurs. Parsons, Garry, illus. 2003. (Flying Foxes Ser.). (ENG.). 48p. (J). lib. bdg. *(978-0-7787-1483-5(7))* Crabtree Publishing Co.
Waldorf, Heather. Leftovers, 1 vol. 2009. (ENG.). 208p. (YA). (gr. 7-12). pap. 12.95 *(978-1-55143-937-2(9))* Orca Bk. Pubs. USA.
Wales, Dirk. Penny House. Kenna, Diane, illus. 2005. 32p. (J). (gr. -1). 16.95 *(978-0-9632459-1-5(0))* Great Plains Pr.
Walker, Anna. I Love Christmas. Walker, Anna, illus. 2009. (ENG., Illus.). 32p. (J). (gr. -1-1). 9.99 *(978-1-4169-8317-0(1),* Simon & Schuster Bks. For Young Readers) Simon & Schuster Bks. For Young Readers.
Walker, Crystal. Maceys Magic Tree. 2009. 28p. pap. 12.49 *(978-1-4490-4916-4(8))* AuthorHouse.
Walker, Doris D. Lucky, the Little Talking Puppy! 2010. 48p. pap. 19.99 *(978-1-4389-5012-9(8))* AuthorHouse.
Walker, Melzina. Little Melvin's Blue Coat. 2007. (Illus.). 32p. (J). pap. 8.00 *(978-0-8059-7389-1(3))* Dorrance Publishing Co., Inc.
Walker, Russell D. Michelle & the Magic Timepiece. 2006. 108p. pap. 19.95 *(978-1-4241-3143-3(X))* PublishAmerica, Inc.
Walker Styles Staff. Something Smells Fishy. Whitehouse, Ben, illus. 2016. (Rider Woofson Ser.: 2). (ENG.). 128p. (J). (gr. k-4). pap. 5.99 *(978-1-4814-5741-5(1),* Little Simon) Little Simon.
Walking the Dogs, 6 Pack. (gr. -1-2). 27.00 *(978-0-7635-9481-7(4))* Rigby Education.
Walko. Amigos: Friends Forever. 2012. (ENG., Illus.). 28p. (J). (gr. -1-k). 16.95 *(978-1-61608-388-5(3),* 608388, Sky Pony Pr.) Skyhorse Publishing Co., Inc.
Wallace, Bill. A Dog Called Kitty. 153p. (J). (gr. 3-5). pap. 3.99 *(978-0-8072-1492-3(2),* Listening Library) Random Hse. Audio Publishing Group.
—The Dog Who Thought He Was Santa. 2007. (ENG., Illus.). 224p. (J). (gr. 4-7). 17.95 *(978-0-8234-2114-5(7))* Holiday Hse., Inc.
—The Dog Who Thought He Was Santa. 2008. (ENG.). 192p. (J). (gr. 3-7). pap. 5.99 *(978-1-4169-4816-2(3),* Aladdin) Simon & Schuster Children's Publishing.
—Goosed! Rogers, Jacqueline, illus. 2004. (ENG.). 128p. (J). (gr. 2-4). pap. 6.99 *(978-0-689-86681-4(X),* Aladdin) Simon & Schuster Children's Publishing.
—No Dogs Allowed! 2004. (ENG.). 214p. (J). (gr. 4-6). tchr. ed. 16.95 *(978-0-8234-1818-3(9))* Holiday Hse., Inc.
—Pick of the Litter. 2005. (ENG.). 160p. (J). (gr. 4-7). 16.95 *(978-0-8234-1921-0(5))* Holiday Hse., Inc.
—Pick of the Litter. 2006. (ENG.). 176p. (J). (gr. 3-7). pap. 5.99 *(978-1-4169-2511-8(2),* Aladdin) Simon & Schuster Children's Publishing.
—That Doggone Calf. Wallace, Carol, illus. 2010. (ENG.). 160p. (J). (gr. 3-7). pap. 6.95 *(978-0-8234-2303-3(4))* Holiday Hse., Inc.
Wallace, Carol. Easter Bunny Blues. Björkman, Steve, illus. 2009. (ENG.). 40p. (J). (gr. k-2). 15.95 *(978-0-8234-2162-6(7))* Holiday Hse., Inc.
—One Nosy Pup. Björkman, Steve, illus. 2004. (ENG.). 40p. (J). 15.95 *(978-0-8234-1917-3(7))* Holiday Hse., Inc.
—The Santa Secret. Björkman, Steve, illus. 2007. (Holiday House Readers: Level 2 Ser.). (ENG.). 40p. (J). (gr. -1-3). 15.95 *(978-0-8234-2022-3(1));* pap. 4.95 *(978-0-8234-2126-8(0))* Holiday Hse., Inc.
—Turkeys Together. Rogers, Jaqueline & Rogers, Jacqueline, illus. 2005. (Holiday House Readers: Level 2 Ser.). (ENG.). 40p. (J). (gr. k-3). 15.95 *(978-0-8234-1895-4(2))* Holiday Hse., Inc.
Wallace, Carol & Wallace, Bill. The Meanest Hound Around. Gurney, John Steven, illus. 2004. 149p. (J). (gr. 2-5). 12.65 *(978-0-7569-3960-1(7))* Perfection Learning Corp.
—The Meanest Hound Around. Gurney, John Steven, illus. 2004. (ENG.). 160p. (J). (gr. 2-5). pap. 5.99 *(978-0-7434-3786-8(1),* Aladdin) Simon & Schuster Children's Publishing.
Wallace, Dillon. Troop One of the Labrador. 2007. (ENG.). 158p. pap. 19.99 *(978-1-4264-9191-7(3));* 178p. pap. 21.99 *(978-1-4264-9248-8(0))* Creative Media Partners, LLC.
Wallace, Karen. Footprints in the Snow, 1 vol. Harland, Jackie, illus. 2013. (Start Reading Ser.). (ENG.). 24p. (gr. k-1). pap. 7.95 *(978-1-4765-4099-3(3))* Capstone Press of Coughlan Cos.
—Lost Kittens. Harland, Jackie, illus. 2013. (Start Reading Ser.). (ENG.). 24p. (gr. k-1). pap. 7.95 *(978-1-4765-4115-0(9))* Capstone Press of Coughlan Cos.
—Stolen Egg. Harland, Jackie, illus. 2013. (Start Reading Ser.). (ENG.). 24p. (gr. k-1). pap. 7.95 *(978-1-4765-4141-9(8))* Capstone Press of Coughlan Cos.
—Treasure Trail, 1 vol. Harland, Jackie, illus. 2013. (Start Reading Ser.). (ENG.). 24p. (gr. k-1). pap. 7.95 *(978-1-4765-4143-3(4))* Capstone Press of Coughlan Cos.
Wallace, Rich. Lost in the Dark. Volpari, Daniela, illus. 2016. (J). *(978-1-62402-148-0(4))* Magic Wagon.
Walsh, Barbara. Sammy in the Sky. Wyeth, Jamie, illus. 2011. (ENG.). 32p. (J). (gr. -1-3). 16.99 *(978-0-7636-4927-2(9))* Candlewick Pr.
Walsh, Bill. The Dog Show. 2010. 32p. pap. 19.95 *(978-0-557-24059-3(X))* Lulu Pr., Inc.
Walsh, Christopher. Tucker's Tale. Lavar, Vanda, illus. 2009. 28p. pap. 11.95 *(978-1-935137-21-4(2))* Guardian Angel Publishing, Inc.
Walsh, Laurence & Walsh, Suella. In the Middle of the Night. 2006. (J). pap. *(978-0-88092-473-3(X))* Royal Fireworks Publishing Co.
Walsleben, Edda Brigitte. Scotty the Little Westie Dog & His Diary. 2013. 268p. 25.00 *(978-1-937911-49-2(7));* pap. 15.00 *(978-1-937911-48-5(9))* Heavenly Realm Publishing.
Walters, Eric. Prince for a Princess, 1 vol. Parkins, David, illus. 2012. (Orca Echoes Ser.). (ENG.). 64p. (J). (gr. 2-3). pap. 6.95 *(978-1-4598-0200-1(4))* Orca Bk. Pubs. USA.
Walters, Janis. Adventures of Libby & Sophie: Sometimes Our Friends Can Get Us into Trouble. 2012. 24p. pap. 15.99 *(978-1-4771-2628-8(7))* Xlibris Corp.
Walton, A. E. What Should I Do with My Love for You? 2009. 24p. pap. 11.49 *(978-1-4389-8532-9(0))* AuthorHouse.
Walton, Evangeline. The Misadventures of Rufus & Misha: Two Dogs Who Are Smart Enough to Go to School. 2013. 24p. pap. 14.93 *(978-1-4669-9970-1(5))* Trafford Publishing.
Wang, Margaret. Five Little Puppies. Haines, Genny, illus. 2006. (ENG.). 12p. (J). (gr. -1-k). 9.95 *(978-1-58117-487-8(X),* Intervisual/Piggy Toes) Bendon, Inc.
Ward, Carla. Emily Finds a Dog. Ward, Megan, illus. 2007. (J). 15.95 *(978-0-9793124-0-3(X))* Tinkertown Museum.
Ward, Helen. Moon Dog. 2005. (Illus.). 40p. (J). *(978-1-84011-864-3(4))* Templar Publishing.
Ward, Jean Elizabeth. A Barbara Anne Bushy Tale: Book #2 in a Series. 2007. 188p. per. 16.95 *(978-0-595-45726-7(6))* iUniverse, Inc.
Ward, Lindsay. Rosco vs. the Baby. Ward, Lindsay, illus. 2016. (ENG., Illus.). 32p. (J). (gr. -1-3). 17.99 *(978-1-4814-3657-1(0),* Simon & Schuster Bks. For Young Readers) Simon & Schuster Bks. For Young Readers.
Ward, Teresa. Blackie's Day Out. Ward, Juliana, illus. 2011. 32p. pap. *(978-1-77067-933-7(2))* FriesenPress.
Warden, Evelyn. Oh, Please, Cricket. 2006. 144p. pap. 24.95 *(978-1-4241-1860-1(3))* America Star Bks.
Wardlaw, Lee. Won Ton & Chopstick. Yelchin, Eugene, illus. 2015. (ENG.). 40p. (J). (gr. -1-3). 17.99 *(978-0-8050-9987-4(5),* 9780805099874, Holt, Henry & Co. Bks. For Young Readers) Holt, Henry & Co.
Wardlow, Lynn. Friends with My Brother. 2012. 28p. pap. 9.95 *(978-1-4787-1384-5(4))* Outskirts Pr., Inc.
Wargin, Kathy-jo. Frank & Beans, 1 vol. Lewis, Anthony, illus. 2010. (I Can Read! / Frank & Beans Ser.). (ENG.). 32p. (J). pap. 3.99 *(978-0-310-71847-5(3))* Zondervan.
—Frank & Beans & the Scary Campout, 1 vol. Lewis, Anthony, illus. 2010. (I Can Read! / Frank & Beans Ser.). (ENG.). 32p. (J). pap. 3.99 *(978-0-310-71850-5(3))* Zonderkidz.
Warner, Cheryl Ware. Chunkerella. 2006. (J). pap. 8.00 *(978-0-8059-7060-9(6))* Dorrance Publishing Co., Inc.
Warner, Jodi. Shia's Tail. 2012. 24p. pap. 10.99 *(978-1-4624-0182-6(1),* Inspiring Voices) Author Solutions, Inc.
Warnes, Tim. Can't You Sleep, Dotty? Warnes, Tim, illus. 2003. (Illus.). 32p. (J). pap. 5.95 *(978-1-58925-376-6(0))* Tiger Tales.
—Can't You Sleep, Little Puppy? Warnes, Tim, illus. 2014. (My First Storybook Ser.). (ENG., Illus.). 32p. (J). (gr. -1). 6.99 *(978-1-58925-508-1(9))* Tiger Tales.
—Chalk & Cheese. Warnes, Tim, illus. 2008. (ENG., Illus.). 32p. (J). (gr. -1-3). 18.99 *(978-1-4169-1378-8(5),* Simon & Schuster Bks. For Young Readers) Simon & Schuster Bks. For Young Readers.
—Happy Birthday, Dotty. Warnes, Tim, illus. 2003. (Illus.). 32p. (J). tchr. ed. 15.95 *(978-1-58925-026-0(5))* Tiger Tales.
Warwaruk, Larry. Brovko's Amazing Journey, 1 vol. 2013. (ENG.). 168p. (J). (gr. 2-6). pap. 8.95 *(978-1-55050-554-2(8))* Coteau Bks. CAN. Dist: Orca Bk. Pubs. USA.
Wasserman, Robin. Search for Scooby Snacks, 1 vol. 2013. (Scooby-Doo! Picture Clue Bks.). (ENG.). 24p. (J). (gr. -1-1). lib. bdg. 24.21 *(978-1-61479-039-6(6),* Essential Library) ABDO Publishing Co.
Wasserman, Robin & Soderberg, Erin. X Marks the Spot. 2015. (Puppy Pirates Ser.: No. 2). (ENG., Illus.). 96p. (J). (gr. 1-4). 4.99 *(978-0-553-51170-3(X),* Random Hse. Bks. for Young Readers) Random Hse. Children's Bks.
Wasserman, Shannon & Wasserman, Curt. The Adventures of Ruff-N-Rescue: Adventures with the Heroes of New Barker Island. Wasserman, Curt et al, illus. 2006. 40p. (J). (gr. -1-3). 16.95 *(978-1-931643-87-0(3))* Seven Locks Pr.
Watkins, Patricia. Boyd-Friend: His Yippie-Skippie Journey to a Forever Home. Watkins, Christopher, illus. l.t. ed. 2004. 44p. 10.95 *(978-0-9753397-0-1(2))* Frayed Pages Publishing.
Watson, Don. Amazing Graci & River Bottom Goats. 2005. 144p. pap. 9.95 *(978-0-9764026-0-2(2))* Longhorn Creek Pr.
Watson, Jane Werner. Walt Disney's the Lucky Puppy (Disney Classic: the Lucky Puppy) Walt Disney Studio et al, illus. 2017. (Little Golden Book Ser.). (ENG.). 24p. (J). (-k). 4.99 ***(978-0-7364-3686-1(3),*** Golden/Disney) Random Hse. Children's Bks.
Watson, Sherri & Abney, Paula. Faith in Fay: The Lost Child. 2009. (Illus.). 112p. (J). (gr. 3-6). pap. 16.95 *(978-1-934812-49-5(8))* Brown Books Publishing Group.
Watson, Tom. Stick Dog. Long, Ethan, illus. 2013. (Stick Dog Ser.: 1). (ENG.). 192p. (J). (gr. 3-7). 12.99 *(978-0-06-211078-7(0))* HarperCollins Pubs.
—Stick Dog & Stick Dog Wants a Hot Dog. 2017. (Stick Dog Ser.). 416p. (J). (gr. 3-7). 25.98 ***(978-0-06-274810-2(6))*** HarperCollins Pubs.
—Stick Dog Chases a Pizza. 2014. (Stick Dog Ser.: 3). (ENG.). 208p. (J). (gr. 3-7). 12.99 *(978-0-06-227805-0(3))* HarperCollins Pubs.
—Stick Dog Craves Candy. 2017. (Stick Dog Ser.: 7). 224p. (J). (gr. 3-7). 12.99 ***(978-0-06-241094-8(6))*** HarperCollins Pubs.
—Stick Dog Dreams of Ice Cream. 2015. (Stick Dog Ser.: 4). (ENG., Illus.). 224p. (J). (gr. 3-7). 12.99 *(978-0-06-227807-4(X))* HarperCollins Pubs.
—Stick Dog Slurps Spaghetti. Long, Ethan, illus. 2016. (Stick Dog Ser.: 6). 240p. (J). (gr. 3-7). 12.99 *(978-0-06-234322-2(X))* HarperCollins Pubs.
—Stick Dog Wants a Hot Dog. Long, Ethan, illus. 2013. 200p. (J). *(978-0-06-229593-4(4))* Harper & Row Ltd.
—Stick Dog Wants a Hot Dog. Long, Ethan, illus. 2013. (Stick Dog Ser.: 2). (ENG.). 224p. (J). (gr. 3-7). 12.99 *(978-0-06-211080-0(2))* HarperCollins Pubs.
Watson, Tom & Long, Ethan, illus. Stick Dog Dreams of Ice Cream. 2015. 216p. (J). *(978-0-06-238092-0(3))* Harper & Row Ltd.
Watt, Fiona. Complete Book of First Experiences. rev. ed. 2011. (First Experiences Ser.). 144p. (J). ring bd. 19.99 *(978-0-7945-2948-2(8),* Usborne) EDC Publishing.
—Este No Es Mi Perrito. 2004.Tr. of That's Not My Puppy. (SPA., Illus.). 10p. (J). (gr. -1-18). 7.95 *(978-0-7460-3898-7(4))* EDC Publishing.
Watts, Jeri. Kizzy Ann Stamps. 2013. (ENG., Illus.). 192p. (J). (gr. 4-7). pap. 5.99 *(978-0-7636-6976-8(8))* Candlewick Pr.
Weakley, David. Rowley to the Rescue. 2009. 72p. pap. 24.00 *(978-1-60860-295-7(8),* Eloquent Bks.) Strategic Book Publishing & Rights Agency (SBPRA).

Weaver, Griz. Along Came Lizzie. 2005. 36p. (J). 12.43 *(978-1-4116-3933-1(2))* Lulu Pr., Inc.
—How It Came to Be Seven Cats, A Woman, A Man & Me. 2005. 55p. (J). 15.28 *(978-1-4116-0630-2(2))* Lulu Pr., Inc.
Weaver, Jack W. Cat & Dog Breath Meet the Last Pirates: How to Fly a Basset Hound. 2012. 164p. 24.95 *(978-1-4626-6652-2(3))* America Star Bks.
Webb, Holly. Harry the Homeless Puppy. Williams, Sophy, illus. 2015. (Pet Rescue Adventures Ser.). (ENG.). 128p. (J). (gr. 2-6). pap. 4.99 *(978-1-58925-474-9(0))*; lib. bdg. 19.99 *(978-1-68010-002-0(5))* Tiger Tales.
—Jessie the Lonely Puppy. Williams, Sophy, illus. 2015. (Pet Rescue Adventures Ser.). (ENG.). 128p. (J). (gr. -1-3). lib. bdg. 19.99 *(978-1-68010-003-7(3))*; (gr. 2-6). pap. 4.99 *(978-1-58925-473-2(2))* Tiger Tales.
—Leo All Alone. Williams, Sophy, illus. 2016. (Pet Rescue Adventures Ser.). (ENG.). 128p. (J). (gr. 2-6). 4.99 *(978-1-58925-482-4(1))* Tiger Tales.
—The Lost Puppy. Williams, Sophy, illus. 2016. (Pet Rescue Adventures Ser.). (ENG.). 128p. (J). (gr. 2-6). pap. 4.99 *(978-1-58925-491-6(0))* Tiger Tales.
—The Rescued Puppy. Williams, Sophy, illus. 2017. (Pet Rescue Adventures Ser.). (ENG.). 128p. (J). (gr. 2-6). 19.99 ***(978-1-68010-051-8(3))*** Tiger Tales.
—The Scruffy Puppy. Williams, Sophy, illus. 2016. (Pet Rescue Adventures Ser.). (ENG.). 128p. (J). (gr. 2-6). pap. 4.99 *(978-1-58925-490-9(2))* Tiger Tales.
—The Secret Puppy. Williams, Sophy, illus. 2016. (Pet Rescue Adventures Ser.). (ENG.). 128p. (J). (gr. 2-6). 4.99 *(978-1-58925-483-1(X))* Tiger Tales.
Webb, Holly. The Tiniest Puppy. Williams, Sophy, illus. 2017. (Pet Rescue Adventures Ser.). (ENG.). 128p. (J). (gr. 2-6). 19.99 ***(978-1-68010-052-5(1))*** Tiger Tales.
Webb, Ryan. Buddy: Dog of the Smoky Mountains. 2013. (Illus.). 34p. (J). pap. 12.00 *(978-0-9847836-3-2(6))* Celtic Cat Publishing.
Weber, Richard D. Elvis & Me. 2004. 511p. (YA). per. 17.41 *(978-1-4116-0549-7(7))* Lulu Pr., Inc.
Weeks, Sarah. Glamourpuss. Small, David, illus. 2015. (ENG.). 40p. (J). (gr. -1-1). 16.99 *(978-0-545-60954-8(2)*, Scholastic Pr.) Scholastic, Inc.
—Honey. 2015. (ENG.). 160p. (J). (gr. 4-7). 16.99 *(978-0-545-46557-1(5)*, Scholastic Pr.) Scholastic, Inc.
Wegman, William. Chip Wants a Dog. 2014. (Penguin Young Readers, Level 2 Ser.). (ENG.). 32p. (J). (gr. 1-2). pap. 3.99 *(978-0-448-48043-5(3)*, Penguin Young Readers) Penguin Young Readers Group.
—Dress up Batty. Wegman, William, illus. 2004. (ENG., Illus.). 18p. (gr. -1-17). 19.99 *(978-0-7868-1849-5(2))* Hyperion Bks. for Children.
—Farm Days. Wegman, William, illus. 2014. (Penguin Young Readers, Level 2 Ser.). (ENG., Illus.). 32p. (J). (gr. 1-3). pap. 3.99 *(978-0-448-48230-9(4)*, Penguin Young Readers) Penguin Young Readers Group.
—3... 2... 1... Circus! 2014. (ENG., Illus.). 24p. (J). (— 1). bds. 6.99 *(978-0-8037-3934-5(6)*, Dial Bks) Penguin Young Readers Group.
Wehrmeijer, Annelien. Anik & Yukon. van de Liejgraaf, Deborah, illus. 2015. (My Best Friend & Me Ser.). (ENG.). 10p. (J). (gr. -1-k). bds. 6.99 *(978-0-7641-6763-8(4))* Barron's Educational Series, Inc.
Weil, Zoe. Claude & Medea: The Hellburn Dogs. 2007. (ENG., Illus.). 103p. (J). (gr. 2-7). per. 12.00 *(978-1-59056-105-8(8))* Lantern Bks.
Weinberg, Jennifer Liberts. Princesses & Puppies. 2013. (Disney Princess Step into Reading Ser.). lib. bdg. 13.55 *(978-0-606-32201-0(9)*, Turtleback) Turtleback Bks.
Wejrmeijer, Annelien. Dan & Max. van de Liejgraaf, Deborah, illus. 2013. (My Best Friend & Me Ser.). (ENG.). 10p. (J). (gr. -1 — 1). bds. 6.99 *(978-0-7641-6634-1(4))* Barron's Educational Series, Inc.
Wells, Angela. Tales of Albie the Talking Dog. 2008. (J). per. 12.95 *(978-0-9767047-0-6(6))* Anystar Publishing.
Wells, Rosemary. Ivy Takes Care. LaMarche, Jim, illus. (ENG.). 208p. (J). (gr. 3-7). 2015. pap. 6.99 *(978-0-7636-7660-5(8))* 2013. 15.99 *(978-0-7636-5352-1(7))* Candlewick Pr.
—McDuff Comes Home. Jeffers, Susan, illus. 2007. 24p. (J). pap. 4.99 *(978-0-7868-1192-2(7))* Hyperion Paperbacks for Children.
—McDuff Comes Home. Jeffers, Susan, illus. rev. ed. 2006. (ENG.). 32p. (gr. -1-k). 9.99 *(978-0-7868-3833-2(7))* Hyperion Pr.
—McDuff's New Friend with Plush Box Set. 2003. (Illus.). 28p. (J). 14.99 *(978-0-7868-1866-2(2)*, Disney Editions) Disney Pr.
—Otto Runs for President. Wells, Rosemary, illus. 2011. (Illus.). (J). (gr. -1-4). 29.95 *(978-0-545-10690-0(7))* Weston Woods Studios, Inc.
Wells, Rosemary & Jeffers, Susan. McDuff Moves In. 2015. 32p. pap. 7.00 *(978-1-61003-538-5(0))* Center for the Collaborative Classroom.
Wenning, Jeremy. Coco & Pebbles: Bath Night. Barrett, Casey, illus. 2013. 20p. pap. 6.99 *(978-1-938768-16-3(7))* Gypsy Pubns.
—Coco & Pebbles: That's My Duck! Barrett, Casey, illus. 2012. 16p. pap. 6.99 *(978-1-938768-04-0(3))* Gypsy Pubns.
—Roscoe the Volunteer Emt. Burns, Sandra, illus. 2013. 24p. pap. 8.99 *(978-1-938768-19-4(1))* Gypsy Pubns.
Wensley, Walter F. Yorkie. 2011. 44p. pap. 19.50 *(978-1-4634-3185-3(6))* AuthorHouse.
Wentz, Lorraine. Who Has Barney. 2013. 38p. pap. 10.99 *(978-1-62697-124-0(2))* Salem Author Services.
Wemer, James R. Dave's Christmas Surprise & a Puppy Named Oxley. 2008. 28p. pap. 14.95 *(978-1-4327-3298-1(6))* Outskirts Pr., Inc.
West, Hadley. Doggie Daycare. 2011. 74p. 24.99 *(978-1-4628-6066-1(4))*; pap. 15.99 *(978-1-4628-6065-4(6))* Xlibris Corp.
West, Nancy. Chips - the War Dog: Based on the True-Life Adventures of the World War II K-9 Hero. 2nd ed. 2004. 183p. (J). per. 8.95 *(978-0-9743659-1-6(2))* Hero Dog Pubns.
West, Tracey. The Audio Files. Harrington, Rich, illus. 2006. 96p. (J). pap. *(978-0-439-90719-4(5))* Scholastic, Inc.
Westfeldt, Linda M. Buttons' Big Ears. l.t. ed. 2004. 32p. (J). spiral bd. *(978-1-59196-686-9(8))* Instant Pub.
Westley, William. Charlie & Crow. 2011. 66p. 24.99 *(978-1-4628-6802-5(9))*; pap. 15.99 *(978-1-4628-6801-8(0))* Xlibris Corp.
Westling, Vicki Diane. Cats Keep Out: Sam & Friends. 2009. 40p. pap. 16.99 *(978-1-4490-3623-2(6))* AuthorHouse.
—Hannibal Breaks His Promise: Sam & Friends. 2009. 32p. pap. 15.99 *(978-1-4490-4711-5(4))* AuthorHouse.
Weston Woods Staff, creator. Angus & the Ducks. 2004. (J). 38.75 *(978-1-55592-370-9(4))*; 18.95 *(978-1-55592-369-3(0))* Weston Woods Studios, Inc.
—Dot the Fire Dog. 2004. (J). (gr. -1-2). 29.95 *(978-1-55592-623-6(1))* Weston Woods Studios, Inc.
—Hondo & Fabian. 2011. 18.95 *(978-0-545-14958-7(4))*; 38.75 *(978-0-545-14959-4(2))* Weston Woods Studios, Inc.
—Madeline's Rescue. 2011. 18.95 *(978-0-439-72770-9(7))*; 38.75 *(978-0-439-72772-3(3))*; 29.95 *(978-0-439-73488-2(6))* Weston Woods Studios, Inc.
—Otto Runs for President. 2011. 18.95 *(978-0-545-31400-8(3))*; 38.75 *(978-0-545-31401-5(1))* Weston Woods Studios, Inc.
—The Pigeon Finds a Hot Dog. 2011. 38.75 *(978-0-545-26298-9(4))* Weston Woods Studios, Inc.
—Pinkerton, Behave! 2011. 18.95 *(978-0-439-72880-5(0))*; 29.95 *(978-0-439-73515-5(7))*; 38.75 *(978-0-439-72881-2(9))* Weston Woods Studios, Inc.
—Whistle for Willie. 2011. 38.75 *(978-1-55592-764-6(5))* Weston Woods Studios, Inc.
Whamond, O. T. Wiffin & Wussell Go Digging. 2009. (Illus.). 16p. pap. 8.49 *(978-1-4389-4236-0(2))* AuthorHouse.
Wharton, Laura Spanton, et al. Mystery at the Phoenix Festival. 2012. 140p. pap. 9.99 *(978-0-9837148-8-0(6))* Broad Creek Pr.
Whatley, Bruce. That Magnetic Dog. 2015. (ENG., Illus.). 32p. (J). (gr. -1-3). pap. 9.99 *(978-0-207-18420-8(8))* HarperCollins Pubs. Australia AUS. Dist: HarperCollins Pubs.
Wheeler-Cribb, Peggy. Madeline Becomes a Star. Bensch, April, illus. 2013. 50p. 29.95 *(978-0-9886194-1-8(5))* ProsePress.
Wheeler, Isabelle. Many a Mickle: Little Things Not to Be Forgotten. 2003. 202p. 24.95 *(978-0-595-66007-0(X))*; pap. 14.95 *(978-0-595-29487-9(1))* iUniverse, Inc.
Wheeler, Lisa. Seadogs: An Epic Ocean Operetta. Siegel, Mark, illus. 2006. (ENG.). 40p. (J). (gr. 2-5). reprint ed. 7.99 *(978-1-4169-4103-3(7)*, Atheneum Bks. for Young Readers) Simon & Schuster Children's Publishing.
Wheiler, Robert. Herphus & the importance of Aroooo. 2010. 68p. pap. 10.00 *(978-0-557-29769-6(9))* Lulu Pr., Inc.
—Snowflake a Christmas Gift. 2010. 39p. pap. 11.50 *(978-0-557-47524-7(4))* Lulu Pr., Inc.
—Wink's , Boo, & Who! 2012. 64p. pap. 13.49 *(978-1-105-49858-9(1))* Lulu Pr., Inc.
Whelan, Gloria. Silver. Marchesi, Stephen, illus. 2004. (Stepping Stone Book(TM) Ser.). (ENG.). 64p. (J). (gr. 1-4). 3.99 *(978-0-394-89611-3(4)*, Random Hse. Bks. for Young Readers) Random Hse. Children's Bks.
Whisler, Barbara. Shag Finds a Home. Jackson, Kay, illus. 2008. 24p. pap. 24.95 *(978-1-60703-730-9(0))* America Star Bks.
Whitaker, Kent. Big Mo's Tennis Ball Hunt. 2007. (Illus.). (J). *(978-0-9779053-8-6(1))* Great American Pubs.
Whitaker, Sue. And Jake Makes Three. Ludlam, Jamie, illus. 2013. 108p. pap. *(978-1-907978-16-6(X))* ETA Publishing Hse.
—And Jake Makes Three & the Secret of Badlands. Ludlam, Jamie, illus. 2013. 92p. pap. *(978-1-907978-26-5(7))* ETA Publishing Hse.
—And Jake Makes Three in the Snow. Ludlam, Jamie, illus. 2013. 104p. pap. *(978-1-907978-21-0(6))* ETA Publishing Hse.
—And Jake Makes Three in the Vampires Den. Thomas-Brown, Cauline, ed. Ludlam, Jamie, illus. 2013. 86p. pap. *(978-1-907978-31-9(3))* ETA Publishing Hse.
White-Adams, Beverly. The Adventures of Rusty: Rusty Goes to Maine Vol. 3. 2012. 40p. pap. 19.57 *(978-1-4669-5442-7(6))* Trafford Publishing.
—The Adventures of Rusty: Rusty Goes to Tennessee the Adventures Continue Vol. 4. 2013. 32p. pap. 17.25 *(978-1-4669-8583-4(6))* Trafford Publishing.
White, Ellen Emerson. Webster: Tale of an Outlaw. (ENG., Illus.). 256p. (J). (gr. 3-7). 2016. pap. 7.99 *(978-1-4814-2202-4(2))* 2015. 17.99 *(978-1-4814-2201-7(4))* Simon & Schuster Children's Publishing. (Aladdin).
White, George. Kirby the Easter Dog: A Pop-up Easter Egg Hunt. 2008. (Illus.). 14p. (J). 14.99 *(978-0-9795441-2-5(2))* Jumping Jack Pr.
White, Herman H. Valley of the Flames. 2004. (ENG.). 96p. 19.95 *(978-1-932278-09-5(5))* Mayhaven Publishing, Inc.
White, J. Scratch & Sniff: The Case of the Stuck Seagull. 2013. 32p. pap. *(978-1-4602-0552-5(9))* FriesenPress.
White, K. B. Adrianna*Angelica*Andrea Mystery Stories: The Case of the Missing Dog. 2012. 20p. pap. 17.99 *(978-1-4772-4549-1(9))* AuthorHouse.
White Marklin, Mary M. I Was Beautiful Once. 2008. 52p. pap. 20.49 *(978-1-4389-1022-2(3))* AuthorHouse.
White, Ruth. The Treasure of Way down Deep. 2013. (ENG.). 176p. (J). (gr. 5-9). 16.99 *(978-0-374-38067-0(8)*, 9780374380670, Farrar, Straus & Giroux (BYR)) Farrar, Straus & Giroux.
Whitmore, G. A. A Place to Call Home: Toby's Tale. 2014. (ENG.). 291p. pap. 18.95 *(978-1-4787-0073-9(4))* Outskirts Pr., Inc.
Whitmore, Gary. Prince Luna & the Space Dreamers. 2011. (ENG.). 204p. pap. 8.50 *(978-1-4565-8438-2(3))* CreateSpace Independent Publishing Platform.
Whittaker, Heather. A Different Little Doggy. Alberts, Scott, illus. 2013. 28p. (J). 9.99 *(978-0-9820962-1-5(6))* Pen-Tech Professional.
Whybrow, Ian. Say Hello to the Snowy Animals! Eaves, Edward, illus. 2012. (J). *(978-0-7607-9675-7(0))* Barnes & Noble, Inc.
Widmayer, Paul. Jake & the Cowboy Hat. 2013. 24p. pap. 12.45 *(978-1-4908-1233-5(4)*, WestBow Pr.) Author Solutions, Inc.
Wight, Eric. Frankie Pickle & the Closet of Doom. Wight, Eric, illus. (Frankie Pickle Ser.). (ENG., Illus.). 96p. (J). (gr. 2-5). 2010. pap. 5.99 *(978-1-4424-1304-7(2))* 2009. 9.99 *(978-1-4169-6484-1(3))* Simon & Schuster Bks. For Young Readers. (Simon & Schuster Bks. For Young Readers).
Wignell, Edel & Argent, Leanne. I Wonder Who Lives Upstairs. (Illus.). 32p. pap. 10.95 *(978-1-875560-55-4(6))* UWA Publishing AUS. Dist: ISBS Publisher Services.
Wild, Kate. Firefight. 2009. (ENG.). 352p. (J). (gr. 3-7). 16.99 *(978-0-439-87176-1(X)*, Chicken Hse., The) Scholastic, Inc.
Wild, Margaret. Fox. Brooks, Ron, illus. 2006. (ENG.). 32p. (J). (gr. 1). pap. 7.99 *(978-1-933605-15-9(4))* Kane Miller.
Wilde, Irma & dePaola, Tomie. The Christmas Puppy. Wilde, Irma, illus. 2015. (G&d Vintage Ser.). (ENG., Illus.). 24p. (J). (-k). bds. 9.99 *(978-0-448-48765-6(9)*, Grosset & Dunlap) Penguin Young Readers Group.
Wilde, Jeanne Wilkins. Two Dogs Long & Half a Dog High. 2013. 20p. pap. 15.99 *(978-1-4817-0594-3(6))* AuthorHouse.
Wildsmith, Brian. Hunter & His Dog, 1 vol. Wildsmith, Brian, illus. 2008. (ENG., Illus.). 32p. (J). 16.95 *(978-1-59572-123-5(1))* Star Bright Bks., Inc.
Wilhelm, Hans. Buddy for President. Wilhelm, Hans, illus. 2016. (Illus.). 32p. (J). (gr. -1-3). 17.99 *(978-0-06-240366-7(4))* HarperCollins Pubs.
—I Love Rainy Days! Wilhelm, Hans, illus. 2011. (Scholastic Reader Level 1 Ser.). (ENG., Illus.). 32p. (J). (gr. -1-2). pap. 3.99 *(978-0-545-24503-6(6)*, Cartwheel Bks.) Scholastic, Inc.
—I Love School! Wilhelm, Hans, illus. 2010. (Scholastic Reader Level 1 Ser.). (ENG., Illus.). 32p. (J). (gr. -1-k). pap. 3.99 *(978-0-545-13474-3(9)*, Cartwheel Bks.) Scholastic, Inc.
—I Love Valentine's Day! 2010. (Illus.). (J). pap. *(978-0-545-13475-0(7)*, Cartwheel Bks.) Scholastic, Inc.
—I Won't Share! Wilhelm, Hans, illus. 2010. (Scholastic Reader Level 1 Ser.). (ENG., Illus.). 32p. (J). (gr. -1-2). pap. 3.99 *(978-0-439-77353-9(9))* Scholastic, Inc.
—Ouch! It Hurts! 2008. (Illus.). (J). pap. *(978-0-545-00093-2(9))* Scholastic, Inc.
Wilkerson, Alison. The Adventures of Tabby Cat. 2009. (Illus.). 104p. pap. 12.49 *(978-1-4389-6695-3(4))* AuthorHouse.
Wilkerson, Grandma. Mac the Stray Dog. 2011. 16p. 11.49 *(978-1-4520-4018-9(4))* AuthorHouse.
Will Mcallister. Sam Rivers & the Night Rustlers. 2009. 88p. pap. 9.95 *(978-0-595-46287-2(1))* iUniverse, Inc.
Willard, Hugh. The Goodwill Vultures Club. Holjes, Kerry, ed. Eason, D. M., illus. 2013. 122p. pap. 9.99 *(978-1-935711-26-1(1))* Peak City Publishing, LLC.
Willems, Mo. City Dog, Country Frog. Muth, Jon J., illus. 2010. (ENG.). 64p. (J). (gr. -1-k). 17.99 *(978-1-4231-0300-4(9))* Hyperion Pr.
—The Story of Diva & Flea. DiTerlizzi, Tony, illus. 2015. (ENG.). 80p. (J). (gr. 1-3). 14.99 *(978-1-4847-2284-8(1))* Disney Pr.
Willems, Mo & Willems, Trixie, narrated by. The Pigeon Finds a Hot Dog! 2011. (J). (gr. -1-1). 29.95 *(978-0-545-23795-6(5))*; 18.95 *(978-0-545-26297-2(6))* Weston Woods Studios, Inc.
Williams, Amanda Schaefer. Sadie in Heaven. 2012. 28p. pap. 24.95 *(978-1-4626-8802-9(0))* America Star Bks.
Williams, Donald & Williams, Ronald. The Adventures of Wacko Rabbit. 2012. (Illus.). (J). 14.95 *(978-1-62086-058-8(9))* Mascot Bks., Inc.
Williams, Emma. The Adventures of Emma & Scruffy. 2010. 50p. 24.99 *(978-1-4500-3908-6(1))*; pap. 15.99 *(978-1-4500-3907-9(3))* Xlibris Corp.
Williams, Eula. Loving Danger. Branch Jr., Robert F., illus. 2012. 20p. pap. 24.95 *(978-1-4626-6954-7(9))* America Star Bks.
Williams, Geoffrey T. Manatees & Mermaids. 2010. (ENG., Illus.). 64p. (J). (gr. 3-7). 8.95 *(978-0-9800444-3-0(X))* Save Our Seas, Ltd.
Williams, Jason & Felt, Jeremy. The Adventures of Sam & Rowdy: Two Best Friends. 2013. 16p. pap. 15.99 *(978-1-4817-1268-2(3))* AuthorHouse.
Williams, Jay & Blickenstaff, Wayne. Puppy Pie. 2016. (ENG., Illus.). 64p. (J). (gr. k-2). pap. 9.99 *(978-0-486-81064-5(X))* Dover Pubns., Inc.
Williams, Renee Pierce. Buck the Good Doog. 2012. 28p. pap. 15.99 *(978-1-4691-5325-4(4))* Xlibris Corp.
Williams, Roberta C. The Lonely Little Puppy. 2011. 28p. pap. 15.99 *(978-1-4568-9304-0(1))* Xlibris Corp.
Williams, Rozanne Lanczak. Cat Can't Write: A Cat & Dog Story. Leary, Catherine, illus. 2007. (Learn to Write Ser.). 16p. (J). (gr. -1-3). pap. 8.99 *(978-1-59198-344-6(4))* Creative Teaching Pr., Inc.
—Cat's Fairy Tale: A Cat & Dog Story. Leary, Catherine, illus. 2006. (Learn to Write Ser.). 16p. (J). (gr. k-2). pap. 3.49 *(978-1-59198-294-4(4)*, 6191) Creative Teaching Pr., Inc.
—Cat's Fairy Tale: A Cat & Dog Story. Maio, Barbara, ed. Leary, Catherine, illus. 2006. (J). per. 8.99 *(978-1-59198-348-4(7))* Creative Teaching Pr., Inc.
—Lost Puppy, Found Puppy. Motoyama, Keiko, illus. 2006. (Learn to Write Ser.). 16p. (J). (gr. k-2). pap. 3.49 *(978-1-59198-296-8(0)*, 6190) Creative Teaching Pr., Inc.
—Lost Puppy, Found Puppy. Maio, Barbara, ed. Motoyama, Keiko, illus. 2006. (J). per. 8.99 *(978-1-59198-347-7(9))* Creative Teaching Pr., Inc.
Williams, Vanessa A. The Missing Penny. 2013. 28p. pap. 9.95 *(978-1-4787-2429-2(3))* Outskirts Pr., Inc.
Willis, Cynthia Chapman. Dog Gone. 2009. (ENG.). 240p. (J). (gr. 3-7). pap. 17.99 *(978-0-312-56113-0(X)*, 9780312561130) Square Fish.
Willis, Jeanne. Dr Xargle's Book of Earth Hounds. Ross, Tony, illus. 2012. (ENG.). 28p. (J). (gr. -1-k). pap. 13.99 *(978-1-84270-170-6(3))* Andersen Pr. GBR. Dist: Independent Pubs. Group.
—Flabby Cat & Slobby Dog. Ross, Tony, illus. 2009. (Andersen Press Picture Bks). (ENG.). 32p. (J). (gr. -1-3). 16.95 *(978-0-7613-5151-1(5)*, Carolrhoda Bks.) Lerner Publishing Group.
—The Pet Person. Ross, Tony, illus. 2015. (ENG.). 32p. (J). (-k). pap. 9.99 *(978-1-78344-242-3(5))* Andersen Pr. GBR. Dist: Independent Pubs. Group.
Willocks, Tim. Doglands. 2012. (ENG.). 324p. (YA). (gr. 7). pap. 9.99 *(978-0-375-85818-5(0)*, Ember) Random Hse. Children's Bks.
Willson, Sarah. Simon Says. Ulrich, George, illus. 2006. (Step-By-Step Readers Ser.). (J). pap. *(978-1-59939-057-4(4)*, Reader's Digest Young Families, Inc.) Studio Fun International.
Wilson, Anna. Pup Idol. 2015. (Top of the Pups Ser.). (ENG., Illus.). 224p. (J). (gr. 4-7). pap. 8.99 *(978-1-4472-7982-2(4))* Pan Macmillan GBR. Dist: Independent Pubs. Group.
—Puppy Party. (ENG., Illus.). 256p. (J). 2015. (Top of the Pups Ser.: 2). (gr. 4-7). pap. 8.99 *(978-1-4472-7615-9(9))*1. 2014. (gr. 2-4). pap. 7.99 *(978-0-330-51881-9(X))* Pan Macmillan GBR. Dist: Independent Pubs. Group.
—The Puppy Plan. 2015. (Top of the Pups Ser.: 1). (ENG., Illus.). 192p. (J). (gr. 4-7). pap. 8.99 *(978-1-4472-7611-1(6))* Pan Macmillan GBR. Dist: Independent Pubs. Group.
—Puppy Power. 2015. (Top of the Pups Ser.: 3). (ENG., Illus.). 288p. (J). (gr. 4-7). pap. 8.99 *(978-1-4472-7613-5(2))* Pan Macmillan GBR. Dist: Independent Pubs. Group.
Wilson, Annemarie. What Could Have Happened to Max? 2008. 56p. pap. 14.95 *(978-1-59858-683-1(1))* Dog Ear Publishing, LLC.
Wilson, Audrey. Dante Goes to the Circus. 2009. 28p. pap. 13.99 *(978-1-4389-6779-0(9))* AuthorHouse.
Wilson, Barbara. Bud the Pup. Caracino, Leah, illus. 2012. (ENG.). 22p. (gr. k-3). pap. 9.00 *(978-1-56778-539-5(5))* Wilson Language Training.
Wilson, Shelliah. Samuel's Little Brother. 2005. 12p. 9.72 *(978-1-4116-4789-3(0))* Lulu Pr., Inc.
Wilson, Wayne L. Kate, the Ghost Dog: Coping with the Death of a Pet. Soud, illus. 2009. 48p. (J). (gr. 3-8). 14.95 *(978-1-4338-0554-7(5))*; pap. 9.95 *(978-1-4338-0555-4(3))* American Psychological Assn. (Magination Pr.).
Wilson Young, Elaine. Butch, the Cape Cod Dog. 2009. 32p. pap. 16.00 *(978-1-4490-0536-8(5))* AuthorHouse.
Wingate, Barbara. Petey the One Lopped Eared Dog, 1 vol. Mignano, Daniel, illus. 2009. 20p. pap. 24.95 *(978-1-60836-931-7(5))* America Star Bks.
Winget, Dianna Dorisi. A Million Ways Home. 2014. (ENG.). 272p. (J). (gr. 3-7). 16.99 *(978-0-545-66706-7(2)*, Scholastic Pr.) Scholastic, Inc.
Wingfield, Hayley. Little Johnny's Book of Wild & Crazy Friends. 2011. 28p. pap. 24.95 *(978-1-4626-2801-8(X))* America Star Bks.
Winkler, Henry & Oliver, Lin. A Short Tale about a Long Dog. Garrett, Scott, illus. 2014. (Here's Hank Ser.: 2). (ENG.). 128p. (J). (gr. 1-3). 14.99 *(978-0-448-48240-8(1))*;No. 2. 5.99 *(978-0-448-47998-9(2))* Penguin Young Readers Group. (Grosset & Dunlap).
—A Short Tale about a Long Dog. 2014. (Here's Hank Ser.: 2). lib. bdg. 16.00 *(978-0-606-34143-1(9)*, Turtleback) Turtleback Bks.
Winkowski, Jackie. Miki's Challenge: One sled dog's Story. Winkowski, Jackie, photos by. 2006. (Illus.). 44p. (J). 10.95 *(978-0-9791367-1-9(7))* Snowy Plains.
Winslow, Barbara. Fancy & Francis. 2012. 32p. (-18). pap. 21.99 *(978-1-4797-4580-7(4))* Xlibris Corp.
Winters, John. Gramps' Children's Stories. 2007. 60p. pap. 6.96 *(978-1-4357-0038-3(4))* Lulu Pr., Inc.
Wirth, Margie & Sherfinski, Julie. BF: the Carrot Monster. 2010. 36p. 15.50 *(978-0-557-27308-9(0))* Lulu Pr., Inc.
Wishinsky, Frieda. Halifax Explodes! Lewis-MacDougall, Patricia Ann & Owlkids Books Inc. Staff, illus. 2011. (Canadian Flyer Adventures Ser.: 17). (ENG.). 96p. (J). (gr. 1-4). pap. 7.95 *(978-1-926818-98-6(9)*, Maple Tree Pr.) Owlkids Bks. Inc. CAN. Dist: Publishers Group West (PGW).
—Please, Louise!, 1 vol. Gay, Marie-Louise, illus. 2007. (ENG.). 32p. (J). (gr. k-k). 17.95 *(978-0-88899-796-8(5))* Groundwood Bks. CAN. Dist: Publishers Group West (PGW).
Witschen, Kay. Clinker's Christmas Star. Witschen, Kay, illus. 2004. (Illus.). 24p. (J). 6.95 *(978-0-9741352-1-2(6))* Dwitt Publishing.
Wittreich, Yvonne M. B. The True Story of Sasha, from Homelessness to Happiness. 2008. 36p. per. 17.95 *(978-1-4327-1502-1(X))* Outskirts Pr., Inc.
Wohnoutka, Mike. Little Puppy & the Big Green Monster. Wohnoutka, Mike, illus. 2014. (ENG., Illus.). 32p. (J). (gr. -1-k). 16.95 *(978-0-8234-3064-2(2))* Holiday Hse., Inc.
Wojtusik, Elizabeth. Kitty Up! Yoshikawa, Sachiko, illus. 2008. (J). *(978-0-8037-3045-8(4)*, Dial) Penguin Publishing Group.
Wolbrueck, Cherri. Amy Finds a Home. 2008. 36p. pap. 21.99 *(978-1-4363-7237-4(2))* Xlibris Corp.
—Chippi's Adopted Dozen. 2012. 40p. pap. 21.99 *(978-1-4691-3528-1(0))* Xlibris Corp.
Wolf, Carol A. Foggy Dog. 2011. 36p. pap. *(978-1-4269-7918-7(5))* Trafford Publishing (UK) Ltd.
—Foggy Dog Discovers Christmas. 2012. 40p. pap. 16.46 *(978-1-4669-6253-8(4))* Trafford Publishing.
Wolfe, Jack & Wolfe, Jennifer. The Tales of Spy Dogs Archie & Hazel. 2011. 44p. pap. 16.59 *(978-1-4567-6244-5(3))* AuthorHouse.
Wolfe, Jane. Noisy Dog. Benham, Tors, illus. 2013. (ENG.). 8p. (J). (gr. -1-k). bds. 6.99 *(978-1-84322-779-3(7)*, Armadillo) Anness Publishing GBR. Dist: National Bk. Network.
Wolfe, Linda, illus. Across the Road. 2008. 32p. (J). 10.00 *(978-0-937179-16-1(7))* Blue Scarab Pr.
Wolfinger, Sheri. Has Anyone Seen Puff? A Billy & Jake Adventure. 2012. 20p. pap. 11.59 *(978-1-4669-1377-6(0))* Trafford Publishing.
Wood, A. J. Slide & Play: Playful Puppy. Pledger, Maurice, illus. 2016. (Slide & Play Ser.). (ENG.). 16p. (J). (gr. -1). bds. 14.99 *(978-1-62686-572-3(8)*, Silver Dolphin Bks.) Readerlink Distribution Services, LLC.
Wood, Audrey. A Dog Needs a Bone! 2007. (J). pap. *(978-0-545-00006-2(8))* Blue Sky Pr.
Wood, Beverley & Wood, Chris. DogStar. 2004. (ENG.). 4p. (J). pap., tchr. ed. *(978-1-55192-608-7(3)*, Polestar Book Pubs.) Raincoast Bk. Distribution CAN. Dist: Publishers Group West (PGW).
wood, fern. Blank, the Dog with No Name. 2010. 34p. pap. 18.95 *(978-1-4457-6889-2(5))* Lulu Pr., Inc.
Woodrow, Allan. The Pet War. 2015. (ENG.). 272p. (J). (gr. 3-7). pap. 6.99 *(978-0-545-51320-3(0)*, Scholastic Paperbacks) Scholastic, Inc.
Woodruff, Liza. Emerson Barks. Woodruff, Liza, illus. 2016. (ENG., Illus.). 32p. (J). 16.99 *(978-1-62779-167-0(1)*, 9781627791670, Holt, Henry & Co. Bks. For Young Readers) Holt, Henry & Co.
Woods, Brenda. Saint Louis Armstrong Beach. 2012. (ENG.). 160p. (J). (gr. 5). pap. 5.99 *(978-0-14-242186-4(3)*, Puffin Books) Penguin Young Readers Group.

C
D

—Saint Louis Armstrong Beach. 2012. lib. bdg. 16.00 *(978-0-606-26661-1(5),* Turtleback) Turtleback Bks.
Woods, Wendy. Welcome Home, Indigeaux: A Louisiana Adventure. Martin, Sherry, illus. 2013. (ENG.). (J). (gr. -1-3). 14.95 *(978-1-62086-246-9(8))* Mascot Bks., Inc.
Woodson, Rick. Poodles & Thunderchicken. 2012. 40p. pap. 24.95 *(978-1-4626-7531-9(X))* America Star Bks.
Woodsonrick. Poodles in Space. 2012. 24p. 24.95 *(978-1-4626-5333-1(2))* America Star Bks.
Woody, John. Ernie Tales. Byars, Bob M., illus. 2012. pap. 13.95 *(978-0-9848019-9-2(5))* Inkwell Books LLC.
Wooster, Devin Ann. Barbie & Her Sisters in the Great Puppy Adventure. 2015. (Barbie Chapters Ser.). (ENG.). 64p. (J). (gr. 1-4). pap. 5.99 *(978-0-553-53764-2(4),* Random Hse. Bks. for Young Readers) Random Hse. Children's Bks.
Worley, Michelle. Buster Goes to the White House, 1 vol. 2009. 48p. pap. 16.95 *(978-1-61546-352-7(6))* PublishAmerica, Inc.
Wormell, Chris. The Wild Girl. Wormell, Chris, illus. 2006. (Illus.). 32p. (J). (gr. -1). 17.00 *(978-0-8028-5311-0(0),* Eerdmans Bks For Young Readers) Eerdmans, William B. Publishing Co.
Worth, Bonnie & Klimo, Kate. Ginger. Jessell, Tim, illus. 2013. (Dog Diaries). (ENG.). 160p. (J). (gr. 2-5). pap. 7.99 *(978-0-307-97899-8(0),* Random Hse. Bks. for Young Readers) Random Hse. Children's Bks.
Worthington, Heather Hill. Miles of Smiles: The Story of Roxey, the Long Island Rail Road Dog. Farnsworth, Bill, illus. 2010. (J). *(978-0-9792918-4-5(4));* pap. *(978-0-9792918-8-3(7))* Blue Marlin Pubns.
Written By Kimberly M Sosnowski; Illustr. Ace's Wish for a Forever Home. Sosnowski, Tiffany, illus. 2011. 28p. pap. 24.95 *(978-1-4626-3031-8(6))* America Star Bks.
Written By Pamela McFarland; Illustrated. Guide Me Home, Sunny. Bates, Bill, illus. 2011. 44p. pap. 24.95 *(978-1-4560-8890-3(4))* America Star Bks.
Wyant, Sharon Kay. The Adventures of Brody. 2011. 56p. pap. 31.99 *(978-1-4568-7560-2(4))* Xlibris Corp.
Wyvill, Grace. Charlie Basset: A Hound's Tail. 2012. 40p. pap. 19.57 *(978-1-4669-3929-5(X))* Trafford Publishing.
Yaccarino, Dan. Unlovable. Yaccarino, Dan, illus. rev. ed. 2004. (ENG., Illus.). 32p. (J). (gr. -1-1). reprint ed. pap. 7.99 *(978-0-8050-7532-8(1),* 9780805075328) Square Fish.
Yang, James. Joey & Jet: Book 1 of Their Adventures. Yang, James, illus. 2012. (ENG., Illus.). 32p. (J). (gr. -1-k). pap. 16.99 *(978-1-4424-5930-4(1),* Atheneum Bks. for Young Readers) Simon & Schuster Children's Publishing.
—Joey & Jet in Space. Yang, James, illus. 2006. (ENG., Illus.). 32p. (J). (gr. -1-k). 17.99 *(978-0-689-86927-3(4),* Atheneum/Richard Jackson Bks.) Simon & Schuster Children's Publishing.
Yasko, Carmen R. Buddy & His Buddies. 2012. 40p. pap. 22.65 *(978-1-4797-4710-8(6))* Xlibris Corp.
Yates, Elizabeth. The Seventh One. 2003. 115p. (J). 8.99 *(978-1-57924-981-6(7))* BJU Pr.
Yates, Louise. Dog Loves Books. 2010. (ENG., Illus.). 32p. (J). (gr. -1-2). 16.99 *(978-0-375-86449-0(0),* Knopf Bks. for Young Readers) Random Hse. Children's Bks.
—Dog Loves Counting. 2013. (ENG.). 32p. (J). (gr. -1-3). 17.99 *(978-0-449-81342-3(8),* Knopf Bks. for Young Readers) Random Hse. Children's Bks.
—Dog Loves Drawing. 2012. (ENG.). 32p. (J). (gr. -1-3). 16.99 *(978-0-375-87067-5(9),* Knopf Bks. for Young Readers) Random Hse. Children's Bks.
—Dog Loves Fairy Tales. 2015. (ENG., Illus.). 32p. (J). (-k). 17.99 *(978-0-85755-017-0(9))* Transworld Publishers Ltd. GBR. Dist: Independent Pubs. Group.
Yee, Paul. Shu-Li & Diego, 1 vol. Wang, Shaoli, illus. 2009. (ENG.). 85p. (J). (gr. 1-4). pap. 7.95 *(978-1-896580-53-1(X))* Tradewind Bks. CAN. Dist: Orca Bk. Pubs. USA.
Yee, Wong Herbert. Did You See Chip? Ovresat, Laura, illus. 2004. (Green Light Readers Level 2 Ser.). (ENG.). 24p. (J). (gr. -1-3). pap. 3.95 *(978-0-15-205096-2(5))* Houghton Mifflin Harcourt Publishing Co.
Yerges, Karen. The Adventures of Scooper the Beagle Dog: Las aventuras de Scooper el perrito Beagle. 2004. (SPA., Illus.). 60p. (J). per. 19.95 *(978-0-9764384-0-3(2))* Mitre's Touch Gallery, The.
Ylvisaker, Anne. Little Klein. 2009. (ENG.). 192p. (J). (gr. 3-7). pap. 6.99 *(978-0-7636-4338-6(6))* Candlewick Pr.
Yobe, Marjorie. The Adventures of Little Tyke: A Loveab. 2006. 48p. pap. 16.95 *(978-1-4241-3920-0(1))* PublishAmerica, Inc.
Yocum, Randi. Cowpie Corgi: A Dog's Tale. Yocum, Sam, 2nd, photos by. 2007. (Illus.). 32p. (J). lib. bdg. 16.98 *(978-0-9663629-3-0(4))* By Grace Enterprises.
Yohn-Rhodes, Phyllis. Abbey & Jakey - Jakey's Happy Tale. 2005. 56p. pap. 27.99 *(978-1-4134-8593-6(6))* Xlibris Corp.
—The Monster. 2005. (Special Kids of Sharon Ser.). (ENG., Illus.). 34p. (J). (gr. -1-3). per. 15.99 *(978-1-4134-8516-5(2))* Xlibris Corp.
—The Wagon. 2005. (Special Kids of Sharon Ser.). (ENG., Illus.). 32p. (J). (gr. -1-3). per. 14.99 *(978-1-4134-8541-7(3))* Xlibris Corp.
Yolen, Jane. How Do Dinosaurs Love Their Dogs? Teague, Mark, illus. 2010. (How Do Dinosaurs... Ser.). (ENG.). 6p. (J). (gr. -1-k). bds. 6.99 *(978-0-545-15352-2(2))* Scholastic, Inc.
Yorinks, Arthur. Flappy & Scrappy. Ivanov, Olga & Ivanov, Aleksey, illus. 2010. (I Can Read Level 2 Ser.). (ENG.). 48p. (J). (gr. k-3). 16.99 *(978-0-06-205117-2(2))* HarperCollins Pubs.
—Flappy & Scrappy. Ivanov, Aleksey & Ivanov, Olga, illus. 2010. (I Can Read Level 2 Ser.). (ENG.). 48p. (J). (gr. k-3). pap. 3.99 *(978-0-06-205913-0(0))* HarperCollins Pubs.
—Harry & Lulu. braille ed. 2004. (Illus.). (J). (gr. k-3). spiral bd. *(978-0-616-07250-9(3));* spiral bd. *(978-0-616-07249-3(X))* Canadian National Institute for the Blind/Institut National Canadien pour les Aveugles.
—Harry & Lulu. Matje, Martin, illus. 32p. (J). pap. 4.99 *(978-0-7868-1221-9(4))* Hyperion Paperbacks for Children.
Young, Franklin. S P O T S. 2012. 198p. pap. *(978-0-9869350-0-8(X))* Awesome Bks.
Young, Helen Ann. Hellie & the Sensational Magic Carpet. Young, Tim, illus. 2013. 106p. pap. *(978-1-908353-02-3(3))* Young Editions.
—Hello to Hellie's World. Young, Tim Blair, illus. 2013. 46p. pap. *(978-1-908353-00-9(7))* Young Editions.
Young, Jessica. All Paws on Deck. Burks, James, illus. 2016. (Haggis & Tank Unleashed Ser.: 1). (ENG.). 80p. (J). (gr. k-2). pap. 4.99 *(978-0-545-81886-5(9))* Scholastic, Inc.
—Digging for Dinos. Burks, James, illus. 2016. (Haggis & Tank Unleashed Ser.: 2). (ENG.). 80p. (J). (gr. k-2). 15.99 *(978-0-545-81889-6(3))* Scholastic, Inc.
Young, Jessica. Howl at the Moon. 2017. (Haggis & Tank Unleashed — Branches Ser.: 3). lib. bdg. 14.75 ***(978-0-606-40190-6(3))*** Turtleback Bks.
Young, Judy. Digger & Daisy Go on a Picnic. Sullivan, Dana, illus. 2014. (I Am a Reader: Digger & Daisy Ser.). (ENG.). 32p. (J). (gr. k-1). 9.99 *(978-1-58536-843-3(1),* 203006) Sleeping Bear Pr.
—Digger & Daisy Go to the Doctor. Sullivan, Dana, illus. 2014. (I AM a READER!: Digger & Daisy Ser.). (ENG.). 32p. (J). (gr. k-2). 9.99 *(978-1-58536-845-7(8),* 203674); pap. 4.99 *(978-1-58536-846-4(6),* 203728) Sleeping Bear Pr.
—Digger & Daisy Go to the Zoo. 2013. (ENG.). (J). *(978-1-58536-841-9(5))* Sleeping Bear Pr.
—Digger & Daisy Plant a Garden. Sullivan, Dana, illus. 2016. (I AM a READER: Digger & Daisy Ser.). (ENG.). 32p. (J). (gr. k-2). 9.99 *(978-1-58536-931-7(4),* 204030) Sleeping Bear Pr.
—Digger et Daisy Vont Au Docteur (Digger & Daisy Go to the Doctor) Sullivan, Dana, illus. 2016. (I AM a READER: Digger & Daisy Ser.). (FRE & ENG.). 32p. (J). (gr. k-2). 12.95 *(978-1-62753-949-4(2),* 204172) Sleeping Bear Pr.
—Digger y Daisy Van a la Ciudad (Digger & Daisy Go to the City) Sullivan, Dana, illus. 2016. (I AM a READER: Digger & Daisy Ser.). (SPA & ENG.). 32p. (J). (gr. k-2). 9.99 *(978-1-62753-954-8(9),* 204177) Sleeping Bear Pr.
—Digger y Daisy Van Al Médico (Digger & Daisy Go to the Doctor) Sullivan, Dana, illus. 2016. (I AM a READER: Digger & Daisy Ser.). (SPA & ENG.). 32p. (J). (gr. k-2). 9.99 *(978-1-62753-953-1(0),* 204176) Sleeping Bear Pr.
—Digger y Daisy Van Al Zoológico (Digger & Daisy Go to the Zoo) Sullivan, Dana, illus. 2016. (I AM a READER: Digger & Daisy Ser.). (SPA & ENG.). 32p. (J). (gr. k-2). 9.99 *(978-1-62753-951-7(4),* 204174) Sleeping Bear Pr.
—Digger y Daisy Van de Picnic (Digger & Daisy Go on a Picnic) Sullivan, Dana, illus. 2016. (I AM a READER: Digger & Daisy Ser.). (SPA & ENG.). 32p. (J). (gr. k-2). 9.99 *(978-1-62753-952-4(2),* 204175) Sleeping Bear Pr.
—Star in a Play. Sullivan, Dana, illus. 2015. (I AM a READER: Digger & Daisy Ser.). (ENG.). 32p. (J). (gr. k-2). 9.99 *(978-1-58536-929-4(2),* 203950) Sleeping Bear Pr.
Young, Judy & Sullivan, Dana. Digger & Daisy Go to the City. 2015. (I AM a READER!: Digger & Daisy Ser.). (ENG., Illus.). 32p. (J). (gr. k-2). pap. 4.99 *(978-1-58536-848-8(2),* 203821) Sleeping Bear Pr.
Young, Leslie. Plaid: A Tale of Compassion. 2006. (Illus.). 15p. 9.00 *(978-1-4120-2793-9(4))* Trafford Publishing.
Young, Ned. Zoomer. Young, Ned, illus. 2010. (ENG., Illus.). 32p. (J). (gr. -1-2). 16.99 *(978-0-06-170088-0(6))* HarperCollins Pubs.
—Zoomer's Out-of-This-World Christmas. Young, Ned, illus. 2013. (ENG., Illus.). 32p. (J). (gr. -1-3). 17.99 *(978-0-06-199959-8(8))* HarperCollins Pubs.
—Zoomer's Summer Snowstorm. Young, Ned, illus. 2011. (ENG., Illus.). 32p. (J). (gr. -1-2). 16.99 *(978-0-06-170092-7(4))* HarperCollins Pubs.
Young, Pershail Catherine. Rusty & Mr. Earlie. 2010. 28p. pap. 12.49 *(978-1-4520-4514-6(3))* AuthorHouse.
Youngs, Kendahl Brooke. Kendahl Gets a Puppy. 2012. (ENG.). (J). pap. 13.95 *(978-0-9836045-8-7(4),* Kendahl Hse. Pr.) Youngs, Bettie Bks.
Yukkie the Yorkie, A. K. A. Marilyn J. Sanders. The Adventures of Yukkie the Yorkie: The Beginning. 2008. (Illus.). 32p. (J). 16.00 *(978-0-8059-7606-9(X))* Dorrance Publishing Co., Inc.
Zail, Suzy. Lulu. Hill, Trish, illus. 2004. iv, 36p. (J). pap. *(978-0-7608-6741-9(0))* Sundance/Newbridge Educational Publishing.
Zalme, Ron, illus. Rainy Day Tales. 2009. (J). *(978-1-59078-734-2(X))* Highlights for Children.
—Sunny Day Tales. 2009. (J). *(978-1-59078-735-9(8))* Highlights for Children.
Zarin, Cynthia. Albert, the Dog Who Liked to Ride in Taxis. Pratt, Pierre, illus. 2004. (ENG.). 32p. (J). (gr. -1-3). 18.99 *(978-0-689-84762-2(9),* Atheneum/Richard Jackson Bks.) Simon & Schuster Children's Publishing.
Zarins, Kim. The Helpful Puppy. McCully, Emily Arnold, illus. 2012. (ENG.). 32p. (J). 16.95 *(978-0-8234-2318-7(2))* Holiday Hse., Inc.
—The Helpful Puppy. McCully, Emily Arnold, illus. 2013. (ENG.). 32p. (J). pap. 6.99 *(978-0-8234-2919-6(9))* Holiday Hse., Inc.
Zeltser, David. Stinker. Patton, Julia, illus. 2017. (ENG.). 32p. (gr. -1-3). 17.99 *(978-1-5124-1792-0(0),* Carolrhoda Bks.) Lerner Publishing Group.
Zera, Beata. Little Puppy Swifty & Elle. 2008. 64p. pap. 21.99 *(978-1-4257-6703-7(6))* Xlibris Corp.
Ziegler-Sullivan, Ursula. Pirate Pups! Petrossi, Fabrizio, illus. 2016. (J). *(978-1-4806-9717-1(6),* Golden Bks.) Random Hse. Children's Bks.
—The Pups Save the Bunnies. 2016. (Illus.). (J). *(978-1-5182-1575-9(0))* Random Hse., Inc.
Zimmerman, Andrea & Clemesha, David. Dig! Rosenthal, Marc, illus. 2014. (ENG.). 30p. (J). (— 1). bds. 7.99 *(978-0-544-17388-0(0),* HMH Books For Young Readers) Houghton Mifflin Harcourt Publishing Co.
Zimmerman, George G. Dougie & the Dane: Chelsea the Great Dane. 2004. (Illus.). 36p. 21.99 *(978-1-4134-4139-0(4))* Xlibris Corp.
Zion, Gene. Harry & the Lady Next Door. Graham, Margaret Bloy, illus. 2003. (I Can Read Level 1 Ser.). (ENG.). 64p. (J). (gr. k-3). pap. 3.99 *(978-0-06-444008-0(7))* HarperCollins Pubs.
—Harry & the Lady Next Door. Graham, Margaret Bloy, illus. 2004. (I Can Read Bks.). 64p. (gr. -1-3). 14.00 *(978-0-7569-3087-5(1))* Perfection Learning Corp.
—Harry & the Lady Next Door. 2003. (I Can Read! Level 1 Ser.). (J). (gr. k-3). lib. bdg. 13.55 *(978-0-8085-2612-4(X),* Turtleback) Turtleback Bks.
—Harry, el Perrito Sucio, 1 vol. Fiol, María A., tr. Graham, Margaret Bloy, illus. 2003. (Harper Arco Iris Ser.).Tr. of Harry the Dirty Dog. (SPA.). 32p. (J). (gr. -1-3). pap. 6.99 *(978-0-06-443443-0(5),* HC0801) HarperCollins Pubs.
—Harry the Dirty Dog. Graham, Margaret Bloy, illus. 50th ed. 2006. (ENG.). (J). (gr. -1-3). 34p. bds. 7.99 *(978-0-06-084244-4(X),* HarperFestival); 32p. 17.99 *(978-0-06-026865-7(4))* HarperCollins Pubs.
—Harry the Dirty Dog. 2006. (J). (gr. -1-2). 17.20 *(978-0-8085-2456-4(9),* Turtleback) Turtleback Bks.
—Harry the Dirty Dog. unabr. ed. 2006. (SPA.). (J). (gr. -1-2). 18.95 *(978-0-439-90593-0(1))* Weston Woods Studios, Inc.
Zion, Gene & Zion. Harry the Dirty Dog. Graham, Margaret Bloy, illus. 50th anniv. ed. 2006. (Trophy Picture Bks.). (ENG.). 32p. (J). (gr. -1-3). pap. 6.99 *(978-0-06-443009-8(X))* HarperCollins Pubs.
Zoellick, Todd. Daniel Harrington Fairbanks the Third & a Day on the Farm. 2012. 40p. pap. 18.58 *(978-1-4772-8408-7(7))* AuthorHouse.
—Daniel Harrington Fairbanks the Third & the Dog That Wouldn't Bark. 2009. 52p. pap. 20.49 *(978-1-4490-1047-8(4))* AuthorHouse.
Zomerdyke, Joy. Polar & Grizzly Find Christmas. 2013. 24p. pap. 17.99 *(978-1-4817-1155-5(5))* AuthorHouse.
Zommer, Yuval. One Hundred Bones. Zommer, Yuval, illus. 2016. (ENG., Illus.). 32p. (J). (gr. -1-2). 16.99 *(978-0-7636-8183-8(0),* Templar) Candlewick Pr.
Zoomer's Out-Of-This-World Christmas. 2013. (Illus.). (J). *(978-0-06-199960-4(1))* Harper & Row Ltd.
Zoss, Lori. A Bed for Fred. 2013. 24p. 15.95 *(978-1-936449-52-1(8))* Roberts & Ross Publishing.
Zsikai-Spiker, Lisa Marie. Buster & Snoopy. Schimmelman, Alex, illus. 2012. 24p. 24.95 *(978-1-4626-7112-0(8))* America Star Bks.
Zuill, Andrea. Wolf Camp. 2016. (ENG., Illus.). 40p. (J). (gr. -1-3). 16.99 *(978-0-553-50912-0(8),* Schwartz & Wade Bks.) Random Hse. Children's Bks.

DOGS—HABITS AND BEHAVIOR

Bailey, Gwen & Whitehead, Sarah. Why Is My Dog Doing That? 2009. (ENG., Illus.). 96p. 9.95 *(978-1-60710-031-7(2),* Thunder Bay Pr.) Readerlink Distribution Services, LLC.
Brett, Flora. A Dog's View of the World. 2015. (Pet Perspectives Ser.). (ENG., Illus.). 24p. (gr. 1-2). lib. bdg. 25.32 *(978-1-4914-5049-9(5))* Capstone Press of Coughlan Cos.
Brooks, Linda. Wait for Me!!!!!!!! The Misadventures of Smokie & Leroy. 2009. 28p. pap. 12.49 *(978-1-4490-1503-9(4))* AuthorHouse.
Daly, Ruth. Dog Walker. 2017. (J). ***(978-1-4896-6086-2(0),*** AV2 by Weigl) Weigl Pubs., Inc.
Dromgoole, Glenn. What Puppies Teach Us: Life's Lessons Learned from Our Little Friends. 2003. (Illus.). 32p. tchr. ed. 12.95 *(978-1-57223-684-4(1),* 6841) Willow Creek Pr., Inc.
George, Jean Craighead. How to Talk to Your Dog. Truesdell, Sue & Meisel, Paul, illus. 2003. (ENG.). 40p. (J). (gr. 1-4). pap. 6.99 *(978-0-06-000623-5(4))* HarperCollins Pubs.
Hibbert, Clare. If You Were a Dog. 2013. (If You Were A... Ser.). 32p. (gr. 2-5). 31.35 *(978-1-59920-960-9(8))* Black Rabbit Bks.
Hoopmann, Kathy. All Dogs Have ADHD. 2008. (ENG., Illus.). 72p. 14.95 *(978-1-84310-651-7(5),* 4468) Kingsley, Jessica Pubs. GBR. Dist: Macmillan Distribution Ltd.
Horowitz, Alexandra. Inside of a Dog: What Dogs See, Smell, & Know. Edgerton, Sean Vidal, illus. 2017. (ENG.). 272p. (J). (gr. 3-7). pap. 7.99 *(978-1-4814-5094-2(6),* Simon & Schuster Bks. For Young Readers) Simon & Schuster Bks. For Young Readers.
—Inside of a Dog: What Dogs See, Smell, & Know (Young Reader's Edition) Edgerton, Sean Vidal, illus. 2016. (ENG.). 256p. (J). (gr. 3-7). 16.99 *(978-1-4814-5093-5(X),* Simon & Schuster Bks. For Young Readers) Simon & Schuster Bks. For Young Readers.
Keay, Loralee. Ear Muffs for Phoebe. 2009. 36p. (J). pap. 13.95 *(978-1-4327-1203-7(9))* Outskirts Pr., Inc.
Kopp, Megan. The Language of Dogs & Other Canines. 2016. (Call of the Wild Ser.). (ENG.). 32p. (J). (gr. 3-3). 28.50 *(978-1-5026-1725-5(0))* Cavendish Square Publishing.
Marlowe, Christie. Dog Groomer. 2013. (Earning $50,000 - $100,000 with a High School Diploma or Less Ser.: 14). 64p. (J). (gr. 7-18). 22.95 *(978-1-4222-2893-7(2))* Mason Crest.
Muntean, Michaela. The True Story of Ten Dogs - Stay. Bailey, K. C., illus. Kazmierski, Stephen, photos by. 2012. (ENG.). 40p. (J). (gr. -1-3). 17.99 *(978-0-545-23497-9(2),* Scholastic Pr.) Scholastic, Inc.
Newman, Aline Alexander. Rascally Rabbits! And More True Stories of Animals Behaving Badly! 2016. (NGK Chapters Ser.). (ENG., Illus.). 112p. (J). (gr. 2-5). pap. 5.99 *(978-1-4263-2308-9(5),* National Geographic Children's Bks.) National Geographic Society.
Pang, Evelyn & Louie, Hilary. Good Dog! Kids Teach Kids about Dog Behavior & Training. 2008. (J). *(978-1-929242-58-0(1))* Dogwise Publishing.
Patent, Dorothy Hinshaw. Super Sniffers: Dog Detectives on the Job. 2014. (ENG., Illus.). 48p. (J). (gr. 2-4). 17.99 *(978-0-8027-3618-5(1),* 9780802736185, Bloomsbury USA Childrens) Bloomsbury Publishing USA.
Pavia, Audrey & Schultz, Jacque Lynn. Having Fun with Your Dog. 2009. (ASPCA Kids Ser.: 3). (ENG., Illus.). 108p. 12.99 *(978-0-470-41085-1(X),* Howell Bk. Hse.) Wiley, John & Sons, Inc.
Petrie, Kristin. Cesky Terriers, 1 vol. 2014. (Dogs Set 11 Ser.). (ENG., Illus.). 24p. (gr. 3-6). 25.65 *(978-1-62403-101-4(3))* ABDO Publishing Co.
Rutherford, Clarice. A Dog Is a Dog: And That's Why He's So Special. 2012. (ENG., Illus.). 106p. (J). pap. 14.95 *(978-1-57779-103-4(7))* Alpine Pubns., Inc.
Spilsbury, Richard & Spilsbury, Louise. Dog Packs. 2013. (Animal Armies Ser.). (ENG., Illus.). 32p. (J). (gr. k-5). pap. 10.00 *(978-1-4777-0330-4(6));* lib. bdg. 25.25 *(978-1-4777-0304-5(7))* Rosen Publishing Group, Inc., The. (PowerKids Pr.).
Wahman, Wendy. Don't Lick the Dog: Making Friends with Dogs. Wahman, Wendy, illus. 2009. (ENG., Illus.). 32p. (J). (gr. -1-2). 17.99 *(978-0-8050-8733-8(8),* 9780805087338, Holt, Henry & Co. Bks. For Young Readers) Holt, Henry & Co.
Wild Canines. 2016. (Wild Canines Ser.). 24p. (gr. 3-3). 94.40 *(978-1-4994-1916-0(3));* pap. 33.00 *(978-1-4994-2465-2(5))* Rosen Publishing Group, Inc., The. (PowerKids Pr.).

DOGS—HISTORY

Hoena, Blake. Stubby the Dog Soldier: World War I Hero, 1 vol. 2014. (Animal Heroes Ser.). (ENG., Illus.). 32p. (gr. k-2). 28.65 *(978-1-4795-5461-4(8))* Picture Window Bks.
Hughes, Trevor. The Oxenholme Hounds. 2009. (ENG., Illus.). 128p. 26.95 *(978-1-84868-608-3(0))* Amberley Publishing GBR. Dist: Independent Pubs. Group.
MacLeod, Elizabeth. Top Dogs: Canines That Changed History. 2017. (ENG., Illus.). 96p. (J). (gr. 3-7). 19.95 *(978-1-55451-907-1(1))* Annick Pr., Ltd. CAN. Dist: Publishers Group West (PGW).
—Top Dogs: Canines That Made History. 2017. (ENG., Illus.). 96p. (J). (gr. 3-7). pap. 12.95 *(978-1-55451-906-4(3))* Annick Pr., Ltd. CAN. Dist: Publishers Group West (PGW).
Myers, Jack. How Dogs Came from Wolves: And Other Explorations of Science in Action. Rice, John, illus. 2004. (ENG.). 64p. (J). (gr. 4-6). pap. 10.95 *(978-1-59078-278-1(X))* Boyds Mills Pr.

DOGS—PICTORIAL WORKS

Aigner-Clark, Julie. Perros. 2004. (Baby Einstein Ser.). (SPA., Illus.). 20p. (J). bds. *(978-970-718-156-4(7),* Silver Dolphin en Español) Advanced Marketing, S. de R. L. de C. V.
Barker Bridges, Rebecca. Meet Stanley: The Reading Dog. 2014. (Illus.). (J). 16.95 *(978-0-9856631-6-2(2))* Golden Gate Publishing.
Brassey, Richard. Greyfriars Bobby. 2010. (ENG., Illus.). 24p. pap. 9.99 *(978-1-4440-0057-3(8))* Orion Publishing Group, Ltd. GBR. Dist: Hachette Bk. Group.
Bruce, Relly. Fun Times with Meekus & Myron. 2011. 16p. pap. 24.95 *(978-1-4489-9171-6(4))* America Star Bks.
Carroll, Colleen. Dogs. 2008. (How Artists See Jr.: Ser.). (ENG., Illus.). 18p. (J). (gr. -1-k). bds. 7.95 *(978-0-7892-0972-6(1),* Abbeville Kids) Abbeville Pr., Inc.
Casteel, Seth. Underwater Doggies 1,2,3. 2014. (ENG., Illus.). 18p. (J). (gr. -1 — 1). bds. 6.99 *(978-0-316-33175-3(9))* Little, Brown Bks. for Young Readers.
—Underwater Doggies Colors. 2014. (ENG., Illus.). 18p. (J). (gr. -1 — 1). bds. 6.99 *(978-0-316-37365-4(6))* Little, Brown Bks. for Young Readers.
Clinker, Gayle. The Very Busy Vizzi. 2011. 52p. pap. 15.95 *(978-1-4567-5615-4(X))* AuthorHouse.
Davidson, Carli, photos by. Heads & Tails. 2017. (ENG., Illus.). 20p. (J). bds. 8.99 *(978-1-4521-5137-3(7))* Chronicle Bks. LLC.
—Shake, Wiggle & Roll. 2017. (ENG., Illus.). 20p. (J). bds. 8.99 *(978-1-4521-5136-6(9))* Chronicle Bks. LLC.
Dorling Kindersley Publishing Staff. Puppy. 2011. (Touch & Feel Ser.). (ENG.). 12p. (J). (gr. -1-k). bds. 6.99 *(978-0-7566-9166-0(4),* DK Children) Dorling Kindersley Publishing, Inc.
epstein, brad M., et al. Dogs ABC: My First Alphabet Book. 2013. (Illus.). 32p. (J). *(978-1-60730-400-5(7),* ABC Bk.) Michaelson Entertainment.
Gamble, Adam & Jasper, Mark. Good Night Puppies. Veno, Joe, illus. 2015. (Good Night Our World Ser.). (ENG.). 20p. (J). (— 1). bds. 9.95 *(978-1-60219-227-0(8))* Good Night Bks.
Glover, Harry. Dogs. 2004. (Spotter's Guides Sticker Bks.). (SPA., Illus.). 32p. (J). pap. 7.95 *(978-0-7945-0212-6(1),* Usborne) EDC Publishing.
Harris, John & Lorenz, Catherine. Discovering Art Dogs. 2009. (ENG., Illus.). 24p. (gr. -1). 4.95 *(978-0-89236-949-2(3))* Oxford Univ. Pr., Inc.
Innovative Kids Staff, creator. Soft Shapes Photo Books: Puppies. 2011. (ENG., Illus.). 8p. (J). (gr. -1 — 1). 10.99 *(978-1-60169-154-5(8))* Innovative Kids.
Kalman, Bobbie. It Looks Like a Dog. 2011. (ENG.). 16p. (J). lib. bdg. *(978-0-7787-9546-9(2));* pap. *(978-0-7787-9571-1(3))* Crabtree Publishing Co.
Laplander, Cheryl. Maximillion. 2011. 48p. pap. 22.50 *(978-1-4269-5211-1(2))* Trafford Publishing.
Medway, Jim. Big Dogs, Little Dogs: A Visual Guide to the World's Dogs. 2016. (ENG., Illus.). 32p. (J). (gr. -1-2). 19.95 *(978-1-77085-828-2(8),* 9781770858282) Firefly Bks., Ltd.
Picthall, Chez. Puppies. 2015. (ENG., Illus.). 10p. (J). 7.99 *(978-1-905503-77-3(6))* Award Pubns. Ltd. GBR. Dist: Parkwest Pubns., Inc.
Publishing, Sterling. Woof. 2008. (Books for Brainy Babies). (Illus.). 12p. (J). bds. *(978-1-934618-33-2(0))* Begin Smart LLC.
Schindel, John & Woodward, Molly. The Babies & Doggies Book. 2015. (ENG., Illus.). 26p. (J). (— 1). bds. 7.99 *(978-0-544-44477-5(9),* HMH Books For Young Readers) Houghton Mifflin Harcourt Publishing Co.
Sforza, Daniella, ed. Savannah Blue's Activity Book/Libro de Actividades de Savannah Azul. Spagnoli, Maria Eugenia, tr. Rakusin, Sudie, illus. 2005.Tr. of Libro de Actividades de Savannah Azul. (SPA & ENG.). 48p. (J). 10.95 *(978-0-9664805-4-2(6))* Winged Willow Pr.
Swinney, Nicola Jane. I Love Dogs & Puppies: Over 50 Breeds. 2014. (Illus.). 119p. (J). *(978-1-4351-5534-3(3))* Barnes & Noble, Inc.
The Wisdom of Zeus. 2005. (J). *(978-0-9765840-0-1(X))* Zeus Media LLC.

DOGS—POETRY

Archer, Peggy. Name That Dog! Buscema, Stephanie, illus. 2010. (ENG.). 32p. (J). (gr. -1-k). 16.99 *(978-0-8037-3322-0(4),* Dial Bks) Penguin Young Readers Group.
Cabrera, Jane. Old Mother Hubbard. 2008. (Jane Cabrera Board Bks.). (ENG., Illus.). 24p. (J). (gr. -1-k). bds. 6.95 *(978-0-8234-2132-9(5))* Holiday Hse., Inc.
Clements, Andrew. Dogku. Bowers, Tim, illus. 2007. (ENG.). 40p. (J). (gr. -1-3). 17.99 *(978-0-689-85823-9(X),* Atheneum Bks. for Young Readers) Simon & Schuster Children's Publishing.
Crawley, Dave. Dog Poems. Petrosino, Tamara, illus. 2007. (ENG.). 32p. (J). (gr. 4-6). 16.95 *(978-1-59078-454-9(5),* Wordsong) Boyds Mills Pr.
D'Onofrio, Sister Alice Marie. Woofs, Whiskers, & Wags: Tales of Rocky's Brave Heart. 2012. 28p. pap. 19.99 *(978-1-4772-8596-1(2))* AuthorHouse.
Flor Ada, Alma & Campoy, F. Isabel. Ten Little Puppies/Diez Perritos. Wensell, Ulises, illus. 2011. (SPA & ENG.). 32p. (J). (gr. -1-3). 16.99 *(978-0-06-147043-1(0),* Rayo) HarperCollins Pubs.

Harrison, David L. Farmer's Dog Goes to the Forest: Rhymes for Two Voices. Johnson-Petrov, Arden, illus. 2005. (ENG.). 32p. (J). (gr. k-3). 15.95 *(978-1-59078-242-2(9))* Boyds Mills Pr.

MacLachlan, Patricia & Charest, Emily MacLachlan. Once I Ate a Pie. Schneider, Katy, illus. (ENG.). 40p. (J). (gr. -1-3). 2010. pap. 6.99 *(978-0-06-073533-3(3))* 2006. 17.99 *(978-0-06-073531-9(7))* HarperCollins Pubs.

—Once I Ate a Pie. 2010. (J). lib. bdg. 17.20 *(978-0-606-12296-2(6),* Turtleback) Turtleback Bks.

Rosen, Michael J. The Hound Dog's Haiku: And Other Poems for Dog Lovers. Azarian, Mary, illus. 2011. (ENG.). 56p. (J). (gr. 1-4). 17.99 *(978-0-7636-4499-4(4))* Candlewick Pr.

Sargent, David M., Jr. Buffy's Anger. 2003. (Doggie Tails Ser.). (Illus.). 23p. (J). pap. 10.95 *(978-1-56763-856-1(2));* lib. bdg. 20.95 *(978-1-56763-855-4(4))* Ozark Publishing.

—Emma's Law, 9 vols. 2003. (Doggie Tails Ser.). (Illus.). 24p. (J). pap. 10.95 *(978-1-56763-862-2(7));* lib. bdg. 20.95 *(978-1-56763-861-5(9))* Ozark Publishing.

—Vera's Talent, 9 vols. 2003. (Doggie Tails Ser.). (Illus.). 25p. (J). pap. 10.95 *(978-1-56763-858-5(9))* Ozark Publishing.

Shields, Gillian. Puppy Love: The Story of Esme & Sam. Harbour, Elizabeth, illus. 2009. (ENG.). 32p. (J). (gr. -1-3). 16.99 *(978-1-4169-8010-0(5),* Simon & Schuster Bks. For Young Readers) Simon & Schuster Bks. For Young Readers.

Williams, Vivienne. Rosie & Her Formidable Bark, Indomitable Nose & Rambunctioustail. Wotton, Jon, illus. 2013. 46p. pap. *(978-0-9576680-4-1(X))* Williams, Vivienne.

DOGS—TRAINING

Barnes, Julia. Dog Training, Vol. 12. 2016. (Understanding & Caring for Your Pet Ser.: Vol. 12). (ENG., Illus.). 128p. (J). (gr. 5-8). 25.95 *(978-1-4222-3694-9(3))* Mason Crest.

Basic Canine Grooming. 2004. (YA). cd-rom 59.00 *(978-1-56918-000-6(8),* CEV70145) Visual Education Productions.

Bates, Dawn. My First Dog Book: 35 Fun Activities to Do with Your Dog, for Children Aged 7 Years + 2015. (ENG., Illus.). 128p. (J). (gr. 7-11). pap. 14.95 *(978-1-78249-197-2(X),* CICO Books) Ryland Peters & Small GBR. Dist: WIPRO.

Bly, Nicole. Liam Goes to Agility School. 2011. 48p. pap. 23.50 *(978-1-4567-5659-8(1))* AuthorHouse.

Bozzo, Linda & Library Association Staff. Fire Dog Heroes. 2010. (Amazing Working Dogs with American Humane Ser.). (Illus.). 48p. (J). (gr. 2-5). 25.27 *(978-0-7660-3202-6(7))* Enslow Pubs., Inc.

Dog School: Individual Title Six-Packs. (Story Steps Ser.). (gr. k-2). 32.00 *(978-0-7635-9834-1(8))* Rigby Education.

Goldish, Meish. Buddy: America's First Guide Dog. 2016. (Dog Heroes Ser.). (ENG., Illus.). 32p. (J). (gr. 2-7). 19.95 *(978-1-943553-09-9(2))* Bearport Publishing Co., Inc.

Goldish, Meish & Aiello, Ron. War Dogs. 2012. (America's Animal Soldiers Ser.). 24p. (J). (gr. 1-6). lib. bdg. 23.93 *(978-1-61772-452-7(1))* Bearport Publishing Co., Inc.

Kabel, Amy. Hank's Visit to the Doggie Store. 2013. 32p. pap. 17.25 *(978-1-4669-9281-8(6))* Trafford Publishing.

Laughlin, Kara L. Search-And-Rescue Dogs. 2014. (Service Dogs Ser.). (ENG.). 24p. (J). (gr. 1-4). 27.07 *(978-1-62687-311-7(9),* 207152) Child's World, Inc., The.

LeTourneau, Anthony Alex, illus. Hanni & Beth: Safe & Sound. 2007. (J). (gr. k-3). 17.95 *(978-0-9792918-0-7(1))* Blue Marlin Pubns.

Miles, Ellen. Guide to Puppies. 2013. (Puppy Place Ser.). lib. bdg. 16.00 *(978-0-606-31503-6(9),* Turtleback) Turtleback Bks.

Pang, Evelyn & Louie, Hilary. Good Dog! Kids Teach Kids about Dog Behavior & Training. 2008. (J). *(978-1-929242-58-0(1))* Dogwise Publishing.

Pavia, Audrey & Schultz, Jacque Lynn. Having Fun with Your Dog. 2009. (ASPCA Kids Ser.: 3). (ENG.). 108p. 12.99 *(978-0-470-41085-1(X),* Howell Bk. Hse.) Wiley, John & Sons, Inc.

Rutherford, Clarice. A Dog Is a Dog: And That's Why He's So Special. 2012. (ENG., Illus.). 106p. (J). pap. 14.95 *(978-1-57779-103-4(7))* Alpine Pubns., Inc.

Simmons-Moake, Jane. Excelling at Dog Agility - Book 3 Advanced Skills Training - Updated Second Edition Bk. 3. 2007. (ENG., Illus.). 192p. 25.95 *(978-0-9674929-2-6(0))* FlashPaws Productions.

Stewart, Gail B. Cesar Milan. 2010. (People in the News Ser.). (Illus.). 128p. (J). 33.95 *(978-1-4205-0231-2(X),* Lucent Bks.) Cengage Gale.

Sundance, Kyra. 101 Dog Tricks, Kids Edition: Fun & Easy Activities, Games, & Crafts. 2014. (ENG., Illus.). 192p. pap. 19.99 *(978-1-59253-893-5(2),* 1592538932, Quarry Books) Quarto Publishing Group USA.

Thornton, Kim Campbell. Train. 2008. (Illus.). 39p. (J). *(978-1-933958-56-9(1))* i-5 Publishing LLC.

Wadsworth, Ginger. Poop Detectives: Working Dogs in the Field. 2016. (ENG., Illus.). 80p. (J). (gr. 3-7). lib. bdg. 17.95 *(978-1-58089-650-4(2))* Charlesbridge Publishing, Inc.

Williams, Christopher. One Incredible Dog! Kizzy. Friedman, Judith, illus. 2006. (One Incredible Dog! Ser.). (ENG.). 32p. (J). (gr. -1-3). lib. bdg. 15.95 *(978-0-9766805-5-0(6))* Keene Publishing.

Wombacher, Michael. There's a Puppy in the House: Surviving the First Five Months. 2003. pap. 16.95 *(978-0-9713033-1-7(2))* Wombacher, Michael.

DOGS—TREATMENT

Bly, Nicole. Liam Visits the Veterinarian. 2013. 48p. pap. 21.99 *(978-1-4772-5583-4(4))* AuthorHouse.

Bozzo, Linda & Library Association Staff. Therapy Dog Heroes. 2010. (Amazing Working Dogs with American Humane Ser.). 48p. (J). (gr. 2-5). 25.27 *(978-0-7660-3200-2(0))* Enslow Pubs., Inc.

Fornaro, Claire. The Puppy Factory Guide to Dog Care: The Absolute to the Zany of Dog Care. 2009. 28p. pap. 13.50 *(978-1-4251-6597-0(4))* Trafford Publishing.

Stories from Black Dog Ranch: Dog Tales about Hope & Second Chances. 2008. (Illus.). 64p. 18.00 *(978-0-9817830-0-0(7))* BRIO Pr.

DOGS FOR THE BLIND

see Guide Dogs

DOLITTLE, DOCTOR (FICTITIOUS CHARACTER)—FICTION

Lofting, Hugh. The Story of Doctor Dolittle. 2005. 26.95 *(978-1-4218-0047-9(0),* 1st World Library - Literary Society) 1st World Publishing, Inc.

—The Story of Doctor Dolittle. unabr. ed. 2011. (Dover Children's Thrift Classics Ser.). (ENG., Illus.). 96p. (J). (gr. 3-8). reprint ed. pap. 4.00 *(978-0-486-29350-9(5))* Dover Pubns., Inc.

—The Story of Doctor Dolittle: Animal Talk. Kanzler, John, illus. 2008. (Easy Reader Classics Ser.). (ENG.). 32p. (gr. 3-7). lib. bdg. 24.21 *(978-1-59961-338-3(7))* Spotlight.

—The Story of Doctor Dolittle: The Circus Crocodile. Kanzler, John, illus. 2008. (Easy Reader Classics Ser.). (ENG.). 32p. (gr. 3-7). lib. bdg. 24.21 *(978-1-59961-339-0(5))* Spotlight.

—The Voyages of Doctor Dolittle. 2004. (Dover Children's Classics Ser.). (ENG., Illus.). 224p. (J). (gr. 3-7). pap. 4.95 *(978-0-486-43491-9(5))* Dover Pubns., Inc.

DOLL

see Dolls

DOLLHOUSES

Carlson, Laurie. Doll Crafts: A Kid's Guide to Making Simple Dolls, Clothing, Accessories, & Houses. 2017. (ENG.). 144p. (J). (gr. 2). pap. 14.99 ***(978-1-61373-778-1(5))*** Chicago Review Pr., Inc.

Hattenhauer, Ina, illus. Dollhouse Sticker Book. 2012. (Sticker Activity Book Ser.). 24p. (J). pap. 8.99 *(978-0-7945-2944-4(5),* Usborne) EDC Publishing.

Hinkler Books, ed. My Designer Doll's House to Make & Decorate. 2012. 12p. (J). pap. 12.99 *(978-1-74184-302-6(2))* Hinkler Bks. Pty, Ltd. AUS. Dist: Ideals Pubns.

Mazurkiewicz, Jessica. Victorian Dollhouse Wallpaper. 2017. (ENG., Illus.). 48p. pap. 12.95 *(978-0-486-81475-9(0))* Dover Pubns., Inc.

Pipe, Jim. Lift, Look & Learn Doll's House: Uncover the Secrets of a Victorian Home. Taylor, Maria, illus. 2014. (ENG.). 24p. (J). (gr. 1). 19.95 *(978-1-78312-082-6(7))* Carlton Bks., Ltd. GBR. Dist: Sterling Publishing Co., Inc.

Priddy, Roger. Doll's House. 2013. (Lift-The-Flap Tab Bks.). (ENG.). 16p. (J). (gr. -1 — 1). bds. 8.99 *(978-0-312-51657-4(6),* 9780312516574, Priddy Bks.) St. Martin's Pr.

Warner, Barbara. The ABC's of Dollhouse Finishing. 2nd ed. 2003. (Illus.). 124p. (YA). per. 19.95 *(978-1-893625-05-1(2))* Scott Pubns., Inc.

DOLLHOUSES—FICTION

Carpenter, Ann. The Slumber Girls & the Mystical Dollhouse. 2006. (J). per. 8.99 *(978-0-9771030-0-3(5))* Kidz By Dezign Pr., Inc.

Godden, Rumer. The Dolls' House. 126p. (J). (gr. 3-5). pap. 4.99 *(978-0-8072-1408-4(6),* Listening Library) Random Hse. Audio Publishing Group.

Keene, Carolyn. The Dollhouse Mystery. Jones, Jan Naimo, illus. 2004. (Nancy Drew Notebooks). 68p. (J). (gr. 1-4). 12.65 *(978-0-7569-5524-3(6))* Perfection Learning Corp.

—The Dollhouse Mystery. Jones, Jan Naimo, illus. 58th ed. 2004. (Nancy Drew Notebooks Ser.: 58). (ENG.). 80p. (J). (gr. 1-4). pap. 6.99 *(978-0-689-86534-3(1),* Aladdin) Simon & Schuster Children's Publishing.

Martin, Ann M. & Godwin, Laura. The Doll People's Christmas. Helquist, Brett, illus. 2016. (ENG.). 48p. (J). (gr. -1-k). 17.99 *(978-1-4847-2339-5(2))* Hyperion Bks. for Children.

Petrucha, Stefan. The Haunted Dollhouse. Murase, Sho, illus. 2005. (Nancy Drew: Girl Detective Ser.). 88p. (gr. 3-7). 24.21 *(978-1-59961-059-7(0))* Spotlight.

Potter, Beatrix. A Tale of Two Bad Mice, 1 vol. McClintock, Barbara, illus. 2007. (Rabbit Ears: A Classic Tale Ser.). (ENG.). 40p. (gr. -1-3). 25.65 *(978-1-59961-314-7(X))* Spotlight.

Potter, Giselle. This Is My Dollhouse. 2016. (ENG., Illus.). 40p. (J). (gr. -1-3). 17.99 *(978-0-553-52153-5(5),* Schwartz & Wade Bks.) Random Hse. Children's Bks.

Ray, Jane. The Dollhouse Fairy. Ray, Jane, illus. 2010. (ENG., Illus.). 32p. (J). (gr. -1-2). 16.99 *(978-0-7636-4411-6(0))* Candlewick Pr.

Reiss, Kathryn. Sweet Miss Honeywell's Revenge: A Ghost Story. 2005. (ENG.). 444p. (YA). (gr. 7-12). pap. 22.95 *(978-0-15-205471-7(5))* Houghton Mifflin Harcourt Publishing Co.

Rudnicki, Richard, illus. A Christmas Dollhouse, 1 vol. 2012. (ENG.). 32p. (J). (gr. -1-3). 18.95 *(978-1-55109-868-5(7))* Nimbus Publishing, Ltd. CAN. Dist: Orca Bk. Pubs. USA.

Swanson, Maggie, illus. The Tale of Two Bad Mice. 2006. (J). 6.99 *(978-1-59939-030-7(2))* Cornerstone Pr.

Wright, Betty Ren. The Dollhouse Murders. 2008. (ENG.). 149p. (J). (gr. 4-7). pap. 7.99 *(978-0-8234-2172-5(4))* Holiday Hse., Inc.

Young, Miriam. Miss Suzy. Lobel, Arnold, illus. (J). 40th anniv. ed. 2004. 44p. 18.95 *(978-1-930900-28-8(7))* 50th ed. 2014. (ENG.). 40p. (gr. -1-3). 18.95 *(978-1-930900-75-2(9))* Purple Hse. Pr.

DOLLS

Adams, Lynn. Penguin Sticker Paper Doll. 2003. (Dover Little Activity Books Paper Dolls Ser.). (ENG., Illus.). 4p. (J). (gr. k-3). pap. 1.50 *(978-0-486-42629-7(7))* Dover Pubns., Inc.

Autumn Publishing, Autumn. Party Animals! — Kitten Paper Dolls. 2014. (ENG.). 16p. (J). (gr. -1). 7.99 *(978-0-486-78029-0(5))* Dover Pubns., Inc.

—Party Animals! — Pony Paper Dolls. 2014. (ENG.). 16p. (J). (gr. -1). 7.99 *(978-0-486-78030-6(9))* Dover Pubns., Inc.

Barbie. Barbie: I Love to Draw! 2015. (Love to Draw Ser.: 5). (ENG.). 48p. (J). (gr. 1-4). pap. 8.99 *(978-0-7944-3314-7(6),* Reader's Digest Children's Bks.) Studio Fun International.

Barker, Cicely Mary & Potter, Beatrix. Flower Fairies Paper Dolls. 2005. (Flower Fairies Ser.). (ENG.). 13p. (J). (gr. -1-2). 6.99 *(978-0-7232-5432-4(X),* Warne) Penguin Young Readers Group.

Byj, Charlot. Six Little Steppers Paper Dolls. Taliadoros, Jenny, ed. Byj, Charlot & Richardson, Doris, illus. 2008. 8p. pap. 12.00 *(978-0-9795053-7-9(2))* Paper Studio Pr.

Carlson, Laurie. Doll Crafts: A Kid's Guide to Making Simple Dolls, Clothing, Accessories, & Houses. 2017. (ENG.). 144p. (J). (gr. 2). pap. 14.99 ***(978-1-61373-778-1(5))*** Chicago Review Pr., Inc.

Cherry, Winky. My First Doll Book: Hand Sewing. 2nd ed. 2011. (My First Sewing Book Kit Ser.). (ENG.). 40p. (J). (gr. 3-7). pap. 16.95 *(978-0-935278-87-3(7))* Palmer-Pletsch Assocs.

Cutting, David, illus. Betty Boop Paper Dolls. 2016. (ENG.). 32p. (J). (gr. 3-6). pap. 11.99 *(978-0-486-80171-1(3))* Dover Pubns., Inc.

Doney, Meryl. Toys. 2004. (Crafts from Many Cultures Ser.). (Illus.). 32p. (gr. 2-5). lib. bdg. 26.00 *(978-0-8368-4048-3(8),* Gareth Stevens Learning Library) Stevens, Gareth Publishing LLLP.

Drews, Judith. Ava: Magnetic Dress-up Doll. 2014. (ENG., Illus.). 1p. (J). (gr. -1-2). 14.95 *(978-3-89955-720-6(4))* Die Gestalten Verlag DEU. Dist: Penguin Random Hse. LLC.

—Lucas: Magnetic Dress-up Doll. 2014. (ENG., Illus.). 1p. (J). (gr. -1-2). 14.95 *(978-3-89955-721-3(2))* Die Gestalten Verlag DEU. Dist: Penguin Random Hse. LLC.

Duck Egg Blue & Autumn Publishing. Press-Out & Make Dolly Dressing — Fashionable Friends. 2013. (Dover Paper Dolls Ser.). (ENG.). 16p. (J). (gr. k-5). 6.99 *(978-0-486-49130-1(7))* Dover Pubns., Inc.

Eagan, Cindy. The Story of Barbie & the Woman Who Created Her. Bates, Amy June, illus. 2017. (ENG.). 40p. (J). (gr. -1-3). 17.99 ***(978-0-399-55378-3(9),*** Random Hse. Bks. for Young Readers) Random Hse. Children's Bks.

Ellis, Erin A. Great Horror Movie Villains Paper Dolls: Psychos, Slashers & Their Unlucky Victims! 2013. (Dover Paper Dolls Ser.). (ENG.). 32p. (gr. 7-12). pap. 9.99 *(978-0-486-49886-7(7))* Dover Pubns., Inc.

Engelbreit, Mary. Mary Engelbreit's Paper Dolls: Fun with Ann Estelle & Mikayla. 2013. (ENG.). 32p. (J). pap. 12.99 *(978-1-4494-3595-0(5))* Andrews McMeel Publishing.

Fairies: Petal People You Make Yourself. 2009. (ENG.). 38p. (J). (gr. 3). spiral bd. 16.95 *(978-1-59174-802-1(X))* Klutz.

Falligant, Erin, et al. American Girl: Ultimate Visual Guide. 2016. (ENG., Illus.). 200p. (J). (gr. 1-4). 24.99 *(978-1-4654-4496-7(3),* DK Children) Dorling Kindersley Publishing, Inc.

Fisher, Phyllis Mae Richardson, illus. Janae, #3 in the 1989 Family Friends Paper Doll Set, Vol. 3. l.t. ed. 2003. 24p. (J). 10.00 *(978-0-9745615-7-8(6))* PJs Corner.

Foley, Tim. New Presidential Paper Doll Inaugural Edition. 2017. (Dover Paper Dolls Ser.). (ENG.). 32p. pap. 9.99 *(978-0-486-81528-2(5))* Dover Pubns., Inc.

Graves, Mab. Little Lost Girls Paper Dolls. 2013. (ENG.). 32p. (J). (gr. 3-8). pap. 9.99 *(978-0-486-49160-8(9))* Dover Pubns., Inc.

Green, Sara. American Girl. 2017. (Brands We Know Ser.). (ENG., Illus.). 24p. (J). (gr. 3-8). lib. bdg. 25.95 *(978-1-62617-553-2(5),* Pilot Bks.) Bellwether Media.

Green, Yuko. Greek Girl & Boy Paper Dolls. 2003. (Dover Paper Dolls Ser.). (ENG.). 16p. (J). (gr. -1-5). pap. 3.95 *(978-0-486-42389-0(1))* Dover Pubns., Inc.

Hall, Patricia. Honest-to-Goodness Story of Raggedy Andy, 1 vol. Wannamaker, Joni Gruelle, illus. 2005. (ENG.). 32p. (J). (gr. k-3). 16.99 *(978-1-58980-251-3(9))* Pelican Publishing Co., Inc.

Henry, Marilyn. Marilyn Monroe Paper Dolls. Henry, Marilyn, illus. 2007. (ENG., Illus.). 16p. pap. 12.00 *(978-0-9790668-8-7(3))* Paper Studio Pr.

Holzer, David. Make & Play Airplanes. Galvani, Maureen, illus. 2005. (Fun Kits (Top That! Ser.). 48p. (J). (gr. -1-3). *(978-1-84510-549-5(4))* Top That! Publishing PLC.

Johnson, Robyn. The Enchanted Dolls' House Wedding. Johnson, Robyn, illus. 2006. (Illus.). 28p. *(978-1-74178-090-1(X))* Bonnier Publishing Australia.

Leonard, Kiri Ostergaard. Vikings of Legend & Lore Paper Dolls. 2013. (ENG.). 32p. (gr. 3-8). pap. 9.99 *(978-0-486-49334-3(2))* Dover Pubns., Inc.

Lum, Kwei-lin. Chinatown Paper Dolls. 2013. (ENG.). 32p. (J). (gr. 6). pap. 9.99 *(978-0-486-49987-1(1))* Dover Pubns., Inc.

—Voodoo Paper Dolls. 2011. (Dover Paper Dolls Ser.). (ENG., Illus.). 32p. (J). (gr. 3-5). pap. 9.99 *(978-0-486-47785-5(1))* Dover Pubns., Inc.

Lunzer, Lee. Betty Grable Paper Dolls. Lunzer, Lee, illus. 2007. (ENG., Illus.). 16p. pap. 12.00 *(978-0-9790668-7-0(5))* Paper Studio Pr.

Madan, Fredric C. Greer Garson Paper Dolls. Madan, Fredric C. & Ernst, Clara, illus. 2007. (ENG.). 16p. pap. 12.00 *(978-0-9790668-6-3(7))* Paper Studio Pr.

Mattox, Brenda Sneathen. Ladies in Red Paper Dolls: Famous Fashions from Great Designers. 2013. (ENG.). 48p. (gr. 6-12). pap. 12.99 *(978-0-486-49159-2(5))* Dover Pubns., Inc.

Mattox, Brenda Sneathen & Paper Dolls for Grownups Staff. Fashion Fads Paper Dolls. 2012. (Dover Paper Dolls Ser.). (ENG., Illus.). 32p. (gr. 3-5). pap. 9.99 *(978-0-486-48704-5(0))* Dover Pubns., Inc.

May, Darcy. Fairy of the Seasons. 2004. (Dover Little Activity Books Paper Dolls Ser.). (ENG., Illus.). 4p. (J). (gr. 1-4). 1.50 *(978-0-486-43312-7(9))* Dover Pubns., Inc.

—Glitter Christmas Fairy Sticker Paper Doll. 2008. (Dover Little Activity Books Paper Dolls Ser.). (ENG., Illus.). 2p. (J). (gr. 1-4). 1.99 *(978-0-486-46536-4(5))* Dover Pubns., Inc.

Mayer, Kirsten. Meet the Ghouls Character Guidebook. 2014. (ENG., Illus.). 96p. (J). (gr. 3-7). 9.99 *(978-0-316-28361-8(4))* Little, Brown Bks. for Young Readers.

McElwee, Renee. Goddesses Paper Dolls. 2013. (Dover Paper Dolls Ser.). (ENG.). 32p. (J). (gr. 3-5). pap. 9.99 *(978-0-486-49000-7(9))* Dover Pubns., Inc.

Menten, Ted. Paper Doll Design Studio. 2013. (Dover Paper Dolls Ser.). (ENG.). 48p. (J). (gr. 2-5). pap. 9.99 *(978-0-486-49004-5(1))* Dover Pubns., Inc.

Miller, Eileen Rudisill. Dream Wedding Paper Dolls with Glitter! 2016. (Dover Paper Dolls Ser.). (ENG.). 32p. (J). (gr. k-3). pap. 12.99 *(978-0-486-80122-3(5))* Dover Pubns., Inc.

—Fairy Paper Doll. 2010. (Dover Paper Dolls Ser.). (ENG.). 16p. (J). (gr. 1-5). pap. 4.99 *(978-0-486-47680-3(4))* Dover Pubns., Inc.

—Glitter Rapunzel Sticker Paper Doll. 2013. (Dover Little Activity Books Paper Dolls Ser.). (ENG.). 2p. (J). (gr. 1-4). pap. 1.50 *(978-0-486-49948-2(0))* Dover Pubns., Inc.

—Glitter Sleeping Beauty Sticker Paper Doll. 2013. (Dover Little Activity Books Paper Dolls Ser.). (ENG.). 2p. (J). (gr. 1-4). pap. 1.50 *(978-0-486-49970-3(7))* Dover Pubns., Inc.

—Glitter Snow Queen Sticker Paper Doll. 2014. (Dover Little Activity Books Paper Dolls Ser.). (ENG.). 2p. (J). (gr. 1-4). pap. 1.99 *(978-0-486-78171-6(2))* Dover Pubns., Inc.

—Glitter Snow White Sticker Paper Doll. 2013. (Dover Little Activity Books Stickers Ser.). (ENG.). 2p. (J). (gr. 1-4). pap. 1.50 *(978-0-486-49975-8(8))* Dover Pubns., Inc.

—Jane Austen Paper Dolls: Four Classic Characters. 2014. (ENG., Illus.). 32p. (gr. 4). pap. 9.99 *(978-0-486-49222-3(2))* Dover Pubns., Inc.

—KATE: the Duchess of Cambridge Paper Dolls. 2014. (Dover Paper Dolls Ser.). (ENG.). 32p. (gr. 3-6). pap. 9.99 *(978-0-486-78073-3(2))* Dover Pubns., Inc.

Mingo, Norman. Alice Faye Paper Dolls: Glamorous Movie Star Paper Dolls & Costumes. Mingo, Norman & Ernst, Clara, illus. 2007. 8p. pap. 12.00 *(978-0-9795053-0-0(5))* Paper Studio Pr.

—Bette Davis Paper Dolls. Taliadoros, Jenny, ed. Mingo, Norman & Ernst, Clara, illus. 2007. (ENG.). 16p. pap. 12.00 *(978-0-9790668-2-5(4))* Paper Studio Pr.

—Deanna Durbin Paper Dolls. Mingo, Norman & Ernt, Clara, illus. 2007. 16p. pap. 12.00 *(978-0-9790668-5-6(9))* Paper Studio Pr.

—Navy Scouts Paper Dolls. Taliadoros, Jenny, ed. Mingo, Norman & Ernst, Clara, illus. 2007. (ENG.). 16p. pap. 12.00 *(978-0-9790668-3-2(2))* Paper Studio Pr.

—Rita Hayworth Paper Dolls. Taliadoros, Jenny, ed. Mingo, Norman & Ernst, Clara, illus. 2006. 16p. pap. 12.00 *(978-0-9790668-0-1(8))* Paper Studio Pr.

Nystrom, Gregg. Golden Age of Hollywood Paper Dolls with Glitter! 2013. (Dover Paper Dolls Ser.). (ENG.). 32p. (gr. 7-4). pap. 10.95 *(978-0-486-49043-4(2))* Dover Pubns., Inc.

Parot, Annelore, illus. Kokeshi Style: Design Your Own Kokeshi Fashions. 2012. (ENG.). 120p. 14.99 *(978-1-4521-1372-2(6))* Chronicle Bks. LLC.

Princess Sweetwater Paper Doll. 2006. 24p. (J). pap. *(978-0-9762071-0-8(9),* 371-010) Big City Publishing.

Reinckens, Sunnhild. Making Dolls, 1 vol. 2nd rev. ed. 2003. (ENG., Illus.). 80p. pap. 15.95 *(978-0-86315-415-7(8))* Floris Bks. GBR. Dist: SteinerBooks, Inc.

Ross, Kathy. Things to Make for Your Doll. Garvin, Elaine, illus. (Girl Crafts Ser.). 48p. 2005. (ENG.). (J). lib. bdg. 26.60 *(978-0-7613-2861-2(0),* Millbrook Pr.) 2003. (J). (gr. k-2). pap. 7.95 *(978-0-7613-1781-4(3),* First Avenue Editions) Lerner Publishing Group.

Schiffer, Nancy N. Contemporary Hopi Kachina Dolls, 1 vol. 2003. (ENG., Illus.). 208p. (gr. 10-13). 39.95 *(978-0-7643-1848-1(9),* 9780764318481) Schiffer Publishing, Ltd.

Schmitz, Mark. Manga Paper Dolls. 2013. (Dover Paper Dolls Ser.). (ENG.). 32p. (J). (gr. 3-8). pap. 7.99 *(978-0-486-49967-3(7))* Dover Pubns., Inc.

Slater, Lee. Barbie Developer: Ruth Handler, 1 vol. 2016. (Toy Trailblazers Ser.). (ENG., Illus.). 32p. (J). (gr. 3-6). lib. bdg. 27.07 *(978-1-62403-974-4(X),* Checkerboard Library) ABDO Publishing Co.

Stardoll. Stardoll: Sticker Red Carpet Dress Up. 2013. (Stardoll Ser.). (ENG.). 24p. (J). (gr. 2-4). pap. 6.99 *(978-0-85751-178-2(5))* Transworld Publishers Ltd. GBR. Dist: Independent Pubs. Group.

—Sticker Catwalk Dress Up. 2013. (Stardoll Ser.). (ENG.). 24p. (J). (gr. 2-4). pap. 6.99 *(978-0-85751-176-8(9))* Transworld Publishers Ltd. GBR. Dist: Independent Pubs. Group.

Steadman, Barbara. Storybook Princess. 2004. (Dover Little Activity Books Paper Dolls Ser.). (ENG., Illus.). 4p. (J). (gr. k-3). pap. 1.50 *(978-0-486-43726-2(4))* Dover Pubns., Inc.

—Sweet Valentine. 2004. (Dover Little Activity Books Paper Dolls Ser.). (ENG., Illus.). 4p. (J). (gr. -1-5). pap. 1.50 *(978-0-486-43751-4(5))* Dover Pubns., Inc.

Stillerman, Robbie. Ballerina Friends Sticker Paper Dolls. 2008. (Dover Little Activity Books Paper Dolls Ser.). (ENG., Illus.). 4p. (J). (gr. k-3). pap. 1.99 *(978-0-486-46574-6(8))* Dover Pubns., Inc.

—Little King & Queen Sticker Paper Dolls. 2003. (Dover Little Activity Books Paper Dolls Ser.). (ENG., Illus.). 4p. (J). (gr. -1-5). pap. 1.50 *(978-0-486-42631-0(9))* Dover Pubns., Inc.

—Wendy Works Out Sticker Paper Doll. 2003. (Dover Little Activity Books Paper Dolls Ser.). (ENG., Illus.). 4p. (J). (gr. -1-5). 1.50 *(978-0-486-42632-7(7))* Dover Pubns., Inc.

Sun, Ming-Ju. Flower Fashion Fantasies Paper Dolls. 2014. (Dover Paper Dolls Ser.). (ENG.). 32p. (gr. 3). pap. 9.99 *(978-0-486-49265-2(2))* Dover Pubns., Inc.

—Traditional Japanese Fashions Paper Dolls. 2003. (Dover Paper Dolls Ser.). (ENG., Illus.). 32p. (J). (gr. 3-8). pap. 6.95 *(978-0-486-42654-9(8))* Dover Pubns., Inc.

Swanson, Maggie & Paper Dolls. Lucky Cats. 2012. (Dover Paper Dolls Ser.). (ENG., Illus.). 32p. (gr. 3-5). pap. 9.99 *(978-0-486-48682-6(6))* Dover Pubns., Inc.

Taliadoros, Jenny, ed. Doris Day Paper Dolls. 2007. (ENG., Illus.). 16p. pap. 12.00 *(978-0-9790668-4-9(0))* Paper Studio Pr.

—The Lollypop Crowd Stand-up Paper Dolls. 2007. (Illus.). 8p. pap. 12.00 *(978-0-9795053-1-7(3))* Paper Studio Pr.

Tierney, Tom. The Dalai Lama Paper Doll. 2006. (Dover Paper Dolls Ser.). (ENG., Illus.). 32p. (gr. 7-8). pap. 6.95 *(978-0-486-45181-7(X))* Dover Pubns., Inc.

—Famous Movie Dance Stars Paper Dolls. 2009. (Dover Celebrity Paper Dolls Ser.). (ENG., Illus.). 32p. (J). (gr. 3-8). pap. 6.99 *(978-0-486-46758-0(9))* Dover Pubns., Inc.

—Ferdinand & Isabella Paper Dolls. 2004. (Dover Royal Paper Dolls Ser.). (ENG., Illus.). 16p. (gr. 3-8). pap. 4.95 *(978-0-486-43345-5(5))* Dover Pubns., Inc.

—Givenchy Paper Dolls. 2013. (Dover Paper Dolls Ser.). (ENG.). 32p. (J). (gr. 6-12). pap. 9.99 *(978-0-486-49959-8(6))* Dover Pubns., Inc.

—Great Costumes from Classic Movies Paper Dolls: 30 Fashions by Adrian, Edith Head, Walter Plunkett & Others. 2003. (Dover Paper Dolls Ser.). (ENG., Illus.). 32p. (gr. 8-8). pap. 6.95 *(978-0-486-42772-0(2))* Dover Pubns., Inc.

—Mae West Paper Doll. 2005. (Dover Celebrity Paper Dolls Ser.). (ENG., Illus.). 32p. (J). (gr. 7-8). pap. 5.95 *(978-0-486-44099-6(0))* Dover Pubns., Inc.

—Mexican Folk Dance Paper Dolls. 2013. (Dover Paper Dolls Ser.). (ENG.). 32p. (gr. 3-8). pap. 9.99 *(978-0-486-48831-8(4))* Dover Pubns., Inc.

—Michelle Obama Paper Dolls. 2014. (Dover Paper Dolls Ser.). (ENG.). 32p. (gr. 3). pap. 9.99 *(978-0-486-49330-5(X))* Dover Pubns., Inc.

—Nelson Mandela Paper Dolls. 2014. (ENG.). 32p. (gr. 3-8). pap. 9.99 *(978-0-486-78573-8(4))* Dover Pubns., Inc.

C
D

—Southern Belle Ball Gowns Paper Dolls. 2006. (Dover Paper Dolls Ser.). (ENG., Illus.). 32p. (gr. 3-8). per. 6.95 *(978-0-486-45365-1(0))* Dover Pubns., Inc.
—Ziegfeld Girls Paper Dolls. 2004. (Dover Paper Dolls Ser.). (ENG., Illus.). 32p. (J). (gr. 6). pap. 5.95 *(978-0-486-43679-1(9))* Dover Pubns., Inc.
Tierney, Tom, illus. Life's a Drag! Paper Dolls. 2012. (Dover Celebrity Paper Dolls Ser.). (ENG.). 32p. (gr. 7-8). pap. 9.99 *(978-0-486-48313-9(4))* Dover Pubns., Inc.
Tierney, Tom & Paper Dolls for Grownups Staff. Betty Grable Paper Dolls. 2012. (Dover Celebrity Paper Dolls Ser.). (ENG.). 32p. (J). (gr. 3-5). pap. 9.99 *(978-0-486-47248-5(5))* Dover Pubns., Inc.
Tierney, Tom, et al. Award-Winning Fashions of Edith Head Paper Dolls. 2014. (ENG.). 32p. (J). (gr. 6-6). pap. 9.99 *(978-0-486-49626-9(0))* Dover Pubns., Inc.
The Trend-Setters: Paper Doll Cut-Out Book. 2006. (J). pap. 8.95 *(978-0-9787319-2-2(1))* Kolluri, Alina M.
Valliant, Regina. Judy Garland Cut-Out Dolls. Valliant, Regina & Lunzer, Lee, illus. 2007. (ENG.). 16p. pap. 12.00 *(978-0-9790668-9-4(1))* Paper Studio Pr.
Ventura, Charles. Paper Dolls in the Style of Mucha. 2012. (Dover Paper Dolls Ser.). (ENG., Illus.). 32p. (J). (gr. 6-8). pap. 9.99 *(978-0-486-47921-7(8))* Dover Pubns., Inc.
Walter Foster Creative Team & Burrell, Norma J. Paper Dolls Fashion Workshop: More Than 40 Inspiring Designs, Projects & Ideas for Creating Your Own Paper Doll Fashions. 2016. (Walter Foster Studio Ser.). (ENG.). 128p. (J). (gr. 5-9). pap. 16.95 *(978-1-63322-165-9(2),* Walter Foster) Quarto Publishing Group USA.
Zourelias, Diana. Celebrity Parents, Celebrity Kids Paper Dolls. 2010. (Dover Celebrity Paper Dolls Ser.). (ENG., Illus.). 32p. (gr. 3-3). pap. 9.99 *(978-0-486-47740-4(1))* Dover Pubns., Inc.

DOLLS—FICTION

Ackelsberg, Amy. The Sweetest Friends. 2013. (Lalaloopsy Ser.). (ENG., Illus.). 24p. (J). (gr. -1-3). 4.99 *(978-0-545-53366-9(X))* Scholastic, Inc.
Alvarado, I. J. The Adventures of Saleiah & Emm: Book 1. Zacker, Sandi, illus. 2009. 16p. pap. 11.99 *(978-1-4490-0515-3(2))* AuthorHouse.
Ashley, Brook, et al. The Lonely Doll Makes New Friends. 2006. (ENG., Illus.). 44p. per. 17.99 *(978-1-4257-0410-0(7))* Xlibris Corp.
Augustin, Yvonne. Rag Doll Tales. 2012. 70p. pap. 13.99 *(978-0-9858398-8-8(0))* Mindstir Media.
Austin, Rikey. Tilly & the Magic Wand: Alice's Bear Shop. 2012. 28p. pap. *(978-1-78092-146-4(2))* MX Publishing, Ltd.
Bailey, Wendy R. Mary the Doll. 2012. 66p. pap. 24.99 *(978-1-300-18820-9(0))* Lulu Pr., Inc.
Barchers, Suzanne I. Get to Bed, Ren!, 1 vol. 2011. (Targeted Phonics Ser.). (ENG.). 16p. (J). (gr. k-2). pap. 5.99 *(978-1-4333-2416-1(4))* Teacher Created Materials, Inc.
Barr, Bitsy. Zock's Adventures: Just for Boys ... 2010. 40p. pap. 16.99 *(978-1-4490-5880-7(9))* AuthorHouse.
—Zock's Counting Book. 2013. (Illus.). 40p. pap. 16.00 *(978-1-300-51038-3(2))* Lulu Pr., Inc.
Batkhuu, Kh. The Doll That Flew Away. Myagmardorj, Enkhtungalag, illus. 2007. 32p. (J). (POL & ENG.). pap. 12.95 *(978-1-60195-098-7(5));* (ARA & ENG.). pap. 12.95 *(978-1-60195-092-5(6))* International Step by Step Assn.
Bauer, Marion Dane. The Red Ghost. Ferguson, Peter, illus. 2009. (Stepping Stone Book Ser.). (ENG.). 96p. (J). (gr. 1-4). 4.99 *(978-0-375-84082-1(6),* Random Hse. Bks. for Young Readers) Random Hse. Children's Bks.
Baxter, Nicola. My Perfect Doll's House: Peek Inside the 3D Windows. Chaffey, Samantha, illus. 2013. (ENG.). 12p. (J). (gr. k-4). 16.99 *(978-1-84322-924-7(2),* Armadillo) Anness Publishing GBR. Dist: National Bk. Network.
Bell, Alex. Frozen Charlotte. 2016. (ENG.). 304p. (J). (gr. 7). 18.99 *(978-0-545-94108-2(3),* Scholastic Pr.) Scholastic, Inc.
Black, Holly. Doll Bones. Wheeler, Eliza, illus. 2013. (ENG.). 256p. (J). (gr. 5-9). 18.99 *(978-1-4169-6398-1(7),* McElderry, Margaret K. Bks.) McElderry, Margaret K. Bks.
—Doll Bones. 2015. lib. bdg. 18.40 *(978-0-606-36308-2(4))* Turtleback Bks.
Bridges, Eunice. A Day Like Mine. Goodwin, Adrienne Annette, illus. 2011. 32p. pap. 24.95 *(978-1-4560-5766-4(9))* America Star Bks.
Brooke, Samantha. Princess Parade. movie tie-in ed. 2013. (Lalaloopsy Ser.). (ENG., Illus.). 24p. (J). (gr. -1-3). 3.99 *(978-0-545-58126-4(5))* Scholastic, Inc.
—Welcome to Lalaloopsy Land. 2011. (Lalaloopsy Ser.). (ENG.). 16p. (J). (gr. -1-3). pap. 6.99 *(978-0-545-37999-1(7))* Scholastic, Inc.
Brown, Marc. Arthur in New York. 2008. (Step into Reading Ser.). (ENG., Illus.). 24p. (J). (gr. k-3). pap. 3.99 *(978-0-375-82976-5(8),* Random Hse. Bks. for Young Readers) Random Hse. Children's Bks.
Burnett, Frances Hodgson. The Racketty-Packetty House. Halperin, Wendy Anderson, illus. 100th anniv. ed. 2006. (ENG.). 96p. (J). (gr. 4-7). 21.99 *(978-0-689-86974-7(6),* Simon & Schuster Bks. For Young Readers) Simon & Schuster Bks. For Young Readers.
—The Racketty-Packetty House. 2006. 128p. per. 12.45 *(978-1-59462-419-3(4),* 455, Book Jungle) Standard Pubns., Inc.
—RackettyPacketty House. l.t. ed. 2006. 52p. pap. *(978-1-84637-262-9(3))* Echo Library.
Calvani, Mayra. A Bad Mad Sad Day for Mama Bear. Snider, K. C., illus. 2013. 24p. 19.95 *(978-1-61633-434-5(7))* Guardian Angel Publishing, Inc.
Canale, Allison. Ella & the Worry Doll. Lefebure, Ingrid, illus. 2013. (ENG.). (J). (gr. -1-3). 14.95 *(978-1-62086-332-9(4))* Mascot Bks., Inc.
Cecil, Lauren. Harmony Takes the Stage. 2013. (Lalaloopsy Ser.). (ENG.). 24p. (J). (gr. -1-3). pap. 3.99 *(978-0-545-53180-1(2))* Math Solutions.
—Lalaloopsy: Cinder Slippers & the Grand Ball. Hill, Prescott, illus. 2013. (Lalaloopsy Ser.). (ENG.). 24p. (J). (gr. -1-3). pap. 3.99 *(978-0-545-47769-7(7))* Scholastic, Inc.
—Lalaloopsy: Here Come the Little Sisters! Hill, Prescott, illus. 2013. (Lalaloopsy Ser.). (ENG.). 5p. (J). (gr. -1-k). bds. 9.99 *(978-0-545-44266-4(4))* Scholastic, Inc.
—Lalaloopsy: Lala-Oopsies: Meet the Lala-Oopsies. 2013. (ENG.). 24p. (J). (gr. -1-3). pap. 3.99 *(978-0-545-57224-8(X))* Scholastic, Inc.
Cheney, Cora. The Doll of Lilac Valley. Cassidy, Nancy White, illus. 2003. 128p. 11.95 *(978-0-9714612-5-3(2))* Green Mansion Pr. LLC.
Christiansen, Sue. Zoey. 2012. 20p. pap. 17.99 *(978-1-4772-6019-7(6))* AuthorHouse.
Church, Alfred J. Three Greek Children. 2008. (Illus.). 160p. pap. 9.95 *(978-1-59915-081-9(6))* Yesterday's Classics.
Chyle, Bonnie. Our Pet Show. 2008. 28p. pap. 24.95 *(978-1-60474-391-3(3))* PublishAmerica, Inc.
Cohen, Leah. Sophie. 2010. 24p. 11.49 *(978-1-4520-1854-6(5))* AuthorHouse.
Cohen, Marina. The Doll's Eye. 2017. (ENG.). 208p. (J). 16.99 *(978-1-62672-204-0(8),* 9781626722040) Roaring Brook Pr.
Conrad. The Tub People. Date not set. 32p. (J). 16.99 *(978-0-694-00604-5(1),* HarperFestival) HarperCollins Pubs.
Las Cosas Del Jardin. (SPA.). 24p. 7.95 *(978-84-488-1109-9(7))* Beascoa, Ediciones S.A. ESP. Dist: Distribooks, Inc.
Las Cosas Del Salon. (SPA.). 24p. 7.95 *(978-84-488-1108-2(9))* Beascoa, Ediciones S.A. ESP. Dist: Distribooks, Inc.
Cowley, Joy. Miss Doll & Friends: A Surprise for Miss Doll. Bordicchia, Gaia, illus. 2014. (ENG.). 8p. pap. *(978-0-927244-52-7(7),* Joy Cowley Club) Flying Start Bks.
—Miss Doll & Friends: Bad Manners. 2014. (ENG., Illus.). 8p. pap. *(978-0-927244-53-4(5),* Joy Cowley Club) Flying Start Bks.
—Miss Doll & Friends: Miss Doll Is Missing. 2014. (ENG., Illus.). 8p. pap. *(978-0-927244-58-9(6),* Joy Cowley Club) Flying Start Bks.
—Miss Doll & Friends: Miss Doll Is Missing BIG BOOK EDITION. 2014. (ENG., Illus.). 8p. pap. *(978-0-927244-67-1(5),* Joy Cowley Club) Flying Start Bks.
—Miss Doll & Friends: Old Jokes. Bordicchia, Gaia, illus. 2014. (ENG.). 8p. pap. *(978-0-927244-60-2(8),* Joy Cowley Club) Flying Start Bks.
—Miss Doll & Friends: Panda¿s Tummy. 2014. (ENG., Illus.). 8p. pap. *(978-0-927244-51-0(9),* Joy Cowley Club) Flying Start Bks.
—Miss Doll & Friends: Panda¿s Tummy BIG BOOK EDITION. 2014. (ENG., Illus.). 8p. pap. *(978-0-927244-68-8(3),* Joy Cowley Club) Flying Start Bks.
—Miss Doll & Friends: Pelican¿s Balloon. 2014. (ENG., Illus.). 8p. pap. *(978-0-927244-54-1(3),* Joy Cowley Club) Flying Start Bks.
—Miss Doll & Friends: Pelican's Balloon BIG BOOK EDITION. 2014. (ENG., Illus.). 8p. pap. *(978-0-927244-66-4(7),* Joy Cowley Club) Flying Start Bks.
—Miss Doll & Friends: Red Lipstick. Bordicchia, Gaia, illus. 2014. (ENG.). 8p. pap. *(978-0-927244-78-7(0),* Joy Cowley Club) Flying Start Bks.
—Miss Doll & Friends: Rocking Race. Bordicchia, Gaia, illus. 2014. (ENG.). 8p. pap. *(978-0-927244-64-0(0),* Joy Cowley Club) Flying Start Bks.
—Miss Doll & Friends: The New Toy. 2014. (ENG., Illus.). 8p. pap. *(978-0-927244-61-9(6),* Joy Cowley Club) Flying Start Bks.
—Miss Doll & Friends: The Rainbow Bird. Bordicchia, Gaia, illus. 2014. (ENG.). 8p. pap. *(978-0-927244-65-7(9),* Joy Cowley Club) Flying Start Bks.
—Miss Doll & Friends: Tin Clown. Bordicchia, Gaia, illus. 2014. (ENG.). 8p. pap. *(978-0-927244-55-8(1),* Joy Cowley Club) Flying Start Bks.
—Miss Doll & Friends: Tin Clown¿s Hat. Bordicchia, Gaia, illus. 2014. (ENG.). 8p. pap. *(978-0-927244-79-4(9),* Joy Cowley Club) Flying Start Bks.
—Miss Doll & Friends: Toy Music. Bordicchia, Gaia, illus. 2014. (ENG.). 8p. pap. *(978-0-927244-59-6(4),* Joy Cowley Club) Flying Start Bks.
—Miss Doll & Friends: Where Is Fire Engine? Bordicchia, Gaia, illus. 2014. (ENG.). 8p. pap. *(978-0-927244-57-2(8),* Joy Cowley Club) Flying Start Bks.
—Miss Doll & Friends: Yellow Duck. Bordicchia, Gaia, illus. 2014. (ENG.). 8p. pap. *(978-0-927244-62-6(4),* Joy Cowley Club) Flying Start Bks.
Criss, Lisa. You Can't Teach a Doll How to Fish! 2008. 36p. per. 24.95 *(978-1-4241-9359-2(1))* America Star Bks.
Cuno, Sabine. Abre, Cierra y Aprende! Caballero, D., tr. Senner, Katja, illus. 2007. 14p. (J). (gr. -1). *(978-970-718-489-3(2),* Silver Dolphin en Español) Advanced Marketing, S. de R. L. de C. V.
Cushman, Jean, et al. Little Golden Book Mommy Stories. Wilkin, Eloise & Meisel, Paul, illus. 2015. (Little Golden Book Favorites Ser.). (ENG.). 80p. (J). (-k). 6.99 *(978-0-385-39273-0(7),* Golden Bks.) Random Hse. Children's Bks.
Dahl, Michael. The Doll That Waved Goodbye: And Other Scary Tales. Bonet, Xavier, illus. 2015. (Michael Dahl's Really Scary Stories Ser.). (ENG.). 72p. (gr. 2-3). lib. bdg. 25.32 *(978-1-4965-0595-8(6))* Stone Arch Bks.
Dahl, Michael. The Girl in the Graveyard: And Other Scary Tales. Bonet, Xavier, illus. 2017. (Michael Dahl's Really Scary Stories Ser.). (ENG.). 72p. (gr. 2-3). lib. bdg. 25.32 ***(978-1-4965-4901-3(5))*** Stone Arch Bks.
Davidson, Susanna. Stories of Dolls. Wanert, Amandine, illus. 2006. 48p. (J). (gr. 2-5). 8.99 *(978-0-7945-1327-6(1),* Usborne) EDC Publishing.
—Usborne Stories of Dolls & Fairies. Wanert, Amandine, illus. 2007. (Usborne Ser.). 96p. (J). 9.99 *(978-0-7945-1779-3(X),* Usborne) EDC Publishing.
DeBellis, Thea. Miss Anne & Her Doll Collection. 2004. pap. 8.00 *(978-0-8059-6407-3(X))* Dorrance Publishing Co., Inc.
Dennett, Kathleen. The 4 Corners Mystery. 2008. 32p. pap. 24.95 *(978-1-4137-2603-9(8))* America Star Bks.
Devany, Betsy. Lucy's Lovey. Denise, Christopher, illus. 2016. (ENG.). 40p. (J). 17.99 *(978-1-62779-147-2(7),* 9781627791472, Holt, Henry & Co. Bks. For Young Readers) Holt, Henry & Co.
Dillard, Mary Gregory. Finding Betsyanna. 2006. (ENG.). 48p. per. 16.95 *(978-1-4241-5492-0(8))* America Star Bks.
Disney Press Editors. Peaches Pie, Take a Bath! 2015. (World of Reading Ser.). (J). lib. bdg. 13.55 *(978-0-606-36900-8(7))* Turtleback Bks.
Dracker, Pune. Doll & Teddy Bear Activity Book. Bart, Kathleen & Hofmann, Ginnie, illus. 2005. 96p. (J). pap. *(978-1-932485-24-0(4))* Reverie Publishing Co.
Dreamworks Animation Publishing, LLC. Olivia Paper Dolls. Kurtz, John, illus. 2015. (Dover Paper Dolls Ser.). (ENG.). 24p. (J). (gr. 2-5). 9.99 *(978-0-486-80278-7(7))* Dover Pubns., Inc.
—Olivia Sticker Paper Doll. Kurtz, John, illus. 2015. (Dover Little Activity Books Stickers Ser.). (ENG.). 4p. (J). (gr. 2-5). 1.99 *(978-0-486-80277-0(9))* Dover Pubns., Inc.
Earl, Janice. Jan Has a Doll. Tusa, Tricia, illus. 2005. (Green Light Readers Level 1 Ser.). (ENG.). 24p. (J). (gr. -1-3). pap. 3.95 *(978-0-15-205167-9(8))* Houghton Mifflin Harcourt Publishing Co.
Emily Reed-Guldin, Reed-Guldin & Emily Reed-Guldin. Sarah & Sammi's Playhouse Bedroom. 2009. 32p. pap. 14.49 *(978-1-4389-5881-1(1))* AuthorHouse.
Fatio, Louise. A Doll for Marie. Duvoisin, Roger, illus. 2015. (ENG.). 32p. (J). (gr. -1-2). 16.99 *(978-0-385-75596-2(1),* Knopf Bks. for Young Readers) Random Hse. Children's Bks.
Feierabend, John M. Momma, Buy Me a China Doll. Norton, Allyssa, illus. 2017. (First Steps in Music Ser.). (ENG.). 32p. (J). (— 1). 16.95 ***(978-1-62277-226-1(1))*** G I A Pubns., Inc.
Ferguson, Sarah & Duchess of York Staff. Little Red's Autumn Adventure. Williams, Sam, illus. 2009. (ENG.). 40p. (J). (gr. -1-1). 16.99 *(978-0-689-84341-9(0),* Simon & Schuster/Paula Wiseman Bks.) Simon & Schuster/Paula Wiseman Bks.
—Little Red's Christmas Story. Williams, Sam, illus. 2011. (ENG.). 40p. (J). (gr. -1-2). pap. 19.99 *(978-1-4424-3076-1(1),* Simon & Schuster/Paula Wiseman Bks.) Simon & Schuster/Paula Wiseman Bks.
—Little Red's Summer Adventure. Williams, Sam, illus. 2006. (ENG.). 40p. (J). (gr. -1-3). 17.99 *(978-0-689-85562-7(1),* Simon & Schuster/Paula Wiseman Bks.) Simon & Schuster/Paula Wiseman Bks.
Ferrante, Elena. The Beach at Night. Goldstein, Ann, tr. from ITA. Cerri, Mara, illus. 2016. (ENG.). 38p. 13.00 *(978-1-60945-370-1(0))* Europa Editions, Inc.
Ford, Lorry. Goodnight Red: A Lesson in Courage. 2007. 20p. per. 12.90 *(978-1-4343-0477-3(9))* AuthorHouse.
—Goodnight Red: A Lesson in Courage, 1 vol. 2009. 15p. pap. 24.95 *(978-1-61582-421-2(9))* PublishAmerica, Inc.
Gates, Josephine Scribner. The April fool Doll. Keep, Virginia, illus. 2007. 152p. (J). lib. bdg. 59.00 *(978-1-60304-009-9(9))* Dollworks.
—Captain Billie: Leads the way to the land of I don't want To. Sichel, Harold, illus. 2007. 96p. (J). lib. bdg. 59.00 *(978-1-60304-019-8(6))* Dollworks.
—The dolls in Fairyland. Keep, Virginia, illus. 2007. 136p. (J). lib. bdg. 59.00 *(978-1-60304-013-6(7))* Dollworks.
—Little girl Blue: Lives in the woods till she learns to say Please. Keep, Virginia, illus. 2007. 54p. (J). lib. bdg. 59.00 *(978-1-60304-012-9(9))* Dollworks.
—Little Girl Blue plays I Spy. 2007. (Illus.). 64p. (J). lib. bdg. 59.00 *(978-1-60304-017-4(X))* Dollworks.
—Little red white & Blue. Keep, Virginia, illus. 2007. 118p. (J). lib. bdg. 59.00 *(978-1-60304-006-8(4))* Dollworks.
—The Live Doll Series, 4 vols., 9bks. 2006. (Illus.). (YA). lib. bdg. 349.00 *(978-0-9760064-4-2(8))* Dollworks.
—The live dolls' busy Days. Keep, Virginia, illus. 2007. 106p. (J). lib. bdg. 59.00 *(978-1-60304-007-5(2))* Dollworks.
—The live dolls' house Party. Keep, Virginia, illus. 2007. 104p. (J). lib. bdg. 59.00 *(978-1-60304-005-1(6))* Dollworks.
—The live dolls in Wonderland. Keep, Virginia, illus. 2007. 150p. (J). lib. bdg. 59.00 *(978-1-60304-015-0(3))* Dollworks.
—The live dolls' play Days. Keep, Virginia, illus. 2007. 110p. (J). lib. bdg. 59.00 *(978-1-60304-008-2(0))* Dollworks.
—More about live Dolls. Keep, Virginia, illus. 2007. 106p. (J). lib. bdg. 59.00 *(978-1-60304-002-0(1))* Dollworks.
—Nannette & the baby Monkey. 2007. (Illus.). 50p. (J). lib. bdg. 59.00 *(978-1-60304-020-4(X))* Dollworks.
—Nannette goes to visit her Grandmother. 2007. (J). lib. bdg. 59.00 *(978-1-60304-021-1(8))* Dollworks.
—One day in Betty¿s Life. Stuart, B. S., illus. 2007. 58p. (J). lib. bdg. 59.00 *(978-1-60304-018-1(8))* Dollworks.
—The secret of the live Dolls. Archibald, A. L., illus. 2007. (J). lib. bdg. 59.00 *(978-1-60304-024-2(2))* Dollworks.
—The Story of Live Dolls: Being an account by Josephine Scribner Gates of how, on a certian June morning, all of the dolls in the Cloverdale came Alive. Keep, Virginia, illus. 2007. 102p. (J). lib. bdg. 59.00 *(978-1-60304-001-3(3))* Dollworks.
—The Story of Live Dolls: Being an Account of How, on a Certain June Morning. unabr. ed. 2012. (Illus.). 104p. 39.99 *(978-1-4622-8158-9(3))* Repressed Publishing LLC.
—The story of the lost Doll. Keep, Virginia, illus. 2007. 108p. (J). lib. bdg. 59.00 *(978-1-60304-003-7(X))* Dollworks.
—The Story of the three Dolls. Keep, Virginia, illus. 2007. 148p. (J). lib. bdg. 59.00 *(978-1-60304-004-4(8))* Dollworks.
—Sunshine Annie. Cory, Fanny Y., illus. 2007. 148p. (J). lib. bdg. 59.00 *(978-1-60304-011-2(0))* Dollworks.
—Tommy Sweet-Tooth & Little girl Blue. Churbuck, Esther V., illus. 2007. 64p. (J). lib. bdg. 59.00 *(978-1-60304-014-3(5))* Dollworks.
—The Turkey Doll. Flass, E. C., illus. 2007. 62p. (J). lib. bdg. 59.00 *(978-1-60304-016-7(1))* Dollworks.
Geddes, Anne. 10 en la Cama. 2005. (SPA & ENG.). 34p. 7.95 *(978-84-406-9855-1(0))* Ediciones B ESP. Dist: Independent Pubs. Group.
Gibson, Marley. The Discovery. 2011. (ENG.). 264p. (YA). (gr. 7-18). pap. 8.99 *(978-0-547-39308-7(3))* Houghton Mifflin Harcourt Publishing Co.
Gipson, Morrell. The Surprise Doll. Lerch, Steffie, illus. 2005. 46p. (J). (gr. -1-2). reprint ed. 15.00 *(978-1-930900-18-9(X))* Purple Hse. Pr.
Godden, Rumer. The Dolls' House. Ray, Jane, illus. 2017. (ENG.). 192p. (J). (gr. 2-6). pap. 8.99 ***(978-1-5098-3669-7(1))*** Pan Macmillan GBR. Dist: Independent Pubs. Group.
—The Dolls' House. 126p. (J). (gr. 3-5). pap. 4.99 *(978-0-8072-1408-4(6),* Listening Library) Random Hse. Audio Publishing Group.
—The Story of Holly & Ivy. Cooney, Barbara, illus. 2006. (ENG.). 32p. (J). (gr. k-3). 17.99 *(978-0-670-06219-5(7),* Viking Books for Young Readers) Penguin Young Readers Group.
Golden Books Staff. Barbie Loves Ballet/Fashion Show Fun!, 2 bks. in 1. Golden Books Staff, illus. 2009. (Pictureback(R) Ser.). (ENG., Illus.). 32p. (J). (gr. -1-2). pap. 4.99 *(978-0-375-85148-3(8),* Golden Bks.) Random Hse. Children's Bks.
Gorey, Edward & Chess, Victoria. Fletcher & Zenobia. Chess, Victoria, illus. 2016. (ENG., Illus.). 72p. (J). (gr. k-2). 14.95 *(978-1-59017-963-5(3),* NYR Children's Collection) New York Review of Bks., Inc., The.
Gruelle, Johnny. Raggedy Andy Stories. 2015. (ENG., Illus.). 96p. (J). (gr. k-3). pap. 9.99 *(978-0-486-79411-2(3))* Dover Pubns., Inc.
—Raggedy Ann & Andy: A Read-Aloud Treasury. 2005. (Raggedy Ann Ser.). (ENG., Illus.). 96p. (J). (gr. -1-3). 14.99 *(978-1-4169-0752-7(1),* Little Simon) Little Simon.
—Raggedy Ann & Andy & the Camel with the Wrinkled Knees. Moerbeek, Kees, illus. collector's ed. 2003. (Raggedy Ann Ser.). (ENG.). 14p. (J). (gr. -1-2). 29.99 *(978-0-689-85775-1(6),* Little Simon) Little Simon.
—Raggedy Ann & Rags. Palmer, Jan, illus. 2010. (Raggedy Ann Ser.). (ENG.). 40p. (J). (gr. -1-2). 19.99 *(978-1-4424-2198-1(3),* Simon & Schuster Bks. For Young Readers) Simon & Schuster Bks. For Young Readers.
—Raggedy Ann in Cookie Land: (Classic) Gruelle, Johnny, illus. 2010. (Raggedy Ann Ser.). (ENG., Illus.). 96p. (J). (gr. k-5). 21.99 *(978-1-4424-2199-8(1),* Simon & Schuster Bks. For Young Readers) Simon & Schuster Bks. For Young Readers.
—Raggedy Ann Stories. 2015. (ENG., Illus.). 96p. (J). (gr. k-3). pap. 9.99 *(978-0-486-79410-5(5))* Dover Pubns., Inc.
Haft, Sheryl. Baby Boo, I Love You. Massey, Jane, illus. 2017. (ENG.). 32p. (J). (-k). 16.99 *(978-0-399-54782-9(7),* Nancy Paulsen Books) Penguin Young Readers Group.
Hahn, Mary Downing. The Doll in the Garden: A Ghost Story. 2007. (ENG.). 144p. (J). (gr. 1-4). pap. 7.99 *(978-0-618-87315-9(5))* Houghton Mifflin Harcourt Publishing Co.
Haxhia, Miranda. The Dolls Nose. Kohler, Ursula, illus. 2007. 32p. (J). (POL & ENG.). pap. 16.95 *(978-1-60195-097-0(7));* (ARA & ENG.). pap. 16.95 *(978-1-60195-087-1(X))* International Step by Step Assn.
Haxhia, Miranda. The Doll's Nose. Kohrer, Ursula, illus. 2014. (ARA.). (J). ***(978-0-9856237-4-6(8))*** East West Discovery Pr.
Hayes-Knoll, Carolyn. Ista Cante. 2004. (Illus.). 32p. (J). *(978-0-9755646-6-0(8))* Westview Publishing Co., Inc.
Henkes, Kevin. Penny & Her Doll. Henkes, Kevin, illus. 2012. (Illus.). 32p. (J). (gr. -1-3). (ENG.). 12.99 *(978-0-06-208199-5(3));* lib. bdg. 14.89 *(978-0-06-208200-8(0))* HarperCollins Pubs. (Greenwillow Bks.).
—Penny & Her Doll. 2013. (I Can Read! Level 1 Ser.). (J). lib. bdg. 13.55 *(978-0-606-27147-9(3),* Turtleback) Turtleback Bks.
Herman, Alison & Grossman, Lynne. Dolly Goes on Vacation. Eve, Lealand, illus. 2007. 22p. (J). 24.95 *(978-0-9746153-2-5(3))* DMH Pr., Inc.
—Dolly Goes to the Beach. Eve, Lealand, illus. 2007. 24p. (J). 24.95 *(978-0-9746153-1-8(5))* DMH Pr., Inc.
—Dolly Goes to the Supermarket. Eve, Lealand, illus. 2007. 22p. (J). 24.96 *(978-0-9746153-0-1(7))* DMH Pr., Inc.
Hill, Eric. Spot's Christmas Plush Doll. Hill, Eric, illus. 2005. (Illus.). (J). 11.00 *(978-0-399-24472-8(7),* Putnam Juvenile) Penguin Publishing Group.
Hobbie, Holly. Fanny & Annabelle. 2009. (Fanny Ser.: 2). (ENG., Illus.). 40p. (J). (gr. -1-3). 16.99 *(978-0-316-16688-1(X))* Little, Brown Bks. for Young Readers.
Hoffmann, E. T. A. The Nutcracker & the Mouse King. Scheiner, A. & Wenckebach, L. W. R., illus. 2013. Orig. Title: Nutcracker & the King of the Mice. 88p. pap. *(978-1-909115-77-4(0))* Planet, The.
How, Barbara. My Friend: Beth. 2010. 52p. pap. 14.99 *(978-1-4269-4707-0(0))* Trafford Publishing.
Innovative Kids Staff. Sugar & Spice - Fashion Girls. Perrett, Lisa, illus. 2006. (ENG.). 10p. (J). (gr. -1-1). 19.99 *(978-1-58476-487-8(2),* IKIDS) Innovative Kids.
Irbinskas, Heather. The Lost Kachina. Albert, Robert & Anthis, Brian, illus. 2004. 32p. (J). 15.95 *(978-1-885772-33-6(5))* Kiva Publishing, Inc.
Itoh, Shimpei. Hyper Dolls. 2003. Vol. 4. 218p. pap. 15.95 *(978-1-929090-44-0(7))* Vol. 5. (Illus.). 208p. pap. 15.95 *(978-1-929090-67-9(6))* International Comics & Entertainment L.L.C.
James, Annabelle. Abigail's Bedtime. Beckes, Shirley, illus. 2004. (J). bds. 12.99 *(978-1-883043-53-7(0),* 6022) Straight Edge Pr., The.
Jane, Pamela. Noelle of the Nutcracker. Brett, Jan, illus. 2003. (ENG.). 64p. (J). (gr. 5-7). pap. 8.95 *(978-0-618-36922-5(8))* Houghton Mifflin Harcourt Publishing Co.
Jones, Debra. Christmas & the Little Dolls. Bullock Jr., Michael A., illus. 2011. 24p. pap. 24.95 *(978-1-4560-6679-6(X))* America Star Bks.
Jordan, Apple & RH Disney Staff. Barbie: On Your Toes. Wolcott, Karen, illus. 2005. (Step into Reading Ser.: No. 1). (ENG.). 32p. (J). (gr. -1-1). pap. 3.99 *(978-0-375-83142-3(8),* Random Hse. Bks. for Young Readers) Random Hse. Children's Bks.
Kane, Sharon. Little Mommy. Kane, Sharon, illus. 2008. (Little Golden Book Ser.). (ENG., Illus.). 24p. (J). (gr. -1-2). 4.99 *(978-0-375-84820-9(7),* Golden Bks.) Random Hse. Children's Bks.
Karpinski, David. Sarah's Christmas Presence. 2006. 58p. pap. 8.95 *(978-0-7414-3411-1(3))* Infinity Publishing.
Kawahara, Yumiko. Dolls, Vol. 2. Kawahara, Yumiko, illus. 2005. (Dolls Ser.: 2). (ENG., Illus.). 216p. pap. 9.99 *(978-1-59116-670-2(5))* Viz Media.
Keene, Carolyn. The Nancy Drew & the Clue Crew Collection: Sleepover Sleuths; Scream for Ice Cream; Pony Problems; the Cinderella Ballet Mystery; Case of the Sneaky Snowman. Pamintuan, Macky, illus. 2014. (Nancy Drew & the Clue Crew Ser.). (ENG.). 480p. (J). (gr. 1-4). pap. 29.99 *(978-1-4814-1472-2(0),* Aladdin) Simon & Schuster Children's Publishing.
—Sleepover Sleuths, 1 vol. Pamintuan, Macky, illus. 2007. (Nancy Drew & the Clue Crew Ser.). (ENG.). 81p. (gr. 1-4). 24.21 *(978-1-59961-348-2(4))* Spotlight.
—Time Thief. Pamintuan, Macky, illus. 2011. (Nancy Drew & the Clue Crew Ser.: 28). (ENG.). 96p. (J). (gr. 1-4). pap. 5.99 *(978-1-4169-9458-9(0),* Aladdin) Simon & Schuster Children's Publishing.

Knights, David. Stumpy the Tree. 2013. 28p. pap. 24.95 *(978-1-62709-375-0(3))* America Star Bks.

Kroll, Steven. The Hand-Me-Down Doll, 0 vols. Andreasen, Dan, illus. 2012. (ENG.). 40p. (J). (gr. k-3). 17.99 *(978-0-7614-6124-1(8),* 9780761461241, Amazon Children's Publishing) Amazon Publishing.

Kunhardt, Dorothy. Kitty's New Doll. 2004. (Little Golden Book Ser.). (ENG., Illus.). 24p. (J). (gr. -1-2). 3.99 *(978-0-375-82936-9(9),* Golden Bks.) Random Hse. Children's Bks.

Larson, Kirby. The Friendship Doll. 2012. (ENG.). 208p. (J). (gr. 4-7). 6.99 *(978-0-375-85089-9(9),* Yearling) Random Hse. Children's Bks.

Leijten, Aileen. Lint Boy. 2017. (ENG., Illus.). 128p. (J). (gr. 2-5). 16.99 *(978-0-544-52860-4(3))* Houghton Mifflin Harcourt Publishing Co.

Lemonade Zoo Monkeys. 2006. (Illus.). 33p. (YA). 10.95 *(978-0-9765321-2-5(3))* Taven Hill Studio.

Liberts, Jennifer. Baby Mcstuffins (Disney Junior: Doc Mcstuffins) RH Disney & Batson, Alan, illus. 2017. (Little Golden Book Ser.). (ENG.). 24p. (J). (-k). 4.99 *(978-0-7364-3567-3(0),* Golden/Disney) Random Hse. Children's Bks.

The live dolls' party Days. 2007. (Illus.). 160p. (J). lib. bdg. 59.00 *(978-1-60304-010-5(2))* Dollworks.

Luna, Danielle. Precious & Loved. 2011. 20p. pap. 24.95 *(978-1-4626-0281-0(9))* America Star Bks.

Lunn, Janet. Double Spell. 2003. (ENG.). 144p. (J). (gr. 3-7). pap. 8.95 *(978-0-88776-660-2(9),* Tundra Bks.) Tundra Bks. CAN. Dist: Penguin Random Hse. LLC.

Man-Kong, Mary. Learning to Save (Barbie) 2016. (Pictureback(R) Ser.). (ENG., Illus.). 16p. (J). (gr. -1-2). 4.99 *(978-0-553-53921-9(3),* Random Hse. Bks. for Young Readers) Random Hse. Children's Bks.

Martin, Ann M. & Godwin, Laura. The Doll People, Set. Selznick, Brian, illus. 2014. (Doll People Ser.: Bk. 1). (ENG.). 944p. (J). (gr. 3-7). pap. 24.99 *(978-1-4847-1299-3(4))* Hyperion Bks. for Children.

—The Doll People. Selznick, Brian, illus. 2003. (Doll People Ser.: Bk. 1). (ENG.). 288p. (J). (gr. 3-7). pap. 7.99 *(978-0-7868-1240-0(0))* Hyperion Pr.

—The Doll People. 2004. (Doll People Ser.: Bk. 1). 288p. (J). (gr. 3-7). pap. 37.00 incl. audio *(978-1-4000-9021-1(0),* Listening Library) Random Hse. Audio Publishing Group.

—The Doll People. Selznick, Brian, illus. pap. *(978-0-439-05648-9(9))* Scholastic, Inc.

—The Doll People. Selznick, Brian, illus. 2003. (Doll People Ser.: 1). (J). (gr. 3-6). lib. bdg. 18.40 *(978-0-613-49623-0(X),* Turtleback) Turtleback Bks.

—The Doll People Book 4 the Doll People Set Sail. Helquist, Brett, illus. 2016. (Doll People Ser.). (ENG.). 304p. (J). (gr. 3-7). pap. 7.99 *(978-1-4231-3998-0(4))* Hyperion Bks. for Children.

—The Doll People Set Sail. Helquist, Brett, illus. 2014. (Doll People Ser.: Bk. 4). (ENG.). 304p. (J). (gr. 3-7). 17.99 *(978-1-4231-3683-5(7))* Hyperion Bks. for Children.

—The Doll People's Christmas. Helquist, Brett, illus. 2016. (ENG.). 48p. (J). (gr. -1-k). 17.99 *(978-1-4847-2339-5(2))* Hyperion Bks. for Children.

—The Meanest Doll in the World. Selznick, Brian, illus. 2005. (Doll People Ser.: Bk. 2). (ENG.). 304p. (J). (gr. 3-7). pap. 7.99 *(978-0-7868-5297-0(6))* Hyperion Pr.

—The Runaway Dolls. Selznick, Brian, illus. (Doll People Ser.: Bk. 3). (ENG.). 352p. (J). (gr. 3-7). 2010. pap. 7.99 *(978-0-7868-5585-8(1))* 2008. 17.99 *(978-0-7868-5584-1(3))* Hyperion Pr.

—The Runaway Dolls. Selznick, Brian, illus. 2010. (Doll People Ser.: 3). (J). lib. bdg. 18.40 *(978-0-606-13987-8(7),* Turtleback) Turtleback Bks.

Mattel Inc. Staff, illus. Barbie Always in Style. 2011. (Storybook & Playset Ser.). (ENG.). 24p. (J). (gr. -1-1). 19.99 *(978-0-7944-2316-2(7))* Reader's Digest Assn., Inc., The.

McDonald, Fiona. Ghost Doll & Jasper. 2012. (ENG., Illus.). 112p. (J). (gr. 2-7). 12.95 *(978-1-62087-174-4(2),* 620174, Sky Pony Pr.) Skyhorse Publishing Co., Inc.

McDonough, Yona Zeldis. The Cats in the Doll Shop. Maione, Heather, illus. 2012. (ENG.). 160p. (J). (gr. 3-7). pap. 5.99 *(978-0-14-242198-7(7),* Puffin Books) Penguin Young Readers Group.

—The Doll Shop Downstairs. Maione, Heather, illus. 2011. (ENG.). 128p. (J). (gr. 2-5). 5.99 *(978-0-14-241691-4(6),* Puffin Books) Penguin Young Readers Group.

McElreath, Kim. Pouring in Love. l.t. ed. 2005. (Illus.). 30p. (J). 13.95 *(978-0-9769271-0-5(1))* McElreath, K.M.

McKissack, Patricia C. The All-I'll-Ever-Want Christmas Doll. Pinkney, Jerry, illus. 2007. (J). *(978-0-375-83615-2(2),* Schwartz & Wade Bks.) Random Hse. Children's Bks.

—The All-I'll-Ever-Want Christmas Doll. Pinkney, Jerry, illus. 2007. (ENG.). 40p. (J). (gr. -1-3). 17.99 *(978-0-375-83759-3(0),* Schwartz & Wade Bks.) Random Hse. Children's Bks.

Medearis, Michael & Medearis, Angela Shelf. Daisy & the Doll. Johnson, Larry, illus. 2005. (Vermont Folklife Center Children's Book Ser.). (ENG.). 32p. (J). (gr. -1-3). reprint ed. pap. 7.95 *(978-0-916718-23-7(9))* Vermont Folklife Ctr.

Mercado-López, Larissa. Esteban de Luna, Baby Rescuer / Esteban de Luna, ¡rescatador de Bebés! Pardo DeLange, Alex, illus. 2017. (ENG & SPA.). 32p. (J). (gr. k-3). 17.95 *(978-1-55885-847-3(4),* Piñata Books) Arte Publico Pr.

Miller, Eileen Rudisill. Fairy Tale Princesses Paper Dolls. 2012. (Dover Paper Dolls Ser.). (ENG.). 32p. (J). (gr. k-3). pap. 7.99 *(978-0-486-48990-2(6))* Dover Pubns., Inc.

Moscoso, Edgar. The Doll Repairman. 2011. 32p. pap. 24.95 *(978-1-4560-4011-6(1))* America Star Bks.

Necochea, Kristi Landry. The First Day of Forever. 2007. (J). *(978-0-9792361-0-5(X))* Inspire U., LLC.

Nelson, Vaunda Micheaux. Almost to Freedom. Bootman, Colin, illus. 2003. (Carolrhoda Picture Books Ser.). (ENG.). 40p. (J). (gr. k-3). 16.95 *(978-1-57505-342-4(X))* Lerner Publishing Group.

Niddrie, June. Quiet Queenie. 2010. 36p. pap. 17.30 *(978-0-557-31868-1(8))* Lulu Pr., Inc.

Night, P. J. Best Friends Forever. 2012. (You're Invited to a Creepover Ser.: 6). (ENG.). 160p. (J). (gr. 3-7). pap. 6.99 *(978-1-4424-4150-7(X),* Simon Spotlight) Simon Spotlight.

—Best Friends Forever. 2012. (Creepover Ser.: 6). lib. bdg. 17.20 *(978-0-606-26336-8(5),* Turtleback) Turtleback Bks.

O'Connor, Jane. Fanciest Doll in the Universe. Glasser, Robin Preiss, illus. 2013. (Fancy Nancy Ser.). 32p. (J). (gr. -1-3). (ENG.). 17.99 *(978-0-06-170384-3(2));* lib. bdg. 18.89 *(978-0-06-170385-0(0))* HarperCollins Pubs.

—Fancy Nancy's Perfectly Posh Paper Doll Book. Glasser, Robin Preiss & Bracken, Carolyn, illus. 2009. (Fancy Nancy Ser.). (ENG.). 16p. (J). (gr. -1-3). pap. 6.99 *(978-0-06-187328-7(4),* HarperFestival) HarperCollins Pubs.

O'Neal-Thorpe, Rochelle. The Doll at the Christmas Bazaar: Christmas Miracles. Penn, Karen V., illus. 2010. 32p. (J). pap. 9.95 *(978-0-9823906-2-7(9))* Wiggles Pr.

O'Reilly, Jane. The Secret of Goldenrod. 2016. (ENG.). (gr. 3-6). 328p. (J). 17.99 *(978-1-5124-0135-6(8));* 376p. 35.99 *(978-1-5124-0894-2(8))* Lerner Publishing Group. (Carolrhoda Bks.).

Parenteau, Shirley. Ship of Dolls. 2014. (ENG.). 272p. (J). (gr. 3-7). 16.99 *(978-0-7636-7003-0(0))* Candlewick Pr.

Parot, Annelore. Kimonos. 2011. (ENG.). 36p. (J). (gr. k-17). 17.99 *(978-1-4521-0493-5(X))* Chronicle Bks. LLC.

Pattison, Darcy. The Journey of Oliver K. Woodman. Cepeda, Joe, illus. 2009. (ENG.). 52p. (J). (gr. -1-3). pap. 7.99 *(978-0-15-206118-0(5))* Houghton Mifflin Harcourt Publishing Co.

Pittar, Gill. Milly & Molly Go Camping (book W/dolls) 2006. 28p. pap. *(978-1-86972-097-1(0))* Milly Molly Bks.

—Milly, Molly & Alf (book W/dolls) 2006. 28p. pap. *(978-1-86972-100-8(4))* Milly Molly Bks.

Plant, Marilyn. Trinka's Magic Bracelet. 2012. 40p. pap. *(978-1-77067-956-6(1))* FriesenPress.

Ponko, Cindy A. Busy Busy Days. 2006. (Illus.). (J). *(978-0-9768230-1-8(2))* Some Kids I Know.

Powell, Jillian. Are We There Yet?, 1 vol. Colnaghi, Stefania, illus. 2013. (Start Reading Ser.). (ENG.). 24p. (gr. k-1). pap. 7.95 *(978-1-4765-4083-2(7))* Capstone Press of Coughlan Cos.

A Prairie Heart. 2007. (Illus.). (J). per. 19.95 *(978-0-9793668-0-2(1))* Prairie Heart Publishing.

Raden, Tammy. Priscilla Play. 2010. 28p. 12.49 *(978-1-4520-0808-0(6))* AuthorHouse.

Randall, Alison L. The Wheat Doll, 1 vol. Farnsworth, Bill, illus. 2008. (ENG.). 32p. (J). (gr. k-3). 16.95 *(978-1-56145-456-3(7))* Peachtree Pubs.

Raybon, Charlotte. Meet the Veggies: What Happens in Miss Mae's Kitchen? 2007. 28p. pap. 11.95 *(978-0-9795935-4-3(9),* Eloquent Bks.) Strategic Book Publishing & Rights Agency (SBPRA).

Reed-Guldin, Emily. Sarah & Sammi's Playhouse: Mermaid Adventure. 2009. 36p. pap. 16.99 *(978-1-4389-9342-3(0))* AuthorHouse.

Regelson, Abraham. The Dolls' Journey to Eretz-yisrael. Sharona, Tel-Oren, tr. 2003.Tr. of Masa Habubot L'eretz-yisrael. pap. *(978-0-9729545-8-7(9))* Biblio Bks. International.

—The Doll's Journey to Eretz Yisrael. Tel-Oren, Sharona, tr. from HEB. 2006. (J). lib. bdg. 25.00 *(978-0-9766681-8-3(1))* Biblio Bks. International.

Robertson, Amber. The Runaway Doll. 2009. 20p. pap. 10.49 *(978-1-4343-9336-4(4))* AuthorHouse.

Robinson, Ida. Sally's Doll. 2004. (J). pap. 15.00 *(978-0-8059-6563-6(7))* Dorrance Publishing Co., Inc.

Roper, Robert, illus. Dolls of Danger. 2005. 32p. (J). lib. bdg. 15.00 *(978-1-59054-989-6(9))* Fitzgerald Bks.

Rosy. Tina's Doll. 2009. 16p. pap. 8.49 *(978-1-4389-4212-4(5))* AuthorHouse.

Rotellar, Carlos. Little Red Monster: Tales of Monica. 2009. 24p. pap. 11.49 *(978-1-4490-2812-1(8))* AuthorHouse.

Rubins, Diane Teitel. Sarah the Best Bridesmaid: Paper Doll Storybook. Shanahan, Sue, illus. 2004. (Dover Paper Dolls Ser.). (ENG.). 24p. (J). (gr. 2-5). pap. 5.95 *(978-0-486-43531-2(8))* Dover Pubns., Inc.

Ruby, Lois. The Doll Graveyard. 2014. (Hauntings Ser.). lib. bdg. 17.20 *(978-0-606-35810-1(2))* Turtleback Bks.

Rupert, Rona. Straw Sense. 2013. (ENG., Illus.). 36p. (J). (gr. k-3). 17.99 *(978-1-4814-0151-7(3),* Simon & Schuster Bks. For Young Readers) Simon & Schuster Bks. For Young Readers.

Russo, Marisabina. The Trouble with Baby. Russo, Marisabina, illus. 2003. (Illus.). 32p. (J). (gr. -1-18). 16.89 *(978-0-06-008925-2(3))* HarperCollins Pubs.

San Souci, Robert D. Zigzag. Czernecki, Stefan, illus. 2005. (ENG.). 32p. (J). (gr. -1-2). 16.95 *(978-0-87483-764-3(2))* August Hse. Pubs., Inc.

Schneider, Josh. Princess Sparkle-Heart Gets a Makeover. 2014. (ENG., Illus.). 32p. (J). (gr. -1-3). 16.99 *(978-0-544-14228-2(4))* Houghton Mifflin Harcourt Publishing Co.

Schwind, Beverly Lahote. Patches & Her Backpack Adventures. 2013. (Illus.). 142p. 14.00 *(978-0-9745810-8-8(9))* Potters Publishing LLC.

Seki, Sunny. Yuko-Chan & the Daruma Doll: The Adventures of a Blind Japanese Girl Who Saves Her Village. 2012. (ENG., Illus.). 32p. (J). (gr. -1-3). 15.95 *(978-4-8053-1187-5(8))* Tuttle Publishing.

Shawver, Amanda Nicole. Lily's Rag Doll. 2012. 24p. pap. 17.99 *(978-1-4772-7459-0(6))* AuthorHouse.

Simon, Jenne. The Ballet Recital. 2012. (Scholastic Reader Level 2 Ser.). lib. bdg. 13.55 *(978-0-606-23962-2(6),* Turtleback) Turtleback Bks.

—Lalaloopsy: Chasing Rainbows. 2014. (Scholastic Reader Level 2 Ser.). lib. bdg. 13.55 *(978-0-606-35402-8(6))* Turtleback Bks.

—Let's Pick Apples. Hill, Prescott, illus. 2013. (Lalaloopsy Ser.). (ENG.). 32p. (J). (gr. -1-3). pap. 3.99 *(978-0-545-53182-5(9))* Scholastic, Inc.

Small, David. Eulalie & the Hopping Head. 2003. (Illus.). (J). 25.95 incl. audio *(978-1-59112-217-3(1))* Live Oak Media.

—Eulalie & the Hopping Head. Small, David, illus. 2003. (Illus.). (J). pap. 33.95 incl. audio *(978-1-59112-218-0(X))* Live Oak Media.

Smith, J. Albert. The Adventures of the Molly Dollys. 2011. 28p. (J). pap. 16.95 *(978-1-4327-4313-0(9))* Outskirts Pr., Inc.

Steadman, Barbara. Little Flower Girls Sticker Paper Dolls. 2003. (Dover Little Activity Books Paper Dolls Ser.). (ENG., Illus.). 4p. (J). (gr. k-3). pap. 1.99 *(978-0-486-43019-5(7))* Dover Pubns., Inc.

Stevenson, James. Night after Christmas. 2003. (ENG.). 32p. (J). pap. 2.95 *(978-0-590-41600-9(6))* Scholastic, Inc.

Stone, Phoebe. Paris for Two. 2016. (ENG.). 272p. (J). (gr. 3-7). 16.99 *(978-0-545-44362-3(8),* Levine, Arthur A. Bks.) Scholastic, Inc.

Stuve-Bodeen, Stephanie. La Muneca de Elizabeti. Sarfatti, Esther, tr. Hale, Christy, illus. braille ed. 2004. (SPA.). (J). (gr. k-3). spiral bd. *(978-0-616-08966-8(X))* Canadian National Institute for the Blind/Institut National Canadien pour les Aveugles.

Stuve-Bodeen, Stephanie & Hale, Christy. Elizabeti's Doll. 2009. (ENG., Illus.). 34p. (J). (gr. -1-3). 16.95 *(978-1-880000-70-0(9))* Lee & Low Bks., Inc.

Thompson, Lauren. A Christmas Gift for Mama. Burke, Jim, illus. 2003. (J). pap. 16.95 *(978-0-590-30726-0(6))* Scholastic, Inc.

Townsend, Vanessa. What's in Molly's... . Bedroom? 2012. (Illus.). 24p. pap. 15.99 *(978-1-4797-3248-7(6))* Xlibris Corp.

Troupe, Thomas Kingsley. Darling Doll. Faber, Rudy, illus. 2016. (Hauntiques Ser.). (ENG.). 128p. (gr. 4-6). lib. bdg. 25.32 *(978-1-4965-3548-1(0))* Stone Arch Bks.

Tudor, Tasha. A Is for Annabelle: A Doll's Alphabet. Tudor, Tasha, illus. 2004. (ENG., Illus.). 64p. (J). (gr. -1-3). reprint ed. 7.99 *(978-0-689-86996-9(7),* Simon & Schuster/Paula Wiseman Bks.) Simon & Schuster/Paula Wiseman Bks.

Ultman, Suzy, illus. Masha & Her Sisters. 2017. (ENG.). 10p. (J). bds. 9.99 *(978-1-4521-5159-5(8))* Chronicle Bks. LLC.

Van Walsum-Quispel, J. M. Tina's Island Home. Leeflang-Oudenarden, C., illus. 36p. (J). (gr. k-5). 12.95 *(978-0-87592-053-5(5))* Scroll Pr., Inc.

Verstraete, Majanka. The Doll Maker: Weirdville. l.t. ed. 2013. 1. (ENG.). 86p. (gr. 2-6). pap. 9.95 *(978-1-62253-065-6(9))* Evolved Publishing.

Wade, Rebecca. The Whispering House. 2012. (ENG.). 272p. (J). (gr. 3-7). 16.99 *(978-0-06-077497-4(5),* Tegen, Katherine Bks) HarperCollins Pubs.

Watt, Fiona. That's Not My Dolly. rev. ed. 2012. (Touchy-Feely Board Bks). 10p. (J). bds. 8.99 *(978-0-7945-3308-3(6),* Usborne) EDC Publishing.

Weston Woods Staff, creator. Elizabeti's Doll. 2011. 18.95 *(978-0-439-73629-9(3));* 38.75 *(978-0-439-84574-8(2))* Weston Woods Studios, Inc.

Williams, Margery. Little Wooden Doll. 2003. (Illus.). 32p. (J). 15.95 *(978-0-06-028277-6(0))* HarperCollins Pubs.

World Syndicate Publishing. Fairy Tales & Other Stories. 2012. 348p. pap. 36.95 *(978-1-258-24351-7(2))* Literary Licensing, LLC.

Wright, Betty Ren. The Dollhouse Murders. 2008. (ENG.). 149p. (J). (gr. 4-7). pap. 7.99 *(978-0-8234-2172-5(4))* Holiday Hse., Inc.

Zendrera, Concepcion. Yaci y Su Muneca. (SPA.). 16p. (J). 9.95 *(978-84-261-5604-4(5),* JV3576) Juventud, Editorial ESP. Dist: AIMS International Bks., Inc., Lectorum Pubns., Inc.

DOLLS—POETRY

Canetti, Yanitzia. A Lullaby for My Doll. 2010. 32p. 6.99 *(978-1-59835-257-3(1),* BrickHouse Education) Cambridge BrickHouse, Inc.

DOLPHINS

Albee, Sarah. Dolphins. 2009. (Amazing Animals Ser.). (ENG.). 48p. (J). (gr. 2-6). pap. 10.50 *(978-1-4339-2120-9(0),* Gareth Stevens Learning Library); (YA). (gr. 3-6). lib. bdg. 28.00 *(978-0-8368-9116-4(3))* Stevens, Gareth Publishing LLLP.

—Dolphins. 2006. (Illus.). 45p. (J). *(978-1-59939-064-2(7),* Reader's Digest Young Families, Inc.) Studio Fun International.

Allen, Judy. Flip the Flaps: Whales & Dolphins. Bostock, Mike, illus. 2011. (Flip the Flaps Ser.). (ENG.). 32p. (J). (gr. -1-1). pap. 6.99 *(978-0-7534-6497-7(7),* 9780753464977, Kingfisher) Roaring Brook Pr.

American Museum of Natural History. Baby Dolphin's First Swim. 2017. (First Discoveries Ser.). (ENG., Illus.). 32p. (J). (gr. -1). 14.95 ***(978-1-4549-2236-0(2))*** Sterling Publishing Co., Inc.

Arlon, Penelope. Dolphins. 2014. (Scholastic Discover More Ser.). (ENG.). 32p. (J). (gr. -1-3). 7.99 *(978-0-545-62738-2(9),* Scholastic Reference) Scholastic, Inc.

Baines, Becky. Explore My World Dolphins. 2016. (Explore My World Ser.). (ENG., Illus.). 32p. (J). (gr. -1-2). pap. 4.99 *(978-1-4263-2318-8(2),* National Geographic Children's Bks.) National Geographic Society.

Baltzer, Rochelle. Dolphins Eat & Grow: Level 2. Keimig, Candice, illus. 2014. (Magic Readers Ser.). (ENG.). 24p. (J). (gr. 5-9). 24.21 *(978-1-62402-067-4(4))* ABDO Publishing Co.

—Dolphins in the Ocean: Level 3. Keimig, Candice, illus. 2014. (Magic Readers Ser.). (ENG.). 24p. (J). (gr. 5-9). 24.21 *(978-1-62402-068-1(2))* ABDO Publishing Co.

Barnes, Julia. The Secret Lives of Dolphins. 2007. (Secret Lives of Animals Ser.). (Illus.). 32p. (gr. 2-6). lib. bdg. 26.00 *(978-0-8368-7656-7(3),* Gareth Stevens Learning Library) Stevens, Gareth Publishing LLLP.

Bell, Samantha. Dolphins Are Awesome. 2018. (ENG.). 32p. (gr. 3-6). 31.35 ***(978-1-63235-434-1(9),*** 12-Story Library) Pr. Room Editions LLC.

Berger, Melvin & Berger, Gilda. Dolphins. 2003. (Scholastic Reader Ser.). (Illus.). 16p. (J). *(978-0-439-47389-7(6))* Scholastic, Inc.

Biard, Philippe, et al. Dolphins. Peyrols, Sylvaine, illus. 2012. (ENG.). 32p. (J). (gr. k-3). pap. 11.99 *(978-1-85103-364-5(5))* Moonlight Publishing, Ltd. GBR. Dist: Independent Pubs. Group.

Blake, Carly. Why Why Why... Do Dolphins Squeak? 2010. (Why Why Why Ser.). 32p. (J). (gr. 1-3). lib. bdg. 18.95 *(978-1-4222-1581-4(4))* Mason Crest.

Bozzo, Linda. When Dolphins Mourn. 2017. (Animal Emotions Ser.). 32p. (J). (gr. 3-3). lib. bdg. 25.27 ***(978-0-7660-8615-9(1))*** Enslow Pubs., Inc.

Brust, Beth Wagner. Dolphins. rev. ed. 2003. (Illus.). 24p. 10.95 *(978-1-888153-94-1(6),* Zoo Bks.) Wildlife Education, Ltd.

Bull, Peter & Ganeri, Anita. Explorers: Whales & Dolphins. 2013. (Explorers Ser.). (ENG., Illus.). 32p. (J). (gr. 2-5). 10.99 *(978-0-7534-6815-9(8),* 9780753468159, Kingfisher) Roaring Brook Pr.

Camm, Martin, illus. Meyers Buch der Wale und Delfine. (GER.). 48p. *(978-3-411-07451-8(5))* Bibliographisches Institut & F. A. Brockhaus AG DEU. Dist: i. b. d., Ltd.

Carney, Elizabeth. Dog Finds Lost Dolphins! And More True Stories of Amazing Animal Heroes. 2012. (NGK Chapters Ser.). (ENG., Illus.). 112p. (J). (gr. 2-5). pap. 5.99 *(978-1-4263-1031-7(5));* lib. bdg. 14.90 *(978-1-4263-1032-4(3))* National Geographic Society. (National Geographic Children's Bks.).

—Dolphins: Dolphin Facts, Photos, & Fun That Will Make You Flip. 2012. (National Geographic Kids Everything Ser.). (ENG., Illus.). 64p. (J). (gr. 3-7). lib. bdg. 25.90 *(978-1-4263-0843-7(4),* National Geographic Children's Bks.) National Geographic Society.

Carney, Elizabeth & National Geographic Kids Staff. Everything Dolphins: Dolphin Facts, Photos, & Fun That Will Make You Flip! 2012. (National Geographic Kids Everything Ser.). (ENG., Illus.). 64p. (J). (gr. 3-7). pap. 12.95 *(978-1-4263-0842-0(6),* National Geographic Children's Bks.) National Geographic Society.

Christopherson, Sara Cohen. Top 50 Reasons to Care about Whales & Dolphins: Animals in Peril. 2010. (Top 50 Reasons to Care about Endangered Animals Ser.). (Illus.). 104p. (J). (gr. 5-9). 33.27 *(978-0-7660-3453-2(4))* Enslow Pubs., Inc.

Clark, Willow. Asian Dolphins & Other Marine Mammals. 2012. (Animals of Asia Ser.). (ENG., Illus.). 24p. (J). (gr. 1-5). 22.60 *(978-1-4488-7419-4(X));* pap. 8.25 *(978-1-4488-7492-7(0))* Rosen Publishing Group, Inc., The. (PowerKids Pr.).

—Dolphins: Delfines: Life in the Pod: Vida en la Manada. 2011. (Animal Families / Familias de animales Ser.). (SPA & ENG., Illus.). 24p. lib. bdg. 22.60 *(978-1-4488-3126-5(1),* PowerKids Pr.) Rosen Publishing Group, Inc., The.

—Dolphins: Life in the Pod. 2011. (Animal Families Ser.). 24p. (J). (ENG.). pap. 8.25 *(978-1-4488-2610-0(1));* (Illus.). lib. bdg. 22.60 *(978-1-4488-2512-7(1))* Rosen Publishing Group, Inc., The. (PowerKids Pr.).

Claybourne, Anna. Dolphins, 1 vol. 2013. (Living in the Wild: Sea Mammals Ser.). (ENG.). 48p. (gr. 4-6). pap. 9.95 *(978-1-4329-7068-0(2));* lib. bdg. 33.32 *(978-1-4329-7061-1(5))* Heinemann-Raintree. (Heinemann InfoSearch).

Coleman, Janet Wyman. Eight Dolphins of Katrina: A True Tale of Survival. Nascimbene, Yan, illus. (ENG.). 40p. (J). (gr. 1-4). 2017. pap. 8.99 *(978-0-544-93261-6(7),* HMH Books For Young Readers) 2013. lib. bdg. 17.99 *(978-0-547-71923-8(X))* Houghton Mifflin Harcourt Publishing Co.

Coleman, Miriam. Swimming with Dolphins. 2009. (Flippers & Fins Ser.). (Illus.). 24p. (J). (ENG.). pap. 8.25 *(978-1-4358-3237-4(X),* PowerKids Pr.); (gr. 1-3). lib. bdg. 22.60 *(978-1-4042-8090-8(1))* Rosen Publishing Group, Inc., The.

Crisp, Marty. Everything Dolphin: What Kids Really Want to Know About Dolphins. 2004. (Kids Faqs Ser.). (ENG., Illus.). 64p. (J). (gr. 3-6). pap. 8.95 *(978-1-55971-049-7(7))* Cooper Square Publishing Llc.

—Everything Dolphin: What Kids Really Want to Know about Dolphins. 2004. (Kids Faqs Ser.). (ENG., Illus.). 64p. (J). (gr. 3-6). 10.95 *(978-1-55971-042-8(X))* Cooper Square Publishing Llc.

Davidson, Margaret & Wilson, Roger. Neuf Histoires Vraies de Dauphins. (FRE.). (J). pap. 4.99 *(978-0-590-71188-3(1))* Scholastic, Inc.

Davidson, Susanna. Whales & Dolphins: Internet-Linked. 2009. (Discovery Nature Ser.). 48p. (YA). (gr. 3-18). 8.99 *(978-0-7945-2376-3(5),* Usborne) EDC Publishing.

Davidson, Susannah. Whales & Dolphins. 2004. (Discovery Program Ser.). (Illus.). 48p. (J). lib. bdg. 16.95 *(978-1-58086-478-7(3))* EDC Publishing.

Davidson, Susannah, et al. Whales & Dolphins. Woodcock, John, illus. 2003. (Usborne Discovery Ser.). 48p. (J). pap. *(978-0-439-56060-3(8));* pap. *(978-0-439-57780-9(2))* Scholastic, Inc.

De Medeiros, James. Dolphins. 2008. (Amazing Animals Ser.). (Illus.). 24p. (J). (gr. 2-4). pap. 8.95 *(978-1-59036-959-3(9));* lib. bdg. 24.45 *(978-1-59036-958-6(0))* Weigl Pubs., Inc.

Dolphin in the Sea. Date not set. (Illus.). (J). bds. 1.98 *(978-0-7525-9840-6(6))* Parragon, Inc.

Dolphins. 2006. (J). 4.95 *(978-1-932396-18-8(7))* Wildlife Education, Ltd.

Dolphins: Level 1. 2014. (Magic Readers Ser.). (ENG., Illus.). 24p. (J). (gr. 5-9). 24.21 *(978-1-62402-066-7(6))* Magic Wagon.

Dolphins: Level L, 6 vols. (Wonder Worldtm Ser.). 16p. 34.95 *(978-0-7802-2895-5(2))* Wright Group/McGraw-Hill.

Dorling Kindersley Publishing Staff. Whales & Dolphins. 2013. (Eye Wonder Ser.). (ENG., Illus.). 56p. (J). (gr. k-4). 10.99 *(978-1-4654-0910-2(6),* DK Children) Dorling Kindersley Publishing, Inc.

Driscoll, Laura. Do Dolphins Really Smile? Wald, Christina, illus. 2006. (Penguin Young Readers, Level 3 Ser.). (ENG.). 48p. (J). (gr. 1-3). mass mkt. 3.99 *(978-0-448-44341-6(4),* Penguin Young Readers) Penguin Young Readers Group.

Drumlin, Sam. Dolphins. 2013. (PowerKids Readers: Sea Friends Ser.). (ENG., Illus.). 24p. (J). (gr. k-2). pap. 8.25 *(978-1-4488-9740-7(8));* lib. bdg. 22.60 *(978-1-4488-9641-7(X))* Rosen Publishing Group, Inc., The. (PowerKids Pr.).

—Dolphins: Los Delfines. Alamán, Eduardo, tr. from ENG. 2013. (PowerKids Readers: Sea Friends / Los Amigos Del Mar Ser.). (SPA & ENG., Illus.). 24p. (J). (gr. k-2). lib. bdg. 22.60 *(978-1-4488-9972-2(9),* PowerKids Pr.) Rosen Publishing Group, Inc., The.

Fact Atlas: Dolphins & Whales. 2009. (FACT ATLAS Ser.). 72p. (J). 14.95 *(978-0-8437-1865-2(X))* Hammond World Atlas Corp.

Fenner, Matthew. A Pod of Dolphins. 2013. (Animal Groups Ser.). (Illus.). 24p. (J). (gr. 1-3). pap. 8.15 *(978-1-4339-8215-6(3));* lib. bdg. 22.60 *(978-1-4339-8214-9(5))* Stevens, Gareth Publishing LLLP.

—A Pod of Dolphins / una Manada de Delfines. 2013. (Animal Groups / Grupos de Animales Ser.). (ENG & SPA., Illus.). 24p. (gr. 1-3). 22.60 *(978-1-4339-8810-3(0))* Stevens, Gareth Publishing LLLP.

Gareth Stevens Editorial Staff. Dolphins. 2004. (All about Wild Animals Ser.). (Illus.). 32p. (gr. k-4). lib. bdg. 26.00

C
D

(978-0-8368-4115-2(8), Gareth Stevens Learning Library) Stevens, Gareth Publishing LLLP.

Gillot, Laurence & Sebaoun, Elisabeth. Half & Half-Swimming with Dolphins. Rocco & Dorémus, Gaëtan, illus. 2010. 32p. (J). 9.95 (978-1-60115-215-2(9)); pap. 4.99 (978-1-60115-216-9(7)) Treasure Bay, Inc.

Glaser, Rebecca Stromstad. Dolphins Play. 2016. (ENG., Illus.). 16p. (J). (gr. -1 — 1). bds. 7.99 (978-1-68152-067-4(2)) Amicus.

Gordon, Sharon. Adivina Quien Cambia. 2006. (Bookworms Ser.). (SPA & ENG., Illus.). 32p. (gr. k-2). lib. bdg. 15.95 (978-0-7614-2380-5(X)) Marshall Cavendish Corp.

—Adivina Quien Se Zambulle. 2006. (Bookworms Ser.). (SPA., Illus.). 32p. (gr. k-2). lib. bdg. 15.95 (978-0-7614-2381-2(8)) Marshall Cavendish Corp.

—Dives. 2007. (J). pap. 6.99 (978-0-7614-3319-4(8)) Marshall Cavendish Corp.

—Guess Who Changes/Adivina Quien Cambia. 2006. (Bookworms Ser.). (ENG & SPA., Illus.). 32p. (gr. k-2). lib. bdg. 15.95 (978-0-7614-2461-1(X)) Marshall Cavendish Corp.

—Guess Who Dives/Adivina Quien Se Zambulle. 2006. (Bookworms Ser.). (SPA & ENG., Illus.). 32p. (gr. k-2). lib. bdg. 15.95 (978-0-7614-2462-8(8)) Marshall Cavendish Corp.

Gray, Susan H. Dolphins Breathe Air. 2015. (Tell Me Why Library). (ENG., Illus.). 24p. (J). (gr. 2-5). pap. 12.79 (978-1-63362-030-8(1), 205877) Cherry Lake Publishing.

Green, Jen. Dolphins. 2009. (Illus.). 52p. (Orig.). (J). (978-0-7172-8064-3(0)) Grolier, Ltd.

Gregory, Josh. Dolphins. 2012. (Nature's Children Ser.). (ENG., Illus.). 48p. (J). pap. 6.95 (978-0-531-21075-8(8)); (gr. 3-5). lib. bdg. 28.00 (978-0-531-20900-4(8)) Scholastic Library Publishing. (Children's Pr.).

Guidoux, Valerie. Little Dolphins. 2005. (Born to Be Wild Ser.). (Illus.). 24p. (gr. k-3). lib. bdg. 23.00 (978-0-8368-4735-2(0), Gareth Stevens Learning Library) Stevens, Gareth Publishing LLLP.

Gunderson, Megan M. Bottlenose Dolphins, 1 vol. 2011. (Dolphins Set 1 *2011 Ser.). (ENG.). 24p. 25.65 (978-1-61613-411-2(9), Checkerboard Library) ABDO Publishing Co.

—Common Dolphins, 1 vol. 2011. (Dolphins Set 1 *2011 Ser.). (ENG.). 24p. 25.65 (978-1-61613-412-9(7), Checkerboard Library) ABDO Publishing Co.

—Freshwater Dolphins, 1 vol. 2011. (Dolphins Set 1 *2011 Ser.). (ENG.). 24p. (J). (gr. 2-5). 25.65 (978-1-61613-413-6(5)) ABDO Publishing Co.

—Spinner Dolphins, 1 vol. 2011. (Dolphins Set 1 *2011 Ser.). (ENG.). 24p. (J). (gr. 2-5). 25.65 (978-1-61613-414-3(3)) ABDO Publishing Co.

—Spotted Dolphins, 1 vol. 2011. (Dolphins Set 1 *2011 Ser.). (ENG.). 24p. (J). (gr. 2-5). 25.65 (978-1-61613-415-0(1)) ABDO Publishing Co.

—White-Sided Dolphins, 1 vol. 2011. (Dolphins Set 1 *2011 Ser.). (ENG.). 24p. (J). (gr. 2-5). 25.65 (978-1-61613-416-7(X)) ABDO Publishing Co.

Gustafson, Sarah. Whales, Dolphins, & More Marine Mammals. 2005. (Illus.). 48p. (J). pap. (978-0-439-71189-0(4)) Scholastic, Inc.

Haney, Johannah. Dolphins. 2010. (Endangered! 2 Ser.). 48p. (gr. 3). lib. bdg. 29.93 (978-0-7614-4049-9(6)) Marshall Cavendish Corp.

Hansen, Grace. Bottlenose Dolphins, 1 vol. 2015. (ENG., Illus.). 24p. (J). 28.50 (978-1-62970-891-1(7)) ABDO Publishing Co.

—Dolphins, 1 vol. 2014. (Ocean Life Ser.). (ENG.). 24p. (J). (gr. 2-4). lib. bdg. 28.50 (978-1-62970-708-2(2)) ABDO Publishing Co.

Hardyman, Robyn. Dolphins. 2008. (World of Animals Ser.). 32p. (gr. 2-5). 31.35 (978-1-933834-35-1(8)) Brown Bear Bks.

Harris, Tim, ed. Dolphins. 2012. (Animal Families Ser.). (ENG., Illus.). 32p. (gr. 2-5). 31.35 **(978-1-78121-002-4(0))** Brown Bear Bks.

Hatkoff, Craig & Yates, David. Hope for Winter: The True Story of a Remarkable Dolphin Friendship. 2014. (ENG.). 40p. (J). (gr. -1-3). 6.99 (978-0-545-68669-3(5), Scholastic Paperbacks) Scholastic, Inc.

Hatkoff, Juliana, et al. Winter's Tail: How One Little Dolphin Learned to Swim Again. 2011. (ENG.). 40p. (J). (gr. -1-3). pap. 6.99 (978-0-545-34830-0(7), Scholastic Paperbacks) Scholastic, Inc.

Herriges, Ann. Dolphins. 2006. (Oceans Alive Ser.). (ENG., Illus.). 24p. (J). (gr. k-3). lib. bdg. 25.95 (978-1-60014-017-4(3)) Bellwether Media.

Hibbert, Clare. If You Were a Dolphin. 2013. (If You Were A... Ser.). 32p. (gr. 2-5). 31.35 (978-1-59920-961-6(6)) Black Rabbit Bks.

Ingram, Scott. Dolphins. 2006. (Smart Animals! Ser.). (Illus.). 32p. (YA). (gr. 2-5). lib. bdg. 25.27 (978-1-59716-161-9(6)) Bearport Publishing Co., Inc.

Jackson, Tom. Inside the Mind of a Clever Dolphin. 2012. (Animal Instincts Ser.). (ENG., Illus.). 32p. (J). (gr. k-5). pap. 10.00 (978-1-4488-7078-3(X)); lib. bdg. 25.25 (978-1-4488-7034-9(8)) Rosen Publishing Group, Inc., The. (PowerKids Pr.).

John, Victoria. Dolphins: Level N, 6 vols. (Raging Rivers Ser.). 128p. (gr. 3-6). 36.95 (978-0-322-05902-3(X)) Wright Group/McGraw-Hill.

Johnson, Jinny & The Born Free Foundation. Dolphin Rescue: A True-Life Story. 2017. (Born Free... Bks.). (ENG.). 96p. (J). (gr. 2-6). pap. 6.99 (978-1-4380-0986-5(0)) Barron's Educational Series, Inc.

Jones, Tracy. Whales & Dolphins. 2011. (Illus.). 16p. (J). (978-0-545-24793-1(4)) Scholastic, Inc.

Jugran, Jan. Baby Dolphins. Larranaga, Ana Martin, illus. 2006. (ENG.). 6p. (J). (gr. -1 — 1). 14.99 (978-1-58476-490-8(2), IKIDS) Innovative Kids.

Kalman, Bobbie. La Famille des Dauphins. 2011. (FRE., Illus.). 32p. (J). pap. 10.95 (978-2-89579-395-3(6)) Bayard Canada CAN. Dist: Crabtree Publishing Co.

Kalz, Jill. Dolphins. 2006. (Wild World of Animals Ser.). (Illus.). 30p. (J). (gr. 5). 18.95 (978-1-58341-432-3(0), Creative Education) Creative Co., The.

Kenan, Tessa. Look, a Dolphin! 2016. (Bumba Books (tm) — I See Ocean Animals Ser.). (ENG., Illus.). 24p. (J). (gr. -1-1). 25.32 (978-1-5124-1424-0(7)) Lerner Publishing Group.

—¡Mira, un Delfín! (Look, a Dolphin!) 2017. (Bumba Books (tm) en Español — Veo Animales Marinos (I See Ocean Animals) Ser.). (SPA., Illus.). 24p. (J). (gr. -1-1). 25.32 (978-1-5124-2865-0(5)) Lerner Publishing Group.

Kerrod, Robin. Exploring Nature: Whales & Dolphins. 2014. (ENG., Illus.). 64p. (J). (gr. 3-7). 12.99 (978-1-84322-912-4(9), Armadillo) Anness Publishing GBR. Dist: National Bk. Network.

—Whales & Dolphins. 2008. (Nature Watch Ser.). (ENG., Illus.). 64p. (J). (gr. 4-7). 14.99 (978-0-7548-1875-5(6)) Anness Publishing GBR. Dist: National Bk. Network.

King, Zelda. Dolphins. 2012. (Illus.). 24p. (J). 49.50 (978-1-4488-5138-6(6), PowerKids Pr.); pap. 8.25 (978-1-4488-5137-9(8), PowerKids Pr.); lib. bdg. 22.60 (978-1-4488-5003-7(7)) Rosen Publishing Group, Inc., The.

Kratt, Chris & Kratt, Martin. Wild Sea Creatures: Sharks, Whales & Dolphins! 2014. (Step into Reading Ser.). (ENG., Illus.). 32p. (J). (gr. -1-1). lib. bdg. 12.99 (978-0-553-49902-5(5), Random Hse. Bks. for Young Readers) Random Hse. Children's Bks.

—Wild Sea Creatures: Sharks, Whales, & Dolphins! 2014. (Step into Reading Ser.). (ENG., Illus.). 32p. (J). (gr. -1-1). 3.99 (978-0-553-49901-8(7), Random Hse. Bks. for Young Readers) Random Hse. Children's Bks.

Kurtz, Kevin. Sharks & Dolphins: A Compare & Contrast Book, 1 vol. 2016. (Compare & Contrast Ser.). (ENG., Illus.). 32p. (J). (gr. k-3). 17.95 (978-1-62855-732-9(X)) Arbordale Publishing.

—Tiburones y Delfines: Un Libro de Comparación y Contraste, 1 vol. 2016. (SPA., Illus.). 32p. (J). (gr. k-3). pap. 9.95 (978-1-62855-746-6(X)) Arbordale Publishing.

Laughlin, Kara L. Dolphins. 2017. (In the Deep Blue Sea Ser.). (ENG.). 24p. (J). (gr. k-3). lib. bdg. 27.07 (978-1-5038-1685-5(0), 211519) Child's World, Inc., The.

Leavitt, Amie. Threat to the Yangtze River Dolphin. 2008. (On the Verge of Extinction Ser.). (Illus.). 32p. (J). (gr. 2-5). lib. bdg. 25.70 (978-1-58415-684-0(8)) Mitchell Lane Pubs., Inc.

Lebloas-Julienne, Renee. The Dolphin. 2004. (Animal Close-Ups Ser.). (ENG., Illus.). 28p. (J). pap. 6.95 (978-1-57091-627-4(6)) Charlesbridge Publishing, Inc.

Lindeen, Carol K. Dolphins [Scholastic]. 2010. (Under the Sea Ser.). 24p. pap. 0.50 (978-1-4296-5063-2(X), Pebble Plus) Capstone Press of Coughlan Cos.

Little & Large Sticker Activity Whales & Dolphins. 2008. 24p. pap. (978-1-84810-064-0(7)) Miles Kelly Publishing, Ltd.

Loh-Hagan, Virginia. Discover Bottlenose Dolphins. 2015. (21st Century Basic Skills Library: Splash! Ser.). (ENG., Illus.). 24p. (J). (gr. 2-4). 24.21 (978-1-63362-597-6(4), 206572) Cherry Lake Publishing.

Lynette, Rachel. Pink River Dolphins. 2013. (Jungle Babies of the Amazon Rain Forest Ser.). 24p. (J). (gr. -1-3). lib. bdg. 21.32 (978-1-61772-758-0(X)) Bearport Publishing Co., Inc.

MacAulay, Kelley & Kalman, Bobbie. Dolphins & Other Marine Mammals. 2005. (What Kind of Animal Is It? Ser.). (ENG., Illus.). 32p. (J). (gr. 1-2). pap. (978-0-7787-2222-9(8)) Crabtree Publishing Co.

Macleod, Steve. Dolphin. 2011. (J). 27.13 (978-1-61690-754-9(1)); pap. 12.95 (978-1-61690-761-7(4)) Weigl Pubs., Inc.

—Soy el Delfín. 2012. (SPA.). (J). (978-1-61913-173-6(0)) Weigl Pubs., Inc.

McAneney, Caitie. Bottlenose Dolphins, 01 vols., 1. 2016. (Ocean Friends Ser.). (ENG., Illus.). 24p. (J). pap. 8.25 (978-1-5081-4165-5(7), PowerKids Pr.) Rosen Publishing Group, Inc., The.

Meinking, Mary. Dolphin vs. Fish, 1 vol. 2011. (Predator vs. Prey Ser.). (ENG., Illus.). 32p. (gr. 1-2). 29.99 (978-1-4109-3940-1(5)); pap. 8.29 (978-1-4109-3949-4(9)) Heinemann-Raintree. (Read Me!).

Meister, Cari. Dolphins. 2012. (Illus.). 24p. (J). lib. bdg. 25.65 (978-1-62031-008-3(2)) Jump! Inc.

Morgan, Sally. Dolphins & Porpoises: Animal Lives Series. 2008. 32p. (J). lib. bdg. 18.95 (978-1-59566-537-9(4)) QEB Publishing Inc.

Murray, Julie. Bottle-Nosed Dolphins, 1 vol. 2005. (Animal Kingdom Set Ii Ser.). (ENG., Illus.). 24p. (gr. k-4). 25.65 (978-1-59197-304-1(X), Buddy Bks.) ABDO Publishing Co.

—Common Dolphins, 1 vol. 2005. (Animal Kingdom Set Ii Ser.). (ENG., Illus.). 24p. (gr. k-4). 25.65 (978-1-59197-308-9(2), Buddy Bks.) ABDO Publishing Co.

—Spotted Dolphins, 1 vol. 2003. (Animal Kingdom Ser.). (ENG.). 24p. (gr. k-4). 25.65 (978-1-57765-707-1(1), Buddy Bks.) ABDO Publishing Co.

National Geographic Editors. Favorite Animals Collection. 2013. (Readers Ser.). (ENG., Illus.). 128p. (J). (gr. -1-1). pap. 7.99 (978-1-4263-1333-2(0), National Geographic Children's Bks.) National Geographic Society.

National Geographic Kids. National Geographic Readers: Dive, Dolphin. 2016. (Readers Ser.). (ENG., Illus.). 24p. (J). (-k). pap. 3.99 (978-1-4263-2440-6(5), National Geographic Children's Bks.) National Geographic Society.

National Geographic Kids Staff. Dive, Dolphin. 2016. (Readers Ser.). (ENG., Illus.). 24p. (J). (-k). lib. bdg. 13.90 (978-1-4263-2441-3(3), National Geographic Children's Bks.) National Geographic Society.

Nicklin, Linda & Nicklin, Flip. Face to Face with Dolphins. 2009. (Face to Face with Animals Ser.). (ENG., Illus.). 32p. (J). (gr. 2-5). pap. 6.95 (978-1-4263-0549-8(4), National Geographic Children's Bks.) National Geographic Society.

Niver, Heather Moore. 20 Fun Facts about Dolphins. 2012. (Fun Fact File: Animals! Ser.). (ENG.). 32p. (J). (gr. 2-5). pap. 10.50 (978-1-4339-6515-9(1)); lib. bdg. 25.25 (978-1-4339-6513-5(5)) Stevens, Gareth Publishing LLLP. (Gareth Stevens Learning Library).

Nuzzolo, Deborah. Dolphin Discovery: Bottlenose Dolphin Training & Interaction. 2nd rev. ed. 2003. (Seaworld Education Ser.). (Illus.). 76p. (gr. 4-12). per. 7.99 (978-1-893698-03-1(3), B03, SeaWorld Education Dept.) SeaWorld, Inc.

Osborne, Mary Pope & Boyce, Natalie Pope. Dolphins & Sharks: Dolphins at Daybreak. Murdocca, Sal, illus. 2003. (Magic Tree House - Fact Tracker Ser.: 9). (ENG.). 128p. (J). (gr. 2-5). 6.99 (978-0-375-82377-0(8), Random Hse. Bks. for Young Readers) Random Hse. Children's Bks.

Our Friend the Dolphin: Level P, 6 vols. (Wonder Worldtm Ser.). 48p. 39.95 (978-0-7802-7078-7(9)) Wright Group/McGraw-Hill.

Owen, Ruth. Dolphins. 2011. (World's Smartest Animals Ser.). (ENG., Illus.). 32p. (J). (gr. k-5). 26.50 (978-1-61533-379-0(7)); pap. 11.75 (978-1-61533-416-2(5)) Windmill Bks.

Parker, Steve. Wales & Dolphins. 2010. (Remarkable Man & Beast Ser.). (Illus.). 48p. (J). (gr. 3-18). lib. bdg. 19.95 (978-1-4222-1978-2(X)) Mason Crest.

—Whales & Dolphins. 2015. (100 Facts You Should Know Ser.). (ENG., Illus.). 48p. (J). (gr. 4-5). pap. 14.05 (978-1-4824-3211-4(0)) Stevens, Gareth Publishing LLLP.

Petersen, Megan Cooley & Rake, Jody Sullivan. Bottlenose Dolphins, 1 vol. 2012. (Marine Mammals Ser.). (ENG.). 24p. (gr. k-1). 26.65 (978-1-4296-8716-4(9), Pebble Plus) Capstone Press of Coughlan Cos.

Petrie, Kristin. Amazon River Dolphins, 1 vol. 2006. (Dolphins Set 2 Ser.). (ENG., Illus.). 24p. (gr. k-6). 25.65 (978-1-59679-299-9(X), Checkerboard Library) ABDO Publishing Co.

—Atlantic Humpbacked Dolphins, 1 vol. 2006. (Dolphins Set 2 Ser.). (ENG., Illus.). 24p. (gr. k-6). 25.65 (978-1-59679-300-2(7), Checkerboard Library) ABDO Publishing Co.

—Chinese River Dolphins, 1 vol. 2006. (Dolphins Set 2 Ser.). (ENG., Illus.). 24p. (gr. k-6). 25.65 (978-1-59679-301-9(5), Checkerboard Library) ABDO Publishing Co.

—Ganges River Dolphins, 1 vol. 2006. (Dolphins Set 2 Ser.). (ENG., Illus.). 24p. (gr. k-6). 25.65 (978-1-59679-302-6(3), Checkerboard Library) ABDO Publishing Co.

—Risso's Dolphins, 1 vol. 2006. (Dolphins Set 2 Ser.). (ENG., Illus.). 24p. (gr. k-6). 25.65 (978-1-59679-303-3(1), Checkerboard Library) ABDO Publishing Co.

—Striped Dolphins, 1 vol. 2006. (Dolphins Set 2 Ser.). (ENG., Illus.). 24p. (gr. k-6). 25.65 (978-1-59679-304-0(X), Checkerboard Library) ABDO Publishing Co.

Pfeffer, Wendy. Dolphin Talk: Whistles, Clicks, & Clapping Jaws. Davie, Helen K., illus. 2003. (Let's-Read-and-Find-Out Science Ser.). 40p. (J). (gr. k-4). (ENG.). 15.99 (978-0-06-028801-3(9)); lib. bdg. 16.89 (978-0-06-028802-0(7)) HarperCollins Pubs.

Pfeffer, Wendy & Pfeffer. Dolphin Talk: Whistles, Clicks, & Clapping Jaws. Davie, Helen K., illus. 2003. (Let's-Read-And-Find-Out Science 2 Ser.). (ENG.). 40p. (J). (gr. k-4). pap. 5.99 (978-0-06-445210-6(7)) HarperCollins Pubs.

Pohl, Kathleen. Dolphins. 2007. (Let's Read about Animals Ser.). (Illus.). 24p. (gr. k-3). lib. bdg. 22.00 (978-0-8368-7816-5(7), Weekly Reader Leveled Readers) Stevens, Gareth Publishing LLLP.

—Dolphins (Delfines) 2007. (Let's Read about Animals/ Conozcamos a los animales Ser.). (ENG & SPA., Illus.). 24p. (gr. k-3). pap. 8.15 (978-0-8368-8012-0(9), Weekly Reader Leveled Readers) Stevens, Gareth Publishing LLLP.

—Dolphins/Delfines. 2007. (Let's Read about Animals/ Conozcamos a los animales Ser.). (ENG & SPA., Illus.). 24p. (gr. k-3). lib. bdg. 22.00 (978-0-8368-8005-2(6), Weekly Reader Leveled Readers) Stevens, Gareth Publishing LLLP.

Rake, Jody Sullivan. Bottlenose Dolphin up Close [Scholastic]. 2011. (Whales & Dolphins up Close Ser.). pap. 0.50 (978-1-4296-6321-2(9), First Facts) Capstone Press of Coughlan Cos.

Riggs, Kate. Amazing Animals - Dolphins. 2011. (J). 25.65 (978-1-58341-989-2(6), Creative Education) Creative Co., The.

—Dolphins. (J). 2015. pap. (978-1-62832-211-8(X), Creative Paperbacks) 2012. (Illus.). 24p. (gr. -1-3). 15.95 (978-1-60818-274-9(6), Creative Education) Creative Co., The.

—Dolphins. 2010. (ENG., Illus.). 24p. (J). (978-1-926853-69-7(5)) Saunders Bk. Co. CAN. Dist: Creative Co., The.

—Seedlings: Dolphins. 2013. (Seedlings Ser.). (ENG.). 24p. (J). (gr. -1-k). pap. 7.99 (978-0-89812-781-2(5), Creative Paperbacks) Creative Co., The.

Ripley's Believe It Or Not! Staff & Ripley's Believe It Or Not! Editors, compiled by. Whales & Dolphins: Believe It or Not! 2014. (Twist Ser.: 11). (ENG., Illus.). 48p. (J). 12.95 (978-1-60991-114-0(8)) Ripley Entertainment, Inc.

Rockwood, Leigh. Dolphins Are Smart! 2010. (Super Smart Animals Ser.). (Illus.). 24p. (J). pap. 8.25 (978-1-4358-9842-4(7), PowerKids Pr.); (YA). (gr. 2-5). lib. bdg. 22.60 (978-1-4358-9398-6(0)) Rosen Publishing Group, Inc., The.

Rodrigo-Gomez, Mike. Dolphins & Calves. 2017. (Animal Family Ser.). 24p. (gr. k-k). pap. 8.15 **(978-1-4824-6377-4(6))** Stevens, Gareth Publishing LLLP.

Rustad, Martha E. Dolphins [Scholastic]. 2009. (Ocean Life Ser.). 24p. (gr. k-1). pap. 2.99 (978-1-4296-3674-2(2), Pebble Bks.) Capstone Press of Coughlan Cos.

Ryndak, Rob. Dolphin or Porpoise? 2015. (Animal Look-Alikes Ser.). (ENG., Illus.). 24p. (J). (gr. 1-2). pap. 8.15 (978-1-4824-2712-7(5)) Stevens, Gareth Publishing LLLP.

Scheunemann, Pam. Dolphins Click!, 1 vol. 2011. (Animal Sounds Set 2 Ser.). (ENG., Illus.). 24p. (J). (gr. k-3). lib. bdg. 24.21 (978-1-61613-570-6(0), SandCastle) ABDO Publishing Co.

Schuetz, Kari. Bottlenose Dolphins. 2016. (Ocean Life up Close Ser.). (ENG., Illus.). 24p. (J). (gr. k-3). 25.95 (978-1-62617-413-9(X), Blastoff! Readers) Bellwether Media.

Sea 3D Whales& Dolphins. 2008. (Illus.). 24p. (J). spiral bd. 19.95 (978-0-9759629-1-6(4)) ETN, Inc.

Shaskan, Trisha Speed. What's the Difference Between a Dolphin & a Porpoise?, 1 vol. Bandelin, Debra et al, illus. 2010. (What's the Difference? Ser.). (ENG.). 24p. (gr. k-3). lib. bdg. 26.65 (978-1-4048-5545-8(9)) Picture Window Bks.

Shaw, Gina. Dolphins & Whales in a Box. 2014. (ENG.). 48p. (J). (gr. k-2). 9.99 (978-0-545-68163-6(4), Scholastic Nonfiction) Scholastic, Inc.

Shivley, Julie. Baby Dolphin. Sharp, Chris & Seaworld, Chris, illus. Seaworld, Chris, photos by. 2005. (Seaworld Animal Library: Vol. 4). 26p. (J). (gr. -1-k). bds. 6.95 (978-0-8249-6614-0(7), Ideal Pubns.) Worthy Publishing.

Silverman, Buffy. Can You Tell a Dolphin from a Porpoise? 2011. (Lightning Bolt Books (tm) — Animal Look-Alikes Ser.). (ENG.). 32p. (gr. k-2). pap. 7.95 (978-0-7613-7848-8(0)); (Illus.). lib. bdg. 26.60 (978-0-7613-6734-5(9)) Lerner Publishing Group.

—Can You Tell A Dolphin from A Porpoise? 2011. (Animal Look-Alikes Ser.). pap. 45.32 (978-0-7613-8385-7(9)) Lerner Publishing Group.

Simon, Seymour. Dolphins. 2011. (ENG.). 32p. (J). (gr. k-4). pap. 6.99 (978-0-06-446220-4(X)) HarperCollins Pubs.

Skog, Jason. Dolphins. 2008. (Living Wild Ser.). (Illus.). 46p. 22.95 (978-1-58341-653-2(6), Creative Education) Creative Co., The.

Spilsbury, Louise. Dolphin, 1 vol. 2010. (Day in the Life: Sea Animals Ser.). (ENG.). 24p. (gr. k-2). 23.32 (978-1-4329-3999-1(8)); pap. 6.79 (978-1-4329-4006-5(6)) Heinemann-Raintree. (Heinemann Read & Learn).

Spilsbury, Richard. A Pod of Dolphins: And Other Sea Mammal Groups, 1 vol. 2012. (Animals in Groups Ser.). (ENG.). 48p. (gr. 4-6). pap. 9.95 (978-1-4329-6490-0(9)); lib. bdg. 33.32 (978-1-4329-6483-2(6)) Heinemann-Raintree. (Heinemann InfoSearch).

Spilsbury, Richard & Spilsbury, Louise. Dolphin & Whale Pods. 2013. (Animal Armies Ser.). (ENG., Illus.). 32p. (J). (gr. k-5). pap. 10.00 (978-1-4777-0332-8(2)); lib. bdg. 25.25 (978-1-4777-0305-2(5)) Rosen Publishing Group, Inc., The. (PowerKids Pr.).

Stewart, Melissa. Dolphins. 2010. (Readers Ser.). (ENG., Illus.). 32p. (J). (gr. k-3). pap. 3.99 (978-1-4263-0652-5(0)); lib. bdg. 13.90 (978-1-4263-0653-2(9)) National Geographic Society. (National Geographic Children's Bks.).

—Dolphins (1 Hardcover/1 CD) 2017. (National Geographic Kids Ser.). (ENG.). (J). 29.95 **(978-1-4301-2665-2(5))** Live Oak Media.

—Dolphins (1 Paperback/1 CD) 2017. (National Geographic Kids Ser.). (ENG.). (J). pap. 19.95 **(978-1-4301-2664-5(7))** Live Oak Media.

—Dolphins (4 Paperbacks/1 CD), 4 vols. 2017. (National Geographic Kids Ser.). (ENG.). (J). pap., pap. 31.95 **(978-1-4301-2666-9(3))** Live Oak Media.

Stewart, Melissa. Shark or Dolphin? How Do You Know? 2011. (Which Animal Is Which? Ser.). (Illus.). 24p. (J). (gr. k-18). pap. 7.95 (978-1-59845-239-6(8), Enslow Elementary); lib. bdg. 22.60 (978-0-7660-3680-2(4)) Enslow Pubs., Inc.

Swift, Christine, illus. Splash, Dolphin! 2014. (Shake, Rattle, Splash Ser.). (ENG.). 8p. (J). (gr. -1 — 1). 6.99 (978-1-4380-0421-1(4)) Barron's Educational Series, Inc.

Taylor, Trace & Sánchez, Lucía M. Delfines: Dolphins. 2010. (2G Animales Marinos Ser.). (SPA.). 12p. (J). (gr. k-2). pap. 6.99 (978-1-61541-282-2(4)) American Reading Co.

Taylor, Trace & Sanchez, Lucia M. Delfines (Dolphins) 2011. (poder de 100 - Animales marinos Ser.). (SPA.). 12p. pap. 39.62 (978-1-61541-283-9(2)) American Reading Co.

Teora, creator. Dolphins. 2007. (My First Sticker Encyclopedia Ser.). (Illus.). 18p. (J). (gr. -1-3). pap. 5.95 (978-1-59496-149-6(2)) Teora USA LLC.

Thomas, Elizabeth. Bottlenose Dolphins. 2014. (21st Century Skills Library: Exploring Our Oceans Ser.). (ENG., Illus.). 32p. (J). (gr. 3-6). 28.50 (978-1-62431-598-5(4), 203176) Cherry Lake Publishing.

Thomson, Sarah L. Amazing Dolphins! Wildlife Conservation Society, photos by. 2008. (I Can Read Level 2 Ser.). (ENG., Illus.). 32p. (J). (gr. k-3). pap. 3.99 (978-0-06-054455-3(4)) HarperCollins Pubs.

Tuchman, Gail & Buckley, James, Jr. Dolphin Dive. 2014. (Scholastic Discover More Readers Ser.). (ENG.). 32p. (J). (gr. 1-2). pap. 3.99 (978-0-545-63632-2(9), Scholastic Reference) Scholastic, Inc.

Turnbull, Stephanie. Dolphin. 2015. (ENG., Illus.). 24p. (J). pap. 8.95 (978-1-77092-212-9(1)) RiverStream Publishing.

—Dolphins. 2013. (Big Beasts Ser.). (Illus.). 24p. (gr. k-3). 28.50 (978-1-62588-169-4(X)) Black Rabbit Bks.

Turner, Pamela S. The Dolphins of Shark Bay. 2016. (Scientists in the Field Ser.). (ENG., Illus.). 80p. (J). (gr. 5-7). pap. 9.99 (978-0-544-80909-3(2), HMH Books For Young Readers) Houghton Mifflin Harcourt Publishing Co.

—The Dolphins of Shark Bay. Tuason, Scott, photos by. 2013. (Scientists in the Field Ser.). (ENG., Illus.). 80p. (J). (gr. 5-7). 18.99 (978-0-547-71638-1(9)) Houghton Mifflin Harcourt Publishing Co.

Vail, Grace. Dolphin Doubles. 2013. (Animal Math Ser.). 24p. (J). (gr. 1-3). 22.60 (978-1-4339-9306-0(6)); pap. 8.15 (978-1-4339-9303-9(1)); pap. 48.90 (978-1-4339-9304-6(X)) Stevens, Gareth Publishing LLLP.

Walker, Sally M. Dolphins. rev. ed. 2007. (Nature Watch Ser.). (ENG., Illus.). 48p. (J). (gr. 4-8). lib. bdg. 27.93 (978-0-8225-6767-7(9), Lerner Pubns.) Lerner Publishing Group.

Wallace, Karen. DK Readers L1: Diving Dolphin: Diving Dolphin. 2015. (DK Readers Ser.). (ENG., Illus.). 48p. (J). (gr. k-2). pap. 3.99 (978-1-4654-2829-5(1), DK Children) Dorling Kindersley Publishing, Inc.

Waxman, Laura Hamilton. Diving Dolphins. (Pull Ahead Bks.). (Illus.). 32p. (gr. k-3). 2005. lib. bdg. 22.60 (978-0-8225-0684-3(X)) 2003. (ENG., (J). pap. 6.95 (978-0-8225-0964-6(4)) Lerner Publishing Group.

Webb, Sophie. Far from Shore: Chronicles of an Open Ocean Voyage. 2011. (ENG., Illus.). 80p. (J). (gr. 5-7). 17.99 (978-0-618-59729-1(8)) Houghton Mifflin Harcourt Publishing Co.

Weber, Valerie J. Dolphins. 2008. (Animals That Live in the Ocean Ser.). (Illus.). 24p. (J). (gr. -1-3). lib. bdg. 22.60 (978-0-8368-9240-6(2), Weekly Reader Leveled Readers) Stevens, Gareth Publishing LLLP.

—Dolphins (Delfines) 2008. (Animals That Live in the Ocean/Animales Que Viven en el Oceano Ser.). (SPA & ENG.). 24p. (gr. -1-3). pap. 8.15 (978-0-8368-9345-8(X), Weekly Reader Leveled Readers) Stevens, Gareth Publishing LLLP.

—Dolphins/Delfines. 2008. (Animals That Live in the Ocean/Animales Que Viven en el Oceano Ser.). (SPA & ENG.). 24p. (J). (gr. -1-3). lib. bdg. 22.60 (978-0-8368-9246-8(1), Weekly Reader Leveled Readers) Stevens, Gareth Publishing LLLP.

Wendorff, Anne. Orcas. 2008. (Oceans Alive Ser.). (ENG., Illus.). 24p. (J). (gr. k-3). lib. bdg. 25.95 (978-1-60014-205-5(2)) Bellwether Media.

Westerskov, Kim, photos by. Dolphins. 2004. (Illus.). 32p. (J). pap. (978-0-7685-2110-8(6)) Dominie Pr., Inc.

Whales & Dolphins. (Eyes on Nature Ser.). 32p. (J). (gr. 1). pap. *(978-1-882210-56-5(5))* Action Publishing, Inc.
Whales & Dolphins. (Eyes on Nature Ser.). (Illus.). 32p. (J). (gr. 1-18). 7.95 *(978-1-56156-423-1(0))* Kidsbooks, LLC.
Whales & Dolphins Pack [Scholastic]. 2011. (Whales & Dolphins up Close Ser.). 24p. pap. 2.00 *(978-1-4296-6325-0(1),* First Facts) Capstone Press of Coughlan Cos.
Wicker, Jan Lee. Those Delightful Dolphins. Weaver, Steve, illus. 2007. (Those Amazing Animals Ser.). (ENG.). 55p. (J). (gr. k). per. 9.95 *(978-1-56164-381-3(5))* Pineapple Pr., Inc.
Wildlife Education, Ltd Staff, contrib. by. Dolphins. (Critters Up Close Ser.). (Illus.). (J). 2006. bds. 5.95 *(978-1-932396-14-0(4))* 2005. 20p. *(978-1-932396-09-6(8))* Wildlife Education, Ltd.
Worth, Bonnie. A Whale of a Tale! All about Porpoises, Dolphins, & Whales. Ruiz, Aristides & Mathieu, Joe, illus. 2006. (Cat in the Hat's Learning Library). (ENG.). 48p. (J). (gr. -1-3). 9.99 *(978-0-375-82279-7(8),* Random Hse. Bks. for Young Readers) Random Hse. Children's Bks.
Yates, David & Hatkoff, Craig. Hope for Winter - The True Story of Two Dolphins' Remarkable Friendship. 2014. (ENG.). 40p. (J). (gr. -1-3). 17.99 *(978-0-545-75037-0(7))* Scholastic, Inc.

DOLPHINS—FICTION

Aldrich, Sandra D. Danny Dolphin. 2012. 30p. 19.95 *(978-1-4626-6594-5(2))* America Star Bks.
Anderson, Lonzo. Arion & the Dolphins. 2017. (ENG.). 32p. (J). (gr. -1-3). 13.99 ***(978-1-5344-1242-2(5),*** Atheneum Bks. for Young Readers) Simon & Schuster Children's Publishing.
Andrews, McKenna. Riding the Storm Out. 2006. 73p. pap. 22.99 *(978-1-4116-7216-1(X))* Lulu Pr., Inc.
Armstrong, Kim. Frosty the Snowbear. 2009. 48p. pap. 12.99 *(978-1-935436-96-6(1))* Rodaian Pr.
Bahhur, Hana T. The Red Dolphin: Looking for a Friend. 2008. 32p. (J). pap. 14.92 *(978-1-4251-7557-3(0))* Trafford Publishing.
Ballantyne, R. M. The World of Ice. 2006. (Illus.). pap. *(978-1-4065-0533-7(1))* Dodo Pr.
Baltazar, Art. Starro & the Space Dolphins, 1 vol. Baltazar, Art, illus. 2012. (DC Super-Pets Ser.). (ENG., Illus.). 56p. (gr. 2-2). pap. 4.95 *(978-1-4048-7217-2(5));* lib. bdg. 23.99 *(978-1-4048-6487-0(3))* Picture Window Bks. (DC Super-Pets).
Belcher, Angie & Belcher, Andy. Swimming with Dolphins. 2005. (Big Cat Ser.). pap. 6.50 *(978-1-60457-102-8(0))* Pacific Learning, Inc.
Bond, Linda. Retishella & the Dolphins. 2006. 50p. pap. 16.95 *(978-1-4241-1868-7(9))* PublishAmerica, Inc.
Book Buddy: Dolphin with Story Book. Orig. Title: Child's Play. (Illus.). 10p. (J). (gr. -1-3). reprint ed. *(978-1-881469-49-0(2))* Safari, Ltd.
Bornemann, Elsa. Cuadernos de un Delfin. 2003. (SPA., Illus.). 125p. (J). (gr. 5-8). pap. 11.95 *(978-950-511-724-6(8))* Santillana USA Publishing Co., Inc.
Burchett, Jan & Vogler, Sara. Ocean S. O. S. Le Feyer, Diane, illus. 2013. (Wild Rescue Ser.). (ENG.). 152p. (gr. 3-6). 9.95 *(978-1-4342-4891-6(7))* Stone Arch Bks.
—Ocean S. O. S. Le Feyer, Diane & Kennedy, Sam, illus. 2012. (Wild Rescue Ser.). (ENG.). 152p. (gr. 3-6). lib. bdg. 25.32 *(978-1-4342-3771-2(0))* Stone Arch Bks.
Butterfield, Moira. Dolphin Finds a Star. (Glitter Books Ser.). 24p. *(978-1-4054-7604-1(4))* Parragon, Inc.
Carris, Joan D. A Ghost of a Chance. 2003. (Legends of the Carolinas Ser.). 155p. (J). 8.95 *(978-1-928556-40-4(X))* Coastal Carolina Pr.
Cavanagh, Peter J. Fungie: The Dingle Dolphin. 2008. 48p. per. 24.95 *(978-1-4241-8356-2(1))* America Star Bks.
Chapman, Karen B. The Marino Mission: One Girl, One Mission, One Thousand Words - 1,000 Need-to-Know New 'SAT Vocabulary Words. 2004. (ENG.). 336p. pap. 15.99 *(978-0-7645-7831-1(6))* Houghton Mifflin Harcourt Publishing Co.
Christen, Dennis H. Lundon's Bridge & the Three Keys. 2008. 221p. (J). pap. 12.95 *(978-0-9718151-5-5(1))* C-It Entertainment Group, LLC.
Colhoun, Sheelah. Elric's Florida Holiday. Cotton, Sue Lynn, illus. 2012. 20p. pap. 13.95 *(978-1-61493-110-2(0))* Peppertree Pr., The.
Cordish, Janet Luckey. Dolly Dolphin. Cordish, Janet Luckey, illus. 2004. (Illus.). 32p. (J). (gr. k-3). 19.95 *(978-0-9661315-6-7(8))* FreeStar Pr.
Craipeau, Jean-Lou & Dutrieux, Brigitte. Half & Half-Giants of the Ocean: Great Story & Cool Facts. Hyman, Miles & Alibert, Eric, illus. 2009. 56p. (J). pap. 4.99 *(978-1-60115-212-1(4))* Treasure Bay, Inc.
Craipeau, Jean-Lou & Dutrieux, Julien. Half & Half-Giants of the Ocean: Great Story & Cool Facts. Hyman, Miles & Alibert, Eric, illus. 2009. 56p. (J). 9.95 *(978-1-60115-211-4(6))* Treasure Bay, Inc.
Crouse, Donna J. The Ruby Ring: The Whispering Cove Kids Club. 2005. 114p. pap. 12.99 *(978-0-9765339-0-0(1))* Crouse, Donna J.
Crowe, Ellie. Go to Sleep, Hide & Seek. Wu, Julie, illus. 2009. 10p. (J). bds. 11.95 *(978-1-59700-759-7(5))* Island Heritage Publishing.
Cruz Garcia, Juanita. Yocumal & Juno. 2009. 16p. pap. 8.99 *(978-1-4490-2631-8(1))* AuthorHouse.
Damitz, Charlie. Diving for el Corazon. Diefendorf, Cathy, illus. 2007. (ENG.). 101p. (J). pap. 7.95 *(978-0-9744446-3-5(4))* All About Kids Publishing.
Daniels, Lucy. Oscar's Best Friends. 2005. 57p. *(978-0-439-68199-5(5))* Scholastic, Inc.
Dell, Scott O. L Isola Dei Delfini Blu. pap. 16.95 *(978-88-09-02504-2(0))* Giunti Gruppo Editoriale ITA. Dist: Distribooks, Inc.
Denver, John. Ancient Rhymes, a Dolphin Lullaby: With Audio CD & Score, 1 vol. Canyon, Christopher, illus. 2004. (Sharing Nature with Children Book Ser.). (ENG.). 36p. (J). (gr. -1-6). 19.95 *(978-1-58469-064-1(X))* Dawn Pubns.
Depken, Kristen L. Little Lost Dolphin. 2014. (Barbie Step into Reading Level 2 Ser.). lib. bdg. 13.55 *(978-0-606-35191-1(4))* Turtleback Bks.
Dipietro, Frances. Eagle & Dolphin: We Are Wonderfully Made. 2010. 28p. 16.09 *(978-1-4269-3315-8(0))* Trafford Publishing.
Dolphin Diaries. 2005. (J). *(978-1-59564-639-2(6))* Steps To Literacy, LLC.
Dolphin Halloween & Elsie's Scrapbook. l.t. ed. 2004. (Illus.). 32p. (J). mass mkt. 4.99 *(978-0-9760868-0-2(8))* Pluegl Bks.
The Dolphin's Gift: El Don Del Delfin. 2005. (J). per. 8.95 *(978-0-9766572-0-0(1))* Tucu Pr.
Donovan, Stacey. Who I Am Keeps Happening. 2004. (YA). *(978-0-7636-1988-6(4))* Candlewick Pr.
Douglas, Babette. Amazing Grace. Rockwell, Barry, illus. 2006. (Kiss a Me Teacher Creature Stories Ser.). (J). (gr. 3-7). 9.99 *(978-1-890343-33-0(1))* Kiss A Me Productions, Inc.
Duey, Kathleen. Tahi: A Baby Dolphin's Story. Gurin, Lara, illus. 2009. (ENG.). 32p. 12.99 *(978-0-8249-1434-9(1),* Ideal Pubns.) Worthy Publishing.
Emmer, E. R. The Dolphin Project. 2004. (Going to Ser.). (ENG., Illus.). 202p. (J). (gr. 4-8). pap. 6.95 *(978-1-893577-12-1(0))* Fruitbearer Publishing, LLC.
Fripp, Deborah & Fripp, Michael. Naya & the Haunted Shipwreck. Fripp, Jean, ed. Barbor, Carol, illus. 2004. 32p. (J). (gr. k-4). pap. 5.99 *(978-0-9701008-7-0(6))* Bicast, Inc.
Galvin, Laura. Baby Dolphin's Busy Day. 2008. (Smithsonian Baby Animals Ser.). (ENG., Illus.). 16p. (gr. -1-k). 13.95 *(978-1-59249-792-8(6))* Soundprints.
Galvin, Laura Gates. Baby Dolphin's Busy Day. 2007. (Baby Animals Ser.). (ENG., Illus.). 16p. (gr. -1-k). 6.95 *(978-1-59249-745-4(4))* Soundprints.
—Baby Dolphins Busy Day. 2011. (Baby Animals (Soundprints) Ser.). (ENG., Illus.). 16p. (gr. -1-k). 15.95 *(978-1-60727-329-5(2))* Soundprints.
Gillingham, Sara. In My Ocean. Siminovich, Lorena, illus. 2011. (ENG.). 12p. (J). (gr. -1 — 1). bds. 8.99 *(978-0-8118-7717-6(5))* Chronicle Bks. LLC.
Gillrie Fraser, Marg. The Dolphin Way. 2011. 156p. (gr. -1 — 1). 22.95 *(978-1-4502-8225-3(3));* pap. 12.95 *(978-1-4502-8224-6(5))* iUniverse, Inc.
Gillrie-Fraser, Margaret. The Dolphin Way. 2011. 120p. pap. 36.99 *(978-1-4634-3638-4(6))* AuthorHouse.
—The Dolphin Way: Learn about the amazing underwater sea world of Mattie the Dolphin as he soars through one exciting adventure after Another! 2011. 152p. pap. 42.21 *(978-1-4634-3635-3(1))* AuthorHouse.
Gold, Rainbow. Dolphin Dreams. 2013. 72p. pap. 18.68 *(978-1-4797-6009-1(9))* Xlibris Corp.
Green, Yuko. Naia & Kohola. 2010. 20p. pap. 6.95 *(978-1-59700-803-7(6))* Island Heritage Publishing.
Grooms, Molly. We Are Dolphins. Oda, Takashi, illus. 2004. (ENG.). 32p. (J). (gr. -1-2). pap. 7.95 *(978-1-55971-904-9(4))* Cooper Square Publishing Llc.
Halfmann, Janet. Dolphin's Rescue: The Story of a Pacific White-Sided Dolphin. Petruccio, Steven James, illus. (Smithsonian Oceanic Collection Ser.). (ENG.). 32p. (J). 2011. (gr. -1-3). 19.95 *(978-1-60727-646-3(1))* 2011. (gr. -1-3). 8.95 *(978-1-60727-647-0(X))* 2005. (gr. -1-3). 19.95 *(978-1-59249-430-9(7),* BC4028) 2005. (gr. -1-3). 4.95 *(978-1-59249-427-9(7),* B4078) 2005. (gr. -1-3). pap. 6.95 *(978-1-59249-428-6(5),* S4028) 2005. (gr. 1-3). 15.95 *(978-1-59249-426-2(9),* B4028) Soundprints.
Hapka, Catherine, pseud. Dolphin Dreams. 2017. (ENG.). 224p. (J). (gr. 3-7). pap. 6.99 ***(978-1-338-13642-5(9))*** Scholastic, Inc.
—Echo's Lucky Charm. Hibbert, Hollie, illus. 2016. (Dolphin School Ser.: 2). (ENG.). 112p. (J). (gr. 2-5). pap. 4.99 *(978-0-545-75025-7(3))* Scholastic, Inc.
—Flip's Surprise Talent. 2016. (Dolphin School Ser.: 4). (ENG., Illus.). 112p. (J). (gr. 2-5). pap. 4.99 *(978-0-545-75027-1(X),* Scholastic Paperbacks) Scholastic, Inc.
—Heart of a Dolphin. 2016. (ENG., Illus.). 192p. (J). (gr. 3-7). pap. 6.99 *(978-0-545-91763-6(8))* Scholastic, Inc.
—Pearl's Ocean Magic. Hibbert, Hollie, illus. 2016. (Dolphin School Ser.: 1). (ENG.). 112p. (J). (gr. 2-5). pap. 4.99 *(978-0-545-75024-0(5))* Scholastic, Inc.
—Splash's Secret Friend. 2016. (Dolphin School Ser.: 3). (ENG., Illus.). 112p. (J). (gr. 2-5). pap. 4.99 *(978-0-545-75026-4(1),* Scholastic Paperbacks) Scholastic, Inc.
Hapka, Cathy, pseud. Heart of a Dolphin. 2016. (Illus.). 186p. (J). pap. ***(978-1-338-03282-6(8))*** Scholastic, Inc.
Harpan, Gaile & DiMarcello, Pete. Another Dolphin's Tale, a Love Story. Baker, Edmund, illus. 2012. 16p. pap. 12.95 *(978-1-61493-057-0(0))* Peppertree Pr., The.
Harrison, Paula. Wishing Pearl. 2013. (Rescue Princesses Ser.: 2). (ENG., Illus.). 128p. (J). (gr. 2-5). pap. 4.99 *(978-0-545-50914-5(9),* Scholastic Paperbacks) Scholastic, Inc.
—Wishing Pearl. 2013. (Rescue Princesses Ser.: 2). lib. bdg. 14.75 *(978-0-606-31987-4(5),* Turtleback) Turtleback Bks.
Hawkins, Nicole. Blue. 2013. 20p. pap. 24.95 *(978-1-4137-3232-0(1))* America Star Bks.
Hesse, Karen. The Music of Dolphins. 244p. (J). pap. 4.50 *(978-0-8072-1542-5(2),* YA113P); 2004. (gr. 5-9). pap. 29.00 incl. audio *(978-0-8072-8135-2(2),* YA113SP) Random Hse. Audio Publishing Group. (Listening Library).
Humphreys, Neil. I Trapped a Dolphin but It Really Wasn't My Fault. Cheng, Puay Koon, illus. 2013. (Abbie Rose & the Magic Suitcase Ser.). (ENG.). 24p. (J). (gr. -1-3). pap. 9.90 *(978-981-4408-51-6(4))* Marshall Cavendish International (Asia) Private Ltd. SGP. Dist: National Bk. Network.
Image Books Staff. Little Dolphin. Put, Klaartje van der, illus. 2012. (Little Finger Puppet Board Bks.: FING). (ENG.). 12p. (J). (gr. -1 — 1). bds. 6.99 *(978-1-4521-0816-2(1))* Chronicle Bks. LLC.
Jalonen, Nicole. Magical Animal Army Adventures. 2012. 28p. pap. 15.99 *(978-1-4691-7544-7(4))* Xlibris Corp.
James, Larry W. Captain Petey: An Adventure at Sea. Ramos, Violet M., ed. James, Larry W. & Freshman, Floris R., illus. 2003. 28p. pap. 6.99 *(978-0-9742154-0-2(6))* Cross Pointe Printing.
Jefferson, Patti Brassard. How Long Will You Love Me? Jefferson, Patti Brassard, illus. 2013. (Illus.). 28p. pap. 12.95 *(978-1-61244-178-8(5))* Halo Publishing International.
Jensen, Kathryn. Splash! 2012. 194p. 29.95 *(978-1-4489-6574-8(8))* America Star Bks.
Johnson, Rebecca. Little Dolphin's Big Leap. Parish, Steve, illus. 2005. (Animal Storybooks Ser.). 24p. (gr. k-3). lib. bdg. 22.00 *(978-0-8368-5973-7(1),* Gareth Stevens Learning Library) Stevens, Gareth Publishing LLLP.
Joy, Eliza. The Yellow Dolphin. 2012. (Illus.). 12p. pap. 18.30 *(978-1-4685-8222-2(4))* AuthorHouse.
Kendall, Sarita H. Al Rescate de Omacha. (SPA.). (YA). (gr. 5-8). 8.95 *(978-958-04-2930-2(8),* NR2139) Norma S.A. COL. Dist: Distribuidora Norma, Inc., Lectorum Pubns., Inc.
Kernan, Martin James. Danger Dolphin. Finley, Thomas Murray, illus. 2012. 28p. pap. 14.95 *(978-1-4675-2428-5(X))* Independent Pub.
King, Alice (Ali). Daisy the Different Dolphin. 2010. 36p. 19.99 *(978-1-4269-1070-8(3))* Trafford Publishing.
Koerner, Miranda Pike. Blue Mermaid. 2013. 210p. pap. 12.99 *(978-1-62237-202-7(6))* Turquoise Morning Pr.
Krulik, Nancy. Going Overboard! John and Wendy Staff, illus. 2012. (Katie Kazoo, Switcheroo Ser.: No. 9). (ENG.). 144p. (J). (gr. 2-4). pap. 5.99 *(978-0-448-45681-2(8),* Grosset & Dunlap) Penguin Young Readers Group.
Lagrou, Patrick. Born among the Dolphins. 2008. (Born among the Dolphins Ser.: 1). (ENG & DUT.). 154p. (J). (gr. 3-18). 19.95 *(978-1-60537-022-4(3))* Clavis Publishing.
Lasky, Kathryn. Shadows in the Water. 2008. (ENG., Illus.). 224p. (J). (gr. 2-5). pap. 14.95 *(978-0-15-205874-6(5))* Houghton Mifflin Harcourt Publishing Co.
Law, Felicia. Darwin the Dolphin: A Tale of Bravery & Courage. Danson, Lesley, illus. 2010. (Animal Fair Values Ser.). 32p. (J). (gr. -1-3). pap. 10.55 *(978-1-60754-810-2(0));* lib. bdg. 22.60 *(978-1-60754-806-5(2))* Windmill Bks.
L'Engle, Madeleine. A Ring of Endless Light. 2006. (Austin Family Ser.: No. 5). 21.75 *(978-0-8446-7285-4(8))* Smith, Peter Pub., Inc.
—A Ring of Endless Light Bk. 4. 2008. (Austin Family Ser.: 4). (ENG.). 352p. (J). (gr. 6-12). pap. 8.99 *(978-0-312-37935-3(8),* 9780312379353) Square Fish.
Lewis, Gill. One White Dolphin. Aparicio, Raquel, illus. 2013. (ENG.). 368p. (J). (gr. 3-7). pap. 8.99 *(978-1-4424-1448-8(0),* Atheneum Bks. for Young Readers) Simon & Schuster Children's Publishing.
Lionheart, Amelia. The Dolphin Heptad. 2009. 200p. (gr. 4-6). pap. 14.95 *(978-1-4401-8028-6(8))* iUniverse, Inc.
Little Dolphin & Friends. (Flocked Soft-to-Touch Board Ser.). 5p. bds. *(978-1-4054-9503-5(0))* Parragon, Inc.
London, C. Alexander. Blood in the Water. 2014. (Tides of War Ser.: 1). (ENG.). 224p. (J). (gr. 5-9). pap. 5.99 *(978-0-545-66298-7(2),* Scholastic Paperbacks) Scholastic, Inc.
Long, Claire Nicole. Dreaming of Dolphins. 2012. (Illus.). 52p. (gr. 4-6). pap. 13.66 *(978-1-4772-3937-7(5))* AuthorHouse.
Lumry, Amanda & Hurwitz, Laura. Adventures of Riley: Dolphins in Danger. McIntyre, Sarah, illus. 2005. 36p. 15.95 *(978-0-9748411-3-0(0))* Eaglemont Pr.
Mabille, Christine. Potato-Kid & the Adventure: Treasures Within, 1 vol. 2009. 76p. pap. 19.95 *(978-1-61582-981-1(4))* America Star Bks.
MacPherson, D. R. The Sport of Kings. 2011. 92p. pap. 25.00 *(978-1-60911-294-3(6),* Strategic Bk. Publishing) Strategic Book Publishing & Rights Agency (SBPRA).
Man-Kong, Mary. Barbie in a Mermaid Tale. Golden Books Staff, illus. 2010. (Little Golden Book Ser.). (ENG.). (J). (gr. -1-2). 24p. 4.99 *(978-0-375-85733-1(8),* Golden Bks.); 16p. pap. 3.99 *(978-0-375-85735-5(4),* Random Hse. Bks. for Young Readers) Random Hse. Children's Bks.
Meister, Cari. The Clever Dolphin, 1 vol. Harpster, Steve, illus. 2012. (Ocean Tales Ser.). (ENG.). 32p. (gr. 2-4). pap. 6.25 *(978-1-4342-4229-7(3))* Stone Arch Bks.
Meyer, Bryce L. Dolphin & Manatee Friends End to End: Formerly Grant's Book of Manatees & Dolphins. 2009. 32p. pap. 16.99 *(978-1-4269-1678-6(7))* Trafford Publishing.
Miki, Roy & Miki, Slavia. Dolphin Sos, 1 vol. Flett, Julie, illus. 2014. (ENG.). 32p. (J). (gr. 1-4). 16.95 *(978-1-896580-76-0(9))* Tradewind Bks. CAN. Dist: Orca Bk. Pubs. USA.
Mogavera, Cyndie Lepori & Richards, Courtland William. Bubbles & Billy Sandwalker. Murrish, Layne Keeton, illus. 2nd ed. 2012. 106p. pap. 19.95 *(978-0-9856754-0-0(3))* IAMPress.
Mohn, Eric A. Ocean Encounter. 2005. 56p. spiral bd. 15.75 *(978-1-4116-6199-8(0))* Lulu Pr., Inc.
Morpurgo, Michael. Dolphin Boy. Foreman, Michael, illus. 2005. (ENG.). 32p. (J). (gr. k-2). pap. 13.99 *(978-1-84270-448-6(6));* 14.99 *(978-1-84270-320-5(X))* Andersen Pr. GBR. Dist: Independent Pubs. Group, Trafalgar Square Publishing.
Nickelodeon Staff & Nickelodeon / LeapFrog. Go Diego Go! Underwater Mystery. 2008. (J). 13.99 *(978-1-59319-925-8(2))* LeapFrog Enterprises, Inc.
Norman, Matthew. Domestic Violets. 2011. (P. S. Ser.). (ENG.). 352p. pap. 14.99 *(978-0-06-206511-7(4),* Harper Perennial) HarperCollins Pubs.
Nyikos, Stacy. Dizzy. Lee, Kary, illus. l.t. ed. 2006. 32p. (J). (gr. -1-3). 15.95 *(978-0-9764199-2-1(0),* 888-867-1927) Stonehorse Publishing, LLC.
O'Dell, Scott. Island of the Blue Dolphins. 2010. lib. bdg. 18.40 *(978-0-606-10724-2(X),* Turtleback) Turtleback Bks.
Ogata, Michael, illus. New Friend for Nai'a. 2009. (J). *(978-1-56647-912-7(6))* Mutual Publishing LLC.
Oliver, Lin & Baker, Theo. Sound Bender. 2011. (ENG.). 272p. (J). (gr. 5-9). 16.99 *(978-0-545-19692-5(2),* Scholastic Pr.) Scholastic, Inc.
O'Rourke, Ryan. Bella, Up, Up & Away. O'Rourke, Ryan, illus. 2016. (Illus.). 40p. (J). (gr. -1-3). 17.99 *(978-0-06-221863-6(8))* HarperCollins Pubs.
Osborne, Mary Pope. Dolphins at Daybreak. unabr. ed. 2004. (Magic Tree House Ser.: No. 9). 67p. (J). (gr. k-3). pap. 17.00 incl. audio *(978-0-8072-0534-1(6),* Listening Library) Random Hse. Audio Publishing Group.
Patenaude, Jeremy, et al. Little Dolphin. 2014. (DK Readers Ser.). (ENG.). 32p. (J). (gr. k-4). pap. 3.99 *(978-1-4654-1997-2(7),* DK Children) Dorling Kindersley Publishing, Inc.
Pavón, Mar. Zaira & the Dolphins. 2012. (ENG., Illus.). 32p. (J). (gr. k-2). *(978-84-15241-07-2(0))* D P & G Military Pubs.
—Zaira y los Delfines. 2012. (SPA & ENG., Illus.). 32p. (J). (gr. k-2). *(978-84-15241-02-7(X))* D P & G Military Pubs.
Peters, Kara L. The Adventures of the Peters Family: A Dolphin of a Time. 2013. 12p. pap. 15.99 *(978-1-4685-4404-6(7))* AuthorHouse.
Pledger, Maurice, illus. Dottie Dolphin Plays Hide-And-Seek. 2015. (Friendship Tales Ser.). (ENG.). 16p. (gr. -1). bds. 10.95 *(978-1-62686-344-6(X),* Silver Dolphin Bks.) Readerlink Distribution Services, LLC.
Posner-Sanchez, Andrea. Ariel's Dolphin Adventure - Snow White's New Friend, 2 bks. in 1. Random House Disney Staff, illus. 2010. (Pictureback(R) Ser.). (ENG.). 32p. (J). (gr. -1-2). pap. 4.99 *(978-0-7364-2654-1(X),* RH/Disney) Random Hse. Children's Bks.
Rabley, Stephen & Pearson Education Staff. Maisie & the Dolphin. 2nd ed. 2009. (ENG.). 20p. pap. 11.99 *(978-1-4058-6954-6(2))* Pearson Education.
Random House Staff. I Can Be... A Zoo Vet/I Can Be... A Cheerleader. Riley, Kellee, illus. 2011. (Pictureback(R) Ser.). (ENG.). 32p. (J). (gr. -1-2). pap. 4.99 *(978-0-375-87265-5(5),* Random Hse. Bks. for Young Readers) Random Hse. Children's Bks.
Reh, Rusalka. The Secret of the Water Knight, 0 vols. Derbyshire, Katy, tr. unabr. ed. 2011. (ENG.). 100p. (J). (gr. 4-7). pap. 9.95 *(978-1-61109-006-2(7),* 9781611090062) Amazon Publishing.
Reyes, Gabrielle. Dolphin Tale 2: The Junior Novel. 2014. (Dolphin Tale 2 Ser.). (ENG.). 144p. (J). (gr. 2-5). pap. 5.99 *(978-0-545-68174-2(X))* Scholastic, Inc.
—Dolphin Tale 2: Movie Reader. 2014. (Dolphin Tale 2 Ser.). (ENG.). 32p. (J). (gr. -1-3). pap. 3.99 *(978-0-545-68175-9(8))* Scholastic, Inc.
Robison, Dan, Jr. Kimo's Escape: The Story of a Hawaiian Boy Who Learns to Believe in Himself. 2005. 100p. (J). per. 19.95 *(978-0-922993-28-4(9))* Marquette Bks., LLC.
Rogers, Jewels. The Princess & the Dolphin. 2011. 28p. pap. 12.50 *(978-1-4567-3278-3(1))* AuthorHouse.
—The Princess & the Dolphin. 2010. 28p. pap. 16.99 *(978-1-4269-3966-2(3))* Trafford Publishing.
Rorby, Ginny. How to Speak Dolphin. (ENG.). 272p. (J). (gr. 3-7). 2017. pap. 6.99 *(978-0-545-67607-6(X))* 2015. 16.99 *(978-0-545-67605-2(3))* Scholastic, Inc. (Scholastic Pr.).
Santillo, LuAnn. Flipper. Santillo, LuAnn, ed. 2003. (Half-Pint Kids Readers Ser.). (Illus.). 7p. (J). (gr. -1-1). pap. 1.00 *(978-1-59256-095-0(4))* Half-Pint Kids, Inc.
Scholastic, Inc. Staff. Dolphin Rescue. 2014. (LEGO Friends Ser.). (ENG., Illus.). 64p. (J). (gr. 2-5). pap. 4.99 *(978-0-545-51655-6(2))* Math Solutions.
—Dolphin Rescue. 2014. (LEGO Friends Chapter Bks.: 5). lib. bdg. 14.75 *(978-0-606-35858-3(7))* Turtleback Bks.
Segal, Douglas. Dolphin's Day. 2007. 5p. 15.95 *(978-1-58117-555-4(8),* Intervisual/Piggy Toes) Bendon, Inc.
Self, Timothy. Davy the Dolphin. l.t. ed. 2003. (Illus.). 22p. (J). per. 8.99 *(978-1-932338-30-0(6))* Lifevest Publishing, Inc.
Seth, Vikram. Arion y el Delfin. Dieguez Dieguez, Remedios, tr. Ray, Jane, illus. 2004. (SPA & ENG.). 40p. (J). (gr. 2-4). 14.95 *(978-84-95939-74-6(6))* Blume ESP. Dist: Independent Pubs. Group.
Sherrow, Victoria. Bottlenose Dolphin. Wertheim, Anne, illus. 2012. (ENG.). 24p. (J). pap. 3.95 *(978-1-60727-724-8(7))* Soundprints.
Smith, Sindy. Dadu the Dolphin. Smith, Sindy, illus. 2012. (Illus.). 24p. 29.95 *(978-1-4626-9862-2(X))* America Star Bks.
Snider, Ann. The Giant Sea & Me. 2008. (Illus.). 24p. pap. 14.99 *(978-1-4389-1720-7(1))* AuthorHouse.
St. John, Lauren. Dolphin Song. 2009. (ENG.). 272p. (J). (gr. 3-7). 7.99 *(978-0-14-241375-3(5),* Puffin Books) Penguin Young Readers Group.
Tate, Suzanne. Danny & Daisy: A Tale of a Dolphin Duo. Melvin, James, illus. 2004. (Suzanne Tate's Nature Ser.: No. 13). 32p. (J). per. 10.95 *(978-1-878405-44-9(6))* Nags Head Art, Inc.
Tovey, Imogen. Maddy's Dolphin. 2009. (Illus.). 108p. pap. *(978-1-84748-532-8(4))* Athena Pr.
Trantham, Cary Gordon. The Saving of Sophi: El Rescate de Sofia. 2012. 28p. pap. 19.99 *(978-1-4772-0799-4(6))* AuthorHouse.
Wallace, Karen & Bostock, Mike. Imagine You Are a Dolphin. (Illus.). 25p. (J). pap. *(978-0-340-67833-6(X))* Hodder & Stoughton.
Waters, Summer. High Tide. 2010. (Silver Dolphins Ser.: 9). (ENG.). 176p. (J). (gr. 2-4). pap. 7.99 *(978-0-00-736749-8(X),* HarperCollins Children's Bks.) HarperCollins Pubs. Ltd. GBR. Dist: HarperCollins Pubs.
—Rising Star. 2011. (Silver Dolphins Ser.). (ENG.). 176p. (J). (gr. 2-4). pap. 7.99 *(978-0-00-734812-1(6))* HarperCollins Pubs. Ltd. GBR. Dist: Independent Pubs. Group.
—River Rescue, 10. 2010. (Silver Dolphins Ser.: 10). (ENG.). 176p. (J). (gr. 2-4). pap. 7.99 *(978-0-00-736750-4(3),* HarperCollins Children's Bks.) HarperCollins Pubs. Ltd. GBR. Dist: HarperCollins Pubs.
—Stormy Skies. 2010. (Silver Dolphins Ser.: 8). (ENG.). 176p. (J). (gr. 2-4). pap. 7.99 *(978-0-00-734813-8(4),* HarperCollins Children's Bks.) HarperCollins Pubs. Ltd. GBR. Dist: HarperCollins Pubs.
Watkins, Sam. Darcy Dolphin Is a Little Bit Magic! Barker, Vicky, illus. 2017. (Darcy Dolphin Ser.). (ENG.). 160p. (J). (gr. 1-3). pap. 9.99 ***(978-1-4052-8423-3(4))*** Egmont Bks., Ltd. GBR. Dist: Independent Pubs. Group.
Webster, Christy. Barbie in a Mermaid Tale. Random House Editors, illus. 2010. (Step into Reading Ser.). (ENG.). 32p. (J). (gr. -1-1). pap. 3.99 *(978-0-375-86450-6(4),* Random Hse. Bks. for Young Readers) Random Hse. Children's Bks.
—Barbie in a Mermaid Tale. 2010. (Barbie Step into Reading Level 2 Ser.). lib. bdg. 13.55 *(978-0-606-07031-7(1),* Turtleback) Turtleback Bks.
Weinberger, Kimberly. Dolphin's Big Leap. Ziss, Debra, illus. 2003. (Hello Reader! Ser.). 30p. (J). *(978-0-439-44159-9(5))* Scholastic, Inc.
Weiss, Shelly. Dillin the Dolphin. 2003. 32p. (J). per. 15.00 *(978-1-59196-454-4(7))* Instant Pub.
Wejrmeijer, Annelien. Lily & Dolly. van de Liejgraaf, Deborah, illus. 2013. (My Best Friend & Me Ser.). (ENG.). 10p. (J). (gr. -1 — 1). bds. 6.99 *(978-0-7641-6636-5(0))* Barron's Educational Series, Inc.
Whispers from the Bay. 2008. 224p. (YA). 22.95 *(978-0-9794454-0-8(X))* Tkac, John Enterprises LLC.
Williams, Jo. The Golden Dolphin. 2011. 28p. pap. 16.95 *(978-1-4626-2951-0(2))* America Star Bks.
Wilson, CeCe. Dolphin's Big Day. 2015. (Rosen REAL Readers: STEM & STEAM Collection). (ENG.). 8p. pap. 5.46 *(978-1-4994-9501-0(3),* Rosen Classroom) Rosen Publishing Group, Inc., The.

C
D

Winton, Tim. The Deep. Louise, Karen, illus. 32p. (YA). pap. 13.95 *(978-1-86368-210-7(4))* Fremantle Pr. AUS. Dist: Independent Pubs. Group.

Wishinsky, Frieda. Avis Dolphin, 1 vol. Dawson, Willow, illus. 2015. (ENG.). 128p. (J). (gr. 3-7). 16.95 *(978-1-55498-489-3(0))* Groundwood Bks. CAN. Dist: Publishers Group West (PGW).

Wlodarski, Loran. If a Dolphin Were a Fish, 1 vol. Klein, Laurie Allen, illus. 2006. (ENG.). 32p. (J). (gr. -1-2). 15.95 *(978-0-9768823-2-9(9))* Arbordale Publishing.

Wright, Mary. Co-Man & Poppa Meet Kanka. Dewitt, Levi, illus. 2013. 24p. pap. 24.95 *(978-1-62709-328-6(1))* America Star Bks.

Wright, Mary F. Co-Man the Dolphin. 2011. 24p. pap. 24.95 *(978-1-4560-2549-6(X))* America Star Bks.

Zoehfeld, Kathleen Weidner. Dolphin's First Day: The Story of a Bottlenose Dolphin. Petruccio, Steven James, illus. (Smithsonian Oceanic Collection). (J). 2009. 24.95 incl. audio compact disk *(978-1-59249-666-2(0))* 2003. (ENG.). 32p. (gr. -1-3). pap. 6.95 *(978-1-59249-056-1(5)*, S4001) Soundprints.

Zoehfeld, Kathleen Weidner & Petruccio, Steven James. Dolphin's First Day: The Story of a Bottlenose Dolphin. 2003. (Smithsonian Oceanic Collection). (ENG., Illus.). 32p. (J). (gr. -1-3). 8.95 *(978-1-59249-064-6(6)*, SC4001) Soundprints.

Zoehfeld, Kathleen Weidner & Smithsonian Institution Staff. Primer Dia del Delfin: La Historia de un Delfin Nariz de Botella. 2008.Tr. of Dolphin's First Day - The Story of a Bottlenose Dolphin. (MUL & SPA.). 16p. 14.95 *(978-1-59249-848-2(5))* Soundprints.

DOMESTIC ANIMALS

see also Animals—Treatment; Camels; Cats; Cattle; Cows; Dogs; Horses; Livestock; Pets; Reindeer; Sheep

Acampora, Courtney & DiPerna, Kaitlyn. Read with Me! Pre, Level 1. 2016. (Smithsonian Readers Ser.). (ENG., Illus.). 200p. (J). (gr. -1). 14.95 *(978-1-62686-571-6(X)*, Silver Dolphin Bks.) Readerlink Distribution Services, LLC.

Ackerman, Jill & Bryan, Beth. Petting Farm, Set. Karp, Ken, photos by. 2007. (Little Scholastic Ser.). (ENG., Illus.). 12p. (J). (gr. k — 1). 12.99 *(978-0-439-88558-4(2)*, Cartwheel Bks.) Scholastic, Inc.

Ackland, Nick. On the Farm. McDonald, Jake, illus. 2017. (Who's Hiding? Bks.). (ENG.). 10p. (J). (gr. -1 — 1). bds. 7.99 *(978-0-7641-6875-8(4))* Barron's Educational Series, Inc.

—What Noise Does a Cow Make? Bee, Bella, illus. 2016. (What Noise Does A... Ser.). (ENG.). 10p. (J). (gr. -1 — 1). bds. 6.99 *(978-0-7641-6843-7(6))* Barron's Educational Series, Inc.

Amery, Heather. La Oveja Rizos. Cartwright, Stephen, illus. 2004. (Titles in Spanish Ser.). (SPA.). 10p. (J). bds. 3.99 *(978-0-7460-6104-6(8)*, Usborne) EDC Publishing.

Andrews, Alexa. On a Farm. Keimig, Candice, illus. 2013. (Penguin Young Readers, Level 1 Ser.). (ENG.). 32p. (J). (gr. k-1). mass mkt. 3.99 *(978-0-448-46376-6(8)*, Penguin Young Readers) Penguin Young Readers Group.

Appleby, Alex. Dinosaurs on the Farm. 2013. (Dinosaur School Ser.). 24p. (J). (gr. k-1). pap. 8.15 *(978-1-4339-9058-8(X))*; pap. 48.90 *(978-1-4339-9059-5(8))*; (ENG., Illus.). lib. bdg. 22.60 *(978-1-4339-9057-1(1))* Stevens, Gareth Publishing LLLP.

Arcturus Publishing Staff. Lots to Spot: Farm. 2017. (ENG., Illus.). 48p. (J). (gr. k-5). 9.99 ***(978-1-78428-476-3(9)***, 9781784284763) Arcturus Publishing GBR. Dist: Bookmasters Distribution.

Armadillo Press Staff. My Book of Baby Animals: A Fun-Packed Picture & Puzzle Book for Little Ones. 2016. (ENG., Illus.). 48p. bds. 9.99 *(978-1-86147-662-3(0)*, Armadillo) Anness Publishing GBR. Dist: National Bk. Network.

AZ Books Staff. Animales - Farm Animals: Farm Animals. Gorbachenok, Ekaterina, ed. 2012. (Spanish for Kids Ser.). (ENG & SPA.). 10p. (J). (gr. -1-k). 11.95 *(978-1-61889-135-8(9))* AZ Bks. LLC.

—Farm Animals. Gorojan, Elena, ed. 2012. (My First Library). (ENG.). 12p. (J). (gr. -1-k). bds. 8.95 *(978-1-61889-123-5(5))* AZ Bks. LLC.

—Loud Farm. Tulup, Natalia, ed. 2012. (How We Speak Ser.). (ENG.). 12p. (J). (-k). bds. 10.95 *(978-1-61889-093-1(X))* AZ Bks. LLC.

—On the Farm. Ulasevich, Olga, ed. 2012. (Animal Sounds Ser.). (ENG.). 14p. (J). (-k). bds. 7.95 *(978-1-61889-129-7(4))* AZ Bks. LLC.

—Sounds of the Farm. Sheljagovich, Yana, ed. 2012. (Sounds Around Us Ser.). (ENG.). 16p. (J). (gr. 1-3). bds. 17.95 *(978-1-61889-029-0(8))* AZ Bks. LLC.

—Visiting the Farm. Zuk, Valentina, ed. 2012. (Lively Pictures Ser.). (ENG.). 10p. (J). (gr. -1-k). bds. 9.95 *(978-1-61889-182-2(0))* AZ Bks. LLC.

Bampton, Bob, illus. Animals on the Farm. 2004. (Look & Learn about Ser.). 18p. (J). bds. 5.99 *(978-1-85854-319-2(3))* Brimax Books Ltd. GBR. Dist: Byeway Bks.

Barraclough, Sue. Farm Animals. 2009. (Me & My World Ser.). (Illus.). 24p. (J). (gr. -1-2). pap. 8.15 *(978-1-60754-060-1(6))*; lib. bdg. 22.60 *(978-1-60754-056-4(8))* Windmill Bks.

Baxter, Nicola. We Love Animals on the Farm. Henson, Gaby, illus. 2013. (ENG.). 12p. (J). (gr. -1-12). 9.99 *(978-1-84322-693-2(6)*, Armadillo) Anness Publishing GBR. Dist: National Bk. Network.

Bicknell, Joanna. Googlies: Funny Farm. 2006. (Illus.). 12p. (gr. -1). per. *(978-1-84610-295-0(2))* Make Believe Ideas.

Bingham, Jane. Animal Heroes, 1 vol. 2011. (War Stories Ser.). (ENG.). 32p. (gr. 3-6). 30.65 *(978-1-4329-4834-4(2)*, NA-h) Heinemann-Raintree.

Blane, Francisco. Farm Animals: Lap Book. 2009. (My First Reader's Theater Set B Ser.). (J). 28.00 *(978-1-4108-8540-1(2))* Benchmark Education Co.

Bloomsbury USA. Baby's First Words: Farm. 2016. (ENG., Illus.). 10p. (J). (— 1). bds. 5.99 *(978-1-61963-825-9(8)*, 9781619638259, Bloomsbury Activity Bks.) Bloomsbury Publishing USA.

Bonforte, Lisa. Farm Animals Coloring Book. 2012. (Dover Little Activity Bks.). (ENG., Illus.). 64p. (J). (gr. k-3). pap. 1.99 *(978-0-486-29781-1(0))* Dover Pubns., Inc.

Borth, Teddy. Animals on the Farm, 1 vol. 2014. (On the Farm Ser.). (ENG.). 24p. (J). (gr. 4-8). lib. bdg. 28.50 *(978-1-62970-050-2(9))* ABDO Publishing Co.

Borth, Teddy, et al. Animales de la Granja. 2015. (En la Granja Ser.). (SPA., Illus.). 24p. (gr. k-1). pap. 7.95 *(978-1-4966-0443-9(1))* Capstone Classroom.

Butterfield, Moira. Farm Animals. 2006. (Illus.). 24p. (YA). (gr. 1-18). lib. bdg. 22.80 *(978-1-931983-61-7(5))* Chrysalis Education.

Cabat, Erni. Erni Cabat's Magical ABC: Animals Around the Farm. Date not set. (Illus.). 64p. (Orig.). (J). (gr. -1-2). 23.00 *(978-0-943173-73-3(6))* Cabat Studio Pubns.

Cambell, Rod & Wen, Dref. Anifeiliaid y Fferm. 2005. (WEL., Illus.). 14p. *(978-1-85596-654-3(9))* Dref Wen.

Campbell, Rod. Farm Animals. Campbell, Rod, illus. 2015. (Dear Zoo & Friends Ser.). (ENG., Illus.). 14p. (J). (gr. -1 — 1). bds. 6.99 *(978-1-4814-4984-7(2)*, Little Simon) Little Simon.

Cardenas, Ernesto A. Baby, Mom, & Dad. 2009. 19.95 *(978-1-60698-002-6(5))*; pap. 3.95 *(978-1-60698-000-2(9))* Milo Educational Bks. & Resources.

Carr, Aaron. Bison. 2014. (Illus.). 24p. (J). *(978-1-62127-230-4(3))* Weigl Pubs., Inc.

—Goose. 2014. (Illus.). 24p. (J). *(978-1-62127-231-1(1))* Weigl Pubs., Inc.

—Horses. 2014. (Illus.). 24p. (J). *(978-1-62127-232-8(X))* Weigl Pubs., Inc.

Casado, Alicia & Casado, Dami. Los Ruidos de la Granja. 2005. (SPA.). 12p. 7.99 *(978-84-272-8291-9(5))* Molino, Editorial ESP. Dist: Santillana USA Publishing Co., Inc.

Children's Press, contrib. by. Piglets Belong to Pigs. 2009. (Rookie Preschool Ser.). (ENG.). 24p. (J). (gr. -1). 23.00 *(978-0-531-24408-1(3)*, Children's Pr.) Scholastic Library Publishing.

Clay, Kathryn & Doyle, Sheri. Farm Animals. 2012. (Farm Animals Ser.). (ENG.). 24p. (gr. k-1). lib. bdg. 159.90 *(978-1-4296-9173-4(5)*, Pebble Plus) Capstone Press of Coughlan Cos.

Cleeves, Frances. Feeding Farm Animals: Use Place Value & Properties of Operation to Add. 2013. (InfoMax Math Readers Ser.). (ENG.). 24p. (J). (gr. 1-2). pap. 8.25 *(978-1-4777-2136-0(3)*, Rosen Classroom) Rosen Publishing Group, Inc., The.

—Feeding Farm Animals: Use Place Value & Properties of Operations to Subtract. 2013. (InfoMax Math Readers Ser.). (ENG.). 24p. (J). (gr. 1-2). pap. 49.50 *(978-1-4777-2137-7(1)*, Rosen Classroom) Rosen Publishing Group, Inc., The.

Cooper, Wade. Farm Animals. Cooper, Wade, illus. 2009. (Scholastic Reader Level 2 Ser.). (ENG., Illus.). 32p. (J). (gr. -1-3). pap. 3.99 *(978-0-545-09993-6(5)*, Cartwheel Bks.) Scholastic, Inc.

Creese, Sarah. Mad about Chicks Lambs & Other Farm Animals. 2009. (Mad About Ser.). (ENG., Illus.). 24p. (J). (gr. -1-3). pap. 3.99 *(978-1-84879-000-1(7))* Make Believe Ideas GBR. Dist: Nelson, Thomas Inc.

Dale, Jay. Baby Farm Animals, 1 vol. 2012. (Engage Literacy Blue Ser.). (ENG.). 32p. (gr. k-2). pap. 5.99 *(978-1-4296-8990-8(0)*, Engage Literacy) Capstone Press of Coughlan Cos.

Daynes, Katie. Farm Animals. Fox, Christyan, illus. 2006. (Beginners Nature: Level 1 Ser.). 32p. (J). (gr. k-2). 4.99 *(978-0-7945-1396-2(4)*, Usborne) EDC Publishing.

—Flip Flap Farm. 2009. (Flip Flap Board Bks). 13p. (J). (gr. -1). bds. 14.99 *(978-0-7945-2348-0(X)*, Usborne) EDC Publishing.

de Lambilly-Bresson, Elisabeth. Animals on the Farm. 2007. (Animal Show & Tell Ser.). (Illus.). 16p. (gr. -1-3). lib. bdg. 19.00 *(978-0-8368-7834-9(5)*, Gareth Stevens Learning Library) Stevens, Gareth Publishing LLLP.

Diaz, Joanne Ruelos. Animals on the Farm, 1 vol. Mendez, Simon, illus. 2014. (Animals All Day! Ser.). (ENG.). 32p. (gr. k-2). 27.27 *(978-1-4795-5699-1(8))* Picture Window Bks.

Dickmann, Nancy. Los Animales de la Granja. 2011. (Mundo de la Granja Ser.). 24p. (gr. -1-1). (SPA & ENG.). 22.65 *(978-1-4329-5306-5(0))*; (ENG & SPA.). pap. 6.29 *(978-1-4329-5313-3(3))* Heinemann-Raintree. (Bellota).

—Farm Animals, 1 vol. 2010. (World of Farming Ser.). (ENG.). 24p. (gr. -1-1). pap. 6.29 *(978-1-4329-3941-0(6)*, Acorn) Heinemann-Raintree.

Dils, Tracey E. Down on the Farm 1,2,3: A Farm Counting Book. 2015. (1, 2, 3... Count with Me Ser.). (ENG., Illus.). 24p. (J). (gr. k-2). 19.95 *(978-1-60753-718-2(4))* Amicus Publishing.

Dorling Kindersley Publishing Staff. Baby Baa Baa! 2009. (ENG.). 16p. (J). (gr. -1 — 1). bds. 6.99 *(978-0-7566-5802-1(0)*, DK Children) Dorling Kindersley Publishing, Inc.

—Farm. 2014. (ENG., Illus.). 10p. (J). (gr. -1 — 1). bds. 6.99 *(978-1-4654-1687-2(0)*, DK Children) Dorling Kindersley Publishing, Inc.

—Farm Animals. (ENG., (J). 2016. Illus.). 32p. (-k). 8.99 *(978-1-4654-4834-7(9))* 2011. 14p. (gr. -1 — 1). bds. 5.99 *(978-0-7566-8986-5(4))* Dorling Kindersley Publishing, Inc. (DK Children).

—Farm Friends. 2013. (Baby Touch & Feel Ser.). (ENG., Illus.). 14p. (J). (gr. -1 — 1). bds. 5.99 *(978-1-4654-1672-8(2)*, DK Children) Dorling Kindersley Publishing, Inc.

—Noisy Farm Peekaboo! 2015. (ENG., Illus.). 12p. (J). (— 1). bds. 12.99 *(978-1-4654-3820-1(3)*, DK Children) Dorling Kindersley Publishing, Inc.

—Noisy Peekaboo! Baa! Baa! 2009. (ENG.). 12p. (J). (gr. -1 — 1). bds. 12.99 *(978-0-7566-4299-0(X)*, DK Children) Dorling Kindersley Publishing, Inc.

—Who Am I? Farm Animals. 2012. (ENG.). 28p. (J). (gr. -1 — 1). bds. 6.99 *(978-0-7566-9017-5(X)*, DK Children) Dorling Kindersley Publishing, Inc.

Douglas, Donna. Miss Donna's Mulberry Acres Farm. Baizer, Gayle Susan, illus. 2011. (Mulberry Acres Farm Ser.). (ENG.). 24p. (J). (gr. -1-3). pap. 10.99 *(978-1-61036-098-2(2))* Bridge-Logos, Inc.

Elliott, David. On the Farm. Meade, Holly, illus. (ENG.). 32p. (J). (gr. -1-2). 2012. pap. 6.99 *(978-0-7636-5591-4(0))* 2008. 16.99 *(978-0-7636-3322-6(4))* Candlewick Pr.

Everyday Animals Classroom Library. (gr. k-2). lib. bdg. 81.95 *(978-0-7368-1821-6(9))* Red Brick Learning.

Facts on File, Inc. Staff. Animals. 2010. (New Discovering Careers for Your Future Ser.). (Illus.). 128p. (gr. 4-9). 24.95 *(978-0-8160-8044-1(5)*, Ferguson Publishing Co.) Facts On File, Inc.

Farm Animals. 2005. (Farm Animals Ser.). (Illus.). 32p. (gr. 2-4). 138.00 *(978-0-7910-8463-2(9)*, Chelsea Hse.) Facts On File, Inc.

Farm Animals. (My Sticker Activity Ser.). (Illus.). 12p. (J). *(978-1-4054-1181-3(3))*; 2008. 32p. *(978-1-4075-0349-3(9))* Parragon, Inc.

Farm Animals. 2007. (Nonfiction Collection). 16p. (J). 8.00 *(978-1-60343-000-5(8))* Pioneer Valley Bks.

Farm Animals. 2004. (Illus.). 10p. (J). *(978-1-59060-332-1(X))* Waldman Publishing Corp.

Farm Animals: KinderFacts Individual Title, 6 packs. (Kinderstarters Ser.). 8p. (gr. -1-1). 21.00 *(978-0-7635-8752-9(4))* Rigby Education.

Farmyard Animals. 2003. 32p. 12.98 *(978-1-4054-1929-1(6))* Parragon, Inc.

Fennell, Clare, illus. Farm Families. 2017. (Push & Pull Ser.). (ENG.). 8p. (J). (gr. -1 — 1). bds. 5.99 *(978-0-7641-6888-8(6))* Barron's Educational Series, Inc.

First Discovery Staff & Peyrols, Sylvaine. Farm Animals. 2005. (ENG., Illus.). 36p. (J). (gr. k-3). pap. 11.99 *(978-1-85103-169-6(3))* Moonlight Publishing, Ltd. GBR. Dist: Independent Pubs. Group.

Fretland VanVoorst, Jenny. Homing Pigeons. 2013. (We Work! Animals with Jobs Ser.). 24p. (J). (gr. -1-3). lib. bdg. 21.32 *(978-1-61772-900-3(0))* Bearport Publishing Co., Inc.

—Pig Detectives. 2013. (We Work! Animals with Jobs Ser.). 24p. (J). (gr. -1-3). lib. bdg. 21.32 *(978-1-61772-899-0(3))* Bearport Publishing Co., Inc.

—Therapy Cats, Dogs, & Rabbits. 2013. (We Work! Animals with Jobs Ser.). 24p. (J). (gr. -1-3). lib. bdg. 21.32 *(978-1-61772-895-2(0))* Bearport Publishing Co., Inc.

Furfur, Christopher. Rebecca & the Great Goat Getaway. Artigas, Alexandra, illus. 2005. 40p. (J). (gr. -1). per. 15.95 *(978-0-9742845-7-6(2))* Mystic Ridge Bks.

Gardiner, Lisa. Farm Animals. Flowerpot Press, ed. 2012. (Illus.). 20p. (J). *(978-1-926988-02-3(7))* Flowerpot Children's Pr. Inc.

Gibbs, Edward. I Spy on the Farm. Gibbs, Edward, illus. 2016. (ENG., Illus.). 22p. (J). (gr. -1-k). bds. 7.99 *(978-0-7636-8530-0(5)*, Templar) Candlewick Pr.

Gibbs, Maddie. Amigos de la Granja / Farmyard Friends, 1 vol. 2015. (Amigos de la Granja / Farmyard Friends Ser.). (ENG & SPA.). 24p. (J). 141.60 *(978-1-4994-0275-9(9)*, PowerKids Pr.) Rosen Publishing Group, Inc., The.

—Chickens, 1 vol. 2015. (ENG., Illus.). 24p. (J). lib. bdg. 23.60 *(978-1-4994-0064-9(0)*, PowerKids Pr.) Rosen Publishing Group, Inc., The.

—Ducks, 1 vol. 2015. (ENG.). 24p. (J). lib. bdg. 23.60 *(978-1-4994-0098-4(5)*, PowerKids Pr.) Rosen Publishing Group, Inc., The.

—Farmyard Friends, 1 vol. 2015. (Farmyard Friends Ser.). (ENG.). 24p. (J). 49.50 *(978-1-4777-7407-6(6)*, PowerKids Pr.) Rosen Publishing Group, Inc., The.

—Goats, 1 vol. 2015. (ENG., Illus.). 24p. (J). lib. bdg. 23.60 *(978-1-4994-0134-9(5)*, PowerKids Pr.) Rosen Publishing Group, Inc., The.

—Horses, 1 vol. 2015. (ENG., Illus.). 24p. (J). lib. bdg. 23.60 *(978-1-4994-0143-1(4)*, PowerKids Pr.) Rosen Publishing Group, Inc., The.

—Las Cabras / Goats, 1 vol. 2015. (Amigos de la Granja / Farmyard Friends Ser.). (ENG & SPA.). 24p. (J). 23.60 *(978-1-4994-0272-8(4)*, PowerKids Pr.) Rosen Publishing Group, Inc., The.

—Las Vacas / Cows, 1 vol. 2015. (Amigos de la Granja / Farmyard Friends Ser.). (ENG & SPA.). 24p. (J). 23.60 *(978-1-4994-0265-0(1)*, PowerKids Pr.) Rosen Publishing Group, Inc., The.

—Los Caballos / Horses, 1 vol. 2015. (Amigos de la Granja / Farmyard Friends Ser.). (ENG & SPA.). 24p. (J). 23.60 *(978-1-4994-0267-4(8)*, PowerKids Pr.) Rosen Publishing Group, Inc., The.

—Los Patos / Ducks, 1 vol. 2015. (Amigos de la Granja / Farmyard Friends Ser.). (ENG & SPA.). 24p. (J). 23.60 *(978-1-4994-0269-8(4)*, PowerKids Pr.) Rosen Publishing Group, Inc., The.

—Pigs, 1 vol. 2015. (ENG., Illus.). 24p. (J). lib. bdg. 23.60 *(978-1-4994-0168-4(X)*, PowerKids Pr.) Rosen Publishing Group, Inc., The.

Greenwell, Jessica. Farm Animals Lift & Look. 2010. (Lift & Look Board Bks). 12p. (J). bds. 9.99 *(978-0-7945-2612-2(8)*, Usborne) EDC Publishing.

Grimm, Sandra. Baby Farm Animals. Sodré, Julie, illus. 2012. (ENG.). 20p. (J). (gr. -1-1). 12.95 *(978-1-61608-654-1(8)*, 608654, Sky Pony Pr.) Skyhorse Publishing Co., Inc.

Group/McGraw-Hill, Wright. Animales Domesticos, 6 vols., Vol. 2. (First Explorers, Primeros Exploradores Nonfiction Sets Ser.). (SPA.). (gr. 1-2). 29.95 *(978-0-7699-1483-1(7))* Shortland Pubns. (U. S. A.) Inc.

Gunzi, Christiane. Farm. 2nd rev. ed. 2015. (ENG., Illus.). 34p. (J). 7.95 *(978-1-906572-28-0(3))* Award Pubns. Ltd. GBR. Dist: Parkwest Pubns., Inc.

Hankin, Rosie. Cut & Paste Farm Animals. 2007. (Cut, Paste, & Create Ser.). (Illus.). 32p. (gr. k-3). lib. bdg. 26.00 *(978-0-8368-7719-9(5)*, Gareth Stevens Learning Library) Stevens, Gareth Publishing LLLP.

Hasselius, Michelle M. Farm Animals. 2016. (Farm Animals Ser.). (ENG.). 24p. (gr. k-1). pap. 27.80 *(978-1-5157-1382-1(2)*, Pebble Plus) Capstone Press of Coughlan Cos.

Hellen, Nancy. A Visit to the Farm: Pop-up. Hellen, Nancy, illus. 2004. (Illus.). 16p. (J). (gr. k-2). reprint ed. 7.00 *(978-0-7567-7063-1(7))* DIANE Publishing Co.

Heritage House, Inc. Staff, ed. Baby Barnyard Animals, 1 vol. 2016. (Kids' Own Nature Book Ser.). (ENG., Illus.). 48p. (J). (gr. k-1). pap. 6.95 ***(978-1-77203-145-4(3))*** Heritage Hse. CAN. Dist: Orca Bk. Pubs. USA.

Herriot, James. James Herriot's Treasury for Children: Warm & Joyful Tales by the Author of All Creatures Great & Small. Brown, Ruth & Barrett, Peter, illus. 2014. (ENG.). 272p. (J). (gr. -1-3). 24.99 *(978-1-250-05813-3(9)*, 9781250058133, St. Martin's Griffin) St. Martin's Pr.

Hileman, Jane. Farms Have Animals. 2016. (1-3Y Animals Ser.). (ENG., Illus.). 12p. (J). pap. 5.99 *(978-1-63437-482-8(7))* American Reading Co.

HOP, LLC. Hooked on Animals on the Farm Super Activity Kit. 2006. (J). (gr. -1). 9.99 *(978-1-933863-19-1(6))* HOP, LLC.

Jackson, Sadara J. Cows Are Not Just for Milk: Las Vacas No Solamente Nos Dan Leche. 2008. 16p. pap. 9.49 *(978-1-4343-9488-0(3))* AuthorHouse.

Johanson, Paula. Money-Making Opportunities for Teens Who Like Pets & Animals. 2013. 80p. (YA). (gr. 7-12). 33.25 *(978-1-4488-9384-3(4))* Rosen Publishing Group, Inc., The.

Johnson, Betty. Farm Animals for Kids: Amazing Pictures & Fun Fact Children Book. 2013. 42p. pap. 9.97 *(978-1-63022-040-2(X))* Speedy Publishing LLC.

Kalman, Bobbie. Baby Pets. 2012. (ENG., Illus.). 24p. (J). *(978-0-7787-4075-9(7))*; pap. *(978-0-7787-4080-3(3))* Crabtree Publishing Co.

Kalz, Jill. Farm Adventure. Cerato, Mattia, illus. 2010. (A-MAZE-Ing Adventures Ser.). (ENG.). 32p. (gr. 1-2). lib. bdg. 26.65 *(978-1-4048-6038-4(X))* Picture Window Bks.

Katirgis, Jane. Baby Farm Animals. 2010. (All about Baby Animals Ser.). (Illus.). 24p. (J). pap. 7.95 *(978-1-59845-157-3(X))*; lib. bdg. 22.60 *(978-0-7660-3794-6(0))* Enslow Pubs., Inc. (Enslow Elementary).

Kids Can Press Staff. This Is Daniel Cook at the Farm. 2006. (This Is Daniel Cook Ser.). (ENG., Illus.). 24p. (J). (gr. -1-1). 4.95 *(978-1-55453-078-6(4))* Kids Can Pr., Ltd. CAN. Dist: Hachette Bk. Group.

Komiya, Teruyuki. Life-Size Farm. 2012. (ENG., Illus.). 48p. (gr. -1). 18.95 *(978-1-934734-58-2(6))* Seven Footer Pr.

Kranking, Kathy. In the Spotlight: Animal Superstars. 2007. (Illus.). 32p. (J). pap. *(978-0-439-02576-8(1))* Scholastic, Inc.

Kummer, Patricia K. Working Horses. 2013. 48p. (J). (gr. 4-8). 29.93 *(978-1-60870-840-6(3))* Cavendish Square Publishing.

Kuskowski, Alex. A Flock of Sheep: Animal Groups on the Farm, 1 vol. 2012. (Animal Groups Ser.). (ENG.). 24p. (J). (gr. k-3). lib. bdg. 24.21 *(978-1-61783-538-4(2)*, SandCastle) ABDO Publishing Co.

—Super Simple Farm Critter Crafts: Fun & Easy Animal Crafts. 2016. (ENG., Illus.). 32p. (J). *(978-1-68078-161-8(8))* ABDO Publishing Co.

Kutner, Merrily. Down on the Farm. Hillenbrand, Will, illus. 2005. (ENG.). 32p. (J). (gr. -1 — 1). pap. 7.99 *(978-0-8234-1985-2(1))* Holiday Hse., Inc.

La Coccinella. Farm Animals. 2015. (Peekaboo! Ser.). (ENG., Illus.). 26p. (J). (gr. -1-k). bds. 6.95 *(978-1-4549-1586-7(2))* Sterling Publishing Co., Inc.

Laval, Thierry. Look & Find on the Farm. 2017. (Mini Look & Find Ser.). (ENG.). 14p. (J). 9.95 ***(978-0-531-23080-0(5)***, Children's Pr.) Scholastic Library Publishing.

Lewin, Ted. Animals Work. Lewin, Ted, illus. 2014. (I Like to Read(r) Ser.). (ENG., Illus.). 24p. (J). (gr. -1-2). 14.95 *(978-0-8234-3040-6(5))* Holiday Hse., Inc.

Lewis, Jan. Farm. 2015. (ENG., Illus.). 24p. bds. 6.99 *(978-1-86147-635-7(3)*, Armadillo) Anness Publishing GBR. Dist: National Bk. Network.

little bee books, little bee & Seal, Julia. Farm. 2016. (ENG., Illus.). 12p. (J). (gr. -1 — 1). bds. 6.99 *(978-1-4998-0260-3(9))* Little Bee Books Inc.

Littlefield, Cindy A. Pop-Out & Paint Farm Animals. 2013. (ENG.). 48p. (J). (gr. 3-8). pap. 12.95 *(978-1-61212-139-0(X))* Storey Publishing, LLC.

Lodge, Jo. Baby's Very First Book: Farm: A Rag/cloth Book about Farm Animals with Mirror, Crinkly Pages & High-Contrast Images. Lodge, Jo, illus. 2017. (Baby's Very First Book Ser.). (ENG., Illus.). 8p. (J). (— 1). 9.99 ***(978-1-5098-0610-2(5))*** Pan Macmillan GBR. Dist: Independent Pubs. Group.

Look Who's Popping Up: On the Farm. 2003. (J). (gr. -1-k). 4.98 *(978-0-7525-8903-9(2))* Parragon, Inc.

Lynch, Annabelle. Farm Animals, 01 vols., 1. 2016. (Nature Explorers Ser.). (ENG.). 24p. (J). pap. 8.25 *(978-1-5081-9065-3(8)*, Windmill Bks.) Rosen Publishing Group, Inc., The.

Lynette, Rachel. Producing Meat, 1 vol. 2012. (Technology of Farming Ser.). (ENG.). 48p. (gr. 4-6). lib. bdg. 33.32 *(978-1-4329-6410-8(0)*, Heinemann InfoSearch) Heinemann-Raintree.

Macken, JoAnn Early. Animals That Live on the Farm;Animales que viven en la granja Complete Series, 6 vols. 2nd rev. ed. 2009. (Animals That Live on the Farm/Animales que viven en la granja Ser.). (ENG & SPA.). 24p. (J). (gr. 1-1). pap. 35.70 *(978-1-4339-2477-4(3)*, Weekly Reader Leveled Readers) Stevens, Gareth Publishing LLLP.

Mark R. Borene, R. Borene & Mark R Borene. Welcome to the Farm: Book 2 of Welcome to the World. 2009. (Illus.). 20p. pap. 10.49 *(978-1-4389-6549-9(4))* AuthorHouse.

Martin, Claudia. Farming. 2010. (Working Animals Ser.). 64p. (gr. 5-18). 28.50 *(978-1-60870-162-9(X))* Marshall Cavendish Corp.

Martin, John David. My Little Farm Book. 2007. (Illus.). 16p. (J). (gr. -1). pap. 1.90 *(978-0-7399-2399-3(4))* Rod & Staff Pubs., Inc.

Martin, Ruth. Noisy Nature: on the Farm. Pledger, Maurice, illus. 2015. (ENG.). 12p. (J). (gr. -1). 16.95 *(978-1-62686-103-9(X)*, Silver Dolphin Bks.) Readerlink Distribution Services, LLC.

Mattern, Joanne. Catahoula Leopard Dogs, 1 vol. 2012. (Dogs Set 9 Ser.). (ENG., Illus.). 24p. (J). (gr. 2-5). 25.65 *(978-1-61714-990-0(X))* ABDO Publishing Co.

—Farm Animals. 2017. (Readers Ser.). (ENG., Illus.). 48p. (J). (-k). pap. 4.99 *(978-1-4263-2687-5(4)*, National Geographic Children's Bks.) National Geographic Society.

McCurry, Kristin. Farm Babies. 2006. (Animal Babies Ser.). (ENG., Illus.). 22p. (J). (gr. -1 — 1). bds. 5.95 *(978-1-55971-941-4(9))* Northland Publishing.

Mercer, Abbie. Goats on a Farm. 2009. (Barnyard Animals Ser.). (ENG.). 24p. (J). pap. 8.25 *(978-1-4042-8056-4(1))*; (Illus.). lib. bdg. 22.60 *(978-1-4042-8049-6(9))* Rosen Publishing Group, Inc., The. (PowerKids Pr.).

Mezzanotte, Jim. Police. 2010. (Working Animals Ser.). 64p. (gr. 5-18). 28.50 *(978-1-60870-166-7(2))* Marshall Cavendish Corp.

Miles, Lisa. Origami Farm Animals. 2013. (Amazing Origami Ser.). 32p. (J). (gr. 2-5). pap. 10.50 *(978-1-4339-9653-5(7))*;

pap. 63.00 *(978-1-4339-9654-2(5))*; (ENG., Illus.). lib. bdg. 26.60 *(978-1-4339-9652-8(9))* Stevens, Gareth Publishing LLLP.

Miniature Farm Animals, 1 vol. 2014. (Mini Animal Marvels Ser.). (ENG., Illus.). 24p. (J). (gr. -1-3). 24.21 *(978-1-62403-066-6(1))* ABDO Publishing Co.

Murray, Julie. Service Animals, 1 vol. 2009. (Going to Work:Animal Edition Ser.). (ENG., Illus.). 32p. (J). (gr. 2-5). 27.07 *(978-1-60453-564-8(4))* ABDO Publishing Co.

Nagle, Jeanne. Working Horses. 2011. (Horsing Around Ser.). (Illus.). 24p. (J). (gr. 2-5). lib. bdg. 22.60 *(978-1-4339-4643-1(2))* Stevens, Gareth Publishing LLLP.

Newman-D'Amico, Fran. Fun Farm Animal Mazes. 2006. (Dover Children's Activity Bks.). (ENG., Illus.). 32p. (J). (gr. -1-3). pap. 2.95 *(978-0-486-45184-8(4))* Dover Pubns., Inc.

Novick, Mary & Hale, Jenny. Farm Animals Jigsaw Book. 2007. bds. *(978-1-921049-99-6(5))* Little Hare Bks. AUS. Dist: HarperCollins Pubs. Australia.

Nunn, Daniel. Farm Animals, 1 vol. 2013. (True or False? Ser.). (ENG.). 20p. (gr. -1-1). bds. 7.99 *(978-1-4109-5084-0(0),* NA-r) Heinemann-Raintree.

—The Farm Animals. 2013. (True or False? Ser.). (ENG.). 24p. (gr. -1-1). pap. 6.29 *(978-1-4109-5073-4(5),* NA-r) Heinemann-Raintree.

—True or False? 2013. (True or False? Ser.). (ENG.). 20p. (gr. -1-1). bds. 15.98 *(978-1-4109-6296-6(2),* NA-r) Heinemann-Raintree.

Ottina, Laura. On the Farm. Ranchetti, Sebastiano, illus. 2009. (Learn with Animals Ser.). (ENG.). 24p. (J). (gr. -1-2). pap. 8.15 *(978-1-4339-2092-9(1))*; lib. bdg. 22.00 *(978-1-4339-1915-2(X))* Stevens, Gareth Publishing LLLP. (Weekly Reader Leveled Readers).

Page, Nick & Page, Claire. Funny Faces Farm Animals. 2006. (Funny Faces Ser.). (Illus.). 10p. (gr. -1-k). bds. *(978-1-84610-117-5(4))* Make Believe Ideas.

Parragon, creator. Oink on the Farm! 2014. (Discovery Kids 10 Button Ser.). (ENG., Illus.). (J). (gr. -1). bds. *(978-1-4723-6107-3(5))* Parragon Bk. Service Ltd.

Pèrols, Sylvaine & Pèrols, Sylvaine. La Granja. (Coleccion Mundo Maravilloso). (SPA., Illus.). 40p. (J). (gr. 2-7). *(978-84-348-3809-3(5),* SM5478) SM Ediciones ESP. Dist: Lectorum Pubns., Inc.

Pettiford, Rebecca. Farm. Fretland VanVoorst, Jenny, ed. 2016. (First Field Trips). 24p. (J). (gr. k-2). lib. bdg. 25.65 *(978-1-62031-295-7(6),* Bullfrog Bks.) Jump! Inc.

—La Granja. 2016. (Los Primeros Viajes Escolares (First Field Trips)).Tr. of Farm. (SPA.). 24p. (J). (gr. k-2). lib. bdg. 25.65 *(978-1-62031-330-5(8),* Bullfrog Bks.) Jump! Inc.

Phillips, Dee. Find It on the Farm. 2006. (Can You Find It? Ser.). (Illus.). 24p. (gr. k-3). lib. bdg. 23.00 *(978-0-8368-6303-1(8),* Gareth Stevens Learning Library) Stevens, Gareth Publishing LLLP.

Phillips, Sarah. Flip, Flap, Match Noisy Farm. 2013. (ENG.). 12p. (J). bds. 7.99 *(978-1-78235-570-0(7))* Make Believe Ideas GBR. Dist: Nelson, Thomas Inc.

Play Bac, creator. Farm Animals. 2006. (Padded Board Bks.). (Illus.). 24p. (J). (gr. 3-7). bds. 7.95 *(978-1-58925-797-9(9))* Tiger Tales.

Plourde, Lynn. Storytime Stickers: Farm Follies. Ferraro Close, Laura, illus. 2010. (Storytime Stickers Ser.). (ENG.). 16p. (J). (gr. k-2). pap. 5.95 *(978-1-4027-7127-9(4))* Sterling Publishing Co., Inc.

Post, Hans. Creepy Crawlies. Goede, Irene, illus. 2006. (ENG.). 32p. (J). (gr. 4-8). 16.95 *(978-1-932425-65-9(9),* Lemniscaat) Boyds Mills Pr.

Priddy Books Staff, creator. Farm. 2005. (ENG., Illus.). 12p. (J). (gr. -1-k). bds. 0.97 *(978-0-312-49618-0(4),* Priddy Bks.) St. Martin's Pr.

Priddy, Roger. Farm. 2016. (Playtown Ser.). (ENG., Illus.). 12p. (J). bds. 9.99 *(978-0-312-51959-9(1),* 9780312519599, Priddy Bks.) St. Martin's Pr.

—Farm: A Noisy Animal Book. 2017. (Baby's First Ser.). (ENG., Illus.). 8p. (J). bds. 8.99 *(978-0-312-52164-6(2),* 9780312521646, Priddy Bks.) St. Martin's Pr.

—Farm Friends. 2013. (My Carry-Along Sound Bks.). (ENG.). 10p. (J). (gr. -1 — 1). bds. 9.99 *(978-0-312-51645-1(2),* 9780312516451, Priddy Bks.) St. Martin's Pr.

—First 100 Farm Words Lift-The-Flap. 2016. (ENG.). 14p. (J). bds. 9.99 *(978-0-312-52019-9(0),* 9780312520199, Priddy Bks.) St. Martin's Pr.

—My Big Farm Book. 2011. (My Big Board Bks.). (ENG., Illus.). 12p. (J). (gr. -1 — 1). bds. 8.99 *(978-0-312-51082-4(9),* 9780312510824, Priddy Bks.) St. Martin's Pr.

—On the Farm. 2006. (Bright Baby Touch & Feel Ser.). (ENG., Illus.). 10p. (J). (gr. -1 — 1). bds. 4.95 *(978-0-312-49859-7(4),* 9780312498597, Priddy Bks.) St. Martin's Pr.

—Treasure Hunt: on the Farm. 2015. (Treasure Hunt Ser.). (ENG., Illus.). 10p. (J). (gr. -1 — 1). bds. 8.99 *(978-0-312-51796-0(3),* 9780312517960, Priddy Bks.) St. Martin's Pr.

Professor Q's Chinese-English Language Books: Sh#275;ng Chù- Farm Animals. 2006. (J). *(978-0-9743359-7-1(5))* Murdock Publishing Co.

Publications International Ltd. Staff, ed. The World of Eric Carle - Baby's First Animal Treasury: Plays Music While You Read! 2015. 20p. (J). *(978-1-4508-8584-3(5),* 1450885845) Publications International, Ltd.

Randall, Jory. My Day at the Farm. 2009. (Kid's Life! Ser.). 24p. (J). (ENG.). pap. 8.25 *(978-1-4358-2473-7(3))*; (Illus.). lib. bdg. 22.60 *(978-1-4042-8077-9(4))* Rosen Publishing Group, Inc., The. (PowerKids Pr.).

Ranson, Erin. Fuzzy Farm. Green, Barry, illus. 2017. (Soft Felt Play Bks.). (ENG.). 10p. (J). (gr. -1-k). 12.99 ***(978-1-78700-066-7(4))*** Top That! Publishing PLC GBR. Dist: Independent Pubs. Group.

Reader, Jack. Working on the Farm. 2017. (Animals in My World Ser.). 24p. (gr. 4-6). pap. 8.25 ***(978-1-5383-2193-5(9),*** PowerKids Pr.) Rosen Publishing Group, Inc., The.

Reasoner, Charles. Animal Friends on the Farm. Pitt, Sarah, illus. 2009. (3D Board Bks.). 12p. (J). (gr. -1-k). bds. 9.99 *(978-1-934650-35-6(8))* Just For Kids Pr., LLC.

Redmond, Shirley Raye. Blind Tom: The Horse Who Helped Build the Great Railroad. Bradley, Lois, illus. 2009. (J). pap. 10.00 *(978-0-87842-558-7(6))* Mountain Pr. Publishing Co., Inc.

Regan, Lisa. Farm Animals. Thompson, Kim, illus. 2010. (I Love Animals Ser.). (ENG.). 24p. (J). (gr. 1-5). pap. 8.15 *(978-1-61533-233-5(2))*; lib. bdg. 22.60 *(978-1-61533-227-4(8))* Windmill Bks.

Remson, Billie. A Mississippi Spring on Bluebird Hill. Garraway, Kym W., illus. 2004. per. 12.95 *(978-1-59571-004-8(3))* Word Association Pubs.

—A Mississippi Winter on Bluebird Hill: A True Story about Our Little Farm in the Hills of Southern Mississippi. Garraway, Kym, illus. 2004. (J). per. 12.95 *(978-1-59571-044-4(2))* Word Association Pubs.

Renaud, Katy. Guess Where I Was. 2011. 52p. pap. 20.26 *(978-1-4634-2352-0(7))* AuthorHouse.

Reyes, Blanca Matilde. Farm Animals. 2006. (Illus.). 16p. (J). act. bk. ed. 0.75 *(978-1-933984-02-5(3))* Two Lands.

Ridley, Sarah. In the Home. 2010. (J). 28.50 *(978-1-59920-328-7(6))* Black Rabbit Bks.

Riggs, Kate. On the Farm. Dogi, Fiammetta & Kubinyi, Laszlo, illus. 2015. (ENG.). 14p. (J). (gr. -1 — 1). bds. 7.99 *(978-1-56846-272-1(7),* Creative Editions) Creative Co., The.

Riipi, Sherida. A Bunny Named Horse. 2010. 24p. 14.95 *(978-1-4490-5271-3(1))* AuthorHouse.

Ring, Susan. On the Farm. Melmon, Deborah, illus. 2008. (ENG.). 10p. (J). (gr. 3-17). 12.99 *(978-1-58476-729-9(4))* Innovative Kids.

Rosa-Mendoza, Gladys. Animals at the Farm/Animales de la Granja Big Book. 2009. (ENG & SPA.). 20p. (J). pap. 19.95 *(978-1-931398-89-3(5))* Me+Mi Publishing.

Rosen Publishing Staff. Farmyard Friends, 1 vol. 2015. (Farmyard Friends Ser.). (ENG.). 24p. (J). 141.60 *(978-1-4777-5730-7(9),* PowerKids Pr.) Rosen Publishing Group, Inc., The.

Ross, Kathy. Crafts for Kids Who Are Learning about Farm Animals. Barger, Jan, illus. 2007. (Crafts for Kids Who Are Learning about Ser.). (ENG.). 48p. (gr. k-3). lib. bdg. 26.60 *(978-0-8225-6366-2(5))* Lerner Publishing Group.

Rotner, Shelley. I Like the Farm. 2017. (I Like to Read(r) Ser.). (ENG.). 32p. (J). (gr. -1-3). 14.95 ***(978-0-8234-3833-4(3))*** Holiday Hse., Inc.

Rudick, Dina. Barnyard Kids: A Family Guide for Raising Animals. 2015. (ENG., Illus.). 160p. (gr. 3-6). pap. 24.99 *(978-1-63159-071-9(5),* Quarry Books) Quarto Publishing Group USA.

Rustad, Martha E. H. Chicks 2, 4, 6: A Baby Animals Counting by Twos Book. 2017. (1, 2, 3 Count with Me Ser.). (ENG., Illus.). 24p. (J). (gr. k-2). pap. 8.99 *(978-1-68152-111-4(3))* Amicus.

—Chicks 2, 4, 6: A Baby Animals Counting by Twos Book. 2016. (1, 2, 3 Count with Me Ser.). (ENG., Illus.). 24p. (J). (gr. k-3). 20.95 *(978-1-60753-920-9(9))* Amicus Publishing.

Sánchez, Isidro. Mi Gato. Ruis, Maria, illus. (Coleccion Mis Animales Preferidos).Tr. of My Cat. (SPA.). 32p. (J). (gr. k-3). 6.36 *(978-84-342-1127-8(0),* PR0482) Parramon Ediciones S.A. ESP. Dist: Lectorum Pubns., Inc.

—Mi Hamster. Ruis, Maria, illus. (Coleccion Mis Animales Preferidos).Tr. of My Hamster. (SPA.). 32p. (J). (gr. k-3). 6.36 *(978-84-342-1129-2(7),* PR0485) Parramon Ediciones S.A. ESP. Dist: Lectorum Pubns., Inc.

—Mi Pajaro. Ruis, Maria, illus. (Coleccion Mis Animales Preferidos).Tr. of My Bird. (SPA.). 32p. (J). (gr. k-3). 6.36 *(978-84-342-1128-5(9),* PR0483) Parramon Ediciones S.A. ESP. Dist: Lectorum Pubns., Inc.

—Mi Perro. Ruis, Maria, illus. (Coleccion Mis Animales Preferidos).Tr. of My Dog. (SPA.). 32p. (J). (gr. k-3). *(978-84-342-1126-1(2),* PR0481) Parramon Ediciones S.A. ESP. Dist: Lectorum Pubns., Inc.

Scholastic, Inc. Staff, contrib. by. Baby Animals on the Farm. 2013. (ENG.). 12p. (J). bds. 6.95 *(978-0-531-27252-7(4))* Scholastic Library Publishing.

Schwartz, Betty Ann & Seresin, Lynn. My Barnyard! A Read & Play Book! Bendall-Brunello, John, illus. 2015. (ENG.). 10p. (J). (gr. -1-k). bds. 7.99 *(978-0-545-69077-5(3),* Cartwheel Bks.) Scholastic, Inc.

Schweitzer, Karen. The Cocker Spaniel. 2011. (J). 34.95 *(978-1-932904-76-5(X))*; *(978-1-932904-82-6(4))* Eldorado Ink.

Scollen, Chris. Busy Kids Farm Animals Sticker Activity Book. 2008. (Busy Kids Ser.). (Illus.). 12p. (gr. -1-3). 4.99 *(978-1-84610-638-5(9))* Make Believe Ideas GBR. Dist: Nelson, Thomas Inc.

Silverstein, Alvin, et al. Ferrets: Cool Pets! Kelley, Gerald, illus. 2011. (Far-Out & Unusual Pets Ser.). 48p. (J). (gr. 2-5). lib. bdg. 25.27 *(978-0-7660-3683-3(9))* Enslow Pubs., Inc.

Sirett, Dawn & Dorling Kindersley Publishing Staff. Farm. Quasha, Jennifer, ed. 2008. (Baby Touch & Feel Ser.). (ENG., Illus.). 14p. (J). (gr. -1 — 1). bds. 5.99 *(978-0-7566-3467-4(9),* DK Children) Dorling Kindersley Publishing, Inc.

Small World Creations. Farm Animals. 2016. (Crinkle Cloth Bks.). (ENG.). 8p. (J). (gr. -1 — 1). 9.99 *(978-1-4380-7752-9(1))* Barron's Educational Series, Inc.

Spilsbury, Louise & Spilsbury, Richard. A Nature Walk on the Farm, 1 vol. 2014. (Nature Walks Ser.). (ENG., Illus.). 24p. (gr. k-2). 23.32 *(978-1-4846-0402-1(4),* Heinemann Read & Learn) Heinemann-Raintree.

Stanos, Dimi, et al. Taking Care of Farm Animals. 2007. (Windows on Literacy Ser.). (ENG., Illus.). 12p. (J). pap. 10.95 *(978-0-7922-8482-5(8))* CENGAGE Learning.

Stead, Emily. On the Farm. 2013. (My First Creativity Activity Bks.). (ENG.). 66p. (J). (gr. -1-2). pap. 9.99 *(978-1-4380-0239-2(4))* Barron's Educational Series, Inc.

Tani, Branca. Baby Farm Animals. 2015. (Rosen REAL Readers: STEM & STEAM Collection). (ENG.). 8p. pap. 5.46 *(978-1-4994-9651-2(6),* Rosen Classroom) Rosen Publishing Group, Inc., The.

Tejido, Jomike. Farm Animals. 2016. (Jumbo Stickers for Little Hands Ser.). (ENG.). 24p. (J). (gr. -1-k). pap. 7.95 *(978-1-63322-122-2(9),* Moondance) Quarto Publishing Group USA.

Teora, creator. Farm Animals. 2007. (My First Sticker Encyclopedia Ser.). (Illus.). 18p. (J). (gr. -1-3). pap. 5.95 *(978-1-59496-150-2(6))* Teora USA LLC.

Teora, ed. Hi Read Stick & Learn about Farm Animals. 2004. (Illus.). 20p. pap. 6.99 *(978-1-59496-049-9(6))* Teora USA LLC.

Thomas Nelson. Farm Animals. 2016. (ENG.). 12p. (gr. -1). bds. *(978-1-78598-136-4(6))* Make Believe Ideas.

—Touch & Sparkle Farm Animals. 2016. (ENG.). 12p. (gr. -1). bds. *(978-1-78598-133-3(1))* Make Believe Ideas.

Time for Dinner: Individual Title Six-Packs. (Chiquilibros Ser.). (gr. k-1). 23.00 *(978-0-7635-0414-4(9))* Rigby Education.

Wald, Christina, illus. The Barnyard. 2006. (ENG.). 12p. (J). (gr. -1). pap. 7.95 *(978-1-58017-640-8(2),* 67640) Storey Publishing, LLC.

Wallace, Karen. Flip the Flaps: Farm Animals. Palin, Nicki, illus. 2012. (Flip the Flaps Ser.). (ENG.). 32p. (J). (gr. -1-1). pap. 6.99 *(978-0-7534-6738-1(0),* 9780753467381, Kingfisher) Roaring Brook Pr.

—I Wonder Why Flip the Flaps Farm Animals. 2009. *(978-0-7534-6222-5(2),* Kingfisher) Roaring Brook Pr.

Watt, Fiona & Wells, Rachel. Anifeiliaid y Fferm. 2005. (WEL., Illus.). 10p. *(978-1-84512-000-9(0))* Cymdeithas Lyfrau Ceredigion.

Watterson, Carol. The Edible Alphabet: 26 Reasons to Love the Farm. Sorrentino, Michela, illus. 2011. (ENG.). 48p. (J). (gr. k-3). 16.99 *(978-1-58246-421-3(9),* Tricycle Pr.) Random Hse. Children's Bks.

Weber, Vicky. Animal Babies on the Farm. Kingfisher Editors, ed. 2005. (Animal Babies Ser.). (ENG., Illus.). 28p. (J). (gr. -1-k). bds. 6.99 *(978-0-7534-5838-9(1),* 9780753458389, Kingfisher) Roaring Brook Pr.

West, David. Farm Animals. (Nora the Naturalist's Animals Ser.). 24p. (gr. k-3). 2014. pap. 8.95 *(978-1-62588-049-9(9))* 2013. 28.50 *(978-1-62588-000-0(6))* Black Rabbit Bks.

Wildsmith, Brian. Brian Wildsmith's Farm Animals, 1 vol. 2004. (NAV., Illus.). 16p. (J). 4.99 *(978-1-932065-26-8(1))* Star Bright Bks., Inc.

—Brian Wildsmith's Farm Animals, 1 vol. Wildsmith, Brian, illus. 2003. (Illus.). 16p. (J). (TAG.). 4.99 *(978-1-932065-29-9(6),* 1-718-784-9112); (KOR., 4.99 *(978-1-932065-19-0(9),* 1-718-784-9112) Star Bright Bks., Inc.

—Farm Animals (Simplified Mandarin), 1 vol. Wildsmith, Brian, illus. 2003. (CHI & ENG., Illus.). 16p. (J). 4.99 *(978-1-932065-22-0(9),* 1-718-784-9112) Star Bright Bks., Inc.

—Farm Animals (Traditional Cantonese) Wildsmith, Brian, illus. 2003. (CHI., Illus.). 16p. (J). bds. 4.99 *(978-1-932065-23-7(7),* 1-718-784-9112) Star Bright Bks., Inc.

Wildsmith, Brian, illus. Brian Wildsmith's Farm Animals. 2003. 16p. (J). (VIE.). bds. 4.95 *(978-1-932065-21-3(0))*; (POR.). bds. 4.95 *(978-1-932065-20-6(2),* 1-718-784-9112) Star Bright Bks., Inc.

Williams, Garth. Baby Farm Animals. 2016. (Little Golden Board Book Ser.). (ENG., Illus.). 26p. (J). (gr. -1-k). bds. 7.99 *(978-0-553-53632-4(X),* Golden Bks.) Random Hse. Children's Bks.

World Book, Inc Staff, contrib. by. Beagles & Other Hounds. 2009. (J). *(978-0-7166-1369-5(7))* World Bk., Inc.

—Portuguese Water Dogs & Other Working Dogs. 2009. (J). *(978-0-7166-1367-1(0))* World Bk., Inc.

—Shih Tzu & Other Toy Dogs. 2009. (J). *(978-0-7166-1372-5(7))* World Bk., Inc.

Yoon, Salina, illus. Peek-a-Boo Farm Animals. 2005. (Peek-a-Boo Guess Who Book Ser.: Vol. 2). 10p. (J). 7.95 *(978-1-58117-158-7(7),* Intervisual/Piggy Toes) Bendon, Inc.

Yoyo Books, creator. Farm Animals. 2011. (ENG., Illus.). 10p. (gr. -1-k). bds. *(978-94-6151-210-9(4))* YoYo Bks.

Yoyo Books Staff. Farm Animals: Animal Jigsaw Fun. 2004. 12p. bds. *(978-90-5843-549-1(0))* YoYo Bks.

Zwemmer, Dominic, des. Farm. 2015. (ENG., Illus.). 16p. (J). pap. 7.99 *(978-1-907604-46-1(4))* Award Pubns. Ltd. GBR. Dist: Parkwest Pubns., Inc.

21st Century Junior Library: Farm Animals. 2011. 24p. lib. bdg. 179.50 *(978-1-60279-999-8(7),* 200932) Cherry Lake Publishing.

DOMESTIC ANIMALS—DISEASES

see Veterinary Medicine

DOMESTIC ANIMALS—FICTION

ABDO Publishing Company Staff. Doreen Cronin: Click-Clack & More. 2006. (Doreen Cronin: Click-Clack & More Ser.). (ENG., Illus.). 30p. (J). (gr. -1-3). lib. bdg. 169.47 *(978-1-59961-087-0(6),* Picture Bk.) Spotlight.

Ackerman, Jill. Old MacDonald: A Hand-Puppet Board Book. Berg, Michelle, illus. 2007. (Little Scholastic Ser.). (ENG.). 6p. (J). (gr. k — 1). bds. 12.99 *(978-0-545-02603-1(2))* Scholastic, Inc.

Albee, Sarah. Where Is Pig? Velez, Walter, illus. 2006. (Step-By-Step Readers Ser.). (J). pap. *(978-1-59939-056-7(6),* Reader's Digest Young Families, Inc.) Studio Fun International.

Alexander, Kwame. Acoustic Rooster & His Barnyard Band. Bowers, Tim, illus. 2011. (ENG.). 32p. (J). (gr. k-5). lib. bdg. 15.95 *(978-1-58536-688-0(9))* Sleeping Bear Pr.

Amerel. The Summer Holidays: A Story for Childre. 2006. pap. *(978-1-4065-0808-6(X))* Dodo Pr.

Amery, H. Where's Curly? Cartwright, Stephen, illus. 2004. (Treasury of Farmyard Tales Ser.). 16p. (J). (gr. 1-18). lib. bdg. 15.95 *(978-1-58086-563-0(1))* EDC Publishing.

Amery, Heather. Farmyard Tales Treasury - Internet Referenced. Cartwright, Stephen, illus. 2007. 96p. (J). 19.99 *(978-0-7945-1440-2(5),* Usborne) EDC Publishing.

—Where's Woolly? Tyler, Jenny, ed. Cartwright, Stephen, illus. 2006. (Treasury of Farmyard Tales Ser.). 16p. (J). (gr. 1-18). 15.95 *(978-1-58086-531-9(3))* EDC Publishing.

And Bean. Pronouns on the Farm. 2011. 32p. pap. 21.99 *(978-1-4568-4235-2(8))* Xlibris Corp.

Anderson, Airlie, illus. Cows in the Kitchen. 2009. (Classic Books with Holes Big Book Ser.). (ENG.). 16p. (J). (gr. -1-1). *(978-1-84643-208-8(1))* Child's Play International Ltd.

—Cows in the Kitchen W/ 2009. (Classic Books with Holes US Soft Cover with CD Ser.). (ENG.). 16p. (J). pap. incl. audio compact disk *(978-1-84643-257-6(X))* Child's Play International Ltd.

Anderson, Carolyn D. Granny's Farm Friends. 2nd ed. 2012. (ENG., Illus.). 102p. (J). pap. *(978-1-77143-007-4(9),* CCB Publishing) CCB Publishing.

Anderson, Peggy Perry. Chuck's Band. 2017. (Green Light Readers Level 1 Ser.). (ENG., Illus.). 32p. (J). (gr. -1-3). 12.99 *(978-0-544-92620-2(X),* HMH Books For Young Readers) Houghton Mifflin Harcourt Publishing Co.

—Chuck's Truck. 2017. (Green Light Readers Level 1 Ser.). (ENG., Illus.). 32p. (J). (gr. -1-3). 12.99 *(978-0-544-92618-9(8),* HMH Books For Young Readers) Houghton Mifflin Harcourt Publishing Co.

Andrews, Julie & Hamilton, Emma Walton. Dumpy to the Rescue! Walton, Tony, illus. 2004. 24p. (J). lib. bdg. 13.85 *(978-1-4242-0707-7(X))* Fitzgerald Bks.

Andrews McMeel Publishing, LLC Staff. Hop, Pop, & Play. 2014. (ENG.). 12p. (J). bds. 5.99 *(978-1-4494-6053-2(4))* Andrews McMeel Publishing.

Angelastro, Yvonne. The Four Lost Chicks. 2013. 28p. pap. 16.99 *(978-1-4808-0292-6(1))* Archway Publishing.

Armstrong, Alan W. Whittington. Schindler, S. D., illus. 2007. 191p. (gr. 3-7). 17.00 *(978-0-7569-7768-9(1))* Perfection Learning Corp.

Auch, Mary Jane. Poultrygeist. Jane, Mary & Auch, Herm, illus. 2004. (ENG.). 32p. (J). (gr. k-3). reprint ed. 6.95 *(978-0-8234-1876-3(6))* Holiday Hse., Inc.

—Souperchicken. Auch, Herm, illus. 2004. (ENG.). 32p. (J). (gr. -1-3). reprint ed. pap. 6.95 *(978-0-8234-1829-9(4))* Holiday Hse., Inc.

Aylesworth, Jim. Cock-a-Doodle-Doo, Creak, Pop-Pop, Moo. Sneed, Brad, illus. 2012. (ENG.). 32p. (J). 16.95 *(978-0-8234-2356-9(5))* Holiday Hse., Inc.

—Cock-a-Doodle Doo, Creak, Pop-Pop, Moo. Sneed, Brad, illus. 2013. (ENG.). 32p. (J). pap. 7.99 *(978-0-8234-2754-3(4))* Holiday Hse., Inc.

AZ Books Staff. Farm Animals Moving & Talking. Harko, Lubov, ed. 2012. (Funny Trails Ser.). (ENG.). 10p. (J). (gr. -1-k). bds. 9.95 *(978-1-61889-174-7(X))* AZ Bks. LLC.

—My Farm. Yaroshevich, Angelica, ed. 2012. (Open the Book-I Am Alive Ser.). (ENG.). 8p. (J). (— 1). bds. 5.95 *(978-1-61889-043-6(3))* AZ Bks. LLC.

—Our Friendly Farm. Zayceva, Irina, ed. 2012. (Hook-And-Loop-Pictures Ser.). (ENG.). 8p. (J). (-k). bds. 11.95 *(978-1-61889-156-3(1))* AZ Bks. LLC.

—Who Lives on a Farm? Gridina, Anna, ed. 2012. (Funny Animals Ser.). (ENG.). 10p. (J). (-k). bds. 8.95 *(978-1-61889-047-4(6))* AZ Bks. LLC.

Bailey, Linda. The Farm Team. Slavin, Bill, illus. 2006. (ENG.). 32p. (J). (gr. -1-2). 16.95 *(978-1-55337-850-1(4))* Kids Can Pr., Ltd. CAN. Dist: Hachette Bk. Group.

Baker, Ken. Cow Can't Sleep, 0 vols. Gray, Steve, illus. 2012. (ENG.). 24p. (J). (gr. -1-3). 12.99 *(978-0-7614-6198-2(1),* 9780761461982, Amazon Children's Publishing) Amazon Publishing.

—Old MacDonald Had a Dragon, 0 vols. Santoro, Christopher, illus. 2012. (ENG.). 32p. (J). (gr. k-3). 16.99 *(978-0-7614-6175-3(2),* 9780761461753, Amazon Children's Publishing) Amazon Publishing.

Balian, Lorna. Humbug Rabbit. 2004. (Illus.). 32p. (J). 15.95 *(978-1-932065-40-4(7))* Star Bright Bks., Inc.

Bardhan-Quallen, Sudipta. Hampire! Fine, Howard, illus. 2011. (ENG.). 32p. (J). (gr. -1-3). 16.99 *(978-0-06-114239-0(5))* HarperCollins Pubs.

Barn Party: Level M, 6 vols. 128p. (gr. 2-3). 49.95 *(978-0-7699-0983-7(3))* Shortland Pubns. (U. S. A.) Inc.

Bateman, Teresa. Job Wanted. Sheban, Chris, illus. 2015. (ENG.). 32p. (J). (gr. k-3). 16.95 *(978-0-8234-3391-9(9))* Holiday Hse., Inc.

Baxter, Nicola. My First Farmyard Tales: Eight Exciting Picture Stories for Little Ones. Lodge, Ali, illus. 2013. (ENG.). 16p. (J). (gr. -1-2). bds. 13.99 *(978-1-84322-990-2(0),* Armadillo) Anness Publishing GBR. Dist: National Bk. Network.

Beaton, Clare & Blackstone, Stella. Cerdota Grandota. Beaton, Clare, illus. 2006.Tr. of How Big Is a Pig. (ENG., Illus.). 24p. (J). (gr. -1-k). bds. 6.99 *(978-1-84686-018-8(0))* Barefoot Bks., Inc.

Beaumont, Karen. Duck, Duck, Goose! (A Coyote's on the Loose!) Aruego, Jose & Dewey, Ariane, illus. 2004. 32p. (J). (gr. -1-2). lib. bdg. 18.89 *(978-0-06-050804-3(3))* HarperCollins Pubs.

—Duck, Duck, Goose! A Coyote's on the Loose! Aruego, Jose & Dewey, Ariane, illus. 2004. (ENG.). 32p. (J). (gr. -1-2). 17.99 *(978-0-06-050802-9(7))* HarperCollins Pubs.

—No Sleep for the Sheep! Urbanovic, Jackie, illus. 2011. (ENG.). 32p. (J). (gr. -1-3). 17.99 *(978-0-15-204969-0(X))* Houghton Mifflin Harcourt Publishing Co.

Bedford, David. Mole's Babies. Beardshaw, Rosalind, illus. 2012. (ENG.). 32p. (J). *(978-1-58925-108-3(3))*; pap. *(978-1-58925-435-0(X))* Tiger Tales.

Bell, Phillip. Ken the Farmer & His Friend Herbie the Talking Goat. 2012. 26p. 24.95 *(978-1-4626-6212-8(9))* America Star Bks.

Benchmark Education Co., LLC. One Frosty Night at the Farm Big Book. 2014. (Shared Reading Foundations Ser.). (J). (gr. -1). *(978-1-4509-9443-9(1))* Benchmark Education Co.

Benjamin, A. H. Baa! Moo! What Will We Do? Chapman, Jane, tr. Chapman, Jane, illus. 2003. 32p. (J). pap. 6.95 *(978-1-58925-381-0(7))* Tiger Tales.

Berkes, Marianne Collins. Over on the Farm. Morrison, Cathy, illus. 2016. (ENG.). 32p. (J). (gr. -1-2). 16.95 *(978-1-58469-548-6(X))* Dawn Pubns.

Bidelman, Jeff. The Adventures of Mr. Chicken Butt. Mozi, Jennifer, illus. 2013. (ENG.). (J). 14.95 *(978-1-62086-354-1(5))* Mascot Bks., Inc.

Bisgrove, Victoria. Wilgrove Farm. 2009. (Illus.). 78p. pap. 24.99 *(978-1-4389-8668-5(8))* AuthorHouse.

Black, Michael Ian. Cock-a-Doodle-Doo-Bop. Myers, Matthew, illus. 2015. (ENG.). 40p. (J). (gr. -1-3). 17.99 *(978-1-4424-9510-4(3),* Simon & Schuster Bks. For Young Readers) Simon & Schuster Bks. For Young Readers.

Blackman, Malorie. Jessica Strange. 2003. (Illus.). 32p. (J). pap. 8.99 *(978-0-340-77964-4(0))* Hodder & Stoughton GBR. Dist: Trafalgar Square Publishing.

Bock, Lee. Oh, Crumps!Tr. of Ay, Caramba. (ENG.). 32p. (J). (gr. 4-7). 2010. pap. 7.95 *(978-1-934960-71-4(3))* 2009. 16.95 *(978-1-934960-70-7(5))* Continental Sales, Inc. (Raven Tree Pr.,Csi).

Bond, Rebecca. Escape from Baxters' Barn. Bond, Rebecca, illus. 2017. (ENG., Illus.). 256p. (J). (gr. 2-5). pap. 7.99 ***(978-1-328-74093-9(5),*** HMH Books For Young Readers) Houghton Mifflin Harcourt Publishing Co.

—Escape from Baxters' Barn. 2015. (ENG., Illus.). 256p. (J). (gr. 2-5). 16.99 *(978-0-544-33217-1(2),* HMH Books For Young Readers) Houghton Mifflin Harcourt Publishing Co.

Boonen, Stefan. When Pigs Fly! Loufane, illus. 2004. 32p. (J). 6.95 *(978-1-58925-384-1(1))* Tiger Tales.

C
D

Bowles, Paula. Scary Mary. 2012. (ENG., Illus.). 24p. (J). *(978-1-58925-110-6(5))* Tiger Tales.

Boynton, Sandra. Barnyard Dance! (Lap Edition) 2011. (ENG., Illus.). 22p. (J). (gr. k — 1). bds. 11.95 *(978-0-7611-6616-0(5),* 16616) Workman Publishing Co., Inc.

Broekstra, Lorette. Baby Bbear Goes to the Farm. 2004. (Baby-Bear Ser.). (Illus.). 32p. (J). 5.99 *(978-1-85854-488-5(2))* Brimax Books Ltd. GBR. Dist: Byeway Bks.

Brooks, Walter R. The Clockwork Twin: A Freddy the Pig Book on Everything. Wiese, Kurt, illus. 2013. (ENG.). 256p. (gr. 4-13). pap. 10.99 *(978-1-4683-0349-0(X),* 460349) Overlook Pr., The.

—Freddy & Mr. Camphor. Wiese, Kurt, illus. 2013. (ENG.). 256p. (gr. 4-13). pap. 10.99 *(978-1-4683-0666-8(9),* 460666) Overlook Pr., The.

—Freddy & the Baseball Team from Mars. Wiese, Kurt, illus. 2011. (ENG.). 256p. 10.99 *(978-1-59020-696-6(7),* 902696) Overlook Pr., The.

—Freddy & the Dragon. Wiese, Kurt, tr. 2012. (ENG., Illus.). 240p. (gr. 4-13). pap. 10.99 *(978-1-59020-866-3(8),* 902866) Overlook Pr., The.

—Freddy & the Flying Saucer Plans. Wiese, Kurt, illus. 2013. (ENG.). 256p. (gr. 4-13). pap. 10.99 *(978-1-4683-0319-3(8),* 460319) Overlook Pr., The.

—Freddy & the Men from Mars. Wiese, Kurt, illus. 2011. (ENG.). 256p. 10.99 *(978-1-59020-695-9(9),* 902695) Overlook Pr., The.

—Freddy & the North Pole. Wiese, Kurt, illus. 2013. (ENG.). 322p. (gr. 4-13). pap. 10.99 *(978-1-4683-0320-9(1),* 460320) Overlook Pr., The.

—Freddy & the Perilous Adventure. Wiese, Kurt, illus. 2012. (ENG.). 256p. 10.99 *(978-1-59020-742-0(4),* 902742) Overlook Pr., The.

—Freddy & the Space Ship. Wiese, Kurt, illus. 2011. (ENG.). 266p. (gr. 2-18). 10.99 *(978-1-59020-469-6(7))* Overlook Pr., The.

—Freddy Goes Camping. Wiese, Kurt, illus. 2014. (ENG.). 272p. (gr. 4-13). pap. 10.99 *(978-1-4683-0831-0(9),* 460831) Overlook Pr., The.

—Freddy Goes to Florida. Wiese, Kurt, illus. 2012. (ENG.). 224p. (gr. 4-13). 10.99 *(978-1-59020-741-3(6),* 902741) Overlook Pr., The.

—Freddy Plays Football. Wiese, Kurt, illus. 2013. (ENG.). 288p. (gr. 4-13). pap. 10.99 *(978-1-4683-0667-5(7),* 460667) Overlook Pr., The.

—Freddy Rides Again. Wiese, Kurt, illus. 2013. (ENG.). 240p. (gr. 4-13). pap. 10.99 *(978-1-4683-0724-5(X),* 460724) Overlook Pr., The.

—Freddy the Cowboy. Wiese, Kurt, illus. 2014. (ENG.). 240p. (gr. 4-13). pap. 10.99 *(978-1-4683-0830-3(0),* 460830) Overlook Pr., The.

—Freddy the Detective. Wiese, Kurt, illus. 2010. (ENG.). 272p. (gr. 4-13). 11.99 *(978-1-59020-418-4(2),* 902418) Overlook Pr., The.

—Freddy the Magician. Wiese, Kurt, illus. 2011. (ENG.). 224p. (gr. 4-13). pap. 10.99 *(978-1-59020-481-8(6),* 902481) Overlook Pr., The.

—Freddy the Pied Piper. Wiese, Kurt, illus. 2014. (ENG.). 272p. (gr. 4-13). pap. 10.99 *(978-1-4683-0915-7(3),* 460915) Overlook Pr., The.

—Freddy the Pilot. Wiese, Kurt, tr. 2012. (ENG., Illus.). 256p. (gr. 4-13). pap. 10.99 *(978-1-59020-867-0(6),* 902867) Overlook Pr., The.

—Freddy's Cousin Weedly. Wiese, Kurt, illus. 2014. (ENG.). 240p. (gr. 4-13). pap. 10.99 *(978-1-4683-0914-0(5),* 460914) Overlook Pr., The.

Broughton, Theresa. Benny's Very Special Trip. Warren, Joyce, illus. 2008. 20p. pap. 24.95 *(978-1-60813-165-5(3))* America Star Bks.

—Three Amazing Farm Animals. 2008. 12p. pap. 24.95 *(978-1-60474-545-0(2))* America Star Bks.

Brown, Jo. Hoppity Skip Little Chick. 2005. (Illus.). 32p. (J). 15.95 *(978-1-58925-045-1(1))* Tiger Tales.

Brown, L. McDougal's Feast. 2013. (ENG.). 24p. (J). pap. 11.95 *(978-1-4787-0596-3(5))* Outskirts Pr., Inc.

Brown, Margaret Wise. Christmas in the Barn. Dewdney, Anna, illus. 2016. 40p. (J). (gr. -1-3). 17.99 *(978-0-06-237986-3(0))* HarperCollins Pubs.

—El Gran Granero Rojo, 1 vol. Bond, Felicia, illus. 2003.Tr. of Big Red Barn. (SPA.). 34p. (J). (gr. -1 — 1). 7.99 *(978-0-06-009107-1(X))* HarperCollins Pubs.

Bugbird, Tim. Farm Friends Peek a Boo! 2009. (Busy Baby Ser.). (ENG., Illus.). 12p. (gr. -1-k). 7.99 *(978-1-84610-859-4(4))* Make Believe Ideas GBR. Dist: Nelson, Thomas Inc.

Bunting, Eve. Hurry! Hurry! Mack, Jeff, illus. (ENG.). (J). 2009. 32p. (gr. k — 1). bds. 6.99 *(978-0-15-206686-4(1))* 2007. 40p. (gr. -1-3). 16.99 *(978-0-15-205410-6(3))* Houghton Mifflin Harcourt Publishing Co.

Cabrera, Jane. One, Two, Buckle My Shoe. 2009. (ENG., Illus.). 32p. (J). (gr. -1-k). 16.95 *(978-0-8234-2230-2(5))* Holiday Hse., Inc.

Capucilli, Alyssa Satin. Biscuit's Day at the Farm. Schories, Pat, illus. 2007. (My First I Can Read Ser.). (ENG.). 32p. (J). (gr. -1 — 1). pap. 3.99 *(978-0-06-074169-3(4));* 16.99 *(978-0-06-074167-9(8))* HarperCollins Pubs.

—Biscuit's Day at the Farm. 2007. (Biscuit: My First I Can Read! Ser.). (J). lib. bdg. 13.55 *(978-1-4177-9810-0(6),* Turtleback) Turtleback Bks.

Carle, Eric. The Very Busy Spider. Carle, Eric, illus. (Penguin Young Readers, Level 2 Ser.). (ENG., Illus.). (J). 2014. 32p. (gr. 1-2). pap. 3.99 *(978-0-448-48052-7(2),* Penguin Young Readers) 2011. 24p. (gr. -1 — 1). bds. 15.99 *(978-0-399-25601-1(6),* Philomel Bks.) Penguin Young Readers Group.

—The Very Busy Spider. 2006. (World of Eric Carle Ser.). (ENG., Illus.). 24p. (J). (gr. -1-k). 6.99 *(978-0-448-44421-5(6),* Grosset & Dunlap) Penguin Young Readers Group.

Carpenter, Tad. Barnyard Friends. 2015. (Who's That? Ser.). (ENG., Illus.). 16p. (J). (— 1). bds. 7.95 *(978-1-4549-1226-2(X))* Sterling Publishing Co., Inc.

Carris, Joan. Wild Times at the Bed & Biscuit. Jones, Noah Z., illus. 2011. (ENG.). 128p. (J). (gr. 1-4). pap. 5.99 *(978-0-7636-5294-4(6))* Candlewick Pr.

Cartwright, Steven, illus. Farmyard Tales Sticker Coloring Book. 2011. (Coloring Bks). 20p. (J). pap. 5.99 *(978-0-7945-2959-8(3),* Usborne) EDC Publishing.

Cazet, Denys. Minnie & Moo: Hooves of Fire. Cazet, Denys, illus. 2014. (ENG., Illus.). 208p. (J). (gr. k-6). 15.95 *(978-1-939547-08-8(3))* Creston Bks.

—Minnie & Moo: The Attack of the Easter Bunnies. Cazet, Denys, illus. 2004. (I Can Read Bks.). (Illus.). 48p. (J). (gr. k-3). (ENG.). 15.99 *(978-0-06-000506-1(8));* lib. bdg. 17.89 *(978-0-06-000507-8(6))* HarperCollins Pubs.

—Minnie & Moo: The Case of the Missing Jelly Donut. Cazet, Denys, illus. 2006. (I Can Read Bks.). (ENG., Illus.). 48p. (J). (gr. k-3). pap. 3.99 *(978-0-06-073009-3(9))* HarperCollins Pubs.

—Minnie & Moo: The Case of the Missing Jelly Donut. Cazet, Denys, illus. 2007. (Minnie & Moo Ser.). (Illus.). 45p. (J). (gr. -1-3). pap. 29.95 incl. audio *(978-1-4301-0088-1(5))* Live Oak Media.

—Minnie & Moo: The Case of the Missing Jelly Donut, 4 bks., Set. 2007. (J). (gr. k-2). pap. 31.95 incl. audio compact disk *(978-1-4301-0091-1(5))* Live Oak Media.

—Minnie & Moo: The Night of the Living Bed. Cazet, Denys, illus. 2003. (I Can Read Bks.). (Illus.). 48p. (J). (gr. k-3). lib. bdg. 16.89 *(978-0-06-000504-7(1))* HarperCollins Pubs.

—Minnie & Moo - The Night of the Living Bed. Cazet, Denys, illus. 2004. (I Can Read Level 3 Ser.). (ENG., Illus.). 48p. (J). (gr. k-3). pap. 3.99 *(978-0-06-000505-4(X))* HarperCollins Pubs.

—Minnie & Moo & the Seven Wonders of the World. Cazet, Denys, illus. 2003. (ENG., Illus.). 144p. (J). (gr. 2-5). 19.99 *(978-0-689-85330-2(0),* Atheneum/Richard Jackson Bks.) Simon & Schuster Children's Publishing.

—Minnie & Moo Meet Frankenswine. Cazet, Denys, illus. 2004. (Readalongs for Beginning Readers Ser.). (Illus.). 28.95 incl. audio compact disk *(978-1-59112-876-2(5));* (J). 25.95 incl. audio *(978-1-59112-262-3(7));* (J). pap. 29.95 incl. audio *(978-1-59112-263-0(5))* Live Oak Media.

—Minnie & Moo Meet Frankenswine, 4 bks. 2004. (Readalongs for Beginning Readers Ser.). (Illus.). 48p. (J). (gr. -1-2). pap. 31.95 incl. audio compact disk *(978-1-59112-877-9(3))* Live Oak Media.

—The Night of the Living Bed. Cazet, Denys, illus. unabr. ed. 2005. (Minnie & Moo Ser.). (Illus.). (J). (gr. k-4). 25.95 incl. audio *(978-1-59519-389-6(8));*Set. pap. 29.95 incl. audio *(978-1-59519-390-2(1));*Set. pap. 31.95 incl. audio compact disk *(978-1-59519-394-0(4))* Live Oak Media.

Cepeda, Joe. Up. Cepeda, Joe, illus. 2016. (I Like to Read(r) Ser.). (ENG., Illus.). 24p. (J). 6.99 *(978-0-8234-3689-7(6));* 14.95 *(978-0-8234-3655-2(1))* Holiday Hse., Inc.

Chaconas, Dori. Coriander the Contrary Hen. Carrington, Marsha Gray, illus. 2007. (Carolrhoda Picture Bks.). (ENG.). 32p. (J). (gr. k-3). lib. bdg. 16.95 *(978-1-57505-749-1(2),* Carolrhoda Bks.) Lerner Publishing Group.

Chall, Marsha Wilson. A Secret Keeps. 2012. (Carolrhoda Picture Bks.). (ENG., Illus.). 32p. (J). (gr. k-3). lib. bdg. 16.95 *(978-0-7613-5593-9(6))* Lerner Publishing Group.

Chapman, Keith. Itsy Bitsy Spider. Tickle, Jack, illus. (Tiger Tales Ser.). (J). 2008. 24p. (gr. -1-2). pap. 6.95 *(978-1-58925-407-7(4))* 2006. 32p. 15.95 *(978-1-58925-055-0(9))* Tiger Tales.

Church, Caroline Jayne. Little Apple Goat. Church, Caroline Jayne, illus. 2007. (ENG., Illus.). 28p. (J). (gr. k-3). 16.00 *(978-0-8028-5320-2(X),* Eerdmans Bks For Young Readers) Eerdmans, William B. Publishing Co.

—Ping Pong Pig. Church, Caroline Jayne, illus. 2008. (ENG., Illus.). 32p. (J). (gr. -1-1). 16.95 *(978-0-8234-2176-3(7))* Holiday Hse., Inc.

Church, Caroline Jayne, illus. The Very Busy Farm. 2016. (ENG.). 10p. (J). (gr. -1-k). bds. 8.99 *(978-0-7944-3752-7(4),* Reader's Digest Children's Bks.) Studio Fun International.

Churchman, Jennifer & Churchman, John. Brave Little Finn. 2016. (Sweet Pea & Friends Ser.). (ENG., Illus.). 40p. (J). (gr. -1-3). 17.99 *(978-0-316-27359-6(7))* Little, Brown Bks. for Young Readers.

Clark, Leslie Ann. Peepsqueak! Clark, Leslie Ann, illus. 2012. (ENG., Illus.). 32p. (J). (gr. -1-k). 12.99 *(978-0-06-207801-8(1))* HarperCollins Pubs.

—Peepsqueak Wants a Friend! Clark, Leslie Ann, illus. 2013. (ENG., Illus.). 32p. (J). (gr. -1-3). 15.99 *(978-0-06-207804-9(6))* HarperCollins Pubs.

Coffin, Douglas. One Maine Christmas Eve, 1 vol. Coffin, Douglas, illus. 2015. (ENG., Illus.). 32p. (gr. -1-12). 16.95 *(978-0-88448-469-1(6),* 884469) Tilbury Hse. Pubs.

Cohen, Caron Lee. Digger Pig & the Turnip. Denise, Christopher, illus. 2003. (Green Light Readers Level 2 Ser.). (ENG.). 24p. (J). (gr. -1-3). pap. 3.95 *(978-0-15-204829-7(4))* Houghton Mifflin Harcourt Publishing Co.

Cole, Henry. Eddie the Bully. 2016. (ENG.). 40p. (J). (gr. -1-3). 17.99 *(978-1-4998-0181-1(5))* Little Bee Books Inc.

Collins, Bert McLemore. Excitement at Double B Acres. 2009. 52p. pap. 22.49 *(978-1-4389-8447-6(2))* AuthorHouse.

Cotton, Katie. And the Cow Said. Gausden, Vicki, illus. 2015. (ENG.). 24p. (J). (gr. -1-1). 12.99 *(978-1-4998-0101-9(7))* Little Bee Books Inc.

Courtin, Thierry. Decouvre les petits de la Ferme. 15.95 *(978-2-09-202273-3(3))* Nathan, Fernand FRA. Dist: Distribooks, Inc.

Cousins, Lucy. Where Does Maisy Live? 2010. 12p. bds. 4.99 *(978-976-3-64668-7(5))* Candlewick Pr.

—Where Does Maisy Live? Cousins, Lucy, illus. 2010. (Maisy Ser.). (ENG., Illus.). 12p. (J). (-k). bds. 5.99 *(978-0-7636-4668-4(7))* Candlewick Pr.

Cowley, Joy. Mrs. WishyWashy & the Big Wash Big Book. 2010. 48.25 *(978-1-60559-247-3(1))* Hameray Publishing Group, Inc.

Cox, Judy. The Case of the Purloined Professor, 0 vols. Rayyan, Omar, illus. 2009. (Tails of Frederick & Ishbu Ser.: 0). (ENG.). 256p. (J). (gr. 5-7). 16.99 *(978-0-7614-5544-8(2),* 9780761455448, Amazon Children's Publishing) Amazon Publishing.

Craig, Lindsey. Farmyard Beat. Brown, Marc, illus. 2012. (ENG.). 32p. (J). (gr. k-k). bds. 6.99 *(978-0-307-93082-8(3),* Knopf Bks. for Young Readers) Random Hse. Children's Bks.

Crofoot, Nancy. Christmas in the Barn, 1 vol. Rawat, Tania, illus. 2009. 37p. pap. 24.95 *(978-1-61582-585-1(1))* America Star Bks.

Cromwell, Daisy. Arthur, the Talking Goat. Paxton, Cameron L., illus. 2007. 52p. (J). pap. 18.99 *(978-0-9800675-1-4(0))* Mirror Publishing.

Cronin, Doreen. A Busy Day at the Farm. Lewin, Betsy, illus. 2009. (Click, Clack Book Ser.). (ENG.). 16p. (J). (gr. -1-k). pap. 6.99 *(978-1-4169-5518-4(6),* Little Simon) Little Simon.

—Click, Clack, Boo! A Tricky Treat. Lewin, Betsy, illus. 2013. (ENG.). 40p. (J). (gr. -1-2). 17.99 *(978-1-4424-6553-4(0))* Simon & Schuster Children's Publishing.

—Click, Clack, Moo: Cows That Type. Lewin, Betsy, illus. (Click, Clack Book Ser.). (ENG.). (J). (gr. -1-3). 2011. 32p. pap. 9.99 *(978-1-4424-3370-0(1))* 2010. 34p. bds. 7.99 *(978-1-4424-0889-0(8))* Little Simon. (Little Simon).

—Click, Clack, Moo: Cows That Type. 2004. 29.95 *(978-1-55592-104-0(3))* Weston Woods Studios, Inc.

—Click, Clack, Peep! Lewin, Betsy, illus. 2015. (Click, Clack Book Ser.). (ENG.). 40p. (J). (gr. -1-3). 17.99 *(978-1-4814-2411-0(4))* Simon & Schuster Children's Publishing.

—Dooby Dooby Moo. Lewin, Betsy, illus. 2010. (Click, Clack Book Ser.). (ENG.). 40p. (J). (gr. -1-k). bds. 7.99 *(978-1-4424-0890-6(1),* Little Simon) Little Simon.

—Dooby Dooby Moo. Lewin, Betsy, illus. 2006. (Click, Clack Book Ser.). (ENG.). 40p. (J). (gr. -1-3). 17.99 *(978-0-689-84507-9(3),* Atheneum Bks. for Young Readers) Simon & Schuster Children's Publishing.

—Dooby Dooby Moo. Lewin, Betsy, illus. 2017. (Click, Clack Book Ser.). (ENG.). 40p. (J). (gr. k-2). 16.99 ***(978-1-5344-0177-8(6));*** pap. 3.99 ***(978-1-5344-0176-1(8))*** Simon Spotlight. (Simon Spotlight).

—Dooby Dooby Moo, 1 vol. Lewin, Betsy, illus. 2008. (Doreen Cronin: Click-Clack & More Ser.). (ENG.). 40p. (gr. -1-3). lib. bdg. 24.21 *(978-1-59961-423-6(5))* Spotlight.

—Dooby Dooby Moo. Lewin, Betsy, illus. 2011. (J). (gr. -1-3). 29.95 *(978-0-545-04281-9(X))* Weston Woods Studios, Inc.

—Dubi Dubi Muu. Jimenez Rioja, Alberto, tr. from ENG. 2007.Tr. of Dooby Dooby Moo. (SPA., Illus.). 35p. (J). (gr. -1-1). 15.95 *(978-1-933032-33-7(2))* Lectorum Pubns., Inc.

—Farmer Brown's Barnyard, Set. Lewin, Betsy, illus. gif. ed. 2008. (Click, Clack Book Ser.). (ENG.). 106p. (J). (gr. -1-k). 18.99 *(978-1-4169-5521-4(6),* Little Simon) Little Simon.

—Giggle, Giggle, Quack. Lewin, Betsy, illus. 2011. (Click, Clack Book Ser.). (ENG.). 34p. (J). (gr. -1-k). bds. 7.99 *(978-1-4424-0891-3(X),* Little Simon) Little Simon.

—Giggle, Giggle, Quack. Lewin, Betsy, illus. 2006. (Doreen Cronin: Click-Clack & More Ser.). (ENG.). 32p. (gr. -1-3). lib. bdg. 24.21 *(978-1-59961-092-4(2))* Spotlight.

—Jaja Jiji, Cuac. Jimenez, Alberto, tr. from ENG. Lewin, Betsy, illus. 2003.Tr. of Giggle, Giggle, Quack. (SPA.). (J). 15.00 *(978-1-930332-46-1(7))* Lectorum Pubns., Inc.

—Thump, Quack, Moo: A Whacky Adventure. Lewin, Betsy, illus. 2008. (Click, Clack Book Ser.). (ENG.). 42p. (J). (gr. -1-2). 16.99 *(978-1-4169-1630-7(X),* Atheneum Bks. for Young Readers) Simon & Schuster Children's Publishing.

Cronin, Doreen & Jiménez Rioja, Alberto. Pum, Cuac, Muu: Una Loca Aventura. Lewin, Betsy, illus. 2008. (SPA.). (J). pap. 5.99 *(978-1-933032-54-2(5));* 36p. 16.99 *(978-1-933032-53-5(7))* Lectorum Pubns., Inc.

Cronin, Doreen & Lewin, Betsy. Click, Clack, Moo: Cows That Type. 2014. 32p. pap. 8.00 *(978-1-61003-342-8(6))* Center for the Collaborative Classroom.

Cronin, Doreen & Simon and Schuster/LeapFrog Staff. Click, Clack, Moo: Cows That Type. Lewin, Betsy, illus. 2008. (J). 13.99 *(978-1-59319-936-4(8))* LeapFrog Enterprises, Inc.

Cuyler, Margery. Purim Chicken. Pinillos, Puy, illus. 2017. (ENG.). 32p. (J). (gr. -1-3). 16.99 *(978-0-8075-3381-9(5))* Whitman, Albert & Co.

Czekaj, Jef. Oink-a-Doodle-Moo. Czekaj, Jef, illus. 2012. (ENG., Illus.). 32p. (J). (gr. -1-1). 16.99 *(978-0-06-206011-2(2))* HarperCollins Pubs.

Dalmatian Press Staff. Mommy, Is That You? 2008. (ENG.). 5p. bds. 4.95 *(978-1-58117-714-5(3),* Intervisual/Piggy Toes) Bendon, Inc.

Deák, Erzsi. Pumpkin Time! Cushman, Doug, illus. 2014. (ENG.). 32p. (J). (-3). 14.99 *(978-1-4022-9526-3(X),* 9781402295263, Sourcebooks Jabberwocky) Sourcebooks, Inc.

Degman, Lori. Cock-A-Doodle-Oops! Zemke, Deborah, illus. 2014. (ENG.). 36p. (J). (gr. -1-4). 16.95 *(978-1-939547-07-1(5))* Creston Bks.

DePrisco, Dorothea. Who's on the Farm? Gilvan-Cartwright, Chris, illus. 2006. (ENG.). 10p. (gr. -1-k). bds. 4.95 *(978-1-58117-508-0(6),* Intervisual/Piggy Toes) Bendon, Inc.

Dillon, Kadi. Babies in the Barnyard, 1 vol. 2010. 26p. pap. 24.95 *(978-1-61546-415-9(8))* PublishAmerica, Inc.

Dobbins, Jan. Driving My Tractor. Sim, David, illus. 2009. (ENG.). 32p. (J). (gr. -1-3). 16.99 incl. audio compact disk *(978-1-84686-358-5(9))* Barefoot Bks., Inc.

Dodd, Emma. On the Farm. 2017. (ENG., Illus.). 12p. (J). (gr. -1-12). bds. 9.99 ***(978-1-86147-838-2(0),*** Armadillo) Anness Publishing GBR. Dist: National Bk. Network.

Donaldson, Julia. A Squash & a Squeeze. Scheffler, Axel, illus. 2016. (ENG.). 32p. (J). (gr. -1-k). 16.99 *(978-1-338-05220-6(9))* Scholastic, Inc.

—What the Ladybug Heard. Monks, Lydia, illus. 2010. (ENG.). 32p. (J). (gr. -1-1). 18.99 *(978-0-8050-9028-4(2),* 9780805090284, Holt, Henry & Co. Bks. For Young Readers) Holt, Henry & Co.

Dooby Dooby Moo. 2014. (Click, Clack Book Ser.). (ENG., Illus.). 40p. (J). (gr. -1-3). pap. 9.99 *(978-1-4814-1456-2(9),* Little Simon) Little Simon.

Dorling Kindersley Publishing Staff. Farm. 2011. (ENG., Illus.). 12p. (J). (gr. -1 — 1). bds. 9.99 *(978-0-7566-7172-3(8),* DK Children) Dorling Kindersley Publishing, Inc.

—Farm - Little Hide & Seek. 2013. (ENG.). 14p. (J). (gr. -1 — 1). bds. 7.99 *(978-1-4654-0932-4(7),* DK Children) Dorling Kindersley Publishing, Inc.

Downing, Sue. Cheep, Cheep! Baby Animal Sounds. 2016. (ENG., Illus.). 10p. (J). bds. 7.99 *(978-1-61963-833-4(9),* 9781619638334, Bloomsbury USA Childrens) Bloomsbury Publishing USA.

Dries, L. M. H. Stella & the Rocks. 2013. 28p. pap. 13.99 *(978-1-4808-0409-8(6))* Archway Publishing.

Driscoll, Amanda. Wally Does Not Want a Haircut. 2016. (ENG., Illus.). 32p. (J). (gr. -1-2). 16.99 *(978-0-553-53579-2(X),* Knopf Bks. for Young Readers) Random Hse. Children's Bks.

Dumbleton, Mike. Muddled-Up Farm, 1 vol. Murphy, Jobi, illus. 2013. (ENG.). 32p. (J). 16.99 *(978-1-59572-630-8(6))* Star Bright Bks., Inc.

Dunbar, Joyce. A Chick Called Saturday. Granström, Brita, illus. 2004. 32p. (J). 16.00 *(978-0-8028-5260-1(2))* Eerdmans, William B. Publishing Co.

Dunn, Phoebe, illus. & photos by. The Little Duck. Dunn, Phoebe, photos by. Dunn, Judy, photos by. 2017. (Step into Reading Ser.). (ENG.). 32p. (J). (gr. -1-1). pap. 3.99 *(978-0-553-53352-1(5),* Random Hse. Bks. for Young Readers) Random Hse. Children's Bks.

Dunrea, Olivier. BooBoo. 2008. (Gossie & Friends Ser.). (ENG., Illus.). 32p. (J). (gr. k — 1). bds. 6.95 *(978-0-618-75505-9(5))* Houghton Mifflin Harcourt Publishing Co.

—Gossie & Friends: A First Flap Book. Dunrea, Olivier, illus. 2006. (Gossie & Friends Ser.). (ENG., Illus.). 8p. (J). (gr. -1 — 1). 11.99 *(978-0-618-70786-7(7))* Houghton Mifflin Harcourt Publishing Co.

Dutton, Stella. Tex the Mockingbird. ed. 2015. (ENG., Illus.). 36p. (J). (gr. -1-5). 15.99 *(978-0-9790832-6-6(5))* 405 Pubns.

Duvoisin, Roger. Donkey-Donkey. 2016. (ENG., Illus.). 56p. (J). (-k). 16.95 *(978-1-59017-964-2(1),* NYR Children's Collection) New York Review of Bks., Inc., The.

Edwards, Pamela Duncan. McGillycuddy Could! Porter, Sue, illus. 2005. 32p. (J). (gr. -1-1). 14.99 *(978-0-06-029001-6(3))* HarperCollins Pubs.

Elliot, David. Henry's Map. Elliot, David, illus. 2013. (ENG., Illus.). 40p. (J). (gr. -1-3). 16.99 *(978-0-399-16072-1(8),* Philomel Bks.) Penguin Young Readers Group.

—Henry's Stars. Elliot, David, illus. 2015. (ENG., Illus.). 40p. (J). (gr. k-3). 16.99 *(978-0-399-17116-1(9),* Philomel Bks.) Penguin Young Readers Group.

Englert, June Scott. My Story by Jake, 1 vol. 2010. 48p. pap. 16.95 *(978-1-4489-5308-0(1))* America Star Bks.

Evensen, Rachelle. Finn's Marching Band: A Story of Counting, Colors, & Playing Together. 2009. 32p. (J). 14.95 *(978-0-8091-6749-4(2),* Ambassador Bks.) Paulist Pr.

Farmyard Tales. 2017. (Farmyard Tales Ser.). 24p. (gr. 4-6). pap. 24.75 ***(978-1-5081-6181-3(X),*** PowerKids Pr.) Rosen Publishing Group, Inc., The.

Fass, Amanda L. Farm Friends. Swope, Brenda, illus. 2011. 28p. pap. 24.95 *(978-1-4560-0894-9(3))* America Star Bks.

Feldman, Thea. Hello, Farm! 2015. (Flap Book Ser.: 3). (ENG.). 14p. (J). (gr. -1-k). 8.99 *(978-0-7944-3298-0(0),* Reader's Digest Children's Bks.) Studio Fun International.

Fischer, Hans. Pitschi. 2010. (ENG., Illus.). 32p. (J). (gr. -1-3). 16.95 *(978-0-7358-2278-8(6))* North-South Bks., Inc.

Fisher, Carolyn. A Twisted Tale. 2004. (Illus.). 33p. (J). (gr. k-4). reprint ed. 16.00 *(978-0-7567-8412-6(3))* DIANE Publishing Co.

Fisher, Pam. Pammy the Pig. 2011. 20p. 13.99 *(978-1-4567-1796-4(0))* AuthorHouse.

Fisher-Price. Fisher-Price Little People Let's Imagine on the Farm. 2014. (Lift-The-Flap Ser.: 28). (ENG.). 10p. (J). (gr. -1-k). bds. 9.99 *(978-0-7944-3114-3(3),* Reader's Digest Children's Bks.) Studio Fun International.

Fleming, Candace. Go Sleep in Your Own Bed. Nichols, Lori, illus. 2017. (ENG.). 40p. (J). (gr. -1-2). 17.99 *(978-0-375-86648-7(5),* Schwartz & Wade Bks.) Random Hse. Children's Bks.

Freedman, Deborah. Blue Chicken. 2011. (ENG.). 40p. (J). (gr. -1-k). 15.99 *(978-0-670-01293-0(9),* Viking Books for Young Readers) Penguin Young Readers Group.

A friend for Flash. 2006. (J). per. 3.99 *(978-1-934004-14-2(6))* Byeway Bks.

Frohmuth, Shawn. The Wiblet. 2005. 200p. (YA). pap. 12.95 *(978-0-595-36956-0(1))* iUniverse, Inc.

Galvin, Laura Gates. My First Trip to the Farm. Rabe, Tish, ed. rev. ed. 2007. (ENG., Illus.). 24p. (J). (gr. -1-3). 5.49 *(978-1-59069-561-6(5))* Studio Mouse LLC.

Gardner, Charlie & Dorling Kindersley Publishing Staff. Farm Peekaboo! King, Dave, photos by. 2007. (ENG., Illus.). 12p. (J). (gr. -1-k). bds. 6.99 *(978-0-7566-3104-8(1),* DK Children) Dorling Kindersley Publishing, Inc.

Garland, Michael. Oh, What a Christmas! Garland, Michael, illus. 2011. (ENG., Illus.). 40p. (J). (gr. -1-3). 16.99 *(978-0-545-24210-3(X),* Scholastic Pr.) Scholastic, Inc.

Gernhart, Cyndi. Gertrude Sees... On the Farm. Gernhart, Cyndi et al, illus. l.t. ed. 2006. 20p. (J). 8.00 *(978-0-9778240-0-7(4))* Prairie Winds Publishing.

Gershator, Phillis. Who's in the Farmyard? McDonald, Jill, illus. 2012. (ENG.). 24p. (J). (gr. -1-k). bds. 14.99 *(978-1-84686-574-9(3))* Barefoot Bks., Inc.

Gershman, Regina. Animals from My Window. 2011. 24p. pap. 16.44 *(978-1-4634-2094-9(3))* AuthorHouse.

Ghigna, Charles. Lucy Goose. East, Jacqueline, illus. 2015. (Tiny Tales Ser.). (ENG.). 64p. (gr. -1-2). lib. bdg. 23.99 *(978-1-4795-6529-0(6))* Tiny Tales.

Ghigna, Charles & Ghigna, Debra. Barn Storm. Greenseid, Diane, illus. 2010. (Step into Reading Ser.). (ENG.). 32p. (J). (gr. -1-1). pap. 3.99 *(978-0-375-86114-7(9),* Random Hse. Bks. for Young Readers) Random Hse. Children's Bks.

Golden Books Staff. Farm Tales. 2007. (Little Golden Book Treasury Ser.). (ENG., Illus.). 224p. (J). (gr. -1-2). 10.99 *(978-0-375-83942-9(9),* Golden Bks.) Random Hse. Children's Bks.

Gondek, Heather J. Who's on the Farm? Lift-the-Flap 'n' Learn Book. Gilvan-Cartwright, Chris, illus. 2005. (Fun with Animals Ser.). 10p. (J). (gr. -1-k). act. bk. ed. 9.95 *(978-1-58117-143-3(9),* Intervisual/Piggy Toes) Bendon, Inc.

Grandpa Dennis, as told by. George Washington's Smallest Army: The Miracle Before Trenton. 2009. 216p. (J). pap. 17.49 *(978-1-4389-3147-0(6))* AuthorHouse.

Grant, Nicola. Don't Be So Nosy, Posy! Warnes, Tim, illus. 2004. 32p. (J). tchr. ed. 15.95 *(978-1-58925-036-9(2))* Tiger Tales.

Green, Kate. A Number of Animals. Wormell, Christopher, illus. 2012. (ENG.). 32p. (J). (gr. -1-k). 15.99 *(978-1-56846-222-6(0),* Creative Editions) Creative Co., The.

Gulbis, Stephen, illus. Old MacDonald Had a Barn. 2003. 22p. (YA). *(978-1-85602-453-2(9),* Pavilion Children's Books) Pavilion Bks.

Hamilton, Arlene. Only a Cow, 1 vol. Griffiths, Dean, illus. 2006. (ENG.). 32p. (J). (gr. -1-2). *(978-1-55041-871-2(8))* Fitzhenry & Whiteside, Ltd.

Hamilton, Martha & Weiss, Mitch. The Hidden Feast: A Folktale from the American South. Tate, Don, illus. 2006. (ENG.). 32p. (J). (gr. k-3). 16.95 (978-0-87483-758-2(8)) August Hse. Pubs., Inc.

Hancock, Dennis. Goodnight on the Farm. Hancock, Uyen, illus. 2012. 28p. pap. 24.95 (978-1-4626-7233-2(7)) America Star Bks.

Happpy Books. A Day at the Farm. 2012. (Day at ... Bks.). (ENG., Illus.). 8p. (J). bds. 6.99 (978-0-7641-6532-0(1)) Barron's Educational Series, Inc.

Harris, Patricia. Everyone Has a Job on the Farm. 2017. (Farmyard Tales Ser.). 24p. (gr. 4-6). pap. 8.25 **(978-1-5383-2182-9(3)**, PowerKids Pr.) Rosen Publishing Group, Inc., The.

Head, Mat. Warduff & the Corn Cob Caper. Head, Mat, illus. 2011. (Andersen Press Picture Books Ser.). (Illus.). 16.95 (978-0-7613-8095-5(7)) Andersen Pr. GBR. Dist: Lerner Publishing Group.

Hill, Eric. Spot Can Count. 2009. (Spot (Chinese) Ser.). (CHI., Illus.). 22p. (978-957-762-468-0(5)) Hsin Yi Pubns.

—Spot Goes to the Farm. Hill, Eric, illus. 2003. (Spot Ser.). (ENG., Illus.). 24p. (J). (gr. -1-k). 7.99 (978-0-14-250123-8(9), Warne) Penguin Young Readers Group.

—Spot Goes to the Farm. 2003. (Spot Ser.). (gr. -1-2). lib. bdg. 18.40 (978-0-613-86708-5(4), Turtleback) Turtleback Bks.

Hillenbrand, Will. Cock-a-Doodle Christmas!, 0 vols. 2010. (ENG.). 32p. (J). (gr. -1-2). pap. 6.99 (978-0-7614-5718-3(6), 9780761457183, Amazon Children's Publishing) Amazon Publishing.

—Down by the Barn, 0 vols. 2014. (ENG.). 32p. (J). (gr. -1-k). 16.99 (978-1-4778-4731-2(6), 9781477847312, Amazon Children's Publishing) Amazon Publishing.

Himmelman, John. Chickens to the Rescue. Himmelman, John, illus. 2006. (Barnyard Rescue Ser.). (ENG., Illus.). 32p. (J). (gr. -1-3). 17.99 (978-0-8050-7951-7(3), 9780805079517, Holt, Henry & Co. Bks. For Young Readers) Holt, Henry & Co.

Hines, Chrissie & Ferreras, Alberto. El Perro y el Gato. Winslow, Justin, illus. 2010.Tr. of Perro y el Gato: la Nieve. (SPA.). 28p. 3.99 (978-0-9828167-1-4(5)) Home Box Office, Inc.

Hodges, Meredith. Jasper: A Fabulous Fourth. Shields, Bonnie, illus. 2006. 83p. (J). (978-1-928624-24-0(3)) Lucky 3 Ranch, Inc.

Hodgson, Christy. Debra's First Day of School. 2011. 40p. pap. 19.95 (978-1-4567-3260-8(9)) AuthorHouse.

Holtfreter, Nastja, illus. Push Puzzles: on the Farm. 2016. (ENG.). 10p. (J). (gr. -1 — 1). bds. 7.99 (978-1-4998-0348-8(6)) Little Bee Books Inc.

Hood, Karen Jean Matsko. Petting Farm Fun, Vol. 3. Whispering Pine Press International, ed. Digital Island, illus. 2014. (Hood Picture Book Ser.). (ENG.). 46p. (J). 24.95 (978-1-59434-885-3(5)) Whispering Pine Pr. International, Inc.

—Petting Farm Fun: Hood Picture Book Series, Vol. 3. Whispering Pine Press International, ed. Digital Island, illus. 2014. (Hood Picture Book Ser.). (ENG.). 46p. (J). 84.99 (978-1-59434-914-0(2)); pap. 15.95 (978-1-59434-618-7(6)) Whispering Pine Pr. International, Inc.

—Petting Farm Fun: Hood Picture Book Series - Book 3, Vol. 3. Whispering Pine Press International Staff, ed. Digital Island, illus. 2015. (Hood Picture Book Ser.). (ENG.). 46p. (J). pap. 15.95 (978-1-59434-905-8(3)) Whispering Pine Pr. International, Inc.

—Petting Farm Fun, Bilingual English & Hindi. Whispering Pine Press International, ed. Artistic Design Services Staff, illus. 2015. (Hood Picture Book Ser.). (ENG & HIN.). 36p. (J). Bk. 3. pap. 29.95 (978-1-59808-646-1(4)) Vol. 3. 34.95 (978-1-59808-641-6(3)) Vol. 3. 94.99 (978-1-59808-642-3(1)) Vol. 3. pap. 25.95 (978-1-59808-657-7(X)) Whispering Pine Pr. International, Inc.

—Petting Farm Fun, Bilingual English & Marathi Edition: Hood Picture Book Series- Book 3. 2014. (ENG & MAR.). (J). 29.95 (978-1-59808-723-9(1)); 80.95 (978-1-59808-724-6(X)); pap. 54.95 (978-1-59808-727-7(4)); pap. 20.95 (978-1-59808-726-0(6)); pap. 24.95 (978-1-59808-725-3(8)) Whispering Pine Pr. International, Inc.

—Petting Farm Fun, Bilingual English & Portuguese. Whispering Pine Press International, ed. Artistic Design Services Staff, illus. 2015. (Hood Picture Book Ser.). (ENG & POR.). 36p. (J). Bk. 3. pap. 29.95 (978-1-59808-813-7(0)) Vol. 3. 94.95 (978-1-59808-812-0(2)) Vol. 3. 34.95 (978-1-59808-811-3(4)) Vol. 3. pap. 25.95 (978-1-59808-814-4(9)) Whispering Pine Pr. International, Inc.

—Petting Farm Fun, Bilingual English & Spanish, Bk. 3. Whispering Pine Press International, ed. Artistic Design Service, illus. 2015. (Hood Picture Book Ser.). (ENG & SPA.). 36p. (J). pap. 29.95 (978-1-59808-824-3(6)) Whispering Pine Pr. International, Inc.

—Petting Farm Fun, Bilingual English & Spanish, Vol. 3. Whispering Pine Press International, ed. Artistic Design Services Staff, illus. 2015. (Hood Picture Book Ser.). (ENG & SPA.). 36p. (J). 94.99 (978-1-59808-823-6(8)); 34.95 (978-1-59808-822-9(X)); pap. 25.95 (978-1-59808-825-0(4)) Whispering Pine Pr. International, Inc.

—Petting Farm Fun, Translated Hindi, bk. 3. Whispering Pine Press International, ed. Artistic Design Services Staff, illus. 2014. (Hood Picture Book Ser.). (HIN.). 46p. (J). 84.99 (978-1-59808-844-1(0)); 24.95 (978-1-59808-843-4(2)); pap. 19.95 (978-1-59808-846-5(7)); pap. 15.95 (978-1-59808-845-8(9)) Whispering Pine Pr. International, Inc.

—Petting Farm Fun, Translated Marathi Edition: Hood Picture Book Series- Book 3. 2014. (MAR.). (J). 29.95 (978-1-59808-712-3(6)); 80.95 (978-1-59808-713-0(4)); pap. 24.95 (978-1-59808-714-7(2)); pap. 20.95 (978-1-59808-715-4(0)) Whispering Pine Pr. International, Inc.

—Petting Farm Fun, Translated Portuguese, bk. 3. Whispering Pine Press International, ed. Artistic Design Services Staff, illus. 2014. (Hood Picture Book Ser.). (POR.). 46p. (J). 84.99 (978-1-59808-865-6(3)); 24.95 (978-1-59808-864-9(5)); pap. 19.95 (978-1-59808-867-0(X)); pap. 15.95 (978-1-59808-866-3(1)) Whispering Pine Pr. International, Inc.

Hopgood, Sally. A Day on the Farm: A Pull-The-Tab Book. Hinton, Stephanie, illus. 2014. (J). (978-1-4351-5688-3(9)) Barnes & Noble, Inc.

—Let's Find Farm Animals. Hinton, Steph, illus. 2017. (Let's Find Pull-The-Tab Bks.). (ENG.). 12p. (J). (gr. -1-5). bds. 9.99 (978-1-78700-057-5(5)) Top That! Publishing PLC GBR. Dist: Independent Pubs. Group.

Howard, Martin. Shaun the Sheep: the Beast of Soggy Moor. Janes, Andy, illus. 2015. (Tales from Mossy Bottom Farm Ser.). (ENG.). (J). (gr. k-3). pap. 4.99 (978-0-7636-7586-8(5), Candlewick Entertainment) Candlewick Pr.

Hudgens, Melica, illus. Flim Flam & Other Such Gobbledygook. 2015. (J). 14.99 (978-1-4621-1684-3(1)) Cedar Fort, Inc./CFI Distribution.

Hunt, Wayne. Zack & the Validators: Good As Gold. 2011. 138p. pap. 19.99 (978-1-4653-5816-5(1)) Xlibris Corp.

Hutchins, Pat. Barn Dance! Hutchins, Pat, illus. 2007. (Illus.). 32p. (J). (gr. -1-k). lib. bdg. 17.89 (978-0-06-089122-0(X), Greenwillow Bks.) HarperCollins Pubs.

Ipcar, Dahlov. Brown Cow Farm: A Counting Book. 2003. (ENG., Illus.). 42p. (J). (gr. -1-17). pap. 10.95 (978-0-89272-602-8(4)) Down East Bks.

Jacobs, Lana. Paint Book. Farley, Rick, illus. 2006. (Charlotte's Web Ser.). 32p. (J). 4.99 (978-0-06-088277-8(8)) HarperCollins Pubs.

Jenkins-Greaves, Shenita. Raptown U. S. A. Rappers. 2013. 24p. pap. 14.95 (978-1-4669-7717-4(5)) Trafford Publishing.

Jeong, SoYun. Lulu the Shy Piglet. Orsolini, Laura, illus. rev. ed. 2014. (MySELF Bookshelf Ser.). (ENG.). 32p. (J). (gr. k-2). pap. 11.94 (978-1-60357-654-3(1)); lib. bdg. 25.27 (978-1-59953-645-3(5)) Norwood Hse. Pr.

Johnson, D. B., illus. Four Legs Bad, Two Legs Good! 2007. (J). (978-1-4287-6423-1(2)) Houghton Mifflin Harcourt Publishing Co.

Jordan, Apple. I Can Be a Farm Vet (Barbie) Riley, Kellee, illus. 2016. (Step into Reading Ser.). (ENG.). 24p. (J). (gr. -1-1). 4.99 (978-1-101-93245-2(7), Random Hse. Bks. for Young Readers) Random Hse. Children's Bks.

Jordan, Karen. On the Farm. Steuerwald, Joy, illus. 2015. (Highlights(tm) Find It! Padded Board Bks.). (ENG.). 14p. (J). (— 1). bds. 7.99 (978-1-62979-413-6(9), Highlights) Boyds Mills Pr.

Jordan, Mary Ellen & Weldon, Andrew. Lazy Daisy, Cranky Frankie: Bedtime on the Farm. Weldon, Andrew, illus. 2013. (ENG., Illus.). 24p. (J). (gr. -1-3). 15.99 (978-0-8075-4400-6(0)) Whitman, Albert & Co.

Katz, Karen. Baby at the Farm. Katz, Karen, illus. 2009. (ENG., Illus.). 12p. (J). (gr. -1 — 1). bds. 7.99 (978-1-4169-8568-6(9), Little Simon) Little Simon.

Kelly, Mij. Preschool Time. McQuillan, Mary, illus. 2014. (ENG.). 32p. (J). (gr. -1 — 1). 14.99 (978-0-7641-6655-6(7)) Barron's Educational Series, Inc.

Kennedy, Kim & Kennedy, Doug. Hee-Haw-Dini & the Great Zambini. 2009. (ENG., Illus.). 32p. (J). (gr. k-2). 15.95 (978-0-8109-7025-0(2), Abrams Bks. for Young Readers) Abrams, Inc.

Klein, Adria F. Max Goes to the Farm, 1 vol. Gallagher-Cole, Mernie, illus. 2007. (Read-It! Readers: the Life of Max Ser.). (ENG.). 24p. (gr. -1-2). lib. bdg. 21.32 (978-1-4048-3678-5(0), Easy Readers) Picture Window Bks.

Klise, Kate. Shall I Knit You a Hat? A Christmas Yarn. Klise, M. Sarah, illus. 2007. (ENG.). 32p. (J). (gr. -1-2). per. 8.99 (978-0-312-37139-5(X), 9780312371395) Square Fish.

Konecny, Linda. Dave's First Christmas. 2011. 26p. pap. 9.99 (978-1-61379-817-1(2)) Salem Author Services.

Krause, John & Chua, Maria. Poco Loco, 0 vols. 2013. (ENG.). 32p. (J). (gr. -1-3). 15.99 (978-1-4778-1649-3(6), 9781477816493, Amazon Children's Publishing) Amazon Publishing.

Kreloff, Elliot, illus. My Little Baby. 2010. 12p. (J). bds. (978-1-60906-008-4(3)) Begin Smart LLC.

Krilanovich, Nadia. Chicken, Chicken, Duck! Krilanovich, Nadia, illus. (ENG., Illus.). (J). (gr. -1-2). 2016. 26p. bds. 7.99 (978-0-553-53806-9(3)) 2011. 32p. 14.99 (978-1-58246-385-8(9)) Random Hse. Children's Bks. (Tricycle Pr.).

Krosoczka, Jarrett J. Punk Farm. (ENG.). 40p. (J). (gr. -1-2). 2010. pap. 7.99 (978-0-440-41793-4(7), Dragonfly Bks.) 2005. (Illus.). 15.95 (978-0-375-82429-6(4), Knopf Bks. for Young Readers) Random Hse. Children's Bks.

—Punk Farm on Tour. 2007. (ENG., Illus.). 40p. (J). (gr. -1-2). 15.99 (978-0-375-83343-4(9), Knopf Bks. for Young Readers) Random Hse. Children's Bks.

Krulik, Nancy. Be Careful What You Sniff For, No. 1. Braun, Sebastien, illus. 2013. (Magic Bone Ser.: 1). (ENG.). 128p. (J). (gr. 1-3). pap. 5.99 (978-0-448-46399-5(7), Grosset & Dunlap) Penguin Young Readers Group.

—Be Careful What You Sniff For. 2013. (Magic Bone Ser.: 1). lib. bdg. 16.00 (978-0-606-31680-4(9), Turtleback) Turtleback Bks.

Kutner, Merrily. Down on the Farm. Hillenbrand, Will, illus. 2016. (ENG.). 24p. (J). (gr. -1 — 1). bds. 7.99 (978-0-8234-2177-0(5)) Holiday Hse., Inc.

Laden, Nina. Peek-A Moo! 2017. (ENG., Illus.). 22p. (J). (gr. -1 — 1). bds. 6.99 **(978-1-4521-5474-9(0))** Chronicle Bks. LLC.

Laínez, René Colato. Señor Pancho Had a Rancho. Smith, Elwood, illus. 2014. (ENG & SPA.). 32p. (J). (gr. -1-1). 6.99 (978-0-8234-3173-1(8)) Holiday Hse., Inc.

—Señor Pancho Had a Rancho. Smith, Elwood H., illus. 2013. (ENG.). 32p. (J). (gr. -1-1). 16.95 (978-0-8234-2632-4(7)) Holiday Hse., Inc.

Lake Press Ltd. Farm Friends. 2016. (Little Grabbers Ser.). (ENG., Illus.). 6p. (J). (gr. -1 — 1). bds. 5.99 (978-0-7641-6834-5(7)) Barron's Educational Series, Inc.

Lambert, Megan Dowd. A Crow of His Own. Costello, David & Costello, David Hyde, illus. 2015. (ENG.). 32p. (J). (gr. -1-1). lib. bdg. 16.95 (978-1-58089-447-0(X)) Charlesbridge Publishing, Inc.

—A Crow of His Own. Costello, David, illus. 2014. (J). pap. (978-1-58089-448-7(8)) Charlesbridge Publishing, Inc.

Law, Jessica. A Farmer's Life for Me. McDonald, Jill, illus. 2013. (SPA.). 24p. (J). pap. 6.99 (978-1-78285-025-0(2)) Barefoot Bks., Inc.

Lawrence, John. This Little Chick. Lawrence, John, illus. 2013. (ENG., Illus.). 32p. (J). (gr. -1-k). 4.99 (978-0-7636-6350-6(6)) Candlewick Pr.

Lewis, Rob. What's up, Jac. 2005. (ENG., Illus.). 32p. pap. 12.95 (978-1-84323-428-9(9)) Beekman Bks., Inc.

Lindemer, C. R. Beauly, the Donkey-Mooing Beltie. Bouthyette, Valerie, illus. 2008. 32p. (J). pap. (978-0-9821058-2-5(7)) Shapato Publishing, LLC.

Litton, Jonathan. I Like to Squeak! How Do You Speak? Galloway, Fhiona, illus. 2015. (My Little World Ser.). (ENG.). 10p. (J). bds. 12.99 (978-1-68010-505-6(1)) Tiger Tales.

Long, Ethan. Good Night! 2015. (Animal Sounds Ser.). (ENG., Illus.). 20p. (J). (gr. -1 — 1). bds. 7.95 (978-1-4197-1366-8(3)) Abrams, Inc.

—Pig Has a Plan. Long, Ethan, illus. 2012. (I Like to Read(r) Ser.). (ENG., Illus.). 24p. (J). (gr. -1-3). 14.95 (978-0-8234-2428-3(6)) Holiday Hse., Inc.

Long, Ethan & McPike, Elizabeth. In, over & on the Farm. Long, Ethan, illus. 2015. (ENG., Illus.). 40p. (J). (gr. -1-k). bds. 15.99 (978-0-399-16907-6(5), G.P. Putnam's Sons Books for Young Readers) Penguin Young Readers Group.

Long, Loren. Otis & the Kittens. Long, Loren, illus. 2016. (Otis Ser.). (ENG., Illus.). 40p. (J). (gr. -1-3). 17.99 (978-0-399-16398-2(0), Philomel Bks.) Penguin Young Readers Group.

—Otis & the Scarecrow. Long, Loren, illus. 2014. (Otis Ser.). (ENG., Illus.). 40p. (J). (gr. k-3). 17.99 (978-0-399-16396-8(4), Philomel Bks.) Penguin Publishing Group.

—Otis & the Tornado. Long, Loren, illus. 2011. (Otis Ser.: 2). (ENG., Illus.). 40p. (J). (gr. -1-2). 17.99 (978-0-399-25477-2(3), Philomel Bks.) Penguin Young Readers Group.

Louise, Cristina & McIlroy, Michelle. Where Is Paco Now? Louise, Cristina & McIlroy, Michelle, illus. 2012. (SPA & ENG., Illus.). (J). (978-1-934370-26-1(6), Campanita Bks.) Editorial Campana.

Ludmila's Way - Teaching Guide. 2003. (J). 17.95 (978-1-55942-192-8(4)) Witcher Productions.

Ludmila's Way: Evaluation Guide. 2006. (J). (978-1-55942-415-8(X)) Witcher Productions.

Macauley, Myron Christian. Modern Man in Search of Soul. 2010. pap. 60.00 (978-0-578-05300-4(4)) Macauley, Myron Christian.

MacDonald, Alan. The Pig in a Wig. Hess, Paul, illus. 2003. 32p. (J). (gr. k-3). pap. 6.95 (978-1-56145-299-6(8), Q32523) Peachtree Pubs.

Mathews, Leslie. The Sheep Go on Strike. Dumont, Jean-françois, illus. 2014. (ENG.). 34p. (J). 16.00 (978-0-8028-5470-4(2), Eerdmans Bks For Young Readers) Eerdmans, William B. Publishing Co.

McDonald, Megan. Hen Hears Gossip. Kim, Joung Un, illus. 2008. 32p. (J). (gr. -1-k). lib. bdg. 17.89 (978-0-06-113877-5(0)); (ENG.). 17.99 (978-0-06-113876-8(2)) HarperCollins Pubs. (Greenwillow Bks.).

McDonnell, Flora & Jones, Gordon. Rwy'n Hoffi Anifeiliaid. 2005. (WEL., Illus.). 32p. pap. 11.99 (978-1-84323-316-9(9)) Gomer Pr. GBR. Dist: Gomer Pr.

McGinley, Phyllis, et al. Little Golden Book Farm Favorites. Rojankovsky, Feodor & Gergely, Tibor, illus. 2012. (Little Golden Book Favorites Ser.). (ENG.). 80p. (J). (gr. k-k). 7.99 (978-0-307-93020-0(3), Golden Bks.) Random Hse. Children's Bks.

Meister, Cari. Tiny on the Farm. Davis, Rich, illus. 2008. (Tiny Ser.). (ENG.). 32p. (J). (gr. -1-1). 16.99 (978-0-670-06246-1(4), Viking Books for Young Readers) Penguin Young Readers Group.

Miller, Janet. Fox Tail Farms. 2011. 172p. pap. 19.95 (978-1-257-85817-0(3)) Lulu Pr., Inc.

Minne, Brigitte. The Best Bottom. Pottie, Marjolein, illus. 2004. 32p. (J). 15.95 (978-0-689-03595-1(0), Milk & Cookies) ibooks, Inc.

Minor, Wendell. My Farm Friends. Minor, Wendell, illus. (ENG., Illus.). (J). (gr. -1-k). 2013. 26p. bds. 7.99 (978-0-399-25799-5(3), Nancy Paulsen Books) 2011. 28p. 17.99 (978-0-399-24477-3(8), G.P. Putnam's Sons Books for Young Readers) Penguin Young Readers Group.

Moncure, Jane Belk. Ice Cream Cows & Mitten Sheep: A Book about Farm Animals. Billin-Frye, Paige, illus. 2013. (Magic Castle Readers Ser.). (ENG.). 32p. (J). (gr. -1-2). 25.64 (978-1-62323-583-3(9), 206319) Child's World, Inc., The.

Moore, Carol Hair. Marvin the Magnificent Nubian Goat. Harrell, Michael, illus. 2009. (I Wish You Ice Cream & Cake Ser.). 28p. (J). lib. bdg. 15.95 (978-1-935083-03-0(1)) CyPress Pubns.

Mortensen, Lori. Chicken Lily. Crittenden, Nina Victor, illus. 2016. (ENG.). 40p. (J). 16.99 (978-1-62779-120-5(5), 9781627791205, Holt, Henry & Co. Bks. For Young Readers) Holt, Henry & Co.

Murphy, Mary. How Kind! Murphy, Mary, illus. 2004. (ENG., Illus.). 24p. (J). (gr. k-k). bds. 6.99 (978-0-7636-2307-4(5)) Candlewick Pr.

Nash, Margaret. Hetty's New Hat. Impey, Martin, illus. 2005. (Reading Corner Ser.). 24p. (J). (gr. k-3). lib. bdg. 22.80 (978-1-59771-007-7(5)) Sea-To-Sea Pubns.

Nees, Diane L. A Bunny Tail. Lueer, Carmen A., illus. 2012. 44p. pap. 24.95 (978-1-4626-9191-3(9)) America Star Bks.

Neimark, Jill & Weiner, Marcella Bakur. Toodles & Teeny: A Story about Friendship. 2012. (J). pap. 9.95 (978-1-4338-1199-9(5)); (Illus.). 14.95 (978-1-4338-1198-2(7)) American Psychological Assn. (Magination Pr.).

Newell, Stephanie Jordy. Nite, Nite Farm. 2009. 24p. pap. 12.98 (978-1-4490-0170-4(X)) AuthorHouse.

Newman, Robin. The Case of the Poached Egg. Zemke, Deborah, illus. 2017. (Wilcox & Griswold Mystery Ser.). (ENG.). 48p. (J). (gr. -1-3). 15.95 (978-1-939547-30-9(X)) Creston Bks.

Newman, Tracy. Sukkot Is Coming! Garófoli, Viviana, illus. 2017. (ENG.). 12p. (gr. -1 — 1). bds. 5.99 (978-1-5124-0828-7(X), Kar-Ben Publishing) Lerner Publishing Group.

Nobisso, Josephine. In English, of Course. Ziborova, Dasha, illus. 2003.Tr. of En Ingles, Por Supuesto. 32p. (J). (gr. -1). (SPA & ENG.). 16.95 (978-0-940112-07-0(8)); (ENG.). pap. 8.95 (978-0-940112-08-7(6)) Gingerbread Hse.

Nosy Crow Staff. Old MacDonald Had a Farm: Sing along with Me! Huang, Yu-Hsuan, illus. 2016. (Sing along with Me! Ser.). (ENG.). (J). (-k). bds. 8.99 (978-0-7636-8652-9(2), Nosy Crow) Candlewick Pr.

Olesen, Demetria Vassiliou. Lambyro. Forcada, Adiela & Giron, Elizabeth, illus. 2011. (ENG.). 32p. (J). 19.00 (978-0-615-47664-3(3)) Elissian Publishing Co.

Oswald, Pete & Thompson, Justin K. Mingo the Flamingo. Oswald, Pete & Thompson, Justin K., illus. 2017. (Illus.). 40p. (J). (gr. -1-3). 17.99 (978-0-06-239198-8(4)) HarperCollins Pubs.

Palatini, Margie. Boo-Hoo Moo. Graves, Keith, illus. 2009. 32p. (J). (gr. -1-3). lib. bdg. 18.89 (978-0-06-114376-2(6)) HarperCollins Pubs.

—Earthquack! Moser, Barry, illus. 2005. (ENG.). 32p. (J). (gr. -1-3). 7.99 (978-1-4169-0260-7(0), Simon & Schuster Bks. For Young Readers) Simon & Schuster Bks. For Young Readers.

—Hogg, Hogg, & Hog. Palatini, Margie, illus. 2011. (ENG., Illus.). 32p. (J). (gr. -1-3). 15.99 (978-1-4424-0322-2(5), Simon & Schuster Bks. For Young Readers) Simon & Schuster Bks. For Young Readers.

—Oink? Cole, Henry, illus. 2006. (ENG.). 40p. (J). (gr. -1-3). 17.99 (978-0-689-86258-8(X), Simon & Schuster Bks. For Young Readers) Simon & Schuster Bks. For Young Readers.

—Piggie Pie!, 1 vol. Fine, Howard, illus. 2008. (Read along Book & CD Ser.). (ENG.). 32p. (J). (gr. -1-3). audio compact disk 10.99 (978-0-547-18178-3(7)) Houghton Mifflin Harcourt Publishing Co.

Parker, Emma. At the Farm. 2010. (Illus.). pap. (978-1-877547-94-2(8)) First Edition Ltd.

Perrin, Martine. Cock-a-Doodle Who? 2012. (ENG., Illus.). 40p. (J). (gr. -1-3). 12.99 (978-0-8075-1107-7(2)) Whitman, Albert & Co.

Peterson, Mary & Rofé, Jennifer. Piggies in the Pumpkin Patch. Peterson, Mary, illus. 2010. (ENG., Illus.). 28p. (J). (gr. -1-2). 16.95 (978-1-57091-460-7(5)); pap. 7.95 (978-1-57091-461-4(3)) Charlesbridge Publishing, Inc.

Pierre Brignaud, Pierre, illus. Baby Caillou: My Farm Friends: A Finger Fun Book. 2015. (Baby Caillou Ser.). (ENG.). 16p. (J). (— 1). bds. 6.99 (978-2-89718-177-2(X)) Caillouet, Gerry.

Pingry, Patricia A. Sounds. Rose, Drew, illus. 2005. (J). (978-0-8249-6596-9(5), Ideal Pubns.) Worthy Publishing.

Pixton, Amy, creator. Farm Charm. 2006. (J). (978-0-9779631-0-2(1)) TyBook.

Pluta, K. There's a Yak in my Bed. Stallop, Christy, illus. 2007. (ENG.). 32p. (J). (gr. -1 — 1). 16.95 (978-0-9769417-4-3(0)) Blooming Tree Pr.

Poitier, Anton. Flippy Floppy Farm Animals. Touliatou, Sophia, illus. 2014. 10p. (J). 12.99 (978-1-61067-310-5(7)) Kane Miller.

Polacco, Patricia. Mommies Say Shhh! Polacco, Patricia, illus. (ENG., Illus.). (J). (gr. -1 — 1). 2007. 32p. bds. 6.99 (978-0-399-24720-0(3)) 2005. 40p. 16.99 (978-0-399-24341-7(0)) Penguin Young Readers Group. (Philomel Bks.).

Priddy, Roger. Barnyard Fun! 2015. (Little Friends Ser.). (ENG., Illus.). 12p. (J). (gr. -1 — 1). bds. 8.99 (978-0-312-51841-7(2), 9780312518417, Priddy Bks.) St. Martin's Pr.

—Farm. (Sticker Friends Ser.). (ENG., (J). 2017. Illus.). 24p. pap. 4.99 (978-0-312-52155-4(3), 9780312521554) 2005. 10p. bds. 0.01 (978-0-312-49643-2(5)) St. Martin's Pr. (Priddy Bks.).

—Night Night Farm. 2017. (ENG., Illus.). 20p. (J). bds. 9.99 (978-0-312-52163-9(4), 9780312521639, Priddy Bks.) St. Martin's Pr.

Prochovnic, Dawn Babb. Famous Fenton Has a Farm: Sign Language for Farm Animals, 1 vol. Bauer, Stephanie, illus. 2009. (Story Time with Signs & Rhymes Ser.). (ENG.). 32p. (gr. -1-3). 28.50 (978-1-60270-669-9(7), Looking Glass Library) ABDO Publishing Co.

Pryor, Bonnie. Greenbrook Farm. 2013. (ENG.). 36p. (J). (gr. -1-3). 14.99 (978-1-4424-8873-1(5), Atheneum Bks. for Young Readers) Simon & Schuster Children's Publishing.

Publications International Ltd. Staff, ed. Me Reader Jr(tm) Old MacDonald's Farm: Electronic Reader & 8-Book Library. 2015. (J). 22.98 (978-1-4508-9401-2(1), 1450894011) Publications International, Ltd.

Publishing, Arcturus. Farm. 2016. (ENG.). 10p. (J). 9.95 (978-1-78599-101-1(9), 9781785991011) Arcturus Publishing GBR. Dist: Bookmasters Distribution.

Random House. Open the Barn Door... Santoro, Christopher, illus. 2016. (ENG.). 22p. (J). (— 1). bds. 6.99 (978-0-399-54948-9(X), Random Hse. Bks. for Young Readers) Random Hse. Children's Bks.

Raschka, Chris. Farmy Farm. Raschka, Chris, illus. 2011. (ENG., Illus.). 8p. (J). (gr. -1 — 1). bds. 8.99 (978-0-545-21981-5(7), Orchard Bks.) Scholastic, Inc.

Reader's Digest Staff. Tractor Trouble Drive Through Storybook. Pitt, Sarah, illus. 2011. (Drive-Through Storybooks Ser.). (ENG.). 10p. (J). (gr. -1-1). bds. 12.99 (978-0-7944-2169-4(5)) Reader's Digest Assn., Inc., The.

Reasoner, Charles. Farm Animals. Doherty, Paula, illus. 2009. (Little Big Flap Bks.). 10p. (J). (gr. -1-k). 9.99 (978-1-934650-23-3(4)) Just For Kids Pr., LLC.

Reece, Eva. Brownie Calf & the Barnyard Babies. Davis, Shelley La, illus. 2012. 24p. pap. 12.99 (978-0-9836641-8-5(8)) Kids At Heart Publishing, LLC.

Reed, Jennifer. Time for a Trim. Mones, Marc, illus. 2012. (ENG.). 24p. (gr. 1-2). pap. 8.95 (978-1-61810-319-2(9)) Rourke Educational Media.

Regan, Dian. Barnyard Slam. Meisel, Paul, illus. 2009. (ENG.). 32p. (J). (gr. -1-3). 16.95 (978-0-8234-1907-4(X)) Holiday Hse., Inc.

Richardson, Lans. A Calf Named Polly. Arndt, Charles T., illus. 2003. 38p. per. 11.95 (978-1-59405-022-0(8)) New Age World Publishing.

Rinaldo, Luana. Sleepy Farm. 2014. (ENG., Illus.). 10p. (J). (— 1). 11.99 (978-1-4472-6765-2(6)) Pan Macmillan GBR. Dist: Independent Pubs. Group.

Robertson, James & Fitt, Matthew. Katie's Ferm: A Hide-and-Seek Book for Wee Folk. Sutherland, Karen, illus. 2007. (ENG.). 18p. (J). (-k). bds. 10.99 (978-1-84502-149-8(5)) Black and White Publishing Ltd. GBR. Dist: Independent Pubs. Group.

Roddie, Shen. You're Too Small! Lavis, Steve, illus. 2004. 32p. (J). 6.95 (978-1-58925-385-8(X)); tchr. ed. 15.95 (978-1-58925-038-3(9)) Tiger Tales.

Rosen, Michael. Farmyard Read & Play Set, 3 vols. Langley, Jonathan, illus. 2008. (ENG.). 96p. (J). (gr. -1-k). bds. 19.95 (978-0-00-725969-4(7)) HarperCollins Pubs. Ltd. GBR. Dist: Independent Pubs. Group.

Rostoker-Gruber, Karen & Isaacs, Ronald H. Farmer Kobi's Hanukkah Match. Decker, C. B., illus. 2015. (J). (978-1-68115-501-2(X)); pap. (978-0-87441-924-5(7)) Behrman Hse., Inc.

Rubino, Tony. Animal Farm. 2013. 24p. pap. 24.95 (978-1-62709-615-7(9)) America Star Bks.

Ruffenach, Jessie, ed. Baby Learns about Animals. Thomas, Peter, tr. from NAV. Blacksheep, Beverly, illus. 2004. (ENG & NAV.). 16p. (J). (gr. -1-12). 7.95 (978-1-893354-49-4(0)) Salina Bookshelf Inc.

Russell, Natalie. Donkey's Busy Day. Russell, Natalie, illus. 2009. (ENG., Illus.). 32p. (J). (gr. k-k). pap. 11.95 (978-0-7475-9547-2(X)) Bloomsbury Publishing Plc GBR. Dist: Independent Pubs. Group.

Rylant, Cynthia. Henry & Mudge & the Wild Goose Chase. Bracken, Carolyn, illus. 2004. (Henry & Mudge Ser.). 40p. (gr. k-2). 14.00 (978-0-7569-3366-1(8)) Perfection Learning Corp.

—Henry & Mudge & the Wild Goose Chase. Bracken, Carolyn, illus. 2004. (Henry & Mudge Ready-To-Read Ser.: 26). 40p. (gr. k-2). lib. bdg. 13.55 (978-1-4176-4340-0(4), Turtleback) Turtleback Bks.

Rylant, Cynthia & Bracken, Carolyn. Henry & Mudge & the Wild Goose Chase. 2004. (Henry & Mudge Ser.: 23). (ENG., Illus.). 40p. (J). (gr. k-2). pap. 3.99 (978-0-689-83450-9(0), Simon Spotlight) Simon Spotlight.

—Henry & Mudge & the Wild Goose Chase. Bracken, Carolyn, illus. 2003. (Henry & Mudge Ser.: 23). (ENG., Illus.). 40p. (J). (gr. k-2). 16.99 (978-0-689-81172-2(1), Simon Spotlight) Simon Spotlight.

Sauer, Tammi. Chicken Dance. Santat, Dan, illus. (ENG.). 40p. (J). (gr. -1-2). 2015. pap. 6.95 (978-1-4549-1477-8(7)) 2009. 14.95 (978-1-4027-5366-4(7)) Sterling Publishing Co., Inc.

—Mr. Duck Means Business. Mack, Jeff, illus. 2011. (ENG.). 32p. (J). (gr. -1-3). 15.99 (978-1-4169-8522-8(0), Simon & Schuster/Paula Wiseman Bks.) Simon & Schuster/Paula Wiseman Bks.

Schaal, Patty. Nighttide on a Vineyard Farm. Datz, Margot, illus. 2010. (J). (978-0-9827146-1-4(0)) Vineyard Stories.

School Zone Staff, ed. Talking Telephone. 2007. (J). 7.99 (978-1-58947-873-2(8)) School Zone Publishing Co.

Schories, Pat, illus. Biscuit Visits the Farm. 2012. (J). (978-1-4351-4383-8(3), HarperFestival) HarperCollins Pubs.

Scollon, William & Disney Book Group Staff. Mickey & Donald Have a Farm. Disney Storybook Art Team, illus. 2012. (ENG.). 32p. (J). (gr. -1-k). pap. 5.99 (978-1-4231-4946-0(7)) Disney Pr.

Seeger, Laura Vaccaro. Bully. Seeger, Laura Vaccaro, illus. 2013. (ENG., Illus.). 40p. (J). (gr. -1-3). 17.99 (978-1-59643-630-5(1), 9781596436305) Roaring Brook Pr.

Shannon, David. Duck on a Tractor. 2016. (ENG.). 40p. (J). (gr. -1-3). 16.99 (978-0-545-61941-7(6), Blue Sky Pr., The) Scholastic, Inc.

Shannon, George. Wise Acres. Zemke, Deborah, illus. 2004. (ENG.). 40p. (J). (gr. -1-7). 15.95 (978-1-59354-041-8(8), Handprint Bks.) Chronicle Bks. LLC.

Shaw, Stephanie. Lullaby Farm. Harry, Rebecca, illus. 2017. (ENG.). 22p. (J). (gr. -1-k). bds. 8.99 **(978-1-68010-512-4(4))** Tiger Tales.

Sickler, Jonas & Pixton, Kaaren, illus. Old Macdonald Had a Farm: Hey Baby! Look at These Animals on the Farm — in Bolivia! 2011. (Indestructibles Ser.). (ENG.). 12p. (J). (gr. k — 1). pap. 5.95 (978-0-7611-5922-3(3), 15922) Workman Publishing Co., Inc.

Silvano, Wendi. Turkey Trouble, 0 vols. 2009. (ENG., Illus.). 32p. (J). (gr. -1-2). 15.99 (978-0-7614-5529-5(9), 9780761455295, Two Lions) Amazon Publishing.

Siminovich, Lorena, illus. You Are My Baby - Farm. 2013. (ENG.). 10p. (J). (gr. -1 — 1). bds. 8.99 (978-1-4521-0643-4(6)) Chronicle Bks. LLC.

Simmons, Lynn Sheffield. Sugar Lump, the Orphan Calf, 1 vol. 2003. (ENG., Illus.). 50p. (J). (gr. k-5). 12.95 (978-1-58980-216-2(0)) Pelican Publishing Co., Inc.

Sio, Betsy Menson. Little Critters. Richter, Hank, illus. 2003. (Books for Young Learners). (ENG.). 16p. (J). 5.75 net. (978-1-57274-532-2(0), 2458, Bks. for Young Learners) Owen, Richard C. Pubs., Inc.

Smethurst, Julia. Finclucky from Kentucky: A Picture Book. 2013. (J). (978-1-938905-36-0(9)) Acclaim Pr., Inc.

Smith, Ian & Julian, Sean. Rooster's Alarm. Smith, Ian, illus. 2009. (Tadpoles Ser.). (ENG., Illus.). 24p. (J). (gr. -1-2). pap. (978-0-7787-3905-0(8)); (gr. k-2). lib. bdg. (978-0-7787-3874-9(4)) Crabtree Publishing Co.

Sommer, Carl. Proud Rooster & Little Hen. Budwine, Greg, illus. 2014. (J). pap. (978-1-57537-964-7(3)) Advance Publishing, Inc.

—Proud Rooster & Little Hen. 2003. (Another Sommer-Time Story Ser.). (Illus.). 48p. (J). (gr. 1-4). 16.95 incl. audio (978-1-57537-559-5(1)) Advance Publishing, Inc.

—Proud Rooster & Little Hen. Budwine, Greg, illus. 2003. (Another Sommer-Time Story Ser.). (ENG.). 48p. (J). (gr. 1-4). 16.95 incl. audio compact disk (978-1-57537-510-6(9)) Advance Publishing, Inc.

—Proud Rooster & Little Hen(Gallito Orgulloso y Gallinita) Budwine, Greg, illus. 2009. (Another Sommer-Time Story Bilingual Ser.). (SPA & ENG.). 48p. (J). 16.95 (978-1-57537-164-1(2)) Advance Publishing, Inc.

Spinelli, Eileen. Silly Tilly, 0 vols. Slonim, David, illus. 2012. (ENG.). 32p. (J). (gr. -1-2). pap. 9.99 (978-0-7614-5990-3(1), 9780761459903, Amazon Children's Publishing) Amazon Publishing.

Star, Ian. Breakfast at the Farm. 2006. (Neighborhood Readers Ser.). (ENG.). 12p. (gr. -1-3). pap. 5.90 (978-1-4042-6473-1(6), Rosen Classroom) Rosen Publishing Group, Inc., The.

Stevens, Carla & Stevens, Chapman. Who's Knocking at the Door?, 1 vol. Chapman, Lee, illus. 2004. (ENG.). 32p. (J). 16.95 (978-0-7614-5168-6(4)) Marshall Cavendish Corp.

Stevens, Janet & Crummel, Susan Stevens. Find a Cow Now! Stevens, Janet, illus. 2012. (ENG., Illus.). 32p. (J). (gr. -1-3). 16.95 (978-0-8234-2218-0(6)) Holiday Hse., Inc.

Stewart, Wilson N. Cock-a-Doodle-Who? 2007. (ENG., Illus.). 6p. (J). 15.99 (978-0-7868-0826-7(8)) Hyperion Bks. for Children.

Stock, Catherine. A Porc in New York. 2007. (ENG., Illus.). 32p. (J). (gr. -1-3). 16.95 (978-0-8234-1994-4(0)) Holiday Hse., Inc.

Swift, Ginger. Little Red Barn. Pavon, David, illus. 2016. (ENG.). 10p. (J). bds. 0.00 (978-1-68052-055-2(5)) Cottage Door Pr.

Sykes, Julie. That Pesky Dragon. Williamson, Melanie, illus. 2007. 32p. (J). (gr. -1-3). 15.95 (978-1-58925-069-7(9)) Tiger Tales.

Tafuri, Nancy. All Kinds of Kisses. 2012. (ENG., Illus.). 32p. (J). (gr. -1-1). 16.99 (978-0-316-12235-1(1)) Little Brown & Co.

—Blue Goose. Tafuri, Nancy, illus. 2010. (Classic Board Bks.). (ENG., Illus.). 34p. (J). (gr. -1 — 1). bds. 7.99 (978-1-4169-2835-5(9), Little Simon) Little Simon.

Talley, Linda. Ludmila's Way. Chase, Andra, illus. 2003. (J). 17.95 (978-1-55942-190-4(8)) Witcher Productions.

Teal, Val. The Little Woman Wanted Noise. Lawson, Robert, illus. 2013. (ENG.). 48p. (J). (gr. -1-2). 14.95 (978-1-59017-711-2(8), NYR Children's Collection) New York Review of Bks., Inc., The.

Tekavec, Heather. Storm Is Coming! Spengler, Margaret, illus. 2004. (ENG.). 32p. (J). (gr. -1-3). reprint ed. pap. 6.99 (978-0-14-240070-8(X), Puffin Books) Penguin Young Readers Group.

Temporin, Elena, illus. The Gingerbread Man. 2007. (Picture Book Classics Ser.). 24p. (J). 9.99 (978-0-7945-1786-1(2), Usborne) EDC Publishing.

Terada, Junzo. Animal Friends: Barnyard Jamboree! 2017. (ENG., Illus.). 10p. (J). bds. 9.99 (978-1-4521-5189-2(X)) Chronicle Bks. LLC.

Terwilliger, Kelly. Barnyard Purim. Newman, Barbara Johansen, illus. 2012. (Purim Ser.). (ENG.). 32p. (J). (gr. k-3). pap. 7.95 (978-0-7613-4514-5(0)); lib. bdg. 17.95 (978-0-7613-4513-8(2)) Lerner Publishing Group. (Kar-Ben Publishing).

Theule, Larissa. Fat & Bones. Doyle, Adam S., illus. 2014. (ENG.). 112p. (J). (gr. 4-12). lib. bdg. 16.95 (978-1-4677-0825-8(9), Carolrhoda Bks.) Lerner Publishing Group.

Thomas, Jan. The Doghouse. (ENG., Illus.). (J). 2015. 36p. (— 1). bds. 7.99 (978-0-544-43063-1(8), HMH Books For Young Readers) 2008. 40p. (gr. -1-k). 12.95 (978-0-15-206533-1(4)) Houghton Mifflin Harcourt Publishing Co.

—Is That Wise, Pig? Thomas, Jan, illus. 2016. (ENG., Illus.). 40p. (J). (gr. -1-3). 15.99 (978-1-4169-8582-2(4), Beach Lane Bks.) Beach Lane Bks.

Thompson, Lauren. Wee Little Chick. Butler, John, illus. 2008. (Wee Little Ser.). (ENG.). 32p. (J). (gr. -1-1). 15.99 (978-1-4169-3468-4(5), Simon & Schuster Bks. For Young Readers) Simon & Schuster Bks. For Young Readers.

Thomson, Pat. It's So Unfair! Allen, Jonathan, illus. 2007. (ENG.). 32p. (J). pap. 10.99 (978-1-84270-594-0(6)) Andersen Pr. GBR. Dist: Independent Pubs. Group.

Ticktock Media, Ltd. Staff. Farm. 2009. (Animal Fun Touch & Feel Ser.). (ENG.). 10p. (J). (gr. -1-k). bds. 4.95 (978-1-84696-827-3(5), TickTock Books) Octopus Publishing Group GBR. Dist: Independent Pubs. Group.

Tiger Tales Staff, creator. Lift & See Farm. 2013. (My First Matching Bks.). (ENG., Illus.). 10p. (gr. -1). bds. 7.99 (978-1-58925-612-5(3)) Tiger Tales.

—5 Minute Farm Tales. 2013. (ENG., Illus.). 292p. (J). (gr. -1-1). 14.95 (978-1-58925-505-0(4)) Tiger Tales.

Tougas, Chris. Mechanimals, 1 vol. 2012. (ENG.). 32p. (J). (gr. -1-3). 9.95 (978-1-4598-0273-5(X)) Orca Bk. Pubs. USA.

Trussell-Cullen, Alan. Shoo! Shoo! Shoo! Woodford-Robinson, Rieko, illus. 2010. (ENG.). 16p. (gr. k-1). pap. 7.95 (978-1-61181-035-6(3), Kaeden Bks.) Kaeden Corp.

—Shoo! Shoo! Shoo! (6 Packs) Woodford-Robinson, Rieko, illus. 2010. (ENG.). 16p. (gr. k-1). pap. (978-1-61181-036-3(1), Kaeden Bks.) Kaeden Corp.

Vamos, Samantha R. The Cazuela That the Farm Maiden Stirred. López, Rafael, illus. (ENG & SPA.). 32p. (J). (gr. k-3). 2013. pap. 8.95 (978-1-58089-243-8(4)) 2011. 17.95 (978-1-58089-242-1(6)) Charlesbridge Publishing, Inc.

Van Fleet, Matthew. Moo. Stanton, Brian, photos by. 2011. (ENG., Illus.). 18p. (J). (gr. -1-1). 18.99 (978-1-4424-3503-2(8), Simon & Schuster/Paula Wiseman Bks.) Simon & Schuster/Paula Wiseman Bks.

—Van Fleet Animal Trio: Moo; Cat; Dog. Stanton, Brian, photos by. 2013. (ENG., Illus.). 58p. (J). (gr. -1-2). 51.99 (978-1-4424-8450-4(0), Simon & Schuster/Paula Wiseman Bks.) Simon & Schuster/Paula Wiseman Bks.

Van Leeuwen, Jean. Chicken Soup. Gavril, David, illus. 2009. (ENG.). 40p. (J). (gr. k-2). 16.95 (978-0-8109-8326-7(5), Abrams Bks. for Young Readers) Abrams, Inc.

Varacchi, Barbara. Desiree's Adventures with Her Friends. 2009. 36p. pap. 16.99 (978-1-4389-1603-3(5)) AuthorHouse.

Voake, Steve. Daisy Dawson on the Farm. Meserve, Jessica, illus. 2013. (Daisy Dawson Ser.). (ENG.). 96p. (J). (gr. 1-4). pap. 5.99 (978-0-7636-6340-7(9)) Candlewick Pr.

Walden, Libby. Noisy Touch & Feel: Cow Says Moo. Enright, Amanda, illus. 2016. (Noisy Touch & Feel Ser.). (ENG.). 12p. (J). bds. 14.99 (978-1-62686-575-4(2), Silver Dolphin Bks.) Readerlink Distribution Services, LLC.

Wallace, Sandra Neil. Little Joe. Elliott, Mark, illus. 2011. (ENG.). 192p. (J). (gr. 3-7). 6.99 (978-0-375-85450-7(9), Yearling) Random Hse. Children's Bks.

Wallin, Betsy. My First Farm Friends, 4 vols. 2011. (ENG., Illus.). 20p. (J). (gr. -1 — 1). bds. 18.95 (978-1-60342-991-7(3), 62991) Storey Publishing, LLC.

Weeks, Sarah & Weeks. Baa-Choo! Manning, Jane K., illus. 2006. (I Can Read Level 1 Ser.). (ENG.). 32p. (J). (gr. k-3). pap. 3.99 (978-0-06-443740-0(X)) HarperCollins Pubs.

Weston, Carrie. What Noise Does a Rabbit Make? Byrne, Richard, illus. 2013. (ENG.). 32p. (J). (gr. -1-3). 16.95 (978-1-4677-2032-8(1)) Lerner Publishing Group.

Weston Woods Staff, creator. Duck on a Bike. 2011. 38.75 (978-0-545-19709-0(0)); 29.95 (978-0-545-19698-7(1)); 18.95 (978-0-545-19704-5(X)) Weston Woods Studios, Inc.

—Giggle, Giggle Quack. 2004. (J). 29.95 (978-1-55592-701-1(7)) Weston Woods Studios, Inc.

Wheeler, Lisa. Farmer Dale's Red Pickup Truck. Bates, Ivan, illus. 2014. (ENG.). 32p. (J). (— 1). bds. 7.99 (978-0-544-24765-9(5), HMH Books For Young Readers) Houghton Mifflin Harcourt Publishing Co.

Whispering Pine Press International, ed. Petting Farm Fun, Translated Amharic, Vol. 3. Artistic Design Service Staff, illus. 2014. (Hood Picture Book Ser.). (AMH.). 42p. (J). per. 19.95 (978-1-59649-554-8(5)) Whispering Pine Pr. International, Inc.

White, E. B. Charlotte's Web. Williams, Garth, illus. 2005. (Charming Classics). 192p. (J). pap. 7.99 (978-0-06-084594-0(5), HarperFestival) HarperCollins Pubs.

—Charlotte's Web. movie tie-in ed. 2006. (Charlotte's Web Ser.). (ENG., Illus.). 192p. (J). (gr. 4-7). per. 7.99 (978-0-06-112026-8(X)) HarperCollins Pubs.

—Charlotte's Web. Williams, Garth, illus. movie tie-in ed. 2006. (Charlotte's Web Ser.). (J). 192p. mass mkt. 7.99 (978-0-06-122874-2(5), Harper Trophy);Set. pap. 19.99 (978-0-06-121502-5(3)) HarperCollins Pubs.

—Charlotte's Web. Williams, Garth, illus. 2004. (CHI.). 158p. (YA). pap. (978-957-08-2568-8(5)) Linking Publishing Co., Ltd.

—Charlotte's Web. Williams, Garth, illus. 184p. (J). pap. 5.95 (978-0-8072-8305-9(3), Listening Library) Random Hse. Audio Publishing Group.

—Charlotte's Web. unabr. ed. 2004. 184p. (J). (gr. 3-7). pap. 36.00 incl. audio (978-0-8072-8304-2(5), YYA156SP, Listening Library) Random Hse. Audio Publishing Group.

—Charlotte's Web. 2012. (J). (gr. 3-6). 18.40 (978-0-8085-3772-4(5), Turtleback) Turtleback Bks.

—The Telarana of Carlota (LaTelarana de Carlota) Williams, Garth, illus. movie tie-in ed. 2006. (Charlotte's Web Ser.). (SPA.). 224p. (J). pap. 7.99 (978-0-06-112522-5(9), Rayo) HarperCollins Pubs.

—Wilbur's Adventure: A Charlotte's Web Picture Book. Kneen, Maggie, illus. 2008. (Charlotte's Web Ser.). 32p. (J). (gr. k-2). lib. bdg. 17.89 (978-0-06-078165-1(3)) HarperCollins Pubs.

White, E. B. & DiCamillo, Kate. Charlotte's Web. Williams, Garth, illus. (ENG.). 192p. (J). (gr. 3-7). 2012. 16.99 (978-0-06-026385-0(7)) 2012. 8.99 (978-0-06-112495-2(8)) 2012. pap. 8.99 (978-0-06-440055-8(7)) 2006. 16.99 (978-0-06-088261-7(1)) HarperCollins Pubs.

Whybrow, Ian. The Noisy Way to Bed. Beeke, Tiphanie, tr. Beeke, Tiphanie, illus. 2004. (J). (978-0-439-55690-3(2), Levine, Arthur A. Bks.) Scholastic, Inc.

Whybrow, Ian & Warnes, Tim. Say Hello to the Animals, 2. 2008. (ENG., Illus.). 20p. (J). (gr. 1-5). bds. 14.95 (978-0-230-52859-8(7), Macmillan) Pan Macmillan GBR. Dist: Trans-Atlantic Pubns., Inc.

Wild, Margaret. Piglet & Granny. King, Stephen Michael, illus. 2009. (ENG.). 32p. (J). (gr. -1-k). 15.95 (978-0-8109-4063-5(9), Abrams Bks. for Young Readers) Abrams, Inc.

Williams, Sue. Let's Go Visiting. Vivas, Julie, illus. 2003. (ENG.). 32p. (J). (gr. k — 1). bds. 6.95 (978-0-15-204638-5(0)) Houghton Mifflin Harcourt Publishing Co.

Willow Creek Press, creator. Secret of the Pasture. 2005. (Children's Adventure Tales Ser.). (ENG., Illus.). 32p. (J). (gr. -1-k). 12.95 (978-1-59543-237-7(X)) Willow Creek Pr., Inc.

Wilson, Douglas. Maude, the Flop-Eared Mule. Fore, Elizabeth, illus. 2012. 38p. 24.95 (978-1-4626-7455-8(0)) America Star Bks.

Wilson, Karma. Beautiful Babies. Wilson, Karma, photos by. 2009. (ENG., Illus.). 14p. (J). (gr. -1 — 1). bds. 6.99 (978-1-4169-1908-7(2), Little Simon) Little Simon.

—The Cow Loves Cookies. Hall, Marcellus, illus. 2010. (ENG.). 40p. (J). (gr. -1-3). 17.99 (978-1-4169-4206-1(6), McElderry, Margaret K. Bks.) McElderry, Margaret K. Bks.

—Duddle Puck: The Puddle Duck. Hall, Marcellus, illus. 2015. (ENG.). 40p. (J). (gr. -1-3). 17.99 (978-1-4424-4927-5(6), McElderry, Margaret K. Bks.) McElderry, Margaret K. Bks.

Winthrop, Elizabeth. Dumpy la Rue. Lewin, Betsy, illus. rev. ed. 2004. (ENG.). 40p. (J). (gr. -1-3). reprint ed. pap. 8.99 (978-0-8050-7535-9(6), 9780805075359, Holt, Henry & Co. Bks. For Young Readers) Holt, Henry & Co.

Wright, Maureen. Barnyard Fun, 0 vols. De Tagyos, Paul Ratz, illus. 2013. (ENG.). 24p. (J). (gr. -1-3). 16.99 (978-1-4778-1643-1(7), 9781477816431, Amazon Children's Publishing) Amazon Publishing.

Wyatt, Cherokee. The Adventures of Margaret Mouse: Hide 'n Seek. Redmon, Angela M., illus. Lt. ed. 2005. 32p. (J). (gr. k-5). 6.95 (978-0-9761326-4-6(8)) www.margaretmouse.com publishing co.

Yocum, Randi. Cowpie Corgi: A Dog's Tale. Yocum, Sam, 2nd, photos by. 2007. (Illus.). 32p. (J). lib. bdg. 16.98 (978-0-9663629-3-0(4)) By Grace Enterprises.

Yoon, Salina. Old MacDonald Had a Farm. 2008. (Salina Yoon Bks.). (ENG., Illus.). 12p. (J). (gr. -1-k). bds. 6.99 (978-0-8431-2817-8(8), Price Stern Sloan) Penguin Young Readers Group.

Young, Pippa, illus. On the Farm. (Match & Twist Ser.). (J). 11.99 (978-0-525-47054-0(9), Dutton Juvenile) Penguin Publishing Group.

Zarins, Kim. The Helpful Puppy. McCully, Emily Arnold, illus. 2012. (ENG.). 32p. (J). 16.95 (978-0-8234-2318-7(2)) Holiday Hse., Inc.

—The Helpful Puppy. McCully, Emily Arnold, illus. 2013. (ENG.). 32p. (J). pap. 6.99 (978-0-8234-2919-6(9)) Holiday Hse., Inc.

DOMESTIC ANIMALS—PICTORIAL WORKS

Baggott, Stella. Baby's Very First Little Book of Farm Animals. 2012. (Baby's Very First Board Book Ser.). 10p. (J). ring bd. 6.99 (978-0-7945-3218-5(7), Usborne) EDC Publishing.

Bergin, Mark. Farm Animals. 2012. (It's Fun to Draw Ser.). (Illus.). 32p. (J). (gr. k-3). lib. bdg. 26.50 (978-1-61533-599-2(4)) Windmill Bks.

Brooks, Felicity. First Word Book on the Farm. 2015. (My First Word Bks.). (ENG.). 20p. (J). 9.99 (978-0-7945-3445-5(7), Usborne) EDC Publishing.

Brown, James. Farm. Brown, James, illus. 2013. (ENG., Illus.). 16p. (J). (gr. -1 — 1). bds. 6.99 (978-0-7636-5931-8(2)) Candlewick Pr.

Chicks. 2003. (Three Minute Tales Ser.). 32p. (J). 5.98 (978-0-7525-8915-2(6)); 7.95 (978-0-7525-4759-6(3)) Parragon, Inc.

Cocoretto, illus. On the Farm. 2016. (Peekaboo! Ser.: 4). (ENG.). 12p. (J). bds. (978-1-84643-864-6(0)) Child's Play International Ltd.

Daynes, Katie. Look Inside a Farm. rev. ed. 2012. (Look Inside Board Bks). 13p. (J). ring bd. 15.99 (978-0-7945-3249-9(7), Usborne) EDC Publishing.

Dorling Kindersley Publishing Staff. Farm Animals. 2004. (DK Readers Ser.). (ENG., Illus.). 32p. (J). (gr. -1-1). pap. 3.99 (978-0-7566-0536-0(9), DK Children) Dorling Kindersley Publishing, Inc.

Farm Animals. Date not set. (Illus.). 16p. (J). 5.98 (978-0-7525-7697-8(6)); 2.98 (978-0-7525-9761-4(2)) Parragon, Inc.

Farm Animals. (Puppet Board Books Ser.). (J). 2.50 Penguin Publishing Group.

Farm Animals. (Illus.). 12p. (J). (978-2-7643-0148-7(0)) Phidal Publishing, Inc./Editions Phidal, Inc.

Guettier, Bénédicte. On the Farm. 2010. (Funny Faces Ser.). (Illus.). 14p. bds. (978-1-84089-646-6(9)) Zero to Ten, Ltd.

Gunzi, Christiane. On the Farm. 2015. (ENG., Illus.). 8p. (J). 9.99 (978-1-909763-09-8(8)) Award Pubns. Ltd. GBR. Dist: Parkwest Pubns., Inc.

Hess, Paul. Farmyard Animals. Hess, Paul, illus. 2009. (Animal Verse Ser.). (ENG., Illus.). 24p. (J). (gr. -1-k). pap. (978-1-84089-559-9(4)) Zero to Ten, Ltd.

Holmes, Stephen. Number Farm. 2003. (J). bds. 5.98 (978-0-7525-8920-6(2)) Parragon, Inc.

Mathews, Sarah. Farm Animals. 2012. (ENG., Illus.). 36p. (J). (gr. -1-k). pap. 12.99 (978-1-85103-381-2(5)) Moonlight Publishing, Ltd. GBR. Dist: Independent Pubs. Group.

Novick, Mary & Hale, Jenny. Farm & Zoo. 2006. (Illus.). 32p. (978-1-921049-26-2(X)) Little Hare Bks. AUS. Dist: HarperCollins Pubs. Australia.

Tai, Elise See. Farm Animal Counting. 2014. (Lumpy Bumpy Ser.). (ENG., Illus.). 10p. (J). (gr. -1 — 1). 5.99 (978-0-7641-6708-9(1)) Barron's Educational Series, Inc.

Tuxworth, Nicola. Farm Animals. (ENG., Illus.). 2016. 20p. bds. 6.99 (978-1-86147-476-6(8), Armadillo) 2013. 12p. (J). (gr. -1-12). bds. 6.99 (978-0-7548-2202-8(8)) Anness Publishing GBR. Dist: National Bk. Network.

Wildsmith, Brian. Brian Wildsmith's Farm Animals, 1 vol. 2007. (ENG., Illus.). 32p. (J). (gr. -1-k). bds. 4.99 (978-1-59572-119-8(3)) Star Bright Bks., Inc.

Wolfe, Jane & Baxter, Nicola. Who's on the Farm? Lawson, Peter, illus. 2013. (ENG.). 8p. bds. 6.99 (978-1-84322-652-9(9), Armadillo) Anness Publishing GBR. Dist: National Bk. Network.

DOMESTIC APPLIANCES

see Household Appliances, Electric; Household Equipment and Supplies

DOMESTIC ARCHITECTURE

see Architecture, Domestic

DOMESTIC ARTS

see Home Economics

DOMESTIC FINANCE

see Home Economics—Accounting

DOMESTIC RELATIONS

see also Divorce; Marriage; Parent and Child

Amato, Mary Anne. Where Are My Pictures, Mommy? 2009. 36p. pap. 16.49 (978-1-4490-2672-1(9)) AuthorHouse.

Bartel, Blaine. Little Black Book on How to Get Along with Your Parents. 2004. (Illus.). 80p. (J). pap. 4.99 (978-1-57794-626-7(X)) Harrison House Pubs.

Bianchi, Anne. Everything You Need to Know about Family Court. 2005. (Need to Know Library). (Illus.). 64p. (YA). (gr. 7-12). lib. bdg. 31.95 (978-0-8239-3163-7(3), NTFACO) Rosen Publishing Group, Inc., The.

Brown, Isobel. Domestic Crime. 2004. (Crime & Detection Ser.). (Illus.). 96p. (YA). (gr. 7-18). lib. bdg. 22.95 (978-1-59084-370-3(3)) Mason Crest.

Cargile, Phillip & Miss Cheryl. The Wagon Man: The Untold Story of the Go-Bum Kids. 2009. 54p. pap. 16.95 (978-1-60703-939-6(7)) America Star Bks.

Head, Honor. Family & Friends. 2013. (Let's Read & Talk about Ser.). (Illus.). 32p. (J). (gr. 2-5). 28.50 (978-1-59771-397-9(X)) Sea-To-Sea Pubns.

Meyer, Brian E. What You Mean to Me. 2010. 20p. 11.99 (978-1-4520-8170-0(0)) AuthorHouse.

Prentzas, G. S. The Law & Your Family: Your Legal Rights, 1 vol. 2015. (ENG., Illus.). 64p. (J). 33.25 (978-1-4777-8012-1(2), Rosen Reference) Rosen Publishing Group, Inc., The.

Schuette, Sarah L. Adoptive Families, 1 vol. 2010. (My Family Ser.). (ENG.). 24p. (gr. k-1). pap. 6.29 (978-1-4296-4836-3(8), Pebble Bks.) Capstone Press of Coughlan Cos.

Slier, Debby. Loving Me, 1 vol. 2013. (ENG., Illus.). 32p. (J). bds. 5.99 (978-1-59572-334-5(X)) Star Bright Bks., Inc.

Smith, Michael. Questions for Kids: A Book to Discover a Child's Imagination & Knowledge. Smith, Crystal & Lin, Albert, illus. 2003. 209p. (J). (gr. k-4). 13.95 (978-0-9669437-3-3(2)) East West Discovery Pr.

—Questions for Kids: A Book to Discover a Child's Imagination & Knowledge. Lin, Albert & Smith, Crystal, illus. 2003. 208p. (J). (gr. k-4). pap. 9.95 (978-0-9669437-1-9(6)) East West Discovery Pr.

Thomas, Gina. Mr Taxi Man Meets Irene. 2009. 48p. pap. 19.99 (978-1-4490-3495-5(0)) AuthorHouse.

DOMINICA—FICTION

Schindel, John. Busy Barnyard. Holt, Steven, photos by. 2006. (Busy Book Ser.). (ENG., Illus.). 20p. (J). (— 1). bds. 7.99 (978-1-58246-168-7(6), Tricycle Pr.) Random Hse. Children's Bks.

DOMINICAN REPUBLIC

Cantor, Rachel Anne. Dominican Republic. 2016. (Countries We Come From Ser.). (ENG., Illus.). 32p. (J). (gr. -1-3). lib. bdg. 19.95 (978-1-943553-33-4(5)) Bearport Publishing Co., Inc.

The Dominican Republic. 2010. (Modern World Nations Ser.). (Illus.). 120p. (gr. 6-12). 35.00 *(978-1-60413-618-0(9),* Chelsea Hse.) Facts On File, Inc.

Foley, Erin & Jermyn, Leslie. Dominican Republic. 2nd rev. ed. 2005. (Cultures of the World Ser.). (Illus.). 144p. (gr. 6-10). lib. bdg. 42.79 *(978-0-7614-1966-2(7),* Benchmark Bks.) Marshall Cavendish Corp.

Frisch, Aaron. Albert Pujols. 2013. (Illus.). 24 p.p. (J). 25.65 *(978-1-60818-336-4(X),* Creative Education) Creative Co., The.

Gaab, Carol. Felipe Alou: From the Valleys to the Mountains. 2012. (Illus.). 98p. (J). *(978-1-935575-79-5(1))* TPRS Publishing, Inc.

Marcus, Amy. Exploring the Dominican Republic with the Five Themes of Geography. (Library of the Western Hemisphere Ser.). 24p. 2009. (gr. 4-4). 42.50 *(978-1-60853-931-4(8),* PowerKids Pr.) 2005. (Illus.). (J). (gr. 3-7). lib. bdg. 22.60 *(978-1-4042-2671-5(0))* 2005. (ENG., Illus.). (gr. 3-8). pap. 8.25 *(978-0-8239-4631-0(2))* Rosen Publishing Group, Inc., The.

McCarthy, Pat. The Dominican Republic: A MyReportLinks.com Book. 2004. (Top Ten Countries of Recent Immigrants Ser.). (Illus.). 48p. (J). lib. bdg. 26.60 *(978-0-7660-5179-9(X),* MyReportLinks.com Bks.) Enslow Pubs., Inc.

Morris, Kerry-Ann & Ismail, Nafisah. Dominican Republic. 2004. (Countries of the World Ser.). (Illus.). 96p. (gr. 5-12). lib. bdg. 31.00 *(978-0-8368-3110-8(1))* Stevens, Gareth Publishing LLLP.

Nagelhout, Ryan. David Ortiz: World Series Champion. 2015. (Living Legends of Sports Ser.). (ENG.). 48p. (J). (gr. 5-6). pap. 14.05 *(978-1-68048-100-6(2),* Britannica Educational Publishing) Rosen Publishing Group, Inc., The.

Oscar de la Renta. 2010. (Great Hispanic Heritage Ser.). (Illus.). 128p. (gr. 6-12). 35.00 *(978-1-60413-733-0(9),* Chelsea Hse.) Facts On File, Inc.

Rinker, Kimberly. Immigration from the Dominican Republic. 2005. (Changing Face of North America Ser.). (Illus.). 112p. (YA). lib. bdg. 24.95 *(978-1-59084-689-6(3))* Mason Crest.

Rodriguez Gonzalez, Tania. Albert Pujols. 2012. (Superstars of Baseball ENGLISH Ser.). 32p. (J). (gr. 4). 19.95 *(978-1-4222-2676-6(X));* (SPA., Illus.). 19.95 *(978-1-4222-2623-0(9))* Mason Crest.

—Alfonso Soriano. 2012. (Superstars of Baseball ENGLISH Ser.). 32p. (J). (gr. 4). 19.95 *(978-1-4222-2673-5(5))* Mason Crest.

—Aramis Ramirez. 2012. (ENG & SPA., Illus.). 32p. (J). *(978-1-4222-2617-9(4))* Mason Crest.

—David Ortiz. 2012. (Superstars of Baseball SPANISH Ser.). 32p. (J). (gr. 4). (SPA.). 19.95 *(978-1-4222-2626-1(3));* 19.95 *(978-1-4222-2679-7(4))* Mason Crest.

—José Reyes. 2012. (Superstars of Baseball ENGLISH Ser.). 32p. (J). (gr. 4). 19.95 *(978-1-4222-2684-1(0));* (SPA., Illus.). 19.95 *(978-1-4222-2631-5(X))* Mason Crest.

—Robinson Canó. 2012. (Superstars of Baseball SPANISH Ser.). (SPA., Illus.). 32p. (J). (gr. 4). 19.95 *(978-1-4222-2630-8(1))* Mason Crest.

Rogers, Lura, et al. Dominican Republic. 2008. (Enchantment of the World Ser.). (ENG., Illus.). 144p. (J). (gr. 5-9). 40.00 *(978-0-531-12097-2(X))* Scholastic Library Publishing.

Simmons, Walter. The Dominican Republic. 2012. (Exploring Countries Ser.). (ENG., Illus.). 32p. (J). (gr. 3-7). lib. bdg. 26.95 *(978-1-60014-729-6(1),* Blastoff! Readers) Bellwether Media.

Tavares, Matt. Growing up Pedro: How the Martinez Brothers Made It from the Dominican Republic All the Way to the Major Leagues. Tavares, Matt, illus. 2015. (ENG., Illus.). 40p. (J). (gr. 3-7). 16.99 *(978-0-7636-6824-2(9))* Candlewick Pr.

Temple, Bob. Dominican Republic. 2010. (Caribbean Today Ser.). (Illus.). 64p. (YA). (gr. 9-12). 21.95 *(978-1-4222-0624-9(6))* Mason Crest.

—Dominican Republic, Vol. 11. Henderson, James D., ed. 2015. (Discovering the Caribbean: History, Politics, & Culture Ser.). (Illus.). 64p. (J). (gr. 7). lib. bdg. 22.95 *(978-1-4222-3311-5(1))* Mason Crest.

Torres, John. We Visit the Dominican Republic. 2010. (Your Land & My Land Ser.). (Illus.). 64p. (J). (gr. 3-6). lib. bdg. 33.95 *(978-1-58415-891-2(3))* Mitchell Lane Pubs., Inc.

Zuchora-Walske, Christine. Dominican Republic in Pictures. 2008. (Visual Geography (Lerner) Ser.). (Illus.). 80p. (YA). (gr. 7-12). lib. bdg. 29.27 *(978-0-8225-8569-5(3))* Twenty First Century Bks.

DOMINICAN REPUBLIC—FICTION

Alvarez, Julia. Antes de Ser Libres. Valenzuela, Liliana, tr. 2004.Tr. of Before We Were Free. (SPA.). 192p. (YA). (gr. 7). mass mkt. 6.99 *(978-0-375-81545-4(7),* Laurel Leaf) Random Hse. Children's Bks.

—Antes de Ser Libres. 2004.Tr. of Before We Were Free. (SPA.). (gr. 7-12). lib. bdg. 17.20 *(978-0-613-71931-5(X),* Turtleback) Turtleback Bks.

—Before We Were Free. 2004. 192p. (J). (gr. 7-18). pap. 38.00 incl. audio *(978-1-4000-9017-4(2),* Listening Library) Random Hse. Audio Publishing Group.

—Before We Were Free. 2004. (ENG.). 192p. (YA). (gr. 7). reprint ed. mass mkt. 6.99 *(978-0-440-23784-6(X),* Laurel Leaf) Random Hse. Children's Bks.

—Before We Were Free. 2004. (gr. 7-12). lib. bdg. 17.20 *(978-0-613-72269-8(8),* Turtleback) Turtleback Bks.

Diaz, Junot. Drown. 2011. 14.45 *(978-0-7848-3428-2(8));* 14.45 *(978-0-7848-3380-3(X))* Marco Bk. Co. (Everbind).

Ellis, Amanda & Block, Maggie. Jwenlapaix in the Bateyes. 2009. 52p. pap. 24.00 *(978-1-4389-4391-6(1))* AuthorHouse.

Joseph, Lynn. El Color de Mis Palabras. Rioja, Alberto Jimenez, tr. 2004. (SPA., Illus.). (YA). (gr. 5-18). ring bd. 15.95 *(978-1-930332-22-5(X),* LC7235) Lectorum Pubns., Inc.

—Flowers in the Sky. 2013. (ENG.). 240p. (YA). (gr. 8). 17.99 *(978-0-06-029794-7(8),* HarperTeen) HarperCollins Pubs.

Julia, Alvarez. Before We Were Free. 2014. (ENG.). 192p. (YA). 11.24 *(978-1-63245-139-2(5))* Lectorum Pubns., Inc.

Lupica, Mike. Point Guard. 2017. (Home Team Ser.). (ENG., Illus.). 272p. (J). (gr. 3-7). 16.99 *(978-1-4814-1003-8(2),* Simon & Schuster Bks. For Young Readers) Simon & Schuster Bks. For Young Readers.

Lynn, Joseph. Color of My Words. 2014. (ENG.). 144p. (J). (gr. 5-12). 10.24 *(978-1-63245-277-1(4))* Lectorum Pubns., Inc.

Mulder, Michelle. Not a Chance, 1 vol. 2013. (ENG.). 160p. (J). (gr. 4-7). pap. 9.95 *(978-1-4598-0216-2(0))* Orca Bk. Pubs. USA.

DOMINION OF THE SEA

see Sea Power

DON QUIXOTE (FICTITIOUS CHARACTER)—FICTION

Cervantes, Miguel de. Don Quijote. Svetlin, illus. 2005. 159p. (J). (gr. 6-8). per. 14.99 *(978-84-316-7637-7(X))* Vicens-Vives, Editorial, S.A. ESP. Dist: Lectorum Pubns., Inc.

Côté, Denis. La Forêt aux Mille et un Périls, Tome 2. Poulin, Stephane, illus. 2004. (Roman Jeunesse Ser.). (FRE.). 96p. (J). (gr. 4-7). pap. *(978-2-89021-696-9(9))* Diffusion du livre Mirabel (DLM).

Shield ARP, Peter J. Don Quixote & the Windmills, 1 vol. 2010. 30p. 24.95 *(978-1-4512-9032-5(2))* PublishAmerica, Inc.

DONALD DUCK (FICTITIOUS CHARACTER)—FICTION

Amano, Shiro. Chain of Memories, Vol. 2. 2nd rev. ed. 2007. (Kingdom Hearts Ser.). (Illus.). 232p. (gr. 4-7). pap. 9.99 *(978-1-59816-638-5(7),* Tokyopop Kids) TOKYOPOP, Inc.

Ambrosio, Stefano. Mouse Magic. Pastrovicchio, Lorenzo, illus. 2010. (ENG.). 112p. (J). 24.99 *(978-1-60886-550-5(9));* Vol. 1. pap. 9.99 *(978-1-60886-541-3(X))* Boom! Studios.

—Wizards of Mickey - Grand Tournament, Vol. 2. Pastrovicchio, Lorenzo & Magic Eye Studios, illus. 2010. (Wizards of Mickey Ser.). (ENG.). 128p. (J). (gr. 3-6). pap. 9.99 *(978-1-60886-564-2(9))* Boom! Studios.

Amerikaner, Susan. Goofy at Bat. 2013. (Mickey & Friends World of Reading Ser.). (J). lib. bdg. 13.55 *(978-0-606-27117-2(1),* Turtleback) Turtleback Bks.

Artibani, Francesco, et al. Donald Duck Adventures, Vol. 19. Clark, John, ed. 2006. (ENG., Illus.). 128p. (YA). pap. 7.95 *(978-1-888472-31-8(6),* 9781888472318) Gemstone Publishing, Inc.

Barks, Carl. The Golden Helmet Starring Walt Disney's Donald Duck. 2015. (ENG., Illus.). 128p. pap. 12.99 *(978-1-60699-852-6(8),* 699852) Fantagraphics Bks.

—Sheriff of Bullet Valley: Starring Walt Disney's Donald Duck. 2015. (ENG., Illus.). 96p. pap. 9.99 *(978-1-60699-820-5(X),* 699820) Fantagraphics Bks.

—Walt Disney's Donald Duck: Trick or Treat. 2015. (Carl Barks Library: 0). (ENG., Illus.). 232p. 29.99 *(978-1-60699-874-8(9),* 699874) Fantagraphics Bks.

Barks, Carl, et al. Uncle Scrooge #387. 2009. 64p. pap. 7.99 *(978-1-60360-087-3(6))* Gemstone Publishing, Inc.

—Uncle Scrooge #389. 2009. 64p. pap. 7.99 *(978-1-60360-089-7(2))* Gemstone Publishing, Inc.

—Walt Disney's Christmas Parade #5. 2008. (Illus.). 80p. pap. 9.50 *(978-1-60360-005-7(1))* Gemstone Publishing, Inc.

—Walt Disney's Comics & Stories #702. 2009. 64p. pap. 7.99 *(978-1-60360-092-7(2))* Gemstone Publishing, Inc.

—Walt Disney's Comics & Stories #704. 2009. 64p. pap. 7.99 *(978-1-60360-094-1(9))* Gemstone Publishing, Inc.

—Walt Disney's Vacation Parade Volume 5. Clark, John, ed. 2008. (ENG., Illus.). 80p. pap. 9.95 *(978-1-60360-031-6(0),* 9781603600316) Gemstone Publishing, Inc.

—Walt Disney's Vacation Parade Volume 6. 2009. 80p. pap. 9.99 *(978-1-60360-096-5(5))* Gemstone Publishing, Inc.

Barosso, Abramo, et al. Uncle Scrooge #386. 2009. 64p. pap. 7.99 *(978-1-60360-086-6(8))* Gemstone Publishing, Inc.

Enna, Bruno. Double Duck. Soffritti, Donald, illus. 2010. (ENG.). 112p. (J). pap. 9.99 *(978-1-60886-545-1(2))* Boom! Studios.

Figuerola, Maite. Los Deportes. 2003. (Disney Collection). (SPA., Illus.). 32p. (J). 5.95 *(978-84-670-0301-7(4))* Espasa Calpe, S.A. ESP. Dist: Planeta Publishing Corp.

Francesc Bargada Studios Staff & Staff, Di I. Around the World in 80 Bucks. 2010. (Uncle Scrooge Ser.). (ENG., Illus.). 128p. (J). (gr. 3-6). pap. 9.99 *(978-1-60886-566-6(5))* Boom! Studios.

Gilbert, Michael T., et al. Walt Disney's Comics & Stories #693. Clark, John, ed. 2008. (ENG., Illus.). 64p. pap. 7.99 *(978-1-60360-038-5(8),* 9781603600385) Gemstone Publishing, Inc.

Gottfredson, Floyd, et al. Walt Disney's Comics & Stories #700. 2008. 80p. pap. 9.99 *(978-1-60360-057-6(4))* Gemstone Publishing, Inc.

Jensen, Lars, et al. Donald Duck Adventures, Vol. 18. Clark, John, ed. 2006. (ENG., Illus.). 128p. (YA). pap. 7.95 *(978-1-888472-30-1(8),* 9781888472301) Gemstone Publishing, Inc.

Jippes, Daan, et al. Donald Duck Family, Vol. 2. 2009. 64p. pap. 8.99 *(978-1-60360-099-6(X))* Gemstone Publishing, Inc.

—Walt Disney's Comics & Stories #703. 2009. 64p. pap. 7.99 *(978-1-60360-093-4(0))* Gemstone Publishing, Inc.

Korhonen, Kari, et al. Walt Disney's Comics & Stories #705. 2009. 64p. pap. 7.99 *(978-1-60360-095-8(7))* Gemstone Publishing, Inc.

Kruse, Jan, et al. Walt Disney's Spring Fever Volume 3. 2009. 80p. pap. 9.99 *(978-1-60360-097-2(3))* Gemstone Publishing, Inc.

Laban, Terry. Donald Duck Adventures, Vol. 17. Clark, John, ed. Andersen, Flemming & Gonzalez, Jose Antonio, illus. 2006. (ENG.). 128p. (YA). (gr. 3-7). pap. 7.95 *(978-1-888472-12-7(X),* 9781888472127) Gemstone Publishing, Inc.

McGreal, Pat & McGreal, Carol. Uncle Scrooge #385. 2008. 64p. pap. 7.99 *(978-1-60360-062-0(0))* Gemstone Publishing, Inc.

McGreal, Pat, et al. Uncle Scrooge #390. 2009. 64p. pap. 7.99 *(978-1-60360-090-3(6))* Gemstone Publishing, Inc.

—Walt Disney's Comics & Stories #701. 2009. 64p. pap. 7.99 *(978-1-60360-091-0(4))* Gemstone Publishing, Inc.

O'Connor, Eddie, et al. Donald Duck Adventures, Vol. 16. Clark, John, ed. 2006. (ENG., Illus.). 128p. (YA). pap. 7.95 *(978-1-888472-11-0(1),* 9781888472110) Gemstone Publishing, Inc.

Pujol, Miquel, et al. Uncle Scrooge #388. 2009. 64p. pap. 7.99 *(978-1-60360-088-0(4))* Gemstone Publishing, Inc.

Rosa, Don. Walt Disney Uncle Scrooge & Donald Duck: Treasure under Glass: The Don Rosa Library Vol. 3. 2015. (Don Rosa Library: 0). (ENG., Illus.). 192p. 29.99 *(978-1-60699-836-6(6),* 699836) Fantagraphics Bks.

Sarda, Bruno. Mickey & Donald: the Search for the Zodiac Stone. Vita, Massimo de & Valussi, Franco, illus. 2016. (Mickey Mouse Ser.). (ENG.). 368p. 39.99 *(978-1-63140-706-2(6),* 9781631407062) Idea & Design Works, LLC.

Scollon, Bill. A Goofy Fairy Tale. 2014. (Mickey Mouse 8x8 Ser.). (J). lib. bdg. 14.75 *(978-0-606-35900-9(1))* Turtleback Bks.

Scollon, William & Disney Book Group Staff. Mickey & Donald Have a Farm. Disney Storybook Art Team, illus. 2012. (ENG.). 32p. (J). (gr. -1-k). pap. 5.99 *(978-1-4231-4946-0(7))* Disney Pr.

Soundprints Staff. Old MacDonald: And Other Favorites. 2005. (Meet Mother Goose Ser.). (ENG., Illus.). 36p. (J). 10.95 *(978-1-931465-30-4(4))* Soundprints.

Various. Donald Duck Adventures, Vol. 2. 2003. (ENG., Illus.). 128p. pap. 7.95 *(978-0-911903-11-9(9),* 9780911903119) Gemstone Publishing, Inc.

Werner, Jane. Mickey Mouse & His Spaceship (Disney: Mickey Mouse) RH Disney, illus. 2016. (Little Golden Book Ser.). (ENG.). 24p. (J). (-k). 4.99 *(978-0-7364-3633-5(2),* Golden/Disney) Random Hse. Children's Bks.

DONATIONS

see Gifts

DONKEYS

Bailer, Darice. Donkeys. 2011. 48p. (gr. 3). lib. bdg. 23.95 *(978-0-7614-4875-4(6),* Benchmark Bks.) Marshall Cavendish Corp.

Chottin, Ariane. Little Donkeys. 2006. (Born to Be Wild Ser.). (Illus.). 24p. (gr. k-3). lib. bdg. 23.00 *(978-0-8368-6165-5(5),* Gareth Stevens Learning Library) Stevens, Gareth Publishing LLLP.

Dickens, Lydia. The Little Donkey Nico / el Burrito Nico. 2012. 32p. pap. 19.99 *(978-1-4772-7026-4(4))* AuthorHouse.

Donkey Work: Level J, 6 vols. (Wonder Worldtm Ser.). 16p. 29.95 *(978-0-7802-4569-3(5))* Wright Group/McGraw-Hill.

Elora, Grace. Foals. 2011. (Cute & Cuddly: Baby Animals Ser.). (Illus.). 24p. (J). (gr. k-2). pap. 8.15 *(978-1-4339-4508-3(8));* lib. bdg. 22.60 *(978-1-4339-4507-6(X))* Stevens, Gareth Publishing LLLP.

Hasselius, Michelle M. Donkeys. 2016. (Farm Animals Ser.). (ENG.). 24p. (gr. k-1). lib. bdg. 26.65 *(978-1-5157-0925-1(6))* Capstone Press of Coughlan Cos.

Kuskowski, Alex. Foals, 1 vol. 2013. (Baby Animals Set 1 Ser.). (ENG.). 24p. (J). (gr. k-3). lib. bdg. 24.21 *(978-1-61783-837-8(3),* SandCastle) ABDO Publishing Co.

Metz, Lorijo. Donkeys: Jennies, Jacks, & Foals. 2010. (On the Farm Ser.). (ENG.). 24p. (J). pap. 8.25 *(978-1-4488-1337-7(9));* lib. bdg. 22.60 *(978-1-4488-0688-1(7))* Rosen Publishing Group, Inc., The. (PowerKids Pr.).

Pearlman, Larry & Pearlman, Esther, illus. Cute Li'l Donkeys: (Raisin' & Grazin') 2014. (J). *(978-0-935047-81-3(6))* Americas Group, The.

Yasuda, Anita. Burros. 2014. (SPA., Illus.). 24p. (J). *(978-1-62127-587-9(6))* Weigl Pubs., Inc.

—Donkeys. 2012. (J). *(978-1-61913-276-4(1));* *(978-1-61913-280-1(X))* Weigl Pubs., Inc.

DONKEYS—FICTION

Adams, Michelle Medlock. Little Colt's Palm Sunday. Parmenter, Wayne, illus. 2005. (ENG.). 28p. (J). 14.95 *(978-0-8249-5503-8(X),* Ideal Pubns.) Worthy Publishing.

Aesop. The Donkey & the Load of Salt. 2012. (J). *(978-1-61913-105-7(6))* Weigl Pubs., Inc.

—The Miller & the Donkey: A Tale about Thinking for Yourself. Branch, Beverly, illus. 2006. (J). *(978-1-59939-087-1(6),* Reader's Digest Young Families, Inc.) Studio Fun International.

Ahokangas, Anne Margit. The Adventures of Velvet Series: I Am Who I Am. 2012. 46p. (-18). pap. 20.99 *(978-1-4525-6154-7(0))* Balboa Pr.

Allen, F. M. Brayhard. 2009. 268p. pap. 30.95 *(978-1-4092-7639-5(2))* Lulu Pr., Inc.

Amery, Heather. Hungry Donkey. Tyler, Jenny, ed. Cartwright, Stephen, illus. rev. ed. 2004. (Farmyard Tales Readers Ser.). 16p. (J). pap. 5.95 *(978-0-7945-0752-7(2),* Usborne) EDC Publishing.

Anderson, James O. Poggy, the Stuffed Donkey. 2006. 16p. 4.95 *(978-1-57258-395-5(9))* TEACH Services, Inc.

Angus, Sam. Captain. Roberto, Anna, ed. 2016. (ENG.). 240p. (J). 16.99 *(978-1-250-06137-9(7),* 9781250061379) Feiwel & Friends.

Atwood, Peggy. Levi Jackson the Littlest Gold Prospector & His Donkey Dilbert. 2010. 24p. 11.49 *(978-1-4490-7831-7(1))* AuthorHouse.

Award, Anna & Aesop. The Lion & the Mouse with the Donkey & the Lapdog. Biro, Val, illus. 2014. (ENG.). 24p. (J). pap. 6.95 *(978-1-84135-953-3(X))* Award Pubns. Ltd. GBR. Dist: Parkwest Pubns., Inc.

Award, Anna, et al. The Farmer & His Sons & the Donkey in the Lion's Den. 2014. (ENG.). 24p. (J). pap. 6.95 *(978-1-84135-960-1(2))* Award Pubns. Ltd. GBR. Dist: Parkwest Pubns., Inc.

—The Fox & the Stork & the Man, His Son & the Donkey. 2014. (ENG.). 24p. (J). pap. 6.95 *(978-1-84135-955-7(6))* Award Pubns. Ltd. GBR. Dist: Parkwest Pubns., Inc.

—Monkey & the Fishermen & the Donkey in the Pond. 2014. (ENG.). 24p. (J). pap. 6.95 *(978-1-84135-956-4(4))* Award Pubns. Ltd. GBR. Dist: Parkwest Pubns., Inc.

Barella, Laura, illus. Donkey Skin. 2011. (Flip-Up Fairy Tales Ser.). (ENG.). 24p. (J). audio compact disk *(978-1-84643-410-5(6));* (gr. 2-2). *(978-1-84643-371-9(1))* Child's Play International Ltd.

Bell, Anthea, ed. & tr. The Bremen Town Musicians. Bell, Anthea, tr. Lai, Hsin-Shih, illus. 2007. 32p. (J). (gr. -1-3). 17.95 *(978-0-88010-583-5(6),* Bell Pond Bks.) SteinerBooks, Inc.

Bell, Cece. I Yam a Donkey! Bell, Cece, illus. 2015. (ENG., Illus.). 32p. (J). (gr. -1-3). 16.99 *(978-0-544-08720-0(8))* Houghton Mifflin Harcourt Publishing Co.

Bennett, Amy Culbertson. The Little Donkey & the Shadow of the Cross. 2008. 15p. pap. 24.95 *(978-1-60563-545-3(6))* America Star Bks.

Bezek, Lyn. Daisy: The Cripple Creek Donkey. 2004. (J). pap. 7.95 *(978-1-932738-09-4(6))* Western Reflections Publishing Co.

Blair, Eric. The Donkey in the Lion's Skin: A Retelling of Aesop's Fable, 1 vol. Silverman, Dianne, illus. 2013. (My First Classic Story Ser.). (ENG.). 24p. (gr. k-3). pap. 7.10 *(978-1-4795-1855-5(7),* My First Classic Story) Picture Window Bks.

Blair, Eric & Aesop Enterprise Inc. Staff. The Donkey in the Lion's Skin: A Retelling of Aesop's Fable, 1 vol. Silverman, Dianne, illus. 2011. (My First Classic Story Ser.). (ENG.). 24p. (gr. k-3). lib. bdg. 22.65 *(978-1-4048-6506-8(3),* My First Classic Story) Picture Window Bks.

Blunt, Julia & Gilbert, Dawn. How Donkey Became GREAT. 2007. 48p. pap. 22.85 *(978-0-615-16220-1(7))* Runamuck Publishing.

A Boy & His Donkey: Individual Title Six-Packs. (Literatura 2000 Ser.). (gr. 2-3). 33.00 *(978-0-7635-0193-8(X))* Rigby Education.

Brabham, Barbara. Donkey Tales — Color with Paco! [English/Spanish Versions]. 2006. (J). 2.95 *(978-1-882185-86-3(2))* Cornerstone Publishing, Inc.

Brannon, Pat. Has a Donkey Ever Brought You Breakfast in Bed? Demming, Karen, illus. 2012. 38p. pap. 10.00 *(978-1-938634-90-1(X))* Freedom of Speech Publishing, Inc.

Brezenoff, Steve. The Grand Canyon Burros That Broke, 1 vol. Calo, Marcos, illus. 2012. (Field Trip Mysteries Ser.). (ENG.). 88p. (gr. 2-3). pap. 6.10 *(978-1-4342-4198-6(X));* lib. bdg. 25.32 *(978-1-4342-3788-0(5))* Stone Arch Bks.

Broome, Errol. The Judas Donkey. Thompson, Sharon, illus. 2003. 144p. pap. 13.50 *(978-1-920731-18-2(0))* Fremantle Pr. AUS. Dist: Independent Pubs. Group.

Broughton, Theresa. Three Amazing Farm Animals. 2008. 12p. pap. 24.95 *(978-1-60474-545-0(2))* America Star Bks.

Brown, Russ. Daisy the Donkey's First Fare. 2011. (Illus.). 24p. 10.96 *(978-1-4567-7323-6(2))* AuthorHouse.

Buchholz, Erwin. Born under a Star, 1 vol. Legg, Barbara, illus. 2009. 44p. pap. 24.95 *(978-1-61546-130-1(2))* America Star Bks.

Calopisis, Dennis. The Lonely Little Donkey. 2010. 26p. 14.98 *(978-0-557-20849-4(1))* Lulu Pr., Inc.

Caplan, Frank A. The Donkey Who Lost His Tail. 2010. (Illus.). 20p. 12.49 *(978-1-4520-2778-4(1))* AuthorHouse.

Cerimele, Ron. Hee, Haw, & a Donkey Named Sam. 2007. (ENG.). 20p. per. 24.95 *(978-1-4241-9013-3(4))* America Star Bks.

Cochrane, Ian. Shian & the Corryvreckan. 2013. (Illus.). 96p. pap. *(978-1-909465-09-1(7))* Cloister Hse. Pr., The.

Cohen, Barbara Berkule. The Donkey That Couldn't Find His Bray. 2011. 28p. pap. 24.95 *(978-1-4560-3737-6(4))* America Star Bks.

Colvin, Adele. The Donkey of Tarsus: His Tales about the Apostle Paul, 1 vol. Carmichael, Peyton, illus. 2010. (Donkey Tales Ser.). (ENG.). 32p. (J). (gr. k-3). 16.99 *(978-1-58980-780-8(4))* Pelican Publishing Co., Inc.

Colvin, Adele Bibb. The Donkey's Easter Tale, 1 vol. Carmichael, Peyton, illus. 2008. (Donkey Tales Ser.). (ENG.). 32p. (J). (gr. k-3). 16.99 *(978-1-58980-593-4(3))* Pelican Publishing Co., Inc.

Cook, Norman. Sam in the Crimea: A Victorian Adventure Based on the Work of Lord Shaftesbury. 2007. (Illus.). 128p. (J). (gr. 4-7). per. 9.00 *(978-1-84625-045-3(5))* DayOne Pubns. GBR. Dist: Send The Light Distribution LLC.

Cooper, Paul Fenimore. Tal, His Marvelous Adventures with Noom-Zor-Noom. Reeves, Ruth, illus. 80th ed. 2009. 305p. (J). pap. 12.95 *(978-1-930900-41-7(4))* Purple Hse. Pr.

Cosgrove, Stephen. Jalopy. 2011. (Orig.). (J). *(978-0-86592-797-1(9))* Rourke Enterprises, Inc.

Cowan, Dolly. Yeehaw, the Chosen Donkey. 2012. 26p. pap. 13.95 *(978-1-4497-6675-7(7),* WestBow Pr.) Author Solutions, Inc.

Cox, Roy. And They Fell Fast Asleep. McCall, Anthony, illus. 2012. 48p. pap. 15.95 *(978-1-61493-045-7(7))* Peppertree Pr., The.

Cunningham, Sarah. The Donkey in the Living Room: A Tradition That Celebrates the Real Meaning of Christmas. Foster, Michael K., illus. 2014. (ENG.). 32p. (J). (gr. -1-3). 14.99 *(978-1-4336-8317-6(2),* B&H Kids) B&H Publishing Group.

—The Donkey in the Living Room Nativity Set: A Tradition That Celebrates the True Meaning of Christmas. Foster, Michael K., illus. 2014. (ENG.). 32p. (J). (gr. -1-3). 29.99 *(978-1-4336-8448-7(9),* B&H Kids) B&H Publishing Group.

Cunningham, Terri Ann. Hillary Hind Hooth Lost Her Tooth. 2009. 28p. pap. 14.49 *(978-1-4389-3959-9(0))* AuthorHouse.

Dahiméne, Adelheid. Donkeys. Stollinger, Heide, illus. 2014. (ENG.). 48p. (J). (gr. k-3). 17.95 *(978-0-7358-4160-4(8))* North-South Bks., Inc.

Daly, Niki. Thank You, Jackson: How One Little Boy Makes a Big Difference. Daly, Jude, illus. 2015. (ENG.). 32p. (J). (gr. -1-3). 17.99 *(978-1-84780-484-6(5),* Frances Lincoln) Quarto Publishing Group UK GBR. Dist: Hachette Bk. Group.

De Segur, Comtesse & Willard, J. H. The Story of a Donkey. 2004. reprint ed. pap. 20.95 *(978-1-4179-4273-2(8))* Kessinger Publishing, LLC.

De Segur, Condesa. Memorias de un Asno. (Torre de Papel Ser.). (SPA.). (YA). (gr. 6-18). 7.95 *(978-958-04-4144-1(8))* Norma S.A. COL. Dist: Distribuidora Norma, Inc.

Dowley, Tim. El Viaje Especial del Burrito - Donkey's Special Ride. (Serie Libros de Carton - Board Bks.). pap. *(978-1-56063-956-5(3))* Editorial Unilit.

Duggan, Janet. The Christmas Story As Told by Assellus the Christmas Donkey. Robertson, Catherine, illus. 2009. (ENG.). 44p. *(978-0-9563389-1-4(7))* Janet Duggan.

Duvoisin, Roger. Donkey-Donkey. 2016. (ENG., Illus.). 32p. (J). (-k). 16.95 *(978-1-59017-964-2(1),* NYR Children's Collection) New York Review of Bks., Inc., The.

Estrada, Pau. Pedro's Burro. Estrada, Pau, illus. 2007. (My First I Can Read Bks.). (Illus.). 32p. (J). (gr. -1-k). lib. bdg. 16.89 *(978-0-06-056032-4(0))* HarperCollins Pubs.

Estrada, Pau & Capucilli, Alyssa Satin. Pedro's Burro. Estrada, Pau, illus. 2008. (My First I Can Read Ser.). (ENG., Illus.). 32p. (J). (gr. -1 — 1). pap. 3.99 *(978-0-06-056033-1(9))* HarperCollins Pubs.

Ferrell, Annie K. Benny the Burro Bears His Burden. 2004. 24p. pap. 24.95 *(978-1-4137-2495-0(7))* PublishAmerica, Inc.

Fry, Debbie, illus. Donkeywise & Otherwise: The Story of Daisy Doo & Dudley Duz. 2004. 44p. (J). (978-0-9759647-0-5(4), 1238040) Fry, Debbie.

Golden Books. Shrek Little Golden Book. Nedelcu, Ovi, illus. 2017. (Little Golden Book Ser.). (ENG.). 24p. (J). (-k). 4.99 (**978-1-5247-6770-9(0)**, Golden Bks.) Random Hse. Children's Bks.

Gorla, Stefano. A Donkey's Tale. Marchetti, Angela, illus. 2013. 64p. (J). pap. 9.95 (978-0-8198-1901-7(8)) Pauline Bks. & Media.

Griffin, Lydia. Prunes & Rupe. Hunt, Judith, illus. 2007. 32p. (J). 16.00 (978-0-86541-086-2(0)) Filter Pr., LLC.

Griggs, Rosemarie. The Adventures of Donkey Tom Volume 2: Crystal Forest. 2012. 40p. pap. 32.70 (978-1-4797-0553-5(5)) Xlibris Corp.

Grindley, Sally, et al. Pam Mae'r Awyr Yn Las? Stori Gan Sally Grindley. 2005. (WEL., Illus.). 25p. (978-1-85596-265-1(9)) Dref Wen.

Guibert, Emmanuel. Just a Donkey Like You & Me. 2013. (Ariol Graphic Novels Ser.). (ENG., Illus.). 124p. (J). (gr. 1-5). pap. 12.99 (978-1-59707-399-8(7), 9781597073998) Papercutz.

—Just a Donkey Like You & Me. 2013. (Ariol Ser.: 1). (J). lib. bdg. 24.50 (978-0-606-28692-3(6), Turtleback) Turtleback Bks.

—The Teeth of the Rabbit. 2016. (Ariol Ser.: 9). (J). lib. bdg. 24.50 (978-0-606-39481-9(8)) Turtleback Bks.

—The Three Donkeys. 2016. (Ariol Ser.: 8). (J). lib. bdg. 24.50 (978-0-606-38372-1(7)) Turtleback Bks.

—Where's Petula? 2015. (Ariol Ser.: 7). (J). lib. bdg. 20.85 (978-0-606-37284-8(9)) Turtleback Bks.

Hamilton, Elizabeth L. Dorrie Donkey's Cooperation Camp. l.t. ed. 2005. (Character Critters Ser.: No. 12). (Illus.). 32p. (J). per. 5.95 (978-0-9754629-9-7(7), Character-in-Action) Quiet Impact, Inc.

Harrinsson, Nelson. Mario, Donkey Cuco & the Mango Tree. 2011. 48p. pap. 24.95 (978-1-4560-4911-9(9)) America Star Bks.

Henry, Marguerite. Brighty of the Grand Canyon. 2015. (ENG., Illus.). 256p. (J). (gr. 3-7). 19.99 (978-1-4814-1582-8(4), Aladdin) Simon & Schuster Children's Publishing.

Hinkelman, Carole & Rebik, Nan. The Herman Chronicles: *Herman the Horrible Trailer Mouse *Herman & the Donkeys * Herman's Midnight Trek * Herman's Vacation. 2012. 84p. (gr. 2-4). pap. 11.50 (978-1-4669-5202-7(4)) Trafford Publishing.

Hipp, Diane. Stuart the Donkey: A Tale of His Tail. Hill, T. J., illus. 2010. 52p. pap. 21.99 (978-1-4520-3420-1(6)) AuthorHouse.

Holliday, Bobby. Hamor: The Road to Jerusalem. 2013. (ENG., Illus.). 32p. (J). 18.99 (978-0-9829082-3-5(7)) Lady Hawk Pr.

Howard, Annabelle. A Father, His Son, & Their Donkey: An Aesop's Fable. 2006. (J). pap. (978-1-4108-7154-1(1)) Benchmark Education Co.

Hunt, Wayne. Zack & the Validators: Good As Gold. 2011. 138p. pap. 19.99 (978-1-4653-5816-5(1)) Xlibris Corp.

Ippolito, Eva Marie. The Donkey's Tale. Ippolito, Eva Marie, illus. 2003. (Illus.). lll, 15p. (J). (gr. -1-3). pap. 1.95 (978-0-9705350-3-0(1)) Ippolito, Eva Marie.

Jaxland, Sheila. Mylo. 2013. 32p. pap. 12.95 (978-0-578-12595-4(1)) Roald Publishing.

Jiménez, Juan Ramón. Platero y Yo. (SPA.). 192p. (J). 13.95 (978-84-206-1851-7(9), AZ1851); (Illus.). 159p. 15.95 (978-84-206-3408-1(5)) Alianza Editorial, S. A. ESP. Dist: Continental Bk. Co., Inc., Distribooks, Inc.

—Platero y Yo. (SPA.). (J). pap. 9.95 (978-968-432-357-5(3), PM223) Editorial Porrua MEX. Dist: Continental Bk. Co., Inc.

—Platero y Yo. annot. ed. (SPA., Illus.). 232p. (J). 15.95 (978-84-207-2636-6(2), ANY010) Grupo Anaya, S.A. ESP. Dist: Continental Bk. Co., Inc.

—Platero y Yo (Platero & I) (SPA.). (J). pap. 9.95 (978-968-416-022-4(4), AOR01) Fernandez USA Publishing.

Johnson, Joanne Gail. Donkey & the Racehorse. Ferris, Carole Anne, illus. 2011. (ENG.). 48p. pap. 12.00 (978-0-230-02552-3(8), Macmillan) Pan Macmillan GBR. Dist: Macmillan.

Johnson, Veronica E. The Donkey Ride. 2006. per. 9.95 (978-0-9779600-0-2(5)) Euphema Press.

Jumbo & the Lost Tail. 2004. (J). per. 15.99 (978-0-9744205-0-9(6)) Golden Eagle Publishing Hse., Inc.

Kilimo, R. The Donkey Who Wanted to Be a Lion. 2004. (Illus.). 16p. pap. (978-9966-25-169-5(3)) Heinemann Kenya, Limited (East African Educational Publishers Ltd E.A.E.P.) KEN. Dist: Michigan State Univ. Pr.

King, Emily. Clopper & the Night Travelers. Olson, Ed, illus. 2007. 32p. (J). (gr. -1-3). 10.99 (978-0-8254-3066-4(6)) Kregel Pubns.

—Clopper the Christmas Donkey. 1 vol. Olson, Ed, illus. 2003. 32p. (J). 12.99 (978-0-8254-3069-5(0)) Kregel Pubns.

Kirkland, Jo. Donald the Donkey. 2011. 28p. (gr. -1). pap. 13.55 (978-1-4567-6892-8(1)) AuthorHouse.

Krueger, T. W. Donkeys Are Special & So Are You! Bohart, Lisa, illus. 2013. (ENG.). 46p. (J). 12.99 (978-0-9887454-0-7(2)) Donkey Publishing.

Leech, Carlyle & Leech, Thirma. Ha-Ha Farm. 2009. (ENG., Illus.). 24p. (J). (gr. -1-1). 14.95 (978-1-59583-396-9(X), 9781595833969, Green Tiger Pr.) Laughing Elephant.

Mackall, Dandi Daley. One Small Donkey. 1 vol. 2016. (ENG., Illus.). 32p. (J). 14.99 (978-0-7180-8747-0(X)) Nelson, Thomas Inc.

—One Small Donkey for Little Ones. 1 vol. 2016. (ENG., Illus.). 20p. (J). bds. 8.99 (978-0-7180-8247-5(8)) Nelson, Thomas Inc.

Meredith, Susan Markowitz, retold by. The Donkey & the Rock. 2016. (Spring Forward Ser.). (J). (gr. 2). (978-1-4900-9447-2(4)) Benchmark Education Co.

Meyer, Diana. Samson's Great Adventure. 2009. 32p. pap. 10.50 (978-1-60693-029-8(X), Eloquent Bks.) Strategic Book Publishing & Rights Agency (SBPRA).

Monks, Lydia. Where's Your Eee-Orrh? 2015. (ENG., Illus.). 32p. (J). (gr. -1-k). pap. 10.99 (978-1-4052-7814-0(5)) Egmont Bks., Ltd. GBR. Dist: Independent Pubs. Group.

Morgan, Vicky S. Jim & Me & Theo T. 2011. 28p. pap. 21.99 (978-1-4568-8124-5(8)) Xlibris Corp.

Mundy, Charlene & Chapline, Jo. David's Donkey Tales. 2007. 73p. pap. 12.50 (978-0-615-16825-8(6)) Knee-High Adventures.

Newton, Jill, illus. Crash Bang Donkey! 2015. 32p. (J). (978-1-4896-3858-8(X)) Weigl Pubs., Inc.

Un nino y su Burro: Individual Title Six-Packs. (Literatura 2000 Ser.). (SPA.). (gr. 2-3). 33.00 (978-0-7635-1097-8(1)) Rigby Education.

Nunes, Ernest. Oh! How I Wish I Could Play Soccer with Ernie & the Dreamers. 2013. 70p. pap. 12.99 (978-1-62509-705-7(0)) Salem Author Services.

O'Donnell, Jane. Hey! There's a Donkey in the Boro. 2011. 16p. pap. 10.70 (978-1-4634-0157-3(4)) AuthorHouse.

Oghenekaro, Elsie Ovhe. The Speaking Donkey & other Bible Stories. 2011. (Illus.). 40p. (gr. 1-2). pap. 18.68 (978-1-4567-7930-6(3)) AuthorHouse.

Orme, David. The Donkey That Went Too Fast. Rivers, Ruth, illus. 2005. 32p. (J). lib. bdg. 9.00 (978-1-4242-0890-6(4)) Fitzgerald Bks.

Parker, Emma. The Spaghetti Tree. 2010. (Illus.). pap. (978-1-877561-02-3(9)) First Edition Ltd.

Pauline Wall & Shelley Smith. What the Owl Saw: (a Christmas Story) 2012. 20p. pap. 15.19 (978-1-4669-2813-8(1)) Trafford Publishing.

Paulk, Earl. Fir for a King: The Story of Obed, the Ugly Donkey. (J). pap. 9.95 (978-0-917595-63-9(7)) Cathedral of the Holy Spirit.

Payot Karpathakis, Emmanuelle. Pixie en Vacaciones. 2013. 40p. pap. (978-1-909193-28-4(3)) Summertime Publishing.

—Pixie's Holidays. 2013. 40p. pap. (978-1-909193-25-3(9)) Summertime Publishing.

Pequeña the Burro: Evaluation Guide. 2006. (J). (978-1-55942-420-2(6)) Witcher Productions.

Phillips, Rachelle. Dinkey the Donkey. Randolph, Carolyn, illus. l.t. ed. 2004. 24p. (J). 7.50 (978-0-9748591-5-6(X), MSP) Main St Publishing, Inc.

Pidutti, Nancy L. José the Donkey. 2013. 36p. pap. 16.99 (978-1-4497-9213-8(8), WestBow Pr.) Author Solutions, Inc.

Pierson, Rich. Adventures of Fred the Donkey. 2012. 48p. pap. 21.99 (978-1-4691-7343-6(3)) Xlibris Corp.

Productions, Donkey Ollie. The Tales of Donkey Ollie. 2012. (ENG.). pap. (978-1-4675-4475-7(2)) Independent Pub.

Ratcliffe, Bob. The Dawn Hee-Haw. 2009. 32p. pap. 13.00 (978-1-60860-508-8(6), Eloquent Bks.) Strategic Book Publishing & Rights Agency (SBPRA).

Rath, Tom H. Donkey Oatie's Christmas Pageant. Townshend, Katie, illus. 2013. 24p. pap. (978-0-9918033-6-1(1)) Wood Islands Prints.

—Donkey Oatie's Fashion Statement. MacAdam, Ian Paul, illus. 2012. 32p. pap. (978-0-9866065-7-1(X)) Wood Islands Prints.

—Donkey Oatie's Field Trip. Gaudet, Christine, illus. 2013. 26p. pap. (978-0-9918033-4-7(5)) Wood Islands Prints.

—Donkey Oatie's Impossible Dream. MacAdam, Reegory, illus. 2012. 24p. pap. (978-0-9866065-5-7(3)) Wood Islands Prints.

Ray, Rhonda. David Donkey Had a Lot of Fun. 2012. 28p. (-18). pap. 24.95 (978-1-4626-9298-9(2)) America Star Bks.

Reid, Pamela Carrington. Little One. Tolman, Tom, illus. 2010. (J). (978-1-59811-574-1(X)) Covenant Communications.

Reviejo Hernandez, Carlos. Platero y Juan Ramon. Wensell, Ulises, illus. 2006. (SPA.). 29p. (J). (gr. 6-8). 12.99 (978-1-933032-10-8(3)) Lectorum Pubns., Inc.

Rizvi, Sobia. Zebra Stripes. 2011. 24p. pap. 15.99 (978-1-4653-4618-6(X)) Xlibris Corp.

Russell, Natalie. Donkey's Busy Day. Russell, Natalie, illus. 2009. (ENG., Illus.). 32p. (J). (gr. k-k). pap. 11.95 (978-0-7475-9547-2(X)) Bloomsbury Publishing Plc GBR. Dist: Independent Pubs. Group.

Schloesser, Natalie, illus. The Donkey's Ear. 2005. 34p. (J). 10.00 (978-0-9743850-1-3(8)) O'Brien, Gerard.

Schmidt, Troy. The Donkey Tells His Side of the Story: Hey God, I'm Sorry to Be Stubborn, but I Just Don't Like Anyone Riding on My Back! Jones, Cory, illus. 2014. (ENG.). 32p. (gr. -1-3). 9.99 (978-1-4336-8309-1(1), B&H Kids) B&H Publishing Group.

Segur, Condesa de. MEMORIAS DE UN BURRITO. (SPA., Illus.). (YA). 11.95 (978-84-7281-087-7(9), AF1087) Auriga, Ediciones S.A. ESP. Dist: Continental Bk. Co., Inc.

Sehlin, Gunhild. Mary's Little Donkey: And the Flight to Egypt. 1 vol. Latham, Hugh & Maclean, Donald, trs. from SWE. Verheijen, Jan, illus. 2nd rev. ed. 2004. (ENG.). 160p. (J). (gr. 3-6). pap. 12.00 (978-0-86315-064-7(0)) Floris Bks. GBR. Dist: SteinerBooks, Inc.

Sharpe, Charlotte. Jasper & Jesus at the Well. Ettinger, Charles, illus. 2012. 16p. pap. 11.99 (978-1-937129-33-0(0)) Faithful Life Pubs.

Simpson, Wanda. Jupiter the Space Donkey. 1 vol. 2009. 17p. pap. 24.95 (978-1-61582-733-6(1)) PublishAmerica, Inc.

Smith, Jimmie. Jonas Little Donkey, Big Job. 2013. 20p. pap. 11.99 (978-1-62509-331-8(4)) Salem Author Services.

Smith, Lane. It's a Book. Smith, Lane, illus. 2010. (ENG., Illus.). 32p. (J). (gr. 1-5). 15.99 (978-1-59643-606-0(9), 9781596436060) Roaring Brook Pr.

—It's a Little Book. 2011. (ENG., Illus.). 24p. (J). (— 1). bds. 7.99 (978-1-59643-758-6(8), 9781596437586) Roaring Brook Pr.

Smith, Pieter Ernst. A Donkey Is Not Stupid, a Donkey Can Think. Shirley-Smith, Sanette, illus. 2011. 24p. pap. 11.50 (978-1-61204-039-4(X), Eloquent Bks.) Strategic Book Publishing & Rights Agency (SBPRA).

Sommer, Carl. The Donkey, Fox, & the Lion. Noé, Ignacio, illus. 2016. (ENG.). 32p. (J). (gr. k-4). lib. bdg. 16.95 (978-1-57537-926-5(0), Another Sommer-Time Story) Advance Publishing, Inc.

Steig, William. Farmer Palmer's Wagon Ride. Steig, William, illus. 2014. (ENG., Illus.). 32p. (J). (gr. -1-3). 6.99 (978-1-250-05791-4(4), 9781250057914) Square Fish.

—Sylvester & the Magic Pebble. Steig, William, illus. 2012. (ENG., Illus.). 32p. (J). (gr. -1-2). pap. 9.99 (978-1-4424-3560-5(7), Little Simon) Little Simon.

—Sylvester & the Magic Pebble. Steig, William, illus. 2005. (ENG., Illus.). 42p. (J). (gr. -1-3). 17.99 (978-1-4169-0206-5(6), Simon & Schuster Bks. For Young Readers) Simon & Schuster Bks. For Young Readers.

—Sylvester & the Magic Pebble. Steig, William, illus. 2006. (Stories to Go! Ser.). (Illus.). 32p. (J). (gr. -1-3). 4.99 (978-1-4169-1857-8(4), Simon & Schuster/Paula Wiseman Bks.) Simon & Schuster/Paula Wiseman Bks.

Stever, Karen Malloy. Jabin, the Talking Donkey: In Jerusalem. 2012. 24p. pap. 24.95 (978-1-4626-8285-0(5)) America Star Bks.

Storck, Patrick. Dreamworks Shrek Comics Collection. 2016. (J). lib. bdg. 20.85 (978-0-606-39427-7(3)) Turtleback Bks.

Tak, Bibi Dumon. Mikis & the Donkey. Hopman, Philip, illus. 2014. (ENG.). 89p. (J). 13.00 (978-0-8028-5430-8(3), Eerdmans Bks For Young Readers) Eerdmans, William B. Publishing Co.

Tarlow, Ellen. Pinwheel Days. 1 vol. Parker, Gretel, illus. 2007. (ENG.). 32p. (J). (gr. -1-3). pap. 6.95 (978-1-59572-059-7(6)) Star Bright Bks., Inc.

Taylor, Sean. Crocodiles Are the Best Animals of All! Shaw, Hannah, illus. 2009. (Time to Read Ser.). (ENG.). 32p. (J). (gr. -1-k). (978-1-84507-904-8(3)) Rough Guides, Ltd.

Terbay, Susan Handle. Jeremiah & the Man. 6 vols., Vol. 1. Mariants, tr. Children-Oln, illus. 2007. 43p. (J). (gr. 1-6). pap. (978-0-9628309-8-3(4)) Marianist Pr.

Thornton, Vera E. The Useless Donkey. 2007. 36p. per. 24.95 (978-1-4241-8736-2(2)) America Star Bks.

Toledo, Leila J. Little Peter & Sela. Davis, Chad L., illus. l.t. ed. 2004. 17p. (J). pap. 8.95 (978-0-9753118-0-6(8)) Bimini Bks.

The Trouble with Patrick: Individual Title Six-Packs. (Action Packs Ser.). 120p. (gr. 3-5). 44.00 (978-0-7635-8431-3(2)) Rigby Education.

Trusler, Heidi Jo. Firecracker the Miniature Donkey: Makes A Marvelous Choice! 2009. 25p. (J). pap. 13.95 (978-1-4327-4153-2(5)) Outskirts Pr., Inc.

Watt, Fiona. That's Not My Donkey. Wells, Rachel, illus. 2011. (Touchy-Feely Board Books Ser.). 10p. (J). ring bd. 8.99 (978-0-7945-3012-9(5), Usborne) EDC Publishing.

Weigl Publishers, creator. The Wild Donkey & the Tame Donkey: Why Should You Not Judge Others by Their Appearance? 2013. (AV2 Animated Storytime Ser.: Vol. 20). (ENG., Illus.). 32p. (J). (gr. -1-3). lib. bdg. 29.99 (978-1-62127-924-2(3), AV2 by Weigl) Weigl Pubs., Inc.

Weston Woods Staff, creator. Sylvester & the Magic Pebble. 2011. 38.75 (978-0-439-72898-0(3)); 29.95 (978-0-439-73522-3(X)) Weston Woods Studios, Inc.

Williams, Emma. The Story of Hurry. Quraishi, Ibrahim, illus. 2014. (ENG.). 38p. (J). (gr. -1-2). 16.95 (978-1-60980-589-0(5), Triangle Square) Seven Stories Pr.

Wohlford, Connie. Joy Comes to Bethlehem. 2012. 38p. pap. 16.99 (978-1-4497-5809-7(6), WestBow Pr.) Author Solutions, Inc.

Woods, Denise M. & McKelvain, Dana. The Legend of the Donkey's Cross. 2004. (Illus.). 32p. (J). per. 12.99 (978-1-58930-112-2(9)) Selah Publishing Group, LLC.

Wright, Boyd. Donkey Tales. 2006. 74p. pap. 16.95 (978-1-4241-1900-4(6)) PublishAmerica, Inc.

DORA THE EXPLORER (FICTITIOUS CHARACTER)—FICTION

A and J Studios Staff. Dora's Three Little Fairy Tales. 2005. (Dora the Explorer Ser.). (ENG., Illus.). 36p. (J). bds. 10.99 (978-1-4169-0640-7(1), Simon Spotlight/Nickelodeon) Simon Spotlight/Nickelodeon.

Aikins, Dave, illus. Big Sister Dora! 2005. (Dora the Explorer Ser.). (ENG.). 24p. (J). pap. 3.99 (978-0-689-87846-6(X), Simon Spotlight/Nickelodeon) Simon Spotlight/Nickelodeon.

—Dora Saves the Snow Princess. 2008. (Dora the Explorer Ser.: 27). (ENG.). 24p. (J). (gr. -1-2). pap. 3.99 (978-1-4169-5866-6(5), Simon Spotlight/Nickelodeon) Simon Spotlight/Nickelodeon.

Artful Doodlers Limited Staff. Dora Salva a las Sirenas. 2007. (Dora la Exploradora Ser.). (SPA., Illus.). 24p. (J). (gr. -1-2). pap. 3.99 (978-1-4169-4725-7(6), Libros Para Ninos) Libros Para Ninos.

Artful Doodlers Ltd Staff. Dora Saves Mermaid Kingdom! 2007. (Dora the Explorer Ser.: 24). (ENG., Illus.). 24p. (J). (gr. -1-2). pap. 3.99 (978-1-4169-3841-5(9), Simon Spotlight/Nickelodeon) Simon Spotlight/Nickelodeon.

Beinstein, Phoebe. ¡A nadar, Boots! (Swim, Boots, Swim!) Roper, Robert, illus. 2009. (Dora la Exploradora Ser.). (SPA.). 24p. (J). pap. 3.99 (978-1-4169-7939-5(5), Libros Para Ninos) Libros Para Ninos.

—Dora. Mangano, Tom, illus. 2003. (Dora the Explorer Ser.). (ENG & SPA.). 12p. (J). bds. 7.99 (978-0-689-85484-2(6), Simon Spotlight/Nickelodeon) Simon Spotlight/Nickelodeon.

—Dora Explora los Colores. Hall, Susan & Hall, Susan, illus. 2007. (Dora la Exploradora Ser.).Tr. of Dora Explores Colors. (SPA & ENG.). 14p. (J). (gr. -1). bds. 4.99 (978-1-4169-4726-4(4), Libros Para Ninos) Libros Para Ninos.

—Dora Goes for a Ride. Fruchter, Jason, illus. 2004. (Dora the Explorer Ser.). (ENG.). 22p. (J). bds. 4.99 (978-0-689-86372-1(1), Simon Spotlight/Nickelodeon) Simon Spotlight/Nickelodeon.

—¿Qué Voy a Ser? Saunders, Zina, illus. 2007. (Dora la Exploradora Ser.).Tr. of What Will I Be? (ENG & SPA.). 14p. (J). (gr. -1). bds. 4.99 (978-1-4169-3366-3(2), Libros Para Ninos) Libros Para Ninos.

—Swim, Boots, Swim! Roper, Robert, illus. 2009. (Dora the Explorer Ser.: 29). (ENG.). 24p. (J). (gr. -1-2). pap. 3.99 (978-1-4169-7195-5(5), Simon Spotlight/Nickelodeon) Simon Spotlight/Nickelodeon.

—¡Vámonos! / Let's Go! Ziegler, Argentina Palacios, tr. Fruchter, Jason, illus. 2007. (Dora la Exploradora Ser.). (SPA & ENG.). 14p. (J). bds. 4.99 (978-1-4169-3367-0(0), Libros Para Ninos) Libros Para Ninos.

Beinstein, Phoebe & A and J Studios Staff. Di "Aaaa"! Dora Va al Médico. 2008. (Dora la Exploradora Ser.). (SPA & ENG., Illus.). 24p. (J). (gr. -1-2). pap. 3.99 (978-1-4169-5492-7(9), Libros Para Ninos) Libros Para Ninos.

—Say Ahhh! Dora Goes to the Doctor. 2008. (Dora the Explorer Ser.: 26). (ENG., Illus.). 24p. (J). (gr. -1-2). pap. 3.99 (978-1-4169-5430-9(9), Simon Spotlight/Nickelodeon) Simon Spotlight/Nickelodeon.

Beinstein, Phoebe & Silverhardt, Lauryn. Dora's Little Library. 2009. (Dora the Explorer Ser.). (ENG.). 70p. (J). 6.99 (978-1-4169-8029-2(6), Simon Spotlight/Nickelodeon) Simon Spotlight/Nickelodeon.

Beinstein, Phoebe, et al. Dora's Stories: A Boxed Set. 2005. (Dora the Explorer Ser.). (ENG.). 56p. (J). bds. 9.99 (978-1-4169-0035-1(7), Simon Spotlight/Nickelodeon) Simon Spotlight/Nickelodeon.

Bergen, Lara Rice & Bergen, Lara. Dora's Sleepover. Miller, Victoria, illus. 2006. (Dora the Explorer Ser.: 12). (ENG.). 24p. (J). (gr. -1-1). pap. 3.99 (978-1-4169-1508-9(7), Simon Spotlight/Nickelodeon) Simon Spotlight/Nickelodeon.

Burroughs, Caleb. Dora the Explorer to the Moon. Miller, Victoria, illus. 2007. (Play a Tune Tale Ser.). 16p. (J). (gr. -1-3). 12.98 (978-1-4127-8830-4(7)) Publications International, Ltd.

David, Erica. The Big Pony Race. Fruchter, Jason, illus. 2006. 27p. (J). (978-0-7172-9869-3(8)) Scholastic, Inc.

Depken, Kristen L. Fairytale Magic. 2014. (Dora the Explorer Step into Reading Ser.). lib. bdg. 13.55 (978-0-606-36011-1(5)) Turtleback Bks.

—Fairytale Magic (Dora the Explorer) Random House & Miller, Victoria, illus. 2014. (Step into Reading Ser.). (ENG.). 24p. (J). (gr. -1-1). 3.99 (978-0-385-37503-0(4), Random Hse. Bks. for Young Readers) Random Hse. Children's Bks.

—Island of the Lost Horses (Dora & Friends) Aikins, David, illus. 2015. (Step into Reading Ser.). (ENG.). 24p. (J). (gr. -1-1). 4.99 (978-0-553-52093-4(8), Random Hse. Bks. for Young Readers) Random Hse. Children's Bks.

—We Love to Dance! 2015. (Dora the Explorer Step into Reading Ser.). lib. bdg. 14.75 (978-0-606-36396-9(3)) Turtleback Bks.

—We Love to Dance! (Dora & Friends) Aikins, David, illus. 2015. (Step into Reading Ser.). (ENG.). 24p. (J). (gr. -1-1). 4.99 (978-0-553-50857-4(1), Random Hse. Bks. for Young Readers) Random Hse. Children's Bks.

Dominguez, Adriana, tr. Dora y la Aventura de Cumpleaños. Roper, Robert, illus. 2010. (Dora la Exploradora Ser.). (SPA.). 24p. (J). 6.99 (978-1-4424-0286-7(5), Libros Para Ninos) Libros Para Ninos.

Dora the Explorer Publishing Staff. Dora the Explorer Dora Loves Easter! 2014. (Hugs Book Ser.: 2). (ENG.). 10p. (J). (gr. -1-k). bds. 10.99 (978-0-7944-3032-0(5)) Reader's Digest Assn., Inc., The.

—Dora the Explorer Holidays Are for Hugs: A Hugs Book. 2013. (Hugs Book Ser.: 1). (ENG.). 10p. (J). (gr. -1-k). bds. 10.99 (978-0-7944-2917-1(3)) Reader's Digest Assn., Inc., The.

Dora's Magical Adventures, Set. 2008. (Dora the Explorer Ser.). (ENG.). 144p. (J). pap. 10.99 (978-1-4169-7583-0(7), Simon Spotlight/Nickelodeon) Simon Spotlight/Nickelodeon.

Driscoll, Laura. Dance to the Rescue. Aikins, Dave, illus. 2005. 24p. (J). lib. bdg. 9.00 (978-1-4242-0981-1(1)) Fitzgerald Bks.

—Where Is Baby Jaguar? Mangano, Tom & Miller, Victoria, illus. 2011. (Dora la Exploradora Ser.). (ENG.). 24p. (J). pap. 3.99 (978-1-4424-1398-6(0), Simon Spotlight/Nickelodeon) Simon Spotlight/Nickelodeon.

Echeverria, Jessica. Dora y el Día lluvioso. Savitsky, Steven, illus. 2009. (Dora la Exploradora Ser.). Orig. Title: Dora & the Rainy Day. (SPA.). 26p. (J). (gr. -1). bds. 5.99 (978-1-4169-7186-3(6), Libros Para Ninos) Libros Para Ninos.

Giddy Up Staff, contrib. by. Dora Surprize Ink Book 3. 2009. (J). 6.99 (978-1-932125-61-0(2)) Giddy Up, LLC.

Golden Books. ABC Animals (Dora the Explorer) McGee, Warner, illus. 2013. (Color Plus Card Stock Ser.). (ENG.). 48p. (J). (gr. -1-2). pap. 3.99 (978-0-307-98218-6(1), Golden Bks.) Random Hse. Children's Bks.

—The Big Ballet Show (Dora the Explorer) Loter, Inc., illus. 2012. (Little Golden Book Ser.). (ENG & SPA.). 24p. (J). (gr. k-k). 4.99 (978-0-307-93094-1(7), Golden Bks.) Random Hse. Children's Bks.

—Dora's Christmas Carol (Dora the Explorer) Goddard, Brenda & Haskett, Dan, illus. 2012. (Big Golden Book Ser.). (ENG.). 48p. (J). (gr. -1-2). 9.99 (978-0-307-97592-8(4), Golden Bks.) Random Hse. Children's Bks.

—Hooray for Dora! (Dora the Explorer) Golden Books, illus. 2012. (Super Jumbo Coloring Book Ser.). (ENG., Illus.). 416p. (J). (gr. -1-2). pap. 10.99 (978-0-307-93093-4(9), Golden Bks.) Random Hse. Children's Bks.

—One Spooky Night (Dora & Friends) Aikins, David, illus. 2015. (Holographic Sticker Book Ser.). (ENG.). 64p. (J). (gr. -1-2). pap. 4.99 (978-0-553-52118-4(7), Golden Bks.) Random Hse. Children's Bks.

—Rainbow Rescue! (Dora the Explorer) Miller, Victoria, illus. 2014. (Color Plus Chunky Crayons Ser.). (ENG.). 48p. (J). (gr. -1-2). pap. 3.99 (978-0-385-37436-1(4), Golden Bks.) Random Hse. Children's Bks.

—Welcome to the City! (Dora & Friends) Sciarrone, Claudio, illus. 2014. (Color Plus Chunky Crayons Ser.). (ENG.). 48p. (J). (gr. -1-2). pap. 3.99 (978-0-385-38412-4(2), Golden Bks.) Random Hse. Children's Bks.

—Welcome to Wonderland! (Dora the Explorer) Miller, Victoria, illus. 2014. (Color Plus Chunky Crayons Ser.). (ENG.). 48p. (J). (gr. -1-2). pap. 3.99 (978-0-449-81760-5(1), Golden Bks.) Random Hse. Children's Bks.

Golden Books, illus. Nickelodeon Little Golden Book Library (Nickelodeon). 5 vols. 2015. (ENG.). 120p. (J). (-k). 24.95 (978-0-553-50797-3(4), Golden Bks.) Random Hse. Children's Bks.

Golden Books Staff. Christmas Is Coming! (Dora the Explorer) McGee, Warner, illus. 2011. (Glitter Sticker Book Ser.). (ENG.). 64p. (J). (gr. -1-2). pap. 4.99 (978-0-375-87393-5(7), Golden Bks.) Random Hse. Children's Bks.

—Dora the Explorer Fun Kit! , Kit. Golden Books Staff, illus. 2010. (Fun Kit Ser.). (ENG., Illus.). 64p. (J). (gr. -1-2). 9.99 (978-0-375-86527-5(6), Golden Bks.) Random Hse. Children's Bks.

—Fairy Magic (Dora the Explorer) Fruchter, Jason, illus. 2012. (Color Plus Chunky Crayons Ser.). (ENG.). 48p. (J). (gr. -1-2). pap. 3.99 (978-0-307-93030-9(0), Golden Bks.) Random Hse. Children's Bks.

Golden Books Staff & Carbone, Courtney. Grandma's House (Dora the Explorer) Goddard, Brenda & Haskett, Dan, illus. 2013. (Little Golden Book Ser.). (ENG.). 24p. (J). (-k). 3.99 (978-0-307-98105-9(3), Golden Bks.) Random Hse. Children's Bks.

Hall, Susan, illus. Dora's Cousin Diego. 2011. (Dora & Diego Ser.). (ENG.). 24p. (J). pap. 3.99 (978-1-4424-1399-3(9), Simon Spotlight/Nickelodeon) Simon Spotlight/Nickelodeon.

Hinkler Studios Staff., ed. Dora the Explorer Story Vision. 2012. (Story Vision Ser.). 96p. (J). 12.99 (978-1-74181-224-4(0)) Hinkler Bks. Pty, Ltd. AUS. Dist: Ideals Pubns.

Inches, Alison. Big Sister Dora! Aikins, Dave, illus. 2005. (Dora the Explorer Ser.: 13). 32p. (J). lib. bdg. 15.00 *(978-1-59054-790-8(X))* Fitzgerald Bks.

—Dora Loves Boots (Dora the Explorer) Random House Beginners Books Staff & MJ Illustrations Staff, illus. 2013. (Pictureback(R) Ser.). (ENG.). 16p. (J). (gr. -1-2). 4.99 *(978-0-385-37345-6(7)*, Random Hse. Bks. for Young Readers) Random Hse. Children's Bks.

—La Quinceañera. Aikins, Dave, illus. 2006. (Dora la Exploradora Ser.). (SPA.). 24p. (J). (gr. -1-3). pap. 3.99 *(978-1-4169-2462-3(0)*, Libros Para Ninos) Libros Para Ninos.

—Súper Bebés! Miller, Victoria, illus. 2006. (Dora la Exploradora Ser.). (SPA.). 24p. (J). (gr. -1-3). pap. 3.99 *(978-1-4169-2461-6(2)*, Libros Para Ninos) Libros Para Ninos.

Inches, Alison & Weiner, Eric. Dora Loves Boots. Saunders, Zina, illus. 2004. (SPA & ENG.). (J). *(978-0-7383-3858-3(3)*, Simon Spotlight/Nickelodeon) Simon Spotlight/Nickelodeon.

Keast, Jennifer H. Dora the Explorer (Giant First Play-a-Sound) 2010. 10p. (J). bds. 17.98 *(978-1-60553-544-9(3))* Publications International, Ltd.

Larsen, Kirsten. Dora's Perfect Pumpkin. Miller, Victoria, illus. 2007. (Dora the Explorer Ser.). (ENG.). 24p. (J). (gr. -1-3). pap. 3.99 *(978-1-4169-3438-7(3)*, Simon Spotlight/Nickelodeon) Simon Spotlight/Nickelodeon.

—It's Sharing Day! Zalme, Ron, illus. 2007. (SPA & ENG.). (J). pap. *(978-0-439-92237-1(2)*, Scholastic) Scholastic, Inc.

—It's Sharing Day! Zalme, Ron, illus. 2007. (Dora the Explorer Ser.: 22). (ENG.). 24p. (J). pap. 3.99 *(978-1-4169-1575-1(3)*, Simon Spotlight/Nickelodeon) Simon Spotlight/Nickelodeon.

Lee, Quinlan B. The Circus Comes to Town. 2005. (Illus.). (J). *(978-0-439-77931-9(6))* Scholastic, Inc.

—A Great Day for Soccer. 2005. (Illus.). (J). *(978-0-439-77921-0(9))* Scholastic, Inc.

—Sail Away. 2005. (Illus.). (J). *(978-0-439-77933-3(2))* Scholastic, Inc.

—Super Spies. 2005. (Illus.). (J). *(978-0-439-77923-4(5))* Scholastic, Inc.

Maher, Alex, illus. El Safari de Diego. 2007. (Go, Diego, Go! Ser.).Tr. of Diego's Safari Rescue. (SPA.). 24p. (J). (gr. -1-2). pap. 3.99 *(978-1-4169-5998-4(X)*, Libros Para Ninos) Libros Para Ninos.

Mangano, Tom, illus. Dora's World Adventure! 2006. (Dora the Explorer Ser.). (ENG.). 24p. (J). (gr. -1-2). pap. 3.99 *(978-1-4169-2447-0(7)*, Simon Spotlight/Nickelodeon) Simon Spotlight/Nickelodeon.

Mawhinney, Art, illus. Diego's Arctic Rescue. 2009. (Go, Diego, Go! Ser.). (ENG.). 24p. (J). (gr. -1-2). pap. 3.99 *(978-1-4169-8504-4(2)*, Simon Spotlight/Nickelodeon) Simon Spotlight/Nickelodeon.

—Dora & Diego Help the Dinosaur. 2011. (Dora & Diego Ser.). (ENG.). 24p. (J). pap. 3.99 *(978-1-4424-1400-6(6)*, Simon Spotlight/Nickelodeon) Simon Spotlight/Nickelodeon.

McMahon, Kara. Dress up Dora! Aikins, Dave, illus. 2009. (Dora the Explorer Ser.). (ENG.). 12p. (J). 8.99 *(978-1-4169-6067-6(8)*, Simon Spotlight/Nickelodeon) Simon Spotlight/Nickelodeon.

Miller, Victoria, illus. Dora & the Unicorn King. 2011. (Dora the Explorer Ser.). (ENG.). 24p. (J). pap. 3.99 *(978-1-4424-1312-2(3)*, Simon Spotlight/Nickelodeon) Simon Spotlight/Nickelodeon.

—Flowers for Mami Unicorn! 2010. (Dora the Explorer Ser.). (ENG.). 24p. (J). (gr. -1-2). pap. 3.99 *(978-1-4169-9064-2(X)*, Simon Spotlight/Nickelodeon) Simon Spotlight/Nickelodeon.

—Super Babies! 2006. (Dora the Explorer Ser.: 18). (ENG.). 24p. (J). (gr. -1-3). pap. 3.99 *(978-1-4169-1485-3(4)*, Simon Spotlight/Nickelodeon) Simon Spotlight/Nickelodeon.

Nickelodeon. Swim, Boots, Swim! 2013. (Dora the Explorer 8X8 Ser.). lib. bdg. 13.55 *(978-0-606-31933-1(6)*, Turtleback) Turtleback Bks.

Nickelodeon Dora the Explorer Staff. Say Boo! 2013. (Guess Who! Book Ser.: 1). (ENG.). 10p. (J). (gr. -1-1). bds. 10.99 *(978-0-7944-2857-0(6))* Reader's Digest Assn., Inc., The.

Nickelodeon Staff & LeapFrog Staff/Nickelodeon. Dora the Explorer: Dora Goes to School. 2008. (J). 13.99 *(978-1-59319-985-2(6))* LeapFrog Enterprises, Inc.

Ottersley, Martha T. Dora & the Winter Games (Dora the Explorer) Hall, Susan, illus. 2013. (Pictureback(R) Ser.). (ENG.). 24p. (J). (gr. -1-2). 3.99 *(978-0-385-37930-4(7)*, Random Hse. Bks. for Young Readers) Random Hse. Children's Bks.

—Guess Who Loves Christmas! Hall, Susan, illus. 2014. (Guess Who Ser.). (ENG.). 10p. (J). (gr. -1-k). 10.99 *(978-0-7944-3210-2(7))* Reader's Digest Assn., Inc., The.

Publications International Ltd. Staff. Dora PNO BK Follow Music. 2008. 10p. (J). 16.98 *(978-1-4127-8996-7(6)*, PIL Kids) Publications International, Ltd.

—Dora the Explorer My First Look & Find. 2006. 18p. (J). 9.98 *(978-1-4127-3909-2(8))* Phoenix International Publications, Inc.

—Little Lift & Listen Sound Dora Go to School. 2007. 12p. (J). 10.98 *(978-1-4127-8575-4(8)*, PIL Kids) Publications International, Ltd.

Publications International Ltd. Staff, creator. Let's Dance!/Vamos a Bailar! 2007. (Play-A-Sound Ser.). (J). 17.98 *(978-1-4127-9276-9(2))* Publications International, Ltd.

Publications International Ltd. Staff, ed. Dance Mat Sound Book Dora Lets Dance. 2007. (J). 17.98 *(978-1-4127-8305-7(4))* Publications International, Ltd.

—Dora Little Stars, Big Adventure. 2013. 14p. (J). bds. 16.98 *(978-1-4127-8950-9(8)*, 1412789508) Phoenix International Publications, Inc.

—Dora Says Good Night. 2011. 12p. (J). bds. 11.98 *(978-1-4508-0764-7(X))* Phoenix International Publications, Inc.

—Dora the Explorer. (J). 2010. 128p. pap. 12.98 *(978-1-60553-793-1(4))* 2007. (Illus.). 4.00 *(978-1-4127-8442-9(5))* Phoenix International Publications, Inc.

—Dora the Explorer: Island Adventure (Talking Look & Find) 2010. 16p. (J). bds. 12.98 *(978-1-60553-471-8(4))* Publications International, Ltd.

—Dora the Explorer: Little Star's Big Adventure. 2010. (J). 10.98 *(978-1-4508-0391-5(1))* Phoenix International Publications, Inc.

—Dora the Explorer: Little Star's Big Adventure (Flashlight Adventure Book & Dora Plush) 2010. (J). 24.98 *(978-1-4508-0129-4(3))* Publications International, Ltd.

—Dora the Explorer: Scavenger Hunt (Little Look & Find) 2010. 24p. (J). 2.98 *(978-1-4127-7113-9(7))* Phoenix International Publications, Inc.

—Dora the Explorer: Sounds All Around! 2011. 24p. (J). 20.98 *(978-1-4508-0011-2(4))* Phoenix International Publications, Inc.

—Dora the Explorer: We Did It! 2010. 10p. (J). bds. 14.98 *(978-1-4508-0384-7(9))* Phoenix International Publications, Inc.

—Dora the Explorer, Ding Dong! It's Dora! 2009. 12p. (J). bds. 11.98 *(978-1-4127-7598-4(1))* Phoenix International Publications, Inc.

—Dora the Explorer Look & Find. 2005. (Illus.). 24p. (J). pap. 24.98 *(978-1-4127-3318-2(9)*, 7241500) Phoenix International Publications, Inc.

—The Enchanted Forest. 2011. 14p. (J). 17.98 *(978-1-4508-0565-0(5))* Phoenix International Publications, Inc.

—It's Riddle Time! 2009. 10p. (J). bds. 11.98 *(978-1-4127-1689-5(6)*, PIL Kids) Publications International, Ltd.

—My First Story Reader Dora the Explorer. 2011. (J). 31.98 *(978-1-4508-0618-3(X))* Phoenix International Publications, Inc.

—Nickelodeon Dora the Explorer: Let's Go! (Musical Treasury) 2011. 40p. (J). bds. 13.98 *(978-1-4508-1525-3(1))* Publications International, Ltd.

—Nickelodeon Dora the Explorer: When I Grow Up. 2011. 14p. (J). bds. 13.98 *(978-1-4508-1439-3(5))* Publications International, Ltd.

—Nickelodeon Dora the Explorer: Choo, Choo, Let's Go! 2014. 12p. (J). bds. 12.98 *(978-1-4508-7591-2(2)*, 9eb3d955-9235-4e60-b5f1-58f6e60ec19b) Publications International, Ltd.

—Nickelodeon Dora the Explorer: Cook with Dora: Abuela's Birthday Fiesta. 2010. 14p. (J). bds. 16.98 *(978-1-4508-0842-2(5))* Phoenix International Publications, Inc.

—Play & Learn Piano Dora. 2011. 24p. (J). 17.98 *(978-1-4508-1165-1(5))* Phoenix International Publications, Inc.

—Potty Time with Big Sister Dora. 2011. 12p. (J). bds. 11.98 *(978-1-4508-1438-6(7))* Phoenix International Publications, Inc.

—Whats That Sound? 2009. 24p. (J). bds. 17.98 *(978-1-4127-3974-0(8)*, PIL Kids) Publications International, Ltd.

Random House. Dora Goes to School/Dora Va a la Escuela (Dora the Explorer) MJ Illustrations, illus. 2014. (Pictureback(R) Ser.). (ENG.). 24p. (J). (gr. -1-2). 3.99 *(978-0-385-37496-5(8)*, Random Hse. Bks. for Young Readers) Random Hse. Children's Bks.

—Dora's Farm Rescue! (Dora the Explorer) Random House, illus. 2014. (Pictureback(R) Ser.). (ENG., Illus.). 24p. (J). (gr. -1-2). 5.99 *(978-0-385-38516-9(1)*, Random Hse. Bks. for Young Readers) Random Hse. Children's Bks.

—Five Playtime Tales (Nick, Jr.) Random House, illus. 2015. (Step into Reading Ser.). (ENG., Illus.). 160p. (J). (gr. -1-1). 7.99 *(978-0-553-50859-8(8)*, Random Hse. Bks. for Young Readers) Random Hse. Children's Bks.

Random House Staff. Dora & the Unicorn King (Dora the Explorer) Random House Staff, illus. 2013. (Step into Reading Ser.). (ENG., Illus.). 24p. (J). (gr. -1-1). pap. 3.99 *(978-0-449-81437-6(8)*, Random Hse. Bks. for Young Readers) Random Hse. Children's Bks.

—Dora Saves the Enchanted Forest/Dora Saves Crystal Kingdom (Dora the Explorer) Random House Staff, illus. 2013. (Pictureback(R) Ser.). (ENG., Illus.). 32p. (J). (gr. -1-2). pap. 4.99 *(978-0-449-81450-5(5)*, Random Hse. Bks. for Young Readers) Random Hse. Children's Bks.

—Dora's Big Birthday Adventure (Dora the Explorer) Random House Staff, illus. 2013. (Pictureback(R) Ser.). (ENG., Illus.). 24p. (J). (gr. -1-2). pap. 3.99 *(978-0-449-81445-1(9)*, Random Hse. Bks. for Young Readers) Random Hse. Children's Bks.

—Dora's Easter Bunny Adventure (Dora the Explorer) Random House Staff, illus. 2013. (Pictureback(R) Ser.). (ENG., Illus.). 16p. (J). (gr. -1-2). pap. 3.99 *(978-0-449-81442-0(4)*, Random Hse. Bks. for Young Readers) Random Hse. Children's Bks.

—Dora's Puppy, Perrito! (Dora the Explorer) Aikins, David, illus. 2013. (Step into Reading Ser.). (ENG.). 32p. (J). (gr. -1-1). 3.99 *(978-0-449-81857-2(8)*, Random Hse. Bks. for Young Readers) Random Hse. Children's Bks.

—Good Night, Dora! (Dora the Explorer) Hall, Susan, illus. 2013. (Pictureback(R) Ser.). (ENG.). 16p. (J). (gr. -1-2). 4.99 *(978-0-449-81781-0(4)*, Random Hse. Bks. for Young Readers) Random Hse. Children's Bks.

—I Love Colors (Dora the Explorer) Random House Staff, illus. 2013. (ENG., Illus.). 24p. (J). (-k). bds. 4.99 *(978-0-449-81481-9(5)*, Random Hse. Bks. for Young Readers) Random Hse. Children's Bks.

—I Love My Mami! (Dora the Explorer) Random House Staff & Aikins, Dave, illus. 2013. (Step into Reading Ser.). (ENG.). 24p. (J). (gr. -1-1). pap. 3.99 *(978-0-449-81439-0(4)*, Random Hse. Bks. for Young Readers) Random Hse. Children's Bks.

—Swim, Boots, Swim! (Dora the Explorer) Random House Staff, illus. 2013. (Pictureback(R) Ser.). (ENG., Illus.). 24p. (J). (gr. -1-2). 3.99 *(978-0-449-81850-3(0)*, Random Hse. Bks. for Young Readers) Random Hse. Children's Bks.

Random House Staff & Roper, Robert. Dora Goes to the Doctor/Dora Goes to the Dentist (Dora the Explorer) Random House Staff, illus. 2013. (Pictureback(R) Ser.). (ENG., Illus.). 32p. (J). (gr. -1-2). 4.99 *(978-0-449-81771-1(7)*, Random Hse. Bks. for Young Readers) Random Hse. Children's Bks.

Reader's Digest Staff. Discover with Dora: Books & Magnetic Playset, Set. Nickelodeon Staff, illus. 2010. (Magnetic Playset Ser.). (ENG.). 16p. (J). (gr. -1-2). bds. 15.99 *(978-0-7944-2003-1(6)*, Reader's Digest Children's Bks.) Studio Fun International.

—Dora the Explorer My Favorite Story. 2013. (ENG.). 32p. (J). 15.99 *(978-0-7944-2795-5(2))* Reader's Digest Assn., Inc., The.

Reisner, Molly. Dora & the Unicorn King (Dora the Explorer) Aikins, David, illus. 2011. (Little Golden Book Ser.). (ENG.). 24p. (J). (gr. -1-2). 4.99 *(978-0-375-87226-6(4)*, Golden Bks.) Random Hse. Children's Bks.

—Dora's Birthday Surprise! Aikins, David, illus. 2010. (Little Golden Book Ser.). (ENG.). 24p. (J). (gr. -1-2). 3.99 *(978-0-375-86163-5(7)*, Golden Bks.) Random Hse. Children's Bks.

—Dora's Princess Party. Aikins, Dave, illus. 2009. (Dora the Explorer Ser.). (ENG.). 12p. (J). (gr. -1-1). 6.99 *(978-1-4169-9045-1(3)*, Simon Spotlight/Nickelodeon) Simon Spotlight/Nickelodeon.

—Halloween Hoedown! 2013. (Dora the Explorer 8X8 Ser.). lib. bdg. 13.55 *(978-0-606-32217-1(5)*, Turtleback) Turtleback Bks.

Reisner, Molly, et al. Nickelodeon Little Golden Book Collection (Nickelodeon) Golden Books, illus. 2012. (Little Golden Book Treasury Ser.). (ENG.). 224p. (J). (gr. -1-2). 10.99 *(978-0-375-85120-9(8)*, Golden Bks.) Random Hse. Children's Bks.

Ricci, Christine. Dora in the Deep Sea. Roper, Robert, illus. 2003. (Dora the Explorer Ser.: Vol. 3). (ENG.). 24p. (J). pap. 3.99 *(978-0-689-85845-1(0)*, Simon Spotlight/Nickelodeon) Simon Spotlight/Nickelodeon.

—Dora's Book of Manners. Hall, Susan, illus. 2005. (Dora the Explorer Ser.: No. 7). 22p. (J). lib. bdg. 15.00 *(978-1-59054-793-9(4))* Fitzgerald Bks.

—Dora's Costume Party! Saunders, Zina, illus. 2005. (Dora the Explorer Ser.). (ENG.). 24p. (J). (gr. -1-2). pap. 3.99 *(978-1-4169-0010-8(1)*, Simon Spotlight/Nickelodeon) Simon Spotlight/Nickelodeon.

—Dora's Nursery Rhyme Adventure. Fruchter, Jason, illus. 2005. (Dora the Explorer Ser.). (J). *(978-0-7172-9819-8(1))* Scholastic, Inc.

—Dora's Starry Christmas. Studios, A&J, illus. 2005. 24p. (J). lib. bdg. 9.00 *(978-1-4242-0980-4(3))* Fitzgerald Bks.

—Dora's Valentine Adventure. A and J Studios Staff, illus. 2006. (Dora the Explorer Ser.). (ENG.). 14p. (J). (gr. -1-k). bds. 6.99 *(978-1-4169-1754-0(3)*, Simon Spotlight/Nickelodeon) Simon Spotlight/Nickelodeon.

—I Love My Abuela! Miller, Victoria, illus. 2009. (Dora the Explorer Ser.: 28). (ENG.). 24p. (J). pap. 3.99 *(978-1-4169-6866-5(0)*, Simon Spotlight/Nickelodeon) Simon Spotlight/Nickelodeon.

—Navidad Estelar de Dora. Ziegler, Argentina Palacios, tr. A and J Studios Staff, illus. 2005. (Dora the Explorer Ser.). (SPA.). 24p. (J). pap. 3.99 *(978-1-4169-1183-8(9)*, Libros Para Ninos) Libros Para Ninos.

—Say Cheese! Savitsky, Steven, illus. 2005. 22p. (J). lib. bdg. 15.00 *(978-1-59054-975-9(9))* Fitzgerald Bks.

—Show Me Your Smile! Roper, Robert, illus. 2005. (Dora the Explorer Ser.: 11). 22p. (J). lib. bdg. 15.00 *(978-1-59054-800-4(0))* Fitzgerald Bks.

Risco, Elle D. Dora Had a Little Lamb. Savitsky, Steve, illus. 2007. (Dora the Explorer Ser.). (J). (gr. -1-2). 11.65 *(978-0-7569-8294-2(4))* Perfection Learning Corp.

Rodriguez, Daynali Flores, tr. from ENG. Dora salva el Reino de Cristal (Dora Saves Crystal Kingdom) Aikins, Dave, illus. 2009. (Dora la Exploradora Ser.). (SPA.). 24p. (J). (gr. -1-2). pap. 3.99 *(978-1-4169-9020-8(8)*, Libros Para Ninos) Libros Para Ninos.

Roper, Robert. Dora Goes to the Doctor. 2013. (Dora the Explorer 8X8 Ser.). lib. bdg. 14.75 *(978-0-606-32216-4(7)*, Turtleback) Turtleback Bks.

Rosebrough, Ellen. Dora's Chilly Day. 2013. (Dora the Explorer 8X8 Ser.). lib. bdg. 13.55 *(978-0-606-32215-7(9)*, Turtleback) Turtleback Bks.

—Dora's Chilly Day (Dora the Explorer) Mogee, Warner & MJ Illustrations Staff, illus. 2013. (Pictureback Ser.). (ENG.). 16p. (J). (gr. -1-2). 3.99 *(978-0-449-81950-0(7)*, Random Hse. Bks. for Young Readers) Random Hse. Children's Bks.

Savitsky, Steve, illus. Dora's Pirate Treasure Hunt. 2010. (Dora the Explorer Ser.). (ENG.). 12p. (J). (gr. -1-1). 6.99 *(978-1-4169-9927-0(2)*, Simon Spotlight/Nickelodeon) Simon Spotlight/Nickelodeon.

Savitsky, Steven, illus. Dora Had a Little Lamb. 2007. (Dora the Explorer Ser.: 23). (ENG.). 24p. (J). (gr. -1-2). pap. 3.99 *(978-1-4169-3368-7(9)*, Simon Spotlight/Nickelodeon) Simon Spotlight/Nickelodeon.

Seiss, Ellie. Dora's Princess Pals. 2011. (Dora the Explorer Ser.). (ENG.). 12p. (J). (gr. -1-k). 5.99 *(978-1-4424-1203-3(8)*, Simon Spotlight/Nickelodeon) Simon Spotlight/Nickelodeon.

Seiss, Ellie & Random House Staff. Dora & the Unicorn King. 2013. (Dora the Explorer Step into Reading Ser.). lib. bdg. 13.55 *(978-0-606-32415-1(1)*, Turtleback) Turtleback Bks.

Silverhardt, Lauryn. Un Dia en la Playa. Ziegler, Argentina Palacios, tr. Fruchter, Jason, illus. 2004. (Dora la Exploradora Ser.).Tr. of Day at the Beach. (SPA.). 22p. (J). bds. 4.99 *(978-0-689-86976-1(2)*, Libros Para Ninos) Libros Para Ninos.

—A Surprise Party. Yee, Josie, illus. 2003. (Dora the Explorer Ser.). (ENG.). 22p. (J). bds. 4.99 *(978-0-689-85483-5(8)*, Simon Spotlight/Nickelodeon) Simon Spotlight/Nickelodeon.

Simon Spotlight, creator. Dora & Diego's Adventures! 2007. (Dora the Explorer Ser.). (ENG., Illus.). 80p. (J). (gr. -1-2). 7.99 *(978-1-4169-3532-2(0)*, Simon Spotlight/Nickelodeon) Simon Spotlight/Nickelodeon.

SoftPlay Staff, contrib. by. Dora's Happy Dance. 2007. 8p. 12.98 *(978-1-59292-229-1(5))* SoftPlay, Inc.

Stevens, Cara. Let's Save Pirate Day! (Dora & Friends) Aikins, David, illus. 2014. (Pictureback(R) Ser.). (ENG.). 24p. (J). (gr. -1-2). 4.99 *(978-0-385-37440-8(2)*, Random Hse. Bks. for Young Readers) Random Hse. Children's Bks.

Storytime with Dora & Diego. 2009. (Dora & Diego Ser.). (ENG.). 192p. (J). (gr. -1-2). 12.99 *(978-1-4169-7093-4(2)*, Simon Spotlight/Nickelodeon) Simon Spotlight/Nickelodeon.

Tarkington, Booth. Ramsey Milholland. 2009. 108p. 22.95 *(978-1-60664-679-3(6))*; 104p. pap. 9.95 *(978-1-60664-308-2(8))* Rodgers, Alan Bks.

Thorpe, Kiki. Dora's Chilly Day. Savitsky, Steven, illus. 2005. (Dora the Explorer Ser.: No. 10). 22p. (J). lib. bdg. 15.00 *(978-1-59054-794-6(2))* Fitzgerald Bks.

—Dora's Chilly Day. Savitsky, Steven, illus. 2004. (Dora the Explorer Ser.). (ENG.). 24p. (J). pap. 3.99 *(978-0-689-86795-8(6)*, Simon Spotlight/Nickelodeon) Simon Spotlight/Nickelodeon.

Tillworth, Mary. Color Fiesta! (Dora & Friends) Random House, illus. 2016. (ENG.). 24p. (J). (gr. -1 — 1). bds. 6.99 *(978-0-553-53839-7(X)*, Random Hse. Bks. for Young Readers) Random Hse. Children's Bks.

—Dora in Magic Land (Dora & Friends) Haskett, Dan & Goddard, Brenda, illus. 2016. (Little Golden Book Ser.). (ENG.). 24p. (J). (gr. -1-2). 4.99 *(978-0-553-53840-3(3)*, Golden Bks.) Random Hse. Children's Bks.

—Dora in Wonderland. 2014. (Dora the Explorer 8X8 Ser.). lib. bdg. 13.55 *(978-0-606-35557-5(X))* Turtleback Bks.

—Dora in Wonderland (Dora the Explorer) Miller, Victoria, illus. 2014. (Pictureback(R) Ser.). (ENG.). 24p. (J). (gr. -1-2). 3.99 *(978-0-385-37119-3(5)*, Random Hse. Bks. for Young Readers) Random Hse. Children's Bks.

—Dora's Christmas Star (Dora the Explorer) Miller, Victoria, illus. 2013. (Pictureback(R) Ser.). (ENG.). 16p. (J). (gr. -1-2). 4.99 *(978-0-449-81780-3(6)*, Random Hse. Bks. for Young Readers) Random Hse. Children's Bks.

—Dragon in the School (Dora & Friends) Goddard, Brenda & Haskett, Dan, illus. 2015. (Little Golden Book Ser.). (ENG.). 24p. (J). (gr. -1-2). 4.99 *(978-0-553-52089-7(X)*, Golden Bks.) Random Hse. Children's Bks.

—A Fairytale Adventure (Dora the Explorer) Jackson, Mike, illus. 2014. (Pictureback(R) Ser.). (ENG.). 24p. (J). (gr. -1-2). 3.99 *(978-0-385-37443-9(7)*, Random Hse. Bks. for Young Readers) Random Hse. Children's Bks.

—Meet My Friends! (Dora & Friends) Aikins, David, illus. 2014. (Step into Reading Ser.). (ENG.). 24p. (J). (gr. -1-1). 3.99 *(978-0-385-38462-9(9)*, Random Hse. Bks. for Young Readers) Random Hse. Children's Bks.

—Mermaid Treasure Hunt (Dora & Friends) Aikins, David, illus. 2015. (Pictureback(R) Ser.). (ENG.). 24p. (J). (gr. -1-2). 3.99 *(978-0-553-51076-8(2)*, Random Hse. Bks. for Young Readers) Random Hse. Children's Bks.

—Nickelodeon 5-Minute Stories Collection. Random House, illus. 2016. (5-Minute Story Collection). (ENG.). 160p. (J). (gr. -1-2). 12.99 *(978-0-399-55314-1(2)*, Random Hse. Bks. for Young Readers) Random Hse. Children's Bks.

—Welcome to Fairy World! (Dora & Friends) Aikins, David, illus. 2015. (Glitter Picturebook Ser.). (ENG.). 16p. (J). (gr. -1-2). 5.99 *(978-0-553-52119-1(5)*, Random Hse. Bks. for Young Readers) Random Hse. Children's Bks.

Valdes, Leslie. Dora Goes to School. Roper, Robert, illus. 2005. (Dora the Explorer Ser.: 8). 22p. (J). lib. bdg. 15.00 *(978-1-59054-791-5(8))* Fitzgerald Bks.

—Meet Diego! Hall, Susan, illus. 2005. (Dora the Explorer Ser.: No. 4). 22p. (J). lib. bdg. 15.00 *(978-1-59054-799-1(3))* Fitzgerald Bks.

Various, illus. Dora's 10 Best Adventures. 2010. (Dora the Explorer Ser.). (ENG.). 248p. (J). 15.99 *(978-1-4424-0967-5(3)*, Simon Spotlight/Nickelodeon) Simon Spotlight/Nickelodeon.

—Let's Read with Dora! 2010. (Dora the Explorer Ser.). (ENG.). 144p. (J). (gr. -1-1). pap. 7.99 *(978-1-4169-9742-9(3)*, Simon Spotlight/Nickelodeon) Simon Spotlight/Nickelodeon.

Various Authors, illus. Dora's Bedtime Adventures. 2005. (Dora the Explorer Ser.). (ENG.). 36p. (J). bds. 10.99 *(978-1-4169-0628-5(2)*, Simon Spotlight/Nickelodeon) Simon Spotlight/Nickelodeon.

Wax, Wendy & A and J Studios Staff. Dora's Camping Trip. 2007. (Dora the Explorer Ser.). (ENG., Illus.). 26p. (J). (gr. -1). bds. 5.99 *(978-1-4169-3434-9(0)*, Simon Spotlight/Nickelodeon) Simon Spotlight/Nickelodeon.

Willson, Sarah. Dora's Halloween Adventure. Savitsky, Steven, illus. 2003. (Dora the Explorer Ser.). (ENG.). 14p. (J). bds. 5.99 *(978-0-689-85844-4(2)*, Simon Spotlight/Nickelodeon) Simon Spotlight/Nickelodeon.

Ziegler, Argentina Palacios, tr. Dora y la Princesa de la Nieve (Dora Saves the Snow Princess) Aikins, Dave, illus. 2008. (Dora la Exploradora Ser.). (SPA.). 24p. (J). (gr. -1-2). pap. 3.99 *(978-1-4169-5870-3(3)*, Libros Para Ninos) Libros Para Ninos.

DOUBLE STARS

see Stars

DOUBLEDAY, ABNER, 1819-1893

Dunham, Montrew. Abner Doubleday: Boy Baseball Pioneer, 11 vols. Underdown, Harold D., ed. Morrison, Cathy, illus. 2nd ed. 2005. (Young Patriots Ser.: 11). (ENG.). 118p. (J). (gr. 4-7). 15.95 *(978-1-882859-49-8(9))*; pap. 9.95 *(978-1-882859-50-4(2))* Patria Pr., Inc. (Young Patriots Series).

DOUBT

see Belief and Doubt

DOUGLAS, STEPHEN A. (STEPHEN ARNOLD), 1813-1861

Porterfield, Jason. The Lincoln-Douglas Senatorial Debates Of 1858: A Primary Source Investigation. 2009. (Great Historic Debates & Speeches Ser.). 64p. (gr. 5-8). 58.50 *(978-1-61513-126-6(4))* Rosen Publishing Group, Inc., The.

DOUGLASS, FREDERICK, 1818-1895

Adler, David A. Frederick Douglass: A Noble Life. 2010. (ENG., Illus.). 144p. (J). (gr. 5-18). 21.95 *(978-0-8234-2056-8(6))* Holiday Hse., Inc.

—A Picture Book of Frederick Douglass. Byrd, Samuel, illus. unabr. ed. 2005. (Picture Book Readalongs Ser.). (J). (gr. k-4). 25.95 incl. audio *(978-1-59519-373-5(1))*; pap. 28.95 incl. audio compact disk *(978-1-59519-377-3(4))*;Set. pap. 37.95 incl. audio *(978-1-59519-374-2(X))*;Set. pap. 39.95 incl. audio compact disk *(978-1-59519-378-0(2))* Live Oak Media.

Archer, Jules. They Had a Dream: The Struggles of Four of the Most Influential Leaders of the Civil Rights Movement, from Frederick Douglass to Marcus Garvey to Martin Luther King Jr. & Malcolm X. 2016. (Jules Archer History for Young Readers Ser.). (ENG., Illus.). 272p. (J). (gr. 6). 16.99 *(978-1-63450-194-1(2)*, Sky Pony Pr.) Skyhorse Publishing Co., Inc.

Berne, Emma. Face of Freedom: How the Photos of Frederick Douglass Celebrated Racial Equality. 2017. (Captured History Ser.). (ENG.). 64p. (gr. 5-7). pap. 9.10

C D

(978-0-7565-5619-8(8), CPB Grades 4-8) Compass Point Bks.

Bodden, Valerie. How to Analyze the Works of Frederick Douglass, 1 vol. 2013. (Essential Critiques Set 4 Ser.). (ENG.). 112p. (J). (gr. 6-12). lib. bdg. 35.64 *(978-1-61783-644-2(3)*, Essential Library) ABDO Publishing Co.

Burchard, Peter. Frederick Douglass: For the Great Family of Man. 2007. (ENG., Illus.). 240p. (YA). (gr. 7). pap. 13.95 *(978-1-4169-6752-1(4)*, Atheneum Bks. for Young Readers) Simon & Schuster Children's Publishing.

Carosella, Melissa. Frederick Douglass: Leader of the Abolitionist Movement, 1 vol. 2011. (Primary Source Readers Ser.). (ENG.). 32p. (J). (gr. 4-4). pap. 8.99 *(978-1-4333-1518-3(1))* Teacher Created Materials, Inc.

Cline-Ransome, Lesa. Words Set Me Free: The Story of Young Frederick Douglass. Ransome, James E., illus. 2012. (ENG.). 32p. (J). (gr. k-4). 17.99 *(978-1-4169-5903-8(3)*, Simon & Schuster/Paula Wiseman Bks.) Simon & Schuster/Paula Wiseman Bks.

Copeland, Greg, illus. The Frederick Douglass You Never Knew. 2004. (You Never Knew Ser.). (ENG.). 80p. (J). (gr. 4-6). pap. 6.95 *(978-0-516-25837-9(0)*, Children's Pr.) Scholastic Library Publishing.

Elliot, Henry. Frederick Douglass: From Slavery to Statesman. 2009. (Voices for Freedom Ser.). (ENG., Illus.). 64p. (J). (gr. 5-8). pap. *(978-0-7787-4836-6(7))*; lib. bdg. *(978-0-7787-4820-5(0))* Crabtree Publishing Co.

Fleming, Alice. Frederick Douglass: From Slave to Statesman. 2009. (Library of American Lives & Times Ser.). 112p. (gr. 5-5). 69.20 *(978-1-60853-482-1(0))* Rosen Publishing Group, Inc., The.

Fleming, Alice Mulcahey. Frederick Douglass: From Slave to Statesman. 2005. (Library of American Lives & Times). (Illus.). 112p. (J). (gr. 4-8). lib. bdg. 34.60 *(978-0-8239-6624-0(0))* Rosen Publishing Group, Inc., The.

Freedman, Russell. Abraham Lincoln & Frederick Douglass: The Story Behind an American Friendship. 2012. (ENG., Illus.). 128p. (J). (gr. 5-7). 18.99 *(978-0-547-38562-4(5))* Houghton Mifflin Harcourt Publishing Co.

Giovanni, Nikki. Lincoln & Douglass: An American Friendship. Collier, Bryan, illus. 2013. (ENG.). 40p. (J). (gr. 2-6). 8.99 *(978-1-250-01869-4(2)*, 9781250018694) Square Fish.

—Lincoln & Douglass: An American Friendship. Collier, Bryan, illus. 2011. (J). (gr. -1-3). 29.95 *(978-0-545-13457-6(9))* Weston Woods Studios, Inc.

Gregory, Josh. Frederick Douglass. 2015. (ENG., Illus.). 48p. (J). lib. bdg. *(978-0-531-21597-5(0)*, Orchard Bks.) Scholastic, Inc.

Group/McGraw-Hill, Wright. Frederick Douglass: A Voice for Civil Rights, 6 vols. (Book2WebTM Ser.). (gr. 4-8). 36.50 *(978-0-322-04464-7(2))* Wright Group/McGraw-Hill.

Haldy, Emma E. Frederick Douglass. Bane, Jeff, illus. 2016. (My Early Library: My Itty-Bitty Bio Ser.). (ENG.). 24p. (J). (gr. k-1). 28.50 *(978-1-63470-479-3(7)*, 207647) Cherry Lake Publishing.

Johnson, Claudia Durst. Slavery & Racism in the Narrative Life of Fredrick Douglass. 2014. (Social Issues in Literature Ser.). (ENG., Illus.). 224p. (gr. 7-12). lib. bdg. 46.40 *(978-0-7377-6986-9(6)*, Greenhaven Pr., Inc.) Cengage Gale.

Kramer, Barbara. Frederick Douglass. 2017. (Readers Bios Ser.). (ENG., Illus.). 32p. (J). (gr. k-3). pap. 3.99 *(978-1-4263-2756-8(0)*, National Geographic Children's Bks.) National Geographic Society.

Maloof, Torrey. True Life: Frederick Douglass. 2017. (J). pap. 9.97 ***(978-1-4938-3634-5(X))*** Teacher Created Materials, Inc.

—True Life: Frederick Douglass. 2017. (Time for Kids Nonfiction Readers Ser.). lib. bdg. 20.85 ***(978-0-606-40287-3(X))*** Turtleback Bks.

Marlowe, Sam. Learning about Dedication from the Life of Frederick Douglass. (Character Building Book Ser.). 24p. 2009. (gr. 2-3). 42.50 *(978-1-60854-970-2(4))* 2004. (Illus.). (J). lib. bdg. 22.60 *(978-0-8239-6928-9(2))* Rosen Publishing Group, Inc., The. (PowerKids Pr.).

Marsh, Carole. Frederick Douglass. 2003. 12p. (gr. k-4). 2.95 *(978-0-635-02125-0(0))* Gallopade International.

Martin, Isabel. Frederick Douglass, 1 vol. 2014. (Great African-Americans Ser.). (ENG., Illus.). 24p. (J). (gr. k-1). pap. 5.95 *(978-1-4914-0507-9(4)*, Pebble Bks.) Capstone Press of Coughlan Cos.

McKissack, Patricia C. & McKissack, Fredrick L. Frederick Douglass: Fighter Against Slavery. 2013. (Famous African Americans Ser.). 24p. (J). (gr. k-3). pap. 7.95 *(978-1-4644-0196-1(9))*; (Illus.). 22.60 *(978-0-7660-4098-4(4))* Enslow Pubs., Inc. (Enslow Elementary).

Miller, Barbara Kiely. Frederick Douglass. 2007. (Great Americans Ser.). 24p. (gr. 1-4). pap. 8.15 *(978-0-8368-8322-0(5))*; (SPA.). pap. 8.15 *(978-0-8368-8335-0(7))*; lib. bdg. 22.00 *(978-0-8368-8315-2(2))*; (SPA., Illus.). lib. bdg. 22.00 *(978-0-8368-8328-2(4))* Stevens, Gareth Publishing LLLP. (Weekly Reader Leveled Readers).

Miller, William & Lucas, Cedric. Frederick Douglass: The Last Day of Slavery. 2005. (ENG., Illus.). 32p. (J). (gr. -1-18). reprint ed. pap. 9.95 *(978-1-880000-42-7(3))* Lee & Low Bks., Inc.

Morretta, Alison. Frederick Douglass & William Garrison. 2015. (Primary Sources of the Abolitionist Movement Ser.). (ENG., Illus.). 64p. (J). (gr. 6-6). lib. bdg. 34.21 *(978-1-5026-0532-0(5))* Cavendish Square Publishing.

Myers, Elisabeth P. Frederick Douglass: Young Defender of Human Rights. Morrison, Cathy, illus. 2nd rev. ed. 2007. (Young Patriots Ser.: 13). Orig. Title: Frederick Douglass Boy Champion of Human Rights. (ENG.). 120p. (J). (gr. 4-7). per. 9.95 *(978-1-882859-58-0(8)*, Young Patriots Series) Patria Pr., Inc.

—Frederick Douglass: Young Defender of Human Rights. Morrison, Cathy, illus. 2nd rev. ed. 2007. (Young Patriots Ser.: 13). (ENG.). 120p. (J). (gr. 4-7). 15.95 *(978-1-882859-57-3(X)*, Young Patriots Series) Patria Pr., Inc.

Myers, Walter Dean. Frederick Douglass: The Lion Who Wrote History. Cooper, Floyd, illus. 2017. 40p. (J). (gr. -1-3). 17.99 *(978-0-06-027709-3(2))* HarperCollins Pubs.

Narrative of Frederick Douglass: Prestwick House Literary Touchstone Edition. 2004. 96p. (YA). per. *(978-1-58049-576-9(1)*, PWH5761) Prestwick Hse., Inc.

Pace, Lorenzo. Frederick Douglass & the North Star, 1 vol. 2015. (African American Quartet Ser.). (ENG., Illus.). 48p. (J). 30.25 *(978-1-4777-9281-0(3)*, Windmill Bks.) Rosen Publishing Group, Inc., The.

Passaro, John. Frederick Douglass. 2009. (Journey to Freedom Ser.). (ENG., Illus.). 32p. (J). (gr. 4-7). 29.93 *(978-1-60253-122-2(6)*, 200388) Child's World, Inc., The.

Porterfield, Jason. Frederick Douglass: Abolitionist & Fighter for Equality. 2017. (J). ***(978-1-5383-0019-0(2))***; pap. ***(978-1-68048-802-9(3))*** Rosen Publishing Group, Inc., The. (Britannica Educational Publishing).

Pressberg, Dava. The Life of Frederick Douglass. 2013. (Rosen Readers Ser.). (ENG.). 24p. (J). (gr. 2-3). pap. 8.25 *(978-1-4777-2348-7(X))*; pap. 49.50 *(978-1-4777-2349-4(8))* Rosen Publishing Group, Inc., The. (Rosen Classroom).

Prince, April Jones. Who Was Frederick Douglass? Squier, Robert & Harrison, Nancy, illus. 2014. (Who Was? Ser.). (ENG.). 112p. (J). (gr. 3-7). 5.99 *(978-0-448-47911-8(7)*, Grosset & Dunlap) Penguin Young Readers Group.

—Who Was Frederick Douglass? 2014. (Who Was... ? Ser.). lib. bdg. 16.00 *(978-0-606-36184-2(7))* Turtleback Bks.

Rappaport, Doreen. Frederick's Journey: The Life of Frederick Douglass. Ladd, London, illus. 2015. (Big Words Ser.). (ENG.). 48p. (J). (gr. 1-3). 17.99 *(978-1-4231-1438-3(8))* Disney Pr.

Roberts, Kayla. Frederick Douglass: Freedom Fighter. 2013. (InfoMax Readers Ser.). (ENG.). 24p. (J). (gr. 2-3). pap. 8.25 *(978-1-4777-2329-6(3))*; pap. 49.50 *(978-1-4777-2330-2(7))* Rosen Publishing Group, Inc., The. (Rosen Classroom).

Roos, Am & Hamilton, A. Turning the Page: Frederick Douglass Learns to Read. Adams, Michael, illus. 2014. (ENG.). 28p. (J). pap. 5.99 *(978-1-61406-683-5(3))* American Reading Co.

Russell, Sharman Apt. Frederick Douglass: Abolitionist Editor. 2004. (Black Americans of Achievement Ser.). (Illus.). 112p. (gr. 6-12). 35.00 *(978-0-7910-8157-0(5)*, Chelsea Hse.) Facts On File, Inc.

Sanders, Nancy I. Frederick Douglass for Kids: His Life & Times, with 21 Activities. 2012. (For Kids Ser.). (ENG., Illus.). 144p. (J). (gr. 4). pap. 16.95 *(978-1-56976-717-3(7))* Chicago Review Pr., Inc.

Schraff, Anne. The Life of Frederick Douglass: Speaking Out Against Slavery. 2014. (Legendary African Americans Ser.). (Illus.). 96p. (J). (gr. 6-12). pap. 10.95 *(978-0-7660-6133-0(7))* Enslow Pubs., Inc.

Schraff, Anne E. The Life of Frederick Douglass: Speaking Out Against Slavery. 2014. (Legendary African Americans Ser.). 96p. (J). (gr. 6-12). 27.94 *(978-0-7660-6132-3(9))* Enslow Pubs., Inc.

Schuman, Michael A. Frederick Douglass: Truth Is of No Color. 2009. (Americans—the Spirit of a Nation Ser.). (Illus.). 128p. (J). (gr. 5-12). lib. bdg. 33.27 *(978-0-7660-3025-1(3))* Enslow Pubs., Inc.

Shaffer, Jody Jensen. What's Your Story, Frederick Douglass? 2016. (Cub Reporter Meets Famous Americans Ser.). (ENG., Illus.). 32p. (J). (gr. k-3). pap. 8.99 *(978-1-4677-9647-7(6)*, Lerner Pubns.) Lerner Publishing Group.

Shea, Nicole. Frederick Douglass in His Own Words, Vol. 1. 2014. (Eyewitness to History Ser.). 32p. (J). (gr. 4-5). (ENG.). 26.60 *(978-1-4339-9898-0(X))*; pap. 10.50 *(978-1-4824-3288-6(9))* Stevens, Gareth Publishing LLLP.

Slade, Suzanne. Friends for Freedom: The Story of Susan B. Anthony & Frederick Douglass. Tadgell, Nicole, illus. 2014. (ENG.). 40p. (J). (gr. 1-4). 16.95 *(978-1-58089-568-2(9))* Charlesbridge Publishing, Inc.

—Friends for Freedom: The Story of Susan B. Anthony & Frederick Douglass. 2014. (Illus.). 39p. *(978-1-60734-651-7(6))* Charlesbridge Publishing, Inc.

Stanley, George E. Frederick Douglass: Abolitionist Hero. Henderson, Meryl, illus. 2008. (Childhood of Famous Americans Ser.). (ENG.). 208p. (J). (gr. 3-7). pap. 6.99 *(978-1-4169-5547-4(X)*, Aladdin) Simon & Schuster Children's Publishing.

Sterngass, Jon. Frederick Douglass. 2009. (Leaders of the Civil War Era Ser.). (Illus.). 160p. (gr. 6-12). 35.00 *(978-1-60413-306-6(6)*, Chelsea Hse.) Facts On File, Inc.

Vander Hook, Sue. Frederick Douglass: Fugitive Slave & Abolitionist, 1 vol. 2010. (Essential Lives Set 5 Ser.). (ENG., Illus.). 112p. (J). (gr. 6-12). lib. bdg. 35.64 *(978-1-61613-513-3(1))* ABDO Publishing Co.

Weidt, Maryann N. & National Geographic Learning Staff. Voice of Freedom: A Story about Frederick Douglass. Reeves, Jeni, illus. 2010. (Rise & Shine Ser.). (ENG.). 64p. (C). (gr. 4-8). pap. 14.95 *(978-1-57505-553-4(8))* National Geographic School Publishing, Inc.

Weiss, Lynne. Frederick Douglass & the Abolitionist Movement. 2013. (Jr. Graphic African American History Ser.). (Illus.). 24p. (J). (gr. 3-6). pap. 63.60 *(978-1-4777-1452-2(9))*; (ENG., pap. 10.60 *(978-1-4777-1451-5(0))*; (ENG., lib. bdg. 25.25 *(978-1-4777-1313-6(1))* Rosen Publishing Group, Inc., The. (PowerKids Pr.).

Welch, Catherine A. Frederick Douglass. 2003. (History Maker Bios Ser.). (Illus.). 48p. (J). (gr. 4-7). pap. 8.95 *(978-0-8225-4802-7(X))*; (gr. 3-5). lib. bdg. 26.60 *(978-0-8225-4672-6(8))* Lerner Publishing Group.

Whiting, Jim. Frederick Douglass. 2010. (Transcending Race in America: Biographies of Biracial Achievers Ser.). (Illus.). 64p. (YA). (gr. 5-18). lib. bdg. 22.95 *(978-1-4222-1611-8(X))* Mason Crest.

Wilson, Camilla. Frederick Douglass: A Voice for Freedom in the 1800s. 2003. (Scholastic Biography Ser.). (Illus.). 90p. (J). pap. *(978-0-439-38082-9(0))* Scholastic, Inc.

Zaboly, Gary. Frederick Douglass Coloring Book. 2014. (ENG.). 32p. (gr. 4). pap. 3.99 *(978-0-486-49215-5(X))* Dover Pubns., Inc.

DOWN SYNDROME

Bowman-Kruhm, Mary. Everything You Need to Know about down Syndrome. 2009. (Need to Know Library). 64p. (gr. 5-5). 58.50 *(978-1-60854-065-5(0))* Rosen Publishing Group, Inc., The.

—Everything You Need to Know about Down Syndrome. rev. ed. 2005. (Need to Know Library). (Illus.). 64p. (YA). (gr. 4-6). lib. bdg. 31.95 *(978-0-8239-3767-7(4))* Rosen Publishing Group, Inc., The.

Brill, Marlene Targ. Down Syndrome. 2006. (Health Alert Ser.). (Illus.). 64p. (YA). (gr. 4-7). lib. bdg. 32.79 *(978-0-7614-2207-5(2))* Marshall Cavendish Corp.

Campos, Maria de Fatima. Victoria's Day. 2015. (ENG., Illus.). 32p. (J). (gr. -1-1). pap. 10.99 *(978-1-84780-424-2(1)*, Frances Lincoln) Quarto Publishing Group UK GBR. Dist: Hachette Bk. Group.

Doering Tourville, Amanda. My Friend Has down Syndrome, 1 vol. Sorra, Kristin, illus. 2010. (Friends with Disabilities Ser.). (ENG.). 24p. (gr. k-3). pap. 7.49 *(978-1-4048-6110-7(6))* Picture Window Bks.

—My Friend Has down Syndrome [Readers World]. Sorra, Kristin, illus. 2010. (Friends with Disabilities Ser.). 24p. pap. 6.00 *(978-1-4048-6703-1(1)*, Nonfiction Picture Bks.) Picture Window Bks.

Dysinger, Stephen. William. Dysinger, Stephen, illus. 2007. (Illus.). 28p. (J). (gr. -1-3). per. 12.99 *(978-1-59879-297-3(0))* Lifevest Publishing, Inc.

Elliott, Elizabeth. Can I Tell You about down Syndrome? A Guide for Friends, Family & Professionals. Thapp, Manjit, illus. 2015. (Can I Tell You About... ? Ser.). (ENG.). 48p. pap. 14.95 *(978-1-84905-501-7(7)*, 2395) Kingsley, Jessica Pubs. GBR. Dist: Macmillan Distribution Ltd.

Evans-Martin, F. Fay. Down Syndrome. 2009. (Genes & Disease Ser.). (Illus.). 128p. (YA). (gr. 7-12). 35.00 *(978-0-7910-9644-4(0))* Facts On File, Inc.

Foster, Dylan. My Friend Sammy. 2011. 28p. (gr. 1-2). pap. 14.95 *(978-1-4634-1063-6(8))* AuthorHouse.

Laney, Dawn. Down Syndrome. 2008. (Perspectives on Diseases & Disorders Ser.). (ENG., Illus.). 128p. (YA). (gr. 10-12). lib. bdg. 38.95 *(978-0-7377-4025-7(6)*, LML02109-239984, Greenhaven Pr., Inc.) Cengage Gale.

Levine, Michelle. Down Syndrome. 2015. (Living With... Ser.). (Illus.). 32p. (J). 28.50 *(978-1-60753-481-5(9))* Amicus Publishing.

Libal, Autumn. Intellectual Disabilities. Albers, Lisa et al, eds. 2014. (Living with a Special Need Ser.: 16). 128p. (J). (gr. 7-18). 25.95 *(978-1-4222-3037-4(6))* Mason Crest.

Margulies, Philip. Down Syndrome. 2006. (Genetic Diseases & Disorders Ser.). (Illus.). 64p. (J). (gr. 3-7). lib. bdg. 31.95 *(978-1-4042-0695-3(7))* Rosen Publishing Group, Inc., The.

Margulies, Phillip. Down Syndrome. 2009. (Genetic Diseases & Disorders Ser.). 64p. (gr. 6-6). 58.50 *(978-1-61512-664-4(3))* Rosen Publishing Group, Inc., The.

Pitzer, Marjorie. Animal Fun for Everyone! 2014. (ENG., Illus.). 14p. (J). pap. *(978-1-60613-188-6(5))* Woodbine Hse.

Pitzer, Marjorie W. My up & down & All Around Book. Pitzer, Marjorie W., photos by. 2008. (ENG., Illus.). 16p. (J). (gr. -1-1). pap. 10.95 *(978-1-890627-90-4(9))* Woodbine Hse.

Ronay, Laura. Kids Like Me... Learn ABCs. Kishimoto, Jon Wayne, illus. 2008. (ENG.). 32p. (J). (gr. -1-1). 12.95 *(978-1-60613-000-1(5))* Woodbine Hse.

—Kids Like Me... Learn Colors. Kishimoto, Jon Wayne, illus. 2008. (ENG.). 16p. (J). (gr. -1-1). 11.95 *(978-1-60613-001-8(3))* Woodbine Hse.

Royston, Angela. Explaining Down's Syndrome. 2009. (Explaining... Ser.). 48p. (gr. 7-12). 37.10 *(978-1-59920-308-9(1))* Black Rabbit Bks.

Skotko, Brian & Levine, Susan P. Fasten Your Seatbelt: A Crash Course on Down Syndrome for Brothers & Sisters. 2008. (ENG.). 192p. (YA). (gr. 4-9). pap. 18.95 *(978-1-890627-86-7(0))* Woodbine Hse.

Tourville, Amanda Doering. My Friend Has down Syndrome, 1 vol. Sorra, Kristin, illus. 2010. (Friends with Disabilities Ser.). (ENG.). 24p. (gr. k-3). lib. bdg. 25.99 *(978-1-4048-5751-3(6))* Picture Window Bks.

Tourville, Amanda Doering & Sorra, Kristin. Mi Amiga Tiene Sindrome de Down. Translations.com Staff, tr. from ENG. Sorra, Kristin, illus. 2012. (Amigos con Discapacidades/Friends with Disabilities Ser.). (MUL & SPA., Illus.). 24p. (gr. k-3). lib. bdg. 25.99 *(978-1-4048-7313-1(9))* Picture Window Bks.

DOWN SYNDROME—FICTION

Flinn, Alex. Fade to Black. 2006. (ENG.). 208p. (YA). (gr. 9-12). pap. 9.99 *(978-0-06-056842-9(9)*, HarperTeen) HarperCollins Pubs.

Galante, Cecilia. Willowood. 2011. (ENG.). 288p. (J). (gr. 4-8). pap. 6.99 *(978-1-4169-8303-3(1)*, Aladdin) Simon & Schuster Children's Publishing.

—Willowood. 2010. (ENG.). 272p. (J). (gr. 4-8). 16.99 *(978-1-4169-8022-3(9)*, Simon & Schuster/Paula Wiseman Bks.) Simon & Schuster/Paula Wiseman Bks.

Goodhart, Pippa. Ginny's Egg. Brouwer, Aafke, illus. 142p. (J). pap. 7.50 *(978-0-7497-4557-8(6))* Egmont Bks., Ltd. GBR. Dist: Trafalgar Square Publishing.

Hubler, Marsha. Blue Ribbon Champ, 1 vol. rev. ed. 2010. (Keystone Stables Ser.). (ENG.). 112p. (J). pap. 7.99 *(978-0-310-71797-3(3))* Zonderkidz.

Hyde, Catherine Ryan. The Year of My Miraculous Reappearance. 2009. (ENG.). 240p. (YA). (gr. 7). pap. 8.99 *(978-0-375-83261-1(0)*, Knopf Bks. for Young Readers) Random Hse. Children's Bks.

Kats, Jewel. Hansel & Gretel: A Fairy Tale with a Down Syndrome Twist. Lenart, Claudia, illus. 2014. 37p. (J). *(978-1-61599-251-5(0))* Loving Healing Pr., Inc.

Lange, Erin Jade. Dead Ends. 2013. (ENG.). 336p. (YA). (gr. 9). 17.99 *(978-1-61963-080-2(X)*, 9781619630802, Bloomsbury USA Childrens); 288p. pap. 17.99 *(978-1-61963-081-9(8))* Bloomsbury Publishing USA.

McMurchy-Barber, Gina & Zweig, Eric. Free as a Bird. 2010. (ENG., Illus.). 176p. (YA). (gr. 6-8). pap. 10.99 *(978-1-55488-447-6(0)*, Dundurn Pr.) Dundurn CAN. Dist: Ingram Publisher Services.

Pick, Alice. Jamey's Promise, 1 vol. 2009. 61p. pap. 19.95 *(978-1-61582-547-9(9))* America Star Bks.

Pitzer, Marjorie W. I Like Berries, Do You? Pitzer, Marjorie W., photos by. 2013. (ENG., Illus.). 14p. (J). 11.95 *(978-1-60613-183-1(4))* Woodbine Hse.

Plucker, Sheri. Me, Hailey. Fargo, Todd, illus. 2005. (Turtle Books). 32p. (J). (gr. k-3). pap. 9.95 *(978-0-944727-49-2(2))*; lib. bdg. 15.95 *(978-0-944727-50-8(6)*, Turtle Bks.) Jason & Nordic Pubs.

Rosen, Chaya & Braverman, Rivkie. Our New Special Baby. 2013. *(978-1-59826-960-4(7))* Feldheim Pubs.

Rottman, S. L. Head above Water, 1 vol. 2003. (ENG.). 192p. (YA). (gr. 7-18). pap. 6.95 *(978-1-56145-238-5(6)*, Q21186) Peachtree Pubs.

Sheldon, Kaylene Kauwila. A Day with Makana. 2007.Tr. of I Kekahi la me Makana. (ENG & HAW.). (J). lib. bdg. *(978-0-9773495-2-4(7))* Na Kamalei Koolauloa Early Education Program.

Smiley, Sophie. Team Trouble. Foreman, Michael, illus. 2007. (ENG.). 64p. (J). (gr. 2-4). pap. 9.95 *(978-1-84270-684-8(5))* Andersen Pr. GBR. Dist: Independent Pubs. Group.

Tompkins, Lisa. Why Are You Looking at Me? I Just Have down Syndrome. 2013. 32p. pap. 19.99 *(978-1-4817-1138-8(5))* AuthorHouse.

Tupper Ling, Nancy. My Sister, Alicia May. Bersani, Shennen, illus. 2009. (ENG.). 32p. (J). (gr. k-2). 16.95 *(978-0-9792035-9-6(7))* Pleasant St. Pr.

Vazquez, Tiziana & Llano, Gabriella. In My World: Down Syndrome. 2013. 108p. 23.99 *(978-1-4772-9274-7(8))*; pap. 14.95 *(978-1-4772-9188-7(1))* AuthorHouse.

Woloson, Eliza. My Friend Isabelle. Gough, Bryan, tr. Gough, Bryan, illus. 2003. (ENG.). 28p. (J). 14.95 *(978-1-890627-50-8(X))* Woodbine Hse.

Wood, June Rae. The Man Who Loved Clowns. 2005. (ENG.). 224p. (J). (gr. 3-7). 6.99 *(978-0-14-240422-5(5)*, Puffin Books) Penguin Young Readers Group.

—The Man Who Loved Clowns. 2005. 224p. (gr. 3-7). 16.00 *(978-0-7569-5516-8(5))* Perfection Learning Corp.

DOWN'S SYNDROME

see Down Syndrome

DOYLE, ARTHUR CONAN, SIR, 1859-1930

Adams, Cynthia. The Mysterious Case of Sir Arthur Conan Doyle. 2004. (World Writers Ser.). (Illus.). 112p. (J). (gr. 5-13). 21.95 *(978-1-883846-34-3(X))* Reynolds, Morgan Inc.

Cosson, M. J. Sherlock Holmes & the Adventure of the Dancing Men. 4th rev. ed. 2010. pap. 39.62 *(978-0-7613-6961-5(9))* Lerner Publishing Group.

Doyle, Arthur Conan & Saddleback Educational Publishing Staff, eds. The Hound of the Baskervilles. 2011. (Timeless Classics Ser.). (ENG.). 48p. (YA). (gr. 9-12). pupil's gde. ed. 19.95 incl. cd-rom *(978-1-61651-137-1(0))* Saddleback Educational Publishing, Inc.

Losure, Mary. The Fairy Ring: Or Elsie & Frances Fool the World. (ENG.). 192p. (J). (gr. 5). 2014. pap. 8.99 *(978-0-7636-7495-3(8))* 2012. (Illus.). 16.99 *(978-0-7636-5670-6(4))* Candlewick Pr.

DRACULA, COUNT (FICTITIOUS CHARACTER)—FICTION

Deutsch, Stacia, adapted by. Hotel Transylvania 2: Movie Novelization. 2015. (Illus.). 141p. (J). *(978-1-4806-9404-0(5)*, Simon Spotlight) Simon Spotlight.

Dracula. (J). 9.95 *(978-1-56156-373-9(0))* Kidsbooks, LLC.

Higginson, Sheila Sweeny & Deutsch, Stacia, adapted by. Hotel Transylvania 2 Movie Novelization. 2015. (Hotel Transylvania 2 Ser.). (ENG., Illus.). 144p. (J). (gr. 3-7). pap. 6.99 *(978-1-4814-4819-2(6)*, Simon Spotlight) Simon Spotlight.

Hill, Will. Darkest Night (Department 19, Book 5) 2016. (Department 19 Ser.: 5). (ENG.). 736p. (J). pap. 9.99 *(978-0-00-815427-1(9)*, HarperCollins Children's Bks.) HarperCollins Pubs. Ltd. GBR. Dist: HarperCollins Pubs.

—The Rising: A Department 19 Novel. 2013. (Department Nineteen Ser.: 2). (ENG.). 592p. (YA). (gr. 9). pap. 9.99 *(978-1-59514-629-8(6)*, Razorbill) Penguin Young Readers Group.

Hoffman, Mary. Dracula's Daughter. 2006. (Yellow Bananas Ser.). (ENG., Illus.). 48p. (J). (gr. -1-3). *(978-0-7787-1000-4(9))*; lib. bdg. *(978-0-7787-0954-1(X))* Crabtree Publishing Co.

Maniscalco, Kerri. Hunting Prince Dracula. 2017. (Stalking Jack the Ripper Ser.: 2). (ENG., Illus.). (YA). (gr. 10-17). 448p. 18.99 ***(978-0-316-55166-3(X))***; 608p. 20.99 ***(978-0-316-43986-2(X))*** Little Brown & Co. (Jimmy Patterson).

Marsh, Carole. The Mystery at Dracula's Castle: Transylvania, Romania. (Around the World in 80 Mysteries Ser.). 133p. (J). 2009. 18.99 *(978-0-635-07039-5(1)*, Marsh, Carole Mysteries) 2008. (Illus.). (gr. 3-5). 14.95 *(978-0-635-06471-4(5))* 2008. (Illus.). (gr. 3-5). per. 5.95 *(978-0-635-06469-1(3)*, Marsh, Carole Mysteries) Gallopade International.

McNaughton, Colin. Dracula's Tomb. McNaughton, Colin, illus. 2009. (ENG., Illus.). 24p. (J). (gr. k-4). 14.99 *(978-0-7636-4488-8(9))* Candlewick Pr.

Medina, Andre, illus. Meet the Monsters. 2015. (Hotel Transylvania 2 Ser.). (ENG.). 16p. (J). (gr. -1-3). pap. 5.99 *(978-1-4814-4802-4(1)*, Simon Spotlight) Simon Spotlight.

Ratnett, Michael. Dracula Steps Out. Goulding, June & Smyth, Iain, illus. 2005. 12p. (J). (gr. k-4). reprint ed. 16.00 *(978-0-7567-8585-7(5))* DIANE Publishing Co.

Rosen, Lucy. Minions: Dracula's Last Birthday. Miller, Ed, illus. 2015. (ENG.). 32p. (J). (gr. -1-3). 7.99 *(978-0-316-26693-2(0))* Little, Brown Bks. for Young Readers.

Stoker, Bram. Count Dracula. 2004. (Fast Track Classics Ser.). (Illus.). 48p. (J). pap. *(978-0-237-52401-2(5))* Evans Brothers, Ltd.

—Dracula. Bryant, Clive, ed. Johnson, Staz et al, illus. 2012. (ENG.). 144p. (gr. 6). pap. 16.95 *(978-1-906332-68-6(1))*; pap. 16.95 *(978-1-906332-67-9(3)*, Classical Comics, Ltd.) Classical Comics GBR. Dist: Publishers Group West (PGW).

—Dracula. Williams, Anthony, illus. 2014. (ENG.). 32p. 8.95 *(978-1-78404-355-1(9))* Arcturus Publishing GBR. Dist: Bookmasters Distribution.

—Dracula. Kliros, Thea, illus. abr. ed. 2011. (Dover Children's Thrift Classics Ser.). (ENG.). 96p. (J). (gr. 3-8). reprint ed. pap. 4.00 *(978-0-486-29567-1(2))* Dover Pubns., Inc.

Thaler, Mike. Hubie Cool: Vampire Hunter. Lee, Jared D., illus. 2015. 64p. (J). pap. ***(978-0-545-85075-9(4))*** Scholastic, Inc.

Thomas, Roy, text. Dracula. 2010. (ENG., Illus.). 208p. (gr. 10-17). 19.99 *(978-0-7851-4905-7(8))* Marvel Worldwide, Inc.

Universal. Mower Minions. Miller, Ed, illus. 2016. (ENG.). 24p. (J). (gr. -1-3). pap. 5.99 *(978-0-316-39297-6(9))* Little, Brown Bks. for Young Readers.

Williams, Anthony, illus. Dracula: A Classic Pop-Up Tale. 2009. (ENG.). 16p. (J). 29.95 *(978-0-7893-2050-6(9))* Universe Publishing.

DRAFT

Wagner, Viqi. Military Draft. 2007. (Opposing Viewpoints Ser.). (Illus.). 238p. (YA). (gr. 10-12). 29.45 *(978-0-7377-3825-4(1),* LML02109-234567, Greenhaven Pr., Inc.); (gr. 9-12). pap. 42.95 *(978-0-7377-3824-7(3),* LML02109-234561) Cengage Gale.

DRAFTING, MECHANICAL

see Mechanical Drawing

DRAG RACING

see Automobile Racing

DRAGONFLIES

Armstrong, Robert H., et al. Dragons in the Pond. 2007. pap. *(978-1-57833-362-2(8))* Todd Communications.

Bodden, Valerie. Creepy Creatures: Dragonflies. 2014. (Creepy Creatures Ser.). (ENG.). 24p. (J). (gr. 1-3). pap. 7.99 *(978-0-89812-933-5(8),* Creative Paperbacks) Creative Co., The.

Dragonfly. 2004. per. 18.00 *(978-0-9749492-2-2(1))* Giant Robot Bks.

Dragonfly. 2003. (J). 36.95 *(978-0-8136-9267-8(9))* Modern Curriculum Pr.

Dragonfly: Big Book. 2003. (J). 38.95 *(978-0-8136-4156-0(X))* Modern Curriculum Pr.

Earley, Chris G. Dragonflies: Find - Identify - Raise Your Own. 2013. (ENG., Illus.). 32p. (J). (gr. 3-6). 19.95 *(978-1-77085-185-6(2),* 9781770851856); pap. 6.95 *(978-1-77085-186-3(0),* 9781770851863) Firefly Bks., Ltd.

Ganeri, Anita & Johnson, Jinny. What's It Like to Be... Dragonfly? Sanzi, Desiderio, illus. 2011. (What's It Like to Be... ? Ser.). 24p. (J). (gr. -1-k). 25.65 *(978-1-60753-186-9(0))* Amicus Publishing.

Glaser, Linda. Dazzling Dragonflies: A Life Cycle Story. Posada, Mia, illus. 2008. (Linda Glaser's Classic Creatures Ser.). (ENG.). 32p. (J). (gr. k-3). lib. bdg. 22.60 *(978-0-8225-6753-0(9),* Millbrook Pr.) Lerner Publishing Group.

Green, Emily K. Dragonflies. 2006. (World of Insects Ser.). (ENG., Illus.). 24p. (J). (gr. k-3). lib. bdg. 25.95 *(978-1-60014-012-9(2))* Bellwether Media.

Green, Jen. Dragonflies. 2009. (Illus.). 52p. (J). ***(978-0-7172-8065-0(9))*** Grolier, Ltd.

Hansen, Grace. Dragonflies, 1 vol. 2014. (Insects Ser.). (ENG.). 24p. (J). (gr. 4-8). lib. bdg. 28.50 *(978-1-62970-040-3(1))* ABDO Publishing Co.

Hansen, Grace, et al. Libélulas. 2015. (Insectos Ser.). (SPA., Illus.). 24p. (gr. k-1). pap. 7.95 *(978-1-4966-0477-4(6))* Capstone Classroom.

Harasymiw, Mark J. Dragonflies Lived with the Dinosaurs! 2016. (Living with the Dinosaurs Ser.). 00024p. (J). pap. 8.15 ***(978-1-4824-5649-3(4))*** Stevens, Gareth Publishing LLLP.

Helget, Nicole. Dragonflies. 2007. (Bugbooks Ser.). (Illus.). 24p. (J). (gr. -1-3). lib. bdg. 24.25 *(978-1-58341-541-2(6),* Creative Education) Creative Co., The.

Hudak, Heather C. Dragonflies. 2008. (World of Wonder Ser.). (Illus.). 24p. (J). (gr. k-3). pap. 8.95 *(978-1-59036-865-7(7))* Weigl Pubs., Inc.

Ipcizade, Catherine. Dazzling Dragonflies. 2017. (Bugs Are Beautiful! Ser.). (ENG., Illus.). 32p. (gr. 1-2). lib. bdg. 27.32 *(978-1-5157-4498-6(1),* Aplus Bks.) Capstone Press of Coughlan Cos.

Lawrence, Ellen. A Dragonfly's Life. 2012. (Science Slam: Animal Diaries-Life Cycles Ser.). 24p. (J). (gr. -1-3). lib. bdg. 23.93 *(978-1-61772-594-4(3))* Bearport Publishing Co., Inc.

Lockwood, Sophie. Dragonflies. 2007. (World of Insects Ser.). (ENG., Illus.). 40p. (J). (gr. 3-6). 31.36 *(978-1-59296-821-3(X),* 200974) Child's World, Inc., The.

Macheske, Felicia. Quick & Quiet: Dragonfly. 2016. (Guess What Ser.). (ENG., Illus.). 24p. (J). (gr. k-2). 28.50 *(978-1-63470-715-2(X),* 207571) Cherry Lake Publishing.

Macken, JoAnn Early. The Life Cycle of a Dragonfly. 2006. (Things with Wings Ser.). (Illus.). 24p. (J). (gr. k-3). lib. bdg. 22.00 *(978-0-8368-6381-9(X),* Weekly Reader Leveled Readers) Stevens, Gareth Publishing LLLP.

McLaughlin, Kari Massie. My Adventure with Dragonflies. 2009. 44p. (J). 8.99 *(978-1-59092-452-5(5))* Blue Forge Pr.

Miller, David. Dragonfly. 2017. (Up Close & Scary Ser.). (Illus.). 32p. (gr. 2-5). 31.35 ***(978-1-911242-05-5(9))*** Book Hse. GBR. Dist: Black Rabbit Bks.

Morris, Neil & Morris, Ting. Dragonfly. 2003. (Illus.). 32p. (J). lib. bdg. 27.10 *(978-1-58340-380-8(9))* Black Rabbit Bks.

Murray, Julie. Dragonflies, 1 vol. 2010. (Big Buddy Bks.). (ENG.). 32p. (J). (gr. 2-5). 28.50 *(978-1-61613-484-6(4))* ABDO Publishing Co.

Nelson, Maria. 20 Fun Facts about Dragonflies. 2013. (Fun Fact File: Bugs! Ser.). (Illus.). 32p. (J). (gr. 2-5). pap. 10.50 *(978-1-4339-8236-1(6));* lib. bdg. 25.25 *(978-1-4339-8235-4(8))* Stevens, Gareth Publishing LLLP.

Nelson, Robin. Darting Dragonflies. 2016. (First Step Nonfiction — Backyard Critters Ser.). (ENG., Illus.). 24p. (J). (gr. k-2). 23.99 *(978-1-5124-0883-6(2))* Lerner Publishing Group.

—Dragonflies. 2009. pap. 34.95 *(978-0-7613-4105-5(6));* (ENG.). 24p. 23.93 *(978-0-7613-4066-9(1),* Lerner Pubns.) Lerner Publishing Group.

Perish, Patric. Dragonflies. 2017. (Insects up Close Ser.). (ENG., Illus.). 24p. (J). (gr. k-3). lib. bdg. 25.95 ***(978-1-62617-662-1(0),*** Blastoff! Readers) Bellwether Media.

Peters, Elisa. It's a Dragonfly! 2009. (Everyday Wonders Ser.). 24p. (gr. 1-1). 42.50 *(978-1-61512-323-0(7));* (Illus.). (J). lib. bdg. 22.60 *(978-1-4042-4460-3(3))* Rosen Publishing Group, Inc., The. (PowerKids Pr.).

—It's a Dragonfly! Es una Libélula! 2009. (Everyday Wonders / Maravillas de Todos Los días Ser.). (SPA & ENG., Illus.). 24p. (J). lib. bdg. 22.60 *(978-1-4358-2525-3(X),* PowerKids Pr.) Rosen Publishing Group, Inc., The.

—It's a Dragonfly! / ¡Es una Libélula! 2009. (Everyday Wonders / Maravillas de todos los días Ser.). (ENG & SPA.). 24p. (gr. 1-1). 42.50 *(978-1-61512-329-2(6),* Editorial Buenas Letras) Rosen Publishing Group, Inc., The.

Rissman, Rebecca. Dragonflies, 1 vol. 2012. (Creepy Critters Ser.). (ENG.). 24p. (gr. -1-k). pap. 9.95 *(978-1-4109-4819-9(6));* lib. bdg. 25.32 *(978-1-4109-4806-9(4))* Heinemann-Raintree.

Romanosky, David. Dragonfly Babies. 2015. (2G Bugs Ser.). (ENG., Illus.). 28p. (J). pap. 5.99 *(978-1-63437-144-5(5))* American Reading Co.

Salzmann, Mary Elizabeth. Dashing Dragonflies, 1 vol. 2012. (Bug Bks.). (ENG.). 24p. (J). (gr. k-3). lib. bdg. 24.21 *(978-1-61783-190-4(5),* SandCastle) ABDO Publishing Co.

Schuh, Mari C. Dragonflies. 2014. (Illus.). 24p. (J). lib. bdg. 25.65 *(978-1-62031-083-0(X),* Bullfrog Bks.) Jump! Inc.

Shaffer, Christy. Shiny Dragonflies Stickers. 2006. (Dover Little Activity Books Stickers Ser.). (ENG., Illus.). 2p. (J). (gr. -1-5). 1.50 *(978-0-486-44926-5(2))* Dover Pubns., Inc.

Slade, Suzanne. Dragonflies. 2009. (Under the Microscope: Backyard Bugs Ser.). 24p. (gr. 2-3). 42.50 *(978-1-60854-614-5(4),* PowerKids Pr.) Rosen Publishing Group, Inc., The.

Smith, Molly. Speedy Dragonflies. 2008. (No Backbone! Ser.). (Illus.). 24p. (J). (gr. k-3). lib. bdg. 21.28 *(978-1-59716-583-9(2))* Bearport Publishing Co., Inc.

Stewart, Melissa. Zoom in on Dragonflies. 2014. (Zoom in on Insects! Ser.). 24p. (J). 22.60 *(978-0-7660-4212-4(X));* pap. 7.95 *(978-1-4644-0367-5(8),* Enslow Elementary) Enslow Pubs., Inc.

Trueit, Trudi Strain. Dragonflies. 2013. 32p. (J). (gr. 6-9). 28.50 *(978-1-60870-244-2(8));* pap. 10.58 *(978-1-62712-028-9(9))* Cavendish Square Publishing.

Vasilyeva, Anastasiya. Dragonfly. 2017. (See Them Grow Ser.). (ENG., Illus.). 24p. (J). (gr. -1-3). 17.95 ***(978-1-68402-039-3(5))*** Bearport Publishing Co., Inc.

Washington, Joi. Dragonflies. 2011. (ARC Press / Predator Bugs Ser.). pap. 39.62 *(978-1-61541-656-1(0));* (ENG., Illus.). 16p. (J). pap. 5.99 *(978-1-61541-228-0(X))* American Reading Co.

—The Dragonfly. 2011. (Power 50 - Predator Bugs Ser.). 32p. (J). (gr. k-2). pap. 7.95 *(978-1-61541-383-6(9))* American Reading Co.

Woodward, John. Dragonfly. 2010. (Garden Minibeasts up Close Ser.). 32p. (gr. 2-4). 30.00 *(978-1-60413-898-6(X),* Chelsea Clubhouse) Facts On File, Inc.

DRAGONS

Abbott, Simon, illus. Learn to Draw: Dragons. 2011. (Learn to Draw Ser.). (ENG.). 24p. (J). (gr. k-2). pap. 6.95 *(978-1-84898-201-7(1),* TickTock Books) Octopus Publishing Group GBR. Dist: Independent Pubs. Group.

Adamson, Heather. Sea Dragons. 2017. (Ocean Life up Close Ser.). (ENG., Illus.). 24p. (J). (gr. k-3). lib. bdg. 25.95 ***(978-1-62617-644-7(2),*** Blastoff! Readers) Bellwether Media.

Boyce, Natalie Pope & Osborne, Mary Pope. Dragons & Mythical Creatures. Molinari, Carlo, illus. 2016. (Magic Tree House - Fact Tracker Ser.: 35). (ENG.). 128p. (J). (gr. 2-5). 6.99 *(978-1-101-93636-8(3),* Random Hse. Bks. for Young Readers) Random Hse. Children's Bks.

Brett, Flora. Get to Know Komodo Dragons. 2015. (Get to Know Reptiles Ser.). (ENG.). 24p. (gr. 1-2). lib. bdg. 25.32 *(978-1-4914-2062-1(6))* Capstone Press of Coughlan Cos.

Broutin, Christian & Delafosse, Claude. Let's Look at Fairies, Witches, Giants & Dragons. 2012. (ENG., Illus.). 38p. (J). (gr. k-3). pap. 11.99 *(978-1-85103-358-4(0))* Moonlight Publishing, Ltd. GBR. Dist: Independent Pubs. Group.

Cain, Patrick G. Komodo Dragon, 1 vol. 2013. (Great Predators Ser.). (ENG., Illus.). 48p. (J). (gr. 3-6). lib. bdg. 32.79 *(978-1-61783-949-8(3),* 1360915) ABDO Publishing Co.

—Komodo Dragon Paperback. 2013. (Illus.). 48p. (J). pap. 15.64 *(978-1-62403-014-7(9),* 1360915, Core Library) ABDO Publishing Co.

Caldwell, S. a. Secrets of the Dragon World: Curiosities, Legends & Lore. 2014. (ENG., Illus.). 80p. (J). (gr. 3). pap. 16.95 *(978-1-78097-098-1(6))* Carlton Bks., Ltd. GBR. Dist: Sterling Publishing Co., Inc.

Castellano, Peter. Dragons. 2016. (Monsters! Ser.). (ENG.). 32p. (J). (gr. 1-2). pap. 10.50 *(978-1-4824-4086-7(5))* Stevens, Gareth Publishing LLLP.

Doeden, Matt. Anatomy of a Dragon. Mayer, Jonathan, illus. 2013. (World of Dragons Ser.). (ENG.). 32p. (gr. 1-2). lib. bdg. 26.65 *(978-1-62065-145-2(9))* Capstone Press of Coughlan Cos.

—Dragon Behavior, 1 vol. Mayer, Jonathan, illus. 2013. (World of Dragons Ser.). (ENG.). 32p. (gr. 1-2). lib. bdg. 26.65 *(978-1-62065-144-5(0))* Capstone Press of Coughlan Cos.

—Dragons in Mythology, 1 vol. 2013. (World of Dragons Ser.). (ENG.). 32p. (gr. 1-2). lib. bdg. 26.65 *(978-1-62065-143-8(2),* Blazers) Capstone Press of Coughlan Cos.

—Real-World Dragons, 1 vol. Pellegrino, Rich, illus. 2013. (World of Dragons Ser.). (ENG.). 32p. (gr. 1-2). lib. bdg. 26.65 *(978-1-62065-146-9(7),* Blazers) Capstone Press of Coughlan Cos.

—The World of Dragons. Mayer, Jonathan & Pellegrino, Rich, illus. 2013. (World of Dragons Ser.). (ENG.). 32p. (gr. 1-2). lib. bdg. 106.60 *(978-1-62065-147-6(5),* Blazers) Capstone Press of Coughlan Cos.

Dragons: Coloring Book. 2007. (Illus.). 20p. (J). 10.00 *(978-0-9795206-5-5(7))* Unseen Gallery.

Gish, Melissa. Komodo Dragons. 2012. (Living Wild Ser.). 48p. (J). (ENG.). (gr. 4-7). pap. 12.00 *(978-0-89812-672-3(X),* Creative Paperbacks); 35.65 *(978-1-60818-080-6(8),* Creative Education) Creative Co., The.

Hallmark, Darla, illus. More Dragons: Coloring Book by Darla Hallmark. 2007. 20p. (YA). 10.00 *(978-0-9795206-8-6(1))* Unseen Gallery.

Hamilton, John. Dragons, 1 vol. 2004. (Fantasy & Folklore Ser.). (ENG., Illus.). 32p. (gr. 4-8). 27.07 *(978-1-59197-711-7(8),* Abdo & Daughters) ABDO Publishing Co.

Hansen, Grace, et al. Dragones de Komodo. 2015. (Reptiles Ser.). (SPA., Illus.). 24p. (gr. k-1). pap. 7.95 *(978-1-4966-0503-0(9))* Capstone Classroom.

Hirsch, Rebecca E. Komodo Dragons: Deadly Hunting Reptiles. 2015. (ENG., Illus.). 32p. (J). (gr. 2-4). 26.65 *(978-1-4677-7977-7(6))* Lerner Publishing Group.

Holcomb, Carrie E. Dragons: A Fantasy Made Real. Holcomb, Carrie E., ed. 2007. (Illus.). 32p. (J). pap. 6.99 *(978-0-696-23693-8(1))* Meredith Bks.

Jeffrey, Gary. Dragons. 2011. (Graphic Mythical Creatures Ser.). (Illus.). 24p. (J). (gr. 3-5). pap. 8.15 *(978-1-4339-6032-1(X),* Gareth Stevens Learning Library); lib. bdg. 23.95 *(978-1-4339-6031-4(1))* Stevens, Gareth Publishing LLLP.

Johnson, Anne Akers & Murphy, Pat. Paper Flying Dragons: Design & Build Your Own Fantastic Flyers. Klutz Editors, ed. 2012. (ENG.). 48p. (J). (gr. 3). pap. 16.99 *(978-0-545-44936-6(7))* Klutz.

Krensky, Stephen. Dragons. 2006. (Monster Chronicles Ser.). (ENG., Illus.). 48p. (gr. 4-7). lib. bdg. 26.60 *(978-0-8225-6543-7(9),* Lerner Pubns.) Lerner Publishing Group.

Libra, Michael W. Dragons of Draegoni: Dragon Black's Revenge Book 2. 2012. (Illus.). 262p. pap. *(978-1-78148-505-7(4))* Grosvenor Hse. Publishing Ltd.

Loh-Hagan, Virginia. Dragons: Magic, Myth, & Mystery. 2016. (Magic, Myth, & Mystery Ser.). (ENG., Illus.). 32p. (J). (gr. 4-8). 29.93 *(978-1-63471-113-5(0),* 208563, 45th Parallel Press) Cherry Lake Publishing.

Mara, Wil. Bearded Dragons. 2017. (Real-Life Dragons Ser.). (ENG., Illus.). 32p. (gr. 3-4). pap. 7.95 *(978-1-5157-5074-1(4));* lib. bdg. 27.99 *(978-1-5157-5070-3(1))* Capstone Press of Coughlan Cos. (Edge Bks.).

Mara, Wil, et al. Real-Life Dragons. 2017. (Real-Life Dragons Ser.). (ENG.). 32p. (gr. 3-4). 111.96 *(978-1-5157-5089-5(2),* Edge Bks.) Capstone Press of Coughlan Cos.

Marsico, Katie. Beastly Monsters: From Dragons to Griffins. 2017. (Monster Mania Ser.). (ENG.). 32p. (J). (gr. 2-5). 12.99 ***(978-1-5124-3818-5(9),*** Lerner Pubns.); 39.99 ***(978-1-5124-3819-2(7),*** Lerner Pubns.); 39.99 ***(978-1-5124-2814-8(0),*** Lerner Pubns.); (Illus.). 26.65 *(978-1-5124-2592-5(3))* Lerner Publishing Group.

Mazurkiewicz, Jessica. Dragons Activity Book. 2011. (Dover Little Activity Bks.). (ENG.). 64p. (J). (gr. k-3). pap. 1.99 *(978-0-486-47521-9(2))* Dover Pubns., Inc.

McCullough, Joseph A. Dragonslayers, 1 vol. 2015. (ENG., Illus.). 80p. (J). 35.60 *(978-1-4777-8136-4(6),* Rosen Young Adult) Rosen Publishing Group, Inc., The.

McDowell, Pamela & Rose, Simon. Sea Dragons. 2011. (J). (gr. 2-4). pap. 12.95 *(978-1-61690-832-4(7),* AV2 by Weigl) Weigl Pubs., Inc.

Medina, Conni. Haz un Dragón del Año Nuevo Chino, 1 vol. 2nd rev. ed. 2012. (Nonfiction Readers Ser.). (SPA.). 20p. (J). (gr. 1-1). pap. 4.99 *(978-1-4333-4426-8(2))* Teacher Created Materials, Inc.

—Make a Chinese New Year Dragon, 1 vol. 2nd rev. ed. 2011. (Nonfiction Readers Ser.). (ENG.). 20p. (J). (gr. 1-1). pap. 4.99 *(978-1-4333-3593-8(X))* Teacher Created Materials, Inc.

Owings, Lisa. The Komodo Dragon. 2011. (Nature's Deadliest Ser.). (ENG., Illus.). 24p. (YA). (gr. 3-8). lib. bdg. 25.95 *(978-1-60014-667-1(8),* Pilot Bks.) Bellwether Media.

Paolini, Christopher. The Official Eragon Coloring Book. Ciruelo, illus. 2017. (Inheritance Cycle Ser.). (ENG.). 96p. (J). (gr. 7-12). pap. 15.99 ***(978-1-5247-1874-9(2),*** Knopf Bks. for Young Readers) Random Hse. Children's Bks.

Passes, David. Dragon Legends. 2012. (ENG., Illus.). 46p. (J). (gr. 4-7). pap. 9.99 *(978-1-84365-212-0(9),* Pavilion) Pavilion Bks. GBR. Dist: Independent Pubs. Group.

—Dragons: Truth, Myth & Legend. Anderson, Wayne, illus. 2007. (ENG.). 46p. (J). (gr. 4-7). pap. 11.95 *(978-1-84458-476-5(3))* Pavilion Bks. GBR. Dist: Independent Pubs. Group.

Perkins, Wendy. Sea Dragons. 2017. (Weird & Unusual Animals Ser.). (ENG.). 24p. (gr. 1-4). 20.95 ***(978-1-68151-159-7(2))*** Amicus Publishing.

Petrini, Catherine & Petrini, Catherine M. Dragons. 2004. (Kidhaven Science Library). (ENG., Illus.). 48p. (J). (gr. 3-7). lib. bdg. 27.50 *(978-0-7377-3163-7(X),* 1256753, Kidhaven) Cengage Gale.

Pringle, Laurence. Imagine a Dragon. Neilan, Eujin Kim, illus. 2008. (ENG.). 32p. (J). (gr. 2-4). 16.95 *(978-1-56397-328-4(6))* Boyds Mills Pr.

Rau, Dana Meachen. Dragons. 2010. (Bookworms Chapter Books: for Real? Ser.). 24p. (gr. 2-3). 22.79 *(978-1-60870-219-0(7))* Marshall Cavendish GBR. Dist: Marshall Cavendish Corp.

Raum, Elizabeth. Bearded Dragons. 2015. (Illus.). 32p. (J). lib. bdg. 28.50 *(978-1-60753-483-9(5))* Amicus Publishing.

—Komodo Dragons. 2015. (Illus.). 32p. (J). lib. bdg. 28.50 *(978-1-60753-488-4(6))* Amicus Publishing.

Renison, Jessica. The Secret History of Dragons. 2008. (Illus.). 96p. *(978-1-904756-96-5(4))* Kandour Ltd.

Riehecky, Janet. Komodo Dragons [Scholastic]: On the Hunt. 2011. (Killer Animals Ser.). 32p. pap. 1.00 *(978-1-4296-6483-7(5),* Blazers) Capstone Press of Coughlan Cos.

Roberts, Steven. Dragons! 2012. (Jr. Graphic Monster Stories Ser.). (ENG., Illus.). 24p. (J). (gr. 3-6). pap. 10.60 *(978-1-4488-8003-4(3));* lib. bdg. 25.25 *(978-1-4488-7903-8(5))* Rosen Publishing Group, Inc., The. (PowerKids Pr.).

Robertson, M. P., et al. Dare to Care: Pet Dragon. 2016. (ENG., Illus.). 32p. (J). (gr. 1-4). 17.99 *(978-1-84780-589-8(2),* Frances Lincoln Children's Bks.) Quarto Publishing Group UK GBR. Dist: Hachette Bk. Group.

Sautter, A. J. A Field Guide to Dragons, Trolls, & Other Dangerous Monsters, 1 vol. Ashcroft, Colin Michael et al, illus. 2014. (Fantasy Field Guides). (ENG.). 32p. (gr. 3-4). lib. bdg. 27.99 *(978-1-4914-0691-5(7))* Capstone Press of Coughlan Cos.

Scarace, Caroly. Dragons. 2014. (Big Book Of... Ser.). (Illus.). 48p. (gr. 3-6). 37.10 *(978-1-907184-90-1(2))* Book Hse. GBR. Dist: Black Rabbit Bks.

Sherman, Jill. Komodo Dragons. 2017. (Real-Life Dragons Ser.). (ENG., Illus.). 32p. (gr. 3-4). lib. bdg. 27.99 *(978-1-5157-5069-7(8),* Edge Bks.) Capstone Press of Coughlan Cos.

Tatchell, Judy. Dragons Lift-the-flap. Scott, Peter, illus. 2005. 16p. (J). (gr. 1-18). 11.99 *(978-0-7945-0968-2(1),* Usborne) EDC Publishing.

Topsell, John. How to Raise & Keep a Dragon. Nigg, Joseph, ed. 2nd rev. ed. 2013. (ENG.). 128p. (J). (gr. 4-7). 18.99 *(978-0-7641-6575-7(5))* Barron's Educational Series, Inc.

Turnbull, Stephanie. Komodo Dragon. 2015. (ENG., Illus.). 24p. (J). pap. 8.95 *(978-1-77092-215-0(6))* RiverStream Publishing.

Weiss, Bobbi Jg & Weiss, David Cody. Phonic Comics - Hiro Dragon Warrior: Fight or Flight Level 2, Issue 3. 2011. (ENG., Illus.). 24p. (J). (gr. 1-17). pap. 3.99 *(978-1-60169-111-8(4))* Innovative Kids.

Whittington, Thea. The Dragon's Back. 2010. (ENG., Illus.). 36p. (J). (gr. -1-3). pap. 9.95 *(978-988-99799-5-9(0))* Blacksmith Bks. HKG. Dist: National Bk. Network.

Yasuda, Anita. Dragon, the Phoenix, & the Beautiful Pearl: A Chinese Dragon Spirit Myth. 2014. (Short Tales Chinese Myths Ser.). 32p. (J). (gr. 3-6). lib. bdg. 24.21 *(978-1-62402-030-8(5),* Short Tales) Magic Wagon.

Yates, Gene. The Dragon Opposites Book. 2005. (Illus.). 14p. (J). *(978-1-58865-283-6(1))* Kidsbooks, LLC.

Yates, Gene, illus. The Dragon Opposites Book. 2006. (J). *(978-1-58865-362-8(5))* Kidsbooks, LLC.

Zhang, Song Nan. A Time of Golden Dragons. 2004. (J). (gr. 3-5). spiral bd. *(978-0-616-07258-5(9))* Canadian National Institute for the Blind/Institut National Canadien pour les Aveugles.

Zhang, Song Nan & Zhang, Hao Yu. A Time of Golden Dragons. Zhang, Song Nan, illus. 2006. (ENG., Illus.). 24p. (J). (gr. 4-7). pap. 11.95 *(978-0-88776-791-3(5),* Tundra Bks.) Tundra Bks. CAN. Dist: Penguin Random Hse. LLC.

DRAGONS—FICTION

Abbott, Tony. The Ice Dragon. Caparó, Antonio Javier, illus. 2012. (Underworlds Ser.: 4). (ENG.). 128p. (J). (gr. 2-5). pap. 4.99 *(978-0-545-30834-2(8),* Scholastic Paperbacks) Scholastic, Inc.

ABDO Publishing Company Staff. Dragon Slayer's Academy. 2006. (Dragon Slayers' Academy Ser.). 112p. (gr. 1-6). 145.26 *(978-1-59961-121-1(X))* Spotlight.

Aceti, Jerome & ASF, Jerome. Bacca & the Riddle of the Diamond Dragon: An Unofficial Minecrafter's Adventure. 2015. (ENG.). 224p. (J). (gr. 2). pap. 9.99 *(978-1-5107-0398-8(5),* Sky Pony Pr.) Skyhorse Publishing Co., Inc.

Ackland, Rachel. Nick the Knight & the Dragon! 2017. (ENG.). 22p. (J). (gr. -1-2). pap. 5.99 *(978-1-4380-0983-4(6))* Barron's Educational Series, Inc.

Adams, Leon. Dragon Pearls. 2008. 176p. pap. 13.95 *(978-1-4357-0395-7(2))* Lulu Pr., Inc.

—Land of the Dragons. 2009. 290p. pap. 18.60 *(978-0-557-00645-8(7))* Lulu Pr., Inc.

Adeney, Anne & Kavanagh, Peter. George & the Dragon. 2009. (Hopscotch Adventures Ser.). (Illus.). 32p. (J). (gr. 1). lib. bdg. 25.65 *(978-1-59771-183-8(7))* Sea-To-Sea Pubns.

Adventures in Flatfrost. 2014. (Kingdom of Wrenly Ser.: 5). (ENG., Illus.). 128p. (J). (gr. k-4). pap. 5.99 *(978-1-4814-1388-6(0),* Little Simon) Little Simon.

Aguirre, Jorge. Dragons Beware! 2015. (Chronicles of Claudette Ser.). (J). lib. bdg. 26.95 *(978-0-606-37298-5(9))* Turtleback Bks.

Allabach, P. R. Dragon & Captain. Turnbloom, Lucas, illus. 2015. (ENG.). 32p. (J). (gr. k-2). 17.95 *(978-1-936261-33-8(2))* Flashlight Pr.

Alongi, Anthony & Davidson, MaryJanice. Jennifer Scales & the Ancient Furnace. 2007. (Jennifer Scales Ser.: 1). (ENG.). 224p. (gr. 12-18). 7.99 *(978-0-441-01474-3(7),* Ace Bks.) Penguin Publishing Group.

—Jennifer Scales & the Messenger of Light. 2007. (Jennifer Scales Ser.: 2). (ENG.). 288p. (gr. 12-18). 7.99 *(978-0-441-01510-8(7),* Ace Bks.) Penguin Publishing Group.

Alva, Kristian. The Balborite Curse: Book Four of the Dragon Stones Saga. 2013. 240p. pap. 9.98 *(978-1-937361-11-2(X),* Defiant Pr.) Passkey Pubns.

Ameet Studio Staff. Dragon Adventures. 2016. (LEGO Elves Ser.). (ENG.). 32p. (J). (gr. 2-5). pap. 8.99 *(978-0-545-92539-6(8))* Scholastic, Inc.

Anders, Lou. Nightborn. 2015. (Thrones & Bones Ser.). (ENG.). 368p. (J). (gr. 3-7). 16.99 *(978-0-385-39036-1(X),* Crown Books For Young Readers) Random Hse. Children's Bks.

Andersen, Izzyana. The Power of the Gemstones: Revealing Her Secret. 2016. (ENG., Illus.). (J). pap. 15.99 *(978-1-59298-594-4(7))* Beaver's Pond Pr., Inc.

Anna, Jennifer. Year of the Dragon. 2nd ed. 2007. (Illus.). 56p. (J). pap. 24.99 *(978-1-59092-155-5(0))* Blue Forge Pr.

Appel, Julie & Guglielmo, Amy. Find King Henry's Treasure. 2010. (Touch the Art Ser.). (ENG., Illus.). 24p. (J). (gr. -1-1). bds. 12.95 *(978-1-4027-6324-3(7))* Sterling Publishing Co., Inc.

Appleton-Smith, Laura. Oh My, It Must Be the Sky! Neel, Preston, illus. 2004. (Book to Remember Ser.). (ENG.). 52p. pap. 8.95 *(978-1-929262-21-2(3),* Books To Remember) Flyleaf Publishing.

Aptekar, Devan. How to Train Your Dragon - Befriending a Foe. 2010. (How to Train Your Dragon Ser.). 24p. (J). (gr. -1-2). pap. 3.99 *(978-0-06-156735-3(3),* HarperFestival) HarperCollins Pubs.

Arato, Rona. Mrs. Kaputnik's Pool Hall & Matzo Ball Emporium. 2010. (ENG., Illus.). 192p. (J). (gr. 4-7). pap. 9.95 *(978-0-88776-967-2(5),* Tundra Bks.) Tundra Bks. CAN. Dist: Penguin Random Hse. LLC.

Archambault, Marc. Hal the Unwashed Dragon. 2009. 28p. pap. 18.98 *(978-0-557-09894-1(7))* Lulu Pr., Inc.

—Hal the Unwashed Dragon (perfect Bound) 2009. 32p. pap. 18.97 *(978-0-557-12009-3(8))* Lulu Pr., Inc.

Aronson, Deborah. Dragons from Mars. Jack, Colin, illus. 2016. 32p. (J). (gr. -1-3). 17.99 *(978-0-06-236850-8(8))* HarperCollins Pubs.

Aumuller, Kimberly. Dragon's Hope: Tale of the Guardians. 2009. 224p. 25.95 *(978-0-595-50945-4(2));* pap. 15.95 *(978-0-595-52209-5(2))* iUniverse, Inc.

Avalon, Dawn. Bubbels. Een Vochtig Draakje. 2006. 60p. pap. 8.23 *(978-1-4116-1193-1(4))* Lulu Pr., Inc.

—Bubbles. A Wet Dragon. 2006. 59p. pap. 8.21 *(978-1-4116-1177-1(2))* Lulu Pr., Inc.

Avanti, Michele. GreeHee the Journey of Five: Tales of Tamoor Book One. 2008. (Illus.). 304p. (J). per. 14.99 *(978-0-9779590-4-4(X))* GreeHee Publishing.

Averbeck, Jim. Oh No, Little Dragon! Averbeck, Jim, illus. 2012. (ENG., Illus.). 40p. (J). (gr. -1-1). 14.99 *(978-1-4169-9545-6(5),* Atheneum Bks. for Young Readers) Simon & Schuster Children's Publishing.

Awdry, Wilbert V. & Random House Editors. Thomas & Percy & the Dragon. 2003. (Thomas & Friends Step into Reading Ser.). (gr. -1-2). lib. bdg. 13.55 *(978-0-613-89791-4(9),* Turtleback) Turtleback Bks.

C
D

Axworthy, Anni. The Dragon Who Couldn't Do Dragony Things. 2008. (Little Dragon Ser.). (ENG., Illus.). 32p. (J). (gr. -1-k). pap. *(978-1-84089-344-1(3))* Zero to Ten, Ltd.

—The Dragon Who Couldn't Do Sporty Things. Axworthy, Anni, illus. 2008. (Little Dragon Ser.). (ENG., Illus.). 32p. (J). (gr. -1-k). *(978-1-84089-533-9(0))* Zero to Ten, Ltd.

—Dragon Who Couldn't Do Sporty Things. Axworthy, Anni, illus. 2010. (Little Dragon Ser.). (ENG., Illus.). 32p. (J). (gr. -1-k). pap. *(978-1-84089-556-8(X))* Zero to Ten, Ltd.

Baccalario, Pierdomenico. Enchanted Emporium, 1 vol. Pernigotti, Chiara, tr. Bruno, Iacopo, illus. 2014. (Enchanted Emporium Ser.). (ENG.). 240p. (gr. 4-8). 53.30 *(978-1-4342-9603-0(2))* Stone Arch Bks.

Bagdanov, Patricia. The Adventures of Charlie & a Dragon Named Trevor. 2013. 26p. pap. 16.95 *(978-1-63004-985-0(9))* PublishAmerica, Inc.

Bailey, Margaret A. Dragonworld & the Room of Strange Hangings. 2009. 172p. pap. 11.99 *(978-1-4389-8252-6(6))* AuthorHouse.

Baillie, Allan. DragonQuest. Harris, Wayne, illus. 2013. (ENG.). 40p. (J). (gr. k-4). 16.99 *(978-0-7636-6617-0(3))* Candlewick Pr.

Baker, E. D. Dragon Kiss. 2nd ed. (Tales of the Frog Princess Ser.). (ENG.). (YA). 2009. 288p. (gr. 5-8). 16.99 *(978-1-59990-348-4(2),* 9781599903484) 2015. 304p. (gr. 3-6). pap. 8.99 *(978-1-61963-623-1(9),* 9781619636231) Bloomsbury Publishing USA. (Bloomsbury USA Childrens).

—The Dragon Princess. (Tales of the Frog Princess Ser.). (ENG.). (YA). 2010. 240p. (gr. 5-8). pap. 7.99 *(978-1-59990-448-1(9),* 9781599904481) 2008. (Illus.). 224p. (gr. 4-8). 16.99 *(978-1-59990-194-7(3),* 9781599901947) Bloomsbury Publishing USA. (Bloomsbury USA Childrens).

—A Prince among Frogs. 2nd ed. 2010. (Tales of the Frog Princess Ser.). (ENG.). 224p. (YA). (gr. 5-8). 16.99 *(978-1-59990-349-1(0),* 9781599903491, Bloomsbury USA Childrens) Bloomsbury Publishing USA.

Baker, Ken. Old MacDonald Had a Dragon, 0 vols. Santoro, Christopher, illus. 2012. (ENG.). 32p. (J). (gr. k-3). 16.99 *(978-0-7614-6175-3(2),* 9780761461753, Amazon Children's Publishing) Amazon Publishing.

Ballou, Kathy. The Tracks Out Back. l.t. ed. 2005. (Illus.). 24p. (J). per. 10.00 *(978-1-932338-50-8(0))* Lifevest Publishing, Inc.

Banks, Kate. Max's Dragon. Kulikov, Boris, illus. 2008. (Max's Words Ser.: 2). (ENG.). 32p. (J). (gr. -1-3). 17.99 *(978-0-374-39921-4(2),* 9780374399214, Farrar, Straus & Giroux (BYR)) Farrar, Straus & Giroux.

Banta, Sandra F. Fancy the Beautiful Little Dragon: Book Number Two Little One's Series. Hecker, Vera, illus. l.t. ed. 2006. 45p. per. 11.99 *(978-1-59879-157-0(5))* Lifevest Publishing, Inc.

—Muffy the Dragon. Hecker, Vera, illus. l.t. ed. 2005. 19p. (J). per. 9.99 *(978-1-59879-060-3(9))* Lifevest Publishing, Inc.

Bar-el, Dan. Not Your Typical Dragon. Bowers, Tim, illus. 2013. (ENG.). 40p. (J). (gr. -1-k). 16.99 *(978-0-670-01402-6(8),* Viking Books for Young Readers) Penguin Young Readers Group.

Barandela, Jeremy. United We Stand. 2007. 376p. per. 20.95 *(978-1-4327-1495-6(3))* Outskirts Pr., Inc.

Barany, Beth. Henrietta the dragon Slayer. 2011. (ENG.). 234p. (YA). pap. 8.99 *(978-0-9832960-4-1(9))* Barany Publishing.

Barchers, Suzanne. Dragonwings. 2015. (Great Works). (ENG., Illus.). 72p. (gr. 4-8). pap. 9.99 *(978-1-4258-8977-7(8))* Shell Educational Publishing.

Barnes, Kenneth Edward. Invasion of the Dregs. 2011. 164p. (gr. 10-12). pap. 13.50 *(978-1-4634-0745-2(9));* (gr. 4-6). 22.23 *(978-1-4634-0726-1(2))* AuthorHouse.

Barnhill, Kelly. Iron Hearted Violet. Bruno, Iacopo, illus. 2014. (ENG.). 448p. (J). (gr. 3-7). pap. 7.00 *(978-0-316-05675-5(8))* Little, Brown Bks. for Young Readers.

Barron, T. A. Doomraga's Revenge. (Merlin Saga Ser.: 7). (ENG.). (J). (gr. 5-18). 2009. 256p. 19.99 *(978-0-399-25212-9(6),* Philomel Bks.)Bk. 7. 2011. 272p. 8.99 *(978-0-14-241925-0(7),* Puffin Books) Penguin Young Readers Group.

—The Dragon of Avalon, Bk. 6. 2011. (Merlin Saga Ser.: 6). (ENG.). 336p. (J). (gr. 5-18). 8.99 *(978-0-14-241924-3(9),* Puffin Books) Penguin Young Readers Group.

—Merlin's Dragon. 2008. (Merlin Saga Ser.: 6). (ENG.). 336p. (J). (gr. 5-18). 19.99 *(978-0-399-24750-7(5),* Philomel Bks.) Penguin Young Readers Group.

—Ultimate Magic, 8 vols., Bk. 8. 2011. (Merlin Saga Ser.: 8). (ENG.). 256p. (J). (gr. 5-18). 8.99 *(978-0-14-241926-7(5),* Puffin Books) Penguin Young Readers Group.

Bartow, Philip. T & the Jello Castle-Book 1. 2013. 252p. (J). pap. 13.30 *(978-0-9835176-2-7(2))* Institute For Outdoor Awareness, Inc.

—T & the Jello Castle-Book 2: Bio Bots. 2013. 264p. (J). pap. 13.30 *(978-0-9835176-3-4(0))* Institute For Outdoor Awareness, Inc.

Bass, Jules. Herb, the Vegetarian Dragon. Harter, Debbie, illus. 2005. 32p. (J). (gr. 1-5). reprint ed. pap. 6.99 *(978-1-84148-127-2(0))* Barefoot Bks., Inc.

—Herb, the Vegetarian Dragon: Book & Bendo Gift Set. Harter, Debbie, illus. 2005. 32p. (J). 14.99 *(978-1-905236-43-5(3))* Barefoot Bks., Inc.

Bass, Jules & Harter, Debbie. Herb the Vegetarian Dragon. (ENG., Illus.). 32p. (J). 2008. 16.99 *(978-1-84686-248-9(5))* 2005. pap. 8.99 *(978-1-905236-47-3(6))* Barefoot Bks., Inc.

Baxter, Nicola. Amazing Dragons: Fiendish Tales of Dastardly Deeds. King, Colin, illus. 2012. (ENG.). 80p. (J). (gr. k-4). pap. 9.99 *(978-1-84322-836-3(X))* Anness Publishing GBR. Dist: National Bk. Network.

Bealer-Wynton, Cheryl. Blinky's Island. 2008. 60p. pap. 6.50 *(978-1-4303-1146-1(0))* Lulu Pr., Inc.

Beck, A. E. Master-E: Travel into Mystical Dragon Dimensions: Collision of Fantasy, Science Fiction & Physics. 2010. 212p. pap. 49.49 *(978-1-4490-3612-6(0))* AuthorHouse.

Beekman, Kelley Lee. Sir Eli & the Halloween Dragon: The Legend of the Toasted Marshmallow. 2006. 55p. pap. 16.95 *(978-1-4241-4047-3(1))* PublishAmerica, Inc.

Bell, Hilari. The Prophecy. 2006. (ENG., Illus.). 208p. (J). (gr. 5-9). 15.99 *(978-0-06-059943-0(X))* HarperCollins Pubs.

Bergsma, Jody. Wizard. 2nd ed. 2008. (Illus.). 32p. (J). 15.95 *(978-0-9740190-9-3(7))* Illumination Arts Publishing Co., Inc.

Bernhardt, William. Princess Alice & the Dreadful Dragon. McGhee, Kerry, illus. 2007. 27p. (J). 19.99 *(978-1-930709-65-2(X))* HAWK Publishing Group.

Biedrzycki, David. Me & My Dragon. Biedrzycki, David, illus. 2011. (ENG., Illus.). 40p. (J). (gr. -1-3). 17.95 *(978-1-58089-278-0(7));* pap. 7.95 *(978-1-58089-279-7(5))* Charlesbridge Publishing, Inc.

—Me & My Dragon: Christmas Spirit. Biedrzycki, David, illus. 2015. (ENG., Illus.). 40p. (J). (gr. -1-3). lib. bdg. 17.95 *(978-1-58089-622-1(7))* Charlesbridge Publishing, Inc.

—Me & My Dragon: Scared of Halloween. Biedrzycki, David, illus. 2013. (ENG., Illus.). 32p. (J). (gr. -1-3). pap. 7.95 *(978-1-58089-659-7(6))* Charlesbridge Publishing, Inc.

Biedrzycki, David & Canetti, Yanitzia. Mi Dragón y Yo. Biedrzycki, David, illus. 2014. (SPA., Illus.). 32p. (J). (gr. -1-3). pap. 7.95 *(978-1-58089-574-3(3));* lib. bdg. 17.95 *(978-1-58089-693-1(6))* Charlesbridge Publishing, Inc.

Bird, Benjamin. Magic Monsters! Levins, Tim, illus. 2015. (Amazing Adventures of Superman! Ser.). (ENG.). 32p. (gr. k-2). pap. 3.95 *(978-1-4795-6525-2(3),* DC Super Heroes) Stone Arch Bks.

Bishop, Debbie. MYST of the Lost Shadow Boys. 2008. (ENG.). 228p. (J). (gr. 4-9). pap. 6.99 *(978-1-932431-79-7(9))* Left Field,Angel Gate.

Black, Robyn Hood. Sir Mike. Murphy, David, illus. 2005. (Rookie Reader Skill Set Ser.). (ENG.). 32p. (J). (gr. k-2). per. 4.95 *(978-0-516-25020-5(5),* Children's Pr.) Scholastic Library Publishing.

Blackford, Ami. Quest for the Dragon Stone: A Duncan Family Adventure. Blackford, Ami, illus. 2006. (Illus.). 48p. (J). (gr. 3-7). 16.95 *(978-1-60108-008-0(5))* Red Cygnet Pr.

Blade, Adam. Vedra & Krimon the Twin Dragons. 2012. (Beast Quest Special Edition Ser.: 2). lib. bdg. 16.00 *(978-0-606-26187-6(7),* Turtleback) Turtleback Bks.

Blanco Moleon, Elena. The Talented Demetri. 2012. 28p. pap. 9.17 *(978-1-61370-003-7(2))* Eriginal Bks. LLC.

Blueraven, Solaris. Mr. Sun & the Halloween Ball. 2010. 20p. 13.99 *(978-1-4520-0431-0(5))* AuthorHouse.

Blum, Vicki. The Dragon Prince. Sourwine, David, illus. 2005. (ENG.). 160p. pap. *(978-0-439-95668-0(4))* Scholastic Canada, Ltd.

Blunden, Alan. Tommy & the Garden Shed. 2008. 104p. pap. *(978-1-84923-111-4(7))* YouWriteOn.

Bosch, Pseudonymous. Bad Luck. (Bad Bks.: 2). (ENG., Illus.). (J). (gr. 3-7). 2017. 304p. pap. 7.99 *(978-0-316-32044-3(7))* 2016. 288p. 17.00 *(978-0-316-32042-9(0))* Little, Brown Bks. for Young Readers.

—Bad Luck. 2017. (Bad Bks.: 2). (J). lib. bdg. 18.40 *(978-0-606-39475-8(3))* Turtleback Bks.

Bow, Patricia. The Prism Blade. 2008. (Passage to Mythrin Ser.: 2). (ENG.). 272p. (YA). (gr. 7-12). pap. 12.99 *(978-1-55002-809-6(X),* Boardwalk Bks.) Dundurn CAN. Dist: Ingram Publisher Services.

Bowles, Paula. What Goes Up. Bowles, Paula, illus. 2013. (ENG., Illus.). 32p. (J). (gr. -1-1). 12.95 *(978-1-58925-119-9(9))* Tiger Tales.

Branson, Terri. Brother Dragon. Taylor, Chet, illus. 2004. (J). 18.99 *(978-0-9755888-5-7(0))* Dragonfly Publishing, Inc.

—A Very Dragon Christmas. 2007. (Illus.). 24p. (J). *(978-0-9797574-0-2(1));* per. *(978-0-9797574-1-9(X))* Dragonfly Publishing, Inc.

Brauner, Susan. The Adventures of Sohi: Mystery of Moon Island. 2011. 207p. 28.95 *(978-1-4327-6752-5(6));* pap. 15.95 *(978-1-4327-6536-1(1))* Outskirts Pr., Inc.

Brennan, Sarah. The Tale of Chester Choi. Harrison, Harry, illus. 2013. (ENG.). 32p. (J). 24.95 *(978-1-937160-16-6(5))* Eliassen Creative.

Briggs-Greenberg, Ruthie. Felicity the Dragon. 2015. (ENG., Illus.). 32p. (J). (gr. -1-2). 15.95 *(978-1-63076-062-5(5))* Taylor Trade Publishing.

Brill, Calista. Little Wing Learns to Fly. Bell, Jennifer A., illus. 2016. (Little Wing Ser.). 32p. (J). (gr. -1-3). 17.99 *(978-0-06-236033-5(7))* HarperCollins Pubs.

Broderick, Paula. The Quest: The First Toby & Sox Adventure. 2011. (ENG., Illus.). 160p. pap. *(978-1-84876-626-6(2))* Troubador Publishing Ltd.

Bröger, Achim. Historia de Dragolina (Story of Little Dragon) 4th ed. (SPA., Illus.). 32p. (J). 14.95 *(978-84-261-1924-7(7))* Juventud, Editorial ESP. Dist: AIMS International Bks., Inc.

Brooks, Charlie. Greystone Valley. Grundy, Jessica, illus. 2013. 166p. 17.99 *(978-1-938821-33-2(5));* 198p. pap. 9.99 *(978-1-938821-41-7(6))* Grey Gecko Pr.

Brooks, Felicity. Jason & the Argonauts. Humphreys, Graham, illus. 2005. 144p. (J). pap. 4.95 *(978-0-7945-0275-1(X),* Usborne) EDC Publishing.

Brown, Alan James. Michael & the Monkey King. 2008. 180p. pap. 16.95 *(978-1-4092-0241-7(0))* Lulu Pr., Inc.

Brown, Kevin. In a Field of Sunflowers. 2006. pap. 9.00 *(978-0-8059-6921-4(7))* Dorrance Publishing Co., Inc.

Brown, Kimberly. Autumn Castles. 2012. 28p. pap. 12.50 *(978-1-61897-032-9(1),* Strategic Bk. Publishing) Strategic Book Publishing & Rights Agency (SBPRA).

Bruchac, Joseph. Dragon Castle. 2011. (ENG.). 352p. (J). (gr. 5-18). 16.99 *(978-0-8037-3376-3(3),* Dial Bks) Penguin Young Readers Group.

Bryan, Jennifer Liu. The Different Dragon. Hosler, Danamarie, illus. 2006. (J). pap. 12.95 *(978-0-9674468-6-8(4))* Two Lives Publishing.

Bryant, Ann. Dragons vs Dinos. 2014. (ENG., Illus.). 32p. (J). *(978-0-7787-1328-9(8))* Crabtree Publishing Co.

Bucher, Heatherly & Menking, Amanda. The Happy Dragon, 1 vol. Menking, Amanda & Fisher, Sean, illus. 2006. 32p. (J). *(978-0-9790920-1-5(9))* MoonRattles.

Buckmaster, Heath L. The Dragons of Tarnack. 2008. 142p. pap. 13.99 *(978-1-4357-4624-4(4))* Lulu Pr., Inc.

Bulla, Lynda. Freedom Rings: An American Parable. 2005. (Illus.). 32p. (J). lib. bdg. 14.99 *(978-0-9724272-3-4(6))* Katydid Publishing LLC.

Burgess, Jennifer. DJ Daring & the Dangerous Dragon. 2013. 20p. pap. 11.97 *(978-1-61204-287-9(2),* Strategic Bk. Publishing) Strategic Book Publishing & Rights Agency (SBPRA).

Burgis, Stephanie. The Dragon with a Chocolate Heart. 2017. (ENG.). 256p. (J). 16.99 *(978-1-68119-343-4(4),* 9781681193434, Bloomsbury USA Childrens) Bloomsbury Publishing USA.

Burnham, Janet Hayward. The Dragoness Mess. 2003. (Illus.). 32p. (J). (gr. k-1). pap. 12.95 *(978-0-9740743-1-3(4))* My Little Jessie Pr.

Cameron, Anne. The Fire Dragon Storm. 2016. (Lightning Catcher Ser.: 4). 464p. (J). (gr. 3-7). 16.99 *(978-0-06-211286-6(4),* Greenwillow Bks.) HarperCollins Pubs.

Campbell, Hannah. Skylanders Universe: Take Flight & Fight! 2015. lib. bdg. 14.75 *(978-0-606-36801-8(9))* Turtleback Bks.

Campbell, R. W. Merrick Tumbledorf: The Last Talcomite Dragon. 2013. (ENG.). 250p. (YA). pap. 15.95 *(978-1-4787-1312-8(7))* Outskirts Pr., Inc.

Cannon, Chris. Trial by Fire. 2016. (ENG., Illus.). 330p. (J). pap. 16.99 *(978-1-68281-140-5(9))* Entangled Publishing, LLC.

Cano, Carles & Carles, Cano. Un Dragon a Dieta. Bravo, Juan & Bravo, Fran, illus. 2006. (Montana Encantada Ser.). (SPA.). 36p. (J). (gr. 1-2). pap. 8.50 *(978-84-241-8747-7(4))* Everest Editora ESP. Dist: Lectorum Pubns., Inc.

Carey, Janet Lee. Dragon's Keep. 2007. 302p. (J). *(978-1-4287-3929-1(7))* Harcourt Trade Pubs.

—Dragon's Keep. 2008. (ENG., Illus.). 320p. (YA). (gr. 7-18). pap. 7.95 *(978-0-15-206401-3(X))* Houghton Mifflin Harcourt Publishing Co.

—Dragonswood. 2013. (ENG.). 416p. (YA). (gr. 7). pap. 9.99 *(978-0-14-242432-2(3),* Firebird) Penguin Young Readers Group.

—In the Time of Dragon Moon. 2015. (ENG.). 480p. (YA). (gr. 7). 17.99 *(978-0-8037-3810-2(2),* Kathy Dawson Books) Penguin Young Readers Group.

Casey, C. A. Dragon Drool. 2nd ed. 2010. (ENG.). 128p. (J). (gr. 4-7). pap. 7.95 *(978-1-934452-47-9(5),* Dragonfeather Bks.) Bedazzled Ink Publishing Co.

Cassidy, Georgina M. The True Make Believe Story: TTMBS Collection. 2011. 64p. pap. 31.99 *(978-1-4628-6236-8(5))* Xlibris Corp.

Cattanach, Ann. Malpas the Dragon. Renouf, Michael, illus. 2007. (ENG.). 28p. (J). (gr. 3-7). per. 15.95 *(978-1-84310-572-5(1),* 1774) Kingsley, Jessica Pubs. GBR. Dist: Macmillan Distribution Ltd.

Cave, Kathryn. You've Got Dragons, 1 vol. Maland, Nick, illus. 2003. (ENG.). 32p. (J). (gr. 1-5). 16.95 *(978-1-56145-284-2(X))* Peachtree Pubs.

Chambers, Melinda. The Day the Snapdragons Snapped Back. Spiker, Sue Ann, illus. 2007. 32p. (J). 16.95 *(978-0-929915-72-2(0))* Headline Bks., Inc.

Chandra, Rohini S. The Dragon in the Candle Jar. 2013. 52p. pap. 16.95 *(978-1-4626-9842-4(5))* America Star Bks.

Chang, Grace. Jin Jin & Rain Wizard. Chang, Chong, illus. 2009. (ENG.). 48p. (J). (gr. -1-3). 16.95 *(978-1-59270-086-8(1))* Enchanted Lion Bks., LLC.

—Jin Jin the Dragon. Chang, Chong, illus. 2008. (ENG.). 48p. (J). (gr. -1-3). 16.95 *(978-1-59270-102-5(7))* Enchanted Lion Bks., LLC.

Chapman, Karean. The Adventures of Northern the Moose & a Dragon Named Zeus. Ciesinka, Izabela, illus. 2010. 38p. pap. 12.95 *(978-1-935268-44-4(9))* Halo Publishing International.

Childress, Jenna Lynn. Dragon Soul: Book One of the Triune Jewels. 2003. 262p. (YA). per. 8.00 *(978-0-9704006-2-8(4))* Bound & Determined Pubs.

Chima, Cinda Williams. The Dragon Heir. 2009. (Heir Chronicles Ser.). (ENG., Illus.). 528p. (J). (gr. 5-9). pap. 9.99 *(978-1-4231-1071-2(4))* Hyperion Pr.

Chin, Oliver. The Year of the Dragon: Tales from the Chinese Zodiac. 2012. (Tales from the Chinese Zodiac Ser.: 7). (ENG., Illus.). 36p. (J). (gr. -1-3). 15.95 *(978-1-59702-028-2(1))* Immedium.

Chipman, Laura. Dragonspeaker. 2005. 76p. pap. 19.95 *(978-1-4241-0136-8(0))* America Star Bks.

Ciccone, Tiziana. Taylor, Please Stop Talking! Cannavicci, Luigi A., illus. 2013. 32p. pap. 12.95 *(978-1-62516-817-7(9),* Strategic Bk. Publishing) Strategic Book Publishing & Rights Agency (SBPRA).

Claire Hamelin Bruyere. Princess Bonnie & the Dragon. Mary Connors, illus. 2009. 16p. pap. 8.49 *(978-1-4389-8731-6(5))* AuthorHouse.

Clark, Gloria. The Little Candy Breathing Dragons. 2008. 36p. per. 12.95 *(978-1-4327-1510-6(0))* Outskirts Pr., Inc.

Clark, Hamish. Mara's Flame. 2006. 191p. spiral bd. 12.99 *(978-1-4116-2768-0(7))* Lulu Pr., Inc.

Clarke, Jane. G. E. M. Parsons, Garry, illus. 2008. (ENG.). 32p. (J). (gr. -1-k). pap. 9.95 *(978-0-09-948012-9(3),* Red Fox) Random House Children's Books GBR. Dist: Independent Pubs. Group.

Coats, Lucy. Dragon Healer. Bean, Brett, illus. 2015. 136p. (J). **(978-1-4806-8442-3(2),** Grosset & Dunlap) Penguin Publishing Group.

—Dragon Healer. 2015. (Beasts of Olympus Ser.: 4). lib. bdg. 16.00 *(978-0-606-38409-4(X))* Turtleback Bks.

—Dragon Healer #4. Bean, Brett, illus. 2015. (Beasts of Olympus Ser.: 4). (ENG.). 144p. (J). (gr. 2-4). 5.99 *(978-0-448-46196-0(X),* Grosset & Dunlap) Penguin Young Readers Group.

Cohen, Lawrence J. The Dragon's Familiar. 2008. 236p. 25.95 *(978-0-595-63430-9(3));* (YA). pap. 15.95 *(978-0-595-51413-7(8))* iUniverse, Inc.

Cohen, Warren Lee. Dragon Baked Bread. Ssebulime, John, illus. 2005. 32p. (J). *(978-1-902636-70-2(8))* Clairview Bks.

Cole, Henry. Bayberry Island. Cole, Henry, illus. 2017. (Brambleheart Ser.: 2). (Illus.). 176p. (J). (gr. 3-7). 16.99 *(978-0-06-224551-9(1),* Tegen, Katherine Bks) HarperCollins Pubs.

—Brambleheart. Cole, Henry, illus. 2016. (Brambleheart Ser.: 1). (Illus.). 272p. (J). (gr. 3-7). 16.99 *(978-0-06-224546-5(5))* HarperCollins Pubs.

Collett, Susan, illus. The Christmas Dragon. Collett, Susan, . 2007. 64p. (J). pap. 5.95 *(978-0-9678115-1-2(1))* Dragonseed Pr.

Collier, Kevin Scott. Diligence the Dragon Vol. 1: A Prebiblical Fable. l.t. ed. 2005. (Illus.). 22p. (J). E-Book 9.95 incl. cd-rom *(978-1-933090-25-2(1))* Guardian Angel Publishing, Inc.

Collins, Christine. The Knight Meets Ole Dragon. 2009. 100p. pap. 28.95 *(978-1-4327-4128-0(4))* Outskirts Pr., Inc.

Connolly, MarcyKate. Monstrous. Young, Skottie, illus. (J). (gr. 3-7). 2016. 448p. pap. 7.99 *(978-0-06-227272-0(1))* 2015. (ENG.). 432p. 16.99 *(978-0-06-227271-3(3))* HarperCollins Pubs.

—Monstrous. 2016. (J). lib. bdg. 18.40 *(978-0-606-38136-9(8))* Turtleback Bks.

Connolly, Tina. Seriously Wicked. 2015. (ENG.). 208p. (YA). (gr. 8-12). 17.99 *(978-0-7653-7516-2(8),* 9780765375162, Tor Teen) Doherty, Tom Assocs., LLC.

Coombs, Kate. The Runaway Princess. l.t. ed. 2007. (Literacy Bridge Middle Reader Ser.). 325p. (J). (gr. 3-7). 22.95 *(978-0-7862-9633-0(X))* Thorndike Pr.

Coons, Susan Anderson. Ibakon, Gretl & the Stinky,Sticky Dragon, Vol.1. rev. ed. 2008. (Illus.). 45p. (J). 10.95 *(978-0-9721410-2-4(2))* Vinland Pr.

Corwin, Katherine A. R. Greg the Bearded Dragon & Thomas the Sea Turtle: A Tale of Adventure, Discovery, & Friendship. 2012. 28p. pap. 19.99 *(978-1-4685-7958-1(4))* AuthorHouse.

Coughlin, Denise. Dragon in My Pocket. Kastan, Bill, illus. 2005. (J). *(978-0-9765905-0-7(6))* Rose Valley Publishing.

Courtauld, Sarah & Burniac, Lauren. The Perilous Princess Plot. 2015. (Buckle & Squash Ser.). (ENG., Illus.). 192p. (J). (gr. 2-5). 14.99 *(978-1-250-05277-3(7),* 9781250052773) Feiwel & Friends.

Coville, Bruce. The Dragon of Doom. Coville, Katherine, illus. 2005. (Moongobble & Me Ser.: Bk. 1). (ENG.). 80p. (J). (gr. 1-5). pap. 5.99 *(978-0-689-85757-7(8),* Aladdin) Simon & Schuster Children's Publishing.

—The Dragonslayers. unabr. ed. 2004. (Words Take Wingtm Ser.). 119p. (J). (gr. 3-6). pap. 29.00 incl. audio *(978-0-8072-7988-5(9),* S YA 958 SP, Listening Library) Random Hse. Audio Publishing Group.

—Jeremy Thatcher, Dragon Hatcher. (Magic Shop Bks.). 148p. (J). (gr. 4-6). pap. 4.50 *(978-0-8072-1471-8(X),* Listening Library) Random Hse. Audio Publishing Group.

—Jeremy Thatcher, Dragon Hatcher: A Magic Shop Book. Lippincott, Gary A., illus. 20th ed. 2007. (Magic Shop Book Ser.: 2). (ENG.). 176p. (J). (gr. 5-7). pap. 7.99 *(978-0-15-206252-1(1))* Houghton Mifflin Harcourt Publishing Co.

Cowell, Cressida. The Complete Book of Dragons: A Guide to Dragon Species. 2014. (How to Train Your Dragon Ser.). (ENG., Illus.). 224p. (J). (gr. 3-7). 15.00 *(978-0-316-24410-7(4))* Little, Brown Bks. for Young Readers.

—A Hero's Guide to Deadly Dragons. 2010. (ENG., Illus.). 272p. (J). *(978-0-340-99913-4(6),* Hodder Children's Books) Hachette Children's Group GBR. Dist: Hachette Bk. Group.

—A Hero's Guide to Deadly Dragons. (How to Train Your Dragon Ser.: 6). (ENG.). (J). (gr. 3-7). 2010. 272p. pap. 8.00 *(978-0-316-08532-8(4))* 2009. 256p. 12.99 *(978-0-316-11779-1(X))* Little, Brown Bks. for Young Readers.

—How to Be a Pirate. 2010. (ENG., Illus.). 240p. (J). *(978-0-340-99908-0(X),* Hodder Children's Books) Hachette Children's Group GBR. Dist: Hachette Bk. Group.

—How to Be a Pirate. (How to Train Your Dragon Ser.: 2). (ENG.). (J). (gr. 3-7). 2010. 240p. pap. 8.99 *(978-0-316-08528-1(6))* 2005. (Illus.). 224p. 13.99 *(978-0-316-15598-4(5))* Little, Brown Bks. for Young Readers.

—How to Betray a Dragon's Hero. 2014. (How to Train Your Dragon Ser.: 11). (J). lib. bdg. 18.45 *(978-0-606-35943-6(5))* Turtleback Bks.

—How to Break a Dragon's Heart. 2012. (How to Train Your Dragon Ser.: 8). (ENG.). 272p. (J). (gr. 3-7). pap. 8.00 *(978-0-316-17617-0(6))* Little, Brown Bks. for Young Readers.

—How to Break a Dragon's Heart. 2012. (How to Train Your Dragon Ser.: 8). (J). lib. bdg. 18.45 *(978-0-606-26163-0(X),* Turtleback) Turtleback Bks.

—How to Cheat a Dragon's Curse. 2010. (ENG., Illus.). 256p. (J). *(978-0-340-99910-3(1),* Hodder Children's Books) Hachette Children's Group GBR. Dist: Hachette Bk. Group.

—How to Cheat a Dragon's Curse. 2010. (How to Train Your Dragon Ser.: 4). (ENG.). 272p. (J). (gr. 3-7). pap. 8.99 *(978-0-316-08530-4(8))* Little, Brown Bks. for Young Readers.

—How to Cheat a Dragon's Curse. Cowell, Cressida, illus. 2007. (How to Train Your Dragon Ser.: 4). (ENG., Illus.). 256p. (J). (gr. 3-7). 14.99 *(978-0-316-11425-7(1))* Little, Brown Bks. for Young Readers.

—How to Fight a Dragon's Fury. 2015. (How to Train Your Dragon Ser.: 12). (ENG., Illus.). 496p. (J). (gr. 3-7). 13.99 *(978-0-316-36515-4(7))* Little, Brown Bks. for Young Readers.

—How to Fight a Dragon's Fury. 2016. (How to Train Your Dragon Ser.: 12). (J). lib. bdg. 18.40 *(978-0-606-39195-5(9))* Turtleback Bks.

—How to Ride a Dragon's Storm. 2010. (ENG., Illus.). 288p. (J). *(978-0-340-99912-7(8),* Hodder Children's Books) Hachette Children's Group GBR. Dist: Hachette Bk. Group.

—How to Ride a Dragon's Storm. (How to Train Your Dragon Ser.: 7). (ENG.). (J). (gr. 3-7). 2011. 288p. pap. 8.99 *(978-0-316-07909-9(X))* 2010. 272p. 12.99 *(978-0-316-07916-7(2))* Little, Brown Bks. for Young Readers.

—How to Seize a Dragon's Jewel. (How to Train Your Dragon Ser.: 10). (ENG., Illus.). 416p. (J). (gr. 3-7). 2014. pap. 8.00 *(978-0-316-24408-4(2))* 2013. 12.99 *(978-0-316-24409-1(0))* Little, Brown Bks. for Young Readers.

—How to Seize a Dragon's Jewel. 2014. (How to Train Your Dragon Ser.: 10). (J). lib. bdg. 18.45 *(978-0-606-35307-6(0))* Turtleback Bks.

—How to Speak Dragonese. 2010. (ENG., Illus.). 256p. (J). *(978-0-340-99909-7(8),* Hodder Children's Books) Hachette Children's Group GBR. Dist: Hachette Bk. Group.

—How to Speak Dragonese. (How to Train Your Dragon Ser.: 3). (ENG.). (J). (gr. 3-7). 2010. 256p. pap. 8.99 *(978-0-316-08529-8(4))* 2006. (Illus.). 240p. 12.99 *(978-0-316-15600-4(0))* Little, Brown Bks. for Young Readers.

—How to Steal a Dragon's Sword. (How to Train Your Dragon Ser.: 9). (ENG.). 384p. (J). (gr. 3-7). 2013. pap. 8.00 *(978-0-316-20570-2(2))* 2012. 12.99 *(978-0-316-20571-9(0))* Little, Brown Bks. for Young Readers.

—How to Steal a Dragon's Sword. 2013. (How to Train Your Dragon Ser.: 9). (J). lib. bdg. 18.45 *(978-0-606-31742-9(2),* Turtleback) Turtleback Bks.

—How to Train Your Dragon. 2010. (ENG., Illus.). (J). 240p. *(978-0-340-99907-3(1));* 240p. pap. *(978-0-340-99716-1(8));*No. 1. 304p. *(978-0-340-99717-8(6))* Hachette Children's Group GBR. (Hodder Children's Books). Dist: Hachette Bk. Group.

—How to Train Your Dragon. (How to Train Your Dragon Ser.: 1). (ENG., (J). (gr. 3-7). 2004. Illus.). 224p. 13.99 *(978-0-316-73737-1(2))*Bk. 1. 2010. 240p. pap. 8.99 *(978-0-316-08527-4(8))* Little, Brown Bks. for Young Readers.

—How to Train Your Dragon: How to Betray a Dragon's Hero. (How to Train Your Dragon Ser.: 11). (ENG., Illus.). 416p. (J). (gr. 3-7). 2014. pap. 8.99 *(978-0-316-24411-4(2))* 2013. 13.99 *(978-0-316-24412-1(0))* Little, Brown Bks. for Young Readers.

—How to Train Your Dragon: How to Fight a Dragon's Fury. 2016. (How to Train Your Dragon Ser.: 12). (ENG., Illus.). 496p. (J). (gr. 3-7). pap. 7.99 *(978-0-316-36516-1(5))* Little, Brown Bks. for Young Readers.

—How to Train Your Dragon Special Edition: With Brand New Short Stories! 2014. (ENG., Illus.). 432p. (J). (gr. 3-7). pap. 10.00 *(978-0-316-40747-2(X))* Little, Brown Bks. for Young Readers.

—How to Twist a Dragon's Tale. 2010. (ENG., Illus.). 272p. (J). *(978-0-340-99911-0(X),* Hodder Children's Books) Hachette Children's Group GBR. Dist: Hachette Bk. Group.

—How to Twist a Dragon's Tale. (How to Train Your Dragon Ser.: 5). (ENG., (J). (gr. 3-7). 2008. Illus.). 256p. 10.99 *(978-0-316-11774-6(9))*Bk. 5. 2010. 272p. pap. 8.99 *(978-0-316-08531-1(6))* Little, Brown Bks. for Young Readers.

—A Journal for Heroes. 2015. (How to Train Your Dragon Ser.). (ENG.). 176p. (J). (gr. 3-7). 10.99 *(978-0-316-30743-7(2))* Little, Brown Bks. for Young Readers.

Cowsert, Sami. Tammi & Her Dragon. 2006. 48p. pap. 16.95 *(978-1-4241-5211-7(9))* America Star Bks.

Cowsert, Sandra. The Continuing Adventures of Tammi & Her Dragon. 2007. 48p. per. 16.95 *(978-1-4241-8313-5(8))* America Star Bks.

Crowley, Jennifer Brasington. Lyndsay & Lainey Lion: E Is for Dragon. 2012. (ENG.). (J). pap. *(978-1-4675-5417-6(0))* Independent Pub.

—Lyndsay & Lainey Lion: F Is for Dragon. 2012. (ENG.). (J). pap. *(978-1-4675-5418-3(9))* Independent Pub.

Crowley, Jennifer Brasington, ed. Lyndsay & Lainey Lion: D Is for Dragon. 2012. (ENG.). (J). pap. *(978-1-4675-5416-9(2))* Independent Pub.

Crowley, Suzanne. The Very Ordered Existence of Merilee Marvelous. 2007. 380p. (J). (gr. 5-9). 16.99 *(978-0-06-123197-1(5),* Greenwillow Bks.) HarperCollins Pubs.

Crum, Shutta. Thomas & the Dragon Queen. Wildish, Lee, illus. 2011. (ENG.). 272p. (J). (gr. 3-7). 6.99 *(978-0-375-84634-2(4),* Yearling) Random Hse. Children's Bks.

Crump, Fred, Jr. Marigold & the Dragon. 2010. 32p. (J). 12.95 *(978-1-934056-73-8(1))* UMI (Urban Ministries, Inc.).

Crump, Marty. Mysteries of the Komodo Dragon: The Biggest, Deadliest Lizard Gives up Its Secrets. 2010. (ENG.). 40p. (J). (gr. 4-6). 18.95 *(978-1-59078-757-1(9))* Boyds Mills Pr.

Curry, Kenneth. The Return of Gamalok: The Return of Gamalok. 2007. (Illus.). 83p. (J). per. 12.95 *(978-0-9798364-2-8(5))* Curry Brothers Publishing Group.

Dahl, Michael. Claws in the Snow, 1 vol. Vue, Tou, illus. 2010. (Dragonblood Ser.). (ENG.). 40p. (gr. 1-3). pap. 6.25 *(978-1-4342-2308-1(6),* Zone Bks.) Stone Arch Bks.

—Claws in the Snow, 1 vol. Evans, Mark & Vue, Tou, illus. 2009. (Dragonblood Ser.). (ENG.). 40p. (gr. 1-3). 23.99 *(978-1-4342-1262-7(9),* Zone Bks.) Stone Arch Bks.

—Dead Wings, 1 vol. Piatti, Federico, illus. 2010. (Dragonblood Ser.). (ENG.). 40p. (gr. 1-3). lib. bdg. 23.99 *(978-1-4342-1926-8(7),* Zone Bks.) Stone Arch Bks.

—Dragon Cowboy, 1 vol. Piatti, Federico, illus. 2010. (Dragonblood Ser.). (ENG.). 40p. (gr. 1-3). lib. bdg. 23.99 *(978-1-4342-1927-5(5),* Zone Bks.) Stone Arch Bks.

—Dragon in the Desert, 1 vol. Vue, Tou, illus. (Dragonblood Ser.). (ENG.). 40p. (gr. 1-3). 2010. pap. 6.25 *(978-1-4342-2309-8(4))* 2009. 23.99 *(978-1-4342-1260-3(2))* Stone Arch Bks. (Zone Bks.).

—Dragon Theft Auto, 1 vol. Rong, Yap Kun, illus. 2010. (Dragonblood Ser.). (ENG.). 40p. (gr. 1-3). pap. 6.25 *(978-1-4342-2310-4(8),* Zone Bks.) Stone Arch Bks.

—Dragon Theft Auto, 1 vol. Evans, Mark & Kun Rong, Yap, illus. 2009. (Dragonblood Ser.). (ENG.). 40p. (gr. 1-3). 23.99 *(978-1-4342-1264-1(5),* Zone Bks.) Stone Arch Bks.

—The Dragon with the Girl Tattoo, 1 vol. Aime, Luigi, illus. 2012. (Dragonborn Ser.). (ENG.). 72p. (gr. 1-3). pap. 7.10 *(978-1-4342-4257-0(9));* lib. bdg. 23.99 *(978-1-4342-4041-5(X))* Stone Arch Bks.

—Eye of the Monster, 1 vol. Piatti, Federico, illus. 2010. (Dragonblood Ser.). (ENG.). 40p. (gr. 1-3). lib. bdg. 23.99 *(978-1-4342-1928-2(3),* Zone Bks.) Stone Arch Bks.

—Fangs in the Mirror, 1 vol. Aime, Luigi, illus. 2012. (Dragonborn Ser.). (ENG.). 72p. (gr. 1-3). pap. 7.10 *(978-1-4342-4255-6(2));* lib. bdg. 23.99 *(978-1-4342-4042-2(8))* Stone Arch Bks.

—The Girl Who Breathed Fire. Piatti, Federico, illus. 2010. (Dragonblood Ser.). (ENG.). 40p. (gr. 1-3). lib. bdg. 23.99 *(978-1-4342-1925-1(9),* Zone Bks.) Stone Arch Bks.

—It Screams at Night, 1 vol. Rong, Yap Kun & Kun Rong, Yap, illus. 2010. (Dragonblood Ser.). (ENG.). 40p. (gr. 1-3). pap. 6.25 *(978-1-4342-2311-1(6),* Zone Bks.) Stone Arch Bks.

—It Screams at Night, 1 vol. Kun Rong, Yap, illus. 2009. (Dragonblood Ser.). (ENG.). 40p. (gr. 1-3). 23.99 *(978-1-4342-1261-0(0),* Zone Bks.) Stone Arch Bks.

—The Missing Fang, 1 vol. Piatti, Federico, illus. 2010. (Dragonblood Ser.). (ENG.). 40p. (gr. 1-3). lib. bdg. 23.99 *(978-1-4342-1923-7(2),* Zone Bks.) Stone Arch Bks.

—Monster Hunter, 1 vol. Aime, Luigi, illus. 2012. (Dragonborn Ser.). (ENG.). 72p. (gr. 1-3). pap. 7.10 *(978-1-4342-4256-3(0));* lib. bdg. 23.99 *(978-1-4342-4040-8(1))* Stone Arch Bks.

—Stowaway Monster, 1 vol. Pellegrino, Richard, illus. (Dragonblood Ser.). (ENG.). 40p. (gr. 1-3). 2010. pap. 6.25 *(978-1-4342-2312-8(4))* 2009. 23.99 *(978-1-4342-1259-7(9))* Stone Arch Bks. (Zone Bks.).

—Terror Beach, 1 vol. Pellegrino, Richard, illus. (Dragonblood Ser.). (ENG.). 40p. (gr. 1-3). 2010. pap. 6.25 *(978-1-4342-2313-5(2))* 2009. 23.99 *(978-1-4342-1263-4(7))* Stone Arch Bks. (Zone Bks.).

—Wings above the Waves, 1 vol. Piatti, Federico, illus. 2010. (Dragonblood Ser.). (ENG.). 40p. (gr. 1-3). lib. bdg. 23.99 *(978-1-4342-1924-4(0),* Zone Bks.) Stone Arch Bks.

Dahl, Michael & Aime, Luigi. Duel of Dragons, 1 vol. 2012. (Dragonborn Ser.). (ENG., Illus.). 72p. (gr. 1-3). pap. 7.10 *(978-1-4342-4254-9(4));* lib. bdg. 23.99 *(978-1-4342-4039-2(8))* Stone Arch Bks.

Daisy, April. The Lonely Dragon. Daisy, April, illus. 2005. (Illus.). (J). per. 7.95 *(978-1-59466-074-0(3),* Little Ones) Port Town Publishing.

Daniels, Jake. Do Dragons Burn Their Tongues? 2010. 41p. pap. 18.95 *(978-0-557-29312-4(X))* Lulu Pr., Inc.

David, Erica. How to Build a Dragon Fort. 2016. (Simon & Schuster Ready-To-Read Level 2 Ser.). lib. bdg. 13.55 *(978-0-606-38244-1(5))* Turtleback Bks.

—How to Track a Dragon. 2016. (Simon & Schuster Ready-To-Read Level 2 Ser.). lib. bdg. 13.55 *(978-0-606-38992-1(X))* Turtleback Bks.

Davidson L. Haworth. The Dragon of Prali. 2010. 168p. 22.95 *(978-1-4502-0147-6(4));* pap. 12.95 *(978-1-4502-0145-2(8))* iUniverse, Inc.

Davidson, MaryJanice & Alongi, Anthony. The Silver Moon Elm, 3 vols. 2008. (Jennifer Scales Ser.: 3). (ENG.). 288p. (gr. 12-18). 7.99 *(978-0-441-01601-3(4),* Ace Bks.) Penguin Publishing Group.

Davies, Christie. Dewi the Dragon. 2006. (ENG.). 96p. (J). pap. 9.95 *(978-0-86243-770-1(9))* Y Lolfa GBR. Dist: Dufour Editions, Inc.

Davis, Bryan. From the Mouth of Elijah. 2012. (Children of the Bard Ser.: 2). (ENG.). 512p. (YA). (gr. 7). pap. 14.99 *(978-0-89957-881-1(0))* AMG Pubs.

Davis, Garfield. The Little Blue Water Dragon. 2013. 24p. pap. 12.56 *(978-1-4669-7033-5(2))* Trafford Publishing.

Davis, Mike. Pirates, Bats, & Dragons. Simpson, William, illus. 2004. 174p. (J). 15.95 *(978-0-9747078-2-2(1))* Perceval Pr.

Davison, Gail. Prince Alexander. PellerinUndo, Joel Ray, illus. 2016. (ENG.). 28p. (J). pap. 28.22 ***(978-1-5245-1787-8(9))*** Xlibris Corp.

de Brunhoff, Laurent. Babar on Paradise Island. 2014. (ENG., Illus.). 48p. (J). (gr. k-2). 18.95 *(978-1-4197-1038-4(9),* Abrams Bks. for Young Readers) Abrams, Inc.

de Bruno, Oanna. Cuentos de Dragones para Ninos. (Stories for Children Ser.).Tr. of Children's Dragon Stories. (SPA.). (J). 7.95 *(978-970-643-264-3(7))* Selector, S.A. de C.V. MEX. Dist: Libros Sin Fronteras.

De Kockere, Geert & Dom, An. Dragon Fire. Van Hemeldonck, Tineke, illus. 2015. (ENG.). 32p. (J). (gr. -1-k). 16.99 *(978-1-63220-599-5(8),* Sky Pony Pr.) Skyhorse Publishing Co., Inc.

De la Cruz, Melissa & Johnston, Michael. Stolen Bk. 2: Heart of Dread. 2014. (Heart of Dread Ser.: 2). (ENG.). 304p. (YA). (gr. 7). 17.99 *(978-0-399-25755-1(1),* G.P. Putnam's Sons Books for Young Readers) Penguin Young Readers Group.

de Las Casas, Dianne. There's a Dragon in the Library, 1 vol. Gentry, Marita, illus. 2011. (ENG.). 32p. (J). (gr. k-3). 16.99 *(978-1-58980-844-7(4))* Pelican Publishing Co., Inc.

Dean, James, illus. Sir Pete the Brave. 2016. 32p. (J). ***(978-1-5182-0881-2(9))*** Harper & Row Ltd.

DeBlois, Dean, et al. The Serpent's Heir. Wheatley, Doug, illus. 2017. (ENG.). 80p. (gr. 4-7). pap. 10.99 *(978-1-61655-931-1(4))* Dark Horse Comics.

Deedy, Carmen Agra. The Library Dragon, 1 vol. White, Michael P., illus. 2012. (ENG.). 32p. (J). 19.95 *(978-1-56145-639-0(X))* Peachtree Pubs.

—Return of the Library Dragon, 1 vol. White, Michael P., illus. 2012. (ENG.). 32p. (J). 16.95 *(978-1-56145-621-5(7))* Peachtree Pubs.

Demi & Demi Staff. The Boy Who Painted Dragons. Demi & Demi Staff, illus. 2007. (ENG., Illus.). 52p. (J). (gr. 2-5). 21.99 *(978-1-4169-2469-2(8),* McElderry, Margaret K. Bks.) McElderry, Margaret K. Bks.

Depken, Kristen L. Castle Caper. Cartobaleno, illus. 2015. (Pictureback(R) Ser.). (ENG.). 24p. (J). (gr. -1-2). 5.99 *(978-0-553-52313-3(9),* Random Hse. Bks. for Young Readers) Random Hse. Children's Bks.

—Dragon Hiccups. Burch, Benjamin, illus. 2015. (Little Golden Book Ser.). (ENG.). 24p. (J). (-k). 4.99 *(978-0-553-52310-2(4),* Golden Bks.) Random Hse. Children's Bks.

—Mighty Troll & Wonder Dragon. Burch, Benjamin, illus. 2016. (Little Golden Book Ser.). (ENG.). 24p. (J). (gr. -1-k). 4.99 *(978-1-101-93149-3(3),* Golden Bks.) Random Hse. Children's Bks.

Depken, Kristen L. Sing Your Song! (Nella the Princess Knight) Myers, Nneka, illus. 2017. (Step into Reading Ser.). (ENG.). 24p. (J). (gr. -1-1). pap. 4.99 ***(978-1-5247-6505-7(8));*** lib. bdg. 12.99 ***(978-1-5247-6506-4(6))*** Random Hse. Children's Bks. (Random Hse. Bks. for Young Readers).

Deutsch, Stacia. The Dragon Queen. 2016. (LEGO Elves Ser.: 2). (ENG.). 128p. (J). (gr. 2-5). pap. 5.99 *(978-0-545-85281-4(1))* Scholastic, Inc.

Diggs, Linda. Gwynepe Slew the Dragon Almost. Hanna, Ellen & Steier, John, eds. Morris, Samuel L., illus. 2004. 49p. (J). (gr. k-6). 17.99 *(978-0-9754126-0-2(4))* Willie & Willie.

Dimpel, Matt. The War of the Serpent Swords. 2011. 230p. pap. 24.95 *(978-1-4626-3169-8(X))* PublishAmerica, Inc.

Dinardo, Jeff. The Fable of the Bully Dragon: Facing Your Fears. Coloji, Livia, illus. 2015. (ENG.). 24p. (J). (gr. k-2). lib. bdg. 19.99 *(978-1-63440-000-8(3))* Red Chair Pr.

Ding, Yuhui Andrew. Warrior Soul. 2009. 28p. pap. 15.99 *(978-1-4415-6734-5(8))* Xlibris Corp.

Dipucchio, Kelly. Dragon Was Terrible. Pizzoli, Greg, illus. 2016. (ENG.). 40p. (J). 16.99 *(978-0-374-30049-4(6),* 9780374300494, Farrar, Straus & Giroux (BYR)) Farrar, Straus & Giroux.

Disney Book Group. Doc Mcstuffins a Dragon's Best Friend. Disney Storybook Art Team, illus. 2015. (ENG.). 40p. (J). (gr. -1-k). 8.99 *(978-1-4847-2388-3(0))* Disney Pr.

—Pete's Dragon Junior Novel: With 8 Pages of Photos from the Movie! 2016. (ENG.). 144p. (J). (gr. 3-7). pap. 5.99 *(978-1-4847-4992-0(8))* Disney Pr.

Disney Book Group & Rudnick, Elizabeth. Pete's Dragon: the Lost Years. Disney Book Group & Kole, Nicholas, illus. 2016. (ENG.). 208p. (J). (gr. 3-7). 16.99 *(978-1-4847-4993-7(6))* Disney Pr.

Disney Book Group Staff & Halbrooks, Toby. Pete's Dragon: Elliot Gets Lost. Disney Book Group Staff, illus. 2016. (ENG., Illus.). 48p. (J). (gr. -1-k). 16.99 *(978-1-4847-5029-2(2))* Disney Pr.

Disney Book Group Staff, et al. World of Reading: Doc Mcstuffins Brave Dragon: Level Pre-1. Disney Storybook Artists Staff, illus. 2014. (World of Reading Ser.). (ENG.). 32p. (J). (gr. -1-k). pap. 3.99 *(978-1-4847-0244-4(1))* Disney Pr.

DiTerlizzi, Tony. Kenny & the Dragon. 2008. (Playaway Children Ser.). (J). (gr. 3-7). 39.99 *(978-1-60640-958-9(1))* Findaway World, LLC.

—Kenny & the Dragon. DiTerlizzi, Tony, illus. (ENG., Illus.). (J). (gr. 3-7). 2012. 176p. pap. 8.99 *(978-1-4424-3651-0(4))* 2008. 160p. 17.99 *(978-1-4169-3977-1(6))* Simon & Schuster Bks. For Young Readers. (Simon & Schuster Bks. For Young Readers).

—Kenny & the Dragon. DiTerlizzi, Tony, illus. 2008. (Illus.). 160p. (J). (gr. 3-7). 15.99 Simon & Schuster Children's Publishing.

Dixon, Andy. Dragon Quest. Brooks, Felicity, ed. Harris, Nick, illus. rev. ed. 2005. (Usborne Fantasy Puzzle Bks.). 32p. (J). (gr. 3-7). per. 7.99 *(978-0-7945-1098-5(1),* Usborne) EDC Publishing.

d'Lacey, Chris. Dark Fire. (Last Dragon Chronicles Ser.: 5). (ENG.). 576p. (J). (gr. 3-7). 2011. pap. 8.99 *(978-0-545-10273-5(1))* 2010. 17.99 *(978-0-545-10272-8(3),* Orchard Bks.) Scholastic, Inc.

—The Fire Ascending. (ENG.). 576p. (J). (gr. 3-7). 2013. pap. 9.99 *(978-0-545-40293-4(X),* Scholastic Paperbacks) 2012. (Last Dragon Chronicles Ser.: 7). 18.99 *(978-0-545-40216-3(6),* Orchard Bks.) Scholastic, Inc.

—The Fire Ascending. 2013. (Last Dragon Chronicles Ser.: 7). lib. bdg. 20.85 *(978-0-606-31958-4(1),* Turtleback) Turtleback Bks.

—The Fire Eternal. (Last Dragon Chronicles Ser.: 4). (ENG.). 512p. (J). (gr. 3-7). 2010. 8.99 *(978-0-545-05164-4(9))* 2008. 17.99 *(978-0-545-05163-7(0))* Scholastic, Inc. (Orchard Bks.).

—The Fire Eternal. 2010. (Last Dragon Chronicles Ser.: 4). lib. bdg. 19.65 *(978-0-606-12558-1(2),* Turtleback) Turtleback Bks.

—Fire Star. 2008. (Last Dragon Chronicles Ser.: 3). (ENG.). 560p. (J). (gr. 3-7). 8.99 *(978-0-439-90185-7(5),* Orchard Bks.) Scholastic, Inc.

—The Fire Within. 2007. (Last Dragon Chronicles Ser.: 1). (ENG.). 352p. (J). (gr. 3-7). pap. 8.99 *(978-0-439-67244-3(9),* Orchard Bks.) Scholastic, Inc.

—Fire World. 2012. (Last Dragon Chronicles Ser.: 6). lib. bdg. 19.65 *(978-0-606-23967-7(7),* Turtleback) Turtleback Bks.

—Gauge. 2010. (Dragons of Wayward Crescent Ser.: No. 2). (ENG.). 112p. (J). (gr. 2-5). 9.99 *(978-0-545-16831-1(7),* Orchard Bks.) Scholastic, Inc.

—Icefire. 2007. (Last Dragon Chronicles Ser.: 2). (ENG.). 432p. (J). (gr. 3-7). pap. 8.99 *(978-0-439-67246-7(5),* Orchard Bks.) Scholastic, Inc.

—Icefire. d'Lacey, Chris, illus. 2007. (Last Dragon Chronicles Ser.: 2). (Illus.). lib. bdg. 19.65 *(978-1-4177-9138-5(1),* Turtleback) Turtleback Bks.

—The Wearle. 2016. (Erth Dragons Ser.: 1). (ENG.). 320p. (J). (gr. 3-7). 16.99 *(978-0-545-90018-8(2),* Scholastic Pr.) Scholastic, Inc.

d'Lacey, Jay & d'Lacey, Chris. Rain & Fire. 2012. (Last Dragon Chronicles Ser.). (ENG.). 304p. (J). (gr. 3-7). 16.99 *(978-0-545-41453-1(9),* Orchard Bks.) Scholastic, Inc.

Dober, Jim. Hickory Woods Adventures: Waiting for A Bubble. 2010. pap. 14.99 *(978-1-61579-688-5(6))* Salem Author Services.

Docherty, Helen. The Storybook Knight. Docherty, Thomas, illus. 2016. (ENG.). 32p. (J). (-4). 16.99 *(978-1-4926-3814-8(5),* 9781492638148, Sourcebooks Jabberwocky) Sourcebooks, Inc.

Doherty, Gillian. Stories of Dragons. Milbourne, Anna, ed. Edwards, Linda, illus. 2007. (Stories for Young Children Ser.). 96p. (J). 16.99 *(978-0-7945-1465-5(0),* Usborne) EDC Publishing.

Dolby, Karen. Dragon in the Cupboard. 2004. (Young Puzzle Adventures Ser.). 32p. (J). (gr. 2-18). pap. 4.95 *(978-0-7945-0232-4(6));* lib. bdg. 12.95 *(978-1-58086-461-9(9))* EDC Publishing.

Donaldson, Julia. A Gold Star for Zog. Scheffler, Axel, illus. 2012. (ENG.). 32p. (J). (gr. -1-3). 17.99 *(978-0-545-41724-2(4),* Levine, Arthur A. Bks.) Scholastic, Inc.

—Room on the Broom. Scheffler, Axel, illus. 2003. (ENG.). 32p. (J). (gr. -1-2). pap. 6.99 *(978-0-14-250112-2(3),* Puffin Books) Penguin Young Readers Group.

Dongweck, James. The Dragon Cant. Baker, Joe, illus. 2004. 32p. (J). per. 16.95 *(978-0-9719632-0-7(7))* Golden Monkey Publishing, LLC.

Donovan, Anna. A Dragon's Tale. 2003. (ENG., Illus.). 12p. (J). pap. 7.95 *(978-0-86278-845-2(5))* O'Brien Pr., Ltd., The IRL. Dist: Dufour Editions, Inc.

Dorris, Peggy. The Dragon. Knox, Dahk, ed. 2013. 54p. pap. 10.95 *(978-1-58275-287-7(7),* Sonnenschein Bks.) Black Forest Pr.

Dove, S. R. Gabriel the First Christmas Dragon, 1 vol. 2009. 39p. pap. 24.95 *(978-1-60836-855-6(6))* America Star Bks.

Downer, Ann. The Dragon of Never-Was. Rayyan, Omar, illus. 2008. (ENG.). 320p. (J). (gr. 3-6). pap. 14.99 *(978-1-4169-5453-8(8),* Atheneum Bks. for Young Readers) Simon & Schuster Children's Publishing.

—Hatching Magic. Rayyan, Omar, illus. 2004. 242p. 16.00 *(978-0-7569-3481-1(8))* Perfection Learning Corp.

—Hatching Magic. 2004. (ENG.). 256p. (J). (gr. 3-7). reprint ed. pap. 15.99 *(978-0-689-87057-6(4),* Atheneum Bks. for Young Readers) Simon & Schuster Children's Publishing.

Dozier, Kim. Where's Dwight Dragon. Dozier, Ashlyn McCauley, illus. l.t. ed. 2004. (ENG.). 32p. (J). 10.00 *(978-0-9745839-2-1(8),* Fun to Read Bks. with Royally Good Morals) MKADesigns.

Dragon: Enter the Realm. 2007. (YA). per. *(978-1-934345-43-6(1))* SouthWest Pubns.

Dragon: The Fantasy Continues. 2007. (YA). per. *(978-1-934345-44-3(X))* SouthWest Pubns.

The Dragon Queen. 2016. 126p. (J). ***(978-1-5182-0562-0(3))*** Scholastic, Inc.

Dragones de Durn: Los Dragones de Durn Saga, Libro Uno. 2013. 206p. pap. 9.50 *(978-1-937361-13-6(6),* Defiant Pr.) Passkey Pubns.

Dragonology: Pocket Adventures, 4 vols. 2007. (Illus.). (J). *(978-0-7636-3698-2(3)); (978-0-7636-3699-9(1)); (978-0-7636-3696-8(7)); (978-0-7636-3697-5(5))* Candlewick Pr.

Dragons in Flight. 2014. (ENG.). 14p. (J). (gr. 1-6). 10.99 *(978-0-7944-3213-3(1))* Studio Fun International.

Dragons, Phantoms, & Secrets: The Best New Fantasy from Arrow Writers. 2005. 63p. (J). *(978-0-439-74432-4(6))* Scholastic, Inc.

Dragon's Tears. 2004. (J). cd-rom *(978-1-84444-458-8(9))* Mantra Lingua.

Drake, Ernest. Dragonology: The Complete Book of Dragons. Steer, Dugald A., ed. 2003. (Ologies Ser.). (ENG., Illus.). 32p. (J). (gr. 3-7). 24.99 *(978-0-7636-2329-6(6))* Candlewick Pr.

—Dragonology Coloring Book. 2016. (Ologies Ser.). (ENG.). 64p. (J). (gr. 3-7). pap. 14.99 *(978-0-7636-9530-9(0))* Candlewick Pr.

Draper, Adrian. Chili Peppers in Oatmeal. 2012. 30p. 24.95 *(978-1-4626-5553-3(X))* America Star Bks.

Draper, Rochelle. The Stone Wall Dragon. Draper, Rochelle, illus. 2007. (ENG., Illus.). 32p. (J). (gr. 1-17). 15.95 *(978-0-89272-690-5(3))* Down East Bks.

Dreamworks How to Train Your Dragon, Dreamworks How. Dreamworks How to Train Your Dragon 2: Time to Race! 2014. (Build It Ser.: 4). (ENG.). 24p. (J). (gr. -1-1). 14.99 *(978-0-7944-3111-2(9),* Reader's Digest Children's Bks.) Studio Fun International.

Drischel, Candy L. Restless with the Dark Moon Rising. 2008. 105p. pap. 19.95 *(978-1-60610-421-7(7))* America Star Bks.

Driscoll, Amanda. Duncan the Story Dragon. 2015. (ENG., Illus.). 40p. (J). (gr. -1-2). 16.99 *(978-0-385-75507-8(4),* Knopf Bks. for Young Readers) Random Hse. Children's Bks.

—Duncan the Story Dragon. 2017. lib. bdg. 18.40 ***(978-0-606-39866-4(X))*** Turtleback Bks.

Du Lac, Leo J. Dogfish on the Moon: Santa Claus & the Flying Carpet 2. Baker, David, illus. 2012. 26p. 24.95 *(978-1-4560-1036-2(0))* America Star Bks.

—Moon Fruit & the Dragons: Santa Claus & the Flying Carpet 3. Washington, Victoria, ed. Baker, David, illus. 2012. 26p. 24.95 *(978-1-4560-1037-9(9))* America Star Bks.

Dube, Pierrette. How to Become a Perfect Knight in Five Days. Hamel, Caroline, illus. 2009. (Rainy Day Readers Ser.). 32p. (J). (gr. -1-3). 22.60 *(978-1-60754-373-2(7));* pap. 10.55 *(978-1-60754-374-9(5))* Windmill Bks.

Duckett, Brenda. The Giggling Purple Dragon. 2006. 84p. pap. 9.99 *(978-1-4116-3826-6(3))* Lulu Pr., Inc.

Dugin, Andrei. Dragon Feathers. Dugina, Olga, illus. 2010. Orig. Title: Die Drachenfedern. 24p. (J). (gr. k-3). 17.95 *(978-0-86315-774-5(2))* Floris Bks. GBR. Dist: SteinerBooks, Inc.

Duk, Lor. The Firestorm Heart: A Dragon Friend Story. 2010. 236p. pap. 15.95 *(978-1-4401-9474-0(2))* iUniverse, Inc.

Durant, Sybrina, et al. Legend of the Blue Unicorn: Return of the Dragons, 3 vols. Johnson, Britt, ed. l.t. ed. 2003. (ENG., Illus.). 25p. (J). (gr. k-5). spiral bd. 8.99 *(978-1-929063-93-2(8),* 331) Moons & Stars Publishing For Children.

Durbin, Amanda. Tree Houses & Treasures. 2013. 24p. pap. 24.95 *(978-1-63004-353-7(2))* America Star Bks.

Eaves, Victor Caleb. Vee's the Chapters of Expudict: Book One. 2008. 128p. pap. 12.00 *(978-1-4389-3385-6(1))* AuthorHouse.

Edwards, Stuart. Dragon Jack. 2006. 42p. 15.99 *(978-1-4116-7499-8(5))* Lulu Pr., Inc.

Elgert, C. J. The Elder Brothers & the Dragon's Portal. 2011. 236p. (gr. 4-6). 25.95 *(978-1-4620-1467-5(4));* pap. 15.95 *(978-1-4620-1466-8(6))* iUniverse, Inc.

Ellery, Amanda. If I Had a Dragon. Ellery, Tom, illus. 2006. (ENG.). 40p. (J). (gr. -1-3). 17.99 *(978-1-4169-0924-8(9),* Simon & Schuster Bks. For Young Readers) Simon & Schuster Bks. For Young Readers.

Ellis, M. Henderson. Petra K & the Blackhearts: A Novel. 2014. (Young Europe Bks.). (ENG., Illus.). 202p. (J). (gr. 9). pap. 11.99 *(978-0-9850623-8-5(X))* New Europe Bks.

Ende, Michael. El Dragon y la Mariposa. De Horna, Luis, illus. 2003.Tr. of Der Lindwurm und der Schmetterling. (SPA.). 48p. (J). (gr. k-3). pap. 8.95 *(978-84-204-3710-1(7))* Santillana USA Publishing Co., Inc.

Ericks, Leonard. The Red Dragon Ryan Learns How to Fly. 2010. 24p. pap. 12.25 *(978-1-60911-201-1(6),* Eloquent Bks.) Strategic Book Publishing & Rights Agency (SBPRA).

—Things We Should All Know about Dragons. 2009. 28p. pap. 12.25 *(978-1-60693-505-7(4),* Eloquent Bks.) Strategic Book Publishing & Rights Agency (SBPRA).

Evans, Cordelia. Live & Let Fly. 2015. (Simon & Schuster Ready-To-Read Ser.). lib. bdg. 13.55 *(978-0-606-37872-7(3))* Turtleback Bks.

Evans, Cordelia, adapted by. The Dragon That Rides on Lightning. 2015. (How to Train Your Dragon TV Ser.). (ENG., Illus.). 24p. (J). (gr. -1-3). 12.99 *(978-1-4814-3613-7(9),* Simon Spotlight) Simon Spotlight.

Evans, Michael. Poggle & the Birthday Present. Evans, Michael, illus. 2011. (Poggle Ser.). (ENG., Illus.). 32p. (J). (gr. k — 1). pap. 8.99 *(978-1-4052-5359-8(2))* Egmont Bks., Ltd. GBR. Dist: Independent Pubs. Group.

—Poggle & the Treasure. Evans, Michael, illus. 2011. (Poggle Ser.). (ENG., Illus.). 32p. (J). (gr. k — 1). pap. 8.99 *(978-1-4052-4812-9(2))* Egmont Bks., Ltd. GBR. Dist: Independent Pubs. Group.

Eversole, Robyn. East Dragon, West Dragon. Campbell, Scott, illus. 2012. (ENG.). 40p. (J). (gr. -1-2). 17.99 *(978-0-689-85828-4(0),* Atheneum Bks. for Young Readers) Simon & Schuster Children's Publishing.

C
D

Fabrizio, T. L. Natalie Bean. 2011. 28p. pap. 24.95 *(978-1-4626-0645-0(8))* America Star Bks.

Falkenstem, Lisa. A Dragon Moves In, 0 vols. 2011. (ENG.). 32p. (J). (gr. -1-3). 16.99 *(978-0-7614-5947-7(2),* 9780761459477, Amazon Children's Publishing) Amazon Publishing.

Farrell, Steve. What Do You Do on a Rainy Day? Bendoly, Lynne, illus. 2013. 48p. pap. 24.95 *(978-1-4626-9685-7(6))* America Star Bks.

Fast, David R. Doctor Dave's Dragon Tales. Ciesinska, Izabela, illus. 2007. 160p. (J). per. 13.95 *(978-0-9793944-8-5(1))* Digi-Tall Media.

Father of Dragons. 2007. (Binding of the Blade Ser.). (Illus.). 486p. per. 16.99 *(978-0-87552-723-9(X))* P & R Publishing.

Fell, K. The Dragon Stones. 2009. 352p. 30.95 *(978-0-595-51644-5(0));* pap. 20.95 *(978-0-595-52712-0(4))* iUniverse, Inc.

Ferrone, John M. Gus & the Golden Dragon. Ferrone, John M., illus. Date not set. (Illus.). 36p. (gr. -1-5). pap. 16.95 *(978-1-928811-02-2(7))* Story Stuff, Inc.

Fforde, Jasper. The Last Dragonslayer. 2011. 352p. pap. *(978-1-4447-0720-5(5),* Hodder Faith) Hodder & Stoughton.

—The Last Dragonslayer. (Chronicles of Kazam Ser.). (ENG.). (gr. 5-9). 2013. 306p. (YA). pap. 7.99 *(978-0-544-10471-6(4))*Bk. 1. 2012. 296p. (J). 16.99 *(978-0-547-73847-5(1))* Houghton Mifflin Harcourt Publishing Co.

Fienberg, Anna & Fienberg, Barbara. Once Tashi Met a Dragon. Gamble, Kim, illus. 2014. (Tashi Ser.). (ENG.). 34p. (J). (gr. k-2). 16.99 *(978-1-74175-887-0(4))* Allen & Unwin AUS. Dist: Independent Pubs. Group.

Fiford, Tanya. Robin & the Pocket Dragon. 2009. (Illus.). 24p. pap. 11.49 *(978-1-4389-9610-3(1))* AuthorHouse.

Fischel, Ana. The Twelve Quests - Book 2, a Dragon's Tooth. 2009. 158p. pap. *(978-1-84923-874-8(X))* YouWriteOn.

Fischer, David. Heir to Oswyn. 2011. 66p. pap. 19.95 *(978-1-4626-2581-9(9))* America Star Bks.

Fletcher, Ralph J. The Sandman. Cowdrey, Richard, illus. rev. ed. 2008. (ENG.). 32p. (J). (gr. -1-1). 17.99 *(978-0-8050-7726-1(X),* 9780805077261, Holt, Henry & Co. Bks. For Young Readers) Holt, Henry & Co.

Fletcher, Susan. Ancient, Strange, & Lovely. (Dragon Chronicles Ser.). (ENG.). 336p. (J). (gr. 3-7). 2011. pap. 10.99 *(978-1-4169-5787-4(1))* 2010. 16.99 *(978-1-4169-5786-7(3))* Simon & Schuster Children's Publishing. (Atheneum Bks. for Young Readers).

—Flight of the Dragon Kyn. 2010. (Dragon Chronicles Ser.). (ENG.). 240p. (J). (gr. 3-7). pap. 10.99 *(978-1-4169-9713-9(X),* Atheneum Bks. for Young Readers) Simon & Schuster Children's Publishing.

—Sign of the Dove. 2010. (Dragon Chronicles Ser.). (ENG.). 240p. (J). (gr. 3-7). pap. 10.99 *(978-1-4169-9714-6(8),* Atheneum Bks. for Young Readers) Simon & Schuster Children's Publishing.

Florian, Douglas. How to Draw a Dragon. Florian, Douglas, illus. 2015. (ENG., Illus.). 42p. (J). (gr. -1-3). 17.99 *(978-1-4424-7399-7(1),* Beach Lane Bks.) Beach Lane Bks.

Floyd, Donyell. The Curious Child. 2008. 16p. per. 11.95 *(978-1-59800-046-7(2))* Outskirts Pr., Inc.

Forbeck, Matt. Dungeonology. 2016. (Ologies Ser.). (ENG.). 30p. (J). (gr. 5). 24.99 *(978-0-7636-9353-4(7))* Candlewick Pr.

Forbes, Anne. Dragonfire, 1 vol. 2006. (ENG.). 256p. (J). per. 11.95 *(978-0-86315-552-9(9))* Floris Bks. GBR. Dist: SteinerBooks, Inc.

Forde, Patricia. Frogs Do Not Like Dragons. Dreidemy, Joëlle, illus. 2nd ed. 2016. (Reading Ladder Ser.). (ENG.). 48p. (J). (gr. k-2). 7.99 *(978-1-4052-8206-2(1))* Egmont Bks., Ltd. GBR. Dist: Independent Pubs. Group.

Forward, Toby. Doubleborn: A Dragonborn Novel. 2016. (Dragonborn Ser.: 3). (ENG.). 352p. (J). pap. 8.99 *(978-1-61963-921-8(1),* 9781619639218, Bloomsbury USA Childrens) Bloomsbury Publishing USA.

—Dragonborn. (Dragonborn Ser.: 1). (ENG.). (YA). (gr. 3-6). 2013. 368p. pap. 8.99 *(978-1-59990-983-7(9),* 9781599909837) 2012. 352p. 16.99 *(978-1-59990-724-6(0),* 9781599907246) Bloomsbury Publishing USA. (Bloomsbury USA Childrens).

—Starborn: A Dragonborn Novel. (Dragonborn Ser.). (ENG.). 448p. (J). 2017. pap. 9.99 *(978-1-68119-277-2(2),* 9781681192772) 2016. 16.99 *(978-1-61963-842-6(8),* 9781619638426) Bloomsbury Publishing USA. (Bloomsbury USA Childrens).

Foulks, Denine. Jimmy Pfeiffer Dragonmeyer. 2013. 44p. pap. 9.00 *(978-1-937260-97-2(6))* Sleepytown Pr.

Fox, Jennifer. We Like Spike! 2015. (Passport to Reading Level 1 Ser.). (J). lib. bdg. 13.55 *(978-0-606-37512-2(0))* Turtleback Bks.

Francis, Azra Daniel. Grampa's Stories. 2013. 232p. *(978-1-4602-2688-9(7))* FriesenPress.

—Grandpa's Stories. 2013. 232p. pap. *(978-1-4602-2689-6(5))* FriesenPress.

French, Jackie. My Dad the Dragon. King, Stephen Michael, illus. 2004. 128p. *(978-0-207-19950-9(7))* HarperCollins Pubs. Australia.

French, Vivian. The Flight of Dragons: The Fourth Tale from the Five Kingdoms. Collins, Ross, illus. 2011. (Tales from the Five Kingdoms Ser.: 4). (ENG.). 208p. (J). (gr. 3-7). 15.99 *(978-0-7636-5083-4(8))* Candlewick Pr.

—The Flight of Dragons: The Fourth Tale from the Five Kingdoms. Collins, Ross, illus. 2012. (Tales from the Five Kingdoms Ser.: 4). (ENG.). 256p. (J). (gr. 3-7). pap. 5.99 *(978-0-7636-5133-6(8))* Candlewick Pr.

Fryer, Samantha. A Sorcerer's Tale. 2008. 116p. pap. 14.95 *(978-1-84799-366-3(4))* Lulu Pr., Inc.

Funk, Josh. Dear Dragon: A Pen Pal Tale. Montalvo, Rodolfo, illus. 2016. (ENG.). 40p. (J). (gr. -1-3). 16.99 *(978-0-451-47230-4(6),* Viking Books for Young Readers) Penguin Young Readers Group.

Funke, Cornelia. Dragon Rider. 2011.Tr. of Drachenreiter. (ENG.). 560p. (J). (gr. 2-5). pap. 9.99 *(978-0-545-31648-4(0),* Chicken Hse., The) Scholastic, Inc.

Furman, Simon. Dragon Down. 2014. lib. bdg. 17.20 *(978-0-606-35605-3(3))* Turtleback Bks.

—Dragons Vol.4: The Stowaway. 2015. (Riders of Berk Ser.). (ENG., Illus.). 64p. (J). (gr. 3-7). pap. 6.99 *(978-1-78276-079-5(2))* Titan Bks. Ltd. GBR. Dist: Penguin Random Hse. LLC.

—Dragons - Defenders of Berk Vol. 1: The Endless Night. Florean, Arianna, illus. 2016. (ENG.). 64p. (J). (gr. 3-7). pap. 6.99 *(978-1-78276-214-0(0))* Titan Bks. Ltd. GBR. Dist: Penguin Random Hse. LLC.

—Dragons: Riders of Berk Collection Volume 3. Nasif, Iwan, illus. 2016. (ENG.). 112p. (J). (gr. 1-4). pap. 12.99 *(978-1-78585-177-3(2))* Titan Bks. Ltd. GBR. Dist: Penguin Random Hse. LLC.

—Riders of Berk - Tales from Berk, Vol. 1. 2016. (ENG., Illus.). 64p. (J). (gr. 3-7). pap. 12.99 *(978-1-78276-696-4(0))* Titan Bks. Ltd. GBR. Dist: Penguin Random Hse. LLC.

Furman, Simon & Nazif, Iwan. Dragons - Riders of Berk, Vol. 2. Lawrence, Jack, illus. 2016. (ENG.). 112p. (J). (gr. 3-7). pap. 12.99 *(978-1-78585-176-6(4))* Titan Bks. Ltd. GBR. Dist: Penguin Random Hse. LLC.

Furman, Simon & Titan Comics Staff. The Legend of Ragnarok, Vol. 5. 2015. (Riders of Berk Ser.). (ENG., Illus.). 64p. (J). (gr. 3-7). pap. 6.99 *(978-1-78276-080-1(6))* Titan Bks. Ltd. GBR. Dist: Penguin Random Hse. LLC.

Gagliardi, Tina. Don't Forget the Knight Light, 1 vol. Girouard, Patrick, illus. 2009. (Carly's Dragon Days Ser.). (ENG.). 32p. (J). (gr. -1-2). 28.50 *(978-1-60270-593-7(3))* ABDO Publishing Co.

—Dragonpox, 1 vol. Girouard, Patrick, illus. 2009. (Carly's Dragon Days Ser.). (ENG.). 32p. (J). (gr. -1-2). 28.50 *(978-1-60270-594-4(1))* ABDO Publishing Co.

—Fire-Breathers' Academy, 1 vol. Girouard, Patrick, illus. 2009. (Carly's Dragon Days Ser.). (ENG.). 32p. (J). (gr. -1-2). 28.50 *(978-1-60270-595-1(X))* ABDO Publishing Co.

—Fire-Breathers' Science Fair, 1 vol. Girouard, Patrick, illus. 2009. (Carly's Dragon Days Ser.). (ENG.). 32p. (J). (gr. -1-2). 28.50 *(978-1-60270-596-8(8))* ABDO Publishing Co.

—The Golden Dragon, 1 vol. Girouard, Patrick, illus. 2009. (Carly's Dragon Days Ser.). (ENG.). 32p. (J). (gr. -1-2). 28.50 *(978-1-60270-597-5(6))* ABDO Publishing Co.

—The Last One Is a Rotten Egg, 1 vol. Girouard, Patrick, illus. 2009. (Carly's Dragon Days Ser.). (ENG.). 32p. (J). (gr. -1-2). 28.50 *(978-1-60270-598-2(4))* ABDO Publishing Co.

Gannett, Ruth Stiles. The Dragons of Blueland. Gannett, Ruth Chrisman, illus. 2007. (My Father's Dragon Ser.). (ENG.). 112p. (J). (gr. 3-7). 6.99 *(978-0-440-42137-5(3),* Yearling) Random Hse. Children's Bks.

—Elmer & the Dragon. Gannett, Ruth Chrisman, illus. (Tales of My Father's Dragon Ser.: Bk. 2). 87p. (J). (gr. 3-6). pap. 4.99 incl. audio *(978-0-8072-1288-2(1),* Listening Library) Random Hse. Audio Publishing Group.

—Elmer & the Dragon. Gannett, Ruth Chrisman, illus. 2007. (My Father's Dragon Ser.). (ENG.). 96p. (J). (gr. 3-7). 6.99 *(978-0-440-42136-8(5),* Yearling) Random Hse. Children's Bks.

—My Father's Dragon. Gannett, Ruth Chrisman, illus. 2014. (ENG.). 96p. (J). (gr. 1-4). pap. 5.99 *(978-0-486-49283-4(4))* Dover Pubns., Inc.

—My Father's Dragon. Gannett, Ruth Chrisman, illus. 2005. (My Father's Dragon Ser.). (ENG.). 96p. (J). (gr. 3-7). 6.99 *(978-0-440-42121-4(7),* Yearling) Random Hse. Children's Bks.

Garcia Iii, Joe. Dragon Boogers. 2010. 40p. pap. 16.99 *(978-1-4490-5639-1(3))* AuthorHouse.

Garland, Sherry. Children of the Dragon: Selected Tales from Vietnam, 1 vol. Hyman, Trina Schart, illus. 2012. (ENG.). 32p. (J). (gr. 3-7). 16.99 *(978-1-4556-1709-8(1))* Pelican Publishing Co., Inc.

Gassman, Julie. Do Not Bring Your Dragon to the Library. Elkerton, Andy, illus. 2016. (Fiction Picture Bks.). (ENG.). 32p. (gr. -1-2). lib. bdg. 21.32 *(978-1-4795-9175-6(0),* Fiction Picture Bks.) Picture Window Bks.

—Do Not Bring Your Dragon to the Library. Elkerton, Andy, illus. 2016. (ENG.). 32p. (gr. -1-2). 14.95 *(978-1-62370-651-7(3))* Capstone Young Readers of Coughlan Cos.

Gassman, Julie. Do Not Take Your Dragon to Dinner. Elkerton, Andy, illus. 2017. (Fiction Picture Bks.). (ENG.). 32p. (gr. -1-2). lib. bdg. 21.32 ***(978-1-4795-9888-5(7))*** Picture Window Bks.

Gelber, Peter Frost. The Dragon Who Lived Next Door. Tucker, Lewis R. & Mosher, Scott, illus. l.t. ed. 2003. 64p. (J). (gr. -1-6). pap. 12.00 *(978-0-9658920-4-9(2))* Fore Angels Pr.

Gelsey, James, adapted by. Opposing Force. 2004. (Illus.). 92p. (J). *(978-1-4156-3935-1(3),* Volo) Hyperion Bks. for Children.

George, Jessica Day. Dragon Flight. 2009. (Dragon Slippers Ser.). (ENG.). 288p. (YA). (gr. 5-8). pap. 8.99 *(978-1-59990-359-0(8),* 9781599903590, Bloomsbury USA Childrens) Bloomsbury Publishing USA.

—Dragon Slippers. (Dragon Slippers Ser.). (ENG., (YA). 2008. Illus.). 352p. (gr. 5). pap. 8.99 *(978-1-59990-275-3(3),* 9781599902753) 2007. 336p. (gr. 4-7). 16.95 *(978-1-59990-057-5(2),* 9781599900575) Bloomsbury Publishing USA. (Bloomsbury USA Childrens).

—Dragon Slippers. l.t. ed. 2008. (Thorndike Literacy Bridge Middle Reader Ser.). 391p. (J). (gr. 4-7). 22.95 *(978-1-4104-0337-7(8))* Thorndike Pr.

—Dragon Spear. (Dragon Slippers Ser.). (ENG.). (YA). (gr. 5-8). 2010. 272p. pap. 8.99 *(978-1-59990-516-7(7),* 9781599905167) 2009. 256p. 16.99 *(978-1-59990-369-9(5),* 9781599903699) Bloomsbury Publishing USA. (Bloomsbury USA Childrens).

George, Kallie. Spark. Côté, Geneviève, illus. 2013. (ENG.). 34p. (J). (gr. -1-3). 12.95 *(978-1-927018-24-8(2))* Simply Read Bks. CAN. Dist: Ingram Publisher Services.

Givens, Terryl L. Escamas de Dragon y Hojas de Sauce. Portwood, Andrew, illus. (SPA.). (J). pap. 7.95 *(978-958-04-4168-7(5))* Norma S.A. COL. Dist: Distribuidora Norma, Inc., Lectorum Pubns., Inc.

Gliori, Debi. Dragon's Extraordinary Egg. 2014. (ENG., Illus.). 32p. (J). (gr. -1-3). 17.99 *(978-0-8027-3759-5(5),* 9780802737595, Bloomsbury USA Childrens) Bloomsbury Publishing USA.

Gloria North. Dragon Dreams: Tales of Fun & Fantasy. 2005. 77p. pap. 10.00 *(978-1-59926-471-4(4))* Xlibris Corp.

Godin, Thelma Lynne. How to Dress a Dragon. Barclay, Eric, illus. 2016. (ENG.). 40p. (J). (gr. -1-k). 16.99 *(978-0-545-67846-9(3),* Scholastic Pr.) Scholastic, Inc.

Golden Books. Purpleberry Surprise! (Nella the Princess Knight) Cespedes-Alicea, Marcela, illus. 2017. (Deluxe Paint Box Book Ser.). (ENG.). 128p. (J). (gr. -1-2). pap. 7.99 ***(978-1-5247-1673-8(1),*** Golden Bks.) Random Hse. Children's Bks.

Golden Books Staff. Welcome to Wally's World! VanTuyle, David, illus. 2015. (Pictureback(R) Ser.). (ENG.). 16p. (J). (gr. -1-2). 3.99 *(978-0-385-38764-4(4),* Golden Bks.) Random Hse. Children's Bks.

Goodhart, Pippa. Dragon Boy. Ursell, Martin, illus. 2nd ed. 2016. (Reading Ladder Ser.). (ENG.). 48p. (J). (gr. k-2). pap. 7.99 *(978-1-4052-8238-3(X))* Egmont Bks., Ltd. GBR. Dist: Independent Pubs. Group.

—Dragon Magic. Danson, Lesley, illus. 2nd ed. 2016. (Reading Ladder Ser.). (ENG.). 48p. (J). (gr. k-2). 7.99 *(978-1-4052-8244-4(4))* Egmont Bks., Ltd. GBR. Dist: Independent Pubs. Group.

Goodman, Alison. Eon: Dragoneye Reborn. 2010. (ENG.). 576p. (YA). (gr. 7-18). 10.99 *(978-0-14-241711-9(4),* Firebird) Penguin Young Readers Group.

—Eon: Dragoneye Reborn. 2010. (Eon Ser.: 1). lib. bdg. 22.10 *(978-0-606-23647-8(3),* Turtleback) Turtleback Bks.

—The Last Dragoneye. 2012. (ENG.). 672p. (YA). (gr. 7-18). 11.99 *(978-0-14-242093-5(X),* Firebird) Penguin Young Readers Group.

—The Last Dragoneye. 2012. (Eon Ser.: 2). lib. bdg. 23.30 *(978-0-606-23648-5(1),* Turtleback) Turtleback Bks.

Gouveia, Keith. Children of the Dragon. 2005. (ENG.). 174p. pap. *(978-1-897217-03-0(X))* Coscom Entertainment.

Graham, L. B. All My Holy Mountain. 2008. (YA). pap. *(978-0-87552-724-6(8))* P & R Publishing.

Grahame, Kenneth. The Reluctant Dragon. Shepard, Ernest H., illus. 2013. (ENG.). 64p. (J). (gr. 1-5). 2nd ed. pap. 6.95 *(978-0-8234-2821-2(4))* 75th ed. 16.95 *(978-0-8234-2820-5(6))* Holiday Hse., Inc.

—The Reluctant Dragon (Illustrated Edition) 2015. (ENG., Illus.). 42p. pap. *(978-1-5154-0330-2(0),* Illustrated Bks.) Jorge Pinto Bks.

Grandpa Peeps. The Squire & the White Dragon. 2011. 24p. 11.95 *(978-1-4567-1872-5(X))* AuthorHouse.

Gravett, Emily. Again! Gravett, Emily, illus. 2013. (ENG., Illus.). 32p. (J). (gr. -1-3). 17.99 *(978-1-4424-5231-2(5),* Simon & Schuster Bks. For Young Readers) Simon & Schuster Bks. For Young Readers.

Gray, Stephen J. For the Love of a Cloud Maker. 2013. 28p. pap. 13.55 *(978-1-4669-8004-4(4))* Trafford Publishing.

Gregory, Manju. Dragon's Tears. Le, Guo, illus. 2004. (ENG & CHI.). 24p. (J). pap. *(978-1-84444-477-9(5))* Mantra Lingua.

—The Dragon's Tears: Lotet e Kucedres. Le, Guo, illus. 2004. (ENG & ALB.). 24p. (J). pap. *(978-1-85269-685-6(0))* Mantra Lingua.

Gregory, the Mean Dragon. (Early Intervention Levels Ser.). 28.38 *(978-0-7362-0409-5(1))* CENGAGE Learning.

Grochowski, Brad. The Secret Weakness of Dragons: And Other Tales a Fairy Whispered in My Ear. 2004. (Illus.). 105p. (YA). per. 12.50 *(978-0-9755606-0-0(3))* Eepie Pr.

Grove, Malachai. Malachai Grove Plunt Solinatry: The Song of Malachai. 2010. 24p. 14.99 *(978-1-4520-6441-3(5))* AuthorHouse.

—The Return of Malachai. 2011. 24p. pap. 14.99 *(978-1-4567-6257-5(5))* AuthorHouse.

Gubernatis, Loretto. Dragons N Things. 2009. 316p. pap. 19.99 *(978-1-4363-9969-2(6))* Xlibris Corp.

Guide to the Dragons Volume 2. 2014. (How to Train Your Dragon TV Ser.: 2). (ENG., Illus.). 24p. (J). (gr. -1-2). pap. 8.99 *(978-1-4814-1987-1(0),* Simon Spotlight) Simon Spotlight.

Guillain, Adam & Guillain, Charlotte. Doughnuts for a Dragon. Wildish, Lee, illus. 2nd ed. 2015. (George's Amazing Adventures Ser.). (ENG.). 32p. (J). (gr. -1-k). pap. 10.99 *(978-1-4052-7054-0(3))* Egmont Bks., Ltd. GBR. Dist: Independent Pubs. Group.

Guthrie, Janelle. Rachel & the Pink & Green Dragon. 2012. 50p. (-18). pap. 11.95 *(978-1-4772-8198-7(3))* AuthorHouse.

Haggarty, Holly. Summer Dragons. 2007. (ENG.). 176p. (J). (gr. 3-18). per. 9.95 *(978-1-894917-52-0(9),* Napoleon & Co.) Dundurn CAN. Dist: Ingram Publisher Services.

Hahn, Rebecca. A Creature of Moonlight. 2014. (ENG.). 224p. (YA). (gr. 7-12). 17.99 *(978-0-544-10935-3(X),* HMH Books For Young Readers) Houghton Mifflin Harcourt Publishing Co.

Hall, Frank. The Prince Who Did Not Want to be King. 2011. 132p. 28.95 *(978-1-4497-1440-6(4));* (J). pap. 11.95 *(978-1-4497-1438-3(2))* Author Solutions, Inc. (WestBow Pr.).

Halloran, Craig. The Chronicles of Dragon: Dragon Bones & Tombstones (Book 2) 2013. 226p. pap. 9.99 *(978-0-9896216-0-1(X))* Two-Ten Bk. Pr.

—The Chronicles of Dragon: Terror at the Temple (Book 3) 2013. 276p. pap. 9.99 *(978-0-9896216-2-5(6))* Two-Ten Bk. Pr.

—The Chronicles of Dragon: The Hero, the Sword & the Dragons (Book 1) 2013. 136p. pap. 9.99 *(978-0-9884642-6-1(8))* Two-Ten Bk. Pr.

Halsted, John David, ed. & compiled by. Dragon's Tales for Boys Only! Halsted, John David, compiled by. 2013. (Illus.). 318p. pap. *(978-1-909302-39-6(2))* Abela Publishing.

Hamel, Mike. Dragon's Lair, 5. 2007. (Matterhorn the Brave Ser.: 5). (ENG.). 192p. (J). (gr. 5-11). per. 9.99 *(978-0-89957-837-8(3))* AMG Pubs.

Hamilton, Seymour. The Laughing Princess. 2012. (ENG.). 146p. (J). pap. 7.99 *(978-1-937291-45-7(6))* Acedrex Publishing.

Hapka, Catherine, pseud. How to Train Your Dragon: Meet the Dragons. Grosvenor, Charles & Gerard, Justin, illus. 2010. (I Can Read Book 1 Ser.). 32p. (J). (gr. k-3). pap. 3.99 *(978-0-06-156733-9(7))* HarperCollins Pubs.

Hardy, Gary D. Pj the Water Breathing Dragon: In Being Different Is a Good Thing. 2012. 28p. pap. 15.99 *(978-1-4691-7742-7(0))* Xlibris Corp.

Hardy, Sarah C. The Silver Winged Dragon. 2011. 32p. pap. 14.49 *(978-1-4634-2565-4(1))* AuthorHouse.

Hargreaves, Roger & Hargreaves, Adam. Mr. Tickle & the Dragon. Hargreaves, Adam, illus. 2008. (Mr. Men & Little Miss Ser.). (ENG., Illus.). 32p. (J). (gr. -1-2). mass mkt. 3.99 *(978-0-8431-3278-6(7),* Grosset & Dunlap) Penguin Young Readers Group.

Harrar, Frank W. Wee Dragonslayers. Galan-Robles, Francisco, illus. 2008. 45p. pap. 24.95 *(978-1-60610-851-2(4))* America Star Bks.

Harris, Christine. Four Tails: An Anthology of Four Tales for Children. 2011. (Illus.). 92p. (gr. -1). pap. 12.10 *(978-1-4520-7643-0(X))* AuthorHouse.

Harrison, Paula. The Baby Firebird. Williams, Sophy, illus. 2017. (Secret Rescuers Ser.: 3). (ENG.). 128p. (J). (gr. 2-5). pap. 5.99 ***(978-1-4814-7613-3(0),*** Aladdin) Simon & Schuster Children's Publishing.

Hart, Derek. Secret of the Dragon's Eye. 2007. 264p. per. 16.95 *(978-0-595-42967-7(X))* iUniverse, Inc.

Hartman, Rachel. Seraphina. (ENG.). (YA). (gr. 7). 2014. 528p. pap. 10.99 *(978-0-375-86622-7(1),* Ember) 2012. 512p. lib. bdg. 20.99 *(978-0-375-96656-9(0),* Random Hse. Bks. for Young Readers) Random Hse. Children's Bks.

—Shadow Scale. 2015. (ENG., Illus.). 608p. (J). (gr. 7). 18.99 *(978-0-375-86657-9(4),* Random Hse. Bks. for Young Readers) Random Hse. Children's Bks.

Harvey, Keith. Tiberius & the Friendly Dragon. Kirk, Heather, illus. 2010. (Tiberius Tales Ser.). 24p. (J). (gr. -1-2). pap. 8.15 *(978-1-60754-834-8(8));* lib. bdg. 22.60 *(978-1-60754-830-0(5))* Windmill Bks.

—Tiberius Meets Sneaky Cat. Hickman, Paula, illus. 2010. (Tiberius Tales Ser.). 24p. (J). (gr. -1-2). pap. 8.15 *(978-1-60754-835-5(6));* lib. bdg. 22.60 *(978-1-60754-831-7(3))* Windmill Bks.

Harvey, Keith & Kirk, Heather. Tiberius & the Friendly Dragon. 2014. (ENG., Illus.). 24p. pap. 8.95 *(978-1-84135-917-5(3))* Award Pubns. Ltd. GBR. Dist: Parkwest Pubns., Inc.

Haskell, Merrie. Handbook for Dragon Slayers. 2013. (ENG.). 336p. (J). (gr. 3-7). 16.99 *(978-0-06-200816-9(1))* HarperCollins Pubs.

Hatke, Ben. Mighty Jack. (Mighty Jack Ser.: 2). (ENG., Illus.). 208p. (J). 2017. 22.99 ***(978-1-62672-267-5(6),*** 9781626722675) 2017. pap. 14.99 ***(978-1-62672-266-8(8),*** 9781626722668) 2016. pap. 14.99 *(978-1-62672-264-4(1),* 9781626722644) Roaring Brook Pr. (First Second Bks.).

—Mighty Jack. 2017. (Mighty Jack Ser.). (J). lib. bdg. 26.95 ***(978-0-606-40540-9(2))*** Turtleback Bks.

Hayes, Geoffrey. A Poor Excuse for a Dragon. 2011. (Step into Reading Ser.). (ENG., Illus.). 48p. (J). (gr. 2-4). pap. 4.99 *(978-0-375-86867-2(4),* Random Hse. Bks. for Young Readers) Random Hse. Children's Bks.

Hayes, Tracey J. Bartina in Trouble Again. 2009. 64p. pap. 15.99 *(978-1-4415-2050-0(3))* Xlibris Corp.

Hazel, Jan. Marshall Meets the Little Dragons. 2013. 38p. pap. 9.99 *(978-1-62509-396-7(9))* Salem Author Services.

Hebert, J. J. Weepy the Dragon. 2012. 36p. pap. 9.99 *(978-0-9853650-7-3(2))* Mindstir Media.

Hecker, Vera, illus. A Home for Rainbow. 2007. 32p. (J). *(978-0-9799729-0-4(6))* Banta, Sandra.

Heeney, Bronwyn. A Dragon Called Wilbur: How a Fire-Breathing Dragon Made Friends. Fekete, Lucy, illus. 2012. 40p. pap. 16.97 *(978-1-61204-803-1(X),* Strategic Bk. Publishing) Strategic Book Publishing & Rights Agency (SBPRA).

Hellier, Lorraine. The Wayward Wagon. 2010. 114p. pap. 10.99 *(978-1-4520-3232-0(7))* AuthorHouse.

Helm, Julie G. Merlin for Sherman. Cary, Debbi G., photos by. 2010. (Illus.). 84p. pap. 26.49 *(978-1-4520-5183-3(6))* AuthorHouse.

Heneghan, Judith. Dragon School Set. 2015. (Dragon School Ser.). (ENG., Illus.). 32p. (J). pap., pap., pap. 40.00 *(978-1-4777-5690-4(6),* Windmill Bks.) Rosen Publishing Group, Inc., The.

Henham, R. D. Black Dragon Codex. 2008. (Dragon Codices Ser.). (ENG.). 256p. (J). (gr. 4-7). 9.95 *(978-0-7869-4972-4(4),* Mirrorstone) Wizards of the Coast.

—Bronze Dragon Codex. 2008. (Dragon Codices Ser.). (ENG., Illus.). 256p. (J). (gr. 4-7). 9.95 *(978-0-7869-4930-4(9),* Mirrorstone) Wizards of the Coast.

—Red Dragon Codex. 2008. (Dragon Codices Ser.). (ENG., Illus.). 256p. (J). (gr. 4-7). 9.95 *(978-0-7869-4925-0(2),* Mirrorstone) Wizards of the Coast.

Herda, Frank A. The Cup of Death: Cronicles of the Dragons of the Magi. 2007. 180p. 16.95 *(978-1-4327-0922-8(4));* 212p. per. 9.95 *(978-1-4327-1412-3(0))* Outskirts Pr., Inc.

Herman, George & Seaton, Kristen. Nine Dragons: A Contemporary Fable. 2003. (ENG., Illus.). 1p. 15.95 *(978-0-8048-3481-0(4))* Tuttle Publishing.

Hess, Brian F. Lynquest & the Search for Greatness. 2006. (ENG.). 116p. per. 19.95 *(978-1-4241-4503-4(1))* PublishAmerica, Inc.

Hicks, Bob. Cornelius, the Little Dragon Book. Hicks, Bob, illus. 2004. (Illus.). (J). ring bd. incl. audio compact disk *(978-0-9722036-5-4(6))* T. E. Publishing, Inc.

Hicks, Michael Christopher. Tales of Drake: The Tale of the Lost Dog. 2011. 40p. pap. 18.99 *(978-1-4634-1823-6(X))* AuthorHouse.

Higginbotham, Liz. Drake the Dragon. 2011. 20p. pap. 24.95 *(978-1-4560-8472-1(0))* America Star Bks.

Higgins, Lawrence. Demons & Dragons: Time, Space & Magic. 2010. (ENG., Illus.). 93p. pap. 20.99 *(978-1-906791-68-1(6))* Arena Bks. GBR. Dist: Lightning Source UK, Ltd.

Highley, Rainey Marie. The Long Lost Tale of the Dragon & the Whale. 2013. 28p. pap. 16.95 *(978-1-4808-0151-6(8))* Archway Publishing.

Hightman, Jason. The Saint of Dragons. 2004. 304p. (J). (gr. 7-18). (ENG.). 16.99 *(978-0-06-054011-1(7));* lib. bdg. 17.89 *(978-0-06-054012-8(5))* HarperCollins Pubs.

Hill, C. J. Slayers. 2011. (Slayers Ser.: 1). (ENG.). 384p. (YA). (gr. 7). 16.99 *(978-0-312-61414-0(4))* Feiwel & Friends.

—Slayers. 2013. (Slayers Ser.: 1). (ENG.). 400p. (YA). (gr. 7). pap. 9.99 *(978-0-312-67514-1(3))* Square Fish.

—Slayers: Friends & Traitors. 2013. (Slayers Ser.: 2). (ENG.). 400p. (YA). (gr. 7). 16.99 *(978-1-250-02461-9(7),* 9781250024619) Feiwel & Friends.

—Slayers: Friends & Traitors. 2014. (Slayers Ser.: 2). (ENG.). 416p. (YA). (gr. 7). pap. 10.99 *(978-1-250-05079-3(0),* 9781250050793) Square Fish.

Hill, Douglas. The Dragon Charmer. Melnyczuk, Peter, illus. 2005. 151p. (J). (gr. -1-k). pap. 4.95 *(978-1-903015-36-0(7))* Barn Owl Bks, London GBR. Dist: Independent Pubs. Group.

Hill, Kevin Kelvin. The Supreme Sorcerer Ollie Tooth Pick & His Two Henchmen versus the Magical Dragons. 2011. 40p. 20.76 *(978-1-4567-3254-7(4))* AuthorHouse.

Hillert, Margaret. Una Amiga para Querido Dragón. Pullan, Jack, illus. 2017. (BeginningtoRead Ser.).Tr. of Friend for Dear Dragon. (ENG & SPA.). 32p. (J). (-2). 22.60 ***(978-1-59953-828-0(8))*** Norwood Hse. Pr.

—Ayuda para Querido Dragón. Pullan, Jack, illus. 2017. (BeginningtoRead Ser.). Orig. Title: Help for Dear Dragon. (ENG & SPA.). 32p. (J). (-2). 22.60 ***(978-1-59953-832-7(6))*** Norwood Hse. Pr.

—Come to School, Dear Dragon. Pullan, Jack, illus. 2016. (BeginningtoRead Ser.). (ENG.). 32p. (J). (-2). lib. bdg. 22.60 *(978-1-59953-764-1(8))*; (gr. -1-2). pap. 11.94 *(978-1-60357-877-6(3))* Norwood Hse. Pr.

—Dear Dragon Eats Out. Schimmell, David, illus. rev. ed. 2014. (BeginningtoRead Ser.). (ENG.). 32p. (J). (gr. k-2). pap. 11.94 *(978-1-60357-637-6(1))*; lib. bdg. 22.60 *(978-1-59953-629-3(3))* Norwood Hse. Pr.

—Dear Dragon Flies a Kite. Pullan, Jack, illus. 2014. (BeginningtoRead Ser.). (ENG.). 32p. (J). (gr. k-2). pap. 11.94 *(978-1-60357-709-0(2))*; lib. bdg. 22.60 *(978-1-59953-674-3(9))* Norwood Hse. Pr.

—Dear Dragon Gets a Hole-In-One. Pullan, Jack, illus. 2015. (BeginningtoRead Ser.). (ENG.). 32p. (J). (gr. k-2). pap. 11.94 *(978-1-60357-790-8(4))*; lib. bdg. 22.60 *(978-1-59953-705-4(2))* Norwood Hse. Pr.

—Dear Dragon Gets a Pet. Pullan, Jack, illus. 2015. (BeginningtoRead Ser.). (ENG.). 32p. (J). (gr. k-2). pap. 11.94 *(978-1-60357-791-5(2))*; lib. bdg. 22.60 *(978-1-59953-706-1(0))* Norwood Hse. Pr.

—Dear Dragon Goes Camping. Schimmell, David, illus. 2010. (BeginningtoRead Ser.). 32p. (J). (gr. k-2). lib. bdg. 22.60 *(978-1-59953-345-2(6))* Norwood Hse. Pr.

—Dear Dragon Goes to Grandpa's Farm. Pullan, Jack, illus. 2014. (BeginningtoRead Ser.). (ENG.). 32p. (J). (gr. k-2). pap. 11.94 *(978-1-60357-710-6(6))*; lib. bdg. 22.60 *(978-1-59953-675-0(7))* Norwood Hse. Pr.

—Dear Dragon Goes to the Aquarium. Pullan, Jack, illus. 2014. (BeginningtoRead Ser.). (ENG.). 32p. (J). (gr. k-2). pap. 11.94 *(978-1-60357-712-0(2))*; lib. bdg. 22.60 *(978-1-59953-677-4(3))* Norwood Hse. Pr.

—Dear Dragon Goes to the Bank. Schimmell, David, illus. 2012. (BeginningtoRead Ser.). 32p. (J). (-2). lib. bdg. 22.60 *(978-1-59953-502-9(5))* Norwood Hse. Pr.

—Dear Dragon Goes to the Beach. Pullan, Jack, illus. 2015. (BeginningtoRead Ser.). (ENG.). 32p. (J). (gr. k-2). pap. 11.94 *(978-1-60357-789-2(0))*; lib. bdg. 22.60 *(978-1-59953-704-7(4))* Norwood Hse. Pr.

—Dear Dragon Goes to the Carnival. Schimmell, David, illus. 2010. (BeginningtoRead Ser.). 32p. (J). (gr. k-2). lib. bdg. 22.60 *(978-1-59953-346-9(4))* Norwood Hse. Pr.

—Dear Dragon Goes to the Dentist. Schimmell, David, illus. rev. ed. 2014. (BeginningtoRead Ser.). (ENG.). 32p. (J). (gr. k-2). lib. bdg. 22.60 *(978-1-59953-577-7(7))* Norwood Hse. Pr.

—Dear Dragon Goes to the Firehouse. Schimmell, David, illus. 2010. (BeginningtoRead Ser.). 32p. (J). (gr. k-2). lib. bdg. 22.60 *(978-1-59953-375-9(8))* Norwood Hse. Pr.

—Dear Dragon Goes to the Hospital. Schimmell, David, illus. rev. ed. 2014. (BeginningtoRead Ser.). (ENG.). 32p. (J). (gr. k-2). pap. 11.94 *(978-1-60357-422-8(0))*; lib. bdg. 22.60 *(978-1-59953-581-4(5))* Norwood Hse. Pr.

—Dear Dragon Goes to the Library. Schimmell, David, illus. 2008. (BeginningtoRead Ser.). 32p. (J). (gr. k-2). lib. bdg. 22.60 *(978-1-59953-160-1(7))* Norwood Hse. Pr.

—Dear Dragon Goes to the Library (Querido Dragon Va a la Biblioteca) Del Risco, Eida, tr. from ENG. Schimmell, David, illus. 2010. (BeginningtoRead Ser.). (SPA & ENG.). 32p. (J). (gr. k-2). lib. bdg. 22.60 *(978-1-59953-361-2(8))* Norwood Hse. Pr.

—Dear Dragon Goes to the Market. Schimmell, David, illus. 2010. (BeginningtoRead Ser.). 32p. (J). (gr. k-2). lib. bdg. 22.60 *(978-1-59953-347-6(2))* Norwood Hse. Pr.

—Dear Dragon Goes to the Police Station. Pullan, Jack, illus. 2014. (BeginningtoRead Ser.). (ENG.). 32p. (J). (gr. k-2). pap. 11.94 *(978-1-60357-711-3(4))*; lib. bdg. 22.60 *(978-1-59953-676-7(5))* Norwood Hse. Pr.

—Dear Dragon Goes to the Zoo. Schimmell, David, illus. 2010. (BeginningtoRead Ser.). 32p. (J). (gr. k-2). lib. bdg. 22.60 *(978-1-59953-348-3(0))* Norwood Hse. Pr.

—Dear Dragon Grows a Garden. Schimmell, David, illus. rev. ed. 2014. (BeginningtoRead Ser.). (ENG.). 32p. (J). (gr. k-2). pap. 11.94 *(978-1-60357-414-3(X))*; lib. bdg. 22.60 *(978-1-59953-578-4(5))* Norwood Hse. Pr.

—Dear Dragon Helps Out. Schimmell, David, illus. 2012. (BeginningtoRead Ser.). 32p. (J). (-2). lib. bdg. 22.60 *(978-1-59953-505-0(X))* Norwood Hse. Pr.

—Dear Dragon Learns to Read. Pullan, Jack, illus. 2015. (BeginningtoRead Ser.). (ENG.). 32p. (J). (gr. k-2). pap. 11.94 *(978-1-60357-792-2(0))*; lib. bdg. 22.60 *(978-1-59953-707-8(9))* Norwood Hse. Pr.

—Dear Dragon's A Is for Apple. Schimmell, David, illus. 2008. (BeginningtoRead Ser.). 32p. (J). (gr. k-2). lib. bdg. 22.60 *(978-1-59953-158-8(5))* Norwood Hse. Pr.

—Dear Dragon's Colors 1, 2, 3. Schimmell, David, illus. 2010. (BeginningtoRead Ser.). 32p. (J). (-2). pap. 11.94 *(978-1-60357-100-5(0))* Norwood Hse. Pr.

—Dear Dragon's Colors 1 ,2, 3. Schimmell, David, illus. 2010. (BeginningtoRead Ser.). 32p. (J). (gr. k-2). lib. bdg. 22.60 *(978-1-59953-376-6(6))* Norwood Hse. Pr.

—Dear Dragon's Day with Father. Schimmell, David, illus. 2008. (BeginningtoRead Ser.). 32p. (J). (-2). (ENG.). pap. 11.94 ***(978-1-68404-010-0(8))***; lib. bdg. 22.60 *(978-1-59953-162-5(3))* Norwood Hse. Pr.

—Dear Dragon's Day with Father (Querido Dragon Pasa el Dia con Papa) Del Risco, Eida, tr. from ENG. Schimmell, David, illus. 2010. (BeginningtoRead Ser.). (SPA & ENG.). 32p. (J). (gr. k-2). lib. bdg. 22.60 *(978-1-59953-360-5(X))* Norwood Hse. Pr.

—Dear Dragon's Fun with Shapes. Schimmell, David, illus. 2015. (BeginningtoRead Ser.). 32p. (J). (-2). lib. bdg. 22.60 *(978-1-59953-544-9(0))* Norwood Hse. Pr.

—Dear Dragon's Fun with Shapes. del Risco, Eida, tr. Schimmell, David, illus. 2015. (BeginningtoRead Ser.). 32p. (J). (-2). pap. 11.94 *(978-1-60357-447-1(6))* Norwood Hse. Pr.

—¿Dónde Está Querido Dragón? Fernandez, Queta, tr. from ENG. Schimmell, David, illus. 2014. (BeginningtoRead Ser.).Tr. of Where Is Dear Dragon? (SPA & ENG.). 32p. (J). (-2). lib. bdg. 22.60 *(978-1-59953-615-6(3))* Norwood Hse. Pr.

—Dragon Goes to the Farm: For the Earliest Reader. Starfall Education, illus. 2006. (ENG.). 32p. (J). *(978-1-59577-032-5(1))*; pap. *(978-1-59577-034-9(8))* Starfall Education.

—Es Halloween, Querido Dragón. Pullan, Jack, illus. 2017. (BeginningtoRead Ser.).Tr. of It's Halloween, Dear Dragon. (ENG & SPA.). 32p. (J). (-2). 22.60 ***(978-1-59953-836-5(9))*** Norwood Hse. Pr.

—Es Hora de Ir a la Cama, Querido Dragón. Fernandez, Queta, tr. from ENG. Schimmell, David, illus. 2014. (BeginningtoRead Ser.).Tr. of It's Bedtime, Dear Dragon. (ENG & SPA.). 32p. (J). (-2). lib. bdg. 22.60 *(978-1-59953-612-5(9))* Norwood Hse. Pr.

—Es Primavera, Querido Dragón/It's Spring, Dear Dragon. Schimmell, David, illus. 2011. (BeginningtoRead Ser.). 32p. (J). (-2). pap. 11.94 *(978-1-60357-555-3(3))* Norwood Hse. Pr.

—Es Primavera, Querido Dragón/It's Spring, Dear Dragon. del Risco, Eida, tr. from ENG. Schimmell, David, illus. 2011. (BeginningtoRead Ser.). 32p. (J). (gr. k-2). lib. bdg. 22.60 *(978-1-59953-471-8(1))* Norwood Hse. Pr.

—Es un Buen Juego, Querido Dragón/It's a Good Game, Dear Dragon. Schimmell, David, illus. 2010. (BeginningtoRead Ser.). 32p. (J). (-2). pap. 11.94 *(978-1-60357-550-8(2))* Norwood Hse. Pr.

—Feliz Cumpleaños, Querido Dragón. Pullan, Jack, illus. 2017. (BeginningtoRead Ser.).Tr. of Happy Birthday, Dear Dragon. (ENG & SPA.). 32p. (J). (-2). 22.60 ***(978-1-59953-830-3(X))*** Norwood Hse. Pr.

—Feliz Navidad, Querido Dragón. Pullan, Jack, illus. 2017. (BeginningtoRead Ser.).Tr. of Merry Christmas, Dear Dragon. (ENG & SPA.). 32p. (J). (-2). 22.60 ***(978-1-59953-838-9(5))*** Norwood Hse. Pr.

—Feliz Pascua, Querido Dragón. Pullan, Jack, illus. 2017. (BeginningtoRead Ser.).Tr. of Happy Easter, Dear Dragon. (ENG & SPA.). 32p. (J). (-2). 22.60 ***(978-1-59953-831-0(8))*** Norwood Hse. Pr.

—A Friend for Dear Dragon. Pullan, Jack, illus. 2016. (BeginningtoRead Ser.). (ENG.). 32p. (J). (-2). lib. bdg. 22.60 *(978-1-59953-765-8(6))*; (gr. 1-2). pap. 11.94 *(978-1-60357-878-3(1))* Norwood Hse. Pr.

—Go to Sleep, Dear Dragon. Pullan, Jack, illus. 2016. (BeginningtoRead Ser.). (ENG.). 32p. (J). (-2). lib. bdg. 22.60 *(978-1-59953-766-5(4))*; (gr. -1-2). pap. 11.94 *(978-1-60357-879-0(X))* Norwood Hse. Pr.

—Happy Birthday, Dear Dragon. Pullan, Jack, illus. 2016. (BeginningtoRead Ser.). (ENG.). 32p. (J). (-2). lib. bdg. 22.60 *(978-1-59953-767-2(2))*; (gr. 1-2). pap. 11.94 *(978-1-60357-880-6(3))* Norwood Hse. Pr.

—Happy Easter, Dear Dragon. Pullan, Jack, illus. 2016. (BeginningtoRead Ser.). (ENG.). 32p. (J). (-2). lib. bdg. 22.60 *(978-1-59953-768-9(0))*; (gr. 1-2). pap. 11.94 *(978-1-60357-881-3(1))* Norwood Hse. Pr.

—Happy Hanukkah, Dear Dragon. Schimmell, David, illus. 2008. (BeginningtoRead Ser.). 32p. (J). (-2). (ENG.). pap. 11.94 ***(978-1-68404-011-7(6))***; lib. bdg. 22.60 *(978-1-59953-159-5(3))* Norwood Hse. Pr.

—Happy Mother's Day, Dear Dragon, 5 bks. Starfall Education, illus. 2005. (ENG.). 32p. (J). 6.95 *(978-1-59577-022-6(4))*; pap. *(978-1-59577-023-3(2))* Starfall Education.

—Help for Dear Dragon. Pullan, Jack, illus. 2016. (BeginningtoRead Ser.). (ENG.). 32p. (J). (-2). lib. bdg. 22.60 *(978-1-59953-769-6(9))* Norwood Hse. Pr.

—I Did It, Dear Dragon. Schimmell, David, illus. 2009. (BeginningtoRead Ser.). 32p. (J). (gr. k-2). lib. bdg. 22.60 *(978-1-59953-295-0(6))* Norwood Hse. Pr.

—I Love You, Dear Dragon. Pullan, Jack, illus. 2016. (BeginningtoRead Ser.). (ENG.). 32p. (J). (-2). lib. bdg. 22.60 *(978-1-59953-770-2(2))*; (gr. 1-2). pap. 11.94 *(978-1-60357-883-7(8))* Norwood Hse. Pr.

—I Need You, Dear Dragon. Pullan, Jack, illus. 2016. (BeginningtoRead Ser.). (ENG.). 32p. (J). (-2). lib. bdg. 22.60 *(978-1-59953-771-9(0))*; (gr. -1-2). pap. 11.94 *(978-1-60357-884-4(6))* Norwood Hse. Pr.

—It's a Good Game, Dear Dragon. Schimmell, David, illus. 2009. (BeginningtoRead Ser.). 32p. (J). (gr. k-2). lib. bdg. 22.60 *(978-1-59953-293-6(X))* Norwood Hse. Pr.

—It's a Good Game, Dear Dragon (Es un Buen Juego, Querido Dragon) Del Risco, Eida, tr. from ENG. Schimmell, David, illus. 2010. (BeginningtoRead Ser.). (SPA & ENG.). 32p. (J). (gr. k-2). lib. bdg. 22.60 *(978-1-59953-362-9(6))* Norwood Hse. Pr.

—It's Bedtime Dear Dragon. Schimmell, David, illus. 2012. (BeginningtoRead Ser.). 32p. (J). (-2). lib. bdg. 22.60 *(978-1-59953-503-6(3))* Norwood Hse. Pr.

—It's Circus Time, Dear Dragon. Pullan, Jack, illus. 2016. (BeginningtoRead Ser.). (ENG.). 32p. (J). (-2). lib. bdg. 22.60 *(978-1-59953-772-6(9))*; (gr. 1-2). pap. 11.94 *(978-1-60357-885-1(4))* Norwood Hse. Pr.

—It's Earth Day, Dear Dragon: For the Earliest Reader. Starfall Education, illus. 2006. (ENG.). 32p. (J). *(978-1-59577-041-7(0))*; pap. *(978-1-59577-042-4(9))* Starfall Education.

—It's Fall, Dear Dragon. Schimmell, David, illus. 2009. (BeginningtoRead Ser.). 32p. (J). (gr. k-2). lib. bdg. 22.60 *(978-1-59953-311-7(1))* Norwood Hse. Pr.

—It's Ground Hog Day Dear Dragon. Schimmell, David, illus. 2012. (BeginningtoRead Ser.). 32p. (J). (-2). lib. bdg. 22.60 *(978-1-59953-504-3(1))* Norwood Hse. Pr.

—It's Groundhog Day, Dear Dragon. Schimmell, David, illus. 2012. (BeginningtoRead Ser.). 32p. (J). (-2). pap. 11.94 *(978-1-60357-384-9(4))* Norwood Hse. Pr.

—It's Halloween, Dear Dragon. Pullan, Jack, illus. 2016. (BeginningtoRead Ser.). (ENG.). 32p. (J). (-2). lib. bdg. 22.60 *(978-1-59953-773-3(7))*; (gr. -1-2). pap. 11.94 *(978-1-60357-886-8(2))* Norwood Hse. Pr.

—It's Spring, Dear Dragon. Schimmell, David, illus. 2009. (BeginningtoRead Ser.). 32p. (J). (gr. k-2). lib. bdg. 22.60 *(978-1-59953-312-4(X))* Norwood Hse. Pr.

—It's St. Patrick's Day, Dear Dragon. Schimmell, David, illus. 2008. (BeginningtoRead Ser.). 32p. (J). (gr. k-2). lib. bdg. 22.60 *(978-1-59953-161-8(5))* Norwood Hse. Pr.

—It's St. Patrick's Day, Dear Dragon. del Risco, Eida, tr. Schimmell, David, illus. 2008. (BeginningtoRead Ser.). 32p. (J). (-2). pap. 11.94 *(978-1-60357-086-2(1))* Norwood Hse. Pr.

—It's Summer, Dear Dragon. Schimmell, David, illus. 2009. (BeginningtoRead Ser.). 32p. (J). (gr. k-2). lib. bdg. 22.60 *(978-1-59953-313-1(8))* Norwood Hse. Pr.

—It's Winter, Dear Dragon. Schimmell, David, illus. 2009. (BeginningtoRead Ser.). 32p. (J). (gr. k-2). lib. bdg. 22.60 *(978-1-59953-314-8(6))* Norwood Hse. Pr.

—Juega, Juega, Juega, Querido Dragón/Play, Play, Play, Dear Dragon. del Risco, Eida, tr. Schimmell, David, illus. 2010. (BeginningtoRead Ser.). 32p. (J). (-2). pap. 11.94 *(978-1-60357-551-5(0))* Norwood Hse. Pr.

—Let's Go, Dear Dragon. Pullan, Jack, illus. 2016. (BeginningtoRead Ser.). (ENG.). 32p. (J). (-2). lib. bdg. 22.60 *(978-1-59953-774-0(5))* Norwood Hse. Pr.

—Merry Christmas, Dear Dragon. Pullan, Jack, illus. 2016. (BeginningtoRead Ser.). (ENG.). 32p. (J). (-2). lib. bdg. 22.60 *(978-1-59953-775-7(3))*; (gr. -1-2). pap. 11.94 *(978-1-60357-888-2(9))* Norwood Hse. Pr.

—Play, Play, Play Dear Dragon. Schimmell, David, illus. 2009. (BeginningtoRead Ser.). 32p. (J). (gr. k-2). lib. bdg. 22.60 *(978-1-59953-294-3(8))* Norwood Hse. Pr.

—Play, Play, Play, Dear Dragon (Juega, Juega, Juega, Querido Dragon) Del Risco, Eida, tr. Schimmell, David, illus. 2010. (BeginningtoRead Ser.). (SPA & ENG.). 32p. (J). (gr. k-2). lib. bdg. 22.60 *(978-1-59953-363-6(4))* Norwood Hse. Pr.

—¿Qué Hay en el Cielo, Querido Dragón? Fernandez, Queta, tr. from ENG. Schimmell, David, illus. 2014. (BeginningtoRead Ser.).Tr. of What's in the Sky, Dear Dragon? (ENG & SPA.). 32p. (J). (-2). lib. bdg. 22.60 *(978-1-59953-610-1(2))* Norwood Hse. Pr.

—¿Qué Hay en el Estanque, Querido Dragón? Fernandez, Queta, tr. from ENG. Schimmell, David, illus. 2014. (BeginningtoRead Ser.).Tr. of What's in the Pond, Dear Dragon? (ENG & SPA.). 32p. (J). (-2). lib. bdg. 22.60 *(978-1-59953-608-8(0))* Norwood Hse. Pr.

—¿Qué Tengo en el Bolsillo, Querido Dragón? Fernandez, Queta, tr. from ENG. Schimmell, David, illus. 2014. (BeginningtoRead Ser.).Tr. of What's in My Pocket, Dear Dragon? (ENG & SPA.). 32p. (J). (-2). lib. bdg. 22.60 *(978-1-59953-611-8(0))* Norwood Hse. Pr.

—Querido Dragón, Los Colores y 1, 2, 3 /Dear Dragon's Colors 1, 2, 3. del Risco, Eida, tr. Schimmell, David, illus. 2011. (BeginningtoRead Ser.). 32p. (J). (-2). pap. 11.94 *(978-1-60357-554-6(5))* Norwood Hse. Pr.

—Querido Dragón, los Colores y 1, 2, 3 /Dear Dragon's Colors 1, 2, 3. del Risco, Eida, tr. from ENG. Schimmell, David, illus. 2011. (BeginningtoRead Ser.). 32p. (J). (gr. k-2). lib. bdg. 22.60 *(978-1-59953-470-1(3))* Norwood Hse. Pr.

—Querido Dragón Quiere Ayudar. Fernandez, Queta, tr. from ENG. Schimmell, David, illus. 2014. (BeginningtoRead Ser.).Tr. of Dear Dragon Helps Out. (ENG & SPA.). 32p. (J). (-2). lib. bdg. 22.60 *(978-1-59953-613-2(7))* Norwood Hse. Pr.

—Querido Dragón Va a la Biblioteca/Dear Dragon Goes to the Library. del Risco, Eida, tr. Schimmell, David, illus. 2010. (BeginningtoRead Ser.). 32p. (J). (-2). pap. 11.94 *(978-1-60357-549-2(9))* Norwood Hse. Pr.

—Querido Dragón Va a la Estación de Bomberos/Dear Dragon Goes to the Firehouse. de', Eida, tr. Schimmell, David, illus. 2011. (BeginningtoRead Ser.). 32p. (J). (-2). pap. 11.94 *(978-1-60357-552-2(9))* Norwood Hse. Pr.

—Querido Dragón Va Al Banco. Fernandez, Queta, tr. from ENG. Schimmell, David, illus. 2014. (BeginningtoRead Ser.).Tr. of Dear Dragon Goes to the Bank. (ENG & SPA.). 32p. (J). (-2). lib. bdg. 22.60 *(978-1-59953-614-9(5))* Norwood Hse. Pr.

—Querido Dragón Va Al Cuartel de Bomberos/Dear Dragon Goes to the Firehouse. del Risco, Eida, tr. from ENG. Schimmell, David, illus. 2011. (BeginningtoRead Ser.). 32p. (J). (gr. k-2). lib. bdg. 22.60 *(978-1-59953-468-8(1))* Norwood Hse. Pr.

—Querido dragón va al mercado. del Risco, Eida, tr. from ENG. Schimmell, David, illus. 2011. (BeginningtoRead Ser.).Tr. of Dear Dragon Goes to the Market. (SPA.). 32p. (J). (gr. k-2). lib. bdg. 22.60 *(978-1-59953-469-5(X))* Norwood Hse. Pr.

—Querido Dragón Va Al Mercado/Dear Dragon Goes to the Market. Schimmell, David, illus. 2011. (BeginningtoRead Ser.). 32p. (J). (-2). pap. 11.94 *(978-1-60357-553-9(7))* Norwood Hse. Pr.

—Te Necesito, Querido Dragón. Pullan, Jack, illus. 2017. (BeginningtoRead Ser.).Tr. of I Need You, Dear Dragon. (ENG & SPA.). 32p. (J). (-2). 22.60 ***(978-1-59953-834-1(2))*** Norwood Hse. Pr.

—Te Quiero, Querido Dragón. Pullan, Jack, illus. 2017. (BeginningtoRead Ser.).Tr. of I Love You, Dear Dragon. (ENG & SPA.). 32p. (J). (-2). 22.60 ***(978-1-59953-833-4(4))*** Norwood Hse. Pr.

—Touchdown! Dear Dragon. Schimmell, David, illus. 2009. (BeginningtoRead Ser.). 32p. (J). (gr. k-2). lib. bdg. 22.60 *(978-1-59953-296-7(4))* Norwood Hse. Pr.

—Up, up, up, Dear Dragon. Schimmell, David, illus. 2012. (BeginningtoRead Ser.). 32p. (J). (-2). lib. bdg. 22.60 *(978-1-59953-545-6(9))* Norwood Hse. Pr.

—Vamos Al Circo, Querido Dragón. Pullan, Jack, illus. 2017. (BeginningtoRead Ser.).Tr. of It's Circus Time, Dear Dragon. (ENG & SPA.). 32p. (J). (-2). 22.60 ***(978-1-59953-835-8(0))*** Norwood Hse. Pr.

—Vamos, Querido Dragón. Pullan, Jack, illus. 2017. (BeginningtoRead Ser.).Tr. of Let's Go, Dear Dragon. (ENG & SPA.). 32p. (J). (-2). 22.60 ***(978-1-59953-837-2(7))*** Norwood Hse. Pr.

—Ve a Dormir, Querido Dragón. Pullan, Jack, illus. 2017. (BeginningtoRead Ser.).Tr. of Go to Sleep, Dear Dragon. (ENG & SPA.). 32p. (J). (-2). 22.60 ***(978-1-59953-829-7(6))*** Norwood Hse. Pr.

—Ven a la Escuela, Querido Dragón. Pullan, Jack, illus. 2017. (BeginningtoRead Ser.).Tr. of Come to School, Dear Dragon. (ENG & SPA.). 32p. (J). (-2). 22.60 ***(978-1-59953-827-3(X))*** Norwood Hse. Pr.

—What's in My Pocket, Dear Dragon? Schimmell, David, illus. 2014. (BeginningtoRead Ser.). (ENG.). 32p. (J). (-2). pap. 11.94 *(978-1-60357-415-0(8))*; lib. bdg. 22.60 *(978-1-59953-579-1(3))* Norwood Hse. Pr.

—What's in the Pond, Dear Dragon? Schimmell, David, illus. 2014. (BeginningtoRead Ser.). (ENG.). 32p. (J). (-2). pap. 11.94 *(978-1-60357-601-7(0))*; lib. bdg. 22.60 *(978-1-59953-607-1(2))* Norwood Hse. Pr.

—What's in the Sky, Dear Dragon? Schimmell, David, illus. 2014. (BeginningtoRead Ser.). (ENG.). 32p. (J). (-2). pap. 11.94 *(978-1-60357-416-7(6))*; lib. bdg. 22.60 *(978-1-59953-580-7(7))* Norwood Hse. Pr.

—What's in the Woods, Dear Dragon? Schimmell, David, illus. 2014. (BeginningtoRead Ser.). (ENG.). 32p. (J). (-2). pap. 11.94 *(978-1-60357-599-7(5))*; lib. bdg. 22.60 *(978-1-59953-606-4(4))* Norwood Hse. Pr.

—Where Is Dear Dragon? Schimmell, David, illus. 2012. (BeginningtoRead Ser.). 32p. (J). (-2). lib. bdg. 22.60 *(978-1-59953-546-3(7))* Norwood Hse. Pr.

—Who Feels Mad, Dear Dragon? Pullan, Jack, illus. 2017. (BeginningtoRead Ser.). (ENG.). 32p. (J). (-2). 22.60 ***(978-1-59953-822-8(9))***; pap. 11.94 ***(978-1-68404-000-1(0))*** Norwood Hse. Pr.

—Who Feels Sad, Dear Dragon? Pullan, Jack, illus. 2017. (BeginningtoRead Ser.). (ENG.). 32p. (J). (-2). 22.60 ***(978-1-59953-823-5(7))***; pap. 11.94 ***(978-1-68404-001-8(9))*** Norwood Hse. Pr.

—Who Feels Surprised, Dear Dragon? Pullan, Jack, illus. 2017. (BeginningtoRead Ser.). (ENG.). 32p. (J). (-2). 22.60 ***(978-1-59953-825-9(3))***; pap. 11.94 ***(978-1-68404-003-2(5))*** Norwood Hse. Pr.

Hillert, Margaret & Fernández, Queta. ¿Que Hay en el Bosque, Querido Dragon? Schimmell, David, illus. 2014. (BeginningtoRead Ser.).Tr. of What's in the Woods, Dear Dragon? (ENG & SPA.). 32p. (J). (-2). lib. bdg. 22.60 *(978-1-59953-609-5(9))* Norwood Hse. Pr.

Hitchcock, Alfred. Misterio del Dragon. (Alfred Hitchcock y los Tres Investigadores Ser.). (SPA.). 176p. (YA). 8.95 *(978-84-272-4914-1(4))*, MO66) Molino, Editorial ESP. Dist: Continental Bk. Co., Inc.

Hlobil, Karel. Forest Friends & the Three-Headed Dragon. 2010. 48p. pap. *(978-1-926582-61-0(6))* Insomniac Pr.

Hoban, Russell. Ace Dragon Ltd. Blake, Quentin, illus. 2015. (ENG.). 48p. (J). (gr. k-3). 16.99 *(978-0-7636-7482-3(6))* Candlewick Pr.

Hodges, Jean A. Drinking Dragon Sam Learns Drinking Doesn't Pay. 2011. 40p. pap. 24.95 *(978-1-4560-5507-3(0))* America Star Bks.

Hodges, Margaret. Saint George & the Dragon. braille ed. 2004. (Illus.). (J). (gr. 2-4). spiral bd. *(978-0-616-01675-6(1))* Canadian National Institute for the Blind/Institut National Canadien pour les Aveugles.

Hodgson, Louise & Jones, Eric. Delyth y Ddraig. 2005. (WEL., Illus.). 20p. pap. *(978-1-85596-220-0(9))* Dref Wen.

Hoel, Charlotte. The Magical Mischief Maker. 2004. (J). spiral bd. *(978-0-9754004-0-1(1))* Magical Mischief Maker.

Hofer, Debra. Kido the Dragon. 2012. 36p. pap. 12.95 *(978-1-936750-07-8(4)*, Total Publishing & Media) Yorkshire Publishing Group.

Hoffman, Cj. The Dragons & the Simmies: A Friendly Story. 2008. 20p. pap. 10.49 *(978-1-4389-1452-7(0))* AuthorHouse.

Holley, M. E. Jonah & the Last Great Dragon: Legend of the Heart Eaters. 2012. (ENG.). 149p. pap. 13.95 *(978-1-78099-541-0(5)*, Our Street Bks.) Hunt, John Publishing Ltd. GBR. Dist: National Bk. Network.

Holm, Jennifer L. Little Babymouse & the Christmas Cupcakes. Holm, Matthew, illus. 2016. (ENG.). 40p. (J). (gr. -1-2). 17.99 *(978-1-101-93743-3(2)*, Random Hse. Bks. for Young Readers) Random Hse. Children's Bks.

Holstein, Ima. A Dragons Daydream. 2011. 24p. pap. 12.99 *(978-1-4634-0430-7(1))* AuthorHouse.

Hook, Carol A. Before There Were Stars: An Orange Dragon. 2009. 48p. pap. 8.95 *(978-1-4401-5475-1(9))* iUniverse, Inc.

Hook, Jason. Where's the Dragon? Hook, Richard, illus. 2004. (Where's The ... ? Ser.). (ENG.). 26p. (J). (gr. -1-2). 14.95 *(978-1-4027-1624-9(9))* Sterling Publishing Co., Inc.

Hooten, K. J. The Egg Nanny Tales. 2008. 98p. pap. 19.95 *(978-1-60563-722-8(X))* America Star Bks.

Hopkins, Howard. The Nightmare Club #2: the Deadly Dragon. 2009. 104p. pap. 9.98 *(978-0-578-00320-7(1))* Golden Perils Pr.

Horns, Scales, Claws, & Tails: Individual Title Six-Packs. (Story Steps Ser.). (gr. k-2). 32.00 *(978-0-7635-9830-3(5))* Rigby Education.

Houck, Colleen. Tiger's Voyage. 2014. (Tiger's Curse Ser.: Bk. 3). (ENG.). 568p. (J). (gr. 7). pap. 9.95 *(978-1-4549-0357-4(0))* Sterling Publishing Co., Inc.

How to Start a Dragon Academy. 2014. (How to Train Your Dragon TV Ser.). (ENG., Illus.). 32p. (J). (gr. k-2). pap. 3.99 *(978-1-4814-1925-3(0)*, Simon Spotlight) Simon Spotlight.

Howard, Cheryl L. Mikhael the Mighty: Be True to Who You Are & You Can Never Go Wrong. 2009. 52p. pap. 18.50 *(978-1-60860-760-0(7)*, Strategic Bk. Publishing) Strategic Book Publishing & Rights Agency (SBPRA).

Howell, Julie Ann. Finnigan the Dragon. Zamboni, David, illus. 2009. 24p. pap. 12.95 *(978-1-936051-61-8(3))* Peppertree Pr., The.

Howell, Troy. The Dragon of Cripple Creek. 2011. (ENG., Illus.). 400p. (J). (gr. 3-7). 16.95 *(978-0-8109-9713-4(4)*, Amulet Bks.) Abrams, Inc.

Hsiao, Christie. Journey to Rainbow Island. 2013. (ENG., Illus.). 400p. (J). (gr. 2-7). 17.95 *(978-1-939529-24-4(7))* BenBella Bks.

Hughan, Judy. The Make Better Story, 1 vol. 2009. 31p. pap. 24.95 *(978-1-60836-754-2(1))* America Star Bks.

Hughes, Rick. The Dream Dragon. 2012. 156p. (gr. 4-6). 23.42 *(978-1-4669-3362-0(3))*; pap. 13.42 *(978-1-4669-3360-6(7))* Trafford Publishing.

Humphreys, Audrey. The Dragon Princess. 2012. 24p. pap. 24.99 *(978-1-4691-6554-7(6))* Xlibris Corp.

Huxman, K. D. Dragon Talk. 2007. (Illus.). 24p. (J). per. 11.99 *(978-0-9797574-9-5(5))* Dragonfly Publishing, Inc.

—Dragon Talk. Farrington, Teresa, illus. l.t. ed. 2006. 24p. (J). pap. 14.99 *(978-0-9765786-7-3(0))* Dragonfly Publishing, Inc.

C
D

Huxman, Karin (K. D.). Dragon Talk. 2006. (Illus.). 24p. (J). lib. bdg. 24.95 (978-0-9778651-7-8(7)) Dragonfly Publishing, Inc.

Ikin, Susan. Alex & the Night-tide Dragon. 2010. (Illus.). 68p. pap. 18.95 (978-1-4461-4894-5(7)) Lulu Pr., Inc.

Irvine, Patricia McCune. Beyond the Greenest Hill: A Fairy Tale. 2003. 136p. (YA). pap. 11.95 (978-0-595-26941-9(9)) iUniverse, Inc.

Irwin, Bindi & Kunz, Chris. Camouflage. 2011. (Bindi's Wildlife Adventures Ser.: 4). (ENG.). 112p. (gr. 3-6). pap. 4.99 (978-1-4022-5523-6(3), Sourcebooks Jabberwocky) Sourcebooks, Inc.

Ivanoff, George. Gamers' Quest. 2009. (Gamers Ser.: Bk. 1). (ENG.). 208p. (YA). pap. (978-1-876462-86-4(8), Ford Street Publishing) Hybrid Pubs.

Jackson, Lyn D. The Perilous Journey Home. 2009. 200p. pap. 14.49 (978-1-4389-4651-1(1)) AuthorHouse.

Janeway, Paul. Dragon Eye Connection. 2011. 202p. pap. 14.95 (978-1-60976-854-6(X), Strategic Bk. Publishing) Strategic Book Publishing & Rights Agency (SBPRA).

Janosch. Just One Apple. 2014. (ENG., Illus.). 32p. (J). 17.95 (978-0-7358-4151-2(9)) North-South Bks., Inc.

Jansson, Tove. Tales from Moominvalley. Warburton, Thomas, tr. Jansson, Tove, illus. 2010. (Moomins Ser.: 6).Tr. of Osynliga Barnet. (ENG., Illus.). 192p. (J). (gr. 4-7). pap. 7.99 (978-0-312-62542-9(1), 9780312625429) Square Fish.

Jay, Annabelle. The Sun Dragon. 2016. (ENG., Illus.). (YA). 24.99 **(978-1-63477-977-7(0))**; 180p. (J). pap. 14.99 (978-1-63476-339-4(4)) Dreamspinner Pr. (Harmony Ink Pr.).

Jenkins, Jerry B. & Fabry, Chris. The Author's Blood. 2008. (Wormling Ser.: 5). (ENG.). 368p. (J). (gr. 5-9). per. 7.99 (978-1-4143-0159-4(6), Tyndale Kids) Tyndale Hse. Pubs.

—The Book of the King. 2007. (Wormling Ser.: 1). (ENG.). 288p. (J). (gr. 5-9). per. 7.99 (978-1-4143-0155-6(3)) Tyndale Hse. Pubs.

—The Changeling. 2007. (Wormling Ser.: 3). (ENG.). 336p. (J). (gr. 5-9). per. 7.99 (978-1-4143-0157-0(X)) Tyndale Hse. Pubs.

—El Libro del Rey. 2008. (Lombricero Ser.: 1).Tr. of Book of the King. (SPA.). 304p. (J). pap. 7.99 (978-1-4143-2216-2(X), Tyndale Espanol) Tyndale Hse. Pubs.

—Sword of the Wormling. 2007. (Wormling Ser.: 2). (ENG.). 336p. (J). (gr. 5-9). per. 7.99 (978-1-4143-0156-3(1)) Tyndale Hse. Pubs.

Jessica Hoel. Adam B Brave. Samantha Nowak, illus. 2009. 20p. pap. 12.49 (978-1-4389-3240-8(5)) AuthorHouse.

Jian, Li. The Water Dragon: A Chinese Legend. 2012. (ENG., Illus.). 42p. (J). (gr. -1-3). 16.95 (978-1-60220-978-7(2)) BetterLink Pr., Inc.

Johnson, Sandi. Jim Elephant: The Nasty Bug, 2 vols. l.t. ed. 2003. (Illus.). 10p. (J). (gr. k-5). spiral bd. 5.99 (978-1-929063-33-8(4), 330) Moons & Stars Publishing For Children.

—1 - Dorp the Scottish Dragon: Scotland, 7 vols. Johnson, Britt & Durant, Sybrina, eds. Trevino, Juan & Johnson, Jim, illus. 2nd rev. ed. 2014. (Lost from Loch Lomond Ser.: 1). 38p. (J). (gr. -1-6). pap. 12.99 (978-1-929063-00-0(8), 101) Moons & Stars Publishing For Children.

—3 - Dorp the Scottish Dragon Bk. 3: Book 3 - Hollywood - the Movie, 7 vols. Johnson, Britt & Durant, Sybrina, eds. Vu, Thi, illus. 2004. (Little Choo-Choo Bks.). 28p. (J). (gr. -1-6). pap. 16.99 (978-1-929063-02-4(4), 103) Moons & Stars Publishing For Children.

—4 - Dorp the Scottish Dragon Bk. 4: New York Christmas. Durant, Sybrina, ed. Johnson, Jim, illus. 2014. (Little Choo-Choo Bks.). 46p. (J). (gr. -1-6). pap. 14.99 (978-1-929063-03-1(2), 104) Moons & Stars Publishing For Children.

Johnston, E. K. Prairie Fire. 2015. (J). 18.99 (978-1-4677-6181-9(8)); (ENG.). 304p. (gr. 6-12). 18.99 (978-1-4677-3909-2(X)) Lerner Publishing Group.

—The Story of Owen: Dragon Slayer of Trondheim. 2014. 312p. (J). (gr. 6-12). 17.95 (978-1-4677-1066-4(0), Carolrhoda Lab™) Lerner Publishing Group.

Jones, Brittany. Drake the Dragon King. Grimes, Kristopher, illus. 2013. (ENG.). (J). 14.95 (978-1-62086-360-2(X)) Mascot Bks., Inc.

Jones, Marcia Thornton & Dadey, Debbie. Dragons Do Eat Homework. Dreidemy, Joëlle, illus. 2007. 64p. (J). (978-0-545-00234-9(6)) Scholastic, Inc.

—This Side of Magic. Stower, Adam, illus. 2009. (Keyholders Ser.: 1). (ENG.). 144p. (J). (gr. 2-5). 3.99 (978-0-7653-5982-7(0), 9780765359827, Starscape) Doherty, Tom Assocs., LLC.

Jones, Nathan Smith. Dragonkyn. 2017. (YA). pap. 14.99 **(978-1-4621-1978-3(6))** Cedar Fort, Inc./CFI Distribution.

Joosse, Barbara M. Evermore Dragon. Cecil, Randy, illus. 2015. (ENG.). 32p. (J). (gr. -1-2). 15.99 (978-0-7636-6882-2(6)) Candlewick Pr.

—Lovabye Dragon. Cecil, Randy, illus. 2012. (ENG.). 32p. (J). (gr. -1-2). 15.99 (978-0-7636-5408-5(6)) Candlewick Pr.

Jordan, Christina. I Wish I Were a Komodo Dragon, 1 vol. Utomo, Gabhor, illus. 2011. (I Wish I Were ... Ser.). (ENG.). 24p. (J). (gr. k-3). 28.50 (978-1-61641-659-1(9)) Magic Wagon.

Jordan, Sophie. Firelight. (Firelight Ser.: 1). (ENG.). (YA). (gr. 8). 2011. 352p. pap. 9.99 (978-0-06-193509-1(3)) 2010. 336p. 16.99 (978-0-06-193508-4(5)) HarperCollins Pubs.

—Hidden. 2013. (Firelight Ser.: 3). (ENG.). 288p. (YA). (gr. 8). pap. 9.99 (978-0-06-193513-8(1)) HarperCollins Pubs.

—Vanish. 2012. (Firelight Ser.: 2). (ENG.). 320p. (YA). (gr. 8). pap. 9.99 (978-0-06-193511-4(5)) HarperCollins Pubs.

Joyce, Sandie May. Little Miss Alice & the Bookworm. 2007. 65p. pap. 24.95 (978-1-4357-0328-5(6)) Lulu Pr., Inc.

Julian, Sean. Sloppy Wants a Hug. 2017. (ENG., Illus.). 32p. (J). (gr. -1-3). 17.95 (978-0-7358-4273-1(6)) North-South Bks., Inc.

Justis, Jon. Pumpkin & the Great Dragon Caper. 2012. 32p. pap. 24.95 (978-1-4626-9733-5(X)) America Star Bks.

K. B. Kendricks. Travis Taylor & the Dragon Quest. 2010. 344p. 29.95 (978-1-4502-0261-9(6)); pap. 19.95 (978-1-4502-0259-6(4)) iUniverse, Inc.

Kananen, Barbara L. Fairies in My Garden. 2007. 106p. (YA). (gr. 2-2). per. 10.95 (978-0-595-45082-4(2)) iUniverse, Inc.

—Fairies in My Garden. 2007. 106p. (YA). (gr. 2-2). 20.95 (978-0-595-91014-4(9)) iUniverse, Inc.

Kaneko, Amanda Bullard. Darza the Little Dragon. Hildebrandt, Lowell, illus. 2010. 28p. 13.99 (978-1-4520-4198-8(9)) AuthorHouse.

Katz, Welwyn Wilton. Beowulf, 1 vol. Gal, Laszlo, illus. 2nd ed. 2007. (ENG.). 96p. (J). (gr. 4-7). 17.95 (978-0-88899-807-1(4)) Groundwood Bks. CAN. Dist: Publishers Group West (PGW).

Kaufman, Jeanne. Young Henry & the Dragon. Tessler, Daria, illus. 2011. (J). (978-1-934860-11-3(5)) Shenanigan Bks.

Kemp, Anna. The Worst Princess. Ogilvie, Sara, illus. 2014. (ENG.). 32p. (J). (gr. -1-2). 16.99 (978-0-385-37125-4(X), Random Hse. Bks. for Young Readers) Random Hse. Children's Bks.

Kennedy, J. Aday. Cobbledom's Curse. Foster, Jack, illus. 2012. 20p. pap. 9.95 (978-1-61633-265-5(4)) Guardian Angel Publishing, Inc.

—Stella, the Fire Farting Dragon. Foster, Jack, illus. 2011. 20p. pap. 10.95 (978-1-61633-149-8(6)) Guardian Angel Publishing, Inc.

Kent, Jack, illus. There's No Such Thing as a Dragon. 2009. (ENG.). 32p. (J). (gr. -1-2). pap. 7.99 (978-0-375-85137-7(2), Dragonfly Bks.) Random Hse. Children's Bks.

Kent, Jaden. #1: the Cave of Aaaaah! Doom! Bodnaruk, Iryna, illus. 2017. (Ella & Owen Ser.: 1). (ENG.). 112p. (J). (gr. 1-3). pap. 5.99 (978-1-4998-0368-6(0)) Little Bee Books Inc.

Kerney, Beth. The Dragonstone Journal. 2016. (ENG.). 165p. (J). pap. 10.95 (978-1-78554-787-4(9), 29d05d9c-117f-40aa-92d9-300f1ca3546b) Austin, Stan AUS. Dist: Bookmasters Distribution.

Kiarie, Vivian W. The Waltz, the Weasel & the Lair. 2008. 50p. pap. 16.95 (978-1-60474-265-7(8)) America Star Bks.

King, Steve. The Stone Dragon. 2005. 80p. pap. 16.95 (978-1-4137-9628-5(1)) PublishAmerica, Inc.

King, Wesley. Enemy of the Realm. 2017. (Dragons vs. Drones Ser.: 2). (ENG.). 256p. (J). (gr. 3-7). 8.99 (978-1-59514-799-8(3), Razorbill) Penguin Young Readers Group.

Kingsley, Kaza. Erec Rex: the Monsters of Otherness. 2007. (Erec Rex Ser.). (Illus.). 344p. (J). (gr. 3-7). 18.99 (978-0-9786555-7-0(5)) Firelight Press, Inc.

—The Monsters of Otherness. Grant, Melvyn, illus. 2009. (Erec Rex Ser.: 2). (ENG.). 352p. (J). (gr. 5-9). pap. 9.99 (978-1-4169-7934-0(4), Simon & Schuster Bks. For Young Readers) Simon & Schuster Bks. For Young Readers.

—The Search for Truth. Jacobus, Tim, illus. (Erec Rex Ser.: 3). (ENG.). (J). (gr. 5-9). 2010. 464p. pap. 9.99 (978-1-4169-7989-0(1)) 2009. 448p. 17.99 (978-1-4169-7988-3(3)) Simon & Schuster Bks. For Young Readers. (Simon & Schuster Bks. For Young Readers).

—The Three Furies. Ng, James & Mohrbacher, Peter, illus. 2011. (Erec Rex Ser.: 4). (ENG.). 576p. (J). (gr. 5-9). pap. 8.99 (978-1-4169-7991-3(3), Simon & Schuster Bks. For Young Readers) Simon & Schuster Bks. For Young Readers.

—The Three Furies. Mohrbacher, Peter, illus. 2010. (Erec Rex Ser.: 4). (ENG.). 576p. (J). (gr. 5-9). 16.99 (978-1-4169-7990-6(5), Simon & Schuster Bks. For Young Readers) Simon & Schuster Bks. For Young Readers.

Kinney, Sarah. Enter the Dragon Mystery. 2013. (Nancy Drew & the Clue Crew Ser.). (ENG., Illus.). 64p. (J). (gr. k-3). pap. 7.99 (978-1-59707-437-7(3), 9781597074377) Papercutz.

—Nancy Drew & the Clue Crew #3: Enter the Dragon Mystery. 2013. (Nancy Drew & the Clue Crew Ser.). (ENG., Illus.). 64p. (J). (gr. k-3). 11.99 (978-1-59707-438-4(1), 9781597074384) Papercutz.

Kirk, David. Oh So Brave Dragon. Kirk, David, illus. 2014. (ENG., Illus.). 40p. (J). (gr. -1-1). 17.99 (978-1-250-01689-8(4), 9781250016898) Feiwel & Friends.

Klement, Jon. Smerd's Book of ABC's. 2009. 32p. pap. 19.85 (978-0-557-19030-0(4)) Lulu Pr., Inc.

Klimo, Kate. The Dragon in the Driveway. Shroades, John, illus. 2010. (Dragon Keepers Ser.). (ENG.). 176p. (J). (gr. 3-7). pap. 6.99 (978-0-375-85590-0(4), Yearling) Random Hse. Children's Bks.

—The Dragon in the Sea. Shroades, John, illus. 2013. (Dragon Keepers Ser.: 5). (ENG.). 224p. (J). (gr. 3-7). 6.99 (978-0-375-87116-0(0), Yearling) Random Hse. Children's Bks.

—The Dragon in the Sock Drawer. Shroades, John, illus. 2009. (Dragon Keepers Ser.). (ENG.). 192p. (J). (gr. 3-7). 6.99 (978-0-375-85588-7(2), Yearling) Random Hse. Children's Bks.

—Dragon Keepers #3: the Dragon in the Library. Shroades, John, illus. 2011. (Dragon Keepers Ser.). (ENG.). 240p. (J). (gr. 3-7). 6.99 (978-0-375-85592-4(0), Yearling) Random Hse. Children's Bks.

—Dragon Keepers #4: the Dragon in the Volcano. Shroades, John, illus. 2012. (Dragon Keepers Ser.). (ENG.). 256p. (J). (gr. 3-7). 6.99 (978-0-375-86688-3(4), Yearling) Random Hse. Children's Bks.

—Dragon Keepers #6: the Dragon at the North Pole. Shroades, John, illus. (Dragon Keepers Ser.). (ENG.). 176p. (J). (gr. 3-7). 2014. 6.99 (978-0-375-87117-7(9), Yearling) 2013. 15.99 (978-0-375-87066-8(0), Random Hse. Bks. for Young Readers) Random Hse. Children's Bks.

K.M. Mohr, John Kelley and. Waking Dalifi. 2005. 72p. pap. 9.95 (978-1-4116-6364-0(0)) Lulu Pr., Inc.

Knight, Aya. The Chronicles of Kale: Dawn of Retribution. 2012. 456p. 28.95 (978-1-938083-13-6(X)); pap. 15.95 (978-1-938083-12-9(1)) Silver Knight Publishing, LLC.

Knudsen, Michelle. Argus. Wesson, Andrea, illus. 2011. (ENG.). 32p. (J). (gr. -1-3). 15.99 (978-0-7636-3790-3(4)) Candlewick Pr.

—The Dragon of Trelian. (Trelian Ser.: 1). (ENG.). 416p. (J). (gr. 5). 2017. pap. 9.99 (978-0-7636-9454-8(1)) 2011. (Illus.). pap. 8.99 (978-0-7636-4993-7(7)) 2009. (Illus.). 16.99 (978-0-7636-3455-1(7)) Candlewick Pr.

—Mage of Trelian. 2016. (Trelian Ser.). (ENG.). 432p. (J). (gr. 5). 17.99 (978-0-7636-7436-6(2)) Candlewick Pr.

—The Princess of Trelian. (Trelian Ser.). (ENG.). 448p. (J). (gr. 5). 2014. pap. 8.99 (978-0-7636-6935-5(0)) 2012. (Illus.). 16.99 (978-0-7636-5062-9(5)) Candlewick Pr.

Kochalka, James. Dragon Puncher Book 1. 2010. (Dragon Puncher Ser.: 1). (ENG., Illus.). 40p. (J). (gr. 2-5). 9.95 (978-1-60309-057-5(6), 9781603090575) Top Shelf Productions.

—Dragon Puncher Book 2: Dragon Puncher Island: Dragon Puncher Island. 2011. (Dragon Puncher Ser.: 2). (ENG., Illus.). 40p. (J). (gr. 2-5). 9.95 (978-1-60309-085-8(1), 9781603090858) Top Shelf Productions.

—Johnny Boo Meets Dragon Puncher. 2015. (Johnny Boo Ser.). (ENG., Illus.). 40p. (J). (gr. 2-5). 9.99 (978-1-60309-368-2(0), 9781603093682) Top Shelf Productions.

Kowalski, Bernard. Alexis & Ralph the Dragon. Phillips, Dawn, illus. 2009. 32p. pap. 24.95 (978-1-60749-167-5(2)) America Star Bks.

—Alexis & Ralph the Dragon, 1 vol. 2010. 32p. 24.95 (978-1-4512-1008-8(6)) PublishAmerica, Inc.

Krause, Ute. Oscar & the Very Hungry Dragon. Krause, Ute, illus. 2015. (ENG., Illus.). 40p. (J). 8.95 (978-0-7358-4230-4(2)) North-South Bks., Inc.

—Oscar & the Very Hungry Dragon. 2010. (ENG., Illus.). 40p. (gr. -1-3). 16.95 (978-0-7358-2306-8(5)) North-South Bks., Inc.

Krensky, Stephen. The Dragon Emperor: A Chinese Folktale. 2009. pap. 40.95 (978-0-7613-4817-7(4)) Lerner Publishing Group.

Kroll, Steven. Super-Dragon, 0 vols. Holgate, Doug, illus. 2011. (ENG.). 32p. (J). (gr. -1-2). 16.99 (978-0-7614-5819-7(0), 9780761458197, Amazon Children's Publishing) Amazon Publishing.

Kroner, David & Du Houx, Ramona. Seasons. Du Houx, E. M. Cornell, illus. 2007. 70p. (J). per. 6.95 (978-1-882190-54-6(8)) Polar Bear & Co.

Kuenzler, Lou. The Dragon Dance. 2017. (Princess DisGrace Ser.). (ENG., Illus.). 272p. (J). (gr. 3-7). 15.99 (978-0-553-53781-9(4), Random Hse. Bks. for Young Readers) Random Hse. Children's Bks.

Kuijpers, Justin. The Dragon Myth & the Mysterious Eyeball. 2010. 58p. pap. 7.90 (978-3-8391-5033-7(7)) Bks. on Demand.

Kurd, Tariq. Gordon the Goblin in Oh My! Is That a Pork Pie? Robertson, Laura, illus. 2012. 36p. pap. (978-1-907762-10-9(8)) Malt Publishing.

Lacey, Josh. The Dragonsitter. Parsons, Garry, illus. 2016. (Dragonsitter Ser.: 4). (ENG.). 96p. (J). (gr. 1-5). pap. 5.99 (978-0-316-29908-4(1)) Little, Brown Bks. for Young Readers.

LaFevers, R. L. The Wyverns' Treasure. Murphy, Kelly, illus. 2012. (Nathanial Fludd, Beastologist Ser.: 3). (ENG.). 160p. (J). (gr. 1-4). pap. 6.99 (978-0-547-85823-4(X)) Houghton Mifflin Harcourt Publishing Co.

—The Wyverns' Treasure. 2012. (Nathaniel Fludd, Beastologist Ser.: 3). lib. bdg. 16.00 (978-0-606-24516-6(2), Turtleback) Turtleback Bks.

Lairamore, Dawn. Ivy & the Meanstalk. 2011. (ENG.). 192p. (J). 16.95 (978-0-8234-2392-7(1)) Holiday Hse., Inc.

—Ivy's Ever After. (ENG.). 192p. (J). 2013. (gr. 2-7). pap. 7.99 (978-0-8234-2937-0(7)) 2010. (gr. 3-7). 16.95 (978-0-8234-2261-6(5)) Holiday Hse., Inc.

Lake, A. J. The Book of the Sword. 2007. (Darkest Age Ser.). (ENG.). 240p. (YA). (gr. 4-7). 16.95 (978-1-59990-039-1(4), 9781599900391, Bloomsbury USA Childrens) Bloomsbury Publishing USA.

—The Coming of Dragons: The Darkest Age. 2007. (Darkest Age Ser.). (ENG., Illus.). 256p. (YA). (gr. 4-7). per. 7.99 (978-1-58234-902-2(9), 9781582349022, Bloomsbury USA Childrens) Bloomsbury Publishing USA.

Lake, Nick. The Betrayal of the Living. 2013. (Blood Ninja Ser.: Bk. 3). (ENG., Illus.). 368p. (YA). (gr. 9). pap. 9.99 (978-1-4424-2680-1(2), Simon & Schuster Bks. For Young Readers) Simon & Schuster Bks. For Young Readers.

Lang, Andrew. The Red Romance Book; Tales of Knights. 2006. 396p. per. (978-1-84664-477-1(1), Obscure Pr.) Read Bks.

—The Violet Fairy Book. 2005. 404p. pap. 16.95 (978-1-4218-0107-0(8), 1st World Library - Literary Society) 1st World Publishing, Inc.

Lang, Andrew & Ford, H. J. The Tale of the Cid: And Other Stories of Knights & Chivalry. Ford, H. J., illus. 2007. (Dover Children's Classics Ser.). (ENG., Illus.). 208p. (J). (gr. 4-7). per. 9.95 (978-0-486-45470-2(3)) Dover Pubns., Inc.

Lang, Heidi & Bartkowski, Kati. A Dash of Dragon. 2017. (ENG., Illus.). 320p. (J). (gr. 3-7). 17.99 **(978-1-4814-7793-2(5)**, Aladdin) Simon & Schuster Children's Publishing.

LaRochelle, David. The Best Pet of All. Wakiyama, Hanako, illus. (ENG.). 32p. (J). (gr. -1-k). 2009. pap. 7.99 (978-0-14-241272-5(4), Puffin Books) 2004. 16.99 (978-0-525-47129-5(4), Dutton Books for Young Readers) Penguin Young Readers Group.

Larsen, Erik. Savage Dragon on Trial TP. 2013. (ENG., Illus.). 128p. (YA). pap. 16.99 (978-1-60706-755-9(2), 9781607067559) Image Comics.

Larson, M. A. Pennyroyal Academy. 2014. (Pennyroyal Academy Ser.: 1). (ENG.). 320p. (J). (gr. 5). 16.99 (978-0-399-16324-1(7), G.P. Putnam's Sons Books for Young Readers) Penguin Young Readers Group.

Lawson, Barbara. Huff the Magicless Dragon, 1 vol. Swope, Brenda, illus. 2009. 35p. pap. 24.95 (978-1-61546-419-7(0)) PublishAmerica, Inc.

Laybourn, Emma. Dungeon Dragon. 2008. (ENG.). 156p. (J). (gr. 3-6). pap. 9.95 (978-1-84270-736-4(1)) Andersen Pr. GBR. Dist: Independent Pubs. Group.

Lee, Deborah Baptiste & Atcheson-Melton, Patty. In the Shade of the Spade: This Tale in a Poetry Format Takes Us on a Journey. the Illustrations Are Bright & Whimsical. You Can Almost Hear Music. Baptiste, Annette Green, illus. 2013. 48p. pap. 14.95 (978-0-9858839-1-1(X)) Lee, Deborah I.

Lehrhaupt, Adam. I Will Not Eat You. Magoon, Scott, illus. 2016. (ENG.). 40p. (J). (gr. -1-3). 17.99 (978-1-4814-2933-7(7), Simon & Schuster Bks. For Young Readers) Simon & Schuster Bks. For Young Readers.

Leloup, Roger. The Dragon of Hong Kong - Yoko Tsuno, Vol. 5. 2010. (Yoko Tsuno Ser.: 5). (ENG., Illus.). 46p. (J). (gr. 3-17). pap. 11.95 (978-1-84918-041-2(5)) CineBook GBR. Dist: National Bk. Network.

Lemmens, Riske. Little Dragon. 2004. (Illus.). 24p. (J). (978-1-85269-482-1(3)); (978-1-85269-537-8(4)); (978-1-85269-577-4(3)); (978-1-85269-575-0(7)); (978-1-85269-576-7(5)) Mantra Lingua.

Leonhard, Herb. Sir Norman & the Dreaming Dragon. Leonhard, Herb, illus. 2008. (ENG., Illus.). 32p. (J). 17.95 (978-0-9763555-1-9(5)) Prancing Pony, The.

Levine, Gail Carson. The Lost Kingdom of Bamarre. 2017. 400p. (J). (gr. 3-7). 16.99 (978-0-06-207466-9(0)) HarperCollins Pubs.

—A Tale of Two Castles. Call, Greg, illus. (ENG.). (J). (gr. 3-7). 2012. 352p. pap. 6.99 (978-0-06-122967-1(9)) 2011. 336p. 16.99 (978-0-06-122965-7(2)) HarperCollins Pubs.

Liess, Claudia Schmidt. Henry the Magical, Mythical Dragon. 2008. 74p. pap. 19.95 (978-1-60672-956-4(X)) America Star Bks.

Lifton, Betty Jean. Taka-Chan & I: A Dog's Journey to Japan by Runcible. Hosoe, Eikoh, photos by. 2012. (ENG., Illus.). 64p. (J). (gr. k-4). 16.95 (978-1-59017-502-6(6), NYR Children's Collection) New York Review of Bks., Inc., The.

Light, Steve. Have You Seen My Dragon? Light, Steve, illus. 2014. (ENG., Illus.). 48p. (J). (-k). 16.99 (978-0-7636-6648-4(3)) Candlewick Pr.

Lillehaug-Collins, Yvonne. Little Dragon. 2009. 70p. pap. 21.00 (978-1-60693-344-2(2), Eloquent Bks.) Strategic Book Publishing & Rights Agency (SBPRA).

Limke, Jeff. Tristan & Isolde: The Warrior & the Princess [A British Legend]. Randall, Ron, illus. 2009. (Graphic Myths & Legends Ser.). (ENG.). 48p. (gr. 4-8). pap. 8.95 (978-1-58013-889-5(6)) Lerner Publishing Group.

Lin, Grace. Where the Mountain Meets the Moon. 2009. (ENG., Illus.). 288p. (J). (gr. 3-7). 18.99 (978-0-316-11427-1(8)) Little Brown & Co.

—Where the Mountain Meets the Moon. 2011. (ENG., Illus.). 320p. (J). (gr. 3-7). pap., pap. 10.99 (978-0-316-03863-8(6)) Little, Brown Bks. for Young Readers.

—Where the Mountain Meets the Moon. 2011. (ENG., Illus.). 278p. (gr. 4-7). 19.00 (978-1-61383-087-1(4)) Perfection Learning Corp.

—Where the Mountain Meets the Moon. 2011. (J). lib. bdg. 22.10 (978-0-606-16233-3(X), Turtleback) Turtleback Bks.

Little Dragon & the Magic Wagon. 2008. (Little Dragon Storybooks Ser.). 32p. (978-1-4075-1289-1(7)) Parragon, Inc.

Little Dragon Catches Colors. 2008. (Little Dragon Tab Board Book Ser.). 6p. bds. (978-1-4075-2666-9(9)) Parragon, Inc.

Little Dragon Counts 1, 2, 3, 4, 5. 2008. (Little Dragon Flying Board Ser.). 7p. bds. (978-1-4075-2665-2(0)) Parragon, Inc.

Little Dragon Makes Friends. 2008. (Little Dragon Storybooks Ser.). 32p. (978-1-4075-1288-4(9)) Parragon, Inc.

Loehr, Mallory. Dragon Egg. Wittwer, Hala, illus. 2007. (Step into Reading Ser.). (ENG.). 32p. (J). (gr. -1-1). pap. 3.99 (978-0-375-84350-1(7), Random Hse. Bks. for Young Readers) Random Hse. Children's Bks.

Long, Ethan. One Drowsy Dragon. 2010. (Illus.). (J). (978-0-545-23412-2(3), Orchard Bks.) Scholastic, Inc.

Lore, Erin, illus. Timmy the Dragon. l.t. ed. 2007. 32p. (J). 8.95 (978-0-9741562-7-9(2)) Yarrow Pr.

Lorentzen, Bent. Krona: Dragons of Nistala. 2009. 266p. (J). pap. 18.95 (978-1-60619-091-3(1)) Twilight Times Bks.

Love, Makada H. Harold's Adventures. Holt, Lindsey, illus. 2008. 92p. pap. 10.99 (978-1-4343-6875-1(0)) AuthorHouse.

Lowenstein, Sallie, illus. Sir Kyle & Lady Madeline. Lowenstein, Sallie, . 2007. 32p. (J). 18.95 (978-0-9658486-6-4(3)) Lion Stone Bks.

Luberto, Bradley. Clide & Druce: A Repulsive Tale of Trolls & Tax Money. 2006. (ENG.). 48p. per. 16.95 (978-1-4241-5012-0(4)) PublishAmerica, Inc.

Lucia encuentra un Dragon: Individual Title, 6 packs. (Literatura 2000 Ser.). (SPA.). (gr. 2-3). 33.00 (978-0-7635-1095-4(5)) Rigby Education.

Lucy Meets a Dragon, 6 Packs. (Literatura 2000 Ser.). (gr. 2-3). 33.00 (978-0-7635-0177-8(8)) Rigby Education.

Luder, Doreen. Dax the Last Dragon. 2012. 24p. pap. 24.95 (978-1-62709-988-2(3)) America Star Bks.

Lyons, Maggie. Dewi & the Seeds of Doom. 2012. 70p. pap. 9.99 (978-1-61244-094-1(0)) Halo Publishing International.

Maelor, Gwawr, et al. Tân Yn y Jyngl. 2005. (WEL., Illus.). 16p. pap. (978-1-85644-842-0(8)) CAA.

Magee, Wes. Little Dragon. Warburton, Sarah, illus. 2004. (ENG.). 24p. (J). lib. bdg. 23.65 (978-1-59646-690-6(1)) Dingles & Co.

Maguire, Thomas Aquinas. Three Little Dreams, 3 vols. 2010. (ENG., Illus.). 36p. (J). (gr. -1). 16.95 (978-1-894965-79-8(5)) Simply Read Bks. CAN. Dist: Ingram Publisher Services.

Mahy, Margaret. A Lion in the Meadow. 2013. (ENG., Illus.). 32p. (gr. 4-13). 17.95 (978-1-4683-0665-1(0), 460665) Overlook Pr., The.

Mancusi, Mari. Scorched. (Scorched Ser.: 1). (ENG.). (YA). (gr. 6-12). 2014. 368p. pap. 9.99 (978-1-4022-9227-9(9)) 2013. 352p. 16.99 (978-1-4022-8458-8(6), 9781402284588) Sourcebooks, Inc.

—Shattered. (Scorched Ser.: 2). (ENG.). (YA). 2015. 416p. (gr. 8-12). pap. 9.99 (978-1-4926-0869-1(6)) 2014. 400p. (gr. 7-12). 16.99 (978-1-4022-8461-8(6), 9781402284618) Sourcebooks, Inc.

Marcus, Richard. What Will Happen in Eragon IV: Who Lives, Who Dies, Who Becomes the Third Dragon Rider & How Will the Inheritance Cycle Finally End? 2009. (ENG.). 180p. (J). (gr. 3). pap. 12.95 (978-1-56975-728-4(3)) Ulysses Pr.

Mariet, Nico & Frawley, Keith, illus. Book of Dragons. 2014. (How to Train Your Dragon TV Ser.). (ENG.). 24p. (J). (gr. -1-5). 16.99 (978-1-4814-2137-9(9), Simon Spotlight) Simon Spotlight.

Martín Anguita, Carmen & Carmen, Martín Anguita. Marta y Su Dragón (Martha & Her Dragon) Cortazar, Alicia Canas, illus. 2008. (SPA.). 32p. (J). 10.99 (978-84-241-5444-8(4)) Everest Editora ESP. Dist: Lectorum Pubns., Inc.

Martin, George R. R. The Ice Dragon. Royo, Luis, illus. 2014. (ENG.). 128p. (YA). (gr. 7-12). 14.99 (978-0-7653-7877-4(9), 9780765378774, Tor Teen) Doherty, Tom Assocs., LLC.

Martinez, Rene. The Journey of the Golden Sword. 2011. 64p. pap. 15.99 (978-1-4535-9187-1(7)) Xlibris Corp.

Matheis, Mickie. Sparkle Fest Showdown! (Nella the Princess Knight) Lew, Steph, illus. 2017. (Pictureback(R) Ser.). (ENG.). 24p. (J). (gr. -1-2). pap. 5.99 **(978-1-5247-1723-0(1)**, Random Hse. Bks. for Young Readers) Random Hse. Children's Bks.

Mathis, Kate. Moon over Monsters. 2013. 318p. pap. 12.95 (978-0-9819789-9-4(1)) PowWow Publishing.

Mattel & Deutsch, Stacia. Ever after High Entertainment Tie-In: the Deluxe Junior Novel. 2016. (ENG.). 144p. (J). (gr. 3-7). 9.99 (978-0-316-27045-8(8)) Little, Brown Bks. for Young Readers.
Mattel & Green, Margaret. Ever after High. 2016. (ENG., Illus.). 24p. (J). (gr. -1-3). pap. 3.99 (978-0-316-30179-4(5)) Little, Brown Bks. for Young Readers.
—Ever after High Entertainment Tie-In: Reader. 2016. (Passport to Reading Level 3 Ser.). (ENG., Illus.). 32p. (J). (gr. -1-3). pap. 3.99 (978-0-316-30180-0(9)) Little, Brown Bks. for Young Readers.
Maxwell, Calvin. American Pool Player. 2012. 168p. 22.99 (978-1-62230-142-3(0)) Salem Author Services.
MaxwellJr, Calvin. American Pool Player. 2012. 168p. pap. 14.99 (978-1-62230-141-6(2)) Salem Author Services.
Mayhall, Robin. The Quest for Dragon Mountain. Martinez, Alitha E., illus. 2010. (Twisted Journeys (r) Ser.: 16). (ENG.). 112p. (J). (gr. 4-7). pap. 7.95 (978-0-8225-9267-9(3), Graphic Universe™); lib. bdg. 27.93 (978-0-8225-9261-7(4)) Lerner Publishing Group.
—The Quest for Dragon Mountain. Martinez, Alitha, illus. 16th rev. ed. 2010. (Twisted Journeys (r) Ser.: 16). (ENG.). (J). (gr. 4-7). pap. 45.32 (978-0-7613-6999-8(6)) Lerner Publishing Group.
Mayher, Lauren. The Legend of Darien: A Hero Rises: Book 1. 2008. 423p. (J). per. 12.95 (978-0-9794545-0-9(6)) Blue Eyed Mayhem Publishing.
McCaffrey, Anne. Dragonsong. 2016. (Harper Hall of Pern Ser.: 1). (ENG., Illus.). 224p. (J). (gr. 5-9). 18.99 (978-1-4814-4860-4(9), Aladdin) Simon & Schuster Children's Publishing.
McCandless Iii, Bruce. Beatrice & the Basilisk. 2012. 66p. pap. 5.99 (978-0-615-60901-0(5)) Ninth Planet Pr.
McClanahan, Teel, 3rd. Dragons' Truth. 2007. 208p. (YA). per. 12.99 (978-1-934516-02-7(3)) Modern Evil Pr.
McCune, Joshua. Invisible Monsters. 2015. (Talker 25 Ser.: 2). (ENG.). 448p. (YA). (gr. 8). 17.99 (978-0-06-212194-3(4), Greenwillow Bks.) HarperCollins Pubs.
—Talker 25. 2014. (Talker 25 Ser.: 1). (ENG.). 432p. (YA). (gr. 9). 17.99 (978-0-06-212191-2(X), Greenwillow Bks.) HarperCollins Pubs.
—Talker 25 #2: Invisible Monsters. 2016. (Talker 25 Ser.: 2). 448p. (YA). (gr. 8). pap. 9.99 (978-0-06-212195-0(2), Greenwillow Bks.) HarperCollins Pubs.
McDaniels, Preston, illus. The Squire & the Scroll: A Tale of the Rewards of a Pure Heart. 2004. (ENG.). 32p. (J). 12.99 (978-1-59317-079-0(3)) Warner Pr., Inc.
McDonald, Ann-Eve. The Dragon's Lair, a Counterpane Story. 2004. (J). (978-0-9770158-3-2(1)) BeachWalk Bks. Inc.
McGlame, Jack. Majik: The Beginning. 2012. 132p. 21.95 (978-1-4759-3289-8(8)) iUniverse, Inc.
McKay, Hilary. Tilly & the Dragon. Shaw, Mick, illus. 2016. (Reading Ladder Ser.). (ENG.). 48p. (J). (gr. k-2). 7.99 (978-1-4052-8251-2(7)) Egmont Bks., Ltd. GBR. Dist: Independent Pubs. Group.
McKay, Laurie. Realm Breaker. 2017. (Last Dragon Charmer Ser.: 3). 368p. (J). (gr. 3-7). 16.99 (978-0-06-230849-8(1)) HarperCollins Pubs.
—The Villain Keeper. 2015. (Last Dragon Charmer Ser.: 1). (ENG.). 352p. (J). (gr. 3-7). 16.99 (978-0-06-230843-6(2)) HarperCollins Pubs.
McKee, David. Melric & the Dragon. McKee, David, illus. 2016. (Melric Ser.: 4). (ENG., Illus.). 32p. (J). (-k). pap. 9.99 (978-1-78344-210-2(7)); (gr. -1-k). 16.99 (978-1-78344-162-4(3)) Andersen Pr. GBR. Dist: Independent Pubs. Group.
McKenna, James. The Mind Traveller. 2013. 212p. pap. (978-0-9569723-8-5(1)) Lone Cloud Publishing.
McKinley, Robin. Dragonhaven. 2009. (ENG.). 368p. (YA). (gr. 7-18). 9.99 (978-0-14-241494-1(8), Firebird) Penguin Young Readers Group.
McLeod, Kris Aro. Hush-a-Bye Counting: A Bedtime Book. Allyn, Virginia, illus. 2008. (ENG.). 20p. (J). (gr. -1). 14.95 (978-1-58117-785-5(2), Intervisual/Piggy Toes) Bendon, Inc.
McMahon, P. J. The Case of the Singing Sea Dragons. Manders, John, illus. 6th ed. 2005. (Freaky Joe Club Ser.: 6). (ENG.). 160p. (J). (gr. 2-5). pap. 8.99 (978-1-4169-0050-4(0), Aladdin) Simon & Schuster Children's Publishing.
McMann, Lisa. Dragon Captives. 2017. (Unwanteds Quests Ser.: 1). (ENG., Illus.). 432p. (J). (gr. 3-7). 17.99 (978-1-4814-5681-4(4), Simon & Schuster/Paula Wiseman Bks.) Simon & Schuster/Paula Wiseman Bks.
—Dragon Captives. 2018. (Unwanteds Quests Ser.: 1). lib. bdg. 18.40 **(978-0-606-40846-2(0))** Turtleback Bks.
—The Island of Dragons. 2017. (Unwanteds Ser.: 7). lib. bdg. 19.65 **(978-0-606-39761-2(2))** Turtleback Bks.
McMilin, Jack. Dodger the Dragon, 1 vol. 2010. 22p. 24.95 (978-1-4512-1508-3(8)) PublishAmerica, Inc.
—Dodger the Dragon, 1 vol. Nevarez, Lisa, illus. 2009. pap. 24.95 (978-1-60703-930-3(3)) PublishAmerica, Inc.
McMullan, Kate. Beware! It's Friday the 13th. Basso, Bill, illus. 2005. (Dragon Slayers' Academy Ser.: 13). (ENG.). 112p. (J). (gr. 2-5). pap. 4.99 (978-0-448-43531-2(4), Grosset & Dunlap) Penguin Young Readers Group.
—Beware! It's Friday the 13th, 1 vol. Basso, Bill, illus. 2006. (Dragon Slayers' Academy Ser.: No. 13). (ENG.). 112p. (gr. 1-7). 24.21 (978-1-59961-122-8(8)) Spotlight.
—Class Trip to the Cave of Doom, 3 vols. Basso, Bill, illus. 2003. (Dragon Slayers' Academy Ser.: 3). (ENG.). 112p. (J). (gr. 2-5). pap. 5.99 (978-0-448-43110-9(6), Grosset & Dunlap) Penguin Young Readers Group.
—Class Trip to the Cave of Doom, 1 vol. Basso, Bill, illus. 2006. (Dragon Slayers' Academy Ser.: No. 3). (ENG.). 112p. (gr. 1-7). 24.21 (978-1-59961-123-5(6)) Spotlight.
—Countdown to the Year 1000. Basso, Bill, illus. 2003. (Dragon Slayers' Academy Ser.: 8). (ENG.). 112p. (J). (gr. 2-5). pap. 5.99 (978-0-448-43508-4(X), Grosset & Dunlap) Penguin Young Readers Group.
—Countdown to the Year 1000, 1 vol. Basso, Bill, illus. 2007. (Dragon Slayers' Academy Ser.: No. 8). (ENG.). 107p. (gr. 2-5). 24.21 (978-1-59961-376-5(X)) Spotlight.
—Double Dragon Trouble. Basso, Bill, illus. 2005. (Dragon Slayers' Academy Ser.: 15). (ENG.). 112p. (J). (gr. 2-5). pap. 5.99 (978-0-448-43821-4(6), Grosset & Dunlap) Penguin Young Readers Group.
—Dragon Slayers' Academy Set 2. Basso, Bill, illus. 2007. (Dragon Slayers' Academy Ser.). (ENG.). 112p. 145.26 (978-1-59961-375-8(1)) Spotlight.
—Help! It's Parent's Day at DSA. Basso, Bill, illus. 2004. (Dragon Slayers' Academy Ser.: 10). (ENG.). 112p. (J). (gr. 2-5). pap. 4.99 (978-0-448-43220-5(X), Grosset & Dunlap) Penguin Young Readers Group.
—Help! It's Parent's Day at DSA, 1 vol. Basso, Bill, illus. 2006. (Dragon Slayers' Academy Ser.: No. 10). (ENG.). 112p. (gr. 1-7). 24.21 (978-1-59961-125-9(2)) Spotlight.
—The New Kid at School. Basso, Bill & Gilpin, Stephen, illus. 2003. (Dragon Slayers' Academy Ser.: 1). (ENG.). 112p. (J). (gr. 2-5). mass mkt. 5.99 (978-0-448-43108-6(4), Grosset & Dunlap) Penguin Young Readers Group.
—The New Kid at School, 1 vol. Basso, Bill, illus. 2006. (Dragon Slayers' Academy Ser.: No. 1). (ENG.). 112p. (gr. 1-7). 24.21 (978-1-59961-126-6(0)) Spotlight.
—Revenge of the Dragon Lady. 2005. (Dragon Slayers Academy Ser.: No. 2). (J). 28.75 (978-1-4193-1910-5(8)) Recorded Bks., Inc.
—School's Out... Forever! Basso, Bill & Gilpin, Stephen, illus. 2012. (Dragon Slayers' Academy Ser.: 20). (ENG.). 112p. (J). (gr. 2-5). pap. 4.99 (978-0-448-44571-7(9), Grosset & Dunlap) Penguin Young Readers Group.
—Wheel of Misfortune. Basso, Bill, illus. 2003. (Dragon Slayers' Academy Ser.: 7). (ENG.). 112p. (J). (gr. 2-5). pap. 5.99 (978-0-448-43507-7(1), Grosset & Dunlap) Penguin Young Readers Group.
—Wheel of Misfortune, 1 vol. Basso, Bill, illus. 2007. (Dragon Slayers' Academy Ser.: No. 7). (ENG.). 109p. (gr. 2-5). 24.21 (978-1-59961-381-9(6)) Spotlight.
—World's Oldest Living Dragon. Basso, Bill, illus. 2006. (Dragon Slayers' Academy Ser.: 16). (ENG.). 112p. (J). (gr. 2-5). pap. 4.99 (978-0-448-44112-2(8), Grosset & Dunlap) Penguin Young Readers Group.
—97 Ways to Train a Dragon. Basso, Bill, illus. 2003. (Dragon Slayers' Academy Ser.: 9). (ENG.). 112p. (J). (gr. 2-5). pap. 5.99 (978-0-448-43177-2(7), Grosset & Dunlap) Penguin Young Readers Group.
McNabb, Linda. Dragons' Bane. 2008. 208p. (978-1-86950-655-1(3)) HarperCollins Pubs. Australia.
McShane, Pol. Return to Animal Land: The Adventures of Johnny & Joey. 2007. 132p. (J). per. 10.95 (978-0-595-45804-2(1)) iUniverse, Inc.
Meadows, Daisy. Ashley the Dragon Fairy. 2012. (Illus.). (J). (Magical Animal Fairies Ser.: 1). (ENG.). 80p. (gr. 2-5). pap. 4.99 (978-0-545-38417-9(6), Scholastic Paperbacks); 65p. (978-0-545-42595-7(6)) Scholastic, Inc.
—Rosie Gigglepip's Lucky Escape. 2016. (Magic Animal Friends Ser.: 8). (ENG., Illus.). 112p. (J). (gr. 2-5). pap. 4.99 (978-0-545-90747-7(0), Scholastic Paperbacks) Scholastic, Inc.
—Sophie Flufftail's Brave Plan. 2016. (Magic Animal Friends Ser.: 5). (ENG., Illus.). 112p. (J). (gr. 2-5). pap. 4.99 (978-0-545-90741-5(1), Scholastic Paperbacks) Scholastic, Inc.
Meeks, Elizbiff. Without Millard's Wings. 2006. 58p. pap. 16.95 (978-1-4241-2199-1(X)) America Star Bks.
Memoirs of Gulis: Growing Up. I.t. ed. 2005. (Illus.). 28p. (J). pap. 14.95 (978-0-9768752-1-5(7)) Open Spaces Publishing (Rupen), LLC.
Mercer, Graham. The Secret Cave. 2009. 52p. pap. 10.50 (978-1-4092-9055-1(7)) Lulu Pr., Inc.
Merrill, Jennifer. The Briar Hill Brats. 2009. 58p. pap. 17.50 (978-1-60860-492-0(6), Eloquent Bks.) Strategic Book Publishing & Rights Agency (SBPRA).
Mertz, Alyssa. The Lucky Farm Boy, 1 vol. Crum, A. M., illus. 2009. 28p. pap. 24.95 (978-1-60813-892-0(5)) PublishAmerica, Inc.
Metz, Diana. Brinn & the Dragons of Pallan Cliffs. 2003. 352p. (J). pap. (978-0-9718431-2-7(0)) M.O.T.H.E.R. Publishing Co., Inc., The.
Meyer, Zachary. The Book Buddies' Adventures the Dragon Story. 2011. 76p. pap. 10.99 (978-0-557-82961-3(5)) Lulu Pr., Inc.
Michael. Bedwin, 1 vol. David, Amanda, illus. 2009. (ENG.). 46p. 24.95 (978-1-60813-258-4(7)) America Star Bks.
Michaelis, Antonia. The Dragons of Darkness. Bell, Anthea, tr. from GER. 2010. (ENG.). 566p. (YA). (gr. 7-11). 18.95 (978-0-8109-4074-1(4), Amulet Bks.) Abrams, Inc.
—Dragons of Darkness. Bell, Anthea, tr. 2011. (ENG.). 576p. (YA). (gr. 7-17). pap. 8.95 (978-1-4197-0085-9(5), Amulet Bks.) Abrams, Inc.
Miles, Colin. Naughty Nicky & the Good Ship Oggy. Miles, Gail, illus. 2013. 24p. pap. (978-1-909202-16-0(9)) Little Acorns Publishing.
Miranda, Edward. The Truth about Dragons & Dinosaurs. Cassetta, Andrea, illus. 2007. 32p. per. 10.95 (978-1-934246-22-1(0)) Peppertree Pr., The.
The Missing Man & the Twenty Dragons. 2nd ed. 2005. (ENG., Illus.). 204p. (J). reprint ed. per. 11.99 (978-0-9760045-1-6(8), Reluctant Reader Bks.) Cronus College.
Mitchell, Devon L. The Candy Dragon: Torchy's Adventures of Starting School. 2009. 40p. pap. 16.99 (978-1-4389-4626-9(0)) AuthorHouse.
Mitchell, Lucinda Orr. Ladon's Lapse: The Story of Draco. 2012. 28p. pap. 17.99 (978-1-4685-5525-7(1)) AuthorHouse.
Mitchell, N. J. W. Saraly & the Dragons. 2003. 124p. pap. 10.95 (978-0-595-30264-2(5)) iUniverse, Inc.
Mitton, Tony. The Somethingosaur. Ayto, Russell, illus. 2014. (ENG.). 32p. (J). 17.99 (978-0-00-758395-9(8), HarperCollins Children's Bks.) HarperCollins Pubs. Ltd. GBR. Dist: HarperCollins Pubs.
Mlawer, Teresa. If I Had a Dragon/Si Yo Tuviera un Dragon. Ellery, Tom & Ellery, Amanda, illus. 2006. (ENG & SPA.). (J). (gr. -1-3). per. 3.99 (978-1-933032-17-7(0)); 32p. (gr. 5-6). 12.99 (978-1-933032-16-0(2)) Lectorum Pubns., Inc.
Moeling, Neil. The Secret Adventures of Prince Justin & the Dragon. 2010. 40p. 17.99 (978-1-4520-4996-0(3)) AuthorHouse.
Molinari, Laurice Elehwany. The Dragon's Descent, 1 vol. 2017. (Ether Novel Ser.). (ENG.). 384p. (J). pap. 8.99 (978-0-310-73563-2(7)) Zonderkidz.
Molnar, Cheri Eplin. Dee Diddly Dragon Is Not a Wimp. Gutwein, Gwendolyn, illus. 2004. 32p. (J). per. 17.95 (978-0-9746330-3-9(8)) Anton Berkshire Publishing.
Moncure, Jane Belk. A Dragon in a Wagon: A Book about Ways to Travel. Regan, Dana, illus. 2013. (Magic Castle Readers Ser.). (ENG.). 32p. (J). (gr. -1-2). 25.64 (978-1-62323-573-4(1), 206307) Child's World, Inc., The.
Montgomery, Anson. Dragon Day. 2011. (Illus.). 80p. (J). (gr. k-3). 7.99 (978-1-933390-61-1(1)) Chooseco LLC.
—Search for the Dragon Queen. 2011. (Illus.). 80p. (J). (gr. k-3). pap. 7.99 (978-1-933390-56-7(5)) Chooseco LLC.
—Your Grandparents Are Spies. 2016. (Illus.). (J). pap. 7.99 (978-1-937133-51-1(6)) Chooseco LLC.
Moore, Jodi. When a Dragon Moves In. McWilliam, Howard, illus. 2011. (When a Dragon Moves In Ser.). (ENG.). 32p. (J). (gr. k-2). 16.95 (978-0-9799746-7-0(4)) Flashlight Pr.
—When a Dragon Moves in Again. McWilliam, Howard, illus. 2015. (When a Dragon Moves In Ser.). (ENG.). 32p. (J). (gr. k-2). 17.95 (978-1-936261-35-2(9)) Flashlight Pr.
Moore, Shawn. Sam & the Tale of the Dragon Prints. Baker, David, illus. 2011. 28p. pap. 24.95 (978-1-4560-7724-2(4)) America Star Bks.
Moredun, P. R. The World of Eldaterra Vol. 1: The Dragon Conspiracy. 2005. (World of Eldaterra Ser.). (Illus.). 304p. (J). (gr. 7-18). lib. bdg. 17.89 (978-0-06-076664-1(6)) HarperCollins Pubs.
Moredun, P.R. The World of Eldaterra: The Dragon Conspiracy, Vol. 1. 2005. (World of Eldaterra Ser.). 304p. (J). (gr. 7-18). 16.99 (978-0-06-076663-4(8)) HarperCollins Pubs.
Morningforest, Chris & Raymond, Rebecca. Princess Underdrawers & the Dragon. 2006. 37p. (J). pap. 15.58 (978-1-4116-8837-7(6)) Lulu Pr., Inc.
Morpurgo, Michael. Mimi & the Mountain Dragon. Stephens, Helen, illus. 2015. (ENG.). 48p. (J). (gr. 2-4). 9.99 (978-1-4052-6934-6(0)) Egmont Bks., Ltd. GBR. Dist: Independent Pubs. Group.
Morris, Jackie. Tell Me a Dragon. 2017. (ENG., Illus.). 40p. (J). (gr. -1-k). 17.99 **(978-1-84780-242-2(7)**, Frances Lincoln) Quarto Publishing Group UK GBR. Dist: Hachette Bk. Group.
Morris, Jackie. Y Tu Dragón, ¿Cómo Es? Morris, Jackie, illus. 2010. (SPA., Illus.). 28p. (J). (gr. k-2). 14.95 (978-84-92595-21-1(3)) Thule Ediciones, S. L. ESP. Dist: Independent Pubs. Group.
Mould, Chris. Fangs 'n' Fire. 2010. (ENG., Illus.). 96p. (J). (978-0-340-94475-2(7), Hodder Children's Books) Hachette Children's Group GBR. Dist: Hachette Bk. Group.
—Fangs 'n' Fire: Ten Dragon Tales. 2011. (ENG., Illus.). 144p. (J). (gr. 4-6). pap. 8.99 (978-1-4449-0616-5(X)) Hodder & Stoughton GBR. Dist: Hachette Bk. Group.
Mulholland, Jane. Ribeye, the Vegetarian Dragon. 2013. 24p. pap. 24.95 (978-1-4626-9935-3(9)) America Star Bks.
Mull, Brandon. Dragonwatch. 2017. (Dragonwatch Ser.: 1). (ENG., Illus.). 384p. (J). (gr. 3). 18.99 (978-1-62972-256-6(1), Shadow Mountain) Shadow Mountain Publishing.
—Dragonwatch. 2018. (Dragonwatch Ser.: 1). lib. bdg. 19.65 **(978-0-606-40838-7(X))** Turtleback Bks.
Mull, Brandon. Secrets of the Dragon Sanctuary. 2009. (Fablehaven Ser.: 4). (ENG., Illus.). 544p. (J). (gr. 3-7). 19.99 (978-1-60641-042-4(3), Shadow Mountain) Shadow Mountain Publishing.
Munoz, Isabel. En el Museo. Mazali, Gustavo, illus. 2011. (Eric & Julieta Ser.).Tr. of At the Museum. (SPA & ENG.). 24p. (J). (gr. -1-3). pap. 3.99 (978-0-545-34512-5(X), Scholastic en Espanol) Scholastic, Inc.
Munsch, Robert. The Paper Bag Princess. Martchenko, Michael, illus. 10th ed. 2009. (ENG.). 28p. (J). (gr. -1-2). bds. 7.99 (978-1-55451-211-9(5), 9781554512119) Annick Pr., Ltd. CAN. Dist: Publishers Group West (PGW).
—The Paper Bag Princess: The Story Behind the Story. Martchenko, Michael, illus. 3rd anniv. ed. 2005. (ENG.). 64p. (J). (gr. -1-12). 19.95 (978-1-55037-915-0(1), 9781550379150) Annick Pr., Ltd. CAN. Dist: Publishers Group West (PGW).
Murakami, Jon & Yeh, Phil. The Winged Tiger & the Dragons of Hawaii. 2005. 48p. pap. 11.95 (978-0-9755635-0-2(5)) Eastwind Studios.
Murillo, Vinicio. Roderick Roach. 2013. 50p. pap. 10.95 (978-1-62516-018-8(6), Strategic Bk. Publishing) Strategic Book Publishing & Rights Agency (SBPRA).
Natori. Josie & the Dragon. 2012. (ENG.). pap. (978-1-4675-4376-7(4)) Independent Pub.
Nelson, James Gary. Smileytooth & the Castle Hassle. Bumstead, Debbie, illus. 2008. 24p. pap. 10.95 (978-1-933090-95-5(2)) Guardian Angel Publishing, Inc.
Nelson, Peter. Creature Keepers & the Burgled Blizzard-Bristles. Rao, Rohitash, illus. 2016. (Creature Keepers Ser.: 3). 336p. (J). (gr. 3-7). 12.99 (978-0-06-223647-0(4)) HarperCollins Pubs.
Nesbit, E. The Book of Dragons. 2008. 108p. 23.95 (978-1-60664-859-9(4)); (gr. 2-13). pap. 9.95 (978-1-60664-106-4(9)) Aegypan.
—The Book of Dragons. Fell, H. Granville & Millar, H. R., illus. unabr. ed. 2004. (Dover Children's Classics Ser.). (ENG.). 176p. (gr. 3-5). pap. 7.95 (978-0-486-43648-7(9)) Dover Pubns., Inc.
—The Seven Dragons & Other Stories. 2006. 140p. 24.95 (978-1-59818-171-5(8)) Aegypan.
—Seven Dragons & Other Stories. 2006. 140p. per. 11.95 (978-1-59818-964-3(6)) Aegypan.
Nettrour, Nelani. Banshees Bk. 2: Dragon Lands. Nettrour, Heather, illus. I.t. ed. 2003. 114p. (J). pap. 11.95 (978-1-932657-03-6(7)) Third Millennium Pubns.
—Meeshu's Keep Bk. 1: Dragon Guardians. Nettrour, Heather, illus. 2005. 113p. pap. 14.95 (978-1-932657-37-1(1)) Third Millennium Pubns.
Neubecker, Robert. Racing the Waves. 2014. (Tales of the Time Dragon Ser.: 2). (ENG.). 32p. (J). (gr. 1-3). 15.99 (978-0-545-54903-5(5)) Scholastic, Inc.
Newberger Speregen, Devra. How to Train Your Dragon. Shimabukuro, Denise, illus. 2017. (Little Golden Book Ser.). (ENG.). 24p. (J). (-k). 4.99 **(978-1-5247-6774-7(3)**, Golden Bks.) Random Hse. Children's Bks.
Newton Driscoll, Ell. The Dragons of Candlewood. 2006. pap. 15.95 (978-1-932196-92-4(7)) WordWright.biz, Inc.
Newton Driscoll, Ellen. The Legend of the Dragon Sword. 2009. 204p. pap. 14.95 (978-1-934335-36-9(3)) WordWright.biz, Inc.
Neyer, Daniel. Bulkington. Wilmot, Anita, illus. 2004. 136p. (YA). pap. 9.95 (978-0-9666701-1-0(6)) One Faithful Harp Publishing Co.
Nez, John, illus. The Dragon Painter. 2006. (First Reading Level 4 Ser.). 48p. (J). (gr. 1-4). 8.99 (978-0-7945-1275-0(5), Usborne) EDC Publishing.
Nick, Barbara. Bella the Dragon. Steckler, Elaine, illus. 2013. 36p. pap. 11.75 (978-1-938078-05-7(5)) Catto Creations, LLC.
Nielsen, Jennifer A. Rise of the Wolf. 2016. (Mark of the Thief Ser.: 2). (ENG.). 352p. (J). (gr. 4-7). pap. 7.99 (978-0-545-56205-8(8)); 17.99 (978-0-545-56204-1(X)) Scholastic, Inc. (Scholastic Pr.).
—Rise of the Wolf. 2016. (Mark of the Thief Ser.: 2). lib. bdg. 18.40 **(978-0-606-39707-0(8))** Turtleback Bks.
Nielsen, Jennifer A. Wrath of the Storm. 2017. (Mark of the Thief Ser.: 3). (ENG.). 352p. (J). (gr. 4-7). 16.99 (978-0-545-56207-2(4), Scholastic Pr.) Scholastic, Inc.
Niemann, Christoph. The Pet Dragon: A Story about Adventure, Friendship, & Chinese Characters. Niemann, Christoph, illus. 2008. (ENG., Illus.). 40p. (J). (gr. -1-3). 16.99 (978-0-06-157776-5(6), Greenwillow Bks.) HarperCollins Pubs.
Nigg, Joe. How to Raise & Keep a Dragon. 2006. (Illus.). 128p. (978-0-7322-8409-1(0)) HarperCollins Pubs. Australia.
Nixon, Tom, illus. Sled Dog Wisdom: Humorous & Heartwarming Tales from Alaska's Mushers. 2006. (ENG.). 64p. 4.95 (978-0-9745014-5-1(X)) Epicenter Pr., Inc.
Nunez, Alonso. El Invencible y Malvado Dragon Curiambro. (SPA.). (J). (gr. 2-4). 18.95 (978-968-494-096-3(3), CI30452) Centro de Informacion y Desarrollo de la Comunicacion y la Literatura MEX. Dist: AIMS International Bks., Inc., Lectorum Pubns., Inc.
Nyikos, Stacy. Dragon Wishes. 2008. (ENG.). 256p. (J). (gr. 2-7). 16.95 (978-1-933831-11-4(1)) Blooming Tree Pr.
Ode, Eric. The Boy & the Dragon, 1 vol. Harris, Jim, illus. 2013. (ENG.). 32p. (J). (gr. k-3). 16.99 (978-1-4556-1813-2(6)) Pelican Publishing Co., Inc.
Offen, Hilda. There Might Be Giants. (Illus.). 25p. (J). pap. (978-0-340-68149-7(7)) Hodder & Stoughton.
Ogilvy, Ian. Measle & the Dragodon. 2006. 344p. (J). (gr. 3-8). per. 6.99 (978-0-06-058690-4(7), Harper Trophy) HarperCollins Pubs.
Oh, Ellen. Warrior. 2013. (Prophecy Ser.: 2). (ENG.). 336p. (YA). (gr. 8). 17.99 (978-0-06-209112-3(3), HarperTeen) HarperCollins Pubs.
Oldaugh, Charles. The Frog Knight. 2011. 28p. (gr. 1-2). pap. 16.99 (978-1-4567-6198-1(6)) AuthorHouse.
Oliver, Gloria. Cross-eyed Dragon Troubles. 2008. 308p. (YA). per. 14.95 (978-0-7599-4466-4(0)) Hard Shell Word Factory.
Oliver, Jan. Heart of Fire. 2009. 176p. pap. 18.95 (978-1-4092-6660-0(5)) Lulu Pr., Inc.
O'Ryan, Ellie. How to Raise Three Dragons. 2015. (Simon & Schuster Ready-To-Read Level 2 Ser.). lib. bdg. 13.55 (978-0-606-37873-4(1)) Turtleback Bks.
Osborne, Mary Pope. Night of the Ninth Dragon. Murdocca, Sal, illus. 2016. (Magic Tree House Merlin Missions Ser.: No. 27). (ENG.). 144p. (J). (gr. 2-5). 13.99 (978-0-553-51089-8(4), Random Hse. Bks. for Young Readers) Random Hse. Children's Bks.
Owen, James A. Here, There Be Dragons. Owen, James A., illus. (Chronicles of the Imaginarium Geographica Ser.: 1). (ENG., Illus.). (YA). (gr. 7-12). 2007. 352p. pap. 11.99 (978-1-4169-1228-6(2)) 2006. 336p. 21.99 (978-1-4169-1227-9(4)) Simon & Schuster Bks. For Young Readers. (Simon & Schuster Bks. For Young Readers).
Palka, Yvonne. Dragon Fire Ocean Mist. 2009. pap. 12.95 (978-0-9817668-0-5(3)) Heartrock Pr.
Paolini, Christopher. Brisingr. 2009. (Inheritance Cycle Ser.: Bk. 3). (CHI., Illus.). 560p. (YA). pap. (978-7-5448-0634-3(0)) Jieli Publishing Hse.
—Brisingr. 2009. (Inheritance Cycle Ser.: Bk. 3). (CHI., Illus.). 822p. (YA). pap. (978-957-08-3421-5(8)) Linking Publishing Co., Ltd.
—Brisingr, Bk. 3. 2011. (ENG., Illus.). 784p. pap. (978-0-552-55212-7(7), Corgi Bks. Ltd.) Random House Children's Books.
—Brisingr. (ENG.). 2010. (Inheritance Cycle Ser.: 3). 800p. (YA). (gr. 7-18). pap. 14.99 (978-0-375-82674-0(2)) 2008. (Inheritance Cycle Ser.: Bk. 3). 784p. (J). 27.50 (978-0-375-85117-9(8)) 2008. (Inheritance Cycle Ser.: Bk. 3). 784p. (YA). (gr. 7). 27.50 (978-0-375-82672-6(6)) 2009. (Inheritance Cycle Ser.: Bk. 3). 800p. (YA). (gr. 7-18). 29.99 (978-0-375-85481-1(9)) Random Hse. Children's Bks. (Knopf Bks. for Young Readers).
—Brisingr, Vol. 1. Isern, Carol & Rizzo, Jorge, trs. 2008. (Inheritance Cycle Ser.: Bk. 3). (SPA.). 704p. (YA). (gr. 7-12). pap. 21.95 (978-84-92429-39-4(9)) Roca Editorial ESP. Dist: Spanish Pubs., LLC.
—Brisingr. 2010. (Inheritance Ser.: 03). lib. bdg. 26.95 (978-0-606-14109-3(X), Turtleback) Turtleback Bks.
—Eldest. abr. ed. 2009. (Inheritance Cycle Ser.: Bk. 2). (SPA.). (J). 59.99 (978-1-60847-564-3(6)) Findaway World, LLC.
—Eldest. (Inheritance Cycle Ser.: Bk. 2). (ENG.). 704p. (YA). (gr. 7-18). 2007. pap. 12.99 (978-0-375-84040-1(0)) 2005. (Illus.). 21.00 (978-0-375-82670-2(X)) Random Hse. Children's Bks. (Knopf Bks. for Young Readers).
—Eldest. de Heriz, Enrique, tr. 2006. (Inheritance Cycle Ser.: Bk. 2). (SPA.). (YA). 832p. (gr. 7-12). 22.95 (978-84-96284-96-8(4)); 831p. (gr. 8-12). per. 22.95 (978-84-96544-07-9(9)) Roca Editorial ESP. Dist: Spanish Pubs., LLC.
—Eldest. 2007. (Inheritance Ser.: 2). 24.50 (978-1-4177-7363-3(4), Turtleback) Turtleback Bks.
—Eragon. 2006. (Inheritance Cycle Ser.: Bk. 1). (YA). cd-rom 39.99 (978-1-59895-406-7(7)) Findaway World, LLC.
—Eragon. (Inheritance Cycle Ser.: Bk. 1). (ENG.). 528p. (YA). (gr. 7-18). 2003. Illus.). 18.95 (978-0-375-82668-9(8)) 2005. reprint ed. pap. 11.99 (978-0-375-82669-6(6)) Random Hse. Children's Bks. (Knopf Bks. for Young Readers).
—Eragon. (Inheritance Cycle Ser.: Bk. 1). (SPA.). (YA). pap. (978-84-96284-44-9(1)) Roca Editorial.
—Eragon; Eldest. (Inheritance Cycle Ser.: Bks. 1-2). (ENG.). (YA). (gr. 7). 2008. 1216p. pap. 19.99

*(978-0-375-85704-1(4))*Set. 2005. 1232p. 39.95 *(978-0-375-83658-9(6))* Random Hse. Children's Bks. (Knopf Bks. for Young Readers).

—Eragon, Eldest, Brisingr, 3 vols., Set. 2010. (Inheritance Cycle Ser.: Bk. 4). (ENG.). 800p. (YA). (gr. 7). pap., pap., pap. 38.97 *(978-0-375-87203-7(5)*, Knopf Bks. for Young Readers) Random Hse. Children's Bks.

—Inheritance. (Inheritance Cycle Ser.: Bk. 4). (ENG.). (YA). (gr. 7). 2012. 880p. pap. 15.99 *(978-0-375-84631-1(X))* 2011. 880p. 27.99 *(978-0-375-85611-2(0))* 2012. (Illus.). 896p. 29.99 *(978-0-449-81319-5(3))* Random Hse. Children's Bks. (Knopf Bks. for Young Readers).

—Inheritance Set: Eragon; Eldest; Brisingr, 3 vols. 2008. (Inheritance Cycle Ser.: Bks. 1-3). (ENG.). (YA). (gr. 7). 67.45 *(978-0-375-84615-1(8)*, Knopf Bks. for Young Readers) Random Hse. Children's Bks.

—The Inheritance Cycle, 3 vols. 2008. (Inheritance Cycle Ser.: Bks. 1-3). (ENG.). (J). (gr. 7). 67.45 *(978-0-375-85141-4(0)*, Knopf Bks. for Young Readers) Random Hse. Children's Bks.

Parker, Emma. Albert & the Dragon. 2010. (Illus.). 20p. pap. *(978-1-877561-50-4(9))* First Edition Ltd.

Parker, Emma & Renaud, Marguerite. Dragon Bowling. 2010. (Illus.). 24p. pap. *(978-1-877561-82-5(7))* First Edition Ltd.

Parker, Vic, compiled by. How the Dragon Was Tricked & Other Silly Stories. 2016. (Silly Stories Ser.). (ENG.). 40p. (J). (gr. 2-3). pap. 14.05 *(978-1-4824-4187-1(X))* Stevens, Gareth Publishing LLLP.

Parker, Vic, ed. The Prince & the Dragon & Other Stories. 2015. (Scary Fairy Tales Ser.). (ENG.). 40p. (J). (gr. 3-4). pap. 14.05 *(978-1-4824-3097-4(5))* Stevens, Gareth Publishing LLLP.

Pau Pau. The Princess' Adventure. 2007. 52p. pap. 16.95 *(978-1-60441-069-3(8))* America Star Bks.

Paul, Donita K. Two Renegade Realms, 1 vol. 2014. (Realm Walkers Ser.). (ENG.). 416p. (YA). pap. 13.99 *(978-0-310-73581-6(5))* Zondervan.

Pavey, Peter. One Dragon's Dream. Pavey, Peter, illus. 2009. (ENG., Illus.). 40p. (J). (gr. -1-2). 17.99 *(978-0-7636-4470-3(6))* Candlewick Pr.

Payton, Nicole. Dragon Savior. 2007. 212p. per. 24.95 *(978-1-4241-5498-2(7))* America Star Bks.

Pendergrass, D. Louis, a Blue Dragon. 2009. 32p. pap. 15.00 *(978-1-4389-9036-1(7))* AuthorHouse.

Pendergrass, Daphne. Riders of Berk: A Fiery Discovery. 2015. lib. bdg. 13.55 *(978-0-606-36311-2(4))* Turtleback Bks.

Pendziwol, Jean E. Once upon a Dragon: Stranger Safety for Kids (and Dragons) Gourbault, Martine, illus. 2006. (ENG.). 32p. (J). (gr. -1-2). 7.95 *(978-1-55337-969-0(1))* Kids Can Pr., Ltd. CAN. Dist: Hachette Bk. Group.

Pepper, Sly. Dugan Peckles & the Keepers of the Crystal Flame. Germano, Nicholas, illus. 2006. 229p. per. 5.99 *(978-0-9747668-1-2(X))* MindMaze Publishing Co.

Peppermint, Aurora. Beneath the Scales. 2016. (ENG., Illus.). (J). 24.99 ***(978-1-63477-940-1(1)***, Harmony Ink Pr.) Dreamspinner Pr.

Perelman, Helen. Gooey Goblins: Halloween Special. Waters, Erica-Jane, illus. 2011. (Candy Fairies Ser.). (ENG.). 176p. (J). (gr. 2-5). pap. 5.99 *(978-1-4424-2213-1(0)*, Aladdin) Simon & Schuster Children's Publishing.

—Gooey Goblins: Halloween Special. Waters, Erica-Jane, illus. 2013. (Candy Fairies Ser.). (ENG.). 176p. (J). (gr. 2-5). 15.99 *(978-1-4424-6495-7(X)*, Simon & Schuster/Paula Wiseman Bks.) Simon & Schuster/Paula Wiseman Bks.

Peretti, Frank E. The Door in the Dragon's Throat. 2004. (Cooper Kids Adventure Ser.: 1). 128p. (J). (gr. 3-6). pap. 6.99 *(978-1-58134-618-3(2))* Crossway.

Perro, Bryan. Amos Daragon #2: the Key of Braha. 2013. (Amos Daragon Ser.). (ENG.). 192p. (J). (gr. 3-7). 6.99 *(978-0-375-85977-9(2))* Random Hse. Children's Bks.

Perry, Dakota. Brim's Journey. 2008. 36p. pap. 24.95 *(978-1-60703-938-9(9))* America Star Bks.

Peters, Andrew Fusek. Dragon & Mousie. Wade, Gini, illus. 2006. (ENG.). 32p. (J). pap. 7.95 *(978-0-86243-650-6(8))* Y Lolfa GBR. Dist: Dufour Editions, Inc.

—Dragon & Mousie & the Snow Factory. Wade, Gini, illus. 2007. (ENG.). 32p. (J). pap. 7.95 *(978-0-86243-945-3(0))* Y Lolfa GBR. Dist: Dufour Editions, Inc.

Philippa & the Dragon, Pk. 6. (Literatura 2000 Ser.). (gr. 1-2). 28.00 *(978-0-7635-0148-8(4))* Rigby Education.

Phillips, Beth Ann. Crystal Kingdom, 1 vol. 2009. 63p. pap. 19.95 *(978-1-60813-003-0(7))* America Star Bks.

Phillips, Kent. The Red Eyed Black Dragon. 2011. 28p. pap. 15.99 *(978-1-4568-3795-2(8))* Xlibris Corp.

Pike, Christopher, pseud. The Hidden Beast. 2016. (Spooksville Ser.: 12). (ENG., Illus.). 112p. (J). (gr. 3-7). 16.99 *(978-1-4814-1095-3(4))*; pap. 7.99 *(978-1-4814-1093-9(8))* Simon & Schuster Children's Publishing. (Aladdin).

Pike, Tabitha R. Dragon Tears: The Legacy. 2011. 232p. pap. 24.95 *(978-1-4560-6664-2(1))* America Star Bks.

Pilkey, Dav. Dragon Gets By. 2008. (Dragon Tales Ser.). (Illus.). 48p. (gr. -1-3). 16.00 *(978-0-7569-8347-5(9))* Perfection Learning Corp.

—Dragon's Fat Cat. 2008. (Illus.). 48p. (gr. -1-3). 16.00 *(978-0-7569-8835-7(7))* Perfection Learning Corp.

—Dragon's Halloween. 2007. (Dragon's Tales Ser.: Bk. 5). (Illus.). 48p. (gr. -1-3). 16.00 *(978-0-7569-7861-7(0))* Perfection Learning Corp.

—Dragon's Halloween. Pilkey, Dav, illus. 2003. (Dragon's Tales Ser.: Bk. 5). (ENG., Illus.). 48p. (J). (gr. -1-3). pap. 5.99 *(978-0-439-54847-2(0)*, Orchard Bks.) Scholastic, Inc.

—A Friend for Dragon. 2008. (Dragon Tales Ser.). (Illus.). (gr. -1-3). 16.00 *(978-0-7569-8299-7(5))* Perfection Learning Corp.

Pope, Cody/Louis Ray. Andy & the Dragons. 2008. (Illus.). 48p. (J). per. *(978-0-9798792-1-0(3))* Scavenger's Pubns.

Porter, Duane. Molly O'Malley & the Leprechaun. 2007. (Illus.). 224p. (J). per. 12.95 *(978-0-9800993-0-0(7))* Buried Treasure Publishing.

Postgate, Oliver. Noggin & the Dragon. Firmin, Peter, illus. 2016. (Noggin the Nog Ser.: 4). (ENG.). 48p. (J). (gr. 1-3). 8.99 *(978-1-4052-8154-6(5))* Egmont Bks., Ltd. GBR. Dist: Independent Pubs. Group.

Press, Pikachu. Super Pokemon Pop-Up! - White Kyurem. 2013. (ENG.). 5p. (J). (gr. 3-6). 9.99 *(978-1-60438-180-1(9))* Pokemon, USA, Inc.

Pretty Little Lilly & the Dragon's Slumber. 2008. (Illus.). 38p. (J). pap. *(978-0-9777241-4-7(X))* Cepia LLC.

Price, Allison W. A. The Dragons & the Words of Knowledge. 2009. 112p. pap. 14.98 *(978-0-557-05766-5(3))* Lulu Pr., Inc.

Prichard, Kathy. Tree Twitters: An Earth Dragons Tale, 1 vol. 2009. 23p. pap. 19.95 *(978-1-61582-620-9(3))* PublishAmerica, Inc.

Princess Madeline & the Dragon. 2013. (Illus.). 118p. (YA). pap. 5.99 *(978-1-62375-070-1(9)*, Caliburn Bks.) MQuills Publishing.

Prior, Natalie. Lily Quench & the Dragon of Ashby, No. 1. Dawson, Janine, illus. 2004. (ENG.). 160p. (J). (gr. 3-7). 6.99 *(978-0-14-240020-3(3)*, Puffin Books) Penguin Young Readers Group.

Prior, Natalie Jane. Lily Quench 6 Hand of Manuelo, Vol. 6. Dawson, Janine, illus. 2004. (ENG.). 176p. (J). (gr. 3-7). 6.99 *(978-0-14-240222-1(2)*, Puffin Books) Penguin Young Readers Group.

—The Search for King Dragon. Dawson, Janine, illus. 2005. (ENG.). 192p. (J). (gr. 3-7). 6.99 *(978-0-14-240267-2(2)*, Puffin Books) Penguin Young Readers Group.

Prior, Natalie Jane & Prior, Natalie. Lily Quench & the Treasure of Mote Ely, Vol. 3. 2004. (ENG., Illus.). 160p. (J). (gr. 3-7). 6.99 *(978-0-14-240022-7(X)*, Puffin Books) Penguin Young Readers Group.

The Prophesied. 2013. 152p. *(978-1-4602-3111-1(2))* FriesenPress.

Provencio, Marta. The Christmas Dragon. 2013. 24p. pap. 12.99 *(978-1-4808-0379-4(0))* Archway Publishing.

Punter, Russell. Danny & the Dragon. 2009. (First Reading Level 3 Ser.). 48p. (J). 6.99 *(978-0-7945-2261-2(0)*, Usborne) EDC Publishing.

Quillen, Carl. Dragon Girl Myra. 2009. 53p. pap. 5.56 *(978-0-557-08268-1(4))* Lulu Pr., Inc.

Quinn, Jordan. Let the Games Begin! McPhillips, Robert, illus. 2015. (Kingdom of Wrenly Ser.: 7). (ENG.). 128p. (J). (gr. k-4). pap. 5.99 *(978-1-4814-2379-3(7)*, Little Simon) Little Simon.

—The Scarlet Dragon. McPhillips, Robert, illus. 2014. (Kingdom of Wrenly Ser.: 2). (ENG.). 128p. (J). (gr. k-4). pap. 5.99 *(978-1-4424-9693-4(2)*, Little Simon) Little Simon.

—The Scarlet Dragon. 2014. (Kingdom of Wrenly Ser.: 2). lib. bdg. 16.00 *(978-0-606-35444-8(1))* Turtleback Bks.

—Sea Monster! McPhillips, Robert, illus. 2014. (Kingdom of Wrenly Ser.: 3). (ENG.). 128p. (J). (gr. k-4). pap. 5.99 *(978-1-4814-0072-5(X)*, Little Simon) Little Simon.

R, J. Ff: The Weedy Sea Dragon Coloring Book (Standard Version) 2013. 38p. (J). pap. 9.95 *(978-1-935734-53-6(9))* Kitanie Bks.

Random House Editors & RH Disney Staff. Aurora & the Helpful Dragon/Tiana & Her Furry Friend. Disney Storybook Artists Staff & Studio Iboix Staff, illus. 2011. (Pictureback(R) Ser.). (ENG.). 32p. (J). (gr. -1-2). pap. 4.99 *(978-0-7364-2757-9(0)*, RH/Disney) Random Hse. Children's Bks.

Raum, Elizabeth. Cedric & the Dragon. Crittenden, Nina Victor, illus. 2010. (J). *(978-1-934617-05-2(9)*, Alma Little) Elva Resa Publishing, LLC.

Rawson, Christopher. Dragons, Stories Of. Cartwright, Stephen, illus. 2004. (Young Reading Series One Ser.). 48p. (J). (gr. 2-18). pap. 5.95 *(978-0-7945-0446-5(9)*, Usborne) EDC Publishing.

Reader's Digest Staff & Roe, David. How to Train Your Dragon Mix & Match. 2010. (Mix & Match Ser.). (ENG., Illus.). 12p. (J). (gr. -1-1). bds. 14.99 *(978-0-7944-1938-7(0)*, Reader's Digest Children's Bks.) Studio Fun International.

Reasor, Teresa J. Willy C. Sparks. 2012. 36p. pap. 9.15 *(978-0-9850069-6-9(X))* Reasor, Teresa J.

Reed, Janet. Brave Dave & the Dragons. Fraser, Kara-Anne, illus. 2009. 12p. (J). *(978-0-545-16142-8(8))* Scholastic, Inc.

Reed, Master Amy. The Adventures of A Dragon Named Ryung: Journey to Black Belt. 2010. 56p. pap. 30.99 *(978-1-4520-0145-6(6))* AuthorHouse.

Reeve, Philip. No Such Thing As Dragons. 2010. (ENG.). 192p. (J). (gr. 3-7). 16.99 *(978-0-545-22224-2(9)*, Scholastic Pr.) Scholastic, Inc.

Regan, Dian. The Dragon Stone, 0 vols. Curtis, Stacy, illus. 2013. (ENG.). 96p. (J). (gr. 2-4). pap. 9.99 *(978-1-4778-1632-5(1)*, 9781477816325, Amazon Children's Publishing) Amazon Publishing.

Regin, Andrew. Guardians: Volume 1. 2012. 286p. pap. 27.95 *(978-1-4626-8856-2(X))* America Star Bks.

Reyes, Yolanda. Una Cama para Tres. Coll, Ivar Da, illus. 2004. (SPA.). 36p. (J). (gr. k-3). 14.95 *(978-958-704-055-5(4))* Santillana USA Publishing Co., Inc.

RH Disney. A Fairy's Fire. RH Disney, illus. 2016. (Never Girls Ser.). (ENG., Illus.). 224p. (J). (gr. 1-4). lib. bdg. 17.99 *(978-0-7364-8175-5(3)*, RH/Disney) Random Hse. Children's Bks.

— Fairy's Fire. RH Disney, illus. 2016. (Never Girls Ser.). (ENG., Illus.). 224p. (J). (gr. 1-4). 14.99 *(978-0-7364-3556-7(5)*, RH/Disney) Random Hse. Children's Bks.

—Pete's Dragon (Disney: Pete's Dragon) RH Disney, illus. 2016. (Little Golden Book Ser.). (ENG., Illus.). 24p. (J). (-k). 4.99 *(978-0-7364-3522-2(0)*, Golden/Disney) Random Hse. Children's Bks.

Rice, Morgan. A Land of Fire. 2014. 196p. 26.99 *(978-1-939416-87-2(6))* Morgan Rice Bks.

—A Land of Fire (Book #12 in the Sorcerer's Ring) 2014. 196p. (YA). pap. 15.99 *(978-1-939416-86-5(8)*, Morgan Rice) Morgan Rice Bks.

—A Reign of Steel (Book #11 in the Sorcerer's Ring) 2014. 216p. (YA). pap. 15.99 *(978-1-939416-76-6(0)*, Morgan Rice) Morgan Rice Bks.

Riddell, Chris. The Emperor of Absurdia. 3rd ed. 2007. (ENG., Illus.). 32p. (J). (gr. -1-k). pap. 11.99 *(978-1-4050-9028-5(6))* Pan Macmillan GBR. Dist: Independent Pubs. Group.

Riggs, Mary L. Dragon Forge the Ballad of Beighn. 2009. 110p. pap. 9.95 *(978-1-60860-499-9(3)*, Strategic Bk. Publishing) Strategic Book Publishing & Rights Agency (SBPRA).

Rinehart, J. D. A Kingdom Rises. 2017. (Crown of Three Ser.: 3). (ENG., Illus.). 432p. (J). (gr. 4-8). 18.99 ***(978-1-4814-2449-3(1)***, Aladdin) Simon & Schuster Children's Publishing.

Ripley's Believe It or Not Editors & Ripley's Believe It Or Not! Staff. The Dragon's Triangle. 2010. (Rbi Ser.: 2). (ENG.). 128p. (J). pap. 4.99 *(978-1-893951-53-2(7))* Ripley Entertainment, Inc.

Ripley's Believe It Or Not! Staff. Secrets of the Deep. 2010. (Rbi Ser.: 4). (ENG.). 128p. (J). pap. 4.99 *(978-1-893951-54-9(5))* Ripley Entertainment, Inc.

Roberts, Daniel. The Dragon, the Princess & the Peanut Butter Sandwiches. 2009. 36p. pap. 16.99 *(978-1-4389-8277-9(1))* AuthorHouse.

Roberts, Esyllt Nest & Owen, Carys Eurwen. Dinas Emrys. 2005. (WEL., Illus.). 36p. pap. *(978-0-86381-439-6(5))* Gwasg Carreg Gwalch.

Robertson, M. P. The Egg. 2004. (ENG., Illus.). 32p. (J). (gr. k-3). pap. 6.99 *(978-0-14-240038-8(6)*, Puffin Books) Penguin Young Readers Group.

—The Great Dragon Rescue. 2009. (ENG., Illus.). 32p. (J). (gr. -1-2). pap. 8.95 *(978-1-84507-379-4(7)*, Frances Lincoln) Quarto Publishing Group UK GBR. Dist: Hachette Bk. Group.

Robinson, Michelle. The Forgetful Knight. Blunt, Fred, illus. 2016. (ENG.). 40p. (J). (gr. -1-3). 16.99 *(978-0-8037-4067-9(0)*, Dial Bks) Penguin Young Readers Group.

Robshaw, Brandon. Georgina & the Dragon. l.t. ed. 2007. pap. *(978-1-905665-65-5(2))* Pollinger In Print.

Rodda, Emily. Isle of the Dead. 2004. (Dragons of Deltora Ser.: No. 3). 195p. (J). lib. bdg. 16.92 *(978-1-4242-0273-7(6))* Fitzgerald Bks.

—Shadowgate. 2004. (Dragons of Deltora Ser.: No. 2). 195p. (J). lib. bdg. 16.92 *(978-1-4242-0274-4(4))* Fitzgerald Bks.

—The Sister of the South. 2004. (Dragons of Deltora Ser.: No. 4). 205p. (J). lib. bdg. 16.92 *(978-1-4242-0275-1(2))* Fitzgerald Bks.

Romey, Elizabeth A. Dragon Magic. (YA). pap. 9.99 *(978-0-88092-625-6(2))* Royal Fireworks Publishing Co.

Rosenberg, Michael. The Story of Bendalot Part: The Return Home. 2009. (Illus.). 36p. pap. 15.49 *(978-1-4389-8294-6(1))* AuthorHouse.

Roth, Judith. Goodnight, Dragons [padded Board Book]. Lemaître, Pascal, illus. 2015. (ENG.). 32p. (J). (gr. -1-k). bds. 8.99 *(978-1-4847-2190-2(X))* Hyperion Bks. for Children.

Rothwell, Tammy. The Adventures of Lewis the Dragon: The journey Begins... 2008. (Illus.). 89p. (J). per. *(978-0-615-18912-3(1))* Rothwell Digital Imagery.

Rotter, Laura. Terratorv. 2009. 32p. pap. 12.99 *(978-1-4490-3092-6(0))* AuthorHouse.

Rouncville, Bibi. Trouble at Binka Bridge. 2010. 52p. pap. 9.50 *(978-0-557-16051-8(0))* Lulu Pr., Inc.

Rovetch, L. Bob & Whitman, Emily. Sir Henry, the Polite Knight. Barnard, Bryn, illus. 2006. (J). *(978-1-58987-204-2(5))* Kindermusik International.

Roy, Alene Adele. The Legend of Dragonfly Pond: Volume One. 2008. 60p. pap. 24.99 *(978-1-4343-6824-9(6))* AuthorHouse.

The Royal Guard Dragons. 2007. (Illus.). 160p. (YA). per. 14.95 *(978-0-9791733-0-1(2))* Royal Guard Dragon Society, The.

Rubin, Adam. Dragons Love Tacos. Salmieri, Daniel, illus. 2012. (ENG.). 40p. (J). (gr. -1-2). 16.99 *(978-0-8037-3680-1(0)*, Dial Bks) Penguin Young Readers Group.

—Dragons Love Tacos 2: The Sequel. Salmieri, Daniel, illus. 2017. (ENG.). 48p. (J). (-k). 18.99 *(978-0-525-42888-6(7)*, Dial Bks) Penguin Young Readers Group.

Rubin, Adam & Salmieri, Daniel. Dragons Love Tacos. 2016. (ENG., Illus.). 40p. (J). (gr. -1-2). 17.99 *(978-0-7352-2823-8(X)*, Dial Bks) Penguin Young Readers Group.

Russell, James. The Dragon Hunters. Choi, Link, illus. 2017. (Dragon Brothers Ser.: 1). (ENG.). 32p. (J). (-4). 16.99 *(978-1-4926-4861-1(2)*, 9781492648611, Sourcebooks Jabberwocky) Sourcebooks, Inc.

Russell, James. The Dragon Riders. Choi, Link, illus. 2017. (Dragon Brothers Ser.: 3). (ENG.). 32p. (J). (-4). 16.99 ***(978-1-4926-4867-3(1)***, Sourcebooks Jabberwocky) Sourcebooks, Inc.

Ryan, Margaret. Littlest Dragon. Smith, Jamie, illus. 2011. (ENG.). 80p. (J). (gr. 2-4). pap. 5.99 *(978-0-00-714163-0(7)*, HarperCollins Children's Bks.) HarperCollins Pubs. Ltd. GBR. Dist: HarperCollins Pubs.

—Littlest Dragon Gets the Giggles. Smith, Jamie, illus. 2011. (ENG.). 80p. (J). pap. 5.99 *(978-0-00-718029-5(2)*, HarperCollins Children's Bks.) HarperCollins Pubs. Ltd. GBR. Dist: HarperCollins Pubs.

—Littlest Dragon Goes for Goal. Smith, Jamie, illus. 2011. (ENG.). 64p. (J). pap. 5.99 *(978-0-00-719294-6(0)*, HarperCollins Children's Bks.) HarperCollins Pubs. Ltd. GBR. Dist: HarperCollins Pubs.

Saltzberg, Barney. Would You Rather Be a Princess or a Dragon? 2016. (ENG., Illus.). 32p. (J). 16.99 *(978-1-62672-358-0(3)*, 9781626723580) Roaring Brook Pr.

Salvatore, R. A. Road of the Patriarch. 2007. (Sellswords Ser.: Bk. 3). (ENG., Illus.). 384p. mass mkt. 7.99 *(978-0-7869-4277-0(0)*, Wizards of the Coast) Wizards of the Coast.

San Souci, Daniel. Rabbit & the Dragon King: Based on a Korean Folk Tale. Neilan, Eujin Kim, illus. 2006. (ENG.). 32p. (J). (gr. 1-4). pap. 9.95 *(978-1-59078-418-1(9))* Boyds Mills Pr.

Sander, Sonia, adapted by. Dragon's Snowy Day. 2005. (Scholastic Reader Ser.). (Illus.). 32p. (J). pap. *(978-0-439-80163-8(X))* Scholastic, Inc.

Sands, Maria. Sanjee & Her Delightful Hats. 2008. 20p. pap. 24.95 *(978-1-60563-700-6(9))* America Star Bks.

Sauer, Tammi. Roar! Starin, Liz, illus. 2015. (ENG.). 32p. (J). (gr. -1-3). 17.99 *(978-1-4814-0224-8(2)*, Simon & Schuster Bks. For Young Readers) Simon & Schuster Bks. For Young Readers.

Savage, J. Scott. Fires of Invention. 2015. (Mysteries of Cove Ser.: Bk. 1). 312p. (J). 17.99 *(978-1-62972-092-0(5)*, Shadow Mountain) Deseret Bk. Co.

—Gears of Revolution. 2016. (Mysteries of Cove Ser.: 2). 342p. (J). 17.99 *(978-1-62972-223-8(5)*, Shadow Mountain) Deseret Bk. Co.

Scharf, J. L. Grace & the Ice Prince: The Diamond Heart Quest. 2006. (ENG.). 262p. (J). per. 16.95 *(978-1-897235-09-6(7))* Thistledown Pr., Ltd. CAN. Dist: Univ. of Toronto Pr.

Schemery, Beau. The Unlikely Hero. 2016. (ENG., Illus.). (J). 24.99 ***(978-1-63477-979-1(7))*** 2013. 160p. pap. 14.99 *(978-1-62380-451-0(5))* Dreamspinner Pr. (Harmony Ink Pr.).

Schemery, Beau. The Unlikely Hero [Library Edition]. 2013. 160p. pap. 14.99 *(978-1-62380-920-1(7)*, Harmony Ink Pr.) Dreamspinner Pr.

Scollon, Bill. Dreamworks Dragons: A Tale of Two Dragons. 2015. (Ultra Build It Ser.: 2). (ENG.). 24p. (J). (gr. -1-3). pap. 10.99 *(978-0-7944-3319-2(7)*, Reader's Digest Children's Bks.) Studio Fun International.

Scollon, William. Doc Mcstuffins: Brave Dragon. 2014. (World of Reading Ser.). (J). lib. bdg. 13.55 *(978-0-606-35268-0(6))* Turtleback Bks.

Scott, Eric. The Day the Rainbow Ended. 2013. 90p. pap. 7.99 *(978-1-78333-419-3(3))* Acorn Bks.

—The Island of Lost Dolls. 2013. 86p. pap. 7.99 *(978-1-78333-403-2(7))* Acorn Bks.

Sellier, Marie. Legend of the Chinese Dragon. Kazeroid, Sibylle, tr. from FRE. Louis, Catherine & Fei, Wang, illus. 2008. (ENG.). 40p. (J). (gr. -1-3). 15.95 *(978-0-7358-2152-1(6))* North-South Bks., Inc.

Seven, John. The Dragon of Rome, 1 vol. Phillips, Craig, illus. 2013. (Time-Tripping Faradays Ser.). (ENG.). 160p. (gr. 4-5). 9.95 *(978-1-62370-012-6(4))*; lib. bdg. 26.65 *(978-1-4342-6029-1(1))* Stone Arch Bks.

Seven, John & Phillips, Craig. The Dragon of Rome, 1 vol. 2013. (ENG.). 160p. (YA). pap. *(978-1-4342-6439-8(4))* Stone Arch Bks.

SFX Fantasy. Tween Tales - Robots, Dragons & the Interworld Machine. 2007. 131p. pap. 12.99 *(978-1-4303-2546-8(1))* Lulu Pr., Inc.

Shah, Idries. Neem el Media Nino. Wirkala, Rita, tr. Mori, Midori & Revels, Robert, illus. 2007. 32p. (J). 18.00 *(978-1-883536-96-1(0))*; pap. 7.99 *(978-1-883536-97-8(9))* I S H K. (Hoopoe Bks.).

—Neem the Half-Boy. Mori, Midori & Revels, Robert, illus. 2007. 32p. (J). (gr. -1). pap. 7.99 *(978-1-883536-95-4(2)*, Hoopoe Bks.) I S H K.

Shanghai Animation Studio Staff & Tang, Sanmu. Nezha Conquers the Dragon King. Yawtsong, Lee, tr. from CHI. 2010. (Favorite Children's Ser.). (ENG., Illus.). 32p. (J). (gr. -1-3). pap. 5.95 *(978-1-60220-975-6(8))* BetterLink Pr., Inc.

Shapiro D., Brian. Plaquetooth. 2008. 28p. pap. 13.99 *(978-1-4343-8913-8(8))* AuthorHouse.

Sharma, Shivan. The Castle, Dragons & a Cricket Ball. 2009. 76p. pap. *(978-1-84549-415-5(6)*, Swirl) arima publishing.

Sharp, Laura. The Key Prince. 2012. 24p. pap. 24.95 *(978-1-4626-8959-0(0))* America Star Bks.

Shaw, Natalie. A Tale of Dragons. 2014. lib. bdg. 13.55 *(978-0-606-35757-9(2))* Turtleback Bks.

Sheldon, Dyan. The Moon Dragons. Blythe, Gary, illus. 2015. (J). 17.32 *(978-1-4677-6318-9(7))* Lerner Publishing Group.

—Moon Dragons. Blythe, Gary, illus. 2015. (ENG.). 32p. (J). (gr. -1-3). 16.95 *(978-1-4677-6314-1(4))* Lerner Publishing Group.

Shrestha, Sophie & Shrestha, Romio. In Search of the Thunder Dragon. Shrestha, Sophie & Shrestha, Romio, illus. 2007. (ENG., Illus.). 32p. (J). (gr. 3). 16.95 *(978-1-60109-100-0(1))* Mandala Publishing.

Shulda, Daron M. Dragon Boots. 2009. 40p. pap. 18.49 *(978-1-4389-7022-6(6))* AuthorHouse.

Sibille, Lucinda. Dragon Swirl: Book II. 2009. 28p. pap. 14.95 *(978-1-4490-1057-7(1))* AuthorHouse.

—Dragon Swirl: Book III. 2009. 32p. pap. 14.95 *(978-1-4490-1072-0(5))* AuthorHouse.

—Dragon Swirl: Book IV. 2009. 32p. pap. 14.95 *(978-1-4490-1075-1(X))* AuthorHouse.

—Dragon Swirl: In the Beginning. 2009. 32p. pap. 14.95 *(978-1-4490-0965-6(4))* AuthorHouse.

Sinden, David, et al. Werewolf Versus Dragon. Duddle, Jonny, illus. 2009. (Awfully Beastly Business Ser.: 1). (ENG.). 192p. (J). (gr. 3-7). 9.99 *(978-1-4169-8649-2(9)*, Aladdin) Simon & Schuster Children's Publishing.

Skye, obert. Choke. 2010. (Pillage Ser.: 2). (ENG., Illus.). 336p. (YA). (gr. 7). 17.99 *(978-1-60641-653-2(7)*, Shadow Mountain) Shadow Mountain Publishing.

—Pillage. (YA). 2010. (Pillage Ser.: 1). (ENG.). 320p. (gr. 7). mass mkt. 7.99 *(978-1-60641-680-8(4))* 2008. (Illus.). 352p. 17.95 *(978-1-59038-922-5(0))* Shadow Mountain Publishing. (Shadow Mountain).

—Pillagy: The Complete Trilogy. 2013. (ENG., Illus.). 712p. (YA). (gr. 6). pap. 17.99 *(978-1-60907-706-8(7)*, Shadow Mountain) Shadow Mountain Publishing.

Slater Iii, John D. The Monkey & the Dragon Meet. 2009. 28p. pap. 12.99 *(978-1-4389-4353-4(9))* AuthorHouse.

Smiley, Diane. Ollie. 2012. (Illus.). 40p. pap. 22.88 *(978-1-4772-1812-9(2))* AuthorHouse.

Smith, C. E. Draupner's Curse. 2009. 208p. 24.95 *(978-1-4401-6797-3(4))*; pap. 14.95 *(978-1-4401-6799-7(0))* iUniverse, Inc.

Smith, Jeff. The Dragonslayer. Smith, Jeff, illus. 2006. (Bone Ser.: 4). (ENG., Illus.). 176p. (J). (gr. 3-7). 26.99 *(978-0-439-70626-1(2))*; pap. 12.99 *(978-0-439-70637-7(8))* Scholastic, Inc. (Graphix).

—Eyes of the Storm. Smith, Jeff & Hamaker, Steve, illus. 2006. (Bone Ser.: 3). (ENG.). 192p. (J). (gr. 3-7). 26.99 *(978-0-439-70625-4(4))*; pap. 12.99 *(978-0-439-70638-4(6))* Scholastic, Inc. (Graphix).

Smith, Lee A. Dobee the Littlest Dragon. 2008. 24p. per. 24.95 *(978-1-60441-165-2(1))* America Star Bks.

Sniegoski, Thomas E. & Golden, Christopher. Dragon Secrets. 2013. (Magic Zero Ser.: 2). (ENG.). 320p. (J). (gr. 3-7). pap. 6.99 *(978-1-4424-7309-6(6)*, Aladdin) Simon & Schuster Children's Publishing.

—Dragon Secrets. 2013. (Magic Zero Ser.: 2). (ENG.). 320p. (J). (gr. 3-7). 17.99 *(978-1-4424-7310-2(X)*, Simon & Schuster/Paula Wiseman Bks.) Simon & Schuster/Paula Wiseman Bks.

Soli, Doris. Jango the Little Dragon: The Wondrous Adventures of Little Dragon. 2011. (Illus.). 36p. pap. 17.07 *(978-1-4567-8487-4(0))* AuthorHouse.

Sorenson, Jack R. Eibhlin & Her Dragon, 1 vol. 2009. 131p. pap. 24.95 *(978-1-60749-634-2(8))* America Star Bks.

Sperring, Mark. The Sunflower Sword. Latimer, Miriam, illus. 2011. (Andersen Press Picture Bks). (ENG.). 32p. (J). (gr.

-1-3). 16.95 *(978-0-7613-7486-2(8))* Lerner Publishing Group.

Springett, Martin. Breakfast on a Dragon's Tail: And Other Book Bites. 2011. (ENG.). 32p. (J). *(978-1-55455-200-9(1))* Fitzhenry & Whiteside, Ltd.

St. Aubin, Anne. Drafus the Daring Dragon. 2008. 24p. pap. 16.49 *(978-1-4343-8875-9(1))* AuthorHouse.

St. John, Justine. Wilbur the Zucchini-Eating Dragon. 2012. (ENG., Illus.). 24p. (J). pap. 9.99 *(978-0-9829256-3-8(8))* SDP Publishing.

Stanek, Robert, pseud. In the Service of Dragons. 2007. (ENG., Illus.). 280p. (YA). 19.99 *(978-1-57545-134-3(4))* RP Media.

—In the Service of Dragons: Keeper Martin's Tales, Book 5. 2005. 252p. (YA). (gr. 4-9). pap. 14.00 *(978-1-57545-089-6(5))* RP Media.

—In the Service of Dragons II. 2007. (ENG., Illus.). 284p. (YA). 19.99 *(978-1-57545-135-0(2))* RP Media.

—In the Service of Dragons II: Keeper Martin's Tales, Book 6. 2005. (Illus.). 256p. (YA). (gr. 4-9). pap. 14.00 *(978-1-57545-090-2(9))* RP Media.

—In the Service of Dragons III. 2007. (ENG., Illus.). 268p. (YA). 19.99 *(978-1-57545-136-7(0))* RP Media.

—In the Service of Dragons IV. 2007. 264p. (YA). 19.99 *(978-1-57545-137-4(9))* RP Media.

—In the Service of Dragons IV: Keeper Martin's Tales, Book 8. 2006. (ENG.). 180p. (YA). (gr. 8-12). per. 11.25 *(978-1-57545-119-0(0),* Reagent Pr. Echo) RP Media.

—The Kingdoms & the Elves of the Reaches: Signature, Keeper Martin's Tales, Bk. 1. 2007. (Illus.). 240p. (YA). 35.00 *(978-1-57545-128-2(X))* RP Media.

—The Kingdoms & the Elves of the Reaches II: Signature, Keeper Martin's Tales, Bk. 2. 2007. (Illus.). 244p. (J). (gr. 4-7). 35.00 *(978-1-57545-129-9(8))* RP Media.

Stanford, K. B. Sixteen Wishes (paperback) 2008. 188p. pap. 15.47 *(978-1-4357-1773-2(2))* Lulu Pr., Inc.

Steer, Dugald A. The Dragon Diary, Vol. 2. Carrel, Douglas, illus. 2010. (Ologies Ser.: Vol. 2). (ENG.). 272p. (J). (gr. 4-7). pap. 7.99 *(978-0-7636-4514-4(1))* Candlewick Pr.

Stef. Be Careful What You Wish For. 2008. 380p. 29.99 *(978-1-4363-5233-8(9));* pap. 19.99 *(978-1-4363-5232-1(0))* Xlibris Corp.

Steinlage, Ben. Bird Boy. 2011. 290p. pap. 17.95 *(978-1-4327-6667-2(8))* Outskirts Pr., Inc.

Steps To Literacy Staff, compiled by. Eragon/Eldest Box Set: Variety Pack (2 Titles, 1 Each) 2010. (ENG.). (J). pap. 23.85 *(978-1-61267-194-9(2))* Steps To Literacy, LLC.

Stewart, Joel. Dexter Bexley & the Big Blue Beastie on the Road. 2010. (ENG., Illus.). 32p. (J). (gr. -1-3). pap. 16.95 *(978-0-8234-2292-0(5))* Holiday Hse., Inc.

Stewart, Justus. Kyle Oaks: A Traitor on Nighta. 2007. 144p. per. 11.95 *(978-0-595-47708-1(9))* iUniverse, Inc.

Stewart, Paul & Riddell, Chris. The Bone Trail. 2013. (Wyrmeweald Trilogy Ser.: 3). (ENG.). 384p. (YA). (gr. 9-12). pap. 16.99 *(978-1-4804-1611-6(8),* Open Road Media E-riginal) Open Road Integrated Media, Inc.

—Dragon's Hoard. Riddell, Chris, illus. 2014. (Knight's Story Ser.: 3). (ENG., Illus.). 144p. (J). (gr. 2-6). pap. 13.99 *(978-1-4814-2890-3(X),* Atheneum Bks. for Young Readers) Simon & Schuster Children's Publishing.

—Returner's Wealth. 2013. (Wyrmeweald Trilogy Ser.: 1). (ENG.). 374p. (YA). (gr. 9-12). pap. 14.99 *(978-1-4804-1610-9(X),* Open Road Media E-riginal) Open Road Integrated Media, Inc.

Stiles, Gannett Ruth. My Father's Dragon. 2014. (My Father's Dragon Ser.). (ENG.). 96p. (J). (gr. 4-7). 11.24 *(978-1-63245-265-8(0))* Lectorum Pubns., Inc.

Stilton, Geronimo. The Dragon of Fortune: An Epic Kingdom of Fantasy Adventure. 2017. (Geronimo Stilton & the Kingdom of Fantasy Ser.: 2). (ENG.). 592p. (J). (gr. 2-5). 19.99 ***(978-1-338-15939-4(9),*** Scholastic Paperbacks) Scholastic, Inc.

—The Dragon Prophecy. 2012. (Geronimo Stilton & the Kingdom of Fantasy Ser.: Bk. 4). (ENG.). 320p. (J). (gr. 2-5). 14.99 *(978-0-545-39351-5(5),* Scholastic Paperbacks) Scholastic, Inc.

—The Quest for Paradise. 2010. (Geronimo Stilton & the Kingdom of Fantasy Ser.: 2). (ENG.). 320p. (J). (gr. 2-5). 14.99 *(978-0-545-25307-9(1))* Scholastic, Inc.

Stilton, Geronimo & Geronimo Stilton Staff. Attack of the Dragons. 2016. (Geronimo Stilton Micekings Ser.: 1). (ENG.). 128p. (J). (gr. 2-5). pap. 6.99 *(978-0-545-87238-6(3),* Scholastic Paperbacks) Scholastic, Inc.

Storm, Falcon. The Persnickety Princess (Tales from upon A. Time - Book 1) l.t. ed. 2013. (ENG.). 94p. pap. 9.95 *(978-1-62253-047-2(0))* Evolved Publishing.

Strickland, Brad. Dragon's Plunder. 2011. (ENG., Illus.). 160p. (J). (gr. -1-12). pap. 9.95 *(978-1-59687-391-9(4))* IBks., Inc.

Stroud, Jonathan. Buried Fire. 2004. 332p. (J). pap. *(978-0-7818-5794-9(5))* Hippocrene Bks., Inc.

Style Guide Staff, illus. Gift of the Night Fury. 2014. (How to Train Your Dragon TV Ser.). (ENG.). 24p. (J). (gr. -1-2). pap. 3.99 *(978-1-4814-0436-5(9),* Simon Spotlight) Simon Spotlight.

—How to Build a Dragon Fort. 2016. (How to Train Your Dragon TV Ser.). (ENG.). 32p. (J). (gr. k-2). pap. 3.99 *(978-1-4814-5215-1(0),* Simon Spotlight) Simon Spotlight.

Style Guide, Style, illus. The Dragon Games. 2015. (How to Train Your Dragon TV Ser.). (ENG.). 24p. (J). (gr. -1-3). pap. 3.99 *(978-1-4814-3288-7(5),* Simon Spotlight) Simon Spotlight.

—A Fiery Discovery. 2015. (How to Train Your Dragon TV Ser.). (ENG.). 24p. (J). (gr. -1-3). pap. 3.99 *(978-1-4814-2768-5(7),* Simon Spotlight) Simon Spotlight.

—How to Defend Your Dragon. 2015. (How to Train Your Dragon TV Ser.). (ENG.). 32p. (J). (gr. k-2). pap. 3.99 *(978-1-4814-3710-3(0),* Simon Spotlight) Simon Spotlight.

Summers, Portia & Rau, Dana Meachen. Are Dragons Real? 2016. (I Want to Know Ser.). (Illus.). 32p. (J). pap. 10.52 *(978-0-7660-8232-8(6))* Enslow Pubs., Inc.

Sunday, Bonnie. Sparkles, Dragons, & Dragonfly Land. 2012. 32p. pap. 19.99 *(978-1-4772-2914-9(0))* AuthorHouse.

Sutherland, Tui T. The Brightest Night. (Wings of Fire Ser.: Bk. 5). (ENG.). 336p. (J). (gr. 3-7). 2015. pap. 6.99 *(978-0-545-34927-7(3),* Scholastic Paperbacks) 2014. (Illus.). 16.99 *(978-0-545-34922-2(2),* Scholastic Pr.) Scholastic, Inc.

—The Dark Secret. (Wings of Fire Ser.: 4). (ENG.). 336p. (J). (gr. 3-7). 2014. pap. 6.99 *(978-0-545-34926-0(5))* 2013. (Illus.). 16.99 *(978-0-545-34921-5(4))* Scholastic, Inc. (Scholastic Pr.).

—The Dark Secret. 2014. (Wings of Fire Ser.: 4). lib. bdg. 17.20 *(978-0-606-36033-3(6))* Turtleback Bks.

—Darkness of Dragons. 2017. (Wings of Fire Ser.: 10). (ENG.). 432p. (J). (gr. 3-7). 16.99 ***(978-0-545-68547-4(8),*** Scholastic Pr.) Scholastic, Inc.

—Darkstalker. 2016. (Wings of Fire Ser.). (ENG., Illus.). 400p. (J). (gr. 3-7). 17.99 *(978-1-338-05361-6(2),* Scholastic Pr.) Scholastic, Inc.

—The Dragonet Prophecy. (Wings of Fire Ser.: 1). 2013. (ENG.). 336p. (J). (gr. 3-7). pap. 6.99 *(978-0-545-34923-9(0))* 2012. (ENG.). 336p. (J). (gr. 3-7). 16.99 *(978-0-545-34918-5(4))* 2012. (Illus.). 304p. pap. *(978-0-545-48603-3(3))* Scholastic, Inc. (Scholastic Pr.).

—The Dragonet Prophecy. 2013. (Wings of Fire Ser.: 1). lib. bdg. 17.20 *(978-0-606-31952-2(2),* Turtleback) Turtleback Bks.

—Escaping Peril. (Wings of Fire Ser.: 8). (ENG.). 336p. (J). (gr. 3-7). 2017. pap. 6.99 ***(978-0-545-68545-0(1))*** 2015. (Illus.). 16.99 *(978-0-545-68544-3(3))* Scholastic, Inc. (Scholastic Pr.).

—Escaping Peril. 2017. (Wings of Fire Ser.: 8). lib. bdg. 17.20 ***(978-0-606-40142-5(3))*** Turtleback Bks.

—The Hidden Kingdom. (Wings of Fire Ser.: 3). (ENG.). 336p. (J). (gr. 3-7). 2014. pap. 6.99 *(978-0-545-34925-3(7))* 2013. (Illus.). 16.99 *(978-0-545-34920-8(6),* Scholastic Pr.) Scholastic, Inc.

—The Lost Heir. 2013. (Wings of Fire Ser.: 2). (ENG.). 336p. (J). (gr. 3-7). pap. 6.99 *(978-0-545-34924-6(9));* 16.99 *(978-0-545-34919-2(2))* Scholastic, Inc. (Scholastic Pr.).

—The Lost Heir. 2013. (Wings of Fire Ser.: 2). lib. bdg. 17.20 *(978-0-606-32341-3(4),* Turtleback) Turtleback Bks.

—Moon Rising. (Wings of Fire Ser.: 6). (ENG.). 336p. (J). (gr. 3-7). 2016. pap. 6.99 *(978-0-545-68536-8(2))* 2014. 16.99 *(978-0-545-68534-4(6),* Scholastic Pr.) Scholastic, Inc.

—Moon Rising. 2016. (Wings of Fire Ser.: 6). lib. bdg. 17.20 *(978-0-606-38815-3(X))* Turtleback Bks.

—Winter Turning. 2015. (Wings of Fire Ser.: Bk. 7). (ENG., Illus.). 336p. (J). (gr. 3-7). 16.99 *(978-0-545-68537-5(0),* Scholastic Pr.) Scholastic, Inc.

—Winter Turning. 2016. (Wings of Fire Ser.: 7). lib. bdg. 17.20 ***(978-0-606-39706-3(X))*** Turtleback Bks.

Sutherland, Tui T. & Sutherland, Kari. Dragon on Trial. (Menagerie Ser.: 2). (ENG.). (J). (gr. 3-7). 2015. 320p. pap. 6.99 *(978-0-06-085145-3(7))* 2014. 304p. 16.99 *(978-0-06-085143-9(0))* HarperCollins Pubs.

Sutton, Laurie S. Sword of the Dragon, 1 vol. Schoening, Dan, illus. (Wonder Woman Ser.). (ENG.). 56p. (gr. 2-3). 2014. pap. 4.95 *(978-1-4342-2760-7(X))* 2010. 26.65 *(978-1-4342-1979-4(8))* Stone Arch Bks. (DC Super Heroes).

Sykes, Julie. That Pesky Dragon. Williamson, Melanie, illus. 2007. 32p. (J). (gr. -1-3). 15.95 *(978-1-58925-069-7(9))* Tiger Tales.

Tatchell, Judy. Dragons. Scott, Peter David & Furnival, Keith, illus. 2006. (J). *(978-0-439-82790-4(6))* Scholastic, Inc.

Tate Kuelling, Judy. The Hitchhiker. 2009. 20p. pap. 10.49 *(978-1-4389-5144-7(2))* AuthorHouse.

Taylor, Dereen. The Dragon's Magic Wish. Hutchinson, Tim, illus. 2012. (ENG.). 12p. (J). (gr. 1-6). 16.99 *(978-1-84322-856-1(4))* Anness Publishing GBR. Dist: National Bk. Network.

Taylor, Dorothea. There's a Dragon in My Closet. Palmer, Charly, illus. 2017. (Denene Millner Bks.). (ENG.). 32p. (J). (gr. -1-3). 17.95 ***(978-1-57284-227-4(X))*** Agate Publishing, Inc.

Taylor, Jennifer. Dragon Sitter. 2005. 36p. (J). 14.99 *(978-1-4116-6449-4(3))* Lulu Pr., Inc.

Teague, Victoria. Dragons, Demons, & Feathers. 2007. 48p. pap. 19.96 *(978-1-4357-0317-9(0))* Lulu Pr., Inc.

Terri, Branson. Brother Dragon. l.t. ed. 2007. (ENG., Illus.). 24p. (J). 14.99 *(978-0-9787421-9-5(2))* Dragonfly Publishing, Inc.

Testa, Maggie. Gift of the Night Fury. 2014. lib. bdg. 13.55 *(978-0-606-36110-1(3))* Turtleback Bks.

—Guide to the Dragons. Style Guide, Style, illus. 2014. (How to Train Your Dragon TV Ser.: 1). (ENG.). 24p. (J). (gr. -1-2). pap. 8.99 *(978-1-4814-1936-9(6),* Simon Spotlight) Simon Spotlight.

Teves, Miles, illus. The Dragon Hunter's Handbook. 2008. (J). *(978-1-4351-0204-0(5))* Metro Bks.

Thomas, Shelley Moore. Get Well, Good Knight. Plecas, Jennifer, illus. 2004. (Penguin Young Readers, Level 3 Ser.). (ENG.). 48p. (J). (gr. 1-3). 3.99 *(978-0-14-240050-0(5),* Penguin Young Readers) Penguin Young Readers Group.

—Get Well, Good Knight. Plecas, Jennifer, illus. 2004. (Easy-to-Read Ser.). 44p. (gr. k-3). 14.00 *(978-0-7569-2923-7(7))* Perfection Learning Corp.

—Get Well, Good Knight. 2004. (Penguin Young Readers Level 3 Ser.). 13.55 *(978-0-613-97291-8(0),* Turtleback) Turtleback Bks.

—Happy Birthday, Good Knight. Plecas, Jennifer, illus. 2014. (Penguin Young Readers, Level 3 Ser.). (ENG.). 48p. (J). (gr. 1-3). pap. 3.99 *(978-0-448-46374-2(1),* Penguin Young Readers) Penguin Young Readers Group.

—Happy Birthday, Good Knight. 2014. (Penguin Young Readers Level 3 Ser.). lib. bdg. 13.55 *(978-0-606-35728-9(9))* Turtleback Bks.

—This Book Is Not about Dragons. Koehler, Fred, illus. 2016. (ENG.). 32p. (J). (gr. -1-2). 16.95 *(978-1-62979-168-5(7))* Boyds Mills Pr.

Thompson, Jill. Magic Trixie & the Dragon. Thompson, Jill, illus. 2009. (ENG., Illus.). 96p. (J). (gr. 3-7). pap. 7.99 *(978-0-06-117050-8(X))* HarperCollins Pubs.

Thomson, Kate. Dragon of Legends. Mendez, Simon, illus. 2016. (Press Out & Build Ser.). (ENG.). 24p. (J). (gr. 2-6). pap. 19.99 *(978-1-84956-795-4(6))* Top That! Publishing PLC GBR. Dist: Independent Pubs. Group.

Thomson, Sarah L. Dragon's Egg. 2007. (ENG.). 272p. (J). (gr. 3-7). 16.99 *(978-0-06-128848-7(9),* Greenwillow Bks.) HarperCollins Pubs.

Tillworth, Mary. Dragon in the School (Dora & Friends) Goddard, Brenda & Haskett, Dan, illus. 2015. (Little Golden Book Ser.). (ENG.). 24p. (J). (gr. -1-2). 4.99 *(978-0-553-52089-7(X),* Golden Bks.) Random Hse. Children's Bks.

Titan Comics Staff. Underworld, Vol. 6. 2015. (Riders of Berk Ser.). (ENG., Illus.). 64p. (J). (gr. 3-7). pap. 6.99 *(978-1-78276-081-8(4))* Titan Bks. Ltd. GBR. Dist: Penguin Random Hse. LLC.

Toby Forward Staff. Doubleborn. 2015. (Dragonborn Ser.: 3). (ENG.). 336p. (YA). (gr. 5-8). 16.99 *(978-1-61963-528-9(3),* 9781619635289, Bloomsbury USA Childrens) Bloomsbury Publishing USA.

Tomasso, Phillip. King Gauthier & the Little Dragon Slayer. l.t. ed. 2003. (Illus.). 61p. (J). per. *(978-0-9740833-5-3(6))* Port Town Publishing.

Toriyama, Akira. Dragon Ball: Chapter Book, Vol. 9. Toriyama, Akira, illus. 2010. (ENG., Illus.). 80p. (J). pap. 4.99 *(978-1-4215-3125-0(9))* Viz Media.

—Strongest under the Heavens. Toriyama, Akira, illus. 2010. (Dragon Ball Ser.: 10). (ENG., Illus.). 80p. (J). pap. 4.99 *(978-1-4215-3126-7(7))* Viz Media.

Torres, J. The Case of the Fractured Fairy Tale, 1 vol. Barberi, Carlo & Beatty, Terry, illus. 2013. (Batman: the Brave & the Bold Ser.). (ENG.). 32p. (gr. 2-3). 22.60 *(978-1-4342-4705-6(8))* Stone Arch Bks.

Toufexis, George. Demonic Dragons Stickers. 2017. (Dover Stickers Ser.). (ENG., Illus.). 8p. pap. 1.99 *(978-0-486-81563-3(3))* Dover Pubns., Inc.

Towler, Grayson. The Dragon Waking. (ENG.). 288p. (J). (gr. 3-7). 2017. pap. 9.99 ***(978-0-8075-1706-2(2))*** 2016. 14.99 *(978-0-8075-1704-8(6))* Whitman, Albert & Co.

Tucker, Kathy. The Seven Chinese Sisters. Lin, Grace, illus. 2003. (ENG.). 32p. (J). (gr. k-3). per. 6.99 *(978-0-8075-7310-5(8))* Whitman, Albert & Co.

Tucker, Kathy & Hong, Lily Toy. The Seven Chinese Sisters, Bk. 2. Hong, Lily Toy & Lin, Grace, illus. 2010. (Book & DVD Packages with Nutmeg Media Ser.). (ENG.). 4p. (J). (gr. -1-3). 69.95 *(978-0-8075-9984-6(0))* Whitman, Albert & Co.

Tulien, Sean. The Not-So-Deadly Dragon. Cunyat, Pol, illus. 2016. (Thud & Blunder Ser.). (ENG.). 56p. (gr. 2-4). pap. 4.95 *(978-1-4965-3224-4(4));* lib. bdg. 23.99 *(978-1-4965-3220-6(1))* Stone Arch Bks.

Tulien, Sean & Hoena, Blake. The Not-So-Heroic Knight. Cunyat, Pol, illus. 2016. (Thud & Blunder Ser.). (ENG.). 56p. (gr. 2-4). pap. 4.95 *(978-1-4965-3223-7(6));* lib. bdg. 23.99 *(978-1-4965-3219-0(8))* Stone Arch Bks.

Turquoise Class. George's Dragon Adventure. 2012. (Illus.). 24p. pap. 19.82 *(978-1-4772-1427-5(5))* AuthorHouse.

Tysinger, Dona. The Cheyenne Dragon & the Dragonfly. 2011. 52p. (gr. 4-6). pap. 10.99 *(978-1-4634-3032-0(9))* AuthorHouse.

Tyson, Leigh Ann. Good Night, Little Dragons. 2012. (Little Golden Book Ser.). (ENG., Illus.). 24p. (J). (gr. k-k). 4.99 *(978-0-307-92957-0(4),* Golden Bks.) Random Hse. Children's Bks.

Urrea, Lourdes, et al. El Dragon Jines. 2005. (Ediciones Castillo Castillo Del Terror Ser.). (SPA.). (J). (gr. 2-6). pap. 7.95 *(978-970-20-0357-1(1))* Castillo, Ediciones, S. A. de C. V. MEX. Dist: Iaconi, Mariuccia Bk. Imports.

Valente, Catherynne M. The Girl Who Circumnavigated Fairyland in a Ship of Her Own Making. Juan, Ana, illus. 2011. (Fairyland Ser.: 1). (ENG.). 256p. (YA). (gr. 5-9). 16.99 *(978-0-312-64961-6(4),* 9780312649616) Feiwel & Friends.

—The Girl Who Circumnavigated Fairyland in a Ship of Her Own Making. 2012. (CHI & ENG., Illus.). 304p. (J). (gr. 5-8). pap. *(978-986-6026-24-9(8))* Muses Publishing Hse.

—The Girl Who Circumnavigated Fairyland in a Ship of Her Own Making. Juan, Ana, illus. 2012. (Fairyland Ser.: 1). (ENG.). 288p. (YA). (gr. 5-9). pap. 7.99 *(978-1-250-01019-3(5),* 9781250010193) Square Fish.

Valois, Rob & Caravan Studios Staff. Spyro & the Giants. 2013. (Penguin Young Readers Level 3 Ser.). lib. bdg. 13.55 *(978-0-606-31693-4(0),* Turtleback) Turtleback Bks.

Vaughn, Carrie. Voices of Dragons. (ENG.). (YA). (gr. 8). 2011. 336p. pap. 8.99 *(978-0-06-154790-4(5))* 2010. 320p. 16.99 *(978-0-06-179894-8(0))* HarperCollins Pubs. (HarperTeen).

Venable, Colleen A. F. Going, Going, Dragon! 2013. 48p. pap. 14.95 *(978-1-4677-0973-6(5))* Lerner Publishing Group.

—Going, Going, Dragon! Yue, Stephanie, illus. 2013. (Guinea Pig, Pet Shop Private Eye Ser.: 6). (ENG.). 48p. (J). (gr. 2-5). pap. 6.95 *(978-1-4677-0726-8(0));* lib. bdg. 27.93 *(978-0-7613-6009-4(3))* Lerner Publishing Group.

—Going, Going, Dragon! Yue, Stephanie, illus. 2013. (Guinea Pig, Pet Shop Private Eye Ser.: 6). (ENG.). 46p. lib. bdg. 17.15 *(978-0-606-33994-0(9),* Turtleback) Turtleback Bks.

Vernon, Ursula. Attack of the Ninja Frogs. 2nd ed. (Dragonbreath Ser.: 2). (ENG.). 208p. (J). (gr. 3-7). 2012. pap. 6.99 *(978-0-14-242066-9(2),* Puffin Books) 2010. 12.99 *(978-0-8037-3365-7(8),* Dial Bks) Penguin Young Readers Group.

—Attack of the Ninja Frogs. 2012. (Dragonbreath Ser.: 2). lib. bdg. 17.20 *(978-0-606-26666-6(6),* Turtleback) Turtleback Bks.

—The Case of the Toxic Mutants. 2013. (Dragonbreath Ser.: 9). (ENG., Illus.). 208p. (J). (gr. 3-7). 12.99 *(978-0-8037-3847-8(1),* Dial Bks) Penguin Young Readers Group.

—Curse of the Were-Wiener. 3rd ed. (Dragonbreath Ser.: 3). (ENG.). 208p. (J). (gr. 3-7). 2014. pap. 6.99 *(978-0-14-751321-2(9),* Puffin Books) 2010. 12.99 *(978-0-8037-3469-2(7),* Dial Bks) Penguin Young Readers Group.

—Curse of the Were-Wiener. 2014. (Dragonbreath Ser.: 3). lib. bdg. 17.20 *(978-0-606-35710-4(6))* Turtleback Bks.

—Dani Bocafuego. la Cueva Del Murcielago Gigante. 2012. (SPA.). 204p. (J). (gr. 4-6). pap. 20.99 *(978-84-246-3599-2(X))* La Galera, S.A. Editorial ESP. Dist: Lectorum Pubns., Inc.

—Dragonbreath. Vernon, Ursula, illus. (Dragonbreath Ser.: 1). (ENG., Illus.). 160p. (J). (gr. 3-7). 2012. pap. 6.99 *(978-0-14-242095-9(6),* Puffin Books) 2009. 12.99 *(978-0-8037-3363-3(1),* Dial Bks) Penguin Young Readers Group.

—Dragonbreath. 2012. (Dragonbreath Ser.: 1). lib. bdg. 17.20 *(978-0-606-26665-9(8),* Turtleback) Turtleback Bks.

—The Frozen Menace. 2016. (Dragonbreath Ser.: 11). (ENG., Illus.). 208p. (J). (gr. 3-7). 12.99 *(978-0-8037-3986-4(9),* Dial Bks) Penguin Young Readers Group.

—Knight-Napped! 2015. (Dragonbreath Ser.: 10). (ENG.). 208p. (J). (gr. 3-7). 12.99 *(978-0-8037-3849-2(8),* Dial Bks) Penguin Young Readers Group.

—Lair of the Bat Monster. 4th ed. (Dragonbreath Ser.: 4). (ENG.). 208p. (J). (gr. 3-7). 2014. pap. 6.99 *(978-0-14-751320-5(0),* Puffin Books) 2011. 12.99 *(978-0-8037-3525-5(1),* Dial Bks) Penguin Young Readers Group.

—Lair of the Bat Monster. 2014. (Dragonbreath Ser.: 4). lib. bdg. 17.20 *(978-0-606-35711-1(4))* Turtleback Bks.

—Nightmare of the Iguana. 2013. (Dragonbreath Ser.: 8). (ENG., Illus.). 208p. (J). (gr. 3-7). 12.99 *(978-0-8037-3846-1(3),* Dial Bks) Penguin Publishing Group.

—No Such Thing as Ghosts. 5th ed. 2011. (Dragonbreath Ser.: 5). (ENG.). 208p. (J). (gr. 3-7). 12.99 *(978-0-8037-3527-9(8),* Dial Bks) Penguin Young Readers Group.

—Revenge of the Horned Bunnies, No. 6. 6th ed. 2012. (Dragonbreath Ser.: 6). (ENG.). 208p. (J). (gr. 3-7). 12.99 *(978-0-8037-3677-1(0),* Dial Bks) Penguin Young Readers Group.

—When Fairies Go Bad, No. 7. 7th ed. 2012. (Dragonbreath Ser.: 7). (ENG.). 208p. (J). (gr. 3-7). 12.99 *(978-0-8037-3678-8(9),* Dial Bks) Penguin Young Readers Group.

Vincent, Patti. The Village Heroes Meet the Dragon. 2008. 44p. pap. 19.95 *(978-1-4389-1764-1(3))* AuthorHouse.

Vyvyan, Taylor. A Dragon's Odyssey. 2012. 120p. pap. *(978-1-78281-021-6(8))* Athena Pr.

Wacker, Eileen. Black Tortoise & the Dynasty Dragon. Low, Alan M., illus. 2012. (Fujimini Adventure Ser.: Vol. 5). (ENG.). 40p. (J). (gr. -1-3). 10.99 *(978-1-4675-1741-6(0))* Oncekids.

Waddilove, Guy. Dancing with the Dragleon. 2013. (Illus.). 222p. pap. *(978-1-78036-196-3(3))* Peach Publishing.

Wallace, Karen. Dragon Hunt, 1 vol. Baines, Nigel, illus. 2013. (Start Reading Ser.). (ENG.). 24p. (gr. k-1). pap. 7.95 *(978-1-4765-4095-5(0))* Capstone Press of Coughlan Cos.

Waltz, Dan. Dragon Fly: A Gnome's Great Adventure. Waltz, Dan, illus. 2007. (Illus.). 360p. (YA). per. 12.49 *(978-0-9741774-7-2(4))* D. W. Publishing.

Ward, Joshua. Eric the Dragon: Gr... Atchoooo!! Dragon Flu! 2012. (Illus.). 20p. pap. 19.82 *(978-1-4772-2712-1(1))* AuthorHouse.

Warden, John. The Chronicles of Zabaduk. 2009. 116p. pap. 13.53 *(978-1-4251-6488-1(9))* Trafford Publishing.

Waring, Rob. Cupid the Dolphin (US) 2008. (Footprint Reading Library: Level 4 Ser.). (ENG.). 32p. (C). pap. 15.95 *(978-1-4240-4463-4(4))* Cengage Heinle.

Watson, M. Desmond & the Challenge on Mudwig Mountain. 2005. 109p. pap. *(978-1-84401-010-3(4))* Athena Pr.

Watt, Fiona. Hide-and-Seek Dragons. Fiorin, Fabiano, illus. 2007. (Touchy-Feely Flap Bks). 10p. (J). (gr. -1-k). bds. 16.99 *(978-0-7945-1590-4(8),* Usborne) EDC Publishing.

—That's Not My Dragon... Wells, Rachel, illus. 2006. (Usborne Touchy-Feely Bks.). 10p. (J). (gr. -1-k). bds. 7.99 *(978-0-7945-1285-9(2),* Usborne) EDC Publishing.

Wealth, Viktoria. Aadom Kingdom of the Dragons' Light: Book-I. 2003. 214p. (YA). pap. 14.95 *(978-0-595-28175-6(3))* iUniverse, Inc.

Webb, Rita. Tears. 2012. 350p. pap. 12.99 *(978-0-615-51355-3(7))* Robot Playground, Inc.

Webster, Christy. Bath Party! Random House Editors & VanTuyle, David, illus. 2015. (Step into Reading Ser.). (ENG.). 24p. (J). (gr. -1-1). pap. 4.99 *(978-0-385-38767-5(9),* Random Hse. Bks. for Young Readers) Random Hse. Children's Bks.

Weiss, Bobbi & Weiss, David. Hiro Dragon Warrior: Battle at Mount Kamado. Short, Robbie, illus. 2008. (ENG.). 24p. (J). (gr. 1-17). pap. 3.99 *(978-1-58476-721-3(9))* Innovative Kids.

—Hiro: Dragon Warrior: Level 2. Short, Robbie, illus. 2007. (ENG.). 24p. (J). (gr. 1-4). per. 3.99 *(978-1-58476-616-2(6),* IKIDS) Innovative Kids.

Welch, Laura. Dragons at Play. 2011. 16p. (gr. 1-2). 9.36 *(978-1-4567-6354-1(7))* AuthorHouse.

Wenzel, Terri. A Dragon Called Leona. 2012. (ENG.). (J). pap. 5.99 *(978-1-4675-4062-9(5))* Independent Pub.

West, David, illus. The Illustrated Guide to Mythical Creatures. 2009. 48p. (J). (gr. 5-18). pap. 15.99 *(978-0-8437-1669-6(X))* Hammond World Atlas Corp.

West, Tracey. Flight of the Moon Dragon. Jones, Damien, illus. 2016. (Dragon Masters Ser.: 6). (ENG.). 96p. (J). (gr. 1-3). pap. 4.99 *(978-0-545-91392-8(6))* Scholastic, Inc.

—Flight of the Moon Dragon: a Branches Book. Jones, Damien, illus. 2016. (Dragon Masters Ser.: 6). (ENG.). 96p. (J). (gr. 1-3). 14.75 *(978-0-606-39155-9(X))* Turtleback Bks.

—Power of the Fire Dragon. Howells, Graham, illus. 2015. (Dragon Masters Ser.: No. 4). (ENG.). 96p. (J). (gr. 1-3). pap. 4.99 *(978-0-545-64631-4(6))* Scholastic, Inc.

—Rise of the Earth Dragon. Howells, Graham, illus. 2014. (Dragon Masters Ser.: 1). (ENG.). 96p. (J). (gr. 1-3). 15.99 *(978-0-545-64624-6(3));* pap. 4.99 *(978-0-545-64623-9(5))* Scholastic, Inc.

—Rise of the Earth Dragon. 2014. (Dragon Masters Ser.: 1). lib. bdg. 14.75 *(978-0-606-36050-0(6))* Turtleback Bks.

—Roar of the Thunder Dragon: a Branches Book. Jones, Damien, illus. 2017. (Dragon Masters Ser.: 8). (ENG.). 96p. (J). (gr. 1-3). lib. bdg. 15.99 ***(978-1-338-04293-1(9));*** pap. 4.99 ***(978-1-338-04292-4(0))*** Scholastic, Inc.

—Saving the Sun Dragon. Howells, Graham & Jones, Damien, illus. 2014. (Dragon Masters Ser.: 2). (ENG.). 96p. (J). (gr. 1-3). 15.99 *(978-0-545-64626-0(X));* pap. 4.99 *(978-0-545-64625-3(1))* Scholastic, Inc.

—Saving the Sun Dragon. 2014. (Dragon Masters Ser.: 2). lib. bdg. 14.75 *(978-0-606-36051-7(4))* Turtleback Bks.

—Search for the Lightning Dragon. 2017. (Dragon Masters Ser.: 7). lib. bdg. 14.75 ***(978-0-606-39713-1(2))*** Turtleback Bks.

—Search for the Lightning Dragon: a Branches Book (Dragon Masters #7) Jones, Damien, illus. 2017. (Dragon Masters Ser.: 7). (ENG.). 96p. (J). (gr. 1-3). pap. 4.99 *(978-1-338-04288-7(2))* Scholastic, Inc.

—Secret of the Water Dragon. Howells, Graham & Jones, Damien, illus. 2015. (Dragon Masters Ser.: 3). (ENG.). 96p. (J). (gr. 1-3). pap. 4.99 *(978-0-545-64628-4(6))* Scholastic, Inc.

C
D

—Song of the Poison Dragon. 2016. (Dragon Masters Ser.: 5). lib. bdg. 14.75 *(978-0-606-38808-5(7))* Turtleback Bks.

—Song of the Poison Dragon: a Branches Book (Dragon Masters #5) Jones, Damien, illus. 2016. (Dragon Masters Ser.: 5). (ENG.). 96p. (J). (gr. 1-3). pap. 4.99 *(978-0-545-91387-4(X))* Scholastic, Inc.

What Flies Beneath. 2014. (How to Train Your Dragon TV Ser.). (ENG., Illus.). 16p. (J). (gr. -1-2). pap. 5.99 *(978-1-4814-2191-1(3),* Simon Spotlight) Simon Spotlight.

White, Wade Albert. The Adventurer's Guide to Dragons (and Why They Keep Biting Me) 2017. (Adventurer's Guide Ser.: 2). (ENG.). 384p. (J). (gr. 3-7). 16.99 ***(978-0-316-30531-0(6))*** Little, Brown Bks. for Young Readers.

Wiggins, Bethany. The Dragon's Price (a Transference Novel) 2017. (Transference Trilogy Ser.: 1). (ENG.). 304p. (YA). (gr. 7). 17.99 *(978-0-399-54981-6(1),* Crown Books For Young Readers) Random Hse. Children's Bks.

Wilcox, Jean A. Diary of Sir Winston Loki, 1 vol. 2010. 34p. 24.95 *(978-1-4512-1813-8(3))* PublishAmerica, Inc.

Wilder, Adrienne. Dragon Unlikely. 2007. 244p. (YA). per. 11.95 *(978-0-9797759-1-8(4))* PageMaster Publishing.

Wilkins, Phil Cole. Dragog & the Seven Weeks of Summer. 2012. 164p. (gr. -1). pap. 15.60 *(978-1-4567-8998-5(8))* AuthorHouse.

Wilkinson, James H. Yang the Dragon Tells His Story, Halloween Train. Blake, Carol, illus. 2013. 32p. pap. 15.99 *(978-0-9886360-0-2(X))* Kids At Heart Publishing, LLC.

Williams, David Morgan. Xcalibur, Merlin & the Teeth of the Dragon. 2015. (ENG.). 160p. (J). pap. 13.00 *(978-1-84771-823-5(X))* Y Lolfa GBR. Dist: Dufour Editions, Inc.

Williams, Lee. Twin Dragons. Johnson, Tamaris, illus. 2012. 32p. (J). 8.99 *(978-1-937493-18-9(0))* Dancing Moon Pr.

Wilson, A. c. & Wilson, A. C. Ambersil - the Legacy of Mr Harrison. 2011. 496p. pap. *(978-1-908105-45-5(3))* Grosvenor Hse. Publishing Ltd.

Wilson, Wendy. The First Book of Red. 2005. 99p. pap. 19.95 *(978-1-4137-5570-1(4))* America Star Bks.

Winkler, Ashley & Winkler, Michael. One Good Quest Deserves Another: A Crown of Amaranth Story. 2009. 292p. 28.95 *(978-0-595-71039-3(5));* pap. 18.95 *(978-0-595-47365-6(2))* iUniverse, Inc.

Wisbauer, Cortney. Rodney, the Ice Dragon. Wisbauer, Cortney, illus. 2006. (Illus.). 48p. (J). 22.95 *(978-1-59879-215-7(6))* Lifevest Publishing, Inc.

Witschen, Kay. Clinker's Dragon. 2006. (J). 6.95 *(978-0-9741352-2-9(4))* Dwitt Publishing.

Wojtowycz, David, illus. Elephant Joe, Brave Firefighter! 2015. (Step into Reading Ser.). (ENG.). 32p. (J). (gr. -1-1). 12.99 *(978-0-375-97203-4(X),* Random Hse. Bks. for Young Readers) Random Hse. Children's Bks.

Wolfe, Carolyn. The Unhappy Little Dragon: Lessons Begin. Mathis, Leslie, illus. 2009. 38p. pap. 12.99 *(978-1-935105-42-8(6))* Avid Readers Publishing Group.

Wong, Benedict Norbert. Lo & Behold. Wong, Benedict Norbert, illus. l.t. ed. 2003. (Illus.). 38p. (gr. 1-18). 16.95 *(978-0-9728192-0-6(7),* LOBE) Taiji Arts Publishing.

—Lo & Behold: A Boy & His Dragon. 2004. (Illus.). 44p. (J). (gr. 1-12). 8.95 *(978-0-9728192-4-4(X))* Taiji Arts Publishing.

—Lo & Behold: Good Enough to Eat. Wong, Benedict Norbert, illus. l.t. ed. 2003. (Illus.). 40p. (J). (gr. 1-12). 16.95 *(978-0-9728192-1-3(5),* 1002LB) Taiji Arts Publishing.

—Lo & Behold: The Millennia Just Roll By. 2004. (Illus.). 40p. (J). (gr. 1-12). 16.95 *(978-0-9728192-3-7(1))* Taiji Arts Publishing.

Wood, Audrey. The Princess & the Dragon. 2010. (Child's Play Library). (ENG., Illus.). 32p. (J). audio compact disk *(978-1-84643-362-7(2))* Child's Play International Ltd.

—The Princess & the Dragon. 2003. (Child's Play Library). (ENG., Illus.). 10p. (J). *(978-0-85953-717-9(X))* Child's Play International Ltd.

—Princess, the Dragon & Scaredy Cats. (J). audio *(978-0-85953-375-1(1))* Child's Play International Ltd.

Woodberry, Gareth. Gakeva Gluntok's New School. 2005. 65p. pap. 16.95 *(978-1-4137-9894-4(2))* PublishAmerica, Inc.

Wrede, Patricia C. Searching for Dragons. unabr. ed. 2004. (Enchanted Forest Chronicles: Bk. 2). 242p. (J). (gr. 5-18). pap. 38.00 incl. audio *(978-0-8072-0670-6(9),* Listening Library) Random Hse. Audio Publishing Group.

Wrede, Patricia C. & Wrede, Patricia. Dealing with Dragons. 2015. (Enchanted Forest Chronicles Ser.: Bk. 1). (gr. 7-12). lib. bdg. 18.40 *(978-0-613-56300-0(X),* Turtleback) Turtleback Bks.

Wright, S. B. Lissa Discovers the Secrets of the Castle, 1 vol. 2010. 62p. pap. 19.95 *(978-1-4489-9692-6(9))* America Star Bks.

Wynn, Thad & Wynn, Juliette. The Tale of a Dragon. 2004. (Illus.). 85p. (gr. k-4). 15.95 *(978-1-57197-140-1(8))* Pentland Pr., Inc.

Xiong, Kim, illus. The Dragon Tribe. 2008. (ENG & CHI.). 33p. (J). 18.95 *(978-1-60603-000-4(0))* Better Chinese LLC.

Yarrow, Peter & Lipton, Lenny. Puff, the Magic Dragon. Puybaret, Eric, illus. 2007. (ENG.). 24p. (J). 16.95 *(978-1-4027-5219-3(9));* 16.95 *(978-1-4027-5279-7(2))* Sterling Publishing Co., Inc.

—Puff, the Magic Dragon Pop-Up. Puybaret, Eric, illus. 2011. (ENG.). 14p. (J). (gr. 1). 26.95 *(978-1-4027-8711-9(1))* Sterling Publishing Co., Inc.

Yep, Laurence. City of Death. 2013. (City Trilogy Ser.: 3). (ENG.). 384p. (J). (gr. 3-7). 17.99 *(978-0-7653-1926-5(8),* 9780765319265, Starscape) Doherty, Tom Assocs., LLC.

—Tiger's Blood. 2005. (Tiger's Apprentice Ser.: Bk. 2). (ENG.). 240p. (J). (gr. 5-18). 15.99 *(978-0-06-001016-4(9))* HarperCollins Pubs.

Yep, Laurence & Ryder, Joanne. A Dragon's Guide to Making Perfect Wishes. 2017. (Dragon's Guide Ser.: 3). (ENG.). 240p. (J). (gr. 3-7). 16.99 *(978-0-385-39236-5(2),* Crown Books For Young Readers) Random Hse. Children's Bks.

—A Dragon's Guide to Making Your Human Smarter. GrandPré, Mary, illus. 2016. (Dragon's Guide Ser.). (ENG.). 304p. (J). (gr. 3-7). 16.99 *(978-0-385-39232-7(X),* Crown Books For Young Readers) Random Hse. Children's Bks.

—A Dragon's Guide to the Care & Feeding of Humans. GrandPré, Mary, illus. 2015. (Dragon's Guide Ser.). (ENG.). 160p. (J). (gr. 3-7). 15.99 *(978-0-385-39228-0(1),* Crown Books For Young Readers) Random Hse. Children's Bks.

Yolen, Jane. Dragon's Blood. 2004. (Pit Dragon Chronicles Ser.: 1). (ENG., Illus.). 320p. (YA). (gr. 7-12). pap. 7.99 *(978-0-15-205126-6(0))* Houghton Mifflin Harcourt Publishing Co.

—Dragon's Heart. Schmidt, Jonathon, ed. 2011. (Pit Dragon Chronicles Ser.: 4). (ENG.). 400p. (YA). (gr. 7). pap. 8.99 *(978-0-547-39862-4(X))* Houghton Mifflin Harcourt Publishing Co.

—Heart's Blood, Vol. 2. 2004. (Pit Dragon Chronicles Ser.: 2). (ENG., Illus.). 368p. (YA). (gr. 7-12). pap. 7.99 *(978-0-15-205118-1(X))* Houghton Mifflin Harcourt Publishing Co.

—The Last Dragon. Guay, Rebecca, illus. 2011. (ENG.). 144p. (J). (gr. 7-7). pap. 29.99 *(978-1-59582-798-2(6))* Dark Horse Comics.

—The Last Dragon. Guay, Rebecca, illus. 2016. (ENG.). 144p. (J). (gr. 3-7). pap. 12.99 *(978-1-61655-874-1(1))* Dark Horse Comics.

—A Sending of Dragons Vol. 3. 2004. (Pit Dragon Chronicles Ser.: 3). (ENG., Illus.). 320p. (YA). (gr. 7-12). pap. 8.99 *(978-0-15-205128-0(7))* Houghton Mifflin Harcourt Publishing Co.

—Waking Dragons. Anderson, Derek, illus. 2012. (ENG.). 32p. (J). (gr. -1-3). 16.99 *(978-1-4169-9032-1(1),* Simon & Schuster Bks. For Young Readers) Simon & Schuster Bks. For Young Readers.

Young, Julie. The Defeat of Gullvieg: Dragon Cliff Trilogy, Book Three. 2012. 132p. (gr. 4-6). pap. 11.95 *(978-1-4759-2585-2(9))* iUniverse, Inc.

Zanzonico, Gaetana. A Magical Dream. 2011. 52p. pap. 31.99 *(978-1-4568-1562-2(8))* Xlibris Corp.

Zee, Amy Van. The Constellation Draco: The Story of the Dragon. Morrow, J. T., illus. 2013. (Constellations Ser.). (ENG.). 32p. (J). (gr. 2-5). 29.93 *(978-1-62323-485-0(9),* 206253) Child's World, Inc., The.

Zimmermann, Andreas. Shard. 2012. 302p. 28.95 *(978-1-4620-8351-0(X));* pap. 18.95 *(978-1-4620-8350-3(1))* iUniverse, Inc.

Zub, Jim. Figment: Journey into Imagination. 2016. (Figment: Journey into Imagination Ser.: 5). (ENG.). 24p. (J). (gr. k-5). lib. bdg. 121.05 *(978-1-61479-444-8(8),* Graphic Planet) Magic Wagon.

—Figment: Journey into Imagination: Volume 1, 1 vol. 2016. (Figment: Journey into Imagination Ser.). (ENG., Illus.). 24p. (J). (gr. k-5). lib. bdg. 24.21 *(978-1-61479-445-5(6),* Graphic Planet) Magic Wagon.

—Figment: Journey into Imagination: Volume 2, 1 vol. 2016. (Figment: Journey into Imagination Ser.). (ENG., Illus.). 24p. (J). (gr. k-5). lib. bdg. 24.21 *(978-1-61479-446-2(4),* Graphic Planet) Magic Wagon.

—Figment: Journey into Imagination: Volume 3, 1 vol. 2016. (Figment: Journey into Imagination Ser.). (ENG., Illus.). 24p. (J). (gr. k-5). lib. bdg. 24.21 *(978-1-61479-447-9(2),* Graphic Planet) Magic Wagon.

—Figment: Journey into Imagination: Volume 4, 1 vol. 2016. (Figment: Journey into Imagination Ser.). (ENG., Illus.). 24p. (J). (gr. k-5). lib. bdg. 24.21 *(978-1-61479-448-6(0),* Graphic Planet) Magic Wagon.

—Figment: Journey into Imagination: Volume 5, 1 vol. 2016. (Figment: Journey into Imagination Ser.). (ENG., Illus.). 24p. (J). (gr. k-5). lib. bdg. 24.21 *(978-1-61479-449-3(9),* Graphic Planet) Magic Wagon.

DRAKE, FRANCIS, SIR, 1540?-1596

Courtauld, Sarah. The Queen's Pirate - Francis Drake. Dutrait, Vincent, illus. 2008. (Usborne Young Reading: Series Three Ser.). 64p. (J). 8.99 *(978-0-7945-2048-9(0),* Usborne) EDC Publishing.

Crompton, Samuel Willard. Francis Drake & the Oceans of the World. Goetzmann, William H., ed. 2005. (Explorers of New Worlds Ser.). (Illus.). 160p. (J). (gr. 5-8). lib. bdg. 30.00 *(978-0-7910-8615-5(1))* Facts On File, Inc.

Guy, John. Drake & the Elizabethan Explorers. 2010. (History of Exploration Ser.). 48p. 32.80 *(978-1-84898-304-5(2))* Black Rabbit Bks.

Hoogenboom, Lynn. Sir Francis Drake. 2009. (Primary Source Library of Famous Explorers Ser.). 24p. (gr. 4-4). 42.50 *(978-1-60854-131-7(2),* PowerKids Pr.) Rosen Publishing Group, Inc., The.

—Sir Francis Drake: A Primary Source Biography. 2006. (Primary Source Library of Famous Explorers Ser.). (Illus.). 24p. (YA). (gr. 2-5). lib. bdg. 22.60 *(978-1-4042-3035-4(1))* Rosen Publishing Group, Inc., The.

Krasner, Barbara. Sir Francis Drake. 2016. (Spotlight on Explorers & Colonization Ser.). 00048p. (J). (gr. 6-6). pap. 11.75 *(978-1-5081-7218-5(8))* Rosen Publishing Group, Inc., The.

Lace, William W. Sir Francis Drake. 2009. (Great Explorers Ser.). (Illus.). 112p. (gr. 6-12). 30.00 *(978-1-60413-417-9(8),* Chelsea Hse.) Facts On File, Inc.

Nick, Charles. Sir Francis Drake: Slave Trader & Pirate. 2010. (ENG., Illus.). 128p. (C). (gr. 6-12). pap. 9.95 *(978-0-531-20740-6(4))* National Geographic School Publishing, Inc.

—Sir Francis Drake: Slave Trader & Pirate. 2009. (Wicked History Ser.). (ENG., Illus.). 128p. (J). (gr. 6-12). 31.00 *(978-0-531-21800-6(7),* Watts, Franklin) Scholastic Library Publishing.

Sheehan, Robert. Francis Drake: Patriot or Pirate? 2013. (Discovery Education: Sensational True Stories Ser.). (ENG., Illus.). 32p. (J). (gr. 3-6). pap. 10.00 *(978-1-4777-0105-8(2));* lib. bdg. 25.25 *(978-1-4777-0060-0(9))* Rosen Publishing Group, Inc., The. (PowerKids Pr.).

Sir Francis Drake. 2013. 56p. 15.95 *(978-0-9897533-0-2(1))* Croce, Pat & Co.

Stewart, David. You Wouldn't Want to Explore with Sir Francis Drake! A Pirate You'd Rather Not Know. Antram, David, illus. 2005. (You Wouldn't Want to... Ser.). (ENG.). 32p. (J). (gr. 2-5). 29.00 *(978-0-531-12413-0(4));* pap. 9.95 *(978-0-531-12393-5(6))* Scholastic Library Publishing. (Watts, Franklin).

DRAKE, FRANCIS, SIR, 1540?-1596—FICTION

Henty, George Alfred. Under Drake's Flag: A Tale of the Spanish Main. 2007. (ENG.). 290p. pap. 21.99 *(978-1-4346-3056-8(0));* 322p. pap. 24.99 *(978-1-4346-3070-4(6))* Creative Media Partners, LLC.

—Under Drake's Flag: A Tale of the Spanish Main. 2011. 316p. pap. 19.95 *(978-1-61179-182-2(0))* Fireship Pr.

Jarman, Julia. Stowaway? Oldroyd, Mark, illus. 2007. (Collins Big Cat Ser.). (ENG.). 48p. (J). (gr. 3-4). pap. 8.99 *(978-0-00-723088-4(5))* HarperCollins Pubs. Ltd. GBR. Dist: Independent Pubs. Group.

Lacey, Josh. Island of Thieves. 2013. (ENG.). 240p. (J). (gr. 5-7). pap. 7.99 *(978-0-544-10485-3(4))* Houghton Mifflin Harcourt Publishing Co.

Lacey, Josh & Pakenham, Sarah. Island of Thieves. 2012. (ENG.). 240p. (J). (gr. 5-7). 15.99 *(978-0-547-76327-9(1))* Houghton Mifflin Harcourt Publishing Co.

DRAMA—COLLECTIONS

see also American Drama—Collections; Christmas Plays

Foxton, David. Sepia & Song. 10th ed. 2003. (Drama Anthologies Ser.). (Illus.). 148p. (Orig.). (YA). (gr. 6-12). pap. 15.00 *(978-0-333-40923-7(X))* Macmillan Education, Ltd. GBR. Dist: Players Pr., Inc.

Garrett, Dan, ed. Friends & Neighbors. 11th ed. 2003. (Drama Workshop Plays Ser.). (Illus.). 96p. (Orig.). (YA). (gr. 6-12). pap. 15.00 *(978-0-333-36054-5(0))* Macmillan Education, Ltd. GBR. Dist: Players Pr., Inc.

—Girls. 11th ed. 2003. (Drama Anthologies Ser.). (Illus.). 86p. (Orig.). (YA). pap. 15.00 *(978-0-333-46708-4(6))* Macmillan Education, Ltd. GBR. Dist: Players Pr., Inc.

—Masks & Faces. 11th ed. 2003. (Drama Workshop Plays Ser.). (Illus.). 96p. (Orig.). (YA). (gr. 6-12). pap. 15.00 *(978-0-333-36056-9(7))* Macmillan Education, Ltd. GBR. Dist: Players Pr., Inc.

—Scapegoats. 11th ed. 2003. (Drama Workshop Plays Ser.). (Illus.). 96p. (Orig.). (YA). (gr. 6-12). pap. 15.00 *(978-0-333-36055-2(9))* Macmillan Education, Ltd. GBR. Dist: Players Pr., Inc.

Hezlep, William, ed. Trouble in the Mountains. 2003. (Players Press Classic Plays Ser.). 20p. (J). (gr. 3-8). pap. 7.50 *(978-0-88734-862-4(9))* Players Pr., Inc.

Lambert, Alan & Scott-Hughes, Brian. Junior Drama Workshop. 10th ed. 2003. (Drama Anthologies Ser.). (Illus.). 96p. (Orig.). (YA). (gr. 4-12). pap. 15.00 *(978-0-333-43459-8(5))* Macmillan Education, Ltd. GBR. Dist: Players Pr., Inc.

DRAMA—HISTORY AND CRITICISM

see also American Drama—History and Criticism

Dramentexte Analysieren. (Duden Abiturhilfen Ser.). (GER.). 112p. (YA). (gr. 12-13). *(978-3-411-70131-5(5))* Bibliographisches Institut & F. A. Brockhaus AG DEU. Dist: International Bk. Import Service, Inc.

McDonnell, Kathleen. Putting on a Show: Theater for Young People, 1 vol. 2005. (ENG., Illus.). 226p. (J). (gr. 4-9). pap. 14.95 *(978-1-896764-89-4(4))* Second Story Pr. CAN. Dist: Orca Bk. Pubs. USA.

Pickering, Kenneth. Drama in the Cathedral: The Twentieth Century Encounter of Church & Stage. 2nd ed. 2003. (Illus.). 384p. (J). pap. 25.00 *(978-0-85343-627-0(4))* Miller, J. Garnet Ltd. GBR. Dist: Empire Publishing Service.

DRAMA—STUDY AND TEACHING

McCaslin, Nellie. Children & Drama. Landes, William Alan, ed. 3rd rev. ed. 2003. (Illus.). 288p. (YA). (gr. 8-12). pap. 40.00 *(978-0-88734-662-0(6))* Players Pr., Inc.

DRAMA—TECHNIQUE

Brecke, Nicole & Stockland, Patricia M. Extinct & Endangered Animals You Can Draw. Brecke, Nicole, illus. 2010. (Ready, Set, Draw! Ser.). (ENG., Illus.). 32p. (gr. 2-4). lib. bdg. 25.26 *(978-0-7613-4165-9(X),* Millbrook Pr.) Lerner Publishing Group.

Cobb, Lisa Kaniut. Literary Ideas & Scripts for Young Playwrights, 1 vol. 2004. (Illus.). 192p. (J). pap. 32.00 *(978-1-59158-071-3(4),* LU0714, Libraries Unlimited) ABC-CLIO, LLC.

Elish, Dan. Plays. 2011. (Craft of Writing Ser.). 96p. (gr. 6). 34.21 *(978-1-60870-499-6(8))* Marshall Cavendish Corp.

Guillain, Charlotte. Writing & Staging Adventure Plays. 2016. (Writing & Staging Plays Ser.). (ENG., Illus.). 48p. (gr. 4-6). lib. bdg. 33.32 *(978-1-4846-2770-9(9),* Heinemann InfoSearch) Heinemann-Raintree.

—Writing & Staging Funny Plays. 2016. (Writing & Staging Plays Ser.). (ENG.). 48p. (gr. 4-6). pap. 8.99 *(978-1-4846-2773-0(3));* (Illus.). lib. bdg. 33.32 *(978-1-4846-2769-3(5))* Heinemann-Raintree. (Heinemann InfoSearch).

—Writing & Staging Myths & Legends. 2016. (Writing & Staging Plays Ser.). (ENG., Illus.). 48p. (gr. 4-6). lib. bdg. 33.32 *(978-1-4846-2772-3(5),* Heinemann InfoSearch) Heinemann-Raintree.

—Writing & Staging Plays. 2016. (Writing & Staging Plays Ser.). (ENG.). 48p. (gr. 4-6). 133.28 *(978-1-4846-2785-3(7),* Heinemann InfoSearch) Heinemann-Raintree.

—Writing & Staging Real-Life Plays. 2016. (Writing & Staging Plays Ser.). (ENG., Illus.). 48p. (gr. 4-6). lib. bdg. 33.32 *(978-1-4846-2771-6(7),* Heinemann InfoSearch) Heinemann-Raintree.

Hubbard, Rita Lorraine. Playwriting. 2016. (Exploring Theater Ser.). 96p. (J). lib. bdg. 42.79 *(978-1-5026-2273-0(4))* Cavendish Square Publishing.

Kenney, Karen Latchana. Cool Scripts & Acting: How to Stage Your Very Own Show, 1 vol. 2010. (Cool Performances Ser.). (ENG., Illus.). 32p. (gr. 3-6). 28.50 *(978-1-60453-717-8(5),* Checkerboard Library) ABDO Publishing Co.

Kopp, Megan. How to Write a Drama. 2014. (ENG., Illus.). 32p. (J). *(978-0-7787-1653-2(8))* Crabtree Publishing Co.

Korty, Carol. Writing Your Own Plays: Creating, Adapting, Improvising. 2nd ed. 2003. (Writing & Publishing Ser.). 192p. (YA). (gr. 6-12). pap. 17.00 *(978-0-88734-668-2(5))* Players Pr., Inc.

Krasner, Barbara. 12 Great Tips on Writing a Script. 2017. (Great Tips on Writing Ser.). (ENG.). 32p. (J). (gr. 3-6). 21.95 *(978-1-63235-276-7(1))* Pr. Room Editions LLC.

Loewen, Nancy. Action! Writing Your Own Play, 1 vol. Beacon, Dawn, illus. 2010. (Writer's Toolbox Ser.). (ENG.). 32p. (gr. 2-4). pap. 8.95 *(978-1-4048-6392-7(3));* lib. bdg. 27.32 *(978-1-4048-6017-9(7))* Picture Window Bks.

Minden, Cecilia & Roth, Kate. How to Write a Play. 2012. (Explorer Junior Library: Language Arts Explorer Junior Ser.). (ENG.). 24p. (gr. 1-4). 25.64 *(978-1-61080-490-5(2),* 202100); pap. 12.79 *(978-1-61080-664-0(6),* 202274) Cherry Lake Publishing.

Poets & Playwrights, 5 vols., Set. Incl. Carl Sandburg. Murcia, Rebecca Thatcher. lib. bdg. 37.10 *(978-1-58415-430-3(6));* Emily Dickinson. Griskey, Michele. lib. bdg. 37.10 *(978-1-58415-429-7(2));* Langston Hughes. Gibson, Karen Bush. lib. bdg. 37.10 *(978-1-58415-431-0(4));* Tennessee Williams. Tracy, Kathleen. lib. bdg. 37.10 *(978-1-58415-427-3(6));* William Shakespeare. Whiting, Jim. lib. bdg. 37.10 *(978-1-58415-426-6(8));* (Illus.). 112p. (J). (gr. 3-7). 2007. 2007. Set lib. bdg. 185.50 *(978-1-58415-284-2(2))* Mitchell Lane Pubs., Inc.

Rooyackers, Paul, et al. 101 Dialogues, Sketches & Skits: Instant Theatre for Teens & Tweens. 2014. (SmartFun Activity Bks.). (ENG., Illus.). 144p. (gr. 1). 28.95 *(978-1-63026-927-2(1),* Hunter Hse.) Turner Publishing Co.

Schwartz, Heather E. Steal the Scene: Writing Amazing Drama. 2015. (Writer's Notebook Ser.). (ENG., Illus.). 64p. (gr. 4-5). lib. bdg. 34.65 *(978-1-4914-5988-1(3))* Capstone Press of Coughlan Cos.

Tyler, Barbara A. Picture Yourself Writing Drama: Using Photos to Inspire Writing. 2011. (See It, Write It Ser.). (ENG.). 32p. (gr. 3-4). pap. 47.70 *(978-1-4296-7204-7(8));* lib. bdg. 27.32 *(978-1-4296-6126-3(7))* Capstone Press of Coughlan Cos. (Fact Finders).

DRAMATIC MUSIC

see Opera

DRAMATISTS

Bailey, Gerry & Foster, Karen. Shakespeare's Quill. Radford, Karen & Noyes, Leighton, illus. 2008. (Stories of Great People Ser.). (ENG.). 40p. (J). (gr. 3-7). lib. bdg. *(978-0-7787-3691-2(1));* pap. *(978-0-7787-3713-1(6))* Crabtree Publishing Co.

Berne, Emma Carlson. William Shakespeare: Playwright & Poet, 1 vol. 2008. (Essential Lives Set 2 Ser.). (ENG., Illus.). 112p. (J). (gr. 6-12). lib. bdg. 35.64 *(978-1-60453-042-1(1))* ABDO Publishing Co.

Bloom, Harold, ed. Tony Kushner. 2005. (Bloom's Modern Critical Views Ser.). (Illus.). 300p. (C). (gr. 9-13). 45.00 *(978-0-7910-8139-6(7),* Chelsea Hse.) Facts On File, Inc.

Bloom, Harold, et al. Bloom's Major Dramatists. 2005. (Bloom's Major Dramatists Ser.). (Illus.). 144p. (C). (gr. 9). 383.40 *(978-0-7910-7376-6(9))* Facts On File, Inc.

Bloom's Major Dramatists Series, 24 vols., Set. Incl. Anton Chekhov. Bloom, Harold. 1999. 31.95 *(978-0-7910-5243-3(5),* 040007); Ben Jonson. Bloom, Harold, ed. & intro. 2001. 31.95 *(978-0-7910-6359-0(3),* 040015); Berthold Brecht. Bloom, Harold, ed. & intro. 2002. 31.95 *(978-0-7910-6363-7(1),* 040013); Eugene Ionesco. Erskine, Robb. Bloom, Harold, ed. (Illus.). 2002. 31.95 *(978-0-7910-7037-6(9),* 040021); Euripides. Albertazzi, Anne Marie. Bloom, Harold, ed. (Illus.). 2002. 31.95 *(978-0-7910-6356-9(9),* 040014); George Bernard Shaw. Bloom, Harold. 1999. 31.95 *(978-0-7910-5237-2(0),* 040001); Luigi Pirandello. Griffin, Patsy. Bloom, Harold, ed. (Illus.). 2003. 31.95 *(978-0-7910-7036-9(0),* 040023); Sam Shepard. Bloom, Harold & Albertazzi, Anne Marie, eds. (Illus.). 2002. 31.95 *(978-0-7910-7035-2(2),* 040024); Shakespeare's Comedies. Bloom, Harold. 1999. 31.95 *(978-0-7910-5238-9(9),* 040002); Shakespeare's Histories. Bloom, Harold. (Illus.). 1999. 31.95 *(978-0-7910-5241-9(9),* 040005); 120p. (C). (gr. 9-18). Set lib. bdg. 550.80 *(978-0-7910-7198-4(7),* 040000S, Chelsea Hse.) Facts On File, Inc.

Carew-Miller, Anna. William Shakespeare: Great English Playwright & Poet. 2013. (People of Importance Ser.: 21). (Illus.). 32p. (J). (gr. 4-18). 19.95 *(978-1-4222-2859-3(2))* Mason Crest.

Dabrowski, Kristen. 111 One-Minute Monologues. 2003. (Ultimate Audition Book for Middle School Actors Ser.: Vol. 1). 116p. (J). (gr. 3-7). pap. 12.95 *(978-1-57525-346-6(1))* Smith & Kraus Pubs., Inc.

Dickins, Rosie. William Shakespeare - Internet Referenced. 2008. (Young Reading Series 3 Gift Books - Famous Lives Ser.). 64p. (J). 8.99 *(978-0-7945-2096-0(0),* Usborne) EDC Publishing.

Fandel, Jennifer. William Shakespeare. 2014. (J). *(978-1-60818-328-9(9),* Creative Education) Creative Co., The.

Fischel, Emma. William Shakespeare. Remphry, Martin, illus. 2010. (Famous People, Famous Lives Ser.). (KOR.). 46p. (J). *(978-89-491-8826-3(0))* Biryongso Publishing Co.

Hill Nettleton, Pamela. William Shakespeare: The Inspiring Life Story of the Playwright Extraordinaire. 2016. (Inspiring Stories Ser.). (ENG., Illus.). 112p. (gr. 5-7). lib. bdg. 35.99 *(978-0-7565-5163-6(3),* CPB Grades 4-8) Compass Point Bks.

Johnson, Robin. William Shakespeare. 2016. (ENG., Illus.). 48p. (J). pap. *(978-0-7787-2229-8(5))* Crabtree Publishing Co.

Maloof, Torrey. Stepping into William Shakespeare's World (Grade 7) 2017. (TIME for KIDS(r) Nonfiction Readers Ser.). (Illus.). 48p. (J). (gr. 7-7). pap. 9.99 ***(978-1-4938-3618-5(8))*** Teacher Created Materials, Inc.

Mannis, Celeste Davidson & Davidson, Mannis. Who Was William Shakespeare? O'brien, John, illus. 2006. (Who Was? Ser.). (ENG.). 112p. (J). (gr. 3-7). pap. 5.99 *(978-0-448-43904-4(2),* Grosset & Dunlap) Penguin Young Readers Group.

Mannis, Celeste Davidson & Kramer, Sydelle. Who Was William Shakespeare? O'Brien, John, illus. 2006. (Who Was... ? Ser.). 105p. (gr. 2-6). 15.00 *(978-0-7569-6952-3(2))* Perfection Learning Corp.

Middleton, Haydn. True Lives Shakespeare. 2009. (True Lives Ser.). (ENG., Illus.). 32p. (J). pap. 6.99 *(978-0-19-911968-4(6))* Oxford Univ. Pr., Inc.

Mittelstaedt, Walt. A Student's Guide to William Shakespeare. 2005. (Understanding Literature Ser.). (Illus.). 192p. (YA). lib. bdg. 29.27 *(978-0-7660-2284-3(6))* Enslow Pubs., Inc.

Padale, Jacinto. Federico García Lorca. 2005. (Protagonistas Ser.). (SPA.). (YA). *(978-987-1129-58-4(0))* Grupo Visor E.A.S.A.

Perrin, Pat & Coleman, Wim. The Mystery of the Murdered Playwright. 2004. (Cover-To-Cover Books). (Illus.). 56p. pap. 9.00 *(978-0-7891-6001-0(3));* (gr. 4-7). lib. bdg. 17.95 *(978-0-7569-1353-3(5))* Perfection Learning Corp.

Raum, Elizabeth. Twenty-First Century Shakespeare. 2010. (Culture in Action Ser.). (ENG.). 32p. (gr. 3-6). 30.65 *(978-1-4109-3920-3(0),* NA-r) Heinemann-Raintree.

Reef, Catherine. Arthur Miller. 2014. (J). *(978-1-59935-400-2(4))* Reynolds, Morgan Inc.

Rocamore, Carol. Acts of Courage: Václav Havel's Life in the Theater. 2005. (Ultimate Audition Book for Middle School Actors Ser.: Vol. 1). (Illus.). xx, 490p. 35.00 *(978-1-57525-344-2(5))* Smith & Kraus Pubs., Inc.

Rosen, Michael. Shakespeare: His Work & His World. Ingpen, Robert R., illus. 2006. (ENG.). 96p. (J). (gr. 7-11). pap. 10.99 *(978-0-7636-3201-4(5))* Candlewick Pr.

Shuter, Paul. William Shakespeare: A Man for All Times, 1 vol. 2014. (Shakespeare Alive Ser.). (ENG.). 80p. (gr. 7-8). lib. bdg. 37.32 *(978-1-4329-9629-1(0))* Heinemann-Raintree.

DRAUGHTS

see Checkers

DRAWING

see also Anatomy, Artistic; Architectural Drawing; Commercial Art; Crayon Drawing; Design, Decorative; Figure Drawing; Geometrical Drawing; Graphic Methods; Illustration of Books; Mechanical Drawing; Pastel Drawing; Pencil Drawing; Perspective; Shadows

Abraham, Philip. How to Draw the Life & Times of George Washington. 2005. (Kid's Guide to Drawing the Presidents of the United States of America Ser.). (Illus.). 32p. (YA). (gr. 2-5). 26.50 *(978-1-4042-2978-5(7))* Rosen Publishing Group, Inc., The.

Ames, Lee J. Draw 50 Boats, Ships, Trucks, & Trains: The Step-by-Step Way to Draw Submarines, Sailboats, Dump Trucks, Locomotives, & Much More... 2013. (ENG., Illus.). 64p. pap. 9.99 *(978-0-8230-8602-3(X)*, Watson-Guptill) Potter/TenSpeed/Harmony.

Anderson, Airlie. What to Doodle? Jr. — Princesses, Fairies, Mermaids & More! 2013. (Dover Doodle Bks.). (ENG.). 128p. (J). (gr. k-3). pap. 4.99 *(978-0-486-49951-2(0))* Dover Pubns., Inc.

Anderson, Graylin. Seeing the Shapes + Drawing the Shapes = Drawing the Object. 2008. (ENG.). 32p. pap. 11.99 *(978-1-4196-9609-1(2))* CreateSpace Independent Publishing Platform.

Angleberger, Tom. Art2-D2's Guide to Folding & Doodling. 2016. (Origami Yoda Ser.). (ENG., Illus.). 192p. (J). (gr. 3-7). pap. 7.95 *(978-1-4197-2028-4(7)*, Amulet Bks.) Abrams, Inc.

Anorak Press Staff & Olmedillas, Cathy, compiled by. Anorak: The Happy Mag For Kids. 2012. (ENG., Illus.). 64p. (J). pap. 9.99 *(978-1-4236-3317-4(2)*, Anorak Pr.) Gibbs Smith, Publisher.

The Art of Drawing the Male Form: Artistic Anatomy Drawing Series. 2003. (Illus.). 60p. 35.00 *(978-0-9747389-5-6(6))*; 20.00 *(978-0-9747389-4-9(8))* Hensley, Michael.

Award Staff & Award, Anna. Sticker Fun & Colouring. 2015. (ENG.). 48p. (J). pap. 7.99 *(978-1-78270-012-8(9))* Award Pubns. Ltd. GBR. Dist: Parkwest Pubns., Inc.

Ayers, Chris. My Daily Zoo: A Drawing Activity Book for All Ages. 2011. (ENG., Illus.). 96p. pap. 9.95 *(978-1-933492-63-6(5))* Design Studio Pr.

Bahbout, Jacky & Rhodes, Peter. Grids: A Drwaing Book for Squares. 2016. (ENG., Illus.). 128p. (J). (gr. 2-6). pap. 14.95 *(978-0-500-29233-4(7)*, 529233) Thames & Hudson.

Baker, Michael. Thinker Doodles A1: Think, Draw, & Color. 2010. (Thinker Doodles Ser.). 45p. (gr. k-1). pap. 8.99 *(978-0-89455-870-2(6))* Critical Thinking Co., The.

—Thinker Doodles Beginning: Think, Draw, & Color. 2010. (Thinker Doodles Ser.). 48p. (gr. -1 — 1). pap. 8.99 *(978-0-89455-869-6(2))* Critical Thinking Co., The.

Bailey, Simon. The Adventures of Sherlock Holmes: Color in Classics. Thunder Bay Press, Editors of, ed. Gordon, Martin & Knight, Kevin, illus. 2016. (ENG.). 144p. pap. 14.99 *(978-1-62686-559-4(0)*, Thunder Bay Pr.) Readerlink Distribution Services, LLC.

Barclay, Adrian. Outdoor Adventure Doodles: Amazing Scenes to Complete & Create. Running Press Staff, ed. 2014. (ENG., Illus.). 160p. (J). (gr. -1-17). pap. 12.95 *(978-0-7624-5218-7(8)*, Running Pr. Kids) Running Pr. Bk. Pubs.

Barefoot Books Staff, et al. Zig Zag Zebra. 2008. (ENG., Illus.). 24p. (J). pap., act. bk. ed. 6.99 *(978-1-84686-233-5(7))* Barefoot Bks., Inc.

Bartch, Lea & Mangrum, Kaylea J. Tucker Goes to Kindergarten. Mangrum, Kaylea J., illus. 2013. (Illus.). 54p. pap. 14.99 *(978-0-9883009-5-8(8))* Mangrum, Kaylea J.

Basford, Johanna. Secret Garden: An Inky Treasure Hunt & Coloring Book. 2013. (J). lib. bdg. 28.10 *(978-0-606-37119-3(2))* Turtleback Bks.

Battaglioli, Peter. What to Doodle? Crazy Faces. 2013. (Dover Doodle Bks.). (ENG.). 48p. (J). (gr. 2-5). pap. 4.99 *(978-0-486-49100-4(5))* Dover Pubns., Inc.

Beaumont, Steve. Drawing Legendary Monsters, 6 vols., Set. Incl. Drawing Dragons: And Other Cold-Blooded Creatures. lib. bdg. 26.50 *(978-1-4488-3324-5(8))*; Drawing Griffins & Other Winged Wonders. lib. bdg. 26.50 *(978-1-4488-3253-8(5))*; Drawing the Kraken & Other Sea Monsters. lib. bdg. 26.50 *(978-1-4488-3252-1(7))*; Drawing the Minotaur & Other Demihumans. lib. bdg. 26.50 *(978-1-4488-3250-7(0))*; Drawing Unicorns & Other Mythical Beasts. lib. bdg. 26.50 *(978-1-4488-3251-4(9))*; Drawing Werewolves & Other Gothic Ghouls. 26.50 *(978-1-4488-3254-5(3))*; (J). (gr. 3-6). (Drawing Legendary Monsters Ser.). (Illus.). 32p. 2011. Set lib. bdg. 151.50 *(978-1-4488-3267-5(5)*, PowerKids Pr.) Rosen Publishing Group, Inc., The.

—How to Draw Magical Kings & Queens. 2009. (Drawing Fantasy Art Ser.). 32p. (gr. 4-5). 50.50 *(978-1-61512-191-5(9)*, PowerKids Pr.) Rosen Publishing Group, Inc., The.

—How to Draw Orcs, Elves, & Dwarves. 2009. (Drawing Fantasy Art Ser.). 32p. (gr. 4-5). 50.50 *(978-1-61512-192-2(7)*, PowerKids Pr.) Rosen Publishing Group, Inc., The.

Beilenson, Suzanne. Rain Forest Scratch & Sketch: An Art Activity Book for Adventurous Artists & Explorers of All Ages. 2007. (Illus.). 64p. (YA). 12.99 *(978-1-59359-862-4(9))* Peter Pauper Pr. Inc.

Bergin, Mark. It's Fun to Draw Monsters. 2013. (ENG., Illus.). 32p. (J). (gr. k-3). pap. 5.95 *(978-1-62087-534-6(9)*, 620534, Sky Pony Pr.) Skyhorse Publishing Co., Inc.

—Safari Animals. 2011. (It's Fun to Draw Ser.). (ENG., Illus.). 32p. (J). (gr. k-3). lib. bdg. 26.50 *(978-1-61533-348-6(7))* Windmill Bks.

Besel, Jennifer M. Holiday Sketchbook. Makuc, Lucy, illus. 2013. (Holiday Sketchbook Ser.). (ENG.). (gr. 1-2). 40p. pap. 19.80 *(978-1-4765-3653-8(8))*; 24p. lib. bdg. 101.28 *(978-1-4765-3652-1(X))* Capstone Press of Coughlan Cos. (First Facts).

The Best Workbook of Drawing Practice for Very Young Children. 2006. (Illus.). (J). (gr. -1-3). pap. 14.95 *(978-0-9773205-0-9(2))* Godinez-Hammermaster Design.

The Big Yellow Drawing Book, Newsprint Edition. 2005. wbk. ed. *(978-0-9675919-4-0(5))* O'Neill, Hugh & Assocs.

Billman, Hilary Barton. How to Draw the Life & Times of William Henry Harrison. 2006. (Kid's Guide to Drawing the Presidents of the United States of America Ser.). (Illus.). 32p. (YA). (gr. 2-5). 26.50 *(978-1-4042-2986-0(8))* Rosen Publishing Group, Inc., The.

Bird, Benjamin. Food Doodles with Scooby-Doo! Neely, Scott, illus. 2017. (Scooby-Doodles! Ser.). (ENG.). 32p. (gr. 3-6). lib. bdg. 27.99 *(978-1-5157-3407-9(2))* Capstone Press of Coughlan Cos.

—Monster Doodles with Scooby-Doo! Neely, Scott, illus. 2017. (Scooby-Doodles! Ser.). (ENG.). 32p. (gr. 3-6). lib. bdg. 27.99 *(978-1-5157-3406-2(4))* Capstone Press of Coughlan Cos.

—Scooby-Doodles! 2017. (Scooby-Doodles! Ser.). (ENG.). 32p. (gr. 3-6). 111.96 *(978-1-5157-3409-3(9))* Capstone Press of Coughlan Cos.

—Scooby-Doodles! Draw, Color, & Create with Scooby-Doo! 2017. (Scooby-Doodles! Ser.). (ENG.). 144p. (gr. 3-6). pap. 14.95 *(978-1-62370-811-5(7))* Capstone Press of Coughlan Cos.

—Vehicle Doodles with Scooby-Doo! Neely, Scott, illus. 2017. (Scooby-Doodles! Ser.). (ENG.). 32p. (gr. 3-6). lib. bdg. 27.99 *(978-1-5157-3408-6(0))* Capstone Press of Coughlan Cos.

Bloomenstein, Susan. Allover Patterns Stained Glass Coloring Book. 2012. (Dover Stained Glass Coloring Book Ser.). (ENG., Illus.). 32p. (gr. 3-5). pap. 6.99 *(978-0-486-49784-6(4))* Dover Pubns., Inc.

Bolte, Mari. All-American Girl Style: Fun Fashions You Can Sketch, 1 vol. Otero, Sole, illus. 2013. (Drawing Fun Fashions Ser.). (ENG.). 32p. (gr. 3-4). lib. bdg. 27.99 *(978-1-62065-039-4(8)*, Snap Bks.) Capstone Press of Coughlan Cos.

—Drawing Fun Fashions. Rzasa, Jennifer et al, illus. 2013. (Drawing Fun Fashions Ser.). (ENG.). 32p. (gr. 3-4). lib. bdg. 167.94 *(978-1-62065-040-0(1)*, Snap Bks.) Capstone Press of Coughlan Cos.

—Girly Girl Style: Fun Fashions You Can Sketch, 1 vol. Hagel, Brooke, illus. 2013. (Drawing Fun Fashions Ser.). (ENG.). 32p. (gr. 3-4). lib. bdg. 27.99 *(978-1-62065-035-6(5)*, Snap Bks.) Capstone Press of Coughlan Cos.

—Harajuku Style: Fun Fashions You Can Sketch, 1 vol. Hagel, Brooke, illus. 2013. (Drawing Fun Fashions Ser.). (ENG.). 32p. (gr. 3-4). lib. bdg. 27.99 *(978-1-62065-034-9(7)*, Snap Bks.) Capstone Press of Coughlan Cos.

—Hollywood Style: Fun Fashions You Can Sketch, 1 vol. Dahl, Sarah, illus. 2013. (Drawing Fun Fashions Ser.). (ENG.). 32p. (gr. 3-4). lib. bdg. 27.99 *(978-1-62065-037-0(1)*, Snap Bks.) Capstone Press of Coughlan Cos.

—Rock Star Style: Fun Fashions You Can Sketch, 1 vol. Dahl, Sarah, illus. 2013. (Drawing Fun Fashions Ser.). (ENG.). 32p. (gr. 3-4). lib. bdg. 27.99 *(978-1-62065-036-3(3)*, Snap Bks.) Capstone Press of Coughlan Cos.

—Skater Chic Style: Fun Fashions You Can Sketch, 1 vol. Rzasa, Jennifer, illus. 2013. (Drawing Fun Fashions Ser.). (ENG.). 32p. (gr. 3-4). lib. bdg. 27.99 *(978-1-62065-038-7(X)*, Snap Bks.) Capstone Press of Coughlan Cos.

Bolte, Marissa. Fashion Drawing Studio: A Guide to Sketching Stylish Fashions, 1 vol. Hagel, Brooke et al, illus. 2013. (Craft It Yourself Ser.). (ENG.). 144p. (gr. 3-4). pap. 14.95 *(978-1-62370-005-8(1))* Capstone Young Readers of Coughlan Cos.

Booth, Scott, illus. How to Draw Superheroes & Super Villains. 2003. 64p. (J). *(978-0-439-55133-5(1))* Scholastic, Inc.

Bowman, Lucy. Drawing, Doodling & Coloring Book Girls. 2012. (Activity Cards Ser.). 128p. (J). pap. 13.99 *(978-0-7945-3297-0(7)*, Usborne) EDC Publishing.

—Spooky Doodles. 2012. (Doodles Cards Ser.). 50p. (J). 9.99 *(978-0-7945-2902-4(X)*, Usborne) EDC Publishing.

Branson, Michelle. Texas Doodles, 1 vol. 2014. (ENG., Illus.). 240p. (J). pap. 9.99 *(978-1-4236-3634-2(1))* Gibbs Smith, Publisher.

Brecke, Nicole & Stockland, Patricia M. Ready, Set, Draw!, 12 vols., Set. Brecke, Nicole, illus. Incl. Airplanes & Ships You Can Draw. 2010. lib. bdg. 25.26 *(978-0-7613-4166-6(8))*; Cars, Trucks, & Motorcycles You Can Draw. 2009. lib. bdg. 25.26 *(978-0-7613-4162-8(5))*; Cats You Can Draw. 2009. lib. bdg. 25.26 *(978-0-7613-4161-1(7))*; Cool Boy Stuff You Can Draw. 2009. lib. bdg. 25.26 *(978-0-7613-4163-5(3))*; Cool Girl Stuff You Can Draw. 2009. lib. bdg. 25.26 *(978-0-7613-4164-2(1))*; Dinosaurs & Other Prehistoric Creatures You Can Draw. 2010. lib. bdg. 25.26 *(978-0-7613-4169-7(2))*; Dogs You Can Draw. 2009. lib. bdg. 25.26 *(978-0-7613-4159-8(5))*; Extinct & Endangered Animals You Can Draw. 2010. lib. bdg. 25.26 *(978-0-7613-4165-9(X))*; Horses You Can Draw. 2009. lib. bdg. 25.26 *(978-0-7613-4160-4(9))*; Insects You Can Draw. (J). 2010. lib. bdg. 25.26 *(978-0-7613-4170-3(6))*; Sea Creatures You Can Draw. 2010. lib. bdg. 25.26 *(978-0-7613-4168-0(4))*; Spaceships, Aliens, & Robots You Can Draw. 2010. lib. bdg. 25.26 *(978-0-7613-4167-3(6))*; (Illus.). 32p. (gr. 2-4). 2009. Set lib. bdg. 303.12 *(978-0-7613-4158-1(7)*, Millbrook Pr.) Lerner Publishing Group.

Brooks, Rosie. What to Doodle? - Jr. Everything! 2011. (Dover Doodle Bks.). (ENG.). 128p. (J). (gr. k-3). pap. 3.99 *(978-0-486-47821-0(1))* Dover Pubns., Inc.

—What to Doodle? Everyday. 2011. (Dover Doodle Bks.). (ENG.). 64p. (J). (gr. k-3). pap. 1.50 *(978-0-486-47816-6(5))* Dover Pubns., Inc.

Brown, Calef, illus. Dragon, Robot, Gatorbunny: Pick one. Draw it. Make it Funny. 2012. (ENG.). 160p. (J). (gr. k-17). 14.99 *(978-1-4521-0364-8(X))* Chronicle Bks. LLC.

Butkus, Michael. Drawing: Learn the Basics of Drawing. 2003. (How to Draw & Paint Ser.). (ENG., Illus.). 32p. (gr. k-6). pap. 8.95 *(978-1-56010-484-1(8)*, 1560104848) Quarto Publishing Group USA.

Campbell, Kathy. Let's Draw a Bear with Squares. 2009. (Let's Draw with Shapes Ser.). 24p. (gr. k-k). 42.50 *(978-1-61514-202-6(9)*, PowerKids Pr.) Rosen Publishing Group, Inc., The.

—Let's Draw a Bear with Squares / Vamos a dibujar un oso usando Cuadrados. 2009. (Let's Draw with Shapes / Vamos a dibujar con figuras Ser.). (ENG & SPA.). 24p. (gr. k-1). 42.50 *(978-1-61514-220-0(7)*, Editorial Buenas Letras) Rosen Publishing Group, Inc., The.

—Let's Draw a Fish with Triangles. 2009. (Let's Draw with Shapes Ser.). 24p. (gr. k-k). 42.50 *(978-1-61514-207-1(X)*, PowerKids Pr.) Rosen Publishing Group, Inc., The.

—Let's Draw a Fish with Triangles / Vamos a dibujar un pez usando Triángulos. 2009. (Let's Draw with Shapes / Vamos a dibujar con figuras Ser.). (ENG & SPA.). 24p. (gr. k-1). 42.50 *(978-1-61514-222-4(3)*, Editorial Buenas Letras) Rosen Publishing Group, Inc., The.

—Let's Draw a Frog with Ovals. 2009. (Let's Draw with Shapes Ser.). 24p. (gr. k-k). 42.50 *(978-1-61514-208-8(8)*, PowerKids Pr.) Rosen Publishing Group, Inc., The.

—Let's Draw a Frog with Ovals / Vamos a dibujar una rana Usando óvalos. 2009. (Let's Draw with Shapes / Vamos a dibujar con figuras Ser.). (ENG & SPA.). 24p. (gr. k-1). 42.50 *(978-1-61514-223-1(1)*, Editorial Buenas Letras) Rosen Publishing Group, Inc., The.

Campbell, Kathy Kuhtz. Let's Draw a Bear with Squares. Muschinske, Emily, illus. 2004. (Let's Draw with Shapes Ser.). 24p. (J). (gr. k-1). lib. bdg. 22.60 *(978-1-4042-2501-5(3)*, PowerKids Pr.) Rosen Publishing Group, Inc., The.

—Let's Draw a Bear with Squares: Vamos a Dibujar un Oso Usando Cuadrados. 2004. (Let's Draw with Shapes / Vamos a Dibujar con Figuras Ser.). (ENG & SPA., Illus.). 24p. (J). (gr. -1-1). lib. bdg. 22.60 *(978-1-4042-7501-0(0)*, PowerKids Pr.) Rosen Publishing Group, Inc., The.

—Let's Draw a Fish with Triangles. 2004. (Let's Draw with Shapes Ser.). (Illus.). 24p. (J). (gr. k-1). lib. bdg. 22.60 *(978-1-4042-2505-3(6)*, PowerKids Pr.) Rosen Publishing Group, Inc., The.

—Let's Draw a Fish with Triangles: Vamos a Dibujar un Pez Usando Triangulos. Muschinske, Emily, tr. Muschinske, Emily, illus. 2004. (Let's Draw with Shapes / Vamos a Dibujar con Figuras Ser.). (ENG & SPA.). 24p. (J). (gr. -1-1). lib. bdg. 22.60 *(978-1-4042-7505-8(3)*, PowerKids Pr.) Rosen Publishing Group, Inc., The.

—Let's Draw a Frog with Ovals. 2004. (Let's Draw with Shapes Ser.). (Illus.). 24p. (J). (gr. k-1). lib. bdg. 22.60 *(978-1-4042-2503-9(X)*, PowerKids Pr.) Rosen Publishing Group, Inc., The.

—Let's Draw a Frog with Ovals: Vamos a Dibujar una Rana Usando Ovalos. Muschinske, Emily, tr. Muschinske, Emily, illus. 2004. (Let's Draw with Shapes / Vamos a Dibujar con Figuras Ser.). (ENG & SPA.). 24p. (J). (gr. -1-1). lib. bdg. 22.60 *(978-1-4042-7503-4(7)*, PowerKids Pr.) Rosen Publishing Group, Inc., The.

Catlow, Nikalas. Do You Doodle? 2007. (ENG., Illus.). 256p. (J). (gr. -1-17). pap. 12.95 *(978-0-7624-2927-1(5))* Running Pr. Bk. Pubs.

Cedar Fort. Hooray for Mom! Drawing My Favorite Moments with Mom. 2017. (ENG.). (J). 14.99 ***(978-1-4621-1990-5(5))*** Cedar Fort, Inc./CFI Distribution.

Celia, Shannon Casey. Nature's Music: Musical Colors Series 2003. (ENG., Illus.). 12p. (J). spiral bd. 10.95 *(978-1-931844-07-9(0)*, PP1019) Piano Pr.

Cerato, Mattia & Sexton, Brenda. Easy-to-Draw Mythical Creatures. Cerato, Mattia & Sexton, Brenda, illus. 2011. (You Can Draw Ser.). (ENG., Illus.). 48p. (gr. 1-2). pap. 5.19 *(978-1-4048-7059-8(8))* Picture Window Bks.

Chorba, April. Thumb Doodles: The Epic Saga at Your Fingertips. Klutz Editors, ed. 2013. (ENG.). 40p. (J). (gr. 3). 16.99 *(978-0-545-49284-3(X))* Klutz.

Chronicle Books. 642 Things to Draw: London (pocket-Size) 2017. (ENG.). 304p. 9.95 *(978-1-4521-4737-6(X))* Chronicle Bks. LLC.

—642 Things to Draw: San Francisco (pocket-Size) 2017. (ENG.). 304p. 9.95 *(978-1-4521-4738-3(8))* Chronicle Bks. LLC.

Cohen, Sheldon & Drawing Staff. How to Draw & Save Your Planet from Alien Invasion! 2011. (Dover How to Draw Ser.). (ENG.). 72p. (J). (gr. 3-5). pap. 4.99 *(978-0-486-47833-3(5))* Dover Pubns., Inc.

Compendium Inc, creator. My Artwork. 2011. 64p. (J). pap. 5.95 *(978-1-932319-98-9(0))* Compendium, Inc., Publishing & Communications.

Corfee, Stephanie. Doodle with Attitude. Corfee, Stephanie, illus. 2016. (Doodle with Attitude Ser.). (ENG., Illus.). 32p. (gr. 4-5). 83.97 *(978-1-4914-7949-0(3))* Capstone Press of Coughlan Cos.

Corporate Contributor, ed. Diary of a Texas Kid. 2011. (State Journal Ser.). (ENG.). 128p. (J). (gr. 4-8). pap. 9.95 *(978-1-58536-608-8(0)*, 202225) Sleeping Bear Pr.

Crawford, K. Michael. Batty Malgoony's Mystic Carnivale. 2009. 60p. pap. 18.95 *(978-0-9817940-1-3(7))* Virtualbookworm.com Publishing, Inc.

Davies, Andy, et al. Boys' World of Doodles: Over 100 Pictures to Complete & Create. 2011. (ENG.). 128p. (J). (gr. -1-17). pap. 12.95 *(978-0-7624-4288-1(3))* Running Pr. Bk. Pubs.

Davies, Carolyn. Josef Herman in Wales. 2004. (ENG., Illus.). 32p. pap. 15.95 *(978-1-85902-999-2(X))* Beekman Bks., Inc.

Deinard, Jenny. How to Draw Illinois's Sights & Symbols. 2009. (Kid's Guide to Drawing America Ser.). 32p. (gr. k-k). 50.50 *(978-1-61511-060-5(7)*, PowerKids Pr.) Rosen Publishing Group, Inc., The.

—How to Draw Indiana's Sights & Symbols. 2009. (Kid's Guide to Drawing America Ser.). 32p. (gr. k-k). 50.50 *(978-1-61511-063-6(1)*, PowerKids Pr.) Rosen Publishing Group, Inc., The.

—How to Draw Iowa's Sights & Symbols. 2009. (Kid's Guide to Drawing America Ser.). 32p. (gr. k-k). 50.50 *(978-1-61511-064-3(X)*, PowerKids Pr.) Rosen Publishing Group, Inc., The.

—How to Draw Kansas's Sights & Symbols. 2009. (Kid's Guide to Drawing America Ser.). 32p. (gr. k-k). 50.50 *(978-1-61511-065-0(8)*, PowerKids Pr.) Rosen Publishing Group, Inc., The.

—How to Draw Kentucky's Sights & Symbols. 2009. (Kid's Guide to Drawing America Ser.). 32p. (gr. k-k). 50.50 *(978-1-61511-066-7(6)*, PowerKids Pr.) Rosen Publishing Group, Inc., The.

—How to Draw Louisiana's Sights & Symbols. 2009. (Kid's Guide to Drawing America Ser.). 32p. (gr. k-k). 50.50 *(978-1-61511-067-4(4)*, PowerKids Pr.) Rosen Publishing Group, Inc., The.

—How to Draw Maine's Sights & Symbols. 2009. (Kid's Guide to Drawing America Ser.). 32p. (gr. k-k). 50.50 *(978-1-61511-068-1(2)*, PowerKids Pr.) Rosen Publishing Group, Inc., The.

—How to Draw Maryland's Sights & Symbols. 2009. (Kid's Guide to Drawing America Ser.). 32p. (gr. k-k). 50.50 *(978-1-61511-069-8(0)*, PowerKids Pr.) Rosen Publishing Group, Inc., The.

—How to Draw Massachusetts's Sights & Symbols. 2009. (Kid's Guide to Drawing America Ser.). 32p. (gr. k-k). 50.50 *(978-1-61511-070-4(4)*, PowerKids Pr.) Rosen Publishing Group, Inc., The.

—How to Draw Michigan's Sights & Symbols. 2009. (Kid's Guide to Drawing America Ser.). 32p. (gr. k-k). 50.50 *(978-1-61511-071-1(2)*, PowerKids Pr.) Rosen Publishing Group, Inc., The.

DeLong, Ron. Crayola (R) Dream-Makers (R) 11: Drawing on Character. DeLong, Ron, ed. 2004. per. 6.00 *(978-0-86696-317-6(0))* Binney & Smith, Inc.

Dickins, Rosie & McCafferty, Jan. Drawing Faces. 2004. (Art Ideas Ser.). (Illus.). (J). (ENG.). 1p. pap. 8.99 *(978-0-7945-0097-9(8)*, Usborne); 64p. lib. bdg. 16.99 *(978-1-58086-382-7(5))* EDC Publishing.

Disney Storybook Artists Staff. Enchanted Princesses: Learn to Draw Ariel, Cinderella, Belle, Rapunzel, & All of Your Favorite Disney Princesses! 2012. (Licensed Learn to Draw Ser.). (ENG., Illus.). 64p. (J). (gr. 1-17). pap. 9.95 *(978-1-60058-305-6(9)*, 1600583059) Quarto Publishing Group USA.

Disney Storybook Artists Staff, ed. Celebrated Characters Collection: Including Your Disney/Pixar Favorites! 2009. (Licensed Learn to Draw Ser.). (ENG.). 144p. (J). (gr. 1-3). pap. 19.95 *(978-1-60058-144-1(7)*, 1600581447) Quarto Publishing Group USA.

Dixon, Margaret Davis. Don't Go Fishing with a Caterpillar! 2012. 16p. pap. 12.68 *(978-1-4669-5166-2(4))* Trafford Publishing.

Donahue, Peter. Cool Cars & Trucks Stained Glass Jr. Coloring Book. 2012. (Dover Stained Glass Coloring Book Ser.). (ENG.). 32p. (J). (gr. -1-3). pap. 3.99 *(978-0-486-49874-4(3))* Dover Pubns., Inc.

—What to Doodle? Jr. - Superheroes & Robots! 2013. (Dover Doodle Bks.). (ENG.). 128p. (J). (gr. 1-5). pap. 4.99 *(978-0-486-49954-3(5))* Dover Pubns., Inc.

Doodle. The Most Amazing Drawing, Doodle, Colouring, Sketchbook in the World. 2009. 98p. pap. 15.95 *(978-1-4452-1310-1(9))* Lulu Pr., Inc.

Dorling Kindersley Publishing Staff. Megadoodle. 2015. (ENG.). 400p. (J). (gr. 1-4). pap. 16.99 *(978-1-4654-3433-3(X)*, DK Children) Dorling Kindersley Publishing, Inc.

—My Art Book. 2011. (ENG., Illus.). 80p. (J). (gr. 2-5). 15.99 *(978-0-7566-7582-0(0)*, DK Children) Dorling Kindersley Publishing, Inc.

Dorling Kindersley Publishing Staff, ed. Doodlepedia - Wow. 2012. (ENG.). 96p. (J). (gr. 2-5). pap. 12.99 *(978-0-7566-9800-3(6)*, DK Children) Dorling Kindersley Publishing, Inc.

Dover & Printworks KMG Staff. Sea Life Field Guide. 2013. (ENG.). 48p. (J). (gr. 3-8). pap. 5.99 *(978-0-486-49157-8(9))* Dover Pubns., Inc.

Dover Publications Inc. Staff. Design Discovery Coloring Book. 2006. (Dover Design Coloring Bks.). (ENG., Illus.). 32p. (gr. 3-8). pap. 3.99 *(978-0-486-45109-1(7))* Dover Pubns., Inc.

Draught Associates. Visual Aid Doodling Book for Creative Kids. 2012. (ENG.). 96p. (J). (gr. k-6). pap. 11.95 *(978-1-907317-70-5(8))* Black Dog Publishing Ltd. GBR. Dist: Two Rivers Distribution.

Draw It! 2014. (Draw It! Ser.). 32p. (J). (gr. 3-6). 165.00 *(978-1-4777-9156-1(6))* Windmill Bks.

Draw Pretty Things. 2013. (ENG.). 144p. (J). pap. 10.95 *(978-1-78212-095-7(5))* Arcturus Publishing GBR. Dist: Bookmasters Distribution.

Drawing Animals Kid Kit. 2004. (Illus.). 64p. (J). 17.95 *(978-1-58086-527-2(5))* EDC Publishing.

Drawing Cartoons. 2004. (I-Quest Ser.). (J). *(978-1-84229-756-8(2))* Top That! Publishing PLC.

Drawing Cool Stuff. 2016. (Drawing Cool Stuff Ser.). (ENG.). 32p. lib. bdg. 139.95 *(978-1-5157-4027-8(7)*, Edge Bks.) Capstone Press of Coughlan Cos.

Drawing on the Go! (Learning Ser.). 22p. (J). bds. *(978-2-7643-0165-4(0))* Phidal Publishing, Inc./Editions Phidal, Inc.

Duggan, John M. The Doodle Book: 187 Fun Drawings You Can Finish Yourself. 2008. (ENG., Illus.). 192p. (J). (gr. -1). pap. 14.95 *(978-1-56975-676-8(7))* Ulysses Pr.

Duggan, John M., illus. The Action-Packed Book of Adventure Doodles: 187 Fun & Exciting Drawings You Can Finish Yourself. 2009. (ENG.). 192p. (gr. -1-3). pap. 12.95 *(978-1-56975-724-6(0))* Ulysses Pr.

Dunn, Ben. How to Draw Manga. 2004. (Illus.). 344p. (YA). pap. 3.25 *(978-1-59412-063-3(3))* Mud Puddle, Inc.

—How to Draw Steampunk. 2011. (ENG.). 128p. (YA). pap., pap. 24.99 *(978-0-9844879-8-1(0)*, 9780984487981) Antarctic Pr., Inc.

Dunn, Ben, et al. How to Draw Manga, Vol. 3. 2003. (ENG.). 128p. (YA). pap. 17.95 *(978-0-9663588-1-0(3)*, 9780966358810) Antarctic Pr., Inc.

Egmont Books. Christmas Doodle & Colouring Book. 2014. (ENG., Illus.). 128p. (J). (gr. -1). pap. 16.99 *(978-1-4052-7351-0(8))* Egmont Bks., Ltd. GBR. Dist: Independent Pubs. Group.

Ellis, Paula. Minnesota Activity Book, 1 vol. Nitzsche, Shane, illus. 2013. (Color & Learn Ser.). (ENG.). 64p. (J). (gr. k-2). pap. 5.95 *(978-1-59193-377-9(3))* Adventure Pubns.

Emberley, Ed. Ed Emberley's Drawing Book of Trucks & Trains. Emberley, Ed, illus. 2005. (ENG., Illus.). 32p. (J). (gr.

C
D

2-17). pap. 6.99 *(978-0-316-78967-7(4))* Little, Brown Bks. for Young Readers.
—Ed Emberley's Fingerprint Drawing Book. Emberley, Ed, illus. 2005. (ENG., Illus.). 48p. (J). (gr. 2-17). pap., pap. 7.99 *(978-0-316-78969-1(0))* Little, Brown Bks. for Young Readers.
Emberley, Edward R. Ed Emberley's Drawing Book of Weirdos. 2005. (ENG., Illus.). 32p. (J). (gr. 2-17). per. 7.00 *(978-0-316-78971-4(2))* Little, Brown Bks. for Young Readers.
—Ed Emberley's Great Thumbprint Drawing Book. Emberley, Edward R., illus. 2005. (ENG., Illus.). 48p. (J). (gr. 2-17). per. 8.99 *(978-0-316-78968-4(2))* Little, Brown Bks. for Young Readers.
Fashion Designs. 2004. (Art Rom Create Your Own... Ser.). (Illus.). 24p. (J). pap. incl. audio compact disk *(978-1-84229-769-8(4))* Top That! Publishing PLC.
Fay, Claire. Color, Snap, App! My First Animated Coloring Book. Fay, Claire, illus. 2017. (ENG., Illus.). 32p. (J). (gr. k-4). pap. 9.99 ***(978-0-7636-9347-3(2))*** Candlewick Pr.
Fazzi, Cindy. How to Draw Ireland's Sights & Symbols. (Kid's Guide to Drawing the Countries of the World Ser.). 48p. 2009. (gr. 4-4). 53.00 *(978-1-61511-114-5(X))* 2005. (Illus.). (J). (gr. k-5). lib. bdg. 29.25 *(978-1-4042-2738-5(5))* Rosen Publishing Group, Inc., The. (PowerKids Pr.).
—How to Draw Pakistan's Sights & Symbols. 2005. (Kid's Guide to Drawing the Countries of the World Ser.). (J). 29.25 *(978-1-4042-2739-2(3),* PowerKids Pr.) Rosen Publishing Group, Inc., The.
—How to Draw Peru's Sights & Symbols. 2005. (Kid's Guide to Drawing the Countries of the World Ser.). (J). 29.25 *(978-1-4042-2740-8(7),* PowerKids Pr.) Rosen Publishing Group, Inc., The.
—How to Draw the Philippines's Sights & Symbols. 2005. (Kid's Guide to Drawing the Countries of the World Ser.). (J). 29.25 *(978-1-4042-2742-2(3),* PowerKids Pr.) Rosen Publishing Group, Inc., The.
Fedhar. Como Dibujar Personajes Magicos. Fedhar, illus. 2003. (SPA., Illus.). 160p. (J). (gr. 4-8). pap. *(978-987-550-281-9(2))* Longseller S.A. ARG. Dist: Bilingual Pubns. Co., The.
Fein, E. How to Draw Nevada's Sights & Symbols. 2009. (Kid's Guide to Drawing America Ser.). 32p. (gr. k-k). 50.50 *(978-1-61511-077-3(1),* PowerKids Pr.) Rosen Publishing Group, Inc., The.
—How to Draw New York's Sights & Symbols. 2009. (Kid's Guide to Drawing America Ser.). 32p. (gr. k-k). 50.50 *(978-1-61511-081-0(X),* PowerKids Pr.) Rosen Publishing Group, Inc., The.
—How to Draw Oklahoma's Sights & Symbols. 2009. (Kid's Guide to Drawing America Ser.). 32p. (gr. k-k). 50.50 *(978-1-61511-089-6(5),* PowerKids Pr.) Rosen Publishing Group, Inc., The.
Fingerprint Fabulous: Create Sweet & Sparkly Thumbprint Art. 2010. (ENG.). 40p. (J). (gr. 1). spiral bd. 14.95 *(978-1-59174-748-2(1))* Klutz.
A First Look at Art. (Illus.). (gr. 3-5). lib. bdg. 59.80 *(978-0-7910-7944-7(9),* Chelsea Hse.) Facts On File, Inc.
Fish, Simon. Alphabet Madness. 2012. (ENG.). (J). pap. *(978-1-4675-0896-4(9))* Independent Pub.
Gaffney, Sean Kevin & Activity Books. AREA 51 UFO Maintenance & Repair Manual Activity Book. 2012. (Dover Children's Activity Bks.). (ENG., Illus.). 48p. (J). (gr. 3-5). pap. 7.99 *(978-0-486-49035-9(1))* Dover Pubns., Inc.
Gage, Kathryn, illus. Wow, I'm a Big Sister. 2011. 48p. (J). spiral bd. 6.25 net. *(978-1-890703-45-5(1))* Penny Laine Papers, Inc.
Gair, Angela. How to Draw Anything: A Complete Guide. 2003. (Essential Art Ser.). 160p. (YA). 19.95 *(978-0-7525-8773-8(0))* Parragon, Inc.
George, Joshua. Space. Green, Barry, illus. 2017. (Scratch & Draw Ser.). (ENG.). 56p. (J). (gr. k-2). 12.99 ***(978-1-78700-070-4(2))*** Top That! Publishing PLC GBR. Dist: Independent Pubs. Group.
Gibson, R. What Shall I Draw? 2004. (What Shall I Do Today? Ser.). 32p. (J). pap. 7.95 *(978-0-7945-0375-8(6))*; lib. bdg. 15.95 *(978-1-58086-504-3(6))* EDC Publishing.
Gibson, Ray. Drawing Animals Pack. 2004. (Activity Kits Ser.). 24p. (J). act. bk. ed. 14.95 *(978-0-7945-0456-4(6))* EDC Publishing.
—I Can Draw People. Watt, Fiona, ed. Barlow, Amanda, illus. 2004. (Usborne Playtime Ser.). (SPA.). (J). (gr. -1-18). 32p. lib. bdg., act. bk. ed. 12.95 *(978-1-58086-223-3(3))*; 1p. pap., act. bk. ed. 4.95 *(978-0-7460-3704-1(X))* EDC Publishing.
Gilpin, Rebecca. Trucks & Tractors. 2005. (ENG.). 32p. (J). pap. 8.95 *(978-0-7945-1134-0(1),* Usborne) EDC Publishing.
Glaser, Byron & Higashi, Sandra, illus. Zolocolor! Doodle Canoodle. 2013. (ENG.). 96p. (J). 7.99 *(978-1-4424-6848-1(3),* Little Simon) Little Simon.
—Zolocolor! Toodle-Oo Doodle-Oo. 2013. (ENG.). 96p. (J). 7.99 *(978-1-4424-6847-4(5),* Little Simon) Little Simon.
Gluck, Larry. The Art of Drawing Pt. 1: Creating Accurate Lines & Shapes. 2003. (YA). spiral bd. 16.95 *(978-1-929473-51-9(6))* Renaissance Pubns.
Gomi, Taro. Story Doodles Place Mats. 2012. (ENG., Illus.). 104p. (J). (gr. -1-17). 12.99 *(978-1-4521-0739-4(4))* Chronicle Bks. LLC.
Gowen, Fiona, illus. Deadly Dinosaurs & Prehistoric Creatures. 2016. (How to Draw Ser.). (ENG.). 32p. (J). (gr. 2-6). pap. 4.99 *(978-1-4380-0852-3(X))* Barron's Educational Series, Inc.
Green, Barry & Green, Dan. How to Draw 101 Animals. 2003. (How to Draw 101... Ser.). (ENG., Illus.). 48p. (J). (gr. k). pap. 4.99 *(978-1-84229-740-7(6))* Top That! Publishing PLC GBR. Dist: Independent Pubs. Group.
—How to Draw 101 Funny People. 2003. (How to Draw 101... Ser.). (ENG., Illus.). 48p. (J). (gr. k). pap. 4.99 *(978-1-84229-739-1(2))* Top That! Publishing PLC GBR. Dist: Independent Pubs. Group.
—How to Draw 101 Monsters. 2003. (How to Draw 101... Ser.). (ENG., Illus.). 48p. (J). (gr. k). pap. 4.99 *(978-1-84229-742-1(2))* Top That! Publishing PLC GBR. Dist: Independent Pubs. Group.
Griffin, Georgene, illus. Dinosaurs, Meat-Eaters. 2004. (J). *(978-1-59203-086-6(6))* Learning Challenge, Inc.
—Endangered Mammals. 2004. (J). *(978-1-59203-089-7(0))* Learning Challenge, Inc.
Griffin, Georgene & Jael, illus. Cool Wheels. 2004. (J). *(978-1-59203-087-3(4))* Learning Challenge, Inc.
Groenendyk, Doretta. I'm Drawing a Story, 1 vol. 2016. (ENG.). 32p. (J). (gr. -1-3). pap. 12.95 *(978-1-927502-50-1(0))* Acorn Pr., The CAN. Dist: Orca Bk. Pubs. USA.
Gross, Miriam. How to Draw the Life & Times of James Monroe. 2006. (Kid's Guide to Drawing the Presidents of the United States of America Ser.). (YA). (gr. 2-5). 26.50 *(978-1-4042-2982-2(5))* Rosen Publishing Group, Inc., The.
Gunnell, Beth. I Heart Drawing. Gunnell, Beth, illus. 2017. (I Heart Ser.). (ENG., Illus.). 128p. (J). (gr. 2). pap. 8.99 ***(978-1-78055-414-3(1))*** O'Mara, Michael Bks., Ltd. GBR. Dist: Independent Pubs. Group.
Gunnell, Beth, et al. Summer Fun Doodles: Sunny Full-Color Pictures to Complete & Create. 2013. (ENG., Illus.). 128p. (J). (gr. -1-17). pap. 12.95 *(978-0-7624-4901-9(2),* Running Pr. Kids) Running Pr. Bk. Pubs.
Hamilton, Sue L. Forensic Artist: Solving the Case with a Face, 1 vol. 2008. (Crime Scene Investigation Ser.). (ENG.). 32p. (gr. 4-8). 27.07 *(978-1-59928-989-2(X),* Abdo & Daughters) ABDO Publishing Co.
Haring, Kay. Keith Haring: The Boy Who Just Kept Drawing. Neubecker, Robert, illus. 2017. (ENG.). 40p. (J). (gr. k-3). 16.99 *(978-0-525-42819-0(4),* Dial Bks) Penguin Young Readers Group.
Harper, Piers. Christmas Doodles: Over 100 Pictures to Complete & Create. 2014. (ENG.). 160p. (J). (gr. 1-17). pap. 12.95 *(978-0-7624-5656-7(6),* Running Pr. Kids) Running Pr. Bk. Pubs.
Hart, Christopher. Draw Manga Villains! 2004. (XTreme Art Ser.). (ENG., Illus.). 64p. (J). (gr. 2-4). pap. 7.95 *(978-0-8230-0370-9(1),* Watson-Guptill) Potter/TenSpeed/Harmony.
—Fashion Design Studio: Learn to Draw Figures, Fashion, Hairstyles & More. 2013. (Creative Girls Draw Ser.). (ENG., Illus.). 128p. (J). pap. 16.95 *(978-1-936096-62-6(5),* Hart, Chris Bks.) Sixth&Spring Bks.
—Kids Draw Animals. 2003. (Kids Draw Ser.). (ENG., Illus.). 64p. (J). (gr. 2-4). pap. 11.95 *(978-0-8230-2631-9(0),* Watson-Guptill) Potter/TenSpeed/Harmony.
—Kids Draw Manga. 2004. (Kids Draw Ser.). (ENG., Illus.). 64p. (J). (gr. 2-4). pap. 11.95 *(978-0-8230-2623-4(X),* Watson-Guptill) Potter/TenSpeed/Harmony.
—You Can Draw Cartoon Animals: A Simple Step-by-Step Drawing Guide! 2009. (ENG., Illus.). 120p. (J). (gr. 1-3). pap., instr.'s gde. ed. 12.95 *(978-1-60058-611-8(2),* 1600586112) Quarto Publishing Group USA.
—Young Artists Draw Animals. 2012. (ENG., Illus.). 144p. pap. 14.99 *(978-0-8230-0718-9(9),* Watson-Guptill) Potter/TenSpeed/Harmony.
Hastings, John. The Drawing Breakthrough Kit: Taking the Mystery Out of Learning to Draw. 2004. (Illus.). spiral bd. 49.95 *(978-0-9749418-0-6(8))* Draw Three Lines Publishing.
Hecht, Kristina. A Bird & a Bee, 1 vol. 2009. 16p. pap. 24.95 *(978-1-60836-408-4(9))* America Star Bks.
Hellman, Charles S. Luckysports Abc's Coloring Book. Tiritilli, Robert A., illus. 2013. 50p. pap. 5.40 *(978-0-935938-46-3(X))* LuckySports.
Henry, Sally. Drawing. 2009. (Make Your Own Art Ser.). 32p. (gr. 2-6). pap. 11.75 *(978-1-4358-2643-4(4),* Rosen Classroom) Rosen Publishing Group, Inc., The.
—Make Your Own Art, 6 vols., Set 1. Incl. Card Making. lib. bdg. 26.50 *(978-1-4358-2506-2(3))*; Clay Modeling. lib. bdg. 26.50 *(978-1-4358-2508-6(X))*; Collage. lib. bdg. 26.50 *(978-1-4358-2509-3(8))*; Drawing. lib. bdg. 26.50 *(978-1-4358-2510-9(1))*; Painting. lib. bdg. 26.50 *(978-1-4358-2511-6(X))*; Paper Folding. lib. bdg. 26.50 *(978-1-4358-2507-9(1))*; (J). (gr. 3-6). 2009. (Make Your Own Art Ser.). (Illus.). 32p. 2008. Set lib. bdg. 151.50 *(978-1-4358-2549-9(7),* PowerKids Pr.) Rosen Publishing Group, Inc., The.
Henry, Sally & Cook, Trevor. Make Your Own Art, 6 vols., Set 2. Incl. Eco Crafts. lib. bdg. 26.50 *(978-1-4488-1582-1(7))*; Making Masks. 26.50 *(978-1-4488-1583-8(5))*; Making Mosaics. 26.50 *(978-1-4488-1585-2(1))*; Making Puppets. 26.50 *(978-1-4488-1584-5(3))*; Papier-Mâché. 26.50 *(978-1-4488-1587-6(8))*; (J). (gr. 3-6). (Make Your Own Art Ser.). (Illus.). 32p. 2010. Set lib. bdg. 151.50 *(978-1-4488-1625-5(4),* PowerKids Pr.) Rosen Publishing Group, Inc., The.
Highlights for Children Editorial Staff. Doodlerama: Oodles of Doodling, Coloring, & Puzzling Fun! 2015. (ENG., Illus.). 144p. (J). (gr. -1). 9.95 *(978-1-62979-330-6(2),* Highlights) Boyds Mills Pr.
Hildebrand, Jens, et al. The Art of Team 002. 2013. 50p. pap. *(978-3-929892-43-7(X))* Hildebrand, Jutta Warped Tomato Publishing.
Hill, Eric. Drawing Fun with Spot. 2005. bds. 7.99 *(978-0-399-24337-0(2),* Putnam Juvenile) Penguin Publishing Group.
Hill, Kevin. A - Z Animal Coloring & Activity Book: English & Spanish. 2012. 60p. (gr. -1). pap. 12.95 *(978-1-4772-0407-8(5))* AuthorHouse.
Houghton Mifflin Harcourt Publishing Company Staff. Draw It! Color It! Creatures. Gravett, Emily et al, illus. 2016. (ENG.). 120p. (J). 11.99 *(978-0-544-77979-2(7),* HMH Books For Young Readers) Houghton Mifflin Harcourt Publishing Co.
How to Draw 101 Things That Go. 2004. (How to Draw... Ser.). (Illus.). 48p. (J). pap. *(978-1-84229-741-4(4))* Top That! Publishing PLC.
How to Draw Shojo Supersize, Vol. 1. 2003. (ENG., Illus.). 144p. (YA). pap. 19.95 *(978-0-9728978-4-6(4),* 9780972897846) Antarctic Pr., Inc.
How to Draw Wings & Wheels. (Illus.). 128p. (J). (gr. 1-18). 14.95 *(978-1-56156-223-7(8))* Kidsbooks, LLC.
Hruby, Patrick. Natural Wonders: A Patrick Hruby Coloring Book. 2011. (ENG.). 32p. pap. 9.95 *(978-1-934429-71-6(6))* AMMO Bks., LLC.
I Can Draw Cartoons. Date not set. (I Can Draw Ser.). (Illus.). 128p. (J). 7.98 *(978-1-4054-0542-3(2))* Parragon, Inc.
Ismail, Yasmeen, illus. Inside, Outside, Upside Down: Draw & Discover. 2017. (ENG.). 56p. (J). (gr. -1-2). pap. 9.99 *(978-1-78067-929-7(7))* King, Laurence Publishing GBR. Dist: Hachette Bk. Group.
—Push, Pull, Empty, Full: Draw & Discover. 2017. (ENG.). 56p. (J). (gr. -1-2). pap. 9.99 *(978-1-78067-931-0(9))* King, Laurence Publishing GBR. Dist: Hachette Bk. Group.
Jackson, Katy. Doodles Movie Star: Sensational, Show-Stopping Pictures to Create & Complete. 2013. (ENG., Illus.). 64p. (J). (gr. k-3). pap. 7.95 *(978-1-62087-530-8(6),* 620530, Sky Pony Pr.) Skyhorse Publishing Co., Inc.
—Doodles Pop Star: Fabulous & Funky Pictures to Create & Complete. 2013. (ENG., Illus.). 64p. (J). (gr. k-3). pap. 7.95 *(978-1-62087-531-5(4),* 620531, Sky Pony Pr.) Skyhorse Publishing Co., Inc.
Kaehler, Lorie King. Chalk on the Wild Side. 2016. (DIY Ser.). (ENG., Illus.). 128p. (J). (gr. 3-8). 34.65 *(978-1-942875-11-6(8),* Walter Foster Jr) Quarto Publishing Group USA.
Khu, Jannel. Let's Draw a Fire Truck with Shapes. 2009. (Let's Draw with Shapes Ser.). 24p. (gr. k-k). 42.50 *(978-1-61514-206-4(1),* PowerKids Pr.) Rosen Publishing Group, Inc., The.
—Let's Draw a Fire Truck with Shapes/Vamos a dibujar un camión de bomberos usando Figuras. 2009. (Let's Draw with Shapes / Vamos a dibujar con figuras Ser.). (ENG & SPA.). 24p. (gr. k-1). 42.50 *(978-1-61514-216-3(9),* Editorial Buenas Letras) Rosen Publishing Group, Inc., The.
—Let's Draw a House with Shapes. 2009. (Let's Draw with Shapes Ser.). 24p. (gr. k-k). 42.50 *(978-1-61514-210-1(X),* PowerKids Pr.) Rosen Publishing Group, Inc., The.
—Let's Draw a House with Shapes/Vamos a dibujar una casa usando Figuras. 2009. (Let's Draw with Shapes / Vamos a dibujar con figuras Ser.). (ENG & SPA.). 24p. (gr. k-1). 42.50 *(978-1-61514-217-0(7),* Editorial Buenas Letras) Rosen Publishing Group, Inc., The.
—Let's Draw a School Bus with Shapes. 2009. (Let's Draw with Shapes Ser.). 24p. (gr. k-k). 42.50 *(978-1-61514-211-8(8),* PowerKids Pr.) Rosen Publishing Group, Inc., The.
—Let's Draw a School Bus with Shapes/Vamos a dibujar un autobus escolar usando Figuras. 2009. (Let's Draw with Shapes / Vamos a dibujar con figuras Ser.). (ENG & SPA.). 24p. (gr. k-1). 42.50 *(978-1-61514-218-7(5),* Editorial Buenas Letras) Rosen Publishing Group, Inc., The.
A Kid's Guide to Drawing: Set 2. (Illus.). (J). (gr. k-5). 127.50 *(978-0-8239-7190-9(2))* Rosen Publishing Group, Inc., The.
A Kid's Guide to Drawing: Set 3. (Illus.). (J). (gr. k-5). 127.50 *(978-0-8239-7256-2(9))* Rosen Publishing Group, Inc., The.
A Kid's Guide to Drawing: Set 4. (Illus.). (J). (gr. k-5). 127.50 *(978-0-8239-7675-1(0))* Rosen Publishing Group, Inc., The.
Kindberg, Sally. Draw It! Monsters: 100 Spooky Things to Doodle & Draw! 2015. (ENG.). 112p. (J). (gr. 2-4). pap. 12.99 *(978-1-61963-366-7(3),* 9781619633667, Bloomsbury USA Childrens) Bloomsbury Publishing USA.
Klutz Editors. Draw It 3D. 2016. (ENG.). 70p. (J). (gr. 3-7). 16.99 *(978-1-338-03748-7(X))* Klutz.
Klutz Editors, ed. Window Art. 4th ed. 2012. (ENG.). 56p. (J). (gr. 3). 21.99 *(978-0-545-45990-7(7))* Klutz.
Kohl, MaryAnn F. & Potter, Jean. Storybook Art: Hands-On Art for Children in the Styles of 100 Great Picture Book Illustrators. Davis, Katheryn & Van Slyke, Rebecca, illus. 2003. (Bright Ideas for Learning Ser.: 7). (ENG.). 144p. (J). (gr. -1-6). pap. 18.95 *(978-0-935607-03-1(X))* Bright Ring Publishing, Inc.
Kronheimer, Ann. Delicious Doodles: Super Sweet Designs to Complete & Create. 2014. (ENG., Illus.). 160p. (J). (gr. -1-17). pap. 12.95 *(978-0-7624-5480-8(6),* Running Pr. Kids) Running Pr. Bk. Pubs.
Kuedee, Jaycee. How to Draw Minnesota's Sights & Symbols. 2009. (Kid's Guide to Drawing America Ser.). 32p. (gr. k-k). 50.50 *(978-1-61511-072-8(0),* PowerKids Pr.) Rosen Publishing Group, Inc., The.
—How to Draw Mississippi's Sights & Symbols. 2009. (Kid's Guide to Drawing America Ser.). 32p. (gr. k-k). 50.50 *(978-1-61511-073-5(9),* PowerKids Pr.) Rosen Publishing Group, Inc., The.
—How to Draw Missouri's Sights & Symbols. 2009. (Kid's Guide to Drawing America Ser.). 32p. (gr. k-k). 50.50 *(978-1-61511-074-2(7),* PowerKids Pr.) Rosen Publishing Group, Inc., The.
—How to Draw Montana's Sights & Symbols. 2009. (Kid's Guide to Drawing America Ser.). 32p. (gr. k-k). 50.50 *(978-1-61511-075-9(5),* PowerKids Pr.) Rosen Publishing Group, Inc., The.
Kurtz, John. What to Doodle? at School. 2013. (ENG.). 64p. (J). (gr. k-3). pap. 1.50 *(978-0-486-49229-2(X))* Dover Pubns., Inc.
Lamb, Stacey, illus. Wipe-Clean Doodles. 2013. (Wipe-Clean Bks). 20p. (J). pap. 7.99 *(978-0-7945-3312-0(4),* Usborne) EDC Publishing.
Lambert, Nat. How to Draw Dinosaurs & Other Cool Stuff! Green, Barry, illus. 2015. (404 Things to Draw Ser.). (ENG.). 192p. (J). (gr. k). pap. 12.99 *(978-1-78445-274-2(2))* Top That! Publishing PLC GBR. Dist: Independent Pubs. Group.
Last, Ian & Smith, Diana, illus. How to Draw. 2005. (Art Tricks Ser.). 48p. (J). (gr. 4-7). *(978-1-84510-676-8(8))* Top That! Publishing PLC.
Lazoo Publishing Staff & ZOO, La. Squiggles! A Drawing Book. Oku, Makiko, tr. 2009. (King of Play Ser.). (ENG., Illus.). 64p. (J). (gr. -1). pap. 7.95 *(978-1-934734-13-1(6))* Seven Footer Pr.
Learn to Draw. (Learning Ser.). (Illus.). 22p. (J). bds. *(978-2-7643-0000-8(X))* Phidal Publishing, Inc./Editions Phidal, Inc.
Lee, Justin. How to Draw Fish. 2009. (Kid's Guide to Drawing Ser.). 24p. (gr. 3-3). 47.90 *(978-1-61511-032-2(1),* PowerKids Pr.) Rosen Publishing Group, Inc., The.
LeLarge, Blandine. Fashion Design Lookbook: More Than 50 Creative Tips & Techniques for the Fashion-Forward Artist. 2014. (ENG., Illus.). 128p. (J). (gr. 5-11). pap. 16.95 *(978-1-60058-436-7(5))* Quarto Publishing Group USA.
Lester, Alison. Alison Lester's Wonderful World: Colour Your Favourite Drawings. 2017. (ENG.). 48p. (J). (gr. k). pap. 9.99 ***(978-1-76029-313-0(X))*** Allen & Unwin AUS. Dist: Independent Pubs. Group.
Levin, Freddie. ABC Fun Stained Glass Jr. Coloring Book. 2012. (Dover Stained Glass Coloring Book Ser.). (ENG.). 32p. (J). (gr. -1-1). pap. 3.99 *(978-0-486-49875-1(1))* Dover Pubns., Inc.
—1-2-3 Draw Horses. Levin, Freddie, illus. 2004. (1-2-3 Draw Ser.). (ENG., Illus.). 64p. (J). pap. 8.99 *(978-0-939217-61-8(9))* Peel Productions, Inc.
—1-2-3 Draw Mythical Creatures: A Step-by-Step Guide. Levin, Freddie, illus. 2014. Orig. Title: 2003. (Illus.). 64p. (J). pap. *(978-0-939217-06-9(6))* Peel Productions, Inc.
Levy, Barbara Soloff. Drawing on the Go! Animals. 2010. (Dover Doodle Bks.). (ENG., Illus.). 64p. (J). (gr. k-3). pap. 1.99 *(978-0-486-47944-6(7))* Dover Pubns., Inc.
—Drawing on the Go! Lots of Things. 2010. (Dover Doodle Bks.). (ENG., Illus.). 64p. (J). (gr. k-3). pap. 1.99 *(978-0-486-47945-3(5))* Dover Pubns., Inc.
—How to Draw Christmas Pictures. 2005. (Dover How to Draw Ser.). (ENG., Illus.). 32p. (J). (gr. 1-5). per. 2.95 *(978-0-486-44008-8(7))* Dover Pubns., Inc.
—How to Draw Forest Animals. 2008. (Dover How to Draw Ser.). (ENG., Illus.). 64p. (J). (gr. k-5). pap. 4.99 *(978-0-486-47199-0(3))* Dover Pubns., Inc.
—How to Draw Musical Instruments. 2009. (Dover How to Draw Ser.). (ENG.). 64p. (J). (gr. 1-5). pap. 4.99 *(978-0-486-46220-2(X))* Dover Pubns., Inc.
—Pets Follow-the-Dots. 2006. (Dover Little Activity Bks.). (ENG., Illus.). 64p. (J). (gr. k-3). per. 1.99 *(978-0-486-44890-9(8))* Dover Pubns., Inc.
Levy, Barbara Soloff & Activity Books. Drawing on the Go! People. 2012. (Dover Little Activity Bks.). (ENG., Illus.). 32p. (J). (gr. k-3). pap. 1.99 *(978-0-486-48882-0(9))* Dover Pubns., Inc.
—Drawing on the Go! under the Sea. 2012. (Dover Little Activity Bks.). (ENG., Illus.). 32p. (J). (gr. k-3). pap. 1.99 *(978-0-486-48883-7(7))* Dover Pubns., Inc.
Levy, Barbara Soloff & Drawing Staff. You Can Draw Animals. 2003. (Dover How to Draw Ser.). (ENG., Illus.). 132p. (J). (gr. k-4). pap. 8.95 *(978-0-486-42899-4(0))* Dover Pubns., Inc.
Levy, Janey. Renaissance Paintings: Using Perspective to Represent Three-Dimensional Objects. (PowerMath Ser.). (Illus.). 32p. 2009. (ENG.). (gr. 5-6). pap. 10.00 *(978-1-4042-5115-1(4))* 2005. (J). (gr. 3-6). lib. bdg. 25.25 *(978-1-4042-2926-6(4),* PowerKids Pr.) Rosen Publishing Group, Inc., The.
Lewis & Clark Hands on Art And. 2004. (J). pap. 14.95 *(978-0-9715970-5-1(7))* Visual Manna.
Lipniewska, Dominika, illus. 100 Coloring Book. 2015. (ENG.). 20p. (gr. -1-2). pap. 12.95 *(978-1-84976-381-3(X))* Tate Publishing, Ltd. GBR. Dist: Abrams, Inc.
Lipsey, Jennifer. I Love to Draw! 2005. (My Very Favorite Art Book Ser.). (ENG., Illus.). 48p. (J). (gr. k-3). 9.95 *(978-1-57990-629-0(X))* Lark Bks.
Lodge, Jo. Colour & Stick, Mr Croc. 2013. (ENG.). 24p. (J). (gr. -1-k). pap. 5.99 *(978-1-4449-1308-8(5))* Hodder & Stoughton GBR. Dist: Hachette Bk. Group.
Low, Susan. Just Draw! 2006. (Illus.). 24p. *(978-2-7643-0295-8(9))* Phidal Publishing, Inc./Editions Phidal, Inc.
MacBeth, Sybil. Praying in Color. 2009. (ENG., Illus.). 40p. (J). (gr. 1-5). pap. 16.99 *(978-1-55725-595-2(4))* Paraclete Pr., Inc.
Maclaine, James. Drawing, Doodling & Coloring Blue Book. 2015. (Doodle Bks.). (ENG.). 128p. (J). (gr. k-5). pap. 13.99 *(978-0-7945-3443-1(0),* Usborne) EDC Publishing.
—Drawing, Doodling & Coloring Book Boys. 2012. (Activity Cards Ser.). 128p. (J). pap. 13.99 *(978-0-7945-3296-3(9),* Usborne) EDC Publishing.
Magruder, Trula & American Girl Editors, eds. Design by Me Tropical: Fancy Art & Fun Display Ideas! 2011. (ENG.). 32p. (J). spiral bd. 14.95 *(978-1-59369-871-3(2))* American Girl Publishing, Inc.
Make Your Own Art, 12 vols., Sets 1-2. Incl. Set 1. 2008. lib. bdg. 151.50 *(978-1-4358-2549-9(7))*; Set 2. 2010. lib. bdg. 151.50 *(978-1-4488-1625-5(4))*; (J). (gr. 3-6). (Make Your Own Art Ser.). (Illus.). 32p. 2010. Set lib. bdg. 303.00 *(978-1-4488-1626-2(2),* PowerKids Pr.) Rosen Publishing Group, Inc., The.
Makowski, Robin Lee. Draw Anything You Like. 2005. (Drawing Made Fun Ser.). (Illus.). 32p. (J). (gr. 2-5). lib. bdg. 20.95 *(978-1-59515-470-5(1),* 1244420) Rourke Educational Media.
Makowski, Robin Lee, illus. Dogs. 2004. (J). *(978-1-59203-088-0(2))* Learning Challenge, Inc.
—Sea Creatures. 2004. (J). *(978-1-59203-090-3(4))* Learning Challenge, Inc.
Masiello, Ralph. Bug Drawing Book: Simple Steps Make Anyone an Artist. Masiello, Ralph, illus. 2004. (ENG., Illus.). 32p. (J). (gr. k-3). 16.95 *(978-1-57091-525-3(3))* Charlesbridge Publishing, Inc.
—Bug Drawing Book: Simple Steps to Make Anyone an Artist. Masiello, Ralph, illus. 2004. (ENG., Illus.). 32p. (J). (gr. k-3). pap. 7.95 *(978-1-57091-526-0(1))* Charlesbridge Publishing, Inc.
—Ralph Masiello's Dinosaur Drawing Book. Masiello, Ralph, illus. 2005. (ENG., Illus.). 48p. (J). (gr. k-3). per. 7.95 *(978-1-57091-528-4(8))* Charlesbridge Publishing, Inc.
Mayer, Kirsten. Monster High. 2015. (ENG., Illus.). 128p. (J). (gr. 1-17). pap. 12.99 *(978-0-316-28721-0(0))* Little, Brown Bks. for Young Readers.
Mazurkiewicz, Jessica. COLORTWIST — Blue Coloring Book. 2013. (Dover Coloring Bks.). (ENG.). 64p. (J). (gr. -1-8). pap. 5.99 *(978-0-486-49971-0(5))* Dover Pubns., Inc.
—COLORTWIST — Green Coloring Book. 2013. (Dover Coloring Bks.). (ENG.). 64p. (J). (gr. -1-8). pap. 5.99 *(978-0-486-49945-1(6))* Dover Pubns., Inc.
—COLORTWIST — Pink Coloring Book. 2013. (Dover Coloring Bks.). (ENG.). 64p. (J). (gr. -1-8). pap. 5.99 *(978-0-486-49946-8(4))* Dover Pubns., Inc.
—COLORTWIST — Purple Coloring Book. 2013. (Dover Coloring Bks.). (ENG.). 64p. (J). (gr. -1-8). pap. 5.99 *(978-0-486-49947-5(2))* Dover Pubns., Inc.
—How to Draw Mandalas. 2013. (ENG., Illus.). 48p. (J). (gr. 6-12). pap. 5.99 *(978-0-486-49179-0(X))* Dover Pubns., Inc.
McCann, Emily. Animal Doodles. McCann, Emily, illus. 2011. (Doodle On! Ser.). (ENG., Illus.). 160p. (J). (gr. k-4). 15.99 *(978-0-230-74485-1(0))* Pan Macmillan GBR. Dist: Independent Pubs. Group.
McClurkan, Rob. What to Doodle? on the Farm. 2013. (ENG.). 64p. (J). (gr. k-3). pap. 1.50 *(978-0-486-49230-8(3))* Dover Pubns., Inc.
McCurry, Kristen. Smithsonian Drawing Books. Edwards, Mat et al, illus. 2013. (Smithsonian Drawing Bks.). (ENG.). 64p. (gr. 3-4). pap. 166.80 *(978-1-62065-732-4(5))*; lib. bdg.

101.97 (978-1-4296-9942-6(6)) Capstone Press of Coughlan Cos.

—Smithsonian Drawing Books. Meschini, Leonardo & Osterhold, Jared, illus. 2012. (Smithsonian Drawing Bks.). (ENG.). 64p. (gr. 3-4). pap. 13.90 (978-1-62065-730-0(9)) Capstone Press of Coughlan Cos.

—Smithsonian Drawing Books. Edwards, Mat et al, illus. 2012. (Smithsonian Drawing Bks.). (ENG.). 64p. (gr. 3-4). pap. 27.80 (978-1-62065-731-7(7)) Capstone Press of Coughlan Cos.

McKee, Karen & Griffin, Georgene, illus. Hot Wings. 2004. (J). (978-1-59203-091-0(2)) Learning Challenge, Inc.

Milbourne, Anna. Drawing Animals. 2004. (Art School Ser.). (Illus.). 64p. (J). lib. bdg. 16.95 (978-1-58086-381-0(7)) EDC Publishing.

Miller, Mona. A Very Busy Coloring Book. Golden Books, illus. 2013. (Jumbo Coloring Book Ser.). (ENG.). 224p. (J). (gr. -1-2). pap. 5.99 (978-0-449-81609-7(5), Golden Bks.) Random Hse. Children's Bks.

Mis, M. S. How to Draw New Jersey's Sights & Symbols. 2009. (Kid's Guide to Drawing America Ser.). 32p. (gr. k-k). 50.50 (978-1-61511-079-7(8), PowerKids Pr.) Rosen Publishing Group, Inc., The.

—How to Draw North Dakota's Sights & Symbols. 2009. (Kid's Guide to Drawing America Ser.). 32p. (gr. k-k). 50.50 (978-1-61511-087-2(9), PowerKids Pr.) Rosen Publishing Group, Inc., The.

Mis, Melody S. How to Draw Australia's Sights & Symbols. 2005. (Kid's Guide to Drawing the Countries of the World Ser.). (Illus.). 48p. (J). (gr. -1-3). lib. bdg. 29.25 (978-1-4042-2731-6(8), PowerKids Pr.) Rosen Publishing Group, Inc., The.

—How to Draw Brazil's Sights & Symbols. 2004. (Kid's Guide to Drawing the Countries of the World Ser.). (Illus.). 48p. (J). lib. bdg. 29.25 (978-0-8239-6667-7(4), PowerKids Pr.) Rosen Publishing Group, Inc., The.

—How to Draw China's Sights & Symbols. 2004. (Kid's Guide to Drawing the Countries of the World Ser.). (Illus.). 48p. (J). lib. bdg. 29.25 (978-0-8239-6664-6(X), PowerKids Pr.) Rosen Publishing Group, Inc., The.

—How to Draw India's Sights & Symbols. (Kid's Guide to Drawing the Countries of the World Ser.). 48p. 2009. (gr. 4-4). 53.00 (978-1-61511-113-8(1)) 2005. (Illus.). (J). (gr. k-5). lib. bdg. 29.25 (978-1-4042-2732-3(6)) Rosen Publishing Group, Inc., The. (PowerKids Pr.).

—How to Draw Kenya's Sights & Symbols. (Kid's Guide to Drawing the Countries of the World Ser.). 48p. 2009. (gr. 4-4). 53.00 (978-1-61511-117-6(4)) 2005. (Illus.). (J). (gr. k-5). lib. bdg. 29.25 (978-1-4042-2733-0(4)) Rosen Publishing Group, Inc., The. (PowerKids Pr.).

—How to Draw Norway's Sights & Symbols. (Kid's Guide to Drawing the Countries of the World Ser.). 48p. 2009. (gr. 4-4). 53.00 (978-1-61511-119-0(0)) 2005. (Illus.). (J). (gr. k-5). lib. bdg. 29.25 (978-1-4042-2734-7(2)) Rosen Publishing Group, Inc., The. (PowerKids Pr.).

—How to Draw Poland's Sights & Symbols. 2004. (Kid's Guide to Drawing the Countries of the World Ser.). (Illus.). 48p. (J). lib. bdg. 29.25 (978-0-8239-6669-1(0), PowerKids Pr.) Rosen Publishing Group, Inc., The.

—How to Draw Portugal's Sights & Symbols. 2005. (Kid's Guide to Drawing the Countries of the World Ser.). (J). 29.25 (978-1-4042-2735-4(0), PowerKids Pr.) Rosen Publishing Group, Inc., The.

—How to Draw Russia's Sights & Symbols. 2004. (Kid's Guide to Drawing the Countries of the World Ser.). (Illus.). 48p. (J). lib. bdg. 29.25 (978-0-8239-6666-0(6), PowerKids Pr.) Rosen Publishing Group, Inc., The.

—How to Draw South Africa's Sights & Symbols. 2004. (Kid's Guide to Drawing the Countries of the World Ser.). (Illus.). 48p. (J). lib. bdg. 29.25 (978-0-8239-6665-3(8), PowerKids Pr.) Rosen Publishing Group, Inc., The.

—How to Draw South Korea's Sights & Symbols. 2005. (Kid's Guide to Drawing the Countries of the World Ser.). (J). 29.25 (978-1-4042-2736-1(9), PowerKids Pr.) Rosen Publishing Group, Inc., The.

—How to Draw the Life & Times of Andrew Jackson. 2006. (Kid's Guide to Drawing the Presidents of the United States of America Ser.). (YA). (gr. 2-5). 26.50 (978-1-4042-2984-6(1)) Rosen Publishing Group, Inc., The.

—How to Draw the Life & Times of Thomas Jefferson. 2006. (Kid's Guide to Drawing the Presidents of the United States of America Ser.). (YA). (gr. 2-5). 26.50 (978-1-4042-2980-8(9)) Rosen Publishing Group, Inc., The.

—A Kid's Guide to Drawing the Countries of the World: Set 2, 6 bks., Set 2003. (Illus.). (J). (gr. k-5). (978-0-8239-8486-2(9), PowerKids Pr.) Rosen Publishing Group, Inc., The.

Mostyn, David. Super Doodles: Complete the Crazy Pictures! 2015. (ENG.). 384p. (J). (gr. 2-6). pap. 9.99 (978-1-4380-0606-2(3)) Barron's Educational Series, Inc.

Mottashed, Susie. Who Lives in Your Backyard? Creating a journal that opens your eyes & heart to nature's nearby Wonders. Mottashed, Susie, illus. 2005. (Illus.). 96p. 24.95 (978-0-9759300-0-7(1)) Sketches From The Heart Publishing.

Muehlenhardt, Amy Bailey. Drawing & Learning about Cars: Using Shapes & Lines, 1 vol. Muehlenhardt, Amy Bailey, illus. 2004. (Sketch It! Ser.). (ENG., Illus.). 24p. (gr. k-4). 26.65 (978-1-4048-0269-8(X)) Picture Window Bks.

—Drawing & Learning about Faces: Using Shapes & Lines. Muehlenhardt, Amy Bailey, illus. 2004. (Sketch It! Ser.). (ENG., Illus.). 24p. (gr. k-4). 26.65 (978-1-4048-0271-1(1), 1229557) Picture Window Bks.

—Sketch It! Set of 6, 6 bks. Muehlenhardt, Amy Bailey, illus. Incl. Drawing & Learning about Cars: Using Shapes & Lines. 26.65 (978-1-4048-0269-8(X)); Drawing & Learning about Faces: Using Shapes & Lines. 26.65 (978-1-4048-0271-1(1), 1229557); (gr. k-4). (Sketch It! Ser.). (ENG., Illus.). 24p. 2004. 159.90 o.p. (978-1-4048-0265-0(7)) Picture Window Bks.

My Little Pony Staff. I Love to Draw! Design & Draw Your Favorite Ponies with Stickers, Stencils, & More! 2013. (Learn Drawing Ser.: 1). (ENG.). 48p. (J). (gr. 1-4). pap. 8.99 (978-0-7944-2852-5(5)) Reader's Digest Assn., Inc., The.

Nash, Mike, et al, illus. Drawing. 2012. (Drawing Ser.). (ENG.). 48p. (gr. 3-4). lib. bdg. 63.98 (978-1-4296-8228-2(0)); lib. bdg. 191.94 (978-1-4296-8229-9(9)) Capstone Press of Coughlan Cos.

Nemmers, Tom. Pirates Scratch & Sketch: For Adventurous Artists & Explorers of All Ages. Zschock, Martha Day, illus. 2007. 64p. (J). 12.99 (978-1-59359-871-6(8)) Peter Pauper Pr. Inc.

Newman-D'Amico, Fran. BOOST Favorite Fairy Tales Coloring Book. 2013. (BOOST Educational Ser.). (ENG.). 32p. (J). (gr. -1-k). pap. 4.99 (978-0-486-49403-6(9)) Dover Pubns., Inc.

Nichols, Kaitlyn. Draw the DC Universe: Learn to Draw the Heroes & the Villains. 2011. (ENG.). 104p. (J). spiral bd. 19.99 (978-0-545-34619-1(3)) Klutz.

Nicholson, Sue. Drawing, 6 vols. 2005. (QEB Let's Start! Art Ser.). (Illus.). 24p. (J). (gr. 2-5). lib. bdg. 16.95 (978-1-59566-083-1(6)) QEB Publishing Inc.

Nissen Samuels, Linda. Draw Water & Other Things. Malvezi, Irene, illus. 2010. 48p. (J). pap. 15.98 (978-1-905941-15-5(3)) Sigel Pr.

Noble, Marty. Fanciful Butterflies Stained Glass Coloring Book. 2012. (Dover Nature Stained Glass Coloring Book Ser.). (ENG., Illus.). 32p. (gr. 3-5). pap. 7.99 (978-0-486-48649-9(4)) Dover Pubns., Inc.

—3-D Coloring Book — Mystic Mandalas. 2011. (Dover 3-D Coloring Book Ser.). (ENG., Illus.). 32p. (J). (gr. 3-5). pap. 5.99 (978-0-486-48102-9(6)) Dover Pubns., Inc.

Odenthal, Ingrid. The Warm Heart. 2009. 20p. pap. 12.49 (978-1-4490-5188-4(X)) AuthorHouse.

Oka, Joseph J. Rosary Reflections for Kids. 2003. (Illus.). 30p. (J). (gr. -1-8). 9.95 (978-0-9729800-0-5(8)) Joseph's Labor.

Olmedillas, Cathy, compiled by. Anorak. 2013. (ENG., Illus.). 64p. (J). pap. 9.99 (978-1-4236-3340-2(7), Anorak Pr.) Gibbs Smith, Publisher.

Owen, Ruth. Goldendoodles. 2012. (Designer Dogs Ser.). (ENG., Illus.). 32p. (J). (gr. k-5). 25.25 (978-1-4488-7856-7(X)); pap. 10.00 (978-1-4488-7909-0(4)) Rosen Publishing Group, Inc., The. (PowerKids Pr.).

—Labradoodles. 2012. (Designer Dogs Ser.). (ENG., Illus.). 32p. (J). (gr. k-5). pap. 10.00 (978-1-4488-7910-6(8), PowerKids Pr.) Rosen Publishing Group, Inc., The.

Papel, Dibujos y Pinturas. (One Hundred One Things to Do Ser.).Tr. of Paper, Drawing & Painting. (SPA.). (J). (gr. 3-5). pap. 4.76 (978-950-724-204-5(X)) Lumen ARG. Dist: Lectorum Pubns., Inc.

Parot, Annelore, illus. Kokeshi Style: Design Your Own Kokeshi Fashions. 2012. (ENG.). 120p. 14.99 (978-1-4521-1372-2(6)) Chronicle Bks. LLC.

Parramore, Helen. Brian's Bird Book. 2009. 32p. pap. 12.99 (978-1-4490-2886-2(1)) AuthorHouse.

Parrish, Emma. Spooky Doodles: Ghostly Designs to Complete & Create. 2014. (ENG.). 128p. (J). (gr. 1-17). pap. 12.95 (978-0-7624-5481-5(4), Running Pr. Kids) Running Pr. Bk. Pubs.

Perry, Fred. Gold Digger, Vol. 10. 2003. (ENG., Illus.). 124p. (gr. 11-18). pap. 12.95 (978-0-9728978-7-7(9), 9780972897877) Antarctic Pr., Inc.

Peters, S. True. How to Draw New Hampshire's Sights & Symbols. 2009. (Kid's Guide to Drawing America Ser.). 32p. (gr. k-k). 50.50 (978-1-61511-078-0(X), PowerKids Pr.) Rosen Publishing Group, Inc., The.

—How to Draw North Carolina's Sights & Symbols. 2009. (Kid's Guide to Drawing America Ser.). 32p. (gr. k-k). 50.50 (978-1-61511-084-1(4), PowerKids Pr.) Rosen Publishing Group, Inc., The.

—How to Draw Oregon's Sights & Symbols. 2009. (Kid's Guide to Drawing America Ser.). 32p. (gr. k-k). 50.50 (978-1-61511-090-2(9), PowerKids Pr.) Rosen Publishing Group, Inc., The.

Phillips, Jillian. What to Doodle? - Jr. Animals! 2011. (Dover Doodle Bks.). (ENG.). 128p. (J). (gr. k-3). pap. 3.99 (978-0-486-47822-7(X)) Dover Pubns., Inc.

—What to Doodle? At the Aquarium. 2011. (Dover Doodle Bks.). (ENG., Illus.). 64p. (J). (gr. k-3). pap. 1.99 (978-0-486-47819-7(X)) Dover Pubns., Inc.

Pinder, Andrew. Icky, Sticky, Slimy Doodles: Gross, Full-Color Pictures to Complete & Create. 2013. (ENG., Illus.). 160p. (J). (gr. -1-17). pap. 12.95 (978-0-7624-4972-9(1), Running Pr. Kids) Running Pr. Bk. Pubs.

Pinnington, Andrea. The Horse & Pony Creativity Book. 2013. (Creativity Bks.). (ENG., Illus.). 80p. (J). (gr. 1-6). pap. 12.99 (978-1-4380-0127-2(4)) Barron's Educational Series, Inc.

Poitier, Anton. Design & Doodle: A Book of Astonishing Invention - Amazing Things to Imagine, Draw, & Discover. Running Press Staff, ed. 2013. (ENG., Illus.). 128p. (gr. k). pap. 12.95 (978-0-7624-5047-3(9), Running Pr. Kids) Running Pr. Bk. Pubs.

Pomaska, Anna & Coloring Books Staff. My First Mandalas - Nature. 2012. (Dover Coloring Bks.). (ENG., Illus.). 32p. (J). (gr. -1-3). pap. 3.99 (978-0-486-48708-3(3)) Dover Pubns., Inc.

Powell, William F. Drawing - Wild Animals: Learn to Draw Step by Step. 2004. (How to Draw & Paint Ser.). (ENG., Illus.). 32p. pap. 8.95 (978-1-56010-815-3(0), 1560108150) Quarto Publishing Group USA.

Prasadam-halls, Smriti. Scary Doodles. Boretzki, Anja, illus. 2011. (Doodle On! Ser.). (ENG.). 160p. (J). (gr. k-4). 15.99 (978-0-230-73624-5(6)) Pan Macmillan GBR. Dist: Independent Pubs. Group.

Priddy, Roger. Pen Control. 2012. (Wipe Clean Ser.). (ENG., Illus.). 24p. (J). (gr. -1-1). bds. 8.95 (978-0-312-51395-5(X), 9780312513955, Priddy Bks.) St. Martin's Pr.

—Super Dinky Doodles. 2014. (Dinky Doodles Ser.). (ENG.). 128p. (J). (gr. k-3). pap. 4.99 (978-0-312-51665-9(7), 9780312516659, Priddy Bks.) St. Martin's Pr.

Princenthal, Nancy. Heide Fasnacht. 2004. (Illus.). 80p. (978-1-878607-54-6(5), 50) Kent Gallery.

Princess & Butterflies Sketchbook. 2005. (J). pap. (978-1-59461-068-4(1)) eeBoo Corp.

Publications International Ltd. Staff, ed. Doodles for Kids. 2011. 100p. (J). spiral bd. 13.98 (978-1-4508-0991-7(X)) Publications International, Ltd.

—Doodles to Go: Razzle Dazzle Doodles. 2011. 146p. (J). spiral bd. 8.98 (978-1-4508-1662-5(2)) Publications International, Ltd.

—Doodles to Go: Super Duper Doodles. 2011. 146p. (J). spiral bd. (978-1-4508-1603-8(7)) Publications International, Ltd.

—Fun to Draw. 2010. 96p. (J). 5.98 (978-1-60553-749-8(7)) Phoenix International Publications, Inc.

Puck. Doodle New York: Create. Imagine. Draw Your Way Through the Big Apple. Lemay, Violet, illus. 2012. (ENG.). 120p. (J). (gr. k-3). pap. 12.95 (978-0-9838121-3-5(6)) Duo Pr. LLC.

QEB Learn Art National Book Stores Edition: Drawing & Sketching. 2006. (J). per. (978-1-59566-280-4(4)) QEB Publishing Inc.

QEB Let's Start! Art National Book Stores Edition: Drawing. 2006. (J). per. (978-1-59566-304-7(5)) QEB Publishing Inc.

Quasha, Jennifer. How to Draw Colorado's Sights & Symbols. 2009. (Kid's Guide to Drawing America Ser.). 32p. (gr. k-k). 50.50 (978-1-61511-050-6(X), PowerKids Pr.) Rosen Publishing Group, Inc., The.

—How to Draw Connecticut's Sights & Symbols. 2009. (Kid's Guide to Drawing America Ser.). 32p. (gr. k-k). 50.50 (978-1-61511-051-3(8), PowerKids Pr.) Rosen Publishing Group, Inc., The.

—How to Draw Delaware's Sights & Symbols. 2009. (Kid's Guide to Drawing America Ser.). 32p. (gr. k-k). 50.50 (978-1-61511-052-0(6), PowerKids Pr.) Rosen Publishing Group, Inc., The.

—How to Draw Florida's Sights & Symbols. 2009. (Kid's Guide to Drawing America Ser.). 32p. (gr. k-k). 50.50 (978-1-61511-054-4(2), PowerKids Pr.) Rosen Publishing Group, Inc., The.

—How to Draw Georgia's Sights & Symbols. 2009. (Kid's Guide to Drawing America Ser.). 32p. (gr. k-k). 50.50 (978-1-61511-057-5(7), PowerKids Pr.) Rosen Publishing Group, Inc., The.

—How to Draw Hawaii's Sights & Symbols. 2009. (Kid's Guide to Drawing America Ser.). 32p. (gr. k-k). 50.50 (978-1-61511-058-2(5), PowerKids Pr.) Rosen Publishing Group, Inc., The.

—How to Draw Idaho's Sights & Symbols. 2009. (Kid's Guide to Drawing America Ser.). 32p. (gr. k-k). 50.50 (978-1-61511-059-9(3), PowerKids Pr.) Rosen Publishing Group, Inc., The.

Radford, Megan. Canada Doodles, 1 vol. Cook, Peter, illus. 2014. (ENG.). 240p. pap. 9.99 (978-1-4236-3621-2(X)) Gibbs Smith, Publisher.

Randolph, Joanne. Let's Draw a Bird with Shapes. 2009. (Let's Draw with Shapes Ser.). 24p. (gr. k-k). 42.50 (978-1-61514-203-3(7), PowerKids Pr.) Rosen Publishing Group, Inc., The.

—Let's Draw a Bird with Shapes. Muschinske, Emily, illus. 2005. (Let's Draw with Shapes Ser.). 24p. (J). (gr. k-1). lib. bdg. 22.60 (978-1-4042-2792-7(X), PowerKids Pr.) Rosen Publishing Group, Inc., The.

—Let's Draw a Bird with Shapes: Vamos a Dibujar un Ave Usando Figuras. Muschinske, Emily, illus. 2005. (Let's Draw with Shapes / Vamos a Dibujar con Figuras Ser.). (J). 22.60 (978-1-4042-7555-3(X), PowerKids Pr.) Rosen Publishing Group, Inc., The.

—Let's Draw a Bird with Shapes/Vamos a dibujar un ave usando Figuras. 2009. (Let's Draw with Shapes / Vamos a dibujar con figuras Ser.). (ENG & SPA.). 24p. (gr. k-1). 42.50 (978-1-61514-214-9(2), Editorial Buenas Letras) Rosen Publishing Group, Inc., The.

—Let's Draw a Butterfly with Circles. 2009. (Let's Draw with Shapes Ser.). 24p. (gr. k-k). 42.50 (978-1-61514-204-0(5), PowerKids Pr.) Rosen Publishing Group, Inc., The.

—Let's Draw a Butterfly with Circles. Muschinske, Emily, illus. 2005. (Let's Draw with Shapes Ser.). 24p. (J). (gr. k-1). lib. bdg. 22.60 (978-1-4042-2500-8(5), PowerKids Pr.) Rosen Publishing Group, Inc., The.

—Let's Draw a Butterfly with Circles: Vamos a Dibujar una Mariposa Usando Circulos. Muschinske, Emily, illus. 2004. (Let's Draw with Shapes / Vamos a Dibujar con Figuras Ser.). (ENG & SPA.). 24p. (J). (gr. -1-1). lib. bdg. 22.60 (978-1-4042-7500-3(2), PowerKids Pr.) Rosen Publishing Group, Inc., The.

—Let's Draw a Butterfly with Circles / Vamos a dibujar una mariposa usando Círculos. 2009. (Let's Draw with Shapes / Vamos a dibujar con figuras Ser.). (ENG & SPA.). 24p. (gr. k-1). 42.50 (978-1-61514-221-7(5), Editorial Buenas Letras) Rosen Publishing Group, Inc., The.

—Let's Draw a Dinosaur with Shapes. 2009. (Let's Draw with Shapes Ser.). 24p. (gr. k-k). 42.50 (978-1-61514-205-7(3), PowerKids Pr.) Rosen Publishing Group, Inc., The.

—Let's Draw a Dinosaur with Shapes. Muschinske, Emily, illus. 2005. (Let's Draw with Shapes Ser.). 24p. (J). (gr. k-1). lib. bdg. 22.60 (978-1-4042-2793-4(8), PowerKids Pr.) Rosen Publishing Group, Inc., The.

—Let's Draw a Dinosaur with Shapes: Vamos a Dibujar un Dinosaurio Usando Figuras. 2005. (Let's Draw with Shapes / Vamos a Dibujar con Figuras Ser.). (ENG & SPA.). (J). 22.60 (978-1-4042-7553-9(3), PowerKids Pr.) Rosen Publishing Group, Inc., The.

—Let's Draw a Dinosaur with Shapes/Vamos a dibujar un dinasaurio usando Figuras. 2009. (Let's Draw with Shapes / Vamos a dibujar con figuras Ser.). (ENG & SPA.). 24p. (gr. k-1). 42.50 (978-1-61514-215-6(0), Editorial Buenas Letras) Rosen Publishing Group, Inc., The.

—Let's Draw a Fire Truck with Shapes. Muschinske, Emily, illus. 2005. (Let's Draw with Shapes Ser.). 24p. (J). (gr. k-1). lib. bdg. 22.60 (978-1-4042-2794-1(6), PowerKids Pr.) Rosen Publishing Group, Inc., The.

—Let's Draw a Fire Truck with Shapes: Vamos a Dibujar un Camion de Bomberos Usando Figuras. Muschinske, Emily, illus. 2005. (Let's Draw with Shapes / Vamos a Dibujar con Figuras Ser.). (ENG & SPA.). (J). 22.60 (978-1-4042-7556-0(8), PowerKids Pr.) Rosen Publishing Group, Inc., The.

—Let's Draw a Horse with Rectangles. 2009. (Let's Draw with Shapes Ser.). 24p. (gr. k-k). 42.50 (978-1-61514-209-5(6), PowerKids Pr.) Rosen Publishing Group, Inc., The.

—Let's Draw a Horse with Rectangles. Muschinske, Emily, tr. Muschinske, Emily, illus. 2004. (Let's Draw with Shapes Ser.). 24p. (gr. -1-1). 22.60 (978-1-4042-2502-2(1), PowerKids Pr.) Rosen Publishing Group, Inc., The.

—Let's Draw a Horse with Rectangles: Vamos a Dibujar un Caballo Usando Rectangulos. 2004. (Let's Draw with Shapes / Vamos a Dibujar con Figuras Ser.). (ENG & SPA., Illus.). 24p. (J). (gr. -1-1). lib. bdg. 22.60 (978-1-4042-7502-7(9), PowerKids Pr.) Rosen Publishing Group, Inc., The.

—Let's Draw a Horse with Rectangles / Vamos a dibujar un caballo usando Rectángulos. 2009. (Let's Draw with Shapes / Vamos a dibujar con figuras Ser.). (ENG & SPA.). 24p. (gr. k-1). 42.50 (978-1-61514-224-8(X), Editorial Buenas Letras) Rosen Publishing Group, Inc., The.

—Let's Draw a House with Shapes. Muschinske, Emily, illus. 2005. (Let's Draw with Shapes Ser.). 24p. (J). (gr. k-1). lib. bdg. 22.60 (978-1-4042-2795-8(4), PowerKids Pr.) Rosen Publishing Group, Inc., The.

—Let's Draw a House with Shapes: Vamos a Dibujar una Casa Usando Figuras. Muschinske, Emily, illus. 2005. (Let's Draw with Shapes / Vamos a Dibujar con Figuras Ser.). (ENG & SPA.). (J). 22.60 (978-1-4042-7558-4(4), PowerKids Pr.) Rosen Publishing Group, Inc., The.

—Let's Draw a School Bus with Shapes. Muschinske, Emily, illus. 2005. (Let's Draw with Shapes Ser.). 24p. (J). (gr. k-1). lib. bdg. 22.60 (978-1-4042-2791-0(1), PowerKids Pr.) Rosen Publishing Group, Inc., The.

—Let's Draw a School Bus with Shapes: Vamos a Dibujar un Autobus Escolar Usando Figuras. Muschinske, Emily, illus. 2005. (Let's Draw with Shapes / Vamos a Dibujar con Figuras Ser.). (ENG & SPA.). (J). 22.60 (978-1-4042-7557-7(6), PowerKids Pr.) Rosen Publishing Group, Inc., The.

—Let's Draw a Truck with Shapes. 2009. (Let's Draw with Shapes Ser.). 24p. (gr. k-k). 42.50 (978-1-61514-212-5(6), PowerKids Pr.) Rosen Publishing Group, Inc., The.

—Let's Draw a Truck with Shapes. Muschinske, Emily, illus. 2005. (Let's Draw with Shapes Ser.). 24p. (J). (gr. k-1). lib. bdg. 22.60 (978-1-4042-2796-5(2), PowerKids Pr.) Rosen Publishing Group, Inc., The.

—Let's Draw a Truck with Shapes: Vamos a Dibujar un Camion Usando Figuras. Muschinske, Emily, illus. 2005. (Let's Draw with Shapes / Vamos a Dibujar con Figuras Ser.). (ENG & SPA.). (J). 22.60 (978-1-4042-7554-6(1), PowerKids Pr.) Rosen Publishing Group, Inc., The.

—Let's Draw a Turtle with Half Circles. 2004. (Let's Draw with Shapes Ser.). (Illus.). 24p. (J). (gr. k-1). lib. bdg. 22.60 (978-1-4042-2504-6(8), PowerKids Pr.) Rosen Publishing Group, Inc., The.

—Let's Draw a Turtle with Half Circles/Vamos a Dibujar una Tortuga Usando Medios Circulos. Brusca, Maria Cristina, tr. 2004. (Let's Draw with Shapes / Vamos a Dibujar con Figuras Ser.). (ENG & SPA., Illus.). 24p. (J). (gr. -1-k). lib. bdg. 22.60 (978-1-4042-7504-1(5), PowerKids Pr.) Rosen Publishing Group, Inc., The.

Raynes, John & Raynes, Jody. How to Draw a Human Figure. 2003. (Essential Art Ser.). 160p. (YA). 19.95 (978-0-7525-8772-1(2)) Parragon, Inc.

Rechlin, Ted. What to Doodle? Manga! 2011. (Dover Doodle Bks.). (ENG., Illus.). 64p. (J). (gr. 2-5). pap. 5.99 (978-0-486-48290-3(1)) Dover Pubns., Inc.

Reynolds, Virginia. Fine Art Scratch & Sketch: A Cool Art Activity Book for Budding Fine Artists of All Ages. 2005. (Activity Journal Ser.). (Illus.). (J). 12.99 (978-0-88088-596-6(3)) Peter Pauper Pr. Inc.

Richardson, Sarah. Make Your Mark: The Drawing Book for Children. 2012. (ENG., Illus.). 80p. pap. 9.95 (978-1-84976-111-6(6)) Tate Publishing, Ltd. GBR. Dist: Abrams, Inc.

Robson, Kirsteen & Clarke, Phil. 1000 Doodles. 2015. (Tear-Off Pads Ser.). (ENG.). 128p. (J). (gr. k-5). pap. 8.99 (978-0-7945-3309-0(4), Usborne) EDC Publishing.

Rogers, Kirsteen. Spooky Coloring Book. 2012. (Coloring Bks). 32p. (J). pap. 5.99 (978-0-7945-2546-0(6), Usborne) EDC Publishing.

Ross, Graham. Bible-Story Doodles: Favorite Scenes to Complete & Create. Running Press Staff, ed. 2014. (ENG., Illus.). 160p. (J). (gr. -1-17). pap. 12.95 (978-0-7624-5217-0(X), Running Pr. Kids) Running Pr. Bk. Pubs.

Rowlands, Caroline. Dare to Doodle: Can You Complete over 100 Drawings & Let Your Pencils Loose? 2015. (Doodle Fun Ser.). (ENG.). 144p. (J). (gr. 1-5). pap. 12.99 (978-1-4380-0642-0(X)) Barron's Educational Series, Inc.

—Daydream Doodles: Let Your Mind Drift & Your Pencil Scribble with over 100 Drawings to Complete & Color. 2015. (Doodle Fun Ser.). (ENG.). 144p. (J). (gr. 1-5). pap. 12.99 (978-1-4380-0641-3(1)) Barron's Educational Series, Inc.

Roytman, Arkady, et al. Build a 3-D Poster Coloring Book — Outer Space. 2012. (Dover 3-D Coloring Book Ser.). (ENG.). 32p. (J). (gr. 3-5). 5.99 (978-0-486-49831-7(X)) Dover Pubns., Inc.

Running Press Staff. The Peanuts Gang Loves to Doodle: Create & Complete Full-Color Pictures with Charlie Brown, Snoopy, & Friends. 2013. (ENG., Illus.). 128p. (J). (gr. -1-17). pap. 12.95 (978-0-7624-5093-0(2), Running Pr. Kids) Running Pr. Bk. Pubs.

Running Press Staff, ed. Hello Kitty Fun, Friendly Doodles: Supercute Full-Color Pictures to Create & Complete. 2013. (ENG., Illus.). 160p. (J). (gr. -1-17). pap. 12.95 (978-0-7624-5092-3(4), Running Pr. Kids) Running Pr. Bk. Pubs.

Russell, Harriet. Drawing in Space. 2017. (ENG.). 64p. (J). (gr. 1-3). pap. 18.95 (978-1-61689-497-9(0)) Princeton Architectural Pr.

Ryan, Nellie. Doodles Dancing: Graceful & Gorgeous Pictures to Create & Complete. 2013. (ENG., Illus.). 64p. (J). (gr. k-3). pap. 7.95 (978-1-62087-529-2(2), 620529, Sky Pony Pr.) Skyhorse Publishing Co., Inc.

—Fabulous Fashion. Ryan, Nellie, illus. 2014. (ENG., Illus.). 160p. (J). (gr. 3-7). pap. 12.99 (978-1-907151-84-2(2)) O'Mara, Michael Bks., Ltd. GBR. Dist: Independent Pubs. Group.

Ryan, Nellie, et al. Girls' World of Doodles: Over 100 Pictures to Complete & Create. 2011. (ENG.). 128p. (J). (gr. -1-17). pap. 12.95 (978-0-7624-4287-4(5)) Running Pr. Bk. Pubs.

—Gorgeous Doodles: Pretty, Full-Color Pictures to Create & Complete. 2013. (ENG., Illus.). 128p. (J). (gr. -1-17). pap. 12.95 (978-0-7624-4971-2(3), Running Pr. Kids) Running Pr. Bk. Pubs.

Sabatino, Chris. City Doodles - Boston. 2013. (ENG., Illus.). 240p. (J). pap. 9.99 (978-1-4236-3207-8(9)) Gibbs Smith, Publisher.

—Pocketdoodles for Boys, 1 vol. 2010. (ENG.). 272p. (J). (gr. 1). 9.99 (978-1-4236-0756-4(2)) Gibbs Smith, Publisher.

—Superhero Doodles for Kids, 1 vol. 2012. (ENG., Illus.). 272p. (J). pap. 9.99 (978-1-4236-2483-7(1)) Gibbs Smith, Publisher.

Sanrio Company, Ltd. Staff. I Heart Hello Kitty Activity Book: Read, Write, Count, & Draw with Hello Kitty & Friends! 2012. (ENG.). 224p. (J). (gr. k-2). pap. 10.95 (978-1-4197-0551-9(2), Abrams Bks. for Young Readers) Abrams, Inc.

Sazaklis, John. Disney Fairies: the Pixie Dust Doodle Book. 2015. (ENG., Illus.). 128p. (J). (gr. -1-3). pap. 12.99 (978-0-316-37859-8(3)) Little, Brown Bks. for Young Readers.

Schimmell, David. Wizard of Oz. 2011. (Dover Children's Activity Bks.). (ENG., Illus.). 48p. (J). (gr. 2-5). pap., act. bk. ed. 4.99 (978-0-486-48095-4(X)) Dover Pubns., Inc.

Schmidt, Roderic. How to Draw the Life & Times of James Madison. 2006. (Kid's Guide to Drawing the Presidents of the United States of America Ser.). (YA). (gr. 2-5). 26.50 (978-1-4042-2981-5(7)) Rosen Publishing Group, Inc., The.

—How to Draw the Life & Times of Martin Van Buren. 2006. (Kid's Guide to Drawing the Presidents of the United States of America Ser.). (YA). (gr. 2-5). 26.50 (978-1-4042-2985-3(X)) Rosen Publishing Group, Inc., The.

—How to Draw the Life & Times of Zachary Taylor. 2006. (Kid's Guide to Drawing the Presidents of the United States of America Ser.). (YA). (gr. 2-5). 26.50 (978-1-4042-2989-1(2)) Rosen Publishing Group, Inc., The.

Scholastic & Klutz Editors. My Super Sweet Scented Sketchbook. 2017. (ENG.). 62p. (J). (gr. 3-7). 18.99 (978-1-338-10638-1(4)) Klutz.

Scholastic, Inc. Staff. Preschool Basic Skills: Visual Perception & Drawing Activities. 2003. (Preschool Basic Skills Ser.). (ENG.). 48p. 6.99 (978-0-439-50026-5(5), Teaching Resources) Scholastic, Inc.

Scholastic Teaching Resources Staff. Preschool Basic Skills: Visual Perception & Drawing. 2012. (Preschool Basic Skills Ser.). (ENG.). 48p. pap. 6.99 (978-0-545-42967-2(6)) Teacher's Friend Pubns., Inc.

Schulz, Charles M. Good Grief! Charlie Brown Doodles: Create & Complete Pictures with the Peanuts Gang. 2012. (ENG.). 64p. (J). (gr. 1-17). pap. 7.95 (978-0-7624-4448-9(7)) Running Pr. Bk. Pubs.

Schulz, Charles M., creator. Snoopy Loves to Doodle: Create & Complete Pictures with the Peanuts Gang. 2011. (ENG.). 64p. (J). (gr. -1-17). pap. 7.95 (978-0-7624-4378-9(2)) Running Pr. Bk. Pubs.

Scott, Linda. How to Be the Best Bubblewriter in the World Ever! 2011. (ENG., Illus.). 160p. (J). (gr. 3-7). pap. 14.95 (978-1-85669-761-3(4)) King, Laurence Publishing GBR. Dist: Hachette Bk. Group.

Scotton, Rob. Doodle & Draw. Scotton, Rob, illus. 2013. (Splat the Cat Ser.). (ENG., Illus.). 64p. (J). (gr. -1-3). pap. 6.99 (978-0-06-211607-9(X), HarperFestival) HarperCollins Pubs.

Sebastiani, Laura, creator. Penny & Drew's Penciltips, Vols. 1-4. 2006. (J). 19.95 (978-0-9766793-4-9(5)) ThoughtRockets, Inc.

—Penny & Drew's Penciltips: Animal Alliteration. 2006. 80p. (J). 4.95 (978-0-9766793-1-8(0)) ThoughtRockets, Inc.

—Penny & Drew's Penciltips: Draw THIS! 2006. 80p. (J). 4.95 (978-0-9766793-0-1(2)) ThoughtRockets, Inc.

—Penny & Drew's Penciltips: Idioms. 2006. 80p. (J). 4.95 (978-0-9766793-2-5(9)) ThoughtRockets, Inc.

—Penny & Drew's Penciltips: Transportation. 2006. 80p. (J). 4.95 (978-0-9766793-3-2(7)) ThoughtRockets, Inc.

Seuss. I Can Draw It Myself, by Me, Myself. 2017. (ENG.). 64p. (J). (gr. -1-2). 16.99 **(978-1-101-93960-4(5)**, Random Hse. Bks. for Young Readers) Random Hse. Children's Bks.

Seuss, Dr. I Can Draw It Myself, by Me, Myself. 2011. (Classic Seuss Ser.). (ENG., Illus.). 36p. (J). (gr. -1-2). pap. 4.99 (978-0-375-86600-5(0), Golden Bks.) Random Hse. Children's Bks.

Shaw-Russell, Susan. Seek, Sketch & Color — Alphabet. 2013. (Dover Children's Activity Bks.). (ENG.). 64p. (J). (gr. 1-3). pap. 5.99 (978-0-486-49772-3(0)) Dover Pubns., Inc.

—Seek, Sketch & Color — Animals. 2013. (Dover Children's Activity Bks.). (ENG.). 64p. (J). (gr. 1-3). pap. 5.99 (978-0-486-49773-0(9)) Dover Pubns., Inc.

Shaw-Russell, Susan, et al. Animals on Parade Find & Color. 2012. (Dover Children's Activity Bks.). (ENG.). 48p. (J). (gr. k-6). pap. 4.99 (978-0-486-48938-4(8)) Dover Pubns., Inc.

Shlomo, Pia. Thank You for Everything: A Book about Thanking Hashem. 2011. (Illus.). 28p. (J). 10.95 (978-1-929628-63-6(3)) Hachai Publishing.

Silver Dolphin en Español Staff, creator. Aprende con Tus Amigas. 2007. (Illus.). 20p. (J). (gr. -1). bds. (978-970-718-467-1(1), Silver Dolphin en Español) Advanced Marketing, S. de R. L. de C. V.

Singh, Asavari. Drawing. 2011. (Drawing Ser.). (ENG.). 48p. (gr. 3-4). lib. bdg. 127.96 (978-1-4296-6597-1(1)) Capstone Press of Coughlan Cos.

Sleeping Bear Press. Diary of a Pennsylvania Kid. 2011. (State Journal Ser.). (ENG.). 128p. (J). (gr. 4-8). pap. 9.95 (978-1-58536-610-1(2), 202226) Sleeping Bear Pr.

Smith, A. & Tatchell, J. Complete Book of Drawing. 2004. (Art Ideas Ser.). (Illus.). (J). (ENG.). 1p. pap. 17.99 (978-0-7945-0015-3(3), Usborne); 128p. lib. bdg. 25.95 (978-1-58086-353-7(1)) EDC Publishing.

Snider, Brandon T. Spider-Man Doodles. Montalvo-Lagos, Tomás, illus. 2017. (Doodle Book Ser.). (ENG.). 128p. (J). (gr. 1-3). pap. 12.99 **(978-1-4847-8771-7(4)**, Marvel Pr.) Disney Publishing Worldwide.

Soltero, Emilio, illus. & text. Draw the Line. Soltero, Emilio, text. 2003. 128p. (YA). per. 15.95 (978-0-9741332-0-1(5)) Pearl Pr.

Songhurst, Hazel & Breeden, Neil. Activators Drawing. (Illus.). 128p. (J). pap. 8.99 (978-0-340-71521-5(9)) Hodder & Stoughton GBR. Dist: Trafalgar Square Publishing.

Sovak, Jan, et al. Build a 3-D Poster Coloring Book — Fairies. 2012. (Dover 3-D Coloring Book Ser.). (ENG.). 16p. (J). (gr. 3-5). pap. 5.99 (978-0-486-49830-0(1)) Dover Pubns., Inc.

Sterling Children's, Sterling. Coloring Book of Visual Tricks & Optical Illusions: Color the Patterns to Reveal Eye-Popping Effects! 2017. (ENG., Illus.). 96p. (J). (gr. 3). pap. 9.95 **(978-1-4549-2565-1(5))** Sterling Publishing Co., Inc.

Stillinger, Doug. Espirales de Colores. 2004. (SPA., Illus.). 56p. (J). spiral bd. 23.95 (978-987-1078-24-0(2)) Klutz Latino MEX. Dist: Independent Pubs. Group.

Sun, Jennie. Fashion. 2011. (Dover Doodle Bks.). (ENG.). 64p. (J). (gr. 3-5). pap. 5.99 (978-0-486-48050-3(X)) Dover Pubns., Inc.

Tai, Elise See. Write & Draw Dinosaurs. 2014. (Wipe-Clean Stencil Bks.). (ENG., Illus.). 24p. (J). (gr. -1-1). bds. 9.99 (978-0-7641-6710-2(3)) Barron's Educational Series, Inc.

Tallarico, Tony J., Jr. Spot-the-Differences Across the USA. 2008. (Dover Children's Activity Bks.). (ENG., Illus.). 48p. (J). (gr. 3-5). pap. 4.99 (978-0-486-46827-3(5)) Dover Pubns., Inc.

Taylor, Adam. George in the UK: The Unknown Kingdom. Taylor, Adam & West, Jeannette, eds. 2011. (Illus.). 28p. (J). 8.99 (978-0-9766062-9-1(1)) Higher Ground Pr.

Tecco, Betsy Dru. How to Draw France's Sights & Symbols. (Kid's Guide to Drawing the Countries of the World Ser.). 48p. 2009. (gr. 4-4). 53.00 (978-1-61511-110-7(7)) 2004. (Illus.). (J). lib. bdg. 29.25 (978-0-8239-6683-7(6)) Rosen Publishing Group, Inc., The. (PowerKids Pr.).

—How to Draw Germany's Sights & Symbols. (Kid's Guide to Drawing the Countries of the World Ser.). 48p. 2009. (gr. 4-4). 53.00 (978-1-61511-111-4(5)) 2004. (Illus.). (J). lib. bdg. 29.25 (978-0-8239-6685-1(2)) Rosen Publishing Group, Inc., The. (PowerKids Pr.).

—How to Draw Hungary's Sights & Symbols. 2005. (Kid's Guide to Drawing the Countries of the World Ser.). (Illus.). 48p. (J). (gr. k-5). lib. bdg. 29.25 (978-1-4042-2737-8(7), PowerKids Pr.) Rosen Publishing Group, Inc., The.

—How to Draw Italy's Sights & Symbols. (Kid's Guide to Drawing the Countries of the World Ser.). 48p. 2009. (gr. 4-4). 53.00 (978-1-61511-115-2(8)) 2004. (Illus.). (J). lib. bdg. 29.25 (978-0-8239-6686-8(0)) Rosen Publishing Group, Inc., The. (PowerKids Pr.).

—How to Draw Japan's Sights & Symbols. (Kid's Guide to Drawing the Countries of the World Ser.). 48p. 2009. (gr. 4-4). 53.00 (978-1-61511-116-9(6)) 2004. (J). lib. bdg. 29.25 (978-0-8239-6681-3(X)) Rosen Publishing Group, Inc., The. (PowerKids Pr.).

—How to Draw Thailand's Sights & Symbols. 2005. (Kid's Guide to Drawing the Countries of the World Ser.). (J). 29.25 (978-1-4042-2741-5(5), PowerKids Pr.) Rosen Publishing Group, Inc., The.

—How to Draw the Life & Times of John Quincy Adams. 2006. (Kid's Guide to Drawing the Presidents of the United States of America Ser.). (YA). (gr. 2-5). 26.50 (978-1-4042-2983-9(3)) Rosen Publishing Group, Inc., The.

—How to Draw the Life & Times of Ulysses S. Grant. 2006. (Kid's Guide to Drawing the Presidents of the United States of America Ser.). (YA). (gr. 2-5). 26.50 (978-1-4042-2995-2(7)) Rosen Publishing Group, Inc., The.

—How to Draw the United Kingdom's Sights & Symbols. 2004. (Kid's Guide to Drawing the Countries of the World Ser.). (Illus.). 48p. (J). lib. bdg. 29.25 (978-0-8239-6684-4(4), PowerKids Pr.) Rosen Publishing Group, Inc., The.

—A Kid's Guide to Drawing the Countries of the World: Set 1, 6 bks., Set 2003. (Illus.). (J). (gr. k-5). (978-0-8239-8485-5(0), PowerKids Pr.) Rosen Publishing Group, Inc., The.

Tell It to a Friend, 6 Packs. (gr. k-1). 23.00 (978-0-7635-8827-4(X)) Rigby Education.

The Museum of Modern Art, contrib. by. MoMA Art While You Eat Place Mats. 2013. (ENG., Illus.). 104p. (J). (gr. -1-17). 12.99 (978-1-4521-0635-9(5)) Chronicle Bks. LLC.

Thomas Nelson. My Butterfly Doodle Pad. 2016. (ENG.). 160p. (J). (gr. -1-7). spiral bd. (978-1-78598-646-8(5)) Make Believe Ideas.

Thomson, Ruth. Creatures. 2003. (First Look at Art Ser.). (Illus.). 32p. (gr. 4-6). 23.00 (978-0-7910-7945-4(7), Chelsea Hse.) Facts On File, Inc.

Thorpe, Scott. Draw a d*ck on It: A Naughty Drawing Game. 2017. (ENG., Illus.). 200p. bds. 9.95 (978-1-4521-5467-1(8)) Chronicle Bks. LLC.

Timms, Diann. Hare & Bear Draw, 5 vols., Set. Date not set. (Illus.). 22p. (J). (978-0-89577-548-1(4)) Reader's Digest Assn., Inc., The.

Top That Publishing Editors, ed. Silly Scribbles. Dahl, Roald, illus. 2005. 24p. (J). pap. (978-1-905359-52-3(7)) Top That! Publishing PLC.

Top That Publishing Staff, ed. Drawing with Pastels. 2005. (Illus.). 48p. (978-1-84510-677-5(6)) Top That! Publishing PLC.

—How to Draw Monster Reptiles. 2005. (Illus.). 48p. pap. (978-1-84510-745-1(4)) Top That! Publishing PLC.

—Sketching with Pencils. 2004. (Art Tricks Ser.). (Illus.). 48p. (978-1-84510-320-0(3)) Top That! Publishing PLC.

Top That!, creator. How to Draw Managa Fantasy Fighters. 2005. (Illus.). 48p. (J). (gr. 4-7). per. (978-1-84510-972-1(4)) Top That! Publishing PLC.

—How to Draw Manga Transforming Robots. 2005. (Illus.). 48p. (J). (gr. 4-7). per. (978-1-84510-973-8(2)) Top That! Publishing PLC.

—Journey to the Bottom of the Sea. 2012. (Draw-on Wipe-off Doodle Storybook Ser.). (ENG., Illus.). 24p. (gr. -1-k). (978-1-84956-656-8(9)) Top That! Publishing PLC.

—Old MacDonald's Farm. 2012. (Draw-on Wipe-off Doodle Storybook Ser.). (ENG., Illus.). 24p. (J). (gr. -1). (978-1-84956-657-5(7)) Top That! Publishing PLC.

Top That!, ed. How to Draw 101 Super Heroes. Griffin, Hedley, illus. 2005. (ENG.). 48p. (J). per. (978-1-84510-738-3(1)) Top That! Publishing PLC.

Trafford, Adrienne. The Journey Coloring Book, 1 vol. 2011. (ENG., Illus.). 48p. pap. 9.99 (978-0-7643-3784-0(X), 9780764337840, Schiffer Publishing Ltd) Schiffer Publishing, Ltd.

Tresco, Betsy Dru. How to Draw Hungary's Sights & Symbols. 2009. (Kid's Guide to Drawing the Countries of the World Ser.). 48p. (gr. 4-4). 53.00 (978-1-61511-112-1(3), PowerKids Pr.) Rosen Publishing Group, Inc., The.

Tuchman, Gail & Gray, Margaret. AddUps Fun for All Seasons! Griego, Tony, illus. 2012. (Dover Little Activity Bks.). (ENG.). 32p. (J). (gr. k-3). pap. 1.50 (978-0-486-49860-7(3)) Dover Pubns., Inc.

—AddUps Going Places! Griego, Tony, illus. 2012. (Dover Little Activity Bks.). (ENG.). 32p. (J). (gr. k-3). pap. 1.50 (978-0-486-49861-4(1)) Dover Pubns., Inc.

—AddUps My Day! Griego, Tony, illus. 2012. (Dover Little Activity Bks.). (ENG.). 32p. (J). (gr. k-3). pap. 1.50 (978-0-486-49862-1(X)) Dover Pubns., Inc.

Tullet, Hervé. The Book with a Hole. 2011. (ENG., Illus.). 96p. (J). (gr. -1-3). pap. 14.50 (978-1-85437-946-7(1)) Tate Publishing, Ltd. GBR. Dist: Abrams, Inc.

—Doodle Cook. Barbour, Susan, tr. from FRE. 2011. (ENG., Illus.). 48p. pap. 14.95 (978-0-7148-6070-1(0)) Phaidon Pr., Inc.

—The Scribble Book. 2008. (ENG., Illus.). 64p. (J). (gr. -1-1). pap. 14.95 (978-1-85437-774-6(4)) Tate Publishing, Ltd. GBR. Dist: Abrams, Inc.

Usborne Books Staff, ed. Pintar Personajes. 2004.Tr. of I Can Draw People. (SPA., Illus.). 32p. (J). (gr. -1-3). lib. bdg. 12.95 (978-1-58086-285-1(3)) EDC Publishing.

Various. How to Draw Super-Powered Heroes. 2011. (ENG.). 128p. (YA). pap., pap. 12.99 (978-0-9831823-1-3(0), 9780983182313) Antarctic Pr., Inc.

Very Very van Gogh. 2004. (J). (978-0-9765917-0-2(7)) EDUKIT, L.L.C.

Visca, Curt & Visca, Kelley. How to Draw Cartoon Careers. 2004. (Kid's Guide to Drawing Ser.). (Illus.). 24p. (YA). (gr. 2-5). lib. bdg. 25.25 (978-0-8239-6725-4(5)) Rosen Publishing Group, Inc., The.

—How to Draw Cartoon Holiday Symbols. 2004. (Kid's Guide to Drawing Ser.). (Illus.). 24p. (YA). (gr. 2-5). lib. bdg. 25.25 (978-0-8239-6726-1(3)) Rosen Publishing Group, Inc., The.

—How to Draw Cartoon Spacecraft & Astronauts in Action. 2004. (Kid's Guide to Drawing Ser.). (Illus.). 24p. (J). lib. bdg. 25.25 (978-0-8239-6729-2(8), PowerKids Pr.) Rosen Publishing Group, Inc., The.

—How to Draw Cartoon Symbols of the United States. 2004. (Kid's Guide to Drawing Ser.). (Illus.). 24p. (J). lib. bdg. 25.25 (978-0-8239-6727-8(1), PowerKids Pr.) Rosen Publishing Group, Inc., The.

—How to Draw Cartoon Symbols of the Wild West. 2004. (Kid's Guide to Drawing Ser.). (Illus.). 24p. (J). lib. bdg. 25.25 (978-0-8239-6728-5(X), PowerKids Pr.) Rosen Publishing Group, Inc., The.

Vision, David & Vision, Mutiya. What Makes Me Beautiful? ¿Qué Es lo Que Me Hace Hermoso? 2013.Tr. of ¿Qué Es lo Que Me Hace Hermoso? (Illus.). 24p. (J). 17.00 (978-0-9816254-1-6(X), Vision Works Publishing) Soul Vision Works Publishing.

Walt Disney Company Staff & Phidal Publishing Staff, contrib. by. Cars. 2006. (Illus.). 24p. (978-2-7643-0261-3(4)) Phidal Publishing, Inc./Editions Phidal, Inc.

Ward, Wendy. My One-of-a-Kind Fashion Design. Neild, Robyn, illus. 2014. (ENG.). 128p. (J). (gr. 4-8). pap. 14.99 (978-1-4022-9541-6(3), Sourcebooks Jabberwocky) Sourcebooks, Inc.

Watkins, Courtney. Dream It! Draw It! Think It! Do It! Activities to Spark Creative Adventures. 2016. (ENG., Illus.). 96p. (J). pap. 9.99 (978-1-4494-8034-9(9)) Andrews McMeel Publishing.

Watt, Fiona. Art Ideas Drawing Pack: Internet-Linked. 2004. (Activity Kits Ser.). (ENG.). 32p. (J). pap., act. bk. ed. 16.95 (978-0-7945-0539-4(2)) EDC Publishing.

—Big Drawing Book. Thompson, Josephine & Day, Caroline, illus. 2013. (Doodle Bks). 95p. (J). pap. 11.99 (978-0-7945-3365-6(5), Usborne) EDC Publishing.

—Drawing, Doodling & Coloring Fashion. Miller, Antonia, illus. 2013. (Activity Bks). 128p. (J). pap. 13.99 (978-0-7945-3336-6(1), Usborne) EDC Publishing.

—How to Draw Ballerinas & Princesses. 2005. (Illus.). 32p. (J). pap. 8.99 (978-0-7945-0956-9(8), Usborne) EDC Publishing.

—How to Draw Dinosaurs. Figg, Non et al, illus. 2005. (Usborne Activities Ser.). 31p. (J). (gr. -1-3). pap. 8.95 (978-0-7945-1056-5(6), Usborne) EDC Publishing.

—How to Draw Fairies & Mermaids. 2005. (Activity Books Ser.). (ENG.). 32p. (J). pap. 8.95 (978-0-7945-0919-4(3), Usborne) EDC Publishing.

—Monster Doodles. 2010. (Doodle Cards Ser.). 50p. (J). 9.99 (978-0-7945-2550-7(4), Usborne) EDC Publishing.

—50 Things to Draw & Paint. (50 Things to Make & Do Ser.). (J). 2009. 104p. spiral bd. 9.99 (978-0-7945-2463-0(X)) 2006. (Illus.). 50p. (gr. 1-4). 9.99 (978-0-7945-1215-6(1)) EDC Publishing. (Usborne).

Webster, Christine. How to Draw Christmas Symbols. 2005. (Kid's Guide to Drawing Ser.). (Illus.). 24p. (YA). (gr. 2-5). lib. bdg. 25.25 (978-1-4042-2725-5(3)) Rosen Publishing Group, Inc., The.

—How to Draw Easter Symbols. (Kid's Guide to Drawing Ser.). 24p. 2009. (gr. 3-3). 47.90 (978-1-61511-031-5(3), PowerKids Pr.) 2005. (Illus.). (YA). (gr. 2-5). lib. bdg. 25.25 (978-1-4042-2726-2(1)) Rosen Publishing Group, Inc., The.

—How to Draw Hanukkah Symbols. (Kid's Guide to Drawing Ser.). 24p. 2009. (gr. 3-3). 47.90 (978-1-61511-033-9(X), PowerKids Pr.) 2005. (Illus.). (YA). (gr. 2-5). lib. bdg. 25.25 (978-1-4042-2727-9(X)) Rosen Publishing Group, Inc., The.

—How to Draw Kwanzaa Symbols. (Kid's Guide to Drawing Ser.). 24p. 2009. (gr. 3-3). 47.90 (978-1-61511-038-4(0), PowerKids Pr.) 2005. (Illus.). (YA). (gr. 2-5). lib. bdg. 25.25 (978-1-4042-2728-6(8)) Rosen Publishing Group, Inc., The.

—How to Draw Passover Symbols. 2005. (Kid's Guide to Drawing Ser.). (Illus.). 24p. (YA). (gr. 2-5). lib. bdg. 25.25 (978-1-4042-2729-3(6)) Rosen Publishing Group, Inc., The.

—How to Draw Thanksgiving Symbols. 2005. (Kid's Guide to Drawing Ser.). (Illus.). 24p. (YA). (gr. 2-5). lib. bdg. 25.25 (978-1-4042-2730-9(X)) Rosen Publishing Group, Inc., The.

Weintraub, A. How to Draw District of Columbia's Sights & Symbols. 2009. (Kid's Guide to Drawing America Ser.). 32p. (gr. k-k). 50.50 (978-1-61511-053-7(4), PowerKids Pr.) Rosen Publishing Group, Inc., The.

—How to Draw Nebraska's Sights & Symbols. 2009. (Kid's Guide to Drawing America Ser.). 32p. (gr. k-k). 50.50 (978-1-61511-076-6(3), PowerKids Pr.) Rosen Publishing Group, Inc., The.

—How to Draw New Mexico's Sights & Symbols. 2009. (Kid's Guide to Drawing America Ser.). 32p. (gr. k-k). 50.50 (978-1-61511-080-3(1), PowerKids Pr.) Rosen Publishing Group, Inc., The.

—How to Draw Ohio's Sights & Symbols. 2009. (Kid's Guide to Drawing America Ser.). 32p. (gr. k-k). 50.50 (978-1-61511-088-9(7), PowerKids Pr.) Rosen Publishing Group, Inc., The.

West, Tracey. How to Draw Pokemon. 2003. (Pokemon Ser.). (ENG., Illus.). 32p. (J). (gr. 2-5). pap. 5.99 (978-0-439-43440-9(8)) Scholastic, Inc.

—How to Draw Pokemon. 2003. (gr. k-3). lib. bdg. 16.00 (978-0-613-72110-3(1), Turtleback) Turtleback Bks.

Whelon, Chuck. What to Doodle? All Sorts of Sports! 2009. (Dover Doodle Bks.). (ENG., Illus.). 64p. (J). (gr. 2-5). pap. 5.99 (978-0-486-47267-6(1)) Dover Pubns., Inc.

—What to Doodle? Amazing Animals! 2009. (Dover Doodle Bks.). (ENG., Illus.). 64p. (J). (gr. 2-5). pap. 5.99 (978-0-486-47266-9(3)) Dover Pubns., Inc.

—What to Doodle? Best Friends Forever! 2011. (Dover Doodle Bks.). (ENG., Illus.). 64p. (J). (gr. 2-5). pap. 5.99 (978-0-486-48527-0(7)) Dover Pubns., Inc.

—What to Doodle? Christmas Creations! 2011. (Dover Doodle Bks.). (ENG., Illus.). 64p. (J). (gr. 2-5). pap. 5.99 (978-0-486-48530-0(7)) Dover Pubns., Inc.

—What to Doodle? Happy Halloween! 2011. (Dover Doodle Bks.). (ENG., Illus.). 64p. (J). (gr. 2-5). pap. 5.99 (978-0-486-48531-7(5)) Dover Pubns., Inc.

White, Kimberly. Mood Music: Musical Colors Series Axford, Elizabeth C., ed. 2003. (Musical Colors Rhyming Story Coloring Book Ser.). (ENG., Illus.). 16p. (J). spiral bd. 10.95 (978-1-931844-06-2(2), PP1018) Piano Pr.

Wild Animals. Date not set. (Illus.). 16p. (J). 5.98 (978-0-7525-7699-2(2)); 2.98 (978-0-7525-9763-8(9)) Parragon, Inc.

Wilde, Cindy, illus. Beautiful Doodling. 2015. (ENG.). 128p. (J). (gr. k-5). pap. 12.95 (978-1-4549-1882-0(9)) Sterling Publishing Co., Inc.

Winter Wonderland. 2014. (Dream Doodle Draw! Ser.). (ENG., Illus.). 96p. (J). (gr. -1-2). pap. 7.99 (978-1-4814-1634-4(0), Little Simon) Little Simon.

Winterberg, Jenna. The Zoo: A Step-by-Step Drawing & Story Book. Fisher, Diana, illus. 2006. (Watch Me Draw Ser.). (ENG.). 24p. (J). (gr. -1-3). pap. 4.95 (978-1-56010-798-9(7), 1560107987) Quarto Publishing Group USA.

Wojick, Luke. I Can Draw Shapes. 2013. (Core Math Skills: Measurement & Geometry Ser.). (Illus.). 24p. (J). (gr. 1-2). 22.60 (978-1-4777-2231-2(9)); (ENG., pap. 8.25 (978-1-4777-2055-4(3)) Rosen Publishing Group, Inc., The. (Rosen Classroom).

—I Can Draw Shapes: Shapes & Their Attributes. 2013. (Rosen Math Readers Ser.). (ENG., Illus.). 24p. (J). (gr. 1-2). pap. 49.50 (978-1-4777-2056-1(1), Rosen Classroom) Rosen Publishing Group, Inc., The.

Wood, Anita. City Doodles San Francisco, 1 vol. 2013. (ENG., Illus.). 240p. (J). pap., pap. 9.99 (978-1-4236-3286-3(9)) Gibbs Smith, Publisher.

—Doodle Your Day, 1 vol. Kalis, Jennifer, illus. 2013. (ENG.). 224p. (J). pap. 16.99 (978-1-4236-2368-7(1)) Gibbs Smith, Publisher.

—Pocketdoodles for Girls, 1 vol. Kalis, Jennifer, illus. 2010. (ENG.). 272p. (J). (gr. 1). 9.99 (978-1-4236-0755-7(4)) Gibbs Smith, Publisher.

—Travel Doodles for Kids, 1 vol. 2012. (ENG., Illus.). 272p. (J). pap. 9.99 (978-1-4236-2454-7(8)) Gibbs Smith, Publisher.

Woodcock, John, illus. Color & Doodle Your Way Across the USA. 2013. 108p. (978-1-78157-023-4(X), Ilex Pr.) Octopus Publishing Group.

Yano, Yuriko. Manga Doodles. Yano, Yuriko, illus. 2010. (ENG., Illus.). 128p. (J). (gr. 3). pap. 12.99 (978-1-906082-70-3(7)) O'Mara, Michael Bks., Ltd. GBR. Dist: Independent Pubs. Group.

You Can Draw, 9 vols., Set. Incl. You Can Draw Construction Vehicles. Cerato, Mattia. Cerato, Mattia, illus. 2011. lib. bdg. 26.65 (978-1-4048-6807-6(0)); You Can Draw Dinosaurs. Bruning, Matt & Cerato, Mattia. Cerato, Mattia, illus. 2010. lib. bdg. 26.65 (978-1-4048-6280-7(3)); You Can Draw Dragons, Unicorns, & Other Magical Creatures. Cerato, Mattia. Cerato, Mattia, illus. 2011. lib. bdg. 26.65 (978-1-4048-6809-0(7)); You Can Draw Fairies & Princesses. Sexton, Brenda. Sexton, Brenda, illus. 2011. lib. bdg. 26.65 (978-1-4048-6808-3(9)); You Can Draw Flowers. Bruning, Matt & Cerato, Mattia. Cerato, Mattia, illus. 2010. lib. bdg. 26.65 (978-1-4048-6279-1(X)); You Can Draw Monsters & Other Scary Things. Bruning, Matt & Ho, Jannie. Ho, Jannie, illus. 2010. lib. bdg. 26.65 (978-1-4048-6276-0(5)); You Can Draw Pets. Sexton, Brenda. Sexton, Brenda, illus. 2010. lib. bdg. 26.65 (978-1-4048-6277-7(3)); You Can Draw Planes, Trains, & Other Vehicles. Bruning, Matt & Sexton, Brenda. Sexton, Brenda, illus. 2010. lib. bdg. 26.65 (978-1-4048-6278-4(1)); You Can Draw Zoo Animals. Bruning, Matt & Ho, Jannie. Ho, Jannie, illus. 2010. lib. bdg. 26.65 (978-1-4048-6275-3(7)); (Illus.). (gr. 1-2). (You Can Draw Ser.). (ENG.). 24p. 2011. Set lib. bdg. 239.85 (978-1-4048-6830-4(5)) Picture Window Bks.

Zamora, Dulce. How to Draw the Life & Times of Franklin Pierce. 2006. (Kid's Guide to Drawing the Presidents of the United States of America Ser.). (YA). (gr. 2-5). 26.50 (978-1-4042-2991-4(4)) Rosen Publishing Group, Inc., The.

—How to Draw the Life & Times of John Tyler. 2006. (Kid's Guide to Drawing the Presidents of the United States of America Ser.). (YA). (gr. 2-5). 26.50 (978-1-4042-2987-7(6)) Rosen Publishing Group, Inc., The.

Zimmerman, Bill. City Doodles New York, 1 vol. 2013. (ENG., Illus.). 240p. (J). pap., pap. 9.99 (978-1-4236-3227-6(3)) Gibbs Smith, Publisher.

—Pocketdoodles for Young Artists, 1 vol. Bloom, Tom, illus. 2010. (ENG.). 272p. (J). (gr. 1). 9.99 (978-1-4236-0466-2(0)) Gibbs Smith, Publisher.

Zschock, Heather. Under the Sea Scratch & Sketch: An Art Activity Book for Imaginative Artists of All Ages. 2005. (Activity Book Ser.). (Illus.). 64p. (J). 12.99 (978-1-59359-905-8(6)) Peter Pauper Pr. Inc.

826 Valencia Writing Center Staff. 642 Things to Draw: Young Artist's Edition. Armstrong, Tymn, illus. 2016. (ENG.). 304p. (J). (gr. 3-7). 16.95 (978-1-4521-5066-6(4)) Chronicle Bks. LLC.

DRAWING—FICTION

Ahlberg, Allan. The Pencil. Ingman, Bruce, illus. 2012. (ENG.). 48p. (J). (gr. -1-3). pap. 6.99 (978-0-7636-6088-8(4)) Candlewick Pr.

—The Pencil. Ingman, Bruce, illus. 2012. lib. bdg. 17.20 (978-0-606-26942-1(8), Turtleback) Turtleback Bks.

Banks, Kate. The Eraserheads. Kulikov, Boris, illus. 2010. (ENG.). 40p. (J). (gr. -1-3). 16.99 (978-0-374-39920-7(4), 9780374399207, Farrar, Straus & Giroux (BYR)) Farrar, Straus & Giroux.

Barshaw, Ruth McNally. Best Friends Fur-Ever. Barshaw, Ruth McNally, illus. 2013. (Ellie Mcdoodle Diaries). (ENG., Illus.). 192p. (YA). (gr. 3-6). 12.99 *(978-1-61963-175-5(X)*, 9781619631755, Bloomsbury USA Childrens) Bloomsbury Publishing USA.

—Ellie McDoodle: Best Friends Fur-Ever. Barshaw, Ruth McNally, illus. 2011. (Ellie Mcdoodle Ser.). (ENG., Illus.). 192p. (YA). (gr. 3-6). pap. 7.99 *(978-1-59990-657-7(0)*, 9781599906577, Bloomsbury USA Childrens) Bloomsbury Publishing USA.

Becker, Aaron. Return. Becker, Aaron, illus. 2016. (ENG., Illus.). 40p. (J). (gr. -1-3). 15.99 *(978-0-7636-7730-5(2))* Candlewick Pr.

Becker, Suzy. Kate the Great: Winner Takes All. Becker, Suzy, illus. 2016. (Kate the Great Ser.). (ENG., Illus.). 256p. (J). (gr. 3-7). 12.99 *(978-0-385-38880-1(2)*, Crown Books For Young Readers) Random Hse. Children's Bks.

Berlan, Kathryn. Andrew's Amazing Monsters. 2013. (ENG., Illus.). 32p. (J). (gr. -1-3). 16.99 *(978-1-4814-2160-7(3)*, Atheneum Bks. for Young Readers) Simon & Schuster Children's Publishing.

Bruna, Dick. Miffy the Artist. 2016. (ENG., Illus.). 12p. (J). (gr. -1-k). bds. 14.50 *(978-1-84976-395-0(X))* Tate Publishing, Ltd. GBR. Dist: Abrams, Inc.

Carter, Denzel T. Demarco's Perfect Circles. 2015. (Rosen REAL Readers: STEM & STEAM Collection). (ENG.). 8p. pap. 5.46 *(978-1-4994-9497-6(1)*, Rosen Classroom) Rosen Publishing Group, Inc., The.

Colón, Raúl. Draw! Colón, Raúl, illus. 2014. (ENG., Illus.). 40p. (J). (gr. -1-3). 17.99 *(978-1-4424-9492-3(1)*, Simon & Schuster/Paula Wiseman Bks.) Simon & Schuster/Paula Wiseman Bks.

Coville, Bruce. Jeremy Thatcher, Dragon Hatcher: A Magic Shop Book. Lippincott, Gary A., illus. 20th ed. 2007. (Magic Shop Book Ser.: 2). (ENG.). 176p. (J). (gr. 5-7). pap. 7.99 *(978-0-15-206252-1(1))* Houghton Mifflin Harcourt Publishing Co.

Cowen-Fletcher, Jane. Nell's Elf. Cowen-Fletcher, Jane, illus. 2006. (ENG., Illus.). 32p. (J). (gr. -1-3). 14.99 *(978-0-7636-2391-3(1))* Candlewick Pr.

Crockett, Johns. Dessin pour Harold. (FRE.). pap. 13.95 *(978-2-266-09597-6(8))* Presses Pocket FRA. Dist: Distribooks, Inc.

Culpepper, Karen. The Homework Monster. 2011. 32p. (J). 23.95 *(978-0-9765641-2-6(2))* Rai Publishing.

Davies, Matt. Ben Draws Trouble. 2015. (ENG., Illus.). 32p. (J). (gr. -1-2). 17.99 *(978-1-59643-795-1(2)*, 9781596437951) Roaring Brook Pr.

Degen, Bruce. I Gotta Draw. Degen, Bruce, illus. 2012. (ENG., Illus.). 40p. (J). (gr. k-4). 16.99 *(978-0-06-028417-6(X))* HarperCollins Pubs.

Demi. The Girl Who Drew a Phoenix. Demi, illus. 2008. (ENG., Illus.). 52p. (J). (gr. 2-5). 24.99 *(978-1-4169-5347-0(7)*, McElderry, Margaret K. Bks.) McElderry, Margaret K. Bks.

Dixon, Amy. Sophie's Animal Parade. Wish, Katia, illus. 2015. (ENG.). 32p. (J). (gr. -1-k). 16.99 *(978-1-63220-403-5(7)*, Sky Pony Pr.) Skyhorse Publishing Co., Inc.

Drescher, Henrik. Simon's Book. 2006. (ENG., Illus.). 32p. (J). (gr. -1-1). *(978-1-59692-135-1(8))* MacAdam/Cage Publishing, Inc.

Dyan, Penelope. The Big Mikey & Me Workbook. Dyan, Penelope, illus. 2011. (Illus.). 48p. pap. 11.95 *(978-1-935630-72-2(5))* Bellissima Publishing, LLC.

—Did You Call? 2011. 34p. pap. 11.95 *(978-1-935630-78-4(4))* Bellissima Publishing, LLC.

—Hush! 2011. 34p. pap. 11.95 *(978-1-935630-53-1(9))* Bellissima Publishing, LLC.

Dyan, Peneope. Bunny Ears. Dyan, Penelope, illus. 2011. 34p. pap. 11.95 *(978-1-935630-68-5(7))* Bellissima Publishing, LLC.

Elliott, Zetta & Strickland, Shadra. Bird. 1 vol. 2008. (ENG., Illus.). 48p. (J). (gr. 3-7). 19.95 *(978-1-60060-241-2(X))* Lee & Low Bks., Inc.

Elliott, Zetta & Terasaki, Stanley Todd. Bird. Shinjo, Shelly, illus. 2016. (ENG.). 32p. (J). (gr. 2-5). pap. 9.95 ***(978-1-62014-350-6(X))*** Lee & Low Bks., Inc.

Fagan, Cary. I Wish I Could Draw. 1 vol. 2014. (ENG., Illus.). 32p. (J). (gr. k-3). 12.95 *(978-1-55498-318-6(5))* Groundwood Bks. CAN. Dist: Publishers Group West (PGW).

Falwell, Cathryn & National Geographic Learning Staff. David's Drawings. 2010. (Rise & Shine Ser.). (ENG., Illus.). 32p. (C). (gr. -1-2). pap. 14.95 *(978-1-58430-261-2(5))* National Geographic School Publishing, Inc.

Florian, Douglas. How to Draw a Dragon. Florian, Douglas, illus. 2015. (ENG., Illus.). 42p. (J). (gr. -1-3). 17.99 *(978-1-4424-7399-7(1)*, Beach Lane Bks.) Beach Lane Bks.

Fulmer, Jeffrey. My Imagination Kit. Pickering, Jimmy, tr. Pickering, Jimmy, illus. 2003. (J). 24p. 15.95 *(978-1-59336-008-5(8))*; 23p. pap. 7.95 *(978-1-59336-009-2(6))* Mondo Publishing.

Gangloff, Sylviane, illus. Zoom the Zebra. 2015. (Talking Back Ser.). (ENG.). 36p. (J). (gr. -1-2). 7.95 *(978-0-7892-1246-7(3)*, Abbeville Kids) Abbeville Pr., Inc.

—Zulka the Wolf. 2015. (Talking Back Ser.). (ENG.). 36p. (J). (gr. -1-2). 7.95 *(978-0-7892-1245-0(5)*, Abbeville Kids) Abbeville Pr., Inc.

Gerstein, Mordicai. The First Drawing. 2013. (ENG., Illus.). 40p. (J). (gr. -1-3). 18.99 *(978-0-316-20478-1(1))* Little, Brown Bks. for Young Readers.

Grosgebauer, Clare Ham. My Snickerdoodle Doodle Book: Creative Writing & Drawing Adventures. 2004. (Illus.). 72p. (J). spiral bd. 3.00 *(978-0-9741888-1-2(6))* Small Wonders Enterprises.

Gurnick, Isabella Grace & Beals, Stephen Naayvek. Girls Have Eyelashes. 2004. 39p. pap. 11.63 *(978-1-4116-1696-7(0))* Lulu Pr., Inc.

Heap, Sue. Danny's Drawing Book. Heap, Sue, illus. 2008. (ENG., Illus.). 32p. (J). (gr. -1-3). 9.99 *(978-0-7636-3654-8(1))* Candlewick Pr.

Jeffers, Susan. My Pony. Jeffers, Susan, illus. 2008. (ENG., Illus.). 32p. (J). (gr. -1-3). 6.99 *(978-1-4231-1295-2(4))* Hyperion Pr.

Johnson, Crockett. Harold's ABC Board Book. Johnson, Crockett, illus. 2015. (ENG., Illus.). 34p. (J). (gr. -1 — 1). bds. 7.99 *(978-0-06-242731-1(8)*, HarperFestival) HarperCollins Pubs.

Johnson, Crockett, illus. Harold et le Crayon Violet: The French Edition of Harold & the Purple Crayon. 2013. (FRE & ENG.). 64p. (J). (gr. -1-3). 10.00 *(978-1-61243-164-2(X))* Ulysses Pr.

Keller, Elinoar & Peleg-Segal, Naama. Just Like I Wanted. Gordon-Noy, Aya, illus. 2015. (ENG.). 26p. (J). 17.00 *(978-0-8028-5453-7(2)*, Eerdmans Bks For Young Readers) Eerdmans, William B. Publishing Co.

Kline, Suzy. Horrible Harry & the Scarlet Scissors. Wummer, Amy, illus. (Horrible Harry Ser.). (ENG.). 80p. (J). (gr. 2-4). 2013. pap. 4.99 *(978-0-14-242671-5(7)*, Puffin Books) 2012. 14.99 *(978-0-670-01306-7(4)*, Viking Books for Young Readers) Penguin Young Readers Group.

Korelitz, Jean Hanff. Interference Powder. 0 vols. 2006. (ENG.). 146p. (J). (gr. 4-7). pap. 7.99 *(978-0-7614-5275-1(3)*, 9780761452751, Amazon Children's Publishing) Amazon Publishing.

Kroll, Steven. Patches Lost & Found. 0 vols. Gott, Barry, illus. 2005. (ENG.). 32p. (J). (gr. k-4). pap. 5.95 *(978-0-7614-5217-1(6)*, 9780761452171, Amazon Children's Publishing) Amazon Publishing.

Larsen, Andrew. A Squiggly Story. Lowery, Mike, illus. 2016. (ENG.). 32p. (J). (gr. -1-2). 16.95 *(978-1-77138-016-4(0))* Kids Can Pr., Ltd. CAN. Dist: Hachette Bk. Group.

Lechner, John. The Clever Stick. Lechner, John, illus. 2009. (ENG., Illus.). 40p. (J). (gr. k-3). 14.99 *(978-0-7636-3950-1(8))* Candlewick Pr.

Lee, Suzy. Lines. Lee, Suzy, illus. 2017. (ENG., Illus.). 40p. (J). (gr. -1-k). 17.99 ***(978-1-4521-5665-1(4))*** Chronicle Bks. LLC.

Lehrer, Damon, illus. Rocket Boy. 2016. (J). ***(978-1-56792-587-6(1))*** Godine, David R. Pub.

Lehrhaupt, Adam. I Don't Draw, I Color! Sala, Felicita, illus. 2017. (ENG.). 32p. (J). (gr. -1-3). 17.99 *(978-1-4814-6275-4(X)*, Simon & Schuster/Paula Wiseman Bks.) Simon & Schuster/Paula Wiseman Bks.

Leoni, Gail. Chalk Dust. 2008. 36p. pap. 24.95 *(978-1-60474-881-9(8))* America Star Bks.

Leopold, Nikia Speliakos Clark. Adam's Crayons. Nemett, Barry & Nemett, Laini, illus. 2011. (J). *(978-0-9817519-1-7(1))* Galileo Pr.

Lewin, Ted. I See & See. Lewin, Ted, illus. 2016. (I Like to Read(r) Ser.). (ENG., Illus.). 24p. (J). (gr. -1-3). 6.99 *(978-0-8234-3545-6(8))*; 14.95 *(978-0-8234-3544-9(X))* Holiday Hse., Inc.

Lewis, K. s. & Lewis, K. S. Happiness: A Charlie Travel Adventure Story. 2009. 28p. pap. 21.20 *(978-0-557-12094-9(2))* Lulu Pr., Inc.

Lichtenheld, Tom. Bridget's Beret. Lichtenheld, Tom, illus. 2010. (ENG., Illus.). 40p. (J). (gr. -1-2). 16.99 *(978-0-8050-8775-8(3)*, 9780805087758, Holt, Henry & Co. Bks. For Young Readers) Holt, Henry & Co.

Light, Kelly. Louise Loves Art. Light, Kelly, illus. 2014. (ENG., Illus.). 40p. (J). (gr. -1-3). 17.99 *(978-0-06-224817-6(0))* HarperCollins Pubs.

Liniers. Written & Drawn by Henrietta. 2015. (ENG., Illus.). 64p. (J). (gr. k). 12.95 *(978-1-935179-90-0(X))* TOON Books / RAW Junior, LLC.

Luyken, Corinna. The Book of Mistakes. Luyken, Corinna, illus. 2017. (ENG., Illus.). 56p. (J). (gr. -1-3). 18.99 *(978-0-7352-2792-7(6)*, Dial Bks) Penguin Young Readers Group.

Lying as Still as I Can: Six-Pack. (Greetings Ser.: Vol. 3). (gr. 2-3). 31.00 *(978-0-7635-9433-6(4))* Rigby Education.

Mangrum, Kaylea J. How to Draw Step-By-Step with Special Kids. Mangrum, Kaylea J., illus. 2013. (Illus.). 38p. pap. 12.49 *(978-0-9883009-3-4(1))* Mangrum, Kaylea J.

McCarty, Peter. The Monster Returns. McCarty, Peter, illus. 2012. (Jeremy & the Monster Ser.). (ENG., Illus.). 40p. (J). (gr. -1-1). 16.99 *(978-0-8050-9030-7(4)*, 9780805090307, Holt, Henry & Co. Bks. For Young Readers) Holt, Henry & Co.

McDonnell, Patrick. Art. 2006. (ENG., Illus.). 48p. (J). (gr. -1-3). 17.99 *(978-0-316-11491-2(X))* Little, Brown Bks. for Young Readers.

—Art. 2011. (J). (gr. -1-3). 29.95 *(978-0-545-10697-9(4))* Weston Woods Studios, Inc.

McLachlan, Edward. Simon in the Land of Chalk Drawings: Four Stories That Inspired the TV Series! 2016. (ENG.). 128p. (J). (gr. 2-4). pap. 14.99 *(978-0-486-80103-2(9))* Dover Pubns., Inc.

McPhail, David. Andrew Draws. McPhail, David, illus. 2014. (ENG., Illus.). 32p. (J). (gr. -1-3). 16.95 *(978-0-8234-3063-5(4))* Holiday Hse., Inc.

McRae, G. c. Pretty Ballerina. Anderson, David, illus. 2013. 44p. pap. *(978-0-9876845-3-0(1))* Warne, MacDonald Media.

Meade, Saci & Nonino, Lila. ABCs for Little Yogis. Meade, Sarah, illus. 2014. (ENG.). 26p. (J). (gr. -1). 16.95 *(978-1-60887-340-1(4))* Mandala Publishing.

Meadows, Daisy. Annabelle the Drawing Fairy. 2015. (Magical Crafts Fairies Ser.: 2). (ENG., Illus.). 80p. (J). (gr. 2-5). pap. 4.99 *(978-0-545-70830-2(3)*, Scholastic Paperbacks) Scholastic, Inc.

Mielcarek, David. Time for your Mind. Mielcarek, David, ed. 2006. (Illus.). 38p. (J). *(978-0-9785480-0-1(0))* Mielcarek, David.

Morimoto, Sango. Taro & the Carnival of Doom. Morimoto, Sango, illus. 2011. (ENG., Illus.). 96p. (J). pap. 7.99 *(978-1-4215-3526-5(2))* Viz Media.

—Taro & the Magic Pencil. Morimoto, Sango, illus. 2010. (ENG., Illus.). 104p. (J). pap. 7.99 *(978-1-4215-3524-1(6))* Viz Media.

Morpurgo, Michael. Meeting Cezanne. Place, Francois, illus. 2013. (ENG.). 80p. (J). (gr. 2-5). 15.99 *(978-0-7636-4896-1(5))* Candlewick Pr.

Myers, Christopher. My Pen. Myers, Christopher, illus. 2015. (ENG., Illus.). 32p. (J). (gr. -1-k). 16.99 *(978-1-4231-0371-4(8))* Hyperion Bks. for Children.

Newell, Jeff. Skimper-Scamper. Hranilovich, Barbara, illus. 2005. (Green Light Readers Level 2 Ser.). (J). (gr. k-2). 11.60 *(978-0-7569-5244-0(1))* Perfection Learning Corp.

Paradis, Anne. Caillou Takes a Nap. Brignaud, Pierre, illus. 2014. (Step by Step Ser.). (ENG.). 24p. (J). (gr. -1 — 1). bds. 5.99 *(978-2-89718-147-5(8))* Caillouet, Gerry.

Parish, Herman. Amelia Bedelia Chalks It Up! Avril, Lynne, illus. 2014. (I Can Read Level 1 Ser.). (ENG.). 32p. (J). (gr. -1-3). 16.99 *(978-0-06-233422-0(0)*, Greenwillow Bks.) HarperCollins Pubs.

—Amelia Bedelia Chalks One Up. Avril, Lynne, illus. 2014. (I Can Read Level 1 Ser.). (ENG.). 32p. (J). (gr. -1-3). pap. 3.99 *(978-0-06-233421-3(2)*, Greenwillow Bks.) HarperCollins Pubs.

—Amelia Bedelia Chalks One Up. 2014. (Amelia Bedelia: I Can Read! Ser.). (J). lib. bdg. 13.55 *(978-0-606-35947-4(8))* Turtleback Bks.

Parkinson, Kate. Grace. Parkinson, Kate, illus. 2015. (ENG., Illus.). 24p. (J). (gr. -1-3). 6.99 *(978-0-8234-3317-9(X))*; 14.95 *(978-0-8234-3207-3(6))* Holiday Hse., Inc.

Pearce, Jacqueline. L' Effet Manga. 1 vol. 2010.Tr. of Manga Touch. (FRE.). 136p. (J). (gr. 5-9). pap. 9.95 *(978-1-55469-379-5(9))* Orca Bk. Pubs. USA.

Power Of The Pencil. Round. 2013. 64p. pap. 24.99 *(978-1-4817-0913-2(5))* AuthorHouse.

Poydar, Nancy. Cool Ali. Poydar, Nancy, illus. 2014. (ENG., Illus.). 32p. (J). (gr. -1-2). 16.99 *(978-1-4814-2531-5(5)*, McElderry, Margaret K. Bks.) McElderry, Margaret K. Bks.

Prosek, James. The Day My Mother Left. Prosek, James, illus. 2009. (ENG., Illus.). 304p. (J). (gr. 4-7). pap. 7.99 *(978-1-4169-0771-8(8)*, Simon & Schuster Bks. For Young Readers) Simon & Schuster Bks. For Young Readers.

R. N., Lavanya. The Bookworm. Suleman, Shilo Shiv, illus. 2013. (ENG.). 32p. (J). (gr. k). pap. 9.95 *(978-81-8190-180-4(0))* Karadi Tales Co. Pvt. Ltd. IND. Dist: Consortium Bk. Sales & Distribution.

Raczka, Bob. Niko Draws a Feeling. Shin, Simone, illus. 2017. (ENG.). 32p. (gr. k-3). 17.99 *(978-1-4677-9843-3(6)*, Carolrhoda Bks.) Lerner Publishing Group.

Raczka, Robert. Niko Draws a Feeling. Shin, Simone, illus. 2017. (Carolrhoda Picture Bks.). (ENG.). 32p. (gr. k-3). (J). 9.99 ***(978-1-5124-3276-3(8))***; 35.99 ***(978-1-5124-3275-6(X))***; 35.99 ***(978-1-5124-2688-5(1))*** Lerner Publishing Group. (Carolrhoda Bks.).

Reynolds, Peter H. Ish. Reynolds, Peter H., illus. unabr. ed. 2005. (Illus.). (J). (gr. -1-4). 24.95 incl. audio *(978-0-439-80428-8(0)*, WHRA676) Scholastic, Inc.

—Ish. Reynolds, Peter H., illus. 2005. (Illus.). (J). (gr. -1-4). 29.95 *(978-0-439-80429-5(9)*, WHCD676) Weston Woods Studios, Inc.

Reynolds, Peter H. & Reynolds, Peter. Ish. Reynolds, Peter H. & Reynolds, Peter, illus. 2004. (Creatrilogy Ser.). (ENG., Illus.). 32p. (J). (gr. k-12). 15.00 *(978-0-7636-2344-9(X))* Candlewick Pr.

Russell, Natalie. Lost for Words. 1 vol. Russell, Natalie, illus. 2014. (ENG., Illus.). 32p. (J). (gr. -1-3). 16.95 *(978-1-56145-739-7(6))* Peachtree Pubs.

Sateren, Shelley Swanson. The Very Best Art Project. Sullivan, Mary, illus. 2013. (Max & Zoe Ser.). (ENG.). 32p. (gr. k-2). lib. bdg. 21.32 *(978-1-4048-7201-1(9)*, Max & Zoe) Picture Window Bks.

Say, Allen. Emma's Rug. 2003. (ENG., Illus.). 32p. (J). pap. 7.99 *(978-0-618-33523-7(4))* Houghton Mifflin Harcourt Publishing Co.

Scieszka, Jon. Kat's Maps. Long, Loren et al, illus. 2011. (Jon Scieszka's Trucktown Ser.). (ENG.). 24p. (J). (gr. -1-1). 15.99 *(978-1-4169-4159-0(2)*, Simon Spotlight) Simon Spotlight.

—Kat's Maps. Shannon, David et al, illus. 2011. (Jon Scieszka's Trucktown Ser.). (ENG.). 24p. (J). (gr. -1-1). pap. 3.99 *(978-1-4169-4148-4(7)*, Simon Spotlight) Simon Spotlight.

Sévigny, Eric, illus. Caillou: the Doodle Artist. 2014. (ENG.). 128p. (J). (gr. -1-1). 7.95 *(978-2-89718-126-0(5))* Caillouet, Gerry.

Stairs-Oberlick, Anita Ruth. Helen the Transartist. 2004. (Illus.). 256p. (J). per. 15.95 *(978-0-9759738-0-6(0))* Carleton Bks.

Stubbs, Lisa. Lily & Bear. Stubbs, Lisa, illus. 2015. (Lily & Bear Ser.). (ENG., Illus.). 32p. (J). (gr. -1-3). 17.99 *(978-1-4814-4416-3(6)*, Simon & Schuster Bks. For Young Readers) Simon & Schuster Bks. For Young Readers.

Sullivan, Dana. Ozzie & the Art Contest. Sullivan, Dana, illus. 2013. (ENG., Illus.). 15.99 *(978-1-58536-820-4(2))* Sleeping Bear Pr.

Thomson, Bill. Chalk. 0 vols. Thomson, Bill, illus. 2010. (ENG., Illus.). 40p. (J). (gr. -1-3). 15.99 *(978-0-7614-5526-4(4)*, 9780761455264, Amazon Children's Publishing) Amazon Publishing.

Waldman, Neil. Al & Teddy. 2013. 48p. 17.95 *(978-0-615-72969-5(X))* Dream Yard Pr.

Wang, Gabrielle. El Jardin de la Emperatriz Casia. Holguin, Magdalena, tr. Cuellar, Olga, illus. 2004. (SPA.). 108p. (YA). 8.95 *(978-958-04-7346-6(3))* Norma S.A. COL. Dist: Distribuidora Norma, Inc.

Wells, Marcia. Doom at Grant's Tomb. Calo, Marcos, illus. 2017. (Eddie Red Undercover Ser.: 3). (ENG.). 208p. (J). (gr. 5-7). pap. 6.99 *(978-0-544-93733-8(3)*, HMH Books For Young Readers) Houghton Mifflin Harcourt Publishing Co.

—Doom at Grant's Tomb. Calo, Marcos, illus. 2017. (Eddie Red Undercover Ser.: 3). (ENG.). (J). (gr. 5-7). lib. bdg. 17.20 ***(978-0-606-39813-8(9))*** Turtleback Bks.

—Mystery in Mayan Mexico. Calo, Marcos, illus. 2016. (Eddie Red Undercover Ser.: 2). (ENG.). 224p. (J). (gr. 5-7). pap. 7.99 *(978-0-544-66850-8(2)*, HMH Books For Young Readers) Houghton Mifflin Harcourt Publishing Co.

—Mystery in Mayan Mexico. 2016. (Eddie Red Undercover Ser.: 2). lib. bdg. 18.40 *(978-0-606-39664-6(0))* Turtleback Bks.

—Mystery on Museum Mile. Calo, Marcos, illus. (Eddie Red Undercover Ser.). (ENG.). 256p. (J). (gr. 5-7). 2015. pap. 7.99 *(978-0-544-43940-5(6))* 2014. 16.99 *(978-0-544-23833-6(8))* Houghton Mifflin Harcourt Publishing Co. (HMH Books For Young Readers).

Weston Woods Staff, creator. Casi. 2011. (SPA.). 29.95 *(978-0-439-90592-3(3))* Weston Woods Studios, Inc.

Williams, Karen Lynn. A Beach Tail. Cooper, Floyd, illus. 2010. (ENG.). 32p. (J). (gr. -1-2). 17.95 *(978-1-59078-712-0(9))* Boyds Mills Pr.

Williams, Vera B. Cherries & Cherry Pits. 2014. 40p. pap. 7.00 *(978-1-61003-324-4(8))* Center for the Collaborative Classroom.

Winters, Kari-Lynn. Jeffrey & Sloth. 1 vol. Hodson, Ben, illus. 2008. (ENG.). 32p. (J). (gr. -1-3). per. 9.95 *(978-1-55143-974-7(3))* Orca Bk. Pubs. USA.

Wooten, Laura. With My Little Box of Crayons. Pennington, Kelly, illus. 2008. 50p. pap. 18.95 *(978-1-4251-7103-2(6))* Trafford Publishing.

Yates, Louise. Dog Loves Drawing. 2012. (ENG.). 32p. (J). (gr. -1-3). 16.99 *(978-0-375-87067-5(9)*, Knopf Bks. for Young Readers) Random Hse. Children's Bks.

Young, Karen Romano. Doodlebug: A Novel in Doodles. 2012. (ENG., Illus.). 128p. (J). (gr. 3-7). pap. 7.99 *(978-1-250-01020-9(9)*, 9781250010209) Square Fish.

—Stuck in the Middle (of Middle School) A Novel in Doodles. 2013. (ENG., Illus.). 112p. (J). (gr. 3-7). 12.99 *(978-0-312-55596-2(2)*, 9780312555962) Feiwel & Friends.

—Stuck in the Middle (of Middle School) A Novel in Doodles. 2014. (ENG., Illus.). 128p. (J). (gr. 3-7). pap. 6.99 *(978-1-250-03997-2(5)*, 9781250039972) Square Fish.

Zemach, Kaethe. Ms. McCaw Learns to Draw. (J). 2008. (ENG., Illus.). 32p. (gr. -1-3). 16.99 *(978-0-439-82914-4(3))* 2006. *(978-0-439-82915-1(1))* Scholastic, Inc. (Levine, Arthur A. Bks.).

Zemke, Deborah. The Curse of Einstein's Pencil. 2017. (Bea Garcia Ser.: 2). (ENG., Illus.). 144p. (J). (gr. 1-4). 15.99 *(978-0-8037-4155-3(3)*, Dial Bks) Penguin Young Readers Group.

—My Life in Pictures. 2016. (Bea Garcia Ser.). (ENG., Illus.). 144p. (J). (gr. 1-3). 14.99 *(978-0-8037-4154-6(5)*, Dial Bks) Penguin Young Readers Group.

—My Life in Pictures. 2017. (Bea Garcia Ser.: 1). lib. bdg. 18.40 ***(978-0-606-40083-1(4))*** Turtleback Bks.

DRAWING—TECHNIQUE

Abbott, Simon, illus. Dinosaurs. 2011. (Learn to Draw Ser.). (ENG.). 24p. (J). (gr. k-2). pap. 6.95 *(978-1-84898-202-4(X)*, TickTock Books) Octopus Publishing Group GBR. Dist: Independent Pubs. Group.

—Learn to Draw: Dragons. 2011. (Learn to Draw Ser.). (ENG.). 24p. (J). (gr. k-2). pap. 6.95 *(978-1-84898-201-7(1)*, TickTock Books) Octopus Publishing Group GBR. Dist: Independent Pubs. Group.

—Learn to Draw: Fairies. 2011. (Learn to Draw Ser.). (ENG.). 24p. (J). (gr. k-2). pap. 6.95 *(978-1-84898-203-1(8)*, TickTock Books) Octopus Publishing Group GBR. Dist: Independent Pubs. Group.

—Learn to Draw: Monsters. 2011. (Learn to Draw Ser.). (ENG.). 24p. (J). (gr. k-2). pap. 6.95 *(978-1-84898-200-0(3)*, TickTock Books) Octopus Publishing Group GBR. Dist: Independent Pubs. Group.

ABDO Publishing Company Staff. First Drawings. 2007. (First Drawings Ser.). 153.90 *(978-1-59679-798-7(3)*, Buddy Bks.) ABDO Publishing Co.

Abraham, Philip. How to Draw the Life & Times of George Washington. 2009. (Kid's Guide to Drawing the Presidents of the United States of America Ser.). 32p. (gr. 4-4). 50.50 *(978-1-61511-140-4(9)*, PowerKids Pr.) Rosen Publishing Group, Inc., The.

Ahmed, Suhel. Monsters. Bassani, Srimalie, illus. 2015. (Doodle Magic Ser.). (ENG.). 64p. (J). (gr. k). spiral bd. 14.95 *(978-1-62686-478-8(0)*, Silver Dolphin Bks.) Readerlink Distribution Services, LLC.

—Princesses. Silver Dolphin Books, Silver Dolphin, ed. Bassani, Srimalie, illus. 2015. (Doodle Magic Ser.). (ENG.). 64p. (J). (gr. k). spiral bd. 14.95 *(978-1-62686-479-5(9)*, Silver Dolphin Bks.) Readerlink Distribution Services, LLC.

Aikins, Dave, illus. Watch Me Draw Dora's Favorite Adventures: Let's Draw! 2012. (J). *(978-1-936309-76-4(9))* Quarto Publishing Group USA.

Allen, Chris, et al. How to Draw Adventure Friends & Other Cartoon Heroes. 2013. (ENG., Illus.). 128p. (YA). pap. 19.95 *(978-0-9850925-8-0(0)*, 9780985092580) Antarctic Pr., Inc.

Ames, Lee J. Draw 50 Airplanes, Aircraft, & Spacecraft. 2012. (Draw 50 Ser.). lib. bdg. 20.85 *(978-0-606-26434-1(5)*, Turtleback) Turtleback Bks.

—Draw 50 Airplanes, Aircraft, & Spacecraft: The Step-by-Step Way to Draw World War II Fighter Planes, Modern Jets, Space Capsules, & Much More... 2012. (ENG., Illus.). 64p. pap. 9.99 *(978-0-8230-8570-5(8)*, Watson-Guptill) Potter/TenSpeed/Harmony.

—Draw 50 Animals. 2012. (Draw 50 Ser.). lib. bdg. 20.85 *(978-0-606-26426-6(4)*, Turtleback) Turtleback Bks.

—Draw 50 Animals: The Step-by-Step Way to Draw Elephants, Tigers, Dogs, Fish, Birds, & Many More... 2012. (ENG., Illus.). 64p. pap. 9.99 *(978-0-8230-8578-1(3)*, Watson-Guptill) Potter/TenSpeed/Harmony.

—Draw 50 Athletes. 2012. (Draw 50 Ser.). lib. bdg. 20.85 *(978-0-606-26428-0(0)*, Turtleback) Turtleback Bks.

—Draw 50 Athletes: The Step-by-Step Way to Draw Wrestlers & Figure Skaters, Baseball & Football Players, & Many More. 2012. (ENG., Illus.). 64p. pap. 9.99 *(978-0-8230-8572-9(4)*, Watson-Guptill) Potter/TenSpeed/Harmony.

—Draw 50 Baby Animals. 2012. (Draw 50 Ser.). lib. bdg. 20.85 *(978-0-606-26427-3(2)*, Turtleback) Turtleback Bks.

—Draw 50 Beasties. 2013. (Draw 50 Ser.). lib. bdg. 20.85 *(978-0-606-26508-9(2)*, Turtleback) Turtleback Bks.

—Draw 50 Beasties: The Step-By-Step Way to Draw 50 Beasties & Yugglies & Turnover Uglies & Things That Go Bump in the Night. 2013. (ENG., Illus.). 64p. pap. 9.99 *(978-0-8230-8582-8(1)*, Watson-Guptill) Potter/TenSpeed/Harmony.

—Draw 50 Boats, Ships, Trucks, & Trains. 2013. (Draw 50 Ser.). lib. bdg. 20.85 *(978-0-606-26510-2(4)*, Turtleback) Turtleback Bks.

—Draw 50 Buildings & Other Structures. 2013. (Draw 50 Ser.). (Illus.). (J). lib. bdg. 20.85 *(978-0-606-26511-9(2)*, Turtleback) Turtleback Bks.

—Draw 50 Buildings & Other Structures: The Step-by-Step Way to Draw Castles & Cathedrals, Skyscrapers & Bridges, & So Much More... 2013. (ENG., Illus.). 64p. pap. 9.99 *(978-0-8230-8604-7(6)*, Watson-Guptill) Potter/TenSpeed/Harmony.

—Draw 50 Cars, Trucks, & Motorcycles. 2012. (Draw 50 Ser.). lib. bdg. 20.85 *(978-0-606-26435-8(3)*, Turtleback) Turtleback Bks.

—Draw 50 Cars, Trucks, & Motorcycles: The Step-by-Step Way to Draw Dragsters, Vintage Cars, Dune Buggies, Mini Coopers, & Many More... 2012. (ENG., Illus.). 64p. pap. 9.99 *(978-0-8230-8576-7(7)*, Watson-Guptill) Potter/TenSpeed/Harmony.

—Draw 50 Cats. 2012. (Draw 50 Ser.). lib. bdg. 20.85 *(978-0-606-26440-2(X)*, Turtleback) Turtleback Bks.

—Draw 50 Cats: The Step-by-Step Way to Draw Domestic Breeds, Wild Cats, Cuddly Kittens, & Famous Felines. 2012.

(ENG., Illus.). 64p. pap. 9.99 *(978-0-8230-8575-0(9),* Watson-Guptill) Potter/TenSpeed/Harmony.

—Draw 50 Dinosaurs & Other Prehistoric Animals. 2012. (Draw 50 Ser.). lib. bdg. 20.85 *(978-0-606-26441-9(8),* Turtleback) Turtleback Bks.

—Draw 50 Dinosaurs & Other Prehistoric Animals: The Step-by-Step Way to Draw Tyrannosauruses, Wooly Mammoths, & Many More... 2012. (ENG., Illus.). 64p. pap. 9.99 *(978-0-8230-8574-3(0),* Watson-Guptill) Potter/TenSpeed/Harmony.

—Draw 50 Dogs. 2012. (Draw 50 Ser.). lib. bdg. 20.85 *(978-0-606-26433-4(7),* Turtleback) Turtleback Bks.

—Draw 50 Endangered Animals. 2013. (Draw 50 Ser.). (Illus.). (J). lib. bdg. 20.85 *(978-0-606-26506-5(6),* Turtleback) Turtleback Bks.

—Draw 50 Horses. 2012. (Draw 50 Ser.). lib. bdg. 20.85 *(978-0-606-26430-3(2),* Turtleback) Turtleback Bks.

—Draw 50 Horses: The Step-by-Step Way to Draw Broncos, Arabians, Thoroughbreds, Dancers, Prancers, & Many More... 2012. (ENG., Illus.). 64p. pap. 9.99 *(978-0-8230-8581-1(3),* Watson-Guptill) Potter/TenSpeed/Harmony.

—Draw 50 Monsters. 2012. (Draw 50 Ser.). lib. bdg. 20.85 *(978-0-606-26432-7(9),* Turtleback) Turtleback Bks.

—Draw 50 Monsters: The Step-by-Step Way to Draw Creeps, Superheroes, Demons, Dragons, Nerds, Ghouls, Giants, Vampires, Zombies, & Other Scary Creatures. 2012. (ENG., Illus.). 64p. pap. 9.99 *(978-0-8230-8584-2(8),* Watson-Guptill) Potter/TenSpeed/Harmony.

—Draw 50 Sharks, Whales, & Other Sea Creatures. 2012. (Draw 50 Ser.). lib. bdg. 20.85 *(978-0-606-26429-7(9),* Turtleback) Turtleback Bks.

—Draw 50 Vehicles: The Step-by-Step Way to Draw Speedboats, Spaceships, Fire Trucks, & Many More... 2012. (ENG., Illus.). 64p. pap. 9.99 *(978-0-8230-8569-9(4),* Watson-Guptill) Potter/TenSpeed/Harmony.

—Draw the Draw 50 Way. 2012. (Draw 50 Ser.). lib. bdg. 20.85 *(978-0-606-26431-0(0),* Turtleback) Turtleback Bks.

Ames, Lee J. & Budd, Warren. Draw 50 Endangered Animals: The Step-by-Step Way to Draw Humpback Whales, Giant Pandas, Gorillas, & More Friends We May Lose... 2013. (ENG., Illus.). 64p. pap. 9.99 *(978-0-8230-8608-5(9),* Watson-Guptill) Potter/TenSpeed/Harmony.

—Draw 50 Sharks, Whales, & Other Sea Creatures: The Step-by-Step Way to Draw Great White Sharks, Killer Whales, Barracudas, Seahorses, Seals, & More... 2012. (ENG., Illus.). 64p. pap. 9.99 *(978-0-8230-8571-2(6),* Watson-Guptill) Potter/TenSpeed/Harmony.

Ames, Lee J. & Burns, Ray. Draw 50 Creepy Crawlies. 2013. (Draw 50 Ser.). (Illus.). (J). lib. bdg. 20.85 *(978-0-606-26512-6(0),* Turtleback) Turtleback Bks.

—Draw 50 Creepy Crawlies: The Step-by-Step Way to Draw Bugs, Slugs, Spiders, Scorpions, Butterflies, & Many More... 2013. (ENG., Illus.). 64p. pap. 9.99 *(978-0-8230-8614-6(3),* Watson-Guptill) Potter/TenSpeed/Harmony.

Ames, Lee J. & D'Adamo, Tony. Draw 50 Birds. 2013. (Draw 50 Ser.). lib. bdg. 20.85 *(978-0-606-26509-6(0),* Turtleback) Turtleback Bks.

—Draw 50 Birds: The Step-By-Step Way to Draw Chickadees, Peacocks, Toucans, Mallards, & Many More of Our Feathered Friends. 2013. (ENG., Illus.). 64p. pap. 9.99 *(978-0-8230-8598-9(8),* Watson-Guptill) Potter/TenSpeed/Harmony.

Ames, Lee J. & Estrada, Ric. Draw 50 Aliens. 2013. (Draw 50 Ser.). lib. bdg. 20.85 *(978-0-606-26507-2(4),* Turtleback) Turtleback Bks.

—Draw 50 Aliens: The Step-by-Step Way to Draw UFOs, Galaxy Ghouls, Milky Way Marauders, & Other Extraterrestrial Creatures. 2013. (ENG., Illus.). 64p. pap. 9.99 *(978-0-8230-8616-0(X),* Watson-Guptill) Potter/TenSpeed/Harmony.

Ames, Lee J. & Harvey, Erin. Draw 50 Deep Space: The Step-By-Step Way to Draw Astronauts, Rockets, Space Stations, Planets, Meteors, Comets, Asteroids, & More. 2017. (ENG., Illus.). 64p. pap. 9.99 ***(978-0-399-58019-2(0),*** Watson-Guptill) Potter/TenSpeed/Harmony.

—Draw 50 Sea Creatures: The Step-By-Step Way to Draw Fish, Sharks, Mollusks, Dolphins, & More. 2017. (ENG., Illus.). 64p. pap. 9.99 ***(978-0-399-58017-8(4),*** Watson-Guptill) Potter/TenSpeed/Harmony.

Ames, Lee J. & Mitchell, Andrew. Draw 50 Magical Creatures. 2013. (Draw 50 Ser.). lib. bdg. 20.85 *(978-0-606-26513-3(9),* Turtleback) Turtleback Bks.

—Draw 50 Magical Creatures: The Step-By-Step Way to Draw Unicorns, Elves, Cherubs, Trolls, & Many More. 2013. (ENG., Illus.). 64p. pap. 9.99 *(978-0-8230-8610-8(0),* Watson-Guptill) Potter/TenSpeed/Harmony.

Ames, Lee J. & Moylan, Holly Handler. Draw 50 Princesses. 2012. (Draw 50 Ser.). lib. bdg. 20.85 *(978-0-606-26438-9(8),* Turtleback) Turtleback Bks.

Ames, Lee J. & Zak, Murray. Draw 50 Baby Animals: The Step-by-Step Way to Draw Kittens, Lambs, Chicks, & Other Adorable Offspring. 2012. (ENG., Illus.). 64p. pap. 9.99 *(978-0-8230-8573-6(2),* Watson-Guptill) Potter/TenSpeed/Harmony.

Andrews McMeel Publishing Staff. Go Fun! Monster Doodle Book. 2015. (Go Fun! Ser.: 8). (ENG.). 88p. (J). pap. 10.99 *(978-1-4494-6807-1(1))* Andrews McMeel Publishing.

Antram, David. Draw Caricatures. David Antram, illus. 2017. (Step-By-Step Ser.). 32p. (gr. 3-8). 31.35 ***(978-1-911242-20-8(2))*** Book Hse. GBR. Dist: Black Rabbit Bks.

—Drawing Manga Pets. 2015. (Art Class: the Art of Drawing Manga Ser.). (ENG., Illus.). 32p. (gr. 2-6). 31.35 *(978-1-62588-353-7(6))* Black Rabbit Bks.

—Extreme Sports. 2012. (How to Draw Ser.). (ENG.). 32p. (J). (gr. 4-6). pap. 11.75 *(978-1-4488-6465-2(8));* lib. bdg. 26.50 *(978-1-4488-6459-1(3))* Rosen Publishing Group, Inc., The. (PowerKids Pr.).

—Fantasy Castles. 2012. (How to Draw Ser.). (ENG.). 32p. (J). (gr. 4-6). pap. 11.75 *(978-1-4488-6467-6(4));* lib. bdg. 26.50 *(978-1-4488-6461-4(5))* Rosen Publishing Group, Inc., The. (PowerKids Pr.).

—How to Draw Fairies. 2012. (Illus.). 32p. (J). 70.50 *(978-1-4488-4529-3(7));* pap. 11.75 *(978-1-4488-4521-7(1));* lib. bdg. 26.50 *(978-1-4488-4513-2(0))* Rosen Publishing Group, Inc., The. (PowerKids Pr.).

—How to Draw Manga Warriors. 2010. (How to Draw Ser.). (Illus.). 32p. (YA). (gr. 6-18). pap. 11.75 *(978-1-4488-1609-5(2));* lib. bdg. 26.50 *(978-1-4488-1581-4(9))* Rosen Publishing Group, Inc., The. (PowerKids Pr.).

—How to Draw Pets. 2012. (Illus.). 32p. (J). 70.50 *(978-1-4488-4523-1(8));* pap. 11.75 *(978-1-4488-4517-0(3));* lib. bdg. 26.50 *(978-1-4488-4511-8(4))* Rosen Publishing Group, Inc., The. (PowerKids Pr.).

—How to Draw Pirates. 2012. (Illus.). 32p. (J). 70.50 *(978-1-4488-4526-2(2));* pap. 11.75 *(978-1-4488-4520-0(3));* lib. bdg. 26.50 *(978-1-4488-4515-6(7))* Rosen Publishing Group, Inc., The. (PowerKids Pr.).

—How to Draw Science Fiction. 2012. (Illus.). 32p. (J). 70.50 *(978-1-4488-4528-6(9));* pap. 11.75 *(978-1-4488-4527-9(0))* Rosen Publishing Group, Inc., The. (PowerKids Pr.).

—How to Draw Vampires, Zombies, & Other Monsters. 2012. (Illus.). 32p. (J). 70.50 *(978-1-4488-4525-5(4));* pap. 11.75 *(978-1-4488-4524-8(6));* lib. bdg. 26.50 *(978-1-4488-4512-5(2))* Rosen Publishing Group, Inc., The. (PowerKids Pr.).

Arcturus Publishing. My Drawing, Doodling & Coloring Book. 2015. (ENG.). 256p. (J). 16.95 *(978-1-78404-796-2(1),* 9781784047962) Arcturus Publishing GBR. Dist: Bookmasters Distribution.

Ard, Catherine. Drawing Zentangle Animals. Geddes, Hannah, illus. 2017. (How to Draw Zentangle Art Ser.). 32p. (gr. 3-3). pap. 63.00 ***(978-1-5382-0705-5(2))*** Stevens, Gareth Publishing LLLP.

—Drawing Zentangle Birds. Geddes, Hannah, illus. 2017. (How to Draw Zentangle Art Ser.). 32p. (gr. 3-3). pap. 63.00 ***(978-1-5382-0706-2(0))*** Stevens, Gareth Publishing LLLP.

—Drawing Zentangle Bugs & Butterflies. Geddes, Hannah, illus. 2017. (How to Draw Zentangle Art Ser.). 32p. (gr. 3-3). pap. 10.50 ***(978-1-5382-0840-3(7))*** Stevens, Gareth Publishing LLLP.

—Drawing Zentangle Fantasy Worlds. Geddes, Hannah, illus. 2017. (How to Draw Zentangle Art Ser.). 32p. (gr. 3-3). pap. 63.00 ***(978-1-5382-0708-6(7))*** Stevens, Gareth Publishing LLLP.

—Drawing Zentangle Holidays. Geddes, Hannah, illus. 2017. (How to Draw Zentangle Art Ser.). 32p. (gr. 3-3). pap. 63.00 ***(978-1-5382-0709-3(5))*** Stevens, Gareth Publishing LLLP.

—Drawing Zentangle Sea Life. Geddes, Hannah, illus. 2017. (How to Draw Zentangle Art Ser.). 32p. (gr. 3-3). pap. 63.00 ***(978-1-5382-0710-9(9))*** Stevens, Gareth Publishing LLLP.

Artell, Mike. Funny Cartooning for Kids. 2014. (ENG., Illus.). 128p. (J). (gr. 3). pap. 9.95 *(978-1-4027-8475-0(9))* Sterling Publishing Co., Inc.

Ashforth, Kate. Zap! Fab Things to Draw. Konye, Paul, illus. 2014. (ENG.). (J). (gr. 4-7). pap. *(978-1-74363-385-4(8))* Hinkler Bks. Pty, Ltd.

Bahbout, Jacky & Kudo, Momoko. Making Faces! Star in Your Own Works of Art. 2015. (ENG., Illus.). 64p. (J). (gr. -1-2). pap. 17.95 *(978-0-500-65052-3(7),* 565052) Thames & Hudson.

Baker, Robin J., et al. Crazy Paisley. 2012. (Adult Coloring Ser.). (ENG., Illus.). 64p. (gr. 3). pap. 5.99 *(978-0-486-49086-1(6))* Dover Pubns., Inc.

Balart, Maïté. Farm Animals. 2016. (Drawing with Your Hand Ser.). (ENG., Illus.). 48p. (J). (gr. -1-1). pap. 9.95 *(978-1-63322-174-1(1),* Walter Foster Jr) Quarto Publishing Group USA.

—Wild Animals. 2016. (Drawing with Your Hand Ser.). (ENG., Illus.). 48p. (J). (gr. -1-1). pap. 9.95 *(978-1-63322-175-8(X),* Walter Foster Jr) Quarto Publishing Group USA.

Baltzer, Rochelle. Dinosaurs & Other Prehistoric Animals, 1 vol. Penfield, James, illus. 2015. (ENG.). 32p. (J). *(978-1-62402-081-0(X))* Magic Wagon.

—Dogs & Cats, 1 vol. Penfield, James, illus. 2015. (ENG.). 32p. (J). *(978-1-62402-080-3(1))* Magic Wagon.

—Monsters & Other Mythical Creatures, 1 vol. Penfield, James, illus. 2015. (ENG.). 32p. (J). *(978-1-62402-083-4(6))* Magic Wagon.

—Pirates on the High Seas, 1 vol. Penfield, James, illus. 2015. (ENG.). 32p. (J). *(978-1-62402-084-1(4))* Magic Wagon.

—A Royal Court in Its Kingdom, 1 vol. Penfield, James, illus. 2015. (ENG.). 32p. (J). *(978-1-62402-085-8(2))* Magic Wagon.

Barbie. Barbie: I Love to Draw! 2015. (Love to Draw Ser.: 5). (ENG.). 48p. (J). (gr. 1-4). pap. 8.99 *(978-0-7944-3314-7(6),* Reader's Digest Children's Bks.) Studio Fun International.

Barcella, Laura. BFF: A Keepsake Journal of Off-the-Wall Q&As. 2015. (ENG., Illus.). 368p. (J). (gr. 3-6). pap. 16.95 *(978-1-4549-1396-2(7))* Sterling Publishing Co., Inc.

—OMG: A Keepsake Journal of Off-the-Wall Q&As. 2015. (ENG., Illus.). 368p. (J). (gr. 3-6). pap. 16.95 *(978-1-4549-1395-5(9))* Sterling Publishing Co., Inc.

Barclay, Adrian. Construction Doodles: On-Site Scenes to Complete & Create. 2015. (ENG., Illus.). 160p. (J). (gr. -1-17). pap. 12.95 *(978-0-7624-5629-1(9),* Running Pr. Kids) Running Pr. Bk. Pubs.

Barr, Steve. Draw Crazy Creatures. 2013. (Kids DIY Ser.). (ENG.). 64p. (J). pap. 12.99 *(978-1-4403-2220-4(1),* Impact) F&W Media, Inc.

—1-2-3 Draw Cartoon People. 2014. 64p. pap. 9.00 *(978-1-61003-322-0(1))* Center for the Collaborative Classroom.

—1-2-3 Draw Cartoon People: A Step-By-Step Guide. 2016. (ENG., Illus.). 66p. (J). (gr. k-5). pap. 6.99 *(978-0-939217-98-4(8))* Peel Productions, Inc.

Barroux, illus. Draw Patterns with Barroux Drawing Book & Kit: Everything You Need to Start Drawing Shapes, Colors, & Patterns! 2014. (ENG.). 64p. (J). (gr. -1-3). 14.95 *(978-1-60058-470-1(5))* Quarto Publishing Group USA.

Barton Billman, Hilary. How to Draw the Life & Times of William Henry Harrison. 2009. (Kid's Guide to Drawing the Presidents of the United States of America Ser.). 32p. (gr. 4-4). 50.50 *(978-1-61511-164-0(6),* PowerKids Pr.) Rosen Publishing Group, Inc., The.

Beasant, Pam. How to Draw Buildings. Tatchell, Judy, ed. Ashman, Iain, illus. 2006. (Young Artist Ser.). 32p. (J). (gr. 4-7). pap. 5.99 *(978-0-7945-1371-9(9),* Usborne) EDC Publishing.

Beaumont, Steve. Drawing Diplodocus & Other Plant-Eating Dinosaurs. 2010. (Drawing Dinosaurs Ser.). (Illus.). 32p. (J). pap. 11.75 *(978-1-4488-0424-5(8));* (gr. 2-5). lib. bdg. 26.50 *(978-1-61531-902-2(6))* Rosen Publishing Group, Inc., The.

—Drawing Dragons: And Other Cold-Blooded Creatures. 2011. (Drawing Legendary Monsters Ser.). 32p. (J). (ENG.). pap. 11.75 *(978-1-4488-3257-6(8));* (Illus.). (gr. 3-6). lib. bdg. 26.50 *(978-1-4488-3324-5(8))* Rosen Publishing Group, Inc., The. (PowerKids Pr.).

—Drawing Giganotosaurus & Other Giant Dinosaurs. 2010. (Drawing Dinosaurs Ser.). (Illus.). 32p. (J). pap. 11.75 *(978-1-4488-0430-6(2));* (gr. 2-5). lib. bdg. 26.50 *(978-1-61531-905-3(0))* Rosen Publishing Group, Inc., The.

—Drawing Griffins & Other Winged Wonders. 2011. (Drawing Legendary Monsters Ser.). (Illus.). 32p. (J). (gr. 3-6). lib. bdg. 26.50 *(978-1-4488-3253-8(5),* PowerKids Pr.) Rosen Publishing Group, Inc., The.

—Drawing Plesiosaurus & Other Ocean Dinosaurs. 2010. (Drawing Dinosaurs Ser.). (Illus.). 32p. (J). pap. 11.75 *(978-1-4488-0426-9(4));* (gr. 2-5). lib. bdg. 26.50 *(978-1-61531-903-9(4))* Rosen Publishing Group, Inc., The.

—Drawing Pteranodon & Other Flying Reptiles. 2010. (Drawing Dinosaurs Ser.). (Illus.). 32p. (J). pap. 11.75 *(978-1-4488-0428-3(0));* (gr. 2-5). lib. bdg. 26.50 *(978-1-61531-904-6(2))* Rosen Publishing Group, Inc., The.

—Drawing T. Rex & Other Meat-Eating Dinosaurs. 2010. (Drawing Dinosaurs Ser.). (Illus.). 32p. (J). pap. 11.75 *(978-1-4488-0434-4(5));* (gr. 2-5). lib. bdg. 26.50 *(978-1-61531-907-7(7))* Rosen Publishing Group, Inc., The.

—Drawing the Kraken & Other Sea Monsters. 2011. (Drawing Legendary Monsters Ser.). 32p. (J). (ENG.). pap. 11.75 *(978-1-4488-3263-7(2));* (Illus.). (gr. 3-6). lib. bdg. 26.50 *(978-1-4488-3252-1(7))* Rosen Publishing Group, Inc., The. (PowerKids Pr.).

—Drawing the Minotaur & Other Demihumans. 2011. (Drawing Legendary Monsters Ser.). 32p. (J). (ENG.). pap. 11.75 *(978-1-4488-3259-0(4));* (Illus.). (gr. 3-6). lib. bdg. 26.50 *(978-1-4488-3250-7(0))* Rosen Publishing Group, Inc., The. (PowerKids Pr.).

—Drawing Triceratops & Other Armored Dinosaurs. 2010. (Drawing Dinosaurs Ser.). (Illus.). 32p. (J). pap. 11.75 *(978-1-4488-0432-0(9));* (gr. 2-5). lib. bdg. 26.50 *(978-1-61531-906-0(9))* Rosen Publishing Group, Inc., The.

—Drawing Unicorns & Other Mythical Beasts. 2011. (Drawing Legendary Monsters Ser.). 32p. (J). (ENG.). pap. 11.75 *(978-1-4488-3261-3(6));* (Illus.). (gr. 3-6). lib. bdg. 26.50 *(978-1-4488-3251-4(9))* Rosen Publishing Group, Inc., The. (PowerKids Pr.).

—Drawing Werewolves & Other Gothic Ghouls. 2011. (Drawing Legendary Monsters Ser.). (Illus.). 32p. (J). pap. 11.75 *(978-1-4488-3255-2(1));* (gr. 3-6). 26.50 *(978-1-4488-3254-5(3))* Rosen Publishing Group, Inc., The. (PowerKids Pr.).

—How to Draw Dark Fantasy Art. 2017. (Creating Fantasy Art Ser.). 48p. (gr. 12-12). 31.75 ***(978-1-4994-6669-0(2),*** Rosen Young Adult) Rosen Publishing Group, Inc., The.

—How to Draw Epic Fantasy Art. 2017. (Creating Fantasy Art Ser.). 48p. (gr. 12-12). 31.75 ***(978-1-4994-6670-6(6),*** Rosen Young Adult) Rosen Publishing Group, Inc., The.

—How to Draw Gothic Fantasy Art. 2017. (Creating Fantasy Art Ser.). 48p. (gr. 12-12). 31.75 ***(978-1-4994-6671-3(4),*** Rosen Young Adult) Rosen Publishing Group, Inc., The.

—How to Draw Magical Kings & Queens. 2007. (Drawing Fantasy Art Ser.: Vol. 2). (Illus.). 32p. (J). (gr. 4-7). lib. bdg. 26.50 *(978-1-4042-3860-2(3))* Rosen Publishing Group, Inc., The.

—How to Draw Orcs, Elves, & Dwarves. 2007. (Drawing Fantasy Art Ser.: Vol. 2). (Illus.). 32p. (J). (gr. 4-7). lib. bdg. 26.50 *(978-1-4042-3859-6(X))* Rosen Publishing Group, Inc., The.

—How to Draw Warriors. (Drawing Fantasy Art Ser.). 32p. (gr. 4-5). 2009. 50.50 *(978-1-61512-194-6(3),* PowerKids Pr.) 2007. (Illus.). (J). lib. bdg. 26.50 *(978-1-4042-3858-9(1))* Rosen Publishing Group, Inc., The.

—How to Draw Weird Fantasy Art. 2017. (Creating Fantasy Art Ser.). 48p. (gr. 12-12). 31.75 ***(978-1-5081-7594-0(2),*** Rosen Young Adult) Rosen Publishing Group, Inc., The.

—How to Draw Witches & Wizards. (Drawing Fantasy Art Ser.). 32p. (gr. 4-5). 2009. 50.50 *(978-1-61512-195-3(1),* PowerKids Pr.) 2007. (Illus.). (J). lib. bdg. 26.50 *(978-1-4042-3857-2(3))* Rosen Publishing Group, Inc., The.

—How to Draw Wizards, Warriors, Orcs & Elves. 2007. (Illus.). 143p. pap. 7.99 *(978-0-7858-2345-2(X),* Chartwell) Book Sales, Inc.

Becker, Ann. Dinosaurs. 2009. (Illus.). 24p. (J). pap. 7.95 *(978-1-60694-834-7(2))* Rourke Educational Media.

—Monster Trucks. 2009. (Illus.). 24p. (J). pap. 7.95 *(978-1-60694-838-5(5))* Rourke Educational Media.

—Wizards, Witches, & Dragons. 2009. (Illus.). 24p. (J). pap. 7.95 *(978-1-60694-832-3(6))* Rourke Educational Media.

Bell, Jennifer. Smoky Joe's Book of Drawing Ponies: Top Tips, Techniques & Pony Stuff - Straight from the Horse's Mouth! 2011. (ENG., Illus.). 48p. (J). (gr. 2-7). pap. *(978-0-85131-978-0(5))* Rough Guides, Ltd.

Bell, Megan. Littlest Pet Shop I Love to Draw. 2015. (Love to Draw Ser.). (ENG.). 48p. (J). (gr. 1-5). pap. 8.99 *(978-0-7944-3525-7(4),* Reader's Digest Children's Bks.) Studio Fun International.

Bellen-Berthézène, Cyndie. Flipping Out! How to Draw Flip Animation. Steck, Jim, illus. 2005. 48p. (J). *(978-0-439-81335-8(2))* Scholastic, Inc.

Bergin, Mark. Boats. 2012. (You Can Draw Ser.). (Illus.). 32p. (J). (gr. 1-3). pap. 10.50 *(978-1-4339-7466-3(5));* lib. bdg. 26.60 *(978-1-4339-7465-6(7))* Stevens, Gareth Publishing LLLP.

—Cars. 2009. (How to Draw Ser.). (ENG., Illus.). 32p. (J). (gr. 4-6). pap. 11.75 *(978-1-4358-2649-6(3),* PowerKids Pr.) Rosen Publishing Group, Inc., The.

—Cars. 2012. (You Can Draw Ser.). (Illus.). 32p. (J). (gr. 1-3). pap. 10.50 *(978-1-4339-7469-4(X));* lib. bdg. 26.60 *(978-1-4339-7468-7(1))* Stevens, Gareth Publishing LLLP.

—Dinosaurs. 2011. (It's Fun to Draw Ser.). (ENG., Illus.). 32p. (J). (gr. k-3). lib. bdg. 26.50 *(978-1-61533-349-3(5))* Windmill Bks.

—Dinosaurs & Other Prehistoric Creatures. 2009. (How to Draw Ser.). (Illus.). 32p. (J). lib. bdg. 26.50 *(978-1-4358-2517-8(9),* PowerKids Pr.) Rosen Publishing Group, Inc., The.

—Draw Cats & Kittens. Mark Bergin, illus. 2017. (Step-By-Step Ser.). 32p. (gr. 3-8). 31.35 ***(978-1-911242-21-5(0))*** Book Hse. GBR. Dist: Black Rabbit Bks.

—Fairies & Mermaids. 2011. (It's Fun to Draw Ser.). (ENG., Illus.). 32p. (J). (gr. k-3). lib. bdg. 26.50 *(978-1-61533-350-9(9))* Windmill Bks.

—Farm Animals. 2012. (It's Fun to Draw Ser.). (Illus.). 32p. (J). (gr. k-3). lib. bdg. 26.50 *(978-1-61533-599-2(4))* Windmill Bks.

—Ghosts & Ghouls. 2012. (It's Fun to Draw Ser.). (Illus.). 32p. (J). (gr. k-3). lib. bdg. 26.50 *(978-1-61533-600-5(1))* Windmill Bks.

—How to Draw Cars. 2009. (How to Draw Ser.). (Illus.). 32p. (J). lib. bdg. 26.50 *(978-1-4358-2520-8(9),* PowerKids Pr.) Rosen Publishing Group, Inc., The.

—How to Draw Dinosaurs & Other Prehistoric Creatures. 2009. (How to Draw Ser.). (Illus.). 32p. (gr. 4-6). pap. 11.75 *(978-1-4358-2646-5(9),* Rosen Classroom) Rosen Publishing Group, Inc., The.

—How to Draw Dragons. 2010. (How to Draw Ser.). (ENG.). 32p. (J). pap. 11.75 *(978-1-4488-1607-1(6));* lib. bdg. 26.50 *(978-1-4488-1580-7(0))* Rosen Publishing Group, Inc., The. (PowerKids Pr.).

—How to Draw Fantasy Art. 2010. (How to Draw Ser.). (Illus.). 32p. (YA). (gr. 6-18). pap. 11.75 *(978-1-4488-1601-9(7));* lib. bdg. 26.50 *(978-1-4488-1578-4(9))* Rosen Publishing Group, Inc., The. (PowerKids Pr.).

—How to Draw Knights & Castles. 2012. (Illus.). 32p. (J). 70.50 *(978-1-4488-4530-9(0));* pap. 11.75 *(978-1-4488-4522-4(X));* lib. bdg. 26.50 *(978-1-4488-4514-9(9))* Rosen Publishing Group, Inc., The. (PowerKids Pr.).

—How to Draw Planes. 2009. (How to Draw Ser.). (Illus.). 32p. (gr. 4-6). pap. 11.75 *(978-1-4358-2648-9(5),* Rosen Classroom); (J). lib. bdg. 26.50 *(978-1-4358-2519-2(5),* PowerKids Pr.) Rosen Publishing Group, Inc., The.

—How to Draw Ships. 2010. (How to Draw Ser.). 32p. (J). (ENG.). pap. 11.75 *(978-1-4488-1599-9(1));* (Illus.). lib. bdg. 26.50 *(978-1-4488-1577-7(0))* Rosen Publishing Group, Inc., The. (PowerKids Pr.).

—It's Fun to Draw Dinosaurs & Other Prehistoric Creatures. 2011. (It's Fun to Draw Ser.). (ENG., Illus.). 32p. (J). (gr. -1-3). pap. 5.95 *(978-1-61608-478-3(2),* 608478, Sky Pony Pr.) Skyhorse Publishing Co., Inc.

—It's Fun to Draw Fairies & Mermaids. 2013. (It's Fun to Draw Ser.). (ENG., Illus.). 32p. (J). (gr. 2-5). pap. 5.95 *(978-1-62087-112-6(2),* 620112, Sky Pony Pr.) Skyhorse Publishing Co., Inc.

—It's Fun to Draw Farm Animals. 2012. (It's Fun to Draw Ser.). (ENG., Illus.). 32p. (J). (gr. -1-3). pap. 5.95 *(978-1-61608-669-5(6),* 608669, Sky Pony Pr.) Skyhorse Publishing Co., Inc.

—It's Fun to Draw Ghosts & Ghouls. 2014. (It's Fun to Draw Ser.). (ENG., Illus.). 32p. (J). (gr. -1-3). 5.95 *(978-1-62914-611-9(0),* Sky Pony Pr.) Skyhorse Publishing Co., Inc.

—It's Fun to Draw Knights & Castles. 2013. (It's Fun to Draw Ser.). (ENG., Illus.). 32p. (J). (gr. -1-3). pap. 5.95 *(978-1-62087-113-3(0),* 620113, Sky Pony Pr.) Skyhorse Publishing Co., Inc.

—It's Fun to Draw Pets. 2014. (ENG., Illus.). 32p. (J). (gr. -1-3). 5.95 *(978-1-62636-385-4(4),* Sky Pony Pr.) Skyhorse Publishing Co., Inc.

—It's Fun to Draw Pirates. 2014. (It's Fun to Draw Ser.). (ENG., Illus.). 32p. (J). (gr. -1-3). 5.95 *(978-1-62914-612-6(9),* Sky Pony Pr.) Skyhorse Publishing Co., Inc.

—It's Fun to Draw Princesses & Ballerinas. 2012. (It's Fun to Draw Ser.). (ENG., Illus.). 32p. (J). (gr. -1-3). pap. 5.95 *(978-1-61608-671-8(8),* 608671, Sky Pony Pr.) Skyhorse Publishing Co., Inc.

—It's Fun to Draw Robots & Aliens. 2014. (ENG., Illus.). 32p. (J). (gr. -1-3). 5.95 *(978-1-62636-386-1(2),* Sky Pony Pr.) Skyhorse Publishing Co., Inc.

—It's Fun to Draw Safari Animals. 2011. (It's Fun to Draw Ser.). (ENG., Illus.). 32p. (J). (gr. -1-3). pap. 5.95 *(978-1-61608-477-6(4),* 608477, Sky Pony Pr.) Skyhorse Publishing Co., Inc.

—It's Fun to Draw Sea Creatures. 2013. (ENG., Illus.). 32p. (J). (gr. k-3). pap. 5.95 *(978-1-62087-535-3(7),* 620535, Sky Pony Pr.) Skyhorse Publishing Co., Inc.

—Knights & Castles. 2011. (It's Fun to Draw Ser.). (ENG., Illus.). 32p. (J). (gr. k-3). lib. bdg. 26.50 *(978-1-61533-352-3(5))* Windmill Bks.

—Magical Creatures & Mythical Beasts. 2009. (How to Draw Ser.). (Illus.). 32p. (J). (ENG.). (gr. 4-6). pap. 11.75 *(978-1-4358-2647-2(7));* lib. bdg. 26.50 *(978-1-4358-2518-5(7))* Rosen Publishing Group, Inc., The. (PowerKids Pr.).

—Mammoths & Other Prehistoric Animals. 2012. (How to Draw Ser.). (ENG.). 32p. (J). (gr. 4-6). pap. 11.75 *(978-1-4488-6471-3(2));* lib. bdg. 26.50 *(978-1-4488-6462-1(3))* Rosen Publishing Group, Inc., The. (PowerKids Pr.).

—Monsters. 2012. (It's Fun to Draw Ser.). (Illus.). 32p. (J). (gr. k-3). lib. bdg. 26.50 *(978-1-61533-601-2(X))* Windmill Bks.

—Pets. 2012. (It's Fun to Draw Ser.). (Illus.). 32p. (J). (gr. k-3). lib. bdg. 26.50 *(978-1-61533-597-8(8))* Windmill Bks.

—Pirates. 2012. (It's Fun to Draw Ser.). (ENG., Illus.). 32p. (J). (gr. k-3). lib. bdg. 26.50 *(978-1-61533-602-9(8))* Windmill Bks.

—Planes. 2012. (You Can Draw Ser.). (Illus.). 32p. (J). (gr. 1-3). pap. 10.50 *(978-1-4339-7472-4(X));* lib. bdg. 26.60 *(978-1-4339-7471-7(1))* Stevens, Gareth Publishing LLLP.

—Princesses & Ballerinas. 2011. (It's Fun to Draw Ser.). (ENG., Illus.). 32p. (J). (gr. k-3). lib. bdg. 26.50 *(978-1-61533-351-6(7))* Windmill Bks.

—Robots. 2009. (How to Draw Ser.). (Illus.). 32p. (J). (ENG.). (gr. 4-6). pap. 11.75 *(978-1-4358-2650-2(7));* lib. bdg. 26.50 *(978-1-4358-2521-5(7))* Rosen Publishing Group, Inc., The. (PowerKids Pr.).

—Robots & Aliens. 2011. (It's Fun to Draw Ser.). (ENG., Illus.). 32p. (J). (gr. k-3). lib. bdg. 26.50 *(978-1-61533-353-0(3))* Windmill Bks.

—Rockets. 2012. (You Can Draw Ser.). (Illus.). 32p. (J). (gr. 1-3). pap. 10.50 *(978-1-4339-7475-5(4));* lib. bdg. 26.60 *(978-1-4339-7474-8(6))* Stevens, Gareth Publishing LLLP.

—Sea Creatures. 2012. (It's Fun to Draw Ser.). (Illus.). 32p. (J). (gr. k-3). lib. bdg. 26.50 *(978-1-61533-598-5(6))* Windmill Bks.

—Soldiers. 2012. (How to Draw Ser.). (ENG.). 32p. (J). (gr. 4-6). pap. 11.75 *(978-1-4488-6473-7(9))*; lib. bdg. 26.50 *(978-1-4488-6463-8(1))* Rosen Publishing Group, Inc., The. (PowerKids Pr.).

—Trains. 2012. (You Can Draw Ser.). (Illus.). 32p. (J). (gr. 1-3). pap. 10.50 *(978-1-4339-7478-6(9))*; lib. bdg. 26.60 *(978-1-4339-7477-9(0))* Stevens, Gareth Publishing LLLP.

Bergin, Mark, illus. It's Fun to Draw Cars, Planes, & Trains. 2015. (It's Fun to Draw Ser.). (ENG.). 32p. (J). (gr. -1-3). 5.99 *(978-1-63220-410-3(X)*, Sky Pony Pr.) Skyhorse Publishing Co., Inc.

—It's Fun to Draw Creepy-Crawlies. 2015. (It's Fun to Draw Ser.). (ENG.). 32p. (J). (gr. -1-3). 5.99 *(978-1-63220-406-6(1)*, Sky Pony Pr.) Skyhorse Publishing Co., Inc.

—It's Fun to Draw Ponies & Horses. 2015. (It's Fun to Draw Ser.). (ENG.). 32p. (J). (gr. -1-3). 5.99 *(978-1-63220-415-8(0)*, Sky Pony Pr.) Skyhorse Publishing Co., Inc.

Bergin, Mark & Antram, David. How to Draw Cartoons. 2010. (How to Draw Ser.). (Illus.). 32p. (YA). (gr. 6-18). pap. 11.75 *(978-1-4488-1597-5(5))*; lib. bdg. 26.50 *(978-1-4488-1576-0(2))* Rosen Publishing Group, Inc., The. (PowerKids Pr.).

Berry, Bob. How to Draw Magical, Monstrous & Mythological Creatures. 2013. (Walter Foster Studio Ser.). 128p. (J). (gr. 3-8). 35.65 *(978-1-936309-92-4(0))* Quarto Publishing Group USA.

Berry, Bob, illus. Ancient Times: Step-by-Step Instructions for 18 Ancient Characters & Civilizations. 2013. (Learn to Draw Ser.). (ENG.). 40p. (J). (gr. 1-3). pap. 4.95 *(978-1-60058-310-0(5)*, 1600583105) Quarto Publishing Group USA.

Berry, Bob & Destefano, Merrie. How to Draw Magical, Monstrous & Mythological Creatures: Discover the Magic of Drawing More Than 20 Legendary Folklore, Fantasy, & Horror Characters. 2011. (Walter Foster Studio Ser.). (ENG., Illus.). 128p. (J). (gr. 5-11). pap. 16.95 *(978-1-60058-228-8(1)*, 1600582281) Quarto Publishing Group USA.

Besel, Jennifer M. Christmas Drawing Wonderland! Makuc, Lucy, illus. 2013. (Holiday Sketchbook Ser.). (ENG.). (gr. 1-2). 40p. pap. 4.95 *(978-1-4765-3447-3(0))*; 24p. 25.32 *(978-1-4765-3092-5(0))* Capstone Press of Coughlan Cos. (First Facts).

—Drawing a Christmas Wonderland: A Step-By-Step Sketchpad, 1 vol. Makuc, Lucy, illus. 2014. (My First Sketchpads Ser.). (ENG.). 48p. (gr. 1-2). pap. 5.95 *(978-1-4914-1748-5(X)*, First Facts) Capstone Press of Coughlan Cos.

—Drawing a Halloween Spooktacular: A Step-By-Step Sketchpad, 1 vol. Makuc, Lucy, illus. 2014. (My First Sketchpads Ser.). (ENG.). 48p. (gr. 1-2). pap. 5.95 *(978-1-4914-1749-2(8)*, First Facts) Capstone Press of Coughlan Cos.

—Halloween Drawing Spooktacular! Makuc, Lucy, illus. 2013. (Holiday Sketchbook Ser.). (ENG.). (gr. 1-2). 40p. pap. 4.95 *(978-1-4765-3446-6(2))*; 24p. 25.32 *(978-1-4765-3091-8(2))* Capstone Press of Coughlan Cos. (First Facts).

—Thanksgiving Drawing Feast! Makuc, Lucy, illus. 2013. (Holiday Sketchbook Ser.). (ENG.). (gr. 1-2). 40p. pap. 4.95 *(978-1-4765-3448-0(9))*; 24p. 25.32 *(978-1-4765-3093-2(9))* Capstone Press of Coughlan Cos. (First Facts).

—Valentine's Day Drawing Treat! Makuc, Lucy, illus. 2013. (Holiday Sketchbook Ser.). (ENG.). (gr. 1-2). 40p. pap. 4.95 *(978-1-4765-3449-7(7))*; 24p. 25.32 *(978-1-4765-3094-9(7))* Capstone Press of Coughlan Cos. (First Facts).

Bishop-Stephens, Will. How to Create Animation in 10 Easy Lessons: Create 2-D, 3-d, & Digital Animation Without a Hollywood Budget. 2016. (Super Skills Ser.). (ENG.). 64p. (J). (gr. 3-7). 12.95 *(978-1-63322-182-6(2)*, Walter Foster Jr) Quarto Publishing Group USA.

Bolte, Mari. Draw Amazing Animal Mash-Ups. 2017. (Drawing Mash-Ups Ser.). (ENG.). 32p. (gr. 3-4). lib. bdg. 27.99 ***(978-1-5157-6936-1(4)***, Edge Bks.) Capstone Press of Coughlan Cos.

—Draw Astonishing Warrior Mash-Ups. 2017. (Drawing Mash-Ups Ser.). (ENG.). 32p. (gr. 3-4). lib. bdg. 27.99 ***(978-1-5157-6937-8(2)***, Edge Bks.) Capstone Press of Coughlan Cos.

—Draw Scary Monster Mash-Ups. 2017. (Drawing Mash-Ups Ser.). (ENG.). 32p. (gr. 3-4). lib. bdg. 27.99 ***(978-1-5157-6935-4(6)***, Edge Bks.) Capstone Press of Coughlan Cos.

—Draw Wild Robot Mash-Ups. 2017. (Drawing Mash-Ups Ser.). (ENG.). 32p. (gr. 3-4). lib. bdg. 27.99 ***(978-1-5157-6934-7(8)***, Edge Bks.) Capstone Press of Coughlan Cos.

—Drawing Faces: A Step-By-Step Sketchbook, 1 vol. Makuc, Lucy & Dynamo Limited Staff, illus. 2014. (My First Sketchbook Ser.). (ENG.). 24p. (gr. 1-2). lib. bdg. 25.32 *(978-1-4914-0284-9(9))* Capstone Press of Coughlan Cos.

—Drawing Faces: A Step-By-Step Sketchpad, 1 vol. Makuc, Lucy & Dynamo Limited Staff, illus. 2014. (My First Sketchpads Ser.). (ENG.). 48p. (gr. 1-2). pap. 5.95 *(978-1-4914-0293-1(8)*, First Facts) Capstone Press of Coughlan Cos.

—Drawing Monsters: A Step-By-Step Sketchbook, 1 vol. Makuc, Lucy & Dynamo Limited Staff, illus. 2014. (My First Sketchbook Ser.). (ENG.). 24p. (gr. 1-2). lib. bdg. 25.32 *(978-1-4914-0282-5(2))* Capstone Press of Coughlan Cos.

—Drawing Monsters: A Step-By-Step Sketchpad, 1 vol. Makuc, Lucy & Dynamo Limited Staff, illus. 2014. (My First Sketchpads Ser.). (ENG.). 48p. (gr. 1-2). pap. 5.95 *(978-1-4914-0291-7(1)*, First Facts) Capstone Press of Coughlan Cos.

—Drawing Pets: A Step-By-Step Sketchbook, 1 vol. Makuc, Lucy & Dynamo Limited Staff, illus. 2014. (My First Sketchbook Ser.). (ENG.). 24p. (gr. 1-2). lib. bdg. 25.32 *(978-1-4914-0281-8(4))* Capstone Press of Coughlan Cos.

—Drawing Pets: A Step-By-Step Sketchpad, 1 vol. Makuc, Lucy & Dynamo Limited Staff, illus. 2014. (My First Sketchpads Ser.). (ENG.). 48p. (gr. 1-2). pap. 5.95 *(978-1-4914-0290-0(3)*, First Facts) Capstone Press of Coughlan Cos.

—Drawing Vehicles: A Step-By-Step Sketchbook, 1 vol. Makuc, Lucy & Dynamo Limited Staff, illus. 2014. (My First Sketchbook Ser.). (ENG.). 24p. (gr. 1-2). lib. bdg. 25.32 *(978-1-4914-0283-2(0))* Capstone Press of Coughlan Cos.

—Drawing Vehicles: A Step-By-Step Sketchpad, 1 vol. Makuc, Lucy & Dynamo Limited Staff, illus. 2014. (My First Sketchpads Ser.). (ENG.). 48p. (gr. 1-2). pap. 5.95 *(978-1-4914-0292-4(X)*, First Facts) Capstone Press of Coughlan Cos.

Bontinck, Helga. All Around Town. 2006. (Simple Steps to Drawing Ser.). (Illus.). 24p. (gr. k-3). lib. bdg. 23.00 *(978-0-8368-6310-9(0)*, Gareth Stevens Learning Library) Stevens, Gareth Publishing LLLP.

—Animal Favorites. 2006. (Simple Steps to Drawing Ser.). (Illus.). 24p. (gr. k-3). lib. bdg. 23.00 *(978-0-8368-6311-6(9)*, Gareth Stevens Learning Library) Stevens, Gareth Publishing LLLP.

—At the Circus. 2006. (Simple Steps to Drawing Ser.). (Illus.). 24p. (gr. k-3). lib. bdg. 23.00 *(978-0-8368-6312-3(7)*, Gareth Stevens Learning Library) Stevens, Gareth Publishing LLLP.

—At the Seashore. 2006. (Simple Steps to Drawing Ser.). (Illus.). 24p. (gr. k-3). lib. bdg. 23.00 *(978-0-8368-6313-0(5)*, Gareth Stevens Learning Library) Stevens, Gareth Publishing LLLP.

Boyds Mills Press Staff. Drawing Activities. 2008. (Highlights Hidden Pictures Ser.). (ENG., Illus.). 32p. (J). (gr. -1-3). pap. 5.49 *(978-1-59078-579-9(7))* Highlights for Children.

Brecke, Nicole & Stockland, Patricia M. Airplanes & Ships You Can Draw. Brecke, Nicole, illus. 2010. (Ready, Set, Draw! Ser.). (ENG., Illus.). 32p. (gr. 2-4). lib. bdg. 25.26 *(978-0-7613-4166-6(8)*, Millbrook Pr.) Lerner Publishing Group.

—Cars, Trucks, & Motorcycles You Can Draw. Brecke, Nicole, illus. 2009. (Ready, Set, Draw! Ser.). (ENG., Illus.). 32p. (gr. 2-4). lib. bdg. 25.26 *(978-0-7613-4162-8(5)*, Millbrook Pr.) Lerner Publishing Group.

—Cats You Can Draw. Brecke, Nicole, illus. 2009. (Ready, Set, Draw! Ser.). (ENG., Illus.). 32p. (gr. 2-4). lib. bdg. 25.26 *(978-0-7613-4161-1(7)*, Millbrook Pr.) Lerner Publishing Group.

—Cool Boy Stuff You Can Draw. Brecke, Nicole, illus. 2009. (Ready, Set, Draw! Ser.). (ENG., Illus.). 32p. (gr. 2-4). lib. bdg. 25.26 *(978-0-7613-4163-5(3)*, Millbrook Pr.) Lerner Publishing Group.

—Cool Girl Stuff You Can Draw. Brecke, Nicole, illus. 2009. (Ready, Set, Draw! Ser.). (ENG., Illus.). 32p. (gr. 2-4). lib. bdg. 25.26 *(978-0-7613-4164-2(1)*, Millbrook Pr.) Lerner Publishing Group.

—Dinosaurs & Other Prehistoric Creatures You Can Draw. Brecke, Nicole, illus. 2010. (Ready, Set, Draw! Ser.). (ENG., Illus.). 32p. (gr. 2-4). lib. bdg. 25.26 *(978-0-7613-4169-7(2)*, Millbrook Pr.) Lerner Publishing Group.

—Dogs You Can Draw. Brecke, Nicole, illus. 2009. (Ready, Set, Draw! Ser.). (ENG., Illus.). 32p. (gr. 2-4). lib. bdg. 25.26 *(978-0-7613-4159-8(5)*, Millbrook Pr.) Lerner Publishing Group.

—Horses You Can Draw. Brecke, Nicole, illus. 2009. (Ready, Set, Draw! Ser.). (ENG., Illus.). 32p. (gr. 2-4). lib. bdg. 25.26 *(978-0-7613-4160-4(9)*, Millbrook Pr.) Lerner Publishing Group.

—Insects You Can Draw. Brecke, Nicole, illus. 2010. (Ready, Set, Draw! Ser.). (ENG., Illus.). 32p. (J). (gr. 2-4). lib. bdg. 25.26 *(978-0-7613-4170-3(6)*, Millbrook Pr.) Lerner Publishing Group.

—Sea Creatures You Can Draw. Brecke, Nicole, illus. 2010. (Ready, Set, Draw! Ser.). (ENG., Illus.). 32p. (gr. 2-4). lib. bdg. 25.26 *(978-0-7613-4168-0(4)*, Millbrook Pr.) Lerner Publishing Group.

—Spaceships, Aliens, & Robots You Can Draw. Brecke, Nicole, illus. 2010. (Ready, Set, Draw! Ser.). (ENG., Illus.). 32p. (gr. 2-4). lib. bdg. 25.26 *(978-0-7613-4167-3(6)*, Millbrook Pr.) Lerner Publishing Group.

Bruning, Matt & Cerato, Mattia. You Can Draw Dinosaurs, 1 vol. Cerato, Mattia, illus. 2010. (You Can Draw Ser.). (ENG., Illus.). 24p. (gr. 1-2). lib. bdg. 26.65 *(978-1-4048-6280-7(3))* Picture Window Bks.

—You Can Draw Flowers, 1 vol. Cerato, Mattia, illus. 2010. (You Can Draw Ser.). (ENG., Illus.). 24p. (gr. 1-2). lib. bdg. 26.65 *(978-1-4048-6279-1(X))* Picture Window Bks.

Bruning, Matt & Ho, Jannie. You Can Draw Monsters & Other Scary Things, 1 vol. Ho, Jannie, illus. 2010. (You Can Draw Ser.). (ENG., Illus.). 24p. (gr. 1-2). lib. bdg. 26.65 *(978-1-4048-6276-0(5))* Picture Window Bks.

—You Can Draw Zoo Animals, 1 vol. Ho, Jannie, illus. 2010. (You Can Draw Ser.). (ENG., Illus.). 24p. (gr. 1-2). lib. bdg. 26.65 *(978-1-4048-6275-3(7))* Picture Window Bks.

Bruning, Matt & Sexton, Brenda. You Can Draw Planes, Trains, & Other Vehicles, 1 vol. Sexton, Brenda, illus. 2010. (You Can Draw Ser.). (ENG., Illus.). 24p. (gr. 1-2). lib. bdg. 26.65 *(978-1-4048-6278-4(1))* Picture Window Bks.

Burklow, Shan Williams. Learn to Draw with Quacker & Friends. 2012. (ENG.). (J). pap. 12.99 *(978-1-4675-4791-8(3))* Independent Pub.

Calver, Paul. Drawing. 2014. (Mini Artist Ser.). (Illus.). 24p. (J). (gr. k-3). lib. bdg. 26.25 *(978-1-4777-9115-8(9))* Windmill Bks.

Campbell, Trenton, ed. Drawing: Materials, Technique, Styles, & Practice. 2016. (Britannica's Practical Guide to the Arts Ser.). 128p. (J). (gr. 10-10). lib. bdg. 36.25 *(978-1-68048-371-0(4))* Rosen Publishing Group, Inc., The.

Capsey, Steve. Let's Draw Cars. 2010. (Let's Draw Ser.). (ENG., Illus.). 32p. (J). (gr. 3-5). pap. 10.55 *(978-1-61533-266-3(9))*; lib. bdg. 22.60 *(978-1-61533-263-2(4))* Windmill Bks.

Cardaci, Diane. Realistic Textures: Discover Your Inner Artist as You Explore the Basic Theories & Techniques of Pencil Drawing. 2007. (Drawing Made Easy Ser.). (ENG., Illus.). 64p. pap. 9.95 *(978-1-56010-997-6(1)*, 1560109971) Quarto Publishing Group USA.

Catlow, Nikalas. Do You Doodle? 2013. (ENG., Illus.). 160p. (J). (gr. -1-17). pap. 12.95 *(978-0-7624-5287-3(0)*, Running Pr. Kids) Running Pr. Bk. Pubs.

—Oodles of Doodles. 2013. (ENG., Illus.). 160p. (J). (gr. -1-17). pap. 12.95 *(978-0-7624-5294-1(3)*, Running Pr. Kids) Running Pr. Bk. Pubs.

Cerato, Mattia. You Can Draw Construction Vehicles, 1 vol. Cerato, Mattia, illus. 2011. (You Can Draw Ser.). (ENG., Illus.). 24p. (gr. 1-2). lib. bdg. 26.65 *(978-1-4048-6807-6(0))* Picture Window Bks.

—You Can Draw Dragons, Unicorns, & Other Magical Creatures, 1 vol. Cerato, Mattia, illus. 2011. (You Can Draw Ser.). (ENG., Illus.). 24p. (gr. 1-2). lib. bdg. 26.65 *(978-1-4048-6809-0(7))* Picture Window Bks.

Cerato, Mattia & Ho, Jannie. Easy-To-Draw Monsters: A Step-By-Step Drawing Book. Cerato, Mattia & Ho, Jannie, illus. 2014. (You Can Draw Ser.). (ENG., Illus.). 64p. (gr. 1-2). pap. 6.95 *(978-1-4795-5512-3(6))* Picture Window Bks.

Cerato, Mattia & Sexton, Brenda. Easy-to-Draw Vehicles. Cerato, Mattia & Sexton, Brenda, illus. 2011. (You Can Draw Ser.). (ENG., Illus.). 48p. (gr. 1-2). pap. 5.19 *(978-1-4048-7058-1(X))* Picture Window Bks.

—Easy-To-Draw Vehicles: A Step-By-Step Drawing Book. Cerato, Mattia & Sexton, Brenda, illus. 2014. (You Can Draw Ser.). (ENG., Illus.). 64p. (gr. 1-2). pap. 6.95 *(978-1-4795-5513-0(4))* Picture Window Bks.

Chambers, Ailin. Animals. 2014. (Ready, Set, Draw! Ser.). (Illus.). 32p. (J). (gr. 2-5). 26.60 *(978-1-4824-0907-9(0))* Stevens, Gareth Publishing LLLP.

—Creepy Crawlies. 2014. (Ready, Set, Draw! Ser.). 32p. (J). (gr. 2-5). 26.60 *(978-1-4824-0911-6(9))* Stevens, Gareth Publishing LLLP.

—Fairies & Princesses. 2014. (Ready, Set, Draw! Ser.). 32p. (J). (gr. 2-5). 26.60 *(978-1-4824-0915-4(1))* Stevens, Gareth Publishing LLLP.

—Robots & Monsters. 2014. (Ready, Set, Draw! Ser.). 32p. (J). (gr. 2-5). 26.60 *(978-1-4824-0922-2(4))* Stevens, Gareth Publishing LLLP.

—Superheroes. 2014. (Ready, Set, Draw! Ser.). 32p. (J). (gr. 2-5). pap. 63.00 *(978-1-4824-0926-0(7))* Stevens, Gareth Publishing LLLP.

Chronicle Books Staff. Draw Bridge: A Draw-Your-Own Adventure. Walsh, Sarah, illus. 2017. (ENG.). 96p. (J). (gr. 1-17). pap. 14.99 ***(978-1-4521-6097-9(X))*** Chronicle Bks. LLC.

Cis, Valeria. ABC & Color Me: The Art of Hand-Lettered Doodling for Kids. 2016. (ENG., Illus.). 96p. (J). (gr. k-6). pap. 12.95 *(978-1-63322-170-3(9)*, Walter Foster Jr) Quarto Publishing Group USA.

Claridge, Marit. How to Draw Dinosaurs & Prehistoric Life. Tatchell, Judy, ed. Biro, Val, illus. 2006. (Young Artist Ser.). 32p. (J). (gr. 4-7). pap. 5.99 *(978-0-7945-1372-6(7)*, Usborne) EDC Publishing.

Clay, Kathryn. Girls' Guide to Drawing: Horses, Flowers, Faces, & Other Cool Stuff. 2009. (Drawing Fun Ser.). (ENG.). 144p. (gr. 3-4). pap. 14.95 *(978-1-4296-3645-2(9)*, Snap Bks.) Capstone Press of Coughlan Cos.

—Girls' Guide to Drawing [LTD Commodities]. 2011. (Drawing Fun Ser.). 144p. pap. 3.00 *(978-1-4296-6640-4(4)*, Snap Bks.) Capstone Press of Coughlan Cos.

Clunes, Rebecca. Drawing Creepy Crawlies. 2011. (Drawing Is Fun Ser.). (Illus.). 32p. (J). (gr. 1-3). pap. 10.50 *(978-1-4339-5940-0(2)*, Gareth Stevens Learning Library); lib. bdg. 26.60 *(978-1-4339-5938-7(0))* Stevens, Gareth Publishing LLLP.

—Drawing Dinosaurs. 2011. (Drawing Is Fun Ser.). (Illus.). 32p. (J). (gr. 1-3). pap. 10.50 *(978-1-4339-5944-8(5)*, 1330713, Gareth Stevens Learning Library); lib. bdg. 26.60 *(978-1-4339-5942-4(9)*, 1330713) Stevens, Gareth Publishing LLLP.

—Drawing Sea Creatures. 2011. (Drawing Is Fun Ser.). (Illus.). 32p. (J). (gr. 1-3). pap. 10.50 *(978-1-4339-5948-6(8)*, 1330714, Gareth Stevens Learning Library); lib. bdg. 26.60 *(978-1-4339-5946-2(1)*, 1330714) Stevens, Gareth Publishing LLLP.

—Drawing Speed Machines. 2011. (Drawing Is Fun Ser.). (Illus.). 32p. (J). (gr. 1-3). pap. 10.50 *(978-1-4339-5952-3(6)*, 1330715, Gareth Stevens Learning Library); lib. bdg. 26.60 *(978-1-4339-5950-9(X)*, 1330715) Stevens, Gareth Publishing LLLP.

Cole, Jeff & Andrews McMeel Publishing, LLC Staff. Eyeball Animation Drawing Book: Underwater Safari Edition. Cole, Jeff, illus. 2009. (ENG., Illus.). 84p. (J). (gr. -1). pap. 14.99 *(978-0-7407-8106-3(5))* Andrews McMeel Publishing.

Colich, Abby. Drawing Amazing Animals. Calle, Juan & Howard, Colin, illus. 2015. (Drawing Amazing Animals Ser.). (ENG.). 32p. (gr. 3-4). lib. bdg. 111.96 *(978-1-4914-2559-6(8)*, Snap Bks.) Capstone Press of Coughlan Cos.

—Drawing Fascinating Animals. Howard, Colin, illus. 2015. (Drawing Amazing Animals Ser.). (ENG.). 32p. (gr. 3-4). 27.99 *(978-1-4914-2133-8(9)*, Snap Bks.) Capstone Press of Coughlan Cos.

—Drawing Ocean Animals. Calle, Juan, illus. 2015. (Drawing Amazing Animals Ser.). (ENG.). 32p. (gr. 3-4). 27.99 *(978-1-4914-2131-4(2)*, Snap Bks.) Capstone Press of Coughlan Cos.

—Drawing Wild Animals. Juta, Jason, illus. 2015. (Drawing Amazing Animals Ser.). (ENG.). 32p. (gr. 3-4). 27.99 *(978-1-4914-2132-1(0)*, Snap Bks.) Capstone Press of Coughlan Cos.

—Drawing Your Pets. Azzalin, Stefano, illus. 2015. (Drawing Amazing Animals Ser.). (ENG.). 32p. (gr. 3-4). 27.99 *(978-1-4914-2134-5(7)*, Snap Bks.) Capstone Press of Coughlan Cos.

—The Ultimate Girls' Guide to Drawing: Puppies, Polar Bears, & Other Adorable Animals. Howard, Colin, illus. 2015. (ENG.). 144p. (gr. 3-4). pap. 14.95 *(978-1-62370-229-8(1))* Capstone Young Readers of Coughlan Cos.

Cook, Janet. How to Draw Robots & Aliens. Tatchell, Judy, ed. 2006. (Illus.). 32p. (J). (gr. 4). lib. bdg. 13.99 *(978-1-58086-897-6(5)*, Usborne) EDC Publishing.

—How to Draw Robots & Aliens. Tatchell, Judy, ed. Chen, Kuo Kang, illus. 2006. (Young Artist Ser.). 32p. (J). (gr. 4-7). pap. 5.99 *(978-0-7945-1370-2(0)*, Usborne) EDC Publishing.

Cook, Trevor & Miles, Lisa. Drawing Fantasy Figures. 2011. (Drawing Is Fun Ser.). (Illus.). 32p. (J). (gr. 1-3). pap. 10.50 *(978-1-4339-5065-0(0)*, Gareth Stevens Learning Library); lib. bdg. 26.60 *(978-1-4339-5022-3(7))* Stevens, Gareth Publishing LLLP.

—Drawing Pets & Farm Animals. 2011. (Drawing Is Fun Ser.). (Illus.). 32p. (J). (gr. 1-3). pap. 10.50 *(978-1-4339-5071-1(5)*, Gareth Stevens Learning Library); lib. bdg. 26.60 *(978-1-4339-5026-1(X))* Stevens, Gareth Publishing LLLP.

—Drawing Sports Figures. 2011. (Drawing Is Fun Ser.). (Illus.). 32p. (J). (gr. 1-3). pap. 10.50 *(978-1-4339-5074-2(X)*, Gareth Stevens Learning Library); lib. bdg. 26.60 *(978-1-4339-5028-5(6))* Stevens, Gareth Publishing LLLP.

—Drawing Vehicles. 2011. (Drawing Is Fun Ser.). (Illus.). 32p. (J). (gr. 1-3). pap. 10.50 *(978-1-4339-5077-3(4)*, Gareth Stevens Learning Library); lib. bdg. 26.60 *(978-1-4339-5030-8(8))* Stevens, Gareth Publishing LLLP.

—Drawing Wild Animals. 2011. (Drawing Is Fun Ser.). (Illus.). 32p. (J). (gr. 1-3). lib. bdg. 26.60 *(978-1-4339-5032-2(4))* Stevens, Gareth Publishing LLLP.

Corfee, Stephanie. Creative Doodling & Beyond. 2011. (Creative... & Beyond Ser.). (ENG., Illus.). 144p. pap. 19.95 *(978-1-60058-247-9(8)*, 1600582478) Quarto Publishing Group USA.

—Free Spirit Doodles. Corfee, Stephanie, illus. 2016. (Doodle with Attitude Ser.). (ENG., Illus.). 32p. (gr. 4-5). lib. bdg. 27.99 *(978-1-4914-7945-2(0))* Capstone Press of Coughlan Cos.

—Girl Plus Pen: Doodle, Draw, Color, & Express Your Individual Style. Corfee, Stephanie, illus. 2016. (Craft It Yourself Ser.). (ENG., Illus.). 144p. (gr. 3-4). pap. 12.95 *(978-1-62370-596-1(7))* Capstone Young Readers of Coughlan Cos.

—Quirky, Cute Doodles. Corfee, Stephanie, illus. 2016. (Doodle with Attitude Ser.). (ENG., Illus.). 32p. (gr. 4-5). lib. bdg. 27.99 *(978-1-4914-7944-5(2))* Capstone Press of Coughlan Cos.

—Twirly Girly Doodles. Corfee, Stephanie, illus. 2016. (Doodle with Attitude Ser.). (ENG., Illus.). 32p. (gr. 4-5). lib. bdg. 27.99 *(978-1-4914-7943-8(4))* Capstone Press of Coughlan Cos.

Correll, Gemma. What I Wore Today. 2012. (ENG., Illus.). 112p. (gr. -1-17). 12.99 *(978-1-84601-395-9(X)*, Spruce) Octopus Publishing Group GBR. Dist: Hachette Bk. Group.

Cousins, Lucy. Doodle with Maisy. 2013. (Maisy Ser.). (ENG.). 80p. (J). (gr. -1-2). pap. 8.99 *(978-0-7636-6490-9(1))* Candlewick Pr.

Coussement, Frank, et al. Go Fun! BrainSnack Draw with Numbers. 2015. (Go Fun! Ser.: 11). (ENG.). 128p. (J). pap. 8.99 *(978-1-4494-7242-9(7))* Andrews McMeel Publishing.

Creative Team at Walter Foster Publishing Staff. How to Draw Teenage Mutant Ninja Turtles: Learn to Draw Leonardo, Raphael, Donatello, & Michelangelo Step by Step! 2013. (Licensed Learn to Draw Ser.). (ENG., Illus.). 64p. (J). (gr. 3-7). pap. 9.95 *(978-1-60058-296-7(6)*, 1600582966) Quarto Publishing Group USA.

—I Love Cats! Activity Book: Meow-velous stickers, trivia, step-by-step drawing projects, & more for the cat lover in You! Fisher, Diana, illus. 2011. (I Love Activity Bks.). (ENG.). 112p. (J). (gr. 1-3). pap. 9.95 *(978-1-60058-224-0(9)*, 1600582249) Quarto Publishing Group USA.

—I Love Dogs! Pup-Tacular Stickers, Trivia, Step-by-Step Drawing Projects, & More for the Dog Lover in You! Fisher, Diana, illus. 2011. (I Love Activity Bks.). (ENG.). 112p. (J). (gr. 1-3). pap., act. bk. ed. 9.95 *(978-1-60058-225-7(7)*, 1600582257) Quarto Publishing Group USA.

—Learn to Draw Angry Birds: Learn to Draw All of Your Favorite Angry Birds & Those Bad Piggies! 2012. (Licensed Learn to Draw Ser.). (ENG., Illus.). 64p. (J). (gr. 1-3). pap. 9.95 *(978-1-60058-306-3(7)*, 1600583067) Quarto Publishing Group USA.

—Learn to Draw Angry Birds Drawing Book & Kit: Includes Everything You Need to Draw Your Favorite Angry Birds Characters! 2013. (Licensed Learn to Draw Ser.). (ENG., Illus.). 32p. (J). (gr. 1-17). pap. 19.99 *(978-1-60058-373-5(3)*, 1600583733) Quarto Publishing Group USA.

—The Legend of Korra: Learn to Draw All Your Favorite Characters, Including Korra, Mako, & Bolin! 2014. (Licensed Learn to Draw Ser.). (ENG., Illus.). 64p. (J). (gr. 3-7). pap. 9.95 *(978-1-60058-379-7(2)*, 1600583792) Quarto Publishing Group USA.

—Spongebob Squarepants - The Bikini Bottom Collection. 2012. (Licensed Learn to Draw Ser.). (ENG., Illus.). 64p. (J). (gr. 1-3). pap. 9.95 *(978-1-60058-297-4(4)*, 1600582974) Quarto Publishing Group USA.

—150 Fun Things to Doodle: An Interactive Adventure in Drawing Lively Animals, Quirky Robots, & Zany Doodads. 2014. (ENG., Illus.). 128p. (J). (gr. 1-3). pap. 14.95 *(978-1-60058-376-6(8)*, 1600583768) Quarto Publishing Group USA.

Criscione, Rachel. How to Draw the Life & Times of Chester A. Arthur. 2006. (Kid's Guide to Drawing the Presidents of the United States of America Ser.). (YA). (gr. 2-5). 26.50 *(978-1-4042-2998-3(1))* Rosen Publishing Group, Inc., The.

Criscon, R. D. How to Draw the Life & Times of Chester A. Arthur. 2009. (Kid's Guide to Drawing the Presidents of the United States of America Ser.). 32p. (gr. 4-4). 50.50 *(978-1-61511-135-0(2)*, PowerKids Pr.) Rosen Publishing Group, Inc., The.

Cuddy, Robbin. All about Drawing: Farm & Forest Animals. Cuddy, Robin, illus. 2014. (All about Drawing Ser.). (ENG.). 80p. (J). (gr. 2-5). lib. bdg. 34.60 *(978-1-939581-10-5(9))* Quarto Publishing Group USA.

—All about Drawing Farm & Forest Animals: Learn to Draw More Than 40 Barnyard Animals & Wildlife Critters Step by Step. 2013. (All about Drawing Ser.). (ENG., Illus.). 80p. (J). (gr. 1-3). pap. 9.95 *(978-1-60058-361-2(X)*, 160058361X) Quarto Publishing Group USA.

—Learn to Draw Birds & Butterflies: Step-by-step Instructions for More Than 25 Winged Creatures. 2016. (Learn to Draw Ser.). (ENG., Illus.). 64p. (J). (gr. 1-3). pap. 8.95 *(978-1-63322-064-5(8))* Quarto Publishing Group USA.

—Learn to Draw Cats & Kittens: Step-by-step Instructions for More Than 25 Favorite Feline Friends. 2015. (Learn to Draw Ser.). (ENG., Illus.). 64p. (J). (gr. 1-3). pap. 8.95 *(978-1-60058-480-0(2)*, Walter Foster Jr) Quarto Publishing Group USA.

—Learn to Draw Dinosaurs: Step-by-step Instructions for More Than 25 Prehistoric Creatures. 2015. (Learn to Draw Ser.). (ENG., Illus.). 64p. (J). (gr. 1-3). pap. 8.95 *(978-1-63322-030-0(3)*, Walter Foster Jr) Quarto Publishing Group USA.

—Learn to Draw Exotic Animals: Step-by-step Instructions for More Than 25 Unusual Animals. 2016. (Learn to Draw Ser.). (ENG., Illus.). 64p. (J). (gr. 1-3). pap. 8.95

(978-1-63322-065-2(6), Walter Foster Jr) Quarto Publishing Group USA.

—Learn to Draw Forest Animals: Step-By-step Instructions for More Than 25 Woodland Creatures. 2015. (Learn to Draw Ser.). (ENG., Illus.). 64p. (J). (gr. 1-3). pap. 8.95 (978-1-60058-482-4(9)) Quarto Publishing Group USA.

—Learn to Draw Safari Animals: Step-By-step Instructions for More Than 25 Exotic Animals. 2015. (Learn to Draw Ser.). (ENG., Illus.). 64p. (J). (gr. 1-3). pap. 8.95 (978-1-60058-481-7(0), Walter Foster Jr) Quarto Publishing Group USA.

—Learn to Draw Zoo Animals: Step-By-step Instructions for More Than 25 Zoo Animals. 2016. (Learn to Draw Ser.). (ENG., Illus.). 64p. (J). (gr. 1-3). pap. 8.95 (978-1-63322-103-1(2)) Quarto Publishing Group USA.

—Polar Animals: Draw More Than 25 Favorite Arctic & Antarctic Wildlife Critters. 2014. (Learn to Draw Ser.). (ENG., Illus.). 64p. (J). (gr. 1-3). pap. 8.95 (978-1-60058-386-5(5), 1600583865) Quarto Publishing Group USA.

Cuddy, Robbin, illus. Learn to Draw Dogs & Puppies: Step-By-Step Instructions for More Than 25 Different Breeds. 2015. (Learn to Draw: Expanded Edition Ser.). (ENG.). 64p. (gr. k-5). 33.27 (978-1-939581-52-5(4)) Quarto Publishing Group USA.

—Learn to Draw Forest Animals & Wildlife: Step-by-Step Instructions for 25 Different Woodland Animals. 2012. (Learn to Draw Ser.). (ENG.). 40p. (J). (gr. 1-3). pap. 4.95 (978-1-60058-308-7(3), 1600583083) Quarto Publishing Group USA.

—Learn to Draw Pets: Step-By-Step Instructions for More Than 25 Cute & Cuddly Animals. 2015. (Learn to Draw: Expanded Edition Ser.). (ENG.). 64p. (J). (gr. k-5). 33.27 (978-1-939581-53-2(2)) Quarto Publishing Group USA.

—Learn to Draw Polar Animals: Draw More Than 25 Favorite Arctic & Antarctic Wildlife Critters. 2015. (Learn to Draw: Expanded Edition Ser.). (ENG.). 64p. (J). (gr. k-5). 33.27 (978-1-939581-51-8(6)) Quarto Publishing Group USA.

—Learn to Draw Rainforest & Jungle Animals: Step-by-Step Drawing Instructions for 25 Exotic Creatures. 2013. (Learn to Draw Ser.). (ENG.). 40p. (J). (gr. 1-3). pap. 4.95 (978-1-60058-309-4(1), 1600583091) Quarto Publishing Group USA.

—Learn to Draw Sea Creatures. 2015. (Learn to Draw: Expanded Edition Ser.). (ENG.). 64p. (J). (gr. k-5). 33.27 (978-1-939581-54-9(0)) Quarto Publishing Group USA.

Cuddy, Robin. Learn to Draw Horses & Ponies: Step-by-Step Instructions for More Than 25 Different Breeds. 2014. (Learn to Draw Ser.). (ENG., Illus.). 64p. (J). (gr. 1-3). pap. 8.95 (978-1-60058-446-6(2)) Quarto Publishing Group USA.

—Learn to Draw Pets: Step-By-step Instructions for More Than 25 Cute & Cuddly Animals. 2014. (Learn to Draw Ser.). (ENG., Illus.). 64p. (J). (gr. 1-3). pap. 8.95 (978-1-60058-444-2(6)) Quarto Publishing Group USA.

—Learn to Draw Sea Creatures: Step-by-Step Instructions for More Than 25 Ocean Animals. 2014. (Learn to Draw Ser.). (ENG., Illus.). 64p. (J). (gr. 1-3). pap. 8.95 (978-1-60058-445-9(4)) Quarto Publishing Group USA.

Cunningham, Kelley, illus. The Ultimate How-To-Draw Real Stuff Book. 2006. 48p. (J). (978-0-439-81336-5(0)) Scholastic, Inc.

Curto, Rosa M. Art from Simple Shapes: Make Amazing Art from 8 Simple Geometric Shapes! Includes a Shape Stencil. 2015. (ENG.). 96p. (J). (gr. 2-5). 12.99 (978-0-486-80221-3(3)) Dover Pubns., Inc.

—Draw the Magic Blue Fairy. 2013. (Draw the Magic Fairy Ser.). 36p. (J). lib. bdg. 23.94 (978-0-7660-4265-0(0)); pap. 7.95 (978-1-4644-0473-3(9)) Enslow Pubs., Inc. (Enslow Elementary).

—Draw the Magic Green Fairy. 2013. (Draw the Magic Fairy Ser.). 36p. (J). (gr. k-3). pap. 7.95 (978-1-4644-0479-5(8), Enslow Elementary) Enslow Pubs., Inc.

—Draw the Magic Pink Fairy. 2013. (Draw the Magic Fairy Ser.). 36p. (J). lib. bdg. 23.94 (978-0-7660-4266-7(9)); pap. 7.95 (978-1-4644-0475-7(5)) Enslow Pubs., Inc. (Enslow Elementary).

—Draw the Magic Red Fairy. 2013. (Draw the Magic Fairy Ser.). 36p. (J). lib. bdg. 23.94 (978-0-7660-4267-4(7)); pap. 7.95 (978-1-4644-0477-1(1)) Enslow Pubs., Inc. (Enslow Elementary).

—Fingerprint Drawing: Art Fun at Your Fingertips! 2015. (ENG.). 96p. (J). (gr. 2-5). 12.99 (978-0-486-80222-0(1)) Dover Pubns., Inc.

—Fun & Easy Drawing at Sea. 2013. (Fun & Easy Drawing Ser.). 36p. (J). lib. bdg. 23.94 (978-0-7660-6039-5(X)); pap. 7.95 (978-0-7660-6040-1(3)) Enslow Pubs., Inc. (Enslow Elementary).

—Fun & Easy Drawing Fantasy Characters. 2013. (Fun & Easy Drawing Ser.). 36p. (J). lib. bdg. 23.94 (978-0-7660-6041-8(1)); pap. 7.95 (978-0-7660-6042-5(X)) Enslow Pubs., Inc. (Enslow Elementary).

—Fun & Easy Drawing on the Farm. 2013. (Fun & Easy Drawing Ser.). 36p. (J). lib. bdg. 23.94 (978-0-7660-6037-1(3)); pap. 7.95 (978-0-7660-6038-8(1)) Enslow Pubs., Inc. (Enslow Elementary).

—Fun & Easy Drawing Storybook Characters. 2013. (Fun & Easy Drawing Ser.). 36p. (J). lib. bdg. 23.94 (978-0-7660-6043-2(8)); pap. 7.95 (978-0-7660-6044-9(6)) Enslow Pubs., Inc. (Enslow Elementary).

Curto, Rosa Maria. Draw the Magic Green Fairy. 2013. (Draw the Magic Fairy Ser.). 36p. (J). lib. bdg. 23.94 (978-0-7660-4268-1(5)) Enslow Pubs., Inc.

Davidson, Mike, et al, illus. Draw What? A Doodling, Drawing, & Coloring Book. 2014. (ENG.). (J). (gr. -1-3). (978-1-74352-285-1(1)) Hinkler Bks. Pty, Ltd.

Davies, Andrew. Simply Drawing: How to Draw from the Beginning. 2017. (ENG., Illus.). 160p. (J). pap. 16.99 (978-1-74257-859-0(4)) New Holland Pubs. Pty, Ltd. AUS. Dist: Midpoint Trade Bks., Inc.

Davis, Rich. The 1-Minute Artist: Learn to Draw Almost Anything in Six Easy Steps. 2016. (ENG.). 176p. (J). (gr. 1-7). pap. 16.99 (978-1-63106-254-4(9), Race Point Publishing) Quarto Publishing Group USA.

Debacque, Pascal. Create Your Own Mandalas — Fantasy. 2013. (ENG.). 32p. (J). (gr. -1-12). 6.99 (978-0-486-49373-2(3)) Dover Pubns., Inc.

—Create Your Own Mandalas — Nature. 2013. (ENG.). 32p. (J). (gr. -1-12). pap. 6.99 (978-0-486-49375-6(X)) Dover Pubns., Inc.

Dicker, Katie. You Can Draw Birds! Saunders, Mike, illus. 2013. (Draw Your Pet! Ser.). 32p. (gr. 3-5). 26.60 (978-1-4339-8723-6(6)); pap. 10.50 (978-1-4339-8724-3(4)) Stevens, Gareth Publishing LLLP. (Gareth Stevens Learning Library).

—You Can Draw Cats! Saunders, Mike, illus. 2013. (Draw Your Pet! Ser.). 32p. (gr. 3-5). 26.60 (978-1-4339-8727-4(9)); pap. 10.50 (978-1-4339-8728-1(7)) Stevens, Gareth Publishing LLLP. (Gareth Stevens Learning Library).

—You Can Draw Exotic Pets! Saunders, Mike, illus. 2013. (Draw Your Pet! Ser.). 32p. (gr. 3-5). 26.60 (978-1-4339-8735-9(X)); pap. 10.50 (978-1-4339-8736-6(8)) Stevens, Gareth Publishing LLLP. (Gareth Stevens Learning Library).

—You Can Draw Fish! Saunders, Mike, illus. 2013. (Draw Your Pet! Ser.). 32p. (gr. 3-5). 26.60 (978-1-4339-8739-7(2)); pap. 10.50 (978-1-4339-8740-3(6)) Stevens, Gareth Publishing LLLP. (Gareth Stevens Learning Library).

—You Can Draw Horses! Saunders, Mike, illus. 2013. (Draw Your Pet! Ser.). 32p. (gr. 3-5). 26.60 (978-1-4339-8743-4(0)); pap. 10.50 (978-1-4339-8744-1(9)) Stevens, Gareth Publishing LLLP. (Gareth Stevens Learning Library).

Dickler, Katie. You Can Draw Dogs! Saunders, Mike, illus. 2013. (Draw Your Pet! Ser.). 32p. (J). (gr. 3-5). pap. 10.50 (978-1-4339-8732-8(5)); lib. bdg. 26.60 (978-1-4339-8731-1(7)) Stevens, Gareth Publishing LLLP.

Disney Enterprises Inc., Staff. Finding Dory: Including Dory, Nemo, Marlin, & All Your Favorite Characters! Loter, John, illus. 2017. (Learn to Draw Favorite Characters: Expanded Edition Ser.). (ENG.). 64p. (J). (gr. 3-5). 33.32 (978-1-942875-18-5(5)) Quarto Publishing Group USA.

Disney Publishing Creative Development (Firm) Staff, et al, contrib. by. Learn to Draw Disney/Pixar Toy Story: Featuring Favorite Characters from Toy Story 2 & Toy Story 3! 2010. (Learn to Draw Favorite Characters Ser.). 32p. (J). (gr. k-3). 28.50 (978-1-936309-00-9(9)) Quarto Publishing Group USA.

Disney Storybook Artists. Classic Animated Movies: Featuring Favorite Characters from Alice in Wonderland, the Jungle Book, 101 Dalmations, Peter Pan, & More! 2016. (Licensed Learn to Draw Ser.). (ENG.). 144p. (J). (gr. 1-3). pap. 19.95 (978-1-63322-135-2(0), Walter Foster Jr) Quarto Publishing Group USA.

—Learn to Draw Disney Pixar's Finding Dory: Including Nemo, Marlin, Dory, & All Your Favorite New Characters! 2016. (Licensed Learn to Draw Ser.). (ENG.). 64p. (J). (gr. 1-3). pap. 9.95 (978-1-63322-073-7(7), Walter Foster Jr) Quarto Publishing Group USA.

—Learn to Draw Disney's Classic Fairy Tales: Featuring Cinderella, Snow White, Belle, & All Your Favorite Fairy Tale Characters! 2017. (Licensed Learn to Draw Ser.). (ENG., Illus.). 64p. (J). (gr. 1-3). pap. 9.95 (978-1-63322-145-1(8), Walter Foster Jr) Quarto Publishing Group USA.

—Learn to Draw Disney's Moana: Learn to Draw Moana, Maui, Chief Tui, Pua, & Other Favorite Characters Step by Step! 2016. (Licensed Learn to Draw Ser.). (ENG.). 64p. (J). (gr. 1-3). pap. 9.95 (978-1-63322-144-4(X), Walter Foster Jr) Quarto Publishing Group USA.

Disney Storybook Artists Staff. Fabulous Fashions: Learn to Draw Minnie, Daisy, & Their Favorite Fashions & Accessories - Step by Step! 2014. (Licensed Learn to Draw Ser.). (ENG., Illus.). 64p. (J). (gr. 1-3). pap. 9.95 (978-1-60058-364-3(4), 1600583644) Quarto Publishing Group USA.

—Favorite Fairies: Learn to Draw the Magical World of Tinker Bell, Silver Mist, Rosetta, & All of Your Favorite Disney Fairies! 2012. (Licensed Learn to Draw Ser.). (ENG., Illus.). 64p. (J). (gr. 1-3). pap. 9.95 (978-1-60058-298-1(2), 1600582982) Quarto Publishing Group USA.

—Finding Nemo. 2011. (Learn to Draw Favorite Characters Ser.). 32p. (J). (gr. k-3). 28.50 (978-1-936309-34-4(3)) Quarto Publishing Group USA.

—Learn to Draw Disney I Pixar Cars. 2011. (Learn to Draw Favorite Characters Ser.). 32p. (J). (gr. k-3). 28.50 (978-1-936309-32-0(7)) Quarto Publishing Group USA.

—Learn to Draw Disney Phineas & Ferb: Featuring Candace, Agent P, Dr. Doofenshmirtz, & Other Favorite Characters from the Hit Show! 2011. (Licensed Learn to Draw Ser.). (ENG., Illus.). 64p. (J). (gr. 1-3). pap. 9.95 (978-1-60058-230-1(3), 1600582303) Quarto Publishing Group USA.

—Learn to Draw Disney Villains: Featuring Favorite Villains, Including Captain Hook, Cruella de Vil, Jafar, & Others! 2012. (Licensed Learn to Draw Ser.). (ENG., Illus.). 144p. (J). (gr. 1-3). pap. 19.95 (978-1-60058-261-5(3), 1600582613, Walter Foster Jr) Quarto Publishing Group USA.

—Learn to Draw Disney's Frozen: Featuring Anna, Elsa, Olaf, & All Your Favorite Characters! 2015. (Licensed Learn to Draw Ser.). (ENG.). 64p. (J). (gr. 1-3). pap. 9.95 (978-1-60058-496-1(9)) Quarto Publishing Group USA.

—Learn to Draw Disney's Phineas & Ferb Drawing Book & Kit: Includes Everything You Need to Draw Candace, Agent P, & Your Other Favorite Characters from the Hit Show! 2012. (Licensed Learn to Draw Ser.). (ENG., Illus.). 32p. (J). (gr. 1-3). pap. 19.99 (978-1-60058-331-5(8), 1600583318) Quarto Publishing Group USA.

—Learn to Draw Disney's Planes: Featuring Dusty Crophopper, Skipper Riley, Ripslinger, el Chupacabra, & All Your Favorite Characters! 2013. (Licensed Learn to Draw Ser.). (ENG., Illus.). 64p. (J). (gr. 1-3). pap. 9.95 (978-1-60058-383-4(0), 1600583830, Walter Foster Jr) Quarto Publishing Group USA.

—Learn to Draw Mickey Mouse & His Friends. 2011. (Licensed Learn to Draw Ser.). (ENG., Illus.). 64p. (J). (gr. 1-3). pap. 9.95 (978-1-60058-253-0(2), 1600582532, Walter Foster Jr) Quarto Publishing Group USA.

—Learn to Draw Winnie the Pooh: Featuring Tigger, Eeyore, Piglet, & Other Favorite Characters of the Hundred Acre Wood! 2011. (Licensed Learn to Draw Ser.). (ENG., Illus.). 64p. (J). (gr. 1-3). pap. 9.95 (978-1-60058-254-7(0), 1600582540) Quarto Publishing Group USA.

—Toy Story. 2011. (Licensed Learn to Draw Ser.). (ENG., Illus.). 64p. (J). (gr. 1-3). pap. 9.95 (978-1-60058-263-9(X), 160058263X) Quarto Publishing Group USA.

—Your Favorite Disney Pixar Characters. 2011. (Learn to Draw Favorite Characters Ser.). (Illus.). 32p. (J). (gr. k-3). 28.50 (978-1-936309-22-1(X)) Quarto Publishing Group USA.

Disney Storybook Artists Staff, contrib. by. Disney/Pixar Cars: Learn to Draw. 2015. (Learn to Draw Favorite Characters: Expanded Edition Ser.). (ENG., Illus.). 64p. (gr. k-5). 33.32 (978-1-939581-44-0(3)) Quarto Publishing Group USA.

—Learn to Draw Disney/Pixar Brave. 2015. (Learn to Draw Favorite Characters: Expanded Edition Ser.). (ENG., Illus.). 64p. (J). (gr. k-5). 33.32 (978-1-939581-45-7(1)) Quarto Publishing Group USA.

—Learn to Draw Disney's Classic Animated Movies. 2017. (Learn to Draw Favorite Characters: Expanded Edition Ser.). (ENG.). 64p. (J). (gr. 3-5). 33.32 (978-1-942875-19-2(3)) Quarto Publishing Group USA.

—Learn to Draw Plus Disney Pixar Toy Story: Featuring Favorite Characters from Toy Story 2 & Toy Story 3! 2012. (J). (978-1-936309-69-6(6)) Quarto Publishing Group USA.

Disney Storybook Artists Staff, ed. Disney/Pixar Finding Nemo Drawing Book & Kit. 2008. pap. 10.95 (978-1-60058-109-0(9)) Quarto Publishing Group USA.

—Disney's Princess - Favorite Princesses: Featuring Tiana, Cinderella, Ariel, Snow White, Belle, & Other Characters! 2010. (Licensed Learn to Draw Ser.). (ENG., Illus.). 144p. (J). (gr. 1-3). pap. 19.95 (978-1-60058-145-8(5), 1600581455) Quarto Publishing Group USA.

Dogs & Puppies. 2006. (Illus.). (J). cd-rom 9.99 (978-0-9795190-0-0(4)) Color & Learn.

Dompierre, Judith. I See Pigs Everywhere. 2012. 32p. pap. 25.00 (978-1-4626-9333-7(4)) America Star Bks.

Donahue, Peter. What to Doodle? Moustaches: Over 60 Drawings to Complete & Color. 2016. (Dover Little Activity Bks.). (ENG., Illus.). 64p. (J). (gr. k-3). pap. 1.99 (978-0-486-80525-2(5)) Dover Pubns., Inc.

Dorling Kindersley Publishing Staff. How to Draw. 2017. (ENG., Illus.). 96p. (J). (gr. 2-4). 14.99 (978-1-4654-5685-4(6), DK Children) Dorling Kindersley Publishing, Inc.

Draw 50 Aliens. 16.28 (978-0-7383-3391-5(3)) Booksource, The.

Drawing Manga. (Illus.). (J). (gr. 3-8). 151.50 (978-1-4042-3385-0(7)) Rosen Publishing Group, Inc., The.

DreamWorks Animation Creative Team. Learn to Draw DreamWorks Animation's Kung Fu Panda: Featuring Po, Tigress, Master Shifu, & All Your Favorite New Characters from Kung Fu Panda 3! 2016. (Licensed Learn to Draw Ser.). (ENG.). 64p. (J). (gr. 1-3). pap. 9.95 (978-1-63322-060-7(5), Walter Foster Jr) Quarto Publishing Group USA.

DreamWorks Animation LLC Staff. Learn to Draw DreamWorks Animation's Kung Fu Panda. Vance, Joe, illus. 2017. (Learn to Draw Favorite Characters: Expanded Edition Ser.). (ENG.). 64p. (J). (gr. 3-5). 33.32 (978-1-942875-21-5(5)) Quarto Publishing Group USA.

Dudziuk, Kasia. Let's Draw Pets & Farm Animals. 2016. (Let's Draw Step by Step Ser.). 00032p. (J). (gr. 1-2). pap. 11.75 (978-1-4994-8179-2(9), Windmill Bks.) Rosen Publishing Group, Inc., The.

—Let's Draw Storybook Characters. 2016. (Let's Draw Step by Step Ser.). 00032p. (J). (gr. 1-2). pap. 11.75 (978-1-4994-8182-2(9), Windmill Bks.) Rosen Publishing Group, Inc., The.

—Let's Draw Things That Go. 2016. (Let's Draw Step by Step Ser.). 00032p. (J). (gr. 1-2). pap. 11.75 (978-1-4994-8185-3(3), Windmill Bks.) Rosen Publishing Group, Inc., The.

—Let's Draw Wild Animals. 2016. (Let's Draw Step by Step Ser.). 00032p. (J). (gr. 1-2). pap. 11.75 (978-1-4994-8188-4(8), Windmill Bks.) Rosen Publishing Group, Inc., The.

Duhig, Lee. Draw Dinosaurs! 2006. (Illus.). 64p. (J). pap. (978-1-59412-158-6(3)) Mud Puddle, Inc.

Eason, Sarah. Drawing Baby Animals. 2013. (Learn to Draw Ser.). 32p. (J). (gr. 2-5). pap. 10.50 (978-1-4339-9525-5(5)); lib. bdg. 26.60 (978-1-4339-9524-8(7)) Stevens, Gareth Publishing LLLP.

—Drawing Baby Animals. Santillan, Jorge, illus. 2013. (Learn to Draw Ser.). 32p. (J). (gr. 2-5). pap. 63.00 (978-1-4339-9526-2(3)) Stevens, Gareth Publishing LLLP.

—Drawing Dinosaurs. Santillan, Jorge, illus. 2013. (Learn to Draw Ser.). 32p. (J). (gr. 2-5). pap. 10.50 (978-1-4339-9529-3(8)); pap. 63.00 (978-1-4339-9530-9(1)) Stevens, Gareth Publishing LLLP.

—Drawing Dragons. Santillan, Jorge, illus. 2013. (Learn to Draw Ser.). 32p. (J). (gr. 2-5). pap. 10.50 (978-1-4339-9533-0(6)); pap. 63.00 (978-1-4339-9534-7(4)) Stevens, Gareth Publishing LLLP.

—Drawing Fairies, Mermaids, & Unicorns. Santillan, Jorge, illus. 2013. (Learn to Draw Ser.). 32p. (J). (gr. 2-5). pap. 10.50 (978-1-4339-9537-8(9)); pap. 63.00 (978-1-4339-9538-5(7)) Stevens, Gareth Publishing LLLP.

—Drawing Knights & Castles. Santillan, Jorge, illus. 2013. (Learn to Draw Ser.). 32p. (J). (gr. 2-5). pap. 10.50 (978-1-4339-9541-5(7)); pap. 63.00 (978-1-4339-9542-2(5)) Stevens, Gareth Publishing LLLP.

—Drawing Pirates & Pirate Ships. Santillan, Jorge, illus. 2013. (Learn to Draw Ser.). 32p. (J). (gr. 2-5). pap. 10.50 (978-1-4339-9545-3(X)); pap. 63.00 (978-1-4339-9546-0(8)) Stevens, Gareth Publishing LLLP.

—Learn to Draw. Santillan, Jorge, illus. 2013. (Learn to Draw Ser.). 32p. (J). (gr. 2-5). 159.60 (978-1-4339-9682-5(0)) Stevens, Gareth Publishing LLLP.

Editors of Kingfisher. I Can Draw: With 40 Easy Step-By-step Pictures. Abbott, Simon, illus. 2016. (ENG.). 96p. (J). pap. 9.99 (978-0-7534-7249-1(X), 9780753472491, Kingfisher) Roaring Brook Pr.

Elliott, Craig. Craig Elliott Sketchbook. 2006. (Illus.). 24p. per. (978-0-9754912-4-9(5)) Aristata Publishing.

Elliott, Rob. Laugh-Out-Loud Doodles for Kids. Hawkins, Jonny, illus. 2014. (ENG.). 240p. (J). pap. 8.99 (978-0-8007-2446-7(1)) Revell.

Elliott, Ruth. See What You're Looking At. Elliott, Ruth, illus. 2008. (Illus.). (J). 27.00 (978-0-9795017-0-8(9)) Edu Designs.

Emberley, Ed. Ed Emberley's Picture Pie: A Cut & Paste Drawing Book. Emberley, Ed, illus. 2006. (ENG., Illus.). 48p. (J). (gr. 2-17). pap. 9.99 (978-0-316-78982-0(8)) Little, Brown Bks. for Young Readers.

Emberley, Edward R. Ed Emberley's Big Green Drawing Book. Emberley, Edward R., illus. 2005. (ENG., Illus.). 96p. (J). (gr. 2-17). pap. 10.99 (978-0-316-78976-9(3)) Little, Brown Bks. for Young Readers.

—Ed Emberley's Big Green Drawing Book. 2005. (Ed Emberley Drawing Books Ser.). (Illus.). 91p. (J). (gr. -1-3). 18.65 (978-0-7569-6519-8(5)) Perfection Learning Corp.

—Ed Emberley's Big Purple Drawing Book. Emberley, Edward R., illus. 2005. (ENG., Illus.). 96p. (J). (gr. 2-17). pap. 10.99 (978-0-316-78973-8(9)) Little, Brown Bks. for Young Readers.

—Ed Emberley's Drawing Book - Make a World: Learn to Draw the Ed Emberley Way! Emberley, Edward R., illus. 2006. (ENG., Illus.). 32p. (J). (gr. 2-17). pap. 7.99 (978-0-316-78972-1(0)) Little, Brown Bks. for Young Readers.

—Ed Emberley's Drawing Book of Animals. Emberley, Edward R., illus. 2006. (ENG., Illus.). 32p. (J). (gr. 2-17). per. 7.99 (978-0-316-78979-0(8)) Little, Brown Bks. for Young Readers.

—Ed Emberley's Drawing Book of Faces. Emberley, Edward R., illus. 2006. (ENG., Illus.). 32p. (J). (gr. 2-17). pap. 7.99 (978-0-316-78970-7(4)) Little, Brown Bks. for Young Readers.

Enchanted Forest. 2014. (Illus.). 32p. (J). (978-1-62127-336-3(9)); pap. (978-1-62127-340-0(7)) Weigl Pubs., Inc.

Eppard, Jon. Aircraft. 2012. (ENG., Illus.). 24p. (J). pap. (978-1-60014-853-8(0)); (gr. 3-8). 25.95 (978-1-60014-808-8(5), Express Bks.) Bellwether Media.

—Big Cats. 2012. (ENG., Illus.). 24p. (J). pap. (978-1-60014-854-5(9)); (gr. 3-8). 25.95 (978-1-60014-809-5(3), Express Bks.) Bellwether Media.

—Dogs. 2012. (You Can Draw It! Ser.). (ENG., Illus.). 24p. (J). (gr. 3-8). 25.95 (978-1-60014-810-1(7), Express Bks.) Bellwether Media.

—Horses. 2012. (ENG., Illus.). 24p. (J). pap. (978-1-60014-856-9(5)); (gr. 3-8). 25.95 (978-1-60014-811-8(5), Express Bks.) Bellwether Media.

—Monsters. 2012. (You Can Draw It! Ser.). (ENG., Illus.). 24p. (J). (gr. 3-8). 25.95 (978-1-60014-813-2(1), Express Bks.) Bellwether Media.

Farrell, Russell, illus. Horses & Ponies: Step-by-Step Insructions for 25 Different Breads. 2011. (Learn to Draw Ser.). 32p. (J). (gr. 1-4). (978-1-936309-16-0(5)) Quarto Publishing Group USA.

Farrell, Russell & Creative Team at Walter Foster Publishing Staff. I Love Horses! Giddy-Up Great Stickers, Trivia, Step-by-Step Drawing Projects, & More for the Horse Lover in You! Fisher, Diana, illus. 2011. (I Love Activity Bks.). (ENG.). 112p. (J). (gr. 1-3). pap. 9.95 (978-1-60058-226-4(5), 1600582265) Quarto Publishing Group USA.

Farrell, Russell & Fisher, Diana, illus. All about Drawing Sea Creatures & Animals. 2010. (All about Drawing Ser.). 80p. (J). 34.25 (978-1-936309-08-5(4)) Quarto Publishing Group USA.

Farrell, Russell & Mueller, Peter. All about Horses & Pets. 2010. (All about Drawing Ser.). 80p. (J). 34.25 (978-1-936309-06-1(8)) Quarto Publishing Group USA.

Fazzi, Cindy. How to Draw Pakistan's Sights & Symbols. 2009. (Kid's Guide to Drawing the Countries of the World Ser.). 48p. (gr. 4-4). 53.00 (978-1-61511-120-6(4), PowerKids Pr.) Rosen Publishing Group, Inc., The.

—How to Draw Peru's Sights & Symbols. 2009. (Kid's Guide to Drawing the Countries of the World Ser.). 48p. (gr. 4-4). 53.00 (978-1-61511-121-3(2), PowerKids Pr.) Rosen Publishing Group, Inc., The.

—How to Draw the Philippines's Sights & Symbols. 2009. (Kid's Guide to Drawing the Countries of the World Ser.). 48p. (gr. 4-4). 53.00 (978-1-61511-128-2(X), PowerKids Pr.) Rosen Publishing Group, Inc., The.

Fein, E. How to Draw Puerto Rico's Sights & Symbols. 2009. (Kid's Guide to Drawing America Ser.). 32p. (gr. k-k). 50.50 (978-1-61511-092-6(5), PowerKids Pr.) Rosen Publishing Group, Inc., The.

—How to Draw Utah's Sights & Symbols. 2009. (Kid's Guide to Drawing America Ser.). 32p. (gr. k-k). 50.50 (978-1-61511-100-8(X), PowerKids Pr.) Rosen Publishing Group, Inc., The.

—How to Draw West Virginia's Sights & Symbols. 2009. (Kid's Guide to Drawing America Ser.). 32p. (gr. k-k). 50.50 (978-1-61511-104-6(2), PowerKids Pr.) Rosen Publishing Group, Inc., The.

Fisher, Diana. Insects: Step-by-Step Instructions for 26 Creepy Crawlies. 2007. (Learn to Draw Ser.). (ENG., Illus.). 40p. (J). (gr. 1-17). per. 4.95 (978-1-60058-507-4(8), 1600585078) Quarto Publishing Group USA.

—Reptiles & Amphibians: Step by Step Intsructions for 29 Reptiles & Amphibians. 2006. (Learn to Draw Ser.). (ENG., Illus.). 40p. (J). (gr. 1-17). per. 4.95 (978-1-56010-994-5(7), 1560109947) Quarto Publishing Group USA.

Fisher, Diana, illus. Learn to Draw Cats & Kittens. 2012. (J). (978-1-936309-51-1(3)) Quarto Publishing Group USA.

—Learn to Draw Insects. 2012. (J). (978-1-936309-52-8(1)) Quarto Publishing Group USA.

—Learn to Draw Reptiles & Amphibians. 2012. (J). (978-1-936309-50-4(5)) Quarto Publishing Group USA.

—Watch Me Draw a Boy's Adventure. 2012. (J). (978-1-936309-79-5(3)) Quarto Publishing Group USA.

—Watch Me Draw a Magical Fairy World. 2013. (Watch Me Draw Ser.). 24p. (J). (gr. -1-2). 25.65 (978-1-936309-91-7(2)) Quarto Publishing Group USA.

—Watch Me Draw Dinosaurs. 2013. (Watch Me Draw Ser.). 24p. (J). (gr. -1-2). 25.65 (978-1-936309-89-4(0)) Quarto Publishing Group USA.

—Watch Me Draw Disney's Little Einsteins Amazing Missions. 2012. (J). (978-1-936309-43-6(2)) Quarto Publishing Group USA.

—Watch Me Draw Favorite Pets. 2012. 24p. (J). (978-1-936309-77-1(7)) Quarto Publishing Group USA.

—Watch Me Draw the Zoo. 2013. (Watch Me Draw Ser.). 24p. (J). (gr. -1-2). 25.65 (978-1-936309-90-0(4)) Quarto Publishing Group USA.

—Watch Me Draw Things Girls Love. 2012. (J). *(978-1-936309-78-8(5))* Quarto Publishing Group USA.

Fisher, Diana & Shelly, Jeff, illus. All about Dinosaurs & Reptiles. 2010. (All about Drawing Ser.). 80p. (J). 34.25 *(978-1-936309-07-8(6))* Quarto Publishing Group USA.

Flying Frog Publishing, ed. Farm Animals. 2012. (Drawing in Color Ser.). 96p. (J). 12.99 *(978-1-60745-373-4(8))* Flying Frog Publishing, Inc.

—Jungle Animals. 2012. (Drawing in Color Ser.). 96p. (J). 12.99 *(978-1-60745-374-1(6))* Flying Frog Publishing, Inc.

—Ocean Animals. 2012. (Drawing in Color Ser.). 96p. (J). 12.99 *(978-1-60745-375-8(4))* Flying Frog Publishing, Inc.

—Safari Animals. 2012. (Drawing in Color Ser.). 96p. (J). 12.99 *(978-1-60745-376-5(2))* Flying Frog Publishing, Inc.

for Young Readers, Racehorse. Learn to Draw People: How to Draw Like an Artist in 5 Quick-And-Easy Steps! 2016. (ENG., Illus.). 80p. (J). (gr. 1-7). pap. 7.99 *(978-1-944686-25-3(8),* Racehorse Publishing) Skyhorse Publishing Co., Inc.

—Learn to Draw Pets: How to Draw Like an Artist in 5 Quick-And-Easy Steps! 2016. (ENG., Illus.). 80p. (J). (gr. 1-7). pap. 7.99 *(978-1-944686-24-6(X),* Racehorse Publishing) Skyhorse Publishing Co., Inc.

Fowler Hicks, Ginny. Mountain Star: A Story about a Mountaineer That Will Teach You How to Draw a Star! Fowler, Charlie, photos by. 2008. (Illus.). 24p. (J). 18.95 *(978-0-9763309-3-6(8))* Mountain World Media LLC.

Franklin, Carolyn. Big Cats. 2009. (How to Draw Ser.). (Illus.). 32p. (J). lib. bdg. 26.50 *(978-1-4358-2516-1(0),* PowerKids Pr.) Rosen Publishing Group, Inc., The.

—How to Draw Big Cats. 2009. (How to Draw Ser.). (Illus.). 32p. (gr. 4-6). pap. 11.75 *(978-1-4358-2645-8(0),* Rosen Classroom) Rosen Publishing Group, Inc., The.

Fun with Fingerprints. 2016. (Fun with Fingerprints Ser.). (ENG.). 24p. (gr. k-1). 106.60 *(978-1-4795-8692-9(7))* Picture Window Bks.

Gamble, Paul. Draw Horrible Pictures. 2014. (Draw It! Ser.). 32p. (J). (gr. 3-6). lib. bdg. 27.50 *(978-1-4777-9140-0(X))* Windmill Bks.

—Draw Horrible Stuff: A Step-by-Step Guide to Drawing All Things Yucky! 2012. (ENG., Illus.). 144p. (J). pap. 10.95 *(978-1-84858-423-5(7))* Arcturus Publishing GBR. Dist: Bookmasters Distribution.

—Draw Scary Pictures. 2014. (Draw It! Ser.). 32p. (J). (gr. 3-6). lib. bdg. 27.50 *(978-1-4777-9148-6(5))* Windmill Bks.

—Draw Weird Pictures. 2014. (Draw It! Ser.). 32p. (J). (gr. 3-6). lib. bdg. 27.50 *(978-1-4777-9152-3(3))* Windmill Bks.

Garbot, Dave. Crazy, Zany Cartoon Characters. 2015. (Cartooning for Kids Ser.). (ENG., Illus.). 64p. (J). (gr. k-5). 33.32 *(978-1-939581-47-1(8))* Quarto Publishing Group USA.

—Fairy Tale Fun. 2015. (Cartooning for Kids Ser.). (ENG., Illus.). 64p. (J). (gr. k-5). 33.32 *(978-1-939581-50-1(8))* Quarto Publishing Group USA.

—Fairy Tale Fun: Learn to Draw More Than 20 Cartoon Princesses, Fairies, & Adventure Characters. 2014. (Cartooning for Kids Ser.). (ENG., Illus.). 64p. (J). (gr. 1-3). pap. 8.95 *(978-1-60058-451-0(9))* Quarto Publishing Group USA.

—Furry & Feathered Friends. 2015. (Cartooning for Kids Ser.). (ENG., Illus.). 64p. (J). (gr. k-5). 33.32 *(978-1-939581-49-5(4))* Quarto Publishing Group USA.

—Furry & Feathered Friends: Learn to Draw More Than 20 Cute Cartoon Critters. 2014. (Cartooning for Kids Ser.). (ENG., Illus.). 64p. (J). (gr. 1-3). pap. 8.95 *(978-1-60058-450-3(0))* Quarto Publishing Group USA.

—Mashup Mania: Learn to Draw More Than 20 Laughable, Loony Characters. Garbot, Dave, illus. 2016. (Cartooning for Kids Ser.). (ENG., Illus.). 64p. (J). (gr. k-5). 33.32 *(978-1-939581-92-1(3),* Walter Foster Jr) Quarto Publishing Group USA.

—Mean 'n' Messy Monsters. 2015. (Cartooning for Kids Ser.). (ENG., Illus.). 64p. (J). (gr. k-5). 33.32 *(978-1-939581-48-8(6))* Quarto Publishing Group USA.

—Mean 'n' Messy Monsters: Learn to Draw 25 Spooky, Kooky Monsters! 2014. (Cartooning for Kids Ser.). (ENG., Illus.). 64p. (J). (gr. 1-3). pap. 8.95 *(978-1-60058-392-6(X),* 160058392X) Quarto Publishing Group USA.

—Silly Sports: Learn to Draw More Than 20 Amazingly Awesome Athletes. Garbot, Dave, illus. 2016. (Cartooning for Kids Ser.). (ENG., Illus.). 64p. (J). (gr. k-5). 33.32 *(978-1-939581-93-8(1),* Walter Foster Jr) Quarto Publishing Group USA.

—Space Aliens. Garbot, Dave, illus. 2016. (Cartooning for Kids Ser.). (ENG., Illus.). 64p. (J). (gr. k-5). 33.32 *(978-1-939581-94-5(X),* Walter Foster Jr) Quarto Publishing Group USA.

—Spectacular Superheroes. Garbot, Dave, illus. 2016. (Cartooning for Kids Ser.). (ENG., Illus.). 64p. (J). (gr. k-5). 33.32 *(978-1-939581-95-2(8),* Walter Foster Jr) Quarto Publishing Group USA.

Geller, Kristin. Follow-the-Directions Draw & Write Activities: Step-by-Step Directions & Writing Prompts That Guide Children to Draw Pictures & Write Stories about Them. 2005. (ENG., Illus.). 48p. (gr. k-2). pap. 10.99 *(978-0-439-47122-0(2),* Teaching Resources) Scholastic, Inc.

Getha, Patricia, et al. Art of Drawing & Painting Horses: Capture the Majesty of Horses & Ponies in Pencil, Oil, Acrylic, Watercolor & Pastel. 2011. (Collector's Ser.). (ENG., Illus.). 144p. pap. 19.95 *(978-1-60058-237-0(0),* 1600582370) Quarto Publishing Group USA.

Giallongo, Zach. Star Wars Doodles. Giallongo, Zach, illus. 2015. (Doodle Book Ser.). (ENG., Illus.). 128p. (J). (gr. 1-3). pap. 12.99 *(978-1-4847-0684-8(6),* Disney Lucasfilm Press) Disney Publishing Worldwide.

Gibson, Ray. I Can Draw Animals Kid Kit. 2007. (Kid Kits Ser.). (Illus.). 32p. (J). (gr. -1). pap. 7.99 *(978-0-60130-018-8(2),* Usborne) EDC Publishing.

Gilbert, Elizabeth T., illus. Watch Me Draw Tiggerific Tales. 2013. (Watch Me Draw Ser.). 24p. (gr. -1-2). 25.65 *(978-1-936309-87-0(4))* Quarto Publishing Group USA.

Goldberg, Barry, illus. Watch Me Draw SpongeBob's Underwater Escapades. 2012. (J). *(978-1-936309-75-7(0))* Quarto Publishing Group USA.

Golding, Elizabeth. How to Draw Animals. Chang, Hui Yuan, illus. 2016. (Draw Around & Astound! Ser.). (ENG.). 32p. (J). (gr. -1-k). 9.99 *(978-0-7641-6839-0(8))* Barron's Educational Series, Inc.

—How to Draw Dinosaurs. Chang, Hui Yuan, illus. 2016. (Draw Around & Astound! Ser.). (ENG.). 32p. (J). (gr. -1-k). 9.99 *(978-0-7641-6840-6(1))* Barron's Educational Series, Inc.

Gowen, Fiona, illus. How to Draw Amazing Animals & Incredible Insects. 2015. (How to Draw Ser.). (ENG.). 32p. (J). (gr. 2-6). pap. 4.99 *(978-1-4380-0583-6(0))* Barron's Educational Series, Inc.

—How to Draw Amazing Birds: From Songbirds to Birds of Prey. 2017. (How to Draw Ser.). (ENG.). 32p. (J). (gr. 2-6). pap. 4.99 ***(978-1-4380-1053-3(2))*** Barron's Educational Series, Inc.

—How to Draw Awesome Vehicles: Land, Sea, & Air. 2015. (How to Draw Ser.). (ENG.). 32p. (J). (gr. 2-6). pap. 4.99 *(978-1-4380-0582-9(2))* Barron's Educational Series, Inc.

—How to Draw Incredible Aliens & Cool Space Stuff. 2015. (How to Draw Ser.). (ENG.). 32p. (J). (gr. 2-6). pap. 4.99 *(978-1-4380-0584-3(9))* Barron's Educational Series, Inc.

Gowen, Fiona, illus. How to Draw Scary Monsters & Other Mythical Creatures. 2017. (How to Draw Ser.). (ENG.). 32p. (J). (gr. 2-6). pap. 4.99 ***(978-1-4380-1055-7(9))*** Barron's Educational Series, Inc.

Graham, Oakley. Vampires vs Werewolves. Pinder, Andrew, illus. 2016. (Doodle Wars Ser.). (ENG.). 100p. (J). (gr. k-3). pap. 12.99 *(978-1-78244-060-4(7))* Top That! Publishing PLC GBR. Dist: Independent Pubs. Group.

Gravel, Élise. How Do You Doodle? 2013. (Illus.). 96p. pap. 12.95 *(978-1-4338-1291-0(6))* American Psychological Assn.

Gray, Peter. How to Draw Butterflies & Other Insects. 2013. (How to Draw Animals Ser.). 32p. (J). (gr. 3-6). 26.50 *(978-1-4777-1299-3(2));* pap. 11.75 *(978-1-4777-1409-6(X));* pap. 70.50 *(978-1-4777-1410-2(3))* Rosen Publishing Group, Inc., The. (PowerKids Pr.).

—How to Draw Cats & Dogs & Other Pets. 2013. (How to Draw Animals Ser.). 32p. (J). (gr. 3-6). 26.50 *(978-1-4777-1300-6(X));* pap. 70.50 *(978-1-4777-1412-6(X));* pap. 11.75 *(978-1-4777-1411-9(1))* Rosen Publishing Group, Inc., The. (PowerKids Pr.).

—How to Draw Dolphins & Other Sea Creatures. 2013. (How to Draw Animals Ser.). 32p. (J). (gr. 3-6). 26.50 *(978-1-4777-1302-0(6));* pap. 11.75 *(978-1-4777-1415-7(4));* pap. 70.50 *(978-1-4777-1416-4(2))* Rosen Publishing Group, Inc., The. (PowerKids Pr.).

—How to Draw Tigers & Other Big Cats. 2013. (How to Draw Animals Ser.). 32p. (J). (gr. 3-6). 26.50 *(978-1-4777-1304-4(2));* pap. 70.50 *(978-1-4777-1420-1(0));* pap. 11.75 *(978-1-4777-1419-5(7))* Rosen Publishing Group, Inc., The. (PowerKids Pr.).

—Let's Draw: Animals, People, Cars, Cartoons. 2012. (ENG., Illus.). 128p. (J). pap. 9.95 *(978-1-84837-839-1(4))* Arcturus Publishing GBR. Dist: Bookmasters Distribution.

—Male Action Figures. 2009. (Drawing Manga Ser.). 32p. (gr. 4-4). 50.50 *(978-1-61512-199-1(4))* Rosen Publishing Group, Inc., The.

Green, Barry, illus. Utterly Awesome 501 Things to Draw. 2017. (ENG.). 256p. (J). (gr. k-2). pap. 14.99 *(978-1-78700-067-4(2))* Top That! Publishing PLC GBR. Dist: Independent Pubs. Group.

Green, Barry & Lambert, Nat. How to Draw 101 Dinosaurs. Green, Dan, illus. 2013. (ENG.). 48p. (J). (gr. k-2). pap. 4.99 *(978-1-78244-612-5(5))* Top That! Publishing PLC GBR. Dist: Independent Pubs. Group.

—How to Draw 101 Spooky Things. Green, Dan, illus. 2013. (How to Draw 101... Ser.). (ENG.). 48p. (J). (gr. k-2). pap. 4.99 *(978-1-78244-613-2(3))* Top That! Publishing PLC GBR. Dist: Independent Pubs. Group.

Green, Dan. Doodle Book. 2016. (ENG.). 128p. (J). pap. 10.99 *(978-1-4059-2652-2(X),* 9781405926522) Penguin Bks., Ltd. GBR. Dist: Diamond Comic Distributors, Inc.

Green, Dan & McMillan, Sue. How to Improve at Drawing. 2010. (How to Improve At... Ser.). (ENG., Illus.). 48p. (J). (gr. 7-18). pap. *(978-0-7787-3598-4(2));* lib. bdg. *(978-0-7787-3576-2(1))* Crabtree Publishing Co.

Green, John & Drawing Staff. How to Draw Horses. 2009. (Dover How to Draw Ser.). (ENG., Illus.). 64p. (J). (gr. 1-4). pap. 4.99 *(978-0-486-46759-7(7))* Dover Pubns., Inc.

Gressman, Carylee Anne. Draw & Write Through History: Creation Through Jonah. Wolf, Aaron D., ed. Dick, Peggy, illus. 2006. (J). per. 12.95 *(978-0-9778597-0-2(3))* CPR Pubng.

Griffiths, Margaret. Doodle Magic: Animals. McDonald, Jake, illus. 2016. (Doodle Magic Ser.). (ENG.). 64p. (J). (gr. k). spiral bd. 14.95 *(978-1-62686-480-1(2),* Silver Dolphin Bks.) Readerlink Distribution Services, LLC.

Gross, M. J. How to Draw the Life & Times of William Jefferson Clinton. 2009. (Kid's Guide to Drawing the Presidents of the United States of America Ser.). 32p. (gr. 4-4). 50.50 *(978-1-61511-166-4(2),* PowerKids Pr.) Rosen Publishing Group, Inc., The.

Gross, Miriam. How to Draw the Life & Times of James Monroe. 2009. (Kid's Guide to Drawing the Presidents of the United States of America Ser.). 32p. (gr. 4-4). 50.50 *(978-1-61511-149-7(2),* PowerKids Pr.) Rosen Publishing Group, Inc., The.

Gross, Miriam J. How to Draw the Life & Times of William Jefferson Clinton. 2007. (Kid's Guide to Drawing the Presidents of the United States of America Ser.). (Illus.). 32p. (YA). (gr. 2-5). 26.50 *(978-1-4042-3018-7(1))* Rosen Publishing Group, Inc., The.

Guillain, Charlotte. Get Drawing!, 1 vol. 2014. (Dream It, Do It! Ser.). (ENG.). 32p. (gr. 1-3). lib. bdg. 29.99 *(978-1-4109-6262-1(8),* Read Me!) Heinemann-Raintree.

Hall, Susan T., illus. Watch Me Draw Diego's Animal Adventures. 2013. (Watch Me Draw Ser.). 24p. (J). (gr. -1-2). 25.65 *(978-1-936309-88-7(2))* Quarto Publishing Group USA.

Hamsters. 2007. (Illus.). (J). cd-rom 9.99 *(978-0-9795190-3-1(9))* Color & Learn.

Hansen, Jim. How to Draw Superheroes. 2009. (Drawing Fantasy Art Ser.). 32p. (gr. 4-5). 50.50 *(978-1-61512-193-9(5),* PowerKids Pr.) Rosen Publishing Group, Inc., The.

Hanson, Anders. Cool Drawing: The Art of Creativity for Kids, 1 vol. 2009. (Cool Art Ser.). (ENG.). 32p. (gr. 3-6). 28.50 *(978-1-60453-142-8(8),* Checkerboard Library) ABDO Publishing Co.

Harpster, Steve. Drawing with Letters the Haunted Creeps & Ghastly Ghouls of Spiderbite. 2012. (ENG., Illus.). 32p. (J). pap. 6.95 *(978-0-615-68599-1(4))* Harptoons Publishing.

—Pencil, Paper, Draw! - Animals. 2014. (Pencil, Paper, Draw!(r) Ser.). (ENG., Illus.). 64p. (J). (gr. k-3). pap. 6.95 *(978-1-4549-1148-7(4))* Sterling Publishing Co., Inc.

—Pencil, Paper, Draw! - Cars & Trucks. 2014. (Pencil, Paper, Draw!(r) Ser.). (ENG., Illus.). 64p. (J). (gr. k-3). pap. 6.95 *(978-1-4549-1150-0(6))* Sterling Publishing Co., Inc.

—Pencil, Paper, Draw!(r) - Dinosaurs. 2014. (Pencil, Paper, Draw!(r) Ser.). (ENG., Illus.). 64p. (J). (gr. k-3). pap. 6.95 *(978-1-4549-1151-7(4))* Sterling Publishing Co., Inc.

—Pencil, Paper, Draw! - Dogs. 2014. (Pencil, Paper, Draw!(r) Ser.). (ENG., Illus.). 64p. (J). (gr. k-3). pap. 6.95 *(978-1-4549-1152-4(2))* Sterling Publishing Co., Inc.

—Pencil, Paper, Draw!(r) - Horses. 2014. (Pencil, Paper, Draw!(r) Ser.). (ENG., Illus.). 64p. (J). (gr. k-3). pap. 6.95 *(978-1-4549-1155-5(7))* Sterling Publishing Co., Inc.

—Pencil, Paper, Draw! - Pirates. 2014. (Pencil, Paper, Draw!(r) Ser.). (ENG., Illus.). 64p. (J). (gr. k-3). pap. 6.95 *(978-1-4549-1156-2(5))* Sterling Publishing Co., Inc.

—Pencil, Paper, Draw!(r) - Sharks. 2014. (Pencil, Paper, Draw!(r) Ser.). (ENG., Illus.). 64p. (J). (gr. k-3). pap. 6.95 *(978-1-4549-1157-9(3))* Sterling Publishing Co., Inc.

Harris, Nathaniel. Wall Paintings. 2009. (Stories in Art Ser.). (Illus.). 30p. (J). (gr. 4-8). lib. bdg. 26.50 *(978-1-4042-4440-5(9),* PowerKids Pr.) Rosen Publishing Group, Inc., The.

Hart, Christopher. How to Draw Chic Fashions Drawing Kit. 2006. (How to Draw Ser.). (Illus.). 24p. (J). (gr. 3-9). 16.99 *(978-0-9776925-7-6(4))* Loew-Cornell, Inc.

—Kids Draw Big Book of Everything Manga. 2009. (ENG., Illus.). 256p. (J). (gr. 4-7). pap. 22.99 *(978-0-8230-9509-4(6),* Watson-Guptill) Potter/TenSpeed/Harmony.

Harwood, Pearl A. Mr. Bumba Draws a Kitten. (Mr. Bumba Bks.). (Illus.). 32p. (J). (gr. k-3). reprint ed. 5.95 *(978-0-8225-0107-7(4),* Lerner Pubns.) Lerner Publishing Group.

Hawkins, Jonny. Doodle Through the Bible for Kids. 2016. (ENG.). 144p. (J). pap. 7.99 *(978-0-7369-6520-0(3))* Harvest Hse. Pubs.

Hayn, Carter. Drawing Dragons. 2013. (Drawing Monsters Step-By-Step Ser.). (ENG., Illus.). 24p. (gr. 3-6). 26.50 *(978-1-61533-689-0(3));* pap. 12.85 *(978-1-61533-698-2(2))* Windmill Bks.

—Drawing Ghosts. 2013. (Drawing Monsters Step-By-Step Ser.). (ENG., Illus.). 24p. (gr. 3-6). 26.50 *(978-1-61533-690-6(7));* pap. 12.85 *(978-1-61533-700-2(8))* Windmill Bks.

—Drawing Vampires. 2013. (Drawing Monsters Step-By-Step Ser.). (ENG., Illus.). 24p. (gr. 3-6). 26.50 *(978-1-61533-691-3(5));* pap. 12.85 *(978-1-61533-702-6(4))* Windmill Bks.

—Drawing Werewolves. 2013. (Drawing Monsters Step-By-Step Ser.). (ENG., Illus.). 24p. (gr. 3-6). 26.50 *(978-1-61533-692-0(3));* pap. 12.85 *(978-1-61533-704-0(0))* Windmill Bks.

—Drawing Witches & Wizards. 2013. (Drawing Monsters Step-By-Step Ser.). (ENG., Illus.). 24p. (gr. 3-6). 26.50 *(978-1-61533-693-7(1));* pap. 12.85 *(978-1-61533-706-4(7))* Windmill Bks.

—Drawing Zombies. 2013. (Drawing Monsters Step-By-Step Ser.). (ENG., Illus.). 24p. (gr. 3-6). 26.50 *(978-1-61533-694-4(X));* pap. 12.85 *(978-1-61533-708-8(3))* Windmill Bks.

Hecht, Kristina. 1, 2, 3, My Daddy & Me. 2007. 16p. per. 24.95 *(978-1-4241-8940-3(3))* America Star Bks.

Henry, Sally. Drawing. 2009. (Make Your Own Art Ser.). (Illus.). 32p. (J). (gr. 3-6). lib. bdg. 26.50 *(978-1-4358-2510-9(1),* PowerKids Pr.) Rosen Publishing Group, Inc., The.

Hinkler Books, ed. Funky Things to Draw. 2012. 192p. (J). spiral bd. 19.99 *(978-1-74182-942-6(9))* Hinkler Bks. Pty, Ltd. AUS. Dist: Ideals Pubns.

—You Can Draw. 2012. 192p. (J). spiral bd. 19.99 *(978-1-74182-944-0(5))* Hinkler Bks. Pty, Ltd. AUS. Dist: Ideals Pubns.

Hodge, Susie. Animals. Roberts, Steve, illus. 2010. (Let's Draw Ser.). (ENG.). 32p. (gr. 3-5). 22.60 *(978-1-61533-269-4(3));* pap. 10.55 *(978-1-61533-270-0(7))* Windmill Bks.

—Dinosaurs. 2010. (Let's Draw Ser.). (ENG., Illus.). 32p. (gr. 3-5). pap. 10.55 *(978-1-61533-267-0(7))* Windmill Bks.

—Dinosaurs. Roberts, Steve, illus. 2010. (Let's Draw Ser.). (ENG.). 32p. (gr. 3-5). 22.60 *(978-1-61533-264-9(2))* Windmill Bks.

—How to Draw Animals. Roberts, Steve, illus. 2008. (How to Draw Ser.). 47p. (J). (gr. 4-7). *(978-1-84810-005-3(1))* Miles Kelly Publishing, Ltd.

—How to Draw Dinosaurs. Roberts, Steve, illus. 2008. (How to Draw Ser.). 47p. (J). (gr. 4-7). *(978-1-84810-006-0(X))* Miles Kelly Publishing, Ltd.

Hoff, Syd. Syd Hoff's Dinosaur Stories & More. 2015. (ENG., Illus.). 160p. (J). (gr. 2-4). pap. 14.99 *(978-0-486-80024-0(5))* Dover Pubns., Inc.

Hosley, Maria. Airplanes, 1 vol. 2007. (First Drawings Ser.). (ENG., Illus.). 24p. (gr. -1-3). 25.65 *(978-1-59679-799-4(1),* Buddy Bks.) ABDO Publishing Co.

—Cars, 1 vol. 2007. (First Drawings Ser.). (ENG., Illus.). 24p. (J). (gr. -1-3). lib. bdg. 25.65 *(978-1-59679-800-7(9),* Buddy Bks.) ABDO Publishing Co.

—Cats, 1 vol. 2007. (First Drawings Ser.). (ENG., Illus.). 24p. (gr. -1-3). 25.65 *(978-1-59679-801-4(7),* Buddy Bks.) ABDO Publishing Co.

—Dogs, 1 vol. 2007. (First Drawings Ser.). (ENG., Illus.). 24p. (gr. -1-3). 25.65 *(978-1-59679-803-8(3),* Buddy Bks.) ABDO Publishing Co.

—People, 1 vol. 2007. (First Drawings Ser.). (ENG., Illus.). 24p. (gr. -1-3). 25.65 *(978-1-59679-812-0(2),* Buddy Bks.) ABDO Publishing Co.

How to Draw a Horse. 2006. (J). *(978-1-933343-13-6(3))* Stabenfeldt Inc.

How to Draw Animals. 2013. (How to Draw Animals Ser.). 32p. (J). (gr. 3-6). 159.00 *(978-1-4777-1545-1(2));* pap. 423.00 *(978-1-4777-2729-4(9));* pap. 70.50 *(978-1-4777-2728-7(0))* Rosen Publishing Group, Inc., The. (PowerKids Pr.).

How to Draw Zentangle Art. 2017. (How to Draw Zentangle Art Ser.). 32p. (gr. 3-3). pap. 63.00 ***(978-1-5382-0832-8(6));*** lib. bdg. 159.60 ***(978-1-5382-0613-3(7))*** Stevens, Gareth Publishing LLLP.

Huff, Abby. Draw Your Own Animal Zendoodles. Scudamore, Angelika et al, illus. 2017. (Draw Your Own Zendoodles Ser.). (ENG.). 48p. (gr. 4-5). lib. bdg. 31.32 *(978-1-5157-4840-3(5))* Capstone Press of Coughlan Cos.

—Draw Your Own Fairy Tale Zendoodles. Preston, Lizzie et al, illus. 2017. (Draw Your Own Zendoodles Ser.). (ENG.). 48p. (gr. 4-5). lib. bdg. 31.32 *(978-1-5157-4842-7(1))* Capstone Press of Coughlan Cos.

—Draw Your Own Nature Zendoodles. Phruapadit, Pimlada et al, illus. 2017. (Draw Your Own Zendoodles Ser.). (ENG.). 48p. (gr. 4-5). lib. bdg. 31.32 *(978-1-5157-4843-4(X))* Capstone Press of Coughlan Cos.

—Draw Your Own Zendoodles. 2017. (Draw Your Own Zendoodles Ser.). (ENG.). 48p. (gr. 4-5). 125.28 *(978-1-5157-4845-8(6))* Capstone Press of Coughlan Cos.

Iguanas & Reptiles. 2007. (Illus.). (J). cd-rom 9.99 *(978-0-9795190-5-5(5))* Color & Learn.

Jackson, Katy. Draw Cute Pictures. 2014. (Draw It! Ser.). 32p. (J). (gr. 3-6). lib. bdg. 27.50 *(978-1-4777-9132-5(9))* Windmill Bks.

—Draw Magical Pictures. 2014. (Draw It! Ser.). 32p. (J). (gr. 3-6). lib. bdg. 27.50 *(978-1-4777-9136-3(1))* Windmill Bks.

—Draw Pretty Pictures. 2014. (Draw It! Ser.). 32p. (J). (gr. 3-6). lib. bdg. 27.50 *(978-1-4777-9144-8(2))* Windmill Bks.

Jantner, Janos, illus. Drawing Fantasy Monsters. 2013. (How to Draw Monsters Ser.). (ENG.). 32p. (J). (gr. 3-6). pap. 11.75 *(978-1-4777-0344-1(6));* lib. bdg. 26.50 *(978-1-4777-0311-3(X))* Rosen Publishing Group, Inc., The. (PowerKids Pr.).

—Drawing Horror-Movie Monsters. 2013. (How to Draw Monsters Ser.). (ENG.). 32p. (J). (gr. 3-6). 26.50 *(978-1-4777-0308-3(X));* pap. 11.75 *(978-1-4777-0338-0(1))* Rosen Publishing Group, Inc., The. (PowerKids Pr.).

—Drawing Monsters from Great Books. 2013. (How to Draw Monsters Ser.). (ENG.). 32p. (J). (gr. 3-6). pap. 11.75 *(978-1-4777-0348-9(9));* lib. bdg. 26.50 *(978-1-4777-0313-7(6))* Rosen Publishing Group, Inc., The. (PowerKids Pr.).

—Drawing Mythological Monsters. 2013. (How to Draw Monsters Ser.). (ENG.). 32p. (J). (gr. 3-6). pap. 11.75 *(978-1-4777-0340-3(3));* lib. bdg. 26.50 *(978-1-4777-0309-0(8))* Rosen Publishing Group, Inc., The. (PowerKids Pr.).

—Drawing Science-Fiction Monsters. 2013. (How to Draw Monsters Ser.). (ENG.). 32p. (J). (gr. 3-6). pap. 11.75 *(978-1-4777-0342-7(X));* lib. bdg. 26.50 *(978-1-4777-0310-6(1))* Rosen Publishing Group, Inc., The. (PowerKids Pr.).

—Drawing Unexplained-Mystery Monsters. 2013. (How to Draw Monsters Ser.). (ENG.). 32p. (J). (gr. 3-6). pap. 11.75 *(978-1-4777-0346-5(2));* lib. bdg. 26.50 *(978-1-4777-0312-0(8))* Rosen Publishing Group, Inc., The. (PowerKids Pr.).

Johansen, H. L. How to Draw the Life & Times of Calvin Coolidge. 2009. (Kid's Guide to Drawing the Presidents of the United States of America Ser.). 32p. (gr. 4-4). 50.50 *(978-1-61511-134-3(4),* PowerKids Pr.) Rosen Publishing Group, Inc., The.

Johansen, Heidi Leigh. How to Draw the Life & Times of Calvin Coolidge. 2007. (Kid's Guide to Drawing the Presidents of the United States of America Ser.). (Illus.). 32p. (YA). (gr. 2-5). 26.50 *(978-1-4042-3006-4(8))* Rosen Publishing Group, Inc., The.

Johnson, Shane. How to Draw Avatar: The Last Airbender. 2011. (Learn to Draw Favorite Characters Ser.). (Illus.). 32p. (J). (gr. k-3). 28.50 *(978-1-936309-37-5(8))* Quarto Publishing Group USA.

Jones, Richard & Santillan, Jorge. Manga Dinosaurs. 2012. (Learn to Draw Manga Ser.). (ENG., Illus.). 32p. (J). (gr. 4-6). pap. 11.75 *(978-1-4488-7944-1(2));* lib. bdg. 26.50 *(978-1-4488-7873-4(X))* Rosen Publishing Group, Inc., The. (PowerKids Pr.).

K-Town Youth Empowerment Network Youth Council, et al. Be True to You: Celebrating the Things that Make Us Unique. 2011. (Illus.). 48p. (J). lib. bdg. 15.95 *(978-0-9816793-1-0(5))* Melton Hill Media.

Kauffman Yaun, Debra. People: Learn to Draw Step by Step. 2007. (How to Draw & Paint Ser.). (ENG., Illus.). 32p. pap. 8.95 *(978-1-56010-795-8(2),* 1560107952) Quarto Publishing Group USA.

A Kid's Guide to Drawing the Countries of the World: Set 3. (Illus.). (J). (gr. k-5). 159.00 *(978-1-4042-2958-7(2))* Rosen Publishing Group, Inc., The.

A Kid's Guide to Drawing the Countries of the World: Set 4. (Illus.). (J). (gr. k-5). 159.00 *(978-1-4042-2959-4(0))* Rosen Publishing Group, Inc., The.

Kindberg, Sally. Draw It! 100 Wacky Things to Doodle & Draw! 2015. (ENG.). 112p. (J). (gr. 2-4). pap. 12.99 *(978-1-61963-761-0(8),* 9781619637610, Bloomsbury USA Childrens) Bloomsbury Publishing USA.

—Draw It! Christmas: 100 Festive Things to Doodle & Draw! 2015. (ENG.). 112p. (J). (gr. 2-4). pap. 12.99 *(978-1-61963-792-4(8),* 9781619637924, Bloomsbury USA Childrens) Bloomsbury Publishing USA.

Kinkade, Thomas, contrib. by. Lifepac Elective Drawing Basics, Bk. 5. 2006. pap. 3.49 *(978-0-7403-0712-6(6))* Alpha Omega Pubns., Inc.

Kissock, Heather. Extreme Sports. 2012. (J). *(978-1-61913-239-9(7));* pap. *(978-1-61913-244-3(3))* Weigl Pubs., Inc.

—Insects. 2012. (J). 28.55 *(978-1-61913-241-2(9))* Weigl Pubs., Inc.

—Military Vehicles. 2012. (J). 28.55 *(978-1-61913-242-9(7));* pap. 13.95 *(978-1-61913-247-4(8))* Weigl Pubs., Inc.

—Structural Wonders. 2012. (J). *(978-1-61913-243-6(5));* pap. *(978-1-61913-248-1(6))* Weigl Pubs., Inc.

—Underwater Life. 2012. (J). *(978-1-61913-240-5(0));* pap. *(978-1-61913-245-0(1))* Weigl Pubs., Inc.

Klutz Editors, ed. Draw Star Wars Rebels. 2014. (ENG.). 74p. (J). (gr. 3). 16.99 *(978-0-545-70324-6(7))* Klutz.

—My Style Studio: Design & Trace Your Own Fashions. 2014. (ENG.). 48p. (J). (gr. 3). 21.99 *(978-0-545-65053-3(4))* Klutz.

C
D

Knowles, Heather. Learn to Draw Tangled. 2011. (Learn to Draw Favorite Characters Ser.). (Illus.). 32p. (J). (gr. k-3). 28.50 (978-1-936309-66-5(1)) Quarto Publishing Group USA.

Kraft, Ellen Christiansen. Doodle Design & Draw DREAM ROOMS. 2012. (Dover Doodle Bks.). (ENG.). 64p. (J). (gr. 3-5). pap. 5.99 (978-0-486-48439-6(4)) Dover Pubns., Inc.

Krefta, Ben. Step by Step Manga. 2013. (ENG., Illus.). 64p. (J). pap. 7.95 (978-1-84858-863-9(1)) Arcturus Publishing GBR. Dist: Bookmasters Distribution.

Kurtz, John. What to Doodle? Jr. — My World. 2013. (Dover Doodle Bks.). (ENG.). 128p. (J). (gr. k-3). pap. 3.99 (978-0-486-49059-5(9)) Dover Pubns., Inc.

La Coccinella. Animals at Play. 2015. (Play & Draw Ser.). (ENG., Illus.). 22p. (J). (gr. k-3). spiral bd. 9.95 (978-1-4549-1556-0(0)) Sterling Publishing Co., Inc.

LaBaff, Stephanie. Draw Aliens & Space Objects in 4 Easy Steps: Then Write a Story. LaBaff, Tom, illus. 2012. (Drawing in 4 Easy Steps Ser.). 48p. (J). (gr. 3-18). lib. bdg. 25.27 (978-0-7660-3841-7(6)) Enslow Pubs., Inc.

Labaff, Stephanie. Draw Aliens & Space Objects in 4 Easy Steps: Then Write a Story. LaBaff, Tom, illus. 2012. (Drawing in 4 Easy Steps Ser.). 48p. (J). (gr. 3-18). pap. 8.95 (978-1-4644-0014-8(8), Enslow Elementary) Enslow Pubs., Inc.

LaBaff, Stephanie. Draw Animals in 4 Easy Steps: Then Write a Story. LaBaff, Tom, illus. 2012. (Drawing in 4 Easy Steps Ser.). 48p. (J). (gr. 3-18). 25.27 (978-0-7660-3840-0(8)) Enslow Pubs., Inc.

Labaff, Stephanie. Draw Animals in 4 Easy Steps: Then Write a Story. LaBaff, Tom, illus. 2012. (Drawing in 4 Easy Steps Ser.). 48p. (J). (gr. 3-18). pap. 8.95 (978-1-4644-0013-1(X), Enslow Elementary) Enslow Pubs., Inc.

LaBaff, Stephanie. Draw Cartoon People in 4 Easy Steps: Then Write a Story. LaBaff, Tom, illus. 2012. (Drawing in 4 Easy Steps Ser.). 48p. (J). (gr. 3-18). 25.27 (978-0-7660-3843-1(2)) Enslow Pubs., Inc.

Labaff, Stephanie. Draw Cartoon People in 4 Easy Steps: Then Write a Story. LaBaff, Tom, illus. 2012. (Drawing in 4 Easy Steps Ser.). 48p. (J). (gr. 3-18). pap. 8.95 (978-1-4644-0016-2(4), Enslow Elementary) Enslow Pubs., Inc.

LaBaff, Stephanie. Draw Pirates in 4 Easy Steps: Then Write a Story. LaBaff, Tom, illus. 2012. (Drawing in 4 Easy Steps Ser.). 48p. (J). (gr. 3-18). pap. 8.95 (978-1-4644-0012-4(1), Enslow Elementary); 25.27 (978-0-7660-3839-4(4)) Enslow Pubs., Inc.

—Draw Princesses in 4 Easy Steps: Then Write a Story. LaBaff, Tom, illus. 2012. (Drawing in 4 Easy Steps Ser.). 48p. (J). (gr. 3-18). 25.27 (978-0-7660-3838-7(6)) Enslow Pubs., Inc.

Labaff, Stephanie. Draw Princesses in 4 Easy Steps: Then Write a Story. LaBaff, Tom, illus. 2012. (Drawing in 4 Easy Steps Ser.). 48p. (J). (gr. 3-18). pap. 8.95 (978-1-4644-0011-7(3), Enslow Elementary) Enslow Pubs., Inc.

LaBaff, Stephanie. Draw Superheroes in 4 Easy Steps: Then Write a Story. LaBaff, Tom, illus. 2012. (Drawing in 4 Easy Steps Ser.). 48p. (J). (gr. 3-18). pap. 8.95 (978-1-4644-0015-5(6), Enslow Elementary) Enslow Pubs., Inc.

Langeler, Gerard. Let's Make Faces. Grindell, Joan & Grindell, Mark, illus. 2009. (ENG.). 24p. (J). (gr. -1-3). spiral bd. 14.95 (978-1-932565-63-8(9)) Future Horizons, Inc.

Lanza, Barbara. How to Draw & Paint Enchanting Fairies. 2008. (ENG., Illus.). 32p. (J). pap. 11.99 (978-1-60061-169-8(9), Impact) F&W Media, Inc.

LaPadula, Tom. Learn to Draw Military Machines: Step-By-step Instructions for More Than 25 High-powered Vehicles. 2016. (Learn to Draw Ser.). (ENG.). 64p. (J). (gr. 1-3). pap. 8.95 (978-1-63322-067-6(2), Walter Foster Jr) Quarto Publishing Group USA.

LaPadula, Tom, illus. Learn to Draw Planes, Choppers & Watercraft. 2013. 40p. (J). (978-1-936309-82-5(3)) Quarto Publishing Group USA.

—Learn to Draw Tanks, Aircraft & Armored Vehicles: Learn to Draw 23 Favorite Subjects, Step by Easy Step, Shape by Simple Shape! 2013. 40p. (J). (978-1-936309-83-2(1)) Quarto Publishing Group USA.

LaPadula, Tom & Shellly, Jeff, illus. All about Drawing: Cool Cars, Fast Planes & Military Machines. 2014. (All about Drawing Ser.). (ENG.). 80p. (J). (gr. 3-7). lib. bdg. 34.60 (978-1-939581-09-9(5)) Quarto Publishing Group USA.

LaPadula, Tom & Shelly, Jeff. All about Drawing Cool Cars, Fast Planes & Military Machines: Learn How to Draw More Than 40 High-Powered Vehicles Step by Step. 2011. (All about Drawing Ser.). (ENG., Illus.). 80p. (J). (gr. 1-3). pap. 9.95 (978-1-60058-235-6(4), 1600582354) Quarto Publishing Group USA.

LBCL & Emberley, Ed. Picture Pie Vol. 2: A Drawing Book & Stencil. Emberley, Ed, illus. 2005. (ENG., Illus.). 32p. (J). (gr. 2-17). pap. 10.00 (978-0-316-78980-6(1)) Little, Brown Bks. for Young Readers.

Learn to Draw. 2013. (Learn to Draw Ser.). 32p. (J). (gr. 2-5). pap. 63.00 (978-1-4339-9807-2(6)); pap. 378.00 (978-1-4339-9808-9(4)) Stevens, Gareth Publishing LLLP.

Learn to Paint & Draw. 2009. (Reference Ser.). 128p. (978-1-4075-2106-0(3)) Parragon, Inc.

Lee, Frank. Drawing Action in Your Graphic Novel. 2012. (How to Draw Your Own Graphic Novel Ser.). (ENG.). 32p. (J). (gr. 4-6). pap. 12.30 (978-1-4488-6451-5(8)); lib. bdg. 26.50 (978-1-4488-6477-5(1)) Rosen Publishing Group, Inc., The. (PowerKids Pr.).

Lee, Justin. How to Draw African Animals. 2009. (Kid's Guide to Drawing Ser.). 24p. (gr. 3-3). 47.90 (978-1-61511-008-7(9), PowerKids Pr.) Rosen Publishing Group, Inc., The.

—How to Draw Animals of the Rain Forest. 2009. (Kid's Guide to Drawing Ser.). 24p. (gr. 3-3). 47.90 (978-1-61511-010-0(0), PowerKids Pr.) Rosen Publishing Group, Inc., The.

—How to Draw Sharks. 2009. (Kid's Guide to Drawing Ser.). 24p. (gr. 3-3). 47.90 (978-1-61511-040-7(2), PowerKids Pr.) Rosen Publishing Group, Inc., The.

—How to Draw Whales. 2009. (Kid's Guide to Drawing Ser.). 24p. (gr. 3-3). 47.90 (978-1-61511-042-1(9), PowerKids Pr.) Rosen Publishing Group, Inc., The.

Legendre, Philippe. I Can Draw! Dinosaurs, Dragons & Prehistoric Creatures. 2015. (I Can Draw Ser.). (ENG., Illus.). 48p. (J). (gr. -1-3). 30.65 (978-1-939581-60-0(5)) Quarto Publishing Group USA.

Let's Draw Step by Step. 2016. (Let's Draw Step by Step Ser.). 00032p. (J). (gr. 1-2). 114.00 (978-1-4994-8140-2(3), Windmill Bks.) Rosen Publishing Group, Inc., The.

Let's Draw with Shapes: Set 2.Tr. of Vamos a dibujar con figuras Set 2. (Illus.). (J). (ENG & SPA.). (gr. -1-1). 103.50 (978-1-4042-7560-7(6), Editorial Buenas Letras); (gr. k-1). 103.50 (978-1-4042-2947-1(7), Powerstart Pr.) Rosen Publishing Group, Inc., The.

Levin, Freddie. Princesses. 2010. (1-2-3 Draw Ser.). (ENG., Illus.). 64p. (J). (gr. 1-7). pap. 8.99 (978-0-939217-65-6(1)) Peel Productions, Inc.

—1-2-3 Draw Ocean Life. 2014. 64p. pap. 9.00 (978-1-61003-323-7(X)) Center for the Collaborative Classroom.

Levy, Barbara Soloff. How to Draw. 2009. (Dover How to Draw Ser.). (ENG., Illus.). 64p. (J). (gr. k-5). pap. 4.99 (978-0-486-47203-4(5)) Dover Pubns., Inc.

—How to Draw Ballet Pictures. 2009. (Dover How to Draw Ser.). (ENG., Illus.). 64p. (J). (gr. 1-5). pap. 4.99 (978-0-486-47055-9(5)) Dover Pubns., Inc.

—How to Draw Bible Figures. 2009. (Dover How to Draw Ser.). (ENG., Illus.). 64p. (J). (gr. -1-2). pap. 4.99 (978-0-486-47237-9(X)) Dover Pubns., Inc.

—How to Draw Circus Pictures. 2007. (Dover How to Draw Ser.). (ENG., Illus.). 32p. (J). (gr. -1-5). pap. 2.95 (978-0-486-45647-8(1)) Dover Pubns., Inc.

—How to Draw Dogs. 2011. (Dover How to Draw Ser.). (ENG.). 64p. (J). (gr. k-5). pap. 4.99 (978-0-486-47201-0(9)) Dover Pubns., Inc.

—How to Draw for All Seasons. 2007. (Dover How to Draw Ser.). (ENG., Illus.). 32p. (J). (gr. -1-5). pap. 3.95 (978-0-486-46219-6(6)) Dover Pubns., Inc.

—How to Draw Halloween Pictures. 2010. (Dover How to Draw Ser.). (ENG., Illus.). 64p. (J). (gr. k-5). pap. 4.99 (978-0-486-47671-1(5)) Dover Pubns., Inc.

—How to Draw Mother Goose Characters. 2006. (Dover How to Draw Ser.). (ENG., Illus.). 32p. (J). (gr. -1-5). pap. 2.95 (978-0-486-44769-8(3)) Dover Pubns., Inc.

—How to Draw Pets. 2006. (Dover How to Draw Ser.). (ENG., Illus.). 64p. (J). (gr. k-5). pap. 4.99 (978-0-486-44710-0(3)) Dover Pubns., Inc.

—How to Draw Sports. 2009. (Dover How to Draw Ser.). (ENG., Illus.). 64p. (J). (gr. k-5). pap. 4.99 (978-0-486-47305-5(8)) Dover Pubns., Inc.

—I Can Draw Wizards, Dragons & Other Magical Creatures. 2007. (Boxed Sets/Bindups Ser.). (ENG., Illus.). 64p. (J). (gr. 1-7). pap. 5.95 (978-0-486-46389-6(3)) Dover Pubns., Inc.

—Sea Creatures: How to Draw with Simple Shapes. 2012. (Dover How to Draw Ser.). (ENG., Illus.). 64p. (J). (gr. k-3). pap. 4.99 (978-0-486-47865-4(3)) Dover Pubns., Inc.

Levy, Barbara Soloff & Dover Publications Inc. Staff. I Can Draw Dogs. 2007. (Boxed Sets/Bindups Ser.). (ENG., Illus.). 64p. (J). (gr. 1-5). pap. 5.95 (978-0-486-46385-8(0)) Dover Pubns., Inc.

Levy, Barbara Soloff & Drawing Staff. ART START Animals: How to Draw with Simple Shapes. 2010. (Dover How to Draw Ser.). (ENG., Illus.). 64p. (J). (gr. k-3). pap. 4.99 (978-0-486-47677-3(4)) Dover Pubns., Inc.

—ART START Funny Characters: How to Draw with Simple Shapes. 2010. (Dover How to Draw Ser.). (ENG., Illus.). 64p. (J). (gr. k-3). pap. 4.99 (978-0-486-47679-7(0)) Dover Pubns., Inc.

—How to Draw Pirates: Captain, Crew, Ships & More. 2008. (Dover How to Draw Ser.). (ENG., Illus.). 64p. (J). (gr. 1-5). per. 4.99 (978-0-486-46548-7(9)) Dover Pubns., Inc.

—How to Draw Princesses & Other Fairy Tale Pictures. 2008. (Dover How to Draw Ser.). (ENG., Illus.). 64p. (J). (gr. 1-5). pap. 4.99 (978-0-486-46813-6(5)) Dover Pubns., Inc.

Levy, Janey. Renaissance Paintings: Using Perspective to Represent Three-Dimensional Objects. (PowerMath: Proficiency Plus Ser.). 32p. 2009. (gr. 4-5). 47.90 (978-1-60851-416-8(1), PowerKids Pr.) 2005. 47.50 (978-1-4042-5220-2(7), Rosen Classroom) Rosen Publishing Group, Inc., The.

Lewis K., Parker. How to Draw the Life & Times of Richard M. Nixon. 2007. (Kid's Guide to Drawing the Presidents of the United States of America Ser.). (Illus.). 32p. (YA). (gr. 2-5). 26.50 (978-1-4042-3013-2(0)) Rosen Publishing Group, Inc., The.

Lifepac Elective Drawing Basics. 2006. Bk. 1. pap. 3.90 (978-0-7403-0708-9(8))Bk. 2. 3.99 (978-0-7403-0710-2(X))Bk. 2. 3.50 (978-0-7403-0709-6(6))Bk. 4. pap. 3.90 (978-0-7403-0711-9(8)) Alpha Omega Pubns., Inc.

Lipniewska, Dominika. Doodle Town. 2016. (ENG., Illus.). 64p. (J). (gr. -1-2). pap. 16.95 (978-1-84976-472-8(7)) Tate Publishing, Ltd. GBR. Dist: Abrams, Inc.

Lo Raso, Carlo, illus. Watch Me Draw the Backyardigans' Incredible Adventures. 2012. (J). (978-1-936309-42-9(4)) Quarto Publishing Group USA.

Lonely Planet Publications Staff, et al. Doodle Spots, 1 vol. 2016. (Lonely Planet Kids Ser.). (ENG., Illus.). 100p. (J). pap. 12.99 (978-1-76034-346-0(3), 5343) Lonely Planet Pubns.

Long, Ethan, illus. Draw with Scribbles & Ink: Draw & Paint Your Own Masterpieces! 2014. (ENG.). 48p. (J). (gr. 1-3). 14.95 (978-1-60058-471-8(3)) Quarto Publishing Group USA.

LTD Finding Nemo: Learn to Draw. 2013. (Learn to Draw Ser.: 3). 32p. (gr. -1-2). 12.75 (978-1-62588-910-2(0)) Black Rabbit Bks.

LTD Pixar/Disney Characters: Learn to Draw. 2013. (Learn to Draw Ser.: 1). 32p. (gr. -1-2). 12.75 (978-1-62588-913-3(5)) Black Rabbit Bks.

LTD Princesses: Learn to Draw. 2013. (Learn to Draw Ser.: 2). 32p. (gr. -1-2). 12.75 (978-1-62588-911-9(9)) Black Rabbit Bks.

LTD Toy Story. 2013. (Learn to Draw Ser.: 4). 32p. (gr. -1-2). 12.75 (978-1-62588-912-6(7)) Black Rabbit Bks.

Luxbacher, Irene. 123 I Can Draw! Luxbacher, Irene, illus. 2008. (Starting Art Ser.). (ENG., Illus.). 24p. (J). (gr. -1-2). 14.95 (978-1-55453-039-7(3)); pap. 5.95 (978-1-55453-152-3(7)) Kids Can Pr., Ltd. CAN. Dist: Hachette Bk. Group.

Makowski, Robin Lee. Cats. 2005. (Drawing Made Fun Ser.). (Illus.). 32p. (J). (gr. 3-7). lib. bdg. 20.95 (978-1-59515-468-2(X), 1244418) Rourke Educational Media.

—Dogs. 2005. (Drawing Made Fun Ser.). (Illus.). 32p. (J). (gr. -1-3). lib. bdg. 20.95 (978-1-59515-469-9(8), 1244419) Rourke Educational Media.

Mangrum, Kaylea J. How to Draw Step-By-Step Using the Alphabet. Mangrum, Kaylea J., illus. 2013. (Illus.). 38p. pap. 12.49 (978-0-9883009-4-1(X)) Mangrum, Kaylea J.

Marbaix, Jane. Zentangle for Kids. 2015. (ENG., Illus.). 96p. (J). (gr. 2). pap. 12.95 (978-1-4549-1902-5(7)) Sterling Publishing Co., Inc.

Marroquin-Burr, Kristina, illus. Learn to Draw Angry Birds Space. 2014. 64p. (J). (gr. 3-5). 33.27 (978-1-939581-33-4(8)) Quarto Publishing Group USA.

Marsocci, Joey & DeBlasio, Allison. How to Draw Steampunk: Discover the Secrets to Drawing, Painting, & Illustrating the Curious World of Science Fiction in the Victorian Age. Berry, Bob, illus. 2011. (Fantasy Underground Ser.). (ENG.). 128p. pap. 19.95 (978-1-60058-240-0(0), 1600582400) Quarto Publishing Group USA.

Marvel Book Group. Marvel Doodles. 2016. (Doodle Book Ser.). (ENG.). 128p. (J). (gr. 1-3). pap. 12.99 (978-1-4847-8636-9(X), Marvel Pr.) Disney Publishing Worldwide.

Masiello, Ralph. Ralph Masiello's Ancient Egypt Drawing Book. Masiello, Ralph, illus. 2008. (Ralph Masiello's Drawing Bks.). (ENG., Illus.). 40p. (J). (gr. 3-7). pap. 7.95 (978-1-57091-534-5(2)) Charlesbridge Publishing, Inc.

—Ralph Masiello's Christmas Drawing Book. Masiello, Ralph, illus. 2013. (ENG., Illus.). 32p. (J). (gr. k-3). 17.95 (978-1-57091-543-7(1)); pap. 7.95 (978-1-57091-544-4(X)) Charlesbridge Publishing, Inc.

—Ralph Masiello's Dragon Drawing Book. Masiello, Ralph, illus. 2007. (Fiery Good Time! Ser.). (ENG., Illus.). 64p. (J). (gr. 3-7). 17.95 (978-1-57091-531-4(8)); pap. 9.95 (978-1-57091-532-1(6)) Charlesbridge Publishing, Inc.

—Ralph Masiello's Fairy Drawing Book. Masiello, Ralph, illus. 2013. (ENG., Illus.). 32p. (J). (gr. k-3). pap. 7.95 (978-1-57091-540-6(7)); lib. bdg. 17.95 (978-1-57091-539-0(3)) Charlesbridge Publishing, Inc.

—Ralph Masiello's Farm Drawing Book. Masiello, Ralph, illus. 2012. (Illus.). (J). (ENG.). 32p. (gr. k-3). 16.95 (978-1-57091-537-6(7)); (ENG., 32p. (gr. k-3). pap. 7.95 (978-1-57091-538-3(5)); (gr. 1-4). pap. 16.95 (978-1-60734-082-9(8)) Charlesbridge Publishing, Inc.

—Ralph Masiello's Halloween Drawing Book. Masiello, Ralph, illus. 2012. (ENG., Illus.). 32p. (J). (gr. k-3). pap. 7.95 (978-1-57091-542-0(3)) Charlesbridge Publishing, Inc.

—Ralph Masiello's Ocean Drawing Book. Masiello, Ralph, illus. 2006. (Ralph Masiello's Drawing Bks.). (ENG., Illus.). 32p. (J). (gr. k-3). pap. 7.95 (978-1-57091-530-7(X), 1258410) Charlesbridge Publishing, Inc.

—Ralph Masiello's Robot Drawing Book. Masiello, Ralph, illus. 2011. (ENG., Illus.). 32p. (J). (gr. 1-4). 7.95 (978-1-57091-536-9(9)); 16.95 (978-1-57091-535-2(0)) Charlesbridge Publishing, Inc.

McArdle, Thaneeya. Draw Groovy: Groovy Girls Do-It-Yourself Drawing & Coloring Book. 2014. (Kids DIY Ser.). (ENG., Illus.). 64p. (J). pap. 12.99 (978-1-4403-2216-7(3), Impact) F&W Media, Inc.

McClurkan, Rob. What to Doodle? Jr. — On the Farm & in the Wild. 2013. (Dover Doodle Bks.). (ENG.). 128p. (J). (gr. k-3). pap. 3.99 (978-0-486-49056-4(4)) Dover Pubns., Inc.

McCurry, Kristen. How to Draw Amazing Airplanes & Spacecraft, 1 vol. Edwards, Mat, illus. 2012. (Smithsonian Drawing Bks.). (ENG.). 64p. (gr. 3-4). pap. 7.19 (978-1-4296-9448-3(3)); 33.99 (978-1-4296-8749-2(5)); pap. 41.70 (978-1-4296-9449-0(1)) Capstone Press of Coughlan Cos.

—How to Draw Amazing Animals, 1 vol. Meschini, Leonardo, illus. 2013. (Smithsonian Drawing Bks.). (ENG.). 64p. (gr. 3-4). pap. 7.19 (978-1-62065-726-3(0)); pap. 41.70 (978-1-62065-727-0(9)) Capstone Press of Coughlan Cos.

—How to Draw Incredible Dinosaurs, 1 vol. Calle, Juan, illus. 2012. (Smithsonian Drawing Bks.). (ENG.). 64p. (gr. 3-4). pap. 7.19 (978-1-4296-9450-6(5)); pap. 41.70 (978-1-4296-9451-3(3)); lib. bdg. 33.99 (978-1-4296-8750-8(9)) Capstone Press of Coughlan Cos.

—How to Draw Incredible Ocean Animals, 1 vol. Osterhold, Jared, illus. 2013. (Smithsonian Drawing Bks.). (ENG.). 64p. (gr. 3-4). pap. 7.19 (978-1-62065-728-7(7)); pap. 41.70 (978-1-62065-729-4(5)); lib. bdg. 33.99 (978-1-4296-9940-2(X)) Capstone Press of Coughlan Cos.

—Smithsonian Drawing Books. 2012. (Smithsonian Drawing Bks.). (ENG.). 64p. (gr. 3-4). lib. bdg. 67.98 (978-1-4296-9177-2(8)) Capstone Press of Coughlan Cos.

—Smithsonian Drawing Books. Edwards, Mat, illus. 2012. (Smithsonian Drawing Bks.). (ENG.). 64p. (gr. 3-4). pap. 83.40 (978-1-4296-9453-7(X)); pap. 13.90 (978-1-4296-9452-0(1)) Capstone Press of Coughlan Cos.

McGill, Jordan. Amazing Animals. 2011. (J). (978-1-61690-985-7(4)) Weigl Pubs., Inc.

—Backyard Animals. 2011. (J). (978-1-61690-987-1(0)) Weigl Pubs., Inc.

—Dinosaurs. 2011. (J). (978-1-61690-990-1(0)) Weigl Pubs., Inc.

—Machines. 2011. (J). (978-1-61690-988-8(9)) Weigl Pubs., Inc.

—Space. 2011. (J). (978-1-61690-989-5(7)) Weigl Pubs., Inc.

McGill, Jordan, ed. Amazing Animals. 2011. (J). (gr. 3-5). pap. 13.95 (978-1-61690-862-1(9), AV2 by Weigl); (Illus.). 32p. 28.55 (978-1-61690-856-0(4)) Weigl Pubs., Inc.

—Backyard Animals. 2011. (J). (gr. 3-5). pap. 13.95 (978-1-61690-863-8(7), AV2 by Weigl); (Illus.). 32p. 28.55 (978-1-61690-857-7(2)) Weigl Pubs., Inc.

—Dinosaurs. 2011. (J). (gr. 3-5). pap. 13.95 (978-1-61690-866-9(1), AV2 by Weigl); (Illus.). 32p. 28.55 (978-1-61690-860-7(2)) Weigl Pubs., Inc.

—Machines. 2011. (gr. 3-5). (J). pap. 13.95 (978-1-61690-864-5(5), AV2 by Weigl); (Illus.). 32p. (YA). 28.55 (978-1-61690-858-4(0)) Weigl Pubs., Inc.

—Pets. 2011. (J). (gr. 3-5). pap. 13.95 (978-1-61690-861-4(0), AV2 by Weigl); (Illus.). 32p. 28.55 (978-1-61690-855-3(6)) Weigl Pubs., Inc.

—Space. 2011. (gr. 3-5). (J). pap. 13.95 (978-1-61690-865-2(3), AV2 by Weigl); (Illus.). 32p. (YA). 28.55 (978-1-61690-859-1(9)) Weigl Pubs., Inc.

McLachlan, Brian & Owlkids Books Inc. Staff. Draw Out the Story: Ten Secrets to Creating Your Own Comics. 2013. (ENG., Illus.). 144p. (J). (gr. 2-7). pap. 11.95 (978-1-77147-003-2(8)); (gr. 3-7). 18.95 (978-1-926973-83-8(6)) Owlkids Bks. Inc. CAN. (Owlkids). Dist: Publishers Group West (PGW).

Meyers, Nancy. Doodles 123. Meyers, Nancy, illus. 2012. (Doodles Ser.). (ENG., Illus.). 64p. (J). (gr. k-5). pap. 7.95 (978-1-61608-664-0(5), 608664, Sky Pony Pr.) Skyhorse Publishing Co., Inc.

—Doodles ABC: Alphabet Fun with Dots to Join & Doodles to Do. Meyers, Nancy, illus. 2012. (Doodles Ser.). (ENG., Illus.). 64p. (J). (gr. -1-1). pap. 7.95 (978-1-61608-666-4(1), 608666, Sky Pony Pr.) Skyhorse Publishing Co., Inc.

—Doodles Shapes. Meyers, Nancy, illus. 2012. (Doodles Ser.). (ENG., Illus.). 64p. (J). (gr. k-5). pap. 7.95 (978-1-61608-668-8(8), 608668, Sky Pony Pr.) Skyhorse Publishing Co., Inc.

—Doodles Time. Meyers, Nancy, illus. 2012. (Doodles Ser.). (ENG., Illus.). 64p. (J). (gr. k-5). pap. 7.95 (978-1-61608-670-1(X), 608670, Sky Pony Pr.) Skyhorse Publishing Co., Inc.

Millidge, Gary Spencer & McKay, James. Draw Fantasy Figures: Basic Drawing Techniques - Develop Characters from Elves to Dragons - Create Fantasy Worlds. 2007. (ENG., Illus.). 96p. pap. (978-1-84537-753-3(2)) New Holland Pubs., Ltd.

Mis, M. S. How to Draw Pennsylvania's Sights & Symbols. 2009. (Kid's Guide to Drawing America Ser.). 32p. (gr. k-k). 50.50 (978-1-61511-091-9(7), PowerKids Pr.) Rosen Publishing Group, Inc., The.

—How to Draw Tennessee's Sights & Symbols. 2009. (Kid's Guide to Drawing America Ser.). 32p. (gr. k-k). 50.50 (978-1-61511-096-4(8), PowerKids Pr.) Rosen Publishing Group, Inc., The.

—How to Draw the Life & Times of Franklin Delano Roosevelt. 2009. (Kid's Guide to Drawing the Presidents of the United States of America Ser.). 32p. (gr. 4-4). 50.50 (978-1-61511-136-7(0), PowerKids Pr.) Rosen Publishing Group, Inc., The.

—How to Draw the Life & Times of Lyndon B. Johnson. 2009. (Kid's Guide to Drawing the Presidents of the United States of America Ser.). 32p. (gr. 4-4). 50.50 (978-1-61511-154-1(9), PowerKids Pr.) Rosen Publishing Group, Inc., The.

—How to Draw the Life & Times of Ronald Reagan. 2009. (Kid's Guide to Drawing the Presidents of the United States of America Ser.). 32p. (gr. 4-4). 50.50 (978-1-61511-158-9(1), PowerKids Pr.) Rosen Publishing Group, Inc., The.

—How to Draw the Life & Times of Woodrow Wilson. 2009. (Kid's Guide to Drawing the Presidents of the United States of America Ser.). 32p. (gr. 4-4). 50.50 (978-1-61511-168-8(9), PowerKids Pr.) Rosen Publishing Group, Inc., The.

—How to Draw Virginia's Sights & Symbols. 2009. (Kid's Guide to Drawing America Ser.). 32p. (gr. k-k). 50.50 (978-1-61511-102-2(6), PowerKids Pr.) Rosen Publishing Group, Inc., The.

—How to Draw Wyoming's Sights & Symbols. 2009. (Kid's Guide to Drawing America Ser.). 32p. (gr. k-k). 50.50 (978-1-61511-106-0(9), PowerKids Pr.) Rosen Publishing Group, Inc., The.

Mis, Melody S. How to Draw Australia's Sights & Symbols. 2009. (Kid's Guide to Drawing the Countries of the World Ser.). 48p. (gr. 4-4). 53.00 (978-1-61511-107-7(7), PowerKids Pr.) Rosen Publishing Group, Inc., The.

—How to Draw Brazil's Sights & Symbols. 2009. (Kid's Guide to Drawing the Countries of the World Ser.). 48p. (gr. 4-4). 53.00 (978-1-61511-108-4(5), PowerKids Pr.) Rosen Publishing Group, Inc., The.

—How to Draw China's Sights & Symbols. 2009. (Kid's Guide to Drawing the Countries of the World Ser.). 48p. (gr. 4-4). 53.00 (978-1-61511-109-1(3), PowerKids Pr.) Rosen Publishing Group, Inc., The.

—How to Draw Poland's Sights & Symbols. 2009. (Kid's Guide to Drawing the Countries of the World Ser.). 48p. (gr. 4-4). 53.00 (978-1-61511-122-0(0), PowerKids Pr.) Rosen Publishing Group, Inc., The.

—How to Draw Portugal's Sights & Symbols. 2009. (Kid's Guide to Drawing the Countries of the World Ser.). 48p. (gr. 4-4). 53.00 (978-1-61511-123-7(9), PowerKids Pr.) Rosen Publishing Group, Inc., The.

—How to Draw Russia's Sights & Symbols. 2009. (Kid's Guide to Drawing the Countries of the World Ser.). 48p. (gr. 4-4). 53.00 (978-1-61511-124-4(7), PowerKids Pr.) Rosen Publishing Group, Inc., The.

—How to Draw South Africa's Sights & Symbols. 2009. (Kid's Guide to Drawing the Countries of the World Ser.). 48p. (gr. 4-4). 53.00 (978-1-61511-125-1(5), PowerKids Pr.) Rosen Publishing Group, Inc., The.

—How to Draw South Korea's Sights & Symbols. 2009. (Kid's Guide to Drawing the Countries of the World Ser.). 48p. (gr. 4-4). 53.00 (978-1-61511-126-8(3), PowerKids Pr.) Rosen Publishing Group, Inc., The.

—How to Draw the Life & Times of Andrew Jackson. 2009. (Kid's Guide to Drawing the Presidents of the United States of America Ser.). 32p. (gr. 4-4). 50.50 (978-1-61511-131-2(X), PowerKids Pr.) Rosen Publishing Group, Inc., The.

—How to Draw the Life & Times of Benjamin Harrison. (Kid's Guide to Drawing the Presidents of the United States of America Ser.). 32p. 2009. (gr. 4-4). 50.50 (978-1-61511-133-6(6), PowerKids Pr.) 2007. (Illus.). (YA). (gr. 2-5). 26.50 (978-1-4042-3000-2(9)) Rosen Publishing Group, Inc., The.

—How to Draw the Life & Times of Franklin Delano Roosevelt. 2007. (Kid's Guide to Drawing the Presidents of the United States of America Ser.). (Illus.). 32p. (YA). (gr. 2-5). 26.50 (978-1-4042-3008-8(4)) Rosen Publishing Group, Inc., The.

—How to Draw the Life & Times of James Buchanan. (Kid's Guide to Drawing the Presidents of the United States of America Ser.). 2009. 32p. (gr. 4-4). 50.50 (978-1-61511-146-6(8), PowerKids Pr.) 2006. (YA). (gr. 2-5).

26.50 *(978-1-4042-2992-1(2))* Rosen Publishing Group, Inc., The.

—How to Draw the Life & Times of James K. Polk. (Kid's Guide to Drawing the Presidents of the United States of America Ser.). 2009. 32p. (gr. 4-4). 50.50 *(978-1-61511-147-3(6),* PowerKids Pr.) 2006. (YA). (gr. 2-5). 26.50 *(978-1-4042-2988-4(4))* Rosen Publishing Group, Inc., The.

—How to Draw the Life & Times of Lyndon B. Johnson. 2007. (Kid's Guide to Drawing the Presidents of the United States of America Ser.). (Illus.). 32p. (YA). (gr. 2-5). 26.50 *(978-1-4042-3012-5(2))* Rosen Publishing Group, Inc., The.

—How to Draw the Life & Times of Ronald Reagan. 2007. (Kid's Guide to Drawing the Presidents of the United States of America Ser.). (Illus.). 32p. (YA). (gr. 2-5). 26.50 *(978-1-4042-3016-3(5))* Rosen Publishing Group, Inc., The.

—How to Draw the Life & Times of Rutherford B. Hayes. (Kid's Guide to Drawing the Presidents of the United States of America Ser.). 2009. 32p. (gr. 4-4). 50.50 *(978-1-61511-159-6(X),* PowerKids Pr.) 2006. (YA). (gr. 2-5). 26.50 *(978-1-4042-2996-9(5))* Rosen Publishing Group, Inc., The.

—How to Draw the Life & Times of Thomas Jefferson. 2009. (Kid's Guide to Drawing the Presidents of the United States of America Ser.). 32p. (gr. 4-4). 50.50 *(978-1-61511-161-9(1),* PowerKids Pr.) Rosen Publishing Group, Inc., The.

—How to Draw the Life & Times of Woodrow Wilson. 2007. (Kid's Guide to Drawing the Presidents of the United States of America Ser.). (Illus.). 32p. (YA). (gr. 2-5). 26.50 *(978-1-4042-3004-0(1))* Rosen Publishing Group, Inc., The.

Monroe, Colleen. The Wonders of Nature Sketchbook: Learn about Nature & How to Draw It. Monroe, Michael Glenn, illus. 2006. 40p. (J). (gr. 4-7). lib. bdg. 15.00 *(978-0-9754942-1-9(X))* Storytime Pr., Inc.

Mosqueda, Olga T. & Tucker, Marianne, illus. Learn to Draw Plus Disney Winnie the Pooh. 2012. (J). *(978-1-936309-68-9(8))* Quarto Publishing Group USA.

Muehlenhardt, Amy Bailey. Beginner's Guide to Drawing: Animals, Bugs, Dinosaurs, & Other Cool Stuff!! Muehlenhardt, Amy Bailey, illus. 2010. (Sketch It! Ser.). (ENG., Illus.). 144p. (gr. k-4). pap. 14.95 *(978-1-4048-6166-4(1))* Picture Window Bks.

Muschinske, Emily, illus. Fingerprint Critters: Turning Your Prints into Fun Art. 2006. 48p. (J). pap. *(978-0-439-81338-9(7))* Scholastic, Inc.

My Little Pony - Equestria Girls. 2014. (Love to Draw Ser.: 4). (ENG.). 48p. (J). (gr. 1-3). pap. 8.99 *(978-0-7944-3209-6(3),* Reader's Digest Children's Bks.) Studio Fun International.

Nash, Mike, et al, illus. How to Draw the Coolest, Most Creative Tattoo Art, 1 vol. 2012. (Drawing Ser.). (ENG.). 48p. (gr. 3-4). lib. bdg. 31.99 *(978-1-4296-7539-0(X))* Capstone Press of Coughlan Cos.

—How to Draw the Meanest, Most Terrifying Monsters, 1 vol. 2012. (Drawing Ser.). (ENG.). 48p. (gr. 3-4). lib. bdg. 31.99 *(978-1-4296-7538-3(1))* Capstone Press of Coughlan Cos.

Nguyen, Angela. How to Draw Cute Stuff: Draw Anything & Everything in the Curest Style Ever. 2017. (ENG., Illus.). 128p. (J). (gr. 1). pap. 12.95 ***(978-1-4549-2564-4(7))*** Sterling Publishing Co., Inc.

Nishida, Masaki. Drawing Manga Animals. 2007. (How to Draw Manga Ser.: Vol. 4). (Illus.). 24p. (J). (gr. 4-7). lib. bdg. 25.25 *(978-1-4042-3846-6(8))* Rosen Publishing Group, Inc., The.

Noble, Marty & Creative Haven Staff. Steampunk Designs. 2013. (Adult Coloring Ser.). (ENG., Illus.). 64p. (gr. 3). pap. 5.99 *(978-0-486-49919-2(7))* Dover Pubns., Inc.

North, B. C. What Small Vertical Line Learned. 2012. 16p. pap. 12.70 *(978-1-4669-5914-9(2))* Trafford Publishing.

Nuytten, Bobbie. Fingerprint Animals. Nuytten, Bobbie, illus. 2016. (Fun with Fingerprints Ser.). (ENG., Illus.). 24p. (gr. k-1). lib. bdg. 26.65 *(978-1-4795-8687-5(0))* Picture Window Bks.

—Fingerprint Bugs. Nuytten, Bobbie, illus. 2016. (Fun with Fingerprints Ser.). (ENG., Illus.). 24p. (gr. k-1). lib. bdg. 26.65 *(978-1-4795-8684-4(6))* Picture Window Bks.

—Fingerprint Characters. Nuytten, Bobbie, illus. 2016. (Fun with Fingerprints Ser.). (ENG., Illus.). 24p. (gr. k-1). lib. bdg. 26.65 *(978-1-4795-8685-1(4))* Picture Window Bks.

—Fingerprint Vehicles. Nuytten, Bobbie, illus. 2016. (Fun with Fingerprints Ser.). (ENG., Illus.). 24p. (gr. k-1). lib. bdg. 26.65 *(978-1-4795-8686-8(2))* Picture Window Bks.

Nyberg, Jeanette. Tangle Art & Drawing Games for Kids: A Silly Book for Creative & Visual Thinking. 2016. (ENG., Illus.). 112p. (J). (gr. 3-7). pap. 19.99 *(978-1-63159-126-6(6),* Quarry Bks.) Quarto Publishing Group USA.

Osle, Janessa. Animals Around the World. Legendre, Philippe, illus. 2015. (I Can Draw Ser.). (ENG.). 48p. (J). (gr. -1-3). 30.65 *(978-1-939581-56-3(7))* Quarto Publishing Group USA.

—Favorite Pets. Legendre, Philippe, illus. 2015. (I Can Draw Ser.). (ENG.). 48p. (J). (gr. -1-3). 30.65 *(978-1-939581-55-6(9))* Quarto Publishing Group USA.

—Planes, Trains & Moving Machines. Legendre, Philippe, illus. 2015. (I Can Draw Ser.). (ENG.). 48p. (J). (gr. -1-3). 30.65 *(978-1-939581-58-7(3))* Quarto Publishing Group USA.

—Princesses, Fairies & Fairy Tales. Legendre, Philippe, illus. 2015. (I Can Draw Ser.). (ENG.). 48p. (J). (gr. -1-3). 30.65 *(978-1-939581-59-4(1))* Quarto Publishing Group USA.

—Sea Creatures & Other Favorite Animals. Legendre, Philippe, illus. 2015. (I Can Draw Ser.). (ENG.). 48p. (J). (gr. -1-3). 30.65 *(978-1-939581-57-0(5))* Quarto Publishing Group USA.

Pallotta, Jerry. How to Draw Icky Bugs. Gee, Bonnie, illus. 2003. (J). mass mkt. *(978-0-439-38916-7(X))* Scholastic, Inc.

Parker, Lewis. How to Draw the Life & Times of George H. W. Bush. 2009. (Kid's Guide to Drawing the Presidents of the United States of America Ser.). 32p. (gr. 4-4). 50.50 *(978-1-61511-138-1(7),* PowerKids Pr.) Rosen Publishing Group, Inc., The.

—How to Draw the Life & Times of Harry S. Truman. 2009. (Kid's Guide to Drawing the Presidents of the United States of America Ser.). 32p. (gr. 4-4). 50.50 *(978-1-61511-143-5(3),* PowerKids Pr.) Rosen Publishing Group, Inc., The.

—How to Draw the Life & Times of James A. Garfield. 2009. (Kid's Guide to Drawing the Presidents of the United States of America Ser.). 32p. (gr. 4-4). 50.50 *(978-1-61511-145-9(X),* PowerKids Pr.) Rosen Publishing Group, Inc., The.

—How to Draw the Life & Times of Richard M. Nixon. 2009. (Kid's Guide to Drawing the Presidents of the United States of America Ser.). 32p. (gr. 4-4). 50.50 *(978-1-61511-157-2(3),* PowerKids Pr.) Rosen Publishing Group, Inc., The.

—How to Draw the Life & Times of Warren G. Harding. 2009. (Kid's Guide to Drawing the Presidents of the United States of America Ser.). 32p. (gr. 4-4). 50.50 *(978-1-61511-163-3(8),* PowerKids Pr.) Rosen Publishing Group, Inc., The.

—How to Draw the Life & Times of William Mckinley. 2009. (Kid's Guide to Drawing the Presidents of the United States of America Ser.). 32p. (gr. 4-4). 50.50 *(978-1-61511-167-1(0),* PowerKids Pr.) Rosen Publishing Group, Inc., The.

Parker, Lewis K. How to Draw the Life & Times of George H. W. Bush. 2007. (Kid's Guide to Drawing the Presidents of the United States of America Ser.). (Illus.). 32p. (YA). (gr. 2-5). 26.50 *(978-1-4042-3017-0(3))* Rosen Publishing Group, Inc., The.

—How to Draw the Life & Times of Harry S. Truman. 2005. (Kid's Guide to Drawing the Presidents of the United States of America Ser.). (Illus.). 32p. (YA). (gr. 2-5). lib. bdg. 26.50 *(978-1-4042-3009-5(2))* Rosen Publishing Group, Inc., The.

—How to Draw the Life & Times of James A. Garfield. 2006. (Kid's Guide to Drawing the Presidents of the United States of America Ser.). (YA). (gr. 2-5). 26.50 *(978-1-4042-2997-6(3))* Rosen Publishing Group, Inc., The.

—How to Draw the Life & Times of Warren G. Harding. 2007. (Kid's Guide to Drawing the Presidents of the United States of America Ser.). (Illus.). 32p. (J). (gr. 2-5). 26.50 *(978-1-4042-3005-7(X))* Rosen Publishing Group, Inc., The.

—How to Draw the Life & Times of William McKinley. 2007. (Kid's Guide to Drawing the Presidents of the United States of America Ser.). (Illus.). 32p. (YA). (gr. 2-5). 26.50 *(978-1-4042-3001-9(7))* Rosen Publishing Group, Inc., The.

Peot, Margaret. Inkblot: Drip, Splat, & Squish Your Way to Creativity. Peot, Margaret, illus. 2011. (ENG., Illus.). 56p. (J). (gr. 6-18). 19.95 *(978-1-59078-720-5(X))* Boyds Mills Pr.

Pepper, Charlotte. What to Draw & How to Draw It for Kids. 2017. (ENG.). 64p. (J). (gr. 2-6). pap. 7.99 ***(978-1-4380-1099-1(0))*** Barron's Educational Series, Inc.

Peter Pauper Press, Inc., creator. Learn to Draw... Animals! Easy Step-By-Step Drawing Guide. 2014. (ENG., Illus.). 48p. (J). 5.99 *(978-1-4413-0270-0(0),* 9781441302700) Peter Pauper Pr. Inc.

—Learn to Draw... Christmas! Easy Step-By-Step Drawing Guide. 2014. (ENG., Illus.). 48p. (J). 5.99 *(978-1-4413-1275-4(7),* 9781441312754) Peter Pauper Pr. Inc.

—Learn to Draw... Dinosaurs! Easy Step-By-Step Drawing Guide. 2014. (ENG., Illus.). 48p. (J). 5.99 *(978-1-4413-1277-8(3),* 9781441312778) Peter Pauper Pr. Inc.

—Learn to Draw... Flower Garden! Easy Step-By-Step Drawing Guide. 2014. (ENG., Illus.). 48p. (J). 5.99 *(978-1-4413-0557-2(2),* 9781441305572) Peter Pauper Pr. Inc.

—Learn to Draw... Ocean Wonders! Easy Step-By-Step Drawing Guide. 2014. (ENG., Illus.). 48p. (J). 5.99 *(978-1-4413-1604-2(3),* 9781441316042) Peter Pauper Pr. Inc.

—Learn to Draw... Princess Kingdom! Easy Step-By-Step Drawing Guide. 2014. (ENG., Illus.). 48p. (J). 5.99 *(978-1-4413-0558-9(0),* 9781441305589) Peter Pauper Pr. Inc.

—Learn to Draw... Things That Go! Easy Step-By-Step Drawing Guide. 2014. (ENG., Illus.). 48p. (J). 5.99 *(978-1-4413-1602-8(7),* 9781441316028) Peter Pauper Pr. Inc.

Peter Pauper Press Staff, creator. Dragons & Mythical Creatures: An Art Activity Book. 2006. (Scratch & Sketch Ser.). (Illus.). 68p. (J). (gr. 4-7). 12.99 *(978-1-59359-937-9(4))* Peter Pauper Pr. Inc.

—Merry Christmas: An Art Activity Book. 2006. (Scratch & Sketch Ser.). (Illus.). 64p. (J). (gr. 4-7). 12.99 *(978-1-59359-943-0(9))* Peter Pauper Pr. Inc.

Peters, S. True. How to Draw South Dakota's Sights & Symbols. 2009. (Kid's Guide to Drawing America Ser.). 32p. (gr. k-k). 50.50 *(978-1-61511-095-7(X),* PowerKids Pr.) Rosen Publishing Group, Inc., The.

—How to Draw Vermont's Sights & Symbols. 2009. (Kid's Guide to Drawing America Ser.). 32p. (gr. k-k). 50.50 *(978-1-61511-101-5(8),* PowerKids Pr.) Rosen Publishing Group, Inc., The.

—How to Draw Wisconsin's Sights & Symbols. 2009. (Kid's Guide to Drawing America Ser.). 32p. (gr. k-k). 50.50 *(978-1-61511-105-3(0),* PowerKids Pr.) Rosen Publishing Group, Inc., The.

Peterson, Scott. Learn to Draw Plus Disney Phineas & Ferb. Guler, Greg & Ulene, Nancy, illus. 2012. (J). *(978-1-936309-71-9(8))* Quarto Publishing Group USA.

Phan, Sandy. Learn to Draw Ancient Times. Berry, Bob, illus. 2014. (Learn to Draw (Walter Foster Library) Ser.). (ENG.). 40p. (J). (gr. 4-7). lib. bdg. 29.27 *(978-1-939581-26-6(5))* Quarto Publishing Group USA.

—Learn to Draw Forest Animals & Wildlife: Learn to Draw 20 Different Woodland Animals, Step by Easy Step, Shape by Simple Shape! Cuddy, Robbin, illus. 2014. 40p. (J). *(978-1-939581-24-2(9))* Quarto Publishing Group USA.

—Learn to Draw Rainforest & Jungle Animals: Learn to Draw & Color 21 Different Exotic Creatures, Step by Easy Step, Shape by Simple Shape! Cuddy, Robbin, illus. 2014. 40p. (J). *(978-1-939581-25-9(7))* Quarto Publishing Group USA.

Pinder, Andrew. The Boys' Doodle Book. 2013. (ENG., Illus.). 160p. (J). (gr. -1-17). pap. 12.95 *(978-0-7624-5291-0(9),* Running Pr. Kids) Running Pr. Bk. Pubs.

—The Girls' Doodle Book. 2013. (ENG., Illus.). 160p. (J). (gr. -1-17). pap. 12.95 *(978-0-7624-5290-3(0),* Running Pr. Kids) Running Pr. Bk. Pubs.

—Journey Through Time Doodles. 2013. (ENG., Illus.). 128p. (J). (gr. -1-17). pap. 12.95 *(978-0-7624-5295-8(1),* Running Pr. Kids) Running Pr. Bk. Pubs.

Pirates. 2014. (Illus.). 32p. (J). *(978-1-62127-339-4(3));* pap. *(978-1-62127-343-1(1))* Weigl Pubs., Inc.

Plaut, Michael. How to Draw the Life & Times of Gerald R. Ford. 2009. (Kid's Guide to Drawing the Presidents of the United States of America Ser.). 32p. (gr. 4-4). 50.50 *(978-1-61511-141-1(7),* PowerKids Pr.) Rosen Publishing Group, Inc., The.

Plaut, Michael F. How to Draw the Life & Times of Gerald R. Ford. 2005. (Kid's Guide to Drawing the Presidents of the United States of America Ser.). (Illus.). 32p. (YA). (gr. 2-5). lib. bdg. 26.50 *(978-1-4042-3014-9(9))* Rosen Publishing Group, Inc., The.

Poitier, Anton. My Big Book of Stencil Drawing for Little Hands: Draw Through the Stencils with Crayons, Pencils or Felt Pens. 2014. (ENG.). 53p. (J). (gr. -1-2). pap. 7.99 *(978-1-4380-0438-9(9))* Barron's Educational Series, Inc.

Porter, Steve. Birds of Prey. 2014. (You Can Draw It! Ser.). (ENG., Illus.). 24p. (J). (gr. 3-8). lib. bdg. 25.95 *(978-1-62617-096-4(7),* Express Bks.) Bellwether Media.

—Fairies. 2014. (You Can Draw It! Ser.). (ENG., Illus.). 24p. (J). (gr. 3-8). lib. bdg. 25.95 *(978-1-62617-097-1(5),* Express Bks.) Bellwether Media.

—Mythical Beasts. 2014. (You Can Draw It! Ser.). (ENG., Illus.). 24p. (J). (gr. 3-8). lib. bdg. 25.95 *(978-1-62617-098-8(3),* Express Bks.) Bellwether Media.

—Sports Cars. 2014. (You Can Draw It! Ser.). (ENG., Illus.). 24p. (J). (gr. 3-8). lib. bdg. 25.95 *(978-1-62617-099-5(1),* Express Bks.) Bellwether Media.

Powell, Marc & Neal, David. How to Draw Fantasy Manga. 2015. (Ultimate Manga Ser.). (ENG., Illus.). 32p. (J). (gr. 3-4). pap. 11.75 *(978-1-4994-1142-3(1),* 1391134, PowerKids Pr.) Rosen Publishing Group, Inc., The.

—How to Draw Manga Adventure. 2015. (Ultimate Manga Ser.). (ENG., Illus.). 32p. (J). (gr. 3-4). pap. 11.75 *(978-1-4994-1144-7(8),* 1391135, PowerKids Pr.) Rosen Publishing Group, Inc., The.

—How to Draw Manga Mecha. 2015. (Ultimate Manga Ser.). (ENG., Illus.). 32p. (J). (gr. 3-4). pap. 11.75 *(978-1-4994-1145-4(6),* 1391136, PowerKids Pr.) Rosen Publishing Group, Inc., The.

Powell, Walter. How to Draw the Life & Times of Andrew Johnson. 2009. (Kid's Guide to Drawing the Presidents of the United States of America Ser.). 32p. (gr. 4-4). 50.50 *(978-1-61511-132-9(8),* PowerKids Pr.) Rosen Publishing Group, Inc., The.

Pratt, Laura. Famous Monsters. 2013. (J). *(978-1-62127-337-0(7));* pap. *(978-1-62127-341-7(5))* Weigl Pubs., Inc.

—Medieval Times. 2013. (Illus.). 32p. (J). *(978-1-62127-338-7(5))* Weigl Pubs., Inc.

Pratt, Leonie & Stowell, Louie. How to Draw Animals. Figg, Non, illus. 2006. (Usborne Activities Ser.). 32p. (J). (gr. 1-4). pap. 8.99 *(978-0-7945-1241-5(0),* Usborne) EDC Publishing.

Priddy, Roger. How to Draw: Includes Wipe-Clean Pen. 2016. (Early Learning Fun Ser.). (ENG.). 48p. (J). spiral bd. 9.99 *(978-0-312-51962-9(1),* 9780312519629, Priddy Bks.) St. Martin's Pr.

—How to Draw - Extended Version. 2016. (Early Learning Fun Ser.). (ENG.). 56p. (J). spiral bd. 12.99 *(978-0-312-52129-5(4),* 9780312521295, Priddy Bks.) St. Martin's Pr.

—My Super Duper Drawing. 2015. (ENG.). 308p. (J). (gr. -1-1). pap., act. bk. ed. 12.99 *(978-0-312-51819-6(6),* 9780312518196, Priddy Bks.) St. Martin's Pr.

Princess Doodle Book. 2016. (ENG., Illus.). 128p. (J). (gr. k-2). pap. 9.99 *(978-1-4052-7732-7(7))* Egmont Bks., Ltd. GBR. Dist: Independent Pubs. Group.

Publications International Ltd. Staff, ed. Sketch That! The Ultimate Scribble Book. 2015. 150p. (J). spiral bd. 10.99 *(978-1-4508-8890-5(9),* 1450888909) Publications International, Ltd.

Publishing, Arcturus. The Complete Guide to Drawing Comics. 2015. (ENG., Illus.). 128p. pap. 12.95 *(978-1-78404-512-8(8),* 25dacec2-20ea-471f-b501-c878db71bbac) Arcturus Publishing GBR. Dist: Bookmasters Distribution.

Quasha, J. How to Draw Alabama's Sights & Symbols. 2009. (Kid's Guide to Drawing America Ser.). 32p. (gr. k-k). 50.50 *(978-1-61511-043-8(7),* PowerKids Pr.) Rosen Publishing Group, Inc., The.

—How to Draw Alaska's Sights & Symbols. 2009. (Kid's Guide to Drawing America Ser.). 32p. (gr. k-k). 50.50 *(978-1-61511-044-5(5),* PowerKids Pr.) Rosen Publishing Group, Inc., The.

Quasha, Jennifer. How to Draw Arizona's Sights & Symbols. 2009. (Kid's Guide to Drawing America Ser.). 32p. (gr. k-k). 50.50 *(978-1-61511-045-2(3),* PowerKids Pr.) Rosen Publishing Group, Inc., The.

—How to Draw Arkansas's Sights & Symbols. 2009. (Kid's Guide to Drawing America Ser.). 32p. (gr. k-k). 50.50 *(978-1-61511-046-9(1),* PowerKids Pr.) Rosen Publishing Group, Inc., The.

—How to Draw California's Sights & Symbols. 2009. (Kid's Guide to Drawing America Ser.). 32p. (gr. k-k). 50.50 *(978-1-61511-047-6(X),* PowerKids Pr.) Rosen Publishing Group, Inc., The.

Radtke, Becky J. Draw It! Animals. 2013. (ENG.). 80p. (J). (gr. 3-8). pap. 3.99 *(978-0-486-49955-0(3))* Dover Pubns., Inc.

—Draw It! Princesses, Mermaids & Fairies. 2013. (ENG.). 80p. (J). (gr. 3-8). pap. 3.99 *(978-0-486-49957-4(X))* Dover Pubns., Inc.

—Draw It! Sea Life. 2013. (ENG.). 80p. (J). (gr. 3-8). pap. 3.99 *(978-0-486-49958-1(8))* Dover Pubns., Inc.

RainbowBrush, creator. RainbowBrush Alphabet. 2007. (Illus.). 48p. *(978-0-9734981-0-3(2))* RainbowBrush, LLC.

Randolph, Joanne. Let's Draw a Truck with Shapes/Vamos a dibujar un camión usando Figuras. 2009. (Let's Draw with Shapes / Vamos a dibujar con figuras Ser.). (SPA.). 24p. (gr. k-1). 42.50 *(978-1-61514-219-4(3),* Editorial Buenas Letras) Rosen Publishing Group, Inc., The.

—Let's Draw a Turtle with Half Circles. 2009. (Let's Draw with Shapes Ser.). 24p. (gr. k-k). 42.50 *(978-1-61514-213-2(4),* PowerKids Pr.) Rosen Publishing Group, Inc., The.

—Let's Draw a Turtle with Half Circles/ Vamos a dibujar una tortuga usando medios Círculos. 2009. (Let's Draw with Shapes / Vamos a dibujar con figuras Ser.). (SPA.). 24p. (gr. k-1). 42.50 *(978-1-61514-225-5(8),* Editorial Buenas Letras) Rosen Publishing Group, Inc., The.

Randolph, Ryan P. How to Draw the Life & Times of Andrew Johnson. 2006. (Kid's Guide to Drawing the Presidents of the United States of America Ser.). (YA). (gr. 2-5). 26.50 *(978-1-4042-2994-5(9))* Rosen Publishing Group, Inc., The.

—How to Draw the Life & Times of Dwight D. Eisenhower. 2007. (Kid's Guide to Drawing the Presidents of the United States of America Ser.). (Illus.). 32p. (YA). (gr. 2-5). 25.25 *(978-1-4042-3010-1(6))* Rosen Publishing Group, Inc., The.

—How to Draw the Life & Times of John Adams. (Kid's Guide to Drawing the Presidents of the United States of America Ser.). 2009. 32p. (gr. 4-4). 50.50 *(978-1-61511-150-3(6),* PowerKids Pr.) 2006. (YA). (gr. 2-5). 26.50 *(978-1-4042-2979-2(5))* Rosen Publishing Group, Inc., The.

—How to Draw the Life & Times of Millard Fillmore. (Kid's Guide to Drawing the Presidents of the United States of America Ser.). 2009. 32p. (gr. 4-4). 50.50 *(978-1-61511-156-5(5),* PowerKids Pr.) 2006. (YA). (gr. 2-5). 26.50 *(978-1-4042-2990-7(6))* Rosen Publishing Group, Inc., The.

—How to Draw the Life & Times of William Howard Taft. 2007. (Kid's Guide to Drawing the Presidents of the United States of America Ser.). (Illus.). 32p. (YA). (gr. 2-5). 26.50 *(978-1-4042-3003-3(3))* Rosen Publishing Group, Inc., The.

Razo, Rebecca J. The Monsters under My Bed. Fisher, Diana, illus. 2014. 24p. (J). (gr. k-2). 23.93 *(978-1-939581-37-2(0))* Quarto Publishing Group USA.

Ready, Set, Draw! 2014. (Ready, Set, Draw! Ser.). 32p. (J). (gr. 2-5). 159.60 *(978-1-4824-0938-3(0));* pap. 63.00 *(978-1-4824-1581-0(X))* Stevens, Gareth Publishing LLLP.

Rechlin, Ted. Superheroes! 2012. (Dover Doodle Bks.). (ENG., Illus.). 64p. (J). (gr. 2-5). pap. 5.99 *(978-0-486-48404-4(1))* Dover Pubns., Inc.

Regan, Lisa. Bugs. Roberts, Steve, illus. 2010. (Let's Draw Ser.). (ENG.). 32p. (J). (gr. 3-5). pap. 10.55 *(978-1-61533-268-7(5));* lib. bdg. 22.60 *(978-1-61533-265-6(0))* Windmill Bks.

—How to Draw Baby Animals. Roberts, Steve, illus. 2008. (How to Draw Ser.). 47p. (J). (gr. 4-7). *(978-1-84810-066-4(3))* Miles Kelly Publishing, Ltd.

—How to Draw Bugs. Roberts, Steve, illus. 2008. (How to Draw Ser.). 47p. (J). (gr. -1-3). *(978-1-84810-065-7(5))* Miles Kelly Publishing, Ltd.

—My Crazy Inventions Sketchbook. Rae, Andrew, illus. 2015. (ENG.). 128p. (J). (gr. 2-6). 15.95 *(978-1-78067-611-1(5))* King, Laurence Publishing GBR. Dist: Hachette Bk. Group.

Robins, Deri. Drawing & Sketching. 2006. (Art Smart Ser.). (ENG., Illus.). 32p. (J). (gr. 2-5). pap. 9.95 *(978-1-58728-543-1(6))* Cooper Square Publishing Llc.

—Drawing & Sketching. 2004. (QEB Learn Art Ser.). (Illus.). 32p. (J). lib. bdg. 18.95 *(978-1-59566-045-9(3))* QEB Publishing Inc.

Root Division. 642 Awesome Things to Draw: Young Artist's Edition. 2017. (ENG.). 304p. (J). (gr. 3-7). 16.95 ***(978-1-4521-5538-8(0))*** Chronicle Bks. LLC.

Rosen Publishing Staff. Drawing Is Awesome!, 1 vol. 2015. (Drawing Is Awesome! Ser.). (ENG.). 24p. (J). 220.00 *(978-1-4777-5455-9(5),* Windmill Bks.) Rosen Publishing Group, Inc., The.

Rosier, Maggie. Aliens. 2013. (You Can Draw It! Ser.). (ENG., Illus.). 24p. (J). (gr. 3-8). lib. bdg. 25.95 *(978-1-60014-898-9(0),* Express Bks.) Bellwether Media.

—Dinosaurs. 2013. (You Can Draw It! Ser.). (ENG., Illus.). 24p. (J). (gr. 3-8). lib. bdg. 25.95 *(978-1-60014-899-6(9),* Express Bks.) Bellwether Media.

—Robots. 2013. (You Can Draw It! Ser.). (ENG., Illus.). 24p. (J). (gr. 3-8). lib. bdg. 25.95 *(978-1-60014-900-9(6),* Express Bks.) Bellwether Media.

—Sharks. 2013. (You Can Draw It! Ser.). (ENG., Illus.). 24p. (J). (gr. 3-8). lib. bdg. 25.95 *(978-1-60014-901-6(4),* Express Bks.) Bellwether Media.

Rosinski, Carol. Getting Started: Discover Your Inner Artist as You Explore the Basic Theories & Techniques of Pencil Drawing. 2007. (Drawing Made Easy Ser.). (ENG., Illus.). 64p. pap. 9.95 *(978-1-56010-995-2(5),* 1560109955) Quarto Publishing Group USA.

Roytman, Arkady. How to Draw Sharks. 2015. (Dover Children's Activity Bks.). (ENG.). 64p. (J). (gr. 2-5). pap. 4.99 *(978-0-486-79963-6(8))* Dover Pubns., Inc.

Ruffin, Frances E. How to Draw the Life & Times of Theodore Roosevelt. (Kid's Guide to Drawing the Presidents of the United States of America Ser.). 32p. 2009. (gr. 4-4). 50.50 *(978-1-61511-160-2(3),* PowerKids Pr.) 2007. (Illus.). (YA). (gr. 2-5). 26.50 *(978-1-4042-3002-6(5))* Rosen Publishing Group, Inc., The.

Runyen, Elizabeth, illus. Watch Me Draw Disney's Mickey Mouse Clubhouse. 2012. 24p. (J). *(978-1-936309-74-0(2))* Quarto Publishing Group USA.

Russell, Harriet. Drawing in the Sea. 2015. (ENG., Illus.). 64p. (J). (gr. 1-3). pap. 18.95 *(978-1-61689-418-4(0))* Princeton Architectural Pr.

Ryan, Nellie. Beautiful Doodles. Ryan, Nellie, illus. 2013. (ENG., Illus.). 160p. (J). (gr. -1-17). pap. 12.95 *(978-0-7624-5289-7(7),* Running Pr. Kids) Running Pr. Bk. Pubs.

—Designer Doodles. 2014. (ENG., Illus.). 160p. (J). (gr. -1-17). pap. 12.95 *(978-0-7624-5315-3(X),* Running Pr. Kids) Running Pr. Bk. Pubs.

—Dream House Doodles. 2013. (ENG., Illus.). 160p. (J). (gr. -1-17). pap. 12.95 *(978-0-7624-5292-7(7),* Running Pr. Kids) Running Pr. Bk. Pubs.

Salvador, Ana & Quarto Generic Staff. Draw with Pablo Picasso. 2008. (ENG., Illus.). 48p. (J). (gr. 1-4). pap. 12.99 *(978-1-84507-819-5(5),* Frances Lincoln Children's Bks.) Quarto Publishing Group UK GBR. Dist: Hachette Bk. Group.

Santillan, Jorge & Eason, Sarah. Drawing Dinosaurs. 2013. (Learn to Draw Ser.). (ENG., Illus.). 32p. (J). (gr. 2-5). lib. bdg. 26.60 *(978-1-4339-9528-6(X))* Stevens, Gareth Publishing LLLP.

—Drawing Dragons. 2013. (Learn to Draw Ser.). (ENG., Illus.). 32p. (J). (gr. 2-5). lib. bdg. 26.60 *(978-1-4339-9532-3(8))* Stevens, Gareth Publishing LLLP.

—Drawing Fairies, Mermaids, & Unicorns. 2013. (Learn to Draw Ser.). (ENG., Illus.). 32p. (J). (gr. 2-5). lib. bdg. 26.60 *(978-1-4339-9536-1(0))* Stevens, Gareth Publishing LLLP.

—Drawing Knights & Castles. 2013. (Learn to Draw Ser.). (ENG., Illus.). 32p. (J). (gr. 2-5). lib. bdg. 26.60 *(978-1-4339-9540-8(9))* Stevens, Gareth Publishing LLLP.
—Drawing Pirates & Pirate Ships. 2013. (Learn to Draw Ser.). (ENG., Illus.). 32p. (J). (gr. 2-5). lib. bdg. 26.60 *(978-1-4339-9544-6(1))* Stevens, Gareth Publishing LLLP.
Santos, D. I Can Draw: Learning the DR Sound. 2009. (PowerPhonics Ser.). 24p. (gr. 1-1). 39.90 *(978-1-60851-446-5(3),* PowerKids Pr.) Rosen Publishing Group, Inc., The.
Sautter, A. J. Drawing Fantasy Creatures. 2016. (Drawing Fantasy Creatures Ser.). (ENG.). 32p. (gr. 3-4). 111.96 *(978-1-4914-8669-6(4),* Edge Bks.) Capstone Press of Coughlan Cos.
—How to Draw Dragons, Trolls, & Other Dangerous Monsters. McGrath, Tom et al, illus. 2016. (Drawing Fantasy Creatures Ser.). (ENG.). 32p. (gr. 3-4). lib. bdg. 27.99 *(978-1-4914-8023-6(8),* Edge Bks.) Capstone Press of Coughlan Cos.
—How to Draw Elves, Dwarves, & Other Magical Folk. Azzalin, Stefano et al, illus. 2016. (Drawing Fantasy Creatures Ser.). (ENG.). 32p. (gr. 3-4). lib. bdg. 27.99 *(978-1-4914-8027-4(0),* Edge Bks.) Capstone Press of Coughlan Cos.
—How to Draw Griffins, Unicorns, & Other Mythical Beasts. Howard, Colin et al, illus. 2016. (Drawing Fantasy Creatures Ser.). (ENG.). 32p. (gr. 3-4). lib. bdg. 27.99 *(978-1-4914-8025-0(4),* Edge Bks.) Capstone Press of Coughlan Cos.
—How to Draw Orcs, Goblins, & Other Wicked Creatures. Azzalin, Stefano et al, illus. 2016. (Drawing Fantasy Creatures Ser.). (ENG.). 32p. (gr. 3-4). lib. bdg. 27.99 *(978-1-4914-8024-3(6),* Edge Bks.) Capstone Press of Coughlan Cos.
Sautter, Aaron. Boys' Guide to Drawing: Aliens, Warriors, Robots & Other Cool Stuff. 2008. (Drawing Cool Stuff Ser.). (ENG., Illus.). 144p. (gr. 3-4). pap. 14.95 *(978-1-4296-2917-1(7),* Edge Bks.) Capstone Press of Coughlan Cos.
—Boys' Guide to Drawing [LTD Commodities]. 2011. (Drawing Cool Stuff Ser.). 144p. pap. 3.00 *(978-1-4296-6639-8(0),* Edge Bks.) Capstone Press of Coughlan Cos.
—Drawing DC Super Heroes. Doescher, Erik & Levins, Tim, illus. 2015. (Drawing DC Super Heroes Ser.). (ENG.). 32p. (gr. 3-6). lib. bdg. 111.96 *(978-1-4914-2553-4(9),* DC Super Heroes) Stone Arch Bks.
—How to Draw Amazing Motorcycles, 1 vol. Smith, Tod, illus. 2007. (Drawing Cool Stuff Ser.). (ENG.). 32p. (gr. 3-4). 27.99 *(978-1-4296-0073-6(X),* Edge Bks.) Capstone Press of Coughlan Cos.
—How to Draw Batman & His Friends & Foes. Doescher, Erik, illus. 2015. (Drawing DC Super Heroes Ser.). (ENG.). 32p. (gr. 3-6). lib. bdg. 27.99 *(978-1-4914-2153-6(3))* Capstone Press of Coughlan Cos.
—How to Draw Batman, Superman, & Other DC Super Heroes & Villains. Doescher, Erik & Levins, Tim, illus. 2015. (DC Super Heroes Ser.). (ENG.). 144p. (gr. 3-6). pap. 14.95 *(978-1-62370-231-1(3))* Capstone Press of Coughlan Cos.
—How to Draw Incredible Cars, 1 vol. Bascle, Brian, illus. 2007. (Drawing Cool Stuff Ser.). (ENG.). 32p. (gr. 3-4). 27.99 *(978-1-4296-0077-4(2),* Edge Bks.) Capstone Press of Coughlan Cos.
—How to Draw Indestructible Tanks, 1 vol. Whigham, Rod, illus. 2008. (Drawing Cool Stuff Ser.). (ENG.). 32p. (gr. 3-4). 27.99 *(978-1-4296-1301-9(7),* Edge Bks.) Capstone Press of Coughlan Cos.
—How to Draw Monster Trucks, 1 vol. Whigham, Rod, illus. 2007. (Drawing Cool Stuff Ser.). (ENG.). 32p. (gr. 3-4). 27.99 *(978-1-4296-0079-8(9),* Edge Bks.) Capstone Press of Coughlan Cos.
—How to Draw Superman & His Friends & Foes. Doescher, Erik, illus. 2015. (Drawing DC Super Heroes Ser.). (ENG.). 32p. (gr. 3-6). lib. bdg. 27.99 *(978-1-4914-2156-7(8))* Capstone Press of Coughlan Cos.
—How to Draw the Joker, Lex Luthor, & Other DC Super-Villains. Levins, Tim, illus. 2015. (Drawing DC Super Heroes Ser.). (ENG.). 32p. (gr. 3-6). lib. bdg. 27.99 *(978-1-4914-2155-0(X))* Capstone Press of Coughlan Cos.
—How to Draw Wonder Woman, Green Lantern, & Other DC Super Heroes. Levins, Tim, illus. 2015. (Drawing DC Super Heroes Ser.). (ENG.). 32p. (gr. 3-6). lib. bdg. 27.99 *(978-1-4914-2154-3(1))* Capstone Press of Coughlan Cos.
—The Young Artist's Guide to Drawing Fantasy Creatures. Bustamante, Martin et al, illus. 2016. (Drawing Fantasy Creatures Ser.). (ENG.). 112p. (gr. 3-4). pap. 9.95 *(978-1-4914-8670-2(8))* Capstone Young Readers of Coughlan Cos.
Schmidt, Roderic. How to Draw the Life & Times of Abraham Lincoln. (Kid's Guide to Drawing the Presidents of the United States of America Ser.). 2009. 32p. (gr. 4-4). 50.50 *(978-1-61511-130-5(1),* PowerKids Pr.) 2006. (YA). (gr. 2-5). 26.50 *(978-1-4042-2993-8(0))* Rosen Publishing Group, Inc., The.
—How to Draw the Life & Times of George W. Bush. (Kid's Guide to Drawing the Presidents of the United States of America Ser.). 32p. 2009. (gr. 4-4). 50.50 *(978-1-61511-139-8(5),* PowerKids Pr.) 2007. (Illus.). (YA). (gr. 2-5). 26.50 *(978-1-4042-3019-4(X))* Rosen Publishing Group, Inc., The.
—How to Draw the Life & Times of James Madison. 2009. (Kid's Guide to Drawing the Presidents of the United States of America Ser.). 32p. (gr. 4-4). 50.50 *(978-1-61511-148-0(4),* PowerKids Pr.) Rosen Publishing Group, Inc., The.
—How to Draw the Life & Times of Martin Van Buren. 2009. (Kid's Guide to Drawing the Presidents of the United States of America Ser.). 32p. (gr. 4-4). 50.50 *(978-1-61511-155-8(7),* PowerKids Pr.) Rosen Publishing Group, Inc., The.
—How to Draw the Life & Times of Zachary Taylor. 2009. (Kid's Guide to Drawing the Presidents of the United States of America Ser.). 32p. (gr. 4-4). 50.50 *(978-1-61511-169-5(7),* PowerKids Pr.) Rosen Publishing Group, Inc., The.
Scrace, Carolyn. Drawing Animals. 2016. (Art Works). 32p. (gr. 2-6). 31.35 *(978-1-62588-343-8(9),* Smart Apple Media) Black Rabbit Bks.
—Drawing Dinosaurs & Other Prehistoric Animals. 2016. (Art Works). 32p. (gr. 2-6). 31.35 *(978-1-62588-344-5(7),* Smart Apple Media) Black Rabbit Bks.
—Drawing Fairies & Mermaids. 2016. (Art Works). 32p. (gr. 2-6). 31.35 *(978-1-62588-345-2(5),* Smart Apple Media) Black Rabbit Bks.
—Drawing Things That Go. 2016. (Art Works). 32p. (gr. 2-6). 31.35 *(978-1-62588-348-3(X),* Smart Apple Media) Black Rabbit Bks.
—Portraits & Animals. 2015. (How to Art Doodle Ser.). (Illus.). 24p. (gr. 3-6). 28.50 *(978-1-909645-49-3(4))* Book Hse. GBR. Dist: Black Rabbit Bks.
—Simple Pattern Building Techniques. 2015. (How to Art Doodle Ser.). (Illus.). 24p. (gr. 3-6). 28.50 *(978-1-909645-50-9(8))* Book Hse. GBR. Dist: Black Rabbit Bks.
Sénac, Jean-Vincent. How to Draw a Chicken. 2013. (ENG., Illus.). 72p. (gr. 3-7). 10.95 *(978-1-84976-068-3(3))* Tate Publishing, Ltd. GBR. Dist: Abrams, Inc.
Sexton, Brenda. You Can Draw Fairies & Princesses, 1 vol. Sexton, Brenda, illus. 2011. (You Can Draw Ser.). (ENG., Illus.). 24p. (gr. 1-2). lib. bdg. 26.65 *(978-1-4048-6808-3(9))* Picture Window Bks.
—You Can Draw Pets, 1 vol. Sexton, Brenda, illus. 2010. (You Can Draw Ser.). (ENG., Illus.). 24p. (gr. 1-2). lib. bdg. 26.65 *(978-1-4048-6277-7(3))* Picture Window Bks.
Sexton, Brenda & Ho, Jannie. Easy-To-Draw Animals: A Step-By-Step Drawing Book. Sexton, Brenda & Ho, Jannie, illus. 2014. (You Can Draw Ser.). (ENG., Illus.). 64p. (gr. 1-2). pap. 6.95 *(978-1-4795-5511-6(8))* Picture Window Bks.
Shelly, Jeff, illus. Learn to Draw Cars & Trucks. 2012. (J). *(978-1-936309-49-8(1))* Quarto Publishing Group USA.
—Learn to Draw Dinosaurs. 2012. (J). *(978-1-936309-48-1(3))* Quarto Publishing Group USA.
Silvani, James. Draw-A-Saurus: Everything You Need to Know to Draw Your Favorite Dinosaurs. 2014. (ENG., Illus.). 160p. (gr. 2-5). pap. 18.99 *(978-0-385-34580-4(1),* Watson-Guptill) Potter/TenSpeed/Harmony.
Silver Dolphin en Español Editors. Serie Aprendizaje: Drawing with Fairies. 2006. (SPA., Illus.). 22p. (J). bds. 16.95 *(978-970-718-331-5(4))* Readerlink Distribution Services, LLC.
—Serie Aprendizaje: Let's Draw with Pixar. 2006. (SPA., Illus.). 22p. (J). bds. 16.95 *(978-970-718-320-9(9))* Readerlink Distribution Services, LLC.
Sims, Steve. Drawing Dungeon Creatures. 2010. (You Can Draw Fantasy Figures Ser.). (ENG., Illus.). 32p. (J). (gr. 3-6). pap. 10.50 *(978-1-4339-4059-0(0));* lib. bdg. 28.00 *(978-1-4339-4058-3(2))* Stevens, Gareth Publishing LLLP. (Gareth Stevens Learning Library).
—Drawing Heroic Warriors. 2010. (You Can Draw Fantasy Figures Ser.). (ENG., Illus.). 32p. (J). (gr. 3-6). pap. 10.50 *(978-1-4339-4053-8(1));* lib. bdg. 28.00 *(978-1-4339-4052-1(3))* Stevens, Gareth Publishing LLLP. (Gareth Stevens Learning Library).
Singh, Asavari. How to Draw the Fastest, Coolest Cars, 1 vol. James, Martin et al, illus. 2011. (Drawing Ser.). (ENG.). 48p. (gr. 3-4). lib. bdg. 31.99 *(978-1-4296-6596-4(3))* Capstone Press of Coughlan Cos.
Sketch It!, 12 vols. 2005. (Sketch It! Ser.). (ENG.). 24p. (gr. k-4). 79.95 *(978-1-4048-1518-6(X))* Picture Window Bks.
SmartLab, creator. Fashion Studio. 2011. (SmartLAB Ser.). (J). (gr. 2). 24.99 *(978-1-60380-127-0(8),* SmartLab) becker&mayer! books.
Smith, Andrea Helen. A Catholic How-to-Draw. 2006. (Illus.). 102p. (J). spiral bd. 14.95 *(978-0-9764691-3-1(8))* Little Way Pr.
Smith, Elwood. How to Draw with Your Funny Bone. Smith, Elwood, illus. 2015. (ENG., Illus.). 40p. (J). (gr. 1-3). 17.99 *(978-1-56846-243-1(3),* Creative Editions) Creative Co., The.
Smith, Lucy. How to Draw Horses. Chapman, Chris et al, illus. 2006. (Young Artist Ser.). 32p. (J). (gr. 4-7). pap. 5.99 *(978-0-7945-1368-9(9),* Usborne) EDC Publishing.
Snider, Brandon T. Draw It Out! Hundreds of Prompts to Inspire Creative Expression. 2016. (ENG.). 248p. (J). (gr. 3). pap. 14.95 *(978-1-4549-1934-6(5))* Sterling Publishing Co., Inc.
Soffer, Ruth. BOOST Arctic & Antarctic Life Coloring Book. 2013. (BOOST Educational Ser.). (ENG.). 48p. (J). (gr. 3-5). pap. 5.99 *(978-0-486-49430-2(6))* Dover Pubns., Inc.
Sokol, Dawn DeVries. Doodle Sketchbook: Art Journaling for Boys, 1 vol. 2011. (ENG., Illus.). 160p. pap. 12.99 *(978-1-4236-2046-4(1))* Gibbs Smith, Publisher.
Sonneman, Alan. Clouds & Skyscapes: Explore Techniques for Painting Splendid Skies. 2011. (How to Draw & Paint Ser.). (ENG., Illus.). 32p. pap. 8.95 *(978-1-60058-241-7(9),* 1600582419) Quarto Publishing Group USA.
Southgate, Anna & Sparrow, Keith. Drawing Manga Boys. 2011. (J). 84.30 *(978-1-4488-4807-2(5));* pap. 14.05 *(978-1-4488-4803-4(2));* lib. bdg. 33.25 *(978-1-4488-4799-0(0))* Rosen Publishing Group, Inc., The. (Rosen Reference).
Sovak, Jan. Deadly Insects & Arachnids. 2013. (Dover Nature Coloring Book Ser.). (ENG.). 32p. (J). (gr. 3-5). pap. 3.99 *(978-0-486-49054-0(8))* Dover Pubns., Inc.
Stegenga, Wil. Pinwheel Designs. 2007. (Dover Design Coloring Bks.). (ENG., Illus.). 32p. (gr. 3-5). pap. 3.99 *(978-0-486-46227-1(7))* Dover Pubns., Inc.
Step-By-Step Drawing Dinosaurs. 2017. (Step-By-Step Drawing Bks.). (ENG.). (J). pap. 9.99 ***(978-0-7945-3934-4(3),*** Usborne) EDC Publishing.
Stillinger, Doug. Spiral Draw. 2nd ed. 2012. (ENG.). 48p. (J). (gr. 3). 19.99 *(978-0-545-45992-1(3))* Klutz.
Sun, Jennie & Kraft, Ellen Christiansen. Doodle Design & Draw GIRL STYLE. 2013. (ENG.). 192p. (J). (gr. 6-8). pap. 9.99 *(978-0-486-49624-5(4))* Dover Pubns., Inc.
Tako, Rony & Seijas, Hugo. Doodlers Anonymous Epic Coloring Book: An Extraordinary Mashup of Doodles & Drawings Begging to Be Filled in with Color. 2015. (ENG.). 96p. pap. 15.95 *(978-1-58093-463-3(3))* Monacelli Pr., Inc.
Tallarico, Tony. Things That Go. 2011. (Dover How to Draw Ser.). (ENG., Illus.). 64p. (J). (gr. 3-8). pap. 4.99 *(978-0-486-48119-7(0))* Dover Pubns., Inc.
Tallarico, Tony, Sr. & Drawing Staff. Drawing & Cartooning Monsters: A Step-by-Step Guide for the Aspiring Monster-Maker. 2010. (Dover How to Draw Ser.). (ENG., Illus.). 96p. (J). (gr. 3-6). pap. 6.99 *(978-0-486-47278-2(7))* Dover Pubns., Inc.
Tallarico, Tony & Drawing Staff. Quick Draw Animals. 2011. (Dover How to Draw Ser.). (ENG., Illus.). 64p. (J). (gr. 3-8). pap. 4.99 *(978-0-486-48118-0(2))* Dover Pubns., Inc.
Tatchell, Judy. How to Draw Cartoons & Caricatures. Round, Graham et al, illus. 2007. 40p. (J). (gr. 4). lib. bdg. 13.99 *(978-1-58086-895-2(9),* Usborne) EDC Publishing.
Tatchell, Judy & Varley, Carol. How to Draw Lettering. Brown, Fiona, illus. 2006. (Young Artist Ser.). 32p. (J). (gr. 4-7). pap. 5.99 *(978-0-7945-1379-5(4),* Usborne) EDC Publishing.
Tecco, Betsy Dru. How to Draw Thailand's Sights & Symbols. 2009. (Kid's Guide to Drawing the Countries of the World Ser.). 48p. (gr. 4-4). 53.00 *(978-1-61511-127-5(1),* PowerKids Pr.) Rosen Publishing Group, Inc., The.
—How to Draw the Life & Times of Grover Cleveland. (Kid's Guide to Drawing the Presidents of the United States of America Ser.). 2009. 32p. (gr. 4-4). 50.50 *(978-1-61511-142-8(5),* PowerKids Pr.) 2006. (YA). (gr. 2-5). 26.50 *(978-1-4042-2999-0(X))* Rosen Publishing Group, Inc., The.
—How to Draw the Life & Times of John Quincy Adams. 2009. (Kid's Guide to Drawing the Presidents of the United States of America Ser.). 32p. (gr. 4-4). 50.50 *(978-1-61511-152-7(2),* PowerKids Pr.) Rosen Publishing Group, Inc., The.
—How to Draw the Life & Times of Ulysses S. Grant. 2009. (Kid's Guide to Drawing the Presidents of the United States of America Ser.). 32p. (gr. 4-4). 50.50 *(978-1-61511-162-6(X),* PowerKids Pr.) Rosen Publishing Group, Inc., The.
—How to Draw the United Kingdom's Sights & Symbols. 2009. (Kid's Guide to Drawing the Countries of the World Ser.). 48p. (gr. 4-4). 53.00 *(978-1-61511-129-9(8),* PowerKids Pr.) Rosen Publishing Group, Inc., The.
Temple, Kathryn. Art for Kids: Drawing: The Only Drawing Book You'll Ever Need to Be the Artist You've Always Wanted to Be. 2014. (Art for Kids Ser.). (ENG., Illus.). 112p. (J). (gr. 3-12). pap. 9.95 *(978-1-4027-8477-4(5))* Sterling Publishing Co., Inc.
Thomas, Isabel. Drawing, 1 vol. 2011. (Start with Art Ser.). (ENG.). 24p. (gr. k-2). 23.32 *(978-1-4329-5016-3(9),* Heinemann Read & Learn) Heinemann-Raintree.
Thomas Nelson. My Perfect Pug Doodle Pet. 2015. (ENG.). 98p. (J). (gr. -1-7). pap. *(978-1-78393-961-9(3))* Make Believe Ideas.
—Scratch & Sparkle Princess Stencil Art. 2016. (ENG.). 80p. (J). (gr. -1-3). *(978-1-78598-073-2(4))* Make Believe Ideas.
Todoro, Carlie. Let's Draw! 2003. (Real Readers - Upper Emergent Ser.). (ENG., Illus.). 12p. (gr. 1-2). pap. 5.90 *(978-0-8239-6359-1(4))* Rosen Publishing Group, Inc., The.
Toll, Damien. Drawing Is Awesome!, 1 vol. 2015. (Drawing Is Awesome! Ser.). (ENG.). 24p. (J). 94.00 *(978-1-4994-8032-0(6),* Windmill Bks.) Rosen Publishing Group, Inc., The.
Top That!, creator. How to Draw Manga Ninja Warriors. 2005. (Illus.). 48p. (J). (gr. 4-7). per. *(978-1-84510-971-4(6))* Top That! Publishing PLC.
Torres, Jickie. Learn to Draw Farm Animals: Step-by-Step Instructions for 21 Favorite Subjects, Including a Horse, Cow & Pig! Cuddy, Robbin, illus. 2011. (Learn to Draw Ser.). (ENG.). 40p. (J). (gr. 1-3). pap. 4.95 *(978-1-60058-213-4(3),* 1600582133) Quarto Publishing Group USA.
Tucker, Marianne & Gilbert, Elizabeth T., illus. Watch Me Draw Cinderella's Enchanted World. 2013. (Watch Me Draw Ser.). 24p. (J). (gr. -1-2). 25.65 *(978-1-936309-86-3(6))* Quarto Publishing Group USA.
Tucker, Marianne & Phillipson, Andy, illus. Learn to Draw Plus Disney Pixar Cars. 2012. *(978-1-936309-70-2(X))* Quarto Publishing Group USA.
Ultimate Manga. 2015. (Ultimate Manga Ser.). (ENG.). 32p. (J). (gr. 3-4). pap., pap., pap. 423.00 *(978-1-4994-1327-4(0),* PowerKids Pr.) Rosen Publishing Group, Inc., The.
Ursell, Martin. You Can Draw Horses. 2014. (You Can Draw Ser.). (ENG., Illus.). 32p. (J). (gr. 1-4). pap. 7.99 *(978-1-902915-21-0(6))* B Small Publishing GBR. Dist: Independent Pubs. Group.
—You Can Draw Monsters. 2014. (You Can Draw Ser.). (ENG., Illus.). 32p. (J). (gr. 1-4). pap. 7.99 *(978-1-902915-26-5(7))* B Small Publishing GBR. Dist: Independent Pubs. Group.
—You Can Draw Wild Animals. 2014. (You Can Draw Ser.). (ENG., Illus.). 32p. (J). (gr. 1-4). pap. 7.99 *(978-1-902915-97-5(6))* B Small Publishing GBR. Dist: Independent Pubs. Group.
Usborne Books Staff, creator. How to Draw Horses Kid Kit. rev. ed. 2006. (Kid Kits Ser.). (Illus.). 32p. (J). (gr. 4). pap. 13.99 *(978-1-58086-970-6(X))* EDC Publishing.
Various Experts, compiled by. Draw It! Learn to Draw from Real Life with This Exciting Step-By-Step Guide. 2012. (ENG., Illus.). 128p. (J). pap. 9.95 *(978-1-84858-132-6(7))* Arcturus Publishing GBR. Dist: Bookmasters Distribution.
ViiZ. Photo Doodles: 200 Photos for You to Complete. 2013. (ENG.). 160p. (J). (gr. 5). pap. 12.95 *(978-1-59474-652-9(4))* Quirk Bks.
Visca, Curt. How to Draw Cartoon Careers. 2009. (Kid's Guide to Drawing Ser.). 24p. (gr. 3-3). 47.90 *(978-1-61511-012-4(7),* PowerKids Pr.) Rosen Publishing Group, Inc., The.
—How to Draw Cartoon Holiday Symbols. 2009. (Kid's Guide to Drawing Ser.). 24p. (gr. 3-3). 47.90 *(978-1-61511-015-5(1),* PowerKids Pr.) Rosen Publishing Group, Inc., The.
—How to Draw Cartoon Spacecraft & Astronauts in Action. 2009. (Kid's Guide to Drawing Ser.). 24p. (gr. 3-3). 47.90 *(978-1-61511-019-3(4),* PowerKids Pr.) Rosen Publishing Group, Inc., The.
—How to Draw Cartoon Symbols of the United States. 2009. (Kid's Guide to Drawing Ser.). 24p. (gr. 3-3). 47.90 *(978-1-61511-020-9(8),* PowerKids Pr.) Rosen Publishing Group, Inc., The.
—How to Draw Cartoon Symbols of the Wild West. 2009. (Kid's Guide to Drawing Ser.). 24p. (gr. 3-3). 47.90 *(978-1-61511-021-6(6),* PowerKids Pr.) Rosen Publishing Group, Inc., The.
Visca, Kelly. How to Draw Cartoon Birds. 2009. (Kid's Guide to Drawing Ser.). 24p. (gr. 3-3). 47.90 *(978-1-61511-011-7(9),* PowerKids Pr.) Rosen Publishing Group, Inc., The.
—How to Draw Cartoon Rodents. 2009. (Kid's Guide to Drawing Ser.). 24p. (gr. 3-3). 47.90 *(978-1-61511-018-6(6),* PowerKids Pr.) Rosen Publishing Group, Inc., The.
Wacholtz, Anthony. Drawing with Sports Illustrated Kids, 1 vol. Haya, Erwin & Ray, Mike, illus. 2013. (Drawing with Sports Illustrated Kids Ser.). (ENG.). 144p. (gr. 5-7). pap. 14.95 *(978-1-4765-3581-4(7))* Capstone Press of Coughlan Cos.
—Drawing with Sports Illustrated Kids. Ray, Mike & Haya, Erwin, illus. 2013. (Drawing with Sports Illustrated Kids Ser.). (ENG.). 64p. (gr. 5-7). 135.96 *(978-1-4765-3741-2(0))* Capstone Press of Coughlan Cos.
—Picture a Home Run: A Baseball Drawing Book, 1 vol. Haya, Erwin, illus. 2013. (Drawing with Sports Illustrated Kids Ser.). (ENG.). 64p. (gr. 5-7). 33.99 *(978-1-4765-3106-9(4))* Capstone Press of Coughlan Cos.
—Picture a Slam Dunk: A Basketball Drawing Book, 1 vol. Haya, Erwin, illus. 2013. (Drawing with Sports Illustrated Kids Ser.). (ENG.). 64p. (gr. 5-7). 33.99 *(978-1-4765-3107-6(2))* Capstone Press of Coughlan Cos.
—Picture a Slap Shot: A Hockey Drawing Book, 1 vol. Ray, Mike, illus. 2013. (Drawing with Sports Illustrated Kids Ser.). (ENG.). 64p. (gr. 5-7). 33.99 *(978-1-4765-3105-2(6))* Capstone Press of Coughlan Cos.
—Picture a Touchdown: A Football Drawing Book, 1 vol. Ray, Mike, illus. 2013. (Drawing with Sports Illustrated Kids Ser.). (ENG.). 64p. (gr. 5-7). 33.99 *(978-1-4765-3104-5(8))* Capstone Press of Coughlan Cos.
Wainwright, Jen, ed. Winter Wonderland Doodles: Festive Full-Color Pictures to Complete & Create. 2012. (ENG., Illus.). 128p. (J). (gr. -1-17). pap. 12.95 *(978-0-7624-4675-9(7),* Running Pr. Kids) Running Pr. Bk. Pubs.
Walter Foster (Firm) Staff, contrib. by. Learn to Draw Walt Disney's Mickey Mouse. 2010. (Learn to Draw Favorite Characters Ser.). (Illus.). 32p. (J). (gr. k-3). 28.50 *(978-1-936309-02-3(5))* Quarto Publishing Group USA.
Walter Foster Creative Team. Animals: Step-by-Step Instructions for 26 Captivating Creatures. Fisher, Diana, illus. 2011. (Learn to Draw Ser.). 32p. (J). (gr. 1-4). 28.50 *(978-1-936309-20-7(3))* Quarto Publishing Group USA.
—Dogs & Puppies: Step-by-Step Insructions for 25 Different Breeds. Fisher, Diana, illus. 2011. (Learn to Draw Ser.). 32p. (J). (gr. 1-4). 28.50 *(978-1-936309-18-4(1))* Quarto Publishing Group USA.
—Frozen: Featuring Anna, Elsa, Olaf, & All Your Favorite Characters! 2015. (Learn to Draw Favorite Characters: Expanded Edition Ser.). (ENG., Illus.). 64p. (J). (gr. k-5). 33.32 *(978-1-939581-64-8(8))* Quarto Publishing Group USA.
—Learn to Draw Angry Birds Space: Learn to Draw All Your Favorite Angry Birds & Those Bad Piggies-In Space! 2013. (Licensed Learn to Draw Ser.). (ENG., Illus.). 64p. (J). (gr. 1-5). pap. 9.95 *(978-1-60058-368-1(7),* 1600583687) Quarto Publishing Group USA.
—Learn to Draw Archie & Friends: Featuring Betty, Veronica, Sabrina the Teenage Witch, Josie & the Pussycats, & More! 2015. (Licensed Learn to Draw Ser.). (ENG., Illus.). 128p. pap. 19.95 *(978-1-60058-391-9(1))* Quarto Publishing Group USA.
—Learn to Draw Birds & Butterflies: Step-By-Step Instructions for More Than 25 Winged Creatures. Cuddy, Robbin, illus. 2016. (Learn to Draw: Expanded Edition Ser.). (ENG.). 64p. (J). (gr. 3-5). 33.32 *(978-1-939581-96-9(6),* Walter Foster Jr) Quarto Publishing Group USA.
—Learn to Draw Cars, Planes & Moving Machines: Step-By-Step Instructions for More Than 25 High-Powered Vehicles. LaPadula, Tom & Shelly, Jeff, illus. 2015. (Learn to Draw: Expanded Edition Ser.). (ENG.). 64p. (J). (gr. 3-5). 33.32 *(978-1-939581-69-3(9))* Quarto Publishing Group USA.
—Learn to Draw Cats & Kittens: Step-By-Step Instructions for More Than 25 Favorite Feline Friends. Cuddy, Robbin, illus. 2015. (Learn to Draw: Expanded Edition Ser.). (ENG.). 64p. (J). (gr. 3-5). 33.32 *(978-1-939581-66-2(4))* Quarto Publishing Group USA.
—Learn to Draw Dinosaurs: Step-By-Step Instructions for More Than 25 Prehistoric Creatures. Cuddy, Robbin, illus. 2015. (Learn to Draw: Expanded Edition Ser.). (ENG.). 64p. (J). (gr. 3-5). 33.32 *(978-1-939581-70-9(2))* Quarto Publishing Group USA.
—Learn to Draw Disney Minnie & Daisy Best Friends Forever Fabulous Fashions. Disney Storybook Artists Staff, illus. 2014. 64p. (J). (gr. 3-5). 33.27 *(978-1-939581-32-7(X))* Quarto Publishing Group USA.
—Learn to Draw Exotic Animals: Step-By-Step Instructions for More Than 25 Unusual Animals. Cuddy, Robbin, illus. 2016. (Learn to Draw: Expanded Edition Ser.). (ENG.). 64p. (J). (gr. 3-5). 33.32 *(978-1-939581-97-6(4),* Walter Foster Jr) Quarto Publishing Group USA.
—Learn to Draw Forest Animals: Step-By-Step Instructions for More Than 25 Woodland Creatures. Cuddy, Robbin, illus. 2015. (Learn to Draw: Expanded Edition Ser.). (ENG.). 64p. (J). (gr. 3-5). 33.32 *(978-1-939581-68-6(0))* Quarto Publishing Group USA.
—Learn to Draw Horses & Ponies: Step-By-Step Instructions for More Than 25 Different Breeds. Cuddy, Robbin, illus. 2015. (Learn to Draw: Expanded Edition Ser.). (ENG.). 64p. (J). (gr. k-5). 33.32 *(978-1-939581-65-5(6))* Quarto Publishing Group USA.
—Learn to Draw Military Machines: Step-By-Step Instructions for More Than 25 High-Powered Vehicles. Walter Foster Creative Team, illus. 2016. (Learn to Draw: Expanded Edition Ser.). (ENG., Illus.). 64p. (J). (gr. 3-5). lib. bdg. 33.32 *(978-1-939581-98-3(2),* Walter Foster Jr) Quarto Publishing Group USA.
—Learn to Draw Safari Animals: Step-By-Step Instructions for More Than 25 Exotic Animals. Cuddy, Robbin, illus. 2015. (Learn to Draw: Expanded Edition Ser.). (ENG.). 64p. (J). (gr. 3-5). 33.32 *(978-1-939581-67-9(2))* Quarto Publishing Group USA.
—Learn to Draw Zoo Animals: Step-By-Step Instructions for More Than 25 Popular Animals. Cuddy, Robbin, illus. 2016. (Learn to Draw: Expanded Edition Ser.). (ENG.). 64p. (J). (gr.

3-5). lib. bdg. 33.32 *(978-1-939581-99-0(0)*, Walter Foster Jr) Quarto Publishing Group USA.
—Madagascar. 2015. (Learn to Draw Favorite Characters: Expanded Edition Ser.). (ENG., Illus.). 64p. (J). (gr. k-5). 33.32 *(978-1-939581-62-4(1))* Quarto Publishing Group USA.
—My Big, Crazy Drawing & Doodle Book: An Interactive Adventure with More Than 100 Creative Ideas for Tons of Doodling Fun. 2015. (ENG., Illus.). 128p. (J). (gr. 1-3). pap. 14.95 *(978-1-60058-475-6(6))* Quarto Publishing Group USA.
—Palace Pets: Featuring Pumpkin, Beauty, Treasure, Blondie & All of Your Favorite Princesses' Pets! 2015. (Learn to Draw Favorite Characters: Expanded Edition Ser.). (ENG., Illus.). 64p. (J). (gr. k-5). 33.32 *(978-1-939581-63-1(X))* Quarto Publishing Group USA.
—Pets: Step-by-Step Insructions for 23 Favorite Animals. Mueller, Peter, illus. 2011. (Learn to Draw Ser.). 32p. (J). (gr. 1-4). 28.50 *(978-1-936309-17-7(3))* Quarto Publishing Group USA.
—Sea Creatures: Step-by-Step Insructions for 25 Ocean Animals. Farrell, Russell, illus. 2011. (Learn to Draw Ser.). 32p. (J). (gr. 1-4). 28.50 *(978-1-936309-19-1(X))* Quarto Publishing Group USA.
Walter Foster Creative Team, creator. Learn to Draw Angry Birds. 2014. (Learn to Draw (Walter Foster Library) Ser.). (ENG., Illus.). 64p. (J). (gr. 4-7). lib. bdg. 33.27 *(978-1-939581-20-4(6))* Quarto Publishing Group USA.
—Learn to Draw Disney/Pixar's Toy Story. 2014. (ENG., Illus.). 64p. (J). (gr. 4-7). lib. bdg. 33.27 *(978-1-939581-12-9(5))* Quarto Publishing Group USA.
—Learn to Draw Disney's Enchanted Princesses. 2014. (Learn to Draw (Walter Foster Library) Ser.). (ENG., Illus.). 64p. (J). (gr. 4-7). lib. bdg. 33.27 *(978-1-939581-14-3(1))* Quarto Publishing Group USA.
—Learn to Draw Disney's Favorite Fairies. 2014. (Learn to Draw (Walter Foster Library) Ser.). (ENG., Illus.). 64p. (J). (gr. 4-7). lib. bdg. 33.27 *(978-1-939581-13-6(3))* Quarto Publishing Group USA.
—Learn to Draw Mickey & His Friends. 2014. (Learn to Draw (Walter Foster Library) Ser.). (ENG., Illus.). 64p. (J). (gr. 4-7). lib. bdg. 33.27 *(978-1-939581-15-0(X))* Quarto Publishing Group USA.
—Learn to Draw Phineas & Ferb. 2014. (Learn to Draw (Walter Foster Library) Ser.). (ENG., Illus.). 64p. (J). (gr. 4-7). lib. bdg. 33.27 *(978-1-939581-11-2(7))* Quarto Publishing Group USA.
—Learn to Draw the Best of Nickelodeon Collection. 2014. (Learn to Draw (Walter Foster Library) Ser.). (ENG., Illus.). 64p. (J). (gr. 4-7). lib. bdg. 33.27 *(978-1-939581-19-8(2))* Quarto Publishing Group USA.
—Learn to Draw Winnie the Pooh. 2014. (Learn to Draw (Walter Foster Library) Ser.). (ENG., Illus.). 64p. (J). (gr. 4-7). lib. bdg. 33.27 *(978-1-939581-16-7(8))* Quarto Publishing Group USA.
Walter Foster Creative Team, ed. All about Drawing Horses & Pets. 2008. (All about Drawing Ser.). (ENG., Illus.). 80p. (J). (gr. 1-3). pap. 9.95 *(978-1-60058-580-7(9)*, 1600585809) Quarto Publishing Group USA.
—How to Draw Transformers. 2008. 32p. pap. 5.95 *(978-1-60058-119-9(6))* Quarto Publishing Group USA.
Walter Foster Creative Team & Garbot, Dave. The Big Book of Cartooning: An Adventurous Journey into the Crazy, Zany World of Cartooning! 2016. (Big Book Ser.). (ENG., Illus.). 128p. (J). (gr. k-3). pap. 14.95 *(978-1-63322-177-2(6)*, Walter Foster Jr) Quarto Publishing Group USA.
Walter Foster Creative Team & Legendre, Philippe. Animals Around the World: Learn to Draw More Than 25 Exotic Animals Step by Step! 2014. (I Can Draw Ser.). (ENG., Illus.). 48p. (J). (gr. -1-3). pap. 6.95 *(978-1-60058-438-1(1))* Quarto Publishing Group USA.
—Dinosaurs, Dragons & Prehistoric Creatures: Learn to Draw More Than 25 Reptilian Beasts & Fantasy Characters Step by Step! 2014. (I Can Draw Ser.). (ENG., Illus.). 48p. (J). (gr. -1-3). pap. 6.95 *(978-1-60058-442-8(X))* Quarto Publishing Group USA.
—Planes, Trains & Moving Machines: Learn to Draw More Than 25 Flying, Locomotive, & Heavy-Duty Machines Step by Step! 2014. (I Can Draw Ser.). (ENG., Illus.). 48p. (J). (gr. -1-3). pap. 6.95 *(978-1-60058-440-4(3))* Quarto Publishing Group USA.
Walter Foster Creative Team Staff & Legendre, Philippe. Favorite Pets: Learn to Draw More Than 25 Furry Friends & Cute Companions Step by Step. 2014. (I Can Draw Ser.). (ENG., Illus.). 48p. (J). (gr. -1-3). pap. 6.95 *(978-1-60058-437-4(3))* Quarto Publishing Group USA.
—Princesses, Fairies & Fairy Tales: Learn to Draw More Than 25 Pretty Princesses & Fairy Tale Characters Step by Step! 2014. (I Can Draw Ser.). (ENG., Illus.). 48p. (J). (gr. -1-3). pap. 6.95 *(978-1-60058-441-1(1))* Quarto Publishing Group USA.
—Sea Creatures & Other Favorite Animals: Learn to Draw More Than 25 Land & Sea Animals Step by Step! 2014. (I Can Draw Ser.). (ENG., Illus.). 48p. (J). (gr. -1-3). pap. 6.95 *(978-1-60058-439-8(X))* Quarto Publishing Group USA.
Walter Foster Jr. Creative Team. 150 Fun Holiday Things to Doodle: An Interactive Adventure in Drawing Holiday Fun! 2015. (ENG.). 128p. (J). (gr. 1-3). pap. 14.95 *(978-1-63322-034-8(6)*, Walter Foster Jr) Quarto Publishing Group USA.
Walter Foster Jr. Creative Team & DreamWorks Animation Creative Team. Madagascar: Featuring the Penguins of Madagascar & Other Favorite Characters! 2015. (Licensed Learn to Draw Ser.). (ENG.). 64p. (J). (gr. 1-3). pap. 9.95 *(978-1-63322-032-4(X)*, Walter Foster Jr) Quarto Publishing Group USA.
Walter Foster Publishing & Berry, Bob. Watch Me Draw Robots. Torres, Jickie, illus. 2014. (ENG.). 24p. (J). (gr. k-2). lib. bdg. 23.93 *(978-1-939581-38-9(9))* Quarto Publishing Group USA.
Watt, Fiona. Christmas Things to Draw. 2011. (Activity Bks). (J). pap. 9.99 *(978-0-7945-2952-9(6)*, Usborne) EDC Publishing.
—Complete Book of Art Ideas. rev. ed. 2011. (Art Ser.). 288p. (J). pap. 19.99 *(978-0-7945-2642-9(X)*, Usborne) EDC Publishing.
—365 Things to Draw & Paint. 2011. (Activity Books Ser.). 128p. (J). pap. 24.99 *(978-0-7945-2707-5(8)*, Usborne) EDC Publishing.
Watt, Fiona, et al. Big Book of Things to Draw. Figg, Non et al, illus. Allman, Howard, photos by. 2007. (Art Ideas Drawing School Ser.). 96p. (J). (gr. 4-7). pap. 15.99 *(978-0-7945-1328-3(X)*, Usborne) EDC Publishing.
Webster, Christine. How to Draw Christmas Symbols. 2009. (Kid's Guide to Drawing Ser.). 24p. (gr. 3-3). 47.90 *(978-1-61511-026-1(7)*, PowerKids Pr.) Rosen Publishing Group, Inc., The.
—How to Draw Passover Symbols. 2009. (Kid's Guide to Drawing Ser.). 24p. (gr. 3-3). 47.90 *(978-1-61511-039-1(9)*, PowerKids Pr.) Rosen Publishing Group, Inc., The.
—How to Draw Thanksgiving Symbols. 2009. (Kid's Guide to Drawing Ser.). 24p. (gr. 3-3). 47.90 *(978-1-61511-041-4(0)*, PowerKids Pr.) Rosen Publishing Group, Inc., The.
Weintraub, A. How to Draw Rhode Island's Sights & Symbols. 2009. (Kid's Guide to Drawing America Ser.). 32p. (gr. k-k). 50.50 *(978-1-61511-093-3(3)*, PowerKids Pr.) Rosen Publishing Group, Inc., The.
—How to Draw South Carolina's Sights & Symbols. 2009. (Kid's Guide to Drawing America Ser.). 32p. (gr. k-k). 50.50 *(978-1-61511-094-0(1)*, PowerKids Pr.) Rosen Publishing Group, Inc., The.
—How to Draw Texas's Sights & Symbols. 2009. (Kid's Guide to Drawing America Ser.). 32p. (gr. k-k). 50.50 *(978-1-61511-097-1(6)*, PowerKids Pr.) Rosen Publishing Group, Inc., The.
—How to Draw Washington's Sights & Symbols. 2009. (Kid's Guide to Drawing America Ser.). 32p. (gr. k-k). 50.50 *(978-1-61511-103-9(4)*, PowerKids Pr.) Rosen Publishing Group, Inc., The.
Whelon, Chuck. What to Doodle? Adventure Stories! Pirates, Robots & More. 2013. (Dover Doodle Bks.). (ENG.). 64p. (J). (gr. 2-5). pap. 5.99 *(978-0-486-48991-9(4))* Dover Pubns., Inc.
—What to Doodle? Fantastic Fantasy! 2009. (Dover Doodle Bks.). (ENG., Illus.). 64p. (J). (gr. 2-5). pap. 5.99 *(978-0-486-47044-3(X))* Dover Pubns., Inc.
—What to Doodle? in the Garden! 2012. (Dover Doodle Bks.). (ENG., Illus.). 64p. (J). (gr. 2-5). pap. 5.99 *(978-0-486-48529-4(3))* Dover Pubns., Inc.
—What to Doodle? Things That Go! 2009. (Dover Doodle Bks.). (ENG., Illus.). 64p. (J). (gr. -1-2). pap. 5.99 *(978-0-486-47045-0(8))* Dover Pubns., Inc.
Williams, Anthony. Creating Superhero Comics, 1 vol. 2015. (Creating Comics Ser.). (ENG.). 32p. (J). 27.50 *(978-1-4777-5934-9(4)*, PowerKids Pr.) Rosen Publishing Group, Inc., The.
Wilson, Natashya. How to Draw the Life & Times of Herbert Hoover. (Kid's Guide to Drawing the Presidents of the United States of America Ser.). 32p. 2009. (gr. 4-4). 50.50 *(978-1-61511-144-2(1)*, PowerKids Pr.) 2007. (Illus.). (YA). (gr. 2-5). 26.50 *(978-1-4042-3007-1(6))* Rosen Publishing Group, Inc., The.
—How to Draw the Life & Times of William Howard Taft. 2009. (Kid's Guide to Drawing the Presidents of the United States of America Ser.). 32p. (gr. 4-4). 50.50 *(978-1-61511-165-7(4)*, PowerKids Pr.) Rosen Publishing Group, Inc., The.
Wilson, Natashya & Natashya, Wilson. How to Draw the Life & Times of James Earl Carter Jr. 2007. (Kid's Guide to Drawing the Presidents of the United States of America Ser.). (Illus.). 32p. (YA). (gr. 2-5). 26.50 *(978-1-4042-3015-6(7))* Rosen Publishing Group, Inc., The.
Winkler, Beate. Zentangle for Kids: 101 Favorite Patterns. 2016. (ENG., Illus.). 80p. (J). (gr. 1-7). pap. 15.99 *(978-1-63159-258-4(0)*, Quarry Bks.) Quarto Publishing Group USA.
Winterberg, Jenna. Dinosaurs. Fisher, Diana & Cerato, Mattia, illus. 2006. (Watch Me Draw Ser.). (ENG.). 24p. (J). (gr. -1-3). pap. 4.95 *(978-1-56010-951-8(3)*, 1560109513) Quarto Publishing Group USA.
—Dolphins, Whales, Fish & More. Fisher, Diana, illus. 2006. (Watch Me Draw Ser.). (ENG.). 24p. (J). (gr. -1-3). pap. 4.95 *(978-1-56010-949-5(1)*, 1560109491) Quarto Publishing Group USA.
—Dolphins, Whales, Fish & More. Fisher, Diana, illus. 2015. (J). *(978-1-939581-34-1(6))* Quarto Publishing Group USA.
—Things Girls Love. Fisher, Diana, illus. 2006. (Watch Me Draw Ser.). (ENG.). 24p. (J). (gr. -1-3). pap. 4.95 *(978-1-56010-950-1(5)*, 1560109505, Walter Foster Jr) Quarto Publishing Group USA.
Winterberg, Jenna, et al. Favorite Pets: A Step-By-step Drawing & Story Book for Preschoolers. Fisher, Diana, illus. 2006. (Watch Me Draw Ser.). (ENG.). 24p. (J). (gr. -1-3). pap. 4.95 *(978-1-56010-948-8(3)*, 1560109483) Quarto Publishing Group USA.
Wood, Anita. Fairy Doodles, 1 vol. Kalis, Jennifer, illus. 2014. (ENG.). 240p. (J). pap. 9.99 *(978-1-4236-3606-9(6))* Gibbs Smith, Publisher.
Young, Rae. Drawing Appaloosas & Other Handsome Horses, 1 vol. Q2AMedia Services Private Ltd, Q2AMedia Services, illus. 2014. (Drawing Horses Ser.). (ENG.). 32p. (gr. 3-4). lib. bdg. 27.99 *(978-1-4765-4001-6(2)*, Snap Bks.) Capstone Press of Coughlan Cos.
—Drawing Arabians & Other Amazing Horses, 1 vol. Q2AMedia Services Private Ltd, Q2AMedia Services, illus. 2014. (Drawing Horses Ser.). (ENG.). 32p. (gr. 3-4). lib. bdg. 27.99 *(978-1-4765-3995-9(2)*, Snap Bks.) Capstone Press of Coughlan Cos.
—Drawing Friesians & Other Beautiful Horses, 1 vol. Q2AMedia Services Private Ltd, Q2AMedia Services, illus. 2014. (Drawing Horses Ser.). (ENG.). 32p. (gr. 3-4). lib. bdg. 27.99 *(978-1-4765-3996-6(0)*, Snap Bks.) Capstone Press of Coughlan Cos.
—Drawing Horses, 1 vol. Q2AMedia Services Private Ltd, Q2AMedia Services, illus. 2014. (Drawing Horses Ser.). (ENG.). 32p. (gr. 3-4). lib. bdg. 167.94 *(978-1-4765-4667-4(3)*, Snap Bks.) Capstone Press of Coughlan Cos.
—Drawing Mustangs & Other Wild Horses, 1 vol. Q2AMedia Services Private Ltd, Q2AMedia Services, illus. 2014. (Drawing Horses Ser.). (ENG.). 32p. (gr. 3-4). lib. bdg. 27.99 *(978-1-4765-4002-3(0)*, Snap Bks.) Capstone Press of Coughlan Cos.
—Drawing Thoroughbreds & Other Elegant Horses, 1 vol. Q2AMedia Services Private Ltd, Q2AMedia Services, illus. 2014. (Drawing Horses Ser.). (ENG.). 32p. (gr. 3-4). lib. bdg. 27.99 *(978-1-4765-3993-5(6)*, Snap Bks.) Capstone Press of Coughlan Cos.
—The Ultimate Guide to Drawing Horses, 1 vol. Q2AMedia Services Private Ltd Staff, illus. 2013. (Drawing Horses Ser.). (ENG.). 144p. (gr. 3-4). pap. 14.95 *(978-1-4765-3992-8(8)*, Snap Bks.) Capstone Press of Coughlan Cos.
Zalme, Ron. How to Draw Johto Heroes. 2010. (Pokemon Ser.). (ENG.). 32p. (J). (gr. 2-5). pap. 4.99 *(978-0-545-24826-6(4))* Scholastic, Inc.
Zalme, Ron, illus. How to Draw Sinnoh Superstars. 2010. 32p. (J). pap. *(978-0-545-22625-7(2))* Scholastic, Inc.
—Pokémon: How to Draw Unova Heroes. 2011. 31p. (J). pap. *(978-0-545-35086-0(7))* Scholastic, Inc.
Zamora, Dulce. How to Draw the Life & Times of Franklin Pierce. 2009. (Kid's Guide to Drawing the Presidents of the United States of America Ser.). 32p. (gr. 4-4). 50.50 *(978-1-61511-137-4(9)*, PowerKids Pr.) Rosen Publishing Group, Inc., The.
—How to Draw the Life & Times of John F. Kennedy. 2005. (Kid's Guide to Drawing the Presidents of the United States of America Ser.). (Illus.). 32p. (YA). (gr. 2-5). lib. bdg. 25.25 *(978-1-4042-3011-8(4))* Rosen Publishing Group, Inc., The.
—How to Draw the Life & Times of John Fitzgerald Kennedy. 2009. (Kid's Guide to Drawing the Presidents of the United States of America Ser.). 32p. (gr. 4-4). 50.50 *(978-1-61511-151-0(4)*, PowerKids Pr.) Rosen Publishing Group, Inc., The.
—How to Draw the Life & Times of John Tyler. 2009. (Kid's Guide to Drawing the Presidents of the United States of America Ser.). 32p. (gr. 4-4). 50.50 *(978-1-61511-153-4(0)*, PowerKids Pr.) Rosen Publishing Group, Inc., The.

DRAWING, ARCHITECTURAL

see Architectural Drawing

DRAWING MATERIALS

see Artists' Materials

DRAWINGS

see Drawing

DREAMS

see also Nightmares

Apel, Melanie Ann. Let's Talk about Nightmares. 2009. (Let's Talk Library). 24p. (gr. 2-3). 42.50 *(978-1-60853-446-3(4)*, PowerKids Pr.) Rosen Publishing Group, Inc., The.
Blum, Renon. Explore Your Dream. 2003. (Musicals for Young Audiences Ser.). 55p. (Orig.). (YA). (gr. k-12). pap. 8.00 *(978-0-88734-528-9(X))* Players Pr., Inc.
Boritzer, Etan. What Is Dreaming? Vernon, Jeff, illus. 2007. 40p. (J). (gr. -1-3). 14.95 *(978-0-9762743-7-7(X))*; pap. 6.95 *(978-0-9762743-6-0(1))* Lane, Veronica Bks.
Collier-Thompson, Kristi. The Girls' Guide to Dreams. Turchyn, Sandie, illus. 2006. 128p. (YA). (gr. 8-11). reprint ed. pap. 13.00 *(978-0-7567-9899-4(X))* DIANE Publishing Co.
Crispin, Gerald W. God Speaks Through Dreams: But Who's Listening?, No. 1. Crispin, Gerald W. & Crispin, Vera G., eds. unabr. ed. 2003. (Illus.). 160p. (gr. 10-18). reprint ed. pap. 19.95 *(978-0-9744015-1-5(X))* Benchmark Book Craft.
DeLong, Ron. Crayola Dream-Makers: Dreams You Can Count On. DeLong, Ron, ed. 14th ed. 2004. (Illus.). 48p. per. 6.00 *(978-0-86696-316-9(2))* Binney & Smith, Inc.
Dyan, Penelope. Happy Birthday! a Book about Birthdays, Dreams & Wishes. Dyan, Penelope, illus. 2009. (Illus.). 42p. pap. 11.95 *(978-1-935118-73-2(0))* Bellissima Publishing, LLC.
—A Royal Residence — A Kid's Guide to Windsor Castle. Weigand, John D., photos by. 2011. (Illus.). 40p. pap. 12.95 *(978-1-935630-65-4(2))* Bellissima Publishing, LLC.
Gaestel, Tiffany & Benchmark Education Co. Staff. The Science of Sleep & Dreams. 2014. (Text Connections Ser.). (J). (gr. 5). *(978-1-4900-1381-7(4))* Benchmark Education Co.
Gee, Allison. Animal Dreams: Coloring Book. 2009. 52p. pap. 14.99 *(978-1-4389-9014-9(6))* AuthorHouse.
Gibson, Clare. The Secret Life of Dreams: Decoding the Messages from Your Subconscious. 2003. (Illus.). 400p. 29.98 *(978-1-59223-101-0(2))* Readerlink Distribution Services, LLC.
Green, Carl R. & Sanford, William R. The Mysterious Secrets of Dreams. Kelley, Gerald, illus. 2011. (Investigating the Unknown Ser.). 48p. (J). (gr. 5-18). pap. 8.95 *(978-1-59845-306-5(8))*; lib. bdg. 25.27 *(978-0-7660-3821-9(1))* Enslow Pubs., Inc.
Guiley, Rosemary Ellen. Dreams & Astral Travel. 2009. (Mysteries, Legends, & Unexplained Phenomena Ser.). (Illus.). 128p. (YA). (gr. 7-12). 29.95 *(978-0-7910-9387-0(5))* Facts On File, Inc.
Guillain, Charlotte & Colson, Mary. Dream It, Do It!, 1 vol. 2014. (Dream It, Do It! Ser.). (ENG.). 32p. (gr. 1-3). lib. bdg. 119.96 *(978-1-4109-6266-9(0)*, Read Me!) Heinemann-Raintree.
Jaskolka, Anna. Teen Dreams & What They Mean. (ENG., Illus.). 1p. 10.95 *(978-0-572-02877-0(6))* Foulsham, W. Co., Ltd. GBR. Dist: APG Sales & Distribution Services.
Mannion, Mary. The Boy & the Fish. Fitzgerald, Brian, illus. 2010. 52p. pap. *(978-1-907276-62-0(9))* Lapwing Pubns.
Mitchell, Arnold. Arnold's Dream. 2009. 32p. pap. 14.95 *(978-1-4092-4776-0(7))* Lulu Pr., Inc.
Moonchild, Karen Davies. Moon Dreams. 2003. 184p. 25.95 *(978-0-595-74890-7(2))*; pap. 15.95 *(978-0-595-28343-9(8))* iUniverse, Inc.
Muhammad, Renay. Dreams Do Come True. 2004. (Illus.). (J). cd-rom *(978-0-9754024-0-5(4))* Doses of Reality, Inc.
Olson, Elsie. Dreams & What They Mean: Facts, Trivia, & Quizzes. 2017. (Mind Games Ser.). (ENG., Illus.). 32p. (J). (gr. 2-5). 27.99 ***(978-1-5124-3417-0(5)***, Lerner Pubns.) Lerner Publishing Group.
Prisco & Benchmark Education Co. Staff. Interpreting Our Dreams. 2014. (Text Connections Ser.). (J). (gr. 5). *(978-1-4900-1382-4(2))* Benchmark Education Co.
Rosen, Marvin. Demystifying Dreams. 2004. 64p. (YA). pap. 9.95 *(978-0-595-30290-1(4))* iUniverse, Inc.
Sonandres, Thomas William & Peterson, Marilyn A. DreamLady.com: Guidance from Your Dreams. 2003. 224p. per. 12.95 *(978-0-9728531-0-1(3))* Spica Bks.
Thomas, Wendy Russell & Ruchman, Laura. Bliss Live It! Bliss Give It! Starmer, Anika & Wertz, Michael, illus. 2010. 60p. (YA). *(978-0-88441-754-5(9))* Girl Scouts of the USA.

DREAMS—FICTION

Abrahams, Alayne. Dreams & Daydreams. 2010. 26p. 14.95 *(978-1-4269-4173-3(0))* Trafford Publishing.
Abshire, Lisa D. Sam's Magical Day. 2006. 48p. pap. 16.95 *(978-1-4241-1484-9(5))* PublishAmerica, Inc.
Adkins, Ryan. Dream Catcher. 2013. 28p. pap. 16.99 *(978-1-4808-0326-8(X))* Archway Publishing.
Ahlers, Oly. Following My Magical Dream, 1 vol. 2010. 48p. pap. 16.95 *(978-1-61582-758-9(7))* America Star Bks.
Ajiri, Ijeoma. Why, Oh Why, Why Must I Be So Shy!?!, 1 vol. Izenwata, Chinwendu, illus. 2010. 16p. 24.95 *(978-1-4512-0928-0(2))* PublishAmerica, Inc.
Albee, Sarah & Hood, Susan. Blue's Bad Dream. Chernichaw, Ian, illus. 2006. (Blue's Clues Ser.: 21). (ENG.). 24p. (J). (gr. -1-2). pap. 3.99 *(978-1-4169-1553-9(2)*, Simon Spotlight/Nickelodeon) Simon Spotlight/Nickelodeon.
Alford-Craig, Lakiesha. Joe's Dreams of Adventure. 2012. 24p. (-18). pap. 10.00 *(978-0-9884237-3-2(1))* CLF Publishing.
Aliaga, Roberto. A Night Time Story. 2012. (ENG., Illus.). 24p. (J). (gr. k-2). *(978-84-15241-98-0(4))* D P & G Military Pubs.
All the Stars. 2008. (Looney Tunes Giant Floor Pad Ser.). 80p. pap. *(978-1-4075-2897-7(1))* Parragon, Inc.
Alloway, Kit. Dreamfever: A Novel. 2016. (Dream Walker Trilogy Ser.: 2). (ENG.). 320p. (J). 19.99 *(978-1-250-07811-7(3)*, 9781250078117, St. Martin's Griffin) St. Martin's Pr.
—Dreamfire. 2015. (Dream Walker Trilogy Ser.: 1). (ENG.). 368p. (YA). (gr. 8-12). 18.99 *(978-1-250-06366-3(3)*, 9781250063663, St. Martin's Griffin) St. Martin's Pr.
Alonso, Fernando. El Arbol de los Suenos. Urberuaga, Emilio, illus. 2005. (Alfaguara Juvenil Ser.).Tr. of Dream Trees. (SPA.). 124p. (J). (gr. 5-8). pap. 10.95 *(978-968-19-0978-9(X))* Santillana USA Publishing Co., Inc.
—Las Fantasias de la Lechera. (Superbks./Superlibros).Tr. of Milkmaid's Daydreams. (J). (gr. k-1). (SPA.). pap. 6.95 *(978-0-88272-473-7(8))*;Big Book. 21.95 *(978-0-88272-464-5(9))*;Big Book. (SPA.). 21.95 *(978-0-88272-463-8(0))* Santillana USA Publishing Co., Inc.
—A Milkmaid's Daydreams. (Superbks./Superlibros). (Illus.). 16p. (J). (gr. k-3). pap. 6.95 *(978-0-88272-474-4(6))* Santillana USA Publishing Co., Inc.
Alumbaugh, Michelle. Dream Away. 2009. 28p. pap. 10.75 *(978-1-4490-0663-1(9))* AuthorHouse.
Anderson, Robert L. Dreamland. 336p. (YA). (gr. 9). 2016. pap. 9.99 *(978-0-06-233868-6(4))* 2015. (ENG.). 17.99 *(978-0-06-233867-9(6))* HarperCollins Pubs. (HarperTeen).
Angel, Embracing. Miranda the Flying Mermaid. 2010. 36p. pap. 18.99 *(978-1-4490-9563-5(1))* AuthorHouse.
Angelina, Laura. A Little Girl's Wish. 2013. 32p. pap. 19.99 *(978-1-4772-9896-1(7))* AuthorHouse.
Arbuthnott, Gill. The Keepers' Tattoo. 2010. (ENG.). 432p. (J). (gr. 3-7). 17.99 *(978-0-545-17166-3(0)*, Chicken Hse., The) Scholastic, Inc.
Argiento, Cindy. Doris in Dreamland. 2007. pap. 8.00 *(978-0-8059-7461-4(X))* Dorrance Publishing Co., Inc.
Armstrong, Ashley Sage-Taylor. The Adventures of Starlight & Sunny: Building a Dream, How to Focus & Make Your Dreams Come to Life, with Positive Conscious Morals. Picture Boo. 2013. 52p. pap. *(978-1-927863-04-6(X))* Armstrong, Ashley.
Arnett, Mindee. The Nightmare Charade. 2015. (Arkwell Academy Ser.: 3). (ENG.). 384p. (YA). (gr. 8-12). 18.99 *(978-0-7653-3335-3(X)*, 9780765333353, Tor Teen) Doherty, Tom Assocs., LLC.
—The Nightmare Dilemma. 2015. (Arkwell Academy Ser.: 2). (ENG.). 400p. (YA). (gr. 8-12). pap. 10.99 *(978-0-7653-3337-7(6)*, 9780765333377, Tor Teen) Doherty, Tom Assocs., LLC.
Arruda, Diane. The Ancient One, Book II in the Dream River Adventure. 2009. 56p. pap. 12.95 *(978-1-60860-397-8(0)*, Eloquent Bks.) Strategic Book Publishing & Rights Agency (SBPRA).
—The Undiscovered River: Golden Fish & a True Dream. 2008. 60p. pap. 12.95 *(978-1-60693-399-2(X)*, Eloquent Bks.) Strategic Book Publishing & Rights Agency (SBPRA).
Aryal, Kusum. The Magic Mermaid Girl. 2011. 36p. pap. *(978-1-4269-8836-3(2))* Trafford Publishing (UK) Ltd.
Asch, Frank. Milk & Cookies. Asch, Frank, illus. 2015. (Frank Asch Bear Book Ser.). (ENG., Illus.). 40p. (J). (gr. -1-3). 17.99 *(978-1-4424-6672-2(3)*, Aladdin) Simon & Schuster Children's Publishing.
Ash. The Thrush's Song. 2011. 20p. pap. 24.95 *(978-1-4626-3720-1(5))* America Star Bks.
Aspesi, Carol. The Tale of the Snail. 2008. 25p. pap. 24.95 *(978-1-60672-794-2(X))* America Star Bks.
Atamer, Billie. A Pocket Full of Dreams. 2009. 32p. pap. 12.99 *(978-1-4490-2924-1(8))* AuthorHouse.
Atnip, Linda. Miranda's Magic Garden. 2004. cd-rom 15.98 *(978-1-885394-25-5(X))* Amber Lotus Publishing.
—Miranda's Magic Garden. Rothan, Ann, illus. 2004. 32p. (gr. -1-7). 19.95 *(978-1-885394-21-7(7))* Amber Lotus Publishing.
Auntie Annie. Knute: Dreams of Africa. 2013. 32p. pap. 17.25 *(978-1-4669-7519-4(9))* Trafford Publishing.
Bach, Shelby. Of Giants & Ice. Loftis, Cory, illus. 2013. (Ever Afters Ser.: 1). (ENG.). 368p. (J). (gr. 3-7). pap. 7.99 *(978-1-4424-3147-8(4)*, Simon & Schuster Bks. For Young Readers) Simon & Schuster Bks. For Young Readers.
—Of Giants & Ice. 2012. (Ever Afters Ser.: 1). (ENG., Illus.). 352p. (J). (gr. 3-7). 15.99 *(978-1-4424-3146-1(6)*, Simon & Schuster Bks. For Young Readers) Simon & Schuster Bks. For Young Readers.
Bailey, Kristin. Average Joe. 2006. 56p. per. *(978-1-84667-004-6(7))* Derwent Pr., The.
Bajpai, Sneha. Grant Me a Wish: Sometimes... you do get exactly what you wish For. 2010. 28p. pap. 12.49 *(978-1-4490-9780-6(4))* AuthorHouse.
Baker, Michelle M. The Geese of Belle Isle: Volume I. 2011. 28p. pap. 24.95 *(978-1-4626-3715-7(9))* America Star Bks.
Balázs, Béla. The Cloak of Dreams: Chinese Fairy Tales. Lydes, Mariette, illus. 2010. (Oddly Modern Fairy Tales Ser.). (ENG.). 208p. 24.95 *(978-0-691-14711-6(6))* Princeton Univ. Pr.

Balzola, Asun. Munia y el Cocolilo Naranja. (SPA.). 32p. (J). (978-84-233-1335-8(2)) Ediciones Destino ESP. Dist: Lectorum Pubns., Inc.

Banks, Kate. Close Your Eyes. Hallensleben, Georg, illus. 2015. (ENG.). 36p. (J). (gr. -1-1). bds. 7.99 (978-0-374-30101-9(8), 9780374301019, Farrar, Straus & Giroux (BYR)) Farrar, Straus & Giroux.

Banks, Rosemary. Moe the Well Dressed Scarecrow. 2013. 20p. pap. 24.95 (978-1-4626-9683-3(X)) America Star Bks.

Barber, Elaine R. Billy's First Flight Lesson. 2010. 36p. (J). 16.95 (978-1-4507-0620-9(7)) Independent Pub.

Barragan, Sophia & Barragan, Ivy. Susana Banana the Fantastic Figure Skater. 2008. 32p. pap. 12.99 (978-1-4389-0169-5(0)) AuthorHouse.

Barry, Bridget. Sweet Dreams. 2010. 24p. pap. 12.99 (978-1-4490-6905-6(3)) AuthorHouse.

Bate, Tharah. White Arrow. 2012. 20p. pap. 13.77 (978-1-4669-0991-5(9)) Trafford Publishing.

Batson, Wayne. The War for the Waking World, 1 vol. 2015. (Dreamtreaders Ser.). (ENG.). 288p. (J). pap. 9.99 (978-1-4003-2368-5(1)) Nelson, Thomas Inc.

Batson, Wayne Thomas. Dreamtreaders, 1 vol. 2014. (Dreamtreaders Ser.). (ENG.). 304p. (J). pap. 9.99 (978-1-4003-2366-1(5)) Nelson, Thomas Inc.

—Search for the Shadow Key, 1 vol. 2014. (Dreamtreaders Ser.). (ENG.). 336p. (J). pap. 9.99 (978-1-4003-2367-8(3)) Nelson, Thomas Inc.

Beard, Robert. Lovenia Little & Her Big Dreams. 2005. 60p. (J). pap. (978-1-886098-16-9(6)) Gye Nyame Hse.

Beck, Andrea. Pierre in the Air!, 1 vol. Beck, Andrea, illus. 2011. (Pierre le Poof Ser.: 3). (ENG., Illus.). 32p. (J). (gr. -1-3). 19.95 (978-1-55469-032-9(3)) Orca Bk. Pubs. USA.

Becker, Savan. Starry Night (2nd Edition) 2008. 60p. pap. 25.95 (978-0-615-23554-7(9)) Becker, Savan C.

Beckman, Amy. The Good Night Book. Ahern, Frank, illus. 2006. 28p. per. 16.95 (978-1-59858-255-0(0)) Dog Ear Publishing, LLC.

Beckstedt, Cynthia. Hopsy. 2008. 24p. pap. 24.95 (978-1-4241-9122-2(X)) America Star Bks.

Beletic, Kittie Nesius. What Color Is Your Dream? 2007. (Illus.). 44p. (J). 16.95 (978-1-933285-56-6(7)) Brown Books Publishing Group.

Bell-Jackson, Sylvia. Bree's Bubble Gum Adventures: The Pajamas from the Bahamas. 2012. 36p. pap. 13.97 (978-1-61204-299-2(6), Strategic Bk. Publishing) Strategic Book Publishing & Rights Agency (SBPRA).

Benevenia, Rose. Dolly & Babe. Benevenia, Rose, illus. l.t. ed. 2004. (Illus.). 9p. (J). (gr. k-2). pap. 9.00 (978-0-9729044-0-7(9)) Cabbage Patch Pr.

Bentley, Dawn. Fuzzy Bear's Bedtime. Nagy, Krisztina, illus. 2005. (Fuzzy Bear Ser.). 10p. (J). (gr. -1-k). act. bk. ed. 10.95 (978-1-58117-055-9(6), Intervisual/Piggy Toes) Bendon, Inc.

Berenstain, Stan & Berenstain, Jan. The Berenstain Bears & the Bad Dream. 2004. (Berenstain Bears First Time Bks.). (J). (gr. -1-2). spiral bd. (978-0-616-01556-8(9)); spiral bd. (978-0-616-01555-1(0)) Canadian National Institute for the Blind/Institut National Canadien pour les Aveugles.

Bernal, Sandra Marie. The Wish: Johnny's Story. Merriman, Christi, illus. 2011. 48p. pap. 24.95 (978-1-4560-4934-8(8)) America Star Bks.

Bier, Andreas. I Wish I Could Fly. Bier, Donna, illus. 2009. 20p. pap. 9.14 (978-1-4269-0271-0(9)) Trafford Publishing.

Biro, Sharon. Snaggleloopus. 2008. (Illus.). 36p. pap. 24.95 (978-1-60474-118-6(X)) America Star Bks.

Black, Robert A. Lunar Pioneers. 2008. 280p. (YA). pap. 14.99 (978-1-59092-397-9(9)) Blue Forge Pr.

Blackstone, Stella. I Dreamt I Was a Dinosaur. Beaton, Clare, illus. 2005. (ENG.). 32p. (J). (gr. -1-3). 15.99 (978-1-84148-238-5(2)) Barefoot Bks., Inc.

Bosak, Susan V. Dream: A Tale of Wonder, Wisdom & Wishes. Dillon, Leo et al, illus. 2004. 40p. (J). (978-1-896232-04-1(3), TCP Pr.) Communication Project, The.

Botelho, R. J. Elizabeth & Equines: G. A. R. T. H. V (Genetically Altered Radically Transformed Human), 1 vol. 2009. 105p. pap. 19.95 (978-1-61582-952-1(0)) America Star Bks.

Boyer, Gregory. My Little Red Book, 1 vol. 2010. 16p. 24.95 (978-1-4512-9251-0(1)) PublishAmerica, Inc.

Braden, Stephanie. The Wishing Well. 2012. 48p. pap. 16.95 (978-1-62709-450-4(4)) America Star Bks.

Braganza, Sheraleen. Butterfly Kisses. 2006. (Illus.). 68p. pap. (978-1-84401-812-3(1)) Athena Pr.

Braswell, Liz. Once upon a Dream. 2017. (Twisted Tale Ser.). (YA). lib. bdg. 20.85 **(978-0-606-39935-7(6))** Turtleback Bks.

Braswell, Liz. Once upon a Dream: A Twisted Tale. 2016. (Twisted Tale Ser.). (ENG.). 448p. (J). (gr. 7-17). 17.99 (978-1-4847-0725-8(7)) Disney Pr.

Bray, Libba. Lair of Dreams. 2015. (Diviners Ser.: 2). (ENG.). 624p. (YA). (gr. 10-17). 19.00 (978-0-316-12604-5(7)); (gr. 7-17). E-Book (978-0-316-36488-1(6)) Little, Brown Bks. for Young Readers.

Breaking Through the Access Barrier: How Academic Capital Formation Can Improve Policy in Higher Education. Date not set. 5.95 (978-0-89868-309-7(2)) ARO Publishing Co.

Brewer, Michelle. Sunrise in My Cup. 2011. 28p. (gr. -1). pap. 13.99 (978-1-4567-3995-9(6)) AuthorHouse.

Briggs, Raymond. The Snowman. 2013. (ENG.). 34p. (J). (— 1). bds. 6.99 (978-0-385-37869-7(6), Random Hse. Bks. for Young Readers) Random Hse. Children's Bks.

Brinegar, R. L. Ron. Pokey: The Fastest Horse on the Ranch. 2007. 33p. pap. 8.95 (978-0-7414-4078-5(4)) Infinity Publishing.

Brock-Jaurequi, Dawn. Dream Big, 1 vol. 2009. 27p. pap. 24.95 (978-1-61582-584-4(3)) America Star Bks.

Brodien-Jones, Christine. The Dreamkeepers. 2009. (ENG.). 148p. (YA). (gr. 7). pap. 8.99 (978-1-4424-0221-8(0), Simon & Schuster Bks. For Young Readers) Simon & Schuster Bks. For Young Readers.

Bronzan, William M., Sr. A Time to Dream. 2006. 41p. (J). pap. 8.95 (978-0-7414-3158-5(0)) Infinity Publishing.

Brooks, Elizabeth. Montefiore's Goddaughter. 2012. (ENG.). 304p. (YA). (gr. 4-6). 15.95 (978-1-84982-099-8(6)) MP Publishing Ltd. GBR. Dist: Midpoint Trade Bks., Inc.

Brooks, Martha. Bone Dance, 1 vol. 2005. (ENG.). 184p. (J). (gr. 6-16). pap. 8.95 (978-0-88899-336-6(6)) Groundwood Bks. CAN. Dist: Publishers Group West (PGW).

Brown, Desirae. A Pumpkin's Dream, 1 vol. 2009. 29p. pap. 24.95 (978-1-60836-364-3(3)) America Star Bks.

Brown, Margaret Wise. Buenas Noches Oso. 2006. (Illus.). 24p. (J). (gr. -1-k). 12.95 (978-1-882077-61-8(X)) Sweetwater Pr.

—The Dream Book. 2005. 32p. (J). (978-0-7868-2097-9(7)) Hyperion Bks. for Children.

—Goodnight Moon. Hurd, Clement, illus. 2012. (ENG.). 8p. (J). (gr. -1 — 1). pap. 14.99 (978-0-06-076224-7(1), HarperFestival) HarperCollins Pubs.

—Wish upon a Dream. Cooke, Charlotte, illus. 2014. (ENG.). 24p. (J). (gr. -1-3). 7.99 (978-1-4723-4531-8(2)) Parragon, Inc.

Brundin, Anders & Dranger, Joanna Rubin. Dudley the Daydreamer. Perry, Frank, tr. from SWE. 2008. (ENG., Illus.). 32p. (J). (gr. k-2). pap. 12.95 (978-1-905341-10-8(5)) WingedChariot Pr. GBR. Dist: Independent Pubs. Group.

Bug, June. The Legend of the Wooden Bowl. 2013. 44p. pap. 20.45 (978-1-4624-0688-3(2), Inspiring Voices) Author Solutions, Inc.

Bulger, Melissa. We Can Dream. 2009. 36p. pap. 15.65 (978-1-4490-1170-3(5)) AuthorHouse.

Burkart, Tammy Jayne. Lillie, 1 vol. 2009. 48p. pap. 16.95 (978-1-60813-680-3(9)) America Star Bks.

Burns, Mary Gore. The Magic Room: Mandy & the Lily Pond. 2011. 48p. pap. 17.30 (978-1-4634-2642-2(9)) AuthorHouse.

Butcher, A. J. & Butcher, Andrew J. Conexión Caos Vol. 2: Spy High, Episodio 2. Morales, Andrea & Yver, Camila, trs. 2004. (SPA., Illus.). 272p. 12.95 (978-84-95618-58-0(3), Umbriel) Ediciones Urano S. A. ESP. Dist: Spanish Pubs., LLC.

Butcher, Kristin. Return to Bone Tree Hill. 2009. (ENG.). 176p. (J). pap. 12.95 (978-1-897235-58-4(5)) Thistledown Pr., Ltd. CAN. Dist: Univ. of Toronto Pr.

Butler, John, illus. If Your Dreams Take off & Fly. 2013. (J). (978-1-4351-4769-0(3)) Barnes & Noble, Inc.

Byun, You. Dream Friends. Byun, You, illus. 2013. (ENG., Illus.). 32p. (J). (gr. -1-k). 16.99 (978-0-399-25739-1(X), Nancy Paulsen Books) Penguin Young Readers Group.

Cabrini, Joe. Chicco's Nicedream Van - Daniel's Winning Goal. Cabrini, Joe, illus. 2007. (Illus.). 32p. per. (978-0-7552-0300-0(3)) Authors OnLine, Ltd.

—Chicco's Nicedream Van - Jessica the Superstar. Cabrini, Joe, illus. 2007. (Illus.). 32p. per. (978-0-7552-0301-7(1)) Authors OnLine, Ltd.

Cadenhead, MacKenzie. Sleeper. 2017. (ENG.). 272p. (YA). (gr. 6-12). pap. 10.99 **(978-1-4926-3614-4(2))** Sourcebooks, Inc.

Capucilli, Alyssa Satin. Biscuit's First Sleepover. Schories, Pat & Berlin, Rose Mary, illus. 2008. (Biscuit Ser.). (ENG.). 24p. (J). (gr. -1-1). pap. 3.99 (978-0-06-112842-4(2), HarperFestival) HarperCollins Pubs.

Carroll, Harlisha. Miracle Mouse & Jesus Book #3: Short Stories 2. 2013. 32p. pap. 24.95 (978-1-4626-6647-8(7)) America Star Bks.

Carter, Larry. Tommie's Bad Dream. 2013. 28p. pap. 24.95 (978-1-4626-9668-0(6)) America Star Bks.

Cavaliere, Katrina. Mom! There's a Monster under My Bed! 2008. 24p. per. 24.95 (978-1-60441-066-2(3)) America Star Bks.

Cazet, Denys. Minnie & Moo: The Night of the Living Bed. Cazet, Denys, illus. 2003. (I Can Read Bks.). (Illus.). 48p. (J). (gr. k-3). lib. bdg. 16.89 (978-0-06-000504-7(1)) HarperCollins Pubs.

—Minnie & Moo - The Night of the Living Bed. Cazet, Denys, illus. 2004. (I Can Read Level 3 Ser.). (ENG., Illus.). 48p. (J). (gr. k-3). pap. 3.99 (978-0-06-000505-4(X)) HarperCollins Pubs.

—The Night of the Living Bed. Cazet, Denys, illus. unabr. ed. 2005. (Minnie & Moo Ser.). (Illus.). (J). (gr. k-4). 25.95 incl. audio (978-1-59519-389-6(8));Set. pap. 29.95 incl. audio (978-1-59519-390-2(1));Set. pap. 31.95 incl. audio compact disk (978-1-59519-394-0(4)) Live Oak Media.

Cefalo, Maria Raffaella. If Dreams Could Talk. 2012. (ENG.). 25p. (J). pap. 17.95 (978-1-4327-9623-5(2)); pap. 27.95 (978-1-4327-9708-9(5)) Outskirts Pr., Inc.

Cerato, Mattia. Sheep in the Closet. Cerato, Mattia, illus. 2014. (Family Snaps Ser.). (ENG., Illus.). 32p. (J). (gr. k-2). pap. 6.95 (978-1-939656-62-9(1)) Red Chair Pr.

Chapman, Karean. Look at Me, a Muscian I Want to Be. Ciesinska, Izabela, illus. 2011. 32p. pap. 12.95 (978-1-935268-75-8(9)) Halo Publishing International.

—Look at Me, a Veterinarian I Want to Be. Ciesinska, Izabela, illus. 2011. 32p. pap. 12.95 (978-1-935268-76-5(7)) Halo Publishing International.

Child, Lauren. I Am Not Sleepy & I Will Not Go to Bed. Child, Lauren, illus. 2008. (Charlie & Lola Ser.). (ENG., Illus.). 16p. (J). (gr. -1-2). 19.99 (978-0-7636-4098-9(0)) Candlewick Pr.

Childress, Story. Blue Moon Cheese. 2008. 28p. pap. 24.95 (978-1-60610-174-2(9)) America Star Bks.

Chriscoe, Sharon. Race Car Dreams. Mottram, Dave, illus. 2016. (ENG.). 32p. (J). (gr. -1 — 1). 16.95 (978-0-7624-5964-3(6), Running Pr. Kids) Running Pr. Bk. Pubs.

Church, Bryan. The Dreamcatcher Bowl. 2009. 54p. pap. 9.99 (978-0-557-07517-1(3)) Lulu Pr., Inc.

Cindy Lou. Boxes & Bows & Wiggling Toes. 2012. 32p. pap. 13.95 (978-1-4525-4553-0(7)) Balboa Pr.

Clark, Matthew. SongrrLines: A Beastie Bedtime Dreaming, & Coloring Book. 2005. 26p. (J). pap. 8.95 net. (978-1-59975-106-1(2)) Independent Pub.

Clark, Terri A. Sleepless. 2008. (ENG.). 288p. (YA). (gr. 9-18). pap. 5.99 (978-0-06-137596-5(9), HarperTeen) HarperCollins Pubs.

Clarkson, Kelly. River Rose & the Magical Lullaby. Hughes, Laura, illus. 2016. 32p. (J). (gr. -1-3). 18.99 (978-0-06-242756-4(3)) HarperCollins Pubs.

Clayton, Dallas. An Awesome Book! Clayton, Dallas, illus. 2012. (Awesome Book Ser.). (ENG., Illus.). 64p. (J). (gr. k-3). 16.99 (978-0-06-211468-6(9)) HarperCollins Pubs.

—An Awesome Book of Love! Clayton, Dallas, illus. 2012. (Awesome Book Ser.). (ENG., Illus.). 56p. (J). (gr. -1-3). 16.99 (978-0-06-211666-6(5)) HarperCollins Pubs.

Clow, Alexine. Jenny's Dreams. Clow, Alexine, illus. 2010. (Illus.). 20p. pap. 10.95 (978-1-936051-89-2(3)) Peppertree Pr., The.

Cnockaert, Cindy. The Magical Stones. 2011. 36p. pap. 16.86 (978-1-4389-8929-7(6)) AuthorHouse.

Coburn, Ann. Mission 1: Flying Solo. Horne, Sarah, illus. 2006. (Dream Team Ser.: Vol. 1). 80p. (J). pap. (978-1-84428-118-3(3)) Walker & Co.

—Showtime. Horne, Sarah, illus. 2006. (Dream Team Mission Ser.: Vol. 2). 80p. (J). pap. (978-1-84428-071-1(3)) Walker Bks., Ltd.

Cohen, Edythe. The Ghetto Garden. 2005. 51p. pap. 16.95 (978-1-4137-9539-4(0)) America Star Bks.

Cole, Joanne & Cole, Michael. Bod's Dream. 2016. (Bod Ser.). (ENG., Illus.). 32p. (J). (gr. -1-1). 9.99 (978-1-4052-7588-0(X)) Egmont Bks., Ltd. GBR. Dist: Independent Pubs. Group.

Collins, Terry. Spongebob NaturePants, Vol. 7. 2004. 64p. (J). (gr. 2-5). pap. 17.00 incl. audio (978-1-4000-8630-6(2), Listening Library) Random Hse. Audio Publishing Group.

Colon, Danny. The Little Caterpillar Who Dreams to Fly. 2012. 40p. pap. 15.99 (978-1-4624-0377-6(8), Inspiring Voices) Author Solutions, Inc.

Colvin, Denise Marie. Suzy's Big Dream Comes True. 2007. 61p. pap. 19.95 (978-1-4241-8157-5(7)) America Star Bks.

Coman, Carolyn. The Memory Bank. Shepperson, Rob, illus. 2010. (J). 263p. pap. (978-0-545-21067-6(4)); (ENG.). 288p. (gr. 3-7). 16.99 (978-0-545-21066-9(6)) Scholastic, Inc. (Levine, Arthur A. Bks.).

Condon, Bill. Riley Versus the Giant Banana. Hopgood, Andrew, illus. 2015. (Legends in Their Own Lunchbox Ser.). (ENG.). 48p. (gr. 1-2). pap. 7.99 (978-1-4966-0246-6(3), Legends in Their Own Lunchbox) Capstone Classroom.

Cooper, Christina. If I Only Had One Wish. 2008. 20p. pap. 12.50 (978-1-60693-304-6(3), Strategic Bk. Publishing) Strategic Book Publishing & Rights Agency (SBPRA).

Cordell, Greg. Doodle Bug: Digging to Reach the Top. Hyun, Jinsun, illus. 2004. (J). (978-0-9759699-0-8(0)) Greenville Family Partnership.

Cordova, Sarah. Arch Angel, 1 vol. 2010. 220p. pap. 24.95 (978-1-4489-9778-7(X)) America Star Bks.

Córdova, Zoraida. The Vicious Deep. 2012. (Vicious Deep Ser.: 1). (ENG.). 384p. (YA). (gr. 7-12). pap. 9.99 (978-1-4022-7441-1(6)) Sourcebooks, Inc.

Corkran, Alice. Down the Snow Stairs: Or, from Goodnight to Goodmorning. Browne, Gordon, illus. 2012. 278p. pap. 14.95 (978-1-934671-12-2(6)) Salem Ridge Press LLC.

Corre, Lorraine. Book #1, Just for Fun. 2009. 116p. pap. 14.95 (978-1-4401-2812-7(X)) iUniverse, Inc.

Costantino, Eric. Beeboo Bear Dreamed A Dream. 2004. 31p. pap. 24.95 (978-1-4137-3649-6(1)) PublishAmerica, Inc.

Cousins, Lucy. Sweet Dreams, Maisy. Cousins, Lucy, illus. 2009. (Maisy Ser.). (ENG., Illus.). 32p. (J). (gr. -1-2). bds. 6.99 (978-0-7636-4532-8(X)) Candlewick Pr.

Cowlard, Irene. Moriarty's Dream. 2007. (Illus.). 52p. per. (978-1-84748-062-0(4)) Athena Pr.

Cronin, Doreen. Diary of a Fly. 2011. (J). (gr. -1-3). 29.95 (978-0-545-09454-2(2)) Weston Woods Studios, Inc.

Cronkhite, Lisa. Disconnected. 2014. (ENG.). 196p. (YA). pap. 10.95 (978-1-929345-02-1(X)) Poisoned Pen Pr.

Culp, Barbara D. An Incredible Dream. 2010. 39p. (J). pap. 21.95 (978-0-615-16593-6(1)) Outskirts Pr., Inc.

Cumming, Wendy. How to Soar Like an Eagle When You Are Standing with the Turkeys. 2012. 32p. pap. 21.99 (978-1-4797-2934-0(5)) Xlibris Corp.

Cuqui. The Little House Without Windows: A Casinha sem Janelas. 2008. 124p. pap. 11.00 (978-1-4343-7876-7(4)) AuthorHouse.

Daddo, Andrew. When I Grow Up. Bentley, Jonathan, illus. 2017. 32p. 17.99 (978-0-7333-3341-5(9)) ABC Bks. AUS. Dist: HarperCollins Pubs.

Dale, Decisive. The Determined Dream Cars. 2008. 48p. pap. 19.95 (978-1-4389-1484-8(9)) AuthorHouse.

Damiron, Anya. Dreamboy. Pino, Pablo, illus. 2010. (SPA.). 26p. (J). (978-9945-421-42-2(5)) Lucia Stories.

Davis, Maggie Steincrohn. A Garden of Whales. O'Connell, Jennifer Barrett, illus. 2008. (ENG.). 32p. (J). (gr. -1-2). reprint ed. pap. 6.95 (978-0-944475-35-5(3), 9780944475355) Firefly Bks., Ltd.

de Lint, Charles. The Blue Girl. 2006. (ENG.). 384p. (YA). (gr. 7-18). reprint ed. 7.99 (978-0-14-240545-1(0), Firebird) Penguin Young Readers Group.

Defilippo, Lauren Frances. Dance with Me, Please. 2009. 24p. pap. 14.99 (978-1-4490-0607-5(8)) AuthorHouse.

Deluca, Laura. Demon. 2013. 298p. pap. 12.95 (978-1-938397-46-2(0), Pagan Writers Pr.) Mroczka Media.

DeMascio, William. Don't Forget to Visit the Moon. 2005. 31p. (J). 13.01 (978-1-4116-1239-6(6)) Lulu Pr., Inc.

Demi. The Magic Pillow. Demi, illus. 2008. (ENG., Illus.). 40p. (J). (gr. 2-5). 24.99 (978-1-4169-2470-8(1), McElderry, Margaret K. Bks.) McElderry, Margaret K. Bks.

Denman, K. L. Stuff We All Get, 1 vol. 2011. (Orca Currents Ser.). (ENG.). 128p. (J). (gr. 5-9). pap. 9.95 (978-1-55469-820-2(0)); lib. bdg. 16.95 (978-1-55469-821-9(9)) Orca Bk. Pubs. USA.

Diamond, Lorraine. I Want a Camel for a Pet, 1 vol. 2009. 13p. pap. 24.95 (978-1-61546-425-8(5)) America Star Bks.

Diaz, Luis. The Dream. 2010. 166p. pap. 12.98 (978-0-557-09653-4(7)) Lulu Pr., Inc.

Dilloway, Margaret. Momotaro Xander & the Dream Thief. Yoon, Choong, illus. 2017. (Momotaro Ser.). (ENG.). 336p. (J). (gr. 3-7). 16.99 (978-1-4847-2488-0(7)) Hyperion Bks. for Children.

Disbro, Laura M. Adventures with Miss Lol: The Magic Paper Ride. 2011. 28p. pap. 15.99 (978-1-4628-9072-9(5)) Xlibris Corp.

Docherty, Thomas. To the Beach. Docherty, Thomas, illus. 2009. (ENG., Illus.). 40p. (J). (gr. -1-2). 15.99 (978-0-7636-4429-1(3), Templar) Candlewick Pr.

Dodd, Emma. Sweet Dreams, Baby. 2017. (Illus.). 12p. (J). bds. **(978-1-4083-3981-7(1))** Barron's Educational Series, Inc.

Doyle, Celia. Lizzie's Dream, 1 vol. 2013. (Fiction Readers Ser.). (ENG., Illus.). 28p. (J). (gr. 2-2). pap. 6.99 (978-1-4333-5563-9(9)) Shell Educational Publishing.

Doyle, Teresa J. The Dream Box: Big Dreams for Little Sleepers. 2008. 84p. pap. 26.95 (978-1-4343-9086-8(1)) AuthorHouse.

Dozier, Mike. The Little Inchworm with the Big Dream. 2009. (J). pap. 12.50 (978-1-61623-365-5(6)) Independent Pub.

Dream Catchers - Evaluation Guide: Evaluation Guide. 2006. (J). (978-1-55942-403-5(6)) Witcher Productions.

Dreaming: Set D Individual Title Six-Packs. (Smart Start Ser.). (gr. k-1). 23.00 (978-0-7635-0451-9(3)) Rigby Education.

Dreams Will Come, Dreams Will Go. 2008. (Illus.). 28p. (J). per. 11.99 (978-0-615-17947-6(9)) Play Ball Publishing.

Dudley, Rebecca. Hank Has a Dream. Dudley, Rebecca, photos by. 2014. (ENG., Illus.). 32p. (J). 16.99 (978-1-4413-1572-4(1), 9781441315724) Peter Pauper Pr. Inc.

Dukoff, K. D. If I Had A Wish. Graham, C. E., illus. 2008. 12p. pap. 24.95 (978-1-60610-241-1(9)) America Star Bks.

Dunbar, Polly. Arthur's Dream Boat. Dunbar, Polly, illus. 2012. (ENG., Illus.). 40p. (J). (gr. -1-k). 15.99 (978-0-7636-5867-0(7)) Candlewick Pr.

Dunn, Hunter S. A Winter's Dream. Ellis, Joey, illus. 2004. 65p. (J). 19.95 (978-0-9761732-0-5(4)) Dunn, Hunter.

Durango, Julia & Trupiano, Katie Belle. Dream Away. Goldstrom, Robert, illus. 2011. (ENG.). 32p. (J). (gr. -1-3). 16.99 (978-1-4169-8702-4(9), Simon & Schuster Bks. For Young Readers) Simon & Schuster Bks. For Young Readers.

Durst, Sarah Beth. The Girl Who Could Not Dream. 2017. (ENG.). 384p. (J). (gr. 5-7). pap. 6.99 (978-0-544-93526-6(8), HMH Books For Young Readers) Houghton Mifflin Harcourt Publishing Co.

—The Girl Who Could Not Dream. 2015. (ENG.). 384p. (J). (gr. 5-7). 16.99 (978-0-544-46497-1(4), Clarion Bks.) Houghton Mifflin Harcourt Trade & Reference Pubs.

—The Girl Who Could Not Dream. 2017. (ENG.). (J). (gr. 5-7). lib. bdg. 17.20 **(978-0-606-39810-7(4))** Turtleback Bks.

Dwyer, Mindy. Sweet Dreams, Polar Bear. 2004. (ENG., Illus.). 32p. (J). 15.95 (978-0-88240-554-4(3)); pap. 8.99 (978-0-88240-555-1(1)) Graphic Arts Ctr. Publishing Co.

Dyan, Penelope. Even More of My Life As I Know It. 2011. 100p. pap. 8.95 (978-1-935630-50-0(4)) Bellissima Publishing, LLC.

—Mermaids & Wishes for Tails Like Fishes. Dyan, Penelope, illus. 2009. (Illus.). 44p. pap. 11.95 (978-1-935118-50-3(1)) Bellissima Publishing, LLC.

—Out of Deepest Africa — -Another of Ben's Big Adventures — -for Boys Only (r). Dyan, Penelope, illus. 2010. (Illus.). 34p. pap. 11.95 (978-1-935630-13-5(X)) Bellissima Publishing, LLC.

—There's No Business Like Bartholomew Bunny's Business. Dyan, Penelope, illus. 2009. (Illus.). 44p. pap. 11.95 (978-1-935118-54-1(4)) Bellissima Publishing, LLC.

Eaton, Kay A. Gleason & the Dewdrop's Dream. 2011. 24p. (gr. -1). pap. 15.00 (978-1-4567-4075-7(X)) AuthorHouse.

Eaton, Kelly Toole. Kellina Makes Her Dreams Come True. 2011. 40p. pap. 21.99 (978-1-4568-8824-4(2)) Xlibris Corp.

Edgren, Elizabeth. Little Tree's Mightiest Deed. Penk, Kathryn, illus. 2009. 36p. pap. 12.95 (978-1-59858-825-5(7)) Dog Ear Publishing, LLC.

Elliott, Odette. Sammy Goes Flying. McIntyre, Georgina, illus. 2011. (ENG.). 32p. (J). (gr. -1-k). pap. 9.99 (978-1-84853-050-8(1)) Transworld Publishers Ltd. GBR. Dist: Independent Pubs. Group.

Elliott, Ruth. Little Blossom, 1 disc. Cullquipuma, Diana y. Jose, tr. Elliott, Ruth, illus. 2008. (ENG & SPA., Illus.). 26p. (J). per. 12.99 incl. DVD (978-0-9795017-2-2(5)) Edu Designs.

Emin, Rebecca. When Dreams Come True. 2012. 164p. pap. (978-1-4710-9204-6(6)) Lulu.com.

Enersen, Adele. When My Baby Dreams. Enersen, Adele, illus. 2012. (ENG., Illus.). 48p. (J). (gr. -1-3). 14.99 (978-0-06-207175-0(0)) HarperCollins Pubs.

—When My Baby Dreams of Fairy Tales. Enersen, Adele, illus. 2013. (ENG., Illus.). 48p. (J). (gr. -1-k). 15.99 (978-0-06-207177-4(7)) HarperCollins Pubs.

Erlandson, Nick. Duncan & the Bone Tree, 1 vol. 2009. 40p. pap. 24.95 (978-1-60813-864-7(X)) America Star Bks.

Erne, Monica. Fantazzzmia: Where Dreams Come From. 2004. 26p. pap. 7.99 (978-0-9745746-0-8(0)) Four Dolphins Pr.

Esenwa, Anthony. Jaja, King of Opobo. 2009. (Illus.). 24p. pap. 11.49 (978-1-4389-5886-6(2)) AuthorHouse.

Evans, Margaret. The Tale of Rainbow's End. 2007. pap. 11.00 (978-0-8059-8716-4(9)) Dorrance Publishing Co., Inc.

Ewert, Marcus. 10,000 Dresses. Ray, Rex, illus. 2008. (ENG.). 32p. (J). (gr. k-4). 14.95 (978-1-58322-850-0(0), Triangle Square) Seven Stories Pr.

Fahy, Thomas. The Unspoken. 2008. (ENG.). 176p. (YA). (gr. 7-18). 15.99 (978-1-4169-4007-4(3), Simon & Schuster Bks. For Young Readers) Simon & Schuster Bks. For Young Readers.

—The Unspoken. 2009. (ENG.). 256p. (YA). (gr. 7). mass mkt. 6.99 (978-1-4169-4008-1(1), Simon Pulse) Simon Pulse.

Fanny, Nanny. Touch the Stars: A Children's Book. Nanny Fanny, illus. 2013. 32p. pap. 12.99 (978-1-61204-275-6(9), Strategic Bk. Publishing) Strategic Book Publishing & Rights Agency (SBPRA).

Fant, Donna. Scotty's Dream: Book & CD. Axford, Elizabeth C., ed. McKeown, David, illus. 2004. (ENG.). 16p. (J). audio compact disk 14.99 (978-1-931844-17-8(8), PP1034) Piano Pr.

Faye Morningstar. Little Dream Athe: The Sand Prince. 2012. 20p. pap. 17.99 (978-1-4772-9540-3(2)) AuthorHouse.

Feierabend, John M. Momma, Buy Me a China Doll. Norton, Allyssa, illus. 2017. (First Steps in Music Ser.). (ENG.). 32p. (J). (— 1). 16.95 **(978-1-62277-226-1(1))** G I A Pubns., Inc.

Fell, K. The Dragon Stones. 2009. 352p. 30.95 (978-0-595-51644-5(0)); pap. 20.95 (978-0-595-52712-0(4)) iUniverse, Inc.

Fischer, David. Heir to Oswyn. 2011. 66p. pap. 19.95 (978-1-4626-2581-9(9)) America Star Bks.

Fisher, Catherine. The Ghost Box. 2012. (Stoke Books Titles Ser.). 72p. (J). (gr. 5-8). pap. 45.32 (978-0-7613-9218-7(1)) Stoke Bks.

Fisher, Henry. When I Dream of ABC. 2014. (Illus.). (J). (978-1-4351-5469-8(X)); 64p. (978-1-84956-102-0(8)) Barnes & Noble, Inc.

Fleischman, Sid. The Dream Stealer. Sís, Peter, illus. (ENG.). (J). 2011. 128p. pap. 6.99 (978-0-06-178729-4(9)) 2009. 96p. (gr. 4-18). 16.99 (978-0-06-175563-7(X)) HarperCollins Pubs. (Greenwillow Bks.).

Fletcher, Susan. Alphabet of Dreams. 2008. (ENG., Illus.). 432p. (YA). (gr. 7-12). mass mkt. 7.99 (978-0-689-85152-0(9), Simon Pulse) Simon Pulse.

Flint-Warren, Cathrine. To Dance with the Yellow Butterfly. 2007. 28p. per. 18.95 *(978-1-4327-0491-9(5))* Outskirts Pr., Inc.

Flodin, Louise E. Sherman the Frog Meets the Snow Princess. l.t. ed. 2006. (Illus.). 24p. (J). (gr. -1-3). 15.95 *(978-0-9745052-5-1(0),* 1) Tree Of Life Publishing.

Floerchinger, Lori Liddic. Ocean of Dreams. Floerchinger, Jeremy, illus. 2008. 36p. pap. 24.95 *(978-1-60703-003-4(9))* America Star Bks.

Foth, Horst. Traumreisen. 2011. 120p. 26.50 *(978-1-4477-2150-5(0))* Lulu Pr., Inc.

Fournier, Elizabeth. Sailboat Dreams: Monkey Island. 2012. 16p. pap. 15.99 *(978-1-4772-7670-9(X))* AuthorHouse.

Frank, Hannah. If I Had Three Wishes. 2008. 56p. pap. 23.99 *(978-1-4343-7529-2(3))* AuthorHouse.

Frederick, Melissa. With a Dream, 1 vol. 2010. 138p. pap. 24.95 *(978-1-4489-5908-2(X))* America Star Bks.

Fricke, Paul. Night of the Bedbugs. 2010. (ENG., Illus.). 32p. (J). 12.99 *(978-1-60706-145-8(7),* 9781607061458) Image Comics.

Friedman, C. S. Dreamwalker. 2014. (Dreamwalker Ser.: 1). (ENG.). 320p. (gr. 12). 19.95 *(978-0-7564-0888-6(1),* DAW) DAW.

Fujii, Jocelyn. Pono the Dog That Dreams. Burns, Donna, illus. 2008. (ENG.). 40p. (YA). 14.95 *(978-0-9794649-2-8(7))* Hula Moon Pr.

Funkhouser, Patricia A. Dripps -. A Little Star's Dream. 2010. 104p. pap. 15.99 *(978-1-4535-3762-6(7))* Xlibris Corp.

Gabolinscy, Jack & Oppatt, Karen. Danny's Dream. 2008. (Rigby Focus Forward: Level O Ser.). (Illus.). 24p. pap. *(978-1-4190-3843-3(5),* Rigby) Pearson Education Australia.

Gall, Allan R. Of Mouse & Magic. 2011. (ENG., Illus.). 269p. (J). (gr. 3-7). pap. 12.95 *(978-1-936401-78-9(9))* Salem Author Services.

Gallo, Tina. Brava OLIVIA. Rose, Drew, illus. 2009. (Olivia TV Tie-In Ser.). (ENG.). 32p. (J). (gr. -1-1). 4.99 *(978-1-4169-8521-1(2),* Simon Scribbles) Simon Scribbles.

Ganges, Montse. Cooper, King of Cushion Island. Urberuaga, Emilio, illus. 2009. (Cooper Ser.). 24p. (J). (gr. -1-3). pap. 8.15 *(978-1-60754-243-8(9))* Windmill Bks.

—Fly Hunter. Urberuaga, Emilio, illus. 2009. (Cooper Ser.). 24p. (J). (gr. -1-3). pap. 8.15 *(978-1-60754-237-7(4))*; lib. bdg. 22.60 *(978-1-60754-236-0(6))* Windmill Bks.

—King of Cushion Island. Urberuaga, Emilio, illus. 2009. (Cooper Ser.). 24p. (J). (gr. -1-3). lib. bdg. 22.60 *(978-1-60754-242-1(0))* Windmill Bks.

Garcia, Kami & Stohl, Margaret. Beautiful Creatures. 2009. (Beautiful Creatures Ser.: 1). (ENG.). 576p. (YA). (gr. 7-17). 17.99 *(978-0-316-04267-3(6))* Little Brown & Co.

—Beautiful Creatures. (Beautiful Creatures Ser.: 1). (ENG.). 592p. (YA). (gr. 7-17). 2010. pap. 12.99 *(978-0-316-07703-3(8))* 2012. mass mkt. 7.99 *(978-0-316-23165-7(7))* 2012. pap. 10.99 *(978-0-316-23167-1(3))* Little, Brown Bks. for Young Readers.

—Beautiful Creatures. 2013. (ENG., Illus.). 240p. (gr. 8-17). 20.00 *(978-0-316-18271-3(0),* Yen Pr.) Orbit.

—Beautiful Creatures. 2010. (Beautiful Creatures Ser.: 1). (YA). lib. bdg. 23.30 *(978-0-606-26699-4(2),* Turtleback) Turtleback Bks.

Gardner, Scot. The Dead I Know. (ENG.). 208p. (YA). (gr. 9). 2016. pap. 8.99 *(978-0-544-67174-4(0))* 2015. 17.99 *(978-0-544-23274-7(7))* Houghton Mifflin Harcourt Publishing Co. (HMH Books For Young Readers).

Gentry, Jennifer Mills. Maria the Cat, 1 vol. 2010. 24p. pap. 24.95 *(978-1-4489-7748-2(7))* PublishAmerica, Inc.

—Maria's Bedtime. 2012. 24p. pap. 24.95 *(978-1-4626-7816-7(5))* America Star Bks.

Geraldi, Michele J. Pennies at Piper Park. 2009. 24p. pap. 12.99 *(978-1-4389-2829-6(7))* AuthorHouse.

Gerry, Bella Bashan. The Sweetest Dreams. 2013. 32p. pap. 19.99 *(978-1-4772-8625-8(X))* AuthorHouse.

Gerstein, Mordicai. The Sleeping Gypsy. Gerstein, Mordicai, illus. 2016. (ENG., Illus.). 32p. (J). 16.95 *(978-0-8234-2142-8(2))* Holiday Hse., Inc.

Gettman, Cheryl. Molly Magee & the Jelly Bean Tree. 2011. 24p. pap. 12.99 *(978-1-4634-3770-1(6))* AuthorHouse.

Gier, Kerstin. Dream a Little Dream. Bell, Anthea, tr. from GER. 2015. (Silver Trilogy Ser.: 1). (ENG.). 336p. (YA). (gr. 7). 17.99 *(978-1-62779-027-7(6),* 9781627790277, Holt, Henry & Co. Bks. For Young Readers) Holt, Henry & Co.

—Dream On. Bell, Anthea, tr. from GER. 2016. (Silver Trilogy Ser.: 2). (ENG.). 336p. (YA). 17.99 *(978-1-62779-079-6(9),* 9781627790796, Holt, Henry & Co. Bks. For Young Readers) Holt, Henry & Co.

—Just Dreaming. Bell, Anthea, tr. from GER. 2017. (Silver Trilogy Ser.). (ENG.). 368p. (YA). 18.99 *(978-1-62779-080-2(2),* 9781627790802, Holt, Henry & Co. Bks. For Young Readers) Holt, Henry & Co.

Giles, Mike, illus. Sleep & Dream of Happy Things. 2009. (Yo Gabba Gabba! Ser.). (ENG.). 26p. (J). (gr. -1 — 1). bds. 5.99 *(978-1-4169-7823-7(2),* Simon Spotlight) Simon Spotlight.

Gilmartin, Mary. Adventures with Easton: The Magical Journey. 2012. (ENG.). (J). pap. 16.95 *(978-1-4675-2418-6(2))* Independent Pub.

Giorgio, Marg. Maxi's Magical Dream. 2011. 24p. pap. 12.79 *(978-1-4634-4491-4(5))* AuthorHouse.

Glass, Graeme. A Bee's Kiss. Trone, Jo, illus. 2012. 60p. pap. 21.50 *(978-1-61897-383-2(5),* Strategic Bk. Publishing) Strategic Book Publishing & Rights Agency (SBPRA).

Glennon, Michelle. Duncan the Circus Dinosaur. Glennon, Michelle, illus. 2008. (Illus.). 21p. (J). 16.95 *(978-0-9796625-5-3(9))* GDG Publishing.

Godbersen, Anna. The Lucky Ones. 2013. (Bright Young Things Ser.: 3). (ENG.). 400p. (YA). (gr. 9). pap. 9.99 *(978-0-06-196271-4(6))* HarperCollins Pubs.

Goerzen, Christy. Farmed Out, 1 vol. 2011. (Orca Currents Ser.). (ENG.). 128p. (J). (gr. 5-9). pap. 9.95 *(978-1-55469-910-0(X))*; lib. bdg. 16.95 *(978-1-55469-911-7(8))* Orca Bk. Pubs. USA.

Goguen, Martha M. Andromed: Dream Believe Achieve Series. Walker, Patricia M., illus. 2011. 36p. pap. *(978-1-897435-35-9(5))* Agio Publishing Hse.

Gómez Cerdá, Alfredo, et al. Dos Plumas de Aguila. Puebla, Teo, illus. 2003. (SPA.). 32p. (gr. 3-5). 14.99 *(978-84-241-8028-7(3))* Everest Editora ESP. Dist: Lectorum Pubns., Inc.

Good, Yvonne & Good, Sr. Bubble Gum & Polka Dot. 2009. 96p. pap. 13.95 *(978-1-4389-6640-3(7))* AuthorHouse.

Gorbachev, Valeri. When Someone Is Afraid, 1 vol. Gorbachev, Kostya, illus. (ENG.). 32p. (J). 2012. pap. 6.95 *(978-1-59572-344-4(7))* 2005. (gr. -1-2). 15.95 *(978-1-932065-99-2(7))* Star Bright Bks., Inc.

Gossett, Susan. A True Superhero. 2009. 28p. pap. 16.50 *(978-1-4490-3147-3(1))* AuthorHouse.

Graham, Lauren N. I Wanna Be a Chef! 2010. 24p. 15.50 *(978-1-4520-2217-8(8))* AuthorHouse.

Graham, Oakley. When I Dream of 123. 2014. (Illus.). (J). *(978-1-4351-5468-1(1))* Barnes & Noble, Inc.

Graham, Sabrina Depina. Breanna & Amber: Help Each Other Achieve Their Dreams (Christian Version) 2012. 92p. 19.99 *(978-1-4691-6411-3(6))*; pap. 12.99 *(978-1-4691-6410-6(8))* Xlibris Corp.

Gray, Rita. When the World Is Dreaming. Pak, Kenard, illus. 2016. (ENG.). 32p. (J). (gr. -1-3). 17.99 *(978-0-544-58262-0(4),* HMH Books For Young Readers) Houghton Mifflin Harcourt Publishing Co.

Greene, Thomas. Whacked Out Wrestling: Memorial - A tale of Headlocks, Hurricanranas, & High School. 2007. 228p. pap. 14.95 *(978-1-60145-175-0(X))* Booklocker.com, Inc.

Greens, Olivia. My Dream. 2012. 28p. pap. 21.99 *(978-1-4797-1305-9(8))* Xlibris Corp.

Grimes, Terri & Timmons, Jasmine. A Pony Named Penny. 2007. 16p. 11.95 *(978-0-615-15990-4(7))* Dm Productions.

Grover, Kuloa A. Charlie the Snake. 2012. 32p. pap. 19.99 *(978-1-4685-5568-4(5))* AuthorHouse.

Guiffre, William A. Eddie, the Elf Who Would Be Elvis. Fannon, Chris, illus. 2011. (ENG.). 40p. (J). 17.95 *(978-0-9830172-0-2(4))*; pap. 9.95 *(978-0-9830172-1-9(2))* Bks. for Children Publishing.

—The Wrong Side of the Bed. Baron, Cheri Ann, illus. 2003. 36p. (J). (gr. -1-3). lib. bdg. 17.95 *(978-1-931650-20-5(9))* Bks. for Children Publishing.

Gutman, Anne & Hallensleben, Georg. Daddy Dreams. 2017. (ENG., Illus.). 14p. (J). (gr. -1 — 1). bds. 5.99 *(978-1-4521-5823-5(1))* Chronicle Bks. LLC.

Haile, Carol J. A Dream Vacation. Miller, Robert, illus. 2003. 32p. (J). per. 19.95 *(978-0-9724699-0-6(7))* Panda Bear Pr.

Halvorson, Michelle. All My Wishes for You. 2013. (ENG.). 26p. (J). 19.95 *(978-1-4787-0145-3(5))* Outskirts Pr., Inc.

Hamblin, Hope. Kyl. 2012. 28p. pap. 17.99 *(978-1-4772-2084-9(4))* AuthorHouse.

Hamilton, Benny. The Goat in the Coat. 2010. 36p. (J). pap. 21.95 *(978-1-4327-4884-5(X))* Outskirts Pr., Inc.

Handelsman, Valerie J. Lobster Monica: Dream, Dream, Dream - Monica Was Always Dreaming. Handelsman, Valerie J., illus. 2004. (Illus.). 31p. (J). pap. 7.95 *(978-0-9748884-0-8(0))* Little Thoughts For Little Ones Publishing, Inc.

Handleman, Philip. A Dream of Pilots, 1 vol. Kodera, Craig, illus. 2009. (ENG.). 128p. (J). (gr. 3-7). 14.95 *(978-1-58980-570-5(4))* Pelican Publishing Co., Inc.

Harris, Charles Edward. Ice Angels. 2007. 60p. pap. 30.50 *(978-1-84799-750-0(3))* Lulu Pr., Inc.

Harris, Diane Banks. The Eagle & the Chickens. 2008. 13p. pap. 24.95 *(978-1-60703-092-8(6))* PublishAmerica, Inc.

Harris, Dorthy. Taylor's Dream Ends Summer School Nightm. 2006. 95p. pap. 16.95 *(978-1-4241-3574-5(5))* PublishAmerica, Inc.

Harrison, S. Infinity Rises, 0 vols. 2016. (Infinity Trilogy Ser.: 2). (ENG.). 261p. (YA). (gr. 9-13). pap. 9.99 *(978-1-5039-5225-6(8),* 9781503952256, Skyscape) Amazon Publishing.

Harrison, Troon. The Dream Collector. 2004. (Illus.). (J). (gr. k-3). spiral bd. *(978-0-616-01671-8(9))* Canadian National Institute for the Blind/Institut National Canadien pour les Aveugles.

Hart, Christine. Best Laid Plans, 1 vol. 2009. (Lorimer SideStreets Ser.). (ENG.). 152p. (YA). (gr. 9-12). 16.95 *(978-1-55277-447-2(3),* 9781552774472); 9.95 *(978-1-55277-446-5(5),* 9781552774465) Lorimer, James & Co., Ltd., Pubs. CAN. Dist: Casemate Pubs. & Bk. Distributors, LLC.

Hartnett, Edmond. Dreams. 2010. 28p. 16.09 *(978-1-4269-3812-2(8))* Trafford Publishing.

Harvey, Gill. Orphan of the Sun. 2006. (ENG., Illus.). 320p. (YA). (gr. 3-7). 16.95 *(978-1-58234-685-4(2),* 9781582346854, Bloomsbury USA Childrens) Bloomsbury Publishing USA.

Hasler, Eveline. En Suenos Puedo Volar. (Barril Sin Fondo Ser.).Tr. of In Dreams I Can Fly. (SPA.). (J). (gr. 3-5). pap. 8.76 *(978-968-6465-04-4(9))* Casa de Estudios de Literatura y Talleres Artisticos Amaquemecan A.C. MEX. Dist: Lectorum Pubns., Inc.

Hatch, Morgan John. Where Dreams Are Made. 2011. 28p. pap. 24.95 *(978-1-4626-2896-4(6))* America Star Bks.

Havran, Melissa. George Washington. 2013. 32p. pap. 19.99 *(978-1-4817-0157-0(6))* AuthorHouse.

Hayes, Gwen. Falling Under. 2011. (ENG.). 336p. (YA). (gr. 7-18). 9.99 *(978-0-451-23268-7(2),* Berkley) Penguin Publishing Group.

Head, Jean. Andrew's Christmas Dream. 2012. 28p. pap. 5.00 *(978-1-937260-19-4(4))* Sleepytown Pr.

Heine, Helme. Wunderbare Reise Durch Die Na. 12.95 *(978-3-7876-9528-7(1))* Middelhauve Verlags GmbH DEU. Dist: Distribooks, Inc.

Hendrix, E. B. Angel & Evie: Catching a Unicorn. 2013. (Illus.). 42p. 19.99 *(978-0-9857367-9-8(8))* Advanced Publishing LLC.

Henkes, Kevin. Old Bear. Henkes, Kevin, illus. 2008. (Illus.). 32p. (J). (gr. -1-5). (ENG.). 17.99 *(978-0-06-155205-2(4))*; lib. bdg. 18.89 *(978-0-06-155206-9(2))* HarperCollins Pubs. (Greenwillow Bks.).

—Old Bear Board Book. Henkes, Kevin, illus. 2011. (ENG., Illus.). 28p. (J). (gr. -1 — 1). bds. 7.99 *(978-0-06-208963-2(3),* Greenwillow Bks.) HarperCollins Pubs.

Hill, Marvin. Playland. 2007. 96p. pap. 14.95 *(978-1-84799-888-0(7))* Lulu Pr., Inc.

Hill, Nancy. If Body Parts Could Grow on Trees. 2010. 32p. pap. 12.99 *(978-1-4520-0661-1(X))* AuthorHouse.

Hillard, Shirley. One Big Hug. 2005. (Illus.). 32p. (J). 13.95 *(978-1-933014-20-3(2))* Mamoo Hse.

Hillert, Margaret. Go to Sleep, Dear Dragon. Pullan, Jack, illus. 2016. (BeginningtoRead Ser.). (ENG.). 32p. (J). (-2). lib. bdg. 22.60 *(978-1-59953-766-5(4))*; (gr. -1-2). pap. 11.94 *(978-1-60357-879-0(X))* Norwood Hse. Pr.

Hillert, Margaret. Ve a Dormir, Querido Dragón. Pullan, Jack, illus. 2017. (BeginningtoRead Ser.).Tr. of Go to Sleep, Dear Dragon. (ENG & SPA.). 32p. (J). (-2). 22.60 ***(978-1-59953-829-7(6))*** Norwood Hse. Pr.

Hladik, Terry L. Timid Timmy the Brave. Bouthyette, Valerie, illus. 2008. 28p. pap. 12.95 *(978-0-9822540-5-9(9))* Peppertree Pr., The.

Hobbs, Will. Beardream. Kastner, Jill, illus. 2014. 32p. pap. 8.00 *(978-1-61003-340-4(X))* Center for the Collaborative Classroom.

Hohl, Valicity. When I Grow Up. 2012. 20p. pap. 17.99 *(978-1-4772-3685-7(6))* AuthorHouse.

Holyoak, Kathleen & Summers, Sherry. Flowers in Heaven. 2009. 32p. pap. 14.49 *(978-1-4389-4607-8(4))* AuthorHouse.

Hondo. Dream World Tales. 2005. pap. 9.99 *(978-0-9773016-0-7(5))* Capital Publishing.

Honigsberg, Peter Jan. Pillow of Dreams. Morse, Tony, illus. 2004. 32p. (gr. k-4). 17.95 *(978-1-57143-076-2(8))* RDR Bks.

Hooper, Leta. The Dream That Saved Grizzly Forest. 2010. 16p. pap. 9.00 *(978-1-4490-5087-0(5))* AuthorHouse.

Hopes & Dreams Series II. 64p. (gr. 6-12). pap., tchr.'s training gde. ed. 32.50 *(978-0-8224-3817-5(8))* Globe Fearon Educational Publishing.

Hopton, Stan. To Dance Beneath a Diamond Sky. 2005. 118p. pap. 19.95 *(978-1-4241-0032-3(1))* PublishAmerica, Inc.

Horne, Glenda Burton & Burton, Beth Windsor. My Daydreams, 1 vol. 2009. 21p. pap. 24.95 *(978-1-60749-284-9(9))* America Star Bks.

Hornsby, Ashley Brooke. Pretty Little Lilly & the Land of Sweet Dreams (Hard Bound) Hranilovich, Barbara, illus. 2007. (J). 15.95 *(978-0-9777241-2-3(3))* Cepia LLC.

—Pretty Little Lilly & the Land of Sweet Dreams (Paperback) Hranilovich, Barbara, illus. 2007. (J). *(978-0-9777241-3-0(1))* Cepia LLC.

Howard, Arthur. My Dream Dog. Howard, Arthur, illus. 2016. (ENG., Illus.). 32p. (J). (gr. -1-3). 17.99 *(978-1-4814-5838-2(8),* Beach Lane Bks.) Beach Lane Bks.

Howard-Hess, Susan. Harriet Higby. Leamer, Vickie, illus. 2006. (ENG.). 20p. (gr. k-2). pap. 8.95 *(978-1-57874-093-2(2),* Kaeden Bks.) Kaeden Corp.

Howard, Juliana. Catie the Copycat. 2010. 32p. (J). 17.00 *(978-1-59298-368-1(5))* Beaver's Pond Pr., Inc.

Hubbard O.D., Kristopher T. Iggie's Telescope. 2011. 32p. pap. 14.95 *(978-1-4634-2160-1(5))* AuthorHouse.

Hughes, Rick. The Dream Dragon. 2012. 156p. (gr. 4-6). 23.42 *(978-1-4669-3362-0(3))*; pap. 13.42 *(978-1-4669-3360-6(7))* Trafford Publishing.

Hunter, Erin. Fading Echoes. Richardson, Owen & Douglas, Allen, illus. (Warriors: Omen of the Stars Ser.: 2). (ENG.). (J). (gr. 3-7). 2011. 368p. pap. 6.99 *(978-0-06-155514-5(2))* 2010. 352p. 16.99 *(978-0-06-155512-1(6))* HarperCollins Pubs.

—Fading Echoes. 2015. (Warriors — Omen of the Stars Ser.: 2). (J). lib. bdg. 18.40 *(978-0-606-37723-2(9))* Turtleback Bks.

—Night Whispers. Richardson, Owen & Douglas, Allen, illus. 2010. (Warriors: Omen of the Stars Ser.: 3). (ENG.). 352p. (J). (gr. 3-7). 16.99 *(978-0-06-155515-2(0))* HarperCollins Pubs.

—Warriors: Omen of the Stars #2: Fading Echoes. Richardson, Owen & Douglas, Allen, illus. 2015. (Warriors: Omen of the Stars Ser.: 2). (ENG.). 384p. (J). (gr. 3-7). pap. 7.99 *(978-0-06-238259-7(4))* HarperCollins Pubs.

Hyde, Margaret E. Mo Smells Sweet Dreams: A Scentsational Journey. Chaudhary, Aman, illus. 2012. (Mo's Nose Ser.). (ENG.). 24p. (J). (-k). 17.95 *(978-0-9816255-8-4(4))* Mo's Nose, LLC.

I Dream of Sleeping Dogs. 2006. (J). 24.95 *(978-0-9789633-0-9(X))* Village Monkey LLC, The.

I Love Dreaming. 2005. (J). bds. *(978-0-9759086-0-0(X))* Twinbrook Publishing.

Irwin, Esther. White Cloud: A Little Boy's Dream. Puett, Gayle, ed. Roberson, Ron, illus. 2006. 61p. (J). spiral bd. 10.00 *(978-0-9778462-0-7(2))* Irwin, Esther L.

Jackson, Bridgett. The Princess & the Pink Palace: Book Two of Tales from the Creek. 2008. 36p. pap. 16.99 *(978-1-4389-2038-2(5))* AuthorHouse.

Jackson, Sue Ann. A Vessel for the King. 2013. (Illus.). 40p. pap. 7.99 *(978-1-936688-55-5(7))* AKA:yoLa.

Jean Emily Myers, Emily Myers & Jean Emily Myers. Mickey's Mini Farm. Tanner Voyles, illus. 2009. 32p. pap. 21.99 *(978-1-4389-5544-5(8))* AuthorHouse.

Jeffers, Dawn. Beautiful Moon. Leick, Bonnie, illus. 2010. (ENG.). 32p. (J). (gr. -1-3). pap. 7.95 *(978-1-934960-06-6(3),* Raven Tree Pr.,Csi) Continental Sales, Inc.

Johansson, J. R. Insomnia. 2013. (Night Walkers Ser.: 1). (ENG.). 360p. (YA). pap. 9.99 *(978-0-7387-3593-1(0),* Flux) North Star Editions.

—Mania. 2015. (Night Walkers Ser.: 3). (ENG.). 408p. (YA). pap. 9.99 *(978-0-7387-4431-5(X),* Flux) North Star Editions.

—Paranoia. 2014. (Night Walkers Ser.: 2). (ENG.). 336p. (YA). pap. 9.99 *(978-0-7387-4018-8(7),* Flux) North Star Editions.

Johnson, Cara. Falling Awake - the Remembering: The Dream Travelers Companion. 2007. 64p. (J). per. 6.99 *(978-0-9768870-2-7(9))* Whirling Dirvish Publishing.

—Looking Forward Back: The Dream Travelers Book Three. 2008. 162p. (J). per. 9.99 *(978-0-9768870-3-4(7))* Whirling Dirvish Publishing.

Johnson, Phyllis. Ben's Dreams. 2013. 24p. 18.95 *(978-1-4575-2277-2(2))* Dog Ear Publishing, LLC.

—Betsy Star Ballerin. 2011. 24p. 16.95 *(978-1-4575-0149-4(X))* Dog Ear Publishing, LLC.

Johnson, Vickey L. The Monster Mix-Up. 2003. (Illus.). (J). pap. 9.00 *(978-0-8059-6125-6(9))* Dorrance Publishing Co., Inc.

Johnston, Jan. Cruiser & the Night Noises. Eugenia, Maria, illus. 2009. (ENG.). 20p. 12.99 *(978-1-934706-51-0(5))* Blue Apple Bks.

Jones, Brandy. Petunia: The Plump Princess, 1 vol. 2010. 32p. 24.95 *(978-1-4489-4874-1(6))* PublishAmerica, Inc.

Jones, H. Lena. Trapped on Planet Liska. 2006. 180p. pap. 19.95 *(978-1-4241-0989-0(2))* America Star Bks.

Jones, Sandy. Anya's Gift: A Tale of Two Christmases, 1 vol. Yourell, Pam, illus. 2009. 48p. pap. 24.95 *(978-1-61546-129-5(9))* America Star Bks.

Kaaberbøl, Lene. The Serpent Gift. 3rd ed. 2007. (Shamer Chronicles Ser.: 3). Orig. Title: Slangens Gave. (ENG.). 384p. (J). (gr. 5-9). pap. 22.99 *(978-0-8050-8655-3(2),* 9780805086553, Holt, Henry & Co. Bks. For Young Readers) Holt, Henry & Co.

Kauzlarich, Jane. Quack: A Two Jane Creation. 2009. 20p. pap. 12.49 *(978-1-4389-6599-4(0))* AuthorHouse.

Keast, Ellen Frances. A Snowy Week. 2010. 16p. pap. 9.99 *(978-1-60911-647-7(X),* Eloquent Bks.) Strategic Book Publishing & Rights Agency (SBPRA).

Keating, Lucy. Dreamology. 2016. 336p. (YA). (gr. 8). 17.99 *(978-0-06-238000-5(1),* HarperTeen) HarperCollins Pubs.

Kelty, Colleen Alyce. I Guess I'll Be, 1 vol. Swope, Brenda, illus. 2010. 24p. 24.95 *(978-1-4489-4937-3(8))* PublishAmerica, Inc.

Ketchen, Susan. Born That Way. 2009. (ENG.). 176p. (YA). (gr. 7-10). pap. 12.95 *(978-0-88982-254-2(9))* Oolichan Bks. CAN. Dist: Univ. of Toronto Pr.

Kidd, Ronald. Dreambender. (ENG.). 256p. (J). (gr. 3-7). 2017. pap. 9.99 ***(978-0-8075-1726-0(7))*** 2016. (Illus.). 16.99 *(978-0-8075-1725-3(9))* Whitman, Albert & Co.

Kiker, Jean. The Story of Misty: The star who became the most famous star of All. 2011. 20p. 11.59 *(978-1-4269-5627-0(4))* Trafford Publishing.

King, A. S. Everybody Sees the Ants. 2011. (ENG.). 288p. (YA). (gr. 10-17). 18.00 *(978-0-316-12928-2(3))* Little Brown & Co.

—Everybody Sees the Ants. 2012. (ENG.). 320p. (YA). (gr. 10-17). pap. 10.00 *(978-0-316-12927-5(5))* Little, Brown Bks. for Young Readers.

Knesek, Marian. Sage & the Peacock. Buehrle, Jackie, illus. 2011. 28p. pap. 24.95 *(978-1-4512-2211-1(4))* America Star Bks.

Knox, Elizabeth. Dreamhunter. 2009. (Dreamhunter Duet Ser.: 1). (ENG.). 384p. (YA). (gr. 7-12). pap. 10.99 *(978-0-312-53571-1(6),* 9780312535711) Square Fish.

—Dreamquake. 2007. (Dreamhunter Duet Ser.: No. 2). 528p. *(978-0-7322-8194-6(6),* Fourth Estate) HarperCollins Pubs. Australia.

—Dreamquake. 2009. (Dreamhunter Duet Ser.: 2). (ENG., Illus.). 464p. (YA). (gr. 7-12). pap. 12.99 *(978-0-312-58147-3(5),* 9780312581473) Square Fish.

Kollin, Dani. My Very Own Dreidel: A Pop-up Hanakkah Celebration! Howard, Juliet, illus. 2007. (ENG.). 12p. 10.95 *(978-1-58117-592-9(2),* Intervisual/Piggy Toes) Bendon, Inc.

Kongyin. Gooby & the Dreamwalker. 2011. 296p. pap. *(978-0-9869858-4-3(8))* Kima Global Pubs.

Kreitz, Tina. Rocky the Sea Turtle. Triplett, Chris Harper, illus. 2013. (ENG.). (J). 14.95 *(978-1-62086-132-5(1))* Mascot Bks., Inc.

Kropik, Linda Kristine. Christopher the Choo Choo Train. Haezer, Jane, illus. 2011. 24p. pap. 11.50 *(978-1-60911-522-7(8),* Strategic Bk. Publishing) Strategic Book Publishing & Rights Agency (SBPRA).

Kushner, Sam. Cinderell. 2012. 34p. 25.99 *(978-1-4582-0684-8(X))*; pap. 16.99 *(978-1-4582-0685-5(8))* Author Solutions, Inc. (Abbott Pr.).

Kusugak, Michael. The Littlest Sled Dog, 1 vol. Krykorka, Vladyana, illus. 2010. (ENG.). 32p. (J). (gr. -1-3). pap. 10.95 *(978-1-55469-174-6(5))* Orca Bk. Pubs. USA.

LaChanze. Little Diva. Pinkney, Brian, illus. 2010. (ENG.). 32p. (J). (gr. -1-3). 16.99 *(978-0-312-37010-7(5),* 9780312370107) Feiwel & Friends.

Lacoursiere, Patrick. Dream Songs Night Songs: From China to Senegal. Bourbonnière, Sylvie, illus. 2006. (ENG.). 36p. (J). (gr. -1-2). 16.95 *(978-2-923163-24-6(9))* La Montagne Secrete CAN. Dist: Independent Pubs. Group.

Lagonegro, Melissa & RH Disney Staff. Ballerina Princess. Harding, Niall, illus. 2007. (Step into Reading Ser.). (ENG.). 32p. (J). (gr. k-3). pap. 3.99 *(978-0-7364-2428-8(8),* RH/Disney) Random Hse. Children's Bks.

Lalich, Nadine. Finding Happiness: A Magical Tale about the Power of Positive Thinking. Lalich, Nadine, illus. 2017. (ENG., Illus.). 68p. (gr. -1-4). reprint ed. per. 14.95 *(978-0-9711776-0-4(0))* HB Publishing, LLC.

Lancett, Peter. The Dark Dreams, 1 vol. unabr. ed. 2010. (Dark Man Ser.). (ENG.). 34p. (YA). (gr. 9-12). pap. 7.95 *(978-1-61651-017-6(X))* Saddleback Educational Publishing, Inc.

—The Dark Never Hides (Blue Series), 1 vol. 2015. (Dark Man Ser.). (ENG.). 36p. (YA). (gr. 9-12). pap. 7.95 *(978-1-68021-124-5(2))* Saddleback Educational Publishing, Inc.

Lawson, Dorie McCullough. Tex: A Book for Little Dreamers. 2011. (ENG., Illus.). 44p. (J). (gr. -1-k). 15.95 *(978-1-57076-501-8(4))* Trafalgar Square Bks.

Layton, Dan. Adventures in the Kingdom, the Dreamer. 2004. 64p. pap. 5.99 *(978-0-9707919-4-8(1))* Mercy Place, Inc.

Lloyd, Natalie. The Key to Extraordinary. (ENG.). 240p. (J). (gr. 3-7). 2017. pap. 6.99 ***(978-0-545-55276-9(1))*** 2016. 16.99 *(978-0-545-55274-5(5))* Scholastic, Inc. (Scholastic Pr.).

Lois, Lowry. Gossamer. 2006. (ENG.). 144p. (J). (gr. 5-7). 17.99 *(978-0-618-68550-9(2))* Houghton Mifflin Harcourt Publishing Co.

—Gossamer. 2008. (ENG.). 176p. (J). (gr. 3-7). 6.99 *(978-0-385-73416-5(6),* Yearling) Random Hse. Children's Bks.

Lopez, C. Pellicer. Juan y Sus Zapatos. (SPA., Illus.). (J). (gr. k-2). pap. 5.95 *(978-970-629-132-5(6),* SI6616) Sistemas Tecnicos de Edicion, S.A. de C.V. MEX. Dist: AIMS International Bks., Inc.

Lore, Erin, illus. Timmy the Dragon. l.t. ed. 2007. 32p. (J). 8.95 *(978-0-9741562-7-9(2))* Yarrow Pr.

Louise, T. See You in My Dreams. 2013. 52p. pap. 14.14 *(978-0-9853560-7-1(3))* TLC.

Lovelady, W. f. The Adventures of Johnny Saturday: Back to the Drawing Board. 2012. 76p. pap. 12.95 *(978-1-4685-5286-7(4))* AuthorHouse.

Luiken, Nicole. Dreamfire. 2009. (Dreamfire Ser.: 1). (ENG.). 192p. pap. 14.95 *(978-1-894283-88-5(0),* Great Plains Teen Fiction) Great Plains Pubns. CAN. Dist: Publishers Group Canada.

Lynch, Kendra. Sweet Dreams Little. 2011. 24p. pap. 12.74 *(978-1-4520-8295-0(2))* AuthorHouse.

C D

Maar, Paul. El Viaje de Lisa. Kasparavicius, Kestutis, illus. 2008. (la Orilla del Viento Ser.). (SPA.). 28p. (J). (gr. -1-3). 12.99 (978-968-16-7452-6(9)) Fondo de Cultura Economica USA.

MacDonald, Anne Louise. Seeing Red. 2009. (ENG.). 224p. (J). (gr. 5-9). 17.95 (978-1-55453-291-9(4)) Kids Can Pr., Ltd. CAN. Dist: Hachette Bk. Group.

MacDonald, Anne Louise & Wahl, Charis. Seeing Red. 2009. (ENG.). 224p. (J). (gr. 5-9). 8.95 (978-1-55453-292-6(2)) Kids Can Pr., Ltd. CAN. Dist: Hachette Bk. Group.

MacHado, Ana Maria. Delantal Que el Viento Lleva. (SPA.). pap. 12.95 (978-950-07-2220-9(8)) Editorial Sudamericana S.A. ARG. Dist: Distribooks, Inc.

Mack, Jeff. Hush Little Polar Bear. Mack, Jeff, illus. (ENG., Illus.). (J). (gr. -1-1). 2013. 36p. bds. 7.99 (978-1-59643-945-0(9), 9781596439450) 2008. 40p. 17.99 (978-1-59643-368-7(X), 9781596433687) Roaring Brook Pr.

Mackall, Deborah. What Happens When I'm Asleep? Mackall, Debbie, illus. 2008. (ENG.). 32p. (J). (gr. -1-k). 15.95 (978-0-9762273-1-1(2)) Dimensions in Media, Inc.

Mackan, Paul. Dream Girl, Dream! A Story for Children to Share with Groan-Ups, 1 vol. 2010. 55p. pap. 16.95 (978-1-4489-7842-7(4)) America Star Bks.

MacKenzie, Ross. Zac & the Dream Stealers. (J). 2013. 297p. (978-0-545-40107-4(0)) 2012. (ENG.). 304p. (gr. 3-7). 16.99 (978-0-545-40106-7(2)) Scholastic, Inc. (Chicken Hse., The).

MacMillan, Dustin. A Place of Dreams. 2008. 20p. pap. 10.49 (978-1-4389-4062-5(9)) AuthorHouse.

MacPherson, D. R. The First Wave. 2009. 68p. pap. 21.00 (978-1-60860-456-2(X), Eloquent Bks.) Strategic Book Publishing & Rights Agency (SBPRA).

Madel, Dan. Cracker the Cat, Almost Caught. 2008. 24p. pap. 24.95 (978-1-4241-9252-6(8)) America Star Bks.

Magee, Dolunay. Perrey's Adventures. 2012. (Illus.). 20p. pap. 19.82 (978-1-4772-3501-0(9)) AuthorHouse.

Maguire, Thomas Aquinas. Three Little Dreams, 3 vols. 2010. (ENG., Illus.). 36p. (J). (gr. -1). 16.95 (978-1-894965-79-8(5)) Simply Read Bks. CAN. Dist: Ingram Publisher Services.

Mair, J. Samia. Amira's Totally Chocolate World. 2010. (ENG., Illus.). 29p. (J). (gr. k-3). 8.95 (978-0-86037-408-4(4)) Kube Publishing Ltd. GBR. Dist: Consortium Bk. Sales & Distribution.

Malik, S. A. Omari's Flight: The Mercy of Love. 2007. (Illus.). 81p. (YA). per. 7.98 (978-0-9794615-0-7(2)) EDR.

Malouf, Ranya. Blue Fish's Secret Wish. 2011. 32p. pap. (978-9963-610-72-3(2)) Rimal Pubns.

Marchessault, Sara J. Pinky the Dreamer & Her Silver Jet. 2009. 36p. pap. 15.49 (978-1-4389-9902-9(X)) AuthorHouse.

Mariolle, Mathieu. Changing Moon. MiniKim et al, illus. 2010. (Nola's Worlds Ser.: 1). (ENG.). 136p. (J). (gr. 6-9). 30.60 (978-0-7613-6502-0(8)) Lerner Publishing Group.

—Changing Moon. Jeffrey, Erica Olson, tr. from FRE. MiniKim et al, illus. 2010. (Nola's Worlds Ser.: 1). (ENG.). 136p. (J). (gr. 6-9). pap. 9.95 (978-0-7613-6538-9(9), Graphic Universe™) Lerner Publishing Group.

—Changing Moon. rev. ed. 2010. pap. 56.72 (978-0-7613-6953-0(8)) Lerner Publishing Group.

Martin, Amy. In Your Dreams. 2012. 254p. pap. 9.99 (978-0-9882051-0-9(6)) Martin, Amy.

Martin, Emily Winfield. Dream Animals: A Bedtime Journey. 2013. (ENG., Illus.). 32p. (J). (gr. -1-k). 17.99 (978-0-449-81080-4(1)); lib. bdg. 20.99 (978-0-375-97149-5(1)) Random Hse. Children's Bks. (Random Hse. Bks. for Young Readers).

Martin, Paige. Daniel Keep Dreaming. Price, Ronnalda, ed. Williams, Angie, photos by. 2011. (Illus.). 48p. (J). pap. 15.00 (978-0-578-08272-1(1)) Paige Martin Bks.

Martone, Ginny. Trapped in Dead Man's Cave. 2007. 61p. pap. 19.95 (978-1-60474-227-5(5)) America Star Bks.

Matas, Carol. Visions. 2nd rev. ed. 2008. (Freak Ser.). (ENG.). 128p. (J). (gr. 7-18). pap. (978-1-55263-932-0(0)) Me to We.

Mathis, Kate. Moon over Monsters. 2013. 318p. pap. 12.95 (978-0-9819789-9-4(1)) PowWow Publishing.

Matott, J. P. & Baker, Margaret. When I Was a Girl ... I Dreamed. Ludy, Mark, illus. 2005. (ENG.). 32p. (J). (gr. -1-4). (978-0-9664276-3-9(7)) Green Pastures Publishing, Inc.

Matthews, Gail. Our Forever Family, 1 vol. 2010. 32p. 24.95 (978-1-4512-1055-2(8)) America Star Bks.

Matthews, Regina Stone. Elizabeth Marie Hutchinson - When I Dream. 2008. 48p. pap. 16.95 (978-1-60563-112-7(4)) America Star Bks.

Mayer, Marvin. Ferdinand Frog's Flight. Macquignon, Stephen, illus. 2011. 32p. pap. 15.55 (978-0-9832740-0-1(2)) 4RV Publishing, LLC.

Mayer, Mercer. Una Pesadilla en Mi Armario. 2003. (SPA., Illus.). 32p. (J). (gr. k-3). 7.95 (978-84-372-1754-3(7), SAN7547) Altea, Ediciones, S.A. - Grupo Santillana ESP. Dist: Santillana USA Publishing Co., Inc.

McAllister, Margaret. Life Shop. 2004. (ENG.). 160p. (YA). (gr. 7). pap. 8.99 (978-0-7459-4906-2(1), Lion Books) Lion Hudson PLC GBR. Dist: Independent Pubs. Group.

McCalla Njee, Lena. Ivan Consigue la Casa de Sus Suenos. Urruela, Maria Cristina, tr. 2013. 46p. pap. 13.99 (978-976-95510-3-9(1)) Minna Pr.

—Ivan Gets a Dream House. 2012. 46p. pap. 13.99 (978-0-9829630-4-3(1)) Minna Pr.

McConchie, Lyn. Winter of Waiting. 2015. (YA). (gr. 5-18). pap. 15.00 (978-1-936021-55-0(2), Banana Oil Bks.) Cyberwizard Productions.

McCullough, Angela. Night Nite. 2008. 24p. pap. 10.00 (978-1-934925-10-2(1), Eloquent Bks.) Strategic Book Publishing & Rights Agency (SBPRA).

McDunn, Rosemary. When Kids Dream & Trucks Fly. 2007. (ENG.). 52p. per. 12.99 (978-0-9792258-6-4(8)) Bezalel Bks.

McEntee, Jackie. Reality & Dreams. 2010. 120p. (gr. -1). pap. 12.49 (978-1-4389-9551-9(2)) AuthorHouse.

McKechnie, Edward. Sweet Dreams for Scotty. Blanding, Allison, illus. 2007. 14p. (J). spiral bd. 14.95 (978-0-9785302-0-4(9)) Beanstalk Pubns.

McKelvain Kite, Karen. I Had a Dream. 2009. (Illus.). 40p. pap. 18.49 (978-1-4490-3539-6(6)) AuthorHouse.

McKenna, Jacqueline & Manarino-Leggett, Priscilla. Sourpuss Sue. Manarino, Mark, illus. 2011. 24p. pap. 24.95 (978-1-4560-8939-9(0)) America Star Bks.

McMann, Lisa. Don't Close Your Eyes: Wake; Fade; Gone. 2013. (ENG., Illus.). 720p. (YA). (gr. 9). pap. 12.99 (978-1-4424-9913-3(3), Simon Pulse) Simon Pulse.

—Fade. (Wake Ser.: Bk. 2). (ENG., (YA). (gr. 9-18). 2010. Illus.). 272p. pap. 10.99 (978-1-4169-7448-2(2)) 2009. 256p. 17.99 (978-1-4169-5358-6(2)) Simon Pulse. (Simon Pulse).

—Gone. (Wake Ser.: Bk. 3). (ENG.). (YA). (gr. 9). 2011. 240p. pap. 9.99 (978-1-4169-7921-0(2)) 2010. 224p. 17.99 (978-1-4169-7918-0(2)) Simon Pulse. (Simon Pulse).

—Wake. 2008. (Wake Ser.: Bk. 1). (ENG.). 224p. (YA). (gr. 9). pap. 11.99 (978-1-4169-7447-5(4)); 17.99 (978-1-4169-5357-9(4)) Simon Pulse. (Simon Pulse).

McMillan, Angelo. The Adventures of W D: The Dreamers Series Vol. 1. 2012. 24p. 24.95 (978-1-4626-5270-9(0)) America Star Bks.

Medina, Sylvia M. & Ballock-Dixon, Saige J. Desert Mirage. Eagle, Joy, illus. 2012. 32p. pap. 11.59 (978-0-9836602-6-2(3)) Green Kids Club, Inc.

Merberg, Julie & Bober, Suzanne. Dreaming with Rousseau. 2007. (Mini Masters Ser.: MINI). (ENG., Illus.). 22p. (J). (gr. -1 — 1). bds. 6.99 (978-0-8118-5712-3(3)) Chronicle Bks. LLC.

Meyer, Victoria. Dream Catcher, 1 vol. 2009. 48p. pap. 16.95 (978-1-61582-998-9(9)) PublishAmerica, Inc.

Michaels, Mishon. The Big Adventures of Little Again Sam. 2012. 28p. pap. 24.95 (978-1-4626-8827-2(6)) America Star Bks.

Middleton, Julian. Rebecca's Book of Dreams. 2013. 110p. pap. (978-1-78407-136-3(6)) FeedARead.com.

A Midsummer Nightrsquo;s Dream by William Shakespeare: The Graphic Novel. 2012. (Classic Graphic Novel Collection). (ENG.). (gr. 7-10). lib. bdg. 34.80 (978-1-4205-0840-6(7), Lucent Bks.) Cengage Gale.

Miller, Janet. DuckDumB. 2010. 32p. pap. 21.95 (978-0-557-57669-2(5)) Lulu Pr., Inc.

Mills, Patricia Anne. Oswald Daydreams. 2010. (Illus.). 32p. pap. 12.99 (978-1-4520-2209-3(7)) AuthorHouse.

Milne, Rg. Quibble Tales: The Adventures of Bobin Hood of Sherworm Forest. 2012. 28p. 24.95 (978-1-4626-6755-0(4)) America Star Bks.

Mitchell, Sherry. Fernando the Veterinarian. 2012. 20p. pap. 17.99 (978-1-4685-8098-3(1)) AuthorHouse.

Mitchell, Todd. The Secret to Lying. (ENG., Illus.). 336p. (YA). (gr. 9). 2011. pap. 7.99 (978-0-7636-5620-1(8)) 2010. 17.99 (978-0-7636-4084-2(0)) Candlewick Pr.

Moffett, Rodney. The Eighth Crest. 2006. (ENG.). 228p. per. 24.95 (978-1-4241-3907-1(4)) PublishAmerica, Inc.

Montgomery, L. M. Anne's House of Dreams. 2011. 228p. 27.95 (978-1-4638-9526-6(7)) Rodgers, Alan Bks.

Moody, Cynthia. Dream, the Big Elephant. 2012. 24p. pap. 14.93 (978-1-4669-2610-3(4)) Trafford Publishing.

Moore, Johnny Ray. But Still, We Dream: (a novel in Verse), 1 vol. 2009. 60p. pap. 16.95 (978-1-60813-491-5(1)) America Star Bks.

Mora, Pat. Sweet Dreams/Dulces Suenos. Suarez, Maribel, illus. 2008. (My Family: Mi Familia Ser.). (SPA & ENG.). 24p. (J). (gr. -1-1). 12.99 (978-0-06-085041-8(8), Rayo) HarperCollins Pubs.

Morden, Daniel. So Hungry. Carpenter, Suzanne, illus. 2004. (ENG.). 32p. pap. 29.95 (978-1-84323-455-5(6)) Beekman Bks., Inc.

Morgan, Allen. Matthew & the Midnight Hospital. 2004. (Illus.). (J). (gr. k-3). spiral bd. (978-0-616-01529-2(1)) Canadian National Institute for the Blind/Institut National Canadien pour les Aveugles.

Morrissey, Dean. Ship of Dreams. 2016. (ENG., Illus.). 40p. (J). (gr. -1-2). 17.95 (978-1-63226-051-2(4), Prospecta Pr.) Easton Studio Pr., LLC.

Moverley, Richard. The Reluctant Rajput. Dean, David, illus. 2005. (Yellow Go Bananas Ser.). (ENG.). 48p. (J). (gr. 3-4). lib. bdg. (978-0-7787-2723-1(8)) Crabtree Publishing Co.

Mulrain, Sabrina. Ultimate Dreamer. 2011. 44p. pap. 24.95 (978-1-4560-3670-6(X)) America Star Bks.

Murguia, Bethanie Deeney. Buglette, the Messy Sleeper. Murguia, Bethanie Deeney, illus. 2011. (ENG., Illus.). 32p. (J). (gr. -1-2). 15.99 (978-1-58246-375-9(1), Tricycle Pr.) Random Hse. Children's Bks.

Murphy, Bobby. Ted the Turtle's Trip to the Moon. 2013. 24p. pap. 11.50 (978-1-62212-431-2(6), Strategic Bk. Publishing) Strategic Book Publishing & Rights Agency (SBPRA).

Musgrave, Susan. Dreams Are More Real Than Bathtubs. braille ed. 2004. (Illus.). (J). (gr. k-3). spiral bd. (978-0-616-01748-7(0)) Canadian National Institute for the Blind/Institut National Canadien pour les Aveugles.

Myers, Walter Dean. The Dream Bearer. 2004. (ENG.). 192p. (YA). (gr. 5-18). reprint ed. pap. 6.99 (978-0-06-447289-0(2), Amistad) HarperCollins Pubs.

Najafi, Imran. Dreams. 2013. 18p. pap. 9.95 (978-1-62857-238-4(8), Strategic Bk. Publishing) Strategic Book Publishing & Rights Agency (SBPRA).

Nason, Seldon E. The Adventures of Otis & Amigo, Book Two - the President's Request. 2016. (ENG., Illus.). 46p. (J). pap. 11.95 (978-1-5069-0207-4(3)) First Edition Design eBook Publishing.

Nave, Jeff. Obama's Pajamas. 2008. 44p. pap. 18.99 (978-1-4389-3150-0(6)) AuthorHouse.

Nelid, Piper. The Big Dream, 01 vols., 1. 2016. (Rosen REAL Readers: Social Studies Nonfiction / Fiction: Family, Community, & the World Ser.). (ENG.). 12p. (J). pap. 6.33 (978-1-5081-1964-7(3), Rosen Classroom) Rosen Publishing Group, Inc., The.

Neuhofer, Sheri L. Courageous Warrior. Amory, Deanna & O'Hara, Cynthia, illus. 2010. 28p. pap. 10.95 (978-0-9787472-7-5(5)) Ajoyin Publishing, Inc.

Neuman, M. Robert. Clawing & Scratching & Thumping About. 2013. 30p. pap. 9.99 (978-0-9898820-0-2(4)) Mindstir Media.

Newland, James P. A Smile Says It All. 2009. 48p. pap. 17.49 (978-1-4490-3438-2(1)) AuthorHouse.

Newton-Perry, Linda. The Little Red Car & Bigfoot. 2009. 70p. pap. 15.95 (978-0-557-08449-4(0)) Lulu Pr., Inc.

Nicely, Adam. Bedtime for Tad. 2009. (ENG., Illus.). 28p. (J). (gr. k — 1). bds. 7.95 (978-1-894965-84-2(1)) Simply Read Bks. CAN. Dist: Ingram Publisher Services.

Nielsen, Gwyn English. Serendipity & the Dream Catcher. Nielsen, Gwyn English, ed. Colby, Devon English, illus. 2003. 176p. (gr. 3-7). pap. 5.95 (978-0-9660726-2-4(6)) C.G.S. Pr.

Night, P. J. Together Forever. 2012. (Creepover Ser.: 8). lib. bdg. 16.00 (978-0-606-26339-9(X), Turtleback) Turtleback Bks.

Noël, Alyson. Dreamland. 2011. (Riley Bloom Book Ser.: 3). (ENG.). 224p. (J). (gr. 4-7). pap. 7.99 (978-0-312-56375-2(2), 9780312563752) Square Fish.

Norton, Tamra. Bearubs & Flutterberries. 2008. (Bearubs Ser.). pap. 3.99 (978-0-9796008-1-4(2)) Lindsley, David Studio.

—Bearubs Clydes New Job. 2008. (Bearubs Ser.). 32p. pap. 3.99 (978-0-9796008-2-1(0)) Lindsley, David Studio.

—Meet Bearubs. 2008. (Bearubs Ser.). 32p. pap. 3.99 (978-0-9796008-0-7(4)) Lindsley, David Studio.

Nowell, Daphne A. Juana Meets Gabriel, the Small Business Angel: What if you Don't Want to Wait Around for a Prince Charming? 2008. (Illus.). 24p. (J). 17.95 (978-0-9798909-1-8(8)) Business Angel Pr.

O'Brien, Caragh M. The Rule of Mirrors. 2016. (Vault of Dreamers Trilogy Ser.: 2). (ENG., Illus.). 432p. (YA). (gr. 7). 17.99 (978-1-59643-940-5(8), 9781596439405) Roaring Brook Pr.

—The Vault of Dreamers. 2014. (ENG., Illus.). 432p. (YA). (gr. 7-12). 17.99 (978-1-59643-938-2(6), 9781596439382) Roaring Brook Pr.

O'Connor, Crystal Ball. Katherine's Quilt. 2007. (J). 18.95 (978-0-9774038-4-4(X)) Monarch Pubs.

Olsen, Gina Ann. I Can't, Even Though I Should, 1 vol. 2010. 18p. pap. 24.95 (978-1-4489-7671-3(5)) PublishAmerica, Inc.

Olvera, Jillann. Christian's Lullaby. 2006. 29p. pap. 24.95 (978-1-4241-1909-7(X)) PublishAmerica, Inc.

Once upon My Summer Camp Dream. 2003. spiral bd. 14.95 (978-0-9744437-1-3(9)) Imagination Workshop, The.

Onwusilikam, Ify Chinedum. The Drama Queen. 2009. 56p. pap. 10.00 (978-1-60860-126-4(9), Strategic Bk. Publishing) Strategic Book Publishing & Rights Agency (SBPRA).

Orgel, Doris. Sarah's Room. Sendak, Maurice, illus. 2003. (Sendak Reissues Ser.). (ENG.). 48p. (J). (gr. -1-3). 15.95 (978-0-06-029727-5(1)) HarperCollins Pubs.

Orser-Mokelky, Jacqueline. If I Had ... 2012. 24p. pap. 10.95 (978-1-4525-5987-2(2)) Balboa Pr.

Ortiz, Tracy. As Dreamtime Unfolds. 2009. 20p. pap. 24.95 (978-1-60749-359-4(4)) America Star Bks.

Owens, Joann. I Have a Dream: A child's view of Martin Luther King Day. 2008. 24p. pap. 14.00 (978-1-4389-0172-5(0)) AuthorHouse.

Paladin, Frank. Hole in My Stocking. Amber, Holly & Lin, Melanie, illus. 2005. 24p. (J). per. 16.95 (978-0-9763635-4-5(2)) Beyond the Stars Pubns.

Palumbo, Mary Lou. Skippy the Dog in the Band. Mikle, Toby, illus. 2009. 48p. pap. 19.49 (978-1-4389-9218-1(1)) AuthorHouse.

Paniagua, Kelly. Bedtime for Sarah Sullivan. Warrick, Jessica, illus. 2012. 36p. (J). 13.95 (978-1-60131-119-1(2)); pap. 10.95 (978-1-60131-120-7(6)) Big Tent Bks. (Castlebridge Bks.).

Pardoe, David. Jasper Tippett's Amazing Journey to Page 42. 2006. (Illus.). 132p. pap. (978-1-84401-785-0(0)) Athena Pr.

Paris, Tom. Tom & Pearl's Udder Stand. 2012. 44p. pap. 17.45 (978-1-4669-4829-7(9)) Trafford Publishing.

Parker, Lisa L. Gray. Princesses Do Not Wear Tattoos. Logan, Desiree, illus. 2011. 48p. pap. 24.95 (978-1-4560-3281-4(X)) America Star Bks.

Parragon Staff. Disney Princess Sparkling Dreams. 2010. (Disney Twinkly Lights Board Bks.). 6p. (J). (gr. -1-k). bds. (978-1-4075-9340-1(4)) Parragon, Inc.

Parsons, Leif. Only Fish Fall from the Sky. 2015. (ENG., Illus.). 32p. (J). (gr. -1-2). 17.95 (978-1-57687-757-9(4), powerHouse Bks.) powerHouse Cultural Entertainment, Inc.

Paul Frank Industries. Only in Dreams. 2011. (ENG., Illus.). 24p. (J). (gr. -1 — 1). bds. 6.99 (978-0-8118-7867-8(8)) Chronicle Bks. LLC.

Paulsen, Gary. The Night the White Deer Died. 2011. (ENG.). 114p. (YA). (gr. 7). pap. 6.99 (978-0-385-74235-1(5), Ember) Random Hse. Children's Bks.

Pavey, Peter. One Dragon's Dream. Pavey, Peter, illus. 2009. (ENG., Illus.). 40p. (J). (gr. -1-2). 17.99 (978-0-7636-4470-3(6)) Candlewick Pr.

Pedraza, M. Eugenia Rueda. Nico's Voyage. 2013. 32p. pap. (978-1-4602-2360-4(8)) FriesenPress.

Pelham, P.J. Hanna Searches for "Me!" 2004. 24p. (J). pap. 15.50 (978-1-4120-3208-7(3)) Trafford Publishing.

Perry, Dakota. Brim's Journey. 2008. 36p. pap. 24.95 (978-1-60703-938-9(9)) America Star Bks.

Peters, Jackie. Mary Maybelieve. 2011. (Illus.). 92p. pap. 30.63 (978-1-4567-7283-3(X)) AuthorHouse.

Phillips, Ruby Ann. Dream Birthday, 1 vol. Isik, Semur, illus. 2014. (Krystal Ball Ser.). (ENG.). 112p. (gr. 2-3). 25.32 (978-1-4795-2178-4(7)) Picture Window Bks.

—Fortune Cookie Fiasco. Isik, Semur, illus. 2015. (Krystal Ball Ser.). (ENG.). 112p. (gr. 2-3). lib. bdg. 25.32 (978-1-4795-5874-2(5)) Picture Window Bks.

—Pet Psychic. Isik, Semur, illus. 2015. (Krystal Ball Ser.). (ENG.). 112p. (gr. 2-3). lib. bdg. 25.32 (978-1-4795-5875-9(3)) Picture Window Bks.

Picard, Barbara Leonie. One Is One. 2006. (ENG.). 286p. (J). (gr. 3-7). per. 9.95 (978-1-58988-027-6(7)) Consortium Bk. Sales & Distribution.

Pippenger, Jack G. The Young Rebel. 2007. 292p. 27.95 (978-0-595-86314-3(0)); per. 17.95 (978-0-595-41077-4(4)) iUniverse, Inc.

Pimot, Karen Hutchins. Night Traveler. Pimot, Karen Hutchins, illus. 2007. (Illus.). 24p. per. 12.95 (978-1-934246-97-9(2)) Peppertree Pr., The.

Plitt, Kay. Why Isn't Bobby Like Me, Mom? 2010. 32p. 14.75 (978-1-4269-4038-5(6)) Trafford Publishing.

Plum, Amy. Dreamfall. 2017. (Dreamfall Ser.: 1). 288p. (YA). (gr. 9). 17.99 (978-0-06-242987-2(6), HarperTeen) HarperCollins Pubs.

Potter, Giselle. Tell Me What to Dream About. 2015. (ENG., Illus.). 40p. (J). (gr. -1-2). 17.99 (978-0-385-37423-1(2), Schwartz & Wade Bks.) Random Hse. Children's Bks.

Potter, Ryan. Perennial, 0 vols. 2014. (ENG.). 296p. (YA). (gr. 7-9). pap. 9.99 (978-1-4778-1818-3(9), 9781477818183, Amazon Children's Publishing) Amazon Publishing.

Preble, Joy. Dreaming Anastasia. 2009. (ENG.). 320p. (YA). (gr. 7-12). pap. 13.99 (978-1-4022-1817-0(6), Sourcebooks Jabberwocky) Sourcebooks, Inc.

Preble, Laura. Lica's Angel. 2003. 142p. (YA). 21.95 (978-0-595-74914-0(3)); pap. 11.95 (978-0-595-28253-1(9)) iUniverse, Inc.

Price, Cheryl A. Follow the Sun. 2010. (Calico Pony Ser.: Bk. 1). 48p. (J). pap. 17.49 (978-1-4490-7217-9(8)) AuthorHouse.

Price, Justine. The Dreams of a Puppy. 2013. 28p. pap. 24.95 (978-1-63000-049-3(3)) America Star Bks.

Price, Mary Ellizabeth. Wallbaby Bumblebees. 2004. (Illus.). 40p. (J). per. 15.75 (978-0-9715402-2-4(5), 410-707-6686) Barnhardt & Ashe Publishing, Inc.

Prochaska, Dan J. Courage, 1 vol. 2009. 48p. pap. 16.95 (978-1-61582-995-8(4)) PublishAmerica, Inc.

Publications International Ltd. Staff, ed. Disney Princess: Enchanted Dreams. 2010. 40p. (J). bds. 14.98 (978-1-60553-685-9(7)) Publications International, Ltd.

Quinn, Susan. Little Bear & the Butterflies. Pedler, Caroline, illus. 2014. 24p. (J). **(978-1-4351-5922-8(5))** Barnes & Noble, Inc.

Quintana, Pamela. Silly Sweet SnuggleBugzzz Dreamzzz. 2010. (J). 14.95 (978-0-615-38169-5(3)) SnuggleBugzzz Pr.

Rader, Jared. Sandy's Dream. Meyers, Sarah, illus. 2007. 16p. (J). (gr. -1-3). 10.99 (978-1-59879-398-7(5)) Lifevest Publishing, Inc.

Randall, Ronne. Before I Go to Sleep. Kerins, Tony, illus. 2010. (Picture Books Ser.). (J). (gr. -1-k). bds. (978-1-4075-8756-1(0)) Parragon, Inc.

Randolph, Robert. Ben the Flying Cat, 1 vol. Sappington, Ray, illus. 2009. 30p. pap. 24.95 (978-1-60749-088-3(9)) America Star Bks.

Rath, Tom H. Donkey Oatie's Impossible Dream. MacAdam, Reegory, illus. 2012. 24p. pap. (978-0-9866065-5-7(3)) Wood Islands Prints.

Reader's Digest Staff & Disney Storybook Artists Staff. Rapunzel's Dream Walmart Edition Storybook with Musical Hairbrush. 2010. (Disney Tangled Ser.). (ENG., Illus.). 32p. (J). bds. 19.99 (978-0-7944-2048-2(6)) Reader's Digest Assn., Inc., The.

RealBuzz Studios Staff. Let There Be Lighten Up! 2007. (Goofyfoot Gurl Ser.: No. 1). 96p. (YA). pap. 4.97 (978-1-59789-573-6(3), Barbour Bks.) Barbour Publishing, Inc.

Reaves, Esther R. Gammy's Snow Queen. 2011. 24p. pap. 12.79 (978-1-4520-7158-9(6)) AuthorHouse.

Rebbie, Kevin. Mr. Stinkas & the Little Cheese Shop. 2011. pap. 23.95 (978-0-7414-6439-2(X)) Infinity Publishing.

Reece, Eva. The Boinking Bubble MacHine. Davis, Shelley L. A., illus. 2013. 24p. pap. 12.99 (978-0-9886360-2-6(6)) Kids At Heart Publishing, LLC.

Rees, Gwyneth. Fairy Dreams Vol. 1: A Magical Journey to Fairyland. 3rd unabr. ed. 2005. (Fairy Dust Ser.: 3). (ENG., Illus.). 224p. (J). (gr. 2-4). pap. 8.99 (978-0-330-43476-8(4)) Pan Macmillan GBR. Dist: Independent Pubs. Group.

Regin, Andrew. Guardians: Volume 1. 2012. 286p. pap. 27.95 (978-1-4626-8856-2(X)) America Star Bks.

Richards, Kitty. SpongeBob AirPants: The Lost Episode, Vol. 8. 2004. 64p. (J). (gr. 2-5). pap. 17.00 incl. audio (978-1-4000-8631-3(0), Listening Library) Random Hse. Audio Publishing Group.

Richey, Denise. The King's Bad Dream. 2009. 32p. pap. 12.99 (978-1-4490-1303-5(1)) AuthorHouse.

Riley, Christine. Chester's Field O'Brien, Laurel, illus. 2004. 296p. (J). per. 17.50 (978-0-9740683-6-7(5)) Authors & Artists Publishers of New York, Inc.

Ritsema van Eck, Patricia. The Dreaming of Paradise. 2005. 62p. (J). pap. 24.70 (978-1-4116-6097-7(8)) Lulu Pr., Inc.

Roberts, Pauline. He Shined on Me. 2010. 20p. pap. 9.95 (978-0-9841991-6-7(0)) Beckham Pubns. Group, Inc.

Robinson, Kathleen Marie. The Magic Doorknob, 1 vol. 2009. 56p. pap. 16.95 (978-1-60813-362-8(1)) America Star Bks.

Robleda, Margarita. Suenos. Suarez, Maribel, illus. (Rana, Rema, Rimas Ser.). (SPA.). 16p. (J). (gr. k-3). 7.95 (978-1-59437-821-8(5)) Santillana USA Publishing Co., Inc.

Robson, Jenny. Savannah 2116 Ad. 2005. 144p. pap. (978-0-624-04230-3(8)) Tafelberg Pubs., Ltd.

Rochester, Mary Frances. The Turquoise Monkey. 2010. 48p. pap. 17.99 (978-1-4490-7260-5(7)) AuthorHouse.

Rockhill, Dennis. Meadow Dance. 2007. (Wonderlands Ser.).Tr. of Danza de la Pradera. (ENG., Illus.). 32p. (J). (gr. -1-3). per. 7.95 (978-1-932748-70-3(9), Raven Tree Pr.,Csi) Continental Sales, Inc.

—Polar Slumber. 2008. (ENG., Illus.). 32p. (J). (gr. -1-3). pap. 7.95 (978-1-932748-73-4(3), Raven Tree Pr.,Csi) Continental Sales, Inc.

—Polar Slumber. Rockhill, Dennis, illus. 2007. (ENG., Illus.). 32p. (J). (gr. -1-3). 16.95 (978-0-9741992-8-3(1), Raven Tree Pr.,Csi) Continental Sales, Inc.

—Sueno Polar. 2008. 32p. (J). (gr. -1-3). (ENG.). 16.95 (978-1-932748-76-5(8)); (SPA & ENG.). pap. 7.95 (978-1-932748-77-2(6)) Continental Sales, Inc. (Raven Tree Pr.,Csi).

—Sueno Polar. 2008. 32p. 16.95 (978-1-932746-76-1(5)) Sacred Garden Fellowship.

Rodríguez-Nora, Tere. En busca de la Paz. Gordo, Aleix, illus. 2005. (SPA & ENG.). 32p. (J). (gr. 2-4). 13.95 (978-84-96046-51-1(6)) Ediciones Norte, Inc.

Roe, D. J. The Impossible Dream. 2008. 59p. pap. 16.95 (978-1-60610-173-5(0)) America Star Bks.

Rogers, Wanda. Polliwog Pete. 2013. 24p. pap. (978-1-77097-968-0(9)) FriesenPress.

Romeo, Fran & Romeo, Fran. Once upon A Dream. 2007. (ENG., Illus.). 18p. 14.99 (978-0-8249-5901-2(9), Ideal Pubns.) Worthy Publishing.

Rose, Jeremy. If I Could Fly... 2013. 36p. pap. 15.99 (978-1-4624-0665-4(3), Inspiring Voices) Author Solutions, Inc.

Rose, Laura Lopez. Chester the Christmas Cookie Jar. 2008. 24p. per. 24.95 (978-1-60441-228-4(3)) PublishAmerica, Inc.

Rosenberg, Madelyn & Crockett, Mary. Dream Boy. 2014. (ENG.). 336p. (YA). (gr. 7-12). pap. 9.99 (978-1-4022-9583-6(9), 9781402295836) Sourcebooks, Inc.

Round, J. The Catcher. 2008. 168p. pap. 14.95 (978-1-4092-0372-8(7)) Lulu Pr., Inc.

Roy, Kasi. Elizabeth Dreams: And the Christmas House Clock. 2011. 96p. pap. 12.10 (978-1-4520-1864-5(2)) AuthorHouse.

Rush, Barbara & Stratton, Jane. The Boat in the Attic. 2012. (ENG.). 30p. pap. 15.00 *(978-1-938002-02-1(4),* Hummingbird World Media) Double Edge Pr.

Russell, John. Sam & Socrates. 2012. 60p. (gr. 4-6). pap. 8.95 *(978-1-4620-6830-2(8))* iUniverse, Inc.

Russell, Rachel Renée. Tales from a Not-So-Happily Ever After. 2014. (Dork Diaries: 8). lib. bdg. 25.75 *(978-0-606-36241-2(X))* Turtleback Bks.

Ryder, Joanne. The Night Flight. Schwartz, Amy, illus. 2014. (ENG.). 32p. (J). (gr. k-2). 16.99 *(978-1-4814-2521-6(8),* Simon & Schuster Bks. For Young Readers) Simon & Schuster Bks. For Young Readers.

Sáenz, Benjamin Alire. Un Tiempo Perfecto para Sonar. Valencia, Esau Andrade, illus. 2008. (SPA & ENG.). 40p. (J). (gr. 1-4). 17.95 *(978-1-933693-01-9(0))* Cinco Puntos Pr.

Salimena, Kathleen Elizabeth. The Royal Yacht. 2008. (Illus.). 24p. (J). (gr. 11-18). 15.95 *(978-0-9798624-0-3(X))* Royal Imprint Pr., Inc.

Salton, Liz. Eelfish, a Rock & Roll King. Hathaway, Karen, illus. 2004. 38p. pap. 24.95 *(978-1-4137-1847-8(7))* PublishAmerica, Inc.

Salvati, Urbano. Anthology of a Childhood Dream. 2012. 92p. pap. 10.95 *(978-1-60976-142-4(1),* Strategic Bk. Publishing) Strategic Book Publishing & Rights Agency (SBPRA).

Samuelson, Jazlyn. Dream Big. 2012. 28p. pap. 15.99 *(978-1-4771-0868-0(8))* Xlibris Corp.

Sanders, Gaye Lynn. Chameleon Girl Again. 2012. 86p. 19.95 *(978-1-4626-7378-0(3))* America Star Bks.

Sandler, Steve. My Uncle Rob. Cunningham, Rob, illus. 2008. 32p. (J). pap. 12.95 *(978-0-9715721-5-7(1))* Washington Pubs.

Sanrio Company, LTD. Hello Kitty Presents the Storybook Collection: Alice's Adventures in Wonderland. 2017. (Hello Kitty Storybook Ser.). (ENG., Illus.). 32p. (J). (gr. -1-k). pap. 6.95 *(978-1-4197-2488-6(6),* Abrams Appleseed) Abrams, Inc.

Sansone, V. K. WANTED: Children for Toys. 2009. 32p. pap. 14.98 *(978-0-557-16717-3(5))* Lulu Pr., Inc.

Santillana USA. Dreams. Suarez, Maribel, illus. (Rowing Frog's Rhymes Ser.). 16p. (J). (gr. k-3). 7.95 *(978-1-59437-842-3(8))* Santillana USA Publishing Co., Inc.

Sasso, Emilie. Cystic Fibrosis & You. 2008. 23p. pap. 24.95 *(978-1-60672-405-7(3))* America Star Bks.

Say, Allen. The Boy in the Garden. 2010. (ENG., Illus.). 32p. (J). (gr. -1-3). 17.99 *(978-0-547-21410-8(3))* Houghton Mifflin Harcourt Publishing Co.

Schaffter, Ehren. Through the Curtain. 2009. 239p. pap. 20.00 *(978-0-557-20001-6(6))* Lulu Pr., Inc.

Schamerhorn, Ronna. Dreamy Navy Boy. 2007. 44p. per. 24.95 *(978-1-4241-8372-2(3))* America Star Bks.

Schneider, Antonie & Bansch, Helga. Leo's Dream. Cole, Alyson, tr. from GER. 2006. (ENG., Illus.). 32p. (J). (gr. -1). 22.95 *(978-0-7475-8184-0(3),* Bloomsbury Childrens) Bloomsbury Publishing Plc GBR. Dist: Independent Pubs. Group.

Schuette, Eva. The Kingdom of the Wild Gootsies: Meet the Wild Gootsies. 2010. 12p. 8.49 *(978-1-4490-8798-2(1))* AuthorHouse.

Scott, Jeff. Becoming the King: Where's my Father? 2006. 222p. (J). per. 17.95 *(978-0-9787624-0-7(1))* TDO Enterprises.

Scotto, Michael. Buck's Bad Dreams. Gabriel, Evette, illus. 2009. (J). *(978-1-935193-46-3(5))* National Network of Digital Schls.

Scotton, Rob. Russell the Sheep. Scotton, Rob, illus. 2007. (ENG., Illus.). 16p. (J). (gr. -1-k). 9.99 *(978-0-06-128434-2(3))* HarperCollins Pubs.

—Splat the Cat Dreams Big. Scotton, Rob, illus. 2013. (Splat the Cat Ser.). (ENG., Illus.). 24p. (J). (gr. -1-3). pap. 3.99 *(978-0-06-209012-6(7),* HarperFestival) HarperCollins Pubs.

Scribner, Don. Bennie & Thomas & the Battle at Worldsend, 1 vol. 2009. 84p. pap. 19.95 *(978-1-60836-630-9(8))* America Star Bks.

Scruggs, Stephanie. Deer Can't Dance. 2009. 36p. pap. 15.95 *(978-1-4490-4535-7(9))* AuthorHouse.

Segel, Jason & Miller, Kirsten. The Sleepwalker Tonic. Kwasny, Karl, illus. 2015. (Nightmares! Ser.). (ENG.). 368p. (J). (gr. 3-7). 16.99 *(978-0-385-74427-0(7));* lib. bdg. 19.99 *(978-0-375-99158-5(1))* Random Hse. Children's Bks. (Delacorte Bks. for Young Readers).

—The Sleepwalker Tonic. Kwasny, Karl, illus. 2016. (Nightmares! Ser.: 2). (ENG.). 384p. (J). (gr. 3-7). 18.40 *(978-0-606-39350-8(1))* Turtleback Bks.

Sendak, Maurice. Kenny's Window. Sendak, Maurice, illus. 2004. (Illus.). 54p. (J). (gr. k-4). reprint ed. 14.00 *(978-0-7567-7767-8(4))* DIANE Publishing Co.

—Kenny's Window. Sendak, Maurice, illus. 2004. (Trophy Picture Bks.). (ENG., Illus.). 64p. (J). (gr. 3-6). pap. 11.95 *(978-0-06-443209-2(2))* HarperCollins Pubs.

Sharpe, Gerald. Tommy's Tales. Moya, Patricia, illus. 2006. (Tommy's Tales Ser.). 300p. (J). per. 7.00 *(978-1-933894-00-3(8))* IJN Publishing, Inc.

—What Lies Beneath the Bed: Tommy's Tales (Revised) 2nd rev. ed. 2008. 320p. pap. 7.95 *(978-1-933894-04-1(0))* IJN Publishing, Inc.

Shepherd-Harvey, M. Neville the Froad. 2011. 32p. pap. 14.95 *(978-1-4634-4651-2(9))* AuthorHouse.

Shields, Gillian & Reed, Nathan. Angel Baby. 2006. (ENG., Illus.). 24p. (J). (gr. -1-k). pap. 9.99 *(978-0-00-718006-6(3),* HarperCollins Children's Bks.) HarperCollins Pubs. Ltd. GBR. Dist: Independent Pubs. Group.

Shinn, Sharon. The Dream-Maker's Magic. 2008. (ENG.). 288p. (YA). (gr. 7-18). pap. 8.99 *(978-0-14-241096-7(9),* Speak) Penguin Young Readers Group.

Shondalae. The Great Giver of Life, No. 8. 2008. 49p. pap. 16.95 *(978-1-60672-071-4(6))* America Star Bks.

Simmonds, Posy. Lulu & the Chocolate Wedding. 2016. (ENG., Illus.). 32p. (J). (-k). pap. 12.99 *(978-1-78344-407-6(X))* Andersen Pr. GBR. Dist: Independent Pubs. Group.

Simpkins, Debra Burke. The Luna Tuna. 2010. 32p. 12.99 *(978-1-4520-0213-2(4))* AuthorHouse.

Simson, Dana & Book Company Staff. Dreamland. Simson, Dana, illus. 2003. (Pop-up Bks.). (Illus.). 14p. (J). 15.95 *(978-1-74047-211-1(X))* Book Co. Publishing Pty, Ltd., The AUS. Dist: Penton Overseas, Inc.

Sinclair, Nicholas, et al. The Cookie Story. Wall, Randy Hugh, ed. Varela, Juan D., tr. Varela, Juan D., illus. l.t. ed. 2005. Tr. of Cuent de Galletas. (SPA.). 33p. (J). 14.95 *(978-0-9764798-1-9(8))* Story Stone Collection Publishing.

Singleton, Clayton. Dream an Awesome Dream. 2007. (J). per. 10.99 *(978-1-59872-828-6(8))* Instant Pub.

Singleton, Glynn. Buddy Boy Brooks Takes the Wheel: A Mile Wide Tale from the Mighty Mississippi. Carisse, Carissa, illus. 2007. 32p. (J). (gr. 2-4). 12.95 *(978-1-57072-320-9(6))* Overmountain Pr.

Sister Flowers. When Boo Boo Wakes Up!, 1 vol. Smith, Brenda, illus. 2009. 36p. pap. 24.95 *(978-1-61546-250-6(3))* America Star Bks.

Skye, obert. The Eyes of the Want. Sowards, Ben, illus. 2008. (Leven Thumps Ser.: 3). (ENG.). 464p. (J). (gr. 3-7). pap. 9.99 *(978-1-4169-4719-6(1),* Aladdin) Simon & Schuster Children's Publishing.

—The Gateway. Sowards, Ben, illus. 2006. (Leven Thumps Ser.: 1). (ENG.). 400p. (J). (gr. 3-7). pap. 9.99 *(978-1-4169-2806-5(5),* Aladdin) Simon & Schuster Children's Publishing.

—Leven Thumps 5 Volume Set. 2009. (ENG.). (J). *(978-1-60641-220-6(5),* Shadow Mountain) Shadow Mountain Publishing.

—Leven Thumps & the Gateway to Foo. (Leven Thumps Ser.: 1). (J). 2008. 74.75 *(978-1-4361-1570-4(1))* 2007. 112.75 *(978-1-4281-4622-8(9))* 2007. 115.75 *(978-1-4281-4620-4(2))* 2007. 85.75 *(978-1-4281-4616-7(4))* 2007. 178.75 *(978-1-4281-4617-4(2))* 2007. 82.75 *(978-1-4281-4618-1(0))* 2007. 1.25 *(978-1-4281-4613-6(X))* Recorded Bks., Inc.

—Leven Thumps & the Gateway to Foo. 2005. (Leven Thumps Ser.: Bk. 1). (Illus.). 384p. (J). 17.95 *(978-1-59038-369-8(9),* Shadow Mountain) Shadow Mountain Publishing.

—The Ruins of Alder. Sowards, Ben, illus. 2010. (Leven Thumps Ser.: 5). (ENG.). 416p. (J). (gr. 4-9). pap. 9.99 *(978-1-4169-9093-2(3),* Aladdin) Simon & Schuster Children's Publishing.

Small, Lily. Daisy the Deer. 2017. (Fairy Animals of Misty Wood Ser.). (ENG., Illus.). 144p. (J). pap. 5.99 *(978-1-62779-738-2(6),* 9781627797382, Holt, Henry & Co. Bks. For Young Readers) Holt, Henry & Co.

Smith, Lane. Abe Lincoln's Dream. Smith, Lane, illus. 2012. (ENG., Illus.). 32p. (J). (gr. k-4). 16.99 *(978-1-59643-608-4(5),* 9781596436084) Roaring Brook Pr.

Smith, Lindsay. Dreamstrider. 2015. (ENG., Illus.). 400p. (YA). (gr. 7). 17.99 *(978-1-62672-042-8(8),* 9781626720428) Roaring Brook Pr.

Sniegoski, Tom. Quest for the Spark. Smith, Jeff, illus. (Bone Ser.). (ENG.). (J). (gr. 3-7). 2012. 240p. pap. 10.99 *(978-0-545-14104-8(4))*Bk. 2. 2012. 240p. 26.99 *(978-0-545-14103-1(6))*Bk. 3. 2013. 288p. pap. 10.99 *(978-0-545-14106-2(0))*No. 3. 2013. 288p. 22.99 *(978-0-545-14105-5(2))* Scholastic, Inc. (Graphix).

—Quest for the Spark. (Bone: Quest for the Spark Ser.: 3). 2013. lib. bdg. 22.10 *(978-0-606-31497-8(0))* 2012. lib. bdg. 22.10 *(978-0-606-23947-9(2))* Turtleback Bks. (Turtleback).

Sniegoski, Tom & Smith, Jeff. Quest for the Spark, Bk. 1. Smith, Jeff, illus. 2011. (BONE: Quest for the Spark Ser.: 1). (ENG., Illus.). 224p. (J). (gr. 3-7). 26.99 *(978-0-545-14101-7(X),* Graphix) Scholastic, Inc.

Snyder, Betsy E. Sweet Dreams Lullaby. 2012. (ENG., Illus.). 32p. (J). (— 1). bds. 6.99 *(978-0-307-98060-1(X),* Random Hse. Bks. for Young Readers) Random Hse. Children's Bks.

Soler, Michael. The Ladybug & Me. Eisenberg, Serge, illus. 2007. 24p. (J). per. 8.99 *(978-0-9795469-0-7(7))* Soler, Michael.

Solomon, Barbara. The Girl Who Wanted to Become a Princess. 2013. 50p. pap. 12.99 *(978-1-62839-354-5(8))* Salem Author Services.

Sommer, Carl. Dare to Dream! Martinez, Jorge et al, illus. 2007. (Another Sommer-Time Story Ser.). (ENG.). 48p. (J). 23.95 incl. audio compact disk *(978-1-57537-723-0(3))* Advance Publishing, Inc.

Sorenson, Margo. Ambrose & the Cathedral Dream. Szegedi, Katalin, illus. 2006. (ENG.). 32p. (J). (gr. -1-3). 4.24 *(978-0-8146-3004-4(9))* Liturgical Pr.

Sosa, Joe. The Lonely Little World. 2006. 48p. pap. 9.95 *(978-1-59800-419-0(0))* Outskirts Pr., Inc.

Spurlock, Jefferson. Clemente's Dream. 2007. 108p. per. 19.95 *(978-1-4241-7483-6(X))* America Star Bks.

Stalling-Patton, Deborah. Shypoodle: Getting to Know You. 2009. 40p. pap. 17.99 *(978-1-4389-3899-8(3))* AuthorHouse.

Stanley, Dan. Danny the Fisherman, 1 vol. LaRue, Athena Mariah, illus. 2010. 46p. 24.95 *(978-1-4512-9695-2(9))* PublishAmerica, Inc.

Stanley, Dean. The Horsosaurus. France, Mark, illus. 2008. 32p. pap. 14.62 *(978-1-4251-8158-1(9))* Trafford Publishing.

Starlight, Cyandria. Daydreams of a Little Girl. 2012. 18p. pap. 16.95 *(978-1-4626-6003-2(7))* America Star Bks.

Stefano, Tony. Tommy & the Dream MacHine — What a Trip! a Boy, a Soda MacHine & a Voyage to Save the Planet. 2012. 138p. pap. 11.95 *(978-1-61897-489-1(0),* Strategic Bk. Publishing) Strategic Book Publishing & Rights Agency (SBPRA).

Stein, A. K. EZEKIEL MAYHILL & the Crystal of God. 2007. 196p. pap. 16.96 *(978-1-4303-2540-6(2))* Lulu Pr., Inc.

Steinberg, Laya. All Around Me, I See. Arbo, Cris, illus. 2005. (Sharing Nature with Children Book Ser.). 32p. (J). 16.95 *(978-1-58469-068-9(2));* pap. 8.95 *(978-1-58469-069-6(0))* Dawn Pubns.

Steiner, Barbara. 23 Shadow Street: Deadly Dreams. 2007. (ENG.). 304p. (J). (gr. -1-12). pert. 8.95 *(978-1-59687-329-2(9))* IBks., Inc.

Stella, Pilar. Seeking Serenity. Cummings, Maris, illus. 2008. (ENG.). (J). (gr. -1-3). pap. 17.95 *(978-1-60037-451-7(4))* Morgan James Publishing.

Stephenson, Mary. Naven's Dream. 2011. 24p. pap. 24.95 *(978-1-4626-0309-1(2))* America Star Bks.

Stevenson, William. Ricky's Dream Trip under the Sea. 2013. 38p. pap. 13.50 *(978-1-936517-85-5(X))* Micro Publishing Media, Inc.

Stiefvater, Maggie. Blue Lily, Lily Blue. (Raven Cycle Ser.: 3). (ENG.). 400p. (J). (gr. 9). 2015. pap. 9.99 *(978-0-545-42497-4(6))* 2014. 18.99 *(978-0-545-42496-7(8))* Scholastic, Inc. (Scholastic Pr.).

—Blue Lily, Lily Blue. 2015. (Raven Cycle Ser.: 3). lib. bdg. 20.85 *(978-0-606-38004-1(3))* Turtleback Bks.

—The Dream Thieves. (Raven Cycle Ser.: 2). (ENG.). 448p. (J). (gr. 9). 2014. pap. 9.99 *(978-0-545-42495-0(X),* Scholastic Paperbacks) 2013. 18.99 *(978-0-545-42494-3(1),* Scholastic Pr.) Scholastic, Inc.

—The Dream Thieves. 2014. (Raven Cycle Ser.: 2). lib. bdg. 20.85 *(978-0-606-36029-6(8))* Turtleback Bks.

Stiefvater, Maggie. The Raven King. 2016. (Raven Cycle Ser.: 4). (ENG.). 400p. (YA). (gr. 9). 18.99 *(978-0-545-42498-1(4));* 439p. (J). ***(978-0-605-90184-1(8))*** Scholastic, Inc. (Scholastic Pr.).

Stoddard, Laura. The Dreamosphere. 2014. pap. 14.99 *(978-1-4621-1444-3(X))* Cedar Fort, Inc./CFI Distribution.

Stolarz, Laurie Faria. Blue Is for Nightmares. Zins, Rebecca, ed. 2nd rev. ed. 2003. (Stolarz Ser.: 1). (ENG.). 312p. (YA). pap. 9.95 *(978-0-7387-0391-6(5),* Flux) North Star Editions.

—Silver Is for Secrets. 2005. (Stolarz Ser.: 3). (ENG.). 288p. (YA). pap. 11.99 *(978-0-7387-0631-3(0),* Flux) North Star Editions.

Stone, Kazuko G. & Keido, Ippo. The Butterfly's Dream: Children's Stories from China. 2003. (ENG., Illus.). 1p. 15.95 *(978-0-8048-3480-3(6))* Tuttle Publishing.

Storr, Catherine. Marianne Dreams. 2014. (ENG., Illus.). 320p. pap. 9.95 *(978-0-571-31327-3(2))* Faber & Faber, Inc.

Stovall, Sue A. Dream Valley. 2008. 30p. pap. 24.95 *(978-1-60672-161-2(5))* America Star Bks.

Stuart, Tara. Tara's Tales: Dream. 2012. 50p. pap. 16.99 *(978-1-4575-0742-7(0))* Dog Ear Publishing, LLC.

Stussy, Virginia. Wishes & Wonder. 2007. (ENG.). 52p. per. 16.95 *(978-1-4241-6086-0(3))* America Star Bks.

Summer of Dreaming. 2010. (Illus.). 157p. (YA). pap. *(978-1-936021-22-2(6),* Banana Oil Bks.) Cyberwizard Productions.

Sunderland, Margot & Hancock, Nicky. A Pea Called Mildred. Armstrong, Nicky, tr. Armstrong, Nicky, illus. 2017. (Helping Children with Feelings Ser.). (ENG.). 32p. (C). pap. 15.95 *(978-0-86388-497-9(0),* Y329771, Routledge) Taylor & Francis Group GBR. Dist: Taylor & Francis Group.

Sunkuli, O. The Hero & the Dream. 2004. (Illus.). 28p. pap. *(978-9966-25-161-9(8))* Heinemann Kenya, Limited (East African Educational Publishers Ltd E.A.E.P.) KEN. Dist: Michigan State Univ. Pr.

Sutherland, Marc. The Waiting Place. Sutherland, Marc, illus. 2004. (Illus.). 24p. (J). (gr. k-4). reprint ed. 15.00 *(978-0-7567-8382-2(8))* DIANE Publishing Co.

Sweeney, Kathleen L. The Dream of a Little Farmer Girl. 2012. 24p. pap. 15.99 *(978-1-4653-7927-6(4))* Xlibris Corp.

Sweet Dreams. 2003. (J). per. *(978-1-57657-876-6(3))* Paradise Pr., Inc.

Sweet Dreams. Date not set. 88p. (J). 7.98 *(978-0-7525-9846-8(5))* Parragon, Inc.

Symington, Martha M. Emily: Dream Believe Achieve. Nolan, Amanda M., illus. 2008. 36p. pap. *(978-1-897435-21-2(5))* Agio Publishing Hse.

—Global Heart Warming: Dream Believe Achieve Series. Sanderson, Jessica B., illus. 2009. 36p. pap. *(978-1-897435-34-2(7))* Agio Publishing Hse.

Tandy, Clive. Quarry Grove. 2008. 60p. per. 11.59 *(978-1-4251-4974-1(X))* Trafford Publishing.

Taylor, Roy. Matilda's Magic Wand: Dreamland Adventure. 2008. 36p. (J). pap. 9.00 *(978-0-8059-7716-5(3))* Dorrance Publishing Co., Inc.

Taylor, Thomas. Haunters. 2013. (J). 327p. *(978-0-545-50253-5(5));* (ENG.). 336p. (gr. 5-9). 17.99 *(978-0-545-49644-5(6))* Scholastic, Inc.

Teare, Nellie. Celia & the Witches. Senkel, Nicholas, illus. 2008. 24p. (J). 13.95 *(978-0-9820852-0-2(6))* Harmon Creek Pr.

Tetlow, Karin. Harry Goes Rowing. Guze, Tessa, illus. 2013. 32p. pap. 11.95 *(978-0-615-75585-4(2))* Juping Horse Pr.

The Poet 174. The Ways of Life. 2011. 130p. pap. 15.95 *(978-1-4327-5135-7(2))* Outskirts Pr., Inc.

Thewes Nicolai, Susan. The Thirteenth Butterfly: A Lizzie's Life Novel. 2009. 192p. pap. 14.49 *(978-1-4389-9975-3(5))* AuthorHouse.

Thomas, Amy Maude. Stories in My Eyes. 2011. 20p. pap. 7.99 *(978-1-936750-04-7(X))* Yorkshire Publishing Group.

Thomas, John Ira. Zoo Force: Dear Eniko. Smith, Jeremy, illus. 2003. 68p. per. 6.95 *(978-0-9743147-1-6(4))* Candle Light Pr.

Thompson, Don. Bunny World: Kindness Is the Key to Happiness. 2009. 28p. pap. 14.99 *(978-1-4389-5475-2(1))* AuthorHouse.

Tibo, Gilles. Le Gardien du Sommeil. Jorisch, Stéphane, illus. 2004. (Mon Roman Ser.). (FRE.). 64p. (J). (gr. 2). pap. *(978-2-89021-691-4(8))* Diffusion du livre Mirabel (DLM).

Toms, Kate. Twinkle Twinkle Box Set. 2007. (Illus.). 26p. (gr. -1). per. *(978-1-84610-672-9(9))* Make Believe Ideas.

Toska, Mary Lou. Ernest's Dream: A Young Boy Wanting to Spend the Summer in the High Alps. 2012. 20p. pap. 24.95 *(978-1-4626-8662-9(1))* America Star Bks.

Townley, Roderick. The Great Good Thing. 2003. (Richard Jackson Books (Econo-Clad) Ser.). 216p. (J). (gr. 5). 16.00 *(978-0-7569-1435-6(3))* Perfection Learning Corp.

—The Great Good Thing. unabr. ed. 2004. (Middle Grade Cassette Librariestm Ser.). 176p. (J). (gr. 4-6). pap. 29.00 incl. audio *(978-0-8072-1001-7(3),* S YA 302 SP, Listening Library) Random Hse. Audio Publishing Group.

Travitzky, Paul Joseph & Travitzky, Brianna Marie. Brianna Marie Wants to Be: A Cowgirl. 2009. 20p. pap. 11.95 *(978-1-4490-2110-8(7))* AuthorHouse.

Trumbo, Stephen. Dreamers, Fantasies & Thrill Seekers. 2011. 26p. pap. 16.95 *(978-1-4560-7319-0(2))* America Star Bks.

Tshionyi, Muabilai. Reach from Within, Dreams Never Die. Date not set. 92p. (Orig.). (YA). (gr. 6-18). pap. *(978-0-9649156-1-9(8))* Calychio Publishing.

Tukan, Jaytoe Anthony, Sr. Kitty cat had a Dream: Kingdom without a King. 2005. (Illus.). 124p. (J). per. 19.95 *(978-0-9665909-7-5(X))* Kalawantis Publishing Services, Inc.

Turner, Corey W. Little Benjamin, the Bugs, & the Holy Spirit. 2010. 40p. 16.99 *(978-1-4490-8498-1(2))* AuthorHouse.

Twitty, Mary F. Ashley Visits Urchin Village. 2008. 92p. pap. 51.99 *(978-1-4363-5578-0(8))* Xlibris Corp.

Van Allsburg, Chris. Just a Dream. Van Allsburg, Chris, illus. 2014. (Illus.). 48p. pap. 9.00 *(978-1-61003-182-0(2))* Center for the Collaborative Classroom.

—Just a Dream 25th Anniversary Edition. 2015. (ENG., Illus.). 48p. (J). (gr. -1-3). 18.99 *(978-0-544-42283-4(X),* HMH Books For Young Readers) Houghton Mifflin Harcourt Publishing Co.

—The Sweetest Fig. 2014. 32p. pap. 9.00 *(978-1-61003-223-0(3))* Center for the Collaborative Classroom.

van Genechten, Guido. Knight Ricky. van Genechten, Guido, illus. 2010. (Ricky Ser.). (ENG., Illus.). 30p. (J). (gr. -1-k). 16.95 *(978-1-60537-059-0(2))* Cobblestone Publishing Co.

Van Zant, Dawn. No More Night Mares: A Dream of Freedom. McElroy, Kim, illus. 2005. (J). pap. 9.99 *(978-0-9761768-1-7(5))* Wild Heart Ranch, Inc.

Vana, Dan. Joey & the Magic Dream Pillow. Ware, Quinton, illus. 2013. 20p. pap. 24.95 *(978-1-4626-7872-3(6))* America Star Bks.

Vande Velde, Vivian. Witch Dreams, 0 vols. 2008. (ENG.). 128p. (YA). (gr. 5-9). pap. 7.99 *(978-0-7614-5460-1(8),* 9780761454601, Amazon Children's Publishing) Amazon Publishing.

von Botefuhr, Andrea & Russel, Angela. The Land of Smaerd. 2008. 40p. 16.95 *(978-0-615-18112-7(0))* Know Wonder Publishing, LLC.

Von, Cristina. Diego y el Monstruo. 2003. (ENG & SPA., Illus.). 24p. pap. 6.95 *(978-85-7416-189-1(6))* Callis Editora Ltda BRA. Dist: Independent Pubs. Group.

Waddell, Martin. Can't You Sleep, Little Bear?: Candlewick Storybook Animations. Firth, Barbara, illus. 2008. (Candlewick Storybook Animations Ser.). (ENG.). 32p. (J). (gr. k-k). 14.99 *(978-0-7636-3537-4(5))* Candlewick Pr.

Wagner, Mckenzie. Keys to the Dream World. 2014. pap. 8.99 *(978-1-4621-1435-1(0))* Cedar Fort, Inc./CFI Distribution.

Wahl, Jan. Elf Night. Weevers, Peter, illus. 2005. (Picture Bks.). 32p. (gr. k-2). 15.25 *(978-1-57505-512-1(0))* Lerner Publishing Group.

Walker, Melzina. Little Melvin's Blue Coat. 2007. (Illus.). 32p. (J). pap. 8.00 *(978-0-8059-7389-1(3))* Dorrance Publishing Co., Inc.

Walter, Chris. Tell Your Dreams to Me. 2008. 32p. pap. 14.95 *(978-1-4389-0162-6(3))* AuthorHouse.

Ward, Nick. Another Rumpus. Ward, Nick, illus. 2015. (ENG., Illus.). 24p. (J). (gr. -1-3). 7.99 *(978-1-85733-728-0(X))* Lerner Publishing Group.

Washington. Jack the Boogey Is My Real Name: The Truth about the Boogeyman. 2014. (ENG.). (J). 18.93 *(978-0-9960916-0-2(2))* Bedford Hse. Bks.

Water, Charles. The Road to Iadore. 2012. 48p. pap. 21.99 *(978-1-4772-4483-8(2))* AuthorHouse.

Waters, Ginny B. The Miracle House. 2011. 36p. pap. 24.95 *(978-1-4560-3510-5(X))* America Star Bks.

Watt, Mélanie. Scaredy Squirrel at Night. Watt, Mélanie, illus. 2009. (ENG., Illus.). 32p. (J). (gr. -1-3). 16.95 *(978-1-55453-288-9(4))* Kids Can Pr., Ltd. CAN. Dist: Hachette Bk. Group.

Weatherbee, Tabatha. Dream Sharers: Love/Hate. 2013. 336p. (J). pap. 19.00 *(978-1-62212-978-2(4),* Strategic Bk. Publishing) Strategic Book Publishing & Rights Agency (SBPRA).

Webb-King, Marian. Sweet Dreams Bear Cub: My Life As a Cricket. 2011. 20p. 11.49 *(978-1-4520-0979-7(1))* AuthorHouse.

Weinberg, Moshe. The Unforgettable Journey. 2004. 142p. (J). 12.95 *(978-1-56871-306-9(1))* Targum Pr., Inc.

Welch, Ginger. The Dream Reader. 2012. 76p. 19.95 *(978-1-4626-7276-9(0));* pap. 19.95 *(978-1-4626-8291-1(X))* America Star Bks.

Wendy Lee Jungling; Illustrated By My Fa. Who Do You Want to Be? 2012. 28p. 24.95 *(978-1-4626-6873-1(9))* America Star Bks.

Weston, Greg. The Man Upstairs. 2007. 212p. pap. 14.95 *(978-1-84799-957-3(3))* Lulu Pr., Inc.

Weston Woods Staff, creator. In the Night Kitchen. 2011. 29.95 *(978-0-439-73480-6(0));* 18.95 *(978-0-439-72723-5(5));* 38.75 *(978-0-439-72728-0(6))* Weston Woods Studios, Inc.

White, Stanley I. & White, Rachael. Absence Abbey, 1 vol. 2009. 21p. pap. 24.95 *(978-1-60749-577-2(5))* America Star Bks.

Wiesner, David. Free Fall. Wiesner, David, illus. 2008. (ENG., Illus.). 32p. (J). (gr. -1-3). 17.99 *(978-0-06-156741-4(8))* HarperCollins Pubs.

Wiggins, D. L. Where Dreams Are Born. Carter, Kelly, illus. 2012. 26p. (J). 16.95 *(978-1-60131-128-3(1),* Castlebridge Bks.) Big Tent Bks.

Wilderness, Dale. Drift in Your Pillow's Eyes. 2013. pap. 9.95 *(978-1-59433-155-8(3))* Publication Consultants.

Wiley, Jean. Sweet Dreams for Sydney: A Book to Help Dissipate Nightmares, 1 vol. Green, Burt, illus. 2009. 25p. pap. 24.95 *(978-1-60703-002-7(0))* America Star Bks.

Williams, Annik. Mr. Mole's Day Off: With Goodnight Little Birdie. 2010. 20p. 15.78 *(978-1-4520-3756-1(6))* AuthorHouse.

Williams, Harland, illus. The Kid with Too Many Nightmares. 2004. (J). *(978-0-8431-1582-6(3),* Price Stern Sloan) Penguin Publishing Group.

Williams, John Joseph. The Frightened Garden. 2013. 98p. (J). pap. *(978-1-78299-167-0(0))* FeedARead.com.

Williams, Valerie. The Funny Dreams of Dennis the Dartmoor Pony. 2010. (Illus.). 24p. 12.99 *(978-1-4520-0504-1(4))* AuthorHouse.

Wilson, Karma. Dormouse Dreams. Liwska, Renata, illus. 2017. (ENG.). 40p. (J). (gr. -1-k). 16.99 *(978-1-4231-7874-3(2))* Disney Pr.

Wilson, N. D. Outlaws of Time: the Legend of Sam Miracle. 2017. (Outlaws of Time Ser.: 1). 352p. (J). (gr. 3-7). pap. 6.99 *(978-0-06-232727-7(5),* Tegen, Katherine Bks) HarperCollins Pubs.

Winn, Don M. Chipper the Clown. 2010. 20p. pap. 7.99 *(978-0-88144-259-5(3))* Yorkshire Publishing Group.

Wise, Anna. The Vala of Trinity: Book One Norse Series, 1 vol. 2009. 195p. pap. 24.95 *(978-1-61582-763-3(3))* America Star Bks.

Witkowski, Teri. Bitty Bear's Snowflake Dreams. Ackley, Peggy Jo, illus. 2006. (J). *(978-1-59369-166-0(1))* American Girl Publishing, Inc.

Wolford, Margo. The Moinks Collection Presents: Sami's Big Day. 2009. (Illus.). 39p. (J). pap. 18.95 *(978-1-4327-3980-5(8))* Outskirts Pr., Inc.

Wolford, Merle & Harvey, Karen. Pau Pua & the Watering Hole. 2013. 40p. pap. *(978-1-4602-1383-4(1))* FriesenPress.

Wood Jr, Richard L. The Stick Family. 2011. 28p. pap. 15.00 *(978-1-4634-2564-7(3))* AuthorHouse.

Wray, Patricia. Sasha, the Dreamer, 1 vol. 2009. 192p. pap. 24.95 *(978-1-60672-885-7(7))* PublishAmerica, Inc.

Wyss, Tyan. Night Flyer. Immelman, Sarita, illus. 2006. 40p. (J). per. 14.95 *(978-1-58939-916-7(1))* Virtualbookworm.com Publishing, Inc.

Yang, Gene Luen. Animal Crackers: A Gene Luen Yang Collection. 2012. (ENG., Illus.). 216p. (YA). pap. 14.95 *(978-1-59362-183-4(3),* 9781593621834) Slave Labor Bks.

Yellowknife, Jessica. Spring Break Adventure. 2011. 84p. pap. 11.11 *(978-1-4269-6952-2(X))* Trafford Publishing.

Yolanda And Reese. The Boy Who Loved to Be Like Michael Jackson. Harrell, Maurice, illus. 2012. 32p. 24.95 *(978-1-4560-8506-3(9))* America Star Bks.

Yonge, Charlotte M. Little Lucy's Wonderful Globe. 2008. 152p. 36.95 *(978-0-548-97272-4(9))* Kessinger Publishing, LLC.

You. My Biggest Secret. 2009. 36p. pap. 17.49 *(978-1-4490-4644-6(4))* AuthorHouse.

Yovanoff, Brenna. Places No One Knows. 2016. (ENG.). 384p. (YA). (gr. 9). 17.99 *(978-0-553-52263-1(9),* Delacorte Pr.) Random Hse. Children's Bks.

Zhou, Carmen. A Tree's Dream. 2012. 24p. pap. 15.99 *(978-1-4691-8958-1(5))* Xlibris Corp.

DRESS

see Clothing and Dress

DRESSMAKING

see also Sewing

Figueroa, Shelly. Ms. Figgy's Garment School for Girls: Learn to Sew 15 Classic Pieces * Tweens & Teens — Sizes 10-16. 2015. (ENG., Illus.). 176p. pap. 19.95 *(978-1-61745-062-4(6),* FunStitch Studio) C & T Publishing.

Lan, Angela. #OOTD Sew & Style: Make Your Dream Wardrobe with Angela. 2016. (ENG., Illus.). 128p. (J). (gr. 6-12). pap. 24.95 *(978-1-61745-136-2(3),* Stash Bks.) C & T Publishing.

Low, Rachel. Girl's Guide to DIY Fashion: Design & Sew 5 Complete Outfits * Mood Boards * Fashion Sketching * Choosing Fabric * Adding Style. 2015. (ENG., Illus.). 192p. (J). (gr. 2-8). pap. 19.95 *(978-1-60705-995-0(9),* FunStitch Studio) C & T Publishing.

Merrill, Amy French. A Day in the Life of a Colonial Dressmaker. 2009. (Library of Living & Working in Colonial Times Ser.). 24p. (gr. 3-3). 42.50 *(978-1-60853-730-3(7),* PowerKids Pr.) Rosen Publishing Group, Inc., The.

Okawa, Junko & Uonca Staff. Carefree Clothes for Girls: 20 Patterns for Outdoor Frocks, Playdate Dresses, & More. 2009. (Make Good: Crafts + Life Ser.). (ENG., Illus.). 96p. pap. 21.95 *(978-1-59030-717-5(8),* Roost Books) Shambhala Pubns., Inc.

Patterns: Individual Title Six-Packs. (Story Steps Ser.). (gr. k-2). 29.00 *(978-0-7635-9569-2(1))* Rigby Education.

Patterns Are Fun!, 6 Packs. (Story Steps Ser.). (gr. k-2). 29.00 *(978-0-7635-9576-0(4))* Rigby Education.

Sullivan, Laura L. The Colonial Dressmaker. 2015. (Colonial People Ser.). (ENG.). 48p. (J). (gr. 4-4). 31.36 *(978-1-5026-0482-8(5))* Cavendish Square Publishing.

Ware, Lesley. Sew Fab: Sewing & Style for Young Fashionistas. 2015. (ENG., Illus.). 80p. (J). (gr. 3-8). 19.95 *(978-1-78067-404-9(X))* King, Laurence Publishing GBR. Dist: Hachette Bk. Group.

DRESSMAKING—FICTION

Beskow, Elsa. Pelle's New Suit, 1 vol. 2007. (ENG., Illus.). 32p. (J). (gr. -1-4). *(978-0-86315-584-0(7))* Floris Bks.

Brightwood, Laura, illus. King's New Suit. Brightwood, Laura, . 2007. (J). DVD *(978-1-934409-05-3(7))* 3-C Institute for Social Development.

Brooks, Felicity. Dress the Teddy Bears Going Shopping. 2015. (Dress the Teddy Bears Sticker Bks.). (ENG.). 16+8p. (J). pap. 6.99 *(978-0-7945-3530-8(5),* Usborne) EDC Publishing.

Burnett, Frances Hodgson. Emily Fox-Seton. 2008. 188p. per. 13.95 *(978-1-60312-503-1(5))* Aegypan.

Chessa, Francesca. A Button Muddle. Chessa, Francesca, illus. 2003. (Illus.). 32p. (YA). pap. *(978-1-85602-461-7(X),* Pavilion Children's Books) Pavilion Bks.

Davies, Katie. Knights Sticker Dressing. 2010. 24p. (J). 8.99 *(978-0-7945-2891-1(0))* EDC Publishing.

Davis, Kerry. Plumple. 2009. (Illus.). 20p. pap. 12.49 *(978-1-4389-9362-1(5))* AuthorHouse.

FLCL T-Shirt - Turn Around - Extra Large: Fooly Cooly. 2004. (YA). mass mkt. 17.99 *(978-1-932480-99-3(4))* Broccoli International USA, Inc.

Floca, Brian, illus. The Hinky-Pink: An Old Tale. 2008. (ENG.). 48p. (J). (gr. -1-3). 16.99 *(978-0-689-87588-5(6),* Atheneum/Richard Jackson Bks.) Simon & Schuster Children's Publishing.

Gay, Marie-Louise. Buenos Dias Samuel. 2004.Tr. of Good Morning Sam. (SPA.). (J). (gr. k-18). pap. 7.99 *(978-980-257-293-9(4))* Ekare, Ediciones VEN. Dist: Lectorum Pubns., Inc.

Markowitz-Meredith, Susan. Frances & the Fairy Dressmaker: Set Of 6. 2011. (Early Connections Ser.). (J). pap. 39.00 net. *(978-1-4108-1557-6(9))* Benchmark Education Co.

Noland, Charles. The Adventures of Drew & Ellie: The Magical Dress. Baker, Sherri, illus. 2006. (J). *(978-0-9789297-1-8(3));* 2nd rev. ed. 84p. per. 7.95 *(978-0-9789297-0-1(5))* TMD Enterprises.

Off to School: Individual Title Six-Packs. (Story Steps Ser.). (gr. k-2). 29.00 *(978-0-7635-9577-7(2))* Rigby Education.

Reader's Digest Staff & Rhodes, Lilly. Guess Who, Minnie! Loter Inc. Staff, illus. 2013. (Guess Who Ser.: 1). (ENG.). 10p. (J). (gr. -1-k). 10.99 *(978-0-7944-2555-5(0))* Reader's Digest Assn., Inc., The.

Stop Knitting, Nina!, 6 Packs. (gr. k-1). 23.00 *(978-0-7635-9028-4(2))* Rigby Education.

Taylor, Chloë. A Tangled Thread. Zhang, Nancy, illus. 2014. (Sew Zoey Ser.: 6). (ENG.). 176p. (J). (gr. 3-7). 16.99 *(978-1-4814-0444-0(X),* Simon Spotlight) Simon Spotlight.

Taylor, Chloe. A Tangled Thread. Zhang, Nancy, illus. 2014. (Sew Zoey Ser.: 6). (ENG.). 176p. (J). (gr. 3-7). pap. 5.99 *(978-1-4814-0443-3(1),* Simon Spotlight) Simon Spotlight.

Tinti, Natalie. Sewing a Friendship. Tinti, Natalie, illus. 2009. (Sewing a Friendship Ser.: 1). (ENG., Illus.). 88p. (J). pap. 12.95 *(978-0-9842625-1-9(2))* Tintinatie Publishing Hse.

Wang, Sarah. My Quilt. 2009. (Illus.). 24p. pap. 11.49 *(978-1-4490-3422-1(5))* AuthorHouse.

DREW, CHARLES RICHARD, 1904-1950

Marsh, Carole. Charles Drew: Dedicated Doctor. 2004. (1000 Readers Ser.). (Illus.). 12p. (J). (gr. k-4). per. 2.95 *(978-0-635-02528-9(0))* Gallopade International.

Schraff, Anne. Charles Drew: Pioneer in Medicine. 2003. (Famous Inventors Ser.). (Illus.). 32p. (J). (gr. 1-4). lib. bdg. 22.60 *(978-0-7660-2008-5(8))* Enslow Pubs., Inc.

—Dr. Charles Drew: Blood Bank Innovator. 2003. (African-American Biographies Ser.). (Illus.). 112p. (J). (gr. 6-12). lib. bdg. 27.94 *(978-0-7660-2117-4(3))* Enslow Pubs., Inc.

—The Life of Dr. Charles Drew: Blood Bank Innovator. 2015. (Legendary African Americans Ser.). 96p. (J). (gr. 6-12). pap. 10.95 *(978-0-7660-6266-5(X))* Enslow Pubs., Inc.

Schraff, Anne E. The Life of Dr. Charles Drew: Blood Bank Innovator. 2015. (Legendary African Americans Ser.). 96p. (J). (gr. 6-12). 27.94 *(978-0-7660-6265-8(1))* Enslow Pubs., Inc.

Venezia, Mike. Charles Drew: Doctor Who Got the World Pumped up to Donate Blood. Venezia, Mike, illus. 2009. (Getting to Know the World's Greatest Inventors & Scientists Ser.). (ENG., Illus.). 32p. (J). (gr. 3-4). pap. 6.95 *(978-0-531-21334-6(X),* Children's Pr.); (gr. 2-5). 28.00 *(978-0-531-23725-0(7))* Scholastic Library Publishing.

DREW, NANCY (FICTITIOUS CHARACTER)—FICTION

ABDO Publishing Company Staff. Nancy Drew - 4 Titles. 2005. (Nancy Drew Ser.). (ENG., Illus.). 88p. (gr. 3-8). 72.63 *(978-1-59961-056-6(6))* Spotlight.

—Nancy Drew & the Clue Crew - 4 Titles. 2007. (Nancy Drew & the Clue Crew Ser.). (ENG., Illus.). 80p. 96.84 *(978-1-59961-344-4(1))* Spotlight.

Conway, Gerry. Nancy Drew: Together with the Hardy Boys. 2011. (Nancy Drew the New Case Files Ser.). (ENG., Illus.). 64p. (J). (gr. 3-7). pap. 7.99 *(978-1-59707-262-5(1),* 9781597072625) Papercutz.

Dixon, Franklin W. & Keene, Carolyn. Bonfire Masquerade. 2011. (Nancy Drew/Hardy Boys Ser.: 5). (ENG.). 176p. (J). (gr. 3-7). pap. 6.99 *(978-1-4424-0328-4(4),* Aladdin) Simon & Schuster Children's Publishing.

Keene, Carolyn. The Apple Bandit. Jones, Jan Naimo, illus. 2005. (Nancy Drew Notebooks). 74p. (J). (gr. 1-4). 11.65 *(978-0-7569-6505-1(5))* Perfection Learning Corp.

—April Fool's Day. Pamintuan, Macky, illus. 2009. (Nancy Drew & the Clue Crew Ser.: 19). (ENG.). 96p. (J). (gr. 1-4). pap. 5.99 *(978-1-4169-7518-2(7),* Aladdin) Simon & Schuster Children's Publishing.

—Babysitting Bandit. Pamintuan, Macky, illus. 2009. (Nancy Drew & the Clue Crew Ser.: 23). (ENG.). 96p. (J). (gr. 1-4). pap. 5.99 *(978-1-4169-7813-8(5),* Aladdin) Simon & Schuster Children's Publishing.

—Bad Times, Big Crimes. 14th ed. 2005. (Nancy Drew (All New) Girl Detective Ser.: 14). (ENG.). 160p. (J). (gr. 3-7). pap. 6.99 *(978-0-689-87883-1(4),* Aladdin) Simon & Schuster Children's Publishing.

—Buggy Breakout. Pamintuan, Macky, illus. 2010. (Nancy Drew & the Clue Crew Ser.: 25). (ENG.). 96p. (J). (gr. 1-4). pap. 5.99 *(978-1-4169-7814-5(3),* Aladdin) Simon & Schuster Children's Publishing.

—The Bungalow Mystery, No. 3. 2014. (Nancy Drew Ser.: 3). (ENG.). 192p. (J). (gr. 3-7). 7.99 *(978-0-448-47971-2(0),* Grosset & Dunlap) Penguin Young Readers Group.

—The Bunny-Hop Hoax. Jones, Jan Naimo, illus. 2005. (Nancy Drew Notebooks). 70p. (J). (gr. 1-4). 11.65 *(978-0-7569-5884-8(9))* Perfection Learning Corp.

—The Bunny-Hop Hoax. Jones, Jan Naimo, illus. Frost, Michael, photos by. 64th ed. 2005. (Nancy Drew Notebooks Ser.: 64). (ENG.). 80p. (J). (gr. 1-4). pap. 3.99 *(978-0-689-87754-4(4),* Simon & Schuster/Paula Wiseman Bks.) Simon & Schuster/Paula Wiseman Bks.

—Butterfly Blues. Francis, Peter, illus. 2015. (Nancy Drew & the Clue Crew Ser.: 40). (ENG.). 96p. (J). (gr. 1-4). pap. 5.99 *(978-1-4814-1470-8(4),* Aladdin) Simon & Schuster Children's Publishing.

—California Schemin' 2011. (Nancy Drew (All New) Girl Detective Ser.: 45). (ENG.). 160p. (J). (gr. 3-7). pap. 5.99 *(978-1-4424-2295-7(5),* Aladdin) Simon & Schuster Children's Publishing.

—Camp Creepy. Pamintuan, Macky, illus. 2010. (Nancy Drew & the Clue Crew Ser.: 26). (ENG.). 96p. (J). (gr. 1-4). pap. 4.99 *(978-1-4169-9438-1(6),* Aladdin) Simon & Schuster Children's Publishing.

—Chick-Napped! Pamintuan, Macky, illus. 13th ed. 2008. (Nancy Drew & the Clue Crew Ser.: 13). (ENG.). 96p. (J). (gr. 1-4). pap. 5.99 *(978-1-4169-5522-1(4),* Aladdin) Simon & Schuster Children's Publishing.

—The Cinderella Ballet Mystery, 1 vol. Pamintuan, Macky, illus. 2007. (Nancy Drew & the Clue Crew Ser.). (ENG.). 83p. (gr. 1-4). 24.21 *(978-1-59961-345-1(X))* Spotlight.

—The Circus Scare, 1 vol. Pamintuan, Macky, illus. 2009. (Nancy Drew & the Clue Crew Set II Ser.). (ENG.). 96p. (gr. 2-4). 24.21 *(978-1-59961-642-1(4))* Spotlight.

—Close Encounters. 21st ed. 2006. (Nancy Drew (All New) Girl Detective Ser.: 21). (ENG.). 176p. (J). (gr. 3-7). pap. 5.99 *(978-1-4169-1245-3(2),* Aladdin) Simon & Schuster Children's Publishing.

—Club Dread. 2009. (Nancy Drew/Hardy Boys Ser.: 3). (ENG.). 192p. (J). (gr. 3-7). pap. 5.99 *(978-1-4169-7871-8(2),* Aladdin) Simon & Schuster Children's Publishing.

—The Clue at Black Creek Farm. 2015. 171p. (J). *(978-1-4806-8613-7(1),* Simon & Schuster/Paula Wiseman Bks.) Simon & Schuster/Paula Wiseman Bks.

—The Clue in the Diary. 2015. (Nancy Drew Ser.: 7). (ENG.). 192p. (J). (gr. 3-7). 8.99 *(978-0-448-48907-0(4),* Grosset & Dunlap) Penguin Young Readers Group.

—Cooking Camp Disaster. Pamintuan, Macky, illus. 2013. (Nancy Drew & the Clue Crew Ser.: 35). (ENG.). 96p. (J). (gr. 1-4). pap. 4.99 *(978-1-4169-9466-4(1),* Aladdin) Simon & Schuster Children's Publishing.

—Cupcake Chaos. Pamintuan, Macky, illus. 2013. (Nancy Drew & the Clue Crew Ser.: 34). (ENG.). 96p. (J). (gr. 1-4). pap. 5.99 *(978-1-4424-5351-7(6),* Aladdin) Simon & Schuster Children's Publishing.

—Curse of the Arctic Star. 2013. (Nancy Drew Diaries: 1). (ENG.). 208p. (J). (gr. 3-7). 15.99 *(978-1-4424-6610-4(3));* pap. 6.99 *(978-1-4169-9072-7(0))* Simon & Schuster Children's Publishing. (Aladdin).

—Designed for Disaster. Pamintuan, Macky, illus. 2011. (Nancy Drew & the Clue Crew Ser.: 29). (ENG.). 96p. (J). (gr. 1-4). pap. 5.99 *(978-1-4169-9439-8(4),* Aladdin) Simon & Schuster Children's Publishing.

—Dressed to Steal. 22nd ed. 2007. (Nancy Drew (All New) Girl Detective Ser.: 22). (ENG.). 160p. (J). (gr. 3-7). pap. 5.99 *(978-1-4169-3385-4(9),* Aladdin) Simon & Schuster Children's Publishing.

—En Garde. 17th ed. 2006. (Nancy Drew (All New) Girl Detective Ser.: 17). (ENG.). 160p. (J). (gr. 3-7). pap. 4.99 *(978-1-4169-0603-2(7),* Aladdin) Simon & Schuster Children's Publishing.

—The Fashion Disaster. Pamintuan, Macky, illus. 6th ed. 2007. (Nancy Drew & the Clue Crew Ser.: 6). (ENG.). 96p. (J). (gr. 1-4). pap. 5.99 *(978-1-4169-3485-1(5),* Aladdin) Simon & Schuster Children's Publishing.

—Fishing for Clues. 26th ed. 2007. (Nancy Drew (All New) Girl Detective Ser.: 26). (ENG.). 144p. (J). (gr. 3-7). pap. 5.99 *(978-1-4169-3525-4(8),* Aladdin) Simon & Schuster Children's Publishing.

—The Flower Show Fiasco. Pamintuan, Macky, illus. 2014. (Nancy Drew & the Clue Crew Ser.: 37). (ENG.). 96p. (J). (gr. 1-4). pap. 5.99 *(978-1-4424-8668-3(6),* Aladdin) Simon & Schuster Children's Publishing.

—Getting Burned. 20th ed. 2006. (Nancy Drew (All New) Girl Detective Ser.: 20). (ENG.). 160p. (J). (gr. 3-7). pap. 5.99 *(978-0-689-87703-2(X),* Aladdin) Simon & Schuster Children's Publishing.

—The Ghost of Grey Fox Inn. 2016. (Nancy Drew Diaries: 13). (ENG., Illus.). 192p. (J). (gr. 3-7). 17.99 *(978-1-4814-6596-0(1),* Simon & Schuster/Paula Wiseman Bks.) Simon & Schuster/Paula Wiseman Bks.

—Ghost Stories. 2008. (Nancy Drew (All New) Girl Detective Ser.). (ENG.). 240p. (J). (gr. 3-7). pap. 5.99 *(978-1-4169-5909-0(2),* Aladdin) Simon & Schuster Children's Publishing.

—Green with Envy: Book Two in the Eco Mystery Trilogy. 2010. (Nancy Drew (All New) Girl Detective Ser.: 40). (ENG.). 160p. (J). (gr. 3-7). pap. 6.99 *(978-1-4169-7842-8(9),* Aladdin) Simon & Schuster Children's Publishing.

—The Hidden Staircase, No. 2. 2014. (Nancy Drew Ser.: 2). (ENG.). 192p. (J). (gr. 3-7). 7.99 *(978-0-448-47970-5(2),* Grosset & Dunlap) Penguin Young Readers Group.

—High Risk. 4th ed. 2004. (Nancy Drew (All New) Girl Detective Ser.: 4). (ENG.). 160p. (J). (gr. 3-7). mass mkt. 5.99 *(978-0-689-86569-5(4),* Aladdin) Simon & Schuster Children's Publishing.

—Identity Revealed. 2009. (Nancy Drew (All New) Girl Detective Ser.: 35). (ENG.). 208p. (J). (gr. 3-7). pap. 5.99 *(978-1-4169-6828-3(8),* Aladdin) Simon & Schuster Children's Publishing.

—Intruder. 27th ed. 2007. (Nancy Drew (All New) Girl Detective Ser.: 27). (ENG.). 160p. (J). (gr. 3-7). pap. 5.99 *(978-1-4169-3526-1(6),* Aladdin) Simon & Schuster Children's Publishing.

—Lights, Camera ... Cats! Pamintuan, Macky, illus. 8th ed. 2007. (Nancy Drew & the Clue Crew Ser.: 8). (ENG.). 96p. (J). (gr. 1-4). pap. 5.99 *(978-1-4169-3957-3(1),* Aladdin) Simon & Schuster Children's Publishing.

—The Magician's Secret. 2015. (Nancy Drew Diaries: 8). (ENG., Illus.). 176p. (J). (gr. 3-7). pap. 6.99 *(978-1-4814-1700-6(2),* Aladdin) Simon & Schuster Children's Publishing.

—The Make-a-Pet Mystery. Pamintuan, Macky, illus. 2012. (Nancy Drew & the Clue Crew Ser.: 31). (ENG.). 96p. (J). (gr. 1-4). pap. 5.99 *(978-1-4169-9464-0(5),* Aladdin) Simon & Schuster Children's Publishing.

—Mall Madness. Pamintuan, Macky, illus. 15th ed. 2008. (Nancy Drew & the Clue Crew Ser.: 15). (ENG.). 96p. (J). (gr. 1-4). pap. 5.99 *(978-1-4169-5900-7(9),* Aladdin) Simon & Schuster Children's Publishing.

—Movie Madness. Francis, Peter, illus. 2016. (Nancy Drew Clue Book Ser.: 5). (ENG.). 96p. (J). (gr. 1-4). pap. 5.99 *(978-1-4814-5820-7(5),* Aladdin) Simon & Schuster Children's Publishing.

—Movie Madness. Francis, Peter, illus. 2016. (Nancy Drew Clue Book Ser.: 5). (ENG.). 96p. (J). (gr. 1-4). 16.99 *(978-1-4814-5821-4(3),* Simon & Schuster/Paula Wiseman Bks.) Simon & Schuster/Paula Wiseman Bks.

—Murder on the Set. 24th ed. 2007. (Nancy Drew (All New) Girl Detective Ser.: 24). (ENG.). 176p. (J). (gr. 3-7). pap. 4.99 *(978-1-4169-3397-7(2),* Aladdin) Simon & Schuster Children's Publishing.

—A Musical Mess. Pamintuan, Macky, illus. 2014. (Nancy Drew & the Clue Crew Ser.: 38). (ENG.). 96p. (J). (gr. 1-4). pap. 5.99 *(978-1-4424-9512-8(X),* Aladdin) Simon & Schuster Children's Publishing.

—The Mystery at Lilac Inn. 2014. (Nancy Drew Ser.: 4). (ENG.). 192p. (J). (gr. 3-7). 7.99 *(978-0-448-47972-9(9),* Grosset & Dunlap) Penguin Young Readers Group.

—Mystery of the Midnight Rider. 2013. (Nancy Drew Diaries: 3). (ENG.). 208p. (J). (gr. 1-7). 15.99 *(978-1-4424-7861-9(6));* pap. 6.99 *(978-1-4424-7860-2(8))* Simon & Schuster Children's Publishing. (Aladdin).

—The Nancy Drew & the Clue Crew Collection: Sleepover Sleuths; Scream for Ice Cream; Pony Problems; the Cinderella Ballet Mystery; Case of the Sneaky Snowman. Pamintuan, Macky, illus. 2014. (Nancy Drew & the Clue Crew Ser.). (ENG.). 480p. (J). (gr. 1-4). pap. 29.99 *(978-1-4814-1472-2(0),* Aladdin) Simon & Schuster Children's Publishing.

—Nancy Drew Diaries: Curse of the Arctic Star; Strangers on a Train; Mystery of the Midnight Rider; Once upon a Thriller. 2013. (Nancy Drew Diaries). (ENG., Illus.). 768p. (J). (gr. 3-7). pap. 27.99 *(978-1-4424-8896-0(4),* Aladdin) Simon & Schuster Children's Publishing.

—Nancy Drew Diaries 3-Books-In-1! Curse of the Arctic Star; Strangers on a Train; Mystery of the Midnight Rider. 2016. (Nancy Drew Diaries). (ENG., Illus.). 592p. (J). (gr. 3-7). pap. 8.99 *(978-1-4814-8554-8(7),* Aladdin) Simon & Schuster Children's Publishing.

—Once upon a Crime. 2nd ed. 2006. (Nancy Drew: Girl Detective Super Mystery Ser.: 2). (ENG.). 192p. (J). (gr. 3-7). pap. 6.99 *(978-1-4169-1248-4(7),* Aladdin) Simon & Schuster Children's Publishing.

—Once upon a Thriller. 2013. (Nancy Drew Diaries: 4). (ENG., Illus.). 144p. (J). (gr. 3-7). 15.99 *(978-1-4424-6612-8(X));* pap. 6.99 *(978-1-4169-9074-1(7))* Simon & Schuster Children's Publishing. (Aladdin).

—The Orchid Thief. 19th ed. 2006. (Nancy Drew (All New) Girl Detective Ser.: 19). (ENG.). 144p. (J). (gr. 3-7). pap. 5.99 *(978-1-4169-0980-4(X),* Aladdin) Simon & Schuster Children's Publishing.

—Pageant Perfect Crime: Book One in the Perfect Mystery Trilogy. 30th ed. 2008. (Nancy Drew (All New) Girl Detective Ser.: 30). (ENG.). 160p. (J). (gr. 3-7). pap. 5.99 *(978-1-4169-5528-3(3),* Aladdin) Simon & Schuster Children's Publishing.

—Perfect Cover. 31st ed. 2008. (Nancy Drew (All New) Girl Detective Ser.: 31). (ENG.). 160p. (J). (gr. 3-7). pap. 5.99 *(978-1-4169-5530-6(5),* Aladdin) Simon & Schuster Children's Publishing.

—Pony Problems. Pamintuan, Macky, illus. 3rd ed. 2006. (Nancy Drew & the Clue Crew Ser.: 3). (ENG.). 96p. (J). (gr. 1-4). pap. 5.99 *(978-1-4169-1815-8(9),* Aladdin) Simon & Schuster Children's Publishing.

—Pony Problems, 1 vol. Pamintuan, Macky, illus. 2007. (Nancy Drew & the Clue Crew Ser.). (ENG.). 80p. (gr. 1-4). 24.21 *(978-1-59961-346-8(8))* Spotlight.

—The Pumpkin Patch Puzzle. Pamintuan, Macky, illus. 2012. (Nancy Drew & the Clue Crew Ser.: 33). (ENG.). 112p. (J). (gr. 1-4). pap. 5.99 *(978-1-4169-9465-7(3),* Aladdin) Simon & Schuster Children's Publishing.

—Real Fake. 3rd ed. 2007. (Nancy Drew: Girl Detective Super Mystery Ser.: 3). (ENG.). 224p. (J). (gr. 3-7). pap. 5.99 *(978-1-4169-3881-1(8),* Aladdin) Simon & Schuster Children's Publishing.

—The Red Slippers. 2015. (Nancy Drew Diaries: 11). (ENG., Illus.). 192p. (J). (gr. 3-7). pap. 6.99 *(978-1-4814-3813-1(1),* Aladdin) Simon & Schuster Children's Publishing.

—Riverboat Ruse. 2005. (Nancy Drew Ser.: 11). 154p. (J). lib. bdg. 15.00 *(978-1-59054-813-4(2))* Fitzgerald Bks.

—Sabotage at Willow Woods. 2014. (Nancy Drew Diaries: 5). (ENG., Illus.). 176p. (J). (gr. 3-7). pap. 6.99 *(978-1-4424-9392-6(5),* Aladdin) Simon & Schuster Children's Publishing.

—Sabotage Surrender: Book Three in the Sabotage Mystery Trilogy. 2011. (Nancy Drew (All New) Girl Detective Ser.: 44). (ENG.). 128p. (J). (gr. 3-7). pap. 6.99 *(978-1-4169-9071-0(2),* Aladdin) Simon & Schuster Children's Publishing.

—The Scarlet Macaw Scandal. Frost, Michael, illus. 8th ed. 2004. (Nancy Drew (All New) Girl Detective Ser.: 8). (ENG.). 160p. (J). (gr. 3-7). pap. 5.99 *(978-0-689-86844-3(8),* Aladdin) Simon & Schuster Children's Publishing.

—Scream for Ice Cream. Pamintuan, Macky, illus. 2nd ed. 2006. (Nancy Drew & the Clue Crew Ser.: 2). (ENG.). 96p. (J). (gr. 1-4). pap. 5.99 *(978-1-4169-1253-8(3),* Aladdin) Simon & Schuster Children's Publishing.

—Scream for Ice Cream, 1 vol. Pamintuan, Macky, illus. 2007. (Nancy Drew & the Clue Crew Ser.). (ENG.). 89p. (gr. 1-4). 24.21 *(978-1-59961-347-5(5))* Spotlight.

—A Script for Danger. 2015. (Nancy Drew Diaries: 10). (ENG., Illus.). 192p. (J). (gr. 3-7). 6.99 *(978-1-4814-3810-0(7),* Aladdin) Simon & Schuster Children's Publishing.

—Secret Identity, Bk. 1. 33rd ed. 2008. (Nancy Drew (All New) Girl Detective Ser.: 33). (ENG.). 176p. (J). (gr. 3-7). pap. 5.99 *(978-1-4169-6827-6(X),* Aladdin) Simon & Schuster Children's Publishing.

—The Secret of Red Gate Farm. 2015. (Nancy Drew Ser.: 6). (ENG.). 192p. (J). (gr. 3-7). 8.99 *(978-0-448-48906-3(6),* Grosset & Dunlap) Penguin Young Readers Group.

—Secret of Shadow Ranch. 2015. (Nancy Drew Ser.: 5). (ENG.). 192p. (J). (gr. 3-7). 8.99 *(978-0-448-48905-6(8),* Grosset & Dunlap) Penguin Young Readers Group.

—The Secret of the Old Clock, Bk. 1. 2014. (Nancy Drew Ser.: 1). (ENG.). 192p. (J). (gr. 3-7). 7.99 *(978-0-448-47969-9(9),* Grosset & Dunlap) Penguin Young Readers Group.

—Seeing Green: Book Three in the Eco Mystery Trilogy. 2010. (Nancy Drew (All New) Girl Detective Ser.: 41). (ENG.). 160p. (J). (gr. 3-7). pap. 6.99 *(978-1-4169-7845-9(3),* Aladdin) Simon & Schuster Children's Publishing.

—The Sign in the Smoke. 2016. (Nancy Drew Diaries: 12). (ENG., Illus.). 272p. (J). (gr. 3-7). pap. 6.99 *(978-1-4814-3816-2(6),* Aladdin) Simon & Schuster Children's Publishing.

—The Singing Suspects. Jones, Jan Naimo, illus. 2005. (Nancy Drew Notebooks). 69p. (J). (gr. 1-4). 11.65 *(978-0-7569-5952-4(7))* Perfection Learning Corp.

—Ski School Sneak. Pamintuan, Macky, illus. 11th ed. 2007. (Nancy Drew & the Clue Crew Ser.: 11). (ENG.). 96p. (J). (gr. 1-4). pap. 5.99 *(978-1-4169-4936-7(4),* Aladdin) Simon & Schuster Children's Publishing.

—Sleepover Sleuths, 1 vol. Pamintuan, Macky, illus. 2007. (Nancy Drew & the Clue Crew Ser.). (ENG.). 81p. (gr. 1-4). 24.21 *(978-1-59961-348-2(4))* Spotlight.

—Snowman Surprise. Casale, Paul, illus. Frost, Michael, photos by. 63rd ed. 2004. (Nancy Drew Notebooks Ser.: 63). (ENG.). 80p. (J). (gr. 1-4). pap. 4.99 *(978-0-689-87411-6(1),* Aladdin) Simon & Schuster Children's Publishing.

—Stage Fright. 2012. (Nancy Drew/Hardy Boys Ser.: 6). (ENG.). 176p. (J). (gr. 3-7). pap. 6.99 *(978-1-4424-5681-5(7),* Aladdin) Simon & Schuster Children's Publishing.

—Stalk, Don't Run. 2012. (Nancy Drew (All New) Girl Detective Ser.: 47). (ENG.). 160p. (J). (gr. 3-7). pap. 5.99 *(978-1-4424-2299-5(8),* Aladdin) Simon & Schuster Children's Publishing.

—The Stolen Relic. 7th ed. 2004. (Nancy Drew (All New) Girl Detective Ser.: 7). (ENG.). 160p. (J). (gr. 3-7). mass mkt. 6.99 *(978-0-689-86843-6(X),* Aladdin) Simon & Schuster Children's Publishing.

—Stop the Clock. 2005. (Nancy Drew Ser.: 12). 160p. (J). lib. bdg. 15.00 *(978-1-59054-815-8(9))* Fitzgerald Bks.

—Strangers on a Train. 2013. (Nancy Drew Diaries: 2). (ENG.). 208p. (J). (gr. 3-7). 15.99 (978-1-4424-6611-1(1), Simon & Schuster/Paula Wiseman Bks.) Simon & Schuster/Paula Wiseman Bks.

—A Taste of Danger. 174th ed. 2003. (Nancy Drew Ser.: 174). (ENG.). 176p. (J). (gr. 3-7). pap. 5.99 (978-0-689-86154-3(0), Aladdin) Simon & Schuster Children's Publishing.

—Ticket Trouble. Pamintuan, Macky, illus. 10th ed. 2007. (Nancy Drew & the Clue Crew Ser.: 10). (ENG.). 96p. (J). (gr. 1-4). pap. 5.99 (978-1-4169-4733-2(7), Aladdin) Simon & Schuster Children's Publishing.

—Time Thief. Pamintuan, Macky, illus. 2011. (Nancy Drew & the Clue Crew Ser.: 28). (ENG.). 96p. (J). (gr. 1-4). pap. 5.99 (978-1-4169-9458-9(0), Aladdin) Simon & Schuster Children's Publishing.

—Trails of Treachery. 2008. (Nancy Drew: Girl Detective Ser.). 136p. (gr. 3-7). 15.00 (978-0-7569-8295-9(2)) Perfection Learning Corp.

—Trails of Treachery. 25th ed. 2007. (Nancy Drew (All New) Girl Detective Ser.: 25). (ENG.). 144p. (J). (gr. 3-7). pap. 5.99 (978-1-4169-3524-7(X), Aladdin) Simon & Schuster Children's Publishing.

—Troubled Waters. 23rd ed. 2007. (Nancy Drew (All New) Girl Detective Ser.: 23). (ENG.). 160p. (J). (gr. 3-7). pap. 5.99 (978-1-4169-2513-2(9), Aladdin) Simon & Schuster Children's Publishing.

—Uncivil Acts. 2005. (Nancy Drew Ser.: 10). 152p. (J). lib. bdg. 15.00 (978-1-59054-818-9(3)) Fitzgerald Bks.

—Valentine's Day Secret. Pamintuan, Macky, illus. 12th ed. 2007. (Nancy Drew & the Clue Crew Ser.: 12). (ENG.). 96p. (J). (gr. 1-4). pap. 5.99 (978-1-4169-4944-2(5), Aladdin) Simon & Schuster Children's Publishing.

—Without a Trace. 2005. (Nancy Drew Ser.: 1). (Illus.). 154p. (J). lib. bdg. 15.00 (978-1-59054-819-6(1)) Fitzgerald Bks.

—Without a Trace. 2004. (Nancy Drew (All New) Girl Detective Ser.: 1). (ENG.). 160p. (J). (gr. 3-7). pap. 5.99 (978-0-689-86566-4(X), Aladdin) Simon & Schuster Children's Publishing.

—Without a Trace Set: A Race Against Time - False Notes - High Risk. 2004. (Nancy Drew (All New) Girl Detective Ser.). (ENG., Illus.). 640p. (J). (gr. 3-7). pap. 23.99 (978-0-689-03691-0(4), Aladdin) Simon & Schuster Children's Publishing.

Keene, Carolyn & Dixon, Franklin W. Danger Overseas. 2008. (Nancy Drew/Hardy Boys Ser.: 2). (ENG., Illus.). 224p. (J). (gr. 3-7). pap. 5.99 (978-1-4169-5777-5(4), Aladdin) Simon & Schuster Children's Publishing.

—Terror on Tour. 2007. (Nancy Drew/Hardy Boys Ser.: 1). (ENG., Illus.). 224p. (J). (gr. 3-7). pap. 5.99 (978-1-4169-2726-6(3), Aladdin) Simon & Schuster Children's Publishing.

Keene, Carolyn & Whelan, Patrick. Danger on the Great Lakes. 173rd ed. 2003. (Nancy Drew Ser.: 173). (ENG., Illus.). 160p. (J). (gr. 3-7). pap. 5.99 (978-0-689-86146-8(X), 53545777, Simon & Schuster/Paula Wiseman Bks.) Simon & Schuster/Paula Wiseman Bks.

Kinney, Sarah. Enter the Dragon Mystery. 2013. (Nancy Drew & the Clue Crew Ser.). (ENG., Illus.). 64p. (J). (gr. k-3). pap. 7.99 (978-1-59707-437-7(3), 9781597074377) Papercutz.

—Nancy Drew & the Clue Crew #3: Enter the Dragon Mystery. 2013. (Nancy Drew & the Clue Crew Ser.). (ENG., Illus.). 64p. (J). (gr. k-3). 11.99 (978-1-59707-438-4(1), 9781597074384) Papercutz.

Kinney, Sarah & Petrucha, Stefan. Secret Sand Sleuths. 2013. (Nancy Drew & the Clue Crew Ser.). (ENG., Illus.). 64p. (J). (gr. k-3). pap. 7.99 (978-1-59707-376-9(8), 9781597073769);Bk. 2. 11.99 (978-1-59707-377-6(6), 9781597073776) Papercutz.

McDonald, Megan. Girl Detective. Reynolds, Peter H., illus. (Judy Moody Ser.: 9). (ENG.). 192p. (J). (gr. 1-4). 2011. pap. 5.99 (978-0-7636-4349-2(1))Bk. 9. 2010. 15.99 (978-0-7636-3450-6(6)) Candlewick Pr.

Petrucha, Stefan. The Demon of River Heights. Murase, Sho, illus. 2005. (Nancy Drew: Girl Detective Ser.). 88p. (gr. 3-8). 24.21 (978-1-59961-057-3(4)) Spotlight.

—Mr. Cheeters Is Missing. 6th rev. ed. 2006. (Nancy Drew Graphic Novels: Girl Detective Ser.: 6). (ENG., Illus.). 96p. (J). (gr. 3-7). pap. 7.95 (978-1-59707-030-0(0), 9781597070300) Papercutz.

—The Nancy Drew Diaries. 2014. (Nancy Drew Diaries). (ENG., Illus.). 176p. (J). (gr. 3-7). pap. 9.99 (978-1-59707-501-5(9), 9781597075015) Papercutz.

Petrucha, Stefan & Kinney, Sarah. City under the Basement. Murase, Sho, illus. 2009. (Nancy Drew Graphic Novels: Girl Detective Ser.: 18). (ENG.). 96p. (J). (gr. 3-7). pap. 7.95 (978-1-59707-154-3(4), 9781597071543); 18th ed. 12.95 (978-1-59707-155-0(2), 9781597071550) Papercutz.

—Cliffhanger. Murase, Sho, illus. 2009. (Nancy Drew Graphic Novels: Girl Detective Ser.: 19). (ENG.). 96p. (J). (gr. 3-7). 12.95 (978-1-59707-166-6(8), 9781597071666) Papercutz.

—High School Musical Mystery. 2010. (Nancy Drew Graphic Novels: Girl Detective Ser.). (ENG., Illus.). 96p. (J). (gr. 3-7). pap. 8.99 (978-1-59707-178-9(1), 9781597071789) Papercutz.

—Nancy Drew: High School Musical Mystery II - "The Lost Verse" 2010. (Nancy Drew Graphic Novels: Girl Detective Ser.). (ENG., Illus.). 96p. (J). (gr. 3-7). pap. 8.99 (978-1-59707-195-6(1), 9781597071956) Papercutz.

—Night of the Living Chatchke. 2009. (Nancy Drew Graphic Novels: Girl Detective Ser.). (ENG., Illus.). 96p. (J). (gr. 3-7). pap. 7.95 (978-1-59707-143-7(9), 9781597071437) Papercutz.

—Night of the Living Chatchke. Murase, Sho, illus. 17th ed. 2009. (Nancy Drew Graphic Novels: Girl Detective Ser.: 17). (ENG.). 96p. (J). (gr. 3-7). 12.95 (978-1-59707-144-4(7), 9781597071444) Papercutz.

—Sleight of Dan. 14th ed. 2008. (Nancy Drew Graphic Novels: Girl Detective Ser.: 14). (ENG., Illus.). 112p. (J). (gr. 3-7). pap. 7.95 (978-1-59707-107-9(2), 9781597071079) Papercutz.

—Small Volcanoes. 2012. (ENG., Illus.). 64p. (J). (gr. 3-7). 10.99 (978-1-59707-355-4(5), 9781597073554);No. 1. pap. 6.99 (978-1-59707-354-7(7), 9781597073547) Papercutz.

—Tiger Counter. 2008. (Nancy Drew Graphic Novels: Girl Detective Ser.: 15). (ENG., Illus.). 96p. (J). (gr. 3-7). 12.95 (978-1-59707-119-2(6), 9781597071192) Papercutz.

—Vampire Slayer, No. 2. 2010. (Nancy Drew the New Case Files Ser.). (ENG., Illus.). 64p. (J). (gr. 3-7). pap. 6.99 (978-1-59707-233-5(8), 9781597072335) Papercutz.

Petrucha, Stefan, et al. The Fake Heir. Ross, Daniel Vaughn, illus. 2006. (J). (978-1-59707-060-7(2)) Papercutz.

DREXEL, KATHARINE, 1858-1955

Wallace, Susan Helen. Saint Katharine Drexel: The Total Gift. Kiwak, Barbara, illus. 2003. (Encounter the Saints Ser.: Vol. 15). 144p. (J). pap. 5.95 (978-0-8198-7068-1(4), 332-365) Pauline Bks. & Media.

DRINKS

see Beverages

DRIVERS, AUTOMOBILE

see Automobile Drivers

DROMEDARIES

see Camels

DROON (IMAGINARY PLACE)—FICTION

Abbott, Tony. City in the Clouds. Jessell, Tim, illus. 2004. (Secrets of Droon Ser.: No. 4). 88p. 15.00 (978-0-7569-3930-4(5)) Perfection Learning Corp.

—Flight of the Genie. Jessell, Tim, illus. 2004. (Secrets of Droon Ser.: No. 21). 122p. (J). lib. bdg. 15.38 (978-1-4242-0314-7(7)) Fitzgerald Bks.

—The Fortress of the Treasure Queen. Merrell, David, illus. 2004. (Secrets of Droon Ser.: No. 23). 115p. (J). lib. bdg. 15.38 (978-1-4242-0312-3(0)) Fitzgerald Bks.

—The Magic Escapes. Jessell, Tim, illus. 2004. (Secrets of Droon Ser.: No. 1). 161p. (gr. 2-5). 16.00 (978-0-7569-3944-1(5)) Perfection Learning Corp.

—The Riddle of Zorfendorf Castle. Merrell, David, illus. 2005. (Secrets of Droon Ser.: No. 25). 124p. (J). lib. bdg. 15.38 (978-1-4242-0310-9(4)) Fitzgerald Bks.

DROPOUTS

Bartos, Judeen. High School Dropouts. 2013. (At Issue Ser.). (ENG.). 128p. (gr. 10-12). pap. 27.80 (978-0-7377-6182-5(2)); lib. bdg. 39.40 (978-0-7377-6181-8(4)) Cengage Gale. (Greenhaven Pr., Inc.).

Gall, Stewart B. Teenage Dropouts. 2013. 96p. (YA). lib. bdg. (978-1-60152-506-2(0)) ReferencePoint Pr., Inc.

Watkins, Heidi. Dropping Out of School. 2012. (Issues That Concern You Ser.). (ENG., Illus.). 144p. (gr. 7-10). lib. bdg. 42.00 (978-0-7377-6289-1(6)) Cengage Gale.

DROPOUTS—FICTION

Abrahams, Peter. Reality Check. 2010. (ENG.). 352p. (YA). (gr. 8). pap. 8.99 (978-0-06-122768-4(4), HarperTeen) HarperCollins Pubs.

Marchetta, Melina. The Piper's Son. (ENG.). 336p. (YA). (gr. 9). 2012. pap. 7.99 (978-0-7636-6062-8(0)) 2011. (Illus.). 17.99 (978-0-7636-4758-2(6)) Candlewick Pr.

van Diepen, Allison. Street Pharm. 2013. (ENG., Illus.). 320p. (YA). (gr. 8). pap. 10.99 (978-1-4424-8166-4(8), Simon Pulse) Simon Pulse.

Velasquez, Gloria. Tyrone's Betrayal. 2006. (Roosevelt High School Series Bks.). 135p. (J). (gr. 3-7). per. 9.95 (978-1-55885-465-9(7), Piñata Books) Arte Publico Pr.

DRUG ABUSE

see also Drug Addiction

Allen, John. The Dangers of Heroin. 2016. (ENG.). 80p. (J). (gr. 5-12). lib. bdg. (978-1-68282-018-6(1)) ReferencePoint Pr., Inc.

—Thinking Critically: Legalizing Marijuana. 2015. (ENG., Illus.). 80p. (J). lib. bdg. (978-1-60152-782-0(9)) ReferencePoint Pr., Inc.

Apel, Melanie Ann. Cocaine & Your Nose: The Incredibly Disgusting Story. 2005. (Incredibly Disgusting Drugs Ser.). (Illus.). 48p. (YA). (gr. 5-8). lib. bdg. 25.25 (978-0-8239-3251-1(6), DDCONO) Rosen Publishing Group, Inc., The.

Auer, Jim. Know How to Say No to Drugs & Alcohol: A Kid's Guide. 2007. (Elf-Help Books for Kids Ser.). (Illus.). (J). (gr. -1-3). per. 7.95 (978-0-87029-407-5(5)) Abbey Pr.

Axelrod-Contrada, Joan. The Facts about Drugs & Society. 2007. (Drugs Ser.). (Illus.). 143p. (J). (gr. 4-7). lib. bdg. 39.93 (978-0-7614-2674-5(4), Benchmark Bks.) Marshall Cavendish Corp.

Bankston, John. Ecstasy = Busted! 2005. (Busted! Ser.). (Illus.). 104p. (J). (gr. 6-13). lib. bdg. 33.27 (978-0-7660-2387-1(7)) Enslow Pubs., Inc.

Barbour, Scott. Should Marijuana Be Legalized? 2010. (In Controversy Ser.). 96p. (YA). (gr. 7-12). 27.95 (978-1-60152-106-4(5)) ReferencePoint Pr., Inc.

Becker, Peggy Daniels. Drugs. 2011. (Issues That Concern You Ser.). (ENG.). 144p. (gr. 10-10). 42.00 (978-0-7377-4951-9(2)) Cengage Gale.

Becnel, Barbara, ed. Gangs & Drugs: Stanley Tookie Williams Street Peace Series, 8 bks., Vol. 1, Bk. 1. 2008. 24p. (J). 6.95 (978-0-9753584-2-9(1)) Damamli Publishing Co.

Being Me & Drug-Free. (J). 29.50 (978-1-56230-034-0(2)); (SPA.). 29.50 (978-1-56230-211-5(6)) Syndistar, Inc.

Benson, Michael. Drug Crime. 2008. (Criminal Investigations Ser.). (Illus.). 128p. (C). (gr. 9-12). 35.00 (978-0-7910-9407-5(3), Chelsea Hse.) Facts On File, Inc.

Berne, Emma Carlson. Methamphetamine. 2007. (Compact Research Ser.). (Illus.). 102p. (YA). (gr. 7-12). lib. bdg. 25.95 (978-1-60152-004-3(2)) ReferencePoint Pr., Inc.

Bigelow, Barbara C. & Edgar, Kathleen J. The UXL Encyclopedia of Drugs & Addictive Substances, 5 vols. 2005. (Illus.). (J). (978-1-4144-0447-9(6)); (978-1-4144-0448-6(4)); (978-1-4144-0449-3(2)); (978-1-4144-0446-2(8)); (978-1-4144-0445-5(X)) Cengage Gale.

Biggers, Jeff. Chemical Dependency. rev. ed. 2005. (Drug Abuse Prevention Library). (Illus.). 64p. (YA). (gr. 7-12). lib. bdg. 31.95 (978-0-8239-3269-6(9)) Rosen Publishing Group, Inc., The.

bjornlund, lydia. Oxycodone. 2011. (Compact Research Ser.). 96p. (YA). (gr. 7-12). lib. bdg. 27.95 (978-1-60152-161-3(8)) ReferencePoint Pr., Inc.

Bodden, Valerie. Club & Prescription Drug Abuse, 1 vol. 2014. (Essential Issues Set 4 Ser.). (ENG.). 112p. (J). (gr. 6-12). lib. bdg. 35.64 (978-1-62403-419-0(5), Essential Library) ABDO Publishing Co.

Brezina, Corona. Heroin: The Deadly Addiction. 2009. (Drug Abuse & Society Ser.). 64p. (gr. 6-6). 58.50 (978-1-61512-222-6(2)) Rosen Publishing Group, Inc., The.

Burlingame, Jeff. Crystal Meth. 2013. 64p. (J). (gr. 6-9). 34.21 (978-1-60870-823-9(3)); pap. 15.28 (978-1-62712-059-3(9)) Cavendish Square Publishing.

Cefrey, Holly. Hallucinogens & Your Neurons: The Incredibly Disgusting Story. (Incredibly Disgusting Drugs Ser.). 48p. 2009. (gr. 5-8). 53.00 (978-1-61513-499-1(9), Rosen Reference) 2005. (Illus.). (J). (gr. k-3). lib. bdg. 29.25 (978-1-4042-0633-5(7), Rosen Reference) 2005. (Illus.). (YA). (gr. 5-8). lib. bdg. 25.25 (978-0-8239-3391-4(1)) Rosen Publishing Group, Inc., The.

Centore, Michael. Causes of Drug Use, Vol. 13. Becker, Sara, ed. 2016. (Drug Addiction & Recovery Ser.). (Illus.). 64p. (J). (gr. 7). 23.95 (978-1-4222-3600-0(5)) Mason Crest.

—Drug Use & Mental Health, Vol. 13. Becker, Sara, ed. 2016. (Drug Addiction & Recovery Ser.). (Illus.). 64p. (J). (gr. 7). 23.95 (978-1-4222-3601-7(3)) Mason Crest.

—Drug Use & the Family, Vol. 13. Becker, Sara, ed. 2016. (Drug Addiction & Recovery Ser.). 64p. (J). (gr. 7). 23.95 (978-1-4222-3603-1(X)) Mason Crest.

—Drug Use & the Law, Vol. 13. Becker, Sara, ed. 2016. (Drug Addiction & Recovery Ser.). (Illus.). 64p. (J). (gr. 7). 23.95 (978-1-4222-3602-4(1)) Mason Crest.

—Drugs & the Law. 2017. (Illus.). 64p. (J). (978-1-4222-3598-0(X)) Mason Crest.

—Intervention & Recovery, Vol. 13. Becker, Sara, ed. 2016. (Drug Addiction & Recovery Ser.). (Illus.). 64p. (J). (gr. 7). 23.95 (978-1-4222-3605-5(6)) Mason Crest.

Chastain, Zachary. Cocaine: The Rush to Destruction. 2012. (Illicit & Misused Drugs Ser.). 128p. (J). (gr. 7). 24.95 (978-1-4222-2429-8(5)) Mason Crest.

—Cocaine: The Rush to Destruction. Henningfield, Jack E., ed. 2012. (Illicit & Misused Drugs Ser.). 128p. (J). (gr. 7). pap. 14.95 (978-1-4222-2448-9(1)) Mason Crest.

Clayton, Lawrence. Amphetamines & Other Stimulants. (Drug Abuse Prevention Library). 64p. 2009. (gr. 5-5). 58.50 (978-1-60853-426-5(X)) 2005. (Illus.). (YA). (gr. 7-12). lib. bdg. 31.95 (978-0-8239-3444-7(6)) Rosen Publishing Group, Inc., The.

—Barbiturates & Other Depressants. (Drug Abuse Prevention Library). 64p. 2009. (gr. 5-5). 58.50 (978-1-60853-427-2(8)) 2005. (Illus.). (YA). (gr. 7-12). lib. bdg. 31.95 (978-0-8239-3442-3(X)) Rosen Publishing Group, Inc., The.

—Coping with a Drug-Abusing Parent. 2003. (C). per. 34.95 (978-0-9709523-6-3(8)) Clayro Corp.

Cobb, Allan B. Heroin & Your Veins: The Incredibly Disgusting Story. (Incredibly Disgusting Drugs Ser.). 48p. (gr. 5-8). 2009. 53.00 (978-1-61513-500-4(6), Rosen Reference) 2005. (Illus.). (J). lib. bdg. 25.25 (978-0-8239-3249-8(4), DDHEVE) Rosen Publishing Group, Inc., The.

Cobb, Allan B., et al. Heroin. 2008. (Junior Drug Awareness Ser.). (Illus.). 112p. (gr. 5-8). 30.00 (978-0-7910-9749-6(8), Chelsea Hse.) Facts On File, Inc.

Collins, Anna & Marcovitz, Hal. Marijuana: Abuse & Legalization. 2017. (Drug Education Library). 104p. (YA). (gr. 7-7). lib. bdg. 37.45 **(978-1-5345-6001-7(7)**, Lucent Pr.) Greenhaven Publishing LLC.

Connelly, Elizabeth Russell. Predatory Drugs = Busted! 2006. (Busted! Ser.). (Illus.). 104p. (J). (gr. 6). lib. bdg. 33.27 (978-0-7660-2474-8(1)) Enslow Pubs., Inc.

Connolly, Sean. Cocaine. 2009. (Straight Talking Ser.). (Illus.). 46p. (YA). (gr. 8-12). pap. (978-1-895058-50-5(3)) Saunders Bk. Co.

—Ecstasy. 2009. (Straight Talking Ser.). (Illus.). 46p. (YA). (gr. 8-12). pap. (978-1-895058-52-9(X)) Saunders Bk. Co.

Conti, Nicolette & Johanson, Paula. The Truth about Amphetamines & Stimulants. 2011. (Drugs & Consequences Ser.). (YA). (gr. 7-12). lib. bdg. 31.95 (978-1-4488-5483-7(0)) Rosen Publishing Group, Inc., The.

Crist, James J. When Someone You Love Abuses Alcohol or Drugs - a Guide for Kids. 2003. 112p. pap. 12.95 (978-1-58741-119-9(9)) Wellness Institute/Self-Help Bks., LLC.

Cunningham, Anne C. Critical Perspectives on Legalizing Marijuana. 2016. (Analyzing the Issues Ser.). 208p. (J). (gr. 8-8). 47.93 (978-0-7660-7669-3(5)) Enslow Pubs., Inc.

Currie-McGhee, Leanne. Teenage Drug Abuse. 2011. (Compact Research Ser.). 96p. (YA). (gr. 7-12). lib. bdg. 27.95 (978-1-60152-165-1(0)) ReferencePoint Pr., Inc.

Diconsiglio, John. True Confessions: Real Stories about Drinking & Drugs. 2008. (Scholastic Choices Ser.). (ENG., Illus.). 112p. (J). (gr. 7-13). pap. 8.95 (978-0-531-14773-3(8), Watts, Franklin) Scholastic Library Publishing.

Dinan, Robert S. Drug Free Teen: The Ultimate Guide for Parents, Teens, Teachers & Friends. 2004. (Illus.). 64p. (YA). per. 12.95 (978-0-9744682-0-4(7)) Red Men Interprises.

Drug Abuse & Society, 6 bks., Set. Incl. Ghb & Analogs: High-Risk Club Drugs. Wolf, Marie. lib. bdg. 31.95 (978-1-4042-0910-7(7)); Ketamine: Dangerous Hallucinogen. Lockwood, Brad. lib. bdg. 31.95 (978-1-4042-0911-4(5)); Methamphetamine: The Dangers of Crystal Meth. Spalding, Frank. lib. bdg. 31.95 (978-1-4042-0912-1(3)); Oxycontin: From Pain Relief to Addiction. Lockwood, Brad. lib. bdg. 31.95 (978-1-4042-0913-8(1)); Prescription Drugs. Ramen, Fred. lib. bdg. 31.95 (978-1-4042-0915-2(8)); (Illus.). 64p. (YA). (gr. 7-12). 2006. 2006. 167.70 (978-1-4042-1016-5(4)) Rosen Publishing Group, Inc., The.

Drug Dangers, 14 bks., Set. (Illus.). (YA). (gr. 4-10). lib. bdg. 279.30 (978-0-7660-1405-3(3)) Enslow Pubs., Inc.

Drug Dangers, 14 bks., Set. Incl. Alcohol Drug Dangers. Clayton, Lawrence. 64p. (YA). 2000. pap. 13.26 (978-0-7660-1735-1(4)); Alcohol Drug Dangers. Clayton, Lawrence. 64p. (YA). 1999. lib. bdg. 27.93 (978-0-7660-1159-5(3)); Amphetamine Drug Dangers. Pellowski, Michael J. 64p. (YA). 2000. lib. bdg. 27.93 (978-0-7660-1321-6(9)); Amphetamine Drug Dangers. Pellowski, Michael J. 64p. (YA). 2001. pap. 13.26 (978-0-7660-1962-1(4)); Crack & Cocaine Drug Dangers. Robbins, Paul R. 64p. (YA). 2000. pap. 13.26 (978-0-7660-1736-8(2)); Crack & Cocaine Drug Dangers. Robbins, Paul R. 64p. (YA). 1999. lib. bdg. 27.93 (978-0-7660-1155-7(0)); Diet Pill Drug Dangers. Clayton, Lawrence. 64p. (YA). 2000. pap. 13.26 (978-0-7660-1737-5(0)); Diet Pill Drug Dangers. Clayton, Lawrence. 64p. (YA). 1999. lib. bdg. 19.95 (978-0-7660-1158-8(5)); Ecstasy & Other Designer Drug Dangers. Weatherly, Myra. 64p. (J). 2000. lib. bdg. 27.93 (978-0-7660-1322-3(7)); Ecstasy & Other Designer Drug Dangers. Weatherly, Myra. 64p. (YA). 2001. pap. 10.95 (978-0-7660-1963-8(2)); Herbal Drug Dangers. Monroe, Judy. 64p. (YA). 2000. lib. bdg. 27.93 (978-0-7660-1319-3(7)); Herbal Drug Dangers. Monroe, Judy. 64p. (YA). 2001. pap. 13.26 (978-0-7660-1964-5(0)); Heroin Drug Dangers. Littell, Mary Ann. 64p. (YA). 2000. pap. 13.26 (978-0-7660-1738-2(9)); Heroin Drug Dangers. Littell, Mary Ann. 64p. (YA). 1999. lib. bdg. 27.93 (978-0-7660-1156-4(9)); Inhalant Drug Dangers. Monroe, Judy. 64p. (YA). 2000. pap. 13.26 (978-0-7660-1739-9(7)); Inhalant Drug Dangers. Monroe, Judy. 64p. (YA). 1999. lib. bdg. 27.93 (978-0-7660-1153-3(4)); LSD, PCP & Hallucinogen Drug Dangers. Monroe, Judy. 64p. (YA). 2001. pap. 13.26 (978-0-7660-1965-2(9)); LSD, PCP & Hallucinogen Drug Dangers. Monroe, Judy. 64p. (YA). 2000. lib. bdg. 27.93 (978-0-7660-1318-6(9)); Marijuana Drug Dangers. Somdahl, Gary L. 64p. (YA). 2000. pap. 13.26 (978-0-7660-1740-5(0)); Marijuana Drug Dangers. Somdahl, Gary L. 64p. (J). 1999. lib. bdg. 27.93 (978-0-7660-1214-1(X)); Speed & Methamphetamine Drug Dangers. Littell, Mary Ann. 64p. (YA). 2000. pap. 13.26 (978-0-7660-1741-2(9)); Speed & Methamphetamine Drug Dangers. Littell, Mary Ann. 64p. (YA). 1999. lib. bdg. 27.93 (978-0-7660-1157-1(7)); Steroid Drug Dangers. Monroe, Judy. 64p. (YA). 2000. pap. 13.26 (978-0-7660-1742-9(7)); Steroid Drug Dangers. Monroe, Judy. 64p. (YA). 1999. lib. bdg. 27.93 (978-0-7660-1154-0(2)); Tobacco & Nicotine Drug Dangers. MacDonald, Joan Vos. 64p. (YA). 2000. lib. bdg. 27.93 (978-0-7660-1317-9(0)); Tobacco & Nicotine Drug Dangers. MacDonald, Joan Vos. 64p. (YA). 2001. pap. 13.26 (978-0-7660-1966-9(7)); Tranquilizer, Barbiturate & Downer Drug Dangers. Houle, Michelle M. 64p. (YA). 2001. pap. 13.26 (978-0-7660-1967-6(5)); Tranquilizer, Barbiturate & Downer Drug Dangers. Houle, Michelle M. 64p. (YA). 2000. lib. bdg. 27.93 (978-0-7660-1320-9(0)); Set. (YA). lib. bdg. 279.30 (978-0-7660-1405-3(3)); (gr. 4-10). (Illus.). Set pap. 153.30 (978-0-7660-1794-8(X)) Enslow Pubs., Inc.

Drugs & Consequences: Set 2. 2013. (Drugs & Consequences Ser.). 64p. (YA). (gr. 7-12). 255.60 (978-1-4777-1910-7(5)) Rosen Publishing Group, Inc., The.

Dudley, William. Synthetic Drug Addiction. 2015. (ENG., Illus.). 96p. (J). lib. bdg. (978-1-60152-764-6(0)) ReferencePoint Pr., Inc.

Edelfield, Bruce & Moosa, Tracey J. Drug Abuse. 2011. (Teen Mental Health Ser.). (Illus.). 48p. (YA). (gr. 7-12). lib. bdg. 29.25 (978-1-4488-4590-3(4)) Rosen Publishing Group, Inc., The.

Ellis, Carol & Grayson, Robert. Drug Cartels & Smugglers. 2013. 96p. (J). 34.95 (978-1-61900-028-5(8)) Eldorado Ink.

Engdahl, Sylvia. Prescription Drugs. 2014. (Current Controversies Ser.). (ENG., Illus.). 224p. (gr. 7-12). lib. bdg. 46.40 (978-0-7377-6888-6(6), Greenhaven Pr., Inc.) Cengage Gale.

Esherick, Joan. Drug - & Alcohol-Related Health Issues. McDonnell, Mary Ann & Forman, Sara, eds. 2013. (Young Adult's Guide to the Science of Health Ser.: 15). 128p. (J). (gr. 7-18). 24.95 (978-1-4222-2808-1(8)) Mason Crest.

Etingoff, Kim. Abusing Over-the-Counter Drugs: Illicit Uses for Everyday Drugs. Henningfield, Jack E., ed. 2012. (Illicit & Misused Drugs Ser.). 128p. (J). (gr. 7). 24.95 (978-1-4222-2425-0(2)); pap. 14.95 (978-1-4222-2444-1(9)) Mason Crest.

—Drugs & Alcohol. Stephens, Ronald, ed. 2014. (Safety First Ser.: 11). 48p. (J). (gr. 5-18). 20.95 (978-1-4222-3046-6(5)) Mason Crest.

—Methamphetamines: Unsafe Speed. 2009. (Illicit & Misused Drugs Ser.). (Illus.). 128p. (YA). (gr. 7-18). lib. bdg. 24.95 (978-1-4222-0159-6(7)) Mason Crest.

Faulkner, Nicholas & Williams, Kara. Conquering Diet Drug Abuse, 01 vols., 1. 2016. (Conquering Eating Disorders Ser.). (ENG.). 64p. (J). 32.95 (978-1-4994-6197-8(6), Rosen Young Adult) Rosen Publishing Group, Inc., The.

Ford, Jean Otto. Rural Crime & Poverty: Violence, Drugs, & Other Issues. 2009. (Youth in Rural North America Ser.). (Illus.). 96p. (YA). (gr. 3-7). lib. bdg. 22.95 (978-1-4222-0016-2(7)) Mason Crest.

Friedman, Lauri S. Athletes & Drug Use. 2008. (Introducing Issues with Opposing Viewpoints Ser.). (ENG., Illus.). 112-144p. (gr. 7-10). 36.95 (978-0-7377-4166-7(X), Greenhaven Pr., Inc.) Cengage Gale.

—Drug Abuse. 2012. (Introducing Issues with Opposing Viewpoints Ser.). (ENG., Illus.). 144p. (gr. 7-10). lib. bdg. 42.00 (978-0-7377-5675-3(6), Greenhaven Pr., Inc.) Cengage Gale.

Friedman, Lauri S. & Des Chenes, Elizabeth, eds. Drug Abuse. 2007. (Writing the Critical Essay Ser.). (ENG., Illus.). 112p. (YA). (gr. 7-12). lib. bdg. 33.75 (978-0-7377-3461-4(2), Greenhaven Pr., Inc.) Cengage Gale.

Frisch, Carlienne A. When a Friend Has a Drug Problem. 2005. (Drug Abuse Prevention Library). (Illus.). 64p. (YA). (gr. 7-12). lib. bdg. 31.95 (978-0-8239-3120-0(X), DRFRPR) Rosen Publishing Group, Inc., The.

Gerber, Larry. The Truth about Steroids. 2013. (Drugs & Consequences Ser.). (Illus.). 64p. (J). (gr. 7-12). 31.95 (978-1-4777-1895-7(8)) Rosen Publishing Group, Inc., The.

Gillard, Arthur. Drug Abuse. 2013. (Issues That Concern You Ser.). (ENG., Illus.). 144p. (gr. 7-10). lib. bdg. 42.00 (978-0-7377-6290-7(X), Greenhaven Pr., Inc.) Cengage Gale.

Goldsmith, Connie. Addiction & Overdose: Confronting an American Crisis. 2017. (ENG.). 128p. (YA). (gr. 8-12). 37.32 **(978-1-5124-0953-6(7)**, Twenty-First Century Bks.) Lerner Publishing Group.

Greek, Joe. Coping with Opioid Abuse. 2017. (Coping Ser.). 112p. (gr. 12-12). 37.10 **(978-1-5081-7394-6(X)**, Rosen Young Adult) Rosen Publishing Group, Inc., The.

Greenhaven Press Staff, ed. Teen Drug Abuse. 2014. (Opposing Viewpoints Ser.). (ENG.). 208p. (gr. 10-12). pap. 30.95 (978-0-7377-7293-7(X)); lib. bdg. 44.95 (978-0-7377-7292-0(1)) Cengage Gale. (Greenhaven Pr., Inc.).

Grosshandler, Janet. Drugs & Driving. 2009. (Drug Abuse Prevention Library). 64p. (gr. 5-5). 58.50 (978-1-60853-429-6(4)) Rosen Publishing Group, Inc., The.

H, prod. Outsmarting Gateway Drugs with Dr. Craniac Workbook. 2006. (ENG.). (J). pap. 4.95 (978-1-55548-001-1(2), 4201) Human Relations Media.

Harris, Nathaniel. Drug Trafficking. 2009. (What If We Do Nothing? Ser.). 48p. (YA). (gr. 4-7). lib. bdg. 31.00 (978-1-4339-1981-7(8)) Stevens, Gareth Publishing LLLP.

Harrow, Jeremy. Crystal Meth. 2009. (Incredibly Disgusting Drugs Ser.). 48p. (gr. 5-8). 53.00 (978-1-61513-495-3(6), Rosen Reference) Rosen Publishing Group, Inc., The.

Hatton, Caroline. The Night Olympic Team: Fighting to Keep Drugs Out of the Games. 2008. (ENG., Illus.). 56p. (YA). (gr. 9-12). 17.95 (978-1-59078-566-9(5)) Boyds Mills Pr.

Haughton, Emma. Drug Abuse? 2005. (Viewpoints (Sea to Sea) Ser.). (Illus.). 32p. (YA). (gr. 5-9). lib. bdg. 27.10 (978-1-932889-60-4(4)) Sea-To-Sea Pubns.

Herscovitch, Arthur. Everything You Need to Know about Drug Abuse. rev. ed. 2005. (Need to Know Library). (Illus.). 64p. (YA). (gr. 7-12). lib. bdg. 31.95 (978-0-8239-3036-4(X), NTGUGU) Rosen Publishing Group, Inc., The.

Honders, Christine & Roleff, Tamara L. Steroids & Other Performance-Enhancing Drugs. 2017. (Drug Education Library). 112p. (YA). (gr. 7-7). lib. bdg. 37.45 **(978-1-5345-6003-1(3)**, Lucent Pr.) Greenhaven Publishing LLC.

Horning, Nicole. Heroin: Killer Drug Epidemic. 2017. (Drug Education Library). 104p. (J). (gr. 7-7). lib. bdg. 37.45 **(978-1-5345-6009-3(2)**, Lucent Pr.) Greenhaven Publishing LLC.

Human Relations Media, prod. Clued in! on Street Drugs. 2005. (ENG.). (J). pap. 4.95 (978-1-55548-148-3(5), 672) Human Relations Media.

Hyde, Margaret O. & Setaro, John F. Drugs 101: An Overview for Teens. 2003. (Teen Overviews Ser.). (ENG., Illus.). 160p. (gr. 7-12). lib. bdg. 27.93 (978-0-7613-2608-3(1), Twenty-First Century Bks.) Lerner Publishing Group.

Illicit & Misused Drugs, 16 vols., Set. Incl. Addiction in America: Society, Psychology, & Heredity. Walker, Ida. (Illus.). (YA). lib. bdg. 24.95 (978-1-4222-0151-0(1)); Addiction Treatment: Escaping the Trap. Walker, Ida. (Illus.). (YA). lib. bdg. 24.95 (978-1-4222-0152-7(X)); Alcohol Addiction: Not Worth the Buzz. Walker, Ida J. (YA). lib. bdg. 24.95 (978-1-4222-0153-4(8)); Hallucinogens: Unreal Visions. Nelson, Sheila. (Illus.). (YA). lib. bdg. 24.95 (978-1-4222-0155-8(4)); Inhalants & Solvents: Sniffing Disaster. Flynn, Noa. (Illus.). (YA). lib. bdg. 24.95 (978-1-4222-0157-2(0)); Marijuana: Mind-Altering Weed. Sanna, E. J. (Illus.). (YA). lib. bdg. 24.95 (978-1-4222-0158-9(9)); Methamphetamines: Unsafe Speed. Etingoff, Kim. (Illus.). (YA). lib. bdg. 24.95 (978-1-4222-0159-6(7)); Sedatives & Hypnotics: Deadly Downers. Walker, Ida J. (Illus.). (J). lib. bdg. 24.95 (978-1-4222-0163-3(5)); Tobacco: Through the Smokescreen. Chastain, Zachary. (YA). lib. bdg. 24.95 (978-1-4222-0165-7(1)); (gr. 7-18). 2009. (Illus.). 128p. 2007. Set lib. bdg. 399.20 (978-1-4222-0149-7(X)) Mason Crest.

Jeffrey, Laura S. Marijuana = Busted! 2006. (Busted! Ser.). (Illus.). 104p. (J). (gr. 6-15). lib. bdg. 33.27 (978-0-7660-2796-1(1)) Enslow Pubs., Inc.

Johanson, Paula. Critical Perspectives on the Opioid Epidemic. 2017. (Analyzing the Issues Ser.). 208p. (J). (gr. 8-8). lib. bdg. 47.93 **(978-0-7660-8487-2(6))** Enslow Pubs., Inc.

Kallen, Stuart A. Heroin: Drugs. 2006. (At Issue Ser.). (ENG., Illus.). 128p. (gr. 10-12). 39.40 (978-0-7377-2715-9(2)); pap. 27.80 (978-0-7377-2716-6(0)) Cengage Gale. (Greenhaven Pr., Inc.).

Kamberg, Mary-Lane. The Truth about Heroin: World's Fastest Bike. 2013. (Motorcycles: a Guide to the World's Best Bikes Ser.). 48p. (J). (gr. 5-8). 29.95 (978-1-4777-1860-5(5), Rosen Reference) Rosen Publishing Group, Inc., The.

Karson, Jill. Club Drugs. 2007. (Compact Research Ser.). (Illus.). 112p. (YA). (gr. 7-12). lib. bdg. 25.95 (978-1-60152-005-0(0)) ReferencePoint Pr., Inc.

Kerrigan, Michael. The War Against Drugs. 2004. (Crime & Detection Ser.). (Illus.). 96p. (J). (gr. 7-18). lib. bdg. 22.95 (978-1-59084-368-0(1)) Mason Crest.

—The War on Drugs, Vol. 20. Gomez, Manny, ed. 2016. (Crime & Detection Ser.). 96p. (J). (gr. 7). 24.95 (978-1-4222-3489-1(4)) Mason Crest.

Knight, Erin. Steroids. 2011. (ENG.). 48p. (J). pap. (978-0-7787-5518-0(5)); (gr. 4-7). (978-0-7787-5511-1(8)) Crabtree Publishing Co.

Knight, S. Black Magic. 2007. (ENG.). 156p. per. (978-1-84747-007-2(6)) Chipmunkapublishing.

Koellhoffer, Tara. Ecstasy & Other Club Drugs. 2008. (Junior Drug Awareness Ser.). (Illus.). 120p. (gr. 5-8). lib. bdg. 30.00 (978-0-7910-9697-0(1), Chelsea Hse.) Facts On File, Inc.

Konieczko, Craig. Intervention: Putting Yourself Between a Friend & Addiction. 2005. (Drug Abuse Prevention Library). (Illus.). 64p. (YA). (gr. 7-12). lib. bdg. 31.95 (978-0-8239-3156-9(0), DRINVE) Rosen Publishing Group, Inc., The.

Kreske, Damian P., et al. Junior Drug Awareness: How to Say No to Drugs. 2008. (Junior Drug Awareness Ser.). (Illus.). 112p. (gr. 5-8). 30.00 (978-0-7910-9699-4(8), Chelsea Hse.) Facts On File, Inc.

Laliberte, Michelle. Marijuana: A MyReportLinks. com Book. 2005. (Drugs Ser.). (Illus.). 48p. (J). lib. bdg. 26.60 (978-0-7660-5281-9(8), MyReportLinks.com Bks.) Enslow Pubs., Inc.

Landau, Elaine. Meth: America's Drug Epidemic. 2007. (Exceptional Social Studies Titles for Upper Grades). (ENG., Illus.). 120p. (gr. 7-12). lib. bdg. 30.60 (978-0-8225-6808-7(X)) Lerner Publishing Group.

Langwith, Jacqueline & Des Chenes, Elizabeth, eds. Drug Abuse. 2006. (Introducing Issues with Opposing Viewpoints Ser.). (ENG., Illus.). 128p. (YA). (gr. 7-12). lib. bdg. 35.75 (978-0-7377-3566-6(X)) Cengage Gale.

Latchana Kenney, Karen. The Hidden Story of Drugs, 1 vol., 1. 2014. (Undercover Story Ser.). (ENG.). 48p. (J). (gr. 5-8). 30.25 (978-1-4777-2803-1(1), Rosen Reference) Rosen Publishing Group, Inc., The.

LeVert, Suzanne & Hendricks, Jeff. Ecstasy. 2009. (Benchmark Rockets Ser.). 32p. (YA). (gr. 5-9). 28.50 (978-0-7614-4349-0(5)) Marshall Cavendish Corp.

LeVert, Suzanne & Whiting, Jim. The Facts about Steroids. 2009. (Benchmark Rockets: Drug Facts Ser.). 32p. (YA). (gr. 5-9). 28.50 (978-0-7614-4352-0(5)) Marshall Cavendish Corp.

Lew, Kristi. The Truth about Oxycodone & Other Narcotics. 2013. (Drugs & Consequences Ser.). (Illus.). 64p. (J). (gr. 7-12). 31.95 (978-1-4777-1894-0(X)) Rosen Publishing Group, Inc., The.

Libal, Joyce. Drug Therapy an Substance-Related Disorders. 2003. (Psychiatric Disorders: Drugs & Psychology for the Mind & Bod Ser.). (Illus.). 124p. (YA). (gr. 8-12). pap. 14.95 (978-1-4222-0401-6(4)) Mason Crest.

Lishak, Antony. Drugs. 2007. (What's That Got to Do with Me?/Watts Ser.). (Illus.). 32p. (YA). (gr. 4-7). lib. bdg. 28.50 (978-1-59920-035-4(X)) Black Rabbit Bks.

Lynette, Rachel. Drugs. 2007. (Illus.). 32p. (J). (978-0-431-90736-9(6)) Steck-Vaughn.

—The Real Deal: Drugs Hardback. 2007. (Illus.). 32p. (J). (978-0-431-90729-1(3)) Steck-Vaughn.

MacGregor, Cynthia. Refuse to Use. 2009. (Reading Room Collection 2 Ser.). 24p. (gr. 3-4). 42.50 (978-1-60851-985-9(6), PowerKids Pr.) Rosen Publishing Group, Inc., The.

MacKay, Jenny. The Dangers of Hallucinogens. 2016. (ENG.). 80p. (YA). (gr. 5-12). (978-1-68282-016-2(5)) ReferencePoint Pr., Inc.

Manley, Claudia B. Crack & Your Circulatory System: The Incredibly Disgusting Story. (Incredibly Disgusting Drugs Ser.). 48p. (gr. 5-8). 2009. 53.00 (978-1-61513-494-6(8), Rosen Reference) 2005. (Illus.). (J). lib. bdg. 29.25 (978-0-8239-3389-1(X)) Rosen Publishing Group, Inc., The.

Marcovitz, Hal. The Dangers of Methamphetamine. 2016. (ENG.). 80p. (J). (gr. 5-12). lib. bdg. (978-1-68282-022-3(X)) ReferencePoint Pr., Inc.

—Drug Abuse. 2008. (Hot Topics Ser.). (ENG., Illus.). 128p. (gr. 7-10). lib. bdg. 39.40 (978-1-4205-0081-3(3), LML02109-242085, Lucent Bks.) Cengage Gale.

—Drug & Alcohol Abuse. 2008. (Gallup Major Trends & Events Ser.). (Illus.). 120p. (YA). (gr. 7-18). lib. bdg. 22.95 (978-1-59084-963-7(9)) Mason Crest.

Marsico, Katie. Drug Abuse. 2013. 80p. (YA). (gr. 7-12). 34.21 (978-1-60870-852-9(7)); pap. 17.64 (978-1-62712-128-6(5)) Cavendish Square Publishing.

—Heroin. 2014. (J). (978-0-7614-8120-1(6)) Marshall Cavendish Corp.

—Heroin. 2014. (Illus.). 64p. (J). (978-1-62712-372-3(5)) Musa Publishing.

Marzilli, Alan. Drugs & Sports. 2008. (Point/Counterpoint Ser.). (Illus.). 144p. (C). (gr. 9). 35.00 (978-0-7910-9553-9(3), Chelsea Hse.) Facts On File, Inc.

Mason, Paul. Know the Facts about Drinking & Smoking. 2009. (Know the Facts Ser.). (ENG.). 48p. (YA). pap. 11.75 (978-1-4358-5462-8(4), Rosen Reference) Rosen Publishing Group, Inc., The.

McCage, Crystal D. Hallucinogens: Drugs. 2007. (Compact Research Ser.). (Illus.). 104p. (YA). (gr. 7-12). lib. bdg. 25.95 (978-1-60152-014-2(X)) ReferencePoint Pr., Inc.

—Inhalants. 2007. (Compact Research Ser.). (Illus.). 104p. (YA). (gr. 7-12). lib. bdg. 25.95 (978-1-60152-015-9(8)) ReferencePoint Pr., Inc.

McIntosh, Kenneth & Livingston, Phyllis. Youth with Alcohol & Drug Addiction: Escape from Bondage. 2009. (Helping Youth with Mental, Physical, & Social Challenges Ser.). (Illus.). 128p. (YA). (gr. 7-18). lib. bdg. 24.95 (978-1-4222-0143-5(0)) Mason Crest.

McKenzie, Precious. Helping a Friend with a Drug Problem. 2016. (How Can I Help? Friends Helping Friends Ser.). 00064p. (J). (gr. 6-6). pap. 12.95 (978-1-4994-6444-3(4)) Rosen Publishing Group, Inc., The.

McMahon, Christina & Marcovitz, Hal. The Dangers of Diet Drugs. 2017. (Drug Education Library Ser.). 104p. (YA). (gr. 7-7). 37.45 **(978-1-5345-6005-5(X)**, Lucent Pr.) Greenhaven Publishing LLC.

McPhee, Edna. Designer Drugs: Deadly Chemistry. 2017. (Drug Education Library). 112p. (YA). (gr. 7-7). lib. bdg. 37.45 **(978-1-5345-6007-9(6)**, Lucent Pr.) Greenhaven Publishing LLC.

McPherson, Stephanie Sammartino. Doping in Sports: Winning at Any Cost? 2016. (Nonfiction - Young Adult Ser.). (ENG., Illus.). 104p. (J). (gr. 7-12). 34.65 (978-1-4677-6148-2(6), Twenty-First Century Bks.) Lerner Publishing Group.

Medina, Sarah. Know the Facts about Drugs. 2009. 48p. (J). 70.50 (978-1-4358-5459-8(4), Rosen Reference); (ENG.). (YA). pap. 11.75 (978-1-4358-5458-1(6), Rosen Reference); (ENG., Illus.). (YA). (gr. 5-9). lib. bdg. 29.25 (978-1-4358-5337-9(7)) Rosen Publishing Group, Inc., The.

Merino, Noël. Gateway Drugs. 2008. (Opposing Viewpoints Ser.). (ENG., Illus.). (gr. 10-12). 224p. 48.80 (978-0-7377-4002-8(7)); 198p. (YA). 29.45 (978-0-7377-4003-5(5)) Cengage Gale. (Greenhaven Pr., Inc.).

Miller, Maia. Drugs & Mental Illness. 2005. (Drug Abuse Prevention Library). (Illus.). 64p. (YA). (gr. 7-12). lib. bdg. 31.95 (978-0-8239-3155-2(2), DRMEIL) Rosen Publishing Group, Inc., The.

Miller, Malinda. Ecstasy: Dangerous Euphoria. Henningfield, Jack E., ed. 2012. (Illicit & Misused Drugs Ser.). 128p. (J). (gr. 7). 24.95 (978-1-4222-2431-1(7)); pap. 14.95 (978-1-4222-2450-2(3)) Mason Crest.

Mintzer, Rich. Meth & Speed = Busted! 2005. (Busted! Ser.). (Illus.). 104p. (J). (gr. 6-13). lib. bdg. 33.27 (978-0-7660-2551-6(9)) Enslow Pubs., Inc.

—Steroids = Busted! 2006. (Busted! Ser.). (Illus.). 112p. (J). (gr. 6). lib. bdg. 33.27 (978-0-7660-2471-7(7)) Enslow Pubs., Inc.

Mirman, Heather Moehn. Issues in Drug Abuse. 2003. (Contemporary Issues Ser.). (ENG., Illus.). 112p. (YA). (gr. 7-10). 30.85 (978-1-59018-035-8(6), Lucent Bks.) Cengage Gale.

Moe, Barbara. Drug Abuse Relapse: Helping Teens to Get Clean Again. 2005. (Drug Abuse Prevention Library). (Illus.). 64p. (YA). (gr. 7-12). lib. bdg. 31.95 (978-0-8239-3157-6(9), DRRELA) Rosen Publishing Group, Inc., The.

Monroe, Judy. Steroids, Sports, & Body Image: The Risks of Performance-Enhancing Drugs. 2004. (Issues in Focus Ser.). (Illus.). 128p. (J). lib. bdg. 26.60 (978-0-7660-2160-0(2)) Enslow Pubs., Inc.

Monroe Peterson, Judy. The Truth about Barbiturates. 2013. (Drugs & Consequences Ser.). (Illus.). 64p. (J). (gr. 7-12). 31.95 (978-1-4777-1896-4(6)) Rosen Publishing Group, Inc., The.

Mooney, Carla. The Dangers of Synthetic Drugs. 2016. (ENG.). 80p. (J). (gr. 5-12). lib. bdg. (978-1-68282-026-1(2)) ReferencePoint Pr., Inc.

Murphy, Patricia J. Avoiding Drugs. (Illus.). 32p. 2006. (J). pap. 6.95 (978-0-8225-2779-4(0), Lerner Pubns.) 2005. (ENG., lib. bdg. 22.60 (978-0-8225-2867-8(3)) Lerner Publishing Group.

—Evitar las Drogas. 2005. (Libros para Avanzar (Pull Ahead Bks.)). (SPA., Illus.). 32p. (J). (gr. 3-7). lib. bdg. 22.60 (978-0-8225-3172-2(0), Ediciones Lerner) Lerner Publishing Group.

Naden, Corinne J. The Facts about the A-Z of Drugs. 2007. (Drugs Ser.). (Illus.). 156p. (J). (gr. 4-7). lib. bdg. 42.79 (978-0-7614-2673-8(6), Benchmark Bks.) Marshall Cavendish Corp.

Nelson, David. Teen Drug Abuse. 2010. (Opposing Viewpoints Ser.). (ENG.). 240p. pap. 29.45 (978-0-7377-4993-9(8)); 224p. (gr. 10-12). 48.80 (978-0-7377-4992-2(X)) Cengage Gale. (Greenhaven Pr., Inc.).

Nelson, Sheila. Hallucinogens: Unreal Visions. Henningfield, Jack E., ed. 2012. (Illicit & Misused Drugs Ser.). 128p. (J). (gr. 7). 24.95 (978-1-4222-2432-8(5)); pap. 14.95 (978-1-4222-2451-9(1)) Mason Crest.

—Hallucinogens: Unreal Visions. 2009. (Illicit & Misused Drugs Ser.). (Illus.). 128p. (YA). (gr. 7-18). lib. bdg. 24.95 (978-1-4222-0155-8(4)) Mason Crest.

Netzley, Patricia D. Is Legalized Marijuana Good for Society? 2015. (ENG., Illus.). 96p. (J). lib. bdg. (978-1-60152-774-5(8)) ReferencePoint Pr., Inc.

Orr, Tamra. Ecstasy. 2009. (Incredibly Disgusting Drugs Ser.). 48p. (gr. 5-8). 53.00 (978-1-61513-497-7(2), Rosen Reference) Rosen Publishing Group, Inc., The.

—The Truth about Cocaine. 2013. (Drugs & Consequences Ser.). (Illus.). 64p. (J). (gr. 7-12). 31.95 (978-1-4777-1897-1(4)) Rosen Publishing Group, Inc., The.

Parks, Peggy. How Serious a Problem Is Synthetic Drug Use? 2015. (In Controversy Ser.). (ENG., Illus.). 96p. (J). (gr. 8-12). lib. bdg. 28.95 (978-1-60152-884-1(1)) ReferencePoint Pr., Inc.

Parks, Peggy J. Heroin Addiction. 2015. (ENG., Illus.). 96p. (J). lib. bdg. (978-1-60152-756-1(X)) ReferencePoint Pr., Inc.

Perritano, John. Hallucinogens: Ecstasy, LSD, & Ketamine, Vol. 13. Becker, Sara, ed. 2016. (Drug Addiction & Recovery Ser.). (Illus.). 64p. (J). (gr. 7). 23.95 (978-1-4222-3604-8(8)) Mason Crest.

—Stimulants: Meth, Cocaine, & Amphetamines, Vol. 13. Becker, Sara, ed. 2016. (Drug Addiction & Recovery Ser.). (Illus.). 64p. (J). (gr. 7). 23.95 (978-1-4222-3611-6(0)) Mason Crest.

Petersen, Christine. Ecstasy. 2013. (J). (978-0-7614-8119-5(2)) Marshall Cavendish Corp.

Pierce, Simon. Prescription Drugs: Opioids That Kill. 2017. (Drug Education Library). 104p. (YA). (gr. 7-7). lib. bdg. 37.45 **(978-1-5345-6011-6(4)**, Lucent Pr.) Greenhaven Publishing LLC.

Poole, H. W. Over-The-Counter Drugs, Vol. 13. Becker, Sara, ed. 2016. (Drug Addiction & Recovery Ser.). (Illus.). 64p. (J). (gr. 7). 23.95 (978-1-4222-3608-6(0)) Mason Crest.

—Prescription Drugs, Vol. 13. Becker, Sara, ed. 2016. (Drug Addiction & Recovery Ser.). (Illus.). 64p. (J). (gr. 7). 23.95 (978-1-4222-3610-9(2)) Mason Crest.

Poolos, Christine. The Truth about Pcp. 2013. (Drugs & Consequences Ser.). (Illus.). 64p. (J). (gr. 7-12). 31.95 (978-1-4777-1899-5(0)) Rosen Publishing Group, Inc., The.

Powell, Jillian & Samanich, John G. Alcohol & Drug Abuse. 2008. (Emotional Health Issues Ser.). (Illus.). 48p. (YA). (gr. 7-12). lib. bdg. 31.00 (978-0-8368-9199-7(6)) Stevens, Gareth Publishing LLLP.

Redmond, Jodee. The Dangers of Drug Abuse. 2017. (Opioids & Opiates: the Silent Epidemic* Ser.: Vol. 5). (ENG.). (YA). (gr. 7-12). 23.95 **(978-1-4222-3824-0(5))** Mason Crest.

Rees, Jonathan. Drugs. 2005. (It's Your Health Ser.). (Illus.). 45p. (J). (gr. 6-9). lib. bdg. 29.95 (978-1-58340-586-4(0)) Black Rabbit Bks.

Roberts, Jeremy. Prescription Drug Abuse. 2005. (Drug Abuse Prevention Library). (Illus.). 64p. (YA). (gr. 7-12). lib. bdg. 31.95 (978-0-8239-3158-3(7), DRPRES) Rosen Publishing Group, Inc., The.

Rodger, Marguerite. Party & Club Drugs. 2011. (ENG.). 48p. (J). pap. (978-0-7787-5517-3(7)); (gr. 4-7). lib. bdg. (978-0-7787-5510-4(X)) Crabtree Publishing Co.

Roleff, Tamara L. Cocaine & Crack. 2007. (Compact Research Ser.). (Illus.). 104p. (YA). (gr. 7-12). lib. bdg. 25.95 (978-1-60152-001-2(8)) ReferencePoint Pr., Inc.

Rooney, Anne. Drugs on the Street. 2010. (Voices Ser.). (Illus.). 48p. pap. (978-0-237-54216-0(1)) Evans Brothers, Ltd.

Sanna, E. J. Marijuana: Mind-Altering Weed. 2009. (Illicit & Misused Drugs Ser.). (Illus.). 128p. (YA). (gr. 7-18). lib. bdg. 24.95 (978-1-4222-0158-9(9)) Mason Crest.

Saying No & Feeling Fine. (J). 29.50 (978-1-56230-078-4(4)) Syndistar, Inc.

Schroeder, Brock E. Ecstasy. 2003. (Drugs Ser.). (Illus.). 112p. (C). (gr. 9-13). 30.00 (978-0-7910-7633-0(4), Chelsea Hse.) Facts On File, Inc.

Schwartzenberger, Tina, ed. Substance Use & Abuse. 2006. (Understanding Global Issues Ser.). (Illus.). 56p. (J). (gr. 3-7). lib. bdg. 28.50 (978-1-59036-232-7(2)) Weigl Pubs., Inc.

Scott, Celicia. Doping: Human Growth Hormone, Steroids, & Other Performance-Enhancing Drugs. Borus, Joshua, ed. 2014. (Downside of Drugs Ser.). (ENG., Illus.). 48p. (J). (gr. 5-18). lib. bdg. 20.95 (978-1-4222-3020-6(1)) Mason Crest.

—Energy Drinks, Coffee, Soda, & Pills. Borus, Joshua, ed. 2014. (Downside of Drugs Ser.). (Illus.). 48p. (J). (gr. 5-18). pap. 10.95 (978-1-4222-3191-3(7)) Mason Crest.

—Hard Drugs: Cocaine, LSD, PCP, & Heroin. Borus, Joshua, ed. 2014. (Downside of Drugs Ser.). (ENG., Illus.). 48p. (J). (gr. 5-18). lib. bdg. 20.95 (978-1-4222-3021-3(X)) Mason Crest.

Sheff, Nic. We All Fall Down: Living with Addiction. 2012. (ENG.). 384p. (YA). (gr. 10-17). pap. 10.99 (978-0-316-08081-1(0)) Little, Brown Bks. for Young Readers.

Sherman, Jill. Drug Trafficking, 1 vol. 2010. (Essential Issues Set 1 Ser.). (ENG.). 112p. (J). (gr. 6-12). lib. bdg. 35.64 (978-1-60453-953-0(4), Essential Library) ABDO Publishing Co.

Sherry, Clifford. Inhalants. rev. ed. 2005. (Drug Abuse Prevention Library). (Illus.). 64p. (YA). (gr. 7-12). lib. bdg. 31.95 (978-0-8239-3443-0(8)) Rosen Publishing Group, Inc., The.

Silverman, Steve. Performance-Enhancing Drugs, 1 vol. 2008. (Essential Viewpoints Set 3 Ser.). (ENG.). 112p. (J). (gr. 6-12). lib. bdg. 35.64 (978-1-60453-111-4(8)) ABDO Publishing Co.

Slade, Suzanne. OxyContin Abuse. 2007. (Incredibly Disgusting Drugs Ser.). (Illus.). 48p. (YA). (gr. 5-9). lib. bdg. 29.25 (978-1-4042-1954-0(4)) Rosen Publishing Group, Inc., The.

Sommers, Michael A. Cocaine. 2008. (Incredibly Disgusting Drugs Ser.). (Illus.). 48p. (J). (gr. 4-7). lib. bdg. 29.25 (978-1-4042-1379-1(1)) Rosen Publishing Group, Inc., The.

Spalding, Frank. Methamphetamine: The Dangers of Crystal Meth. 2009. (Drug Abuse & Society Ser.). 64p. (gr. 6-6). 58.50 (978-1-61512-224-0(9)) Rosen Publishing Group, Inc., The.

Tina, Schwartzenberger. Substance Use & Abuse. 2007. (Understanding Global Issues Ser.). 56p. (J). pap. 11.95 (978-1-59036-506-9(2)) Weigl Pubs., Inc.

Triggle, David J., ed. Drugs: The Straight Facts. (Illus.). (gr. 9-13). lib. bdg. (978-0-7910-8397-0(7)); lib. bdg. 275.40 (978-0-7910-7632-3(6)) Facts On File, Inc. (Chelsea Hse.).

Wagner, Heather Lehr. Alcohol. 2003. (Drugs Ser.). (Illus.). 112p. (C). (gr. 9-13). 30.00 (978-0-7910-7259-2(2), Chelsea Hse.) Facts On File, Inc.

Walker, Ida. Natural & Everyday Drugs: A False Sense of Security. 2012. (J). pap. (978-1-4222-2456-4(2)) Mason Crest.

—Natural & Everyday Drugs: A False Sense of Security. Henningfield, Jack E., ed. 2012. (Illicit & Misused Drugs Ser.). 128p. (J). (gr. 7). 24.95 (978-1-4222-2437-3(6)) Mason Crest.

—Painkillers: Prescription Dependency. 2012. (J). pap. (978-1-4222-2457-1(0)) Mason Crest.

—Painkillers: Prescription Dependency. Henningfield, Jack E., ed. 2012. (Illicit & Misused Drugs Ser.). 128p. (J). (gr. 7). 24.95 (978-1-4222-2438-0(4)) Mason Crest.

Walker, Pam & Wood, Elaine. Stimulants. 2004. (Drug Education Library). (Illus.). 112p. lib. bdg. 32.45 (978-1-59018-044-0(5), Lucent Bks.) Cengage Gale.

Warburton, Lianne & Callfas, Diana. Amphetamines & Other Stimulants. 2007. (Junior Drug Awareness Ser.). (Illus.). 120p. (gr. 5-8). lib. bdg. 30.00 (978-0-7910-9712-0(9), Chelsea Hse.) Facts On File, Inc.

Waters, Rosa. Legal & Developmental Consequences. Borus, Joshua, ed. 2014. (Downside of Drugs Ser.). 48p. (J). (gr. 5-18). pap. 10.95 (978-1-4222-3192-0(5)) Mason Crest.

—Marijuana: Legal & Developmental Consequences. Borus, Joshua, ed. 2014. (Downside of Drugs Ser.). (ENG., Illus.). 48p. (J). (gr. 5-18). lib. bdg. 20.95 (978-1-4222-3022-0(8)) Mason Crest.

—Methamphetamine & Other Amphetamines. Borus, Joshua, ed. 2014. (Downside of Drugs Ser.). (ENG., Illus.). 48p. (J). (gr. 5-18). lib. bdg. 20.95 (978-1-4222-3023-7(6)) Mason Crest.

—Oxycontin(r), Percocet(r), Vicodin(r), & Other Addictive Analgesics. Borus, Joshua, ed. 2014. (Downside of Drugs Ser.). 48p. (J). (gr. 5-18). pap. 10.95 (978-1-4222-3194-4(1)) Mason Crest.

—Ritalin(r), Adderall(r), & Other Addictive Stimulants. Borus, Joshua, ed. 2014. (Downside of Drugs Ser.). 48p. (J). (gr. 5-18). pap. 10.95 (978-1-4222-3189-0(5)) Mason Crest.

Weaver, David J. Only Mortals Can Be Heroes: A True Story about Drug Addiction. 2005. 200p. 23.95 (978-0-9770916-0-7(0)) Cambria Creations, LLC.

West, Krista. Cocaine & Crack. 2008. (Junior Drug Awareness Ser.). (Illus.). 119p. (gr. 5-8). lib. bdg. 30.00 (978-0-7910-9704-5(8), Chelsea Hse.) Facts On File, Inc.

Wilkins, Jessica. Street Pharma. 2011. (ENG.). 48p. (J). pap. (978-0-7787-5519-7(3)); (gr. 4-7). lib. bdg. (978-0-7787-5512-8(6)) Crabtree Publishing Co.

Wilkinson Brown, Valerie. Me & My Faith. 2010. 48p. pap. 28.40 (978-0-557-14705-2(0)) Lulu Pr., Inc.

Willett, Edward. Speed. 2009. (Incredibly Disgusting Drugs Ser.). 48p. (gr. 5-8). 53.00 (978-1-61513-505-9(7), Rosen Reference) Rosen Publishing Group, Inc., The.

Williams, Mary E. Synthetic Drugs. Gale, G., ed. 2014. (Introducing Issues with Opposing Viewpoints Ser.). (ENG., Illus.). 144p. (gr. 10-12). lib. bdg. 42.00 (978-0-7377-6929-6(7), Greenhaven Pr., Inc.) Cengage Gale.

Wolny, Philip. Abusing Prescription Drugs. (Incredibly Disgusting Drugs Ser.). 48p. (gr. 5-8). 2009. 53.00 (978-1-61513-492-2(1), Rosen Reference) 2007. (Illus.). (YA). lib. bdg. 29.25 (978-1-4042-1955-7(2)) Rosen Publishing Group, Inc., The.

—The Truth about Heroin. 2013. (Drugs & Consequences Ser.). (Illus.). 64p. (J). (gr. 7-12). 31.95 (978-1-4777-1898-8(2)) Rosen Publishing Group, Inc., The.

DRUG ABUSE—FICTION

Anaya, Rudolfo. Curse of the ChupaCabra. 2013. (ENG.). 176p. (YA). pap. 19.95 (978-0-8263-4115-0(2)) Univ. of New Mexico Pr.

Andrews, Emily. The Finer Points of Becoming Machine. 2008. (Cutting Edge Ser.). (ENG.). 200p. pap. (978-1-84167-714-9(0)) Ransom Publishing Ltd.

Anonymous. Go Ask Alice. 2006. (ENG.). 224p. (YA). (gr. 7). pap. 9.99 (978-1-4169-1463-1(3), Simon Pulse) Simon Pulse.

—Go Ask Alice/Jay's Journal. Sparks, Beatrice, ed. 2010. (ENG.). 480p. (YA). (gr. 9). pap. 16.99 (978-1-4424-2310-7(2), Simon Pulse) Simon Pulse.

—Lucy in the Sky. 2012. (ENG.). 288p. (YA). (gr. 9). 19.99 (978-1-4424-5187-2(4)); pap. 10.99 (978-1-4424-5185-8(8)) Simon Pulse. (Simon Pulse).

Arcos, Carrie. Out of Reach. (ENG., (YA). (gr. 9). 2013. Illus.). 272p. pap. 9.99 (978-1-4424-4054-8(6)) 2012. 256p. 16.99 (978-1-4424-4053-1(8)) Simon Pulse. (Simon Pulse).

Atwood, Megan. The Terror of Black Eagle Tavern. 2012. (Paranormalists Ser.: 2). (ENG.). 104p. (YA). (gr. 6-12). pap. 7.95 (978-0-8225-9078-1(6), Darby Creek); lib. bdg. 27.93 (978-0-7613-8333-8(6)) Lerner Publishing Group.

Brian, Kate, pseud. Private. 2009. (Private Ser.: No. 1). (ENG.). 240p. (YA). pap. 9.99 (978-1-4169-9946-1(9), Simon & Schuster Bks. For Young Readers) Simon & Schuster Bks. For Young Readers.

Brockmann, Suzanne & Brockmann, Melanie. Wild Sky: A Night Sky Novel. 2015. (Night Sky Ser.: 2). (ENG.). 448p. (YA). (gr. 8-12). 16.99 (978-1-4926-0484-6(4)); pap. 9.99 (978-1-4926-2314-4(8)) Sourcebooks, Inc.

Burgess, Melvin. Smack. 2010. (ENG.). 352p. (YA). (gr. 9-13). pap. 13.99 (978-0-312-60862-0(4), 9780312608620) Square Fish.

Carlson, Melody. Playing with Fire. 2007. (Secret Life of Samantha Mcgregor Ser.: No. 3). (ENG.). 256p. (YA). (gr. 7-12). per. 12.99 (978-1-59052-694-1(5), Multnomah Bks.) Crown Publishing Group.

—Road Trip. 2003. (Diary of a Teenage Girl Ser.: Bk. 7). (ENG.). 304p. (J). (gr. 7). pap. 14.99 (978-1-59052-142-7(0), Multnomah) Doubleday Religious Publishing Group, The.

Cotugno, Katie. How to Love. 2015. (ENG.). 416p. (YA). (gr. 9). pap. 9.99 (978-0-06-221636-6(8)) HarperCollins Pubs.

Coy, John. Crackback. 2007. 201p. (gr. 7-12). 17.00 (978-0-7569-8274-4(X)) Perfection Learning Corp.

Denman, K. L. Spiral, 1 vol. 2008. (Orca Soundings Ser.). (ENG.). (YA). (gr. 8-12). 112p. 16.95 (978-1-55143-932-7(8)); 128p. pap. 9.95 (978-1-55143-930-3(1)) Orca Bk. Pubs. USA.

Elliott, Zetta & Strickland, Shadra. Bird, 1 vol. 2008. (ENG., Illus.). 48p. (J). (gr. 3-7). 19.95 (978-1-60060-241-2(X)) Lee & Low Bks., Inc.

Elliott, Zetta & Terasaki, Stanley Todd. Bird. Shinjo, Shelly, illus. 2016. (ENG.). 32p. (J). (gr. 2-5). pap. 9.95 **(978-1-62014-350-6(X))** Lee & Low Bks., Inc.

Flinn, Alex. Towering. 2013. (YA). (Kendra Chronicles Ser.: 3). (ENG.). 304p. (gr. 9). 17.99 (978-0-06-202417-6(5), HarperTeen); (Kendra Chronicles Ser.: 3). 304p. (gr. 9). lib. bdg. 18.89 (978-0-06-202418-3(3), HarperTeen); 296p. (978-0-06-227632-2(8)) HarperCollins Pubs.

Gaetz, Dayle Campbell. No Problem. 2004. (Orca Soundings Ser.). 87p. 19.95 (978-0-7569-4317-2(5)) Perfection Learning Corp.

Garsee, Jeannine. Before, after, & Somebody in Between. 2008. (ENG., Illus.). 368p. (YA). (gr. 9-12). pap. 8.99 (978-1-59990-292-0(3), 9781599902920, Bloomsbury USA Childrens) Bloomsbury Publishing USA.

Going, K. L. Fat Kid Rules the World. 2004. (ENG.). 224p. (YA). (gr. 7-18). reprint ed. pap. 9.99 (978-0-14-240208-5(7), Speak) Penguin Young Readers Group.

—Saint Iggy. 2008. (ENG., Illus.). 272p. (YA). (gr. 9-18). pap. 9.99 (978-0-15-206248-4(3)) Houghton Mifflin Harcourt Publishing Co.

Grosso, Alissa. Ferocity Summer. 2012. (ENG., Illus.). 288p. (YA). pap. 9.95 (978-0-7387-3070-7(X), Flux) North Star Editions.

Hardrick, Jackie. Imani in Never Say Goodbye. 2004. 272p. (YA). per. 15.00 (978-0-9706226-2-4(7)) Enlighten Pubns.

Hearn, Julie. Ivy. (ENG.). (YA). (gr. 7). 2009. 384p. pap. 9.99 (978-1-4169-2507-1(4)) 2008. 368p. 17.99 (978-1-4169-2506-4(6)) Simon & Schuster Children's Publishing. (Atheneum Bks. for Young Readers).

Helfand, Lewis. Photo Booth. Nagar, Sachin, illus. 2011. (Campfire Graphic Novels Ser.). (ENG.). 80p. (YA). (gr. 3-7). pap. 9.99 (978-93-80028-65-1(2), Campfire) Steerforth Pr.

Hernandez, David. Suckerpunch. 2007. (ENG.). 224p. (YA). (gr. 9-18). 17.99 (978-0-06-117330-1(4), HarperTeen) HarperCollins Pubs.

Holubitsky, Katherine. Tweaked, 1 vol. 2008. (ENG.). 192p. (YA). (gr. 8-12). pap. 12.95 (978-1-55143-851-1(8)) Orca Bk. Pubs. USA.

Hopkins, Ellen. Crank. (ENG., (YA). (gr. 9). 2013. Illus.). 576p. pap. 12.99 (978-1-4424-7181-8(6)) 2010. 544p. 21.99 (978-1-4169-9513-5(7)) McElderry, Margaret K. Bks. (McElderry, Margaret K. Bks.).

—Crank. 2013. lib. bdg. 24.50 (978-0-606-35118-8(3)) Turtleback Bks.

—The Crank Trilogy: Crank; Glass; Fallout. 2013. (ENG., Illus.). 1952p. (YA). (gr. 9). pap. 38.99 (978-1-4424-9959-1(1), McElderry, Margaret K. Bks.) McElderry, Margaret K. Bks.

—Fallout. (ENG., (YA). (gr. 9). 2013. Illus.). 720p. pap. 12.99 (978-1-4424-7180-1(8)) 2010. 672p. 18.99 (978-1-4169-5009-7(5)) McElderry, Margaret K. Bks. (McElderry, Margaret K. Bks.).

—Glass. (ENG., (YA). (gr. 9). 2013. Illus.). 720p. pap. 12.99 (978-1-4424-7182-5(4)) 2007. 688p. 21.99 (978-1-4169-4090-6(1)) McElderry, Margaret K. Bks. (McElderry, Margaret K. Bks.).

Horowitz, Lena. Dancing with Molly. 2016. (ENG.). 272p. (YA). (gr. 9). pap. 10.99 (978-1-4814-1551-4(4), Simon Pulse) Simon Pulse.

Johnson, Alaya Dawn. Love Is the Drug. 2014. (YA). pap. (978-0-545-41782-2(1)); (ENG.). 352p. (J). (gr. 9). 17.99 (978-0-545-41781-5(3), Levine, Arthur A. Bks.) Scholastic, Inc.

Jones, Patrick. Body Shot. 2013. (Dojo Ser.). (ENG.). 112p. (YA). (gr. 6-12). pap. 7.95 (978-1-4677-1490-7(9)); lib. bdg. 27.93 (978-1-4677-0633-9(7)) Lerner Publishing Group. (Darby Creek).

—Freedom Flight. 2015. (ENG.). 112p. (YA). (gr. 6-12). lib. bdg. 27.99 (978-1-4677-8051-3(0), Darby Creek) Lerner Publishing Group.

Kern, Peggy. Little Peach. 2015. (ENG.). 208p. (YA). (gr. 9). 17.99 (978-0-06-226695-8(0)) HarperCollins Pubs.

Koertge, Ron. Now Playing: Stoner & Spaz II. 2011. (ENG., Illus.). 224p. (YA). (gr. 9-18). 16.99 (978-0-7636-5081-0(1)) Candlewick Pr.

—Stoner & Spaz. 2011. (ENG., Illus.). 192p. (YA). (gr. 9). pap. 7.99 (978-0-7636-5757-4(3)) Candlewick Pr.

Kropp, Paul. Student Narc. Melanson, Matt, illus. 2004. (New Series Canada). 94p. (J). pap. (978-1-897039-05-2(0)) High Interest Publishing (HIP).

Leavitt, Martine. My Book of Life by Angel. 2012. (ENG.). 256p. (YA). (gr. 9-13). 17.99 (978-0-374-35123-6(6), 9780374351236, Farrar, Straus & Giroux (BYR)) Farrar, Straus & Giroux.

—My Book of Life by Angel. 2014. (ENG.). 272p. (YA). (gr. 9-13). pap. 11.99 (978-1-250-04003-9(5), 9781250040039) Square Fish.

Lipsyte, Robert. Raiders Night. (YA). (gr. 9-12). 2007. (ENG.). 256p. pap. 9.99 (978-0-06-059948-5(0)) 2006. 232p. 15.99 (978-0-06-059946-1(4)) 2006. 232p. lib. bdg. 16.89 (978-0-06-059947-8(2)) HarperCollins Pubs. (HarperTeen).

Mac, Carrie. Pain & Wastings, 1 vol. 2008. (Orca Soundings Ser.). (ENG.). (YA). (gr. 8-12). 128p. 16.95 (978-1-55143-906-8(9)); 152p. pap. 9.95 (978-1-55143-904-4(2)) Orca Bk. Pubs. USA.

Madison, Ron. Ned Learns to Say No: A Lesson about Drugs. Covolo, David, illus. l.t. ed. 2003. (Health & Safety Ser.). 24p. pap. 4.95 (978-1-887206-23-5(X)) Ned's Head Productions.

Martinez, Jessica. Virtuosity. (ENG.). (YA). (gr. 9). 2012. 320p. pap. 9.99 (978-1-4424-2053-3(7)) 2011. 304p. 16.99 (978-1-4424-2052-6(9)) Simon Pulse. (Simon Pulse).

Moses, Shelia P. Joseph. (ENG.). (YA). (gr. 7). 2010. 208p. pap. 8.99 (978-1-4169-9442-8(4)) 2008. (Illus.). 176p. 16.99 (978-1-4169-1752-6(7)) McElderry, Margaret K. Bks. (McElderry, Margaret K. Bks.).

—Joseph's Grace. 2011. (ENG.). 160p. (YA). (gr. 7-18). 16.99 (978-1-4169-3942-9(3), McElderry, Margaret K. Bks.) McElderry, Margaret K. Bks.

Murray, Jaye. Bottled Up. 2004. (ENG.). 224p. (YA). (gr. 7-12). reprint ed. 6.99 (978-0-14-240240-5(0), Speak) Penguin Young Readers Group.

Myers, Jason. Run the Game: Play or Be Played. 2012. (ENG.). 544p. (YA). (gr. 10). pap. 9.99 (978-1-4424-1432-7(4), Simon Pulse) Simon Pulse.

Myers, Walter Dean. The Beast. 2005. 17.00 (978-0-7569-5107-8(0)) Perfection Learning Corp.

—Dope Sick. (ENG.). 208p. (YA). (gr. 9). 2010. pap. 9.99 (978-0-06-121479-0(5)) 2009. 17.99 (978-0-06-121477-6(9)) HarperCollins Pubs. (Amistad).

Oates, Joyce Carol. After the Wreck, I Picked Myself Up, Spread My Wings, & Flew Away. 2006. (YA). (gr. 9-12). 304p. 16.99 (978-0-06-073525-8(2)); 292p. lib. bdg. 17.89 (978-0-06-073526-5(0)) HarperCollins Pubs. (HarperTeen).

Orme, Helen. Who Can I Tell? 2008. (Siti's Sisters Ser.). (ENG., Illus.). 36p. pap. (978-1-84167-744-6(2)) Ransom Publishing Ltd.

Rapp, Adam. The Children & the Wolves. Ering, Timothy Basil, illus. 2012. (ENG.). 160p. (YA). (gr. 9). 16.99 (978-0-7636-5337-8(3)) Candlewick Pr.

Reed, Amy. Beautiful. 2010. (ENG.). 256p. (YA). (gr. 9). pap. 10.99 (978-1-4169-7831-2(3), Simon Pulse) Simon Pulse.

—Clean. (ENG.). (YA). (gr. 9). 2012. 304p. pap. 10.99 (978-1-4424-1345-0(X)) 2011. 288p. 16.99 (978-1-4424-1344-3(1)) Simon Pulse. (Simon Pulse).

Reed, Amy Lynn. Beautiful. 2009. (ENG.). 240p. (YA). (gr. 9-18). 16.99 (978-1-4169-7830-5(5), Simon Pulse) Simon Pulse.

Reisfeld, Randi. Rehab. 2008. (ENG.). 256p. (YA). (gr. 9-18). pap. 8.99 (978-1-4169-6121-5(6), Simon Pulse) Simon Pulse.

Rivers, Karen. What Is Real, 1 vol. 2011. (ENG.). 304p. (YA). (gr. 7-12). pap. 12.95 (978-1-55469-356-6(X)) Orca Bk. Pubs. USA.

Ross, Jeff. Coming Clean, 1 vol. 2012. (Orca Soundings Ser.). (ENG.). 128p. (YA). (gr. 8-12). lib. bdg. 16.95 (978-1-4598-0332-9(9)) Orca Bk. Pubs. USA.

Rowley, Melissa. The Falcon Shield. 2009. (J). 6.99 (978-1-60641-103-2(9)) Deseret Bk. Co.

Sharpe, Tess. Far from You. 2014. (ENG.). 352p. (YA). (gr. 9-17). 17.99 (978-1-4231-8462-1(9)) Hyperion Bks. for Children.

Shinoda, Anna. Learning Not to Drown. 2014. (ENG., Illus.). 352p. (YA). (gr. 9). 17.99 (978-1-4169-9393-3(2), Atheneum Bks. for Young Readers) Simon & Schuster Children's Publishing.

Stoehr, Shelley. Crosses. 2003. 161p. (YA). pap. 13.95 (978-0-595-26952-5(4), Writers Club Pr.) iUniverse, Inc.

Storti, Kara. Tripping Back Blue. 2016. (ENG.). 368p. (YA). (gr. 9-12). 17.99 (978-1-5124-0308-4(3), Carolrhoda Bks.); 35.99 (978-1-5124-0444-9(6), Carolrhoda Lab™) Lerner Publishing Group.

Vega, Danielle & Loftin, Nikki. Survive the Night. 2015. (DUT & ENG.). 272p. (YA). (gr. 9). 17.99 (978-1-59514-724-0(1), Razorbill) Penguin Young Readers Group.

Voigt, Cynthia. Orfe. 2009. (ENG.). 162p. (YA). (gr. 7). pap. 8.99 (978-1-4169-9842-6(X), Simon Pulse) Simon Pulse.

Volponi, Paul. Rooftop. 2007. (ENG.). 224p. (YA). (gr. 7-18). 6.99 (978-0-14-240844-5(1), Puffin Books) Penguin Young Readers Group.

—Rooftop. 2007. 199p. 17.00 (978-0-7569-7958-4(7)) Perfection Learning Corp.

Vrettos, Adrienne Maria. Burnout. (ENG., 208p. (YA). (gr. 7). 2012. Illus.). pap. 8.99 (978-1-4169-9470-1(X)) 2011. 16.99 (978-1-4169-9469-5(6)) McElderry, Margaret K. Bks. (McElderry, Margaret K. Bks.).

Williams, Katie. Absent. 2013. (ENG.). 180p. (YA). (gr. 7-12). 16.99 (978-0-8118-7150-1(9)) Chronicle Bks. LLC.

Woodson, Jacqueline. Beneath a Meth Moon: An Elegy. (ENG.). (YA). (gr. 7). 2013. 240p. pap. 8.99 (978-0-14-242392-9(0), Speak) 2013. 240p. pap. 8.99 (978-0-14-242392-9(0), Speak) 2012. 144p. 16.99 (978-0-399-25250-1(9), Nancy Paulsen Books) Penguin Young Readers Group.

Zei, Alki. Tina's Web. Thornley, John, tr. from GRE. 2007. (ENG.). 300p. per. 18.95 (978-0-9551566-1-8(0)) Aurora Metro Pubns. Ltd. GBR. Dist: Consortium Bk. Sales & Distribution.

DRUG ADDICTION

Beal, Eileen J. Ritalin: Its Use & Abuse. 2005. (Drug Abuse Prevention Library). (Illus.). 64p. (YA). (gr. 7-12). lib. bdg. 31.95 (978-0-8239-3759-2(3)) Rosen Publishing Group, Inc., The.

Benton, John. New Hope Series, 10 bks., Set. 2004p. (J). (gr. 3-12). 35.00 (978-0-9635411-1-6(0)) Benton, John Bks.

Centore, Michael. Causes of Drug Use, Vol. 13. Becker, Sara, ed. 2016. (Drug Addiction & Recovery Ser.). (Illus.). 64p. (J). (gr. 7). 23.95 (978-1-4222-3600-0(5)) Mason Crest.

—Drug Use & the Family, Vol. 13. Becker, Sara, ed. 2016. (Drug Addiction & Recovery Ser.). 64p. (J). (gr. 7). 23.95 (978-1-4222-3603-1(X)) Mason Crest.

Colligan, L. H. Drug Dependence. 2010. (Health Alert 7 Ser.). (Illus.). 64p. (J). (gr. 4-7). 32.79 (978-0-7614-4818-1(7)) Marshall Cavendish GBR. Dist: Marshall Cavendish Corp.

Currie-McGhee, L. K. Drug Addiction. 2010. (Compact Research Ser.). (YA). (gr. 7-12). 26.95 (978-1-60152-109-5(X)) ReferencePoint Pr., Inc.

Decoded. Hooked: When Addiction Hits Home. Shantz-Hilkes, Chloe, ed. 2013. (ENG., Illus.). 128p. (YA). (gr. 7-12). pap. 12.95 (978-1-55451-474-8(6), 9781554514748) Annick Pr., Ltd. CAN. Dist: Publishers Group West (PGW).

Drug & Alcohol Prevention. (J). (gr. 2-3). 3.80 (978-0-8374-1262-7(5), 211); (gr. 3). 3.80 (978-0-8374-0120-1(8), 212); (gr. 4). 3.80 (978-0-8374-0121-8(6), 213); (gr. 5-6). 5.95 (978-0-8374-1266-5(8), 267); (gr. 7-9). 3.80 (978-0-8374-0080-8(5), 411) Weekly Reader Corp.

Elferr, Aluney. Lives Discolored: How Paul Was Lost to Drugs. 2012. 112p. (gr. -1). pap. 14.95 (978-1-4817-0087-0(1)) AuthorHouse.

Etler, Cyndy. We Can't Be Friends. 2017. (ENG.). 304p. (YA). (gr. 8-12). 17.99 **(978-1-4926-3576-5(6))** Sourcebooks, Inc.

Friedman, Lauri S. Addiction. Haugen, David M., ed. 2013. (Introducing Issues with Opposing Viewpoints Ser.). (ENG., Illus.). 144p. (gr. 7-10). 42.00 (978-0-7377-4164-3(3), Greenhaven Pr., Inc.) Cengage Gale.

Goldsmith, Connie. Addiction & Overdose: Confronting an American Crisis. 2017. (ENG.). 128p. (YA). (gr. 8-12). 37.32 **(978-1-5124-0953-6(7)**, Twenty-First Century Bks.) Lerner Publishing Group.

Greenwood, Carmel & Taylor, Chris. Wake up Mum: A Mother & Son's True Crisis Story of Overcoming Drug Addiction with Love, Laughter & Miraculous Insights. (Illus.). (Orig.). (YA). 16.95 (978-0-9646285-0-2(3)); pap. 12.95 (978-0-9646285-1-9(1)) Carmel Concepts, Ltd.

Hunter, David. Born to Smoke: Nicotine & Genetics. (Tobacco: the Deadly Drug Ser.). 2009. (Illus.). 112p. (YA). (gr. 7-12). 26.95 (978-1-4222-0243-2(7)) 2008. (J). pap. 26.95 (978-1-4222-1325-4(0)) Mason Crest.

Keegan, Kyle, et al. Chasing the High: A Firsthand Account of One Young Person's Experience with Substance Abuse. 2008. (ENG., Illus.). 208p. per. 11.95 (978-0-19-531472-4(7)) Oxford Univ. Pr., Inc.

Klosterman, Lorrie. The Facts about Drug Dependence to Treatment. 2007. (Drugs Ser.). (Illus.). 126p. (J). lib. bdg. 42.79 (978-0-7614-2676-9(0), Benchmark Bks.) Marshall Cavendish Corp.

Konieczko, Craig. Recovery from Drug Addiction. 2005. (Drug Abuse Prevention Library). (Illus.). 64p. (YA). (gr. 7-12). lib. bdg. 31.95 (978-0-8239-3284-9(2), DRRECO) Rosen Publishing Group, Inc., The.

Krinard, Susan. Dark of the Moon. l.t. ed. 2008. 475p. (J). 23.95 (978-1-4104-0956-0(2)) Thorndike Pr.

McKenzie, Precious. Helping a Friend with a Drug Problem. 2016. (How Can I Help? Friends Helping Friends Ser.). 00064p. (J). (gr. 6-6). pap. 12.95 (978-1-4994-6444-3(4)) Rosen Publishing Group, Inc., The.

Moe, Barbara. Drug Abuse Relapse: Helping Teens to Get Clean Again. 2005. (Drug Abuse Prevention Library). (Illus.). 64p. (YA). (gr. 7-12). lib. bdg. 31.95 (978-0-8239-3157-6(9), DRRELA) Rosen Publishing Group, Inc., The.

Perritano, John. Marijuana & Synthetics, Vol. 13. Becker, Sara, ed. 2016. (Drug Addiction & Recovery Ser.). (Illus.). 64p. (J). (gr. 7). 23.95 (978-1-4222-3606-2(4)) Mason Crest.

—Opioids: Heroin, Oxycontin, & Painkillers, Vol. 13. Becker, Sara, ed. 2016. (Drug Addiction & Recovery Ser.). (Illus.). 64p. (J). (gr. 7). 23.95 (978-1-4222-3607-9(2)) Mason Crest.

Petersen, Christine. Vicodin & Oxycontin. 2013. 64p. (J). (gr. 6-9). 34.21 (978-1-60870-827-7(6)) Cavendish Square Publishing.

—Vicodin & OxyContin. 2013. (Dangerous Drugs Ser.). 64p. (J). (gr. 6-9). pap. 15.28 (978-1-62712-063-0(7)) Cavendish Square Publishing.

Poole, H. W. Drug & Alcohol Dependence, Vol. 13. Walters, Anne S., ed. 2015. (Mental Illnesses & Disorders: Awareness & Understanding Ser.). (Illus.). 48p. (J). (gr. 5). 20.95 (978-1-4222-3371-9(5)) Mason Crest.

Rundquist, Thomas J., ed. The Drug Addict Trials Before the US Supreme Court: An Educational Prevention Game. 2003. (Illus.). 66p. (gr. 9-12). pap. 29.95 (978-1-884239-65-6(X)) Nova Media, Inc.

Shantz-Hilkes, Chloe, ed. Hooked: When Addiction Hits Home. 2013. (ENG., Illus.). 128p. (YA). (gr. 7-12). 21.95 (978-1-55451-475-5(4), 9781554514755) Annick Pr., Ltd. CAN. Dist: Publishers Group West (PGW).

Sheff, Nic. Tweak: Growing up on Methamphetamines. 2009. (ENG.). (YA). (gr. 9). lib. bdg. 23.60 **(978-1-61383-809-9(3))** Perfection Learning Corp.

—Tweak: Growing up on Methamphetamines. (ENG., Illus.). (YA). (gr. 9-18). 2009. 352p. pap. 13.99 (978-1-4169-7219-8(6)) 2008. 336p. 16.99 (978-1-4169-1362-7(9)) Simon & Schuster Children's Publishing. (Atheneum Bks. for Young Readers).

—We All Fall Down: Living with Addiction. 2011. (ENG.). 368p. (YA). (gr. 10-17). 17.99 (978-0-316-08082-8(9)) Little, Brown Bks. for Young Readers.

Sheva, Marie, mem. The Year of the Dogs: A Chronicle of Redemption, a Story of Love. 2003. (Illus.). 247p. (YA). per. 15.95 (978-0-9741736-0-3(6), 9900) Sheva, Marie.

Walker, Ida. Addiction Treatment: Escaping the Trap. 2009. (Illicit & Misused Drugs Ser.). (Illus.). 128p. (YA). (gr. 7-18). lib. bdg. 24.95 (978-1-4222-0152-7(X)) Mason Crest.

—Painkillers: Prescription Dependency. 2012. (J). pap. (978-1-4222-2457-1(0)) Mason Crest.

—Painkillers: Prescription Dependency. Henningfield, Jack E., ed. 2012. (Illicit & Misused Drugs Ser.). 128p. (J). (gr. 7). 24.95 (978-1-4222-2438-0(4)) Mason Crest.

DRUG ADDICTION—FICTION

Gibbons, Alan. Blood Pressure. 2005. (ENG.). 208p. (gr. 7-17). per. 11.99 (978-1-84255-199-8(X)) Orion Publishing Group, Ltd. GBR. Dist: Hachette Bk. Group.

Iacovone, Lauren Marie. Here Lies Thomas Crawford, 1 vol. 2010. 252p. pap. 27.95 (978-1-61582-690-2(4)) America Star Bks.

Javier's Sister - A Family's Struggle with Drug Addiction: One Day the Sun Will Shine Again Series. 2005. (J). pap. 16.95 (978-0-9768827-8-7(7)) Prevention Through Puppetry, Inc.

Kendal, Penny. Broken. 2003. (ENG., Illus.). 192p. (YA). pap. 9.99 (978-1-84270-174-4(6)) Andersen Pr. GBR. Dist: Independent Pubs. Group.

Mikulencak, Mandy. Burn Girl. 2015. (ENG.). 288p. (J). (gr. 8-12). 16.99 (978-0-8075-2217-2(1)) Whitman, Albert & Co.

Orme, Helen. Who Cares? 2004. (Shades Ser.). 64p. (J). pap. (978-0-237-52625-2(5)) Evans Brothers, Ltd.

Padula, Stacy A. The Aftermath. 2013. 176p. pap. 13.00 (978-1-62857-057-1(1), Strategic Bk. Publishing) Strategic Book Publishing & Rights Agency (SBPRA).

Patton, Cristina. On My Way to School. 2013. 28p. pap. 24.95 (978-1-4626-8240-9(5)) America Star Bks.

DRUG HABIT

see Drug Addiction

DRUGS

see also Materia Medica; Pharmacy; Poisons

also names of individual drugs, and groups of drugs, e.g. Narcotics

Adamec, Christine & Triggle, David J. Amphetamines & Methamphetamine. 2011. (Understanding Drugs Ser.). (Illus.). 108p. (C). (gr. 9-12). 34.95 (978-1-60413-530-5(1)) Facts On File, Inc.

—Barbiturates & Other Depressants. 2012. (Understanding Drugs Ser.). 118p. (C). (gr. 9-12). 34.95 (978-1-60413-534-3(4)) Facts On File, Inc.

Aretha, David. Cocaine & Crack: A MyReportLinks. com Book. 2005. (Drugs Ser.). (Illus.). 48p. (J). lib. bdg. 26.60 (978-0-7660-5276-5(1), MyReportLinks.com Bks.) Enslow Pubs., Inc.

—Ecstasy & Other Party Drugs: A MyReportLinks. com Book. 2005. (Drugs Ser.). (Illus.). 48p. (J). lib. bdg. 25.26 (978-0-7660-5278-9(8), MyReportLinks.com Bks.) Enslow Pubs., Inc.

—Methamphetamine & Amphetamines: A MyReportLinks. com Book. 2005. (Drugs Ser.). (Illus.). 48p. (J). lib. bdg. 26.60 (978-0-7660-5279-6(6), MyReportLinks.com Bks.) Enslow Pubs., Inc.

Becker, Peggy Daniels. Drugs. 2011. (Issues That Concern You Ser.). (ENG.). 144p. (gr. 10-10). 42.00 (978-0-7377-4951-9(2)) Cengage Gale.

Bell, Suzanne. Drugs, Poisons, & Chemistry. 2008. (Essentials of Forensic Science Ser.). (Illus.). 124p. (gr. 6-12). 35.00 (978-0-8160-5510-4(6)) Facts On File, Inc.

Breguet, Amy E., et al. Diet Pills. 2008. (Junior Drug Awareness Ser.). (Illus.). 112p. (J). (gr. 5-8). 30.00 (978-0-7910-9750-2(1), Chelsea Hse.) Facts On File, Inc.

—Junior Drug Awareness: Vicodin, OxyContin, & Other Pain Relievers. 2008. (Junior Drug Awareness Ser.). (Illus.). 112p. (gr. 5-8). 30.00 (978-0-7910-9700-7(5), Chelsea Hse.) Facts On File, Inc.

Brinkerhoff, Shirley. Anxiety Disorders. McDonnell, Mary Ann & Esherick, Donald, eds. 2013. (State of Mental Illness & Its Therapy Ser.: 19). 128p. (J). (gr. 7-18). 24.95 (978-1-4222-2821-0(5)) Mason Crest.

—Drug Therapy & Childhood & Adolescent Disorders. 2003. (Psychiatric Disorders: Drugs & Psychology for the Mind & Bod Ser.). (Illus.). 125p. (YA). (gr. 4-7). pap. 14.95 (978-1-4222-0386-6(7)) Mason Crest.

Brogan, Ronald J., intro. Junior Drug Awareness, 14 Vols., Set. 2008. (Junior Drug Awareness Ser.). (gr. 5-8). 420.00 (978-0-7910-9880-6(X), Chelsea Hse.) Facts On File, Inc.

Chambers, Catherine. Living Forever: The Pharmaceutical Industry. 2012. (Big-Buck Business Ser.). (Illus.). 48p. (J). (gr. 6-8). 31.95 (978-1-4339-7755-8(9)); pap. 14.05 (978-1-4339-7756-5(7)) Stevens, Gareth Publishing LLLP. (Gareth Stevens Secondary Library).

Cobb, Allan B. Heroin & Your Veins: The Incredibly Disgusting Story. 2005. (Incredibly Disgusting Drugs Ser.). (Illus.). 48p. (J). (gr. 5-8). lib. bdg. 25.25 (978-0-8239-3249-8(4), DDHEVE) Rosen Publishing Group, Inc., The.

Cobb, Allan B., et al. Heroin. 2008. (Junior Drug Awareness Ser.). (Illus.). 112p. (gr. 5-8). 30.00 (978-0-7910-9749-6(8), Chelsea Hse.) Facts On File, Inc.

Conti, Nicolette & Johanson, Paula. The Truth about Amphetamines & Stimulants. 2011. (Drugs & Consequences Ser.). (YA). (gr. 7-12). lib. bdg. 31.95 (978-1-4488-5483-7(0)) Rosen Publishing Group, Inc., The.

Crist, James J. When Someone You Love Abuses Alcohol or Drugs - a Guide for Kids. 2003. 112p. pap. 12.95 (978-1-58741-119-9(9)) Wellness Institute/Self-Help Bks., LLC.

Custom Curricul Staff. What about Sex, Drugs, And... ? 2004. (Custom Curriculum Ser.). 256p. pap., pap. 19.99 (978-0-7814-4093-6(9), 0781440939) Cook, David C.

Docalavich, Heather. Antidepressants & Psychology: Talk Therapy vs. Medication. (Antidepressants Ser.). (Illus.). 104p. (YA). (gr. 7-18). 2008. lib. bdg. 24.95 (978-1-4222-0096-4(5)) 2007. pap. 14.95 (978-1-4222-0405-4(7)) Mason Crest.

—The Future of Antidepressants: the New Wave of Research. 2007. (Antidepressants Ser.). (Illus.). 104p. (YA). (gr. 7). pap. 14.95 (978-1-4222-0412-2(X)) Mason Crest.

Drugs & Consequences: Set 2. 2013. (Drugs & Consequences Ser.). 64p. (YA). (gr. 7-12). 255.60 (978-1-4777-1910-7(5)) Rosen Publishing Group, Inc., The.

Drugs Group 3, 5 bks., Set. Incl. Facts about Antidepressants. LeVert, Suzanne. lib. bdg. 42.79 (978-0-7614-2241-9(2)); Facts about Caffeine. Klosterman, Lorrie. lib. bdg. 42.79 (978-0-7614-2242-6(0)); Facts about Nicotine. LeVert, Suzanne. lib. bdg. 42.79 (978-0-7614-2244-0(7)); (Illus.). 112p. (YA). (gr. 9-12). 2006. 2007. Set lib. bdg. 199.64 (978-0-7614-2240-2(4), Benchmark Bks.) Marshall Cavendish Corp.

Dudley, William. Antidepressants. 2008. (Compact Research Ser.). (Illus.). 112p. (YA). (gr. 3-7). lib. bdg. (978-1-60152-041-8(7)) ReferencePoint Pr., Inc.

Egendorf, Laura K. Performance Enhancing Drugs. 2007. (Compact Research Ser.). (Illus.). 96p. (YA). (gr. 7-12). lib. bdg. 25.95 (978-1-60152-003-6(4)) ReferencePoint Pr., Inc.

Engdahl, Sylvia. Prescription Drugs. 2014. (Current Controversies Ser.). (ENG., Illus.). 224p. (gr. 7-12). lib. bdg. 46.40 (978-0-7377-6888-6(6), Greenhaven Pr., Inc.) Cengage Gale.

Esherick, Joan. Drug Therapy & Mood Disorders. 2003. (Psychiatric Disorders: Drugs & Psychology for the Mind & Bod Ser.). (Illus.). 126p. (YA). (gr. 4-7). pap. 14.95 (978-1-4222-0392-7(1)) Mason Crest.

—Dying for Acceptance: A Teen's Guide to Drug- & Alcohol-Related Health Issues. 2006. (Science of Health Ser.). (Illus.). 128p. (YA). lib. bdg. 24.95 (978-1-59084-847-0(0)) Mason Crest.

—The FDA & Psychiatric Drugs: How a Drug Is Approved. McDonnell, Mary Ann & Esherick, Donald, eds. 2013. (State of Mental Illness & Its Therapy Ser.: 19). 128p. (J). (gr. 7-18). 24.95 (978-1-4222-2826-5(6)) Mason Crest.

—The FDA & Psychiatric Drugs: How a Drug Is Approved. 2004. (Encyclopedia of Psychiatric Drugs & Their Disorders Ser.). (Illus.). 128p. (YA). lib. bdg. 24.95 (978-1-59084-578-3(1)) Mason Crest.

—How a Drug Is Approved: The FDA & Psychiatric Drugs. 2003. (Psychiatric Disorders: Drugs & Psychology for the Mind & Bod Ser.). (Illus.). 124p. (YA). (gr. 7). pap. 14.95 (978-1-4222-0402-3(2)) Mason Crest.

—Prozac: North American Culture & the Wonder Drug. 2008. (Antidepressants Ser.). (Illus.). 120p. (YA). (gr. 7-18). lib. bdg. 24.95 (978-1-4222-0106-0(6)) Mason Crest.

—Prozac: North American Culture & the Wonder Drug. 2007. (Antidepressants Ser.). (Illus.). 120p. (YA). (gr. 7). pap. 14.95 (978-1-4222-0415-3(4)) Mason Crest.

Espejo, Roman & Mur, Cindy. Drug Testing. annot. ed. 2006. (At Issue Ser.). (ENG.). 128p. (gr. 10-12). 39.40 (978-0-7377-3093-7(5), Greenhaven Pr., Inc.) Cengage Gale.

Etingoff, Kim. Methamphetamines: Unsafe Speed. 2009. (Illicit & Misused Drugs Ser.). (Illus.). 128p. (YA). (gr. 7-18). lib. bdg. 24.95 (978-1-4222-0159-6(7)) Mason Crest.

Gagne, Tammy & Mangor, Jodie. Battling Against Drug-Resistant Bacteria. 2016. (Science Frontiers Ser.). (ENG., Illus.). 32p. (J). pap. 9.95 (978-1-63235-390-0(3)) Pr. Room Editions LLC.

Gerber, Larry. The Truth about Steroids. 2013. (Drugs & Consequences Ser.). (Illus.). 64p. (J). (gr. 7-12). 31.95 (978-1-4777-1895-7(8)) Rosen Publishing Group, Inc., The.

Gogerly, Liz. Taking Medicine. Gordon, Mike, illus. 2008. (Looking after Me Ser.). (ENG.). 32p. (J). (gr. -1-3). pap. (978-0-7787-4121-3(4)); lib. bdg. (978-0-7787-4114-5(1)) Crabtree Publishing Co.

Gold, Susan Dudley. Vernonia School District V. Action: Drug Testing in the Schools. 2005. (Supreme Court Milestones Ser.). (Illus.). 142p. (J). (gr. 3-7). lib. bdg. (978-0-7614-1941-9(1), Benchmark Bks.) Marshall Cavendish Corp.

Hager, Holly J. Heroin = Busted! 2005. (Busted! Ser.). (Illus.). 104p. (J). (gr. 6-12). lib. bdg. 33.27 (978-0-7660-2386-4(9)) Enslow Pubs., Inc.

Harris, Nathaniel. Drug Trafficking. 2009. (What If We Do Nothing? Ser.). 48p. (YA). (gr. 4-7). lib. bdg. 31.00 (978-1-4339-1981-7(8)) Stevens, Gareth Publishing LLLP.

Hecht, Alan. Antidepressants & Antianxiety Drugs. 2010. (Understanding Drugs Ser.). (Illus.). 112p. (YA). (gr. 9-12). 34.95 (978-1-60413-532-9(8)) Facts On File, Inc.

Holt, Rinehart and Winston Staff. Decisions for Health Blue, Chptr. 16: Medicine & Illegal Drugs. 4th ed. 2004. pap. 11.20 (978-0-03-068051-9(4)) Holt McDougal.

—Decisions for Health Green Chptr. 13: Understanding Drugs. 4th ed. 2004. pap. 11.20 (978-0-03-068034-2(4)) Holt McDougal.

—Decisions for Health Red Chptr. 13: Teens & Drugs. 4th ed. 2004. pap. 11.20 (978-0-03-068039-7(5)) Holt McDougal.

—A Lifetime of Health Chptr. 12: Illegal Drugs. 4th ed. Date not set. pap. 11.20 (978-0-03-068104-2(9)) Holt McDougal.

Hunter, David. Antidepressants & Advertising: Marketing Happiness. (Antidepressants Ser.). (Illus.). 112p. 2008. (J). (gr. 7-18). 24.95 (978-1-4222-0095-7(7)) 2007. (YA). pap. 14.95 (978-1-4222-0404-7(9)) Mason Crest.

—Antidepressants & the Pharmaceutical Companies: Corporate Responsibilities. (Antidepressants Ser.). (Illus.). 112p. (YA). 2008. (gr. 7-18). lib. bdg. 24.95 (978-1-4222-0101-5(5)) 2007. (gr. 8-12). pap. 14.95 (978-1-4222-0409-2(X)) Mason Crest.

Hyde, Margaret O. & Setaro, John F. Drugs 101: An Overview for Teens. 2003. (Teen Overviews Ser.). (ENG., Illus.). 160p. (gr. 7-12). lib. bdg. 27.93 (978-0-7613-2608-3(1), Twenty-First Century Bks.) Lerner Publishing Group.

Incredibly Disgusting Drugs. 2005. (Illus.). 48p. (gr. 5-8). lib. bdg. 227.40 (978-0-8239-3918-3(9)) Rosen Publishing Group, Inc., The.

Kehner, George B. Date Rape Drugs. 2004. (Drugs Ser.). (Illus.). 96p. (YA). (gr. 9-13). 30.00 (978-0-7910-7634-7(2), Chelsea Hse.) Facts On File, Inc.

Klosterman, Lorrie. The Facts about Caffeine. 2006. (Drugs Ser.). (Illus.). 112p. (YA). (gr. 9-12). lib. bdg. 42.79 (978-0-7614-2242-6(0)) Marshall Cavendish Corp.

—The Facts about Drugs & the Body. 2007. (Drugs Ser.). (Illus.). 112p. (gr. 6-7). lib. bdg. 42.79 (978-0-7614-2675-2(2), Benchmark Bks.) Marshall Cavendish Corp.

Knowles, Johanna, et al. Junior Drug Awareness: Over-the-Counter Drugs. 2008. (Junior Drug Awareness Ser.). (Illus.). 112p. (gr. 5-8). 30.00 (978-0-7910-9759-5(5), Chelsea Hse.) Facts On File, Inc.

Koellhoffer, Tara. Ecstasy & Other Club Drugs. 2008. (Junior Drug Awareness Ser.). (Illus.). 120p. (gr. 5-8). lib. bdg. 30.00 (978-0-7910-9697-0(1), Chelsea Hse.) Facts On File, Inc.

Koellhoffer, Tara, et al. Prozac & Other Antidepressants. 2nd rev. ed. 2008. (Junior Drug Awareness Ser.). (Illus.). 120p. (gr. 5-8). 30.00 (978-0-7910-9747-2(1), Chelsea Hse.) Facts On File, Inc.

Kovacs, Vic. Vaccines. 2016. (Miracles of Medicine Ser.). 00048p. (J). pap. 14.05 **(978-1-4824-6102-2(1))** Stevens, Gareth Publishing LLLP.

Laliberte, Michelle. Marijuana: A MyReportLinks. com Book. 2005. (Drugs Ser.). (Illus.). 48p. (J). lib. bdg. 26.60 (978-0-7660-5281-9(8), MyReportLinks.com Bks.) Enslow Pubs., Inc.

Latchana Kenney, Karen. The Hidden Story of Drugs, 1 vol., 1. 2014. (Undercover Story Ser.). (ENG.). 48p. (J). (gr. 5-8). 30.25 (978-1-4777-2803-1(1), Rosen Reference) Rosen Publishing Group, Inc., The.

Legalizing Marijuana. 2nd rev. ed. 2010. (Point/Counterpoint Ser.). (Illus.). 128p. (C). (gr. 9). 35.00 (978-1-60413-690-6(1), Chelsea Hse.) Facts On File, Inc.

Leonard, Basia & Roberts, Jeremy. The Truth about Prescription Drugs. 2011. (Drugs & Consequences Ser.). (Illus.). 64p. (YA). (gr. 7-12). lib. bdg. 31.95 (978-1-4488-4642-9(0)) Rosen Publishing Group, Inc., The.

LeVert, Suzanne. The Facts about Antidepressants. 2006. (Drugs Ser.). (Illus.). 112p. (YA). (gr. 9-12). lib. bdg. 42.79 (978-0-7614-2241-9(2)) Marshall Cavendish Corp.

LeVert, Suzanne & Hendricks, Jeff. Ecstasy. 2009. (Benchmark Rockets Ser.). 32p. (YA). (gr. 5-9). 28.50 (978-0-7614-4349-0(5)) Marshall Cavendish Corp.

Libal, Joyce. Antidepressants & Social Anxiety: A Pill for Shyness? (Antidepressants Ser.). (Illus.). 112p. (YA). (gr. 7-18). 2008. lib. bdg. 24.95 (978-1-4222-0098-8(1)) 2007. pap. 14.95 (978-1-4222-0406-1(5)) Mason Crest.

—Antidepressants & Suicide: When Treatment Kills. 2007. (Antidepressants Ser.). (Illus.). 112p. (YA). (gr. 7). pap. 14.95 (978-1-4222-0407-8(3)) Mason Crest.

Llewellyn, Claire. Me Hace Bien o Mal? Aprender Sobre Medicamentos, Drogas y Salud. Gordon, Mike, illus. (SPA.). (J). (gr. k-2). pap. (978-950-24-0946-7(9)) Albatros ARG. Dist: Lectorum Pubns., Inc.

Lockwood, Brad. Ketamine: Dangerous Hallucinogen. 2006. (Drug Abuse & Society Ser.). (Illus.). 64p. (YA). (gr. 7-12). lib. bdg. 31.95 (978-1-4042-0911-4(5)) Rosen Publishing Group, Inc., The.

Lovegrove, Ray. Health - Ethical Debates in Modern Medicine. 2008. (Dilemmas in Modern Science Ser.). (ENG., Illus.). 48p. (J). 23.99 (978-0-237-53368-7(5)) Evans Brothers, Ltd. GBR. Dist: Independent Pubs. Group.

Marcovitz, Hal. Marijuana. 2006. (Drug Education Library). (ENG., Illus.). 104p. (J). (gr. 3-7). lib. bdg. 34.80 (978-1-59018-959-7(0), Lucent Bks.) Cengage Gale.

Marsico, Katie. Heroin. 2014. (J). (978-0-7614-8120-1(6)) Marshall Cavendish Corp.

Mayo Clinic Staff, contrib. by. Getting the Most from Your Medications. 2004. (Mayo Clinic on Health Ser.). (Illus.). 36,52p. (YA). (gr. 8-18). lib. bdg. 15.95 (978-1-59084-251-5(0)) Mason Crest.

McIntosh, Kenneth. The History of Depression: the Mind-Body Connection. 2008. (Antidepressants Ser.). (Illus.). 120p. (YA). (gr. 8-12). pap. 14.95 (978-1-4222-0413-9(8)) Mason Crest.

—Natural Alternatives to Antidepressants: St. John's Wort, Kava Kava, & Others. 2008. (Antidepressants Ser.). (Illus.). 104p. (YA). (gr. 7-18). lib. bdg. 24.95 (978-1-4222-0105-3(8)) Mason Crest.

McMahon, Christina & Marcovitz, Hal. The Dangers of Diet Drugs. 2017. (Drug Education Library Ser.). 104p. (YA). (gr. 7-7). 37.45 **(978-1-5345-6005-5(X)**, Lucent Pr.) Greenhaven Publishing LLC.

McPhee, Edna. Designer Drugs: Deadly Chemistry. 2017. (Drug Education Library). 112p. (YA). (gr. 7-7). lib. bdg. 37.45 **(978-1-5345-6007-9(6)**, Lucent Pr.) Greenhaven Publishing LLC.

McPherson, Stephanie Sammartino. Doping in Sports: Winning at Any Cost? 2016. (ENG., Illus.). 104p. (YA). (gr. 7-12). 51.99 (978-1-4677-9576-0(3), Twenty-First Century Bks.) Lerner Publishing Group.

Merino, Noël, ed. Drug Legalization. 2015. (Current Controversies Ser.). (ENG.). 224p. (gr. 10-12). pap. 32.00 (978-0-7377-7216-6(6), Greenhaven Pr., Inc.) Cengage Gale.

Mitchell, E. Siobhan. Anti-Depressants. 2003. (Drugs Ser.). (Illus.). 112p. (C). (gr. 9-13). 30.00 (978-0-7910-7635-4(0), Chelsea Hse.) Facts On File, Inc.

Mooney, Carla. The Dangers of Synthetic Drugs. 2016. (ENG.). 80p. (J). (gr. 5-12). lib. bdg. (978-1-68282-026-1(2)) ReferencePoint Pr., Inc.

Mur, Cindy. Drug Testing. 2006. (At Issue Ser.). (ENG.). 91p. (gr. 10-12). pap. 24.45 (978-0-7377-3094-4(3), Greenhaven Pr., Inc.) Cengage Gale.

Murphy, Patricia J. Avoiding Drugs. 2006. (Illus.). 32p. (J). pap. 6.95 (978-0-8225-2779-4(0), Lerner Pubns.) Lerner Publishing Group.

—Evitar las Drogas. 2005. (Libros para Avanzar (Pull Ahead Bks.)). (SPA., Illus.). 32p. (J). (gr. 3-7). lib. bdg. 22.60 (978-0-8225-3172-2(0), Ediciones Lerner) Lerner Publishing Group.

Murray, Julie. The Body, 1 vol. 2009. (That's Gross! A Look at Science Ser.). (ENG., Illus.). 32p. (J). (gr. 2-5). 28.50 (978-1-60453-554-9(7)) ABDO Publishing Co.

Newton, David E. Chemistry of Drugs. 2007. (New Chemistry Ser.). 192p. (gr. 6-12). 35.00 (978-0-8160-5276-9(X)) Facts On File, Inc.

Newton, Michael. Drug Enforcement Administration. 2011. (Law Enforcement Agencies Ser.). (Illus.). 128p. (gr. 6-12). 35.00 (978-1-60413-641-8(3), Chelsea Hse.) Facts On File, Inc.

Nichols, Katherine. Deep Water. 2017. (Simon True Ser.). (ENG., Illus.). 288p. (YA). (gr. 9). pap. 10.99 **(978-1-4814-8106-9(1)**, Simon Pulse) Simon Pulse.

Olive, M. Foster. Sleep AIDS. Triggle, David J., ed. 2005. (Drugs: the Straight Facts Ser.). (Illus.). 112p. (C). (gr. 9-12). 30.00 (978-0-7910-8200-3(8), Chelsea Hse.) Facts On File, Inc.

—Understanding Drugs: Ecstasy. 2010. (Understanding Drugs Ser.). (Illus.). 112p. (YA). (gr. 9-12). 34.95 (978-1-60413-538-1(7)) Facts On File, Inc.

Orr, Tamra. Ecstasy. 2009. (Incredibly Disgusting Drugs Ser.). 48p. (gr. 5-8). 53.00 (978-1-61513-497-7(2), Rosen Reference) Rosen Publishing Group, Inc., The.

Palenque, Stephanie Maher. Crack & Cocaine = Busted! 2005. (Busted! Ser.). (Illus.). 104p. (J). (gr. 6-12). lib. bdg. 33.27 (978-0-7660-2169-3(6)) Enslow Pubs., Inc.

Paris, Stephanie. Drugs & Alcohol, 1 vol. 2nd rev. ed. 2012. (Nonfiction Readers Ser.). (ENG., Illus.). 48p. (J). (gr. 4-4). pap. 9.99 (978-1-4333-4859-4(4)) Teacher Created Materials, Inc.

—Hablemos Claro: Alcohol y Drogas. 2017. (TIME for Kids en Español - Level 4 Ser.). (SPA.). 48p. (gr. 4-4). lib. bdg. 31.99 (978-1-5157-5140-3(6)) Time for Kids Inc AUS. Dist: Capstone Pub.

—Straight Talk: Drugs & Alcohol, 1 vol. 2nd rev. ed. 2013. (Nonfiction Readers Ser.). (ENG., Illus.). 48p. (J). (gr. 4-4). pap. 29.96 (978-1-4807-1111-2(X)) Shell Educational Publishing.

Petersen, Christine. Ecstasy. 2013. (J). (978-0-7614-8119-5(2)) Marshall Cavendish Corp.

Pierce, Simon. Prescription Drugs: Opioids That Kill. 2017. (Drug Education Library). 104p. (YA). (gr. 7-7). lib. bdg. 37.45 **(978-1-5345-6011-6(4)**, Lucent Pr.) Greenhaven Publishing LLC.

Pomere, Jonas. Drug Testing. 2007. (FAQ: Teen Life Ser.). (Illus.). 64p. (YA). (gr. 7-12). lib. bdg. 31.95 (978-1-4042-1973-1(0), 1267045) Rosen Publishing Group, Inc., The.

Poole, H. W. Over-The-Counter Drugs, Vol. 13. Becker, Sara, ed. 2016. (Drug Addiction & Recovery Ser.). (Illus.). 64p. (J). (gr. 7). 23.95 (978-1-4222-3608-6(0)) Mason Crest.

—Prescription Drugs, Vol. 13. Becker, Sara, ed. 2016. (Drug Addiction & Recovery Ser.). (Illus.). 64p. (J). (gr. 7). 23.95 (978-1-4222-3610-9(2)) Mason Crest.

Porterfield, Jason. Downers: Depressant Abuse. (Incredibly Disgusting Drugs Ser.). 48p. (gr. 5-8). 2009. 53.00 (978-1-61513-496-0(4), Rosen Reference) 2007. (Illus.). (YA). lib. bdg. 29.25 (978-1-4042-1957-1(9)) Rosen Publishing Group, Inc., The.

Ramen, Fred. Prescription Drugs. 2009. (Drug Abuse & Society Ser.). 64p. (gr. 6-6). 58.50 (978-1-61512-226-4(5)) Rosen Publishing Group, Inc., The.

Rees, Jonathan. Drugs. 2005. (It's Your Health Ser.). (Illus.). 45p. (J). (gr. 6-9). lib. bdg. 29.95 (978-1-58340-586-4(0)) Black Rabbit Bks.

Reese, Jon. Critical World Issues: Drugs, Vol. 16. 2016. (Critical World Issues Ser.: Vol. 16). (ENG., Illus.). 112p. (J). (gr. 7-12). 25.95 (978-1-4222-3651-2(X)) Mason Crest.

Roberts, Jeremy. Prescription Drug Abuse. 2005. (Drug Abuse Prevention Library). (Illus.). 64p. (YA). (gr. 7-12). lib. bdg. 31.95 (978-0-8239-3158-3(7), DRPRES) Rosen Publishing Group, Inc., The.

Rooney, Anne. Dealing with Drugs. 2010. (Healthy Lifestyles Ser.). 48p. (J). 35.65 (978-1-60753-084-8(8)) Amicus Publishing.

Rosinsky, Natalie M. The Story of Pharmaceuticals: How They Changed the World, 1 vol. 2010. (World Transformed Ser.). (ENG.). 64p. (gr. 6-7). lib. bdg. 33.99 (978-0-7565-4315-0(0), CPB Grades 4-8) Compass Point Bks.

Russell, Craig. Antidepressants & Side Effects: Managing the Risks. 2007. (Antidepressants Ser.). (Illus.). 112p. (YA). (gr. 8-12). pap. 14.95 (978-1-4222-0410-8(3)) Mason Crest.

—Psychostimulants as Antidepressants: Worth the Risk? 2008. (Antidepressants Ser.). (Illus.). 112p. (YA). (gr. 7-18). lib. bdg. 24.95 (978-1-4222-0107-7(4)) Mason Crest.

—Psychostimulants as Antidepressants: Worth the Risk? 2007. (Antidepressants Ser.). (Illus.). 112p. (YA). (gr. 7). pap. 14.95 (978-1-4222-0416-0(2)) Mason Crest.

Schroeder, Brock E. Ecstasy. 2003. (Drugs Ser.). (Illus.). 112p. (C). (gr. 9-13). 30.00 (978-0-7910-7633-0(4), Chelsea Hse.) Facts On File, Inc.

Scott, Celicia. Dangerous Depressants & Sedatives. Borus, Joshua, ed. 2014. (Downside of Drugs Ser.). (ENG., Illus.). 48p. (J). (gr. 5-18). lib. bdg. 20.95 (978-1-4222-3019-0(8)) Mason Crest.

—New Drugs: Bath Salts, Spice, Salvia, & Designer Drugs. Borus, Joshua, ed. 2014. (Downside of Drugs Ser.). (ENG., Illus.). 48p. (J). (gr. 5-18). lib. bdg. 20.95 (978-1-4222-3024-4(4)) Mason Crest.

Senker, Cath. Avoiding Harmful Substances. 2008. (Healthy Choices Ser.). (Illus.). 24p. (J). (gr. 3-7). lib. bdg. 22.60 (978-1-4042-4304-0(6), PowerKids Pr.) Rosen Publishing Group, Inc., The.

Shoup, Kate. Rohypnol. 2015. (Dangerous Drugs Ser.). (ENG.). 64p. (J). (gr. 6-6). lib. bdg. 34.21 (978-1-5026-0562-7(7)) Cavendish Square Publishing.

Slade, Suzanne. OxyContin Abuse. 2007. (Incredibly Disgusting Drugs Ser.). (Illus.). 48p. (YA). (gr. 5-9). lib. bdg. 29.25 (978-1-4042-1954-0(4)) Rosen Publishing Group, Inc., The.

Somerville, Clive. The Drug Enforcement Administration. 2004. (Rescue & Prevention Ser.). (Illus.). 96p. (YA). (gr. 7-18). lib. bdg. 22.95 (978-1-59084-413-7(0)) Mason Crest.

Sommers, Annie. College Athletics: Steroids & Supplement Abuse. 2009. (Disgraced! the Dirty History of Performance-Enhancing Drugs in Sports Ser.). (Illus.). 48p. (YA). (gr. 5-9). 29.25 (978-1-4358-5303-4(2)) Rosen Publishing Group, Inc., The.

Sommers, Michael. Cocaine. 2009. (Incredibly Disgusting Drugs Ser.). 48p. (gr. 5-8). 53.00 (978-1-61513-493-9(X), Rosen Reference) Rosen Publishing Group, Inc., The.

Stewart, Jan. How Drugs & Alcohol Affect Us. 2004. (ENG., Illus.). 32p. (J). pap. 9.95 (978-0-89793-314-8(1), Hunter Hse.) Turner Publishing Co.

Toufexis, Donna & Hammack, Sayamwong E. Anti-Anxiety Drugs. Triggle, David J., ed. 2006. (Drugs Ser.). (Illus.). 128p. (C). (gr. 9-12). lib. bdg. 30.00 (978-0-7910-8556-1(2), Chelsea Hse.) Facts On File, Inc.

Triggle, David J., ed. Drugs: The Straight Facts Set, 32-Volumes. 2009. (Drugs: the Straight Facts Ser.). (C). (gr. 9-18). 900.00 (978-0-7910-9909-4(1), Chelsea Hse.) Facts On File, Inc.

—The Straight Facts. (Drugs Ser.). (Illus.). (J). 137.70 (978-0-7910-7258-5(4), Chelsea Hse.) Facts On File, Inc.

Tsaioun, Katya. ADMET for Medicinal Chemists: A Practical Guide. Kates, Steven A., ed. 2011. (ENG., Illus.). 512p. 153.00 (978-0-470-48407-4(1), Wiley) Wiley, John & Sons, Inc.

Walker, Ida J. Sedatives & Hypnotics: Deadly Downers. 2009. (Illicit & Misused Drugs Ser.). (Illus.). 128p. (J). (gr. 7-18). lib. bdg. 24.95 (978-1-4222-0163-3(5)) Mason Crest.

Walker, Maryalice. The Development of Antidepressants: The Chemistry of Depression. 2007. (Antidepressants Ser.). (Illus.). 112p. (YA). (gr. 7). pap. 14.95 (978-1-4222-0411-5(1)) Mason Crest.

Warburton, Lianne & Callfas, Diana. Amphetamines & Other Stimulants. 2007. (Junior Drug Awareness Ser.). (Illus.). 120p. (gr. 5-8). lib. bdg. 30.00 (978-0-7910-9712-0(9), Chelsea Hse.) Facts On File, Inc.

Whittaker, Helen. How Toys Spin. 2012. (Toys & Forces Ser.). 32p. (gr. 1-4). lib. bdg. 27.10 (978-1-59920-467-3(3)) Black Rabbit Bks.

Willett, Edward. Speed. 2009. (Incredibly Disgusting Drugs Ser.). 48p. (gr. 5-8). 53.00 (978-1-61513-505-9(7), Rosen Reference) Rosen Publishing Group, Inc., The.

Williams, Mary E. Synthetic Drugs. Gale, G., ed. 2014. (Introducing Issues with Opposing Viewpoints Ser.). (ENG., Illus.). 144p. (gr. 10-12). lib. bdg. 42.00 (978-0-7377-6929-6(7), Greenhaven Pr., Inc.) Cengage Gale.

Winters, Adam & Sommers, Michael A. Tobacco & Your Mouth: The Incredibly Disgusting Story. 2005. (Incredibly Disgusting Drugs Ser.). (Illus.). 48p. (YA). (gr. 5-8). lib. bdg. 29.25 (978-0-8239-3250-4(8), DDTOMO) Rosen Publishing Group, Inc., The.

Wolf, Marie. Ghb & Analogs: High-Risk Club Drugs. 2006. (Drug Abuse & Society Ser.). (Illus.). 64p. (YA). (gr. 7-12). lib. bdg. 31.95 (978-1-4042-0910-7(7)) Rosen Publishing Group, Inc., The.

Wolf, Marie E. GHB & Analogs: High-Risk Club Drugs. 2009. (Drug Abuse & Society Ser.). 64p. (gr. 6-6). 58.50 (978-1-61512-220-2(6)) Rosen Publishing Group, Inc., The.

Worth, Richard. Weight Control Drugs. 2011. (Understanding Drugs Ser.). (YA). (gr. 9-12). 34.95 (978-1-60413-553-4(0)) Facts On File, Inc.

Yomtov, Nel. From African Plant to Vaccine Preservation. 2014. (21st Century Skills Innovation Library: Innovations from Nature Ser.). (ENG., Illus.). 32p. (J). (gr. 4-8). 28.50 (978-1-62431-753-8(7), 203280); pap. 14.21 (978-1-62431-759-0(6), 203281) Cherry Lake Publishing.

DRUGS—FICTION

Badger, Hilary. State of Grace. 2015. (ENG.). 304p. 17.95 (978-1-63079-015-8(X)) Switch Pr.

Burgess, Melvin. The Hit. 2014. (ENG.). 304p. (J). (gr. 9). 17.99 (978-0-545-55699-6(6), Chicken Hse., The) Scholastic, Inc.

Cadenhead, MacKenzie. Sleeper. 2017. (ENG.). 272p. (YA). (gr. 6-12). pap. 10.99 **(978-1-4926-3614-4(2))** Sourcebooks, Inc.

Carlson, Melody. Playing with Fire. 2007. (Secret Life of Samantha Mcgregor Ser.: No. 3). (ENG.). 256p. (YA). (gr. 7-12). per. 12.99 (978-1-59052-694-1(5), Multnomah Bks.) Crown Publishing Group.

Cortés, Ricardo, illus. It's Just a Plant: A Children's Story about Marijuana. 2013. (ENG.). 48p. (J). 20.00 (978-1-61775-186-8(3)) Akashic Bks.

Cousineau, Craig S. Skippy & Oaf Explore the Battles of the Immune System. 2010. (ENG., Illus.). 180p. (J). (gr. 2-4). pap. 9.95 (978-1-933255-56-9(0)) DNA Pr.

De la Cruz, Melissa. Angels on Sunset Boulevard. 2008. (Angels on Sunset Boulevard Ser.: Bk. 1). (ENG.). 240p. (YA). (gr. 9-18). pap. 8.99 (978-1-4169-3991-7(1), Simon & Schuster Bks. For Young Readers) Simon & Schuster Bks. For Young Readers.

Elkeles, Simone. Rules of Attraction. 2015. (Perfect Chemistry Novel Ser.). (ENG.). 352p. (YA). (gr. 9). pap. 9.99 (978-1-61963-702-3(2), 9781619637023, Bloomsbury USA Childrens) Bloomsbury Publishing USA.

Flowers, J. J. Juan Pablo & the Butterflies. 2017. (ENG., Illus.). 224p. (YA). (gr. 9-12). 17.99 (978-1-5072-0214-2(8), Simon Pulse) Simon Pulse.

Gaetz, Dayle Campbell. No Problem, 1 vol. 2003. (Orca Soundings Ser.). (ENG.). 128p. (YA). (gr. 8-12). pap. 9.95 (978-1-55143-231-1(5)) Orca Bk. Pubs. USA.

—No Problem. 2004. (Orca Soundings Ser.). 87p. 19.95 (978-0-7569-4317-2(5)) Perfection Learning Corp.

Hankins, M. Lil' Mikie Tells It Like It Is. 2007. 20p. per. 24.95 (978-1-4137-0168-5(X)) America Star Bks.

Haydu, Corey Ann. Rules for Stealing Stars. 2017. 352p. (J). (gr. 3-7). pap. 6.99 (978-0-06-235273-6(3), Tegen, Katherine Bks) HarperCollins Pubs.

Heather, Cherry. Surviving High School: The Journey of an Angst Filled Teen, 1 vol. 2010. 74p. pap. 19.95 (978-1-4489-4145-2(8)) PublishAmerica, Inc.

Hinton, S. E. Esto Ya Es Otra Historia. (SPA.). (J). 6.95 (978-84-204-4121-4(X)) Santillana USA Publishing Co., Inc.

Horowitz, Lena. Dancing with Molly. 2016. (ENG.). 272p. (YA). (gr. 9). pap. 10.99 (978-1-4814-1551-4(4), Simon Pulse) Simon Pulse.

Ketchedjian, Armen G. & Ketch. Golden Apples. 2007. 12.95 (978-0-9778274-0-4(2)) Parental Interventional Tools, Inc.

Layboume, Emmy. Sweet. 2015. (ENG.). 288p. (YA). (gr. 8). 17.99 (978-1-250-05519-4(9)) Feiwel & Friends.

Mac, Carrie. Charmed, 1 vol. 2006. (Orca Soundings Ser.). (ENG.). 112p. (YA). (gr. 8-12). 14.95 (978-1-55143-578-7(0)) Orca Bk. Pubs. USA.

Marois, André & Norman, Taylor. The Poisoned Cake. Doyon, Patrick, illus. 2017. (J). **(978-1-4521-4660-7(8))** Chronicle Bks. LLC.

Marshall, Wendolyn. Buzzbee Warnings about Drugs. 2010. 32p. pap. 19.99 (978-1-4389-9980-7(1)) AuthorHouse.

McRae, David. Blood of the Donnellys. 2007. (ENG.). 144p. (J). (gr. 8). pap. 11.99 (978-1-55002-754-9(9)) Dundurn CAN. Dist: Ingram Publisher Services.

Newberry, Geoffrey C. The Cape Don Adventure. 2011. 48p. pap. 6.99 (978-1-61667-262-1(5)) Raider Publishing International.

Night, P. J. Don't Drink the Punch! 2012. (Creepover Ser.: 11). lib. bdg. 16.00 (978-0-606-26901-8(0), Turtleback) Turtleback Bks.

Orme, Helen. She's My Friend Now. 2008. (Siti's Sisters Ser.). (ENG., Illus.). 36p. pap. (978-1-84167-740-8(X)) Ransom Publishing Ltd.

Patrick, Cat. Revived. 2013. (ENG.). 368p. (YA). (gr. 7-17). pap. 10.99 (978-0-316-09463-4(3)) Little, Brown Bks. for Young Readers.

Reihs, Linda. The Adventures of Maddy Morphis. 2012. 34p. pap. 9.99 (978-0-9819648-1-2(8)) Mindstir Media.

Richards, Elizabeth. Black City. 2013. (Black City Novel Ser.: 1). (ENG., Illus.). 400p. (YA). (gr. 9). pap. 9.99 (978-0-14-242722-4(5), Speak) Penguin Young Readers Group.

—Phoenix. 2nd ed. 2014. (Black City Novel Ser.: 2). (ENG.). 368p. (YA). (gr. 9). pap. 9.99 (978-0-14-751137-9(2), Speak) Penguin Young Readers Group.

—Rise Above. 2014. (Red Zone Ser.: 6). (ENG.). 104p. (YA). (gr. 6-12). lib. bdg. 27.93 (978-1-4677-2127-1(1)) Lerner Publishing Group.

Robinson, Gwen G. The Jensen Case. 2010. (Illus.). 228p. pap. *(978-0-7552-0496-0(4))* Authors OnLine, Ltd.
Rodriguez, Paul. Don't Do Drugs! Do Dance! Character Education/Prevention. Rodriguez, Paul, illus. 2003. (Illus.). 32p. (J). lib. bdg. 15.99 *(978-0-9744770-1-5(X))* Rodro.
Runaway-A Survivor, 1. 2004. 365p. 14.99 *(978-0-9753252-0-9(5))* IndieArtz, Inc.
Smith, Sandra. Dilemm. 2011. 28p. pap. 15.99 *(978-1-4628-6213-9(6))* Xlibris Corp.
Stone, Jeff. Five Ancestors Out of the Ashes #3: Jackal. 2014. (Five Ancestors Out of the Ashes Ser.). (ENG.). 192p. (J). (gr. 4-7). 16.99 *(978-0-375-87020-0(2),* Random Hse. Bks. for Young Readers) Random Hse. Children's Bks.
Swain, H. A. Hungry. 2014. (ENG.). 384p. (YA). (gr. 8). 16.99 *(978-1-250-02829-7(9),* 9781250028297) Feiwel & Friends.
Thunder Brook: Escape from the Land of Huffra, Adam & the Valley of the Weedgrass. 2005. (Illus.). 136p. (J). 14.95 *(978-0-9768152-0-4(6))* Buttercup Media.
Vaval, Fisepe. The Blueprint. Bubsy, Nancy, ed. 2003. 270p. (YA). pap. 15.00 *(978-0-9743207-0-0(6))* Tayes Bks.
Wilson, Lynn. Ava & Drew Join the Cheese Heroin Patrol, 1 vol. 2010. 30p. 24.95 *(978-1-4489-5210-6(7))* PublishAmerica, Inc.

DRUGS—HISTORY

Weintraub, Aileen. Heroin: A MyReportLinks. com Book. 2005. (Drugs Ser.). (Illus.). 48p. (J). lib. bdg. 26.60 *(978-0-7660-5275-8(3),* MyReportLinks.com Bks.) Enslow Pubs., Inc.

DRUGS—LAW AND LEGISLATION

Allen, John. Thinking Critically: Legalizing Marijuana. 2015. (ENG., Illus.). 80p. (J). lib. bdg. *(978-1-60152-782-0(9))* ReferencePoint Pr., Inc.
Barbour, Scott. Should Marijuana Be Legalized? 2010. (In Controversy Ser.). 96p. (YA). (gr. 7-12). 27.95 *(978-1-60152-106-4(5))* ReferencePoint Pr., Inc.
Brezina, Corona. Alcohol & Drug Offenses: Your Legal Rights, 1 vol. 2015. (ENG., Illus.). 64p. (J). 33.25 *(978-1-4777-8032-9(7),* Rosen Reference) Rosen Publishing Group, Inc., The.
Centore, Michael. Drug Use & the Law, Vol. 13. Becker, Sara, ed. 2016. (Drug Addiction & Recovery Ser.). (Illus.). 64p. (J). (gr. 7). 23.95 *(978-1-4222-3602-4(1))* Mason Crest.
Croft, Jennifer. Drugs & the Legalization Debate. rev. ed. 2005. (Drug Abuse Prevention Library). (Illus.). 64p. (YA). (gr. 7-12). lib. bdg. 31.95 *(978-0-8239-3206-1(0),* DRLEDE) Rosen Publishing Group, Inc., The.
Goldstein, Margaret. Legalizing Marijuana: Promises & Pitfalls. 2016. (ENG., Illus.). 104p. (YA). (gr. 7-12). 35.99 *(978-1-4677-9243-1(8),* Twenty-First Century Bks.) Lerner Publishing Group.
Goldstein, Margaret J. Legalizing Marijuana: Promises & Pitfalls. 2016. (ENG., Illus.). 104p. (YA). (gr. 7-12). 53.32 *(978-1-5124-1144-7(2),* Twenty-First Century Bks.) Lerner Publishing Group.
Harmon, Daniel E. New Medicines: Issues of Approval, Access, & Product Safety. 2009. (Science & Society Ser.). 64p. (gr. 5-6). 58.50 *(978-1-60853-010-6(8));* (Illus.). (YA). (gr. 7-12). lib. bdg. 31.95 *(978-1-4358-5026-2(2))* Rosen Publishing Group, Inc., The.
Kerrigan, Michael. The War on Drugs, Vol. 20. Gomez, Manny, ed. 2016. (Crime & Detection Ser.). 96p. (J). (gr. 7). 24.95 *(978-1-4222-3489-1(4))* Mason Crest.
Merino, Noel. Drug Legalization. Greenhaven Press Editors, ed. 2013. (Introducing Issues with Opposing Viewpoints Ser.). (ENG.). 144p. (gr. 10-12). lib. bdg. 42.00 *(978-0-7377-6275-4(6),* Greenhaven Pr., Inc.) Cengage Gale.
—Drugs. Greenhaven Press Staff, ed. 2014. (Teen Rights & Freedoms Ser.). (ENG., Illus.). 176p. (gr. 10-12). lib. bdg. 42.00 *(978-0-7377-6998-2(X),* Greenhaven Pr., Inc.) Cengage Gale.
Morgan, Kayla. Legalizing Marijuana, 1 vol. 2010. (Essential Viewpoints Set 5 Ser.). (ENG.). 112p. (J). (gr. 6-12). lib. bdg. 35.64 *(978-1-61613-523-2(9),* Essential Library) ABDO Publishing Co.
Ruschmann, Paul. Prescription & Non-Prescription Drugs. 2007. (Point/Counterpoint Ser.). (Illus.). 120p. (YA). (gr. 9-12). lib. bdg. 35.00 *(978-0-7910-9552-2(5))* Facts On File, Inc.
Somerville, Clive. The Drug Enforcement Administration. 2017. (J). ***(978-1-4222-3765-6(6))*** Mason Crest.

DRUGSTORES

Petersen, Christine. The Apothecary. 2010. (Colonial People Ser.). 48p. (gr. 3-18). 29.93 *(978-0-7614-4795-5(4))* Marshall Cavendish Corp.

DRUIDS AND DRUIDISM

Hamilton, John. Witches, 1 vol. 2007. (World of Horror Ser.). (ENG., Illus.). 32p. (gr. 4-8). 27.07 *(978-1-59928-776-8(5),* Abdo & Daughters) ABDO Publishing Co.

DRUIDS AND DRUIDISM—FICTION

Farmer, Nancy. The Islands of the Blessed. 2012. (ENG., Illus.). 496p. (YA). (gr. 7). pap. 11.99 *(978-1-4169-0738-1(6),* Atheneum Bks. for Young Readers) Simon & Schuster Children's Publishing.
—The Islands of the Blessed. Foster, Jon, illus. 2009. (ENG.). 496p. (YA). (gr. 7-9). 18.99 *(978-1-4169-0737-4(8),* Atheneum/Richard Jackson Bks.) Simon & Schuster Children's Publishing.
—The Islands of the Blessed. l.t. ed. 2010. (Sequel to the Land of the Silver Apples Ser.). (ENG.). 520p. (J). 23.95 *(978-1-4104-2253-8(4))* Thorndike Pr.
—The Land of the Silver Apples. 2009. (ENG., Illus.). 528p. (YA). (gr. 7). pap. 11.99 *(978-1-4169-0736-7(X),* Atheneum Bks. for Young Readers) Simon & Schuster Children's Publishing.
—The Land of the Silver Apples. Sardinha, Rick, illus. 2007. (ENG.). 512p. (J). (gr. 5-9). 18.99 *(978-1-4169-0735-0(1),* Atheneum/Richard Jackson Bks.) Simon & Schuster Children's Publishing.
—The Sea of Trolls. (ENG., Illus.). 480p. 2004. (J). (gr. 5-8). 19.99 *(978-0-689-86744-6(1),* Atheneum/Richard Jackson Bks.) 2006. (YA). (gr. 9-8). reprint ed. pap. 11.99 *(978-0-689-86746-0(8),* Atheneum Bks. for Young Readers) Simon & Schuster Children's Publishing.

Fisher, Catherine. Circle of Stones. 2014. (ENG.). 304p. (YA). (gr. 7). 17.99 *(978-0-8037-3819-5(6),* Dial Bks) Penguin Young Readers Group.
—Darkhenge. 2006. 340p. (YA). (gr. 7-12). 15.99 *(978-0-06-078582-6(9))* HarperCollins Pubs.
Freeman, Martha. The Spy Wore Shades. Date not set. 160p. (YA). (gr. 3-18). pap. 4.99 *(978-0-06-440957-5(0))* HarperCollins Pubs.
L'Engle, Madeleine. An Acceptable Time. 2007. (Wrinkle in Time Quintet Ser.: 5). (ENG.). 384p. (J). (gr. 5-9). per. 6.99 *(978-0-312-36858-6(5),* 9780312368586) Square Fish.

DRUM

Adams, Ian. Drumming. 2012. (Master This! Ser.). (Illus.). 32p. (J). lib. bdg. 25.25 *(978-1-4488-5284-0(6),* PowerKids Pr.) Rosen Publishing Group, Inc., The.
Amoroso, Cynthia & Noyed, Robert B. Drums. 2010. (Music Makers Ser.). (ENG., Illus.). 24p. (J). (gr. -1-2). 27.07 *(978-1-60253-353-0(9),* 200504) Child's World, Inc., The.
Black, Dave. Kids Drumset Course. 2005. (Kid's Drumset Course Ser.). (ENG.). 48p. pap. 15.99 *(978-0-7390-3825-3(7))* Alfred Publishing Co., Inc.
Feldstein, Sandy & Clark, Larry. Barcarolle - Snare Drum Solo with Piano Acc. 2005. (YA). pap. 10.95 *(978-1-932895-96-4(5))* PlayinTime Productions, Inc.
Gutner, Howard. Drums: The World's Heartbeat. 2003. (ENG., Illus.). 32p. (J). (gr. 6-8). pap. 8.47 net. *(978-0-7652-3273-1(1),* Celebration Pr.) Pearson Schl.
Landau, Elaine. Are the Drums for You? 2010. (Ready to Make Music Ser.). (ENG.). 40p. (gr. 4-6). lib. bdg. 27.93 *(978-0-7613-5426-0(3),* Lerner Pubns.) Lerner Publishing Group.
Riggs, Kate. Making Music: Drums. 2014. (Making Music Ser.). (ENG.). 24p. (J). (gr. 1-3). pap. 9.99 *(978-0-89812-945-8(1),* Creative Paperbacks) Creative Co., The.
Riley, Peter D. & Walker, Mark. Xtreme Drums. 2006. (ENG., Illus.). 80p. pap. 11.95 incl. audio compact disk *(978-1-84492-019-8(4),* 1844920194) Music Sales Corp.
Salzmann, Mary Elizabeth. What in the World Is a Drum?, 1 vol. 2012. (ENG.). 24p. 25.65 *(978-1-61783-204-8(9),* Super SandCastle) ABDO Publishing Co.

DRUM—FICTION

Allan, Patsy. The Boy Who Loved Drums. 2012. 36p. pap. 32.70 *(978-1-4797-1938-9(2))* Xlibris Corp.
Bass, Karen. Drummer Girl, 1 vol. 2011. (ENG.). 192p. (YA). (gr. 8-12). pap. 14.95 *(978-1-55050-462-0(2))* Coteau Bks. CAN. Dist: Orca Bk. Pubs. USA.
Berry, Ron & Mead, David. The Little Drummer Boy. Sharp, Chris, illus. 2009. (ENG.). 16p. 12.99 *(978-0-8249-1429-5(5),* Ideal Pubns.) Worthy Publishing.
Bootman, Colin, illus. The Steel Pan Man of Harlem. 2009. (Carolrhoda Picture Bks.). 32p. (J). (gr. 1-3). 16.95 *(978-0-8225-9026-2(3))* Lerner Publishing Group.
Darden, Floyd. Drumdee makes a Drum. 2007. 15.95 *(978-1-59526-711-5(5))* Aeon Publishing Inc.
Dole, Mayra L. Drum, Chavi, Drum! Tonel, illus. 2013.Tr. of ¡Toca, Chavi, Toca! (ENG & SPA.). 32p. (J). pap. 9.95 *(978-0-89239-302-2(5),* Children's Book Press) Lee & Low Bks., Inc.
Donegan, Noel & Donegan, Luz. The Noisy Blue Drum. 2013. (Magical Mozart & His Musical Ser.). (ENG.). 32p. (J). pap. 8.95 *(978-1-84730-391-2(9))* Veritas Pubns. IRL. Dist: Dufour Editions, Inc.
Gorg, Gwyn. I Am the Blues. Alfandolo, Koffi, illus. 2012. 26p. pap. 19.95 *(978-0-9840204-2-3(X))* Pacific Raven Pr.
Guidone, Thea. Drum City. Newton, Vanessa, illus. 2015. (ENG.). 32p. (J). (gr. -1-2). 7.99 *(978-0-553-52350-8(3),* Dragonfly Bks.) Random Hse. Children's Bks.
Mayer, Mercer. Just a Little Music. 2009. (Little Critter Ser.). (J). lib. bdg. 13.55 *(978-0-606-12258-0(3),* Turtleback) Turtleback Bks.
Meadows, Daisy. Danni the Drum Fairy #4. 2010. (ENG.). 80p. (J). lib. bdg. 15.39 *(978-1-4242-4729-5(2))* Fitzgerald Bks.
Patricelli, Leslie. Be Quiet, Mike! 2011. (ENG., Illus.). 40p. (J). (gr. -1-2). 14.99 *(978-0-7636-4477-2(3))* Candlewick Pr.
Redding, LaTisha. Calling the Water Drum, 1 vol. Boyd, Aaron, illus. 2016. (ENG.). 32p. (J). (gr. 1-4). 17.95 *(978-1-62014-194-6(9))* Lee & Low Bks., Inc.
Todd, Traci N. The Drum Circle. Reisch, Jesse, illus. 2006. (J). *(978-1-58987-023-9(9))* Kindermusik International.
Top That! Playtime Shapes (large Version) Parry, Jo, illus. 2007. 10p. (J). (gr. -1). *(978-1-84666-555-4(8),* Tide Mill Pr.) Top That! Publishing PLC.
Vernick, Audrey. Teach Your Buffalo to Play Drums. Jennewein, Daniel, illus. 2011. (ENG.). 32p. (J). (gr. -1-3). 16.99 *(978-0-06-176253-6(9))* HarperCollins Pubs.

DRUM MAJORS—FICTION

Echols, Jennifer. The One That I Want. 2012. (ENG.). 288p. (YA). (gr. 7). pap. 9.99 *(978-1-4424-5236-7(6),* Simon Pulse) Simon Pulse.

DRUNKENNESS

see Alcoholism

DRY GOODS

see Textile Industry

DUBLIN (IRELAND)

Mac a'Bháird, Natasha. Dublin: My Ireland Activity Book. Nolan, Alan, illus. 2017. (ENG.). 24p. (J). pap. 12.00 ***(978-1-84717-892-3(8))*** O'Brien Pr., Ltd., The. IRL. Dist: Dufour Editions, Inc.

DUBLIN (IRELAND)—FICTION

Carroll, Sarah. The Girl in Between. 2017. (ENG.). 256p. (YA). (gr. 7). 16.99 ***(978-0-7352-2860-3(4),*** Kathy Dawson Books) Penguin Young Readers Group.
Colton, Nicola. A Dublin Fairytale. 2016. (ENG., Illus.). 32p. (J). 18.00 *(978-1-84717-774-2(3))* O'Brien Pr., Ltd., The. IRL. Dist: Dufour Editions, Inc.
Cusack, Geraldine O'Connell. Wrecker's Cove. 2013. 100p. pap. *(978-1-78407-081-6(5))* FeedARead.com.
Doyle, Roddy. Brilliant. Hughes, Emily, illus. 2015. (ENG.). 192p. (J). (gr. 3-7). 16.95 *(978-1-4197-1479-5(1),* Amulet Bks.) Abrams, Inc.
—A Greyhound of a Girl. 2013. (ENG.). 224p. (YA). (gr. 3-7). pap. 7.95 *(978-1-4197-0798-8(1),* Amulet Bks.) Abrams, Inc.
Gallagher, Brian. Secrets & Shadows: Two Friends in a World at War. 2013. (ENG.). 224p. (J). pap. 13.95 *(978-1-84717-350-8(0))* O'Brien Pr., Ltd., The. IRL. Dist: Dufour Editions, Inc.
—Taking Sides: A Boy, a Girl, a Nation Torn Apart. 2012. (ENG.). 224p. (J). pap. 13.95 *(978-1-84717-279-2(2))* O'Brien Pr., Ltd., The. IRL. Dist: Dufour Editions, Inc.
MacAndrew, Richard. A Little Trouble in Dublin Level 1 Beginner/Elementary. 2010. (ENG., Illus.). 46p. pap. 11.00 *(978-84-8323-695-6(8))* Cambridge Univ. Pr.
Massey, Eithne. Where the Stones Sing: Who Are the Mysterious Voices in Christ Church? 2012. (ENG., Illus.). 208p. (J). pap. 12.95 *(978-1-84717-277-8(6))* O'Brien Pr., Ltd., The. IRL. Dist: Dufour Editions, Inc.
McDonnell, Vincent. The Knock Airport Mystery. 2006. (ENG., Illus.). 203p. (J). pap. 11.95 *(978-1-903464-87-8(0))* Collins Pr., The. IRL. Dist: Dufour Editions, Inc.
Murray, E. R. The Book of Learning. 2015. (Nine Lives Trilogy Ser.: 1). (ENG.). 352p. (J). pap. 12.00 ***(978-1-78117-362-6(1))*** Mercier Pr., Ltd., The. IRL. Dist: Dufour Editions, Inc.
O'Brien, Joe. Legends' Lair. 2016. (ENG., Illus.). 192p. (J). pap. 13.00 *(978-1-84717-826-8(X))* O'Brien Pr., Ltd., The. IRL. Dist: Dufour Editions, Inc.
Regan, Peter. Riverside: The Curse. Myler, Terry, illus. 2004. (Riverside Ser.). (ENG.). 127p. (J). pap. 11.95 *(978-1-901737-46-2(2))* Anvil Bks., Ltd. IRL. Dist: Dufour Editions, Inc.
Sirr, Peter. Black Wreath: The Stolen Life of James Lovett. 2015. (ENG.). 320p. (J). pap. 13.00 *(978-1-84717-560-1(0))* O'Brien Pr., Ltd., The. IRL. Dist: Dufour Editions, Inc.
Taylor, Marilyn. 17 Martin Street. 2012. (ENG.). 208p. (J). pap. 12.95 *(978-1-84717-286-0(5))* O'Brien Pr., Ltd., The. IRL. Dist: Dufour Editions, Inc.
Thompson, Kate. Switchers. 220p. (J). (gr. 4-7). pap. 5.99 *(978-0-8072-1553-1(8));* 2004. (Switchers Ser.: Vol. 1). (gr. 5-9). pap. 38.00 incl. audio *(978-0-8072-8138-3(7),* YA115SP) Random Hse. Audio Publishing Group. (Listening Library).

DU BOIS, W. E. B. (WILLIAM EDWARD BURGHARDT), 1868-1963

Hinman, Bonnie. A Stranger in My Own House: The Story of W. E. B. du Bois. 2005. (Civil Rights Leaders Ser.). (Illus.). 176p. (gr. 6-12). 28.95 *(978-1-931798-45-7(1))* Reynolds, Morgan Inc.
Lochte, Hilary. W. E. B. du Bois. 2015. (Heroes of Black History Ser.). (ENG., Illus.). 32p. (J). (gr. 3-4). 26.60 *(978-1-4824-2922-0(5))* Stevens, Gareth Publishing LLLP.
Rowh, Mark. The Life of W. E. B. du Bois: Civil Rights Champion. 2015. (Legendary African Americans Ser.). 96p. (J). (gr. 6-12). 27.94 *(978-0-7660-6280-1(5));* pap. 10.95 *(978-0-7660-6281-8(3))* Enslow Pubs., Inc.
Stafford, Mark & Davenport, John, texts. W. E. B. Du Bois: Scholar & Activist. 2004. (Black Americans of Achievement Ser.). (Illus.). 112p. (gr. 6-12). 35.00 *(978-0-7910-8158-7(3),* Chelsea Hse.) Facts On File, Inc.
Warren, Nagueyalti. Grandfather of Black Studies: W.E.B. du Bois. 2011. (J). *(978-1-59221-821-9(0));* (ENG., Illus.). 258p. pap. *(978-1-59221-822-6(9))* Africa World Pr.
Whiting, Jim. W. E. B. du Bois: Civil Rights Activist, Author, Historian. 2009. (Transcending Race in America: Biographies of Biracial Achievers Ser.). 64p. (YA). (gr. 5-18). pap. 9.95 *(978-1-4222-1632-3(2))* Mason Crest.
Wittrock, Jeni. W. E. B. du Bois. 2014. (Great African-Americans Ser.). (ENG., Illus.). 24p. (gr. k-1). lib. bdg. 21.99 *(978-1-4914-0505-5(8),* Pebble Bks.) Capstone Press of Coughlan Cos.

DUCKS

Aspen-Baxter, Linda. Patos. 2012. (SPA.). (J). *(978-1-61913-187-3(0))* Weigl Pubs., Inc.
Blake, Joseph D. This Little Village: It Took A Village to Rescue These Little Ducks. 2011. 32p. (gr. 1-2). pap. 12.77 *(978-1-4490-4093-2(4))* AuthorHouse.
Bygrave, Linda. Duck. (Illus.). 24p. (YA). (gr. 1-18). lib. bdg. 22.80 *(978-1-931983-48-8(8))* Chrysalis Education.
Carpenter, Tom. Duck Hunting, 1 vol. 2015. (ENG., Illus.). 48p. (J). 32.79 *(978-1-62403-834-1(4),* 1391419) ABDO Publishing Co.
Childrens Press Staff & Scholastic, Inc. Staff, contrib. by. 5 Busy Ducklings. 2010. (Rookie Toddler: First Concepts Ser.). (ENG.). 12p. (J). bds. 6.95 *(978-0-531-25232-1(9),* Children's Pr.) Scholastic Library Publishing.
Cox, Phil Roxbee, ed. Find the Duck. Cartwright, Stephen, illus. 2004. (Find It Board Bks.). (ENG.). 1p. (J). (gr. -1-18). bds. 3.95 *(978-0-7460-3821-5(6))* EDC Publishing.
Davies, Nicola. Just Ducks! 2014. (Read & Wonder Ser.). lib. bdg. 17.20 *(978-0-606-35167-6(1))* Turtleback Bks.
Dicker, Katie. Ducks. 2014. (Farm Animals Ser.). (Illus.). 24p. (gr. 2-5). 28.50 *(978-1-62588-020-8(0))* Black Rabbit Bks.
Dieker, Wendy. Ducks. 2012. (Illus.). 24p. (J). lib. bdg. 25.65 *(978-1-62031-002-1(3))* Jump! Inc.
Doeden, Matt. Duck Hunting. 2017. (Great Outdoors Ser.). (ENG., Illus.). 32p. (J). (gr. 1-3). pap. 9.99 *(978-1-68152-077-3(X))* Amicus.
Duck. 2004. (J). per. *(978-1-57657-354-9(0))* Paradise Pr., Inc.
Ducks. Date not set. (Old MacDonald Stickers Ser.). (Illus.). 16p. (J). 2.98 *(978-0-7525-7061-7(7));* 5.98 *(978-0-7525-9967-0(4))* Parragon, Inc.
Endres, Hollie. Ducks. 2007. (Farm Animals Ser.). (ENG., Illus.). 24p. (J). (gr. k-3). lib. bdg. 25.95 *(978-1-60014-112-6(9))* Bellwether Media.
Ganeri, Anita. Ducks & Ducklings. Axworthy, Ani, illus. 2010. (Animal Families Ser.). (ENG.). 14p. (J). bds. 10.99 *(978-1-84089-643-5(4))* Evans Brothers, Ltd. GBR. Dist: Independent Pubs. Group.
Gibbs, Maddie. Ducks, 1 vol. 2015. (ENG.). 24p. (J). lib. bdg. 23.60 *(978-1-4994-0098-4(5),* PowerKids Pr.) Rosen Publishing Group, Inc., The.
—Los Patos / Ducks, 1 vol. 2015. (Amigos de la Granja / Farmyard Friends Ser.). (ENG & SPA.). 24p. (J). 23.60 *(978-1-4994-0269-8(4),* PowerKids Pr.) Rosen Publishing Group, Inc., The.
Glaser, Rebecca Stromstad. Ducks Quack. 2016. (ENG., Illus.). 14p. (J). (gr. -1 — 1). bds. 7.99 *(978-1-68152-127-5(X))* Amicus.
Hall, Margaret. Ducks & Their Ducklings [Scholastic]. 2011. (Animal Offspring Ser.). 24p. pap. 0.50 *(978-1-4296-6295-6(6),* Pebble Plus) Capstone Press of Coughlan Cos.

Hasselius, Michelle M. Ducks. 2016. (Farm Animals Ser.). (ENG.). 24p. (gr. k-1). lib. bdg. 26.65 *(978-1-5157-0926-8(4))* Capstone Press of Coughlan Cos.
Hédelin, Pascale. Face-to-Face with the Duck. 2005. (Illus.). 28p. (J). 9.95 *(978-1-57091-457-7(5))* Charlesbridge Publishing, Inc.
Hills, Tad. What's up, Duck? A Book of Opposites. Hills, Tad, illus. 2008. (Duck & Goose Ser.). (ENG., Illus.). 22p. (J). (gr. k — 1). bds. 6.99 *(978-0-375-84738-7(3),* Schwartz & Wade Bks.) Random Hse. Children's Bks.
Hipp, Andrew. The Life Cycle of a Duck. 2009. (Life Cycles Library). 24p. (gr. 3-4). 42.50 *(978-1-60853-994-9(6),* PowerKids Pr.) Rosen Publishing Group, Inc., The.
Ho, Cammie. Duckling Duckling. 2016. (Life Cycle Bks.). (ENG., Illus.). 33p. (J). (gr. k-2). pap. 7.99 *(978-1-943241-00-2(7))* Phonic Monic.
Hudak, Heather C. Ducks. 2006. (Farm Animals Ser.). (Illus.). 24p. (J). (gr. 3-7). lib. bdg. 24.45 *(978-1-59036-504-5(6));* per. 8.95 *(978-1-59036-505-2(4))* Weigl Pubs., Inc.
Johnson, Jinny. Duck. Woods, Michael, illus. 2010. (J). 28.50 *(978-1-59920-353-9(7))* Black Rabbit Bks.
Kavanagh, James. Ducks Nature Activity Book. Leung, Raymond, illus. 2nd ed. 2011. (Nature Activity Book Ser.). (ENG.). 32p. (J). (gr. 4-7). 6.95 *(978-1-58355-579-8(X))* Western National Parks Assn.
Kawa, Katie. Ducklings. 2011. (Cute & Cuddly: Baby Animals Ser.). (Illus.). 24p. (gr. k-2). (J). 22.60 *(978-1-4339-5538-9(5));* (J). pap. 8.15 *(978-1-4339-5540-2(7));* 69.20 *(978-1-4339-6895-2(9))* Stevens, Gareth Publishing LLLP.
Kissock, Heather & Aspen-Baxter, Linda. Ducks. 2011. (J). *(978-1-61690-572-9(7)); (978-1-61690-926-0(9))* Weigl Pubs., Inc.
Lambert, Hines. Hunting Ducks. 2013. (Let's Go Hunting Ser.). (ENG., Illus.). 32p. (J). (gr. 4-6). 25.25 *(978-1-4488-9661-5(4));* pap. 10.00 *(978-1-4488-9780-3(7))* Rosen Publishing Group, Inc., The. (PowerKids Pr.).
Leaf, Christina. Baby Ducks. 2014. (Super Cute! Ser.). (ENG., Illus.). 24p. (J). (gr. k-3). lib. bdg. 25.95 *(978-1-60014-973-3(1),* Blastoff! Readers) Bellwether Media.
Little Ducks Don't Fly. (Illus.). 32p. (J). (gr. -1-3). *(978-0-914082-27-9(2))* Syentek, Inc.
Llewellyn, Claire. Duck. Mendez, Simon, tr. Mendez, Simon, illus. 2004. (Starting Life Ser.). (ENG.). 24p. (J). (gr. k-3). 16.95 *(978-1-55971-878-3(1))* Cooper Square Publishing Llc.
Mara, Wil. Ducks. 2008. (Animals Animals Ser.). (Illus.). 48p. (gr. 3-18). lib. bdg. 29.93 *(978-0-7614-2927-2(1),* Benchmark Bks.) Marshall Cavendish Corp.
Minden, Cecilia. Farm Animals: Ducks. 2009. (21st Century Junior Library: Farm Animals Ser.). (ENG., Illus.). 24p. (gr. 2-4). lib. bdg. 25.64 *(978-1-60279-546-4(0),* 200269) Cherry Lake Publishing.
Mitchell, Melanie S. Ducks. 2005. (First Step Nonfiction Ser.). (Illus.). 24p. (gr. k-2). lib. bdg. 17.27 *(978-0-8225-4602-3(7))* Lerner Publishing Group.
Morgan, Sally. Ducks. 2008. (Down on the Farm (N.Y.) Ser.). (ENG., Illus.). 24p. (J). (gr. 3-7). pap. *(978-0-7787-4052-0(8))* Crabtree Publishing Co.
National Geographic Kids & Delano, Marfe Ferguson. Explore My World: Ducklings. 2017. (Explore My World Ser.). (ENG., Illus.). 32p. (J). (gr. -1-2). pap. 4.99 *(978-1-4263-2715-5(3),* National Geographic Children's Bks.) National Geographic Society.
Omoth, Tyler. Duck Hunting for Kids, 1 vol. 2012. (Into the Great Outdoors Ser.). (ENG.). 32p. (gr. 3-4). lib. bdg. 27.99 *(978-1-4296-8616-7(2),* Edge Bks.) Capstone Press of Coughlan Cos.
Omoth, Tyler Dean. Duck Hunting for Kids, 1 vol. 2012. (Into the Great Outdoors Ser.). (ENG.). 32p. (gr. 3-4). pap. 7.95 *(978-1-4296-9268-7(5),* Edge Bks.) Capstone Press of Coughlan Cos.
Randolph, Joanne. A Family of Ducks. 2015. (Rosen REAL Readers: STEM & STEAM Collection). (ENG.). 8p. pap. 5.46 *(978-1-4994-9633-8(8),* Rosen Classroom) Rosen Publishing Group, Inc., The.
Royer, Anne. Little Ducks. 2006. (Born to Be Wild Ser.). (Illus.). 24p. (gr. k-3). lib. bdg. 23.00 *(978-0-8368-6697-1(5),* Gareth Stevens Learning Library) Stevens, Gareth Publishing LLLP.
—Patitos. 2006. (Nacidos para Ser Salvajes Ser.). (SPA., Illus.). 24p. (J). (gr. k-3). lib. bdg. 23.00 *(978-0-8368-7425-9(0),* Gareth Stevens Learning Library) Stevens, Gareth Publishing LLLP.
Rustad, Martha E. H. A Baby Duck Story, 1 vol. 2011. (Baby Animals Ser.). (ENG.). 24p. (gr. k-1). pap. 7.29 *(978-1-4296-7091-3(6));* pap. 41.70 *(978-1-4296-7097-5(5))* Capstone Press of Coughlan Cos. (Pebble Plus).
—A Baby Duck Story (La Historia de un Pato Bebé) Strictly Spanish Translation Services Staff, tr. from ENG. 2012. (Animales Bebé/Baby Animals Ser.). (ENG & MUL.). 24p. (gr. k-1). lib. bdg. 26.65 *(978-1-4296-9219-9(7))* Capstone Press of Coughlan Cos.
Sanoja, Kira Shanell. The Ducks from the Block. 2010. 28p. 13.99 *(978-1-4520-5040-9(6))* AuthorHouse.
Savage, Stephen. Duck. 2009. (Animal Neighbors Ser.). (Illus.). 32p. (J). (gr. 3-6). lib. bdg. 25.25 *(978-1-4358-4988-4(4),* PowerKids Pr.) Rosen Publishing Group, Inc., The.
Savage, Steven. Duck. 2009. (Animal Neighbors Ser.). 32p. (gr. k-5). pap. 10.60 *(978-1-4042-4565-5(0),* Rosen Classroom) Rosen Publishing Group, Inc., The.
Scheunemann, Pam. Ducks Quack!, 1 vol. 2009. (Animal Sounds Set 1 Ser.). (ENG., Illus.). 24p. (J). (gr. k-3). lib. bdg. 24.21 *(978-1-60453-571-6(7),* SandCastle) ABDO Publishing Co.
Seaver Keith, Emily. A Home for Webby. Seaver Keith, Emily, illus. 2008. (Illus.). 23p. (J). (gr. -1-3). 16.95 *(978-0-9728646-1-9(X))* Bangzoom Pubs.
Sexton, Colleen. Ducklings. 2008. (Watch Animals Grow Ser.). (ENG., Illus.). 24p. (J). (gr. k-3). lib. bdg. 25.95 *(978-1-60014-167-6(6))* Bellwether Media.
Sherman, Rose. Danielle the Duck. 2006. 17.00 *(978-0-8059-9890-0(X))* Dorrance Publishing Co., Inc.
Sing along Rhymes Five Little Ducks. 2010. (J). *(978-85-312-5232-7(6))* Children's Pr., Ltd.

CD

Steinkraus, Kyla. Ducks on the Farm. 2010. (Farm Animals Ser.). (Illus.). 24p. (J). (gr. k-3). 22.79 (978-1-61590-269-9(4)) Rourke Educational Media.
Stockland, Patricia M. On the Duck Pond, 1 vol. Ouren, Todd, illus. 2007. (Barnyard Buddies Ser.). (ENG.). 24p. (gr. -1-2). 27.07 (978-1-60270-027-7(3), Looking Glass Library-Nonfiction) Magic Wagon.
Tapp, Karen J. Molly the Mallard Duck: The True Story of Kathy & the Mallard Duck She Named Molly. 2013. 32p. pap. 17.25 (978-1-4669-8524-7(0)) Trafford Publishing.
Top That Publishing Staff, ed. Wacky Duck. 2004. (Wacky Animals Ser.). (Illus.). 10p. (J). pap. (978-1-84510-086-5(7)) Top That! Publishing PLC.
Troupe, Thomas Kingsley. Wild Weather: Science Adventures with Sonny the Origami Bird, 1 vol. Christoph, Jamey, illus. 2014. (Origami Science Adventures Ser.). (ENG.). 24p. (gr. 3-4). lib. bdg. 27.32 (978-1-4795-2188-3(4)) Picture Window Bks.
Twine, Alice. Ducks. (Baby Animals Ser.). 24p. 2009. (gr. 1-1). 42.50 (978-1-61511-489-4(0)) 2007. (Illus.). (J). (gr. -1-3). lib. bdg. 22.60 (978-1-4042-3771-1(2)) Rosen Publishing Group, Inc., The. (PowerKids Pr.).
—Ducks/Patos. 2009. (Baby Animals/Animales bebé Ser.). (ENG & SPA.). 24p. (gr. 1-1). 42.50 (978-1-61511-500-6(5), Editorial Buenas Letras) Rosen Publishing Group, Inc., The.
—Ducks/Patos. Obregon, Jose Maria, tr. 2007. (Baby Animals / Animales Bebé Ser.). (ENG & SPA., Illus.). 24p. (J). (gr. -1-3). lib. bdg. 22.60 (978-1-4042-7633-8(5), Editorial Buenas Letras) Rosen Publishing Group, Inc., The.
Wilsdon, Christina. Ducks. 2007. (J). (978-1-59939-119-9(8), Reader's Digest Young Families, Inc.) Studio Fun International.
Yoon, Salina. Duck, Duck, Porcupine! 2016. (Duck, Duck, Porcupine Book Ser.). (ENG., Illus.). 64p. (J). 9.99 (978-1-61963-723-8(5), 9781619637238, Bloomsbury USA Childrens) Bloomsbury Publishing USA.
—Duck, Duck, Porcupine! 2017. (J). lib. bdg. 16.00 (978-0-606-40593-5(3)) Turtleback Bks.
Zemlicka, Shannon. Mallard Ducks. (Pull Ahead Bks.). 32p. (J). 2004. 22.60 (978-0-8225-3773-1(7), Carolrhoda Bks.) 2003. pap. 5.95 (978-0-8225-9888-6(4)) Lerner Publishing Group.
Zobel, Derek. Ducks. 2011. (Backyard Wildlife Ser.). (ENG., Illus.). 24p. (J). (gr. k-3). lib. bdg. 25.95 (978-1-60014-596-4(5), Blastoff! Readers) Bellwether Media.

DUCKS—FICTION

Abedí, Isabel & Neuendorf, Abedi -. No Quiero Verte Mas! Neuendorf, Silvio, illus. 2003. (SPA.). 196p. (J). (gr. -1-3). 17.99 (978-84-261-3303-8(7)) Juventud, Editorial ESP. Dist: Lectorum Pubns., Inc.
Abrahams, Peter. Quacky Baseball. Morrison, Frank, illus. 2011. (ENG.). 32p. (J). (gr. -1-3). 16.99 (978-0-06-122978-7(4)) HarperCollins Pubs.
Acreman, Hayley. Found You Rabbit! Acreman, Hayley, illus. 2011. (ENG., Illus.). 34p. (J). (gr. k-2). pap. 9.95 (978-1-905762-87-3(9)) Parthian Bks. GBR. Dist: Independent Pubs. Group.
Adams, Diane. Love Is. Keane, Claire, illus. 2017. (ENG.). 32p. (J). 15.99 (978-1-4521-3997-5(0)) Chronicle Bks. LLC.
Alder, Charlie. Daredevil Duck. 2015. (ENG., Illus.). 48p. (J). (gr. -1-17). 16.95 (978-0-7624-5456-3(3), Running Pr. Kids) Running Pr. Bk. Pubs.
Allan, Jayne. PC Polly to the Rescue. Mercer, Lynn, illus. 2003. (ENG.). 32p. (J). (gr. 1-18). pap. 10.95 (978-0-9535413-8-6(X)) iynx publishing GBR. Dist: Dufour Editions, Inc.
Allen, Elaine. Mallory the Forgetful Duck, 1 vol. Nash, Kelli, illus. 2012. (ENG.). 40p. (J). 16.99 (978-0-7643-4069-7(7), 9780764340697) Schiffer Publishing, Ltd.
Ana, Moh. Kookaburra Tales # 3: Laugh Not at Others. 2013. 16p. pap. 16.81 (978-1-4669-3477-1(8)) Trafford Publishing.
Andersen, Hans Christian & Kurt, Robert. Ugly Duckling. Watts, Bernadette, illus. 2008. (ENG.). 32p. (J). (gr. -1-3). pap. 7.95 (978-0-7358-2146-0(1)) North-South Bks., Inc.
Angelique, Janice. Ducky Grows Up. 2009. 40p. pap. 18.49 (978-1-4389-5963-4(X)) AuthorHouse.
Ashby, Gaylene. STORY TIME A Collection of Three Children's Stories. 2008. 28p. 14.95 (978-1-4357-1929-3(8)) Lulu Pr., Inc.
Austin, Heather. Boatyard Ducklings. Austin, Heather, illus. 2008. (ENG., Illus.). 32p. (J). (gr. -1-3). 15.95 (978-0-89272-663-9(6)) Down East Bks.
Award, Anna & Biro, Val. The Bear & the Travellers & the Ducks & the Tortoise. 2014. (ENG.). 24p. (J). pap. 6.95 (978-1-84135-959-5(9)) Award Pubns. Ltd. GBR. Dist: Parkwest Pubns., Inc.
Backman, Laura. Lemon the Duck. l.t. ed. 2012. 64p. (J). pap. (978-1-4596-3450-3(0)) ReadHowYouWant.com, Ltd.
Badenhop, Faye D. 'Quacking' the 'Pair O' Ducks' Case. 2008. 32p. pap. 13.75 (978-1-4343-7956-6(6)) AuthorHouse.
Baker, Harriet Lila. Boyduck Goose: His Life & Times, Bk. II. 2005. (J). pap. 9.00 (978-0-8059-6694-7(3)) Dorrance Publishing Co., Inc.
Bardhan-Quallen, Sudipta. Duck, Duck, Moose! Jones, Noah Z., illus. 2014. (ENG.). 32p. (J). (gr. -1-k). 16.99 (978-1-4231-7110-2(1)) Hyperion Bks. for Children.
—Quackenstein Hatches a Family. Jones, Brian T., illus. 2010. (ENG.). 32p. (J). (gr. k-2). 15.95 (978-0-8109-8973-3(5), Abrams Bks. for Young Readers) Abrams, Inc.
Bardoe, Cheryl. The Ugly Duckling Dinosaur: A Prehistoric Tale. Kennedy, Doug & Kennedy, Roy D., illus. 2011. (ENG.). 32p. (J). (gr. -1-3). 16.95 (978-0-8109-9739-4(8), Abrams Bks. for Young Readers) Abrams, Inc.
Barham, Paul Richard. The Adventures of Damen the Duck. 2012. 72p. pap. 41.99 (978-1-4691-5476-3(5)) Xlibris Corp.
Barnes, Charlotte. Stella Ducktropolis. 2008. 36p. pap. 11.95 (978-1-4327-1806-0(1)) Outskirts Pr., Inc.
Barrows, Marjorie. Little Duck. Myers, Marie Honre, illus. 2011. 50p. 35.95 (978-1-258-08897-2(5)) Literary Licensing, LLC.
Batson, Priscilla. Big Dig Ducks. 2010. 68p. pap. 23.49 (978-1-4389-9249-5(1)) AuthorHouse.
Batson, Susann. A Duck at the Dog Pound. 2007. (Illus.). 32p. (J). E-Book 5.00 incl. cd-rom (978-1-933090-23-8(5)) Guardian Angel Publishing, Inc.
Beatty, Cherie B. Meet Lewis the Duck. 2009. 24p. pap. 12.99 (978-1-4389-5116-4(7)) AuthorHouse.
Behn, Rosa & Graham, Dora. The Adventures of Jenny Duck. 2006. 109p. pap. 19.95 (978-1-4137-9450-2(5)) PublishAmerica, Inc.
Beiser, Tim. Little Chicken Duck. Slavin, Bill, illus. 2013. (ENG.). 24p. (J). (gr. -1-2). 17.95 (978-1-77049-392-6(1), Tundra Bks.) Tundra Bks. CAN. Dist: Penguin Random Hse. LLC.
Benson, Ken. Leela's Great Life. 2012. 28p. pap. 15.99 (978-1-4771-2713-1(5)) Xlibris Corp.
Berg, Ray. Sailing Duck. 2005. 15p. (J). 9.33 (978-1-4116-3554-8(X)) Lulu Pr., Inc.
The Big Rain. 2003. (Illus.). 32p. (J). mass mkt. (978-0-9740599-2-1(7), 3) Omnibus Publishing.
Bills, Taylor, illus. The Ugly Duckling. 2009. 24p. 12.95 (978-0-9776845-1-9(2)) 3D Alley, Inc.
Blackaby, Susan. El Patito Feo. Ruíz, Carlos, tr. from ENG. Delage, Charlene, illus. 2006. (Read-It! Readers en Español: Cuentos de Hadas Ser.). (SPA.). 32p. (gr. k-3). 21.32 (978-1-4048-1644-2(5), Easy Readers) Picture Window Bks.
Blazek, Frank. Phil & His Fabulous Feathers, 1 vol. Thomas, Wes, illus. 2005. (ENG.). 32p. (J). (gr. k-3). 16.99 (978-1-58980-280-3(2)) Pelican Publishing Co., Inc.
Blount, Willie And Ebony. Super Duck Goes Green. 2011. 44p. pap. 16.59 (978-1-4634-1909-7(0)) AuthorHouse.
Blum, Geoffrey & Barks, Carl. Uncle Scrooge #377. Clark, John, ed. 2008. (ENG., Illus.). 64p. pap. 7.99 (978-1-60360-033-0(7), 9781603600330) Gemstone Publishing, Inc.
A Book of Babies. (ENG.). 24p. (J). (— 1). 2015. bds. 6.99 (978-0-553-50779-9(6)) 2014. 15.99 (978-0-385-75290-9(3)) Random Hse. Children's Bks. (Knopf Bks. for Young Readers).
Bowser, Ken. Homesick Penguin: Empathy/Caring for Others. Bowser, Ken, illus. 2014. (Funny Bone Readers: Being a Friend Ser.). (Illus.). 24p. (gr. -1-1). pap. 4.99 (978-1-939656-03-2(6)) Red Chair Pr.
Bramsen, Carin. Hey, Duck! (ENG., Illus.). (J). 2017. 32p. (— 1). bds. 7.99 (978-1-5247-1581-6(6)) 2013. 40p. (gr. -1-2). 17.99 (978-0-375-86990-7(5)) Random Hse. Children's Bks. (Random Hse. Bks. for Young Readers).
—Just a Duck? 2015. (ENG., Illus.). 40p. (J). (gr. -1-2). 17.99 (978-0-385-38415-5(7)); lib. bdg. 20.99 (978-0-375-97344-4(3)) Random Hse. Children's Bks. (Random Hse. Bks. for Young Readers).
Branen, Kathy. My Life By: D. D. Duck. Robinson, Marcus, illus. 2012. 24p. pap. 12.95 (978-0-9845904-1-4(2)) Joshua Tree Publishing.
Briggs-Anderson, Naomi. Mattie & Percy: The Story of a Chicken & a Duck. Wooten, Vernon Lee, illus. 2011. 32p. pap. 24.95 (978-1-4560-5319-2(1)) America Star Bks.
Bromley, Nick. Open Very Carefully: A Book with Bite. O'Byrne, Nicola, illus. 2013. (ENG.). 32p. (J). (gr. -1-2). 15.99 (978-0-7636-6163-2(5), Nosy Crow) Candlewick Pr.
Brooks, Felicity. This Is My Duck. 2008. (NoisyTouchy-Feely Board Bks). 10p. (J). (gr. -1). bds. 16.99 (978-0-7945-2187-5(8), Usborne) EDC Publishing.
Brost, April. Luckyduck Luckyduck. 2013. 24p. pap. 24.95 (978-1-63004-104-5(1)) America Star Bks.
Brown, Alan James. Love-a-Duck. Chessa, Francesca, illus. 2010. (ENG.). 32p. (J). (gr. -1-1). pap. 16.95 (978-0-8234-2263-0(1)) Holiday Hse., Inc.
Brown, J. A. Scaredy Duck. Knight, Paula, illus. 2004. (Funny Faces Ser.). 10p. (J). 3.95 (978-1-58925-716-0(2)) Tiger Tales.
Brown, Margaret Wise. The Golden Egg Book. Weisgard, Leonard, illus. 2004. (Big Little Golden Book Ser.). (ENG.). 32p. (J). (gr. -1-2). 8.99 (978-0-375-82717-4(X), Golden Bks.) Random Hse. Children's Bks.
—The Golden Egg Book. Weisgard, Leonard, illus. 2015. (Little Golden Book Ser.). (ENG.). 24p. (J). (-k). 4.99 (978-0-385-38476-6(9), Golden Bks.) Random Hse. Children's Bks.
Brown, Rosie L. Zach & Rob's Journey: The Lost Eggs. 2007. 24p. per. 24.95 (978-1-4241-8401-9(0)) America Star Bks.
Bruckner, Tai. Lemon Path Encounter, 1 vol. Bruckner, Wes, illus. 2009. 15p. pap. 24.95 (978-1-60836-407-7(0)) America Star Bks.
Buchanan, Darlene. Smiley's World. 2009. 64p. pap. 11.49 (978-1-4490-2675-2(3)) AuthorHouse.
Bunting, Eve. Ducky. Wisniewski, David, illus. 2004. (ENG.). 32p. (J). (gr. k — 1). 6.99 (978-0-618-43240-0(X)) Houghton Mifflin Harcourt Publishing Co.
—Have You Seen My New Blue Socks? Ruzzier, Sergio, illus. 2013. (ENG.). 32p. (J). (gr. -1-3). 16.99 (978-0-547-75267-9(9)) Houghton Mifflin Harcourt Publishing Co.
Burgess, Thornton W. The Adventures of Poor Mrs Quack. 2007. 124p. 23.95 (978-1-60312-595-6(7)) Aegypan.
—The Adventures of Poor Mrs Quack. 2011. 124p. 24.95 (978-1-4638-9562-4(3)) Rodgers, Alan Bks.
—The Adventures of Poor Mrs. Quack. 2004. reprint ed. pap. 1.99 (978-1-4192-5160-3(0)); pap. 15.95 (978-1-4191-5160-6(6)) Kessinger Publishing, LLC.
Bush, Emilie P. Steamduck Learns to Fly! Petty, William Kevin, illus. 2012. 36p. pap. 11.95 (978-0-9849028-1-1(3)) Coal City Stories.
Butterfield, Moira. Wake up, Magic Duck! Child, Jeremy, illus. 2010. (Magic Bath Bks.). (ENG.). 8p. (J). (gr. -1-k). 5.99 (978-0-7641-9792-5(4)) Barron's Educational Series, Inc.
Callen, Sharon. Duck Pond Fun, 1 vol. rev. ed. 2013. (Fiction Readers Ser.). (ENG., Illus.). 12p. (J). (gr. 1-1). pap. 12.96 (978-1-4807-1124-2(1)); pap. 4.99 (978-1-4333-5445-8(4)) Shell Educational Publishing.
The Can Do Duck: A Story about Believing in Yourself. 2005. (J). pap. (978-0-9768384-1-8(9)) Can Do Duck Publishing.
Candlewick Press, Candlewick. Peppa Pig & the Lucky Ducks. 2016. (Peppa Pig Ser.). (ENG.). 32p. (J). (-k). 12.99 (978-0-7636-8740-3(5), Candlewick Entertainment) Candlewick Pr.
Capucilli, Alyssa Satin. Adventures of Katy Duck. Cole, Henry, illus. 2016. (J). (978-1-4814-8110-6(X), Simon Spotlight) Simon Spotlight.
—Bizcocho Encuentra un Amigo, 1 vol. Pasternac, Susana, tr. Schories, Pat, illus. 2008. (My First I Can Read Ser.).Tr. of Biscuit Finds a Friend. (SPA.). 32p. (J). (gr. -1 — 1). pap. 4.99 (978-0-06-143526-3(0)) HarperCollins Pubs.
—Katy Duck. Cole, Henry, illus. 2007. (Katy Duck Ser.). (ENG.). 16p. (J). (gr. -1-k). bds. 7.99 (978-1-4169-1901-8(5), Little Simon) Little Simon.
—Katy Duck & the Tip-Top Tap Shoes. Cole, Henry, illus. 2013. (Katy Duck Ser.). (ENG.). 24p. (J). (gr. -1-1). 16.99 (978-1-4424-5246-6(3)); pap. 3.99 (978-1-4424-5245-9(5)) Simon Spotlight. (Simon Spotlight).
—Katy Duck, Big Sister. Cole, Henry, illus. 2007. (ENG.). 14p. (J). (gr. -1-k). bds. 7.99 (978-1-4169-4209-2(2), Little Simon) Little Simon.
—Katy Duck, Center Stage. Cole, Henry, illus. 2008. (Katy Duck Ser.). (ENG.). 16p. (J). (gr. -1-k). bds. 7.99 (978-1-4169-3338-0(7), Little Simon) Little Simon.
—Katy Duck, Dance Star. Cole, Henry, illus. 2008. (Katy Duck Ser.). (ENG.). 16p. (J). (gr. -1-k). bds. 7.99 (978-1-4169-3337-3(9), Little Simon) Little Simon.
—Katy Duck, Dance Star/Katy Duck, Center Stage. Cole, Henry, illus. 2009. (Katy Duck Ser.). (ENG.). 24p. (J). (gr. -1-k). pap. 3.99 (978-1-4169-8279-1(5), Little Simon) Little Simon.
—Katy Duck, Flower Girl. Cole, Henry, illus. 2013. (Katy Duck Ser.). (ENG.). 24p. (J). (gr. -1-1). 16.99 (978-1-4424-7279-2(0)); pap. 3.99 (978-1-4424-7278-5(2)) Simon Spotlight. (Simon Spotlight).
—Katy Duck Goes to Work. Cole, Henry, illus. 2014. (Katy Duck Ser.). (ENG.). 24p. (J). (gr. -1-1). pap. 3.99 (978-1-4424-7281-5(2), Simon Spotlight) Simon Spotlight.
—Katy Duck Goes to Work. 2014. (Simon & Schuster Ready-To-Read Level 1 Ser.). lib. bdg. 13.55 (978-0-606-35455-4(7)) Turtleback Bks.
—Katy Duck Makes a Friend. Cole, Henry, illus. 2012. (Katy Duck Ser.). (ENG.). 24p. (J). (gr. -1-1). 16.99 (978-1-4424-1977-3(6)); pap. 3.99 (978-1-4424-1976-6(8)) Simon Spotlight. (Simon Spotlight).
—Katy Duck Meets the Babysitter. Cole, Henry, illus. 2012. (Katy Duck Ser.). (ENG.). 24p. (J). (gr. -1-1). 15.99 (978-1-4424-5242-8(0)); pap. 3.99 (978-1-4424-5241-1(2)) Simon Spotlight. (Simon Spotlight).
—Katy Duck Ready-To-Read Value Pack: Starring Katy Duck; Katy Duck Makes a Friend; Katy Duck Meets the Babysitter; Katy Duck & the Tip-Tip Tap Shoes; Katy Duck, Flower Girl; Katy Duck Goes to Work. Cole, Henry, illus. 2014. (Katy Duck Ser.). (ENG.). 144p. (J). (gr. -1-1). pap. 15.96 (978-1-4814-2600-8(1), Simon Spotlight) Simon Spotlight.
—Katy Duck's Happy Halloween. Cole, Henry, illus. 2014. (Katy Duck Ser.). (ENG.). 24p. (J). (gr. -1-1). pap. 3.99 (978-1-4424-9806-8(4), Simon Spotlight) Simon Spotlight.
—Starring Katy Duck. Cole, Henry, illus. 2011. (Katy Duck Ser.). (ENG.). 24p. (J). (gr. -1-1). pap. 3.99 (978-1-4424-1974-2(1)); lib. bdg. 15.99 (978-1-4424-1975-9(X)) Simon Spotlight. (Simon Spotlight).
Capucilli, Alyssa Satin & Cole, Henry. Katy Duck Is a Caterpillar. 2009. (Katy Duck Ser.). (ENG., Illus.). 32p. (J). (gr. -1-k). 14.99 (978-1-4169-6061-4(9), Little Simon) Little Simon.
Carle, Eric. 10 Little Rubber Ducks. Carle, Eric, illus. 2005. (ENG., Illus.). 36p. (J). (gr. -1-1). 21.99 (978-0-06-074075-7(2)) HarperCollins Pubs.
—10 Little Rubber Ducks Board Book. Carle, Eric, illus. 2010. (ENG., Illus.). 34p. (J). (gr. -1-k). bds. 7.99 (978-0-06-196428-2(X), HarperFestival) HarperCollins Pubs.
Carpenter, Chad. Morry Moose's Time-Traveling Outhouse Adventure. 2013. (ENG.). 48p. (J). pap. 12.95 (978-1-62343-163-1(8)) Willow Creek Pr., Inc.
Carter, Maureen, illus. The Tale of Jemima Puddle-Duck: A Story about Trust. 2006. (J). 6.99 (978-1-59939-000-0(0)) Cornerstone Pr.
Carter, Tammy. My Friend, Dinner. 2013. 28p. pap. 24.95 (978-1-4241-0629-5(X)) America Star Bks.
Cartwright, Stephen, illus. Find the Duck. 2007. (Find-its Board Bks). 12p. (J). (gr. -1-k). bds. 6.99 (978-0-7945-1804-2(4), Usborne) EDC Publishing.
Castellucci, Cecil. Odd Duck. Varon, Sara, illus. 2013. (ENG.). 96p. (J). (gr. 1-5). 15.99 (978-1-59643-557-5(7), 9781596435575, First Second Bks.) Roaring Brook Pr.
Cater, Angela. A Perfect Nest for Mrs Mallard. Cater, Angela, illus. 2009. (Illus.). 32p. pap. (978-0-9555725-2-4(5)) Tabby Cat Pr.
Catherine, Rose. Fido the Duck: A Short Tale. 2006. (J). 9.43 (978-0-9786276-5-2(2)) Mentzer Printing Ink.
Cecil, Randy. Duck. Cecil, Randy, illus. 2008. (ENG., Illus.). 40p. (J). (gr. -1-2). 15.99 (978-0-7636-3072-0(1)) Candlewick Pr.
Cerimele, Ron. Hee, Haw, & a Donkey Named Sam. 2007. (ENG.). 20p. per. 24.95 (978-1-4241-9013-3(4)) America Star Bks.
Chaconas, Dori. The Collectors, 4 vols. McCue, Lisa, illus. 2010. (Cork & Fuzz Ser.: 4). (ENG.). 32p. (J). (gr. 1-3). mass mkt. 3.99 (978-0-14-241714-0(9), Penguin Young Readers) Penguin Young Readers Group.
—Cork & Fuzz - The Collectors. McCue, Lisa, illus. 2008. (Cork & Fuzz Ser.: 4). (ENG.). 32p. (J). (gr. k-3). 13.99 (978-0-670-06286-7(3), Viking Books for Young Readers) Penguin Young Readers Group.
Chambers, Sally, et al. Waldo'n Ennill y Dydd. 2005. (WEL., Illus.). 32p. pap. (978-1-85596-658-1(1)) Dref Wen.
Choi, JeongIm. Who's Coming Tonight? Gang, MinJeong, illus. rev. ed. 2014. (MySELF Bookshelf Ser.). (ENG.). 32p. (J). (gr. k-2). lib. bdg. 25.27 (978-1-59953-653-8(6)) Norwood Hse. Pr.
Church, Caroline Jayne. Ruff! And the Wonderfully Amazing Busy Day. Church, Caroline Jayne, illus. 2013. (ENG., Illus.). 32p. (J). (gr. k-3). 17.99 (978-0-06-201498-6(6)) HarperCollins Pubs.
Churchill, Jill. Five Little Ducks. Yaccarino, Dan, illus. 2005. 26p. (J). (gr. -1 — 1). bds. 5.99 (978-0-06-073465-7(5), HarperFestival) HarperCollins Pubs.
Claflin, Willy. The Uglified Ducky. Stimson, James, illus. 2011. (ENG.). 32p. (J). (gr. -1-3). pap. 9.95 (978-0-87483-953-1(X)) August Hse. Pubs., Inc.
Clarke, Jane. The Amazing Adventures of Batbird. Schon, Nick, illus. 2005. (Collins Big Cat Ser.). (ENG.). 32p. (J). (gr. 2-3). pap. 7.99 (978-0-00-718637-2(1)) HarperCollins Pubs. Ltd. GBR. Dist: Independent Pubs. Group.
Cloke, Rene, illus. The Ugly Duckling. 2012. (ENG.). 24p. (J). pap. 6.50 (978-1-84135-543-6(7)) Award Pubns. Ltd. GBR. Dist: Parkwest Pubns., Inc.
Cole, Stacey. Fluffy's Very Special Christmas. 2010. (Illus.). 32p. (J). pap. 26.95 (978-1-4327-4569-1(7)) Outskirts Pr., Inc.
Conlon, Mara, adapted by. Bill Hatches an Egg. 2005. (Sitting Ducks Ser.). (J). (978-0-8431-1343-3(X), Price Stern Sloan) Penguin Publishing Group.
Conrad, Liz, illus. Little Duck. 2009. (My Sparkling Springtime Friends Ser.). (ENG.). 10p. (J). bds. 3.95 (978-1-58117-867-8(0), Intervisual/Piggy Toes) Bendon, Inc.
Cooper, Helen S. Delicious! Cooper, Helen S., illus. 2007. (ENG., Illus.). 32p. (J). (gr. -1-3). 16.99 (978-0-374-31756-0(9), 9780374317560, Farrar, Straus & Giroux (BYR)) Farrar, Straus & Giroux.
—Pumpkin Soup, Set. unabr. ed. 2009. (ENG., Illus.). 32p. (J). (gr. -1-3). 9.99 (978-1-4272-0740-1(2), 9781427207401) Macmillan Audio.
Copp, Raymond. Carolyn Quimby. Manning, Mary, illus. 2013. 110p. pap. 30.95 (978-1-4575-2364-9(7)) Dog Ear Publishing, LLC.
Cordone Warner, Debra. A Busy Day for Baby Duck & Little Boy Blue. 2010. 34p. pap. 19.99 (978-0-557-59587-7(8)) Lulu Pr., Inc.
Cowley, Joy. Miss Doll & Friends: Yellow Duck. Bordicchia, Gaia, illus. 2014. (ENG.). 8p. pap. (978-0-927244-62-6(4), Joy Cowley Club) Flying Start Bks.
—Mrs. Wishy-Washy's Farm. Fuller, Elizabeth, illus. (ENG.). 32p. (J). (gr. -1-k). 2006. 5.99 (978-0-14-240299-3(0), Puffin Books) 2003. 16.99 (978-0-399-23872-7(7), Philomel Bks.) Penguin Young Readers Group.
Cox, Phil Roxbee & Cartwright, S. Ted in a Red Bed. 2004. (Phonics Board Bks.). 10p. (J). 4.95 (978-0-7945-0061-0(7), Usborne) EDC Publishing.
—Toad Makes a Road. 2004. (Phonics Board Bks.). (ENG.). 1p. (J). bds. 4.99 (978-0-7945-0062-7(5), Usborne) EDC Publishing.
Craig, Deborah Anne. Paddle, the Extraordinary Duck. Glueck, Michael Wells, ed. Karcz, Katherine, illus. 2011. 42p. pap. 19.95 (978-1-4583-6916-1(1)) Lulu Pr., Inc.
Crane, Venessa. Duck down Under. 2008. 70p. pap. 29.95 (978-1-4092-2376-4(0)) Lulu Pr., Inc.
Cronin, Doreen. Click, Clack, Ho! Ho! Ho! Lewin, Betsy, illus. 2015. (Click, Clack Book Ser.). (ENG.). 40p. (J). (gr. -1-2). 17.99 (978-1-4424-9673-6(8)) Simon & Schuster Children's Publishing.
—Click, Clack, Peep! Lewin, Betsy, illus. 2015. (Click, Clack Book Ser.). (ENG.). 40p. (J). (gr. -1-3). 17.99 (978-1-4814-2411-0(4)) Simon & Schuster Children's Publishing.
—Click, Clack, Surprise! Lewin, Betsy, illus. 2016. (Click, Clack Book Ser.). (ENG.). 40p. (J). (gr. -1-3). 17.99 (978-1-4814-7031-5(0), Atheneum/Caitlyn Dlouhy Books) Simon & Schuster Children's Publishing.
—Duck for President. Lewin, Betsy, illus. 2004. (Click, Clack Book Ser.). (ENG.). 32p. (J). (gr. -1-3). 17.99 (978-0-689-86377-6(2), Atheneum Bks. for Young Readers) Simon & Schuster Children's Publishing.
—Duck for President. Lewin, Betsy, illus. 2006. (Doreen Cronin: Click-Clack & More Ser.). (ENG.). 32p. (gr. -1-3). lib. bdg. 24.21 (978-1-59961-091-7(4)) Spotlight.
—Giggle, Giggle, Quack. Lewin, Betsy, illus. 2011. (Click, Clack Book Ser.). (ENG.). 34p. (J). (gr. -1-k). bds. 7.99 (978-1-4424-0891-3(X), Little Simon) Little Simon.
—Giggle, Giggle, Quack. Lewin, Betsy, illus. 2006. (Doreen Cronin: Click-Clack & More Ser.). (ENG.). 32p. (gr. -1-3). lib. bdg. 24.21 (978-1-59961-092-4(2)) Spotlight.
—Jaja Jiji, Cuac. Jimenez, Alberto, tr. from ENG. Lewin, Betsy, illus. 2003.Tr. of Giggle, Giggle, Quack. (SPA.). (J). 15.00 (978-1-930332-46-1(7)) Lectorum Pubns., Inc.
—Pato para Presidente. Lewin, Betsy, illus. 2008.Tr. of Duck for President. (SPA.). (J). (gr. k-2). pap. 7.99 (978-1-930332-74-4(2), LC32509) Lectorum Pubns., Inc.
—Thump, Quack, Moo: A Whacky Adventure. Lewin, Betsy, illus. 2008. (Click, Clack Book Ser.). (ENG.). 42p. (J). (gr. -1-2). 16.99 (978-1-4169-1630-7(X), Atheneum Bks. for Young Readers) Simon & Schuster Children's Publishing.
Cronin, Doreen & Jiménez Rioja, Alberto. Pum, Cuac, Muu: Una Loca Aventura. Lewin, Betsy, illus. 2008. (SPA.). (J). pap. 5.99 (978-1-933032-54-2(5)); 36p. 16.99 (978-1-933032-53-5(7)) Lectorum Pubns., Inc.
Crown Peak Publishing. Just Be You. Crown Peak Publishing, illus. 2008. (ENG., Illus.). 40p. (J). 19.95 (978-0-9645663-5-4(4)) Crown Peak Publishing.
Cuentecitos- El Patito Feo. 2003. (SPA.). 1.75 (978-970-607-787-5(1)) Larousse, Ediciones, S. A. de C. V. MEX. Dist: Giron Bks.
Cuthand, Beth. The Little Duck Sikihpsis. Cuthand, Stan, tr. Longman, Mary, illus. ed. 2013. (ENG.). 34p. 18.00 (978-1-894778-10-7(3)) Theytus Bks., Ltd. CAN. Dist: Univ. of Toronto Pr.
—Sikihpsis. Cuthand, Stan, tr. Longman, Mary, illus. ed. 2007. (Little Duck Ser.). (CRE & ENG.). 28p. 17.00 (978-1-894778-44-2(8)) Theytus Bks., Ltd. CAN. Dist: Univ. of Toronto Pr.
Dahl, Michael. Duck Goes Potty, 1 vol. Vidal, Oriol, illus. 2010. (Hello Genius Ser.). (ENG.). 20p. (gr. 1-2). bds. 7.99 (978-1-4048-5726-1(5)) Picture Window Bks.
—No More Pacifier, Duck. Vidal, Oriol, illus. 2015. (Hello Genius Ser.). (ENG.). 20p. (gr. 1-2). bds. 7.99 (978-1-4795-5793-6(5)) Picture Window Bks.
Dale, Jenny. Blossom & Beany. Hellard, Susan, illus. 2004. 60p. (J). (978-0-439-66991-7(X)) Scholastic, Inc.
Daley-Prado, M. J. Baby Duck Gets A New Grandma. 2008. 40p. pap. 17.95 (978-1-4357-1312-3(5)) Lulu Pr., Inc.
Dalmatian Press Staff. Fuzzy Ducky's Birthday! 2008. (ENG.). 5p. bds. 4.95 (978-1-58117-725-1(9), Intervisual/Piggy Toes) Bendon, Inc.
Danny the Duck. 2003. (Chunky Animal Shaped Boards Ser.). (J). 10p. bds. 9.95 (978-0-7525-7853-8(7)); (Illus.). bds. 1.98 (978-0-7525-7774-6(3)) Parragon, Inc.
Das, Christina. Coo Coo Duckling. l.t. ed. 2005. (Illus.). 32p. (J). 15.95 (978-0-9763082-4-9(X), A JuneOne Production) JuneOne Publishing Hub.
Davies, Caroline, illus. Duck. 2013. (Shake & Play Bath Bks.). (ENG.). 8p. (J). (gr. -1 — 1). 5.99 (978-1-4380-7339-2(9)) Barron's Educational Series, Inc.

Davies, Nicola. Just Ducks! Rubbino, Salvatore, illus. 2012. (ENG.). 32p. (J). (gr. k-4). 15.99 (978-0-7636-5936-3(3)) Candlewick Pr.

Davis, Melissa. Denny the Duck. 2008. 25p. pap. 24.95 (978-1-60672-712-6(5)) America Star Bks.

Day, Alexandra. Carl & the Baby Duck. 2011. (My Readers Ser.). (ENG., Illus.). 32p. (J). (gr. -1-1). pap. 4.99 (978-0-312-62485-9(9), 9780312624859) Square Fish.

Dean, James. Pete the Cat: Five Little Ducks. Dean, James, illus. 2017. (Pete the Cat Ser.). (Illus.). 32p. (J). (gr. -1-3). 9.99 (978-0-06-240448-0(2)) HarperCollins Pubs.

Delaronde, Deborah L. Duck's Bay. Dawson, Sheldon, illus. 2004. 48p. (J). pap. (978-1-894717-24-3(4), Spotlight Poets) Pemmican Pubns., Inc.

Dexter Rescues Matt the Duckling. 2004. (J). per. 15.99 (978-0-9753533-3-2(0)) Golden Eagle Publishing Hse., Inc.

Disney Book Group & Ritchey, Kate. Mickey & Friends Huey, Dewey, & Louie's Rainy Day. Loter, Inc. Staff, illus. 2014. (World of Reading Ser.). (ENG.). 32p. (J). (gr. 1-3). pap. 3.99 (978-1-4231-6965-9(4)) Disney Pr.

Disney Book Group Staff & Driscoll, Laura. Thumper & the Noisy Ducky. Disney Storybook Art Team, illus. 2014. (ENG.). 12p. (J). (gr. -1 — 1). bds. 6.99 (978-1-4231-8487-4(4)) Disney Pr.

Dodd, Lynley. Zachary Quack Minimonster. Dodd, Lynley, illus. 2006. (Gold Star First Readers Ser.). (Illus.). 32p. (gr. -1-3). lib. bdg. 23.00 (978-0-8368-6187-7(6), Gareth Stevens Learning Library) Stevens, Gareth Publishing LLLP.

Dodge, Jim. Fup. 2011. pap. 9.95 (978-1-59714-158-1(5)) Heyday.

Dolan, Penny. The Lovely Duckling. 2014. (ENG., Illus.). 32p. (J). (978-0-7787-0445-4(9)); pap. (978-0-7787-0480-5(7)) Crabtree Publishing Co.

Dormer, Frank W. Firefighter Duckies! Dormer, Frank W., illus. 2017. (ENG., Illus.). 40p. (J). (gr. -1-3). 17.99 (978-1-4814-6090-3(0), Atheneum Bks. for Young Readers) Simon & Schuster Children's Publishing.

Douglas, Ryke Leigh. Sam's Surprise. 2008. 28p. per. 12.95 (978-1-4327-0850-4(3)) Outskirts Pr., Inc.

Dreisbach, Kristin Wolf. Winston the Duck & His Big Orange Bill. Dreisbach, Kristin Wolf & Foreman, Austin Lee, illus. 2013. 20p. pap. 13.97 (978-1-62212-897-6(4), Strategic Bk. Publishing) Strategic Book Publishing & Rights Agency (SBPRA).

The Duck: Duck Learns to Make Friends. 2004. (J). per. 17.00 (978-0-9758861-0-6(X)) Zest Publishing.

Duck on a Bike. 2017. 59.95 **(978-1-338-18702-1(3))** Scholastic, Inc.

Dunn, Judy. The Little Duck. Dunn, Phoebe, photos by. 2014. (ENG., Illus.). 14p. (J). (— 1). bds. 6.99 (978-0-385-38521-3(8), Random Hse. Bks. for Young Readers) Random Hse. Children's Bks.

Dunn, Phoebe, illus. & photos by. The Little Duck. Dunn, Phoebe, photos by. Dunn, Judy, photos by. 2017. (Step into Reading Ser.). (ENG.). 32p. (J). (gr. -1-1). pap. 3.99 (978-0-553-53352-1(5), Random Hse. Bks. for Young Readers) Random Hse. Children's Bks.

Dussling, Jennifer. Picky Peggy. Adams, Lynn, tr. Adams, Lynn, illus. 2004. (Science Solves It! Ser.). 32p. (J). pap. 5.95 (978-1-57565-138-5(6)) Kane Press, Inc.

Eaton, Maxwell, III. Two Dumb Ducks. 2010. (ENG.). 32p. (J). (gr. -1-2). 12.99 (978-0-375-84576-5(3), Knopf Bks. for Young Readers) Random Hse. Children's Bks.

Edwards, Hazel, et al. Duckstar / Cyberfarm. l.t. ed. 2012. 156p. pap. (978-1-4596-3429-9(2)) ReadHowYouWant.com, Ltd.

—Operatic Duck / Duck on Tour. l.t. ed. 2012. 123p. pap. (978-1-4596-3430-5(6)) ReadHowYouWant.com, Ltd.

Egan, Tim. Dodsworth in London. Egan, Tim, illus. (Dodsworth Book Ser.). (ENG., Illus.). 48p. (J). 2010. (gr. 2-5). pap. 3.99 (978-0-547-41440-9(4)) 11th ed. 2009. (gr. 1-4). 15.00 (978-0-547-13816-9(4)) Houghton Mifflin Harcourt Publishing Co.

—Dodsworth in New York. 2009. (Dodsworth Book Ser.). (ENG., Illus.). 48p. (J). (gr. 2-5). pap. 3.99 (978-0-547-24831-8(8)) Houghton Mifflin Harcourt Publishing Co.

—Dodsworth in Paris. Egan, Tim, illus. 2010. (Dodsworth Book Ser.). (ENG., Illus.). 48p. (J). (gr. 1-4). pap. 3.99 (978-0-547-33192-8(4)) Houghton Mifflin Harcourt Publishing Co.

—Dodsworth in Tokyo. Egan, Tim, illus. 2014. (Green Light Readers Level 3 Ser.). (ENG., Illus.). 48p. (J). (gr. 1-4). pap. 3.99 (978-0-544-33915-6(0), HMH Books For Young Readers) Houghton Mifflin Harcourt Publishing Co.

Elizabeth, Shelby. Dabby's Pond. 2006. (Neighborhood Readers Ser.). (ENG.). 16p. (gr. 1-3). pap. 6.50 (978-1-4042-7148-7(1), Rosen Classroom) Rosen Publishing Group, Inc., The.

Ellens, Brenda L. The Duckling Pond. 2008. 32p. pap. 16.49 (978-1-4343-9566-5(9)) AuthorHouse.

Elsdale, Bob & PQ Blackwell, Ltd. Staff. Mom: I'm a Lucky Duck! 2008. (ENG., Illus.). 84p. 9.99 (978-0-7407-7279-5(1)) Andrews McMeel Publishing.

Ericson, Nora. Dill & Bizzy: An Odd Duck & a Strange Bird. Ericson, Lisa, illus. 2016. 40p. (J). (gr. -1-3). 17.99 (978-0-06-230452-0(6)) HarperCollins Pubs.

—Dill & Bizzy: Opposite Day. Ericson, Lisa, illus. 2017. 40p. (J). (gr. -1-3). 17.99 (978-0-06-230453-7(4)) HarperCollins Pubs.

Ering, Timothy Basil. The Unexpected Love Story of Alfred Fiddleduckling. Ering, Timothy Basil, illus. 2017. (ENG., Illus.). 48p. (J). (-k). 15.99 (978-0-7636-6432-9(4)) Candlewick Pr.

Erlbruch, Wolf. Duck, Death & the Tulip. Erlbruch, Wolf, illus. 2011. (ENG., Illus.). 38p. (J). 17.95 (978-1-877579-02-8(5)) Gecko Pr. NZL. Dist: Lerner Publishing Group.

Erlbruch, Wolf & Chidgey, Catherine. Duck, Death & the Tulip. Erlbruch, Wolf, illus. 2016. (ENG., Illus.). 38p. (gr. 4-12). 16.99 (978-1-877467-14-1(6)) Gecko Pr. NZL. Dist: Lerner Publishing Group.

Escoffier, Michaël. Me First! Di Giacomo, Kris, illus. 2013. (ENG.). 24p. (J). 14.00 (978-1-59270-136-0(1)) Enchanted Lion Bks., LLC.

Evensen, Rachelle. Finn's Marching Band: A Story of Counting, Colors, & Playing Together. 2009. 32p. (J). 14.95 (978-0-8091-6749-4(2), Ambassador Bks.) Paulist Pr.

Falconer, Ian, et al. Olivia & Her Great Adventures. Osterhold, Jared & Johnson, Shane L., illus. 2012. (J). (978-1-4351-4316-6(7), Simon Spotlight) Simon Spotlight.

Fares, Laura. Glow: The Duck with the Golden Ring. 2011. 28p. pap. 15.99 (978-1-4634-2017-8(X)) AuthorHouse.

Fazenbaker, Jo Ann. Daisy & Duke, 1 vol. 2010. 18p. 24.95 (978-1-4512-1483-3(9)) PublishAmerica, Inc.

Fierstein, Harvey. The Sissy Duckling. Cole, Henry, illus. 2014. (ENG.). 40p. (J). (gr. -1-3). pap. 9.99 (978-1-4424-9817-4(X), Little Simon) Little Simon.

—The Sissy Duckling. Cole, Henry, illus. 2005. (ENG.). 40p. (J). (gr. k-3). reprint ed. 8.99 (978-1-4169-0313-0(5), Simon & Schuster Bks. For Young Readers) Simon & Schuster Bks. For Young Readers.

Filipek, Nina & Andersen, Hans Christian. The Ugly Duckling. O'Toole, Jeanette, illus. 2009. (Fairy Tale Firsts Ser.). 12p. (J). (gr. -1-k). bds. 11.40 (978-1-60754-692-4(2)) Windmill Bks.

Filoche, Eric. Hey ! We're Talking about Ourselves ! 2013. 68p. pap. (978-2-9538737-4-0(0)) Koshkindom.

Finn, Rebecca, illus. Little Ducky. (Cuddly Cuffstm Ser.). 6p. (J). 6.95 (978-1-58925-766-5(9)) Tiger Tales.

Fisk, Cindy. Melvin Pickles. Fisk, David, illus. 2013. 26p. pap. 11.95 (978-1-938743-03-0(2)) Reimann Bks.

Fitzpatrick, Heather. Chuck: The Chicken That Thought He Was a Duck. 2012. 24p. pap. 17.99 (978-1-4772-6012-8(9)) AuthorHouse.

Fleming, Denise, illus. 5 Little Ducks. 2016. (ENG.). 40p. (J). (gr. -1-3). 17.99 (978-1-4814-2422-6(X), Beach Lane Bks.) Beach Lane Bks.

Ford, Bernette. No More Blanket for Lambkin! Williams, Sam, illus. 2010. (Ducky & Piggy Ser.). (ENG.). 26p. (J). (gr. k — 1). bds. 6.95 (978-1-906250-47-8(2)) Boxer Bks., Ltd. GBR. Dist: Sterling Publishing Co., Inc.

—No More Diapers for Ducky! Williams, Sam, illus. 2007. (Ducky & Piggy Ser.). (ENG.). 26p. (J). (gr. -1 — 1). bds. 7.95 (978-1-905417-38-4(1)) Boxer Bks., Ltd. GBR. Dist: Sterling Publishing Co., Inc.

Foreman, Michael. Tufty. Foreman, Michael, illus. 2016. (ENG., Illus.). 32p. (gr. -1-3). (J). 17.99 (978-1-5124-0425-8(X)); 35.99 (978-1-5124-0448-7(9)) Lerner Publishing Group.

Frank Alvarado Madrigal, Alvarado Madrig & Frank Alvarado Madrigal. Las Increíbles Aventuras Del Patito Kuak Kuak: The Incredible Adventures of Kuack Kuack, the Little Duck. 2010. 32p. pap. (978-1-4269-2540-5(9)) Trafford Publishing (UK) Ltd.

Frankenhuyzen, Robbyn Smith van. I Love You Just Enough. Frankenhuyzen, Gijsbert van, illus. 2014. (Hazel Ridge Farm Stories Ser.). (ENG.). 36p. (J). (gr. 1-4). 16.95 (978-1-58536-839-6(3), 203009) Sleeping Bear Pr.

Frati, Dorothy. Friendly Bubbles. 2012. 24p. pap. 17.99 (978-1-4772-6447-8(7)) AuthorHouse.

Freedman, Claire. A Cuddle for Little Duck. Pedler, Caroline, illus. 2009. (ENG.). 20p. (J). (gr. -1-k). bds. 8.99 (978-0-545-07797-2(4), Cartwheel Bks.) Scholastic, Inc.

—Silly Dilly Duckling. Chapman, Jane, illus. 2014. (ENG.). 22p. (J). (gr. -1-k). bds. 8.99 (978-1-58925-578-4(X)) Tiger Tales.

Freymann-Weyr, Garret. French Ducks in Venice. McGuire, Erin, illus. 2011. (ENG.). 56p. (J). (gr. k-4). 16.99 (978-0-7636-4173-3(1)) Candlewick Pr.

Furukawa, Masumi, illus. The Ugly Duckling. 2007. (Flip-Up Fairy Tales Ser.). (ENG.). 24p. (J). (gr. -1-2). audio compact disk (978-1-84643-095-4(X)) Child's Play International Ltd.

Galvin, Laura. Baby Duck Gets Lost. 2008. (Smithsonian Baby Animals Ser.). (ENG., Illus.). 16p. (gr. -1-k). 13.95 (978-1-59249-789-8(6)) Soundprints.

Galvin, Laura Gates. Baby Duck Gets Lost. 2007. (Baby Animals Ser.). (ENG., Illus.). 16p. (gr. -1-k). 6.95 (978-1-59249-747-8(0)) Soundprints.

Garis, Howard Roger. Lulu, Alice & Jammie Wibble Wobble. 2005. 152p. pap. 11.95 (978-1-4218-1564-0(8), 1st World Library - Literary Society) 1st World Publishing, Inc.

—Lulu, Alice & Jimmie Wibblewobble. 2005. 26.95 (978-1-4218-1464-3(1), 1st World Library - Literary Society) 1st World Publishing, Inc.

Gavin, Ciara. Bear Is Not Tired. 2016. (ENG., Illus.). 32p. (J). (gr. -1-2). 16.99 (978-0-385-75476-7(0), Knopf Bks. for Young Readers) Random Hse. Children's Bks.

—Bear Likes Jam. 2017. (ENG., Illus.). 32p. (J). (gr. -1-2). 16.99 (978-0-399-55179-6(4), Knopf Bks. for Young Readers) Random Hse. Children's Bks.

—Room for Bear. 2015. (ENG., Illus.). 32p. (J). (gr. -1-2). 16.99 (978-0-385-75473-6(6), Knopf Bks. for Young Readers) Random Hse. Children's Bks.

George, Jean Craighead. Goose & Duck. Lamont, Priscilla, illus. 2008. (I Can Read Level 2 Ser.). (ENG.). 48p. (J). (gr. k-3). 16.99 (978-0-06-117076-8(3)) HarperCollins Pubs.

George, Kallie. Duck, Duck, Dinosaur. Vidal, Oriol, illus. 2016. 40p. (J). (gr. -1-3). 17.99 (978-0-06-235308-5(X)) HarperCollins Pubs.

—Duck, Duck, Dinosaur: Bubble Blast. Vidal, Oriol, illus. 2017. (My First I Can Read Ser.). 32p. (J). (gr. -1-3). pap. 3.99 (978-0-06-235311-5(X)) HarperCollins Pubs.

George, Kallie. Duck, Duck, Dinosaur: Perfect Pumpkin. Vidal, Oriol, illus. 2017. (My First I Can Read Ser.). 32p. (J). (gr. -1-3). 16.99 **(978-0-06-235315-3(2))**; pap. 3.99 **(978-0-06-235314-6(4))** HarperCollins Pubs.

Gerstein, Mordicai. You Can't Have Too Many Friends! Gerstein, Mordicai, illus. 2014. (ENG., Illus.). 32p. (J). (gr. -1-2). 16.95 (978-0-8234-2393-4(X)) Holiday Hse., Inc.

Giacomoni, Carol A. I can ski despite these Ducky feet on Me. 2010. 24p. 14.95 (978-1-4269-3187-1(5)) Trafford Publishing.

Gibson, Betty & Denton, Kady MacDonald. Couac, la Petite Cane (Little Quack) (FRE., Illus.). (J). pap. 7.99 (978-0-590-73575-9(6)) Scholastic, Inc.

Ginsburg, Mirra. The Chick & the Duckling. Russian of V. Êsuteyev Publishing Staff, tr. Aruego, Jose & Dewey, Ariane, illus. 2010. (Rise & Shine Ser.). (ENG.). 32p. (C). (gr. -1-3). reprint ed. 11.95 (978-0-689-71226-5(X)) National Geographic School Publishing, Inc.

Gober, Thomas. Dandylion the Duck. Gillen, Rosemarie, illus. 2012. 26p. (J). 16.95 (978-1-60131-126-9(5), Castlebridge Bks.) Big Tent Bks.

Godby, Giovanna. Quaddles, Dwaddles, & Elizabeth: The Tale of a Very Confused Chicken. 2013. 40p. (J). (gr. -1-3). pap. 12.95 (978-0-9890975-0-5(1)) Caledonia Pr., LLC.

Goldstein, Sol. A Baby Crane's Tale. 2012. 40p. pap. 21.99 (978-1-4797-3928-8(6)) Xlibris Corp.

Goodspeed, Judy. Perky Turkey Finds a Friend. Taylor, Chet, illus. l.t. ed. 2006. 24p. (J). pap. 14.99 (978-0-9765786-6-6(2)) Dragonfly Publishing, Inc.

Grandreams Staff. Deborah the Dozy Duckling: A Squeaky Storybook. (Illus.). 16p. (J). bds. (978-0-7554-1170-2(6)) Grandreams Bks., Inc.

Graves, Susan Elaine. Lily the Lucky Ducky, 1 vol. 2010. 44p. 24.95 (978-1-4489-4433-0(3)) PublishAmerica, Inc.

Gravett, Emily. The Odd Egg. Gravett, Emily, illus. 2009. (ENG., Illus.). 32p. (J). (gr. -1-3). 16.99 (978-1-4169-6872-6(5), Simon & Schuster Bks. For Young Readers) Simon & Schuster Bks. For Young Readers.

Greenhalgh, Miranda. Rapid Duck. 2007. (Illus.). 38p. (J). per. 14.99 (978-1-59879-348-2(9), Lifevest) Lifevest Publishing, Inc.

Groethe, Kd. The Boy Who Would Walk on Air. 2012. 118p. (gr. -1). 23.99 (978-1-4772-9164-1(4)); pap. 14.95 (978-1-4772-9165-8(2)) AuthorHouse.

Gross, S. D. Freddie. 2007. (Illus.). 22p. (J). per. 12.99 (978-1-59879-342-0(X)) Lifevest Publishing, Inc.

Groves. Duck in the Box, Bk. 4A. Date not set. (Illus.). 16p. (J). pap. 129.15 (978-0-582-18795-5(8)) Addison-Wesley Longman, Ltd. GBR. Dist: Trans-Atlantic Pubns., Inc.

Hahn, Phil. Henrietta: The Homely Duckling. Coker, Paul, Jr., illus. 2004. (Weewisdom Bks.). 47p. (J). 16.95 (978-0-87159-293-4(2), 168, Unity Hse.) Unity Schl. of Christianity.

Haines, Genny, illus. Five Little Ducks. 2016. (ENG.). 10p. (J). (gr. -1 — 1). bds. 8.99 (978-1-4998-0217-7(X)) Little Bee Books Inc.

Hall, Kirsten. Duck, Duck, Goose! 2004. (My First Reader Ser.). (ENG., Illus.). 32p. (J). (gr. k-1). pap. 3.95 (978-0-516-24627-7(5), Children's Pr.) Scholastic Library Publishing.

Hall, Terri L. Denny & Denise: A Story of Two Ducks: Introducing Pretty Boy & Fella, 1 vol. Hall, Terri L. & Babeaux, Dennis, photos by. 2009. (Illus.). 42p. pap. 24.95 (978-1-60749-609-0(7)) America Star Bks.

Hamburg, Jennifer. Monkey & Duck Quack Up! Fotheringham, Edwin, illus. 2015. (ENG.). 32p. (J). (gr. -1-3). 17.99 (978-0-545-64514-0(X), Scholastic Pr.) Scholastic, Inc.

Hamm, Lisa. Buddy the Duck. 2010. 39p. pap. 8.50 (978-0-557-28251-7(9)) Lulu Pr., Inc.

Happy Quacky Lucky Duck. 2005. (J). per. 4.95 (978-0-9761763-1-2(9)) Banana Bunch Publishing.

Harnish, Jeannette. The Duck Who Drove a Boat. Harnish, Alexander, illus. 2008. 31p. pap. 24.95 (978-1-60610-665-5(1)) America Star Bks.

Harris, Polly. Peep Peep, You're a Duck, Not a People! 2nd ed. 2004. Orig. Title: Peep Peep. . You're a Duck! Not a Peeple! (Illus.). 43p. (J). 10.95 (978-0-9749375-0-2(9), 73032) Harris, Polly.

Hattaway, Carol. Dinky Duck's Adventure. Cotton, Sue Lynn, illus. 2012. 16p. pap. 12.95 (978-1-61493-128-7(3)) Peppertree Pr., The.

Hazelton, Jack W. Charlie Duck. Hazelton, Jack W., illus. l.t. ed. 2003. (Illus.). 24p. (J). 12.95 (978-1-928907-54-1(7)) Jack's Bookshelf, Inc.

Hello, Duck! (Early Intervention Levels Ser.). 21.30 (978-0-7362-2118-4(2)) CENGAGE Learning.

Henderson, Barbara. Down in Mr Brown's Garden. 2009. 40p. pap. 14.75 (978-1-60860-703-7(8), Strategic Bk. Publishing) Strategic Book Publishing & Rights Agency (SBPRA).

Hest, Amy. Guess Who, Baby Duck! Barton, Jill, illus. 2004. (ENG.). 32p. (J). (gr. k-k). 15.99 (978-0-7636-1981-7(7)) Candlewick Pr.

Hiebert, Elfrieda H. & Juel, Connie. The Lucky Duck. (Little Book Practice Reader). (J). (gr. k-6). 9.90 (978-0-8136-2012-1(0)) Modern Curriculum Pr.

Hillert, Margaret. The Funny Baby. Wendland, Paula, illus. 2016. (BeginningtoRead Ser.). (ENG.). 32p. (J). (gr. -1-2). pap. 11.94 (978-1-60357-907-0(9)) Norwood Hse. Pr.

Hills, Tad. Duck & Goose. Hills, Tad, illus. 2006. (Duck & Goose Ser.). (ENG., Illus.). 40p. (J). (gr. -1-2). 17.99 (978-0-375-83611-4(X), Schwartz & Wade Bks.) Random Hse. Children's Bks.

—Duck & Goose, 1, 2, 3. Hills, Tad, illus. 2008. (Duck & Goose Ser.). (ENG., Illus.). 22p. (J). (gr. k — 1). bds. 7.99 (978-0-375-85621-1(8), Schwartz & Wade Bks.) Random Hse. Children's Bks.

—Duck & Goose Go to the Beach. 2014. (Duck & Goose Ser.). (ENG., Illus.). 40p. (J). (gr. -1-2). 17.99 (978-0-385-37235-0(3), Schwartz & Wade Bks.) Random Hse. Children's Bks.

—Duck & Goose, Goose Needs a Hug. Hills, Tad, illus. 2012. (Duck & Goose Ser.). (ENG., Illus.). 22p. (J). (-k). bds. 6.99 (978-0-307-98293-3(9), Schwartz & Wade Bks.) Random Hse. Children's Bks.

—Duck & Goose, Here Comes the Easter Bunny! Hills, Tad, illus. 2012. (Duck & Goose Ser.). (ENG., Illus.). 22p. (J). (gr. k-k). bds. 7.99 (978-0-375-87280-8(9), Schwartz & Wade Bks.) Random Hse. Children's Bks.

—Duck & Goose, How Are You Feeling? Hills, Tad, illus. 2009. (Duck & Goose Ser.). (ENG., Illus.). 22p. (J). (gr. -1 — 1). bds. 7.99 (978-0-375-84629-8(8), Schwartz & Wade Bks.) Random Hse. Children's Bks.

—Duck, Duck, Goose. Hills, Tad, illus. 2007. (Duck & Goose Ser.). (ENG., Illus.). 40p. (J). (gr. -1-2). 17.99 (978-0-375-84068-5(0), Schwartz & Wade Bks.) Random Hse. Children's Bks.

—Find a Pumpkin. Hills, Tad, illus. 2009. (Duck & Goose Ser.). (ENG., Illus.). 22p. (J). (gr. k — 1). bds. 7.99 (978-0-375-85813-0(X), Schwartz & Wade Bks.) Random Hse. Children's Bks.

—It's Time for Christmas! Hills, Tad, illus. (Duck & Goose Ser.). (ENG., Illus.). 22p. (J). 2011. (gr. -1 — 1). bds. 10.99 (978-0-375-87112-2(8)) 2010. (gr. k — 1). bds. 7.99 (978-0-375-86484-1(9)) Random Hse. Children's Bks. (Schwartz & Wade Bks.).

Hills, Tad & Hills, Tad. Duck & Goose, Honk! Quack! Boo! 2017. (Duck & Goose Ser.). (ENG., Illus.). 40p. (J). (gr. -1-2). 16.99 **(978-1-5247-0175-8(0))**; lib. bdg. 19.99 **(978-1-5247-0176-5(9))** Random Hse. Children's Bks. (Schwartz & Wade Bks.).

Himmelman, John. Duck to the Rescue. Himmelman, John, illus. 2014. (Barnyard Rescue Ser.). (ENG., Illus.). 32p. (J). (gr. -1-3). 16.99 (978-0-8050-9485-5(7), 9780805094855, Holt, Henry & Co. Bks. For Young Readers) Holt, Henry & Co.

Hindley, Judy. Do Like a Duck Does! Bates, Ivan, illus. 2007. (ENG.). 40p. (J). (gr. -1-2). 4.99 (978-0-7636-3284-7(8)) Candlewick Pr.

—Do Like a Duck Does! Bates, Ivan, illus. 2007. (gr. -1-k). 15.00 (978-0-7569-8127-3(1)) Perfection Learning Corp.

—Do Like A Duck Does! 2007. 14.75 (978-1-4177-8331-1(1), Turtleback) Turtleback Bks.

Hinson, Paw Paw. Country Days: Duck Pond. 2010. 12p. 11.95 (978-1-4490-7030-4(2)) AuthorHouse.

Hiranandani, Veera. Olivia & Her Ducklings. 2010. (Olivia Ready-To-Read Level 1 Ser.). lib. bdg. 13.55 (978-0-606-10663-4(4), Turtleback) Turtleback Bks.

Hoercher, Donald F. The Duckie Walk. Zaharias, Terrilynn, illus. 2011. 28p. pap. 12.50 (978-1-60976-912-3(0), Eloquent Bks.) Strategic Book Publishing & Rights Agency (SBPRA).

Hopgood, Sally. Five Little Ducklings. Piwowarski, Marcin, illus. 2012. (Five Little Counting Bks.). (ENG.). 10p. (J). (gr. -1). 7.99 (978-1-84956-658-2(5)) Top That! Publishing PLC GBR. Dist: Independent Pubs. Group.

Horne, Jane, et al. Five Noisy Ducks: An Action-Packed Counting Book. 2014. (Illus.). (J). (978-1-4351-6034-7(7)) Barnes & Noble, Inc.

Horowitz, Dave. Duck Duck Moose. Horowitz, Dave, illus. 2009. (ENG., Illus.). 32p. (J). (gr. k-3). 16.99 (978-0-399-24782-8(3), G.P. Putnam's Sons Books for Young Readers) Penguin Young Readers Group.

Hudgins, Mary Jane. Quacker Jack the Duck, 1 vol. 2010. 20p. pap. 24.95 (978-1-4489-8188-5(3)) PublishAmerica, Inc.

Hudson, Katy. Bear & Duck. Hudson, Katy, illus. 2015. (ENG., Illus.). 32p. (J). (gr. -1-3). 17.99 (978-0-06-232051-3(3)) HarperCollins Pubs.

Hulst, W. G. van de & Hulst, Willem G. van de, illus. Herbie, the Runaway Duck. 2014. (J). (978-1-928136-19-4(2)) Inheritance Pubns.

I Can Hear S/s -Duck. 2005. (J). bds. (978-1-4194-0057-5(6)) Paradise Pr., Inc.

Ikids. Soft Shapes: Ducks: (Baby's First Book + Puzzle) 2011. (ENG., Illus.). 8p. (J). (gr. -1 — 1). 10.99 (978-1-60169-112-5(2)) Innovative Kids.

Irvin-Marston, Hope. My Little Book of Wood Ducks. Magdalena-Brown, Maria, illus. 2nd ed. 2004. 32p. (J). pap. 7.95 (978-0-89317-053-0(4), WW-0534, Windward Publishing) Finney Co., Inc.

Ives, Penny. Celestine, Drama Queen. 2009. (J). (978-0-545-08715-5(5)); pap. (978-0-545-08714-8(7)) Scholastic, Inc. (Levine, Arthur A. Bks.).

—5 Little Ducks W. 2007. (Classic Books with Holes 8x8 with CD Ser.). (ENG., Illus.). 16p. (J). audio compact disk (978-1-84643-137-1(9)) Child's Play International Ltd.

Ives, Penny, illus. Five Little Ducks. 2004. (Classic Books with Holes Giant Board Book Ser.). (ENG.). 16p. (J). bds. (978-0-85953-204-4(6)) Child's Play International Ltd.

Jackson, G. A. Twelve Yellow Ducks. 2011. 28p. (gr. -1 — 1). pap. 13.59 (978-1-4567-4268-3(X)) AuthorHouse.

Jacobs, Leslie. The Adventure of the Tall giraffe & the Short Duck. 2009. (J). 14.99 (978-1-61584-646-7(8)) Independent Pub.

James, Simon. Little One Step. James, Simon, illus. (ENG., Illus.). (J). (-k). 2016. 32p. 7.99 (978-0-7636-8176-0(8)) 2007. 24p. bds. 6.99 (978-0-7636-3520-6(0)) Candlewick Pr.

Jennings, Sharon, et al, adapted by. Franklin & the Duckling. 2007. (Kids Can Read Ser.). (ENG., Illus.). 32p. (J). (gr. 1-2). 14.95 (978-1-55337-888-4(1)) Kids Can Pr., Ltd. CAN. Dist: Hachette Bk. Group.

Johansen, Hanna & Barrett, John S. The Duck & the Owl. Bhend, Käthi, illus. 2005. (ENG.). 72p. (J). 17.95 (978-1-56792-285-1(6)) Godine, David R. Pub.

John, Jory. Goodnight Already! Davies, Benji, illus. 2014. (ENG.). 32p. (J). (gr. -1-3). 17.99 (978-0-06-228620-8(X)) HarperCollins Pubs.

—I Love You Already! Davies, Benji, illus. 2015. 32p. (J). (gr. -1-3). 17.99 (978-0-06-237095-2(2)) HarperCollins Pubs.

John Philip Duck. 2004. (J). 27.95 incl. audio (978-0-8045-6932-3(0)); 29.95 incl. audio compact disk (978-0-8045-4127-5(2)) Spoken Arts, Inc.

Johnson, Gerald J. J. Officer Buck MacDuck. Miltenberger, Dave & Jeri, illus. 2013. 24p. pap. 24.95 (978-1-62709-429-0(6)) America Star Bks.

Johnson, Shane L., illus. Olivia & Her Ducklings. 2010. (Olivia TV Tie-In Ser.). (ENG.). 24p. (J). (gr. -1-1). 16.99 (978-1-4424-1382-5(4), Simon Spotlight) Simon Spotlight.

Jones, Bedo. The Adventures of Rodeo Duck. 2008. 37p. pap. 24.95 (978-1-60610-554-2(X)) America Star Bks.

Jones, Cloteal Mae. The Five Little Ducks Went to the Forest. 2012. 24p. (-18). pap. 15.99 (978-1-4797-0274-9(9)) Xlibris Corp.

—The Five Little Ducks Went to the Forest: The Work Book. 2012. 44p. (-18). pap. 21.99 (978-1-4797-1000-3(8)) Xlibris Corp.

Jones, Noah Z. Little Red Quacking Hood. 2014. (Princess Pink & the Land of Fake-Believe Ser.: 2). (ENG.). 80p. (J). (gr. k-2). 15.99 (978-0-545-63842-5(9)) Scholastic, Inc.

—Little Red Quacking Hood. Jones, Noah Z., illus. 2014. (Princess Pink & the Land of Fake-Believe Ser.: 2). (ENG., Illus.). 80p. (J). (gr. k-2). pap. 4.99 (978-0-545-63841-8(0)) Scholastic, Inc.

—Little Red Quacking Hood. 2014. (Princess Pink & the Land of Fake-Believe Ser.: 2). lib. bdg. 14.75 (978-0-606-36048-7(4)) Turtleback Bks.

Joyce, William. Bently & Egg. Joyce, William, illus. 2017. (World of William Joyce Ser.). (ENG., Illus.). 32p. (J). (gr. -1-3). 17.99 (978-1-4814-8949-2(6), Atheneum/Caitlyn Dlouhy Books) Simon & Schuster Children's Publishing.

Kaldor, Connie. A Duck in New York City. Fil and Julie Staff, illus. 2005. (ENG.). 36p. (J). (gr. -1-2). 16.95 (978-2-923163-02-4(8)) La Montagne Secrete CAN. Dist: Independent Pubs. Group.

Kanninen, Barbara. A Story with Pictures. Reed, Lynn Rowe, illus. 2007. (ENG.). 32p. (J). (gr. -1-3). 16.95 (978-0-8234-2049-0(3)) Holiday Hse., Inc.

Katy Duck & the Secret Valentine. 2014. (Katy Duck Ser.). (ENG., Illus.). 24p. (J). (gr. -1-1). pap. 3.99 (978-1-4424-9809-9(9), Simon Spotlight) Simon Spotlight.

Kauzlarich, Jane. Quack: A Two Jane Creation. 2009. 20p. pap. 12.49 (978-1-4389-6599-4(0)) AuthorHouse.

Kayaalp, Suzan. The Adventures of Lucky the Duck. 2010. 90p. pap. 9.95 (978-1-60693-716-7(2), Eloquent Bks.) Strategic Book Publishing & Rights Agency (SBPRA).

Keith, Patty J. Hank the Honking Goose Learns to Listen. Wright, Brent A., illus. Keith, Patty J., photos by. 2013. 36p. pap. 12.95 (978-0-9893303-1-2(1)) Patty's Blooming Words.

—I Wish I Was a Mallard but God Made Me a Pekin Instead. Keith, Patty J., photos by. 2013. (Illus.). 32p. pap. 12.95 (978-0-9893303-0-5(3)) Patty's Blooming Words.

—Will You Be My Friend? Even If I Am Different from You. Keith, Patty J., photos by. 2013. (Illus.). 36p. pap. 12.95 (978-0-615-78050-4(4)) Patty's Blooming Words.

Kennedy. Dabbling Doezee. 2014. (ENG., Illus.). (J). 16.95 (978-0-9915194-0-8(X)) Fabula.

Kids Can Press Staff, ed. Franklin & the Duckling. 2007. (Kids Can Read Ser.). (ENG., Illus.). 32p. (J). (gr. 1-2). 3.95 (978-1-55337-889-1(X)) Kids Can Pr., Ltd. CAN. Dist: Hachette Bk. Group.

Kieslich, Anita Hilliker. Friends Forever: Adventures of Henderson. 2010. 32p. pap. 14.49 (978-1-4490-7997-0(0)) AuthorHouse.

King-smith, Dick. Funny Frank. Eastwood, John, illus. 2003. (ENG.). 112p. (J). (gr. 1-4). 5.99 (978-0-440-41880-1(1), Yearling) Random Hse. Children's Bks.

Kinross, Robin. No! Go Away! 2013. 40p. pap. 16.95 (978-1-4525-0979-2(4)) Balboa Pr.

Kohuth, Jane. Ducks Go Vroom. Garofoli, Viviana, illus. 2011. (Step into Reading Ser.). (ENG.). 32p. (J). (gr. -1-1). pap. 3.99 (978-0-375-86560-2(8), Random Hse. Bks. for Young Readers) Random Hse. Children's Bks.

Kompelien, Tracy. Duck Bills, 1 vol. Haberstroh, Anne, illus. 2006. (Animal Tales Ser.). 24p. (J). (gr. k-3). (ENG.). lib. bdg. 24.21 (978-1-59679-933-2(1), SandCastle); pap. 48.42 (978-1-59679-934-9(X)) ABDO Publishing Co.

Krilanovich, Nadia. Chicken, Chicken, Duck! Krilanovich, Nadia, illus. (ENG., Illus.). (J). (gr. -1-2). 2016. 26p. bds. 7.99 (978-0-553-53806-9(3)) 2011. 32p. 14.99 (978-1-58246-365-8(9)) Random Hse. Children's Bks. (Tricycle Pr.).

Krommenacker, Mark. Dave the Duck Gets Active, 1 vol. 2010. 20p. 24.95 (978-1-4512-1231-0(3)) PublishAmerica, Inc.

Lamb Ii, James. Jimmy Jimmy el Cordero Salto Cumple Phil el Pato. 2012. 28p. pap. 17.99 (978-1-4685-5036-8(5)) AuthorHouse.

Lamb, Lenny. Moving Blues: Greener Grass. 2011. 32p. pap. 24.95 (978-1-4626-4398-1(1)) America Star Bks.

Langhans, Bob. Disney's DuckTales: the Gold Odyssey: The Gold Odyssey. Clark, John, ed. 2008. (ENG., Illus.). 184p. pap. 15.99 (978-1-60360-065-1(5), 9781603600651) Gemstone Publishing, Inc.

Lansdowne, Marcella. The Adventures of Patty & Annabel: Apache Lake & the Chakras. 2009. 28p. pap. 15.95 (978-1-4389-1643-9(4)) AuthorHouse.

Lawson, Barbara Spilman. Lucky Duck. 2016. (Spring Forward Ser.). (J). (gr. 2). (978-1-4900-9433-5(4)) Benchmark Education Co.

Leech, Carlyle & Leech, Thirma. Ha-Ha Farm. 2009. (ENG., Illus.). 24p. (J). (gr. -1-1). 14.95 (978-1-59583-396-9(X), 9781595833969, Green Tiger Pr.) Laughing Elephant.

Leonard, Barry, ed. The Ugly Duckling. 2003. (Illus.). 12p. (J). (gr. k-4). reprint ed. 17.00 (978-0-7567-6858-4(6)) DIANE Publishing Co.

Levy, Janice. Diva Duck Dreams, 1 vol. Madden, Colleen M., illus. 2012. (Diva Duck Ser.). (ENG.). 32p. (J). (gr. -1-4). 28.50 (978-1-61641-886-1(9)) Magic Wagon.

—Diva Duck Goes to Hollywood, 1 vol. Madden, Colleen M., illus. 2012. (Diva Duck Ser.). (ENG.). 32p. (J). (gr. -1-4). 28.50 (978-1-61641-887-8(7)) Magic Wagon.

—Diva Duck Travels the World, 1 vol. Madden, Colleen M., illus. 2012. (Diva Duck Ser.). (ENG.). 32p. (J). (gr. -1-4). 28.50 (978-1-61641-888-5(5)) Magic Wagon.

—School Rules for Diva Duck, 1 vol. Madden, Colleen M., illus. 2012. (Diva Duck Ser.). (ENG.). 32p. (J). (gr. -1-4). 28.50 (978-1-61641-889-2(3)) Magic Wagon.

Lewis, Kim. Seymour & Henry. Lewis, Kim, illus. 2009. (ENG., Illus.). 32p. (J). (gr. k-k). 15.99 (978-0-7636-4243-3(6)) Candlewick Pr.

Lewis-Wells, Helen. Sad Duck. 2012. 16p. pap. 12.68 (978-1-4669-2277-8(X)) Trafford Publishing.

Liette, Chad. The Downy Duck. 2013. 16p. pap. 12.70 (978-1-4669-8469-1(4)) Trafford Publishing.

Lo, Yer Jenny. The Disobedient Ducklings. Lo, Talthau, photos by. 2008. (Illus.). 44p. pap. 24.95 (978-1-60441-576-6(2)) America Star Bks.

Lodge, Yvette. Rainbow Duck. Abel, Simone, illus. 2006. 8p. (J). (gr. -1-k). bds. 9.99 (978-1-57791-263-7(2)) Brighter Minds Children's Publishing.

London, Adam. Lucky the Rubber Ducky. Atherton, Jim, illus. 2009. 14p. (J). pap. 14.95 (978-0-578-00865-3(3)) AthertonCustoms.

Losey, Tori. The Ducks of Congress Park. Liguori, Kathy, illus. 2004. 36p. (J). (978-0-925168-97-9(1)) North Country Bks., Inc.

Lowery, Mike. The Rise of the Rusty Robo-Cat! 2017. (Doodle Adventures Ser.). (ENG., Illus.). 112p. (J). (gr. 2). 12.95 (978-0-7611-8721-9(9)) Workman Publishing Co., Inc.

Lowrey-Christian, Jane. Quackless Duck Finds His Pals. 2009. 36p. pap. 21.99 (978-1-4415-1374-8(4)) Xlibris Corp.

—Quakless Duck Prays for a New Voice. 2009. 44p. pap. 21.99 (978-1-4415-1846-0(0)) Xlibris Corp.

Luckritz, Gratti C. Christopher's Duck. 2012. (ENG.). (J). pap. 0.99 (978-1-4675-2999-0(0)) Independent Pub.

Lurie, Susan. Swim, Duck, Swim! Head, Murray, photos by. (ENG., Illus.). 32p. (J). 2016. bds. 7.99 (978-1-250-07740-0(0), 9781250077400) 2014. (gr. -1-2). 16.99 (978-1-250-04642-0(4), 9781250046420) Feiwel & Friends.

Luthardt, Kevin. Peep!, 1 vol. Luthardt, Kevin, illus. (ENG., Illus.). 36p. (J). 2013. (gr. -1-1). 7.95 (978-1-56145-682-6(9)) 2003. (gr. k-1). 15.95 (978-1-56145-046-6(4)) Peachtree Pubs.

Lynne, Kimberlee, illus. The Frog & the Mouse. 2011. (First Steps in Music Ser.). (ENG.). 32p. (J). (gr. k-2). 16.95 (978-1-57999-802-8(X)) G I A Pubns., Inc.

Mack, Jeff. Duck in the Fridge, 0 vols. 2014. (ENG.). 40p. (J). (gr. 1-3). 16.99 (978-1-4778-4776-3(6), 9781477847763, Amazon Children's Publishing) Amazon Publishing.

Magona, Sindiwe. The Ugly Duckling. Hinrichsen, Natalie, illus. 2011. (Best Loved Tales for Africa Ser.). (ENG.). 32p. (J). (gr. k-2). pap. 10.95 (978-1-77009-823-7(2)) Jacana Media ZAF. Dist: Independent Pubs. Group.

Mallat, Kathy. Just Ducky. 2004. (Illus.). 24p. (J). (gr. -1-1). 16.85 (978-0-8027-8825-2(4)) Walker & Co.

Marcoux, Tom. Crystal Pegasus. 2012. 92p. pap. 18.24 (978-0-9800511-9-3(3)) Marcoux, Tom Media, LLC.

Martin, C. L. Ducky Goes to the Dentist. 2013. 16p. pap. 24.95 (978-1-62709-742-0(2)) America Star Bks.

Martin, David. Peep & Ducky. Walker, David, illus. (ENG.). (J). (— 1). 2015. 24p. bds. 6.99 (978-0-7636-7243-0(2)) 2013. 32p. 14.99 (978-0-7636-5039-1(0)) Candlewick Pr.

—Peep & Ducky Rainy Day. Walker, David, illus. 2015. (ENG.). 32p. (J). (— 1). 14.99 (978-0-7636-6884-6(2)) Candlewick Pr.

Mastrud, Karen. Fucious. 2012. 34p. 24.95 (978-1-61863-419-1(4)) Bookstand Publishing.

—Fucious: The True Story of the Ugly Duckling. Margolis, Al, illus. 2012. 32p. (J). 24.95 (978-1-61863-414-6(3)) Bookstand Publishing.

Mattern, Carrie. Welcome Little Leo. 2010. 28p. 15.99 (978-1-4490-9924-4(6)) AuthorHouse.

Maxwell, Wayne F., Jr. The Miracle of Sandy Duck: A True Story. McCabe, Jane M., illus. 2003. 32p. (gr. k-4). lib. bdg. 15.00 (978-0-9747023-0-8(7)) Pegasus Pubns.

Mayberry, Becky. Always Listen to Your Mom, Even If She Is a Duck: Even If She Is A Duck. 2011. 28p. pap. 21.99 (978-1-4628-7175-9(5)) Xlibris Corp.

Mazurke, Rachel. Mr. & Mrs. Duck: Busy Day, The Accident, New Home or the Brook, Dirty Water Again. 2008. (Illus.). 62p. (J). pap. 9.00 (978-0-8059-7762-2(7)) Dorrance Publishing Co., Inc.

McCloskey, Robert. Abran Paso a los Patitos. Blanco, Osvaldo, tr. from ENG. 2005.Tr. of Make Way for Ducklings. (SPA., Illus.). 62p. (J). (gr. k-4). reprint ed. 15.00 (978-0-7567-8841-4(2)) DIANE Publishing Co.

—Make Way for Ducklings, 1 vol. (Puffin Storytime Ser.). (ENG.). (J). (gr. -1-2). 2010. 15p. 9.99 (978-0-14-241386-9(0), Puffin Books) 75th anniv. ed. 2016. (Illus.). 68p. 24.99 (978-1-101-99795-6(8), Viking Books for Young Readers) Penguin Young Readers Group.

McCully, Emily Arnold. Little Ducks Go. McCully, Emily Arnold, illus. (I Like to Read(r) Ser.). (ENG., Illus.). 24p. (J). (gr. -1-2). 2015. 6.99 (978-0-8234-3300-1(5)) 2014. 14.95 (978-0-8234-2941-7(5)) Holiday Hse., Inc.

McGann, Amber Ann. Windrush the Crooked Llama. 2008. 34p. pap. 24.95 (978-1-60563-728-0(9)) PublishAmerica, Inc.

McGhee, Patti Gray. Ducky Bill's Great Race. Vermillion, Danny, illus. 2013. 46p. 24.95 (978-1-63000-424-8(3)); 48p. pap. 24.95 (978-1-62709-522-8(5)) America Star Bks.

McKinlay, Meg. Duck for a Day. Rudge, Leila, illus. 2012. (ENG.). 96p. (J). (gr. 2-4). 12.99 (978-0-7636-5784-0(0)) Candlewick Pr.

McMurtrie, Kevin. Have You Seen My Duck? 2012. 20p. pap. 13.77 (978-1-4669-4847-1(7)) Trafford Publishing.

McNeil, Niki, et al. HOCPP 1079 All about Ping. 2006. spiral bd. 15.00 (978-1-60308-079-8(1)) In the Hands of a Child.

McPhail, David. Waddles. 2011. (ENG., Illus.). 32p. (J). (gr. k-2). 16.95 (978-0-8109-8415-8(6), Abrams Bks. for Young Readers) Abrams, Inc.

Melinda, Braun. Luella. 2007. (Illus.). 32p. (J). lib. bdg. 14.95 (978-1-886028-85-2(0)) Savage Pr.

Melling, David. Splish, Splash, Splosh! Melling, David, illus. 2013. (ENG., Illus.). 22p. (J). (gr. -1). bds. 8.95 (978-1-58925-643-9(3)) Tiger Tales.

Merer, Laura, illus. Fuzzy Ducky's Birthday: A Touch-and-Feel Pop-up Book. 2005. 10p. (J). 8.95 (978-1-58117-324-6(5), Intervisual/Piggy Toes) Bendon, Inc.

Meyrick, Judith. Gracie: The Public Gardens Duck, 1 vol. Rudnicki, Richard, illus. 2008. (ENG.). 32p. (J). (gr. -1-3). 10.95 (978-1-55109-645-2(5)) Nimbus Publishing, Ltd. CAN. Dist: Orca Bk. Pubs. USA.

Michiko Florence, Debbi. The Hunt for the Perfect Present. Roe, Monika, illus. 2016. (Dorothy & Toto Ser.). (ENG.). 40p. (gr. k-2). lib. bdg. 21.32 (978-1-4795-8703-2(6)) Capstone Press of Coughlan Cos.

Middleditch, Susan. Monty the Mountain Duck. 2013. (Illus.). 145p. pap. 9.50 (978-1-78035-394-4(4), Fastprint Publishing) Upfront Publishing Ltd. GBR. Dist: Printondemand-worldwide.com.

Miguel, Angela. Harold the Duck. 2009. 52p. pap. 19.50 (978-1-60693-658-0(1), Eloquent Bks.) Strategic Book Publishing & Rights Agency (SBPRA).

Miller, Al. Patricia the Duck. 2013. 20p. pap. 14.95 (978-1-4669-7798-3(1)) Trafford Publishing.

Miller, David. Refugees. 2005. (Illus.). 32p. (J). (978-0-7344-0633-0(9), Lothian Children's Bks.) Hachette Australia.

Miller, Janet. DuckDumB. 2010. 32p. pap. 21.95 (978-0-557-57669-2(5)) Lulu Pr., Inc.

Milne, Rg. Quibble Tales: Davey Sprocket & the Alamo Alamode Pie Factory. 2013. 24p. pap. 24.95 (978-1-63000-727-0(7)) America Star Bks.

Mitchell, Sheena. Out of the Ark. 2012. 48p. pap. 18.41 (978-1-4669-1489-6(0)) Trafford Publishing.

Moeckel, Christine. Dick the Duck. Moeckel, Christine, illus. I.t. ed. 2004. (Illus.). 31p. (J). spiral bd. 9.98 (978-0-9720350-2-6(8)) Duckpond Publishing, Inc.

Moerbeek, Kees. The Ugly Duckling. 2014. (My Secret Scrapbook Diary Ser.). (ENG., Illus.). 10p. (J). (978-1-84643-593-5(5)) Child's Play International Ltd.

Moore, Angela. Rebecca's Ducks, 1 vol. Keating, Nancy, illus. 2007. (ENG.). 32p. (J). (gr. -1-2). pap. 8.95 (978-1-897174-00-5(4), Tuckamore Bks) Creative Bk. Publishing CAN. Dist: Orca Bk. Pubs. USA.

Moore, Eva. Lucky Ducklings. Carpenter, Nancy, illus. 2013. (ENG.). 32p. (J). (gr. k-2). 16.99 (978-0-439-44861-1(1), Orchard Bks.) Scholastic, Inc.

Moran, Mary C. Digby's Rescue. 2012. 28p. pap. 15.95 (978-1-105-96859-4(6)) Lulu Pr., Inc.

Morgan, Mary. Pip Sits. 2017. (I Like to Read(r) Ser.). (ENG.). 24p. (J). (gr. -1-3). 6.99 (978-0-8234-3778-8(7)); (Illus.). 14.95 (978-0-8234-3676-7(4)) Holiday Hse., Inc.

Morrison, Marianne. The Saddleshoe Quackers Present Lucky's Adventure. 2004. 17p. (J). 5.95 (978-0-9709575-3-5(X)) Singing River Pubns.

Morton, Jane & Dreier, Ted. Moozie's Cow Wisdom for Loving to the "Uddermost" Royse, Jane, illus. 2003. (J). pap. 4.95 (978-0-9662268-3-6(6)) Children's Kindness Network.

Muir-Chase, Marlene. Miranda the Mallard from Moose Jaw, 1 vol. 2009. 31p. pap. 24.95 (978-1-60749-255-9(5)) America Star Bks.

Muller, Lisa M. Master smokey & mr. Duck. 2006. 15p. (J). 9.99 (978-1-4276-0027-1(9)) Aardvark Global Publishing.

Mulryan, Doreen. Lucky Ducky. 2016. (ENG., Illus.). 32p. (J). (gr. k-2). 14.95 (978-1-4197-1467-2(8), Abrams Bks. for Young Readers) Abrams, Inc.

Murphy, Mary. Quick Duck! Murphy, Mary, illus. 2013. (ENG., Illus.). 16p. (J). (— 1). bds. 6.99 (978-0-7636-6022-2(1)) Candlewick Pr.

Murphy, Mary Elizabeth. I Kissed the Baby! Murphy, Mary Elizabeth, illus. 2004. (ENG., Illus.). 24p. (J). (— 1). bds. 6.99 (978-0-7636-2443-9(8)) Candlewick Pr.

Nagle, Barbara. Duck & Spider, 1 vol. 2009. 37p. pap. 24.95 (978-1-60749-980-0(0)) America Star Bks.

Newth, Rebecca. Tinkum's Dog. Primm, Thomas, illus. 2005. 32p. (J). 15.00 (978-0-9630310-7-5(4)) Will Hall Bks.

Niddrie, June. Great Scott & Otis. 2010. 56p. pap. 23.30 (978-0-557-31863-6(7)) Lulu Pr., Inc.

—Quiet Queenie. 2010. 36p. pap. 17.30 (978-0-557-31868-1(8)) Lulu Pr., Inc.

Nolan, J. & Moffatt, J. Floaties: Five Little Ducks. 2003. (J). 9.95 (978-1-929766-59-8(9)) Handprint Bks.

Nolan, Lucy & Nolan. Jack Quack, 1 vol. Wesson, Andrea, illus. 2003. (ENG.). 32p. (J). (gr. k-3). pap. 5.95 (978-0-7614-5153-2(6)) Marshall Cavendish Corp.

O'Toole, Detra. Ty-Ty Quackers & the Hidden Treasure: Biblical Lessons with Barnyard Fun. 2009. 32p. pap. 13.99 (978-1-4343-6799-0(1)) AuthorHouse.

Page, Claire. Five Noisy Ducks: An Action-Packed Counting Book. 2008. (Illus.). 18p. (J). (gr. -1-k). bds. (978-1-84610-587-6(0)) Make Believe Ideas.

Pascucci, Adele. Duck on a Dock. 2012. 20p. pap. 13.95 (978-1-105-40403-0(X)) Lulu Pr., Inc.

Pate, Ginger. Look Left, Look Right, Look Left Again. Pennell, Rhett / R., illus. 2013. 28p. (J). 8.50 (978-1-880851-30-2(X)) Greene Bark Pr., Inc.

Paterson, Katherine. The Tale of the Mandarin Ducks. Dillon, Leo & Dillon, Diane, illus. 2004. 32p. (J). (gr. k-4). reprint ed. 15.00 (978-0-7567-7698-5(8)) DIANE Publishing Co.

—The Tale of the Mandarin Ducks. 2009. 9.00 (978-0-7848-3652-1(3), Everbind) Marco Bk. Co.

PC Treasures Staff, prod. The Ugly Duckling. 2007. (J). (978-1-60072-018-5(8)) PC Treasures, Inc.

Pellerin, Mona. Peetie & the Marsh Aliens, 1 vol. 2010. 58p. pap. 16.95 (978-1-4489-7017-9(2)) America Star Bks.

—Peetie, the Thinking Dabbler Duck. 2009. 32p. pap. 18.95 (978-1-4389-6303-7(3)) AuthorHouse.

Perry, Shelly. Duckling's First Adventure. Loebel, Bonnie, illus. 2006. (ENG.). 56p. (J). per. 9.95 (978-0-9787740-3-5(5)) Peppertree Pr., The.

Petsch, Maggie, photos by & text. Dora the A-Dora-ble Duck. Petsch, Maggie, text. 2004. (Illus.). (J). per. 9.95 (978-0-9715860-4-8(7)) From the Asylum Bks. & Pr.

Pfeffer, Wendy. Mallard Duck at Meadow View Pond. Oughton, Taylor, illus. (Smithsonian's Backyard Ser.). (ENG.). 32p. (J). (gr. -1-2). 2005. 19.95 (978-1-56899-958-6(5), BC5021) 2005. pap. 4.95 (978-1-56899-957-9(7), B5071) 2003. 9.95 (978-1-56899-961-6(5), PB5071) 2003. 8.95 (978-1-59249-063-9(8), SC5021) Soundprints.

—Mallard Duck at Mountain View Pond. Oughton, Taylor, illus. 2005. (Smithsonian's Backyard Ser.). (ENG.). 32p. (J). (gr. -1-2). 15.95 (978-1-56899-956-2(9), B5021) Soundprints.

Pierro, Rita. The Duck Who Couldn't Swim, 1 vol. French, David, illus. 2010. 26p. 24.95 (978-1-4489-6405-5(9)) PublishAmerica, Inc.

Piper, Danny W. Skinny Boy's Close Call. 2008. 28p. per. 24.95 (978-1-60441-534-6(7)) America Star Bks.

Pokas, Dora. Muriel's Red Sweater. (J). 15.95 (978-0-8118-3771-2(8)) Chronicle Bks. LLC.

Polacco, Patricia. John Philip Duck. Polacco, Patricia, illus. 2004. (ENG., Illus.). 48p. (J). (gr. k-4). 17.99 (978-0-399-24262-5(7), Philomel Bks.) Penguin Young Readers Group.

Posner-Sanchez, Andrea & Weinberg, Jennifer Liberts. Bow-Bot Robot (Disney Junior: Minnie's Bow Toons) RH Disney Staff, illus. 2014. (Little Golden Book Ser.). (ENG.). 24p. (J). (-k). 4.99 (978-0-7364-3078-4(4), Golden/Disney) Random Hse. Children's Bks.

Postgate, Daniel, illus. The Ugly Duckling. 2006. (First Reading Level 4 Ser.). 48p. (J). (gr. 1-4). 8.99 (978-0-7945-1274-3(7), Usborne) EDC Publishing.

Potter, Beatrix. Conte de Sophie Canetang. pap. 18.95 (978-2-07-054701-2(9)) Gallimard, Editions FRA. Dist: Distribooks, Inc.

—Hello, Jemima! 2012. (Peter Rabbit Ser.). (ENG.). 10p. (J). (gr. -1-k). bds. 5.99 (978-0-7232-6749-2(9), Warne) Penguin Young Readers Group.

—The Tale of Jemima Puddle-Duck. 2012. (Peter Rabbit Ser.: 9). (ENG., Illus.). 64p. (J). (gr. -1-2). 6.99 (978-0-7232-6778-2(2), Warne) Penguin Young Readers Group.

Powell, Richard. Duck. Gardner, Louise, illus. 2014. (Bathing Beauties Ser.). (ENG.). 8p. (J). (gr. -1 — 1). 7.99 (978-1-4380-7442-9(5)) Barron's Educational Series, Inc.

Prasadam-halls, Smriti. Have You Seen Duck? Berg, Michelle, illus. 2012. (ENG.). 12p. (J). (gr. -1-k). 7.99 (978-1-4083-1500-2(9)) Hodder & Stoughton GBR. Dist: Hachette Bk. Group.

Priddy, Roger. Little Friends: Splish Splash. 2014. (Little Friends Ser.). (ENG.). 6p. (J). (gr. -1 — 1). 7.99 (978-0-312-51682-6(7), 9780312516826, Priddy Bks.) St. Martin's Pr.

Publications International Ltd. Staff, ed. Record Story Ugly Duckling. 2011. 18p. 17.98 (978-1-4508-1912-1(5)) Phoenix International Publications, Inc.

Q., Bev. Diddly Duck & His Goosie Friends. 2010. 32p. 13.54 (978-1-4269-4518-2(3)) Trafford Publishing.

Quack, Quack, Goodmorning Ducks. 2005. (J). 9.95 (978-1-59352-177-6(4)) Christian Services Publishing.

Quackenbush, Robert. Henry's Awful Mistake. Quackenbush, Robert, illus. rev. deluxe ed. 2005. (Illus.). 40p. (J). (gr. k-2). reprint ed. 12.95 (978-0-9712757-0-6(X)) Quackenbush, Robert Studios.

Qualls, Shirley. Marigold Duck Comes to Our School. 2009. 28p. pap. 12.49 (978-1-4389-8386-8(7)) AuthorHouse.

Quinlan, Divya Maureen. The Baggy Duck of Rainbow's End. 2010. 16p. 10.00 (978-1-4490-3694-2(5)) AuthorHouse.

The Rainy Day: Individual Title Two-Packs. (Chiquilibros Ser.). (gr. -1-1). 12.00 (978-0-7635-8532-7(7)) Rigby Education.

Redmond, Diane, contrib. by. Roley & the Rock Star. 2003. (Bob the Builder Ser.). (Illus.). (J). 11.15 (978-0-7569-2097-5(3)) Perfection Learning Corp.

Reinoso, Carlos. Little Ducky Jr. & the Whirlwind Storm: A Tale of Loss, Hope,and Renewal. Reinoso, Carlos, illus. I.t. ed. 2005. (Illus.). 50p. (J). 8.99 (978-0-9777672-0-5(5)) Behavioral Health & Human Development Ctr.

Reisinger, John. The Duckworth Chronicles. 2005. pap. 11.95 (978-1-59330-269-6(X)) Aventine Pr.

Reva Jean Rohe. Adventures of Tomtom the Duck. 2009. 52p. pap. 22.49 (978-1-4343-7811-8(X)) AuthorHouse.

Rey, H. A. Curious George & the Dump Truck. 2010. (Curious George Ser.). (ENG., Illus.). 24p. (J). (gr. -1-3). pap. 4.99 (978-0-547-50425-4(X)) Houghton Mifflin Harcourt Publishing Co.

Rey, H. A. & Rey, Margret. Lost & Found. 2008. (Curious George Ser.). (ENG., Illus.). 24p. (J). (gr. -1-3). pap. 3.99 (978-0-618-89197-9(8)) Houghton Mifflin Harcourt Publishing Co.

RH Disney. Walt Disney's the Ugly Duckling (Disney Classic: the Ugly Duckling) RH Disney, illus. 2017. (Little Golden Book Ser.). (ENG., Illus.). 24p. (J). (-k). 4.99 (978-0-7364-3571-0(9), Golden/Disney) Random Hse. Children's Bks.

Richards, Dawn. Duck's Easter Egg Hunt. D'hamers, Heidi, illus. 2014. (J). (978-1-4351-5243-4(3)) Barnes & Noble, Inc.

RIGBY. Mother Duck's Walk: First Grade Big Books. 2003. (Rigby on Our Way to English Ser.). (ENG.). 24p. (gr. 1-1). pap. 50.70 (978-0-7578-1509-6(X)) Rigby Education.

Rigby Education Staff. Fat Ducks. (Sails Literacy Ser.). (Illus.). 16p. (gr. 1-2). 27.00 (978-0-7635-9917-1(4), 699174C99) Rigby Education.

—The Robbers. (Sails Literacy Ser.). (Illus.). 16p. (gr. 1-2). 27.00 (978-0-7635-9913-3(1), 699131C99) Rigby Education.

Rigo, L., illus. Little Duckling. (Mini Look at Me Bks.). 10p. (J). 2012. (ENG.). bds. 4.99 (978-0-7641-6510-8(0)) 2011. bds. 7.99 (978-0-7641-6425-5(2)) Barron's Educational Series, Inc.

Riley, Penelope A. Christmas Away! A Duckie Dan Adventure Book. 2012. 48p. pap. 21.99 (978-1-4772-7554-2(1)) AuthorHouse.

—Duckie Dan the Traveling Man. 2009. 44p. pap. 16.99 (978-1-4490-4634-7(7)) AuthorHouse.

Ritchey, Kate. Huey, Dewey, & Louie's Rainy Day. 2014. (Mickey & Friends World of Reading Ser.). (J). lib. bdg. 13.55 (978-0-606-34122-6(6), Turtleback) Turtleback Bks.

Rivers-Moore, Debbie. Scrub-A-Dub Ducky: Bath Mitt & Bath Book Set. Jones, Anna, illus. 2014. (ENG.). 8p. (J). (gr. -1 — 1). 9.99 (978-1-4380-7530-3(8)) Barron's Educational Series, Inc.

Robert, Quackenbush & Robert Quackenbush. Calling Doctor Quack. 2010. 68p. (J). (gr. k-4). pap. 8.95 (978-1-4502-1379-0(0)) iUniverse, Inc.

Robinson, Michelle. Yak Yuk. Sim, David, illus. 2012. (ENG.). 12p. (J). (gr. -1-k). 10.99 (978-1-4088-1703-2(9), 9781408817032, Bloomsbury USA Childrens) Bloomsbury Publishing USA.

Robinson, Nikki Slade. Muddle & Mo. 2017. (ENG., Illus.). 32p. (J). (gr. -1-3). 14.99 (978-0-544-71612-4(4)) Houghton Mifflin Harcourt Publishing Co.

Rock, Brian. The Deductive Detective, 1 vol. Rogers, Sherry, illus. 2013. (SPA.). 32p. (J). (gr. -1-2). pap. 9.95 (978-1-62855-347-5(2)) Arbordale Publishing.

Rock, Brian & Rogers, Sherry. El Detective Deductivo, 1 vol. Rogers, Sherry, illus. 2013. (SPA., Illus.). 32p. (J). (gr. -1-2). 17.95 (978-1-60718-708-0(6)) Arbordale Publishing.

Romeo, Angelina, et al. Gooda & Goda. 2010. 23p. 15.90 (978-1-4452-2788-7(6)) Lulu Pr., Inc.

Root, Phyllis. One Duck Stuck. 2003. (gr. k-3). 17.20 (978-0-613-60361-4(3), Turtleback) Turtleback Bks.

—One Duck Stuck: A Mucky Ducky Counting Book. Chapman, Jane, illus. 2003. (ENG.). 40p. (J). (gr. k-k). pap. 6.99 (978-0-7636-1566-6(8)) Candlewick Pr.

—One Duck Stuck: A Mucky Ducky Counting Book. Chapman, Jane, illus. 2008. (Candlewick Press Big Book Ser.). (ENG.). 40p. (J). (gr. k-k). pap. 24.99 (978-0-7636-3817-7(X)) Candlewick Pr.

Rosenthal, Amy Krouse. Duck! Rabbit! Lichtenheld, Tom, illus. aut. ed. 2009. (J). 16.99 (978-0-8118-8332-0(9)) Chronicle Bks. LLC.

Roth, Carol. Five Little Ducklings Go to Bed. Julian, Sean, illus. 2014. (ENG.). 32p. (J). (gr. k-3). 17.95 (978-0-7358-4128-4(4)) North-South Bks., Inc.

—Five Little Ducklings Go to School. Julian, Sean, illus. 2015. (ENG.). 32p. (J). (gr. -1-2). 17.95 (978-0-7358-4132-1(2)) North-South Bks., Inc.

Roth, Carol & Julian, Sean. Five Little Ducklings Go to Bed. 2013. (Illus.). 32p. (J). pap. (978-0-7358-4153-6(5)) North-South Bks., Inc.

Roy, Alene Adele. The Legend of Dragonfly Pond: Volume One. 2008. 60p. pap. 24.99 (978-1-4343-6824-9(6)) AuthorHouse.

Roy, Ron. May Magic. Gurney, John Steven, illus. 2011. (Calendar Mysteries Ser.: 5). (ENG.). 80p. (J). (gr. 1-4). 4.99 (978-0-375-86111-6(4), Random Hse. Bks. for Young Readers) Random Hse. Children's Bks.

Rustrian, Edvin E. The Adventures of Timmy & Jay. 2010. 24p. pap. 15.99 (978-1-4535-3792-3(9)) Xlibris Corp.

Ruzzier, Sergio. This Is Not a Picture Book! 2016. (ENG., Illus.). 40p. (J). (gr. -1-k). 16.99 *(978-1-4521-2907-5(X))* Chronicle Bks. LLC.
Rylant, Cynthia. The Case of the Desperate Duck, 4 bks., Set. 2007. (High-Rise Private Eyes Ser.: Bk. 8). (J). (gr. k-2). pap. 31.95 incl. audio compact disk *(978-1-4301-0067-6(2))*; pap. 29.95 incl. audio *(978-1-4301-0065-2(6))* Live Oak Media.
Salinas, Veronica. The Voyage, 1 vol. Eirheim, Jeanne, tr. from NOR. Engman, Camilla, illus. 2013. (ENG.). 40p. (J). (gr. -1-2). 16.95 *(978-1-55498-386-5(X))* Groundwood Bks. CAN. Dist: Publishers Group West (PGW).
Salzano, Tammi. One Rainy Day. Wood, Hannah, illus. 2011. (ENG.). 24p. (J). (gr. -1-k). bds. 8.95 *(978-1-58925-860-0(6))* Tiger Tales.
Santa Elena, Antonio E. Babba Has Golden Feathers. (Illus.). (J). (gr. 4-6). *(978-0-89626-019-1(4))* Alchemy Bks.
Santillo, LuAnn. The Duck. Santillo, LuAnn, ed. 2003. (Half-Pint Kids Readers Ser.). (Illus.). 7p. (J). (gr. -1-1). pap. 1.00 *(978-1-59256-069-1(5))* Half-Pint Kids, Inc.
Sarfatti, Esther, tr. El Patito Feo. Bordoy, Irene, illus. 2006. (Bilingual Tales Ser.). (SPA.). 24p. (J). (gr. -1-3). pap. 3.99 *(978-0-439-77376-8(8),* Scholastic en Espanol) Scholastic, Inc.
Sargent, Dave & Sargent, David M., Jr. Dinky Duck: Be Prompt, 19 vols., Vol. 7. Lenoir, Jane, illus. 2003. (Feather Tales Ser.: 7). 42p. (J). pap. 10.95 *(978-1-56763-732-8(9))* Ozark Publishing.
Sargent, Dave & Sargent, David M. Dinky Duck: Be Prompt, 20 vols., Vol. 7. Lenoir, Jane, illus. 2nd ed. 2003. (Feather Tales Ser.: 7). 42p. (J). lib. bdg. 20.95 *(978-1-56763-731-1(0))* Ozark Publishing.
Sargent, Dave & Sargent, Pat. Do All Ducks Quack?, 10 vols., Vol. 14. Robinson, Laura, illus. 2004. (Learn to Read Ser.: 10). 18p. (J). lib. bdg. 20.95 *(978-1-56763-823-3(6))*; lib. bdg. 10.95 *(978-1-56763-824-0(4))* Ozark Publishing.
—Do All Ducks Quack?/¿Granznan todos los Patos?, 10 vols., Vol. 14. Robinson, Laura, illus. 2004. (Learn to Read Ser.: 10). (ENG & SPA.). 18p. (J). pap. 10.95 *(978-1-56763-988-9(7))*; lib. bdg. 20.95 *(978-1-56763-987-2(9))* Ozark Publishing.
Sauer, Tammi. Mr. Duck Means Business. Mack, Jeff, illus. 2011. (ENG.). 32p. (J). (gr. -1-3). 15.99 *(978-1-4169-8522-8(0),* Simon & Schuster/Paula Wiseman Bks.) Simon & Schuster/Paula Wiseman Bks.
Saveley, Barb. Curse of Moonstone Island. 2009. (Illus.). 36p. pap. 16.99 *(978-1-4389-4938-3(3))* AuthorHouse.
Schiller, Pam. Five Little Ducks. Newsom, Carol, illus. 2014. 19p. (J). ***(978-1-60128-879-0(4))*** Frog Street Pr.
Scott-Branagan, Bronwen. Chips Quackety. 2012. 36p. pap. 15.95 *(978-1-61204-719-5(X),* Strategic Bk. Publishing) Strategic Book Publishing & Rights Agency (SBPRA).
Scotton, Rob. Splat the Cat & the Duck with No Quack. Scotton, Rob, illus. 2011. (I Can Read Level 1 Ser.). (ENG., Illus.). 32p. (J). (gr. k-3). 16.99 *(978-0-06-197858-6(2))*; pap. 3.99 *(978-0-06-197857-9(4))* HarperCollins Pubs.
—Splat the Cat Treasure Box. Scotton, Rob, illus. 2011. (Splat the Cat Ser.). (ENG., Illus.). (J). (gr. k-3). pap. 15.99 *(978-0-06-210010-8(6))* HarperCollins Pubs.
Screech! Individual Title Six-Packs. (Literatura 2000 Ser.). (gr. 1-2). 28.00 *(978-0-7635-0109-9(3))* Rigby Education.
Seuss, Dr. Sneetches on Beaches. 2011. (Dr. Seuss Nursery Collection). (ENG., Illus.). 14p. (J). (— 1). 10.99 *(978-0-375-87318-8(X),* Random Hse. Bks. for Young Readers) Random Hse. Children's Bks.
Shannon, David. Duck & a Book. 2005. (Illus.). (J). pap. *(978-0-439-80288-8(1))* Scholastic, Inc.
Shannon, David. Duck on a Tractor. 2017. 59.95 ***(978-1-338-16188-5(1))*** 2016. (ENG.). 40p. (J). (gr. -1-3). 16.99 *(978-0-545-61941-7(6),* Blue Sky Pr., The) Scholastic, Inc.
Shaw, Patricia. Gilly the Duck Meets the Magical Lady. 2013. 36p. pap. 20.99 *(978-1-4817-0288-1(2))* AuthorHouse.
Shelton, Ricky V. Quacker Meets His Dad the Squirrel: Tales from a Duck Named Quacker. Williams, Shan, illus. Date not set. (J). (gr. -1-1). pap. 7.00 *(978-0-9634257-3-7(0))* RVS Bks., Inc.
Simmons, Jane. Come On. 2005. (Daisy Ser.). (Illus.). (Orig.). (J). (ARA, ENG, VIE, CHI & BEN.). 36p. pap. 11.95 *(978-1-84059-217-7(6))*; (VIE, ENG, CHI, ARA & BEN., 3p. (gr. -1-1). pap. 11.95 *(978-1-84059-183-5(8))*; (URD, ENG, VIE, CHI & ARA., 36p. (gr. -1-1). pap. 11.95 *(978-1-84059-182-8(X))* Milet Publishing.
—Daisy & the Egg. 2005. (Daisy Ser.). (Illus.). 36p. (J). (gr. -1-1). (ARA, ENG, VIE, CHI & BEN.). pap. 11.95 *(978-1-84059-216-0(8))*; (VIE, ENG, CHI, ARA & BEN., pap. 11.95 *(978-1-84059-176-7(5))* Milet Publishing.
—Ven Aqui, Daisy! (SPA., Illus.). 32p. (J). (gr. -1). *(978-84-488-0649-5(5),* BS5842) Beascoa, Ediciones S.A. ESP. Dist: Lectorum Pubns., Inc.
Simmons, Martha. Grandma Perkido & Sidney. 2007. (Illus.). 24p. (J). 14.95 *(978-0-9777041-4-9(9))* Third Dimension Publishing.
Simon, Mary Manz. Duckling Is Patient. Clearwater, Linda, illus. 2006. (First Virtues for Toddlers Ser.). 20p. (J). 5.99 *(978-0-7847-1410-2(X),* 04038) Standard Publishing.
Skandle, D. L. Little Duckie's Day. 2010. 28p. pap. 15.49 *(978-1-4490-9705-9(7))* AuthorHouse.
Skiles, Janet. Just Ducky! Stickers. 2017. (Dover Little Activity Books Stickers Ser.). (ENG., Illus.). 8p. (J). (gr. k-3). pap. 1.99 *(978-0-486-81455-1(6))* Dover Pubns., Inc.
Smith, Carrie. The Ugly Duckling: Classic Tales Edition. Rogers, Jacqueline, illus. 2011. (Classic Tales Ser.). (J). *(978-1-936258-63-5(3))* Benchmark Education Co.
Smith, Michelle. Duck in the Hedge: Jeremy & the Big Pond. 2011. (Illus.). 36p. pap. 15.66 *(978-1-4567-8818-6(3))* AuthorHouse.
Smith, Nancy. The Christmas Duck. 2012. (ENG.). (J). pap. *(978-1-4675-1988-5(X))* Independent Pub.
Soffer, Gilad. Duck's Vacation. 2015. (ENG., Illus.). 48p. (J). (gr. -1-k). 17.99 *(978-1-250-05647-4(0),* 9781250056474) Feiwel & Friends.
Spafford, Suzy. Helping-Out Day? Hooray! Spafford, Suzy, illus. 2003. (Tales from Duckport Ser.). (ENG., Illus.). 40p. (J). (gr. k-3). pap. 3.99 *(978-0-439-38358-5(7))* Scholastic, Inc.
—Witzy's Fall Collection. 2010. (Illus.). (J). *(978-1-4037-9599-1(1))* Creative Edge.
Spikes, James L. The Adventures of LemonHead & Mudd Duck: What to do if Someone Tries to Grab You. 2005. 36p. (J). lib. bdg. 19.95 net. *(978-0-9749202-7-6(4))* Excel Digital Pr.
Stanley, David J. A Lovely Day for Knitting. 2010. 28p. pap. 12.50 *(978-1-60911-773-3(5),* Eloquent Bks.) Strategic Book Publishing & Rights Agency (SBPRA).
Starfall Education. Gus the Duck. Starfall Education, ed. 2004. (ENG., Illus.). 8p. (J). pap. *(978-1-59577-005-9(4))* Starfall Education.
Stephenson, Nancy Ann. The Ducks' New Friends. Coffin, Marilyn, illus. l.t. ed. 2006. 34p. (J). per. 9.99 *(978-1-59879-164-8(8))* Lifevest Publishing, Inc.
Sullivan, Chris Mann. Oh No, Not the Shot! 2011. 24p. pap. 11.98 *(978-1-4490-8392-2(7))* AuthorHouse.
Supples, Lottie K. Happy, the Red Duck. 2011. 24p. pap. 15.99 *(978-1-4568-7931-0(6))* Xlibris Corp.
Swenson, Jamie. Woof & Quack in Winter (reader) Sias, Ryan, illus. 2017. (Green Light Readers Level 1 Ser.). (ENG.). 32p. (J). (gr. -1-3). 12.99 ***(978-0-544-95949-1(3)***, HMH Books For Young Readers) Houghton Mifflin Harcourt Publishing Co.
Swimming Lessons with Stewie the Duck. 2005. (J). 9.95 *(978-0-9668611-3-6(2))* Kimberly Pr., LLC.
Tafuri, Nancy. Have You Seen My Duckling? Tafuri, Nancy, illus. 2007. (Illus.). (J). (gr. -1-k). 17.00 *(978-0-7569-7869-3(6))* Perfection Learning Corp.
Taylor, Douglas. Downtown Ducks. Taylor, Catherine, illus. 2005. 62p. (J). per. 22.99 *(978-1-4134-3803-1(2))* Xlibris Corp.
Teddy Bear-Duck. 2003. (J). per. *(978-1-57657-160-6(2))* Paradise Pr., Inc.
Ten Little Ducks & Other Stories: Individual Title Six-Pack. (Story Steps Ser.). (gr. k-2). 48.00 *(978-0-7635-9798-6(8))* Rigby Education.
Tenbeth, Kate. Burly & Grum & the Secret City. Jones, Rob, illus. 2012. 108p. pap. *(978-0-9572119-5-7(3))* Magic Toy Bks.
Thank You, Meiling: Evaluation Guide. 2006. (J). *(978-1-55942-423-3(0))* Witcher Productions.
Thomas, Jan. Pumpkin Trouble. Thomas, Jan, illus. 2011. (ENG., Illus.). 40p. (J). (gr. -1-3). 9.99 *(978-0-06-169284-0(0))* HarperCollins Pubs.
—What Is Chasing Duck? 2017. (Giggle Gang Ser.). (ENG., Illus.). 48p. (J). (gr. -1-3). 9.99 *(978-0-544-93907-3(7),* HMH Books For Young Readers) Houghton Mifflin Harcourt Publishing Co.
Thomas, Kate. Mother Duck Knows the Way. Larkins, Mona, illus. 2005. 32p. (J). 8.95 *(978-1-58374-122-1(4))* Chicago Spectrum Pr.
Thomasson, Daniel E. The Lion & the Egg. 2012. 56p. pap. 24.20 *(978-1-4669-1303-5(7))* Trafford Publishing.
Thompson, Lauren. Cuaquito (Little Quack) Anderson, Derek, illus. 2010. (SPA.). 34p. (J). (gr. -1-1). bds. 7.99 *(978-1-4169-9894-5(2),* Libros Para Ninos) Libros Para Ninos.
—Little Quack. Anderson, Derek, illus. 2005. (Classic Board Bks.). (ENG.). 32p. (J). (gr. -1-k). bds. 7.99 *(978-0-689-87645-5(9),* Little Simon) Little Simon.
—Little Quack's ABC's. Anderson, Derek, illus. 2010. (Super Chubbies Ser.). (ENG.). 26p. (J). (gr. -1 — 1). bds. 5.99 *(978-1-4169-6091-1(0),* Little Simon) Little Simon.
—Little Quack's Bath Book. Anderson, Derek, illus. 2006. (ENG.). 8p. (J). (gr. -1 — 1). 8.99 *(978-1-4169-0803-6(X),* Little Simon) Little Simon.
—Little Quack's Bedtime. Anderson, Derek, illus. 2005. (ENG.). 32p. (J). (gr. -1-3). 17.99 *(978-0-689-86894-8(4),* Simon & Schuster Bks. For Young Readers) Simon & Schuster Bks. For Young Readers.
—Little Quack's New Friend. Anderson, Derek, illus. 2008. (Classic Board Bks.). (ENG.). 34p. (J). (gr. -1-1). bds. 7.99 *(978-1-4169-4923-7(2),* Little Simon) Little Simon.
—Little Quack's New Friend. Anderson, Derek, illus. 2006. (ENG.). 32p. (J). (gr. -1-3). 17.99 *(978-0-689-86893-1(6),* Simon & Schuster Bks. For Young Readers) Simon & Schuster Bks. For Young Readers.
—Little Quack's Opposites. Anderson, Derek, illus. 2010. (Super Chubbies Ser.). (ENG.). 26p. (J). (gr. -1 — 1). bds. 5.99 *(978-1-4169-6092-8(9),* Little Simon) Little Simon.
Thompson, Lauren & Anderson, Derek. Little Quack. 2003. (ENG., Illus.). 32p. (J). (gr. -1-3). 17.99 *(978-0-689-84723-3(8),* Simon & Schuster Bks. For Young Readers) Simon & Schuster Bks. For Young Readers.
—Little Quack's Bedtime. 2009. (Classic Board Bks.). (ENG., Illus.). 34p. (J). (gr. -1-k). bds. 7.99 *(978-1-4169-6873-3(3),* Little Simon) Little Simon.
—Little Quack's Hide & Seek. 2007. (Classic Board Bks.). (ENG., Illus.). 34p. (J). (gr. -1-k). bds. 7.99 *(978-1-4169-0325-3(9),* Little Simon) Little Simon.
—Little Quack's Hide & Seek. 2004. (ENG., Illus.). 32p. (J). (gr. -1-3). 17.99 *(978-0-689-85722-5(5),* Simon & Schuster Bks. For Young Readers) Simon & Schuster Bks. For Young Readers.
Tiger Tales, Tiger, ed. The Ugly Duckling. Eastland, Sue, illus. 2017. (My First Fairy Tales Ser.). (ENG.). 32p. (J). (gr. -1-2). pap. 7.99 ***(978-1-58925-497-8(X))*** Tiger Tales.
Tilert, Heather R. Ming-Ming Saves the Day: Follow the Reader Level 1. 2008. (Wonder Pets! Ser.). (ENG.). 24p. (J). 24.99 *(978-1-4169-6459-9(2),* Simon Scribbles) Simon Scribbles.
Toms, Kate. Duckie Duck. 2009. (Kate Toms Ser.). (Illus.). 26p. (gr. -1-k). bds. 7.99 *(978-1-84610-726-9(1))* Make Believe Ideas GBR. Dist: Nelson, Thomas Inc.
—Duckie Duck Boxed Set. 2008. (Illus.). 26p. (gr. -1-k). bds. *(978-1-84610-740-5(7))* Make Believe Ideas.
Trimoglie, Mario. The Story of Ocos: King of the Sky, Master of the Water. Buehrle, Jacquelyn, illus. 2011. 28p. pap. 24.95 *(978-1-4560-2015-6(3))* America Star Bks.
Twohy, Mike. Outfoxed. Twohy, Mike, illus. 2013. (ENG., Illus.). 40p. (J). (gr. -1-3). 16.99 *(978-1-4424-7392-8(4),* Simon & Schuster Bks. For Young Readers) Simon & Schuster Bks. For Young Readers.
Tyler, Jenny & Cartwright, S. Duck by the Sea. 2004. (SPA.). 6p. (J). vinyl bd. 7.95 *(978-0-7945-0569-1(4))* EDC Publishing.
Ugly Duckling. 2004. (My First Fairy Tales Ser.). (Illus.). 24p. (J). pap. 3.99 *(978-1-85854-685-8(0))* Brimax Books Ltd. GBR. Dist: Byeway Bks.
Urbanovic, Jackie. Duck & Cover. Urbanovic, Jackie, illus. 2009. (Max the Duck Ser.: 3). (ENG., Illus.). 32p. (J). (gr. -1-2). 17.99 *(978-0-06-121444-8(2))* HarperCollins Pubs.
—Duck at the Door. Urbanovic, Jackie, illus. (Max the Duck Ser.: 1). (ENG., Illus.). 32p. (J). (gr. -1-2). 2011. pap. 6.99 *(978-0-06-121440-0(X))* 2007. 17.99 *(978-0-06-121438-7(8))* HarperCollins Pubs.
—Duck Soup. Urbanovic, Jackie, illus. 2008. (Max the Duck Ser.: 2). (Illus.). 32p. (J). (gr. -1-2). (ENG.). 17.99 *(978-0-06-121441-7(8))*; lib. bdg. 18.89 *(978-0-06-121442-4(6))* HarperCollins Pubs.
—Ducks in a Row. Urbanovic, Jackie & Mathieu, Joe, illus. 2011. (I Can Read Level 1 Ser.). (ENG.). 32p. (J). (gr. k-3). 16.99 *(978-0-06-186438-4(2))*; pap. 3.99 *(978-0-06-186437-7(4))* HarperCollins Pubs.
—Happy Go Ducky. Urbanovic, Jackie & Mathieu, Joe, illus. 2012. (I Can Read Level 1 Ser.). (ENG.). 32p. (J). (gr. k-3). 16.99 *(978-0-06-186440-7(4))*; pap. 3.99 *(978-0-06-186439-1(0))* HarperCollins Pubs.
—Sitting Duck. Urbanovic, Jackie, illus. 2010. (Illus.). 40p. (J). (gr. -1-2). (ENG.). 17.99 *(978-0-06-176583-4(X))*; lib. bdg. 18.89 *(978-0-06-176584-1(8))* HarperCollins Pubs.
Valdez, Joseph G. Lean on Me, Lee. Martinez, Gayle Denise, illus. 2012. 24p. pap. *(978-1-77067-670-1(8))* FriesenPress.
Valentine, Victoria. The Cutest Little Duckie. Tucker, Amanda, illus. 2007. 80p. (J). per. 15.00 *(978-0-9723493-4-5(0),* Water Forest Pr.) Skyline Pubn.
van der Put, Klaartje, et al. Little Duck: Finger Puppet. 2005. (Little Finger Puppet Board Bks.: FING). (ENG., Illus.). 12p. (J). (gr. -1 — 1). bds. 6.99 *(978-0-8118-4847-3(7))* Chronicle Bks. LLC.
Van Scoyoc, Pam. The Ballerina with Webbed Feet/la Bailarina Palmipeda. Teichman, Diane E., tr. from ENG. Lewis, R. J., illus. l.t. ed. 2004. (ENG & SPA.). 40p. (J). (gr. k-2). lib. bdg. 16.98 *(978-0-9663629-2-3(6))* By Grace Enterprises.
Verdick, Elizabeth. Peep Leap, 0 vols. Bendall-Brunello, John, illus. 2013. (ENG.). 32p. (J). (gr. -1-2). 16.99 *(978-1-4778-1640-0(2),* 9781477816400, Amazon Children's Publishing) Amazon Publishing.
Verrett, Michael. The White Alligator Crown Quatro. 2010. 147p. pap. 13.95 *(978-0-557-58121-4(4))* Lulu Pr., Inc.
—The White Alligator (paper Back) 2010. 116p. pap. 17.30 *(978-0-557-28042-1(7))* Lulu Pr., Inc.
—The White Alligator (paperback full Color) 2010. 116p. pap. 42.00 *(978-0-557-36924-9(X))* Lulu Pr., Inc.
Verville, Claudia J. Little Duckie Doodle. 2013. 26p. pap. 14.25 *(978-1-4817-0407-6(9))* AuthorHouse.
Victoria & the Baby Tree. 2005. pap. 14.95 *(978-1-59526-525-8(2))* Aeon Publishing Inc.
Volker, Kerstin. Lilly's Birthday Party. 2003. (Funny Friends Lift-and-Learn Bks.). (Illus.). 14p. (J). 5.99 *(978-1-59384-022-8(5))* Parklane Publishing.
Volp, Denise. Gregory the Greedy Duck. 2013. 32p. pap. 23.35 *(978-1-4669-3216-6(3))* Trafford Publishing.
Waddell, Martin. Farmer Duck. Oxenbury, Helen, illus. 2008. (Candlewick Storybook Animations Ser.). (ENG.). 40p. (J). (gr. -1-k). 14.99 *(978-0-7636-3512-1(X))* Candlewick Pr.
Walker, Lane. The Day It Rained Ducks. 2014. (Hometown Hunters Collection: Vol. 5). (ENG.). 151p. (J). (gr. 4-7). pap. 9.99 *(978-1-58169-564-9(0),* Evergreen Pr.) Genesis Communications, Inc.
Wallen, Virginia. Amanda: Duck or Chicken? 2007. 17.00 *(978-0-8059-8828-4(9))* Dorrance Publishing Co., Inc.
Walsh, Meg. Mama, Won't You Play with Me? 2009. 28p. pap. 13.99 *(978-1-4490-1424-7(0))* AuthorHouse.
Wan, Joyce. Frog & Friends. Wan, Joyce, illus. 2013. (ENG., Illus.). 14p. (J). (gr. -1-k). bds. 6.99 *(978-0-8431-7277-5(0),* Price Stern Sloan) Penguin Young Readers Group.
Watt, Fiona. Quack, Quack, Quack. 2008. (Bath Bks). 8p. (J). 14.99 *(978-0-7945-2304-6(8),* Usborne) EDC Publishing.
—That's Not My Duck... Wells, Rachel, illus. 2014. (ENG.). (gr. -1). bds. 9.99 *(978-0-7945-3193-5(6),* Usborne) EDC Publishing.
Weidner, Teri. Always Twins. Weidner, Teri, illus. 2015. (ENG., Illus.). 32p. (J). (gr. -1-k). 16.95 *(978-0-8234-3159-5(2))* Holiday Hse., Inc.
Weiss, Ellen. Lucky Duck. Lies, Brian, illus. 2004. (Ready-to-Read Ser.). 31p. (J). (gr. -1-1). 11.65 *(978-0-7569-5618-9(8))* Perfection Learning Corp.
Welch, Fred. The Little Duck Who Lost His Quack. 2009. 20p. pap. 11.99 *(978-1-4389-9644-8(6))* AuthorHouse.
Wells, Rosemary. A Visit to Dr. Duck. Wells, Rosemary, illus. 2014. (ENG., Illus.). 30p. (J). (-k). bds. 7.99 *(978-0-7636-7229-4(7))* Candlewick Pr.
West-Pratt, Judy Lea. Just Like Me! 2013. 40p. pap. *(978-1-4602-0325-5(9))* FriesenPress.
Weston Woods Staff, creator. Angus & the Ducks. 2004. (J). 18.95 *(978-1-55592-369-3(0))*; 38.75 *(978-1-55592-370-9(4))* Weston Woods Studios, Inc.
—Duck for President. 2004. 29.95 *(978-0-7882-0540-8(4))* Weston Woods Studios, Inc.
—Duck on a Bike. 2011. 18.95 *(978-0-545-19704-5(X))*; 29.95 *(978-0-545-19698-7(1))*; 38.75 *(978-0-545-19709-0(0))* Weston Woods Studios, Inc.
—Giggle, Giggle Quack. 2004. (J). 29.95 *(978-1-55592-701-1(7))* Weston Woods Studios, Inc.
—Make Way for Ducklings. 2011. 18.95 *(978-0-439-72774-7(X))*; 29.95 *(978-0-439-73489-9(4))*; 38.75 *(978-0-439-72776-1(6))* Weston Woods Studios, Inc.
—The Story about Ping. 2011. 38.75 *(978-0-439-72894-2(0))*; 18.95 *(978-0-439-72893-5(2))*; 29.95 *(978-0-439-73519-3(X))* Weston Woods Studios, Inc.
—The Tale of the Mandarin Ducks. 2004. 18.95 *(978-1-55592-742-4(4))*; 38.75 *(978-1-55592-750-9(5))* Weston Woods Studios, Inc.
—The Ugly Duckling. 2011. 29.95 *(978-0-439-72909-3(2))* Weston Woods Studios, Inc.
When Aunt Mattie Got Her Wings. 2014. (ENG., Illus.). 32p. (J). (gr. -1-3). 17.99 *(978-1-4814-1044-1(X),* Beach Lane Bks.) Beach Lane Bks.
White, Cathy. The Duck Named Dean. 2009. 24p. pap. 14.00 *(978-1-4389-9569-2(X))* AuthorHouse.
Wildsmith, Brian. Hunter & His Dog, 1 vol. Wildsmith, Brian, illus. 2008. (ENG., Illus.). 32p. (J). 16.95 *(978-1-59572-123-5(1))* Star Bright Bks., Inc.
—The Little Wood Duck, 1 vol. 2007. (ENG., Illus.). 32p. (J). (gr. -1-3). 16.95 *(978-1-59572-042-9(1))* Star Bright Bks., Inc.
—The Little Wood Duck, 1 vol. Wildsmith, Brian, illus. 2006. (ENG., Illus.). 32p. (J). pap. 6.95 *(978-1-59572-049-8(9))* Star Bright Bks., Inc.
Willems, Mo. The Duckling Gets a Cookie!? Willems, Mo, illus. 2012. (ENG., Illus.). 40p. (J). (gr. -1-k). 16.99 *(978-1-4231-5128-9(3))* Hyperion Pr.
—The Pigeon Finds a Hot Dog! Willems, Mo, illus. 2004. (Pigeon Ser.). (ENG., Illus.). 40p. (J). (gr. -1-k). 16.99 *(978-0-7868-1869-3(7))* Hyperion Pr.
Willems, Mo & Campoy, F. Isabel. ¡La Paloma Encuentra un Perro Caliente! Willems, Mo, illus. 2011. (SPA & ENG., Illus.). 40p. (J). (gr. -1-k). pap. 9.99 *(978-1-4231-4051-1(6))* Hyperion Pr.
Williamgoldenpen. Quacker's Bedtime Stories. 2006. 49p. pap. 16.95 *(978-1-4241-2236-3(8))* PublishAmerica, Inc.
—Quacker's Bedtime Stories... Continued. 2007. (ENG.). 68p. per. 19.95 *(978-1-4241-7448-5(1))* America Star Bks.
Williams, Dan. The Duck That Lost His Waddle. 2010. 40p. pap. 24.99 *(978-1-60957-538-0(5))* Salem Author Services.
Williams, Greg. Dudley the Duck. 2011. 32p. pap. 19.00 *(978-1-60746-368-9(7))* FastPrncil, Inc.
—Puggley Wuggley & the Three-Legged Chicken. 2011. 40p. pap. 19.00 *(978-1-60746-233-0(8))* FastPrncil, Inc.
Williams, Quatessa. The Little Fritter Counters. 2012. 48p. pap. 21.99 *(978-1-4691-8686-3(1))* Xlibris Corp.
Wilson, Karma. Duddle Puck: The Puddle Duck. Hall, Marcellus, illus. 2015. (ENG.). 40p. (J). (gr. -1-3). 17.99 *(978-1-4424-4927-5(6),* McElderry, Margaret K. Bks.) McElderry, Margaret K. Bks.
Wilson, Pamela J. Tales from Tubblewood Too. 2009. (Illus.). 164p. 23.50 *(978-1-4389-4064-9(5))* AuthorHouse.
—Tales from Tubblewood Too: Miss Duck to the Rescue. 2009. (Illus.). 164p. pap. 13.50 *(978-1-4389-4063-2(7))* AuthorHouse.
Wilson, Troy. The Duck Says. Boldt, Mike, illus. 2016. 29p. (J). ***(978-1-338-03466-0(9))*** Scholastic, Inc.
Windsor, Jo. Lazy Duck. Webb, Philip, illus. (Sails Literacy Ser.). 24p. (gr. k-18). 27.00 *(978-0-7635-6989-1(5))* Rigby Education.
—Lazy Duck: 3-in-1 Package. Webb, Philip, illus. (Sails Literacy Ser.). 24p. (gr. k-18). 57.00 *(978-0-7578-3199-7(0))* Rigby Education.
Witte, Jessica Pierce. Dexter the Duck Gets His Quack. York, Shane, illus. 2012. 30p. 24.95 *(978-1-4626-6592-1(6))* America Star Bks.
Wolfe, Jane. Dizzy Duck. Benham, Tors, illus. 2016. (ENG.). 8p. (J). (gr. -1-12). bds. 6.99 *(978-1-84322-719-9(3),* Armadillo) Anness Publishing GBR. Dist: National Bk. Network.
Wolff, Susan. Quackers Wants to Fly. Currie, Justin, illus. 2013. 32p. pap. 8.95 *(978-1-60653-074-0(7))* High Hill Pr.
Wong, Liz. Quackers. 2016. (ENG.). 40p. (J). (gr. -1-2). 15.99 *(978-0-553-51154-3(8),* Knopf Bks. for Young Readers) Random Hse. Children's Bks.
Woods, Emily. Thingamafig B Quaxindehouse: Best Friends. 2011. 24p. pap. 12.99 *(978-1-4634-4853-0(8))* AuthorHouse.
Yoon, Salina. Duck, Duck, Porcupine! 2017. (Duck, Duck, Porcupine Book Ser.). (ENG., Illus.). 64p. (J). pap. 5.99 ***(978-1-61963-724-5(3)***, 9781619637245, Bloomsbury USA Childrens) Bloomsbury Publishing USA.
—My Kite Is Stuck! & Other Stories. 2017. (Duck, Duck, Porcupine Book Ser.). (ENG.). 64p. (J). 9.99 *(978-1-61963-887-7(8),* 9781619638877, Bloomsbury USA Childrens) Bloomsbury Publishing USA.
Yoon, Salina. That's My Book! & Other Stories. 2017. (Duck, Duck, Porcupine Book Ser.). (ENG., Illus.). 64p. (J). 9.99 ***(978-1-61963-891-4(6)***, 9781619638914, Bloomsbury USA Childrens) Bloomsbury Publishing USA.
Yzaguirre, Ricky. The Day I Turned into a Duck. 2012. 8p. pap. 15.99 *(978-1-4772-1275-2(2))* AuthorHouse.
Ziefert, Harriet & National Geographic Learning Staff. The Ugly Duckling. 2010. (Rise & Shine Ser.). (ENG., Illus.). 32p. (C). (gr. k-3). mass mkt. 14.95 *(978-0-14-038352-2(2))* National Geographic School Publishing, Inc.
Zoller, Jayson D. The Laziest Duck. l.t. ed. 2004. (Illus.). 13p. (J). lib. bdg. 12.95 *(978-1-932338-55-3(1))*; per. 7.99 *(978-1-932338-52-2(7))* Lifevest Publishing, Inc.
Zschock, Martha Day & Zschock, Martha. Hello, Cape Cod! 2009. (Hello! Ser.). (ENG., Illus.). 16p. (gr. -1-k). bds. 9.95 *(978-0-9819430-1-5(2),* Commonwealth Editions) Applewood Bks.

DUMB (DEAF MUTES)

see Deaf

DUNBAR, PAUL LAURENCE, 1872-1906

Reef, Catherine. The Life of Paul Laurence Dunbar: Portrait of a Poet. 2014. (Legendary African Americans Ser.). (Illus.). 96p. (J). (gr. 6-12). 27.94 *(978-0-7660-6152-1(3))*; pap. 10.95 *(978-0-7660-6153-8(1))* Enslow Pubs., Inc.

DUNES

see Sand Dunes

DUNGEONS

see Prisons

DUNHAM, KATHERINE, 1909-2006

O'Connor, Barbara. Katherine Dunham: Pioneer of Black Dance. 2005. (Trailblazers Biographies Ser.). (Illus.). 112p. (gr. 5-9). 27.93 *(978-1-57505-353-0(5))* Lerner Publishing Group.

DUST

Dust Bunnies. 2007. 13.95 *(978-1-4218-9932-9(9))* 1st World Publishing, Inc.
Sayre, April Pulley. Stars Beneath Your Bed: The Surprising Story of Dust. Jonas, Ann, illus. 2005. 32p. (J). lib. bdg. 17.89 *(978-0-06-057189-4(6))*; (ENG.). 17.99 *(978-0-06-057188-7(8),* Greenwillow Bks.) HarperCollins Pubs.

DUSTLAND (IMAGINARY PLACE)—FICTION

Marsh, Carole. Adventure to the Pioneer Prairie! 2007. (Field Trips (Gallopade International) Ser.). (Illus.). 114p. (J). (gr. 2-9). pap. 14.95 *(978-0-635-06393-9(X))* Gallopade International.

DUTCH—UNITED STATES

Gibson, Karen Bush. New Netherland: The Dutch Settle the Hudson Valley. 2006. (Building America Ser.). (Illus.). 48p.

C D

(J). (gr. 3-7). lib. bdg. 29.95 *(978-1-58415-461-7(6))* Mitchell Lane Pubs., Inc.

Huey, Lois Miner. American Archaeology Uncovers the Dutch Colonies. 2009. (American Archaeology Ser.). 64p. (gr. 5-6). 31.36 *(978-0-7614-4263-9(4))* Marshall Cavendish Corp.

Parker, Lewis K. Dutch Colonies in the Americas. 2009. (European Colonies in the Americas Ser.). 24p. (gr. 2-2). 42.50 *(978-1-61512-316-2(4)*, PowerKids Pr.) Rosen Publishing Group, Inc., The.

Schimel, Kate & Levy, Janey. New York: The Dutch Colony of New Amsterdam. 2012. (Illus.). 24p. (J). 60.00 *(978-1-4488-5758-6(9))*; pap. 10.00 *(978-1-4488-5757-9(0))*; lib. bdg. 22.60 *(978-1-4488-5742-5(2))* Rosen Publishing Group, Inc., The. (PowerKids Pr.).

DUTCH—UNITED STATES—FICTION

The Little Dutch Boy: 6 Small Books. (gr. k-2). 23.00 *(978-0-7635-8509-9(2))* Rigby Education.

DWARFS

Beaumont, Steve. How to Draw Orcs, Elves, & Dwarves. 2007. (Drawing Fantasy Art Ser.: Vol. 2). (Illus.). 32p. (J). (gr. 4-7). lib. bdg. 26.50 *(978-1-4042-3859-6(X))* Rosen Publishing Group, Inc., The.

—How to Draw Wizards, Warriors, Orcs & Elves. 2007. (Illus.). 143p. pap. 7.99 *(978-0-7858-2345-2(X)*, Chartwell) Book Sales, Inc.

Kortenkamp, Steve. The Dwarf Planets. 2011. (Solar System & Beyond Ser.). (ENG.). 32p. (gr. 3-4). pap. 47.70 *(978-1-4296-6406-6(1)*, Fact Finders) Capstone Press of Coughlan Cos.

Krensky, Stephen. Watchers in the Woods. 2008. pap. 52.95 *(978-0-8225-9892-3(2))* 2007. (ENG., Illus.). 48p. (gr. 4-7). lib. bdg. 26.60 *(978-0-8225-6763-6(6)*, Lerner Pubns.) Lerner Publishing Group.

Sautter, A. J. A Field Guide to Elves, Dwarves, & Other Magical Folk, 1 vol. Ashcroft, Colin Michael et al, illus. 2014. (Fantasy Field Guides). (ENG.). 32p. (gr. 3-4). lib. bdg. 27.99 *(978-1-4914-0692-2(5))* Capstone Press of Coughlan Cos.

DWARFS—FICTION

Abbott, Ellen Jensen. Watersmeet, 0 vols. 2012. (Watersmeet Ser.: 1). (ENG.). 352p. (YA). (gr. 7-11). pap. 8.99 *(978-0-7614-5992-7(8)*, 9780761459927, Amazon Children's Publishing) Amazon Publishing.

Akihiro. Light of Love, Forever. 2009. 76p. pap. 8.99 *(978-0-557-03693-6(3))* Lulu Pr., Inc.

Alfaro Sifontes, Manuel Guillermo. Alboroto en un Lugar Remoto. 2005. (Illus.). 32p. (J). *(978-1-58018-052-8(3))* Cambridge BrickHouse, Inc.

Allen, Mike. A Little on a Road Trip. 2009. 144p. pap. 12.95 *(978-1-4327-3942-3(5))* Outskirts Pr., Inc.

Alva, Kristian. The Balborite Curse: Book Four of the Dragon Stones Saga. 2013. 240p. pap. 9.98 *(978-1-937361-11-2(X)*, Defiant Pr.) Passkey Pubns.

AZ Books, creator. Snow White & the Seven Dwarfs. 2012. (Musical Fairy Tales Ser.). (ENG., Illus.). 12p. (J). (gr. -1-3). bds. 15.95 *(978-1-61889-068-9(9))* AZ Bks. LLC.

Becker, Jaqueline H. Listen, There Are More Than Seven Dwarfs. 2012. pap. 11.95 *(978-0-7414-7037-9(3))* Infinity Publishing.

Berrios, Frank & RH Disney Staff. Snow White & the Seven Dwarfs. Disney Storybook Artists Staff, illus. 2006. (Read-Aloud Board Book Ser.). (ENG.). 24p. (J). (gr. k — 1). bds. 4.99 *(978-0-7364-2426-4(1)*, RH/Disney) Random Hse. Children's Bks.

Black, Holly & DiTerlizzi, Tony. The Ironwood Tree. DiTerlizzi, Tony, illus. 2013. (Spiderwick Chronicles Ser.: 4). (ENG., Illus.). (J). (gr. 1-5). 128p. 15.99 *(978-1-4424-8702-4(X))*; 144p. pap. 7.99 *(978-1-4424-8701-7(1))* Simon & Schuster Bks. For Young Readers. (Simon & Schuster Bks. For Young Readers).

Bray, Libba. Going Bovine. 2010. (ENG.). 496p. (YA). (gr. 9). pap. 10.99 *(978-0-385-73398-4(4)*, Ember) Random Hse. Children's Bks.

Brown, Carron, ed. Sleeping Beauty & Snow White & the Seven Dwarfs: Two Tales & Their Histories. 2009. (World of Fairy Tales Ser.). (Illus.). 32p. (J). (gr. -1-2). pap. 10.55 *(978-1-60754-635-1(3))*; lib. bdg. 22.60 *(978-1-60754-634-4(5))* Windmill Bks.

Crump, Fred, Jr. Ebonita & the Seven Boyz. 2010. 32p. (J). 12.95 *(978-1-934056-71-4(5))* UMI (Urban Ministries, Inc.).

DiTerlizzi, Tony & Black, Holly. The Ironwood Tree. DiTerlizzi, Tony, illus. 4th ed. 2004. (Spiderwick Chronicles Ser.: 4). (ENG., Illus.). 128p. (J). (gr. 2-6). 10.99 *(978-0-689-85939-7(2)*, Simon & Schuster Bks. For Young Readers) Simon & Schuster Bks. For Young Readers.

—The Ironwood Tree. l.t. ed. 2006. (Spiderwick Chronicles: Bk. 4). 90p. (YA). (gr. 2-18). 23.95 *(978-0-7862-8583-9(4))* Thorndike Pr.

Frabetti, Carlo. La Magia Mas Poderosa. 11th ed. 2003. (SPA., Illus.). 120p. (J). 15.95 *(978-84-204-4844-2(3))* Ediciones Alfaguara ESP. Dist: Santillana USA Publishing Co., Inc.

French, Vivian. The Heart of Glass: The Third Tale from the Five Kingdoms. Collins, Ross, illus. 2010. (Tales from the Five Kingdoms Ser.: 3). (ENG.). 256p. (J). (gr. 3-7). 14.99 *(978-0-7636-4814-5(0))* Candlewick Pr.

Frizzell, Sally Parker. The Adventures in the Secret Valley. 2007. 40p. pap. 9.00 *(978-0-8059-7615-1(9))* Dorrance Publishing Co., Inc.

Godfrey, Jessica E. Night Hamster. 2012. 28p. pap. 15.99 *(978-1-4691-5083-3(2))* Xlibris Corp.

Graff, Lisa. The Thing about Georgie. 2008. (ENG.). 224p. (J). (gr. 3-7). pap. 6.99 *(978-0-06-087591-6(7))* HarperCollins Pubs.

Hub, Ulrich & Ragg-Kirkby, Helena. Becoming the Wolf. Mühle, Jörg, illus. 2012. (ENG.). 64p. (YA). 12.00 *(978-0-8028-5409-4(5)*, Eerdmans Bks For Young Readers) Eerdmans, William B. Publishing Co.

Hubbard, L. Ron. If I Were You: Literature Guide for Teachers & Librarians, Based on Common Core ELA Standards for Classrooms 6-9, Kit. 2014. (gr. 6-10). 22.95 *(978-1-61986-295-1(6))* Galaxy Pr., LLC.

Hubbard, L. Ron, contrib. by. If I Were You: Literature Guide for Teachers & Librarians, Based on Common Core ELA Standards for Classrooms 6-9. 2013. (Stories from the Golden Age Ser.). (ENG.). 35p. (gr. 6-9). pap., tchr. ed. 14.95 *(978-1-61986-201-2(8))* Galaxy Pr., LLC.

Lagonegro, Melissa. Friends for a Princess. 2004. (Disney Princess Step into Reading Ser.). (gr. -1-2). lib. bdg. 13.55 *(978-0-613-73713-5(X)*, Turtleback) Turtleback Bks.

Lake, Susan. Ebony & the Five Dwarfs. 2007. 56p. per. 10.00 *(978-1-4257-7841-5(0))* Xlibris Corp.

Laura Grey Wahl. The Magic Town of Stuart Easterly. 2009. 16p. pap. 15.00 *(978-1-4389-4703-7(8))* AuthorHouse.

Marsh, Katherine. Jepp, Who Defied the Stars. 2013. (ENG.). 400p. (J). (gr. 5-9). pap. 9.99 *(978-1-4231-3786-3(8))* Hyperion Pr.

Morgan, C. M. Silver Doorway #1: A Gnome Away from Home. 2003. 104p. (J). pap. 6.99 *(978-0-9702189-2-6(3))* Sabledrake Enterprises.

—Silver Doorway #2: Dwarves in the Dark. 2003. 104p. (J). pap. *(978-0-9702189-3-3(1))* Sabledrake Enterprises.

Morris, Gerald. The Savage Damsel & the Dwarf. 2008. (Squire's Tales Ser.: 3). (ENG.). 224p. (J). (gr. 5-7). pap. 7.99 *(978-0-547-01437-1(6))* Houghton Mifflin Harcourt Publishing Co.

Page, Nick & Claire. Snow White. 2006. (Read with Me (Make Believe Ideas) Ser.). (Illus.). 32p. (J). (gr. k-2). *(978-1-84610-163-2(8))* Make Believe Ideas.

PC Treasures Staff, prod. Snow White & the Seven Dwarfs. 2007. (J). *(978-1-60072-033-8(1))* PC Treasures, Inc.

Poole, Josephine. BLANCANIEVES. 2007. (SPA., Illus.). 30p. (J). (gr. -1-5). 24.95 *(978-84-96629-17-2(1))* S.A. Kokinos ESP. Dist: Lectorum Pubns., Inc.

Posner-Sanchez, Andrea. Ariel's Dolphin Adventure - Snow White's New Friend, 2 bks. in 1. Random House Disney Staff, illus. 2010. (Pictureback(R) Ser.). (ENG.). 32p. (J). (gr. -1-2). pap. 4.99 *(978-0-7364-2654-1(X)*, RH/Disney) Random Hse. Children's Bks.

Ruzzier, Sergio. The Little Giant. 2004. (Illus.). 32p. (J). (gr. -1-2). 16.89 *(978-0-06-052952-9(0)*, Geringer, Laura Book) HarperCollins Pubs.

Snow White & the Seven Dwarfs. 2008. (Read & Learn Sticker Books Ser.). 48p. pap. *(978-1-4075-3197-7(2))* Parragon, Inc.

Spinner, Stephanie. Damosel: In Which the Lady of the Lake Renders a Frank & Often Startling Account of Her Wondrous Life & Times. 2010. (ENG.). 208p. (YA). (gr. 7). pap. 8.99 *(978-0-553-49511-9(9)*, Knopf Bks. for Young Readers) Random Hse. Children's Bks.

Van Stockum, Hilda. King Oberon's Forest. 2012. 164p. pap. 11.95 *(978-0-7414-6693-8(7))* Infinity Publishing.

Waltz, Dan. Dragon Fly: A Gnome's Great Adventure. Waltz, Dan, illus. 2007. (Illus.). 360p. (YA). per. 12.49 *(978-0-9741774-7-2(4))* D. W. Publishing.

DWELLINGS

see Architecture, Domestic; Houses

DYES AND DYEING

dePaola, Tomie. Charlie Needs a Cloak. 2015. 32p. pap. 7.00 *(978-1-61003-601-6(8))* Center for the Collaborative Classroom.

Kassinger, Ruth. Dyes: From Sea Snails to Synthetics. 2003. (Material World Ser.). (Illus.). 80p. (gr. 6-8). lib. bdg. 25.90 *(978-0-7613-2112-5(8)*, Twenty-First Century Bks.) Lerner Publishing Group.

Senisi, Ellen B. Berry Smudges & Leaf Prints: Finding & Making Colors from Nature. Senisi, Ellen B., photos by. 2005. (Illus.). 40p. (J). (gr. 4-8). reprint ed. 17.00 *(978-0-7567-9707-2(1))* DIANE Publishing Co.

Weston Woods Staff, creator. Charlie Needs a Cloak. 2004. 18.95 *(978-1-55592-382-2(8))*; 38.75 *(978-1-55592-383-9(6))* Weston Woods Studios, Inc.

DYLAN, BOB, 1941-

Golio, Gary. When Bob Met Woody: The Story of the Young Bob Dylan. Burckhardt, Marc, illus. 2011. (ENG.). 40p. (J). (gr. 3-7). 17.99 *(978-0-316-11299-4(2))* Little, Brown Bks. for Young Readers.

Manzella, Teresa Ryan. How to Analyze the Music of Bob Dylan, 1 vol. 2011. (Essential Critiques Set 2 Ser.). (ENG., Illus.). 112p. (J). (gr. 6-12). lib. bdg. 35.64 *(978-1-61783-090-7(9))* ABDO Publishing Co.

O'Connor, Jim. Who Is Bob Dylan? Harrison, Nancy & O'brien, John, illus. 2013. (Who Was? Ser.). (ENG.). 112p. (J). (gr. 3-7). pap. 5.99 *(978-0-448-46461-9(6)*, Grosset & Dunlap) Penguin Young Readers Group.

—Who Is Bob Dylan? 2013. (Who Is...? Ser.). lib. bdg. 16.00 *(978-0-606-31685-9(X)*, Turtleback) Turtleback Bks.

Roberts, Jeremy. Bob Dylan: Voice of a Generation. 128p. (J). (gr. 6-18). 18.95 *(978-1-58013-155-1(7)*, Kar-Ben Publishing); 2005. (ENG., Illus.). 27.93 *(978-0-8225-1368-1(4)*, Lerner Pubns.) Lerner Publishing Group.

Schuman, Michael. Bob Dylan. 2017. (J). ***(978-0-7660-9206-8(2))*** Enslow Pubs., Inc.

Schuman, Michael A. Bob Dylan: The Life & Times of an American Icon. 2003. (People to Know Ser.). (Illus.). 112p. (J). lib. bdg. 26.60 *(978-0-7660-2108-2(4))* Enslow Pubs., Inc.

DYNAMICS

see also Aerodynamics; Force and Energy; Matter; Motion; Physics; Quantum Theory; Thermodynamics

Bailey, Gerry & Law, Felicia. Energy & Movement. 2015. (Stone Age Science Ser.). (ENG., Illus.). 32p. (J). (gr. 3-7). lib. bdg. *(978-0-7787-1888-8(3))* Crabtree Publishing Co.

Berger, Melvin & Berger, Gilda. Are Mountains Getting Taller? Questions & Answers about the Changing Earth. Carter, Robin, illus. 2003. (Question & Answer Ser.). (ENG.). 48p. (J). pap. 5.95 *(978-0-439-26673-4(4)*, Scholastic Reference) Scholastic, Inc.

Cavell-Clarke, Steffi. Pushes & Pulls. 2017. (First Science Ser.). 24p. (J). (gr. 1-1). pap. 8.25 ***(978-1-5345-2080-6(5))***; lib. bdg. 24.60 ***(978-1-5345-2082-0(1))*** Greenhaven Publishing LLC. (KidHaven Publishing).

Holt, Rinehart and Winston Staff. Holt Science & Technology Chapter 6: Physical Science: Forces in Motion. 5th ed. 2004. (Illus.). pap. 12.86 *(978-0-03-030381-4(8))* Holt McDougal.

Kenney, Karen Latchana. The Science of Race Cars: Studying Forces & Motion, 1 vol. 2016. (Science in Action Ser.). (ENG., Illus.). 32p. (J). (gr. 3-6). 27.07 *(978-1-62403-963-8(4))* ABDO Publishing Co.

Petersen, Kristen. Understanding Kinetic Energy. 2015. (J). lib. bdg. *(978-1-62713-435-4(2))*; (ENG.). 48p. (gr. 7-7). 31.36 *(978-1-5026-0144-5(3))* Cavendish Square Publishing.

—Understanding the Laws of Motion. 2015. (J). lib. bdg. *(978-1-62713-427-9(1))* Cavendish Square Publishing.

Rees, Peter. Why Do Swings Swing? Level 4 Factbook. 2010. (Cambridge Young Readers Ser.). (ENG., Illus.). 16p. pap. 6.00 *(978-0-521-13720-1(9))* Cambridge Univ. Pr.

The Science of Energy. 2016. (Illus.). 48p. (J). *(978-1-4222-3513-3(0))* Mason Crest.

Silverman, Buffy. Pull It, Push It. 2012. (ENG.). 24p. (gr. 3-4). pap. 8.95 *(978-1-61810-229-4(X))* Rourke Educational Media.

Stoyles, Pennie & Pentland, Peter. Earth & Space. 2011. (Energy in Action Ser.). (Illus.). 32p. (J). (gr. 4). 28.50 *(978-1-60870-566-5(8))* Marshall Cavendish Corp.

VanVoorst, Jenny Fretland. Bicycles. 2016. (Early Physics Fun). 24p. (J). (gr. 2-5). lib. bdg. 25.65 *(978-1-62031-314-5(6)*, Pogo) Jump! Inc.

Viegas, Jennifer. Kinetic & Potential Energy: Understanding Changes Within Physical Systems. (Library of Physics Ser.). 48p. (gr. 7-7). 2009. 53.00 *(978-1-60853-802-7(8))* 2004. (Illus.). (J). lib. bdg. 29.25 *(978-1-4042-0333-4(8))* Rosen Publishing Group, Inc., The.

Weakland, Mark. Zoom! Wile E. Coyote Experiments with Speed & Velocity. Sordo, Paco, illus. 2017. (Wile E. Coyote, Physical Science Genius Ser.). (ENG.). 32p. (gr. 3-5). lib. bdg. 30.65 *(978-1-5157-3734-6(9))* Capstone Press of Coughlan Cos.

DYNAMOS

see Electric Generators

DYSLEXIA

Doering Tourville, Amanda. My Friend Has Dyslexia [Readers World]. Sorra, Kristin, illus. 2010. (Friends with Disabilities Ser.). 24p. pap. 6.00 *(978-1-4048-6704-8(X)*, Nonfiction Picture Bks.) Picture Window Bks.

Donnelly, Karen J. Coping with Dyslexia. 2005. (Coping Ser.). (Illus.). 192p. (YA). (gr. 7-12). lib. bdg. 34.60 *(978-0-8239-2850-7(0)*, CODYSL) Rosen Publishing Group, Inc., The.

Goldish, Meish. Everything You Need to Know about Dyslexia. 2009. (Need to Know Library). 64p. (gr. 5-5). 58.50 *(978-1-60854-066-2(9))* Rosen Publishing Group, Inc., The.

Landau, Elaine. Dyslexia. 2004. (Life Balance Ser.). (ENG.). 80p. (YA). (gr. 5-8). pap. 6.95 *(978-0-531-16612-3(0)*, Watts, Franklin) Scholastic Library Publishing.

Moody, Sylvia. Dyslexia. 2004. (ENG., Illus.). 176p. pap. 19.95 *(978-0-09-190001-4(8))* Random Hse. GBR. Dist: Independent Pubs. Group.

Silverstein, Virginia. Handy Health Guide to Dyslexia. 2013. (Handy Health Guides). 48p. (J). (gr. 5-12). pap. 8.95 *(978-1-4644-0495-5(X))* Enslow Pubs., Inc.

Silverstein, Virginia & Nunn, Laura Silverstein. Handy Health Guide to Dyslexia. 2013. (Handy Health Guides). 48p. (J). lib. bdg. 25.27 *(978-0-7660-4276-6(6))* Enslow Pubs., Inc.

Squire, Ann O. Dyslexia. 2016. (True Book(tm), A — Health Ser.). (ENG., Illus.). 48p. (J). lib. bdg. 31.00 *(978-0-531-22843-2(6)*, Children's Pr.) Scholastic Library Publishing.

Tourville, Amanda Doering. My Friend Has Dyslexia, 1 vol. Sorra, Kristin, illus. 2010. (Friends with Disabilities Ser.). (ENG.). 24p. (gr. k-3). lib. bdg. 25.99 *(978-1-4048-5752-0(4))* Picture Window Bks.

DYSLEXIA—FICTION

Alexander, Claire, illus. Back to Front & Upside Down. 2012. (ENG.). 26p. (J). 16.00 *(978-0-8028-5414-8(1)*, Eerdmans Bks For Young Readers) Eerdmans, William B. Publishing Co.

Beckhorn, Susan Williams. Sarey by Lantern Light. 2003. (ENG., Illus.). 150p. (J). (gr. 4-17). pap. 9.95 *(978-0-89272-612-7(1))* Down East Bks.

Chambers, Aidan. Dying to Know You. 2013. (ENG.). 288p. (YA). (gr. 9-17). pap. 9.95 *(978-1-4197-0794-0(9)*, Amulet Bks.) Abrams, Inc.

Clarke, Kevin & Dutton, Demi. Jenny Can't Read: A Story about Dyslexia & Its Effect on Self-Esteem. 2012. 90p. pap. 13.66 *(978-1-4772-1909-6(9))* AuthorHouse.

DeClements, Barthe & Declements, Barthe. Sixth Grade Can Really Kill You. 2008. (ENG.). 160p. (J). (gr. 3-7). 5.99 *(978-0-14-241380-7(1)*, Puffin Books) Penguin Young Readers Group.

Draper, Sharon M. Double Dutch. 2004. 183p. (gr. 6-9). 17.00 *(978-0-7569-2934-3(2))* Perfection Learning Corp.

Engle, Margarita. The Wild Book. 2014. (ENG., Illus.). 144p. (J). (gr. 5-7). pap. 7.99 *(978-0-544-02275-1(0))* Houghton Mifflin Harcourt Publishing Co.

Goodhart, Pippa. Rescued by a Dog Called Flow. Lewis, Anthony, illus. 2006. 121p. (J). (gr. 4-7). pap. 6.95 *(978-1-903015-47-6(2))* Barn Owl Bks, London GBR. Dist: Independent Pubs. Group.

Hansen, Joyce. Yellow Bird & Me. 2005. (163rd Street Ser.). 155p. (gr. 5-9). 16.95 *(978-0-7569-6228-9(5))* Perfection Learning Corp.

Hodge, Deborah. Lily & the Mixed-Up Letters. Brassard, France, illus. 2007. (ENG.). 32p. (J). (gr. 1-4). 18.95 *(978-0-88776-757-9(5)*, Tundra Bks.) Tundra Bks. CAN. Dist: Penguin Random Hse. LLC.

Hoffman, Mary. City of Secrets. (Stravaganza Ser.). (ENG.). (YA). 2010. 416p. (gr. 7). pap. 8.99 *(978-1-59990-451-1(9)*, 9781599904511) 2008. 400p. (gr. 5-18). 17.99 *(978-1-59990-202-9(8)*, 9781599902029) Bloomsbury Publishing USA. (Bloomsbury USA Childrens).

Hudson, Ella. Hudson Hates School. 2014. (ENG., Illus.). 32p. (J). (gr. k-3). pap. 8.99 *(978-1-84780-375-7(X)*, Frances Lincoln) Quarto Publishing Group UK GBR. Dist: Hachette Bk. Group.

Hunt, Lynda Mullaly. COMO PEZ EN EL ÁRBOL: UNA NOVELA SOBRE LA DISLEXIA. 2016. (SPA.). 240p. (J). (gr. 4). pap. 13.95 *(978-84-15594-69-7(0)*, Nube De Tinta) Penguin Random House Grupo Editorial ESP. Dist: Two Rivers Distribution.

—Fish in a Tree. (ENG.). (J). (gr. 5). 2017. 304p. 8.99 *(978-0-14-242642-5(3)*, Puffin Books) 2015. 288p. 16.99 *(978-0-399-16259-6(3)*, Nancy Paulsen Books) Penguin Young Readers Group.

—Fish in a Tree. 2017. lib. bdg. 19.65 ***(978-0-606-39991-3(7))*** Turtleback Bks.

Kear, Nicole C. The Fix-It Friends: the Show Must Go On. Dockray, Tracy, illus. 2017. (Fix-It Friends Ser.: 3). (ENG.). 160p. (J). pap. 5.99 ***(978-1-250-08668-6(X)***, 9781250086686) Imprint IND. Dist: Macmillan.

Lupica, Mike. Two-Minute Drill, 1 vol. 2012. (Comeback Kids Ser.). (ENG.). 192p. (J). (gr. 4-8). lib. bdg. 27.07 *(978-1-59961-179-2(1))* Spotlight.

Mackall, Dandi Daley. Natalie & the Bestest Friend Race, 1 vol. Blakeslee, Lys, illus. 2009. (That's Nat! Ser.). (ENG.). 96p. (J). (gr. 1-4). pap. 4.99 *(978-0-310-71570-2(9))* Zonderkidz.

Martin, Ann M. Family Tree Book Three: Best Kept Secret. 2014. (ENG.). 224p. (J). (gr. 3-7). 16.99 *(978-0-545-35944-3(9)*, Scholastic Pr.) Scholastic, Inc.

Mixon, Donovan. Ahgottahandleonit. 2017. (ENG.). 288p. (J). (gr. 6). 16.95 *(978-1-941026-46-5(X))* Cinco Puntos Pr.

Oelschlager, Vanita. Knees: The Mixed up World of a Boy with Dyslexia. Rossi, Joe, illus. 2012. (ENG.). 128p. (J). (gr. k-5). pap. 9.95 *(978-0-9826366-9-5(5))* VanitaBooks.

Robb, Diane Burton. The Alphabet War: A Story about Dyslexia. Piazza, Gail, illus. 2004. (ENG.). 32p. (J). (gr. 2-3). 16.99 *(978-0-8075-0302-7(9))* Whitman, Albert & Co.

Steinkraus, Kyla. Case of the Uncrackable Code. 2015. (ENG.). 64p. (gr. 3-6). 29.95 *(978-1-63430-388-0(1))* Rourke Educational Media.

Ventura, Marne. Anxious Adam Braves the Test. Trinidad, Leo, illus. 2016. (Worry Warriors Ser.). (ENG.). 96p. (gr. 2-4). pap. 5.95 *(978-1-4965-3650-1(9))*; lib. bdg. 25.99 *(978-1-4965-3611-2(8))* Stone Arch Bks.

Winkler, Henry & Oliver, Lin. Holy Enchilada! Heyer, Carol et al, illus. 2004. (Hank Zipzer Ser.: 6). (ENG.). 160p. (J). (gr. 3-7). pap. 5.99 *(978-0-448-43353-0(2)*, Grosset & Dunlap) Penguin Young Readers Group.

—The Zippity Zinger, 4 vols. Heitz, Tim, illus. 2004. (Hank Zipzer Ser.: 4). (ENG.). 160p. (J). (gr. 3-7). mass mkt. 5.99 *(978-0-448-43193-2(9)*, Grosset & Dunlap) Penguin Young Readers Group.

E

EAGLES

Avett, Harper. I See the Bald Eagle. 2016. (Symbols of Our Country Ser.). 00024p. (J). (gr. 1-1). pap. 8.25 *(978-1-4994-2763-9(8)*, PowerKids Pr.) Rosen Publishing Group, Inc., The.

Bald Eagles: Individual Title Six-Packs. (Action Packs Ser.). 120p. (gr. 3-5). 44.00 *(978-0-7635-8422-1(3))* Rigby Education.

Barnes, Julia. 101 Facts about Eagles. 2004. (One Hundred One Facts about Predators Ser.). (Illus.). 32p. (gr. 1-4). lib. bdg. 26.00 *(978-0-8368-4036-0(4)*, Gareth Stevens Learning Library) Stevens, Gareth Publishing LLLP.

Bechtold, Phyliss. Seymour Bluffs & the Legend of the Piasa Bird. 2007. 26p. 9.95 *(978-0-9728532-8-6(6))* New Horizons Christian Ctr.

Bechtold, Phyllis. Seymour Bluffs Activities Coloring Book. 2006. 32p. spiral bd. 5.95 *(978-0-9728538-3-5(9))* Amica Publishing.

Blazeman, Christopher. Eagles up Close, 1 vol. 2nd rev. ed. 2014. (TIME for KIDS(r) Nonfiction Readers Ser.). (ENG., Illus.). 28p. (J). (gr. 2-2). pap. 23.96 *(978-1-4807-1043-6(1))* Shell Educational Publishing.

—Eagles up Close, 1 vol. 2nd rev. ed. 2011. (Nonfiction Readers Ser.). (ENG.). 28p. (J). (gr. 2-2). pap. 6.99 *(978-1-4333-3616-4(2))* Teacher Created Materials, Inc.

Bodden, Valerie. Eagle. 2014. (J). *(978-1-60818-405-7(6)*, Creative Education) Creative Co., The.

—Grow with Me: Eagle. 2015. (Grow with Me Ser.). (ENG.). 32p. (J). (gr. 3-5). pap. 9.99 *(978-0-89812-991-5(5)*, Creative Paperbacks) Creative Co., The.

Bowman, Chris. Bald Eagles. 2015. (North American Animals Ser.). (ENG., Illus.). 24p. (J). (gr. k-3). lib. bdg. 25.95 *(978-1-62617-185-5(8)*, Blastoff! Readers) Bellwether Media.

Butterfield, Moira. Golden Eagle. (Who Am I? Ser.). (Illus.). 32p. (J). lib. bdg. 24.25 *(978-1-930643-90-1(X))* Chrysalis Education.

Calhoun, Kelly. Feathered & Fierce: Bald Eagle. 2015. (Guess What Ser.). (ENG., Illus.). 24p. (J). (gr. k-2). 28.50 *(978-1-63362-624-9(5)*, 206668) Cherry Lake Publishing.

—Valientes Plumíferos (Feathered & Fierce) Águila (Bald Eagle) 2016. (Adivina (Guess What) Ser.). (SPA., Illus.). 24p. (J). (gr. k-2). 28.50 *(978-1-63471-447-1(4)*, 208851) Cherry Lake Publishing.

Cosson, M. J. Golden Eagle Migration. 2012. (Animal Migrations Ser.). (ENG., Illus.). 32p. (J). (gr. 2-5). lib. bdg. 29.93 *(978-1-60973-620-0(6)*, 201197) Child's World, Inc., The.

—Golden Eagles: A Solo Journey. 2016. (Illus.). 32p. (J). *(978-1-4896-4515-9(2))* Weigl Pubs., Inc.

DeFries, Cheryl L. The Bald Eagle: A MyReportLinks. com Book. 2003. (Endangered & Threatened Animals Ser.). (Illus.). 48p. (J). (gr. 4-10). lib. bdg. 26.60 *(978-0-7660-5057-0(2)*, MyReportLinks.com Bks.) Enslow Pubs., Inc.

Dolbear, Emily J. Bald Eagles. 2012. (Nature's Children Ser.). (ENG., Illus.). 48p. (J). pap. 6.95 *(978-0-531-21076-5(6))*; (gr. 3-5). lib. bdg. 28.00 *(978-0-531-20901-1(6))* Scholastic Library Publishing. (Children's Pr.).

Domm, Kristin Bieber. Eagle of the Sea, 1 vol. Domm, Jeffrey C., illus. 2011. (ENG.). 32p. (J). (gr. -1-3). 9.95 *(978-1-55109-749-7(4))* Nimbus Publishing, Ltd. CAN. Dist: Orca Bk. Pubs. USA.

Douglas, Lloyd G. The Bald Eagle. 2003. (Welcome Bks.). 24p. (J). 19.00 *(978-0-516-25851-5(6))*; (ENG.). (gr. -1-2). pap. 4.95 *(978-0-516-27874-2(6))* Scholastic Library Publishing. (Children's Pr.).

Edwards, Rhonda S. A Living Mascot. Owens, Alana, illus. 2013. (ENG.). 38p. (J). pap. 9.99 *(978-0-7443-2013-8(5))* SynergEbks.

Eldridge, Alison & Eldridge, Stephen. The Bald Eagle: An American Symbol. 2012. (All about American Symbols Ser.). 24p. (J). (gr. -1-16). 22.60 *(978-0-7660-4058-8(5)*, Enslow Elementary) Enslow Pubs., Inc.

Fleischer, Jayson. Bald Eagles. Johnson, Gee, illus. 2011. (2G Predator Animals Ser.). (ENG.). 32p. (J). (gr. k-2). pap. 5.99 *(978-1-61541-492-5(4))* American Reading Co.
Furgang, Kathy. Saving the Bald Eagles. (Early Connections Ser.). (J). *(978-1-61672-598-3(2))* Benchmark Education Co.
—Saving the Bald Eagles: Set Of 6. 2011. (Early Connections Ser.). (J). pap. 37.00 net. *(978-1-4108-1089-2(5))* Benchmark Education Co.
—Saving the Bald Eagles & ¡Salvemos al águila cabeza Blanca! 6 English, 6 Spanish Adaptations. 2011. (ENG & SPA.). (J). 75.00 net. *(978-1-4108-5652-4(6))* Benchmark Education Co.
Gagne, Tammy. Eagles: Built for the Hunt. 2016. (Predator Profiles Ser.). (ENG., Illus.). 24p. (gr. 1-2). lib. bdg. 25.32 *(978-1-4914-8842-3(5))* Capstone Press of Coughlan Cos.
George, Jean Craighead. The Eagles Are Back. Minor, Wendell, illus. 2013. (ENG.). 32p. (J). (gr. 1-3). 17.99 *(978-0-8037-3771-6(8)*, Dial Bks) Penguin Young Readers Group.
Gilkerson, Patricia. My Adventure with Eagles. 2009. (ENG.). 44p. (J). 8.99 *(978-1-59092-453-2(3))* Blue Forge Pr.
Gish, Melissa. Eagles. (Living Wild Ser.). 2011. (ENG., Illus.). 48p. (J). (gr. 4-7). pap. 12.00 *(978-0-89812-551-1(0)*, Creative Paperbacks) 2010. 46p. (YA). (gr. 5-18). 23.95 *(978-1-58341-968-7(3)*, Creative Education) Creative Co., The.
Goldish, Meish. Bald Eagles: A Chemical Nightmare. 2007. (America's Animal Comebacks Ser.). (Illus.). 32p. (YA). (gr. 2-5). lib. bdg. 25.27 *(978-1-59716-505-1(0))* Bearport Publishing Co., Inc.
Gove-Berg, Christie. Esther the Eaglet: A True Story of Rescue & Rehabilitation. 2015. (Wildlife Rescue Stories Ser.). (ENG.). 32p. (J). 12.95 *(978-1-59193-542-1(3))* Adventure Pubns.
Gray, Susan H. Harpy Eagle. 2015. (21st Century Skills Library: Exploring Our Rainforests Ser.). (ENG., Illus.). 32p. (gr. 3-6). 29.93 *(978-1-63188-976-9(1)*, 205816) Cherry Lake Publishing.
Guillain, Charlotte. Soaring Eagles, 1 vol. 2013. (Walk on the Wild Side Ser.). (ENG.). 32p. (gr. 1-3). 29.99 *(978-1-4109-5220-2(7))*; pap. 8.95 *(978-1-4109-5227-1(4))* Heinemann-Raintree. (Read Me!).
Harris, Tim. Eagles. 2008. (Nature's Children Ser.). (Illus.). 52p. (J). *(978-0-7172-6222-9(7))* Grolier, Ltd.
Haywood, Karen. Eagles. 2008. (Endangered! Ser.). 48p. (gr. 3-18). lib. bdg. 29.93 *(978-0-7614-2991-3(3)*, Benchmark Bks.) Marshall Cavendish Corp.
Herrington, Lisa M. The Bald Eagle. 2014. (Rookie Read-About(r) American Symbols Ser.). (ENG., Illus.). 32p. (J). pap. 5.95 *(978-0-531-21837-2(6))* Scholastic Library Publishing.
—Totally Fierce Animals. 2017. (Rookie Amazing America(tm) Ser.). (ENG., Illus.). 32p. (J). pap. 5.95 *(978-0-531-22590-5(9)*, Children's Pr.) Scholastic Library Publishing.
Hudak, Heather C. Eagles. 2008. (Backyard Animals Ser.). (Illus.). 24p. (J). (gr. 4-7). lib. bdg. 24.45 *(978-1-60596-002-9(0))* Weigl Pubs., Inc.
Hudak, Heather C., ed. Eagles. 2008. (Backyard Animals Ser.). (Illus.). 24p. (J). (gr. 4-7). pap. 8.95 *(978-1-60596-008-1(X))* Weigl Pubs., Inc.
Jango-Cohen, Judith. The Bald Eagle. 2003. (Pull Ahead Books-American Symbols Ser.). (ENG.). 32p. (gr. k-3). pap. 7.95 *(978-0-8225-4750-1(3))*; (Illus.). lib. bdg. 22.60 *(978-0-8225-3645-1(5))* Lerner Publishing Group.
Jennings, Rosemary. Eagles, 01 vols., 1. 2016. (Raptors! Ser.). (ENG., Illus.). 24p. (J). pap. 8.25 *(978-1-5081-4240-9(8)*, PowerKids Pr.) Rosen Publishing Group, Inc., The.
Johnson, Gee & Fleischer, Jayson. Bald Eagles. 2011. (ARC Press / Power 100 - Predator Animals Ser.). pap. 45.32 *(978-1-61541-493-2(2))* American Reading Co.
Kalz, Jill. Eagles. 2003. (Birds Ser.). (Illus.). 23p. (J). 21.35 *(978-1-58340-129-3(6))* Black Rabbit Bks.
Kenney, Karen Latchana. The Bald Eagle, 1 vol. Hunt, Judith A., illus. 2011. (Our Nation's Pride Set 2 Ser.). (ENG.). 32p. (J). (gr. 1-4). 28.50 *(978-1-61641-149-7(X))* Magic Wagon.
Kissock, Heather. Bald Eagles. 2016. (J). **(978-1-4896-5387-1(2))** Weigl Pubs., Inc.
Landau, Elaine. The Bald Eagle. 2008. (True Bks.). (ENG., Illus.). 48p. (J). (gr. 3-5). pap. 6.95 *(978-0-531-14776-4(2)*, Children's Pr.) Scholastic Library Publishing.
Leighton, Christina. Golden Eagles. 2017. (North American Animals Ser.). (ENG., Illus.). 24p. (J). (gr. k-3). lib. bdg. 25.95 *(978-1-62617-567-9(5)*, Blastoff! Readers) Bellwether Media.
Llanas, Sheila Griffin. Bald Eagles, 1 vol. 2013. (Animal Icons Ser.). (ENG.). 32p. (J). (gr. 3-6). lib. bdg. 27.07 *(978-1-61783-568-1(4)*, Checkerboard Library) ABDO Publishing Co.
Lundgren, Julie. Eagles. 2009. (Illus.). 24p. (J). pap. 7.95 *(978-1-60694-772-2(9))* Rourke Educational Media.
Macken, JoAnn Early. Golden Eagles. 2nd rev. ed. 2009. (Animals That Live in the Mountains Ser.). 24p. (J). (gr. -1-3). (ENG.). pap. 8.15 *(978-1-4339-2496-5(X))*; lib. bdg. 22.60 *(978-1-4339-2413-2(7))* Stevens, Gareth Publishing LLLP. (Weekly Reader Leveled Readers).
—Golden Eagles;Águila Real. 2nd rev. ed. 2009. (Animals That Live in the Mountains/Animales de las montañas Ser.). (SPA & ENG.). 24p. (J). (gr. -1-3). pap. 8.15 *(978-1-4339-2503-0(6))*; lib. bdg. 22.60 *(978-1-4339-2445-3(5))* Stevens, Gareth Publishing LLLP. (Weekly Reader Leveled Readers).
Magby, Meryl. Bald Eagles. 2012. (American Animals Ser.). (ENG., Illus.). 24p. (J). (gr. k-3). lib. bdg. 22.60 *(978-1-4488-6180-4(2))*; pap. 8.25 *(978-1-4488-6319-8(8)*, PowerKids Pr.) Rosen Publishing Group, Inc., The.
Marcovitz, Hal. The Bald Eagle. 2004. (American Symbols & Their Meanings Ser.). (Illus.). 48p. (J). (gr. 4-18). lib. bdg. 19.95 *(978-1-59084-032-0(1))* Mason Crest.
—Bald Eagle: The Story of Our National Bird. Moreno, Barry, ed. 2014. (Patriotic Symbols of America Ser.: 20). 48p. (J). (gr. 4-18). 20.95 *(978-1-4222-3120-3(8))* Mason Crest.
Markle, Sandra. Eagles. 2009. (Animal Predators Ser.). (ENG.). 40p. (gr. 3-6). 26.60 *(978-1-58013-519-1(6))* Lerner Publishing Group.
McDowell, Pamela. Aguilas de Cabeza Blanca. 2013. (Animales en Mi Patio Ser.). (SPA., Illus.). 24p. (J). (gr. -1-3). lib. bdg. 27.13 *(978-1-62127-593-0(0)*, AV2 by Weigl) Weigl Pubs., Inc.
—Bald Eagle. 2012. (J). *(978-1-61913-268-9(0))*; pap. 12.95 *(978-1-61913-272-6(9))* Weigl Pubs., Inc.
Miller, Sara Swan. Eagles. (Paws & Claws Ser.). 24p. 2009. (gr. 2-3). 42.50 *(978-1-60851-150-1(2))* 2008. (Illus.). (J). (gr. 3-7). lib. bdg. 22.60 *(978-1-4042-4163-3(9))* Rosen Publishing Group, Inc., The. (PowerKids Pr.).
Morgan, Sally. Eagles. 2011. (Amazing Animal Hunters Ser.). (Illus.). 32p. (J). 28.50 *(978-1-60753-045-9(7))* Amicus Publishing.
—Eagles. 2012. (Illus.). 32p. (gr. 3-5). pap. 8.95 *(978-1-926722-49-8(3))* Saunders Bk. Co. CAN. Dist: RiverStream Publishing.
Morgan, Sally & Molnar, Michael. Eagles. 2011. (Life Cycles of Marine Animals Ser.). 32p. (YA). (gr. 3-6). lib. bdg. 28.50 *(978-1-59920-485-7(1))* Black Rabbit Bks.
Murray, Julie. Eagles, 1 vol. 2003. (Buddy Book Ser.). (ENG.). 24p. (gr. k-4). 25.65 *(978-1-57765-703-3(9)*, Buddy Bks.) ABDO Publishing Co.
Nobleman, Marc Tyler. Eagles. 2006. (Animals Animals Ser.). (Illus.). 48p. (J). (gr. 3-7). lib. bdg. 28.50 *(978-0-7614-2236-5(6)*, Benchmark Bks.) Marshall Cavendish Corp.
Omoth, Tyler. Bald Eagles. 2017. (Animals of North America (hardcover) Ser.). (ENG., Illus.). 32p. (J). (gr. 3-5). lib. bdg. 28.50 ***(978-1-63517-031-3(1)**, Focus Readers)* North Star Editions.
Pearl, Norman. The Bald Eagle, 1 vol. Skeens, Matthew, illus. 2007. (American Symbols Ser.). (ENG.). 24p. (gr. 1-2). 9.95 *(978-1-4048-2645-8(9))* Picture Window Bks.
—The Great Seal of the United States, 1 vol. Skeens, Matthew, illus. 2006. (American Symbols Ser.). (ENG.). 24p. (gr. 1-2). per. 9.95 *(978-1-4048-2220-7(8))* Picture Window Bks.
Priebe, Mac. EagleQuest CD-ROM + the Bald Eagle Book 2003. (Illus.). (J). 29.95 incl. cd-rom *(978-0-9669551-6-3(1)*, 1) Mindfull Publishing.
Read, Tracy C. Exploring the World of Eagles. 2010. (Exploring the World Of Ser.). (ENG., Illus.). 24p. (J). (gr. 3-6). 16.95 *(978-1-55407-647-5(1)*, 9781554076475); pap. 6.95 *(978-1-55407-656-7(0)*, 9781554076567) Firefly Bks., Ltd.
Rice, Dona. America's Eagle (Foundations) 2015. (TIME for KIDS(r) Nonfiction Readers Ser.). (ENG., Illus.). 12p. (gr. k-k). 4.99 *(978-1-4938-2056-6(7))* Teacher Created Materials, Inc.
Riggs, Kate. Amazing Animals: Eagles. 2012. (Amazing Animals Ser.). (ENG., Illus.). 24p. (J). (gr. 1-3). pap. 8.99 *(978-0-89812-691-4(6)*, Creative Paperbacks) Creative Co., The.
—Eagles. 2014. (J). *(978-1-60818-453-8(6)*, Creative Education) Creative Co., The.
—Seedlings: Eagles. 2015. (Seedlings Ser.). (ENG.). 24p. (J). (gr. -1-1). pap. 7.99 *(978-1-62832-041-1(9)*, Creative Paperbacks) Creative Co., The.
Rustad, Martha. Is a Bald Eagle Really Bald? Conger, Holli, illus. 2014. (Cloverleaf Books — Our American Symbols Ser.). 24p. (gr. k-2). (J). lib. bdg. 23.93 *(978-1-4677-2138-7(7))*; pap. 6.95 *(978-1-4677-4466-9(2))* Lerner Publishing Group. (Millbrook Pr.).
Salzmann, Mary Elizabeth. Baby Eagles, 1 vol. 2014. (Baby Animals Set 2 Ser.). (ENG.). 24p. (J). (gr. -1-3). 24.21 *(978-1-62403-508-1(6))* ABDO Publishing Co.
Schuetz, Kari. Eagles. 2012. (Backyard Wildlife Ser.). (ENG., Illus.). 24p. (J). (gr. k-3). lib. bdg. 25.95 *(978-1-60014-721-0(6)*, Blastoff! Readers) Bellwether Media.
Schuh, Mari. Bald Eagles. 2016. (My First Animal Library). 24p. (J). (gr. k-2). lib. bdg. 25.65 *(978-1-62031-287-2(5)*, Bullfrog Bks.) Jump! Inc.
Silate, Jennifer. The Bald Eagle. 2005. (Primary Sources of American Symbols Ser.). (Illus.). 24p. (J). lib. bdg. 22.60 *(978-1-4042-2697-5(4))* Rosen Publishing Group, Inc., The.
Stone, Lynn M. Bald Eagles. 2003. (Early Bird Nature Bks.). (ENG., Illus.). 48p. (J). (gr. 2-5). lib. bdg. 26.60 *(978-0-8225-3034-3(1))* Lerner Publishing Group.
Taylor, Trace. Bald Eagles. 2011. (1G Predator Animals Ser.). (ENG., Illus.). 32p. (J). pap. 5.99 *(978-1-61406-031-4(2))* American Reading Co.
Taylor, Trace & Sánchez, Lucía M. Águilas Calvas. 2009. (1G Animales Depredador Ser.). (SPA., Illus.). 32p. (J). (gr. k-2). pap. 6.99 *(978-1-61541-059-0(7))* American Reading Co.
Troupe, Thomas Kingsley. I Want to Be a Bald Eagle. Rodriguez, Christina Ann, illus. 2015. (I Want to Be... Ser.). (ENG.). 24p. (gr. k-3). lib. bdg. 26.65 *(978-1-4795-6858-1(9))* Capstone Press of Coughlan Cos.
Turnbull, Stephanie. Eagle. 2013. (Big Beasts Ser.). (Illus.). 24p. (gr. k-3). 28.50 *(978-1-59920-832-9(6))* Black Rabbit Bks.
Vaughn, Royce, illus. Seymour Bluffs & the Legend of the Piasa Bird. 2006. 24p. (J). pap. 9.95 *(978-0-9728538-2-8(0))* Amica Publishing.
Waxman, Laura Hamilton. Bald Eagles: Prey-Snatching Birds. 2016. (Comparing Animal Traits Ser.). (ENG., Illus.). 32p. (J). (gr. 2-4). 26.65 *(978-1-4677-9507-4(0)*, Lerner Pubns.) Lerner Publishing Group.
Wechsler, Doug. Bald Eagles. 2009. (Really Wild Life of Animals Ser.). 24p. (gr. 3-4). 42.50 *(978-1-60854-182-9(7)*, PowerKids Pr.) Rosen Publishing Group, Inc., The.
Wendorff, Anne. Eaglets. 2009. (Watch Animals Grow Ser.). (ENG., Illus.). 24p. (J). (gr. k-3). lib. bdg. 25.95 *(978-1-60014-239-0(7))* Bellwether Media.
—Eaglets. 2009. (Blastoff! Readers Ser.). (ENG., Illus.). 24p. (J). (gr. k-3). 20.00 *(978-0-531-21627-9(6)*, Children's Pr.) Scholastic Library Publishing.
Wexo, John Bonnett. Eagles. rev. ed. 2003. (Illus.). 24p. (J). (gr. 1-7). 10.95 *(978-1-888153-98-9(9)*, Zoo Bks.) Wildlife Education, Ltd.
Wicker, Jan L. Those Excellent Eagles. Weaver, Steve, illus. Moore, H G, III, photos by. 2006. (Those Amazing Animals Ser.). (ENG.). 55p. (J). (gr. 5-9). lib. bdg. 14.95 *(978-1-56164-360-8(2))* Pineapple Pr., Inc.
Wicker, Jan Lee. Those Excellent Eagles. Weaver, Steve, illus. Moore, H G, III, photos by. 2006. (Those Amazing Animals Ser.). (ENG.). 55p. (J). (gr. -1-3). pap. 9.95 *(978-1-56164-355-4(6))* Pineapple Pr., Inc.
Worsley, Arlene. Bald Eagles. 2006. (Amazing Animals Ser.). (Illus.). 24p. (J). (gr. 3-7). pap. 8.95 *(978-1-59036-394-2(9))*; lib. bdg. 24.45 *(978-1-59036-388-1(4))* Weigl Pubs., Inc.

EAGLES—FICTION

Aldrick, Shirley H. F. Hazel, the Hoppity Kangaroo. 2010. 28p. pap. 12.50 *(978-1-60860-743-3(7)*, Strategic Bk. Publishing) Strategic Book Publishing & Rights Agency (SBPRA).
Anrias, Donnan. Targ - the King of Eagles. 2005. 138p. (YA). per. 23.00 *(978-1-4116-1923-4(4))* Lulu Pr., Inc.
Award, Anna, et al. The Eagle & the Man with the Town Mouse & the Country Mouse. 2014. (ENG.). 24p. (J). pap. 6.95 *(978-1-84135-958-8(0))* Award Pubns. Ltd. GBR. Dist: Parkwest Pubns., Inc.
Baird Wireman, Ginger. If Wishes Had Wings: A Fall Flight of Fancy. 2009. 40p. pap. 16.99 *(978-1-4490-0262-6(5))* AuthorHouse.
Bettenberg, Barbie. Edgar, the Near-Sighted Eagle. Clement, Marilyn, illus. 2008. 27p. (J). *(978-0-9822534-0-3(0))* Cricket XPress of Minnesota.
Burke, Maria. The Ark of Dun Ruah. 2013. (Ark of Dun Ruah Ser.: 01). (ENG., Illus.). 256p. (J). pap. 23.95 *(978-1-85607-794-1(2))* Currach Pr. IRL. Dist: Dufour Editions, Inc.
Burns, Joanne. How & Why Eagles Fly. 2005. 27p. (J). 9.99 *(978-1-4116-3387-2(3))* Lulu Pr., Inc.
Butchart, Francis & Smith, Ron. Elf the Eagle. Campbell, Ruth, illus. 2007. (ENG.). 40p. 19.95 *(978-0-88982-241-2(7))* Oolichan Bks. CAN. Dist: Univ. of Toronto Pr.
Casanova, Mary. When Eagles Fall. 2014. (Fesler-Lampert Minnesota Heritage Ser.). (ENG.). 160p. pap. 9.95 *(978-0-8166-9211-8(4))* Univ. of Minnesota Pr.
Charles, Novalyn. Wagabuibui, the Four Eyed Eagle. Manasau, Amos, illus. 2012. 38p. pap. *(978-9980-945-66-2(4))* University of Papua New Guinea Press.
Cortinas, Suzanne. A Tale of Red Feather. 2009. 16p. pap. 8.49 *(978-1-4389-7566-5(X))* AuthorHouse.
Cumming, Wendy. How to Soar Like an Eagle When You Are Standing with the Turkeys. 2012. 32p. pap. 21.99 *(978-1-4797-2934-0(5))* Xlibris Corp.
Dell, Pamela. The Eagle Nest. Corbalán, Begoña, illus. 2016. (Spring Forward Ser.). (J). (gr. 1). *(978-1-4900-9382-6(6))* Benchmark Education Co.
Dipietro, Frances. Eagle & Dolphin: We Are Wonderfully Made. 2010. 28p. 16.09 *(978-1-4269-3315-8(0))* Trafford Publishing.
Dyas, Amy. The Robins of St Lawrence Church. 2009. 128p. pap. 29.96 *(978-0-9786567-8-2(4))* Parson Place Pr., LLC.
Echols, Larry. When the Eagles Fly. 2004. (YA). per. 11.95 *(978-1-932496-11-6(4))* Penman Publishing, Inc.
Edwards, Carol. Jacy's Search for Jesus Frey, Daniel J., illus. 2005. 31p. (J). (gr. -1-3). 15.95 *(978-0-9755314-0-2(9))* Majestic Publishing, LLC.
Edwards, Melvin Neal. Blakee the Bald Eagle. 2012. 64p. (gr. -1). 20.43 *(978-1-4669-5077-1(3))*; pap. 10.43 *(978-1-4669-5075-7(7))* Trafford Publishing.
Farshtey, Greg. Beware of the Wolves. 2013. (LEGO Legends of Chima Chapter Bks.: 2). lib. bdg. 14.75 *(978-0-606-32014-6(8)*, Turtleback) Turtleback Bks.
Ferer, Whitney H. The Owl Who Thinks He Is an Eagle. McCaslin, Anna, illus. 2003. 20p. (J). 14.95 *(978-0-9729975-0-8(4)*, OWL1) Graphically Speaking, Inc.
Flanagan, Liz. Oni & the Eagle. Docampo, Valeria, illus. 2014. (J). *(978-1-84686-876-4(9))* Barefoot Bks., Ltd.
Gault, Linda Fulford. Help Is on the Way: The Adventures of Madame Flutterby Book Iii. 2012. 36p. (-18). pap. 17.46 *(978-1-4772-8746-0(9))* AuthorHouse.
Gómez Cerdá, Alfredo, et al. Dos Plumas de Aguila. Puebla, Teo, illus. 2003. (SPA.). 32p. (gr. 3-5). 14.99 *(978-84-241-8028-7(3))* Everest Editora ESP. Dist: Lectorum Pubns., Inc.
Gregorowski, Christopher. Fly, Eagle, Fly: An African Tale. Daly, Niki, illus. 2008. (ENG.). 36p. (J). (gr. -1-3). 12.99 *(978-1-4169-7599-1(3)*, Aladdin) Simon & Schuster Children's Publishing.
Harris, Diane Banks. The Eagle & the Chickens. 2008. 13p. pap. 24.95 *(978-1-60703-092-8(6))* PublishAmerica, Inc.
Hobbs, Brice Edward. Beth's Woodpecker. 2004. 108p. 26.45 *(978-1-4208-0135-4(X))* AuthorHouse.
Hoog, Mark. Your Song: A Growing Field Adventure. Aukerman, Robert J., illus. 2007. (ENG.). 43p. (J). (gr. -1-3). 16.95 *(978-0-9770391-2-8(9))* Growing Field Bks.
Hoover, T. A. The Last Eagle. Kaths, Kathy, illus. 2004. 38p. (J). 16.00 *(978-0-9702216-3-6(0))* Sport Story Publishing.
Jarman, Julia. The Time-Travelling Cat & the Roman Eagle. 2008. (Time-Travelling Cat Ser.: 3). (ENG., Illus.). 156p. (J). (gr. 4-7). pap. 13.99 *(978-1-84270-617-6(9))* Andersen Pr. GBR. Dist: Independent Pubs. Group.
Jones, Steven E. The Ballad of Blue Eagle. Jones, Steven E., Jr., illus. 2011. (Blue Eagle Ser.). (ENG.). 48p. (J). (gr. -1-2). 18.95 *(978-0-9794655-1-2(6))* Blue Eagle Bks., Inc.
Kehret, Peg. Screaming Eagles. 2008. (ENG.). 128p. (J). (gr. 3-7). pap. 7.99 *(978-1-4169-9106-9(9)*, Simon & Schuster/Paula Wiseman Bks.) Simon & Schuster/Paula Wiseman Bks.
King III, Dudley Allen. Skye's High Fly'n Adventures: How Skye Gets His Name. 2012. 28p. pap. 10.95 *(978-1-4626-7445-9(3))* America Star Bks.
Kvalvasser, Leonid. Eagle - Proud Bird. 2004. (RUS.). bds. *(978-0-9753110-0-4(X))* Kvalvasser, Leonid.
Leinberger, Judy. The Man Who Talks with Eagles. 2010. 60p. pap. 14.00 *(978-1-4269-3396-7(7))* Trafford Publishing.
Lochmandy, Sandy. Kids & Critters on an Adventure. 2009. 36p. pap. 14.95 *(978-1-60860-387-9(3)*, Eloquent Bks.) Strategic Book Publishing & Rights Agency (SBPRA).
MacKie, Ian. The Adventures of Hamish the Sea Eagle. Mackie, Marie-Anne, illus. 2013. 24p. *(978-1-78148-614-6(X))* Grosvenor Hse. Publishing Ltd.
Mahoney, Tammy. Eddie the Eagle Learns to Fly. 2012. 24p. pap. 19.99 *(978-1-4772-1747-4(9))* AuthorHouse.
Manning, Jack. The Eagle Inside. Bancroft, Bronwyn, illus. 2016. (ENG.). 32p. (J). (gr. -1-k). 18.99 *(978-1-74297-469-9(4))* Little Hare Bks. AUS. Dist: Independent Pubs. Group.
Marlin, Peggy. Wackydoodle. 2009. 20p. pap. 12.49 *(978-1-4389-7573-3(2))* AuthorHouse.
Matson, Rob. Pickles Eyrie. 2010. 28p. pap. 12.95 *(978-1-4490-6088-6(9))* AuthorHouse.
McAuliffe, Nichola. Attila, Loolagax & the Eagle. Collins, Ross, tr. Collins, Ross, illus. 2003. (ENG.). 128p. (J). pap. 10.99 *(978-0-7475-6499-7(X))* Bloomsbury Publishing Plc GBR. Dist: Independent Pubs. Group.
Mirhady, Irandought. Thorn-Bush Boy: Pesare Tigh. Mirhady, Irandought, illus. 2004. Orig. Title: Pesare Tigh. (PEO., Illus.). 63p. (YA). per. *(978-0-9760323-0-4(9))* Mirhady, Farhad.
Moore, Wendy Leptien. Eaglet & the River. 2011. 108p. 21.92 *(978-1-4269-5478-8(6))*; pap. 11.92 *(978-1-4269-5477-1(8))* Trafford Publishing.
Munté, Marta. KUKU AND MWEWE: A SWAHILI FOLKTALE. 2013. (ENG., Illus.). 30p. (J). (gr. -1-k). 16.95 *(978-84-15619-97-0(9))* Eastern National.
O'Kane, George & Weikert, Dana, illus. Baldwin's Colorful Campus Tour - Boston College A-Z. 2004. (J). 9.99 *(978-1-933069-00-5(7))* Odd Duck Ink, Inc.
Oliver, Lin. Secret of the Super-Small Superstar. Gilpin, Stephen, illus. 2010. (Who Shrunk Daniel Funk? Ser.: 4). (ENG.). 160p. (J). (gr. 3-7). 14.99 *(978-1-4169-0963-7(X)*, Simon & Schuster Bks. For Young Readers) Simon & Schuster Bks. For Young Readers.
Pappas, Charles. The Tree That Loved the Eagle. Schlueter, Rachel, illus. 2013. 56p. (J). 19.95 *(978-1-58790-175-1(7))* Regent Pr.
Parrish, Edith. Sarah the Purple Goose Gets Lost. Odom, Kelly, illus. 2011. 34p. 23.95 *(978-1-60844-930-9(0))* Dog Ear Publishing, LLC.
Pedraza, M. Eugenia Rueda. Nico's Voyage. 2013. 32p. pap. *(978-1-4602-2360-4(8))* FriesenPress.
Previn, Alicia L. The Strange Disappearance of Walter Tortoise. Previn, Alicia L., illus. 2013. (Illus.). 36p. pap. 12.99 *(978-0-9847107-1-3(X))* Previn, Lovely Pubns.
Rexroth, Sharon. America from the Sky. 2006. (J). 9.95 *(978-1-57166-429-7(7))*; per. 22.95 *(978-1-57166-430-3(0))* Quixote Pr.
—Ohio. 2006. (ENG., Illus.). (J). per. 19.95 *(978-1-57166-421-1(1))* Quixote Pr.
Rhodes, Shayla. I Know Who I Am. 2012. 30p. pap. 15.00 *(978-0-9705008-7-8(4))* J & J Publishing Co.
Ruiz, John. The Squirrel, the Eagle & the Red Hawk. 2012. 32p. pap. 21.99 *(978-1-4691-7970-4(9))* Xlibris Corp.
Rylant, Cynthia. The Eagle. McDaniels, Preston, illus. 2004. (Lighthouse Family Ser.: 3). (ENG.). 64p. (J). (gr. 1-5). 15.99 *(978-0-689-86243-4(1)*, Simon & Schuster Bks. For Young Readers) Simon & Schuster Bks. For Young Readers.
Salazar, L. J. Chin & the Magic Stones: Book One - Becoming Guardians. 2009. 108p. 20.95 *(978-0-595-63627-3(6))*; pap. 10.95 *(978-0-595-53157-8(1))* iUniverse, Inc.
Sargent, Dave. Baldy Eagle: Honor. 2003. (Feather Tales Ser.: 1). (Illus.). 42p. (J). lib. bdg. 20.95 *(978-1-56763-719-9(1))* Ozark Publishing.
—Baldy Eagle: Honor. Lenoir, Jane, illus. 2003. (Feather Tales Ser.: 1). 42p. (J). pap. 6.95 *(978-1-56763-720-5(5))* Ozark Publishing.
Shannon, Terry Miller. The Boy & the Eagle. 2016. (Spring Forward Ser.). (J). (gr. 1). *(978-1-4900-2241-3(4))* Benchmark Education Co.
Sinclair, Howard. Ego: And the Chocolate-Covered Worms. 2013. (ENG.). 28p. (J). pap. 9.95 *(978-1-4787-0089-0(0))* Outskirts Pr., Inc.
Skinner, Teresa. Casaq the Eagle. 2012. 29.95 *(978-0-7414-7075-1(6))*; pap. 19.95 *(978-0-7414-7313-4(5))* Infinity Publishing.
Smith, Margaret Ann. A New Kind of Life for Eddie Eagle. 2008. 36p. pap. 24.95 *(978-1-60441-168-3(6))* America Star Bks.
Sobol, Donald J. Encyclopedia Brown & the Case of the Dead Eagles. Shortall, Leonard W., illus. 2008. (Encyclopedia Brown Ser.: 12). (ENG.). 96p. (J). (gr. 3-7). 4.99 *(978-0-14-241135-3(3)*, Puffin Books) Penguin Young Readers Group.
Sommer, Carl. The Eagle & the Chickens. Noé, illus. 2016. (J). *(978-1-57537-945-6(7))* Advance Publishing, Inc.
Steams, Carolyn. Quiet Please - Eaglets Growing. Aiken, David, illus. 2009. (ENG.). 30p. (J). 11.95 *(978-0-87033-541-9(3)*, 9780870335419, Cornell Maritime Pr./Tidewater Pubs.) Schiffer Publishing, Ltd.
.T. Ozzie the Spider. 2013. 24p. pap. 11.95 *(978-1-4575-2025-9(7))* Dog Ear Publishing, LLC.
Tata, Cb. Ernie the Eagle Goes to Maine. Hanley, Zachary, illus. 2012. 42p. 24.95 *(978-1-4626-4545-9(3))* America Star Bks.
—Ernie the Eagle Goes to Texas. Hanley, Zachary, illus. 2012. 44p. 24.95 *(978-1-4626-5374-4(X))* America Star Bks.
Thiele, Colin. Brahminy: The Story of a Boy & a Sea Eagle. (Illus.). 196p. pap. *(978-0-7344-0402-2(6)*, Lothian Children's Bks.) Hachette Australia.
Vaughan, Richard Lee. Eagle Boy: A Pacific Northwest Native Tale. Christiansen, Lee, illus. 2008. (ENG.). 32p. (J). (gr. -1-3). pap. 10.99 *(978-1-57061-592-4(6)*, Little Bigfoot) Sasquatch Bks.
Vaughn, Royce, illus. Seymour Bluffs & Robert Wadlow, the Tallest Man in the World: A Story about Diversity & Tolerance. 2007. 28p. (J). 12.95 *(978-0-9728538-4-2(7))* Amica Publishing.
Wargin, Kathy-jo. The Legend of Old Abe: A Civil War Eagle. Caple, Laurie, illus. 2006. (Legend (Sleeping Bear) Ser.). (ENG.). 40p. (J). (gr. 3-7). 17.95 *(978-1-58536-232-5(8))* Sleeping Bear Pr.
Wheeler, Jordan. Just a Walk. 2009. (ENG., Illus.). 32p. (J). (gr. -1-k). pap. 8.95 *(978-1-894778-82-4(0))* Theytus Bks., Ltd. CAN. Dist: Univ. of Toronto Pr.
Zschock, Martha Day. Hello, Philadelphia! 2011. (Hello! Ser.). (ENG., Illus.). 16p. (J). (gr. -1-k). bds. 9.95 *(978-1-933212-64-7(0)*, Commonwealth Editions) Applewood Bks.

EAR

see also Hearing

Acampora, Courtney. Eyes & Ears. Kushnir, Hilli, illus. 2016. (ENG.). 22p. (J). (gr. -1). bds. 12.99 *(978-1-62686-749-9(6)*, Silver Dolphin Bks.) Readerlink Distribution Services, LLC.
Arif, Amrana. Allah Gave Me Two Ears to Hear. Clarke, Asiya, illus. 2015. (ENG.). 32p. (J). 8.95 *(978-0-86037-353-7(3))* Kube Publishing Ltd. GBR. Dist: Consortium Bk. Sales & Distribution.

Ashley, Michele. Who Has Ears Like These? 2014. (Little Books of Answers: Level C Ser.). (Illus.). 16p. (gr. k-2). pap. 7.95 *(978-1-927136-27-0(X))* Three Crows Media NZL. Dist: RiverStream Publishing.

Ballard, Carol. How Your Ears Work. 2010. (Your Body at Work Ser.). (ENG.). 32p. (YA). (gr. 2-5). lib. bdg. 26.60 *(978-1-4339-4106-1(6))* Stevens, Gareth Publishing LLLP.

Burton, Margie, et al. Animals' Eyes & Ears. 2011. (Early Connections Ser.). (J). *(978-1-61672-479-5(X))* Benchmark Education Co.

Canetti, Yanitzia. La Adaptación, ¡qué Sensación! 2010. (SPA.). (J). *(978-1-59835-171-2(0))* Cambridge BrickHouse, Inc.

—Amazing Adaptations! 2010. (J). *(978-1-59835-195-8(8))* Cambridge BrickHouse, Inc.

Carr, Aaron. El Oido. 2013. (Mis Sentidos Ser.). (SPA., Illus.). 24p. (J). (gr. -1-3). lib. bdg. 27.13 *(978-1-62127-575-6(2)*, AV2 by Weigl) Weigl Pubs., Inc.

Cobb, Vicki. Your Body Battles an Earache. 2009. pap. 40.95 *(978-0-7613-4618-0(X))* Lerner Publishing Group.

Corsaro, Nicola. What Are Sound Waves? 2013. (Rosen Readers Ser.). (ENG.). 24p. (J). (gr. 2-3). pap. 49.50 *(978-1-4777-2398-2(6))*; pap. 8.25 *(978-1-4777-2397-5(8))* Rosen Publishing Group, Inc., The. (Rosen Classroom).

Dayton, Connor. El Oido / Hearing. De La Vega, Eida, ed. 2014. (Tus Cinco Sentidos y Tu Sexto Sentido / Your Five Senses & Your Sixth Sense Ser.). (SPA & BYN.). 24p. (J). (gr. k-2). 23.60 *(978-1-4777-3268-7(3)*, PowerKids Pr.) Rosen Publishing Group, Inc., The.

Douglas, Lloyd G. My Ears. 2004. (Wel-My Body Ser.). (J). 19.00 *(978-0-516-24062-6(5)*, Children's Pr.) Scholastic Library Publishing.

Ears. (Early Intervention Levels Ser.). 23.10 *(978-0-7362-0026-4(6))* CENGAGE Learning.

Enslow, Brian. My Ears. 2010. (All about My Body Ser.). (Illus.). 24p. (J). 22.60 *(978-0-7660-3812-7(2))*; pap. 7.95 *(978-1-59845-168-9(5))* Enslow Pubs., Inc. (Enslow Elementary).

Equipo Staff & Delafosse, Claude. El Oido. (Coleccion Mundo Maravilloso). (SPA., Illus.). 22p. (J). (gr. 2-4). *(978-84-348-5096-5(6)*, SM7493) SM Ediciones.

Eyes & Ears Sets: 1 Each of 3 Big Books. (Sunshinetm Science Ser.). (gr. 1-2). 111.50 *(978-0-7802-1445-3(5))* Wright Group/McGraw-Hill.

Eyes & Ears Sets: 1 Each of 3 Student Books. (Sunshinetm Science Ser.). (gr. 1-2). 20.95 *(978-0-7802-1747-8(0))* Wright Group/McGraw-Hill.

Faulkner, Nicholas & Sherman, Josepha. The Ear in 3D. 2015. (Human Body In 3D Ser.). (ENG., Illus.). 64p. (J). (gr. 5-6). 32.95 *(978-1-4994-3585-6(1)*, Rosen Central) Rosen Publishing Group, Inc., The.

Fernandez, A. & Fernandez, Q. Hooray for My Ears. (Hooray for My Senses Ser.). (Illus.). (J). 19.27 *(978-1-58952-373-9(3))* Rourke Educational Media.

Fullick, Ann. Why Do My Ears Pop? Hearing, 1 vol. 2011. (Inside My Body Ser.). (ENG.). 32p. (gr. 3-5). 30.65 *(978-1-4109-4016-2(0)*, NA-r) Heinemann-Raintree.

Furgang, Kathy. My Ears. 2009. (My Body Ser.). 24p. (gr. 3-3). 42.50 *(978-1-61514-687-1(3)*, PowerKids Pr.) Rosen Publishing Group, Inc., The.

Ganeri, Anita. Hearing. 2013. (Senses Ser.). (Illus.). 24p. (gr. k-3). 28.50 *(978-1-59920-851-0(2))* Black Rabbit Bks.

Gordon, Sharon. Earaches. 2003. (Rookie Read-About Health Ser.). (ENG., Illus.). 32p. (J). 20.50 *(978-0-516-22584-5(7)*, Children's Pr.) Scholastic Library Publishing.

Halvorson, Karin. Inside the Ears, 1 vol. 2013. (Super Simple Your Body Ser.). (ENG.). 32p. (J). (gr. k-4). 27.07 *(978-1-61783-610-7(9))* ABDO Publishing Co.

Hengel, Katherine. Ears Are for Earrings: The Sense of Hearing, 1 vol. 2012. (All about Your Senses Ser.). (ENG.). 24p. (J). (gr. k-3). lib. bdg. 24.21 *(978-1-61783-196-6(4)*, SandCastle) ABDO Publishing Co.

Hidalgo, Maria. Hearing. 2003. 24p. (J). lib. bdg. 21.35 *(978-1-58340-304-4(3))* Black Rabbit Bks.

Klingel, Cynthia & Noyed, Robert B. Ears / Los Oídos. 2010. (Let's Read about Our Bodies / Hablemos del cuerpo humano Ser.). (SPA., Illus.). 24p. (gr. k-3). pap. 8.15 *(978-1-4339-3730-9(1))* Stevens, Gareth Publishing LLLP.

—Ears (Los Oidos) 2010. (Let's Read about Our Bodies Ser.). (Illus.). 24p. (gr. k-3). pap. 8.15 *(978-1-4339-3354-7(3))*; (J). lib. bdg. 22.00 *(978-1-4339-3353-0(5))* Stevens, Gareth Publishing LLLP.

—Ears/Los Oidos. 2010. (Let's Read about Our Bodies / Hablemos del cuerpo humano Ser.). (SPA., Illus.). 24p. (J). (gr. k-3). lib. bdg. 22.00 *(978-1-4339-3729-3(8))* Stevens, Gareth Publishing LLLP.

Libra, Anna. Why Does Loud Music Hurt My Ears? An Inside Look at the Ear. 2003. (J). pap. *(978-1-58417-072-3(7))*; lib. bdg. *(978-1-58417-009-9(3))* Lake Street Pubs.

Markle, Sandra. What If You Had Animal Ears? McWilliam, Howard, illus. 2016. (ENG.). 32p. (J). (gr. -1-3). pap. 4.99 *(978-0-545-85926-4(3)*, Scholastic Nonfiction) Scholastic, Inc.

Meachen Rau, Dana. Shhhh... [Scholastic]: A Book about Hearing. Peterson, Rick, illus. 2010. (Amazing Body: the Five Senses Ser.). 24p. pap. 0.56 *(978-1-4048-6541-9(1)*, Nonfiction Picture Bks.) Picture Window Bks.

Mitchell, Melanie S. Ears. 2008. (First Step Nonfiction - Animal Traits Ser.). (ENG., Illus.). 8p. (gr. -1-1). pap. 4.95 *(978-0-8225-3910-0(1)*, Lerner Pubns.) Lerner Publishing Group.

Murphy, Patricia J. Hearing: Your Ears are the Key to Your Sense of Hearing. 2003. (True Bks.). (ENG.). 48p. (gr. 3-5). pap. 6.95 *(978-0-516-26970-2(4)*, Children's Pr.) Scholastic Library Publishing.

Nelson, Kristen Rajczak. What Is Earwax Made Of? And Other FAQs about Your Body. 2016. (Q & a: Life's Mysteries Solved! Ser.). (Illus.). 32p. (J). (gr. 4-3). pap. 10.50 *(978-1-4824-4764-4(9))* Stevens, Gareth Publishing LLLP.

Nelson, Robin. Hearing. 2005. (First Step Nonfiction Ser.). (Illus.). 24p. (gr. k-2). lib. bdg. 17.27 *(978-0-8225-1264-6(5))* Lerner Publishing Group.

—Seeing & Hearing Well. 2006. (Pull Ahead Bks.). (Illus.). 32p. (J). (gr. -1-3). lib. bdg. 22.60 *(978-0-8225-3488-4(6)*, Lerner Pubns.) Lerner Publishing Group.

Ollhoff, Jim. Ear, Nose, & Throat. 2012. (J). *(978-1-61783-254-3(5))* ABDO Publishing Co.

Olson, Karen W. Eyes, Ears, Nose & Mouth. George, Leonard, Jr., illus. (ENG.). 20p. 2005. (J). pap. 10.95 *(978-1-894778-34-3(0))* 2009. pap. 9.95 *(978-1-894778-52-7(9))* Theytus Bks., Ltd. CAN. Dist: Univ. of Toronto Pr.

Phillips, Jillian. The World Around Us! Hearing. 2010. (Dover Coloring Bks.). (ENG., Illus.). 32p. (J). (gr. k-3). pap. 4.99 *(978-0-486-47730-5(4))* Dover Pubns., Inc.

Pryor, Kimberley Jane. Hearing. 2003. (Senses Ser.). (Illus.). 32p. (gr. 2-4). 23.00 *(978-0-7910-7554-8(0)*, Chelsea Hse.) Facts On File, Inc.

Rustad, Martha E. H. Hearing. 2014. (Illus.). 24p. (J). lib. bdg. 25.65 *(978-1-62031-115-8(1)*, Bullfrog Bks.) Jump! Inc.

Simon, Seymour. Eyes & Ears. (ENG., Illus.). 32p. (J). (gr. k-5). 2005. pap. 6.99 *(978-0-06-073302-5(0))* 2003. 15.99 *(978-0-688-15303-8(8))* HarperCollins Pubs.

—Eyes & Ears. 2005. (Illus.). (gr. k-3). 17.00 *(978-0-7569-5398-0(7))* Perfection Learning Corp.

Stewart, Melissa. Incredible Ears up Close. 2012. (Animal Bodies up Close Ser.). 24p. (J). (gr. k-3). (Illus.). pap. 7.95 *(978-1-4644-0081-0(4))*; 22.60 *(978-0-7660-3891-2(2))* Enslow Pubs., Inc. (Enslow Elementary).

—Now Hear This! The Secrets of Ears & Hearing. Hamlin, Janet, illus. 2009. (Gross & Goofy Body Ser.). 48p. (gr. 3-4). 29.93 *(978-0-7614-4161-8(1))* Marshall Cavendish Corp.

Stone, Lynn. How Do Animals Use Their Ears? 2007. (How Do Animals Use (Discovery Library) Ser.). (Illus.). 24p. (J). (gr. -1-3). lib. bdg. 22.79 *(978-1-60044-503-3(9))* Rourke Educational Media.

Tekiela, Stan. Floppers & Loppers, 1 vol. 2013. (Adventure Boardbook Ser.). (ENG.). 22p. (J). (gr. -1-k). bds. 6.95 *(978-1-59193-424-0(9))* Adventure Pubns.

VanVoorst, Jenny Fretland. Take a Closer Look at Your Ears. 2013. (Take a Closer Look Ser.). (ENG.). 24p. (J). (gr. 2-5). 28.50 *(978-1-62323-545-1(6)*, 206350) Child's World, Inc., The.

Vogel, Julia. Your Sensational Sense of Hearing. Squier, Robert, illus. 2011. (Sensational Senses Ser.). (ENG.). 32p. (J). (gr. k-3). lib. bdg. 27.07 *(978-1-60954-286-3(X)*, 200815) Child's World, Inc., The.

Wheeler-Toppen, Jodi Lyn. Our Ears Can Hear. 2017. (Our Amazing Senses Ser.). (ENG.). 24p. (gr. k-1). lib. bdg. 21.99 ***(978-1-5157-6713-8(2)***, Pebble Bks.) Capstone Press of Coughlan Cos.

EARHART, AMELIA, 1898-1937

Adler, David A. A Picture Book of Amelia Earhart. Fisher, Jeff, illus. 2015. 32p. pap. 8.00 *(978-1-61003-403-6(1))* Center for the Collaborative Classroom.

Amelia Earhart: Individual Title Six-Packs. (Action Packs Ser.). 120p. (gr. 3-5). 44.00 *(978-0-7635-8395-8(2))* Rigby Education.

Barton, Jen. What's Your Story, Amelia Earhart? 2016. (Cub Reporter Meets Famous Americans Ser.). (ENG.). 32p. (J). (gr. k-3). 26.65 *(978-1-4677-8783-3(3))*; (Illus.). pap. 8.99 *(978-1-4677-9645-3(X))* Lerner Publishing Group.

BourkeKenna. LOST: THE MYSTERY OF AMELIA EARHART HIGH BEGINNING BOOK WITH ONLINE ACCESS. 2014. (ENG.). 24p. (J). pap. 9.50 *(978-1-107-69335-7(7))* Cambridge Univ. Pr.

Brown, Jeremy K. Amelia Earhart. 2011. (Women of Achievement Ser.). (Illus.). 132p. (gr. 6-12). 35.00 *(978-1-60413-910-5(2)*, Chelsea Hse.) Facts On File, Inc.

Brown, Jonatha A. Amelia Earhart. 2005. (Gente que hay que conocer (People We Should Know- Spanish) Ser.). (SPA.). 24p. (gr. 1-4). lib. bdg. 22.00 *(978-0-8368-4581-5(1)*, Weekly Reader Leveled Readers) Stevens, Gareth Publishing LLLP.

Buckley, A. M. The Disappearance of Amelia Earhart, 1 vol. 2012. (Unsolved Mysteries (el) Ser.). (ENG.). 112p. (J). (gr. 6-12). lib. bdg. 35.64 *(978-1-61783-302-1(9)*, Essential Library) ABDO Publishing Co.

Burke, John. Amelia Earhart: Flying Solo. 2017. (Great Leaders & Events Ser.). (ENG.). (J). (gr. 4-8). lib. bdg. 35.99 ***(978-1-942875-45-1(2))*** Quarto Publishing Group USA.

Cain, Marie Mowery. Who Was Amelia Earhart? 2013. (Big Books, Red Ser.). (ENG & SPA., Illus.). 16p. pap. 33.00 *(978-1-59246-227-8(8))* Big Books, by George!

Cooke, Tim. Amelia Earhart. 2016. (Meet the Greats Ser.). 00048p. (J). pap. 14.05 ***(978-1-4824-5944-9(2))*** Stevens, Gareth Publishing LLLP.

Dakers, Diane. Amelia Earhart: Pioneering Aviator & Force for Women's Rights. 2016. (ENG.). 112p. (J). *(978-0-7787-2562-6(6))* Crabtree Publishing Co.

Doak, Robin S. Amelia Earhart, 1 vol. 2012. (American Biographies Ser.). (ENG.). 48p. (gr. 4-6). pap. 9.95 *(978-1-4329-6462-7(3)*, NA-h) Heinemann-Raintree.

Dunn, Joeming W. Amelia Earhart, 1 vol. Dunn, Ben, illus. 2008. (Bio-Graphics Ser.). (ENG.). 32p. (gr. 3-5). 28.50 *(978-1-60270-173-1(3)*, Graphic Planet- Nonfiction) ABDO Publishing Co.

Feinstein, Stephen. Read about Amelia Earhart. 2006. (I Like Biographies! Ser.). (Illus.). 24p. (J). (gr. 1-3). lib. bdg. 22.60 *(978-0-7660-2582-0(9)*, Enslow Elementary) Enslow Pubs., Inc.

Fleming, Candace. Amelia Lost: The Life & Disappearance of Amelia Earhart. 2011. (ENG., Illus.). 128p. (J). (gr. 3-7). 19.99 *(978-0-375-84198-9(9))*; lib. bdg. 21.99 *(978-0-375-94598-4(9))* Random Hse. Children's Bks. (Schwartz & Wade Bks.).

Freedman, Lew. All about Amelia Earhart. 2015. (ENG., Illus.). 128p. (J). pap. 4.99 *(978-1-935628-44-6(5))* Blue River Pr.

Gilpin, Caroline. Amelia Earhart. 2013. (Readers Bios Ser.). (ENG.). 32p. (J). (gr. -1-1). pap. 3.99 *(978-1-4263-1350-9(0)*, National Geographic Children's Bks.) National Geographic Society.

—National Geographic Readers: Amelia Earhart. 2013. (Readers Bios Ser.). (ENG.). 32p. (J). (gr. -1-1). lib. bdg. 13.90 *(978-1-4263-1351-6(9)*, National Geographic Children's Bks.) National Geographic Society.

Golightly, Anne. Amelia Earhart: Female Aviator. 2012. (Beginning Biographies Ser.). (ENG., Illus.). 24p. (J). (gr. 1-3). 22.60 *(978-1-4488-8601-2(5)*, PowerKids Pr.) Rosen Publishing Group, Inc., The.

Harmon, Daniel E. Amelia Earhart: Aviation Pioneer. 2017. (J). ***(978-1-5383-0020-6(6))*** Rosen Publishing Group, Inc., The.

Inventions & Discovery, Set. 2006. (Inventions & Discovery Ser.). (ENG., Illus.). 32p. (gr. 3-4). pap. 89.10 *(978-0-7368-7532-5(8)*, Graphic Library) Capstone Press of Coughlan Cos.

Jones, Victoria Garrett. Amelia Earhart: A Life in Flight. 2009. (Sterling Biographies(r) Ser.). (ENG., Illus.). 128p. (J). (gr. 5-18). pap. 5.95 *(978-1-4027-5157-8(5))* Sterling Publishing Co., Inc.

Klingel, Cynthia Fitterer & Klingel, Cynthia. Amelia Earhart: Aviation Pioneer. 2003. (Our People Ser.). (ENG., Illus.). 32p. (J). (gr. 3-6). 29.93 *(978-1-59296-000-2(6)*, 200627) Child's World, Inc., The.

Lakin, Patricia, et al. Amelia Earhart: More Than a Flier. Daniel, Alan & Daniel, Lea, illus. 2003. (Ready-To-read SOFA Ser.). (ENG.). 48p. (J). (gr. 1-3). pap. 3.99 *(978-0-689-85575-7(3)*, Simon Spotlight) Simon Spotlight.

Leavitt, Amie Jane. Amelia Earhart. 2007. (What's So Great About...? Ser.). (Illus.). 32p. (J). (gr. 2-4). lib. bdg. 25.70 *(978-1-58415-576-8(0))* Mitchell Lane Pubs., Inc.

Londoño, Patricia Torres. Amelia Earhart. 2005. (SPA.). 136p. (YA). *(978-958-30-1680-6(2))* Panamericana Editorial.

Mallory, Mark. Amelia Earhart: Queen of the Sky. 2009. (Real Life Readers Ser.). 16p. (gr. 2-3). pap. 7.05 *(978-1-4358-0053-3(2)*, Rosen Classroom) Rosen Publishing Group, Inc., The.

Mara, Wil. Amelia Earhart. 2014. (Rookie Biographies(tm) Ser.). (ENG.). 32p. (J). lib. bdg. 25.00 *(978-0-531-21059-8(6))* Scholastic Library Publishing.

Marsh, Carole. Amelia Earhart. 2003. 12p. (gr. k-4). 2.95 *(978-0-635-02131-1(5))* Gallopade International.

Meltzer, Brad. I Am Amelia Earhart. Eliopoulos, Christopher, illus. 2014. (Ordinary People Change World Ser.). (ENG.). 40p. (J). (gr. k-3). 14.99 *(978-0-8037-4082-2(4)*, Dial Bks) Penguin Publishing Group.

Micklos, John & Micklos, John, Jr. Unsolved: What Really Happened to Amelia Earhart? 2006. (Prime (Middle/Senior) Ser.). (Illus.). 144p. (J). (gr. 5-9). lib. bdg. 34.60 *(978-0-7660-2365-9(6))* Enslow Pubs., Inc.

Miklowitz, Gloria D. Amelia Earhart. 2004. (ENG., Illus.). 31p. (J). (gr. 2-5). pap. 7.33 *(978-0-7685-1213-7(1)*, Dominie Elementary) Pearson Schl.

Mills, Nathan & Golightly, Anne. Amelia Earhart: Female Aviator. 2012. (Rosen Readers Ser.). (ENG., Illus.). 24p. (J). (gr. 1-2). pap. 8.25 *(978-1-4488-8854-2(9)*, Rosen Classroom) Rosen Publishing Group, Inc., The.

Pflueger, Lynda. Amelia Earhart: Legend of Flight. 2003. (Historical American Biographies Ser.). (Illus.). 128p. (J). lib. bdg. 27.94 *(978-0-7660-1976-8(4))* Enslow Pubs., Inc.

Reyburn, Susan. Amelia Earhart. 2006. (Women Who Dare Ser.). (Illus.). 64p. 12.95 *(978-0-7649-3545-9(3)*, A111) Pomegranate Communications, Inc.

Rinaldo, Denise. Amelia Earhart: With a Discussion of Courage. 2004. (Values in Action Ser.). (J). *(978-1-59203-068-2(8))* Learning Challenge, Inc.

Saddleback Educational Publishing Staff, ed. Amelia Earhart, 1 vol. unabr. ed. 2008. (Graphic Biographies Ser.). (ENG., Illus.). 25p. (YA). (gr. 9-12). pap. 7.95 *(978-1-59905-214-4(8))* Saddleback Educational Publishing, Inc.

Sanchez Vegara, Ma Isabel. Amelia Earhart. Mariadiamantes, illus. 2016. (Little People, Big Dreams Ser.). (ENG.). 32p. (J). (gr. k-3). 14.99 *(978-1-84780-888-2(3)*, Frances Lincoln Children's Bks.) Quarto Publishing Group UK GBR. Dist: Hachette Bk. Group.

Sutcliffe, Jane. Amelia Earhart. 2003. (History Maker Bios Ser.). (Illus.). 48p. (J). (gr. 3-5). lib. bdg. 26.60 *(978-0-8225-0396-5(4))* Lerner Publishing Group.

Thiel, Kristin. Amelia Earhart: First Woman to Fly Solo Across the Atlantic. 2017. (J). ***(978-1-5026-2749-0(3))*** Cavendish Square Publishing.

Valentin, Jean. The Bravery of Amelia Earhart. 2012. (InfoMax Readers Ser.). (ENG., Illus.). 24p. (J). (gr. 1-2). pap. 8.25 *(978-1-4488-9067-5(5)*, Rosen Classroom) Rosen Publishing Group, Inc., The.

Weakland, Mark. When Amelia Earhart Built a Roller Coaster. Grivina, Oksana, illus. 2017. 31p. (J). *(978-1-5158-0142-9(X))* 2016. (ENG.). 32p. (gr. 2-3). pap. 7.95 *(978-1-5158-0138-2(1))* Picture Window Bks.

Wearing, Judy. Amelia Earhart. 2010. pap. 9.95 *(978-1-61690-060-1(1))*; 24p. (J). (gr. 2-4). lib. bdg. 25.70 *(978-1-61690-059-5(8))* Weigl Pubs., Inc.

EARHART, AMELIA, 1898-1937—FICTION

Lakin, Patricia. Amelia Earhart: Amelia Earhart: More Than A Flier. Daniel, Alan & Daniel, Lea, illus. 2005. 48p. (J). lib. bdg. 15.00 *(978-1-59054-957-5(0))* Fitzgerald Bks.

Wickham, Martha. Mysterious Journey. 2011. (ENG.). 32p. (J). 9.95 *(978-1-60727-179-6(6))* Soundprints.

EARP, WYATT, 1848-1929

Alagna, Magdalena. Wyatt Earp: Lawman of the American West. (Primary Sources of Famous People in American History Ser.). 32p. 2009. (gr. 2-3). 47.90 *(978-1-60851-747-3(0))* 2004. (ENG., Illus.). (J). (gr. 4-8). pap. 10.00 *(978-0-8239-4195-7(7))* 2004. (Illus.). (J). (gr. 3-7). 22.50 *(978-0-8239-4123-0(X)*, Rosen Reference) Rosen Publishing Group, Inc., The.

—Wyatt Earp: Lawman of the American West / Sheriff del oeste Americano. 2009. (Famous People in American History/Grandes personajes en la historia de los Estados Unidos Ser.). (ENG & SPA.). 32p. (gr. 2-3). 47.90 *(978-1-61512-558-6(2)*, Editorial Buenas Letras) Rosen Publishing Group, Inc., The.

—Wyatt Earp: Sheriff del legano Oeste. 2004. (Grandes personajes en la historia de los Estados Unidos Ser.). (SPA.). 32p. (gr. 3-6). pap. 10.00 *(978-0-8239-4241-1(4)*, Rosen Classroom) Rosen Publishing Group, Inc., The.

—Wyatt Earp: Sheriff del oeste americano (Wyatt Earp: Lawman of the American West) 2009. (Grandes personajes en la historia de los Estados Unidos (Famous People in American History) Ser.). (SPA.). 32p. (gr. 2-3). 47.90 *(978-1-61512-811-2(5)*, Editorial Buenas Letras) Rosen Publishing Group, Inc., The.

Goodman, Michael E. Wyatt Earp. 2005. (Legends of the West Ser.). (Illus.). 48p. (J). (gr. 5-9). lib. bdg. 21.95 *(978-1-58341-339-5(1)*, Creative Education) Creative Co., The.

Green, Carl R. & Sanford, William R. Wyatt Earp. rev. ed. 2008. (Outlaws & Lawmen of the Wild West, Revised Edition Ser.). (Illus.). 48p. (J). (gr. 5-18). lib. bdg. 25.27 *(978-0-7660-3174-6(8))* Enslow Pubs., Inc.

Landau, Elaine. Wyatt Earp: Wild West Lawman. 2004. (Best of the West Biographies Ser.). (Illus.). 48p. (YA). lib. bdg. 23.93 *(978-0-7660-2217-1(X))* Enslow Pubs., Inc.

Urban, William. Wyatt Earp: The O. K. Corral & the Law of the American West. 2009. (Library of American Lives & Times Ser.). 112p. (gr. 5-5). 69.20 *(978-1-60853-512-5(6))* Rosen Publishing Group, Inc., The.

—Wyatt Earp: The OK Corral & the Law of the American West. 2005. (Library of American Lives & Times). (Illus.). 112p. (YA). (gr. 4-8). lib. bdg. 34.60 *(978-0-8239-5740-8(3))* Rosen Publishing Group, Inc., The.

Waldman, Scott. Gunfight at the O. K. Corral: Wyatt Earp Upholds the Law. 2009. (Great Moments in American History Ser.). 32p. (gr. 3-3). 47.90 *(978-1-61513-143-3(4))* Rosen Publishing Group, Inc., The.

Wyatt Earp. 2010. (Legends of the Wild West Ser.). (Illus.). 112p. (gr. 6-12). 35.00 *(978-1-60413-597-8(2)*, Chelsea Hse.) Facts On File, Inc.

EARP, WYATT, 1848-1929—FICTION

Breault, Christie Merriman. Logan West, Printer's Devil. Archembault, Matthew, illus. 2006. 142p. (J). pap. *(978-1-59336-762-6(7))* Mondo Publishing.

EARTH (PLANET)

see also Antarctica; Arctic Regions; Atmosphere; Creation; Earthquakes; Geodesy; Geography; Geology; Geophysics; Glacial Epoch; Meteorology; Ocean; Oceanography; Physical Geography; Universe

Adamson, Thomas K. Earth [Scholastic]: Revised Edition. 2010. (Exploring the Galaxy Ser.). (ENG.). 24p. pap. 0.49 *(978-1-4296-5809-6(6)*, Pebble Plus) Capstone Press of Coughlan Cos.

Aguilar, David A. Cosmic Catastrophes. 2016. (Smithsonian Ser.). (ENG., Illus.). 80p. (J). (gr. 3-7). 18.99 *(978-0-451-47684-5(0)*, Viking Books for Young Readers) Penguin Young Readers Group.

Allen, Heather. Earth Day Is Every Day! 2011. (Dover Children's Activity Bks.). (ENG.). 48p. (J). (gr. 1-5). pap. 4.99 *(978-0-486-47765-7(7))* Dover Pubns., Inc.

Allyn, Daisy. Earth: The Blue Planet. 2010. (Our Solar System Ser.). 24p. (J). (gr. k-3). (ENG.). pap. 8.15 *(978-1-4339-3819-1(7))*; (Illus.). lib. bdg. 22.60 *(978-1-4339-3818-4(9))* Stevens, Gareth Publishing LLLP.

Andersen, Jill. Respect for Planet Earth. 2016. (Rosen REAL Readers: STEM & STEAM Collection). 8p. (gr. 1-k). pap. 5.46 *(978-1-5081-2401-6(9)*, Rosen Classroom) Rosen Publishing Group, Inc., The.

Anderson, Michael. Earth & Its Moon. 2011. lib. bdg. 31.70 *(978-1-61530-515-5(7))* Rosen Publishing Group, Inc., The.

Appleton-Smith, Laura & Harris, Greg. Plates, Quakes, & Glowing Magma. 2014. (Book to Remember Ser.). (ENG., Illus.). 24p. (J). pap. 8.95 *(978-1-60541-154-5(X)*, Books To Remember) Flyleaf Publishing.

Arnov Jr., Boris & Mindlin, Helen Mather-Smith. Inside Our Earth. Mather-Smith, Charles, illus. 2011. 160p. 41.95 *(978-1-258-07682-5(9))* Literary Licensing, LLC.

Ashby, Ruth. The Earth & Its Moon. 2003. (New Solar System Ser.). (J). lib. bdg. 28.50 *(978-1-58340-287-0(X))* Black Rabbit Bks.

Asimov, Isaac. The Solar System: Earth. 2004. (ENG., Illus.). 32p. (J). (gr. -1-3). pap. 15.99 *(978-1-59102-177-3(4))* Prometheus Bks., Pubs.

Asimov, Isaac & Hantula, Richard. La Tierra. Porras, Carlos & D'Andrea, Patricia, trs. from ENG. 2003. (Isaac Asimov's Biblioteca del Universo del Siglo XXI). (SPA., Illus.). 32p. (gr. 2-6). lib. bdg. 26.00 *(978-0-8368-3862-6(9)*, Gareth Stevens Learning Library) Stevens, Gareth Publishing LLLP.

Atkinson, Mary. The Earth Is Flat! 2007. (Shockwave: Science in Practice Ser.). (ENG., Illus.). 36p. (J). (gr. 3-5). 25.00 *(978-0-531-17580-4(4)*, Children's Pr.) Scholastic Library Publishing.

Austen, Mary. Exploring Earth. 2017. ***(978-1-5345-2247-3(6)***, KidHaven Publishing) Greenhaven Publishing LLC.

AZ Books. Our Planet. 2013. (Sounds Around Us Ser.). (ENG.). 16p. (J). (gr. 1-3). bds. 17.95 *(978-1-61889-282-9(7))* AZ Bks. LLC.

AZ Books Staff. About Planet Earth. Petrovskaya, Olga, ed. 2012. (Million Whys Ser.). (ENG.). 12p. (J). (gr. -1-4). bds. 18.95 *(978-1-61889-061-0(1))* AZ Bks. LLC.

Baker, David. Satellites. 2008. (Exploring Space Ser.). (Illus.). 32p. (J). (gr. 4-6). lib. bdg. 26.00 *(978-1-59036-777-3(4))* Weigl Pubs., Inc.

Baker, David & Kissock, Heather. Satellites. 2008. (Exploring Space Ser.). (Illus.). 32p. (J). (gr. 4-6). pap. 9.95 *(978-1-59036-778-0(2))* Weigl Pubs., Inc.

Ball, Jacqueline A. & Ball, Jacqueline A. Earth's History. 2004. (Discovery Channel School Science Ser.). (Illus.). 32p. (gr. 4-8). lib. bdg. 26.00 *(978-0-8368-3379-9(1)*, Gareth Stevens Learning Library) Stevens, Gareth Publishing LLLP.

Banqueri, Eduardo. Secrets of Earth. 2005. (Our Planet Ser.). (Illus.). 32p. (gr. 4-6). lib. bdg. 28.00 *(978-0-7910-9011-4(6)*, Chelsea Clubhouse) Facts On File, Inc.

Basher, Simon & Gilpin, Dan. Planet Earth: What Planet Are You On? Basher, Simon, illus. 2010. (Basher Science Ser.). (ENG., Illus.). 128p. (J). (gr. 5-9). 14.99 *(978-0-7534-6616-2(3)*, 9780753466162, Kingfisher) Roaring Brook Pr.

Bell, Trudy E. Earth's Journey Through Space. 2007. (Scientific American Ser.). (Illus.). 80p. (YA). (gr. 5-9). lib. bdg. 30.00 *(978-0-7910-9050-3(7))* Facts On File, Inc.

Bellisario, Gina. To Planet Earth! Becker, Paula, illus. 2017. (Cloverleaf Books (tm) — Space Adventures Ser.). (ENG.). 24p. (J). (gr. k-2). 25.32 *(978-1-5124-2535-2(4)*, Millbrook Pr.) Lerner Publishing Group.

—To Planet Earth! Becker, Paula J., illus. 2017. (Cloverleaf Books (tm) — Space Adventures Ser.). (ENG.). 24p. (J). (gr. k-2). 6.99 ***(978-1-5124-3891-8(X))***; 38.65 ***(978-1-5124-2831-5(0))***; 38.65 ***(978-1-5124-3890-1(1))*** Lerner Publishing Group. (Millbrook Pr.).

Benchmark Education Co., LLC Staff & Furgang, Kathy. Wind & Water Change Earth. 2015. (Content Connections Ser.). (J). (gr. 2). *(978-1-4900-0486-0(6))* Benchmark Education Co.

—Wind & Water Change Earth: Big Book Edition. 2015. (Content Connections Ser.). (J). (gr. 2). *(978-1-4900-0480-8(7))* Benchmark Education Co.

Benchmark Education Company, LLC Staff, compiled by. Earth the Inside Story & Earth Systems. 2005. spiral bd. 225.00 (978-1-4108-5823-8(5)) Benchmark Education Co.

—Earth the Inside Story & Earth's HIST. 2005. spiral bd. 225.00 (978-1-4108-5822-1(7)) Benchmark Education Co.

—Our Changing Earth: Theme Set. 2006. (J). 147.00 (978-1-4108-7081-0(2)) Benchmark Education Co.

Bennett, Jeffrey. I, Humanity. 2016. (ENG., Illus.). 32p. (J). (gr. 2-4). 15.00 (978-1-937548-52-0(X)) Big Kid Science.

Berger, Melvin & Berger, Gilda. Are Mountains Getting Taller? Questions & Answers about the Changing Earth. Carter, Robin, illus. 2003. (Question & Answer Ser.). (ENG.). 48p. (J). pap. 5.95 (978-0-439-26673-4(4), Scholastic Reference) Scholastic, Inc.

Berne, Emma Carlson. The Secrets of Earth. 2015. (Planets Ser.). (ENG., Illus.). 32p. (gr. 2-4). lib. bdg. 31.99 (978-1-4914-5863-1(1)) Capstone Press of Coughlan Cos.

Besel, Jennifer M. The Hottest Places on Earth. 2010. (Extreme Planet Ser.). (ENG.). 24p. (gr. 1-2). lib. bdg. 25.32 (978-1-4296-3964-4(4), First Facts) Capstone Press of Coughlan Cos.

Bethea, Nikole Brooks, et al. Our World: the Next 100 Years. Pota, Giovanni, illus. 2016. (Our World: the Next 100 Years Ser.). (ENG.). 32p. (gr. 3-4). 122.60 (978-1-4914-8272-8(9), Graphic Library) Capstone Press of Coughlan Cos.

Birch, Robin. Earth's Climate. 2009. (Weather & Climate Ser.). 32p. (gr. 3). 28.50 (978-0-7614-4471-8(8)) Marshall Cavendish Corp.

Bloom, J. P. Earth, 1 vol. 2014. (Planets Ser.). (ENG.). 24p. (J). (gr. 2-4). lib. bdg. 28.50 (978-1-62970-715-0(5)) ABDO Publishing Co.

The Blue Planet, Earth: Alien Technical Research. 2004. (YA). cd-rom 15.00 (978-0-934269-60-5(2)) UFO Photo Archives.

Bluthenthal, Todd. Earth's Hemispheres. 2017. (Where on Earth? Mapping Parts of the World Ser.). 24p. (gr. 1-2). pap. 8.15 **(978-1-4824-6417-7(9))** Stevens, Gareth Publishing LLLP.

Bourgoing, Pascale De, et al. Earth & Sky. Peyrols, Sylvaine, illus. 2006. (ENG.). 39p. (J). (gr. k-3). pap. 11.99 (978-1-85103-110-8(3)) Moonlight Publishing, Ltd. GBR. Dist: Independent Pubs. Group.

Bow, James. Earth Mysteries Revealed. 2010. (ENG., Illus.). 32p. (J). pap. (978-0-7787-7428-0(7)); (gr. 4-7). lib. bdg. (978-0-7787-7413-6(9)) Crabtree Publishing Co.

Braun, Eric. Curious Pearl Identifies the Reason for Seasons: 4D an Augmented Reality Science Experience. Dehennin, Stephanie, illus. 2017. (Curious Pearl, Science Girl 4D Ser.). (ENG.). 24p. (gr. k-2). lib. bdg. 20.65 **(978-1-5158-1343-9(6))** Picture Window Bks.

Bredeson, Carmen. What Do You Know about Earth? 2008. (I Like Space! Ser.). (Illus.). 32p. (J). (gr. 1-3). lib. bdg. 23.94 (978-0-7660-2945-3(X), Enslow Elementary) Enslow Pubs., Inc.

Bredeson, Carmen & Dyson, Marianne. Exploring Earth. 2015. (Launch into Space! Ser.). (ENG.). 32p. (J). (gr. 3-4). pap. 10.52 (978-0-7660-6817-9(X)) Enslow Pubs., Inc.

Bredeson, Carmen, et al. Exploring Earth. 2015. (Launch into Space! Ser.). (ENG., Illus.). 32p. (J). (gr. 3-4). 25.27 (978-0-7660-6819-3(6)) Enslow Pubs., Inc.

Bright, Michael. Planet Earth Explained, 1 vol., 1. 2014. (Guide for Curious Minds Ser.). (ENG.). 136p. (YA). (gr. 7-12). 38.25 (978-1-4777-2968-7(2)) Rosen Publishing Group, Inc., The.

Brinkman, Patricia. Discover Earth. 2006. (J). pap. (978-1-4108-6479-6(0)) Benchmark Education Co.

—Earth. 2006. (J). pap. (978-1-4108-6476-5(6)) Benchmark Education Co.

Britannica, Learning Library. Planet Earth. 2003. (Illus.). 64p. 14.95 (978-1-59339-032-7(7)) Encyclopaedia Britannica, Inc.

Broadbent, Paul. Beneath Our Feet. 2007. (Trackers-Math Ser.). (gr. 2-5). pap. 5.00 (978-1-59055-929-1(0)) Pacific Learning, Inc.

Brown, Don & Perfit, Michael R. Older Than Dirt. 2017. (ENG., Illus.). 112p. (J). (gr. 5-7). 18.99 (978-0-544-80503-3(8), HMH Books For Young Readers) Houghton Mifflin Harcourt Publishing Co.

Buchanan, Shelly. Our Ever-Changing Environment. rev. ed. 2014. (Primary Source Readers Content & Literacy Ser.). (ENG., Illus.). 32p. (gr. 3-3). pap. 8.99 (978-1-4333-7369-5(6)) Teacher Created Materials, Inc.

Bullard, Lisa. Earth Day Every Day. Xin, Xiao, illus. 2011. (Cloverleaf Books (tm) — Planet Protectors Ser.). (ENG.). 24p. (gr. k-2). lib. bdg. 23.93 (978-0-7613-6109-1(X)) Lerner Publishing Group.

Butterfield, Moira. Superstats: Extreme Planet. 2015. (Superstats Ser.). (ENG., Illus.). 64p. (J). (gr. 2-4). 11.99 (978-1-4998-0084-5(3)) Little Bee Books Inc.

Butterfield, Moira & Jacobs, Pat. Planet Earth. 2016. (Know It All Ser.). (ENG., Illus.). 32p. (J). (gr. 5-5). pap. 10.58 (978-1-5026-0886-4(3), 1398904) Cavendish Square Publishing.

Canavan, Thomas. Does It Really Rain Frogs? Questions & Answers about Planet Earth. 2013. (Science F. A. Q. Ser.). (Illus.). 32p. (gr. 3-6). 31.35 (978-1-78212-393-4(8)) Arcturus Publishing GBR. Dist: Black Rabbit Bks.

Cane, Ella. Continents in My World, 1 vol. 2013. (My World Ser.). (ENG.). 24p. (gr. k-1). 21.99 (978-1-4765-3123-6(4)); pap. 6.95 (978-1-4765-3465-7(9)) Capstone Press of Coughlan Cos. (Pebble Bks.).

Carson, Mary Kay. Far-Out Guide to Earth. 2010. (Far-Out Guide to the Solar System Ser.). (Illus.). 48p. (J). pap. 8.95 (978-1-59845-183-2(9), Enslow Elementary); (gr. 2-5). 25.27 (978-0-7660-3182-1(9)) Enslow Pubs., Inc.

—Why Does the Earth Spin? And Other Questions about ... Our Planet. Bull, Peter, illus. 2014. (Good Question! Ser.). (ENG.). 40p. (J). (gr. 1). 12.95 (978-1-4549-0674-2(X)) Sterling Publishing Co., Inc.

Cartwright, Pauline. About Earth (Paperback) Copyright 2016. 2015. (ENG.). (gr. k-6). pap. 6.97 (978-0-328-83287-3(1), Scott Foresman) Addison Wesley Schl.

Cella, Clara. Earth Day. 2012. (Let's Celebrate Ser.). (ENG.). 24p. (gr. k-1). pap. 41.70 (978-1-4296-9385-1(1), Pebble Plus) Capstone Press of Coughlan Cos.

Chambers, Catherine. Stickmen's Guide to Earth's Atmosphere in Layers. Dean, Venitia & De Quay, John Paul, illus. 2016. (Stickmen's Guides to This Incredible Earth Ser.). (ENG.). 32p. (J). (gr. 3-6). 26.65 (978-1-5124-0617-7(1)) Lerner Publishing Group.

—Stickmen's Guide to Mountains & Valleys in Layers. Dean, Venitia & de Quay, John Paul, illus. 2016. (Stickmen's Guides to This Incredible Earth Ser.). (ENG.). 32p. (J). (gr. 3-6). 26.65 (978-1-5124-0618-4(X)) Lerner Publishing Group.

Channing, Margot. Planet Earth. 2014. (Closer Look At... Ser.). (Illus.). 32p. (gr. 3-6). 31.35 (978-1-904642-69-5(1)) Book Hse. GBR. Dist: Black Rabbit Bks.

Charner, Kathy, ed. Learn Every Day about Our Green Earth: 100 Best Ideas from Teachers. 2010. (Learn Every Day Ser.). (ENG.). 128p. pap. 12.95 (978-0-87659-127-7(6), Gryphon House Inc) Gryphon Hse., Inc.

Claybourne, A. Encyclopedia of Planet Earth. 2004. (Geography Ser.). (Illus.). 160p. (J). lib. bdg. 27.95 (978-1-58086-573-9(9)) EDC Publishing.

Claybourne, Anna. Enciclopedia del Planeta Tierra. 2004. (SPA.). 160p. (J). 19.95 (978-0-7460-4526-8(3)) EDC Publishing.

—Extreme Earth. 2010. (Discovery of Life Ser.). (Illus.). 48p. (YA). lib. bdg. 19.95 (978-1-4222-1520-3(2)) Mason Crest.

Close, Edward. Earth's Place in Space, 1 vol., 1. 2014. (Discovery Education: Earth & Space Science Ser.). (ENG.). 32p. (gr. 3-6). 26.25 (978-1-4777-6174-8(8), PowerKids Pr.) Rosen Publishing Group, Inc., The.

—Earth's Treasures: Rocks & Minerals: Rocks & Minerals, 1 vol., 1. 2014. (Discovery Education: Earth & Space Science Ser.). (ENG.). 32p. (gr. 3-6). 26.25 (978-1-4777-6170-0(5), PowerKids Pr.) Rosen Publishing Group, Inc., The.

Cobb, Allan B. Earth Chemistry. 2008. (Essential Chemistry Ser.). 136p. (YA). (gr. 7-12). 35.00 (978-0-7910-9677-2(7)) Facts On File, Inc.

Cobie, Charles. Earth Science. 3rd ed. (J). 33.47 (978-0-13-982109-7(0)) Prentice Hall (Schl. Div.).

Cole, Joanna. Planet Earth. 2014. (Magic School Bus Presents Ser.). lib. bdg. 17.20 (978-0-606-35813-2(7)) Turtleback Bks.

Cole, Joanna & Jackson, Tom. Planet Earth. Degen, Bruce & Bracken, Carolyn, illus. 2014. (Magic School Bus Presents Ser.). (ENG.). 32p. (J). (gr. 1-3). pap. 6.99 (978-0-545-68012-7(3)) Scholastic, Inc.

Conklin, Wendy. Earth's Cycles. 2015. (Science Readers: Content & Literacy Ser.). (ENG., Illus.). 32p. (gr. 4-4). pap. 8.99 (978-1-4807-4686-2(X)) Teacher Created Materials, Inc.

Coote, Roger. Earth. 2003. (Knowledge Masters Ser.). (Illus.). 32p. (YA). pap. incl. cd-rom (978-1-903954-11-9(8), Pavilion Children's Books) Pavilion Bks.

Dakers, Diane. Earth's Cycles. 2014. (ENG., Illus.). 48p. (J). pap. (978-0-7787-0619-9(2)) Crabtree Publishing Co.

Dal Fuoco, Gina. Spaceship Earth, 1 vol. 2007. (Science Readers Ser.). (ENG., Illus.). 32p. (J). (gr. 4-4). pap. 8.99 (978-0-7439-0565-7(2)) Shell Educational Publishing.

Davis, Barbara J. Earth's Core & Crust. 2007. (Gareth Stevens Vital Science: Earth Science Ser.). (Illus.). 48p. (gr. 5-12). pap. 14.05 (978-0-8368-7873-8(6), Gareth Stevens Secondary Library) Stevens, Gareth Publishing LLLP.

Davis, Kenneth C. Don't Know Much about Planet Earth. unabr. ed. 2004. (Don't Know Much about Ser.). 144p. (J). (gr. 4-7). pap. 29.00 incl. audio (978-0-8072-0660-7(1), Listening Library) Random Hse. Audio Publishing Group.

Daynes, Katie & Allen, Peter. See Inside Planet Earth - Internet Referenced. 2008. (See Inside Board Bks). 16p. (J). bds. 12.99 (978-0-7945-2070-0(7), Usborne) EDC Publishing.

¿De Que Esta Hecha la Tierra? (Coleccion Primeros Pasos en la Ciencia). (SPA., Illus.). (J). (gr. 1-3). pap. (978-950-724-689-0(4), LMA8230) Lumen ARG. Dist: Lectorum Pubns., Inc.

DeCristofano, Carolyn. National Geographic Kids Ultimate Space Atlas. 2017. (ENG.). 160p. (J). (gr. 3-7). lib. bdg. 22.90 **(978-1-4263-2803-9(6))**; (Illus.). pap. 12.99 **(978-1-4263-2802-2(8))** National Geographic Society. (National Geographic Children's Bks.).

DeCristofano, Carolyn Cinami. The Sun & the Moon. Morley, Taia, illus. 2016. (Let's-Read-And-Find-Out Science 1 Ser.). 40p. (J). (gr. -1-3). pap. 6.99 (978-0-06-233803-7(X)) HarperCollins Pubs.

DePrisco, Dorothea. Smithsonian Discover: Earth. 2015. (Smithsonian Discover Ser.). (ENG., Illus.). 64p. (J). (gr. 2). spiral bd. 16.95 (978-1-62686-163-3(3), Silver Dolphin Bks.) Readerlink Distribution Services, LLC.

Desonie, Dana. Our Fragile Planet Set, 8-Volumes. 2008. (Our Fragile Planet Ser.). (gr. 6-12). 280.00 (978-0-8160-7424-2(0), Chelsea Hse.) Facts On File, Inc.

Dickmann, Nancy. Exploring Planet Earth & the Moon. 2015. (Spectacular Space Science Ser.). (ENG., Illus.). 48p. (J). (gr. 5-6). 30.25 (978-1-4994-3625-9(4), Rosen Central) Rosen Publishing Group, Inc., The.

Dobeck, Maryann. Circling the Sun. 2004. (Reading PowerWorks Ser.). (Illus.). 16p. (gr. 1-3). pap. 6.10 (978-0-7608-8917-6(1)) Sundance/Newbridge Educational Publishing.

Dorling Kindersley Publishing Staff. First Earth Encyclopedia. 2010. (ENG.). 128p. (J). (gr. k-4). 16.99 (978-0-7566-7139-6(6), DK Children) Dorling Kindersley Publishing, Inc.

—My Tourist Guide to the Centre of the Earth. 2013. (ENG., Illus.). 64p. (J). (978-1-4093-2443-0(5)) Dorling Kindersley Publishing, Inc.

—Pocket Genius: Earth. 2016. (Pocket Genius Ser.). (ENG., Illus.). 160p. (J). (gr. 3-7). pap. 4.99 (978-1-4654-4586-5(2), DK Children) Dorling Kindersley Publishing, Inc.

—Super Earth Encyclopedia. 2017. (ENG.). 208p. (J). (gr. 4-7). 24.99 **(978-1-4654-6187-2(6)**, DK Children) Dorling Kindersley Publishing, Inc.

—Utterly Amazing Earth. 2017. (ENG., Illus.). 32p. (J). (gr. 2-4). 19.99 (978-1-4654-5867-4(0), DK Children) Dorling Kindersley Publishing, Inc.

—When on Earth? 2015. (ENG.). 160p. (J). (gr. 3-7). 19.99 (978-1-4654-2940-7(9), DK Children) Dorling Kindersley Publishing, Inc.

Dorling Kindersley Publishing Staff & Green, Jen. Big Fantastic Earth. 2016. (DK Readers Ser.). (ENG., Illus.). 96p. (J). (gr. 3-7). 14.99 (978-1-4654-4413-4(0), DK Children) Dorling Kindersley Publishing, Inc.

Draper, Allison Stark. Earth. (Library of Planets Ser.). 2009. 48p. (gr. 5-8). 55.90 (978-1-60853-815-7(X), Rosen Reference) 2008. (J). lib. bdg. 29.25 (978-1-4358-5074-3(2)) 2005. (ENG., Illus.). 48p. (J). lib. bdg. 27.95 (978-1-4042-0167-5(X)) Rosen Publishing Group, Inc., The.

Duhamel, Megan. The Earth. 2007. (Illus.). 16p. (J). 3.95 (978-0-545-00731-3(3)) Scholastic, Inc.

Dunn, Mary R. A Look at Earth. (Astronomy Now! Ser.). 24p. 2009. (gr. 2-3). 42.50 (978-1-61511-467-2(X)) 2007. (Illus.). (J). (gr. 3-7). lib. bdg. 21.25 (978-1-4042-3827-5(1)) Rosen Publishing Group, Inc., The. (PowerKids Pr.).

Earth. (Make it Work Ser.). 42p. (J). (gr. 4-8). pap. (978-1-882210-44-2(1)) Action Publishing, Inc.

Earth. 2014. (Four Elements Ser.). 32p. (J). (gr. k-3). pap. 10.00 (978-1-4777-9273-5(2)) Windmill Bks.

Earth, Module C. 2003. (Scott Foresman Science Ser.). (gr. 3-18). suppl. ed. 15.50 (978-0-328-03437-6(1)); (gr. 4-18). suppl. ed. 15.50 (978-0-328-03441-3(X)); (gr. 5-18). suppl. ed. 16.00 (978-0-328-03445-1(2)); (gr. 6-18). suppl. ed. 16.00 (978-0-328-03449-9(5)) Addison-Wesley Educational Pubs., Inc.

Earth. 2nd rev. ed. 2008. (New Solar System Ser.). 32p. (YA). (gr. 3-6). 23.00 (978-1-60413-210-6(8)) Facts On File, Inc.

Earth & Space. (Illus.). (J). Date not set. 48p. 5.98 (978-1-4054-0206-4(7)) 2003. 256p. 12.98 (978-1-4054-1543-9(6)) Parragon, Inc.

Earth Features, Set. 2003. (Earth Features Ser.). (ENG.). 24p. (gr. k-1). pap. 249.90 (978-0-7368-3282-3(3), Pebble Bks.) Capstone Press of Coughlan Cos.

Earth in Action [Capstone Sole Source]. 2010. (Earth in Action Ser.). 24p. lib. bdg. 191.92 (978-1-4296-5853-9(3), Pebble Plus) Capstone Press of Coughlan Cos.

Earth in Action Pack [Scholastic]. 2010. (Earth in Action Ser.). 24p. pap. 1.96 (978-1-4296-5803-4(7), Pebble Plus) Capstone Press of Coughlan Cos.

Earth Instructional Guide. 2009. (Grade 8: Science Exit Project Kits Ser.). spiral bd. (978-1-4042-4022-3(5), Rosen Classroom) Rosen Publishing Group, Inc., The.

Earth's Crust. 2007. (Illus.). 48p. (J). (gr. 2-5). pap. 8.95 (978-0-8225-6585-7(4)) Lerner Publishing Group.

Earth's Most Extreme Places. 2015. (Earth's Most Extreme Places Ser.). (ENG.). 24p. (J). (gr. 2-3). 135.60 (978-1-4824-1639-8(5)) Stevens, Gareth Publishing LLLP.

Earth's Spheres, 6 bks., Set. Incl. Atmosphere: Planetary Heat Engine. Vogt, Gregory. (gr. 6-8). 2007. lib. bdg. 29.27 (978-0-7613-2841-4(6), Twenty-First Century Bks.); Biosphere: Realm of Life. Vogt, Gregory. (gr. 6-8). 2007. lib. bdg. 29.27 (978-0-7613-2840-7(8)); Earth's Core & Mantle: Heavy Metal, Moving Rock. Vogt, Gregory L. (YA). (gr. 7-12). 2006. lib. bdg. 29.27 (978-0-7613-2837-7(8)); Earth's Outer Atmosphere: Bordering Space. Vogt, Gregory. (YA). (gr. 7-12). 2007. lib. bdg. 29.27 (978-0-7613-2842-1(4)); Hydrosphere: Agent of Change. Vogt, Gregory. (gr. 6-8). 2007. lib. bdg. 29.27 (978-0-7613-2839-1(4)); Lithosphere: Earth's Crust. Vogt, Gregory L. (gr. 6-8). 2007. lib. bdg. 29.27 (978-0-7613-2838-4(6)); (Illus.). 80p. 2007. Set lib. bdg. 175.62 (978-0-8225-8058-4(6), Twenty-First Century Bks.) Lerner Publishing Group.

Editors of TIME For Kids Magazine. Stellar Space. 2014. (TIME for Kids Big Books of WHY Ser.). (ENG., Illus.). 48p. (J). (gr. 3-17). pap. 4.99 (978-1-60320-985-4(9)) Time Inc. Bks.

Enz, Tammy. Dynamic Planet: Exploring Changes on Earth with Science Projects. 2015. (Discover Earth Science Ser.). (ENG., Illus.). 32p. (gr. 3-4). lib. bdg. 27.32 (978-1-4914-4815-1(6)) Capstone Press of Coughlan Cos.

—Liquid Planet: Exploring Water on Earth with Science Projects. (Illus.). 32p. 2016. (J). lib. bdg. (978-1-4747-0325-3(9)) 2015. (ENG., (gr. 3-4). lib. bdg. 27.32 (978-1-4914-4817-5(2)) Capstone Press of Coughlan Cos.

Essential Atlas of the World. (Illus.). 159p. reprint ed. pap. (978-0-681-50234-5(7)) Borders Pr.

Evans, Shira. Day & Night. 2016. (Readers Ser.). (ENG., Illus.). 48p. (J). (-k). pap. 4.99 (978-1-4263-2470-3(7), National Geographic Children's Bks.) National Geographic Society.

Exploration. 2010. (Discovering the Earth Ser.). (Illus.). 256p. (C). (gr. 9-18). 39.95 (978-0-8160-6103-7(3)) Facts On File, Inc.

Exploring Earth's Treasures. (Eyes on Adventure Ser.). (Illus.). 32p. (J). (gr. 1-18). 7.95 (978-1-56156-485-9(0)) Kidsbooks, LLC.

Exploring Wonders of the World. (Eyes on Adventure Ser.). (Illus.). 32p. (J). (gr. 1-18). 7.95 (978-1-56156-486-6(9)) Kidsbooks, LLC.

Facts on File, Inc. Staff, creator. The Hazardous Earth Set, 8-Volumes. 2008. (Hazardous Earth Ser.). (gr. 6-12). 316.00 (978-0-8160-7828-8(9)) Facts On File, Inc.

Farndon, John & Walshaw, Rodney. Planet Earth: Continents, Oceans, Climate, Geology. 2015. (ENG., Illus.). 64p. (J). (gr. k-6). 12.99 (978-1-86147-402-5(4), Armadillo) Anness Publishing GBR. Dist: National Bk. Network.

Faust, Daniel R. After Earth: Living on a Different Planet. 2008. (Jr. Graphic Environmental Dangers Ser.). (ENG.). 24p. (J). 47.90 (978-1-61532-099-8(7), PowerKids Pr.); (Illus.). (gr. 3-6). lib. bdg. 25.25 (978-1-4042-4229-6(5)) Rosen Publishing Group, Inc., The.

Feinstein, Stephen. Earth: A MyReportLinks. com Book. 2005. (Solar System Ser.). (Illus.). 48p. (J). lib. bdg. 26.60 (978-0-7660-5301-4(6), MyReportLinks.com Bks.) Enslow Pubs., Inc.

Flores, Mina. Lakes, Rivers, & Streams. 2016. (Spotlight on Earth Science Ser.). 00024p. (J). (gr. 4-6). pap. 10.00 (978-1-4994-2522-2(8), PowerKids Pr.) Rosen Publishing Group, Inc., The.

Ford, Adam. Stars: A Family Guide to the Night Sky. 2016. (Discover Together Guides). (ENG., Illus.). 48p. 16.95 (978-1-61180-283-2(0), Roost Books) Shambhala Pubns., Inc.

Frith, Alex & King, Colin. See under the Ground. 2007. (See Inside Science Ser.). (Illus.). 15p. (J). bds. 12.99 (978-0-7945-1600-0(9), Usborne) EDC Publishing.

Fry, Erin. Earth Fast Changes: Set Of 6. 2011. (Navigators Ser.). (J). pap. 48.00 net. (978-1-4108-5078-2(1)) Benchmark Education Co.

Gaff, Jackie. Looking at Earth: How Does It Change? 2008. (Looking at Science: How Things Change Ser.). (Illus.). 32p. (J). (gr. 3-7). lib. bdg. 23.94 (978-0-7660-3088-6(1), Enslow Elementary) Enslow Pubs., Inc.

Galvin, Laura Gates. ABCDEarth. 2010. (Sesame Street Alphabet Bks.). (Illus.). 40p. (J). (gr. -1). 17.95 (978-1-59069-875-4(4)); 17.95 (978-1-59069-874-7(6)) Studio Mouse LLC.

Ganeri, Anita. I Wonder Why the Wind Blows. 2011. (I Wonder Why Ser.). (ENG., Illus.). 32p. (J). (gr. k-3). pap. 6.99 (978-0-7534-6522-6(1), 9780753465226, Kingfisher) Roaring Brook Pr.

—Record-Breaking Earth. 2010. (ENG.). 32p. (J). (978-0-7787-9908-5(5)); pap. (978-0-7787-9929-0(8)) Crabtree Publishing Co.

Ganeri, Anita & Oxlade, Chris. Introducing Continents. 2013. (Introducing Continents Ser.). (ENG.). 32p. (gr. 1-3). pap. 47.94 (978-1-4329-8053-5(X)); lib. bdg. 191.24 (978-1-4329-8045-0(9)) Heinemann-Raintree. (Heinemann First Library).

Gardner, Robert. Earth-Shaking Science Projects about Planet Earth. LaBaff, Tom, illus. 2007. (Rockin' Earth Science Experiments Ser.). 48p. (J). (gr. 3-4). lib. bdg. 25.27 (978-0-7660-2733-6(3), Enslow Elementary) Enslow Pubs., Inc.

Geatches, Hazel, ed. Earth. 2012. (ENG., Illus.). 40p. pap., act. bk. ed. 10.00 (978-0-19-464679-6(3)) Oxford Univ. Pr., Inc.

Gendell, Megan & Connolly, Rachel. Your Home in Space: Everything You Wanted to Know about Earth, the Sun, & the Moon. 2008. (Illus.). 32p. (J). (978-0-545-04457-8(X)) Scholastic, Inc.

George, Jean Craighead. La Tierra Que Habla.Tr. of Talking Earth. (SPA.). 136p. (J). 9.95 (978-84-204-3699-9(2)) Santillana USA Publishing Co., Inc.

Gerard, James H. The Blue Marble: How a Photograph Revealed Earth's Fragile Beauty, 1 vol. 2014. (Captured World History Ser.). (ENG., Illus.). 64p. (gr. 5-7). pap. 8.95 (978-0-7565-4788-2(1), CPB Grades 4-8) Compass Point Bks.

Gilpin, Dan & Bull, Peter. Explorers: Planet Earth. 2014. (Explorers Ser.). (ENG., Illus.). 32p. (J). (gr. 2-5). 6.99 (978-0-7534-7169-2(8), 9780753471692, Kingfisher) Roaring Brook Pr.

Gladstone, James. When Planet Earth Was New. Diemert, Katherine, illus. 2017. (ENG.). 40p. (J). (gr. -1-5). 18.95 **(978-1-77147-203-6(0))** Owlkids Bks. Inc. CAN. Dist: Publishers Group West (PGW).

Global Guardians. 2016. (Global Guardians Ser.). 00024p. (J). (gr. 3-3). 141.60 (978-1-4994-2645-8(3), PowerKids Pr.) Rosen Publishing Group, Inc., The.

Goldsmith, Mike. Flip the Flaps: Planet Earth. Palin, Nicki, illus. 2012. (Flip the Flaps Ser.). (ENG.). 32p. (J). (gr. -1-1). pap. 6.99 (978-0-7534-6860-9(3), 9780753468609, Kingfisher) Roaring Brook Pr.

Goldsmith, Mike & Taylor, Barbara. Earth & Space: A Thrilling Adventure from Planet Earth into the Universe. 2016. (ENG., Illus.). 80p. 15.99 (978-0-7534-7279-8(1), 9780753472798, Kingfisher) Roaring Brook Pr.

Goldstein, Margaret J. Earth. 2003. (Our Universe Ser.). (ENG., Illus.). 32p. (gr. 2-4). lib. bdg. 22.60 (978-0-8225-4650-4(7)) Lerner Publishing Group.

Gottlieb. The Earth & Beyond. 2004. (Wonders of Science Ser.). (ENG., Illus.). 144p. (gr. 7-12). pap. 24.55 (978-0-7398-9181-0(2)) Houghton Mifflin Harcourt Publishing Co.

—Earth & Beyond. 2004. (Wonders of Science Ser.). (ENG.). 176p. (gr. 7-12). pap., tchr. ed. 27.70 (978-0-7398-9187-2(1)) Houghton Mifflin Harcourt Publishing Co.

Graf, Mike & Snedden, Robert. Mapping Earth from Space, 1 vol. 2011. (Science Missions Ser.). (ENG.). 56p. (gr. 3-3). 34.65 (978-1-4109-3994-4(4)); pap. 9.95 (978-1-4109-4001-8(2)) Heinemann-Raintree. (Raintree Freestyle Express).

Graham, Ian. Earth & the Universe. 2008. (World of Wonder Ser.). (ENG.). 32p. (J). 29.00 (978-0-531-24025-0(8), Children's Pr.) Scholastic Library Publishing.

Granger, Ronald. Exploring Earth's Surface. 2012. (Exploring Earth & Space Ser.). (ENG., Illus.). 24p. (J). (gr. 1-3). 22.60 (978-1-4488-8570-1(1), PowerKids Pr.) Rosen Publishing Group, Inc., The.

Green, Dan. The Adventures of Earth. Sims, Sean, illus. 2016. (ENG.). 14p. (J). (gr. k). 14.95 (978-1-4549-2143-1(9)) Sterling Publishing Co., Inc.

Green, Jen. Big Fantastic Earth. 2016. (Illus.). 96p. (J). (978-1-5182-1730-2(3)) Dorling Kindersley Publishing, Inc.

—Frozen Extremes. 2008. (Extreme Nature Ser.). (ENG., Illus.). 32p. (J). (gr. 2-3). pap. (978-0-7787-4519-8(8)) Crabtree Publishing Co.

Greer, Eileen. Plate Tectonics. 2016. (Spotlight on Earth Science Ser.). 00024p. (J). (gr. 4-6). 26.25 (978-1-4994-2535-2(X)); pap. 10.00 (978-1-4994-2532-1(5)) Rosen Publishing Group, Inc., The. (PowerKids Pr.).

Group/McGraw-Hill, Wright. Dreams of Flight, 6 vols. (Book2WebTM Ser.). (gr. 4-8). 36.50 (978-0-322-04433-3(2)) Wright Group/McGraw-Hill.

—La Erosion de la Tierra, 6 vols., Vol. 2. (First Explorers. Primeros Exploradores Nonfiction Sets Ser.). (SPA.). (gr. 1-2). 34.95 (978-0-7699-1481-7(0)) Shortland Pubns. (U. S. A.) Inc.

—Rocks & Minerals Tell Earth's Story, 6 vols. (Book2WebTM Ser.). (gr. 4-8). 36.50 (978-0-322-04426-5(X)) Wright Group/McGraw-Hill.

Haelle, Tara. Seasons, Tides, & Lunar Phases. 2016. (Let's Explore Science Ser.). (ENG., Illus.). 48p. (gr. 5-8). 35.64 (978-1-68191-395-7(X)) Rourke Educational Media.

Hammond World Atlas Corporation Staff, ed. Planet Earth: Our Planet as You've Never Seen It Before. 2008. 168p. (J). (gr. 3-7). 19.99 (978-0-8437-1834-8(X)) Hammond World Atlas Corp.

Hansen, Amy S. Where Does the Sun Go at Night? An Earth Science Mystery, 1 vol. Scott, Korey, illus. 2011. (First Graphics: Science Mysteries Ser.). (ENG.). 24p. (gr. 1-2). lib. bdg. 23.99 (978-1-4296-6098-3(8)) Capstone Press of Coughlan Cos.

Harcourt School Publishers Staff. Looking at the Earth, Unit 3. 3rd ed. 2003. (Horizons Ser.). (Illus.). pap. 166.70 (978-0-15-340229-6(6)) Harcourt Schl. Pubs.

—Looking at the Earth Big Book No. 3. 2nd ed. 2003. (Illus.). pap. 139.70 (978-0-15-337568-2(X)) Harcourt Schl. Pubs.

Harman, Alice. Earth, 01 vols., 1. 2016. (Fact Finders: Space Ser.). (ENG., Illus.). 24p. (J). pap. 8.25

(978-1-5081-9125-4(5), Windmill Bks.) Rosen Publishing Group, Inc., The.

Harris, Irene. Earth's Continents. 2016. (Spotlight on Earth Science Ser.). 00024p. (J). (gr. 4-6). pap. 10.00 (978-1-4994-2496-6(5), PowerKids Pr.) Rosen Publishing Group, Inc., The.

Hartley, Susan. We Can Help Our Earth. 2016. (Spring Forward Ser.). (J). (gr. k). (978-1-4900-6013-2(8)) Benchmark Education Co.

Haskell, J. P. Earth's Many Landforms. 2012. (InfoMax Readers Ser.). (ENG., Illus.). 24p. (J). (gr. 1-2). pap. 8.25 (978-1-4488-9052-1(7), Rosen Classroom) Rosen Publishing Group, Inc., The.

Haslam, Andrew, et al. Earth. (Make It Work! Ser.). (Illus.). 48p. (J). pap. 7.99 (978-0-590-24617-0(8)) Scholastic, Inc.

Helbrough, Emma. Great Planet Earth Search. Milbourne, Anna, ed. Jackson, Ian, illus. 2005. (Great Searches Ser.). 32p. (J). (gr. 3). lib. bdg. 15.95 (978-1-58086-827-3(4)) EDC Publishing.

—Great Planet Earth Search. Jackson, Ian, illus. 2006. 32p. (J). (978-0-439-83402-5(3)) Scholastic, Inc.

Hicks, Terry Allan. Earth & the Moon. 2009. (Space!). 64p. (gr. 5-18). lib. bdg. 32.79 (978-0-7614-4254-7(5)) Marshall Cavendish Corp.

Hill, Christina. Earth's Moon, 1 vol. 2015. (Science Readers: Content & Literacy Ser.). (ENG., Illus.). 32p. (gr. 3-3). pap. 8.99 (978-1-4807-4651-0(7)) Teacher Created Materials, Inc.

Hill, E. C. Earth the Water Planet: Set Of 6. 2011. (Navigators Ser.). (J). pap. 48.00 net. (978-1-4108-5083-6(8)) Benchmark Education Co.

Holt, Rinehart and Winston Staff. Holt Science & Technology Level F: Inside the Restless Earth. 5th ed. 2004. tchr. ed. 46.66 (978-0-03-025571-7(6)) Holt McDougal.

—Holt Science Spectrum Chptr. 21: Planet Earth. 4th ed. Date not set. pap. 11.20 (978-0-03-068059-5(X)) Holt McDougal.

How to Be Earth Friendly, 6 vols., Set. Incl. Earth-Friendly Buildings. Coleman, Miriam. lib. bdg. 25.25 (978-1-4488-2588-2(1)); Earth-Friendly Energy. Gosman, Gillian. lib. bdg. 25.25 (978-1-4488-2587-5(3)); Earth-Friendly Food. Gosman, Gillian. lib. bdg. 25.25 (978-1-4488-2589-9(X)); Earth-Friendly Living. Coleman, Miriam. lib. bdg. 25.25 (978-1-4488-2592-9(X)); Earth-Friendly Shopping. Gosman, Gillian. lib. bdg. 25.25 (978-1-4488-2591-2(1)); Earth-Friendly Transportation. Coleman, Miriam. lib. bdg. 25.25 (978-1-4488-2590-5(3)); (YA). (gr. 3-6). (How to Be Earth Friendly Ser.). (Illus.). 32p. 2011. Set lib. bdg. 143.70 (978-1-4488-2794-7(9), PowerKids Pr.) Rosen Publishing Group, Inc., The.

Howard, Fran. Earth, 1 vol. 2007. (Planets Ser.). (ENG.). 32p. (gr. 3-7). 27.07 (978-1-59928-825-3(7), Buddy Bks.) ABDO Publishing Co.

Howell, Laura & Rogers, Kirsteen. Earth & Space. 2004. (Library of Science Ser.). 64p. (J). lib. bdg. 17.95 (978-1-58086-373-5(6)) EDC Publishing.

Hughes, Tom. Day & Night. 2016. (All about Opposites Ser.). (Illus.). 24p. (J). pap. 9.35 (978-0-7660-8082-9(X)) Enslow Pubs., Inc.

Hunter, Nick. Earth, 1 vol. 2012. (Astronaut Travel Guides). (ENG.). 48p. (gr. 3-6). pap. 9.95 (978-1-4109-4577-8(4)); lib. bdg. 32.65 (978-1-4109-4568-6(5)) Heinemann-Raintree. (NA-r).

Hutmacher, Kimberly. Studying Our Earth, Inside & Out. 2012. (ENG.). 24p. (gr. 3-4). pap. 8.95 (978-1-61810-224-9(9)) Rourke Educational Media.

Ikids Staff. Green Start - Little Helpers. Phillips, Jillian, illus. 2010. (ENG.). 20p. (J). (gr. -1-17). 6.99 (978-1-60169-007-4(X)) Innovative Kids.

In the World. (J). (gr. 6). 3.80 (978-0-8374-1455-3(5), 406) Weekly Reader Corp.

Jackson, Ellen B. The Spring Equinox: The Greening of the Earth. 2003. (Illus.). 32p. (J). (gr. 3-6). pap. 7.95 (978-0-7613-1983-2(2), Millbrook Pr.) Lerner Publishing Group.

Jackson, Tom. Destination Earth. (Illus.). 32p. (J). 2010. pap. 10.00 (978-1-4358-3471-2(2)) 2009. (ENG., lib. bdg. 25.25 (978-1-4358-3450-7(X)) Rosen Publishing Group, Inc., The. (PowerKids Pr.).

Jefferis, David. The Earth: Our Home Planet. 2008. (Exploring Our Solar System Ser.). (ENG., Illus.). 32p. (J). (gr. 3-7). pap. (978-0-7787-3746-9(2)) Crabtree Publishing Co.

Jones, Tammy. Look at the Sky. 2009. (Sight Word Readers Set A Ser.). (J). 3.49 net. (978-1-60719-141-4(5)) Newmark Learning LLC.

Kalman, Bobbie. Explore Earth's Seven Continents. 2010. (Explore the Continents Ser.). (ENG., Illus.). 32p. (J). (gr. 1-5). lib. bdg. (978-0-7787-3078-1(6)) Crabtree Publishing Co.

—Looking at Earth. 2008. (ENG.). 32p. (J). pap. (978-0-7787-3210-5(X)) Crabtree Publishing Co.

—La Tierra y el Sol. 2009. (SPA.). 32p. (J). (978-0-7787-8241-4(7)); pap. (978-0-7787-8258-2(1)) Crabtree Publishing Co.

—We Are the Earth. 2009. (Our Multicultural World Ser.). (ENG., Illus.). 32p. (J). (gr. 1-4). pap. (978-0-7787-4649-2(6)); lib. bdg. (978-0-7787-4634-8(8)) Crabtree Publishing Co.

Kalman, Bobbie & MacAulay, Kelley. Earth & the Sun. 2008. (Looking at Earth Ser.). (ENG., Illus.). 32p. (J). (gr. 3-7). pap. (978-0-7787-3212-9(6)); lib. bdg. (978-0-7787-3202-0(9)) Crabtree Publishing Co.

Karas, G. Brian. On Earth. Karas, G. Brian, illus. 2008. (ENG., Illus.). 32p. (J). (gr. k-3). pap. 7.99 (978-0-14-241063-9(2), Puffin Books) Penguin Young Readers Group.

—On Earth. Karas, G. Brian, illus. 2008. (Illus.). (gr. k-3). 18.00 (978-0-7569-8926-2(4)) Perfection Learning Corp.

Kenney, Karen Latchana. Peeking Underground. Wood, Steven, illus. 2016. (What's Beneath Ser.). (ENG.). 32p. (gr. -1-3). lib. bdg. 27.32 (978-1-4795-8666-0(8)) Picture Window Bks.

Kenny, Natalie. Earth Day: Taking Care of Our Planet. 2009. (Real Life Readers Ser.). 16p. (gr. 2-3). pap. 7.05 (978-1-4358-0103-5(2), Rosen Classroom) Rosen Publishing Group, Inc., The.

Kerrod, Robin. Planet Earth. 2005. (Planet Library). (Illus.). 32p. (gr. 3-8). lib. bdg. 21.27 (978-0-8225-3902-5(0)) Lerner Publishing Group.

Khanduri, K. The Great World Search. rev. ed. 2004. (Great Searches Ser.). (SPA., Illus.). 48p. (J). lib. bdg. 17.95 (978-1-58086-596-8(8)) EDC Publishing.

Ladybird. Planet Earth. 2016. (Read It Yourself with Ladybird Ser.). (ENG., Illus.). 48p. (J). 5.99 (978-0-241-23740-3(8)) Penguin Bks., Ltd. GBR. Dist: Independent Pubs. Group.

—Planet Earth, Level 3. 2016. (Read It Yourself with Ladybird Ser.). (ENG., Illus.). 48p. (J). (gr. 2-4). pap. 9.99 (978-0-241-23738-0(6)) Penguin Bks., Ltd. GBR. Dist: Independent Pubs. Group.

Larson, Paul. The Four Spheres of the Earth. 2015. (Science Readers: Content & Literacy Ser.). 32p. (gr. 5-5). pap. 8.99 (978-1-4807-4725-8(4)) Teacher Created Materials, Inc.

Lawrence, Ellen. Earth: Our Home in the Solar System. 2013. (Zoom into Space Ser.). 24p. (J). (gr. -1-3). lib. bdg. 23.93 (978-1-909673-06-9(4)) Ruby Tuesday Books Limited GBR. Dist: Bearport Publishing Co., Inc.

Leavitt, Amie Jane. The Science Behind Wonders of the Earth: Cave Crystals, Balancing Rocks, & Snow Donuts. 2016. (Science Behind Natural Phenomena Ser.). (ENG., Illus.). 32p. (gr. 3-4). lib. bdg. 27.99 (978-1-5157-0773-8(3), Edge Bks.) Capstone Press of Coughlan Cos.

LernerClassroom Editors. Pull Ahead Books-Continents Teaching Guide. 2009. pap. 7.95 (978-0-8225-2349-9(3)) Lerner Publishing Group.

Lewis, J. Patrick. Earth & Us-Continuous: Earth's Past & Future. Canyon, Christopher, illus. 2004. (Sharing Nature with Children Book Ser.). 36p. (J). 16.95 (978-1-58469-024-5(0)); pap. 7.95 (978-1-58469-023-8(2)) Dawn Pubns.

Linde, Barbara M. Earth Measuring Its Changes: Set Of 6. 2011. (Navigators Ser.). (J). pap. 48.00 net. (978-1-4108-5080-5(3)) Benchmark Education Co.

little bee books, little bee. Listopia: Planet Earth. 2016. (ENG., Illus.). 208p. (J). (gr. 2-4). pap. 9.99 (978-1-4998-0279-5(X)) Little Bee Books Inc.

Litton, Jonathan. The Earth Book. Hegbrook, Thomas, illus. 2017. (360 Degrees Ser.). (ENG.). 64p. (J). (gr. 3-12). 29.99 **(978-1-944530-06-8(1)**, 360 Degrees) Tiger Tales.

Loewen, Nancy. Our Home Planet: Earth, 1 vol. Yesh, Jeff, illus. 2008. (Amazing Science: Planets Ser.). (ENG.). 24p. (gr. k-4). lib. bdg. 26.65 (978-1-4048-3951-9(8), 1278903) Picture Window Bks.

Lonely Planet Publications Staff. Not for Parents Extreme Planet, 1 vol. 2012. (Lonely Planet Kids Ser.). (ENG., Illus.). 192p. (J). 19.99 (978-1-74321-424-4(3), 4355) Lonely Planet Pubns.

Looye, Juliette, text. I Live on the Earth. 2004. (Illus.). 16p. (J). pap. (978-0-7367-1931-5(8)) Zaner-Bloser, Inc.

Lowery, Linda. Earth Day. Bergherr, Mary, illus. rev. ed. 2003. (On My Own Holidays Ser.). (ENG.). 48p. (gr. 2-4). (J). lib. bdg. 25.26 (978-1-57505-700-2(X)); pap. 6.95 (978-1-57505-620-3(8)) Lerner Publishing Group.

Lundgren, Julie K. Earth: The Living Planet. 2014. (ENG.). 24p. (gr. k-3). 28.50 (978-1-62717-724-5(8)) Rourke Educational Media.

MacDonald, Margaret. Tell Me about the Continents. 2011. (Learn-Abouts Ser.). (Illus.). 16p. (J). pap. 7.95 (978-1-59920-630-1(7)) Black Rabbit Bks.

Maloof, Torrey. Earth & Moon, 1 vol. (Science Readers: Content & Literacy Ser.). (ENG., Illus.). 24p. (gr. 1-1). 2015. pap. 22.96 (978-1-4938-1158-8(4)) 2014. pap. 8.99 (978-1-4807-4571-1(5)) Teacher Created Materials, Inc.

Mariner, Tom, ed. The Land. (Illus.). 32p. (J). (978-0-7451-5316-2(X)) Cherrytree Bks.

Markovics, Joyce. La Tierra: QuÉ Bien Se EstÁ en Casa. 2015. (Fuera de Este Mundo Ser.). (SPA., Illus.). 24p. (J). (gr. -1-3). lib. bdg. 23.93 (978-1-62724-588-3(X)) Bearport Publishing Co., Inc.

Markovics, Joyce L. Earth: No Place Like Home. 2015. (Out of This World Ser.). (ENG.). 24p. (J). (gr. -1-3). lib. bdg. 23.93 (978-1-62724-563-0(4)) Bearport Publishing Co., Inc.

Marquardt, Meg. Earth Myths, Busted! 2017. (Science Myths, Busted! Ser.). (ENG., Illus.). 32p. (J). (gr. 3-6). 21.95 (978-1-63235-302-3(4)) Pr. Room Editions LLC.

Martin, Bill, Jr. & Sampson, Michael. I Love Our Earth. Lipow, Dan, photos by. 2009. (Rise & Shine Ser.). (ENG., Illus.). 32p. (J). (gr. -1-2). pap. 7.95 (978-1-58089-107-3(1)) Charlesbridge Publishing, Inc.

Martin, Justin McCory. Earth. 2010. (Illus.). 16p. (J). (978-0-545-13727-0(6)) Scholastic, Inc.

Martin, Michael. Extreme Earth. 2015. (ENG., Illus.). 448p. 85.00 (978-1-4197-1791-8(X)) Abrams, Inc.

Mason Crest. Our Home Planet, Vol. 7. 2016. (Solar System Ser.: Vol. 7). (ENG., Illus.). 48p. (J). (gr. 5-8). 20.95 (978-1-4222-3549-2(1)) Mason Crest.

Mattern, Joanne. Our Earth, 1 vol. (Solar System & Beyond Ser.). (ENG., 32p. (gr. 3-4). 2011. Illus.). pap. 8.10 (978-1-4296-6240-6(9)) 2011. pap. 47.70 (978-1-4296-6407-3(X)) 2010. lib. bdg. 27.32 (978-1-4296-5395-4(7)) Capstone Press of Coughlan Cos. (Fact Finders).

McDaniel, Melissa. Earth Slow Changes: Set Of 6. 2010. (Navigators Ser.). (J). pap. 48.00 net. (978-1-4108-5079-9(X)) Benchmark Education Co.

McKenzie, Precious. Cleaning up the Earth. 2011. (ENG., Illus.). 24p. (gr. k-2). pap. 8.95 (978-1-61741-970-6(2)) Rourke Educational Media.

Miles Kelly Staff. Our Planet. 2003. (Ask Me a Question Ser.). (Illus.). 20p. (J). spiral bd. 7.95 (978-1-84236-128-3(7)) Miles Kelly Publishing, Ltd. GBR. Dist: Independent Pubs. Group.

Miller, Derek L. Earth, Sun, & Moon: Cyclic Patterns of Lunar Phases, Eclipses, & the Seasons. 2016. (Space Systems Ser.). 112p. (J). 42.79 (978-1-5026-2291-4(2)) Cavendish Square Publishing.

Miller, Kelley. Funny Fill-In: Inside the Earth Adventure. 2014. (NG Kids Funny Fill In Ser.). (ENG.). 48p. (J). (gr. 3-7). pap. 4.99 (978-1-4263-1737-8(9), National Geographic Children's Bks.) National Geographic Society.

Miller, Patti. Mother Earth Has Seven Kids! 2009. 44p. pap. 21.99 (978-1-4415-8454-0(4)) Xlibris Corp.

Miller, Ron. Earth & the Moon. 2003. (Worlds Beyond Ser.). (Illus.). 96p. (gr. 7-18). lib. bdg. 27.93 (978-0-7613-2358-7(9), Twenty-First Century Bks.) Lerner Publishing Group.

Mills, Nathan & Granger, Ronald. Exploring Earth's Surface. 2012. (Rosen Readers Ser.). (ENG., Illus.). 24p. (J). (gr. 1-2). pap. 8.25 (978-1-4488-8839-9(5), Rosen Classroom) Rosen Publishing Group, Inc., The.

Mitchell, Melanie S. Earth. 2004. (First Step Nonfiction Ser.). (Illus.). 24p. (J). (gr. k-2). lib. bdg. 18.60 (978-0-8225-5137-9(3)) Lerner Publishing Group.

—The Earth. 2003. (First Step Nonfiction Ser.). (Illus.). 22p. (J). pap. 5.95 (978-0-8225-3590-4(4), Lerner Pubns.) Lerner Publishing Group.

Mitten, Ellen. Counting the Continents. 2009. (ENG., Illus.). 24p. (gr. k-2). pap. 8.95 (978-1-60694-538-4(6)) Rourke Educational Media.

Moignot, Daniel. Atlas of the Earth. 2012. (ENG., Illus.). 36p. (J). (gr. -1-k). spiral bd. 14.99 (978-1-85103-406-2(4)) Moonlight Publishing, Ltd. GBR. Dist: Independent Pubs. Group.

Monier, Eric M., ed. How Life on Earth Is Affected by Earth's Unique Placement & Orientation in Our Solar System: An Anthology of Current Thought. 2009. (Contemporary Discourse in the Field of Astronomy Ser.). 240p. (gr. 10-10). 63.90 (978-1-61511-903-5(5)) Rosen Publishing Group, Inc., The.

Moon, Walt K. Let's Explore Earth. 2017. (Bumba Books (tm) — a First Look at Space Ser.). (ENG.). 24p. (J). (gr. -1-1). 25.32 **(978-1-5124-3345-6(4))** Lerner Publishing Group.

Morey, Allan. The Science Behind Wonders of the Sky: Aurora Borealis, Moonbows, & St. Elmo's Fire. 2016. (Science Behind Natural Phenomena Ser.). (ENG., Illus.). 32p. (gr. 3-4). lib. bdg. 27.99 (978-1-5157-0777-6(6), Edge Bks.) Capstone Press of Coughlan Cos.

Morgan, Jennifer. From Lava to Life: The Universe Tells Our Earth Story. Andersen, Dana Lynne, illus. (Sharing Nature with Children Book Ser.: Vol. 2). 48p. (YA). 2004. 19.95 (978-1-58469-043-6(7)) 2003. (ENG.). pap. 9.95 (978-1-58469-042-9(9)) Dawn Pubns.

Mullins, Matt & Plummer, Todd. Super Cool Science Experiments: Planet Earth. 2009. (Explorer Library: Science Explorer Ser.). (ENG., Illus.). 32p. (gr. 4-8). lib. bdg. 28.50 (978-1-60279-515-0(0), 200302) Cherry Lake Publishing.

Murphy, Patricia J. Why Is Earth Round? (Library of Why Ser.). 24p. 2009. (gr. 3-4). 42.50 (978-1-60853-965-9(2)) 2004. (Illus.). (J). lib. bdg. 22.60 (978-0-8239-6236-5(9)) Rosen Publishing Group, Inc., The. (PowerKids Pr.).

My Very First Our World Book IR. 2017. (My Very First Bks.). (ENG.). (J). bds. 11.99 **(978-0-7945-3879-8(7)**, Usborne) EDC Publishing.

My World. 2004. 80p. (YA). per. 15.00 (978-0-9754834-6-6(3)) Standing For Christ, Inc.

Nagelhout, Ryan. Earth Borers. 2016. (Technology Takes on Nature Ser.). 00032p. (J). pap. 10.50 **(978-1-4824-5783-4(0))** Stevens, Gareth Publishing LLLP.

Nash, Geoffrey H., frwd. The Extreme Earth Set, 8-Volumes. 2008. (Extreme Earth Ser.). (gr. 6-12). 280.00 (978-0-8160-7423-5(2), Chelsea Hse.) Facts On File, Inc.

National Geographic Kids Staff. National Geographic Readers: Planet Earth Collection: Readers That Grow with You. 2014. (ENG., Illus.). 128p. (J). (gr. k-3). pap. 7.99 (978-1-4263-1813-9(8), National Geographic Children's Bks.) National Geographic Society.

Nelson, Maria. Earth's Minerals. 2013. (That Rocks! Ser.). 24p. (J). (gr. 2-5). pap. 48.90 (978-1-4339-8311-5(7)); (Illus.). pap. 8.15 (978-1-4339-8310-8(9)); (Illus.). lib. bdg. 22.60 (978-1-4339-8309-2(5)) Stevens, Gareth Publishing LLLP.

Nelson, Robin. Estaciones (Seasons) 2012. (Mi Primer Paso Al Mundo Real - Descubriendo Los Ciclos de la Naturaleza (First Step Nonfiction - Discovering Nature's Cycles) Ser.). (Illus.). 24p. (gr. k-2). (ENG & SPA.). pap. 6.95 (978-0-7613-9357-3(9)); (SPA., lib. bdg. 23.93 (978-0-7613-9339-9(0)) Lerner Publishing Group. (Ediciones Lerner).

—Seasons. 2010. (First Step Nonfiction - Discovering Nature's Cycles Ser.). (ENG.). 24p. (gr. k-2). pap. 6.95 (978-0-7613-5684-4(3)); (Illus.). lib. bdg. 23.93 (978-0-7613-4578-7(7)) Lerner Publishing Group.

Nemeth, Jason D. Earth's Layers. 2012. (Our Changing Earth Ser.). (ENG., Illus.). 24p. (J). (gr. 3-6). pap. 8.25 (978-1-4488-6296-2(5), PowerKids Pr.); lib. bdg. 22.60 (978-1-4488-6169-9(1)) Rosen Publishing Group, Inc., The.

Nicolson, Cynthia Pratt & Slavin, Bill. Starting with Space: The Earth.Tr. of Destination Univers: La Terre. (FRE., Illus.). 40p. (J). pap. 8.99 (978-0-590-16009-4(5)) Scholastic, Inc.

Nuestro Planeta: La Tierra. (SPA.). (J). 10.00 (978-84-342-1813-0(5)) Parramon Ediciones S.A. ESP. Dist: Distribuidora Norma, Inc.

Oates, Betsy. Journey to Earth, 1 vol. 2014. (Spotlight on Space Science Ser.). (ENG.). 32p. (J). (gr. 5-5). pap. 11.75 (978-1-4994-0368-8(2), PowerKids Pr.) Rosen Publishing Group, Inc., The.

Olien, Rebecca. Exploring Earth. (Objects in the Sky Ser.). 24p. (gr. 3-3). 2009. 42.50 (978-1-60851-138-9(3), PowerKids Pr.) 2007. (Illus.). (J). lib. bdg. 22.60 (978-1-4042-3465-9(9)) Rosen Publishing Group, Inc., The.

Orme, Helen & Orme, David. Let's Explore Earth. 2007. (Space Launch! Ser.). (Illus.). 24p. (gr. 1-4). pap. 8.15 (978-0-8368-8124-0(9)); lib. bdg. 23.00 (978-0-8368-7939-1(2)) Stevens, Gareth Publishing LLLP. (Gareth Stevens Learning Library).

O'Shaughnessy, Tam E. The Inside Story of Earth. 2006. (J). 7.80 (978-1-933798-09-7(2)) Sally Ride Science.

Owen, Ruth. Earth. 2013. (Explore Outer Space Ser.). 32p. (J). (gr. 3-6). 25.25 (978-1-61533-724-8(5)); pap. 60.00 (978-1-61533-766-8(0)); pap. 10.00 (978-1-61533-765-1(2)) Windmill Bks.

Owens, L. L. Earth. McGeehan, Dan, illus. 2011. (Space Neighbors Ser.). (ENG.). 32p. (J). (gr. 1-4). lib. bdg. 27.07 (978-1-60954-381-5(5), 200885) Child's World, Inc., The.

Oxlade, Chris. Earth & Its Moon. 2007. (Earth & Space Ser.). (Illus.). 48p. (YA). (gr. 5-9). lib. bdg. 29.25 (978-1-4042-3734-6(8)) Rosen Publishing Group, Inc., The.

—Space Watch: The Sun. 2010. (Eye on Space Ser.). 24p. (J). pap. 8.25 (978-1-61532-544-3(1), PowerKids Pr.); (ENG.). lib. bdg. 22.60 (978-1-61532-540-5(9)) Rosen Publishing Group, Inc., The.

Palmer, Kristen. Wild Weather Trivia. 2013. (Ultimate Trivia Challenge Ser.). (Illus.). 32p. (J). (gr. 2-5). pap. 10.50 (978-1-4339-8305-4(2)); lib. bdg. 25.25 (978-1-4339-8304-7(4)) Stevens, Gareth Publishing LLLP.

Palmer, Kristin. Wild Weather Trivia. 2013. (Ultimate Trivia Challenge Ser.). 32p. (J). (gr. 2-5). pap. 63.00 (978-1-4339-8306-1(0)) Stevens, Gareth Publishing LLLP.

Parker, Steve. Complete Guides Our World. 2012. (ENG.). 144p. (J). (978-1-4351-4406-4(6)) Barnes & Noble, Inc.

Parker, Steve & Oxlade, Chris. Earth & Space. 2007. (J). 159.00 (978-1-4042-1103-2(9), Rosen Reference) Rosen Publishing Group, Inc., The.

Parr, Todd. The Earth Book. 2010. (ENG., Illus.). 40p. (J). (gr. -1-1). 11.99 (978-0-316-04265-9(X)) Little, Brown Bks. for Young Readers.

Pasricha, Neil. Awesome Is Everywhere. 2015. (ENG., Illus.). 32p. (J). (-k). 17.99 (978-0-670-06933-0(7), Puffin Canada) Penguin Random House Canada Young Readers CAN. Dist: Penguin Random Hse. LLC.

Payne, Jan, et al. It Can Rain Frogs & Fish: And Other Facts about Planet Earth. 2016. (True or False? Ser.). 48p. (J). (gr. 3-3). pap. 11.70 (978-0-7660-7732-4(2)) Enslow Pubs., Inc.

Peter, Carsten & Phelan, Glen. Extreme Planet: Carsten Peter's Wild Adventures in Volcanoes, Caves, Canyons, Deserts, & Ice! 2015. (ENG., Illus.). 112p. (J). (gr. 3-7). pap. 12.99 (978-1-4263-2100-9(7), National Geographic Children's Bks.) National Geographic Society.

Peters, Elisa. Earth. 2012. (PowerKids Readers: the Universe Ser.). (ENG., Illus.). 24p. (J). (gr. k-2). pap. 8.25 (978-1-4488-7467-5(X)); lib. bdg. 22.60 (978-1-4488-7387-6(8)) Rosen Publishing Group, Inc., The. (PowerKids Pr.).

—Earth: La Tierra. 2012. (PowerKids Readers: the Universe / el universo Ser.). (SPA & ENG., Illus.). 24p. (J). (gr. k-2). lib. bdg. 22.60 (978-1-4488-7823-9(3), PowerKids Pr.) Rosen Publishing Group, Inc., The.

PH Inc. Staff. PH Science Ecology Earth. (J). pap., act. bk. ed. (978-0-13-225582-0(0)) Prentice Hall (Schl. Div.).

Phelan, Glen. Earth in Space. 2007. (Language, Literacy, & Vocabulary - Reading Expeditions Ser.). (ENG., Illus.). 36p. (J). pap. 18.95 (978-0-7922-5428-7(7)) CENGAGE Learning.

—Earth, Sun, Moon. 2007. (Reading Expeditions Ser.). (ENG., Illus.). 32p. (J). pap. 17.95 (978-0-7922-4573-5(3)) CENGAGE Learning.

Pifer, Joanne. EarthWise: Environmental Learning Series, Vol. II. (Illus.). 192p. (J). (gr. 5-8). 24.95 (978-0-9633019-6-3(9)) WP Pr., Inc.

Pipe, Jim. Wonderful World. 2009. (ENG.). 112p. (J). (gr. 4-7). pap. 12.95 (978-1-84696-204-2(8), TickTock Books) Octopus Publishing Group GBR. Dist: Independent Pubs. Group.

Planet Earth. 2017. (Planet Earth Ser.). 32p. (gr. 9-10). 157.50 **(978-1-4994-3406-4(5))**; pap. 60.00 **(978-1-4994-3408-8(1))** Rosen Publishing Group, Inc., The. (PowerKids Pr.).

Planet Earth/Inside Out. (Lexile Levels Ser.). 9.09 (978-1-56334-748-1(2)) CENGAGE Learning.

Playhouse Disney Encyclopedia. 2009. (ENG.). 196p. (gr. -1-k). 19.99 (978-1-4231-1921-0(5)) Disney Pr.

Prentice-Hall Staff. Exploring Planet Earth. (J). tchr. ed. (978-0-13-400607-9(0)); pap., act. bk. ed. (978-0-13-400615-4(1)); 2nd ed. stu. ed. (978-0-13-400599-7(6)) Prentice Hall (Schl. Div.).

Prokos, Anna. Star Light, Star Bright: Exploring Our Solar System. Clegg, Dave, illus. 2017. (Imagine That! Ser.). (ENG.). 32p. (J). (gr. 2-4). lib. bdg. 26.65 (978-1-63440-152-4(2)); 39.99 **(978-1-63440-164-7(6))** Red Chair Pr.

Publishers, Chelsea House, creator. The Restless Earth Set, 6-Volumes. 2009. (Restless Earth Ser.). (gr. 5-8). 210.00 (978-0-7910-9878-3(6), Chelsea Hse.) Facts On File, Inc.

¿Que Hay Debajo de la Tierra? (Coleccion Primeros Pasos en la Ciencia). (SPA., Illus.). (J). (gr. 1-3). pap. (978-950-724-015-7(2), LMA8214) Lumen ARG. Dist: Lectorum Pubns., Inc.

Rapp, Valerie. Protecting Earth's Air Quality. 2015. (Saving Our Living Earth Ser.). (ENG., Illus.). 72p. (gr. 4-7). 30.65 (978-1-5124-1048-8(9), Lerner Pubns.) Lerner Publishing Group.

Reher, Matt. Life on the Blue Planet. 2016. (2R Science Ser.). (ENG., Illus.). 40p. (J). pap. 5.99 **(978-1-63437-730-0(3))** American Reading Co.

Reynolds, Toby & Calver, Paul. Extreme Earth. 2015. (Visual Explorers Ser.). (ENG., Illus.). 32p. (J). (gr. 3-7). pap. 6.99 (978-1-4380-0578-2(4)) Barron's Educational Series, Inc.

Rice, William B. Landforms, 1 vol. rev. ed. 2014. (Science Readers: Content & Literacy Ser.). (ENG.). 32p. (gr. 2-2). pap. 8.99 (978-1-4807-4608-4(8)) Teacher Created Materials, Inc.

Richard, Orlin. Investigating Seasons. 2015. (ENG., Illus.). 40p. (J). (gr. 3-5). 29.32 (978-1-4677-8059-9(6), Lerner Pubns.) Lerner Publishing Group.

Richards, Jon. Planet Earth. Simkins, Ed, illus. 2013. (World in Infographics Ser.). (ENG.). 32p. (J). (gr. 3-7). 15.95 (978-1-926973-75-3(5)) Owlkids Bks. Inc. CAN. Dist: Publishers Group West (PGW).

Richards, Jon & Simkins, Ed. The Natural World. 2016. 32p. (J). (978-0-7787-2658-6(4)) Crabtree Publishing Co.

—Record-Breaking Earth & Space Facts. 2015. (Infographic Top 10s Ser.). (ENG., Illus.). 32p. (J). (gr. 4-6). 26.65 (978-1-4677-8595-2(4), Lerner Pubns.) Lerner Publishing Group.

Ride, Sally & O'Shaughnessy, Tam E. The Third Planet: Exploring the Earth from Space. 2nd rev. ed. 2004. (J). per. 20.00 (978-0-9753920-0-3(X)) Sally Ride Science.

RIGBY. Our Changing Earth: Fourth Grade Class Collection Books. 2003. (Rigby on Our Way to English Ser.). (ENG.). 32p. (gr. 4-4). pap. 48.75 (978-0-7578-4339-6(5)) Rigby Education.

Riley, Peter. Earth, Moon & Sun. 2007. (Essential Science/Watts Ser.). (Illus.). 32p. (YA). (gr. 3-6). lib. bdg. 28.50 (978-1-59920-025-5(2)) Black Rabbit Bks.

Ring, Susan. Earth. 2013. (J). (978-1-62127-263-2(X)); pap. (978-1-62127-272-4(9)) Weigl Pubs., Inc.

Ring, Susan & Roumanis, Alexis. Earth. 2016. (Illus.). 24p. (J). (978-1-5105-0971-9(2)) SmartBook Media, Inc.

Roca, Núria, et al. The Earth. 2014. (Solar System Ser.). (ENG., Illus.). 36p. (J). (gr. -1-2). pap. 7.99 (978-1-4380-0475-4(3)) Barron's Educational Series, Inc.

Rockett, Paul. Seven Quintillion, Five Hundred Quadrillion Grains of Sand on Planet Earth. Ruffle, Mark, illus. 2015.

(Big Countdown Ser.). (ENG.). 32p. (gr. 3-5). 29.99 *(978-1-4109-6880-7(4),* Raintree Perspectives) Heinemann-Raintree.
Rooney, Anne. A Math Journey Through Planet Earth. 2014. (ENG.). 32p. (J). *(978-0-7787-0728-8(8))* Crabtree Publishing Co.
Roumanis, Alexis. Earth. 2016. (J). ***(978-1-5105-2045-5(7))*** SmartBook Media, Inc.
—Earth. 2015. (J). *(978-1-4896-3280-7(8))* Weigl Pubs., Inc.
Royston, Angela. Planet Earth. 2017. (Discover & Share Ser.). (ENG., Illus.). 24p. (J). (gr. k-2). 16.99 *(978-1-4451-3809-1(3),* Franklin Watts) Hachette Children's Group GBR. Dist: Hachette Bk. Group.
Roza, Greg. Beneath Earth's Surface. 2009. (Reading Room Collection 2 Ser.). 24p. (gr. 3-4). 42.50 *(978-1-60851-958-3(9),* PowerKids Pr.) Rosen Publishing Group, Inc., The.
Rushworth, Gary. Our Solar System Earth: Set Of 6. 2011. (Navigators Ser.). (J). pap. 44.00 net. *(978-1-4108-6222-8(4))* Benchmark Education Co.
—Our Solar System: Earth: Text Pairs. 2008. (Bridges/Navigators Ser.). (J). (gr. 3). 89.00 *(978-1-4108-8369-8(8))* Benchmark Education Co.
—What Makes a Human a Human: Text Pairs. 2008. (Bridges/Navigators Ser.). (J). (gr. 4). 89.00 *(978-1-4108-8399-5(X))* Benchmark Education Co.
Rustad, Martha E. H. Earth. 2016. (Space Ser.). (ENG., Illus.). 24p. (gr. k-1). lib. bdg. 21.99 *(978-1-4914-8321-3(0),* Pebble Bks.) Capstone Press of Coughlan Cos.
Salas, Laura Purdie. Home on the Earth: A Song about Earth's Layers, 1 vol. Garofoli, Viviana, illus. 2009. (Science Songs Ser.). (ENG.). 24p. (gr. 1-3). lib. bdg. 26.65 *(978-1-4048-5296-9(4))* Picture Window Bks.
Schimmel, Schim, illus. Magic Planet: Pop-Up Fun. 2003. 12p. (J). (gr. k-5). 20.00 *(978-0-7567-6651-1(6))* DIANE Publishing Co.
Schorr, Titus. Earth Day, 01 vols., 1. 2016. (Rosen REAL Readers: Social Studies Nonfiction / Fiction: Family, Community, & the World Ser.). (ENG.). 12p. (J). pap. 6.33 *(978-1-5081-1803-9(5),* Rosen Classroom) Rosen Publishing Group, Inc., The.
Schwacber, Barbie Heit. Alphabet of Earth. Vitsky, Sally, illus. 2009. (ENG.). 40p. (J). 9.95 *(978-1-59249-997-7(X))* Soundprints.
Schwaeber, Barbie. Alphabet of Earth. Vitsky, Sally, illus. 2009. (ENG.). 40p. 17.95 *(978-1-59249-996-0(1))* Soundprints.
Scott, Elaine. Our Moon: New Discoveries about Earth's Closest Companion. 2016. (ENG., Illus.). 72p. (J). (gr. 5-7). 18.99 *(978-0-547-48394-8(5),* Clarion Bks.) Houghton Mifflin Harcourt Trade & Reference Pubs.
Senior, Kathryn. What on Earth? - Wild Weather, 5 bks., Set. Incl. Volcanoes. (Illus.). 32p. (J). (gr. 2-4). 2005. lib. bdg. 25.50 *(978-0-516-25324-4(7),* Children's Pr.); (What on Earth? Ser.). 2005. 127.50 o.p. *(978-0-516-25224-7(0),* Children's Pr.) Scholastic Library Publishing.
Shepherd, Donna Walsh. Earth. 2003. (Watts Library). (ENG., Illus.). 64p. (J). (gr. 5-7). pap. 8.95 *(978-0-531-15559-2(5),* Watts, Franklin) Scholastic Library Publishing.
Sherman, Jill. Continents: What You Need to Know. 2017. (Fact Files Ser.). (ENG.). 24p. (gr. 1-2). lib. bdg. 25.32 ***(978-1-5157-8110-3(0),*** First Facts) Capstone Press of Coughlan Cos.
Sian revision our changing Earth. 2004. (Science in A Nutshell Ser.). (J). *(978-1-59242-053-7(2))* Delta Education, LLC.
Silverman, Buffy. Saving Energy: Earth's Resources. 2016. (Do It Yourself Ser.). (ENG.). 48p. pap. 8.99 *(978-1-4846-3816-3(6),* NA-h) Heinemann-Raintree.
Simon, Charnan. Earth. 2011. (21st Century Junior Library: Solar System Ser.). (ENG.). 24p. (gr. 2-5). lib. bdg. 25.64 *(978-1-61080-081-5(8),* 201072) Cherry Lake Publishing.
Simon, Seymour. Earth: Our Planet in Space. rev. ed. 2003. (ENG., Illus.). 32p. (J). (gr. 2-6). 19.99 *(978-0-689-83562-9(0),* Simon & Schuster Bks. For Young Readers) Simon & Schuster Bks. For Young Readers.
—Extreme Earth Records. 2014. 52p. pap. 9.00 *(978-1-61003-327-5(2))* Center for the Collaborative Classroom.
—Seymour Simon's Extreme Earth Records. 2012. (ENG., Illus.). 60p. (J). (gr. 1-4). 17.99 *(978-1-4521-0785-1(8))* Chronicle Bks. LLC.
Smith, Paula. Earthquakes, Eruptions, & Other Events That Change Earth. 2015. (Earth's Processes Close-Up Ser.). (ENG., Illus.). 24p. (J). (gr. k-3). *(978-0-7787-1725-6(9))* Crabtree Publishing Co.
Soll, Karen. Extreme Earth. 2016. (Extreme Earth Ser.). (ENG.). 24p. (gr. k-1). 106.60 *(978-1-4914-8356-5(3),* Pebble Plus) Capstone Press of Coughlan Cos.
—Hottest Places on the Planet. 2016. (Extreme Earth Ser.). (ENG., Illus.). 24p. (gr. k-1). lib. bdg. 26.65 *(978-1-4914-8341-1(5),* Pebble Plus) Capstone Press of Coughlan Cos.
Solway, Andrew. Why Is There Life on Earth?, 1 vol. 2011. (Earth, Space, & Beyond Ser.). (ENG.). 48p. (gr. 3-3). pap. 9.49 *(978-1-4109-4184-8(1),* Raintree Freestyle Express); (gr. 3-3). 34.65 *(978-1-4109-4178-7(7),* Raintree Freestyle Express); (Illus.). (gr. 6-6). 34.65 *(978-1-4109-4160-2(4),* Raintree Freestyle) Heinemann-Raintree.
Sparrow, Giles. Earth & the Inner Planets. 2011. (Exploring Space: Space Travel Guides). 32p. (gr. 3-6). 31.35 *(978-1-59920-663-9(3))* Black Rabbit Bks.
Spotlight on the Continents, 7 vols., Set. Incl. Spotlight on Africa. Schaefer, A. R. lib. bdg. 25.32 *(978-1-4296-6624-4(2));* Spotlight on Asia. Schaefer, A. R. lib. bdg. 25.32 *(978-1-4296-6623-7(4));* Spotlight on Australia. Niz, Xavier. lib. bdg. 25.32 *(978-1-4296-6627-5(7));* Spotlight on Europe. Gibson, Karen Bush. lib. bdg. 25.32 *(978-1-4296-6625-1(0));* Spotlight on South America. Gibson, Karen Bush. lib. bdg. 25.32 *(978-1-4296-6622-0(6));* (gr. 1-2). (Spotlight on the Continents Ser.). (ENG.). 24p. 2010. Set lib. bdg. 126.60 *(978-1-4296-6511-7(4),* First Facts) Capstone Press of Coughlan Cos.
Steele, Philip, et al. Extreme Planet. 2014. (Illus.). 128p. (J). *(978-1-4351-5523-7(8))* Barnes & Noble, Inc.
Steloff, Rebecca. Flat Earth & Round Earth. 2014. 48p. pap. 29.93 *(978-1-62712-512-3(4))* Cavendish Square Publishing.
—The Sun & the Earth. 2014. 48p. pap. 29.93 *(978-1-62712-521-5(3))* Cavendish Square Publishing.
Steinkraus, Kyla. Rocky Planets: Mercury, Venus, Earth, & Mars. 2014. (ENG.). 24p. (gr. k-3). 28.50 *(978-1-62717-727-6(2))* Rourke Educational Media.
Stewart, Kathy & Effe Team. Earth Facts for Earthlings Bk. 1: The World. 2005. (Earth Facts for Earthlings Ser.). (Illus.). 64p. (J). (gr. 3-7). per. 12.95 *(978-0-9773583-0-4(5),* EFFE01) EFFE Bks.
Storad, Conrad J. Earth's Changing Surface. 2011. (ENG., Illus.). 24p. (gr. 1-2). pap. 8.95 *(978-1-61741-938-6(9))* Rourke Educational Media.
—Earth's Crust. 2006. (Early Bird Earth Science Ser.). (ENG., Illus.). 48p. (gr. 2-5). lib. bdg. 26.60 *(978-0-8225-5944-3(7),* Lerner Pubns.) Lerner Publishing Group.
—Uncovering Earth's Crust. 2013. (Searchlight Books (tm) — Do You Dig Earth Science? Ser.). (ENG., Illus.). 40p. (gr. 3-5). pap. 8.95 *(978-1-4677-0789-3(9));* lib. bdg. 27.93 *(978-1-4677-0020-7(7),* Lerner Pubns.) Lerner Publishing Group.
Sundance/Newbridge LLC Staff. Circling the Sun. 2004. (Reading PowerWorks Ser.). (gr. 1-3). 37.50 *(978-0-7608-8916-9(3))* Sundance/Newbridge Educational Publishing.
Tanaka, Shelley. A Great Round Wonder: My Book of the World. Perna, Debi, illus. (J). 4.99 *(978-1-55054-213-4(3))* Da Capo Pr., Inc.
Taylor, Barbara & Chancellor, Deborah. Discover Science: Planet Earth. 2014. (Discover Science Ser.). (ENG., Illus.). 56p. (J). (gr. -1-3). 7.99 *(978-0-7534-6780-0(1),* 9780753467800, Kingfisher) Roaring Brook Pr.
Taylor-Butler, Christine. Earth. 2008. (Scholastic News Nonfiction Readers Ser.). (ENG., Illus.). 24p. (J). (gr. 1-2). pap. 6.95 *(978-0-531-14760-3(6))* Scholastic Library Publishing.
Terry, Paul. Top 10 for Kids Nature. 2015. (ENG., Illus.). 96p. (J). (gr. 3-6). pap. 9.95 *(978-1-77085-563-2(7),* 9781770855632) Firefly Bks., Ltd.
Thompson, Luke. Earth. 2009. (Library of the Planets Ser.). 24p. (gr. 3-3). 42.50 *(978-1-60853-917-8(2),* PowerKids Pr.) Rosen Publishing Group, Inc., The.
Throp, Claire. Fantasy Science Field Trips, 1 vol. 2014. (Fantasy Science Field Trips Ser.). (ENG.). 32p. (gr. 1-3). lib. bdg. 119.96 *(978-1-4109-6201-0(6),* Read Me!) Heinemann-Raintree.
—A Journey to the Center of the Earth: Fantasy Science Field Trips, 1 vol. 2014. (Fantasy Science Field Trips Ser.). (ENG.). 32p. (gr. 1-3). pap. 8.95 *(978-1-4109-6205-8(9));* lib. bdg. 29.99 *(978-1-4109-6200-3(8))* Heinemann-Raintree. (Read Me!).
Todoro, Carlie. Our Earth. 2003. (Real Readers - Upper Emergent Ser.). (ENG., Illus.). 12p. (gr. 1-2). pap. 5.90 *(978-0-8239-6360-7(8))* Rosen Publishing Group, Inc., The.
Top That Publishing Staff, ed. Our Planet. 2004. (Know How Know Why Ser.). (Illus.). 48p. (J). pap. *(978-1-84510-028-5(X))* Top That! Publishing PLC.
Twist, Clint. Extreme Earth. 2010. (Ripley Twists Ser.). (Illus.). 48p. (J). (gr. 3-18). lib. bdg. 19.95 *(978-1-4222-1829-7(5),* 1318258) Mason Crest.
Twist, Clint, et al. Extreme Earth. 2009. (Ripley Twists Ser.). (Illus.). 48p. (J). (gr. 3-18). pap. 8.95 *(978-1-4222-2067-2(2),* 1318258) Mason Crest.
Two-Can Publishing Ltd. Staff, contrib. by. Planet Earth. 2004. (Illus.). 192p. (J). (gr. 3-6). 24.95 *(978-1-58728-049-8(3),* Two-Can Publishing) T&N Children's Publishing.
Valencia, Vanessa. Mamma's Planet Earth. 2011. 24p. pap. 10.95 *(978-1-4525-3921-8(9))* Balboa Pr.
Vogt, Gregory L. Earth's Core & Mantle: Heavy Metal, Moving Rock. 2006. (Earth's Spheres Ser.). (Illus.). 80p. (YA). (gr. 7-12). lib. bdg. 29.27 *(978-0-7613-2837-7(8))* Lerner Publishing Group.
—The Lithosphere: Earth's Crust. 2007. (Earth's Spheres Ser.). (ENG., Illus.). 80p. (gr. 6-8). lib. bdg. 29.27 *(978-0-7613-2838-4(6))* Lerner Publishing Group.
Voiland, Adam. ABCs from Space: A Discovered Alphabet. 2017. (ENG., Illus.). 40p. (J). (gr. -1-3). 18.99 ***(978-1-4814-9428-1(7),*** Simon & Schuster Bks. For Young Readers) Simon & Schuster Bks. For Young Readers.
Volke, Gordon. Our Planet. 2006. (Illus.). 48p. (J). lib. bdg. 29.95 *(978-1-60044-261-2(7))* Rourke Educational Media.
Walsh, Kenneth. Our Earth, 1 vol. 2nd rev. ed. 2011. (Nonfiction Readers Ser.). (ENG.). 28p. (J). (gr. 2-2). pap. 6.99 *(978-1-4333-3631-7(6))* Teacher Created Materials, Inc.
Wells, Robert E. What's So Special about Planet Earth? 2012. (J). *(978-1-61913-154-5(4))* Weigl Pubs., Inc.
—What's So Special about Planet Earth? Wells, Robert E., illus. (Wells of Knowledge Science Ser.). (ENG., Illus.). 32p. (J). (gr. 2-3). 2010. pap. 7.99 *(978-0-8075-8816-1(4))* 2009. 16.99 *(978-0-8075-8815-4(6))* Whitman, Albert & Co.
West, Krista. Layers of the Earth. 2009. (Restless Earth Ser.). (Illus.). 112p. (YA). (gr. 5-9). 35.00 *(978-0-7910-9706-9(4))* Facts On File, Inc.
What on Earth? - It's Alive!, 5 bks., Set. Incl. Life in a Rain Forest. Senior, Kathryn. lib. bdg. 25.50 *(978-0-516-25315-2(8));* Life in the Wetlands. Scrace, Carolyn. 25.50 *(978-0-516-25318-3(2));* (Illus.). 32p. (J). (gr. 2-4). 2005. (What on Earth? Ser.). 2005. 127.50 o.p. *(978-0-516-25223-0(2),* Children's Pr.) Scholastic Library Publishing.
Where on Earth? 2016. (Where on Earth? Ser.). 32p. (gr. 5-4). 105.00 *(978-1-5081-5042-8(7));* pap. 40.00 *(978-1-4994-2463-8(9))* Rosen Publishing Group, Inc., The. (PowerKids Pr.).
Wilkins, Mary-Jane. Earth. 2017. (Fast Track: Our Solar System Ser.). 24p. (gr. k-3). 28.50 ***(978-1-78121-364-3(X))*** Brown Bear Bks.
Williams, Brian. What about Planet Earth. 2008. 40p. pap. *(978-1-84810-073-2(6))* Miles Kelly Publishing, Ltd.
Williams, Zella. Experiments about Planet Earth. (Do-It-Yourself Science Ser.). 24p. (gr. 2-3). 2009. 47.90 *(978-1-61512-185-4(4),* PowerKids Pr.) 2007. (Illus.). (J). lib. bdg. 25.25 *(978-1-4042-3662-2(7))* Rosen Publishing Group, Inc., The.
Wimmer, Teresa. Earth. 2007. (My First Look at: Planets Ser.). (Illus.). 24p. (J). (gr. -1-3). lib. bdg. 24.25 *(978-1-58341-516-0(5),* Creative Education) Creative Co., The.
World Book, contrib. by. Earth & Earth's Moon. 2nd ed. 2007. (World Book's Solar System & Space Exploration Library). (Illus.). 64p. (J). *(978-0-7166-9512-7(X))* World Bk., Inc.
World Book, Inc Staff, contrib. by. Earth. 2014. (Illus.). 319p. *(978-0-7166-7519-8(6))* World Bk., Inc.
—Earth & Earth's Moon. (J). 2010. *(978-0-7166-9540-0(5))* 2006. 63p. *(978-0-7166-9503-5(0))* World Bk., Inc.
The World's Deadliest, 6 vols. 2010. (World's Deadliest Ser.). (ENG.). 32p. (gr. 1-2). lib. bdg. 133.25 *(978-1-4296-4418-1(4),* Blazers) Capstone Press of Coughlan Cos.
The World's Deadliest [Capstone Sole Source]. 2010. (World's Deadliest Ser.). 32p. lib. bdg. 151.92 *(978-1-4296-5890-4(8),* Blazers) Capstone Press of Coughlan Cos.
Woyt, Barbara A. Geology. 2016. (Study of Science Ser.). 00104p. (YA). (gr. 8-8). 36.25 *(978-1-5081-0426-1(3))* Rosen Publishing Group, Inc., The.
Zobel, Derek. Earth. 2010. (Exploring Space Ser.). (ENG., Illus.). 24p. (J). (gr. k-3). lib. bdg. 25.95 *(978-1-60014-404-2(7),* Blastoff! Readers) Bellwether Media.
Zuchora-Walske, Christine & Burroughs, Scott. Your Mission on Earth, 1 vol. 2011. (Planets Ser.). (ENG., Illus.). 32p. (J). (gr. k-3). 28.50 *(978-1-61641-677-5(7))* Magic Wagon.
Zuehlke, Jeffrey. Earth. 2009. (Early Bird Astronomy Ser.). (ENG.). 48p. (gr. 2-5). pap. 8.95 *(978-0-7613-4978-5(2));* lib. bdg. 26.60 *(978-0-7613-4149-9(8))* Lerner Publishing Group.

EARTH (PLANET)—DICTIONARIES

Allaby, Michael. Visual Encyclopedia of Earth. 2008. (ENG., Illus.). 256p. (J). (gr. 5-18). lib. bdg. 32.90 *(978-1-4263-0367-8(X));* 24.95 *(978-1-4263-0366-1(1))* National Geographic Society. (National Geographic Children's Bks.).
Brooks, Felicity. First Encyclopedia of Our World. 2004. (First Encyclopedias Ser.). (SPA., Illus.). 64p. (J). (gr. 3-18). lib. bdg. 17.95 *(978-1-58086-427-5(9))* EDC Publishing.
Dell, Pamela. Show Me the Continents. 2013. (My First Picture Encyclopedias Ser.). (ENG., Illus.). 32p. (gr. 1-2). 7.95 *(978-1-4765-3344-5(X),* Aplus Bks.) Capstone Press of Coughlan Cos.
Malam, John & Hincks, Gary. Extraordinary World: Highest, Longest, Deepest - An Exploration of the World's Most Fantastic Features. (Illus.). 44p. (J). pap. 19.99 *(978-0-590-24956-0(8))* Scholastic, Inc.
Punter, Russell. Encyclopedia of Planet Earth: Internet-Linked. Harvey, Gil, illus. 2009. (Geography Ser.). 160p. (YA). (gr. 4-18). 9.99 *(978-0-7945-2469-2(9),* Usborne) EDC Publishing.

EARTH (PLANET)—ROTATION

Bernhard, Durga. While You Are Sleeping. 2011. (J). pap. 14.95 *(978-1-57091-474-4(5))* Charlesbridge Publishing, Inc.
—While You Are Sleeping. Bernhard, Durga, illus. 2011. (ENG., Illus.). 24p. (J). (gr. k-3). 14.95 *(978-1-57091-473-7(7))* Charlesbridge Publishing, Inc.
Branley, Franklyn M. What Makes Day & Night? 2015. (Let's Read & Find Out Science Stage 2 Ser.). (J). lib. bdg. 17.20 *(978-0-606-37738-6(7))* Turtleback Bks.
Brasch, Nicolas. Times, Tides, & Revolutions. 2010. (Science Behind Ser.). 32p. lib. bdg. 28.50 *(978-1-59920-563-2(7))* Black Rabbit Bks.
Brennan, Linda Crotta. There Is Day & Night. 2014. (Tell Me Why Library). (ENG., Illus.). 24p. (J). (gr. 2-5). 25.64 *(978-1-63188-007-0(1),* 205435) Cherry Lake Publishing.
Clark, Claire. How Long Is a Day?, 1 vol. 2012. (Calendar Ser.). (ENG.). 24p. (gr. k-1). lib. bdg. 26.65 *(978-1-4296-7591-8(8),* Pebble Plus) Capstone Press of Coughlan Cos.
—How Long Is a Year?, 1 vol. 2012. (Calendar Ser.). (ENG., Illus.). 24p. (gr. k-1). lib. bdg. 26.65 *(978-1-4296-7594-9(2),* Pebble Plus) Capstone Press of Coughlan Cos.
Green, Jen. Day & Night. 2008. (Our Earth Ser.). (Illus.). 24p. (J). (gr. 1-4). lib. bdg. 22.60 *(978-1-4042-4275-3(9))* Rosen Publishing Group, Inc., The.
Hansen, Amy S. Where Does the Sun Go at Night? An Earth Science Mystery, 1 vol. Scott, Korey, illus. 2011. (First Graphics: Science Mysteries Ser.). (ENG.). 24p. (gr. 1-2). pap. 6.29 *(978-1-4296-7176-7(9));* pap. 35.70 *(978-1-4296-7180-4(7))* Capstone Press of Coughlan Cos.
Hicks, Terry Allan. Why Does the Sun Set? 2009. (Tell Me Why, Tell Me How Ser.). 32p. (gr. 3-18). 29.93 *(978-0-7614-3993-6(5))* Marshall Cavendish Corp.
Llewellyn, Claire. Day & Night. 2006. (I Know That, Cycles of Nature Set Ser.). (Illus.). 24p. (J). (gr. -1-3). lib. bdg. 22.80 *(978-1-59771-018-3(0))* Sea-To-Sea Pubns.
Meachen Rau, Dana. Space & Time/El Tiempo y Espacio. 2008. (Earth Matters/El Planeta Es Importante Ser.). (SPA & ENG.). 32p. (gr. k-1). lib. bdg. 15.95 *(978-0-7614-3496-2(8),* Benchmark Bks.) Marshall Cavendish Corp.
—El Tiempo y el Espacio. 2008. (Planeta Es Importante Ser.). (SPA.). 32p. (gr. 1-2). lib. bdg. 15.95 *(978-0-7614-3470-2(4),* Benchmark Bks.) Marshall Cavendish Corp.
Morgan, Emily R. Next Time You See a Sunset. 2012. (Next Time You See Ser.). (ENG., Illus.). 32p. (J). (gr. k-5). pap. 12.95 *(978-1-936959-16-7(X))* National Science Teachers Assn.
National Geographic Learning Staff. Why Do the Seasons Change? 2010. (ENG., Illus.). 32p. (C). (gr. -1-3). pap. 12.95 *(978-0-7614-3367-5(8))* National Geographic School Publishing, Inc.
Nelson, Robin. Day & Night. 2010. pap. 33.92 *(978-0-7613-6912-7(0));* (ENG.). 24p. pap. 6.95 *(978-0-7613-5679-0(7));* (ENG., Illus.). 24p. lib. bdg. 23.93 *(978-0-7613-4576-3(0))* Lerner Publishing Group.
—Día y Noche (Day & Night) 2012. (Mi Primer Paso Al Mundo Real - Descubriendo Los Ciclos de la Naturaleza (First Step Nonfiction - Discovering Nature's Cycles) Ser.). (Illus.). 24p. (gr. k-2). (ENG & SPA.). pap. 6.95 *(978-0-7613-9345-0(5));* (SPA., lib. bdg. 23.93 *(978-0-7613-9340-5(4))* Lerner Publishing Group. (Ediciones Lerner).
Pendergast, George. A Year of Seasons. 2015. (Cycles in Nature Ser.). (ENG., Illus.). 24p. (J). (gr. 1-2). lib. bdg. 22.60 *(978-1-4824-1654-1(9))* Stevens, Gareth Publishing LLLP.
Rau, Dana Meachen. Day & Night. 2009. (Bookworms Ser.). 32p. (gr. 1-2). 15.95 *(978-0-7614-4094-9(1))* Marshall Cavendish Corp.
—Day & Night/El Día y la Noche. 2009. (Bookworms Ser.). (SPA & ENG.). 32p. (gr. 1-2). lib. bdg. 15.95 *(978-0-7614-4788-7(1))* Marshall Cavendish Corp.
Slade, Suzanne. The Four Seasons. (Cycles in Nature Ser.). (gr. 3-3). 2009. 24p. 42.50 *(978-1-61512-111-3(0))* 2007. 28p. pap. 21.25 *(978-1-4358-3827-7(0))* Rosen Publishing Group, Inc., The. (PowerKids Pr.).
Stewart, Melissa. Why Do the Seasons Change? 2006. (Tell Me Why, Tell Me How Ser.). (Illus.). 32p. (gr. 3-7). lib. bdg. 29.93 *(978-0-7614-2112-2(2),* Benchmark Bks.) Marshall Cavendish Corp.
Storad, Conrad J. Day & Night. 2011. (ENG., Illus.). 24p. (gr. k-1). pap. 8.95 *(978-1-61741-926-3(5))* Rourke Educational Media.
—Earth Is Tilting! 2011. (ENG., Illus.). 24p. (gr. 2-3). pap. 8.95 *(978-1-61741-952-2(4))* Rourke Educational Media.
Upgrade kit dsm-3 earth Movement. (J). 2004. *(978-1-59242-529-7(1))* 2003. *(978-1-59242-412-2(0))* Delta Education, LLC.

EARTH SCIENCES

ABDO Publishing Company. Earth's Treasures. 2013. (Earth's Treasures Ser.: 6). 32p. (J). (gr. 3-6). lib. bdg. 162.42 *(978-1-61783-869-9(1),* Checkerboard Library) ABDO Publishing Co.
Achieve Now Institute Staff. ESR Student Resource Book. 2004. pap. 8.12 *(978-0-7398-9881-9(7))* Steck-Vaughn.
Adams, Simon, et al. Discover the Savage World. 2013. (Illus.). 224p. (J). *(978-1-4351-4990-8(4))* Barnes & Noble, Inc.
Allaby, Michael. Earth Science: A Scientific History of the Solid Earth. Garratt, Richard, illus. 2009. (Discovering the Earth Ser.). 224p. (C). (gr. 9-18). 39.95 *(978-0-8160-6097-9(5))* Facts On File, Inc.
Allen, Nancy Kelly. Earth's Rock Cycle. 2009. (Rock It! Ser.). 24p. (gr. 3-6). (ENG.). (J). pap. 8.25 *(978-1-4358-3185-8(3));* 42.50 *(978-1-60852-480-8(9),* PowerKids Pr.) Rosen Publishing Group, Inc., The.
Arthus, Yann B. Tierra explicada a los ninos. 2005. 34p. *(978-970-651-910-8(6))* Editorial Oceano De Mexico, S.A. DE C.V.
Banqueri, Eduardo. Our Planet. 2005. (Our Planet Ser.). (Illus.). 32p. (gr. 4-6). 112.00 *(978-0-7910-9087-9(6),* Chelsea Clubhouse) Facts On File, Inc.
Benchmark Education Company, LLC Staff, compiled by. Earth & Space Science. 2006. spiral bd. 235.00 *(978-1-4108-6934-0(2))* 2006. spiral bd. 365.00 *(978-1-4108-6946-3(6))* 2006. spiral bd. 695.00 *(978-1-4108-6942-5(3))* 2006. spiral bd. 365.00 *(978-1-4108-6939-5(3))* 2006. spiral bd. 80.00 *(978-1-4108-6927-2(X))* 2006. spiral bd. 365.00 *(978-1-4108-6925-8(3))* 2005. spiral bd. 405.00 *(978-1-4108-5852-8(9))* 2005. spiral bd. 675.00 *(978-1-4108-5851-1(0))* 2005. spiral bd. 950.00 *(978-1-4108-5441-4(8))* 2005. spiral bd. 1025.00 *(978-1-4108-5440-7(X))* 2005. spiral bd. 55.00 *(978-1-4108-3874-2(9))* 2005. spiral bd. 75.00 *(978-1-4108-3870-4(6))* 2005. spiral bd. 220.00 *(978-1-4108-3859-9(5))* 2005. spiral bd. 370.00 *(978-1-4108-3858-2(7))* 2005. spiral bd. 220.00 *(978-1-4108-3851-3(X))* 2005. spiral bd. 305.00 *(978-1-4108-3850-6(1))* 2005. spiral bd. 335.00 *(978-1-4108-3829-2(3))* 2005. spiral bd. 580.00 *(978-1-4108-3826-1(9))* 2005. spiral bd. 870.00 *(978-1-4108-4518-4(4))* Benchmark Education Co.
—Learning about Earth's Past. 2006. (J). 206.00 *(978-1-4108-7059-9(6))* Benchmark Education Co.
—Life on Earth: Theme Set. 2006. (J). 259.00 *(978-1-4108-7119-0(3))* Benchmark Education Co.
—Science Theme: Earth & Space Science. 2005. spiral bd. 340.00 *(978-1-4108-5314-1(4))* Benchmark Education Co.
—Science Theme: Life on Earth. 2005. spiral bd. 115.00 *(978-1-4108-5320-2(9))* Benchmark Education Co.
—Science Theme: What Changes Our Earth. 2005. spiral bd. 115.00 *(978-1-4108-5315-8(2))* Benchmark Education Co.
—What Changes Our Earth. 2006. spiral bd. 330.00 *(978-1-4108-7017-9(0))* 2005. (J). spiral bd. 265.00 *(978-1-4108-5762-0(X))* Benchmark Education Co.
Bone, Emily. Storms & Hurricanes. Weston, Paul, illus. 2013. (Beginner's Science Ser.). 32p. (J). ring bd. 4.99 *(978-0-7945-3350-2(7),* Usborne) EDC Publishing.
Bow, James. Earth Mysteries Revealed. 2010. (ENG., Illus.). 32p. (J). pap. *(978-0-7787-7428-0(7));* (gr. 4-7). lib. bdg. *(978-0-7787-7413-6(9))* Crabtree Publishing Co.
—Earth's Secrets. 2010. (Invisible Worlds Ser.). 48p. (gr. 4). 28.50 *(978-0-7614-4196-0(4))* Marshall Cavendish GBR. Dist: Marshall Cavendish Corp.
Brasch, Nicolas. Why Do Volcanoes Erupt? Level 4 Factbook. 2010. (Cambridge Young Readers Ser.). (ENG., Illus.). 16p. pap. 6.00 *(978-0-521-13838-3(8))* Cambridge Univ. Pr.
Brown, Don & Perfit, Michael R. Older Than Dirt. 2017. (ENG., Illus.). 112p. (J). (gr. 5-7). 18.99 *(978-0-544-80503-3(8),* HMH Books For Young Readers) Houghton Mifflin Harcourt Publishing Co.
Butterfield, Moira. Superstats: Extreme Planet. 2015. (Superstats Ser.). (ENG., Illus.). 64p. (J). (gr. 2-4). 11.99 *(978-1-4998-0084-5(3))* Little Bee Books Inc.
Calhoun, Yael. Earth Science Fair Projects: Using Rocks, Minerals, Magnets, Mud, & More. 2005. (Earth Science! Best Science Projects Ser.). (Illus.). 128p. (J). (gr. 6-12). lib. bdg. 27.94 *(978-0-7660-2363-5(X))* Enslow Pubs., Inc.
—Earth Science Fair Projects, Revised & Expanded Using the Scientific Method. LaBaff, Stephanie & LaBaff, Tom, illus. 2010. (Earth Science Projects Using the Scientific Method Ser.). 160p. (J). (gr. 5-18). 35.94 *(978-0-7660-3425-9(9))* Enslow Pubs., Inc.
Canavan, Thomas. Does It Really Rain Frogs? Questions & Answers about Planet Earth. 2013. (Science F. A. Q. Ser.). (Illus.). 32p. (gr. 3-6). 31.35 *(978-1-78212-393-4(8))* Arcturus Publishing GBR. Dist: Black Rabbit Bks.
Chambers, Catherine. Earth Debates. 2015. (Earth Debates Ser.). (ENG.). 48p. (gr. 4-6). lib. bdg. 133.28 *(978-1-4846-0999-6(9),* Heinemann InfoSearch) Heinemann-Raintree.
Chandler, Kimberley L., et al. The Earth Beneath Our Feet: An Earth Science Unit for High-Ability Learners in Grades 3-4. 2014. (William & Mary Units Ser.). (ENG.). 100p. (gr. 3-4). pap. 39.95 *(978-1-61821-045-6(9))* Prufrock Pr.
Channing, Margot. Planet Earth. 2014. (Closer Look At... Ser.). (Illus.). 32p. (gr. 3-6). 31.35 *(978-1-904642-69-5(1))* Book Hse. GBR. Dist: Black Rabbit Bks.

Children's Planet Earth Encyclopedia. 2008. (1st Encyclopedia Ser.). 224p. *(978-1-4075-1310-2(9))* Parragon, Inc.

Clarke, Phillip. Planet Earth Facts & Lists - Internet Linked. 2004. (Facts & Lists Internet-Linked Ser.). (ENG., Illus.). 64p. (J). pap. 7.95 *(978-0-7945-0644-5(5)*, Usborne) EDC Publishing.

Claybourne, Anna. Extreme Earth. 2010. (Discovery of Life Ser.). (Illus.). 48p. (YA). lib. bdg. 19.95 *(978-1-4222-1520-3(2))* Mason Crest.

Close, Edward. All about the Weather, 1 vol., 1. 2014. (Discovery Education: Earth & Space Science Ser.). (ENG.). 32p. (gr. 3-6). 26.25 *(978-1-4777-6190-8(X)*, PowerKids Pr.) Rosen Publishing Group, Inc., The.

Conklin, Wendy. Earth's Cycles. 2015. (Science Readers: Content & Literacy Ser.). (ENG., Illus.). 32p. (gr. 4-4). pap. 8.99 *(978-1-4807-4686-2(X))* Teacher Created Materials, Inc.

Conoce las Nubes. 2006. (Real Readers en español Ser.). (J). pap. 24.95 *(978-1-4042-2486-5(6)*, Rosen Classroom) Rosen Publishing Group, Inc., The.

Crawford, Gerald. The Magic in the Mud. Date not set. (Illus.). 48p. (J). (gr. 1-4). 14.95 *(978-0-9672996-0-0(8))* Red Mud Pr.

Cullen, Katherine. Earth Science. 2006. (Science News for Kids Ser.). (Illus.). 144p. (gr. 4-6). 30.00 *(978-0-7910-9124-1(4)*, Chelsea Clubhouse) Facts On File, Inc.

Dakers, Diane. Earth's Cycles. 2014. (ENG., Illus.). 48p. (J). pap. *(978-0-7787-0619-9(2))* Crabtree Publishing Co.

Davis, Barbara J. Minerals, Rocks, & Soil. 2016. (Sci-Hi: Earth & Space Science Ser.). (ENG.). 48p. (gr. 4-4). pap. 8.99 *(978-1-4109-8521-7(0)*, Sci-Hi) Heinemann-Raintree.

DeCristofano, Carolyn. National Geographic Kids Ultimate Space Atlas. 2017. (ENG.). 160p. (J). (gr. 3-7). lib. bdg. 22.90 ***(978-1-4263-2803-9(6))***; (Illus.). pap. 12.99 ***(978-1-4263-2802-2(8))*** National Geographic Society. (National Geographic Children's Bks.).

Denecke, Edward J., Jr. & Long, Lynette. Painless Earth Science. 2011. (Painless Ser.). (ENG., Illus.). 320p. pap. 11.99 *(978-0-7641-4601-5(7))* Barron's Educational Series, Inc.

Diagram Group Staff. Earth Science: An Illustrated Guide to Science. 2006. (Science Visual Resources Ser.). (Illus.). 208p. (gr. 6-12). 49.50 *(978-0-8160-6164-8(5))* Facts On File, Inc.

Diagram Group Staff, contrib. by. The Facts on File Earth Science Handbook. 2nd rev. ed. 2006. (Science Handbks.). (Illus.). 272p. (gr. 6-12). 40.00 *(978-0-8160-5879-2(2))* Facts On File, Inc.

Dickmann, Nancy. Habitats & Biomes. 2016. (Earth Figured Out Ser.). (ENG.). 32p. (J). (gr. 4-4). pap. 10.58 *(978-1-5026-0878-9(2))* Cavendish Square Publishing.

Discovering the Earth, 7 vols., Set. 2010. (Discovering the Earth Ser.). (Illus.). 208p. (C). (gr. 9-18). 279.65 *(978-0-8160-6096-2(7))* Facts On File, Inc.

Discovery Education Staff, creator. DE Science Techbook for National - Grades 3-5: Earth Science. 2011. (J). *(978-1-61828-183-8(6))* Discovery Education.

Dorion, Christiane. How the World Works: A Hands-On Guide to Our Amazing Planet. Young, Beverley, illus. 2010. (Explore the Earth Ser.). (ENG.). 18p. (J). (gr. 2-5). 18.99 *(978-0-7636-4801-5(9)*, Templar) Candlewick Pr.

Dumit, Sharon & Nowak, Jeffrey. Cool Science Matters with Molly Cool & Atom: A - Air. 2009. 32p. pap. 7.95 *(978-0-9822262-0-9(9))* Sow Forth Publishing LLC.

Earth & Space Science. 2011. (Earth & Space Science Ser.). (ENG.). 24p. (gr. k-1). pap. 27.80 *(978-1-4296-7147-7(5))*; pap. 166.80 *(978-1-4296-7148-4(3))*; lib. bdg. 53.30 *(978-1-4296-6836-1(9))* Capstone Press of Coughlan Cos. (Pebble Plus).

Earth Features. 2005. (Earth & Outer Space Ser.). (YA). (gr. k-3). 237.60 *(978-0-7368-4212-9(8))*, Pebble Bks.) Capstone Press of Coughlan Cos.

Earth Science, Set. 2010. (Extreme! Ser.). (ENG.). 32p. (gr. 3-4). pap. 286.20 *(978-1-4296-5137-0(7)*, Fact Finders) Capstone Press of Coughlan Cos.

Earth Science: Visualizations. 2003. (gr. 6-12). cd-rom *(978-0-618-16400-4(6)*, 2-01601) Holt McDougal.

Earth Science Detectives. 2015. (Earth Science Detectives Ser.). (ENG.). 24p. (J). (gr. 3-3). pap., pap., pap. 297.00 *(978-1-4994-1284-0(3)*, PowerKids Pr.) Rosen Publishing Group, Inc., The.

Earth Science Experiments. 2010. (Facts on File Science Experiments Ser.). (Illus.). 192p. (gr. 6-12). 40.00 *(978-0-8160-8170-7(0))* Facts On File, Inc.

Earth Science Sets: 1 Each of 3 Big Books. (Sunshinetm Science Ser.). (gr. 1-2). 111.50 *(978-0-7802-2810-8(3))* Wright Group/McGraw-Hill.

Earth Science Sets: 1 Each of 3 Student Books. (Sunshinetm Science Ser.). (gr. 1-2). 20.95 *(978-0-7802-2811-5(1))* Wright Group/McGraw-Hill.

Earth Watch: Clouds & Weather. (J). (gr. 4-6). 75.00 *(978-0-669-15105-3(X))* Houghton Mifflin Harcourt School Pubs.

Earth Watch: The Light in the Sky. (J). (gr. 1-3). *(978-0-669-15104-6(1))* Houghton Mifflin Harcourt School Pubs.

Earth Watch: Tracks. (J). (gr. 4-6). *(978-0-669-15101-5(7))*; *(978-0-669-15884-7(4))* Houghton Mifflin Harcourt School Pubs.

Ebner, Aviva. Earth Science Experiments. 2011. (Experiments for Future Scientists Ser.). (Illus.). 156p. (gr. 5-8). 35.00 *(978-1-60413-854-2(8))* Facts On File, Inc.

Enchantment of the World, Second Series. 2011. (Enchantment of the World Ser.). 234.00 *(978-0-531-21850-1(3)*, Children's Pr.) Scholastic Library Publishing.

Encyclopaedia Britannica Publishers, Inc. Staff. Earth's Changing Environment. 2008. (Illus.). 128p. (YA). (gr. 8-18). 29.95 *(978-1-59339-429-5(2))* Encyclopaedia Britannica, Inc.

Enderle, Dotti. Storytime Discoveries: Earth Science. 2003. (Illus.). 64p. (J). pap. 9.95 *(978-1-57310-412-8(4)*, 1200741) Teaching & Learning Co.

Enz, Tammy. Dynamic Planet: Exploring Changes on Earth with Science Projects. 2015. (Discover Earth Science Ser.). (ENG., Illus.). 32p. (gr. 3-4). lib. bdg. 27.32 *(978-1-4914-4815-1(6))* Capstone Press of Coughlan Cos.

Enz, Tammy, et al. Discover Earth Science. 2015. (Discover Earth Science Ser.). (ENG.). 32p. (gr. 3-4). 109.28 *(978-1-4914-6701-5(0)*, Fact Finders) Capstone Press of Coughlan Cos.

Erickson, John R., et al. AfterSchool KidzScience: Earth & Space Science: Sunlight Science Kit. 2013. (J). 225.00 *(978-1-61003-142-4(3))* Center for the Collaborative Classroom.

Farndon, John. Planet Earth. 2008. (1000 Things You Should Know about Ser.). (Illus.). 61p. (J). pap. *(978-1-84236-628-8(9))* Miles Kelly Publishing, Ltd.

Ferguson, creator. Earth Science. 2nd rev. ed. 2008. (Careers in Focus Ser.). (Illus.). 188p. (gr. 6-12). 32.95 *(978-0-8160-7272-9(8)*, Ferguson Publishing Co.) Facts On File, Inc.

Flaechen und Ihre Berechnung I. 2nd ed. (Duden-Schuelerhilfen Ser.). (GER.). 112p. (YA). (gr. 5-8). *(978-3-411-04412-2(8))* Bibliographisches Institut & F. A. Brockhaus AG DEU. Dist: International Bk. Import Service, Inc.

Flaechen und Ihre Berechnung II. (Duden-Schuelerhilfen Ser.). (GER.). 96p. (YA). (gr. 9-10). *(978-3-411-04711-6(9))* Bibliographisches Institut & F. A. Brockhaus AG DEU. Dist: International Bk. Import Service, Inc.

Fontana, Lynn & Hoge, Patricia, eds. Education Station Reading Anthology, Volume One: F-H, Band 6-8. 2004. (Illus.). 141p. spiral bd. 12.32 *(978-0-7398-9891-8(4))* Steck-Vaughn.

—Education Station Reading, Volume Two: F-H: Student Resource Book. 2004. (Illus.). 248p. per. 12.32 *(978-0-7398-9886-4(8))* Steck-Vaughn.

Franklin, Kent. Exploring Earth & Space Systems. 2006. 96p. pap. 9.95 *(978-1-4116-3469-5(1))* Lulu Pr., Inc.

Friend, Sandra. Exploring Planet Earth, 5 bks. Incl. Earth's Wild Winds. (Illus.). 64p. (gr. 5-9). 2002. lib. bdg. 25.26 *(978-0-7613-2673-1(1)*, Twenty-First Century Bks.); (Illus.). 64p. Set lib. bdg. 124.50 *(978-0-7613-3021-9(6)*, Twenty-First Century Bks.) Lerner Publishing Group.

Friesen, Helen Lepp. Who Lives Here? 2008. (Discovering & Exploring Science Ser.). (Illus.). 16p. (J). (gr. -1-3). lib. bdg. 12.95 *(978-0-7569-8425-0(4))* Perfection Learning Corp.

Gallavotti, Barbara. La Vida en la Tierra. (SPA.). 88p. (YA). (gr. 5-8). *(978-84-7131-936-4(5))* Editex, Editorial S.A. ESP. Dist: Lectorum Pubns., Inc.

Ganeri, Anita. La Lluvia. 2004. (tiempo de aqui (Weather Around You- Spanish) Ser.). (SPA.). 24p. (gr. 1-4). lib. bdg. 22.00 *(978-0-8368-4367-5(3)*, Weekly Reader Leveled Readers) Stevens, Gareth Publishing LLLP.

—La Nieve (Snow) 2004. (tiempo de aqui (Weather Around You- Spanish) Ser.). (SPA.). 24p. (gr. 1-4). lib. bdg. 22.00 *(978-0-8368-4368-2(1)*, Weekly Reader Leveled Readers) Stevens, Gareth Publishing LLLP.

—Ocean Divers, 1 vol. 2011. (Landform Adventurers Ser.). (ENG.). 32p. (gr. 1-2). 29.99 *(978-1-4109-4140-4(X)*, Read Me!) Heinemann-Raintree.

—El Viento. 2004. (tiempo de aqui (Weather Around You- Spanish) Ser.). (SPA.). 24p. (gr. 1-4). lib. bdg. 22.00 *(978-0-8368-4366-8(5)*, Weekly Reader Leveled Readers) Stevens, Gareth Publishing LLLP.

Garbe, Suzanne. Living Earth: Exploring Life on Earth with Science Projects. 2016. (Illus.). 32p. (J). lib. bdg. *(978-1-4747-0326-0(7))* Capstone Press of Coughlan Cos.

Gardner, Robert. Science Fair Projects about Planet Earth. 2016. (Hands-On Science Ser.). 48p. (J). 27.93 *(978-0-7660-8219-9(9))* Enslow Pubs., Inc.

Geiger, Beth & National Geographic Learning (Firm) Staff. Earth's Changing Land. 2007. (Avenues Ser.). (ENG., Illus.). 36p. (J). pap. 18.95 *(978-0-7922-5427-0(9))* CENGAGE Learning.

Gilpin, Dan & Bull, Peter. Explorers: Planet Earth. 2014. (Explorers Ser.). (ENG., Illus.). 32p. (J). (gr. 2-5). 6.99 *(978-0-7534-7169-2(8)*, 9780753471692, Kingfisher) Roaring Brook Pr.

Glencoe McGraw-Hill Staff. The Water Planet. 2nd ed. 2004. (Glen Sci: the Water Planet Ser.). (ENG.). (gr. 6-8). stu. ed. 32.40 *(978-0-07-861755-3(3)*, 0078617553) McGraw-Hill Higher Education.

Glencoe McGraw-Hill Staff, creator. The Changing Surface of Earth. 2nd ed. 2004. (Glen Sci: Changing Surface Ear Ser.). (ENG., Illus.). 256p. (gr. 6-8). lib. bdg., stu. ed. 31.12 *(978-0-07-861752-2(9)*, 0078617529) McGraw-Hill Higher Education.

Gonzales, Doreen & Graham, Amy. What Are the 7 Wonders of the Natural World? 2013. (What Are the Seven Wonders of the World? Ser.). 48p. (J). (gr. 4-18). 25.27 *(978-0-7660-4153-0(0))* Enslow Pubs., Inc.

Graf, Mike & Snedden, Robert. Mapping Earth from Space, 1 vol. KJA Artists Staff, illus. 2010. (Science Missions Ser.). (ENG.). 56p. (gr. 6-6). 34.65 *(978-1-4109-3826-8(3)*, Raintree Freestyle) Heinemann-Raintree.

Graham, Amy. What Are the 7 Wonders of the Natural World? 2013. (What Are the Seven Wonders of the World? Ser.). 48p. (J). (gr. 4-10). pap. 8.95 *(978-1-4644-0232-6(9))* Enslow Pubs., Inc.

Great Earth Science Projects. (Illus.). (J). (gr. k-5). 119.70 *(978-0-8239-7141-1(4))* Rosen Publishing Group, Inc., The.

Great Record Breakers in Nature. (Illus.). (J). (gr. k-5). 112.50 *(978-0-8239-7065-0(5))* Rosen Publishing Group, Inc., The.

Group/McGraw-Hill, Wright. Earth & Physical Science: Exploring Electricity, 6 vols. (Book2WebTM Ser.). (gr. 4-8). 36.50 *(978-0-322-04428-9(6))* Wright Group/McGraw-Hill.

Harcourt School Publishers Staff. Harcourt Ciencias, Grade 3 Unit C&D: Earth Science. 2003. (Harcourt Ciencias Ser.). (SPA.). (gr. 3-18). tchr. ed. 67.40 *(978-0-15-314809-5(8))* Harcourt Schl. Pubs.

—Harcourt Ciencias, Grade 4 Unit C&D: Earth Science. 2003. (Harcourt Ciencias Ser.). (SPA.). (gr. 4-18). tchr. ed. 67.40 *(978-0-15-314812-5(8))* Harcourt Schl. Pubs.

—Harcourt Ciencias, Grade 5 Unit C&D: Earth Science. 2003. (Harcourt Ciencias Ser.). (SPA.). (gr. 5-18). tchr. ed. 70.00 *(978-0-15-314815-6(2))* Harcourt Schl. Pubs.

—Harcourt Science: Earth Instant Reader CD-ROM Teacher's Guide. 2nd ed. 2003. (Harcourt Science Ser.). (gr. k-18). tchr. ed. 8.00 incl. cd-rom *(978-0-15-324956-3(0))* Harcourt Schl. Pubs.

Harris, Tim. Earth Science. 2015. (Science Q & A Ser.). (ENG., Illus.). 32p. (J). (gr. 5-5). pap. 10.58 *(978-1-5026-0615-0(1)*, 1389977) Cavendish Square Publishing.

Haslam, Andrew. Earth. 2004. (Make It Work! Science Ser.). (Illus.). 48p. (J). (gr. 3-6). 12.95 *(978-1-58728-376-5(X)*, Two-Can Publishing) T&N Children's Publishing.

Hewitt, Sally. Earth & Space. (Illus.). 32p. (YA). (gr. 2-18). lib. bdg. 27.10 *(978-1-932333-31-2(2))* Chrysalis Education.

Hodge, Bodie & Welch, Laura. Big Book of Earth & Sky: A 15 Foot Chart Showing the Inner Core to Outer Atmosphere. 2017. (Illus.). 21p. (J). pap. 17.99 ***(978-1-68344-028-4(5))*** Master Bks.

Hodge, Judith. Riches from Earth: Set Of 6. 2011. (Navigators Ser.). (J). pap. 48.00 net. *(978-1-4108-0429-7(1))* Benchmark Education Co.

Holt, Rinehart and Winston Staff. Earth Science. 2004. (Holt Science & Technology Ser.). (Illus.). (gr. 7-7). 4th ed. (ENG.). 824p. 104.80 *(978-0-03-073167-9(4))* 5th ed. (SPA & ENG., 880p. 110.60 *(978-0-03-021213-0(8))* Houghton Mifflin Harcourt Publishing Co.

—Earth Science: Directed Reading & Vocabulary Workbook. 5th ed. 2004. (Holt Science & Technology Ser.). (SPA., Illus.). pap., wbk. ed. 17.13 *(978-0-03-036058-9(7))* Holt McDougal.

—Earth Science: Study Guide. 5th ed. 2004. (Holt Science & Technology Ser.). (SPA., Illus.). pap., stu. ed. 17.13 *(978-0-03-030156-8(4))* Holt McDougal.

—Earth Science No. 2: Earth & It's Systems. 6th ed. 2006. pap. 11.73 incl. cd-rom *(978-0-03-036892-9(8))* Harcourt Schl. Pubs.

—Earth Science No. 3: Models of Earth. 6th ed. 2006. pap. 11.73 incl. cd-rom *(978-0-03-036893-6(6))* Harcourt Schl. Pubs.

—Earth Science No. 4: Earth Chemistry. 6th ed. 2006. pap. 11.73 incl. cd-rom *(978-0-03-036894-3(4))* Harcourt Schl. Pubs.

—Earth Science No. 5: Minerals & Earth's Crust. 6th ed. 2006. pap. 11.73 incl. cd-rom *(978-0-03-036896-7(0))* Harcourt Schl. Pubs.

—Earth Science No. 7: Resources & Energy. 6th ed. 2006. pap. 11.73 incl. cd-rom *(978-0-03-036898-1(7))* Harcourt Schl. Pubs.

—Earth Science No. 8: The Rock Record. 6th ed. 2006. pap. 11.73 incl. cd-rom *(978-0-03-036899-8(5))* Harcourt Schl. Pubs.

—Holt Science & Technology: Earth Science. 5th ed. 2004. tchr. ed. 128.80 *(978-0-03-066479-3(9))* Holt McDougal.

—Holt Science & Technology: Earth Science: Enhanced Online Edition. 4th ed. 2004. 17.26 *(978-0-03-037151-6(1))* Holt McDougal.

—Holt Science & Technology: Earth Science: Reading & Comprehension Guide. 5th ed. 2004. (Holt Middle School Math Ser.). pap. 17.13 *(978-0-03-036062-6(5))* Holt McDougal.

—Holt Science & Technology: Earth Science: Special Needs Workbook. 5th ed. 2004. (Holt Science & Technology Ser.). pap., wbk. ed. 17.13 *(978-0-03-036054-1(4))* Holt McDougal.

—Holt Science & Technology: Earth Science Study Guide. 5th ed. 2004. (Holt Science & Technology Ser.). (Illus.). pap., stu. ed. 17.13 *(978-0-03-030159-9(9))* Holt McDougal.

—Holt Science & Technology Chapter 1: Earth Science: The World of Earth Science. 5th ed. 2004. (Illus.). pap. 12.86 *(978-0-03-030266-4(8))* Holt McDougal.

—Holt Science & Technology Chapter 20: Life Science: Earth's Ecosystems. 5th ed. 2004. (Illus.). pap. 12.86 *(978-0-03-030231-2(5))* Holt McDougal.

Horner, Katie. Brainstorming Creative Guide to Help Parents & Children Through Severe Weather. 2008. 32p. 19.95 *(978-1-933466-73-6(1))* Kansas City Star Bks.

Hunter, Dru. What Is Out There? 2015. (Illus.). 48p. (J). *(978-1-60818-594-8(X)*, Creative Education) Creative Co., The.

—What Is Out There? Think Like a Scientist. 2016. (Think Like a Scientist Ser.). (ENG.). 48p. (J). (gr. 5-9). pap. 12.00 *(978-1-62832-199-9(7)*, Creative Paperbacks) Creative Co., The.

Iyer, Rani & Rake, Jody Sullivan. Endangered Earth. 2015. (Endangered Earth Ser.). (ENG.). 32p. (gr. 3-4). lib. bdg. 109.28 *(978-1-4914-2451-3(6)*, Fact Finders) Capstone Press of Coughlan Cos.

Jennings, Terry. Wood. 2006. (Illus.). 32p. (YA). (gr. 1-18). lib. bdg. 27.10 *(978-1-932333-00-8(2))* Chrysalis Education.

Johnson, J. Angelique & Porter, Esther. Earth Matters. 2013. (Earth Matters Ser.). (ENG.). 32p. (gr. 1-2). pap. 190.80 *(978-1-62065-748-5(1))*; pap. 31.80 *(978-1-62065-747-8(3))*; lib. bdg. 109.28 *(978-1-62065-050-9(9))* Capstone Press of Coughlan Cos. (Aplus Bks.).

Johnson, Rose. Discoveries in Earth & Space Science That Changed the World, 1 vol. 2015. (ENG.). 48p. (YA). 30.25 *(978-1-4777-8609-3(0)*, Rosen Reference) Rosen Publishing Group, Inc., The.

Kalman, Bobbie. Introducción a los Accidentes Geográficos. 2009. (SPA.). 32p. (J). *(978-0-7787-8242-1(5))*; pap. *(978-0-7787-8259-9(X))* Crabtree Publishing Co.

—What Shapes the Land? 2008. (Looking at Earth Ser.). (ENG., Illus.). 32p. (J). (gr. 1-4). pap. *(978-0-7787-3219-8(3))* Crabtree Publishing Co.

Kalman, Bobbie & MacAulay, Kelley. Introducing Landforms. 2008. (Looking at Earth Ser.). (ENG., Illus.). 32p. (J). (gr. 3-7). pap. *(978-0-7787-3213-6(4))* Crabtree Publishing Co.

Katherine, Cullen. Earth Science: The People Behind the Science. 2005. (Pioneers in Science Ser.). (Illus.). 170p. (gr. 6-12). 29.95 *(978-0-8160-5464-0(9))* Facts On File, Inc.

Kids Can Press Staff & Forbes, Scott. How to Make a Planet: A Step-by-Step Guide to Building the Earth. Camden, Jean, illus. 2014. (ENG.). 64p. (J). (gr. 3-7). 17.95 *(978-1-894786-88-1(2))* Kids Can Pr., Ltd. CAN. Dist: Hachette Bk. Group.

Koontz, Robin Michal. Composting: Nature's Recyclers, 1 vol. Harrad, Matthew, illus. 2006. (Amazing Science Ser.). (ENG.). 24p. (gr. k-4). per. 8.95 *(978-1-4048-2200-9(3))* Picture Window Bks.

Korb, Rena. Science Rocks! CD + Book Set. Reibeling, Brandon, illus. 2008. (Science Rocks! (CD+Book) Ser.). (J). (gr. 3). lib. bdg. 324.84 *(978-1-60270-210-3(1))* ABDO Publishing Co.

Latta, Sara L. All about Earth: Exploring the Planet with Science Projects. (Illus.). 32p. 2016. (J). lib. bdg. *(978-1-4747-0323-9(2))* 2015. (ENG., (gr. 3-4). lib. bdg. 27.32 *(978-1-4914-4814-4(8))* Capstone Press of Coughlan Cos.

Lerner Publishing Group Staff, ed. Time Nature's Wonders: The Science & Splendor of Earth's Most Fascinating Places. 2008. (Time Inc. Home Entertainment Library-Bound Titles Ser.). (ENG.). 128p. (gr. 5-12). lib. bdg. 39.93 *(978-0-7613-4228-1(1)*, Twenty-First Century Bks.) Lerner Publishing Group.

LernerClassroom Editors, ed. Early Bird Earth Science: Classroom Set. 2008. pap. 52.95 *(978-0-8225-8982-2(6))* Lerner Publishing Group.

—Early Bird Earth Science: Complete Set. 2008. pap. 316.95 *(978-0-8225-9206-8(1))* Lerner Publishing Group.

Linde, Barbara M. Earth: Measuring Its Changes: Text Pairs. 2008. (Bridges/Navigators Ser.). (J). (gr. 4). 94.00 *(978-1-4108-8383-4(3))* Benchmark Education Co.

Long, John. The Big Picture Book. Choo, Brian, illus. 2005. (ENG.). 48p. (J). (gr. 4-7). 24.99 *(978-1-74114-328-7(4))* Allen & Unwin AUS. Dist: Independent Pubs. Group.

Lyon, George Ella. All the Water in the World. Tillotson, Katherine, illus. 2011. (ENG.). 40p. (J). (gr. -1-3). 17.99 *(978-1-4169-7130-6(0)*, Atheneum/Richard Jackson Bks.) Simon & Schuster Children's Publishing.

Make & Learn. 2014. (Make & Learn Ser.). 32p. (J). (gr. 3-6). pap. 70.50 *(978-1-4777-7230-0(8)*, PowerKids Pr.) Rosen Publishing Group, Inc., The.

Marquardt, Meg. Earth Myths, Busted! 2017. (Science Myths, Busted! Ser.). (ENG., Illus.). 32p. (J). (gr. 3-6). 21.95 *(978-1-63235-302-3(4))* Pr. Room Editions LLC.

McDaniel, Melissa. Earth: Slow Changes: Text Pairs. 2008. (Bridges/Navigators Ser.). (J). (gr. 4). 81.00 *(978-1-4108-8384-1(1))* Benchmark Education Co.

McDougal-Littell Publishing Staff. The Changing Earth. 2004. (McDougal Littell Science Ser.). (ENG.). (gr. 6-8). 64p. pap. 15.30 *(978-0-618-43735-1(5)*, 2-01228); (Illus.). 288p. lib. bdg. 21.80 *(978-0-618-33424-7(6)*, 2-01013) Great Source Education Group, Inc.

—Earth Science. I.t. ed. 2004. (McDougal Littell Middle School Science Ser.). (ENG.). 960p. (gr. 6-8). 84.85 *(978-0-618-30368-7(5)*, 2-01003) Great Source Education Group, Inc.

—Earth's Surface. 2004. (McDougal Littell Science Ser.). (ENG.). 80p. (gr. 6-8). pap., lab manual ed. 14.70 *(978-0-618-43726-9(6)*, 2-01219) Great Source Education Group, Inc.

—Modules: Earth Science - Earth's Waters PE. 2004. (McDougal Littell Middle School Science Ser.). (ENG.). 64p. (gr. 6-8). 21.80 *(978-0-618-33417-9(3)*, 2-01007) Great Source Education Group, Inc.

—Modules: Physical Science - Earth's Atmosphere. 2004. (McDougal Littell Science Ser.). (ENG.). 64p. (gr. 6-8). pap., lab manual ed. 15.30 *(978-0-618-43725-2(8)*, 2-01218) Great Source Education Group, Inc.

—Modules: Physical Science; Earth's Waters. 2004. (McDougal Littell Science Ser.). (ENG.). 56p. (gr. 6-8). pap., lab manual ed. 15.30 *(978-0-618-43727-6(4)*, 2-01220) Great Source Education Group, Inc.

—Space Science. 2004. (McDougal Littell Middle School Science Ser.). (ENG., Illus.). 80p. (gr. 6-8). lib. bdg. 21.80 *(978-0-618-33421-6(1)*, 2-01011) Great Source Education Group, Inc.

McGill, Jordan. Earth Science Fair Projects. 2011. (gr. 3-5). pap. 12.95 *(978-1-61690-655-9(3)*, AV2 by Weigl); (Illus.). 24p. (J). 27.13 *(978-1-61690-651-1(0))* Weigl Pubs., Inc.

Meachen Rau, Dana. Earth Matters, 6 bks., Set. Incl. Air. lib. bdg. 15.95 *(978-0-7614-3042-1(3))*; Land. lib. bdg. 15.95 *(978-0-7614-3043-8(1))*; Life. lib. bdg. 15.95 *(978-0-7614-3044-5(X))*; Maps. lib. bdg. 15.95 *(978-0-7614-3046-9(6))*; Oceans. lib. bdg. 15.95 *(978-0-7614-3048-3(2))*; Space & Time. lib. bdg. 15.95 *(978-0-7614-3049-0(0))*; 32p. (gr. 1-2). (Bookworms: Earth Matters Ser.). 2008. Set lib. bdg. 95.70 *(978-0-7614-3040-7(7)*, Benchmark Bks.) Marshall Cavendish Corp.

—Earth Matters/El Planeta Es Importante, 6 bks., Set. Incl. Land/La Tierra. lib. bdg. 15.95 *(978-0-7614-3490-0(9))*; Life. lib. bdg. 15.95 *(978-0-7614-3491-7(7))*; Maps/Los Mapas. lib. bdg. 15.95 *(978-0-7614-3493-1(3))*; Oceans/Los Oceanos. lib. bdg. 15.95 *(978-0-7614-3494-8(1))*; Space & Time/El Tiempo y Espacio. lib. bdg. 15.95 *(978-0-7614-3496-2(8))*; 32p. (gr. k-1). (Bookworms — Bilingual Editions: Earth Matters/el Planeta Es Importante Ser.). (ENG & SPA.). 2008. Set lib. bdg. 95.70 *(978-0-7614-3487-0(9)*, Benchmark Bks.) Marshall Cavendish Corp.

Media, Cont. The Earth. 2008. (ENG., Illus.). 96p. (YA). 17.99 *(978-1-931703-00-0(0))* Contmedia Inc.

Medina, Phil. Homework Helpers: Earth Science. 2005. (Homework Helpers Ser.). (ENG., Illus.). 1p. (gr. 9-12). pap. 14.99 *(978-1-56414-767-7(3))* Career Pr., Inc.

Milbourne, Anna. Under the Ground. Riglietti, Serena, illus. 2006. 24p. (J). (gr. -1-3). 9.99 *(978-0-7945-1264-4(X)*, Usborne) EDC Publishing.

Miles Kelly Staff. Larger Than Life: Gigantic Views of the Microscopic. 2003. (Illus.). 48p. (J). 12.95 *(978-1-84236-020-0(5))* Miles Kelly Publishing, Ltd. GBR. Dist: Independent Pubs. Group.

Misztal, Fred. What I See in the Sky. 2012. (InfoMax Readers Ser.). (ENG., Illus.). 24p. (J). (gr. 1-2). pap. 8.25 *(978-1-4488-9061-3(6)*, Rosen Classroom) Rosen Publishing Group, Inc., The.

Modules: Earth Science; Earth's Atmosphere PE. 2005. (Module: Earth Science Ser.). (gr. 6-12). *(978-0-618-33415-5(7)*, 2-01005) Holt McDougal.

Modules: Physical Science. 2005. (Module: Physical Science Ser.). (gr. 6-12). cd-rom *(978-0-618-42030-8(4)*, 2-01144) Holt McDougal.

Mullins, Matt. Geoscientist. 2013. (21st Century Skills Library: Cool STEM Careers Ser.). (ENG.). 32p. (J). (gr. 4-8). 28.50 *(978-1-62431-004-1(4)*, 202467); pap. 14.21 *(978-1-62431-028-7(1)*, 202469) Cherry Lake Publishing.

Nadeau, Isaac. Learning about the Water Cycle with Graphic Organizers. 2009. (Graphic Organizers in Science Ser.). 24p. (gr. 3-4). 42.50 *(978-1-61513-052-8(7)*, PowerKids Pr.) Rosen Publishing Group, Inc., The.

Natural Wonders. (Natural Wonders Ser.). (ENG.). 24p. (gr. k-1). 2011. pap. 333.60 *(978-1-4296-6391-5(X))* 2010. pap. 43.74 *(978-1-4296-6222-2(0))* Capstone Press of Coughlan Cos. (Pebble Plus).

Navarro, Jose, et al. El Enorme Pequenoz de la Abuela Tierra.Tr. of Enormous Smallness of Grandmother Earth. (SPA.). 142p. (J). 10.95 *(978-84-7960-107-2(8))* Ediciones de la Torre ESP. Dist: Libros Sin Fronteras.

Ohanesian, Diane. Rocks, Rocks, Rocks. 2nd rev. ed. 2003. (BuildUp Ser.). (J). pap. 22.00 *(978-1-4108-0756-4(8))* Benchmark Education Co.

O'Shaughnessy, Tam E. Totally Amazing Careers in Earth Science. 2006. (J). 7.80 *(978-1-933798-02-8(5))* Sally Ride Science.

Over 1000 Fantastic Earth Facts. 2012. (Illus.). 512p. (J). pap. *(978-1-4351-4418-7(X))* Barnes & Noble, Inc.

Oxlade, Chris. Earth: Find Out about the Planet, Earthquakes, Volcanoes & Weather with 50 Great Experiments & Projects. 2009. (ENG., Illus.). 64p. (J). (gr. 4-7). pap. 7.99 *(978-1-84476-712-0(4))* Anness Publishing GBR. Dist: National Bk. Network.

Pebble Books: Earth & Outer Space. 2005. (YA). (gr. k-3). 594.00 *(978-0-7368-4222-8(5),* Pebble Bks.) Capstone Press of Coughlan Cos.

Phelan, Glen. Forces & Motion on Earth: Text Pairs. 2008. (Bridges/Navigators Ser.). (J). (gr. 6). 94.00 *(978-1-4108-8436-7(8))* Benchmark Education Co.

Pipe, Jim. Wonderful World. 2009. (ENG.). 112p. (J). (gr. 4-7). pap. 12.95 *(978-1-84696-204-2(8),* TickTock Books) Octopus Publishing Group GBR. Dist: Independent Pubs. Group.

Pratt, Leonie. Planet Earth: Level 2. Tudor, Andy & Haggerty, Tim, illus. 2007. (Beginners Nature Ser.). 32p. (J). 4.99 *(978-0-7945-1707-6(2),* Usborne) EDC Publishing.

Quinlan, Julia J. Latitude, Longitude, & Direction. 2012. (How to Use Maps Ser.). (ENG., Illus.). 24p. (J). (gr. 3-6). pap. 8.25 *(978-1-4488-6272-6(8),* PowerKids Pr.); lib. bdg. 22.60 *(978-1-4488-6157-6(8))* Rosen Publishing Group, Inc., The.

Quinlan, Julia J. Plate Tectonics. 2017. (J). ***(978-1-5383-0029-9(X))***; pap. ***(978-1-68048-832-6(5))*** Rosen Publishing Group, Inc., The.

Redmond, Stephanie L. Earth & Space. Taylor, David W., Jr. & Northcutt, Leslie L., illus. 2006. (Christian Kids Explore Ser.). 363p. (J). (gr. 3-7). per. *(978-1-892427-19-9(2))* Bright Ideas! Educational Resources.

Reed, Christina. Earth Science: Decade by Decade. 2008. (Twentieth-Century Science Ser.). (Illus.). 272p. (gr. 6-12). 49.50 *(978-0-8160-5533-3(5))* Facts On File, Inc.

Reilly, Kathleen M. Planet Earth: 25 Environmental Projects You Can Build Yourself. Rizvi, Farah, illus. 2008. (Build It Yourself Ser.). (ENG.). 128p. (J). (gr. 3-7). 21.95 *(978-1-934670-05-7(7))*; pap. 15.95 *(978-1-934670-04-0(9))* Octavio Publishing.

Reynolds, Shaye. Volcanoes. 2016. (Spotlight on Earth Science Ser.). 00024p. (J). (gr. 4-6). pap. 10.00 *(978-1-4994-2537-6(6),* PowerKids Pr.) Rosen Publishing Group, Inc., The.

Reynolds, Toby & Calver, Paul. Extreme Earth. 2015. (Visual Explorers Ser.). (ENG., Illus.). 32p. (J). (gr. 3-7). pap. 6.99 *(978-1-4380-0578-2(4))* Barron's Educational Series, Inc.

Rice, Dona Herweck, et al. Let's Explore Earth & Space Science, Grades 4-5. 2015. (Science Readers: Content & Literacy Ser.). (ENG., Illus.). 32p. (gr. 4-5). 89.90 *(978-1-4938-1423-7(0))* Shell Educational Publishing.

Ripley's Believe It Or Not! Staff, et al. Extreme Earth: Fun, Facts, & Earth-Shattering Stories... 2010. (Twist Ser.: 7). (ENG., Illus.). 48p. (J). 12.95 *(978-1-893951-78-5(2))* Ripley Entertainment, Inc.

Rockett, Paul. Seven Quintillion, Five Hundred Quadrillion Grains of Sand on Planet Earth. Ruffle, Mark, illus. 2015. (Big Countdown Ser.). (ENG.). 32p. (gr. 3-5). 29.99 *(978-1-4109-6880-7(4),* Raintree Perspectives) Heinemann-Raintree.

Royston, Angela. Planet Earth. 2017. (Discover & Share Ser.). (ENG., Illus.). 24p. (J). (gr. k-2). 16.99 *(978-1-4451-3809-1(3),* Franklin Watts) Hachette Children's Group GBR. Dist: Hachette Bk. Group.

Roza, Greg. Beneath Earth's Surface. 2009. (Reading Room Collection 2 Ser.). 24p. (gr. 3-4). 42.50 *(978-1-60851-958-3(9),* PowerKids Pr.) Rosen Publishing Group, Inc., The.

Rudenko, Dennis. Mountains & Canyons. 2016. (Spotlight on Earth Science Ser.). 00024p. (J). (gr. 4-6). pap. 10.00 *(978-1-4994-2527-7(9),* PowerKids Pr.) Rosen Publishing Group, Inc., The.

Saddleback, creator. Earth. 2008. (Factoscope Ser.). (Illus.). 64p. (YA). (gr. 8-12). per. 10.95 *(978-1-59905-233-5(4))* Saddleback Educational Publishing, Inc.

Saddleback Educational Publishing Staff, ed. Earth Science, 1 vol. 2013. (Science Ser.). (ENG.). 110p. (gr. 9-12). pap. 44.95 *(978-1-62250-034-5(2))* Saddleback Educational Publishing, Inc.

Salas, Laura Purdie. Home on the Earth: A Song about Earth's Layers, 1 vol. Garofoli, Viviana, illus. 2009. (Science Songs Ser.). (ENG.). 24p. (gr. 1-3). lib. bdg. 26.65 *(978-1-4048-5296-9(4))* Picture Window Bks.

Sally Ride Science Editors, Sally Ride Science. What Do You Want to Be? Explore Earth Sciences. 2004. (J). 6.00 *(978-0-9753920-2-7(6))* Sally Ride Science.

Scholastic Library Publishing. A True Book—Earth Science. 2012. (J). 116.00 *(978-0-531-26775-2(X),* Children's Pr.) Scholastic Library Publishing.

Schuh, Mari C. Compost Basics. 2011. (Science Builders Ser.). (ENG.). 24p. (gr. k-1). pap. 41.70 *(978-1-4296-7112-5(2),* Pebble Plus) Capstone Press of Coughlan Cos.

—Earthquakes [Scholastic]. 2010. (Earth in Action Ser.). (ENG.). 24p. pap. 0.49 *(978-1-4296-5799-0(5),* Pebble Plus) Capstone Press of Coughlan Cos.

Science & Technology for Books, Life & Earth Sciences Library Set, 6 vols. 2004. (Illus.). 64p. (J). *(978-1-933008-25-7(3))* Smithsonian Science Education Ctr. (SSEC).

Seuling, Barbara. Earth Is Like a Giant Magnet: And Other Freaky Facts about Planets, Oceans, & Volcanoes. Skeens, Matthew, illus. (Freaky Facts Ser.). 40p. 2010. pap. 0.50 *(978-1-4048-6202-9(1))* 2008. (gr. 3-5). pap. 3.00 *(978-1-4048-5289-1(1))* Picture Window Bks. (Nonfiction Picture Bks.).

Skelton, Renee. Forecast Earth: The Story of Climate Scientist Inez Fung. 2006. (ENG., Illus.). 128p. (gr. 7-9). per. 19.95 *(978-0-309-09554-9(9),* Joseph Henry Pr.) National Academies Pr.

Slade, Suzanne. The Rock Cycle. 2009. (Cycles in Nature Ser.). 24p. (gr. 3-3). 42.50 *(978-1-61512-116-8(1),* PowerKids Pr.) Rosen Publishing Group, Inc., The.

Socías, Marcel. Secretos de la Tierra. 2005. (Nuestro Planet Ser.). (SPA., Illus.). 31p. (J). (gr. 4-7). 10.40 *(978-84-342-2692-0(8),* PR33937) Parramon Ediciones S.A. ESP. Dist: Lectorum Pubns., Inc.

Sohn, Emily. Experiments in Earth Science & Weather with Toys & Everyday Stuff. 2015. (Fun Science Ser.). (ENG., Illus.). 24p. (gr. 1-2). lib. bdg. 25.32 *(978-1-4914-5035-2(5))* Capstone Press of Coughlan Cos.

Stephens, Catherine. Volcanoes. 2007. (Language, Literacy, & Vocabulary - Reading Expeditions Ser.). (ENG., Illus.). 36p. (J). pap. 18.95 *(978-0-7922-5434-8(1))* CENGAGE Learning.

Stradling, Jan. Earth Materials: Level I, 6 vols. (First Explorers Ser.). 24p. (gr. 1-2). 29.95 *(978-0-7699-1444-2(6))* Shortland Pubns. (U. S. A.) Inc.

Strother, Ruth. B Is for Blue Planet: An Earth Science Alphabet. Marstall, Robert, illus. 2011. (Sleeping Bear Alphabets Ser.). (ENG.). 40p. (J). (gr. k-6). lib. bdg. 16.95 *(978-1-58536-454-1(1))* Sleeping Bear Pr.

Sundance/Newbridge LLC Staff. Earth's Changing Surface. 2004. (Reading PowerWorks Ser.). (gr. 1-3). 37.50 *(978-0-7608-7807-1(2))*; pap. 6.10 *(978-0-7608-7808-8(0))* Sundance/Newbridge Educational Publishing.

—Sink or Float? 2007. (Early Science Ser.). (gr. k-3). 18.95 *(978-1-4007-6269-9(3))*; pap. 6.10 *(978-1-4007-6265-1(0))* Sundance/Newbridge Educational Publishing.

Teacher Created Materials Staff, ed. Earth & Space Science: Add-on Pack. 2007. (Science Readers Ser.). 89.99 *(978-1-4333-0067-7(2))* Teacher Created Materials, Inc.

Terp, Gail. What Is a Solstice? 2016. (Everyday Earth Science Ser.). (ENG.). 24p. (J). (gr. k-3). 27.07 *(978-1-5038-0792-1(4),* 210628) Child's World, Inc., The.

Thompson, Gare & National Geographic Learning Staff. Kids Care for the Earth. 2006. (Nonfiction Reading & Writing Workshops Ser.). (ENG.). 32p. (J). (gr. 3-6). pap. 17.95 *(978-0-7922-8675-2(8))* CENGAGE Learning.

La Tierra Increible. (SPA.). (YA). (gr. 5-8). pap. 13.56 *(978-950-04-1967-3(X))* Emecé Editores S.A. ARG. Dist: Lectorum Pubns., Inc.

A True Book: Earth Science, 6 vols., Set. Incl. Earthquakes. Than, Ker. 31.00 *(978-0-531-16882-0(4))*; Floods. Koponen, Libby. 31.00 *(978-0-531-16883-7(2))*; Thunderstorms. Stiefel, Chana. (Illus.). 31.00 *(978-0-531-16884-4(0))*; Tsunamis. Stiefel, Chana. (Illus.). 31.00 *(978-0-531-16885-1(9))*; Volcanoes. Landau, Elaine. (Illus.). 31.00 *(978-0-531-16886-8(7))*; Wildfires. Trammel, Howard K. 31.00 *(978-0-531-16887-5(5))*; 48p. (J). (gr. 2-5). 2009. Set lib. bdg. 464.00 *(978-0-531-27903-8(0),* Children's Pr.) Scholastic Library Publishing.

A True Book-Earth Science Spring 2012 Set Of 6. 2012. (True Book Ser.). 168.00 *(978-0-531-25914-6(5),* Children's Pr.) Scholastic Library Publishing.

Twist, Clint. Extreme Earth. 2010. (Ripley Twists Ser.). (Illus.). 48p. (J). (gr. 3-18). lib. bdg. 19.95 *(978-1-4222-1829-7(5),* 1318258) Mason Crest.

Twist, Clint, et al. Extreme Earth. 2009. (Ripley Twists Ser.). (Illus.). 48p. (J). (gr. 3-18). pap. 8.95 *(978-1-4222-2067-2(2),* 1318258) Mason Crest.

Two-Can Publishing Ltd. Staff, contrib. by. Planet Earth. 2004. (Illus.). 192p. (J). (gr. 3-6). 24.95 *(978-1-58728-049-8(3),* Two-Can Publishing) T&N Children's Publishing.

Van Gorp, Lynn. Pioneers of Earth Science, 1 vol. 2007. (Science Readers Ser.). (ENG., Illus.). 32p. (J). (gr. 3-3). pap. 8.99 *(978-0-7439-0558-9(X))* Shell Educational Publishing.

van Rose, Susanna & Dorling Kindersley Publishing Staff. Earth. 2013. (DK Eyewitness Bks.). (ENG.). 72p. (J). (gr. 3-7). 16.99 *(978-1-4654-0897-6(5),* DK Children) Dorling Kindersley Publishing, Inc.

VanCleave, Janice. Even More of Janice VanCleave's Wild, Wacky, & Weird Earth Science Experiments. 2017. (Janice VanCleave's Wild, Wacky, & Weird Science Experiments Ser.). 64p. (J). (gr. 10-10). 34.45 ***(978-1-4994-6689-8(7)***, Rosen Central) Rosen Publishing Group, Inc., The.

VanCleave, Janice. Step-by-Step Science Experiments in Earth Science. 2012. (Janice VanCleave's First-Place Science Fair Projects Ser.). (ENG., Illus.). 80p. (J). (gr. 5-8). 33.25 *(978-1-4488-6983-1(8))*; pap. 14.15 *(978-1-4488-8467-4(5))* Rosen Publishing Group, Inc., The. (Rosen Reference).

VanCleave, Janice Pratt. Janice VanCleave's Wild, Wacky, & Weird Earth Science Experiments. 2016. (Janice VanCleave's Wild, Wacky, & Weird Science Experiments Ser.). (ENG., Illus.). 64p. (J). (gr. 5-5). pap. 12.95 *(978-1-4777-8973-5(1),* Rosen Reference) Rosen Publishing Group, Inc., The.

VanCleave, Janice Pratt. Many More of Janice Vancleave's Wild, Wacky, & Weird Earth Science Experiments. 2017. (J). ***(978-1-4994-3951-9(2)***, Rosen Reference) Rosen Publishing Group, Inc., The.

Walsh, Kenneth. Our Earth, 1 vol. 2nd rev. ed. 2013. (Nonfiction Readers Ser.). (ENG., Illus.). 28p. (J). (gr. 2-2). pap. 23.96 *(978-1-4807-1052-8(0))* Shell Educational Publishing.

Warhol, Tom. Earth's Biomes, 6 bks., Set. Incl. Chaparral & Scrub. (gr. 6-7). lib. bdg. 34.21 *(978-0-7614-2195-5(5))*; Desert. (gr. 6-7). lib. bdg. 34.21 *(978-0-7614-2194-8(7))*; Forest. (J). lib. bdg. 32.79 *(978-0-7614-2189-4(0))*; Grassland. (J). (gr. 3-7). lib. bdg. 32.79 *(978-0-7614-2196-2(3))*; Tundra. (gr. 6-7). lib. bdg. 34.21 *(978-0-7614-2193-1(9))*; Water. (gr. 6-7). lib. bdg. 34.21 *(978-0-7614-2192-4(0))*; (Illus.). 80p. 2006. 2007. Set lib. bdg. 196.71 *(978-0-7614-2188-7(2),* Benchmark Bks.) Marshall Cavendish Corp.

Williams, Brian. Planet Earth: Biggest & Best. 2004. (Biggest & Best Ser.). (Illus.). 40p. (J). pap. 7.95 *(978-1-84236-029-3(9))* Miles Kelly Publishing, Ltd. GBR. Dist: Independent Pubs. Group.

Williams, Zella. Experiments about Planet Earth. (Do-It-Yourself Science Ser.). 24p. (gr. 2-3). 2009. 47.90 *(978-1-61512-185-4(4),* PowerKids Pr.) 2007. (Illus.). (J). lib. bdg. 25.25 *(978-1-4042-3662-2(7))* Rosen Publishing Group, Inc., The.

Wolny, Philip, ed. Earth Science, 1 vol., 1. 2016. (Study of Science Ser.). (ENG.). 00104p. (YA). (gr. 8-8). 36.25 *(978-1-68048-226-3(2),* Britannica Educational Publishing) Rosen Publishing Group, Inc., The.

Woyt, Barbara A. Geology. 2016. (Study of Science Ser.). 00104p. (YA). (gr. 8-8). 36.25 *(978-1-5081-0426-1(3))* Rosen Publishing Group, Inc., The.

Zuchora-Walske, Christine. Key Discoveries in Earth & Space Science. 2015. (Science Discovery Timelines Ser.). (ENG., Illus.). 48p. (J). (gr. 6-8). pap. 8.99 *(978-1-4677-6157-4(5))*; lib. bdg. 30.65 *(978-1-4677-5787-4(X))* Lerner Publishing Group. (Lerner Pubns.).

20 Questions: Earth Science. 2013. (20 Questions: Earth Science Ser.). 24p. (J). (gr. 3-6). 135.60 *(978-1-4488-9965-4(6))*; pap. 297.00 *(978-1-4777-1250-4(X))*; pap. 49.50 *(978-1-4777-1249-8(6))* Rosen Publishing Group, Inc., The. (PowerKids Pr.).

EARTHQUAKES

see also San Francisco Earthquake and Fire, Calif., 1906; Volcanoes

Anderson, Michael. Investigating Plate Tectonics, Earthquakes, & Volcanoes. 2011. (Illus.). 87p. (J). lib. bdg. 31.70 *(978-1-61530-504-9(1))* Rosen Publishing Group, Inc., The.

Armour, Cy. Earthquakes!, 1 vol. 2nd rev. ed. 2014. (TIME for KIDS(r) Nonfiction Readers Ser.). (ENG., Illus.). 24p. (J). (gr. 2-2). pap. 23.96 *(978-1-4807-1040-5(7))* Shell Educational Publishing.

—Earthquakes!, 1 vol. 2nd rev. ed. 2011. (Nonfiction Readers Ser.). (ENG.). 24p. (J). (gr. 2-2). pap. 6.99 *(978-1-4333-3613-3(8))* Teacher Created Materials, Inc.

Aronin, Miriam. Earthquake in Haiti. 2010. (Code Red Ser.). 32p. (YA). (gr. 2-5). lib. bdg. 25.27 *(978-1-936088-66-9(5))* Bearport Publishing Co., Inc.

Baker, John R. The World's Worst Earthquakes. 2016. (World's Worst Natural Disasters Ser.). (ENG., Illus.). 32p. (gr. 1-2). lib. bdg. 26.65 *(978-1-5157-1786-7(0))* Capstone Press of Coughlan Cos.

Ball, Jacqueline A. & Ball, Jacqueline A. Earthquakes. 2004. (Discovery Channel School Science Ser.). (Illus.). 32p. (gr. 4-8). lib. bdg. 26.00 *(978-0-8368-3378-2(3),* Gareth Stevens Learning Library) Stevens, Gareth Publishing LLLP.

Baltzer, Rochelle. Earthquakes, 1 vol. 2011. (Natural Disasters Ser.). (ENG., Illus.). 32p. (J). (gr. 2-5). 28.50 *(978-1-61783-031-0(3))* ABDO Publishing Co.

Bauer, Marion Dane. Earthquake! Wallace, John, illus. 2010. (Rise & Shine Ser.). (ENG.). 32p. (C). (gr. -1-1). pap. 6.95 *(978-1-4169-2551-4(1))* National Geographic School Publishing, Inc.

Baxter, Roberta. Seismology: Our Violent Earth, 1 vol. 2014. (History of Science Ser.). (ENG.). 112p. (J). (gr. 6-12). lib. bdg. 35.64 *(978-1-62403-565-4(5),* Essential Library) ABDO Publishing Co.

Benchmark Education Company. Earthquake! (Teacher Guide) 2005. *(978-1-4108-4641-9(5))* Benchmark Education Co.

Benoit, Peter. The Haitian Earthquake of 2010. 2011. (True Bk Ser.). (ENG., Illus.). 48p. (J). pap. 6.95 *(978-0-531-26625-0(7))*; (gr. 3-5). lib. bdg. 29.00 *(978-0-531-25420-2(8))* Scholastic Library Publishing. (Children's Pr.).

Berger, Susan J. Earthquake! Ruble, Eugene, illus. 28p. 2013. 19.95 *(978-1-61633-430-7(4))* 2009. pap. 11.95 *(978-1-933090-66-5(9))* Guardian Angel Publishing, Inc.

Bone, Emily. Earthquakes & Tsunamis. 2012. (Beginner's Science Ser.). 32p. (J). bds. 4.99 *(978-0-7945-3281-9(0),* Usborne) EDC Publishing.

Branley, Franklyn M. Earthquakes. Lloyd, Megan, illus. 2015. (Let's-Read-And-Find-Out Science 2 Ser.). (ENG.). 40p. (J). (gr. -1-3). pap. 6.99 *(978-0-06-238202-3(0))* HarperCollins Pubs.

—Earthquakes. 2015. (Let's Read & Find Out Science Stage 2 Ser.). (J). lib. bdg. 17.20 *(978-0-606-37642-6(9))* Turtleback Bks.

—Earthquakes. Lloyd, Megan, illus. rev. ed. 2005. (Let's-Read-and-Find-Out Science Ser.). 40p. (J). (gr. k-4). (ENG.). 15.99 *(978-0-06-028008-6(5))*; lib. bdg. 16.89 *(978-0-06-028009-3(3))* HarperCollins Pubs.

Brannon, Barbara. Discover Earthquakes. 2005. (J). pap. *(978-1-4108-5132-1(X))* Benchmark Education Co.

Brennan, Linda Crotta. We Have Earthquakes. 2014. (Tell Me Why Library). (ENG., Illus.). 24p. (J). (gr. 2-5). 25.64 *(978-1-63188-011-7(X),* 205451) Cherry Lake Publishing.

Brooks, Susie. Earthquakes & Volcanoes. 2016. (Where on Earth? Ser.). 32p. (gr. 5-4). 26.25 *(978-1-4994-2256-6(3),* PowerKids Pr.) Rosen Publishing Group, Inc., The.

Bulletpoints Volcanoes & Earthquakes. 2005. (Illus.). (J). per. 4.99 *(978-1-933581-06-4(9))* Byeway Bks.

Burgan, Michael. Surviving Earthquakes, 1 vol. 2011. (Children's True Stories: Natural Disasters Ser.). (ENG.). 32p. (gr. 3-3). pap. 8.29 *(978-1-4109-4097-1(7))*; 30.65 *(978-1-4109-4090-2(X))* Heinemann-Raintree. (Raintree Perspectives).

Clarke, Catriona. Living in an Earthquake Zone. 2017. (ENG., Illus.). 32p. (J). pap. 8.99 ***(978-0-00-820878-3(6))*** HarperCollins Pubs. Ltd. GBR. Dist: Independent Pubs. Group.

Cole, Joanna. Volcanoes & Earthquakes. 2014. (Magic School Bus Presents Ser.). lib. bdg. 17.20 *(978-0-606-36333-4(5))* Turtleback Bks.

Cole, Joanna & Jackson, Tom. Volcanoes & Earthquakes. Degen, Bruce & Bracken, Carolyn, illus. 2014. (Magic School Bus Presents Ser.). (ENG.). 32p. (J). (gr. 1-3). pap. 6.99 *(978-0-545-68584-9(2),* Scholastic Paperbacks) Scholastic, Inc.

Collins. Collins Fascinating Facts - Earthquakes & Volcanoes. rev. ed. 2016. (Collins Fascinating Facts Ser.). (ENG., Illus.). 72p. (J). (gr. 1-3). pap. 10.99 *(978-0-00-816927-5(6))* HarperCollins Pubs. Ltd. GBR. Dist: Independent Pubs. Group.

Collins, Terry. Buried in Rubble: True Stories of Surviving Earthquakes. Chater, Mack, illus. 2015. (True Stories of Survival Ser.). (ENG.). 32p. (gr. 3-4). lib. bdg. 30.65 *(978-1-4914-6570-7(0),* Graphic Library) Capstone Press of Coughlan Cos.

Connolly, Sean. Earthquakes. 2003. (Illus.). 32p. (J). lib. bdg. 27.10 *(978-1-58340-388-4(4))* Black Rabbit Bks.

Cooke, Tim. 1906 San Francisco Earthquake. 2005. (Disasters Ser.). (Illus.). 32p. (gr. 2-6). lib. bdg. 26.00 *(978-0-8368-4494-8(7),* Gareth Stevens Learning Library) Stevens, Gareth Publishing LLLP.

Dahlstrom, Kathryn. Trapped by an Earthquake. Date not set. (Good News Club Ser.). (J). (gr. 4-11). pap. 4.99 *(978-1-55976-827-6(4))* CEF Pr.

Davis, Graeme. Earthquakes. 2012. (21st Century Skills Library: Real World Math Ser.). (ENG., Illus.). 32p. (J). (gr. 4-8). pap. 14.21 *(978-1-61080-411-0(2),* 201343); lib. bdg. 28.50 *(978-1-61080-323-6(X),* 201308) Cherry Lake Publishing.

Dwyer, Helen. Earthquakes. 2010. (Eyewitness Disaster Ser.). 32p. (J). (gr. 2-5). 28.50 *(978-1-60870-001-1(1))* Marshall Cavendish Corp.

Earthquake! Individual Title Six-Packs. (Bookweb Ser.). 32p. (gr. 5-18). 34.00 *(978-0-7635-3785-2(3))* Rigby Education.

Earthquake Experts: 6 Small Books. (Greetings Ser.: Vol. 2). 32p. (gr. 3-5). 31.00 *(978-0-7635-2060-1(8))* Rigby Education.

Earthquake Experts: Big Book. (Greetings Ser.: Vol. 2). 32p. (gr. 3-5). 31.00 *(978-0-7635-3236-9(3))* Rigby Education.

Earthquakes: Level Q, 6 vols., Vol. 3. (Explorers Ser.). 32p. (gr. 3-6). 44.95 *(978-0-7699-0622-5(2))* Shortland Pubns. (U. S. A.) Inc.

Earth's Crust. 2007. (Illus.). 48p. (J). (gr. 2-5). pap. 8.95 *(978-0-8225-6585-7(4))* Lerner Publishing Group.

Elkins, Elizabeth. Investigating Earthquakes. 2017. (Investigating Natural Disasters Ser.). (ENG., Illus.). 32p. (gr. 3-4). lib. bdg. 27.99 *(978-1-5157-4038-4(2),* Edge Bks.) Capstone Press of Coughlan Cos.

Englar, Mary. The Worst Earthquakes of All Time. 2012. (Epic Disasters Ser.). (ENG.). 32p. (gr. 3-4). pap. 47.70 *(978-1-4296-8507-8(7))*; pap. 8.29 *(978-1-4296-8013-4(X))* Capstone Press of Coughlan Cos. (Edge Bks.).

Expertas en Terremotos: 6 Small Books. (Saludos Ser.: Vol. 2). (SPA.). (gr. 3-5). 31.00 *(978-0-7635-2066-3(7))* Rigby Education.

Farndon, John. Extreme Earthquakes & Tsunamis. 2017. (When Nature Attacks Ser.). (ENG., Illus.). 32p. (J). (gr. 3-6). 26.65 ***(978-1-5124-3222-0(9))*** Lerner Publishing Group.

Farndon, John & Riley, Peter D. Volcanoes & Earthquakes & Other Facts about Planet Earth: Bulletpoints. 2003. (Bulletpoints Ser.). (Illus.). 40p. (J). pap. 6.95 *(978-1-84236-238-9(0))* Miles Kelly Publishing, Ltd. GBR. Dist: Independent Pubs. Group.

Freeburg, Jessica. Collapse & Chaos: The Story of the 2010 Earthquake in Haiti. 2017. (Tangled History Ser.). (ENG., Illus.). 112p. (gr. 3-4). lib. bdg. 31.99 *(978-1-5157-3606-6(7))* Capstone Press of Coughlan Cos.

Freed, Kira. The Day the Earth Shook. 2017. (Text Connections Guided Close Reading Ser.). (J). (gr. 2). *(978-1-4900-1837-9(9))* Benchmark Education Co.

—Surviving the 2011 Japanese Earthquake & Tsunami. 2015. (Surviving Disaster Ser.). (ENG., Illus.). 48p. (J). (gr. 5-6). 30.25 *(978-1-4994-3645-7(9),* Rosen Central) Rosen Publishing Group, Inc., The.

Ganeri, Anita. Shaky Ground. 2004. (Turbulent Planet Ser.). (Illus.). 48p. (J). 28.56 *(978-1-4109-0589-5(6))* Heinemann-Raintree.

—Volcanes y terremotos/Earthquakes & Volcanoes. 2011. 16p. pap. *(978-607-404-319-8(1),* Silver Dolphin en Español) Advanced Marketing, S. de R. L. de C. V.

Gates, Alexander E. & Ritchie, David. Encyclopedia of Earthquakes & Volcanoes. 3rd rev. ed. 2007. (Science Encyclopedia Ser.). 368p. pap. 21.95 *(978-0-8160-7120-3(9),* Checkmark Bks.) Facts On File, Inc.

Gonzales, Doreen. Earthquakes. 2012. (Killer Disasters Ser.). (ENG., Illus.). 24p. (J). (gr. 3-6). 22.60 *(978-1-4488-7442-2(4))*; pap. 8.25 *(978-1-4488-7515-3(3))* Rosen Publishing Group, Inc., The. (PowerKids Pr.).

Graham, Ian. Earthquakes. 2013. (21st Century Science Ser.). (ENG.). 64p. (J). (gr. 4-7). pap. 7.95 *(978-1-84898-192-8(9),* TickTock Books) Octopus Publishing Group GBR. Dist: Independent Pubs. Group.

Gray-Wilburn, Renée. Earthquakes!, 1 vol. Sotirovski, Aleksandar, illus. 2012. (First Graphics: Wild Earth Ser.). (ENG.). 24p. (gr. 1-2). pap. 6.29 *(978-1-4296-7950-3(6))*; pap. 35.70 *(978-1-4296-8370-8(8))*; lib. bdg. 23.99 *(978-1-4296-7605-2(1))* Capstone Press of Coughlan Cos.

Green, Jen. Understanding Volcanoes & Earthquakes. 2008. (Our Earth Ser.). (Illus.). 24p. (YA). (gr. 1-4). lib. bdg. 22.60 *(978-1-4042-4276-0(7))* Rosen Publishing Group, Inc., The.

Griffey, Harriet. Earthquakes & Other Natural Disasters, Level 4. 2010. (DK Readers Ser.). (ENG.). 48p. (J). (gr. 2-5). 3.99 *(978-0-7566-5932-5(9),* DK Children) Dorling Kindersley Publishing, Inc.

Group/McGraw-Hill, Wright. Forces of Nature: Level K, 6 vols., Vol. 2. (First Explorers Ser.). 24p. (gr. 1-2). 34.95 *(978-0-7699-1458-9(6))* Shortland Pubns. (U. S. A.) Inc.

Gullard, Pamela & Lund, Nancy. Life on the San Andreas Fault: A History of Portola Valley. 2003. (Illus.). 288p. 60.00 *(978-0-942087-19-2(4))* Scottwall Assocs.

Hamilton, S. L. Earthquakes. 2012. 32p. 27.07 *(978-1-61783-259-8(6),* Abdo & Daughters) ABDO Publishing Co.

Hanel, Rachael. Can You Survive an Earthquake? An Interactive Survival Adventure, 1 vol. 2013. (You Choose: Survival Ser.). (ENG.). 112p. (gr. 3-4). pap. 6.95 *(978-1-62065-709-6(0))*; pap. 41.70 *(978-1-62065-710-2(4))*; lib. bdg. 31.99 *(978-1-4296-9979-2(5))* Capstone Press of Coughlan Cos. (You Choose Bks.).

Harkins, William & Harkins, Susan. Earthquake in Loma Prieta, California 1989. 2005. (Natural Disasters Ser.). (Illus.). 32p. (J). (gr. 1-4). lib. bdg. 25.70 *(978-1-58415-417-4(9))* Mitchell Lane Pubs., Inc.

Harper, Kathryn. Earthquakes White Band. Dean, Venitia, illus. 2016. (Cambridge Reading Adventures Ser.). (ENG.). 24p. pap. 7.19 *(978-1-316-50342-3(9))* Cambridge Univ. Pr.

Harris, Nicolas. Earthquakes Through Time. 2009. (Fast Forward Ser.). 32p. (YA). (gr. 2-5). lib. bdg. 25.25 *(978-1-4358-2803-2(8))* Rosen Publishing Group, Inc., The.

Harrison, David L. Earthquakes: Earth's Mightiest Moments. Nathan, Cheryl, illus. 2004. (Earth Works). (ENG.). 32p. (J). (gr. 1-2). 15.95 *(978-1-59078-243-9(7))* Boyds Mills Pr.

Hawkins, John. Earthquake Disasters. 2011. (Catastrophe! Ser.). (ENG., Illus.). 48p. (J). (gr. 5-9). lib. bdg. 29.25 *(978-1-4488-6003-6(2))* Rosen Publishing Group, Inc., The.

Henningfeld, Diane Andrews, ed. The Haiti Earthquake. 2012. (Perspectives on Modern World History Ser.). (ENG., Illus.). 224p. (J). (gr. 10-12). lib. bdg. 42.45 *(978-0-7377-6367-6(1),* Greenhaven Pr., Inc.) Cengage Gale.

Hodgkins, Fran. Half & Half-Earthquake! Hunt, Judith, illus. 2011. (ENG.). 52p. (J). 9.95 *(978-1-60115-217-6(5));* pap. 4.99 *(978-1-60115-218-3(3))* Treasure Bay, Inc.

Hoffman, Steven M. Volcanoes & Earthquakes: Making & Moving Rock. 2011. (Rock It! Ser.). (Illus.). 24p. (J). pap. 8.25 *(978-1-4488-2704-6(3));* lib. bdg. 22.60 *(978-1-4488-2559-2(8))* Rosen Publishing Group, Inc., The. (PowerKids Pr.).

Holt, Rinehart and Winston Staff. Holt Science & Technology Chapter 8: Earth Science: Earthquakes. 5th ed. 2004. (Illus.). pap. 12.86 *(978-0-03-030301-2(X))* Holt McDougal.

Hoobler, Dorothy & Hoobler, Thomas. What Was the San Francisco Earthquake? Hammond, Ted, illus. 2016. (What Was? Ser.). (ENG.). 112p. (J). (gr. 3-7). 5.99 *(978-0-399-54159-9(4));* lib. bdg. 15.99 *(978-0-399-54212-1(4))* Penguin Young Readers Group. (Grosset & Dunlap).

—What Was the San Francisco Earthquake? Hammond, Ted, illus. 2016. (What Was... ? Ser.). (ENG.). 112p. (J). (gr. 3-7). 16.00 *(978-0-606-39329-4(3))* Turtleback Bks.

Jennings, Terry J. Earthquakes & Tsunamis. 2009. (Amazing Planet Earth Ser.). 32p. (gr. 4-7). 31.35 *(978-1-59920-372-0(3))* Black Rabbit Bks.

Jerome, Kate Boehm & National Geographic Learning Staff. Volcanoes & Earthquakes. 2007. (Language, Literacy, & Vocabulary - Reading Expeditions Ser.). (ENG., Illus.). 32p. (J). pap. 17.95 *(978-0-7922-8874-9(2))* CENGAGE Learning.

Johnson, Rebecca L. & National Geographic Learning Staff. The San Francisco Earthquake. 2007. (Content-Based Chapter Bks.). (ENG., Illus.). 68p. (C). pap. 26.95 *(978-0-7922-5864-3(9))* National Geographic School Publishing, Inc.

Katirgis, Jane & Drohan, Michele Ingber. Eerie Earthquakes. 2015. (Earth's Natural Disasters Ser.). (ENG., Illus.). 32p. (J). (gr. 3-4). 25.27 *(978-0-7660-6795-0(5))* Enslow Pubs., Inc.

Katirgis, Jane & Ingber Drohan, Michele. Eerie Earthquakes. 2015. (Earth's Natural Disasters Ser.). (ENG.). 32p. (J). (gr. 3-4). pap. 10.52 *(978-0-7660-6793-6(9))* Enslow Pubs., Inc.

Koontz, Robin. The Science of a Tsunami. 2015. (21st Century Skills Library: Disaster Science Ser.). (ENG., Illus.). 32p. (J). (gr. 4-8). 29.93 *(978-1-63362-483-2(8),* 206840) Cherry Lake Publishing.

Krensky, Stephen. Lizzie Newton & the San Francisco Earthquake. 2010. pap. 56.72 *(978-0-7613-6928-8(7))* Lerner Publishing Group.

Krohn, Katherine. The Earth-Shaking Facts about Earthquakes with Max Axiom, Super Scientist, 1 vol. Smith, Tod G. & Milgrom, Al, illus. 2008. (Graphic Science Ser.). (ENG.). 32p. (gr. 3-4). per. 8.10 *(978-1-4296-1759-8(4),* Graphic Library) Capstone Press of Coughlan Cos.

Krohn, Katherine E. The Earth-Shaking Facts about Earthquakes with Max Axiom, Super Scientist. Smith, Tod G. & Milgrom, Al, illus. 2008. (Graphic Science Ser.). (ENG.). 32p. (gr. 3-4). 30.65 *(978-1-4296-1328-6(9),* Graphic Library) Capstone Press of Coughlan Cos.

Latimer, Kiki. Heal of the Hand. Griffeth, Bunny, illus. 2012. 44p. (J). pap. 19.50 *(978-1-58432-851-3(7))* Educa Vision Inc.

Levy, Janey. World's Worst Earthquakes. 2009. (Deadly Disasters Ser.). 24p. (gr. 2-6). pap. 9.40 *(978-1-4042-4537-2(5),* Rosen Classroom); (gr. 2-3). 42.50 *(978-1-61512-138-0(2),* PowerKids Pr.); (Illus.). (J). lib. bdg. 22.60 *(978-1-4042-4513-6(8))* Rosen Publishing Group, Inc., The.

Levy, Matthys & Salvadori, Mario. Earthquakes, Volcanoes, & Tsunamis: Projects & Principles for Beginning Geologists. 2009. (ENG., Illus.). 160p. (J). (gr. 4). pap. 14.95 *(978-1-55652-801-9(9))* Chicago Review Pr., Inc.

Lies, Anne. The Earthquake in Haiti, 1 vol. 2010. (Essential Events Set 5 Ser.). (ENG., Illus.). 112p. (J). (gr. 6-12). lib. bdg. 35.64 *(978-1-61613-682-6(0))* ABDO Publishing Co.

Los Terremotos, 6 vols., Vol. 3. (Explorers. Exploradores Nonfiction Sets Ser.). (SPA.). (gr. 3-6). *(978-0-7699-0658-4(3))* Shortland Pubns. (U. S. A.) Inc.

Lusted, Marcia Amidon. 2011 Japan Disasters, 1 vol. 2011. (Essential Events Set 7 Ser.). (ENG.). 112p. (J). (gr. 6-12). lib. bdg. 35.64 *(978-1-61783-179-9(4))* ABDO Publishing Co.

Mara, Wil. How Do Earthquakes Happen? 2010. (Tell Me Why, Tell Me How 4 Ser.). 32p. (gr. 3-5). 29.93 *(978-0-7614-4826-6(8))* Marshall Cavendish GBR. Dist: Marshall Cavendish Corp.

Markovics, Joyce. Earthquake. 2014. (It's a Disaster! Ser.). (Illus.). 24p. (J). (gr. -1-3). lib. bdg. 23.93 *(978-1-62724-128-1(0))* Bearport Publishing Co., Inc.

Markovics, Joyce L. Terremoto. 2014. (Pedacitos Primeros Lectores: Que Desastre! Ser.). (SPA., Illus.). 24p. (J). (gr. -1-2). lib. bdg. 23.93 *(978-1-62724-247-9(3))* Bearport Publishing Co., Inc.

Martin, Claudia. My Little Book of Volcanoes & Earthquakes. 2014. (Illus.). 64p. (J). *(978-1-4351-5531-2(9))* Barnes & Noble, Inc.

McCay, William. After the Earthquake & Después del Terremoto: 6 English, 6 Spanish Adaptations, 122 vols., Vol. 2. 2011. (Navigators Ser.). (J). instr.'s gde. ed. 97.00 net. *(978-1-4108-1776-1(8),* 17768) Benchmark Education Co.

McDougall, Chros. San Francisco Earthquake & Fire, 1 vol. 2013. (History's Greatest Disasters Ser.). (ENG.). 48p. (J). (gr. 3-6). lib. bdg. 32.79 *(978-1-61783-959-7(0))* ABDO Publishing Co.

McDougall, Chris. San Francisco Earthquake & Fire Paperback. 2013. (J). pap. 15.64 *(978-1-62403-024-6(6),* Core Library) ABDO Publishing Co.

McFadzean, Lesley. Earthquakes: on Shaky Ground: On Shaky Ground, 1 vol., 1. 2014. (Discovery Education: Earth & Space Science Ser.). (ENG.). 32p. (gr. 3-6). 26.25 *(978-1-4777-6182-3(9),* PowerKids Pr.) Rosen Publishing Group, Inc., The.

McLeish, Ewan. Earthquakes in Action. 2009. (Natural Disasters in Action Ser.). (Illus.). 48p. (gr. 5-8). pap. 11.75 *(978-1-4358-5135-1(8),* Rosen Classroom) Rosen Publishing Group, Inc., The.

Mehta-Jones, Shilpa. Earthquake Alert! 3rd rev. ed. 2011. (ENG., Illus.). 32p. (J). *(978-0-7787-1590-0(6));* (Disaster Alert! Ser.: No. 15). pap. *(978-0-7787-1623-5(6))* Crabtree Publishing Co.

Meister, Cari. Earthquakes. 2015. (Illus.). 24p. (J). lib. bdg. 25.65 *(978-1-62031-220-9(4))* Jump! Inc.

Miller, Petra. Earthquakes. 2015. (J). lib. bdg. *(978-1-62713-519-1(7))* Cavendish Square Publishing.

Minden, Cecilia. Earthquakes! 2010. (21st Century Basic Skills Library: Natural Disasters Ser.). (ENG.). 24p. (gr. k-3). lib. bdg. 22.79 *(978-1-60279-864-9(8),* 200594) Cherry Lake Publishing.

Mooney, Carla. Earthquakes. 2013. (J). pap. 15.64 *(978-1-62403-002-4(5));* (ENG.). 48p. (gr. 3-6). lib. bdg. 32.79 *(978-1-61783-937-5(X))* ABDO Publishing Co.

Morris, Neil & Steele, Philip. Inside Earthquakes. 2006. (Inside Nature's Disasters Ser.). (Illus.). 36p. (gr. 3-7). lib. bdg. 26.00 *(978-0-8368-7247-7(9),* Gareth Stevens Learning Library) Stevens, Gareth Publishing LLLP.

Murdico, Suzanne. Earthquakes: A Practical Survival Guide. 2009. (Library of Emergency Preparedness Ser.). 64p. (gr. 6-6). 58.50 *(978-1-60853-593-4(2),* Rosen Reference) Rosen Publishing Group, Inc., The.

Murdico, Suzanne J. Earthquakes: A Practical Survival Guide. 2005. (Library of Emergency Preparedness Ser.). (Illus.). 64p. (YA). (gr. 5-9). lib. bdg. 31.95 *(978-1-4042-0531-4(4))* Rosen Publishing Group, Inc., The.

Murray, Peter. Earthquakes. 2015. (Forces of Nature Ser.). (ENG.). 24p. (J). (gr. 2-5). 27.07 *(978-1-63143-764-9(X),* 208604) Child's World, Inc., The.

Nault, Jennifer. Earthquakes. 2016. (Illus.). 24p. (J). *(978-1-5105-1148-4(2))* SmartBook Media, Inc.

—Earthquakes. (Focus on Earth Science Ser.). 2015. (ENG.). (J). (gr. 3-7). lib. bdg. 27.13 *(978-1-4896-4077-2(0),* AV2 by Weigl) 2010. (Illus.). 24p. (J). (gr. 3-5). pap. 11.95 *(978-1-60596-965-7(6))* 2010. (Illus.). 24p. (YA). (gr. 3-6). lib. bdg. 25.70 *(978-1-60596-964-0(8))* 2004. (Illus.). 24p. (J). lib. bdg. 24.45 *(978-1-59036-212-9(8))* Weigl Pubs., Inc.

Nuttall, Gina. Volcanoes & Earthquakes. 2004. (QEB Start Writing Ser.). (Illus.). 24p. (J). lib. bdg. 15.95 *(978-1-59566-018-3(6))* QEB Publishing Inc.

O'Neal, Claire. A Project Guide to Earthquakes. 2010. (Earth Science Projects for Kids Ser.). (Illus.). 48p. (J). (gr. 4-7). lib. bdg. 29.95 *(978-1-58415-870-7(0))* Mitchell Lane Pubs., Inc.

Owens, Meredith P. Earthquakes. 2016. (Spotlight on Earth Science Ser.). 00024p. (J). (gr. 4-6). 26.25 *(978-1-4994-2616-8(X),* PowerKids Pr.) Rosen Publishing Group, Inc., The.

Parks, Peggy J. Predicting Earthquakes. 2006. (Kidhaven Science Library). (Illus.). 48p. (J). (gr. 3-7). lib. bdg. 26.20 *(978-0-7377-3602-1(X),* 1256754, Kidhaven) Cengage Gale.

Penny, Sam. Broken River: Book 2 of the 7. 9 Scenario. 2004. (Illus.). 238p. (YA). pap. 16.99 *(978-0-9755671-1-1(X))* TwoPenny Pubns.

Perish, Patric. Survive an Earthquake. 2017. (Survival Zone Ser.). (ENG., Illus.). 24p. (J). (gr. 3-7). lib. bdg. 25.95 *(978-1-62617-584-6(5),* Torque Bks.) Bellwether Media.

Ponzio, Richard, ed. Earthquake! Beyond Duck, Cover, & Hold. 2006. (Illus.). 115p. (J). (gr. 3-6). reprint ed. pap. 35.00 *(978-1-4223-0756-4(5))* DIANE Publishing Co.

Prager, Ellen. Earthquakes & Volcanoes. 2008. (Restless Earth Ser.). (Illus.). 120p. (YA). (gr. 5-9). 35.00 *(978-0-7910-9705-2(6))* Facts On File, Inc.

Prager, Ellen J. Earthquakes. 2017. (Jump into Science Ser.). (ENG., Illus.). 32p. (J). (gr. -1-3). pap. 7.99 ***(978-1-4263-2833-6(8),*** National Geographic Children's Bks.) National Geographic Society.

—Earthquakes. Greenstein, Susan, illus. 2007. (Jump into Science Ser.). (ENG.). 32p. (J). (gr. -1-3). per. 6.95 *(978-1-4263-0090-5(5),* National Geographic Children's Bks.) National Geographic Society.

Prager, Ellen J. Jump into Science: Earthquakes. 2017. (Jump into Science Ser.). (ENG.). 32p. (J). (gr. -1-3). lib. bdg. 17.90 ***(978-1-4263-2834-3(6),*** National Geographic Children's Bks.) National Geographic Society.

Prokos, Anna. Earthquakes. 2008. (Ultimate 10 Ser.). 48p. (YA). (gr. 5-9). lib. bdg. 31.00 *(978-0-8368-9151-5(1))* Stevens, Gareth Publishing LLLP.

QEB Start Reading & Writing National Book Stores Edition: Volcanoes & Earthquakes. 2006. (J). per. *(978-1-59566-265-1(0))* QEB Publishing Inc.

Raum, Elizabeth. Earthquake! 2017. (Natural Disasters Ser.). (ENG., Illus.). 32p. (J). (gr. 1-3). pap. 9.99 *(978-1-68152-082-7(6))* Amicus.

—Earthquake! 2016. (Natural Disasters Ser.). (ENG., Illus.). 32p. (J). (gr. k-3). 20.95 *(978-1-60753-989-6(5))* Amicus Publishing.

Rebman, Renée C. Anatomy of an Earthquake, 1 vol. (Disasters Ser.). (ENG.). 48p. (gr. 3-4). 2011. pap. 9.95 *(978-1-4296-7363-1(X))* 2011. pap. 59.70 *(978-1-4296-7364-8(8))* 2010. lib. bdg. 31.99 *(978-1-4296-4797-7(3))* Capstone Press of Coughlan Cos.

Reed, Jennifer. Earthquakes: Disaster & Survival. 2005. (Deadly Disasters Ser.). (Illus.). 48p. (J). lib. bdg. 25.27 *(978-0-7660-2381-9(8))* Enslow Pubs., Inc.

Reingold, Adam. Leveled by an Earthquake! 2010. (Disaster Survivors Ser.). (Illus.). 32p. (YA). (gr. 4-7). lib. bdg. 25.27 *(978-1-936087-53-2(7))* Bearport Publishing Co., Inc.

Rice, William B. Earthquakes, 1 vol. 2009. (Science Readers: a Closer Look Ser.). (ENG.). 32p. (J). (gr. 3-3). pap. 8.99 *(978-1-4333-0309-8(4))* Teacher Created Materials, Inc.

—Los Terremotos, 1 vol. rev. ed. 2010. (Science Readers: a Closer Look Ser.). (SPA., Illus.). 32p. (J). (gr. 2-3). pap. 8.99 *(978-1-4333-2153-5(X))* Shell Educational Publishing.

Riley, Joelle. Earthquakes. 2008. pap. 40.95 *(978-0-8225-9441-3(2));* (ENG.). 32p. pap. 7.95 *(978-0-8225-9015-6(8));* (ENG., Illus.). 32p. lib. bdg. 22.60 *(978-0-8225-7905-2(7),* Lerner Pubns.) Lerner Publishing Group.

Rooney, Anne. Earthquake: Perspectives on Earthquake Disasters, 1 vol. 2014. (Disaster Dossiers Ser.). (ENG., Illus.). 56p. (gr. 7-8). 34.65 *(978-1-4846-0180-8(7))* Heinemann-Raintree.

Rooney, Anne, et al. Disaster Dossiers, 1 vol. 2014. (Disaster Dossiers Ser.). 56p. (gr. 7-8). 173.25 *(978-1-4846-0185-3(8))* Heinemann-Raintree.

Roza, Greg. Earthquake: True Stories of Survival. 2009. (Survivor Stories Ser.). 48p. (gr. 5-5). 53.00 *(978-1-60853-253-7(4),* Rosen Reference) Rosen Publishing Group, Inc., The.

—The Indian Ocean Tsunami. 2007. (Nature in the News Ser.). (Illus.). 32p. (YA). (gr. 2-5). lib. bdg. 23.95 *(978-1-4042-3538-0(8))* Rosen Publishing Group, Inc., The.

—Powerful Earthquakes. 2012. (Angry Earth Ser.). (ENG.). 32p. (gr. 3-6). (J). pap. 10.50 *(978-1-4339-6547-0(X),* Gareth Stevens Learning Library); (YA). lib. bdg. 26.60 *(978-1-4339-6545-6(3))* Stevens, Gareth Publishing LLLP.

Rubin, Ken. Volcanoes & Earthquakes. 2007. (Insiders Ser.). (ENG., Illus.). 64p. (J). (gr. 3-7). 17.99 *(978-1-4169-3862-0(1),* Simon & Schuster Bks. For Young Readers) Simon & Schuster Bks. For Young Readers.

Rusch, Elizabeth. Will It Blow? Lewis, K. E., illus. 2017. (ENG.). 48p. (J). (gr. 1-4). pap. 14.99 *(978-1-63217-110-8(4),* Little Bigfoot) Sasquatch Bks.

Schuh, Mari C. Earthquakes. 2016. (Earth in Action Ser.). (ENG.). 24p. pap. 6.95 *(978-1-5157-6224-9(6),* Pebble Plus) Capstone Press of Coughlan Cos.

The Science of an Earthquake. 2014. (21st Century Skills Library: Disaster Science Ser.). (ENG., Illus.). 32p. (J). (gr. 4-8). 28.50 *(978-1-63137-629-0(2),* 205299) Cherry Lake Publishing.

Sengupta, Monalisa. Volcanoes & Earthquakes. (Wild Nature Ser.). 48p. 2009. (gr. 4-5). 53.00 *(978-1-60854-795-1(7),* PowerKids Pr.) 2007. (Illus.). (YA). (gr. 3-6). lib. bdg. 29.25 *(978-1-4042-3901-2(4))* Rosen Publishing Group, Inc., The.

Shofner, Melissa Raé. Earthquake-Proof Buildings. 2016. (Technology Takes on Nature Ser.). 00032p. (J). pap. 10.50 *(978-1-4824-5767-4(9))* Stevens, Gareth Publishing LLLP.

Shone, Rob. Earthquakes. 2009. (Graphic Natural Disasters Ser.). (ENG.). 48p. (YA). (gr. 5-5). 58.50 *(978-1-61512-997-3(9),* Rosen Reference) Rosen Publishing Group, Inc., The.

Shulman, Mark. Super Storms That Rocked the World: Hurricanes, Tsunamis, & Other Disasters. 2007. (Illus.). 40p. (J). *(978-0-696-23702-7(4))* Meredith Bks.

Sillet, Helen. The Awesome Power of Volcanoes & Earthquakes. 2005. (YA). pap. 12.95 *(978-1-4105-0421-0(2));* cd-rom *(978-1-4105-0423-4(9))* Johnston, Don Inc.

—Understanding Volcanoes & Earthquakes. 2005. (YA). pap. 12.95 *(978-1-4105-0417-3(4));* cd-rom *(978-1-4105-0419-7(0))* Johnston, Don Inc.

Silverstein, Alvin, et al. Earthquakes: The Science Behind Seismic Shocks & Tsunamis. 2009. (Science Behind Natural Disasters Ser.). (Illus.). 48p. (J). (gr. 5-9). lib. bdg. 25.27 *(978-0-7660-2975-0(1))* Enslow Pubs., Inc.

Simon, Seymour. Earthquakes. 2006. (ENG., Illus.). 32p. (J). (gr. k-4). 7.99 *(978-0-06-087715-6(4))* HarperCollins Pubs.

—Earthquakes. 2006. (Illus.). 30p. (gr. k-4). 17.00 *(978-0-7569-6742-0(2))* Perfection Learning Corp.

Smith, Paula. Earthquakes, Eruptions, & Other Events That Change Earth. 2015. (Earth's Processes Close-Up Ser.). (ENG., Illus.). 24p. (J). (gr. k-3). *(978-0-7787-1725-6(9))* Crabtree Publishing Co.

Spilsbury, Louise & Spilsbury, Richard. Shattering Earthquakes, 1 vol. 2nd ed. 2010. (Awesome Forces of Nature Ser.). (ENG., Illus.). 32p. (gr. 3-6). 33.32 *(978-1-4329-3784-3(7));* pap. 8.29 *(978-1-4329-3791-1(X))* Heinemann-Raintree. (Heinemann InfoSearch).

—Top 10 Worst Earthquakes. 2016. (Nature's Ultimate Disasters Ser.). 00032p. (J). (gr. 3-4). pap. 10.00 *(978-1-4994-3066-0(3),* PowerKids Pr.) Rosen Publishing Group, Inc., The.

Stamper, Judith Bauer. Earthquakes. 2010. (Illus.). 32p. (J). *(978-0-545-28547-6(X))* Scholastic, Inc.

Steele, Philip, et al. Extreme Planet. 2014. (Illus.). 128p. (J). *(978-1-4351-5523-7(8))* Barnes & Noble, Inc.

Stewart, Melissa. Earthquakes & Volcanoes. 2008. (For Your Information Ser.). (Illus.). 80p. (J). (gr. 3-7). pap. 7.99 *(978-0-06-089950-9(6))* HarperCollins Pubs.

Suen, Anastasia. Earthquakes. 2015. (ENG.). 48p. (gr. 3-6). 35.64 *(978-1-63430-425-2(X))* Rourke Educational Media.

Tanaka, Shelley. Earthquake! A Day That Changed America. Craig, David, illus. 2006. 48p. (J). (gr. 4-8). reprint ed. 17.00 *(978-1-4223-5635-7(3))* DIANE Publishing Co.

Taylor, Chad. All about Earthquakes. 2016. (Rosen REAL Readers: STEM & STEAM Collection). 12p. (gr. 1-k). pap. 6.33 *(978-1-5081-2470-2(1),* Rosen Classroom) Rosen Publishing Group, Inc., The.

Than, Ker. Earthquakes. 2009. (True Book(tm), a — Earth Science Ser.). (ENG.). 48p. (J). (gr. 2-5). 31.00 *(978-0-531-16882-0(4));* (Illus.). (gr. 3-5). pap. 6.95 *(978-0-531-21350-6(1),* Children's Pr.) Scholastic Library Publishing.

Thoron, Joe. Earthquakes. 2006. (Kaleidoscope Natural Disasters Ser.). (Illus.). 48p. (gr. 3-7). lib. bdg. 20.95 *(978-0-7614-2102-3(5),* Benchmark Bks.) Marshall Cavendish Corp.

Ticktock Media, Ltd. Staff. Violent Planet. 2008. (ENG.). 128p. (J). (gr. 4-7). pap. 12.95 *(978-1-84696-813-6(5),* TickTock Books) Octopus Publishing Group GBR. Dist: Independent Pubs. Group.

Time for Kids Editors. Earthquakes! 2006. (Time for Kids Ser.). (ENG., Illus.). 32p. (J). (gr. 1-3). pap. 3.99 *(978-0-06-078211-5(0))* HarperCollins Pubs.

Time for Kids Magazine Staff. Earthquakes! 2006. (Time for Kids Science Scoops Ser.). (Illus.). 32p. (gr. 1-3). 14.00 *(978-0-7569-6675-1(2))* Perfection Learning Corp.

Trumbauer, Lisa. Earthquake! 2005. (J). pap. *(978-1-4108-4593-1(1))* Benchmark Education Co.

U. S. National Geographic Society Staff & Furgang, Kathy. National Geographic Kids Everything Volcanoes & Earthquakes: Earthshaking Photos, Facts, & Fun! 2013. (National Geographic Kids Everything Ser.). (ENG.). 64p. (J). (gr. 3-7). lib. bdg. 21.90 *(978-1-4263-1365-3(9),* National Geographic Children's Bks.) National Geographic Society.

U. S. National Geographic Society Staff, et al. Everything Volcanoes & Earthquakes: Earthshaking Photos, Facts, & Fun! 2013. (National Geographic Kids Everything Ser.). (ENG., Illus.). 64p. (J). (gr. 3-7). pap. 12.95 *(978-1-4263-1364-6(0),* National Geographic Children's Bks.) National Geographic Society.

Vail, Grace. Earthquakes: Energy in Motion. 2009. (Real Life Readers Ser.). 32p. (gr. 4-6). pap. 10.00 *(978-1-4358-0232-2(2),* Rosen Classroom) Rosen Publishing Group, Inc., The.

Ventura, Marne. Detecting Earthquakes. 2017. (Detecting Disasters (paperback) Ser.). (ENG., Illus.). 32p. (J). (gr. 4-7). pap. 9.95 ***(978-1-63517-057-3(5),*** Focus Readers) North Star Editions.

Walker, Sally M. Earthquakes. 2008. pap. 52.95 *(978-0-8225-9109-2(X))* 2007. (ENG., Illus.). 48p. (gr. 2-5). lib. bdg. 26.60 *(978-0-8225-6735-6(0),* Lerner Pubns.) Lerner Publishing Group.

Walsh, Kenneth C. H. You Are There! San Francisco 1906. 2017. (J). pap. 8.97 *(978-1-4938-3617-8(X))* Teacher Created Materials, Inc.

—You Are There! San Francisco 1906. 2017. (Time for Kids Nonfiction Readers Ser.). lib. bdg. 19.65 ***(978-0-606-40271-2(3))*** Turtleback Bks.

Watt, Fiona. Earthquakes & Volcanoes. Stockley, Corinne & Brooks, Felicity, eds. Gower, Jeremy & Shields, Chris, illus. rev. ed. 2007. (Geography Ser.). 32p. (YA). (gr. 8-12). pap. 7.99 *(978-0-7945-1531-7(2),* Usborne) EDC Publishing.

Weil, Ann. Earthquakes, 1 vol. unabr. ed. 2012. (Disasters Ser.). (ENG.). 92p. (YA). (gr. 9-12). 8.95 *(978-1-61651-929-2(0))* Saddleback Educational Publishing, Inc.

Winchester, Simon & Wells, Rosemary. When the Earth Shakes: Earthquakes, Volcanoes, & Tsunamis. 2015. (Smithsonian Ser.). (ENG., Illus.). 80p. (J). (gr. 5). bds. 18.99 *(978-0-670-78536-0(9),* Viking Books for Young Readers) Penguin Young Readers Group.

Woods, Michael & Woods, Mary B. Earthquakes. 2006. (Disasters up Close Ser.). (ENG., Illus.). 64p. (gr. 4-8). lib. bdg. 27.93 *(978-0-8225-4711-2(2),* Lerner Pubns.) Lerner Publishing Group.

World Book, Inc Staff, contrib. by. Earthquakes. (J). 2007. *(978-0-7166-9804-3(8))* 2nd ed. 2009. (Illus.). 47p. *(978-0-7166-9820-3(X))* World Bk., Inc.

Worth, Richard. The San Francisco Earthquake. 2005. (Environmental Disasters Ser.). (Illus.). 112p. (gr. 6-12). 35.00 *(978-0-8160-5756-6(7))* Facts On File, Inc.

Young, Jacob. Examining Earthquakes. 2015. (ENG., Illus.). 48p. (J). lib. bdg. 24.95 net. *(978-1-934545-63-8(5))* Oliver Pr., Inc.

EARTHQUAKES—FICTION

Acton, Vanessa. Aftershock. 2017. (Day of Disaster Ser.). (ENG.). 112p. (gr. 6-12). (J). 26.65 *(978-1-5124-2777-6(2));* (YA). 12.99 ***(978-1-5124-3502-3(3),*** Darby Creek); (YA). 39.99 ***(978-1-5124-3500-9(7),*** Darby Creek); (YA). 39.99 ***(978-1-5124-2785-1(3),*** Darby Creek) Lerner Publishing Group.

Ali, Amani Elcheikh. Under the Rubble. 2011. 56p. 24.99 *(978-1-4568-4267-3(6));* pap. 15.99 *(978-1-4568-4266-6(8))* Xlibris Corp.

Bean, Raymond. Benji Franklin: Kid Zillionaire: Money Troubles. Vimislik, Matthew, illus. 2016. (Benji Franklin: Kid Zillionaire Ser.). (ENG.). 160p. (gr. 2-3). pap. 6.95 *(978-1-4965-4137-6(5))* Stone Arch Bks.

—Buying Stocks (and Solid Gold Submarines!) Vimislik, Matthew, illus. 2015. (Benji Franklin: Kid Zillionaire Ser.). (ENG.). 88p. (gr. 2-3). lib. bdg. 22.65 *(978-1-4965-0367-1(8))* Stone Arch Bks.

—Money Troubles. Vimislik, Matthew, illus. 2015. (Benji Franklin: Kid Zillionaire Ser.). (ENG.). 160p. (gr. 2-3). 9.95 *(978-1-4965-0369-5(4))* Stone Arch Bks.

Block, Francesca Lia. Love in the Time of Global Warming. 2013. (ENG.). 240p. (YA). (gr. 9-13). 16.99 *(978-0-8050-9627-9(2),* 9780805096279, Holt, Henry & Co. Bks. For Young Readers) Holt, Henry & Co.

Bordiglioni, Stephen & Bordiglioni, Stefano. Earthquake! Bertolucci, Federico, illus. 2009. (Dinodino's Dinosaur Adventures Ser.). 56p. (J). (gr. k-4). 27.95 *(978-1-60754-713-6(9));* pap. 12.85 *(978-1-60754-719-8(8))* Windmill Bks.

Brunson, Emma. Survivor Spirit Book: Megan's Ark. 2010. 204p. pap. 13.50 *(978-1-60911-834-1(0),* Eloquent Bks.) Strategic Book Publishing & Rights Agency (SBPRA).

Burg, Ann E. Serafina's Promise. (ENG.). 304p. (J). (gr. 3-7). 2015. pap. 7.99 *(978-0-545-53567-0(0))* 2013. 16.99 *(978-0-545-53564-9(6))* Scholastic, Inc. (Scholastic Pr.).

Carman, Patrick. The House of Power. 2008. (Atherton Ser.: 1). (ENG., Illus.). 384p. (J). (gr. 3-7). pap. 9.99 *(978-0-316-16671-3(5))* Little, Brown Bks. for Young Readers.

—Rivers of Fire. 2009. (Atherton Ser.: 2). (ENG., Illus.). 336p. (J). (gr. 3-7). pap. 9.99 *(978-0-316-16673-7(1))* Little Brown & Co.

Cook, Sherry & Johnson, Terri. Quincy Quake. 26. Kuhn, Jesse, illus. l.t. ed. 2006. (Quirkles — Exploring Phonics through Science Ser.: 17). 32p. (J). 7.99 *(978-1-933815-16-9(7),* Quirkles, The) Creative 3, LLC.

Crofford, Emily. When the River Ran Backward. (Adventures in Time Ser.). (gr. 4-8). 2005. (Illus.). 84p. 15.95 *(978-1-57505-305-9(5))* 2003. 80p. (J). pap. 6.95 *(978-1-57505-488-9(4))* Lerner Publishing Group.

deRubertis, Barbara. Quentin Quokka's Quick Questions. Alley, R. W., illus. 2011. (Animal Antics A to Z Ser.). 32p. (J). pap. 45.32 *(978-0-7613-7663-7(1));* lib. bdg. 22.60 *(978-1-57565-338-9(9));* (gr. -1-3). pap. 7.95 *(978-1-57565-329-7(X))* Kane Press, Inc.

deRubertis, Barbara & DeRubertis, Barbara. Quentin Quokka's Quick Questions. Alley, R. W., illus. 2012. (Animal Antics A to Z Ser.). 32p. (J). (gr. 2 — 1). cd-rom 7.95 *(978-1-57565-410-2(5))* Kane Press, Inc.

Dharma Publishing Staff. The Rabbit Who Overcame Fear: A Story about Wise Action. 2nd ed. 2013. (ENG.). 36p. (gr. -1-7). pap. 8.95 *(978-0-89800-492-2(6))* Dharma Publishing.

Duey, K. & Bale, K. A. Salvados! Terremoto. 2003. (Survival Ser.). Tr. of Survival! Earthquake. (SPA.). (J). pap. 9.95 *(978-0-9715256-5-8(X))* Planeta Publishing Corp.

Duey, Kathleen & Bale, Karen A. Earthquake: San Francisco 1906. 2014. (Survivors Ser.). (ENG., Illus.). 160p. (J). (gr. 3-7). pap. 6.99 *(978-1-4814-0079-4(7),* Aladdin) Simon & Schuster Children's Publishing.

Figley, Marthy Rhodes & Figley, Marty Rhodes. The Night the Chimneys Fell. Marshall, Felicia, illus. 2011. 48p. (J). pap. 6.95 (978-0-7613-3939-7(6), First Avenue Editions) Lerner Publishing Group.

Figley, Marty Rhodes. The Night the Chimneys Fell. Marshall, Felicia, illus. 2011. (On My Own History Ser.). 48p. (J). pap. 39.62 (978-0-7613-7622-4(4), First Avenue Editions) Lerner Publishing Group.

—The Night the Chimneys Fell. Marshall, Felicia, illus. 2009. (On My Own History Ser.). (ENG.). 48p. (gr. 2-4). 25.26 (978-0-8225-7894-9(8)) Lerner Publishing Group.

Garretson, Dee. Wildfire Run. 2011. (ENG.). 288p. (J). (gr. 3-7). pap. 6.99 (978-0-06-195350-7(4)) HarperCollins Pubs.

Gregory, Kristiana & Campbell, Mary Exa Atkins. Earthquake at Dawn. 2003. (Great Episodes Ser.). (ENG., Illus.). 224p. (J). (gr. 5-7). pap. 13.95 (978-0-15-204681-1(X)) Houghton Mifflin Harcourt Publishing Co.

Groth, Darren. Are You Seeing Me?, 1 vol. 2015. (ENG., Illus.). 288p. (YA). (gr. 8-12). 19.95 (978-1-4598-1079-2(1)) Orca Bk. Pubs. USA.

Herzog, Arthur. Earthsound. 2003. 192p. pap. 13.95 (978-0-595-27073-6(5), Authors Choice Pr.) iUniverse, Inc.

Hopkinson, Deborah. Into the Firestorm: A Novel of San Francisco 1906. 2008. (Yearling Bks.). (ENG.). 208p. (J). (gr. 3-7). per. 6.99 (978-0-440-42129-0(2), Yearling) Random Hse. Children's Bks.

Johnson, Elizabeth. And Then Nicholas Sang: The Story of the Trisagion Hymn. Lobastov, Masha, illus. 2010. 32p. (J). 18.95 (978-1-936270-05-7(6)) Ancient Faith Publishing.

Johnson, Kristin F. Wall of Water. 2017. (Day of Disaster Ser.). (ENG.). 112p. (gr. 6-12). (J). 26.65 (978-1-5124-2778-3(0)); (YA). 12.99 **(978-1-5124-3516-0(3)**, Darby Creek); (YA). 39.99 **(978-1-5124-2786-8(1)**, Darby Creek); (YA). 39.99 **(978-1-5124-3515-3(5)**, Darby Creek) Lerner Publishing Group.

Kehret, Peg. Escaping the Giant Wave. 2004. (ENG., Illus.). 160p. (J). (gr. 3-7). pap. 7.99 (978-0-689-85273-2(8), Aladdin) Simon & Schuster Children's Publishing.

Kennedy, Marlane. Disaster Strikes #1: Earthquake Shock. 2014. (Disaster Strikes Ser.: 1). (ENG.). 128p. (J). (gr. 2-5). pap. 4.99 (978-0-545-53044-6(X), Scholastic Paperbacks) Scholastic, Inc.

—Earthquake Shock. 2014. (Disaster Strikes Ser.: 1). lib. bdg. 14.75 (978-0-606-35827-9(7)) Turtleback Bks.

Lawrence, Margaret. Earthshakers, Top Blowers & High Rollers. 2012. 170p. pap. 36.95 (978-1-937600-74-7(2)) Salem Author Services.

Lee, Milly, et al. Earthquake. Choi, Yangsook, illus. 2003. (Avenues Ser.). (ENG.). 32p. (C). (gr. k-2). pap. 21.95 (978-0-374-39964-1(6)) National Geographic School Publishing, Inc.

Lee, Stacey. Outrun the Moon. 2016. (ENG.). 400p. (YA). (gr. 7). 17.99 (978-0-399-17541-1(5), G.P. Putnam's Sons Books for Young Readers) Penguin Young Readers Group.

—Outrun the Moon. 2017. lib. bdg. 22.10 **(978-0-606-40097-8(4))** Turtleback Bks.

Lowell, Susan. I Am Lavina Cumming: A Novel of the American West. 2005. (Historical Fiction for Young Readers Ser.). (ENG., Illus.). 200p. (J). pap. 8.00 (978-1-57131-655-4(8)) Milkweed Editions.

Lowitz, Leza. Up from the Sea. 2016. (ENG.). 272p. (YA). (gr. 7). 17.99 (978-0-553-53474-0(2), Crown Books For Young Readers) Random Hse. Children's Bks.

McKee, David, illus. Elmer & the Birthday Quake. 2013. (ENG.). 32p. (J). (gr. -1-3). 16.95 (978-1-4677-1117-3(9)) Lerner Publishing Group.

McKinlay, Meg. A Single Stone. 2017. (ENG.). 272p. (J). (gr. 5). 17.99 (978-0-7636-8837-0(1)) Candlewick Pr.

Mein eigenes Auto. 2005. (GER.). 4.95 net. (978-0-929724-89-8(5)) Command Performance Language Institute.

Messner, Kate. Escape from the Great Earthquake. McMorris, Kelley, illus. 2017. (Ranger in Time Ser.: 6). (ENG.). 160p. (J). (gr. 2-5). pap. 5.99 **(978-0-545-90983-9(X))** Scholastic, Inc.

Miller, Bobbi. Big River's Daughter. 2013. (ENG.). 224p. (J). (gr. 2-7). 16.95 (978-0-8234-2752-9(8)) Holiday Hse., Inc.

Moonshower, Candie. The Legend of Zoey. 2007. (ENG.). 224p. (J). (gr. 3-7). 6.99 (978-0-440-23924-6(9), Yearling) Random Hse. Children's Bks.

Mortenson, Greg & Husain, Farzana. Listen to the Children: The Story of Dr. Greg & Stones into Schools. Roth, Susan L., illus. 2011. (ENG.). 32p. (J). (gr. 1-3). 17.99 (978-0-8037-3593-4(6), Dial) Penguin Publishing Group.

Mother Earth Quake's. 2004. (Illus.). 33p. (J). per. 11.95 (978-0-9716721-0-9(5), 2000) Marker, Margaret Penfield.

Nelson, Karen, creator. Crystal Brave: Literature Theme Unit. 2012. (Illus.). 48p. spiral bd. 19.99 (978-1-930584-02-0(4)) Progreso Publishing Group, LLC.

Ohi, Ruth. Kenta & the Big Wave. 2nd ed. 2013. (ENG., Illus.). 32p. (J). (gr. -1-2). pap. 9.95 (978-1-55451-576-9(9), 9781554515769) Annick Pr., Ltd. CAN. Dist: Publishers Group West (PGW).

Olsen, Erik. Cobble Cavern. 2012. (J). pap. 16.99 (978-1-4621-1009-4(6)) Cedar Fort, Inc./CFI Distribution.

Osborne, Mary Pope. Earthquake in the Early Morning. unabr. ed. 2004. (Magic Tree House Ser.: No. 24). 71p. (J). (gr. k-3). pap. 17.00 incl. audio (978-0-8072-0933-2(3), S FTR 256 SP, Listening Library) Random Hse. Audio Publishing Group.

Osorio, Rick. The Great Adventure of Sally Rock & the Cretaceous Chicken. 2006. 65p. pap. 16.95 (978-1-4241-0971-5(X)) PublishAmerica, Inc.

Reiss, Kathryn. The Strange Case of Baby H. 2009. (Mysteries Through Time Ser.). 144 - 176p. (YA). (gr. 4-8). 31.95 (978-1-60754-423-4(7)); pap. 15.25 (978-1-60754-424-1(5)) Windmill Bks.

Richter, Danny. The Big Gozonga. 2006. 16.95 (978-0-9786107-0-8(9)) Arbor Bks.

Rockwood, Roy. On a Torn-Away World: Or, the Captives of the Great Earthquake. 2007. 252p. 32.95 (978-1-4344-9622-5(8)); per. 22.95 (978-1-4344-9621-8(X)) Wildside Pr., LLC.

Rucker, Mike. Terry & the Earthquake. 2006. (Terry the Tractor Ser.: Vol. 14). 72p. (J). (gr. k-4). pap. 4.95 (978-0-9711659-5-3(5)) Univ. Editions.

Salisbury, Graham. Night of the Howling Dogs. 2009. (ENG.). 208p. (YA). (gr. 7-7). mass mkt. 6.99 (978-0-440-23839-3(0), Laurel Leaf) Random Hse. Children's Bks.

Salisbury, Linda. Earthquake Surprise: A Bailey Fish Adventure. Tornatore, Carol, illus. 2012. 192p. (J). pap. 8.95 (978-1-881539-65-0(2)) Tabby Hse. Bks.

Salkey, Andrew. Earthquake. 2011. (Caribbean Modern Classics Ser.). (ENG., Illus.). 108p. (J). (gr. 7). pap. 13.95 (978-1-84523-182-8(1)) Peepal Tree Pr., Ltd. GBR. Dist: Independent Pubs. Group.

San Francisco Shake-Up, 6 Packs. (Greetings Ser.: Vol. 3). (gr. 3-5). 31.00 (978-0-7635-2075-5(6)) Rigby Education.

Smith, Roland. Eruption. 2012. (Storm Runners Ser.: 3). (ENG.). 160p. (J). (gr. 3-7). 16.99 (978-0-545-08174-0(2), Scholastic Pr.) Scholastic, Inc.

Tarshis, Lauren. I Survived the Japanese Tsunami 2011. 2013. (I Survived Ser.: No. 8). (ENG., Illus.). 112p. (J). (gr. 2-5). pap. 4.99 (978-0-545-45937-2(0)) Scholastic, Inc.

—I Survived the Japanese Tsunami 2011. Dawson, Scott, illus. 2013. (I Survived Ser.: No. 8). 83p. (J). (978-0-545-62981-2(0)) Scholastic, Inc.

—I Survived the Japanese Tsunami 2011. 2013. (I Survived Ser.: No. 8). lib. bdg. 14.75 (978-0-606-32390-1(2), Turtleback) Turtleback Bks.

—I Survived the San Francisco Earthquake 1906. 2012. (I Survived Ser.: 5). (ENG.). 112p. (J). (gr. 2-5). pap. 4.99 (978-0-545-20699-0(5), Scholastic Paperbacks) Scholastic, Inc.

—I Survived the San Francisco Earthquake 1906. 2012. (I Survived . Ser.: No. 5). lib. bdg. 14.75 (978-0-606-23936-3(7), Turtleback) Turtleback Bks.

Taylor, Janet B. Into the Dim. 2017. lib. bdg. 20.85 **(978-0-606-39929-6(1))** Turtleback Bks.

Veldkamp, Debby. Quake! Six Point Five: The Cat Survived. Van Den Berg, Helen, illus. 2004. (J). lib. bdg. 16.95 (978-1-930401-25-9(6)) Central Coast Bks./Pr.

Wagner, Laura Rose. Hold Tight, Don't Let Go. 2015. (ENG.). 272p. (YA). (gr. 9-17). 17.95 (978-1-4197-1204-3(7), Amulet Bks.) Abrams, Inc.

Yep, Laurence. The Earth Dragon Awakes: The San Francisco Earthquake of 1906. (ENG., Illus.). 128p. (J). (gr. 3-7). 2008. pap. 6.99 (978-0-06-000846-8(6)) 2006. 14.99 (978-0-06-027524-2(3)) HarperCollins Pubs.

EARTHWORKS (ARCHEOLOGY)

see Excavations (Archaeology)

EARTHWORMS

Amstutz, Lisa J. Earthworms. 2016. (Little Critters Ser.). (ENG., Illus.). 24p. (gr. k-1). lib. bdg. 21.99 (978-1-5157-1938-0(3), Pebble Bks.) Capstone Press of Coughlan Cos.

Appelhof, Mary, et al. Worms Eat Our Garbage: Classroom Activities for a Better Environment. Fenton, Mary Frances & Kostecke, Nancy, illus. 2004. 232p. (Orig.). (gr. 4-18). pap., stu. ed. 22.95 (978-0-942256-05-5(0)) Flowerfield Enterprises.

Bishop, Celeste. Wiggly Worms. 2015. (Icky Animals! Small & Gross Ser.). (ENG., Illus.). 24p. (J). (gr. 1-1). pap. 8.25 (978-1-4994-0732-7(7), PowerKids Pr.) Rosen Publishing Group, Inc., The.

Carr, Aaron. Earthworms. 2014. (Illus.). 24p. (J). (978-1-62127-211-3(7)) Weigl Pubs., Inc.

Clapper, Nikki Bruno. Earthworms. 2015. (Creepy Crawlers Ser.). (ENG., Illus.). 24p. (gr. k-1). lib. bdg. 26.65 (978-1-4914-6215-7(9)) Capstone Press of Coughlan Cos.

Dell'Oro, Suzanne Paul. Let's Look at Earthworms. 2010. (Lightning Bolt Books — Animal Close-Ups Ser.). (ENG., Illus.). 32p. (J). (gr. k-2). pap. 7.95 (978-0-7613-6040-7(9), 1312737); lib. bdg. 26.60 (978-0-7613-5458-1(1), 1312737, Lerner Pubns.) Lerner Publishing Group.

—Tunneling Earthworms. 2003. (Pull Ahead Bks.). (Illus.). 32p. (J). (gr. k-2). pap. 5.95 (978-0-8225-3768-7(0)) Lerner Publishing Group.

Dixon, Norma. The Lowdown on Earthworms, 1 vol. 2005. (ENG., Illus.). 32p. (J). (gr. 2-5). (978-1-55005-114-8(8)) Fitzhenry & Whiteside, Ltd.

Earthworms & their Food: 6 Each of 1 Student Book, 6 vols. (Sunshinetm Science Ser.). 24p. (gr. 1-2). 41.95 (978-0-7802-2708-8(5)) Wright Group/McGraw-Hill.

Earthworms & their Food: Big Book. (Sunshinetm Science Ser.). 24p. (gr. 1-2). 37.50 (978-0-7802-2788-0(3)) Wright Group/McGraw-Hill.

Earthworms Sets: 1 Each of 3 Big Books. (Sunshinetm Science Ser.). (gr. 1-2). 111.50 (978-0-7802-2812-2(X)) Wright Group/McGraw-Hill.

Earthworms Sets: 1 Each of 3 Student Books. (Sunshinetm Science Ser.). (gr. 1-2). 20.95 (978-0-7802-2813-9(8)) Wright Group/McGraw-Hill.

Goldish, Meish. Inside the Worm's Hole. 2013. (Science Slam: Snug As a Bug-Where Bugs Live Ser.). 24p. (J). (gr. -1-3). lib. bdg. 23.93 (978-1-61772-904-1(3)) Bearport Publishing Co., Inc.

Group/McGraw-Hill, Wright. Earthworms: Level E, 6 vols. (Take Twostm Ser.). 16p. 29.95 (978-0-322-08959-4(X)) Wright Group/McGraw-Hill.

Hayes, Amy. We Need Worms. 2015. (Creatures We Can't Live Without Ser.). (ENG., Illus.). 24p. (J). (gr. 3-4). pap. 8.25 (978-1-4994-0986-4(9), PowerKids Pr.) Rosen Publishing Group, Inc., The.

Hipp, Andrew. The Life Cycle of an Earthworm. 2009. (Life Cycles Library). 24p. (gr. 3-4). 42.50 (978-1-60853-998-7(9), PowerKids Pr.) Rosen Publishing Group, Inc., The.

How Earthworms Grow: 6 Each of 1 Student Book, 6 vols. (Sunshinetm Science Ser.). 24p. (gr. 1-2). 41.95 (978-0-7802-2706-4(9)) Wright Group/McGraw-Hill.

How Earthworms Grow: Big Book. (Sunshinetm Science Ser.). 24p. (gr. 1-2). 37.50 (978-0-7802-2787-3(5)) Wright Group/McGraw-Hill.

How Earthworms Life: 6 Each of 1 Student Book, 6 vols. (Sunshinetm Science Ser.). 24p. (gr. 1-2). 41.95 (978-0-7802-2710-1(7)) Wright Group/McGraw-Hill.

How Earthworms Life: Big Book. (Sunshinetm Science Ser.). 24p. (gr. 1-2). 37.50 (978-0-7802-2789-7(1)) Wright Group/McGraw-Hill.

Kalman, Bobbie. El Ciclo de Vida de la Lombriz de Tierra. 2006. (Libro de Bobbie Kalman Ser.). (SPA., Illus.). 32p. (J). (gr. 3-7). pap. (978-0-7787-8716-7(8)); lib. bdg. (978-0-7787-8670-2(6)) Crabtree Publishing Co.

—The Life Cycle of an Earthworm. 2003. (Life Cycle Ser.). (ENG., Illus.). 32p. (J). pap. (978-0-7787-0696-0(6)) Crabtree Publishing Co.

—Les Vers de Terre. 2009. (Petit Monde Vivant Ser.). (FRE., Illus.). 32p. (J). pap. 9.95 (978-2-89579-228-4(3)) Bayard Canada Livres CAN. Dist: Crabtree Publishing Co.

Loewen, Nancy. Garden Wigglers: Earthworms in Your Backyard. Peterson, Rick, illus. 2005. (Backyard Bugs Ser.). (ENG.). 24p. (gr. -1-3). lib. bdg. 26.65 (978-1-4048-1144-7(3)) Picture Window Bks.

Lunis, Natalie. Wiggly Earthworms. (No Backbone! Creepy Crawlers Ser.). 24p. (J). (gr. k-3). 2016. (ENG.). pap. 7.95 (978-1-944998-43-1(8)) 2009. (Illus.). lib. bdg. 21.28 (978-1-59716-751-2(7)) Bearport Publishing Co., Inc.

McCloskey, Kevin. We Dig Worms! 2015. (Giggle & Learn Ser.). (ENG., Illus.). 40p. (J). (gr. -1-3). 12.95 (978-1-935179-80-1(2)) TOON Books / RAW Junior, LLC.

Meachen Rau, Dana. Serpentea Lombriz, Serpentea! 2007. (¡Vamos Criaturita, Vamos! Ser.). (SPA & ENG., Illus.). 24p. (gr. k-1). lib. bdg. 15.95 (978-0-7614-2791-9(0), Benchmark Bks.) Marshall Cavendish Corp.

—Squirm, Earthworm, Squirm! 2007. (Bookworms Go, Critter, Go! Ser.). (Illus.). 23p. (J). (gr. -1-3). pap. 6.99 (978-0-7614-3267-8(1)); 24p. (gr. k-1). lib. bdg. 15.95 (978-0-7614-2650-9(7)) Marshall Cavendish Corp. (Benchmark Bks.).

—Squirm, Earthworm, Squirm!/Serpentea Lombriz, Serpentea! 2007. (Go, Critter, Go!/¡Vamos Criaturita, Vamos! Ser.). (SPA & ENG., Illus.). 24p. (gr. k-1). lib. bdg. 15.95 (978-0-7614-2815-2(1), Benchmark Bks.) Marshall Cavendish Corp.

Owens, L. L. The Life Cycle of an Earthworm. 2011. (Life Cycles Ser.). (ENG., Illus.). 32p. (J). (gr. k-3). lib. bdg. 29.93 (978-1-60973-148-9(4), 201179) Child's World, Inc., The.

Pfeffer, Wendy. Wiggling Worms at Work. Jenkins, Steve, illus. 2003. (Let's-Read-And-Find-Out Science 2 Ser.). (ENG.). 40p. (J). (gr. k-4). 16.99 (978-0-06-028448-0(X), Collins) HarperCollins Pubs.

—Wiggling Worms at Work. Jenkins, Steve, illus. 2004. (Let's-Read-and-Find-Out Science Ser.). 31p. (gr. -1-3). 16.00 (978-0-7569-3095-0(2)) Perfection Learning Corp.

Pfeffer, Wendy & Pfeffer. Wiggling Worms at Work. Jenkins, Steve, illus. 2003. (Let's-Read-And-Find-Out Science 2 Ser.). (ENG.). 40p. (J). (gr. k-4). pap. 5.99 (978-0-06-445199-4(2)) HarperCollins Pubs.

Shepherd, Jodie. It's a Good Thing There Are Earthworms. 2014. (Rookie Read-About(r) Science — It's a Good Thing... Ser.). (ENG., Illus.). 32p. (J). pap. 5.95 (978-0-531-22836-4(3)); lib. bdg. 25.00 (978-0-531-22364-2(7)) Scholastic Library Publishing.

Smith, Sian. Worms, 1 vol. 2012. (Creepy Critters Ser.). (ENG.). 24p. (gr. -1-k). pap. 9.95 (978-1-4109-4825-0(0)); lib. bdg. 25.32 (978-1-4109-4812-0(9)) Heinemann-Raintree.

Watts, Barrie. Earthworms. (Illus.). 32p. (YA). (gr. 2-18). lib. bdg. 27.10 (978-1-932889-20-8(5)) Sea-To-Sea Pubns.

Waxman, Laura Hamilton. Wiggling Earthworms. 2016. (First Step Nonfiction — Backyard Critters Ser.). (ENG., Illus.). 24p. (J). (gr. k-2). 23.99 (978-1-5124-0878-2(6)) Lerner Publishing Group.

Yasuda, Anita. Earthworms. 2011. (gr. 2-4). (J). pap. 12.95 (978-1-61690-625-2(1), AV2 by Weigl); (Illus.). 24p. (YA). 27.13 (978-1-61690-619-1(7)) Weigl Pubs., Inc.

EAST (FAR EAST)

see East Asia

EAST AFRICA

see Africa, East

EAST ASIA

Here are entered works dealing collectively with China, Japan, Korea, Taiwan, and Macao.

Ashcroft, Minnie & National Geographic Learning Staff. East Asia. 2007. (Reading Expeditions Ser.). (ENG., Illus.). 64p. (J). pap. 25.95 (978-0-7922-4377-9(3)) CENGAGE Learning.

—East Asia - Geography & Environments. 2007. (Reading Expeditions Ser.). (ENG., Illus.). 64p. (J). pap. 25.95 (978-0-7922-4376-2(5)) CENGAGE Learning.

Chandler, Julia. The Colonial & Postcolonial Experience in East & Southeast Asia. 2016. (Colonial & Postcolonial Experience Ser.). 00128p. (J). (gr. 10-10). 54.00 (978-1-5081-0438-4(7)) Rosen Publishing Group, Inc., The.

Hamashita, Takeshi. China, East Asia & the Global Economy: Regional & Historical Perspectives. Grove, Linda & Selden, Mark, eds. 2008. (Asia's Transformations/Critical Asian Scholarship Ser.). (ENG., Illus.). 224p. (C). 50.95 (978-0-415-46459-8(5), RU53282) Routledge.

—China, East Asia & the Global Economy: Regional & Historical Perspectives. Selden, Mark & Grove, Linda, eds. 2008. (Asia's Transformations/Critical Asian Scholarship Ser.). (ENG., Illus.). 224p. (C). 185.00 (978-0-415-46458-1(7), RU53281) Routledge.

Rauf, Don. Eurasia, Vol. 10. 2016. (Social Progress & Sustainability Ser.). (Illus.). 80p. (J). (gr. 7). 24.95 (978-1-4222-3495-2(9)) Mason Crest.

EAST INDIANS

Brierley, Saroo. Lion: A Long Way Home Young Readers' Edition. 2017. (ENG.). 272p. (J). (gr. 5). 8.99 **(978-0-425-29176-4(6)**, Puffin Books) Penguin Young Readers Group.

Hickman, Pamela & Taraschi-Carr, Gola. Righting Canada's Wrongs: the Komagata Maru & Canada's Anti-Indian Immigration Policies in the Twentieth Century. 2014. (Righting Canada's Wrongs Ser.). (ENG., Illus.). 104p. (YA). (gr. 8-12). 34.95 (978-1-4594-0437-3(8), 9781459404373) Lorimer, James & Co., Ltd., Pubs. CAN. Dist: Casemate Pubs. & Bk. Distributors, LLC.

Thomson, Ruth. Living in India. Hampton, David, illus. 2006. (Living In- Ser.). 32p. (J). (gr. 4-7). lib. bdg. 27.10 (978-1-59771-046-6(6)) Sea-To-Sea Pubns.

EAST INDIANS—UNITED STATES

Aalgaard, Wendy. East Indians in America. 2005. (In America Ser.). (ENG., Illus.). 80p. (gr. 5-8). lib. bdg. 27.93 (978-0-8225-4871-3(2), Lerner Pubns.) Lerner Publishing Group.

Brennan, Kristine. Indian Americans. (Successful Americans Ser.). 64p. (YA). 2009. (gr. 9-12). 22.95 (978-1-4222-0521-1(5)) 2007. (gr. 7-18). pap. 9.95 (978-1-4222-0862-5(1)) Mason Crest.

Doak, Robin Santos. Indian Americans. 2007. (American Immigrants Ser.). (Illus.). 48p. (J). (gr. 4-6). lib. bdg. (978-1-60044-612-2(4)) Rourke Educational Media.

McDaniel, Jan. Indian Immigration. 2005. (Changing Face of North America Ser.). (Illus.). 112p. (YA). lib. bdg. 24.95 (978-1-59084-683-4(4)) Mason Crest.

Park, Ken. Americans from India & Other South Asian Countries. 2009. (New Americans Ser.). 80p. (gr. 5-8). 35.64 (978-0-7614-4305-6(3)) Marshall Cavendish Corp.

Pelham, Lawrence & National Geographic Learning Staff. I Am Indian American. 2010. (Rise & Shine Ser.). (ENG.). 24p. (C). (gr. k-3). lib. bdg. 37.95 (978-0-8239-5008-9(5)) National Geographic School Publishing, Inc.

EASTER

Adams, Michelle Medlock. What Is Easter? Wummer, Amy, illus. (ENG.). 26p. (J). 2007. bds. 12.99 (978-0-8249-6691-1(0)) 2005. (gr. -1-k). bds. 6.95 (978-0-8249-6639-3(2)) Worthy Publishing. (Ideal Pubns.).

Alary, Laura. Make Room: A Child's Guide to Lent & Easter. Boyajian, Ann, illus. 2016. (ENG.). 32p. (J). pap. 15.99 (978-1-61261-659-9(3)) Paraclete Pr., Inc.

Anders, Isabel. Easter ABCs. 2007. (Illus.). 32p. (J). (gr. -1-1). per. 6.49 (978-0-7586-1204-5(4)) Concordia Publishing Hse.

—Easter ABCs. Rasche, Shelly, illus. 2004. 32p. (J). tchr. ed. 9.49 (978-0-570-07020-7(1), 56-2040) Concordia Publishing Hse.

B&H Kids Editorial Staff. Easter (board Book) Conger, Holli, illus. 2017. (Little Words Matter(tm) Ser.). (ENG.). 24p. (J). (gr. -1 — 1). bds. 8.99 (978-1-4336-4453-5(3), B&H Kids) B&H Publishing Group.

Beaton, Clare. Easter. 2007. (Pocket Money Ser.). (ENG., Illus.). 24p. (J). (gr. 1-4). pap. 7.99 (978-1-905710-01-0(1)) B Small Publishing GBR. Dist: Independent Pubs. Group.

—Easter Activity Book. 2011. (Seasonal Activity Ser.). (ENG., Illus.). 24p. (J). (gr. 1-4). reprint ed. pap., act. bk. ed. 7.99 (978-1-874735-46-5(8)) B Small Publishing GBR. Dist: Independent Pubs. Group.

Bentley, Joyce. Happy Easter: The Festival of New Life. 2017. (Let's Celebrate Ser.). (ENG., Illus.). 24p. (J). (gr. k-2). 16.99 (978-0-7502-9568-0(6), Wayland) Hachette Children's Group GBR. Dist: Hachette Bk. Group.

Bickico Enterprises, concept. BabyKids: Easter Book. 2005. 16p. (J). pap. 2.95 (978-0-9746508-8-3(9)) Bickico Enterprises, Inc.

Bohnet, Eric C. Arch Books: The Centurion at the Cross. Murphy, Terri, illus. 2007. (Arch Bks.). (J). 1.99 (978-0-7586-1260-1(5)) Concordia Publishing Hse.

Bradford, Amy L. & Larmoyeux, Mary. Resurrection Eggs Activity Book. Wadkins, Fran, illus. 2006. 58p. (J). (gr. 4-7). pap. 6.99 (978-1-57229-790-6(5)) FamilyLife.

Broslavick, Chris & Pichler, Tony. Totally Lent! A Teen's Journey to Easter 2004. Cannizzo, Karen, ed. Jones, Doug, illus. 2003. 64p. (J). 5.95 (978-0-89837-233-5(X), 3564) Pflaum Publishing Group.

—Totally Lent! A Teen's Journey to Easter 2006. Cannizzo, Karen A., ed. 2005. (Illus.). 64p. (J). 5.95 (978-1-933178-24-0(8), 3566) Pflaum Publishing Group.

—Totally Lent! A Teen's Journey to Easter 2007. 2006. (Illus.). 64p. pap. 5.95 (978-1-933178-44-8(2)) Pflaum Publishing Group.

—Totally Lent! A Teen's Journey to Easter 2008. 2007. (Illus.). 64p. (YA). (gr. 8-12). pap. 5.95 (978-1-933178-72-1(8)) Pflaum Publishing Group.

Buck, Deanna. My First Story of the First Easter. 2008. 32p. (J). 13.95 (978-1-59038-871-6(2)) Deseret Bk. Co.

Burkart, Jeffrey, narrated by. The Week That Led to Easter/Jesus Washes Peter's Feet. 2005. (Arch Books on CD Ser.). (Illus.). 16p. (J). (gr. -1-3). pap. 7.99 incl. audio compact disk (978-5-559-30143-3(4)) Concordia Publishing Hse.

Cosgrove, Stephen. Easter Bunnies. Edelson, Wendy, illus. 32p. (J). pap. 4.95 (978-0-8249-5371-3(1), Ideal Pubns.) Worthy Publishing.

Cosson, M. J. Easter Traditions Around the World. Chavarri, Elisa, illus. 2013. (World Traditions Ser.). (ENG.). 32p. (J). (gr. k-3). 28.50 (978-1-61473-426-0(7), 205131) Child's World, Inc., The.

David, Juliet. The Easter Story, 1 vol. Parry, Jo, illus. 2015. (ENG.). 12p. (J). bds. 3.99 (978-1-85985-992-6(5), Candle Bks.) Lion Hudson PLC GBR. Dist: Kregel Pubns.

David, Juliet & Ayliffe, Alex. Easter Story, 1 vol. Ellis, Elina, illus. 2014. (ENG.). 40p. (J). 8.99 (978-1-78128-177-2(7), Candle Bks.) Lion Hudson PLC GBR. Dist: Kregel Pubns.

DeGezelle, Terri. Simon of Cyrene & the Legend of the Easter Egg. Utomo, Gabhor, illus. 2017. 25p. (J). pap. (978-0-8198-9070-2(7)) Pauline Bks. & Media.

Derico, Laura Ring. Jesus Lives! the Easter Story. Krum, Ronda, illus. 2015. (Faith That Sticks Bks.). (ENG.). 26p. (J). pap. 3.99 (978-1-4964-0310-0(X)) Tyndale Hse. Pubs.

Dickmann, Nancy. Easter, 1 vol. 2010. (Holidays & Festivals Ser.). (ENG., Illus.). 24p. (gr. -1-1). pap. 6.29 (978-1-4329-4067-6(8), Acorn) Heinemann-Raintree.

—Pascua, 1 vol. 2011. (Fiestas Ser.). (ENG & SPA., Illus.). 24p. (gr. -1-1). pap. 6.29 (978-1-4329-5397-3(4), Bellota) Heinemann-Raintree.

Dingles, Molly. On Easter Morning. Wallis, Rebecca, illus. 2005. (Holiday Happenings Ser.). 32p. (J). per. 10.95 (978-1-59646-193-2(4)) Dingles & Co.

Donner, Candie. Easter Activity Book. Kinney, Cyndi, ed. 2013. (J). pap. 22.99 (978-1-61625-617-3(6)); cd-rom 12.99 (978-1-61625-616-6(8)) Knowledge Box Central.

Dowley, Tim. My First Story of Easter. Langton, Roger, illus. 2005. (My First Story Ser.). (ENG.). 24p. (J). 7.99 (978-0-8024-1767-1(1)) Moody Pubs.

—Would You Like to Know the Story of Easter?, 1 vol. Reeves, Eira, illus. 2016. (ENG.). 28p. (J). pap. 2.99 (978-1-78128-198-7(X), Candle Bks.) Lion Hudson PLC GBR. Dist: Kregel Pubns.

Down, Hayley & Make Believe Ideas Staff. My Easter Basket. Ede, Lara, illus. 2014. (ENG.). 12p. (J). (gr. -1). bds. 8.99 (978-1-78235-074-3(8)) Make Believe Ideas GBR. Dist: Nelson, Thomas Inc.

Doyle, Christopher. The Story of Easter. Haysom, John, illus. (J). (gr. k-3). 2008. 29p. pap. 7.49 (978-0-7586-1495-7(0))

E F G

2005. 32p. 13.49 *(978-0-7586-0837-6(3))* Concordia Publishing Hse.

Dreyer, Nicole. Easter Stranger. 2009. (Arch Bks.). (Illus.). 16p. (J). (gr. k-4). pap. 2.49 *(978-0-7586-1610-4(4))* Concordia Publishing Hse.

Easter. (Illus.). (gr. 1-4). 3.00 *(978-0-570-05524-2(5),* 54-1034) Concordia Publishing Hse.

Easter: 400 Reusable Stickers. 2015. (Eyelike Stickers Ser.). (ENG.). 12p. (J). 6.95 *(978-0-7611-8183-5(0),* 18183) Workman Publishing Co., Inc.

The Easter Activity Book. 2013. (ENG.). 144p. (J). pap. 9.95 *(978-1-78212-147-3(1))* Arcturus Publishing GBR. Dist: Bookmasters Distribution.

Ellis, Gwen. Read & Share: the Story of Easter, 0 vols. 2010. 36p. (J). 10.99 *(978-1-4003-1461-4(5))* Nelson, Thomas Inc.

—The Story of Easter, 1 vol. Smallman, Steve, illus. 2008. (Read & Share (Tommy Nelson) Ser.). (ENG.). 32p. (gr. -1-2). 7.99 *(978-1-4003-0855-2(0))* Nelson, Thomas Inc.

Engelbrecht, Edward A. & Pawlitz, Gail E., eds. The Easter Story: Drawn Directly from the Bible. 2011. (ENG., Illus.). 32p. (J). (gr. 4-7). 6.99 *(978-0-7586-1907-5(3))* Concordia Publishing Hse.

Fogle, Robin. The Easter Story Coloring Book. 2007. (Illus.). 16p. (J). pap. 1.89 *(978-1-59317-190-2(0))* Warner Pr., Inc.

Frisch, Aaron. Easter. 2005. (My First Look at Holidays Ser.). (Illus.). 24p. (J). (gr. k-3). lib. bdg. 15.95 *(978-1-58341-367-8(7),* Creative Education) Creative Co., The.

Fryar, Jane L. The Easter Day Surprise. Dorenkamp, Michelle, illus. 2008. 32p. (Orig.). (J). (gr. k-4). 13.49 *(978-0-7586-1445-2(4))* Concordia Publishing Hse.

Galvin, Jennifer. My Catholic Lent & Easter. 2003. 32p. act. bk. ed. 8.95 *(978-0-8091-6706-7(9),* 6706-9) Paulist Pr.

Ganeri, Anita. The Easter Story. Phillips, Rachael, illus. 2003. (Festival Stories Ser.). 24p. (J). pap. *(978-0-237-52475-3(9))* Evans Brothers, Ltd.

Gibson, C. R., Company Staff. Story of Easter. (Illus.). (J). 9.95 *(978-0-8378-2838-1(4))* Gibson, C. R. Co.

Glaser, Rebecca. The Holy Moly Easter Story. Ferenc, Bill, illus. 2016. (Holy Moly Bible Storybooks Ser.). (ENG.). 32p. (J). (gr. k-3). 12.99 *(978-1-5064-0256-7(9),* Sparkhouse Family) Augsburg Fortress, Pubs.

Godfrey, Jan. The Road to Easter Day. Piwowarski, Marcin, illus. 2009. 32p. (J). (gr. -1-1). 14.95 *(978-0-8198-6486-4(2))* Pauline Bks. & Media.

Grabowski, Leo. Nathan's Thread. Hale, Pattie, illus. 2009. 32p. (J). pap. 14.95 *(978-0-9822375-1-9(0))* Relevant Graces Productions.

Grack, Rachel. Easter. 2017. (Easter Ser.). 24p. (J). (gr. k-3). pap. 6.99 ***(978-1-61891-273-2(9))***; (ENG., Illus.). lib. bdg. 25.95 *(978-1-62617-594-5(2))* Bellwether Media. (Blastoff! Readers).

Greenwell, Jessica. First Sticker Book Easter. 2012. (First Sticker Bks). 16p. (J). pap. 8.99 *(978-0-7945-3266-6(7),* Usborne) EDC Publishing.

Hallinan, P. K. Today Is Easter! 2009. (ENG.). 26p. (J). bds. 6.99 *(978-0-8249-1822-4(3),* Ideal Pubns.) Worthy Publishing.

Hayes, Don, illus. The Easter. 24p. (Orig.). (J). pap., act. bk. ed. 4.95 *(978-0-8249-5368-3(1),* Ideal Pubns.) Worthy Publishing.

Heiligman, Deborah. Celebrate Easter: With Colored Eggs, Flowers, & Prayer. (Holidays Around the World Ser.). (ENG., Illus.). 32p. (J). (gr. 1-4). 2010. pap. 6.95 *(978-1-4263-0628-0(8))* 2007. 23.90 *(978-1-4263-0021-9(2))* 2007. 15.95 *(978-1-4263-0020-2(4))* National Geographic Society. (National Geographic Children's Bks.).

He's Alive! The Story of Easter. (Illus.). 16p. (J). pap. 1.50 *(978-0-87162-859-6(7),* E4572) Warner Pr., Inc.

Heyer, Carol. The First Easter. Heyer, Carol, illus. 2008. (ENG., Illus.). 28p. (J). (gr. -1-3). 8.99 *(978-0-8249-5576-2(5),* Ideal Pubns.) Worthy Publishing.

Heyer, Carol, illus. The First Easter. 2003. (ENG.). 32p. (J). 14.95 *(978-0-8249-5463-5(7),* Ideal Pubns.) Worthy Publishing.

Heyer, Carol, illus. & retold by. The Easter Story. Heyer, Carol, retold by. 32p. (J). 12.95 *(978-0-8249-5363-8(0),* Ideal Pubns.) Worthy Publishing.

Highlights. Easter Fun. 2017. (Highlights(tm) Carry-And-Play Board Bks.). (ENG.). 22p. (J). (gr. -1-k). bds. 8.99 *(978-1-62979-758-8(8),* Highlights) Boyds Mills Pr.

Highlights for Children Editorial Staff, creator. Easter Puzzles. 2017. (Highlights(tm) Puzzlemania(r) Activity Bks.). (ENG.). 144p. (J). (gr. k-4). pap. 9.95 *(978-1-62979-700-7(6),* Highlights) Boyds Mills Pr.

Houghton, Gillian. Easter. 2009. (My Library of Holidays Ser.). 24p. (gr. 1-1). 37.50 *(978-1-61514-693-2(8),* PowerKids Pr.) Rosen Publishing Group, Inc., The.

Howie, Vickie & MacLean, Moira. Easter Surprise: A Lift-the-Flap Board Book. 2006. (Illus.). 32p. (J). (gr. -1-k). bds. 9.49 *(978-0-7586-1148-2(X))* Concordia Publishing Hse.

Jander, Martha Streufert. The Easter Gift. 2008. (Arch Bks.). 16p. (J). (gr. k-4). pap. 1.99 *(978-0-7586-1450-6(0))* Concordia Publishing Hse.

Kennedy, Pamela. An Easter Celebration: Traditions & Customs from Around the World. 10.95 *(978-0-8249-5364-5(9),* Ideal Pubns.) Worthy Publishing.

—Prayers at Eastertime. Britt, Stephanie, illus. 2009. (ENG.). 24p. (J). 8.99 *(978-0-8249-5609-7(5),* Ideal Pubns.) Worthy Publishing.

Knighton, Kate. 50 Easter Things to Make & Do. 2009. (50 Easter Things to Make & Do Ser.). 104p. (J). (gr. 1). spiral bd. 9.99 *(978-0-7945-2206-3(8),* Usborne) EDC Publishing.

Knudsen, Michelle. Easter Fun. Starace, Tom, illus. 2006. (ENG.). 12p. (J). bds. 4.99 *(978-0-689-87894-7(X),* Little Simon) Little Simon.

Knudsen, Michelle & Yoon, Salina. Happy Easter! Yoon, Salina, illus. 2003. (Sparkle 'n' Shimmer Ser.). (ENG., Illus.). 14p. (J). (gr. -1-k). bds. 5.99 *(978-0-689-85311-1(4),* Little Simon) Little Simon.

Knudsen, Shannon. Easter Around the World. Erickson, David, illus. 2005. (On My Own Holidays Ser.). (ENG.). 48p. (gr. 2-4). 25.26 *(978-1-57505-655-5(0))* Lerner Publishing Group.

—La Pascua en Todo el Mundo. Erickson, David L., illus. 2007. (Yo Solo - Festividades (on My Own - Holidays) Ser.). 48p. (J). (gr. k-5). (SPA.). lib. bdg. 25.26 *(978-0-8225-7791-1(7))*; per. 6.95 *(978-0-8225-7794-2(1))* Lerner Publishing Group.

—La Pascua en Todo el Mundo; Easter Around the World. 2008. pap. 40.95 *(978-0-8225-9677-6(6))* Lerner Publishing Group.

Kovacs, Victoria. Christmas/Easter Flip-Over Book. Krome, Mike, illus. 2015. (Little Bible Heroes(tm) Ser.). (ENG.). 32p. (J). (gr. k-2). pap. 3.99 *(978-1-4336-8711-2(9),* B&H Kids) B&H Publishing Group.

Kueker, Donald, illus. The Easter Story According to Matthew. 2007. 32p. (J). per. 7.49 *(978-0-7586-1008-9(4))* Concordia Publishing Hse.

Landau, Elaine. Easter: Parades, Chocolates, & Celebration. 2004. (Finding Out about Holidays Ser.). (Illus.). 48p. (J). lib. bdg. 25.27 *(978-0-7660-2172-3(6))* Enslow Pubs., Inc.

Lane, Leena. Easter Days: My First Bible Activity Book. 2008. (Illus.). 31p. (J). pap. 6.95 *(978-1-59325-123-9(8))* Word Among Us Pr.

Larkin, Jean. Totally Lent! A Child's Journey to Easter 2007. 2006. (Illus.). 64p. pap. 5.95 *(978-1-933178-46-2(9))* Pflaum Publishing Group.

—Totally Lent! A Child's Journey to Easter 2008. 2007. (Illus.). 64p. (J). (gr. 4-7). pap. 5.95 *(978-1-933178-70-7(1))* Pflaum Publishing Group.

—Totally Lent! A Kid's Journey to Easter 2007. 2006. (Illus.). 64p. pap. 5.95 *(978-1-933178-45-5(0))* Pflaum Publishing Group.

Let's Celebrate Jesus on Easter. 2004. 24p. (J). 2.49 *(978-0-7847-1582-6(3))* Standard Publishing.

Lewis, Anne Margaret. What Am I? Easter. Mills, Tom, illus. 2012. (ENG.). 24p. (J). (gr. -1 — 1). 9.99 *(978-0-8075-8963-2(2))* Whitman, Albert & Co.

Liguori Publications, creator. Every Day of Lent & Easter, Year C: A Book of Activities for Children. 2007. (Illus.). 47p. (J). (gr. 4-7). pap. 3.95 *(978-0-7648-1499-0(0))* Liguori Pubns.

Mackall, Dandi Daley. Easter Colors Sticker Book. Fyffe, Brian, illus. 2004. 10p. (J). (gr. -1-18). bds. 4.99 *(978-1-57151-723-4(5))* Playhouse Publishing.

—Easter Is for Me! 2007. (Illus.). 24p. (J). (gr. -1-2). 13.49 *(978-0-7586-1299-1(0))* Concordia Publishing Hse.

Maier, Paul L. The Very First Easter. Ordaz, Francisco, illus. (J). 2005. 20p. bds. 7.49 *(978-0-7586-0717-1(2))* 2004. 32p. 13.49 *(978-0-570-07053-5(8))* Concordia Publishing Hse.

Malone, Jean M. The Miracle of Easter. Lango, Bryan, illus. 2010. (Penguin Young Readers, Level 3 Ser.). (ENG.). 48p. (J). (gr. 1-3). pap. 3.99 *(978-0-448-45265-4(0),* Penguin Young Readers) Penguin Young Readers Group.

Matters, Print & Morrill, Ann. Easter, Passover, & Other Spring Festivals. 2009. (Holidays & Celebration Ser.). (Illus.). 112p. (gr. 5-8). 40.00 *(978-1-60413-099-7(7),* Chelsea Hse.) Facts On File, Inc.

McGee, Randel. Paper Crafts for Easter. 2011. (Paper Craft Fun for Holidays Ser.). (Illus.). 48p. (J). (gr. 3-18). pap. 8.95 *(978-1-59845-335-5(1),* Enslow Elementary) Enslow Pubs., Inc.

McGrath, Barbara Barbieri. The M & M's(r) Brand Easter Egg Hunt. Tagel, Peggy, illus. 2004. 12p. (J). (gr. -1-3). bds. 6.95 *(978-1-57091-423-2(0))* Charlesbridge Publishing, Inc.

Meade, Jean McCurdy. The Tale of Rebekah Rabbit. Clark, Barbara Hoseman, illus. 2009. 28p. pap. 12.95 *(978-1-59658-970-2(9))* Dog Ear Publishing, LLC.

Miller, Claire. The Easter Surprise. 2015. (Arch Books Ser.). (ENG.). 16p. (J). pap. 2.49 *(978-0-7586-4820-4(0))* Concordia Publishing Hse.

Miller, Eileen Rudisill. Happy Easter Stained Glass Coloring Book. 2010. (Holiday Stained Glass Coloring Book Ser.). (ENG., Illus.). 32p. (J). (gr. -1-8). pap. 6.99 *(978-0-486-47296-6(5))* Dover Pubns., Inc.

Mitchell, Alison. Easter Unscrambled: Bible Discovery for Children & Families. 2010. 41p. (J). pap. *(978-1-873166-89-5(3))* Good Bk. Co.

Molloy, Bonnie G. When the Rock Rocked... 2011. 24p. pap. 14.93 *(978-1-4269-4890-9(5))* Trafford Publishing.

Morrison, Jessica. Easter. 2010. (Illus.). 24p. *(978-1-55388-610-5(0))*; pap. *(978-1-55388-611-2(9))* Weigl Educational Pubs. Ltd.

Murray, Julie. Easter, 1 vol. 2011. (Holidays Set 3 Ser.). (ENG., Illus.). 24p. (J). (gr. 1-4). 25.65 *(978-1-61783-038-9(0))* ABDO Publishing Co.

One Room Sunday School Leader's Guide (Spring 2010) 2009. 12.50 *(978-1-4267-0141-2(1))* Abingdon Pr.

O'Neal, Debbie Trafton. I Is for Jesus: An Easter Alphabet & Activity Book. Bryan-Hunt, Jan, illus. 2005. 32p. (J). (gr. 3-7). per., act. bk. ed. 11.99 *(978-0-8066-5123-1(7),* Augsburg Bks.) Augsburg Fortress, Pubs.

Owen, Ruth. Easter Origami. 2012. (Holiday Origami Ser.). (ENG., Illus.). 32p. (J). (gr. 3-6). 26.50 *(978-1-4488-7861-1(6))*; pap. 11.75 *(978-1-4488-7920-5(5))* Rosen Publishing Group, Inc., The. (PowerKids Pr.).

Packard, Mary & Croll, Carolyn. The Great Easter Egg Hunt. (Muppets Ser.). (ENG., Illus.). 1p. (J). bds. 77.70 *(978-0-7611-1036-1(4),* 21036) Workman Publishing Co., Inc.

Payne, Martyn. Footsteps to the Feast: 12 Two-Hour Children's Programmes for Christian Festivals & Special Times of the Year. 2007. (ENG., Illus.). 240p. pap. *(978-1-84101-464-7(8),* Barnabas) Bible Reading Fellowship.

Peppas, Lynn. Easter. 2009. (Celebrations in My World Ser.). (ENG., Illus.). 32p. (J). (gr. 1-3). pap. *(978-0-7787-4307-1(1))* Crabtree Publishing Co.

Pettiford, Rebecca. Easter. 2014. (Illus.). 24p. (J). lib. bdg. 25.65 *(978-1-62031-129-5(1),* Bullfrog Bks.) Jump! Inc.

Pfeifer, Alice Ann. Totally Lent! A Kid's Journey to Easter 2008. 2007. (Illus.). 64p. pap. 5.95 *(978-1-933178-71-4(X))* Pflaum Publishing Group.

—Totally Lent! My Journey to Easter 2005! Larkin, Jean K., ed. 2004. (Illus.). 64p. (J). 5.95 *(978-0-89837-248-9(8),* 3575) Pflaum Publishing Group.

Pienkowski, Jan. Easter. 2015. (ENG.). 32p. (J). (gr. k-12). 15.99 *(978-0-385-39277-8(X),* Knopf Bks. for Young Readers) Random Hse. Children's Bks.

Pingry, Patricia A. The Easter Story. Utt, Mary Ann, illus. (ENG.). (J). 2008. 26p. (gr. -1-3). bds. 12.99 *(978-0-8249-6731-4(3))* 2006. 32p. (gr. -1-3). per. 3.95 *(978-0-8249-5531-1(5))* 2003. 26p. bds. 6.95 *(978-0-8249-4231-1(0))* Worthy Publishing. (Ideal Pubns.).

—On Easter Sunday. Johnson, Meredith, illus. 2007. (ENG.). 26p. (J). (gr. -1-3). bds. 6.99 *(978-0-8249-6692-8(9),* Ideal Pubns.) Worthy Publishing.

—The Story of Easter. Thornburgh, Rebecca McKillip & Thornburgh, Rebecca, illus. 2011. 22p. (J). bds. 6.99 *(978-0-8249-1844-6(4),* Ideal Pubns.) Worthy Publishing.

—The Story of Easter. Wells, Lorraine, illus. (ENG.). (gr. -1-3). 2008. 22p. (J). pap. 3.99 *(978-0-8249-5560-1(9))* 2006. 26p. 12.95 *(978-0-8249-6649-2(X))* Worthy Publishing. (Ideal Pubns.).

Pirotta, Saviour. Easter. 2007. (We Love Holidays Ser.). (Illus.). 24p. (J). (gr. -1-3). lib. bdg. 22.60 *(978-1-4042-3705-6(4),* PowerKids Pr.) Rosen Publishing Group, Inc., The.

Priddy, Roger. Baby Touch & Feel Easter Bunny. 2008. (Baby Touch & Feel Ser.). (ENG.). 14p. (J). (gr. -1 — 1). bds. 8.95 *(978-0-312-50580-6(9),* 9780312505806, Priddy Bks.) St. Martin's Pr.

—Bright Baby Touch & Feel Easter. 2012. (Bright Baby Touch & Feel Ser.). (ENG., Illus.). 12p. (J). (gr. -1 — 1). bds. 4.95 *(978-0-312-51375-7(5),* 9780312513757, Priddy Bks.) St. Martin's Pr.

—Slide & Find Easter. 2011. (Slide & Find Ser.). (ENG., Illus.). 8p. (J). (gr. -1 — 1). bds. 8.99 *(978-0-312-51001-5(2),* 9780312510015, Priddy Bks.) St. Martin's Pr.

Publications International Ltd. Staff, ed. Sesame Street(r) Happy Easter, Elmo! 2014. 12p. (J). bds. *(978-1-4508-3302-8(0),* c726526e-0586-4bbf-a70d-c1093f5cc14b) Phoenix International Publications, Inc.

Radtke, Becky. Easter Spot-the-Differences. 2004. (Dover Little Activity Bks.). (ENG., Illus.). 64p. (J). (gr. 3-5). pap. 1.99 *(978-0-486-43852-8(X))* Dover Pubns., Inc.

Randall, Ronne. Happy Easter. Davis, Caroline, illus. 2016. (Create & Celebrate Ser.). (ENG.). 48p. (J). (gr. -1-2). pap. 6.99 *(978-1-4380-0764-9(7))* Barron's Educational Series, Inc.

Robertson, Brynn, compiled by. Standard Easter Program Book. annuals 2005. (New Easter Program Bks.). (Illus.). 48p. pap. 5.99 *(978-0-7847-1618-2(8),* 08716) Standard Publishing.

Roche, Maite. My First Pictures of Easter. 2012. 14p. 6.99 *(978-1-58617-653-2(6))* Ignatius Pr.

Ross, Kathy. All New Crafts for Easter. Holm, Sharon Lane, tr. Holm, Sharon Lane, illus. 2005. (All New Holiday Crafts for Kids Ser.). (ENG.). 48p. (gr. k-3). pap. 7.95 *(978-0-7613-2392-1(9))*; lib. bdg. 25.26 *(978-0-7613-2921-3(8))* Lerner Publishing Group. (Millbrook Pr.).

Rottmann, Erik. The Easter Victory. Billin-Frye, Paige, illus. 2006. (Arch Bks.). (ENG.). 16p. (J). (gr. -1-3). 2.49 *(978-0-7586-0869-7(1))* Concordia Publishing Hse.

Savitskas, Margaret. Totally Lent! A Kid's Journey to Easter 2006. Larkin, Jean K., ed. 2005. (Illus.). 64p. (J). 5.95 *(978-1-933178-25-7(6),* 3576) Pflaum Publishing Group.

Savitskas, Margaret & Behe, Mary. Totally Lent! A Child's Journey to Easter 2006. Larkin, Jean K., ed. 2005. (Illus.). 64p. (J). 5.95 *(978-1-933178-26-4(4),* 3586) Pflaum Publishing Group.

Schroeder, Doug. Does the Bunny Lay Easter Eggs. 2004. pap. 4.99 *(978-0-570-04953-1(9))* Concordia Publishing Hse.

Schulman, Janet. 10 Easter Egg Hunters: A Holiday Counting Book. Davick, Linda, illus. 2015. (ENG.). 32p. (J). (— 1). 4.99 *(978-0-553-50784-3(2),* Dragonfly Bks.) Random Hse. Children's Bks.

Schultz, Joani, et al. Easter Extras: Faith-Filled Ideas for Easter Week. Creyts, Patrick, illus. 2007. 24p. pap. 6.99 *(978-0-7644-3694-9(5))* Group Publishing, Inc.

Sebra, Richard. It's Easter! 2017. (Bumba Books (tm) — It's a Holiday! Ser.). (ENG.). 24p. (J). (gr. -1-1). 12.99 ***(978-1-5124-3699-0(2),*** Lerner Pubns.); 38.65 ***(978-1-5124-3698-3(4),*** Lerner Pubns.); (Illus.). 25.32 *(978-1-5124-2564-2(8))*; (Illus.). 38.65 ***(978-1-5124-2743-1(8),*** Lerner Pubns.) Lerner Publishing Group.

Simon, Mary Manz. My Easter Basket: The True Story of Easter. Clearwater, Linda, illus. 2016. (ENG.). 14p. (J). (gr. -1 — 1). bds. 12.99 *(978-1-4336-8990-1(1),* B&H Kids) B&H Publishing Group.

Smith, Martina. The Story of Easter: A Spark Bible Story. Grosshauser, Peter, illus. 2016. (Spark Bible Stories Ser.). (ENG.). 32p. (J). (gr. -1-2). 12.99 *(978-1-5064-0230-7(5),* Sparkhouse Family) Augsburg Fortress, Pubs.

Smith, Mary Lou. Celebrate Easter. 2015. (Our Holidays Ser.). (ENG., Illus.). 24p. (J). (gr. 1-1). pap. 8.22 *(978-1-5026-0421-7(3))* Cavendish Square Publishing.

Sourcebooks, Inc Staff. Easter Bunny Coupons. 2012. (ENG.). 48p. (J). (-4). pap. 5.99 *(978-1-4022-6821-2(1))* Sourcebooks, Inc.

Spear, Kevin. Itty-bitty Bible Activity Book, Easter. 2007. (Illus.). 48p. (J). pap. 1.49 *(978-1-59317-196-4(X))* Warner Pr., Inc.

Standard Publishing Staff & Bookworks Staff. Tell Me about Easter. 2010. (ENG.). 8p. (J). (gr. -1 — 1). bds. 12.99 *(978-0-7847-2394-4(X),* B&H Kids) B&H Publishing Group.

Steigemeyer, Julie. My Little Easter Book. Regan, Dana, illus. 2008. 20p. (J). (gr. -1-k). bds. 6.49 *(978-0-7586-1444-5(6))* Concordia Publishing Hse.

Stiegemeyer, Julie. Things I See at Easter. Mitter, Kathy, illus. 2005. 20p. (J). bds. 5.49 *(978-0-7586-0797-3(0))* Concordia Publishing Hse.

Trueit, Trudi Strain. Easter. Huang, Benrei, illus. 2013. (Holidays & Celebrations Ser.). (ENG.). 32p. (J). (gr. k-3). 27.07 *(978-1-62323-515-4(4),* 206278) Child's World, Inc., The.

Twin Sisters(r), et al. Celebrate Easter! Prayer & Activity Book. 2017. (I'm Learning the Bible Activity Book Ser.). (ENG.). 32p. (J). pap. 4.99 *(978-1-68322-073-2(0))* Barbour Publishing, Inc.

—The Story of Easter: Read-Along Book with CD. 2017. (Let's Share a Story Ser.). (ENG.). 16p. (J). (-5). bds. 9.99 *(978-1-68322-077-0(3))* Barbour Publishing, Inc.

Vidrine, Beverly Barras. Easter Day Alphabet, 1 vol. Lyne, Alison Davis, illus. 2003. (ENG.). 32p. (J). (gr. k-k). pap. 8.95 *(978-1-58980-076-2(1))* Pelican Publishing Co., Inc.

Walker, Joni, illus. & contrib. by. Tell Me the Easter Story. Walker, Joni, contrib. by. 2004. 14p. (J). bds. 5.49 *(978-0-7586-0629-7(X))* Concordia Publishing Hse.

Watt, Fiona. Easter Activities. 2004. (Activity Bks.). (Illus.). 32p. (J). pap., act. bk. ed. 6.95 *(978-0-7945-0344-4(6),* Usborne) EDC Publishing.

—Easter Fun. 2009. (Preschool Activities Ser.). (Illus.). 24p. (J). (gr. -1). spiral bd. 12.99 *(978-0-7945-2482-1(6),* Usborne) EDC Publishing.

Wedeven, Carol. The Easter Cave. 2007. (Illus.). 28p. (J). (gr. -1). per. 7.49 *(978-0-7586-1213-7(3))* Concordia Publishing Hse.

—The Easter Cave. Ebert, Len, illus. 2004. 32p. (J). (gr. -1-2). 10.49 *(978-0-570-07135-8(6))* Concordia Publishing Hse.

Wesley, Misty Lynn. The Dancing Easter Lilies. 2012. 36p. pap. 16.95 *(978-1-4626-6819-9(4))* America Star Bks.

Wildsmith, Brian. The Easter Story. Wildsmith, Brian, illus. 2004. (Illus.). 24p. (gr. -1-7). 18.00 *(978-0-8028-5189-5(4))* Eerdmans, William B. Publishing Co.

Williams, Colleen Madonna Flood. My Adventure on Easter. 2007. 44p. (J). 8.99 *(978-1-59092-546-1(7))* Blue Forge Pr.

Williamson, Karen. Easter, 1 vol. Embleton-Hall, Chris, illus. 2015. (Candle Tabs Ser.). (ENG.). 12p. (J). bds. 7.99 *(978-1-78128-157-4(2),* Candle Bks.) Lion Hudson PLC GBR. Dist: Kregel Pubns.

—The First Easter, 1 vol. Conner, Sarah, illus. 2016. (Candle Little Lambs Ser.). (ENG.). 24p. (J). pap. 2.99 *(978-1-78128-243-4(9),* Candle Bks.) Lion Hudson PLC GBR. Dist: Kregel Pubns.

Wolf, Jackie. Sparkle Basket. 2003. (Illus.). 10p. (J). (gr. -1-18). bds. 6.99 *(978-1-57151-713-5(8))* Playhouse Publishing.

Yasuda, Anita. Easter Crafts. Gallagher-Cole, Memie, illus. 2016. (Holiday Crafts Ser.). (ENG.). 24p. (J). (gr. k-3). 28.50 *(978-1-5038-0817-1(3),* 210653) Child's World, Inc., The.

Zemlicka, Shannon. Easter Around the World. Erickson, David, illus. 2005. (On My Own Holidays Ser.). 48p. (J). (gr. k-3). pap. 6.95 *(978-1-57505-765-1(4))* Lerner Publishing Group.

Zocchi, Judy. On Easter Morning. Wallis, Rebecca, illus. 2005. (Holiday Happenings Ser.). 32p. (J). pap. 10.95 *(978-1-59646-192-5(6))*; (ENM.). lib. bdg. 21.65 *(978-1-891997-41-9(6))* Dingles & Co.

—On Easter Morning/la mañana de Pascua. Wallis, Rebecca, illus. 2005. (Holiday Happenings Ser.).Tr. of mañana de Pascua. (ENG & SPA.). 32p. (J). pap. 10.95 *(978-1-59646-194-9(2))*; lib. bdg. 21.65 *(978-1-891997-42-6(4))*; per. 10.95 *(978-1-59646-195-6(0))* Dingles & Co.

Zondervan. Ready, Set, Find Easter, 1 vol. 2017. (Ready, Set, Find Ser.). (ENG.). 12p. (J). bds. 8.99 *(978-0-310-75769-6(X))* Zonderkidz.

Zondervan Bibles Staff. The Beginner's Bible Come Celebrate Easter, 1 vol. Pulley, Kelly, illus. 2015. (Beginner's Bible Ser.). (ENG.). 16p. (J). pap., act. bk. ed. 3.99 *(978-0-310-74733-8(3))* Zonderkidz.

Zondervan Staff. The First Easter Ever, 1 vol. Jones, Dennis, illus. 2015. (ENG.). 32p. (J). pap. 1.99 *(978-0-310-74084-1(3))* Zonderkidz.

—Jesus God's Only Son, 1 vol. Jones, Dennis, illus. 2010. (I Can Read! / Dennis Jones Ser.). (ENG.). 32p. (J). (gr. -1-2). pap. 3.99 *(978-0-310-71880-2(5))* Zonderkidz.

—The Very First Easter, 1 vol. Pulley, Kelly, illus. 2009. (Beginner's Bible Ser.). (ENG.). 32p. (J). pap. 47.76 *(978-0-310-71817-8(1))*; pap. 1.99 *(978-0-310-71827-7(9))* Zonderkidz.

EASTER—FICTION

Ackelsberg, Amy. Easter Surprise. Thomas, Laura, illus. 2011. (Strawberry Shortcake Ser.). (ENG.). 24p. (J). (gr. -1-k). mass mkt. 4.99 *(978-0-448-45547-1(1),* Grosset & Dunlap) Penguin Young Readers Group.

Adams, Adrienne. The Easter Egg Artists. 2017. (ENG.). 32p. (J). (gr. -1-3). 13.99 ***(978-1-5344-1245-3(X),*** Aladdin) Simon & Schuster Children's Publishing.

Adams, Michelle Medlock. Hooray for Easter! Devaney, Adam, illus. 2010. 16p. (J). (gr. -1-k). 12.99 *(978-0-8249-1840-8(1),* Ideal Pubns.) Worthy Publishing.

—The Sparrow's Easter Song. Eldridge, Marion, illus. (ENG.). 32p. (J). 2009. pap. 7.99 *(978-0-8249-5608-0(7))* 2003. 14.95 *(978-0-8249-5470-3(X))* Worthy Publishing. (Ideal Pubns.).

Albee, Sarah. The Bunny Hop. Swanson, Maggie, illus. 2004. (Big Bird's Favorites Board Bks.). (ENG.). 24p. (J). (gr. k — 1). bds. 4.99 *(978-0-375-82693-1(9),* Random Hse. Bks. for Young Readers) Random Hse. Children's Bks.

Amant, Kathleen. Anna & the Chocolate Easter Bunny. 2010. (ENG., Illus.). 32p. (J). (gr. k-k). 12.95 *(978-1-60537-028-6(2))* Cobblestone Publishing Co.

Amery, Heather. The Easter Story. 2004. (Bible Tales Readers Ser.). (Illus.). (J). (ENG.). 16p. pap. 4.95 *(978-0-7945-0254-6(7),* Usborne); 6p. lib. bdg. 12.95 *(978-1-58086-456-5(2))* EDC Publishing.

Anderson, R. P., et al. Happy Easter, Curious George. Young, Mary O'Keefe, illus. 2010. (Curious George Ser.). (ENG.). 24p. (J). (gr. -1-3). 9.99 *(978-0-547-04825-3(4))* Houghton Mifflin Harcourt Publishing Co.

Anna. The Magic Money Tree. 2009. (Illus.). 20p. pap. 15.49 *(978-1-4389-0472-6(X))* AuthorHouse.

Aragón, Carla, et al. Dance of the Eggshells: Baile de los Cascarones. Saville, Kathy Dee, illus. 2010. (SPA & ENG.). 32p. (J). (gr. 1). 18.95 *(978-0-8263-4770-1(3))* Univ. of New Mexico Pr.

Auer, Chris. The Legend of the Sand Dollar: An Inspirational Story of Hope for Easter, 1 vol. Johnson, Rick, illus. 2005. (ENG.). 32p. (J). 16.99 *(978-0-310-70780-6(3))* Zonderkidz.

—The Legend of the Sand Dollar, Newly Illustrated Edition: An Inspirational Story of Hope for Easter, 1 vol. Cowdrey, Richard, illus. 2017. (ENG.). 32p. (J). 16.99 *(978-0-310-74980-6(8))* Zonderkidz.

Awdry, Wilbert V. Easter Engines. 2012. (Thomas & Friends Step into Reading Ser.). lib. bdg. 13.55 *(978-0-606-23717-8(8),* Turtleback) Turtleback Bks.

Baker, Stacy. Sammy's Secret. 2005. (J). lib. bdg. 19.95 *(978-1-933732-03-9(2))* Big Ransom Studio.

Balian, Lorna. Humbug Rabbit. 2004. (Illus.). 32p. (J). 15.95 *(978-1-932065-40-4(7))* Star Bright Bks., Inc.

Banks, Steven. Show Me the Bunny! Greenblatt, C. H. & Reiss, William, illus. 2004. (Spongebob Squarepants Ser.).

32p. (J). 11.65 *(978-0-7569-5643-1(9))* Perfection Learning Corp.
—Show Me the Bunny! Random House, illus. 2014. (Step into Reading Ser.). (ENG.). 24p. (J). (gr. -1-1). 4.99 *(978-0-385-37608-2(1),* Random Hse. Bks. for Young Readers) Random Hse. Children's Bks.
Banks, Steven & Hillenburg, Stephen. Show Me the Bunny! Greenblatt, C. H. & Reiss, William, illus. 2004. (SpongeBob SquarePants Ser.: 3). (ENG.). 32p. (J). pap. 3.99 *(978-0-689-86485-8(X),* Simon Spotlight/Nickelodeon) Simon Spotlight/Nickelodeon.
Benoist, Cathy & Gilmore, Cathy. El Conejito de Pascua: El Cuento de un Dia Extraordinario. Sundy, Jonathan, illus. 2014. (SPA.). 40p. (J). (gr. 4-7). 16.99 *(978-0-7648-2456-2(2),* Libros Liguori) Liguori Pubns.
Berenstain, Jan. The Berenstain Bears Easter Fun Sticker & Activity Book, 1 vol. Berenstain, Mike, illus. 2017. (Berenstain Bears/Living Lights Ser.). (ENG.). 32p. (J). pap. 6.99 *(978-0-310-75381-0(3))* Zonderkidz.
Berenstain, Jan & Berenstain, Mike. The Berenstain Bears Bear Country Fun Sticker & Activity Book, 1 vol. 2016. (Berenstain Bears/Living Lights Ser.). (ENG., Illus.). 32p. (J). pap. 6.99 *(978-0-310-75336-0(8))* Zonderkidz.
Berenstain, Mike. The Berenstain Bears' Easter Parade. Berenstain, Mike, illus. 2014. (Berenstain Bears Ser.). (ENG., Illus.). 24p. (J). (gr. -1-3). pap. 3.99 *(978-0-06-207554-3(3),* HarperFestival) HarperCollins Pubs.
—The Berenstain Bears' Easter Sunday, 1 vol. 2016. (Berenstain Bears/Living Lights Ser.). (ENG.). 24p. (J). pap. 3.99 *(978-0-310-74902-8(6))* Zonderkidz.
Berenstain, Mike, illus. The Berenstain Bears: Easter Blessings. 2016. (J). *(978-0-8249-1967-2(X),* Ideal Pubns.) Worthy Publishing.
Berrios, Frank. The Easter Buggy. 2014. lib. bdg. 14.75 *(978-0-606-35543-8(X))* Turtleback Bks.
—The Easter Buggy (Disney/Pixar Cars) Random House Disney Staff, illus. 2014. (Pictureback(R) Ser.). (ENG.). 16p. (J). (gr. -1-2). 4.99 *(978-0-7364-3139-2(X),* RH/Disney) Random Hse. Children's Bks.
Berry, Ron. The Easter Bunny's Colorful Day! 2008. (Slide-N-Color Bks.). (Illus.). 10p. (J). (gr. -1). bds. 6.99 *(978-0-8249-6698-0(8),* Ideal Pubns.) Worthy Publishing.
Bickel, Karla. Easter Lights. Bickel, Karla, illus. l.t. ed. 2004. (Illus.). 16p. (J). (gr. -1-6). pap. 5.00 *(978-1-891452-14-7(2),* 7) Heart Arbor Bks.
Bohlken, Bob. How the Rabbit Became the Easter Bunny. Hogue, Ann, illus. 2016. (ENG.). 32p. (J). pap. 10.95 *(978-0-930643-36-2(4),* Snaptail Pr.) Images Unlimited Publishing.
Bostrom, Kathleen Long. Rufus & Ryan Celebrate Easter! Thornburgh, Rebecca, illus. 2014. (Rufus & Ryan Ser.). 20p. (J). bds. 7.99 *(978-0-8249-1919-1(X),* Ideal Pubns.) Worthy Publishing.
Bowman, Crystal. The Story of the Resurrection Eggs, 1 vol. Johnson, Richard G., illus. 2013. (ENG.). 40p. (J). 7.99 *(978-0-310-72595-4(X))* Zonderkidz.
Bratley, Colleen m. The Easter Spirit Eggs. 2012. (ENG.). (J). pap. 15.50 *(978-1-4675-2523-7(5))* Independent Pub.
Brett, Jan. The Easter Egg. Brett, Jan, illus. (ENG., Illus.). 32p. (J). 2017. (-k). bds. 8.99 *(978-0-399-54733-1(9))* 2010. (gr. -1-k). 17.99 *(978-0-399-25238-9(X))* Penguin Young Readers Group. (G.P. Putnam's Sons Books for Young Readers).
Bridwell, Norman. Clifford's First Easter. Bridwell, Norman, illus. 2010. (Clifford Ser.). (ENG., Illus.). 14p. (J). (gr. k — 1). bds. 6.99 *(978-0-545-20010-3(5),* Cartwheel Bks.) Scholastic, Inc.
—Clifford's Happy Easter. 2011. (Clifford's Big Ideas Ser.). (Illus.). (gr. -1). 14.00 *(978-1-60686-966-6(3))* Perfection Learning Corp.
—Clifford's Happy Easter. Bridwell, Norman, illus. 2011. (Clifford 8x8 Ser.). (ENG., Illus.). 32p. (J). (gr. -1-k). pap. 3.99 *(978-0-545-21587-9(0),* Cartwheel Bks.) Scholastic, Inc.
Bullard, Lisa. Emma's Easter. Basaluzzo, Constanza, illus. 2012. (Holidays & Special Days Ser.). 24p. (gr. k-2). (J). pap. 39.62 *(978-0-7613-9248-4(3));* (ENG.). pap. 6.95 *(978-0-7613-8581-3(9))* Lerner Publishing Group. (Millbrook Pr.).
Candlewick Press. Peppa Pig & the Easter Rainbow. 2017. (Peppa Pig Ser.). (ENG.). 32p. (J). (-k). 12.99 *(978-0-7636-9438-8(X),* Candlewick Entertainment) Candlewick Pr.
Capucilli, Alyssa Satin. Biscuit's Pet & Play Easter. Berlin, Rose Mary & Schories, Pat, illus. 2008. (Biscuit Ser.). (ENG.). 12p. (J). (gr. -1 — 1). bds. 7.99 *(978-0-06-112839-4(2),* HarperFestival) HarperCollins Pubs.
Carbone, Courtney. Somebunny Special (SpongeBob SquarePants) Golden Books Staff, illus. 2013. (Hologramatic Sticker Book Ser.). (ENG.). 48p. (J). (gr. -1-2). pap. 3.99 *(978-0-307-98104-2(5),* Golden Bks.) Random Hse. Children's Bks.
Carlson, Melody. Benjamin's Box: The Story of the Resurrection Eggs, 1 vol. Stockman, Jack, illus. rev. ed. 2008. (ENG.). 40p. (J). (gr. -1-3). 8.99 *(978-0-310-71505-4(9))* Zonderkidz.
Cazet, Denys. Minnie & Moo: The Attack of the Easter Bunnies. Cazet, Denys, illus. 2004. (I Can Read Bks.). (Illus.). 48p. (J). (gr. k-3). (ENG.). 15.99 *(978-0-06-000506-1(8));* lib. bdg. 17.89 *(978-0-06-000507-8(6))* HarperCollins Pubs.
Chaconas, Dori. Looking for Easter. Moore, Margie, illus. 2012. (J). 34.28 *(978-1-61913-120-0(X))* Weigl Pubs., Inc.
Cocca-Leffler, Maryann. Easter Bunny in Training. Cocca-Leffler, Maryann, illus. 2009. (Sneak a Peek Ser.). (Illus.). 16p. (J). (gr. -1-3). pap. 6.99 *(978-0-06-125673-8(0))* HarperCollins Pubs.
Coffelt, Soraya. It's Not about You Mr. Easter Bunny: A Love Letter about the True Meaning of Easter. Seroya, Tea, illus. 2017. (Love Letters Book Ser.). (ENG.). 36p. (J). pap. 8.99 *(978-1-68350-063-6(6))* Morgan James Publishing.
Coven, Wanda. Heidi Heckelbeck & the Tie-Dyed Bunny. 2014. (Heidi Heckelbeck Ser.: 10). lib. bdg. 16.00 *(978-0-606-35429-5(8))* Turtleback Bks.
Cummings, Alicia. The Adventures of Jayda. 2010. 44p. pap. 16.99 *(978-1-4520-2564-3(9))* AuthorHouse.
Dales, Cindy. Autumn's First Easter. 2009. 28p. pap. 12.99 *(978-1-4343-1433-8(2))* AuthorHouse.
Davidson, Alice Joyce. My Day with Jesus, 1 vol. Clar, David Austin, illus. 2005. (Easter Board Bks.). (ENG.). 16p. (J). bds. 3.99 *(978-0-310-70843-8(5))* Zonderkidz.
Davis, Chasta. The Easter Bunny & His Famous Painted Eggs. 2011. 28p. pap. 24.95 *(978-1-4512-1649-3(1))* America Star Bks.
Dean, James & Dean, Kimberly. Big Easter Adventure. Dean, James & Dean, Kimberly, illus. 2014. (Pete the Cat Ser.). (ENG., Illus.). 24p. (J). (gr. -1-3). 9.99 *(978-0-06-219867-9(X))* HarperCollins Pubs.
Dean, Kim & Dean, James. Big Easter Adventure. 2014. (Pete the Cat Ser.). (Illus.). (J). *(978-1-4844-1829-1(8))* HarperCollins Pubs.
DeBoer, Jesslyn. The First Easter, 1 vol. Clar, David Austin, illus. 2005. (Easter Board Bks.). (ENG.). 12p. (J). bds. 3.99 *(978-0-310-70842-1(7))* Zonderkidz.
deGroat, Diane. Last One in Is a Rotten Egg! deGroat, Diane, illus. 2011. (Gilbert Ser.). (ENG., Illus.). 32p. (J). (gr. -1-3). pap. 6.99 *(978-0-06-089296-8(X))* HarperCollins Pubs.
dePaola, Tomie. My First Easter. dePaola, Tomie, illus. 2008. (ENG., Illus.). 14p. (J). (gr. -1-k). bds. 5.99 *(978-0-448-44790-2(8),* Grosset & Dunlap) Penguin Young Readers Group.
Depken, Kristen L. Here Comes Peter Cottontail. 2012. (Step into Reading Level 2 Ser.). lib. bdg. 13.55 *(978-0-606-23719-2(4),* Turtleback) Turtleback Bks.
—Here Comes Peter Cottontail (Peter Cottontail) Karl, Linda, illus. 2012. (Step into Reading Ser.). (ENG.). 32p. (J). (gr. -1-1). pap. 3.99 *(978-0-307-93032-3(7),* Random Hse. Bks. for Young Readers) Random Hse. Children's Bks.
Derico, Laura Ring. Easter Surprises. Harris, Phyllis, illus. 2015. (Faith That Sticks Bks.). (ENG.). 26p. (J). pap. 3.99 *(978-1-4964-0311-7(8))* Tyndale Hse. Pubs.
DeVogt, Rindia M. Tommy Hare & the Color Purple, 1 vol. Trogdon, Kathryn, illus. 2009. (ENG.). 22p. pap. 24.95 *(978-1-61582-827-2(3))* America Star Bks.
Disney Book Group. Whisker Haven Tales with the Palace Pets: Nuzzles & the Easter Egg Mix-Up: Read-along Storybook & CD. Disney Storybook Art Team, illus. 2016. (Read-Along Storybook & CD Ser.). (ENG.). 32p. (J). (gr. -1-k). pap. 6.99 *(978-1-4847-8695-6(5))* Disney Pr.
Disney Book Group Staff. The Easter Egg Hunt. 2010. (Read-Along Storybook & CD Ser.). (ENG.). 32p. (J). (gr. -1-2). pap. 6.99 *(978-1-4231-2087-2(6))* Disney Pr.
Disney Book Group Staff & Higginson, Sheila Sweeny. Doc Mcstuffins Bunny in a Basket. Disney Storybook Art Team, illus. 2015. (ENG.). 12p. (J). (gr. -1-k). bds. 7.99 *(978-1-4847-0679-4(X))* Disney Pr.
Donovan, Dan. Holiday Tails! 2011. 48p. pap. 19.26 *(978-1-4520-9628-5(7))* AuthorHouse.
Dora the Explorer Publishing Staff. Dora the Explorer Dora Loves Easter! 2014. (Hugs Book Ser.: 2). (ENG.). 10p. (J). (gr. -1-k). bds. 10.99 *(978-0-7944-3032-0(5))* Reader's Digest Assn., Inc., The.
Dunn, Robert, illus. The Littlest Bunny in Michigan: An Easter Adventure. 2015. (ENG.). 32p. (J). (-3). 9.99 *(978-1-4926-1117-2(4),* Sourcebooks Jabberwocky) Sourcebooks, Inc.
—The Littlest Bunny in Rhode Island: An Easter Adventure. 2015. (ENG.). 32p. (J). (-3). 9.99 *(978-1-4926-1189-9(1),* Sourcebooks Jabberwocky) Sourcebooks, Inc.
Dunrea, Olivier. Ollie's Easter Eggs. 2010. (Gossie & Friends Ser.). (ENG., Illus.). 32p. (J). (gr. -1 — 1). 9.99 *(978-0-618-53243-8(9))* Houghton Mifflin Harcourt Publishing Co.
—Ollie's Easter Eggs Board Book. 2013. (Gossie & Friends Ser.). (ENG., Illus.). 30p. (J). (gr. k — 1). bds. 6.99 *(978-0-547-85918-7(X))* Houghton Mifflin Harcourt Publishing Co.
—Ollie's Easter Eggs (reader) 2017. (Gossie & Friends Ser.). (ENG., Illus.). 32p. (J). (gr. -1-3). pap. 3.99 *(978-0-544-80911-6(4),* HMH Books For Young Readers) Houghton Mifflin Harcourt Publishing Co.
Dyan, Penelope. Easter Eggs & Bunny Wishes. 2011. (Illus.). 34p. pap. 11.95 *(978-1-935630-61-6(X))* Bellissima Publishing, LLC.
—Hoppy Easter! 2011. (Illus.). 34p. pap. 11.95 *(978-1-935630-49-4(0))* Bellissima Publishing, LLC.
—Hoppy Go Lucky Little Easter Bunny. 2011. 34p. pap. 11.95 *(978-1-935630-60-9(1))* Bellissima Publishing, LLC.
Dyess, Hal. The Night the Rabbits Dance: An Easter Story. 2011. 20p. pap. 10.00 *(978-1-4567-3613-2(2))* AuthorHouse.
East, Jacqueline, illus. Easter Hop. 2008. (ENG.). 16p. (gr. -1-k). bds. 5.95 *(978-1-58117-686-5(4),* Intervisual/Piggy Toes) Bendon, Inc.
Elliott, Ann. GypsyBridge Friends: The Surprise. 2003. 40p. pap. 12.95 *(978-0-9721825-2-2(7))* Open Vision Entertainment Corp.
Ende, Michael & Fushubert, Annegert. Tragasuenos. 5th ed. (SPA., Illus.). 32p. (J). 15.95 *(978-84-261-1740-3(6))* Juventud, Editorial ESP. Dist: AIMS International Bks., Inc.
Eubank, Patricia Reeder. ABCs of Easter. 2010. 40p. (J). (gr. k-3). 8.99 *(978-0-8249-5617-2(6),* Ideal Pubns.) Worthy Publishing.
Evans, Cordelia. Olivia & the Easter Egg Hunt. 2013. (Olivia 8x8 Ser.). lib. bdg. 14.75 *(978-0-606-27062-5(0),* Turtleback) Turtleback Bks.
Evans, Kristina. The Best Easter Prize. Wallace, John, illus. 2010. (ENG.). 32p. (J). (gr. -1-3). pap. 3.99 *(978-0-545-05112-5(6),* Cartwheel Bks.) Scholastic, Inc.
First Easter Story. Date not set. (Illus.). (J). bds. 9.98 *(978-0-7525-9172-8(X))* Parragon, Inc.
Fisch, Sarah & Bridwell, Norman. The Little Blue Easter Egg. Goldberg, Barry, illus. 2006. (Clifford's Puppy Days Ser.). 23p. (J). *(978-0-439-81617-5(3))* Scholastic, Inc.
Frazer, Rebecca. An Egg-Cellent Easter! (Barbie) Riley, Kellee, illus. 2012. (Pictureback(R) Ser.). (ENG.). 16p. (J). (gr. -1-2). pap. 3.99 *(978-0-307-93025-5(4),* Random Hse. Bks. for Young Readers) Random Hse. Children's Bks.
Froeb, Lori C. Fisher-Price Little People Easter Is Here! 2016. (Lift-The-Flap Ser.). (ENG.). 10p. (J). (gr. -1-k). bds. 9.99 *(978-0-7944-3580-6(7),* Reader's Digest Children's Bks.) Studio Fun International.
Fronis, Aly. This Little Bunny. Rescek, Sanja, illus. 2016. (ENG.). 16p. (J). (gr. -1-1). bds. 5.99 *(978-1-4998-0105-7(X))* Little Bee Books Inc.
Gardner, Louise, illus. Five Little Easter Eggs. 2009. (ENG.). 10p. (J). (gr. -1). 5.95 *(978-1-58117-849-4(2),* Intervisual/Piggy Toes) Bendon, Inc.
Garton, Sam. Otter Loves Easter! Garton, Sam, illus. 2017. (Illus.). 32p. (J). (gr. -1-3). 9.99 *(978-0-06-236667-2(X))* HarperCollins Pubs.
Gaster, Valerie Land. Jesus Loves the Easter Bunny. 2011. 20p. 14.50 *(978-1-4567-4418-2(6))* AuthorHouse.
Giacomo, Renee San. Lily's Rainbow. Fernandez, Carina, illus. 2013. 28p. pap. 24.95 *(978-1-63004-174-8(2))* America Star Bks.
Giles, Lisa. The Adventures of Sunny the Bunny: The Easter Egg Hunt. 2010. 20p. 10.49 *(978-1-4520-1842-3(1))* AuthorHouse.
Gilmore, Cathy & Benoist, Carol. Easter Bunny's AMAZING Day. Sundy, Jonathan, illus. 2011. (ENG.). 40p. (J). 15.99 *(978-0-9847656-1-4(1))* I.H.S. Pubs.
Glover, Dennis W. The Cat in the Woods. 2010. 20p. pap. 10.49 *(978-1-4389-8492-6(8))* AuthorHouse.
Golden Books. Here Comes Peter Cottontail. Golden Books, illus. 2014. (Little Golden Book Ser.). (ENG., Illus.). 24p. (J). (-k). 4.99 *(978-0-385-37839-0(4),* Golden Bks.) Random Hse. Children's Bks.
Golden Books Staff. A Big Easter Adventure (Peter Cottontail) 2012. (Big Coloring Book Ser.). (ENG.). 48p. (J). (gr. -1-2). pap. 6.99 *(978-0-375-86557-2(8),* Golden Bks.) Random Hse. Children's Bks.
—Easter Deliveries. Golden Books Staff, illus. 2010. (Color Plus Chunky Crayons Ser.). (ENG., Illus.). 48p. (J). (gr. -1-2). pap. 3.99 *(978-0-375-85747-8(8),* Golden Bks.) Random Hse. Children's Bks.
—Here Comes Bubble Bunny! (Bubble Guppies) MJ Illustrations Staff, illus. 2014. (Hologramatic Sticker Book Ser.). (ENG.). 48p. (J). (gr. -1-2). pap. 3.99 *(978-0-385-37497-2(6),* Golden Bks.) Random Hse. Children's Bks.
Gomez, Rebecca. Happy Easter, Hello Kitty! 2005. (Illus.). 32p. *(978-0-439-67637-3(1))* Scholastic, Inc.
Goodings, Christina. My Look & Point First Easter. Hudson, Annabel, illus. 2015. (ENG.). 16p. (J). (gr. -1-k). 6.99 *(978-0-7459-6453-9(2))* Lion Hudson PLC GBR. Dist: Independent Pubs. Group.
Gordon, Janice Knuth. The Eager Bunny. 2009. 60p. (J). pap. 27.95 *(978-1-4327-3673-6(6))* Outskirts Pr., Inc.
Grambling, Lois G. Here Comes T. Rex Cottontail. Davis, Jack E., illus. 2010. (ENG.). 32p. (J). (gr. -1-1). pap. 6.99 *(978-0-06-053134-8(7),* Tegen, Katherine Bks) HarperCollins Pubs.
Gutman, Dan. Bunny Double, We're in Trouble! Paillot, Jim, illus. 2014. (My Weird School Special Ser.). 144p. (J). (gr. 1-5). (ENG.). pap. 5.99 *(978-0-06-228400-6(2));* lib. bdg. 16.89 *(978-0-06-228401-3(0))* HarperCollins Pubs.
Hale, Rachael. Somebunny Loves You. 2009. (Paw Pals Ser.). (ENG., Illus.). 20p. (J). (gr. -1 — 1). bds. 6.99 *(978-0-316-11370-0(0))* Little, Brown Bks. for Young Readers.
Hallinan, P. K. Easter at Our House. 2007. (ENG., Illus.). 28p. (J). (gr. -1-3). 8.99 *(978-0-8249-5552-6(8),* Ideal Pubns.) Worthy Publishing.
Hardie, Jill. The Sparkle Egg. Kornacki, Christine, illus. 2014. 32p. (J). 16.99 *(978-0-8249-5664-6(8),* Ideal Pubns.) Worthy Publishing.
Harimann, Sierra. Easter Egg Hunt. 2014. (Illus.). 30p. (J). pap. *(978-0-545-59212-3(7))* Scholastic, Inc.
Hartman, Bob. Easter Angels. Williams, Sophy, illus. 2010. (ENG.). 32p. (J). (gr. 2-4). 14.99 *(978-0-7459-6922-0(4))* Lion Hudson PLC GBR. Dist: Independent Pubs. Group.
Heyward, DuBose. The Country Bunny & the Little Gold Shoes 75th Anniversary Edition. Flack, Marjorie, illus. 2014. (ENG.). 56p. (J). (gr. -1-3). 14.99 *(978-0-544-25197-7(0),* HMH Books For Young Readers) Houghton Mifflin Harcourt Publishing Co.
—The Country Bunny & the Little Gold Shoes Gift Edition with Charm. Flack, Marjorie, illus. 2010. (ENG.). 56p. (J). (gr. -1-3). 9.99 *(978-0-547-14418-4(0))* Houghton Mifflin Harcourt Publishing Co.
High, Linda. Lap Talks with Granny at Easter. 2003. (J). pap. 9.95 *(978-0-9661186-9-8(3))* Bks. for Children of the World.
Hill, Eric. Spot's Easter Surprise. Hill, Eric, illus. 2007. (Spot Ser.). (ENG., Illus.). 10p. (J). (gr. -1-k). bds. 5.99 *(978-0-399-24743-9(2),* Warne) Penguin Young Readers Group.
Hillert, Margaret. Feliz Pascua, Querido Dragón. Pullan, Jack, illus. 2017. (BeginningtoRead Ser.).Tr. of Happy Easter, Dear Dragon. (ENG & SPA.). 32p. (J). (-2). 22.60 ***(978-1-59953-831-0(8))*** Norwood Hse. Pr.
Hillert, Margaret. Happy Easter, Dear Dragon. Pullan, Jack, illus. 2016. (BeginningtoRead Ser.). (ENG.). 32p. (J). (-2). lib. bdg. 22.60 *(978-1-59953-768-9(0));* (gr. 1-2). pap. 11.94 *(978-1-60357-881-3(1))* Norwood Hse. Pr.
Hills, Tad. Duck & Goose, Here Comes the Easter Bunny! Hills, Tad, illus. 2012. (Duck & Goose Ser.). (ENG., Illus.). 22p. (J). (gr. k-k). bds. 7.99 *(978-0-375-87280-8(9),* Schwartz & Wade Bks.) Random Hse. Children's Bks.
Hughes, Laura. We're Going on an Egg Hunt. Hughes, Laura, illus. 2017. (ENG., Illus.). 24p. (J). 17.99 *(978-1-68119-314-4(0),* 9781681193144, Bloomsbury USA Childrens) Bloomsbury Publishing USA.
Hulme, Joy N. Easter Babies: A Springtime Counting Book. Andreasen, Dan, illus. 2012. (ENG.). 22p. (J). (gr. k — 1). bds. 6.95 *(978-1-4027-9763-7(X))* Sterling Publishing Co., Inc.
Ivanke, illus. Sparkling Easter Eggs: A Glittery Counting Book. 2008. (ENG.). 10p. (J). bds. 7.95 *(978-1-58117-685-8(6),* Intervisual/Piggy Toes) Bendon, Inc.
Jacobs, Lily. The Littlest Bunny: An Easter Adventure. Dunn, Robert, illus. 2015. (ENG.). 32p. (J). (-3). 9.99 *(978-1-4926-1012-0(7),* Sourcebooks Jabberwocky) Sourcebooks, Inc.
—The Littlest Bunny in Alabama: An Easter Adventure. 2015. (ENG.). 32p. (J). (-3). 9.99 *(978-1-4926-1015-1(1),* Sourcebooks Jabberwocky) Sourcebooks, Inc.
—The Littlest Bunny in Alaska: An Easter Adventure. 2015. (ENG.). 32p. (J). (-3). 9.99 *(978-1-4926-1018-2(6),* Sourcebooks Jabberwocky) Sourcebooks, Inc.
—The Littlest Bunny in Arizona: An Easter Adventure. 2015. (ENG.). 32p. (J). (-3). 9.99 *(978-1-4926-1024-3(0),* Sourcebooks Jabberwocky) Sourcebooks, Inc.
—The Littlest Bunny in Austin. Dunn, Robert, illus. 2016. (ENG.). 32p. (J). (-7). 9.99 *(978-1-4926-3347-1(X),* 9781492633471, Sourcebooks Jabberwocky) Sourcebooks, Inc.
—The Littlest Bunny in Boise: An Easter Adventure. 2015. (ENG.). 32p. (J). (-3). 9.99 *(978-1-4926-1033-5(X),* Sourcebooks Jabberwocky) Sourcebooks, Inc.
—The Littlest Bunny in Boston: An Easter Adventure. 2015. (ENG.). 32p. (J). (-3). 9.99 *(978-1-4926-1036-6(4),* Sourcebooks Jabberwocky) Sourcebooks, Inc.
—The Littlest Bunny in Buffalo. Dunn, Robert, illus. 2016. (ENG.). 32p. (J). (-7). 9.99 *(978-1-4926-3346-4(1),* 9781492633464, Sourcebooks Jabberwocky) Sourcebooks, Inc.
—The Littlest Bunny in California: An Easter Adventure. Dunn, Robert, illus. 2015. (ENG.). 32p. (J). (-3). 9.99 *(978-1-4926-1042-7(9),* Sourcebooks Jabberwocky) Sourcebooks, Inc.
—The Littlest Bunny in Canada: An Easter Adventure. Dunn, Robert, illus. 2015. (ENG.). 32p. (J). (-3). 11.99 *(978-1-4926-1045-8(3),* Sourcebooks Jabberwocky) Sourcebooks, Inc.
—The Littlest Bunny in Charleston: An Easter Adventure. 2015. (ENG.). 32p. (J). (-3). 9.99 *(978-1-4926-1048-9(8),* Sourcebooks Jabberwocky) Sourcebooks, Inc.
—The Littlest Bunny in Chicago: An Easter Adventure. 2015. (ENG.). 32p. (J). (-3). 9.99 *(978-1-4926-1051-9(8),* Sourcebooks Jabberwocky) Sourcebooks, Inc.
—The Littlest Bunny in Cincinnati: An Easter Adventure. Dunn, Robert, illus. 2015. (ENG.). 32p. (J). (-3). 9.99 *(978-1-4926-1054-0(2),* Sourcebooks Jabberwocky) Sourcebooks, Inc.
—The Littlest Bunny in Cleveland. Dunn, Robert, illus. 2016. (ENG.). 32p. (J). (-7). 9.99 *(978-1-4926-3353-2(4),* 9781492633532, Sourcebooks Jabberwocky) Sourcebooks, Inc.
—The Littlest Bunny in Colorado: An Easter Adventure. 2015. (ENG.). 32p. (J). (-3). 9.99 *(978-1-4926-1057-1(7),* Sourcebooks Jabberwocky) Sourcebooks, Inc.
—The Littlest Bunny in Connecticut: An Easter Adventure. 2015. (ENG.). 32p. (J). (-3). 9.99 *(978-1-4926-1060-1(7),* Sourcebooks Jabberwocky) Sourcebooks, Inc.
—The Littlest Bunny in Dallas. Dunn, Robert, illus. 2016. (ENG.). 32p. (J). (-7). 9.99 *(978-1-4926-3349-5(6),* 9781492633495, Sourcebooks Jabberwocky) Sourcebooks, Inc.
—The Littlest Bunny in Delaware: An Easter Adventure. Dunn, Robert, illus. 2015. (ENG.). 32p. (J). (-3). 9.99 *(978-1-4926-1063-2(1),* Sourcebooks Jabberwocky) Sourcebooks, Inc.
—The Littlest Bunny in Edmonton: An Easter Adventure. Dunn, Robert, illus. 2015. (ENG.). 32p. (J). (-3). 11.99 *(978-1-4926-1066-3(6),* Sourcebooks Jabberwocky) Sourcebooks, Inc.
—The Littlest Bunny in Florida: An Easter Adventure. Dunn, Robert, illus. 2015. (ENG.). 32p. (J). (-3). 9.99 *(978-1-4926-1069-4(0),* Sourcebooks Jabberwocky) Sourcebooks, Inc.
—The Littlest Bunny in Georgia: An Easter Adventure. 2015. (ENG.). 32p. (J). (-3). 9.99 *(978-1-4926-1072-4(0),* Sourcebooks Jabberwocky) Sourcebooks, Inc.
—The Littlest Bunny in Hawaii: An Easter Adventure. 2015. (ENG.). 32p. (J). (-3). 9.99 *(978-1-4926-1075-5(5),* Sourcebooks Jabberwocky) Sourcebooks, Inc.
—The Littlest Bunny in Idaho: An Easter Adventure. 2015. (ENG.). 32p. (J). (-3). 9.99 *(978-1-4926-1078-6(X),* Sourcebooks Jabberwocky) Sourcebooks, Inc.
—The Littlest Bunny in Illinois: An Easter Adventure. Dunn, Robert, illus. 2015. (ENG.). 32p. (J). (-3). 9.99 *(978-1-4926-1081-6(X),* Sourcebooks Jabberwocky) Sourcebooks, Inc.
—The Littlest Bunny in Indiana: An Easter Adventure. Dunn, Robert, illus. 2015. (ENG.). 32p. (J). (-3). 9.99 *(978-1-4926-1084-7(4),* Sourcebooks Jabberwocky) Sourcebooks, Inc.
—The Littlest Bunny in Iowa: An Easter Adventure. 2015. (ENG.). 32p. (J). (-3). 9.99 *(978-1-4926-1087-8(9),* Sourcebooks Jabberwocky) Sourcebooks, Inc.
—The Littlest Bunny in Kansas: An Easter Adventure. 2015. (ENG.). 32p. (J). (-3). 9.99 *(978-1-4926-1090-8(9),* Sourcebooks Jabberwocky) Sourcebooks, Inc.
—The Littlest Bunny in Kansas City: An Easter Adventure. Dunn, Robert, illus. 2015. (ENG.). 32p. (J). (-3). 9.99 *(978-1-4926-1093-9(3),* Sourcebooks Jabberwocky) Sourcebooks, Inc.
—The Littlest Bunny in Kentucky: An Easter Adventure. Dunn, Robert, illus. 2015. (ENG.). 32p. (J). (-3). 9.99 *(978-1-4926-1096-0(8),* Sourcebooks Jabberwocky) Sourcebooks, Inc.
—The Littlest Bunny in Las Vegas: An Easter Adventure. 2015. (ENG.). 32p. (J). (-3). 9.99 *(978-1-4926-1099-1(2),* Sourcebooks Jabberwocky) Sourcebooks, Inc.
—The Littlest Bunny in Los Angeles: An Easter Adventure. 2015. (ENG.). 32p. (J). (-3). 9.99 *(978-1-4926-1102-8(6),* Sourcebooks Jabberwocky) Sourcebooks, Inc.
—The Littlest Bunny in Louisiana: An Easter Adventure. Dunn, Robert, illus. 2015. (ENG.). 32p. (J). (-3). 9.99 *(978-1-4926-1105-9(0),* Sourcebooks Jabberwocky) Sourcebooks, Inc.
—The Littlest Bunny in Maine: An Easter Adventure. 2015. (ENG.). 32p. (J). (-3). 9.99 *(978-1-4926-1108-0(5),* Sourcebooks Jabberwocky) Sourcebooks, Inc.
—The Littlest Bunny in Maryland: An Easter Adventure. Dunn, Robert, illus. 2015. (ENG.). 32p. (J). (-3). 9.99 *(978-1-4926-1111-0(5),* Sourcebooks Jabberwocky) Sourcebooks, Inc.
—The Littlest Bunny in Massachusetts: An Easter Adventure. 2015. (ENG.). 32p. (J). (-3). 9.99 *(978-1-4926-1114-1(X),* Sourcebooks Jabberwocky) Sourcebooks, Inc.
—The Littlest Bunny in Minnesota: An Easter Adventure. Dunn, Robert, illus. 2015. (ENG.). 32p. (J). (-3). 9.99 *(978-1-4926-1120-2(4),* Sourcebooks Jabberwocky) Sourcebooks, Inc.

E
F
G

—The Littlest Bunny in Mississippi: An Easter Adventure. Dunn, Robert, illus. 2015. (ENG.). 32p. (J). (-3). 9.99 *(978-1-4926-1123-3(9),* Sourcebooks Jabberwocky) Sourcebooks, Inc.

—The Littlest Bunny in Missouri: An Easter Adventure. Dunn, Robert, illus. 2015. (ENG.). 32p. (J). (-3). 9.99 *(978-1-4926-1126-4(3),* Sourcebooks Jabberwocky) Sourcebooks, Inc.

—The Littlest Bunny in Montana: An Easter Adventure. Dunn, Robert, illus. 2015. (ENG.). 32p. (J). (-3). 9.99 *(978-1-4926-1129-5(8),* Sourcebooks Jabberwocky) Sourcebooks, Inc.

—The Littlest Bunny in Nashville. Dunn, Robert, illus. 2016. (ENG.). 32p. (J). (-7). 9.99 *(978-1-4926-3351-8(8),* 9781492633518, Sourcebooks Jabberwocky) Sourcebooks, Inc.

—The Littlest Bunny in Nebraska: An Easter Adventure. Dunn, Robert, illus. 2015. (ENG.). 32p. (J). (-3). 9.99 *(978-1-4926-1132-5(8),* Sourcebooks Jabberwocky) Sourcebooks, Inc.

—The Littlest Bunny in Nevada: An Easter Adventure. Dunn, Robert, illus. 2015. (ENG.). 32p. (J). (-3). 9.99 *(978-1-4926-1135-6(2),* Sourcebooks Jabberwocky) Sourcebooks, Inc.

—The Littlest Bunny in New England: An Easter Adventure. Dunn, Robert, illus. 2015. (ENG.). 32p. (J). (-3). 9.99 *(978-1-4926-1138-7(7),* Sourcebooks Jabberwocky) Sourcebooks, Inc.

—The Littlest Bunny in New Hampshire: An Easter Adventure. Dunn, Robert, illus. 2015. (ENG.). 32p. (J). (-3). 9.99 *(978-1-4926-1141-7(7),* Sourcebooks Jabberwocky) Sourcebooks, Inc.

—The Littlest Bunny in New Jersey: An Easter Adventure. Dunn, Robert, illus. 2015. (ENG.). 32p. (J). (-3). 9.99 *(978-1-4926-1144-8(1),* Sourcebooks Jabberwocky) Sourcebooks, Inc.

—The Littlest Bunny in New Mexico: An Easter Adventure. Dunn, Robert, illus. 2015. (ENG.). 32p. (J). (-3). 9.99 *(978-1-4926-1147-9(6),* Sourcebooks Jabberwocky) Sourcebooks, Inc.

—The Littlest Bunny in New Orleans. Dunn, Robert, illus. 2016. (ENG.). 32p. (J). (-7). 9.99 *(978-1-4926-3350-1(X),* 9781492633501, Sourcebooks Jabberwocky) Sourcebooks, Inc.

—The Littlest Bunny in New York: An Easter Adventure. Dunn, Robert, illus. 2015. (ENG.). 32p. (J). (-3). 9.99 *(978-1-4926-1150-9(6),* Sourcebooks Jabberwocky) Sourcebooks, Inc.

—The Littlest Bunny in New York City: An Easter Adventure. Dunn, Robert, illus. 2015. (ENG.). 32p. (J). (-3). 9.99 *(978-1-4926-1153-0(0),* Sourcebooks Jabberwocky) Sourcebooks, Inc.

—The Littlest Bunny in North Carolina: An Easter Adventure. Dunn, Robert, illus. 2015. (ENG.). 32p. (J). (-3). 9.99 *(978-1-4926-1156-1(5),* Sourcebooks Jabberwocky) Sourcebooks, Inc.

—The Littlest Bunny in North Dakota: An Easter Adventure. Dunn, Robert, illus. 2015. (ENG.). 32p. (J). (-3). 9.99 *(978-1-4926-1159-2(X),* Sourcebooks Jabberwocky) Sourcebooks, Inc.

—The Littlest Bunny in Ohio: An Easter Adventure. Dunn, Robert, illus. 2015. (ENG.). 32p. (J). (-3). 9.99 *(978-1-4926-1162-2(X),* Sourcebooks Jabberwocky) Sourcebooks, Inc.

—The Littlest Bunny in Oklahoma: An Easter Adventure. Dunn, Robert, illus. 2015. (ENG.). 32p. (J). (-3). 9.99 *(978-1-4926-1165-3(4),* Sourcebooks Jabberwocky) Sourcebooks, Inc.

—The Littlest Bunny in Omaha: An Easter Adventure. Dunn, Robert, illus. 2015. (ENG.). 32p. (J). (-3). 9.99 *(978-1-4926-1168-4(9),* Sourcebooks Jabberwocky) Sourcebooks, Inc.

—The Littlest Bunny in Oregon: An Easter Adventure. Dunn, Robert, illus. 2015. (ENG.). 32p. (J). (-3). 9.99 *(978-1-4926-1171-4(9),* Sourcebooks Jabberwocky) Sourcebooks, Inc.

—The Littlest Bunny in Ottawa: An Easter Adventure. Dunn, Robert, illus. 2015. (ENG.). 32p. (J). (-3). 11.99 *(978-1-4926-1174-5(3),* Sourcebooks Jabberwocky) Sourcebooks, Inc.

—The Littlest Bunny in Pennsylvania: An Easter Adventure. Dunn, Robert, illus. 2015. (ENG.). 32p. (J). (-3). 9.99 *(978-1-4926-1177-6(8),* Sourcebooks Jabberwocky) Sourcebooks, Inc.

—The Littlest Bunny in Philadelphia: An Easter Adventure. Dunn, Robert, illus. 2015. (ENG.). 32p. (J). (-3). 9.99 *(978-1-4926-1180-6(8),* Sourcebooks Jabberwocky) Sourcebooks, Inc.

—The Littlest Bunny in Pittsburgh: An Easter Adventure. Dunn, Robert, illus. 2015. (ENG.). 32p. (J). (-3). 9.99 *(978-1-4926-1183-7(2),* Sourcebooks Jabberwocky) Sourcebooks, Inc.

—The Littlest Bunny in Portland: An Easter Adventure. Dunn, Robert, illus. 2015. (ENG.). 32p. (J). (-3). 9.99 *(978-1-4926-1186-8(7),* Sourcebooks Jabberwocky) Sourcebooks, Inc.

—The Littlest Bunny in San Diego. Dunn, Robert, illus. 2016. (ENG.). 32p. (J). (-7). 9.99 *(978-1-4926-3348-8(8),* 9781492633488, Sourcebooks Jabberwocky) Sourcebooks, Inc.

—The Littlest Bunny in San Francisco: An Easter Adventure. Dunn, Robert, illus. 2015. (ENG.). 32p. (J). (-3). 9.99 *(978-1-4926-1192-9(1),* Sourcebooks Jabberwocky) Sourcebooks, Inc.

—The Littlest Bunny in South Carolina: An Easter Adventure. Dunn, Robert, illus. 2015. (ENG.). 32p. (J). (-3). 9.99 *(978-1-4926-1195-0(6),* Sourcebooks Jabberwocky) Sourcebooks, Inc.

—The Littlest Bunny in South Dakota: An Easter Adventure. Dunn, Robert, illus. 2015. (ENG.). 32p. (J). (-3). 9.99 *(978-1-4926-1198-1(0),* Sourcebooks Jabberwocky) Sourcebooks, Inc.

—The Littlest Bunny in St. Louis: An Easter Adventure. Dunn, Robert, illus. 2015. (ENG.). 32p. (J). (-3). 9.99 *(978-1-4926-1201-8(4),* Sourcebooks Jabberwocky) Sourcebooks, Inc.

—The Littlest Bunny in Tampa Bay: An Easter Adventure. Dunn, Robert, illus. 2015. (ENG.). 32p. (J). (-3). 9.99 *(978-1-4926-1204-9(9),* Sourcebooks Jabberwocky) Sourcebooks, Inc.

—The Littlest Bunny in Tennessee: An Easter Adventure. Dunn, Robert, illus. 2015. (ENG.). 32p. (J). (-3). 9.99 *(978-1-4926-1207-0(3),* Sourcebooks Jabberwocky) Sourcebooks, Inc.

—The Littlest Bunny in Texas: An Easter Adventure. Dunn, Robert, illus. 2015. (ENG.). 32p. (J). (-3). 9.99 *(978-1-4926-1210-0(3),* Sourcebooks Jabberwocky) Sourcebooks, Inc.

—The Littlest Bunny in Toronto: An Easter Adventure. Dunn, Robert, illus. 2015. (ENG.). 32p. (J). (-3). 11.99 *(978-1-4926-1213-1(8),* Sourcebooks Jabberwocky) Sourcebooks, Inc.

—The Littlest Bunny in Tulsa: An Easter Adventure. Dunn, Robert, illus. 2015. (ENG.). 32p. (J). (-3). 9.99 *(978-1-4926-1216-2(2),* Sourcebooks Jabberwocky) Sourcebooks, Inc.

—The Littlest Bunny in Utah: An Easter Adventure. Dunn, Robert, illus. 2015. (ENG.). 32p. (J). (-3). 9.99 *(978-1-4926-1219-3(7),* Sourcebooks Jabberwocky) Sourcebooks, Inc.

—The Littlest Bunny in Vancouver: An Easter Adventure. Dunn, Robert, illus. 2015. (ENG.). 32p. (J). (-3). 11.99 *(978-1-4926-1222-3(7),* Sourcebooks Jabberwocky) Sourcebooks, Inc.

—The Littlest Bunny in Vermont: An Easter Adventure. Dunn, Robert, illus. 2015. (ENG.). 32p. (J). (-3). 9.99 *(978-1-4926-1225-4(1),* Sourcebooks Jabberwocky) Sourcebooks, Inc.

—The Littlest Bunny in Virginia: An Easter Adventure. Dunn, Robert, illus. 2015. (ENG.). 32p. (J). (-3). 9.99 *(978-1-4926-1228-5(6),* Sourcebooks Jabberwocky) Sourcebooks, Inc.

—The Littlest Bunny in Washington: An Easter Adventure. 2015. (ENG.). 32p. (J). (-3). 9.99 *(978-1-4926-1231-5(6),* Sourcebooks Jabberwocky) Sourcebooks, Inc.

—The Littlest Bunny in Washington, DC: An Easter Adventure. Dunn, Robert A., illus. 2015. (ENG.). 32p. (J). (-3). 9.99 *(978-1-4926-1234-6(0),* Sourcebooks Jabberwocky) Sourcebooks, Inc.

—The Littlest Bunny in West Virginia: An Easter Adventure. 2015. (ENG.). 32p. (J). (-3). 9.99 *(978-1-4926-1237-7(5),* Sourcebooks Jabberwocky) Sourcebooks, Inc.

—The Littlest Bunny in Wisconsin: An Easter Adventure. 2015. (ENG.). 32p. (J). (-3). 9.99 *(978-1-4926-1240-7(5),* Sourcebooks Jabberwocky) Sourcebooks, Inc.

—The Littlest Bunny in Wyoming: An Easter Adventure. 2015. (ENG.). 32p. (J). (-3). 9.99 *(978-1-4926-1243-8(X),* Sourcebooks Jabberwocky) Sourcebooks, Inc.

Jaeger, Elizabeth. It's Easter, Little Bunny! Boyer, Robin, illus. 2015. (ENG.). 16p. (J). bds. 12.99 *(978-0-8249-1949-8(1),* Ideal Pubns.) Worthy Publishing.

James, Brian. Easter Bunny's on His Way! 2005. pap. *(978-0-439-74530-7(6))* Scholastic, Inc.

Jenisch, Betty. Rennie. 2007. 9.00 *(978-0-8059-8947-2(1))* Dorrance Publishing Co., Inc.

Jensen, Bonnie Rickner & DaySpring Staff. Really Woolly Easter Blessings, 1 vol. 2017. (Really Woolly Ser.). (ENG., Illus.). 40p. (J). bds. 9.99 *(978-0-7180-9256-6(2))* Nelson, Thomas Inc.

Johnson, Shane L., illus. OLIVIA & the Easter Egg Hunt. 2013. (Olivia TV Tie-In Ser.). (ENG.). 24p. (J). (gr. -1-2). pap. 4.99 *(978-1-4424-6022-5(9),* Simon Spotlight) Simon Spotlight.

Jones, Ernest, illus. The Great Mix Up. 2005. (ENG.). 42p. (J). 17.99 *(978-0-9772282-0-1(7))* B. T. Brooks.

Jordan, Apple. The Bunny Surprise. 2012. (Step into Reading Level 1 Ser.). lib. bdg. 13.55 *(978-0-606-23723-9(2),* Turtleback) Turtleback Bks.

Joyce, William. The True Story of E. Astor Bunnyman. 2004. (J). 15.99 *(978-0-06-050831-9(0));* (Illus.). lib. bdg. 16.89 *(978-0-06-050832-6(9))* HarperCollins Pubs. (Geringer, Laura Book).

Kann, Victoria. Pinkalicious - Eggstraordinary Easter. Kann, Victoria, illus. 2014. (Pinkalicious Ser.). (ENG., Illus.). 24p. (J). (gr. -1-3). pap. 4.99 *(978-0-06-218772-7(4),* HarperFestival) HarperCollins Pubs.

Kaplan, Michael B. Betty Bunny Loves Easter. Jorisch, Stéphane, illus. 2015. (Betty Bunny Ser.). (ENG.). 32p. (J). (gr. -1-k). 16.99 *(978-0-8037-4061-7(1),* Dial Bks) Penguin Young Readers Group.

Karl, Linda. Hooray for Easter! (Peter Cottontail) Random House, illus. 2017. (Tabbed Board Book Ser.). (ENG.). 16p. (J). (-k). bds. 7.99 *(978-0-399-55787-3(3),* Random Hse. Bks. for Young Readers) Random Hse. Children's Bks.

Karr, Lily. Easter Parade! Richards, Kirsten, illus. 2013. (ENG.). 24p. (J). (gr. -1-k). pap. 4.99 *(978-0-545-45824-5(2),* Cartwheel Bks.) Scholastic, Inc.

—Easter Parade! 2013. lib. bdg. 14.75 *(978-0-606-31494-7(6),* Turtleback) Turtleback Bks.

—Five Bouncing Bunnies. Rogers, Jacqueline, illus. 2013. (ENG.). 10p. (J). (gr. -1 — 1). bds. 6.99 *(978-0-545-45825-2(0),* Cartwheel Bks.) Scholastic, Inc.

—My Easter Bunny! Johnson, Jay B., illus. 2012. (ENG.). 12p. (J). (gr. -1-k). bds. 4.99 *(978-0-545-37117-9(1),* Cartwheel Bks.) Scholastic, Inc.

Katz, Karen. Where Are Baby's Easter Eggs? Katz, Karen, illus. 2008. (ENG., Illus.). 14p. (J). (gr. -1 — 1). bds. 7.99 *(978-1-4169-4924-4(0),* Little Simon) Little Simon.

Kelman, Marcy & Disney Book Group Staff. Hoppy Clubhouse Easter. Disney Storybook Art Team, illus. 2011. (ENG.). 12p. (J). (gr. -1-k). bds. 6.99 *(978-1-4231-3910-2(0))* Disney Pr.

Kennedy, Pamela. Easter in the Garden. Wenzel, David T., illus. 2008. (ENG.). 32p. (J). (gr. -1-3). 12.99 *(978-0-8249-5577-9(3),* Ideal Pubns.) Worthy Publishing.

King, Trey. Follow That Easter Egg! 2015. (LEGO City 8X8 Ser.). lib. bdg. 13.55 *(978-0-606-36359-4(9))* Turtleback Bks.

Kinnear, Kay. Deedee's Easter Surprise. Park, Julie, illus. 2003. 25p. (J). pap. 9.99 *(978-0-7459-4443-2(4),* Lion Books) Lion Hudson PLC GBR. Dist: Trafalgar Square Publishing.

Kleinberg, Naomi. In Elmo's Easter Parade. Moroney, Christopher, illus. 2009. (ENG.). 12p. (J). (gr. k — 1). bds. 4.99 *(978-0-375-84460-5(5),* Random Hse. Bks. for Young Readers) Random Hse. Children's Bks.

Knapman, Timothy. The Great Easter Egg Scramble. Walker, David, illus. 2013. (J). *(978-1-4351-4594-8(1))* Barnes & Noble, Inc.

Krensky, Stephen. Milo the Really Big Bunny. Suber, Melissa, illus. 2010. (ENG.). 32p. (J). (gr. -1-1). 11.99 *(978-1-4424-1434-1(0),* Simon & Schuster Bks. For Young Readers) Simon & Schuster Bks. For Young Readers.

Kroll, Steven. The Biggest Easter Basket Ever. Bassett, Jeni, illus. 2008. (ENG.). 32p. (J). (gr. -1-3). pap. 4.99 *(978-0-545-01702-2(5),* Cartwheel Bks.) Scholastic, Inc.

Larsen, Kirsten, et al. Mater & the Easter Buggy. Disney Storybook Art Team, illus. 2012. (ENG.). 48p. (J). (gr. -1-k). 12.99 *(978-1-4231-3875-4(9))* Disney Pr.

Latimer, Sandi. Bunny Bob: The Bumbling Easter Bunny. 2016. (ENG., Illus.). (J). 14.95 ***(978-1-61984-552-7(0))*** Price World Publishing.

Little Fish Easter Merchandiser. (J). 128.16 *(978-0-8307-2908-1(9),* Gospel Light) Gospel Light Pubns.

Lorini, Andrea. Bunny's Easter Surprise. 2015. (ENG., Illus.). 8p. (J). (gr. -1 — 1). bds. 6.99 *(978-0-7641-6782-9(0))* Barron's Educational Series, Inc.

—Easter Egg Party. Rigo, Laura, illus. 2014. (ENG.). 8p. (J). (gr. -1 — 1). bds. 6.99 *(978-0-7641-6716-4(2))* Barron's Educational Series, Inc.

Mackall, Dandi. The Super Gifts of Spring: Easter. 2015. (Seasons Ser.). (ENG., Illus.). 32p. (J). (gr. -1-3). 9.99 *(978-1-4336-8233-9(8),* B&H Kids) B&H Publishing Group.

Mackall, Dandi Daley. The Story of the Easter Robin, 1 vol. Vojtech, Anna, illus. 2010. (ENG.). 32p. (J). (gr. -1-2). 15.99 *(978-0-310-71331-9(5))* Zonderkidz.

—That's My Colt: An Easter Tale. Ellison, Chris, illus. 2008. 24p. (J). (gr. -1). 13.49 *(978-0-7586-1423-0(3))* Concordia Publishing Hse.

Man-Kong, Mary. Easter Surprises! Golden Books, illus. 2015. (Deluxe Coloring Book Ser.). (ENG.). 96p. (J). (gr. -1-2). pap. 3.99 *(978-0-553-50820-8(2),* Golden Bks.) Random Hse. Children's Bks.

—Here Comes Peter Cottontail. Random House, illus. 2015. (Pictureback(R) Ser.). (ENG.). 16p. (J). (gr. -1-2). 4.99 *(978-0-553-50821-5(0),* Random Hse. Bks. for Young Readers) Random Hse. Children's Bks.

Marciano, John Bemelmans. Madeline at the White House. (Madeline Ser.). (ENG., (J). (gr. -1-2). 2016. Illus.). 48p. 8.99 *(978-1-101-99780-2(X),* Puffin Books) 2011. 45p. 17.99 *(978-0-670-01228-2(9),* Viking Books for Young Readers) Penguin Young Readers Group.

—Madeline at the White House. 2016. (Madeline Ser.). lib. bdg. 19.65 *(978-0-606-38845-0(1))* Turtleback Bks.

Markarian, Marianne. Mariam's Easter Parade. Wasielewski, Margaret, illus. 2015. 32p. (J). 16.00 *(978-0-9767377-1-1(X))* Pomegranate Publishing.

Matthews, Elli. The Everyday Easter Dress. Matthews, John, illus. 2011. 24p. pap. 24.95 *(978-1-4560-9411-9(4))* America Star Bks.

Mayer, Mercer. It's Easter, Little Critter! Mayer, Mercer, illus. 2007. (Little Critter Ser.). (ENG., Illus.). 20p. (J). (gr. -1-1). pap. 6.99 *(978-0-06-053974-0(7),* HarperFestival) HarperCollins Pubs.

McGuirk, Leslie. Tucker Digs Easter! McGuirk, Leslie, illus. 2017. (ENG., Illus.). 28p. (J). (-k). bds. 7.99 *(978-0-7636-8536-2(4))* Candlewick Pr.

McInnes, Lisa. Evelyn's Special Eggs. Duersch, Gretchen, ed. Schlund, Mackenzie, illus. 2011. 32p. pap. *(978-1-77067-394-6(6))* FriesenPress.

McIntyre, Sasha & Ghione, Yvette. Franklin's Easter: A Sticker Activity Book. 2004. (ENG., Illus.). 16p. (J). 6.95 *(978-1-55337-521-0(1))* Kids Can Pr., Ltd. CAN. Dist: Hachette Bk. Group.

McIntyre, Sasha & Sinkner, Alice, adapted by. Franklin's Easter: A Sticker Activity Book. 2004. (Franklin Ser.). (ENG., Illus.). 16p. (J). (gr. k-3). 4.95 *(978-1-55337-690-3(0))* Kids Can Pr., Ltd. CAN. Dist: Hachette Bk. Group.

Meadows, Daisy. Bella the Bunny Fairy. Ripper, Georgie, illus. 2008. (Rainbow Magic — the Pet Fairies Ser.). 65p. (gr. 7). lib. bdg. 14.75 *(978-1-4178-2996-5(6),* Turtleback) Turtleback Bks.

—Emma the Easter Fairy. 2011. (Rainbow Magic Ser.). (ENG.). 192p. (J). (gr. 2-5). pap. 6.99 *(978-0-545-27051-9(0),* Scholastic Paperbacks) Scholastic, Inc.

—Pet Parade. 2013. (Rainbow Magic — Scholastic Reader Ser.). lib. bdg. 13.55 *(978-0-606-31973-7(5),* Turtleback) Turtleback Bks.

Metzger, Steve. The Easter Bunny Is Missing! Spurll, Barbara, illus. 2007. (J). pap. *(978-0-439-92959-2(8))* Scholastic, Inc.

Mitter, Matt. Sesame Street Guess Who, Easter Elmo! Guess Who Easter Elmo! Mathieu, Joe, illus. 2015. (Guess Who Ser.: 6). (ENG.). 10p. (J). (gr. -1-k). 10.99 *(978-0-7944-3331-4(6),* Reader's Digest Children's Bks.) Studio Fun International.

Morgan, Ruth. The Funny Easter Bunny. 2003. (Illus.). 22p. per. 1.95 *(978-1-932338-10-2(1))* Lifevest Publishing, Inc.

Mortimer, Anne. Bunny's Easter Egg. Mortimer, Anne, illus. 2010. (ENG., Illus.). 32p. (J). (gr. -1-2). 12.99 *(978-0-06-136664-2(1),* Tegen, Katherine Bks) HarperCollins Pubs.

Mussenbrock, Anne. Easter Notes. 2004. 12p. (J). (gr. -1-k). 5.99 *(978-1-59384-037-2(3));* bds. 5.99 *(978-1-59384-038-9(1))* Parklane Publishing.

Nelson, Steve & Rollins, Jack. Here Comes Peter Cottontail! Levy, Pamela R., illus. 2007. (ENG.). 26p. (gr. -1-k). bds. 12.99 *(978-0-8249-6690-4(2),* Ideal Pubns.) Worthy Publishing.

—Here Comes Peter Cottontail, Set. Levy, Pamela R., illus. 2007. (ENG.). 26p. 16.99 *(978-0-8249-6689-8(9),* Ideal Pubns.) Worthy Publishing.

Nelson, Sue Ellen. The Missing Easter Bunny. 2010. 36p. pap. 15.00 *(978-1-60844-439-7(2))* Dog Ear Publishing, LLC.

Niddrie, June. E. B. & the Bees. 2010. 32p. pap. 16.10 *(978-0-557-31873-5(4))* Lulu Pr., Inc.

Nosy Crow Staff. Can You Say It, Too? Cheep! Cheep! Braun, Sebastien, illus. 2017. (Can You Say It, Too? Ser.). (ENG.). 10p. (J). (— 1). bds. 8.99 *(978-0-7636-9329-9(4),* Nosy Crow) Candlewick Pr.

—Cutie Pie Looks for the Easter Bunny: A Tiny Tab Book. Ho, Jannie, illus. 2015. (Tiny Tab Ser.). (ENG.). 8p. (J). (— 1). bds. 7.99 *(978-0-7636-7599-8(7),* Nosy Crow) Candlewick Pr.

Oceanak, Karla. Kerfuffle: An Aldo Zelnick Comic Novel. Spanjer, Kendra, illus. 2016. (Aldo Zelnick Comic Novel Ser.: 11). (ENG.). 160p. (J). (gr. 1-8). pap. 8.95 *(978-1-934649-75-6(9))* Bailiwick Pr.

O'Connor, Jane. Fancy Nancy's Elegant Easter. Bracken, Carolyn & Glasser, Robin Preiss, illus. 2009. (Fancy Nancy Ser.). (ENG.). 16p. (J). (gr. -1-3). pap. 6.99 *(978-0-06-170379-9(6),* HarperFestival) HarperCollins Pubs.

O'Ryan, Ray. A Galactic Easter! Jack, Colin, illus. 2014. (Galaxy Zack Ser.: 7). (ENG.). 128p. (J). (gr. k-4). pap. 5.99 *(978-1-4424-9357-5(7),* Little Simon) Little Simon.

—A Galactic Easter! 2014. (Galaxy Zack Ser.: 7). lib. bdg. 16.00 *(978-0-606-35428-8(X))* Turtleback Bks.

Pagnoni, Roberta, illus. It's Easter Time. 2010. (ENG.). 10p. (J). (gr. -1-k). bds. 6.99 *(978-0-7641-6334-0(5))* Barron's Educational Series, Inc.

Pagnoni, Roberta & Rigo, Laura, illus. My Easter Basket. 2016. (ENG.). 10p. (J). (gr. -1 — 1). bds. 6.99 *(978-0-7641-6822-2(3))* Barron's Educational Series, Inc.

Pandanas, Ms L. A. Zar-Zar the Russian Ladybeetle: Easter Beetle. 2013. 26p. pap. *(978-0-9870702-4-1(X))* Reed, Laura.

Paquette, Ammi-Joan. Bunny Bus. Withrow, Lesley Breen, illus. 2017. (ENG.). 32p. (J). 16.99 *(978-0-374-30225-2(1),* 9780374302252, Farrar, Straus & Giroux (BYR)) Farrar, Straus & Giroux.

Park, Barbara. Dumb Bunny. Brunkus, Denise, illus. 2009. (Junie B. Jones Ser.). (ENG.). 128p. (J). (gr. 1-4). 4.99 *(978-0-375-83810-1(4),* Random Hse. Bks. for Young Readers) Random Hse. Children's Bks.

Petretti, Silvia I. Rachel's Easter Vacation in Mexico. James, Elizabeth, ed. 2011. (Illus.). 50p. (J). pap. 14.99 *(978-1-931671-37-8(0))* FM Publishing Co.

Pilkey, Dav. Dumb Bunnies' Easter. Pilkey, Dav, illus. 2009. (Dumb Bunnies Ser.). (ENG., Illus.). 32p. (J). (gr. -1-3). 16.99 *(978-0-545-03946-8(0))* Scholastic, Inc.

Piper, Sophie. The Angel & the Dove: A Story for Easter. Stephenson, Kristina, illus. 2010. (ENG.). 28p. (J). (gr. -1-k). 12.99 *(978-0-7459-6123-1(1))* Lion Hudson PLC GBR. Dist: Independent Pubs. Group.

Polacco, Patricia. Chicken Sunday. 2015. 32p. pap. 8.00 *(978-1-61003-527-9(5))* Center for the Collaborative Classroom.

Posner-Sanchez, Andrea. A Royal Easter. 2014. (Disney Princess 8x8 Ser.). lib. bdg. 14.75 *(978-0-606-35553-7(7))* Turtleback Bks.

—A Royal Easter (Disney Princess) RH Disney Staff et al, illus. 2014. (Pictureback(R) Ser.). (ENG.). 16p. (J). (gr. -1-2). 4.99 *(978-0-7364-3084-5(9),* RH/Disney) Random Hse. Children's Bks.

—The Sweetest Easter (Peeps) Random House, illus. 2017. (Pictureback(R) Ser.). (ENG.). 16p. (J). (-k). pap. 4.99 *(978-1-5247-1905-0(6),* Random Hse. Bks. for Young Readers) Random Hse. Children's Bks.

Price, Roger & Stern, Leonard. Easter Eggstravaganza Mad Libs. 2013. (Mad Libs Ser.). (ENG.). 48p. (J). (gr. 3-7). 4.99 *(978-0-8431-7252-2(5),* Mad Libs) Penguin Young Readers Group.

Priddy, Roger. Chunky Pack: Easter. 2016. (Chunky 3 Pack Ser.). (ENG., Illus.). 12p. (J). bds. 4.99 *(978-0-312-51953-7(2),* 9780312519537, Priddy Bks.) St. Martin's Pr.

—Easter Fun! 2017. (Alphaprints Ser.). (ENG.). 12p. (J). bds. 7.99 *(978-0-312-52156-1(1),* 9780312521561, Priddy Bks.) St. Martin's Pr.

—Easter Surprise. 2011. (ENG., Illus.). (J). (gr. -1-k). bds. 9.99 *(978-0-312-51002-2(0),* 9780312510022, Priddy Bks.) St. Martin's Pr.

—Funny Faces: Easter Parade. 2015. (Funny Faces Ser.). (ENG.). 10p. (J). (gr. -1-1). bds. 8.99 *(978-0-312-51785-4(8),* 9780312517854, Priddy Bks.) St. Martin's Pr.

—Lift-The-Tab: Easter. 2017. (ENG., Illus.). 18p. (J). bds. 8.99 *(978-0-312-52158-5(8),* 9780312521585, Priddy Bks.) St. Martin's Pr.

—Mini Tab: Easter. 2017. (Mini Tab Ser.). (ENG., Illus.). 16p. (J). bds. 5.99 *(978-0-312-52157-8(X),* 9780312521578, Priddy Bks.) St. Martin's Pr.

—Shiny Shapes: Easter Surprise. 2017. (Shiny Shapes Ser.). (ENG., Illus.). 10p. (J). bds. 7.99 *(978-0-312-52159-2(6),* 9780312521592, Priddy Bks.) St. Martin's Pr.

Quail, Jane. Easter Bunny's Journey. 2010. 32p. pap. 21.99 *(978-1-4535-0329-4(3))* Xlibris Corp.

Rabe, Tish & Yaccarino, Dan. Five Little Bunnies. Yaccarino, Dan, illus. 2016. (Illus.). 16p. (J). (gr. -1 — 1). bds. 6.99 *(978-0-06-225339-2(5))* HarperCollins Pubs.

Randolph, Tammy. Cricket Hunts for the Easter Bunny. 2011. 28p. pap. 15.99 *(978-1-4568-6786-7(5))* Xlibris Corp.

Random House. Follow That Egg! (Team Umizoomi) Aikins, David, illus. 2014. (Glitter Board Book Ser.). (ENG.). 12p. (J). (-k). bds. 6.99 *(978-0-385-37518-4(2),* Random Hse. Bks. for Young Readers) Random Hse. Children's Bks.

—Peter Cottontail: the Great Easter Egg Hunt (Peter Cottontail) Random House, illus. 2016. (Lift-The-Flap Ser.). (ENG., Illus.). 12p. (J). (gr. -1-k). bds. 6.99 *(978-1-101-93169-1(8),* Random Hse. Bks. for Young Readers) Random Hse. Children's Bks.

Random House Staff. An Egg-Stra Special Easter! (Barbie) Duarte, Pamela, illus. 2014. (Color Plus Card Stock Ser.). (ENG.). 48p. (J). (gr. -1-2). pap. 3.99 *(978-0-385-37319-7(8),* Random Hse. Bks. for Young Readers) Random Hse. Children's Bks.

—SpongeBob's Easter Parade (SpongeBob SquarePants) Random House Staff, illus. 2013. (Pictureback(R) Ser.). (ENG., Illus.). 24p. (J). (gr. -1-2). pap. 3.99 *(978-0-449-81444-4(0),* Random Hse. Bks. for Young Readers) Random Hse. Children's Bks.

Reader's Digest Staff & Gold, Gina. Bunny Hugs. 2013. (Hugs Book Ser.). (ENG.). 10p. (J). (gr. -1-k). bds. 4.99 *(978-0-7944-2784-9(7))* Studio Fun International.

La Reina Ester. (Libros Arco Ser.) Tr. of Just in Time Esther. (SPA.). 24p. (J). 2.49 *(978-0-7586-0497-2(1))* Concordia Publishing Hse.

Reitze, Glenn Logan. Ernie the Easter Hippopotamus: A Comic Adventure for Anytime. Reitze, Glenn Logan, illus. 2007. (ENG., Illus.). 48p. (J). lib. bdg. 19.95

(978-0-88265-040-1(8), Fine Art Editions) North American International.

Reitze, Glenn Logan, illus. & text. Ernie the Easter Hippotamus: A Comic Adventure for Anytime. Reitze, Glenn Logan, text. 2007. (J). pap. (978-0-88265-041-8(6)) North American International.

Rescek, Sanja, illus. Easter Bunny's Helpers. 2009. (ENG.). 12p. (J). 6.95 (978-1-58117-870-8(0), Intervisual/Piggy Toes) Bendon, Inc.

Richards, Dawn. Duck's Easter Egg Hunt. D'hamers, Heidi, illus. 2014. (J). (978-1-4351-5243-4(3)) Barnes & Noble, Inc.

Ritchie, Joseph R. An Easter Basket Peek-A-Boo! Halverson, Lydia, illus. 2007. (Lift-the-Flap Books (Candycane Press) Ser.). (ENG.). 14p. (gr. -1-1). bds. 7.99 (978-0-8249-6688-1(0), Ideal Pubns.) Worthy Publishing.

—Peter Cottontail's Busy Day. Halverson, Lydia, illus. 2006. (ENG.). 26p. (J). (gr. -1-k). 12.95 (978-0-8249-6652-2(X), Ideal Pubns.) Worthy Publishing.

—Peter Cottontail's Easter Egg Hunt. Thornburgh, Rebecca McKillip, illus. 2004. (ENG.). 12p. (J). (gr. -1-k). bds. 9.95 (978-0-8249-6522-8(1), Ideal Pubns.) Worthy Publishing.

—Peter Cottontail's Easter Surprise. Halverson, Lydia, illus. 2006. (ENG.). 18p. (J). (gr. -1-k). bds. 9.95 (978-0-8249-6627-0(9), Ideal Pubns.) Worthy Publishing.

—Peter Cottontaol's Easter Egg Hunt. Thornburgh, Rebecca, illus. 2006. (ENG.). 26p. (J). (gr. -1-k). 12.95 (978-0-8249-6653-9(8), Ideal Pubns.) Worthy Publishing.

Rowley, Deborah Pace. Easter Walk: A Treasure Hunt for the Real Meaning of Easter. Burr, Dan, illus. 2010. (J). (978-1-60641-055-4(5)) Deseret Bk. Co.

Roy, Ron. April Adventure. Gurney, John Steven, illus. 2010. (Calendar Mysteries Ser.: 4). (ENG.). 80p. (J). (gr. 1-4). 4.99 (978-0-375-86116-1(5), Random Hse. Bks. for Young Readers) Random Hse. Children's Bks.

—April Adventure. 2010. (Calendar Mysteries Ser.: 4). lib. bdg. 14.75 (978-0-606-12465-2(9), Turtleback) Turtleback Bks.

Rudel-Tessier, Melanie. Caillou: Happy Easter! Brignaud, Pierre, illus. 2012. (Confetti Ser.). (ENG.). 24p. (J). (gr. -1-1). pap. 4.99 (978-2-89450-947-0(2)) Caillouet, Gerry.

Ruelle, Karen Gray. Easter Egg Disaster: A Harry & Emily Adventure. Ruelle, Karen Gray, illus. 2003. (Holiday House Readers Ser.). (ENG., Illus.). 32p. (J). (gr. k-3). pap. 4.95 (978-0-8234-1823-7(5)) Holiday Hse., Inc.

—Easter Egg Disaster: A Harry & Emily Adventure. 2003. (ENG., Illus.). 32p. (J). (gr. k-3). tchr. ed. 14.95 (978-0-8234-1806-0(5)) Holiday Hse., Inc.

Rumbaugh, Melinda. The Great Easter Egg Hunt. Reed, Lisa, illus. 2014. (VeggieTales Bk Ser.). 16p. (J). 12.99 (978-0-8249-1928-3(9), Ideal Pubns.) Worthy Publishing.

Rusu, Meredith. A Kooky Easter Surprise (Shopkins) 2017. (Shopkins Ser.). (ENG.). 24p. (J). (gr. -1-3). pap. 4.99 (978-1-338-10882-8(4)) Scholastic, Inc.

Saccheri, Josephine. The Secret to Easter Eggs. Saccheri, Briana, illus. 2008. 28p. pap. 24.95 (978-1-60474-210-7(0)) America Star Bks.

Sander, Sonia. Easter Egg Dash! A Lift-The-Flap Book with Stickers. Shannon, David et al, illus. 2010. (Jon Scieszka's Trucktown Ser.). (ENG.). 12p. (J). (gr. -1-k). bds. 7.99 (978-1-4169-4183-5(5), Little Simon) Little Simon.

Sanrio. Easter Bonnet Surprise. 2013. (ENG., Illus.). 24p. (J). (gr. k-2). pap. 6.99 (978-1-4197-0910-4(0), Abrams Bks. for Young Readers) Abrams, Inc.

Schaefer, Lola M. & McCue, Lisa. Easter Surprises. 2009. (ENG., Illus.). 18p. (J). (gr. -1-1). 7.99 (978-1-4169-6476-6(2), Little Simon) Little Simon.

Scholastic Editors. Peppa's Easter Egg Hunt. 2015. (Peppa Pig 8X8 Ser.). lib. bdg. 13.55 (978-0-606-38112-3(0)) Turtleback Bks.

Scholastic, Inc. Staff. Peppa's Easter Egg Hunt (Peppa Pig) Eone, illus. 2015. (Peppa Pig Ser.). (ENG.). 24p. (J). (gr. -1-k). 3.99 (978-0-545-88130-2(7)) Scholastic, Inc.

Schulman, Janet. 10 Easter Egg Hunters. 2015. lib. bdg. 14.75 (978-0-606-36379-2(3)) Turtleback Bks.

—10 Easter Egg Hunters: A Holiday Counting Book. Davick, Linda, illus. (ENG.). (J). (gr. -1 — 1). 2012. 26p. bds. 6.99 (978-0-375-86637-1(X)) 2011. 32p. 8.99 (978-0-375-86787-3(2)) Random Hse. Children's Bks. (Knopf Bks. for Young Readers).

Schulz, Charles M. It's the Easter Beagle, Charlie Brown, 1 vol. 2013. (Peanuts Picture Bks.). (ENG.). 48p. (J). (gr. -1-4). lib. bdg. 24.21 (978-1-61479-031-0(0)) ABDO Publishing Co.

—It's the Easter Beagle, Charlie Brown. Scott, Vicki, illus. 2016. (Peanuts Ser.). (ENG.). 32p. (J). (gr. -1). 7.99 (978-1-4814-6159-7(1), Simon Spotlight) Simon Spotlight.

—It's the Easter Beagle, Charlie Brown: with Sound & Music. 2013. (ENG., Illus.). 48p. (J). (gr. -1-17). 19.95 (978-0-7624-4608-7(0), Running Pr. Kids) Running Pr. Bk. Pubs.

Scollon, William, et al. Easter Bonnet Parade. Disney Storybook Artists Staff, illus. 2013. (ENG.). 24p. (J). (gr. -1-k). pap. 5.99 (978-1-4231-6416-6(4)) Disney Pr.

Scotton, Rob. Where's the Easter Bunny? Scotton, Rob, illus. 2011. (Splat the Cat Ser.). (ENG., Illus.). 16p. (J). (gr. -1-1). pap. 6.99 (978-0-06-197861-6(2), HarperFestival) HarperCollins Pubs.

Sesame Workshop. The Great Easter Race! 2017. (Sesame Street Scribbles Ser.: 0). (ENG.). 40p. (J). (-4). 10.99 (978-1-4926-3837-7(4), 9781492638377, Sourcebooks Jabberwocky) Sourcebooks, Inc.

Sherwood, C. A. Aj's Easter Surprise. 2008. 56p. pap. 24.29 (978-1-4343-7583-4(8)) AuthorHouse.

Silverhardt, Lauryn. Happy Easter, Sprinkles! Kanemoto, Dan, illus. 2008. (Blue's Clues Ser.). (ENG.). 12p. (J). (gr. -1-k). bds. 5.99 (978-1-4169-4775-2(2), Simon Spotlight/Nickelodeon) Simon Spotlight/Nickelodeon.

Simon, Jenne. Lalaloopsy: Easter Eggs-Travaganza. Hill, Prescott, illus. 2014. (ENG.). 24p. (J). (gr. -1-3). pap. 4.99 (978-0-545-60802-2(3)) Scholastic, Inc.

Slegers, Liesbet. Happy Easter! Slegers, Liesbet, illus. 2012. (ENG., Illus.). 30p. (J). (gr. k — 1). 15.95 (978-1-60537-114-6(9)) Cobblestone Publishing Co.

Smith, Jane. It's Easter, Chloe Zoe! Smith, Jane, illus. 2016. (Chloe Zoe Ser.). (ENG., Illus.). 32p. (J). (gr. -1-3). 12.99 (978-0-8075-2460-2(3)) Whitman, Albert & Co.

Smythe, Theresa. Chester's Colorful Easter Eggs. Smythe, Theresa, illus. 2013. (ENG., Illus.). 24p. (J). (gr. -1-k). 12.99 (978-0-8050-9326-1(5), 9780805093261, Holt, Henry & Co. Bks. For Young Readers) Holt, Henry & Co.

Speed, Evelyn. Digger Rabbit & the First Easter. 2009. (Illus.). 24p. pap. 11.49 (978-1-4389-6105-7(7)) AuthorHouse.

Stone Arch Books. St. Patrick's Day & Easter, 1 vol. Nguyen, Dustin, illus. 2014. (Batman: Li'l Gotham Ser.). (ENG.). 32p. (gr. 2-3). 22.60 (978-1-4342-9219-3(3)) Stone Arch Bks.

Stuart, Janet. What? No Easter Eggs? 2011. 24p. pap. 12.79 (978-1-4567-6770-9(4)) AuthorHouse.

Sypolt, Carl W. Fibber Lygood at Christmas, Easter, & St. Patrick's Day. 2006. 108p. (J). pap. 10.95 (978-0-7414-2982-7(9)) Infinity Publishing.

Taplin, Sam. Easter Bunny Flap Book. 2012. (Flap Bks). 10p. (J). ring bd. 7.99 (978-0-7945-3256-7(X), Usborne) EDC Publishing.

Tegen, Katherine. The Story of the Easter Bunny. Lambert, Sally Anne, illus. (ENG.). 40p. (J). (gr. -1-3). 2007. pap. 6.99 (978-0-06-058781-9(4)) 2005. 12.99 (978-0-06-050711-4(X)) HarperCollins Pubs.

—The Story of the Easter Bunny Board Book. Lambert, Sally Anne, illus. 2017. 32p. (J). (gr. -1-3). bds. 7.99 (978-0-06-238155-2(5), HarperFestival) HarperCollins Pubs.

Thaler, Mike. Easter Egg Haunt, 1 vol. Lee, Jared, illus. 2009. (Tales from the Back Pew Ser.). (ENG.). 32p. (J). (gr. 1-4). pap. 3.99 (978-0-310-71591-7(1)) Zonderkidz.

Thomas, Jan. The Easter Bunny's Assistant. Thomas, Jan, illus. 2012. (ENG., Illus.). 40p. (J). (gr. -1-3). 12.99 (978-0-06-169286-4(7)) HarperCollins Pubs.

Tiger Tales Staff, ed. Easter Surprise: My First Lift & Learn. 2014. (ENG.). 10p. (J). bds. 7.99 (978-1-58925-580-7(1)) Tiger Tales.

Tildes, Phyllis Limbacher. The Magic Babushka. Tildes, Phyllis Limbacher, illus. 2009. (ENG., Illus.). 32p. (J). (gr. k-3). pap. 7.95 (978-1-58089-225-4(6)) Charlesbridge Publishing, Inc.

Tisserand, Jean-Louis. That Easter Morn. 2007. (Illus.). 32p. (J). 13.49 (978-0-7586-1264-9(8)) Concordia Publishing Hse.

Tudor, Tasha. A Tale for Easter. Tudor, Tasha, illus. 2014. (Classic Board Bks.). (ENG., Illus.). 34p. (J). (gr. -1 — 1). bds. 7.99 (978-1-4424-8857-1(3), Little Simon) Little Simon.

—A Tale for Easter. Tudor, Tasha, illus. 2004. (ENG., Illus.). 32p. (J). (gr. -1-3). 6.99 (978-0-689-86694-4(1), Aladdin) Simon & Schuster Children's Publishing.

Underwood, Deborah. Here Comes the Easter Cat. Rueda, Claudia, illus. 2014. (ENG.). 80p. (J). (gr. -1-k). 16.99 (978-0-8037-3939-0(7), Dial Bks) Penguin Publishing Group.

Vail, Rachel. Piggy Bunny. Tankard, Jeremy, illus. 2012. (ENG.). 32p. (J). (gr. -1-1). 14.99 (978-0-312-64988-3(6), 9780312649883) Feiwel & Friends.

Vokey, Jessica. Chester the Easter Chicken. 2012. 28p. pap. 15.99 (978-1-4771-4276-9(2)) Xlibris Corp.

Wall, Pauline & Smith, Shelley. What the Mouse Saw: An Easter Story. 2013. 20p. pap. 16.82 (978-1-4669-3503-7(0)) Trafford Publishing.

Wallace, Adam. How to Catch the Easter Bunny. Elkerton, Andy, illus. 2017. (ENG.). 40p. (J). (-6). 10.99 (978-1-4926-3817-9(X), 9781492638179, Sourcebooks Jabberwocky) Sourcebooks, Inc.

Wallace, Carol. Easter Bunny Blues. Björkman, Steve, illus. 2009. (ENG.). 40p. (J). (gr. k-2). 15.95 (978-0-8234-2162-6(7)) Holiday Hse., Inc.

Wallace, Sally. Peter's Puzzling Purple Easter Egg. 2010. 44p. pap. 16.99 (978-1-4490-3032-2(7)) AuthorHouse.

Wang, Margaret. Easter Egg Hunt. Johnson, Richard, illus. 2005. (ENG.). 10p. (J). bds. 9.95 (978-1-58117-375-8(X), Intervisual/Piggy Toes) Bendon, Inc.

Watson, Myrtle. Kite Flying in the Village: A Guyanese Girl's Story. 2011. 20p. 10.03 (978-1-4520-8632-3(X)) AuthorHouse.

Weninger, Brigitte. Happy Easter, Davy! Tharlet, Eve, illus. 2014. (ENG.). 32p. (J). (gr. k-3). 15.95 (978-0-7358-4161-1(6)) North-South Bks., Inc.

Wheelie, P. Tommy's Triumph: The tales of Tommy the tortoise & Friends. 2009. (Illus.). 28p. pap. 12.49 (978-1-4389-2718-3(5)) AuthorHouse.

White, George. Kirby the Easter Dog: A Pop-up Easter Egg Hunt. 2008. (Illus.). 14p. (J). 14.99 (978-0-9795441-2-5(2)) Jumping Jack Pr.

Whitney, A. D. T. Patience Strong's Outings by Mrs a D T Whitney. 2006. 236p. per. 20.99 (978-1-4255-2007-6(3)) Michigan Publishing.

Wolf, Jackie, et al. My Sparkle Egg Book. 2005. (Illus.). (J). (978-1-57151-750-0(2)) Playhouse Publishing.

Wolif, T. Hal & His Pal Al: The Easter Bunny's Helpers. 2007. (Illus.). 36p. per. 12.97 (978-1-932344-93-6(4)) Thornton Publishing, Inc.

Woods, Denise M. & McKelvain, Dana. The Legend of the Donkey's Cross. 2004. (Illus.). 32p. (J). per. 12.99 (978-1-58930-112-2(9)) Selah Publishing Group, LLC.

Zabrosky, Joseph. Sunny & Hunny, 2 vols., 4 bks. l.t. ed. 2005. (Illus.). 32p. (J). per. (978-0-9768831-1-1(2)) Elohim Bks.

EASTER—POETRY

Grimes, Nikki. At Jerusalem's Gate: Poems of Easter. Frampton, David, illus. 2005. 48p. (J). 20.00 (978-0-8028-5183-3(5)) Eerdmans, William B. Publishing Co.

Stiegemeyer, Julie. Bright Easter Day. Spellman, Susan, illus. 2005. 32p. (J). 10.49 (978-0-7586-0818-5(7)) Concordia Publishing Hse.

EASTER ISLAND

Moore Niver, Heather. 20 Fun Facts about Easter Island, Vol. 1. 2014. (Fun Fact File: World Wonders! Ser.). (ENG.). 32p. (J). (gr. 2-3). 25.25 (978-1-4824-0447-0(8)) Stevens, Gareth Publishing LLLP.

Pfeil, Susan. Professor Kiwi, Explorer of the Seven Seas: The Eye of Easter Island. 2005. (J). per. 6.95 (978-1-59094-062-4(8)) Jawbone Publishing Corp.

Raum, Elizabeth. Easter Island. 2015. (Ancient Wonders Ser.). (Illus.). 32p. (J). 28.50 (978-1-60753-465-5(7)) Amicus Publishing.

Reis, Ronald A. Easter Island. 2011. (Lost Worlds & Mysterious Civilizations Ser.). (Illus.). 116p. (gr. 6-12). 35.00 (978-1-60413-972-3(2), Chelsea Hse.) Facts On File, Inc.

Riggs, Kate. Easter Island. 2009. (Places of Old Ser.). 24p. (J). (gr. 1-5). lib. bdg. 24.25 (978-1-58341-710-2(9), Creative Education) Creative Co., The.

Simmons, Alex. Mysteries of the Past: A Chapter Book. 2005. (True Tales Ser.). (ENG., Illus.). 48p. (J). (gr. 2-4). lib. bdg. 22.50 (978-0-516-25184-4(8), Children's Pr.) Scholastic Library Publishing.

Torres, John A. The Ancient Mystery of Easter Island. 2006. (Natural Disasters Ser.). (Illus.). 32p. (J). (gr. 1-4). lib. bdg. 25.70 (978-1-58415-495-2(0)) Mitchell Lane Pubs., Inc.

Waxman, Laura Hamilton. Mysteries of Easter Island. 2017. (Ancient Mysteries Ser.). (ENG.). 32p. (J). (gr. 3-6). 27.99 **(978-1-5124-4015-7(9))** Lerner Publishing Group.

World Book, Inc Staff, contrib. by. The Mysteries of Easter Island. 2014. (J). (978-0-7166-2665-7(9)) World Bk., Inc.

EASTERN EUROPE

see Europe, Eastern

EASTERN SEABOARD

see Atlantic States

EASTMAN, GEORGE, 1854-1932

Aller, Susan Bivin. George Eastman. 2003. (History Maker Biographies Ser.). (ENG., Illus.). 48p. (gr. 3-6). lib. bdg. 27.93 (978-0-8225-0200-5(3)) Lerner Publishing Group.

Davis, Lynn. George Eastman, 1 vol. 2016. (ENG., Illus.). 24p. (J). (978-1-62403-722-1(4)) ABDO Publishing Co.

Fandel, Jennifer & Milgrom, Al. George Eastman & the Kodak Camera, 1 vol. Purcell, Gordon & Milgrom, Al, illus. 2007. (Inventions & Discovery Ser.). (ENG.). 32p. (gr. 3-4). 30.65 (978-0-7368-6848-8(8), Graphic Library) Capstone Press of Coughlan Cos.

—George Eastman & the Kodak Camera, 1 vol. Purcell, Gordon, illus. 2007. (Inventions & Discovery Ser.). (ENG.). 32p. (gr. 3-4). pap. 8.10 (978-0-7368-7900-2(5), Graphic Library) Capstone Press of Coughlan Cos.

Ford, Carin T. George Eastman: The Kodak Camera Man. 2004. (Famous Inventors Ser.). (Illus.). 32p. (J). lib. bdg. 22.60 (978-0-7660-2247-8(1)) Enslow Pubs., Inc.

Kulling, Monica. It's a Snap! George Eastman's First Photograph. Slavin, Bill, illus. (Great Idea Ser.). (ENG.). 32p. (J). (gr. k-3). 2013. pap. 7.95 (978-1-77049-513-5(4)) 2009. 17.95 (978-0-88776-881-1(4)) Tundra Bks. CAN. (Tundra Bks.). Dist: Penguin Random Hse. LLC.

Mattern, Joanne. George Eastman & Photographic Film. 2004. (Uncharted, Unexplored, & Unexplained Ser.). (Illus.). 48p. (J). (gr. 4-8). lib. bdg. 29.95 (978-1-58415-258-3(3)) Mitchell Lane Pubs., Inc.

Rausch, Monica L. George Eastman & the Camera. 2007. (Inventors & Their Discoveries Ser.). (Illus.). 24p. (gr. 1-4). pap. 8.15 (978-0-8368-7730-4(6)); lib. bdg. 22.00 (978-0-8368-7499-0(4)) Stevens, Gareth Publishing LLLP. (Weekly Reader Leveled Readers).

—George Eastman y la Cámara. 2007. (Inventores y sus descubrimientos (Inventors & Their Discoveries) Ser.). (ENG & SPA., Illus.). 24p. (gr. 1-4). pap. 8.15 (978-0-8368-7999-5(6)); lib. bdg. 22.00 (978-0-8368-7994-0(5)) Stevens, Gareth Publishing LLLP. (Weekly Reader Leveled Readers).

EATING DISORDERS

Here are entered works on gross disturbances in eating behavior as a subclass of mental disorders. .

Ambrose, Marylou & Deisler, Veronica. Eating Disorders: Examining Anorexia, Bulimia, & Binge Eating. 2014. (Diseases, Disorders, Symptoms Ser.). (Illus.). 96p. (gr. 9-12). (J). 27.94 (978-1-62293-070-8(3)); pap. 10.95 (978-1-62293-071-5(1)) Enslow Pubs., Inc.

Bellenir, Karen, ed. Eating Disorders Information for Teens. 3rd rev. ed. 2013. (Teen Health Ser.). 424p. lib. bdg. 69.00 (978-0-7808-1269-7(7)) Omnigraphics, Inc.

Bjorklund, Ruth. Eating Disorders. 2005. (Health Alert Ser.). (Illus.). 64p. (gr. 4-7). lib. bdg. 32.79 (978-0-7614-1914-3(4), Benchmark Bks.) Marshall Cavendish Corp.

Brinkerhoff, Shirley. Drug Therapy & Eating Disorders. (Encyclopedia of Psychiatric Drugs & Their Disorders Ser.). (Illus.). (YA). 2004. 128p. lib. bdg. 24.95 (978-1-59084-565-3(X)) 2003. 124p. (gr. 7-12). pap. 14.95 (978-1-4222-0389-7(1)) Mason Crest.

—Eating Disorders. McDonnell, Mary Ann & Esherick, Donald, eds. 2013. (State of Mental Illness & Its Therapy Ser.: 19). 128p. (J). (gr. 7-18). 24.95 (978-1-4222-2825-8(8)) Mason Crest.

Clarke, Julie & Kirby-Payne, Ann. Understanding Weight & Depression. 2005. (Teen Eating Disorder Prevention Book Ser.). (Illus.). 192p. (J). (gr. 7-12). lib. bdg. 34.60 (978-0-8239-2994-8(9), E2WEDE) Rosen Publishing Group, Inc., The.

Cooperman, Sheila & Gilbert, Sara. Living with Eating Disorders. 2009. (Teen's Guides). 192p. (gr. 6-12). pap. 14.95 (978-0-8160-7743-4(6), Checkmark Bks.) Facts On File, Inc.

Cooperman, Sheila & Gilbert, Sara Dulaney. Living with Eating Disorders. 2009. (Teen's Guides). 192p. (gr. 6-12). 34.95 (978-0-8160-7328-3(7)) Facts On File, Inc.

Crabtree Publishing Company Staff & Iorizzo, Carrie. Eating Disorders. 2012. (ENG., Illus.). 48p. (J). (978-0-7787-2183-3(3)); pap. (978-0-7787-2190-1(6)) Crabtree Publishing Co.

Danger Zone: Dieting & Eating Disorders, 6 bks., Set. Incl. Anorexia. Watson, Stephanie. 2006. lib. bdg. 31.95 (978-1-4042-1996-0(X)); Binge Eating. Watson, Stephanie. 2006. lib. bdg. 31.95 (978-1-4042-1998-4(6)); Bulimia. Watson, Stephanie. 2007. lib. bdg. 31.95 (978-1-4042-1997-7(8)); Diet Drugs. Williams, Kara. 2006. lib. bdg. 31.95 (978-1-4042-1994-6(3)); Diet Fads. Zahensky, Barbara A. 2007. lib. bdg. 31.95 (978-1-4042-1999-1(4)); Negative Body Image. Willett, Edward. 2006. lib. bdg. 31.95 (978-1-4042-1995-3(1)); (Illus.). 64p. (YA). (gr. 7-12). 2007. Set lib. bdg. 167.70 (978-1-4042-1061-5(X)) Rosen Publishing Group, Inc., The.

Drew, Ursula & Watson, Stephanie. Conquering Bulimia, 01 vols., 1. 2016. (Conquering Eating Disorders Ser.). (ENG.). 64p. (J). 32.95 (978-1-4994-6201-2(8), Rosen Young Adult) Rosen Publishing Group, Inc., The.

Dunkle, Elena & Dunkle, Clare B. Elena Vanishing. 2015. (ENG.). 288p. (YA). (gr. 9-17). 17.99 (978-1-4521-2151-2(6)) Chronicle Bks. LLC.

Esherick, Joan. Diet & Your Emotions: The Comfort Food Falsehood. 2004. (Obesity Ser.). (Illus.). 104p. (J). (gr. 4-7). lib. bdg. 23.95 (978-1-59084-950-7(7)) Mason Crest.

—Emotions & Eating. Garcia, Victor, ed. 2014. (Understanding Obesity Ser.: 10). 104p. (J). (gr. 7-18). lib. bdg. 24.95 (978-1-4222-3059-6(7)) Mason Crest.

Espejo, Roman, ed. Eating Disorders. 2012. (Opposing Viewpoints Ser.). (ENG., Illus.). 240p. (J). (gr. 10-12). pap. 29.45 (978-0-7377-5724-8(8), Greenhaven Pr., Inc.); (YA). (gr. 9-12). lib. bdg. 42.95 (978-0-7377-5723-1(X)) Cengage Gale.

Favor, Lesli J. & Freed, Kira. Food As Foe: Nutrition & Eating Disorders. 2009. (Benchmark Rockets Ser.). 32p. (gr. 5-18). 28.50 (978-0-7614-4364-3(9)) Marshall Cavendish Corp.

Flynn, Noa. Youth with Eating Disorders: When Food Is an Enemy. 2007. (Helping Youth with Mental, Physical, & Social Challenges Ser.). (Illus.). 128p. (YA). pap. 14.95 (978-1-4222-0444-3(8)) Mason Crest.

Friedman, Lauri S. Eating Disorders. 2008. (Introducing Issues with Opposing Viewpoints Ser.). (ENG., Illus.). 112-144p. (gr. 7-10). 36.95 (978-0-7377-4168-1(6), Greenhaven Pr., Inc.) Cengage Gale.

Friedman, Lauri S., ed. Eating Disorders. 2006. (Writing the Critical Essay Ser.). (ENG., Illus.). 102p. (J). (gr. 3-7). lib. bdg. 33.75 (978-0-7377-3641-0(0), Greenhaven Pr., Inc.) Cengage Gale.

Garbus, Julia. Eating Disorders. Greenhaven Press Staff, ed. 2014. (Issues That Concern You Ser.). (ENG.). 144p. (gr. 7-10). lib. bdg. 42.00 (978-0-7377-7239-5(5), Greenhaven Pr., Inc.) Cengage Gale.

Gay, Kathlyn. Am I Fat? The Obesity Issue for Teens. 2006. (Issues in Focus Today Ser.). (Illus.). 112p. (J). (gr. 8-12). lib. bdg. 33.27 (978-0-7660-2527-1(6)) Enslow Pubs., Inc.

—Are You Fat? The Obesity Issue for Teens. 2014. (Got Issues? Ser.). (Illus.). 112p. (J). (gr. 6-12). lib. bdg. 33.27 (978-0-7660-4322-0(3)) Enslow Pubs., Inc.

—Eating Disorders: Anorexia, Bulimia & Binge Eating. 2003. (Diseases & People Ser.). (Illus.). 112p. (J). (gr. 6-12). lib. bdg. 27.94 (978-0-7660-1894-5(6)) Enslow Pubs., Inc.

Haerens, Margaret. Eating Disorders. 2012. (Global Viewpoints Ser.). (ENG., Illus.). 224p. (gr. 10-12). pap. 31.70 (978-0-7377-6439-0(2), Greenhaven Pr., Inc.) Cengage Gale.

Haerens, Margaret, ed. Eating Disorders. 2012. (Global Viewpoints Ser.). (ENG., Illus.). 224p. (J). (gr. 10-12). lib. bdg. 40.45 (978-0-7377-6263-1(2), Greenhaven Pr., Inc.) Cengage Gale.

Hidalgo-Robert, Alberto. Fat No More: A Teenager's Victory over Obesity. 2012. (J). pap. 16.95 (978-1-55885-745-2(1), Piñata Books) Arte Publico Pr.

Hillstrom, Kevin, ed. Eating Disorders. 2012. (Nutrition & Health Ser.). (ENG., Illus.). 80p. (gr. 7-10). lib. bdg. 30.95 (978-1-4205-0719-5(2), Lucent Bks.) Cengage Gale.

Jones, Keith. Eating Disorders Information for Teens. 4th ed. 2017. (Teen Health Ser.). 400p. lib. bdg. 69.00 **(978-0-7808-1559-9(9))** Omnigraphics, Inc.

Kalodner, Cynthia R. Too Fat or Too Thin? A Reference Guide to Eating Disorders, 1 vol. 2003. (Illus.). 240p. (C). 64.00 (978-0-313-31581-7(7), GR1581, Greenwood) ABC-CLIO, LLC.

Kolodny, Nancy J. The Beginner's Guide to Eating Disorders Recovery. 2004. (ENG., Illus.). 224p. pap. 14.95 (978-0-936077-45-1(X)) Gurze Bks.

Lai, Rozalli. Lethal Light. 2008. 52p. pap. 8.95 (978-0-595-50975-1(4)) iUniverse, Inc.

Landau, Jennifer. Teens Talk about Body Image & Eating Disorders. 2017. (J). **(978-1-5081-7648-0(5))**; **(978-1-5081-7632-9(9))** Rosen Publishing Group, Inc., The. (Rosen Young Adult).

Laser, Tammy & Watson, Stephanie. Eating Disorders. 2011. (Girls' Health Ser.). (Illus.). 48p. (YA). (gr. 5-9). lib. bdg. 29.25 (978-1-4488-4573-6(4)) Rosen Publishing Group, Inc., The.

Lask, Bryan & Watson, Lucy. Can I Tell You about Eating Disorders? A Guide for Friends, Family & Professionals. Field, Fiona, illus. 2014. (Can I Tell You About... ? Ser.). (ENG.). 56p. pap. 14.95 (978-1-84905-421-8(5), 5857) Kingsley, Jessica Pubs. GBR. Dist: Macmillan Distribution Ltd.

Levete, Sarah. The Hidden Story of Eating Disorders, 1 vol., 1. 2014. (Undercover Story Ser.). (ENG.). 48p. (J). (gr. 5-8). 30.25 (978-1-4777-2795-9(7), Rosen Reference) Rosen Publishing Group, Inc., The.

Lew, Kristi. I Have an Eating Disorder, Now What?, 1 vol. 2015. (ENG., Illus.). 112p. (J). 35.60 (978-1-4777-7972-9(8), Rosen Young Adult) Rosen Publishing Group, Inc., The.

Mallick, Nita & Watson, Stephanie. Conquering Binge Eating, 01 vols., 1. 2016. (Conquering Eating Disorders Ser.). (ENG.). 64p. (J). 32.95 (978-1-4994-6199-2(2), Rosen Young Adult) Rosen Publishing Group, Inc., The.

Marsico, Katie. Eating Disorders. 2013. 80p. (YA). (gr. 7-12). 34.21 (978-1-60870-853-6(5)); pap. 17.64 (978-1-62712-129-3(3)) Cavendish Square Publishing.

Meisel, Abigail, et al. Investigating Eating Disorders (Anorexia, Bulimia, & Binge Eating) Real Facts for Real Lives. 2010. (Investigating Diseases Ser.). (Illus.). 160p. (YA). (gr. 9-12). 35.94 (978-0-7660-3339-9(2)) Enslow Pubs., Inc.

Moehn, Heather. Understanding Eating Disorder Support Groups. 2005. (Teen Eating Disorder Prevention Book Ser.). (Illus.). 192p. (YA). (gr. 7-12). lib. bdg. 34.60 (978-0-8239-2992-4(2), E2UGR) Rosen Publishing Group, Inc., The.

Nelson, Kristen Rajczak & Allman, Toney. Eating Disorders: When Food Is an Obsession. 2017. (Hot Topics Ser.). 112p. (YA). (gr. 7-7). lib. bdg. 39.40 **(978-1-5345-6014-7(9)**, Lucent Pr.) Greenhaven Publishing LLC.

Owens, Peter. Teens Health & Obesity. 2008. (Gallup Youth Survey, Major Issues & Trends Ser.). (Illus.). 112p. (YA). (gr. -1-7). lib. bdg. 22.95 (978-1-59084-872-2(1)) Mason Crest.

Parks, Peggy J. Teenage Eating Disorders. 2011. (Compact Research Ser.). 96p. (YA). (gr. 7-12). lib. bdg. 27.95 (978-1-60152-166-8(9)) ReferencePoint Pr., Inc.

Parys, Sabrina. Helping a Friend with an Eating Disorder. 2016. (How Can I Help? Friends Helping Friends Ser.). 00064p. (J). (gr. 6-6). 34.45 (978-1-4994-6435-1(5)) Rosen Publishing Group, Inc., The.

Piehl, Norah. Eating Disorders. 2008. (Social Issues Firsthand Ser.). (ENG., Illus.). 192p. (gr. 10-12). lib. bdg. 38.30 (978-0-7377-4252-7(6), LML02109-243164, Greenhaven Pr., Inc.) Cengage Gale.

Poole, H. W. Eating Disorders, Vol. 13. Walters, Anne S., ed. 2015. (Mental Illnesses & Disorders: Awareness & Understanding Ser.). (Illus.). 48p. (J). (gr. 5). 20.95 (978-1-4222-3372-6(3)) Mason Crest.

Sayer, Melissa & Naik, Anita. Too Fat? Too Thin? The Healthy Eating Handbook. 2009. (Really Useful Handbooks Ser.). (ENG., Illus.). 48p. (J). (gr. 5-11). pap. (978-0-7787-4405-4(1)); lib. bdg. (978-0-7787-4392-7(6)) Crabtree Publishing Co.

Silverstein, Alvin, et al. The Eating Disorders Update: Understanding Anorexia, Bulimia, & Binge Eating. 2008. (Disease Update Ser.). (Illus.). 128p. (J). (gr. 5-18). lib. bdg. 33.27 (978-0-7660-2802-9(X)) Enslow Pubs., Inc.

Silverthorne, Elizabeth. Anorexia & Bulimia. 2009. (Diseases & Disorders Ser.). (ENG., Illus.). 128p. (YA). (gr. 7-12). 34.95 (978-1-4205-0141-4(0)) Cengage Gale.

Simons, Rae. I Eat When I'm Sad: Food & Feelings. 2010. (Kids & Obesity Ser.). 48p. (YA). lib. bdg. 19.95 (978-1-4222-1714-6(0)) Mason Crest.

Simpson, Carolyn. Understanding Compulsive Eating. 2005. (Teen Eating Disorder Prevention Book Ser.). (Illus.). 192p. (YA). (gr. 7-12). lib. bdg. 34.60 (978-0-8239-2989-4(2), E2COEA) Rosen Publishing Group, Inc., The.

Smith, Rita & Baish, Vanessa. Self-Image & Eating Disorders. 2012. (Teen Mental Health Ser.). (ENG., Illus.). 48p. (J). (gr. 7-12). 27.95 (978-1-4488-6894-0(7)) Rosen Publishing Group, Inc., The.

Smolin, Lori A. & Grosvenor, Mary B. Nutrition & Eating Disorders. 2nd rev. ed. 2010. (Healthy Eating: A Guide to Nutrition Ser.). 136p. (C). (gr. 9). 35.00 (978-1-60413-802-3(5), Chelsea Hse.) Facts On File, Inc.

Stewart, Gail B. Anorexia. 2008. (21st Century Skills Library: Health at Risk Ser.). (ENG., Illus.). 32p. (gr. 4-8). lib. bdg. 28.50 (978-1-60279-281-4(X), 200130) Cherry Lake Publishing.

—Bulimia. 2008. (21st Century Skills Library: Health at Risk Ser.). (ENG., Illus.). 32p. (gr. 4-8). lib. bdg. 28.50 (978-1-60279-282-1(8), 200131) Cherry Lake Publishing.

A Teen Eating Disorder Prevention Book. 2005. (Illus.). 192p. (gr. 7-12). lib. bdg. 227.40 (978-0-8239-3904-6(9)) Rosen Publishing Group, Inc., The.

A Teen Eating Disorder Prevention Book: Set 1: Finding Answers, 6 bks. Incl. Understanding Compulsive Eating. Simpson, Carolyn. (YA). lib. bdg. 34.60 (978-0-8239-2989-4(2), E2COEA); Understanding Eating Disorder Support Groups. Moehn, Heather. (YA). lib. bdg. 34.60 (978-0-8239-2992-4(2), E2UGR); Understanding Exercise Addiction. Johnson, Marlys. (YA). lib. bdg. 34.60 (978-0-8239-2990-0(6), E2EXAD); Understanding Sports & Eating Disorders. Stanley, Debbie. (YA). lib. bdg. 34.60 (978-0-8239-2993-1(0), E2SPEA); Understanding Weight & Depression. Clarke, Julie & Kirby-Payne, Ann. (J). lib. bdg. 34.60 (978-0-8239-2994-8(9), E2WEDE); 192p. (gr. 7-12). (Illus.). 2005. Set lib. bdg. 151.50 (978-0-8239-9052-8(4), E2FIAN) Rosen Publishing Group, Inc., The.

The Teen Health Library of Eating Disorder Prevention. 2005. (Illus.). 64p. (gr. 7-12). lib. bdg. 219.45 (978-0-8239-3905-3(7)) Rosen Publishing Group, Inc., The.

Trueit, Trudi Strain. Eating Disorders. 2004. (Life Balance Ser.). (ENG.). 80p. (YA). (gr. 5-8). pap. 6.95 (978-0-531-16610-9(4), Watts, Franklin) Scholastic Library Publishing.

Wagner, Viqi. Eating Disorders. 2007. (Opposing Viewpoints Ser.). (ENG.). 244p. (YA). (gr. 7-12). 27.50 (978-0-7377-3349-5(7), Greenhaven Pr., Inc.); (Illus.). (gr. 9-12). pap. 39.70 (978-0-7377-3348-8(9)) Cengage Gale.

Walden, Katherine & Watson, Stephanie. Conquering Anorexia, 01 vols., 1. 2016. (Conquering Eating Disorders Ser.). (ENG.). 64p. (J). 32.95 (978-1-4994-6203-6(4), Rosen Young Adult) Rosen Publishing Group, Inc., The.

Warbrick, Caroline. Taking Action Against Eating Disorders. 2009. (Taking Action Ser.). (ENG.). 48p. (YA). pap. 11.75 (978-1-4358-5472-7(1), Rosen Reference); (Illus.). (gr. 5-9). lib. bdg. 29.25 (978-1-4358-5344-7(X)) Rosen Publishing Group, Inc., The.

Watson, Stephanie. Anorexia. (Danger Zone: Dieting & Eating Disorders Ser.). 64p. 2009. (gr. 5-6). 55.90 (978-1-61512-120-5(X)) 2006. (Illus.). (YA). (gr. 7-12). lib. bdg. 31.95 (978-1-4042-1996-0(X)) Rosen Publishing Group, Inc., The.

—Binge Eating. (Danger Zone: Dieting & Eating Disorders Ser.). 64p. 2009. (gr. 5-6). 55.90 (978-1-61512-121-2(8)) 2006. (Illus.). (YA). (gr. 7-12). lib. bdg. 31.95 (978-1-4042-1998-4(6)) Rosen Publishing Group, Inc., The.

—Bulimia. (Danger Zone: Dieting & Eating Disorders Ser.). 64p. 2009. (gr. 5-6). 55.90 (978-1-61512-122-9(6)) 2007. (Illus.). (YA). (gr. 7-12). lib. bdg. 31.95 (978-1-4042-1997-7(8)) Rosen Publishing Group, Inc., The.

Willett, Edward. Frequently Asked Questions about Exercise Addiction. (FAQ: Teen Life Ser.). 64p. 2009. (gr. 5-6). 58.50 (978-1-61512-577-7(9)) 2008. (Illus.). (YA). (gr. 7-12). lib. bdg. 31.95 (978-1-4042-1806-2(8)) Rosen Publishing Group, Inc., The.

—Negative Body Image. (Danger Zone: Dieting & Eating Disorders Ser.). 64p. 2009. (gr. 5-6). 55.90 (978-1-61512-125-0(0)) 2006. (Illus.). (YA). (gr. 7-12). lib. bdg. 31.95 (978-1-4042-1995-3(1)) Rosen Publishing Group, Inc., The.

Zeckhausen, Dina. Full Mouse, Empty Mouse: A Tale of Food & Feelings. Boyd, Brian, illus. 2007. 40p. (J). (gr. 2-7). 14.95 (978-1-4338-0132-7(9), 4418003); pap. 9.95 (978-1-4338-0133-4(7), 4418004) American Psychological Assn. (Magination Pr.).

EATING DISORDERS—FICTION

Anderson, Laurie Halse. Frío, Vol. 1. 2010.Tr. of Wintergirls. (SPA.). 240p. (YA). pap. 19.95 (978-84-9918-137-0(6)) Roca Editorial ESP. Dist: Spanish Pubs., LLC.

—Wintergirls. 2009. 11.04 (978-0-7848-3717-7(1), Everbind) Marco Bk. Co.

—Wintergirls. (ENG.). (YA). (gr. 7-18). 2010. 304p. 10.99 (978-0-14-241557-3(X), Speak) 2009. 288p. 17.99 (978-0-670-01110-0(X), Viking Books for Young Readers) Penguin Young Readers Group.

—Wintergirls. 2009. 278p. 20.00 (978-1-60686-532-3(3)) Perfection Learning Corp.

—Wintergirls. 2010. lib. bdg. 22.10 (978-0-606-15195-5(8), Turtleback) Turtleback Bks.

Antieau, Kim. Mercy, Unbound. 2006. (ENG., Illus.). 176p. (YA). (gr. 9). pap. 9.99 (978-1-4169-0893-7(5), Simon Pulse) Simon Pulse.

Believarexic, 1 vol. 2015. (ENG.). 464p. (YA). (gr. 8-11). 18.95 (978-1-56145-771-7(X)) Peachtree Pubs.

Berne, Emma Carlson. Under Pressure. 2013. (Counterattack Ser.). (ENG.). 104p. (YA). (gr. 6-12). pap. 7.95 (978-1-4677-0718-3(X)); lib. bdg. 27.93 (978-1-4677-0303-1(6)) Lerner Publishing Group.

Burton-Hupp, Lynne. Venus the Very Proper Fly Trap. 2009. 28p. pap. 24.95 (978-1-60563-993-2(1)) America Star Bks.

Burton, Rebecca. Leaving Jetty Road. 2004. 272p. (978-0-207-20015-1(7)) HarperCollins Pubs. Australia.

Carlson, Melody. New York Debut, 1 vol. 2014. (Carter House Girls Ser.). (ENG.). 224p. (YA). pap. 9.99 (978-0-310-74779-6(1)) Zondervan.

Condie, Ally. Being Sixteen. 2010. (YA). (978-1-60641-233-6(7)) Deseret Bk. Co.

Davenport, Jennifer. Anna Begins. 2008. (ENG.). 150p. 21.95 (978-0-930773-83-0(7)) Black Heron Pr.

Friend, Natasha. Perfect. 2004. (ENG.). 232p. (J). pap. 7.95 (978-1-57131-651-6(5)) Milkweed Editions.

Gonzalez, Rafael. Cookie Boy! 2011. 20p. pap. 11.99 (978-1-4634-0324-9(0)) AuthorHouse.

Halse Anderson, Laure. FRÍO. 2015. (SPA.). 240p. (YA). pap. 18.95 (978-84-9918-925-3(3)) Roca Editorial ESP. Dist: Spanish Pubs., LLC.

Halse Anderson, Laurie. FRÍO. (SPA.). (YA). pap. 13.95 (978-84-92833-70-2(X)) Roca Bolsillo ESP. Dist: Spanish Pubs., LLC.

Hersey, Jodi. Achy Ali. Peabody, Rob, illus. 2011. pap. 5.00 (978-1-4276-5272-0(4)) Aardvark Global Publishing.

Jaden, Denise. Never Enough. 2012. (ENG.). 400p. (YA). (gr. 9). pap. 9.99 (978-1-4424-2907-9(0), Simon Pulse) Simon Pulse.

Johnson, J. J. Believarexic, 1 vol. 2017. (ENG.). 464p. (YA). (gr. 8-11). pap. 9.95 **(978-1-68263-007-5(2))** Peachtree Pubs.

Kessler, Jackie Morse. Hunger. 2010. (Riders of the Apocalypse Ser.: 1). (ENG.). 192p. (YA). (gr. 7-18). pap. 9.99 (978-0-547-34124-8(5)) Houghton Mifflin Harcourt Publishing Co.

Lange, Erin Jade. Butter. (ENG.). (YA). (gr. 9). 2013. 320p. pap. 9.99 (978-1-61963-121-2(0), 9781619631212) 2012. 304p. 16.99 (978-1-59990-780-2(1), 9781599907802) Bloomsbury Publishing USA. (Bloomsbury USA Childrens).

Littman, Sarah Darer. Purge. 2010. (ENG.). 240p. (J). (gr. 7). 8.99 (978-0-545-05237-5(8), Scholastic Paperbacks) Scholastic, Inc.

Mcgill, Leslie. Running Scared. 2014. (Cap Central Ser.: 2). (YA). lib. bdg. 20.80 (978-0-606-35738-8(6)) Turtleback Bks.

McGowan, Sharlene. Macaroni Monday. 2007. 112p. (YA). per. 10.95 (978-0-595-45984-1(6)) iUniverse, Inc.

mendelsohn, martha. Bromley Girls. 2015. (ENG.). 192p. (YA). pap. 14.95 (978-0-89672-922-3(2)) Texas Tech Univ. Pr.

Metzger, Lois. A Trick of the Light. (ENG.). 208p. (YA). (gr. 9). 2014. pap. 9.99 (978-0-06-213309-0(8)) 2013. 17.99 (978-0-06-213308-3(X)) HarperCollins Pubs.

Morrall, Heather. Echo Glass. 2006. 192p. (YA). (gr. 7-18). pap. (978-0-9554252-0-2(4)) Rubery Pr.

Moskowitz, Hannah. Not Otherwise Specified: A Novel. 2015. (ENG., Illus.). 304p. (YA). (gr. 9). pap. 11.99 (978-1-4814-0595-9(0), Simon Pulse) Simon Pulse.

Myers, Lily. This Impossible Light. 2017. (ENG.). 352p. (YA). (gr. 7). 17.99 (978-0-399-17372-1(2), Philomel Bks.) Penguin Young Readers Group.

Padian, Maria. Jersey Tomatoes Are the Best. 2012. (ENG.). 352p. (YA). (gr. 7). pap. 9.99 (978-0-375-86563-3(2), Ember) Random Hse. Children's Bks.

Rosoff, Meg. How I Live Now. 2013. (ENG.). 208p. (YA). (gr. 7). pap. 8.99 (978-0-449-81960-9(4), Ember) Random Hse. Children's Bks.

Schraff, Anne. Going for Gold. 2008. 124p. lib. bdg. 13.95 (978-0-7569-8403-8(3)) Perfection Learning Corp.

Shahan, Sherry. Skin & Bones. 2014. (ENG.). 272p. (YA). (gr. 8-12). 16.99 (978-0-8075-7397-6(3)) Whitman, Albert & Co.

Shapiro, Lawrence E. Freddy Fights Fat: An Emotional Literacy Book. Harpster, Steve, illus. 2004. (Emotional Literacy Ser.). 54p. (J). (gr. 2-18). 14.95 (978-0-9747789-5-2(8), 67873) CTC Publishing.

Shaw, Liane. Thinandbeautiful. Com, 1 vol. 2009. (ENG.). 216p. (YA). (gr. 8-12). pap. 11.95 (978-1-897187-62-3(9)) Second Story Pr. CAN. Dist: Orca Bk. Pubs. USA.

Sobat, Gail Sidonie. Gravity Journal. 2008. (ENG.). 162p. (YA). (gr. 15-18). pap. 14.95 (978-1-894283-78-6(3)) Great Plains Pubns. CAN. Dist: Publishers Group Canada.

Stine, R. L. The Boy Who Ate Fear Street. 2011. (R. L. Stine's Ghosts of Fear Street Ser.). (ENG.). 128p. (J). (gr. 3-7). pap. 5.99 (978-1-4424-1719-9(6), Aladdin) Simon & Schuster Children's Publishing.

A Story in the Life of the Shapette Family. 2004. (J). 17.95 (978-0-9747509-0-3(5)) Del Gatto, Maria.

Tokio, Marnelle. More Than You Can Chew. 2003. (ENG., Illus.). 240p. (J). (gr. 9-18). pap. 12.95 (978-0-88776-639-8(0), Tundra Bks.) Tundra Bks. CAN. Dist: Penguin Random Hse. LLC.

Vrettos, Adrienne Maria. Skin. 2007. (ENG.). 272p. (YA). (gr. 7-12). pap. 9.99 (978-1-4169-0656-8(8), McElderry, Margaret K. Bks.) McElderry, Margaret K. Bks.

Wasserman, Robin. Gluttony. 2007. (Seven Deadly Sins Ser.: 6). (ENG.). 256p. (YA). (gr. 9). pap. 8.99 (978-1-4169-0719-0(X), Simon Pulse) Simon Pulse.

ECCLESIASTICAL ARCHITECTURE

see Church Architecture

ECCLESIASTICAL ART

see Christian Art and Symbolism

ECCLESIASTICAL BIOGRAPHY

see Christian Biography

ECCLESIASTICAL FASTS AND FEASTS

see Fasts and Feasts

ECCLESIASTICAL HISTORY

see Church History

ECCLESIASTICAL RITES AND CEREMONIES

see Funeral Rites and Ceremonies; Rites and Ceremonies

ECOLOGY

see also Adaptation (Biology); Forest Ecology; Human Ecology; Marine Ecology; Plant Ecology; Wetland Ecology

El Agua en Peligro. (Coleccion Operacion Tierra). (SPA.). 46p. (YA). (gr. 5-18). pap. 12.95 (978-950-11-0976-4(3), SGM799) Sigmar ARG. Dist: Continental Bk. Co., Inc.

El Aire Contaminado. (Coleccion Operacion Tierra). (SPA.). 46p. (YA). (gr. 5-18). pap. 12.95 (978-950-11-0975-7(5), SGM801) Sigmar ARG. Dist: Continental Bk. Co., Inc.

Allaby, Michael. Ecology: Plants, Animals, & the Environment. Garratt, Richard, illus. 2009. (Discovering the Earth Ser.). 256p. (C). (gr. 9-18). 39.95 (978-0-8160-6100-6(9)) Facts On File, Inc.

—The Environment. 2012. (ENG., Illus.). 48p. (J). 15.00 (978-1-899762-83-5(3)) Award Pubns. Ltd. GBR. Dist: Parkwest Pubns., Inc.

Allaby, Michael, et al. Biomes of the Earth Set. 2006. (Biomes of the Earth Ser.). 144p. (gr. 6-12). 395.00 (978-0-8160-5319-3(7)) Facts On File, Inc.

—Deserts & Semideserts, 1 vol. 2nd ed. 2010. (Biomes Atlases Ser.). (ENG.). 64p. (gr. 6-9). 34.65 (978-1-4329-4175-8(5)) Heinemann-Raintree.

Allaire, Caroline & Krawczyk, Sabine. Let's Look at the Hedge. Hugo, Pierre de, illus. 2012. (ENG.). 38p. (J). (gr. 1-4). pap. 11.99 (978-1-85103-339-3(4)) Moonlight Publishing, Ltd. GBR. Dist: Independent Pubs. Group.

Allgor, Marie. Endangered Desert Animals. 2012. (Save Earth's Animals! Ser.). (ENG., Illus.). 24p. (J). (gr. k-5). 22.60 (978-1-4488-7423-1(8)); pap. 8.25 (978-1-4488-7496-5(3)) Rosen Publishing Group, Inc., The. (PowerKids Pr.).

Allred, Sylvester. The DesertAlphabet Encyclopedia. Iverson, Diane, illus. 2006. 50p. (YA). pap. 7.95 (978-0-88045-168-0(8), NaturEncyclopedia) Stemmer Hse. Pubs.

—The Freshwater Alphabet. Iverson, Diane, illus. 2009. 48p. (J). (gr. 4-7). pap. 8.95 (978-0-916144-48-7(8)) Stemmer Hse. Pubs.

Aloian, Molly. The Yangtze: China's Majestic River. 2010. (Rivers Around the World Ser.). (ENG., Illus.). 32p. (J). (gr. 5-8). pap. (978-0-7787-7472-3(4)); lib. bdg. (978-0-7787-7449-5(X)) Crabtree Publishing Co.

Aloian, Molly & Kalman, Bobbie. The Antarctic Habitat. 2006. (Introducing Habitats Ser.). (ENG., Illus.). 32p. (J). (gr. -1-3). lib. bdg. (978-0-7787-2956-3(7)) Crabtree Publishing Co.

—El Hábitat de la Antárdia. 2007. (Introduction a Los Habitats Ser.). (SPA & ENG., Illus.). 32p. (J). (gr. k-3). lib. bdg. (978-0-7787-8332-9(4)) Crabtree Publishing Co.

—El Habitat de la Antardia. rev. ed. 2007. (Introduction a Los Habitats Ser.). (SPA & ENG., Illus.). 32p. (J). (gr. k-3). pap. (978-0-7787-8356-5(1)) Crabtree Publishing Co.

—El Hábitat de la Antártida. 2007. (Libro de Bobbie Kalman Ser.). (SPA., Illus.). 32p. (J). (978-1-4287-3159-2(8)) Crabtree Publishing Co.

—El Habitat del Artico. 2007. (Introduccion A los Habitats Ser.). (SPA & ENG., Illus.). 32p. (J). (gr. k-3). lib. bdg. (978-0-7787-8330-5(8)) Crabtree Publishing Co.

—El Habitat del Artico. rev. ed. 2007. (Introduction a Los Habitats Ser.). (SPA & ENG., Illus.). 32p. (J). (gr. k-3). pap. (978-0-7787-8354-1(5)) Crabtree Publishing Co.

—Habitats Subterráneos. 2007. (Introduccion A los Habitats Ser.). (SPA., Illus.). 32p. (J). (gr. -1-3). lib. bdg. (978-0-7787-8331-2(6)) Crabtree Publishing Co.

—Hábitats Subterraneos. rev. ed. 2007. (Introduction a Los Habitats Ser.). (SPA., Illus.). 32p. (J). (gr. k-3). pap. (978-0-7787-8355-8(3)) Crabtree Publishing Co.

Anderson, Michael, ed. Pioneers of the Green Movement: Environmental Solutions. 2012. (Inventors & Innovators Ser.). (ENG., Illus.). 112p. (gr. 7-12). (J). 32.90 (978-1-61530-698-5(6)); (YA). 65.80 (978-1-61530-788-3(5)) Rosen Publishing Group, Inc., The.

Anderson, Sheila. Coasts. 2008. (First Step Nonfiction - Landforms Ser.). (Illus.). 23p. (J). (gr. -1). lib. bdg. 18.60 (978-0-8225-8595-4(2), Lerner Pubns.); pap. 34.95 (978-0-8225-9935-7(X)) Lerner Publishing Group.

Animal Habitats. 2014. (Illus.). 256p. (J). (978-1-4351-5619-7(6)) Barnes & Noble, Inc.

Apel, Melanie Ann. The Yellowstone Park Fire of 1988. 2004. (Tragic Fires Throughout History Ser.). (Illus.). 48p. (gr. 5-8). lib. bdg. 29.25 (978-0-8239-4490-3(5), Rosen Reference) Rosen Publishing Group, Inc., The.

—The Yellowstone Park Fire Of 1988. 2009. (Tragic Fires Throughout History Ser.). 48p. (gr. 5-8). 53.00 (978-1-60854-585-8(7), Rosen Reference) Rosen Publishing Group, Inc., The.

Arctic & Antarctic Habitats. 2013. (Discovery Education: Habitats Ser.). 32p. (J). (gr. 3-6). pap. 60.00 (978-1-4777-1482-9(0), PowerKids Pr.) Rosen Publishing Group, Inc., The.

Arms. Environmental Science: Enhanced Online Edition. 4th ed. 2004. 17.26 (978-0-03-037156-1(2)) Holt McDougal.

Arnold, Caroline. A Warmer World. Hogan, Jamie, illus. 2012. (ENG.). 32p. (J). (gr. 2-5). pap. 7.95 (978-1-58089-267-4(1)) Charlesbridge Publishing, Inc.

Arnold, Quinn M. Deserts. 2016. (Illus.). 24p. (J). (978-1-60818-741-6(1), Creative Education) Creative Co., The.

—Mountains. 2016. (Illus.). 24p. (J). (978-1-60818-742-3(X), Creative Education) Creative Co., The.

Arnosky, Jim. Crinkleroot's Guide to Knowing Animal Habitats. Arnosky, Jim, illus. 2014. (ENG., Illus.). 32p. (J). (gr. -1-3). pap. 14.99 (978-1-4814-2599-5(4), Simon & Schuster Bks. For Young Readers) Simon & Schuster Bks. For Young Readers.

Aspen-Baxter, Linda. Fresh Water. 2016. (Illus.). 32p. (J). (978-1-5105-0867-5(8)) SmartBook Media, Inc.

—Fresh Water. 2013. (Illus.). 32p. (J). 13.95 (978-1-61913-234-4(6)); 28.55 (978-1-61913-071-5(8)) Weigl Pubs., Inc.

Auch, Alison. Life in the Desert. 2011. (Habitats Around the World Ser.). (ENG.). 24p. (gr. k-1). pap. 41.70 (978-1-4296-7154-5(8)); lib. bdg. 26.65 (978-1-4296-6817-0(2)) Capstone Press of Coughlan Cos. (Pebble Plus).

Avery, Sebastian. Habitats. 2016. (Spotlight on Ecology & Life Science Ser.). 00024p. (J). (gr. 4-6). 26.25 (978-1-4994-2567-3(8)); pap. 10.00 (978-1-4994-2564-2(3)) Rosen Publishing Group, Inc., The. (PowerKids Pr.).

Backyard Biomes. 2016. (Backyard Biomes Ser.). 00024p. (J). pap. 48.90 **(978-1-4824-5840-4(3))** Stevens, Gareth Publishing LLLP.

Bailey, Diane. Arctic Wildlife. 2017. (J). **(978-1-4222-3863-9(6))** Mason Crest.

Ballance, Alison. Habitats of the World, 6 vols. (ENG., Illus.). (J). (gr. 2-2). 2005. pap. 7.47 net. (978-0-7685-0547-4(X)) 2004. pap. 7.47 net. (978-0-7685-0544-3(5)) 2004. pap. 7.47 net. (978-0-7685-0546-7(1)) 2004. pap. 7.47 net. (978-0-7685-0548-1(8)) 2004. pap. 7.47 net. (978-0-7685-0549-8(6)) Pearson Schl. (Dominie Elementary).

Ballard, Carol. Food Relationships & Webs. 2017. (Living Processes Ser.). (ENG., Illus.). 48p. (J). (gr. 7-11). pap. 11.99 (978-0-7502-9624-3(0), Wayland) Hachette Children's Group GBR. Dist: Hachette Bk. Group.

—Food Webs. 2010. (Living Processes Ser.). (Illus.). 48p. (J). pap. 11.75 (978-1-61532-351-7(1)); (YA). (gr. 5-8). lib. bdg. 29.25 (978-1-61532-340-1(6)) Rosen Publishing Group, Inc., The. (Rosen Reference).

Banting, Erinn. Caves. 2011. (J). (gr. 5-8). pap. 13.95 (978-1-61690-645-0(6), AV2 by Weigl); (Illus.). 32p. (gr. 2-5). 28.55 (978-1-61690-639-9(1)) Weigl Pubs., Inc.

—Deserts. 2011. (J). (gr. 5-8). pap. 13.95 (978-1-61690-650-4(2), AV2 by Weigl); (Illus.). 32p. (gr. 2-5). 28.55 (978-1-61690-644-3(8)) Weigl Pubs., Inc.

—Mountains. 2016. (Illus.). 32p. (J). (978-1-5105-0873-6(2)) SmartBook Media, Inc.

—Tundras. 2016. (Illus.). 32p. (J). (978-1-5105-0879-8(1)) SmartBook Media, Inc.

—Tundras. (J). 2012. 28.55 (978-1-61913-075-3(0)) 2012. 13.95 (978-1-61913-238-2(9)) 2005. (Illus.). 32p. (gr. 4-6). lib. bdg. 26.00 (978-1-59036-347-8(7)) Weigl Pubs., Inc.

Barnes, Julia. 101 Facts about Lakes. 2003. (One Hundred One Facts about Our World Ser.). (Illus.). 32p. (gr. 1-4). lib. bdg. 26.00 (978-0-8368-3707-0(X), Gareth Stevens Learning Library) Stevens, Gareth Publishing LLLP.

—101 Facts about Rivers. 2003. (One Hundred One Facts about Our World Ser.). (Illus.). 32p. (gr. 1-4). lib. bdg. 26.00 (978-0-8368-3711-7(8), Gareth Stevens Learning Library) Stevens, Gareth Publishing LLLP.

Baur, Laura, illus. The Riverbank. 2012. (ENG.). 36p. (J). (gr. -1-k). spiral bd. 12.99 (978-1-85103-393-5(9)) Moonlight Publishing, Ltd. GBR. Dist: Independent Pubs. Group.

Becker, Helaine. The Big Green Book of the Big Blue Sea. Dawson, Willow, illus. 2012. (ENG.). 80p. (J). (gr. 3-7). 15.95 (978-1-55453-746-4(0)); pap. 9.95 (978-1-55453-747-1(9)) Kids Can Pr., Ltd. CAN. Dist: Hachette Bk. Group.

Benbow, Ann & Mably, Colin. Nature's Secret Habitats Science Projects. LaBaff, Tom, illus. 2009. (Real Life Science Experiments Ser.). 48p. (J). (gr. 2-5). lib. bdg. 25.27 (978-0-7660-3150-0(0)) Enslow Pubs., Inc.

Benchmark Education Company, LLC Staff, compiled by. Cactus & Canyons & Ecosystems. 2005. spiral bd. 225.00 (978-1-4108-5806-1(5)) Benchmark Education Co.

—The Environment. 2006. spiral bd. 330.00 (978-1-4108-7019-3(7)) 2005. (J). spiral bd. 265.00 (978-1-4108-5764-4(6)) Benchmark Education Co.

—The Environment: Theme Set. 2006. (J). 226.00 (978-1-4108-7147-3(9)) Benchmark Education Co.

—Habitats. 2006. spiral bd. 330.00 (978-1-4108-7015-5(4)) Benchmark Education Co.

—Our Environment. 2006. (J). 305.00 (978-1-4108-7058-2(8)) Benchmark Education Co.

—Science Theme: Habitats. 2005. spiral bd. 115.00 (978-1-4108-5319-6(5)) Benchmark Education Co.

—Science Theme: The Environment. 2005. spiral bd. 115.00 (978-1-4108-5317-2(9)) Benchmark Education Co.

—Watery World & Ecosystems. 2005. spiral bd. 225.00 (978-1-4108-5815-3(4)) Benchmark Education Co.

Bennett, Doraine. Atlantic Ocean. 2009. (J). pap. (978-1-935077-39-8(2)) State Standards Publishing, LLC.

—Marsh & Swamp. 2009. (J). (978-1-935077-36-7(8)); pap. (978-1-935077-41-1(4)) State Standards Publishing, LLC.

—Mountains. 2009. (J). (978-1-935077-37-4(6)); pap. (978-1-935077-42-8(2)) State Standards Publishing, LLC.

—Piedmont. 2009. (J). (978-1-935077-38-1(4)); pap. (978-1-935077-43-5(0)) State Standards Publishing, LLC.

Benoit, Peter. Deserts. 2011. (True Bks.). 48p. (J). (gr. 3-5). 29.00 (978-0-531-20555-6(X), Children's Pr.); (ENG.). pap. 6.95 (978-0-531-28104-8(3)) Scholastic Library Publishing.

—A True Book: Ecosystems, 7 vols., Set. Incl. Climate Change. 29.00 (978-0-531-20557-0(6)); Deserts. 29.00 (978-0-531-20555-6(X)); Oceans. 29.00 (978-0-531-20556-3(8)); Temperate Forests. (Illus.). 29.00 (978-0-531-20552-5(5)); Tropical Rain Forests. 29.00 (978-0-531-20554-9(1)); Tundra. 29.00 (978-0-531-20553-2(3)); Wetlands. 29.00 (978-0-531-20551-8(7)); 48p. (J). (gr. 3-5). 2011. Set lib. bdg. 203.00 (978-0-531-26849-0(7), Children's Pr.) Scholastic Library Publishing.

Berne, Emma Carlson. Coyotes. 2014. (Scavengers: Eating Nature's Trash Ser.). (Illus.). 24p. (J). (gr. k-5). lib. bdg. 23.60 (978-1-4777-6607-1(3), PowerKids Pr.) Rosen Publishing Group, Inc., The.

—Flesh Flies. 2014. (Scavengers: Eating Nature's Trash Ser.). (Illus.). 24p. (J). (gr. k-5). lib. bdg. 23.60 (978-1-4777-6588-3(3), PowerKids Pr.) Rosen Publishing Group, Inc., The.

—Opossums. 2014. (Scavengers: Eating Nature's Trash Ser.). (Illus.). 24p. (J). (gr. k-5). lib. bdg. 23.60 (978-1-4777-6602-6(2), PowerKids Pr.) Rosen Publishing Group, Inc., The.

—Ravens. 2014. (Scavengers: Eating Nature's Trash Ser.). (Illus.). 24p. (J). (gr. k-5). lib. bdg. 23.60 (978-1-4777-6612-5(X), PowerKids Pr.) Rosen Publishing Group, Inc., The.

Bernhard, Durga Yael. Just Like Me, Climbing a Tree: Exploring Trees Around the World, Vol. 2015. (ENG., Illus.). 32p. (J). (gr. k-2). 16.95 (978-1-937786-34-2(X), Wisdom Tales) World Wisdom, Inc.

Bethune, Helen. Why Do Glaciers Grind? 2010. (Solving Science Mysteries Ser.). (Illus.). 24p. (YA). (gr. 3-6). lib. bdg. 22.60 (978-1-4488-0391-0(8)) Rosen Publishing Group, Inc., The.

Bingham, Jane. The Amazon, 1 vol. 2012. (Explorer Tales Ser.). (ENG.). 32p. (gr. 1-3). 29.99 *(978-1-4109-4780-2(7),* Read Me!) Heinemann-Raintree.

Biomes. (Illus.). (J). (gr. 3-6). 103.50 *(978-0-8239-7288-3(7),* Reading Power) Rosen Publishing Group, Inc., The.

Biomes Atlases, Set. 2nd ed. Incl. Arctic Tundra & Polar Deserts. Woodford, Chris. 34.65 *(978-1-4329-4172-7(0));* Deserts & Semideserts. Allaby, Michael. 34.65 *(978-1-4329-4175-8(5));* Mountains & Highlands. Harris, Tim. 34.65 *(978-1-4329-4174-1(7));* Shrublands. Burnie, David. 34.65 *(978-1-4329-4178-9(X));* Taiga. Day, Trevor. 34.65 *(978-1-4329-4179-6(8));* Temperate Forests. Woodward, John. (Illus.). 34.65 *(978-1-4329-4180-2(1));* Temperate Grasslands. Hoare, Ben. 34.65 *(978-1-4329-4181-9(X));* Tropical Forests. Jackson, Tom. 34.65 *(978-1-4329-4177-2(1));* Tropical Grasslands. Morgan, Ben. 34.65 *(978-1-4329-4182-6(8));* Wetlands. Beatty, Richard. 34.65 *(978-1-4329-4183-3(6));* (gr. 6-9). (Biomes Atlases Ser.). (ENG.). 64p. 2010. Set lib. bdg. 346.50 *(978-1-4329-4184-0(4))* Heinemann-Raintree.

Biomes of North America. 2004. (Illus.). lib. bdg. 7.95 *(978-0-8225-4518-7(7))*Set. 2006. (J). (gr. 3-6). 84.95 *(978-0-8225-5304-5(X))* Lerner Publishing Group.

Biskup, Agnieszka. Explorar Ecosistemas con Max Axiom, Supercientífico. Strictly Spanish Translation Services Staff, tr. from ENG. Smith, Tod G., illus. 2012. (Ciencia Gráfica Ser.). (SPA.). 32p. (gr. 3-4). 30.65 *(978-1-4296-9238-0(3))* Capstone Press of Coughlan Cos.

—Exploring Ecosystems with Max Axiom, Super Scientist, 1 vol. Smith, Todd Aaron & Smith, Tod G., illus. 2007. (Graphic Science Ser.). (ENG.). 32p. (gr. 3-4). 30.65 *(978-0-7368-6842-6(9),* Graphic Library) Capstone Press of Coughlan Cos.

—Exploring Ecosystems with Max Axiom, Super Scientist, 1 vol. Smith, Tod G., illus. 2007. (Graphic Science Ser.). (ENG.). 32p. (gr. 3-4). per. 8.10 *(978-0-7368-7894-4(7),* Graphic Library) Capstone Press of Coughlan Cos.

Blackaby, Susan. Nest, Nook & Cranny. Hogan, Jamie, illus. 2010. (ENG.). 60p. (J). (gr. 4-7). 15.95 *(978-1-58089-350-3(3))* Charlesbridge Publishing, Inc.

Bockol, Leslie & Ikids Staff. One Tree. Phillips, Jillian, illus. 2009. (ENG.). 20p. (J). (gr. -1-1). 6.99 *(978-1-58476-811-1(8))* Innovative Kids.

Booth, Edison. Animals & Their Environments. 2016. (Spotlight on Ecology & Life Science Ser.). 00024p. (J). (gr. 4-6). 26.25 *(978-1-4994-2558-1(9));* pap. 10.00 *(978-1-4994-2556-7(2))* Rosen Publishing Group, Inc., The. (PowerKids Pr.).

Boothroyd, Jennifer. Animals & the Environment. 2008. pap. 34.95 *(978-0-8225-9356-0(4))* Lerner Publishing Group.

—Ecology: Classroom Set. 2008. pap. 16.95 *(978-0-8225-9137-5(5))* Lerner Publishing Group.

—Ecology: Complete Set. 2008. pap. 103.95 *(978-0-8225-9192-4(8))* Lerner Publishing Group.

—Let's Visit the Tundra. 2016. (Lightning Bolt Books (tm) — Biome Explorers Ser.). (ENG., Illus.). 32p. (J). (gr. 1-3). 26.65 *(978-1-5124-1196-6(5))* Lerner Publishing Group.

Bosques en Extincion. (Coleccion Operacion Tierra). (SPA.). 46p. (YA). (gr. 5-18). pap. 12.95 *(978-950-11-0977-1(1),* SGM800) Sigmar ARG. Dist: Continental Bk. Co., Inc.

Bow, James. Mountains Inside Out. 2015. (ENG.). 32p. (J). *(978-0-7787-1498-9(5))* Crabtree Publishing Co.

—Tundras Inside Out. 2014. (ENG.). 32p. (J). *(978-0-7787-0639-7(7))* Crabtree Publishing Co.

Brasch, Nicolas. Why Do Spiders Live in Webs? 2010. (Solving Science Mysteries Ser.). (Illus.). 24p. (J). pap. 8.25 *(978-1-4488-0398-9(5),* PowerKids Pr.); (YA). (gr. 3-6). lib. bdg. 22.60 *(978-1-4488-0397-2(7))* Rosen Publishing Group, Inc., The.

—Why Do Spiders Live in Webs? Level 4 Factbook. 2010. (Cambridge Young Readers Ser.). (ENG., Illus.). 16p. pap. 6.00 *(978-0-521-13725-6(X))* Cambridge Univ. Pr.

Bredeson, Carmen. Baby Animals of the World. 2011. (Nature's Baby Animals Ser.). (Illus.). 112p. (J). (gr. k-18). pap. 11.99 *(978-1-59845-218-1(5),* Enslow Elementary) Enslow Pubs., Inc.

—Weird but True Animal Homes. 2011. (Weird but True Science Ser.). (Illus.). 24p. (J). (gr. k-18). pap. 7.95 *(978-1-59845-368-3(8),* Enslow Elementary); (gr. 5-9). lib. bdg. 22.60 *(978-0-7660-3861-5(0))* Enslow Pubs., Inc.

Brenneman, Kimberly. Let's Visit a Coral Reef. 2016. (Illus.). 32p. (J). pap. *(978-0-87659-708-8(8))* Gryphon Hse., Inc.

Brenner, Barbara. One Small Place by the Sea. Leonard, Tom, illus. 2004. (One Small Place Ser.). (ENG.). 32p. (J). (gr. k-3). 16.99 *(978-0-688-17182-7(6))* HarperCollins Pubs.

Broom, Jenny. The Wonder Garden: Wander Through 5 Habitats to Discover 80 Amazing Animals. Williams, Kristjana S., illus. 2015. (ENG.). 48p. (J). 30.00 *(978-1-84780-647-5(3),* Wide Eyed Editions) Quarto Publishing Group UK GBR. Dist: Littlehampton Bk Services, Ltd.

Brown, Carron. Secrets of the Apple Tree. Nassner, Alyssa, illus. 2014. (ENG.). 36p. (J). 12.99 *(978-1-61067-243-6(7))* Kane Miller.

Bull, Schuyler. Crocodile Crossing. Male, Alan, illus. 2005. (Amazing Animal Adventures Ser.). (ENG.). 36p. (J). (gr. -1-2). 15.95 *(978-1-59249-051-6(4),* B7104); (gr. -1-2). pap. 6.95 *(978-1-59249-052-3(2),* S7104); (gr. -1-2). 19.95 *(978-1-59249-390-6(4),* BC7104); (gr. 2-2). 8.95 *(978-1-59249-391-3(2),* SC7104) Soundprints.

Bull, Schuyler M. Crocodile Crossing. Male, Alan, illus. 2003. (Soundprints' Amazing Animal Adventures! Ser.). (ENG.). 36p. (J). (gr. -1-3). 9.95 *(978-1-59249-060-8(3),* PS7154) Soundprints.

Burnie, David. Shrublands, 1 vol. 2nd ed. 2010. (Biomes Atlases Ser.). (ENG.). 64p. (gr. 6-9). 34.65 *(978-1-4329-4178-9(X))* Heinemann-Raintree.

Burton, L. DeVere. Fish & Wildlife: Principles of Zoology & Ecology. 3rd ed. 2009. (ENG.). 416p. (C). 197.95 *(978-1-4354-1963-6(4))* Delmar Cengage Learning.

Burton, Margie, et al. Are We Hurting the Earth? 2011. (Early Connections Ser.). (J). *(978-1-61672-480-1(3))* Benchmark Education Co.

Butterworth, Nick & Inkpen, Mick. Wonderful Earth. 2003. (Illus.). 32p. 14.99 *(978-1-85608-005-7(6))* Hunt, John Publishing Ltd. GBR. Dist: Send The Light Distribution LLC.

Byers, Ann. Jobs As Green Builders & Planners. 2010. (Green Careers Ser.). (Illus.). 80p. (YA). (gr. 7-12). lib. bdg. 33.25 *(978-1-4358-3566-5(2))* Rosen Publishing Group, Inc., The.

Byles, Monica. Los Polos. (Coleccion Tierra Viva).Tr. of Polar Lands. (SPA.). 32p. (YA). (gr. 5-8). *(978-84-348-3372-2(7))* SM Ediciones.

Capeci, Anne. Food Chain Frenzy. Speirs, John, illus. 2010. (ENG.). 96p. (C). (gr. 2-5). pap. 7.95 *(978-0-439-56050-4(0))* National Geographic School Publishing, Inc.

Capon, Brian. Plant Survival: Adapting to a Hostile World. Capon, Brian, illus. 2009. (ENG., Illus.). 144p. pap. 15.95 *(978-0-88192-287-5(0),* 682287) Timber Pr., Inc.

Cardenas, Ernesto A. Habitats. 2009. pap. 4.95 *(978-1-60698-080-4(7))* Milo Educational Bks. & Resources.

Cassidy, Henry. Backyard Ecosystems. 2013. (Rosen Readers Ser.). (ENG.). 24p. (J). (gr. 3-4). pap. 49.50 *(978-1-4777-2552-8(0));* pap. 8.25 *(978-1-4777-2551-1(2))* Rosen Publishing Group, Inc., The. (Rosen Classroom).

Cefrey, Holly. Coniferous Forests. 2003. (Biomes Ser.). (Illus.). 24p. (J). lib. bdg. 22.60 *(978-0-8239-6455-0(8),* PowerKids Pr.) Rosen Publishing Group, Inc., The.

—The Deciduous Forest. 2003. (Biomes Ser.). (Illus.). 24p. (J). lib. bdg. 22.60 *(978-0-8239-6454-3(X),* PowerKids Pr.) Rosen Publishing Group, Inc., The.

—Deserts. (Biomes Ser.). 24p. 2009. (gr. 2-3). 42.50 *(978-1-61511-591-4(9))* 2003. (Illus.). (J). lib. bdg. 22.60 *(978-0-8239-6456-7(6))* Rosen Publishing Group, Inc., The. (PowerKids Pr.).

—Grasslands. 2003. (Biomes Ser.). (Illus.). 24p. (J). lib. bdg. 22.60 *(978-0-8239-6457-4(4),* PowerKids Pr.) Rosen Publishing Group, Inc., The.

—Oceans. 2003. (Biomes Ser.). (Illus.). 24p. (J). lib. bdg. 22.60 *(978-0-8239-6453-6(1),* PowerKids Pr.) Rosen Publishing Group, Inc., The.

—Tundra. 2009. (Biomes Ser.). 24p. (gr. 2-3). 42.50 *(978-1-61511-595-2(1),* PowerKids Pr.) Rosen Publishing Group, Inc., The.

Chambers, Catherine. Go Green! Lead the Way. 2010. (Crabtree Connections Ser.). (ENG.). 24p. (J). (gr. 3-6). *(978-0-7787-9947-4(6));* pap. *(978-0-7787-9969-6(7))* Crabtree Publishing Co.

Channing, Margot. Planet Earth. 2014. (Closer Look At... Ser.). (Illus.). 32p. (gr. 3-6). 31.35 *(978-1-904642-69-5(1))* Book Hse. GBR. Dist: Black Rabbit Bks.

Cheung, Lisa. The 10 Most Destructive Ecosystem Invaders. 2008. 14.99 *(978-1-55448-489-8(8))* Scholastic Library Publishing.

Clarke, Nadine. Get Bushwise: on Safari Desert, River, Bushveld: A Young Explorer's Guide. 2013. 192p. pap. 23.00 *(978-1-4317-0206-0(4))* Penguin Random House Grupo Editorial ESP. Dist: Casemate Pubs. & Bk. Distributors, LLC.

Claybourne, Anna. I Love This Tree: Discover the Life, Beauty & Importance of Trees. 2017. (ENG., Illus.). 64p. (J). (gr. 4-6). pap. 12.99 *(978-1-4451-5265-3(7),* Franklin Watts) Hachette Children's Group GBR. Dist: Hachette Bk. Group.

—Mountains. 2004. (Geography Fact Files Ser.). (Illus.). (J). lib. bdg. 28.50 *(978-1-58340-426-3(0))* Black Rabbit Bks.

Close, Edward. Endangered Animals. 2013. (Discovery Education: Habitats Ser.). 32p. (J). (gr. 3-6). 25.25 *(978-1-4777-1325-9(5));* pap. 10.00 *(978-1-4777-1485-0(5));* pap. 60.00 *(978-1-4777-1486-7(3))* Rosen Publishing Group, Inc., The. (PowerKids Pr.).

Cobb, Allan B. Looking at the Interdependence of Plants, Animals, & the Environment with Graphic Organizers. (Using Graphic Organizers to Study the Living Environment Ser.). 48p. 2009. (gr. 6-6). 53.00 *(978-1-60854-715-9(9),* Rosen Reference) 2005. (Illus.). (YA). (gr. 5-9). 29.25 *(978-1-4042-0615-1(9))* Rosen Publishing Group, Inc., The.

Cohen, Marina. Deserts Inside Out. 2014. (ENG.). 32p. (J). *(978-0-7787-0627-4(3))* Crabtree Publishing Co.

Cole, Melissa S. Desert. 2003. (Wild America Habitats Ser.). (Illus.). 24p. (J). 24.94 *(978-1-56711-799-8(6),* Blackbirch Pr., Inc.) Cengage Gale.

—Mountain. 2003. (Wild America Habitats Ser.). (Illus.). 24p. (J). 21.20 *(978-1-56711-806-3(2),* Blackbirch Pr., Inc.) Cengage Gale.

Colich, Abby. Protecting Food Chains, 1 vol., Set. Incl. Desert Food Chains. Silverman, Buffy. 33.32 *(978-1-4329-3856-7(8));* Grassland Food Chains. Silverman, Buffy. 33.32 *(978-1-4329-3857-4(6));* Mountain Food Chains. Lynette, Rachel. 33.32 *(978-1-4329-3858-1(4));* Ocean Food Chains. Moore, Heidi. (Illus.). 33.32 *(978-1-4329-3859-8(2));* Rain Forest Food Chains. Moore, Heidi. (Illus.). 33.32 *(978-1-4329-3860-4(6));* River Food Chains. Lynette, Rachel. 33.32 *(978-1-4329-3861-1(4));* (gr. 3-6). (Protecting Food Chains Ser.). (ENG.). 48p. 2010. Set lib. bdg. 199.92 *(978-1-4329-3862-8(2),* Heinemann InfoSearch) Heinemann-Raintree.

Collard, Sneed B., III. Fire Birds. 2015. (Illus.). 48p. (J). *(978-0-9844460-7-0(9))* Bucking Horse Bks.

—Many Biomes, One Earth. Needham, James M., illus. 2009. (ENG.). 32p. (J). (gr. k-3). pap. 7.95 *(978-1-57091-632-8(2))* Charlesbridge Publishing, Inc.

Como? (Coleccion Mil Preguntas). (SPA., Illus.). 24p. (J). pap. 5.50 *(978-950-11-0612-1(8),* SGM128) Sigmar ARG. Dist: Continental Bk. Co., Inc.

Connors, Kathleen. Plants & Animals of the Chesapeake Bay. 2013. 32p. (J). (gr. 3-6). 26.60 *(978-1-4339-9780-8(0));* pap. 63.00 *(978-1-4339-9782-2(7));* pap. 10.50 *(978-1-4339-9781-5(9))* Stevens, Gareth Publishing LLLP.

Coss, Lauren. Life in Estuaries. 2014. (Life in Water Biomes Ser.). (ENG.). 24p. (J). (gr. 2-5). 28.50 *(978-1-62687-294-3(5),* 207135) Child's World, Inc., The.

Cowcher, Helen. Desert Elephants, 1 vol. Cowcher, Helen, illus. 2011. (ENG., Illus.). 40p. (J). (gr. k-3). 16.99 *(978-0-374-31774-4(7),* 9780374317744, Farrar, Straus & Giroux (BYR)) Farrar, Straus & Giroux.

Craighead, Shirley A. Bugling Elk & Sleeping Grizzlies: The Who, What, & When of Yellowstone & Grand Teton National Parks. 2004. (ENG., Illus.). 48p. pap. 9.95 *(978-0-7627-2864-0(7),* Falcon Guides) Globe Pequot Pr., The.

Cram101 Textbook Reviews Staff & L. DeVere Burton. Studyguide for Fish & Wildlife: Principles of Zoology & Ecology by L. Devere Burton, Isbn 9781435419636. 3rd ed. 2014. (ENG.). 216p. (C). pap. 30.95 *(978-1-4784-1055-3(8))* Cram101 Inc.

Crenson, Victoria. Horseshoe Crabs & Shorebirds: The Story of a Food Web, 1 vol. Cannon, Annie, illus. 2003. (ENG.). 32p. (J). (gr. 3-5). 16.95 *(978-0-7614-5115-0(3))* Marshall Cavendish Corp.

Crossingham, John & Kalman, Bobbie. Seashore Food Chains. 2005. (Food Chains Ser.). (ENG., Illus.). 32p. (J). lib. bdg. *(978-0-7787-1949-6(9));* (gr. 1-5). pap. *(978-0-7787-1995-3(2))* Crabtree Publishing Co.

Cuando? (Coleccion Mil Preguntas). (SPA., Illus.). 24p. (J). pap. 5.50 *(978-950-11-0610-7(1),* SGM101) Sigmar ARG. Dist: Continental Bk. Co., Inc.

Curran, Christine Perdan, ed. Metabolic Processes & Energy Transfers: An Anthology of Current Thought. (Contemporary Discourse in the Field of Biology Ser.). 2009. 224p. (gr. 10-12). 63.90 *(978-1-61511-911-0(6))* 2005. (Illus.). 192p. (YA). (gr. 7-12). lib. bdg. 35.95 *(978-1-4042-0399-0(0))* Rosen Publishing Group, Inc., The.

Currie, Stephen. Ecosystems. 2009. (21st Century Skills Library: Real World Science Ser.). (ENG.). 32p. (gr. 4-8). lib. bdg. 28.50 *(978-1-60279-458-0(8),* 200229) Cherry Lake Publishing.

Cuthbert, Megan. Africa. 2014. (J). *(978-1-4896-0934-2(2))* Weigl Pubs., Inc.

—Europe. 2014. (J). *(978-1-4896-0950-2(4))* Weigl Pubs., Inc.

Dakers, Diane. The Carbon Cycle. 2014. (ENG., Illus.). 48p. (J). pap. *(978-0-7787-0621-2(4))* Crabtree Publishing Co.

—Earth's Water Cycle. 2014. (ENG., Illus.). 48p. (J). *(978-0-7787-0617-5(6))* Crabtree Publishing Co.

—The Nitrogen Cycle. 2014. (ENG., Illus.). 48p. (J). *(978-0-7787-0599-4(4))* Crabtree Publishing Co.

Daly, Ruth. North America. 2014. (J). *(978-1-4896-0954-0(7))* Weigl Pubs., Inc.

Davenport, Jefferson. What Lives in Your Backyard? 2013. (InfoMax Readers Ser.). (ENG.). 24p. (J). (gr. 3-4). pap. 8.25 *(978-1-4777-2608-2(X));* pap. 49.50 *(978-1-4777-2609-9(8))* Rosen Publishing Group, Inc., The. (Rosen Classroom).

Davidson, Avelyn. Tundras of the World. 2009. (Our Planet Ser.). (YA). (gr. 3-6). lib. bdg. 25.25 *(978-1-4358-2817-9(8))* Rosen Publishing Group, Inc., The.

Davis, Barbara J. Biomes & Ecosystems. 2007. (Gareth Stevens Vital Science: Earth Science Ser.). (Illus.). 48p. (gr. 5-12). pap. 14.05 *(978-0-8368-7872-1(8));* lib. bdg. 27.00 *(978-0-8368-7761-8(6))* Stevens, Gareth Publishing LLLP. (Gareth Stevens Secondary Library).

Dawson, Emily C. Birds & Trees. 2010. (Our Animal World Ser.). 24p. (J). 25.65 *(978-1-60753-010-7(4))* Amicus Publishing.

Day, Trevor. Taiga, 1 vol. 2nd ed. 2010. (Biomes Atlases Ser.). (ENG.). 64p. (gr. 6-9). 34.65 *(978-1-4329-4179-6(8))* Heinemann-Raintree.

De Medeiros, Michael. Chaparrals. 2016. (Illus.). 32p. (J). *(978-1-5105-0864-4(3))* SmartBook Media, Inc.

—Chaparrals. 2012. (J). *(978-1-61913-233-7(8));* *(978-1-61913-070-8(X))* Weigl Pubs., Inc.

deMarin, Layne. Amazon Adventure, 1 vol. 2011. (Wonder Readers: Science Ser.). (ENG.). (gr. -1-2). 20p. lib. bdg. 22.65 *(978-1-4296-8634-1(0));* 16p. pap. 35.94 *(978-1-4296-8069-1(5));* 32p. pap. 5.99 *(978-1-4296-7907-7(7))* Capstone Press of Coughlan Cos. (Wonder Readers).

—Desert Seasons. 2011. (Wonder Readers Fluent Level Ser.). (ENG.). 16p. (gr. -1-2). pap. 35.94 *(978-1-4296-8082-0(2),* Wonder Readers) Capstone Press of Coughlan Cos.

Dewin, Howard & Corwin, Jeff. Habitat Is Where It's At! A Sticker Book Experience. 2003. (Illus.). 31p. (J). *(978-0-439-43595-6(1))* Scholastic, Inc.

Diagram Group Staff. Environment: An Illustrated Guide to Science. 2006. (Science Visual Resources Ser.). (Illus.). 208p. (gr. 6-12). 49.50 *(978-0-8160-6165-5(3))* Facts On File, Inc.

Do You Really Want to Visit a Desert? 2015. (Do You Really Want to Visit... ? Ser.). (Illus.). 24p. (J). 27.10 *(978-1-60753-450-1(9))* Amicus Publishing.

Donald, Rhonda Lucas. Deep in the Desert, 1 vol. Neidigh, Sherry, illus. 2011. (ENG.). 32p. (J). (gr. -1-3). 16.95 *(978-1-60718-125-5(8));* pap. 8.95 *(978-1-60718-135-4(5))* Arbordale Publishing.

Donde? (Coleccion Mil Preguntas). (SPA., Illus.). 24p. (J). pap. 5.50 *(978-950-11-0609-1(8),* SGM098) Sigmar ARG. Dist: Continental Bk. Co., Inc.

Donnelly, Karen. Biomes of the Past & the Future. 2009. (Earth's Changing Weather & Climate Ser.). 24p. (gr. 4-4). 42.50 *(978-1-61512-243-1(5),* PowerKids Pr.) Rosen Publishing Group, Inc., The.

Downer, Ann. Wild Animal Neighbors: Sharing Our Urban World. 2013. 64p. pap. 24.95 *(978-1-4677-1663-5(4))* Lerner Publishing Group.

Drake, Jane & Love, Ann. Cool Woods: A Trip Around the World's Boreal Forest. Kiss, Andrew, illus. 2003. (ENG.). 80p. (J). (gr. 4-7). 19.95 *(978-0-88776-608-4(0),* Tundra Bks.) Tundra Bks. CAN. Dist: Penguin Random Hse. LLC.

Duffield, Katy S. Earth's Biomes. 2009. (21st Century Skills Library: Real World Science Ser.). (ENG.). 32p. (gr. 4-8). lib. bdg. 28.50 *(978-1-60279-457-3(X),* 200231) Cherry Lake Publishing.

Duke, Shirley Smith. Herbivores & Carnivores Explained. 2016. (Distinctions in Nature Ser.). 32p. (J). (gr. 3-3). 28.50 *(978-1-5026-1745-3(5))* Cavendish Square Publishing.

Dunne, Abbie. Food Chains & Webs. 2016. (Life Science Ser.). (ENG., Illus.). 24p. (gr. k-1). lib. bdg. 26.65 *(978-1-5157-0941-1(8),* Pebble Plus) Capstone Press of Coughlan Cos.

Dunphy, Madeleine. Here Is the Coral Reef. Leonard, Tom, illus. 2006. (Web of Life Ser.). (ENG.). 32p. (J). (gr. -1-3). 16.95 *(978-0-9773795-5-2(8));* pap. 9.95 *(978-0-9773795-4-5(X))* Web of Life Children's Bks.

—Here Is the Southwestern Desert. Coe, Anne, illus. 2006. (Web of Life Ser.). (ENG.). 32p. (J). (gr. -1-3). 16.95 *(978-0-9773795-7-6(4));* pap. 9.95 *(978-0-9773795-6-9(6))* Web of Life Children's Bks.

Dutton, Michael. Exploring Ecosystems! An Environmentally Friendly Coloring Book. 2009. (Dover Nature Coloring Book Ser.). (ENG., Illus.). 32p. (J). (gr. k-2). pap. 3.99 *(978-0-486-46988-1(3))* Dover Pubns., Inc.

Eason, Sarah, ed. Ecology. 2011. (FAYFT: Introducing Biology Ser.). 64p. (gr. 4-10). lib. bdg. 39.95 *(978-1-936333-04-2(X))* Brown Bear Bks.

Eboch, M. M. The 12 Biggest Breakthroughs in Energy Technology. 2014. (ENG.). 32p. (J). *(978-1-63235-013-8(0))* Pr. Room Editions LLC.

La Ecologia: Las Mil Caras de la Vida. (Coleccion Bravo). (SPA., Illus.). (YA). (gr. 5-8). pap. *(978-84-7131-911-1(X),* EDI30263) Editex, Editorial S.A. ESP. Dist: Lectorum Pubns., Inc.

Ecology Experiments. 2010. (Facts on File Science Experiments Ser.). (Illus.). 184p. (J). (gr. 6-12). 40.00 *(978-0-8160-8169-1(7))* Facts On File, Inc.

Ecosystem Set, 6-Volumes. 2008. (Ecosystems Ser.). (C). (gr. 9). 420.00 *(978-0-8160-7376-4(7))* Facts On File, Inc.

Eggleton, Jill. Invasive Species. 2007. (Connectors Ser.). (gr. 2-5). pap. *(978-1-877453-04-5(8))* Global Education Systems Ltd.

Encyclopaedia Britannica, Inc. Staff, compiled by. Britannica Illustrated Science Library Print: Ecology. 2010. 37.43 *(978-1-61535-341-5(0))* Encyclopaedia Britannica, Inc.

—Britannica Illustrated Science Library Print: Environment. 2010. 37.43 *(978-1-61535-343-9(7))* Encyclopaedia Britannica, Inc.

Endres, Hollie. Prairies. 2011. (Blastoff! Readers Ser.). 24p. (J). pap. 5.95 *(978-0-531-26034-0(8),* Children's Pr.) Scholastic Library Publishing.

Environment. 2nd rev. ed. 2010. (What Can I Do Now? Ser.). 224p. (gr. 6-12). 32.95 *(978-0-8160-8073-1(9),* Ferguson Publishing Co.) Facts On File, Inc.

Esbaum, Jill & National Geographic Kids Staff. Angry Birds Playground: Animals: An Around-The-World Habitat Adventure. 2016. (ENG.). 128p. (J). (gr. -1-3). pap. 9.99 *(978-1-4263-2457-4(X),* National Geographic Children's Bks.) National Geographic Society.

Evans, Shira. National Geographic Readers: at the Beach. 2017. (Readers Ser.). (ENG., Illus.). 24p. (J). (-k). lib. bdg. 13.90 *(978-1-4263-2808-4(7),* National Geographic Children's Bks.) National Geographic Society.

Exploring the Great Lakes. 2014. (Exploring the Great Lakes Ser.). 32p. (J). (gr. 3-6). 159.60 *(978-1-4824-1171-3(7))* Stevens, Gareth Publishing LLLP.

Falchetta, Drew. Who Lives Here? 2017. (1-3Y Ecosystems Ser.). (ENG.). 28p. pap. 5.99 ***(978-1-63437-820-8(2))*** American Reading Co.

Farquhar, Jackie, et al. Try This at Home: Planet-Friendly Projects for Kids. 2008. (ENG., Illus.). 96p. (J). (gr. 3-4). pap. 10.95 *(978-2-89579-192-8(9))* Owlkids Bks. Inc. CAN. Dist: Publishers Group West (PGW).

Fiedler, Julie. Learning about Food Chains & Food Webs with Graphic Organizers. 2007. (Graphic Organizers in Science Ser.: Vol. 3). (ENG., Illus.). 24p. (J). (gr. 3-7). lib. bdg. 22.60 *(978-1-4042-3412-3(8))* Rosen Publishing Group, Inc., The.

Fleisher, Paul. Desert Food Webs. 2008. pap. 52.95 *(978-0-8225-9348-5(3))* 2007. (Illus.). 48p. (J). (gr. 2-5). lib. bdg. 26.60 *(978-0-8225-6728-8(8),* Lerner Pubns.) Lerner Publishing Group.

—Desert Food Webs in Action. 2013. (Searchlight Books What Is a Food Web Ser.). (ENG., Illus.). 40p. (gr. 3-5). (J). lib. bdg. 27.93 *(978-1-4677-1294-1(9),* Lerner Pubns.); pap. 8.95 *(978-1-4677-1552-2(2))* Lerner Publishing Group.

—Forest Food Webs. 2008. pap. 52.95 *(978-0-8225-9349-2(1))* Lerner Publishing Group.

—Lake & Pond Food Webs. 2007. (Early Bird Food Webs Ser.). (ENG., Illus.). 48p. (gr. 2-5). lib. bdg. 26.60 *(978-0-8225-6731-8(8),* Lerner Pubns.) Lerner Publishing Group.

—Lake & Pond Food Webs in Action. 2013. (Searchlight Books What Is a Food Web Ser.). (ENG., Illus.). 40p. (gr. 3-5). pap. 8.95 *(978-1-4677-1555-3(7));* lib. bdg. 27.93 *(978-1-4677-1256-9(6),* Lerner Pubns.) Lerner Publishing Group.

—Tundra Food Webs. 2008. pap. 52.95 *(978-0-8225-9354-6(8))* Lerner Publishing Group.

—Tundra Food Webs. Schultz, Gary, photos by. 2007. (Early Bird Food Webs Ser.). (ENG., Illus.). 48p. (gr. 2-5). lib. bdg. 26.60 *(978-0-8225-6727-1(X),* Lerner Pubns.) Lerner Publishing Group.

—Webs of Life - Group 2, 4 bks., Set. Incl. Alpine Meadow. lib. bdg. 22.79 *(978-0-7614-0836-9(3));* Mountain Stream. lib. bdg. 22.79 *(978-0-7614-0838-3(X));* Pond. lib. bdg. 22.79 *(978-0-7614-0835-2(5));* Salt Marsh. Cassels, Jean, illus. lib. bdg. 22.79 *(978-0-7614-0834-5(7));* 40p. (J). (gr. 2-5). 1998. Set lib. bdg. 91.14 *(978-0-7614-0833-8(9),* Benchmark Bks.) Marshall Cavendish Corp.

Flounders, Anne. Friends in the Wild. 2014. (Our Green Earth Ser.). (Illus.). 32p. (gr. 2-4). pap. 8.95 *(978-1-939656-29-2(X))* Red Chair Pr.

Franchino, Vicky. Antarctic Tundra. 2016. (Community Connections: Getting to Know Our Planet Ser.). (ENG., Illus.). 24p. (J). (gr. 2-5). 27.07 *(978-1-63470-514-1(9),* 207787) Cherry Lake Publishing.

—Canadian Taiga. 2016. (Community Connections: Getting to Know Our Planet Ser.). (ENG., Illus.). 24p. (J). (gr. 2-5). 27.07 *(978-1-63470-515-8(7),* 207791) Cherry Lake Publishing.

Fredericks, Anthony D. Desert Night Desert Day. Spengler, Kenneth J., illus. 2011. 32p. (J). 15.95 *(978-1-933855-70-7(3))* Rio Nuevo Pubs.

Fretland VanVoorst, Jenny. Ecosystems, 1 vol. 2014. (Science of Life Ser.). (ENG.). 48p. (gr. 3-6). lib. bdg. 32.79 *(978-1-62403-159-5(5))* ABDO Publishing Co.

Friedman, Lauri S., ed. Environmentalism. 2011. (Introducing Issues with Opposing Viewpoints Ser.). (Illus.). 144p. (YA). (gr. 9-12). 35.75 *(978-0-7377-5677-7(2))* Cengage Gale.

Frisch, Aaron. Tundra. 2008. (Our World Ser.). (Illus.). 24p. (J). (gr. -1-3). lib. bdg. 24.25 *(978-1-58341-574-0(2),* Creative Education) Creative Co., The.

Fronczak, Emerson. There's a Food Chain in Your Garden! 2013. (InfoMax Readers Ser.). (ENG.). 24p. (J). (gr. 2-3). pap. 8.25 *(978-1-4777-2360-9(9));* pap. 49.50 *(978-1-4777-2362-3(5))* Rosen Publishing Group, Inc., The. (Rosen Classroom).

Gaff, Jackie. I Wonder Why the Sahara Is Cold at Night. 2014. 32p. pap. 7.00 *(978-1-61003-351-0(5))* Center for the Collaborative Classroom.

E
F
G

Ganeri, Anita. Exploring Coasts: A Benjamin Blog & His Inquisitive Dog Investigation, 1 vol. 2014. (Exploring Habitats with Benjamin Blog & His Inquisitive Dog Ser.). (ENG., Illus.). 32p. (gr. 1-3). lib. bdg. 29.99 *(978-1-4329-8777-0(1)*, NA-h) Heinemann-Raintree.

—Exploring Deserts: A Benjamin Blog & His Inquisitive Dog Investigation, 1 vol. 2014. (Exploring Habitats with Benjamin Blog & His Inquisitive Dog Ser.). (ENG.). 32p. (gr. 1-3). lib. bdg. 29.99 *(978-1-4329-8778-7(X)*, NA-h) Heinemann-Raintree.

—Exploring Habitats, with Benjamin Blog & His Inquisitive Dog, 1 vol. 2014. (Exploring Habitats with Benjamin Blog & His Inquisitive Dog Ser.). (ENG.). 32p. (gr. 1-3). lib. bdg. 179.94 *(978-1-4329-8781-7(X)*, NA-h) Heinemann-Raintree.

—Exploring Mountains: A Benjamin Blog & His Inquisitive Dog Investigation, 1 vol. 2014. (Exploring Habitats with Benjamin Blog & His Inquisitive Dog Ser.). (ENG.). 32p. (gr. 1-3). lib. bdg. 29.99 *(978-1-4329-8776-3(3)*, NA-h) Heinemann-Raintree.

—Exploring Rivers: A Benjamin Blog & His Inquisitive Dog Investigation, 1 vol. 2014. (Exploring Habitats with Benjamin Blog & His Inquisitive Dog Ser.). (ENG., Illus.). 32p. (gr. 1-3). lib. bdg. 29.99 *(978-1-4329-8775-6(5)*, NA-h) Heinemann-Raintree.

Gardner, Jane. Animal Science, Vol. 11. Lewin, Russ, ed. 2015. (Science 24/7 Ser.). (Illus.). 48p. (J). (gr. 5). lib. bdg. 20.95 *(978-1-4222-3405-1(3))* Mason Crest.

Gardner, Jane P. Environmental Science. 2015. (Illus.). 48p. (J). *(978-1-4222-3404-4(5))* Mason Crest.

Gardner, Robert. Desert Experiments: 11 Science Experiments in One Hour or Less. 2014. (Last Minute Science Projects with Biomes Ser.). (Illus.). 48p. (YA). (gr. 5-12). pap. 8.95 *(978-0-7660-5918-4(9)*, Enslow Elementary) Enslow Pubs., Inc.

—Earth's Cycles: Great Science Projects about the Water Cycle, Photosynthesis, & More. 2011. (Team Green Science Projects Ser.). (Illus.). 112p. (J). (gr. 5-9). lib. bdg. 33.27 *(978-0-7660-3644-4(8))* Enslow Pubs., Inc.

—Tundra Experiments: 14 Science Experiments in One Hour or Less. 2014. (Last Minute Science Projects with Biomes Ser.). (Illus.). 48p. (J). (gr. 5-12). lib. bdg. 25.27 *(978-0-7660-5942-9(1))* Enslow Pubs., Inc.

Gardner, Robert, et al. Ace Your Ecology & Environmental Science Project: Great Science Fair Ideas. 2009. (Ace Your Science Project Ser.). (Illus.). 112p. (J). (gr. 5-9). lib. bdg. 33.27 *(978-0-7660-3216-3(7))* Enslow Pubs., Inc.

Geozonen und Landschaftsoekologie. (Duden Abiturhilfen Ser.). (GER.). 96p. (YA). (gr. 12-13). *(978-3-411-04471-9(3))* Bibliographisches Institut & F. A. Brockhaus AG DEU. Dist: International Bk. Import Service, Inc.

Gerber, Carole. Tundra Food Chains. 2003. (What Eats What? Ser.). (J). pap. *(978-1-58417-221-5(5))*; lib. bdg. *(978-1-58417-220-8(7))* Lake Street Pubs.

Gibbons, Gail. Coral Reefs. Gibbons, Gail, illus. 2009. (ENG., Illus.). 32p. (J). (gr. -1-3). pap. 7.99 *(978-0-8234-2278-4(X))* Holiday Hse., Inc.

Golde, Evie. Freshwater & Saltwater Habitats. 2013. (Rosen Readers Ser.). (ENG.). 24p. (J). (gr. 2-3). pap. 8.25 *(978-1-4777-2379-1(X))*; pap. 49.50 *(978-1-4777-2380-7(3))* Rosen Publishing Group, Inc., The. (Rosen Classroom).

Goldsworthy, Steve. Antarctica. 2014. (J). *(978-1-4896-0938-0(5))* Weigl Pubs., Inc.

Gowan, Barbara. D Is for Desert: A World Deserts Alphabet. 2012. (ENG., Illus.). 32p. (J). (gr. 1-5). 16.95 *(978-1-58536-501-2(7))* Sleeping Bear Pr.

Gray, Leon. Food Webs. 2013. (Life Science Stories Ser.). (Illus.). 32p. (gr. 3-5). 26.60 *(978-1-4339-8707-6(4))*; pap. 10.50 *(978-1-4339-8708-3(2))* Stevens, Gareth Publishing LLLP. (Gareth Stevens Learning Library).

—Life in Extreme Places. 2013. (Life Science Stories Ser.). (Illus.). 32p. (gr. 3-5). 26.60 *(978-1-4339-8715-1(5))*; pap. 10.50 *(978-1-4339-8716-8(3))* Stevens, Gareth Publishing LLLP. (Gareth Stevens Learning Library).

—Rivers. 2011. (Geography Wise Ser.). (Illus.). 32p. (YA). (gr. 2-5). lib. bdg. 26.50 *(978-1-4488-3282-8(9))* Rosen Publishing Group, Inc., The.

Gray, Susan H. Ecology: The Study of Ecosystems. 2012. (True Book Ser.). (ENG., Illus.). 48p. (J). lib. bdg. 29.00 *(978-0-531-24675-7(2)*, Children's Pr.) Scholastic Library Publishing.

Gray, Susan Heinrichs. Ecology: The Study of Ecosystems. 2012. (True Book Ser.). (ENG., Illus.). 48p. (J). (gr. 3-5). pap. 6.95 *(978-0-531-28269-4(4)*, Children's Pr.) Scholastic Library Publishing.

Greathouse, Lisa E. Food Webs, 1 vol. 2015. (Science Readers: Content & Literacy Ser.). (ENG., Illus.). 32p. (gr. 3-3). pap. 8.99 *(978-1-4807-4638-1(X))* Teacher Created Materials, Inc.

—The Nutrient Cycle. 2015. (Science Readers: Content & Literacy Ser.). (ENG., Illus.). 32p. (J). (gr. 4-4). pap. 8.99 *(978-1-4807-4680-0(0))* Teacher Created Materials, Inc.

Greeley, August. Fading Forests: The Destruction of Our Rainforests. 2009. (Man-Made Disasters Ser.). 24p. (gr. 3-3). 42.50 *(978-1-61514-347-4(5)*, PowerKids Pr.) Rosen Publishing Group, Inc., The.

Green, Jen. Big Fantastic Earth. 2016. (Illus.). 96p. (J). *(978-1-5182-1730-2(3))* Dorling Kindersley Publishing, Inc.

—Caring for Habitats. 2011. (Sherlock Bones Looks at the Environment Ser.). (ENG., Illus.). 32p. (YA). (gr. 3-6). lib. bdg. 25.25 *(978-1-61533-344-8(4))* Windmill Bks.

—Coasts. 2011. (Geography Wise Ser.). (Illus.). 32p. (YA). (gr. 2-5). lib. bdg. 26.50 *(978-1-4488-3279-8(9))* Rosen Publishing Group, Inc., The.

—Life in the Desert. 2010. (Nature in Focus Ser.). (Illus.). 32p. (gr. 2-5). (J). pap. 10.50 *(978-1-4339-3421-6(3)*, Gareth Stevens Learning Library); (YA). lib. bdg. 26.00 *(978-1-4339-3420-9(5)*, 1309291) Stevens, Gareth Publishing LLLP.

—Life on the Tundra. 2010. (Nature in Focus Ser.). (Illus.). 32p. (gr. 2-5). (J). pap. 10.50 *(978-1-4339-3418-6(3)*, Gareth Stevens Learning Library); (YA). lib. bdg. 26.00 *(978-1-4339-3417-9(5)*, 1309292) Stevens, Gareth Publishing LLLP.

Green, Mary. Rivers in Action. 2004. (Earth's Changing Landscape Ser.). (Illus.). 46p. (YA). (gr. 7-12). lib. bdg. 28.50 *(978-1-58340-477-5(5))* Black Rabbit Bks.

Greenberger, Robert. Deserts: The Living Landscape. 2009. (Biomes of the World Ser.). 48p. (gr. 5-8). (ENG., Illus.). (J). pap. 11.75 *(978-1-4358-5431-4(4))*; 53.00 *(978-1-61511-602-7(8)*, Rosen Reference); (YA). lib. bdg. 29.25 *(978-1-4358-5005-7(X))* Rosen Publishing Group, Inc., The.

Gregoire, Maryellen. Life in a Desert, 1 vol. 2012. (Wonder Readers Emergent Level Ser.). (ENG.). 32p. (gr. -1-1). pap. 5.99 *(978-1-4296-9194-9(8)*, Wonder Readers) Capstone Press of Coughlan Cos.

—We All Need Plants. 2011. (Wonder Readers Emergent Level Ser.). (ENG.). (gr. -1-1). 16p. pap. 35.94 *(978-1-4296-8200-8(0))*; 32p. pap. 5.99 *(978-1-4296-7878-0(X))* Capstone Press of Coughlan Cos. (Wonder Readers).

Gregory, Josh. African Savanna. 2016. (Community Connections: Getting to Know Our Planet Ser.). (ENG., Illus.). 24p. (J). (gr. 2-5). 27.07 *(978-1-63470-512-7(2)*, 207779) Cherry Lake Publishing.

Halsey, Megan. 3 Pandas Planting, 0 vols. Halsey, Megan, illus. rev. ed. 2011. (ENG., Illus.). 34p. (J). (gr. -1-3). pap. 6.99 *(978-0-7614-5844-9(1)*, 9780761458449, Amazon Children's Publishing) Amazon Publishing.

Hanks, Karoline. Exploring Our Biomes (Boxed Set) South Africa, 5 vols. 2010. (ENG., Illus.). 370p. (J). (gr. 4-7). pap. 108.00 *(978-1-77009-679-0(5))* Jacana Media ZAF. Dist: Independent Pubs. Group.

Harmon, Daniel E. Jobs in Environmental Cleanup & Emergency Hazmat Response. 2010. (Green Careers Ser.). (Illus.). 80p. (YA). (gr. 7-12). lib. bdg. 33.25 *(978-1-4358-3570-2(0))* Rosen Publishing Group, Inc., The.

Harper, Judith E. Unique Places. 2005. (Real Deal Ser.). (Illus.). 32p. (J). pap. *(978-0-7608-9635-8(6))* Sundance/Newbridge Educational Publishing.

Harris, Tim. Mountains & Highlands, 1 vol. 2nd ed. 2010. (Biomes Atlases Ser.). (ENG.). 64p. (gr. 6-9). 34.65 *(978-1-4329-4174-1(7))* Heinemann-Raintree.

Haus, Robyn. Create a Year-Round Wildlife Habitat: For Urban & Suburban Small Spaces. 2004. (Quick Starts for Kids! Ser.). (Illus.). 64p. (J). pap. 8.95 *(978-1-885593-97-9(X)*, Ideal Pubns.) Worthy Publishing.

Hawes, Alison. Extreme Places: Could You Live Here? 2010. (Crabtree Connections Ser.). (ENG.). 24p. (J). (gr. 3-6). *(978-0-7787-9940-5(9))*; pap. *(978-0-7787-9962-7(X))* Crabtree Publishing Co.

Hawley, Ella. Exploring Ecosystems. 2012. (Let's Explore Life Science Ser.). (ENG., Illus.). 24p. (J). (gr. 3-6). pap. 8.25 *(978-1-4488-6314-3(7))*; lib. bdg. 22.60 *(978-1-4488-6175-0(6))* Rosen Publishing Group, Inc., The. (PowerKids Pr.).

—Exploring Food Chains & Food Webs. 2012. (Let's Explore Life Science Ser.). (ENG.). 24p. (J). (gr. 3-6). pap. 8.25 *(978-1-4488-6304-4(X))*; lib. bdg. 22.60 *(978-1-4488-6173-6(X))* Rosen Publishing Group, Inc., The. (PowerKids Pr.).

Hawley, Linda Gallo. Nature Adventures: A Guidebook of Nature Facts, Songs, & Hikes in San Diego County. 2017. (ENG., Illus.). (J). (gr. 3-7). pap. 12.95 ***(978-1-941384-28-2(5))*** Sunbelt Pubns., Inc.

Helbrough, Emma. Great Planet Earth Search. Jackson, Ian, illus. 2006. 32p. (J). *(978-0-439-83402-5(3))* Scholastic, Inc.

Heos, Bridget. Do You Really Want to Visit a Coral Reef? Fabbri, Daniele, illus. 2014. (Do You Really Want to Visit... ? Ser.). (ENG.). 24p. (J). (gr. 1-4). 27.10 *(978-1-60753-449-5(5))* Amicus Publishing.

—Do You Really Want to Visit a Prairie? Fabbri, Daniele, illus. 2014. (Do You Really Want to Visit... ? Ser.). (ENG.). 24p. (J). (gr. 1-4). lib. bdg. 27.10 *(978-1-60753-452-5(5))* Amicus Publishing.

Hess, Paul. Animal Worlds. 2006. (Animal Verse Ser.). (ENG., Illus.). 96p. (J). (gr. -1-k). pap. *(978-1-84089-408-0(3))* Zero to Ten, Ltd.

Hibbert, Clare. Pond Wildlife, 01 vols., 1. 2016. (Adventures in Nature Ser.). (ENG.). 32p. (J). pap. 10.00 *(978-1-5081-4587-5(3)*, PowerKids Pr.) Rosen Publishing Group, Inc., The.

High Tide for Horseshoe Crabs. 2015. (ENG., Illus.). 40p. (J). (gr. -1-2). lib. bdg. 16.95 *(978-1-58089-604-7(9))* Charlesbridge Publishing, Inc.

Himmelman, John. Frog in a Bog. Himmelman, John, illus. 2004. (ENG., Illus.). 32p. (J). (gr. -1-2). pap. 7.95 *(978-1-57091-518-5(0))* Charlesbridge Publishing, Inc.

Hirsch, Rebecca E. Birds vs. Blades? Offshore Wind Power & the Race to Protect Seabirds. 2016. (ENG., Illus.). 48p. (gr. 4-6). 33.32 *(978-1-4677-9520-3(8)*, Millbrook Pr.) Lerner Publishing Group.

Hoe, Susan C. Habitats. 2008. (Maps & Mapping Ser.). 32p. (gr. 1-5). (J). lib. bdg. 26.00 *(978-0-8368-9205-5(4))*; pap. 10.50 *(978-0-8368-9332-8(8))* Stevens, Gareth Publishing LLLP. (Gareth Stevens Learning Library).

Hollar, Sherman. Investigating Earth's Polar Biomes. 2011. (J). lib. bdg. 31.70 *(978-1-61530-501-8(7))* Rosen Publishing Group, Inc., The.

Holt, Rinehart and Winston Staff. Environmental Science. 4th ed. 2004. (Holt Environmental Science Ser.). (ENG.). 48p. (gr. 9-9). pap., pupil's gde. ed. 13.50 *(978-0-03-066602-5(3))* Houghton Mifflin Harcourt Publishing Co.

—Environmental Science Chptr. 21: Economics, Policy & the Future. 4th ed. Date not set. (YA). pap. 11.20 *(978-0-03-068083-0(2))* Holt McDougal.

—Holt Science & Technology: Ecolabs & Field Activities. 5th ed. 2004. (Illus.). pap. 11.60 *(978-0-03-035189-1(8))* Holt McDougal.

—Holt Science & Technology Chapter 18: Life Science: Interactions with Living Things. 5th ed. 2004. (Illus.). pap. 12.86 *(978-0-03-030228-2(5))* Holt McDougal.

Housel, Debra J. Inside Ecosystems & Biomes, 1 vol. 2007. (Science Readers Ser.). (ENG., Illus.). 32p. (J). (gr. 4-4). pap. 8.99 *(978-0-7439-0591-6(1))* Shell Educational Publishing.

—Pioneering Ecologists, 1 vol. 2007. (Science Readers Ser.). (SPA & ENG.). 32p. (J). (gr. 3-3). pap. 8.99 *(978-0-7439-0592-3(X))* Shell Educational Publishing.

Housel, Debra J. & Rice, Dona. The Right Environment, 1 vol. 2015. (Science Readers: Content & Literacy Ser.). (ENG., Illus.). 32p. (gr. 3-3). pap. 8.99 *(978-1-4807-4641-1(X))* Teacher Created Materials, Inc.

Howard, Fran. Grasslands, 1 vol. 2006. (Habitats Ser.). (ENG., Illus.). 32p. (gr. -1-3). 27.07 *(978-1-59679-778-9(9)*, Buddy Bks.) ABDO Publishing Co.

Hugo, Pierre de, illus. The Seashore. 2012. (My First Discoveries Ser.: 13). (ENG.). 38p. (J). (gr. -1-k). spiral bd. 14.99 *(978-1-85103-394-2(7))* Moonlight Publishing, Ltd. GBR. Dist: Independent Pubs. Group.

Hunter, Nick. Deserts: An Explorer Travel Guide, 1 vol. HL Studios Staff, illus. 2013. (Explorer Travel Guides). (ENG.). 48p. (gr. 3-6). 29.99 *(978-1-4109-5429-9(3))*; pap. 8.95 *(978-1-4109-5436-7(6))* Heinemann-Raintree. (NA-r).

Hurst, Donna L. & Taylor, Allison Wagner. The Green Alphabet - a First Look at Ecology. 2010. (Illus.). 60p. pap. 18.75 *(978-1-60911-642-2(9)*, Eloquent Bks.) Strategic Book Publishing & Rights Agency (SBPRA).

Hutt, Sarah. Animals Are Delicious. Ladd, Dave & Anderson, Stephanie, illus. 2016. (ENG.). 48p. (gr. -1 — 1). 17.95 *(978-0-7148-7144-8(3))* Phaidon Pr., Inc.

Hyde, Natalie. Desert Extremes. 2008. (Extreme Nature Ser.). (ENG., Illus.). 32p. (J). (gr. 2-3). pap. *(978-0-7787-4517-4(1))*; lib. bdg. *(978-0-7787-4500-6(7))* Crabtree Publishing Co.

Hyde, Natalie. Rocky Mountains Research Journal. 2017. (Illus.). 32p. (J). ***(978-0-7787-3471-0(4))***; pap. ***(978-0-7787-3496-3(X))*** Crabtree Publishing Co.

Hynes, Margaret. Discover Science: Polar Lands. 2017. (Discover Science Ser.). (ENG.). 56p. (J). pap. 7.99 *(978-0-7534-7334-4(8)*, 9780753473344, Kingfisher) Roaring Brook Pr.

Ikids Staff. Animals Everywhere. Phillips, Jillian, illus. 2010. (ENG.). 20p. (J). (gr. -1-17). 6.99 *(978-1-60169-006-7(1))* Innovative Kids.

Invasion de la Basura. (Coleccion Operacion Tierra). (SPA.). 46p. (YA). (gr. 5-18). pap. 12.95 *(978-950-11-0979-5(8)*, SGM798) Sigmar ARG. Dist: Continental Bk. Co., Inc.

El Investigador Verde. (SPA.). 25p. (J). pap. 7.95 *(978-950-11-0934-4(8)*, SGM348) Sigmar ARG. Dist: Continental Bk. Co., Inc.

Jang, Ki-hwa. Good Friends: Symbiotic Relationships. Cowley, Joy, ed. Oh, Seung-min, illus. 2015. (Science Storybooks Ser.). (ENG.). 32p. (J). (gr. k-3). 26.65 *(978-1-925233-58-2(8))* Lerner Publishing Group.

Jang, Ki-hwa & Kim, In-sook. Good Friends: Symbiotic Relationships. Cowley, Joy, ed. Oh, Seung-min, illus. 2015. (Science Storybooks Ser.). (ENG.). 32p. (gr. k-3). 26.65 *(978-1-925246-20-9(5))*; 7.99 *(978-1-925246-72-8(8))* ChoiceMaker Pty. Ltd., The AUS. (Big and SMALL). Dist: Lerner Publishing Group.

Jankowski, Matt. Attack of the Burmese Pythons. 2016. (Animal Invaders: Destroying Native Habitats Ser.). 00024p. (J). pap. 8.15 ***(978-1-4824-5659-2(1))*** Stevens, Gareth Publishing LLLP.

Janning, Scarlett. Therese's Terrarium. 2013. (Rosen Readers Ser.). (ENG.). 24p. (J). (gr. 3-4). pap. 8.25 *(978-1-4777-2536-8(9))*; pap. 49.50 *(978-1-4777-2537-5(7))* Rosen Publishing Group, Inc., The. (Rosen Classroom).

Jaworski, Sarah. Gabe's Garden Food Chain. 2013. (Rosen Readers Ser.). (ENG.). 24p. (J). (gr. 2-3). pap. 8.25 *(978-1-4777-2368-5(4))*; pap. 49.50 *(978-1-4777-2369-2(2))* Rosen Publishing Group, Inc., The. (Rosen Classroom).

Jenkins, Steve & Page, Robin. I See a Kookaburra! Discovering Animal Habitats Around the World. 2005. (ENG., Illus.). 32p. (J). (gr. -1-3). 17.99 *(978-0-618-50764-1(7))* Houghton Mifflin Harcourt Publishing Co.

Jerome, Kate Boehm. Science at the Aquarium. 2006. (Reading Expeditions Ser.). (ENG., Illus.). 24p. (J). pap. 14.95 *(978-0-7922-8625-7(1))* CENGAGE Learning.

Johansson, Philip. The Coral Reef: A Colorful Web of Life. 2007. (Wonderful Water Biomes Ser.). (Illus.). 48p. (J). (gr. 3-7). lib. bdg. 25.27 *(978-0-7660-2813-5(5)*, Enslow Elementary) Enslow Pubs., Inc.

—The Desert: Discover This Dry Biome. 2015. (Discover the World's Biomes Ser.). 48p. (J). (gr. 3-4). 25.27 *(978-0-7660-6400-3(X))*; pap. 8.95 *(978-0-7660-6401-0(8))* Enslow Pubs., Inc. (Enslow Elementary).

—The Dry Desert: A Web of Life. 2004. (World of Biomes Ser.). (Illus.). 48p. (J). (gr. 3-4). lib. bdg. 25.27 *(978-0-7660-2200-3(5))* Enslow Pubs., Inc.

—The Forested Taiga: A Web of Life. 2004. (World of Biomes Ser.). (Illus.). 48p. (J). lib. bdg. 25.27 *(978-0-7660-2197-6(1))* Enslow Pubs., Inc.

—The Frozen Tundra: A Web of Life. 2004. (World of Biomes Ser.). (Illus.). 48p. (J). lib. bdg. 25.27 *(978-0-7660-2176-1(9))* Enslow Pubs., Inc.

—Lakes & Rivers: A Freshwater Web of Life. 2007. (Wonderful Water Biomes Ser.). (Illus.). 48p. (J). (gr. 3-7). lib. bdg. 25.27 *(978-0-7660-2812-8(7)*, Enslow Elementary) Enslow Pubs., Inc.

—The Taiga: Discover This Forested Biome. 2015. (Discover the World's Biomes Ser.). 48p. (J). (gr. 3-4). 25.27 *(978-0-7660-6410-2(7)*, Enslow Elementary) Enslow Pubs., Inc.

—The Temperate Forest: A Web of Life. 2004. (World of Biomes Ser.). (Illus.). 48p. (J). lib. bdg. 25.27 *(978-0-7660-2198-3(X))* Enslow Pubs., Inc.

—The Tundra: Discover This Frozen Biome. 2015. (Discover the World's Biomes Ser.). 48p. (J). (gr. 3-4). 25.27 *(978-0-7660-6425-6(5))*; pap. 8.95 *(978-0-7660-6426-3(3))* Enslow Pubs., Inc. (Enslow Elementary).

—The Wide Open Grasslands: A Web of Life. 2004. (World of Biomes Ser.). (Illus.). 48p. (J). lib. bdg. 25.27 *(978-0-7660-2201-0(3))* Enslow Pubs., Inc.

Johnson, J. Angelique. The Eco-Student's Guide to Being Green at School, 1 vol. Poling, Kyle, illus. 2010. (Point It Out! Tips for Green Living Ser.). (ENG.). 24p. (gr. 2-3). lib. bdg. 26.65 *(978-1-4048-6027-8(4))* Picture Window Bks.

Johnson, Rebecca. Chernobyl's Wild Kingdom: Life in the Dead Zone. 2014. (Illus.). 64p. (J). (gr. 6-12). lib. bdg. 34.60 *(978-1-4677-1154-8(3)*, Twenty-First Century Bks.) Lerner Publishing Group.

Johnson, Rebecca L. A Journey into a Lake. Saroff, Phyllis V., illus. 2004. (Biomes of North America Ser.). (J). pap. 6.95 *(978-0-8225-2043-6(5))*; 48p. (gr. 3-6). lib. bdg. 23.93 *(978-1-57505-594-7(5))* Lerner Publishing Group.

—A Journey into a River. Saroff, Phyllis V., illus. 2004. (Biomes of North America Ser.). (J). pap. 8.95 *(978-0-8225-2044-3(3))*; 48p. (gr. 3-6). 23.93 *(978-1-57505-595-4(3))* Lerner Publishing Group.

—A Journey into a Wetland. Saroff, Phyllis V., illus. 2004. (Biomes of North America Ser.). (J). pap. 8.95 *(978-0-8225-2047-4(8))*; 48p. (gr. 3-6). lib. bdg. 23.93 *(978-1-57505-593-0(7))* Lerner Publishing Group.

—A Journey into an Estuary. Saroff, Phyllis V., illus. 2004. (Biomes of North America Ser.). (J). pap. 6.95 *(978-0-8225-2045-0(1))*; (ENG.). 48p. (gr. 3-6). lib. bdg. 23.93 *(978-1-57505-592-3(9))* Lerner Publishing Group.

—Journey into the Deep: Discovering New Ocean Creatures. 2015. (ENG., Illus.). 64p. (gr. 4-8). 34.65 *(978-1-4677-5923-6(6)*, Lerner Digital) Lerner Publishing Group.

—A Journey into the Ocean. Saroff, Phyllis V., illus. 2004. (Biomes of North America Ser.). (ENG.). 48p. (gr. 3-6). pap. 8.95 *(978-0-8225-2046-7(X)*, I); lib. bdg. 23.93 *(978-1-57505-591-6(0))* Lerner Publishing Group.

Johnson, Robin. Sonoran Desert Research Journal. 2017. (Illus.). 32p. (J). ***(978-0-7787-3491-8(9))***; pap. ***(978-0-7787-3497-0(8))*** Crabtree Publishing Co.

Kalman, Bobbie. The ABCs of Habitats. 2007. (ABCs of the Natural World Ser.). (ENG., Illus.). 32p. (J). (gr. 1-4). pap. *(978-0-7787-3431-4(5))* Crabtree Publishing Co.

—Baby Animals in Cities. 2013. (ENG., Illus.). 24p. (J). *(978-0-7787-1017-2(3))*; pap. *(978-0-7787-1029-5(7))* Crabtree Publishing Co.

—Baby Animals in Land Habitats. 2011. (ENG.). 24p. (J). pap. *(978-0-7787-7744-1(8))*; *(978-0-7787-7731-1(6))* Crabtree Publishing Co.

—Baby Animals in Rivers. 2013. (ENG., Illus.). 24p. (J). *(978-0-7787-1019-6(X))*; pap. *(978-0-7787-1033-2(5))* Crabtree Publishing Co.

—Baby Animals in Savanna Habitats. 2011. (ENG.). 24p. (J). pap. *(978-0-7787-7746-5(4))*; *(978-0-7787-7733-5(2))* Crabtree Publishing Co.

—¿Dónde Viven los Animales? 2010. (SPA.). 24p. (J). pap. *(978-0-7787-8591-0(2))*; lib. bdg. *(978-0-7787-8565-1(3))* Crabtree Publishing Co.

—Food Chains & You. 2004. (Food Chains Ser.). (ENG., Illus.). 32p. (J). pap. *(978-0-7787-1988-5(X))* Crabtree Publishing Co.

—How Do Living Things Find Food? 2010. (Introducing Living Things Ser.). (ENG.). 24p. (J). (gr. 1-4). pap. *(978-0-7787-3258-7(4))*; lib. bdg. *(978-0-7787-3234-1(7))* Crabtree Publishing Co.

—Las Cadenas Alimentarias y Tu. 2006. (Cadenas Alimentarias Ser.). (SPA., Illus.). 32p. (J). (gr. 3-7). pap. *(978-0-7787-8544-6(0))* Crabtree Publishing Co.

—Las Cadenas Alimentarias y Tú. 2006. (Cadenas Alimentarias Ser.). (SPA., Illus.). 32p. (J). (gr. 3-7). lib. bdg. *(978-0-7787-8528-6(9))* Crabtree Publishing Co.

—¿Qué Son Las Redes y Cadenas Alimentarias? 2005. (Ciencia de los Seres Vivos Ser.). (SPA., Illus.). 32p. (J). lib. bdg. *(978-0-7787-8756-3(7))* Crabtree Publishing Co.

—¿Qué Son los Biomas? 2005. (Ciencia de los Seres Vivos Ser.). (SPA., Illus.). 32p. (J). lib. bdg. *(978-0-7787-8755-6(9))* Crabtree Publishing Co.

—La Toundra. 2011. (FRE., Illus.). 32p. (J). pap. 10.95 *(978-2-89579-396-0(4))* Bayard Canada CAN. Dist: Crabtree Publishing Co.

—What Are Earth's Biomes? 2009. (Big Science Ideas Ser.). (ENG., Illus.). 32p. (J). (gr. 1-4). pap. *(978-0-7787-3304-1(1))*; (gr. 2-4). *(978-0-7787-3284-6(3))* Crabtree Publishing Co.

—What Are Food Chains & Webs? 2008. (ENG.). 32p. (J). *(978-0-7787-7638-3(7))*; *(978-0-7787-7637-6(9))* Crabtree Publishing Co.

—What Do I See? 2010. (ENG., Illus.). 16p. (J). (gr. k-2). *(978-0-7787-9419-6(9))*; pap. *(978-0-7787-9463-9(6))* Crabtree Publishing Co.

—What Is a Biome? 2008. (ENG.). 32p. (J). *(978-0-7787-7641-3(7))*; *(978-0-7787-7640-6(9))* Crabtree Publishing Co.

—What Is a Food Chain? 2011. (ENG.). 24p. (J). pap. *(978-0-7787-9592-6(6))* Crabtree Publishing Co.

Kalman, Bobbie & Aloian, Molly. Underground Habitats. 2006. (Introducing Habitats Ser.). (ENG., Illus.). 32p. (J). (gr. 3-7). pap. *(978-0-7787-2982-2(6))* Crabtree Publishing Co.

Kalman, Bobbie & Burns, Kylie. Cadenas Alimentarias de los Pantanos. 2007. (Cadenas Alimentarias Ser.). (SPA., Illus.). 32p. (J). (gr. 3-7). lib. bdg. *(978-0-7787-8532-3(7))*; (gr. 4-7). pap. *(978-0-7787-8548-4(3))* Crabtree Publishing Co.

Kalman, Bobbie & Crossingham, John. Hábitats Terrestres. 2007. (Introduction a Los Habitats Ser.). (SPA & ENG., Illus.). 32p. (J). (gr. k-3). lib. bdg. *(978-0-7787-8324-4(3))* Crabtree Publishing Co.

—Habitats Terrestres. rev. ed. 2007. (Introduction a Los Habitats Ser.). (SPA & ENG., Illus.). 32p. (J). (gr. k-3). pap. *(978-0-7787-8348-0(0))* Crabtree Publishing Co.

—Land Habitats. 2006. (Introducing Habitats Ser.). (ENG., Illus.). 32p. (J). (gr. k-3). pap. *(978-0-7787-2976-1(1))* Crabtree Publishing Co.

Kalman, Bobbie & Dyer, Hadley. Australian Outback Food Chains. 2006. (Food Chains Ser.). (ENG., Illus.). 32p. (J). (gr. -1-3). pap. *(978-0-7787-1996-0(0))*; lib. bdg. *(978-0-7787-1950-2(2))* Crabtree Publishing Co.

Kalman, Bobbie & MacAulay, Kelley. Cadenas Alimentarias del Desierto. 2006. (Cadenas Alimentarias Ser.). (SPA., Illus.). 32p. (J). (gr. 3-7). lib. bdg. *(978-0-7787-8530-9(0))* Crabtree Publishing Co.

—Meadow Food Chains. 2004. (Food Chains Ser.). (ENG., Illus.). 32p. (J). pap. *(978-0-7787-1991-5(X))* Crabtree Publishing Co.

Kalman, Bobbie & Sjonger, Rebecca. Un Habitat de Sabana. 2007. (Libro de Bobbie Kalman Ser.). (SPA., Illus.). 32p. (J). (gr. 3-7). lib. bdg. *(978-0-7787-8329-9(4))*; (gr. k-3). pap. *(978-0-7787-8353-4(7))* Crabtree Publishing Co.

Kaner, Etta. Friend or Foe: The Whole Truth about Animals That People Love to Hate. Anderson, David, illus. 2015. (ENG.). 48p. (J). (gr. 3-7). 16.95 *(978-1-77147-064-3(X)*, Owlkids) Owlkids Bks. Inc. CAN. Dist: Publishers Group West (PGW).

Kapchinske, Pam. Hey Diddle Diddle: A Food Chain Tale, 1 vol. Rogers, Sherry, illus. 2011. (ENG.). 32p. (J). (gr. -1-3). 16.95 *(978-1-60718-130-9(4))*; pap. 8.95 *(978-1-60718-140-8(1))* Arbordale Publishing.

Katirgis, Jane & Ingber Drohan, Michele. Fearsome Forest Fires. 2015. (Earth's Natural Disasters Ser.). (ENG.). 32p. (J). (gr. 3-4). pap. 10.52 *(978-0-7660-6809-4(9))* Enslow Pubs., Inc.

Kavanagh, James. Great Lakes Wildlife Nature Activity Book. Leung, Raymond, illus. 2nd ed. 2011. (Nature Activity Book Ser.). (ENG.). 32p. (J). (gr. 4-7). 6.95 *(978-1-58355-580-4(3))* Western National Parks Assn.

Kawa, Katie. Exploring Food Chains & Food Webs, 1 vol. 2015. (Exploring Food Chains & Food Webs Ser.). (ENG.). 24p. (J). 49.50 *(978-1-4994-0346-6(1),* PowerKids Pr.) Rosen Publishing Group, Inc., The.

—Meadow Food Chains, 1 vol. 2015. (Exploring Food Chains & Food Webs Ser.). (ENG.). 24p. (J). 23.60 *(978-1-4994-0155-4(8),* PowerKids Pr.) Rosen Publishing Group, Inc., The.

Kelsey, Elin. You Are Stardust. Kim, Soyeon, illus. 2012. (ENG.). 32p. (J). (gr. 1-4). 18.95 *(978-1-926973-35-7(6))* Owlkids Bks. Inc. CAN. Dist: Publishers Group West (PGW).

The Kid's Book of Awesome Stuff. 2004. (J). spiral bd. *(978-0-9762568-0-9(0))* Brotman-Marshfield Curriculums.

King, Zelda. Examining Backyard Habitats. 2009. (Graphic Organizers: Habitats Ser.). 24p. (gr. 2-4). (Illus.). (J). pap. 8.25 *(978-1-4358-3124-7(1));* 42.50 *(978-1-61513-088-7(8));* (J). lib. bdg. 22.60 *(978-1-4358-2720-2(1))* Rosen Publishing Group, Inc., The. (PowerKids Pr.).

—Examining Desert Habitats. 2009. (Graphic Organizers: Habitats Ser.). 24p. (gr. 2-4). (Illus.). (J). pap. 8.25 *(978-1-4358-3125-4(X),* 1291756); 42.50 *(978-1-61513-091-7(8));* (J). lib. bdg. 22.60 *(978-1-4358-2721-9(X))* Rosen Publishing Group, Inc., The. (PowerKids Pr.).

—Examining Meadow Habitats. 2009. (Graphic Organizers: Habitats Ser.). (Illus.). 24p. (J). (gr. 2-4). pap. 8.25 *(978-1-4358-3126-1(8),* PowerKids Pr.) Rosen Publishing Group, Inc., The.

—Examining Pond Habitats. 2009. (Graphic Organizers: Habitats Ser.). 24p. (gr. 2-3). 42.50 *(978-1-61513-100-6(0),* PowerKids Pr.) Rosen Publishing Group, Inc., The.

—Examining Tide Pool Habitats. 2009. (Graphic Organizers: Habitats Ser.). 24p. (J). (gr. 2-4). (Illus.). pap. 8.25 *(978-1-4358-3123-0(3));* lib. bdg. 22.60 *(978-1-4358-2719-6(8))* Rosen Publishing Group, Inc., The. (PowerKids Pr.).

Knight, M. J. Why Should I Care about Nature? 2009. (One Small Step Ser.). (YA). (gr. 2-5). 27.10 *(978-1-59920-266-2(2))* Black Rabbit Bks.

Knowlton, Laurie Lazzaro. Come on Down. Brown, Kevin, illus. 2005. (J). *(978-1-933248-07-3(6))* World Quest Learning.

Kochanoff, Peggy. Be a Pond Detective, 1 vol. 2016. (ENG., Illus.). 40p. (J). (gr. -1-4). pap. 14.95 *(978-1-77108-394-2(8))* Nimbus Publishing, Ltd. CAN. Dist: Orca Bk. Pubs. USA.

Koellhoffer, Tara, ed. The Environment. 2006. (Science News for Kids Ser.). (Illus.). 144p. (gr. 4-6). lib. bdg. 30.00 *(978-0-7910-9123-4(6),* Chelsea Clubhouse) Facts On File, Inc.

Koerner, Sandy, et al. Water Adventures Around the World, 10 vols. 2008. (ENG.). 30p. (J). (gr. 3-5). pap. 25.00 *(978-1-58321-558-6(1))* American Water Works Assn.

Kopp, Megan. Rivers & Lakes Inside Out. 2015. (ENG., Illus.). 32p. (J). *(978-0-7787-1499-6(3))* Crabtree Publishing Co.

—What Do You Find in a Tide Pool? 2016. (ENG., Illus.). 24p. (J). *(978-0-7787-2263-2(5))* Crabtree Publishing Co.

Kroll, Jennifer. Counting: Earth's Biomes (Level 2) 2017. (Exploring Reading Ser.). (Illus.). 28p. (J). (gr. 2-2). pap. 6.99 ***(978-1-4258-4968-9(7))*** Teacher Created Materials, Inc.

Labrecque, Ellen. Arctic Tundra, 1 vol. 2014. (Earth's Last Frontiers Ser.). (ENG.). 32p. (gr. 1-3). lib. bdg. 29.99 *(978-1-4109-6177-8(X),* Read Me!) Heinemann-Raintree.

—Earth's Last Frontiers, 1 vol. 2014. (Earth's Last Frontiers Ser.). (ENG.). 32p. (gr. 1-3). lib. bdg. 119.96 *(978-1-4109-6181-5(8),* Read Me!) Heinemann-Raintree.

—Jungle Worlds, 1 vol. 2014. (Earth's Last Frontiers Ser.). (ENG.). 32p. (gr. 1-3). lib. bdg. 29.99 *(978-1-4109-6180-8(X),* Read Me!) Heinemann-Raintree.

—Living Beside a River. 2015. (Places We Live Ser.). (ENG., Illus.). 32p. (gr. 1-3). 27.32 *(978-1-4846-0801-2(1),* Heinemann First Library) Heinemann-Raintree.

—Living in a Desert. 2015. (Places We Live Ser.). (ENG., Illus.). 32p. (gr. 1-3). 27.32 *(978-1-4846-0802-9(X),* Heinemann First Library) Heinemann-Raintree.

—Living on a Mountain. 2015. (Places We Live Ser.). (ENG., Illus.). 32p. (gr. 1-3). 27.32 *(978-1-4846-0806-7(2),* Heinemann First Library) Heinemann-Raintree.

Lane, Brian, et al. Ecology. 2005. (DK Eyewitness Bks.). (ENG., Illus.). 72p. (J). (gr. 3-7). 16.99 *(978-0-7566-1387-7(6),* DK Children) Dorling Kindersley Publishing, Inc.

Lantz, Peggy Sias & Hale, Wendy A. The Coastlines of Florida. 2014. (Florida Water Story Ser.). (ENG., Illus.). 34p. (J). (gr. 4). pap. 6.95 *(978-1-56164-702-6(0))* Pineapple Pr., Inc.

Laplante, Walter. Conserving the Great Lakes. 2014. (Exploring the Great Lakes Ser.). 32p. (J). (gr. 3-6). pap. 63.00 *(978-1-4824-1190-4(3))* Stevens, Gareth Publishing LLLP.

—Plants & Animals of the Great Lakes. 2014. (Exploring the Great Lakes Ser.). 32p. (J). (gr. 3-6). pap. 63.00 *(978-1-4824-1193-5(8))* Stevens, Gareth Publishing LLLP.

LaPlante, Walter. There Are Grasslands in My Backyard! 2016. (Backyard Biomes Ser.). 00024p. (J). pap. 8.15 *(978-1-4824-5551-9(X))* Stevens, Gareth Publishing LLLP.

Latham, Donna. Amazing Biome Projects. Rizvi, Farah, illus. 2009. (Build It Yourself Ser.). (ENG.). 128p. (J). (gr. 3-7). 21.95 *(978-1-934670-40-8(5))* Octavio Publishing.

—Amazing Biome Projects: You Can Build Yourself. Rizvi, Farah, illus. 2009. (Build It Yourself Ser.). (ENG.). 128p. (J). (gr. 3-7). pap. 15.95 *(978-1-934670-39-2(1))* Octavio Publishing.

Latou, Pierre. Who Eats Who in A Food Chain? 2014. (Little Books of Answers: Level F Ser.). (Illus.). 16p. (gr. k-2). pap. 7.95 *(978-1-927136-58-4(X))* Three Crows Media NZL. Dist: RiverStream Publishing.

—Why Can Plants Grow in the Desert? 2014. (Little Books of Answers: Level e Ser.). (Illus.). 16p. (gr. k-2). pap. 7.95 *(978-1-927136-48-5(2))* Three Crows Media NZL. Dist: RiverStream Publishing.

Lauber, Patricia. Who Eats What? Food Chains & Food Webs. Keller, Holly, illus. 2016. (Let's-Read-And-Find-Out Science 2 Ser.). 32p. (J). (gr. -1-3). pap. 6.99 *(978-0-06-238211-5(X))* HarperCollins Pubs.

Lawrence, Debbie & Lawrence, Richard. Properties of Ecosystems. 2009. (God's Design for Chemistry & Ecology Ser.). (Illus.). 144p. (J). pap. 24.99 *(978-1-60092-213-8(9))* Answers in Genesis Ministries.

Lawrence, Ellen. Roseate Spoonbill. 2016. (Swamp Things: Animal Life in a Wetland Ser.). (ENG.). 24p. (J). (gr. -1-3). lib. bdg. 17.95 *(978-1-944102-53-1(1))* Bearport Publishing Co., Inc.

Lawrence, Katherine. Life in the Desert. 2009. (Life in Extreme Environments Ser.). 64p. (gr. 5-8). 53.00 *(978-1-61514-271-2(1),* Rosen Reference) Rosen Publishing Group, Inc., The.

Lawrence, Katherine Drobot. Life in the Desert. 2004. (Life in Extreme Environments Ser.). (Illus.). 64p. (gr. 5-8). lib. bdg. 31.95 *(978-0-8239-3985-5(5),* Rosen Reference) Rosen Publishing Group, Inc., The.

Lazor, Stephanie. Life on the Equator. (Life in Extreme Environments Ser.). 64p. (gr. 5-8). 2009. 53.00 *(978-1-61514-275-0(4))* 2004. (Illus.). lib. bdg. 31.95 *(978-0-8239-3986-2(3))* Rosen Publishing Group, Inc., The. (Rosen Reference).

Leardi, Jeanette. Making Cities Green. 2009. (Going Green Ser.). (Illus.). 32p. (YA). (gr. 3-6). lib. bdg. 25.27 *(978-1-59716-961-5(7))* Bearport Publishing Co., Inc.

Leeson, Cole. Arctic. 2003. (Wild America Habitats Ser.). (Illus.). 24p. (J). 21.20 *(978-1-56711-798-1(8),* Blackbirch Pr., Inc.) Cengage Gale.

—Tidal Flat/Coastal. 2003. (Wild America Habitats Ser.). (Illus.). 24p. (J). 24.94 *(978-1-56711-809-4(7),* Blackbirch Pr., Inc.) Cengage Gale.

Lerner Publishing Group Staff. Habitats: Classroom Set. 2005. (Illus.). (J). (gr. k-2). 16.95 *(978-0-8225-5369-4(4))* Lerner Publishing Group.

LernerClassroom Editors. First Step Nonfiction-Habitats Teaching Guide. 2009. pap. 7.95 *(978-0-8225-5396-0(1))* Lerner Publishing Group.

Leslie, Clare Walker. The Curious Nature Guide: Explore the Natural Wonders All Around You. 2015. (ENG., Illus.). 144p. pap. 14.95 *(978-1-61212-509-1(3))* Storey Publishing, LLC.

Levete, Sarah. Habitats & Wildlife in Danger. 2010. (Protecting Our Planet Ser.). (ENG., Illus.). 32p. (J). (gr. 3-6). *(978-0-7787-5213-4(5));* pap. *(978-0-7787-5230-1(5))* Crabtree Publishing Co.

—Jungle Crash! 2011. (ENG.). 24p. (J). pap. *(978-0-7787-7871-4(1));* (gr. 3-6). *(978-0-7787-7849-3(5))* Crabtree Publishing Co.

—Rain Forest. 2011. (ENG.). 24p. (J). pap. *(978-0-7787-7865-3(7));* (gr. 3-6). *(978-0-7787-7843-1(6))* Crabtree Publishing Co.

Levin, Judy. Life at a High Altitude. (Life in Extreme Environments Ser.). 64p. (gr. 5-8). 2009. 53.00 *(978-1-61514-268-2(1))* 2004. (Illus.). (J). lib. bdg. 31.95 *(978-0-8239-3987-9(1))* Rosen Publishing Group, Inc., The. (Rosen Reference).

Levy, Janey. Discovering Mountains. (World Habitats Ser.). 32p. 2009. (gr. 4-5). 47.90 *(978-1-60854-835-4(X),* PowerKids Pr.) 2007. (Illus.). (YA). (gr. 3-6). lib. bdg. 25.25 *(978-1-4042-3785-8(2))* Rosen Publishing Group, Inc., The.

—Discovering the Arctic Tundra. 2007. (World Habitats Ser.). (Illus.). 32p. (YA). (gr. 3-6). lib. bdg. 25.25 *(978-1-4042-3787-2(9))* Rosen Publishing Group, Inc., The.

—Discovering the Tropical Savanna. 2009. (World Habitats Ser.). 32p. (gr. 4-5). 47.90 *(978-1-60854-837-8(6),* PowerKids Pr.) Rosen Publishing Group, Inc., The.

Lewin, Ted. What Am I? Where Am I? 2013. (I Like to Read(r) Ser.). (ENG.). 24p. (J). (gr. -1-3). 14.95 *(978-0-8234-2856-4(7))* Holiday Hse., Inc.

Lewis, J. Patrick. Earth & You - A Closer View: Nature's Features. Canyon, Christopher, illus. 2004. (Sharing Nature with Children Book Ser.). 36p. (J). (gr. -1-3). 16.95 *(978-1-58469-016-0(X));* (gr. 4-7). pap. 7.95 *(978-1-58469-015-3(1))* Dawn Pubns.

—My Home on the Ice. 2017. (Rookie Poetry(tm) — Animal Homes Ser.). (ENG., Illus.). 24p. (J). lib. bdg. 25.00 *(978-0-531-22872-2(X),* Children's Pr.) Scholastic Library Publishing.

Linda Bartlett & Wen Marcec. Keby the Earth-Friendly Bear. 2009. 36p. pap. 21.32 *(978-1-4415-3989-2(1))* Xlibris Corp.

Lindeen, Mary. Ecosystems. 2017. (BeginningtoRead Ser.). (ENG.). 32p. (J). (-2). 22.60 ***(978-1-59953-878-5(4));*** pap. 11.94 ***(978-1-68404-097-1(3))*** Norwood Hse. Pr.

Lion, David C. La Vida en el Pantano. 2008. (Scholastic News Nonfiction Readers en Espanol Ser.). 24p. (J). pap. 6.95 *(978-0-531-20648-5(3),* Children's Pr.) Scholastic Library Publishing.

Llewellyn, Bridget McGovern. One Child, One Planet: Inspiration for the Young Conservationist. Sams, Carl R., 2nd & Stoick, Jean, photos by. 2009. (Illus.). 48p. (J). 19.95 *(978-0-9841880-0-0(2))* Emerald Shamrock Pr. LLC.

Llewellyn, Claire. Food Webs: Who Eats What?, 1 vol. 2014. (Show Me Science Ser.). (ENG., Illus.). 32p. (gr. 3-5). pap. 8.95 *(978-1-4329-8757-2(7));* lib. bdg. 30.65 *(978-1-4329-8750-3(X))* Heinemann-Raintree. (Raintree Perspectives).

Lorbiecki, Marybeth. Planet Patrol: A Kids' Action Guide to Earth Care. Meyers, Nancy, illus. 2005. (ENG.). 48p. (J). (gr. 4-7). 15.95 *(978-1-58728-514-1(2))* Cooper Square Publishing Llc.

Lovejoy, Sharon. The Little Green Island with a Little Red House: A Book of Colors & Critters. 2015. (ENG., Illus.). 32p. (J). (gr. -1-2). 10.95 *(978-1-60893-464-5(0))* Down East Bks.

Lowery, Lawrence F. Environments of Our Earth: I Wonder Why. 2013. (I Wonder Why Ser.). (ENG., Illus.). 23p. (J). (gr. k-3). pap. 11.95 *(978-1-938946-15-8(4))* National Science Teachers Assn.

Lunde, Darrin P. After the Kill. Stock, Catherine, illus. 2011. (ENG.). 32p. (J). (gr. 1-4). 16.95 *(978-1-57091-743-1(4));* pap. 7.95 *(978-1-57091-744-8(2))* Charlesbridge Publishing, Inc.

Lundgren, Julie K. How Ecosystems Work. 2012. (ENG.). 24p. (gr. 3-4). pap. 8.95 *(978-1-61810-220-1(6))* Rourke Educational Media.

—What's on the Food Chain Menu? 2011. (ENG., Illus.). 24p. (gr. 2-3). pap. 8.95 *(978-1-61741-947-8(8))* Rourke Educational Media.

Lynch, Seth. There's a Swamp in My Backyard! 2016. (Backyard Biomes Ser.). 00024p. (J). pap. 8.15 ***(978-1-4824-5571-7(4))*** Stevens, Gareth Publishing LLLP.

Lynch, Wayne. Arctic Alphabet: Exploring the North from A to Z. Lynch, Wayne, photos by. 2006. (Illus.). 32p. (J). (gr. k-4). reprint ed. 20.00 *(978-1-4223-5190-1(4))* DIANE Publishing Co.

—Sonoran Desert. 2009. (ENG.). 64p. (J). (gr. 3-7). 16.95 *(978-1-58979-389-7(7))* Taylor Trade Publishing.

Lynette, Rachel. Mountain Food Chains, 1 vol. 2010. (Protecting Food Chains Ser.). (ENG.). 48p. (gr. 3-6). 33.32 *(978-1-4329-3858-1(4));* pap. 9.95 *(978-1-4329-3865-9(7))* Heinemann-Raintree. (Heinemann InfoSearch).

—River Food Chains, 1 vol. 2010. (Protecting Food Chains Ser.). (ENG.). 48p. (gr. 3-6). 33.32 *(978-1-4329-3861-1(4));* pap. 9.95 *(978-1-4329-3868-0(1))* Heinemann-Raintree. (Heinemann InfoSearch).

MacAulay, Kelley. Les Récifs Coralliens. 2009. (Petit Monde Vivant Ser.). (FRE., Illus.). 32p. (J). pap. 9.95 *(978-2-89579-229-1(1))* Bayard Canada Livres CAN. Dist: Crabtree Publishing Co.

MacAulay, Kelley & Kalman, Bobbie. A Backyard Habitats. 2006. (Introducing Habitats Ser.). (ENG., Illus.). 32p. (J). (gr. -1-3). pap. *(978-0-7787-2985-3(0))* Crabtree Publishing Co.

—Coral Reef Food Chains. 2005. (Food Chains Ser.). (ENG., Illus.). 32p. (J). lib. bdg. *(978-0-7787-1948-9(0));* (gr. 1-5). pap. *(978-0-7787-1994-6(4))* Crabtree Publishing Co.

—Habitats de Jardín. 2007. (Introduction a Los Habitats Ser.). (SPA., Illus.). 32p. (J). (gr. 3-7). lib. bdg. *(978-0-7787-8335-0(9))* Crabtree Publishing Co.

—Hábitats de Jardín. rev. ed. 2007. (Introduction a Los Habitats Ser.). (SPA., Illus.). 32p. (J). (gr. k-3). pap. *(978-0-7787-8359-6(6))* Crabtree Publishing Co.

—Prairie Food Chains. 2005. (Food Chains Ser.). (ENG., Illus.). 32p. (J). pap. *(978-0-7787-1993-9(6))* Crabtree Publishing Co.

—Tundra Food Chains. 2005. (Food Chains Ser.). (ENG., Illus.). 32p. (J). (gr. 1-5). pap. *(978-0-7787-1992-2(8))* Crabtree Publishing Co.

Macken, JoAnn Early. Coral Reefs. 2005. (Water Habitats Ser.). (Illus.). 24p. (gr. k-3). pap. 8.15 *(978-0-8368-4890-8(X));* lib. bdg. 22.00 *(978-0-8368-4883-0(7))* Stevens, Gareth Publishing LLLP. (Weekly Reader Leveled Readers).

—Rivers. 2005. (Water Habitats Ser.). (Illus.). 24p. (gr. k-3). pap. 8.15 *(978-0-8368-4893-9(4));* lib. bdg. 22.00 *(978-0-8368-4886-1(1))* Stevens, Gareth Publishing LLLP. (Weekly Reader Leveled Readers).

Mani, Anamika & Mani, Anu. Grooming Is Fun! 2013. 26p. 22.00 *(978-0-9893751-6-0(1))* CuriousDots.

Mann, Charles. 1493 for Young People: From Columbus's Voyage to Globalization. 2016. (For Young People Ser.). (ENG., Illus.). 416p. (J). (gr. 7). pap. 18.95 *(978-1-60980-663-7(8),* Triangle Square) Seven Stories Pr.

Markle, Sandra. The Great Monkey Rescue: Saving the Golden Lion Tamarins. 2015. (ENG., Illus.). 40p. (gr. 4-6). (J). 30.65 *(978-1-4677-8030-8(8));* 30.65 *(978-1-4677-8850-2(3))* Lerner Publishing Group. (Millbrook Pr.).

Mason, Adrienne. Planet Ark: Preserving Earth's Biodiversity. Thompson, Margot, illus. 2013. (CitizenKid Ser.). (ENG.). 32p. (J). (gr. 3-7). 18.95 *(978-1-55453-753-2(3))* Kids Can Pr., Ltd. CAN. Dist: Hachette Bk. Group.

Mattern, Joanne. Que Comen los Animales del Bosque?/What Forest Animals Eat. 2006. (Nature's Food Chains/ Las cadenas alimentarias en la naturaleza Ser.). (SPA., Illus.). 24p. (gr. k-3). lib. bdg. 22.00 *(978-0-8368-7372-6(6),* Weekly Reader Leveled Readers) Stevens, Gareth Publishing LLLP.

—What Desert Animals Eat. 2006. (Nature's Food Chains Ser.). (Illus.). 24p. (gr. k-3). pap. 8.15 *(978-0-8368-6877-7(3));* lib. bdg. 22.00 *(978-0-8368-6870-8(6))* Stevens, Gareth Publishing LLLP. (Weekly Reader Leveled Readers).

—What Desert Animals Eat (¿Qué comen los animales del Desierto?) 2006. (Nature's Food Chains/ Las cadenas alimentarias en la naturaleza Ser.). (SPA., Illus.). 24p. (gr. k-3). lib. bdg. 22.00 *(978-0-8368-7371-9(8),* Weekly Reader Leveled Readers) Stevens, Gareth Publishing LLLP.

—What Desert Animals Eat/Que Comen los Animales Del Desierto? Qué Comen los Animales Del Desierto? 2006. (Nature's Food Chains/ Las cadenas alimentarias en la naturaleza Ser.). (ENG & SPA., Illus.). 24p. (gr. k-3). pap. 8.15 *(978-0-8368-7378-8(5),* Weekly Reader Leveled Readers) Stevens, Gareth Publishing LLLP.

—What Forest Animals Eat. 2006. (Nature's Food Chains Ser.). (Illus.). 24p. (gr. k-3). pap. 8.15 *(978-0-8368-6878-4(1));* lib. bdg. 22.00 *(978-0-8368-6871-5(4))* Stevens, Gareth Publishing LLLP. (Weekly Reader Leveled Readers).

—What Forest Animals Eat/¿Qué Comen los Animales del Bosque? 2006. (Nature's Food Chains/ Las cadenas alimentarias en la naturaleza Ser.). (ENG & SPA., Illus.). 24p. (gr. k-3). pap. 8.15 *(978-0-8368-7379-5(3),* Weekly Reader Leveled Readers) Stevens, Gareth Publishing LLLP.

—What Grassland Animals Eat. 2006. (Nature's Food Chains Ser.). (Illus.). 24p. (gr. k-3). lib. bdg. 22.00 *(978-0-8368-6872-2(2),* Weekly Reader Leveled Readers) Stevens, Gareth Publishing LLLP.

—What Grassland Animals Eat: Qué Comen los Animales de Las Praderas? 2006. (Nature's Food Chains/ Las cadenas alimentarias en la naturaleza Ser.). (ENG & SPA., Illus.). 24p. (gr. k-3). pap. 8.15 *(978-0-8368-7380-1(7),* Weekly Reader Leveled Readers) Stevens, Gareth Publishing LLLP.

—What Grassland Animals Eat (¿Qué Comen Los Animales de Las Praderas?) 2006. (Nature's Food Chains/ Las cadenas alimentarias en la naturaleza Ser.). (SPA., Illus.). 24p. (gr. k-3). lib. bdg. 22.00 *(978-0-8368-7373-3(4),* Weekly Reader Leveled Readers) Stevens, Gareth Publishing LLLP.

—What Polar Animals Eat: Qué Comen los Animales de los Polos? 2006. (Nature's Food Chains/ Las cadenas alimentarias en la naturaleza Ser.). (ENG & SPA., Illus.). 24p. (gr. k-3). pap. 8.15 *(978-0-8368-7381-8(5),* Weekly Reader Leveled Readers) Stevens, Gareth Publishing LLLP.

—What Polar Animals Eat/¿Qué Comen los Animales de los Polos? 2006. (Nature's Food Chains/ Las cadenas alimentarias en la naturaleza Ser.). (SPA., Illus.). 24p. (gr. k-3). lib. bdg. 22.00 *(978-0-8368-7374-0(2),* Weekly Reader Leveled Readers) Stevens, Gareth Publishing LLLP.

—What River Animals Eat (¿Qué comen los animales de los Ríos?) 2006. (Nature's Food Chains/ Las cadenas alimentarias en la naturaleza Ser.). (Illus.). 24p. (gr. k-3). (ENG & SPA.). pap. 8.15 *(978-0-8368-7382-5(3));* (SPA., lib. bdg. 22.00 *(978-0-8368-7375-7(0))* Stevens, Gareth Publishing LLLP. (Weekly Reader Leveled Readers).

—What Sea Animals Eat: Qué Comen los Animales del Mar? 2006. (Nature's Food Chains/ Las cadenas alimentarias en la naturaleza Ser.). (ENG & SPA., Illus.). 24p. (gr. k-3). pap. 8.15 *(978-0-8368-7383-2(1),* Weekly Reader Leveled Readers) Stevens, Gareth Publishing LLLP.

—What Sea Animals Eat/¿Qué Comen los Animales del Mar? 2006. (Nature's Food Chains/ Las cadenas alimentarias en la naturaleza Ser.). (SPA., Illus.). 24p. (gr. k-3). lib. bdg. 22.00 *(978-0-8368-7376-4(9),* Weekly Reader Leveled Readers) Stevens, Gareth Publishing LLLP.

Matthews, Sheelagh. Canadian Shield. 2010. (Illus.). 32p. *(978-1-55388-628-0(3));* pap. *(978-1-55388-629-7(1))* Weigl Educational Pubs. Ltd.

McAllan, Kate. Arctic & Antarctic Habitats. 2013. (Discovery Education: Habitats Ser.). 32p. (J). (gr. 3-6). 25.25 *(978-1-4777-1323-5(9));* pap. 10.00 *(978-1-4777-1481-2(2))* Rosen Publishing Group, Inc., The. (PowerKids Pr.).

McCarthy, Cecilia Pinto. Tundra Ecosystems. 2018. (ENG.). 32p. (gr. 3-6). ***(978-1-63235-459-4(4),*** 12-Story Library) Pr. Room Editions LLC.

McDonald, Megan. Judy Moody Salva el Planeta. Reynolds, Peter H., illus. 2005. (SPA.). 74p. (J). (gr. 3-5). pap. 7.95 *(978-1-59437-838-6(X))* Ediciones Alfaguara ESP. Dist: Two Rivers Distribution.

McKissack, Fredrick L. & McKissack, Lisa Beringer. Counting in the Desert. 2008. (Counting in the Biomes Ser.). (Illus.). 32p. (J). (gr. 3-7). lib. bdg. 23.94 *(978-0-7660-2988-0(3),* Enslow Elementary) Enslow Pubs., Inc.

Meachen Rau, Dana. Deserts. 2007. (Wonders of Nature Ser.). (SPA & ENG.). 32p. (gr. 1-2). lib. bdg. 15.95 *(978-0-7614-2667-7(1),* Benchmark Bks.) Marshall Cavendish Corp.

—En la Playa. 2007. (¡A Divertirnos! Ser.). (SPA., Illus.). 24p. (gr. k-1). lib. bdg. 15.95 *(978-0-7614-2748-3(1),* Benchmark Bks.) Marshall Cavendish Corp.

Medina, Nico. Where Is the Great Barrier Reef? Hinderliter, John, illus. 2016. (Where Is? Ser.). (ENG.). 112p. (J). (gr. 3-7). pap. 5.99 *(978-0-448-48699-4(7),* Grosset & Dunlap) Penguin Young Readers Group.

Meredith, Susan Markowitz. Environmentally Friendly World. 2011. (Early Connections Ser.). (J). *(978-1-61672-661-4(X))* Benchmark Education Co.

Messner, Kate. Over & under the Pond. Neal, Christopher Silas, illus. 2017. (ENG.). 48p. (J). 16.99 *(978-1-4521-4542-6(3))* Chronicle Bks. LLC.

Miché, Mary. Nature's Patchwork Quilt: Understanding Habitats. Powell, Consie, illus. 2012. 32p. (J). (gr. k-6). 16.95 *(978-1-58469-169-3(7));* (ENG.). pap. 8.95 *(978-1-58469-170-9(0))* Dawn Pubns.

Miller, Mirella S. Desert Ecosystems. 2018. (ENG.). 32p. (gr. 3-6). ***(978-1-63235-454-9(3),*** 12-Story Library) Pr. Room Editions LLC.

Miller-Schroeder, Patricia. The Science of the Environment. 2003. (Living Science Ser.). (Illus.). 32p. (J). (gr. 1-3). pap. 9.95 *(978-1-930954-21-2(2))* Weigl Pubs., Inc.

Mis, Melody S. Exploring Caves. 2009. (Geography Zone: Landforms Ser.). (J). lib. bdg. 22.60 *(978-1-4358-2713-4(9),* PowerKids Pr.) Rosen Publishing Group, Inc., The.

—Exploring Glaciers. 2009. (Geography Zone: Landforms Ser.). (Illus.). 24p. (J). (gr. 2-4). pap. 8.25 *(978-1-4358-3112-4(8));* 24p. (gr. 2-3). 42.50 *(978-1-61512-698-9(8));* (J). lib. bdg. 22.60 *(978-1-4358-2714-1(7))* Rosen Publishing Group, Inc., The. (PowerKids Pr.).

Monroe, Elliot. Interdependence of Species. 2016. (Spotlight on Ecology & Life Science Ser.). 00024p. (J). (gr. 4-6). pap. 10.00 *(978-1-4994-2595-6(3),* PowerKids Pr.) Rosen Publishing Group, Inc., The.

Montgomery, Heather L. How Is Soil Made? 2010. (Everybody Digs Soil Ser.). (ENG., Illus.). 32p. (J). (gr. 3-6). pap. *(978-0-7787-5414-5(6))* Crabtree Publishing Co.

Montgomery, Sy. Amazon Adventure: How Tiny Fish Are Saving the World's Largest Rainforest. Ellenbogen, Keith, photos by. 2017. (Scientists in the Field Ser.). (ENG., Illus.). 80p. (J). (gr. 5-7). 18.99 *(978-0-544-35299-5(8),* HMH Books For Young Readers) Houghton Mifflin Harcourt Publishing Co.

Mooney, Carla. Explore Rivers & Ponds! With 25 Great Projects. Stone, Bryan, illus. 2012. (Explore Your World Ser.). (ENG.). 96p. (J). (gr. k-4). pap. 12.95 *(978-1-936749-80-5(7))* Open City Bks.

Moore Niver, Heather. A Trip Through a Coral Reef. 2015. (Fantastic Science Journeys Ser.). (ENG., Illus.). 32p. (J). (gr. 2-3). pap. 10.50 *(978-1-4824-2002-9(3))* Stevens, Gareth Publishing LLLP.

—Viaje Dentro de un Arrecife de Coral (a Trip Through a Coral Reef) 2015. (Maravillosos Viajes a Través de la Ciencia (Fantastic Science Journeys) Ser.). (SPA.). 32p. (J). (gr. 2-3). 25.25 *(978-1-4824-2019-7(8))* Stevens, Gareth Publishing LLLP.

Moore, Peter D. Tundra. Garratt, Richard, illus. 2007. (Ecosystems Ser.). 224p. (C). (gr. 9). 70.00 *(978-0-8160-5933-1(0))* Facts On File, Inc.

Morgan, Sally. Food Chains. 2016. (ENG.). 48p. (J). pap. 9.95 *(978-0-00-816389-1(8))* HarperCollins Pubs. Ltd. GBR. Dist: Independent Pubs. Group.

—The Food Cycle. 2009. (Nature's Cycles Ser.). (J). (ENG.). 32p. (gr. 4-6). pap. 10.00 *(978-1-4358-2948-0(4));* lib. bdg. 26.50 *(978-1-4358-2866-7(6))* Rosen Publishing Group, Inc., The. (PowerKids Pr.).

—Under a Stone & Other Rocky Places. 2006. (Hidden Habitats Ser.). (J). *(978-1-59389-285-2(3))* Chrysalis Education.

Morrison, Jessica. Cordillera. 2010. (Illus.). 32p. *(978-1-55388-634-1(8));* pap. *(978-1-55388-635-8(6))* Weigl Educational Pubs. Ltd.

—Maritimes. 2010. (Illus.). 32p. (978-1-55388-637-2(2)); pap. (978-1-55388-638-9(0)) Weigl Educational Pubs. Ltd.

Morrison, Yvonne. Earth Matters. 2007. (Shockwave: People & Communities Ser.). (ENG., Illus.). 36p. (J). (gr. 4-6). lib. bdg. 25.00 (978-0-531-17747-1(5), Children's Pr.) Scholastic Library Publishing.

Mullins, Matt. Super Cool Science Experiments: Ecosystems. 2009. (Explorer Library: Science Explorer Ser.). (ENG.). 32p. (gr. 4-8). lib. bdg. 28.50 (978-1-60279-516-7(9), 200300) Cherry Lake Publishing.

Munro, Roxie. Desert Days, Desert Nights. 2010. (ENG.). 32p. (J). 17.95 (978-1-933979-77-9(1), 7eb1e541-2180-4d1b-847f-abe71cd7cdcd) Bright Sky Pr.

Murray, Aaron R. Counting in the Tundra 1-2-3. 2012. (All about Counting in the Biomes Ser.). (Illus.). (J). 24p. pap. 7.95 (978-1-4644-0064-3(4)); 24p. (gr. -1-1). 22.60 (978-0-7660-4056-4(9)); 23p. E-Book (978-1-4645-0971-1(9)) Enslow Pubs., Inc.

Murray, Julie. Home, 1 vol. 2009. (That's Gross!:A Look at Science Ser.). (ENG., Illus.). 32p. (J). (gr. 2-5). 28.50 (978-1-60453-555-6(5)) ABDO Publishing Co.

Myers, Jenna. Australia. 2014. (J). (978-1-4896-0946-5(6)) Weigl Pubs., Inc.

Nadeau, Isaac. Interdependence of Organisms & Environments. 2006. (Life Science Library). (Illus.). 24p. (YA). (gr. 3-6). 22.60 (978-1-4042-2819-1(5)) Rosen Publishing Group, Inc., The.

—Interdependence of Organisms & the Environment. 2009. (Life Science Library). 24p. (gr. 3-4). 42.50 (978-1-60854-007-5(3), PowerKids Pr.) Rosen Publishing Group, Inc., The.

National Geographic Kids Staff. Explore the World! Packed with Animals Fun Facts, Games, Maps, & More! 2014. (ENG., Illus.). 104p. (J). (gr. 3-7). pap. 9.99 (978-1-4263-1810-8(3), National Geographic Children's Bks.) National Geographic Society.

National Geographic Learning Staff. Saguaro Moon: A Desert Journal. Pratt-Serafini, Kristin Joy, illus. 2010. (Rise & Shine Ser.). (ENG.). 32p. (C). pap. 14.95 (978-1-58469-036-8(4)) National Geographic School Publishing, Inc.

New Careers for the 21st Century: Finding Your Role in the Global Renewal, 15 vols., Set. Incl. Environmental Science & Protection: Keeping Our Planet Green. Strange, Cordelia. pap. 9.95 (978-1-4222-2034-4(6)); Freelance & Technical Writers: Words for Sale. Flath, Camden. pap. 9.95 (978-1-4222-2035-1(4)); Green Construction: Creating Energy-Efficient, Low-Impact Buildings. Miller, Malinda. pap. 9.95 (978-1-4222-2036-8(2)); Medical Technicians: Health-Care Support for the 21st Century. Strange, Cordelia. pap. 9.95 (978-1-4222-2038-2(9)); Modern Mechanics: Maintaining Tomorrow's Green Vehicles. Miller, Malinda. pap. 9.95 (978-1-4222-2039-9(7)); Pharmaceutical Industry: Better Medicine for the 21st Century. Miller, Malinda. pap. 9.95 (978-1-4222-2040-5(0)); Physicians Assistants & Nurses: New Opportunities in the 21st-Century Health System. Strange, Cordelia. pap. 9.95 (978-1-4222-2041-2(9)); Social Workers: Finding Solutions for Tomorrow's Society. Flath, Camden. (Illus.). pap. 9.95 (978-1-4222-2042-9(7)); Therapy Jobs in Educational Settings: Speech, Physical, Occupational & Audiology. Flath, Camden. (Illus.). pap. 9.95 (978-1-4222-2047-4(8)); Tomorrow's Enterprising Scientists: Computer Software Designers & Specialists. Flath, Camden. pap. 9.95 (978-1-4222-2043-6(5)); Tomorrow's Teachers: Urban Leadership, Empowering Students & Improving Lives. Miller, Malinda. pap. 9.95 (978-1-4222-2044-3(3)); Tomorrow's Transportation: Green Solutions for Air, Land, & Sea. Miller, Malinda. pap. 9.95 (978-1-4222-2045-0(1)); 21st-Century Counselors: New Approaches to Mental Health & Substance Abuse. Flath, Camden. pap. 9.95 (978-1-4222-2046-7(X)); 64p. (YA). (gr. 7-18). 2010. 2011. Set pap. 149.25 (978-1-4222-2032-0(X)) Mason Crest.

Nicole, Heather. What Is a Food Chain? 2006. (Science Leveled Readers Ser.). (ENG., Illus.). 8p. (gr. k-k). pap. 5.40 (978-0-15-365337-7(X)) Harcourt Schl. Pubs.

Niver, Heather Moore. Tributaries of the Chesapeake Bay. 2013. (Exploring the Chesapeake Bay Ser.). (Illus.). 32p. (J). (gr. 3-6). pap. 10.50 (978-1-4339-9793-8(2)); lib. bdg. 26.60 (978-1-4339-9792-1(4)) Stevens, Gareth Publishing LLLP.

Nsrc. Science & Technology for Children Books: Land & Water. 2004. (Illus.). 64p. (J). (978-1-933008-01-1(6)) Smithsonian Science Education Ctr. (SSEC).

O'Donnell, Kerri. Denali National Park: An Alaskan Ecosystem: Creating Graphical Representations of Data. 2009. (PowerMath: Advanced Proficiency Plus Ser.). 32p. (gr. 5-5). 47.90 (978-1-60851-353-6(X), PowerKids Pr.) Rosen Publishing Group, Inc., The.

—Denali National Park, an Alaskan Ecosystem: Creating Graphical Representations of Data. (Math for the Real World Ser.). (Illus.). 32p. 2009. (ENG.). (gr. 6-7). pap. 10.00 (978-1-4042-6083-2(8)) 2006. (J). lib. bdg. 23.95 (978-1-4042-3365-2(2)) Rosen Publishing Group, Inc., The.

O'Donnell, Liam & Anderson, Bill. The World of Food Chains with Max Axiom, Super Scientist. Martin, Cynthia, illus. 2016. (Graphic Science Ser.). (ENG.). 32p. (gr. 3-4). pap. 8.10 (978-1-5157-4642-3(9), Graphic Library) Capstone Press of Coughlan Cos.

Die Oekologie. (Duden-Schuelerduden Ser.). (GER., Illus.). 368p. (YA). 27.95 (978-3-411-02240-3(X)) Bibliographisches Institut & F. A. Brockhaus AG DEU. Dist: Continental Bk. Co., Inc.

Orme, Helen. Habitat Destruction. 2008. (Earth in Danger Ser.). (Illus.). 32p. (YA). (gr. 3-6). lib. bdg. 25.27 (978-1-59716-725-3(8), 1284353) Bearport Publishing Co., Inc.

Owen, Ruth. How Do Animals Help Plants Reproduce? 2014. (World of Plants Ser.). 32p. (J). (gr. 2-5). 26.25 (978-1-4777-7141-9(7), PowerKids Pr.) Rosen Publishing Group, Inc., The.

—Welcome to the Backyard. 2016. (Nature's Neighborhoods: All about Ecosystems Ser.: 4). (ENG.). 32p. (J). (gr. -1-3). lib. bdg. 19.95 (978-1-910549-62-9(2)) Bearport Publishing Co., Inc.

—Zoologists & Ecologists. 2013. (Out of the Lab: Extreme Jobs in Science Ser.). 32p. (J). (gr. 3-6). 25.25 (978-1-4777-1293-1(3)); pap. 10.00 (978-1-4777-1384-6(0)) Rosen Publishing Group, Inc., The. (PowerKids Pr.).

Oxlade, Chris. Environment Infographics, 1 vol. 2014. (Infographics Ser.). (ENG.). 32p. (gr. 1-3). lib. bdg. 29.99 (978-1-4109-6217-1(2), Read Me!) Heinemann-Raintree.

Parker, Steve. Survival & Change. (Life Processes Ser.). 32p. pap. 7.50 (978-1-4034-4076-1(X)) Heinemann-Raintree.

Pascoe, Elaine. The Ecosystem of a Garden. (Library of Small Ecosystems Ser.). 24p. 2009. (gr. 3-4). 47.90 (978-1-60853-852-2(4)) 2003. (Illus.). (J). lib. bdg. 25.25 (978-0-8239-6306-5(3)) Rosen Publishing Group, Inc., The. (PowerKids Pr.).

—The Ecosystem of a Grassy Field. 2003. (Library of Small Ecosystems Ser.). (Illus.). 24p. (J). lib. bdg. 25.25 (978-0-8239-6305-8(5), PowerKids Pr.) Rosen Publishing Group, Inc., The.

—The Ecosystem of a Milkweed Patch. (Library of Small Ecosystems Ser.). 24p. 2009. (gr. 3-4). 47.90 (978-1-60853-854-6(0), PowerKids Pr.) 2003. (Illus.). (J). lib. bdg. 25.25 (978-0-8239-6309-6(8)) Rosen Publishing Group, Inc., The.

—The Ecosystem of a Stream. 2009. (Library of Small Ecosystems Ser.). (ENG., Illus.). 32p. (J). (gr. k-5). pap. 9.40 (978-1-4358-3269-5(8), PowerKids Pr.) Rosen Publishing Group, Inc., The.

—The Ecosystem of an Apple Tree. (Library of Small Ecosystems Ser.). 24p. 2009. (gr. 3-4). 47.90 (978-1-60853-860-7(5)) 2003. (Illus.). (J). lib. bdg. 25.25 (978-0-8239-6304-1(7)) Rosen Publishing Group, Inc., The. (PowerKids Pr.).

Patent, Dorothy Hinshaw. Life in a Desert. Muñoz, William, illus. Muñoz, William, photos by. 2003. (Ecosystems in Action Ser.). (ENG.). 72p. (gr. 5-9). 26.60 (978-0-8225-2140-2(7)) Lerner Publishing Group.

Patkau, Karen. Who Needs a Desert? A Desert Ecosystem. 2014. (Ecosystem Ser.). (ENG., Illus.). 32p. (J). (gr. 2-5). 17.99 (978-1-77049-386-5(7), Tundra Bks.) Tundra Bks. CAN. Dist: Penguin Random Hse. LLC.

—Who Needs a Prairie? A Grassland Ecosystem. 2014. (Ecosystem Ser.). (ENG., Illus.). 32p. (J). (gr. 2-5). 17.99 (978-1-77049-388-9(3), Tundra Bks.) Tundra Bks. CAN. Dist: Penguin Random Hse. LLC.

—Who Needs a Reef? A Coral Reef Ecosystem. 2014. (Ecosystem Ser.). (ENG., Illus.). 32p. (J). (gr. 2-5). 17.99 (978-1-77049-390-2(5), Tundra Bks.) Tundra Bks. CAN. Dist: Penguin Random Hse. LLC.

—Who Needs an Iceberg? 2012. (Ecosystem Ser.). (ENG., Illus.). 32p. (J). (gr. 2-5). 17.95 (978-0-88776-993-1(4), Tundra Bks.) Tundra Bks. CAN. Dist: Penguin Random Hse. LLC.

Pelletier, Mia. Avati: Discovering Arctic Ecology, 1 vol. Otterstätter, Sara, illus. 2013. (ENG.). 46p. (J). (gr. 2-5). 14.95 (978-1-927095-13-3(1)) Inhabit Media Inc. CAN. Dist: Independent Pubs. Group.

Pemberton, Rose. Inheritance & Variation of Traits. 2016. (Spotlight on Ecology & Life Science Ser.). 00024p. (J). (gr. 4-6). pap. 10.00 (978-1-4994-2569-7(4), PowerKids Pr.) Rosen Publishing Group, Inc., The.

Penguin Books Staff, ed. Ecology. (Learners Ser.). (Illus.). 48p. (J). 3.50 (978-0-7214-1710-3(8), Dutton Juvenile) Penguin Publishing Group.

Pennybacker, Mindy & Streep, Meryl. Do One Green Thing: Saving the Earth Through Simple, Everyday Choices. 2010. (ENG.). 288p. pap. 21.99 (978-0-312-55976-2(3), 9780312559762, St. Martin's Griffin) St. Martin's Pr.

Pettiford, Rebecca. Arctic Food Chains. 2016. (Who Eats What?). 24p. (J). (gr. 2-5). lib. bdg. 25.65 (978-1-62031-300-8(6), Pogo) Jump! Inc.

—Prairie Food Chains. 2016. (Who Eats What?). 24p. (J). (gr. 2-5). lib. bdg. 25.65 (978-1-62031-303-9(0), Pogo) Jump! Inc.

PH Inc. Staff. PH Science Ecology Earth. (J). pap., act. bk. ed. (978-0-13-225582-0(0)) Prentice Hall (Schl. Div.).

Pifer, Joanne. EarthWise: Environmental Learning Series, Vol. II. (Illus.). 192p. (J). (gr. 5-8). 24.95 (978-0-9633019-6-3(9)) WP Pr., Inc.

Piper, Ross. Surviving in the World's Most Extreme Places. 2010. (Extreme! Ser.). (ENG.). 32p. (gr. 3-4). pap. 47.70 (978-1-4296-5121-9(0), Fact Finders) Capstone Press of Coughlan Cos.

Pollan, Michael. The Omnivore's Dilemma: The Secrets Behind What You Eat. 2015. (ENG., Illus.). 400p. (J). (gr. 5). 18.99 (978-1-101-99382-8(0)); pap. 9.99 (978-1-101-99383-5(9)) Penguin Young Readers Group. (Dial Bks).

Porterfield, Jason. Looking at How Species Compete Within Environments with Graphic Organizers. 2009. (Using Graphic Organizers to Study the Living Environment Ser.). 48p. (gr. 6-6). 53.00 (978-1-60854-711-1(6), Rosen Reference) Rosen Publishing Group, Inc., The.

Powell, Debbie. Make It Grow. 2016. (ENG., Illus.). 16p. (J). (gr. -1-2). 14.99 (978-1-84780-789-2(5), Frances Lincoln Children's Bks.) Quarto Publishing Group UK GBR. Dist: Hachette Bk. Group.

Prasadam-Halls, Smriti. In the Garden. Scobie, Lorna, illus. 2017. (Pairs Ser.). (ENG.). 12p. (J). (gr. -1-k). bds. 9.99 (978-1-84780-883-7(2), Frances Lincoln Children's Bks.) Quarto Publishing Group UK GBR. Dist: Hachette Bk. Group.

Pratt, Laura. Arctic. 2010. (Illus.). 32p. (978-1-55388-631-0(3)); pap. (978-1-55388-632-7(1)) Weigl Educational Pubs. Ltd.

—Plains. 2010. (Illus.). 32p. (978-1-55388-625-9(9)); pap. (978-1-55388-626-6(7)) Weigl Educational Pubs. Ltd.

Pratt-Serafini, Kristin Joy. Salamander Rain: A Lake & Pond Journal. 2004. (Sharing Nature with Children Book Ser.). (Illus.). 32p. (YA). (gr. 4-7). 16.95 (978-1-58469-018-4(6)) Dawn Pubns.

Pratt-Serafini, Kristin Joy, illus. Saguaro Moon: A Desert Journal. 2004. (Sharing Nature with Children Book Ser.). 32p. (YA). 16.95 (978-1-58469-037-5(2)) Dawn Pubns.

Pressberg, Dava. Producers, Consumers, & Decomposers. 2016. (Spotlight on Ecology & Life Science Ser.). 00024p. (J). (gr. 4-6). 26.25 (978-1-4994-2594-9(5), PowerKids Pr.) Rosen Publishing Group, Inc., The.

Price, Jane. Underworld: Exploring the Secret World Beneath Your Feet, 0 vols. Hancock, James Gulliver, illus. 2014. (ENG.). 96p. (J). (gr. 3-7). 18.95 (978-1-894786-89-8(0)) Kids Can Pr., Ltd. CAN. Dist: Hachette Bk. Group.

Proujan, Carl & National Geographic Learning Staff. South America - Geography & Environments. 2007. (Reading Expeditions Ser.). (ENG., Illus.). 64p. (J). pap. 25.95 (978-0-7922-4382-3(X)) CENGAGE Learning.

Pyers, Greg. Biodiversity of Alpine Regions. 2011. (Biodiversity 2 Ser.). 32p. (gr. 4). 28.50 (978-1-60870-528-3(5)) Marshall Cavendish Corp.

—Biodiversity of Coasts. 2010. (Biodiversity Ser.). 32p. (gr. 4-18). 28.50 (978-1-60870-069-1(0)) Marshall Cavendish Corp.

—Biodiversity of Coral Reefs. 2010. (Biodiversity Ser.). 32p. (gr. 4-18). 28.50 (978-1-60870-070-7(4)) Marshall Cavendish Corp.

—Biodiversity of Polar Regions. 2010. (Biodiversity Ser.). 32p. (gr. 4-18). 28.50 (978-1-60870-072-1(0)) Marshall Cavendish Corp.

Quattlebaum, Mary. Jo MacDonald Saw a Pond. Bryant, Laura J., illus. 2011. 32p. (J). 16.95 (978-1-58469-150-1(6)); (ENG.). pap. 8.95 (978-1-58469-151-8(4)) Dawn Pubns.

Rabe, Tish. Why Oh Why Are Deserts Dry? All about Deserts. Ruiz, Aristides & Mathieu, Joe, illus. 2011. (Cat in the Hat's Learning Library). (ENG.). 48p. (J). (gr. -1-3). 9.99 (978-0-375-85868-0(7), Random Hse. Bks. for Young Readers) Random Hse. Children's Bks.

Radford, Tracey. Animal Fun Where Do I Live? 2016. (ENG., Illus.). 10p. (J). (gr. 1-4). 6.95 (978-1-78249-399-0(9), 1782493999, CICO Books) Ryland Peters & Small GBR. Dist: WIPRO.

Rafferty, John P. Biomes & Ecosystems. 2011. (Living Earth Ser.). (Illus.). 240p. (YA). (gr. 9-12). lib. bdg. 51.70 (978-1-61530-302-1(2)) Rosen Publishing Group, Inc., The.

Rake, Jody Sullivan. Meerkats, Moles, & Voles: Animals of the Underground. 2015. (Underground Safari Ser.). (ENG., Illus.). 24p. (gr. 1-2). lib. bdg. 25.32 (978-1-4914-5060-4(6)) Capstone Press of Coughlan Cos.

—Soil, Silt, & Sand: Layers of the Underground. 2015. (Underground Safari Ser.). (ENG., Illus.). 24p. (gr. 1-2). lib. bdg. 25.32 (978-1-4914-5063-5(0)) Capstone Press of Coughlan Cos.

Rau, Dana Meachen. Food Chains. 2009. (Bookworms Ser.). 32p. (gr. 1-2). 15.95 (978-0-7614-4095-6(X)) Marshall Cavendish Corp.

—Food Chains/Las Cadenas Alimentarias. 2009. (Bookworms Ser.). (SPA & ENG.). 32p. (gr. 1-2). lib. bdg. 15.95 (978-0-7614-4789-4(X)) Marshall Cavendish Corp.

Reilly, Kathleen M. Planet Earth: 25 Environmental Projects You Can Build Yourself. Rizvi, Farah, illus. 2008. (Build It Yourself Ser.). (ENG.). 128p. (J). (gr. 3-7). 21.95 (978-1-934670-05-7(7)); pap. 15.95 (978-1-934670-04-0(9)) Octavio Publishing.

Rice, Dona. Environment: A World of Change, 1 vol. rev. ed. 2014. (Science Readers: Content & Literacy Ser.). (ENG.). 32p. (gr. 2-2). pap. 8.99 (978-1-4807-4602-2(9)) Teacher Created Materials, Inc.

—Interdependence of Living Things, 1 vol. rev. ed. 2014. (Science Readers: Content & Literacy Ser.). (ENG.). 32p. (gr. 2-2). pap. 8.99 (978-1-4807-4599-5(5)) Teacher Created Materials, Inc.

Rice, William B. Ecosystems, 1 vol. rev. ed. 2014. (Science Readers: Content & Literacy Ser.). (ENG.). 32p. (gr. 2-2). pap. 8.99 (978-1-4807-4600-8(2)) Teacher Created Materials, Inc.

—Habitats, 1 vol. rev. ed. 2014. (Science Readers: Content & Literacy Ser.). (ENG.). 32p. (gr. 2-2). pap. 8.99 (978-1-4807-4601-5(0)) Teacher Created Materials, Inc.

—Life & Non-Life in an Ecosystem. 2015. (Science Readers: Content & Literacy Ser.). (Illus.). 32p. (gr. 5-5). pap. 8.99 (978-1-4807-4716-6(5)) Teacher Created Materials, Inc.

—Life & the Flow of Energy. 2015. (Science Readers: Content & Literacy Ser.). (Illus.). 32p. (J). (gr. 5-5). pap. 8.99 (978-1-4807-4715-9(7)) Teacher Created Materials, Inc.

—Producers & Consumers. 2015. (Science Readers: Content & Literacy Ser.). (ENG., Illus.). 32p. (gr. 4-4). pap. 8.99 (978-1-4807-4677-0(0)) Teacher Created Materials, Inc.

Richardson, Gillian. Ecosystems. 2016. (J). **(978-1-5105-2235-0(2))** SmartBook Media, Inc.

—Ecosystems. 2008. (Science Q & A Ser.). (Illus.). 48p. (YA). (gr. 5-10). lib. bdg. 29.05 (978-1-59036-954-8(8)); pap. 10.95 (978-1-59036-955-5(6)) Weigl Pubs., Inc.

—Ecosystems QandA. 2014. (J). (978-1-62127-413-1(6)) Weigl Pubs., Inc.

—Mountain Extremes. 2008. (Extreme Nature Ser.). (ENG., Illus.). 32p. (J). (gr. 2-3). pap. (978-0-7787-4520-4(1)); lib. bdg. (978-0-7787-4503-7(1)) Crabtree Publishing Co.

Ridley, Kimberly & Raye, Rebekah. The Secret Bay, 1 vol. 2015. (Tilbury House Nature Book Ser.: 0). (ENG., Illus.). 40p. (gr. 1-6). 17.95 (978-0-88448-433-2(5), 884433) Tilbury Hse. Pubs.

Riggs, Kate. Amazing Animals: Vultures. 2015. (Amazing Animals Ser.). (ENG.). 24p. (J). (gr. 1-3). pap. 7.99 (978-1-62832-092-3(3), Creative Paperbacks) Creative Co., The.

—Arctic Tundra. 2010. (Food for Life Ser.). 24p. (J). 16.95 (978-1-58341-831-4(8), Creative Education) Creative Co., The.

—Deserts. 2010. (Food for Life Ser.). 24p. (J). (gr. 1-4). 16.95 (978-1-58341-826-0(1), Creative Education) Creative Co., The.

—Food for Life: Arctic Tundra. 2015. (Food for Life Ser.). (ENG.). 24p. (J). (gr. 1-3). pap. 9.99 (978-1-62832-105-0(9), Creative Paperbacks) Creative Co., The.

—Food for Life: Deserts. 2015. (Food for Life Ser.). (ENG.). 24p. (J). (gr. 1-3). pap. 9.99 (978-1-62832-100-5(8), Creative Paperbacks) Creative Co., The.

—Food for Life: Mountains. 2015. (Food for Life Ser.). (ENG.). 24p. (J). (gr. 1-3). pap. 9.99 (978-1-62832-101-2(6), Creative Paperbacks) Creative Co., The.

—Mountains. 2010. (Food for Life Ser.). 24p. (J). (gr. 1-4). 16.95 (978-1-58341-827-7(X), Creative Education) Creative Co., The.

—Prairies. 2010. (Food for Life Ser.). 24p. (J). 16.95 (978-1-58341-830-7(X), Creative Education) Creative Co., The.

—Vultures. 2015. (Illus.). 24p. (J). (978-1-60818-492-7(7), Creative Education) Creative Co., The.

Riley, Peter. Habitats. 2017. (Ways into Science Ser.). (ENG., Illus.). 32p. (J). (gr. k-2). pap. 11.99 (978-1-4451-3482-6(9), Franklin Watts) Hachette Children's Group GBR. Dist: Hachette Bk. Group.

Rissman, Rebecca. Habitats. 2013. (Look Inside Ser.). (ENG.). 32p. (gr. 1-3). 24.99 (978-1-4329-7214-1(6), NA-h) Heinemann-Raintree.

Rockwell, Anne F. Who Lives in an Alligator Hole? Rockwell, Lizzy, illus. 2006. (Let's-Read-and-Find-Out Science Ser.). 33p. (gr. k-4). 16.00 (978-0-7569-6953-0(0)) Perfection Learning Corp.

Rodger, Ellen. Arctic Research Journal. 2017. (Illus.). 32p. (J). **(978-0-7787-3468-0(4))**; pap. **(978-0-7787-3493-2(5))** Crabtree Publishing Co.

Rose, Naomi C. Where Snow Leopard Prowls: Wild Animals of Tibet. Rose, Naomi C., illus. 2013. (ENG., Illus.). 32p. (J). 17.95 (978-0-9836333-0-3(4)) Dancing Dakini Pr.

Rose, Simon. Estuaries. 2014. (Illus.). 32p. (J). (978-1-62127-485-8(3)) Weigl Pubs., Inc.

—Polar Ice Caps. 2014. (Illus.). 32p. (J). (978-1-62127-486-5(1)) Weigl Pubs., Inc.

Rose, Simon. Polar Regions. 2017. (J). **(978-1-5105-2173-5(9))** SmartBook Media, Inc.

Rosen Publishing Staff. Exploring Food Chains & Food Webs, 1 vol. 2015. (Exploring Food Chains & Food Webs Ser.). (ENG.). 24p. (J). 141.60 (978-1-4777-5738-3(4), PowerKids Pr.) Rosen Publishing Group, Inc., The.

Rosenberg, Pam. Ack! Icky, Sticky, Gross Stuff Underground. Ramos, Beatriz Helena, illus. 2007. (Icky, Sticky, Gross-Out Bks.). (ENG.). 24p. (J). (gr. 3-6). 27.07 (978-1-59296-900-5(3), 200353) Child's World, Inc., The.

Ross, Mandy. Rivers. 2004. (Geography Fact Files Ser.). (J). lib. bdg. 28.50 (978-1-58340-429-4(5)) Black Rabbit Bks.

Roumanis, Alexis. Coral Reefs. 2014. (Illus.). 24p. (J). (978-1-4896-2998-2(X)) Weigl Pubs., Inc.

—Deserts. 2014. (Illus.). 24p. (978-1-4896-3002-5(3)) Weigl Pubs., Inc.

—Mountains. 2014. (Illus.). 24p. (J). (978-1-4896-3010-0(4)) Weigl Pubs., Inc.

Royston, Angela. Desert Food Chains, 1 vol. 2014. (Food Chains & Webs Ser.). (ENG., Illus.). 32p. (gr. 1-3). 27.32 (978-1-4846-0521-9(7), Heinemann First Library) Heinemann-Raintree.

—Food Chains & Webs, 1 vol. 2014. (Food Chains & Webs Ser.). (ENG.). 32p. (gr. 1-3). 163.92 (978-1-4846-0523-3(3), Heinemann First Library) Heinemann-Raintree.

—Hostile Homes: Extreme Habitats. 2015. (Extreme Biology Ser.). (ENG., Illus.). 48p. (J). (gr. 4-4). lib. bdg. 31.95 (978-1-4824-2242-9(5)) Stevens, Gareth Publishing LLLP.

—Mountain Food Chains, 1 vol. 2014. (Food Chains & Webs Ser.). (ENG., Illus.). 32p. (gr. 1-3). 27.32 (978-1-4846-0519-6(5), Heinemann First Library) Heinemann-Raintree.

—River Food Chains, 1 vol. 2014. (Food Chains & Webs Ser.). (ENG., Illus.). 32p. (gr. 1-3). 27.32 (978-1-4846-0520-2(9), Heinemann First Library) Heinemann-Raintree.

Roza, Greg. An Arctic Ecosystem. 2009. (Real Life Readers Ser.). 32p. (gr. 4-5). pap. 10.00 (978-1-4358-0149-3(0), Rosen Classroom); 32p. (gr. 4-4). 47.90 (978-1-60853-033-5(7), PowerKids Pr.); (J). lib. bdg. 25.25 (978-1-4358-2983-1(2), PowerKids Pr.) Rosen Publishing Group, Inc., The.

—Tundra: Life in a Frozen Landscape. 2009. (Biomes of the World Ser.). 48p. (gr. 5-8). (ENG., Illus.). (J). pap. 11.75 (978-1-4358-5428-4(4)); 53.00 (978-1-61511-611-9(7), Rosen Reference); (YA). lib. bdg. 29.25 (978-1-4358-5002-6(5)) Rosen Publishing Group, Inc., The.

Rustad, Martha E. H. Animal Camouflage in the Snow [Scholastic]. 2010. (Hidden in Nature Ser.). pap. 0.52 (978-1-4296-5049-6(4), Pebble Plus) Capstone Press of Coughlan Cos.

—The Driest Places on Earth. 2010. (Extreme Planet Ser.). (ENG.). 24p. (gr. 1-2). lib. bdg. 25.32 (978-1-4296-3962-0(8), First Facts) Capstone Press of Coughlan Cos.

—What's in the Dirt? 2015. (What's in There? Ser.). (ENG., Illus.). 24p. (gr. k-1). lib. bdg. 21.99 (978-1-4914-6012-2(1), Pebble Bks.) Capstone Press of Coughlan Cos.

Ruurs, Margriet. A Mountain Alphabet. Kiss, Andrew, illus. 2009. (ABC Our Country Ser.). (ENG.). 32p. (J). (gr. 1-4). pap. 7.95 (978-0-88776-940-5(3), Tundra Bks.) Tundra Bks. CAN. Dist: Penguin Random Hse. LLC.

Rybolt, Thomas R. & Mebane, Robert C. Science Experiments for Young People, 5 bks., Set. (Illus.). (YA). (gr. 4-9). lib. bdg. 99.75 (978-0-89490-448-6(5)) Enslow Pubs., Inc.

S. Surges, Carol. Food Chains, 1 vol. 2014. (Science of Life Ser.). (ENG.). 48p. (gr. 3-6). lib. bdg. 32.79 (978-1-62403-160-1(9)) ABDO Publishing Co.

Sayre, April Pulley. Exploring Earth's Biomes, 7 vols. Incl. Coral Reef. 80p. lib. bdg. 25.90 (978-0-8050-4087-6(0)); Tundra. 64p. lib. bdg. (978-0-8050-2829-4(3)); (gr. 5-18). 1997. (Illus.). 2004. 310.80 o.p. (978-0-7613-3020-2(8), Twenty-First Century Bks.) Lerner Publishing Group.

—Good Morning, Africa! 2003. 32p. (J). (gr. 2-5). pap. 7.95 (978-0-7613-1993-1(X)); (Celebrate the Continents Ser.: 4). (Illus.). lib. bdg. 21.90 (978-0-7613-2121-7(7)) Lerner Publishing Group. (Millbrook Pr.).

—Trout Are Made of Trees. Endle, Kate, illus. 2008. (ENG.). 32p. (J). (gr. -1-3). 6.95 (978-1-58089-138-7(1)) Charlesbridge Publishing, Inc.

Scherer, Glenn & Fletcher, Marty. Who on Earth Is Aldo Leopold? Father of Wildlife Ecology. 2009. (Scientists Saving the Earth Ser.). (Illus.). 112p. (J). (gr. 5-9). lib. bdg. 33.27 (978-1-59845-115-3(4)) Enslow Pubs., Inc.

Schomp, Virginia. 24 Hours in a Tropical Rain Forest. 2013. 48p. (J). (gr. 4-8). 29.93 (978-1-60870-895-6(0)) Cavendish Square Publishing.

—24 Hours in the Desert. 2013. 48p. (J). (gr. 4-8). 29.93 (978-1-60870-893-2(4)) Cavendish Square Publishing.

—24 Hours on a Coral Reef. 2013. 48p. (J). (gr. 4-8). 29.93 (978-1-60870-892-5(6)) Cavendish Square Publishing.

Schuetz, Kari. Life in a Desert. 2016. (Biomes Alive! Ser.). (ENG., Illus.). 24p. (J). (gr. k-3). lib. bdg. 25.95 (978-1-62617-316-3(8), Blastoff! Readers) Bellwether Media.

—Life in a Tundra. 2016. (Biomes Alive! Ser.). (ENG., Illus.). 24p. (J). (gr. k-3). lib. bdg. 25.95 (978-1-62617-321-7(4), Blastoff! Readers) Bellwether Media.

Schwacber, Barbie Heit. Alphabet of Earth. Vitsky, Sally, illus. 2009. (ENG.). 40p. (J). 9.95 (978-1-59249-997-7(X)) Soundprints.

Schwaeber, Barbie. Alphabet of Earth. Vitsky, Sally, illus. 2009. (ENG.). 40p. 17.95 *(978-1-59249-996-0(1))* Soundprints.

Science & Technology for Children Books, Land & Water Set, 8 vols. 2004. (Illus.). 64p. (J). *(978-1-933008-13-4(X))* Smithsonian Science Education Ctr. (SSEC).

Science Stories Foss Spanish Environments EA CR05. 2005. (J). *(978-1-59242-593-8(3))* Delta Education, LLC.

A Seaside Ecosystem. 2012. (Nature Trail Ser.). (ENG., Illus.). 32p. (J). (gr. k-5). 23.95 *(978-1-4488-6628-1(6)*, PowerKids Pr.) Rosen Publishing Group, Inc., The.

Senker, Cath, et al. Eco Guides. 2013. (Eco Guides). (ENG.). 56p. (gr. 6-8). lib. bdg. 138.60 *(978-1-4329-7048-2(8))* Heinemann-Raintree.

Sévigny, Eric, illus. Caillou Plants a Tree. 2012. (Ecology Club Ser.). (ENG.). 24p. (J). (gr. -1-1). pap. 5.99 *(978-2-89450-834-3(4))* Caillouet, Gerry.

Sexton, Colleen. Ponds. 2011. (Blastoff! Readers Ser.). 24p. (J). pap. 5.95 *(978-0-531-26033-3(X)*, Children's Pr.) Scholastic Library Publishing.

—Tundra. 2011. (Blastoff! Readers: Learning about the Earth: Level 3 Ser.). (ENG., Illus.). 24p. (J). pap. 5.95 *(978-0-531-26038-8(0)*, Children's Pr.) Scholastic Library Publishing.

Shaw, Daniel. Eco-Tracking: On the Trail of Habitat Change. 2010. (World's of Wonder Ser.). (ENG., Illus.). 98p. (J). (gr. 4-18). 34.95 *(978-0-8263-4531-8(X))* Univ. of New Mexico Pr.

—Southwest Aquatic Habitats: On the Trail of Fish in a Desert. 2013. (Barbara Guth Worlds of Wonder Science Series for Young Readers Ser.). (ENG., Illus.). 112p. (J). 34.95 *(978-0-8263-5309-2(6))* Univ. of New Mexico Pr.

Shields, Mary & Grace, Susan. What's a Shrew to You? Van Zyle, Jon, illus. 2008. (J). *(978-0-9618348-7-6(0))* Pyrola Publishing.

Sill, Cathryn. About Habitats: Polar Regions, 1 vol. Sill, John, illus. 2015. (About Habitats Ser.). (ENG.). 48p. (J). (gr. -1-2). 16.95 *(978-1-56145-832-5(5))* Peachtree Pubs.

Sill, Cathryn & Sill, John. Seashores, 1 vol. Sill, John, illus. 2017. (About Habitats Ser.). (ENG., Illus.). 48p. (J). (gr. -1-2). 16.95 *(978-1-56145-968-1(2))* Peachtree Pubs.

Silverman, Buffy. Desert Food Chains, 1 vol. 2010. (Protecting Food Chains Ser.). (ENG.). 48p. (gr. 3-6). 33.32 *(978-1-4329-3856-7(8))*; pap. 9.95 *(978-1-4329-3863-5(0))* Heinemann-Raintree. (Heinemann InfoSearch).

—Let's Visit the Lake. 2016. (Lightning Bolt Books (tm) — Biome Explorers Ser.). (ENG., Illus.). 32p. (J). (gr. 1-3). lib. bdg. 26.65 *(978-1-5124-1193-5(0))* Lerner Publishing Group.

Silverstein, Alvin, et al. Food Chains. rev. ed. 2007. (Science Concepts, Second Ser.). (ENG., Illus.). 96p. (J). (gr. 6-8). lib. bdg. 31.93 *(978-0-8225-6797-4(0))* Lerner Publishing Group.

Simon, Seymour. Coral Reefs. 2013. (ENG.). 32p. (J). (gr. 1-5). 17.99 *(978-0-06-191495-9(9)*, Collins) HarperCollins Pubs. Ltd. GBR. Dist: HarperCollins Pubs.

Sirota, Lyn A. South America. 2014. (J). *(978-1-4896-0958-8(X))* Weigl Pubs., Inc.

Sivertsen, Linda & Sivertsen, Tosh. Generation Green: The Ultimate Teen Guide to Living an Eco-Friendly Life. 2008. (ENG.). 272p. (YA). (gr. 7-18). pap. 15.99 *(978-1-4169-6122-2(4)*, Simon Pulse) Simon Pulse.

Slade, Suzanne. What Do You Know about Food Chains & Food Webs? (20 Questions: Science Ser.). 24p. (gr. 2-3). 2009. 42.50 *(978-1-60854-962-7(3)*, PowerKids Pr.) 2008. (Illus.). (J). lib. bdg. 22.60 *(978-1-4042-4202-9(3))* Rosen Publishing Group, Inc., The.

—What Do You Know about World Habitats? (20 Questions: Science Ser.). 24p. (gr. 2-3). 2009. 42.50 *(978-1-60854-966-5(6)*, PowerKids Pr.) 2008. (Illus.). (YA). lib. bdg. 22.60 *(978-1-4042-4198-5(1))* Rosen Publishing Group, Inc., The.

—What If There Were No Lemmings? A Book about the Tundra Ecosystem, 1 vol. Schwartz, Carol, illus. 2010. (Food Chain Reactions Ser.). (ENG.). 24p. (gr. 2-4). pap. 9.95 *(978-1-4048-6396-5(6))*; lib. bdg. 26.65 *(978-1-4048-6021-6(5))* Picture Window Bks.

Smalley, Carol. Exploring Earth's Biomes. 2010. (Life Science Projects for Kids Ser.). (Illus.). 48p. (J). (gr. 4-8). lib. bdg. 29.95 *(978-1-58415-878-3(6))* Mitchell Lane Pubs., Inc.

Smith, Andrea Claire Harte. The Effects of Farming. 2004. (Earth's Changing Landscape Ser.). (Illus.). 45p. (J). lib. bdg. 28.50 *(978-1-58340-475-1(9))* Black Rabbit Bks.

Smith, Bill D. Freshwater or Salt Water? 2013. (InfoMax Readers Ser.). (ENG.). 24p. (J). (gr. 2-3). pap. 49.50 *(978-1-4777-2373-9(0)*, Rosen Classroom) Rosen Publishing Group, Inc., The.

Smith, Bill D. & Machajewski, Sarah. Freshwater or Salt Water? 2013. (InfoMax Readers Ser.). (ENG.). 24p. (J). (gr. 2-3). pap. 8.25 *(978-1-4777-2372-2(2)*, Rosen Classroom) Rosen Publishing Group, Inc., The.

Smith-Llera, Danielle. River Communities Past & Present, 1 vol. 2014. (Who Lived Here? Ser.). (ENG.). 24p. (gr. 1-2). lib. bdg. 25.32 *(978-1-4765-4058-0(6)*, First Facts) Capstone Press of Coughlan Cos.

Smith, Natalie. Habitat Protection. 2008. (Saving Our World Ser.). 32p. (gr. 4-18). lib. bdg. 28.50 *(978-0-7614-3225-8(6)*, Benchmark Bks.) Marshall Cavendish Corp.

Sohn, Emily & Kentor Schmauss, Judy. Structures of Life: What Is this Fossil? 2011. (IScience Readers Ser.). 32p. (J). (gr. 3-4). lib. bdg. 22.60 *(978-1-59953-420-6(7))* Norwood Hse. Pr.

Sohn, Emily & Linde, Barbara. Environments: Beetles in the Garden. 2011. (IScience Readers Ser.). 48p. (J). (gr. 5-6). lib. bdg. 23.94 *(978-1-59953-423-7(1))* Norwood Hse. Pr.

Solway, Andrew. Food Chains & Webs, 1 vol. 2012. (Web of Life Ser.). (ENG.). 48p. (gr. 6-10). pap. 9.49 *(978-1-4109-4404-7(2))*; lib. bdg. 34.65 *(978-1-4109-4397-2(6))* Heinemann-Raintree. (Raintree Freestyle).

—Secrets of Habitats. 2010. (Science Secrets Ser.). 32p. (gr. 4). 28.50 *(978-1-60870-137-7(9))* Marshall Cavendish Corp.

—Transportation, 1 vol. 2012. (Impact of Environmentalism Ser.). (ENG.). 64p. (gr. 6-10). lib. bdg. 35.99 *(978-1-4329-6520-4(4))* Heinemann-Raintree.

Souza, Dorothy M. Plant Invaders. 2003. (Watts Library). (Illus.). 64p. (J). 25.50 *(978-0-531-12211-2(5)*, Watts, Franklin) Scholastic Library Publishing.

Spilsbury, Louise. Eat or Be Eaten: Extreme Food Chains. 2015. (Extreme Biology Ser.). (ENG., Illus.). 48p. (J). (gr. 4-4). lib. bdg. 31.95 *(978-1-4824-2238-2(7))* Stevens, Gareth Publishing LLLP.

—Garbage Can. Hanna, Gary, illus. 2013. (Look Inside Ser.). (ENG.). 32p. (gr. 1-3). 27.32 *(978-1-4329-7195-3(6))*; pap. 8.29 *(978-1-4329-7202-8(2))* Heinemann-Raintree. (Heinemann First Library).

—How to Survive on a Mountain. 2012. (Tough Guides). (ENG., Illus.). 32p. (J). (gr. 4-6). pap. 10.00 *(978-1-4488-7936-6(1))*; lib. bdg. 25.25 *(978-1-4488-7871-0(3))* Rosen Publishing Group, Inc., The. (PowerKids Pr.).

—Tide Pool. Hanna, Gary, illus. 2013. (Look Inside Ser.). (ENG.). 32p. (gr. 1-3). 27.32 *(978-1-4329-7197-7(2))*; pap. 8.29 *(978-1-4329-7204-2(9))* Heinemann-Raintree. (Heinemann First Library).

—What Are Food Chains & Food Webs?, 1 vol., 1. 2014. (Let's Find Out! Ser.). (ENG., Illus.). 32p. (J). (gr. 3-6). 23.45 *(978-1-62275-236-2(8))* Rosen Publishing Group, Inc., The.

—What Are Habitats & Biomes?, 1 vol., 1. 2014. (Let's Find Out! Ser.). (ENG.). 32p. (gr. 3-6). 23.45 *(978-1-62275-241-6(4))* Rosen Publishing Group, Inc., The.

Spilsbury, Louise & Spilsbury, Richard. A Nature Walk in the City, 1 vol. 2014. (Nature Walks Ser.). (ENG., Illus.). 24p. (gr. k-2). 23.32 *(978-1-4846-0401-4(6)*, Heinemann Read & Learn) Heinemann-Raintree.

—A Nature Walk on the Farm, 1 vol. 2014. (Nature Walks Ser.). (ENG., Illus.). 24p. (gr. k-2). 23.32 *(978-1-4846-0402-1(4)*, Heinemann Read & Learn) Heinemann-Raintree.

Spilsbury, Richard. Adaptation & Survival. 2010. (Living Processes Ser.). (Illus.). 48p. (J). pap. 11.75 *(978-1-61532-348-7(1))*; (YA). (gr. 5-8). lib. bdg. 29.25 *(978-1-61532-343-2(0))* Rosen Publishing Group, Inc., The. (Rosen Reference).

—Burrow. Hanna, Gary, illus. 2013. (Look Inside Ser.). (ENG.). 32p. (gr. 1-3). 27.32 *(978-1-4329-7193-9(X))*; pap. 8.29 *(978-1-4329-7200-4(6))* Heinemann-Raintree. (Heinemann First Library).

—Cave. Hanna, Gary, illus. 2013. (Look Inside Ser.). (ENG.). 32p. (gr. 1-3). 27.32 *(978-1-4329-7194-6(8))*; pap. 8.29 *(978-1-4329-7201-1(4))* Heinemann-Raintree. (Heinemann First Library).

—Tree. Hanna, Gary, illus. 2013. (Look Inside Ser.). (ENG.). 32p. (gr. 1-3). 27.32 *(978-1-4329-7198-4(0))*; pap. 8.29 *(978-1-4329-7205-9(7))* Heinemann-Raintree. (Heinemann First Library).

Spilsbury, Richard & Spilsbury, Louise. At Home in a Coral Reef, 01 vols., 1. 2016. (Home in the Biome Ser.). (ENG.). 32p. (J). pap. 10.00 *(978-1-5081-4552-3(0)*, PowerKids Pr.) Rosen Publishing Group, Inc., The.

—At Home in the Desert, 01 vols., 1. 2016. (Home in the Biome Ser.). (ENG.). 32p. (J). pap. 10.00 *(978-1-5081-4560-8(1)*, PowerKids Pr.) Rosen Publishing Group, Inc., The.

Stanek, Linda. Erase un Elefante, 1 vol. Bersani, Shennen, illus. 2016. (SPA.). 32p. (J). (gr. k-3). pap. 9.95 *(978-1-62855-745-9(1))* Arbordale Publishing.

—Once upon an Elephant, 1 vol. Bersani, Shennen, illus. 2016. (ENG.). 32p. (J). (gr. k-3). 17.95 *(978-1-62855-731-2(1))* Arbordale Publishing.

Staub, Frank. The Food Chain. 2003. (Illus.). 32p. (J). lib. bdg. *(978-1-58341-269-5(7)*, Creative Education) Creative Co., The.

Stephens, David. Coastal Habitats. 2013. (Discovery Education: Habitats Ser.). 32p. (J). (gr. 3-6). 25.25 *(978-1-4777-1321-1(2))*; pap. 10.00 *(978-1-4777-1477-5(4))* Rosen Publishing Group, Inc., The. (PowerKids Pr.).

Stetson, Emily. Create a Wildlife Habitat for Urban & Suburban Small Spaces. 2004. (ENG., Illus.). 128p. (J). pap. 12.95 *(978-0-8249-8665-0(2)*, Ideal Pubns.) Worthy Publishing.

Stienecker, David. Blast Zone: The Eruption & Recovery of Mount St. Helens. 2003. (ENG., Illus.). 32p. (J). (gr. 6-8). pap. 7.97 net. *(978-0-7652-3265-6(0)*, Celebration Pr.) Pearson Schl.

Stille, Darlene R. Protecting Animals. 2011. (Go Green! Ser.). (ENG.). 32p. (J). (gr. 1-4). lib. bdg. 28.50 *(978-1-60973-174-8(3)*, 201153) Child's World, Inc., The.

Stockland, Patricia M. Sand, Leaf, or Coral Reef: A Book about Animal Habitats. Ouren, Todd, illus. 2005. (Animal Wise Ser.). (ENG.). 24p. (gr. k-2). 26.65 *(978-1-4048-0932-1(5))* Picture Window Bks.

Stone, Lynn M. Deserts. 2003. (Rourke Discovery Library). (Illus.). 24p. (J). 20.64 *(978-1-58952-683-9(X))* Rourke Educational Media.

—Forests. 2003. (Rourke Discovery Library). (Illus.). 24p. (J). 20.64 *(978-1-58952-684-6(8))* Rourke Educational Media.

—Grasslands. 2003. (Rourke Discovery Library). (Illus.). 24p. (J). 20.64 *(978-1-58952-685-3(6))* Rourke Educational Media.

Stone, Omar. Ecology. 2016. (Spotlight on Ecology & Life Science Ser.). 00024p. (J). (gr. 4-6). pap. 10.00 *(978-1-4994-2560-4(0)*, PowerKids Pr.) Rosen Publishing Group, Inc., The.

Sturm, Jeanne. Understanding Biomes. 2011. (ENG., Illus.). 48p. (gr. 4-6). pap. 10.95 *(978-1-61741-985-0(0))* Rourke Educational Media.

Summers, Portia & Grady, Colin. The Coniferous Forest Biome. 2016. (Zoom in on Biomes Ser.). 24p. (J). (gr. 2-2). pap. 9.35 *(978-0-7660-7743-0(8))* Enslow Pubs., Inc.

—The Desert Biome. 2016. (Zoom in on Biomes Ser.). 24p. (J). (gr. 2-2). pap. 9.35 *(978-0-7660-7758-4(6))* Enslow Pubs., Inc.

—The Grassland Biome. 2016. (Zoom in on Biomes Ser.). 24p. (J). (gr. 2-2). pap. 9.35 *(978-0-7660-7778-2(0))* Enslow Pubs., Inc.

—The Tundra Biome. 2016. (Zoom in on Biomes Ser.). 24p. (J). (gr. 2-2). pap. 9.35 *(978-0-7660-7794-2(2))* Enslow Pubs., Inc.

Suzuki, David & Vanderlinden, Kathy. Eco-Fun: Projects, Experiments & Games for a Greener Earth. Kurisu, Jane, illus. 2003. (ENG.). 128p. (J). (gr. 3-6). pap. 14.95 *(978-1-55054-823-5(9))* Greystone Books Ltd. CAN. Dist: Publishers Group West (PGW).

Tarbox, A. D. An Arctic Tundra Food Chain. (Nature's Bounty Ser.). (Illus.). (gr. 5-17). 2011. (ENG.). 48p. (J). pap. 9.99 *(978-1-897563-08-3(6)*, Creative Paperbacks) 2008. 43p. (YA). lib. bdg. 22.95 *(978-1-58341-596-2(3)*, Creative Education) Creative Co., The.

—An Arctic Tundra Food Chain: Nature's Bounty. 2nd ed. 2015. (Illus.). 80p. (J). *(978-1-60818-538-2(9)*, Creative Education) Creative Co., The.

—A Desert Food Chain. 2016. (Odysseys in Nature Ser.). (ENG.). 80p. (J). (gr. 7-10). pap. 12.00 *(978-1-62832-404-4(X)*, Creative Paperbacks) Creative Co., The.

—A Desert Food Chain: Nature's Bounty. 2nd ed. 2015. (Illus.). 80p. *(978-1-60818-539-9(7)*, Creative Education) Creative Co., The.

—A Desert Food Chain: Odysseys in Nature. 2016. (Odysseys in Nature Ser.). (ENG.). 80p. (J). (gr. 7-10). pap. 14.99 *(978-1-62832-140-1(7)*, Creative Paperbacks) Creative Co., The.

—A Mountain Food Chain. 2016. (Odysseys in Nature Ser.). (ENG.). 80p. (J). (gr. 7-10). pap. 12.00 *(978-1-62832-405-1(8)*, Creative Paperbacks) Creative Co., The.

—A Mountain Food Chain: Nature's Bounty. 2nd ed. 2015. (Illus.). 80p. (J). *(978-1-60818-540-5(0)*, Creative Education) Creative Co., The.

—Nature's Bounty: A\Mountain Food Chain. 2008. (Nature's Bounty Ser.). (Illus.). 43p. (YA). (gr. 5-8). lib. bdg. 22.95 *(978-1-58341-598-6(X)*, Creative Education) Creative Co., The.

—An Ocean Food Chain. 2008. (Nature's Bounty Ser.). (Illus.). 46p. (J). (gr. 5-8). lib. bdg. 22.95 *(978-1-58341-599-3(8)*, Creative Education) Creative Co., The.

—A Pairie Food Chain. 2008. (Nature's Bounty Ser.). (Illus.). 43p. 22.95 *(978-1-58341-600-6(5)*, Creative Education) Creative Co., The.

—A Prairie Food Chain. 2016. (Odysseys in Nature Ser.). (ENG.). 80p. (J). (gr. 7-10). pap. 12.00 *(978-1-62832-406-8(6)*, Creative Paperbacks) Creative Co., The.

—A Prairie Food Chain: Nature's Bounty. 2015. (Illus.). 80p. (J). *(978-1-60818-542-9(7)*, Creative Education) Creative Co., The.

—A Rain Forest Food Chain. 2008. (Nature's Bounty Ser.). (Illus.). 43p. 22.95 *(978-1-58341-601-3(3)*, Creative Education) Creative Co., The.

Taylor, Trace & Zorzi, Gina. This Is a Prairie. 2011. (Power 100 - Ecosystems Ser.). 28p. pap. 45.32 *(978-1-61541-285-3(9))* American Reading Co.

Taylor, Trace, et al. This Is a Savannah. Washington, Joi, illus. 2011. (1-3Y Ecosystems Ser.). (ENG.). 20p. (J). (gr. k-2). pap. 5.99 *(978-1-61541-226-6(3))* American Reading Co.

Terry, Michael, illus. Who Lives Here? 2012. (ENG.). 12p. (J). (gr. -1-k). 14.99 *(978-1-4088-1943-2(0)*, 9781408819432, Bloomsbury USA Childrens) Bloomsbury Publishing USA.

Thiessen, Mark. Extreme Wildfire: Smoke Jumpers, High-Tech Gear, Survival Tactics, & the Extraordinary Science of Fire. 2016. (ENG., Illus.). 112p. (J). (gr. 3-7). pap. 12.99 *(978-1-4263-2530-4(4)*, National Geographic Children's Bks.) National Geographic Society.

Thomas, Keltie. Do Fish Fart? Answers to Kids' Questions about Lakes. Ouseley, Deryk, illus. 2016. (ENG.). 48p. (J). (gr. 3-7). pap. 9.95 *(978-1-77085-727-8(3)*, 9781770857278) Firefly Bks., Ltd.

Tocci, Salvatore. The Chaparral: Life on the Scrubby Coast. 2005. (Watts Library). (ENG., Illus.). 64p. (J). (gr. 5-7). pap. 8.95 *(978-0-531-16671-0(6)*, Watts, Franklin) Scholastic Library Publishing.

Toft, Barbara. The Complete Guide to Animals. 2015. (Illus.). 144p. (J). *(978-1-4351-6160-3(2))* Barnes & Noble, Inc.

Toft, Kim Michelle. The World That We Want. 2005. (Illus.). 32p. (J). (gr. -1 — 1). pap. 6.95 *(978-1-58089-115-8(2))*; bds. 16.95 *(978-1-58089-114-1(4))* Charlesbridge Publishing, Inc.

—The World That We Want. Toft, Kim Michelle, illus. 2005. (Illus.). 32p. (J). pap. *(978-0-7022-3482-8(6))* Univ. of Queensland Pr.

Trefil, James, et al. Ecology. 2005. (Illus.). 112p. (gr. 6-12). *(978-0-618-33429-2(7)*, 2-01017) Holt McDougal.

Tributaries of the Chesapeake Bay. 2013. (Exploring the Chesapeake Bay Ser.). 32p. (J). (gr. 3-6). pap. 63.00 *(978-1-4339-9794-5(0))* Stevens, Gareth Publishing LLLP.

Tribuzi, Luke. What's the Difference Between Forests & Prairies? 2013. (Rosen Readers Ser.). (ENG.). 24p. (J). (gr. 3-4). pap. 49.50 *(978-1-4777-2450-7(8))*; pap. 8.25 *(978-1-4777-2449-1(4))* Rosen Publishing Group, Inc., The. (Rosen Classroom).

U-X-L Encyclopedia of Biomes, 3 vols. 2nd ed. 2010. (ENG.). (J). 286.00 *(978-1-4144-5516-7(X)*, UXL) Cengage Gale.

VanCleave, Janice. Step-by-Step Science Experiments in Ecology. 2012. (Janice VanCleave's First-Place Science Fair Projects Ser.). (ENG., Illus.). 80p. (J). (gr. 5-8). 33.25 *(978-1-4488-6980-0(3))*; pap. 14.15 *(978-1-4488-8469-8(1))* Rosen Publishing Group, Inc., The. (Rosen Reference).

Viendo. (Coleccion Mil Preguntas). (SPA., Illus.). 24p. (J). pap. 5.50 *(978-950-11-0658-9(6)*, SGM626) Sigmar ARG. Dist: Continental Bk. Co., Inc.

Vogel, Julia. City Food Chains, 1 vol. Adams, Hazel, illus. 2010. (Fascinating Food Chains Ser.). (ENG.). 32p. 28.50 *(978-1-60270-791-7(X)*, Looking Glass Library- Nonfiction) Magic Wagon.

—Desert Food Chains, 1 vol. Adams, Hazel, illus. 2010. (Fascinating Food Chains Ser.). (ENG.). 32p. 28.50 *(978-1-60270-794-8(4)*, Looking Glass Library- Nonfiction) Magic Wagon.

—What Are Food Chains & Food Webs?, 1 vol. Adams, Hazel, illus. 2010. (Fascinating Food Chains Ser.). (ENG.). 32p. 28.50 *(978-1-60270-796-2(0)*, Looking Glass Library- Nonfiction) Magic Wagon.

Wadsworth, Pamela. Cynefinoedd. 2005. (WEL., Illus.). 24p. pap. *(978-1-85596-229-3(2))* Dref Wen.

—Golwg Gyntaf Ar Ble Mae Pethau'n Byw. 2005. (WEL., Illus.). 24p. pap. *(978-1-85596-256-9(X))* Dref Wen.

—Pethau Byw Ar Waith. 2005. (WEL., Illus.). 24p. pap. *(978-1-85596-233-0(0))* Dref Wen.

—Rhagor Am Gynefinoedd. 2005. (WEL., Illus.). 24p. pap. *(978-1-85596-230-9(6))* Dref Wen.

Walker, Pam & Wood, Elaine. Ecosystem Science Fair Projects, Revised & Expanded Using the Scientific Method. 2010. (Biology Science Projects Using the Scientific Method Ser.). (Illus.). 160p. (J). (gr. 5-18). 35.94 *(978-0-7660-3419-8(4))* Enslow Pubs., Inc.

—Ecosystem Science Fair Projects Using Worms, Leaves, Crickets, & Other Stuff. 2005. (Biology! Best Science Projects Ser.). (Illus.). 128p. (J). lib. bdg. 27.94 *(978-0-7660-2367-3(2)*, 1238537) Enslow Pubs., Inc.

Walker, Sally M. Life in an Estuary. 2003. (American Ecosystems Ser.). (Illus.). 72p. (J). (gr. 6-12). 26.60 *(978-0-8225-2137-2(7))* Lerner Publishing Group.

Wallace, Holly. Food Chains & Webs. (Life Processes Ser.). 32p. pap. 7.50 *(978-1-4034-4074-7(3))* Heinemann-Raintree.

Wanjie, Anne, ed. The Basics of Ecology. 2013. (Core Concepts Ser.). (ENG., Illus.). 96p. (YA). (gr. 7-12). lib. bdg. 34.60 *(978-1-4777-0551-3(1)*, Rosen Classroom) Rosen Publishing Group, Inc., The.

Warhol, Tom. Desert. 2006. (Earth's Biomes Ser.). (Illus.). 80p. (gr. 6-7). lib. bdg. 34.21 *(978-0-7614-2194-8(7)*, Benchmark Bks.) Marshall Cavendish Corp.

—Smart Car. 2010. (Green Cars Ser.). (Illus.). 48p. (J). (gr. 3-6). 28.50 *(978-1-60870-012-7(7))* Marshall Cavendish Corp.

—Tundra. 2006. (Earth's Biomes Ser.). (Illus.). 80p. (gr. 6-7). lib. bdg. 34.21 *(978-0-7614-2193-1(9)*, Benchmark Bks.) Marshall Cavendish Corp.

—Water. 2006. (Earth's Biomes Ser.). (Illus.). 80p. (gr. 6-7). lib. bdg. 34.21 *(978-0-7614-2192-4(0)*, Benchmark Bks.) Marshall Cavendish Corp.

Watson, Stephanie. The Tundra. 2003. (Biomes Around the World Ser.). (J). pap. *(978-1-58417-305-2(X))*; lib. bdg. *(978-1-58417-304-5(1))* Lake Street Pubs.

Waxman, Laura Hamilton. Life in a Wetland. 2016. (Biomes Alive! Ser.). (ENG., Illus.). 24p. (J). (gr. k-3). lib. bdg. 25.95 *(978-1-62617-322-4(2)*, Blastoff! Readers) Bellwether Media.

Webb, Barb. What Does Green Mean? 2011. (ENG., Illus.). 24p. (gr. k-2). pap. 8.95 *(978-1-61741-973-7(7))* Rourke Educational Media.

Weigel, Marlene. U-X-L Encyclopedia of Biomes. 2nd ed. 2009. (J). *(978-1-4144-5519-8(4))*; *(978-1-4144-5518-1(6))*; *(978-1-4144-5517-4(8))* Cengage Gale. (UXL).

Weldon-Owe. Shifting Sands. 2003. (Rigby InfoQuest Ser.). (ENG.). 24p. (gr. 4-4). pap. 9.50 *(978-0-7578-5718-8(3))* Rigby Education.

Whittaker, Helen. Water. 2011. (Living Green Ser.). 32p. (gr. 3). 28.50 *(978-1-60870-576-4(5))* Marshall Cavendish Corp.

Whizpops, The. Forest Communities: Living in Harmony with Fire. Lawson, Glory, illus. 2017. (J). 14.00 ***(978-0-87842-674-4(4))*** Mountain Pr. Publishing Co., Inc.

Wicks, Maris. Science Comics: Coral Reefs. 2016. (Science Comics Ser.). (ENG., Illus.). 128p. (J). pap. 12.99 *(978-1-62672-145-6(9)*, 9781626721456, First Second Bks.) Roaring Brook Pr.

Wild Earth. 2007. (Illus.). 32p. (J). *(978-0-696-24002-7(5))* Meredith Bks.

Wiley, G. D. Tropical Rain Forests. 2003. (Biomes Around the World Ser.). (J). pap. *(978-1-58417-301-4(7))*; lib. bdg. *(978-1-58417-300-7(9))* Lake Street Pubs.

Wilkins, Mary-Jane. Grasslands. 2017. (Fast Track: Who Lives Here? Ser.). (Illus.). 24p. (gr. k-3). 28.50 ***(978-1-78121-362-9(3))*** Brown Bear Bks.

Wilson, Brenda. Totally Amazing Careers in Environmental Sciences. 2006. (J). 7.80 *(978-1-933798-01-1(7))* Sally Ride Science.

Winner, Cherie. Life in the Tundra. 2003. (Ecosystems in Action Ser.). (ENG., Illus.). 72p. (gr. 5-9). lib. bdg. 26.60 *(978-0-8225-4686-3(8))* Lerner Publishing Group.

Winnick, Nick. Reduce Waste. 2010. (Being Green Ser.). (Illus.). 32p. (YA). (gr. 3-6). lib. bdg. 27.13 *(978-1-61690-100-4(4))*; (J). (gr. 4-6). pap. 12.95 *(978-1-61690-101-1(2))* Weigl Pubs., Inc.

Wojahn, Rebecca Hogue & Donald. An Australian Outback Food Chain: A Who-Eats-What Adventure. 2009. pap. 58.95 *(978-0-7613-4662-3(7))* Lerner Publishing Group.

—A Desert Food Chain: A Who-Eats-What Adventures in North America. 2009. pap. 58.95 *(978-0-7613-4665-4(1))* Lerner Publishing Group.

Wojahn, Rebecca Hogue & Wojahn, Donald. An Australian Outback Food Chain: A Who-Eats-What Adventure. 2009. (Follow That Food Chain Ser.). (ENG.). 64p. (gr. 3-5). 30.60 *(978-0-8225-7499-6(3))* Lerner Publishing Group.

—A Coral Reef Food Chain: A Who-Eats-What Adventure in the Caribbean Sea. 2009. (Follow That Food Chain Ser.). (ENG.). 64p. (gr. 3-5). 30.60 *(978-0-8225-7611-2(2))* Lerner Publishing Group.

—A Desert Food Chain: A Who-Eats-What Adventure in North America. 2009. (Follow That Food Chain Ser.). (ENG.). 64p. (gr. 3-5). 30.60 *(978-0-8225-7501-6(9))* Lerner Publishing Group.

—A Galápagos Island Food Chain: A Who-Eats-What Adventure. 2009. (Follow That Food Chain Ser.). (ENG.). 64p. (gr. 3-5). 30.60 *(978-0-8225-7613-6(9))* Lerner Publishing Group.

—A Mangrove Forest Food Chain: A Who-Eats-What Adventure in Asia. 2009. (Follow That Food Chain Ser.). (ENG.). 64p. (gr. 3-5). 30.60 *(978-0-8225-7615-0(5))* Lerner Publishing Group.

—A Nile River Food Chain: A Who-Eats-What Adventure. 2009. (Follow That Food Chain Ser.). (ENG.). 64p. (gr. 3-5). 30.60 *(978-0-8225-7614-3(7))* Lerner Publishing Group.

—A Rain Forest Food Chain: A Who-Eats-What Adventure in South America. 2009. (Follow That Food Chain Ser.). (ENG.). 64p. (gr. 3-5). 30.60 *(978-0-8225-7497-2(7))* Lerner Publishing Group.

—A Savanna Food Chain: A Who-Eats-What Adventure in Africa. 2009. (Follow That Food Chain Ser.). (ENG.). 64p. (gr. 3-5). 30.60 *(978-0-8225-7498-9(5))* Lerner Publishing Group.

—A Tundra Food Chain: A Who-Eats-What Adventure in the Arctic. 2009. (Follow That Food Chain Ser.). (ENG.). 64p. (gr. 3-5). 30.60 *(978-0-8225-7500-9(0))* Lerner Publishing Group.

Wood, Jenny. Los Desiertos. (Coleccion Tierra Viva).Tr. of Deserts. (SPA.). 32p. (YA). (gr. 5-8). *(978-84-348-3266-4(6))* SM Ediciones.

Woodford, Chris. Arctic Tundra & Polar Deserts, 1 vol. 2nd ed. 2010. (Biomes Atlases Ser.). (ENG.). 64p. (gr. 6-9). 34.65 *(978-1-4329-4172-7(0))* Heinemann-Raintree.

Woolf, Alex. Expedition to the Arctic. 2014. (Traveling Wild Ser.). 32p. (J). (gr. 3-6). pap. 63.00 (978-1-4824-1250-5(0)) Stevens, Gareth Publishing LLLP.

—Journey along the Amazon. 2014. (Traveling Wild Ser.). 32p. (J). (gr. 3-6). pap. 63.00 (978-1-4824-1251-2(9)) Stevens, Gareth Publishing LLLP.

World Book, Inc Staff, contrib. by. Deserts & Scrublands. 2012. (J). (978-0-7166-0445-7(0)) World Bk., Inc.

—Nature's Places. 2010. (J). (978-0-7166-7741-3(5)) World Bk., Inc.

—Seasonal Forests. 2012. (J). (978-0-7166-0444-0(2)) World Bk., Inc.

Wynne, Patricia J. My First Book about Backyard Nature: Ecology for Kids! 2016. (Dover Children's Science Bks.). (ENG., Illus.). 48p. (J). (gr. 3-6). pap. 4.99 (978-0-486-80949-6(8)) Dover Pubns., Inc.

Yasuda, Anita. Asia. 2014. (J). (978-1-4896-0942-7(3)) Weigl Pubs., Inc.

—Green Ideas. 2010. (Being Green Ser.). (Illus.). 32p. (YA). (gr. 3-6). lib. bdg. 27.13 (978-1-61690-094-6(6)); (J). (gr. 4-6). pap. 12.95 (978-1-61690-095-3(4)) Weigl Pubs., Inc.

Zoologists & Ecologists. 2013. (Out of the Lab: Extreme Jobs in Science Ser.). 32p. (J). (gr. 3-6). pap. 60.00 (978-1-4777-1385-3(9), PowerKids Pr.) Rosen Publishing Group, Inc., The.

Zoom in on Biomes. 2016. (Zoom in on Biomes Ser.). 24p. (gr. 2-2). pap. 56.10 (978-0-7660-7974-8(0)); lib. bdg. 135.60 (978-0-7660-7494-1(3)) Enslow Pubs., Inc.

Zorzi, Gina & Sánchez, Lucía M. Desiertos: This Is a Desert. 2011. (2G Ecosistemas Ser.). (SPA.). 36p. (J). (gr. k-2). pap. 6.99 (978-1-61541-424-6(X)) American Reading Co.

Zorzi, Gina & Sanchez, Lucia M. Praderas: This Is a Prairie. 2011. (poder de 100 - Ecosistemas (Power 100 - Ecosystems) Ser.). (SPA.). 28p. (J). pap. 7.95 (978-1-61541-430-7(4)) American Reading Co.

ECOLOGY—FICTION

A Boy And His Dog & Bozak, Jon. Demo: The Story of the Junkyard Dog. 2007. 56p. (J). 19.99 (978-0-9794769-1-4(7)) Adibooks.com.

Alemayehu, Tsehay. Bee-Come! A Collection of Short Stories. 2012. 58p. pap. 20.95 (978-1-4525-4816-6(1)) Balboa Pr.

Baer, Julie. Love Me Later. 2005. (Illus.). 28p. (J). (gr. -1-3). 16.99 (978-1-932188-03-5(7)) Bollix Bks.

Bains-Fort. It's Keen to Be Green. 2009. 40p. pap. 23.49 (978-1-4389-9145-0(2)) AuthorHouse.

Branford, Anna. Violet Mackerel's Natural Habitat. Allen, Elanna, illus. 2013. (Violet Mackerel Ser.). (ENG.). 112p. (J). (gr. 1-5). 15.99 (978-1-4424-3594-0(1)); pap. 5.99 (978-1-4424-3595-7(X)) Simon & Schuster Children's Publishing.

Brooks, John. Balloons, Sea Creatures, & Me. 2006. 34p. (J). 14.58 (978-0-9661789-3-7(9)) Lulu Pr., Inc.

Capeci, Anne. Food Chain Frenzy. Speirs, John, illus. 2004. (Magic School Bus Science Chapter Bks.). 91p. (gr. 2-5). 15.00 (978-0-7569-2206-1(2)) Perfection Learning Corp.

Carmody, Isobelle. A Mystery of Wolves. 2009. (Little Fur Ser.: Bk. 3). (ENG., Illus.). 256p. (J). (gr. 3-7). 6.99 (978-0-375-83859-0(7), Yearling) Random Hse. Children's Bks.

—A Riddle of Green. 2009. (Little Fur Ser.: Bk. 4). (J). (978-0-375-83860-6(0)) Random House Children's Books.

Casey, Dawn. The Barefoot Book of Earth Tales. Wilson, Anne, illus. 2009. (ENG.). 96p. (J). (gr. 1-5). 19.99 (978-1-84686-224-3(8)) Barefoot Bks., Inc.

Casey, Dawn, et al. The Barefoot Book of Ballet Stories. Wilson, Anne & Guay, Rebecca, illus. 2009. (ENG.). 80p. (J). (gr. 2-6). 23.99 (978-1-84686-262-5(0)) Barefoot Bks., Inc.

Choyce, Lesley. Big Burn. 2006. (ENG.). 215p. mass mkt. 9.95 (978-1-895449-43-3(X)) Thistledown Pr., Ltd. CAN. Dist: Univ. of Toronto Pr.

Cochard, David, illus. The Legend of Honey Hollow. 2008. 46p. (J). 16.99 (978-0-9799444-0-6(6)) Joey Publishing.

Collard, Sneed B., III. Flash Point, 1 vol. (ENG.). 256p. (YA). 2011. (gr. 5-9). pap. 7.95 (978-1-56145-577-5(6)) 2006. (Illus.). (gr. 7-18). 16.95 (978-1-56145-385-6(4)) Peachtree Pubs.

Crew, Gary. The Cat on the Island. Warden, Gillian, illus. 2008. 32p. (978-0-207-20070-0(X)) HarperCollins Pubs. Australia.

Crocker, Carter & Snyder, Carrie A. The Tale of the Swamp Rat. 2005. (ENG.). 240p. (J). (gr. 3-7). reprint ed. 6.99 (978-0-14-240314-3(8), Puffin Books) Penguin Young Readers Group.

Day, Robert O. & Day, Linda S. There's a Frog on a Log in the Bog. Day, Linda S., illus. 2003. (Illus.). (J). (gr. 3-6). 212p. pap. 8.95 (978-1-890905-50-7(X), Writers Collective, The); (Just So Wild Ser.: Vol. 1). 14.95 (978-1-890905-51-4(8), Eco Fiction Bks.) Day to Day Enterprises.

De Fombelle, Timothée. Toby & the Secrets of the Tree. Ardizzone, Sarah, tr. from FRE. Place, Francois, illus. 2010. (ENG.). 432p. (J). (gr. 4-7). 16.99 (978-0-7636-4655-4(5)) Candlewick Pr.

Dembicki, Carol & Dembicki, Matt. Mr. Big: A Tale of Pond Life. 2012. (ENG., Illus.). 160p. (J). (gr. 1-7). pap. 12.95 (978-1-61608-967-2(9), 608967, Sky Pony Pr.) Skyhorse Publishing Co., Inc.

Dennard, Deborah. Hedgehog Haven: A Story of a British Hedgerow Community. 2005. (Soundprints' Wild Habitats Ser.). (ENG., Illus.). 32p. (J). (gr. 1-4). 8.95 (978-1-59249-108-7(1), SC7020) Soundprints.

—Hedgehog Haven: The Story of an English Hedgerow Community. Hynes, Robert, illus. 2005. (ENG.). (J). (gr. 1-4). 32p. 19.95 (978-1-56899-989-0(5), BC7020); 36p. 15.95 (978-1-56899-987-6(9), B7020); 36p. pap. 6.95 (978-1-56899-988-3(7), S7020) Soundprints.

Douglas, Babette. Amazing Grace. Rockwell, Barry, illus. 2006. (Kiss a Me Teacher Creature Stories Ser.). (J). (gr. 3-7). 9.99 (978-1-890343-33-0(1)) Kiss A Me Productions, Inc.

Ducote, Billie Seaon. The Adventures of Artie Eco Part One: The Problem with Greed, 2 vols, Vol. 1. Ducote, Billie Seaon, illus. 2007. (ENG., Illus.). 26p. (J). 18.95 (978-0-9787597-5-9(3)) PureLight Pubns.

—The Adventures of Artie Eco Part Two: The Problem with Greed Artie Eco Goes to Dirtyville, 2 vols., Vol. 2. Ducote, Billie Seaon, illus. 2007. (Illus.). 26p. (J). act. bk. ed. 18.95 (978-0-9787597-1-1(0)) PureLight Pubns.

Dyer, Hadley. Les Savanes. 2012. (FRE.). 32p. (J). pap. 9.95 (978-2-89579-443-1(X)) Bayard Canada CAN. Dist: Crabtree Publishing Co.

Earhart, Kristin. Outback All-Stars (Race the Wild #5) 2016. (Race the Wild Ser.: 5). (ENG., Illus.). 144p. (J). (gr. 2-5). pap. 4.99 (978-0-545-94064-1(8), Scholastic Paperbacks) Scholastic, Inc.

—Savanna Showdown. 2016. (Illus.). 138p. (J). **(978-1-5182-0302-2(7))** Scholastic, Inc.

—Savanna Showdown. 2015. (Race the Wild Ser.: 4). (ENG., Illus.). 144p. (J). (gr. 2-5). lib. bdg. 14.75 (978-0-606-38080-5(9)) Turtleback Bks.

Ellis, Brian. The Web at Dragonfly Pond. Maydak, Michael S., illus. 2006. (Sharing Nature with Children Book Ser.). 32p. (J). (gr. 1-7). 16.95 (978-1-58469-078-8(X)); pap. 8.95 (978-1-58469-079-5(8)) Dawn Pubns.

Ellis, Sarah & Suzuki, David. Salmon Forest. Lott, Sheena, illus. 2006. (ENG.). 32p. (J). (gr. k-3). pap. 9.95 (978-1-55365-163-5(4)) Greystone Books Ltd. CAN. Dist: Publishers Group West (PGW).

Foreman, Michael. One World. 2012. (ENG., Illus.). 32p. (J). (gr. -1-k). pap. 12.99 (978-1-84939-304-1(4)) Andersen Pr. GBR. Dist: Independent Pubs. Group.

Franco, Betsy. Pond Circle. Vitale, Stefano, illus. 2009. (ENG.). 32p. (J). (gr. -1-3). 17.99 (978-1-4169-4021-0(9), McElderry, Margaret K. Bks.) McElderry, Margaret K. Bks.

Fredericks, Anthony D. Mountain Night Mountain Day. Spengler, Kenneth, illus. 2014. (ENG.). 32p. (J). 15.95 (978-1-933855-98-1(3), Rio Nuevo Pubs.) Rio Nuevo Pubs.

Grigsby, Susan. In the Garden with Dr. Carver. Tadgell, Nicole, illus. 2012. (J). (978-1-61913-157-6(9)) Weigl Pubs., Inc.

—In the Garden with Dr. Carver. Tadgell, Nicole, illus. 2010. (ENG.). 32p. (J). (gr. 2-3). 16.99 (978-0-8075-3630-8(X)) Whitman, Albert & Co.

Harley, Bill. Night of the Spadefoot Toads, 1 vol. 2008. (ENG.). 192p. (J). (gr. 3-7). 15.95 (978-1-56145-459-4(1)) Peachtree Pubs.

Hatton, Libby. Pete Puffin's Wild Ride Cruising Alaska's Currents. Hatton, Libby, illus. 2008. (Illus.). (J). pap. 16.95 (978-0-930931-92-6(0)) Alaska Geographic Assn.

Heim, Barbara. The Hudson Beavers Build a Lodge. 2013. (ENG.). 44p. (J). 13.95 (978-1-938586-45-3(X)) Writer's Cramp, Inc.

Johnson, Grant. Big Tree Bob. 2012. 20p. pap. 12.50 (978-1-61897-208-8(1), Strategic Bk. Publishing) Strategic Book Publishing & Rights Agency (SBPRA).

Keene, Carolyn. Green with Envy: Book Two in the Eco Mystery Trilogy. 2010. (Nancy Drew (All New) Girl Detective Ser.: 40). (ENG.). 160p. (J). (gr. 3-7). pap. 6.99 (978-1-4169-7842-8(9), Aladdin) Simon & Schuster Children's Publishing.

—Seeing Green: Book Three in the Eco Mystery Trilogy. 2010. (Nancy Drew (All New) Girl Detective Ser.: 41). (ENG.). 160p. (J). (gr. 3-7). pap. 6.99 (978-1-4169-7845-9(3), Aladdin) Simon & Schuster Children's Publishing.

Klass, David. Firestorm. 2008. (Caretaker Trilogy Ser.: 1). (ENG.). 320p. (YA). (gr. 9-13). pap. 11.99 (978-0-312-38018-2(6), 9780312380182) Square Fish.

—Firestorm. rev. l.t. ed. 2007. (Caretaker Trilogy: Bk. 1). 435p. (YA). (gr. 9). 23.95 (978-0-7862-9364-3(0)) Thorndike Pr.

—Timelock. 2009. (Caretaker Trilogy Ser.: 3). (ENG.). 256p. (YA). (gr. 9-12). 17.99 (978-0-374-32309-7(7), 9780374323097, Farrar, Straus & Giroux (BYR)) Farrar, Straus & Giroux.

—Timelock. 2010. (Caretaker Trilogy Ser.: 3). (ENG.). 272p. (YA). (gr. 9-12). pap. 8.99 (978-0-312-60863-7(2), 9780312608637) Square Fish.

—Whirlwind. 2009. (Caretaker Trilogy Ser.: 2). (ENG.). 320p. (YA). (gr. 9-12). pap. 18.99 (978-0-312-38429-6(7), 9780312384296) Square Fish.

Kleven, Elisa. The Dancing Deer & the Foolish Hunter. 2013. 34p. 16.99 (978-1-62352-040-3(1)); pap. 9.99 (978-1-62352-038-0(X)) IntoPrint Publishing LLC.

LaMarche, Jim. Pond. LaMarche, Jim, illus. 2016. (ENG., Illus.). 40p. (J). (gr. -1-3). 17.99 (978-1-4814-4735-5(1), Simon & Schuster/Paula Wiseman Bks.) Simon & Schuster/Paula Wiseman Bks.

Lamstein, Sarah Marwil. Big Night for Salamanders. Benioff, Carol, illus. 2010. (ENG.). 40p. (J). (gr. 3-7). 17.95 (978-1-932425-98-7(5)) Boyds Mills Pr.

Langeland, Deirdre. Kangaroo Island: A Story of an Australian Mallee Forest. 2005. (Soundprints' Wild Habitats Ser.). (ENG., Illus.). 32p. (J). (gr. 1-4). 8.95 (978-1-59249-095-0(6)) Soundprints.

Lewis, Gill. One White Dolphin. Aparicio, Raquel, illus. 2013. (ENG.). 368p. (J). (gr. 3-7). pap. 8.99 (978-1-4424-1448-8(0), Atheneum Bks. for Young Readers) Simon & Schuster Children's Publishing.

Lumry, Amanda & Hurwitz, Laura. Riddle of the Reef. 2009. (Illus.). 32p. (J). (978-0-545-06848-2(7), Scholastic Pr.) Scholastic, Inc.

MacDonald, Margaret Read. Surf War! A Folktale from the Marshall Islands. Valério, Geraldo, illus. 2009. (ENG.). 32p. (J). (gr. -1-3). 16.95 (978-0-87483-889-3(4)) August Hse. Pubs., Inc.

Mason, Cherie. Everybody's Somebody's Lunch, 1 vol. Moore, Gustav, illus. 2005. (ENG.). 40p. (J). (gr. 3-6). 7.95 (978-0-88448-200-0(6)) Tilbury Hse. Pubs.

McDiarmid, Gail S. & McGee, Marilyn S. Running for Home. Coffey, Durwood, illus. 2013. 76p. pap. 15.95 (978-0-9854677-0-8(3)) SunDog Enterprises.

Mills, Judith Christine. Carew. rev. ed. 2007. (ENG., Illus.). 248p. (J). (gr. 6). per. 7.95 (978-1-55263-788-3(3)) Leaf Storm Pr.

Nelson, Blake. Destroy All Cars. 2011. (ENG.). 224p. (J). (gr. 9-10). pap. 9.99 (978-0-545-10475-3(0), Scholastic Paperbacks) Scholastic, Inc.

Oliver, Narelle. The Best Beak in Boonaroo Bay. Oliver, Narelle, illus. (Illus.). 48p. (YA). pap. (978-0-85091-671-3(2), Lothian Children's Bks.) Hachette Australia.

Ouchley, Amy Griffin. Swamper: Letters from a Louisiana Swamp Rabbit. 2013. (ENG., Illus.). 72p. (gr. 4-7). 22.50 (978-0-8071-5074-0(6), 9780807150740) Louisiana State Univ. Pr.

Pandell, Karen. Te Amo, Sol - Te Amo, Luna. dePaola, Tomie, illus. 2003.Tr. of I Love You, Sun - I Love You, Moon. (SPA & ENG.). 12p. (J). (gr. -1 — 1). bds. 7.99 (978-0-399-24165-9(5), G.P. Putnam's Sons Books for Young Readers) Penguin Young Readers Group.

Pauli, Gunter. Shiitake Love Caffeine. 2007. (Zeri Fables Ser.). (ENG & SPA., Illus.). 32p. (J). (gr. k-3). pap. 9.95 (978-958-692-833-5(0)) Fondo Editorial Grania, Fundacion Hogares Juveniles Campesinos COL. Dist: Chelsea Green Publishing.

Pfister, Marcus. Milo & the Magical Stones. Pfister, Marcus, illus. 2010. (Milo Ser.). (ENG., Illus.). 32p. (J). (gr. k-3). 17.95 (978-0-7358-2253-5(0)) North-South Bks., Inc.

Phillips, Joanne M. Angelique & the Green Planet. 2013. 112p. 28.99 (978-1-4525-7587-2(8)); pap. 11.99 (978-1-4525-7585-8(1)) Author Solutions, Inc. (Balboa Pr.).

Random House Disney Staff. Big Trouble in Little Rodentia. Random House Disney Staff, illus. 2016. (Pictureback(R) Ser.). (ENG., Illus.). 24p. (J). (gr. -1-2). 4.99 (978-0-7364-3531-4(X), RH/Disney) Random Hse. Children's Bks.

Ranson, Erin. Ocean Wonders. Top That! Staff, ed. Mahoney, Daniel & Wood, Hannah, illus. 2007. (Sparkling Slide Nature Bks.). (ENG.). 12p. (J). (gr. -1). 9.99 (978-1-84666-167-9(6)) Top That! Publishing PLC GBR. Dist: Independent Pubs. Group.

Reynolds, Aaron. Carnivores. Newman, Jeff & Santat, Dan, illus. 2013. (ENG.). 40p. (J). (gr. -1-3). 16.99 (978-0-8118-6690-3(4)) Chronicle Bks. LLC.

Rihani, Ina. Song to the Sun. 2012. 56p. pap. 31.99 (978-1-4653-1123-8(8)) Xlibris Corp.

Ripley's Believe It Or Not! Staff. Secrets of the Deep. 2010. (Rbi Ser.: 4). (ENG.). 128p. (J). pap. 4.99 (978-1-893951-54-9(5)) Ripley Entertainment, Inc.

Samuels, Linda Nissen. Cuando Elly Fue a la Reserva Ecologica. Samuels, Linda Nissen, illus. 2013. (Illus.). 40p. pap. (978-0-9511751-8-7(1)) Samuels, Linda Y.

Saxon, Victoria. Big Trouble in Little Rodentia. 2016. (Illus.). (J). **(978-1-5182-0883-6(5))** Random House Children's Books.

Seuss, Dr. The Lorax. Seuss, Dr., illus. 2010. (ENG., Illus.). 24p. bds. (978-0-00-732618-1(1), HarperCollins Children's Bks.) HarperCollins Pubs. Ltd.

Seven, John. The Ocean Story, 1 vol. Christy, Jana, illus. 2011. (Fiction Picture Bks.). (ENG.). 32p. (gr. k-2). lib. bdg. 23.99 (978-1-4048-6785-7(6), Fiction Picture Bks.) Picture Window Bks.

Shelby, Anne. The Man Who Lived in a Hollow Tree. Hazelaar, Cor, illus. 2009. (ENG.). 40p. (J). (gr. -1-2). 17.99 (978-0-689-86169-7(9), Atheneum/Richard Jackson Bks.) Simon & Schuster Children's Publishing.

Simonet, Evan, illus. Jake & the Sailing Tree. 2009. (J). (978-1-60108-019-6(0)) Red Cygnet Pr.

Smith, Timothy R. The Owls Don't Give a Hoot. 2007. (Buck Wilder's Adventure Ser.: 4). (Illus.). 80p. (J). (gr. -1-3). per. 5.95 (978-1-934133-11-8(6), Mackinac Island Press, Inc.) Charlesbridge Publishing, Inc.

Sommer, Carl. King of the Pond. 2003. (Another Sommer-Time Story Ser.). (Illus.). 48p. (J). (gr. k-4). lib. bdg. 23.95 incl. audio (978-1-57537-766-7(7)); (gr. 1-4). 16.95 incl. audio (978-1-57537-565-6(6)) Advance Publishing, Inc.

—King of the Pond. Budwine, Greg, illus. 2003. (Another Sommer-Time Story Ser.). (ENG.). 48p. (J). (gr. k-4). lib. bdg. 23.95 incl. audio compact disk (978-1-57537-716-2(0)); (gr. 1-4). 16.95 incl. audio compact disk (978-1-57537-516-8(8)) Advance Publishing, Inc.

Spurlin, Barbara & Bernhardt, Michael J. Jellyfish on the Menu. 2011. (Illus.). 120p. (J). pap. (978-0-692-01277-2(X)) Kan sasana Printer.

Steinkraus, Kyla. La Casita Del Arbol. 2012. (SPA & ENG.). 24p. (gr. 2-3). pap. 8.95 (978-1-61810-539-4(6)) Rourke Educational Media.

Ter Haar, Carol. Chris T. Saves the Wetlands. 2008. (J). 20.00 (978-0-9768310-2-0(3)) BIC Alliance.

Terry & the Ecological Disaster. pap. (978-1-56002-792-8(4)) Univ. Editions.

Trout, Richard. Eclipse of the Jaguar, 1 vol. 2011. (ENG., Illus.). 224p. (YA). (gr. 8-12). 16.99 (978-1-58980-872-0(X)) Pelican Publishing Co., Inc.

—Sign of the Dragon, 1 vol. 2007. (MacGregor Family Adventure Ser.: 5). (ENG.). 272p. (YA). (gr. 5-12). 16.99 (978-1-58980-476-0(7)) Pelican Publishing Co., Inc.

Vernon, Ursula. Dragonbreath. 2012. (Dragonbreath Ser.: 1). lib. bdg. 17.20 (978-0-606-26665-9(8), Turtleback) Turtleback Bks.

Villeneuve, Kevin J. The Adventures of Nick the Ecologist & His Robot O-Zone: The Mystery of the Missing Trees. 2007. 96p. per. 9.95 (978-0-595-42362-0(0)) iUniverse, Inc.

Ward, Jennifer. The Seed & the Giant Saguaro. Rangner, Mike K., illus. 2003. (ENG.). 32p. (J). (gr. -1-3). 15.95 (978-0-87358-845-4(2)) Cooper Square Publishing Llc.

Weston Woods Staff, creator. In the Small, Small Pond. 2011. 38.75 (978-0-439-84578-6(5)) Weston Woods Studios, Inc.

White, Carolyn. Snowff & the Rowdy-Cloudy Bunch. 2006. (Snowff the Snowflake Kid Adventure Ser.). (J). 24.95 (978-1-893563-05-6(7)) AARO Publishing.

—Snowff Visits Razorteeth Village. 2006. (Illus.). 72p. (J). 24.95 (978-1-893563-10-0(3)) AARO Publishing.

—Snowff's MIST.erious Journey (Snowff the Snowflake Kid Adventure, 1) 2006. (J). 24.95 (978-1-893563-00-1(6)) AARO Publishing.

Wildsmith, Brian. Professor Noah's Spaceship, 1 vol. Wildsmith, Brian, illus. 2008. (ENG., Illus.). 32p. (J). 16.95 (978-1-59572-124-2(X)) Star Bright Bks., Inc.

Ziskind, Hélio & Duchesne, Christiane. Le Géant de la Forêt: Un Voyage Musical. Pratt, Pierre, illus. 2014. (FRE.). 48p. (J). (gr. k-2). 16.95 (978-2-923163-36-9(2)) La Montagne Secrete CAN. Dist: Independent Pubs. Group.

Zoehfeld, Kathleen Weidner. Secrets of the Garden: Food Chains & the Food Web in Our Backyard. Lamont, Priscilla, illus. 2014. (ENG.). 40p. (J). (gr. k-3). 7.99 (978-0-385-75364-7(0), Dragonfly Bks.) Random Hse. Children's Bks.

ECOLOGY, MARINE

see Marine Ecology

ECONOMIC ASSISTANCE

Bojang, Ali Brownlie. Aid & Development. 2009. (J). 32.80 (978-1-59920-099-6(6)) Black Rabbit Bks.

Connolly, Sean. International Aid & Loans. 2010. (World Economy Explained Ser.). 48p. (YA). (gr. 7-12). 35.65 (978-1-60753-079-4(1)) Amicus Publishing.

—International Aid & Loans. 2012. (Illus.). 48p. (gr. 6-10). pap. 9.95 (978-1-926722-77-1(9)) Saunders Bk. Co. CAN. Dist: RiverStream Publishing.

Connolly, Sean & Morgan, Sally. International Aid & Loans. 2011. (Earth Cycles Ser.). 32p. (YA). (gr. 3-6). lib. bdg. 28.50 (978-1-59920-521-2(1)) Black Rabbit Bks.

Haugen, David M., ed. Is Foreign Aid Necessary? 2012. (At Issue Ser.). (ENG.). 128p. (gr. 10-12). pap. 24.45 (978-0-7377-6188-7(1)); lib. bdg. 39.40 (978-0-7377-6187-0(3)) Cengage Gale. (Greenhaven Pr., Inc.).

Marsico, Katie. Oxfam International. 2016. (Community Connections: How Do They Help? Ser.). (ENG., Illus.). 24p. (J). (gr. 2-5). 27.07 (978-1-63471-052-7(5), 208288) Cherry Lake Publishing.

—United Way. 2016. (Community Connections: How Do They Help? Ser.). (ENG., Illus.). 24p. (J). (gr. 2-5). 27.07 (978-1-63471-054-1(1), 208296) Cherry Lake Publishing.

Prentzas, G. S. The Marshall Plan. 2011. (Milestones in Modern World History Ser.). 128p. (C). (gr. 9). 35.00 (978-1-60413-460-5(7), Chelsea Hse.) Facts On File, Inc.

Shah, Anup. Helping Africa Help Itself: A Global Effort. Ojakorotu, Victor & Rotberg, Robert I., eds. 2013. (Africa: Progress & Problems Ser.: 13). (Illus.). 112p. (J). (gr. 7-18). 24.95 (978-1-4222-2941-5(6)) Mason Crest.

Smith, Paula. Be the Change in the World. 2014. (ENG., Illus.). 24p. (J). (978-0-7787-0622-9(2)) Crabtree Publishing Co.

ECONOMIC BOTANY

see Botany, Economic

ECONOMIC CONDITIONS

see Economic History

ECONOMIC DEPRESSIONS

see Depressions

ECONOMIC DEVELOPMENT

see Economic History

ECONOMIC ENTOMOLOGY

see Insect Pests

ECONOMIC GEOGRAPHY

Maurer, Tracy Nelson. Using Economic & Resource Maps. 2016. (Searchlight Books (tm) — What Do You Know about Maps? Ser.). (ENG., Illus.). 40p. (J). (gr. 3-5). 30.65 (978-1-5124-0951-2(0)) Lerner Publishing Group.

Sheppard, Paul. Access to Geography: Economic Activity & Change. 2004. (Access to Geography Ser.). (Illus.). 128p. pap. 32.50 (978-0-340-81500-7(0), Hodder Education) Hodder Education Group GBR. Dist: Trans-Atlantic Pubns., Inc.

ECONOMIC HISTORY

Berlatsky, Noah. The Global Financial Crisis. 2010. (Global Viewpoints Ser.). (Illus.). 224p. (J). 40.45 (978-0-7377-4725-6(0)); pap. 27.95 (978-0-7377-4726-3(9)) Cengage Gale. (Greenhaven Pr., Inc.).

Bojang, Ali Brownlie. Aid & Development. 2009. (J). 32.80 (978-1-59920-099-6(6)) Black Rabbit Bks.

Dakers, Diane. Green Ways of Getting Around: Careers in Transportation. 2011. (ENG., Illus.). 64p. (J). pap. (978-0-7787-4867-0(7), 1331598); (gr. 5-9). (978-0-7787-4856-4(1), 1331598) Crabtree Publishing Co.

Davidson, Avelyn. Dollars & Sense: Economics & Science. 2007. (Shockwave: Economics & Geography Ser.). (ENG., Illus.). 36p. (J). (gr. 3-5). 25.00 (978-0-531-17750-1(5), Children's Pr.) Scholastic Library Publishing.

Docalavich, Heather. Economic Globalization & Sustainable Development, Vol. 10. Russett, Bruce, ed. 2015. (United Nations: Leadership & Challenges in a Global World Ser.). (Illus.). 88p. (J). (gr. 7). lib. bdg. 24.95 (978-1-4222-3431-0(2)) Mason Crest.

Furgang, Kathy. Understanding Economic Indicators: Predicting Future Trends in the Economy. 2011. (Real World Economics Ser.). (ENG.). 80p. (YA). (gr. 7-12). lib. bdg. 33.25 (978-1-4488-5571-1(3)) Rosen Publishing Group, Inc., The.

Grant, R. G. The Great Depression. 2005. (How Did It Happen? Ser.). (ENG., Illus.). 48p. (YA). (gr. 7-10). lib. bdg. 32.10 (978-1-59018-606-0(0), Lucent Bks.) Cengage Gale.

The Great Depression 1929-1938. 2010. (Discovering U. S. History Ser.). (Illus.). 136p. (gr. 5-8). 35.00 (978-1-60413-357-8(0), Chelsea Hse.) Facts On File, Inc.

Henneberg, Susan. The Wealth Gap. 2017. (Opposing Viewpoints Ser.). 224p. (J). (gr. 10-12). lib. bdg. 48.80 **(978-1-5345-0024-2(3)**, Greenhaven Publishing) Greenhaven Publishing LLC.

Henneberg, Susan, ed. The Wealth Gap. 2017. (Opposing Viewpoints Ser.). 224p. (J). (gr. 10-12). pap. 33.80 **(978-1-5345-0034-1(0)**, Greenhaven Publishing) Greenhaven Publishing LLC.

Mann, Charles. 1493 for Young People: From Columbus's Voyage to Globalization. 2016. (For Young People Ser.). (ENG., Illus.). 416p. (J). (gr. 7). pap. 18.95 (978-1-60980-663-7(8), Triangle Square) Seven Stories Pr.

Marfa, Isabelle. The Land & Resources of Texas: Shaping the Growth of the State. 2010. (Spotlight on Texas Ser.). (ENG., Illus.). 32p. (J). (gr. 3-4). pap. 11.75 (978-1-61532-478-1(X)); lib. bdg. 26.25 (978-1-61532-480-4(1)) Rosen Publishing Group, Inc., The.

McDaniel, Melissa. The Industrial Revolution. 2011. (Cornerstones of Freedom, Third Ser.). (Illus.). 64p. (J). (ENG.). pap. 8.95 (978-0-531-26562-8(5)); lib. bdg. 30.00 (978-0-531-25037-2(7)) Scholastic Library Publishing. (Children's Pr.).

McPherson, Stephanie Sammartino. Arctic Thaw: Climate Change & the Global Race for Energy Resources. 2014. (Illus.). 64p. (J). (gr. 6-12). lib. bdg. 34.60 (978-1-4677-2043-4(7), Twenty-First Century Bks.) Lerner Publishing Group.

Merino, Noël. The World Economy. 2010. (Current Controversies Ser.). (Illus.). 240p. pap. 28.45 (978-0-7377-4714-0(5), Greenhaven Pr., Inc.) Cengage Gale.

Mooney, Carla. The Economy of Latin America. 2017. (Exploring Latin America Ser.). 48p. (gr. 10-12). 84.30 **(978-1-68048-678-0(0)**, Britannica Educational Publishing) Rosen Publishing Group, Inc., The.

Moore, Jess. The Economy of Texas. 2014. (Spotlight on Texas Ser.). (ENG.). 32p. (J). (gr. 3-4). pap. 11.75

(978-1-4777-4512-0(2), Rosen Classroom) Rosen Publishing Group, Inc., The.
Moriarty, J. T. The Birth of American Capitalism: The Growth of American Banks. 2004. (America's Industrial Society in the 19th Century Ser.). (Illus.). 32p. (gr. 5-8). pap. 10.00 (978-0-8239-4280-0(5)) Rosen Publishing Group, Inc., The.
The New Global Society. 2005. (New Global Society Ser.). (Illus.). 112p. (C). (gr. 9-12). 120.00 (978-0-7910-9094-7(9), Chelsea Hse.) Facts On File, Inc.
Schimel, Kate & Collins, Kathleen. The Economic Growth of New York. 2012. (Illus.). 24p. (J). 60.00 (978-1-4488-5766-1(X)); pap. 10.00 (978-1-4488-5765-4(1)); lib. bdg. 22.60 (978-1-4488-5746-3(5)) Rosen Publishing Group, Inc., The. (PowerKids Pr.).
Steele, Philip. Global Financial Crisis. 2016. (Illus.). 48p. (J). (978-0-7787-2586-2(3)) Crabtree Publishing Co.
Wilson, John. Failed Hope: The Story of the Lost Peace. 2012. (Stories of Canada Ser.: 14). (ENG., Illus.). 120p. (J). pap. 18.99 (978-1-4597-0345-2(6)) Dundurn CAN. Dist: Ingram Publisher Services.
—Failed Hope: The Story of the Lost Peace (Large Print 16pt) 2013. 180p. pap. (978-1-4596-6314-5(4)) ReadHowYouWant.com, Ltd.
Winters, Adam. Destruction of Earth's Resources: The Need for Sustainable Development. (Extreme Environmental Threats Ser.). 64p. 2009. (gr. 6-6). 58.50 (978-1-61512-425-1(X)) 2006. (Illus.). (YA). (gr. 5-9). lib. bdg. 31.95 (978-1-4042-0746-2(5)) Rosen Publishing Group, Inc., The.
World Book, Inc Staff, contrib. by. Economics. 2009. (J). (978-0-7166-0392-4(6)) World Bk., Inc.
—Living with Climate Change. 2015. (Illus.). 47p. (J). (978-0-7166-2713-5(2)) World Bk., Inc.

ECONOMIC PLANNING

see Economic Policy

ECONOMIC POLICY

see also International Economic Relations; Manpower Policy

Brezina, Corona. How the Group of 20 Works: Cooperation among the World's Major Economic Powers. 2012. (Real World Economics Ser.). (ENG., Illus.). 80p. (J). (gr. 7-12). 33.25 (978-1-4488-6788-2(6)) Rosen Publishing Group, Inc., The.
—Understanding the Federal Reserve & Monetary Policy. 2011. (Real World Economics Ser.). (ENG.). 80p. (J). (gr. 7-12). lib. bdg. 33.25 (978-1-4488-5567-4(5)) Rosen Publishing Group, Inc., The.
—Understanding the Gross Domestic Product & the Gross National Product. 2011. (Real World Economics Ser.). (ENG.). 80p. (YA). (gr. 7-12). lib. bdg. 33.25 (978-1-4488-5569-8(1)) Rosen Publishing Group, Inc., The.
Crayton, Lisa A. & Nagle, Jeanne. Recession: What It Is & How It Works. 2016. (Economics in the 21st Century Ser.). (ENG., Illus.). 96p. (J). (gr. 8-8). lib. bdg. 34.60 (978-0-7660-7356-2(4), 1399425) Enslow Pubs., Inc.
Nichols, Clive & Bussing-Burks, Marie. Taxes & Government Spending. 2011. (J). pap. 12.95 (978-1-4488-4725-9(7)); (YA). (gr. 5-9). lib. bdg. 31.95 (978-1-4488-4714-3(1)) Rosen Publishing Group, Inc., The.
Orr, Tamra. Understanding Economic Systems. 2011. (Real World Economics Ser.). (ENG.). 80p. (YA). (gr. 7-12). lib. bdg. 33.25 (978-1-4488-5568-1(3)) Rosen Publishing Group, Inc., The.
Schimel, Kate & Cefrey, Holly. New York's Industrial Growth. 2012. (Illus.). 24p. (J). 60.00 (978-1-4488-5774-6(0)); pap. 10.00 (978-1-4488-5773-9(2)); lib. bdg. 22.60 (978-1-4488-5750-0(3)) Rosen Publishing Group, Inc., The. (PowerKids Pr.).
Spilsbury, Richard. The Debate about Energy Resources. 2010. (Ethical Debates Ser.). (ENG.). 48p. (YA). lib. bdg. 29.25 (978-1-4358-9651-2(3), Rosen Reference) Rosen Publishing Group, Inc., The.
Young, Mitchell. Government Spending. 2009. (Opposing Viewpoints Ser.). (ENG., Illus.). 240p. (YA). (gr. 10-12). 29.45 (978-0-7377-4005-9(1), LML02109-239969); pap. 42.95 (978-0-7377-4004-2(3), LML02109-239976) Cengage Gale. (Greenhaven Pr., Inc.).

ECONOMIC RELATIONS, FOREIGN

see International Economic Relations

ECONOMIC ZOOLOGY

see Zoology, Economic

ECONOMICS

see also Business; Capitalism; Commerce; Consumption (Economics); Credit; Depressions; Economic History; Economic Policy; Finance; Income; Industries; Land Use; Money; Population; Socialism; Waste (Economics)

Adler, David A. Prices! Prices! Prices! Why They Go up & Down. Miller, Edward, illus. 2016. (ENG.). 32p. (J). 7.99 (978-0-8234-3574-6(1)) Holiday Hse., Inc.
Anderson, Holly. Global Trade Organizations, Vol. 7. 2016. (Understanding Global Trade & Commerce Ser.: Vol. 7). (ENG., Illus.). 80p. (J). (gr. 7-12). 24.95 (978-1-4222-3668-0(4)) Mason Crest.
Andrews, Carolyn & Thompson, Gare. What Is Importing & Exporting? 2009. (Economics in Action Ser.). (ENG., Illus.). 32p. (J). (gr. 3-7). pap. (978-0-7787-4454-2(X)) Crabtree Publishing Co.
Antell, Gerson & Harris, Walter. Economics for Everybody. 3rd ed. 2003. 592p. (gr. 11-12). pap., tchr. ed. (978-0-87720-874-7(3), R753T) AMSCO Schl. Pubns., Inc.
Bailey, Gerry & Law, Felicia. World Money. Beech, Mark, illus. 2015. (How Money Works). (ENG.). 64p. (J). (gr. 4-6). lib. bdg. 29.27 (978-1-59953-720-7(6)) Norwood Hse. Pr.
Ball, Madeline K. & Seidman, David. Supply & Demand. 2011. (Dollars & Sense: a Guide to Financial Literacy Ser.). (YA). (gr. 5-8). (ENG.). 64p. pap. 12.95 (978-1-4488-4724-2(9)); lib. bdg. 31.95 (978-1-4488-4716-7(8)) Rosen Publishing Group, Inc., The.
Benchmark Education Company, LLC Staff, compiled by. Economics: Theme Set. 2006. (J). 109.00 (978-1-4108-7086-5(3)); 105.00 (978-1-4108-7070-4(7)) Benchmark Education Co.
—Production, Distribution, & Consumption. 2005. spiral bd. 345.00 (978-1-4108-3749-3(1)); spiral bd. 180.00 (978-1-4108-3940-4(0)); spiral bd. 90.00 (978-1-4108-3941-1(9)); spiral bd. 165.00 (978-1-4108-3965-7(6)); spiral bd. 110.00 (978-1-4108-3966-4(4)); spiral bd. 230.00 (978-1-4108-4498-9(6)); spiral bd. 225.00 (978-1-4108-5838-2(3)); spiral bd. 375.00 (978-1-4108-5422-3(1)) Benchmark Education Co.
Berry, Rob & Duey, Kathleen. The Smart Kids Allowance System: Step-by-Step Money Management Guidebook. Bartholomew, illus. Date not set. (Family Skill Builders Ser.). (J). (gr. k-6). pap. 9.95 (978-1-883761-34-9(4)) Family Life Productions.
Boyes, William. Microeconomics. 6th ed. 2004. (ENG.). 512p. (C). pap., pupil's gde. ed. 82.95 (978-0-618-37255-3(5), 305003) Cengage South-Western.
Brezina, Corona. Understanding the Gross Domestic Product & the Gross National Product. 2011. (Real World Economics Ser.). (ENG.). 80p. (YA). (gr. 7-12). lib. bdg. 33.25 (978-1-4488-5569-8(1)) Rosen Publishing Group, Inc., The.
Britton, Tamara L. Eye on Economics, 1 vol. 2012. (Economy in Action! Ser.). (ENG.). 32p. (J). (gr. 3-6). lib. bdg. 27.07 (978-1-61783-487-5(4), Checkerboard Library) ABDO Publishing Co.
Catel, Patrick. Graphing Money, 1 vol. 2010. (Real World Data Ser.). (ENG., Illus.). 32p. (gr. 3-5). lib. bdg. 29.99 (978-1-4329-2618-2(7), NA-h) Heinemann-Raintree.
Challen, Paul. What Is Supply & Demand? 2009. (ENG., Illus.). 32p. (J). (gr. 2-5). lib. bdg. (978-0-7787-4446-7(9)); (gr. 3-7). pap. (978-0-7787-4457-3(4)) Crabtree Publishing Co.
Clayton, Gary E. Economics: Principles & Practices. 2007. (Illus.). 528p. (J). (gr. 4-7). stu. ed. 96.80 (978-0-07-874764-9(3), 9780078747649) Glencoe/McGraw-Hill.
Cohn, Jessica. What Is Scarcity of Resources? 2008. (Economics in Action Ser.). (ENG., Illus.). 32p. (J). (gr. 3-7). pap. (978-0-7787-4261-6(X)) Crabtree Publishing Co.
Corporate Contributor Staff. The Economics of a Video Game. 2013. (ENG.). 48p. (J). (978-0-7787-7970-4(X)); pap. (978-0-7787-7975-9(0)) Crabtree Publishing Co.
Corporate Contributor Staff & Flatt, Lizann. The Economics of the Super Bowl. 2013. (ENG.). 48p. (J). (978-0-7787-7972-8(6)); pap. (978-0-7787-7977-3(7)) Crabtree Publishing Co.
Corporate Contributor Staff & Johnson, Robin. The Economics of Making a Movie. 2013. (ENG.). 48p. (J). (978-0-7787-7971-1(8)); pap. (978-0-7787-7976-6(9)) Crabtree Publishing Co.
Corporate Contributor Staff & Perl, Sheri. The Economics of a Rock Concert. 2013. (ENG.). 48p. (J). (978-0-7787-7969-8(6)); pap. (978-0-7787-7974-2(2)) Crabtree Publishing Co.
Cost Benefit Jr. Stories in Microeconomics. 2003. (J). spiral bd. 29.95 (978-0-9746242-2-8(5)) Consilient Pubns.
Crabtree Publishing Company Staff. Economics of Entertainment. 2013. (ENG.). 48p. (J). (978-0-7787-7968-1(8)); pap. (978-0-7787-7973-5(4)) Crabtree Publishing Co.
Economics: New Ways of Thinking. 54.95 (978-0-8219-3401-2(5)) EMC/Paradigm Publishing.
Economics: Student Technology Package. 4th ed. 2004. (gr. 6-12). (978-0-618-38192-0(9), 3-52024) Holt McDougal.
Economics: Test Bank, Macroeconomics. 4th ed. 2004. (gr. 6-12). (978-0-618-23007-5(6), 3-52016) CENGAGE Learning.
Facts on File, Inc. Staff. Top Careers for Economics Graduates. 2004. (Top Careers Ser.). (Illus.). 368p. (gr. 9). pap. 14.95 (978-0-8160-5566-1(1), Checkmark Bks.) Facts On File, Inc.
Forstater, Mathew. Trailblazers in Economics, 1 vol. 2015. (ENG.). 192p. (J). 40.95 (978-1-4777-8146-3(3), Rosen Young Adult) Rosen Publishing Group, Inc., The.
Gale, ed. U-X-L Money: Making Sense of Economics & Personal Finance, Teacher's Guide. 2015. (U-X-L Money Ser.). (ENG.). 5.00 (978-1-4103-3437-4(6), UXL) Cengage Gale.
Garbus, Julia. UXL Money: Making Sense of Economics & Personal Finance. 2015. (Illus.). (J). (978-1-57302-980-3(7)) Cengage Gale.
Garey, Marita & National Geographic Learning Staff. Kids Are Consumers. 2007. (Reading Expeditions Ser.). (ENG., Illus.). 32p. (J). pap. 17.95 (978-0-7922-8700-1(2)) CENGAGE Learning.
Gilman, Laura Anne. Economics. 2005. (How Economics Works). (Illus.). 48p. (J). (gr. 3-7). lib. bdg. 25.26 (978-0-8225-2662-9(X), Lerner Pubns.) Lerner Publishing Group.
Glencoe McGraw-Hill Staff, creator. Economics, Principles & Practices. 5th ed. 2004. (ECONOMICS PRINCIPLES & PRACTIC Ser.). (ENG.). (gr. 9-12). 145.16 (978-0-07-865056-7(9), 0078650569) McGraw-Hill Higher Education.
—Economics Today & Tomorrow: Spanish Reading Essentials & Study Guide: Student Workbook. 3rd ed. 2004. (ECONOMICS TODAY & TOMORROW Ser.). (SPA., Illus.). 186p. (gr. 9-12). pap., stu. ed., wbk. ed. 12.80 (978-0-07-864044-5(X), 007864044X) McGraw-Hill Higher Education.
—Economics Today & Tomorrow StudentWorks. 3rd ed. 2004. (ECONOMICS TODAY & TOMORROW Ser.). (ENG.). (gr. 9-12). stu. ed. 145.16 (978-0-07-865073-4(9), 0078650739) McGraw-Hill Higher Education.
Glencoe McGraw-Hill Staff & McGraw-Hill Education Editors. Economics: Today & Tomorrow, Spanish Reading Essentials. 2007. (ECONOMICS TODAY & TOMORROW Ser.). (ENG & SPA.). 208p. (gr. 9-12). pap. 12.04 (978-0-07-878590-0(1), 0078785901) McGraw-Hill Higher Education.
Glencoe McGraw-Hill Staff & McGraw-Hill Education Staff. Economics: Today & Tomorrow. 2007. (ECONOMICS TODAY & TOMORROW Ser.). (ENG., Illus.). 208p. (gr. 9-12). per. 12.04 (978-0-07-878351-7(8), 0078783518) McGraw-Hill Higher Education.
Grant, Susan. Cambridge IGCSE Economics. 2014. (Cambridge International IGCSE Ser.). (ENG.). 1224p. pap., wbk. ed. 15.31 (978-1-107-61231-0(4)) Cambridge Univ. Pr.
—[Cambridge IGCSE Economics. 2014. (Cambridge International IGCSE Ser.). (ENG.). 582p. pap., stu. ed. 33.13 (978-1-107-61233-4(0)) Cambridge Univ. Pr.
—Cambridge o Level Economics Student's Book. 2014. (ENG.). 581p. pap. 33.13 (978-1-107-61235-8(7)) Cambridge Univ. Pr.
Gunderson, Megan M. Labor & Management, 1 vol. 2012. (Economy in Action! Ser.). (ENG.). 32p. (J). (gr. 3-6). lib. bdg. 27.07 (978-1-61783-488-2(2), Checkerboard Library) ABDO Publishing Co.
Here's the Scoop: Follow an Ice-Cream Cone Around the World. 2003. (One & Only Common Sense/ents Ser.). 344.95 (978-0-8136-4211-6(6)); 167.95 (978-0-8136-4570-4(0)) Modern Curriculum Pr.
Herman, Stephanie. Cost Benefit Jr Bk. 1: Bound Text with Looseleaf Q & A - Answer Key: How Free Markets Work. 2003. spiral bd. 29.95 (978-0-9746242-0-4(9)) Consilient Pubns.
—Cost Benefit Jr Bk. 1: Self-Contained: How Free Markets Work. 2003. spiral bd., wbk. ed. 29.95 (978-0-9746242-1-1(7)) Consilient Pubns.
Hollander, Barbara. Money Matters: An Introduction to Economics. 2010. (Global Marketplace Ser.). (ENG.). 56p. (gr. 6-9). 34.65 (978-1-4329-3929-8(7), NA-h) Heinemann-Raintree.
How Economics Works, 6 bks., Set. Incl. Banking. Allman, Barbara. (gr. 4-6). lib. bdg. 25.26 (978-0-8225-2148-8(2)); Budgeting. Donovan, Sandy. (gr. 4-6). lib. bdg. 25.26 (978-0-8225-2665-0(4)); Earning Money. Murphy, Patricia J. (J). (gr. 3-7). lib. bdg. 25.26 (978-0-8225-2149-5(0)); Economics. Gilman, Laura Anne. (J). (gr. 3-7). lib. bdg. 25.26 (978-0-8225-2662-9(X)); Saving Money. Heckman, Philip. (gr. 4-6). lib. bdg. 25.26 (978-0-8225-2664-3(6)); Stock Market. Fuller, Donna Jo. (gr. 3-5). lib. bdg. 25.26 (978-0-8225-2635-3(2)); (Illus.). 48p. 2005. Set lib. bdg. 151.56 (978-0-8225-0034-6(5), Lerner Pubns.) Lerner Publishing Group.
Huberman, Leo. Man's Worldly Goods - the Story of the W. 2006. 368p. per. (978-1-4067-9820-3(7), Hesperides Pr.) Read Bks.
Hudak, Heather C. Spending. 2017. (J). **(978-1-5105-1949-7(1))** SmartBook Media, Inc.
Kates, Steven. Economics for Infants. Cappello, Liam, illus. 2017. (ENG.). (J). **(978-1-925501-43-8(4))** Connor Court Publishing Pty Ltd.
Kenney, Karen. Economics Through Infographics. Stankiewicz, Steven, illus. 2014. (Super Social Studies Infographics Ser.). 32p. (gr. 3-5). (J). lib. bdg. 26.60 (978-1-4677-3460-8(8), Lerner Pubns.); pap. 8.95 (978-1-4677-4564-2(2)) Lerner Publishing Group.
La Bella, Laura. What Are Goods & Services? 2016. (Let's Find Out! Ser.). (ENG.). 32p. (J). (gr. 3-2). lib. bdg. 24.45 (978-1-68048-400-7(1)) Rosen Publishing Group, Inc., The.
—What Are Supply & Demand? 2016. (Let's Find Out! Ser.). (ENG., Illus.). 32p. (J). (gr. 3-2). lib. bdg. 24.45 (978-1-68048-406-9(0)) Rosen Publishing Group, Inc., The.
—What Is Supply & Demand? 2016. (Let's Find Out! Ser.). 32p. (J). (gr. 3-2). pap. 12.90 (978-1-68048-414-4(1), Britannica Educational Publishing) Rosen Publishing Group, Inc., The.
Let's Find Out! Community Economics. 2016. (Let's Find Out! Ser.). 32p. (gr. 3-2). 195.60 (978-1-5081-0221-2(X)); pap. 103.20 (978-1-68048-596-7(2)) Rosen Publishing Group, Inc., The. (Britannica Educational Publishing).
Lightning Bolt Books: Exploring Economics, 6 vols., Set. Incl. Do I Need It? or Do I Want It? Making Budget Choices. Larson, Jennifer S. lib. bdg. 26.60 (978-0-7613-3914-4(0)); What Can You Do with Money? Earning, Spending, & Saving. Larson, Jennifer S. lib. bdg. 26.60 (978-0-7613-3910-6(8)); What Do We Buy? A Look at Goods & Services. Nelson, Robin. lib. bdg. 26.60 (978-0-7613-3913-7(2)); What Is Money, Anyway? Why Dollars & Coins Have Value. Larson, Jennifer S. lib. bdg. 26.60 (978-0-7613-3915-1(9)); Where Do We Keep Money? How Banks Work. Larson, Jennifer S. lib. bdg. 26.60 (978-0-7613-3911-3(6)); Who's Buying? Who's Selling? Understanding Consumers & Producers. Larson, Jennifer S. lib. bdg. 26.60 (978-0-7613-3912-0(4)); (Illus.). 32p. (gr. k-2). 2010. 2009. Set lib. bdg. 151.56 (978-0-7613-3909-0(4), Lerner Pubns.) Lerner Publishing Group.
Loughran, Donna. Carnival Coins: How Will We Count Our Money? 2013. (iMath Ser.). (Illus.). 24p. (J). (gr. k-2). lib. bdg. 21.27 (978-1-59953-552-4(1)) Norwood Hse. Pr.
Luh, Shu Shin. The Economy of China. Wang, Jianwei, ed. 2012. (China: the Emerging Superpower Ser.). 128p. (J). (gr. 7). 24.95 (978-1-4222-2157-0(1)) Mason Crest.
—The Economy of China. 2011. (J). pap. (978-1-4222-2168-6(7)) Mason Crest.
Lüsted, Marcia Amidon. What Are Jobs & Earnings? 2016. (Let's Find Out! Ser.). 32p. (J). (gr. 3-2). lib. bdg. 24.45 (978-1-68048-401-4(X)) Rosen Publishing Group, Inc., The.
Mapua, Jeff. Making the Most of Crowdfunding, 1 vol. 2015. (ENG.). 48p. (YA). 30.25 (978-1-4777-7942-2(6), Rosen Reference) Rosen Publishing Group, Inc., The.
Marsh, Carole. Pass the Test! Civics & Economics. (Virginia Experience! Ser.). lab manual ed. 195.00 incl. cd-rom (978-0-635-01593-8(5), 15935); cd-rom 395.00 (978-0-635-01594-5(3), 15943); 2004. cd-rom 24.95 (978-0-635-01592-1(7), 15927) Gallopade International.
Maybury, Richard J. Uncle Eric Talks about Personal, Career, & Financial Security. Williams, Jane A. & Daniels, Kathryn, eds. 2nd ed. 2004. ("Uncle Eric" Bk.: 1). (ENG., Illus.). 187p. pap. 14.95 (978-0-942617-38-2(X)) Bluestocking Pr.
McGraw-Hill Editors. Economics: Principles & Practices. 2004. (ECONOMICS PRINCIPLES & PRACTIC Ser.). (ENG., Illus.). 210p. (gr. 9-12). per., wbk. ed., pupil's gde. ed. 15.52 (978-0-07-865040-6(2), 0078650402) McGraw-Hill Higher Education.
McGraw-Hill Education Editors. Economics: Today & Tomorrow, Interactive Tutor: Self Assessment. 2007. (ECONOMICS TODAY & TOMORROW Ser.). (ENG.). (gr. 9-12). cd-rom 107.12 (978-0-07-878359-3(3), 0078783593) McGraw-Hill Higher Education.
McGraw-Hill Education Staff. Economics: Principles & Practices. 2007. (ECONOMICS TODAY & TOMORROW Ser.). (ENG.). 168p. (gr. 9-12). pap. 12.04 (978-0-07-878593-1(6), 0078785936) McGraw-Hill Higher Education.
—Economics: Principles & Practices, Interactive Tutor. 2007. (ECONOMICS TODAY & TOMORROW Ser.). (ENG.). (gr. 9-12). cd-rom 107.12 (978-0-07-878602-0(9), 0078786029) McGraw-Hill Higher Education.
—Economics: Today & Tomorrow, StudentWorks with Audio. 2007. (ECONOMICS TODAY & TOMORROW Ser.). (ENG.). (gr. 9-12). cd-rom 167.68 (978-0-07-878355-5(0), 0078783550) McGraw-Hill Higher Education.
—Economics Spanish Reading Essentials & Note-Taking Guide Student Workbook: Principles & Practices. 2007. (ECONOMICS TODAY & TOMORROW Ser.). (ENG & SPA., Illus.). 162p. (gr. 9-12). per. 12.04 (978-0-07-878595-5(2), 0078785952) McGraw-Hill Higher Education.
McGraw-Hill Staff. Economics: Principles & Practices. 3rd ed. 2004. (ECONOMICS PRINCIPLES & PRACTIC Ser.). (ENG.). 704p. (gr. 9-12). stu. ed. 129.24 (978-0-07-860693-9(4), 0078606934) McGraw-Hill Higher Education.
—Economics Today & Tomorrow: Reading Essentials & Study Guide. 3rd ed. 2004. (ECONOMICS TODAY & TOMORROW Ser.). (ENG., Illus.). 186p. (gr. 9-12). stu. ed., per., wbk. ed. 12.80 (978-0-07-865063-5(1), 0078650631) McGraw-Hill Higher Education.
Merino, Noël. The World Economy. 2010. (Current Controversies Ser.). (Illus.). 240p. 40.95 (978-0-7377-4713-3(7), Greenhaven Pr., Inc.) Cengage Gale.
Michele, Tracey. Why Is it Expensive? 2014. (Little Books of Answers: Level a Ser.). (Illus.). 16p. (gr. k-2). pap. 7.95 (978-1-927136-02-7(4)) Three Crows Media NZL. Dist: RiverStream Publishing.
Miller, Debra A. Nuclear Energy. Gale Editors, ed. 2010. (Current Controversies Ser.). (ENG.). 224p. (gr. 10-12). 46.40 (978-0-7377-4917-5(2)); pap. 32.00 (978-0-7377-4918-2(0)) Cengage Gale. (Greenhaven Pr., Inc.).
Miller, Roger LeRoy & McGraw-Hill Staff. Economics Today & Tomorrow. 3rd ed. 2004. (ECONOMICS TODAY & TOMORROW Ser.). (ENG., Illus.). 704p. (gr. 9-12). stu. ed. 129.24 (978-0-07-860696-0(9), 0078606969) McGraw-Hill Higher Education.
O'Neal, Claire. Ways to Help in Your Community: A Guide to Giving Back. 2010. (How to Help Ser.). (Illus.). 48p. (J). (gr. 4-8). lib. bdg. 29.95 (978-1-58415-921-6(9)) Mitchell Lane Pubs., Inc.
Orr, Tamra. A Kid's Guide to the Economy. 2009. (Money Matters Ser.). 48p. (YA). (gr. 3-6). 29.95 (978-1-58415-836-3(0)) Mitchell Lane Pubs., Inc.
—Understanding Economic Systems. 2011. (Real World Economics Ser.). (ENG.). 80p. (YA). (gr. 7-12). lib. bdg. 33.25 (978-1-4488-5568-1(3)) Rosen Publishing Group, Inc., The.
Perritano, John. The Making of the Modern World: 1945 to the Present: Trade, Economic Life & Globalization, Vol. 9. van Dijk, Ruud, ed. 2016. (Making of the Modern World: 1945 to the Present Ser.: Vol. 9). (ENG., Illus.). 64p. (J). (gr. 7-12). 23.95 (978-1-4222-3642-0(0)) Mason Crest.
Petechuk, David. The Global Economy & the Environment, Vol. 7. 2016. (Understanding Global Trade & Commerce Ser.: Vol. 7). (ENG., Illus.). 80p. (J). (gr. 7-12). 24.95 (978-1-4222-3669-7(2)) Mason Crest.
Polette, Nancy J. Teaching Economic Concepts with Picture Books & Junior Novels, 1 vol. 2013. 311p. (C). 50.00 (978-1-61069-502-2(X), A4198H) Pearson Education GBR. Dist: ABC-CLIO, LLC.
Political & Economic Systems. 2014. (Political & Economic Systems Ser.). 312p. (YA). (gr. 9-12). 315.00 (978-1-62275-365-9(8)) Rosen Publishing Group, Inc., The.
Prior, Jennifer. Capital Resources & the Economy. rev. ed. 2014. (Primary Source Readers Content & Literacy Ser.). (ENG., Illus.). 32p. (gr. 3-3). pap. 8.99 (978-1-4333-7372-5(6)) Teacher Created Materials, Inc.
Real World Economics, 4 vols., Set. Incl. How a Depression Works. Porterfield, Jason. lib. bdg. 33.25 (978-1-4358-5322-5(9)); How a Recession Works. Nagle, Jeanne M. lib. bdg. 33.25 (978-1-4358-5321-8(0)); How Globalization Works. La Bella, Laura. lib. bdg. 33.25 (978-1-4358-5323-2(7)); How Inflation Works. Hart, Joyce. lib. bdg. 33.25 (978-1-4358-5320-1(2)); (Illus.). 80p. (YA). (gr. 7-12). 2009. 2009. Set lib. bdg. 122.40 (978-1-4358-5642-4(2)) Rosen Publishing Group, Inc., The.
Roome, Anne Ross. The Global Economy. 2013. (True Book(tm), a — Great American Business Ser.). (ENG.). 48p. (J). 31.00 (978-0-531-24776-1(7)) Scholastic Library Publishing.
Roome, Hugh & Roome, Anne Ross. The Global Economy. 2013. (ENG.). 48p. (J). pap. 6.95 (978-0-531-28462-9(X)) Scholastic Library Publishing.
Seth, Shaun. Economics: The Study of Production, Distribution, & Consumption, 01 vols., 1. 2016. (Britannica Guide to the Social Sciences Ser.). (ENG.). 128p. (J). 35.25 (978-1-62275-542-4(1), Britannica Educational Publishing) Rosen Publishing Group, Inc., The.
Shoulders, Michael & Shoulders, Debbie. M Is for Money: An Economics Alphabet. Kelley, Marty, illus. 2015. (Science Alphabet Ser.). (ENG.). 32p. (J). (gr. 3-6). 16.99 (978-1-58536-817-4(2), 203953) Sleeping Bear Pr.
Student Courseware: Applying the Principles. wbk. ed. 12.95 (978-0-8219-3404-3(X)) EMC/Paradigm Publishing.
Sylvester, Kevin & Hlinka, Michael. Follow Your Money: Who Gets It, Who Spends It, Where Does It Go? Sylvester, Kevin, illus. 2nd ed. 2013. (ENG., Illus.). 60p. (J). (gr. 5-12). 24.95 (978-1-55451-481-6(9), 9781554514816); pap. 14.95 (978-1-55451-480-9(0), 9781554514809) Annick Pr., Ltd. CAN. Dist: Publishers Group West (PGW).
Taylor, John B. Study Guide: Used with ... Taylor-Economics. 4th ed. 2003. (ENG.). 368p. (YA). (gr. 6-12). pap., stu. ed. 39.16 (978-0-618-23004-4(1), 352013) CENGAGE Learning.
Turner, Donald R. & Tillema, Juliana O. Production of Goods & Services. 2011. (J). 244.80 (978-1-4488-4860-7(1)); (J). pap. 12.95 (978-1-4488-4721-1(4)); (YA). (gr. 5-9). lib. bdg. 31.95 (978-1-4488-4711-2(7)) Rosen Publishing Group, Inc., The.
U X L, ed. UXL Money, Banking & Trading, 3 vols. 2015. (ENG., Illus.). (J). 286.00 (978-1-57302-979-7(3), UXL) Cengage Gale.
Unidad 4 Superlibro: Economia: Superlibros. 2003. (MacMillan/McGraw-Hill. Estudios Sociales Ser.). (ENG &

SPA.). (gr. 1-18). *(978-0-02-149437-8(1))* Macmillan/McGraw-Hill Schl. Div.
Unidad 4 Superlibro: Economía: Vivimos Juntos: Superlibros (Big Books) 2003. (MacMillan/McGraw-Hill. Estudios Sociales Ser.). (ENG & SPA.). (gr. 2-18). *(978-0-02-149444-6(4))* Macmillan/McGraw-Hill Schl. Div.
Whitehead, William, et al. Country Money. Beech, Mark, illus. 2015. (How Money Works). (ENG.). 64p. (J). (gr. 4-6). lib. bdg. 29.27 *(978-1-59953-719-1(2))* Norwood Hse. Pr.
Williams, Jane A. & Daniels, Kathryn, eds. Economics - A Free Market Reader. 2004. (ENG.). 127p. (YA). pap. 12.95 *(978-0-942617-44-3(4))* Bluestocking Pr.
Wirtschaft. (Duden-Schuelerduden Ser.). (GER., Illus.). 428p. (YA). 27.95 *(978-3-411-04892-2(1),* B4892E) Bibliographisches Institut & F. A. Brockhaus AG DEU. Dist: Continental Bk. Co., Inc.
World Book, Inc Staff, contrib. by. Economics. 2009. (J). *(978-0-7166-0392-4(6))* World Bk., Inc.

ECONOMISTS

Bussing-Burks, Marie. Influential Economists. 2003. (Illus.). 160p. (gr. 5-18). lib. bdg. 19.95 *(978-1-881508-72-4(2))* Oliver Pr., Inc.
Crain, Cynthia D. & Lee, Dwight R. Milton Friedman. 2009. (Profiles in Economics Ser.). (Illus.). 144p. (YA). lib. bdg. 28.95 *(978-1-59935-108-7(0))* Reynolds, Morgan Inc.
Forstater, Mathew. Trailblazers in Economics, 1 vol. 2015. (ENG.). 192p. (J). 40.95 *(978-1-4777-8146-3(3),* Rosen Young Adult) Rosen Publishing Group, Inc., The.
Marini, Matt. Analytics: Sports Stats & More, Vol. 10. Ferrer, Al, ed. 2015. (Careers off the Field Ser.). (Illus.). 64p. (J). (gr. 7). lib. bdg. 23.95 *(978-1-4222-3265-1(4))* Mason Crest.
Yoo, Paula. Twenty-Two Cents: Muhammad Yunus & the Village Bank. Akib, Jamel, illus. 2014. (ENG.). 40p. (J). 18.95 *(978-1-60060-658-8(X))* Lee & Low Bks., Inc.

ECUADOR

Barghoorn, Linda. A Refugee's Journey from Colombia. 2017. 32p. (J). ***(978-0-7787-3672-1(5))*** Crabtree Publishing Co.
Behnke, Alison. Ecuador in Pictures. 2008. (Visual Geography Ser.). (YA). (gr. 7-12). lib. bdg. 31.93 *(978-0-8225-8573-2(1))* Twenty First Century Bks.
Colleen Madonna Flood Williams. Ecuador, Vol. 13. Henderson, James D., ed. 2015. (Discovering South America: History, Politics, & Culture Ser.). (Illus.). 64p. (J). (gr. 7). lib. bdg. 22.95 *(978-1-4222-3299-6(9))* Mason Crest.
Crespi, Jess. Exploring Ecuador with the Five Themes of Geography. (Library of the Western Hemisphere Ser.). 24p. 2009. (gr. 4-4). 42.50 *(978-1-60853-926-0(1),* PowerKids Pr.) 2005. (Illus.). (J). (gr. 5-7). lib. bdg. 22.60 *(978-1-4042-2675-3(3),* PowerKids Pr.) 2005. (ENG., Illus.). (gr. 3-8). pap. 8.25 *(978-0-8239-4635-8(5))* Rosen Publishing Group, Inc., The.
Foley, Erin & Jermyn, Leslie. Ecuador. 2nd rev. ed. 2005. (Cultures of the World Ser.). (Illus.). 144p. (gr. 6-10). lib. bdg. 42.79 *(978-0-7614-2050-7(9),* Benchmark Bks.) Marshall Cavendish Corp.
Foley, Erin, et al. Ecuador. 2016. (Cultures of the World (r) Ser.). (Illus.). 144p. (J). (gr. 5-5). 47.07 *(978-1-5026-1701-9(3))* Cavendish Square Publishing.
Lomberg, Michelle. Ecuador. 2016. (J). ***(978-1-4896-5408-3(9))*** Weigl Pubs., Inc.
Markovics, Joyce L. Ecuador. 2016. (Countries We Come From Ser.). (ENG.). 32p. (J). (gr. -1-3). lib. bdg. 19.95 *(978-1-944102-71-5(X))* Bearport Publishing Co., Inc.
Owings, Lisa. Ecuador. 2015. (Exploring Countries Ser.). (ENG., Illus.). 32p. (J). (gr. 3-7). lib. bdg. 26.95 *(978-1-62617-174-9(2),* Blastoff! Readers) Bellwether Media.
Williams, Colleen Madonna Flood. Ecuador. 2009. (South America Today Ser.). (Illus.). 64p. (J). (gr. 4-7). 21.95 *(978-1-4222-0636-2(X))* Mason Crest.

ECUADOR—FICTION

Cohn, Diana. Roses for Isabella. Córdova, Amy, illus. 2011. 32p. (J). 17.95 *(978-0-88010-731-0(6))* SteinerBooks, Inc.
Farinango, Maria Virginia & Resau, Laura. The Queen of Water. 2012. (ENG.). 368p. (YA). (gr. 7). pap. 9.99 *(978-0-375-85963-2(2),* Ember) Random Hse. Children's Bks.
Hering, Marianne. In Fear of the Spear. 2016. (AIO Imagination Station Bks.: 17). (ENG.). 144p. (J). pap. 4.99 *(978-1-58997-804-1(8))* Focus on the Family Publishing.
Lunn, Carolyn. Tomas & the Galapagos Adventure. Rades, Ashley, illus. 2016. (ENG.). 28p. (J). (gr. 3-4). 15.99 *(978-0-692-58289-3(4),* Little Adventures) Amberjack Publishing Co.
Resau, Laura. The Indigo Notebook. 2010. (ENG.). 336p. (YA). (gr. 7). pap. 9.99 *(978-0-375-84524-6(0),* Ember) Random Hse. Children's Bks.
Saddleback Educational Publishing, ed. Treasure, 1 vol. 2013. (Heights Ser.). (ENG.). 52p. (gr. 5-8). 7.95 *(978-1-62250-048-2(2))* Saddleback Educational Publishing, Inc.
Stilton, Thea. Thea Stilton & the Chocolate Sabotage. 2014. (Thea Stilton Ser.: 19). (ENG., Illus.). 176p. (J). (gr. 2-5). pap. 8.99 *(978-0-545-64656-7(1),* Scholastic Paperbacks) Scholastic, Inc.
Young, Judy. Tuki & Moka: A Tale of Two Tamarins. Madsen, Jim, illus. 2013. (ENG.). 32p. 16.99 *(978-1-58536-795-5(8))* Sleeping Bear Pr.

EDDY, MARY BAKER, 1821-1910

Ferguson, Isabel, et al. A World More Bright: The Life of Mary Baker Eddy. 2013. (Illus.). vi, 279p. (J). *(978-0-87510-494-2(0))* Christian Science Publishing Society.

EDIBLE PLANTS

see Plants, Edible

EDINBURGH (SCOTLAND)

Doeden, Matt. Edinburgh Castle: A Chilling Interactive Adventure. 2017. (You Choose: Haunted Places Ser.). (ENG., Illus.). 112p. (gr. 3-4). lib. bdg. 31.99 *(978-1-5157-3648-6(2),* You Choose Bks.) Capstone Press of Coughlan Cos.
Gordon, Nick. Edinburgh Castle. 2013. (Scariest Places on Earth Ser.). (ENG., Illus.). 24p. (J). (gr. 3-7). lib. bdg. 25.95 *(978-1-60014-948-1(0),* Torque Bks.) Bellwether Media.
Haunted! Edinburgh Castle. 2013. (History's Most Haunted Ser.). 32p. (J). (gr. 3-6). pap. 63.00 *(978-1-4339-9255-1(8))* Stevens, Gareth Publishing LLLP.
Knox, Barbara. Edinburgh Castle: Scotland's Haunted Fortress. 2006. (Castles, Palaces, & Tombs Ser.). (Illus.). 32p. (YA). (gr. 2-5). lib. bdg. 25.27 *(978-1-59716-248-7(5))* Bearport Publishing Co., Inc.
Nagelhout, Ryan. Haunted! Edinburgh Castle. 2013. 32p. (J). (gr. 3-6). 26.60 *(978-1-4339-9253-7(1))* Stevens, Gareth Publishing LLLP.
Sasek, Miroslav. This Is Edinburgh. 2006. (This Is ... Ser.). (ENG., Illus.). 64p. (J). (gr. 2-12). 17.95 *(978-0-7893-1387-4(1))* Universe Publishing.

EDINBURGH (SCOTLAND)—FICTION

Brown, Ruth. Greyfriars Bobby. Brown, Ruth, illus. 2013. (ENG., Illus.). 32p. (J). (gr. -1-k). pap. 12.99 *(978-1-84939-632-5(9))* Andersen Pr. GBR. Dist: Independent Pubs. Group.
Cole, Steve. Z. Rex. 2009. (ENG.). 256p. (J). (gr. 5-9). 16.99 *(978-0-399-25253-2(3),* Philomel Bks.) Penguin Young Readers Group.
Forbes, Anne. Dragonfire, 1 vol. 2006. (ENG.). 256p. (J). per. 11.95 *(978-0-86315-552-9(9))* Floris Bks. GBR. Dist: SteinerBooks, Inc.
—The Underground City. 2008. (Contemporary Kelpies Ser.). (ENG.). 272p. (J). pap. *(978-0-86315-637-3(1))* Floris Bks.
Forrester, Margaret. The Cat Who Decided: The Almost True Story of an Edinburgh Cat, 1 vol. Klaassen, Sandra, illus. 2007. (Young Kelpies Ser.). (ENG.). 112p. (J). per. *(978-0-86315-612-0(6))* Floris Bks.
Goodwin, Vincent. Body-Snatcher, 1 vol. 2014. (Graphic Horror Set 3 Ser.). (ENG.). 32p. (J). (gr. 5-8). lib. bdg. 28.50 *(978-1-62402-013-1(5),* Graphic Planet) Magic Wagon.
Hendry, Frances. Quest for a Queen: The Falcon. 2006. pap. *(978-1-905665-06-8(7))* Pollinger In Print.
Hutton, Alasdair. The Tattoo Fox, 1 vol. Stref, illus. 2013. (ENG.). 96p. (J). (gr. 2-3). pap. 9.95 *(978-1-908373-93-9(8),* 9781908373939) Luath Pr. Ltd. GBR. Dist: Midpoint Trade Bks., Inc.
Lightwood, Donald. The Long Revenge. 128p. pap. 7.95 *(978-1-899827-94-7(3))* Scottish Children's Pr. GBR. Dist: Wilson & Assocs.
Lingard, Joan. Odd Girl Out. 187p. (J). pap. *(978-0-340-75735-2(3))* Hodder & Stoughton.
May, Elizabeth. The Fallen Kingdom: Book Three of the Falconer Trilogy. 2017. (Falconer Ser.: 3). (ENG.). 400p. (YA). 18.99 ***(978-1-4521-2883-2(9))*** Chronicle Bks. LLC.
Spirn, Michele Sobel. The Bridges in Edinburgh. 2004. (Going to Ser.). 144p. (J). pap. 6.95 *(978-1-893577-11-4(2))* Fruitbearer Publishing, LLC.

EDISON, THOMAS A. (THOMAS ALVA), 1847-1931

Adkins, Jan. Thomas Edison. 2009. (DK Biography Ser.). (ENG., Illus.). 128p. (J). (gr. 5-12). 6.99 *(978-0-7566-5207-4(3),* DK Children) Dorling Kindersley Publishing, Inc.
Auch, Allison. Electrifying Personalities & Personalidades Electrizantes: 6 English, 6 Spanish Adaptations. 2011. (ENG & SPA.). (J). 97.00 net. *(978-1-4108-5713-2(1))* Benchmark Education Co.
Barnham, Kay. Thomas Edison, 1 vol. 2014. (Science Biographies Ser.). (ENG.). 32p. (gr. 2-4). lib. bdg. 30.65 *(978-1-4109-6239-3(3),* Raintree Perspectives) Heinemann-Raintree.
Barretta, Gene. Timeless Thomas: How Thomas Edison Changed Our Lives. Barretta, Gene, illus. 2012. (ENG., Illus.). 40p. (J). (gr. 1-5). 18.99 *(978-0-8050-9108-3(4),* 9780805091083, Holt, Henry & Co. Bks. For Young Readers) Holt, Henry & Co.
Benge, Janet & Benge, Geoff. Heroes of History - Thomas Edison: Inspiration & Hard Work. 2007. (Heroes of History Ser.). (ENG.). 208p. (YA). (gr. 3-7). pap. 9.99 *(978-1-932096-37-8(X))* Emerald Bks.
Brown, Don. A Wizard from the Start: The Incredible Boyhood & Amazing Inventions of Thomas Edison. Brown, Don, illus. 2010. (ENG., Illus.). 32p. (J). (gr. -1-3). 17.99 *(978-0-547-19487-5(0))* Houghton Mifflin Harcourt Publishing Co.
Bryant, Tamera. Thomas Alva Edison. 2003. (World Was Never the Same Ser.). (J). *(978-1-58417-260-4(6))*; pap. *(978-1-58417-261-1(4))* Lake Street Pubs.
Carlson, Laurie M. & Carlson, Laurie. Thomas Edison for Kids: His Life & Ideas, 21 Activities. 2006. (For Kids Ser.). (ENG., Illus.). 160p. (J). (gr. 4-7). pap. 17.99 *(978-1-55652-584-1(2),* 1248637) Chicago Review Pr., Inc.
Cefrey, Holly. The Inventions of Thomas Alva Edison: Father of the Light Bulb & the Motion Picture Camera. 2009. (19th Century American Inventors Ser.). 24p. (gr. 2-3). 42.50 *(978-1-60854-954-2(2),* PowerKids Pr.) Rosen Publishing Group, Inc., The.
—The Inventions of Thomas Alva Edison: Father of the Lightbulb & the Motion Picture Camera. 2003. (19th Century American Inventors Ser.). (Illus.). 24p. (J). lib. bdg. 22.60 *(978-0-8239-6440-6(X),* PowerKids Pr.) Rosen Publishing Group, Inc., The.
Colbert, David. Thomas Edison. 2008. (10 Days Ser.). (ENG.). 160p. (J). (gr. 3-8). pap. 8.99 *(978-1-4169-6444-5(4),* Simon & Schuster/Paula Wiseman Bks.) Simon & Schuster/Paula Wiseman Bks.
Cregan, Elizabeth R. C. Thomas Edison & the Pioneers of Electromagnetism, 1 vol. 2007. (Science Readers Ser.). (ENG.). 32p. (J). (gr. 4-4). pap. 8.99 *(978-0-7439-0576-3(8))* Shell Educational Publishing.
Davis, Lynn. Thomas Edison, 1 vol. 2016. (ENG., Illus.). 24p. (J). 25.65 *(978-1-62403-723-8(2))* ABDO Publishing Co.
Delano, Marfe Ferguson. Inventing the Future: A Photobiography of Thomas Alva Edison. 2006. (Photobiographies Ser.). (ENG., Illus.). 64p. (J). (gr. 5-7). per. 7.95 *(978-0-7922-5934-3(3),* National Geographic Children's Bks.) National Geographic Society.
Delano, Marfe Ferguson & National Geographic Kids Staff. Inventing the Future: A Photobiography of Thomas Alva Edison. 2015. (Photobiographies Ser.). (ENG., Illus.). 64p. (J). (gr. 5). pap. 7.99 *(978-1-4263-2220-4(8),* National Geographic Children's Bks.) National Geographic Society.
DeMauro, Lisa. Thomas Edison A Brilliant Inventor. 2005. 44p. (J). lib. bdg. 15.00 *(978-1-4242-0854-8(8))* Fitzgerald Bks.
Demuth, Patricia Brennan. Thomas Edison & His Bright Idea. Tuya, Jez, illus. 2016. (Penguin Young Readers, Level 3 Ser.). (ENG.). 32p. (J). (gr. 1-3). pap. 3.99 *(978-0-448-48830-1(2),* Penguin Young Readers) Penguin Young Readers Group.
Dolan, Ellen M. Thomas Alva Edison: American Inventor & Businessman. 2015. (Legendary American Biographies Ser.). 96p. (J). (gr. 6-12). 27.94 *(978-0-7660-6510-9(3))*; pap. 10.95 *(978-0-7660-6511-6(1))* Enslow Pubs., Inc.
Dooling, Michael. Young Thomas Edison. Dooling, Michael, illus. 2005. (ENG., Illus.). 40p. (J). (gr. -1-3). 17.95 *(978-0-8234-1868-8(5))* Holiday Hse., Inc.
Fandel, Jennifer. The Light Bulb. 2004. (What in the World? Ser.). (Illus.). 48p. 19.95 *(978-1-58341-271-8(9),* Creative Education) Creative Co., The.
Frith, Margaret. Who Was Thomas Alva Edison? O'Brien, John A. et al, illus. 2005. (Who Was? Ser.). (ENG.). 112p. (J). (gr. 3-7). pap. 5.99 *(978-0-448-43765-1(1),* Grosset & Dunlap) Penguin Young Readers Group.
—Who Was Thomas Alva Edison? O'brien, John, illus. 2005. (Who Was... ? Ser.). 106p. (gr. 3-7). 15.00 *(978-0-7569-5830-5(X))* Perfection Learning Corp.
Garcia, Tracy J. Thomas Edison. 2013. (Jr. Graphic American Inventors Ser.). (ENG., Illus.). 24p. (J). (gr. 3-6). pap. 10.60 *(978-1-4777-0137-9(0))*; lib. bdg. 25.25 *(978-1-4777-0076-1(5))* Rosen Publishing Group, Inc., The. (PowerKids Pr.).
Goldsmith, Howard. Thomas Edison to the Rescue! DiVito, Anna, illus. 2003. (Ready-To-read COFA Ser.). (ENG.). 32p. (J). (gr. k-2). pap. 3.99 *(978-0-689-85331-9(9),* Simon Spotlight) Simon Spotlight.
Gomez, Rebecca. Thomas Edison, 1 vol. 2003. (First Biographies Ser.). (ENG., Illus.). 32p. (gr. k-4). 27.07 *(978-1-57765-945-7(7),* Buddy Bks.) ABDO Publishing Co.
Graham, Amy. Thomas Edison: Wizard of Light & Sound. 2007. (Inventors Who Changed the World Ser.). (Illus.). 128p. (J). (gr. 5-9). lib. bdg. 34.60 *(978-1-59845-052-1(2),* MyReportLinks.com Bks.) Enslow Pubs., Inc.
Hantula, Richard. Thomas Edison. 2004. (Trailblazers of the Modern World Ser.). (Illus.). 48p. (J). (gr. 5-12). pap. 14.05 *(978-0-8368-5265-3(6))*; lib. bdg. 31.00 *(978-0-8368-5496-1(9))* Stevens, Gareth Publishing LLLP. (Gareth Stevens Secondary Library).
Hardyman, Robyn. Nikola Tesla & Thomas Edison. 2014. (Dynamic Duos of Science Ser.). 48p. (YA). (gr. 5-8). pap. 84.30 *(978-1-4824-1285-7(3))* Stevens, Gareth Publishing LLLP.
Jenner, Caryn & Dorling Kindersley Publishing Staff. Thomas Edison - The Great Inventor, Level 4. 2007. (DK Readers Ser.). (ENG.). 48p. (J). (gr. 3-7). pap. 3.99 *(978-0-7566-2946-5(2),* DK Children) Dorling Kindersley Publishing, Inc.
Kobayashi, Tatsuyoshi, illus. Thomas Edison: Genius of the Electric Age. 2011. (Biographical Comic Ser.). (ENG.). 152p. (J). (gr. 2-6). 18.99 *(978-1-4215-4236-2(6))* Shogakukan JPN. Dist: Simon & Schuster, Inc.
Krieg, Katherine. Thomas Edison: World-Changing Inventor, 1 vol. 2014. (Great Minds of Science Ser.). (ENG.). 48p. (gr. 8-12). lib. bdg. 32.79 *(978-1-62403-378-0(4))* ABDO Publishing Co.
Kulling, Monica & Slavin, Bill. Zap! Nikola Tesla Takes Charge. 2016. (Great Idea Ser.). (ENG., Illus.). 32p. (J). (gr. k-3). 17.99 *(978-1-77049-522-7(3),* Tundra Bks.) Tundra Bks. CAN. Dist: Penguin Random Hse. LLC.
Lee, T. S. The Thomas Edison Story: The First Thomas Edison Comic Biography. 2010. 179p. (J). pap. 14.95 *(978-0-9819542-5-7(1))* DASANBOOKS.
MacLeod, Elizabeth. Thomas Edison. Krystoforski, Andrej, illus. 2008. (ENG.). 32p. (J). (gr. 1-3). 14.95 *(978-1-55453-057-1(1))*; pap. 3.95 *(978-1-55453-058-8(X))* Kids Can Pr., Ltd. CAN. Dist: Hachette Bk. Group.
Mara, Wil & National Geographic Learning Staff. Thomas Alva Edison. 2010. (Rise & Shine Ser.). (ENG.). 32p. (C). (gr. 1-2). pap. 8.95 *(978-0-516-25822-5(2))* National Geographic School Publishing, Inc.
McLaughlin, Kari Massie. My Adventure with Thomas Edison. 2007. 44p. (J). 8.99 *(978-1-59092-472-3(X))* Blue Forge Pr.
McPherson, Stephanie Sammartino. War of the Currents: Thomas Edison vs. Nikola Tesla. 2012. (Scientific Rivalries & Scandals Ser.). (ENG., Illus.). 64p. (J). (gr. 6-12). lib. bdg. 33.27 *(978-0-7613-5487-1(5))* Lerner Publishing Group.
Miller, Francis Trevel. Thomas A Edison an Inspiring Story for B. 2006. pap. 31.95 *(978-1-4286-5329-0(5))* Kessinger Publishing, LLC.
Mortensen, Lori & Picture Window Books Staff. Thomas Edison: Inventor, Scientist, & Genius, 1 vol. Thompson, Jeffrey, illus. 2007. (Biographies Ser.). (ENG.). 24p. (gr. k-3). 26.65 *(978-1-4048-3105-6(3))* Picture Window Bks.
National Geographic Kids Staff & Kramer, Barbara. National Geographic Readers: Thomas Edison. 2014. (Readers Bios Ser.). (ENG., Illus.). 32p. (J). (gr. k-3). pap. 3.99 *(978-1-4263-1476-6(0))*; lib. bdg. 13.90 *(978-1-4263-1477-3(9))* National Geographic Society. (National Geographic Children's Bks.).
National Geographic Learning Staff. Thomas Edison, Level 3 - World Windows. 2011. (World Windows Ser.). (ENG., Illus.). 16p. (J). stu. ed. 9.95 *(978-1-133-49279-5(7))* Cengage Heinle.
North, Sterling. Young Thomas Edison. 2009. (ENG., Illus.). 192p. (J). (gr. 3-7). pap. 6.99 *(978-0-14-241210-7(4),* Puffin Books) Penguin Young Readers Group.
Pederson, Charles E. Thomas Edison, 1 vol. 2007. (Essential Lives Set 1 Ser.). (ENG., Illus.). 112p. (J). (gr. 6-12). lib. bdg. 35.64 *(978-1-59928-845-1(1))* ABDO Publishing Co.
Rausch, Monica L. Thomas Edison & the Light Bulb. 2007. (Inventors & Their Discoveries Ser.). (Illus.). 24p. (gr. 1-4). pap. 8.15 *(978-0-8368-7732-8(2),* Weekly Reader Leveled Readers) Stevens, Gareth Publishing LLLP.
—Thomas Edison & the Lightbulb. 2007. (Inventors & Their Discoveries Ser.). (Illus.). 24p. (gr. 1-4). lib. bdg. 22.00 *(978-0-8368-7501-0(X),* Weekly Reader Leveled Readers) Stevens, Gareth Publishing LLLP.
—Thomas Edison y la bombilla Eléctrica. 2007. (Inventores y sus descubrimientos (Inventors & Their Discoveries) Ser.). (SPA., Illus.). 24p. (gr. 1-4). lib. bdg. 22.00 *(978-0-8368-7997-1(X),* Weekly Reader Leveled Readers) Stevens, Gareth Publishing LLLP.
—Thomas Edison y la Bombilla Eléctrica. 2007. (Inventores y sus descubrimientos (Inventors & Their Discoveries) Ser.). (SPA., Illus.). 24p. (gr. 1-4). pap. 8.15 *(978-0-8368-8002-1(1),* Weekly Reader Leveled Readers) Stevens, Gareth Publishing LLLP.
Roza, Greg. Thomas Alva Edison, 1 vol. 2015. (ENG., Illus.). 32p. (J). 23.45 *(978-1-62275-693-3(2),* Britannica Educational Publishing) Rosen Publishing Group, Inc., The.
Sabin, Louis & Macken, JoAnn Early. Thomas Edison: Incredible Inventor. 2006. (Illus.). 52p. (J). *(978-0-439-88006-0(8))* Scholastic, Inc.
Saddleback Educational Publishing Staff, ed. Thomas Edison, 1 vol. unabr. ed. 2008. (Graphic Biographies Ser.). (ENG., Illus.). 25p. (YA). (gr. 9-12). pap. 7.95 *(978-1-59905-228-1(8))* Saddleback Educational Publishing, Inc.
Silver, Tony. What's the Big Idea? The Story of Thomas Edison. (Illus.). 16p. *(978-0-7367-2880-5(5))* Zaner-Bloser, Inc.
Slade, Suzanne. The Inventor's Secret: What Thomas Edison Told Henry Ford. Reinhardt, Jennifer Black, illus. 2015. (ENG.). 48p. (J). (gr. 1-4). lib. bdg. 16.95 *(978-1-58089-667-2(7))* Charlesbridge Publishing, Inc.
Sonneborn, Liz. The Electric Light: Thomas Edison's Illuminating Invention. 2007. (Milestones in American History Ser.). (Illus.). 120p. (YA). (gr. 7-12). lib. bdg. 35.00 *(978-0-7910-9350-4(6))* Facts On File, Inc.
Sprunger, Reed. Thomas Edison: Incredible Inventor, 1 vol. 2013. (Beginner Biographies Set 2 Ser.). (ENG.). 32p. (J). (gr. -1-4). lib. bdg. 28.50 *(978-1-61641-936-3(9),* Looking Glass Library) Magic Wagon.
Tagliaferro, Linda. Thomas Edison: Inventor of the Age of Electricity. 2003. (Lerner Biographies Ser.). (ENG., Illus.). 128p. (gr. 6-12). 27.93 *(978-0-8225-4689-4(2),* Lerner Pubns.) Lerner Publishing Group.
Thatcher Murcia, Rebecca. Thomas Edison: Great Inventor. 2004. (Uncharted, Unexplored, & Unexplained Ser.). (Illus.). 48p. (J). (gr. 4-8). lib. bdg. 29.95 *(978-1-58415-306-1(7))* Mitchell Lane Pubs., Inc.
Time for Kids Editors. Time for Kids - Thomas Edison: A Brilliant Inventor. 2005. (Time for Kids Ser.). (ENG., Illus.). 48p. (J). (gr. 2-4). pap. 3.99 *(978-0-06-057611-0(1))* HarperCollins Pubs.
Venezia, Mike. Thomas Edison: Inventor with a Lot of Bright Ideas. Venezia, Mike, illus. (Getting to Know the World's Greatest Inventors & Scientists Ser.). (ENG., Illus.). 32p. (J). 2009. (gr. 3-4). pap. 6.95 *(978-0-531-22209-6(8),* Children's Pr.) 2008. (gr. 2-5). 28.00 *(978-0-531-14978-2(1))* Scholastic Library Publishing.
Weakland, Mark. When Thomas Edison Fed Someone Worms. Radcliffe, Thomas, illus. 2017. (J). *(978-1-5158-0139-9(X))* Picture Window Bks.
—When Thomas Edison Fed Someone Worms. Radcliffe, Thomas, illus. 2016. (Leaders Doing Headstands Ser.). (ENG.). 32p. (gr. 2-3). pap. 7.95 *(978-1-5158-0135-1(7))* Picture Window Bks.
Welvaert, Scott R. Thomas Edison & the Lightbulb, 1 vol. Miller, Phil et al, illus. 2006. (Inventions & Discovery Ser.). (ENG.). 32p. (gr. 3-4). 30.65 *(978-0-7368-6489-3(X),* Graphic Library) Capstone Press of Coughlan Cos.
Woodside, Martin. Thomas Edison: The Man Who Lit up the World. 2007. (Sterling Biographies(r) Ser.). (ENG., Illus.). 128p. (J). (gr. 5-9). pap. 5.95 *(978-1-4027-3229-4(5))* Sterling Publishing Co., Inc.
Zemlicka, Shannon. Thomas Edison. 2003. (History Maker Biographies Ser.). (ENG., Illus.). 48p. (J). (gr. 3-6). lib. bdg. 27.93 *(978-0-8225-0239-5(9),* Lerner Pubns.) Lerner Publishing Group.

EDISON, THOMAS A. (THOMAS ALVA), 1847-1931—FICTION

Helfand, Lewis. They Changed the World: Bell, Edison & Tesla. Kumar, Naresh, illus. 2014. (Campfire Graphic Novels Ser.). (ENG.). 102p. (YA). (gr. 8-12). pap. 12.99 *(978-93-80741-87-1(1),* Campfire) Steerforth Pr.
Moriarty, Chris. The Inquisitor's Apprentice. Geyer, Mark Edward, illus. 2013. (ENG.). 352p. (J). (gr. 5-7). pap. 7.99 *(978-0-547-85084-9(0))* Houghton Mifflin Harcourt Publishing Co.
Sargent, Dave & Sargent, Pat. Ginger: (Lilac Roan) Be Likeable, 30 vols., Vol. 27. Lenoir, Jane, illus. 2003. (Saddle up Ser.: Vol. 27). 42p. (J). pap. 10.95 *(978-1-56763-812-7(0))*; lib. bdg. 23.60 *(978-1-56763-811-0(2))* Ozark Publishing.
Shafer, Susan. Thomas Edison Invents the Lightbulb. 2005. (J). pap. *(978-1-4108-4188-9(X))* Benchmark Education Co.
Steinkraus, Kyla. Toffee with Thomas Edison. 2016. (Time Hop Sweets Shop Ser.). (ENG.). 32p. (gr. k-3). 25.65 *(978-1-68191-372-8(0))* Rourke Educational Media.

EDITORIALS

Harper, Leslie. Cómo Escribir un Artículo de Opinión. 2014. (Sé un líder de la Comunidad (Be a Community Leader) Ser.). (SPA.). 32p. (J). (gr. 4-6). lib. bdg. 26.25 *(978-1-4777-6905-8(6),* PowerKids Pr.) Rosen Publishing Group, Inc., The.
—Cómo Escribir un Artículo Editorial. 2014. (Sé un líder de la Comunidad (Be a Community Leader) Ser.). (SPA.). 32p. (J). (gr. 4-6). pap. 60.00 *(978-1-4777-6907-2(2),* PowerKids Pr.) Rosen Publishing Group, Inc., The.
—How to Write an Op-Ed Piece. 2014. (Be a Community Leader Ser.). (Illus.). 32p. (J). (gr. 4-6). lib. bdg. 26.25 *(978-1-4777-6685-9(5),* PowerKids Pr.) Rosen Publishing Group, Inc., The.
Loewen, Nancy. Writing Outstanding Opinion Pieces. 2015. (ENG., Illus.). 56p. (gr. 6-8). 33.32 *(978-1-4677-7905-0(9),* Lerner Pubns.) Lerner Publishing Group.

EDITORS AND EDITING

see Journalism; Journalists; Publishers and Publishing

EDMONDS, S. EMMA E. (SARAH EMMA EVELYN), 1841-1898

Jones, Carrie. Sarah Emma Edmonds Was a Great Pretender: The True Story of a Civil War Spy. Oldroyd, Mark, illus. 2011. (Carolrhoda Picture Bks.). (ENG.). 32p. (J). (gr. 2-5). 17.95 *(978-0-7613-5399-7(2))* Lerner Publishing Group.
Moss, Marissa. Nurse, Soldier, Spy: The Story of Sarah Edmonds, a Civil War Hero. Hendrix, John, illus. (ENG.). 48p. (J). 2016. (gr. 1-4). pap. 9.95 *(978-1-4197-2065-9(1))* 2011. (gr. 3-7). 19.95 *(978-0-8109-9735-6(5))* Abrams, Inc. (Abrams Bks. for Young Readers).

EDUCATION

see also Audio-Visual Education; Books and Reading; Business Education; Culture; Educators; Learning and Scholarship; Libraries; Literacy; Military Education; Moral Education; Physical Education and Training; Religious Education; Scholarships; Schools; Self-Culture; Study Skills; Teachers; Teaching; Technical Education; Universities and Colleges

also names of classes of people and social and ethnic groups with the subdivision Education, (e.g. African Americans—Education); subjects with the subdivision Study and Teaching (e.g. Science—Study and Teaching); and headings beginning with the words Education and Educational

Agassi, Martine. Hands Are Not for Hitting. Heinlen, Marieka, illus. rev. ed. 2009. (Best Behavior Ser.). (ENG.). 40p. (J). (gr. -1-2). pap. 11.95 (978-1-57542-308-1(1)) Free Spirit Publishing, Inc.

Agassi, Martine & Verdick, Elizabeth. Las Manos No Son para Pegar. Heinlen, Marieka, illus. 2009. (Best Behavior Ser.).Tr. of Hands Are Not for Hitting. (SPA & ENG.). 40p. (J). (gr. -1-2). pap. 11.95 (978-1-57542-310-4(3)) Free Spirit Publishing, Inc.

Agassi, Martine, et al. Las Manos No Son para Pegar. Heinlen, Marieka, illus. 2009. (Best Behavior Ser.).Tr. of Hands Are Not for Hitting. (SPA, ENG & MUL.). 24p. (J). (gr. -1 — 1). bds. 7.95 (978-1-57542-309-8(X)) Free Spirit Publishing, Inc.

Bartos, Judeen. Do Schools Prepare Students for a Global Economy? 2012. (At Issue Ser.). (ENG., Illus.). 128p. (gr. 10-12). pap. 27.80 (978-0-7377-4095-0(7), Greenhaven Pr., Inc.) Cengage Gale.

—Do U. S. Schools Prepare Students for a Global Economy? 2012. (At Issue Ser.). (ENG., Illus.). 128p. (gr. 10-12). 39.40 (978-0-7377-4094-3(9), Greenhaven Pr., Inc.) Cengage Gale.

Bickico Enterprises Staff, concept. BabyKids: The Shapes Book. 2003. 16p. (J). pap. 2.95 (978-0-9746508-3-8(8)) Bickico Enterprises, Inc.

Blue Sky Ink Staff. Congratulations Graduate You Did It! 2004. (Illus.). 128p. 9.99 (978-1-59475-010-6(6)) Blue Sky Ink.

Boothroyd, Jennifer. From Chalkboards to Computers: How Schools Have Changed. 2011. (Lightning Bolt Books Comparing Past & Present Ser.). (ENG., Illus.). 32p. (gr. k-2). lib. bdg. 26.60 (978-0-7613-6744-4(6)) Lerner Publishing Group.

Borgnon, Liselotte & Olsson, Liselott Mariett. Movement & Experimentation in Young Children's Learning: Deleuze & Guattari in Early Childhood Education. 2009. (Contesting Early Childhood Ser.). (ENG., Illus.). 264p. (C). pap. 54.95 (978-0-415-46867-1(1), RU53864) Routledge.

Boritzer, Etan. What Is True? Vernon, Jeff, illus. 2010. (J). (978-0-9637597-0-2(1)) Lane, Veronica Bks.

Boyd, Anne A. Help Me Decide! 2004. (Illus.). 192p. pap. 13.95 (978-0-673-58663-6(4)) Good Year Bks.

Bozzo, Linda & Library. Schools of the Past, Present, & Future. 2010. (Imagining the Future Ser.). (Illus.). 24p. (J). lib. bdg. 22.60 (978-0-7660-3434-1(8), Enslow Elementary) Enslow Pubs., Inc.

Bumcrot, Curt & Bumcrot, Jenny. Achieving Peak Performance New Edition. Krischke, Nikki, ed. 2nd rev. ed. 2003. 21p. (gr. 3-18). pap. 5.00 (978-1-888786-42-2(6)) Basic Skills Assessment & Educational Services.

Carder, Ken & LaRoy, Sue. Kindergarten: Ages 5-6. Johnson, Mike et al, illus. 2005. 95p. (J). (gr. -1-3). pap. 12.99 incl. audio compact disk (978-1-57583-818-2(4)) Twin Sisters IP, LLC.

Carson-Dellosa Publishing Staff, ed. Actividades de Tercer Grado. 2004. (Home Workbooks Ser.). 64p. 3.49 (978-0-88724-263-2(4), CD-4552) Carson-Dellosa Publishing, LLC.

Chomet, Natalie. How to Create Digital Portfolios to Apply for College & Jobs. 2017. (Project Learning Using Digital Portfolios Ser.). 64p. (J). (gr. 12-12). 34.45 (978-1-5081-7528-5(4), Rosen Young Adult) Rosen Publishing Group, Inc., The.

Collins Easy Learning, Collins Easy. English Quick Quizzes Ages 5-7. 2017. (Collins Easy Learning KS1 Ser.). (ENG., Illus.). 32p. (J). (gr. k-2). pap. 6.99 (978-0-00-821253-7(8)) HarperCollins Pubs. Ltd. GBR. Dist: Independent Pubs. Group.

—English Quick Quizzes Ages 7-9. 2017. (Collins Easy Learning KS2 Ser.). (ENG., Illus.). 32p. (J). (gr. 2-4). pap. 6.99 (978-0-00-821263-6(5)) HarperCollins Pubs. Ltd. GBR. Dist: Independent Pubs. Group.

—Fractions & Decimals Quick Quizzes Ages 7-9. 2017. (Collins Easy Learning KS2 Ser.). (ENG., Illus.). 32p. (J). (gr. 2-4). pap. 6.99 (978-0-00-821260-5(0)) HarperCollins Pubs. Ltd. GBR. Dist: Independent Pubs. Group.

—Fractions Quick Quizzes Ages 5-7. 2017. (Collins Easy Learning KS1 Ser.). (ENG., Illus.). 32p. (J). (gr. k-2). pap. 6.99 (978-0-00-821250-6(3)) HarperCollins Pubs. Ltd. GBR. Dist: Independent Pubs. Group.

—Grammar & Punctuation Quick Quizzes Ages 7-9. 2017. (Collins Easy Learning KS2 Ser.). (ENG., Illus.). 32p. (J). (gr. 2-4). pap. 6.99 (978-0-00-821255-1(4)) HarperCollins Pubs. Ltd. GBR. Dist: Independent Pubs. Group.

Culham, Ruth. Trait Crate, Grade 6: Mentor Texts, Model Lessons, & More to Teach Writing with the 6 Traits. 2011. (Trait Crate(r) Ser.). (ENG.). (gr. 6-6). 125.00 (978-0-545-31862-4(9), Teaching Resources) Scholastic, Inc.

—Trait Crate, Grade 7: Mentor Texts, Model Lessons, & More to Teach Writing with the 6 Traits. 2011. (Trait Crate(r) Ser.). (ENG.). (gr. 7-7). 125.00 (978-0-545-31863-1(7), Teaching Resources) Scholastic, Inc.

—Trait Crate Grade 8: Mentor Texts, Model Lessons, & More to Teach Writing with the 6 Traits. 2011. (Trait Crate(r) Ser.). (ENG.). (gr. 8-8). 125.00 (978-0-545-31864-8(5), Teaching Resources) Scholastic, Inc.

Cullum, Albert, ed. Geranium on the Windowsill Just Died, but Teacher You Went Right On. 2003. (Illus.). 40p. (YA). (gr. 4-7). 15.95 (978-0-8252-0500-2(X)) Harvard Business Review Pr.

Curatola Knowles, Carmela N. Piano & Laylee Learn about Acceptable Use Policies. Lewellen, Emily, illus. 2011. 34p. (J). pap. (978-1-56484-281-7(9)) International Society for Technology in Education.

Daily Core Curriculum, Grade 1. 2003. (J). pap. 19.95 (978-1-56911-123-9(5)) Learning Resources, Inc.

Daily Core Curriculum, Grade 2. 2003. (J). pap. 19.95 (978-1-56911-124-6(3)) Learning Resources, Inc.

Daily Core Curriculum, Grade 3. 2003. (J). pap. 19.95 (978-1-56911-125-3(1)) Learning Resources, Inc.

Daily Core Curriculum, Grade 4. 2003. (J). pap. 19.95 (978-1-56911-126-0(X)) Learning Resources, Inc.

Daily Core Curriculum, Grade 5. 2003. (J). pap. 19.95 (978-1-56911-127-7(8)) Learning Resources, Inc.

Data Mania. 2011. (Data Mania Ser.). (ENG.). 24p. (gr. 1-2). pap. 166.80 (978-1-4296-6469-1(X), First Facts) Capstone Press of Coughlan Cos.

Degelman, Charles, et al. Active Citizenship Today Field Guide. 2nd ed. 2005. (J). pap. (978-1-886253-31-5(5)) Constitutional Rights Foundation.

Dodge, Judith & Duarte, Blanca. 25 Quick Formative Assessments for a Differentiated Classroom, 2nd Edition: Easy, Low-Prep Assessments That Help You Pinpoint Students' Needs. 2017. (ENG.). 128p. (gr. 4-4). pap. 21.99 (978-1-338-13516-9(3)) Scholastic, Inc.

Douglas, Vincent. Everything for Early Learning. 2004. (Everything for Early Learning Ser.). (ENG., Illus.). 320p. (gr. 1-1). pap. 7.95 (978-0-7696-3348-0(X)) Carson-Dellosa Publishing, LLC.

Drakeford, Luther D. Quiet Please. 2012. 44p. pap. 11.99 (978-1-4575-1337-4(4)) Dog Ear Publishing, LLC.

Duckworth, Katie. Education. 2004. (Children's Rights Ser.). (J). lib. bdg. 27.10 (978-1-58340-419-5(8)) Black Rabbit Bks.

Dyan, Penelope. The Big Mikey & Me Workbook. 2011. 48p. pap. 11.95 (978-1-935630-70-8(9)) Bellissima Publishing, LLC.

Emmer, Rae. School Newspaper: Periodico Escolar. 2004. (School Activities / Actividades Escolares Ser.). (SPA & ENG., Illus.). 24p. (J). lib. bdg. 22.60 (978-0-8239-6901-2(0), Editorial Buenas Letras) Rosen Publishing Group, Inc., The.

Esparza, Thomas, Jr., prod. Esther's Playhouse, Disk B. 2004. (Illus.). (J). cd-rom (978-1-879817-43-2(8), Children) Star Light Pr.

—Esther's Playhouse, Disk F. 2004. (Illus.). (J). cd-rom (978-1-879817-47-0(0), Children) Star Light Pr.

Evan-Moor. Early Learning Centers, Grades PreK-K. 2005. (Take It to Your Seat Learning Centers). (ENG., Illus.). 192p. (J). (gr. -1-k). pap., suppl. ed. 24.99 (978-1-55799-838-5(8), EMC 2401) Evan-Moor Educational Pubs.

Everett, Reese. Homework, Yes or No. 2016. (Seeing Both Sides Ser.). (ENG.). 32p. (gr. 3-6). 32.79 (978-1-68191-380-3(1)) Rourke Educational Media.

Feldman, Jean & Karapetkova, Holly. I Know an Old Lady. 2010. (ENG.). 16p. (gr. -1-k). bds. 5.99 (978-1-61741-591-3(X)) Rourke Educational Media.

—Mulberry Bush. 2010. (ENG.). 16p. (gr. -1-k). bds. 5.99 (978-1-61741-590-6(1)) Rourke Educational Media.

Felicia, Phyllis. I Count for Something. 2005. (Illus.). 32p. 13.99 (978-0-615-26902-3(8)) Country Girl Publishing.

Fetty, Margaret & Jasinski, Diane, eds. Three Cheers for December: PreK-K. 2004. (Three Cheers For... ! Ser.). (ENG., Illus.). 96p. (gr. -1 — 1). per. 12.99 (978-0-7398-9311-1(4)) Houghton Mifflin Harcourt Publishing Co.

—Three Cheers for February. 2004. (Three Cheers For... ! Ser.). (ENG., Illus.). 96p. per. 12.99 (978-0-7398-9313-5(0)) Houghton Mifflin Harcourt Publishing Co.

—Three Cheers for January. 2004. (Three Cheers For... ! Ser.). (ENG., Illus.). 96p. per. 12.99 (978-0-7398-9312-8(2)) Houghton Mifflin Harcourt Publishing Co.

Fisher, Ann Richmond. Seasons to Celebrate: January to Summer. 2003. (Illus.). 320p. (J). pap. 29.95 (978-1-57310-408-1(6)) Teaching & Learning Co.

Flemmings, Tyrone. Home Schooled Boss. 2011. 12p. pap. 12.99 (978-1-4567-5157-9(3)) AuthorHouse.

Foran, Jill. La Petite école: Le Début de la Colonie. Karvonen, Tanjah, tr. from ENG. 2011. (FRE., Illus.). 24p. (gr. 3-6). (978-1-77071-421-2(9)) Weigl Educational Pubs. Ltd.

Fridell, Ron. Education for All: Floating Schools, Cave Classrooms, & Backpacking Teachers. 2003. (In a Perfect World Ser.). (Illus.). 80p. (gr. 5-8). lib. bdg. 26.90 (978-0-7613-2624-3(3), Twenty-First Century Bks.) Lerner Publishing Group.

Gareis, Elisabeth. A Novel Approach: The Color Purple. (Illus.). (C). pap., stu. ed. (978-0-472-08543-9(3)) Univ. of Michigan Pr.

Ghigna, Charles. My Little School House. Jatkowska, Ag, illus. 2013. (My Little School House Ser.). (ENG.). 24p. (gr. -1-2). lib. bdg. 65.97 (978-1-4048-8143-3(3)) Picture Window Bks.

Gibbons, Susan. Love Grows: El Amor Crece. 2012. 32p. (-18). pap. 19.99 (978-1-4772-6732-5(8)) AuthorHouse.

Ginn, Janel D. Bilingual Education. 2007. (At Issue Ser.). (ENG., Illus.). 128p. (gr. 10-12). pap. 27.80 (978-0-7377-3913-8(4), Greenhaven Pr., Inc.) Cengage Gale.

Gordon, Carol. Super Smart Information Strategies: Make the Grade. 2010. (Explorer Library: Information Explorer Ser.). (ENG.). 32p. (gr. 4-8). pap. 14.21 (978-1-61080-259-8(4), 200907); lib. bdg. 28.50 (978-1-60279-642-3(4), 200345) Cherry Lake Publishing.

Gordon, Sharon. Escuchamos. 2006. (Bookworms Ser.). (SPA & ENG., Illus.). 24p. (gr. k-1). lib. bdg. 15.95 (978-0-7614-2359-1(1), Benchmark Bks.) Marshall Cavendish Corp.

—We Listen. (J). 2007. pap. 6.99 (978-0-7614-3274-6(4)) 2005. (ENG & SPA., Illus.). 24p. (gr. 3-7). lib. bdg. 22.79 (978-0-7614-1991-4(8), Benchmark Bks.) Marshall Cavendish Corp.

—We Listen/Escuchamos. 2006. (Bookworms Ser.). (ENG & SPA., Illus.). 24p. (gr. k-1). lib. bdg. 15.95 (978-0-7614-2439-0(3)) Marshall Cavendish Corp.

Graves, Karen M. School in Pioneer Times. 2016. (It's Back to School ... Way Back! Ser.). (ENG., Illus.). 32p. (gr. 3-4). lib. bdg. 27.32 (978-1-5157-2096-6(9), Fact Finders) Capstone Press of Coughlan Cos.

Graves, Kerry A. School in the Great Depression. 2016. (It's Back to School ... Way Back! Ser.). (ENG., Illus.). 32p. (gr. 3-4). lib. bdg. 27.32 (978-1-5157-2098-0(5), Fact Finders) Capstone Press of Coughlan Cos.

Greenhaven Press Editors. Education. 2012. (Global Viewpoints Ser.). (ENG., Illus.). 224p. (J). (gr. 10-12). pap. 27.95 (978-0-7377-5649-4(7)); lib. bdg. 40.45 (978-0-7377-5648-7(9)) Cengage Gale. (Greenhaven Pr., Inc.).

Greenhaven Press Editors, ed. Education. 2011. (Teen Rights & Freedoms Ser.). (Illus.). 176p. (YA). (gr. 9-12). 37.45 (978-0-7377-5824-5(4)) Cengage Gale.

Gutman, Dan. Dr. Brad Has Gone Mad! Paillot, Jim, illus. 2009. (My Weird School Daze Ser.: 7). (ENG.). 112p. (J). (gr. 1-5). pap. 4.99 (978-0-06-155412-4(X)) HarperCollins Pubs.

Hamilton, Robert M. I Learn from My Teacher. 2016. (Things I Learn Ser.). (Illus.). 24p. (gr. 1-1). pap. 8.25 (978-1-4994-2375-4(6), PowerKids Pr.) Rosen Publishing Group, Inc., The.

Harper, Sandy. Educational Toys for Kids of All Ages. 2013. 56p. pap. 12.55 (978-1-63022-577-3(0)) Speedy Publishing LLC.

Hart, Susan. A Teacher's Guide to Motor Development: Essential For. rev. ed. 2006. (ENG.). 82p. 39.22 (978-0-7575-3967-1(X)) Kendall Hunt Publishing Co.

Hauser, Jill Frankel. Kindergarten Success. Hauser, Salvan, illus. 2005. (Little Hands! Ser.). 128p. (J). (gr. k-18). pap. 12.95 (978-0-8249-6751-2(8), Ideal Pubns.) Worthy Publishing.

Herweck Rice, Dona. La Escuela Alrededor Del Mundo. 2017. (TIME for Kids en Español - Level 3 Ser.). (SPA.). 32p. (gr. 3-3). lib. bdg. 31.99 (978-1-5157-5166-3(X)) Time for Kids Inc AUS. Dist: Capstone Pub.

Hoffman, Joan. First Grade Basics. 2008. (ENG.). 32p. (J). pap. 2.99 (978-1-58947-437-6(6)) School Zone Publishing Co.

Hood, Karen Jean Matsko. Girls Can Do Journal: A Daily Journal, bk. 5. Whispering Pine Press International, ed. Artistic Design Services, illus. 2014. (Educational Activity & Coloring Book Ser.). 164p. (J). spiral bd. 15.95 (978-1-59649-361-2(5)) Whispering Pine Pr. International, Inc.

Hubbard, Rita L. Getting the Most Out of MOOC: Massive Open Online Courses, 1 vol. 2015. (ENG.). 48p. (YA). 30.25 (978-1-4777-7950-7(7), Rosen Reference) Rosen Publishing Group, Inc., The.

Hudson, David L., Jr. Educational Standards. 2007. (Point/Counterpoint Ser.). (Illus.). 110p. (YA). (gr. 9-12). lib. bdg. 35.00 (978-0-7910-9278-1(X)) Facts On File, Inc.

Issues, Evidence & You - Energy Mega Module Complete Materials Package. 2003. (Illus.). (YA). tchr. ed., ring bd. (978-1-887725-48-4(2)) Lab-Aids, Inc.

Issues, Evidence & You - Material Science Mega Module Complete Materials Package. 2003. (Illus.). (YA). tchr. ed., stu. ed., per. (978-1-887725-61-3(X)); tchr. ed., ring bd. (978-1-887725-45-3(8)) Lab-Aids, Inc.

Jackson, Ellen B. It's Back to School We Go! First Day Stories Fro Around the World. Ellis, Jan Davey, illus. 2003. 32p. lib. bdg. 23.90 (978-0-7613-2562-8(X), Millbrook Pr.) Lerner Publishing Group.

—It's Back to School We Go! First Day Stories from Around the World. Ellis, Jan Davey, illus. 2003. (ENG.). 32p. (J). (gr. k-3). 17.99 (978-0-7613-1948-1(4), Millbrook Pr.) Lerner Publishing Group.

Jessen, Lynn Lillard & Lillard, Paula Polk. Montessori from the Start: The Child at Home, from Birth to Age Three. 2003. (ENG., Illus.). 304p. pap. 16.00 (978-0-8052-1112-2(8), Schocken) Knopf Doubleday Publishing Group.

JIST Publishing Staff. Instructor's Guide for Creating Your High School Portfolio & Creating Your High School Resume. 2nd ed. 112p. (YA). pap. 14.95 (978-1-56370-908-1(2)) JIST Publishing.

Kahn, William A. The Student's Guide to Successful Project Teams. 2008. (ENG., Illus.). 256p. (C). 65.00 (978-1-84169-893-9(8), RT8938X) Routledge.

Katz, David Bar. DC Super Heroes ABC 123. 2012. (DC Super Heroes Ser.). (ENG.). 20p. (J). bds. 9.99 (978-1-935703-65-5(X)) Downtown Bookworks.

Kenney, Karen Latchana. Cool School Dance: Fun Ideas & Activities to Build School Spirit, 1 vol. 2011. (Cool School Spirit Ser.). (ENG., Illus.). 32p. (J). (gr. 3-6). 28.50 (978-1-61714-667-1(6), Checkerboard Library) ABDO Publishing Co.

Kilgore, James. Pedagogic Logic. 2005. 224p. (J). pap. 12.00 (978-0-9770405-4-4(2)) Infinite Visions Forum.

Kistler, Marguerite A. Working in Education. 2018. (ENG.). 32p. (gr. 3-6). (978-1-63235-443-3(8), 12-Story Library) Pr. Room Editions LLC.

Klein, Rebecca T. Your Legal Rights in School, 1 vol. 2015. (ENG., Illus.). 64p. (J). 33.25 (978-1-4777-8048-0(3), Rosen Reference) Rosen Publishing Group, Inc., The.

Koestler-Grack, Rachel A. School in the Civil Rights Movement. 2016. (It's Back to School ... Way Back! Ser.). (ENG., Illus.). 32p. (gr. 3-4). lib. bdg. 27.32 (978-1-5157-2099-7(3), Fact Finders) Capstone Press of Coughlan Cos.

La Bella, Laura. Getting a Job in Education. 2016. (Job Basics: Getting the Job You Need Ser.). 80p. (J). (gr. 8-8). 35.75 (978-1-4777-8566-9(3)) Rosen Publishing Group, Inc., The.

Leograndis, Denise. Launching the Writing Workshop: A Step-by-Step Guide in Photographs. 2008. (ENG.). 144p. (gr. 1-6). pap. 19.99 (978-0-545-02121-0(9), Teaching Resources) Scholastic, Inc.

Lewis, Susan Grant. Education in Africa. Rotberg, Robert I. & Ojakorotu, Victor, eds. 2013. (Africa: Progress & Problems Ser.: 13). (Illus.). 112p. (J). (gr. 7-18). 24.95 (978-1-4222-2938-5(6)) Mason Crest.

The Life of a Colonial Schoolteacher. 2013. (Jr. Graphic Colonial America Ser.). 24p. (J). (gr. 3-6). pap. 63.60 (978-1-4777-1428-7(6), PowerKids Pr.) Rosen Publishing Group, Inc., The.

Lindeen, Mary. Robot Competitions. 2017. (Cutting-Edge Robotics Ser.). (ENG.). 32p. (J). (gr. 3-6). 27.99 (978-1-5124-4010-2(8)) Lerner Publishing Group.

Lindeen, Mary. Wonder Readers. 2011. (Wonder Readers Ser.). (ENG.). 20p. (gr. k-1). lib. bdg. 271.80 (978-1-4296-8644-0(8), Wonder Readers) Capstone Press of Coughlan Cos.

Lindsay, Norene. Dream Catchers. 3rd ed. 88p. pap., tchr. ed. 19.95 (978-1-59357-004-0(X)) JIST Publishing.

Loeb, Jason & Green, Robert. Education. 2008. (21st Century Skills Library: Global Perspectives Ser.). (ENG.). 32p. (gr. 4-8). lib. bdg. 28.50 (978-1-60279-124-4(4), 200095) Cherry Lake Publishing.

Lovell, Nadine. Children Around the World: Passport to Adventure. (Illus.). 89p. (J). (gr. 1-6). pap. 9.95 (978-1-56861-058-0(0)) Swift Learning Resources.

Mabry-Gordon, Sherri. How to Create Digital Portfolios to Develop Communication Skills. 2017. (Project Learning Using Digital Portfolios Ser.). 64p. (J). (gr. 12-12). 34.45 (978-1-5081-7530-8(6), Rosen Young Adult) Rosen Publishing Group, Inc., The.

McKenzie, Precious. Group Projects. 2014. (ENG.). 24p. (gr. 3-5). 28.50 (978-1-62717-691-0(8)) Rourke Educational Media.

McMahon, Philip & Collins UK Staff. 11+ Cloze Results Booster for the CEM Tests. 2016. (Letts 11+ Success Ser.). (ENG.). 80p. (J). (gr. 5-6). pap., wbk. ed. 14.95 (978-1-84419-900-6(2)) HarperCollins Pubs. Ltd. GBR. Dist: Independent Pubs. Group.

McMahon, Philip, et al. Non-Verbal Reasoning. 2016. (Letts 11+ Success Ser.). (ENG.). 80p. (J). (gr. 4-5). pap. 11.95 (978-1-84419-892-4(8)) HarperCollins Pubs. Ltd. GBR. Dist: Independent Pubs. Group.

—Verbal Reasoning. 2016. (Letts 11+ Success Ser.). (ENG.). 80p. (J). (gr. 4-5). pap. 11.95 (978-1-84419-891-7(X)) HarperCollins Pubs. Ltd. GBR. Dist: Independent Pubs. Group.

Meese, Ruth Lyn. Family Matters: Adoption & Foster Care in Children's Literature, 1 vol. 2009. 147p. (C). pap. 35.00 (978-1-59158-782-8(4), TIP8782, Libraries Unlimited) ABC-CLIO, LLC.

Meiners, Cheri J. Listen & Learn. 2015. (Learning to Get Along(r) Ser.). (ENG & SPA., Illus.). 48p. (J). (gr. -1-3). pap. 12.45 (978-1-63198-039-8(4)) Free Spirit Publishing, Inc.

Merino, Noel. Education. Greenhaven Press Editors & Gale Editors, eds. 2014. (Opposing Viewpoints Ser.). (ENG., Illus.). 224p. (gr. 7-12). pap. 33.80 (978-0-7377-6433-8(3)); lib. bdg. 48.80 (978-0-7377-6434-5(1)) Cengage Gale. (Greenhaven Pr., Inc.).

Meyer, Terry. Navigating a New School. 2012. (Middle School Survival Handbook Ser.). (ENG., Illus.). 64p. (YA). (gr. 5-8). lib. bdg. 31.95 (978-1-4488-8312-7(1), Rosen Reference) Rosen Publishing Group, Inc., The.

Meyer, Terry Teague. Navigating a New School. 2012. (Middle School Survival Handbook Ser.). (ENG., Illus.). 64p. (YA). (gr. 5-8). pap. 12.95 (978-1-4488-8319-6(9), Rosen Reference) Rosen Publishing Group, Inc., The.

Miller, Karen. The Achievement Gap. 2010. (Opposing Viewpoints Ser.). (Illus.). 240p. (J). 42.95 (978-0-7377-4749-2(8)); pap. 29.45 (978-0-7377-4750-8(1)) Cengage Gale. (Greenhaven Pr., Inc.).

Modoc Press Editors. Directory of Distance Learning Opportunities: K-12, 1 vol. 2003. 432p. (C). (gr. k-12). 96.00 (978-1-57356-515-8(6), OXDLK-12, Greenwood) ABC-CLIO, LLC.

Mortenson, Greg & Relin, David Oliver. Three Cups of Tea: One Man's Journey to Change the World... One Child at a Time. 2009. (ENG.). 240p. (J). (gr. 3-7). 8.99 (978-0-14-241412-5(3), Puffin Books) Penguin Young Readers Group.

—Three Cups of Tea: One Man's Journey to Change the World... One Child at a Time. ed. 2009. lib. bdg. 19.65 (978-0-606-07164-2(4), Turtleback) Turtleback Bks.

Mortenson, Greg, et al. Three Cups of Tea: One Man's Journey to Change the World... One Child at a Time. adapted ed. 2009. 10.36 (978-0-7848-3360-5(5), Everbind) Marco Bk. Co.

Nagle, Jeanne M. Great Lifelong Learning Skills. 2008. (Work Readiness Ser.). (Illus.). 64p. (YA). (gr. 8-12). lib. bdg. 31.95 (978-1-4042-1424-8(0), 1277025) Rosen Publishing Group, Inc., The.

Naik, Anita & Croke, Liam. Beat Stress! The Exam Handbook. 2009. (Really Useful Handbooks Ser.). (ENG., Illus.). 48p. (J). (gr. 5-11). lib. bdg. (978-0-7787-4387-3(X), 1294158) Crabtree Publishing Co.

Nakaya, Andrea C. Growin up in Japan. 2017. (ENG.). 80p. (YA). (gr. 5-12). (978-1-68282-219-7(2)) ReferencePoint Pr., Inc.

Nesbitt, Shawntelle. The Kids' Power Series Teacher Resource, 1 vol. 2011. (Kids' Power Ser.). (ENG.). 125p. (J). spiral bd. 29.95 (978-1-926920-35-1(X)) Second Story Pr. CAN. Dist: Orca Bk. Pubs. USA.

NJMUSST 2004 Anthology. 2004. 112p. (J). per. 10.00 (978-0-9744744-4-1(4), 0-9744744-4-4) Cloonfad Pr.

Painter, Carol. Friends Helping Friends: A Handbook for Helpers. 2nd ed. 2003. (ENG., Illus.). 224p. (J). pap. 10.95 (978-1-930572-21-8(2)) Educational Media Corp.

Palmer, Erin. Summer School, Yes or No. 2016. (Seeing Both Sides Ser.). (ENG.). 32p. (gr. 3-6). 32.79 (978-1-68191-385-8(2)) Rourke Educational Media.

Parker, Harvey C. Listen, Look & Think: A Self-Regulation Program for Children. 2003. 8p. (J). pap., tchr. ed. 22.00 (978-1-886941-12-0(2), 0955) Specialty Pr., Inc.

Pelleschi, Andrea. The Life of a Colonial Schoolteacher. 2013. (Jr. Graphic Colonial America Ser.). 24p. (J). (gr. 3-6). 25.25 (978-1-4777-1305-1(0)); pap. 10.60 (978-1-4777-1427-0(8)) Rosen Publishing Group, Inc., The. (PowerKids Pr.).

Phillips, Vivian A. Education: Show & Tell. Date not set. (Illus.). 10p. (Orig.). (J). pap. (978-1-888413-05-2(0)) Seasoning Quilting (Arts & Crafts).

Poole, Hilary W. School Fears. 2017. (J). (978-1-4222-3729-8(X)) Mason Crest.

Poston, Valerie Williams, illus. ArbeZ ZebrA Teaches A to Z, 3 vols., Vol. 1. 2007. 33p. (J). spiral bd. 39.99 (978-0-9779063-0-7(2)) Gain Literacy Skills / Lynette Gain Williams.

Rasinski, Timothy V., et al. The Fluent Reader in Action, Grades 5 & Up: A Rich Collection of Research-Based, Classroom-Tested Lessons & Strategies for Improving Fluency & Comprehension. 2011. (ENG.). 128p. (gr. 5-5). pap. 18.99 (978-0-439-63340-6(0), Teaching Resources) Scholastic, Inc.

—The Fluent Reader in Action, Grades Prek-4: A Rich Collection of Research-Based, Classroom-Tested Lessons & Strategies for Improving Fluency & Comprehension. 2011. (ENG.). 128p. (gr. -1-4). pap. 18.99 (978-0-439-63341-3(9), Teaching Resources) Scholastic, Inc.

Read, Marya, creator & contrib. by. An Educated Choice Journal. Read, Marya, contrib. by. 2003. 133p. (YA). (978-1-929931-11-8(5)) Intrepid Films, LLC.
Rissman, Rebecca. We All Learn. 2016. (Disabilities & Differences Ser.). (ENG.). 24p. (gr. -1-1). pap. 6.29 (978-1-4846-3626-8(0), Acorn) Heinemann-Raintree.
Romain, Trevor. How to Do Homework Without Throwing Up. Mark, Steve, illus. 2017. (Laugh & Learn(r) Ser.). (ENG.). 80p. (J). (gr. 3-8). pap. 8.95 **(978-1-63198-066-4(1))** Free Spirit Publishing, Inc.
Rosen Publishing Staff. Service Learning for Teens, 1 vol. 2015. (Service Learning for Teens Ser.). (ENG.). 80p. (YA). 276.80 (978-1-4777-7971-2(X), Rosen Young Adult) Rosen Publishing Group, Inc., The.
Sanna, Ellyn. Special Education Teacher. Riggs, Ernestine G. & Gholar, Cheryl, eds. 2013. (Careers with Character Ser.: 18). 96p. (J). (gr. 7-18). 22.95 (978-1-4222-2767-1(7)) Mason Crest.
Scandiffio, Laura. Fight to Learn: The Struggle to Go to School. 2016. (ENG., Illus.). 176p. (J). (gr. 4-9). pap. 14.95 (978-1-55451-797-8(4)) Annick Pr., Ltd. CAN. Dist: Publishers Group West (PGW).
Scholastic, Inc. Staff, contrib. by. Entering Kindergarten. 2004. (Jumpstart Ser.). (ENG., Illus.). 96p. (J). (gr. k-18). pap. 6.99 (978-0-439-38233-5(5)) Scholastic, Inc.
Scholastic Teaching Resources Staff. The Essential Questions Handbook, Grades 4-8: Hundreds of Guiding Questions That Help You Plan & Teach Successful Lessons in the Content Areas. 2011. (ENG.). 96p. (gr. 4-8). pap. 14.99 (978-0-545-30585-3(3), Teaching Resources) Scholastic, Inc.
Schumacher, Bev. Play Action/ Juego en Accion: Juego en Acción. 2005.Tr. of Juego en Acción. (SPA & ENG., Illus.). 20p. (J). lib. bdg. 9.95 (978-0-9741549-5-4(4)) Learning Props.
—Which Way? / Por Donde? 2005. (SPA & ENG.). 20p. lib. bdg. 9.95 (978-0-9741549-3-0(8)) Learning Props.
Schwartz, Tina P. Writing & Publishing: The Ultimate Teen Guide. 2009. (It Happened to Me Ser.: 27). (ENG.). 282p. (gr. 9-18). instr.'s gde. ed. 50.00 (978-0-8108-5647-9(6)) Scarecrow Pr., Inc.
Sellmeyer, Susan. Time for Preschool: An Early Developmental Tool Designed for Toddlers. 2013. 62p. pap. 9.95 (978-1-4620-4470-2(0)) iUniverse, Inc.
Shumsky, Ron, et al. The Survival Guide for School Success: Use Your Brain's Built-In Apps to Sharpen Attention, Battle Boredom, & Build Mental Muscle. 2014. (ENG., Illus.). 128p. (J). (gr. 5-8). pap. 14.99 (978-1-57542-482-8(7)) Free Spirit Publishing, Inc.
Smith, Paula. Schools in Different Places. 2015. (Learning about Our Global Community Ser.). (ENG., Illus.). 24p. (J). (978-0-7787-2013-3(6)) Crabtree Publishing Co.
Stewart, Faith. Teens & Rural Education: Opportunities & Challenges. 2009. (Youth in Rural North America Ser.). (Illus.). 96p. (YA). (gr. 3-7). lib. bdg. 22.95 (978-1-4222-0015-5(9)) Mason Crest.
Stewart, Tobi Stanton. Colonial Teachers. 2006. (Reading Room Collection: Social Studies). (Illus.). 16p. (J). (gr. 3-7). lib. bdg. 17.25 (978-1-4042-3351-5(2), PowerKids Pr.) Rosen Publishing Group, Inc., The.
Stradling, Jan. Handle with Care: Level I, 6 vols., Vol. 2. (First Explorers Ser.). 24p. (gr. 1-2). 29.95 (978-0-7699-1459-6(4)) Shortland Pubns. (U. S. A.) Inc.
Strayer, Troy & Strayer, Beverly. Check-In Assessments for Differentiated Lessons: Quick, Engaging Activities That Help You Find Out What Students Know at the Beginning & End of Your Lessons So You Can Plan Your Next Instructional Steps. 2012. (ENG.). 96p. (gr. 5-5). pap. 16.99 (978-0-545-29682-3(X), Teaching Resources) Scholastic, Inc.
Sullivan, Mary. Lessons for Guided Writing: Whole-Class Lessons & Dozens of Student Samples with Teacher Comments to Effectively Scaffold the Writing Process. 2008. (ENG.). 128p. pap. 18.99 (978-0-545-05401-0(X), Teaching Resources) Scholastic, Inc.
Suzuki, David T. & Hehner, Barbara. Descubre los Insectos. 2004. (Juego de la Ciencia Ser.). (SPA., Illus.). 96p. 14.99 (978-84-9754-051-3(4), 87816) Ediciones Oniro S.A. ESP. Dist: Lectorum Pubns., Inc.
Swan, Richard. The Pardoner's Prologue & Tale. 2011. (Philip Allan Literature Guide for A-Level Ser.). (Illus.). 96p. (gr. 10-12). pap. 24.95 (978-1-4441-2159-9(6)) Trans-Atlantic Pubns., Inc.
Swanson Sateren, Shelley. School in Colonial America. 2016. (It's Back to School ... Way Back! Ser.). (ENG., Illus.). 32p. (gr. 3-4). lib. bdg. 27.32 (978-1-5157-2097-3(7), Fact Finders) Capstone Press of Coughlan Cos.
Tanner, Dawn Leasman. A Kitty Named Indra/Una Gata Llamada Indra. Leasman, Nancy Packard, illus. I.t. ed. 2003. (SPA & ENG.). 36p. (J). per. 6.95 (978-0-9741725-0-7(2)) Leatherwood Publishing.
Teal, Joyce Willard. Clifford's War & A. E. P. 2004. 152p. (YA). per. 13.95 (978-1-932196-32-0(3)) WordWright.biz, Inc.
A Teen's Guide to the Power of Social Networking. 2013. (Teen's Guide to the Power of Social Networking Ser.). 80p. (YA). (gr. 7-12). 133.00 (978-1-4777-1689-2(0)); pap. 56.60 (978-1-4777-7809-8(8)); pap. 339.60 (978-1-4777-7808-1(X)) Rosen Publishing Group, Inc., The.
The Administrator. Holes in the Eagles Wings: Churches are Marxism holes per Separation of Church & State. 2011. 48p. pap. 25.99 (978-1-4520-0352-8(1)) AuthorHouse.
Thiessen, Karen J. World Landmark Books, A Homeschoolers' Guide: Select, Find, & Use World Landmarks in Homeschool Curriculum. 2004. (Illus.). 216p. per. 24.95 (978-0-9749578-5-2(2)) Pure Joy Pubns.
Thinking Kids & Carson-Dellosa Publishing, compiled by. Second Grade Essentials. 2017. (ENG.). 256p. (gr. 2-2). pap. 5.99 **(978-1-4838-3819-9(6)**, Thinking Kids) Carson-Dellosa Publishing, LLC.
Tomlinson, Carol Ann & Imbeau, Marcia B. Managing a Differentiated Classroom: A Practical Guide. 2011. (ENG.). 96p. (gr. k-8). pap. 19.99 (978-0-545-30584-6(5), Teaching Resources) Scholastic, Inc.
Top That Publishing Staff, ed. My First Library. 2005. 180p. (978-1-84510-658-4(X)) Top That! Publishing PLC.
Trumbauer, Lisa. Lighthouses of North America! Exploring Their History, Lore & Science. Kline, Michael, illus. 2007. (Kaleidoscope Kids Bks.). (ENG.). 96p. (J). (gr. 3-7). 16.99 (978-0-8249-6791-8(7)); pap. 12.99 (978-0-8249-6790-1(9)) Worthy Publishing. (Ideal Pubns.).
Understein, Adam L. Learn2study Student Pocket Guide. 2003. 72p. (C). per. 6.99 (978-0-9729557-1-3(2)) Learn2study.
User Manual. 2003. ring bd. (978-1-932166-07-1(6)) Achieve3000.
Watkins, Heidi. Homeschooling. 2013. (Issues That Concern You Ser.). (ENG., Illus.). 144p. (gr. 7-10). lib. bdg. 42.00 (978-0-7377-6296-9(9), Greenhaven Pr., Inc.) Cengage Gale.
West, Tracey. Lunchbox Words. Hindle, James K., illus. 2017. (Scripps National Spelling Bee Ser.). (ENG.). 144p. (J). pap. 10.99 **(978-1-62672-718-2(X)**, 9781626727182) Roaring Brook Pr.
Wilson, Janet. Shannen & the Dream for a School, 1 vol. 2011. (Kids' Power Ser.). (ENG & CRE., Illus.). 132p. (J). (gr. 6-8). pap. 14.95 (978-1-926920-30-6(9)) Second Story Pr. CAN. Dist: Orca Bk. Pubs. USA.
Young, Jay, creator. The Amazing Magic Fact Machine. 2004. (Illus.). 30p. (978-1-903174-16-6(3), Pavilion Children's Books) Pavilion Bks.
Zeng, Sunny. Student Workbook: To Accompany Videos 1 & 2. 2003. (CHI & ENG.). stu. ed., wbk. ed. 14.95 (978-0-9707332-9-0(1), NIHALIWO) Chinasprout, Inc.
The 7 Character Strengths of Highly Successful Students. 2013. (7 Character Strengths of Highly Successful Students Ser.). 64p. (J). (gr. 5-8). 223.65 (978-1-4488-9554-0(5)); pap. 543.90 (978-1-4777-1242-9(9)); pap. 90.65 (978-1-4777-1241-2(0)) Rosen Publishing Group, Inc., The.
500 Palabras (500 Words) (SPA., Illus.). (J). pap. 6.95 (978-950-11-0122-5(3), SGM122) Sigmar ARG. Dist: Continental Bk. Co., Inc.

EDUCATION—AIMS AND OBJECTIVES

Character Strength. 2013. (Character Strength Ser.). 24p. (J). (gr. 3-6). 158.20 (978-1-4488-9962-3(1)); pap. 346.50 (978-1-4777-1254-2(2)); pap. 57.75 (978-1-4777-1253-5(4)) Rosen Publishing Group, Inc., The. (PowerKids Pr.).
Friedman, Ian C. Education Reform. 2nd rev. ed. 2010. (Library in a Book Ser.). 280p. (C). (gr. 9). 45.00 (978-0-8160-8238-4(3)) Facts On File, Inc.
Green, Robert. Expect the Most - Provide the Best: How High Expectations & Outstanding Instruction Help All Learners Succeed. 2014. (ENG.). 96p. (-12). pap. 24.99 (978-0-545-58885-0(5), Teaching Resources) Scholastic, Inc.

EDUCATION, BUSINESS

see Business Education

EDUCATION, CHARACTER

see Moral Education

EDUCATION, CHRISTIAN

see Religious Education

EDUCATION—DATA PROCESSING

Boardman Moen, Christine. Instant PowerPoint Lessons & Activities: Literary Elements: 16 Model Lessons That Guide Students to Create Easy PowerPoint Presentations That Help Them Analyze Literary Elements in the Books They Read. 2012. (ENG., Illus.). 64p. (gr. 4-8). 19.99 (978-0-545-33280-4(X), Teaching Resources) Scholastic, Inc.
Curatola Knowles, Carmela N. Piano & Laylee Learn about Acceptable Use Policies. Lewellen, Emily, illus. 2011. 40p. (J). (978-1-56484-296-1(7)) International Society for Technology in Education.
Kidspiration 2 US 10-Pack License. 2004. (J). cd-rom (978-1-932463-33-0(X)) Inspiration Software, Inc.
Kidspiration 2 US 20-Pack License. 2004. (J). cd-rom (978-1-932463-34-7(8)) Inspiration Software, Inc.
Kidspiration 2 US 5-Pack License. 2004. (J). cd-rom (978-1-932463-32-3(1)) Inspiration Software, Inc.
Kidspiration 2 US Exploring CD. 2004. (J). cd-rom 24.95 (978-1-932463-36-1(4)) Inspiration Software, Inc.
Kidspiration 2 US Personal Edition. 2004. (J). cd-rom (978-1-932463-29-3(1)) Inspiration Software, Inc.
Kidspiration 2 US Upgrade Single. 2004. (J). cd-rom 39.95 (978-1-932463-31-6(3)) Inspiration Software, Inc.
Kidspiration in the Classroom. 2004. (J). per. 29.95 (978-1-932463-51-4(8)) Inspiration Software, Inc.
Kidspiration in the Classroom School License. 2004. (J). per. 199.00 (978-1-932463-52-1(6)) Inspiration Software, Inc.
Lesson Express, Minimum Of 10. 2005. cd-rom (978-0-9740533-1-8(7)) Maestro Learning.
Lesson Express, Minimum Of 100. 2005. cd-rom (978-0-9740533-2-5(5)) Maestro Learning.
Lesson Express, Single User. 2005. cd-rom (978-0-9740533-0-1(9)) Maestro Learning.

EDUCATION, DISCRIMINATION IN

see Discrimination in Education

EDUCATION, ELEMENTARY

Al-Kinani, Maarja. All in One. 2010. 167p. pap. 81.95 (978-1-4461-5903-3(5)) Lulu Pr., Inc.
Angela's Ashes: Response Journal. 2003. 40p. (YA). (978-1-58049-991-0(0), RJ91) Prestwick Hse., Inc.
Around the World in Eighty Days: Response Journal. 2003. 40p. (YA). (978-1-58049-987-3(2), RJ87) Prestwick Hse., Inc.
Atkinson, Sue. Supermaths: Age 4-5. 2003. (Illus.). 32p. pap. (978-0-340-80559-6(5), Hodder Children's Books) Hachette Children's Group.
—Supermaths 3: Age 3-6. 2003. (Illus.). 32p. pap. (978-0-340-80561-9(7), Hodder Children's Books) Hachette Children's Group.
Boyd, Kassandra, et al. Kids on the Move: Creative Movement for Children of All Ages, 1. 2003. (Illus.). 68p. 21.95 (978-0-9744833-0-6(3)) Creative Publishing.
Boykin, Timothy. Timster's World: So What Makes You So Special? 2010. 36p. pap. 16.99 (978-1-4389-8506-0(1)) AuthorHouse.
Bridges, Doreen. Music, Young Children & You: A Parent-Teacher Guide to Music for 0 -5 Year Olds. (Illus.). 160p. (J). (gr. -1-k). pap. (978-0-86806-530-4(7), Hale & Iremonger) GHR Pr., The.
Brown, Robin. Practice Papers: Advanced Maths. 2nd ed. (Illus.). 32p. (YA). pap. (978-0-340-72690-7(3)) Hodder & Stoughton.
—Practice Papers: Advanced Non-Verbal Reasoning. 2nd ed. (Illus.). 32p. (YA). pap. 6.99 (978-0-340-72686-0(5)) Hodder & Stoughton GBR. Dist: Trafalgar Square Publishing.
—Practice Papers: English. 2nd ed. (Illus.). 32p. (YA). pap. 6.99 (978-0-340-72687-7(3)) Hodder & Stoughton GBR. Dist: Trafalgar Square Publishing.
—Practice Papers: Maths. 2nd ed. (Illus.). 32p. (YA). pap. (978-0-340-72689-1(X)) Hodder & Stoughton.
Castellano, Marie. Simply Super Storytimes: Programming Ideas. 2003. (Illus.). 104p. (J). pap. 16.95 (978-1-57950-005-4(6), Upstart Bks.) Highsmith Inc.
Cheva, Cherry. DupliKate. 2009. (ENG.). 256p. (YA). (gr. 9-18). 16.99 (978-0-06-128854-8(3), HarperTeen) HarperCollins Pubs.
Collins, Meg. Twinkle, Twinkle Starry Sky. 2010. 36p. 15.49 (978-1-4520-4453-8(8)) AuthorHouse.
Cryer, Debby, et al. Active Learning for Fives. 2003. (Illus.). 450p. (Orig.). (gr. -1). 28.50 net. (978-0-201-49401-3(9)) Seymour, Dale Pubns.
Ebner, Aviva. Environmental Science Experiments. 2011. (Experiments for Future Scientists Ser.). (Illus.). 160p. (gr. 5-8). 35.00 (978-1-60413-851-1(3)) Facts On File, Inc.
Encyclopaedia Britannica, Inc. Staff, compiled by. The Arts. 2003. (Britannica Learning Library). (Illus.). (gr. 2-5). 14.95 (978-1-59339-004-4(1), 049905-EN-REF) Encyclopaedia Britannica, Inc.
—Emcyclopaedia Britannica Children's Learning Suite 2007. 2007. (gr. 7-14). DVD, cd-rom 29.95 (978-1-59339-538-4(8)) Encyclopaedia Britannica, Inc.
Evans, Carol Wolfe. The No Thank You Bite, 1 vol. Williams, G. L., illus. 2010. 16p. 24.95 (978-1-4512-2132-9(0)) PublishAmerica, Inc.
Fences. 2003. 44p. (YA). tchr. ed., ring bd. (978-1-58049-468-7(4), TU224) Prestwick Hse., Inc.
Ferrisi, Kevin. Kids Can Too. 2010. 32p. pap. 23.99 (978-0-557-61196-6(2)) Lulu Pr., Inc.
Fletcher, Terri. Scrumpy's Educational Kid Songs. 2003. (Illus.). 16p. (J). (gr. -1-1). pap. 12.95 incl. audio compact disk (978-0-9672279-1-7(7)) Scrumps Entertainment, Inc.
Gillham, Bill, et al. Essential Skills, 4 bks. (Illus.). 128p. (YA). pap. 15.99 (978-0-340-71583-3(9)) Hodder & Stoughton GBR. Dist: Trafalgar Square Publishing.
Hall, M. C. First Grade Scholar. Boyer, Robin, illus. 2004. (ENG.). 32p. (J). pap. 2.99 (978-1-58947-456-7(2)) School Zone Publishing Co.
—Second Grade Scholar. Boyer, Robin, illus. 2005. (ENG.). 32p. (J). pap., wbk. ed. 2.99 (978-1-58947-457-4(0)) School Zone Publishing Co.
Hauser, Jill Frankel. Little Hands Celebrate America: Learning about the U. S. A. through Crafts & Activities. Kline, Michael, illus. 2012. (Little Hands! Book Ser.). 128p. (J). pap. 12.99 (978-0-8249-6836-6(0), Ideal Pubns.) Worthy Publishing.
Kalman, Bobbie. What Is It Made From? 2011. (ENG.). 16p. (J). lib. bdg. (978-0-7787-9562-9(4)); (My World Ser.: No. 60). pap. (978-0-7787-9587-2(X)) Crabtree Publishing Co.
Ladybird. I'm Ready... for School! 2016. (Ladybird I'm Ready Ser.). (ENG., Illus.). 40p. (J). (— 1). pap. 11.99 **(978-0-241-21597-5(8))** Penguin Bks., Ltd. GBR. Dist: Independent Pubs. Group.
Learning Co Bks Staff. Reader Rabbit Comprehensive Workbook: First Grade. 2005. (J). (gr. 1). pap., wbk. ed. 19.99 (978-0-7630-8150-8(7)) Houghton Mifflin Harcourt Learning Technology.
—Reader Rabbit Comprehensive Workbook: Kindergarten. 2005. (J). (gr. k). pap., wbk. ed. 19.99 (978-0-7630-8151-5(5)) Houghton Mifflin Harcourt Learning Technology.
—Reader Rabbit Comprehensive Workbook: Preschool. 2005. (J). (gr. -1). pap., wbk. ed. 19.99 (978-0-7630-8149-2(3)) Houghton Mifflin Harcourt Learning Technology.
Marsh, Carole. Electricity: Common Core Lessons & Activities. 2013. (Common Core Ser.). (ENG., Illus.). 24p. (J). (gr. 4-7). pap. 4.99 (978-0-635-10614-8(0)) Gallopade International.
Matthews, John. Interactive Whiteboards. 2008. (21st Century Skills Library: Global Products Ser.). (ENG.). 32p. (gr. 4-8). 28.50 (978-1-60279-254-8(2), 200121) Cherry Lake Publishing.
Modoc Press Editors. Directory of Distance Learning Opportunities: K-12, 1 vol. 2003. 432p. (C). (gr. k-12). 96.00 (978-1-57356-515-8(6), OXDLK-12, Greenwood) ABC-CLIO, LLC.
NCPTA Staff, et al. Maths for the Brighter Child. (Illus.). 24p. pap. 6.99 (978-0-340-71680-9(0), Coronet) Hodder & Stoughton GBR. Dist: Trafalgar Square Publishing.
—SATs Practice in Science Age 11. (Illus.). 32p. pap. 6.99 (978-0-340-71046-3(2), Coronet) Hodder & Stoughton GBR. Dist: Trafalgar Square Publishing.
Press, Judy & Trezzo-Braren, Loretta. Big Fun Craft Book: Creative Fun for 2 to 6 Year Olds. Trezzo-Braren, Loretta, illus. 2008. (ENG., Illus.). (J). (gr. -1-1). 160p. 16.99 (978-0-8249-6826-7(3)); 142p. pap. 12.99 (978-0-8249-6827-4(1)) Worthy Publishing. (Ideal Pubns.).
Rainbow Bridge Publishing Staff. Deep Space Division Fission. 2004. (Ready, Set... Flashcards! Ser.). 8.95 (978-1-932210-90-3(3)) Rainbow Bridge Publishing.
—World Vacation Multiplication. 2004. (Ready, Set... Flashcards! Ser.). 8.95 (978-1-932210-89-7(X)) Rainbow Bridge Publishing.
Rayner, Amanda. Going to School. 2005. (One World (Smart Apple Media) Ser.). (Illus.). 30p. (J). (gr. 3-6). lib. bdg. 27.10 (978-1-58340-697-7(2)) Black Rabbit Bks.
Reis, Ronald A. Christopher Columbus & the Age of Exploration for Kids: With 21 Activities. 2013. (For Kids Ser.). (ENG., Illus.). 160p. (J). (gr. 4). pap. 16.95 (978-1-61374-674-5(1)) Chicago Review Pr., Inc.
Schiller, Melissa. 100th Day of School. 2013. (Rookie Read-About(tm) Holidays Ser.). (ENG.). 32p. (J). 25.00 (978-0-531-27200-8(1)); pap. 5.95 (978-0-531-27350-0(4)) Scholastic Library Publishing.
School Zone Interactive Staff. Preschool. 2006. (ENG.). (J). cd-rom 24.99 (978-1-58947-681-3(6)) School Zone Publishing Co.
The Story of My Life: Response Journal. 2003. 40p. (YA). (978-1-58049-990-3(2), RJ90) Prestwick Hse., Inc.
Stout, Mary A. Native American Boarding Schools, 1 vol. 2012. (Landmarks of the American Mosaic Ser.). (Illus.). 214p. (C). 64.00 (978-0-313-38676-3(5), A3118C, Greenwood) ABC-CLIO, LLC.
Thalhamer, Ellen Viola. Let's Play Doctor: I Love to Pretend! 2010. 36p. pap. 15.99 (978-1-4490-7487-6(1)) AuthorHouse.
Through the Looking Glass: Response Journal. 2003. 32p. (YA). (978-1-58049-989-7(9), RJ89) Prestwick Hse., Inc.
Twain, Mark, pseud. The Prince & the Pauper: Response Journal. 2003. 35p. 19.95 (978-1-58049-986-6(4), RJ86) Prestwick Hse., Inc.
Van Leeuwen, Michele D., creator. Summer Bridge Activities: Grades PK to K. 2012. (Summer Bridge Activities Ser.). (ENG., Illus.). 150p. pap. 14.95 (978-1-60996-440-5(3)) Carson-Dellosa Publishing, LLC.
Walker, Kevin. Field Trips, Yes or No. 2016. (Seeing Both Sides Ser.). (ENG.). 32p. (gr. 3-6). 32.79 (978-1-68191-387-2(9)) Rourke Educational Media.
Whiteford, Rhona & Hachette Children's Group. Complete English, 3 bks. in 1. (Illus.). 96p. (YA). pap. 15.99 (978-0-340-71582-6(0)) Hodder & Stoughton GBR. Dist: Trafalgar Square Publishing.
Whiteford, Rhona, et al. Complete English, 4 bks. in 1. (Illus.). 96p. (YA). pap. 15.99 (978-0-340-71580-2(4)) Hodder & Stoughton GBR. Dist: Trafalgar Square Publishing.
—Complete Maths, 4 bks. in 1. (Illus.). 96p. (YA). pap. 15.99 (978-0-340-71581-9(2)) Hodder & Stoughton GBR. Dist: Trafalgar Square Publishing.
The Witch of Blackbird Pond: Response Journal. 2003. 36p. (YA). (978-1-58049-993-4(7), RJ93) Prestwick Hse., Inc.
Wolshon, Brian. Harry's Healthy Heart. 2009. 28p. pap. 14.99 (978-1-4389-8230-4(5)) AuthorHouse.

EDUCATION, ETHICAL

see Moral Education; Religious Education

EDUCATION—FICTION

Adams, Chanelle. Myra. 2006. 22p. 12.16 (978-1-4116-9426-2(0)) Lulu Pr., Inc.
Adler, David A. Bones & the Math Test Mystery. Newman, Barbara Johansen, illus. 2010. (Bones Ser.: 6). (ENG.). 32p. (J). (gr. 1-3). mass mkt. 3.99 (978-0-14-241519-1(7), Penguin Young Readers) Penguin Young Readers Group.
Amelia Asks Why... Book of Fun. 2007. (J). 1.09 (978-0-9726075-7-5(9)) EPI Bks.
Anton, Maggie. Secret Scholar. 2008. (ENG.). 160p. (gr. 4-7). pap. 14.00 (978-0-8276-0869-6(1)) Jewish Pubn. Society.
Aulbach, Kathy. ABC's. 2008. 29p. 15.95 (978-0-615-21180-0(1)) Flower Sprouts.
BELTEI, Nadia. Emily's BOOKS: Coloring & Activity book, age Level: 2-3. 2010. 39p. pap. 19.99 (978-0-557-32843-7(8)) Lulu Pr., Inc.
Besterman, Catherine. The Extraordinary Education of Johnny Longfoot in His Search for the Magic Hat. Chappell, Warren, illus. 2011. 160p. 41.95 (978-1-258-08544-5(5)) Literary Licensing, LLC.
Bickico Enterprises Staff, concept. BabyKids Bk. 1: El Libro Para Contar. 2003. (SPA.). 16p. (J). pap. 2.95 (978-0-9746508-4-5(6)) Bickico Enterprises, Inc.
—BabyKids Bk. 2: El Libro de los Colores. 2003. (SPA.). 16p. (J). pap. (978-0-9746508-5-2(4)) Bickico Enterprises, Inc.
Black, Jessica L. Why Have Rules? Gillen, Lisa P., illus. I.t. ed. 2003. (HRL Little Book Ser.). 8p. (J). (gr. -1). pap. 10.95 (978-1-57332-271-3(7)); pap. 10.95 (978-1-57332-270-6(9)); pap. 10.95 (978-1-57332-270-6(9)) Carson-Dellosa Publishing, LLC. (HighReach Learning, Incorporated).
Brezenoff, Steve. Cheaters. 2013. (Ravens Pass Ser.). (ENG.). 96p. (gr. 2-3). pap. 35.70 (978-1-4342-6291-2(X)) Stone Arch Bks.
Bruchac, Joseph. Walking Two Worlds. 2015. (ENG.). 152p. (YA). pap. (978-1-939053-10-7(2)) Book Publishing Co.
Buzzeo, Toni. Fire up with Reading! Yoshikawa, Sachiko, illus. 2007. 32p. 17.95 (978-1-60213-019-7(1), Upstart Bks.) Highsmith Inc.
Carey, Benedict. Island of the Unknowns. 2011. (ENG., Illus.). 288p. (YA). (gr. 3-7). pap. 6.95 (978-0-8109-9663-2(4), Amulet Bks.) Abrams, Inc.
Carr, Crystal. Ram, Ham, Strawberry Jam: Identifying Nouns. 2007. 24p. per. 13.95 (978-1-4327-0512-1(1)) Outskirts Pr., Inc.
Carr, Jan. Greedy Apostrophe: A Cautionary Tale. Long, Ethan, illus. 2007. (ENG.). 32p. (J). (gr. 1-3). 17.95 (978-0-8234-2006-3(X)) Holiday Hse., Inc.
Cook, Barbara L. Families. Cress, Michelle H., illus. I.t. ed. 2004. (HRL Board Book Ser.). 8p. (J). (gr. -1-1). pap. 10.95 (978-1-57332-280-5(6), HighReach Learning, Incorporated) Carson-Dellosa Publishing, LLC.
Cooper, Barbara. Hannah Hyphen-Hyphen. Raynor, Maggie, illus. 2004. (Meet the Puncs: A Remarkable Punctuation Family Ser.). 32p. (gr. 1-4). lib. bdg. 26.00 (978-0-8368-4226-5(X), Gareth Stevens Learning Library) Stevens, Gareth Publishing LLLP.
Cordoza, Sandra Sandlin. Smarticus & the Abc's. 2010. 24p. pap. 11.50 (978-1-60860-407-4(1), Eloquent Bks.) Strategic Book Publishing & Rights Agency (SBPRA).
Courtin, Thierry. Decouvre les nombres Avec. (FRE.). pap. (978-2-09-202149-1(4)) Editions Rouge et Or.
Cush, Don. School of the Future: The Dawning of Aquarius. 2013. 28p. pap. 16.95 (978-1-63004-619-4(1)) America Star Bks.
Desjardins, Margaret M. Murky, Quirky, Beserky Math. Bohart, Lisa, illus. 2013. 24p. pap. 13.95 (978-1-61493-210-9(7)) Peppertree Pr., The.
Dickens, Charles. Hard Times. 2009. (Real Reads Ser.). (Illus.). 64p. (J). (gr. 4-8). lib. bdg. 29.25 (978-1-60754-385-5(0)) Windmill Bks.
Dyan, Penelope. My Two Cents Worth! 2011. 34p. pap. 11.95 (978-1-935630-69-2(5)) Bellissima Publishing, LLC.
Elkeles, Simone. How to Ruin Your Boyfriend's Reputation. 2009. (How to Ruin a Summer Vacation Novel Ser.: 3). (ENG.). 264p. (YA). (gr. 7-18). pap. 9.95 (978-0-7387-1879-8(3), Flux) North Star Editions.
Elvgren, Jennifer. Josias, Hold the Book. Tadgell, Nicole, illus. 2011. (ENG.). 32p. (J). (gr. 2-4). pap. 10.95 (978-1-59078-856-1(7)) Boyds Mills Pr.
Epstein, Brad M. Auburn University 101: My First Text-Board-Book. I.t. ed. 2003. (My First Text Board Bks.).

(Illus.). 20p. (J). bds. *(978-0-9727702-7-9(5))* Michaelson Entertainment.
—Dartmouth College 101. l.t. ed. 2003. (My First Text Board Bks.). (Illus.). 20p. (J). bds. *(978-0-9727702-5-5(9))* Michaelson Entertainment.
Esprit, Keisha. Serena Goes to School. 2013. 24p. pap. 24.95 *(978-1-62709-460-3(1))* America Star Bks.
Farshtey, Greg. Cole - Ninja of Earth. 2012. (Lego Ninjago Ser.). (ENG.). 80p. (J). (gr. 2-5). pap. 4.99 *(978-0-545-36993-0(2))* Scholastic, Inc.
Fine, Edith Hope & Josephson, Judith Pinkerton. Armando & the Blue Tarp School, 1 vol. Sosa, Hernan, illus. 2007. (ENG.). 32p. (J). (gr. -1-3). lib. bdg. 16.95 *(978-1-58430-278-0(X))* Lee & Low Bks., Inc.
—Armando y la Escuela de Lona Azul. Sosa, Hernan, illus. 2015.Tr. of Armando & the Blue Tarp School. (SPA & ENG.). 32p. (J). (gr. k-4). pap. 10.95 *(978-1-60060-449-2(8))* Lee & Low Bks., Inc.
Fukui, Isamu. Truancy. 2010. (Truancy Ser.: 1). (ENG.). 432p. (YA). (gr. 8-12). pap. 24.99 *(978-0-7653-2258-6(7),* 9780765322586, Tor Teen) Doherty, Tom Assocs., LLC.
—Truancy Origins. 2011. (Truancy Ser.: 2). (ENG.). 384p. (YA). (gr. 8-12). pap. 19.99 *(978-0-7653-2264-7(1),* 9780765322647, Tor Teen) Doherty, Tom Assocs., LLC.
Gambini, Josephine. Poetino Piccolino Saves the Day. Stafford, Jordan, illus. 2011. (ENG.). (J). pap. 19.95 *(978-0-9829496-3-4(4))* Giusti-Gambini, J.M. Publishing, LLC.
Gantos, Jack. What Would Joey Do? 2004. (Joey Pigza Ser.). 229p. (J). (gr. 5-9). 13.65 *(978-0-7569-2597-0(5))* Perfection Learning Corp.
George, Bobby & George, June. Montessori: Letter Work. Nassner, Alyssa, illus. 2012. (Montessori Ser.). (ENG.). 24p. (J). (gr. -1-k). bds., bds. 9.95 *(978-1-4197-0411-6(7),* Abrams Appleseed) Abrams, Inc.
—Montessori: Number Work. Nassner, Alyssa, illus. 2012. (Montessori Ser.). (ENG.). 24p. (J). (gr. -1-k). bds., bds. 9.95 *(978-1-4197-0412-3(5),* Abrams Appleseed) Abrams, Inc.
Giannasi, Maddalena. Bianca & Her Alphabet Soup. 2011. 32p. 18.99 *(978-1-4520-9908-8(1))* AuthorHouse.
Gomes, Julie. ABC Exercise with Me. Dungan, Julia, illus. 2005. (J). per. 7.50 *(978-0-9770207-0-6(3))* JCCJ Pr.
Goncalves, Regina. Mathematics - what beast Is This? 2008. 214p. pap. 15.95 *(978-1-4092-2673-4(5))* Lulu Pr., Inc.
Goodman, Gabriel. The Alliance. 2013. (Surviving Southside Ser.). (ENG.). 104p. (YA). (gr. 6-12). pap. 7.95 *(978-1-4677-0708-4(2),* Darby Creek); lib. bdg. 27.93 *(978-1-4677-0595-0(0))* Lerner Publishing Group.
Hartman, Judith Allen. Upside down Harry. 2012. 44p. pap. 21.99 *(978-1-4772-9194-8(6))* AuthorHouse.
Hayes, Larry. My Name Starts with K. Anderson, Airlie, illus. 2005. (My Name Starts With Ser.). 31p. (J). 12.95 *(978-0-9725292-6-6(8))* Inspire Pubns.
Hensley, Sarah M. I Want to Ride. Gray, Stacy A., illus. l.t. ed. 2004. (HRL Board Book Ser.). 10p. (J). (gr. -1-1). pap. 10.95 *(978-1-57332-282-9(2),* HighReach Learning, Incorporated) Carson-Dellosa Publishing, LLC.
Hide & Seek. Date not set. (Magic Windows Ser.). (Illus.). (J). Vol. 1. *(978-0-7624-1983-8(0))* Vol. 2. *(978-0-7624-1984-5(9))* Running Pr. Bk. Pubs. (Running Pr. Kids).
Hilton, Charlotte. Adventure of the Pen Pot Pals. 2009. 36p. pap. 16.99 *(978-1-4389-4434-0(9))* AuthorHouse.
Hopkinson, Deborah. Steamboat School. Husband, Ron, illus. 2016. (ENG.). 40p. (J). (gr. -1-k). 17.99 *(978-1-4231-2196-1(1))* Disney Pr.
Howat, Irene, et al. Gweni Gweld Bob Dim. 2005. (Storiau Crefyddol Religious Stories Ser.). (WEL., Illus.). 24p. *(978-1-85994-522-3(8))* Cyhoeddiadau'r Gair.
—Huw Helpu Pawb. 2005. (Storiau Crefyddol Religious Stories Ser.). (WEL., Illus.). 24p. *(978-1-85994-519-3(8))* Cyhoeddiadau'r Gair.
Hughes, Huw John, tr. from ENG. Cadi Deud Celwydd. 2005. (Storiau Crefyddol Religious Stories Ser.). (WEL., Illus.). 24p. pap. *(978-1-85994-517-9(1))* Cyhoeddiadau'r Gair.
Hutchins, Hazel J. & Hutchins, Hazel. Robyn Makes the News, 1 vol. Cathcart, Yvonne, illus. 2003. (Formac First Novels Ser.: 27). (ENG.). 64p. (J). (gr. 1-5). 4.95 *(978-0-88780-593-6(0),* 9780887805936) Formac Publishing Co., Ltd. CAN. Dist: Casemate Pubs. & Bk. Distributors, LLC.
Isdell, Wendy. The Chemy Called Al by Wendy Isdell. 2nd ed. 2004. 150p. (YA). per. 10.99 *(978-1-4116-1095-8(4))* Lulu Pr., Inc.
Jackson, Ovetta. Beanie & Skooda & the Buddifly Gang. 2012. 32p. pap. 19.99 *(978-1-4685-3131-2(X))* AuthorHouse.
Jarrell, Pamela R. Caillou Finds a Caterpillar. Storch, Ellen N., illus. l.t. ed. 2005. (HRL Board Book Ser.). (J). (gr. -1-1). pap. 10.95 *(978-1-57332-292-8(X),* HighReach Learning, Incorporated) Carson-Dellosa Publishing, LLC.
Jenkins, Donna. When I Grow up, I Want to Be a Doctor. 2010. 16p. 10.49 *(978-1-4490-8303-8(X))* AuthorHouse.
Jones, Patrick & Chartier, Brent. The Franchise. 2013. (Opportunity Ser.). (ENG.). 104p. (YA). (gr. 6-12). pap. 7.95 *(978-1-4677-1496-9(8));* lib. bdg. 27.93 *(978-1-4677-1375-7(9))* Lerner Publishing Group. (Darby Creek).
Karre, Elizabeth. The Campaign. 2013. (Opportunity Ser.). (ENG.). 104p. (YA). (gr. 6-12). pap. 7.95 *(978-1-4677-1498-3(4));* lib. bdg. 27.93 *(978-1-4677-1374-0(0))* Lerner Publishing Group. (Darby Creek).
Konigsburg, E. L. The View from Saturday. 280p. (YA). (gr. 5-18). pap. 4.95 *(978-0-8072-1511-1(2),* Listening Library) Random Hse. Audio Publishing Group.
Krulik, Nancy. Something's Fishy, No. 26. John and Wendy Staff, illus. 2007. (Katie Kazoo, Switcheroo Ser.: 26). (ENG.). 80p. (J). (gr. 2-4). pap. 4.99 *(978-0-448-44442-0(9),* Grosset & Dunlap) Penguin Young Readers Group.
Lakes, Lofton & Metu, illus. The Dream Team. 2007. 48p. (YA). pap. *(978-0-9799320-0-7(9))* Pinkney, Gail.
Latham, Irene. Don't Feed the Boy. Graegin, Stephanie, illus. 2012. (ENG.). 288p. (J). (gr. 3-7). 17.99 *(978-1-59643-755-5(3),* 9781596437555) Roaring Brook Pr.
Laurie, Cook, illus. Amelia Asks Why. 2007. (J). 3.99 *(978-0-9726075-4-4(4))* EPI Bks.
Leblanc, Louise. Maddie's Big Test. Cummins, Sarah, tr. from FRE. Gay, Marie-Louise, illus. 2006. (Formac First Novels Ser.: 58). (ENG.). 64p. (J). (gr. 2-5). 14.95 *(978-0-88780-718-3(6),* 9780887807183) Formac Publishing Co., Ltd. CAN. Dist: Casemate Pubs. & Bk. Distributors, LLC.
—Maddie's Big Test, 1 vol. Cummins, Sarah, tr. from FRE. Gay, Marie-Louise, illus. 2006. (Formac First Novels Ser.). (ENG.). 64p. (J). (gr. 2-5). 4.95 *(978-0-88780-714-5(3),* 9780887807145) Formac Publishing Co., Ltd. CAN. Dist: Casemate Pubs. & Bk. Distributors, LLC.
Lee, Karen. ABC Safari, 1 vol. Lee, Karen, illus. 2007. (ENG., Illus.). 32p. (J). (gr. -1-3). 15.95 *(978-0-9777423-0-1(X));* pap. 8.95 *(978-0-9777423-6-3(9))* Arbordale Publishing.
Lewis, Caryl & Lolfa, Y. lawn Boi? 2005. (WEL.). 80p. pap. *(978-0-86243-699-5(0))* Y Lolfa.
Lichtman, Wendy. The Writing on the Wall. 2008. (Do the Math Ser.: 2). (ENG.). 224p. (YA). (gr. 8-9). 16.99 *(978-0-06-122958-9(X),* Greenwillow Bks.) HarperCollins Pubs.
Lieberman, Leanne. The Book of Trees, 1 vol. 2010. (ENG.). 256p. (YA). (gr. 8-12). pap. 12.95 *(978-1-55469-265-1(2))* Orca Bk. Pubs. USA.
Lipp, Frederick. Running Shoes. Gaillard, Jason, illus. 2008. 32p. (J). (gr. 2-5). 16.95 *(978-1-58089-175-2(6));* pap. 7.95 *(978-1-58089-176-9(4))* Charlesbridge Publishing, Inc.
MacDonald, George. The History of Gutta-Percha Willie. 2006. 116p. per. 9.95 *(978-1-59818-578-2(0))* Aegypan.
—The History of Gutta-Percha Willie. 2007. 136p. per. *(978-1-4065-2998-2(2))* Dodo Pr.
MacHado, Ana Maria. De carta en Carta. Basulto, Rita, illus. 2004. (SPA.). 44p. (gr. 3-5). pap. 7.95 *(978-968-19-1483-7(X))* Santillana USA Publishing Co., Inc.
Mack, Iris Marie. Mama Says, Money Doesn't Grow on Trees! 2004. (World of Dr. Mackamatix Mathematics Edutainment Book Ser.). (Illus.). 48p. (J). per. 18.99 *(978-1-4134-0891-1(5))* Xlibris Corp.
Malaspina, Ann. Yasmin's Hammer. Chayka, Doug, illus. 2010. (ENG.). 40p. (J). (gr. k-6). 18.95 *(978-1-60060-359-4(9))* Lee & Low Bks., Inc.
Markel, Michelle. The Shark That Taught Me English/El Tiburon Que Me Enseno Ingles. Kim, Bo Young, illus. 2008. 28p. (J). pap. 8.95 *(978-1-60448-003-0(3))* Lectura Bks.
Masterson, Carla & Druckman, Mike. Memory Emory & His Hiding Places. 2005. (J). per. 16.95 *(978-1-59858-052-5(3))* Dog Ear Publishing, LLC.
McGoldrick, Bernita. Pretty Pretty Picky Penelope. McGoldrick, Bernita, illus. 2010. (Illus.). 32p. pap. 12.95 *(978-1-935268-49-9(X))* Halo Publishing International.
McKee, Ruby. The Land of Phonicia: An Enchanted Tale to Learn Phonics. Allen, Timothy, illus. l.t. ed. 2003. 52p. (J). per. 39.95 *(978-0-9744944-0-1(2))* Jewel Publishing.
Meg. The Adventures of Meg: Wiggles Learns about Making Good Choices. 2010. 24p. pap. 9.99 *(978-1-60911-892-1(8),* Eloquent Bks.) Strategic Book Publishing & Rights Agency (SBPRA).
Mitchard, Jacquelyn & Lewis, Michael S. Eagle Eyes. 2009. (ENG.). 128p. (gr. 4-7). pap. 9.99 *(978-0-9790072-2-4(4))* MAHVL Publishing.
Muench-Williams, Heather. At the Circus. Storch, Ellen N., illus. l.t. ed. 2005. (HRL Board Book Ser.). 10p. (J). (gr. -1-1). bds. 10.95 *(978-1-57332-285-0(7),* HighReach Learning, Incorporated) Carson-Dellosa Publishing, LLC.
Mullican, Judy. A Big Mess. Gray, Stacy A., illus. l.t. ed. 2003. (HRL Little Book Ser.). 8p. (J). (gr. -1). pap. 10.95 *(978-1-57332-273-7(3),* HighReach Learning, Incorporated) Carson-Dellosa Publishing, LLC.
—Caillou Is Healthy. Gray, Stacy A., illus. l.t. ed. 2004. (HRL Board Book Ser.). (J). (gr. -1-1). pap. 10.95 *(978-1-57332-287-4(3),* HighReach Learning, Incorporated) Carson-Dellosa Publishing, LLC.
Mullican, Judy & Williams, Heather L. Building a Sand Castle. Storch, Ellen N., illus. l.t. ed. 2004. (HRL Big Book Ser.). (J). (gr. -1). pap. 10.95 *(978-1-57332-297-3(0));* pap. 10.95 *(978-1-57332-298-0(9))* Carson-Dellosa Publishing, LLC. (HighReach Learning, Incorporated).
Murphy, Eileen. 3 Big Steps. Montgomery, Violet, illus. 2008. 25p. pap. 24.95 *(978-1-60563-310-7(0))* America Star Bks.
Olker, Constance. The Punctuation Pals Go to the Beach. Guzman, Minerva, illus. 2005. (Punctuation Pals Ser.). 36p. (J). per. 18.95 *(978-1-933449-12-8(8))* Nightengale Pr.
—The Punctuation Pals Go to the Beach. l.t. ed. 2005. (Illus.). 22p. (J). per. 17.95 *(978-0-9761289-5-3(0))* Nightengale Pr.
—The Punctuation Pals Go to the Moon. 2005. (Illus.). (J). 64p. per. 24.95 *(978-1-933449-13-5(6));* per. 19.95 *(978-0-9761289-6-0(9))* Nightengale Pr.
—The Punctuation Pals Meet at School. 2005. (Illus.). (J). 40p. per. 18.95 *(978-1-933449-07-4(1));* 18p. per. 16.95 *(978-0-9761289-4-6(2))* Nightengale Pr.
Orme, Helen. New Boy. 2008. (Backstreet Ser.). (ENG., Illus.). 36p. pap. *(978-1-84167-770-5(1))* Ransom Publishing Ltd.
—No More School. 2008. (Backstreet Ser.). (ENG., Illus.). 36p. pap. *(978-1-84167-771-2(X))* Ransom Publishing Ltd.
—Out to Work. 2008. (Backstreet Ser.). (ENG., Illus.). 35p. pap. *(978-1-84167-760-4(9))* Ransom Publishing Ltd.
—Rats! 2008. (Backstreet Ser.). (ENG., Illus.). 36p. pap. *(978-1-84167-772-9(8))* Ransom Publishing Ltd.
Page, Lynda. Caley's Secret Garden. 2012. 28p. pap. 32.70 *(978-1-4771-0605-1(7))* Xlibris Corp.
Parker, David. I Can Listen. Allen, Joy, illus. 2005. (J). *(978-0-439-79208-0(8))* Scholastic, Inc.
Patton, Katherine. Bam Bam the Bandage. 2010. 16p. pap. 10.99 *(978-1-4343-4967-5(5))* AuthorHouse.
Peck, Richard. The Teacher's Funeral. 2006. (ENG.). 224p. (J). (gr. 3-7). reprint ed. 7.99 *(978-0-14-240507-9(8),* Puffin Books) Penguin Young Readers Group.
Pellowski. The Story Vine. 2008. (ENG.). 132p. (J). (gr. -1-3). 7.99 *(978-1-4169-7578-6(0),* Simon & Schuster/Paula Wiseman Bks.) Simon & Schuster/Paula Wiseman Bks.
Penn, M. W. Sidney the Silly Who Only Eats 6. Tommer, Sarah, illus. 2007. 32p. (J). *(978-0-9784047-2-7(6))* Pays et Terroirs.
Ponti, Claude & Desarthe, Agnes. El Principito Puf. 2003. (SPA.). 102p. *(978-84-8470-063-0(1))* Corimbo, Editorial S.L.
Preller, James. A Pirate's Guide to First Grade. Ruth, Greg, illus. 2013. (ENG.). 48p. (J). (gr. -1-1). 7.99 *(978-1-250-02721-4(7),* 9781250027214) Square Fish.
Priddy, Roger & Crimi-Trent, Ellen. My First Day at School. 2013. (Schoolies Ser.). (ENG., Illus.). 28p. (J). (gr. -1-1). 4.99 *(978-0-312-51612-3(6),* 9780312516123, Priddy Bks.) St. Martin's Pr.
Richards, Laura Elizabeth Howe. Queen Hildegarde. 2007. 92p. per. *(978-1-4068-3867-1(5))* Echo Library.
Rowen, Amy & Rowen, Tyla Marie. Waggin' Tails. 2003. 182p. 23.95 *(978-0-595-65740-7(0));* pap. 13.95 *(978-0-595-28171-8(0))* iUniverse, Inc.
Scaglione, Joanne & Small, Gail. The Big Squeal: A Wild, True, & Twisted Tail, Vol. Endelman, David, illus. 2005. (ENG.). 56p. pap. 35.00 *(978-1-57886-256-6(6))* Rowman & Littlefield Education.
Sempe & Goscinny. Los Recreos del Pequeno Nicolas. 2003. (SPA., Illus.). 116p. (J). (gr. 3-5). pap. 9.95 *(978-84-204-4814-5(1))* Santillana USA Publishing Co., Inc.
Shiloh, Ramon. Guidance Through an Illustrative Alphabet: Written & Illustrated by Ramon Shiloh. Shiloh, Ramon, illus. 2006. (Illus.). 64p. (J). per. 29.95 *(978-1-4259-5132-0(5))* AuthorHouse.
Simon, Sandy. Sylvie. 2012. 16p. pap. 15.99 *(978-1-4772-4899-7(4))* AuthorHouse.
Sleator, William. Test. 2010. (ENG.). 320p. (YA). (gr. 7-11). pap. 7.95 *(978-0-8109-8989-4(1),* Amulet Bks.) Abrams, Inc.
Standiford, Natalie. The Boy on the Bridge. 2013. (ENG.). 256p. (J). (gr. 9). 17.99 *(978-0-545-33481-5(0),* Scholastic Pr.) Scholastic, Inc.
Tavner, Gill & Dickens, Charles. Hard Times. Donnelly, Karen, illus. 2009. (Real Reads Ser.). 64p. (J). (gr. 4-8). pap. 13.55 *(978-1-60754-386-2(9))* Windmill Bks.
Thielbar, Melinda. The Hundred-Dollar Robber: A Mystery with Money. Pantoja, Maria Kristina, illus. 2009. (Manga Math Mysteries Ser.: 2). (ENG.). 48p. (gr. 3-5). 29.27 *(978-0-7613-3854-3(3))* Lerner Publishing Group.
—The Kung Fu Puzzle: A Mystery with Time & Temperature. Ota, Yuko & Helmer, Der-Shing, illus. 2009. (Manga Math Mysteries Ser.: No. 4). 48p. (J). (gr. 2-5). 29.27 *(978-0-7613-3856-7(X))* Lerner Publishing Group.
Vicario, Evelyn. Mathematics for Life - Moses Meets the Triangles. Vicario, Evelyn, illus. 2013. (Illus.). 48p. (J). pap. 7.99 *(978-0-9826276-6-2(1),* Bibia Publishing) Bibia, LLC.
—Mathematics for Life - Moses Teaches Properties of Addition. 2013. 48p. (J). pap. 7.99 *(978-0-9826276-7-9(X),* Bibia Publishing) Bibia, LLC.
Villoro, Juan. El Profesor Ziper y la Fabulosa Guitarra Electrica. El Fisgsn, illus. 2005. (Infantil Ser.). (SPA.). 96p. (J). (gr. 5-8). pap. 9.95 *(978-968-19-0206-3(8))* Santillana USA Publishing Co., Inc.
White, Andrea. Surviving Antarctica: Reality TV 2083. 2006. (ENG.). 448p. (YA). (gr. 8). pap. 8.99 *(978-0-06-055456-9(8),* HarperTeen) 2005. 336p. (J). (gr. 7-18). 16.99 *(978-0-06-055454-5(1),* HarperCollins) HarperCollins Pubs.
Williams, Delphine. Freckles with All the Speckles. 2008. 36p. pap. 24.95 *(978-1-60703-402-5(6))* America Star Bks.
Williams, Heather L. Andy & Jerome. Crowell, Knox, illus. l.t. ed. 2004. (HRL Little Book Ser.). 8p. (J). (gr. -1-1). pap. 10.95 *(978-1-57332-276-8(8));* pap. 10.95 *(978-1-57332-277-5(6))* Carson-Dellosa Publishing, LLC. (HighReach Learning, Incorporated).
—Brians Garden. Gillen, Lisa P., illus. l.t. ed. 2004. (HRL Big Book Ser.). (J). (gr. -1-1). pap. 10.95 *(978-1-57332-299-7(7));* pap. 10.95 *(978-1-57332-300-0(4))* Carson-Dellosa Publishing, LLC. (HighReach Learning, Incorporated).
Williams, Rozanne Lanczak. I Love to Write! Schuett, Stacey, illus. 2006. (Learn to Write Ser.). 8p. (J). (gr. k-2). pap. 3.49 *(978-1-59198-283-8(9),* 6177) Creative Teaching Pr., Inc.
—I Love to Write! Maio, Barbara & Faulkner, Stacey, eds. Schuett, Stacey, illus. 2006. (J). per. 6.99 *(978-1-59198-334-7(7))* Creative Teaching Pr., Inc.
—This Is My Story. Burris, Priscilla, illus. 2006. (Learn to Write Ser.). 8p. (J). (gr. k-2). pap. 3.49 *(978-1-59198-280-7(4),* 6174) Creative Teaching Pr., Inc.
—Writing about Books. Schneider, Christine, illus. 2006. (Learn to Write Ser.). 8p. (J). (gr. k-2). pap. 3.49 *(978-1-59198-289-0(8),* 6183) Creative Teaching Pr., Inc.
Wilson, Bryan M. Benjamin's Report Card Blues. 2011. 28p. pap. 12.95 *(978-1-4567-3530-2(6))* AuthorHouse.
Winfield, Arthur M. Putnam Hall Rivals. 2006. pap. 27.95 *(978-1-4286-1948-7(8))* Kessinger Publishing, LLC.
—The Rover Boys in the Mountains. 2005. 216p. pap. 12.95 *(978-1-4218-1109-3(X),* 1st World Library - Literary Society) 1st World Publishing, Inc.
—The Rover Boys in the Mountains: Or, A Hunt for Fun & Fortune. 2007. 170p. pap. 19.99 *(978-1-4264-7052-3(5))* 2006. (ENG.). 188p. pap. 21.99 *(978-1-4264-7128-5(9))* Creative Media Partners, LLC.
Wood, Audrey. Alphabet Rescue. Wood, Bruce, illus. 2006. (ENG.). 40p. (J). (gr. -1-k). 17.99 *(978-0-439-85316-3(8),* Blue Sky Pr., The) Scholastic, Inc.
Wyckoff, Joanne Francis. Wally the Spelling Whiz. 2009. 36p. pap. 17.99 *(978-1-4389-5141-6(8))* AuthorHouse.
Young, Judy. The Lucky Star. Ellison, Chris, illus. 2008. (Tales of Young Americans Ser.). (ENG.). 32p. (J). (gr. 3-7). 17.95 *(978-1-58536-348-3(0))* Sleeping Bear Pr.

EDUCATION, HIGHER

see also Technical Education

Espejo, Roman. What Is the Future of Higher Education? Greenhaven Press Staff, ed. 2015. (At Issue Ser.). (ENG.). 128p. (gr. 10-12). lib. bdg. 39.40 *(978-0-7377-7201-2(8),* Greenhaven Pr., Inc.) Cengage Gale.
Jordan, Keith. Don't Stress the Process: The College Plan. 2005. (J). lib. bdg. 18.95 *(978-0-9761218-0-0(8))* Knowledge College Planning.
McCormick, Lisa Wade. Financial Aid Smarts: Getting Money for School. 2012. (Get Smart with Your Money Ser.). (ENG., Illus.). 64p. (J). (gr. 7-12). pap. 12.95 *(978-1-4488-8266-3(4));* lib. bdg. 31.95 *(978-1-4488-8252-6(4))* Rosen Publishing Group, Inc., The.
Prentzas, G. S. Smart Strategies for Paying for College. 2014. (Financial Security & Life Success for Teens Ser.). (Illus.). 80p. (J). (gr. 7-12). 34.25 *(978-1-4777-7614-8(1))* Rosen Publishing Group, Inc., The.
Watkins, Boyce. Everything You Ever Wanted to Know about College: A Guide for Minority Students. 2004. xiii, 330p. (YA). per. 25.00 *(978-0-9742632-0-5(6))* Blue Boy Publishing Co.
Watkins, Dewhite. Quick & Dirty Secrets of College Success: A Professor Tells It All. 2004. 128p. (YA). per. 14.95 *(978-0-9742632-1-2(4))* Blue Boy Publishing Co.
Williams, Rozalia. College FAQ Book: Over 5,000 Not Frequently Asked Questions about College! 2005. (Illus.). 494p. (YA). per. 24.95 *(978-0-9755103-0-8(4))* Hidden Curriculum Education.
Young, Mitchell. For-Profit Education. 2011. (Opposing Viewpoints Ser.). (ENG., Illus.). 224p. (gr. 10-12). 48.80 *(978-0-7377-5836-8(8))* Cengage Gale.
Young, Mitchell, ed. For-Profit Education. 2011. (Opposing Viewpoints Ser.). (Illus.). 240p. pap. 29.45 *(978-0-7377-5837-5(6),* Greenhaven Pr., Inc.) Cengage Gale.

EDUCATION—HISTORY

Feldman, Ruth Tenzer. Don't Whistle in School: The History of America's Public Schools. 2005. (People's History Ser.). (Illus.). 96p. (gr. 6-12). lib. bdg. 26.60 *(978-0-8225-1745-0(0))* Lerner Publishing Group.
Foran, Jill. The School House: Pioneers of Canada. 2011. 24p. (YA). (gr. 2-4). *(978-1-77071-680-3(7));* pap. *(978-1-77071-684-1(X))* Weigl Educational Pubs. Ltd.
Hinman, Bonnie. The Scoop on School & Work in Colonial America, 1 vol. 2012. (Life in the American Colonies Ser.). (ENG.). 32p. (gr. 3-4). pap. 8.10 *(978-1-4296-7986-2(7),* Fact Finders) Capstone Press of Coughlan Cos.
Lee, Sally. School Long Ago & Today, 1 vol. 2014. (Long Ago & Today Ser.). (ENG.). 24p. (gr. 1-2). 25.32 *(978-1-4914-0296-2(2))* Capstone Press of Coughlan Cos.
Meachen Rau, Dana. La Escuela en la Historia de América. 2006. (Como era la vida en America (How People Lived in America) Ser.). (SPA., Illus.). 24p. (gr. 1-4). pap. 8.15 *(978-0-8368-7439-6(0),* Weekly Reader Leveled Readers) Stevens, Gareth Publishing LLLP.
—La Escuela en la Historia de America. 2006. (Como era la vida en America (How People Lived in America) Ser.). (SPA., Illus.). 24p. (gr. 1-4). lib. bdg. 22.00 *(978-0-8368-7432-7(3),* Weekly Reader Leveled Readers) Stevens, Gareth Publishing LLLP.
—Going to School in American History. 2006. (How People Lived in America Ser.). 24p. (gr. 1-4). pap. 8.15 *(978-0-8368-7214-9(2));* (Illus.). lib. bdg. 22.00 *(978-0-8368-7207-1(X))* Stevens, Gareth Publishing LLLP. (Weekly Reader Leveled Readers).
Platt, Richard. In 1400, Reading Could Save Your Life?! And Other Academic Advantages. 2015. (ENG., Illus.). 48p. pap. 12.95 *(978-0-19-911870-0(1))* Oxford Univ. Pr., Inc.
Randolph, Ryan P. Frontier Schools & Schoolteachers. (Library of the Westward Expansion Ser.). 24p. 2009. (gr. 3-4). 42.50 *(978-1-60853-935-2(0))* 2003. (Illus.). (J). lib. bdg. 22.60 *(978-0-8239-6295-2(4))* Rosen Publishing Group, Inc., The. (PowerKids Pr.).
Reef, Catherine. Education & Learning in America. 2008. (American Experience Ser.). 424p. (C). (gr. 9). 85.00 *(978-0-8160-7024-4(5))* Facts On File, Inc.
Remember: The Journey to School Integration-Display. 2004. (ENG.). 1p. (J). tchr. ed. 162.00 *(978-0-618-45334-4(2))* Houghton Mifflin Harcourt Publishing Co.
Rissman, Rebecca. Going to School: Comparing Past & Present, 1 vol. 2014. (Comparing Past & Present Ser.). (ENG., Illus.). 24p. (gr. -1-1). pap. 6.95 *(978-1-4329-9025-1(X));* lib. bdg. 22.65 *(978-1-4329-8991-0(X))* Heinemann-Raintree. (Acorn).
Stewart, Tobi. Colonial Teachers. 2009. (Reading Room Collection 1 Ser.). 16p. (gr. 2-3). 37.50 *(978-1-60851-942-2(2),* PowerKids Pr.) Rosen Publishing Group, Inc., The.

EDUCATION, INDUSTRIAL

see Technical Education

EDUCATION, INTERCULTURAL

see Multicultural Education

EDUCATION, MILITARY

see Military Education

EDUCATION, MORAL

see Moral Education

EDUCATION, MUSICAL

see Music—Study and Teaching

EDUCATION—PERSONNEL SERVICE

see Educational Counseling

EDUCATION, PHYSICAL

see Physical Education and Training

EDUCATION, PRESCHOOL

see Nursery Schools

EDUCATION, PRIMARY

see Education, Elementary

EDUCATION, RELIGIOUS

see Religious Education

EDUCATION, SCIENTIFIC

see Science—Study and Teaching

EDUCATION, SECONDARY

Gumm, Merry L. Help! I'm in Middle School... How Will I Survive? 2005. (Illus.). 80p. (J). per. 9.95 *(978-0-9761724-5-1(3),* B-HMS) NSR Pubns.
Hoffman, Joan. Second Grade Basics. 2008. (ENG.). 32p. (J). pap. 2.99 *(978-1-58947-438-3(4))* School Zone Publishing Co.
Human Body Experiments. 2010. (Facts on File Science Experiments Ser.). (Illus.). 192p. (gr. 6-12). 40.00 *(978-0-8160-8171-4(9))* Facts On File, Inc.
Kiesbye, Stefan. Can Busy Teens Succeed Academically? 2009. (At Issue Ser.). (ENG., Illus.). 128p. (gr. 10-12). pap. 27.80 *(978-0-7377-4285-5(2),* Greenhaven Pr., Inc.) Cengage Gale.
Modoc Press Editors. Directory of Distance Learning Opportunities: K-12, 1 vol. 2003. 432p. (C). (gr. k-12). 96.00 *(978-1-57356-515-8(6),* OXDLK-12, Greenwood) ABC-CLIO, LLC.
Roselius, J. Chris. Surviving School: Managing School & Career Paths, 1 vol. 2010. (Essential Health: a Guy's Guide Ser.). (ENG.). 112p. (J). (gr. 6-12). lib. bdg. 35.64 *(978-1-61613-544-7(1))* ABDO Publishing Co.
Silverthorne, Sandy. Surviving Middle School: How to Manage the Maze. 2006. (Illus.). 96p. (YA). (gr. 3-6). pap. 5.99 *(978-0-7847-1433-1(9),* 42175) Standard Publishing.

E
F
G

Zaroulis, Christina. Tackling Your High School Term Paper. 2003. (Students Helping Students Ser.). 80p. (gr. 9-12). pap. 8.95 *(978-0-9719392-1-9(7))* Natavi Guides.

EDUCATION, SEGREGATION IN

see Segregation in Education

EDUCATION—STUDY AND TEACHING

see also Teachers—Training of

The Chocolate War: Response Journal. 2003. 36p. (YA). *(978-1-58049-995-8(3)*, RJ95) Prestwick Hse., Inc.

Myers, Walter Dean. Monster. 2008. 45p. tchr. ed., ring bd. 29.99 *(978-1-58049-469-4(2)*, TU225) Prestwick Hse., Inc.

O'Neill, Elizabeth. Alfred Visits Connecticut. 2009. 24p. (J). pap. 12.00 *(978-0-9822288-9-0(9))* Global Business Information Strategies, Inc.

—Alfred Visits Idaho. 2009. 24p. (J). pap. 12.00 *(978-0-9822288-8-3(0))* Global Business Information Strategies, Inc.

—Alfred Visits New Mexico. 2009. (ENG.). 24p. (J). pap. 12.00 *(978-0-9822288-7-6(2))* Global Business Information Strategies, Inc.

—Alfred Visits Wisconsin. 2009. 24p. (J). pap. 12.00 *(978-0-9841507-0-0(6))* Lipp, G. Douglas & Assocs.

School Zone Interactive Staff. Preschool. 2003. (On-Track Software Ser.). (ENG.). (J). (gr. -1-18). cd-rom 24.99 *(978-1-58947-539-7(9))* School Zone Publishing Co.

Thompson, Karen. Preschool. 2003. (Software Ser.). (ENG.). (J). 29.99 *(978-1-58947-534-2(8))*; (Illus.). 24.99 *(978-1-58947-529-8(1))* School Zone Publishing Co.

EDUCATION, TECHNICAL

see Technical Education

EDUCATION, THEOLOGICAL

see Religious Education

EDUCATION—VOCATIONAL GUIDANCE

Blackwell, Amy Hackney. Personal Care Services, Fitness & Education. 2008. (Great Careers with a High School Diploma Ser.). 114p. (C). (gr. 9). 32.95 *(978-0-8160-7045-9(8)*, Ferguson Publishing Co.) Facts On File, Inc.

Cohn, Jessica. On the Job at School. Scheuer, Lauren, illus. 2016. (Core Content Social Studies — on the Job Ser.). (ENG.). 32p. (J). (gr. 2-5). lib. bdg. 26.65 *(978-1-63440-108-1(5))* Red Chair Pr.

Communication, Education, & Travel. 2010. (Green Careers Ser.). (Illus.). 160p. (C). (gr. 9-18). 32.95 *(978-0-8160-8154-7(9)*, Ferguson Publishing Co.) Facts On File, Inc.

Education. 2010. (What Can I Do Now? Ser.). 224p. (gr. 6-12). 32.95 *(978-0-8160-8079-3(8)*, Ferguson Publishing Co.) Facts On File, Inc.

Kampff, Joseph. What Degree Do I Need to Pursue a Career in Education?, 1 vol. 2015. (ENG., Illus.). 80p. (J). 34.60 *(978-1-4777-7873-9(X)*, Rosen Young Adult) Rosen Publishing Group, Inc., The.

Matters, Print & Kirk, Amanda. Education. 2009. (Field Guides to Finding a New Career Ser.). (C). (gr. 9-18). 152p. pap. 16.95 *(978-0-8160-7621-5(9)*, Checkmark Bks.); (Illus.). 134p. 39.95 *(978-0-8160-7597-3(2)*, Ferguson Publishing Co.) Facts On File, Inc.

Pitches, Neale & Hollingsworth, Toni. CSI Comprehensive Strategies Instruction Kit: Grade 6. 2008. (CSI). (gr. 6). 895.00 *(978-1-60457-111-0(X))* Pacific Learning, Inc.

Reeves, Diane Lindsey. Career Ideas for Teens in Education & Training. 2006. (Career Ideas for Teens Ser.). (Illus.). 192p. (gr. 7-12). per. 16.95 *(978-0-8160-6919-4(0)*, Checkmark Bks.) Facts On File, Inc.

Reeves, Diane Lindsey & Karlitz, Gail. Career Ideas for Teens in Education & Training. 2005. (Career Ideas for Teens Ser.). (Illus.). 192p. (gr. 6-12). 40.00 *(978-0-8160-5295-0(6)*, Ferguson Publishing Co.) Facts On File, Inc.

Sheen, Barbara. Careers in Education. 2015. (ENG., Illus.). 80p. (J). lib. bdg. *(978-1-60152-808-7(6))* ReferencePoint Pr., Inc.

Silivanch, Annalise. A Career as a Teacher. 2010. (Essential Careers Ser.). (ENG.). 80p. (YA). lib. bdg. 33.25 *(978-1-4358-9468-6(5))* Rosen Publishing Group, Inc., The.

The Vo-Tech Track to Success in Business. 2014. (Learning a Trade, Preparing for a Career Ser.). (Illus.). 80p. (J). (gr. 7-12). 34.25 *(978-1-4777-7722-0(9))* Rosen Publishing Group, Inc., The.

Wigu Publishing. When I Grow up I Want to Be... a Teacher! Carlee Learns a Surprising Lesson! 2013. (When I Grow Up I Want To Be....Ser.). (Illus.). 62p. pap. 12.95 *(978-1-939973-08-5(2)*, Wigu Publishing) Wigu Publishing.

EDUCATION AND STATE

see also Scholarships

Kowalski, Kathiann M. Lemon V. Kurtzman & the Separation of Church & State Debate. 2005. (Debating Supreme Court Decisions Ser.). (Illus.). 128p. (J). (gr. 7-12). lib. bdg. 27.94 *(978-0-7660-2391-8(5))* Enslow Pubs., Inc.

Ruffin, David C. The Duties & Responsibilities of the Secretary of Education. 2009. (Your Government in Action Ser.). 32p. (gr. 3-3). 43.90 *(978-1-60854-916-0(X)*, PowerKids Pr.) Rosen Publishing Group, Inc., The.

EDUCATION OF CHILDREN

see Education, Elementary

EDUCATION OF GIRLS

see Women—Education

EDUCATION OF THE BLIND

see Blind—Education

EDUCATION OF THE DEAF

see Deaf—Education

EDUCATIONAL ADMINISTRATION

see School Management And Organization

EDUCATIONAL COUNSELING

see also Counseling; Dropouts; Vocational Guidance

Crow, Anne & Miller, Arthur. Death of a Salesman. 2011. (Philip Allan Literature Guide for A-Level Ser.). (Illus.). 96p. (gr. 10-12). pap. 39.50 *(978-1-4441-2158-2(8))* Hodder Education Group GBR. Dist: Trans-Atlantic Pubns., Inc.

Murray, Julie. Counselors, 1 vol. 2010. (Going to Work Ser.). (ENG.). 32p. (J). (gr. 2-5). 27.07 *(978-1-61613-505-8(0))* ABDO Publishing Co.

Onyett, Nicola & Williams, Tennessee. A Streetcar Named Desire. 2011. (Philip Allan Literature Guide for A-Level Ser.). (Illus.). 96p. (gr. 10-12). pap. 24.95 *(978-1-4441-2156-8(1))* Trans-Atlantic Pubns., Inc.

Rutherford, David B. A Navy SEAL's Guide for Helping Kids Get Squared Away: Field Manuals for Kids, Vol. 1. 2007. (ENG.). 118p. (J). per. 15.00 *(978-0-9801464-0-0(2))* Leadline Publishing.

EDUCATIONAL FILMS

see Motion Pictures In Education

EDUCATIONAL GUIDANCE

see Educational Counseling

EDUCATIONAL MEASUREMENTS

see Educational Tests and Measurements

EDUCATIONAL PSYCHOLOGY

see also Imagination; Perception; Psychology, Applied; Thought and Thinking

Kulman, Randy. Train Your Brain for Success: A Teenager's Guide to Executive Functions. 2012. (ENG., Illus.). 100p. (J). (gr. 7). pap. 17.95 *(978-1-886941-76-2(9))* Specialty Pr., Inc.

McPherson, Stephanie Sammartino. Are You Stressed Out in School? 2015. (Got Issues? Ser.). (ENG., Illus.). 128p. (J). (gr. 7-7). 37.27 *(978-0-7660-6983-1(4))* Enslow Pubs., Inc.

Nunn, Daniel. I Can Listen, 1 vol. 2014. (Me & My Friends Ser.). (ENG.). 24p. (gr. -1-1). pap. 5.99 *(978-1-4846-0246-1(3)*, Acorn) Heinemann-Raintree.

EDUCATIONAL TESTS AND MEASUREMENTS

ACT Reading Victory Student Textbook. 2nd ed. 2005. per. *(978-1-58894-033-9(0))* Cambridge Educational Services, Inc.

ACT Science Reasoning Victory Student Textbook. 2nd ed. 2005. per. *(978-1-58894-034-6(9))* Cambridge Educational Services, Inc.

Avenues Language & Literacy Tests: Level D Posttest Booklet (10-Pack) (Avenues Ser.). 30.00 *(978-0-7362-2516-8(1))* CENGAGE Learning.

Bender, Janet M. Tyler Tames the Testing Tiger. 2004. (Illus.). 70p. per. 19.95 *(978-1-931636-27-8(3))* National Ctr. For Youth Issues.

Berry, Joy. Get Good Grades. 2009. (Fun & Easy Way Ser.). (ENG.). 52p. (J). (gr. 2-5). pap. 7.95 *(978-1-60577-311-7(5))* Berry, Joy Enterprises.

Blaisdell, Shele. The L. A. Teen Project. 2010. 183p. pap. 16.00 *(978-0-557-59078-0(7))* Lulu Pr., Inc.

Bodden, Valerie. Preparing for an Exam. 2015. (Classroom How-To Ser.). (ENG.). 48p. (J). (gr. 5-8). pap. 12.00 *(978-0-89812-988-5(5)*, Creative Paperbacks) Creative Co., The.

Book Builders, Inc. Staff & Chin, Beverly. How to Ace Any Test. 2004. (ENG., Illus.). 120p. pap. 16.95 *(978-0-471-43156-5(7)*, Jossey-Bass) Wiley, John & Sons, Inc.

Brams, Jolie S. How to Do Your Best on Every Test: Test-Taking Skills for Elementary Students. 2003. 172p. per. 12.95 *(978-1-59230-027-3(8))* Englefield & Assocs., Inc.

Bumcrot, Curt, et al. Achieving Peak Performance Practice Test: Grade 10. 2003. 23p. (YA). (gr. 10-18). pap. 5.00 *(978-1-888786-37-8(X))* Basic Skills Assessment & Educational Services.

—Achieving Peak Performance Practice Test New Edition. 2nd rev. ed. 2003. 20p. (J). (gr. 2-18). pap. 5.00 *(978-1-888786-40-8(X))* Basic Skills Assessment & Educational Services.

—Achieving Peak Performance Practice Test New Edition. Finley, Mavion, ed. 2nd rev. ed. 2003. 30p. (J). (gr. 3-18). pap. 5.00 *(978-1-888786-41-5(8))* Basic Skills Assessment & Educational Services.

Carson-Dellosa Publishing Staff & Spectrum Staff. Georgia Test Prep, Grade 4. 2004. (Spectrum Ser.). (ENG., Illus.). 208p. (gr. 4-4). per. 15.95 *(978-0-7696-3474-6(5)*, Spectrum) Carson-Dellosa Publishing, LLC.

Douglas, Vincent, et al. California Test Practice, Grade 3. 2003. (Spectrum Ser.). (ENG., Illus.). 176p. (gr. 3-3). pap. 15.95 *(978-0-7696-3003-8(0))* Carson-Dellosa Publishing, LLC.

—California Test Practice, Grade 5. 2003. (Spectrum Ser.). (ENG., Illus.). 168p. (gr. 5-5). pap. 15.95 *(978-0-7696-3005-2(7))* Carson-Dellosa Publishing, LLC.

—California Test Practice, Grade 6. 2003. (Spectrum Ser.). (ENG., Illus.). 208p. (gr. 6-6). pap. 15.95 *(978-0-7696-3006-9(5))* Carson-Dellosa Publishing, LLC.

—Florida Test Prep, Grade 4. 2003. (Spectrum Ser.). (ENG., Illus.). 160p. (gr. 4-4). pap. 15.95 *(978-0-7696-3014-4(6))* Carson-Dellosa Publishing, LLC.

—Florida Test Prep, Grade 5. 2003. (Spectrum Ser.). (ENG., Illus.). 160p. (gr. 5-5). pap. 15.95 *(978-0-7696-3015-1(4))* Carson-Dellosa Publishing, LLC.

—Florida Test Prep, Grade 6. 2003. (Spectrum Ser.). (ENG., Illus.). 160p. (gr. 6-6). pap. 15.95 *(978-0-7696-3016-8(2))* Carson-Dellosa Publishing, LLC.

—Illinois Test Prep, Grade 3. 2004. (Spectrum Ser.). (ENG., Illus.). 208p. (gr. 3-3). pap. 15.95 *(978-0-7696-3483-8(4))* Carson-Dellosa Publishing, LLC.

—Illinois Test Prep, Grade 4. 2004. (Spectrum Ser.). (ENG., Illus.). 272p. (gr. 4-4). pap. 15.95 *(978-0-7696-3484-5(2))* Carson-Dellosa Publishing, LLC.

—Illinois Test Prep, Grade 5. 2004. (ENG., Illus.). 216p. (gr. 5-5). pap. 15.95 *(978-0-7696-3485-2(0))* Carson-Dellosa Publishing, LLC.

—Illinois Test Prep, Grade 6. 2004. (Spectrum Ser.). (ENG., Illus.). 208p. (gr. 6-6). pap. 15.95 *(978-0-7696-3486-9(9))* Carson-Dellosa Publishing, LLC.

—New York Test Prep, Grade 6. 2004. (Spectrum Ser.). (ENG., Illus.). 184p. (gr. 6-6). pap. 15.95 *(978-0-7696-3496-8(6))* Carson-Dellosa Publishing, LLC.

—Texas Test Prep, Grade 3. 2003. (Spectrum Ser.). (ENG., Illus.). 168p. (gr. 3-3). pap. 15.95 *(978-0-7696-3023-6(5))* Carson-Dellosa Publishing, LLC.

—Texas Test Prep, Grade 4. 2003. (Spectrum Ser.). (ENG., Illus.). 168p. (gr. 4-4). pap. 15.95 *(978-0-7696-3024-3(3))* Carson-Dellosa Publishing, LLC.

—Texas Test Prep, Grade 5. 2003. (Spectrum Ser.). (ENG., Illus.). 208p. (gr. 5-5). pap. 15.95 *(978-0-7696-3025-0(1))* Carson-Dellosa Publishing, LLC.

—Texas Test Prep, Grade 6. 2003. (Spectrum Ser.). (ENG., Illus.). 160p. (gr. 6-6). pap. 15.95 *(978-0-7696-3026-7(X))* Carson-Dellosa Publishing, LLC.

DynaNotes Test Taking Tips. 2006. (J). pap. *(978-1-933854-37-3(5))* DynaStudy, Inc.

DynaNotes Test Taking Tips Transparency Set. 2006. (J). trans. *(978-1-933854-38-0(3))* DynaStudy, Inc.

Greenhaven Press Editors & Bryfonski, Dedria. Standardized Testing. 2012. (At Issue Ser.). (ENG.). 128p. (J). (gr. 10-12). pap. 27.80 *(978-0-7377-5599-2(7)*, Greenhaven Pr., Inc.) Cengage Gale.

Grossberg, Blythe. Test Success: Test-Taking & Study Strategies for All Students, Including Those with ADD & LD. 2009. (ENG., Illus.). 125p. (J). (gr. 5-13). pap. 21.95 *(978-1-886941-72-4(6))* Specialty Pr., Inc.

Harcourt School Publishers Staff. Harcourt Language Arts: Standardized Test Preparation. 2nd ed. 2003. (Harcourt Language Ser.). (Illus.). (gr. 2-18). 7.60 *(978-0-15-321223-9(3))*; (gr. 3-18). 7.60 *(978-0-15-321224-6(1))*; (gr. 4-18). 7.60 *(978-0-15-321225-3(X))*; (gr. 5-18). 7.60 *(978-0-15-321226-0(8))* Harcourt Schl. Pubs.

Holt, Rinehart and Winston Staff. Are You Ready? Intervention. 4th ed. 2003. (Illus.). (J). 73.60 incl. cd-rom *(978-0-03-073076-4(7))* Holt McDougal.

—Holt Handbook: Activities & Tests. 3rd ed. 2003. cd-rom 38.53 *(978-0-03-073133-4(X))* Holt McDougal.

—Holt Handbook: Activities & Tests Online. 3rd ed. 2003. cd-rom 38.53 *(978-0-03-073132-7(1))* Holt McDougal.

Letts 11+, Letts. 11+ Practice Test Papers. 2017. (Letts 11+ Success Ser.). (ENG.). 104p. (J). (gr. 4). pap. 15.99 ***(978-1-84419-896-2(0))*** HarperCollins Pubs. Ltd. GBR. Dist: Independent Pubs. Group.

Madison, Lynda. All about You Quiz Book: Discover More about Yourself & How to Be Your Best! Laskey, Shannon, illus. 2009. (ENG.). 64p. (YA). (gr. 3-18). spiral bd. 9.95 *(978-1-59369-598-9(5))* American Girl Publishing, Inc.

Mooney, Carla. Standardized Testing. 2015. (Hot Topics Ser.). (ENG., Illus.). 128p. (J). (gr. 7-10). 39.40 *(978-1-4205-1241-0(2)*, Lucent Bks.) Cengage Gale.

Naik, Anita & Croke, Liam. Beat Stress! The Exam Handbook. 2009. (Really Useful Handbooks Ser.). (ENG., Illus.). 48p. (J). (gr. 5-11). pap. *(978-0-7787-4400-9(0)*, 1294158) Crabtree Publishing Co.

Preparing Your 3rd Grader to Succeed on the MEAP. 2005. *(978-0-9789612-0-6(X))* Excellence Student Incentives.

Preparing Your 4th Grader to Succeed on the MEAP. 2005. *(978-0-9789612-1-3(8))* Excellence Student Incentives.

Preparing Your 5th Grader to Succeed on the MEAP. 2005. *(978-0-9789612-2-0(6))* Excellence Student Incentives.

Rozakis, Laurie. Get Test Smart! The Ultimate Guide to Middle School Standardized Tests. 2007. 144p. (J). *(978-1-4287-1884-5(2)*, Scholastic Reference) Scholastic, Inc.

Short, Deborah J., et al. Avenues Language & Literacy Tests: Level C Posttest Booklet (10-Pack) 2004. (Avenues Ser.). (ENG.). (C). pap. 66.95 *(978-0-7362-2514-4(5))* CENGAGE Learning.

—Avenues Language & Literacy Tests: Level D Pretest Booklet (10-Pack) 2004. (Avenues Ser.). (ENG.). (C). pap. 66.95 *(978-0-7362-2515-1(3))* CENGAGE Learning.

—Avenues Language & Literacy Tests: Level E Posttest Booklet (10-Pack) 2004. (Avenues Ser.). (ENG.). (C). pap. 66.95 *(978-0-7362-2518-2(8))* CENGAGE Learning.

—Avenues Language & Literacy Tests: Level E Pretest Booklet (10-Pack) 2004. (Avenues Ser.). (ENG.). (C). pap. 66.95 *(978-0-7362-2517-5(X))* CENGAGE Learning.

—Avenues Language & Literacy Tests: Level F Posttest Booklet (10-Pack) 2004. (Avenues Ser.). (ENG.). (C). pap. 66.95 *(978-0-7362-2520-5(X))* CENGAGE Learning.

—Avenues Language & Literacy Tests: Level F Pretest Booklet (10-Pack) 2004. (Avenues Ser.). (ENG.). (C). pap. 66.95 *(978-0-7362-2519-9(6))* CENGAGE Learning.

—Avenues Unit Progress Tests: Level A Progress Test Booklets (10-Pack) 2004. (Avenues Ser.). (ENG.). (C). (gr. k-18). pap. 86.95 *(978-0-7362-2227-3(8))* CENGAGE Learning.

—Avenues Unit Progress Tests: Level B Progress Test Booklets (10-Pack) 2004. (Avenues Ser.). (ENG.). (C). (gr. 1-18). pap. 162.95 *(978-0-7362-2230-3(8))* CENGAGE Learning.

—Avenues Unit Progress Tests: Level C Progress Test Booklets - Advanced (10-Pack) 2004. (Avenues Ser.). (ENG.). (C). (gr. 2-18). pap. 162.95 *(978-0-7362-2241-9(3))* CENGAGE Learning.

—Avenues Unit Progress Tests: Level C Progress Test Booklets - Beginning (10-Pack) 2004. (Avenues Ser.). (ENG.). (C). (gr. 2-18). pap. 162.95 *(978-0-7362-2235-8(9))* CENGAGE Learning.

—Avenues Unit Progress Tests: Level C Progress Test Booklets - Intermediate (10-Pack) 2004. (Avenues Ser.). (ENG.). (C). (gr. 2-18). pap. 162.95 *(978-0-7362-2238-9(3))* CENGAGE Learning.

—Avenues Unit Progress Tests: Level D Progress Test Booklets - Advanced (10-Pack) 2004. (Avenues Ser.). (ENG.). (C). (gr. 3-18). pap. 162.95 *(978-0-7362-2252-5(9))* CENGAGE Learning.

—Avenues Unit Progress Tests: Level D Progress Test Booklets - Beginning (10-Pack) 2004. (Avenues Ser.). (ENG.). (C). (gr. 3-18). pap. 162.95 *(978-0-7362-2246-4(4))* CENGAGE Learning.

—Avenues Unit Progress Tests: Level D Progress Test Booklets - Intermediate (10-Pack) 2004. (Avenues Ser.). (ENG.). (C). (gr. 3-18). pap. 162.95 *(978-0-7362-2249-5(9))* CENGAGE Learning.

—Avenues Unit Progress Tests: Level E Progress Test Booklets - Advanced (10-Pack) 2004. (Avenues Ser.). (ENG.). (C). (gr. 4-18). pap. 162.95 *(978-0-7362-2263-1(4))* CENGAGE Learning.

—Avenues Unit Progress Tests: Level E Progress Test Booklets - Beginning (10-Pack) 2004. (Avenues Ser.). (ENG.). (C). (gr. 4-18). pap. 162.95 *(978-0-7362-2257-0(X))* CENGAGE Learning.

—Avenues Unit Progress Tests: Level E Progress Test Booklets - Intermediate (10-Pack) 2004. (Avenues Ser.). (ENG.). (C). (gr. 4-18). pap. 162.95 *(978-0-7362-2260-0(X))* CENGAGE Learning.

—Avenues Unit Progress Tests: Level F Progress Test Booklets - Advanced (10-Pack) 2004. (Avenues Ser.). (ENG.). (C). (gr. 5-18). pap. 162.95 *(978-0-7362-2284-6(7))* CENGAGE Learning.

—Avenues Unit Progress Tests: Level F Progress Test Booklets - Beginning (10-Pack) 2004. (Avenues Ser.). (ENG.). (C). (gr. 5-18). pap. 162.95 *(978-0-7362-2278-5(2))* CENGAGE Learning.

—Avenues Unit Progress Tests: Level F Progress Test Booklets - Intermediate (10-Pack) 2004. (Avenues Ser.). (ENG.). (C). (gr. 5-18). pap. 162.95 *(978-0-7362-2281-5(2))* CENGAGE Learning.

Show What You Know on the TAKS for Grade 4, Spanish Student Workbook. 2006. (J). per. 12.95 *(978-1-59230-207-9(6))* Englefield & Assocs., Inc.

Show What You Know on the TAKS for Grade 5, Student Workbook, Second Edition. 2006. (J). per. 16.95 *(978-1-59230-197-3(5))* Englefield & Assocs., Inc.

Show What You Know Publishing, creator. Show What You Know on the TAKS, Grade 3 Spanish Math Flash Cards. 2004. (SPA.). (J). 15.95 *(978-1-59230-102-7(9))* Englefield & Assocs., Inc.

—Show What You Know on the TAKS, Grade 3 Spanish Reading Flash Cards. 2004. (SPA.). (J). 15.95 *(978-1-59230-103-4(7))* Englefield & Assocs., Inc.

Steck-Vaughn Staff. Pre-GED Complete Preparation. 2004. (Steck-Vaughn Pre-GED Ser.). (ENG., Illus.). 768p. (gr. 5-8). pap. 21.75 *(978-0-7398-8785-1(8))* Houghton Mifflin Harcourt Publishing Co.

EDUCATORS

see also Teachers

Asim, Jabari. Fifty Cents & a Dream: Young Booker T. Washington. 2012. (ENG., Illus.). 48p. (J). (gr. -1-3). 16.99 *(978-0-316-08657-8(6))* Little Brown & Co.

Bertrand, Diane Gonzales. Ricardo's Race/la Carrera de Ricardo. Viegas-Barros, Rocio, tr. from ENG. Accardo, Anthony, illus. 2007. (SPA.). 32p. (J). (gr. -1-2). 16.95 *(978-1-55885-481-9(9))* Arte Publico Pr.

Braun, Eric. Booker T. Washington: Great American Educator, 1 vol. Martin, Cynthia, illus. (Graphic Biographies Ser.). (ENG.). 32p. (gr. 3-4). 2006. per. 8.10 *(978-0-7368-6190-8(4))* 2005. 30.65 *(978-0-7368-4630-1(1))* Capstone Press of Coughlan Cos. (Graphic Library).

Brimner, Larry Dane. Booker T. Washington: Getting into the Schoolhouse. 2008. (American Heroes Ser.). 48p. (YA). (gr. 3-18). lib. bdg. 29.93 *(978-0-7614-3063-6(6)*, Benchmark Bks.) Marshall Cavendish Corp.

Dunn, Joeming W. Booker T. Washington, 1 vol. Allen, Chris, illus. 2008. (Bio-Graphics Ser.). (ENG.). 32p. 28.50 *(978-1-60270-177-9(6)*, Graphic Planet- Nonfiction) ABDO Publishing Co.

Fern, Tracey. W Is for Webster: Noah Webster & His American Dictionary. Kulikov, Boris, illus. 2015. (ENG.). 40p. (J). 17.99 *(978-0-374-38240-7(9)*, 9780374382407, Farrar, Straus & Giroux (BYR)) Farrar, Straus & Giroux.

Ferris, Jeri Chase. Demanding Justice: A Story about Mary Ann Shadd Cary. Smith, Kimanne, illus. 2003. (Creative Minds Biographies Ser.). (ENG.). 64p. (gr. 4-8). 22.60 *(978-1-57505-177-2(X))*; pap. 8.95 *(978-0-87614-928-7(X)*, Carolrhoda Bks.) Lerner Publishing Group.

—Noah Webster & His Words. Kirsch, Vincent X., illus. (ENG.). 32p. (J). (gr. -1-3). 2015. 6.99 *(978-0-544-58242-2(X)*, HMH Books For Young Readers) 2012. 16.99 *(978-0-547-39055-0(6))* Houghton Mifflin Harcourt Publishing Co.

Flynn, Riley. Booker T. Washington, 1 vol. 2014. (Great African-Americans Ser.). (ENG.). 24p. (gr. k-1). lib. bdg. 21.99 *(978-1-4765-3952-2(9)*, Pebble Bks.) Capstone Press of Coughlan Cos.

Gould, Jane H. George Washington Carver. 2013. (Jr. Graphic American Inventors Ser.). (ENG., Illus.). 24p. (J). (gr. 3-6). pap. 10.60 *(978-1-4777-0141-6(9))*; lib. bdg. 25.25 *(978-1-4777-0078-5(1))* Rosen Publishing Group, Inc., The. (PowerKids Pr.).

Haldy, Emma E. Booker T. Washington. Bane, Jeff, illus. 2016. (My Early Library: My Itty-Bitty Bio Ser.). (ENG.). 24p. (J). (gr. k-1). 28.50 *(978-1-63471-018-3(5)*, 208152) Cherry Lake Publishing.

Hally, Ashleigh. Martha Berry. 2012. (Illus.). 24p. (J). *(978-1-935884-73-6(5))*; pap. *(978-1-935884-79-8(4))* State Standards Publishing, LLC.

Hinman, Bonnie. Eternal Vigilance: The Story of Ida B. Wells-Barnett. 2011. (Civil Rights Leaders Ser.). 128p. (gr. 6-10). lib. bdg. 28.95 *(978-1-59935-111-7(0))* Reynolds, Morgan Inc.

Lawson, Sabina. Taking Action to Improve Schools. 2016. (Who's Changing the World? Ser.). (ENG., Illus.). 48p. (J). (gr. 4-6). 50.65 *(978-1-4677-9666-8(2)*, Lerner Pubns.) Lerner Publishing Group.

Massie, Elizabeth. African American Educators. 2012. (J). pap. *(978-1-4222-2386-4(8))* Mason Crest.

—African American Educators. Hill, Marc Lamont, ed. 2012. (Major Black Contributions from Emancipation to Civil Rights Ser.). 64p. (J). (gr. 5). 22.95 *(978-1-4222-2373-4(6))* Mason Crest.

Maurer, Tracy Nelson. Noah Webster's Fighting Words. Catusanu, Mircea, illus. 2017. (ENG.). 40p. (gr. 2-5). 19.99 *(978-1-4677-9410-7(4))*; 30.65 ***(978-1-5124-2839-1(6)**,* Millbrook Pr.) Lerner Publishing Group.

McKissack, Patricia C. & McKissack, Fredrick L. Booker T. Washington: African-American Leader. 2013. (Famous African Americans Ser.). 24p. (J). (gr. k-3). pap. 7.95 *(978-1-4644-0194-7(2))*; (Illus.). lib. bdg. 22.60 *(978-0-7660-4100-4(X))* Enslow Pubs., Inc. (Enslow Elementary).

Melis, Luisanna Fodde. Noah Webster & the First American Dictionary. 2009. (Library of American Lives & Times Ser.). 112p. (gr. 5-5). 69.20 *(978-1-60853-495-1(2))* Rosen Publishing Group, Inc., The.

Mitchell, Melanie. Principals. 2005. (Pull Ahead Bks.). (Illus.). 32p. (J). lib. bdg. 22.60 *(978-0-8225-1694-1(2))* Lerner Publishing Group.

Myers, Walter Dean. Ida B. Wells: Let the Truth Be Told. Christensen, Bonnie, illus. 2008. (ENG.). 40p. (J). (gr. -1-3). 16.99 *(978-0-06-027705-5(X)*, Amistad) HarperCollins Pubs.

Nelson, Robin. George Washington Carver: A Life of Devotion. 2007. (Pull Ahead Books-Biographies Ser.). (ENG.). 32p. (gr. k-3). pap. 7.95 *(978-0-8225-6455-3(6))* Lerner Publishing Group.

Proudfit, Isabel. Noah Webster, Father of the Dictionary. 2008. (Illus.). 224p. (J). pap. 15.95 *(978-0-9801563-0-0(0))* Bradford Pr., Inc.

Reef, Catherine. Noah Webster: Man of Many Words. 2015. (ENG., Illus.). 224p. (J). (gr. 5-7). 18.99 *(978-0-544-12983-2(0),* Clarion Bks.) Houghton Mifflin Harcourt Trade & Reference Pubs.

Schraff, Anne E. Booker T. Washington: Character Is Power. 2006. (African-American Biography Library). (Illus.). 128p. (J). (gr. 3-7). lib. bdg. 33.27 *(978-0-7660-2535-6(7))* Enslow Pubs., Inc.

Schroeder, Alan. Booker T. Washington: Educator & Racial Spokesman. 2004. (Black Americans of Achievement Ser.). (Illus.). 112p. (gr. 6-12). 35.00 *(978-0-7910-8253-9(9),* Chelsea Hse.) Facts On File, Inc.

Sharpe, Paula A. Maria Montessori. Ward, Patricia R. & Pigford, Grady A., illus. 2010. 51p. (J). *(978-1-892142-47-4(3))* Cedar Tree Bks.

Shea, Pegi Deitz. Noah Webster: Weaver of Words. Vachula, Monica, illus. 2009. (ENG.). 40p. (J). (gr. 4-18). 18.95 *(978-1-59078-441-9(3),* Calkins Creek) Boyds Mills Pr.

Slade, Suzanne. With Books & Bricks: How Booker T. Washington Built a School. Tadgell, Nicole, illus. 2014. (ENG.). 32p. (J). (gr. 2-3). 16.99 *(978-0-8075-0897-8(7))* Whitman, Albert & Co.

Spielman, Gloria. Janusz Korczak's Children. Archambault, Matthew, illus. 2007. (Kar-Ben for Older Readers Ser.). 40p. (J). (gr. 3-7). lib. bdg. 17.95 *(978-1-58013-255-8(3));* (ENG.). pap. 7.95 *(978-0-8225-7050-9(5))* Lerner Publishing Group. (Kar-Ben Publishing).

Swain, Gwenyth. A Hunger for Learning: A Story about Booker T. Washington. Johnson, Larry, illus. (Creative Minds Biographies Ser.). (ENG.). 64p. (gr. 4-8). 2006. pap. 8.95 *(978-0-8225-3090-9(2))* 2005. lib. bdg. 22.60 *(978-1-57505-754-5(9))* Lerner Publishing Group.

Trent, Tererai. The Girl Who Buried Her Dreams in a Can. Gilchrist, Jan Spivey, illus. 2015. (ENG.). 34p. (J). (gr. 1-3). 17.99 *(978-0-670-01654-9(3),* Viking Books for Young Readers) Penguin Young Readers Group.

Troy, Don. Booker T. Washington. 2009. (Journey to Freedom Ser.). (ENG., Illus.). 32p. (J). (gr. 4-7). 29.93 *(978-1-60253-118-5(8),* 200384) Child's World, Inc., The.

Watson, Stephanie & Lawson, Sabina. Taking Action to Improve Schools. 2016. (Who's Changing the World? Ser.). (ENG., Illus.). 48p. (J). (gr. 4-6). 33.32 *(978-1-4677-9393-3(0))* Lerner Publishing Group.

Whiting, Jim. Booker T. Washington. 2010. (Transcending Race in America Ser.). (Illus.). 64p. (YA). (gr. 4-8). lib. bdg. 22.95 *(978-1-4222-1608-8(X))* Mason Crest.

Wilds, Mary. I Dare Not Fail: Notable African American Women Educators. 2004. (Avisson Young Adult Ser.). 139p. (J). pap. 19.95 *(978-1-888105-64-3(X))* Avisson Pr., Inc.

Wolff, Ariana. Khan Academy & Salman Khan, 1 vol. 2015. (ENG.). 128p. (YA). 35.60 *(978-1-4777-7927-9(2),* Rosen Young Adult) Rosen Publishing Group, Inc., The.

EDWARD VI, KING OF ENGLAND, 1537-1553—FICTION

Twain, Mark, pseud. The Prince & the Pauper. (J). 19.95 *(978-0-8488-0849-5(5))* Amereon Ltd.

—The Prince & the Pauper. 2008. (Bring the Classics to Life Ser.). (Illus.). 72p. (gr. 2-12). pap., act. bk. ed. 10.95 *(978-1-55576-096-0(1),* EDCTR-206B) EDCON Publishing Group.

—The Prince & the Pauper. (J). 9.95 *(978-1-56156-311-1(0))* Kidsbooks, LLC.

—The Prince & the Pauper. 2003. (Modern Library Classics Ser.). (ENG., Illus.). 240p. pap. 11.00 *(978-0-375-76112-6(8),* Modern Library) Random House Publishing Group.

—The Prince & the Pauper. 2006. (Aladdin Classics Ser.). (ENG.). 352p. (J). pap. 7.99 *(978-1-4169-2805-8(7),* Aladdin) Simon & Schuster Children's Publishing.

—The Prince & the Pauper. Akib, Jamel, illus. 2007. (Classic Starts(tm) Ser.). (ENG.). 160p. (J). (gr. 2-4). 6.95 *(978-1-4027-3687-2(8))* Sterling Publishing Co., Inc.

—The Prince & the Pauper: With a Discussion of Respect. 2003. (Values in Action Illustrated Classics Ser.). (J). *(978-1-59203-052-1(1))* Learning Challenge, Inc.

Twain, Mark, pseud & Clemens, Samuel L. The Prince & the Pauper. 2013. (Works of Mark Twain). 425p. reprint ed. lthr. 79.00 *(978-0-7812-1120-8(4))* Reprint Services Corp.

Twain, Mark, pseud, et al. The Prince & the Pauper. Kliros, Thea, illus. abr. ed. 2011. (Dover Children's Thrift Classics Ser.). (ENG.). 112p. (J). (gr. 3-8). reprint ed. pap. 4.00 *(978-0-486-29383-7(1))* Dover Pubns., Inc.

EDWARDS, JONATHAN, 1703-1758

Carr, Simonetta. Jonathan Edwards. Abraxas, Matt, illus. 2014. (ENG.). 60p. (J). 18.00 *(978-1-60178-354-7(X))* Reformation Heritage Bks.

Crompton, Samuel Willard. Jonathan Edwards. 2004. (Spiritual Leaders & Thinkers Ser.). (Illus.). 120p. (J). (gr. 9-13). 30.00 *(978-0-7910-8103-7(6),* Chelsea Hse.) Facts On File, Inc.

EEYORE (FICTITIOUS CHARACTER)—FICTION

Studio Mouse Staff. Pooh & Eeyore. 2008. (ENG., Illus.). 36p. (J). (gr. -1). 7.99 *(978-1-59069-418-3(X))* Studio Mouse LLC.

Winnie the Pooh: Party in the Wood. 2011. 32p. pap. 4.99 *(978-1-4231-5386-3(3))* Disney Pr.

EGGS

Here are entered works on animal eggs in general as well as chicken eggs.

Abraham, Chuck. Intricate Eggs: 45 Easter Designs to Color. 2008. (ENG., Illus.). 96p. (J). (gr. -1-17). pap. 6.95 *(978-0-7624-3178-6(4))* Running Pr. Bk. Pubs.

Amazing Eggs: Individual Title Six-Packs. (Discovery World Ser.). 16p. (gr. 1-2). 28.00 *(978-0-7635-8455-9(X))* Rigby Education.

Amstutz, Lisa J. Whose Egg Is This? 2012. (Nature Starts Ser.). (ENG.). 32p. (gr. 1-2). pap. 47.70 *(978-1-4296-8299-2(X));* (Illus.). pap. 8.10 *(978-1-4296-7854-4(2));* (Illus.). lib. bdg. 27.32 *(978-1-4296-7554-3(3))* Capstone Press of Coughlan Cos. (Aplus Bks.).

Arnold, Caroline. Hatching Chicks in Room 6. 2017. (ENG., Illus.). 40p. (J). (gr. -1-2). lib. bdg. 16.99 *(978-1-58089-735-8(5))* Charlesbridge Publishing, Inc.

Aston, Dianna Hutts. An Egg Is Quiet. Long, Sylvia, illus. 2006. (J). 16.95 *(978-0-8118-5554-9(6));* (ENG.). 36p. (gr. -1-7). 16.99 *(978-0-8118-4428-4(5))* Chronicle Bks. LLC.

—An Egg Is Quiet. 2014. (J). lib. bdg. 18.40 *(978-0-606-35292-5(9))* Turtleback Bks.

Baines, Becky. What's in That Egg? A Book about Life Cycles. 2009. (ZigZag Ser.). (ENG., Illus.). 32p. (J). (gr. k-3). 16.95 *(978-1-4263-0408-8(0));* lib. bdg. 25.90 *(978-1-4263-0409-5(9))* National Geographic Society. (National Geographic Children's Bks.).

Bingham, Jane. Producing Dairy & Eggs, 1 vol. 2012. (Technology of Farming Ser.). (ENG.). 48p. (gr. 4-6). lib. bdg. 33.32 *(978-1-4329-6406-1(2),* Heinemann InfoSearch) Heinemann-Raintree.

Budai, Joan. What's in an Egg? 2011. 32p. pap. 14.99 *(978-1-4634-1050-6(6))* AuthorHouse.

Caughey, Melissa. A Kid's Guide to Keeping Chickens: Best Breeds, Creating a Home, Care & Handling, Outdoor Fun, Crafts & Recipes. 2015. (ENG., Illus.). 144p. (J). (gr. 2-8). pap. 16.95 *(978-1-61212-418-6(6),* 622418) Storey Publishing, LLC.

—A Kid's Guide to Keeping Chickens: Best Breeds, Creating a Home, Care & Handling, Outdoor Fun, Crafts & Treats. 2015. (ENG., Illus.). 144p. (J). (gr. 2-8). 26.95 *(978-1-61212-648-7(0))* Storey Publishing, LLC.

Chicken & Egg. 2003. (J). 36.95 *(978-0-8136-9274-6(1));* 38.95 *(978-0-8136-4195-9(0))* Modern Curriculum Pr.

Cusick, Dawn & O'Sullivan, Joanne. Animal Eggs: An Amazing Clutch of Mysteries & Marvels. Greenelsh, Susan, illus. (ENG.). 48p. (J). (gr. -1-3). 2012. pap. 8.95 *(978-0-9832014-9-6(8))* 2011. 14.95 *(978-0-9797455-3-9(5))* EarlyLight Bks., Inc.

Della Casa, Chef Luca. No Egg on Your Face! Easy & Delecious Egg-Free Recipes for Kids with Allergies. 2016. (Allergy Aware Cookbooks Ser.). (ENG.). 32p. (gr. 3-4). lib. bdg. 27.99 *(978-1-4914-8055-7(6),* Edge Bks.) Capstone Press of Coughlan Cos.

Eggs! (Little Book Practice Reader). (J). *(978-0-8136-5350-1(9))* Modern Curriculum Pr.

Eggs, Eggs, Eggs: 3-in-1 Package. (Sails Literacy Ser.). 24p. (gr. 1-18). 57.00 *(978-0-7578-3206-2(7))* Rigby Education.

Eggs, Eggs, Eggs: 6 Small Books. (Sails Literacy Ser.). 24p. (gr. 1-18). 25.00 *(978-0-7578-3182-9(6))* Rigby Education.

Eggs, Eggs, Eggs: Big Book Only. (Sails Literacy Ser.). 24p. (gr. 1-18). 27.00 *(978-0-7635-5930-4(X))* Rigby Education.

Eggs, Eggs, Eggs: Level L, 6 vols. (Wonder Worldtm Ser.). 16p. 34.95 *(978-0-7802-1990-8(2))* Wright Group/McGraw-Hill.

Esbaum, Jill. Angry Birds Playground - Animals: An Around-the-World Habitat Adventure. 2012. (ENG.). 128p. (J). (gr. -1-3). lib. bdg. 21.90 *(978-1-4263-1323-3(3),* National Geographic Children's Bks.) National Geographic Society.

Esbaum, Jill & National Geographic Kids Staff. Animals: An Around-the-World Habitat Adventure. 2012. (ENG., Illus.). 128p. (J). (gr. -1-3). 14.95 *(978-1-4263-1266-3(0),* National Geographic Children's Bks.) National Geographic Society.

Etingoff, Kim. Eggs. 2013. (Feeding the World Ser.: 8). (Illus.). 48p. (J). (gr. 4-18). 19.95 *(978-1-4222-2744-2(8))* Mason Crest.

Faltross, Rick. An Easter Egg Hunt. 2016. (We Love Spring! Ser.). 00024p. (J). pap. 8.15 *(978-1-4824-5454-3(8))* Stevens, Gareth Publishing LLLP.

Gibson. Sail Yel Nf Out of the Egg. 2003. (Rigby Sails Early Ser.). (ENG.). 16p. (gr. 1-2). pap. 6.95 *(978-0-7578-8892-2(5))* Rigby Education.

Head, Honor. Milk, Cheese, & Eggs. 2010. (J). 24.25 *(978-1-59920-335-5(9))* Black Rabbit Bks.

Heller, Ruth. Chickens Aren't the Only Ones. l.t. ed. (FRE., Illus.). (J). ring bd. 29.95 *(978-0-590-73732-6(5))* Scholastic, Inc.

Hobbes, Elena. How Do Eggs Hatch? 2013. (Nature's Super Secrets Ser.). (Illus.). 24p. (gr. 1-3). 22.60 *(978-1-4339-8160-9(2));* pap. 8.15 *(978-1-4339-8161-6(0))* Stevens, Gareth Publishing LLLP.

Ikids Staff & Schimel, Lawrence. What's in the Egg? Perez, Sara, illus. 2009. (ENG.). 22p. (J). (gr. -1-1). 9.99 *(978-1-58476-821-0(5),* IKIDS) Innovative Kids.

Jenkins, Priscilla Belz. A Nest Full of Eggs. Rockwell, Lizzy, illus. 2015. (Let's-Read-And-Find-Out Science 1 Ser.). (ENG.). 32p. (J). (gr. -1-3). pap. 6.99 *(978-0-06-238193-4(8))* HarperCollins Pubs.

Kalman, Bobbie. What Is Hatching? 2010. (My World Ser.). (ENG.). 16p. (J). (gr. k-3). *(978-0-7787-9509-4(8));* pap. *(978-0-7787-9534-6(9))* Crabtree Publishing Co.

Kant, Tanya. How an Egg Grows into a Chicken. Franklin, Carolyn, illus. 2008. (Amaze Ser.). (ENG.). 32p. (J). (gr. -1-3). pap. 8.95 *(978-0-531-23801-1(6));* (gr. k-3). 27.00 *(978-0-531-24047-2(9))* Scholastic Library Publishing. (Children's Pr.).

Lanning, Andrea J. The Imposturous Egg. Lanning, Andrea J., illus. Corcacas, Maria, photos by. 2012. (Illus.). 32p. *(978-0-9571677-0-4(9));* pap. *(978-0-9571677-4-2(1))* Ginnal Creatives Ltd.

Marks, Jennifer L. How to Make a Bouncing Egg, 1 vol. (Hands-On Science Fun Ser.). (ENG., 24p. (gr. k-1). 2011. Illus.). pap. 7.29 *(978-1-4296-6214-7(X))* 2011. pap. 41.70 *(978-1-4296-6384-7(7))* 2010. lib. bdg. 26.65 *(978-1-4296-5291-9(8))* Capstone Press of Coughlan Cos. (Pebble Plus).

Martineau, Susan & James, Hel. Meat, Fish, & Eggs. 2012. (Healthy Eating Ser.). (Illus.). 32p. (gr. 2-6). pap. 8.95 *(978-1-59920-244-0(1))* Black Rabbit Bks.

Martinneau, Susan & James, Hel. Meat Fish & Eggs. 2006. (Healthy Eating Ser.). (Illus.). 32p. (YA). (gr. 1-4). lib. bdg. 28.50 *(978-1-58340-893-3(2),* 1262657) Black Rabbit Bks.

Mathews, Sarah & Mettler, René. The Egg. Mettler, René, illus. 2012. (ENG., Illus.). 34p. (J). (gr. -1-k). pap. 13.99 *(978-1-85103-380-5(7))* Moonlight Publishing, Ltd. GBR. Dist: Independent Pubs. Group.

Mettler, Ren'e, et al. El Huevo. (Coleccion Mundo Maravilloso). (SPA., Illus.). 40p. (J). (gr. 2-4). *(978-84-348-3468-2(5),* SM5468) SM Ediciones.

Metz, L. Every Egg: Learning the Short E Sound. 2009. (PowerPhonics Ser.). 24p. (gr. 1-1). 39.90 *(978-1-60851-440-3(4),* PowerKids Pr.) Rosen Publishing Group, Inc., The.

Morley, Margaret W. Seed-Babies. 2009. (Illus.). 88p. pap. 7.95 *(978-1-59915-316-2(5))* Yesterday's Classics.

Owen, Ruth. Eggs! Life on a Chicken Farm. 2012. (Food from Farmers Ser.). (ENG., Illus.). 32p. (J). (gr. k-3). pap. 11.75 *(978-1-61533-536-7(6));* lib. bdg. 26.50 *(978-1-61533-529-9(3))* Windmill Bks.

Page, Robin & Jenkins, Steve. Egg: Nature's Perfect Package. 2015. (ENG., Illus.). 32p. (J). (gr. -1-3). 17.99 *(978-0-547-95909-2(5),* HMH Books For Young Readers) Houghton Mifflin Harcourt Publishing Co.

Patchett, Fiona. Eggs & Chicks. Kushii, Tetsuo & Wray, Zoe, illus. 2007. (Usborne Beginners Ser.). 32p. (J). (gr. -1). 4.99 *(978-0-7945-1342-9(5),* Usborne) EDC Publishing.

—Eggs & Chicks. 2004. (Beginners Ser.). (Illus.). 32p. (J). (gr. 1-18). (ENG.). pap. 4.95 *(978-0-7945-0166-2(4),* Usborne); lib. bdg. 12.95 *(978-1-58086-482-4(1))* EDC Publishing.

Posada, Mia. Adivina Qué Está Creciendo Dentro de Este Huevo. Translations.com Staff, tr. from ENG. Posada, Mia, illus. 2008. (SPA., Illus.). 32p. (J). (gr. k-3). 16.95 *(978-0-7613-3906-9(X))* Lerner Publishing Group.

—Guess What Is Growing Inside This Egg. Posada, Mia, illus. 2007. (ENG., Illus.). 32p. (J). (gr. k-3). 15.95 *(978-0-8225-6192-7(1),* Millbrook Pr.) Lerner Publishing Group.

Rabe, Tish. Who Hatches the Egg? All about Eggs. Ruiz, Aristides & Mathieu, Joe, illus. 2017. (Cat in the Hat's Learning Library). (ENG.). 48p. (J). (gr. k-3). lib. bdg. 13.99 *(978-0-375-97171-6(8),* Random Hse. Bks. for Young Readers) Random Hse. Children's Bks.

Rau, Dana Meachen. Decorating Eggs. 2012. (How-To Library). (ENG.). 32p. (gr. 3-6). 28.50 *(978-1-61080-474-5(0),* 202084); pap. 14.21 *(978-1-61080-648-0(4),* 202258) Cherry Lake Publishing.

Rigby Education Staff. Discovery World Org Amazing Egg Big Book. (Discovery World Ser.). (Illus.). 12p. (gr. 1-2). 27.00 *(978-0-7635-2699-3(1))* Rigby Education.

—What's in an Egg? (Illus.). 16p. (J). pap. 3.95 *(978-0-7635-6459-9(1),* 764591C99) Rigby Education.

Sklansky, Amy E. Where Do Chicks Come From? Paparone, Pam, illus. 2005. (Let's-Read-and-Find-Out-Science Ser.). 40p. (J). (gr. -1-1). (ENG.). 15.99 *(978-0-06-028892-1(2));* lib. bdg. 16.89 *(978-0-06-028893-8(0))* HarperCollins Pubs.

—Where Do Chicks Come From? Paparone, Pamela, illus. 2005. (Let's-Read-And-Find-Out Science 1 Ser.). (ENG.). 40p. (J). (gr. -1-3). pap. 5.99 *(978-0-06-445212-0(3))* HarperCollins Pubs.

Spilsbury, Louise. One Egg. 2011. (ENG.). 24p. (J). pap. *(978-0-7787-7869-1(X));* (gr. 3-6). *(978-0-7787-7847-9(9))* Crabtree Publishing Co.

The Swamp Eggs: 3-in-1 Package. (Sails Literacy Ser.). 24p. (gr. k-18). 57.00 *(978-0-7578-3202-4(4))* Rigby Education.

The Swamp Eggs: Big Book Only. (Sails Literacy Ser.). 24p. (gr. k-18). 27.00 *(978-0-7635-6991-4(7))* Rigby Education.

Teckentrup, Britta. The Egg. 2017. (ENG., Illus.). 96p. (J). (gr. k-4). 16.95 ***(978-3-7913-7294-5(7))*** Prestel Verlag GmbH & Co KG. DEU. Dist: Penguin Random Hse. LLC.

Thompson, Kim. Caillou, Easter Egg Surprise. Sévigny, Eric, illus. 2016. (Clubhouse Ser.). (ENG.). 24p. (J). (gr. -1-k). 9.99 *(978-2-89718-256-4(3))* Caillouet, Gerry.

Tuminelly, Nancy. Let's Cook with Eggs! Delicious & Fun Egg Dishes Kids Can Make, 1 vol. 2012. (Super Simple Recipes Ser.). (ENG.). 32p. (J). (gr. k-4). 27.07 *(978-1-61783-421-9(1))* ABDO Publishing Co.

Ward, Jennifer. What Will Hatch? Ghahremani, Susie, illus. (ENG.). (J). 2016. 30p. bds. 8.99 *(978-1-61963-943-0(2),* 9781619639430) 2013. 40p. (gr. -1-1). 14.99 *(978-0-8027-2311-6(X),* 9780802723116) Bloomsbury Publishing USA. (Bloomsbury USA Childrens).

Wearing, Judy. Chickens. 2010. pap. 9.95 *(978-1-60596-914-5(1));* 24p. (J). (gr. 2-4). lib. bdg. 25.70 *(978-1-60596-913-8(3))* Weigl Pubs., Inc.

EGGS—FICTION

Ailes, Mark Cusco. The Snow Dargles: Book Two: the Chronicles of Weekland. 2010. 244p. pap. 16.95 *(978-1-4327-5223-1(5))* Outskirts Pr., Inc.

Anderson, R. P., et al. Happy Easter, Curious George. Young, Mary O'Keefe, illus. 2010. (Curious George Ser.). (ENG.). 24p. (J). (gr. -1-3). 9.99 *(978-0-547-04825-3(4))* Houghton Mifflin Harcourt Publishing Co.

Archer, Dosh. Humpty's Fall. Archer, Dosh, illus. (Urgency Emergency! Ser.). (ENG., Illus.). 48p. (J). (gr. -1-3). 2016. pap. 9.99 *(978-0-8075-8362-3(6))* 2015. 12.99 *(978-0-8075-8356-2(1))* Whitman, Albert & Co.

Averbeck, Jim. Except If. Averbeck, Jim, illus. 2011. (ENG., Illus.). 40p. (J). (gr. -1-1). 12.99 *(978-1-4169-9544-9(7),* Atheneum Bks. for Young Readers) Simon & Schuster Children's Publishing.

Banks, Steven. Show Me the Bunny! Greenblatt, C. H. & Reiss, William, illus. 2004. (Spongebob Squarepants Ser.). 32p. (J). 11.65 *(978-0-7569-5643-1(9))* Perfection Learning Corp.

Beskow, Elsa. The Sun Egg, 1 vol. 2007. Orig. Title: Solägget. (ENG., Illus.). 32p. (J). (gr. -1-k). *(978-0-86315-585-7(5))* Floris Bks.

Blackwell, Nancy. Andy the Ant in Precious Cargo. Ettinger, Charles, illus. 2011. 40p. pap. 14.99 *(978-1-937129-03-3(9))* Faithful Life Pubs.

Blevins, Wiley & Bader, Bonnie. Max Finds an Egg. Clanton, Ben, illus. 2015. (Penguin Young Readers, Level 1 Ser.). (ENG.). 32p. (J). (gr. k-1). 3.99 *(978-0-448-47993-4(1),* Penguin Young Readers) Penguin Young Readers Group.

Bodach, Vijaya. Ten Easter Eggs. Logan, Laura, illus. 2015. (ENG.). 22p. (J). (gr. -1-k). bds. 8.99 *(978-0-545-74730-1(9),* Cartwheel Bks.) Scholastic, Inc.

Bonnell, Kris. Robins in the Spring. 2007. (J). pap. 5.95 *(978-1-933727-53-0(5))* Reading Reading Bks., LLC.

Braffet, Holly, illus. Kekoa & the Egg Mystery. 2010. (ENG.). 32p. (J). (gr. -1-2). 14.95 *(978-1-933067-35-3(7))* Beachhouse Publishing, LLC.

Branson, Terri. Brother Dragon. Taylor, Chet, illus. 2004. (J). 18.99 *(978-0-9755888-5-7(0))* Dragonfly Publishing, Inc.

Brett, Jan. The Easter Egg. Brett, Jan, illus. (ENG., Illus.). 32p. (J). 2017. (-k). bds. 8.99 *(978-0-399-54733-1(9))* 2010. (gr. -1-k). 17.99 *(978-0-399-25238-9(X))* Penguin Young Readers Group. (G.P. Putnam's Sons Books for Young Readers).

Brown, Margaret Wise. The Golden Egg Book. Weisgard, Leonard, illus. 2004. (Big Little Golden Book Ser.). (ENG.). 32p. (J). (gr. -1-2). 8.99 *(978-0-375-82717-4(X),* Golden Bks.) Random Hse. Children's Bks.

—The Golden Egg Book. Weisgard, Leonard, illus. 2015. (Little Golden Book Ser.). (ENG.). 24p. (J). (-k). 4.99 *(978-0-385-38476-6(9),* Golden Bks.) Random Hse. Children's Bks.

Brown, Rosie L. Zach & Rob's Journey: The Lost Eggs. 2007. 24p. per. 24.95 *(978-1-4241-8401-9(0))* America Star Bks.

Bunting, Eve. Hurry! Hurry! Mack, Jeff, illus. (ENG.). (J). 2009. 32p. (gr. k — 1). bds. 6.99 *(978-0-15-206686-4(1))* 2007. 40p. (gr. -1-3). 16.99 *(978-0-15-205410-6(3))* Houghton Mifflin Harcourt Publishing Co.

Burgess, Thornton W. Blacky the Crow. 2011. 132p. 25.95 *(978-1-4638-9575-4(5))* Rodgers, Alan Bks.

Butterworth, Oliver. The Enormous Egg. 188p. (J). (gr. 3-5). pap. 4.95 *(978-0-8072-1393-3(4),* Listening Library) Random Hse. Audio Publishing Group.

Chandra, Rohini S. The Dragon in the Candle Jar. 2013. 52p. pap. 16.95 *(978-1-4626-9842-4(5))* America Star Bks.

Cohen, Miriam. Eggy Meggy & Peggy. 2003. (Illus.). 16p. (J). bds. 5.95 *(978-1-932065-09-1(1))* Star Bright Bks., Inc.

Conlon, Mara, adapted by. Bill Hatches an Egg. 2005. (Sitting Ducks Ser.). (J). *(978-0-8431-1343-3(X),* Price Stern Sloan) Penguin Publishing Group.

Cowley, Joy. Big Bear & Little Bear: Egg. Lam, Amy, illus. 2013. (ENG.). 8p. pap. *(978-1-927186-32-9(3),* Joy Cowley Club) Flying Start Bks.

Cutbill, Andy. The Cow That Laid an Egg. Ayto, Russell, illus. 2008. (ENG.). 32p. (J). (gr. -1-3). 17.99 *(978-0-06-137295-7(1))* HarperCollins Pubs.

Dahl, Michael. Terror Beach, 1 vol. Pellegrino, Richard, illus. (Dragonblood Ser.). (ENG.). 40p. (gr. 1-3). 2010. pap. 6.25 *(978-1-4342-2313-5(2))* 2009. 23.99 *(978-1-4342-1263-4(7))* Stone Arch Bks. (Zone Bks.).

Dales, Cindy. Autumn's First Easter. 2009. 28p. pap. 12.99 *(978-1-4343-1433-8(2))* AuthorHouse.

Daniel, Claire. The Chick That Wouldn't Hatch. Ernst, Lisa Campbell, illus. 2003. (Green Light Readers Level 2 Ser.). (ENG.). 24p. (J). (gr. -1-3). pap. 3.95 *(978-0-15-204831-0(6))* Houghton Mifflin Harcourt Publishing Co.

Daniel, Claire & Ernst, Lisa Campbell. El Pollito Que No Quería Salir del Huevo. Flor Ada, Alma & Campoy, F. Isabel, trs. from ENG. Ernst, Lisa Campbell, illus. 2009. (Green Light Readers Level 2 Ser.).Tr. of Chick That Wouldn't Hatch. (SPA & ENG., Illus.). 28p. (J). (gr. -1-3). pap. 3.99 *(978-0-15-206446-4(X))* Houghton Mifflin Harcourt Publishing Co.

Daviess, Maria Thompson. The Golden Bird. 2007. 92p. per. *(978-1-4068-1853-6(4))* Echo Library.

Denslow, W. W., illus. & adapted by. Humpty Dumpty. Denslow, W. W., adapted by. 2007. (Rare Book Collections). (ENG.). 16p. (J). (gr. -1-3). 9.95 *(978-1-55709-077-5(7))* Applewood Bks.

Derubertis, Barbara. Eddie Elephant's Exciting Egg-Sitting. 2010. pap. 45.32 *(978-0-7613-6507-5(9))* Kane Press, Inc.

deRubertis, Barbara. Eddie Elephant's Exciting Egg-Sitting. Alley, R. W., illus. 2010. (Animal Antics A to Z Ser.). 32p. (J). (gr. -1-3). pap. 7.95 *(978-1-57565-309-6(5));* lib. bdg. 22.60 *(978-1-57565-316-7(8))* Kane Press, Inc.

deRubertis, Barbara & DeRubertis, Barbara. Eddie Elephant's Exciting Egg-Sitting. Alley, R. W., illus. 2012. (Animal Antics A to Z Ser.). 32p. (J). (gr. 2 — 1). cd-rom 7.95 *(978-1-57565-398-3(2))* Kane Press, Inc.

Devine, Ginger. The Missing Goose Egg: A Sam the Lamb Mystery. 2009. 32p. pap. 14.95 *(978-1-4389-8839-9(7))* AuthorHouse.

DeVogt, Rindia M. Tommy Hare & the Color Purple, 1 vol. Trogdon, Kathryn, illus. 2009. (ENG.). 22p. pap. 24.95 *(978-1-61582-827-2(3))* America Star Bks.

Disney Book Group. Disney Bunnies an Eggcellent Day. Disney Book Group, illus. 2017. (ENG., Illus.). 12p. (J). (gr. -1-k). bds. 7.99 *(978-1-4847-7369-7(1))* Disney Pr.

Douglas, Erin. Get That Pest! Yee, Wong Herbert, illus. 2003. (Green Light Readers Level 2 Ser.). (ENG.). 24p. (J). (gr. -1-3). pap. 3.95 *(978-0-15-204833-4(2))* Houghton Mifflin Harcourt Publishing Co.

—Get That Pest! / ¡Agarren a Ése! Campoy, F. Isabel & Flor Ada, Alma, trs. Yee, Wong Herbert, illus. 2008. (Green Light Readers Level 2 Ser.). (SPA & ENG.). 28p. (J). (gr. k-2). pap. 3.95 *(978-0-15-206269-9(6))* Houghton Mifflin Harcourt Publishing Co.

Driscoll, Laura & Disney Book Group Staff. Thumper Finds an Egg. Tyminski, Lori et al, illus. 2009. (ENG.). 24p. (J). (gr. -1-k). pap. 3.99 *(978-1-4231-1717-9(4))* Disney Pr.

Dudley, Rebecca. Hank Finds an Egg. Dudley, Rebecca, photos by. 2013. (ENG., Illus.). 40p. (J). 16.99 *(978-1-4413-1158-0(0))* Peter Pauper Pr. Inc.

Dunrea, Olivier. Oli/Ollie Bilingual Board Book. 2015. (Gossie & Friends Ser.). (ENG & SPA., Illus.). 32p. (J). (— 1). bds. 4.99 *(978-0-544-31684-3(3),* HMH Books For Young Readers) Houghton Mifflin Harcourt Publishing Co.

—Ollie. 2007. (Gossie & Friends Ser.). (ENG., Illus.). 32p. (J). (gr. -1 — 1). bds. 6.99 *(978-0-618-75503-5(9))* Houghton Mifflin Harcourt Publishing Co.

—Ollie. Dunrea, Olivier, illus. 2003. (Gossie & Friends Ser.). (ENG., Illus.). 32p. (J). (gr. -1 — 1). tchr. ed. 9.95 *(978-0-618-33928-0(0))* Houghton Mifflin Harcourt Publishing Co.

—Ollie (Reader) 2014. (Gossie & Friends Ser.). (ENG., Illus.). 32p. (J). (gr. -1 — 1). pap. 3.99 *(978-0-544-14671-6(9),* HMH Books For Young Readers) Houghton Mifflin Harcourt Publishing Co.

—Ollie's Easter Eggs. 2010. (Gossie & Friends Ser.). (ENG., Illus.). 32p. (J). (gr. -1 — 1). 9.99 *(978-0-618-53243-8(9))* Houghton Mifflin Harcourt Publishing Co.

—Ollie's Easter Eggs Board Book. 2013. (Gossie & Friends Ser.). (ENG., Illus.). 30p. (J). (gr. k — 1). bds. 6.99 *(978-0-547-85918-7(X))* Houghton Mifflin Harcourt Publishing Co.

Echeverria-Bis, Olivia. The EGGbees. Echeverria Gyorkos, Charmaine, illus. 2009. (ENG & SPA.). 32p. (J). (gr. -1-3). 16.95 *(978-1-55885-529-8(7),* Piñata Books) Arte Publico Pr.

Edwards, Sherri L. Sally the Platypus. 2009. 48p. pap. 18.95 *(978-1-4389-5930-6(3))* AuthorHouse.

Ellis, Barbara A. The Eggs Are Talking: Book 2. 2012. 114p. pap. 14.95 *(978-1-4772-8787-3(6))* AuthorHouse.

Evans, Cordelia. Olivia & the Easter Egg Hunt. 2013. (Olivia 8x8 Ser.). lib. bdg. 14.75 *(978-0-606-27062-5(0),* Turtleback) Turtleback Bks.

EFG

Evans, Kristina. The Best Easter Prize. Wallace, John, illus. 2010. (ENG.). 32p. (J). (gr. -1-3). pap. 3.99 (978-0-545-05112-5(6), Cartwheel Bks.) Scholastic, Inc.

Fisch, Sarah & Bridwell, Norman. The Little Blue Easter Egg. Goldberg, Barry, illus. 2006. (Clifford's Puppy Days Ser.). 23p. (J). (978-0-439-81617-5(3)) Scholastic, Inc.

Fitzgerald, Kevin. The EGG-Cellent Adventure. Fitzgerald, Anita, illus. 2005. (J). (978-0-9765987-3-2(6)) Foundation, Pr. The.

Flor Ada, Alma. Daniel's Mystery Egg. Karas, G. Brian, illus. 2003. (Green Light Readers Level 2 Ser.). (ENG.). 24p. (J). (gr. -1-3). pap. 3.95 (978-0-15-204845-7(6)) Houghton Mifflin Harcourt Publishing Co.

—El Misterioso Huevo de Daniel. Flor Ada, Alma, tr. from ENM. Karas, G. Brian, illus. 2007. (Green Light Readers Level 2 Ser.).Tr. of Daniel's Mystery Egg. (SPA & ENG.). 28p. (J). (gr. 1-4). pap. 3.95 (978-0-15-205971-2(7)) Houghton Mifflin Harcourt Publishing Co.

Franceschelli, Christopher. Oliver. 2011. (ENG., Illus.). 16p. (J). (gr. -1). 12.95 (978-1-935954-01-9(6), 9781935954019) Lemniscaat USA.

Frazer, Rebecca. An Egg-Cellent Easter! (Barbie) Riley, Kellee, illus. 2012. (Pictureback(R) Ser.). (ENG.). 16p. (J). (gr. -1-2). pap. 3.99 (978-0-307-93025-5(4), Random Hse. Bks. for Young Readers) Random Hse. Children's Bks.

Gannon, Patty. Desdemona & the Eggs. 2011. 52p. pap. 23.00 (978-1-4567-1581-6(X)) AuthorHouse.

Gardner, Louise, illus. Five Little Easter Eggs. 2009. (ENG.). 10p. (J). (gr. -1). 5.95 (978-1-58117-849-4(2), Intervisual/Piggy Toes) Bendon, Inc.

Garza, R. Baby Blue Egg's Big Adventure. 2008. 16p. pap. 24.95 (978-1-60441-880-4(X)) America Star Bks.

Gehl, Laura. I'm Not Hatching. Wan, Joyce, illus. 2016. (Peep & Egg Ser.). (ENG.). 40p. (J). 16.99 (978-0-374-30121-7(2), 9780374301217, Farrar, Straus & Giroux (BYR)) Farrar, Straus & Giroux.

—I'm Not Trick-Or-Treating. Wan, Joyce, illus. 2016. (Peep & Egg Ser.). (ENG.). 40p. (J). 16.99 (978-0-374-30122-4(0), 9780374301224, Farrar, Straus & Giroux (BYR)) Farrar, Straus & Giroux.

—Peep & Egg: I'm Not Hatching. Wan, Joyce, illus. 2017. (Peep & Egg Ser.). (ENG.). 32p. (J). bds. 7.99 (978-0-374-30542-0(0), 9780374305420, Farrar, Straus & Giroux (BYR)) Farrar, Straus & Giroux.

George, Kallie. The Enchanted Egg. Boiger, Alexandra, illus. 2015. (Magical Animal Adoption Agency Ser.). (ENG.). 138p. (J). (gr. 3-7). 14.99 (978-1-4231-8383-9(5)) Disney Pr.

—The Enchanted Egg. Boiger, Alexandra, illus. 2016. (Magical Animal Adoption Agency Ser.). (ENG.). 160p. (J). (gr. 2-5). pap. 5.99 (978-1-4847-0146-1(1)) Hyperion Bks. for Children.

Gemhart, Cyndi. The Adventures of Gertrude Mccluck, Chicken in Charge Vol. 1: The Missing Eggs, 4 vols. Gemhart, Carlie, illus. l.t. ed. 2005. 32p. (J). 8.00 (978-0-9778240-1-4(2)) Prairie Winds Publishing.

Giles, Lisa. The Adventures of Sunny the Bunny: The Easter Egg Hunt. 2010. 20p. 10.49 (978-1-4520-1842-3(1)) AuthorHouse.

Glass, Susan. The Great Eggscape, 1 vol. Van Wright, Cornelius, illus. 2011. 32p. (J). (gr. k-5). (ENG.). 16.95 (978-1-59572-261-4(0)); pap. 6.95 (978-1-59572-253-9(X)) Star Bright Bks., Inc.

Golden Books Staff. Easter Deliveries. Golden Books Staff, illus. 2010. (Color Plus Chunky Crayons Ser.). (ENG., Illus.). 48p. (J). (gr. -1-2). pap. 3.99 (978-0-375-85747-8(8), Golden Bks.) Random Hse. Children's Bks.

—Egg Surprise. Roper, Bob, illus. 2003. (Paint Box Book Ser.). (ENG.). 32p. (J). (gr. -1-2). pap. 3.99 (978-0-307-10043-6(X), Golden Bks.) Random Hse. Children's Bks.

Goldstein, Sol. A Baby Crane's Tale. 2012. 40p. pap. 21.99 (978-1-4797-3928-8(6)) Xlibris Corp.

Graves, Annie. The Hatching. McElhinney, Glenn, illus. 2015. (Nightmare Club Ser.: 8). (ENG.). 64p. (J). (gr. 2-5). pap. 6.99 (978-1-4677-6045-4(5), Darby Creek); lib. bdg. 25.32 (978-1-4677-4354-9(2)) Lerner Publishing Group.

Gravett, Emily. The Odd Egg. Gravett, Emily, illus. 2009. (ENG., Illus.). 32p. (J). (gr. -1-3). 16.99 (978-1-4169-6872-6(5), Simon & Schuster Bks. For Young Readers) Simon & Schuster Bks. For Young Readers.

The Great Bird Adventure. 2003. (J). lib. bdg. (978-0-9725485-1-9(3)) Waterfall Ridge.

The Great Egg Problem: Individual Title Six-Packs. (Bookweb Ser.). 32p. (gr. 5-18). 34.00 (978-0-7635-3789-0(6)) Rigby Education.

Greve, Meg. Humpty Dumpty. Poole, Helen, illus. 2012. (ENG.). 24p. (gr. 1-2). pap. 8.95 (978-1-61810-313-0(X)) Rourke Educational Media.

Griffin, Adele. Oona Finds an Egg. Wu, Mike, illus. 2016. (Oodlethunks Ser.: Bk. 1). (ENG.). 160p. (J). (gr. 3-7). 12.99 (978-0-545-73279-6(4), Scholastic Pr.) Scholastic, Inc.

Grimes, Janice D. Before You Were Born - Our Wish for A Baby - Egg Donation: Version 3: Egg Donation. 2004. (Illus.). 18p. (J). 17.95 (978-0-9755028-2-2(4)) X, Y, & Me LLC.

Gummer, Chlele. A Family of Geese. 2013. 34p. pap. 16.95 (978-1-4808-0026-7(0)) Archway Publishing.

Hardy, Cindy & Masterman, Lorrine A. Egg Island Reader, 1 vol. 2003. (ENG., Illus.). 76p. pap. 14.95 (978-1-55059-246-7(7)) Brush Education CAN. Dist: Univ. of Toronto Pr.

Harimann, Sierra. Easter Egg Hunt. 2014. (Illus.). 30p. (J). pap. (978-0-545-59212-3(7)) Scholastic, Inc.

Hendricks, Linda K. The Rainbow Egg. 2012. 26p. pap. 12.95 (978-1-4497-7539-1(X), WestBow Pr.) Author Solutions, Inc.

Henkes, Kevin. Egg. Henkes, Kevin, illus. 2017. (Illus.). 40p. (J). (gr. -1-3). 17.99 (978-0-06-240872-3(0), Greenwillow Bks.) HarperCollins Pubs.

Higgins, Ryan T. Mother Bruce. Higgins, Ryan T., illus. 2015. (Mother Bruce Ser.). (ENG., Illus.). 48p. (J). (gr. -1-k). 17.99 (978-1-4847-3088-1(7)) Disney Pr.

Hooten, K. J. The Egg Nanny Tales. 2008. 98p. pap. 19.95 (978-1-60563-722-8(X)) America Star Bks.

Howard, Reginald. The Big, Big Wall. Dewey, Ariane & Aruego, Jose, illus. 2003. (Green Light Readers — Level 1 Ser.). (J). (gr. -1-3). 13.50 (978-0-613-66350-2(0), Turtleback) Turtleback Bks.

—The Big, Big Wall/No Puedo Bajar. Flor Ada, Alma & Campoy, F. Isabel, trs. Dewey, Ariane & Aruego, Jose, illus. 2009. (Green Light Readers Level 1 Ser.). (SPA & ENG.). 28p. (J). (gr. -1-3). pap. 3.99 (978-0-547-25548-4(9)) Houghton Mifflin Harcourt Publishing Co.

Howarth, Daniel, illus. The Goose That Laid the Golden Eggs. 2006. (First Reading Level 3 Ser.). 48p. (J). (gr. 1-4). 8.99 (978-0-7945-1378-8(6), Usborne) EDC Publishing.

Hudson, Katy. The Runaway Egg. 2017. (ENG., Illus.). 32p. (J). (gr. -1-2). 16.99 (978-0-553-52319-5(8), Random Hse. Bks. for Young Readers) Random Hse. Children's Bks.

Hund, Thomas. Toby T-Rex: Lightning Strikes. 2012. 46p. pap. 21.99 (978-1-4685-5305-5(4)) AuthorHouse.

Huxley, Aldous. The Crows of Pearblossom. Blackall, Sophie, illus. 2011. (ENG.). 40p. (J). (gr. k-2). 17.95 (978-0-8109-9730-1(4), Abrams Bks. for Young Readers) Abrams, Inc.

Image Books Staff. Little Chicken. Put, Klaartje van der, illus. 2012. (Little Finger Puppet Board Bks.: FING). (ENG.). 12p. (J). (gr. -1 — 1). bds. 6.99 (978-1-4521-0811-7(0)) Chronicle Bks. LLC.

Ivanke, illus. Sparkling Easter Eggs: A Glittery Counting Book. 2008. (ENG.). 10p. (J). bds. 7.95 (978-1-58117-685-8(6), Intervisual/Piggy Toes) Bendon, Inc.

Jacobs, Lily. The Littlest Bunny: An Easter Adventure. Dunn, Robert, illus. 2015. (ENG.). 32p. (J). (-3). 9.99 (978-1-4926-1012-0(7), Sourcebooks Jabberwocky) Sourcebooks, Inc.

Jenkins, Amanda. George & Grace Find an Egg. Zolotic, Aleksander, illus. 2017. (Text Connections Guided Close Reading Ser.). (J). (gr. 2). (978-1-4900-1846-1(8)) Benchmark Education Co.

Johnson, Shane L., illus. The Chickens & the Eggs. 2014. (Rabbids Invasion Ser.). (ENG.). 40p. (J). (gr. 1-3). pap. 3.99 (978-1-4814-0042-8(8), Simon Spotlight) Simon Spotlight.

Joyce, William. Bently & Egg. Joyce, William, illus. 2017. (World of William Joyce Ser.). (ENG., Illus.). 32p. (J). (gr. -1-3). 17.99 (978-1-4814-8949-2(6), Atheneum/Caitlyn Dlouhy Books) Simon & Schuster Children's Publishing.

—E. Aster Bunnymund & the Warrior Eggs at the Earth's Core!, Bk. 2. Joyce, William, illus. 2012. (Guardians Ser.: 2). (ENG., Illus.). 272p. (J). (gr. 2-6). 15.99 (978-1-4424-3050-1(8), Atheneum Bks. for Young Readers) Simon & Schuster Children's Publishing.

Karr, Lily. My Easter Bunny! Johnson, Jay B., illus. 2012. (ENG.). 12p. (J). (gr. -1-k). bds. 4.99 (978-0-545-37117-9(1), Cartwheel Bks.) Scholastic, Inc.

Katz, Karen. Where Are Baby's Easter Eggs? Katz, Karen, illus. 2008. (ENG., Illus.). 14p. (J). (gr. -1 — 1). bds. 7.99 (978-1-4169-4924-4(0), Little Simon) Little Simon.

King, Trey. Follow That Easter Egg! 2015. (LEGO City 8X8 Ser.). lib. bdg. 13.55 (978-0-606-36359-4(9)) Turtleback Bks.

Kirby, Stan. Captain Awesome & the Easter Egg Bandit. O'Connor, George, illus. 2015. (Captain Awesome Ser.: 13). (ENG.). 128p. (J). (gr. k-4). pap. 5.99 (978-1-4814-2558-2(7), Little Simon) Little Simon.

Klimo, Kate. The Dragon in the Sea. Shroades, John, illus. 2013. (Dragon Keepers Ser.: 5). (ENG.). 224p. (J). (gr. 3-7). 6.99 (978-0-375-87116-0(0), Yearling) Random Hse. Children's Bks.

—The Dragon in the Sock Drawer. Shroades, John, illus. 2009. (Dragon Keepers Ser.). (ENG.). 192p. (J). (gr. 3-7). 6.99 (978-0-375-85588-7(2), Yearling) Random Hse. Children's Bks.

—Dragon Keepers #4: the Dragon in the Volcano. Shroades, John, illus. 2012. (Dragon Keepers Ser.). (ENG.). 256p. (J). (gr. 3-7). 6.99 (978-0-375-86688-3(4), Yearling) Random Hse. Children's Bks.

Knapman, Timothy. The Great Easter Egg Scramble. Walker, David, illus. 2013. (J). (978-1-4351-4594-8(1)) Barnes & Noble, Inc.

Krauss, Ruth. The Happy Egg. Johnson, Crockett, illus. (J). (gr. -1-3). 2016. 40p. 14.99 (978-0-06-243031-1(9)) 2005. (ENG.). 32p. 12.99 (978-0-06-076005-2(2)) HarperCollins Pubs.

Landeman, Tanya. The Little Egg. 2006. (Collins Big Cat Ser.). (ENG., Illus.). 16p. (J). (gr. 1-1). pap. 5.99 (978-0-00-718677-8(0)) HarperCollins Pubs. Ltd. GBR. Dist: Independent Pubs. Group.

LaRose, Melinda & Disney Book Group Staff. Jake Hatches a Plan, Pre-Level 1. Disney Storybook Art Team, illus. 2012. (World of Reading Ser.). (ENG.). 32p. (J). (gr. -1-k). pap. 3.99 (978-1-4231-5542-3(4)) Disney Pr.

Lemke, Amy J. Dinosaurs for Breakfast, 1 vol. Bradley, Jessica, illus. 2013. (Comics Land Ser.). (ENG.). 32p. (gr. k-2). 7.95 (978-1-4342-4270-9(6)); lib. bdg. 25.32 (978-1-4342-4029-3(0)) Stone Arch Bks.

Levey, Emma, illus. Hattie Peck. 2016. (ENG.). 32p. (J). (gr. -1-k). 16.99 (978-1-63450-170-5(5), Sky Pony Pr.) Skyhorse Publishing Co., Inc.

Little Spring Eggs. 2003. per. 8.99 (978-0-89610-792-2(2)) Island Heritage Publishing.

Loehr, Mallory. Dragon Egg. Wittwer, Hala, illus. 2007. (Step into Reading Ser.). (ENG.). 32p. (J). (gr. -1-1). pap. 3.99 (978-0-375-84350-1(7), Random Hse. Bks. for Young Readers) Random Hse. Children's Bks.

Lord, Bruce & Richards, Elisabeth. Humpty Dumpty Was Pushed: And Other Cracked Tales. 2008. 196p. 24.95 (978-0-595-71559-6(1)); pap. 14.95 (978-0-595-47691-6(0)) iUniverse, Inc.

Lucero, Jaime. One Little Egg. Kennedy, Kelly, illus. 2005. (Number Tales Ser.). (ENG.). 16p. (J). (gr. -1-1). pap. 2.99 (978-0-439-68997-7(X)) Scholastic, Inc.

Mancusi, Mari. Scorched. (Scorched Ser.: 1). (ENG.). (YA). (gr. 6-12). 2014. 368p. pap. 9.99 (978-1-4022-9227-9(9)) 2013. 352p. 16.99 (978-1-4022-8458-8(6), 9781402284588) Sourcebooks, Inc.

Mann, Jennifer K. Two Speckled Eggs. Mann, Jennifer K., illus. 2014. (ENG., Illus.). 32p. (J). (gr. k-3). 14.99 (978-0-7636-6168-7(6)) Candlewick Pr.

McCarthy, Jon-Paul. Eddie the Egg. 2010. (Illus.). 32p. pap. 12.99 (978-1-4490-4125-0(6)) AuthorHouse.

McGrath, Barbara Barbieri. Easter Counting. Tagel, Peggy, illus. 2017. (First Celebrations Ser.). (ENG.). 12p. (J). (— 1). bds. 6.99 (978-1-58089-535-4(2)) Charlesbridge Publishing, Inc.

Merrick, Patrick. Easter Bunnies. 2015. (Our Holiday Symbols Ser.). (ENG.). 24p. (J). (gr. 1-4). 25.64 (978-1-63143-743-4(7), 208552) Child's World, Inc., The.

Miles, Brenda & Sweet, Susan D. Chicken or Egg: Who Comes First? 2017. (J). **(978-1-4338-2719-8(0))** American Psychological Assn.

Mitaro, S. Ciara. The Good Eggs. 2013. 104p. pap. 16.95 (978-1-4575-1837-9(6)) Dog Ear Publishing, LLC.

Mitter, Matt. Sesame Street Guess Who, Easter Elmo! Guess Who Easter Elmo! Mathieu, Joe, illus. 2015. (Guess Who Ser.: 6). (ENG.). 10p. (J). (gr. -1-k). 10.99 (978-0-7944-3331-4(6), Reader's Digest Children's Bks.) Studio Fun International.

Morales, Rose. Mary's Egg, 1 vol. 2009. 13p. pap. 24.95 (978-1-61546-912-3(5)) America Star Bks.

Mortimer, Anne. Bunny's Easter Egg. Mortimer, Anne, illus. 2010. (ENG., Illus.). 32p. (J). (gr. -1-2). 12.99 (978-0-06-136664-2(1), Tegen, Katherine Bks) HarperCollins Pubs.

My hard-boiled Egg: Individual Title Six-Packs. (gr. 1-2). 22.00 (978-0-7635-9186-1(6)) Rigby Education.

Nesbit, E. The Phoenix & the Carpet. 2009. 156p. pap. 4.95 (978-1-60459-693-9(7)) Wilder Pubns., Corp.

Newman, Robin. The Case of the Poached Egg. Zemke, Deborah, illus. 2017. (Wilcox & Griswold Mystery Ser.). (ENG.). 48p. (J). (gr. -1-3). 15.95 (978-1-939547-30-9(X)) Creston Bks.

Park, Barbara. Dumb Bunny. Brunkus, Denise, illus. 2009. (Junie B. Jones Ser.). (ENG.). 128p. (J). (gr. 1-4). 4.99 (978-0-375-83810-1(4), Random Hse. Bks. for Young Readers) Random Hse. Children's Bks.

Paschkis, Julie. P. Zonka Lays an Egg, 1 vol. Paschkis, Julie, illus. 2015. (ENG., Illus.). 32p. (J). (gr. 1-3). 16.95 (978-1-56145-819-6(8)) Peachtree Pubs.

Perelman, Helen. A Candy Fairies Sweet Collection: Chocolate Dreams; Rainbow Swirl; Caramel Moon; Cool Mint. Waters, Erica-Jane, illus. 2013. (Candy Fairies Ser.). (ENG.). 512p. (J). (gr. 2-5). pap. 23.99 (978-1-4424-9390-2(9), Aladdin) Simon & Schuster Children's Publishing.

Petreman, Gwen. Who Laid Those Eggs? 2013. 20p. pap. 11.59 (978-1-4669-7633-7(0)) Trafford Publishing.

Peyo. Smurf Cake. Peyo, illus. 2013. (Smurfs Classic Ser.). (ENG., Illus.). 32p. (J). (gr. k-2). 16.99 (978-1-4424-8493-1(4)); pap. 3.99 (978-1-4424-8492-4(6)) Simon Spotlight. (Simon Spotlight).

—The Smurfs & the Magic Egg. Peyo, illus. 2014. (Smurfs Classic Ser.). (ENG., Illus.). 32p. (J). (gr. k-2). pap. 3.99 (978-1-4424-9570-8(7), Simon Spotlight) Simon Spotlight.

Pixton, Kaaren & Sickler, Jonas. Humpty Dumpty: Hey, Bay Look at the Humpty Dumpty - On the Great Wall of China! 2010. (Indestructibles Ser.). (ENG., Illus.). 12p. (J). (gr. k — 1). pap. 5.95 (978-0-7611-5861-5(8), 15861) Workman Publishing Co., Inc.

Polhemus, Coleman. The Crocodile Blues. Polhemus, Coleman, illus. 2007. (ENG., Illus.). 48p. (J). (gr. -1-2). 16.99 (978-0-7636-3543-5(X)) Candlewick Pr.

Rabe, Tish. Thump!/The Lost Egg (Cat in the Hat/Seuss) Ruiz, Aristides & Mathieu, Joe, illus. 2013. (Pictureback(R) Ser.). (ENG.). 32p. (J). (gr. -1-2). pap. 4.99 (978-0-307-98063-2(4), Random Hse. Bks. for Young Readers) Random Hse. Children's Bks.

Rand, Betseygail & Rand, Colleen. Big Bunny. Rand, Colleen, illus. 2011. (ENG., Illus.). 32p. (J). (gr. -1-2). 14.99 (978-1-58246-376-6(X), Tricycle Pr.) Random Hse. Children's Bks.

Randolph, Joanne. Bella: A Butterfly's Story. 2009. (Nature Stories Ser.). (Illus.). 24p. (J). (gr. -1-2). pap. 8.15 (978-1-60754-099-1(1)); lib. bdg. 22.60 (978-1-60754-098-4(3)) Windmill Bks.

Reitze, Glenn Logan. Ernie the Easter Hippopotamus: A Comic Adventure for Anytime. Reitze, Glenn Logan, illus. 2007. (ENG., Illus.). 48p. (J). lib. bdg. 19.95 (978-0-88265-040-1(8), Fine Art Editions) North American International.

Reitze, Glenn Logan, illus. & text. Ernie the Easter Hippotamus: A Comic Adventure for Anytime. Reitze, Glenn Logan, text. 2007. (J). pap. (978-0-88265-041-8(6)) North American International.

Rex, Michael. The Egg of Misery. Rex, Michael, illus. 2012. (Fangbone! Third Grade Barbarian Ser.). (ENG., Illus.). 128p. (J). (gr. 2-4). E-Book (978-1-101-55043-4(0), G.P. Putnam's Sons Books for Young Readers) Penguin Young Readers Group.

—The Egg of Misery: Fangbone, Third Grade Barbarian. Rex, Michael, illus. 2012. (Fangbone! Third Grade Barbarian Ser.: 2). (ENG., Illus.). 128p. (J). (gr. 2-4). 7.99 (978-0-399-25522-9(2), G.P. Putnam's Sons Books for Young Readers) Penguin Young Readers Group.

Rey, H. A. Curious George Colors Eggs. 2012. (Curious George Ser.). (ENG., Illus.). 24p. (J). (gr. -1-3). pap. 3.99 (978-0-547-31585-0(6)) Houghton Mifflin Harcourt Publishing Co.

—Curious George Colors Eggs (CGTV Reader) 2012. (Curious George Ser.). (ENG., Illus.). 24p. (J). (gr. -1-3). 12.99 (978-0-547-55904-9(6)) Houghton Mifflin Harcourt Publishing Co.

Richards, Dawn. Duck's Easter Egg Hunt. D'hamers, Heidi, illus. 2014. (J). (978-1-4351-5243-4(3)) Barnes & Noble, Inc.

Ridgell, Regina. Baby Loggerhead's Long Journey. 2008. 28p. pap. 15.99 (978-1-4363-2087-0(9)) Xlibris Corp.

Rigby Education Staff. The Egg Saga. (Sails Literacy Ser.). (Illus.). 16p. (gr. 2-3). 27.00 (978-0-7635-9935-5(2), 699352C99) Rigby Education.

Ritchie, Joseph R. Peter Cottontail's Busy Day. Halverson, Lydia, illus. 2009. 14p. (J). (gr. -1-k). bds. 6.99 (978-0-8249-1842-2(8), Ideal Pubns.) Worthy Publishing.

—Peter Cottontaol's Easter Egg Hunt. Thornburgh, Rebecca, illus. 2006. (ENG.). 26p. (J). (gr. -1-k). 12.95 (978-0-8249-6653-9(8), Ideal Pubns.) Worthy Publishing.

Rumbaugh, Melinda. The Great Easter Egg Hunt. Reed, Lisa, illus. 2014. (VeggieTales Bk Ser.). 16p. (J). 12.99 (978-0-8249-1928-3(9), Ideal Pubns.) Worthy Publishing.

Rushall, Chris. Do Cows Lay Eggs? 2012. 24p. pap. 28.03 (978-1-4797-2624-0(9)) Xlibris Corp.

Saccheri, Josephine. The Secret to Easter Eggs. Saccheri, Briana, illus. 2008. 28p. pap. 24.95 (978-1-60474-210-7(0)) America Star Bks.

Saltzberg, Barney. Good Egg. 2009. (ENG., Illus.). 16p. (J). (gr. -1-k). 9.95 (978-0-7611-5406-8(X), 15406) Workman Publishing Co., Inc.

Sander, Sonia. Easter Egg Dash! A Lift-The-Flap Book with Stickers. Shannon, David et al, illus. 2010. (Jon Scieszka's Trucktown Ser.). (ENG.). 12p. (J). (gr. -1-k). bds. 7.99 (978-1-4169-4183-5(5), Little Simon) Little Simon.

Santillo, LuAnn. The Eggs. Santillo, LuAnn, ed. 2003. (Half-Pint Kids Readers Ser.). (Illus.). 7p. (J). (gr. -1-1). pap. (978-1-59256-061-5(X)) Half-Pint Kids, Inc.

Sargent, Dave & Sargent, David M., Jr. Glenda Goose: Sharing, 19 vols., Vol. 8. Lenoir, Jane, illus. 2003. (Feather Tales Ser.: 8). 42p. (J). pap. 10.95 (978-1-56763-734-2(5)); 2nd ed. lib. bdg. 20.95 (978-1-56763-733-5(7)) Ozark Publishing.

Scarry, Richard. Egg in the Hole. Golden Books Staff, illus. 2011. (Shaped Board Book Ser.). (ENG.). 20p. (J). (gr. k — 1). bds. 8.99 (978-0-375-86291-5(9), Golden Bks.) Random Hse. Children's Bks.

Schulman, Janet. 10 Easter Egg Hunters: A Holiday Counting Book. Davick, Linda, illus. (ENG.). (J). (gr. -1 — 1). 2012. 26p. bds. 6.99 (978-0-375-86637-1(X)) 2011. 32p. 8.99 (978-0-375-86787-3(2)) Random Hse. Children's Bks. (Knopf Bks. for Young Readers).

Scotton, Rob. Splat the Cat & the Quick Chicks. Scotton, Rob, illus. 2016. (I Can Read Level 1 Ser.). (Illus.). 32p. (J). (gr. -1-3). pap. 3.99 (978-0-06-229424-1(5)) HarperCollins Pubs.

Scotton, Rob. Splat the Cat & the Quick Chicks. Eberz, Robert, illus. 2016. 30p. (J). **(978-1-4844-7139-5(3))** Harper & Row Ltd.

Serban, Milica. Little Bag with Two Gold Coins. 2012. 20p. pap. 17.99 (978-1-4772-1132-8(2)) AuthorHouse.

Sesen, Cihan. Stop the Rain, Issue #1. 2010. 45p. pap. 12.99 (978-0-557-48426-3(X)) Lulu Pr., Inc.

Seuss, Dr. Green Eggs & Ham, 1 vol. 2005. (Book & CD Ser.). (ENG., Illus.). 64p. (J). (gr. -1-2). 9.95 (978-0-375-83495-0(8), Random Hse. Bks. for Young Readers) Random Hse. Children's Bks.

—Tonho Choca o Ovo. pap. 23.95 (978-85-7406-098-9(4)) Schwarcz, Editora Ltda, Companhia das Letrinhas BRA. Dist: Distribooks, Inc.

Simmons, Jane. Daisy & the Egg. 2005. (Daisy Ser.). (Illus.). 36p. (J). (gr. -1-1). (ARA, ENG, VIE, CHI & BEN.). pap. 11.95 (978-1-84059-216-0(8)); (VIE, ENG, CHI, ARA & BEN., pap. 11.95 (978-1-84059-176-7(5)) Milet Publishing.

Smith, Alex T. Foxy & Egg: Starring Vivien Vixen As Foxy Dubois - Introducing Edward l'Ouef As Egg. Smith, Alex T., illus. 2011. (Illus.). 32p. (J). (gr. -1-3). 17.95 (978-0-8234-2330-9(1)) Holiday Hse., Inc.

Smith, Clyde. The Hen That Couldn't Lay an Egg. Bainbridge, Shane & Bainbridge, Bob, illus. 2011. 32p. pap. 24.95 (978-1-4626-3796-6(5)) America Star Bks.

Smith, J. L. The Blue & Purple Egg. Baker, David, illus. 2012. 28p. pap. 24.95 (978-1-4626-6789-5(9)) America Star Bks.

Smith, Jane. It's Easter, Chloe Zoe! Smith, Jane, illus. 2016. (Chloe Zoe Ser.). (ENG., Illus.). 32p. (J). (gr. -1-3). 12.99 (978-0-8075-2460-2(3)) Whitman, Albert & Co.

Smith, Paul. The Little Lost Egg. Smith, Steven, illus. 2017. (ENG.). (gr. 1). pap. **(978-1-78222-500-3(5))** Paragon Publishing, Rothersthorpe.

Smythe, Theresa. Chester's Colorful Easter Eggs. Smythe, Theresa, illus. 2013. (ENG., Illus.). 24p. (J). (gr. -1-k). 12.99 (978-0-8050-9326-1(5), 9780805093261, Holt, Henry & Co. Bks. For Young Readers) Holt, Henry & Co.

Speceal, Edetha. The Lost Egg & Other Stories. 2006. (Illus.). 144p. pap. (978-1-84401-644-0(7)) Athena Pr.

Stileman, Kali. Roly Poly Egg. 2011. (ENG.). 26p. (J). (gr. -1-k). 12.95 (978-1-58925-852-5(5)) Tiger Tales.

Strader, Irm. What Came First. 2012. 32p. pap. (978-1-77067-828-6(X)) FriesenPress.

Stuart, Janet. What? No Easter Eggs? 2011. 24p. pap. 12.79 (978-1-4567-6770-9(4)) AuthorHouse.

Sutton, Jane. What's up with This Chicken?, 1 vol. Welling, Peter, illus. 2015. (ENG.). 32p. (J). (gr. k-3). 16.99 (978-1-4556-2085-2(8)) Pelican Publishing Co., Inc.

Sykes, Julie. Dora's Eggs. Chapman, Jane, illus. 2007. (Storytime Board Bks.). (J). (gr. -1-3). bds. 6.95 (978-1-58925-801-3(0)) Tiger Tales.

Tafuri, Nancy. Whose Chick Are You? Tafuri, Nancy, illus. 2007. (ENG., Illus.). 40p. (J). (gr. -1-k). 16.99 (978-0-06-082514-0(6), Greenwillow Bks.) HarperCollins Pubs.

Thaler, Mike. Easter Egg Haunt, 1 vol. Lee, Jared, illus. 2009. (Tales from the Back Pew Ser.). (ENG.). 32p. (J). (gr. 1-4). pap. 3.99 (978-0-310-71591-7(1)) Zonderkidz.

Thiele, Colin. Danny's Egg. (Illus.). 160p. pap. (978-0-7344-0403-9(4), Lothian Children's Bks.) Hachette Australia.

Thomas, Dee. Silly, Silly, Eggleton Egg: Meet the Egg's of Eggville. 2012. 28p. pap. 21.99 (978-1-4771-5325-3(X)) Xlibris Corp.

Thomas, Jan. The Easter Bunny's Assistant. Thomas, Jan, illus. 2012. (ENG., Illus.). 40p. (J). (gr. -1-3). 12.99 (978-0-06-169286-4(7)) HarperCollins Pubs.

Thomson, Sarah L. Dragon's Egg. 2007. (ENG.). 272p. (J). (gr. 3-7). 16.99 (978-0-06-128848-7(9), Greenwillow Bks.) HarperCollins Pubs.

Tillworth, Mary. Zeg & the Egg. Foley, Niki, illus. 2016. 18p. (J). **(978-1-4806-9878-9(4))** Random Hse., Inc.

Wallace, Carol. Turkeys Together. Rogers, Jaqueline & Rogers, Jacqueline, illus. 2005. (Holiday House Readers: Level 2 Ser.). (ENG.). 40p. (J). (gr. k-3). 15.95 (978-0-8234-1895-4(2)) Holiday Hse., Inc.

Wallace, Karen. Flash Harriet & the Outrageous Ostrich Egg Mystery. (Illus.). 64p. (J). pap. (978-0-340-61961-2(9)) Hodder & Stoughton.

—Stolen Egg. Harland, Jackie, illus. 2013. (Start Reading Ser.). (ENG.). 24p. (gr. k-1). pap. 7.95 (978-1-4765-4141-9(8)) Capstone Press of Coughlan Cos.

Wallace, Sally. Peter's Puzzling Purple Easter Egg. 2010. 44p. pap. 16.99 (978-1-4490-3032-2(7)) AuthorHouse.

Wang, Margaret. Easter Egg Hunt. Johnson, Richard, illus. 2005. (ENG.). 10p. (J). bds. 9.95 (978-1-58117-375-8(X), Intervisual/Piggy Toes) Bendon, Inc.

Ward, Lindsay. When Blue Met Egg. 2012. (ENG.). 32p. (J). (gr. -1-k). 16.99 (978-0-8037-3718-1(1), Dial Bks) Penguin Young Readers Group.

Washington, LaVonne & Washington, LaShawn. The Parables of Humpty Dumpty: Volume 1. 2011. 40p. pap. 24.95 (978-1-4626-0989-5(9)) America Star Bks.

Weeks, Sarah. Two Eggs, Please. Lewin, Betsy, illus. 2007. (ENG.). 32p. (J). (gr. -1-1). reprint ed. 7.99 *(978-1-4169-2714-3(X)*, Atheneum Bks. for Young Readers) Simon & Schuster Children's Publishing.

Weeks, Sarah & Lewin, Betsy. Two Eggs, Please. 2003. (ENG., Illus.). 32p. (J). (gr. -1-3). 18.99 *(978-0-689-83196-6(X)*, Atheneum Bks. for Young Readers) Simon & Schuster Children's Publishing.

Weinberg, Steven. Rex Finds an Egg! Egg! Egg! Weinberg, Steven, illus. 2015. (ENG., Illus.). 40p. (J). (gr. -1-3). 17.99 *(978-1-4814-0308-5(7)*, McElderry, Margaret K. Bks.) McElderry, Margaret K. Bks.

Whose Egg Is This? Individual Title Six-Packs. (Story Steps Ser.). (gr. k-2). 32.00 *(978-0-7635-9607-1(8))* Rigby Education.

Williams, Lori. Henrietta Peddles Her Eggs. 2010. 36p. pap. 15.49 *(978-1-4490-6810-3(3))* AuthorHouse.

Wilson, Karma. What's in the Egg, Little Pip? Chapman, Jane, illus. 2010. (ENG.). 40p. (J). (gr. -1-3). 17.99 *(978-1-4169-4204-7(1)*, McElderry, Margaret K. Bks.) McElderry, Margaret K. Bks.

Wolf, Jackie, et al. My Sparkle Egg Book. 2005. (Illus.). (J). *(978-1-57151-750-0(2))* Playhouse Publishing.

Zuniga, Elisabeth. A Friend for Bo. 2016. (ENG., Illus.). 40p. (J). (gr. -1-2). 16.99 *(978-0-553-50998-4(5)*, Random Hse. Bks. for Young Readers) Random Hse. Children's Bks.

EGYPT

AZ Books Staff. Ancient Egypt. Ulasevich, Olga, ed. 2012. (Mysteries of History Ser.). (ENG.). 18p. (J). (gr. 1-3). bds. 17.95 *(978-1-61889-092-4(1))* AZ Bks. LLC.

Benge, Janet & Benge, Geoff. Christian Heroes - Then & Now - Lillian Trasher: The Greatest Wonder in Egypt. 2003. (Christian Heroes Ser.). (ENG.). 190p. (YA). pap. 9.99 *(978-1-57658-305-0(8))* YWAM Publishing.

Broyles, Janell. Egyptian Mythology. 2005. (Mythology Around the World Ser.). (Illus.). 64p. (YA). (gr. 5-9). lib. bdg. 31.95 *(978-1-4042-0770-7(8))* Rosen Publishing Group, Inc., The.

Dorling Kindersley Publishing Staff. Ancient Egypt. 2012. (Pocket Genius Ser.). (ENG., Illus.). 160p. (J). (gr. 3-7). 7.99 *(978-0-7566-9813-3(8)*, DK Children) Dorling Kindersley Publishing, Inc.

—DK Findout! Ancient Egypt. 2017. (DK Find Out! Ser.). (ENG.). 64p. (J). (gr. 1-4). pap. 10.99 *(978-1-4654-5753-0(4)*, DK Children) Dorling Kindersley Publishing, Inc.

Fact Atlas: Ancient Egypt. 2009. (FACT ATLAS Ser.). 72p. (J). 14.95 *(978-0-8437-0862-2(X))* Hammond World Atlas Corp.

Fiscus, James W. The Suez Crisis. 2004. (War & Conflict in the Middle East Ser.). (Illus.). 64p. (gr. 7-12). lib. bdg. 31.95 *(978-0-8239-4550-4(2))* Rosen Publishing Group, Inc., The.

Furstinger, Nancy. Cairo, 1 vol. 2005. (Cities Set 1 Ser.). (ENG., Illus.). 32p. (gr. k-6). 27.07 *(978-1-59197-856-5(4)*, Checkerboard Library) ABDO Publishing Co.

Green, Jen. Focus on Egypt. 2007. (World in Focus Ser.). (Illus.). 64p. (gr. 5-12). pap. 14.05 *(978-0-8368-6741-1(6))*; lib. bdg. 34.00 *(978-0-8368-6734-3(3))* Stevens, Gareth Publishing LLLP. (Gareth Stevens Secondary Library).

Gutner, Howard. Egypt. 2009. (True Book(tm), A — Countries Ser.). (ENG., 48p. (J). Illus.). (gr. 2-5). 31.00 *(978-0-531-16889-9(1))*; pap. 6.95 *(978-0-531-21356-8(0)*, Children's Pr.) Scholastic Library Publishing.

Hall, Brianna. Mummies of Ancient Egypt. 2012. (Ancient Egyptian Civilization Ser.). (ENG.). 32p. (gr. 3-4). pap. 47.70 *(978-1-4296-8403-3(8)*, Fact Finders) Capstone Press of Coughlan Cos.

Hardwick, Susan, ed. Egypt. 2005. (World-Wise Kids Project Guides). (Illus.). 96p. *(978-1-59258-078-1(5))* Hylas Publishing.

Hardyman, Robyn. Horrible Jobs in Ancient Egypt, Vol. 1. 2014. (History's Most Horrible Jobs Ser.). (ENG.). 48p. (J). (gr. 5-6). 31.95 *(978-1-4824-0324-4(2))* Stevens, Gareth Publishing LLLP.

Harris, Nicolas. Pyramids Through Time. 2009. (Fast Forward Ser.). 32p. (YA). (gr. 2-5). lib. bdg. 25.25 *(978-1-4358-2801-8(1))* Rosen Publishing Group, Inc., The.

Haskins, James & Benson, Kathleen. Count Your Way Through Egypt. Rama, Sue, illus. 2006. (Count Your Way Ser.). 24p. (J). (gr. -1-3). lib. bdg. 19.93 *(978-1-57505-882-5(0)*, Millbrook Pr.) Lerner Publishing Group.

Heinrichs, Ann. Egypt. 2012. (Enchantment of the World, Second Ser.). (ENG., Illus.). 144p. (J). (gr. 5-9). lib. bdg. 40.00 *(978-0-531-25309-0(0)*, Children's Pr.) Scholastic Library Publishing.

Hinds, Kathryn. The City. 2006. (Life in Ancient Egypt Ser.). (Illus.). 80p. (gr. 6-7). lib. bdg. 34.21 *(978-0-7614-2184-9(X)*, Benchmark Bks.) Marshall Cavendish Corp.

Hobbs, Joseph J. Egypt. 2nd rev. ed. 2007. (Modern World Nations Ser.). (Illus.). 118p. (YA). (gr. 7-12). lib. bdg. 35.00 *(978-0-7910-9515-7(0))* Facts On File, Inc.

Jackson, Elaine. Egypt. 2004. (QEB Travel Through Ser.). (Illus.). 32p. (J). lib. bdg. 18.95 *(978-1-59566-059-6(3))* QEB Publishing Inc.

Jankowski, Susan. Egypt in the News: Past, Present, & Future. 2006. (Middle East Nations in the News Ser.). (Illus.). 128p. (J). (gr. 5-9). lib. bdg. 34.60 *(978-1-59845-031-6(X)*, MyReportLinks.com Bks.) Enslow Pubs., Inc.

Kalman, Bobbie. Spotlight on Egypt. 2010. (Spotlight on My Country Ser.). (ENG.). 32p. (J). (gr. 2-5). lib. bdg. *(978-0-7787-3457-4(9))* Crabtree Publishing Co.

Kaplan, Leslie C. Home Life in Ancient Egypt. 2004. (Primary Sources of Ancient Civilizations Ser.). (ENG., Illus.). 24p. (gr. 4-8). pap. 8.25 *(978-0-8239-8935-5(6)*, PowerKids Pr.) Rosen Publishing Group, Inc., The.

—Politics & Government in Ancient Egypt. 2004. (Primary Sources of Ancient Civilizations Ser.). (Illus.). 24p. (ENG.). (gr. 4-8). pap. 8.25 *(978-0-8239-8933-1(X))*; (J). lib. bdg. 22.60 *(978-0-8239-6783-4(2))* Rosen Publishing Group, Inc., The. (PowerKids Pr.).

Karlsson, Val. Egypt, 1 vol. 2011. (Countries of the World Set 1 Ser.). (ENG., Illus.). 144p. (J). (gr. 6-12). lib. bdg. 37.07 *(978-1-61783-108-9(5))* ABDO Publishing Co.

A Kid's Guide to Drawing the Countries of the World: Set 3. (Illus.). (J). (gr. k-5). 159.00 *(978-1-4042-2958-7(2))* Rosen Publishing Group, Inc., The.

A Kid's Guide to Drawing the Countries of the World: Set 4. (Illus.). (J). (gr. k-5). 159.00 *(978-1-4042-2959-4(0))* Rosen Publishing Group, Inc., The.

Levy, Janey. The Great Pyramid of Giza: Measuring Length, Area, Volume, & Angles. (Math for the Real World Ser.). (Illus.). 32p. 2009. (ENG.). (gr. 6-7). pap. 10.00 *(978-1-4042-6059-7(5))* 2006. (YA). (gr. 5-9). lib. bdg. 25.25 *(978-1-4042-3353-9(9))* Rosen Publishing Group, Inc., The.

Malam, John. Pyramids. 2010. (100 Things You Should Know About Ser.). (Illus.). 32p. (YA). (gr. 4-6). lib. bdg. 19.95 *(978-1-4222-1525-8(3))* Mason Crest.

Manning, Paul. Nile River. 2014. (River Adventures Ser.). (J). lib. bdg. 31.35 *(978-1-59920-917-3(9))* Black Rabbit Bks.

Marsh, Carole. Egypt: An Ancient Land of Lore; a Modern Land of Oil & More! 2009. (It's Your World Ser.). 48p. (J). (gr. 2-9). pap. 7.99 *(978-0-635-06820-0(6))* Gallopade International.

Maule, David. What Makes a Place Special? Moscow, Egypt, Australia. 2014. (ENG., Illus.). 24p. (J). pap. 9.50 *(978-1-107-63317-9(6))* Cambridge Univ. Pr.

McLaughlin, Kari Massie. My Adventure in Ancient Egypt. 2007. 44p. (J). 8.99 *(978-1-59092-421-1(5))* Blue Forge Pr.

Millard, Anne. The Great Pyramid of Giza. 2005. (Places in History Ser.). (Illus.). 48p. (gr. 5-12). pap. 14.05 *(978-0-8368-5818-1(2)*, World Almanac Library) Stevens, Gareth Publishing LLLP.

Morris, Ann. Grandma Hekmat Remembers: An Arab-American Family Story. Linenthal, Peter, photos by. 2003. (What Was It Like, Grandma? Ser.). (ENG., Illus.). 32p. (gr. 2-5). lib. bdg. 22.60 *(978-0-7613-2864-3(5)*, Millbrook Pr.) Lerner Publishing Group.

—Grandma Hekmat Remembers: An Egyptian - American Family Story. Linenthal, Peter, photos by. 2003. (Illus.). 32p. (J). (gr. 5-18). pap. 7.95 *(978-0-7613-1944-3(1)*, Millbrook Pr.) Lerner Publishing Group.

Moscovitch, Arlene. Egypt - The Land. 3rd rev. ed. 2007. (Lands, People & Cultures Ser.). (ENG., Illus.). 32p. (J). (gr. 4-9). pap. *(978-0-7787-9673-2(6))*; lib. bdg. *(978-0-7787-9305-2(2))* Crabtree Publishing Co.

—Egypt - The People. 3rd rev. ed. 2007. (Lands, Peoples & Cultures Ser.). (ENG., Illus.). 32p. (J). (gr. 4-9). pap. *(978-0-7787-9674-9(4))*; lib. bdg. *(978-0-7787-9306-9(0))* Crabtree Publishing Co.

Nicolotti, Muriel. Madhi: A Child of Egypt. 2005. (Children of the World Ser.). (ENG., Illus.). 24p. (J). (gr. 2-4). 24.35 *(978-1-4103-0288-5(1)*, Blackbirch Pr., Inc.) Cengage Gale.

Parkes, Elle. Let's Explore Egypt. 2017. (Bumba Books (tm) — Let's Explore Countries Ser.). (ENG.). 24p. (J). (gr. -1-1). 25.32 ***(978-1-5124-3363-0(2))*** Lerner Publishing Group.

Pateman, Robert & El Hamamsy, Salwa. Egypt. 2nd rev. ed. 2003. (Cultures of the World Ser.). (Illus.). 144p. (gr. 6-18). lib. bdg. 42.79 *(978-0-7614-1670-8(6)*, Marshall Cavendish Reference Bks.) Marshall Cavendish Corp.

Peppas, Lynn. Cultural Traditions in Egypt. 2012. (ENG., Illus.). 32p. (J). pap. *(978-0-7787-7522-5(4))* Crabtree Publishing Co.

Popper, Garry. Ali in Egypt. Johnson, Andi, illus. 2004. 36p. (gr. -1-7). 4.00 *(978-1-84161-078-8(X))* Ravette Publishing, Ltd. GBR. Dist: Parkwest Pubns., Inc.

Putnam, James. Pyramid. 2011. (DK Eyewitness Bks.). (ENG.). 72p. (J). (gr. 3-7). 16.99 *(978-0-7566-5832-8(2)*, DK Children) Dorling Kindersley Publishing, Inc.

Rajczak, Kristen. 20 Fun Facts about the Great Pyramid, Vol. 1. 2014. (Fun Fact File: World Wonders! Ser.). (ENG., Illus.). 32p. (J). (gr. 2-3). pap. 10.50 *(978-1-4824-0470-8(2))* Stevens, Gareth Publishing LLLP.

Reynolds, Jeff E. Egypt. 2004. (A to Z Ser.). (ENG., Illus.). 40p. (J). 24.50 *(978-0-516-23652-0(0)*, Children's Pr.) Scholastic Library Publishing.

Rumford, James. Seeker of Knowledge: The Man Who Deciphered Egyptian Hieroglyphs. 2003. (Rise & Shine Ser.). (ENG., Illus.). 32p. (C). (gr. -1-3). pap. 11.95 *(978-0-618-33345-5(2))* National Geographic School Publishing, Inc.

Shakespeare, William. Antony & Cleopatra. Heims, Neil & Bloom, Harold, eds. 2008. (Bloom's Shakespeare Through the Ages Ser.). 290p. (YA). (gr. 9-12). 50.00 *(978-0-7910-9630-7(0))* Facts On File, Inc.

Streissguth, Thomas. Egypt. 2008. (Country Explorers Ser.). (ENG., Illus.). 48p. (gr. 2-4). lib. bdg. 29.27 *(978-0-8225-8660-9(6))* Lerner Publishing Group.

Streissguth, Tom. Egypt. 2008. pap. 40.95 *(978-0-8225-9301-0(7))* Lerner Publishing Group.

Time-Life Audiobooks Staff, contrib. by. Egypt. (J). tchr. ed. 41.95 *(978-0-382-40665-2(6))* Cobblestone Publishing Co.

Westphal, Jeremy. The Mummy's Curse. 2011. (Unexplained Ser.). (ENG., Illus.). 24p. (J). (gr. 3-7). lib. bdg. 25.95 *(978-1-60014-643-5(0)*, Torque Bks.) Bellwether Media.

Williams, Colleen Madonna Flood. My Adventure in Ancient Egypt: Advanced My Adventure. 2007. 44p. (J). pap. 8.99 *(978-1-59092-422-8(3))* Blue Forge Pr.

Wood, Selina. Egypt. 2009. (Countries of the World Ser.). (ENG., Illus.). 64p. (J). (gr. 5). pap. 12.95 *(978-1-4263-0572-6(9)*, National Geographic Children's Bks.) National Geographic Society.

—National Geographic Countries of the World - Egypt. 2007. (Countries of the World Ser.). (ENG., Illus.). 64p. (J). (gr. 5-5). lib. bdg. 27.90 *(978-1-4263-0027-1(1)*, National Geographic Children's Bks.) National Geographic Society.

Zuehlke, Jeffrey. Egypt in Pictures. 2nd rev. ed. 2003. (Visual Geography Series, Second Ser.). (ENG., Illus.). 80p. (gr. 5-12). 31.93 *(978-0-8225-0367-5(0))* Lerner Publishing Group.

EGYPT—ANTIQUITIES

Biskup, Agnieszka. Egypt's Mysterious Pyramids: An Isabel Soto Archaeology Adventure. Stewart, Roger, illus. 2012. (Graphic Expeditions Ser.). (ENG.). 32p. (gr. 3-4). pap. 47.70 *(978-1-4296-8472-9(0)*, Graphic Library) Capstone Press of Coughlan Cos.

Burgan, Michael. The Curse of King Tut's Tomb, 1 vol. Schulz, Barbara, illus. 2005. (Graphic History Ser.). (ENG.). 32p. (gr. 3-4). per. 8.10 *(978-0-7368-5244-9(1)*, Graphic Library) Capstone Press of Coughlan Cos.

Burgan, Michael & Hoena, Blake A. The Curse of King Tut's Tomb, 1 vol. Lohse, Otha Zackariah Edward & Schulz, Barbara, illus. 2005. (Graphic History Ser.). (ENG.). 32p. (gr. 3-4). 30.65 *(978-0-7368-3833-7(3)*, Graphic Library) Capstone Press of Coughlan Cos.

Chambers, Catherine. Egyptian Treasures. 2010. (Crabtree Connections Ser.). (ENG.). 24p. (J). (gr. 3-6). *(978-0-7787-9946-7(8))*; pap. *(978-0-7787-9968-9(9))* Crabtree Publishing Co.

Cohn, Jessica. The Ancient Egyptians. 2012. (Crafts from the Past Ser.). (Illus.). 48p. (J). (gr. 4-6). 31.95 *(978-1-4339-7701-5(X))*; pap. 14.05 *(978-1-4339-7702-2(8))* Stevens, Gareth Publishing LLLP.

Doeden, Matt. Tools & Treasures of Ancient Egypt. 2014. (Searchlight Books: What Can We Learn from Early Civilizations? Ser.). (ENG., Illus.). 40p. (gr. 3-5). lib. bdg. 27.93 *(978-1-4677-1429-7(1)*, Lerner Pubns.) Lerner Publishing Group.

Fletcher, J. Exploring the Life, Myth, & Art of Ancient Egypt. 2009. (Civilizations of the World Ser.). (YA). (gr. 7-12). 42.60 *(978-1-4358-5616-5(3))* Rosen Publishing Group, Inc., The.

Gaff, Jackie. Ancient Egypt. 2016. (Excavating the Past Ser.). (ENG.). 48p. (gr. 4-6). pap. 8.99 *(978-1-4846-3646-6(5)*, NA-h) Heinemann-Raintree.

george, charles. The pyramids of Giza. 2012. (ENG., Illus.). 80p. (YA). lib. bdg. *(978-1-60152-258-0(4))* ReferencePoint Pr., Inc.

Harvey, Gill. Tutankhamun. McNee, Ian, illus. 2006. (Usborne Young Reading Ser.). 64p. (J). (gr. 3-7). 8.99 *(978-0-7945-1271-2(2)*, Usborne) EDC Publishing.

Hawass, Zahi. The Curse of the Pharaohs: My Adventures with Mummies. 2004. (ENG., Illus.). 160p. (J). (gr. 5). 29.90 *(978-0-7922-6963-2(2))*; 19.95 *(978-0-7922-6665-5(X))* National Geographic Society. (National Geographic Children's Bks.).

Henzel, Cynthia Kennedy. Pyramids of Egypt, 1 vol. 2011. (Troubled Treasures: World Heritage Sites Ser.). (ENG., Illus.). 32p. (YA). (gr. 3-6). 27.07 *(978-1-61613-566-9(2))* ABDO Publishing Co.

Hinds, Kathryn. Life in Ancient Egypt, 4 bks., Set. Incl. City. 80p. (gr. 6-7). lib. bdg. 34.21 *(978-0-7614-2184-9(X))*; Countryside. 70p. (J). (gr. 4-7). lib. bdg. 32.79 *(978-0-7614-2185-6(8))*; Pharaoh's Court. 80p. (gr. 6-7). lib. bdg. 34.21 *(978-0-7614-2183-2(1))*; (Illus.). 2006. 2007. Set lib. bdg. 131.14 *(978-0-7614-2182-5(3)*, Benchmark Bks.) Marshall Cavendish Corp.

Holm, Kirsten C. Everyday Life in Ancient Egypt. 2012. (Jr. Graphic Ancient Civilizations Ser.). (ENG.). 24p. (J). (gr. 3-6). pap. 10.60 *(978-1-4488-6391-4(0))*; lib. bdg. 25.25 *(978-1-4488-6216-0(7))* Rosen Publishing Group, Inc., The. (PowerKids Pr.).

Hoobler, Dorothy & Hoobler, Thomas. Where Are the Great Pyramids? 2015. (Where Is... ? Ser.). lib. bdg. 16.00 *(978-0-606-37547-4(3))* Turtleback Bks.

Hoobler, Dorothy, et al. Where Are the Great Pyramids? Hoare, Jerry, illus. 2015. (Where Is? Ser.). (ENG.). 112p. (J). (gr. 3-7). 5.99 *(978-0-448-48409-9(9)*, Grosset & Dunlap) Penguin Young Readers Group.

Hooper, Meredith. Who Built the Pyramid? Heighway-Bury, Robin, illus. 2014. (ENG.). 40p. (J). (gr. 2-5). pap. 7.99 *(978-0-7636-7380-2(3))* Candlewick Pr.

Hyman, Teresa L. The Pyramids of Giza. 2004. (Great Structures in History Ser.). (ENG., Illus.). 48p. (J). (gr. 3-7). lib. bdg. 27.50 *(978-0-7377-1560-6(X)*, Greenhaven Pr., Inc.) Cengage Gale.

Jordan, Shirley J. Egypt, 1 vol. 2007. (Primary Source Readers Ser.). (ENG.). 32p. (J). (gr. 5-5). pap. 8.99 *(978-0-7439-0428-5(1))* Shell Educational Publishing.

Lace, William W. The Curse of King Tut. 2007. (Mysterious & Unknown Ser.). (Illus.). 104p. (YA). (gr. 7-12). lib. bdg. 25.95 *(978-1-60152-024-1(7))* ReferencePoint Pr., Inc.

Malam, John. The Egyptians. 2011. (Dig It: History from Objects Ser.). (Illus.). 32p. (YA). (gr. 2-5). lib. bdg. 26.50 *(978-1-4488-3283-5(7))* Rosen Publishing Group, Inc., The.

McCall, Henrietta. Egyptian Mummies. 2015. (ENG., Illus.). 32p. (J). pap. 9.95 *(978-1-910184-26-4(8))* RiverStream Publishing.

Meachen Rau, Dana. Pyramid. 2006. (Bookworms Ser.). (Illus.). 32p. (gr. k-2). lib. bdg. 15.95 *(978-0-7614-2275-4(7)*, Benchmark Bks.) Marshall Cavendish Corp.

Millard, Anne. The Great Pyramid of Giza. 2005. (Places in History Ser.). (Illus.). 48p. (gr. 5-12). pap. 14.05 *(978-0-8368-5818-1(2)*, World Almanac Library) Stevens, Gareth Publishing LLLP.

Morley, Jacqueline. Inside the Tomb of Tutankhamun. James, John, illus. 2005. (ENG.). 48p. (J). (gr. 3-7). 19.95 *(978-1-59270-042-4(X))* Enchanted Lion Bks., LLC.

Naden, Corinne J. & Blue, Rose. Ancient Egyptians & the Pyramids. 2003. (J). *(978-1-58417-310-6(6))*; pap. *(978-1-58417-311-3(4))* Lake Street Pubs.

O'Donnell, Kerri. The Pyramids of Egypt. (Reading Room Collection 2 Ser.). 24p. (gr. 3-4). 2009. 42.50 *(978-1-60851-996-5(1)*, PowerKids Pr.) 2003. (ENG.). 43.95 *(978-0-8239-8730-6(2))* Rosen Publishing Group, Inc., The.

The Pyramids of Giza. 2014. (Great Idea Ser.). (ENG.). 48p. (J). (gr. 4-6). lib. bdg. 26.60 *(978-1-59953-593-7(9))* Norwood Hse. Pr.

Rajczak, Kristen. 20 Fun Facts about the Great Pyramid, Vol. 1. 2014. (Fun Fact File: World Wonders! Ser.). (Illus.). 32p. (J). (gr. 2-5). 25.25 *(978-1-4824-0467-8(2))* Stevens, Gareth Publishing LLLP.

Rau, Dana Meachen. Pyramid. 2007. (J). pap. 6.99 *(978-0-7614-3302-6(3))* Marshall Cavendish Corp.

Raum, Elizabeth. Egyptian Pyramids. 2014. (Ancient Wonders Ser.). (Illus.). 32p. (J). 28.50 *(978-1-60753-466-2(5))* Amicus Publishing.

Rodger, Ellen. Ancient Egypt Inside Out. 2017. (Ancient Worlds Inside Out Ser.). (ENG.). 32p. (J). ***(978-0-7787-2874-0(9))***; (Illus.). pap. ***(978-0-7787-2888-7(9))*** Crabtree Publishing Co.

Sands, Emily. Egyptology Coloring Book. 2017. (Ologies Ser.). (ENG.). 64p. (J). (gr. 5). pap. 14.99 *(978-0-7636-9531-6(9))* Candlewick Pr.

—The Egyptology Handbook: A Course in the Wonders of Egypt. Steer, Dugald A., ed. 2005. (Ologies Ser.). (ENG., Illus.). 80p. (J). (gr. 4-7). 12.99 *(978-0-7636-2932-8(4))* Candlewick Pr.

Shea, Therese. Discovering Egyptian Dynasties. 2013. (Exploring African Civilizations Ser.). (Illus.). 64p. (J). (gr. 5-8). 31.95 *(978-1-4777-1881-0(8)*, Rosen Reference) Rosen Publishing Group, Inc., The.

—Mummies of Ancient Egypt. 2009. (Real Life Readers Ser.). 24p. (gr. 3-4). pap. 8.25 *(978-1-4358-0052-6(4)*, Rosen Classroom) Rosen Publishing Group, Inc., The.

Stewart, David. You Wouldn't Want to Be Tutankhamen! (Revised Edition) 2017. (You Wouldn't Want to... Ancient Civilizations Ser.). (ENG., Illus.). 32p. (J). lib. bdg. 29.00 *(978-0-531-23837-0(7)*, Watts, Franklin) Scholastic Library Publishing.

Strom, Laura Layton. The Egyptian Science Gazette. 2008. (Illus.). 36p. (J). pap. *(978-0-531-18813-2(2))* Children's Pr., Ltd.

The Treasures of Tutankhamun. (Butterfly Bks.). (ARA.). 48p. (YA). (gr. 5-8). 9.95 *(978-0-86685-485-6(1))* International Bk. Ctr., Inc.

Weil, Ann. The World's Most Amazing Pyramids, 1 vol. 2011. (Landmark Top Tens Ser.). (ENG., Illus.). 32p. (gr. 3-5). 30.65 *(978-1-4109-4240-1(6)*, Raintree Perspectives) Heinemann-Raintree.

Wood, Alix. Uncovering the Culture of Ancient Egypt, 01 vols., 1. 2016. (Archaeology & Ancient Cultures Ser.). (ENG.). 32p. (J). pap. 10.00 *(978-1-5081-4651-3(9)*, PowerKids Pr.) Rosen Publishing Group, Inc., The.

Woods, Michael & Woods, Mary B. The Tomb of King Tutankhamen. 2008. (Unearthing Ancient Worlds Ser.). (ENG., Illus.). 80p. (gr. 5-8). lib. bdg. 30.60 *(978-0-8225-7506-1(X))* Lerner Publishing Group.

Zoehfeld, Kathleen Weidner. The Curse of King Tut's Mummy. Nelson, Jim, illus. 2007. (Totally True Adventures Ser.). (ENG.). 112p. (J). (gr. 2-5). per. 4.99 *(978-0-375-83862-0(7)*, Random Hse. Bks. for Young Readers) Random Hse. Children's Bks.

EGYPT—CIVILIZATION

Ancient Egyptians. 2013. (Ladybird Histories Ser.). (ENG., Illus.). 64p. (J). (gr. 2-4). pap. 13.99 ***(978-0-7181-9622-6(8))*** Penguin Bks., Ltd. GBR. Dist: Independent Pubs. Group.

Asselin, Kristine Carlson. Pharaohs & Dynasties of Ancient Egypt, 1 vol. 2012. (Ancient Egyptian Civilization Ser.). (ENG., Illus.). 32p. (gr. 3-4). lib. bdg. 27.32 *(978-1-4296-7631-1(0)*, Fact Finders) Capstone Press of Coughlan Cos.

Barnham, Kay. Mangy Mummies, Menacing Pharaohs, & the Awful Afterlife: A Moth-Eaten History of the Extraordinary Egyptians! 2015. (Awfully Ancient Ser.). (ENG., Illus.). 32p. (J). (gr. 5-5). pap. 10.50 *(978-1-4824-3125-4(4))* Stevens, Gareth Publishing LLLP.

Bedwin, Christa & Kissock, Heather. Egyptians. 2016. (Illus.). 32p. *(978-1-5105-1098-2(2))* SmartBook Media, Inc.

Bell, Michael & Quie, Sarah. Ancient Egyptian Civilization. D'Ottavi, Francesca, illus. 2009. (Ancient Civilizations & Their Myths & Legends Ser.). 48p. (YA). (gr. 5-9). lib. bdg. 29.25 *(978-1-4042-8034-2(0))* Rosen Publishing Group, Inc., The.

Benchmark Education Company, LLC Staff. Pharaohs, Pyramids & Mummies Teacher's Guide. 2004. *(978-1-4108-2583-4(3))* Benchmark Education Co.

Benduhn, Tea. Ancient Egypt. 2007. (Life Long Ago Ser.). (Illus.). 24p. (gr. 1-4). pap. 8.15 *(978-0-8368-7786-1(1))*; lib. bdg. 22.00 *(978-0-8368-7781-6(0))* Stevens, Gareth Publishing LLLP. (Weekly Reader Leveled Readers).

Bodden, Valerie. Ancient Civilization: Egypt. 2015. (Ancient Civilization Ser.). (ENG.). 48p. (J). (gr. 5-8). pap. 12.00 *(978-0-89812-979-3(6)*, Creative Paperbacks) Creative Co., The.

—Egypt. 2014. (J). *(978-1-60818-392-0(0)*, Creative Education) Creative Co., The.

Boyer, Crispin. National Geographic Kids Everything Ancient Egypt: Dig into a Treasure Trove of Facts, Photos, & Fun. 2012. (National Geographic Kids Everything Ser.). (ENG., Illus.). 64p. (J). (gr. 3-7). lib. bdg. 25.90 *(978-1-4263-0841-3(8)*, National Geographic Children's Bks.) National Geographic Society.

Boyer, Crispin & National Geographic Kids Staff. Ancient Egypt: Dig into a Treasure Trove of Facts, Photos, & Fun! 2012. (National Geographic Kids Everything Ser.). (ENG., Illus.). 64p. (J). (gr. 3-7). pap. 12.95 *(978-1-4263-0840-6(X)*, National Geographic Children's Bks.) National Geographic Society.

Bramwell, Neil D. Ancient Egypt: A MyReportLinks. com Book. 2004. (Civilizations of the Ancient World Ser.). (Illus.). 48p. (J). lib. bdg. 26.60 *(978-0-7660-5252-9(4)*, MyReportLinks.com Bks.) Enslow Pubs., Inc.

—Discover Ancient Egypt. 2014. (Discover Ancient Civilizations Ser.). 104p. (J). pap. 10.95 *(978-1-4644-0333-0(3))*; (gr. 5-18). 33.27 *(978-0-7660-4195-0(6))* Enslow Pubs., Inc.

Burrell, Carol M. Scavella. Did Greek Soldiers Really Hide Inside the Trojan Horse? And Other Questions about the Ancient World. 2010. (Is That a Fact? Ser.). (ENG.). 40p. (gr. 4-6). lib. bdg. 26.60 *(978-0-7613-4912-9(X))* Lerner Publishing Group.

Catel, Patrick. What Did the Ancient Egyptians Do for Me?, 1 vol. 2010. (Linking the Past & Present Ser.). (ENG., Illus.). 32p. (gr. 3-6). 33.32 *(978-1-4329-3742-3(1))*; pap. 8.29 *(978-1-4329-3749-2(9))* Heinemann-Raintree. (Heinemann InfoSearch).

Challen, Paul C. & Challen, Paul. Life in Ancient Egypt. 2004. (Peoples of the Ancient World Ser.). (ENG., Illus.). 32p. (J). pap. *(978-0-7787-2068-3(3))*; lib. bdg. *(978-0-7787-2038-6(1))* Crabtree Publishing Co.

Chambers, Catherine. Egyptian Treasures. 2010. (Crabtree Connections Ser.). (ENG.). 24p. (J). (gr. 3-6). *(978-0-7787-9946-7(8))*; pap. *(978-0-7787-9968-9(9))* Crabtree Publishing Co.

Chrisp, Peter. Explore 360° the Tomb of Tutankhamen: Be Transported Back in Time with a Breathtaking 3D Tour. 2016. (ENG., Illus.). 48p. (J). (gr. 3-9). 18.99 *(978-0-7641-6821-5(5))* Barron's Educational Series, Inc.

Cohn, Jessica. The Ancient Egyptians. 2012. (Crafts from the Past Ser.). (Illus.). 48p. (J). (gr. 4-6). 31.95 *(978-1-4339-7701-5(X))*; pap. 14.05 *(978-1-4339-7702-2(8))* Stevens, Gareth Publishing LLLP.

Conklin, Wendy. You Are There! Ancient Egypt 1535 BC. 2016. (TIME for KIDS(r) Nonfiction Readers Ser.). (Illus.). 32p. (J). (gr. 6-6). 8.99 *(978-1-4938-3602-4(1))* Teacher Created Materials, Inc.

E
F
G

Cooke, Tim. The Ancient Egyptians. 2015. (At Home With... Ser.). (Illus.). 32p. (gr. 5-9). lib. bdg. 31.35 (978-1-78121-083-3(7), Brown Bear Bks.) Windmill Bks. Ltd. GBR. Dist: Black Rabbit Bks.

Corrick, James A. Gritty, Stinky Ancient Egypt: The Disgusting Details about Life in Ancient Egypt. 2010. (Disgusting History Ser.). (ENG.). 32p. (gr. 3-4). lib. bdg. 27.32 (978-1-4296-5406-7(6), Fact Finders) Capstone Press of Coughlan Cos.

Costain, Meredith. Ancient Egypt. 2013. (Discovery Education: Ancient Civilizations Ser.). (ENG., Illus.). 32p. (J). (gr. 3-6). pap. 10.00 (978-1-4777-0087-7(0)); lib. bdg. 25.25 (978-1-4777-0051-8(X)) Rosen Publishing Group, Inc., The. (PowerKids Pr.).

Coupe, Robert. Antiguo Egipto/Acient Egypt. 2011. 16p. pap. (978-607-404-320-4(5), Silver Dolphin en Español) Advanced Marketing, S. de R. L. de C. V.

Deady, Kathleen W. Ancient Egypt: Beyond the Pyramids, 1 vol. 2011. (Great Civilizations Ser.). (ENG.). 32p. (gr. 3-4). pap. 8.10 (978-1-4296-7235-1(8)); pap. 47.70 (978-1-4296-7236-8(6)); lib. bdg. 27.32 (978-1-4296-6830-9(X)) Capstone Press of Coughlan Cos. (Fact Finders).

Der Manuelian, Peter. 30-Second Ancient Egypt: The 50 Most Important Achievements of a Timeless Civilization, Each Explained in Half a Minute. 2014. (Illus.). 160p. (J). (978-1-4351-5178-9(X)) Metro Bks.

Dickinson, Clive. Mummies, Temples, & Tombs: More Real-Life Tales from Ancient Egypt. 2011. (Ancient Egyptians Ser.: 4). (ENG., Illus.). 96p. (J). (gr. 7). pap. 5.99 (978-0-00-715378-7(3), HarperCollins Children's Bks.) HarperCollins Pubs. Ltd. GBR. Dist: HarperCollins Pubs.

Doeden, Matt. Tools & Treasures of Ancient Egypt. 2014. (Searchlight Books: What Can We Learn from Early Civilizations? Ser.). (ENG., Illus.). 40p. (gr. 3-5). lib. bdg. 27.93 (978-1-4677-1429-7(1), Lerner Pubns.) Lerner Publishing Group.

Dorling Kindersley Publishing Staff. Pocket Genius: Ancient Egypt. 2016. (Pocket Genius Ser.). (ENG., Illus.). 160p. (J). (gr. 3-7). pap. 4.99 (978-1-4654-4524-7(2), DK Children) Dorling Kindersley Publishing, Inc.

England, Victoria. Top 10 Worst Things about Ancient Egypt. Antram, David, illus. 2012. (Top 10 Worst Ser.). (ENG.). 32p. (J). (gr. 3-6). pap. 10.50 (978-1-4339-6689-7(1)); lib. bdg. 26.60 (978-1-4339-6688-0(3)) Stevens, Gareth Publishing LLLP. (Gareth Stevens Learning Library).

Evan-Moor. History Pockets: Ancient Egypt, Grades 4-6+ 2003. (History Pockets Ser.). (ENG., Illus.). 96p. (J). (gr. 4-6). pap., suppl. ed. (978-1-55799-904-7(X), EMC 3706) Evan-Moor Educational Pubs.

Fine, Jil. Writing in Ancient Egypt. 2003. (Writing in the Ancient World Ser.). (Illus.). 24p. (J). lib. bdg. 22.60 (978-0-8239-6506-9(6), PowerKids Pr.) Rosen Publishing Group, Inc., The.

Fletcher, J. Exploring the Life, Myth, & Art of Ancient Egypt. 2009. (Civilizations of the World Ser.). (YA). (gr. 7-12). 42.60 (978-1-4358-5616-5(3)) Rosen Publishing Group, Inc., The.

Forest, Christopher, et al. Ancient Egyptian Civilization. 2012. (Ancient Egyptian Civilization Ser.). (ENG.). 32p. (gr. 3-4). pap. 286.20 (978-1-4296-8407-1(0)); pap. 16.20 (978-1-4296-8406-4(2)); lib. bdg. 163.92 (978-1-4296-8161-2(6)) Capstone Press of Coughlan Cos. (Fact Finders).

Gaff, Jackie. Ancient Egypt. 2016. (Excavating the Past Ser.). (ENG.). 48p. (gr. 4-6). pap. 8.99 (978-1-4846-3646-6(5), NA-h) Heinemann-Raintree.

Gallagher, Belinda. Why Why Why... Were the Pyramids Built? 2010. (Why Why Why Ser.). (Illus.). 32p. (J). (gr. 1-3). lib. bdg. 18.95 (978-1-4222-1590-6(3)) Mason Crest.

Ganeri, Anita. Mummies & Ancient Egypt. 2009. (History Explorers Ser.). (ENG.). 24p. (J). (gr. k-2). pap. 5.95 (978-1-84696-210-3(2), TickTock Books) Octopus Publishing Group GBR. Dist: Independent Pubs. Group.

—Pharaohs, Heros & Thieves: More Real-Life Tales from Ancient Egypt. 2003. (Ancient Egyptians Ser.: 3). (ENG., Illus.). 112p. (J). (gr. 7). pap. 7.99 (978-0-00-715377-0(5), HarperCollins Children's Bks.) HarperCollins Pubs. Ltd. GBR. Dist: HarperCollins Pubs.

Green, Jen. Egyptians. 2009. (Flashback History Ser.). (Illus.). 48p. (ENG.). (J). pap. 11.75 (978-1-4358-5511-3(6), 1300548, PowerKids Pr.); (YA). (gr. 3-6). lib. bdg. 29.25 (978-1-4358-5510-6(8)) Rosen Publishing Group, Inc., The.

—Hail! Ancient Egyptians. 2010. (ENG.). 32p. (J). (978-0-7787-6622-3(5)); pap. (978-0-7787-6629-2(2)) Crabtree Publishing Co.

Greenberg, Imogen. The Ancient Egyptians. Greenberg, Isabel, illus. 2016. (Discover... Ser.). (ENG.). 32p. (J). (gr. 3-7). 14.99 (978-1-84780-855-4(7), Frances Lincoln Children's Bks.) Quarto Publishing Group UK GBR. Dist: Hachette Bk. Group.

Gunderson, Jessica. Your Life As a Pharaoh in Ancient Egypt, 1 vol. Ebbeler, Jeff, illus. 2012. (Way It Was Ser.). (ENG.). 32p. (gr. 2-3). lib. bdg. 26.65 (978-1-4048-7371-1(6)) Picture Window Bks.

Gunderson, Jessica Sarah. Your Life As a Pharaoh in Ancient Egypt, 1 vol. Ebbeler, Jeff, illus. 2012. (Way It Was Ser.). (ENG.). 32p. (gr. 2-3). pap. 8.95 (978-1-4048-7744-3(4)) Picture Window Bks.

Guy, John. Egyptian Life. 2006. (Illus.). 29p. (J). per. (978-1-59905-052-2(8)) Saddleback Educational Publishing, Inc.

Hardyman, Robyn. Horrible Jobs in Ancient Egypt, Vol. 1. 2014. (History's Most Horrible Jobs Ser.). (ENG.). 48p. (J). (gr. 5-6). 31.95 (978-1-4824-0324-4(2)) Stevens, Gareth Publishing LLLP.

Harness, Cheryl. Ghosts of the Nile. Harness, Cheryl, illus. 2010. (ENG., Illus.). 32p. (J). (gr. 2-5). 13.99 (978-1-4424-2200-1(9), Simon & Schuster Bks. For Young Readers) Simon & Schuster Bks. For Young Readers.

Hewitt, Sally. The Egyptians. 2007. (Starting History/Watts Ser.). (Illus.). 30p. (J). (gr. 4-7). lib. bdg. 28.50 (978-1-59920-044-6(9)) Black Rabbit Bks.

Hibbert, Clare. Rich & Poor in Ancient Egypt. 2005. (Rich & Poor in Ser.). (Illus.). 32p. (YA). (gr. 4-7). lib. bdg. 27.10 (978-1-58340-720-2(0)) Black Rabbit Bks.

Hinds, Kathryn. Life in Ancient Egypt, 4 bks., Set. Incl. City. 80p. (gr. 6-7). lib. bdg. 34.21 (978-0-7614-2184-9(X)); Countryside. 70p. (J). (gr. 4-7). lib. bdg. 32.79 (978-0-7614-2185-6(8)); Pharaoh's Court. 80p. (gr. 6-7). lib. bdg. 34.21 (978-0-7614-2183-2(1)); (Illus.). 2006. 2007. Set lib. bdg. 131.14 (978-0-7614-2182-5(3), Benchmark Bks.) Marshall Cavendish Corp.

Hollar, Sherman. Ancient Egypt. 2011. (J). lib. bdg. 31.70 (978-1-61530-523-0(8)) Rosen Publishing Group, Inc., The.

Holm, Kirsten C. Everyday Life in Ancient Egypt. 2012. (Jr. Graphic Ancient Civilizations Ser.). (ENG.). 24p. (J). (gr. 3-6). pap. 10.60 (978-1-4488-6391-4(0)); lib. bdg. 25.25 (978-1-4488-6216-0(7)) Rosen Publishing Group, Inc., The. (PowerKids Pr.).

Hoobler, Dorothy & Hoobler, Thomas. Where Are the Great Pyramids? 2015. (Where Is... ? Ser.). lib. bdg. 16.00 (978-0-606-37547-4(3)) Turtleback Bks.

Hoobler, Dorothy, et al. Where Are the Great Pyramids? Hoare, Jerry, illus. 2015. (Where Is? Ser.). (ENG.). 112p. (J). (gr. 3-7). 5.99 (978-0-448-48409-9(9), Grosset & Dunlap) Penguin Young Readers Group.

Hunt, Norman Bancroft. Living in Ancient Egypt. 2008. (Living in the Ancient World Ser.). 96p. (YA). (gr. 7-12). 35.00 (978-0-8160-6338-3(9)) Facts On File, Inc.

Hurdman, Charlotte, et al. Find Out about Ancient Egypt, Rome & Greece: Exploring the Great Classical Civilizations, with 60 Step-By-Step Projects & 1500 Exciting Images. 2013. (ENG., Illus.). 256p. (J). (gr. 3-7). 17.99 (978-1-84322-804-2(1), Armadillo) Anness Publishing GBR. Dist: National Bk. Network.

Hyde, Natalie. King Tut. 2013. (ENG., Illus.). 48p. (J). (978-0-7787-1172-8(2)); pap. (978-0-7787-1181-0(1)) Crabtree Publishing Co.

Jennings, Ken. Ancient Egypt. Lowery, Mike, illus. 2015. (Ken Jennings' Junior Genius Guides). (ENG.). 160p. (J). (gr. 3-5). 19.99 (978-1-4814-2953-5(1), Little Simon) Little Simon.

Jordan, Shirley J. Egypt, 1 vol. 2007. (Primary Source Readers Ser.). (ENG.). 32p. (J). (gr. 5-5). pap. 8.99 (978-0-7439-0428-5(1)) Shell Educational Publishing.

Kaplan, Leslie C. Art & Religion in Ancient Egypt. 2004. (Primary Sources of Ancient Civilizations Ser.). (ENG.). 24p. (gr. 4-8). pap. 8.25 (978-0-8239-8932-4(1), PowerKids Pr.) Rosen Publishing Group, Inc., The.

—Land & Resources in Ancient Egypt. 2004. (Primary Sources of Ancient Civilizations Ser.). (Illus.). 24p. (J). lib. bdg. 22.60 (978-0-8239-6781-0(6), PowerKids Pr.) Rosen Publishing Group, Inc., The.

—Land & Resources of Ancient Egypt. (Primary Sources of Ancient Civilizations Ser.). 24p. 2009. (gr. 3-3). 42.50 (978-1-60851-560-8(5)) 2004. (ENG., Illus.). (gr. 4-8). pap. 8.25 (978-0-8239-8931-7(3)) Rosen Publishing Group, Inc., The. (PowerKids Pr.).

—Technology of Ancient Egypt. 2004. (Primary Sources of Ancient Civilizations Ser.). (ENG., Illus.). 24p. (gr. 4-8). pap. 8.25 (978-0-8239-8934-8(8), PowerKids Pr.) Rosen Publishing Group, Inc., The.

Kerrigan, Michael. Egyptians. 2010. (Ancients in Their Own Words Ser.). 64p. (gr. 5). 32.79 (978-1-60870-064-6(X)) Marshall Cavendish Corp.

Keyes, Anna. Pharaohs, Pyramids & Mummies: Set Of 6. 2011. (Navigators Ser.). (J). pap. 50.00 net. (978-1-4108-2568-1(X)) Benchmark Education Co.

King, David C. Projects about Ancient Egypt. 2006. (Hands-On History Ser.). (Illus.). 48p. (gr. 3-7). lib. bdg. 21.95 (978-0-7614-2258-7(7), Benchmark Bks.) Marshall Cavendish Corp.

Krieger, Emily. National Geographic Kids Funny Fill-In: My Ancient Egypt Adventure. 2014. (NG Kids Funny Fill In Ser.). (ENG.). 48p. (J). (gr. 3-7). pap. 4.99 (978-1-4263-1707-1(7), National Geographic Children's Bks.) National Geographic Society.

Lace, William W. Mummification & Death Rituals of Ancient Egypt. 2012. (ENG., Illus.). 80p. (J). lib. bdg. (978-1-60152-254-2(1)) ReferencePoint Pr., Inc.

Laidlaw, Jill A. Quick Expert: Ancient Egypt. 2010. (Crabtree Connections Ser.). (ENG.). 24p. (J). (gr. 3-6). (978-0-7787-9942-9(5)); pap. (978-0-7787-9964-1(6)) Crabtree Publishing Co.

—Visit Egypt! 2010. (Crabtree Connections Ser.). (ENG.). 24p. (J). (gr. 3-6). (978-0-7787-9956-6(5)); pap. (978-0-7787-9978-8(6)) Crabtree Publishing Co.

Landau, Elaine. Exploring Ancient Egypt with Elaine Landau. 2005. (Exploring Ancient Civilizations with Elaine Landau Ser.). (Illus.). 48p. (J). (gr. 4-7). lib. bdg. 25.27 (978-0-7660-2339-0(7), Enslow Elementary) Enslow Pubs., Inc.

MacDonald, Fiona. Ancient Egyptians: An Epic Lost Civilisation Brought Vividly to Life. 2004. (ENG., Illus.). 64p. (J). (gr. 4-7). 17.99 (978-0-00-715376-3(7)) HarperCollins Pubs. Ltd. GBR. Dist: Independent Pubs. Group.

—The Ancient Egyptians: Dress, Eat, Write & Play Just Like the Egyptians. 2008. (Hands-on History Ser.). (ENG., Illus.). 32p. (J). (gr. 3-7). pap. (978-0-7787-4069-8(2)) Crabtree Publishing Co.

Mahmoud, Zaki Naguib. The Land & People of Egypt. 2012. 142p. 40.95 (978-1-258-23287-0(1)); pap. 25.95 (978-1-258-24914-4(6)) Literary Licensing, LLC.

Malam, John. The Egyptians. 2011. (Dig It: History from Objects Ser.). (Illus.). 32p. (YA). (gr. 2-5). lib. bdg. 26.50 (978-1-4488-3283-5(7)) Rosen Publishing Group, Inc., The.

Manning, Mick & Granström, Brita. Pharaoh's Egypt. Manning, Mick & Granström, Brita, illus. 2015. (Fly on the Wall Ser.). (ENG., Illus.). 40p. (J). (gr. k-3). pap. 9.99 (978-1-84780-623-9(6), Frances Lincoln) Quarto Publishing Group UK GBR. Dist: Hachette Bk. Group.

Masiello, Ralph. Ralph Masiello's Ancient Egypt Drawing Book. Masiello, Ralph, illus. 2008. (Ralph Masiello's Drawing Bks.). (ENG., Illus.). 40p. (J). (gr. 3-7). pap. 7.95 (978-1-57091-534-5(2)) Charlesbridge Publishing, Inc.

McCall, Henrietta. Pyramid. 2015. (Time Shift History Ser.). (Illus.). 32p. (gr. 3-6). 31.35 (978-1-905638-63-5(9)) Book Hse. GBR. Dist: Black Rabbit Bks.

Millard, Anne. The Great Pyramid of Giza. 2005. (Places in History Ser.). (Illus.). 48p. (gr. 5-12). pap. 14.05 (978-0-8368-5818-1(2), World Almanac Library) Stevens, Gareth Publishing LLLP.

Morley, Jacqueline. How to Be an Egyptian Princess. Hewetson, Nicholas J., illus. (How to Be Ser.). (ENG.). 32p. (J). (gr. 4-7). 2008. pap. 5.95 (978-1-4263-0246-6(0)) 2006. 14.95 (978-0-7922-7494-0(6)) 2006. lib. bdg. 21.90 (978-0-7922-7548-0(9)) National Geographic Society. (National Geographic Children's Bks.).

—Inside the Tomb of Tutankhamun. James, John, illus. 2005. (ENG.). 48p. (J). (gr. 3-7). 19.95 (978-1-59270-042-4(X)) Enchanted Lion Bks., LLC.

—You Wouldn't Want to Be a Pyramid Builder! A Hazardous Job You'd Rather Not Have. 2004. (You Wouldn't Want to Ser.). (ENG., Illus.). 32p. (J). 29.00 (978-0-531-12351-5(0)) Scholastic Library Publishing.

Morris, Neil. Ancient Egypt. 2003. (Uncovering History Ser.). (Illus.). 46p. (J). lib. bdg. 28.50 (978-1-58340-247-4(0)) Black Rabbit Bks.

Moscovitch, Arlene. Egypt - The Culture. 3rd rev. ed. 2007. (Lands, Peoples & Cultures Ser.). (ENG., Illus.). 32p. (J). (gr. 4-9). pap. (978-0-7787-9675-6(2)) Crabtree Publishing Co.

Murray, Laura K. Exploring Ancient Egypt. 2018. (ENG.). 32p. (gr. 3-6). **(978-1-63235-462-4(4)**, 12-Story Library) Pr. Room Editions LLC.

Naden, Corinne J. & Blue, Rose. Ancient Egyptians & the Pyramids. 2003. (J). (978-1-58417-310-6(6)); pap. (978-1-58417-311-3(4)) Lake Street Pubs.

Nardo, Don. Ancient Egypt. 2006. (World History Ser.). (ENG., Illus.). 104p. (J). (gr. 3-5). lib. bdg. 33.45 (978-1-59018-857-6(8), 1256847, Lucent Bks.) Cengage Gale.

—Ancient Greece, 1 vol. 2012. (Exploring the Ancient World Ser.). (ENG., Illus.). 48p. (gr. 5-6). 29.32 (978-0-7565-4566-6(8)) Compass Point Bks.

—Cause & Effect: Ancient Egypt. 2017. (ENG.). 80p. (YA). (gr. 5-12). 39.93 **(978-1-68282-150-3(1))** ReferencePoint Pr., Inc.

Nardo, Don. Daily Life in Ancient Egypt. 2015. (Daily Life in Ancient Civilizations Ser.). (ENG., Illus.). 48p. (gr. 3-6). pap. 8.99 (978-1-4846-0834-0(8), Heinemann InfoSearch) Heinemann-Raintree.

National Geographic Learning, National Geographic Learning. Secrets of the Mummies. 2005. (Reader's Workshop Ser.). (ENG.). (C). pap. 21.95 (978-0-7362-2809-1(8)) National Geographic School Publishing, Inc.

Ohlin, Nancy. Ancient Egypt. Larkum, Adam, illus. 2016. (Blast Back! Ser.). (ENG.). 112p. (J). (gr. 2-5). pap. 5.99 (978-1-4998-0116-3(5)) Little Bee Books Inc.

Orr, Tamra. Ancient Egypt. (Explore Ancient Worlds Ser.). (J). 2012. (gr. 3-6). lib. bdg. 29.95 (978-1-61228-279-4(2)) 2009. (Illus.). 64p. (gr. 4-8). lib. bdg. 33.95 (978-1-58415-821-9(2)) Mitchell Lane Pubs., Inc.

Owings, Lisa. What We Get from Egyptian Mythology. 2015. (21st Century Skills Library: Mythology & Culture Ser.). (ENG., Illus.). 32p. (J). (gr. 3-6). pap. 14.21 (978-1-63188-928-8(1), 205973) Cherry Lake Publishing.

Pavan, Toni. Egypt, Nubia, & Kush: Set Of 6. 2011. (Navigators Ser.). (J). pap. 50.00 net. (978-1-4108-5113-0(3)) Benchmark Education Co.

—Egypt, Nubia, & Kush: Text Pairs. 2008. (Bridges/Navigators Ser.). (J). (gr. 6). 94.00 (978-1-4108-8434-3(1)) Benchmark Education Co.

Payne, Elizabeth. Pharaohs of Ancient Egypt. 2014. 16.00 (978-1-63419-724-3(0)) Perfection Learning Corp.

Pemberton, Delia. The Civilization of Ancient Egypt. 2012. (Illustrated History of the Ancient World Ser.). (ENG., Illus.). 232p. (J). (gr. 7-12). 53.25 (978-1-4488-8500-8(0)) Rosen Publishing Group, Inc., The.

Perl, Lila. The Ancient Egyptians. 2005. (People of the Ancient World Ser.). (ENG., Illus.). 112p. (J). (gr. 6-8). pap. 9.95 (978-0-531-16738-0(0), Watts, Franklin) Scholastic Library Publishing.

Phipps, Liza & Thompson, Avril. Ancient Egyptians. 2017. (History Showtime Ser.). (ENG., Illus.). 32p. (J). (gr. 2-4). pap. 11.99 (978-1-4451-1486-6(0), Franklin Watts) Hachette Children's Group GBR. Dist: Hachette Bk. Group.

Platt, Richard. The Egyptians. Lawrence, David, illus. 2011. (How They Made Things Work! Ser.). 32p. (J). (gr. 2-5). lib. bdg. 28.50 (978-1-59771-287-3(6)) Sea-To-Sea Pubns.

Powell, Jillian. The Egyptians. 2010. (Gruesome Truth about Ser.). (ENG.). 32p. (J). (gr. 4-6). lib. bdg. 22.60 (978-1-61533-217-5(0)) Windmill Bks.

Randolph, Joanne, ed. Living & Working in Ancient Egypt. 2017. (Back in Time Ser.). 48p. (J). (gr. 5-6). 27.93 **(978-0-7660-8967-9(3))** Enslow Pubs., Inc.

Ridley, Sarah. Life in Ancient Egypt. 2015. (Everyday History Ser.). (Illus.). 32p. (J). 31.35 (978-1-59920-949-4(7)) Black Rabbit Bks.

Riggs, Sandy. Three Ancient Communities: Text Pairs. 2008. (Bridges/Navigators Ser.). (J). (gr. 3). 89.00 (978-1-4108-8374-2(4)) Benchmark Education Co.

Rockwood, Leigh. Ancient Egyptian Culture. 2013. (Spotlight on Ancient Civilizations: Egypt Ser.). (ENG.). 24p. (J). (gr. 3-4). pap. 10.00 (978-1-4777-0859-0(6)); lib. bdg. 23.60 (978-1-4777-0763-0(8)) Rosen Publishing Group, Inc., The. (PowerKids Pr.).

—Ancient Egyptian Technology. 2013. (Spotlight on Ancient Civilizations: Egypt Ser.). (ENG.). 24p. (J). (gr. 3-4). 23.60 (978-1-4777-0768-5(9)); pap. 10.00 (978-1-4777-0869-9(3)) Rosen Publishing Group, Inc., The. (PowerKids Pr.).

Rodger, Ellen. Ancient Egypt Inside Out. 2017. (Ancient Worlds Inside Out Ser.). (ENG.). 32p. (J). **(978-0-7787-2874-0(9))**; (Illus.). pap. **(978-0-7787-2888-7(9))** Crabtree Publishing Co.

Ross, Stewart. Ancient Egypt. 2006. (Ancient Civilizations Ser.). (Illus.). 48p. (gr. 5-12). lib. bdg. 31.00 (978-0-8368-6189-1(2), Gareth Stevens Secondary Library) Stevens, Gareth Publishing LLLP.

Samuels, Charlie. Technology in Ancient Egypt. 2013. (Technology in the Ancient World Ser.). 48p. (J). (gr. 4-6). pap. 14.05 (978-1-4339-9629-0(4)); pap. 84.30 (978-1-4339-9630-6(8)); (ENG., Illus.). lib. bdg. 31.95 (978-1-4339-9628-3(6)) Stevens, Gareth Publishing LLLP.

Santillian, Beatriz & Thomas, Susanna. Snefru: Pharaoh of the 4th Dynasty. 2017. (Leaders of the Ancient World Ser.). 112p. (J). (gr. 12-11). 37.10 **(978-1-5081-7491-2(1)**, Rosen Young Adult) Rosen Publishing Group, Inc., The.

Schimel, Lawrence. If You Were a Kid Building a Pyramid. 2017. (If You Were a Kid Ser.). (ENG.). 32p. (J). lib. bdg. 26.00 **(978-0-531-23748-9(6)**, Children's Pr.) Scholastic Library Publishing.

—If You Were a Kid Building a Pyramid. Ely, Jennifer W., illus. 2017. (If You Were a Kid Ser.). (ENG.). 32p. (J). pap. 7.95 **(978-0-531-23949-0(7)**, Children's Pr.) Scholastic Library Publishing.

Sharp, Anne Wallace. Women of Ancient Egypt. 2005. (Women in History Ser.). (ENG., Illus.). 112p. (YA). (gr. 7-10). lib. bdg. 33.45 (978-1-59018-361-8(4), Lucent Bks.) Cengage Gale.

Shea, Therese. Discovering Egyptian Dynasties. 2013. (Exploring African Civilizations Ser.). (Illus.). 64p. (J). (gr. 5-8). 31.95 (978-1-4777-1881-0(8), Rosen Reference) Rosen Publishing Group, Inc., The.

Shuter, Jane. Ancient Egypt. 2010. (Exploring the Ancient World Ser.). (Illus.). 64p. (YA). (gr. 6-8). lib. bdg. 34.60 (978-1-4339-4158-0(9), Gareth Stevens Secondary Library) Stevens, Gareth Publishing LLLP.

—How the Ancient Egyptians Lived. 2010. (Life in Ancient Times Ser.). (ENG.). 32p. (J). (gr. 3-6). lib. bdg. 26.60 (978-1-4339-4088-0(4), Gareth Stevens Learning Library) Stevens, Gareth Publishing LLLP.

Smith, Miranda & Steele, Philip. Ancient Worlds: A Thrilling Adventure Through the Ancient Worlds. 2016. (Navigators Ser.). (ENG., Illus.). 80p. (J). 15.99 (978-0-7534-7239-2(2), 9780753472392, Kingfisher) Roaring Brook Pr.

Snedden, Robert. Ancient Egypt. 2009. (Technology in Times Past Ser.). (Illus.). 46p. (J). (gr. 4-7). pap. (978-1-897563-61-8(2)) Saunders Bk. Co.

Solodky, M. The Technology of Ancient Egypt. (Technology of the Ancient World Ser.). 48p. 2009. (gr. 6-6). 61.20 (978-1-60854-239-0(4), Rosen Reference) 2005. (Illus.). (J). (gr. 5-8). lib. bdg. 29.25 (978-1-4042-0557-4(8)) Rosen Publishing Group, Inc., The.

Somerville, Charles C. E Is for Egypt. Somerville, Charles C., illus. 2015. (Is for Alphabet Ser.). (ENG., Illus.). 32p. (J). (gr. -1-3). pap. 9.99 (978-1-907432-15-6(9)) Hogs Back Bks. GBR. Dist: Independent Pubs. Group.

Spotlight on Ancient Civilizations: Egypt. 2013. (Spotlight on Ancient Civilizations: Egypt Ser.). 24p. (J). (gr. 3-4). (ENG.). 141.60 (978-1-4777-1142-2(2)); (ENG.). pap. 60.00 (978-1-4777-1243-6(7)); pap. 297.00 (978-1-4777-1244-3(5)) Rosen Publishing Group, Inc., The. (PowerKids Pr.).

Springer, Lisa & Morris, Neil. Art & Culture of Ancient Egypt. 2010. (Ancient Art & Cultures Ser.). (Illus.). 40p. (J). pap. 11.75 (978-1-61532-881-9(5)); (YA). (gr. 5-8). lib. bdg. 26.50 (978-1-4358-3589-4(1)) Rosen Publishing Group, Inc., The. (Rosen Reference).

Stanborough, Rebecca. Great Pyramid of Giza. 2016. (Engineering Wonders Ser.). (ENG., Illus.). 32p. (gr. 3-4). lib. bdg. 27.32 (978-1-4914-8195-0(1), Fact Finders) Capstone Press of Coughlan Cos.

Steedman, Scott. History News: the Egyptian News. 2009. (History News Ser.). (ENG., Illus.). 32p. (J). (gr. 4-7). pap. 7.99 (978-0-7636-4198-6(7)) Candlewick Pr.

Steele, Philip. Ancient Egypt. 2009. (Passport to the Past Ser.). (Illus.). 64p. (J). (gr. 4-7). lib. bdg. 31.95 (978-1-4358-5173-3(0)) Rosen Publishing Group, Inc., The.

—Hands-On History! Ancient Egypt: Find Out about the Land of the Pharaohs, with 15 Step-by-Step Projects & over 400 Exciting Pictures. 2013. (ENG., Illus.). 64p. 12.99 (978-1-84322-963-6(3)) Anness Publishing GBR. Dist: National Bk. Network.

—I Wonder Why Pyramids Were Built. 2011. (I Wonder Why Ser.). (ENG., Illus.). 32p. (J). (gr. k-3). pap. 6.99 (978-0-7534-6527-1(2), 9780753465271, Kingfisher) Roaring Brook Pr.

Thomas, Susanna. Snefru: The Pyramid Builder. 2009. (Ancient Leaders Ser.). 112p. (gr. 5-8). 66.50 (978-1-61511-428-3(9), Rosen Reference) Rosen Publishing Group, Inc., The.

Turnbull, Stephanie. Egyptians. (Beginners Social Studies). 32p. (J). (gr. 1-18). lib. bdg. 12.99 (978-1-58086-656-9(5), Usborne) EDC Publishing.

—Egyptians. King, Colin, illus. 2007. (Usborne Beginners Ser.). 32p. (J). 4.99 (978-0-7945-1344-3(1), Usborne) EDC Publishing.

—Egyptians Kid Kit. 2007. (Kid Kits Ser.). (Illus.). (J). 32p. 9.99 (978-1-60130-028-7(X)); 9.99 (978-1-60130-029-4(8)) EDC Publishing.

Van Vleet, Carmella. Explore Ancient Egypt! 25 Great Projects, Activities, Experiments. Kim, Alex, illus. 2006. (Explore Your World Ser.). (ENG.). 96p. (J). (gr. k-4). pap. 12.95 (978-0-9792268-3-0(X)) Octavio Publishing.

Waldron, Melanie. Geography Matters in Ancient Egypt. 2015. (Geography Matters in Ancient Civilizations Ser.). (ENG., Illus.). 48p. (gr. 3-6). 33.32 (978-1-4846-0962-0(X), Heinemann InfoSearch) Heinemann-Raintree.

Walker, Jane. Ancient Egypt. 2013. (Illus.). 48p. (J). (978-1-4351-5081-2(3)) Barnes & Noble, Inc.

West, David. The Ancient Egyptians. 2016. (Discovering Ancient Civilizations Ser.). (ENG.). 32p. (J). (gr. 3-3). pap. 10.50 (978-1-4824-5067-5(4)) Stevens, Gareth Publishing LLLP.

Winters, Kay. Voices of Ancient Egypt. Moser, Barry, illus. 2003. (ENG.). 32p. (J). (gr. 3-7). 16.95 (978-0-7922-7560-2(8), National Geographic Children's Bks.) National Geographic Society.

Wood, Alix. Uncovering the Culture of Ancient Egypt, 01 vols., 1. 2016. (Archaeology & Ancient Cultures Ser.). (ENG.). 32p. (J). pap. 10.00 (978-1-5081-4651-3(9), PowerKids Pr.) Rosen Publishing Group, Inc., The.

World Book, Inc Staff, contrib. by. Ancient Egyptians. 2009. (978-0-7166-2129-4(0)) World Bk., Inc.

—The Mystery of Tutankhamun. 2015. (Illus.). 48p. (J). (978-0-7166-2678-7(0)) World Bk., Inc.

Wroble, Lisa A. Kids in Ancient Egypt. (Kids Throughout History Ser.). 24p. 2009. (gr. 3-3). 42.50 (978-1-61513-894-4(3)) 2004. (J). 22.60 (978-0-8239-6931-9(2)) Rosen Publishing Group, Inc., The. (PowerKids Pr.).

Yomtov, Nelson. Ancient Egypt. 2012. (Ancient World Ser.). (ENG., Illus.). 112p. (J). pap. 9.95 (978-0-531-25977-1(3)); lib. bdg. 34.00 (978-0-531-25177-5(2)) Scholastic Library Publishing.

EGYPT—FICTION

Adler, David A. Brothers in Egypt. abr. ed. (Prince of Egypt Ser.). (ENG.). 64p. pap. (978-0-582-36482-0(5)) Addison-Wesley Longman, Inc.

Adlington, L. J. Glittering Eye. 2009. (ENG.). 320p. (J). (gr. 4-6). pap. 8.99 *(978-0-340-95681-6(X))* Hodder & Stoughton GBR. Dist: Hachette Bk. Group.
Al Kalifa & the Nile, 6, Pack. (Bookweb Ser.). 32p. (gr. 5-18). 34.00 *(978-0-7635-3788-3(8))* Rigby Education.
Alrawi, Karim. The Mouse Who Saved Egypt. Willey, Bee, illus. 2011. 32p. (J). (gr. -1-3). 16.95 *(978-1-56656-856-2(0),* Crocodile Bks.) Interlink Publishing Group, Inc.
Ames, Heidi L. Gisselle's Adventures in Color. del Valle, Clara J., photos by. 2010. (Illus.). 36p. pap. 14.95 *(978-1-60844-436-6(8))* Dog Ear Publishing, LLC.
Angel, Ido. Vipo in Egypt: A Pyramid Mystery. 2015. (AV2 Animated Storytime Ser.). (ENG.). (J). lib. bdg. 29.99 *(978-1-4896-3922-6(5),* AV2 by Weigl) Weigl Pubs., Inc.
Arnold, Edward Ronny. Rashida. 2003. 110p. (YA). pap. 7.99 *(978-0-9721216-6-8(8),* 0972121668) Computer Classics (R).
Arnold, George. Pharaohs' Follies: Kits of the CIA Adventures in Egypt. Kablaoui, Rasmia, tr. Eckhardt, Jason C., illus. 2016. (Cats of the CIA Ser.). (ENG.). (YA). (gr. 7-12). pap. 19.95 ***(978-1-68179-074-9(2),*** Eakin Pr.) Eakin Pr.
Bargellini, Demetrio, et al. The Secret of the Sphinx. Cooper-McGuinness, Nanette, tr. 2009. (Geronimo Stilton Graphic Novels Ser.). (ENG., Illus.). 56p. (J). (gr. 2-6). 9.99 *(978-1-59707-159-8(5),* 9781597071598) Papercutz.
Barrett, Tracy. The Case That Time Forgot. 2011. (Sherlock Files Ser.: 3). (ENG., Illus.). 176p. (J). (gr. 3-7). pap. 7.99 *(978-0-312-56358-5(2),* 9780312563585) Square Fish.
Bastet - Evaluation Guide: Evaluation Guide. 2006. (J). *(978-1-55942-400-4(1))* Witcher Productions.
Baum, L. Frank. The Boy Fortune Hunters in Egypt. 2013. (Dover Children's Classics Ser.). (ENG., Illus.). 304p. (J). (gr. 3-8). pap. 12.99 *(978-0-486-49085-4(8))* Dover Pubns., Inc.
Bradbury, Jennifer. Wrapped. 2011. (ENG., Illus.). 320p. (YA). (gr. 7-18). 16.99 *(978-1-4169-9007-9(0),* Atheneum Bks. for Young Readers) Simon & Schuster Children's Publishing.
Bradman, Tony. The Mummy Family Find Fame. 2006. (Red Bananas Ser.). (ENG., Illus.). 48p. (J). (gr. -1-3). lib. bdg. *(978-0-7787-1076-9(9))* Crabtree Publishing Co.
Bright, J. E. Savage Sands, 1 vol. Schoening, Dan, illus. 2011. (Green Lantern Ser.). (ENG.). 56p. (gr. 2-3). pap. 4.95 *(978-1-4342-3405-6(3));* lib. bdg. 26.65 *(978-1-4342-2619-8(0))* Stone Arch Bks. (DC Super Heroes).
Brisland, Toni. DemiChat & the Lost Mummy. de los reyes Cruz, Cheryl, illus. 2013. 142p. (J). pap. 14.95 *(978-1-60131-173-3(7))* Big Tent Bks.
Buchanan, Penelope. In the Spell of an Ibis: The Education of Minemheb the Scribe. Barnet, Nancy, illus. 2004. 80p. pap. *(978-0-940717-82-4(4))* Cleveland Museum of Art.
Classic Goosebumps & Stine, R. L. The Curse of the Mummy's Tomb. 2009. (Classic Goosebumps Ser.: 6). (ENG.). 160p. (J). (gr. 3-7). 6.99 *(978-0-545-03523-1(6),* Scholastic Paperbacks) Scholastic, Inc.
Cole, Frank L. The Guardians of the Finisher's Fury (Guardians 3) 2013. pap. 16.99 *(978-1-4621-1221-0(8),* Horizon Pubs.) Cedar Fort, Inc./CFI Distribution.
Corwin, Susan Simon. The Cryptic Cat. Corwin, Stuart, illus. 2006. 99p. (YA). *(978-0-9790632-0-6(5))* Lucky Duck Designs.
Crow, Stanford. Lazy Hero Cat of Egypt. Hemmingson, Nancy S., illus. 2013. 24p. 24.00 *(978-1-940021-01-0(4))* Bliss Group.
Cuentos Egipcios. (SPA., Illus.). (YA). 11.95 *(978-84-7281-068-6(2),* AF1068) Auriga, Ediciones S.A. ESP. Dist: Continental Bk. Co., Inc.
The Curse of the Nile. 2008. (Looney Tunes 8*8 Ser.). 24p. pap. *(978-1-4075-2639-3(1));* pap. *(978-1-4075-2629-4(4))* Parragon, Inc.
Davie, Jan. Stairway to the Stars. 2005. 76p. pap. *(978-1-84401-569-6(6))* Athena Pr.
De Gieter, Lucien. The Evil Mummies. Spear, Luke, tr. from FRE. 2010. (Papyrus Ser.: 4). (ENG., Illus.). 46p. (J). (gr. 4-7). pap. 11.95 *(978-1-84918-027-6(X))* CineBook GBR. Dist: National Bk. Network.
—The Rameses' Revenge. Spear, Luke, tr. from FRE. 2007. (Papyrus Ser.: 1). (ENG., Illus.). 48p. (J). (gr. 4-7). pap. 11.95 *(978-1-905460-35-9(X))* CineBook GBR. Dist: National Bk. Network.
De la Cruz, Melissa. Lost in Time. 2012. (Blue Bloods Ser.). (ENG.). 368p. (J). (gr. 5-9). pap. 8.99 *(978-1-4231-3413-8(3))* Hyperion Pr.
Dewees-Gilger, Connie. Isla Saves Egypt. Bouthyette, Valerie, illus. 2013. (ENG.). (J). 14.95 *(978-1-62086-375-6(8))* Mascot Bks., Inc.
Diaz, S. Jemmy & the Little Spider of Hope. 2012. 40p. pap. 20.99 *(978-1-4772-7032-5(9))* AuthorHouse.
Diedrich, Ann Goshia. Randal the Flannel Camel. 2012. 24p. pap. 17.99 *(978-1-4685-8822-4(2))* AuthorHouse.
Dolan, Penny. The Egyptian Cat Mystery. 2015. (Race Further with Reading Ser.). (ENG., Illus.). 48p. (J). *(978-0-7787-2060-7(8))* Crabtree Publishing Co.
Doller, Trish. In a Perfect World. 2017. (ENG., Illus.). 304p. (YA). (gr. 7). 18.99 ***(978-1-4814-7988-2(1),*** Simon Pulse) Simon Pulse.
Doyle, Arthur Conan. A Desert Drama: Being the Tragedy of the Korosko. 2007. (ENG.). 160p. pap. 19.99 *(978-1-4346-4997-3(0));* 172p. pap. 21.99 *(978-1-4346-4998-0(9))* Creative Media Partners, LLC.
Doyle, Bill. Trapped! The 2031 Journal of Otis Fitzmorgan. 6th ed. 2006. (ENG., Illus.). 144p. (J). (gr. 3-7). per. 16.99 *(978-0-316-05754-7(1))* Little, Brown Bks. for Young Readers.
Doyle, Bill H. Betrayed! The 1977 Journal of Zeke Moorie. 4th ed. 2006. (ENG., Illus.). 144p. (J). (gr. 3-7). per. 16.99 *(978-0-316-05741-7(X))* Little, Brown Bks. for Young Readers.
Duey, Kathleen. Rex. Epstein, Eugene, illus. Epstein, Eugene, photos by. 2006. (Time Soldiers Ser.: Bk. 1). (ENG.). 96p. (gr. 4-7). 24.21 *(978-1-59961-225-6(9))* Spotlight.
Foley, Ryan. The Treasured Thief. Nagar, Sachin, illus. 2012. (Campfire Graphic Novels Ser.). (ENG.). 64p. (YA). (gr. 3-7). pap. 9.99 *(978-93-80741-11-6(1),* Campfire) Steerforth Pr.
Francia, Giada. Alex & Penny in Egypt Jigsaw Book. 2011. (ENG., Illus.). 14p. 14.95 *(978-88-544-0240-9(0))* White Star ITA. Dist: Random Hse., Inc.
François, André, creator. Crocodile Tears. 2017. (ENG.). 44p. (J). (-3). 16.95 *(978-1-59270-227-5(9))* Enchanted Lion Bks., LLC.
Gantos, Jack. Rotten Ralph Helps Out. Rubel, Nicole, illus. (Rotten Ralph Rotten Readers Ser.: 1). (ENG.). 48p. (J). (gr. 1-3). 2012. 15.99 *(978-0-312-64172-6(9),* 9780312641726) 2012. pap. 3.99 *(978-0-312-67281-2(0),* 9780312672812) 2004. pap. 6.99 *(978-0-374-46355-7(7),* 9780374463557) Square Fish.
Gill, Heidi. Egypt. Carter, Kris, illus. 2012. (2 Kurious Kids Ser.: Vol. 5). (ENG.). 24p. (J). (gr. -1-5). 14.95 *(978-1-936319-93-0(4))* Mascot Bks., Inc.
Grant, Joan Marshall. Scarlet Fish & Other Stories. Lavers, Ralph, illus. 2010. (J). pap. *(978-1-59731-554-8(0))* Perennis, Sophia.
Green, Robert James. Hawk of the Nile. Miller, Shane, illus. 2012. 222p. 44.95 *(978-1-258-25119-2(1));* pap. 29.95 *(978-1-258-25551-0(0))* Literary Licensing, LLC.
Greer, Hannah. The Gift of Re, the Adventures of the Whiz Kids. 2009. 200p. 24.50 *(978-1-60860-466-1(7),* Eloquent Bks.) Strategic Book Publishing & Rights Agency (SBPRA).
—The Pharos Legacy Book: The Whiz Kids Adventures. 2010. 122p. 21.95 *(978-1-60860-902-4(2),* Strategic Bk. Publishing) Strategic Book Publishing & Rights Agency (SBPRA).
Gubernatis, Loretto. Dimitrius & the Gladiolas. 2011. 356p. pap. 19.99 *(978-1-4568-2907-0(6))* Xlibris Corp.
Hamilton, Martha & Weiss, Mitch. The Well of Truth: A Folktale from Egypt. Wrenn, Tom, illus. 2008. (Story Cove Ser.). (ENG.). 32p. (J). (gr. -1-3). pap. 4.95 *(978-0-87483-880-0(0))* August Hse. Pubs., Inc.
Harvey, M. A. The Scorpion Secret: Dare to Take the Test. 2004. (Illus.). 128p. (J). pap. *(978-1-84458-050-7(4),* Pavilion Children's Books) Pavilion Bks.
Hayes, Celeste. The Puzzle Box of Nefertiti: A Sphinx & Trevi Adventure. Bishop, Christina, illus. 2011. 42p. (J). pap. 19.95 *(978-0-9785695-3-2(9))* Adam's Creations Publishing, LLC.
Hergé. Cigars of the Pharaoh.Tr. of Cigares du Pharaon. (Illus.). 62p. (J). 19.95 *(978-0-8288-5021-6(6))* French & European Pubns., Inc.
Hofmeyr, Dianne. Zeraffa Giraffa. Ray, Jane, illus. 2015. (ENG.). 40p. (J). pap. 9.99 *(978-1-84780-661-1(9),* Frances Lincoln Children's Bks.) Quarto Publishing Group UK GBR. Dist: Littlehampton Bk Services, Ltd.
Hotchkiss, Gerry. Emily & the Lost City of Urgup: An Adventure in Arabia. 2012. 112p. 20.95 *(978-1-4759-3764-0(4));* pap. 10.95 *(978-1-4759-3762-6(8))* iUniverse, Inc.
Houck, Colleen. Reawakened. 2015. (Reawakened Ser.: Bk. 1). (ENG.). 400p. (YA). (gr. 9-12). 17.99 *(978-0-385-37656-3(1),* Delacorte Pr.) Random Hse. Children's Bks.
Howe, James. Screaming Mummies of the Pharaoh's Tomb II. Helquist, Brett, illus. 2004. (Tales from the House of Bunnicula Ser.: 4). (ENG.). 112p. (J). (gr. 2-5). pap. 6.99 *(978-0-689-83954-2(5),* Atheneum Bks. for Young Readers) Simon & Schuster Children's Publishing.
Hulme-Cross, Benjamin. The Egyptian Warrior. 2016. (Warrior Heroes Ser.). (ENG., Illus.). 176p. (J). (gr. 6-9). *(978-0-7787-2864-1(1))* Crabtree Publishing Co.
Hunt, Elizabeth Singer. Secret Agent Jack Stalwart: Book 14: the Mission to Find Max: Egypt. 2011. (Secret Agent Jack Stalwart Ser.: 14). (ENG.). 144p. (J). (gr. 1-4). pap. 5.99 *(978-1-60286-152-7(8),* Weinstein Bks.) Perseus Bks. Group.
Ingram, Fiona. The Secret of the Sacred Scarab. 2008. 272p. (gr. -1 — 1). 27.95 *(978-0-595-71977-8(5));* pap. 17.95 *(978-0-595-45716-8(9))* iUniverse, Inc.
Jablonski, Carla. Shadow of the Sphinx. 2007. (Charmed Ser.). (ENG.). 192p. (YA). pap. 14.95 *(978-1-4169-6756-9(7),* Gallery Bks.) Gallery Bks.
Jacobson, Jennifer Richard. Andy Shane & the Queen of Egypt. Carter, Abby, illus. 2009. (Andy Shane Ser.: 3). (ENG.). 64p. (J). (gr. k-3). 4.99 *(978-0-7636-4404-8(8))* Candlewick Pr.
Jaxland, Sheila. Mylo. 2013. 32p. pap. 12.95 *(978-0-578-12595-4(1))* Roald Publishing.
Johnston-Thomas, Lee Ann. The Hidden Treasure of the Forgotten Pharaoh. 2008. 136p. 21.95 *(978-0-595-71157-4(X));* pap. 11.95 *(978-0-595-47552-0(3))* iUniverse, Inc.
Jones, Allan Frewin. Legend of the Pharaoh's Tomb. 2005. 191p. pap. *(978-0-439-80373-1(X))* Scholastic, Inc.
Kato, Shakila Maria Inviolata & Kato, Sharifa Maria Inviolata. The Adventures by the Magic Bicycle. 2012. 134p. 24.95 *(978-1-4137-5716-3(2))* America Star Bks.
KG, Mav. Angeline: the Catacombs of Egypt. 2009. 316p. pap. 25.64 *(978-1-4092-8950-0(8))* Lulu Pr., Inc.
Kirby, Matthew J. The Rogue World. 2017. (Dark Gravity Sequence Ser.: 3). 400p. (J). (gr. 3-7). 16.99 *(978-0-06-222493-4(X))* HarperCollins Pubs.
Kraljic, Helena. Cleopatra. 2017. (SPA.). 32p. (J). (gr. 1-4). 16.95 ***(978-84-9145-008-5(4),*** Picarona Editorial) Ediciones Obelisco ESP. Dist: Spanish Pubs., LLC.
Krebs, Laurie. We're Sailing down the Nile: A Journey Through Egypt. Wilson, Anne, illus. 2007. (ENG.). 40p. (J). (gr. -1-3). 16.99 *(978-1-84686-040-9(7))* Barefoot Bks., Inc.
Lardone, Lilia. Papiros. (SPA.). (YA). 9.95 *(978-958-04-6874-5(5))* Norma S.A. COL. Dist: Distribuidora Norma, Inc.
Lay, Kathryn. Book 3: the Curse of Time. 2016. (Time Twisters Ser.). (ENG.). (J). (gr. 2-6). lib. bdg. 27.07 ***(978-1-62402-179-4(4))*** ABDO Publishing Co.
Lester, Julius. Pharaoh's Daughter: A Novel of Ancient Egypt. 2009. (ENG., Illus.). 192p. (J). (gr. 7). pap. 6.99 *(978-0-15-206662-8(4))* Houghton Mifflin Harcourt Publishing Co.
Limke, Jeff. Isis y Osiris: Hasta el Fin del Mundo: Un Mito Egipcio. Witt, David, illus. 2007. (Mitos y leyendas en viñetas (Graphic Myths & Legends) Ser.). (SPA & ENG.). 48p. (J). (gr. 4-7). per. 8.95 *(978-0-8225-7971-7(5),* Ediciones Lerner) Lerner Publishing Group.
Lopez, David Mark. Walk Like an Egyptian. 2006. (J). (gr. 3-7). *(978-0-9744097-0-2(7))* Lopez, David.
Luedtke, Courtney. Baby Boo: The Happy Beginning. 2009. (Illus.). 72p. pap. 27.49 *(978-1-4389-2696-4(0))* AuthorHouse.
Malaghan, Michael. The Lost Prophecies. 2014. (ENG.). 256p. (J). (gr. 4-6). pap. 9.99 *(978-1-84939-574-8(8))* Andersen Pr. GBR. Dist: Independent Pubs. Group.
Marsh, Carole. The Mystery of the Ancient Pyramid: Cairo, Egypt. 2006. (Around the World in 80 Mysteries Ser.). (Illus.). 128p. (J). lib. bdg. 18.99 *(978-0-635-07006-7(5),* Marsh, Carole Mysteries); (gr. 4-7). 14.95 *(978-0-635-03473-1(5))* Gallopade International.
McBrier, Page. Abracadabra Tut. 2014. (ENG.). (J). pap. 9.99 *(978-0-9960794-0-2(8))* Palm Canyon Pr.
McCaughrean, Geraldine. Casting the Gods Adrift: A Tale of Ancient Egypt. Ludlow, Patricia D., illus. 2003. (ENG.). 112p. (J). (gr. 4-7). 15.95 *(978-0-8126-2684-1(2))* Cricket Bks.
Metcalf, Dan. The Curse of the Cairo Cat: A Lottie Lipton Adventure. Panagarry, Rachelle, illus. 2017. (Adventures of Lottie Lipton Ser.). (ENG.). (J). (gr. 2-5). 80p. pap. 6.99 ***(978-1-5124-8186-0(6));*** lib. bdg. 25.32 ***(978-1-5124-8179-2(3))*** Lerner Publishing Group. (Darby Creek).
—The Egyptian Enchantment: A Lottie Lipton Adventure. Panagarry, Rachelle, illus. 2017. (Adventures of Lottie Lipton Ser.). (ENG.). (J). (gr. 2-5). 96p. pap. 6.99 ***(978-1-5124-8188-4(2));*** lib. bdg. 25.32 ***(978-1-5124-8182-2(3))*** Lerner Publishing Group. (Darby Creek).
Meyer, William. The Secret of the Scarab Beetle. 2016. (Horace J. Edwards & the Time Keepers Ser.). (ENG., Illus.). 230p. (J). (gr. 4-6). pap. 9.99 *(978-1-58536-939-3(X),* 204089); 16.99 *(978-1-58536-938-6(1),* 204031) Sleeping Bear Pr.
Miguel Carbonell. King Tut's Tomb Robbers. 2010. 180p. 23.95 *(978-1-4502-1638-8(2));* pap. 13.95 *(978-1-4502-1637-1(4))* iUniverse, Inc.
Monson, Marianne. Escape from Egypt. 2010. (J). *(978-1-60641-670-9(7))* Deseret Bk. Co.
Nayeri, Daniel & Nayeri, Dina. Another Pan. 2011. (ENG., Illus.). 400p. (YA). (gr. 9). pap. 8.99 *(978-0-7636-5664-5(X))* Candlewick Pr.
Nayeri, Daniel and Dina. Another Pan. 2010. (ENG., Illus.). 400p. (YA). (gr. 9-18). 16.99 *(978-0-7636-3712-5(2))* Candlewick Pr.
Northrop, Michael. Amulet Keepers. 2015. (TombQuest Ser.: 2). (ENG., Illus.). 192p. (J). (gr. 3-7). 12.99 *(978-0-545-72339-8(6),* Scholastic Pr.) Scholastic, Inc.
—The Final Kingdom. 2016. (TombQuest Ser.: 5). (ENG.). 192p. (J). (gr. 3-7). 16.99 *(978-0-545-87111-2(5),* Scholastic Pr.) Scholastic, Inc.
—The Stone Warriors. 2015. (TombQuest Ser.: 4). (ENG.). 192p. (J). (gr. 3-7). 12.99 *(978-0-545-72341-1(8),* Scholastic Pr.) Scholastic, Inc.
—Valley of Kings. 2015. (TombQuest Ser.: 3). (ENG.). 192p. (J). (gr. 3-7). 16.99 *(978-0-545-87104-4(2));* 12.99 *(978-0-545-72340-4(X),* Scholastic Pr.) Scholastic, Inc.
Obi Shaaim Maa. Kheru Nefer (Beautiful Night) A Khamitic (Ancient Egyptian) Lullaby. 2006. (Illus.). (J). 21.95 incl. audio compact disk *(978-0-9770967-0-1(X))* Spirit Publishing LLC.
O'Neill, Katrina & Thompson, Lisa. Missing among the Pyramids. 2007. (Illus.). 56p. (J). pap. *(978-1-4207-0720-5(5))* Sundance/Newbridge Educational Publishing.
Paulsen, Gary & Roberts, Esyllt Nest. Plygu Amser. 2005. (WEL.). 80p. pap. *(978-0-86381-683-3(5))* Gwasg Carreg Gwalch.
Pavanello, Roberto. King Tut's Grandmother, 1 vol. Zeni, Marco, tr. from ITA. Pisapia, Blasco & Brughera, Pamela, illus. 2012. (Echo & the Bat Pack Ser.). (ENG.). 128p. (gr. 2-3). 9.95 *(978-1-4342-4245-7(5));* lib. bdg. 25.32 *(978-1-4342-3823-8(7),* Echo & the Bat Pack) Stone Arch Bks.
Pekkalainen, Leena. Mummies, Monsters, & the Ship of Millions. 2017. (ENG., Illus.). 128p. pap. 18.95 ***(978-977-416-851-2(8))*** American Univ. in Cairo Pr.
Pennypacker, Sara & Brown, Jeff. The Great Egyptian Grave Robbery. Pamintuan, Macky, illus. 2009. (Flat Stanley's Worldwide Adventures Ser.: 2). (ENG.). 96p. (J). (gr. 2-5). pap. 4.99 *(978-0-06-142992-7(9))* HarperCollins Pubs.
—The Great Egyptian Grave Robbery No. 2. Pamintuan, Macky, illus. 2009. (Flat Stanley's Worldwide Adventures Ser.: 2). (ENG.). 96p. (J). (gr. 2-5). 15.99 *(978-0-06-142993-4(7))* HarperCollins Pubs.
Perkins, TJ. Trade Secret: A Kim & Kelly Mystery. 2004. (Illus.). 175p. (YA). 10.99 *(978-0-9777538-2-6(4))* GumShoe Press.
Perritano, John. The Egyptian Prophecy, 1 vol. Laughead, Mike, illus. 2014. (Kid Squad Saves the World Ser.). (ENG.). 112p. (J). (gr. 8-12). 27.07 *(978-1-62402-039-1(9))* Magic Wagon.
Platt, Richard. Egyptian Diary: The Journal of Nakht. Parkins, David, illus. 2014. (ENG.). 128p. (J). (gr. 4-7). pap. 6.99 *(978-0-7636-7054-2(5))* Candlewick Pr.
Richards, Jane. Tombs, Temples, & Thrones. 2005. 125p. pap. 19.95 *(978-1-4137-9084-9(4))* PublishAmerica, Inc.
Riggs, Sandy. Three Ancient Communities: Set Of 6. 2011. (Navigators Ser.). (J). pap. 44.00 net. *(978-1-4108-5093-5(5))* Benchmark Education Co.
Robbins, Trina. The Maltese Mummy. Page, Tyler, illus. 2011. (Chicagoland Detective Agency Ser.: 2). (ENG.). 64p. (gr. 4-8). 29.27 *(978-0-7613-4615-9(5))* Lerner Publishing Group.
Rollins, James. Jake Ransom & the Howling Sphinx. 2012. (Jake Ransom Ser.: 2). (ENG.). 384p. (J). (gr. 5). pap. 7.99 *(978-0-06-147384-5(7))* HarperCollins Pubs.
Rosenstock, Barb. The Littlest Mountain. Hall, Melanie, illus. 2011. (ENG.). 24p. (J). (gr. -1-2). 17.95 *(978-0-7613-4495-7(0));* pap. 7.95 *(978-0-7613-4497-1(7))* Lerner Publishing Group. (Kar-Ben Publishing).
Sands, Emily & Anderson, Wayne. Egyptology: Search for the Tomb of Osiris. Andrew, Ian P. et al, illus. 2004. 32p. *(978-1-84011-852-0(0))* Templar Publishing.
Sarrasin, Alex. The Guardians of Neoegypti: Book One. 2007. 300p. per. 18.95 *(978-0-595-45710-6(X))* iUniverse, Inc.
Sayle, Stephen. Cam & Zara the Travel Bugs: Egypt. 2011. 36p. pap. 15.25 *(978-1-4567-6978-9(2))* AuthorHouse.
Schaenen, Inda. All the Cats of Cairo. 2007. 225p. (J). (gr. -1-10). per. 8.95 *(978-0-9768126-5-4(7))* Brown Barn Bks.
Scherer, Catherine W. Simon & Barklee in Egypt. Richardson, Kara, illus. 2006. (Another Country Calling Ser.). 65p. (J). per. 15.00 *(978-0-9714502-3-3(4),* Explorer Media) Simon & Barklee, Inc./ExplorerMedia.
Scholastic, Inc. Staff & Duendes Del Sur Staff, contrib. by. Scooby-Doo! & the Mummy's Curse. 2005. (Illus.). 24p. (J). *(978-1-4156-3913-9(2))* Scholastic, Inc.
Scieszka, Jon. Tu Mama Era Neanderthal. Smith, Lane, illus. (SPA.). (J). (gr. 5-8). 7.95 *(978-958-04-5045-0(5),* NR3076) Norma S.A. COL. Dist: Distribuidora Norma, Inc., Lectorum Pubns., Inc.
—Tut, Tut. Smith, Lane, illus. 2004. (Time Warp Trio Ser.: No. 6). 74p. (gr. 4-7). 15.00 *(978-0-7569-4050-8(8))* Perfection Learning Corp.
Shecter, Vicky Alvear. Cleopatra's Moon. 2011. (ENG.). 368p. (J). (gr. 9-7). 18.99 *(978-0-545-22130-6(7),* Levine, Arthur A. Bks.) Scholastic, Inc.
Shreve, Steve. The Adventures of Benny, 0 vols. 2013. (ENG.). 160p. (J). (gr. 3-6). pap. 9.99 *(978-1-4778-1607-3(0),* 9781477816073, Amazon Children's Publishing) Amazon Publishing.
Shultz, D. B. The World Adventures of Sahara the Mummy: The Magical Exploration of Ancient Egypt. 2012. 28p. pap. 17.99 *(978-1-4772-3310-8(5))* AuthorHouse.
Snyder, Laurel. The Longest Night: A Passover Story. Chien, Catia, illus. 2013. (ENG.). 40p. (J). (gr. -1-3). 17.99 *(978-0-375-86942-6(5),* Schwartz & Wade Bks.) Random Hse. Children's Bks.
Snyder, Zilpha Keatley. The Egypt Game. 2011. 9.00 *(978-0-7848-3470-1(9),* Everbind) Marco Bk. Co.
—The Egypt Game. Raible, Alton, illus. 2007. (ENG.). 224p. (J). (gr. 3-7). 17.99 *(978-1-4169-6065-2(1),* Atheneum Bks. for Young Readers) Simon & Schuster Children's Publishing.
star, celina. Paw Prints on the Road. 2008. 79p. pap. 9.96 *(978-0-557-02420-9(X))* Lulu Pr., Inc.
Stephens, Sarah Hines. Catwoman's Purrfect Plot. Vecchio, Luciano, illus. 2017. (Batman & Robin Adventures Ser.). (ENG.). 88p. (gr. 2-3). lib. bdg. 26.65 ***(978-1-4965-5349-2(7),*** DC Super Heroes) Stone Arch Bks.
Stevenson, Steve. The Curse of the Pharaoh. Turconi, Stefano, illus. 2013. (Agatha: Girl of Mystery Ser.: 1). (ENG.). 144p. (J). (gr. 2-5). pap. 6.99 *(978-0-448-46217-2(6),* Grosset & Dunlap) Penguin Young Readers Group.
Stevenson, William. Ricky's Dream Trip to Ancient Egypt. 2012. 30p. (J). pap. 12.99 *(978-1-936517-71-8(X),* Pop Pop Pr.) Micro Publishing Media, Inc.
Stilton, Geronimo. The Curse of the Cheese Pyramid. Wolf, Matt & Keys, Larry, illus. 2004. (Geronimo Stilton Ser.: 2). (ENG.). 128p. (J). (gr. 2-5). pap. 7.99 *(978-0-439-55964-5(2))* Scholastic, Inc.
Stilton, Thea. Thea Stilton & the Blue Scarab Hunt. 2012. (Thea Stilton Ser.: 11). lib. bdg. 19.65 *(978-0-606-26183-8(4),* Turtleback) Turtleback Bks.
Stoker, Bram. Mummy, 1 vol. Miroglio, Brian, illus. 2007. (Graphic Horror Ser.). (ENG.). 32p. (gr. 3-7). 28.50 *(978-1-60270-061-1(3),* Graphic Planet- Fiction) ABDO Publishing Co.
Storm, Zed. Will Solvit & the Mummy's Curse. 2010. (Will Solvit Ser.: Bk. 3). (Illus.). 128p. (J). (gr. 1-7). pap. *(978-1-4075-8979-4(2))* Parragon, Inc.
Sumerak, Marc. Ororo: Before the Storm. Barberi, Carlo, illus. 2012. (Ororo: Before the Storm Ser.). 24p. (J). (gr. 2-6). lib. bdg. 24.21 *(978-1-61479-026-6(4));* lib. bdg. 24.21 *(978-1-61479-027-3(2));* lib. bdg. 24.21 *(978-1-61479-025-9(6));* lib. bdg. 24.21 *(978-1-61479-024-2(8))* Spotlight.
Surget, Alain. Tirya y el Complot del Nilo. 2004.Tr. of Tirya & the Conspiracy in the Nile. (SPA.). 208p. (YA). 14.95 *(978-84-95618-50-4(8),* Umbriel) Ediciones Urano S. A. ESP. Dist: Spanish Pubs., LLC.
Teacher Created Resources Staff & Collins, Susan. A Guide for Using Time Soldiers in the Classroom. 2009. (ENG.). 48p. pap. 9.99 *(978-1-4206-2003-0(7))* Teacher Created Resources, Inc.
Teitelbaum, Michael. The Phantom Pharaoh. 2015. (Cold Whispers Ser.). (ENG., Illus.). 32p. (J). (gr. 2-6). lib. bdg. 26.60 *(978-1-62724-810-5(2))* Bearport Publishing Co., Inc.
Terrell, Brandon. Unearthed, Vol. 10. Tortosa, Wilson, illus. 2013. (Tony Hawk's 900 Revolution Ser.). (ENG.). 128p. (gr. 3-4). lib. bdg. 26.65 *(978-1-4342-3841-2(5))* Stone Arch Bks.
—Unearthed: Volume Ten, 1 vol. Tortosa, Wilson, illus. 2013. (Tony Hawk's 900 Revolution Ser.). (ENG.). 128p. (gr. 3-4). pap. 7.19 *(978-1-4342-4897-8(6),* Tony Hawk's 900 Revolution) Stone Arch Bks.
Time, Nicholas O. Stay a Spell. 2016. (In Due Time Ser.: 2). lib. bdg. 17.20 *(978-0-606-38986-0(5))* Turtleback Bks.
Travis, Alva. Secret of the Hidden Chamber. 2006. pap. 16.95 *(978-1-4241-2071-0(3))* PublishAmerica, Inc.
Trout, Richard E. Falcon of Abydos: Oracle of the Nile, 1 vol. 2005. (MacGregor Family Adventure Ser.: 3). (ENG.). 288p. (YA). (gr. 6-12). 16.99 *(978-1-58980-327-5(2))* Pelican Publishing Co., Inc.
VanArsdale, Anthony, illus. The Clue in the Papyrus Scroll. 2017. (Boxcar Children Great Adventure Ser.: 2). (ENG.). 160p. (J). (gr. 1-5). 6.99 ***(978-0-8075-0699-8(0));*** 12.99 ***(978-0-8075-0698-1(2))*** Whitman, Albert & Co.
Vegas, Peter. The Iron Tomb. 2016. (Pyramid Hunters Ser.: 1). (ENG., Illus.). 304p. (J). (gr. 5-9). 16.99 *(978-1-4814-4578-8(2),* Aladdin) Simon & Schuster Children's Publishing.
Warner, Gertrude Chandler. The Clue in the Papyrus Scroll. 2017. (Boxcar Children Great Adventure Ser.: 2). (J). lib. bdg. 17.20 ***(978-0-606-40316-0(7))*** Turtleback Bks.
Warner, Penny. The Code Busters Club, Case #4: the Mummy's Curse. 2014. (ENG., Illus.). 224p. (J). (gr. 3-7). 16.99 *(978-1-60684-459-5(8),* Darby Creek) Lerner Publishing Group.
Wax, Wendy & Weiss, Bobbi. A Tale of Too Many Cities - Egypt. Vargus, Nanci, ed. Slocum, Bradley, illus. 2008. (ENG.). 24p. (J). (gr. 1-17). pap. 3.99 *(978-1-58476-722-0(7))* Innovative Kids.
Weyn, Suzanne. The Cursed Scarab. 2015. (Hauntings: the Haunted Museum Ser.: 4). lib. bdg. 17.20 *(978-0-606-37076-9(5))* Turtleback Bks.
—The Haunted Museum - The Cursed Scarab. 2015. (Haunted Museum Ser.: 4). (ENG.). 208p. (J). (gr. 3-7). pap. 6.99 *(978-0-545-58849-2(9),* Scholastic Paperbacks) Scholastic, Inc.

Wilde, Oscar. Le Prince Hereux. (FRE.). (J). pap. 15.95 *(978-2-07-051629-2(6))* Gallimard, Editions FRA. Dist: Distribooks, Inc.

Wynne-Jones, Tim. Zoom, 1 vol. Beddows, Eric, illus. 2009. (ENG.). 96p. (J). (gr. -1-2). 25.00 *(978-0-88899-936-8(4))* Groundwood Bks. CAN. Dist: Publishers Group West (PGW).

Zindel, Paul. Egyptian Mystery. Date not set. 192p. (YA). (gr. 6-18). lib. bdg. 16.89 *(978-0-06-028509-8(5))* HarperCollins Pubs.

Zucker, Jonny. Mission 4: Grave Danger. Woodman, Ned, illus. 2013. (Max Flash Ser.: 4). (ENG.). 144p. (gr. 2-5). lib. bdg. 27.93 *(978-1-4677-1210-1(8)*, Darby Creek) Lerner Publishing Group.

Zwald, John & DesRochers, Diane O. Mahmoud Meets Moses. Zwald, John, illus. 2012. (Illus.). 26p. pap. 14.99 *(978-0-9838832-9-6(7))* WRB Pub.

EGYPT—HISTORY

Adams, Michelle Medlock. The Life & Times of Cleopatra. 2005. (Biography from Ancient Civilizations Ser.). (Illus.). 48p. (J). (gr. 4-8). lib. bdg. 29.95 *(978-1-58415-335-1(0))* Mitchell Lane Pubs., Inc.

Adamson, Heather. Ancient Egypt: An Interactive History Adventure. 2016. (You Choose: Historical Eras Ser.). (ENG.). 112p. (gr. 3-4). pap. 6.95 *(978-1-5157-4249-4(0)*, You Choose Bks.) Capstone Press of Coughlan Cos.

Allen, Kathy. Ancient Egyptian Hieroglyphs. 2012. (Ancient Egyptian Civilization Ser.). (ENG.). 32p. (gr. 3-4). pap. 47.70 *(978-1-4296-8401-9(1)*, Fact Finders) Capstone Press of Coughlan Cos.

Amstutz, L. J. Ancient Egypt, 1 vol. 2014. (Ancient Civilizations Ser.). (ENG.). 112p. (J). (gr. 6-12). lib. bdg. 35.64 *(978-1-62403-537-1(X)*, Essential Library) ABDO Publishing Co.

Ancient Egypt DBA. 2003. spiral bd. 16.95 *(978-1-56004-151-1(X))* Social Studies Schl. Service.

Ancient Egyptians. 2013. (Ladybird Histories Ser.). (ENG., Illus.). 64p. (J). (gr. 2-4). pap. 13.99 ***(978-0-7181-9622-6(8))*** Penguin Bks., Ltd. GBR. Dist: Independent Pubs. Group.

Asselin, Kristine Carlson. Pharaohs & Dynasties of Ancient Egypt. 2012. (Ancient Egyptian Civilization Ser.). (ENG.). 32p. (gr. 3-4). pap. 47.70 *(978-1-4296-8404-0(6)*, Fact Finders) Capstone Press of Coughlan Cos.

Aykroyd, Clarissa. Egypt. (Major Muslim Nations Ser.). (Illus.). 112p. (J). 2010. (gr. 5-18). lib. bdg. 25.95 *(978-1-4222-1381-0(1))* Vol. 13. 2015. (gr. 7). lib. bdg. 25.95 *(978-1-4222-3440-2(1))* Mason Crest.

Baikie, James & Baikie, Constance N. Peeps at Many Lands: Ancient Egypt (Yesterday's Classics) 2008. 124p. pap. 8.95 *(978-1-59915-288-2(6))* Yesterday's Classics.

Baum, Margaux & Thomas, Susanna. Hatshepsut. 2016. (Leaders of the Ancient World Ser.). 00112p. (J). (gr. 6-6). 37.10 *(978-1-5081-7250-5(1))* Rosen Publishing Group, Inc., The.

Beilenson, Suzanne. Ancient Egypt Scratch & Sketch. 2006. (Activity Book Ser.). 64p. (J). 12.99 *(978-1-59359-915-7(3))* Peter Pauper Pr. Inc.

Benchmark Education Company. The Empire of Egypt (Teacher Guide) 2005. *(978-1-4108-4647-1(4))* Benchmark Education Co.

Berg, Elizabeth. Egypt. 2010. (Festivals of the World Ser.). 32p. (gr. 3). 28.50 *(978-1-60870-097-4(6))* Marshall Cavendish Corp.

Bingham, Jane. How People Lived in Ancient Egypt. (How People Lived Ser.). (Illus.). 2009. 32p. (gr. 4-8). pap. 10.60 *(978-1-4358-2623-6(X)*, Rosen Classroom) 2008. 30p. (J). lib. bdg. 26.50 *(978-1-4042-4433-7(6))* Rosen Publishing Group, Inc., The.

Blackaby, Susan. Cleopatra: Egypt's Last & Greatest Queen. 2009. (Sterling Biographies(r) Ser.). (ENG., Illus.). 128p. (J). (gr. 5-18). pap. 5.95 *(978-1-4027-5710-5(7))* Sterling Publishing Co., Inc.

Bolton, Anne. Pyramids & Mummies. 2008. (ENG., Illus.). 32p. (J). (gr. 3-8). 21.99 *(978-1-4169-5873-4(8)*, Simon & Schuster Bks. For Young Readers) Simon & Schuster Bks. For Young Readers.

Bowden, Rob & Maconachie, Roy. Cairo. 2004. (Great Cities of the World Ser.). (Illus.). 48p. (gr. 5-12). lib. bdg. 31.00 *(978-0-8368-5035-2(1)*, Gareth Stevens Secondary Library) Stevens, Gareth Publishing LLLP.

Bower, Tamara. The Mummy-Makers of Egypt. 2016. (ENG., Illus.). 42p. (J). (gr. 2-5). 17.95 *(978-1-60980-600-2(X)*, Triangle Square) Seven Stories Pr.

Boyer, Crispin. National Geographic Kids Everything Ancient Egypt: Dig into a Treasure Trove of Facts, Photos, & Fun. 2012. (National Geographic Kids Everything Ser.). (ENG., Illus.). 64p. (J). (gr. 3-7). lib. bdg. 25.90 *(978-1-4263-0841-3(8)*, National Geographic Children's Bks.) National Geographic Society.

Boyer, Crispin & National Geographic Kids Staff. Ancient Egypt: Dig into a Treasure Trove of Facts, Photos, & Fun! 2012. (National Geographic Kids Everything Ser.). (ENG., Illus.). 64p. (J). (gr. 3-7). pap. 12.95 *(978-1-4263-0840-6(X)*, National Geographic Children's Bks.) National Geographic Society.

Bramwell, Neil D. Discover Ancient Egypt. 2014. (Discover Ancient Civilizations Ser.). 104p. (J). pap. 10.95 *(978-1-4644-0333-0(3))*; (gr. 5-18). 33.27 *(978-0-7660-4195-0(6))* Enslow Pubs., Inc.

Brannon, Barbara. Discover the Empire of Egypt. 2005. (J). pap. *(978-1-4108-5159-8(1))* Benchmark Education Co.

Brownlie Bojang, Ali. Egypt in Our World. 2011. (Countries in Our World Ser.). 32p. (gr. 4-7). lib. bdg. 31.35 *(978-1-59920-386-7(3))* Black Rabbit Bks.

Cain, Marie Mowery. George Takes a Road Trip, Egypt. 2013. (Big Books, Red Ser.). (ENG & SPA., Illus.). 16p. pap. 33.00 *(978-1-59246-208-7(1))* Big Books, by George!

Caldwell, Stella. Egyptworld: Discover the Ancient Land of Tutankhamun & Cleopatra. 2016. (ENG., Illus.). 80p. (J). (gr. 3). 19.95 *(978-1-78312-009-3(6))* Carlton Kids GBR. Dist: Sterling Publishing Co., Inc.

Caravantes, Peggy. Cleopatra: Powerful Leader or Ruthless Pharaoh? 2015. (Perspectives on History Ser.). (ENG.). 32p. (gr. 3-4). lib. bdg. 27.32 *(978-1-4914-2042-3(1))* Capstone Press of Coughlan Cos.

Challen, Paul. The Culture & Crafts of Egypt. 2015. (Cultural Crafts Ser.). (ENG., Illus.). 32p. (J). (gr. 4-6). pap. 11.75 *(978-1-4994-1120-1(0)*, 1391363, PowerKids Pr.) Rosen Publishing Group, Inc., The.

Chambers, Catherine. A Pharaoh's Guide. Pentney, Ryan, illus. 2017. (How-To Guides for Fiendish Rulers Ser.). (ENG.). 32p. (J). (gr. 3-6). 26.65 *(978-1-5124-1549-0(9))*; 7.99 ***(978-1-5124-3627-3(5))***; 39.99 ***(978-1-5124-3626-6(7))***; 39.99 ***(978-1-5124-2705-9(5))*** Lerner Publishing Group.

Chisholm, Jane & Reid, Straun. Who Built the Pyramids? Stitt, Sue, illus. 2004. (Starting Point History Ser.). 32p. (J). (gr. 1). lib. bdg. 12.95 *(978-1-58086-629-3(8)*, Usborne) EDC Publishing.

Christensen, Wendy. Empire of Ancient Egypt, Revised Edition. 2nd rev. ed. 2009. (Great Empires of the Past Ser.). (Illus.). 160p. (J). (gr. 6-12). 35.00 *(978-1-60413-160-4(8)*, Chelsea Hse.) Facts On File, Inc.

Conklin, Wendy. You Are There! Ancient Egypt 1535 BC. 2016. (TIME for KIDS(r) Nonfiction Readers Ser.). (Illus.). 32p. (J). (gr. 6-6). 8.99 *(978-1-4938-3602-4(1))* Teacher Created Materials, Inc.

Conklin, Wendy & Conklin, Blane Conklin. You Are There! Ancient Egypt 1336 BC. 2016. (Time for Kids Nonfiction Readers Ser.). (ENG.). (J). (gr. 5-8). lib. bdg. 19.65 ***(978-0-606-39538-0(5))*** Turtleback Bks.

Connors, Kathleen. The Life of Cleopatra, Vol. 1. 2014. (Famous Lives Ser.). (ENG.). 24p. (J). (gr. 1-2). 22.60 *(978-1-4824-0384-8(6))* Stevens, Gareth Publishing LLLP.

Cont Media Staff, ed. The Ancient Egyptains. 2008. (Illus.). 48p. (YA). 12.99 *(978-1-931703-25-3(6))* Contmedia Inc.

Cooke, Tim. The Ancient Egyptians. 2015. (At Home With... Ser.). (Illus.). 32p. (gr. 5-9). lib. bdg. 31.35 *(978-1-78121-083-3(7)*, Brown Bear Bks.) Windmill Bks. Ltd. GBR. Dist: Black Rabbit Bks.

Cricket Books Staff & Cobblestone Publishing, Inc. Staff. If I Were a Kid in Ancient Egypt: Children of the Ancient World. Sheldon, Ken, ed. 2007. (If I Were a Kid In... Ser.). (ENG., Illus.). 32p. (J). (gr. 1-5). 17.95 *(978-0-8126-7932-8(6))* Cricket Bks.

Dawson, Ian. Prehistoric & Egyptian Medicine. 2005. (ENG., Illus.). 64p. (J). (gr. 4). 19.95 *(978-1-59270-035-6(7))* Enchanted Lion Bks., LLC.

Deady, Kathleen W. Ancient Egypt: Beyond the Pyramids, 1 vol. 2011. (Great Civilizations Ser.). (ENG.). 32p. (gr. 3-4). pap. 8.10 *(978-1-4296-7235-1(8))*; pap. 47.70 *(978-1-4296-7236-8(6))*; lib. bdg. 27.32 *(978-1-4296-6830-9(X))* Capstone Press of Coughlan Cos. (Fact Finders).

Dell, Pamela Jain. Ancient Egypt, 1 vol. 2012. (Exploring the Ancient World Ser.). (ENG.). 48p. (gr. 5-6). pap. 9.10 *(978-0-7565-4580-2(3)*, CPB Grades 4-8) Compass Point Bks.

Demi. Tutankhamun, 0 vols. 2009. (ENG., Illus.). 64p. (J). (gr. 2-3). 19.99 *(978-0-7614-5558-5(2)*, 9780761455585, Amazon Children's Publishing) Amazon Publishing.

Der Manuelian, Peter. Hieroglyphs from A to Z: A Rhyming Book with Ancient Egyptian Stencils for Kids. 2010. 48p. (J). 17.95 *(978-0-7649-5306-4(0))* Pomegranate Communications, Inc.

—30-Second Ancient Egypt: The 50 Most Important Achievements of a Timeless Civilization, Each Explained in Half a Minute. 2014. (Illus.). 160p. (J). *(978-1-4351-5178-9(X))* Metro Bks.

Dickinson, Clive. Mummies, Temples, & Tombs: More Real-Life Tales from Ancient Egypt. 2011. (Ancient Egyptians Ser.: 4). (ENG., Illus.). 96p. (J). (gr. 7). pap. 5.99 *(978-0-00-715378-7(3)*, HarperCollins Children's Bks.) HarperCollins Pubs. Ltd. GBR. Dist: HarperCollins Pubs.

Dickmann, Nancy. Ancient Egypt. 2016. (History Hunters Ser.). (ENG.). 32p. (gr. 3-4). lib. bdg. 27.99 *(978-1-5157-2531-2(6)*, Edge Bks.) Capstone Press of Coughlan Cos.

Dorling Kindersley Publishing Staff & Putnam, James. Mummy. 2009. (DK Eyewitness Bks.). (ENG., Illus.). 72p. (J). (gr. 3-7). 16.99 *(978-0-7566-4541-0(7)*, DK Children) Dorling Kindersley Publishing, Inc.

Draper, Allison Stark. A Historical Atlas of Egypt. 2009. (Historical Atlases of South Asia, Central Asia, & the Middle East Ser.). 64p. (gr. 6-6). 61.20 *(978-1-61513-317-8(8))* Rosen Publishing Group, Inc., The.

Duke, Shirley. Pyramids of Egypt. 2015. (ENG.). 48p. (gr. 3-6). 35.64 *(978-1-63430-415-3(2))* Rourke Educational Media.

Edgar, Sherra G. Egypt. 2015. (One World, Many Countries Ser.). (ENG.). 32p. (J). (gr. 1-4). 28.50 *(978-1-63407-042-3(9)*, 208881) Child's World, Inc., The.

Editors of Kingfisher. Exotic Egyptians. 2017. (It's All About... Ser.). (ENG.). 32p. pap. 5.99 *(978-0-7534-7271-2(6)*, 9780753472712, Kingfisher) Roaring Brook Pr.

Egipto. 2005. (Coleccion Las Grandes Aventuras Ser.). (SPA.). (J). *(978-968-7381-53-4(1))*; pap. 17.95 *(978-968-7381-49-7(3))* Tecolote, Ediciones, S.A. de C.V. MEX. Dist: Iaconi, Mariuccia Bk. Imports.

Etheredge, Laura S., ed. Egypt. 2011. (Middle East: Region in Transition Ser.). (Illus.). 208p. (YA). (gr. 9-12). 40.00 *(978-1-61530-325-0(1))* Rosen Publishing Group, Inc., The.

Fiscus, James. The Suez Crisis. 2009. (War & Conflict in the Middle East Ser.). 64p. (gr. 5-5). 58.50 *(978-1-60854-741-8(8))* Rosen Publishing Group, Inc., The.

Forest, Christopher. Pyramids of Ancient Egypt. 2012. (Ancient Egyptian Civilization Ser.). (ENG.). 32p. (gr. 3-4). pap. 47.70 *(978-1-4296-8405-7(4)*, Fact Finders) Capstone Press of Coughlan Cos.

Forest, Christopher & Wegner, Jennifer Houser. Pyramids of Ancient Egypt, 1 vol. 2012. (Ancient Egyptian Civilization Ser.). (ENG.). 32p. (gr. 3-4). lib. bdg. 27.32 *(978-1-4296-7632-8(9)*, Fact Finders) Capstone Press of Coughlan Cos.

Galford, Ellen. Hatshepsut: The Princess Who Became King. (National Geographic World History Biographies Ser.). (ENG., Illus.). 64p. (J). (gr. 3-7). 2007. pap. 7.99 *(978-1-4263-0133-9(2))* 2005. lib. bdg. 27.90 *(978-0-7922-3646-7(7))* National Geographic Society. (National Geographic Children's Bks.).

Galford, Ellen & National Geographic Learning Staff. Hatshepsut: The Princess Who Became King. 2005. (National Geographic World History Biographies Ser.). (ENG., Illus.). 64p. (J). (gr. 3-7). 17.95 *(978-0-7922-3645-0(9)*, National Geographic Children's Bks.) National Geographic Society.

Ganeri, Anita. Ancient Egypt: The Complete Homework Solution. 2010. (Study Buddies Ser.). (ENG.). 32p. (J). (gr. 4-7). pap. 6.95 *(978-1-84898-183-6(X)*, TickTock Books) Octopus Publishing Group GBR. Dist: Independent Pubs. Group.

—Egypt: A Benjamin Blog & His Inquisitive Dog Guide, 1 vol. Isik, Semur, illus. 2014. (Country Guides, with Benjamin Blog & His Inquisitive Dog Ser.). (ENG.). 32p. (gr. 1-3). pap. 7.99 *(978-1-4109-6672-8(0)*, Read Me!) Heinemann-Raintree.

—Pharaohs, Heros & Thieves: More Real-Life Tales from Ancient Egypt. 2003. (Ancient Egyptians Ser.: 3). (ENG., Illus.). 112p. (J). (gr. 7). pap. 7.99 *(978-0-00-715377-0(5)*, HarperCollins Children's Bks.) HarperCollins Pubs. Ltd. GBR. Dist: HarperCollins Pubs.

Gifford, Clive. Food & Cooking in Ancient Egypt. 2010. (Cooking in World Cultures Ser.). (Illus.). 32p. (J). (ENG.). pap. 10.60 *(978-1-61532-359-3(7))*; (gr. 3-5). lib. bdg. 26.50 *(978-1-61532-337-1(6))* Rosen Publishing Group, Inc., The. (PowerKids Pr.).

Greeley, August. Writing in Ancient Egypt. 2009. (Writing in the Ancient World Ser.). 24p. (gr. 3-3). 42.50 *(978-1-60854-905-4(4)*, PowerKids Pr.) Rosen Publishing Group, Inc., The.

Greenberg, Imogen. The Ancient Egyptians. Greenberg, Isabel, illus. 2016. (Discover... Ser.). (ENG.). 32p. (J). (gr. 3-7). 14.99 *(978-1-84780-855-4(7)*, Frances Lincoln Children's Bks.) Quarto Publishing Group UK GBR. Dist: Hachette Bk. Group.

Gregory, Stefan. Life along the Nile. 2009. (Real Life Readers Ser.). 16p. (gr. 2-4). pap. 7.05 *(978-1-4358-0226-1(8)*, Rosen Classroom) Rosen Publishing Group, Inc., The.

Group/McGraw-Hill, Wright. Ancient Egypt: The Realm of Pharaohs, 6 vols. (Book2WebTM Ser.). (gr. 4-8). 36.50 *(978-0-322-04451-7(0))* Wright Group/McGraw-Hill.

Guy, John. Egyptian Life. 2006. (Illus.). 29p. (J). per. *(978-1-59905-052-2(8))* Saddleback Educational Publishing, Inc.

Habeeb, William Mark. Egypt. 2012. (J). pap. *(978-1-4222-2206-5(3))* Mason Crest.

—Egypt. Rotberg, Robert I., ed. 2012. (Evolution of Africa's Major Nations Ser.). (Illus.). 88p. (J). (gr. 7). 22.95 *(978-1-4222-2178-5(4))* Mason Crest.

Hall, Brianna. Mummies of Ancient Egypt, 1 vol. 2012. (Ancient Egyptian Civilization Ser.). (ENG.). 32p. (gr. 3-4). pap. 8.10 *(978-1-4296-7978-7(6))*; lib. bdg. 27.32 *(978-1-4296-7629-8(9))* Capstone Press of Coughlan Cos. (Fact Finders).

Harkins, Susan Sales & Harkins, William H. King Tut. 2008. (What's So Great About... ? Ser.). (Illus.). 32p. (YA). (gr. 2-4). lib. bdg. 25.70 *(978-1-58415-681-9(3))* Mitchell Lane Pubs., Inc.

Harris, Geraldine. Ancient Egypt. 3rd rev. ed. 2007. (Cultural Atlas for Young People Ser.). (Illus.). 96p. (YA). (gr. 5-9). 35.00 *(978-0-8160-6823-4(2))* Facts On File, Inc.

Hart, George. Ancient Egypt. 2014. (DK Eyewitness Bks.). (ENG.). 72p. (J). (gr. 3-7). pap. 9.99 *(978-1-4654-2048-0(7)*, DK Children) Dorling Kindersley Publishing, Inc.

Harvey, Gill. Tutankhamun. McNee, Ian, illus. 2006. (Usborne Young Reading Ser.). 64p. (J). (gr. 3-7). 8.99 *(978-0-7945-1271-2(2)*, Usborne) EDC Publishing.

Harvey, Gill & Reid, Struan. Encyclopedia of Ancient Egypt. 2004. (History Encyclopedias Ser.). (Illus.). 144p. (J). (gr. 4-18). lib. bdg. 27.95 *(978-1-58086-387-2(6))* EDC Publishing.

—Encyclopedia of Ancient Egypt - Internet Linked. rev. ed. 2007. (History Encyclopedias Ser.). 128p. (J). 16.99 *(978-0-7945-2212-4(2)*, Usborne) EDC Publishing.

Helbrough, Emma. A Day in the Life of a Pharaoh. (Day in the Life Ser.). 32p. 2009. (gr. 4-5). 47.90 *(978-1-61511-006-3(2)*, PowerKids Pr.) 2007. (J). (gr. 5-8). 25.25 *(978-1-4042-3852-7(2))* Rosen Publishing Group, Inc., The.

Hinds, Kathryn. The Countryside. 2006. (Life in Ancient Egypt Ser.). (Illus.). 70p. (J). (gr. 4-7). lib. bdg. 32.79 *(978-0-7614-2185-6(8)*, Benchmark Bks.) Marshall Cavendish Corp.

—The Pharaoh's Court. 2006. (Life in Ancient Egypt Ser.). (Illus.). 80p. (gr. 6-7). lib. bdg. 34.21 *(978-0-7614-2183-2(1)*, Benchmark Bks.) Marshall Cavendish Corp.

—Religion. 2006. (Life in Ancient Egypt Ser.). (Illus.). 80p. (gr. 6-7). lib. bdg. 34.21 *(978-0-7614-2186-3(6)*, Benchmark Bks.) Marshall Cavendish Corp.

Hirsch, E. D., Jr., ed. Ancient Egypt. 2003. tchr. ed. 9.95 *(978-0-7690-5037-9(9))*; stu. ed. 49.95 *(978-0-7690-2942-9(6))* Pearson Learning.

Hollar, Sherman. Ancient Egypt. 2011. (J). lib. bdg. 31.70 *(978-1-61530-523-0(8))* Rosen Publishing Group, Inc., The.

Hooper, Meredith. An Egyptian Tomb: The Tomb of Nebamun. 2008. (ENG., Illus.). 32p. (J). (gr. 5-8). 19.95 *(978-1-55407-374-0(X)*, 9781554073740) Firefly Bks., Ltd.

Hubbard, Margaret Ann. Saint Louis & the Last Crusade. Barton, Harry, illus. 2013. (ENG.). 157p. pap. 9.95 *(978-1-58617-647-1(1))* Ignatius Pr.

Hurdman, Charlotte, et al. Find Out about Ancient Egypt, Rome & Greece: Exploring the Great Classical Civilizations, with 60 Step-By-Step Projects & 1500 Exciting Images. 2013. (ENG., Illus.). 256p. (J). (gr. 3-7). 17.99 *(978-1-84322-804-2(1)*, Armadillo) Anness Publishing GBR. Dist: National Bk. Network.

Hynson, Colin. Be an Inca Mummy! A One-Way Journey You'D Rather Not Make. Antram, David, illus. 2007. (You Wouldn't Want to...: Ancient Civilization Ser.). (ENG.). 32p. (J). (gr. 2-5). 29.00 *(978-0-531-18744-9(6)*, Watts, Franklin) Scholastic Library Publishing.

—You Wouldn't Want to Be an Inca Mummy! A One-Way Journey You'd Rather Not Make. Antram, David, illus. 2007. (You Wouldn't Want to...: Ancient Civilization Ser.). (ENG.). 32p. (J). (gr. 2-5). pap. 9.95 *(978-0-531-13926-4(3)*, Watts, Franklin) Scholastic Library Publishing.

Jeffrey, Gary. Cleopatra: The Life of an Egyptian Queen. 2009. (Graphic Nonfiction Biographies Ser.). (Illus.). 48p. (YA). (gr. 4-5). 58.50 *(978-1-61513-015-3(2)*, Rosen Reference) Rosen Publishing Group, Inc., The.

Jeffrey, Gary & Ganeri, Anita. Cleopatra: The Life of an Egyptian Queen. 2005. (Graphic Nonfiction Biographies Ser.). (Illus.). 48p. (YA). (gr. 4-7). lib. bdg. 31.95 *(978-1-4042-0242-9(0))* Rosen Publishing Group, Inc., The.

Jestice, Phyllis G. Ancient Egyptian Warfare. 2009. (Ancient Warfare Ser.). (Illus.). 32p. (J). (gr. 5-8). lib. bdg. 26.00 *(978-1-4339-1971-8(0)*, Gareth Stevens Learning Library) Stevens, Gareth Publishing LLLP.

Kalman, Bobbie. Spotlight on Egypt. 2010. (Spotlight on My Country Ser.). (ENG.). 32p. (J). (gr. 2-5). pap. *(978-0-7787-3483-3(8))* Crabtree Publishing Co.

Kaplan, Leslie C. Politics & Government in Ancient Egypt. 2009. (Primary Sources of Ancient Civilizations Ser.). 24p. (gr. 3-3). 42.50 *(978-1-60851-561-5(3)*, PowerKids Pr.) Rosen Publishing Group, Inc., The.

Kenison, Misti, illus. Egypt - The Tiny Traveler: A Book of Shapes. 2015. (ENG.). 24p. (J). (— 1). bds. 5.95 *(978-1-62914-607-2(2)*, Sky Pony Pr.) Skyhorse Publishing Co., Inc.

Kissock, Heather. Pyramids. 2011. (J). *(978-1-61690-435-7(6))* Weigl Pubs., Inc.

Kissock, Heather, ed. Pyramids. 2011. (J). (gr. 4-6). pap. 12.95 *(978-1-61690-771-6(1)*, AV2 by Weigl); (Illus.). 24p. (gr. 2-5). 27.13 *(978-1-61690-767-9(3))* Weigl Pubs., Inc.

Kramer, Ann. Egyptian Myth: A Treasury of Legends, Art, & History. 2007. (Myth Ser.). (Illus.). 96p. (J). (gr. 4-7). pap. 7.99 *(978-0-7858-2347-6(6)*, Chartwell) Book Sales, Inc.

—Egyptian Myth: A Treasury of Legends, Art, & History. 2007. (ENG., Illus.). 96p. (C). (gr. 6-18). lib. bdg. 158.00 *(978-0-7656-8105-8(6)*, Y182128) Routledge.

Kramer, Barbara. National Geographic Readers: Cleopatra. 2015. (Readers Bios Ser.). (ENG., Illus.). 48p. (J). (gr. 1-4). pap. 3.99 *(978-1-4263-2137-5(6)*, National Geographic Children's Bks.) National Geographic Society.

Learning Works, creator. Ancient Egypt. 2006. (Museum Ser.). (Illus.). 64p. (J). (gr. 5-8). pap. 13.99 *(978-0-88160-386-6(4)*, LW442, Learning Works, The) Creative Teaching Pr., Inc.

Leonard, Barry, ed. Treasure Trove of an Ancient Egyptian Child. 2005. (Illus.). 24p. (J). (gr. 4-8). 27.00 *(978-0-7567-8939-8(7))* DIANE Publishing Co.

Lloyd Jones, Rob. See Inside Ancient Egypt. Hancock, David, illus. 2008. (Usborne Flap Book Ser.). 14p. (J). (gr. -1-3). bds. 12.99 *(978-0-7945-2037-3(5)*, Usborne) EDC Publishing.

MacDonald, Fiona. The Amazing History of Mummies & Tombs: Uncover the Secrets of the Egyptian Pyramids & Other Ancient Burial Sites, Shown in over 350 Exciting Pictures. 2016. (ENG., Illus.). 64p. (J). (gr. -1-12). 12.99 *(978-1-86147-735-4(X)*, Armadillo) Anness Publishing GBR. Dist: National Bk. Network.

—Ancient Egyptians: An Epic Lost Civilisation Brought Vividly to Life. 2004. (ENG., Illus.). 64p. (J). (gr. 4-7). 17.99 *(978-0-00-715376-3(7))* HarperCollins Pubs. Ltd. GBR. Dist: Independent Pubs. Group.

—The Egyptian Mummy. 2011. (History Detectives Ser.). (ENG.). 32p. (J). (gr. 4-7). spiral bd. 9.95 *(978-1-84898-186-7(4)*, TickTock Books) Octopus Publishing Group GBR. Dist: Independent Pubs. Group.

Mahmoud, Zaki Naguib. The Land & People of Egypt. 2012. 142p. 40.95 *(978-1-258-23287-0(1))*; pap. 25.95 *(978-1-258-24914-4(6))* Literary Licensing, LLC.

Malam, John. Ancient Egypt. Malam, John, illus. 2004. (Picturing the Past Ser.). (Illus.). 32p. (J). 15.95 *(978-1-59270-021-9(7))* Enchanted Lion Bks., LLC.

—Pyramids. 2015. (100 Facts You Should Know Ser.). (ENG., Illus.). 48p. (J). (gr. 4-5). lib. bdg. 31.95 *(978-1-4824-2185-9(2))* Stevens, Gareth Publishing LLLP.

Manning, Mick & Granström, Brita. Pharaoh's Egypt. Manning, Mick & Granström, Brita, illus. 2015. (Fly on the Wall Ser.). (ENG., Illus.). 40p. (J). (gr. k-3). pap. 9.99 *(978-1-84780-623-9(6)*, Frances Lincoln) Quarto Publishing Group UK GBR. Dist: Hachette Bk. Group.

Marsico, Katie. Egypt. 2011. (Explorer Library: Social Studies Explorer Ser.). (ENG.). 48p. (gr. 4-8). lib. bdg. 31.36 *(978-1-61080-100-3(8)*, 201094) Cherry Lake Publishing.

Morley, Jacqueline. You Wouldn't Want to Be a Pyramid Builder! A Hazardous Job You'd Rather Not Have. Antram, David, illus. rev. ed. 2013. (ENG.). (J). 32p. 29.00 *(978-0-531-27101-8(3))*; 40p. pap. 9.95 *(978-0-531-23852-3(0))* Scholastic Library Publishing. (Watts, Franklin).

Morris, Neil. Everyday Life in Ancient Egypt. 2008. (Uncovering History Ser.). (ENG., Illus.). 48p. (J). (gr. 2-7). 19.95 *(978-88-89272-55-8(4))* McRae Bks. Srl ITA. Dist: Independent Pubs. Group.

Murray, Julie. Egypt, 1 vol. 2013. (Explore the Countries Ser.). (ENG.). 40p. (J). (gr. 2-5). lib. bdg. 29.93 *(978-1-61783-809-5(8)*, Big Buddy Bks.) ABDO Publishing Co.

Nardo, Don. Arts, Leisure, & Sport in Ancient Egypt. 2005. (Lucent Library of Historical Eras Ser.). (ENG., Illus.). 112p. (YA). (gr. 7-12). lib. bdg. 33.45 *(978-1-59018-706-7(7))* Cengage Gale.

—Cause & Effect: Ancient Egypt. 2017. (ENG.). 80p. (YA). (gr. 5-12). 39.93 ***(978-1-68282-150-3(1))*** ReferencePoint Pr., Inc.

—Cleopatra. 2016. (ENG.). 80p. (J). 38.60 *(978-1-60152-948-0(1))* ReferencePoint Pr., Inc.

—Daily Life in Ancient Egypt. 2015. (Daily Life in Ancient Civilizations Ser.). (ENG., Illus.). 48p. (gr. 3-6). pap. 8.99 *(978-1-4846-0834-0(8)*, Heinemann InfoSearch) Heinemann-Raintree.

—Ramesses II: Ruler of Ancient Egypt. 2006. (Rulers of the Ancient World Ser.). (Illus.). 160p. (YA). (gr. 6). lib. bdg. 29.27 *(978-0-7660-2562-2(4))* Enslow Pubs., Inc.

Norwich, Grace. Cleopatra. 2014. (I Am Ser.: 10). (ENG., Illus.). 128p. (J). (gr. 2-5). pap. 5.99 *(978-0-545-58753-2(0)*, Scholastic Paperbacks) Scholastic, Inc.

Orr, Tamra. Ancient Egypt. 2012. (Explore Ancient Worlds Ser.). (J). (gr. 3-6). lib. bdg. 29.95 *(978-1-61228-279-4(2))* Mitchell Lane Pubs., Inc.

—Egyptian Islamic Jihad. 2009. (Inside the World's Most Infamous Terrorist Organizations Ser.). 64p. (gr. 5-5). 58.50 *(978-1-61513-574-5(X))* Rosen Publishing Group, Inc., The.

Owen, Ruth. How to Make an Egyptian Mummy. 2015. (It's a Fact Ser.). (ENG.). 32p. (J). (gr. 3-6). lib. bdg. 26.60 *(978-1-909673-94-6(3))* Bearport Publishing Co., Inc.

Pack, Mary Fisk. Cleopatra: "Serpent of the Nile" Malone, Peter, illus. 2011. (Thinking Girl's Treasury of Dastardly Dames Ser.). (ENG.). 32p. (J). (gr. 3-8). 18.95 *(978-0-9834256-0-1(4))* Goosebottom Bks. LLC.

Park, Louise. The Pharaohs' Armies. 2009. (Ancient & Medieval People Ser.). 32p. (gr. 5). 28.50 *(978-0-7614-4451-0(3))* Marshall Cavendish Corp.

Parks, Peggy J. Aswan High Dam. (Building World Landmarks Ser.). (J). 2004. 26.19 *(978-1-4103-0204-5(0))* 2003. (Illus.). 48p. 24.95 *(978-1-56711-329-7(X))* Cengage Gale. (Blackbirch Pr., Inc.).

Pateman, Robert, et al. Egypt. 2014. (Cultures of the World (r) Ser.). 144p. (J). (gr. 5-10). lib. bdg. 47.07 *(978-0-7614-4992-8(2))* Cavendish Square Publishing.

Phipps, Liza & Thompson, Avril. Ancient Egyptians. 2017. (History Showtime Ser.). (ENG., Illus.). 32p. (J). (gr. 2-4). pap. 11.99 *(978-1-4451-1486-6(0),* Franklin Watts) Hachette Children's Group GBR. Dist: Hachette Bk. Group.

Pipe, Jim. You Wouldn't Want to Be Cleopatra! An Egyptian Ruler You'd Rather Not Be. Antram, David, illus. 2007. (You Wouldn't Want to... Ser.). (ENG.). 32p. (J). (gr. 2-5). pap. 9.95 *(978-0-531-18923-8(6),* Watts, Franklin) Scholastic Library Publishing.

—You Wouldn't Want to Be Cleopatra! An Egyptian Ruler You'D Rather Not Be. Antram, David, illus. 2007. (You Wouldn't Want to... Ser.). (ENG.). 32p. (J). (gr. 2-5). 29.00 *(978-0-531-18726-5(8),* Watts, Franklin) Scholastic Library Publishing.

—You Wouldn't Want to Be Cleopatra! (Revised Edition) 2017. (You Wouldn't Want to... Ancient Civilizations Ser.). (ENG., Illus.). 32p. (J). lib. bdg. 29.00 *(978-0-531-23834-9(2),* Watts, Franklin) Scholastic Library Publishing.

Powell, Jillian. Egypt. 2014. (My Country Ser.). 24p. (gr. k-3). lib. bdg. 28.50 *(978-1-59920-904-3(7))* Black Rabbit Bks.

Rajczak, Kristen. 20 Fun Facts about Women in Ancient Egypt. 2015. (Fun Fact File: Women in History Ser.). (ENG., Illus.). 32p. (J). (gr. 2-3). pap. 10.50 *(978-1-4824-2812-4(1))* Stevens, Gareth Publishing LLLP.

Reid, S. & Chisholm, J. Who Built the Pyramids? rev. ed. 2004. (Starting Point History Ser.). (Illus.). 32p. (J). pap. 4.95 *(978-0-7945-0343-7(8),* Usborne) EDC Publishing.

Rice Jr., Earle. Muslim Brotherhood. 2017. lib. bdg. 29.95 ***(978-1-68020-057-7(7))*** Mitchell Lane Pubs., Inc.

Ridgley, Sara & Mole, Gavin. Sing It & Say - Ancient Egypt. (J). 10.95 incl. audio *(978-1-85909-391-7(4),* Warner Bros. Pubns.) Alfred Publishing Co., Inc.

Riggs, Kate. Egyptian Pyramids. 2009. (Places of Old Ser.). 24p. (J). (gr. 1-5). lib. bdg. 24.25 *(978-1-58341-707-2(9),* Creative Education) Creative Co., The.

Robinson, Tony. Egyptians. unabr. ed. 2015. (Weird World of Wonders Ser.). (ENG., Illus.). 160p. (J). (gr. 4-6). pap. 7.99 *(978-0-330-53387-4(8))* Pan Macmillan GBR. Dist: Independent Pubs. Group.

Rockwood, Leigh. Ancient Egyptian Daily Life. 2013. (Spotlight on Ancient Civilizations: Egypt Ser.). (ENG.). 24p. (J). (gr. 3-4). 23.60 *(978-1-4777-0766-1(2),* PowerKids Pr.); (Illus.). pap. 10.00 *(978-1-4777-0865-1(0),* Rosen Classroom) Rosen Publishing Group, Inc., The.

—The Ancient Egyptian Economy. 2013. (Spotlight on Ancient Civilizations: Egypt Ser.). (ENG., Illus.). 24p. (J). (gr. 3-4). pap. 10.00 *(978-1-4777-0863-7(4));* lib. bdg. 23.60 *(978-1-4777-0765-4(4))* Rosen Publishing Group, Inc., The. (PowerKids Pr.).

—Ancient Egyptian Geography. 2013. (Spotlight on Ancient Civilizations: Egypt Ser.). (ENG., Illus.). 24p. (J). (gr. 3-4). pap. 10.00 *(978-1-4777-0867-5(7),* PowerKids Pr.) Rosen Publishing Group, Inc., The.

—V Ancient Egyptian Geography. 2013. (Spotlight on Ancient Civilizations: Egypt Ser.). (ENG.). 24p. (J). (gr. 3-4). 23.60 *(978-1-4777-0767-8(0),* PowerKids Pr.) Rosen Publishing Group, Inc., The.

Ross, Stewart. Clever Cleo. Shields, Sue, illus. 32p. pap. 9.99 *(978-0-7502-2853-4(9))* Hodder & Stoughton GBR. Dist: Trafalgar Square Publishing.

Roth, Susan L. & Abouraya, Karen Leggett. Hands Around the Library: Protecting Egypt's Treasured Books. Roth, Susan L., illus. 2012. (ENG., Illus.). 32p. (J). (gr. -1-k). 16.99 *(978-0-8037-3747-1(5),* Dial Bks) Penguin Young Readers Group.

Roxburgh, Ellis. Cleopatra vs. the Roman Empire: Power, Conquest, & Tragedy. 2016. (History's Greatest Rivals Ser.). (ENG., Illus.). 48p. (J). (gr. 6-8). pap. 14.05 *(978-1-4824-4223-6(X))* Stevens, Gareth Publishing LLLP.

—The Egyptian Empire. 2015. (Great Empires Ser.). (ENG., Illus.). 48p. (J). (gr. 7-7). 31.36 *(978-1-5026-0632-7(1))* Cavendish Square Publishing.

Rubalcaba, Jill. Ancient Egypt: Archaeology Unlocks the Secrets of Egypt's Past. 2006. (National Geographic Investigates Ser.). (ENG., Illus.). 64p. (J). (gr. 3-7). 17.95 *(978-0-7922-7784-2(8));* (gr. 4-7). 27.90 *(978-0-7922-7857-3(7))* National Geographic Society. (National Geographic Children's Bks.).

Ryall, Michael. The Empire of Egypt. 2005. (J). pap. *(978-1-4108-4599-3(0))* Benchmark Education Co.

Sands, Emily. Egyptology: Search for the Tomb of Osiris. Steer, Dugald A., ed. Andrew, Ian et al, illus. 2004. (Ologies Ser.). (ENG.). 32p. (J). (gr. 3-7). 24.99 *(978-0-7636-2638-9(4))* Candlewick Pr.

Santillian, Beatriz & Thomas, Susanna. Ahmose I: Pharaoh of the 18th Dynasty. 2017. (Leaders of the Ancient World Ser.). 112p. (J). (gr. 12-11). 37.10 ***(978-1-5081-7480-6(6),*** Rosen Young Adult) Rosen Publishing Group, Inc., The.

—Ramses II: The Most Powerful Pharaoh of Ancient Egypt. 2017. (Leaders of the Ancient World Ser.). 112p. (J). (gr. 12-11). 37.10 ***(978-1-5081-7489-9(X),*** Rosen Young Adult) Rosen Publishing Group, Inc., The.

Segal Block, Marta. Egypt, 1 vol. 2012. (Countries Around the World Ser.). (ENG.). 48p. (gr. 3-6). pap. 9.95 *(978-1-4329-6123-7(3));* lib. bdg. 33.32 *(978-1-4329-6097-1(0))* Heinemann-Raintree. (NA-h).

Sexton, Colleen & Simmons, Walter. Egypt. 2010. (Exploring Countries Ser.). (ENG., Illus.). 32p. (J). (gr. 3-7). lib. bdg. 26.95 *(978-1-60014-478-3(0),* Blastoff! Readers) Bellwether Media.

Shea, Therese. Discovering Egyptian Dynasties. 2013. (Exploring African Civilizations Ser.). (Illus.). 64p. (J). (gr. 5-8). 31.95 *(978-1-4777-1881-0(8),* Rosen Reference) Rosen Publishing Group, Inc., The.

Sheafer, Silvia Anne. Ramses the Great. 2008. (Ancient World Leaders Ser.). 136p. (gr. 6-12). 30.00 *(978-0-7910-9637-6(8),* Chelsea Hse.) Facts On File, Inc.

Shecter, Vicky Alvear. Anubis Speaks! A Guide to the Afterlife by the Egyptian God of the Dead. Revoy, Antoine, illus. 2013. (Secrets of the Ancient Gods Ser.). (ENG.). 128p. (J). (gr. 4-6). 16.95 *(978-1-59078-995-7(4))* Boyds Mills Pr.

—Cleopatra Rules! The Amazing Life of the Original Teen Queen. 2013. (ENG., Illus.). 176p. (J). (gr. 6-9). pap. 9.95 *(978-1-62091-032-0(2))* Boyds Mills Pr.

Sheen, Barbara. Foods of Egypt. 2010. (Taste of Culture Ser.). (Illus.). 64p. (J). 30.45 *(978-0-7377-4843-7(5),* Kidhaven) Cengage Gale.

Shoup, Kate. Egypt. 2015. (Exploring World Cultures Ser.). (ENG., Illus.). 32p. (J). (gr. 3-4). pap. 10.58 *(978-1-5026-0582-5(1))* Cavendish Square Publishing.

Shuter, Jane. Ancient Egypt. 2010. (Exploring the Ancient World Ser.). (Illus.). 64p. (YA). (gr. 6-8). lib. bdg. 34.60 *(978-1-4339-4158-0(9),* Gareth Stevens Secondary Library) Stevens, Gareth Publishing LLLP.

Simmons, Walter. Egypt. 2011. (ENG., Illus.). 32p. (J). *(978-0-531-26459-1(9),* Blastoff! Readers) Bellwether Media.

Smith, Miranda & Steele, Philip. Ancient Worlds: A Thrilling Adventure Through the Ancient Worlds. 2016. (Navigators Ser.). (ENG., Illus.). 160p. (J). 15.99 *(978-0-7534-7239-2(2),* 9780753472392, Kingfisher) Roaring Brook Pr.

Snedden, Robert. Ancient Egypt. 2009. (Technology in Times Past Ser.). (Illus.). 46p. (J). (gr. 4-7). pap. *(978-1-897563-61-8(2))* Saunders Bk. Co.

Sohn, Ruth H. Crossing Cairo: A Jewish Woman's Encounter with Egypt. 2013. 272p. pap. 18.95 *(978-1-935604-50-1(3))* Gaon Bks.

Somerville, Charles C. E Is for Egypt. Somerville, Charles C., illus. 2015. (Is for Alphabet Ser.). (ENG., Illus.). 32p. (J). (gr. -1-3). pap. 9.99 *(978-1-907432-15-6(9))* Hogs Back Bks. GBR. Dist: Independent Pubs. Group.

Spilsbury, Richard. Ramesses II, 1 vol. 2013. (Hero Journals). (ENG., Illus.). 48p. (J). (gr. 4-6). 33.32 *(978-1-4109-5358-2(0));* pap. 9.95 *(978-1-4109-5365-0(3))* Heinemann-Raintree. (NA-r).

Stewart, David. Creepy Egyptian Mummies. 2010. (Top 10 Worst Ser.). (Illus.). 32p. (J). (gr. 3-6). (ENG.). pap. 10.50 *(978-1-4339-4080-4(9));* lib. bdg. 26.60 *(978-1-4339-4079-8(5))* Stevens, Gareth Publishing LLLP. (Gareth Stevens Learning Library).

—Tutankhamen! A Mummy Who Really Got Meddled With. Antram, David, illus. 2007. (You Wouldn't Want to... Ser.). (ENG.). 32p. (J). (gr. 2-5). 29.00 *(978-0-531-18725-8(X))* Scholastic Library Publishing.

—You Wouldn't Want to Be an Egyptian Mummy! Disgusting Things You'd Rather Not Know. Antram, David, illus. rev. ed. 2012. (You Wouldn't Want to...: Ancient Civilization Ser.). (ENG.). 40p. (J). pap. 9.95 *(978-0-531-28026-3(8))* Scholastic Library Publishing.

Strom, Laura Layton. The Egyptian Science Gazette. 2008. (Illus.). 36p. (J). pap. *(978-0-531-18813-2(2))* Children's Pr., Ltd.

Thomas, Susanna. Akhenaten & Tutankhamen: The Religious Revolution. 2009. (Ancient Leaders Ser.). 112p. (gr. 5-8). 66.50 *(978-1-61511-417-7(3),* Rosen Reference) Rosen Publishing Group, Inc., The.

—Snefru: The Pyramid Builder. 2003. (Ancient Leaders Ser.). (Illus.). 112p. (J). (gr. 5-8). lib. bdg. 34.60 *(978-0-8239-3598-7(1),* Rosen Reference) Rosen Publishing Group, Inc., The.

Thomas, Sylvia A. Moses & the Exodus from Egypt. 2012. 34p. pap. 19.99 *(978-1-61904-669-6(5))* Salem Author Services.

Turnbull, Stephanie. Egyptians. (Beginners Social Studies). 32p. (J). (gr. 1-18). lib. bdg. 12.99 *(978-1-58086-656-9(5),* Usborne) EDC Publishing.

—Egyptians Kid Kit. King, Colin, illus. 2005. 32p. (J). 9.99 *(978-1-58086-844-0(4),* Usborne) EDC Publishing.

Turner, Tracey. Hard As Nails in Ancient Egypt. Lenman, Jamie, illus. 2015. (ENG.). 64p. (J). *(978-0-7787-1511-5(6))* Crabtree Publishing Co.

Tyldesley, Joyce A. Egypt. 2007. (Insiders Ser.). (ENG., Illus.). 64p. (J). (gr. 3-7). 17.99 *(978-1-4169-3858-3(3),* Simon & Schuster Bks. For Young Readers) Simon & Schuster Bks. For Young Readers.

Uhl, Xina M. Cleopatra: Queen of Egypt. 2017. (Women Who Changed History Ser.). 48p. (gr. 10-12). 26.85 ***(978-1-68048-639-1(X),*** Britannica Educational Publishing) Rosen Publishing Group, Inc., The.

Van Vleet, Carmella. Explore Ancient Egypt! 25 Great Projects, Activities, Experiments. Kim, Alex, illus. 2006. (Explore Your World Ser.). (ENG.). 96p. (J). (gr. k-4). pap. 12.95 *(978-0-9792268-3-0(X))* Octavio Publishing.

—Great Ancient Egypt Projects. 2006. (Build It Yourself Ser.). (ENG., Illus.). 128p. (J). (gr. 3-7). pap. 15.95 *(978-0-9771294-5-4(4))* Northern Trails Pr.

Whiting, Jim. The Life & Times of Rameses the Great. 2005. (Biography from Ancient Civilizations Ser.). (Illus.). 48p. (J). (gr. 5-8). lib. bdg. 29.95 *(978-1-58415-341-2(5))* Mitchell Lane Pubs., Inc.

Whiting, Jim & Nabil, Muhammad. My Teenage Life in Egypt. 2017. (J). ***(978-1-4222-3899-8(7))*** Mason Crest.

Worth, Richard. Cleopatra: Queen of Ancient Egypt. 2006. (Rulers of the Ancient World Ser.). (Illus.). 160p. (YA). (gr. 6-12). lib. bdg. 29.27 *(978-0-7660-2559-2(4))* Enslow Pubs., Inc.

Wroble, Lisa A. Kids in Ancient Egypt. 2009. (Kids Throughout History Ser.). 24p. (gr. 3-3). 42.50 *(978-1-61513-894-4(3),* PowerKids Pr.) Rosen Publishing Group, Inc., The.

Yomtov, Nelson. Ancient Egypt. 2012. (Ancient World Ser.). (ENG., Illus.). 112p. (J). pap. 9.95 *(978-0-531-25977-1(3));* lib. bdg. 34.00 *(978-0-531-25177-5(2))* Scholastic Library Publishing.

EGYPT—HISTORY—FICTION

Berard, Robin M. King Tut & the Girl Who Loved Him: The Strange Adventures of Johanna Wilson. 2007. 212p. per. 12.95 *(978-1-58348-477-7(9),* iUniverse Star) iUniverse, Inc.

Booth, Bradley. Plagues in the Palace. 2006. 159p. (J). 10.99 *(978-0-8163-2143-8(4))* Pacific Pr. Publishing Assn.

Branzei, Sylvia. Ickstory - Unraveling the Icky History of Mummies. Keely, Jack, illus. 2009. (Penguin Young Readers, Level 4 Ser.). (ENG.). 48p. (J). (gr. 3-4). mass mkt. 3.99 *(978-0-448-45033-9(X),* Penguin Young Readers) Penguin Young Readers Group.

Collins, Tim. Diary of Dorkius Maximus in Egypt. Pinder, Andrew, illus. 2014. (Diary of Dorkius Maximus Ser.: 2). (ENG.). 192p. (J). (gr. 4-6). pap. 8.99 *(978-1-78055-028-2(6))* O'Mara, Michael Bks., Ltd. GBR. Dist: Independent Pubs. Group.

Dennard, Susan. Strange & Ever After. 2014. (Something Strange & Deadly Trilogy Ser.: 3). (ENG.). 400p. (YA). (gr. 9). 17.99 *(978-0-06-208332-6(5))* HarperCollins Pubs.

Durant, Alan. Spider Mcdrew & the Egyptians: Band 12. Hopman, Philip, illus. 2007. (Collins Big Cat Ser.). (ENG.). 32p. (J). (gr. 2-3). pap. 7.99 *(978-0-00-723076-1(1))* HarperCollins Pubs. Ltd. GBR. Dist: Independent Pubs. Group.

Ewert, Marcus. Mummy Cat. Brown, Lisa, illus. 2015. (ENG.). 48p. (J). (gr. 1-4). 16.99 *(978-0-544-34082-4(5),* Clarion Bks.) Houghton Mifflin Harcourt Trade & Reference Pubs.

Frazier, Angie. The Eternal Sea. 2011. (ENG.). 368p. (J). (gr. 7-7). 17.99 *(978-0-545-11475-2(6),* Scholastic Pr.) Scholastic, Inc.

Friesner, Esther M. Sphinx's Princess. 2010. (Princesses of Myth Ser.). (ENG.). 400p. (YA). (gr. 7). pap. 9.99 *(978-0-375-85655-6(2),* Random Hse. Bks. for Young Readers) Random Hse. Children's Bks.

—Sphinx's Queen. 2011. (Princesses of Myth Ser.). (ENG., Illus.). 368p. (YA). (gr. 7). pap. 9.99 *(978-0-375-85658-7(7),* Ember) Random Hse. Children's Bks.

Gantos, Jack. Rotten Ralph Helps Out. Rubel, Nicole, illus. unabr. ed. 2006. (Readalongs for Beginning Readers Ser.). (J). (gr. -1-3). 28.95 incl. audio compact disk *(978-1-59519-679-8(X));* 24.95 incl. audio *(978-1-59519-678-1(1))* Live Oak Media.

—Rotten Ralph Helps Out, 4 bks., Set. unabr. ed. 2006. (Readalongs for Beginning Readers Ser.). (Illus.). (J). (gr. -1-3). pap. 29.95 incl. audio *(978-1-59519-676-7(5));* pap. 31.95 incl. audio compact disk *(978-1-59519-677-4(3))* Live Oak Media.

Hamel, Mike. Pyramid Scheme. 2007. (Matterhorn the Brave Ser.: 3). (ENG.). 176p. (J). (gr. 5-7). per. 9.99 *(978-0-89957-835-4(7))* AMG Pubs.

Harvey, Gill. Orphan of the Sun. 2006. (ENG., Illus.). 320p. (YA). (gr. 3-7). 16.95 *(978-1-58234-685-4(2),* 9781582346854, Bloomsbury USA Childrens) Bloomsbury Publishing USA.

Henty, George Alfred. At Aboukir & Acre: A Story of Napoleon's Invasion of Egypt (Henty Homeschool History Series) 2010. 344p. pap. 19.95 *(978-1-935585-23-7(1))* Fireship Pr.

—The Cat of Bubastes. 2006. (ENG.). pap. 33.95 *(978-1-4286-0382-0(4))* Kessinger Publishing, LLC.

—The Cat of Bubastes: A Tale of Ancient Egypt. 2011. 344p. pap. 19.95 *(978-1-61179-125-9(1))* Fireship Pr.

Hernandez, David. Land of the Pharaohs, 1 vol. 2003. (Adventures of Toby Digz Ser.: 1). (ENG., Illus.). 96p. pap. 5.99 *(978-1-4003-0195-9(5))* Nelson, Thomas Inc.

Hofmeyr, Dianne. Eye of the Moon. 2011. (ENG.). 336p. (J). (gr. 3-7). pap. 9.99 *(978-1-4424-1188-3(0),* Aladdin) Simon & Schuster Children's Publishing.

—Eye of the Sun. 2011. (ENG.). 336p. (J). (gr. 3-7). pap. 6.99 *(978-1-4424-1186-9(4),* Aladdin) Simon & Schuster Children's Publishing.

Jones, Ruth Fosdick. Boy of the Pyramids: A Mystery of Ancient Egypt. Morse, Dorothy Bayley, illus. 2011. 150p. 40.95 *(978-1-258-06798-4(6))* Literary Licensing, LLC.

Kimmel, Eric A. Scarlett & Sam: Escape from Egypt. Stevanovic, Ivica, illus. 2015. (J). 6.99 *(978-1-4677-6207-6(5));* (ENG.). 168p. (gr. 1-3). lib. bdg. 15.95 *(978-1-4677-3850-7(6))* Lerner Publishing Group. (Kar-Ben Publishing).

Kramer, Alan. Ramses & Nefertari. 2005. (J). pap. *(978-1-4108-4224-4(X))* Benchmark Education Co.

LaFevers, R. L. Theodosia & the Serpents of Chaos. Tanaka, Yoko, illus. 2008. (ENG.). 352p. (J). (gr. 2-5). pap. 7.99 *(978-0-618-99976-7(0))* Houghton Mifflin Harcourt Publishing Co.

Meyer, Carolyn. Cleopatra Confesses. (ENG.). 304p. (YA). (gr. 7). 2012. pap. 11.99 *(978-1-4169-8728-4(2))* 2011. 16.99 *(978-1-4169-8727-7(4))* Simon & Schuster/Paula Wiseman Bks. (Simon & Schuster/Paula Wiseman Bks.).

Moss, Marissa. The Pharaoh's Secret. 2009. (ENG., Illus.). 320p. (J). (gr. 3-7). 16.95 *(978-0-8109-8378-6(8),* Amulet Bks.) Abrams, Inc.

Napoli, Donna Jo. Lights on the Nile. 2011. (ENG.). 288p. (J). (gr. 3-7). 16.99 *(978-0-06-166793-0(5))* HarperCollins Pubs.

Northrop, Michael. The Final Kingdom. 2016. (TombQuest Ser.: 5). (ENG.). 192p. (J). (gr. 3-7). 12.99 *(978-0-545-72342-8(6),* Scholastic Pr.) Scholastic, Inc.

Rubalcaba, Jill. The Wadjet Eye. 2006. (ENG.). 160p. (J). (gr. 5-7). pap. 7.99 *(978-0-618-68927-9(3))* Houghton Mifflin Harcourt Publishing Co.

Scieszka, Jon. Tut, Tut, No. 6. Smith, Lane, illus. 2004. (Time Warp Trio Ser.: 6). (ENG.). 80p. (J). (gr. 2-4). pap. 5.99 *(978-0-14-240047-0(5),* Puffin Books) Penguin Young Readers Group.

Shecter, Vicky Alvear. Cleopatra's Moon. 2013. (ENG.). 368p. (J). (gr. 9). pap. 9.99 *(978-0-545-22131-3(5),* Levine, Arthur A. Bks.) Scholastic, Inc.

Snyder, Zilpha Keatley. The Egypt Game. 2014. (ENG.). 240p. (J). (gr. 3-7). 11.24 *(978-1-63245-327-3(4))* Lectorum Pubns., Inc.

—The Egypt Game. Raible, Alton, illus. 2009. (ENG.). 240p. (J). (gr. 3-7). pap. 8.99 *(978-1-4169-9051-2(8),* Atheneum Bks. for Young Readers) Simon & Schuster Children's Publishing.

Stevenson, Steve. The Curse of the Pharaoh. 2013. (Agatha Girl of Mystery Ser.: 1). lib. bdg. 17.20 *(978-0-606-29986-2(6),* Turtleback) Turtleback Bks.

Surget, Alain & Yeardley, Glynne. Caesar, Who's He? Parme, Fabrice, illus. 2014. 95p. (J). *(978-1-4351-5328-8(6))* Barnes & Noble, Inc.

—Cleopatra Must Be Saved! Parme, Fabrice, illus. 2014. 95p. (J). *(978-1-4351-5329-5(4))* Barnes & Noble, Inc.

—Danger at the Circus! Parme, Fabrice, illus. 2014. 95p. (J). *(978-1-4351-5334-9(0))* Barnes & Noble, Inc.

—Prisoners in the Pyramid. Parme, Fabrice, illus. 2014. 94p. (J). *(978-1-4351-5326-4(X))* Barnes & Noble, Inc.

Thompson, James A., Jr. The Amarna Experiment. 2003. 128p. (YA). 21.95 *(978-0-595-65753-7(2));* pap. 11.95 *(978-0-595-28296-8(2))* iUniverse, Inc.

Thompson, Lisa. In Search of the Egyptian Queen. Cantell, Brenda, illus. 2006. (Treasure Trackers Ser.). 80p. (J). (gr. 3-4). lib. bdg. 19.00 *(978-0-7910-8874-6(X))* Facts On File, Inc.

Turetsky, Bianca. The Time-Traveling Fashionista & Cleopatra, Queen of the Nile. 2014. (Time-Traveling Fashionista Ser.: 3). (ENG.). 256p. (J). (gr. 3-7). pap. 10.00 *(978-0-316-22490-1(1),* Poppy) Little, Brown Bks. for Young Readers.

Twist, Clint. Cleopatra: Queen of Egypt. Andrew, Ian, illus. 2012. (Historical Notebooks Ser.). (ENG.). 30p. (J). (gr. 3-7). 19.99 *(978-0-7636-6095-6(7),* Templar) Candlewick Pr.

EGYPT—KINGS AND RULERS

Adams, Michelle Medlock. The Life & Times of Cleopatra. 2005. (Biography from Ancient Civilizations Ser.). (Illus.). 48p. (J). (gr. 4-8). lib. bdg. 29.95 *(978-1-58415-335-1(0))* Mitchell Lane Pubs., Inc.

Asselin, Kristine Carlson. Pharaohs & Dynasties of Ancient Egypt, 1 vol. 2012. (Ancient Egyptian Civilization Ser.). (ENG., Illus.). 32p. (gr. 3-4). lib. bdg. 27.32 *(978-1-4296-7631-1(0),* Fact Finders) Capstone Press of Coughlan Cos.

Barnham, Kay. Mangy Mummies, Menacing Pharaohs, & the Awful Afterlife: A Moth-Eaten History of the Extraordinary Egyptians! 2015. (Awfully Ancient Ser.). (ENG., Illus.). 32p. (J). (gr. 5-5). pap. 10.50 *(978-1-4824-3125-4(4))* Stevens, Gareth Publishing LLLP.

Baum, Margaux & Thomas, Susanna. Hatshepsut. 2016. (Leaders of the Ancient World Ser.). 00112p. (J). (gr. 6-6). 37.10 *(978-1-5081-7250-5(1))* Rosen Publishing Group, Inc., The.

Caravantes, Peggy. Cleopatra: Powerful Leader or Ruthless Pharaoh? 2015. (Perspectives on History Ser.). (ENG.). 32p. (gr. 3-4). lib. bdg. 27.32 *(978-1-4914-2042-3(1))* Capstone Press of Coughlan Cos.

Geyer, Flora. Saladin: The Warrior Who Defended His People. 2006. (National Geographic World History Biographies Ser.). (ENG., Illus.). 64p. (J). (gr. 3-7). 17.95 *(978-0-7922-5535-2(6));* lib. bdg. 27.90 *(978-0-7922-5536-9(4))* National Geographic Society. (National Geographic Children's Bks.).

Gunderson, Jessica. Your Life As a Pharaoh in Ancient Egypt, 1 vol. Ebbeler, Jeff, illus. 2012. (Way It Was Ser.). (ENG.). 32p. (gr. 2-3). lib. bdg. 26.65 *(978-1-4048-7371-1(6))* Picture Window Bks.

Gunderson, Jessica Sarah. Your Life As a Pharaoh in Ancient Egypt, 1 vol. Ebbeler, Jeff, illus. 2012. (Way It Was Ser.). (ENG.). 32p. (gr. 2-3). pap. 8.95 *(978-1-4048-7744-3(4))* Picture Window Bks.

Harvey, Gill. Tutankhamun. McNee, Ian, illus. 2006. (Usborne Young Reading Ser.). 64p. (J). (gr. 3-7). 8.99 *(978-0-7945-1271-2(2),* Usborne) EDC Publishing.

Helbrough, Emma. A Day in the Life of a Pharaoh. (Day in the Life Ser.). 32p. 2009. (gr. 4-5). 47.90 *(978-1-61511-006-3(2),* PowerKids Pr.) 2007. (J). (gr. 5-8). 25.25 *(978-1-4042-3852-7(2))* Rosen Publishing Group, Inc., The.

Marsh, Laura. Pyramids. 2017. (Readers Ser.). (ENG., Illus.). 32p. (J). (gr. -1-1). pap. 3.99 *(978-1-4263-2690-5(4),* National Geographic Children's Bks.) National Geographic Society.

Morley, Jacqueline. How to Be an Egyptian Princess. Hewetson, Nicholas J., illus. (How to Be Ser.). (ENG.). 32p. (J). (gr. 4-7). 2008. pap. 5.95 *(978-1-4263-0246-6(0))* 2006. 14.95 *(978-0-7922-7494-0(6))* 2006. lib. bdg. 21.90 *(978-0-7922-7548-0(9))* National Geographic Society. (National Geographic Children's Bks.).

Nardo, Don. Ramesses II: Ruler of Ancient Egypt. 2006. (Rulers of the Ancient World Ser.). (Illus.). 160p. (YA). (gr. 6). lib. bdg. 29.27 *(978-0-7660-2562-2(4))* Enslow Pubs., Inc.

Payne, Elizabeth. Pharoahs of Ancient Egypt. 2014. 16.00 *(978-1-63419-724-3(0))* Perfection Learning Corp.

Rockwood, Leigh. Ancient Egyptian Government. 2013. (Spotlight on Ancient Civilizations: Egypt Ser.). (ENG., Illus.). 24p. (J). (gr. 3-4). pap. 10.00 *(978-1-4777-0861-3(8));* lib. bdg. 23.60 *(978-1-4777-0764-7(6))* Rosen Publishing Group, Inc., The. (PowerKids Pr.).

Ross, Stewart. Clever Cleo. Shields, Sue, illus. 32p. pap. 9.99 *(978-0-7502-2853-4(9))* Hodder & Stoughton GBR. Dist: Trafalgar Square Publishing.

Santillian, Beatriz & Thomas, Susanna. Ahmose I: Pharaoh of the 18th Dynasty. 2017. (Leaders of the Ancient World Ser.). 112p. (J). (gr. 12-11). 37.10 ***(978-1-5081-7480-6(6),*** Rosen Young Adult) Rosen Publishing Group, Inc., The.

—Ramses II: The Most Powerful Pharaoh of Ancient Egypt. 2017. (Leaders of the Ancient World Ser.). 112p. (J). (gr. 12-11). 37.10 ***(978-1-5081-7489-9(X),*** Rosen Young Adult) Rosen Publishing Group, Inc., The.

Sheafer, Silvia Anne. Ramses the Great. 2008. (Ancient World Leaders Ser.). 136p. (gr. 6-12). 30.00 *(978-0-7910-9637-6(8),* Chelsea Hse.) Facts On File, Inc.

Spilsbury, Richard. Ramesses II, 1 vol. 2013. (Hero Journals). (ENG., Illus.). 48p. (gr. 4-6). 33.32 *(978-1-4109-5358-2(0));* pap. 9.95 *(978-1-4109-5365-0(3))* Heinemann-Raintree. (NA-r).

Streissguth, Tom. Queen Cleopatra. 2007. (Illus.). 112p. (J). pap. 9.95 *(978-0-8225-7061-5(0))* Lerner Publishing Group.

Uhl, Xina M. Cleopatra: Queen of Egypt. 2017. (Women Who Changed History Ser.). 48p. (gr. 10-12). 26.85 ***(978-1-68048-639-1(X),*** Britannica Educational Publishing) Rosen Publishing Group, Inc., The.

Whiting, Jim. The Life & Times of Rameses the Great. 2005. (Biography from Ancient Civilizations Ser.). (Illus.). 48p. (J). (gr. 5-8). lib. bdg. 29.95 *(978-1-58415-341-2(5))* Mitchell Lane Pubs., Inc.

World Book, Inc Staff, contrib. by. The Secrets of the Pharaohs. 2014. (J). *(978-0-7166-2666-4(7))* World Bk., Inc.

Worth, Richard. Saladin: Sultan of Egypt & Syria. 2007. (Rulers of the Middle Ages Ser.). (Illus.). 160p. (YA). (gr. 6-12). lib. bdg. 35.94 *(978-0-7660-2712-1(0))* Enslow Pubs., Inc.

EGYPTOLOGY

see Egypt—Antiquities

E F G

EINSTEIN, ALBERT, 1879-1955

Anderson, Jennifer Joline. Albert Einstein: Revolutionary Physicist, 1 vol. 2014. (Great Minds of Science Ser.). (ENG., Illus.). 48p. (J). (gr. 8-12). lib. bdg. 32.79 *(978-1-62403-379-7(2))* ABDO Publishing Co.

Berger, Melvin & Berger, Gilda. Did It Take Creativity to Find Relativity, Albert Einstein? Dorman, Brandon, illus. 2007. (Scholastic Science Supergiants Ser.). (ENG.). 48p. (J). (gr. 2-5). pap. 4.99 *(978-0-439-83384-4(1),* Scholastic Nonfiction) Scholastic, Inc.

Berne, Jennifer. On a Beam of Light: A Story of Albert Einstein. Radunsky, Vladimir, illus. (ENG.). 56p. (J). 2016. (gr. k-3). 7.99 *(978-1-4521-5211-0(X))* 2013. (gr. 1-4). 17.99 *(978-0-8118-7235-5(1))* Chronicle Bks. LLC.

Brallier, Jess M. Who Was Albert Einstein? Parker, Robert Andrew, illus. 2003. (Who Was... ? Ser.). 105p. (gr. 4-7). 15.00 *(978-0-7569-1586-5(4))* Perfection Learning Corp.

Brown, Don. Odd Boy Out: Young Albert Einstein. 2008. (ENG., Illus.). 32p. (J). (gr. -1-3). pap. 7.99 *(978-0-547-01435-7(X))* Houghton Mifflin Harcourt Publishing Co.

Colson, Mary. Albert Einstein & Sir Arthur Eddington. 2014. (Dynamic Duos of Science Ser.). 48p. (YA). (gr. 5-8). pap. 84.30 *(978-1-4824-1276-5(4))* Stevens, Gareth Publishing LLLP.

Cugota, Lluís, et al. Albert Einstein. 2004. (Me Llamo Ser.). (SPA., Illus.). 60p. (J). (gr. 4-7). pap. *(978-84-342-2603-6(0),* PR33293) Parramon Ediciones S.A.

Dakers, Diane. Albert Einstein: Forging the Path of Modern Physics. 2013. (ENG., Illus.). 112p. (J). *(978-0-7787-1188-9(9));* pap. *(978-0-7787-1190-2(0))* Crabtree Publishing Co.

Delano, Marfe Ferguson. Genius. 2008. (Photobiographies Ser.). (ENG., Illus.). 64p. (J). (gr. 5). 7.95 *(978-1-4263-0294-7(0),* National Geographic Children's Bks.) National Geographic Society.

Delano, Marfe Ferguson & National Geographic Kids Staff. Genius: A Photobiography of Albert Einstein. 2015. (Photobiographies Ser.). (ENG.). 64p. (J). (gr. 5). pap. 7.99 *(978-1-4263-2219-8(4),* National Geographic Children's Bks.) National Geographic Society.

Forman, Lillian E. Albert Einstein: Physicist & Genius, 1 vol. 2009. (Essential Lives Set 3 Ser.). (ENG., Illus.). 112p. (J). (gr. 6-12). lib. bdg. 35.64 *(978-1-60453-524-2(5))* ABDO Publishing Co.

Frisch, Aaron. Albert Einstein. 2005. (Genius Ser.). (Illus.). 48p. (J). (gr. 5-9). lib. bdg. 21.95 *(978-1-58341-328-9(6),* Creative Education) Creative Co., The.

Goldenstern, Joyce. Albert Einstein: Genius of the Theory of Relativity. 2015. (Genius Scientists & Their Genius Ideas Ser.). 96p. (J). (gr. 5-12). 27.94 *(978-0-7660-6515-4(4));* pap. 10.95 *(978-0-7660-6516-1(2))* Enslow Pubs., Inc.

—Albert Einstein: Physicist & Genius. rev. ed. 2007. (Great Minds of Science Ser.). (Illus.). 128p. (J). (gr. 4-10). lib. bdg. 33.27 *(978-0-7660-2838-8(0))* Enslow Pubs., Inc.

Gomez, Rebecca. Albert Einstein, 1 vol. 2003. (First Biographies Ser.). (ENG., Illus.). 32p. (J). (gr. 1-4). 27.07 *(978-1-57765-946-4(5))* ABDO Publishing Co.

Gordon, Fernando. Albert Einstein, 1 vol. 2016. (ENG., Illus.). 24p. (J). *(978-1-68078-155-7(3))* ABDO Publishing Co.

Hanson-Harding, Alexandra. Albert Einstein, 01 vols., 1. 2016. (Britannica Beginner Bios Ser.). (ENG., Illus.). 32p. (J). pap. 12.90 *(978-1-5081-0060-7(6),* Britannica Educational Publishing) Rosen Publishing Group, Inc., The.

Hasday, Judy L. Albert Einstein: The Giant of 20th Century Science. 2004. (Nobel Prize-Winning Scientists Ser.). (Illus.). 128p. (J). lib. bdg. 26.60 *(978-0-7660-2185-3(8))* Enslow Pubs., Inc.

Herweck, Don. Albert Einstein: Gentle Genius, 1 vol. 2007. (Science Readers Ser.). (ENG.). 32p. (J). (gr. 3-3). pap. 8.99 *(978-0-7439-0572-5(5))* Shell Educational Publishing.

Hunter, Nick. Gravity. 2017. (Great Scientific Theories Ser.). (ENG.). 32p. (gr. 4-6). lib. bdg. 30.65 ***(978-1-4109-8729-7(9),*** Raintree Perspectives) Heinemann-Raintree.

James, Emily. Albert Einstein. 2017. (Great Scientists & Inventors Ser.). (ENG., Illus.). 24p. (gr. k-1). lib. bdg. 26.65 *(978-1-5157-3884-8(1),* Pebble Plus) Capstone Press of Coughlan Cos.

Kleiner, Mariela. Meet Einstein. Garofoli, Viviana, illus. 2011. 28p. (J). (gr. -1-1). lib. bdg. *(978-0-615-31579-9(8))* Meet Bks., LLC.

Krull, Kathleen. Albert Einstein. Kulikov, Boris, illus. (Giants of Science Ser.). (ENG.). 144p. (J). (gr. 3-7). 2015. 7.99 *(978-0-14-751464-6(9),* Puffin Books) 2009. 15.99 *(978-0-670-06332-1(0),* Viking Books for Young Readers) Penguin Young Readers Group.

Lakin, Patricia. Albert Einstein: Genius of the Twentieth Century. Daniel, Alan & Daniel, Lea, illus. 2005. (Ready-To-read SOFA Ser.). (ENG.). 48p. (J). (gr. 1-3). pap. 3.99 *(978-0-689-87034-7(5),* Simon Spotlight) Simon Spotlight.

Lassieur, Allison. Albert Einstein: Genius of the Twentieth Century. 2005. (Great Life Stories Ser.). (ENG., Illus.). 127p. (J). (gr. 6-8). 30.50 *(978-0-531-12401-7(0),* Watts, Franklin) Scholastic Library Publishing.

MacLeod, Elizabeth. Albert Einstein: A Life of Genius. 2003. (Snapshots: Images of People & Places in History Ser.). (ENG., Illus.). 32p. (J). (gr. 3-7). 6.95 *(978-1-55337-397-1(9))* Kids Can Pr., Ltd. CAN. Dist: Hachette Bk. Group.

Marsh, Carole. Albert Einstein. 2003. 12p. (gr. k-4). 2.95 *(978-0-635-02352-0(0))* Gallopade International.

Marsico, Katie. Genius Physicist Albert Einstein. 2017. (STEM Trailblazer Bios Ser.). (ENG.). 32p. (J). (gr. 2-5). pap. 8.99 ***(978-1-5124-5629-5(2));*** (Illus.). 26.65 ***(978-1-5124-3451-4(5),*** Lerner Pubns.) Lerner Publishing Group.

Mattern, Joanne & Santrey, Laurence. Albert Einstein, Creative Genius. Beier, Ellen, illus. 2005. 45p. (J). pap. *(978-0-439-80152-2(4))* Scholastic, Inc.

May, Andrew. Albert Einstein: Scientist. 2016. (History Makers Ser.). 144p. (J). 45.64 *(978-1-5026-2441-3(9))* Cavendish Square Publishing.

McLeese, Don. Albert Einstein. 2005. (Inventores Famosos Ser.). (SPA & ENG., Illus.). 24p. (J). 22.79 *(978-1-59515-673-0(9))* Rourke Educational Media.

McPherson, Stephanie Sammartino. Albert Einstein. 48p. (J). (gr. 2-5). 18.95 *(978-1-58013-094-3(1),* Kar-Ben Publishing); 2004. (Illus.). (gr. 3-5). lib. bdg. 26.60 *(978-0-8225-0350-7(6))* Lerner Publishing Group.

Meltzer, Brad. I Am Albert Einstein. Eliopoulos, Christopher, illus. 2014. (Ordinary People Change the World Ser.). (ENG.). 40p. (J). (gr. k-3). 14.99 *(978-0-8037-4084-6(0),* Dial Bks) Penguin Young Readers Group.

Meltzer, Milton. Albert Einstein: A Biography. 2007. (ENG., Illus.). 48p. (J). (gr. 1-5). 16.95 *(978-0-8234-1966-1(5))* Holiday Hse., Inc.

Miklowitz, Gloria D. Albert Einstein. 2004. (ENG., Illus.). 32p. (J). (gr. 2-5). pap. 5.97 net. *(978-0-7685-1212-0(3),* Dominie Elementary) Pearson Schl.

Morton, Alan. Einstein's Theories of Relativity. 2005. (Milestones in Modern Science Ser.). 48p. (gr. 6-12). pap. 14.05 *(978-0-8368-5860-0(3));* (Illus.). lib. bdg. 31.00 *(978-0-8368-5853-2(0))* Stevens, Gareth Publishing LLLP. (Gareth Stevens Secondary Library).

Norwich, Grace. Albert Einstein. Simon, Ute, illus. 2012. (I Am Ser.). (ENG.). 112p. (J). (gr. 3-7). pap. 5.99 *(978-0-545-40575-1(0),* Scholastic Paperbacks) Scholastic, Inc.

Novelli, Luca. Einstein & the Time Machine. 2017. (Flashes of Genius Ser.). (ENG., Illus.). 112p. (J). (gr. 3). pap. 9.99 ***(978-1-61373-865-8(X))*** Chicago Review Pr., Inc.

Peare, Catherine Owens. Albert Einstein: A Biography for Young People. 2011. 168p. 41.95 *(978-1-258-01618-0(4))* Literary Licensing, LLC.

Pohlen, Jerome. Albert Einstein & Relativity for Kids: His Life & Ideas with 21 Activities & Thought Experiments. 2012. (For Kids Ser.). (ENG., Illus.). 144p. (J). (gr. 4). pap. 16.95 *(978-1-61374-028-6(X))* Chicago Review Pr., Inc.

Renn, Jürgen, ed. Einstein's Annalen Papers (Annalen der Physik) The Complete Collection, 1901-1922. 2005. (ENG & GER., Illus.). 590p. 176.00 *(978-3-527-40564-0(X),* Wiley-VCH) Wiley, John & Sons, Inc.

Romero, Libby & National Geographic Kids Staff. Albert Einstein. 2016. (Readers Bios Ser.). (ENG., Illus.). 48p. (J). (gr. 1-4). pap. 3.99 *(978-1-4263-2536-6(3),* National Geographic Children's Bks.) National Geographic Society.

Rooney, Anne. Albert Einstein & His Theory of Relativity. 2012. (Miracle Makers Ser.). (ENG.). 48p. (YA). (gr. 5-8). 27.95 *(978-1-4488-6038-8(5),* Rosen Reference) Rosen Publishing Group, Inc., The.

Saddleback Educational Publishing Staff, ed. Albert Einstein, 1 vol. unabr. ed. 2008. (Graphic Biographies Ser.). (ENG., Illus.). 25p. (YA). (gr. 9-12). pap. 7.95 *(978-1-59905-212-0(1))* Saddleback Educational Publishing, Inc.

Santrey, Laurence & Mattern, Joanne. Un Genio Creativo. Beier, Ellen, illus. 2007.Tr. of Albert Einstein. (SPA & ENG.). 48p. (J). (gr. k-2). pap. 4.99 *(978-0-439-87479-3(3),* Scholastic en Espanol) Scholastic, Inc.

Slade, Suzanne. Albert Einstein: Scientist & Genius. Schultz, Jolene, illus. 2007. (Biographies Ser.). (ENG.). 24p. (gr. k-3). 25.99 *(978-1-4048-3730-0(2),* Nonfiction Picture Bks.) Picture Window Bks.

Sprunger, Reed. Albert Einstein: Brilliant Scientist, 1 vol. 2013. (Beginner Biographies Set 2 Ser.). (ENG.). 32p. (J). (gr. -1-4). lib. bdg. 28.50 *(978-1-61641-937-0(7),* Looking Glass Library) Magic Wagon.

Sullivan, Anne Marie. Albert Einstein: Great Scientist. 2013. (Illus.). (J). *(978-1-4222-2839-5(8));* (People of Importance Ser.: 21). 32p. (gr. 4-18). 19.95 *(978-1-4222-2840-1(1))* Mason Crest.

Venezia, Mike. Albert Einstein: Universal Genius. Venezia, Mike, illus. (Getting to Know the World's Greatest Inventors & Scientists Ser.). (ENG., Illus.). 32p. (J). 2009. (gr. 3-4). pap. 6.95 *(978-0-531-22206-5(3),* Children's Pr.) 2008. (gr. 2-5). 28.00 *(978-0-531-14975-1(7))* Scholastic Library Publishing.

Wade McCormick, Lisa. Albert Einstein. 2014. (Great Science Writers Ser.). (Illus.). 112p. (J). (gr. 7-12). 35.60 *(978-1-4777-7687-2(7))* Rosen Publishing Group, Inc., The.

Yasuda, Anita. Albert Einstein. 2013. (J). *(978-1-62127-305-9(9));* pap. *(978-1-62127-311-0(3))* Weigl Pubs., Inc.

Yeatts, Tabatha. Albert Einstein: The Miracle Mind. 2007. (Sterling Biographies(r) Ser.). (ENG., Illus.). 128p. (J). (gr. 5-9). pap. 5.95 *(978-1-4027-3228-7(7))* Sterling Publishing Co., Inc.

EISENHOWER, DWIGHT D. (DWIGHT DAVID), 1890-1969

Adler, David A. A Picture Book of Dwight David Eisenhower. 2004. (ENG., Illus.). 32p. (J). (gr. -1-3). per. 6.95 *(978-0-8234-1830-5(8))* Holiday Hse., Inc.

Alphin, Elaine Marie & Alphin, Arthur B. Dwight D. Eisenhower. 2005. (History Maker Bios Ser.). (Illus.). 48p. (J). (gr. 3-5). lib. bdg. 26.60 *(978-0-8225-1544-9(X))* Lerner Publishing Group.

Aronin, Miriam. Dwight D. Eisenhower. 2016. (First Look at America's Presidents Ser.). (ENG., Illus.). 24p. (J). (gr. -1-3). 17.95 *(978-1-943553-31-0(9))* Bearport Publishing Co., Inc.

Britton, Tamara L. Dwight D. Eisenhower, 1 vol. 2009. (United States Presidents Ser.). (ENG., Illus.). 40p. (YA). (gr. 3-6). 27.07 *(978-1-60453-449-8(4))* ABDO Publishing Co.

Darby, Jean. Dwight D. Eisenhower. 2004. (Presidential Leaders Ser.). (Illus.). 112p. (J). (gr. 6-12). lib. bdg. 29.27 *(978-0-8225-0813-7(3))* Lerner Publishing Group.

Mara, Wil. Dwight Eisenhower. 2010. (Presidents & Their Times 4 Ser.). 96p. (gr. 6). 34.21 *(978-0-7614-4812-9(8))* Marshall Cavendish GBR. Dist: Marshall Cavendish Corp.

Miller, Mirella S. Dwight D. Eisenhower. 2017. (Premier Presidents Ser.). (ENG.). 24p. (J). (gr. 1-4). lib. bdg. 27.07 *(978-1-5038-1644-2(3),* 211487) Child's World, Inc., The.

Randolph, Ryan P. How to Draw the Life & Times of Dwight D. Eisenhower. 2007. (Kid's Guide to Drawing the Presidents of the United States of America Ser.). (Illus.). 32p. (YA). (gr. 2-5). 25.25 *(978-1-4042-3010-1(6))* Rosen Publishing Group, Inc., The.

Schuetz, Randy. Dwight D. Eisenhower: A MyReportLinks. Com Book. 2003. (Presidents Ser.). (Illus.). 48p. (J). (gr. 5-10). lib. bdg. 25.26 *(978-0-7660-5102-7(1),* MyReportLinks.com Bks.) Enslow Pubs., Inc.

Venezia, Mike. Dwight D. Eisenhower: Thirty-Fourth President 1953-1961. Venezia, Mike, illus. 2007. (Getting to Know the U. S. Presidents Ser.). (Illus.). 32p. (J). (gr. 3-4). 28.00 *(978-0-516-22638-5(X),* Children's Pr.) Scholastic Library Publishing.

Young, Jeff C. Dwight D. Eisenhower: Soldier & President. 2004. (Notable Americans Ser.). (Illus.). 128p. (YA). (gr. 6-12). 23.95 *(978-1-883846-76-3(5),* First Biographies) Reynolds, Morgan Inc.

EL GRECO, 1541?-1614

see Greco, 1541?-1614

EL NINO CURRENT

Bredeson, Carmen. Deadly Storm Alert! The Dangerous el Niño & la Niña. 2012. (Disasters — People in Peril Ser.). (Illus.). 48p. (J). (gr. 5-18). 25.27 *(978-0-7660-4014-4(3))* Enslow Pubs., Inc.

EL SALVADOR

Deem, James M. El Salvador: A MyReportLinks. com Book. 2004. (Top Ten Countries of Recent Immigrants Ser.). (Illus.). 48p. (J). lib. bdg. 26.60 *(978-0-7660-5241-3(9),* MyReportLinks.com Bks.) Enslow Pubs., Inc.

DiPiazza, Francesca Davis. El Salvador in Pictures. 2007. (Visual Geography (Lerner) Ser.). (Illus.). 80p. (YA). (gr. 7-12). lib. bdg. 31.93 *(978-0-8225-7145-2(5))* Twenty First Century Bks.

Foley, Erin & Hapipi, Rafiz. El Salvador. 2nd rev. ed. 2005. (Cultures of the World Ser.). (Illus.). 144p. (gr. 6-10). lib. bdg. 42.79 *(978-0-7614-1967-9(5),* Benchmark Bks.) Marshall Cavendish Corp.

Markovics, Joyce L. El Salvador. 2015. (Countries We Come From Ser.). (ENG., Illus.). 32p. (J). (gr. k-3). lib. bdg. 26.60 *(978-1-62724-859-4(5))* Bearport Publishing Co., Inc.

Shields, Charles J. El Salvador. 2010. (Central America Today Ser.). 63p. (YA). (gr. 7-18). pap. 9.95 *(978-1-4222-0714-7(5));* (Illus.). (gr. 9-12). 21.95 *(978-1-4222-0647-8(5))* Mason Crest.

—El Salvador, Vol. 8. Henderson, James D., ed. 2015. (Discovering Central America: History, Politics, & Culture Ser.). (Illus.). 64p. (J). (gr. 7). lib. bdg. 22.95 *(978-1-4222-3288-0(3))* Mason Crest.

Simmons, Walter. El Salvador. 2012. (Exploring Countries Ser.). (ENG., Illus.). 32p. (J). (gr. 3-7). lib. bdg. 26.95 *(978-1-60014-730-2(5),* Blastoff! Readers) Bellwether Media.

EL SALVADOR—FICTION

Argueta, Jorge. Alfredito Flies Home, 1 vol. Amado, Elisa, tr. from SPA. Garay, Luis, illus. 2007. (ENG.). 40p. (J). (gr. -1-4). 17.95 *(978-0-88899-585-8(7))* Groundwood Bks. CAN. Dist: Publishers Group West (PGW).

—La Fiesta de Las Tortillas: The Fiesta of the Tortillas. Hayes, Joe & Franco, Sharon, trs. from SPA. Alvarez, Maria Jesus, illus. 2006. (Bilingual Bks). (ENG & SPA.). 32p. (gr. 3-5). 15.95 *(978-1-59820-094-2(1),* Alfaguara) Santillana USA Publishing Co., Inc.

Bencastro, Mario. A Promise to Keep. Giersbach-Rascon, Susan, tr. from SPA. 2005. 134p. (J). (gr. 3-7). pap. 9.95 *(978-1-55885-457-4(6),* Piñata Books) Arte Publico Pr.

Harrell, Deborah A. Pintos Hope. 2003. 124p. (YA). pap. 10.95 *(978-0-595-26514-5(6),* Writers Club Pr.) iUniverse, Inc.

ELECTIONEERING

see Politics, Practical

ELECTIONS

see also Presidents—United States—Election; Suffrage

Allen, Nancy Kelly. What's an Election? 2012. (ENG.). 24p. (gr. k-2). pap. 8.95 *(978-1-61810-277-5(X))* Rourke Educational Media.

Barnaton, Paul. Elections: Choosing Our Leaders. 2009. (Real Life Readers Ser.). 24p. (gr. 3-4). pap. 8.25 *(978-1-4358-0084-7(2),* Rosen Classroom); 42.50 *(978-1-61512-341-4(5),* PowerKids Pr.); (J). 22.60 *(978-1-4358-2979-4(4),* PowerKids Pr.) Rosen Publishing Group, Inc., The.

Behrens, Janice. Let's Vote on It! 2009. (Scholastic News Nonfiction Readers Ser.). (ENG.). 24p. (J). (gr. 1-2). pap. 6.95 *(978-0-531-21445-9(1),* Children's Pr.); lib. bdg. 22.00 *(978-0-531-21346-9(3))* Scholastic Library Publishing.

Berlatsky, Noah. Voting Rights. Greenhaven Press Staff, ed. 2015. (Opposing Viewpoints Ser.). (ENG.). 224p. (gr. 10-12). pap. 33.80 *(978-0-7377-7301-9(4),* Greenhaven Pr., Inc.) Cengage Gale.

Boothroyd, Jennifer. What Are Elections? 2015. (ENG., Illus.). 24p. (J). (gr. k-2). 23.99 *(978-1-4677-8576-1(8),* Lerner Pubns.) Lerner Publishing Group.

Bright-Moore, Susan & Bedesky, Baron. How Is a Government Elected? 2008. (Your Guide to Government Ser.). (ENG.). 32p. (J). (gr. k-5). lib. bdg. *(978-0-7787-4325-5(X));* (Illus.). pap. *(978-0-7787-4330-9(6))* Crabtree Publishing Co.

Burgan, Michael. Voting & Elections, 1 vol. 2012. (Ethics of Politics Ser.). (ENG.). 64p. (gr. 6-10). pap. 10.95 *(978-1-4329-6557-0(3));* lib. bdg. 35.99 *(978-1-4329-6552-5(2))* Heinemann-Raintree.

Christelow, Eileen. Vote! 2008. (ENG., Illus.). 48p. (J). (gr. 1-4). pap. 9.99 *(978-0-547-05973-0(6))* Houghton Mifflin Harcourt Publishing Co.

—Vote! Christelow, Eileen, illus. 2004. (Illus.). 48p. (J). (gr. 1-5). 47.60 *(978-0-618-51723-7(5),* Clarion Bks.) Houghton Mifflin Harcourt Trade & Reference Pubs.

Cunningham, Kevin. How Political Campaigns & Elections Work, 1 vol. 2014. (How the US Government Works). (ENG.). 48p. (gr. 3-6). lib. bdg. 32.79 *(978-1-62403-633-0(3))* ABDO Publishing Co.

De Capua, Sarah. Running for Public Office. 2012. (True Book Ser.). (ENG., Illus.). 48p. (J). pap. 6.95 *(978-0-531-26213-9(8));* lib. bdg. 29.00 *(978-0-531-26041-8(0))* Scholastic Library Publishing.

—Voting. 2012. (True Book(tm), A — Civics Ser.). (ENG., Illus.). 48p. (J). lib. bdg. 31.00 *(978-0-531-26043-2(7));* pap. 6.95 *(978-0-531-26215-3(4))* Scholastic Library Publishing.

Deitch, JoAnne Weisman, ed. Voting in America. 2003. (Researching American History Ser.). (ENG., Illus.). 52p. (J). pap. 8.95 *(978-1-57960-092-1(1))* History Compass, LLC.

Dillies, Lyn. Your Vote Is Magic! 2012. 184p. pap. 14.95 *(978-0-615-66530-6(6))* Dillies, Lyn.

Donovan, Sandy. Running for Office: A Look at Political Campaigns. 2003. (How Government Works). (ENG., Illus.). 56p. (gr. 4-8). lib. bdg. 25.26 *(978-0-8225-4700-6(7))* Lerner Publishing Group.

—Special Interests: From Lobbyists to Campaign Funding. 2015. (ENG.). 64p. (J). (gr. 6-8). 26.65 *(978-1-4677-7912-8(1),* Lerner Pubns.) Lerner Publishing Group.

Election Reform. 2nd rev. ed. 2010. (Point/Counterpoint Ser.). (Illus.). 128p. (C). (gr. 9). 35.00 *(978-1-60413-691-3(X),* Chelsea Hse.) Facts On File, Inc.

Engdahl, Sylvia. Amendment XXVI — Lowering the Voting Age. 2009. (CONSTITUTIONAL AMENDMENTS Ser.). (ENG., Illus.). 144p. (YA). (gr. 9-12). 37.90 *(978-0-7377-4453-8(7))* Cengage Gale.

Espejo, Roman. Voter Fraud. 2010. (At Issue Ser.). (Illus.). 128p. 34.45 *(978-0-7377-4693-8(9));* pap. 24.45 *(978-0-7377-4694-5(7))* Cengage Gale. (Greenhaven Pr., Inc.).

Fleischer, Jeff. Votes of Confidence: A Young Person's Guide to American Elections. 2016. (YA). lib. bdg. 25.75 *(978-0-606-37982-3(7))* Turtleback Bks.

Ford, Jeanne Marie. How Elections Work. 2016. (How America Works). (ENG.). 24p. (J). (gr. 3-6). 28.50 *(978-1-5038-0902-4(1),* 210659) Child's World, Inc., The.

Gagne, Tammy. A Kid's Guide to the Voting Process. 2012. (J). lib. bdg. 29.95 *(978-1-61228-260-2(1))* Mitchell Lane Pubs., Inc.

Goodman, Susan E. See How They Run: Campaign Dreams, Election Schemes, & the Race to the White House. Smith, Elwood, illus. 2nd rev. ed. 2012. (ENG.). 96p. (J). (gr. 3-12). pap. 9.99 *(978-1-59990-897-7(2),* 9781599908977, Bloomsbury USA Childrens) Bloomsbury Publishing USA.

Gorman, Jacqueline Laks. Por Qué Son Importantes Las Elecciones? 2008. (Conoce tu gobierno (Know Your Government) Ser.). (SPA.). 24p. (gr. 1-4). pap. 8.15 *(978-0-8368-8857-7(X),* Weekly Reader Leveled Readers) Stevens, Gareth Publishing LLLP.

—Por Que Son Importantes las Elecciones? 2008. (Conoce tu gobierno (Know Your Government) Ser.). (SPA., Illus.). 24p. (gr. 1-4). lib. bdg. 22.00 *(978-0-8368-8852-2(9),* Weekly Reader Leveled Readers) Stevens, Gareth Publishing LLLP.

—Why Are Elections Important? 2008. (Know Your Government Ser.). 24p. (gr. 1-4). pap. 8.15 *(978-0-8368-8847-8(2));* (Illus.). lib. bdg. 22.00 *(978-0-8368-8842-3(1))* Stevens, Gareth Publishing LLLP. (Weekly Reader Leveled Readers).

Graham, Roland & National Geographic Learning Staff. Let's Vote! Learning to Use Simple Bar Graphs. 2010. (Rise & Shine Ser.). (ENG.). 12p. (C). (gr. 1-2). pap. 9.95 *(978-0-8239-8864-8(3))* National Geographic School Publishing, Inc.

Grayson, Robert. Voters: From Primaries to Decision Night. 2015. (ENG.). 64p. (J). (gr. 6-8). 26.65 *(978-1-4677-7911-1(3))* Lerner Publishing Group.

Harper, Leslie. How Do Elections Work? 2012. (Civics Q & A Ser.). (ENG., Illus.). 24p. (J). (gr. 3-6). pap. 8.25 *(978-1-4488-7505-4(6));* lib. bdg. 22.60 *(978-1-4488-7432-3(7))* Rosen Publishing Group, Inc., The. (PowerKids Pr.).

Hudak, Heather C. Election Day. (American Celebrations Ser.). (Illus.). 24p. (J). (gr. 3-5). 2012. (ENG.). lib. bdg. 27.13 *(978-1-61913-863-6(8),* AV2 by Weigl) 2006. per. 8.95 *(978-1-59036-407-9(4))* 2006. lib. bdg. 24.45 *(978-1-59036-404-8(X))* Weigl Pubs., Inc.

—Election Day with Code. 2012. (American Celebrations Ser.). (ENG., Illus.). 24p. (J). (gr. 3-5). pap. 12.95 *(978-1-61913-866-7(2),* AV2 by Weigl) Weigl Pubs., Inc.

Hunt, Santana. Why Do We Vote? 2017. (Look at Your Government Ser.). 32p. (J). (gr. 2-2). pap. 10.50 ***(978-1-4824-6067-4(X))*** Stevens, Gareth Publishing LLLP.

Jackson, Richelle. Running for Class President: Represent & Solve Problems Involving Division. 2014. (Rosen Common Core Math Readers Ser.). 24p. (J). (gr. 3-4). (ENG.). pap. 49.50 *(978-1-4777-4960-9(8),* Rosen Classroom); (ENG., Illus.). pap. 8.25 *(978-1-4777-4959-3(4),* PowerKids Pr.); (Illus.). lib. bdg. 23.60 *(978-1-4777-6448-0(8),* PowerKids Pr.) Rosen Publishing Group, Inc., The.

Jennett, Pamela & Marchant, Sherry. Electing Our President: The Process to Elect the Nation's Leader. Jennett, Pamela, ed. Hillam, Corbin & Grayson, Rick, illus. 2004. 48p. pap. 8.99 *(978-0-88160-379-8(1),* LW-436) Creative Teaching Pr., Inc.

Kafer, Kathy, et al. Opinions about the Voting Age. 2014. (Text Connections Ser.). (J). (gr. 3). *(978-1-4509-9661-7(2))* Benchmark Education Co.

Kowalski, Kathiann M. Campaign Politics: What's Fair, What's Foul? 2005. (Pro/Con Ser.). (Illus.). 144p. (gr. 6-12). lib. bdg. 25.26 *(978-0-8225-2630-8(1))* Lerner Publishing Group.

Lankford, Ronald D., ed. Should the Voting Age Be Lowered? 2007. (At Issue Ser.). (ENG., Illus.). 114p. (YA). (gr. 8-12). 24.45 *(978-0-7377-3937-4(1),* Greenhaven Pr., Inc.); (gr. 9-12). pap. 34.45 *(978-0-7377-3936-7(3))* Cengage Gale.

Lansford, Tom. Voting Rights. 2008. (Opposing Viewpoints Ser.). (ENG., Illus.). 225p. (YA). (gr. 10-12). 29.45 *(978-0-7377-4015-8(9),* LML02109-239974, Greenhaven Pr., Inc.) Cengage Gale.

Lansford, Tom, ed. Voting Rights. 2008. (Opposing Viewpoints Ser.). (ENG., Illus.). 186p. (gr. 10-12). 46.45 *(978-0-7377-4014-1(0),* LML02109-239981, Greenhaven Pr., Inc.) Cengage Gale.

Liljeblad, Fredrik. Voting. 2007. (21st Century Skills Library: Citizens & Their Governments Ser.). (ENG., Illus.). 32p. (gr. 4-8). lib. bdg. 28.50 *(978-1-60279-062-9(0),* 200009) Cherry Lake Publishing.

Maloof, Torrey. Understanding Elections, Levels K-2. 2015. (Elections Ser.). (ENG., Illus.). 112p. (gr. k-2). pap. 15.99 *(978-1-4258-1352-9(6))* Shell Educational Publishing.

Mann, Juda, et al. My Vote Counts! 2014. (Text Connections Ser.). (J). (gr. 3). *(978-1-4509-9659-4(0))* Benchmark Education Co.

Manning, Jack. Voting in Elections, 1 vol. 2014. (Our Government Ser.). (ENG.). 24p. (gr. 1-2). lib. bdg. 25.32 *(978-1-4914-0334-1(9))* Capstone Press of Coughlan Cos.

Mara, Wil. Electing Leaders. 2016. (21st Century Skills Library: a Citizen's Guide Ser.). (ENG., Illus.). 32p. (J). (gr. 4-7). 29.93 *(978-1-63471-066-4(5),* 208343) Cherry Lake Publishing.

—Voting. 2016. (21st Century Skills Library: a Citizen's Guide Ser.). (ENG., Illus.). 32p. (J). (gr. 4-7). 29.93 *(978-1-63471-072-5(X),* 208367) Cherry Lake Publishing.

Martin, Bobi. What Are Elections? 2015. (Let's Find Out! Government Ser.). (ENG., Illus.). 32p. (J). (gr. 2-3). 23.45 *(978-1-62275-966-8(4),* Britannica Educational Publishing) Rosen Publishing Group, Inc., The.

McGraw, Earl. Electing Our Leaders. 2012. (I'm an American Citizen Ser.). (ENG., Illus.). 24p. (J). (gr. 1-3). 22.60 *(978-1-4488-8583-1(3)*, PowerKids Pr.) Rosen Publishing Group, Inc., The.

McNamara, Margaret. Election Day. Gordon, Mike, illus. 2004. (Robin Hill School Ser.). (ENG.). 32p. (J). (gr. -1-1). pap. 3.99 *(978-0-689-86425-4(6)*, Simon Spotlight) Simon Spotlight.

Merino, Noël. The Election Process. 2012. (Introducing Issues with Opposing Viewpoints Ser.). (ENG., Illus.). 144p. (gr. 7-10). lib. bdg. 42.00 *(978-0-7377-6276-1(4)*, Greenhaven Pr., Inc.) Cengage Gale.

Miller, Davis Worth & Brevard, Katherine M. Political Elections, 1 vol. Barnett, Charles, III, illus. 2008. (Cartoon Nation Ser.). (ENG.). 32p. (gr. 3-4). 30.65 *(978-1-4296-1333-0(5)*, Graphic Library) Capstone Press of Coughlan Cos.

Mills, Nathan & McGraw, Earl. Electing Our Leaders. 2012. (Rosen Readers Ser.). (ENG., Illus.). 24p. (J). (gr. 1-2). pap. 8.25 *(978-1-4488-8842-9(5))*; pap. 49.50 *(978-1-4488-8843-6(3))* Rosen Publishing Group, Inc., The. (Rosen Classroom).

Moran, Lisa. Making a Difference SB3 I Want Your Vote! 2010. (Connect to Literacy Ser.). 8p. pap. *(978-1-4334-0505-1(9))* Millmark Education.

Nelson, Robin & Donovan, Sandra. Getting Elected: A Look at Running for Office. 2012. (Searchlight Books How Does Government Work Ser.). (ENG., Illus.). 40p. (gr. 3-5). lib. bdg. 27.93 *(978-0-7613-6519-8(2))* Lerner Publishing Group.

Nelson, Robin & Donovan, Sandy. Getting Elected: A Look at Running for Office. 2012. (Searchlight Books How Does Government Work Ser.). (ENG., Illus.). 40p. (gr. 3-5). pap. 51.01 *(978-0-7613-9232-3(7))*; pap. 8.95 *(978-0-7613-8561-5(4))* Lerner Publishing Group.

Orr, Tamra. Electing Leaders. 2007. (21st Century Skills Library: Citizens & Their Governments Ser.). (ENG., Illus.). 32p. (gr. 4-8). lib. bdg. 28.50 *(978-1-60279-063-6(9)*, 200004) Cherry Lake Publishing.

—A History of Voting Rights. 2012. (J). lib. bdg. 29.95 *(978-1-61228-262-6(8))* Mitchell Lane Pubs., Inc.

Peppas, Lynn. Election Day. 2010. (Celebrations in My World Ser.). (ENG.). 32p. (J). (gr. k-3). *(978-0-7787-4925-7(8))*; pap. *(978-0-7787-4932-5(0))* Crabtree Publishing Co.

Rissman, Rebecca. Día de las Elecciones. 2011. (Fiestas Ser.). (SPA & ENG., Illus.). 24p. (gr. -1-1). 22.65 *(978-1-4329-5393-5(1))*; pap. 6.29 *(978-1-4329-5412-3(1))* Heinemann-Raintree. (Bellota).

—Election Day, 1 vol. 2010. (Holidays & Festivals Ser.). (ENG.). 24p. (gr. -1-1). 22.65 *(978-1-4329-4063-8(5))*; pap. 6.29 *(978-1-4329-4082-9(1))* Heinemann-Raintree. (Acorn).

Ross, Katherine. One Vote, Two Votes, I Vote, You Vote. Ruiz, Aristides, illus. 2016. (Cat in the Hat's Learning Library). (ENG.). 48p. (J). (gr. k-3). 9.99 *(978-0-399-55598-5(6))*; lib. bdg. 13.99 *(978-0-399-55599-2(4))* Random Hse. Children's Bks. (Random Hse. Bks. for Young Readers).

Scholastic. Election Activity Kit, Revised Edition. 2016. (ENG., Illus.). 32p. (J). (gr. 1-3). pap. 15.99 *(978-1-338-03836-1(2))* Scholastic, Inc.

See, Betty. Electing the President: The Electoral Process in Action. 2005. 48p. pap. 14.95 *(978-1-59363-067-6(0))* Prufrock Pr.

Shea, Therese. America's Electoral College: Choosing the President Comparing & Analyzing Charts, Graphs, & Tables. 2009. (Math for the Real World Ser.). (ENG., Illus.). 32p. (gr. 6-7). pap. 10.00 *(978-1-4042-6069-6(2))* Rosen Publishing Group, Inc., The.

—America's Electoral College: Choosing the President: Comparing & Analyzing Charts, Graphs, & Tables. 2007. (PowerMath: Advanced Proficiency Plus Ser.). (ENG., Illus.). 32p. (J). (gr. 4-7). lib. bdg. 25.25 *(978-1-4042-3358-4(X))* Rosen Publishing Group, Inc., The.

Steck-Vaughn, creator. Cast Your Vote!: High School: National, State, & Local Government. 2007. (Illus.). 72p. (J). (gr. 4-7). pap. 12.99 *(978-1-4190-3637-8(8))* Steck-Vaughn.

Steck-Vaughn Staff, creator. Cast Your Vote! Grades 3-5: National, State, & Local Government. 2007. (Illus.). 72p. (J). (gr. 4-7). pap. 12.99 *(978-1-4190-3635-4(1))* Steck-Vaughn.

Sundance/Newbridge LLC Staff. America Is Voting. 2004. (Reading PowerWorks Ser.). (gr. 1-3). 37.50 *(978-0-7608-9723-2(9))*; pap. 6.10 *(978-0-7608-9724-9(7))* Sundance/Newbridge Educational Publishing.

Thomas, Ray aka The Bull Cutter. What's Wrong in America. 2008. 216p. pap. 14.95 *(978-1-4327-2531-0(9))* Outskirts Pr., Inc.

Thomas, William David. Como Elegimos a Nuestros Lideres? 2008. (Mi gobierno de Estados Unidos (My American Government) Ser.). (SPA & ENG., Illus.). 32p. (gr. 3-7). lib. bdg. 26.00 *(978-0-8368-8870-6(7)*, Gareth Stevens Learning Library) Stevens, Gareth Publishing LLLP.

—¿Cómo Elegimos a Nuestros Líderes? 2008. (Mi gobierno de Estados Unidos (My American Government) Ser.). (SPA & ENG.). 32p. (gr. 3-7). pap. 10.50 *(978-0-8368-8875-1(8)*, Gareth Stevens Learning Library) Stevens, Gareth Publishing LLLP.

—How Do We Elect Our Leaders? 2008. (My American Government Ser.). (Illus.). 32p. (gr. 3-7). pap. 10.50 *(978-0-8368-8865-2(0))*; lib. bdg. 26.00 *(978-0-8368-8860-7(X))* Stevens, Gareth Publishing LLLP. (Gareth Stevens Learning Library).

Venter, Sahm. Freedom Day: 27 April. 2008. (Exploring Our National Days Ser.). (ENG.). 70p. 20.95 *(978-1-77009-349-2(4))* Jacana Media ZAF. Dist: Independent Pubs. Group.

Whiting, Jim. Election Firsts. 2008. (Illus.). 64p. (J). *(978-0-7367-5284-8(6))* Zaner-Bloser, Inc.

Wilson, Mike. The Election Process. 2008. (Introducing Issues with Opposing Viewpoints Ser.). (ENG., Illus.). 112-144p. (YA). (gr. 7-10). 36.95 *(978-0-7377-3975-6(4)*, Greenhaven Pr., Inc.) Cengage Gale.

Wingate, Kate. Political Reforms: American Citizens Gain More Control over Their Government. 2009. (Progressive Movement 1900-1920: Efforts to Reform America's New Industrial Society Ser.). 32p. (gr. 3-4). 47.90 *(978-1-60854-167-6(3))* Rosen Publishing Group, Inc., The.

Wingate, Katherine. Political Reforms: American Citizens Gain More Control over Their Government. 2006. (Progressive Movement, 1900-1920 — Efforts to Reform America's New Industrial Society Ser.). (ENG., Illus.). 32p. (gr. 4-8). pap. 10.00 *(978-1-4042-0853-7(4))* Rosen Publishing Group, Inc., The.

ELECTIONS—FICTION

Alberto, Daisy. Pete for President! Sims, Blanche, illus. 2004. (Social Studies Connects). 32p. (J). (gr. 1-3). pap. 5.95 *(978-1-57565-142-2(4))* Kane Press, Inc.

Bailey, Michael. Cartoon Nation, 6 bks., Set. Incl. Citizenship. Skog, Jason. Brown, Kelly, illus. 30.65 *(978-1-4296-1331-6(9))*; Political Elections. Miller, Davis Worth & Brevard, Katherine M. Barnett, Charles, III, illus. 30.65 *(978-1-4296-1333-0(5))*; Political Parties. Burgan, Michael & Hoena, Blake A. Barnett, Charles et al, illus. lib. bdg. 30.65 *(978-1-4296-1334-7(3))*; 32p. (gr. 3-4). (Cartoon Nation Ser.). (ENG.). 2008. 91.95 *(978-1-4296-1675-1(X)*, Graphic Library) Capstone Press of Coughlan Cos.

Barnes, Peter W. & Barnes, Cheryl. Woodrow for President: A Tail of Voting, Campaigns, & Elections. 2012. (ENG.). 32p. (J). (gr. k-3). 16.95 *(978-1-59698-786-9(3))* Regnery Publishing, Inc., An Eagle Publishing Co.

Barshaw, Ruth McNally. The Ellie McDoodle Diaries: Ellie for President. Barshaw, Ruth McNally, illus. 2014. (Ellie Mcdoodle Ser.). (ENG., Illus.). 176p. (J). (gr. 3-6). 12.99 *(978-1-61963-061-1(3)*, 9781619630611, Bloomsbury USA Childrens) Bloomsbury Publishing USA.

Benton, Jim. The Frandidate. Benton, Jim, illus. 2009. (Franny K. Stein, Mad Scientist Ser.: 7). (ENG., Illus.). 112p. (J). (gr. 2-5). pap. 5.99 *(978-1-4169-0234-8(1)*, Simon & Schuster Bks. For Young Readers) Simon & Schuster Bks. For Young Readers.

—The Frandidate, 1 vol. Benton, Jim, illus. 2011. (Franny K. Stein, Mad Scientist Ser.). (ENG., Illus.). 128p. (gr. 3-6). 24.21 *(978-1-59961-823-4(0))* Spotlight.

Bowe, Julie. Vicka for President! 2016. (Victoria Torres, Unfortunately Average Ser.). (ENG., Illus.). 160p. (gr. 4-4). lib. bdg. 26.65 *(978-1-4965-3800-0(5))* Stone Arch Bks.

Bruel, Nick. Bad Kitty for President. 2012. (Bad Kitty Ser.). (ENG., Illus.). 144p. (J). (gr. 2-5). 15.99 *(978-1-59643-669-5(7)*, 9781596436695) Roaring Brook Pr.

—Bad Kitty for President. 2012. (Bad Kitty Ser.). (ENG., Illus.). 160p. (J). (gr. 2-5). pap. 6.99 *(978-1-250-01016-2(0)*, 9781250010162) Square Fish.

—Bad Kitty for President. 2012. (Bad Kitty Chapter Bks.). (J). lib. bdg. 17.20 *(978-0-606-26568-3(6)*, Turtleback) Turtleback Bks.

Bryant, Annie. Promises, Promises. 2008. (Beacon Street Girls Ser.: 5). (ENG.). 304p. (J). (gr. 4-8). pap. 8.99 *(978-1-4169-6430-8(4)*, Aladdin) Simon & Schuster Children's Publishing.

Copeland, Cynthia L. Dilly for President. 2005. (Illus.). 64p. (J). (gr. -1-k). pap. 6.95 *(978-0-7613-2442-3(9)*, First Avenue Editions) Lerner Publishing Group.

Cotler, Steve. Cheesie Mack Is Running Like Crazy! Holgate, Douglas, illus. (Cheesie Mack Ser.). (ENG.). (J). (gr. 3-7). 2014. 256p. pap. 6.99 *(978-0-307-97716-8(1)*, Yearling) 2013. 240p. 15.99 *(978-0-307-97713-7(7)*, Random Hse. Bks. for Young Readers) Random Hse. Children's Bks.

Cronin, Doreen. Duck for President. Lewin, Betsy, illus. 2004. (Click, Clack Book Ser.). (ENG.). 32p. (J). (gr. -1-3). 17.99 *(978-0-689-86377-6(2)*, Atheneum Bks. for Young Readers) Simon & Schuster Children's Publishing.

—Duck for President. Lewin, Betsy, illus. 2006. (Doreen Cronin: Click-Clack & More Ser.). (ENG.). 32p. (gr. -1-3). lib. bdg. 24.21 *(978-1-59961-091-7(4))* Spotlight.

—Pato para Presidente. Lewin, Betsy, illus. 2008.Tr. of Duck for President. (SPA.). (J). (gr. k-2). pap. 7.99 *(978-1-930332-74-4(2)*, LC32509) Lectorum Pubns., Inc.

Czajak, Paul. Monster Needs Your Vote. Grieb, Wendy, illus. 2015. (Monster & Me Ser.). (ENG.). 32p. (J). (gr. -1-3). 16.95 *(978-1-938063-63-3(5)*, Mighty Media Kids) Mighty Media Pr.

Czekaj, Jef. A Call for a New Alphabet. Czekaj, Jef, illus. 2011. (ENG., Illus.). 48p. (J). (gr. 1-4). pap. 5.95 *(978-1-58089-229-2(9))* Charlesbridge Publishing, Inc.

Defoe, Daniel & Perry, John Jasiel. Atalantis Major. 2011. 54p. 15.95 *(978-1-4638-9670-6(0))* Rodgers, Alan Bks.

Delporte, Yvan & Peyo. The Smurf King. 2010. (Smurfs Graphic Novels Ser.). (ENG., Illus.). 64p. (J). (gr. 2-5). 10.99 *(978-1-59707-225-0(7)*, 9781597072250) Papercutz.

Dipucchio, Kelly. Grace for President. Pham, LeUyen, illus. 2012. (ENG.). 40p. (J). (gr. 1-3). 16.99 *(978-1-4231-3999-7(2))* Hyperion Pr.

Double or Nothing. 2014. (It Takes Two Ser.: 3). (ENG., Illus.). 160p. (J). (gr. 3-7). pap. 6.99 *(978-1-4814-1652-8(9)*, Simon Spotlight) Simon Spotlight.

Dowell, Frances O'Roark. Phineas L. MacGuire... Gets Slimed! McDaniels, Preston, illus. (From the Highly Scientific Notebooks of Phineas L. MacGuire Ser.). (ENG.). (J). (gr. 3-7). 2010. 224p. pap. 6.99 *(978-1-4169-9775-7(X))* 2007. 208p. 16.99 *(978-1-4169-0196-9(5))* Simon & Schuster Children's Publishing. (Atheneum Bks. for Young Readers).

—Phineas L. MacGuire... Gets Slimed! McDaniels, Preston, illus. l.t. ed. 2008. (From the Highly Scientific Notebooks of Phineas L. MacGuire Ser.). 159p. (J). (gr. 3-7). 22.95 *(978-1-4104-0440-4(4))* Thorndike Pr.

Edwards, Nancy. Mom for Mayor. Chesworth, Michael D., illus. 2006. (ENG.). 96p. (J). (gr. 1-5). 16.95 *(978-0-8126-2743-5(1))* Cricket Bks.

Gallagher, Diana G. Vote! The Complicated Life of Claudia Cristina Cortez, 1 vol. Garvey, Brann, illus. 2008. (Claudia Cristina Cortez Ser.). (ENG.). 88p. (gr. 2-3). pap. 6.10 *(978-1-4342-0866-8(4))*; lib. bdg. 26.65 *(978-1-4342-0770-8(6))* Stone Arch Bks. (Claudia Cristina Cortez).

Gutman, Dan. The Kid Who Ran for President. 2012. (ENG.). 176p. (J). (gr. 3-7). pap. 6.99 *(978-0-545-44213-8(3)*, Scholastic Paperbacks) Scholastic, Inc.

—The Kid Who Ran for President. 2012. (gr. 3-6). 17.20 *(978-0-613-03562-0(3)*, Turtleback) Turtleback Bks.

Hansen, Henry. Mayor Teddy. 2012. 52p. pap. 19.50 *(978-1-61897-498-3(X)*, Strategic Bk. Publishing) Strategic Book Publishing & Rights Agency (SBPRA).

Hapka, Catherine A. & Vandenberg, Ellen. How Not to Run for Class President. Palen, Debbie, illus. 2016. (Step into Reading Ser.). (ENG.). 48p. (J). (gr. k-3). 3.99 *(978-1-101-93362-6(3)*, Random Hse. Bks. for Young Readers) Random Hse. Children's Bks.

Holliday, S. L. My Identity Christ-Is: Stay in the Game. 2012. (ENG.). 166p. (J). pap. 12.95 *(978-1-4787-1827-7(7))* Outskirts Pr., Inc.

Honeyman, Kay. Interference. 2016. (ENG.). 352p. (YA). (gr. 7). 17.99 *(978-0-545-81232-0(1)*, Levine, Arthur A. Bks.) Scholastic, Inc.

Howe, James. The Complete Misfits Collection: The Misfits; Totally Joe; Addie on the Inside; Also Known As Elvis. 2015. (Misfits Ser.). (ENG., Illus.). 1072p. (J). (gr. 5-9). pap. 27.99 *(978-1-4814-2898-9(5)*, Atheneum Bks. for Young Readers) Simon & Schuster Children's Publishing.

—The Misfits. 2003. (Misfits Ser.). (ENG.). 304p. (J). (gr. 5-9). mass mkt. 7.99 *(978-0-689-83956-6(1)*, Atheneum Bks. for Young Readers) Simon & Schuster Children's Publishing.

James, Howe. The Misfits. 2014. (Misfits Ser.). (ENG.). 304p. (J). 11.24 *(978-1-63245-171-2(9))* Lectorum Pubns., Inc.

Johnson, Varian. The Great Greene Heist. 2014. (ENG.). 240p. (J). (gr. 4-7). 16.99 *(978-0-545-52552-7(7)*, Levine, Arthur A. Bks.) Scholastic, Inc.

Jones, Marcia Thornton & Dadey, Debbie. Red, White, & Boo! Francis, Guy, illus. 2007. (Ghostville Elementary Ser.: Bk. 16). 64p. (J). *(978-0-439-88364-1(4))* Scholastic, Inc.

Kravitz, Danny. Tommy Mcknight & the Great Election. 2016. (Presidential Politics Ser.). (ENG.). 96p. (gr. 3-4). lib. bdg. 26.65 *(978-1-4965-2585-7(X)*, Connect) Stone Arch Bks.

—Tommy McKnight & the Great Election. 2016. (J). pap. *(978-1-4965-2752-3(6))* Stone Arch Bks.

Krosoczka, Jarrett J. Max for President. 2008. (ENG.). 40p. (J). (gr. -1-2). pap. 6.99 *(978-0-440-41789-7(9)*, Dragonfly Bks.) Random Hse. Children's Bks.

Krulik, Nancy. How I Survived Middle School: Madame President. 2006. 104p. pap. *(978-0-439-90090-4(5))* Scholastic, Inc.

—Vote for Suzanne. John and Wendy Staff, illus. 2008. (Katie Kazoo, Switcheroo Ser.: No. 7). (ENG.). 160p. (J). (gr. 2-4). pap. 4.99 *(978-0-448-44678-3(2)*, Grosset & Dunlap) Penguin Young Readers Group.

Levithan, David. Wide Awake. 2008. (ENG.). 240p. (YA). (gr. 9). pap. 8.99 *(978-0-375-83467-7(2)*, Knopf Bks. for Young Readers) Random Hse. Children's Bks.

Limbaugh, Rush H., III & Limbaugh, Kathryn Adams. Rush Revere & the Presidency. 2016. (Rush Revere Ser.: 5). (ENG., Illus.). 272p. (gr. 4-7). 19.99 *(978-1-5011-5689-2(6)*, Threshold Editions) Threshold Editions.

Liu, Carol & Caldarone, Marybeth Sidoti. Arlene on the Scene. 2010. 206p. (J). (gr. 3-5). pap. 7.95 *(978-1-934572-54-2(3))* Emerald Bk. Co.

Madonna, pseud. Ready, Set, Vote! 2009. (English Roses Ser.: 10). (ENG., Illus.). 128p. (J). (gr. 3-7). 9.99 *(978-0-14-241127-8(2)*, Puffin Books) Penguin Young Readers Group.

Manushkin, Fran. Elect Me!, 1 vol. Demski, James, Jr., illus. 2008. (Read-It! Readers: Social Studies). (ENG.). 32p. (gr. k-2). 21.32 *(978-1-4048-4911-2(4)*, Easy Readers) Picture Window Bks.

—Pedro for President. Lyon, Tammie, illus. 2016. (Pedro Ser.). (ENG.). 32p. (gr. k-2). lib. bdg. 21.32 *(978-1-5158-0087-3(3))* Pedro Pubns. GBR. Dist: Capstone Pub.

May, Eleanor. Mac & Cheese, Pleeeeeeze! 2008. pap. 34.95 *(978-1-58013-780-5(6))* Kane Press, Inc.

—Mac & Cheese, Pleeeeze! Palmisciano, Diane, illus. 2008. (Math Matters Ser.). (ENG.). 32p. (J). (gr. -1-3). pap. 5.95 *(978-1-57565-260-3(9))* Kane Press, Inc.

McNamara, Margaret. Election Day. Gordon, Mike, illus. 2008. (Robin Hill School Ser.). (J). (gr. -1-1). pap. 16.95 *(978-1-4301-0598-5(4))* Live Oak Media.

—A Tooth Story. Gordon, Mike, illus. 2004. (Robin Hill School Ser.). (ENG.). 32p. (J). (gr. -1-1). pap. 3.99 *(978-0-689-86423-0(X)*, Simon Spotlight) Simon Spotlight.

McVeigh, Mark, et al. Clifford for President. LaPadula, Tom, illus. 2004. (Clifford's Big Red Reader Ser.). (ENG.). 32p. (J). (gr. -1-3). pap. 3.99 *(978-0-439-69391-2(8))* Scholastic, Inc.

Montgomery, Lewis B. The Case of the Crooked Campaign. Wummer, Amy, illus. 2012. (Milo & Jazz Mysteries (r) Ser.: 9). (ENG.). 112p. (J). (gr. 2-5). pap. 6.95 *(978-1-57565-436-2(9))*; lib. bdg. 22.60 *(978-1-57565-435-5(0))* Kane Press, Inc.

Moss, Marissa. Amelia's Back-to-School Survival Guide: Vote 4 Amelia - Amelia's Guide to Babysitting. Moss, Marissa, illus. 2012. (Amelia Ser.). (ENG., Illus.). 160p. (J). (gr. 5-8). 12.99 *(978-1-4424-4349-5(9)*, Simon & Schuster/Paula Wiseman Bks.) Simon & Schuster/Paula Wiseman Bks.

—Vote 4 Amelia. Moss, Marissa, illus. 2007. (Amelia Ser.). (ENG., Illus.). 80p. (J). (gr. 4-7). 9.99 *(978-1-4169-2789-1(1)*, Simon & Schuster/Paula Wiseman Bks.) Simon & Schuster/Paula Wiseman Bks.

Neff, Ethel Maxine. Packy: The Runaway Elephant. 2004. (Illus.). 39p. (J). 5.99 *(978-0-8163-2061-5(6))* Pacific Pr. Publishing Assn.

Nigro, D. M. The Wolfman, the Shrink & the Eighth-Grade Election. 2006. 116p. (J). pap. 13.50 *(978-1-931201-66-7(8))* Twilight Times Bks.

Peschke, Marci. Daisy for President, 1 vol., Bk. 2. Pilz, M. H., illus. 2011. (Growing up Daisy Ser.). (ENG.). 80p. (gr. 3-8). 27.07 *(978-1-61641-115-2(5)*, Calico Chapter Bks) Magic Wagon.

Pollock, Hal. Monster for President. Parisi, Anthony, illus. 2008. 28p. 14.95 *(978-0-9816554-1-3(6))* Esquire Publishing, Inc.

Pratts, Christine. Tabby Wise for School Secretary. 2005. 61p. pap. 8.99 *(978-1-4116-4935-4(4))* Lulu Pr., Inc.

Press, J. Double Trouble #2. Kline, Michael, illus. 2013. (Doodles of Sam Dibble Ser.: 2). (ENG.). 128p. (J). (gr. 1-3). pap. 4.99 *(978-0-448-46108-3(0)*, Grosset & Dunlap) Penguin Young Readers Group.

Robertson, J. Jean. Vote for Me! Mones, Marc, illus. 2012. (ENG.). 24p. (gr. 1-2). pap. 8.95 *(978-1-61810-316-1(4))* Rourke Educational Media.

Robins, Eleanor. Friend or Foe?, 1 vol. unabr. ed. 2011. (Choices Ser.). (ENG.). 52p. (YA). (gr. 9-12). 7.95 *(978-1-61651-593-5(7))* Saddleback Educational Publishing, Inc.

Roland, Timothy. Our Crazy Class Election. 2007. (Illus.). 90p. (J). *(978-0-545-00401-5(2))* Scholastic, Inc.

Rolle Williams, Joyce. Chris's Story: A Family Voting Secret Revealed. 2008. 24p. pap. 12.99 *(978-1-4389-4258-2(3))* AuthorHouse.

Roy, Ron. The Election-Day Disaster. Bush, Timothy, illus. 2008. (Capital Mysteries Ser.: No. 10). 87p. (gr. 1-4). 15.00 *(978-0-7569-8802-9(0))* Perfection Learning Corp.

—The Election-Day Disaster. Bush, Timothy, illus. 2008. (Capital Mysteries Ser.: No. 10). (ENG.). 96p. (J). (gr. 1-4). 4.99 *(978-0-375-84805-6(3)*, Random Hse. Bks. for Young Readers) Random Hse. Children's Bks.

Schmidt, Gary D. First Boy. 2007. (ENG.). 224p. (YA). (gr. 5-9). per. 10.99 *(978-0-312-37149-4(7)*, 9780312371494) Square Fish.

Schraff, Anne. Time of Courage, 1 vol. unabr. ed. 2011. (Urban Underground Ser.). (ENG.). 197p. (YA). (gr. 9-12). pap. 9.95 *(978-1-61651-270-5(9))* Saddleback Educational Publishing, Inc.

Sonneborn, Scott. Attack of the Zom-Bees! Esparza, Andres et al, illus. 2013. (Tiger Moth Ser.). (ENG.). 48p. (gr. 1-3). pap. 6.19 *(978-1-4342-3871-9(7))* Stone Arch Bks.

—Tiger Moth: Attack of the Zom-Bees!, 1 vol. Esparza, Andres, illus. 2013. (Tiger Moth Ser.). (ENG.). 48p. (gr. 1-3). lib. bdg. 23.99 *(978-1-4342-3283-0(2))* Stone Arch Bks.

Sonnenblick, Jordan. Dodger for President. 2010. (Dodger & Me Ser.: 2). (ENG.). 192p. (J). (gr. 3-7). pap. 8.99 *(978-0-312-61112-5(9)*, 9780312611125) Square Fish.

Stier, Catherine. If I Ran for President. Avril, Lynne, illus. 2007. (ENG.). 32p. (J). (gr. 1-3). pap. 6.99 *(978-0-8075-3544-8(3))* Whitman, Albert & Co.

Suen, Anastasia. Vote for Isaiah! A Citizenship Story, 1 vol. Ebbeler, Jeff, illus. 2008. (Main Street School - Kids with Character Ser.). (ENG.). 32p. (gr. -1-4). 28.50 *(978-1-60270-274-5(8)*, Looking Glass Library) ABDO Publishing Co.

Swaab, Neil. Class Election. 2016. (Secrets to Ruling School Ser.: 2). (ENG., Illus.). 240p. (YA). (gr. 5-9). 13.95 *(978-1-4197-2126-7(7)*, Amulet Bks.) Abrams, Inc.

Tashjian, Janet. Vote for Larry. 2008. (Larry Ser.: 2). (ENG.). 256p. (YA). (gr. 7-12). pap. 9.99 *(978-0-312-38446-3(7)*, 9780312384463) Square Fish.

Tayleur, Karen. Promises! Vote for David Mortimore Baxter. Garvey, Brann, illus. 2007. (David Mortimore Baxter Ser.). (ENG.). 96p. (gr. 2-3). per. 6.05 *(978-1-59889-208-6(8)*, David Mortimore Baxter) Stone Arch Bks.

Thaler, Mike. The Class Election from the Black Lagoon. Lee, Jared, illus. 2004. (Black Lagoon Adventures Ser.: 3). (ENG.). 64p. (J). (gr. 2-5). 4.99 *(978-0-439-55716-0(X)*, Scholastic Paperbacks) Scholastic, Inc.

—The Class Election from the Black Lagoon, 1 vol. Lee, Jared, illus. 2011. (Black Lagoon Adventures Ser.: No. 1). (ENG.). 64p. (gr. 3-6). 24.21 *(978-1-59961-810-4(9))* Spotlight.

Van Dolzer, Krista. Don't Vote for Me. 2016. (ENG.). 240p. (J). (gr. 5-8). pap. 7.99 *(978-1-4926-3184-2(1)*, 9781492631842, Sourcebooks Jabberwocky) Sourcebooks, Inc.

—Don't Vote for Me. 2015. (ENG.). 240p. (J). (gr. 5-8). 15.99 *(978-1-4926-0941-4(2)*, 9781492609414, Sourcebooks Jabberwocky) Sourcebooks, Inc.

Vote for Us! Individual Title Six-Packs. (Bookweb Ser.). 32p. (gr. 6-18). 34.00 *(978-0-7578-0907-1(3))* Rigby Education.

Walters, Eric. Laggan Lard Butts, 1 vol. 2006. (Orca Currents Ser.). (ENG.). 112p. (J). (gr. 5-9). per. 9.95 *(978-1-55143-518-3(7))* Orca Bk. Pubs. USA.

Warner, Gertrude Chandler, creator. The Election Day Dilemma. 2016. (Boxcar Children Mysteries Ser.: 145). (ENG.). 128p. (J). (gr. 1-5). 15.99 *(978-0-8075-0721-6(0))* Whitman, Albert & Co.

Weston Woods Staff, creator. Duck for President. 2004. 29.95 *(978-0-7882-0540-8(4))* Weston Woods Studios, Inc.

Wilhelm, Hans. Buddy for President. Wilhelm, Hans, illus. 2016. (Illus.). 32p. (J). (gr. -1-3). 17.99 *(978-0-06-240366-7(4))* HarperCollins Pubs.

Winston, Sherri. President of the Whole Fifth Grade. 2012. (President Ser.: 1). (ENG.). 288p. (J). (gr. 3-7). pap. 8.00 *(978-0-316-11433-2(2))* Little, Brown Bks. for Young Readers.

Winter, Jonah. Lillian's Right to Vote: A Celebration of the Voting Rights Act of 1965. Evans, Shane W., illus. 2015. (ENG.). 40p. (J). (gr. k-4). 17.99 *(978-0-385-39028-6(9)*, Schwartz & Wade Bks.) Random Hse. Children's Bks.

Wise, Rachel. Cast Your Ballot! 2013. (Dear Know-It-All Ser.: 9). (ENG., Illus.). 160p. (J). (gr. 3-7). 15.99 *(978-1-4424-8793-2(3))*; pap. 5.99 *(978-1-4424-8792-5(5))* Simon Spotlight. (Simon Spotlight).

ELECTORAL COLLEGE

see Presidents—United States—Election

ELECTRIC APPLIANCES

see Electric Apparatus and Appliances; Household Appliances, Electric

ELECTRIC APPARATUS AND APPLIANCES

see also Electric Batteries; Electric Generators; Electric Lamps; Electric Motors; Electromagnets; Household Appliances, Electric

Christensen, Victoria G. How Conductors Work. 2016. (Connect with Electricity Ser.). (ENG., Illus.). 40p. (J). (gr. 4-6). 46.65 *(978-1-5124-1008-2(X)*, Lerner Pubns.) Lerner Publishing Group.

—How Sensors Work. 2016. (Connect with Electricity Ser.). (ENG., Illus.). 40p. (J). (gr. 4-6). 46.65 *(978-1-5124-1010-5(1)*, Lerner Pubns.) Lerner Publishing Group.

Deane-Pratt, Ade. Electrical Gadgets. 2012. (How Things Work Ser.). (Illus.). 32p. (YA). (gr. 3-6). lib. bdg. 26.50 *(978-1-4488-5290-1(0))* Rosen Publishing Group, Inc., The.

—Sensors. 2012. (How Things Work Ser.). (Illus.). 32p. (YA). (gr. 3-6). lib. bdg. 26.50 *(978-1-4488-5281-9(1))* Rosen Publishing Group, Inc., The.

Famighetti, Robert, et al. How Do Refrigerators Work? 2009. (Science in the Real World Ser.). (Illus.). 32p. (gr. 4-6). 28.00 *(978-1-60413-473-5(9)*, Chelsea Clubhouse) Facts On File, Inc.

Good, Keith. Zap It: Exciting Electricity Activities. 2008. (Design It! Ser.). pap. 6.95 *(978-0-8225-9926-5(0))* Lerner Publishing Group.

Goodrich, Juliette. The Little Light Shines Bright: A True Story about the World's Longest Burning Lightbulb. 2008. 28p. pap. 12.95 *(978-1-4343-6524-8(7))* AuthorHouse.

Koontz, Robin. TV Remotes. 2014. (ENG.). 24p. (gr. k-3). 28.50 *(978-1-62717-642-2(X))* Rourke Educational Media.

Lee, Ji Sun & Dec, Jaymes. Tech DIY: Easy Electronics Projects for Parents & Kids. 2016. (ENG., Illus.). 192p. pap. 19.99 (978-1-68045-177-1(4)) Maker Media, Inc.

Oxlade, Chris. Gadgets & Games, 1 vol. 2013. (Design & Engineering for STEM Ser.). (ENG., Illus.). 56p. (gr. 6-8). pap. 9.99 (978-1-4329-7036-9(4), NA-h); lib. bdg. 34.65 (978-1-4329-7031-4(3)) Heinemann-Raintree.

Reed, Cristie. Microwave Ovens. 2014. (ENG.). 24p. (gr. k-3). 28.50 (978-1-62717-646-0(2)) Rourke Educational Media.

ELECTRIC BATTERIES

Christensen, Victoria G. How Batteries Work. 2016. (Connect with Electricity Ser.). (ENG., Illus.). 40p. (J). (gr. 4-6). 30.65 (978-1-5124-0781-5(X)); 46.65 (978-1-5124-1006-8(3), Lerner Pubns.) Lerner Publishing Group.

Flaherty, Michael. Electricity & Batteries. (Science Factory Ser.). 32p. (gr. 4-5). 2009. 50.50 (978-1-60853-020-5(5), PowerKids Pr.) 2008. (Illus.). (YA). lib. bdg. 26.50 (978-1-4042-3905-0(7)) Rosen Publishing Group, Inc., The.

Grossblatt, Ben & Klutz Editors. Gotcha Gadgets. 2015. (ENG.). 32p. (J). (gr. 4-7). spiral bd. 24.99 (978-0-545-80593-3(7)) Klutz.

Oxlade, Chris. Using Batteries, 1 vol. 2012. (It's Electric! Ser.). (ENG.). 32p. (gr. 2-4). pap. 8.95 (978-1-4329-5680-6(9)); lib. bdg. 26.65 (978-1-4329-5675-2(2)) Heinemann-Raintree. (NA-h).

Tiner, John Hudson. Water, Acid, & a Metal Make Battery Power. 2003. (From Resource to Energy Source Ser.). (J). (978-1-58417-290-1(8)); pap. (978-1-58417-291-8(6)) Lake Street Pubs.

Wilson, Roman. How Does a Battery Work? 2013. (Electrified! Ser.). (Illus.). 24p. (gr. 2-5). 22.60 (978-1-4339-8399-3(0)); pap. 8.15 (978-1-4339-8400-6(8)) Stevens, Gareth Publishing LLLP. (Gareth Stevens Learning Library).

ELECTRIC CURRENTS

Cooper, Christopher. The Basics of Electric Current. 2014. (Core Concepts Ser.). 96p. (YA). (gr. 7-12). 35.60 (978-1-4777-7758-9(X)) Rosen Publishing Group, Inc., The.

McPherson, Stephanie Sammartino. War of the Currents: Thomas Edison vs. Nikola Tesla. 2012. (Scientific Rivalries & Scandals Ser.). (ENG., Illus.). 64p. (J). (gr. 6-12). lib. bdg. 33.27 (978-0-7613-5487-1(5)) Lerner Publishing Group.

Shea, C. O. Conductors & Insulators. 2013. (Electrified! Ser.). (Illus.). 24p. (gr. 2-5). 22.60 (978-1-4339-8389-4(3)); pap. 8.15 (978-1-4339-8390-0(7)) Stevens, Gareth Publishing LLLP. (Gareth Stevens Learning Library).

ELECTRIC DISTRIBUTION

see Electric Lines

ELECTRIC ENGINEERING

see also Electric Apparatus and Appliances; Radio; Telegraph; Telephone

Benge, Janet & Benge, Geoff. Heroes of History - Thomas Edison: Inspiration & Hard Work. 2007. (Heroes of History Ser.). (ENG.). 208p. (YA). (gr. 3-7). pap. 9.99 (978-1-932096-37-8(X)) Emerald Bks.

Bow, James. Electrical Engineering & the Science of Circuits. 2012. (ENG.). 32p. (J). (978-0-7787-7497-6(X)) Crabtree Publishing Co.

Crabtree Staff & Bow, James. Electrical Engineering & the Science of Circuits. 2012. (ENG., Illus.). 32p. (J). pap. (978-0-7787-7502-7(X)) Crabtree Publishing Co.

Fitzpatrick, Anne. Electricity. 2003. 24p. (J). lib. bdg. 21.35 (978-1-58340-320-4(5)) Black Rabbit Bks.

Freedman, Jeri. Electrician. 2016. (Careers in Construction Ser.). (ENG., Illus.). 112p. (J). (gr. 7-7). lib. bdg. 42.79 (978-1-5026-0980-9(0)) Cavendish Square Publishing.

Garcia, Tracy J. Thomas Edison. 2013. (Jr. Graphic American Inventors Ser.). (ENG., Illus.). 24p. (J). (gr. 3-6). pap. 10.60 (978-1-4777-0137-9(0)); lib. bdg. 25.25 (978-1-4777-0076-1(5)) Rosen Publishing Group, Inc., The. (PowerKids Pr.).

Harmon, Daniel E. A Career As an Electrician. 2010. (Essential Careers Ser.). (Illus.). 80p. (YA). lib. bdg. 33.25 (978-1-4358-9470-9(7)) Rosen Publishing Group, Inc., The.

Hayes, Amy. Freaky Stories about Electricity. 2016. (Freaky True Science Ser.). (Illus.). 32p. (J). (gr. 5-4). pap. 10.50 (978-1-4824-4812-2(2)) Stevens, Gareth Publishing LLLP.

Hinton, Kerry. A Career As an Operating & Stationary Engineer, 01 vols., 1. 2016. (Essential Careers Ser.). (ENG.). 80p. (J). 34.25 (978-1-4994-6223-4(9), Rosen Young Adult) Rosen Publishing Group, Inc., The.

Latta, Sara L. Microwave Man: Percy Spencer & His Sizzling Invention. 2014. (Inventors at Work! Ser.). 48p. (J). 25.27 (978-0-7660-4201-8(4), Enslow Elementary) Enslow Pubs., Inc.

Linde, Barbara M. Computer Network Architect. 2017. (Behind the Scenes with Coders Ser.). 32p. (gr. 9-10). 60.00 **(978-1-5081-5560-7(7)**, PowerKids Pr.) Rosen Publishing Group, Inc., The.

Loria, Laura. Solving Real World Problems with Electrical Engineering, 01 vols., 1. 2016. (Let's Find Out! Ser.). (ENG., Illus.). 32p. (J). pap. 12.90 (978-1-5081-0065-2(9), Britannica Educational Publishing) Rosen Publishing Group, Inc., The.

Luz, Oscar. A Day at Work with an Electrical Engineer, 01 vols., 1. 2016. (Super STEM Careers Ser.). (ENG., Illus.). 24p. (J). pap. 8.25 (978-1-5081-4422-9(2), PowerKids Pr.) Rosen Publishing Group, Inc., The.

Martin, Bobi. Working As an Electrician in Your Community. 2015. (Careers in Your Community Ser.). (ENG., Illus.). 80p. (YA). (gr. 7-8). 34.25 (978-1-4994-6111-4(9), Rosen Young Adult) Rosen Publishing Group, Inc., The.

Minden, Cecilia. Electricians. 2014. (People in Our Community Ser.). (ENG.). 24p. (J). (gr. k-3). 27.07 (978-1-62687-012-3(8), 206802) Child's World, Inc., The.

Nsrc. Science & Technology for Children Books: Electric Circuits. 2004. (Illus.). 64p. (J). (978-1-933008-02-8(4)) Smithsonian Science Education Ctr. (SSEC).

O'Shei, Tim. Marconi & Tesla: Pioneers of Radio Communication. 2008. (Inventors Who Changed the World Ser.). (Illus.). 128p. (J). (gr. 3-7). lib. bdg. 34.60 (978-1-59845-076-7(X), MyReportLinks.com Bks.) Enslow Pubs., Inc.

Rohan, Rebecca Carey. Working with Electricity: Electrical Engineers, 01 vols., 1. 2016. (Engineers Rule Ser.). (ENG.). 32p. (J). pap. 11.75 (978-1-5081-4548-6(2), PowerKids Pr.) Rosen Publishing Group, Inc., The.

Science & Technology for Children Books, Electric Circuits Set, 8 vols. 2004. (Illus.). 64p. (J). (978-1-933008-14-1(8)) Smithsonian Science Education Ctr. (SSEC).

Suen, Anastasia. Ipod & Electronics Visionary Tony Fadell. 2014. (STEM Trailblazer Bios Ser.). (ENG., Illus.). 32p. (gr. 2-5). lib. bdg. 26.60 (978-1-4677-2456-2(4), Lerner Pubns.) Lerner Publishing Group.

Swanson, Jennifer. Amazing Feats of Electrical Engineering, 1 vol. 2014. (Great Achievements in Engineering Ser.). (ENG.). 112p. (J). (gr. 6-12). lib. bdg. 35.64 (978-1-62403-428-2(4), Essential Library) ABDO Publishing Co.

Tagliaferro, Linda. Thomas Edison: Inventor of the Age of Electricity. 2003. (Lerner Biographies Ser.). (ENG., Illus.). 128p. (gr. 6-12). 27.93 (978-0-8225-4689-4(2), Lerner Pubns.) Lerner Publishing Group.

Teitelbaum, Michael. Electrician. 2010. (21st Century Skills Library: Cool Careers Ser.). (ENG.). 32p. (gr. 4-8). lib. bdg. 28.50 (978-1-60279-936-3(9), 200617) Cherry Lake Publishing.

Thatcher Murcia, Rebecca. Thomas Edison: Great Inventor. 2004. (Uncharted, Unexplored, & Unexplained Ser.). (Illus.). 48p. (J). (gr. 4-8). lib. bdg. 29.95 (978-1-58415-306-1(7)) Mitchell Lane Pubs., Inc.

Time for Kids Editors. Time for Kids - Thomas Edison: A Brilliant Inventor. 2005. (Time for Kids Ser.). (ENG., Illus.). 48p. (J). (gr. 2-4). pap. 3.99 (978-0-06-057611-0(1)) HarperCollins Pubs.

Welvaert, Scott R. Thomas Edison & the Lightbulb, 1 vol. Miller, Phil et al, illus. 2006. (Inventions & Discovery Ser.). (ENG.). 32p. (gr. 3-4). 30.65 (978-0-7368-6489-3(X), Graphic Library) Capstone Press of Coughlan Cos.

Yount, Lisa. Nikola Tesla. 2011. (Trailblazers in Science & Technology Ser.). 146p. (gr. 6-12). 35.00 (978-1-60413-670-8(7), Chelsea Hse.) Facts On File, Inc.

Zerbe, J. S. Electricity for Boys. 2008. 140p. pap. 13.95 (978-1-4357-4133-1(1)) Lulu Pr., Inc.

ELECTRIC GENERATORS

Vail, Grace. Motors & Generators. 2013. (Electrified! Ser.). (Illus.). 24p. (J). (gr. 2-5). pap. 8.15 (978-1-4339-8405-1(9)); lib. bdg. 22.60 (978-1-4339-8404-4(0)) Stevens, Gareth Publishing LLLP.

ELECTRIC HOUSEHOLD APPLIANCES

see Household Appliances, Electric

ELECTRIC LAMPS

Flashlights, 6 vols. (Sunshinetm Science Ser.). 24p. (gr. 1-2). 36.95 (978-0-7802-0557-4(X)); 31.50 (978-0-7802-0306-8(2)) Wright Group/McGraw-Hill.

Jackson, Demi. How Does a Light Bulb Work? 2016. (Everyday Mysteries Ser.). (ENG., Illus.). 24p. (J). (gr. 1-2). pap. 8.15 (978-1-4824-3817-8(8)) Stevens, Gareth Publishing LLLP.

Mattern, Joanne. Lightbulbs. 2015. (Rookie Read-About(tm) Science: How Things Work Ser.). (ENG.). 32p. (J). lib. bdg. 25.00 (978-0-531-21368-1(4), Children's Pr.) Scholastic Library Publishing.

Matthews, John R. The Light Bulb. 2005. (Inventions That Shaped the World Ser.). (Illus.). 80p. (J). (gr. 5-8). 17.60 (978-0-7569-6858-8(5)) Perfection Learning Corp.

Nolan, Janet. The Firehouse Light. Lafrance, Marie, illus. 2010. (ENG.). 32p. (J). (gr. k-3). 15.99 (978-1-58246-298-1(4), Tricycle Pr.) Random Hse. Children's Bks.

Oxlade, Chris. The Light Bulb, 1 vol. 2011. (Tales of Invention Ser.). (ENG.). 32p. (gr. 3-5). pap. 8.95 (978-1-4329-4889-4(X)); 30.65 (978-1-4329-4880-1(6)) Heinemann-Raintree. (NA-h).

ELECTRIC LINES

Here are entered works on general transmission systems, their construction and properties.

Hynes, Patricia. The Electric Power Grid. 2007. (21st Century Skills Library: Power Up! Ser.). (ENG.). 32p. (gr. 4-8). pap. 14.21 (978-1-60279-101-5(5), 200662) Cherry Lake Publishing.

Kantrowitz, Joseph & Moran, Jeffrey B. Discovering Thermodynamics. 2011. (Scientist's Guide to Physics Ser.). (YA). (gr. 7-12). lib. bdg. 34.60 (978-1-4488-4701-3(X)) Rosen Publishing Group, Inc., The.

Mezzanotte, Jim. Cómo Funcionan las Palancas. 2006. (Como funcionan las maquinas simples (How Simple Machines Work) Ser.). (SPA., Illus.). 24p. (gr. 1-4). lib. bdg. 22.00 (978-0-8368-7443-3(9), Weekly Reader Leveled Readers) Stevens, Gareth Publishing LLLP.

Monroe, Ron. What Are Electrical Circuits? 2012. (ENG.). 32p. (J). (978-0-7787-2077-5(2)); pap. (978-0-7787-2082-9(9)) Crabtree Publishing Co.

Randolph, Joanne. Pulleys in My World. 2007. (Journeys Ser.). (ENG.). 24p. (gr. k-8). pap. 7.05 (978-1-4042-8425-8(7), Rosen Classroom) Rosen Publishing Group, Inc., The.

ELECTRIC MOTORS

Hannon, Robert A. J. L. Cowen's Postwar Lionel Trains: O-Gauge Reference Manual II, Motorized Units, Rolling Stock & Accessories. 2003. (Illus.). 160p. per. 29.95 (978-0-9710225-2-2(6), 0-9710225-2-6) CrowsNest Publishing.

Sobey, Ed, ed. Electric Motor Experiments. 2011. (Cool Science Projects with Technology Ser.). (Illus.). 128p. (J). (gr. 5-18). lib. bdg. 33.27 (978-0-7660-3306-1(6)) Enslow Pubs., Inc.

Vail, Grace. Motors & Generators. 2013. (Electrified! Ser.). (Illus.). 24p. (J). (gr. 2-5). pap. 8.15 (978-1-4339-8405-1(9)); lib. bdg. 22.60 (978-1-4339-8404-4(0)) Stevens, Gareth Publishing LLLP.

ELECTRIC POWER

Benduhn, Tea. Energía Solar. 2008. (Energía para el presente (Energy for Today) Ser.). (SPA.). 24p. (gr. 2-6). (J). lib. bdg. 22.00 (978-0-8368-9269-7(0)); pap. 8.15 (978-0-8368-9368-7(9)) Stevens, Gareth Publishing LLLP. (Weekly Reader Leveled Readers).

Byers, Ann. Blackouts: A Practical Survival Guide. (Library of Emergency Preparedness Ser.). 64p. 2009. (gr. 6-6). 58.50 (978-1-60853-591-0(6), Rosen Reference) 2005. (Illus.). (YA). (gr. 5-9). lib. bdg. 31.95 (978-1-4042-0535-2(7)) Rosen Publishing Group, Inc., The.

Byrne, Eileen. Electricity for the Future. 2013. (Electrified! Ser.). (Illus.). 24p. (gr. 2-5). 22.60 (978-1-4339-8394-8(X)); pap. 8.15 (978-1-4339-8395-5(8)) Stevens, Gareth Publishing LLLP. (Gareth Stevens Learning Library).

Carlson Berne, Emma. Shocking! Electricity. 2013. (Energy Everywhere Ser.). (ENG., Illus.). 24p. (J). (gr. 3-6). 22.60 (978-1-4488-9650-9(9)); pap. 8.25 (978-1-4488-9758-2(0)) Rosen Publishing Group, Inc., The. (PowerKids Pr.).

Friend, Robyn & Cohen, Judith. Electricity & You: Be Smart, Be Safe. Katz, David, illus. l.t. ed. 2012. (ENG.). 40p. (J). pap. 7.00 (978-1-935999-02-7(8)) Cascade Pass, Inc.

Furgang, Kathy. Zoom in on Power Grids. 2017. (Zoom in on Engineering Ser.). 24p. (gr. 2-2). lib. bdg. 22.60 **(978-0-7660-8707-1(7))** Enslow Pubs., Inc.

Geatches, Hazel, contrib. by. Electricity. 2013. (ENG.). 40p. pap. 9.38 (978-0-19-464685-7(8)) Oxford Univ. Pr., Inc.

Gray, Leon. Electricity. 2013. (Physical Science Ser.). 48p. (J). (gr. 4-6). pap. 14.05 (978-1-4339-9501-9(8)); pap. 84.30 (978-1-4339-9502-6(6)); (ENG., Illus.). lib. bdg. 31.95 (978-1-4339-9500-2(X)) Stevens, Gareth Publishing LLLP.

Greek, Joe. What Is Electrical Energy? 2017. (Let's Find Out! Forms of Energy Ser.). 32p. (gr. 6-8). pap. 12.90 **(978-1-68048-697-1(7)**, Britannica Educational Publishing) Rosen Publishing Group, Inc., The.

Hord, Colleen. From Power Plant to House. 2015. (ENG.). 24p. (gr. k-2). 28.50 (978-1-63430-061-2(0)) Rourke Educational Media.

Kamkwamba, William. The Boy Who Harnessed the Wind: Creating Currents of Electricity & Hope. 2009. 14.44 (978-0-7848-3872-3(0), Everbind) Marco Bk. Co.

—The Boy Who Harnessed the Wind: Creating Currents of Electricity & Hope. Hymas, Anna, illus. 2015. (ENG.). 304p. (J). (gr. 5). 18.99 (978-0-8037-4080-8(8), Dial Bks) Penguin Young Readers Group.

Kamkwamba, William & Mealer, Bryan. The Boy Who Harnessed the Wind: Young Readers Edition. Zunon, Elizabeth, illus. (ENG.). (J). 2016. 304p. (gr. 5). 8.99 (978-0-14-751042-6(2), Puffin Books) 2012. 32p. (gr. 1-3). 17.99 (978-0-8037-3511-8(1), Dial Bks) Penguin Young Readers Group.

Knight M J. Why Should I Switch off the Light? 2009. (One Small Step Ser.). (Illus.). 32p. (J). (gr. -1-3). pap. (978-1-897563-48-9(5)) Saunders Bk. Co.

Law, Felicia. Electricity. 2009. (Simply Science Ser.). (Illus.). 32p. (YA). (gr. 3-6). lib. bdg. 26.00 (978-1-4339-0031-0(9)) Stevens, Gareth Publishing LLLP.

Mahaney, Ian F. Electricity. (Energy in Action Ser.). 24p. 2009. (gr. 3-3). 42.50 (978-1-61512-257-8(5), PowerKids Pr.) 2007. (ENG.). (gr. 3-8). pap. 7.05 (978-1-4042-2187-1(5), PowerKids Pr.) 2007. (Illus.). (YA). (gr. 4-7). lib. bdg. 22.60 (978-1-4042-3478-9(0)) Rosen Publishing Group, Inc., The.

Mason, Jennifer. 10 Things You Can Do to Save Electricity. 2016. (Rookie Star — Make a Difference Ser.). (ENG., Illus.). 32p. (J). lib. bdg. 25.00 (978-0-531-22653-7(0), Children's Pr.) Scholastic Library Publishing.

Mason, Jenny. 10 Cosas Que Puedes Hacer para Ahorrar Electricidad. 2017. (Rookie Star — Make a Difference (Spanish Translation) Ser.). (SPA.). 32p. (J). pap. 5.95 **(978-1-338-18780-9(5))**; lib. bdg. 25.00 **(978-0-531-22859-3(2))** Scholastic Library Publishing. (Children's Pr.).

Masters, Nancy Robinson. How Did That Get to My House? Electricity. 2009. (Community Connections: How Did That Get to My House? Ser.). (ENG.). 24p. (gr. 2-5). lib. bdg. 25.64 (978-1-60279-474-0(X), 200245) Cherry Lake Publishing.

Miller, Debra A. Energy Production & Alternative Energy. 2010. (Confronting Global Warming Ser.). 112p. (YA). (gr. 10-12). lib. bdg., lib. bdg. 38.95 (978-0-7377-5106-2(1), Greenhaven Pr., Inc.) Cengage Gale.

Parker, Russ. Energy Supplies in Crisis. 2009. (Planet in Crisis Ser.). 32p. (YA). (gr. 5-8). lib. bdg. 25.25 (978-1-4358-5251-8(6), Rosen Reference) Rosen Publishing Group, Inc., The.

Parker, Steve & Dorling Kindersley Publishing Staff. Electricity. 2013. (DK Eyewitness Bks.). (ENG.). 72p. (J). (gr. 3-7). 16.99 (978-1-4654-0899-0(1), DK Children) Dorling Kindersley Publishing, Inc.

Peterson, Megan Cooley. How Electricity Gets from Power Plants to Homes. 2016. (Here to There Ser.). (ENG., Illus.). 24p. (gr. k-1). lib. bdg. 26.65 (978-1-4914-8434-0(9), Pebble Plus) Capstone Press of Coughlan Cos.

Seuling, Barbara. Flick a Switch: How Electricity Gets to Your Home. Tobin, Nancy, illus. 2003. (ENG.). 32p. (J). (gr. k-3). tchr. ed. 16.95 (978-0-8234-1729-2(8)) Holiday Hse., Inc.

Steinkraus, Kyla. Money down the Drain. Myer, Ed, illus. 2012. (ENG.). 24p. (gr. 2-3). pap. 8.95 (978-1-61810-329-1(6)) Rourke Educational Media.

Suen, Anastasia. Wired. Carrick, Paul, illus. 2007. (ENG.). 32p. (J). (gr. 1-4). 16.95 (978-1-57091-599-4(7)); pap. 7.95 (978-1-57091-494-2(X)) Charlesbridge Publishing, Inc.

Swanson, Jennifer. The Shocking Truth about Electricity. Lum, Bernice, illus. 2012. (LOL Physical Science Ser.). (ENG.). 32p. (gr. 3-4). pap. 47.70 (978-1-4296-9301-1(0), Fact Finders) Capstone Press of Coughlan Cos.

Westrup, Hugh. Electricity. 2015. (Science Readers: Content & Literacy Ser.). (ENG., Illus.). 32p. (gr. 4-4). pap. 8.99 (978-1-4807-4681-7(9)) Teacher Created Materials, Inc.

Wybomy, Sheila. Electricity. 2003. (Kidhaven Science Library). (Illus.). 48p. (J). (gr. 3-5). 23.70 (978-0-7377-1535-4(9), Kidhaven) Cengage Gale.

Zwerger, Lisbeth, et al. The Sandman. 2010. (Illus.). 25p. (978-1-85618-020-7(4)) Butterworth-Heinemann, Ltd.

ELECTRIC POWER-PLANTS—FICTION

Parker, Russ. Energy Supplies in Crisis. 2009. (Planet in Crisis Ser.). (ENG., Illus.). 32p. (J). (gr. 5-8). pap. 10.00 (978-1-4358-0681-8(6), Rosen Reference) Rosen Publishing Group, Inc., The.

ELECTRIC TRANSMISSIONS

see Electric Lines

ELECTRIC UTILITIES

see Public Utilities

ELECTRICAL

see headings beginning with the word Electric

Labrecque, Ellen. Electrician. 2016. (21st Century Skills Library: Cool Vocational Careers Ser.). (ENG., Illus.). 32p. (J). (gr. 4-7). 29.93 (978-1-63471-062-6(2), 208327) Cherry Lake Publishing.

ELECTRICITY

see also Electrons; Lightning; Magnetism; Radioactivity; Telegraph; Telephone; X-Rays

Alpert, Barbara. Electricity All Around, 1 vol. 2011. (Science Builders Ser.). (ENG.). 24p. (gr. k-1). pap. 7.29 (978-1-4296-7107-1(6)); pap. 41.70 (978-1-4296-7113-2(0)); lib. bdg. 26.65 (978-1-4296-6070-9(8)) Capstone Press of Coughlan Cos. (Pebble Plus).

Anderson, Michael, ed. Electricity. 2011. (Introduction to Physics Ser.). (ENG.). 80p. (YA). (gr. 7-12). lib. bdg. 31.70 (978-1-61530-665-7(X)) Rosen Publishing Group, Inc., The.

Arbuthnott, Gill. Your Guide to Electricity & Magnetism. 2017. (Illus.). 64p. (J). **(978-0-7787-3398-0(X))** Crabtree Publishing Co.

Bailey, Jacqui. Charged Up: The Story of Electricity. Lilly, Matthew, illus. 2004. (Science Works). (ENG.). 32p. (gr. 3-6). per. 7.95 (978-1-4048-1129-4(X)) Picture Window Bks.

Baker, Wendy & Haslam, Andrew. Electricity. (Make It Work! Ser.). (Illus.). 48p. (J). 15.95 (978-0-590-74521-5(2)) Scholastic, Inc.

Baker, Wendy, et al. Electricity. (Make It Work! (Eureka!) Ser.). (FRE., Illus.). (J). pap. 9.99 (978-0-590-74806-3(8)) Scholastic, Inc.

Ballard, Carol. Exploring Electricity. 2008. (How Does Science Work? Ser.). (Illus.). 32p. (J). (gr. 3-7). lib. bdg. 26.50 (978-1-4042-4281-4(3)) Rosen Publishing Group, Inc., The.

Bateman, Graham, ed. Electricity & Electronics. 2011. (Facts at Your Fingertips: Introducing Physics Ser.). 64p. (YA). (gr. 7-12). lib. bdg. 35.65 (978-1-936333-07-3(4)) Brown Bear Bks.

Benchmark Education Company, LLC Staff, compiled by. Electricity & Magnetism. 2006. (J). 91.00 (978-1-4108-7035-3(9)) Benchmark Education Co.

—Electricity & Magnetism: Theme Set. 2006. (J). 131.00 (978-1-4108-7136-7(3)) Benchmark Education Co.

Bliss, Pamela. The Mystery of Magnets. 2007. (Nonfiction Reading & Writing Workshops Ser.). (ENG., Illus.). 32p. (J). pap. 17.95 (978-0-7922-4581-0(4)) CENGAGE Learning.

Bodach, Vijaya Khisty. Electricity. 2008. (Discovering & Exploring Science Ser.). (Illus.). 16p. (J). (gr. -1-3). lib. bdg. 12.95 (978-0-7569-8430-4(0)) Perfection Learning Corp.

Boothroyd, Jennifer. All Charged Up: A Look at Electricity. 2011. (Lightning Bolt Books Exploring Physical Science Ser.). 32p. pap. 45.32 (978-0-7613-7646-0(1)); (ENG.). 26.60 (978-0-7613-6094-0(8)); (ENG.). pap. 7.95 (978-0-7613-7102-1(8)) Lerner Publishing Group.

Buchanan, Theodore. Circuits. 2015. (Science Readers: Content & Literacy Ser.). (ENG., Illus.). 32p. (gr. 4-4). pap. 8.99 (978-1-4807-4682-4(7)) Teacher Created Materials, Inc.

Bushell, Nick & Martineau, Susan. Cool Circuits & Wicked Wires. Ursell, Martin, illus. 2005. (Gruesome Ser.). (ENG.). 24p. (J). (gr. 1-4). pap. 8.99 (978-1-902915-33-3(X)) B Small Publishing GBR. Dist: Independent Pubs. Group.

Byrne, Eileen. Electricity for the Future. 2013. (Electrified! Ser.). (Illus.). 24p. (gr. 2-5). 22.60 (978-1-4339-8394-8(X)); pap. 8.15 (978-1-4339-8395-5(8)) Stevens, Gareth Publishing LLLP. (Gareth Stevens Learning Library).

Canavan, Thomas. Excellent Experiments with Electricity & Magnetism. 2017. (Mind-Blowing Science Experiments Ser.). 32p. (gr. 4-5). pap. 63.00 **(978-1-5382-0730-7(3))** Stevens, Gareth Publishing LLLP.

Carlson Berne, Emma. Shocking! Electricity. 2013. (Energy Everywhere Ser.). (ENG., Illus.). 24p. (J). (gr. 3-6). 22.60 (978-1-4488-9650-9(9)); pap. 8.25 (978-1-4488-9758-2(0)) Rosen Publishing Group, Inc., The. (PowerKids Pr.).

Cheshire, Gerard. Electricity & Magnetism. 2006. (Fundamental Physics Ser.). (Illus.). 48p. (YA). (gr. 5-9). lib. bdg. 34.25 (978-1-58340-994-7(7), 1262672) Black Rabbit Bks.

Christensen, Victoria G. How Batteries Work. 2016. (Connect with Electricity Ser.). (ENG., Illus.). 40p. (J). (gr. 4-6). 30.65 (978-1-5124-0781-5(X)); 46.65 (978-1-5124-1006-8(3), Lerner Pubns.) Lerner Publishing Group.

Clark, John O. E. The Basics of Electric Charges. 2014. (Core Concepts Ser.). 96p. (YA). (gr. 7-12). 35.60 (978-1-4777-7768-8(7)) Rosen Publishing Group, Inc., The.

Claybourne, Anna. Electric Shocks & Other Energy Evils. 2013. (ENG., Illus.). 32p. (J). (978-0-7787-0926-8(4)); pap. (978-0-7787-0953-4(1)) Crabtree Publishing Co.

—Electricity. 2012. (Illus.). 24p. (gr. k-4). pap. 7.95 (978-1-926853-56-7(3)) Saunders Bk. Co. CAN. Dist: RiverStream Publishing.

—Electricity & Magnetism. 2016. (Mind Webs Ser.). (ENG., Illus.). 32p. (J). (gr. 4-6). pap. 11.99 (978-0-7502-8971-9(6), Wayland) Hachette Children's Group GBR. Dist: Hachette Bk. Group.

—The Shocking Story of Electricity. Hopgood, Kevin, illus. 2006. (Young Reading Series 2 Ser.). 63p. (J). (gr. 2-5). pap. 5.99 (978-0-7945-1248-4(8), Usborne) EDC Publishing.

Cobb, Vicki. Sources of Forces: Science Fun with Force Fields. Haefele, Steve, illus. 2007. (Science Fun with Vicki Cobb Ser.). 48p. (J). (gr. 4-7). per. 7.95 (978-0-8225-7023-3(8), First Avenue Editions) Lerner Publishing Group.

Cohen, Judith L. & Friend, Robyn. Los Angeles' Clean Energy Future. Katz, David A., illus. 2015. 40p. (J). pap. 7.00 (978-1-935999-09-6(5)) Cascade Pass, Inc.

Community Connections: How Did They Build That? 2011. 24p. lib. bdg. 179.50 (978-1-61080-001-3(X), 200926) Cherry Lake Publishing.

Cook, Sherry & Johnson, Terri. Ellie Electricity, 26 vols. Kuhn, Jesse, illus. l.t. ed. 2006. (Quirkles — Exploring Phonics through Science Ser.: 5). 32p. (J). 7.99 (978-1-933815-04-6(3), Quirkles, The) Creative 3, LLC.

Cook, Trevor M. Experiments with Electricity & Magnetism. 2009. (Science Lab Ser.). (J). (ENG., Illus.). 32p. (gr. 4-6). pap. 10.00 (978-1-4358-3220-6(5)); lib. bdg. 26.50 (978-1-4358-2807-0(0)) Rosen Publishing Group, Inc., The. (PowerKids Pr.).

Cooper, Christopher. The Basics of Electric Current. 2014. (Core Concepts Ser.). 96p. (YA). (gr. 7-12). 35.60 (978-1-4777-7758-9(X)) Rosen Publishing Group, Inc., The.

Dawson, Patricia. An Electrician's Job. 2014. (Community Workers Ser.). 24p. (J). (gr. k-2). pap. 8.22 (978-1-62712-994-7(4)); lib. bdg. 24.21 (978-1-62712-993-0(6)) Cavendish Square Publishing.

¿De Donde Viene la Electricidad? (Coleccion Primeros Pasos en la Ciencia). (SPA., Illus.). (J). (gr. 1-3). pap.

(978-950-724-016-4(0), LMA8213) Lumen ARG. Dist: Lectorum Pubns., Inc.
Donaldson, Valeria. My Electricity Experiments. 2013. (InfoMax Readers Ser.). (ENG.). 24p. (J). (gr. 3-4). pap. 49.50 (978-1-4777-2475-0(3)); (Illus.). pap. 8.25 (978-1-4777-2474-3(5)) Rosen Publishing Group, Inc., The. (Rosen Classroom).
Dunne, Abbie. Electricity. 2016. (Physical Science Ser.). (ENG., Illus.). 24p. (gr. k-1). lib. bdg. 26.65 (978-1-5157-0935-0(3), Pebble Plus) Capstone Press of Coughlan Cos.
Electric & Magnetic Phenomena. 2011. (Science Made Simple Ser.). (ENG.). 64p. (YA). pap. 12.95 (978-1-4488-2239-3(4), Rosen Reference) Rosen Publishing Group, Inc., The.
Electricidad e Imanes. (Coleccion Jugando Con la Ciencia). (SPA., Illus.). 39p. (J). pap. 9.95 (978-950-11-0828-6(7), SGM309) Sigmar ARG. Dist: Continental Bk. Co., Inc.
Electricity. (Make it Work Ser.). 42p. (J). (gr. 4-8). pap. (978-1-882210-38-1(7)) Action Publishing, Inc.
Electricity. 2011. (Introduction to Physics Ser.). (ENG.). 80p. (YA). (gr. 7-12). 63.40 (978-1-61530-774-6(5)) Rosen Publishing Group, Inc., The.
Elektrizitaetslehre I: Felder. (Duden Abiturhilfen Ser.). (GER.). 96p. (YA). (gr. 12-13). (978-3-411-04461-0(6)) Bibliographisches Institut & F. A. Brockhaus AG DEU. Dist: International Bk. Import Service, Inc.
Else, Mark, et al. Electricity & Thermal Physics. 2nd rev. ed. 2004. (Nelson Advanced Science Ser.). (ENG., Illus.). 152p. (YA). pap. 39.50 (978-0-7487-7663-4(X)) Nelson Thornes Ltd. GBR. Dist: Trans-Atlantic Pubns., Inc.
Fairley, Peter. Electricity & Magnetism. 2007. (Great Ideas of Science Ser.). (Illus.). 80p. (YA). (gr. 9-12). lib. bdg. 27.93 (978-0-8225-6605-2(2)) Twenty First Century Bks.
Famighetti, Robert, et al. Why Do Lights Turn On? 2009. (Science in the Real World Ser.). (Illus.). 32p. (gr. 4-6). 28.00 (978-1-60413-471-1(2), Chelsea Clubhouse) Facts On File, Inc.
Farndon, John. Electricity: An Investigation. 2008. (Science Investigations Ser.). (Illus.). 32p. (YA). (gr. 4-7). lib. bdg. 26.50 (978-1-4042-4287-6(2)) Rosen Publishing Group, Inc., The.
Felix, Rebecca. Cool Battery & Electricity Projects: Fun & Creative Workshop Activities. 2016. (ENG., Illus.). 32p. (J). (978-1-68078-125-0(1)) ABDO Publishing Co.
—Electricity at Work, 1 vol. 2016. (ENG., Illus.). 24p. (J). (978-1-68078-139-7(1)) ABDO Publishing Co.
Fitzpatrick, Anne. Electricity. 2003. 24p. (J). lib. bdg. 21.35 (978-1-58340-320-4(5)) Black Rabbit Bks.
Flaherty, Michael. Electricity & Batteries. 2009. (Science Factory Ser.). 32p. (gr. 4-5). 50.50 (978-1-60853-020-5(5), PowerKids Pr.) Rosen Publishing Group, Inc., The.
French, Cathy. Snap, Crackle, & Flow & Chasquea, cruje y Fluye: 6 English, 6 Spanish Adaptations. 2011. (ENG & SPA.). (J). 97.00 net. (978-1-4108-5697-5(6)) Benchmark Education Co.
Friend, Robyn & Cohen, Judith. Electricity & You: Be Smart, Be Safe. Katz, David, illus. l.t. ed. 2012. (ENG.). 40p. (J). pap. 7.00 (978-1-935999-02-7(8)) Cascade Pass, Inc.
Furgang, Kathy. Working with Electricity & Magnetism & Trabajar con la electricidad y el Magnetismo: 6 English, 6 Spanish Adaptations. 2011. (ENG & SPA.). (J). 97.00 net. (978-1-4108-5719-4(0)) Benchmark Education Co.
Galiano, Dean. Electric & Magnetic Phenomena. 2011. (Science Made Simple Ser.). (Illus.). 64p. (YA). (gr. 5-8). lib. bdg. 31.95 (978-1-4488-1231-8(3), Rosen Reference) Rosen Publishing Group, Inc., The.
Gangemi, Angelo. Where Does Electricity Come From? 2012. (Everyday Mysteries Ser.). (ENG., Illus.). 24p. (J). (gr. 2-4). pap. 8.15 (978-1-4339-6315-5(9)); lib. bdg. 22.60 (978-1-4339-6313-1(2)) Stevens, Gareth Publishing LLLP.
Gardner, Robert. Easy Genius Science Projects with Electricity & Magnetism: Great Experiments & Ideas. 2009. (Easy Genius Science Projects Ser.). (Illus.). 128p. (J). (gr. 5-9). lib. bdg. 33.27 (978-0-7660-2923-1(9)) Enslow Pubs., Inc.
—Electricity & Magnetism Experiments Using Batteries, Bulbs, Wires, & More: One Hour or Less Science Experiments. 2012. (Last-Minute Science Projects Ser.). (Illus.). 48p. (J). (gr. 5-18). 25.27 (978-0-7660-3960-5(9)) Enslow Pubs., Inc.
—Electricity & Magnetism Science Fair Projects, Revised & Expanded Using the Scientific Method. LaBaff, Stephanie & LaBaff, Tom, illus. 2010. (Physics Science Projects Using the Scientific Method Ser.). 160p. (J). (gr. 5-18). 35.94 (978-0-7660-3418-1(6)) Enslow Pubs., Inc.
—Electricity & Magnetism Science Fair Projects Using Batteries, Balloons, & Other Hair-Raising Stuff. 2004. (Physics! Best Science Projects Ser.). (Illus.). 128p. (J). lib. bdg. 27.94 (978-0-7660-2127-3(0)) Enslow Pubs., Inc.
—Energizing Science Projects with Electricity & Magnetism. LaBaff, Tom, illus. 2006. (Fantastic Physical Science Experiments Ser.). 48p. (J). (gr. 4-7). lib. bdg. 25.27 (978-0-7660-2584-4(5), Enslow Elementary) Enslow Pubs., Inc.
Gardner, Robert. Experiments with Electricity & Magnetism. 2017. (Science Whiz Experiments Ser.). 128p. (gr. 5-5). 37.27 **(978-0-7660-8678-4(X))** Enslow Pubs., Inc.
Geatches, Hazel, contrib. by. Electricity. 2013. (ENG.). 40p. pap. 9.38 (978-0-19-464685-7(8)) Oxford Univ. Pr., Inc.
Goldsworthy, Kaite. Electricity. 2017. (Illus.). 24p. (J). **(978-1-5105-1123-1(7))** SmartBook Media, Inc.
—Electricity. 2011. (J). (gr. 4-6). pap. 12.95 (978-1-61690-731-0(2), AV2 by Weigl); (Illus.). 24p. (YA). (gr. 3-6). 27.13 (978-1-61690-727-3(4)) Weigl Pubs., Inc.
—Studying Electricity. 2016. (Illus.). 24p. (J). (978-1-5105-1122-4(9)) SmartBook Media, Inc.
Good, Keith. Zap It! Exciting Electricity Activities. 2008. (Design It! Ser.). pap. 6.95 (978-0-8225-9926-5(0)) Lerner Publishing Group.
Graham, Ian. Electricity! Walker, Rory, illus. 2014. (You Wouldn't Want to Live Without... Ser.). (ENG.). 32p. (J). lib. bdg. 29.00 (978-0-531-21216-5(5), Watts, Franklin) Scholastic Library Publishing.
—From Falling Water to Electric Car: An Energy Journey Through the World of Electricity. 2015. (Energy Journeys Ser.). (ENG.). 48p. (gr. 3-6). 33.32 (978-1-4846-0884-5(4), Heinemann InfoSearch) Heinemann-Raintree.
Gray, Leon. Electricity. 2013. (Physical Science Ser.). 48p. (J). (gr. 4-6). pap. 84.30 (978-1-4339-9502-6(6)); pap. 14.05 (978-1-4339-9501-9(8)); (ENG., Illus.). lib. bdg. 31.95 (978-1-4339-9500-2(X)) Stevens, Gareth Publishing LLLP.
Gray, Susan H. Experiments with Electricity. 2011. (True Bk Ser.). (ENG., Illus.). 48p. (J). pap. 6.95 (978-0-531-26644-1(3), Children's Pr.) Scholastic Library Publishing.
Greek, Joe. What Is Electrical Energy? 2017. (Let's Find Out! Forms of Energy Ser.). 32p. (gr. 6-8). pap. 12.90 **(978-1-68048-697-1(7)**, Britannica Educational Publishing) Rosen Publishing Group, Inc., The.
Green, Joey. The Electric Pickle: 50 Experiments from the Periodic Table, from Aluminum to Zinc. 2017. (ENG.). 272p. pap. 19.99 **(978-1-61373-959-4(1))** Chicago Review Pr., Inc.
H. Gray, Susan. Experiments with Electricity. 2011. (True Book-Experiments Ser.). (Illus.). 48p. (J). lib. bdg. 29.00 (978-0-531-26344-0(4), Children's Pr.) Scholastic Library Publishing.
Hagler, Gina. Electricity. 2016. (J). (978-1-4896-5274-4(4)) Weigl Pubs., Inc.
—Step-by-Step Experiments with Electricity. Ostrom, Bob, illus. 2012. (Step-By-Step Experiments Ser.). (ENG.). 32p. (J). (gr. 1-4). lib. bdg. 29.93 (978-1-60973-338-4(X), 201230) Child's World, Inc., The.
Hantula, Richard. Electricity & Forces. 2006. (Real World Science Ser.). (Illus.). 32p. (gr. 2-6). lib. bdg. 26.00 (978-0-8368-6305-5(4), Gareth Stevens Learning Library) Stevens, Gareth Publishing LLLP.
Harcourt School Publishers, creator. Invisible Pull: Electricity & Magnets. 2009. (ENG., Illus.). 16p. (J). pap. 14.95 (978-0-15-362219-9(9)) Harcourt Schl. Pubs.
Hayes, Amy. Freaky Stories about Electricity. 2016. (Freaky True Science Ser.). (Illus.). 32p. (J). (gr. 5-4). pap. 10.50 (978-1-4824-4812-2(2)) Stevens, Gareth Publishing LLLP.
Hewitt, Sally. Amazing Electricity. 2007. (Amazing Science Ser.). (ENG.). 32p. (J). pap. (978-0-7787-3624-0(5)) Crabtree Publishing Co.
Higgins, Nadia. Electricity Is Everywhere, 1 vol. Ricci, Andres Martinez, illus. 2008. (Science Rocks Ser.). (ENG.). 32p. (gr. -1-4). 28.50 (978-1-60270-276-9(4), 1287324, Looking Glass Library- Nonfiction) Magic Wagon.
—Electricity Is Everywhere CD+Book. Martinez Ricci, Andres, illus. 2010. (Science Rocks! Set 2 CD+Book Ser.). 32p. lib. bdg. 54.14 incl. cd-rom (978-1-60270-991-1(2)) ABDO Publishing Co.
—Electricity Is Everywhere Site CD+Book. Martinez Ricci, Andres, illus. 2010. (Science Rocks! Set 2 Site CD+Book Ser.). 32p. lib. bdg. 84.14 incl. cd-rom (978-1-61641-008-7(6)) ABDO Publishing Co.
—Excited about Energy Site CD+Book. Martinez Ricci, Andres, illus. 2010. (Science Rocks! Set 2 Site CD+Book Ser.). 32p. lib. bdg. 84.14 incl. cd-rom (978-1-61641-009-4(4)) ABDO Publishing Co.
Holt, Rinehart and Winston Staff. Holt Science & Technology Chapter 17: Physical Science: Introduction to Electricity. 5th ed. 2004. (Illus.). pap. 12.86 (978-0-03-030416-3(4)) Holt McDougal.
—Holt Science & Technology Pt. N: Electricity & Magnetism. 3rd ed. 2003. (Holt Science & Technology Ser.). (SPA.). 18.60 (978-0-03-069329-8(2)) Holt McDougal.
Holzweiss, Kristina. Amazing MakerSpace DIY with Electricity. 2017. (True Book — MakerSpace Projects Ser.). (ENG.). 48p. (J). lib. bdg. 31.00 **(978-0-531-23845-5(8)**, Children's Pr.) Scholastic Library Publishing.
Holzweiss, Kristina A. Electricity. 2017. (True Book — MakerSpace Projects Ser.). (ENG.). 48p. (J). pap. 7.95 **(978-0-531-24096-0(7)**, Children's Pr.) Scholastic Library Publishing.
Hunter, Rebecca. The Facts about Electricity. 2004. (Illus.). 32p. (J). lib. bdg. 27.10 (978-1-58340-453-9(8)) Black Rabbit Bks.
Ives, Rob. Fun Experiments with Electricity: Mini Robots, Micro Lightning Strikes, & More. Sassin, Eva, illus. 2017. (Amazing Science Experiments Ser.). (ENG.). (J). (gr. 3-6). lib. bdg. 26.65 **(978-1-5124-3219-0(9))** Lerner Publishing Group.
Jango-Cohen, Judith. Ben Franklin's Big Shock. Lepp, Kevin, illus. 2006. (On My Own Science Ser.). 48p. (J). (gr. k-3). per. 5.95 (978-0-8225-6450-8(5), First Avenue Editions); lib. bdg. 25.26 (978-1-57505-873-3(1), Millbrook Pr.) Lerner Publishing Group.
Jennings, Terry. Electricidad y Magnetismo (Electricity & Magnetism) (SPA.). 32p. (J). 6.95 (978-84-348-1741-8(1)) SM Ediciones ESP. Dist: AIMS International Bks., Inc.
Kessler, Colleen. A Project Guide to Electricity & Magnetism. 2011. (Physical Science Projects for Kids Ser.). (Illus.). 48p. (J). (gr. 3-6). lib. bdg. 29.95 (978-1-58415-966-7(9), 1327821) Mitchell Lane Pubs., Inc.
Lachner, Elizabeth. The History of Electricity. 2009. (Real Life Readers Ser.). 32p. (gr. 4-5). pap. 10.00 (978-1-4358-0143-1(1), Rosen Classroom); 32p. (gr. 4-4). 47.90 (978-1-60853-040-3(X), PowerKids Pr.); (J). lib. bdg. 25.25 (978-1-4358-2980-0(8), PowerKids Pr.) Rosen Publishing Group, Inc., The.
Law, Felicia. Electricity. 2009. (Simply Science Ser.). (Illus.). 32p. (YA). (gr. 3-6). lib. bdg. 26.00 (978-1-4339-0031-0(9)) Stevens, Gareth Publishing LLLP.
Leavitt, Amie Jane. Who Really Discovered Electricity?, 1 vol. (Race for History Ser.). (ENG., 32p. (gr. 3-4). 2011. Illus.). pap. 8.10 (978-1-4296-6248-2(4)) 2011. pap. 47.70 (978-1-4296-6416-5(9)) 2010. lib. bdg. 27.32 (978-1-4296-3345-1(X)) Capstone Press of Coughlan Cos. (Fact Finders).
Lockwood, Sophie. Super Cool Science Experiments: Electricity. 2009. (Explorer Library: Science Explorer Ser.). (ENG., Illus.). 32p. (gr. 4-8). lib. bdg. 28.50 (978-1-60279-533-4(9), 200289) Cherry Lake Publishing.
Lopez, Andre. Emily's Electricity Experiments. 2013. (Rosen Readers Ser.). (ENG.). 24p. (J). (gr. 3-4). pap. 49.50 (978-1-4777-2459-0(1)); pap. 8.25 (978-1-4777-2458-3(3)) Rosen Publishing Group, Inc., The. (Rosen Classroom).
Lyons, Suzanne. Electricity Adds Up: Set Of 6. 2011. (Navigators Ser.). (J). 48.00 net. (978-1-4108-0439-6(9)) Benchmark Education Co.
—Electricity Adds up & Electricidad Lógica: 6 English, 6 Spanish Adaptations. 2011. (ENG & SPA.). (J). 97.00 net. (978-1-4108-5711-8(5)) Benchmark Education Co.
Madgwick, Wendy. Magnets & Sparks: 16 Easy-to-Follow Experiments for Learning Fun - Find Out How Electricity & Magnetism Works! 2014. (ENG., Illus.). 270p. (J). (gr. -1-12). 8.99 (978-1-86147-352-3(4), Armadillo) Anness Publishing GBR. Dist: National Bk. Network.
Magnetism & Electricity. (Jump Ser.). (Illus.). 32p. (J). (gr. 2-7). pap. (978-1-882210-27-5(1)) Action Publishing, Inc.
Mahaney, Ian F. Electricity. (Energy in Action Ser.). 24p. 2009. (gr. 3-3). 42.50 (978-1-61512-257-8(5), PowerKids Pr.) 2007. (ENG.). (gr. 3-8). pap. 7.05 (978-1-4042-2187-1(5), PowerKids Pr.) 2007. (Illus.). (YA). (gr. 4-7). lib. bdg. 22.60 (978-1-4042-3478-9(0)) Rosen Publishing Group, Inc., The.
Marsh, Carole. Electricity: Common Core Lessons & Activities. 2013. (Common Core Ser.). (ENG., Illus.). 24p. (J). (gr. 4-7). pap. 4.99 (978-0-635-10614-8(0)) Gallopade International.
Marsico, Katie. Electricity Investigations. 2017. (Key Questions in Physical Science Ser.). (ENG.). 32p. (J). (gr. 3-6). 27.99 **(978-1-5124-4007-2(8))** Lerner Publishing Group.
Martineau, Susan & Bushell, Nick. Cool Circuits. 2011. (Awesome Activities Ser.). (ENG., Illus.). 24p. (J). (gr. 3-6). pap. 10.60 (978-1-61533-404-9(1)); lib. bdg. 25.25 (978-1-61533-366-0(5)) Windmill Bks.
Masters, Nancy Robinson. How Did That Get to My House? Electricity. 2009. (Community Connections: How Did That Get to My House? Ser.). (ENG.). 24p. (gr. 2-5). lib. bdg. 25.64 (978-1-60279-474-0(X), 200245) Cherry Lake Publishing.
Mayes, Susan. Where Does Electricity Come From? Shackell, John & Scorey, John, illus. 2006. (Usborne Starting Point Science Ser.). 23p. (J). (gr. 1-4). pap. 4.99 (978-0-7945-1411-2(1), Usborne) EDC Publishing.
—Where Does Electricity Come From? Shackell, John, illus. 2006. (Usborne Starting Point Science Ser.). 23p. (J). (gr. 4-7). lib. bdg. 12.99 (978-1-58086-938-6(6), Usborne) EDC Publishing.
McGregor, Harriet. Electricity. 2010. (Sherlock Bones Looks at Physical Science Ser.). (ENG.). 32p. (YA). (gr. 3-6). lib. bdg. 25.25 (978-1-61533-210-6(3)) Windmill Bks.
McNeil, Niki, et al. HOCPP 1087 Electricity. 2006. spiral bd. 24.50 (978-1-60308-087-3(2)) In the Hands of a Child.
McWilliams, Eileen. Pioneers of Electricity. 2013. (Electrified! Ser.). (Illus.). 24p. (gr. 2-5). 22.60 (978-1-4339-8412-9(1)); pap. 8.15 (978-1-4339-8409-9(1)) Stevens, Gareth Publishing LLLP. (Gareth Stevens Learning Library).
Monroe, Ron. What Is Electricity? 2012. (ENG.). 32p. (J). (978-0-7787-2079-9(9)); pap. (978-0-7787-2084-3(5)) Crabtree Publishing Co.
Monroe, Tilda. What Do You Know about Electricity? 2010. (20 Questions: Physical Science Ser.). (ENG.). 24p. (J). pap. 8.25 (978-1-4488-1248-6(8), PowerKids Pr.); (YA). (gr. 2-5). lib. bdg. 22.60 (978-1-4488-0671-3(2)) Rosen Publishing Group, Inc., The.
Mooney, Carla. It's Electric! Currents. 2014. (ENG.). 48p. (gr. 4-6). 35.64 (978-1-62717-750-4(7)) Rourke Educational Media.
Moore, Rob. Why Does Electricity Flow? 2010. (Illus.). 24p. (J). 49.50 (978-1-61531-918-3(2), PowerKids Pr.); (J). pap. 8.25 (978-1-61531-917-6(4), PowerKids Pr.); (YA). (gr. 3-6). lib. bdg. 22.60 (978-1-61531-893-3(3)) Rosen Publishing Group, Inc., The.
—Why Does Electricity Flow? Level 6 Factbook. 2010. (Cambridge Young Readers Ser.). (ENG., Illus.). 24p. pap. 7.16 (978-0-521-13748-5(9)) Cambridge Univ. Pr.
Mullins, Matt. Electricity. 2011. (True Book-Physical Science Ser.). (ENG., Illus.). 48p. (J). 29.00 (978-0-531-26319-8(3)); pap. 6.95 (978-0-531-26581-9(1)) Scholastic Library Publishing. (Children's Pr.).
Murray, Julie. Electricity, 1 vol. 2006. (First Science Ser.). (ENG., Illus.). 24p. (gr. k-4). 25.65 (978-1-59679-822-9(X), Buddy Bks.) ABDO Publishing Co.
National Geographic Learning Staff. Electricity & Magnetism. 2010. (ENG., Illus.). 32p. (C). (gr. 7-13). pap. 12.95 (978-0-7945-2217-9(3)) National Geographic School Publishing, Inc.
Navarro, Paula & Jimenez, Angels. Amazing Experiments with Electricity & Magnetism. Cuxart, Bernadette, illus. 2014. (Magic Science Ser.). (ENG.). 36p. (J). (gr. 1-6). pap. 7.99 (978-1-4380-0428-0(1)) Barron's Educational Series, Inc.
Nemzer, Marilyn, ed. Energy for Keeps: An Illustrated Guide for Everyone Who Uses Electricity 2005. (Illus.). 176p. 24.95 (978-0-9744765-3-7(6)) Energy Education Group.
Newson, Lesley & Wadsworth, Pamela. Trydan a Magnetedd. 2005. (WEL., Illus.). 24p. pap. (978-1-85596-225-5(X)) Dref Wen.
Norlander, Britt. I've Discovered Electricity! 2008. (Eureka! Ser.). 32p. (gr. 4-18). lib. bdg. 28.50 (978-0-7614-3195-4(0), Benchmark Bks.) Marshall Cavendish Corp.
Norman, Penny. Science One Two Three Electricity. Einstein, Ann, ed. 2005. 31p. 15.95 (978-1-886978-65-2(4)) Norman & Globus, Inc.
O'Donnell, Liam & Barnett III, Charles. The Shocking World of Electricity with Max Axiom, Super Scientist, 1 vol. Barnett, Charles, III & Dominguez, Richard, illus. 2007. (Graphic Science Ser.). (ENG.). 32p. (gr. 3-4). 30.65 (978-0-7368-6835-8(6), Graphic Library) Capstone Press of Coughlan Cos.
—The Shocking World of Electricity with Max Axiom, Super Scientist, 1 vol. Dominguez, Richard, illus. 2007. (Graphic Science Ser.). (ENG.). 32p. (gr. 3-4). pap. 8.10 (978-0-7368-7888-3(2), 1264936, Graphic Library) Capstone Press of Coughlan Cos.
Oxlade, Chris. Conductors & Insulators, 1 vol. 2012. (It's Electric! Ser.). (ENG., Illus.). 32p. (gr. 2-4). pap. 8.95 (978-1-4329-5678-3(7)); lib. bdg. 26.65 (978-1-4329-5673-8(6)) Heinemann-Raintree. (NA-h).
—Electricity, 1 vol. 2012. (How Does My Home Work? Ser.). (ENG.). 24p. (gr. k-1). pap. 6.79 (978-1-4329-6570-9(0), Heinemann Read & Learn) Heinemann-Raintree.
—Experiments with Electricity & Magnets, 1 vol. 2015. (ENG., Illus.). 32p. (J). pap. 11.75 (978-1-4777-5962-2(X), PowerKids Pr.) Rosen Publishing Group, Inc., The.
—Making a Circuit, 1 vol. 2012. (It's Electric! Ser.). (ENG., Illus.). 32p. (gr. 2-4). pap. 8.95 (978-1-4329-5679-0(5)); lib. bdg. 26.65 (978-1-4329-5674-5(4)) Heinemann-Raintree. (NA-h).
—Using Electricity, 1 vol. 2012. (It's Electric! Ser.). (ENG.). 32p. (gr. 2-4). pap. 8.95 (978-1-4329-5681-3(7), NA-h) Heinemann-Raintree.
Parker, Steve. DK Eyewitness Books: Electricity: Electricity. 2013. (DK Eyewitness Bks.). (ENG.). 72p. (J). (gr. 3-7). 19.99 (978-1-4654-0900-3(9), DK Children) Dorling Kindersley Publishing, Inc.
Parker, Steve & Dorling Kindersley Publishing Staff. Electricity. 2013. (DK Eyewitness Bks.). (ENG.). 72p. (J). (gr. 3-7). 16.99 (978-1-4654-0899-0(1), DK Children) Dorling Kindersley Publishing, Inc.
Pegis, Jessica. What Are Insulators & Conductors? 2012. (ENG.). 32p. (J). (978-0-7787-2078-2(0)); pap. (978-0-7787-2083-6(7)) Crabtree Publishing Co.
Peterson, Megan Cooley. Scooby-Doo! a Science of Electricity Mystery: The Mutant Crocodile. Cornia, Christian, illus. 2017. (Scooby-Doo Solves It with S. T. E. M. Ser.). (ENG.). 32p. (gr. 3-4). pap. 7.95 (978-1-5157-3702-5(0)) Capstone Press of Coughlan Cos.
—Scooby-Doo! a Science of Light Mystery: The Angry Alien. Brizuela, Dario, illus. 2017. (Scooby-Doo Solves It with S. T. E. M. Ser.). (ENG.). 32p. (gr. 3-4). pap. 7.95 (978-1-5157-3704-9(7)) Capstone Press of Coughlan Cos.
Polinsky, Paige V. & Craig, Diane. Super Simple Experiments with Electricity: Fun & Innovative Science Projects. 2016. (ENG., Illus.). 32p. (978-1-68078-167-0(7)) ABDO Publishing Co.
Randolph, Joanne. Electricity in My World. (My World of Science Ser.). 24p. 2009. (gr. 2-2). 37.50 (978-1-61514-720-5(9), PowerKids Pr.) 2007. (ENG.). (gr. k-8). pap. 7.05 (978-1-4042-8418-0(4), Rosen Classroom) 2006. (Illus.). (J). (gr. 3-7). lib. bdg. 18.75 (978-1-4042-3288-4(5), PowerKids Pr.) Rosen Publishing Group, Inc., The.
—Electricity in My World / la Electricidad en Mi Mundo. Brusca, Maria Cristina, tr. from ENG. 2006. (My World of Science/ Mi mundo y la Ciencia Ser.). (ENG & SPA., Illus.). 24p. (J). (gr. k-3). lib. bdg. 16.00 (978-1-4042-3319-5(9)) Rosen Publishing Group, Inc., The.
—Electricity in My World/la electricidad en mi Mundo. 2009. (My World of Science/la ciencia en mi mundo Ser.). (ENG & SPA.). 48p. (gr. 2-2). 37.50 (978-1-61514-732-8(2), Editorial Buenas Letras) Rosen Publishing Group, Inc., The.
Rau, Dana Meachen. Electricity & Magnetism. 2009. (21st Century Skills Library: Real World Science Ser.). (ENG.). 32p. (gr. 4-8). lib. bdg. 28.50 (978-1-60279-459-7(6), 200236) Cherry Lake Publishing.
Riley, Gail Blasser. Benjamin Franklin & Electricity. 2004. (Cornerstones of Freedom Ser.). (ENG., Illus.). 48p. (YA). (gr. 4-7). 26.00 (978-0-516-24240-8(7)) Scholastic Library Publishing.
Riley, Peter. Electricity. 2016. (Moving up with Science Ser.). 00032p. (J). (gr. 3-4). pap. 10.00 (978-1-4994-3137-7(6), PowerKids Pr.) Rosen Publishing Group, Inc., The.
Riley, Peter D. Electricity. 2011. (Real Scientist Investigates Ser.). 32p. (J). (gr. 3-5). lib. bdg. 28.50 (978-1-59771-279-8(5)) Sea-To-Sea Pubns.
Rogers, K. Light, Sound & Electricity. 2004. (Library of Science Ser.). 64p. (J). lib. bdg. 17.95 (978-1-58086-376-6(0)) EDC Publishing.
Roland, James. How Circuits Work. 2016. (Connect with Electricity Ser.). (ENG., Illus.). 40p. (J). (gr. 4-6). 30.65 (978-1-5124-0778-5(X)); 46.65 (978-1-5124-1007-5(1), Lerner Pubns.) Lerner Publishing Group.
Royston, Angela. Electricity. 2012. (Science Corner Ser.). (Illus.). 24p. (J). (gr. 1-4). lib. bdg. 22.60 (978-1-4488-5257-4(9)) Rosen Publishing Group, Inc., The.
—Using Electricity. 2016. (My World of Science Ser.). (ENG.). 32p. (gr. 1-3). pap. 7.99 (978-1-4846-3823-1(9), Heinemann First Library) Heinemann-Raintree.
Roza, Greg. It's Electric! (Reading Room Collection 2 Ser.). 24p. 2009. (gr. 3-4). 42.50 (978-1-60851-975-0(9), PowerKids Pr.) 2003. (ENG.). (gr. 3-4). 43.95 (978-0-8239-8727-6(2)) 2003. (Illus.). (J). lib. bdg. 22.60 (978-0-8239-3708-0(9)) Rosen Publishing Group, Inc., The.
Samuels, Charlie. The Advent of Electricity, 1800-1900. 2010. (Science Highlights: A Gareth Stevens Timeline Ser.). (ENG.). 48p. (J). (gr. 6-8). pap. 14.05 (978-1-4339-4149-8(X)); lib. bdg. 31.95 (978-1-4339-4148-1(1)) Stevens, Gareth Publishing LLLP. (Gareth Stevens Secondary Library).
Scholastic & Klutz Editors. Circuit Clay. 2017. (ENG.). 52p. (J). (gr. 2-7). 21.99 (978-1-338-10636-7(8)) Klutz.
Schuh, Mari. Electricity. 2007. (First Science Ser.). (ENG., Illus.). 24p. (J). (gr. 2-5). lib. bdg. 25.95 (978-1-60014-095-2(5)) Bellwether Media.
Schuh, Mari C. Electricity. (Blastoff! Readers Ser.). 24p. (J). 2011. (Illus.). pap. 5.95 (978-0-531-28452-0(2)) 2007. (ENG.). 20.00 (978-0-531-14723-8(1)) Scholastic Library Publishing. (Children's Pr.).
Seaver, C. H. American Boys' Book of Electricity. 2013. 400p. (978-1-62583-553-6(1)) Textbook Pubs.
Seuling, Barbara. Flick a Switch: How Electricity Gets to Your Home. Tobin, Nancy, illus. 2003. (ENG.). 32p. (J). (gr. k-3). tchr. ed. 16.95 (978-0-8234-1729-2(8)) Holiday Hse., Inc.
Sganga, Francis. Essentials of Electricity for Gifted Students: Preparation for High School Physics, Grades 4-8. 2003. (Illus.). 70p. (978-0-910609-46-3(2)) Gifted Education Pr.
Sherman, Patrice. Electricity. 2017. (J). **(978-1-5026-2772-8(8))** Cavendish Square Publishing.
Silverman, Buffy. Zap! It's Electricity! 2011. (ENG., Illus.). 24p. (gr. 2-3). pap. 8.95 (978-1-61741-955-3(9)) Rourke Educational Media.
Snedden, Robert. How Does a Waterfall Become Electricity? 2016. (How Does It Happen Ser.). (ENG.). 32p. (gr. 3-5). pap. 8.29 (978-1-4109-8527-9(X), Raintree Perspectives) Heinemann-Raintree.
Sohn, Emily & Brennan, Joseph. Magnetism & Electricity: The Broken Toy Car. 2011. (IScience Readers Ser.). 32p. (J). (gr. 3-4). lib. bdg. 22.60 (978-1-59953-415-2(0)) Norwood Hse. Pr.
Solway, Andrew. Exploring Electricity & Magnetism. 2007. (Exploring Physical Science Ser.). (Illus.). 48p. (YA). (gr. 5-9). lib. bdg. 29.25 (978-1-4042-3749-0(6)) Rosen Publishing Group, Inc., The.
Spilsbury, Louise. The Science of Electricity. 2016. (Flowchart Smart Ser.). (ENG.). 48p. (J). (gr. 4-5). pap. 14.05 (978-1-4824-4131-4(4)) Stevens, Gareth Publishing LLLP.
Spilsbury, Louise & Spilsbury, Richard. Electricity, 1 vol. 2013. (Essential Physical Science Ser.). (ENG.). 48p. (gr. 4-6).

33.32 *(978-1-4329-8143-3(9)*, Heinemann InfoSearch) Heinemann-Raintree.

Spilsbury, Richard & Spilsbury, Louise. Sparks, Shocks, & Secrets. 2015. (Science Adventures Ser.). (ENG., Illus.). 32p. (J). (gr. 3-7). 31.35 *(978-1-62588-148-9(7))* Black Rabbit Bks.

—What Is Electricity & Magnetism? Exploring Science with Hands-on Activities. 2008. (In Touch with Basic Science Ser.). (Illus.). 32p. (J). (gr. 3-4). lib. bdg. 23.94 *(978-0-7660-3096-1(2)*, Enslow Elementary) Enslow Pubs., Inc.

Stille, Darlene R. Electricity: Bulbs, Batteries, & Sparks. Boyd, Sheree, illus. 2004. (Amazing Science Ser.). (ENG.). 24p. (gr. k-4). 26.65 *(978-1-4048-0245-2(2))* Picture Window Bks.

Suen, Anastasia. Wired. Carrick, Paul, illus. 2007. (ENG.). 32p. (J). (gr. 1-4). 16.95 *(978-1-57091-599-4(7))*; pap. 7.95 *(978-1-57091-494-2(X))* Charlesbridge Publishing, Inc.

Sundance/Newbridge LLC Staff. How We Use Electricity. 2007. (Early Science Ser.). (gr. k-3). 18.95 *(978-1-4007-6368-9(1))*; pap. 6.10 *(978-1-4007-6364-1(9))* Sundance/Newbridge Educational Publishing.

Swanson, Jennifer. The Shocking Truth about Electricity. Lum, Bernice, illus. 2012. (LOL Physical Science Ser.). (ENG.). 32p. (gr. 3-4). pap. 47.70 *(978-1-4296-9301-1(0))*; lib. bdg. 27.32 *(978-1-4296-8602-0(2))* Capstone Press of Coughlan Cos. (Fact Finders).

Swanson, Jennifer Ann. The Shocking Truth about Electricity. 1 vol. Lum, Bernice, illus. 2012. (LOL Physical Science Ser.). (ENG.). 32p. (gr. 3-4). pap. 8.10 *(978-1-4296-9300-4(2)*, Fact Finders) Capstone Press of Coughlan Cos.

Thomas, Isabel. Experiments with Electricity. 2015. (Read & Experiment Ser.). (ENG., Illus.). 32p. (gr. 2-4). 30.65 *(978-1-4109-6838-8(3)*, Raintree Perspectives) Heinemann-Raintree.

—Experiments with Sound. 2015. (Read & Experiment Ser.). (ENG., Illus.). 32p. (gr. 2-4). pap. 7.99 *(978-1-4109-7900-1(8)*, Raintree Perspectives) Heinemann-Raintree.

Troupe, Thomas Kingsley. Glowing with Electricity: Science Adventures with Glenda the Origami Firefly. 1 vol. Christoph, Jamey, illus. 2014. (Origami Science Adventures Ser.). (ENG.). 24p. (gr. 3-4). lib. bdg. 27.32 *(978-1-4795-2189-0(2))* Picture Window Bks.

Trumbauer, Lisa. What Is Electricity? 2004. (Rookie Read-About Science Ser.). (ENG.). 32p. (J). (gr. 1-2). pap. 4.95 *(978-0-516-25845-4(1)*, Watts, Franklin) Scholastic Library Publishing.

Twist, Clint. Electricity. 2010. (Science Everywhere! Ser.). 24p. 24.25 *(978-1-84898-295-6(X))* Black Rabbit Bks.

Valkenburgh. Electricidad Basica. 2006. 160p. Vol. 1. 10.95 *(978-968-26-0378-5(1))* Vol. 2. (SPA.). pap. 10.95 *(978-968-26-0382-2(X))* Vol. 3. (SPA.). pap. 10.95 *(978-968-26-0383-9(8))* Vol. 5. (SPA.). pap. 10.95 *(978-968-26-0433-1(8))* Compania Editorial Continental MEX. Dist: Fondo de Cultura Economica USA.

Valkenburgh, Van & Nooger & Neville. Electricidad Basica, Volume 4, Vol. 4. 2004. (SPA., Illus.). 170p. per. 10.95 *(978-968-26-0395-2(1))* Compania Editorial Continental MEX. Dist: Fondo de Cultura Economica USA.

Van Vleet, Carmella. Explore Electricity! With 25 Great Projects. Stone, Bryan, illus. 2013. (Explore Your World Ser.). (ENG.). 96p. (J). (gr. k-4). pap. 13.95 *(978-1-61930-180-1(6))* Open City Bks.

Vogel, Julia. Discover Electricity. Yamada, Jane, illus. 2014. (Science Around Us Ser.). (ENG.). 24p. (J). (gr. -1-2). 25.64 *(978-1-62687-302-5(X)*, 207143) Child's World, Inc., The.

Wadsworth, Pamela. Golwg Gyntaf Ar Drydan a Magnetau. 2005. (WEL., Illus.). 24p. pap. *(978-1-85596-255-2(1))* Dref Wen.

Walker, Sally M. La Electricidad. King, Andy, photos by. 2007. (Libros de Energía para madrugadores (Early Bird Energy) Ser.). (SPA., Illus.). 48p. (J). (gr. 4-7). lib. bdg. 26.60 *(978-0-8225-7717-1(8)*, Ediciones Lerner) Lerner Publishing Group.

—La Electricidad; Electricity. 2008. pap. 52.95 *(978-0-8225-9868-8(X))* Lerner Publishing Group.

—Electricity. King, Andy, photos by. 2005. (Early Bird Energy Ser.). (ENG., Illus.). 48p. (gr. 2-5). lib. bdg. 26.60 *(978-0-8225-2919-4(X)*, Lerner Pubns.) Lerner Publishing Group.

—Investigating Electricity. 2011. (Searchlight Books How Does Energy Work Ser.). (ENG., Illus.). (gr. 3-5). pap. 51.01 *(978-0-7613-8405-2(7))*; 40p. pap. 8.95 *(978-0-7613-7871-6(5))*; 40p. lib. bdg. 27.93 *(978-0-7613-5772-8(6))* Lerner Publishing Group.

Ward, Sarah E. Electricity in the Real World. 2013. (Science in the Real World EBook Ser.). (ENG.). 48p. (J). pap. 15.64 *(978-1-61783-788-3(1)*, Core Library); (gr. 3-6). lib. bdg. 32.79 *(978-1-61783-738-8(5))* ABDO Publishing Co.

Weakland, Mark. Zombies & Electricity. 1 vol. Jok, Diego, illus. 2013. (Monster Science Ser.). (ENG.). 32p. (gr. 3-4). pap. 8.10 *(978-1-62065-822-2(4)*, Graphic Library) Capstone Press of Coughlan Cos.

—Zombies & Electricity. 6 vols. Jok, illus. 2013. (Monster Science Ser.). (ENG.). 32p. (gr. 3-4). 47.70 *(978-1-62065-823-9(2)*, Graphic Library) Capstone Press of Coughlan Cos.

—Zombies & Electricity. 1 vol. Jok, Diego, illus. 2013. (Monster Science Ser.). (ENG.). 32p. (gr. 3-4). lib. bdg. 30.65 *(978-1-4296-9929-7(9)*, Graphic Library) Capstone Press of Coughlan Cos.

Weingarten, Ethan. What Is a Circuit? 2013. (Electrified! Ser.). (Illus.). 24p. (J). (gr. 2-5). 22.60 *(978-1-4339-8414-3(8))*; pap. 8.15 *(978-1-4339-8415-0(6))* Stevens, Gareth Publishing LLLP. (Gareth Stevens Learning Library).

Westrup, Hugh. Electricity. 2015. (Science Readers: Content & Literacy Ser.). (ENG., Illus.). 32p. (gr. 4-4). pap. 8.99 *(978-1-4807-4681-7(9))* Teacher Created Materials, Inc.

Whiting, Jim. The Science of Lighting a City: Electricity in Action. 2010. (Action Science Ser.). (ENG.). 32p. (gr. 3-4). pap. 47.70 *(978-1-4296-5077-9(X)*, Fact Finders) Capstone Press of Coughlan Cos.

Wilson, Roman. How Does a Battery Work? 2013. (Electrified! Ser.). (Illus.). 24p. (J). (gr. 2-5). 22.60 *(978-1-4339-8399-3(0))*; pap. 8.15 *(978-1-4339-8400-6(8))* Stevens, Gareth Publishing LLLP. (Gareth Stevens Learning Library).

Woodford, Chris. Electricity: Investigating the Presence & Flow of Electric Charge. 2012. (Scientific Pathways Ser.). (ENG., Illus.). 48p. (J). (gr. 5-8). lib. bdg. 27.95 *(978-1-4488-7197-1(2)*, Rosen Reference) Rosen Publishing Group, Inc., The.

—Experiments with Electricity & Magnetism. 2010. (Cool Science Ser.). (Illus.). 32p. (J). (gr. 5-6). pap. 10.50 *(978-1-4339-3445-2(0))*; lib. bdg. 28.00 *(978-1-4339-3444-5(2)*, 1309301) Stevens, Gareth Publishing LLLP. (Gareth Stevens Learning Library).

World Book, Inc Staff, contrib. by. Electricity. 2011. (Illus.). 32p. (J). *(978-0-7166-1421-0(9))* World Bk., Inc.

Wright, Russell G. Blackout! Investigations in Electricity. (Event-Based Science Ser.). (YA). (gr. 5-9). 66p. pap., stu. ed. 11.50 *(978-0-7690-2346-5(0))*; 56p. pap., tchr.'s training gde. ed. 25.95 incl. VHS *(978-0-7690-2347-2(9))* Seymour, Dale Pubns.

Wyborny, Sheila. Electricity. 2003. (Kidhaven Science Library). (Illus.). 48p. (J). (gr. 3-5). 23.70 *(978-0-7377-1535-4(9)*, Kidhaven) Cengage Gale.

ELECTRICITY—DISTRIBUTION

see Electric Lines

ELECTRICITY—FICTION

Ballantyne, Robert Michael. The Battery & the Boiler: Adventures in Laying of Submarine Electric Cables. 2007. 254p. pap. 21.99 *(978-1-4346-3754-3(9))*; (ENG.). 282p. pap. 23.99 *(978-1-4346-3768-0(9))* Creative Media Partners, LLC.

Baum, L. Frank. The Master Key. 2004. reprint ed. pap. 1.99 *(978-1-4192-7199-1(7))*; pap. 15.95 *(978-1-4191-7199-4(2))* Kessinger Publishing, LLC.

Collins, Suzanne. When Charlie McButton Lost Power. Lester, Mike, illus. 2007. (ENG.). 32p. (J). (gr. -1-3). pap. 6.99 *(978-0-14-240857-5(3)*, Puffin Books) Penguin Young Readers Group.

—When Charlie McButton Lost Power. Lester, Mike, illus. 2009. 32p. 16.00 *(978-1-60686-529-3(3))* Perfection Learning Corp.

Deubreau, Sharon. Heather & Avery & the Magic Kite. Pileggi, Steve, illus. l.t. ed. 2006. 23p. (J). per. 11.99 *(978-1-59879-143-3(5))* Lifevest Publishing, Inc.

d'Lacey, Chris. Frankin's Bear. Taylor, Thomas, illus. 2005. (Red Go Bananas Ser.). (ENG.). 48p. (J). (gr. 2-3). lib. bdg. *(978-0-7787-2674-6(6))* Crabtree Publishing Co.

Evans, Richard. Battle of the Ampere. (Michael Vey Ser.: 3). (ENG., Illus.). 320p. (YA). (gr. 7). 2014. pap. 11.99 *(978-1-4424-7512-0(9))* 2013. 17.99 *(978-1-4424-7511-3(0))* Simon Pulse/Mercury Ink. (Simon Pulse/Mercury Ink).

—An Electrifying Michael Vey Set. 2013. (Michael Vey Ser.). (ENG., Illus.). 1008p. (YA). (gr. 7). 53.99 *(978-1-4424-9550-0(2)*, Simon Pulse/Mercury Ink) Simon Pulse/Mercury Ink.

—Hunt for Jade Dragon. 2015. (Michael Vey Ser.: 4). (ENG., Illus.). 336p. (YA). (gr. 7). pap. 11.99 *(978-1-4814-2439-4(4))* Simon & Schuster, Inc.

—Michael Vey 5. 2015. (Michael Vey Ser.: 5). (ENG., Illus.). 288p. (YA). (gr. 7). 18.99 *(978-1-4814-4410-1(7)*, Simon Pulse/Mercury Ink) Simon Pulse/Mercury Ink.

—Michael Vey Books One & Two: The Prisoner of Cell 25; Rise of the Elgen. 2014. (Michael Vey Ser.). (ENG., Illus.). 720p. (YA). (gr. 7). pap. 13.99 *(978-1-4814-2034-1(8)*, Simon Pulse/Mercury Ink) Simon Pulse/Mercury Ink.

—The Prisoner of Cell 25. (Michael Vey Ser.: 1). (ENG., Illus.). (YA). (gr. 7). 2012. 352p. pap. 11.99 *(978-1-4424-6812-2(2))* 2011. 336p. 19.99 *(978-1-4516-5650-3(5))* Simon Pulse/Mercury Ink. (Simon Pulse/Mercury Ink).

—Rise of the Elgen. (Michael Vey Ser.: 2). (ENG., Illus.). 352p. (YA). (gr. 7). 2013. pap. 11.99 *(978-1-4424-7510-6(2))* 2012. 17.99 *(978-1-4424-5414-9(8))* Simon Pulse/Mercury Ink. (Simon Pulse/Mercury Ink).

Hunt for Jade Dragon. 2014. (Michael Vey Ser.: No. 4). (ENG., Illus.). 336p. (YA). (gr. 7). 19.99 *(978-1-4814-2438-7(6)*, Simon Pulse/Mercury Ink) Simon Pulse/Mercury Ink.

Michael Vey, the Electric Collection: Michael Vey; Michael Vey 2; Michael Vey 3. 2014. (Michael Vey Ser.). (ENG., Illus.). 1024p. (YA). (gr. 7). pap. 35.99 *(978-1-4814-1411-1(9)*, Simon Pulse/Mercury Ink) Simon Pulse/Mercury Ink.

Nicodemus, Laura Konger. Growing up on the Farm in The 1930s' 2011. 60p. pap. 24.20 *(978-1-4269-3201-4(4))* Trafford Publishing.

Waring, Geoff. Oscar & the Bird: A Book about Electricity. Waring, Geoff, illus. 2011. (Start with Science Ser.). (ENG., Illus.). 32p. (J). (gr. -1-3). pap. 6.99 *(978-0-7636-5302-6(0))* Candlewick Pr.

Woods, Rebecca. Rising Winds of Silver Falls. 2012. (Silver Falls Ser.: Vol. 3). (ENG.). 191p. (J). pap. 15.99 *(978-1-59955-998-8(6)*, Sweetwater Bks.) Cedar Fort, Inc./CFI Distribution.

ELECTRICITY IN THE HOME

see Household Appliances, Electric

ELECTROCHEMISTRY

see also Electric Batteries

Hirsch, Rebecca E. Hydrogen & Fuel Cells. 1 vol. 2013. (Innovative Technologies Ser.). (ENG.). 112p. (J). (gr. 6-12). 35.64 *(978-1-61783-464-6(5))* ABDO Publishing Co.

ELECTROMAGNETISM

Cregan, Elizabeth R. C. Investigating Electromagnetism. 1 vol. 2007. (Science Readers Ser.). (ENG.). 32p. (J). (gr. 4-4). pap. 8.99 *(978-0-7439-0575-6(X))* Shell Educational Publishing.

—Thomas Edison & the Pioneers of Electromagnetism. 1 vol. 2007. (Science Readers Ser.). (ENG.). 32p. (J). (gr. 4-4). pap. 8.99 *(978-0-7439-0576-3(8))* Shell Educational Publishing.

Holt, Rinehart and Winston Staff. Holt Science & Technology Chapter 18: Physical Science: Electromagnetism. 5th ed. 2004. (Illus.). pap. 12.86 *(978-0-03-030421-7(0))* Holt McDougal.

Lachner, Elizabeth. Magnetic Forces. 2009. (Real Life Readers Ser.). 32p. (gr. 4-5). pap. 10.00 *(978-1-4358-0155-4(5)*, Rosen Classroom); 47.90 *(978-1-60853-037-3(X)*, PowerKids Pr.) Rosen Publishing Group, Inc., The.

Petersen, Kristen. Understanding Forces of Nature: Gravity, Electricity, & Magnetism. 2015. (Mastering Physics Ser.). (ENG.). 48p. (J). (gr. 7-7). 31.36 *(978-1-5026-0142-1(7))* Cavendish Square Publishing.

Randolph, Ryan P. Robotics. 2009. (Science Kaleidoscope Ser.). (J). lib. bdg. 25.25 *(978-1-4358-2986-2(7)*, PowerKids Pr.) Rosen Publishing Group, Inc., The.

Reader dsm-3 electromagnetism Ea. 2004. (J). *(978-1-59242-522-8(4))* Delta Education, LLC.

Sandner, Lionel. What Is Electromagnetism? 2012. (ENG.). 32p. (J). *(978-0-7787-2080-5(2))*; pap. *(978-0-7787-2085-0(3))* Crabtree Publishing Co.

Sonneborn, Liz. Forces in Nature: Understanding Gravitational, Electrical, & Magnetic Force. 2009. (Planet Earth Ser.). 48p. (gr. 5-8). pap. 8.25 *(978-1-4358-5160-3(9)*, Rosen Classroom) Rosen Publishing Group, Inc., The.

Tomecek, Stephen M. Electromagnetism, & How It Works. 2007. (Scientific American Ser.). (Illus.). 72p. (YA). (gr. 5-9). lib. bdg. 30.00 *(978-0-7910-9052-7(3))* Facts On File, Inc.

Winterberg, Jenna. Electromagnetism. 1 vol. 2015. (Science Readers: Content & Literacy Ser.). (ENG., Illus.). 32p. (gr. 3-3). pap. 8.99 *(978-1-4807-4645-9(2))* Teacher Created Materials, Inc.

Zannos, Susan. Michael Faraday & the Discovery of Electromagnetism. 2004. (Uncharted, Unexplored, & Unexplained Ser.). (Illus.). 48p. (J). (gr. 4-8). lib. bdg. 29.95 *(978-1-58415-307-8(5))* Mitchell Lane Pubs., Inc.

ELECTROMAGNETS

Bliss, Pamela. The Mystery of Magnets. 2007. (Nonfiction Reading & Writing Workshops Ser.). (ENG., Illus.). 32p. (J). pap. 17.95 *(978-0-7922-4581-0(4))* CENGAGE Learning.

ELECTRONIC CIRCUITS

Basic Introduction to PLCs: Student Kit. (Dvd Training Ser.). 138.00 net. *(978-0-8269-9208-6(0))* American Technical Pubs., Inc.

Dahl, Øyvind Nydal. Electronics for Kids: A Lighthearted Introduction. 2016. (ENG., Illus.). 328p. (J). (gr. 5). pap. 24.95 *(978-1-59327-725-3(3))* No Starch Pr., Inc.

Flaherty, Michael. Electricity & Batteries. 2009. (Science Factory Ser.). 32p. (gr. 4-5). 50.50 *(978-1-60853-020-5(5)*, PowerKids Pr.) Rosen Publishing Group, Inc., The.

Kopp, Megan. Maker Projects for Kids Who Love Electronics. 2016. (Be a Maker! Ser.). (ENG.). 32p. (J). (gr. 5-8). *(978-0-7787-2575-6(8))* Crabtree Publishing Co.

Martineau, Susan & Bushell, Nick. Cool Circuits. 2011. (Awesome Activities Ser.). (ENG., Illus.). 24p. (J). (gr. 3-6). pap. 10.60 *(978-1-61533-404-9(1))*; lib. bdg. 25.25 *(978-1-61533-366-0(5))* Windmill Bks.

Ng, Sandy. Makey Makey. 2016. (21st Century Skills Innovation Library: Makers As Innovators Ser.). (ENG.). 32p. (J). (gr. 4-8). lib. bdg. 29.93 *(978-1-63471-414-3(8)*, 208435) Cherry Lake Publishing.

ELECTRONIC COMPUTERS

see Computers

ELECTRONIC DATA PROCESSING

Bryan, Dale-Marie. Smartphone Safety & Privacy. 2013. (21st Century Safety & Privacy Ser.). 64p. (J). (gr. 5-8). pap. 12.95 *(978-1-4488-9586-1(3))*; pap. 77.70 *(978-1-4488-9587-8(1))* Rosen Publishing Group, Inc., The.

Burstein, John. Usar Computadoras: Una máquina con ratón. 2006. (Monstruos Matematicos Ser.). (ENG & SPA., Illus.). 24p. (J). (gr. k-4). lib. bdg. 21.00 *(978-0-8368-6679-7(7)*, Weekly Reader Leveled Readers) Stevens, Gareth Publishing LLLP.

—Using Computers: Machine with a Mouse. 2003. (Weekly Reader Early Learning Library). (Illus.). 24p. (J). (gr. k-4). pap. 8.15 *(978-0-8368-3832-9(7)*, Weekly Reader Leveled Readers) Stevens, Gareth Publishing LLLP.

Computing: From the Abacus to the Ipad. 2011. (Computing & Connecting in the 21st Century Ser.). (ENG.). 168p. (YA). (gr. 10-12). 70.50 *(978-1-61530-772-2(9))* Rosen Publishing Group, Inc., The.

Curley, Robert, ed. Computing: From the Abacus to the IPad. 2011. (Computing & Connecting in the 21st Century Ser.). (ENG.). 168p. (YA). (gr. 10-12). lib. bdg. 35.25 *(978-1-61530-660-2(9))* Rosen Publishing Group, Inc., The.

Freedman, Jeri. Intellectual Property. 2009. (Cyber Citizenship & Cyber Safety Ser.). 48p. (gr. 5-5). 53.00 *(978-1-61512-104-5(8)*, Rosen Reference) Rosen Publishing Group, Inc., The.

Gerber, Larry. Cloud-Based Computing. 2013. (Digital & Information Literacy Ser.). 48p. (J). (gr. 5-8). 29.25 *(978-1-4488-9516-8(2))* Rosen Publishing Group, Inc., The.

Grayson, Robert. Careers in Network Engineering. 2011. (Careers in Computer Technology Ser.). (ENG.). 80p. (YA). lib. bdg. 33.25 *(978-1-4488-1313-1(1))* Rosen Publishing Group, Inc., The.

McAlpine, Margaret. Working with Computers. 2004. (My Future Career Ser.). (Illus.). 64p. (gr. 3-7). lib. bdg. 27.00 *(978-0-8368-4242-5(1)*, Gareth Stevens Learning Library) Stevens, Gareth Publishing LLLP.

McGuire, Erin K. Careers in Database Design. 2011. (Careers in Computer Technology Ser.). (ENG.). 80p. (YA). lib. bdg. 33.25 *(978-1-4488-1317-9(4))* Rosen Publishing Group, Inc., The.

Miller, Deborah J. Careers with Internet Service Providers. 2009. (Library of E-Commerce & Internet Careers Ser.). 64p. (gr. 5-5). 58.50 *(978-1-60853-583-5(5))* Rosen Publishing Group, Inc., The.

Mozer, Mindy. Big Data & You. 2014. (Digital & Information Literacy Ser.). 48p. (YA). (gr. 5-8). 30.25 *(978-1-4777-7643-8(5))* Rosen Publishing Group, Inc., The.

Suen, Anastasia. Downloading & Online Shopping Safety & Privacy. 2013. (21st Century Safety & Privacy Ser.). (Illus.). 64p. (J). (gr. 5-8). 31.95 *(978-1-4488-9571-7(5))*; pap. 77.70 *(978-1-4488-9583-0(9))*; pap. 12.95 *(978-1-4488-9582-3(0))* Rosen Publishing Group, Inc., The.

Wilkinson, Colin. Twitter & Microblogging: Instant Communication with 140 Characters or Less. 2011. (Digital & Information Literacy Ser.). (ENG.). 48p. (YA). (gr. 5-8). pap. 11.75 *(978-1-4488-5617-6(5))*; lib. bdg. 29.25 *(978-1-4488-5555-1(1))* Rosen Publishing Group, Inc., The. (Rosen Reference).

Woog, Adam. Zuckerberg. 2009. (Innovators Ser.). (ENG., Illus.). 64p. (J). 29.95 *(978-0-7377-4566-5(5))* Cengage Gale.

ELECTRONIC DATA PROCESSING—KEYBOARDING

Johnson, Jack E., et al. Glencoe Keyboarding with Computer Applications. 2nd ed. 2003. (Johnson: Gregg Micro Keyboard Ser.). (ENG., Illus.). 291p. (gr. 9-12). stu. ed., spiral bd. 127.80 *(978-0-07-861075-2(3)*, 0078610753) McGraw-Hill Higher Education.

McGraw-Hill Staff. Glencoe Keyboarding Connections: Projects & Applications with Office 2000. 2nd ed. 2003. (ENG.). (gr. 6-12). stu. ed., spiral bd. 82.80 *(978-0-07-861074-5(5)*, 0078610745) McGraw-Hill Higher Education.

Napier, H. Albert, et al. Learning with Computers I. 2nd ed. 2011. (Middle School Solutions Ser.). (ENG & ABK., Illus.). 464p. (C). 70.95 *(978-0-538-45070-6(3))* Cengage South-Western.

—Learning with Computers II. 2nd ed. 2011. (Middle School Solutions Ser.). (ENG & ABK., Illus.). 512p. (C). pap. 87.95 *(978-0-538-45071-3(1))* Cengage South-Western.

ELECTRONIC SPREADSHEETS

Johnson, Rebecca L. Crunching Numbers. 2007. (Reading Expeditions Ser.). (ENG., Illus.). 24p. (J). pap. 14.95 *(978-0-7922-4592-6(X))* CENGAGE Learning.

Patchett, Fiona. An Introduction to Spreadsheets: Using Microsoft Excel 2000 or Microsoft Office 2000. 2004. (Computer Guides Ser.). (Illus.). (YA). (gr. 5-18). (ENG.). 1p. pap. 10.95 *(978-0-7460-4146-8(2))*; 64p. lib. bdg. 18.95 *(978-1-58086-323-0(X))* EDC Publishing.

Wolny, Philip. Constructing, Using, & Interpreting Spreadsheets. 2010. (Digital & Information Literacy Ser.). (ENG.). 48p. (YA). pap. 11.75 *(978-1-4488-0595-2(3))*; lib. bdg. 29.25 *(978-1-4358-9427-3(8))* Rosen Publishing Group, Inc., The. (Rosen Reference).

ELECTRONICS

see also Electronic Circuits; High-Fidelity Sound Systems; Transistors

Bateman, Graham, ed. Electricity & Electronics. 2011. (Facts at Your Fingertips: Introducing Physics Ser.). 64p. (YA). (gr. 7-12). lib. bdg. 35.65 *(978-1-936333-07-3(4))* Brown Bear Bks.

Bdeir, Ayah & Richardson, Matt. Getting Started with LittleBits: Learning & Inventing with Modular Electronics. 2015. (ENG., Illus.). 190p. (J). pap. 19.99 *(978-1-4571-8670-7(5))* Maker Media, Inc.

The Boy Mechanic, Bk. 1. 470p. (J). (gr. 5-18). reprint ed. pap. 18.95 *(978-0-917914-88-1(0))* Lindsay Pubns., Inc.

Christensen, Victoria G. How Conductors Work. 2016. (Connect with Electricity Ser.). (ENG., Illus.). 40p. (J). (gr. 4-6). 30.65 *(978-1-5124-0782-2(8))* Lerner Publishing Group.

—How Sensors Work. 2016. (Connect with Electricity Ser.). (ENG., Illus.). 40p. (J). (gr. 4-6). 30.65 *(978-1-5124-0779-2(8))* Lerner Publishing Group.

Cooper, Christopher. The Basics of Electronics. 2014. (Core Concepts Ser.). 96p. (YA). (gr. 7-12). 35.60 *(978-1-4777-7756-5(3))* Rosen Publishing Group, Inc., The.

Dahl, Øyvind Nydal. Electronics for Kids: A Lighthearted Introduction. 2016. (ENG., Illus.). 328p. (J). (gr. 5). pap. 24.95 *(978-1-59327-725-3(3))* No Starch Pr., Inc.

Electronics. 2011. (Introduction to Physics Ser.). (ENG.). 80p. (YA). (gr. 7-12). 63.40 *(978-1-61530-775-3(3))* Rosen Publishing Group, Inc., The.

Felix, Rebecca. Cool Battery & Electricity Projects: Fun & Creative Workshop Activities. 2016. (ENG., Illus.). 32p. (J). *(978-1-68078-125-0(1))* ABDO Publishing Co.

Frisch, Aaron. The Story of Sony. 2003. (Built for Success Ser.). (Illus.). 48p. (J). 28.50 *(978-1-58340-296-2(9))* Black Rabbit Bks.

Graham, Ian & Morris, Neil. Handheld Gadgets. 1 vol. 2011. (Sci-Hi: Science & Technology Ser.). (ENG., Illus.). 48p. (gr. 4-4). 33.32 *(978-1-4109-4276-0(7)*, Sci-Hi) Heinemann-Raintree.

Greathead, Helen. My Smartphone & Other Digital Accessories. 2016. (Illus.). 32p. (J). *(978-0-7787-2715-6(7))* Crabtree Publishing Co.

Harmon, Daniel E. 21st-Century Surveillance Technologies. 2017. (J). ***(978-1-5026-2674-5(8))*** Cavendish Square Publishing.

Hollar, Sherman, ed. Electronics. 2011. (Introduction to Physics Ser.). (ENG.). 80p. (YA). (gr. 7-12). lib. bdg. 31.70 *(978-1-61530-664-0(1))* Rosen Publishing Group, Inc., The.

Holt, Rinehart and Winston Staff. Holt Science & Technology Chapter 19: Physical Science: Electronic Technology. 5th ed. 2004. (Illus.). x, 262p. pap. 12.86 *(978-0-03-030426-2(1))* Holt McDougal.

Holzweiss, Kristina & Barth, Amy. I Can Make Exciting Electronics. 2017. (Rookie Star — MakerSpace Projects Ser.). (ENG.). 32p. (J). pap. 5.95 ***(978-0-531-23880-6(6))***; lib. bdg. 25.00 ***(978-0-531-23411-2(8))*** Scholastic Library Publishing. (Children's Pr.).

Jackson, Tom. Digital Technology. 2015. (Technology Timelines Ser.). (Illus.). 32p. (gr. 3-6). 31.35 *(978-1-78121-238-7(4))* Brown Bear Bks.

Jugendhandbuch Naturwissen: Bausteine des Lebens, 6 vols., Vol. 1. (GER.). 144p. (J). pap. 750.00 *(978-3-499-16203-9(2)*, M-7486) French & European Pubns., Inc.

Kopp, Megan. Maker Projects for Kids Who Love Electronics. 2016. (Be a Maker! Ser.). (ENG.). 32p. (J). (gr. 5-8). *(978-0-7787-2575-6(8))* Crabtree Publishing Co.

Lee, Ji Sun & Dec, Jaymes. Tech DIY: Easy Electronics Projects for Parents & Kids. 2016. (ENG., Illus.). 192p. pap. 19.99 *(978-1-68045-177-1(4))* Maker Media, Inc.

Lovett, Amber. LittleBits. 2016. (21st Century Skills Innovation Library: Makers As Innovators Ser.). (ENG., Illus.). 32p. (J). (gr. 4-8). lib. bdg. 29.93 *(978-1-63471-415-0(6)*, 208439) Cherry Lake Publishing.

Murphy, Maggie. High-Tech DIY Projects with Electronics, Sensors, & LEDs. 2014. (Maker Kids Ser.). 32p. (J). (gr. 3-6). pap. 70.50 *(978-1-4777-6659-0(6)*, PowerKids Pr.) Rosen Publishing Group, Inc., The.

Parker, Steve. Gadgets. 2010. (How It Works Ser.). 40p. (J). (gr. 3-18). lib. bdg. 19.95 *(978-1-4222-1795-5(7))* Mason Crest.

Polinsky, Paige V. & Craig, Diane. Super Simple Experiments with Electricity: Fun & Innovative Science Projects. 2016. (ENG., Illus.). 32p. *(978-1-68078-167-0(7))* ABDO Publishing Co.

Rauf, Don. Getting the Most Out of Makerspaces to Explore Arduino & Electronics. 2014. (Makerspaces Ser.). 64p. (J). (gr. 6-12). 32.95 *(978-1-4777-7815-9(2)*, Rosen Reference) Rosen Publishing Group, Inc., The.

La Revolucion Digital. 2003. (Essential Science Ser.). (SPA.). (J). pap. *(978-970-690-598-7(7))* Planeta Mexicana Editorial S. A. de C. V.

Roland, James. How Transistors Work. 2016. (Connect with Electricity Ser.). (ENG., Illus.). 40p. (J). (gr. 4-6). lib. bdg. 30.65 *(978-1-5124-0783-9(6))* Lerner Publishing Group.

Shamieh, Cathleen. Getting Started with Electronics. 2016. (Dummies Junior Ser.). (ENG.). 128p. pap. 9.99 ***(978-1-119-31380-9(5)***, For Dummies) Wiley, John & Sons, Inc.

Stillinger, Doug, ed. Battery Science: Make Widgets That Work & Gadgets That Go. 2003. (ENG., Illus.). 56p. (J). (gr. 3-7). 21.95 *(978-1-59174-251-7(X)*, 53643124) Klutz.

ELECTRONS

Bateman, Graham, ed. Electricity & Electronics. 2011. (Facts at Your Fingertips: Introducing Physics Ser.). 64p. (YA). (gr. 7-12). lib. bdg. 35.65 *(978-1-936333-07-3(4))* Brown Bear Bks.

Bortz, Alfred B. The Electron. 2004. (Library of Subatomic Particles Ser.). (Illus.). 64p. (gr. 7-12). lib. bdg. 29.25 *(978-0-8239-4528-3(6))* Rosen Publishing Group, Inc., The.

Bortz, Fred. The Electron. 2009. (Library of Subatomic Particles Ser.). 64p. (gr. 6-6). 58.50 *(978-1-60853-876-8(1))* Rosen Publishing Group, Inc., The.

Bortz, Fred & Fields, B. H. Understanding Electrons. 2015. (Exploring the Subatomic World Ser.). (ENG., Illus.). 64p. (J). (gr. 8-8). lib. bdg. 34.21 *(978-1-5026-0538-2(4))* Cavendish Square Publishing.

Ferrie, Chris. Quantum Physics for Babies. 2017. (Baby University Ser.: 0). (ENG., Illus.). 24p. (J). bds. 9.99 ***(978-1-4926-5622-7(4)***, Sourcebooks Jabberwocky) Sourcebooks, Inc.

ELECTROSTATICS

Clark, John O. E. The Basics of Electric Charges. 2014. (Core Concepts Ser.). 96p. (YA). (gr. 7-12). 35.60 *(978-1-4777-7768-8(7))* Rosen Publishing Group, Inc., The.

Mahaney, Ian F. Electricity. (Energy in Action Ser.). 24p. 2009. (gr. 3-3). 42.50 *(978-1-61512-257-8(5)*, PowerKids Pr.) 2007. (ENG.). (gr. 3-8). pap. 7.05 *(978-1-4042-2187-1(5)*, PowerKids Pr.) 2007. (Illus.). (YA). (gr. 4-7). lib. bdg. 22.60 *(978-1-4042-3478-9(0))* Rosen Publishing Group, Inc., The.

Seaver, C. H. American Boys' Book of Electricity. 2013. 400p. 179.00 *(978-1-62583-553-6(1))* Textbook Pubs.

ELEMENTARY EDUCATION

see Education, Elementary

ELEMENTS, CHEMICAL

see Chemical Elements

ELEPHANTS

Albee, Sarah. Elephants. (Amazing Animals Ser.). 48p. 2009. (gr. 2-6). pap. 10.50 *(978-1-4339-2013-4(1)*, Gareth Stevens Learning Library) 2008. (YA). (gr. 3-6). lib. bdg. 28.00 *(978-0-8368-9096-9(5))* Stevens, Gareth Publishing LLLP.

—Elephants. 2006. (All about Animals Ser.). (J). *(978-1-59939-063-5(9)*, Reader's Digest Young Families, Inc.) Studio Fun International.

Allen, Kathy. Elephants under Pressure: A Cause & Effect Investigation, 1 vol. 2010. (Animals on the Edge Ser.). (ENG.). 32p. (gr. 3-4). lib. bdg. 27.32 *(978-1-4296-4534-8(2)*, Fact Finders) Capstone Press of Coughlan Cos.

Anderson, W. M. Action Literacy: Elephants. 2008. (Action Literacy Upper Primary Ser.). 32p. pap. 9.95 *(978-0-86431-679-0(8))* ACER Pr. AUS. Dist: ISBS Publisher Services.

Antill, Sara. An Elephant's Life. 2012. (Illus.). 24p. (J). 49.50 *(978-1-4488-5107-2(6)*, PowerKids Pr.); pap. 8.25 *(978-1-4488-5106-5(8)*, PowerKids Pr.); lib. bdg. 22.60 *(978-1-4488-4979-6(9))* Rosen Publishing Group, Inc., The.

Arnold, Katya R. & Arnold, Katya. Elephants Can Paint Too! Arnold, Katya R. & Arnold, Katya, photos by. 2005. (ENG., Illus.). 40p. (J). (gr. -1-3). 18.99 *(978-0-689-86985-3(1)*, Atheneum Bks. for Young Readers) Simon & Schuster Children's Publishing.

Atlantic, Leonard. 80-Year-Old Elephants! 2016. (World's Longest-Living Animals Ser.). 00024p. (J). pap. 8.15 ***(978-1-4824-5609-7(5))*** Stevens, Gareth Publishing LLLP.

Badescu, Ramona. Pomelo's Opposites. Chaud, Benjamin, illus. 2013. (Pomelo the Garden Elephant Ser.). (ENG.). 120p. (J). 15.95 *(978-1-59270-132-2(9))* Enchanted Lion Bks., LLC.

Barnes, Julia. Elephants at Work. 2006. (Animals at Work Ser.). (Illus.). 32p. (J). (gr. 3-6). lib. bdg. 26.00 *(978-0-8368-6224-9(4)*, Gareth Stevens Learning Library) Stevens, Gareth Publishing LLLP.

—The Secret Lives of Elephants. 2007. (Secret Lives of Animals Ser.). (Illus.). 32p. (gr. 2-6). lib. bdg. 26.00 *(978-0-8368-7657-4(1)*, Gareth Stevens Learning Library) Stevens, Gareth Publishing LLLP.

Barr, Catherine & Clulow, Hanako. 10 Reasons to Love an Elephant. 2017. (10 Reasons to Love A... Ser.). (ENG.). 24p. (J). (gr. -1-1). 12.99 ***(978-1-84780-942-1(1)***, Frances Lincoln Children's Bks.) Quarto Publishing Group UK GBR. Dist: Hachette Bk. Group.

Bell, Samantha S. Meet a Baby Elephant. 2015. (ENG., Illus.). 32p. (J). (gr. k-2). 26.65 *(978-1-4677-7976-0(8))* Lerner Publishing Group.

Blewett, Ashlee Brown. National Geographic Kids Mission: Elephant Rescue: All about Elephants & How to Save Them. 2014. (NG Kids Mission: Animal Rescue Ser.). (ENG., Illus.). 128p. (J). (gr. 5). 21.90 *(978-1-4263-1730-9(1)*, National Geographic Children's Bks.) National Geographic Society.

Blewett, Ashlee Brown & National Geographic Kids Staff. Elephant Rescue: All about Elephants & How to Save Them. 2014. (NG Kids Mission: Animal Rescue Ser.). (ENG., Illus.). 128p. (J). (gr. 5). pap. 12.99 *(978-1-4263-1729-3(8)*, National Geographic Children's Bks.) National Geographic Society.

Bloom, Steve & Wilson, David Henry. Elephants. 2015. (ENG., Illus.). 64p. (J). (gr. -1-k). pap. 14.95 *(978-0-500-65055-4(1)*, 565055) Thames & Hudson.

Books Are Fun 8 Title Animal Lives Set: Elephants. 2006. (J). *(978-1-59566-309-2(6))* QEB Publishing Inc.

Brennan, Francis. Elephants. 2012. (ENG., Illus.). 48p. (J). lib. bdg. 28.00 *(978-0-531-26833-9(0))*; (gr. 3-5). pap. 6.95 *(978-0-531-25478-3(X))* Scholastic Library Publishing.

Buckley, Carol. Tarra & Bella: The Elephant & Dog Who Became Best Friends. Buckley, Carol, photos by. 2009. (ENG., Illus.). 32p. (J). (gr. -1-k). 16.99 *(978-0-399-25443-7(9)*, G.P. Putnam's Sons Books for Young Readers) Penguin Young Readers Group.

—Travels with Tarra, 1 vol. 2005. (ENG., Illus.). 40p. (J). (gr. 3-7). 16.95 *(978-0-88448-241-3(3))* Tilbury Hse. Pubs.

Buzzeo, Toni. A Passion for Elephants: The Real Life Adventure of Field Scientist Cynthia Moss. Berry, Holly, illus. 2015. (ENG.). 32p. (J). (gr. k-3). E-Book *(978-0-399-18600-4(X)*, Dial Bks) Penguin Young Readers Group.

Canetti, Yanitzia. 1-2-3, Do, Re, Mi Elephants. 2010. (J). *(978-1-59835-151-4(6))* Cambridge BrickHouse, Inc.

Carr, Aaron. Soy el Elefante. 2012. (SPA.). (J). *(978-1-61913-174-3(9))* Weigl Pubs., Inc.

Clarke, Ginjer L. Baby Elephant. Cuddy, Robin & Wummer, Amy, illus. 2009. (Penguin Young Readers, Level 3 Ser.). (ENG.). 48p. (J). (gr. 1-3). mass mkt. 3.99 *(978-0-448-44825-1(4)*, Penguin Young Readers) Penguin Young Readers Group.

Claybourne, Anna. Elephant. 2012. (Animals on the Edge Ser.). (ENG., Illus.). 48p. (gr. 3-8). pap. 12.00 *(978-1-4081-4958-4(3)*, 9781408149584, Bloomsbury USA Childrens) Bloomsbury Publishing USA.

Costain, Meredith. Elephant. Hanna, Gary, illus. 2016. (Wild World Ser.). 00032p. (J). (gr. 1-2). pap. 10.00 *(978-1-4994-8206-5(X)*, Windmill Bks.) Rosen Publishing Group, Inc., The.

Cowcher, Helen. Desert Elephants, 1 vol. Cowcher, Helen, illus. 2011. (ENG., Illus.). 40p. (J). (gr. k-3). 16.99 *(978-0-374-31774-4(7)*, 9780374317744, Farrar, Straus & Giroux (BYR)) Farrar, Straus & Giroux.

Cox, Lynne. Elizabeth, Queen of the Seas. Floca, Brian, illus. 2014. (ENG.). 48p. (J). (gr. -1-3). 17.99 *(978-0-375-85888-8(1))*; 20.99 *(978-0-375-95888-5(6))* Random Hse. Children's Bks. (Schwartz & Wade Bks.).

Crossingham, John & Kalman, Bobbie. Les Éléphants. 2004. (Petit Monde Vivant Ser.). (FRE., Illus.). 32p. (J). pap. 9.95 *(978-2-89579-015-0(9))* Bayard Canada Livres CAN. Dist: Crabtree Publishing Co.

Cussen, Sarah. Those Enormous Elephants. Weaver, Steve, illus. 2012. (Those Amazing Animals Ser.). (ENG.). 56p. (J). 14.95 *(978-1-56164-515-2(X))*; pap. 9.95 *(978-1-56164-516-9(8))* Pineapple Pr., Inc.

Daley, Sofia. Elephant: From Trunk to Tail. 2009. (Real Life Readers Ser.). 12p. (gr. 1-3). pap. 5.90 *(978-1-4042-7952-0(0)*, Rosen Classroom) Rosen Publishing Group, Inc., The.

Davies, Katie. Elephants: Internet-Referenced. 2009. (First Reading Level 4 Ser.). 48p. (J). 6.99 *(978-0-7945-2291-9(2)*, Usborne) EDC Publishing.

De la Bédoyère, Camilla. Elephants. 2010. (Remarkable Man & Beast Ser.). (Illus.). 48p. (J). (gr. 3-18). lib. bdg. 19.95 *(978-1-4222-1968-3(2))* Mason Crest.

Deluxe...Spirit of the Elephant. 2008. 256p. *(978-1-4075-3951-5(5))* Parragon, Inc.

Dineen, Jacqueline. Elephants. (Amazing Animals Ser.). (Illus.). 24p. (J). 2009. (gr. 2-4). pap. 8.95 *(978-1-60596-155-2(8))* 2009. (gr. 2-4). lib. bdg. 24.45 *(978-1-60596-154-5(X))* 2003. lib. bdg. 21.35 *(978-1-58340-227-6(6))* Weigl Pubs., Inc.

Dorling Kindersley Publishing Staff & Murphy, Patricia J. Hope for the Elephants. 2014. (DK Readers Ser.). (ENG.). 64p. (J). (gr. 2-4). pap. 3.99 *(978-1-4654-2842-4(9)*, DK Children) Dorling Kindersley Publishing, Inc.

Doudna, Kelly. It's a Baby African Elephant!, 1 vol. 2009. (Baby African Animals Ser.). (ENG., Illus.). 24p. (J). (gr. k-3). lib. bdg. 24.21 *(978-1-60453-149-7(5)*, SandCastle) ABDO Publishing Co.

Downer, Ann. Elephant Talk: The Surprising Science of Elephant Communication. 2015. (ENG., Illus.). 112p. (gr. 6-12). 34.65 *(978-1-4677-5988-5(0)*, Lerner Digital) Lerner Publishing Group.

Downer, Anna. Elephant Talk: The Surprising Science of Elephant Communication. 2011. (Single Titles Ser.). (ENG.). 112p. (gr. 6-12). 33.26 *(978-0-7613-5766-7(1))* Lerner Publishing Group.

Elephants. (Early Intervention Levels Ser.). 21.30 *(978-0-7362-0379-1(6))* CENGAGE Learning.

Elephants. 2003. (J). per. *(978-1-57657-943-5(3))* Paradise Pr., Inc.

Elephants. 2006. (Zootles Ser.). (J). 4.95 *(978-1-932396-21-8(7))* Wildlife Education, Ltd.

Elephant's Trunk. Date not set. (Touch & Feel Ser.). (Illus.). (J). 4.98 *(978-0-7525-9568-9(7))* Parragon, Inc.

Ellis, Gerry & Novesky, Amy. Natumi Takes the Lead: The True Story of an Orphan Elephant Who Finds Family. 2016. (ENG., Illus.). 32p. (J). (gr. -1-3). 16.99 *(978-1-4263-2561-8(4))*; lib. bdg. 26.90 *(978-1-4263-2562-5(2))* National Geographic Society. (National Geographic Children's Bks.).

En Donde Marchan los Elefantes? (Pebble Soup Exploraciones Ser.). (SPA.). 16p. (gr. -1-18). 31.00 *(978-0-7578-1679-6(7))* Rigby Education.

En donde marchan los Elefantes? Small Book. (Pebble Soup Exploraciones Ser.). (SPA.). 16p. (gr. -1-18). 5.00 *(978-0-7578-1719-9(X))* Rigby Education.

Enormous Elephants. 2013. (Great Big Animals Ser.). 24p. (J). (gr. k-2). pap. 48.90 *(978-1-4339-9426-5(7))* Stevens, Gareth Publishing LLLP.

Eszterhas, Suzi, photos by. Elephant. 2014. (Eye on the Wild Ser.). (ENG., Illus.). 32p. (J). (gr. -1-2). 15.99 *(978-1-84780-518-8(3)*, Frances Lincoln) Quarto Publishing Group UK GBR. Dist: Hachette Bk. Group.

Feldman, Thea. Tembo Takes Charge. 2006. (Illus.). (J). *(978-0-696-23289-3(8))* Meredith Bks.

Firestone, Mary. Top 50 Reasons to Care about Elephants: Animals in Peril. 2010. (Top 50 Reasons to Care about Endangered Animals Ser.). (Illus.). 104p. (J). (gr. 5-9). 33.27 *(978-0-7660-3454-9(2))* Enslow Pubs., Inc.

Fog City Press Staff, contrib. by. Elephants. 2010. (Illus.). (J). *(978-1-74089-954-3(7))* Fog City Pr.

Franks, Katie. Elephants. 2014. (Zoo's Who's Who Ser.). 24p. (J). (gr. k-2). pap. 8.25 *(978-1-4777-6568-5(9)*, PowerKids Pr.) Rosen Publishing Group, Inc., The.

Furstinger, Nancy. African Elephants. 2015. (Endangered Animals Ser.). (ENG.). 24p. (J). (gr. 1-4). 27.07 *(978-1-63143-963-6(4)*, 208798) Child's World, Inc., The.

Gagne, Tammy. Elephants, 1 vol. 2014. (Smartest Animals Ser.). (ENG.). 48p. (gr. 3-6). 32.79 *(978-1-62403-167-0(6))* ABDO Publishing Co.

Galvin, Laura. Elephant & Mommy. Cohen, Jesse, photos by. 2003. (Let's Go to the Zoo Ser.). (ENG., Illus.). 16p. (J). (gr. -1-k). 5.95 *(978-1-56899-911-1(9)*, B9007) Soundprints.

Gareth Stevens Editorial Staff. Elephants. 2004. (All about Wild Animals Ser.). (Illus.). 32p. (gr. k-4). lib. bdg. 26.00 *(978-0-8368-4183-1(2)*, Gareth Stevens Learning Library) Stevens, Gareth Publishing LLLP.

Gibbons, Gail. Elephants of Africa. Gibbons, Gail, illus. (ENG., Illus.). 32p. (J). (gr. -1-3). 2010. pap. 7.99 *(978-0-8234-2299-9(2))* 2008. 16.95 *(978-0-8234-2168-8(6))* Holiday Hse., Inc.

Gilbert, Sara. Ice Age Mega Beasts: Mammoths. 2017. (Ice Age Mega Beasts Ser.). (ENG., Illus.). 24p. (J). (gr. 1-3). pap. 8.99 ***(978-1-62832-375-7(2)***, Creative Paperbacks) Creative Co., The.

Gilbert, Sara. Mammoths. 2017. (Illus.). 24p. (J). *(978-1-60818-767-6(5)*, Creative Education) Creative Co., The.

Gish, Melissa. Elephants. 2009. (Living Wild Ser.). 48p. 22.95 *(978-1-58341-739-3(7)*, Creative Education) Creative Co., The.

Glaser, Rebecca Stromstad. Elephants Spray. 2016. (ENG., Illus.). 16p. (J). (gr. -1 — 1). bds. 7.99 *(978-1-68152-068-1(0))* Amicus.

Green, Jen. Elephants. 2009. (Illus.). 52p. (J). *(978-0-7172-6292-2(8))* Grolier, Ltd.

Gregory, Josh. Elephants. 2012. (21st Century Basic Skills Library: Baby Zoo Animals Ser.). (ENG.). 24p. (gr. k-3). 22.79 *(978-1-61080-452-3(X)*, 202062); pap. 12.79 *(978-1-61080-626-8(3)*, 202236) Cherry Lake Publishing.

Guillain, Charlotte. Amazing Elephants, 1 vol. 2013. (Walk on the Wild Side Ser.). (ENG.). 32p. (gr. 1-3). 29.99 *(978-1-4109-5216-5(9))*; pap. 8.95 *(978-1-4109-5223-3(1))* Heinemann-Raintree. (Read Me!).

—Elephants, 1 vol. 2013. (Animal Abilities Ser.). (ENG., Illus.). 32p. (gr. 2-4). 29.99 *(978-1-4109-5238-7(X))*; pap. 8.95 *(978-1-4109-5245-5(2))* Heinemann-Raintree. (Raintree Perspectives).

Hall, Kirsten. African Elephant: The World's Biggest Land Mammal. 2007. (SuperSized! Ser.). (Illus.). 24p. (J). (gr. k-3). lib. bdg. 21.28 *(978-1-59716-387-3(2)*, 1265929) Bearport Publishing Co., Inc.

Hall, Margaret. Elephants & Their Calves. 2016. (Animal Offspring Ser.). (ENG.). 24p. (gr. k-1). pap. 7.29 *(978-1-5157-4236-4(9)*, Pebble Plus) Capstone Press of Coughlan Cos.

Hanson, Anders. Elephant, 1 vol. 2014. (Giant Animals Ser.). (ENG., Illus.). 24p. (J). (gr. -1-3). lib. bdg. 24.21 *(978-1-62403-057-4(2)*, SandCastle) ABDO Publishing Co.

Harris, Tim, ed. Elephants. 2012. (Animal Families Ser.). (ENG., Illus.). 32p. (gr. 2-5). 31.35 *(978-1-78121-003-1(9)*, Brown Bear Bks.) Windmill Bks. Ltd. GBR. Dist: Black Rabbit Bks.

Haugen, Brenda. African Elephants, 1 vol. 2012. (Endangered & Threatened Animals Ser.). (ENG., Illus.). 32p. (gr. 3-4). lib. bdg. 27.99 *(978-1-4296-8664-8(2)*, Snap Bks.) Capstone Press of Coughlan Cos.

Hibbert, Clare. Elephant Orphans, 1 vol. 2015. (ENG.). 32p. (J). pap. 10.00 *(978-1-4777-5896-0(8)*, PowerKids Pr.) Rosen Publishing Group, Inc., The.

Hirsch, Rebecca E. African Elephants: Massive Tusked Mammals. 2015. (Comparing Animal Traits Ser.). (ENG.). 32p. (J). (gr. 3-3). E-Book 39.99 *(978-1-4677-6215-1(6)*, 9781467762151); (Illus.). (gr. 2-4). lib. bdg. 26.65 *(978-1-4677-5576-4(1))* Lerner Publishing Group. (Lerner Pubns.).

Hurt, Avery. Elephants. 2016. (Readers Ser.). (ENG., Illus.). 48p. (J). (-k). pap. 4.99 *(978-1-4263-2618-9(1)*, National Geographic Children's Bks.) National Geographic Society.

I Like Elephants: Individual Title, 6 Packs. (Sails Literacy Ser.). 16p. (gr. k-18). 27.00 *(978-0-7635-4403-4(5))* Rigby Education.

Johnson, Jinny. Elephant. Rosewarne, Graham, illus. 2005. (Zoo Animals in the Wild Ser.). 32p. (J). (gr. 2-5). lib. bdg. 27.10 *(978-1-58340-643-4(3))* Black Rabbit Bks.

Jonas, Anne. Little Elephants. 2005. (Born to Be Wild Ser.). (Illus.). 24p. (gr. k-3). lib. bdg. 23.00 *(978-0-8368-4434-4(3)*, Gareth Stevens Learning Library) Stevens, Gareth Publishing LLLP.

Kalman, Bobbie. Baby Elephants. 2010. (ENG.). 24p. (J). *(978-0-7787-3959-3(7))*; pap. *(978-0-7787-3978-4(3))* Crabtree Publishing Co.

—Endangered Elephants. 2005. (Earth's Endangered Animals Ser.). (ENG., Illus.). 32p. (J). (gr. 1-5). pap. *(978-0-7787-1906-9(5))* Crabtree Publishing Co.

Keller, Susanna. Meet the Elephant. 2010. (At the Zoo Ser.). 24p. (J). (ENG.). pap. 8.25 *(978-1-4358-9736-6(9))*; (Illus.). (gr. -1-1). lib. bdg. 22.60 *(978-1-4358-9312-2(3))* Rosen Publishing Group, Inc., The. (PowerKids Pr.).

Kimiko. EL ELEFANTE. (SPA.). 24p. *(978-84-95150-55-4(7))* Corimbo, Editorial S.L.

King, Corinne & Fenton, Corinne. Queenie: One Elephant's Story. Gouldthorpe, Peter, illus. 2013. (ENG.). 24p. (J). (gr. k-3). 16.99 *(978-0-7636-6375-9(1))* Candlewick Pr.

Kleinhenz, Sydnie M. Elephants. 2010. (African Animals Ser.). (ENG.). 24p. (gr. k-1). pap. 41.70 *(978-1-4296-5079-3(6)*, Pebble Plus) Capstone Press of Coughlan Cos.

—Elephants [Scholastic]. 2010. (African Animals Ser.). 24p. pap. 0.49 *(978-1-4296-5783-9(9)*, Pebble Plus) Capstone Press of Coughlan Cos.

Knudsen, Shannon. African Elephants. 2006. (Pull Ahead Bks.). (Illus.). 32p. (J). (gr. 3-7). lib. bdg. 22.60 *(978-0-8225-3483-9(5)*, Lerner Pubns.) Lerner Publishing Group.

Laidlaw, Rob. Elephant Journey: The True Story of Three Zoo Elephants & Their Rescue from Captivity. Deines, Brian, illus. 2016. (ENG.). 40p. (J). (gr. 1-4). 19.95 *(978-1-927485-77-4(0))* Pajama Pr. CAN. Dist: Ingram Publisher Services.

Latta, Jan. Elisa la Elefanta. 2007. (Familias de animales salvajes (Wild Animal Families) Ser.). (SPA., Illus.). 24p. (gr. 1-4). lib. bdg. 24.00 *(978-0-8368-7966-7(X)*, Gareth Stevens Learning Library) Stevens, Gareth Publishing LLLP.

—Ella the Elephant. 2007. (Wild Animal Families Ser.). (Illus.). 24p. (gr. 1-4). pap. 8.15 *(978-0-8368-7775-5(6))*; lib. bdg. 24.00 *(978-0-8368-7768-7(3))* Stevens, Gareth Publishing LLLP. (Gareth Stevens Learning Library).

Leaf, Christina. Baby Elephants. 2015. (Super Cute! Ser.). (ENG., Illus.). 24p. (J). (gr. k-3). lib. bdg. 25.95 *(978-1-62617-169-5(6))* Bellwether Media.

Leaman, Louisa & The Born Free Foundation. Elephant Rescue: A True-Life Story. 2017. (Born Free... Bks.). (ENG.). 96p. (J). (gr. 2-6). pap. 6.99 *(978-1-4380-0987-2(9))* Barron's Educational Series, Inc.

Lewin, Betsy & Lewin, Ted. Elephant Quest, 1 vol. 2014. (ENG., Illus.). 48p. (J). pap. 11.95 *(978-1-62014-183-0(3))* Lee & Low Bks., Inc.

Lewin, Ted & Lewin, Betsy. Balarama: A Royal Elephant, 1 vol. 2014. (Adventures Around the World Ser.). (ENG.). 48p. (J). pap. 11.95 *(978-1-62014-186-1(8))* Lee & Low Bks., Inc.

—Balarama: A Royal Elephant. Lewin, Ted & Lewin, Betsy, illus. 2009. (Adventures Around the World Ser.). (ENG., Illus.). 56p. (J). (gr. 1-6). 19.95 *(978-1-60060-265-8(7))* Lee & Low Bks., Inc.

Lindeen, Mary. Elephants. 2013. (ENG., Illus.). 24p. (J). lib. bdg. 25.65 *(978-1-62031-062-5(7))* Jump! Inc.

Louie the Miracle Elephant. 2006. (J). 9.37 *(978-0-9776974-0-3(1))* Toledo Zoo, The.

Macheske, Felicia. Nifty Noses: Elephant. 2017. (Guess What Ser.). (ENG., Illus.). 24p. (J). (gr. k-2). lib. bdg. 28.50 *(978-1-63472-176-9(4)*, 209276) Cherry Lake Publishing.

Maclaine, James. Elephants IR. 2011. (Beginner's Nature Ser.). 32p. (J). ring bd. 4.99 *(978-0-7945-3122-5(9)*, Usborne) EDC Publishing.

Macleod, Steve. Elephants. 2011. (J). 27.13 *(978-1-61690-753-2(3))*; pap. 12.95 *(978-1-61690-760-0(6))* Weigl Pubs., Inc.

Marsh, Laura. Great Migrations - Elephants. 2010. (Readers Ser.). (ENG., Illus.). 48p. (J). (gr. 2-4). 13.90 *(978-1-4263-0744-7(6))*; pap. 3.99 *(978-1-4263-0743-0(8))* National Geographic Society. (National Geographic Children's Bks.).

Marsico, Katie. Elephants. 2017. (True Book(tm) — The Most Endangered Ser.). (ENG., Illus.). 48p. (J). lib. bdg. 31.00 *(978-0-531-22727-5(8)*, Children's Pr.) Scholastic Library Publishing.

—Elephants Have Trunks. 2014. (Tell Me Why Library). (ENG.). 24p. (J). (gr. 2-5). 25.64 *(978-1-63188-002-5(0)*, 205415) Cherry Lake Publishing.

May, Paul. Elephants. 2009. (Wild Reads Ser.). (ENG., Illus.). 32p. (YA). (gr. k). pap. 4.95 *(978-0-19-911928-8(7))* Oxford Univ. Pr., Inc.

Meister, Cari. Do You Really Want to Meet an Elephant? Fabbri, Daniele, illus. 2015. (Do You Really Want to Meet ... ? Ser.). (ENG.). 24p. (J). (gr. 1-3). 19.95 *(978-1-60753-733-5(8))* Amicus Publishing.

Moldovo, Eustacia. Baby Elephants at the Zoo. 2015. (J). *(978-0-7660-6613-7(4))*; (ENG., Illus.). 24p. (gr. -1-1). pap. 9.35 *(978-0-7660-7089-9(1))* Enslow Pubs., Inc.

Moller, Jonathan R. Bath Time: Picture Book. l.t. ed. 2003. (Illus.). 71p. pap. 19.95 *(978-0-9740169-0-0(X))* Lemonflavor Productions.

Moore Niver, Heather. When Elephants Cry. 2017. (Animal Emotions Ser.). 32p. (J). (gr. 3-3). pap. 10.52 ***(978-0-7660-8860-3(X))*** Enslow Pubs., Inc.

Morgan, Jody. Elephant Rescue: Changing the Future for Endangered Wildlife. 2004. (Firefly Animal Rescue Ser.). (ENG., Illus.). 64p. (J). (gr. 5-8). 19.95 *(978-1-55297-595-4(9)*, 9781552975954); pap. 9.95 *(978-1-55297-594-7(0)*, 9781552975947) Firefly Bks., Ltd.

Morgan, Sally. Elephants. 2004. (QEB Animal Lives Ser.). (Illus.). 32p. (J). lib. bdg. 18.95 *(978-1-59566-032-9(1))* QEB Publishing Inc.

—Elephants. 2015. (ENG.). 24p. (J). (gr. 3-5). 23.99 *(978-1-939581-85-3(0))* QEB Publishing Inc.

Moses: The True Story of an Elephant Baby. 2014. (ENG., Illus.). 48p. (J). (gr. -1-3). 17.99 *(978-1-4424-9603-3(7)*, Atheneum Bks. for Young Readers) Simon & Schuster Children's Publishing.

Murray, Julie. Elephants, 1 vol. (ENG.). 2012. 32p. 28.50 *(978-1-61783-218-5(9)*, Big Buddy Bks.) 2005. (Illus.). 24p. 25.65 *(978-1-59197-314-0(7)*, Buddy Bks.) ABDO Publishing Co.

Nagelhout, Ryan. Enormous Elephants. 2013. (Great Big Animals Ser.). 24p. (J). (gr. k-2). pap. 8.15 *(978-1-4339-9425-8(9))*; (ENG., Illus.). lib. bdg. 22.60 *(978-1-4339-9424-1(0))* Stevens, Gareth Publishing LLLP.

Nagelhout, Ryan, ed. Enormous Elephants / Elefantes Enormes. 2013. (Great Big Animals / Superanimales Ser.). (SPA.). 24p. (J). (gr. k-2). 22.60 *(978-1-4339-9446-3(1))* Stevens, Gareth Publishing LLLP.

Niver, Heather Moore. When Elephants Cry. 2017. (Animal Emotions Ser.). 32p. (J). (gr. 3-3). lib. bdg. 25.27 ***(978-0-7660-8617-3(8))*** Enslow Pubs., Inc.

O'Connell, Caitlin. A Baby Elephant in the Wild. O'Connell, Caitlin & Rodwell, Timothy, illus. 2014. (ENG.). 40p. (J). (gr. -1-3). 17.99 *(978-0-544-14944-1(0)*, HMH Books For Young Readers) Houghton Mifflin Harcourt Publishing Co.

O'Connell, Caitlin & Jackson, Donna M. The Elephant Scientist. Rodwell, Timothy, illus. 2016. (Scientists in the Field Ser.). (ENG.). 80p. (J). (gr. 5-7). 9.99 *(978-0-544-66830-0(8)*, HMH Books For Young Readers) Houghton Mifflin Harcourt Publishing Co.

—The Elephant Scientist. Rodwell, Timothy, illus. O'Connell, Caitlin & Rodwell, Timothy, photos by. 2011. (Scientists in the Field Ser.). (ENG.). 80p. (J). (gr. 5-7). 18.99 *(978-0-547-05344-8(4))* Houghton Mifflin Harcourt Publishing Co.

Orme, Helen. Elephants in Danger. 2006. (Wildlife Survival Ser.). (Illus.). 32p. (YA). (gr. 2-5). lib. bdg. 25.27 *(978-1-59716-260-9(4))* Bearport Publishing Co., Inc.

Owen, Ruth. Elephants. 2011. (World's Smartest Animals Ser.). (ENG., Illus.). 32p. (J). (gr. k-5). pap. 11.75 *(978-1-61533-415-5(7))*; lib. bdg. 26.50 *(978-1-61533-377-6(0))* Windmill Bks.

Owens, Henry. How to Track an Elephant, 1. 2014. (Scatalog: a Kid's Field Guide to Animal Poop Ser.). (ENG.). 24p. (J). (gr. k-5). 23.60 *(978-1-61533-887-0(X)*, Windmill Bks.) Rosen Publishing Group, Inc., The.

Pelusey, Michael & Pelusey, Jane. Elephants. 2008. (Zoo Animals Ser.). 32p. (gr. 2-3). lib. bdg. 18.56 *(978-0-7614-3148-0(9),* Benchmark Bks.) Marshall Cavendish Corp.
Perkins, Wendy. Elephant. Longhi, Katya, illus. 2015. (J). pap. *(978-1-68152-074-2(5))* Amicus Publishing.
Read, Tracy. Exploring the World of Elephants. 2017. (Exploring the World Of Ser.). (ENG., Illus.). 24p. (J). (gr. 3-7). 16.95 ***(978-1-77085-944-9(6),*** 9781770859449); pap. 6.95 ***(978-1-77085-945-6(4),*** 9781770859456) Firefly Bks., Ltd.
Rigby Education Staff. Where Do Elephants Stomp? (Pebble Soup Explorations Ser.). (Illus.). 16p. (gr. -1-18). 31.00 *(978-0-7635-6462-9(1),* 764621C99) Rigby Education.
Riggs, Kate. Amazing Animals - Elephants. 2011. (Amazing Animals Ser.). (J). (gr. 2-5). 24.25 *(978-1-58341-990-8(X))* Creative Co., The.
—Elephants. (Seedlings Ser.). 24p. (J). 2012. (Illus.). (gr. -1-3). 15.95 *(978-1-60818-275-6(4),* Creative Education) 2011. (ENG.). (gr. 1-3). pap. 8.99 *(978-0-89812-563-4(4),* Creative Paperbacks) Creative Co., The.
—Elephants. 2010. (Amazing Animals Ser.). (ENG., Illus.). 24p. (J). 8.95 *(978-1-926853-70-3(9))* Saunders Bk. Co. CAN. Dist: J.Appleseed.
—Seedlings: Elephants. 2013. (Seedlings Ser.). (ENG.). 24p. (J). (gr. -1-k). pap. 7.99 *(978-0-89812-782-9(3),* Creative Paperbacks) Creative Co., The.
Ring, Susan. Project Elephant. Kissock, Heather & Marshall, Diana, eds. 2003. (Zoo Life Ser.). 24p. (J). pap. 8.95 *(978-1-59036-056-9(7))* Weigl Pubs., Inc.
Roy, Katherine. How to Be an Elephant: Growing up in the African Wild. 2017. (ENG., Illus.). 48p. (J). 18.99 ***(978-1-62672-178-4(5),*** 9781626721784, Macaulay, David Studio) Roaring Brook Pr.
Rustad, Martha E. H. Elephants Are Awesome! 2015. (Awesome African Animals! Ser.). (ENG.). 32p. (gr. 1-2). lib. bdg. 27.32 *(978-1-4914-1760-7(9))* Capstone Press of Coughlan Cos.
Sally & the Elephant: Level B, 6 vols. (Wonder Worldtm Ser.). 16p. 24.95 *(978-0-7802-1047-9(6))* Wright Group/McGraw-Hill.
Scheele, William E. Ancient Elephants. 2011. 66p. 36.95 *(978-1-258-01254-0(5))* Literary Licensing, LLC.
Scheunemann, Pam. Elephants Trumpet!, 1 vol. 2011. (Animal Sounds Set 2 Ser.). (ENG., Illus.). 24p. (J). (gr. k-3). lib. bdg. 24.21 *(978-1-61613-571-3(9),* SandCastle) ABDO Publishing Co.
Schuetz, Kari. African Elephants. 2011. (Animal Safari Ser.). (ENG., Illus.). 24p. (J). (gr. k-3). lib. bdg. 25.95 *(978-1-60014-600-8(7),* Blastoff! Readers) Bellwether Media.
Schwabacher, Martin & Mortensen, Lori. Elephants. 2009. (Benchmark Rockets Ser.). 24p. (gr. 1-18). 24.21 *(978-0-7614-4343-8(6))* Marshall Cavendish Corp.
Scott, Jonathan & Scott, Angela. Africa's Big Three. Scott, Jonathan & Scott, Angela, illus. 2006. (Collins Big Cat Ser.). (ENG., Illus.). 56p. (J). (gr. 2-2). pap. 6.99 *(978-0-00-718693-8(2))* HarperCollins Pubs. Ltd. GBR. Dist: Independent Pubs. Group.
Searl, Duncan. Elephants. 2006. (Smart Animals! Ser.). (Illus.). 32p. (J). (gr. 2-5). lib. bdg. 25.27 *(978-1-59716-162-6(4))* Bearport Publishing Co., Inc.
Sexton, Colleen. The African Elephant. 2011. (Nature's Deadliest Ser.). (ENG., Illus.). 24p. (YA). (gr. 3-8). lib. bdg. 25.95 *(978-1-60014-662-6(7),* Pilot Bks.) Bellwether Media.
Shea, Mary Molly. Intimidating Elephants. 2016. (Cutest Animals... That Could Kill You! Ser.). 24p. (J). (gr. 3-2). lib. bdg. 22.60 *(978-1-4824-4912-9(9))* Stevens, Gareth Publishing LLLP.
Shively, Julie. Baby Elephant. Johnson, Meredith, illus. 2005. (San Diego Zoo Animal Library: Vol. 11). (ENG.). 24p. (J). bds. 6.95 *(978-0-8249-6577-8(9),* Ideal Pubns.) Worthy Publishing.
Smith, Lucy Sackett. Elephants: From Trunk to Tail. 2009. (Mighty Mammals Ser.). 24p. (J). (ENG.). pap. 8.25 *(978-1-4358-3261-9(2),* PowerKids Pr.); (Illus.). lib. bdg. 22.60 *(978-1-4042-8102-8(9))* Rosen Publishing Group, Inc., The.
Sobol, Richard, photos by. An Elephant in the Backyard. 2004. (Illus.). (J). *(978-0-525-46970-4(2),* Dutton Juvenile) Penguin Publishing Group.
Soundprints Staff. Elephant & Mommy. 2011. (Let's Go to the Zoo! Ser.). (ENG., Illus.). 16p. (gr. -1). 5.95 *(978-1-60727-452-0(3))* Soundprints.
Stanek, Linda. Beco's Big Year: A Baby Elephant Turns One. 2010. 48p. (J). (gr. 3-7). pap. 8.95 *(978-0-9841554-3-9(0));* lib. bdg. 18.95 *(978-0-9841554-2-2(2))* Columbus Zoo & Aquarium, The.
—Erase un Elefante, 1 vol. Bersani, Shennen, illus. 2016. (SPA.). 32p. (J). (gr. k-3). pap. 9.95 *(978-1-62855-745-9(1))* Arbordale Publishing.
—Once upon an Elephant, 1 vol. Bersani, Shennen, illus. 2016. (ENG.). 32p. (J). (gr. k-3). 17.95 *(978-1-62855-731-2(1))* Arbordale Publishing.
Stone, Tanya Lee. Elephants. 2003. (Wild Wild World Ser.). 24p. (YA). 24.94 *(978-1-56711-825-4(9),* Blackbirch Pr., Inc.) Cengage Gale.
Swanson, Diane. Elephants. 2004. (Welcome to the World of Animals Ser.). (Illus.). 32p. (gr. 1-4). lib. bdg. 24.00 *(978-0-8368-4022-3(4),* Gareth Stevens Learning Library) Stevens, Gareth Publishing LLLP.
Takeuchi, Mayuko. Circle, Triangle, Elephant! A Book of Shapes & Surprises. 2017. (ENG., Illus.). 22p. (gr. -1 — 1). bds. 9.95 ***(978-0-7148-7411-1(6))*** Phaidon Pr., Inc.
Taylor, Barbara. Incredible Elephants: A Fascinating Guide to the Gentle Giants That Dominate Africa & Asia, Shown in More Than 190 Pictures. 2014. (ENG., Illus.). 64p. (J). (gr. -1-3). 12.99 *(978-1-86147-328-8(1),* Armadillo) Anness Publishing GBR. Dist: National Bk. Network.
Taylor, Trace. Asian Elephants. 2008. (1-3Y Wild Animals Ser.). (ENG.). 24p. (J). (gr. k-2). pap. 5.99 *(978-1-59301-263-2(2))* American Reading Co.
Thomas, Isabel. Elephant vs. Rhinoceros. 2017. (Animal Rivals Ser.). (ENG.). 24p. (gr. k-2). lib. bdg. 23.32 ***(978-1-4846-4072-2(1),*** Heinemann Read & Learn) Heinemann-Raintree.
Thompson, Susan C. Elephants Are Wrinkly: Integrated Science Activities for Young Children. 2008. pap. 14.95 *(978-1-59647-267-9(7))* Good Year Bks.
Three Elephants: Big Book. (Pebble Soup Explorations Ser.). 16p. (gr. -1-18). 31.00 *(978-0-7578-1657-4(6))* Rigby Education.
Three Elephants: Small Book. (Pebble Soup Explorations Ser.). 16p. (gr. -1-18). 5.00 *(978-0-7578-1697-0(5))* Rigby Education.
Torres, John Albert. The African Elephant: A MyReportLinks.com Book. 2004. (Endangered & Threatened Animals Ser.). (Illus.). 48p. (J). lib. bdg. 25.26 *(978-0-7660-5174-4(9),* MyReportLinks.com Bks.) Enslow Pubs., Inc.
Tres Elefantes: Big Book. (Pebble Soup Exploraciones Ser.). (SPA.). 16p. (gr. -1-18). 31.00 *(978-0-7578-1676-5(2))* Rigby Education.
Tres Elefantes: Small Book. (Pebble Soup Exploraciones Ser.). (SPA.). 16p. (gr. -1-18). 5.00 *(978-0-7578-1716-8(5))* Rigby Education.
Turnbull, Stephanie. Elephant. 2013. (Big Beasts Ser.). (Illus.). 24p. (gr. k-3). 28.50 *(978-1-59920-833-6(4))* Black Rabbit Bks.
Twine, Alice. Baby Elephants. (Baby Animals Ser.). 24p. 2009. (gr. 1-1). 42.50 *(978-1-61511-486-3(6))* 2008. (Illus.). (J). (gr. -1-3). lib. bdg. 22.60 *(978-1-4042-4148-0(5))* Rosen Publishing Group, Inc., The. (PowerKids Pr.).
—Baby Elephants/Elefantes Bebe. Obregon, Jose Maria, tr. from ENG. 2008. (Baby Animals / Animales Bebé Ser.). (SPA., Illus.). 24p. (J). (gr. k-3). lib. bdg. 22.60 *(978-1-4042-7683-3(1))* Rosen Publishing Group, Inc., The.
—Elephants/Elefantes Bebé. 2009. (Baby Animals/Animales bebé Ser.). (ENG & SPA.). 24p. (gr. 1-1). 42.50 *(978-1-61511-501-3(3),* Editorial Buenas Letras) Rosen Publishing Group, Inc., The.
Vastola, P. Huge Animals: Learning the Long U Sound. 2009. (PowerPhonics Ser.). 24p. (gr. 1-1). 39.90 *(978-1-60851-445-8(5),* PowerKids Pr.) Rosen Publishing Group, Inc., The.
Von Zumbusch, Amelie. Elephants. 2007. (Safari Animals Ser.). (Illus.). 24p. (J). (gr. 3-7). lib. bdg. 22.60 *(978-1-4042-3616-5(3),* PowerKids Pr.) Rosen Publishing Group, Inc., The.
von Zumbusch, Amelie. Elephants. 2009. (Safari Animals Ser.). 24p. (gr. 1-1). 42.50 *(978-1-60852-950-6(9),* PowerKids Pr.) Rosen Publishing Group, Inc., The.
Von Zumbusch, Amelie. Elephants/Elefantes. Sanz, Pilar, tr. 2007. (Safari Animals / Animales de Safari Ser.: Vol. 1). (ENG & SPA., Illus.). 24p. (J). (gr. k-3). lib. bdg. 22.60 *(978-1-4042-7605-5(X))* Rosen Publishing Group, Inc., The.
von Zumbusch, Amelie. Elephants/Elefantes. 2009. (Safari Animals/Animales de safari Ser.). (ENG & SPA.). 24p. (gr. 1-1). 42.50 *(978-1-60852-973-5(8),* Editorial Buenas Letras) Rosen Publishing Group, Inc., The.
Ward, Finn. Elefantes / Elephants at the Zoo. 2015. (Animales Del Zoológico / Zoo Animals Ser.). (ENG & SPA.). 24p. (J). (gr. k-k). lib. bdg. 22.60 *(978-1-4824-3227-5(7))* Stevens, Gareth Publishing LLLP.
—Elephants at the Zoo. 2015. (Zoo Animals Ser.). (ENG., Illus.). 24p. (J). (gr. k-k). pap. 8.15 *(978-1-4824-2589-5(0))* Stevens, Gareth Publishing LLLP.
Wexo, John Bonnett. Elefantes. Rountree, Monica, tr. 2003. (Zoobooks Ser.). Orig. Title: Elephants. (SPA., Illus.). 24p. (J). (gr. k-6). lib. bdg. 15.95 *(978-1-888153-76-7(8))* Wildlife Education, Ltd.
—Elephants. rev. ed. 2003. (Illus.). 24p. 10.95 *(978-1-888153-95-8(4),* Zoo Bks.) Wildlife Education, Ltd.
Where Do Elephants Stomp? Small Book. (Pebble Soup Explorations Ser.). 16p. (gr. -1-18). 5.00 *(978-0-7635-7046-0(X))* Rigby Education.
White Elephants & Yellow Jackets: Individual Title Six-Packs. (Action Packs Ser.). 120p. (gr. 3-5). 44.00 *(978-0-7635-8428-3(2))* Rigby Education.
Wildlife Education. Elephants. 2007. (Illus.). (J). 5.99 *(978-1-932396-34-8(9),* Critters Up Close) Wildlife Education, Ltd.
World Book, Inc. Staff, contrib. by. Lizzy the Elephant. 2017. (J). ***(978-0-7166-3521-5(6))*** World Bk., Inc.
Wrinkles: Individual Title Six-Packs. (Literatura 2000 Ser.). (gr. 1-2). 28.00 *(978-0-7635-0119-8(0))* Rigby Education.
Yates, Gene. The Elephant Alphabet Book. 2003. (Illus.). (J). *(978-1-58865-106-8(1))* Kidsbooks, LLC.
Yates, Gene, illus. The Elephant Alphabet Book. 2006. (J). *(978-1-58865-363-5(3))* Kidsbooks, LLC.

ELEPHANTS—FICTION

Abedi, Isabel. Farewell, Grandpa Elephant: What Happens When a Loved One Dies? Cordes, Miriam, illus. 2012. (ENG.). 28p. (J). (gr. -1-k). 16.95 *(978-1-61608-655-8(6),* 608655, Sky Pony Pr.) Skyhorse Publishing Co., Inc.
Allende, Isabel. Forest of the Pygmies. 2009. (City of the Beasts Ser.: Bk. 3).Tr. of Bosque de los Pigmeos. (ENG.). 320p. pap. 14.99 *(978-0-06-182510-1(7),* Harper Perennial) HarperCollins Pubs.
—Forest of the Pygmies. Peden, Margaret Sayers, tr. from SPA. (City of the Beasts Ser.: Bk. 3).Tr. of Bosque de los Pigmeos. 304p. (J). (gr. 5-12). 2006. (ENG.). pap. 10.99 *(978-0-06-076198-1(9))* 2005. 19.99 *(978-0-06-076196-7(2))* HarperCollins Pubs. (Rayo).
—Forest of the Pygmies. l.t. ed. 2005. (City of the Beasts Ser.: Bk. 3).Tr. of Bosque de los Pigmeos. 304p. (J). (gr. 5-18). pap. 19.99 *(978-0-06-076200-1(4),* Rayo) HarperCollins Pubs.
Amenii, Nehprii. Memories of the Little Elephant. 2008. (Illus.). 60p. (J). 24.95 *(978-0-9797010-0-9(7))* Khunum Productions, Inc.
Anderson, Michael. The Elephants Are Coming. 2012. 32p. pap. 21.99 *(978-1-4653-8254-2(2))* Xlibris Corp.
Andreasen, Dan. Saturday with Daddy. Andreasen, Dan, illus. (ENG., Illus.). (J). 2017. 26p. bds. 7.99 *(978-1-250-11265-1(6),* 9781250112651) 2013. 24p. (gr. -1-2). 12.99 *(978-0-8050-8687-4(0),* 9780805086874) Holt, Henry & Co. (Holt, Henry & Co. Bks. For Young Readers).
Angel, Ido. Vipo in India: The Elephant with Bad Memory. 2015. (AV2 Animated Storytime Ser.). (ENG.). (J). lib. bdg. 29.99 *(978-1-4896-3899-1(7),* AV2 by Weigl) Weigl Pubs., Inc.
Applegate, Katherine. The One & Only Ivan. Castelao, Patricia, illus. (Harper Classic Ser.). (J). (gr. 3-7). 2017. 336p. 16.99 *(978-0-06-264194-6(8))* 2015. (ENG.). 352p. 24.99 *(978-0-06-242524-9(2))* 2015. (ENG.). 272p. pap. 7.99 *(978-0-06-199227-8(5))* 2012. (ENG.). 305p. 17.99 *(978-0-06-199225-4(9))* HarperCollins Pubs.
—The One & Only Ivan. Castelao, Patricia, illus. 2015. (ENG.). (J). (gr. 3-7). lib. bdg. 18.60 ***(978-1-62765-963-5(3))*** Perfection Learning Corp.
—The One & Only Ivan. Castelao, Patricia, illus. 2015. (J). lib. bdg. 18.40 *(978-0-606-35481-3(6))* Turtleback Bks.
Archer, Dosh. Little Elephant's Blocked Trunk. Archer, Dosh, illus. (Urgency Emergency! Ser.). (ENG., Illus.). 48p. (J). (gr. -1-3). 2015. pap. 9.99 *(978-0-8075-8361-6(8))* 2014. 12.99 *(978-0-8075-8354-8(5))* Whitman, Albert & Co.
Arnold, George "Speedy". What's an Elephant Doing in the Ausable River?!! Arnold, George "Speedy", illus. 2012. (ENG., Illus.). 64p. (J). 20.00 *(978-0-9836925-5-3(6))* Bloated Toe Publishing.
Ashley, Elana. Splunkunio Splunkey Detective & Peacemaker: Case One: The Missing Friendship Bracelet. 2003. (ENG & SPA., Illus.). 32p. (J). 17.95 *(978-0-9744812-0-3(3))* Dream Image Pr., LLC.
—Splunkunio Splunkey Detective & Peacemaker Detective y Pacificador: Case One: The Missing Friendship Bracelet Caso Primero: El Brazalete de la Amistad Desaparecido. Nikolov, Stefan V., tr. Ashley, Elana, photos by. 2005. (SPA & ENG., Illus.). 32p. (J). (gr. k-3). 17.95 *(978-0-9744812-1-0(1))* Dream Image Pr., LLC.
Awdry, Wilbert V. Henry & the Elephant. 2007. (Thomas & Friends Step into Reading Ser.). 13.55 *(978-1-4177-7088-5(0),* Turtleback) Turtleback Bks.
Baczynski, Jolanta. Ricky, the Little Elephant. 2012. 34p. pap. *(978-0-9877632-3-5(7))* Flower Pr.
Badescu, Ramona. Pomelo Explores Color. Chaud, Benjamin, illus. 2012. (Pomelo the Garden Elephant Ser.). (ENG.). 120p. (J). (gr. -1). 15.95 *(978-1-59270-126-1(4))* Enchanted Lion Bks., LLC.
—Pomelo's Big Adventure. Chaud, Benjamin, illus. 2014. (Pomelo the Garden Elephant Ser.). (ENG.). 40p. (J). (gr. -1-3). 17.95 *(978-1-59270-158-2(2))* Enchanted Lion Bks., LLC.
Badescu, Ramona & Bedrick, Claudia Z. Pomelo Begins to Grow. Chaud, Benjamin, illus. 2011. (Pomelo the Garden Elephant Ser.). (ENG.). 48p. (J). (gr. -1-2). 16.95 *(978-1-59270-111-7(6))* Enchanted Lion Bks., LLC.
Bailey, Mark & Oatman, Michael. Tiny Pie. Hemingway, Edward, illus. 2013. (ENG.). 32p. (J). (gr. -1-17). 15.95 *(978-0-7624-4482-3(7),* Running Pr. Kids) Running Pr. Bk. Pubs.
Bajaj, Varsha. This Is Our Baby, Born Today. Wheeler, Eliza, illus. 2016. (ENG.). 32p. (J). (-k). 16.99 *(978-0-399-16684-6(X),* Nancy Paulsen Books) Penguin Young Readers Group.
Baker, Ed. The Story of Kitten Cuckoo. Baker, Ed, illus. 2007. (ENG., Illus.). 32p. (J). (gr. -1-17). 15.95 *(978-1-933572-04-8(3))* Centro Bks., LLC.
Ballesta, Juan. Tommy y el Elefante. (SPA., Illus.). 28p. (J). (gr. k-3). *(978-84-264-3578-1(5),* LM1605) Editorial Lumen ESP. Dist: Lectorum Pubns., Inc.
Bansch, Helga. Petra. 2010. (SPA., Illus.). 48p. (J). 15.95 *(978-84-9871-003-8(0))* OQO, Editora ESP. Dist: Baker & Taylor Bks.
Barba, Ale. When Your Elephant Comes to Play. Barba, Ale, illus. 2016. (ENG., Illus.). 32p. (J). (gr. -1-2). 16.99 *(978-0-399-16312-8(3),* Philomel Bks.) Penguin Young Readers Group.
Barbari, Nader. Eddy the Elephant. 2010. 32p. pap. 13.99 *(978-1-4490-9430-0(9))* AuthorHouse.
Barclay, Eric. Hiding Phil. 2013. (Illus.). (J). *(978-0-545-60456-7(7),* Scholastic Pr.) Scholastic, Inc.
Barry, Cotter. The Rhymester Morgan Morgan In: Elephants Don't Fly. 2010. 16p. 12.99 *(978-1-4520-0115-9(4))* AuthorHouse.
Base, Graeme. Little Elephants. 2012. (ENG., Illus.). 40p. (J). (gr. k-2). 17.95 *(978-1-4197-0463-5(X),* Abrams Bks. for Young Readers) Abrams, Inc.
Bass, Joy Wine. The Flamingephants: Story, Songs, & Illustrations. 2011. 96p. 24.99 *(978-1-4568-8553-3(7));* pap. 15.99 *(978-1-4568-8552-6(9))* Xlibris Corp.
Beake, Lesley. Home Now. Littlewood, Karin, illus. 2007. 32p. (J). (ENG.). (gr. -1-3). pap. 6.95 *(978-1-58089-163-9(2));* (gr. k-3). 16.95 *(978-1-58089-162-2(4))* Charlesbridge Publishing, Inc.
Beard, Alex. Monkey See, Monkey Draw. 2011. (ENG., Illus.). 48p. (J). (gr. k-2). 17.95 *(978-0-8109-8970-2(0),* Abrams Bks. for Young Readers) Abrams, Inc.
Bell, Hazel. When Silly the Elephant Done His Tricks. 2013. 16p. (J). pap. 24.95 *(978-1-4626-8888-3(8))* America Star Bks.
Bently, Peter. National Geographic Kids Wild Tales: Ella's Bath: A Lift-The-flap Story about Elephants. 2013. (ENG.). 20p. (J). (gr. -1-2). bds. 9.99 *(978-1-4263-1360-8(8),* National Geographic Children's Bks.) National Geographic Society.
Bildner, Phil. Twenty-One Elephants. Pham, LeUyen, illus. 2004. (ENG.). 40p. (J). (gr. -1-3). 17.99 *(978-0-689-87011-8(6),* Simon & Schuster Bks. For Young Readers) Simon & Schuster Bks. For Young Readers.
Biro, Val. Gumdrop & the Elephant. Biro, Val, illus. 2015. (ENG., Illus.). 32p. (J). pap. 9.99 *(978-1-78270-049-4(8))* Award Pubns. Ltd. GBR. Dist: Parkwest Pubns., Inc.
—Gumdrops & the Elephant. (Illus.). 32p. (J). *(978-0-340-71442-3(5))* Hodder & Stoughton.
Bloomfield, Kevin. Mr. Biggs at the Circus / el Sr. Grande en el Circo. 2012. (ENG.). 32p. 16.95 *(978-1-936299-98-0(4),* Raven Tree Pr.,Csi) Continental Sales, Inc.
Bonanno, Joseph T. Monutza the Firefighting Elephant. 2012. 36p. pap. 15.49 *(978-1-4669-6222-4(4))* Trafford Publishing.
Bornemann, Elsa. Un Elefante Ocupa Mucho Espacio. (SPA.). (YA). (gr. 5-8). pap. 7.95 *(978-958-04-3453-5(0),* NR7780) Norma S.A. COL. Dist: Distribuidora Norma, Inc., Lectorum Pubns., Inc.
Bray, Pamela. Elephant & Ant. 2012. 36p. 24.95 *(978-1-4626-5986-9(1))* America Star Bks.
Breathed, Berkeley. Pete & Pickles. Breathed, Berkeley, illus. 2008. (ENG., Illus.). 48p. (J). (gr. -1-k). 17.99 *(978-0-399-25082-8(4),* Philomel Bks.) Penguin Young Readers Group.
Brewster, Benjamin & dePaola, Tomie. The Baby Elephant. Burchard, Peter, illus. 2015. (G&d Vintage Ser.). (ENG.). 32p. (J). (-k). bds. 7.99 *(978-0-448-48448-8(X),* Grosset & Dunlap) Penguin Young Readers Group.
Brightwood, Laura. Elephant's Trunk of Confidence. Pifer, Kimberly, ed. Brightwood, Laura, illus. 2012. (Illus.). (J). *(978-1-934409-33-6(2))* 3-C Institute for Social Development.
Brown, J. A. Hurray for Elephant. 2003. (Funny Faces Ser.). (Illus.). (J). 3.95 *(978-1-58925-717-7(0))* Tiger Tales.
Browne, Anthony. The Little Bear Book. Browne, Anthony, illus. 2014. (ENG., Illus.). 24p. (J). (gr. -1-2). 15.99 *(978-0-7636-7007-8(3))* Candlewick Pr.
Browne, Anthony & Bartholin, Hanne. Frida & Bear Play the Shape Game! 2016. (ENG.). 32p. (J). (gr. -1-2). 15.99 *(978-0-7636-7837-1(6))* Candlewick Pr.
Bryant, Phoebe. What Is That in the Air? A play date with Sayde. 2009. (Illus.). 28p. pap. 12.99 *(978-1-4490-2209-9(X))* AuthorHouse.
Bunting, Eve. Tweak Tweak. Ruzzier, Sergio, illus. 2011. (ENG.). 40p. (J). (gr. -1-3). 14.99 *(978-0-618-99851-7(9))* Houghton Mifflin Harcourt Publishing Co.
Burch, Sharon. Freddie the Frog & the Mysterious Wahooooo: 3rd Adventure: Tempo Island. 2010. (ENG.). 34p. 24.99 incl. audio compact disk *(978-0-9747454-7-3(2),* 0974745472) Mystic Publishing.
—Freddie the Frog & the Mysterious Wahooooo (DIGITAL EDITION) Digital Storybook with Step-By-Step Lessons for Interactive Whiteboard. 2015. (ENG.). 2p. pap. 29.99 *(978-1-4950-1092-7(9),* 1495010929) Leonard, Hal Corp.
Burch, Sharon, et al. Freddie the Frog & the Secret of Crater Island: 4th Adventure: Crater Island. 2010. (ENG.). 48p. 24.99 incl. audio compact disk *(978-0-9747454-6-6(4),* 0974745464) Mystic Publishing.
Burchett, Jan & Vogler, Sara. Safari Survival, 1 vol. Le Feyer, Diane, illus. 2013. (Wild Rescue Ser.). (ENG.). 152p. (gr. 3-6). 9.95 *(978-1-4342-4890-9(9))* Stone Arch Bks.
—Safari Survival, 1 vol. Le Feyer, Diane & Kennedy, Sam, illus. 2012. (Wild Rescue Ser.). (ENG.). 152p. (gr. 3-6). lib. bdg. 25.32 *(978-1-4342-3770-5(2))* Stone Arch Bks.
Burningham, John. Tug-of-War. Burningham, John, illus. 2013. (ENG., Illus.). 32p. (J). (gr. k-3). 16.99 *(978-0-7636-6575-3(4))* Candlewick Pr.
Busch, Janice. The Elephant That Fell. 2012. 48p. (gr. 1-2). pap. 8.99 *(978-1-4525-0513-8(6),* Balboa Pr.) Author Solutions, Inc.
Buzzeo, Toni. My Bibi Always Remembers. Wohnoutka, Mike, illus. 2014. (ENG.). 32p. (J). (gr. -1-k). 16.99 *(978-1-4231-8385-3(1))* Hyperion Bks. for Children.
Byrne, Richard. I Want to Go First! Byrne, Richard, illus. 2017. (ENG., Illus.). 32p. (J). 16.99 ***(978-1-250-12771-6(8),*** 9781250127716, Holt, Henry & Co. Bks. For Young Readers) Holt, Henry & Co.
Caletti, Deb. The Nature of Jade. 2008. (ENG.). 320p. (YA). (gr. 7-12). pap. 10.99 *(978-1-4169-1006-0(9),* Simon Pulse) Simon Pulse.
Cali, Davide. When an Elephant Falls in Love. Lotti, Alice, illus. 2016. (ENG.). 32p. (J). (gr. k-3). 14.99 *(978-1-4521-4727-7(2))* Chronicle Bks. LLC.
Campbell, Jennifer. Elise the Elephant. Cox, Nancy, illus. 2012. 32p. pap. 16.99 *(978-1-4567-9920-5(7))* AuthorHouse.
Castleton, Chaffee. Runty's Adventure: A Story of Love. Queen, Dana, illus. 2010. 97p. (J). pap. 17.95 *(978-0-578-06109-2(0))* Castleton, Julia J.
Chamber, Catherine. The Elephants' Ears. Mockford, Caroline, illus. 2004. 32p. (J). pap. 6.99 *(978-1-84148-249-1(8))* Barefoot Bks., Inc.
Chambers, Catherine. Elephants' Ears. 2016. (Illus.). 32p. (J). (gr. -1-2). pap. 8.99 *(978-1-78285-282-7(4))* Barefoot Bks., Inc.
Chase, Kit. Oliver's Tree. Chase, Kit, illus. 2014. (ENG., Illus.). 32p. (J). (gr. -1-k). 16.99 *(978-0-399-25700-1(4),* G.P. Putnam's Sons Books for Young Readers) Penguin Young Readers Group.
Choi, SeoYun. Let's Be Friends. Furukawa, Masumi, illus. rev. ed. 2014. (MySELF Bookshelf Ser.). (ENG.). 32p. (J). (gr. k-2). pap. 11.94 *(978-1-60357-658-1(4));* lib. bdg. 25.27 *(978-1-59953-649-1(8))* Norwood Hse. Pr.
Chorao, Kay. Ed & Kip. Chorao, Kay, illus. (I Like to Read(r) Ser.). (ENG., Illus.). 24p. (J). (gr. -1-3). 2015. 6.99 *(978-0-8234-3398-8(6))* 2014. 14.95 *(978-0-8234-2903-5(2))* Holiday Hse., Inc.
Clough, Lisa. Petal & Poppy. Briant, Ed, illus. 2014. (Green Light Readers Level 2 Ser.). (ENG.). 32p. (J). (gr. -1-3). pap. 3.99 *(978-0-544-11380-0(2),* HMH Books For Young Readers) Houghton Mifflin Harcourt Publishing Co.
—Petal & Poppy & the Penguin. Briant, Ed, illus. 2014. (Green Light Readers Level 2 Ser.). (ENG.). 32p. (J). (gr. -1-3). 12.99 *(978-0-544-13770-7(1));* pap. 3.99 *(978-0-544-13330-3(7))* Houghton Mifflin Harcourt Publishing Co. (HMH Books For Young Readers).
Collins, Ross. The Elephantom. Collins, Ross, illus. 2015. (ENG., Illus.). 40p. (J). (gr. -1-2). 16.99 *(978-0-7636-7591-2(1),* Templar) Candlewick Pr.
Conway, David. Errol & His Extraordinary Nose. Angaramo, Roberta, illus. 2010. (ENG.). 32p. (J). (gr. -1-3). 16.95 *(978-0-8234-2262-3(3))* Holiday Hse., Inc.
Corman, Clifford L. & Trevino, Esther. Eukee the Jumpy Jumpy Elephant. DiMatteo, Richard A., illus. (J). 2009. (ENG.). 26p. (gr. -1-1). pap. 10.95 *(978-1-886941-75-5(0))* 2003. 24p. (gr. 1-4). 15.00 *(978-0-9621629-8-5(1))* Specialty Pr., Inc.
Côté, Geneviève. What Elephant? Côté, Geneviève, illus. 2008. (ENG., Illus.). 32p. (J). (gr. -1-2). pap. 7.95 *(978-1-55453-270-4(1))* Kids Can Pr., Ltd. CAN. Dist: Hachette Bk. Group.
Coulton, Mia. Lunch for Baby Elephant. Campbell, D. B., illus. 2009. (ENG.). 12p. pap. 5.50 *(978-1-933624-49-5(3));* pap. 5.35 *(978-1-933624-42-6(6))* Maryruth Bks., Inc.
Cousins, Lucy. Maisy Learns to Swim. Cousins, Lucy, illus. 2013. (Maisy Ser.). (ENG., Illus.). 32p. (J). (gr. -1-k). 12.99 *(978-0-7636-6480-0(4))* Candlewick Pr.
—La Nochebuena de Maisy. 2004.Tr. of Maisy's Christmas Eve. (SPA., Illus.). 32p. (J). 16.99 *(978-84-8488-106-3(7))* Serres, Ediciones, S. L. ESP. Dist: Lectorum Pubns., Inc.
Cowan, Charlotte. The Little Elephant with the Big Earache. Garvin, Elaine, illus. 2007. (Dr. Hippo Ser.). (ENG.). 32p. (J). (gr. -1-3). 17.95 *(978-0-9753516-0-4(5))* Hippocratic Pr., The.

Cross, Frances. The Mystery of the Green Elephant. 2007. (Blobber Ser.). (ENG.). 84p. (J). per. *(978-1-84167-559-6(8))* Ransom Publishing Ltd.

Curato, Mike. Little Elliot, Big City. Curato, Mike, illus. (Little Elliot Ser.). (ENG., Illus.). (J). 2016. 34p. bds. 7.99 *(978-1-62779-698-9(3)*, 9781627796989) 2014. 40p. (gr. -1-3). 16.99 *(978-0-8050-9825-9(9)*, 9780805098259) Holt, Henry & Co. (Holt, Henry & Co. Bks. For Young Readers).

—Little Elliot, Big Family. Curato, Mike, illus. 2015. (Little Elliot Ser.). (ENG., Illus.). 40p. (J). (gr. -1-3). 17.99 *(978-0-8050-9826-6(7)*, 9780805098266, Holt, Henry & Co. Bks. For Young Readers) Holt, Henry & Co.

—Little Elliot, Big Fun. Curato, Mike, illus. 2016. (Little Elliot Ser.). (ENG., Illus.). 40p. (J). 17.99 *(978-0-8050-9827-3(5)*, 9780805098273, Holt, Henry & Co. Bks. For Young Readers) Holt, Henry & Co.

Cushway, Rosemary Lester. The Angel & the Elephant. 2015. (ENG.). 94p. (J). (gr. 2-3). mass mkt. 11.95 *(978-1-78612-047-2(X)*, 14a88a22-ec2b-4701-9a84-b4fc34b4a6b4) Austin, Stan AUS. Dist: Bookmasters Distribution.

D'Amico, Carmela. Ella Sets the Stage. D'Amico, Steven, illus. 2006. 41p. (J). pap. 16.99 *(978-0-439-83153-6(9)*, Levine, Arthur A. Bks.) Scholastic, Inc.

D'Amico, Carmela & D'Amica, Steve. Ella the Elegant Elephant. 2005. (J). (gr. k-3). 29.95 incl. audio compact disk *(978-0-8045-4128-2(0)*, SACD4128) Spoken Arts, Inc.

D'Amico, Carmela & D'Amico, Steven. Ella: The Elegant Elephant. D'Amico, Carmela & D'Amico, Steven, illus. unabr. ed. 2006. (ENG., Illus.). (J). (gr. -1-3). 9.99 *(978-0-439-87589-9(7))* Scholastic, Inc.

—Ella Sets Sail. 2008. (J). *(978-0-439-83156-7(3)*, Levine, Arthur A. Bks.) Scholastic, Inc.

—Ella the Elegant Elephant. 2004. (Illus.). (J). (ENG.). 56p. (gr. -1-3). 17.99 *(978-0-439-62792-4(3))*; *(978-0-439-62793-1(1))* Scholastic, Inc. (Levine, Arthur A. Bks.).

—Ella the Elegant Elephant. 2005. (J). (gr. k-3). 27.95 incl. audio *(978-0-8045-6933-0(9)*, SAC6933) Spoken Arts, Inc.

Davies, Gill. A Special Wish: A Story of Confidence. O'Neill, Rachael, illus. 2009. (Let's Grow Together Ser.). 32p. (J). (gr. -1-2). pap. 10.55 *(978-1-60754-769-3(4))*; lib. bdg. 22.60 *(978-1-60754-760-0(0))* Windmill Bks.

Davies, Timothy, Sr. The Polka-Dotted Elephant. 2007. (J). per. 12.00 *(978-0-9793207-0-5(4))* Wildlife Tales Publishing.

Davis, Lois A. 5 Silly Elephants. 2013. 28p. pap. 24.95 *(978-1-63000-530-6(4))* America Star Bks.

Day, Alexandra. Frank & Ernest. 2010. (ENG., Illus.). 40p. (J). 15.95 *(978-1-59583-424-9(9)*, 9781595834249, Green Tiger Pr.) Laughing Elephant.

—Frank & Ernest Play Ball. 2011. (ENG., Illus.). 40p. 15.95 *(978-1-59583-438-6(9)*, 9781595834386, Green Tiger Pr.) Laughing Elephant.

de Brunhoff, Jean. The Babar Collection: Five Classic Stories. 2017. (ENG., Illus.). 240p. (J). (gr. -1-k). pap. 22.99 ***(978-1-4052-7989-5(3))*** Egmont Bks., Ltd. GBR. Dist: Independent Pubs. Group.

de Brunhoff, Jean. Classic Tales of Babar. 2014. (ENG., Illus.). 112p. (J). (gr. -1-1). 19.99 *(978-1-4052-6420-4(9))* Egmont Bks., Ltd. GBR. Dist: Independent Pubs. Group.

de Brunhoff, Laurent. L' Anniversaire de Babar. (Babar Ser.). (FRE., Illus.). (J). (gr. -1-3). pap. *(978-2-01-002551-8(2))* Hachette Groupe Livre.

—B Is for Babar: An Alphabet Book. 2012. (ENG., Illus.). 30p. (J). (gr. -1 — 1). bds. 7.95 *(978-1-4197-0298-3(X)*, Abrams Appleseed) Abrams, Inc.

—Babar & the Ghost. 2012. (ENG., Illus.). 40p. (J). (gr. k-2). 15.95 *(978-1-4197-0380-5(3)*, Abrams Bks. for Young Readers) Abrams, Inc.

—Babar & the Ghost. 2004. (Illus.). (J). (gr. k-3). spiral bd. *(978-0-616-14570-8(5))*; spiral bd. *(978-0-616-14571-5(3))* Canadian National Institute for the Blind/Institut National Canadien pour les Aveugles.

—Babar & the Wully-Wully. 2012. (ENG., Illus.). 40p. (J). (gr. k-2). 15.95 *(978-1-4197-0381-2(1)*, Abrams Bks. for Young Readers) Abrams, Inc.

—Babar dans l'Ile aux Oiseaux.Tr. of Babar in the Jungle. (FRE., Illus.). (J). pap. 16.95 *(978-2-211-09806-9(1))* Archimede Editions FRA. Dist: Distribooks, Inc.

—Babar dans l'Ile aux Oiseaux. (Babar Ser.).Tr. of Babar in the Jungle. (FRE., Illus.). 29p. (J). (gr. -1-3). 15.95 *(978-0-7859-0681-0(9)*, F2002) French & European Pubns., Inc.

—Babar et la Vieille Dame. (Babar Ser.). (FRE., Illus.). (J). (gr. -1-3). pap. 15.95 *(978-0-7859-0614-8(2)*, FC254) French & European Pubns., Inc.

—Babar et le Wouly-Wouly. (Babar Ser.).Tr. of Babar & the Wully-Wully. (FRE., Illus.). 26p. (J). (gr. -1-3). 15.95 *(978-0-7859-0682-7(7)*, M11805) French & European Pubns., Inc.

—Babar et ses Amis a la Ferme. (Babar Ser.). (FRE., Illus.). 48p. (J). (gr. -1-3). 19.95 *(978-0-7859-8805-2(X))* French & European Pubns., Inc.

—Babar et ses Amis a la Fete. (Babar Ser.). (FRE., Illus.). 48p. (J). (gr. -1-3). 19.95 *(978-0-7859-8806-9(8))* French & European Pubns., Inc.

—Babar et ses Amis a la Maison. (Babar Ser.). (FRE., Illus.). 48p. (J). (gr. -1-3). 19.95 *(978-0-7859-8804-5(1))* French & European Pubns., Inc.

—Babar et ses Amis a la Ville. (Babar Ser.). (FRE., Illus.). 48p. (J). (gr. -1-3). 19.95 *(978-0-7859-8809-0(2))* French & European Pubns., Inc.

—Babar et ses Amis a L'Ecole. (Babar Ser.). (FRE., Illus.). 48p. (J). (gr. -1-3). 19.95 *(978-0-7859-8802-1(5))* French & European Pubns., Inc.

—Babar et ses Amis au Spectacle. (Babar Ser.). (FRE., Illus.). 48p. (J). (gr. -1-3). 19.95 *(978-0-7859-8803-8(3))* French & European Pubns., Inc.

—Babar et ses Amis en Foret. (Babar Ser.). (FRE., Illus.). 48p. (J). (gr. -1-3). 19.95 *(978-0-7859-8811-3(4))* French & European Pubns., Inc.

—Babar et ses Amis en Vacances. (Babar Ser.). (FRE., Illus.). 48p. (J). (gr. -1-3). 19.95 *(978-0-7859-8808-3(4))* French & European Pubns., Inc.

—Babar et ses Amis Font les Courses. (Babar Ser.). (FRE., Illus.). 48p. (J). (gr. -1-3). 19.95 *(978-0-7859-8810-6(6))* French & European Pubns., Inc.

—Babar et ses Amis Visitent le Royaume. (Babar Ser.). (FRE., Illus.). 48p. (J). (gr. -1-3). 19.95 *(978-0-7859-8807-6(6))* French & European Pubns., Inc.

—Babar in Famiglia. pap. 12.95 *(978-88-04-46271-2(X))* Mondadori ITA. Dist: Distribooks, Inc.

—Babar les 500 Premiers Mots. (Babar Ser.). (FRE., Illus.). 48p. (J). (gr. -1-3). 19.95 *(978-0-7859-8812-0(2))* French & European Pubns., Inc.

—Babar on Paradise Island. 2014. (ENG., Illus.). 48p. (J). (gr. k-2). 18.95 *(978-1-4197-1038-4(9)*, Abrams Bks. for Young Readers) Abrams, Inc.

—Babar Raconte Flore Reporter. (Babar Ser.). (FRE., Illus.). 48p. (J). (gr. -1-3). 19.95 *(978-0-7859-8813-7(0))* French & European Pubns., Inc.

—Babar Raconte Halte a la Pollution. (Babar Ser.). (FRE., Illus.). 48p. (J). (gr. -1-3). 19.95 *(978-0-7859-8816-8(5))* French & European Pubns., Inc.

—Babar Raconte la Course a la Lune. (Babar Ser.). (FRE., Illus.). 48p. (J). (gr. -1-3). 19.95 *(978-0-7859-8820-5(3))* French & European Pubns., Inc.

—Babar Raconte l'Affaire de la Couronne. (Babar Ser.). (FRE., Illus.). 48p. (J). (gr. -1-3). 19.95 *(978-0-7859-8818-2(1))* French & European Pubns., Inc.

—Babar Raconte l'Arrivee du Bebe Elephant. (Babar Ser.). (FRE., Illus.). 48p. (J). (gr. -1-3). 19.95 *(978-0-7859-8815-1(7))* French & European Pubns., Inc.

—Babar Raconte le Fantome. (Babar Ser.). (FRE., Illus.). 48p. (J). (gr. -1-3). 19.95 *(978-0-7859-8819-9(X))* French & European Pubns., Inc.

—Babar Raconte le Meilleur Ami des Elephants. (Babar Ser.). (FRE., Illus.). 48p. (J). (gr. -1-3). 19.95 *(978-0-7859-8823-6(8))* French & European Pubns., Inc.

—Babar Raconte le Pianiste. (Babar Ser.). (FRE., Illus.). 48p. (J). (gr. -1-3). 19.95 *(978-0-7859-8822-9(X))* French & European Pubns., Inc.

—Babar Raconte le Plus Beau Cadeau du Monde. (Babar Ser.). (FRE., Illus.). 48p. (J). (gr. -1-3). 19.95 *(978-0-7859-8821-2(1))* French & European Pubns., Inc.

—Babar Raconte Que la Fete Continue. (Babar Ser.). (FRE., Illus.). 48p. (J). (gr. -1-3). 19.95 *(978-0-7859-8824-3(6))* French & European Pubns., Inc.

—Babar Raconte un Diner Chez Rataxes. (Babar Ser.). (FRE., Illus.). 48p. (J). (gr. -1-3). 19.95 *(978-0-7859-8817-5(3))* French & European Pubns., Inc.

—Babar Raconte Zephir Fait le Singe. (Babar Ser.). (FRE., Illus.). 48p. (J). (gr. -1-3). 19.95 *(978-0-7859-8814-4(9))* French & European Pubns., Inc.

—Babar Visits Another Planet. rev. ed. 2012. (ENG., Illus.). 40p. (J). (gr. k-2). 16.95 *(978-1-4197-0342-3(0)*, Abrams Bks. for Young Readers) Abrams, Inc.

—Babar's Birthday Surprise. 2012. (ENG., Illus.). 40p. (J). (gr. k-2). 16.95 *(978-1-4197-0383-6(8)*, Abrams Bks. for Young Readers) Abrams, Inc.

—Babar's Guide to Paris. 2017. (ENG., Illus.). 48p. (J). (gr. k-2). 19.95 *(978-1-4197-2289-9(1)*, Abrams Bks. for Young Readers) Abrams, Inc.

—Babar's Museum of Art, 65 vols. 2003. (ENG., Illus.). 48p. (J). (gr. -1-17). 19.99 *(978-0-8109-4597-5(5))* Abrams, Inc.

—Babar's USA. 2008. (ENG., Illus.). 64p. (J). (gr. -1-k). 17.95 *(978-0-8109-7096-0(1)*, Abrams Bks. for Young Readers) Abrams, Inc.

—Meet Babar & His Family. (Babar Ser.). (Illus.). 32p. (J). (gr. -1-3). Random Hse. Children's Bks.

—Il Re Babar. pap. 12.95 *(978-88-04-44195-3(X))* Mondadori ITA. Dist: Distribooks, Inc.

—Le Roi Babar.Tr. of Babar the King. (FRE.). (J). pap. 14.95 *(978-2-211-06483-5(3))* Archimede Editions FRA. Dist: Distribooks, Inc.

de Brunhoff, Laurent & Rose, Phyllis. Babar & His Family. 2012. (ENG., Illus.). 24p. (J). (gr. -1 — 1). bds. 7.95 *(978-1-4197-0263-1(7)*, Abrams Appleseed) Abrams, Inc.

—Babar Comes to America. 2008. (ENG., Illus.). 72p. (J). (gr. -1-k). 18.95 *(978-0-8109-7244-5(1)*, Abrams Bks. for Young Readers) Abrams, Inc.

De Luca, Daniela. Lizzie the Elephant. 2008. (It's a Wildlife, Buddy! Ser.). (ENG., Illus.). 30p. (J). (gr. -1-1). 12.95 *(978-88-89272-25-1(2))* McRae Bks. Srl ITA. Dist: Independent Pubs. Group.

Delval, Marie-Hélène. Elephants est toujours Conten. (FRE.). pap. 14.95 *(978-2-227-75601-4(2))* Bayard Editions FRA. Dist: Distribooks, Inc.

Derrick, Patricia. Riley the Rhinoceros. Martinez, J-P Loppo, illus. 2007. 32p. (J). 18.95 incl. audio compact disk *(978-1-933818-15-3(8))* Animalations.

Derubertis, Barbara. Eddie Elephant's Exciting Egg-Sitting. 2010. pap. 45.32 *(978-0-7613-6507-5(9))* Kane Press, Inc.

deRubertis, Barbara. Eddie Elephant's Exciting Egg-Sitting. Alley, R. W., illus. 2010. (Animal Antics A to Z Ser.). 32p. (J). (gr. -1-3). pap. 7.95 *(978-1-57565-309-9(5))*; lib. bdg. 22.60 *(978-1-57565-316-7(8))* Kane Press, Inc.

deRubertis, Barbara & DeRubertis, Barbara. Eddie Elephant's Exciting Egg-Sitting. Alley, R. W., illus. 2012. (Animal Antics A to Z Ser.). (J). (gr. 2 — 1). cd-rom 7.95 *(978-1-57565-398-3(2))* Kane Press, Inc.

DiCamillo, Kate. The Magician's Elephant. Tanaka, Yoko, illus. (ENG.). (J). (gr. 3-7). 2015. 224p. pap. 7.99 *(978-0-7636-8088-6(5))* 2009. 208p. 16.99 *(978-0-7636-4410-9(2))* Candlewick Pr.

—The Magician's Elephant. l.t. ed. 2010. (ENG.). 242p. 23.95 *(978-1-4104-2493-8(6))* Thorndike Pr.

—The Magician's Elephant. 2015. lib. bdg. 17.20 *(978-0-606-37891-8(X))* 2011. lib. bdg. 17.20 *(978-0-606-15375-1(6)*, Turtleback) Turtleback Bks.

Dinerstein, Eric. What Elephants Know. 2016. (ENG.). 288p. (J). (gr. 3-7). 16.99 *(978-1-4847-2854-3(8))* Disney Publishing Worldwide.

—What Elephants Know. 2017. (ENG.). 288p. (J). (gr. 3-7). pap. 7.99 *(978-1-4847-4647-9(3))* Hyperion Bks. for Children.

Disney Staff. Dumbo. (FRE.). 96p. (J). (gr. k-5). pap. 9.95 *(978-0-7859-8849-6(1))* French & European Pubns., Inc.

Dodd, Emma. Always. Dodd, Emma, illus. 2014. (Emma Dodd's Love You Bks.). (ENG., Illus.). 24p. (J). (-k). 12.99 *(978-0-7636-7544-8(X)*, Templar) Candlewick Pr.

—Cinderelephant. Dodd, Emma, illus. 2013. (ENG., Illus.). 32p. (J). (gr. -1-3). 16.99 *(978-0-545-53285-3(X)*, Levine, Arthur A. Bks.) Scholastic, Inc.

Dolan, Penny. Princess Rani, 1 vol. Robert, Bruno, illus. 2013. (Start Reading Ser.). (ENG.). 24p. (gr. k-1). pap. 7.95 *(978-1-4765-4131-0(0))* Capstone Press of Coughlan Cos.

Donald, Margaret. Eli the Elephant: A Tsunami Story. Grant, Sophia & Noble, Stuart, illus. 2007. (ENG.). 25p. (gr. 3-7). *(978-81-8386-024-6(9))* India Research Pr. IND. Dist: Independent Pubs. Group.

Drachman, Eric. Ellison the Elephant. Muscarello, James, illus. 2005. (ENG.). 32p. (J). (gr. -1-2). 18.95 incl. audio compact disk *(978-0-9703809-1-3(7))* Kidwick Bks.

Duey, Kathleen. Ella the Baby Elephant: A Baby Elephant's Story. Gurin, Lara, illus. 2008. (My Animal Family Ser.). (ENG.). 32p. (J). (gr. -1-3). 12.99 *(978-0-8249-5584-7(6)*, Ideal Pubns.) Worthy Publishing.

Dyan, Penelope. The White Elephant No One Wants. Dyan, Penelope, illus. 2012. (Illus.). 34p. pap. 11.95 *(978-1-61477-024-4(7))* Bellissima Publishing, LLC.

Eggleton, Jill. Elephant Is Stuck! 3-in-1 Package. (Sails Literacy Ser.). 24p. (gr. k-18). 57.00 *(978-0-7578-8616-4(7))* Rigby Education.

—Elephant Is Stuck! 6 Small Books. (Sails Literacy Ser.). 24p. (gr. k-18). 25.00 *(978-0-7578-7729-2(X))* Rigby Education.

—Elephant Is Stuck! Big Book Only. (Sails Literacy Ser.). 24p. (gr. k-18). 27.00 *(978-0-7578-6199-4(7))* Rigby Education.

Eide, Scott M. Chicago Bob & the Case of the Missing Elephant. 2006. 20p. pap. 3.99 net. *(978-1-59975-649-3(8))* Independent Pub.

An Elephant in the House: Individual Title Six-Pack. (Story Steps Ser.). (gr. k-2). 23.00 *(978-0-7635-9852-5(6))* Rigby Education.

An Elephant's Tail. 2010. 47p. pap. 6.00 *(978-81-7806-190-0(2))* Unicorn Bks. Pvt Ltd. IND. Dist: Mahal, Pustak Pubs., Booksellers & Order Suppliers.

Ella & the Halloween Mystery. 2016. (Illus.). 24p. (J). ***(978-1-5182-3174-2(8))*** Baker & Taylor, CATS.

Ellis, Mary. Elephant Child. Denton, Kady MacDonald, illus. 2010. (ENG.). 128p. (J). (gr. 2-4). pap. 7.99 *(978-0-00-712820-4(7)*, HarperCollins Children's Bks.) HarperCollins Pubs. Ltd. GBR. Dist: HarperCollins Pubs.

Elwell, Telva & Kelley, Barbara. Ellasense Misses the Train. Elwell, Telva, illus. 2004. (Illus.). 48p. (J). per. 12.95 *(978-0-9754591-0-2(4))* Cubby Hole Tales.

Encyclopaedia Britannica, Inc. Staff, compiled by. How the Elephant Got His Trunk. 2008. 49.95 *(978-1-59339-556-8(6))* Encyclopaedia Britannica, Inc.

Engler, Michael. Elephantastic! Tourlonias, Joëlle, illus. 2014. (ENG.). 32p. (J). 16.99 *(978-1-4413-0841-2(5)*, 9781441308412) Peter Pauper Pr. Inc.

Eschberger, Beverly. The Elephants in the City of Light: An Elephant Family Adventure. Gower, Jim, illus. 2010. (J). per. 3.99 *(978-1-932926-28-6(3)*, Kinkajou Pr.) Artemesia Publishing, LLC.

—The Elephants in the Land of Enchantment: An Elephant Family Adventure. Gower, Jim, illus. 2009. 96p. (J). pap. 3.99 *(978-1-932926-02-6(X)*, Kinkajou Pr.) Artemesia Publishing, LLC.

—The Elephants Tour England: An Elephant Family Adventure. Gower, Jim, illus. 2009. 86p. (J). per. 3.99 *(978-1-932926-29-3(1)*, Kinkajou Pr.) Artemesia Publishing, LLC.

—The Elephants Visit London: An Elephant Family Adventure. Gower, Jim, illus. l.t. ed. 2007. 96p. (J). per. 3.99 *(978-1-932926-30-9(5)*, Kinkajou Pr.) Artemesia Publishing, LLC.

Esperanza, Charles George, illus. Red, Yellow, Blue, & a Dash of White, Too! 2015. (ENG.). 40p. (J). (gr. -1-k). 16.99 *(978-1-62914-624-9(2)*, Sky Pony Pr.) Skyhorse Publishing Co., Inc.

Faul, Nicole. The Great Animal Race & Trap the Angry Elephant Finds a Friend. 2009. (Illus.). 44p. pap. 18.49 *(978-1-4389-3320-7(7))* AuthorHouse.

Fenske, Jonathan. Woodward & Mctwee. Fenske, Jonathan, illus. 2014. (Penguin Young Readers, Level 2 Ser.). (ENG., Illus.). 32p. (J). (gr. 1-2). pap. 3.99 *(978-0-448-47991-0(5)*, Penguin Young Readers) Penguin Young Readers Group.

Fleischman, Sid. The White Elephant. McGuire, Robert, illus. 2006. 112p. (J). (gr. 3-6). lib. bdg. 16.89 *(978-0-06-113137-0(7))*; 15.99 *(978-0-06-113136-3(9))* HarperCollins Pubs. (Greenwillow Bks.).

Forssén Ehrlin, Carl-Johan. The Little Elephant Who Wants to Fall Asleep: A New Way of Getting Children to Sleep. Hanson, Sydney, illus. 2016. (ENG.). 40p. (J). (gr. -1-2). 16.99 *(978-0-399-55423-0(8)*, Crown Books For Young Readers) Random Hse. Children's Bks.

Foust, Cindy. Elephant emma Lou. 2006. (J). 12.94 *(978-0-9749220-4-1(8))* Alpha-kidZ.

French, Vivian. Cave-Baby & the Mammoth. Williams, Lisa, illus. 2010. 32p. pap. *(978-1-84089-635-0(3))* Zero to Ten, Ltd.

French, Vivian & Terry, Michael. Ellie & Elvis. 2007. (Bloomsbury Paperbacks Ser.). (ENG., Illus.). 32p. (J). (gr. k-2). 9.99 *(978-0-7475-8403-2(6))* Bloomsbury Publishing Plc GBR. Dist: Independent Pubs. Group.

Friden, Chris & Rodriguez Braojos, Alberto. Storytime with Paige. Jaraiz, David, illus. 2008. (J). *(978-0-9758785-8-3(1))*; *(978-0-9801849-4-5(0))* Haydenburn Lane.

Frost, Adam. Run! The Elephant Weighs a Ton! Chambers, Mark, illus. 2012. (ENG.). 128p. (J). (gr. -1-k). pap. 8.99 *(978-1-4088-2707-9(7)*, 9781408827079, Bloomsbury USA Childrens) Bloomsbury Publishing USA.

Gabriel, Elizabeth P. & Gabriel, Pamela P. Ziccah Blows Her Horn. 2008. 24p. pap. 12.99 *(978-1-4389-2447-2(X))* AuthorHouse.

Galvin, Laura Gates. Judy the Elephant. Denman, Michael & Huiett, William, illus. 2005. (African Wildlife Foundation Ser.). (ENG.). 36p. (J). (gr. -1-2). 2.95 *(978-1-59249-171-1(5)*, S6552); 9.95 *(978-1-59249-172-8(3)*, PS6552) Soundprints.

—Judy the Elephant. Denman, Michael L. & Huiett, William J., trs. Denman, Michael L. & Huiett, William J., illus. 2005. (African Wildlife Foundation Ser.). (ENG.). 36p. (J). (gr. -1-2). 14.95 *(978-1-59249-169-8(3)*, H6502); 6.95 *(978-1-59249-170-4(7)*, S6502) Soundprints.

—Judy the Elephant. Denman, Michael & Huiett, William, illus. 2004. (African Wildlife Foundation Ser.). (ENG.). 36p. (J). (gr. -1-2). 8.95 *(978-1-59249-198-8(7)*, SD6502) Soundprints.

Garis, Howard R. Umboo, the Elephant. 2008. 108p. 22.95 *(978-1-60664-782-0(2))*; pap. 9.95 *(978-1-60664-156-9(5))* Aegypan.

—Umboo, the Elephant. 2007. 100p. per. *(978-1-4065-2771-1(8))* Dodo Pr.

Garis, Howard Roger. Umboo the Elephant. 2004. reprint ed. pap. 15.95 *(978-1-4191-9168-8(3))*; pap. 1.99 *(978-1-4192-9168-5(8))* Kessinger Publishing, LLC.

Garland, Michael. Big & Little: A Story of Two Friends. 2017. (ENG., Illus.). 32p. (J). (gr. -1-k). 14.99 *(978-0-545-87097-9(6))* Scholastic, Inc.

Garstang, Michael. Ntombazana: A Story of an African Elephant Family. 2008. (ZUL., Illus.). 208p. pap. 17.50 *(978-0-615-18904-8(0))* Angel Applications.

Garza, Lois Ann. Lellie the Different Elephant. Martinez-Neal, Juana, illus. 2011. 36p. pap. 11.95 *(978-1-60047-592-4(2))* Wasteland Pr.

Gerstier, J. C. My Elephant Likes to Read. Alley, Ashleigh & Norona, Bill, illus. 2013. 30p. pap. 12.00 *(978-1-4349-3548-9(5)*, RoseDog Bks.) Dorrance Publishing Co., Inc.

Getting Ready for the Ball: Individual Title Six-Packs. (Literatura 2000 Ser.). (gr. -1-1). 28.00 *(978-0-7635-0005-4(4))* Rigby Education.

Gillies, Mark. Imvula, Child of the Rain. 2007. (Illus.). 80p. per. *(978-1-84401-965-6(9))* Athena Pr.

Gingrich, Callista. Hail to the Chief. Arciero, Susan, illus. 2016. (Ellis the Elephant Ser.). (ENG.). 40p. (J). (gr. -1-4). 16.99 *(978-1-62157-479-8(2)*, Regnery Kids) Regnery Publishing, Inc., An Eagle Publishing Co.

—Land of the Pilgrims Pride. Arciero, Susan, illus. 2012. (Ellis the Elephant Ser.). (ENG.). 28p. (J). (gr. k-3). 14.95 *(978-1-59698-829-3(0)*, Little Patriot Pr.) Regnery Publishing, Inc., An Eagle Publishing Co.

Gingrich, Callista & Arciero, Susan. Yankee Doodle Dandy. 2013. (Ellis the Elephant Ser.). (ENG., Illus.). 40p. (J). (gr. -1-3). 14.95 *(978-1-62157-087-5(8)*, Regnery Kids) Regnery Publishing, Inc., An Eagle Publishing Co.

Ginkel, Anne. I've Got an Elephant, 1 vol. Bynum, Janie, illus. (ENG.). (J). 2013. (gr. -1-3). 7.95 *(978-1-56145-685-7(3))* 2006. (gr. k-3). 16.95 *(978-1-56145-373-3(0))* Peachtree Pubs.

Glass, Calliope. Disney Tails Dumbo & Mama. Disney Storybook Art Team, illus. 2016. (Disney Tails Ser.). (ENG.). 10p. (J). (gr. -1 — 1). bds. 6.99 *(978-1-4847-2955-7(2))* Disney Pr.

Gokhale, Ruby. Emma & Kelly. 2011. 20p. pap. 11.99 *(978-1-4567-5288-0(X))* AuthorHouse.

Goodhart, Pippa. Little Nelly's Big Book. Rowland, Andy, illus. 2012. (ENG.). 32p. (J). (gr. -1-3). 16.99 *(978-1-59990-779-6(8)*, 9781599907796, Bloomsbury USA Childrens) Bloomsbury Publishing USA.

Gorman, DI. Pudgy Wudgy: Pudgy Wudgy Meets a Friend. 2008. 32p. pap. 12.99 *(978-1-4389-2151-8(9))* AuthorHouse.

Grambling, Lois G. Can I Bring Woolly to the Library, Ms. Reeder? Love, Judy, illus. 2012. (Prehistoric Pets Ser.). (ENG.). 32p. (J). (gr. k-3). lib. bdg. 16.95 *(978-1-58089-281-0(7))* Charlesbridge Publishing, Inc.

Grant, Carrie and David. Elephant's Birthday Bells: Jump up & Join In. Busby, Ailie, illus. 2013. 32p. (J). pap. 7.99 *(978-1-61067-181-1(3))* Kane Miller.

Gregar, Steve. The Littlest Elephant. 2004. 13p. pap. 9.98 *(978-1-4116-1148-1(9))* Lulu Pr., Inc.

Grosset & Dunlap. Meet Ella the Elephant! Sticker Stories. 2015. (Ella the Elephant Ser.). (ENG.). 16p. (J). (-k). pap. 6.99 *(978-0-448-48926-1(0)*, Grosset & Dunlap) Penguin Young Readers Group.

Grosset & Dunlap & Adler, Eve. Ella & the Halloween Mystery. 2016. (Ella the Elephant Ser.). (ENG., Illus.). 24p. (J). (gr. -1-k). pap. 3.99 *(978-1-101-99591-4(2)*, Grosset & Dunlap) Penguin Young Readers Group.

Gunderson, Jessica. The Elephant Dancer: A Story of Ancient India, 1 vol. Hu, Caroline, illus. 2009. (Read-It! Chapter Books: Historical Tales Ser.). (ENG.). 64p. (gr. 2-4). 22.65 *(978-1-4048-5219-8(0)*, Chapter Readers) Picture Window Bks.

Gwent (Wales), Staff Development Unit Staff & Acen Staff, contrib. by. Nos Da, Arthur. 2005. (WEL., Illus.). 8p. pap. *(978-1-874049-31-9(9))* Acen Limited.

Haile, Carol J. Elephant Overboard! Haile, Carol J., illus. 2007. (Illus.). (J). lib. bdg. 19.95 *(978-0-9711236-3-2(2))* Firenze Pr.

Hamilton, Elizabeth L. Little Zoh's Submissive Trunk. 2003. (Character Critters Ser.: No. 3). (Illus.). 32p. (J). (gr. -1-3). per. 5.95 *(978-0-9713749-9-7(6)*, Character-in-Action) Quiet Impact, Inc.

Hao, K. T. The Magic Book. Ferri, Giuliano, illus. 2008. (ENG.). 32p. (J). (gr. -1). 16.50 *(978-1-933327-44-0(8))*; 15.95 *(978-1-933327-43-3(X))* Purple Bear Bks., Inc.

Harris, Erin & National Geographic Learning Staff. Elephant on My Roof. Harris, Erin, illus. 2010. (Rise & Shine Ser.). (ENG., Illus.). 32p. (C). (gr. -1-3). 26.95 *(978-1-60108-002-8(6))* National Geographic School Publishing, Inc.

Harris, R. P. Tua & the Elephant. Yoo, Taeeun, illus. 2012. (ENG.). 204p. (J). (gr. 3-7). 16.99 *(978-0-8118-7781-7(7))* Chronicle Bks. LLC.

Harris, Shelly Jones. Little Elephant Is a Lifesaver. 2012. 24p. pap. 10.99 *(978-1-4497-6092-2(9)*, WestBow Pr.) Author Solutions, Inc.

Harrison, Paul. Elephant Rides Again. Million, Liz, illus. 2009. (Get Ready (Windmill Books) Ser.). 32p. (J). (gr. k-2). lib. bdg. 22.60 *(978-1-60754-259-9(5))* Windmill Bks.

Harvey, Autumn. Putty. 2009. 16p. pap. 8.99 *(978-1-4389-4421-0(7))* AuthorHouse.

Heide, Florence Parry & Clief, Sylvia Van. That's What Friends Are For. Meade, Holly, illus. 2007. 30p. (gr. -1-3). 17.00 *(978-0-7569-8126-6(3))* Perfection Learning Corp.

Heine, Theresa. El Baile del Elefante: Recuerdos de la India. Moxley, Sheila, illus. 2005. (SPA.). 44p. (gr. 2-3). 22.99 *(978-84-8452-356-7(X))* Fundacion Intermon ESP. Dist: Lectorum Pubns., Inc.

—Elephant Dance: A Journey to India. Moxley, Sheila, illus. 2006. (ENG.). 40p. (J). (gr. -1-2). 8.99 *(978-1-905236-79-4(4))* Barefoot Bks., Inc.

Henrichs, Wendy. When Anju Loved Being an Elephant. Butler, John, illus. 2011. (ENG.). 32p. (gr. k-5). lib. bdg. 16.95 *(978-1-58536-533-3(5))* Sleeping Bear Pr.

Henry, Mandy. Elephants in Our House. 2010. (Illus.). 20p. pap. 10.49 *(978-1-4490-7086-1(8))* AuthorHouse.

Hensel, Boots. The Zoopendous Surprise! Gabriel, Andrea, illus. 2009. (ENG.). 32p. (J). (gr. -1-k). 16.95 *(978-0-9792035-5-8(4))* Pleasant St. Pr.

Herman, Gail. Enterrado en el Jardin; Buried in the Backyard. 2008. pap. 34.95 *(978-1-58013-768-3(7))* Kane Press, Inc.

High, Linda Oatman. One Amazing Elephant. 2017. 272p. (J). (gr. 3-7). 16.99 *(978-0-06-245583-3(4))* HarperCollins Pubs.

Hjertaas, Trevor. Elephant, Elephant, 1 vol. 2009. 31p. pap. 24.95 *(978-1-60749-780-6(8))* America Star Bks.

Hockerman, Dennis, illus. The Little Seed: A Tale about Integrity. 2006. (J). *(978-1-59939-094-9(9)*, Reader's Digest Young Families, Inc.) Studio Fun International.

Hofmann-Maniyar, Ariane. That's NOT How You Do It! Hofmann-Maniyar, Ariane, illus. 2016. (Child's Play Library). (ENG., Illus.). 32p. (J). pap. *(978-1-84643-928-5(0))* Child's Play International Ltd.

Holden, Pam. Thirsty Baby Elephant. 2015. (ENG., Illus.). 16p. (-1). pap. *(978-1-77654-076-1(X)*, Red Rocket Readers) Flying Start Bks.

—Too Big & Heavy, 6 pack. Hatam, Samer, illus. 2009. (Red Rocket Readers Ser.). (ENG.). 16p. (gr. 2-2). pap. *(978-1-877363-70-2(7))* Flying Start Bks.

Holmes, Mary Tavener & Harris, John. The Elephant from Baghdad, 0 vols. Cannell, Jon, illus. 2012. (ENG.). 40p. (J). (gr. k-3). 17.99 *(978-0-7614-6111-1(6)*, 9780761461111, Amazon Children's Publishing) Amazon Publishing.

House, Catherine. Little Elephant. Whelan, Olwyn, illus. 2007. 32p. pap. 11.95 *(978-1-59325-093-5(2))* Word Among Us Pr.

Huang, Yu-Hsuan, illus. Baby Elephant: Finger Puppet Book. 2016. (ENG.). 12p. (J). (gr. -1 — 1). 6.99 *(978-1-4521-4237-1(8))* Chronicle Bks. LLC.

Hudson, Marilyn A. Elephant Hips Are Expensive! A Tale of the Sooner State. Fulco, Haley, illus. 2007. 50p. (J). per. *(978-0-9778850-2-2(X)*, WhorlBooks Thumbprints) Whorl Bks.

Hueber, Jolene Samanatha. Trunkels. 2010. 32p. pap. 14.99 *(978-1-4520-5647-0(1))* AuthorHouse.

Hughes, Mónica. More Little Mouse Deer Tales. Clementson, John, illus. 2005. 24p. (J). lib. bdg. 23.65 *(978-1-59646-730-9(4))* Dingles & Co.

Hunter, Sally. Humphrey's Playtime. 2013. (Illus.). (J). *(978-1-4351-4766-9(9))* Barnes & Noble, Inc.

Huskins, Suzanne Hallier, illus. No Matter What! 2004. (J). *(978-1-887905-93-0(6))* Parkway Pubs., Inc.

Jackson, Colter & dePaola, Tomie. Elephants Make Fine Friends. 2015. (ENG., Illus.). 32p. (J). (gr. -1-k). bds. 3.99 *(978-0-448-48505-8(2)*, Grosset & Dunlap) Penguin Young Readers Group.

Jackson, Kathryn & Jackson, B. The Saggy Baggy Elephant. Tenggren, Gustaf, illus. deluxe ed. Date not set. (J). (gr. -1-2). reprint ed. *(978-1-929566-60-0(3))* Cronies.

—The Saggy Baggy Elephant: Classic Edition. Tenggren, Gustaf, illus. Date not set. 23p. (J). (gr. -1-1). *(978-1-929566-54-9(9))* Cronies.

Jahn-Clough, Lisa, et al. Petal & Poppy & the Mystery Valentine. Briant, Ed, illus. 2015. (Green Light Readers Level 2 Ser.). (ENG.). 32p. (J). (gr. 1-4). pap. 3.99 *(978-0-544-55549-5(X)*, HMH Books For Young Readers) Houghton Mifflin Harcourt Publishing Co.

James, Robert. How the Elephant Got Its Trunk. 2012. (ENG., Illus.). 24p. (J). *(978-0-7787-7891-2(6))*; pap. *(978-0-7787-7903-2(3))* Crabtree Publishing Co.

Jarkins, Sheila. The Adventures of Marco Flamingo in the Jungle. Jarkins, Sheila, illus. 2012. (Illus.). 32p. (J). 1.99 *(978-1-936299-31-7(3)*, Raven Tree Pr.) Delta Systems Company, Inc.

Jarvis. Fred Forgets. Jarvis, illus. 2016. (Illus.). 32p. (J). (gr. -1-3). 17.99 *(978-0-06-234916-3(3))* HarperCollins Pubs.

Javaherbin, Mina & Jalal al-Din Rumi. Elephant in the Dark. Yelchin, Eugene, illus. 2015. (ENG.). 40p. (J). (gr. -1-3). 17.99 *(978-0-545-63670-4(1)*, Scholastic Pr.) Scholastic, Inc.

Jenkins, Martin. Grandma Elephant's in Charge. Bates, Ivan, illus. 2014. (Read & Wonder Ser.). (ENG.). 32p. (J). (gr. k-3). 6.99 *(978-0-7636-7381-9(1))* Candlewick Pr.

Johnson, Gerald J. J. Ellie Saves the Day, 1 vol. Funke, Peggy, illus. 2009. 12p. pap. 24.95 *(978-1-60836-709-2(6))* America Star Bks.

Johnson, Lydia Sue. Chester, the Pink Elephant. 2011. 28p. pap. 21.99 *(978-1-4568-9692-2(2))* Xlibris Corp.

Jomo & Mata: Evaluation Guide. 2006. (J). *(978-1-55942-411-0(7))* Witcher Productions.

Jones, Allan Frewin. Legends of the Golden Elephant. 2006. 188p. *(978-0-439-85671-3(X))* Scholastic, Inc.

Jordan, Christina. I Wish I Were an Enormous Elephant, 1 vol. Utomo, Gabhor, illus. 2011. (I Wish I Were ... Ser.). (ENG.). 24p. (J). (gr. k-3). 28.50 *(978-1-61641-661-4(0))* Magic Wagon.

Jumbo 3. 2004. (J). per. *(978-1-57657-008-1(8))* Paradise Pr., Inc.

Jumbo 4. 2004. (J). per. *(978-1-57657-009-8(6))* Paradise Pr., Inc.

Kadohata, Cynthia. A Million Shades of Gray. (ENG., Illus.). (J). (gr. 5-9). 2011. 240p. pap. 7.99 *(978-1-4424-2919-2(4))* 2010. 224p. 16.99 *(978-1-4169-1883-7(3))* Simon & Schuster Children's Publishing. (Atheneum Bks. for Young Readers).

Kasza, Keiko. The Mightiest. 2003. (ENG., Illus.). 32p. (J). (gr. -1-k). pap. 5.99 *(978-0-14-250185-6(9)*, Puffin Books) Penguin Young Readers Group.

—When the Elephant Walks. Kasza, Keiko, illus. 2004. (ENG., Illus.). 30p. (J). (gr. -1 — 1). bds. 6.99 *(978-0-399-24261-8(9)*, G.P. Putnam's Sons Books for Young Readers) Penguin Young Readers Group.

Kavanagh, Peter. I Love My Mama. Chapman, Jane, tr. Chapman, Jane, illus. 2003. 32p. (J). 12.95 *(978-1-85430-806-1(8)*, Simon & Schuster Bks. For Young Readers) Simon & Schuster Bks. For Young Readers.

Keller, John E. The Emperor's Elephant. 2006. 127p. (YA). per. 12.95 *(978-0-942566-45-1(9))* LinguaText, LLC.

Kelly, Lynne. Chained, 1 vol. 2012. (ENG.). 256p. (J). (gr. 5-9). 17.99 *(978-0-374-31237-4(0)*, 9780374312374, Farrar, Straus & Giroux (BYR)) Farrar, Straus & Giroux.

Kernan, Martin James. Entertaining Elephant. Finley, Thomas Murray, illus. 2012. (ENG.). 28p. (J). pap. 9.95 *(978-1-4675-4149-7(4))* Independent Pub.

Kipling, Rudyard. The Elephant's Child: From the Just So Stories, 1 vol. Raglin, Tim, illus. 2005. (Rabbit Ears: A Classic Tale Ser.). (ENG.). 40p. (gr. -1-3). 25.65 *(978-1-59679-343-9(0))* Spotlight.

—El Hijo del Elefante. Mogensen, Jan, illus. (Baril Sin Fondo Ser.).Tr. of Elephant's Child. (SPA.). (J). (gr. 3-5). pap. 8.76 *(978-968-6465-06-8(5))* Casa de Estudios de Literatura y Talleres Artisticos Amaquemecan A.C. MEX. Dist: Lectorum Pubns., Inc.

—How the Elephant Got His Trunk: The Graphic Novel, 1 vol. Rodriguez, Pedro, illus. 2012. (Graphic Spin Ser.). (ENG.). 40p. (gr. 1-3). pap. 5.95 *(978-1-4342-3880-1(6))*; lib. bdg. 23.99 *(978-1-4342-3222-9(0))* Stone Arch Bks. (Graphic Revolve).

—Rikki-Tikki-Tavi & Toomai of the Elephants. 2008. (Unabridged Classics (in Audio) Ser.). (J). pap. 36.00 incl. audio compact disk *(978-1-58472-431-5(5)*, In Audio) Sound Room Pubs., Inc.

Kirby, Stan. Captain Awesome & the Missing Elephants. O'Connor, George, illus. 2014. (Captain Awesome Ser.: 10). (ENG.). 128p. (J). (gr. k-4). 16.99 *(978-1-4424-8995-0(2))*; pap. 5.99 *(978-1-4424-8994-3(4))* Little Simon. (Little Simon).

—Captain Awesome & the Missing Elephants. 2014. (Captain Awesome Ser.: 10). lib. bdg. 16.00 *(978-0-606-35440-0(9))* Turtleback Bks.

Kirkpatrick, Kevin. Francisco's Friends: The Pachyderm Predicamen. 2012. 40p. pap. 24.95 *(978-1-4626-8881-4(0))* America Star Bks.

Knapman, Timothy. Soon. Benson, Patrick, illus. 2015. (ENG.). 33p. (J). (-k). 16.99 *(978-0-7636-7478-6(8))* Candlewick Pr.

Kneisley, Amy. The Gentle Elephant. Tina, Dunnier, illus. 2013. 24p. pap. 8.99 *(978-1-938768-21-7(3))* Gypsy Pubns.

Kockere, Geert De. Willy. Cneut, Carll, illus. 2011. (ENG.). 32p. (YA). (gr. -1-3). 14.00 *(978-0-8028-5395-0(1)*, Eerdmans Bks For Young Readers) Eerdmans, William B. Publishing Co.

Kodiath, Alex. Elephant Escapes to an Island. 2012. 104p. pap. 31.99 *(978-1-4685-8138-6(4))* AuthorHouse.

Koehler, Fred. How to Cheer up Dad. 2014. (ENG.). 32p. (J). (gr. -1-k). 16.99 *(978-0-8037-3922-2(2)*, Dial Bks) Penguin Young Readers Group.

—Super Jumbo. Koehler, Fred, illus. 2016. (ENG., Illus.). 32p. (J). (-k). 16.99 *(978-0-8037-3923-9(0)*, Dial Bks) Penguin Young Readers Group.

Kompelien, Tracy. Elephant Trunks, 1 vol. Nobens, Cheryl A., illus. 2006. (Animal Tales Ser.). (ENG.). 24p. (J). (gr. k-3). lib. bdg. 24.21 *(978-1-59679-935-6(8)*, SandCastle) ABDO Publishing Co.

—Elephant Trunks. Nobens, C. A., illus. 2006. (Fact & Fiction Ser.). 24p. (J). pap. 48.42 *(978-1-59679-936-3(6))* ABDO Publishing Co.

Krosoczka, Jarrett J. Ollie the Purple Elephant. 2011. (ENG.). 40p. (J). (gr. -1-2). 16.99 *(978-0-375-86654-8(X)*, Knopf Bks. for Young Readers) Random Hse. Children's Bks.

Kuenzler, Lou. How the Elephant Got His Trunk. 2015. (Collins Big Cat Ser.). (ENG.). 24p. (J). (gr. 1-1). pap. 6.95 *(978-0-00-759101-5(2))* HarperCollins Pubs. Ltd. GBR. Dist: Independent Pubs. Group.

Laiz, Jana. Elephants of the Tsunami. Cafiero, Tara, illus. 2005. (J). 10.00 *(978-0-9771818-3-4(9))* EarthBound Bks.

Lamb, Jowana. Makhi & the Run Away Elephant. 2012. 28p. pap. 15.99 *(978-1-4771-3820-5(X))* Xlibris Corp.

Lambert, Jonny. Special You. Lambert, Jonny, illus. 2016. (ENG., Illus.). 24p. (J). (gr. -1-1). bds. 9.99 *(978-1-58925-238-7(1))* Tiger Tales.

Larsa, Angela. Norman PhartEphant. 2009. (J). pap. *(978-1-61623-643-4(4))* Independent Pub.

Larson, Angela. Norman PhartEphant: The coloring Book. 2009. pap. *(978-1-61623-787-5(2))* Independent Pub.

Lee, Karen. An Instrument for Eddie. The, Tienny, illus. 2012. 30p. pap. 12.97 *(978-1-61204-302-9(X)*, Strategic Bk. Publishing) Strategic Book Publishing & Rights Agency (SBPRA).

Lee, P. Janet. Ella Elephant: And Her Fear of Mice. 2007. (ENG., Illus.). 36p. (J). per. 15.95 *(978-1-59800-713-8(0))* Outskirts Pr., Inc.

The Legend of the Great Salt Mountain. 2005. (J). pap. *(978-0-9771804-1-7(7))* Terra Tales.

Lemon, Keith. The Beaver & the Elephant. 2016. (Anholt Family Favourites Ser.). (ENG.). 96p. (J). (gr. -1-k). 12.99 *(978-1-4440-1300-9(9))* Orion Publishing Group, Ltd. GBR. Dist: Hachette Bk. Group.

Lester, Helen. Hurty Feelings. Munsinger, Lynn, illus. 2007. (ENG.). 32p. (J). (gr. -1-3). 7.99 *(978-0-618-84062-5(1))* Houghton Mifflin Harcourt Publishing Co.

—Hurty Feelings. Munsinger, Lynn, illus. 2014. (Laugh-Along Lessons Ser.). (ENG.). 32p. (J). (gr. -1-3). 8.99 *(978-0-544-10622-2(9))* Houghton Mifflin Harcourt Publishing Co.

Lewis, Kim. Hooray for Harry. 2006. (Illus.). (J). *(978-1-4156-7111-5(7))* Candlewick Pr.

Lindahl, Inger. Bertil & the Bathroom Elephants. Dyssegaard, Elisabeth Kallick, tr. Lindstrom, Eva, illus. 2003. 28p. (J). 15.00 *(978-91-29-65944-3(2))* R & S Bks. SWE. Dist: Macmillan.

Little Elephant & Friends. (Flocked Soft-to-Touch Board Ser.). 5p. bds. *(978-1-4054-9445-8(X))* Parragon, Inc.

Lobel, Arnold. Tio Elefante. (SPA.). 68p. (J). 9.95 *(978-84-204-3716-3(6))* Santillana USA Publishing Co., Inc.

Lodding, Linda Ravin. Wakey, Wakey, Elephant! Robertson, Michael, illus. 2017. (ENG.). 32p. (J). (gr. -1). 16.95 ***(978-1-4549-1999-5(X))*** Sterling Publishing Co., Inc.

Long, Olivia. The Elephant Who Forgot. Long, Olivia, illus. Date not set. (Kaleidoscope Ser.). (Illus.). 32p. (J). (gr. -1-4). *(978-1-880042-05-2(3))* Shelf-Life Bks.

Louthain, J. A. Ame the Elephant: Terrorized by Evil Mice. Eberbach, Andrea, illus. 2nd ll.t. ed. 2003. 48p. (J). 12.97 *(978-0-9679416-2-2(8)*, 0-9679416-2-8) Alexie Bks.

Lujan, Jorge. Trunk to Trunklet. Sadat, Madana, illus. 2016. (ENG.). 32p. (J). (gr. -1-2). 16.95 *(978-1-59270-194-0(9))* Enchanted Lion Bks., LLC.

Lumley, Brian. The Nonesuch & Others. 2009. (Illus.). 122p. (J). (gr. 4-7). 35.00 *(978-1-59606-210-8(X))* Subterranean Pr.

MacMillan, Ian C. Khala Maninge - the Little Elephant That Cried a Lot: An African Fable. MacMillan, Eric G., illus. 2nd ed. 2003. lib. bdg. 5.00 *(978-0-9729698-0-2(2))* Maninge Mali.

Majumdar, Debu. Viku & the Elephant: A Story from the Forests of India. Wolfe, Lynn, illus. 2011. (ENG.). 54p. (J). pap. 12.99 *(978-0-9832227-0-5(3))* Bo-Tree Hse.

Mantchev, Lisa. Strictly No Elephants. Yoo, Taeeun, illus. 2015. (ENG.). 32p. (J). (gr. -1-3). 17.99 *(978-1-4814-1647-4(2)*, Simon & Schuster Bks. For Young Readers) Simon & Schuster Bks. For Young Readers.

Marinaro, Stacy. Carter Meets Ella the Elephant. 2008. 20p. pap. 10.95 *(978-0-615-20883-1(5))* Marinaro, Stacy.

Marino, Gianna. Meet Me at the Moon. 2012. (ENG.). 32p. (J). (gr. -1-k). 16.99 *(978-0-670-01313-5(7)*, Viking Books for Young Readers) Penguin Young Readers Group.

Marlee. Harry the Elephant & His New Found Friends. 2009. 16p. pap. 9.49 *(978-1-4490-5305-5(X))* AuthorHouse.

Marsh, Laura. Toot's Tour of India. 2009. (Toot & Puddle Ser.). (ENG., Illus.). 24p. (J). (gr. -1-2). lib. bdg. 11.90 *(978-1-4263-0419-4(6)*, National Geographic Children's Bks.) National Geographic Society.

Marsh, Laura F. Big Enough. 2009. (Mama Mirabelle Ser.). (ENG., Illus.). 24p. (J). (gr. -1-2). lib. bdg. 11.90 *(978-1-4263-0433-0(1)*, National Geographic Children's Bks.) National Geographic Society.

—What's in a Tail? 2009. (Mama Mirabelle Ser.). (ENG., Illus.). 24p. (J). (gr. -1-2). pap. 3.99 *(978-1-4263-0430-9(7))*; lib. bdg. 11.90 *(978-1-4263-0431-6(5))* National Geographic Society. (National Geographic Children's Bks.).

Martin, J. P. Uncle. Blake, Quentin, illus. 2017. (ENG.). 176p. (J). (gr. 4-7). pap. 9.99 ***(978-1-68137-185-6(5)**, NYRB Kids)* New York Review of Bks., Inc., The.

Martin, J. P. Uncle Cleans Up. Blake, Quentin, illus. 2008. (ENG.). 184p. (J). (gr. 4-7). 17.95 *(978-1-59017-276-6(0)*, NYR Children's Collection) New York Review of Bks., Inc., The.

Mary, Nanette. Ashby, the Happy Little Elephant. 2007. (Illus.). 40p. (J). per. 12.95 *(978-0-9787112-7-6(0)*, 01002) New World Publishing.

Mayhew, James. Bubble & Squeak. Vulliamy, Clara, illus. 2013. (J). *(978-1-4351-4770-6(7))* Barnes & Noble, Inc.

McCurry, Meryl. Monto. 2009. 28p. pap. 13.99 *(978-1-4490-1403-2(8))* AuthorHouse.

McDonnell, Flora. Splash! 2004. (Illus.). (J). 25p. *(978-1-85269-488-3(2))*; 25p. *(978-1-85269-489-0(0))*; (ENG & BEN., 28p. pap. *(978-1-85269-486-9(6))*; (ENG & URD., 28p. pap. *(978-1-85269-492-0(0))* Mantra Lingua.

—Splash. 2004. (Illus.). 28p. (J). *(978-1-85269-497-5(1))*; (ENG & SPA., *(978-1-85269-498-2(X))*; *(978-1-85269-499-9(8))*; *(978-1-85269-544-6(7))*; *(978-1-85269-546-0(3))*; *(978-1-85269-490-6(4))*; *(978-1-85269-491-3(2))*; *(978-1-85269-493-7(9))*; *(978-1-85269-494-4(7))*; *(978-1-85269-495-1(5))*; *(978-1-85269-496-8(3))*; (ENG & POR., pap. *(978-1-85269-545-3(5))*; (KOR & ENG., pap. *(978-1-85269-547-7(1))* Mantra Lingua.

McDonnell, Flora & Habashi, Azza. Splash. 2004. (Illus.). 28p. (J). *(978-1-85269-485-2(8))* Mantra Lingua.

Mcevoy, Ariane. Little Monkey Learns to Share. 2012. 28p. pap. 15.99 *(978-1-4691-5830-3(2))* Xlibris Corp.

McGuire, Barry. An Elephant in the Room. 2013. 30p. pap. 8.00 *(978-1-940136-09-7(1))* Vilnius Pr.

McKee, David. Elmer & Butterfly. McKee, David, illus. 2015. (ENG., Illus.). 32p. (J). (gr. -1-3). 16.99 *(978-1-4677-6326-4(8))* Lerner Publishing Group.

—Elmer & Grandpa Eldo. McKee, David, illus. 2016. (ENG., Illus.). 32p. (J). (gr. -1-3). 17.99 *(978-1-5124-0509-9(8))* Lerner Publishing Group.

—Elmer & Rose. McKee, David, illus. 2010. (ENG., Illus.). 32p. (J). (gr. -1-3). 16.95 *(978-0-7613-5493-2(X))* Lerner Publishing Group.

—Elmer & Snake. McKee, David, illus. 2013. (ENG., Illus.). 32p. (J). (gr. -1-3). 16.95 *(978-1-4677-2033-5(X))* Lerner Publishing Group.

Mckee, David. Elmer & Super El. McKee, David, illus. 2012. (Andersen Press Picture Bks). (ENG.). 32p. (J). (gr. -1-3). 16.95 *(978-0-7613-8989-7(X))* Lerner Publishing Group.

McKee, David. Elmer & the Big Bird. McKee, David, illus. 2012. (Andersen Press Picture Bks.). (ENG., Illus.). 32p. (J). (gr. -1-3). 16.95 *(978-1-4677-0319-2(2))* Lerner Publishing Group.

—Elmer & the Flood. McKee, David, illus. 2015. (ENG., Illus.). 32p. (J). (gr. -1-3). 17.99 *(978-1-4677-9314-8(0))*; 17.99 *(978-1-4677-9312-4(4))* Lerner Publishing Group.

—Elmer & the Lost Teddy. McKee, David, illus. 2004. (Elmer Bks.). (Illus.). 32p. (J). 9.99 *(978-0-06-075243-9(2))* HarperCollins Pubs.

—Elmer & the Monster. McKee, David, illus. 2014. (Illus.). 32p. (J). (gr. -1-3). 16.95 *(978-1-4677-4200-9(7))* Lerner Publishing Group.

—Elmer & the Rainbow. McKee, David, illus. 2011. (Andersen Press Picture Bks). (ENG., Illus.). 32p. (J). (gr. -1-3). 16.95 *(978-0-7613-7410-7(8))* Lerner Publishing Group.

—Elmer & the Whales. McKee, David, illus. 2014. (ENG., Illus.). 32p. (J). (gr. -1-3). 16.95 *(978-1-4677-3453-0(5))* Lerner Publishing Group.

—Elmer & Wilbur. McKee, David, illus. 2004. (Elmer Bks.). (Illus.). 32p. (J). 9.99 *(978-0-06-075239-2(4))* HarperCollins Pubs.

—Elmer Board Book. McKee, David, illus. 2014. (Illus.). 32p. (J). (gr. -1 — 1). bds. 7.99 *(978-0-06-232405-4(5)*, HarperFestival) HarperCollins Pubs.

—Elmer in the Snow. McKee, David, illus. 2004. (Elmer Bks.). (Illus.). 32p. (J). 9.99 *(978-0-06-075240-8(8))* HarperCollins Pubs.

—Elmer's Colours. Mo'Allim, Nur M., tr. 2004. (Elmer Ser.). (ENG & SOM., Illus.). 14p. (J). (gr. -1). bds. 8.95 *(978-1-84059-397-6(0))* Milet Publishing.

—Elmer's Day. Mo'Allim, Nur M., tr. 2004. (Elmer Ser.). (ENG & SOM., Illus.). 14p. (J). (gr. -1). bds. 8.95 *(978-1-84059-400-3(4))* Milet Publishing.

—Elmer's Special Day. McKee, David, illus. 2009. (Andersen Press Picture Bks). (ENG., Illus.). 32p. (J). (gr. -1-3). 16.95 *(978-0-7613-5154-2(X)*, Carolrhoda Bks.) Lerner Publishing Group.

—Tusk Tusk. McKee, David, illus. 2007. (ENG., Illus.). 32p. (J). (gr. -1-2). pap. 13.99 *(978-1-84270-579-7(2))* Andersen Pr. GBR. Dist: Independent Pubs. Group.

McKee, David, illus. Elmer & Butterfly. 2015. (J). 17.32 *(978-1-4677-6327-1(6))* Lerner Publishing Group.

—Elmer & the Birthday Quake. 2013. (ENG.). 32p. (J). (gr. -1-3). 16.95 *(978-1-4677-1117-3(9))* Lerner Publishing Group.

—Elmer's Christmas. 2011. (Andersen Press Picture Books Ser.). (J). 16.95 *(978-0-7613-8088-7(4))* Andersen Pr. GBR. Dist: Lerner Publishing Group.

McKown, Martha. An Elephant Story for Alex. Pfisterer Clark, Pem, illus. 2009. 24p. pap. 11.99 *(978-1-4389-4435-7(7))* AuthorHouse.

Mcpherson, Missie & O'Neill, Elizabeth. Alfred Visits Alaska. 2006. (Illus.). 24p. (J). pap. 12.00 *(978-0-9771836-3-0(7))* Global Business Information Strategies, Inc.

McPherson, Missie & O'Neill, Elizabeth. Alfred Visits Washington, D. C. 2005. (ENG., Illus.). 24p. (J). (gr. -1-3). pap. 12.00 *(978-0-9771836-1-6(0))* Lipp, G. Douglas & Assocs.

Medina, Sylvia M. & Ballock-Dixon, Saige J. Jade Elephant. Eagle, Joy, illus. 2012. 36p. pap. 11.49 *(978-0-9836602-4-8(7))* Green Kids Club, Inc.

Meintjes, Chris. Angel's Flight. 2009. 156p. 25.99 *(978-1-4269-0843-9(1))*; pap. 15.99 *(978-1-4269-0842-2(3))* Trafford Publishing.

Merrill, Jean. The Elephant Who Liked to Smash Small Cars. Solbert, Ronni, illus. 2015. (ENG.). 40p. (J). (gr. -1-2). 14.95 *(978-1-59017-872-0(6)*, NYR Children's Collection) New York Review of Bks., Inc., The.

Micchelli, Lauren. I Love My Pet Elephant. 2015. (ENG., Illus.). 28p. (J). pap. 14.95 *(978-1-62287-880-2(9))* First Edition Design eBook Publishing.

Michie, Brandon J. Eddie the Elephant: Animal Lessons. 2011. 20p. pap. 10.71 *(978-1-4634-0381-2(X))* AuthorHouse.

Mike. New Pet. Mike, illus. l.t. ed. 2005. (ENG., Illus.). 32p. (J). lib. bdg. 14.95 *(978-0-9658365-8-6(4))* Beetle Bug Bks.

Milgrim, David. Ride, Otto, Ride! Milgrim, David, illus. 2016. (Adventures of Otto Ser.). (ENG., Illus.). 32p. (J). (gr. -1-k). pap. 3.99 *(978-1-4814-6793-3(X)*, Simon Spotlight) Simon Spotlight.

Mills, Joyce C. & Crowley, Richard J. Sammy the Elephant & Mr. Camel: A Story to Help Children Overcome Bedwetting. Pillo, Cary, illus. 2nd ed. 2005. 32p. (J). 14.95 *(978-1-59147-247-6(4))*; pap. 9.95 *(978-1-59147-248-3(2))* American Psychological Assn. (Magination Pr.).

Miramontes, Arturo J. & Miramontes, Arthur J. There's an Elephant in My Bathtub. 2010. 28p. pap. 16.95 *(978-1-4520-7522-8(0))* AuthorHouse.

Mistretta, Jay. Joe E, 1 vol. Gallet, Karl, illus. 2009. 19p. pap. 24.95 *(978-1-60749-850-6(2))* America Star Bks.

Monroe, Chris. Monkey with a Tool Belt & the Maniac Muffins. Monroe, Chris, illus. 2016. (ENG., Illus.). 32p. (J). (gr. -1-2). 17.99 *(978-1-4677-2155-4(7)*, Carolrhoda Bks.) Lerner Publishing Group.

—Monkey with a Tool Belt & the Noisy Problem. Monroe, Chris, illus. 2009. (Carolrhoda Picture Bks.). (ENG., Illus.). 32p. (J). (gr. -1-2). 16.95 *(978-0-8225-9247-1(9))* Lerner Publishing Group.

—Monkey with a Tool Belt & the Seaside Shenanigans. Monroe, Chris, illus. 2011. (Carolrhoda Picture Books Ser.). (ENG., Illus.). 32p. (J). (gr. -1-2). lib. bdg. 16.95 *(978-0-7613-5616-5(9)*, Carolrhoda Bks.) Lerner Publishing Group.

Moody, Cynthia. Dream, the Big Elephant. 2012. 24p. pap. 14.93 *(978-1-4669-2610-3(4))* Trafford Publishing.

Moon, Nicola. Margarine & Marbles. 2005. (Red Go Bananas Ser.). (ENG., Illus.). 48p. (J). (gr. 2-3). *(978-0-7787-2698-2(3))* Crabtree Publishing Co.

Moonbeam: The Little Elephant. 2005. (Illus.). 32p. (J). 16.95 *(978-0-9763596-0-9(X))* BOOKGEMSFORKIDS.

Morpurgo, Michael. An Elephant in the Garden. 2013. (ENG.). 224p. (J). (gr. 5-9). pap. 7.99 *(978-1-250-03414-4(0)*, 9781250034144) Square Fish.

Morris, April. Eldon the Elephant. 2004. (J). lib. bdg. 25.95 *(978-1-893595-49-1(8))* Four Seasons Bks., Inc.

Morrone Pedowitz, Laura. The Elephant Who Couldn't Eat Peanuts. 2009. 24p. pap. 11.49 *(978-1-4389-4760-0(7))* AuthorHouse.

Mueller, Doris. Small One's Adventure. Fulton, Parker, illus. 2004. 32p. (J). (gr. k-5). 16.95 *(978-0-9710278-1-7(1))* All About Kids Publishing.

Mukluks for Annabelle. 2005. 14.95 *(978-0-9673915-0-2(4))* Alaska Zoo, The.

Murphy, Jill. Five Minutes' Peace. Murphy, Jill, illus. 2012. (ENG., Illus.). 24p. (J). (gr. -1 — 1). bds. 7.99 *(978-0-399-25707-0(1)*, G.P. Putnam's Sons Books for Young Readers) Penguin Young Readers Group.

—Mr. Large in Charge. Murphy, Jill, illus. 2007. (ENG., Illus.). 40p. (J). (gr. -1-3). 16.99 *(978-0-7636-3504-6(9))* Candlewick Pr.

Muthu, Antony M. Athim. 2008. 48p. pap. 19.49 *(978-1-4389-3074-9(7))* AuthorHouse.

Nasser, Amal. Falfoul's Trunk. Abul-Maati, Rania, illus. 2016. (Stories & Fables from Around the World Ser.). (ENG.). 24p. (J). (gr. 2-1). lib. bdg. 24.60 *(978-1-4777-5693-5(0)*, Windmill Bks.) Rosen Publishing Group, Inc., The.

Neher, Anna-Luise. A Tale from the Trunk No. 2: With Words! Words! Words! 2009. 56p. pap. 10.82 *(978-1-4251-8284-7(4))* Trafford Publishing.

Neilson, Ginger. Gunter the Underwater Elephant. Neilson, Ginger, illus. 2011. (Illus.). 32p. pap. 15.99 *(978-0-9832740-2-5(9))* 4RV Publishing, LLC.

Nelson, Sean. Bungles Does the Bunny Op. 2012. 36p. pap. 16.95 *(978-1-4575-1106-6(1))* Dog Ear Publishing, LLC.

Nguyen, Llustrated By Luan. Story of an Ant: Ant & an Elephant. 2008. 36p. pap. 16.99 *(978-1-4389-1534-0(9))* AuthorHouse.

Nielson, Ginger. Willow, an Elephant's Tale. Nielson, Ginger, illus. 2012. (Illus.). 32p. pap. 11.65 *(978-0-9852661-1-0(2))* 4RV Publishing, LLC.

Nosy Crow Staff. Get Out of My Bath! Teckentrup, Britta, illus. 2015. (ENG.). 24p. (J). (gr. -1-2). 15.99 *(978-0-7636-8006-0(0)*, Nosy Crow) Candlewick Pr.

Oelschlager, Vanita. Elefante. Blackwood, Kristin, illus. 2011. 20p. (J). (gr. k-k). (SPA.). bds. 6.95 *(978-0-9826366-5-7(2))*; (ENG.). bds. 6.95 *(978-0-9826366-4-0(4))* VanitaBooks.

Okeke, Paulicap Okechukwu. Biribamba the Lonely Elephant. 2011. (Illus.). 28p. pap. 13.50 *(978-1-4634-2992-8(4))* AuthorHouse.

O'Neill, Elizabeth. Alfred Visits Arizona. 2006. (Illus.). 24p. pap. 12.00 *(978-0-9790240-0-9(5))* Global Business Information Strategies, Inc.
—Alfred Visits California. 2006. (Illus.). 24p. (J). (gr. -1-3). pap. 12.00 *(978-0-9771836-9-2(6))* Global Business Information Strategies, Inc.
—Alfred Visits Georgia. 2007. (Illus.). 24p. (gr. -1-3). pap. 12.00 *(978-0-9799121-0-8(5))* Global Business Information Strategies, Inc.
—Alfred Visits Hawaii. 2009. 24p. (J). pap. 12.00 *(978-0-9822288-5-2(6))* Global Business Information Strategies, Inc.
—Alfred Visits Maine. 2008. (Illus.). 24p. (J). pap. 12.00 *(978-0-9799121-3-9(X))* Funny Bone Bks.
—Alfred Visits Massachusetts. 2006. (Illus.). 24p. (J). (gr. -1-3). pap. 12.00 *(978-0-9771836-7-8(X))* Global Business Information Strategies, Inc.
—Alfred Visits Michigan. 2006. (Illus.). 24p. pap. 12.00 *(978-0-9771836-6-1(1))* Global Business Information Strategies, Inc.
—Alfred Visits Minnesota. 2007. (Illus.). 24p. (J). pap. 12.00 *(978-0-9799121-2-2(1))* Global Business Information Strategies, Inc.
—Alfred Visits Missouri. 2008. 24p. (J). pap. 12.00 *(978-0-9799121-4-6(8))* Global Business Information Strategies, Inc.
—Alfred Visits Montana. 2009. 24p. pap. 12.00 *(978-0-9822288-6-9(4))* Global Business Information Strategies, Inc.
—Alfred Visits Nevada. 2007. (ENG., Illus.). 24p. (J). pap. 12.00 *(978-0-9799121-1-5(3))* Global Business Information Strategies, Inc.
—Alfred Visits New Jersey. 2007. 24p. (J). pap. 12.00 *(978-0-9790240-7-8(2))* Global Business Information Strategies, Inc.
Oneill, Elizabeth. Alfred Visits Ohio. 2006. 24p. pap. 12.00 *(978-0-9771836-4-7(5))* Global Business Information Strategies, Inc.
—Alfred Visits Oregon. 2008. 24p. pap. 12.00 *(978-0-9799121-8-4(0))* Global Business Information Strategies, Inc.
O'Neill, Elizabeth. Alfred Visits Rhode Island. 2007. (Illus.). 24p. (J). pap. 12.00 *(978-0-9790240-6-1(4))* Global Business Information Strategies, Inc.
—Alfred Visits Tennessee. 2006. (Illus.). 24p. 12.00 *(978-0-9771836-5-4(3))* Global Business Information Strategies, Inc.
—Alfred Visits Texas. 2007. 24p. (J). pap. 12.00 *(978-0-9790240-9-2(9))* Global Business Information Strategies, Inc.
—Alfred Visits Utah. 2009. 24p. (J). pap. 12.00 *(978-0-9822288-3-8(X))* Global Business Information Strategies, Inc.
Oneill, Elizabeth. Alfred Visits Vermont. 2008. 24p. pap. 12.00 *(978-0-9799121-9-1(9))* Global Business Information Strategies, Inc.
O'Neill, Elizabeth. Alfred Visits Washington State. 2009. 24p. (J). pap. 12.00 *(978-0-9822288-4-5(8))* Global Business Information Strategies, Inc.
Oneill, Elizabeth. Alfred Visits West Virginia. 2009. 24p. (J). pap. 12.00 *(978-0-9822288-2-1(1))* Global Business Information Strategies, Inc.
—Alfred Visits Wyoming. 2008. 24p. (J). pap. 12.00 *(978-0-9822288-1-4(3))* Global Business Information Strategies, Inc.
Opal, Paola. Ollie. 2010. (ENG., Illus.). 24p. (J). (gr. -1 — 1). bds. 7.95 *(978-1-897476-12-3(4))* Simply Read Bks. CAN. Dist: Ingram Publisher Services.
Ormerod, Jan. When an Elephant Comes to School. 2005. (ENG., Illus.). 32p. (J). (gr. -1-1). pap. 8.99 *(978-1-84507-431-9(9)*, Frances Lincoln) Quarto Publishing Group UK GBR. Dist: Hachette Bk. Group.
Owens, Bettina. Athena, Never A Bite. 2010. 32p. 18.99 *(978-1-4520-6381-2(8))* AuthorHouse.
Paradis, Linzy. Fanny's Walk. 2008. 28p. pap. 24.95 *(978-1-60672-714-0(1))* America Star Bks.
Parker, Vic, compiled by. The Blind Men & the Elephant & Other Silly Stories. 2016. (Silly Stories Ser.). (ENG.). 40p. (J). (gr. 2-3). pap. 14.05 *(978-1-4824-4195-6(0))* Stevens, Gareth Publishing LLLP.
Parragon Staff. Dumbo. 2010. (Disney Diecut Classics). 72p. (J). (gr. -1-1). *(978-1-4075-8935-0(0))* Parragon, Inc.
—Dumbo: The Magical Story. 2010. (Disney Padded Magical Storybks.). (Illus.). 32p. (J). (gr. -1-1). *(978-1-4075-8452-2(9))* Parragon, Inc.
Paterson, Andrew Barton 'Banjo'. Three Elephant Power & Other Stories. 2004. reprint ed. pap. 1.99 *(978-1-4192-8979-8(9))*; pap. 15.95 *(978-1-4191-8979-1(4))* Kessinger Publishing, LLC.
Paul & Lady Jan. Mako in My Backyard. Beeson, Jan, illus. 2013. 34p. pap. 12.99 *(978-0-9890482-3-1(3))* Beeson, Jan.
Pavlova, Elena. Adventures at Tall Oaks: New Friends. 2004. (Illus.). 80p. (J). 19.95 *(978-0-9755839-0-6(5))* Read 2 Children.
Pearson, Tracey Campbell. Elephant's Story. Pearson, Tracey Campbell, illus. 2013. (ENG., Illus.). 40p. (J). (gr. -1-3). 17.99 *(978-0-374-39913-9(1)*, 9780374399139, Farrar, Straus & Giroux (BYR)) Farrar, Straus & Giroux.
Peattie, Cindy & Benchmark Education Co. Staff. The Secret Language of Elephants. 2014. (Text Connections Ser.). (J). (gr. 5). *(978-1-4900-1367-1(9))* Benchmark Education Co.
Pedigo, Kim Tran. Having Fun with Kandai the Elephant. 2nd ed. 2013. (Illus.). 34p. pap. 11.95 *(978-0-9885603-1-4(3))* Outrival Publishing.
—Kandai the Elephant Goes Bananas. 2013. 32p. pap. 11.95 *(978-0-9885603-0-7(5))*; 2nd ed. 17.95 *(978-0-9885603-2-1(1))* Outrival Publishing.
Perera, Hilda. Mumu. (SPA.). (YA). (gr. 5-8). 100p. *(978-84-216-2557-6(8)*, BU1696); 64p. 8.76 *(978-84-216-1611-6(0)*, BU4757); 128p. 8.95 *(978-84-216-1207-1(7)*, BU3780) Bruño, Editorial ESP. Dist: Lectorum Pubns., Inc.
Petrlik, Andrea, illus. Shoo, Fly! 2008. (J). *(978-0-545-03046-5(3))* Scholastic, Inc.
Pien, Lark. Mr. Elephanter. Pien, Lark, illus. 2010. (ENG., Illus.). 32p. (J). (gr. k-4). 14.99 *(978-0-7636-4409-3(9))* Candlewick Pr.
Piercy, Jennifer. Ellie's Math Adventure. 2013. 28p. pap. 16.09 *(978-1-4669-1909-9(4))* Trafford Publishing.
Platt, Kin. Big Max & the Mystery of the Missing Giraffe. Cravath, Lynne Avril, illus. 2006. (I Can Read Level 2 Ser.). (ENG.). 64p. (J). (gr. k-3). pap. 3.99 *(978-0-06-009920-6(8))* HarperCollins Pubs.
Polacco, Patricia. Emma Kate. Polacco, Patricia, illus. (ENG., Illus.). (J). (gr. -1-k). 2008. 32p. pap. 6.99 *(978-0-14-241196-4(5)*, Puffin Books) 2005. 40p. 17.99 *(978-0-399-24452-0(2)*, Philomel Bks.) Penguin Young Readers Group.
Porque los elefantes tienen narices Largas: Individual Title Six-Packs. (Literatura 2000 Ser.). (SPA.). (gr. 1-2). 28.00 *(978-0-7635-1073-2(4))* Rigby Education.
Postgate, Oliver. Nogbad & the Elephants. Firmin, Peter, illus. 2017. (Noggin the Nog Ser.: 6). (ENG.). 48p. (J). (gr. 1-4). 8.99 ***(978-1-4052-8142-3(1))*** Egmont Bks., Ltd. GBR. Dist: Independent Pubs. Group.
Price, Reynolds. A Perfect Friend. 2013. (ENG.). (J). pap. 4.99 *(978-0-689-83148-5(X)*, Simon & Schuster/Paula Wiseman Bks.) Simon & Schuster/Paula Wiseman Bks.
Prince, April Jones. Twenty-One Elephants & Still Standing. Roca, François, illus. 2005. (ENG.). 32p. (J). (gr. -1-3). 17.99 *(978-0-618-44887-6(X))* Houghton Mifflin Harcourt Publishing Co.
Probsdorfer, Maria-Antoinette. Elephant World. 2010. 94p. pap. *(978-3-8391-5497-7(9))* Books on Demand GmbH.
Qahhaar El-Amin, Mary M. Baby Ears: The Littlest Elephant. 2010. 37p. (J). pap. 20.95 *(978-1-4327-2369-9(3))* Outskirts Pr., Inc.
Raines, Jennifer. Laughs for Porcupine, 1 vol. 2009. 18p. pap. 24.95 *(978-1-60836-784-9(3))* America Star Bks.
Random House Disney Staff. Dumbo. Disney Storybook Artists Staff, illus. 2004. (Little Golden Book Ser.). (ENG.). 24p. (J). (gr. -1-2). 4.99 *(978-0-7364-2309-0(5)*, Golden/Disney) Random Hse. Children's Bks.
Redbank, Tennant & Jackson, Kathryn. The Saggy Baggy Elephant. DiCicco, Sue & Hathi, Garva, illus. 2016. (Step into Reading Ser.). (ENG.). 32p. (J). (gr. -1-1). pap. 3.99 *(978-0-553-53588-4(9)*, Random Hse. Bks. for Young Readers) Random Hse. Children's Bks.
Redmond, E. S. Felicity Floo Visits the Zoo. Redmond, E. S., illus. 2009. (ENG., Illus.). 32p. (J). (gr. -1-k). 15.99 *(978-0-7636-3444-5(1))* Candlewick Pr.
Regholec, C. A. T. The Elephant That Forgot to Remember. 2012. 28p. pap. 24.95 *(978-1-4626-9060-2(2))* America Star Bks.
Rettore. Elephant & Friends. 2014. (Friends Cloth Bks.). (ENG.). 8p. (J). (gr. -1 — 1). 9.99 *(978-1-4380-0527-0(X))* Barron's Educational Series, Inc.
Rešcek, Sanja, illus. One Elephant Went Out to Play. 2009. (Classic Books with Holes US Soft Cover with CD Ser.). (ENG.). 16p. (J). (gr. -1-1). pap. incl. audio compact disk *(978-1-84643-258-3(8))* Child's Play International Ltd.
—One Elephant Went Out to Play. 2009. (Classic Books with Holes Big Book Ser.). (ENG.). 16p. (J). (gr. -1-1). *(978-1-84643-209-5(X))* Child's Play International Ltd.
Rhine, Linda H. The Ivory Buttons. 2008. 32p. per. 24.95 *(978-1-4241-8949-6(7))* America Star Bks.
—The Ivory Buttons, 1 vol. 2010. 30p. 24.95 *(978-1-4512-1745-2(5))* PublishAmerica, Inc.
Riedl, Sheila. Elijah & the Elephant. 2011. 24p. pap. 15.99 *(978-1-4653-5796-0(3))* Xlibris Corp.
Rigby Education Staff. The Egg Saga. (Sails Literacy Ser.). (Illus.). 16p. (gr. 2-3). 27.00 *(978-0-7635-9935-5(2)*, 699352C99) Rigby Education.
Rigo, L., illus. Little Elephant. 2011. (Look at Me Bks.). 10p. (J). bds. 8.99 *(978-0-7641-6426-2(0))* Barron's Educational Series, Inc.
Rigo, Laura, illus. Little Elephant. 2017. (Mini Look at Me Bks.). (ENG.). 10p. (J). (gr. -1 — 1). bds. 4.99 *(978-0-7641-6879-6(7))* Barron's Educational Series, Inc.
Robinson, Michelle. Elephant's Pyjamas. Fox, Emily, illus. 2016. (ENG.). 32p. (J). 17.99 *(978-0-00-816479-9(7)*, HarperCollins Children's Bks.) HarperCollins Pubs. Ltd. GBR. Dist: HarperCollins Pubs.
Rolt-Wheeler, Francis. TuskHunters. 2006. pap. 31.95 *(978-1-4286-5352-8(X))* Kessinger Publishing, LLC.
Rose, Phyllis & de Brunhoff, Laurent. Babar & the New Baby. 2013. (ENG., Illus.). 22p. (J). (gr. -1 — 1). bds. 7.95 *(978-1-4197-0620-2(9)*, Abrams Appleseed) Abrams, Inc.
—Babar's Lost & Found. 2013. (ENG., Illus.). 22p. (J). (gr. -1 — 1). bds. 7.95 *(978-1-4197-0981-4(X)*, Abrams Appleseed) Abrams, Inc.
Rouse, W. H. D. The Giant Crab & Other Tales from Old Indi. 2011. 90p. 20.95 *(978-1-4638-9898-4(3))* Rodgers, Alan Bks.
Rouse, W. H. D., ed. The Giant Crab & Other Tales from Old Indi. 2011. 90p. pap. 9.95 *(978-1-4638-0139-7(4))* Rodgers, Alan Bks.
Roza, Greg. El Día de San Valentín (Valentines for Vinnie) 2007. (Lecturas del barrio (Neighborhood Readers) Ser.). (SPA.). 12p. 33.50 *(978-1-4042-7301-6(8)*, Rosen Classroom) Rosen Publishing Group, Inc., The.
Rubinger, Ami. I Dream of an Elephant. Rubinger, Ami, illus. 2010. (ENG., Illus.). 28p. (J). (gr. k-k). 13.95 *(978-0-7892-1058-6(4)*, Abbeville Kids) Abbeville Pr., Inc.
Rucker, Mike. Terry & the Elephant. pap. *(978-1-56002-746-1(0))* Univ. Editions.
Ryan, Jone. Sadie the Little Elephant. 2009. 28p. pap. 12.49 *(978-1-4389-1389-6(3))* AuthorHouse.
Ryan, Meg. A Hat for Markie. 2004. 45p. pap. 24.95 *(978-1-4137-2027-3(7))* PublishAmerica, Inc.
Sabatini, Clare Barone. Stevielephant. 2011. 36p. 16.99 *(978-1-4520-6931-9(X))* AuthorHouse.
Safari Press Staff, ed. Book Buddy - Elephant with Story Book. (Illus.). 10p. (J). (gr. -1-3). pap. *(978-1-881469-83-4(2))* Safari, Ltd.
Salerno, Steven. Little Tumbo, 1 vol. 2003. (ENG., Illus.). 32p. (J). 14.95 *(978-0-7614-5136-5(6))* Marshall Cavendish Corp.
Sanguedolce, Patty & Cowne, Chris. In the Belly of an Elephant. 2013. 28p. 19.99 *(978-1-940136-01-1(6))* Vilnius Pr.
Santos, Antonio. El Viaje de Pancho. 2006. (Coleccion Libros para Sonar Ser.). (Illus.). (J). (gr. -1-3). *(978-84-96388-08-6(5))* Kalandraka Editora, S.L.
Sargent, Mandy And Ben. Best Ted & Ben. 2012. (Illus.). 40p. pap. 20.99 *(978-1-4678-8532-4(0))* AuthorHouse.
Scarry, Patsy, et al. Richard Scarry's Best Little Golden Books Ever! Scarry, Richard, illus. 2014. (Little Golden Book Treasury Ser.). (ENG.). 224p. (J). (-k). 12.99 *(978-0-385-37912-0(9)*, Golden Bks.) Random Hse. Children's Bks.
Scarry, Richard. Richard Scarry's Polite Elephant. Scarry, Richard, illus. 2016. (Little Golden Book Ser.). (ENG., Illus.). 24p. (J). (-k). 4.99 *(978-1-101-93090-8(X)*, Golden Bks.) Random Hse. Children's Bks.
Schaefer, Carole Lexa. Monkey & Elephant. Bernstein, Galia, illus. 2013. (Candlewick Sparks Ser.). (ENG.). 48p. (J). (gr. k-4). pap. 3.99 *(978-0-7636-6261-5(5))* Candlewick Pr.
—Monkey & Elephant & a Secret Birthday Surprise. Bernstein, Galia, illus. (Candlewick Sparks Ser.). (ENG.). 48p. (J). (gr. k-4). 2016. pap. 3.99 *(978-0-7636-8744-1(8))* 2015. 14.99 *(978-0-7636-6131-1(7))* Candlewick Pr.
—Monkey & Elephant & the Babysitting Adventure. Bernstein, Galia, illus. 2016. (ENG.). 48p. (J). (gr. k-4). 14.99 *(978-0-7636-6535-7(5))* Candlewick Pr.
—Monkey & Elephant Get Better. Bernstein, Galia, illus. (Candlewick Sparks Ser.). (ENG.). 48p. (J). (gr. k-4). 2014. pap. 3.99 *(978-0-7636-7180-8(0))* 2013. 14.99 *(978-0-7636-4841-1(8))* Candlewick Pr.
—Monkey & Elephant Go Gadding. Bernstein, Galia, illus. 2015. (Candlewick Sparks Ser.). (ENG.). 48p. (J). (gr. k-4). pap. 3.99 *(978-0-7636-8030-5(3))* Candlewick Pr.
Schindel, John. Busy Elephants. Harvey, Martin, photos by. 2011. (Busy Book Ser.). (ENG., Illus.). 20p. (J). (— 1). bds. 6.99 *(978-1-58246-383-4(2)*, Tricycle Pr.) Random Hse. Children's Bks.
Schneider, Josh. The Meanest Birthday Girl. (ENG., Illus.). 48p. (J). (gr. 1-4). 2015. pap. 5.99 *(978-0-544-45597-9(5)*, HMH Books For Young Readers) 2013. 14.99 *(978-0-547-83814-4(X))* Houghton Mifflin Harcourt Publishing Co.
Scotford, Groenewald & Scotford, Tina. The Mighty Elephant in the Land of Kachoo: The Land of Kachoo Series. Groenewald, Frans, illus. 2014. (Land of Kachoo Ser.). (ENG.). 32p. (J). (gr. k-2). pap. 10.95 *(978-1-4314-0759-0(3))* Jacana Media ZAF. Dist: Independent Pubs. Group.
Seuss, Dr. Horton Hears a Who Pop-Up! 2008. (ENG., Illus.). 22p. (J). (gr. k-12). 25.99 *(978-0-375-84194-1(6)*, Robin Corey Bks.) Random Hse. Children's Bks.
—Tonho Choca o Ovo. pap. 23.95 *(978-85-7406-098-9(4))* Schwarcz, Editora Ltda, Companhia das Letrinhas BRA. Dist: Distribooks, Inc.
Shields, Gillian. Elephantantrum! Johnson-Isaacs, Cally, illus. 2013. (ENG.). 32p. (J). (gr. -1-3). 14.99 *(978-1-58925-126-7(1))* Tiger Tales.
Silver Dolphin Staff, creator. Disney Caritas Felices: Dumbo. 2007. (Illus.). 8p. (J). (gr. -1). bds. *(978-970-718-394-0(2)*, Silver Dolphin en Español) Advanced Marketing, S. de R. L. de C. V.
Slack, Michael. Elecopter. Slack, Michael, illus. 2013. (ENG., Illus.). 32p. (J). (gr. -1 — 1). 15.99 *(978-0-8050-9304-9(4)*, 9780805093049, Holt, Henry & Co. Bks. For Young Readers) Holt, Henry & Co.
Slaughter, Charles E. Golden Tusk. Horvath, Ferdinand H., illus. 2011. 180p. 42.95 *(978-1-258-09834-6(2))* Literary Licensing, LLC.
Smith, E. The Adventures of Sir Ambrose Elephant: A Visit to the City. Apa, Ivy Marie, illus. 2012. 19p. pap. 9.95 *(978-1-4691-8378-7(1))* Xlibris Corp.
Smith, Nicole. Allie the Allergic Elephant: A Children's Story of Peanut Allergies. 2006. (J). 14.95 *(978-1-58628-053-6(8))* Allergic Child Publishing Group.
Smith, Roland. Elephant Run. 2009. (ENG.). 336p. (J). (gr. 5-6). pap. 6.99 *(978-1-4231-0401-8(3))* Hyperion Pr.
Snyder, Marilyn. A Second Chance for Tina. Shiffman, Lena, illus. 2003. (Hello Reader! Ser.). (J). *(978-0-439-44154-4(4))* Scholastic, Inc.
Soli, Doris. Jango the Little Dragon: The Wondrous Adventures of Little Dragon. 2011. (Illus.). 36p. pap. 17.07 *(978-1-4567-8487-4(0))* AuthorHouse.
Sosa, Cynthia. Sebastian, the Small Trunk Elephant. 2013. 32p. pap. 13.00 *(978-1-62516-622-7(2)*, Strategic Bk. Publishing) Strategic Book Publishing & Rights Agency (SBPRA).
Soundprints Staff. Pat-a-Cake: And Othe Favorites. 2005. (Meet Mother Goose Ser.). (ENG., Illus.). 36p. (J). 14.95 *(978-1-931465-48-9(7)*, MPD1104) Soundprints.
—Pat-a-Cake: And Other Favorites. 2005. (Meet Mother Goose Ser.). (ENG., Illus.). 36p. (J). 10.95 *(978-1-931465-28-1(2)*, MD1104) Soundprints.
Sparks, David. Flat-Top Sam & the Junkyard Elephant. Sparks, David, illus. 2008. (Illus.). 36p. pap. 12.95 *(978-1-59858-587-2(8))* Dog Ear Publishing, LLC.
Spooner, Joe. The Elephant Walk. McCann, Michelle, ed. Spooner, Joe, illus. 2005. (ENG., Illus.). 36p. (J). (gr. -1-3). 15.00 *(978-0-9745686-3-8(5))* ACS, LLC Amica Creative Services.
St. John, Lauren. The Elephant's Tale. 2011. (ENG.). 240p. (J). (gr. 3-7). 6.99 *(978-0-14-241879-6(X)*, Puffin Books) Penguin Young Readers Group.
Stanislaus, Justin. The Purple Elephant in the Room. 2008. 44p. pap. 24.95 *(978-1-60474-707-2(2))* America Star Bks.
Stead, Philip C. Special Delivery. Cordell, Matthew, illus. 2015. (ENG.). 40p. (J). (gr. -1-2). 17.99 *(978-1-59643-931-3(9)*, 9781596439313) Roaring Brook Pr.
Steinkraus, Kyla. Nobody's Watching. Dufalla, Anita, illus. 2012. (ENG.). 24p. (gr. 2-3). pap. 8.95 *(978-1-61810-328-4(8))* Rourke Educational Media.
Stockland, Patricia M. Anthill Home Repair, 1 vol. Haugen, Ryan, illus. 2008. (Safari Friends Ser.). (ENG.). 32p. (gr. -1-3). 28.50 *(978-1-60270-082-6(6)*, Looking Glass Library) ABDO Publishing Co.
—The Big Banana Hunt, 1 vol. Haugen, Ryan, illus. 2008. (Safari Friends Ser.). (ENG.). 32p. (gr. -1-3). 28.50 *(978-1-60270-083-3(4)*, Looking Glass Library) ABDO Publishing Co.
—Clean up the Watering Hole!, 1 vol. Haugen, Ryan, illus. 2008. (Safari Friends Ser.). (ENG.). 32p. (gr. -1-3). 28.50 *(978-1-60270-084-0(2)*, Looking Glass Library) ABDO Publishing Co.
—Peanut Picking, 1 vol. Haugen, Ryan, illus. 2008. (Safari Friends Ser.). (ENG.). 32p. (gr. -1-3). 28.50 *(978-1-60270-085-7(0)*, Looking Glass Library) ABDO Publishing Co.
—Stop the Grassfires!, 1 vol. Haugen, Ryan, illus. 2008. (Safari Friends Ser.). (ENG.). 32p. (gr. -1-3). 28.50 *(978-1-60270-086-4(9)*, Looking Glass Library) ABDO Publishing Co.
—Tiger Toothache, 1 vol. Haugen, Ryan, illus. 2008. (Safari Friends Ser.). (ENG.). 32p. (gr. -1-3). 28.50 *(978-1-60270-087-1(7)*, Looking Glass Library) ABDO Publishing Co.
Stoh, Emily. Roger Meets Sam. Stoh, Judy, illus. 2009. 24p. pap. 9.95 *(978-1-935105-41-1(8))* Avid Readers Publishing Group.
Strady, Sophie. The Memory of an Elephant: An Unforgettable Journey. Martin, Jean-Francois, illus. 2014. (ENG.). 38p. (J). (gr. k-3). 18.99 *(978-1-4521-2903-7(7))* Chronicle Bks. LLC.
Suen, Anastasia. In the Big City. Myer, Ed, illus. 2012. (ENG.). 24p. (gr. k-1). pap. 8.95 *(978-1-61810-302-4(4))* Rourke Educational Media.
Suritsch, Gina. Magical Tales from India: The Secret of the White Elephant & Mukti the Lion Finds Himself. 2013. 44p. pap. 22.99 *(978-1-4828-1435-4(8))* Partridge Pub.
Susan, Paradis. Edna. Susan, Paradis, illus. 2013. (Illus.). 32p. pap. 11.95 *(978-1-60898-153-3(3))* namelos llc.
Teall, Wayne. Bong the Bouncing Elephant & His Fantastic Friends. 2012. (Illus.). 68p. pap. 32.03 *(978-1-4772-2994-1(9))* AuthorHouse.
Teis, Sean P. After the Ark: Eli & Ella the Little Elephants - Children of the King! Boutheyette, Valerie, illus. 2013. 32p. pap. 14.99 *(978-1-937129-84-2(5))* Faithful Life Pubs.
Tierney, Melissa. Elly's True Colors. 2009. 32p. pap. 14.99 *(978-1-4389-3901-8(9))* AuthorHouse.
Townsend, Una Belle. The Great Elephant Escape, 1 vol. Hechter, Janice, illus. 2012. (ENG.). 32p. (J). (gr. k-3). 16.99 *(978-1-4556-1582-7(X))* Pelican Publishing Co., Inc.
Trammell, Menlia Moss. Rob & Rex Prevent a Poaching. 2012. 36p. pap. 16.95 *(978-1-4626-7811-2(4))* America Star Bks.
Tres Elefantes: Big Book. (Pebble Soup Exploraciones Ser.). (SPA.). 16p. (gr. -1-18). 31.00 *(978-0-7578-1676-5(2))* Rigby Education.
Tres Elefantes: Small Book. (Pebble Soup Exploraciones Ser.). (SPA.). 16p. (gr. -1-18). 5.00 *(978-0-7578-1716-8(5))* Rigby Education.
Tresh, Doreene. Elephants, Aren't They Great? 2003. (Illus.). 28p. (J). per. 9.95 *(978-1-59405-028-2(7))* New Age World Publishing.
Turin, Adela. Rosa Caramelo. Bosnia, Nella, illus. (SPA.). 40p. (J). (gr. 2-4). *(978-84-264-3800-3(8))* Editorial Lumen ESP. Dist: Lectorum Pubns., Inc.
Van Dusen, Ross, illus. Lyle Got Stuck in a Tree & Became an Honorary Fireman. 2015. (J). *(978-1-936744-45-9(7)*, Rio Grande Bks.) LPD Pr.
Van Straaten, Harmen. Little trunk Late. 2008. (ENG.). 32p. (J). (gr. 1-7). 12.95 *(978-1-60136-004-5(5))* Audio Holdings, LLC.
VanArsdale, Anthony, illus. The Detour of the Elephants. 2017. (Boxcar Children Great Adventure Ser.: 3). (ENG.). 144p. (J). (gr. 1-5). 6.99 ***(978-0-8075-0685-1(0))***; 12.99 ***(978-0-8075-0684-4(2))*** Whitman, Albert & Co.
Velvin, Ellen. Rataplan. 2004. reprint ed. pap. 20.95 *(978-1-4191-4398-4(0))*; pap. 1.99 *(978-1-4192-4398-1(5))* Kessinger Publishing, LLC.
Vere, Ed. Everyone's Little. 2003. (ENG., Illus.). 12p. (J). bds. 6.95 *(978-0-333-78039-8(6))* Macmillan Pubs., Ltd. GBR. Dist: Trafalgar Square Publishing.
Viagem de Babar. pap. 19.95 *(978-85-85466-78-7(2))* Companhia das Letras BRA. Dist: Distribooks, Inc.
Viswanath, Shobha. An Elephant in My Backyard. Jawa, Sadhvi, illus. 2013. (ENG.). 28p. (J). (gr. -1). 11.95 *(978-81-8190-240-5(8))* Karadi Tales Co. Pvt, Ltd. IND. Dist: Consortium Bk. Sales & Distribution.
Voyager, Beatrice Nambouy. Mama Minko: A Survival Quest. 2010. (Illus.). 28p. pap. 15.49 *(978-1-4490-5797-8(7))* AuthorHouse.
Walsh, Kim Carmen. Safari Finn. 2009. 28p. pap. 12.49 *(978-1-4389-0361-3(8))* AuthorHouse.
Walsh, Maria Elena. Dailan Kifki. Lavandeira, Sandra, illus. 2003. (SPA.). 248p. (YA). (gr. 5-8). 18.95 *(978-950-511-629-4(2))* Alfaguara S.A. de Ediciones ARG. Dist: Santillana USA Publishing Co., Inc.
Walsh, Vivian. June & August. McCauley, Adam, illus. 2009. (ENG.). 32p. (J). (gr. k-2). 16.95 *(978-0-8109-8410-3(5)*, Abrams Bks. for Young Readers) Abrams, Inc.
Watt, Fiona. That's Not My Elephant. Wells, Rachel, illus. 2012. (Touchy-Feely Board Bks). 10p. (J). ring bd. 8.99 *(978-0-7945-3167-6(9)*, Usborne) EDC Publishing.
Wehrmeijer, Annelien. Tariq & Mika. van de Liejgraaf, Deborah, illus. 2015. (My Best Friend & Me Ser.). (ENG.). 10p. (J). (gr. -1-k). bds. 6.99 *(978-0-7641-6764-5(2))* Barron's Educational Series, Inc.
Weinberg, Jennifer Liberts. Fly, Dumbo, Fly! Kurtz, John & Lo Raso, Carlo, illus. 2012. (Step into Reading Ser.). (ENG.). 32p. (J). (gr. -1-1). pap. 3.99 *(978-0-7364-2044-0(4)*, RH/Disney) Random Hse. Children's Bks.
Weiss, Ellen. Babar: Four Stories to Read & Share. Gibert, Jean Claude & Gray, J. M. L., illus. 2006. (J). 9.99 *(978-0-8109-9308-2(2)*, Abrams Bks. for Young Readers) Abrams, Inc.
Western, Colleen. Why Elephants Don't Ride School Buses. 2011. 16p. (gr. 1-2). pap. 10.67 *(978-1-4269-6865-5(5))* Trafford Publishing.
Weston Woods Staff, creator. Seven Blind Mice. 2011. 38.75 *(978-0-439-02777-9(2))* Weston Woods Studios, Inc.
Wiley, Gordon. Through the Eyes of Imagination. 2004. 108p. 22.95 *(978-1-4140-0758-8(2))* AuthorHouse.
Willems, Mo. A Big Guy Took My Ball! Willems, Mo, illus. 2013. (Elephant & Piggie Ser.). (ENG., Illus.). 64p. (J). (gr. 1-3). 9.99 *(978-1-4231-7491-2(7))* Hyperion Bks. for Children.
—Can I Play Too? 2012. (Elephant & Piggie Bks.). (CHI & JPN.). (J). (gr. -1-3). pap. ***(978-986-189-329-7(6))*** Grimm Cultural Ent., Co., Ltd.
—Can I Play Too? Willems, Mo, illus. 2010. (Elephant & Piggie Book Ser.). (ENG., Illus.). 64p. (J). (gr. -1-k). 9.99 *(978-1-4231-1991-3(6))* Hyperion Pr.
—An Elephant & Piggie Biggie! Willems, Mo, illus. 2017. (Elephant & Piggie Book Ser.). (ENG., Illus.). 320p. (J). (gr.

1-3). 16.99 ***(978-1-4847-9967-3(4))*** Hyperion Bks. for Children.

—Elephants Cannot Dance! 2012. (Elephant & Piggie Bks.). (CHI & ENG.). (J). pap. ***(978-986-189-325-9(3))*** Grimm Cultural Ent., Co., Ltd.

—Elephants Cannot Dance! Willems, Mo, illus. 2009. (Elephant & Piggie Book Ser.). (ENG., Illus.). 64p. (J). (gr. -1-k). 9.99 *(978-1-4231-1410-9(8))* Hyperion Pr.

—Elephants Cannot Dance! 2011. (ENG & KOR.). (J). ***(978-89-7184-930-9(4))*** Pu-Reun-Sup Publishing Co., Ltd.

—¡Esperar No Es Fácil! Willems, Mo, illus. 2017. (Elephant & Piggie Book Ser.). (ENG & SPA., Illus.). 64p. (J). (gr. 1-3). 9.99 *(978-1-4847-8698-7(X))* Hyperion Bks. for Children.

—Happy Pig Day! Willems, Mo, illus. 2011. (Elephant & Piggie Book Ser.). (ENG., Illus.). 64p. (J). (gr. -1-k). 9.99 *(978-1-4231-4342-0(6))* Hyperion Pr.

—I Am Going! Willems, Mo, illus. 2010. (Elephant & Piggie Book Ser.). (ENG., Illus.). 64p. (J). (gr. -1-k). 9.99 *(978-1-4231-1990-6(8))* Hyperion Pr.

—I Am Invited to a Party! Willems, Mo, illus. rev. ed. 2007. (Elephant & Piggie Book Ser.). (ENG., Illus.). 64p. (J). (gr. -1-k). 9.99 *(978-1-4231-0687-6(3))* Hyperion Pr.

—I Broke My Trunk! Willems, Mo, illus. 2011. (Elephant & Piggie Book Ser.). (ENG., Illus.). 64p. (J). (gr. -1-k). 9.99 *(978-1-4231-3309-4(9))* Hyperion Pr.

—I Love My New Toy! Willems, Mo, illus. 2008. (Elephant & Piggie Book Ser.). (ENG., Illus.). 64p. (J). (gr. -1-k). 9.99 *(978-1-4231-0961-7(9))* Hyperion Pr.

—I Really Like Slop! Willems, Mo, illus. 2015. (Elephant & Piggie Book Ser.). (ENG., Illus.). 64p. (J). (gr. 1-3). 9.99 *(978-1-4847-2262-6(0))* Hyperion Bks. for Children.

—I Will Surprise My Friend! Willems, Mo, illus. 2008. (Elephant & Piggie Book Ser.). (ENG., Illus.). 64p. (J). (gr. -1-k). 9.99 *(978-1-4231-0962-4(7))* Hyperion Pr.

—I Will Take a Nap! Willems, Mo, illus. 2015. (Elephant & Piggie Ser.). (ENG., Illus.). 64p. (J). (gr. 1-3). 9.99 *(978-1-4847-1630-4(2))* Hyperion Bks. for Children.

—I'm a Frog! Willems, Mo, illus. 2013. (Elephant & Piggie Ser.). (ENG., Illus.). 64p. (J). (gr. 1-3). 9.99 *(978-1-4231-8305-1(3))* Hyperion Pr.

—Let's Go for a Drive! Willems, Mo, illus. 2012. (Elephant & Piggie Book Ser.). (ENG., Illus.). 64p. (J). (gr. -1-k). 9.99 *(978-1-4231-6482-1(2))* Hyperion Pr.

—Listen to My Trumpet! Willems, Mo, illus. 2012. (Elephant & Piggie Book Ser.). (ENG., Illus.). 64p. (J). (gr. -1-k). 9.99 *(978-1-4231-5404-4(5))* Hyperion Pr.

—My Friend Is Sad. Willems, Mo, illus. 2007. (Elephant & Piggie Book Ser.). (ENG., Illus.). 64p. (J). (gr. -1-k). 9.99 *(978-1-4231-0297-7(5))* Hyperion Pr.

—Pigs Make Me Sneeze! Willems, Mo, illus. 2009. (Elephant & Piggie Book Ser.). (ENG., Illus.). 64p. (J). (gr. -1-k). 9.99 *(978-1-4231-1411-6(6))* Hyperion Pr.

—Should I Share My Ice Cream? Willems, Mo, illus. 2011. (Elephant & Piggie Book Ser.). (ENG., Illus.). 64p. (J). (gr. -1-k). 9.99 *(978-1-4231-4343-7(4))* Hyperion Pr.

—The Thank You Book. Willems, Mo, illus. 2016. (Elephant & Piggie Book Ser.). (ENG., Illus.). 64p. (J). (gr. 1-3). 9.99 *(978-1-4231-7828-6(9))* Hyperion Bks. for Children.

—There Is a Bird on Your Head! Willems, Mo, illus. rev. ed. 2007. (Elephant & Piggie Book Ser.). (ENG., Illus.). 64p. (J). (gr. -1-k). 9.99 *(978-1-4231-0686-9(5))* Hyperion Pr.

—¡Tienes un Pájaro en la Cabeza! Willems, Mo, illus. 2017. (Elephant & Piggie Book Ser.). (ENG & SPA., Illus.). 64p. (J). (gr. 1-3). 9.99 *(978-1-4847-8697-0(1))* Hyperion Bks. for Children.

—Today I Will Fly! Willems, Mo, illus. 2007. (Elephant & Piggie Book Ser.). (ENG., Illus.). 64p. (J). (gr. -1-k). 9.99 *(978-1-4231-0295-3(9))* Hyperion Pr.

—Waiting Is Not Easy! Willems, Mo, illus. 2014. (Elephant & Piggie Ser.). (ENG., Illus.). 64p. (J). (gr. 1-3). 9.99 *(978-1-4231-9957-1(X))* Hyperion Bks. for Children.

—Watch Me Throw the Ball! Willems, Mo, illus. 2009. (Elephant & Piggie Book Ser.). (ENG., Illus.). 64p. (J). (gr. -1-k). 9.99 *(978-1-4231-1348-5(9))* Hyperion Pr.

—We Are in a Book! Willems, Mo, illus. 2010. (Elephant & Piggie Book Ser.). (ENG., Illus.). 64p. (J). (gr. -1-k). 9.99 *(978-1-4231-3308-7(0))* Hyperion Pr.

Willems, Mo & Campoy, F. Isabel. ¿Debo Compartir Mi Helado? Willems, Mo, illus. 2015. (Elephant & Piggie Book Ser.). (SPA., Illus.). 64p. (J). (gr. -1-k). 9.99 *(978-1-4847-2291-6(4))* Disney Publishing Worldwide.

—!Estamos en un Libro! Willems, Mo, illus. 2015. (Elephant & Piggie Book Ser.). (SPA., Illus.). 64p. (J). (gr. 1-3). 9.99 *(978-1-4847-2288-6(4))* Hyperion Bks. for Children.

—¡Hoy Volaré! Willems, Mo, illus. 2015. (Elephant & Piggie Book Ser.). (SPA., Illus.). 64p. (J). (gr. 1-3). 9.99 *(978-1-4847-2287-9(6))* Disney Publishing Worldwide.

—¡Un Tipo Grande Se Llevó Mi Pelota! Willems, Mo, illus. 2015. (Elephant & Piggie Book Ser.). (SPA., Illus.). 64p. (J). (gr. 1-3). 9.99 *(978-1-4847-2285-5(X))* Disney Publishing Worldwide.

Willis, Jeanne. Elephants Can't Jump! Reynolds, Adrian, illus. 2015. (J). (ENG.). 32p. (gr. -1-3). 16.99 *(978-1-4677-6316-5(0))*; 17.32 *(978-1-4677-6320-2(9))* Lerner Publishing Group.

—Mammoth Pie. Ross, Tony, illus. 2008. (ENG.). 32p. (J). (gr. -1-k). 19.99 *(978-1-84270-659-6(4))* Andersen Pr. GBR. Dist: Independent Pubs. Group.

Winkler, Henry, et al. How to Hug an Elephant #6. Garrett, Scott, illus. 2015. (Here's Hank Ser.: 6). (ENG.). 128p. (J). (gr. 1-3). bds. 5.99 *(978-0-448-48656-7(3))*; bds. 14.99 *(978-0-448-48657-4(1))* Penguin Young Readers Group. (Grosset & Dunlap).

Winstanley, Liz. The Adventures of Abra & His Magic Carpet. 2012. 32p. pap. 14.97 *(978-1-62212-406-0(5)*, Strategic Bk. Publishing) Strategic Book Publishing & Rights Agency (SBPRA).

Wojtowycz, David, illus. Elephant Joe, Brave Firefighter! 2015. (Step into Reading Ser.). (ENG.). 32p. (J). (gr. -1-1). 12.99 *(978-0-375-97203-4(X)*, Random Hse. Bks. for Young Readers) Random Hse. Children's Bks.

Wolfson, Steve. Elephants at the Airport. Brulot, Heleen, illus. 2013. 32p. pap. 11.95 *(978-0-9798324-5-1(4))* Argami Productions, LLC.

Won, Brian. Hooray for Hat! 2014. (ENG., Illus.). 40p. (J). (gr. -1-3). 16.99 *(978-0-544-15903-7(9)*, HMH Books For Young Readers) Houghton Mifflin Harcourt Publishing Co.

—Hooray for Hat! (Board Book) 2016. (ENG., Illus.). 32p. (J). (— 1). bds. 7.99 *(978-0-544-78988-3(1)*, HMH Books For Young Readers) Houghton Mifflin Harcourt Publishing Co.

Wonder Forge Staff, creator. Horton Hears a Who! - You to the Rescue! Game. 2007. (J). *(978-0-9797123-1-9(9))* Wonder Forge, Inc.

Work, Rhoda O. Mr Dawson Had an Elephant. Maas, Dorothy, illus. 2011. 128p. 40.95 *(978-1-258-07973-4(9))* Literary Licensing, LLC.

Wu, Mike. Ellie. Wu, Mike, illus. 2015. (ENG., Illus.). 40p. (J). (gr. -1-k). 16.99 *(978-1-4847-1239-9(0))* Disney Publishing Worldwide.

—Ellie in Concert. Wu, Mike, illus. 2017. (ENG., Illus.). 40p. (J). (gr. -1-k). 16.99 *(978-1-4847-1238-2(2))* Hyperion Bks. for Children.

Wundram, Bill. Finnius: The Tale of a Lost Little Elephant. Tucker, Eric, illus. 2003. (J). *(978-1-59152-011-5(8)*, Sweetgrass Bks.) Farcountry Pr.

Yamada, Rikako. The Unordinary Elephant. States, Anna, illus. 2005.Tr. of Chiisana mimi no Kozou. (JPN.). 26p. (J). per. 14.99 *(978-0-9761606-0-1(9))* WonderToast.

Yoon, Salina. Where's Ellie? 2012. (ENG., Illus.). 18p. (J). (gr. k — 1). bds. 6.99 *(978-0-307-97806-6(0)*, Random Hse. Bks. for Young Readers) Random Hse. Children's Bks.

Youcha, Geraldine. How Does an Elephant Say Hello? Date not set. (J). 15.95 *(978-0-8050-7197-9(0)*, Holt, Henry & Co. Bks. For Young Readers) Holt, Henry & Co.

Young, Ed. Seven Blind Mice. Young, Ed, illus. 2012. (ENG., Illus.). 36p. (J). (gr. -1 — 1). bds. 8.99 *(978-0-399-25742-1(X)*, Philomel Bks.) Penguin Young Readers Group.

—Seven Blind Mice. Young, Ed, illus. 2007. (Illus.). pap. 14.95 incl. audio *(978-0-439-02784-7(5))*; (J). 24.95 incl. audio *(978-0-439-02782-3(9))* Scholastic, Inc.

—Seven Blind Mice. Young, Ed, illus. 2011. (Illus.). 18.95 *(978-0-439-02785-4(3))*; (J). 29.95 *(978-0-439-02783-0(7))* Weston Woods Studios, Inc.

Zaretsky, Evan. Ashley's Elephant: The Pond Hockey Challenge. Spurll, Barbara, illus. 2005. (ENG.). 32p. (gr. k-2). pap. 9.95 *(978-1-57874-095-6(9)*, Kaeden Bks.) Kaeden Corp.

ELEVATORS

Kulling, Monica. Going Up! Elisha Otis's Trip to the Top. Parkins, David, illus. 2014. (Great Idea Ser.). (ENG.). 32p. (J). (gr. k-3). pap. 7.99 *(978-1-77049-516-6(9)*, Tundra Bks.) Tundra Bks. CAN. Dist: Penguin Random Hse. LLC.

Kulling, Monica & Parkins, David. Going Up! Elisha Otis's Trip to the Top. 2012. (Great Idea Ser.). (ENG., Illus.). 32p. (J). (gr. k-3). 17.95 *(978-1-77049-240-0(2)*, Tundra Bks.) Tundra Bks. CAN. Dist: Penguin Random Hse. LLC.

ELIJAH (BIBLICAL PROPHET)

Aderman, James A. Elijah: Fiery Prophet. 2003. (God's People Ser.). pap. 6.99 *(978-0-8100-1339-1(8))* Northwestern Publishing Hse.

Lashbrook, Marilyn. God, Please Send Fire. Sharp, Chris, illus. 2012. 32p. (J). pap. 8.00 *(978-1-935014-42-3(0))* Hutchings, John Pubs.

MacKenzie, Carine. Bible Heroes Elijah. 2005. (Bible Art Ser.). (ENG.). 16p. (J). act. bk. ed. 1.99 *(978-1-84550-089-4(X)*, 7336c626-8c11-4b07-8c54-3f395d9c105e) Christian Focus Pubns. GBR. Dist: Bookmasters Distribution.

—Elijah: God's Miracle Man. 2012. (Bible Wise Ser.). (ENG., Illus.). 32p. (J). (gr. -1-3). pap. 3.99 *(978-1-85792-097-0(X)*, 9781857920970) Christian Focus Pubns. GBR. Dist: Bookmasters Distribution.

Miles, David, illus. Elijah, God's Mighty Prophet, 1 vol. 2016. (I Can Read! / Adventure Bible Ser.). (ENG.). 32p. (J). pap. 3.99 *(978-0-310-75081-9(4))* Zonderkidz.

ELIOT, GEORGE, 1819-1880

Findlay, Clare, ed. Silas Marner. 2003. (ENG., Illus.). 96p. pap. 15.00 *(978-0-582-77271-7(0))* Pearson Education, Ltd. GBR. Dist: Trans-Atlantic Pubns., Inc.

ELIOT, T. S. (THOMAS STEARNS), 1888-1965

Pasachoff, Naomi. Reading & Interpreting the Works of T. S. Eliot. 2016. (Lit Crit Guides). 176p. (J). lib. bdg. 39.93 *(978-0-7660-8356-1(X))* Enslow Pubs., Inc.

Pasachoff, Naomi E. A Student's Guide to T. S. Eliot. 2008. (Understanding Literature Ser.). (Illus.). 160p. (YA). (gr. 9-12). lib. bdg. 29.27 *(978-0-7660-2881-4(X))* Enslow Pubs., Inc.

ELIZABETH I, QUEEN OF ENGLAND, 1533-1603

Adams, Simon. Elizabeth I: The Outcast Who Became England's Queen. (National Geographic World History Biographies Ser.). (ENG., Illus.). 64p. (J). (gr. 3-7). 2008. pap. 7.99 *(978-1-4263-0172-8(3))* 2005. 17.95 *(978-0-7922-3649-8(1))* 2005. lib. bdg. 27.90 *(978-0-7922-3654-2(8))* National Geographic Society. (National Geographic Children's Bks.).

Bailey Publishing Staff & Elgin, Kathy. Elizabethan England. 2009. (Costume Source Bks). (Illus.). 64p. (gr. 6-12). 35.00 *(978-1-60413-379-0(1)*, Chelsea Hse.) Facts On File, Inc.

Courtauld, Sarah. The Queen's Pirate - Francis Drake. Dutrait, Vincent, illus. 2008. (Usborne Young Reading: Series Three Ser.). 64p. (J). 8.99 *(978-0-7945-2048-9(0)*, Usborne) EDC Publishing.

Crompton, Samuel Willard. Queen Elizabeth: And England's Golden Age. 2005. (Makers of the Middle Ages & Renaissance Ser.). (Illus.). 160p. (J). (gr. 5-8). lib. bdg. 32.95 *(978-0-7910-8632-2(1)*, Chelsea Hse.) Facts On File, Inc.

Eding, June. Who Was Queen Elizabeth? Harrison, Nancy & Harrison, illus. 2008. (Who Was? Ser.). (ENG.). 112p. (J). (gr. 3-7). pap. 5.99 *(978-0-448-44839-8(4)*, Grosset & Dunlap) Penguin Young Readers Group.

Guy, John. Elizabeth: The Forgotten Years. 2004. (Illus.). 32p. (J). (gr. 4-7). pap. 5.95 *(978-1-86007-029-7(9)*, TickTock Books) Octopus Publishing Group GBR. Dist: Independent Pubs. Group.

Hilliam, Paul. Elizabeth I: Queen of England's Golden Age. (Rulers, Scholars, & Artists of the Renaissance Ser.). 112p. 2009. (gr. 5-8). 66.50 *(978-1-60852-940-7(1)*, Rosen Reference) 2004. (Illus.). (YA). lib. bdg. 34.60 *(978-1-4042-0313-6(3))* Rosen Publishing Group, Inc., The.

Hinds, Kathryn. Elizabeth & Her Court. 2007. (Life in Elizabethan England Ser.). (Illus.). 80p. (J). (gr. 4-7). lib. bdg. 34.21 *(978-0-7614-2542-7(X)*, Benchmark Bks.) Marshall Cavendish Corp.

Hollander, Barbara Gottfried. Elizabeth I: Queen of England. 2017. (Women Who Changed History Ser.). 48p. (gr. 10-12). lib. bdg. 26.85 ***(978-1-68048-643-8(8)***, Britannica Educational Publishing) Rosen Publishing Group, Inc., The.

Hollihan, Kerrie Logan. Elizabeth I, the People's Queen: Her Life & Times, 21 Activities. 2011. (For Kids Ser.). (ENG., Illus.). 144p. (J). (gr. 4-18). pap. 16.95 *(978-1-56976-349-0(6))* Chicago Review Pr., Inc.

Newbery, Elizabeth. First Elizabeth. 2003. (ENG., Illus.). 32p. (J). (gr. 2-4). pap. 12.95 *(978-0-948065-46-0(X))* National Maritime Museum GBR. Dist: Independent Pubs. Group.

Olson, Steven P. Sir Walter Raleigh: Explorer for the Court of Queen Elizabeth. 2009. (Library of Explorers & Exploration Ser.). 112p. (gr. 5-8). 66.50 *(978-1-60853-612-2(2)*, Rosen Reference) Rosen Publishing Group, Inc., The.

Pascal, Francine. Principe para Elisabeth. Orig. Title: Princess Elizabeth. (SPA.). 112p. (J). 6.95 *(978-84-272-3591-5(7))* Molino, Editorial ESP. Dist: AIMS International Bks., Inc.

Pratt, Mary K. Elizabeth I: English Renaissance Queen, 1 vol. 2011. (Essential Lives Set 7 Ser.). (ENG., Illus.). 112p. (J). (gr. 6-12). lib. bdg. 35.64 *(978-1-61783-003-7(8))* ABDO Publishing Co.

Rasheed, Leila. Collins Big Cat - Sister Queens: The Lives & Reigns of Mary & Elizabeth: Band 15/Emerald. 2015. (Collins Big Cat Ser.). (ENG., Illus.). 48p. (J). (gr. 3-4). pap. 9.95 *(978-0-00-812785-5(9))* HarperCollins Pubs. Ltd. GBR. Dist: Independent Pubs. Group.

Roxburgh, Ellis. Elizabeth I of England vs. Mary, Queen of Scots: Battle for the Throne. 2016. (History's Greatest Rivals Ser.). (ENG., Illus.). 48p. (J). (gr. 6-8). pap. 14.05 *(978-1-4824-4227-4(2))* Stevens, Gareth Publishing LLLP.

Sapet, Kerrily. Elizabeth I of England. 2005. (Illus.). 176p. (J). (gr. 4-7). lib. bdg. 26.95 *(978-1-931798-70-9(2))* Reynolds, Morgan Inc.

Shone, Rob. Elizabeth I: The Life of England's Renaissance Queen. 2009. (Graphic Nonfiction Biographies Ser.). (Illus.). 48p. (YA). (gr. 4-5). 58.50 *(978-1-61513-016-0(0)*, Rosen Reference) Rosen Publishing Group, Inc., The.

Shone, Rob & Ganeri, Anita. Elizabeth I: The Life of England's Renaissance Queen. 2005. (Graphic Nonfiction Biographies Ser.). (Illus.). 48p. (YA). (gr. 4-7). lib. bdg. 31.95 *(978-1-4042-0246-7(3))* Rosen Publishing Group, Inc., The.

Turnbull, Stephanie. Elizabeth I Internet Referenced. King, Colin, illus. 2004. 32p. (J). (gr. 1-18). pap. 4.95 *(978-0-7945-0808-1(1)*, Usborne) EDC Publishing.

White-Thomson, Stephen. Elizabeth I. 2017. (Popcorn: People in History Ser.). (ENG., Illus.). 24p. (J). (gr. k-2). pap. 10.99 *(978-0-7502-8412-7(9)*, Wayland) Hachette Children's Group GBR. Dist: Hachette Bk. Group.

ELIZABETH I, QUEEN OF ENGLAND, 1533-1603—FICTION

Klein, Lisa. Cate of the Lost Colony. 2012. (ENG.). 336p. (YA). (gr. 9-12). pap. 9.99 *(978-1-59990-739-0(9)*, 9781599907390, Bloomsbury USA Childrens) Bloomsbury Publishing USA.

MacDonald, Bailey. Wicked Will: A Mystery of Young William Shakespeare. 2009. (ENG.). 208p. (J). (gr. 4-7). 16.99 *(978-1-4169-8660-7(X)*, Simon & Schuster/Paula Wiseman Bks.) Simon & Schuster/Paula Wiseman Bks.

Maid of Deception. 2014. (Maids of Honor Ser.). (ENG., Illus.). 416p. (YA). (gr. 7). 17.99 *(978-1-4424-4141-5(0)*, Simon & Schuster Bks. For Young Readers) Simon & Schuster Bks. For Young Readers.

Malkus, Alida Sims. The Story of Good Queen Bess. Meadowcroft, Enid Lamonte, ed. Gorsline, Douglas W., illus. 2011. 192p. 42.95 *(978-1-258-09564-2(5))* Literary Licensing, LLC.

McGowan, Jennifer. Maid of Secrets. (Maids of Honor Ser.). (ENG.). (YA). (gr. 7). 2014. 432p. pap. 9.99 *(978-1-4424-4139-2(9))* 2013. 416p. 17.99 *(978-1-4424-4138-5(0))* Simon & Schuster Bks. For Young Readers. (Simon & Schuster Bks. For Young Readers).

—Maid of Wonder. 2015. (Maids of Honor Ser.). (ENG., Illus.). 336p. (YA). (gr. 7). 17.99 *(978-1-4814-1826-3(2))* Simon & Schuster Children's Publishing.

O'Brien, Johnny. Day of Deliverance. Hardcastle, Nick, illus. 2010. (Jack Christie Adventure Ser.: 2). (ENG.). 192p. (J). (gr. 4-7). 15.99 *(978-0-7636-5075-9(7)*, Templar) Candlewick Pr.

Rinaldi, Ann. The Redheaded Princess. 2008. (ENG.). 224p. (J). (gr. 3-7). 15.99 *(978-0-06-073374-2(8))* HarperCollins Pubs.

Thomas, Jane Resh. The Counterfeit Princess. 2005. 197p. (J). *(978-0-618-93780-6(3)*, Clarion Bks.) Houghton Mifflin Harcourt Trade & Reference Pubs.

ELIZABETH II, QUEEN OF GREAT BRITAIN, 1926-

H. M. Queen Elizabeth II: 90th Birthday Celebration. 2016. (ENG., Illus.). 32p. (J). (gr. k-2). 9.99 ***(978-0-241-24032-8(8))*** Penguin Bks., Ltd. GBR. Dist: Independent Pubs. Group.

Malam, John. Queen Elizabeth II: Her Story. 2017. (ENG., Illus.). 24p. (J). (gr. 4-6). pap. 9.99 *(978-0-7502-9878-0(2)*, Wayland) Hachette Children's Group GBR. Dist: Hachette Bk. Group.

Zeiger, Jennifer. Queen Elizabeth II. 2015. (ENG., Illus.). 48p. (J). lib. bdg. *(978-0-531-21599-9(7)*, Orchard Bks.) Scholastic, Inc.

ELK

Gish, Melissa. Elk. 2017. (J). ***(978-1-60818-829-1(9)***, Creative Education) Creative Co., The.

—Living Wild: Elk. 2017. (Living Wild Ser.). (ENG.). 48p. (J). (gr. 5-7). pap. 12.00 ***(978-1-62832-432-7(5)***, Creative Paperbacks) Creative Co., The.

Goecke, Michael P. Irish Elk, 1 vol. 2003. (Prehistoric Animals Set II Ser.). (ENG.). 24p. (gr. k-4). 25.65 *(978-1-57765-975-4(9)*, Buddy Bks.) ABDO Publishing Co.

Jackson, Tom. Elk. 2008. (Nature's Children Ser.). (Illus.). 52p. (J). *(978-0-7172-6223-6(5))* Grolier, Ltd.

Jeffries, Joyce. Elk, 01 vols., 1. 2016. (North America's Biggest Beasts Ser.). (ENG., Illus.). 24p. (J). 23.60 *(978-1-5081-4292-8(0)*, PowerKids Pr.) Rosen Publishing Group, Inc., The.

Love, Donna. The Wild Life of Elk. Wald, Christina, illus. 2011. (J). pap. *(978-0-87842-579-2(9))* Mountain Pr. Publishing Co., Inc.

Macken, JoAnn Early. Elk. 2nd rev. ed. 2009. (Animals That Live in the Mountains Ser.). (ENG.). 24p. (J). (gr. -1-3). pap. 8.15 *(978-1-4339-2495-8(1))*; lib. bdg. 22.60 *(978-1-4339-2412-5(9))* Stevens, Gareth Publishing LLLP. (Weekly Reader Leveled Readers).

—Elk;Venado. 2nd rev. ed. 2009. (Animals That Live in the Mountains/Animales de las montañas Ser.). (ENG & SPA.). 24p. (J). (gr. -1-3). pap. 8.15 *(978-1-4339-2502-3(8))*; lib. bdg. 22.60 *(978-1-4339-2444-6(7))* Stevens, Gareth Publishing LLLP. (Weekly Reader Leveled Readers).

Meinking, Mary. Wolf vs. Elk, 1 vol. 2011. (Predator vs. Prey Ser.). (ENG., Illus.). 32p. (gr. 1-2). pap. 8.29 *(978-1-4109-3950-0(2)*, Read Me!) Heinemann-Raintree.

ELK—FICTION

Clapp. Eloy the Elk & His Desert Friends. Clapp, ed. Drotar, illus. 2009. (J). pap. 9.95 *(978-0-9825181-0-6(2))* Arizona Elk Society.

Dahlstrom, S. J. The Elk Hunt: The Adventure Begins. 2013. (Adventures of Wilder Good Ser.). (ENG., Illus.). 110p. (J). (gr. 3). pap. 8.95 *(978-1-58988-087-0(0))* Dry, Paul Bks., Inc.

ELLINGTON, DUKE, 1899-1974

Bankston, John. The Life & Times of Duke Ellington. 2004. (Masters of Music Ser.). (Illus.). 48p. (gr. 4-8). lib. bdg. 20.95 *(978-1-58415-248-4(6))* Mitchell Lane Pubs., Inc.

Ford, Carin T. Duke Ellington: I Live with Music. 2007. (African-American Biography Library). (Illus.). 128p. (J). (gr. 6-12). lib. bdg. 33.27 *(978-0-7660-2702-2(3))* Enslow Pubs., Inc.

Old, Wendie C. The Life of Duke Ellington: Giant of Jazz. 2014. (Legendary African Americans Ser.). (Illus.). 96p. (J). (gr. 6-12). 27.94 *(978-0-7660-6127-9(2))* Enslow Pubs., Inc.

Pinkney, Andrea Davis. Duke Ellington. Pinkney, Brian, illus. 2006. (ENG.). 32p. (J). (gr. k-4). pap. 6.99 *(978-0-7868-1420-6(9)*, Jump at the Sun) Hyperion Bks. for Children.

Venezia, Mike. Duke Ellington (Revised Edition) 2017. (Getting to Know the World's Greatest Composers Ser.). (ENG.). 40p. (J). pap. 7.95 ***(978-0-531-23036-7(8))***; lib. bdg. 29.00 ***(978-0-531-22658-2(1))*** Scholastic Library Publishing. (Children's Pr.).

Weston Woods Staff, creator. Duke Ellington. 2011. 38.75 *(978-0-545-02759-5(4))*; 18.95 *(978-0-545-02757-1(8))* Weston Woods Studios, Inc.

ELLIS ISLAND IMMIGRATION STATION (N.Y. AND N.J.)

Aloian, Molly. Ellis Island. 2013. (ENG., Illus.). 48p. (J). *(978-0-7787-1168-1(4))*; pap. *(978-0-7787-1176-6(5))* Crabtree Publishing Co.

Arnéz, Lynda. My Journey Through Ellis Island. 2016. (My Place in History Ser.). (ENG., Illus.). 24p. (J). (gr. 2-3). 22.60 *(978-1-4824-4000-3(8))* Stevens, Gareth Publishing LLLP.

DeGezelle, Terri. Ellis Island. 2007. (American Symbols Ser.). (ENG.). 24p. (gr. 1-2). pap. 41.70 *(978-1-4296-1630-0(X)*, First Facts) Capstone Press of Coughlan Cos.

—Ellis Island. 16.30 *(978-1-60686-101-1(8))* Perfection Learning Corp.

Demuth, Patricia Brennan. What Was Ellis Island? McVeigh, Kevin & Groff, David, illus. 2014. (What Was? Ser.). (ENG.). 112p. (J). (gr. 3-7). 5.99 *(978-0-448-47915-6(X)*, Penguin Workshop) Penguin Young Readers Group.

—What Was Ellis Island? 2014. (What Was... ? Ser.). lib. bdg. 16.00 *(978-0-606-34156-1(0)*, Turtleback) Turtleback Bks.

Doherty, Ellen. Ellis Island: Set Of 6. 2011. (Early Connections Ser.). (J). pap. 39.00 net. *(978-1-4108-1546-0(3))* Benchmark Education Co.

Faria, Joseph D. The Statue of Liberty & Ellis Island: A MyReportLinks.com Book. 2005. (Virtual Field Trips Ser.). (Illus.). 48p. (J). (gr. 4-10). lib. bdg. 26.60 *(978-0-7660-5226-0(5)*, MyReportLinks.com Bks.) Enslow Pubs., Inc.

Hicks, Terry Allan. Ellis Island. 2007. (Symbols of America Ser.). (Illus.). 40p. (J). pap. 6.99 *(978-0-7614-3377-4(5)*, Benchmark Bks.) Marshall Cavendish Corp.

Houghton, Gillian. Ellis Island: A Primary Source History of an Immigrant's Arrival in America. (Primary Sources in American History Ser.). 64p. (gr. 5-8). 2009. 58.50 *(978-1-60851-489-2(7))* 2004. (Illus.). (YA). lib. bdg. 31.95 *(978-0-8239-4003-5(9)*, Rosen Reference) Rosen Publishing Group, Inc., The.

Kenney, Karen Latchana. Ellis Island, 1 vol. Hunt, Judith A., illus. 2011. (Our Nation's Pride Set 2 Ser.). (ENG.). 32p. (J). (gr. 1-4). 28.50 *(978-1-61641-150-3(3))* Magic Wagon.

Kroll, Steven. Ellis Island: Doorway to Freedom. 2009. (ENG.). 31p. (J). 18.00 *(978-1-4379-6699-2(3))* DIANE Publishing Co.

Landau, Elaine & National Geographic Learning Staff. Ellis Island. 2012. (ENG., Illus.). 48p. (C). (gr. 3-5). pap. 10.95 *(978-0-531-14781-8(9))* National Geographic School Publishing, Inc.

Marcovitz, Hal. Ellis Island. 2003. (ENG., Illus.). 48p. (YA). pap. 8.95 *(978-1-4222-0975-2(X))* Mason Crest.

McDaniel, Melissa & National Geographic Learning Staff. Ellis Island. 3rd ed. 2011. (ENG., Illus.). 64p. (J). pap. 14.95 *(978-0-531-26556-7(0))* National Geographic School Publishing, Inc.

Mortensen, Lori. Ellis Island, 1 vol. Skeens, Matthew, illus. 2008. (American Symbols Ser.). (ENG.). 24p. (gr. 1-2). 26.65 *(978-1-4048-4705-7(7))* Picture Window Bks.

Peacock, Louise. At Ellis Island: A History in Many Voices. Krudop, Walter Lyon, illus. 2007. (ENG.). 48p. (J). (gr. 2-5). 19.99 *(978-0-689-83026-6(2)*, Atheneum Bks. for Young Readers) Simon & Schuster Children's Publishing.

RJF Publishing Staff & Staton, Hilarie. Ellis Island. 2009. (Symbols of American Freedom Ser.). 48p. (gr. 4-6). 30.00 *(978-1-60413-519-0(0)*, Chelsea Clubhouse) Facts On File, Inc.

Ruffin, Frances E. Ellis Island. 2006. (Places in American History Ser.). (Illus.). 24p. (gr. 1-4). pap. 8.15 *(978-0-8368-6415-1(8))*; lib. bdg. 22.00 *(978-0-8368-6408-3(5))* Stevens, Gareth Publishing LLLP. (Weekly Reader Leveled Readers).

Townsend, Dana E. Ellis Island. (Illus.). 32p. (J). *(978-0-7367-2944-4(5))* Zaner-Bloser, Inc.

Young, Robert. A Personal Tour of Ellis Island. 64p. (J). (gr. 3-6). 6.95 *(978-1-58013-154-4(9))*; 2003. (Illus.). 18.95 *(978-1-58013-079-0(8))* Lerner Publishing Group. (Kar-Ben Publishing).

ELLIS ISLAND IMMIGRATION STATION (N.Y. AND N.J.)—FICTION

Horender, Philip M. A Brave New Mouse: Ellis Island Approved Immigrant, 1 vol. Wolek, Guy, illus. 2013. (Maximilian P. Mouse, Time Traveler Ser.). (ENG.). 112p. (J). (gr. 3-6). lib. bdg. 27.07 *(978-1-61641-961-5(X),* Calico Chapter Bks) Magic Wagon.

Leighton, Maxinne Rhea. An Ellis Island Christmas. Nolan, Dennis, illus. 2005. (ENG.). 32p. (J). (gr. k-3). pap. 6.99 *(978-0-14-240506-2(X),* Puffin Books) Penguin Young Readers Group.

Rhema, Dan. One Tiny Twig, 1. Leonard, Michael, illus. 2003. 32p. (J). per. 19.95 *(978-0-9729835-0-1(3))* Mesquite Tress Pr., LLC.

ELMER (FICTITIOUS CHARACTER: MCKEE)—FICTION

McKee, David. Elmer & Aunt Zelda. McKee, David, illus. 2017. (ENG., Illus.). 32p. (J). (gr. -1-3). 17.99 *(978-1-5124-3945-8(2))* Andersen Pr. GBR. Dist: Lerner Publishing Group.

—Elmer & the Hippos. McKee, David, illus. 2010. (Andersen Press Picture Bks). (ENG., Illus.). 32p. (J). (gr. -1-3). 16.95 *(978-0-7613-6442-9(0))* Lerner Publishing Group.

—Elmer & the Race. McKee, David, illus. 2016. (ENG., Illus.). 32p. (J). (gr. -1-3). 17.99 *(978-1-5124-1624-4(X))* Andersen Pr. GBR. Dist: Lerner Publishing Group.

—Elmer & the Rainbow. 2016. (Elmer Ser.). (ENG., Illus.). 30p. (J). (-k). ring bd. 9.99 *(978-1-78344-424-3(X))* Andersen Pr. GBR. Dist: Independent Pubs. Group.

—Elmer & Wilbur. McKee, David, illus. 2004. (Elmer Bks.). (Illus.). 32p. (J). 9.99 *(978-0-06-075239-2(4))* HarperCollins Pubs.

—Elmer's Colours. Umicini, Roberta, tr. 2004. (Elmer Ser.). (ENG & ITA., Illus.). 14p. (J). (gr. -1). bds. 8.95 *(978-1-84059-396-9(2))* Milet Publishing.

—Elmer's Colours. Al-Hamdi, Ahmed, tr. 2004. (Elmer Ser.). (ARA & ENG., Illus.). 14p. (J). (gr. -1). bds. 8.95 *(978-1-84059-395-2(4))* Milet Publishing.

—Elmer's Colours (English-Polish) 2010. (Elmer Ser.). (POL & ENG., Illus.). 16p. (J). (gr. k — 1). bds. 8.95 *(978-1-84059-531-4(0))* Milet Publishing.

—Elmer's Day. McKee, David, illus. 2014. (Elmer Ser.). (ENG., Illus.). 16p. (J). (-k). 8.99 *(978-0-86264-496-3(8))* Andersen Pr. GBR. Dist: Independent Pubs. Group.

—Elmer's Day. 2010. (Elmer Ser.). (ENG & POL., Illus.). 16p. (J). (gr. k — 1). 8.95 *(978-1-84059-532-1(9))* Milet Publishing.

—Elmer's Day. Umicini, Roberta, tr. 2004. (Elmer Ser.). (ENG & ITA., Illus.). 14p. (J). (gr. -1). bds. 8.95 *(978-1-84059-399-0(7))* Milet Publishing.

—Elmer's Day. Al-Hamdi, Ahmed, tr. 2004. (Elmer Ser.). (ARA & ENG., Illus.). 14p. (J). (gr. -1). bds. 8.95 *(978-1-84059-398-3(9))* Milet Publishing.

—Elmer's Day. Mo'Allim, Nur M., tr. 2004. (Elmer Ser.). (ENG & SOM., Illus.). 14p. (J). (gr. -1). bds. 8.95 *(978-1-84059-400-3(4))* Milet Publishing.

—Elmer's First Counting Book. McKee, David, ed. 2012. (Andersen Press Board Bks). (ENG., Illus.). 10p. (J). (gr. -1-2). bds. 7.95 *(978-0-7613-8999-6(7))* Lerner Publishing Group.

—Elmer's Friends. 2010. (Elmer Ser.).Tr. of Amigos de Elmer. (ENG & POL., Illus.). 16p. (J). (gr. k — 1). 8.95 *(978-1-84059-533-8(7))* Milet Publishing.

—Elmer's Special Day. McKee, David, illus. 2009. (Andersen Press Picture Bks). (ENG., Illus.). 32p. (J). (gr. -1-3). 16.95 *(978-0-7613-5154-2(X),* Carolrhoda Bks.) Lerner Publishing Group.

—Elmer's Weather. 2010. (Elmer Ser.). (ENG & POL., Illus.). 16p. (J). (gr. k — 1). 8.95 *(978-1-84059-534-5(5))* Milet Publishing.

McKee, David & L'Ecole des loisirs/LeapFrog. Elmer. 2008. (J). 20.79 *(978-1-59319-950-0(3))* LeapFrog Enterprises, Inc.

ELMO (FICTITIOUS CHARACTER: HENSON)—FICTION

Albee, Sarah. Elmo Says... Leigh, Tom, illus. 2009. (Big Bird's Favorites Board Bks.). (ENG.). 24p. (J). (gr. k — 1). bds. 4.99 *(978-0-375-84540-6(2),* Random Hse. Bks. for Young Readers) Random Hse. Children's Bks.

—Elmo's Tricky Tongue Twisters. Swanson, Maggie, illus. 2011. (Big Bird's Favorites Board Bks.). (ENG.). 24p. (J). (gr. k — 1). bds. 4.99 *(978-0-375-87249-5(3),* Random Hse. Bks. for Young Readers) Random Hse. Children's Bks.

—Elmo's Tricky Tongue Twisters (Sesame Street) Swanson, Maggie, illus. 2016. (Little Golden Book Ser.). (ENG.). 24p. (J). (gr. -1-k). 4.99 *(978-1-101-93138-7(8),* Golden Bks.) Random Hse. Children's Bks.

Albee, Sarah, et al. Elmo's Little Library (Sesame Street) Swanson, Maggie & Leigh, Tom, illus. 2013. (ENG.). 24p. (J). (— 1). bds. 14.99 *(978-0-449-81740-7(7),* Random Hse. Bks. for Young Readers) Random Hse. Children's Bks.

Alexander, Liza. Splish-Splash Spring! (Sesame Street) Ewers, Joe, illus. 2016. (Pictureback Ser.). (ENG.). 24p. (J). (gr. -1-3). 4.99 *(978-1-101-93429-6(8),* Random Hse. Bks. for Young Readers) Random Hse. Children's Bks.

Allen, Constance. My Name Is Elmo (Sesame Street) Swanson, Maggie, illus. (Little Golden Board Book Ser.). (ENG.). (J). (— 1). 2016. 26p. bds. 7.99 *(978-1-101-93746-4(7))* 2013. 24p. 4.99 *(978-0-449-81066-8(6))* Random Hse. Children's Bks. (Golden Bks.).

—Peekaboo, Elmo! (Sesame Street) Prebenna, David, illus. 2014. (Big Bird's Favorites Board Bks.). (ENG.). 24p. (J). (— 1). bds. 4.99 *(978-0-449-81483-3(1),* Random Hse. Bks. for Young Readers) Random Hse. Children's Bks.

Brannon, Tom, illus. Elmo's Merry Christmas. 2011. (Lift-The-Flap Ser.). (ENG.). 10p. (J). (gr. -1-k). bds. 10.99 *(978-0-7944-2326-1(4),* Reader's Digest Children's Bks.) Studio Fun International.

Flying Frog Pub, creator. ABC Fun with Elmo & Friends. 2011. (Sesame Street (Publications International) Ser.). (ENG., Illus.). 14p. (J). (gr. -1). bds. 3.99 *(978-1-60745-030-6(5))* Flying Frog Publishing.

—Big & Small Fun with Elmo & Friends. 2011. (ENG., Illus.). 14p. (gr. -1-k). bds. 3.99 *(978-1-60745-033-7(X))* Flying Frog Publishing.

—Color Fun with Elmo & Friends. 2011. (ENG., Illus.). 14p. (gr. -1-k). bds. 3.99 *(978-1-60745-031-3(3))* Flying Frog Publishing.

—Counting Fun with Elmo & Friends. 2011. (Sesame Street (Publications International) Ser.). (ENG., Illus.). 14p. (J). (gr. -1). bds. 3.99 *(978-1-60745-032-0(1))* Flying Frog Publishing.

Froeb, Lori C. Elmo's Bedtime Countdown. 2016. (ENG.). 12p. (J). (gr. -1-k). bds. 10.99 *(978-0-7944-3587-5(4),* Reader's Digest Children's Bks.) Studio Fun International.

Furman, Eric. Sesame Street: Elmo (Giant First Play-a-Sound) 2010. 10p. (J). bds. 17.98 *(978-1-60553-546-3(X))* Publications International, Ltd.

Galvin, Laura Gates. My First Pet. Schwaeber, Barbie Heit & Halpenny, Karen, eds. 2008. (ENG., Illus.). 24p. (J). (gr. -1). 4.99 *(978-1-59069-654-5(9))* Studio Mouse LLC.

—My First Trip to the Farm. Rabe, Tish, ed. rev. ed. 2007. (ENG., Illus.). 24p. (J). (gr. -1-3). 5.49 *(978-1-59069-561-6(5))* Studio Mouse LLC.

Kleinberg, Naomi. Elmo's Christmas Snowman (Sesame Street) Brannon, Tom, illus. 2013. (ENG.). 12p. (J). (— 1). bds. 6.99 *(978-0-449-81257-0(X),* Random Hse. Bks. for Young Readers) Random Hse. Children's Bks.

—Elmo's Colors (Sesame Street) 2016. (Pictureback(R) Ser.). (ENG., Illus.). 24p. (J). (gr. -1-2). 4.99 *(978-1-101-93200-1(7),* Random Hse. Bks. for Young Readers) Random Hse. Children's Bks.

—Elmo's Super-Duper Birthday (Sesame Street) Mathieu, Joe, illus. 2016. (Pictureback(R) Ser.). (ENG.). 24p. (J). (gr. -1-2). pap. 5.99 *(978-0-399-55216-8(2),* Random Hse. Bks. for Young Readers) Random Hse. Children's Bks.

—In Elmo's Easter Parade. Moroney, Christopher, illus. 2009. (ENG.). 12p. (J). (gr. k — 1). bds. 4.99 *(978-0-375-84480-5(5),* Random Hse. Bks. for Young Readers) Random Hse. Children's Bks.

Kleinberg, Naomi. Who's Hiding (Sesame Street) 2017. (Pictureback(R) Ser.). (ENG., Illus.). 16p. (J). (gr. -1-2). pap. 5.99 ***(978-1-5247-1634-9(0),*** Random Hse. Bks. for Young Readers) Random Hse. Children's Bks.

Kwiat, Ernie, illus. Sesame Street Boo! Guess Who, Elmo! 2015. (Guess Who! Book Ser.). (ENG.). 10p. (J). (gr. -1-k). bds. 10.99 *(978-0-7944-3475-5(4))* Reader's Digest Assn., Inc., The.

Mitter, Matt. Sesame Street Guess Who, Easter Elmo! Guess Who Easter Elmo! Mathieu, Joe, illus. 2015. (Guess Who Ser.: 6). (ENG.). 10p. (J). (gr. -1-k). 10.99 *(978-0-7944-3331-4(6),* Reader's Digest Children's Bks.) Studio Fun International.

Monica, Carol. Elmo's Easy as 1 2 3. 2006. (Sesame Street Ser.). (ENG., Illus.). 10p. (J). (gr. -1-2). 15.99 *(978-0-7944-1018-6(9))* Reader's Digest Assn., Inc., The.

Monica, Carol & Mathieu, Joe. Elmo's Favorite Places. 2007. (Lift-The-Flap Ser.). (ENG., Illus.). 10p. (J). (gr. -1-k). 11.99 *(978-0-7944-1357-6(9))* Studio Fun International.

Muntean, Michaela. Elmo Can... Taste! Touch! Smell! See! Hear! (Sesame Street) Swanson, Maggie, illus. 2013. (Big Bird's Favorites Board Bks.). (ENG.). 24p. (J). (— 1). bds. 4.99 *(978-0-307-98078-6(2),* Random Hse. Bks. for Young Readers) Random Hse. Children's Bks.

November, Deborah. Elmo's ABC Book. Nicklaus, Carol, illus. 2007. (Big Bird's Favorites Board Bks.). (ENG.). 24p. (J). (gr. k — 1). bds. 4.99 *(978-0-375-84037-1(0),* Random Hse. Bks. for Young Readers) Random Hse. Children's Bks.

November, Deborah, et al. Let's Visit Sesame Street. Mathieu, Joe, illus. 2010. (ENG.). 24p. (J). bds. 14.99 *(978-0-7944-2101-4(6))* Reader's Digest Assn., Inc., The.

Publications International Ltd. Staff. Elmo PNO BK. 2008. 10p. (J). 16.98 *(978-1-4127-8995-0(8))* Phoenix International Publications, Inc.

—Giant Look & Find Elmo. 2008. 24p. (J). 15.98 *(978-1-4127-8975-2(3),* PIL Kids) Publications International, Ltd.

Publications International Ltd. Staff, creator. Hello Elmo! 2007. (Sesame Street Ser.). (Illus.). 10p. (J). (gr. -1-3). bds. 19.98 *(978-1-4127-8724-6(6))* Publications International, Ltd.

Publications International Ltd. Staff, ed. Come along, Sing a Song! 2010. 12p. (J). bds. 12.98 *(978-1-60553-438-1(2),* PIL Kids) Publications International, Ltd.

—Elmo. 2007. (J). 9.98 *(978-1-4127-8301-9(1))* Phoenix International Publications, Inc.

—Elmo Goes to the Doctor. 2010. 14p. (J). bds. 16.98 *(978-1-4127-4609-0(4))* Phoenix International Publications, Inc.

—Elmo's Neighborhood Lights & Music Treasury. 2009. 160p. (J). bds. 17.98 *(978-1-4127-2388-6(4),* PIL Kids) Publications International, Ltd.

—Monsters Can Share. 2010. 20p. bds. 10.98 *(978-1-60553-464-0(1),* PIL Kids) Publications International, Ltd.

—Potty Time with Elmo. 2011. 12p. (J). 4.69 net. *(978-1-4508-1353-2(4),* 1450813534) Phoenix International Publications, Inc.

—Record a Story Elmo'S Bedtime Wish. 2011. 20p. 19.98 *(978-1-4508-1876-6(5))* Phoenix International Publications, Inc.

—Rock & Roll with Elmo. 2010. 24p. (J). bds. 19.98 *(978-1-4127-4475-1(X),* PIL Kids) Publications International, Ltd.

—Sesame St Let's Go to School First Look & Find. 2013. 18p. (J). bds. 7.98 *(978-1-4508-2933-5(3),* 1450829333) Phoenix International Publications, Inc.

—Sesame Street: Elmo's Potty Book (First Look & Find) 2011. 18p. (J). bds. 7.98 *(978-1-60553-840-2(X))* Phoenix International Publications, Inc.

—Sesame Street: Monsters in the Bathroom. 2009. 18p. (J). bds. 10.98 *(978-1-4127-1734-2(5),* PIL Kids) Publications International, Ltd.

—Sesame Street, Ding Dong, Elmo's Here! 2009. 12p. (J). bds. 11.98 *(978-1-4127-9613-2(X))* Phoenix International Publications, Inc.

—Sesame Street(r) Elmo's Valentine. 2013. 12p. (J). bds. 7.98 *(978-1-4508-7410-6(X),* 95d0f5ac-f093-4d77-bf25-5caf2a717091) Phoenix International Publications, Inc.

Random House. Elmo's 123. 2015. (Pictureback(R) Ser.). (ENG., Illus.). 24p. (J). (gr. -1-2). 4.99 *(978-0-553-53679-9(6),* Random Hse. Bks. for Young Readers) Random Hse. Children's Bks.

Reader's Digest Staff. Sesame Street Gift Set. 2012. (ENG.). 22p. (J). 24.98 *(978-0-7944-2679-8(4))* Reader's Digest Assn., Inc., The.

Reader's Digest Staff & Gold, Gina. Night, Night, Elmo! 2013. (Guess Who Ser.). (ENG.). 10p. (J). (gr. -1-k). 10.99 *(978-0-7944-2798-6(7))* Reader's Digest Assn., Inc., The.

Sesame Street Staff. Sesame Street Count with Elmo! A Look, Lift, & Learn Book. 2013. (Look, Lift & Learn Bks.: 1). (ENG.). 10p. (J). (gr. -1-k). 10.99 *(978-0-7944-2861-7(4))* Reader's Digest Assn., Inc., The.

—Sesame Street Hide & Seek, Elmo! 2014. (ENG.). 12p. (J). (gr. -1-k). bds. 10.99 *(978-0-7944-3037-5(6))* Reader's Digest Assn., Inc., The.

Sesame Street Staff & Studio Mouse Staff. Learning Fun. 2008. (ENG.). 60p. (J). 4.99 *(978-1-59069-671-2(9))* Studio Mouse LLC.

Sesame Workshop. Just One You! 2015. (Sesame Street Scribbles Elmo Ser.: 0). (ENG.). 32p. (J). (-3). 10.99 *(978-1-4022-9735-9(1),* Sourcebooks Jabberwocky) Sourcebooks, Inc.

—Off to School! 2015. (Sesame Street Scribbles Elmo Ser.: 0). (ENG.). 32p. (J). (-3). 10.99 *(978-1-4022-9745-8(9),* Sourcebooks Jabberwocky) Sourcebooks, Inc.

Sesame Workshop Staff. Let's Make a Friend! 2016. (Sesame Street Scribbles Ser.: 0). (ENG., Illus.). 32p. (J). (-2). 10.99 *(978-1-4926-4139-1(1),* 9781492641391, Sourcebooks Jabberwocky) Sourcebooks, Inc.

Shepherd, Jodie. Sesame Street Elmo Goes to School. Moroney, Christopher, illus. 2012. (Lift-The-Flap Ser.: 1). (ENG.). 10p. (J). (gr. -1-k). bds. 10.99 *(978-0-7944-2585-2(2),* Reader's Digest Children's Bks.) Studio Fun International.

Stone, Jon. Another Monster at the End of This Book (Sesame Street) Smollin, Michael, illus. 2016. (Little Golden Board Book Ser.). (ENG.). 26p. (J). (-k). bds. 7.99 *(978-1-101-93137-0(X),* Golden Bks.) Random Hse. Children's Bks.

Studio Mouse Staff. Sesame Street My First Instrument. 2008. (ENG.). 24p. (J). (gr. -1). 4.99 *(978-1-59069-737-5(5))* Studio Mouse LLC.

—Sesame Street Share & Care, It's Only Fair. 2009. (ENG.). 60p. (J). (gr. -1). 12.99 *(978-1-59069-739-9(1))* Studio Mouse LLC.

Tabby, Abigail. Hokey Pokey Elmo (Sesame Street) Brannon, Tom, illus. 2016. (Little Golden Book Ser.). (ENG.). 24p. (J). (-k). 4.99 *(978-1-101-93725-9(4),* Golden Bks.) Random Hse. Children's Bks.

Twin Sister Produtions. Sesame Street What Did Elmo Say? 2008. (ENG.). 20p. (J). (gr. -1-3). 9.99 *(978-1-59069-657-6(3))* Studio Mouse LLC.

Twin Sister Produtions & Galvin, Laura Gates. Sesame Street What Did Elmo Say? 2010. (J). (gr. k-2). 14.99 *(978-1-59922-633-0(2))* Twin Sisters IP, LLC.

Twin Sister Produtions Staff & Galvin, Laura Gates. Sesame Street What Did Elmo Say? 2010. (J). (gr. k-2). 14.99 *(978-1-59922-524-1(7))* Twin Sisters IP, LLC.

Wax, Wendy & Kwiat, Ernie. Guess Who, Elmo! 2007. (Guess Who Ser.). (ENG., Illus.). 10p. (J). (gr. -1-k). bds. 10.99 *(978-0-7944-1211-1(4),* Reader's Digest Children's Bks.) Studio Fun International.

ELOCUTION

see Public Speaking

ELOISE (FICTITIOUS CHARACTER)—FICTION

Cheshire, Marc. Eloise Dresses Up: 50 Reusable Stickers! Hahner, Chris, illus. 2005. (Eloise Ser.). (ENG.). 12p. (J). (gr. -1-1). pap. 6.99 *(978-0-689-87455-0(3),* Little Simon) Little Simon.

—Merry Christmas, Eloise! Bracken, Carolyn, illus. 2006. (Eloise Ser.). (ENG.). 18p. (J). (gr. -1-1). pap. 6.99 *(978-0-689-87155-9(4),* Little Simon) Little Simon.

Fry, Sonali. Eloise Takes a Trip. Bracken, Carolyn, illus. 2007. (Eloise Ser.). (ENG.). 16p. (J). (gr. -1-1). 6.99 *(978-1-4169-3343-4(3),* Little Simon) Little Simon.

Fry, Sonali & Knight, Hilary. Eloise Goes to the Beach. Lyon, Tammie Speer & Lyon, Tammie, illus. 2007. (Eloise Ser.). (ENG.). 12p. (J). (gr. -1-2). 9.99 *(978-1-4169-3344-1(1),* Little Simon) Little Simon.

Knight, Hilary. Eloise Throws a Party! Lyon, Tammie, illus. 2008. (Eloise Ser.). (ENG.). 32p. (J). (gr. -1-1). pap. 3.99 *(978-1-4169-6172-7(0),* Simon Spotlight) Simon Spotlight.

McClatchy, Lisa. Eloise's Mother's Day Surprise. Lyon, Tammie, illus. 2009. (Eloise Ser.). (ENG.). 32p. (J). (gr. -1-1). pap. 3.99 *(978-1-4169-7889-3(5),* Simon Spotlight) Simon Spotlight.

McClatchy, Lisa & Thompson, Kay. Eloise & the Big Parade. Lyon, Tammie, illus. 2007. (Eloise Ser.). (ENG.). 32p. (J). (gr. -1-1). pap. 3.99 *(978-1-4169-3523-0(1),* Simon Spotlight) Simon Spotlight.

—Eloise's Summer Vacation. Lyon, Tammie Speer, illus. 2007. (Eloise Ser.). (ENG.). 32p. (J). (gr. -1-1). pap. 3.99 *(978-0-689-87454-3(5),* Simon Spotlight) Simon Spotlight.

McNamara, Margaret & Thompson, Kay. Eloise Breaks Some Eggs. Lyon, Tammie, illus. 2005. (Eloise Ser.). (ENG.). 32p. (J). (gr. -1-1). pap. 3.99 *(978-0-689-87368-3(9),* Simon Spotlight) Simon Spotlight.

—Eloise Has a Lesson. Mitter, Kathryn, illus. 2005. (Eloise Ser.). (ENG.). 32p. (J). (gr. -1-1). pap. 3.99 *(978-0-689-87367-6(0),* Simon Spotlight) Simon Spotlight.

Thompson, Kay. Eloise at the Wedding, Pack. 2012. (Eloise Ser.). (ENG.). 192p. (J). (gr. -1-1). pap. 15.96 *(978-1-4424-4949-7(7),* Simon Spotlight) Simon Spotlight.

—Eloise's What I Absolutely Love Love Love. 2005. (Eloise Ser.). (ENG., Illus.). 32p. (J). 12.99 *(978-0-689-84965-7(6),* Simon & Schuster Bks. For Young Readers) Simon & Schuster Bks. For Young Readers.

Thompson, Kay & Knight, Hilary. Eloise Ready-To-Read Value Pack #2: Eloise Breaks Some Eggs; Eloise & the Dinosaurs; Eloise at the Ball Game; Eloise Has a Lesson; Eloise Skates!; Eloise's New Bonnet. 2013. (Eloise Ser.). (ENG.). 192p. (J). (gr. -1-1). pap. 15.96 *(978-1-4424-9439-8(5),* Simon Spotlight) Simon Spotlight.

Thompson, Kay & McClatchy, Lisa. Eloise Visits the Zoo. Lyon, Tammie, illus. 2009. (Eloise Ser.). (ENG.). 32p. (J). (gr. -1-1). pap. 3.99 *(978-1-4169-8642-3(1),* Simon Spotlight) Simon Spotlight.

ELVES

see Fairies

EMANCIPATION OF SLAVES

see Slavery—United States

EMANCIPATION PROCLAMATION

Armentrout, David & Armentrout, Patricia. The Emancipation Proclamation. 2005. (Documents that Shaped the Nation Ser.). (Illus.). 48p. (gr. 4-6). 20.95 *(978-1-59515-233-6(4))* Rourke Educational Media.

Carey, Charles W., Jr. The Emancipation Proclamation. 2009. (Journey to Freedom Ser.). (ENG., Illus.). 32p. (J). (gr. 4-7). 29.93 *(978-1-60253-137-6(4),* 200403) Child's World, Inc., The.

Gilder Lehrman Institute of American History. Abraham Lincoln & the Emancipation Proclamation. 2nd ed. 2010. (ENG.). pap. 0.00 *(978-1-932821-83-3(X))* Gilder Lehrman Institute of American History, The.

King, Wilma. Children of the Emancipation. 2005. (Picture the American Past Ser.). (Illus.). 48p. (gr. 2-5). 22.60 *(978-1-57505-396-7(9))* Lerner Publishing Group.

Knudsen, Shannon. When Were the First Slaves Set Free During the Civil War? And Other Questions about the Emancipation Proclamation. 2010. (Six Questions of American History Ser.). (ENG.). (gr. 4-6). pap. 56.72 *(978-0-7613-6948-6(1))* Lerner Publishing Group.

—When Were the First Slaves Set Free During the Civil War? And Other Questions about the Emancipation Proclamation. 2010. (Six Questions of American History Ser.). (ENG.). 48p. (gr. 4-6). pap. 9.95 *(978-0-7613-6121-3(9))* Lerner Publishing Group.

Landau, Elaine. The Emancipation Proclamation: Would You Do What Lincoln Did? (What Would You Do? Ser.). (Illus.). 48p. (J). 2010. pap. 8.95 *(978-1-59845-194-8(4))* 2008. (gr. 3-7). lib. bdg. 25.27 *(978-0-7660-2899-9(2))* Enslow Pubs., Inc. (Enslow Elementary).

Prentzas, G. S. The Emancipation Proclamation. 2011. (Cornerstones of Freedom, Third Ser.). (ENG., Illus.). 64p. (J). pap. 8.95 *(978-0-531-26557-4(9),* Children's Pr.) Scholastic Library Publishing.

Sherman, Patrice. Ben & the Emancipation Proclamation. Cooper, Floyd, illus. 2009. (ENG.). 32p. (J). (gr. 3-7). 17.00 *(978-0-8028-5319-6(6),* Eerdmans Bks For Young Readers) Eerdmans, William B. Publishing Co.

Sterling, Dorothy. Forever Free: The Story of the Emancipation Proclamation. Crichlow, Ernest, illus. 2012. 216p. 44.95 *(978-1-258-25034-8(9))*; pap. 29.95 *(978-1-258-25547-3(2))* Literary Licensing, LLC.

Woog, Adam. The Emancipation Proclamation: Ending Slavery in America. 2009. (Milestones in American History Ser.). (Illus.). 128p. (gr. 6-12). 35.00 *(978-1-60413-307-3(4),* Chelsea Hse.) Facts On File, Inc.

EMBLEMS

see Heraldry; Symbolism

EMBROIDERY

see also Beadwork

Buckley, Claire. Start to Embroider. 2009. (Start to Ser.). (ENG., Illus.). 48p. (J). (gr. 4). pap. 10.95 *(978-1-84448-390-7(8))* Stone Ridge Publishing.

Cherry, Winky. My First Embroidery Book: A Name Sampler. 2nd ed. 2011. (My First Sewing Book Kit Ser.). (ENG., Illus.). 40p. (J). (gr. k-3). pap. 16.95 *(978-0-935278-86-6(9))* Palmer-Pletsch Assocs.

Kuskowski, Alex. Cool Embroidery for Kids: A Fun & Creative Introduction to Fiber Art, 1 vol. 2014. (Cool Fiber Art Ser.). (ENG.). 32p. (gr. 8-12). lib. bdg. 28.50 *(978-1-62403-307-0(5),* Checkerboard Library) ABDO Publishing Co.

Marigolds for Dona Remedios, 6 vols. (Multicultural Programs Ser.). 16p. (gr. 1-6). 31.95 *(978-0-7802-8310-7(4))* Wright Group/McGraw-Hill.

Marzollo, Jean. I Spy Little Hearts. Wick, Walter, illus. 2009. (I Spy Ser.). (ENG.). 26p. (J). (gr. -1-k). bds. 6.99 *(978-0-545-08917-3(4),* Cartwheel Bks.) Scholastic, Inc.

Miles, L. Hair Braiding Kid Kit. rev. ed. 2005. 32p. (J). 10.99 *(978-1-58086-858-7(4),* Usborne) EDC Publishing.

Nicholas, Kristin. The Amazing Stitching Handbook for Kids: 17 Embroidery Stitches * 15 Fun & Easy Projects. 2015. (ENG., Illus.). 128p. pap. 16.95 *(978-1-60705-973-8(8),* FunStitch Studio) C & T Publishing.

Sadler, Judy Ann. Embroidery. Bradford, June, illus. 2006. 40p. (J). pap. *(978-0-439-89943-7(5))* Scholastic, Inc.

Switzer, Chris. Projects for Alpaca & Llama. 2004. 16.00 *(978-0-9642663-2-2(6))* Switzer Land Enterprises.

Weller, Alan. Celtic Clip Art for Machine Embroidery. 2010. (Dover Clip Art Embroidery Ser.). (ENG., Illus.). 112p. pap. 24.95 incl. cd-rom *(978-0-486-99111-5(3))* Dover Pubns., Inc.

—Chinese Butterfly Clip Art for Machine Embroidery. 2010. (Dover Clip Art Embroidery Ser.). (ENG., Illus.). 128p. pap. 24.95 incl. cd-rom *(978-0-486-99112-2(1))* Dover Pubns., Inc.

EMBRYOLOGY

see also Cells; Reproduction

Aston, Dianna Hutts. An Egg Is Quiet. Long, Sylvia, illus. 2006. (J). 16.95 *(978-0-8118-5554-9(6))* Chronicle Bks. LLC.

Kalman, Bobbie. La Metamorfosis: Cuerpos Que Cambian. 2006. (Cambios Que Suceden en la Naturaleza Ser.). (SPA., Illus.). 32p. (J). lib. bdg. *(978-0-7787-8373-2(1))*; (gr. 3). pap. *(978-0-7787-8387-9(1))* Crabtree Publishing Co.

Kalman, Bobbie & Sjonger, Rebecca. Metamorphosis: Changing Bodies. 2008. (ENG.). 32p. (J). *(978-0-7787-7714-4(6))*; *(978-0-7787-7713-7(8))* Crabtree Publishing Co.

Monroe, Mary Alice. A Butterfly Called Hope, 1 vol. Bergwerf, Barbara J., illus. 2013. (ENG.). 32p. (J). (gr. -1-4). 17.95 *(978-1-60718-854-4(6))*; pap. 9.95 *(978-1-60718-856-8(2))* Arbordale Publishing.

Rosen, Michael J. Girls vs. Guys: Surprising Differences Between the Sexes. 2014. (Illus.). 72p. (J). (gr. 6-12). lib. bdg. 33.27 *(978-1-4677-1610-9(3),* Twenty-First Century Bks.) Lerner Publishing Group.

West, David & Ganeri, Anita. Werewolves & Other Shape-Shifters. West, David & Ganeri, Anita, illus. 2010. (Dark Side Ser.). (ENG., Illus.). 32p. (J). pap. 10.50 *(978-1-4488-1572-2(X))*; lib. bdg. 26.50

(978-1-61531-900-8(X)) Rosen Publishing Group, Inc., The. (PowerKids Pr.).
Zayamy, Jack. Metamorphosis. (Illus.). 24p. (J). 2017. **(978-1-5105-0929-0(1))** 2016. (978-1-5105-0927-6(5)) SmartBook Media, Inc.
Zerucha, Ted. Human Development. 2009. (Human Body: How It Works Ser.). (Illus.). 160p. (C). (gr. 9-18). 35.00 (978-1-60413-371-4(6), Chelsea Hse.) Facts On File, Inc.

EMERSON, RALPH WALDO, 1803-1882

Bloom, Harold, ed. Emerson's Essays. 2006. (Bloom's Modern Critical Interpretations Ser.). 150p. (C). (gr. 9). lib. bdg. 45.00 (978-0-7910-8118-1(4), Chelsea Hse.) Facts On File, Inc.
Kerley, Barbara. A Home for Mr. Emerson. Fotheringham, Edwin, illus. 2014. (ENG.). 48p. (J). (gr. 3-7). 18.99 (978-0-545-35088-4(3), Scholastic Pr.) Scholastic, Inc.
Keyes, Charlotte E. & Waldo Emerson, Ralph. The Experimenter: A Biography of Ralph Waldo Emerson. 2011. 156p. 41.95 (978-1-258-08635-0(2)) Literary Licensing, LLC.
Self Reliance: The Story of Ralph Waldo Emerson. 2011. (World Writers Ser.). lib. bdg. 28.95 (978-1-59935-124-7(2)) Reynolds, Morgan Inc.

EMIGRANTS

see Immigrants

EMIGRATION AND IMMIGRATION

Here are entered works on migration from one country to another. Works on the movement of population within a country for permanent settlements are entered under Migration, internal.
see also Assimilation (Sociology); Human Geography; Immigrants; Refugees
also names of countries with the subdivision Emigration and Immigration; names of countries, cities, etc. with the subdivision Foreign Population; and names of nationalities

Adasiewicz, Sue. Your Papers, Please: Crossing Borders. 2007. (Shockwave: People & Communities Ser.). (ENG., Illus.). 36p. (J). (gr. 3-5). 25.00 (978-0-531-17572-9(3), Children's Pr.) Scholastic Library Publishing.
Aldridge, Rebecca. Italian Americans. 2003. (Immigrants in America Ser.). (Illus.). 112p. (gr. 6-12). 30.00 (978-0-7910-7129-8(4), Chelsea Hse.) Facts On File, Inc.
Allan, Tony. The Irish Famine: The Birth of Irish America. 2003. (Point of Impact Ser.). (Illus.). 32p. (J). (gr. 5-7). per. 7.50 (978-1-4034-4113-3(8)) Heinemann-Raintree.
Allen, Nancy Kelly. My Life As an Immigrant. 2012. (ENG.). 24p. (gr. k-2). pap. 8.95 (978-1-61810-275-1(3)) Rourke Educational Media.
Aloian, Molly. Ellis Island. 2013. (ENG., Illus.). 48p. (J). (978-0-7787-1168-1(4)); pap. (978-0-7787-1176-6(5)) Crabtree Publishing Co.
Baer, M. Teresa. Indianapolis: A City of Immigrants. 2012. (J). pap. (978-0-87195-299-8(8)) Indiana Historical Society.
Balog, Tom. Immigration to North America: Indian Immigrants, Vol. 11. Anderson, Stuart, ed. 2016. (Immigration to North America Ser.: Vol. 11). (ENG., Illus.). 112p. (J). (gr. 7-12). 25.95 (978-1-4222-3687-1(0)) Mason Crest.
Behnke, Alison. Mexicans in America. 2004. (In America Ser.). (ENG., Illus.). 80p. (gr. 5-8). lib. bdg. 27.93 (978-0-8225-3955-1(1)) Lerner Publishing Group.
Benchmark Education Co., LLC. Immigration. 2014. (PRIME Ser.). (J). (gr. 6-8). pap. (978-1-4509-9494-1(6)) Benchmark Education Co.
Benchmark Education Company, LLC Staff. Coming to America: Immigration from 1840 to 1930 Teacher's Guide. 2004. (978-1-4108-2580-3(9)) Benchmark Education Co.
Benoit, Peter. Immigration. 2012. (Cornerstones of Freedom, Third Ser.). (ENG., Illus.). 64p. (J). pap. 8.95 (978-0-531-28157-4(4)); (gr. 4-6). lib. bdg. 30.00 (978-0-531-23057-2(0)) Scholastic Library Publishing. (Children's Pr.).
Blohm, Judith M. & Lapinksy, Terri. Kids Like Me: Voices of the Immigrant Experience. 2006. (ENG., Illus.). 228p. per. 24.95 (978-1-931930-21-5(X)) Brealey, Nicholas Publishing.
Braun, Eric. Colombians in America. 2005. (J). lib. bdg. 27.93 (978-0-8225-2113-6(X), Lerner Pubns.) Lerner Publishing Group.
Bryan, Nichol. Cuban Americans, 1 vol. 2004. (One Nation Set 1 Ser.). (ENG.). 32p. (gr. k-6). 27.07 (978-1-57765-980-8(5), Checkerboard Library) ABDO Publishing Co.
—Italian Americans, 1 vol. 2004. (One Nation Set 1 Ser.). (ENG.). 32p. (gr. k-6). 27.07 (978-1-57765-985-3(6), Checkerboard Library) ABDO Publishing Co.
—Korean Americans, 1 vol. 2004. (One Nation Set 2 Ser.). (ENG.). 32p. (gr. k-6). 27.07 (978-1-59197-530-4(1), Checkerboard Library) ABDO Publishing Co.
—Mexican Americans, 1 vol. 2004. (One Nation Set 1 Ser.). (ENG.). 32p. (gr. k-6). 27.07 (978-1-57765-987-7(2), Checkerboard Library) ABDO Publishing Co.
—Puerto Rican Americans, 1 vol. 2004. (One Nation Set 2 Ser.). (ENG.). 32p. (gr. k-6). 27.07 (978-1-59197-532-8(8), Checkerboard Library) ABDO Publishing Co.
—Russian Americans, 1 vol. 2004. (One Nation Set 2 Ser.). (ENG.). 32p. (gr. k-6). 27.07 (978-1-59197-533-5(6), Checkerboard Library) ABDO Publishing Co.
—Somali Americans, 1 vol. 2004. (One Nation Set 1 Ser.). (ENG.). 32p. (gr. k-6). 27.07 (978-1-57765-989-1(9), Checkerboard Library) ABDO Publishing Co.
Burgan, Michael. Italian Immigrants. 2004. (Immigration to the United States Ser.). (Illus.). 96p. (gr. 4-9). 35.00 (978-0-8160-5681-1(1)) Facts On File, Inc.
Challen, Paul C. Migration in the 21st Century: How Will Globalization & Climate Change Affect Migration & Settlement? 2010. (Investigating Human Migration & Settlement Ser.). (ENG., Illus.). 48p. (J). (gr. 5-8). (978-0-7787-5181-6(3)); pap. (978-0-7787-5196-0(1)) Crabtree Publishing Co.
Christopher, Nick. The Industrial Revolution, Migration, & Immigration, 01 vols., 1. 2016. (Spotlight on Immigration & Migration Ser.). (ENG., Illus.). 24p. (J). pap. 10.00 (978-1-5081-4086-3(3), PowerKids Pr.) Rosen Publishing Group, Inc., The.
Clare, John D. A Nation of Immigrants? 2010. (Illus.). 48p. pap. 48.50 (978-0-340-95772-1(7)) Pearson Education, Ltd. GBR. Dist: Trans-Atlantic Pubns., Inc.
Cohen, Marina. Changing Cultural Landscapes: How Are People & Their Communities Affected by Migration & Settlement? 2010. (Investigating Human Migration & Settlement Ser., Illus.). 48p. (J). (gr. 5-8). (978-0-7787-5178-6(3)); pap. (978-0-7787-5193-9(7)) Crabtree Publishing Co.
Coming to America. (Illus.). (J). (gr. 3-6). 103.50 (978-0-8239-7282-1(8), Reading Power) Rosen Publishing Group, Inc., The.
Cruz, Bárbara C. Triumphs & Struggles for Latino Civil Rights. 2008. (From Many Cultures, One History Ser.). (Illus.). 128p. (J). (gr. 5-18). lib. bdg. 33.27 (978-0-7660-2804-3(6)) Enslow Pubs., Inc.
Demuth, Patricia Brennan. What Was Ellis Island? McVeigh, Kevin & Groff, David, illus. 2014. (What Was? Ser.). (ENG.). 112p. (J). (gr. 3-7). 5.99 (978-0-448-47915-6(X), Penguin Workshop) Penguin Young Readers Group.
DePietro, Frank. Central American Immigrants. 2012. (J). pap. (978-1-4222-2334-5(5)) Mason Crest.
—Central American Immigrants. Limón, José E., ed. 2012. (Hispanic Americans: Major Minority Ser.). 64p. (J). (gr. 4). 22.95 (978-1-4222-2317-8(5)) Mason Crest.
—South American Immigrants. 2013. (Illus.). 64p. (J). pap. (978-1-4222-2346-8(9)) Mason Crest.
—South American Immigrants. Limón, José E., ed. 2012. (Hispanic Americans: Major Minority Ser.). (Illus.). 64p. (J). (gr. 4). 22.95 (978-1-4222-2329-1(9)) Mason Crest.
Doak, Robin Santos. Fighting for American Values: 1941-1985. Overmyer-Velazquez, Mark, ed. 2007. (Latino-American History Ser.). (Illus.). 106p. (YA). (gr. 5-9). lib. bdg. 35.00 (978-0-8160-6444-1(X)) Facts On File, Inc.
Doherty, Ellen. Ellis Island. 2011. (Early Connections Ser.). (J). (978-1-61672-660-7(1)) Benchmark Education Co.
Donovan, Sandra. Iranians in America. 2005. (J). lib. bdg. 27.93 (978-0-8225-2680-3(8), Lerner Pubns.) Lerner Publishing Group.
Everett-Camplin, Helen. Two Worlds Level 4 Intermediate. 2010. (ENG.). 96p. pap. 16.50 (978-84-8323-566-9(8)) Cambridge Univ. Pr.
Flotz, Katherine Haeger. A Pebble in My Shoe: A Memoir. 2004. (Illus.). 185p. lib. bdg. 29.95 (978-0-9657793-2-6(7)) Pannonia Pr.
For Gold & Blood (Chinese) 76p. (YA). (gr. 6-12). pap. 9.95 (978-0-8224-3679-9(5)) Globe Fearon Educational Publishing.
Frank, Sarah. Greeks in America. 2006. (J). lib. bdg. 27.93 (978-0-8225-2686-5(7), Lerner Pubns.) Lerner Publishing Group.
Freedman, Russell. Angel Island: Gateway to Gold Mountain. 2016. (ENG., Illus.). 96p. (J). (gr. 5-7). pap. 10.99 (978-0-544-81089-1(9), HMH Books For Young Readers) Houghton Mifflin Harcourt Publishing Co.
Friedman, Michael. Settlement Houses: Improving the Social Welfare of America's Immigrants. 2009. (Progressive Movement 1900-1920: Efforts to Reform America's New Industrial Society Ser.). 32p. (gr. 3-4). 47.90 (978-1-60854-170-6(3)) Rosen Publishing Group, Inc., The.
Friedman, Michael & Friedman, Brett. Settlement Houses: Improving the Social Welfare of America's Immigrants. 2006. (Progressive Movement, 1900-1920 — Efforts to Reform America's New Industrial Society Ser.). (ENG., Illus.). 32p. (gr. 4-8). pap. 10.00 (978-1-4042-0859-9(3)) Rosen Publishing Group, Inc., The.
Gagne, Tammy. Immigration in the United States. 2013. (My Guide to U.S. Citizenship Ser.). (ENG.). 48p. (J). (gr. 4-6). lib. bdg. 29.95 (978-1-61228-446-0(9)) Mitchell Lane Pubs., Inc.
Gagne, Tammy & Willis, John. Immigration & Settlement. 2017. (J). **(978-1-5105-2179-7(8)**, Berkley) Penguin Publishing Group.
Gaines, Jena. Haitian Immigration. 2003. (Changing Face of North America Ser.). (Illus.). 112p. (J). lib. bdg. (978-1-59084-691-9(5)) Mason Crest.
Gan, Jiao. Immigration to North America: Chinese Immigrants, Vol. 11. Anderson, Stuart, ed. 2016. (Immigration to North America Ser.: Vol. 11). (ENG., Illus.). 112p. (J). (gr. 7-12). 25.95 (978-1-4222-3684-0(6)) Mason Crest.
Goldstein, Margaret J. British in America. 2006. (In America Ser.). (ENG., Illus.). 80p. (gr. 5-8). lib. bdg. 27.93 (978-0-8225-4875-1(5), Lerner Pubns.) Lerner Publishing Group.
Greenhaven Press Staff. Slavery & Human Trafficking. 2016. (Opposing Viewpoints Ser.). (ENG.). 224p. (gr. 10-12). 48.80 (978-0-7377-7530-3(0), Greenhaven Pr., Inc.) Cengage Gale.
Hamilton, Janice. Canadians in America. 2006. (In America Ser.). (ENG., Illus.). 72p. (gr. 5-8). 27.93 (978-0-8225-2681-0(6), Lerner Pubns.) Lerner Publishing Group.
Hasler, Brian. Casper & Catherine Move to America: An Immigrant Family's Adventures, 1849-1850. Gouge, Angela, tr. Gouge, Angela, illus. 2003. 32p. 17.95 (978-0-87195-168-7(1)) Indiana Historical Society.
Haugen, David. The Children of Undocumented Immigrants. Greenhaven Press Editors, ed. 2013. (At Issue Ser.). (ENG.). 128p. (gr. 10-12). 39.40 (978-0-7377-6159-7(8)); pap. 27.80 (978-0-7377-6160-3(1)) Cengage Gale. (Greenhaven Pr., Inc.).
Hazen, Walter A. Immigration. 2004. (Everyday Life Ser.). (Illus.). 96p. pap. 12.95 (978-0-673-58665-0(0)) Good Year Bks.
Hearn, Emily & Milne, Marywinn, eds. Our New Home: Immigrant Children Speak, 1 vol. 2008. (ENG., Illus.). 128p. (J). (gr. 4-8). pap. 13.95 (978-1-897187-32-6(7)) Orca Bk. Pubs. USA.
Hernández, Roger E. Cuban Immigration. 2005. (Changing Face of North America Ser.). (Illus.). 112p. (YA). lib. bdg. 24.95 (978-1-59084-681-0(8)) Mason Crest.
Hernandez, Roger E. Immigration. 2008. (Gallup Major Trends & Events Ser.). (Illus.). 120p. (YA). (gr. 7-18). lib. bdg. 22.95 (978-1-59084-965-1(5)) Mason Crest.
Hirsch, E. D., Jr., ed. Immigration, Level 6. tchr. ed. 9.95 (978-0-7690-5091-1(3)); stu. ed. 49.95 (978-0-7690-2856-9(X)) Pearson Learning.
Hirsch, Rebecca E. Climate Migrants: On the Move in a Warming World. 2016. (ENG., Illus.). 88p. (YA). (gr. 7-12). 35.99 (978-1-4677-9341-4(8)); 53.32 (978-1-5124-1145-4(0)) Lerner Publishing Group. (Twenty-First Century Bks.).
Hodge, Deborah. The Kids Book of Canadian Immigration. Mantha, John, illus. 2006. (Kids Book Of Ser.). (ENG.). 64p. (J). (gr. 3-7). 19.95 (978-1-55337-484-8(3)) Kids Can Pr., Ltd. CAN. Dist: Hachette Bk. Group.
Hoffman, Betty N. Liberation: Stories of Survival from the Holocaust. 2011. (Holocaust Through Primary Sources Ser.). (Illus.). 128p. (J). (gr. 6-18). pap. 10.95 (978-1-59845-348-5(3)); (gr. 9-12). lib. bdg. 33.27 (978-0-7660-3319-1(8)) Enslow Pubs., Inc.
Holtei, Christa & Woofter, Susi. In the New World: A Family in Two Centuries. Raidt, Gerda, illus. 2015. (ENG.). 40p. (J). (gr. k-3). lib. bdg. 17.95 (978-1-58089-630-6(8)) Charlesbridge Publishing, Inc.
Honovich, Nancy. Immigration from the Former Yugoslavia. 2005. (Changing Face of North America Ser.). (Illus.). 112p. (YA). lib. bdg. 24.95 (978-1-59084-690-2(7)) Mason Crest.
Housel, Debra J. Immigration, 1 vol. 2007. (Primary Source Readers Ser.). (ENG.). 32p. (J). (gr. 5-5). pap. 8.99 (978-0-7439-0662-3(4)) Shell Educational Publishing.
Housel, Debra J. & National Geographic Learning Staff. Famous Immigrants. 2012. (ENG., Illus.). 32p. (C). (gr. 4-4). pap. 14.95 (978-0-7439-0663-0(2)) National Geographic School Publishing, Inc.
Howell, Sara. El Camino a la Ciudadania. 2014. (Mosaico Americano: la Inmigración Hoy en día (the American Mosaic: Immigration Today) Ser.). (SPA., Illus.). 24p. (J). (gr. 3-6). pap. 8.25 (978-1-4777-6825-9(4), PowerKids Pr.) Rosen Publishing Group, Inc., The.
—Famous Immigrants & Their Stories. 2014. (American Mosaic: Immigration Today Ser.). 24p. (J). (gr. 3-6). pap. 49.50 (978-1-4777-6652-1(9)) Rosen Publishing Group, Inc., The.
—Los Refugiados. 2014. (Mosaico Americano: la Inmigración Hoy en día (the American Mosaic: Immigration Today) Ser.). (SPA & ENG., Illus.). 24p. (J). (gr. 3-6). pap. 8.25 (978-1-4777-6817-4(3), PowerKids Pr.) Rosen Publishing Group, Inc., The.
—The Path to Citizenship. 2014. (American Mosaic: Immigration Today Ser.). 24p. (J). (gr. 3-6). 23.60 (978-1-4777-6736-8(3)); pap. 49.50 (978-1-4777-6648-4(0)) Rosen Publishing Group, Inc., The. (PowerKids Pr.).
Hunter, Miranda. Latino Americans & Immigration Laws: Crossing the Border. 2007. (Hispanic Heritage Ser.). (Illus.). 112p. (YA). (gr. 4-7). lib. bdg. 22.95 (978-1-59084-939-2(6)) Mason Crest.
Huthmacher, J. Joseph. A Nation of Newcomers. (J). 17.95 (978-0-88411-651-6(4)) Amereon Ltd.
Hyde, Natalie. Immigration. 2015. (ENG.). 48p. (J). (978-0-7787-1550-4(7)) Crabtree Publishing Co.
Immigration & Migration Instructional Guide. 2009. (Grade 8: Social Studies Exit Project Kits Ser.). spiral bd. (978-1-4042-4038-4(1), Rosen Classroom) Rosen Publishing Group, Inc., The.
Ingram, Scott. Greek Immigrants. 2004. (Immigration to the United States Ser.). (Illus.). 96p. (gr. 4-9). 35.00 (978-0-8160-5689-7(7)) Facts On File, Inc.
—Japanese Immigrants. 2004. (Immigration to the United States Ser.). (Illus.). 96p. (gr. 4-9). 35.00 (978-0-8160-5688-0(9)) Facts On File, Inc.
Ingram, Scott & Asher, Robert. Polish Immigrants. 2004. (Immigration to the United States Ser.). (Illus.). 96p. (gr. 4-9). 35.00 (978-0-8160-5686-6(2)) Facts On File, Inc.
Janssen-Mathes, Mieke M. E. Unlocking the Secret of Otherland: A Story & Activity Book for Children Living Abroad. Kwakkenbos, Frans, illus. 2007. 96p. pap. (978-90-6832-587-4(6)) Royal Tropical Institute Pr. (KIT (Koninklijk Instituut voor de Tropen).
Jeffrey, Gary. The Oregon Trail. Poluzzi, Allesandro, illus. 2012. (Graphic History of the American West Ser.). (ENG.). 24p. (J). (gr. 3-8). pap. 8.15 (978-1-4339-6745-0(6), Gareth Stevens Learning Library); (gr. 4-7). lib. bdg. 23.95 (978-1-4339-6743-6(X)) Stevens, Gareth Publishing LLLP.
Kittinger, Jo S., et al. Un Aliento de Esperanza. Galey, Chuck, illus. 2013. (SPA.). (J). (978-1-61438-868-5(7)) American Bar Assn.
Kowalski, Kathiann M. Salvadorans in America. 2005. (In America Ser.). (Illus.). 80p. (J). (gr. 4-7). lib. bdg. 27.93 (978-0-8225-2424-3(4), Lerner Pubns.) Lerner Publishing Group.
Kramer, Nash. Where Did My Grandparents Come From? 2014. (Little Books of Answers: Level C Ser.). (Illus.). 16p. (gr. k-2). pap. 7.95 (978-1-927136-21-8(0)) Three Crows Media NZL. Dist: RiverStream Publishing.
Kroll, Steven. Barbarians! Byrd, Robert, illus. 2009. (ENG.). 48p. (J). (gr. 3-7). 20.99 (978-0-525-47958-1(9), Dutton Books for Young Readers) Penguin Young Readers Group.
Kurelek, William & Engelhart, Margaret S. They Sought a New World: The Story of European Immigration to North America. Kurelek, William, illus. 2005. (Illus.). 48p. (J). (gr. 4-8). reprint ed. 20.00 (978-0-7567-8682-3(7)) DIANE Publishing Co.
Lacivita, Michael J. Rag Man, Rag Man. 2004. (Mahoning Valley Writers Ser.). (Illus.). 262p. (YA). 26.95 (978-0-917530-80-2(2)); pap. 15.95 (978-0-917530-81-4(0)) Pig Iron Pr.
Lansford, Tom. Citizenship & Immigration, Vol. 8. Lansford, Tom, ed. 2016. (Foundations of Democracy Ser.). (Illus.). 64p. (J). (gr. 7). 23.95 (978-1-4222-3626-0(9)) Mason Crest.
Laurel Corona. Jewish Americans. 2004. (Immigrants in America Ser.). (ENG., Illus.). 112p. (J). 30.85 (978-1-59018-431-8(9)) Cengage Gale.
Leavitt, Amie Jane. United States Immigration Services. 2013. (My Guide to U.S. Citizenship Ser.). (ENG.). 48p. (J). (gr. 4-6). lib. bdg. 29.95 (978-1-61228-447-7(7)) Mitchell Lane Pubs., Inc.
Lüsted, Marcia Amidon. What You Need to Know about Your Status As an Immigrant under the Law. 2015. (Know Your Rights Ser.). (ENG., Illus.). 64p. (J). (gr. 6-6). 33.25 (978-1-4777-8102-9(1), Rosen Young Adult) Rosen Publishing Group, Inc., The.
Lusted, Marcia Amidon. Your Legal Rights As an Immigrant. 2015. (Know Your Rights Ser.). (ENG., Illus.). 64p. (J). (gr. 6-6). pap. 12.95 (978-1-4777-8618-5(X), Rosen Young Adult) Rosen Publishing Group, Inc., The.
Marin-Guzman, Roberto & Zéraoui, Zidane. Arab Immigration in Mexico in the Nineteenth & Twentieth Centuries: Assimilation & Arab Heritage. 2003. (Illus.). 208p. per. 18.95 (978-0-9636882-2-4(7)) Augustine Pr.
Martin, Jennifer C. The Korean Americans. 2003. (Immigrants in America Ser.). (ENG., Illus.). 112p. (J). (gr. 4-7). lib. bdg. 30.85 (978-1-59018-079-2(8), Lucent Bks.) Cengage Gale.
Martinez, Luis. Immigration to North America: Central American Immigrants, Vol. 11. Anderson, Stuart, ed. 2016. (Immigration to North America Ser.: Vol. 11). (ENG., Illus.). 112p. (J). (gr. 7-12). 25.95 (978-1-4222-3686-4(2)) Mason Crest.
Mason, Helen. A Refugee's Journey from Afghanistan. 2017. (Leaving My Homeland Ser.). (ENG., Illus.). 32p. (J). **(978-0-7787-3125-2(1))** Crabtree Publishing Co.
—A Refugee's Journey from Syria. 2017. (Leaving My Homeland Ser.). (ENG., Illus.). 32p. (J). **(978-0-7787-3128-3(6))** Crabtree Publishing Co.
Mattern, Joanne. Japanese Americans. 2003. (Immigrants in America Ser.). (Illus.). 112p. (gr. 6-12). 30.00 (978-0-7910-7130-4(8), Chelsea Hse.) Facts On File, Inc.
McCaffrey, Larry. Immigration to North America: South American Immigrants, Vol. 11. Anderson, Stuart, ed. 2016. (Immigration to North America Ser.: Vol. 11). (ENG., Illus.). 112p. (J). (gr. 7-12). 25.95 (978-1-4222-3690-1(0)) Mason Crest.
Moran, Margaret. Coming to America Immigration from 1840 To 1930: Set Of 6. 2011. (Navigators Ser.). (J). pap. 50.00 net. (978-1-4108-2565-0(5)) Benchmark Education Co.
Moreno, Barry, ed. & intro. We Came to America, 16 vols., Set. Moreno, Barry, intro. 2003. (Illus.). 64p. (YA). lib. bdg. (978-1-59084-100-6(X)) Mason Crest.
Morgan, Sally. Changing Planet: What Is the Environmental Impact of Human Migration & Settlement? 2010. (Investigating Human Migration & Settlement Ser.). (ENG., Illus.). 48p. (J). (gr. 5-8). (978-0-7787-5179-3(1)); pap. (978-0-7787-5194-6(5)) Crabtree Publishing Co.
Moynihan, Daniel Patrick, intro. Immigrants in America. (Illus.). (gr. 6-12). lib. bdg. 39.80 (978-0-7910-8470-0(1), Chelsea Hse.) Facts On File, Inc.
Nagle, Jack. Immigration to North America: Rights & Responsibilities of Citizenship, Vol. 11. Anderson, Stuart, ed. 2016. (Immigration to North America Ser.: Vol. 11). (ENG., Illus.). 112p. (J). (gr. 7-12). 25.95 (978-1-4222-3682-6(X)) Mason Crest.
National Geographic Learning. Jari's Year. 2009. (Inside the USA Ser.). (ENG., Illus.). 16p. (C). pap. 13.95 (978-0-7362-7065-6(5)) CENGAGE Learning.
Nichol, Bryan. Norwegian Americans, 1 vol. 2004. (One Nation Set 2 Ser.). (ENG.). 32p. (gr. k-6). 27.07 (978-1-59197-531-1(X), Checkerboard Library) ABDO Publishing Co.
Noonan, Sheila Smith. Korean Immigration. 2005. (Changing Face of North America Ser.). (Illus.). 112p. (YA). lib. bdg. 24.95 (978-1-59084-693-3(1)) Mason Crest.
Oeppen, Ceri. Hopes, Needs, Rights, & Laws: How Do Governments & Citizens Manage Migration & Settlement? 2010. (Investigating Human Migration & Settlement Ser.). (ENG., Illus.). 48p. (J). (gr. 5-8). (978-0-7787-5180-9(5)); pap. (978-0-7787-5195-3(3)) Crabtree Publishing Co.
Owens, Sharon. Immigration & Migration in Texas. 2014. (Spotlight on Texas Ser.). (ENG.). 32p. (J). (gr. 3-4). 26.25 (978-1-4777-4522-9(X), Rosen Classroom) Rosen Publishing Group, Inc., The.
Owens, Tom. Immigrants & Neighbors. 2003. (Illus.). 40p. pap. 8.00 (978-0-7891-5850-5(7)) Perfection Learning Corp.
Park, Ken. Americans from India & Other South Asian Countries. 2009. (New Americans Ser.). 80p. (gr. 5-8). 35.64 (978-0-7614-4305-6(3)) Marshall Cavendish Corp.
Parker, Lewis K. Why German Immigrants Came to America. (Coming to America Ser.). 24p. 2009. (gr. 2-3). 42.50 (978-1-61511-883-0(7)) 2003. (Illus.). (J). lib. bdg. 22.60 (978-0-8239-6458-1(2)) Rosen Publishing Group, Inc., The. (PowerKids Pr.).
—Why Irish Immigrants Came to America. 2003. (Coming to America Ser.). (Illus.). 24p. (J). lib. bdg. 22.60 (978-0-8239-6462-8(0), PowerKids Pr.) Rosen Publishing Group, Inc., The.
—Why Italian Immigrants Came to America. 2003. (Coming to America Ser.). (Illus.). 24p. (J). lib. bdg. 22.60 (978-0-8239-6460-4(4), PowerKids Pr.) Rosen Publishing Group, Inc., The.
—Why Japanese Immigrants Came to America. 2003. (Coming to America Ser.). (Illus.). 24p. (J). lib. bdg. 22.60 (978-0-8239-6463-5(9), PowerKids Pr.) Rosen Publishing Group, Inc., The.
—Why Vietnamese Immigrants Came to America. 2003. (Coming to America Ser.). (Illus.). 24p. (J). lib. bdg. 22.60 (978-0-8239-6461-1(2), PowerKids Pr.) Rosen Publishing Group, Inc., The.
Paulson, Timothy J. Irish Immigrants. Asher, Robert, ed. 2004. (Immigration to the United States Ser.). (Illus.). 96p. (gr. 4-9). 35.00 (978-0-8160-5682-8(X)) Facts On File, Inc.
Peacock, Louise. At Ellis Island: A History in Many Voices. Krudop, Walter Lyon, illus. 2007. (ENG.). 48p. (J). (gr. 2-5). 19.99 (978-0-689-83026-6(2), Atheneum Bks. for Young Readers) Simon & Schuster Children's Publishing.
Perritano, John. The Making of the Modern World: 1945 to the Present: Migration & Refugees, Vol. 9. van Dijk, Ruud, ed. 2016. (Making of the Modern World: 1945 to the Present Ser.: Vol. 9). (ENG.). 64p. (J). (gr. 7-12). 23.95 (978-1-4222-3640-6(4)) Mason Crest.
Poole, H. W. Immigrant Families, Vol. 12. 2016. (Families Today Ser.). (Illus.). 48p. (J). (gr. 5). 20.95 (978-1-4222-3617-8(X)) Mason Crest.
Richardson, Gillian. 10 Routes That Crossed the World. Rosen, Kim, illus. 2017. (ENG.). 164p. (J). (gr. 3-7). pap. 12.95 (978-1-55451-875-3(X)) Annick Pr., Ltd. CAN. Dist: Publishers Group West (PGW).
Rodger, Ellen. A Refugee's Journey from Iraq. 2017. (Leaving My Homeland Ser.). (ENG., Illus.). 32p. (J). **(978-0-7787-3127-6(8))** Crabtree Publishing Co.
—A Refugee's Journey from the Democratic Republic of the Congo. 2017. (Leaving My Homeland Ser.). (ENG., Illus.). 32p. (J). **(978-0-7787-3126-9(X))** Crabtree Publishing Co.
Rossi, Ann & National Geographic Learning Staff. Immigrants Today. 2007. (Reading Expeditions Ser.). (ENG., Illus.). 40p. (J). pap. 19.95 (978-0-7922-4560-5(1)) CENGAGE Learning.

Rothstein, Evelyn. Clara Becomes a Citizen. Uhlig, Elizabeth, illus. 2009. (ENG.). (J). pap. 12.95 *(978-0-9786745-7-1(X))* Marble Hse. Editions.

Ruiz, Jose. Immigration to North America: Mexican Immigrants, Vol. 11. Anderson, Stuart, ed. 2016. (Immigration to North America Ser.: Vol. 11). (ENG., Illus.). 112p. (J). (gr. 7-12). 25.95 *(978-1-4222-3688-8(9))* Mason Crest.

Ruiz, José. Mexican Immigrants. 2017. (Illus.). 112p. (J). ***(978-1-4222-3679-6(X))*** Mason Crest.

Samuels, Barbara. Canada's Immigrant Cultures: Multiculturalism in Canada. 2011. 32p. (gr. 5-8). *(978-1-77071-705-3(6))*; pap. *(978-1-77071-708-4(0))* Weigl Educational Pubs. Ltd.

—Canada's Multicultural Society Today: Multiculturalism in Canada. 2011. 32p. (gr. 5-8). *(978-1-77071-706-0(4))*; pap. *(978-1-77071-709-1(9))* Weigl Educational Pubs. Ltd.

—Multiculturalism in Early Canada: Multiculturalism in Canada. 2011. 32p. (gr. 5-8). *(978-1-77071-704-6(8))* Weigl Educational Pubs. Ltd.

Schmerhorn, Rick. Immigration to North America: Undocumented Immigration & Homeland Security, Vol. 11. Anderson, Stuart, ed. 2016. (Immigration to North America Ser.: Vol. 11). (ENG., Illus.). 112p. (J). (gr. 7-12). 25.95 *(978-1-4222-3683-3(8))* Mason Crest.

Schwartz, Eric. Central American Immigrants to the United States: Refugees from Unrest. 2007. (Hispanic Heritage Ser.). (Illus.). 112p. (YA). (gr. 4-7). lib. bdg. 22.95 *(978-1-59084-929-3(9))* Mason Crest.

Senker, Cath. The Debate about Immigration. 2007. (Ethical Debates Ser.). (Illus.). 48p. (YA). (gr. 5-9). lib. bdg. 29.25 *(978-1-4042-3755-1(0))* Rosen Publishing Group, Inc., The.

—Mapping Global Issues: Immigrants & Refugees. 2004. (21st Century Issues Ser.). (Illus.). 48p. (gr. 5-12). lib. bdg. 31.00 *(978-0-8368-5644-6(9)*, Gareth Stevens Secondary Library) Stevens, Gareth Publishing LLLP.

—Migration & Refugees. 2009. (J). 32.80 *(978-1-59920-101-6(1))* Black Rabbit Bks.

Shea, Therese. Immigration to America: Identifying Different Points of View about an Issue. 2009. (Critical Thinking in American History Ser.). 48p. (gr. 5-8). 53.00 *(978-1-61512-093-2(9)*, Rosen Reference) Rosen Publishing Group, Inc., The.

Sioux, Tracee. Immigrants & the Westward Expansion. 2009. (Primary Sources of Immigration & Migration in America Ser.). 24p. (gr. 3-4). 42.50 *(978-1-60851-776-3(4)*, PowerKids Pr.) Rosen Publishing Group, Inc., The.

—Immigrants, Migration, & the Industrial Revolution. 2004. (Primary Sources of Immigration & Migration in America Ser.). (Illus.). 24p. (J). lib. bdg. 22.60 *(978-0-8239-6826-8(X)*, PowerKids Pr.) Rosen Publishing Group, Inc., The.

—Native American Migration. 2009. (Primary Sources of Immigration & Migration in America Ser.). 24p. (gr. 3-4). 42.50 *(978-1-60851-781-7(0)*, PowerKids Pr.) Rosen Publishing Group, Inc., The.

Solway, Andrew. Graphing Immigration, 1 vol. 2010. (Real World Data Ser.). (ENG.). 32p. (gr. 3-5). lib. bdg. 29.99 *(978-1-4329-2617-5(9)*, NA-h) Heinemann-Raintree.

Sonnebom, Liz. German Americans. 2003. (Immigrants in America Ser.). (Illus.). 112p. (gr. 6-12). 30.00 *(978-0-7910-7127-4(8)*, Chelsea Hse.) Facts On File, Inc.

Spranger, Pete. Immigration to North America: Cuban Immigrants, Vol. 11. Anderson, Stuart, ed. 2016. (Immigration to North America Ser.: Vol. 11). (ENG., Illus.). 112p. (J). (gr. 7-12). 25.95 *(978-1-4222-3685-7(4))* Mason Crest.

Staeger, Rob. Deported Aliens. 2005. (Changing Face of North America Ser.). (Illus.). 112p. (J). lib. bdg. 24.95 *(978-1-59084-686-5(9))* Mason Crest.

Stein, Robert. Jewish Americans: Coming to America. 2006. (Illus.). 128p. (J). (gr. 4-8). reprint ed. 15.00 *(978-1-4223-5576-3(4))* DIANE Publishing Co.

Stewart, Gail B. Defending the Borders: The Role of Border & Immigration Control. 2003. (Lucent Library of Homeland Security). (Illus.). 112p. (J). 29.95 *(978-1-59018-376-2(2)*, Lucent Bks.) Cengage Gale.

Swain, Gwenyth. Hope & Tears: Ellis Island Voices. 2012. (ENG., Illus.). 128p. (J). (gr. 3). 17.95 *(978-1-59078-765-6(X))* Boyds Mills Pr.

Taus-Bolstad, Stacy. Pakistanis in America. 2006. (In America Ser.). (ENG., Illus.). 80p. (gr. 5-8). lib. bdg. 27.93 *(978-0-8225-4872-0(0)*, Lerner Pubns.) Lerner Publishing Group.

Teichmann, Iris. Immigration & Asylum. 2003. (In the News Ser.). (J). lib. bdg. 16.95 *(978-1-58340-396-9(5))* Black Rabbit Bks.

—Life as an Immigrant. 2006. (Understanding Immigration Ser.). (Illus.). 44p. (YA). (gr. 5-9). lib. bdg. 31.35 *(978-1-58340-968-8(8))* Black Rabbit Bks.

—A Multicultural World. 2006. (Understanding Immigration Ser.). (Illus.). 44p. (YA). (gr. 5-9). lib. bdg. 31.35 *(978-1-58340-969-5(6))* Black Rabbit Bks.

Teitelbaum, Michael. Chinese Immigrants. 2004. (Immigration to the United States Ser.). (Illus.). 96p. (gr. 4-9). 35.00 *(978-0-8160-5687-3(0))* Facts On File, Inc.

Thomas, Zachary & Wilson, Natashya. The Melting Pot: The People & Cultures of New York. 2012. (Illus.). 24p. (J). 60.00 *(978-1-4488-5768-5(6))*; pap. 10.00 *(978-1-4488-5767-8(8))*; lib. bdg. 22.60 *(978-1-4488-5747-0(3))* Rosen Publishing Group, Inc., The. (PowerKids Pr.).

Thornton, Jeremy. New Industries, New Jobs: British Immigrants Come to America(1830s-1890s) 2009. (Primary Sources of Immigration & Migration in America Ser.). 24p. (gr. 3-4). 42.50 *(978-1-60851-782-4(9)*, PowerKids Pr.) Rosen Publishing Group, Inc., The.

—Religious Intolerance: Jewish Immigrants Come to America (1881-1914) 2009. (Primary Sources of Immigration & Migration in America Ser.). 24p. (gr. 3-4). 42.50 *(978-1-60851-783-1(7)*, PowerKids Pr.) Rosen Publishing Group, Inc., The.

Trumbauer, Lisa. German Immigrants. 2004. (Immigration to the United States Ser.). (Illus.). 96p. (gr. 4-9). 35.00 *(978-0-8160-5683-5(8))* Facts On File, Inc.

—Hopes Fulfilled: The Irish Immigrants in Boston. 2005. (Illus.). 32p. (J). pap. *(978-0-7367-2881-2(3))* Zaner-Bloser, Inc.

—Russian Immigrants. 2004. (Immigration to the United States Ser.). (Illus.). 96p. (gr. 4-9). 35.00 *(978-0-8160-5685-9(4))* Facts On File, Inc.

Venettone, Mike. Immigration to North America: Refugees, Vol. 11. Anderson, Stuart, ed. 2016. (Immigration to North America Ser.: Vol. 11). (ENG., Illus.). 112p. (J). (gr. 7-12). 25.95 *(978-1-4222-3681-9(1))* Mason Crest.

Wachtel, Alan. Southeast Asian Americans. 2009. (New Americans Ser.). 80p. (gr. 5-8). 35.64 *(978-0-7614-4312-4(6))* Marshall Cavendish Corp.

Walker, Robert. Pushes & Pulls: Why Do People Migrate? 2010. (Investigating Human Migration & Settlement Ser.). (ENG., Illus.). 48p. (J). (gr. 5-8). *(978-0-7787-5183-0(X))*; pap. *(978-0-7787-5198-4(8))* Crabtree Publishing Co.

Welldon, Christine. Pier 21 - Listen to My Story, 1 vol. 2012. (ENG.). 96p. (J). (gr. 2-5). pap. 15.95 *(978-1-55109-909-5(8))* Nimbus Publishing, Ltd. CAN. Dist: Orca Bk. Pubs. USA.

Wong, Li Keng. Good Fortune: My Journey to Gold Mountain, 1 vol. 2008. (ENG., Illus.). 144p. (J). (gr. 3-7). pap. 8.95 *(978-1-56145-464-8(8))* Peachtree Pubs.

Worth, Richard. Mexican Immigrants. 2004. (Immigration to the United States Ser.). (Illus.). 96p. (gr. 4-9). 35.00 *(978-0-8160-5690-3(0))* Facts On File, Inc.

—1950s to 1960s. 2009. (Hispanic America 2 Ser.). 80p. (gr. 5). 34.21 *(978-0-7614-4177-9(8))* Marshall Cavendish GBR. Dist: Marshall Cavendish Corp.

—The 1970s to the 1980s. 2009. (Hispanic America 2 Ser.). 80p. (gr. 5). 34.21 *(978-0-7614-4178-6(6))* Marshall Cavendish Corp.

Wright, Frank. Immigration to North America: Asylum Seekers, Vol. 11. Anderson, Stuart, ed. 2016. (Immigration to North America Ser.: Vol. 11). (ENG., Illus.). 112p. (J). (gr. 7-12). 25.95 *(978-1-4222-3680-2(3))* Mason Crest.

EMIGRATION AND IMMIGRATION—FICTION

Abdel-Fattah, Randa. The Lines We Cross. 2017. (ENG.). 400p. (J). (gr. 7-7). 18.99 ***(978-1-338-11866-7(8)***, Scholastic Pr.) Scholastic, Inc.

Acheson, A. S. Fighting Words. 2014. (Bareknuckle Ser.). 96p. (YA). (gr. 6-12). lib. bdg. 27.93 *(978-1-4677-1461-7(5)*, Darby Creek) Lerner Publishing Group.

Aksomitis, Linda. Adeline's Dream, 1 vol. 2005. (From Many Peoples Ser.). (ENG.). 216p. (J). (gr. 4-7). per. 7.95 *(978-1-55050-323-4(5))* Coteau Bks. CAN. Dist: Orca Bk. Pubs. USA.

Arkadina, Mina. Nesmotrya Mina Chto. Arkadina, Mina, ed. 2003.Tr. of No Matter What.... (RUS.). 178p. (YA). *(978-0-9728301-0-2(3))* Publishing Hse. Gelany.

Auch, Mary Jane. Ashes of Roses. 2004. 250p. (YA). (gr. 8-12). 14.15 *(978-0-7569-4069-0(9))* Perfection Learning Corp.

Avi. City of Orphans. Ruth, Greg, illus. 2011. (ENG.). 368p. (J). (gr. 5-9). 17.99 *(978-1-4169-7102-3(5)*, Atheneum/Richard Jackson Bks.) Simon & Schuster Children's Publishing.

—Escape from Home. 2012. (ENG.). 304p. (J). (gr. 3-7). pap. 7.99 *(978-0-545-37927-4(X)*, Scholastic Pr.) Scholastic, Inc.

—Into the Storm. 2012. (Beyond the Western Sea Ser.: 2). (ENG.). 400p. (J). (gr. 3-7). pap. 7.99 *(978-0-545-39845-9(2)*, Scholastic Paperbacks) Scholastic, Inc.

—Silent Movie. Mordan, C. B., illus. 2003. (ENG.). 48p. (J). (gr. -1-3). 19.99 *(978-0-689-84145-3(0)*, Atheneum Bks. for Young Readers) Simon & Schuster Children's Publishing.

Ayres, Katherine. Under Copp's Hill. 2009. (Mysteries Through Time Ser.). 176p. (YA). (gr. 4-8). 31.95 *(978-1-60754-185-1(8))*; pap. 15.25 *(978-1-60754-186-8(6))* Windmill Bks.

Barbara, Cohen. Molly's Pilgrim. 97th rev. ed. 2014. (ENG.). 32p. (J). (gr. 1-5). 8.24 *(978-1-63245-244-3(8))* Lectorum Pubns., Inc.

Barbieri, Gladys. A Charmed Life / una Vida con Suerte. Field, Lisa, illus. 2016. (MUL, ENG & SPA.). 32p. (J). (gr. k-3). 17.95 *(978-1-55885-827-5(X)*, Piñata Books) Arte Publico Pr.

Bennett, Carolyn Hart. Seven Sisters: The Voyage. 2008. 232p. 25.95 *(978-0-595-51213-3(5))*; pap. 15.95 *(978-0-595-52242-2(4))* iUniverse, Inc.

Bernardo, Anilu. Quedando Bien. Sanmiguel, Rosario, tr. from ENG. 2006. (SPA., Illus.). 236p. (J). (gr. 6). per. 9.95 *(978-1-55885-474-1(6)*, Piñata Books) Arte Publico Pr.

Black, Robert. Liberty Girl. (YA). pap. 9.99 *(978-0-88092-488-7(8))* Royal Fireworks Publishing Co.

Blasi, Kathleen McAlpin. A Name of Honor. Bowman, Leslie W., illus. 2006. (J). *(978-1-59336-692-6(2))* Mondo Publishing.

Boissery, Beverley. Sophie's Exile. 2008. (ENG.). 280p. (J). (gr. 5-8). pap. 12.99 *(978-1-55002-810-2(3)*, Boardwalk Bks.) Dundurn CAN. Dist: Ingram Publisher Services.

Boyce, Frank Cottrell. The Unforgotten Coat. Hunter, Carl & Heney, Clare, illus. Hunter, Carl & Heney, Clare, photos by. 2011. (ENG.). 112p. (J). (gr. 3-7). 16.99 *(978-0-7636-5729-1(8))* Candlewick Pr.

—The Unforgotten Coat. 2011. (Playaway Children Ser.). (ENG.). (J). (gr. 4-7). 39.99 *(978-1-4558-4539-2(6))* Findaway World, LLC.

Bruce, Mary Grant. Back to Billabong. l.t. ed. 2006. 200p. pap. 21.99 *(978-1-4264-2197-6(4))* Creative Media Partners, LLC.

Burack, Emilie Christie. The Runaway's Gold. 2015. (ENG., Illus.). 320p. (YA). (gr. 3-9). 16.95 *(978-1-4197-1369-9(8)*, Amulet Bks.) Abrams, Inc.

Caraballo, Samuel & Torrecilla, Pablo. Estrellita in the Big City/Estrellita en la Ciudad Grande. Caraballo, Samuel & Torrecilla, Pablo, illus. 2008. (SPA & ENG., Illus.). 32p. (J). (gr. -1-4). 16.95 *(978-1-55885-498-7(3)*, Piñata Books) Arte Publico Pr.

Castilla, Julia Mercedes. Strange Parents. 2009. 144p. (J). (gr. 6-18). pap. 9.95 *(978-1-55885-590-8(4)*, Piñata Books) Arte Publico Pr.

Chan, Gillian. An Ocean Apart: The Gold Mountain Diary of Chin Mei-Ling. 2004. (Dear Canada Ser.). (ENG., Illus.). 224p. (J). *(978-0-7791-1353-8(5))* Scholastic Canada, Ltd.

Cheng, Andrea. Goldfish & Chrysanthemums. Chang, Michelle, illus. 2003. (ENG.). 32p. (J). pap. 8.95 *(978-1-60060-889-6(2))* Lee & Low Bks., Inc.

Cohen, Barbara. Molly's Pilgrim. Duffy, Daniel Mark & Deraney, Michael J., illus. 97th rev. ed. 2005. (ENG.). 32p. (J). (gr. 2-5). pap. 3.99 *(978-0-688-16280-1(0))* HarperCollins Pubs.

—Molly's Pilgrim. (Literature to Go Ser.). pap., tchr. ed. incl. VHS *(978-0-7919-2685-7(0))* Phoenix Films & Video.

Colon, Edie. Good-Bye, Havana! Hola, New York! Colón, Raúl, illus. 2011. (ENG.). 32p. (J). (gr. -1-3). 17.99 *(978-1-4424-0674-2(7)*, Simon & Schuster/Paula Wiseman Bks.) Simon & Schuster/Paula Wiseman Bks.

Corey, Shana. Milly & the Macy's Parade. Helquist, Brett, illus. 2006. 38p. (J). (gr. 4-8). reprint ed. 17.00 *(978-1-4223-5174-1(2))* DIANE Publishing Co.

Currier, Katrina Saltonstall. Kai's Journey to Gold Mountain: An Angel Island Story. 2004. 40p. 16.95 *(978-0-9667352-7-7(7))*; (Illus.). 44p. (J). pap. 10.95 *(978-0-9667352-4-6(2))* Angel Island Assoc.

Curtis, Christopher Paul. The Madman of Piney Woods. (Illus.). (J). 2016. (ENG.). 384p. (gr. 3-7). pap. 7.99 *(978-0-545-15665-3(3))* 2014. 363p. *(978-0-545-63376-5(1))* 2014. (ENG., 384p. (gr. 3-7). 16.99 *(978-0-545-15664-6(5))* Scholastic, Inc. (Scholastic Pr.).

Curtis, Jamie Lee. This Is Me: A Story of Who We Are & Where We Came From. Cornell, Laura, illus. 2016. (ENG.). 32p. (J). (gr. -1-3). 16.95 *(978-0-7611-8011-1(7))*; 17.89 *(978-1-5235-0005-5(0))* Workman Publishing Co., Inc.

Danticat, Edwidge. Behind the Mountains. 2004. (First Person Fiction Ser.). (ENG.). 192p. (J). (gr. 7-10). pap. 6.99 *(978-0-439-37300-5(X)*, Orchard Bks.) Scholastic, Inc.

—Mama's Nightingale: A Story of Immigration & Separation. Staub, Leslie, illus. 2015. (ENG.). 32p. (J). (gr. k-3). 17.99 *(978-0-525-42809-1(7)*, Dial Bks) Penguin Young Readers Group.

Dembar Greene, Jacqueline. Speak up, Tommy! Melmon, Deborah, illus. 2012. (Kar-Ben Favorites Ser.). (ENG.). 32p. (J). (gr. -1-3). 7.95 *(978-0-7613-7498-5(1)*, Kar-Ben Publishing) Lerner Publishing Group.

Diaz, Alexandra. The Only Road. 2016. (ENG., Illus.). 320p. (J). (gr. 3-7). 16.99 *(978-1-4814-5750-7(0)*, Simon & Schuster/Paula Wiseman Bks.) Simon & Schuster/Paula Wiseman Bks.

—El Unico Destino. 2016. (SPA., Illus.). 320p. (J). (gr. 3-7). 16.99 *(978-1-4814-8441-1(9)*, Simon & Schuster/Paula Wiseman Bks.) Simon & Schuster/Paula Wiseman Bks.

—El único Destino (the Only Road) 2016. (SPA., Illus.). 320p. (J). (gr. 3-7). pap. 7.99 *(978-1-4814-8442-8(7)*, Simon & Schuster/Paula Wiseman Bks.) Simon & Schuster/Paula Wiseman Bks.

Doherty, Ellen. William's Journal. 2011. (Early Connections Ser.). (J). *(978-1-61672-680-5(6))* Benchmark Education Co.

Dueck, Adele. Nettie's Journey, 1 vol. 2005. (From Many Peoples Ser.). (ENG., Illus.). 216p. (J). (gr. 4-7). per. 7.95 *(978-1-55050-322-7(7))* Coteau Bks. CAN. Dist: Orca Bk. Pubs. USA.

Durbin, William. The Darkest Evening. 2011. (Fesler-Lampert Minnesota Heritage Ser.). (ENG.). 248p. pap. 11.95 *(978-0-8166-7568-5(6))* Univ. of Minnesota Pr.

Farish, Terry. The Good Braider, 0 vols. 2014. (ENG.). 224p. (YA). (gr. 9-12). pap. 9.99 *(978-1-4778-1628-8(3)*, 9781477816288, Amazon Children's Publishing) Amazon Publishing.

Fleischman, Paul. The Matchbox Diary. Ibatoulline, Bagram, illus. 2013. (ENG.). 40p. (J). (gr. 1-4). 16.99 *(978-0-7636-4601-1(6))* Candlewick Pr.

—The Matchbox Diary. Ibatoulline, Bagram, illus. 2016. (ENG.). 40p. (J). (gr. 1-4). 18.40 *(978-0-606-39097-2(9))* Turtleback Bks.

Flor Ada, Alma. El Vuelo de los Colibries. Jacobson, Judith, illus. 32p. (J). (gr. 3-6). pap. 9.95 *(978-1-56492-211-3(1))* Laredo Publishing Co., Inc.

Flor Ada, Alma & Campoy, F. Isabel. Yes! We Are Latinos. Diaz, David, illus. 2013. (SPA & ENG.). 96p. (J). (gr. 5). 18.95 *(978-1-58089-383-1(X))* Charlesbridge Publishing, Inc.

Flowers, J. J. Juan Pablo & the Butterflies. 2017. (ENG., Illus.). 224p. (YA). (gr. 9-12). 17.99 *(978-1-5072-0214-2(8)*, Simon Pulse) Simon Pulse.

French, Simon. Where in the World. 2003. 208p. (J). (gr. 3-7). 14.95 *(978-1-56145-292-7(0)*, Q34443) Peachtree Pubs.

Gallo, Donald R. First Crossing: Stories about Teen Immigrants. Gallo, Donald R., ed. 2007. (ENG.). 240p. (YA). (gr. 7-12). per. 8.99 *(978-0-7636-3291-5(0))* Candlewick Pr.

Giff, Patricia Reilly. A House of Tailors. 2006. (ENG.). 160p. (J). (gr. 3-7). per. 6.99 *(978-0-440-23800-3(5)*, Yearling) Random Hse. Children's Bks.

—Maggie's Door. 2005. 158p. (gr. 3-7). 17.00 *(978-0-7569-5102-3(X))* Perfection Learning Corp.

—Until I Find Julian. 2015. (ENG.). 160p. (J). (gr. 3-7). 16.99 *(978-0-385-74482-9(X)*, Lamb, Wendy Bks.) Random Hse. Children's Bks.

—Wild Girl. 2011. (ENG.). 160p. (J). (gr. 3-7). pap. 6.99 *(978-0-440-42177-1(2)*, Yearling) Random Hse. Children's Bks.

Griffith, Gretchen. When Christmas Feels Like Home. Farias, Carolina, illus. 2013. (ENG.). 32p. (J). (gr. -1-3). 16.99 *(978-0-8075-8872-7(5))* Whitman, Albert & Co.

Gunderson, Jessica. Emma's New Beginning. Foti, Anthony J., illus. 2015. (U. S. Immigration in The 1900s Ser.). (ENG.). 96p. (gr. 3-4). pap. 7.95 *(978-1-4965-0501-9(8))* Stone Arch Bks.

Hermdorf, Wolfgang. Why We Took the Car. Mohr, Tim, tr. from GER. 2014. (ENG.). 256p. (J). (gr. 9). 17.99 *(978-0-545-48180-9(5)*, Levine, Arthur A. Bks.) Scholastic, Inc.

—You, Me, & a Russian Jeep. 2013. (YA). pap. *(978-0-545-48181-6(3)*, Levine, Arthur A. Bks.) Scholastic, Inc.

Hesse, Karen. Letters from Rifka. 2009. 9.00 *(978-0-7848-2599-0(8)*, Everbind) Marco Bk. Co.

—Letters from Rifka. 2008. (ENG.). 148p. 17.00 *(978-1-60686-224-7(3))* Perfection Learning Corp.

—Letters from Rifka. 2009. (ENG.). 176p. (J). (gr. 5-9). pap. 6.99 *(978-0-312-53561-2(9)*, 9780312535612) Square Fish.

Hest, Amy. When Jessie Came Across the Sea. Lynch, P. J., illus. 2003. (ENG.). 40p. (J). (gr. 1-4). pap. 6.99 *(978-0-7636-1274-0(X))* Candlewick Pr.

—When Jessie Came Across the Sea. 2003. 17.20 *(978-0-613-69484-1(8)*, Turtleback) Turtleback Bks.

Ho & Ho, Minfong. The Stone Goddess. 2006. (Reader's Workshop Ser.). (ENG., Illus.). 200p. (C). pap. 19.95 *(978-0-7362-3160-2(9))* CENGAGE Learning.

Hohn, Nadia L. & Luxbacher, Irene. Malaika's Costume, 1 vol. 2016. (ENG., Illus.). 32p. (J). (gr. -1-2). 18.95 *(978-1-55498-754-2(7))* Groundwood Bks. CAN. Dist: Publishers Group West (PGW).

Honeyman, Kay. The Fire Horse Girl. 2016. (ENG.). 336p. (J). (gr. 7). pap. 9.99 *(978-0-545-40311-5(1)*, Levine, Arthur A. Bks.) Scholastic, Inc.

Horender, Philip M. A Brave New Mouse: Ellis Island Approved Immigrant, 1 vol. Wolek, Guy, illus. 2013. (Maximilian P. Mouse, Time Traveler Ser.). (ENG.). 112p. (J). (gr. 3-6). lib. bdg. 27.07 *(978-1-61641-961-5(X)*, Calico Chapter Bks) Magic Wagon.

Hyde, Heidi Smith. Shanghai Sukkah. Tsong, Jing Jing, illus. 2015. (ENG.). 32p. (J). (gr. k-4). 17.99 *(978-1-4677-3474-5(8))*; pap. 7.99 *(978-1-4677-3475-2(6))* Lerner Publishing Group. (Kar-Ben Publishing).

James, Helen Foster & Loh, Virginia Shin-Mui. Paper Son: Lee's Journey to America. Ong, Wilson, illus. 2013. (Tales of Young Americans Ser.). (ENG.). 32p. (J). (gr. 1-4). 16.99 *(978-1-58536-833-4(4)*, 202366) Sleeping Bear Pr.

Jaramillo, Ann. La Linea. 2008. (ENG.). 144p. (J). (gr. 5-9). pap. 8.99 *(978-0-312-37354-2(6)*, 9780312373542) Square Fish.

Johnson, Annabel. A Rock Candy Dream. 2009. 140p. 22.49 *(978-1-4389-4233-9(8))*; pap. 11.99 *(978-1-4389-4234-6(6))* AuthorHouse.

Kazerooni, Abbas. The Boy with Two Lives. 2016. (ENG.). 256p. (YA). (gr. 7). 12.99 *(978-1-74331-483-8(3))* Allen & Unwin AUS. Dist: Independent Pubs. Group.

Kerz, Anna. The Gnome's Eye, 1 vol. 2010. (ENG.). 224p. (J). (gr. 4-7). pap. 9.95 *(978-1-55469-195-1(8))* Orca Bk. Pubs. USA.

Kobald, Irena. My Two Blankets. Blackwood, Freya, illus. 2015. (ENG.). 32p. (J). (gr. 1-4). 17.99 *(978-0-544-43228-4(2)*, HMH Books For Young Readers) Houghton Mifflin Harcourt Publishing Co.

Krishnaswami, Uma. Chachaji's Cup. Sitaraman, Soumya, illus. 2013. (ENG.). 32p. (J). (gr. 1-18). 16.95 *(978-0-89239-178-3(2))* Lee & Low Bks., Inc.

Lai, Thanhha. Inside Out & Back Again. (ENG.). (J). (gr. 3-7). 2013. 288p. pap. 8.99 *(978-0-06-196279-0(1))* 2011. 272p. 16.99 *(978-0-06-196278-3(3))* HarperCollins Pubs.

—Inside Out & Back Again. 2014. (ENG.). 288p. (J). (gr. 3-7). 12.24 *(978-1-63245-350-1(9))* Lectorum Pubns., Inc.

—Inside Out & Back Again. 2009. 9.68 *(978-0-7848-3887-7(9)*, Everbind) Marco Bk. Co.

—Inside Out & Back Again. 2013. 18.00 *(978-1-61383-970-6(7))* Perfection Learning Corp.

—Inside Out & Back Again. 2013. (J). lib. bdg. 18.40 *(978-0-606-27126-4(0)*, Turtleback) Turtleback Bks.

Lai, Thanhha. Inside Out & Back Again: a Harper Classic. 2017. (Harper Classic Ser.). 288p. (J). (gr. 3-7). 16.99 ***(978-0-06-257402-2(7))*** HarperCollins Pubs.

Lainez, René Colato. From North to South. Cepeda, Joe, illus. 2013.Tr. of Del Norte Al Sur. (ENG & SPA.). 32p. (J). pap. 9.95 *(978-0-89239-304-6(1)*, Children's Book Press) Lee & Low Bks., Inc.

—My Shoes & I. Broeck, Fabricio Vanden, illus. 2010. (ENG.). 32p. (J). (gr. 2-4). 16.95 *(978-1-59078-385-6(9))* Boyds Mills Pr.

—Waiting for Papá/Esperando a Papá. Accardo, Anthony, illus.Tr. of Esperando a Papa. (ENG & SPA.). 32p. (gr. 1-3). 16.95 *(978-1-55885-403-1(7)*, Piñata Books) Arte Publico Pr.

Lantigua, Lizette M. Mission Libertad. 2012. (ENG.). 192p. (YA). pap. 9.95 *(978-0-8198-4900-7(6))* Pauline Bks. & Media.

Lawson, Robert. The Great Wheel. Lawson, Robert, illus. 2004. (ENG., Illus.). 192p. (YA). (gr. 5). pap. 9.99 *(978-0-8027-7705-8(8)*, 9780802777058, Bloomsbury USA Childrens) Bloomsbury Publishing USA.

Leighton, Maxinne Rhea. An Ellis Island Christmas. Nolan, Dennis, illus. 2005. (ENG.). 32p. (J). (gr. k-3). pap. 6.99 *(978-0-14-240506-2(X)*, Puffin Books) Penguin Young Readers Group.

Littman, Sarah Darer. Life, After. 2010. (ENG.). 288p. (J). (gr. 7-18). 17.99 *(978-0-545-15144-3(9)*, Scholastic Pr.) Scholastic, Inc.

Lombard, Jenny. Drita, My Homegirl. 2008. (ENG.). 144p. (J). (gr. 3-7). 5.99 *(978-0-14-240905-3(7)*, Puffin Books) Penguin Young Readers Group.

—Drita, My Homegirl. 2008. 135p. (J). (gr. 4-6). 13.65 *(978-0-7569-8919-4(1))* Perfection Learning Corp.

Look, Lenore. Ruby Lu, Empress of Everything. Wilsdorf, Anne, illus. 2006. (ENG.). 176p. (J). (gr. 1-5). 16.99 *(978-0-689-86460-5(4)*, Atheneum Bks. for Young Readers) Simon & Schuster Children's Publishing.

Lorraine, Nancy. Tatty, the Lonely Monarch. Herron, Dorothy, illus. 2013. 48p. pap. 17.50 *(978-0-9893063-8-6(0))* ProsePress.

Loughrey, Eithne. Annie Moore: First in Line for America. l.t. ed. 2006. (Dales Ser.). 224p. (J). (gr. 4-7). 23.99 *(978-1-84262-446-3(6))* Magna Large Print Bks. GBR. Dist: Ulverscroft Large Print Bks., Ltd.

—Annie Moore: The Golden Dollar Girl. l.t. ed. 2006. (Dales Ser.). 208p. (J). 23.99 *(978-1-84262-447-0(4))* Magna Large Print Bks. GBR. Dist: Ulverscroft Large Print Bks., Ltd.

The Magic Paper (Mexicans) 76p. (YA). (gr. 6-12). pap. 9.95 *(978-0-8224-3686-7(8))* Globe Fearon Educational Publishing.

Magrane, Mijares. Grandma Garcia: La Abuela Garcia - An Intimate Journey into the Past. 2004. (SPA & ENG., Illus.). 96p. pap. 13.95 *(978-0-9741167-0-9(X))* Magrane, Etna International.

Mak, Kam. My Chinatown. Mak, Kam, illus. 2016. (Illus.). 32p. (J). (gr. -1-3). pap. 6.99 *(978-0-06-443732-5(9))* HarperCollins Pubs.

Making Heaven (Koreans) 76p. (YA). (gr. 6-12). pap. 9.95 *(978-0-8224-3801-4(1))* Globe Fearon Educational Publishing.

Manivong, Laura. Escaping the Tiger. 2010. (ENG.). 224p. (J). (gr. 5-18). 15.99 *(978-0-06-166177-8(5))* HarperCollins Pubs.

Mateo, José Manual. Migrant. Pedro, Javier Martínez, illus. 2014. (ENG & SPA.). 22p. (J). (gr. 3-7). 19.95

E
F
G

(978-1-4197-0957-9(7), Abrams Bks. for Young Readers) Abrams, Inc.

McClintock, Norah. Trial by Fire, 1 vol. 2016. (Riley Donovan Ser.). (ENG.). 240p. (YA). (gr. 8-12). pap. 10.95 (978-1-4598-0936-9(X)) Orca Bk. Pubs. USA.

Meyrick, Rich. Jaspa's Journey: The Great Migration. 2015. (ENG., Illus.). 276p. (J). (gr. 4-6). pap. (978-1-62815-313-2(X)) Speaking Volumes, LLC.

Mikaelsen, Ben. Red Midnight. 2003. (ENG.). 224p. (J). (gr. 5-18). pap. 6.99 (978-0-380-80561-7(8), Rayo) HarperCollins Pubs.

—Red Midnight. 2003. 212p. (gr. 5-9). 17.00 (978-0-7569-1550-6(3)) Perfection Learning Corp.

Mohammed, Khadra & Williams, Karen Lynn. My Name Is Sangoel. Stock, Catherine, illus. 2009. (ENG.). 36p. (J). (gr. 1-5). 17.00 (978-0-8028-5307-3(2), Eerdmans Bks For Young Readers) Eerdmans, William B. Publishing Co.

Moore, Julianne. My Mom Is a Foreigner, but Not to Me. So, Meilo, illus. 2013. (ENG.). 40p. (J). (gr. k-3). 16.99 (978-1-4521-0792-9(0)) Chronicle Bks. LLC.

Morpurgo, Michael. Twist of Gold. 2nd ed. 2009. (ENG.). 304p. (J). (gr. 4-7). pap. 10.99 (978-1-4052-2928-9(4)) Egmont Bks., Ltd. GBR. Dist: Independent Pubs. Group.

Nanji, Shenaaz. Child of Dandelions. 2008. (ENG., Illus.). 208p. (J). (gr. 6-9). 17.95 (978-1-932425-93-2(4), Front Street) Boyds Mills Pr.

Napoli, Donna Jo. The King of Mulberry Street. 2007. 245p. (gr. 3-7). 17.00 (978-0-7569-7945-4(5)) Perfection Learning Corp.

—The King of Mulberry Street. 2007. (ENG.). 256p. (J). (gr. 3-7). 6.99 (978-0-553-49416-7(3), Yearling) Random Hse. Children's Bks.

Neale, Cynthia G. The Irish Dresser: A Story of Hope During the Great Hunger (an Gorta Mor, 1845-1850) 2003. 148p. (J). pap. 7.95 (978-1-57249-344-5(5), White Mane Kids) White Mane Publishing Co., Inc.

Never So Good (Jamaicans) 76p. (YA). (gr. 6-12). pap. 9.95 (978-0-8224-3806-9(2)) Globe Fearon Educational Publishing.

Nislick, June Levitt. Zayda Was a Cowboy. 2005. (ENG.). 88p. pap. 11.95 (978-0-8276-0817-7(9)) Jewish Pubn. Society.

Nobisso, Josephine. En Ingles, por Supuesto. Ziborova, Dasha, illus. 2003. Orig. Title: In English, of Course. (SPA & ENG.). 32p. (J). (gr. k-2). 16.95 (978-0-940112-14-8(0)) Gingerbread Hse.

—En ingles, por Supuesto. Ziborova, Dasha, illus. 2003. Orig. Title: In English, of Course. (SPA & ENG.). 32p. (J). (gr. k-2). pap. 8.95 (978-0-940112-16-2(7)) Gingerbread Hse.

Nobody Knows (Africans) 76p. (YA). (gr. 6-12). pap. 9.95 (978-0-8224-3683-6(3)) Globe Fearon Educational Publishing.

O Little Town (Germans) 76p. (YA). (gr. 6-12). pap. 9.95 (978-0-8224-3681-2(7)) Globe Fearon Educational Publishing.

O'Brien, Anne Sibley. I'm New Here. O'Brien, Anne Sibley, illus. 2015. (ENG., Illus.). 32p. (J). (gr. k-3). lib. bdg. 16.95 (978-1-58089-612-2(X)) Charlesbridge Publishing, Inc.

Oh, Jina, reader. A Step from Heaven. 2004. 160p. (J). (gr. 6-18). pap. 36.00 incl. audio (978-0-8072-2287-4(9), Listening Library) Random Hse. Audio Publishing Group.

Old Ways, New Ways (Eastern European Jews) 76p. (YA). (gr. 6-12). pap. 9.95 (978-0-8224-3682-9(5)) Globe Fearon Educational Publishing.

Paterson, Katherine. Bread & Roses, Too. 2008. (ENG.). 288p. (J). (gr. 5-7). pap. 7.99 (978-0-547-07651-5(7)) Houghton Mifflin Harcourt Publishing Co.

Paulding, Steve. The Wonderful Adventures of Bradley the Bat. Schmidt, Caleb & Schmidt, Carter, illus. 2013. 70p. pap. 18.95 (978-0-615-74591-6(1)) Slow on the Draw Productions.

Pérez, Amada Irma. Mi Diario de Aquí Hasta Allá. Gonzalez, Maya Christina, illus. 2013.Tr. of My Diary from Here to There. (ENG & SPA.). 32p. (J). (gr. k). pap. 9.95 (978-0-89239-230-8(4)) Lee & Low Bks., Inc.

Pogue, Carolyn. Gwen, 1 vol. 2009. (ENG.). 160p. (YA). (gr. 9-12). pap. (978-1-894549-80-6(5), Sumach Pr.) Canadian Scholars.

Polacco, Patricia. Fiona's Lace. Polacco, Patricia, illus. 2014. (ENG., Illus.). 48p. (J). (gr. -1-3). 17.99 (978-1-4424-8724-6(0), Simon & Schuster/Paula Wiseman Bks.) Simon & Schuster/Paula Wiseman Bks.

—The Keeping Quilt. 2007. 18.00 (978-0-7569-1720-3(4)) Perfection Learning Corp.

—The Keeping Quilt: 25th Anniversary Edition. Polacco, Patricia, illus. 25th ed. 2013. (ENG., Illus.). 64p. (J). (gr. -1-3). 17.99 (978-1-4424-8237-1(0), Simon & Schuster/Paula Wiseman Bks.) Simon & Schuster/Paula Wiseman Bks.

Preus, Margi. West of the Moon. 2014. (ENG., Illus.). 224p. (J). (gr. 3-7). 16.95 (978-1-4197-0896-1(1), Amulet Bks.) Abrams, Inc.

Pryor, Bonnie. The Iron Dragon: The Courageous Story of Lee Chin. 2010. (Historical Fiction Adventures (HFA) Ser.). (Illus.). 160p. (J). (gr. 3-6). 29.27 (978-0-7660-3389-4(9)); (gr. 4-6). pap. 10.95 (978-1-59845-215-0(0)) Enslow Pubs., Inc.

Push to the West (Norwegians) 76p. (YA). (gr. 6-12). pap. 9.95 (978-0-8224-3678-2(7)) Globe Fearon Educational Publishing.

Pushker, Gloria Teles. Toby Belfer Visits Ellis Island, 1 vol. Hierstein, Judith, illus. 2003. (Toby Belfer Ser.). (ENG.). 32p. (J). (gr. k-3). 16.99 (978-1-58980-117-2(2)) Pelican Publishing Co., Inc.

Pyke, Helen Godfrey. Pinch River: Growing up Hard & Fast on the Michigan Frontier. 2008. (J). pap. 7.97 (978-0-8163-2250-3(3)) Pacific Pr. Publishing Assn.

Recorvits, Helen. My Name Is Yoon. Swiatkowska, Gabi, illus. 2003. (ENG.). 32p. (J). (gr. -1-3). 17.99 (978-0-374-35114-4(7), 9780374351144, Farrar, Straus & Giroux (BYR)) Farrar, Straus & Giroux.

—My Name Is Yoon. Swiatkowska, Gabi, illus. 2014. (ENG.). 32p. (J). (gr. -1-3). 6.99 (978-1-250-05711-2(6), 9781250057112) Square Fish.

Rollason, Jane. Alone! Level 3 Lower-Intermediate. 2011. (ENG.). 80p. pap. 12.75 (978-84-8323-682-6(6)) Cambridge Univ. Pr.

Ryan, Pam Muñoz. Esperanza Rising. 2016. (gr. 5-8). lib. bdg. 17.20 (978-0-613-53807-7(2), Turtleback) Turtleback Bks.

Saldana, Rene, Jr. A Mystery Bigger Than Big / un Misterio Mas Grande Que Grandisimo: A Mickey Rangel Mystery / Colección Mickey Rangel, Detective Privado. 2016. (Mickey Rangel Mystery / Coleccion Mickey Rangel, Detective P Ser.). (MUL, ENG & SPA., Illus.). 64p. (J). (gr. 3-6). pap. 9.95 (978-1-55885-824-4(5), Piñata Books) Arte Publico Pr.

Saturen, Myra. Journey to a New World: Mystic River of the West. 2006. (J). pap. (978-0-88092-495-5(0)) Royal Fireworks Publishing Co.

Schneider, Mical. Annie Quinn in America. 2003. (Adventures in Time Ser.). (Illus.). 252p. (J). (gr. 4-7). 15.95 (978-1-57505-510-7(4), Carolrhoda Bks.) Lerner Publishing Group.

Schuman, Burt E. Chanukah on the Prairie. Kaye, Rosalind Charney, illus. 2004. (gr. k-3). 13.95 (978-0-8074-0814-8(X), 381780) URJ Pr.

Senzai, N. H. Shooting Kabul. (Kabul Chronicles Ser.). (ENG.). (J). (gr. 3-7). 2011. 288p. pap. 7.99 (978-1-4424-0195-2(8)) 2010. 272p. 18.99 (978-1-4424-0194-5(X)) Simon & Schuster/Paula Wiseman Bks. (Simon & Schuster/Paula Wiseman Bks.).

Simpson, Lesley. Yuvi's Candy Tree. Porter, Janice Lee, illus. 2011. (ENG.). 32p. (J). (gr. k-3). pap. 7.95 (978-0-7613-5652-3(5)); lib. bdg. 17.95 (978-0-7613-5651-6(7)) Lerner Publishing Group. (Kar-Ben Publishing).

Sleator, William. Test. 2010. (ENG.). 320p. (YA). (gr. 7-11). pap. 7.95 (978-0-8109-8989-4(1), Amulet Bks.) Abrams, Inc.

Stewart, Sarah. The Quiet Place, 1 vol. Small, David, illus. 2012. (ENG.). 44p. (J). (gr. k-4). 17.99 (978-0-374-32565-7(0), 9780374325657, Farrar, Straus & Giroux (BYR)) Farrar, Straus & Giroux.

Stier, Catherine. Welcome to America, Champ. Ettlinger, Doris, illus. 2013. (Tales of the World Ser.). (ENG.). 32p. (J). (gr. 1-4). 17.95 (978-1-58536-606-4(4), 202360) Sleeping Bear Pr.

Tal, Eve. Double Crossing: A Jewish Immigration Story. 2005. (ENG.). 216p. (J). (gr. 7-9). 16.95 (978-0-938317-94-4(6)) Cinco Puntos Pr.

Tan, Shaun. The Arrival. Tan, Shaun, illus. 2007. (ENG., Illus.). 128p. (J). (gr. 7-12). 21.99 (978-0-439-89529-3(4), Levine, Arthur A. Bks.) Scholastic, Inc.

—The Arrival. 2007. (J). (978-0-439-89530-9(8), Levine, Arthur A. Bks.) Scholastic, Inc.

Ties to the Past (Poles) 76p. (YA). (gr. 6-12). pap. 9.95 (978-0-8224-3803-8(8)) Globe Fearon Educational Publishing.

Volponi, Paul. Game Seven. 2016. lib. bdg. 20.85 (978-0-606-38392-9(1)) Turtleback Bks.

Volponi, Paul & Wells, Rosemary. Game Seven. 2015. (ENG.). 256p. (YA). (gr. 7). bds. 17.99 (978-0-670-78518-6(0), Viking Books for Young Readers) Penguin Young Readers Group.

Walfish, Miriam. The Jewel & the Journey. 2007. 208p. (J). 16.95 (978-1-932443-81-3(9)) Judaica Pr., Inc., The.

Wulf, Linda Press. The Night of the Burning. 2007. (ENG.). 224p. pap. (978-0-7475-9051-4(6)) Bloomsbury Publishing Plc.

Yee, Paul. The Jade Necklace. Lin, Grace, illus. 2006. 29p. (J). (gr. 4-8). reprint ed. 16.00 (978-1-4223-5135-2(1)) DIANE Publishing Co.

—Learning to Fly, 1 vol. 2008. (Orca Soundings Ser.). (ENG.). (YA). (gr. 8-12). 112p. 16.95 (978-1-55143-955-6(7)); 136p. pap. 9.95 (978-1-55143-953-2(0)) Orca Bk. Pubs. USA.

—Shu-Li & Tamara, 1 vol. Wang, Shaoli, illus. 2008. (ENG.). 72p. (J). (gr. 1-4). per. 7.95 (978-1-896580-93-7(9)) Tradewind Bks. CAN. Dist: Orca Bk. Pubs. USA.

Yep, Laurence & Yep, Kathleen S. The Dragon's Child: A Story of Angel Island. 2011. (ENG.). 160p. (J). (gr. 3-7). pap. 5.99 (978-0-06-201815-1(9)) HarperCollins Pubs.

Yin. Coolies. Soentpiet, Chris K., illus. 2003. (ENG.). 40p. (J). (gr. 2-5). 7.99 (978-0-14-250055-2(0), Puffin Books) Penguin Young Readers Group.

Young, Rebecca. Teacup. Ottley, Matt, illus. 2016. (ENG.). 40p. (J). (gr. -1-3). 17.99 (978-0-7352-2777-4(2), Dial Bks) Penguin Young Readers Group.

Zeiss, Joyce Burns. Out of the Dragon's Mouth. 2015. (ENG., Illus.). 240p. (YA). pap. 11.99 (978-0-7387-4196-3(5), Flux) North Star Editions.

EMILY THE STRANGE (FICTITIOUS CHARACTERS)—FICTION

McDuke, Doc. Emily, the Brave. Morse, Michelle, illus. 2010. 20p. pap. 10.95 (978-1-61633-065-1(1)) Guardian Angel Publishing, Inc.

Reger, Rob. Emily the Strange, Vol. 1. Reger, Rob & Brooks, Brian, illus. 2006. (Emily the Strange (Spanish) Ser.). (SPA.). 64p. 19.95 (978-1-59497-188-4(9)) Public Square Bks.

—Emily the Strange Vol. 3: The 13th Hour. 2011. (ENG., Illus.). 104p. (J). (gr. 5-12). pap. 14.99 (978-1-59582-700-5(5)) Dark Horse Comics.

—Emily the Strange Vol. 4: Las apariencias Engañan. 2007. (SPA., Illus.). 64p. reprint ed. 19.95 (978-1-59497-336-9(9)) Public Square Bks.

—El Libro Secreto de las Cosas Extranas. Reger, Rob, illus. 2006. (Emily the Strange (Spanish) Ser.). (SPA., Illus.). 64p. reprint ed. 19.95 (978-1-59497-189-1(7)) Public Square Bks.

Reger, Rob & Huehner, Mariah. Breaking the Record, Vol. 2. Farris, Cat, illus. 2015. (ENG.). 1p. (J). (gr. 5-12). 12.99 (978-1-61655-598-6(X)) Dark Horse Comics.

EMOTIONALLY DISTURBED CHILDREN

see Problem Children

EMOTIONS

see also Attitude (Psychology); Belief and Doubt; Fear; Grief; Jealousy; Love; Prejudices; Self-confidence

Abrams Appleseed. Making Faces: A First Book of Emotions. 2017. (ENG., Illus.). 14p. (J). bds. 7.95 (978-1-4197-2383-4(9), Abrams Appleseed) Abrams, Inc.

Agassi, Martine. Hands Are Not for Hitting. Heinlen, Marieka, illus. rev. ed. 2009. (Best Behavior Ser.). (ENG.). 40p. (J). (gr. -1-2). pap. 11.95 (978-1-57542-308-1(1)) Free Spirit Publishing, Inc.

Agassi, Martine & Verdick, Elizabeth. Las Manos No Son para Pegar. Heinlen, Marieka, illus. 2009. (Best Behavior Ser.).Tr. of Hands Are Not for Hitting. (SPA & ENG.). 40p. (J). (gr. -1-2). pap. 11.95 (978-1-57542-310-4(3)) Free Spirit Publishing, Inc.

Agassi, Martine, et al. Las Manos No Son para Pegar. Heinlen, Marieka, illus. 2009. (Best Behavior Ser.).Tr. of Hands Are Not for Hitting. (SPA, ENG & MUL.). 24p. (J). (gr. -1 — 1). bds. 7.95 (978-1-57542-309-8(X)) Free Spirit Publishing, Inc.

Amos, Janine. Thank You. 2009. (Best Behavior Ser.). (Illus.). 32p. (J). (gr. -1-2). pap. 10.55 (978-1-60754-042-7(8)); lib. bdg. 22.60 (978-1-60754-025-0(8)) Windmill Bks.

Anderson, George. Controlling Ourselves. 2003. (YA). 27.00 net. (978-0-9743682-5-2(3)) Anderson, George.

Andrews, Linda Wasmer. Emotional Intelligence. (Life Balance Ser.). (ENG., Illus.). 80p. (J). 2005. (gr. 5-8). pap. 6.95 (978-0-531-16688-8(0)) 2004. 20.50 (978-0-531-12335-5(9)) Scholastic Library Publishing. (Watts, Franklin).

Antill, Sara. Curiosity. 2013. (Character Strength Ser.). 24p. (J). (gr. 3-6). pap. 49.50 (978-1-4488-9825-1(0)); pap. 8.25 (978-1-4488-9824-4(2)); lib. bdg. 22.60 (978-1-4488-9683-7(5)) Rosen Publishing Group, Inc., The. (PowerKids Pr.).

—Zest. 2013. (Character Strength Ser.). 24p. (J). (gr. 3-6). lib. bdg. 22.60 (978-1-4488-9677-6(0), PowerKids Pr.) Rosen Publishing Group, Inc., The.

Apel, Melanie Ann. Let's Talk about Feeling Confused. 2009. (Let's Talk Library). 24p. (gr. 2-3). 42.50 (978-1-60853-439-5(1), PowerKids Pr.) Rosen Publishing Group, Inc., The.

—Let's Talk about Feeling Defeated. 2009. (Let's Talk Library). 24p. (gr. 2-3). 42.50 (978-1-60853-440-1(5), PowerKids Pr.) Rosen Publishing Group, Inc., The.

—Let's Talk about Feeling Embarrassed. 2009. (Let's Talk Library). 24p. (gr. 2-3). 42.50 (978-1-60853-441-8(3), PowerKids Pr.) Rosen Publishing Group, Inc., The.

—Let's Talk about Feeling Worried. 2009. (Let's Talk Library). 24p. (gr. 2-3). 42.50 (978-1-60853-443-2(X), PowerKids Pr.) Rosen Publishing Group, Inc., The.

Bartels, Lowell. Little Robert: A True Story. Bartels, Mark, illus. 2011. 36p. pap. 19.95 (978-1-4137-7171-8(8)) America Star Bks.

Bender, Janet. Don't Pop Your Balloon! Get a Grip on Anger. 2006. 32p. (J). per. 12.95 (978-1-931636-29-2(X)) National Ctr. For Youth Issues.

Benson, Edmund F. & Benson, Susan. Life Skills Curriculum: ARISE Work in Progress, Book 1. 2011. (Work in Progress Ser.). (Illus.). 78p. (J). (gr. 3-4). pap., wbk. ed. 14.95 (978-1-58614-015-1(9)) Arise Foundation.

Berendes, Mary. Feelings/Las Emociones. Petelinsek, Kathleen, illus. 2007. (WordBooks/Libros de Palabras Ser.). (SPA & ENG.). 24p. (J). (gr. k-3). 25.64 (978-1-59296-797-1(3), 201091) Child's World, Inc., The.

Berry, Joy. Help Me Be Good about Throwing Tantrums. 2009. (Help Me Be Good Ser.). 32p. pap. 7.95 (978-1-60577-117-5(1)) Berry, Joy Enterprises.

—Let's Talk about Feeling Angry. Smith, Maggie, illus. 2010. (Let's Talk About Ser.). (ENG.). 32p. (J). (gr. -1-k). pap. 4.99 (978-1-60577-207-3(0)) Berry, Joy Enterprises.

—Let's Talk about Feeling Disappointed. Smith, Maggie, illus. 2010. (Let's Talk About Ser.). (ENG.). 32p. (J). (gr. -1-k). pap. 4.99 (978-1-60577-204-2(6)) Berry, Joy Enterprises.

—Let's Talk about Feeling Sad. Smith, Maggie, illus. 2010. (Let's Talk About Ser.). (ENG.). 32p. (J). (gr. -1-k). pap. 4.99 (978-1-60577-206-6(2)) Berry, Joy Enterprises.

—Let's Talk about Feeling Worried. Smith, Maggie, illus. 2010. (Let's Talk About Ser.). (ENG.). 32p. (J). (gr. -1-k). pap. 4.99 (978-1-60577-221-9(6)) Berry, Joy Enterprises.

—Let's Talk about Getting Hurt. Smith, Maggie, illus. 2010. (Let's Talk About Ser.). (ENG.). 32p. (J). (gr. -1-k). pap. 4.99 (978-1-60577-203-5(8)) Berry, Joy Enterprises.

Berry, Joy Wilt. A Book about Throwing Tantrums. 2005. (Illus.). (J). (978-0-7172-8586-0(3)) Scholastic, Inc.

Bicknell, Joanna, ed. Baby Fun Baby Faces. 2005. 12p. (978-1-905051-15-1(8)) Make Believe Ideas.

Big Feelings: A Book Filled with Emotions. 2009. 24p. (J). 16.99 (978-0-9742761-1-3(1)) Talaris Research Institute.

Bingham, Jane. Everybody Feels Scared. 2007. (QEB Everybody Feels Ser.). (Illus.). 24p. (J). (gr. -1-3). lib. bdg. 17.95 (978-1-59566-216-3(2)) QEB Publishing Inc.

Bingham, Jane & Turner, Helen. Angry. 2007. (QEB Everybody Feels Ser.). (Illus.). 24p. (J). lib. bdg. 17.95 (978-1-59566-215-6(4)) QEB Publishing Inc.

—Happy. 2006. (QEB Everybody Feels Ser.). (Illus.). 24p. (J). lib. bdg. 17.95 (978-1-59566-213-2(8)) QEB Publishing Inc.

—Sad. 2006. (QEB Everybody Feels Ser.). (Illus.). 24p. (J). lib. bdg. 17.95 (978-1-59566-214-9(6)) QEB Publishing Inc.

Bligh, Deirdre. Perfect World: I Was Soooo Embarrassed! Martini, Angela, illus. 2005. 62p. (J). (978-0-439-80069-3(2)) Scholastic, Inc.

Bober, Suzanne & Merberg, Julie. How Is Mona Lisa Feeling? 2010. (ENG.). 22p. (J). bds. 6.99 (978-1-935703-02-0(1)) Downtown Bookworks.

Bohensky, Anita. Anger Management Workbook for Kids & Teens. 2005. (Illus.). 106p. (YA). pap. 54.00 (978-1-893505-06-3(5)) Growth Publishing.

Boye, B. D. The Look Book. Boye, B. D., illus. l.t. ed. 2004. (Illus.). 20p. (J). per. 4.99 (978-0-9768078-1-0(5), 100001) Innerchild Publishing, Inc.

Brooks, Felicity. My First Sticker Book about Me. 2017. (Trivia Bks.). (ENG.). 24p. pap. 12.99 **(978-0-7945-3951-1(3)**, Usborne) EDC Publishing.

Brownjohn, Emma. All Kinds of Feelings. 2004. (Illus.). (J). (BEN & ENG.). 32p. bds. (978-1-84444-303-1(5)); (978-1-84444-302-4(7)); (978-1-84444-304-8(3)); (978-1-84444-305-5(1)); (978-1-84444-306-2(X)); (978-1-84444-307-9(8)); (978-1-84444-308-6(6)); (978-1-84444-309-3(4)); (978-1-84444-310-9(8)); 12p. (978-1-84444-311-6(6)) Mantra Lingua.

—All Kinds of Feelings. 2004. (URD & ENG., Illus.). (J). 17.95 (978-1-84444-312-3(4)) Mantra Lingua GBR. Dist: Chinasprout, Inc.

—All Kinds of Feelings: A Lift-The-Flap Book. 2003. (All Kinds Of Ser.). (ENG., Illus.). 16p. (J). (gr. -1-k). 12.99 (978-1-85707-596-0(X)) Tango Bks. GBR. Dist: Independent Pubs. Group.

Brownlie, Marion. Spirit of Self. 2013. 36p. pap. (978-0-9875551-5-1(4)) Aurora House.

Brukner, Lauren. How to Be a Superhero Called Self-Control! Super Powers to Help Younger Children to Regulate Their Emotions & Senses. Phillips-Smith, Anthony & Apsley House, London Staff, illus. 2015. (ENG.). 112p. 19.95 (978-1-84905-717-2(6), 8140) Kingsley, Jessica Pubs. GBR. Dist: Macmillan Distribution Ltd.

—The Keep-Calm Guru's Guide to Staying Awesome & in Control. Phillips-Smith, Anthony & Apsley House, London Staff, illus. 2016. (ENG.). 136p. 19.95 (978-1-78592-714-0(0), 8410) Kingsley, Jessica Pubs. GBR. Dist: Macmillan Distribution Ltd.

Brukner, Lauren. Self-Control to the Rescue! Super Powers to Help Kids Through the Tough Stuff in Everyday Life. Apsley, illus. 2017. (ENG.). 112p. 19.95 **(978-1-78592-759-1(0)**, 9279) Kingsley, Jessica Pubs. GBR. Dist: Macmillan Distribution Ltd.

Burton, Neel. Heaven & Hell: Psychology of Emotions. 2015. (ENG.). 250p. 24.99 (978-0-9929127-2-7(5), Acheron Pr.) Scion Publishing Ltd. GBR. Dist: Chicago Distribution Ctr.

Caballero, D., tr. Esa Eres Tu y Este Soy Yo. Rubel, Doris, illus. 2006. (Junior (Silver Dolphin) Ser.). (SPA.). 16p. (J). (gr. -1). 9.95 (978-970-718-346-9(2)) Readerlink Distribution Services, LLC.

Cain, Janan. The Way I Feel. Cain, Janan, illus. 2005. (ENG., Illus.). 18p. (J). (— 1). bds. 8.99 (978-1-884734-72-4(3)) Parenting Pr., Inc.

Carpenter, Tad. I Say, You Say Feelings! 2014. (ENG., Illus.). 18p. (J). (gr. -1 — 1). bds. 6.99 (978-0-316-20074-5(3)) Little, Brown Bks. for Young Readers.

Cavaciuti, Susan. Someone Hurt Me. Cavaciuti, Susan, illus. 2004. (Illus.). 222p. pap. 8.95 (978-1-890995-20-1(7), Vital Health Publishing) Square One Pubs.

Cerebellum Academic Team. Lesson Booster 8 Series Set. 2010. (Lesson Booster Ser.). cd-rom 574.98 (978-1-58565-363-8(2)) Cerebellum Corp.

—Lesson Booster Middle School Series. 2010. (Lesson Booster Ser.). cd-rom 454.95 (978-1-58565-365-2(9)) Cerebellum Corp.

Chapus, Julie. Your Feelings. 2013. 102p. (J). pap. 12.00 (978-1-935018-83-4(3)) International Localization Network.

Ciarrochi, Joseph V., et al. Get Out of Your Mind & into Your Life for Teens: A Guide to Living an Extraordinary Life. 2012. (ENG., Illus.). 152p. (YA). (gr. 6-12). pap. 15.95 (978-1-60882-193-8(5), Instant Help Books) New Harbinger Pubns.

Clark, Rosalyn. Feeling Angry. 2017. (Bumba Books (tm) — Feelings Matter Ser.). (ENG.). (J). (gr. -1-1). pap. 6.99 **(978-1-5124-5546-5(6))**; (Illus.). lib. bdg. 25.32 **(978-1-5124-3370-8(5))** Lerner Publishing Group.

—Feeling Happy. 2017. (Bumba Books (tm) — Feelings Matter Ser.). (ENG.). (J). (gr. -1-1). pap. 6.99 **(978-1-5124-5545-8(8))**; (Illus.). lib. bdg. 25.32 **(978-1-5124-3368-5(3))** Lerner Publishing Group.

—Feeling Sad. 2017. (Bumba Books (tm) — Feelings Matter Ser.). (ENG.). 24p. (J). (gr. -1-1). pap. 6.99 **(978-1-5124-5547-2(4))**; (Illus.). 25.32 **(978-1-5124-3367-8(5)**, Lerner Pubns.) Lerner Publishing Group.

Clark, Travis & Belfield, Annie. A Guys' Guide to Stress. 2008. (Flip-It-Over Guides to Teen Emotions Ser.). (Illus.). 128p. (J). (gr. 8-13). lib. bdg. 33.27 (978-0-7660-2857-9(7)) Enslow Pubs., Inc.

Cleary, Brian P. Skin Like Milk, Hair of Silk: What Are Similes & Metaphors? Gable, Brian, illus. (Words Are CATegorical (r) Ser.). (ENG.). (gr. 2-5). 2011. 32p. pap. 6.95 (978-0-7613-3945-8(0)) 2007. pap. 39.62 (978-0-7613-8361-1(1)) Lerner Publishing Group. (Millbrook Pr.).

Cody, Jacquelyne. How to Be Happy. 2008. 192p. 25.50 (978-1-60693-312-1(4), Strategic Bk. Publishing) Strategic Book Publishing & Rights Agency (SBPRA).

Collins-Donnelly, Kate. Starving the Anger Gremlin: A Cognitive Behavioural Therapy Workbook on Anger Management for Young People. 2012. (Gremlin & Thief CBT Workbooks Ser.). (ENG., Illus.). 88p. (C). pap. 19.95 (978-1-84905-286-3(7), 2414) Kingsley, Jessica Pubs. GBR. Dist: Macmillan Distribution Ltd.

—Starving the Anxiety Gremlin for Children Aged 5-9: A Cognitive Behavioural Therapy Workbook on Anxiety Management. 2014. (Gremlin & Thief CBT Workbooks Ser.). (ENG., Illus.). 192p. (C). pap. 19.95 (978-1-84905-492-8(4), 2358) Kingsley, Jessica Pubs. GBR. Dist: Macmillan Distribution Ltd.

Collins, Savina. Sad. DuFalla, Anita, illus. 2017. (I Have Feelings Ser.). (ENG.). (J). (gr. k-1). 28.51 **(978-1-68342-142-9(6))** Rourke Educational Media.

Cosson, M. J. The Smart Kid's Guide to Feeling Sad or Angry. Rooney, Ronnie, illus. 2014. (Smart Kid's Guide to Everyday Life Ser.). (ENG.). 32p. (J). (gr. 2-5). 28.50 (978-1-62687-341-4(0), 207181) Child's World, Inc., The.

Crist, J. J. Como Superar los Miedos y Preocupaciones. 2004. (SPA., Illus.). 128p. (978-84-9754-125-1(1), 87443) Ediciones Oniro S.A.

Crist, James J. What to Do When You're Cranky & Blue. 2013. (ENG., Illus.). 128p. (J). (gr. 4-8). pap. 10.99 (978-1-57542-430-9(4)) Free Spirit Publishing, Inc.

Curriculum in a Box: Managing Emotions. 2004. (YA). 699.95 incl. DVD (978-1-55548-194-0(9), 605) Human Relations Media.

Del Moral, Susana. Como Me Siento. Zaidi, Nadeem, illus. 2005. (Baby Einstein: Libros de Carton Ser.). (SPA.). 14p. (J). (gr. -1). bds. (978-970-718-308-7(X), Silver Dolphin en Español) Advanced Marketing, S. de R. L. de C. V.

Dijk, Sheri Van. Relationship Skills 101 for Teens: Your Guide to Dealing with Daily Drama, Stress & Difficult Emotions Using Dbt. 2015. (Instant Help Solutions Ser.). (ENG.). 208p. (YA). (gr. 5-12). pap. 17.95 (978-1-62625-052-9(9)) New Harbinger Pubns.

Ditta-Donahue, Gina. Josh's Smiley Faces: A Story about Anger. Blake, Anne Catharine, illus. 2003. 32p. (J). pap. 9.95 (978-1-59147-001-4(3)); 14.95 (978-1-59147-000-7(5)) American Psychological Assn. (Magination Pr.).

Dixon, Thomas. From Passions to Emotions: The Creation of a Secular Psychological Category. 2003. (ENG.). 300p. 129.00 (978-0-521-82729-4(9)) Cambridge Univ. Pr.

Dolphin, Colleen. Adventurous to Zealous: All about Me from A to Z, 1 vol. 2009. (Let's Learn A to Z Ser.). (ENG., Illus.). 32p. (J). (gr. -1-2). 27.07 (978-1-60453-490-0(7), 1293204) ABDO Publishing Co.

Dombrower, Jan. Getting to Know Your Emotional Needs. Sorba, Richard, illus. Date not set. (J). (978-1-55864-021-4(5)) Kidsrights.

Dorling Kindersley Publishing Staff. Disney Pixar Inside Out: the Essential Guide: The Essential Guide. 2015. (ENG., Illus.). 64p. (J). (gr. 1-4). 12.99 (978-1-4654-3547-7(6), DK Children) Dorling Kindersley Publishing, Inc.

—Inside Out. 2015. (Ultimate Sticker Bks.). (ENG.). 16p. (J). (gr. k-4). pap. 6.99 (978-1-4654-3532-3(8), DK Children) Dorling Kindersley Publishing, Inc.

Drescher, Joan. A Journey in the Moon Balloon: When Images Speak Louder Than Words. Drescher, Joan, illus. 2015. (ENG., Illus.). 72p. (J). 19.95 (978-1-84905-730-1(3), 7701) Kingsley, Jessica Pubs. GBR. Dist: Macmillan Distribution Ltd.

Dyan, Penelope. Thou Shalt Not Covet! Dyan, Penelope, illus. 2012. (Illus.). 34p. pap. 11.95 (978-1-61477-042-8(5)) Bellissima Publishing, LLC.

Edwards, Dianna. It's Not Easy Being Patou - Book One. 2004. (J). (978-0-9767756-1-4(1)) Patou Bks., LLC.

—Meet Patou. 2006. (J). pap. 29.95 (978-0-9767756-0-7(3)) Patou Bks., LLC.

—My Journal & Drawings. 2004. (J). spiral bd. (978-0-9767756-4-5(6)) Patou Bks., LLC.

—When Niki Got Sick, Bk. 2. 2004. (J). (978-0-9767756-2-1(X)) Patou Bks., LLC.

—Why Can't Everything Just Stay the Same? Book Three. 2004. (J). (978-0-9767756-3-8(8)) Patou Bks., LLC.

Equipo Staff. El Gusto. (Coleccion Mundo Maravilloso). (SPA., Illus.). 36p. (J). (gr. 2-4). (978-84-348-4779-8(5), SM2722) SM Ediciones.

Etingoff, Kim. Embarrassment, Shame, & Guilt. Croft, Cindy, ed. 2014. (Causes & Effects of Emotions Ser.: 13). 64p. (J). (gr. 7-18). 23.95 (978-1-4222-3069-5(4)) Mason Crest.

—Fear & Anxiety. Croft, Cindy, ed. 2014. (Causes & Effects of Emotions Ser.: 13). 64p. (J). (gr. 7-18). 23.95 (978-1-4222-3073-2(2)) Mason Crest.

Evans, Jane. Kit Kitten & the Topsy-Turvy Feelings: A Story about Parents Who Aren't Always Able to Care. Bean, Izzy, illus. 2015. (ENG.). 32p. (J). 16.95 (978-1-84905-602-1(1), 3206) Kingsley, Jessica Pubs. GBR. Dist: Macmillan Distribution Ltd.

Everthing Changes Interactive Packages: Feelings. (Pebble Soup Explorations Ser.). (gr. -1-18). 52.00 (978-0-7578-5242-8(4)) Rigby Education.

Fiedler, Julie. How to Deal with Anger. (Let's Work It Out Ser.). 24p. (gr. 2-3). 2009. 42.50 (978-1-61514-256-9(8), PowerKids Pr.) 2007. (Illus.). (J). lib. bdg. 22.60 (978-1-4042-3671-4(6)) Rosen Publishing Group, Inc., The.

Finn, Carrie. Kids Talk about Fairness, 1 vol. Muehlenhardt, Amy Bailey, illus. 2006. (Kids Talk Jr Ser.). (ENG.). 32p. (gr. -1-2). lib. bdg. 26.65 (978-1-4048-2316-7(6)) Picture Window Bks.

First Step Nonfiction - Feelings, 4 bks., Set. 2006. (J). (gr. -1-k). 12.95 (978-0-8225-3899-8(7)) Lerner Publishing Group.

Fowler, Leona. I Don't Want to Be Grumpy Anymore! Martins, Ann-Kathrin & Fowler, Romana, illus. 2011. 19p. (J). 12.95 (978-1-58909-804-6(8)) Bookstand Publishing.

Franzen, Lenore. Anger. 2004. (My Feelings Ser.). (Illus.). 24p. (J). lib. bdg. 15.95 (978-1-58341-318-0(9), Creative Education) Creative Co., The.

—Sadness. 2004. (My Feelings Ser.). (Illus.). 24p. (J). lib. bdg. 15.95 (978-1-58341-321-0(9), Creative Education) Creative Co., The.

Freigruber, Amy Elizabeth. At the Top of the Toboggan Hill. 2007. 60p. per. 9.95 (978-0-595-42728-4(6)) iUniverse, Inc.

Fukumoto, Jan. It's Hard Not to Stare: Helping Children Understand Disabilities. Huff, Tim, illus. 2013. 38p. pap. (978-1-927355-28-2(1)) BayRidge Bks.

George, Liz. Empathy: I Know How You Feel! 2015. (Rookie Talk about It(tm) Ser.). (ENG., Illus.). 32p. (J). pap. 5.95 (978-0-531-21380-3(3), Children's Pr.) Scholastic Library Publishing.

Gibs, Leighanne. Emo Poetry & Prose. 2011. 44p. pap. 16.95 (978-1-4626-3803-1(1)) America Star Bks.

Glassman, Bruce S. Caring. 2008. (Illus.). 48p. (J). pap. 9.95 (978-1-60108-501-6(X), Bearing Bks.); (YA). (gr. 3-6). lib. bdg. 29.25 (978-1-60108-500-9(1)) Red Cygnet Pr.

Gootman, Marilyn E. When a Friend Dies: A Book for Teens about Grieving & Healing. Espeland, Pamela, ed. 2004. 120p. (YA). (gr. 6-18). pap. 9.95 (978-0-915793-66-2(0), FS209) Free Spirit Publishing, Inc.

Gravel, Élise. How Do You Doodle? 2013. (Illus.). 96p. pap. 12.95 (978-1-4338-1291-0(6)) American Psychological Assn.

Graves, Sue. I Hate Everything! Guicciardini, Desideria, illus. 2013. (Our Emotions & Behavior Ser.). (ENG.). 32p. (J). (gr. -1-3). 12.99 (978-1-57542-443-9(6)) Free Spirit Publishing, Inc.

Hale, Natalie. So Many Feelings. 2003. (J). spiral bd. 9.95 (978-0-9702698-6-7(2)) Special Reads for Special Needs.

Hall, Pamela. A Bully-Free Playground, 1 vol. Ostrom, Bob, illus. 2012. (Bully-Free World Ser.). (ENG.). 24p. (J). (gr. -1-4). 27.07 (978-1-61641-846-5(X)) Magic Wagon.

—Making a Bully-Free World, 1 vol. Ostrom, Bob, illus. 2012. (Bully-Free World Ser.). (ENG.). 24p. (J). (gr. -1-4). 27.07 (978-1-61641-848-9(6)) Magic Wagon.

Hallinan, P. K. Holidays & Special Feelings, 8 bks. (Illus.). (J). lib. bdg. 108.60 (978-1-56674-909-1(3)) Forest Hse. Publishing Co., Inc.

Hamilton, Prissy. A Rainbow Within: An Introduction to the Emotional Energies for Children. Hamilton, Prissy, ed. Hamilton, Prissy, illus. 2005. (Illus.). (J). pap. 14.00 (978-0-9655933-1-1(2)) IGMI Publishing.

Hill, Z. B. Loneliness. Croft, Cindy, ed. 2014. (Causes & Effects of Emotions Ser.: 13). 64p. (J). (gr. 7-18). 23.95 (978-1-4222-3075-6(9)) Mason Crest.

—Sadness. Croft, Cindy, ed. 2014. (Causes & Effects of Emotions Ser.: 13). 64p. (J). (gr. 7-18). 23.95 (978-1-4222-3078-7(3)) Mason Crest.

Huebner, Dawn. What to Do When Your Temper Flares: A Kid's Guide to Overcoming Problems with Anger. Matthews, Bonnie, illus. 2007. (What-to-Do Guides for Kids Ser.). 95p. (J). (gr. 3-7). per. 15.95 (978-1-4338-0134-1(5), 4418005, Magination Pr.) American Psychological Assn.

Humphrey, Mary. The Kids' Yoga Book of Feelings, 1 vol. Hamlin, Janet, illus. Frost, Michael, photos by. 2008. (ENG.). 40p. (J). (gr. 3-7). 15.99 (978-0-7614-5424-3(1)) Marshall Cavendish Corp.

Hyde, Margaret O. & Forsyth, Elizabeth H. Stress 101: An Overview for Teens. 2008. (Teen Overviews Ser.). (ENG., Illus.). 120p. (gr. 7-12). lib. bdg. 27.93 (978-0-8225-6788-2(1)) Lerner Publishing Group.

Ismail, Yasmeen, illus. Happy, Sad, Feeling Glad: Yasmeen Ismail's Draw & Discover. 2017. (ENG.). 56p. (J). (gr. -1-2). pap. 9.99 (978-1-78067-933-4(5)) King, Laurence Publishing GBR. Dist: Hachette Bk. Group.

Jaffe, Amy V. & Gardner, Luci. My Book Full of Feelings: How to Control & React to the Size of Your Emotions. 2006. (Illus.). 70p. spiral bd. 27.95 (978-1-931282-83-3(8)) Autism Asperger Publishing Co.

Jarvis. Who Is Happy? 2016. (ENG.). 22p. (J). (gr. -1-k). 16.99 (978-1-84780-842-4(5), Frances Lincoln Children's Bks.) Quarto Publishing Group UK GBR. Dist: Hachette Bk. Group.

Jarvis, illus. Who Is Happy? 2016. (ENG.). 22p. (J). 16.99 (978-1-84780-722-9(4), Frances Lincoln Children's Bks.) Quarto Publishing Group UK GBR. Dist: Littlehampton Bk Services, Ltd.

Jeffers, Susan & Gradstein, Donna. I Can Handle It! 50 Confidence-Building Stories to Empower Your Child. 2006. (ENG., Illus.). 160p. per. 9.95 (978-0-9777618-0-7(0)) Jeffers Pr.

Jennings, Sarah, illus. My Feelings. 2017. (ENG.). 14p. (J). bds. 9.99 (978-1-68119-539-1(9), 9781681195391, Bloomsbury Activity Bks.) Bloomsbury Publishing USA.

Johansen, Heidi. What I Look Like When I Am Angry. 2004. (Let's Look at Feelings / un Vistazo a Los Sentimientos Ser.).Tr. of What I Look Like When I am Angry. (SPA., Illus.). 24p. (gr. -1-1). lib. bdg. 22.60 (978-1-4042-7508-9(8), Editorial Buenas Letras) Rosen Publishing Group, Inc., The.

—What I Look Like When I am Angry / Cómo me veo cuando estoy Enojado. 2009. (Let's Look at Feelings / un vistazo a los sentimientos Ser.). (ENG & SPA.). 24p. (gr. k-1). 42.50 (978-1-61514-245-3(2), Editorial Buenas Letras) Rosen Publishing Group, Inc., The.

Johansen, Heidi Leigh. What I Look Like When I Am Angry. 2004. (Let's Look at Feelings Ser.). (Illus.). 24p. (gr. -1-1). 22.60 (978-1-4042-2508-4(0), Editorial Buenas Letras) Rosen Publishing Group, Inc., The.

Johnson, Kimberly. The Things in Your Head: The Adventures of Bulu. 2012. 30p. pap. 13.99 (978-1-4525-6073-1(0)) Balboa Pr.

Johnson, Lakishi. Smiles. 2009. 34p. pap. 14.60 (978-0-557-04782-6(X)) Lulu Pr., Inc.

Johnston, Marianne. Dealing with Anger / Qué hacer con la Ira. 2009. (Conflict Resolution Library / Biblioteca solución de conflictos Ser.). (ENG & SPA.). 24p. (gr. 2-3). 42.50 (978-1-60853-412-8(X), Editorial Buenas Letras) Rosen Publishing Group, Inc., The.

—Dealing with Anger/Que Hacer con la Ira. De Leon, Mauricio Velzaquez, tr. from ENG. 2008. (Conflict Resolution Library / Biblioteca Solución de Conflictos Ser.). (SPA., Illus.). 24p. (J). (gr. k-3). lib. bdg. 22.60 (978-1-4042-7659-8(9)) Rosen Publishing Group, Inc., The.

Johnstone, Michael. My Special Friend. 2003. (Forever Friends Ser.). (Illus.). 64p. pap. 3.95 (978-1-84357-028-8(9)) Contender Entertainment Group GBR. Dist: Independent Pubs. Group.

—Together Forever. 2003. (Forever Friends Ser.). (Illus.). 64p. pap. 3.95 (978-1-84357-006-6(8)) Contender Entertainment Group GBR. Dist: Independent Pubs. Group.

Jones, Frankie. Faces: A Follow-the-Trail Book. Galloway, Fhiona, illus. 2016. (ENG.). 10p. (J). (gr. -1 — 1). bds. 7.99 (978-1-4998-0268-9(4)) Little Bee Books Inc.

Jones, Grace. My Feelings. 2017. (Illus.). 24p. (J). **(978-0-7787-3246-4(0))** Crabtree Publishing Co.

Jones, Viola & Aydt, Rachel. Divorce & Your Feelings. 2016. (Divorce & Your Family Ser.). 64p. (J). (gr. 7-7). 34.45 (978-1-5081-7128-7(9)) Rosen Publishing Group, Inc., The.

Jones, Viola, et al. Life in a Blended Family. 2016. (Divorce & Your Family Ser.). 64p. (J). (gr. 7-7). 34.45 (978-1-5081-7129-4(7)) Rosen Publishing Group, Inc., The.

Just Kidding! 2014. (Just Kidding! Ser.). 24p. (J). (gr. 2-3). 135.60 (978-1-4824-0558-3(X)) Stevens, Gareth Publishing LLLP.

Kalman, Bobbie. I Have Feelings. 2014. 16p. pap. 6.00 (978-1-61003-347-3(7)) Center for the Collaborative Classroom.

—I Have Feelings. 2010. (ENG., Illus.). 16p. (J). (gr. k-2). (978-0-7787-9417-2(2)); pap. (978-0-7787-9461-5(X)) Crabtree Publishing Co.

—I Have Feelings: Tengo Sentimientos. 2010. (My World Ser.). (SPA, ENG & MUL.). 16p. (J). (gr. k-3). pap. (978-0-7787-8265-0(4)); lib. bdg. (978-0-7787-8272-8(7)) Crabtree Publishing Co.

—Tengo Sentimientos. 2010. (SPA.). 16p. (J). pap. (978-0-7787-8580-4(7)); lib. bdg. (978-0-7787-8554-5(8)) Crabtree Publishing Co.

—When I Am Happy. 2010. (My World Ser.). (ENG.). 16p. (J). (gr. k-3). (978-0-7787-9503-2(9)) Crabtree Publishing Co.

Kaplan, Arie. Gratitude. 2013. (7 Character Strengths of Highly Successful Students Ser.). 64p. (J). (gr. 5-8). pap. 77.70 (978-1-4488-9558-8(8)); (Illus.). 31.95 (978-1-4488-9544-1(8)); (Illus.). pap. 12.95 (978-1-4488-9557-1(X)) Rosen Publishing Group, Inc., The.

Karim, Joseph & Karim, Silvana. What Does Happy Look Like? Karim, Joseph & Karim, Silvana, illus. 2009. (Illus.). 47p. (J). pap. 18.95 (978-1-934575-54-3(2)) Autism Asperger Publishing Co.

Kennedy, Debi. The Angry Monster Book. Kennedy, Debi, illus. 2005. (Illus.). 30p. (J). 8.99 (978-0-9769959-0-6(5)) nJoy Bks.

Kimmelman, Leslie & Shepherd, Jodie. How Do You Feel? 2014. (Rookie Toddler(r) Ser.). (ENG.). 12p. (J). bds. 6.95 (978-0-531-20493-1(6)) Scholastic Library Publishing.

Kirberger, Kimberly & Kirberger, Jesse. I Don't Know What I Want but I Want to Be Happy. 2009. (ENG., Illus.). 148p. (gr. 7-18). pap. 14.95 (978-0-7573-0674-7(8)) Health Communications, Inc.

Know Your Emotions. 2011. (Know Your Emotions Ser.). (ENG.). 24p. (gr. 1-2). lib. bdg. 81.96 (978-1-4296-6046-4(5), Aplus Bks.) Capstone Press of Coughlan Cos.

Kravetz, Jonathan. How to Deal with Fighting. 2007. (Let's Work It Out Ser.). (Illus.). 24p. (J). (gr. 2-5). lib. bdg. 22.60 (978-1-4042-3672-1(4)) Rosen Publishing Group, Inc., The.

Lamia, Mary C. Emotions! Making Sense of Your Feelings. 2012. 146p. (J). pap. 14.95 (978-1-4338-1193-7(6), Magination Pr.) American Psychological Assn.

—Understanding Myself: A Kid's Guide to Intense Emotions & Strong Feelings. 2010. (Illus.). 112p. (J). (gr. 3-8). 14.95 (978-1-4338-0889-0(7)); pap. 9.95 (978-1-4338-0890-6(0)) American Psychological Assn. (Magination Pr.).

Langensiepen, Julia. Deeno's Dream Journeys in the Big Blue Bubble: A Relaxation Programme to Help Children Manage Their Emotions. 2009. (ENG., Illus.). 128p. pap. 28.95 **(978-1-84905-039-5(2)**, 3581) Kingsley, Jessica Pubs. GBR. Dist: Macmillan Distribution Ltd.

Larsen, Carolyn. It's Okay to Feel Sad: A Book about Sadness. O'Connor, Tim, illus. 2017. (Growing God's Kids Ser.). (ENG.). 32p. (J). pap. 4.99 (978-0-8010-0988-4(X)) Baker Bks.

—Keeping Your Cool: A Book about Anger. O'Connor, Tim, illus. 2016. (Growing God's Kids Ser.). (ENG.). 32p. (J). pap. 4.99 (978-0-8010-0912-9(X)) Baker Bks.

Larson, Elaine Marie. The Chameleon Kid: Controlling Meltdown Before He Controls You. 2008. (ENG.). 41p. (J). 17.95 (978-1-934575-22-2(4)) Autism Asperger Publishing Co.

Lecoy, Denise. Looking after Me. Hamelin, Marie-Micheline, illus. 2nd rev. ed. 2009. (Caring for Me Ser.). (ENG.). 20p. pap. 9.95 (978-1-894778-54-1(5)) Theytus Bks., Ltd. CAN. Dist: Univ. of Toronto Pr.

Lennon, Liz. I Don't Hit. 2013. (Illus.). (J). 25.65 (978-1-59771-411-2(9)) Sea-To-Sea Pubns.

Leonard, Marcia. I Feel Angry. Bartholomew, illus. 2003. 24p. (J). bds. 2.95 (978-0-8249-6526-6(4), Ideal Pubns.) Worthy Publishing.

—I Feel Sad. Bartholomew, illus. 2003. 24p. (J). bds. 2.95 (978-0-8249-6524-2(8), Ideal Pubns.) Worthy Publishing.

The Let's Talk Set 11: Comforting Information. (Illus.). (J). (gr. k-5). 112.50 (978-0-8239-7140-4(6)) Rosen Publishing Group, Inc., The.

Leventhal-Belfer, Laurie. Why Do I Have To? A Book for Children Who Find Themselves Frustrated by Everyday Rules. Montaini-Klovdahl, Luisa, illus. 2008. (ENG.). 80p. pap. 10.95 (978-1-84310-891-7(7), 5918) Kingsley, Jessica Pubs. GBR. Dist: Macmillan Distribution Ltd.

Levin, Judith. Anxiety & Panic Attacks. 2008. (Teen Mental Health Ser.). (Illus.). 48p. (YA). (gr. 7-12). lib. bdg. 29.25 (978-1-4042-1797-3(5)) Rosen Publishing Group, Inc., The.

Lewis, Anthony, illus. Carrbts or Peas? 2008. (Pick & Choose Ser.). (ENG.). 12p. (J). (gr. -1). bds. (978-1-84643-242-2(1)) Child's Play International Ltd.

—Teddy or Train? 2008. (Pick & Choose Ser.). (ENG.). 12p. (J). (gr. -1). bds. (978-1-84643-241-5(3)) Child's Play International Ltd.

—Wind or Rain? 2008. (Pick & Choose Ser.). (ENG.). 12p. (J). (gr. -1). bds. (978-1-84643-240-8(5)) Child's Play International Ltd.

L'Heureux, Christine. Play with Me! Brignaud, Pierre, illus. 2009. (Big Dipper Ser.). (ENG.). 24p. (J). (gr. -1-k). pap. 3.95 (978-2-89450-679-0(1)) Caillouet, Gerry.

Licata, Renora. Todo lo que necesitas saber sobre la ira (Everything You Need to Know about Anger) 2009. (Todo lo que necesitas (the Need to Know Library) Ser.). (SPA.). 64p. (gr. 6-6). 58.50 (978-1-60854-409-7(5), Editorial Buenas Letras) Rosen Publishing Group, Inc., The.

Light, Steve. I Am Happy: A Touch-and-Feel Book of Feelings. Light, Steve, illus. 2005. (Illus.). 10p. (J). (gr. k-4). reprint ed. 13.00 (978-0-7567-9630-3(X)) DIANE Publishing Co.

Lite, Lori. Children's Wellness Curriculum: Lessons, Stories & Techniques Designed to Decrease Bullying, Anxiety, Anger & Obesity While Promoting Self-Esteem & Healthy Food Choices. 2007. (J). (gr. k-5). 89.95 incl. audio compact disk (978-0-9787781-2-5(X), 5) Stress Free Pubs.

Llenas, Anna. The Color Monster: A Pop-Up Book of Feelings. 2015. (ENG., Illus.). 20p. (J). (gr. -1-2). 19.95 (978-1-4549-1729-8(6)) Sterling Publishing Co., Inc.

Lo Bosco, Maryellen. David Hume & a Treatise of Human Nature. 2016. (J). lib. bdg. (978-1-68048-547-9(4)) Windmill Bks.

Logan, John & Kavanaugh, Dorothy. A Guys' Guide to Love. 2008. (Flip-It-Over Guides to Teen Emotions Ser.). (Illus.). 128p. (J). (gr. k-5). lib. bdg. 33.27 (978-0-7660-2855-5(0)) Enslow Pubs., Inc.

Lohmann, Raychelle Cassada. The Anger Workbook for Teens: Activities to Help You Deal with Anger & Frustration. 2009. (Instant Help Ser.). (ENG.). 144p. (YA). (gr. 6-12). pap. 16.95 (978-1-57224-699-7(5), Instant Help Books) New Harbinger Pubns.

Ludwig, Ashley. You Tickle My Heart: and other ways you make me laugh. 2008. (Illus.). 18p. (J). (gr. k-1). bds. 11.50 (978-0-9800630-0-4(0)) Beachcomber Press.com.

Lynette, Rachel. How to Deal with Hurt Feelings. 2009. (Let's Work It Out Ser.). 24p. (gr. 2-3). 42.50 (978-1-61514-262-0(2), PowerKids Pr.); (Illus.). (J). lib. bdg. 22.60 (978-1-4042-4522-8(7), 1284658) Rosen Publishing Group, Inc., The.

MacGregor, Cynthia. How Do You Feel Today? 2009. (Reading Room Collection 2 Ser.). 24p. (gr. 3-4). 42.50 (978-1-60851-970-5(8), PowerKids Pr.) Rosen Publishing Group, Inc., The.

Maisel, Gail. Feelings Can Be Friends. 2014. (ENG.). 28p. (978-1-909623-26-2(1)) Panoma Pr. Ltd.

Marcovitz, Hal. An Angry Guy's Guide: How to Deal. 2014. (Guy's Guide Ser.). (ENG.). 64p. (J). (gr. 5-12). pap. 9.95 (978-1-62293-000-5(2)) Enslow Pubs., Inc.

Marcovitz, Hal & Snyder, Gail. A Guys' Guide to Anger. 2008. (Flip-It-Over Guides to Teen Emotions Ser.). (Illus.). 128p. (J). (gr. 8-13). lib. bdg. 33.27 (978-0-7660-2853-1(4)) Enslow Pubs., Inc.

Marsico, Katie. I Cry. 2014. (Tell Me Why Library). (ENG., Illus.). 24p. (J). (gr. 2-5). 25.64 (978-1-63188-004-9(7), 205423) Cherry Lake Publishing.

Martin, Martha. Live It: Empathy. 2009. (ENG., Illus.). 32p. (J). (gr. 3-6). lib. bdg. (978-0-7787-4882-3(0)) Crabtree Publishing Co.

McCloud, Carol. Baby's Bucket Book. Zimmer, Glenn, illus. 2014. (ENG.). 16p. (J). (— 1). bds. 7.95 (978-0-9960999-2-9(1)) Bucket Fillers, Inc.

McDonald-Mitchell, Carolyn. The Secret Hiding Place. 2006. 73p. 10.99 (978-1-4116-9140-7(7)) Lulu Pr., Inc.

McNulty John. I Am Your Emotions. Gilmour, Karen, illus. 2006. 32p. (J). (978-0-9769580-4-8(X)) I Am Your Playground LLC.

Meiners, Cheri J. Cool down & Work Through Anger. 2010. (Learning to Get Along(r) Ser.). (ENG., Illus.). 40p. (J). (gr. -1-3). pap. 11.99 (978-1-57542-346-3(4)) Free Spirit Publishing, Inc.

—Cool down & Work Through Anger/Cálmate y Supera la Ira. 2014. (Learning to Get Along(r) Ser.). (SPA, ENG & MUL., Illus.). 48p. (J). (gr. -1-3). pap. 12.45 (978-1-57542-473-6(8)) Free Spirit Publishing, Inc.

—The Learning to Get along Series Interactive Software. Johnson, Meredith, illus. 2008. (Learning to Get Along Ser.). (ENG.). 24p. (gr. k-3). cd-rom 99.99 (978-1-57542-281-7(6)) Free Spirit Publishing, Inc.

—Understand & Care. 2003. (Learning to Get Along(r) Ser.). (ENG., Illus.). 40p. (J). (gr. -1-3). pap. 10.95 (978-1-57542-131-5(3)) Free Spirit Publishing, Inc.

Meister, Cari. Everyone Feels Angry Sometimes, 1 vol. Ward, Damian, illus. 2010. (Everyone Has Feelings Ser.). (ENG.). 24p. (gr. k-2). lib. bdg. 25.99 (978-1-4048-5753-7(2)) Picture Window Bks.

Miles, Lisa & Chown, Xanna Eve. How to Survive Online Embarrassment. 2013. (Girl Talk Ser.). (Illus.). 48p. (J). (gr. 5-8). (ENG.). pap. 11.75 (978-1-4777-0723-4(9), Rosen Classroom); pap. 70.50 (978-1-4777-0726-5(3), Rosen Reference); (ENG., lib. bdg. 29.25 (978-1-4777-0708-1(5), Rosen Reference) Rosen Publishing Group, Inc., The.

Millar, Goldie & Berger, Lisa. F Is for Feelings. Mitchell, Hazel, illus. 2014. (ENG.). 40p. (J). (gr. -1-3). 15.99 (978-1-57542-475-0(4)) Free Spirit Publishing, Inc.

Millar, Goldie, et al. F Is for Feelings. 2014. (ENG., Illus.). 40p. (J). (gr. -1-3). pap. 9.99 (978-1-57542-476-7(2)) Free Spirit Publishing, Inc.

Miller, Connie Colwell. Angry Is... 2011. (Know Your Emotions Ser.). (ENG.). 24p. (gr. 1-2). pap. 8.10 (978-1-4296-7044-9(4)); pap. 47.70 (978-1-4296-7055-5(X)); lib. bdg. 27.32 (978-1-4296-6044-0(9)) Capstone Press of Coughlan Cos. (Aplus Bks.).

—Enojo Es... Strictly Spanish LLC. Staff, tr. from ENG. 2013. (Reconoce Tus Emociones/Know Your Emotions Ser.).Tr. of Angry Is.... (ENG, SPA & MUL.). 24p. (gr. 1-2). lib. bdg. 27.32 (978-1-62065-154-4(8)) Capstone Press of Coughlan Cos.

—Happy Is... 2011. (Know Your Emotions Ser.). (ENG.). 24p. (gr. 1-2). lib. bdg. 27.32 (978-1-4296-6042-6(2), Aplus Bks.) Capstone Press of Coughlan Cos.

Miller, Connie Colwell & Nichols, Cheyenne. Know Your Emotions. 2011. (Know Your Emotions Ser.). (ENG.). 24p. (gr. 1-2). pap. 190.80 (978-1-4296-7066-1(5), Aplus Bks.) Capstone Press of Coughlan Cos.

Miller, Connie Colwell, et al. Reconoce Tus Emociones/Know Your Emotions. Strictly Spanish, LLC., tr. 2013. (Reconoce Tus Emociones/Know Your Emotions Ser.). (MUL.). 24p. (gr. 1-2). lib. bdg. 109.28 (978-1-62065-156-8(4), A+ Bilingue/Bilingual) Capstone Press of Coughlan Cos.

Miller, J. Philip & Greene, Sheppard M. We All Sing with the Same Voice. Meisel, Paul, illus. 2005. (ENG.). 32p. (J). (gr. -1-2). reprint ed. pap. 6.99 (978-0-06-073900-3(2)) HarperCollins Pubs.

Miller, Margaret. Baby Faces. Miller, Margaret, photos by. 2009. (Look Baby! Bks.). (ENG., Illus.). 14p. (J). (gr. -1 — 1). bds. 4.99 (978-1-4169-7887-9(9), Little Simon) Little Simon.

Mitchard, Jacquelyn. Now You See Her. 2008. (ENG.). 224p. (YA). (gr. 7-12). pap. 7.99 (978-0-06-111686-5(6), Harper Trophy) HarperCollins Pubs.

Moe, Barbara. Coping with Rejection. (Coping Ser.). 192p. (gr. 7-12). 2009. 63.90 (978-1-61512-010-9(6)) 2005. (Illus.). (YA). lib. bdg. 34.60 (978-0-8239-3362-4(8)) Rosen Publishing Group, Inc., The.

Moehn, Heather. Coping with Social Anxiety. 2009. (Coping Ser.). 192p. (gr. 7-12). 63.90 (978-1-61512-012-3(2)) Rosen Publishing Group, Inc., The.

Montgormary, Beverly. In Deep Thought. 2004. (J). per. (978-0-9763093-5-2(1)) Creative Bk. Pubs.

Musgrave, Susan. Kiss, Tickle, Cuddle, Hug, 1 vol. 2012. (ENG., Illus.). 24p. (J). (gr. -1-k). bds. 9.95 (978-1-4598-0163-9(6)) Orca Bk. Pubs. USA.

Nemiroff, Marc A. & Annunziata, Jane. Shy Spaghetti & Excited Eggs: A Kid's Menu of Feelings. Battuz, Christine, illus. 2011. 48p. (J). (gr. -1-3). 15.95 (978-1-4338-0956-9(7)); pap. 10.95 (978-1-4338-0957-6(5)) American Psychological Assn. (Magination Pr.).

A New House. 2004. (J). pap. 6.95 (978-0-9760646-0-2(X)) Grape Elephant MarketPr.

Nichols, Cheyenne. Miedo Es... Strictly Spanish Translation Services Staff, tr. from ENG. 2013. (Reconoce Tus Emociones/Know Your Emotions Ser.).Tr. of Scared Is.... (ENG, SPA & MUL.). 24p. (gr. 1-2). lib. bdg. 27.32 (978-1-62065-153-7(X)) Capstone Press of Coughlan Cos.

—Sad Is... 2011. (Know Your Emotions Ser.). (ENG.). 24p. (gr. 1-2). pap. 47.70 (978-1-4296-7060-9(6), Aplus Bks.) Capstone Press of Coughlan Cos.

Nichols, Cheyenne & Miller, Connie Colwell. Know Your Emotions. 2011. (Know Your Emotions Ser.). (ENG.). 24p. (gr. 1-2). pap. 31.80 (978-1-4296-7065-4(7), Aplus Bks.) Capstone Press of Coughlan Cos.

Nilsen, Erika. The Blessing of Feelings. Nilsen, Mary Ylvisaker, photos by. 2007. (Illus.). 32p. (J). 10.95 (978-0-9627147-4-0(7)) Zion Publishing.

Nolan, Tammy. Smiles: It's Really Amazing What They Can Do. 2009. 44p. pap. 16.99 (978-1-4490-3055-1(6)) AuthorHouse.

O'Connor, Frances. Frequently Asked Questions about Academic Anxiety. 2009. (FAQ: Teen Life Ser.). 64p. (gr. 5-6). 58.50 (978-1-61512-560-9(4)) Rosen Publishing Group, Inc., The.

Orr, Tamra B. Anger. 2016. (21st Century Basic Skills Library: Feelings Ser.). (ENG., Illus.). 24p. (J). (gr. k-3). 24.21 (978-1-63471-041-1(X), 208244) Cherry Lake Publishing.

—Excitement. 2016. (21st Century Basic Skills Library: Feelings Ser.). (ENG., Illus.). 24p. (J). (gr. k-3). 24.21 (978-1-63471-042-8(8), 208248) Cherry Lake Publishing.

—Joy. 2016. (21st Century Basic Skills Library: Feelings Ser.). (ENG., Illus.). 24p. (J). (gr. k-3). 24.21 *(978-1-63471-044-2(4)*, 208256) Cherry Lake Publishing.
—Sadness. 2016. (21st Century Basic Skills Library: Feelings Ser.). (ENG., Illus.). 24p. (J). (gr. k-3). 24.21 *(978-1-63471-045-9(2)*, 208260) Cherry Lake Publishing.
—Surprise. 2016. (21st Century Basic Skills Library: Feelings Ser.). (ENG., Illus.). 24p. (J). (gr. k-3). 24.21 *(978-1-63471-048-0(7)*, 208272, Blackbirch Pr., Inc.) Cherry Lake Publishing.
Palmer, Pat. Liking Myself. Shondeck, Betty, illus. 2010. 102p. (J). pap. 12.99 *(978-0-9622834-2-0(8))* Uplift Pr.
Parenting Press Staff & Cain, Janan. Así Me Siento Yo. Canetti, Yanitzia, tr. from ENG. Cain, Janan, illus. 2009.Tr. of Way I Feel. (SPA & ENG., Illus.). 32p. (J). (gr. -1-3). 16.95 *(978-1-884734-83-0(9))* Parenting Pr., Inc.
Patricelli, Leslie. Baby Happy Baby Sad. Patricelli, Leslie, illus. 2008. (Leslie Patricelli Board Bks.). (ENG., Illus.). 24p. (J). (— 1). bds. 6.99 *(978-0-7636-3245-8(7))* Candlewick Pr.
Perritano, John. The Most Disgusting Animals on the Planet, 1 vol. 2012. (Disgusting Stuff Ser.). (ENG., Illus.). 48p. (gr. 3-4). lib. bdg. 31.99 *(978-1-4296-7535-2(7))* Capstone Press of Coughlan Cos.
—The Most Disgusting Foods on the Planet, 1 vol. 2012. (Disgusting Stuff Ser.). (ENG.). 48p. (gr. 3-4). lib. bdg. 31.99 *(978-1-4296-7534-5(9))* Capstone Press of Coughlan Cos.
—The Most Disgusting Places on the Planet, 1 vol. 2012. (Disgusting Stuff Ser.). (ENG.). 48p. (gr. 3-4). lib. bdg. 31.99 *(978-1-4296-7533-8(0))* Capstone Press of Coughlan Cos.
—The Science of Emotions. 2010. (Cool Science Ser.). 48p. (J). (gr. 3-6). 28.50 *(978-1-60870-079-0(8))* Marshall Cavendish Corp.
Peters, Diane. Privacy: Deal with It Like Nobody's Business, 1 vol. Tankard, Jeremy, illus. 2006. (Lorimer Deal with It Ser.). (ENG.). 32p. (J). (gr. 4-6). pap. 12.95 *(978-1-55028-907-1(1)*, 9781550289077) Lorimer, James & Co., Ltd., Pubs. CAN. Dist: Casemate Pubs. & Bk. Distributors, LLC.
Power Pals. (J). 29.50 *(978-1-56230-357-0(0))* Syndistar, Inc.
Raatma, Lucia. Caring. 2013. (21st Century Junior Library: Character Education Ser.). (ENG.). 24p. (J). (gr. 1-4). 25.64 *(978-1-62431-153-6(9)*, 202932); pap. 12.79 *(978-1-62431-285-4(3)*, 202934) Cherry Lake Publishing.
—Trustworthiness. 2013. (21st Century Junior Library: Character Education Ser.). (ENG.). 24p. (J). (gr. 1-4). 25.64 *(978-1-62431-159-8(8)*, 202956); pap. 12.79 *(978-1-62431-291-5(8)*, 202958) Cherry Lake Publishing.
Randolph, Joanne. What I Look Like When I Am Confused. (Let's Look at Feelings Ser.).Tr. of What I Look Like When I am Confused. 24p. 2009. (gr. k-1). 42.50 *(978-1-61514-239-2(8)*, PowerKids Pr.) 2004. (ENG & SPA., Illus.). (gr. -1-1). lib. bdg. 22.60 *(978-1-4042-7510-2(X)*, Editorial Buenas Letras) Rosen Publishing Group, Inc., The.
—What I Look Like When I am Confused / Cómo me veo cuando estoy Confundido. 2009. (Let's Look at Feelings / un vistazo a los sentimientos Ser.). (ENG & SPA.). 24p. (gr. k-1). 42.50 *(978-1-61514-246-0(0)*, Editorial Buenas Letras) Rosen Publishing Group, Inc., The.
—What I Look Like When I Am Sad. (Let's Look at Feelings Ser.). 24p. 2009. (gr. k-1). 42.50 *(978-1-61514-241-5(X)*, PowerKids Pr.) 2004. (Illus.). (gr. -1-1). 22.60 *(978-1-4042-2507-7(2)*, PowerKids Pr.) 2004. (ENG & SPA., Illus.). (gr. -1-1). lib. bdg. 22.60 *(978-1-4042-7507-2(X)*, Editorial Buenas Letras) Rosen Publishing Group, Inc., The.
—What I Look Like When I am Sad / Cómo me veo cuando estoy Triste. 2009. (Let's Look at Feelings / un vistazo a los sentimientos Ser.). (ENG & SPA.). 24p. (gr. k-1). 42.50 *(978-1-61514-247-7(9)*, Editorial Buenas Letras) Rosen Publishing Group, Inc., The.
Ray, Dale Marie. Moody Mae. Ray, Dale Marie & Ray, Joli, illus. 2013. 22p. (J). pap. 7.95 *(978-1-935018-86-5(8))* International Localization Network.
Real Life Issues, 6 vols., Set. Incl. Coping with Absent Parents. Colson, Mary. 32.65 *(978-1-4329-4760-6(5))*; Coping with Bullying. Guillain, Charlotte. 32.65 *(978-1-4329-4761-3(3))*; Coping with Moving Away. Guillain, Charlotte. 32.65 *(978-1-4329-4764-4(8))*; Coping with Unemployment. Colson, Mary. 32.65 *(978-1-4329-4765-1(6))*. (gr. 6-8). (Real Life Issues Ser.). (ENG., Illus.). 48p. 2011. Set lib. bdg. 130.60 *(978-1-4329-4766-8(4))* Heinemann-Raintree.
Rebman, Nick. Who Is Happy? A Book about Emotions. 2016. (Concept Fun Ser.). (ENG.). 16p. (J). (gr. -1-2). 25.64 *(978-1-5038-0767-9(3)*, 210615) Child's World, Inc., The.
Regan, Lisa. Don't Be Sad, Sam: It's Ok. 2017. (You Choose Ser.). 32p. (J). (gr. 2-2). lib. bdg. 25.27 ***(978-0-7660-8698-2(4))*** Enslow Pubs., Inc.
Reid, Stephanie. Feelings, 1 vol. 2012. (Early Childhood Themes Ser.). (ENG.). 16p. (J). (gr. -1-2). pap. 6.99 *(978-1-4333-3478-8(X))*; pap. 19.99 *(978-1-4333-3479-5(8))* Teacher Created Materials, Inc.
RH Disney Staff. Meet the Emotions. RH Disney Staff, illus. 2015. (Glitter Board Book Ser.). (ENG., Illus.). 12p. (J). (gr. -1-2). bds. 8.99 *(978-0-7364-3438-6(0)*, RH/Disney) Random Hse. Children's Bks.
Rhodes, Corey L. Keep Your Head Up! 2010. 24p. 16.99 *(978-1-4490-7580-4(0))* AuthorHouse.
Rice, Dona Herweck. I Wear My Feelings, 1 vol. 2012. (Early Childhood Themes Ser.). (ENG.). 16p. (J). (gr. -1-2). pap. 6.99 *(978-1-4333-3480-1(1))*; pap. 19.99 *(978-1-4333-3481-8(X))* Teacher Created Materials, Inc.
Rosa-Mendoza, Gladys. When I Am/Cuando Estoy. Regan, Dana, illus. 2007. (English Spanish Foundations Ser.). 20p. (gr. -1-k). pap. 19.95 *(978-1-931398-83-1(6))* Me+Mi Publishing.
Ross, Tracey. My Book of Feelings: A Book to Help Children with Attachment Difficulties, Learning or Developmental Disabilities Understand Their Emotions. Salaman, Rosy, illus. 2017. (ENG.). 40p. (J). 16.95 *(978-1-78592-192-6(4)*, 8799) Kingsley, Jessica Pubs. GBR. Dist: Macmillan Distribution Ltd.
Rotner, Shelley. Feeling Thankful. 2013. (Shelley Rotner's World Ser.). (ENG.). 24p. (gr. 1-2). pap. 47.70 *(978-1-62065-753-9(8)*, Aplus Bks.) Capstone Press of Coughlan Cos.
—Feeling Thankful, 1 vol. Rotner, Shelley, photos by. 2013. (Shelley Rotner's World Ser.). (ENG., Illus.). 24p. (gr. 1-2). pap. 8.10 *(978-1-62065-752-2(X))*; lib. bdg. 27.32 *(978-1-62065-068-4(1))* Capstone Press of Coughlan Cos. (Aplus Bks.).
—Lots of Feelings. 2003. 32p. lib. bdg. 22.60 *(978-0-7613-2896-4(3)*, Millbrook Pr.) Lerner Publishing Group.
—Shelley Rotner's World. 2013. (Shelley Rotner's World Ser.). (ENG.). (gr. 1-2). pap. 190.80 *(978-1-62065-759-1(7))*; pap. 31.80 *(978-1-62065-758-4(9))*; lib. bdg. 109.28 *(978-1-62065-070-7(3))* Capstone Press of Coughlan Cos. (Aplus Bks.).
Rotner, Shelley & Kelly, Sheila. Lots of Feelings. Rotner, Shelley, photos by. 2003. (Shelley Rotner's Early Childhood Library Ser.). (ENG., Illus.). 32p. (gr. k-3). pap. 7.95 *(978-0-7613-2377-8(5))* Lerner Publishing Group.
Rubenstein, Lauren. Visiting Feelings. Hehenberger, Shelly, illus. 2014. (J). pap. *(978-1-4338-1340-5(8)*, Magination Pr.) American Psychological Assn.
Rubenstein, Laurence Z. Visiting Feelings. Hehenberger, Shelly, illus. 2013. 32p. (J). 14.95 *(978-1-4338-1339-9(4))* American Psychological Assn.
Salas, Laura Purdie & Nichols, Cheyenne. Sad Is... 2011. (Know Your Emotions Ser.). (ENG.). 24p. (gr. 1-2). pap. 8.10 *(978-1-4296-7052-4(5)*, Aplus Bks.) Capstone Press of Coughlan Cos.
—Scared Is... 2011. (Know Your Emotions Ser.). (ENG.). 24p. (gr. 1-2). pap. 47.70 *(978-1-4296-7063-0(0))*; lib. bdg. 27.32 *(978-1-4296-6045-7(7))* Capstone Press of Coughlan Cos. (Aplus Bks.).
—Scared Is ... 2011. (Know Your Emotions Ser.). (ENG.). 24p. (gr. 1-2). pap. 8.10 *(978-1-4296-7053-1(3)*, Aplus Bks.) Capstone Press of Coughlan Cos.
Sanchez, Chani. There Are No Animals in This Book (Only Feelings) 2013. (ENG., Illus.). 40p. (J). (gr. -1-2). 17.95 *(978-1-57687-644-2(6)*, powerHouse Bks.) powerHouse Cultural Entertainment, Inc.
Scheunemann, Pam. Coping with Anger, 1 vol. 2004. (Keeping the Peace Ser.). (ENG., Illus.). 24p. (J). (gr. k-3). lib. bdg. 24.21 *(978-1-59197-559-5(X)*, SandCastle) ABDO Publishing Co.
Sedley, Ben. Stuff That Sucks: A Teen's Guide to Accepting What You Can't Change & Committing to What You Can. 2017. (Instant Help Solutions Ser.). (ENG., Illus.). 96p. (YA). (gr. 6-12). pap. 12.95 *(978-1-62625-865-5(1))* New Harbinger Pubns.
Segalove, Ilene. List Your Self: Discover Your Own True Self by Making Lists. 2013. (ENG.). 128p. (J). pap. 12.99 *(978-1-4494-3718-3(4))* Andrews McMeel Publishing.
Seven, John. Happy, Sad, Silly, Mad. Christy, Jana, illus. 2012. (ENG.). 26p. (J). (-k). bds. 6.99 *(978-1-4494-2229-5(2))* Andrews McMeel Publishing.
Shapiro, Lawrence E., et al. I'm Not Bad, I'm Just Mad: A Workbook to Help Kids Control Their Anger. 2008. (Instant Help Ser.). (ENG.). 152p. (J). (gr. k-5). pap., wbk. ed. 32.95 *(978-1-57224-665-2(0)*, Instant Help Books) New Harbinger Pubns.
Shepherd, Joanne. What I Look Like When I Am Scared. 2009. (Let's Look at Feelings Ser.). 24p. (gr. k-1). 42.50 *(978-1-61514-242-2(8)*, PowerKids Pr.) Rosen Publishing Group, Inc., The.
—What I Look Like When I Am Scared: Como Me Veo Cuando Estoy Asustado. 2004. (Let's Look at Feelings / un Vistazo a Los Sentimientos Ser.). (ENG., Illus.). 24p. (J). (gr. -1-1). lib. bdg. 22.60 *(978-1-4042-7509-6(6)*, Editorial Buenas Letras) Rosen Publishing Group, Inc., The.
—What I Look Like When I am Scared / Cómo me veo cuando estoy Asustado. 2009. (Let's Look at Feelings / un vistazo a los sentimientos Ser.). (ENG & SPA.). 24p. (gr. k-1). 42.50 *(978-1-61514-248-4(7)*, Editorial Buenas Letras) Rosen Publishing Group, Inc., The.
—What I Look Like When I Am Surprised. (Let's Look at Feelings Ser.). 24p. 2009. (gr. k-1). 42.50 *(978-1-61514-243-9(6)*, PowerKids Pr.) 2004. (Illus.). (gr. -1-1). 22.60 *(978-1-4042-2511-4(0)*, Editorial Buenas Letras) Rosen Publishing Group, Inc., The.
—What I Look Like When I Am Surprised: Como Me Veo Cuando Estoy Sorprendido. 2004. (Let's Look at Feelings / un Vistazo a Los Sentimientos Ser.). (ENG., Illus.). 24p. (J). (gr. -1-1). lib. bdg. 22.60 *(978-1-4042-7511-9(8)*, Editorial Buenas Letras) Rosen Publishing Group, Inc., The.
—What I Look Like When I am Surprised / Cómo me veo cuando estoy Sorprendido. 2009. (Let's Look at Feelings / un vistazo a los sentimientos Ser.). (ENG & SPA.). 24p. (gr. k-1). 42.50 *(978-1-61514-249-1(5)*, Editorial Buenas Letras) Rosen Publishing Group, Inc., The.
Simon, Mary Manz. First Feelings (padded Cover) Twelve Stories for Toddlers. Stott, Dorothy, illus. rev. ed. 2017. (ENG.). 256p. (J). (gr. -1-k). 12.99 *(978-1-4336-4384-2(7)*, B&H Kids) B&H Publishing Group.
Smith, Carrie. Las emociones Humanas. Hanner, Albert, illus. 2011. (SPA.). 32p. (J). pap. 49.00 net. *(978-1-4108-2345-8(8)*, A23458) Benchmark Education Co.
Smith, Paula. Understanding Similes. 2015. (Figuratively Speaking Ser.). (ENG., Illus.). 32p. (J). *(978-0-7787-1775-1(5))* Crabtree Publishing Co.
Snow, Todd & Snow, Peggy. Feelings to Share from a to Z. Hartman, Carrie, illus. 2007. (ENG.). 32p. (J). pap. 9.99 *(978-1-934277-00-3(2))* Marn Green Publishing, Inc.
Snyder, Gail. Angry Girl? Girls Dealing with Feelings. 2014. (ENG.). 64p. (J). (gr. 5-12). 15.95 *(978-1-62293-030-2(4))* Enslow Pubs., Inc.
Spencer, Anne & Lee, Jordan. I Get Panic Attacks. Now What? 2011. (Teen Life 411 Ser.). (YA). (gr. 7-12). lib. bdg. 34.60 *(978-1-4488-4655-9(2))* Rosen Publishing Group, Inc., The.
Sportelli-Rehak, Angela. Uncle Sam's Kids: When Duty Calls. Hinlicky, Gregg, illus. 2004. (Uncle Sam's Kids Ser.: Bk. 1). 40p. (gr. k-6). 15.95 *(978-0-9714515-1-3(6))* Abidenme Bks.
Stefoff, Rebecca. How Is a Simile Similar to a Metaphor? 2017. (Why Do We Say That? Ser.). (ENG.). 32p. (gr. 3-4). lib. bdg. 27.32 ***(978-1-5157-6389-5(7)***, Fact Finders) Capstone Press of Coughlan Cos.
Stewart, Jan. Learning about Anger. 2004. (ENG., Illus.). 32p. (J). pap. 9.95 *(978-0-89793-309-4(5)*, Hunter Hse.) Turner Publishing Co.
—Learning More about Anger. 2004. (ENG., Illus.). 32p. (J). pap. 9.95 *(978-0-89793-310-0(9)*, Hunter Hse.) Turner Publishing Co.
Stewart, Whitney. Meditation Is an Open Sky: Mindfulness for Kids. Rippin, Sally, illus. 2015. (ENG.). 32p. (J). (gr. -1-3). 12.99 *(978-0-8075-4908-7(8))* Whitman, Albert & Co.
Students & Teachers at Christian Academy. Cutting Class: The St. Baldrick's Story of Christian Academy of Louisville Rock Creek. 2008. (Illus.). 32p. 16.95 *(978-0-929915-77-7(1))* Headline Bks., Inc.
Stump, Chuck & Strawn, Jim. Another Sad Mad Glad Book: The Anatomy of Your Attitude. 2008. 104p. (J). pap. 14.50 *(978-0-9799315-2-9(5))* Four Dolphins Pr., LLC.
Surrey, Ellen, illus. Giving Thanks: 150 Ways to Say Thank You. 2016. (ENG.). 32p. (J). (gr. 1-4). 19.99 *(978-1-84780-879-0(4)*, Frances Lincoln Children's Bks.) Quarto Publishing Group UK GBR. Dist: Hachette Bk. Group.
Talaris Institute. Baby Feelings. 2010. (J). 7.99 *(978-0-9742761-2-0(X))* Talaris Research Institute.
Taylor, Damon J. Aprende de las Emociones con la Biblia. 2004. (Mis Calcetines Ser.). (SPA., Illus.). 24p. 5.99 *(978-0-8254-0775-8(3)*, Editorial Portavoz) Kregel Pubns.
Taylor, Jo. My Happiness Journal. 2016. (ENG.). 64p. (J). (gr. 2-5). pap. 5.99 *(978-0-486-80028-8(8))* Dover Pubns., Inc.
That's Mine: Social/Emotional Lap Book. (Pebble Soup Explorations Ser.). (gr. -1-18). 16.00 *(978-0-7635-7565-6(8))* Rigby Education.
Thomas, Isabel. Dealing with Feeling... 2013. (Dealing with Feeling... Ser.). (ENG.). 24p. (gr. 1-2). pap. 51.92 *(978-1-4329-7120-5(4))*; lib. bdg. 163.24 *(978-1-4329-7111-3(5))* Heinemann-Raintree. (Heinemann Read & Learn).
—Dealing with Feeling... Worried. 2013. (Dealing with Feeling... Ser.). (ENG.). 24p. (gr. 1-2). pap. 6.79 *(978-1-4329-7119-9(0))*; lib. bdg. 23.32 *(978-1-4329-7110-6(7))* Heinemann-Raintree. (Heinemann Read & Learn).
Thornborough, Kathy. Feelings & Emotions. Petelinsek, Kathleen, illus. 2014. (Talking Hands Ser.). (ENG.). 24p. (J). (gr. k-3). 25.64 *(978-1-62687-318-6(6)*, 207158) Child's World, Inc., The.
Tieck, Sarah. Manage Feelings, 1 vol. 2012. (ENG.). 32p. 27.07 *(978-1-61783-235-2(9)*, Buddy Bks.) ABDO Publishing Co.
Van Dijk, Sheri. Don't Let Your Emotions Run Your Life for Teens: Dialectical Behavior Therapy Skills for Helping You Manage Mood Swings, Control Angry Outbursts, & Get along with Others. 2011. (Instant Help Ser.). (ENG.). 160p. (YA). (gr. k-12). pap. 16.95 *(978-1-57224-883-0(1)*, Instant Help Books) New Harbinger Pubns.
—Surviving the Emotional Roller Coaster: DBT Skills to Help Teens Manage Emotions. 2016. (Instant Help Solutions Ser.). (ENG.). 224p. (YA). (gr. 5-12). pap. 16.95 *(978-1-62625-240-0(8))* New Harbinger Pubns.
Van Hout, Mies. Happy. 2012. (ENG., Illus.). 52p. (J). (gr. -1). 17.95 *(978-1-935954-14-9(8)*, 9781935954149) Lemniscaat USA.
A veces estamos felices, a veces estamos Tristes: Social/Emotional Lap Book. (Pebble Soup Exploraciones Ser.). (SPA.). (gr. -1-18). 16.00 *(978-0-7578-1789-2(0))* Rigby Education.
Verdick, Elizabeth. Calm-Down Time. Heinlen, Marieka, illus. 2010. (Toddler Tools Ser.). (ENG.). 24p. (J). (gr. -1). 7.95 *(978-1-57542-316-6(2))* Free Spirit Publishing, Inc.
—Calm-Down Time/Momento para Calmarse. Heinlen, Marieka, illus. 2016. (Toddler Tools Ser.). (ENG, SPA & MUL.). 24p. (J). 7.95 *(978-1-63198-093-0(9))* Free Spirit Publishing, Inc.
—Feet Are Not for Kicking. Heinlen, Marieka, illus. 2004. (Best Behavior Ser.). (ENG.). 24p. (J). 7.95 *(978-1-57542-158-2(5))* Free Spirit Publishing, Inc.
Vescia, Monique & Judson, Karen. Do You Get into Arguments? 2016. (Got Issues? Ser.). (ENG.). 128p. (J). (gr. 7-8). lib. bdg. 37.27 *(978-0-7660-7189-6(8))* Enslow Pubs., Inc.
Vo, Dzung X. The Mindful Teen: Powerful Skills to Help You Handle Stress One Moment at a Time. 2015. (Instant Help Solutions Ser.). (ENG., Illus.). 248p. (YA). (gr. 6-12). pap. 17.95 *(978-1-62625-080-2(4))* New Harbinger Pubns.
Wasserman, Robin. Oops! I Did It (Again)! Martini, Angela, illus. 2003. 96p. (J). *(978-0-439-55608-8(2))* Scholastic, Inc.
Waters, Rosa. Anger. Croft, Cindy, ed. 2014. (Causes & Effects of Emotions Ser.: 13). 64p. (J). (gr. 7-18). 23.95 *(978-1-4222-3068-8(6))* Mason Crest.
—Empathy & Compassion. Croft, Cindy, ed. 2014. (Causes & Effects of Emotions Ser.: 13). 64p. (J). (gr. 7-18). 23.95 *(978-1-4222-3071-8(6))* Mason Crest.
—Surprise & Flexibility. Croft, Cindy, ed. 2014. (Causes & Effects of Emotions Ser.: 13). 64p. (J). (gr. 7-18). 23.95 *(978-1-4222-3080-0(5))* Mason Crest.
Weiss, Ellen. Feeling Happy: A Turn-and-Learn Emotions Book. Bennett, Andy, illus. 2006. (PBS Kids Ser.). 10p. (J). bds. 6.95 *(978-1-57791-311-5(6))* Brighter Minds Children's Publishing.
Welbourn, Shannon. Step Forward with Gratitude. 2016. (Step Forward! Ser.). (ENG., Illus.). 24p. (J). (gr. 2-5). *(978-0-7787-2784-2(X))* Crabtree Publishing Co.
What Is Scary?, 6 Packs. (gr. 1-2). 22.00 *(978-0-7635-9105-2(X))* Rigby Education.
White-Johnson, Adair F. Get over It! How to Bounce Back after Hitting Rock Bottom for Teens. 2013. 132p. pap. 12.95 *(978-0-9896733-0-3(8))* Johnson Tribe Publishing.
Wigand, Molly. Being Mad: A Book about Anger... Just for Me! Fitzgerald, Anne, illus. 2012. 32p. (J). pap. 7.95 *(978-0-87029-502-7(0))* Abbey Pr.
Willard, Baron And Mary. Hugs Are for Every One... Willard, Mary, illus. 2013. 54p. pap. 19.99 *(978-0-9896257-0-8(2))* Blue Botte.
Wright, Rebecca. Ups & Downs: Elementary Monologues That Explore Emotions. 2016. (ENG.). 192p. (J). pap. 15.95 *(978-1-56608-209-9(9)*, Meriwether Publishing) Meriwether Publishing, Ltd.
Wroble, Lisa A. Dealing with Stress. 2011. (Life—a How-To Guide Ser.). (Illus.). 128p. (J). lib. bdg. 33.27 *(978-0-7660-3439-6(9))* Enslow Pubs., Inc.
Yankee, Kris & Nelson, Marian. Are You Grateful Today? 2015. (ENG., Illus.). 32p. (J). pap. 9.95 *(978-1-938326-28-8(8))* Nelson Publishing & Marketing.

EMOTIONS—FICTION

Abbott, Roz. A Bump in the Road. Seltzer, Jerry Joe, illus. 2013. 26p. (J). 16.95 *(978-1-60131-179-5(6))* Big Tent Bks.
Accord Publishing Staff. Where Does Love Come From? Kirkova, Milena, illus. 2011. (ENG.). 18p. (J). 9.99 *(978-1-4494-0839-8(7))* Andrews McMeel Publishing.
Adams, Michael. The Little King & the Honeybee. 2005. (J). per. 9.95 *(978-1-58597-327-9(0))* Leathers Publishing.
Adel, Deborah. Tiego's Love. 2008. 24p. per. 24.95 *(978-1-4241-9506-0(3))* America Star Bks.
Adler, David A. The Many Troubles of Andy Russell. 2008. (J). (gr. 2-4). pap. 24.95 incl. audio *(978-1-4301-0479-7(1))* Live Oak Media.
Al-Ghani, K.I. The Red Beast: Controlling Anger in Children with Asperger's Syndrome. Al-Ghani, Haitham, illus. 2008. (K. I. Al-Ghani Children's Colour Story Bks.). (ENG.). 48p. (gr. 3-7). 21.95 *(978-1-84310-943-3(3)*, 1138) Kingsley, Jessica Pubs. GBR. Dist: Macmillan Distribution Ltd.
Ale, Leandra. Spoiled by Grandp. 2008. 28p. pap. 14.51 *(978-1-4389-0461-0(4))* AuthorHouse.
Allen, Constance. Happy & Sad, Grouchy & Glad (Sesame Street) Brannon, Tom, illus. 2017. (Little Golden Book Ser.). (ENG.). 24p. (J). (-k). 4.99 ***(978-1-5247-1576-2(X)***, Golden Bks.) Random Hse. Children's Bks.
Allen, Kathryn Madeline. Show Me Happy. Futran, Eric, photos by. 2015. (ENG., Illus.). 24p. (J). (gr. -1-3). 15.99 *(978-0-8075-7349-5(3))* Whitman, Albert & Co.
Almada, Ariel Andres. Walking Through a World of Aromas. 2013. (ENG., Illus.). 24p. (J). (gr. k-2). 16.95 *(978-84-15619-48-2(0))* Eastern National.
Alonso, Manuel L. Extrano, Muy Extrano. Schubert, Karin, illus. 2003. (SPA.). 124p. (J). (gr. 3-5). pap. 10.95 *(978-84-204-4906-7(7))* Santillana USA Publishing Co., Inc.
Altebrando, Tara. My Life in Dioramas. 2015. (ENG., Illus.). 256p. (J). (gr. 2-7). 14.95 *(978-0-7624-5681-9(7)*, Running Pr. Kids) Running Pr. Bk. Pubs.
Amatangelo, Sergio Lino. Forever Four, Finally Five. 2008. (Illus.). 32p. (J). pap. 8.00 *(978-0-8059-7680-9(9))* Dorrance Publishing Co., Inc.
Amato, Anne McCoy. Moving Shelly: A Novel. 2010. 148p. (gr. 4-6). pap. 12.95 *(978-1-4502-2584-7(5))* iUniverse, Inc.
Amazing Mallika - Evaluation Guide: Evaluation Guide. 2006. (J). *(978-1-55942-398-4(6))* Witcher Productions.
Anastasiu, Heather. Glitch. 2012. (Glitch Novel Ser.: 1). (ENG.). 336p. (YA). (gr. 7-12). pap. 12.99 *(978-1-250-00299-0(0)*, 9781250002990, St. Martin's Griffin) St. Martin's Pr.
—Override. 2013. (Glitch Novel Ser.: 2). (ENG.). 320p. (YA). (gr. 7-12). pap. 9.99 *(978-1-250-00300-3(8)*, 9781250003003, St. Martin's Griffin) St. Martin's Pr.
—Shutdown. 2013. (Glitch Novel Ser.: 3). (ENG.). 320p. (YA). (gr. 7-12). pap. 9.99 *(978-1-250-00301-0(6)*, 9781250003010, St. Martin's Griffin) St. Martin's Pr.
Anderson, Airlie, illus. Cows in the Kitchen. 2009. (Classic Books with Holes Big Book Ser.). (ENG.). 16p. (J). (gr. -1-1). *(978-1-84643-208-8(1))* Child's Play International Ltd.
—Cows in the Kitchen W/ 2009. (Classic Books with Holes US Soft Cover with CD Ser.). (ENG.). 16p. (J). pap. incl. audio compact disk *(978-1-84643-257-6(X))* Child's Play International Ltd.
Anderson, Laurie Halse. Speak. 2006. 24.50 *(978-0-8446-7292-2(0))* Smith, Peter Pub., Inc.
—Speak. 2011. (ENG.). 224p. (YA). (gr. 7-12). pap. 10.99 *(978-0-312-67439-7(2)*, 9780312674397) Square Fish.
Anderson, Libby. The Richest Boy on Earth. 2008. 20p. pap. 24.95 *(978-1-60563-109-7(4))* America Star Bks.
Anderson, R. J. Ultraviolet. 2011. (Carolrhoda YA Ser.). (ENG.). 312p. (YA). (gr. 7-12). 17.95 *(978-0-7613-7408-4(6)*, Carolrhoda Lab™) Lerner Publishing Group.
Andreae, Giles. Leo, the Lovable Lion. 2004. (Illus.). *(978-0-439-65567-5(6))* Scholastic, Inc.
Angelo, Linda. The Three Secrets of Happiness. 2012. (ENG.). 31p. (J). pap. 14.95 *(978-1-4327-9349-4(7))* Outskirts Pr., Inc.
Anholt, Laurence. A Kiss Like This. Anholt, Catherine, illus. 2009. (ENG.). 32p. (J). (gr. -1-1). pap. 7.95 *(978-1-84507-862-1(4)*, Frances Lincoln) Quarto Publishing Group UK GBR. Dist: Hachette Bk. Group.
Apostolina, M. Hazing Meri Sugarman. 2005. (ENG.). 272p. (YA). pap. 8.99 *(978-1-4169-0610-0(X)*, Simon Pulse) Simon Pulse.
Arkangel, Brian. Cow Story. Moffat, Ross, illus. 2009. 24p. pap. 24.95 *(978-1-60703-272-4(4))* America Star Bks.
Armistead, Cal. Being Henry David. 2013. (ENG.). 312p. (YA). (gr. 8-12). 16.99 *(978-0-8075-0615-8(X))* Whitman, Albert & Co.
Ashburn, Boni. The Class. Gee, Kimberly, illus. 2016. (ENG.). 40p. (J). (gr. -1-3). 17.99 *(978-1-4424-2248-3(3)*, Beach Lane Bks.) Beach Lane Bks.
Ashford Frame, Jeron & Christie, R. Gregory. Yesterday I Had the Blues. 2nd rev. ed. 2008. (ENG., Illus.). 32p. (J). (gr. -1-2). pap. 7.99 *(978-1-58246-260-8(7)*, Tricycle Pr.) Random Hse. Children's Bks.
Athena Smiles. 2005. (J). *(978-0-9758714-1-6(2))* Eveready Letter & Advertising Inc.
Audibert, Tara. Matthew Loses His Laugh. 2009. 32p. pap. 16.00 *(978-0-557-09385-4(6))* Lulu Pr., Inc.
Auseon, Andrew. Freak Magnet. 2010. (ENG.). 304p. (YA). (gr. 9-18). 16.99 *(978-0-06-113926-0(2)*, HarperTeen) HarperCollins Pubs.
Azore, Barbara. Wanda's Freckles. Graham, Georgia, illus. 2009. (ENG.). 24p. (J). (gr. -1-2). 19.95 *(978-0-88776-862-0(8)*, Tundra Bks.) Tundra Bks. CAN. Dist: Penguin Random Hse. LLC.
Bailey, Tressie. The Little Box Kittens. 2009. 37p. pap. 20.50 *(978-0-557-02639-5(3))* Lulu Pr., Inc.
Bajaj, Varsha. How Many Kisses Do You Want Tonight? Bates, Ivan, illus. 2007. (ENG.). 26p. (J). (gr. -1 — 1). bds. 6.99 *(978-0-316-06735-5(0))* Little, Brown Bks. for Young Readers.
Baker, Jennifer. Sworn to Silence. 2014. (ENG., Illus.). 192p. (YA). (gr. 7). pap. 13.99 *(978-1-4814-2877-4(2)*, Simon Pulse) Simon Pulse.
Baker, Keith. Sometimes. 2003. (Green Light Readers Level 1 Ser.). (ENG., Illus.). 24p. (J). (gr. -1-3). pap. 3.95 *(978-0-15-204847-1(2))* Houghton Mifflin Harcourt Publishing Co.

—Sometimes. 2003. (Green Light Readers — Level 1 Ser.). (gr. -1-2). lib. bdg. 13.50 *(978-0-613-64597-3(9),* Turtleback) Turtleback Bks.

—Sometimes/Algunas Veces. Flor Ada, Alma & Campoy, F. Isabel, trs. from ENG. 2007. (Green Light Readers Level 1 Ser.). (ENG & SPA., Illus.). 28p. (J). (gr. -1-3). pap. 3.95 *(978-0-15-205961-3(X))* Houghton Mifflin Harcourt Publishing Co.

Bang, Molly. When Sophie Gets Angry - Really, Really Angry. 2014. 40p. pap. 7.00 *(978-1-61003-317-6(5))* Center for the Collaborative Classroom.

—When Sophie Gets Angry - Really, Really Angry. 2004. (Scholastic Bookshelf Ser.). (Illus.). 36p. (gr. -1-3). 17.00 *(978-0-7569-3206-0(8))* Perfection Learning Corp.

—When Sophie Gets Angry - Really, Really Angry. (ENG.). (J). (gr. -1-3). 2007. 9.99 *(978-0-439-92493-1(6))* 2004. (Illus.). 40p. reprint ed. pap. 6.99 *(978-0-439-59845-3(1),* Scholastic Paperbacks) Scholastic, Inc.

—When Sophie's Feelings Are Really, Really Hurt. 2015. (ENG., Illus.). 40p. (J). (gr. -1-3). 17.99 *(978-0-545-78831-1(5),* Blue Sky Pr., The) Scholastic, Inc.

Bar-Lev, Rotem. No More Tears. 2009. (Illus.). 23p. (J). pap. 13.95 *(978-1-4327-3989-8(1))* Outskirts Pr., Inc.

Barcelo, François. My Daddy's Footsteps. Mongeau, Marc, illus. 2009. (My First Stories Ser.). 24p. (J). (gr. -1-3). 22.60 *(978-1-60754-359-6(1));* pap. 8.15 *(978-1-60754-360-2(5))* Windmill Bks.

—My Mommy's Hands. Mongeau, Marc, illus. 2009. (My First Stories Ser.). 24p. (J). (gr. -1-3). 22.60 *(978-1-60754-362-6(1));* pap. 8.15 *(978-1-60754-365-7(6))* Windmill Bks.

Barclift, Betty. Gypsy Summer: A Novel. 2003. 160p. (J). pap. 7.99 *(978-0-8254-2038-2(5))* Kregel Pubns.

Barnett, Mac. I Love You Like a Pig. Pizzoli, Greg, illus. 2017. 40p. (J). (gr. -1-3). 17.99 ***(978-0-06-235483-9(3))*** HarperCollins Pubs.

Barry, Debra R. The Loneliest Leaf. Baker, David, illus. 2011. 28p. pap. 24.95 *(978-1-4560-1002-7(6))* America Star Bks.

Beam, Cris. I Am J. 2012. (ENG.). 352p. (YA). (gr. 10-17). pap. 10.99 *(978-0-316-05360-0(0))* Little, Brown Bks. for Young Readers.

Beaty, Andrea. Secrets of the Cicada Summer. 2010. (ENG.). 176p. (YA). (gr. 3-7). pap. 6.95 *(978-0-8109-8419-6(9),* Amulet Bks.) Abrams, Inc.

Beck, Adrian. Stuff Happens: Dale. 11th ed. 2016. (Stuff Happens Ser.). (ENG.). 96p. (J). (gr. 2-4). 8.99 ***(978-0-14-330896-6(3))*** Random Hse. Australia AUS. Dist: Independent Pubs. Group.

Becker Holstein, Barbara. Secrets: Diary of a Gutsy Teen. 2015. (ENG.). 144p. (J). (gr. 2-7). 12.95 *(978-1-62914-626-3(9),* Sky Pony Pr.) Skyhorse Publishing Co., Inc.

—The Truth: Diary of a Gutsy Tween. 2014. (ENG.). 176p. (J). (gr. 2-7). 12.95 *(978-1-62873-611-3(9),* Sky Pony Pr.) Skyhorse Publishing Co., Inc.

Becker, Shelly. Even Superheroes Have Bad Days. Kaban, Eda, illus. 2016. (ENG.). 40p. (J). (gr. -1-4). 14.95 *(978-1-4549-1394-8(0))* Sterling Publishing Co., Inc.

Beitler, Stacey Ann. Willy Helps a Friend. 2010. 30p. pap. 14.50 *(978-1-60911-355-1(1),* Eloquent Bks.) Strategic Book Publishing & Rights Agency (SBPRA).

Bell, Lucy J. God Made Feelings. Rimmington, Natasha, illus. 2017. 10p. (J). 6.99 ***(978-1-5064-1782-0(5),*** Sparkhouse Family) Augsburg Fortress, Pubs.

Bellingham, Brenda. Lilly Takes the Lead. MacDonald, Clarke, illus. 2006. (Formac First Novels Ser.: 34). (ENG.). 64p. (gr. 2-5). 14.95 *(978-0-88780-703-9(8),* 9780887807039) Formac Publishing Co., Ltd. CAN. Dist: Casemate Pubs. & Bk. Distributors, LLC.

Bennett, Diane. Put a Smile on Your Face. 2008. 24p. per. 24.95 *(978-1-4241-9895-5(X))* America Star Bks.

Bennion, Jay B. From Here to There. 2013. 136p. pap. 9.99 *(978-0-9826175-0-2(X))* Pearl Publishing, LLC.

Benson, Linda Sue. It's Okay, Leon, 1 vol. 2009. 74p. pap. 19.95 *(978-1-4489-2173-7(2))* America Star Bks.

Bentley, Sue. Riding Rescue #6. Swan, Angela, illus. 2013. (Magic Ponies Ser.: 6). (ENG.). 128p. (J). (gr. 1-3). 4.99 *(978-0-448-46735-1(6),* Grosset & Dunlap) Penguin Young Readers Group.

Berenstain, Stan, et al. God Loves You!, 1 vol. 2008. (Berenstain Bears/Living Lights Ser.). (ENG., Illus.). 32p. (J). pap. 3.99 *(978-0-310-71250-3(5))* Zonderkidz.

Berry, Joy. Feeling Angry. 2009. (ENG.). 40p. (J). (gr. -1-k). pap. 7.95 *(978-1-60577-208-0(9))* Berry, Joy Enterprises.

Berry, Ron. Charlie the Can-Do Choo-Choo! Sharp, Chris, illus. 2006. (ENG.). 7p. (J). (gr. -1). bds. 12.95 *(978-0-8249-6678-2(3),* Ideal Pubns.) Worthy Publishing.

Bick, Ilsa J. Draw the Dark. 2010. (ENG.). 344p. (YA). (gr. 9-12). 16.95 *(978-0-7613-5686-8(X),* Carolrhoda Lab™) Lerner Publishing Group.

—Drowning Instinct. 2013. (ENG.). 352p. (YA). (gr. 9-12). pap. 9.95 *(978-1-4677-0912-5(3),* Carolrhoda Lab™) Lerner Publishing Group.

The Biggest Kiss. 2014. (ENG., Illus.). 28p. (J). (gr. -1 — 1). bds. 7.99 *(978-1-4814-1751-8(7),* Little Simon) Little Simon.

Bingham, Frances. Bedtime Stories for the Inner Child: Reuniting with & Nurturing Your Inner Child. 2009. 68p. pap. 10.49 *(978-1-4389-3185-2(9))* AuthorHouse.

Birdseye, Tom. Attack of the Mutant Underwear. 2006. (ENG., Illus.). 208p. (J). (gr. 3-7). 7.99 *(978-0-14-240734-9(8),* Puffin Books) Penguin Young Readers Group.

Bishop, Michele. Mummy's Happy Tears. Sharp, Craig, illus. 2013. 18p. pap. *(978-1-78148-186-8(5))* Grosvenor Hse. Publishing Ltd.

Blakemore, Megan Frazer. Good & Gone. 2017. 304p. (YA). (gr. 8). 17.99 ***(978-0-06-234842-5(6),*** HarperTeen) HarperCollins Pubs.

Blevins, James. The Crones. Whittaker, Stephen, illus. 2008. 36p. pap. 24.95 *(978-1-60610-259-6(1))* America Star Bks.

Bloom, Amy. Little Sweet Potato. Jones, Noah Z., illus. 2012. (ENG.). 32p. (J). (gr. -1-2). 16.99 *(978-0-06-180439-7(8),* Tegen, Katherine Bks) HarperCollins Pubs.

Blume, Judy. Double Fudge. 2007. (ENG.). 240p. (J). (gr. 3-7). 7.99 *(978-0-14-240878-0(6),* Puffin Books) Penguin Young Readers Group.

—Double Fudge. 2004. (Fudge Ser.). 160p. (J). (gr. 3-7). pap. 36.00 incl. audio *(978-0-8072-2036-8(1),* Listening Library) Random Hse. Audio Publishing Group.

—Double Fudge. 2007. (Fudge Bks.: 5). lib. bdg. 18.40 *(978-1-4177-8371-7(0),* Turtleback) Turtleback Bks.

Boos, Marcela. Oh No, It's Bedtime! 2009. 23p. (J). pap. 11.95 *(978-1-4327-3338-4(9))* Outskirts Pr., Inc.

Borris, Albert. Crash into Me. (ENG.). 272p. (YA). (gr. 9). 2010. pap. 9.99 *(978-1-4169-9827-3(6))* 2009. 16.99 *(978-1-4169-7435-2(0))* Simon Pulse. (Simon Pulse).

Bott, Paula. Fighting el Fuego. 2013. (Av2 Audio Chapter Bks.). (ENG.). 113p. (J). (gr. 4-7). lib. bdg. 27.13 *(978-1-62127-975-4(8),* AV2 by Weigl) Weigl Pubs., Inc.

Bouldin, Anthony Roth & Bouldin, Morshica. Tag along with Momo & Jojo: You're It! Series #2. 2012. 16p. pap. 15.99 *(978-1-4772-6797-4(2))* AuthorHouse.

—Tag along with Momo & Jojo: You're IT! Series #1 Jojo's 1st day of School. 2011. 16p. 14.95 *(978-1-4567-2077-3(5))* AuthorHouse.

Bourgeois, Paulette & Clark, Brenda. Franklin & the Contest. 2004. (Kids Can Read Ser.). (ENG., Illus.). 32p. (J). (gr. 1-2). 3.95 *(978-1-55337-492-3(4));* 14.95 *(978-1-55337-491-6(6))* Kids Can Pr., Ltd. CAN. Dist: Hachette Bk. Group.

—Franklin & the Scooter. 2004. (Kids Can Read Ser.). (ENG., Illus.). 32p. (J). (gr. 1-2). 3.95 *(978-1-55337-494-7(0));* 14.95 *(978-1-55337-493-0(2))* Kids Can Pr., Ltd. CAN. Dist: Hachette Bk. Group.

Boyd, David. Closer to Hamlet. 2003. 120p. (YA). (gr. 6-9). pap. *(978-0-921156-93-2(6))* Rubicon Publishing, Inc.

Boynton, Sandra. Happy Hippo, Angry Duck: A Book of Moods. Boynton, Sandra, illus. 2011. (ENG., Illus.). 16p. (J). (gr. -1-k). bds. 5.99 *(978-1-4424-1731-1(5),* Little Simon) Little Simon.

Bracken, Beth. Too Shy for Show-and-Tell. Bell, Jennifer A., illus. 2011. (Little Boost Ser.). (ENG.). 32p. (gr. k-3). lib. bdg. 23.99 *(978-1-4048-6654-6(X),* Little Boost) Picture Window Bks.

Bradman, Tony. Mr. Bear Gets Alarmed, 1 vol. Warburton, Sarah, illus. 2014. (After Happily Ever After Ser.). (ENG.). 56p. (gr. 2-3). lib. bdg. 25.32 *(978-1-4342-7948-4(0),* After Happily Ever After) Stone Arch Bks.

—Mr. Giant & the Beastly Baron, 1 vol. Warburton, Sarah, illus. 2014. (After Happily Ever After Ser.). (ENG.). 56p. (gr. 2-3). lib. bdg. 25.32 *(978-1-4342-7949-1(9),* After Happily Ever After) Stone Arch Bks.

Bradshaw, Dustin W. Counting Candles. 2014. (Illus.). 231p. pap. 15.99 *(978-1-4621-1433-7(4))* Cedar Fort, Inc./CFI Distribution.

Bramwell, Wendie, et al. The Friendship Alphabet. Ziegler, Michael, illus. Ziegler, Michael, photos by. 2003. 32p. (J). pap. *(978-0-9741388-3-1(5))* Committee for Children.

Branford, Anna. Violet Mackerel's Possible Friend. Allen, Elanna, illus. 2014. (Violet Mackerel Ser.). (ENG.). 128p. (J). (gr. 1-5). 15.99 *(978-1-4424-9455-8(7),* Atheneum Bks. for Young Readers) Simon & Schuster Children's Publishing.

Brian, Kate, pseud. Private. 2009. (Private Ser.: No. 1). (ENG.). 240p. (YA). pap. 9.99 *(978-1-4169-9946-1(9),* Simon & Schuster Bks. For Young Readers) Simon & Schuster Bks. For Young Readers.

Brochmann, Holly & Bowen, Leah. A Feel Better Book for Little Worriers. Ng-Benitez, Shirley, illus. 2017. 32p. (J). 15.95 ***(978-1-4338-2718-1(2),*** Magination Pr.) American Psychological Assn.

Brooks, Kevin. Dawn. (ENG.). (J). (gr. 9). 2010. 272p. pap. 8.99 *(978-0-545-06092-9(3),* PUSH) 2009. 256p. 17.99 *(978-0-545-06090-5(7),* Chicken Hse., The) Scholastic, Inc.

Brown, Ilknur. Faces of Little Robert. l.t. ed. 2006. (Illus.). 38p. (J). per. 13.99 *(978-1-59879-191-4(5))* Lifevest Publishing, Inc.

Brown, Ivorine. Don't Cry but Smile & Remember. Wilson, Teddy, illus. 2009. 20p. pap. 24.95 *(978-1-60836-808-2(4))* America Star Bks.

Brown, Jahla. Nathan Is Nathan. 2009. (ENG., Illus.). 20p. (J). pap. 19.95 *(978-0-9778083-8-0(6))* Everlasting Publishing.

Brown, Jennifer. Hate List. 2017. (ENG.). 528p. (YA). (gr. 10-17). pap. 11.99 ***(978-0-316-55678-1(5))*** Little, Brown Bks. for Young Readers.

—Hate List. 2011. 10.36 *(978-0-7848-3563-0(2),* Everbind) Marco Bk. Co.

Brown Lcsw, Jennifer. Star Realizes She Is Not Alone. 2013. 28p. pap. 19.99 *(978-1-4772-7043-1(4))* AuthorHouse.

Brown, Ruby. Cuddles for Mommy. Macnaughton, Tina, illus. 2016. (ENG.). 32p. (J). (gr. -1-3). 16.99 *(978-1-4998-0203-0(X))* Little Bee Books Inc.

Brown, Tori. Today, Every Day, for Always. 2012. 28p. 22.99 *(978-1-4582-0558-2(4));* pap. 16.99 *(978-1-4582-0559-9(2))* Author Solutions, Inc. (Abbott Pr.).

Browne, Anthony. How Do You Feel? Browne, Anthony, illus. 2012. (ENG., Illus.). 32p. (J). (gr. -1-2). 14.99 *(978-0-7636-5862-5(6))* Candlewick Pr.

Brownlie, Marion. Star Is Happy. 2013. 36p. pap. *(978-0-9875551-4-4(6))* Aurora House.

Brueggemann, Mindy. Who Is Lilly? Brueggemann, Mindy, photos by. 2013. (Illus.). 44p. pap. 9.95 *(978-0-9855676-1-3(9))* Dankworth Publishing.

Bryant Sr., Lydia. I Love Lydia, 1 vol. 2009. 20p. pap. 24.95 *(978-1-60703-488-9(3))* America Star Bks.

Buchholz, Chris. Beckett 81. 2010. 147p. pap. 10.00 *(978-0-557-27451-2(6))* Lulu Pr., Inc.

Buck Young. The Men of Lesbos. 2006. 71p. pap. 10.00 *(978-1-4257-1630-1(X))* Xlibris Corp.

Buckley, Michael. The Unusual Suspects. 2006. (Sisters Grimm Ser.: Bk. 2). 1.00 *(978-1-4237-8623-8(8))* Recorded Bks., Inc.

—A Very Grimm Guide. Ferguson, Peter, illus. 2012. (Sisters Grimm Ser.). (ENG.). 128p. (J). (gr. 3-7). 16.95 *(978-1-4197-0201-3(7),* Amulet Bks.) Abrams, Inc.

Bundrick, Lisa. Learning about Feelings, 1 vol. 2010. 18p. pap. 24.95 *(978-1-4489-6338-6(9))* PublishAmerica, Inc.

Bunting, Eve. The Presence: A Ghost Story. 2010. (ENG.). 204p. (YA). (gr. 7). pap. 12.99 *(978-0-547-48032-9(6))* Houghton Mifflin Harcourt Publishing Co.

Burgess, Melvin. El Fantasma tras la Pared. (SPA.). (J). 8.95 *(978-958-04-6483-9(9))* Norma S.A. COL. Dist: Distribuidora Norma, Inc.

—Sara's Face. 2008. (ENG.). 288p. (YA). (gr. 9-12). pap. 7.99 *(978-1-4169-5815-4(0),* Simon Pulse) Simon Pulse.

Burk, Mark Simon. Saddy & Gladdy. 2003. (J). 26.00 *(978-0-9743619-0-1(9))* Ivy Hill Bunch, LLC.

Burkhart, Jessica. Rival Revenge. 2010. (Canterwood Crest Ser.: 7). (ENG.). 240p. (J). (gr. 4-8). pap. 7.99 *(978-1-4169-9039-0(9),* Aladdin) Simon & Schuster Children's Publishing.

Burrows, Ailsa. Jar of Happiness. Burrows, Ailsa, illus. (Child's Play Library). (ENG., Illus.). 32p. (J). 2016. *(978-1-84643-729-8(6))* 2015. pap. *(978-1-84643-728-1(8))* Child's Play International Ltd.

Bush, Don. Little Brook Series, 3 bks. (Illus.). (J). (gr. 3). lib. bdg. 16.50 *(978-0-943978-03-1(3))* Rolling Hills Pr.

Butler, Dori Hillestad. Yes, I Know Monkey Man, 1 vol. 2009. (ENG.). 224p. (YA). (gr. 5-9). 16.95 *(978-1-56145-479-2(6))* Peachtree Pubs.

Cakal, Kimberly. Today I Hugged a Porcupine. 2007. 20p. per. 24.95 *(978-1-4241-8561-0(0))* America Star Bks.

Caletti, Deb. Love Is All You Need: Wild Roses - The Nature of Jade. 2013. (ENG.). 608p. (YA). (gr. 7-7). pap. 11.99 *(978-1-4424-6636-4(7),* Simon Pulse) Simon Pulse.

Callahan, Sean. The Bear Hug. 2015. (Illus.). 24p. (J). *(978-1-4896-3852-6(0))* Weigl Pubs., Inc.

Cannon, A. E. Sophie's Fish. White, Lee, illus. 2012. (ENG.). 32p. (J). (gr. -1-k). 15.99 *(978-0-670-01291-6(2),* Viking Books for Young Readers) Penguin Young Readers Group.

Capdevila, Roser & Vendrell, Maria Martinez. Reir y Llorar. 2003.Tr. of Laugh & Cry. (SPA.). 24p. (J). 7.95 *(978-84-233-1458-4(8))* Ediciones Destino ESP. Dist: Planeta Publishing Corp.

Carlson, Nancy. Life Is Fun. Carlson, Nancy, illus. 2012. (Nancy Carlson Picture Bks). (ENG., Illus.). 32p. (J). (gr. k-2). 9.95 *(978-0-7613-8945-3(8),* Carolrhoda Bks.) Lerner Publishing Group.

—Smile a Lot! Carlson, Nancy, illus. 2012. (Nancy Carlson Picture Bks). (Illus.). 32p. (J). (gr. k-2). (ENG.). 9.95 *(978-0-7613-9173-9(8));* 56.72 *(978-0-7613-9310-8(2))* Lerner Publishing Group. (Carolrhoda Bks.).

—¡Sonrie! Translations.com Staff, tr. from ENG. Carlson, Nancy, illus. 2007. (Ediciones Lerner Single Titles Ser.).Tr. of Smile a Lot! (SPA., Illus.). 32p. (J). (gr. k-2). 15.95 *(978-0-8225-7817-8(4),* Ediciones Lerner) Lerner Publishing Group.

—Think Happy! Carlson, Nancy, illus. 2012. (Nancy Carlson Picture Bks). (Illus.). 32p. (J). (gr. k-3). (ENG.). 9.95 *(978-0-7613-9175-3(4));* 56.72 *(978-0-7613-9312-2(9))* Lerner Publishing Group. (Carolrhoda Bks.).

—What If It Never Stops Raining? Carlson, Nancy, illus. 2012. (Nancy Carlson Picture Bks). (ENG., Illus.). 32p. (J). (gr. k-2). 9.95 *(978-0-7613-8951-4(2),* Carolrhoda Bks.) Lerner Publishing Group.

Carmichael, Katrina. Back Together Again. 2008. 20p. pap. 7.95 *(978-0-9814650-5-0(6))* G Publishing LLC.

Cassidy, Anne. Looking for JJ. 2009. (ENG., Illus.). 336p. (J). (gr. 7). pap. 20.95 *(978-0-15-206638-3(1))* Houghton Mifflin Harcourt Publishing Co.

Cauvin, Raoul. Cedric 1 - High-Risk Class. Laudec, Calvinaoul, illus. 2008. (Cedric Ser.: 1). (ENG.). 48p. pap. 11.95 *(978-1-905460-68-7(6))* CineBook GBR. Dist: National Bk. Network.

Cavanaugh, Natalie. Somebody Loves You. 2012. 24p. pap. 15.99 *(978-1-4771-3787-1(4))* Xlibris Corp.

Chambers, Aidan. The Toll Bridge. 2009. (ENG.). 288p. (YA). (gr. 9-17). pap. 9.95 *(978-0-8109-8358-8(3),* Amulet Bks.) Abrams, Inc.

Chbosky, Stephen. The Perks of Being a Wallflower. 2014. (ENG.). 224p. (gr. 7-12). 18.25 *(978-1-63245-042-5(9))* Lectorum Pubns., Inc.

—The Perks of Being a Wallflower. 2012. (ENG.). 224p. 21.00 *(978-1-4516-9620-2(5));* pap. 14.99 *(978-1-4516-9619-6(1))* MTV Books. (MTV Bks.).

—The Perks of Being a Wallflower. 2009. 13.77 *(978-0-7848-1530-4(5),* Everbind) Marco Bk. Co.

—The Perks of Being a Wallflower. 2008. (ENG.). 24.30 *(978-1-60686-308-4(8),* Covercraft) Perfection Learning Corp.

—The Perks of Being a Wallflower. 2007. 1.25 *(978-1-4281-3271-9(6))* Recorded Bks., Inc.

Chen, Wei Dong. Rage & Rebellion, Vol. 11. Liang, Xiao Long, illus. 2015. (Outlaws of the Marsh Ser.). (ENG.). 176p. (YA). (gr. 6-12). pap. 9.99 *(978-89-98341-95-4(6))* Lerner Publishing Group.

Chichester Clark, Emma. Find a Smile, Vol. 1. 2009. (Melrose & Croc Ser.). (ENG., Illus.). 32p. (J). (gr. -1-2). pap. 8.95 *(978-0-00-718241-1(4))* HarperCollins Pubs. Ltd. GBR. Dist: Independent Pubs. Group.

Child, Lauren. Charlie Is Broken! 2009. (Charlie & Lola Ser.). (ENG.). 24p. (J). (gr. k-3). mass mkt. 3.99 *(978-0-448-45237-1(5),* Grosset & Dunlap) Penguin Young Readers Group.

—Help! I Really Mean It! 2009. (Charlie & Lola Ser.). (ENG.). 24p. (J). (gr. k-3). mass mkt. 3.99 *(978-0-448-45049-0(6),* Grosset & Dunlap) Penguin Young Readers Group.

Christopher, Matt. Football Double Threat. 2008. (ENG.). 128p. (J). (gr. 3-7). pap. 5.99 *(978-0-316-01632-2(2))* Little, Brown Bks. for Young Readers.

—The Spy on Third Base. Ulrich, George, illus. 2009. (New Peach Street Mudders Sports Library). 64p. (J). (gr. 2-4). lib. bdg. 23.93 *(978-1-59953-321-6(9))* Norwood Hse. Pr.

Clark, Maria. Lousy Luck Lucy. 2012. 32p. pap. 13.50 *(978-1-61897-699-4(0),* Strategic Bk. Publishing) Strategic Book Publishing & Rights Agency (SBPRA).

Clark, Sandra. My Tears Count Too. 2009. 84p. pap. 28.99 *(978-1-4389-8357-8(3))* AuthorHouse.

Clemson, C. J. Charlie Mcbly & his Curiosity. 2010. 24p. pap. 14.93 *(978-1-4269-4770-4(4))* Trafford Publishing.

Cocca-Leffler, Maryann. Theo's Mood: A Book of Feelings. Cocca-Leffler, Maryann, illus. 2013. (ENG., Illus.). 24p. (J). (gr. -1-3). 15.99 *(978-0-8075-7778-3(2))* Whitman, Albert & Co.

Cochard, Nadège. Grandma & Grandpa Visit Connor. Fanny, illus. 2009. (My First Stories Ser.). 24p. (J). (gr. -1-3). 22.60 *(978-1-60754-357-2(5))* Windmill Bks.

Cochard, Nadège. Grandma & Grandpa Visit Connor. Fanny, illus. 2009. (My First Stories Ser.). 24p. (J). (gr. -1-3). pap. 8.15 *(978-1-60754-356-5(7))* Windmill Bks.

Colasanti, Susane. Take Me There. 2009. (ENG.). 320p. (YA). (gr. 7-18). 9.99 *(978-0-14-241435-4(2),* Speak) Penguin Young Readers Group.

Colbert, Brandy. Pointe. 2015. (ENG.). 352p. (YA). (gr. 9). pap. 9.99 *(978-0-14-751441-7(X),* Speak) Penguin Young Readers Group.

Coleman-Veach, Marti. Balloons in Heaven. 2013. 32p. pap. *(978-1-4602-1826-6(4))* FriesenPress.

Collins, C. B. Where's My Face? A Simon-the-Cat Tale. Holgren, Anna C., illus. 2008. 36p. pap. 24.95 *(978-1-60441-009-9(4))* America Star Bks.

Collins, Savina. Angry. DuFalla, Anita, illus. 2017. (I Have Feelings Ser.). (ENG.). (J). (gr. k-1). 28.51 ***(978-1-68342-141-2(8))*** Rourke Educational Media.

—Happy. DuFalla, Anita, illus. 2017. (I Have Feelings Ser.). (ENG.). (J). (gr. k-1). 28.51 ***(978-1-68342-143-6(4))*** Rourke Educational Media.

—Scared. DuFalla, Anita, illus. 2017. (I Have Feelings Ser.). (ENG.). (J). (gr. k-1). 28.51 ***(978-1-68342-140-5(X))*** Rourke Educational Media.

Conlin, Christine. Who Sees Your Scrunchy Face? Marroquin, Melissa, illus. 2016. (ENG.). (J). 18.95 *(978-1-59298-658-3(7))* Beaver's Pond Pr., Inc.

Cook, Julia. I Just Don't Like the Sound of No! My Story about Accepting No for an Answer & Disagreeing the Right Way. De Weerd, Kelsey, illus. 2011. (ENG.). 32p. (J). *(978-1-934490-26-6(1))* Boys Town Pr.

—I Just Don't Like the Sound of No! My Story about Accepting 'No' for an Answer & Disagreeing the Right Way!: My Story about Accepting 'No' for an Answer & Disagreeing... the Right Way! De Weerd, Kelsey, illus. 2011. (ENG.). 32p. (J). 10.95 *(978-1-934490-25-9(3))* Boys Town Pr.

Cooper, Christina. If I Only Had One Wish. 2008. 20p. pap. 12.50 *(978-1-60693-304-6(3),* Strategic Bk. Publishing) Strategic Book Publishing & Rights Agency (SBPRA).

Cooper, Ilene. Look at Lucy! Merrell, David, illus. 2009. (Lucy Ser.: No. 3). (ENG.). 112p. (J). (gr. 1-4). 4.99 *(978-0-375-85558-0(0),* Random Hse. Bks. for Young Readers) Random Hse. Children's Bks.

Cooper, Lyn Anne. Henry the Prickly Porcupine. 2010. 44p. pap. 20.10 *(978-1-4251-3175-3(1))* Trafford Publishing.

Corderoy, Tracey. The Grunt & the Grouch. 2013. (Grunt & the Grouch Ser.). (ENG.). 112p. (gr. 1-3). 50.64 *(978-1-4342-4851-0(8));* 101.28 *(978-1-4342-4852-7(6))* Stone Arch Bks.

Cordoba, Jax. Fate Lends a Leg. 2016. (ENG., Illus.). (YA). 24.99 ***(978-1-63533-013-7(0),*** Harmony Ink Pr.) Dreamspinner Pr.

Cormack, Kim. Being. 2011. 26p. pap. 12.00 *(978-1-60911-891-4(X),* Eloquent Bks.) Strategic Book Publishing & Rights Agency (SBPRA).

Cowley, Joy. The Hungry Giant's Baby. 2009. pap. 8.25 *(978-1-60559-221-3(8))* Hameray Publishing Group, Inc.

Crespo, Ana. JP & the Bossy Dinosaur: Feeling Unhappy. Sirotich, Erica, illus. 2016. (My Emotions & Me Ser.). (ENG.). 32p. (J). (gr. -1-3). 16.99 *(978-0-8075-3981-1(3))* Whitman, Albert & Co.

—JP & the Polka-Dotted Aliens: Feeling Angry. Sirotich, Erica, illus. 2015. (My Emotions & Me Ser.). (ENG.). 32p. (J). (gr. -1-3). 16.99 *(978-0-8075-3977-4(5))* Whitman, Albert & Co.

Cresse, Peter. The Bloody Hand. 2009. (Illus.). 40p. pap. 18.95 *(978-1-4389-2161-7(6))* AuthorHouse.

Cronin, Doreen. Cyclone. Sfetsios-Conover, Debra, illus. 2017. (J). pap. ***(978-1-4814-3526-0(4))*** Simon & Schuster Children's Publishing.

Crutcher, Chris. Angry Management. 2011. (ENG.). 256p. (YA). (gr. 9). pap. 8.99 *(978-0-06-050248-5(7),* Greenwillow Bks.) HarperCollins Pubs.

Cuchna, Reid. Out of Love, 1 vol. 2009. 327p. pap. 29.95 *(978-1-60836-345-2(7))* America Star Bks.

Curry, Cicero. The Tickle Man. Ledbetter, John'el, illus. 2013. 44p. 24.95 *(978-1-63004-279-0(X))* America Star Bks.

Curtis, Jamie Lee. Today I Feel Silly & Other Moods That Make My Day. Cornell, Laura, illus. 2007. (ENG.). 40p. (J). (gr. -1-3). 17.99 *(978-0-06-024560-3(3))* HarperCollins Pubs.

Curtis, Vanessa & Quarto Generic Staff. The Taming of Lilah May. 2012. (ENG.). 192p. (J). (gr. 7-9). pap. 8.99 *(978-1-84780-149-4(8),* Frances Lincoln) Quarto Publishing Group UK GBR. Dist: Hachette Bk. Group.

Cutler, Dave. When I Wished I Was Alone. Cutler, Dave, illus. 2003. (Illus.). 36p. (J). 16.95 *(978-0-9671851-0-1(6))* GreyCore Pr.

Cuyler, Margery. 100th Day Worries. Howard, Arthur, illus. 2006. (ENG.). 32p. (J). (gr. k-3). reprint ed. 7.99 *(978-1-4169-0789-3(0),* Simon & Schuster Bks. For Young Readers) Simon & Schuster Bks. For Young Readers.

Danic, Chantelle. To Smile a Smile. 2011. 28p. pap. 28.03 *(978-1-4628-5126-3(6))* Xlibris Corp.

D'Argenzio, Gertilyn Elinor. What Color Is Your Happiness? 2012. 24p. pap. 15.99 *(978-1-4669-1443-8(2))* Trafford Publishing.

Davies, Rocky. Harvey Happy Bee. 2005. (Bee Attitude Board Books). (Illus.). (J). *(978-1-59156-775-2(0))* Covenant Communications.

Davis, Helen J. Good Times with Gregory: Airplanes: A Visit to A 747. Davis, Robyn L., illus. 2008. (Good Times with Gregory Ser.). 37p. (J). (gr. -1-4). 12.95 *(978-1-935122-11-1(8))* K&B Products.

Davis, Jacky & Soman, David. Ladybug Girl Feels Happy. Soman, David, illus. 2012. (Ladybug Girl Ser.). (ENG., Illus.). 12p. (J). (gr. -1 — 1). bds. 5.99 *(978-0-8037-3890-4(0),* Dial Bks) Penguin Young Readers Group.

De la Peña, Matt. I Will Save You. 2011. (ENG.). 320p. (YA). (gr. 9). pap. 9.99 *(978-0-385-73828-6(5),* Ember) Random Hse. Children's Bks.

Dean, Carolee. Forget Me Not. 2013. (ENG.). 400p. (YA). (gr. 9). pap. 11.99 *(978-1-4424-3255-0(1),* Simon Pulse) Simon Pulse.

—Take Me There. 2010. (ENG.). 336p. (YA). (gr. 9-18). pap. 8.99 *(978-1-4169-8950-9(1),* Simon Pulse) Simon Pulse.

DeFelice, Cynthia C. Signal. 2011. (ENG.). 176p. (J). (gr. 5-8). pap. 8.99 *(978-0-312-61776-9(3),* 9780312617769) Square Fish.

Degnan, Robert W. Fife's Lessons: The Tao of Cool. 2013. 38p. 24.99 *(978-1-4575-2081-5(8))* Dog Ear Publishing, LLC.

EFG

Dehghanpisheh, Corine. Can We Play Again? Dehghanpisheh, Corine, illus. 2012. (Illus.). 32p. pap. 12.95 *(978-0-9851930-1-0(8))* Dehghanpisheh, Corine.

Dellicurti, Dana. Christopher's Little Blue Backpack. 2007. 32p. per. 12.95 *(978-1-59800-806-7(4))* Outskirts Pr., Inc.

DeMeo, Kimberly F. One Little Egg. 2013. (ENG.). 25p. (J). pap. 20.95 *(978-1-4787-1084-4(5))* Outskirts Pr., Inc.

Dessen, Sarah. How to Deal: Someone Like You & That Summer. movie tie-in ed. 2003. (ENG.). 496p. (YA). (gr. 7-7). pap. 8.99 *(978-0-14-250103-0(4),* Puffin Books) Penguin Young Readers Group.

—Lock & Key. 2009. (ENG.). 448p. (YA). (gr. 7-18). 10.99 *(978-0-14-241472-9(7),* Speak) Penguin Young Readers Group.

—Lock & Key. 2009. lib. bdg. 22.10 *(978-0-606-14396-7(3),* Turtleback) Turtleback Bks.

Dew, Rachel. The Big Bunny Bed. 2009. 12p. pap. 11.50 *(978-1-60693-316-9(7),* Eloquent Bks.) Strategic Book Publishing & Rights Agency (SBPRA).

Dibani, Robyn. The People in My Life. 2011. 12p. pap. 9.95 *(978-1-4634-1942-4(2))* AuthorHouse.

DiCamillo, Kate. Great Joy. Ibatoulline, Bagram, illus. 2010. (ENG.). 32p. (J). (gr. -1-3). 8.99 *(978-0-7636-4996-8(1))* Candlewick Pr.

DiCicco, Sue. Feelings. DiCicco, Sue, illus. 2010. (Illus.). 10p. 9.95 *(978-1-60747-743-3(2),* Pickwick Pr.) Phoenix Bks., Inc.

Diggs, Taye. Chocolate Me! Evans, Shane W., illus. 2011. (ENG.). 40p. (J). (gr. -1-3). 17.99 *(978-0-312-60326-7(6),* 9780312603267) Feiwel & Friends.

Disney. Inside Out #2. 2015. (Step into Reading Level 3 Ser.). lib. bdg. 14.75 *(978-0-606-36388-4(2))* Turtleback Bks.

—Inside Out Junior Novel. 2015. lib. bdg. 16.00 *(978-0-606-37272-5(5))* Turtleback Bks.

Disney Book Group Staff. Inside Out - Driven by Emotions. Disney Storybook Art Team, illus. 2015. (ENG.). 240p. (J). (gr. 3-7). 10.99 *(978-1-4847-2203-9(5))* Disney Pr.

—Inside Out - Sadly Ever After? Purchase Includes Disney Ebook! 2015. (ENG., Illus.). 40p. (J). (gr. 1-3). 17.99 *(978-1-4847-1280-1(3))* Disney Pr.

—Inside Out Box of Mixed Emotions. 2015. (ENG.). 120p. (J). (gr. -1-k). 12.99 *(978-1-4847-1671-7(X))* Disney Pr.

Disney Inside Out, Disney Inside. Disney Pixar Inside Out - Joy's Journey. 2015. (ENG.). 24p. (J). (gr. -1-2). 19.99 *(978-0-7944-3386-4(3))* Studio Fun International.

—So Many Feelings: Riley's World Inside & Out. 2015. (ENG.). 64p. (J). (gr. 1-3). 11.99 *(978-0-7944-3387-1(1),* Reader's Digest Children's Bks.) Studio Fun International.

Disney Staff & Glumm, Felicity. Inside Out 8x8 Pictureback. 2015. lib. bdg. 14.75 *(978-0-606-36386-0(6))* Turtleback Bks.

Divine, Miss Jill. Miles Smiles. 2008. 88p. pap. 15.95 *(978-1-4092-5052-4(0))* Lulu Pr., Inc.

Dix, Catherine R. Rosetta Stones. 2009. (ENG.). 213p. pap. 14.95 *(978-0-9798452-2-2(X))* Central Ave. Pr.

Doney, Meryl. The Very Worried Sparrow. Hansen, Gaby, illus. 2008. (J). (gr. -1-3). 12.95 *(978-0-8198-8038-3(8))* Pauline Bks. & Media.

Donnelly, Jennifer. Revolution. 2011. (ENG.). 512p. (YA). (gr. 9). pap. 9.99 *(978-0-385-73764-7(5),* Ember) Random Hse. Children's Bks.

Doyle, Sheldon. Purple Mountain's Majesty. 2008. 224p. pap. 21.95 *(978-1-4357-2017-6(2))* Lulu Pr., Inc.

Dressel, Toni Ankeney. Sophie Smiles, 1 vol. 2010. 22p. 24.95 *(978-1-4489-7234-0(5))* PublishAmerica, Inc.

Drum, Emily. Happy Trails Horse Ranch. 2007. 16.95 *(978-1-58117-639-1(2),* Intervisual/Piggy Toes) Bendon, Inc.

Du Bist Spat Aufgewacht, Mein Schatz: Eine Abenteuergeschichte. 2003. (Illus.). 284p. (YA). 15.00 *(978-0-9712545-0-3(8))* Privatgaeste Verlag.

Duksta, Laura. I'll Hug You More. Iwai, Melissa, illus. 2017. (ENG.). 32p. (J). (-4). 16.99 *(978-1-4926-2618-3(X),* 9781492626183, Sourcebooks Jabberwocky) Sourcebooks, Inc.

Dumas, Alexandre. The Count of Monte Cristo, 1 vol. Fisher, Scott, illus. 2011. (Calico Illustrated Classics Ser.). (ENG.). 112p. (YA). (gr. 3-6). 27.07 *(978-1-60270-744-3(8))* Magic Wagon.

Durocher, Amelia. 3 Steps to Happy: Stop, Snap & Smile. 2011. 28p. pap. 13.95 *(978-1-4525-2970-7(1))* Balboa Pr.

Dvok, Eduard & Dvorák, Eduard. Bobek, the Cat with a Pompon Tail. Dvorák, Jaroslav, illus. 2010. 52p. pap. 17.00 *(978-1-60911-734-4(4),* Eloquent Bks.) Strategic Book Publishing & Rights Agency (SBPRA).

Dyan, Penelope. My Life As I Know It — Part Iv. 2011. 104p. pap. 8.95 *(978-1-935630-51-7(2))* Bellissima Publishing, LLC.

Edwards, Glenna S. Rainbow Bed: A child's perspective on coping with Grief. 2009. 20p. pap. 17.95 *(978-1-4327-2422-1(3))* Outskirts Pr., Inc.

Edwards, Meinir Wyn. Red Bandits of Mawddwy. Wade, Gini, illus. 2008. (ENG.). 24p. (J). pap. 4.95 *(978-1-84771-023-9(9))* Y Lolfa GBR. Dist: Dufour Editions, Inc.

Edwards, Wysteria. Bethany Bubbles Makes a Mistake. Abbott, Jason, illus. 2011. 34p. pap. 14.50 *(978-1-60911-353-7(5),* Strategic Bk. Publishing) Strategic Book Publishing & Rights Agency (SBPRA).

Eisenson, Adam. Hope. 2005. (Illus.). 35p. (J). 14.95 *(978-0-9766157-0-5(3))* Lone Star Pubns.

Elffers, Joost & Freymann, Saxton. How Are You Peeling? Foods with Moods. 2004. (ENG.). 48p. (J). (gr. -1-3). reprint ed. pap. 6.99 *(978-0-439-59841-5(9),* Scholastic Paperbacks) Scholastic, Inc.

Eliason, Scott. Andy's Magic Marble. 2008. 40p. per. 24.95 *(978-1-4241-8774-4(5))* America Star Bks.

Ellefson, Benjamin. The Land Without Color. 2015. (ENG.). (J). 16.95 *(978-1-59298-844-0(X))* Beaver's Pond Pr., Inc.

Elliott, David. Finn Throws a Fit! Ering, Timothy Basil, illus. 2011. (ENG.). 32p. (J). (gr. k-k). pap. 6.99 *(978-0-7636-5604-1(6))* Candlewick Pr.

Ellison, Joy D. Carol & Connie. 2008. 28p. per. 24.95 *(978-1-4241-9276-2(5))* America Star Bks.

Ernst, Kathleen. Highland Fling. 2006. (ENG.). 192p. (J). (gr. 3-8). 15.95 *(978-0-8126-2742-8(3))* Cricket Bks.

Ernst, Lisa Campbell. Snow Surprise. 2008. (Green Light Readers Level 2 Ser.). (ENG., Illus.). 24p. (J). (gr. k-2). pap. 3.95 *(978-0-15-206559-1(8))* Houghton Mifflin Harcourt Publishing Co.

Falligant, Erin. A Surprise Find. Studios, Arcana, illus. 2011. (ENG.). 120p. (J). pap. 8.95 *(978-1-59369-908-6(5))* American Girl Publishing, Inc.

Fanning, Meghan. Mrs. Kisses. Judah, Nathan, illus. 2013. 28p. pap. 9.99 *(978-1-61225-227-8(3))* Mirror Publishing.

Fault Line. 2014. (ENG., Illus.). 256p. (YA). (gr. 10). pap. 11.99 *(978-1-4424-6073-7(3),* Simon Pulse) Simon Pulse.

Fessler, Jennifer. Precious Is Worried. 2008. 16p. 11.30 *(978-0-615-24258-3(8))* Twin Sisters Publishing Co.

Fickey, Brenda. Beckoning Shadows, 1 vol. 2009. (ENG.). 179p. pap. 24.95 *(978-1-61546-330-5(5))* America Star Bks.

Filigenzi, Courtney & Bersani, Shennen. Let My Colors Out. Bersani, Shennen, illus. 2009. (ENG., Illus.). 16p. (J). (gr. -1-k). pap. 11.95 *(978-1-60443-011-0(7),* 1604430117) American Cancer Society, Inc.

Fiori, Natalie. Lobsters in Seacliff. 2009. 52p. pap. 20.99 *(978-1-4490-1811-5(4))* AuthorHouse.

Fitzmaurice, Kathryn. A Diamond in the Desert. 2013. (ENG.). 272p. (J). (gr. 5). pap. 6.99 *(978-0-14-242437-7(4),* Puffin Books) Penguin Young Readers Group.

Flanery, Alicia & Stephenson, Caitlin. Wow: We Wrote a Book! 2003. 140p. (YA). pap. 13.95 *(978-0-595-28056-8(0))* iUniverse, Inc.

The Flower Child. 2013. (Illus.). 28p. 17.99 *(978-0-9891510-1-6(8))* Zebra Ginkgo.

Foley, Greg. Willoughby & the Lion. Foley, Greg, illus. 2009. (ENG., Illus.). 40p. (J). (gr. -1-2). 17.99 *(978-0-06-154750-8(6))* HarperCollins Pubs.

Foley, Monica. The Four of Us. 2008. pap. 9.00 *(978-0-8059-8628-0(6))* Dorrance Publishing Co., Inc.

Forler, Nan. Bird Child. Thisdale, Francois, illus. 2009. (ENG.). 32p. (J). (gr. k-3). 19.95 *(978-0-88776-894-1(6),* Tundra Bks.) Tundra Bks. CAN. Dist: Penguin Random Hse. LLC.

Forman, Gayle. Where She Went. l.t. ed. 2015. (If I Stay Ser.: BK.2). (ENG.). 288p. (YA). 23.99 *(978-1-4104-7562-6(X))* Cengage Gale.

—Where She Went. (If I Stay Ser.: BK.2). (ENG.). (YA). (gr. 9-18). 2012. 304p. 10.99 *(978-0-14-242089-8(1),* Speak) 2011. 272p. 17.99 *(978-0-525-42294-5(3),* Dutton Books for Young Readers) Penguin Young Readers Group.

—Where She Went. 2012. (If I Stay Ser.: BK.2). (YA). 21.00 *(978-1-61383-394-0(6))* Perfection Learning Corp.

—Where She Went. l.t. ed. 2015. (If I Stay Ser.: BK.2). (ENG.). 286p. (YA). pap. 12.99 *(978-1-59413-855-3(9),* Large Print Pr.) Thorndike Pr.

—Where She Went. 2012. (If I Stay Ser.: BK.2). (YA). lib. bdg. 22.10 *(978-0-606-23644-7(9),* Turtleback) Turtleback Bks.

Fortner, Tama. God Is Always Good: Comfort for Kids Facing Grief, Fear, or Change, 1 vol. Vasylenko, Veronica, illus. 2014. (ENG.). 32p. (J). 12.99 *(978-0-7180-1145-1(7))* Nelson, Thomas Inc.

Fox, Mem. Harriet, You'll Drive Me Wild! Frazee, Marla, illus. 2003. (ENG.). 32p. (J). (gr. -1-3). pap. 7.99 *(978-0-15-204598-2(8))* Houghton Mifflin Harcourt Publishing Co.

Friday, Mary Ellen. It's a Bad Day. 2006. (ENG., Illus.). 32p. (J). (gr. -1-3). 15.95 *(978-0-87358-904-8(1))* Cooper Square Publishing Llc.

Friend, Gaythel Boggs & Miller, Dalton. Foundation of a Clown, 1 vol. 2010. 58p. pap. 19.95 *(978-1-4489-8253-0(7))* America Star Bks.

Friesen, Jonathan. Rush. 2010. (ENG.). 320p. (YA). (gr. 7-18). 9.99 *(978-0-14-241258-9(9),* Speak) Penguin Young Readers Group.

Fruchter, Jason, illus. Daniel Feels Left Out. 2015. (Daniel Tiger's Neighborhood Ser.). (ENG.). 32p. (J). (gr. -1-k). 16.99 *(978-1-4814-3836-0(0),* Simon Spotlight) Simon Spotlight.

—How Is Daniel Feeling? 2015. (Daniel Tiger's Neighborhood Ser.). (ENG.). 14p. (J). (gr. -1-k). bds. 10.99 *(978-1-4814-3856-8(5),* Simon Spotlight) Simon Spotlight.

Fucile, Tony. Poor Louie. Fucile, Tony, illus. 2017. (ENG., Illus.). 40p. (J). (gr. -1-2). 16.99 *(978-0-7636-5828-1(6))* Candlewick Pr.

Fujishima, Kosuke. Oh My Goddess! Volume 36. 2010. (ENG., Illus.). 152p. pap. 10.99 *(978-1-59582-581-0(9))* Dark Horse Comics.

Furniss, Alice. The Happiest Mommy Ever. 2009. (Illus.). 32p. (J). 17.95 *(978-1-60641-056-1(3))* Deseret Bk. Co.

Furraway, Bec. Sarah Meets a Bully. 2008. 36p. pap. 18.50 *(978-1-60693-214-8(4),* Eloquent Bks.) Strategic Book Publishing & Rights Agency (SBPRA).

Fusco, Kimberly Newton. Tending to Grace. 2005. 175p. (gr. 7-12). 16.50 *(978-0-7569-5478-9(9))* Perfection Learning Corp.

Galante, Cecilia. The Summer of May. Carpenter, Tad, illus. 2012. (ENG.). 256p. (J). (gr. 4-8). pap. 6.99 *(978-1-4169-8304-0(X),* Simon & Schuster/Paula Wiseman Bks.) Simon & Schuster/Paula Wiseman Bks.

Galliez, Roxane Marie. Farewell Sadness. Lhomme, Sandrine, illus. 2010. 24p. (J). 9.99 *(978-0-8416-7139-3(7))* Hammond World Atlas Corp.

Galvin, Laura Gates. Angry, Brave & Cheerful: An Alphabet of Feelings. 123 Sesame Street, ed. 2009. 20p. (J). (gr. -1). 8.99 incl. audio compact disk *(978-1-59069-833-4(9))* Studio Mouse LLC.

—Mickey Mouse Clubhouse Teamwork: Let's Do It Together. 2008. (ENG.). 40p. (J). (gr. -1). 12.99 *(978-1-59069-738-2(3))* Studio Mouse LLC.

Gardner, Graham. Finn Finds Fun! LeBlanc, Nancy, illus. 2015. 32p. (J). (gr. -1-2). 17.95 *(978-1-939930-41-5(3),* Belle Isle Bks.) Brandylane Pubs., Inc.

Garrett, Troy. Kramer's World. 204p. 2010. pap. 12.50 *(978-1-60693-155-4(5))* 2008. 23.50 *(978-1-60693-518-7(6))* Strategic Book Publishing & Rights Agency (SBPRA). (Eloquent Bks.).

Gassman, Julie A. You Get What You Get, 1 vol. Horne, Sarah, illus. (Little Boost Ser.). (ENG.). 32p. (gr. k-3). 2013. 14.95 *(978-1-4795-2157-9(4))* 2012. lib. bdg. 23.99 *(978-1-4048-6794-9(5))* Picture Window Bks. (Little Boost).

Gemeinhart, Dan. The Honest Truth. 2015. (ENG.). 240p. (J). (gr. 3-7). 16.99 *(978-0-545-66573-5(6),* Scholastic Pr.) Scholastic, Inc.

George, Kallie. Flare. Cote, Genevieve, illus. 2014. (ENG.). 34p. (J). (gr. -1-3). 12.95 *(978-1-927018-50-7(1))* Simply Read Bks. CAN. Dist: Ingram Publisher Services.

Geras, Adèle. Watching the Roses: The Egerton Hall Novels, Volume Two, Vol. 2. 2005. (ENG.). 192p. (YA). (gr. 7-12). pap. 11.95 *(978-0-15-205531-8(2))* Houghton Mifflin Harcourt Publishing Co.

Gibson, Amy. Catching Kisses. van Lieshout, Maria, illus. 2013. (ENG.). 32p. (J). (gr. -1-1). 16.99 *(978-0-312-37647-5(2),* 9780312376475) Feiwel & Friends.

Gidali, Orit. Nora the Mind Reader. Gordon-Noy, Aya, illus. 2012. (ENG.). 32p. (J). (gr. -1-3). 15.95 *(978-1-59270-120-9(5))* Enchanted Lion Bks., LLC.

Gingras, Charlotte. Pieces of Me. Ouriou, Susan, tr. from FRE. 2009. (ENG.). 144p. (J). (gr. 7-9). 8.95 *(978-1-55453-432-6(1))* Kids Can Pr., Ltd. CAN. Dist: Hachette Bk. Group.

Giordano, Anthony. Another Boring Summer... Again! 2009. 154p. (YA). pap. 11.25 *(978-1-60695-077-7(0))* Callanish Pr.

Glasgow, Kathleen. Girl in Pieces. 2016. (ENG.). 416p. (YA). (gr. 9). lib. bdg. 21.99 *(978-1-101-93473-9(5),* Delacorte Pr.) Random House Publishing Group.

—Girl in Pieces. 2016. (ENG.). 416p. (YA). (gr. 9). 18.99 *(978-1-101-93471-5(9),* Delacorte Pr.) Random Hse. Children's Bks.

Goldblatt, Rob, illus. The Boy Who Didn't Want to Be Sad. 2004. 32p. (J). 14.95 *(978-1-59147-134-9(6),* Magination Pr.) American Psychological Assn.

Goldblatt, Robert. The Boy Who Didn't Want to Be Sad. 2004. (Illus.). 32p. (J). pap. 9.95 *(978-1-59147-135-6(4),* Magination Pr.) American Psychological Assn.

Gomez, Sally. Too Many Freckles! Mitchell, Hazel, illus. 2008. (ENG.). 32p. pap. *(978-1-934363-32-4(4))* Zoe Life Publishing.

Gownley, Jimmy. What Makes You Happy. Gownley, Jimmy, illus. 2009. (Amelia Rules! Ser.). (ENG., Illus.). 176p. (J). (gr. 2-7). pap. 12.99 *(978-1-4169-8605-8(7),* Atheneum Bks. for Young Readers) Simon & Schuster Children's Publishing.

Grace, Amanda. But I Love Him. 2011. (ENG.). 264p. (YA). (gr. 7-18). pap. 9.95 *(978-0-7387-2594-9(3),* Flux) North Star Editions.

Graff, Lisa. Lost in the Sun. 2015. (ENG.). 304p. (J). (gr. 5). 16.99 *(978-0-399-16406-4(5),* Philomel Bks.) Penguin Young Readers Group.

—Umbrella Summer. 2011. (ENG.). 240p. (J). (gr. 3-7). pap. 6.99 *(978-0-06-143189-0(3))* HarperCollins Pubs.

Graham-Morgan, Ivet. Peter the Parrot Misses Home: Misses Home. 2011. 16p. 9.98 *(978-1-4343-9791-1(2))* AuthorHouse.

Grant, Alice. Dear Mr President, Please Send My Daddy Home. 2008. 23p. pap. 24.95 *(978-1-60441-293-2(3))* America Star Bks.

Grant, Katy. Pranked. 2008. (Summer Camp Secrets Ser.). (ENG.). 240p. (J). (gr. 3-7). pap. 7.99 *(978-1-4169-3576-6(2),* Aladdin) Simon & Schuster Children's Publishing.

Gray, Kes. Worries Go Away! Wildish, Lee, illus. 2015. (ENG.). 32p. (J). (gr. -1-k). pap. 9.99 *(978-1-4449-0017-0(X))* Hodder & Stoughton GBR. Dist: Hachette Bk. Group.

Gregori, Anthony, illus. Meet the Itslts. l.t. ed. 2007. 40p. (J). lib. bdg. 9.99 *(978-0-9769360-1-5(1))* Adam Hill Pubns.

Gregory, Dee. The Accidental Daughter: A Children's Story about Hope. 2008. 96p. pap. 10.49 *(978-1-4389-3338-2(X))* AuthorHouse.

Griffin, Adele. Amandine. 2003. (ENG.). 208p. (gr. 5-9). pap. 6.99 *(978-0-7868-1441-1(1))* Disney Pr.

Grimes, Nikki. Garvey's Choice. 2016. (ENG.). 120p. (J). (gr. 2-7). 16.95 *(978-1-62979-740-3(5),* Wordsong) Boyds Mills Pr.

Grimshaw, Kath. Frankie's Foibles: A Story about a Boy Who Worries. 2015. (ENG., Illus.). 32p. (J). 16.95 *(978-1-84905-695-3(1),* 8167) Kingsley, Jessica Pubs. GBR. Dist: Macmillan Distribution Ltd.

Grossman, David. The Hug. Schoffman, Stuart, tr. Rovner, Michal, illus. 2013. (ENG.). 32p. (gr. 4-13). 19.95 *(978-1-4683-0273-8(6),* 460273) Overlook Pr., The.

Grover, Lorie Ann. Hold Me Tight. 2007. (ENG.). 352p. (J). (gr. 5-9). pap. 16.95 *(978-1-4169-6753-8(2),* McElderry, Margaret K. Bks.) McElderry, Margaret K. Bks.

Guest, Elissa Haden. Iris & Walter, the Sleepover. Davenier, Christine, illus. 2006. (Iris & Walter Ser.). 44p. (gr. 1-4). 15.95 *(978-0-7569-6681-2(7))* Perfection Learning Corp.

Guiffre, William. The Wrong Side of the Bed. Baron, Cheri Ann, illus. 2008. 32p. (J). (gr. -1-3). pap. 9.95 *(978-1-931650-34-2(9))* Bks. for Children Publishing.

Gunderson, Jessica. There's a Hurricane in the Pool!, 1 vol. Santillan, Jorge H., illus. 2011. (Sports Illustrated Kids Victory School Superstars Ser.). (ENG.). 56p. (gr. 1-3). 26.65 *(978-1-4342-2230-5(6))* Stone Arch Bks.

Gutierrez-Green, Sandra. The Colors in My Garden. 2005. 36p. per. 19.25 *(978-1-4208-4266-1(8))* AuthorHouse.

Haddix, Margaret Peterson. Claim to Fame. (ENG.). 272p. (YA). (gr. 7). 2010. pap. 9.99 *(978-1-4169-3918-4(0))* 2009. 16.99 *(978-1-4169-3917-7(2))* Simon & Schuster Bks. For Young Readers. (Simon & Schuster Bks. For Young Readers).

Haesche, Richard, Sr. The Big Race. 2007. (ENG.). 222p. (J). per. 10.49 *(978-0-9796536-1-6(3))* Kreative X-Pressions Pubns.

Half a World Away. 2014. (ENG., Illus.). 240p. (J). (gr. 5-9). 17.99 *(978-1-4424-1275-0(5),* Atheneum Bks. for Young Readers) Simon & Schuster Children's Publishing.

Hall, Mary Kathleen. Marland's Mysterious Mazes: Past the Mailbox. 2010. 40p. pap. 16.99 *(978-1-4490-7824-9(9))* AuthorHouse.

Hall, Michael. My Heart Is Like a Zoo. Hall, Michael, illus. (Illus.). (J). (gr. -1-k). 2013. (ENG.). 34p. bds. 7.99 *(978-0-06-191512-3(2))* 2009. (ENG.). 32p. 16.99 *(978-0-06-191510-9(6))* 2009. 32p. lib. bdg. 17.89 *(978-0-06-191511-6(4))* HarperCollins Pubs. (Greenwillow Bks.).

—Perfect Square. Hall, Michael, illus. 2011. (ENG., Illus.). 40p. (J). (gr. -1-k). 16.99 *(978-0-06-191513-0(0),* Greenwillow Bks.) HarperCollins Pubs.

Hall, Rocky Lane. Fan, 1 vol. 2010. 38p. pap. 24.95 *(978-1-4489-8498-5(X))* PublishAmerica, Inc.

Hancock, Dennis & Uyen. The Tree House on the Bluff. Hancock, Uyen, illus. 2012. 36p. pap. 24.95 *(978-1-4626-7318-6(X))* America Star Bks.

Hardgrave, Gayle. Daniel Goes to Pre-K. 2009. 32p. pap. 12.99 *(978-1-4389-7090-5(0))* AuthorHouse.

Hardinge, Frances. A Face Like Glass. 2017. (ENG.). 496p. (YA). (gr. 7-17). 19.95 *(978-1-4197-2484-8(3),* Amulet Bks.) Abrams, Inc.

Hargreaves, Adam. Little Miss Hug. Hargreaves, Adam, illus. 2014. (Mr. Men & Little Miss Ser.). (ENG., Illus.). 32p. (J). (gr. -1-2). 4.99 *(978-0-8431-8059-6(5),* Price Stern Sloan) Penguin Young Readers Group.

Hargreaves, Adam & Sloan, Price Stern. Little Miss Hug. 2015. (Mr. Men & Little Miss Ser.). (ENG., Illus.). 32p. (J). (gr. -1-2). bds. 7.99 *(978-1-101-99523-5(8),* Price Stern Sloan) Penguin Young Readers Group.

Hargreaves, Roger. Little Miss Giggles. 2011. (Mr. Men & Little Miss Ser.). (ENG.). 32p. (J). (gr. -1-2). mass mkt. 4.99 *(978-0-8431-9890-4(7),* Price Stern Sloan) Penguin Young Readers Group.

Harper, Charise Mericle. Just Grace & the Snack Attack. 2010. (Just Grace Ser.: 5). (ENG., Illus.). 176p. (J). (gr. 1-4). pap. 5.99 *(978-0-547-40629-9(0))* Houghton Mifflin Harcourt Publishing Co.

Harper, Jessica. Lizzy's Ups & Downs: NOT an Ordinary School Day. Dupont, Lindsay Harper, illus. 2004. 32p. (J). (gr. -1-3). 15.99 *(978-0-06-052063-2(9))* HarperCollins Pubs.

Harpster, Steve, illus. Arnold Gets Angry: An Emotional Literacy Book. 2004. (Emotional Literacy Ser.). 45p. (J). (gr. 2-18). 14.95 *(978-0-9747789-0-7(7),* 67312) CTC Publishing.

Harris, Robie H. When Lions Roar. Raschka, Chris, illus. 2013. (ENG.). 32p. (J). (gr. -1-k). 16.99 *(978-0-545-11283-3(4),* Orchard Bks.) Scholastic, Inc.

Harris-Wyrick, Wayne. Kimmy Finds Her Key. Liz Warren, illus. 2013. 28p. pap. 11.99 *(978-0-9852661-8-9(X))* 4RV Publishing, LLC.

Harrison, Lisi. Revenge of the Wannabes. 2005. (Clique Ser.: 3). (ENG.). 304p. (YA). (gr. 7-17). pap. 9.99 *(978-0-316-70133-4(5),* Poppy) Little, Brown Bks. for Young Readers.

Hartman, Brett. Cadillac Chronicles. 2012. (ENG.). 304p. (J). (gr. 10). 16.95 *(978-1-935955-41-2(1))* Cinco Puntos Pr.

Hartman, Carrie. Child of Mine. 2007. (ENG., Illus.). 32p. (J). lib. bdg. 11.99 *(978-1-934277-12-6(6))* Mam Green Publishing, Inc.

Hartt-Sussman, Heather. Noni Is Nervous. Côté, Geneviève, illus. 2013. (ENG.). 24p. (J). (gr. -1-2). 17.95 *(978-1-77049-323-0(9),* Tundra Bks.) Tundra Bks. CAN. Dist: Penguin Random Hse. LLC.

Hastings, Suanne. Many Moods of Maddie: Bossy Boots. Crabtree, Andy, illus. 2006. (Baby Sitter Ser.). 24p. (J). (gr. -1-3). pap. 9.99 *(978-0-9769348-0-6(9))* Tastica, Suanne Creations Inc.

Hawa, Christine Elias. Joy the Girl How Never Smiled. 2011. 32p. pap. 16.19 *(978-1-4634-3636-0(X))* AuthorHouse.

Hawes, Dorothy. Invisible Julian. Reaves, Daniel, illus. 2011. 24p. pap. 24.95 *(978-1-4560-9583-3(8))* America Star Bks.

Hays, Anna. Portia's Ultra Mysterious Double Life. 2008. (Mix Ser.). (ENG.). 224p. (J). (gr. 4-8). pap. 5.99 *(978-1-4169-4893-3(7),* Aladdin) Simon & Schuster Children's Publishing.

Heartfelt Hugs. 2009. 8p. 12.99 *(978-1-4231-1882-4(0))* Disney Pr.

Heiss, Renee. Somebody Cares! 2010. 32p. 16.95 *(978-1-4497-0758-3(0),* WestBow Pr.) Author Solutions, Inc.

Helen, Grace. Vicky Sticky Lips: Putting Others to the Test. 2012. 24p. 24.95 *(978-1-4626-5975-3(6))* America Star Bks.

Helfenbein, DeWayne. The Treasure Hunt. 2006. pap. 9.99 *(978-1-60034-562-3(X))* Salem Author Services.

Helmore, Jim. Letterbox Lil: A Cautionary Tale. 2006. (Illus.). (J). *(978-1-4156-4110-1(2))* Book Wholesalers, Inc.

Henderson, Sara. Howie Finds a Hug, 1 vol. Zenz, Aaron, illus. 2008. (I Can Read! / Howie Ser.). (ENG.). 32p. (J). (gr. -1-3). pap. 3.99 *(978-0-310-71607-5(1))* Zonderkidz.

Henkes, Kevin. Wemberly Worried. Henkes, Kevin, illus. 2010. (ENG., Illus.). 32p. (J). (gr. -1-4). pap. 6.99 *(978-0-06-185776-8(9),* Greenwillow Bks.) HarperCollins Pubs.

—Wemberly Worried. 2010. (J). lib. bdg. 17.20 *(978-0-606-14757-6(8),* Turtleback) Turtleback Bks.

Henson, Heather. Dream of Night. 2010. (ENG.). 224p. (J). (gr. 3-7). 15.99 *(978-1-4169-4899-5(6),* Atheneum Bks. for Young Readers) Simon & Schuster Children's Publishing.

Higesanbon. Mo Mo Mo Mo Monster: Mon Monster. 2011. 56p. pap. 34.95 *(978-1-4327-4149-5(7))* Outskirts Pr., Inc.

Higgins, F. E. The Eyeball Collector. 2011. (ENG.). 272p. (J). (gr. 5-9). pap. 9.99 *(978-0-312-66097-0(9),* 9780312660970) Square Fish.

Hillert, Margaret. Who Feels Mad, Dear Dragon? Pullan, Jack, illus. 2017. (BeginningtoRead Ser.). (ENG.). 32p. (J). (-2). 22.60 **(978-1-59953-822-8(9))**; pap. 11.94 ***(978-1-68404-000-1(0))*** Norwood Hse. Pr.

—Who Feels Sad, Dear Dragon? Pullan, Jack, illus. 2017. (BeginningtoRead Ser.). (ENG.). 32p. (J). (-2). 22.60 ***(978-1-59953-823-5(7))***; pap. 11.94 ***(978-1-68404-001-8(9))*** Norwood Hse. Pr.

—Who Feels Surprised, Dear Dragon? Pullan, Jack, illus. 2017. (BeginningtoRead Ser.). (ENG.). 32p. (J). (-2). 22.60 ***(978-1-59953-825-9(3))***; pap. 11.94 ***(978-1-68404-003-2(5))*** Norwood Hse. Pr.

Hills, Tad. Duck & Goose, How Are You Feeling? Hills, Tad, illus. 2009. (Duck & Goose Ser.). (ENG., Illus.). 22p. (J). (gr. -1 — 1). bds. 7.99 *(978-0-375-84629-8(8),* Schwartz & Wade Bks.) Random Hse. Children's Bks.

Hinton, Amber. Mister Ego & the Bubble of Love. Zintoll, Gabreyhl, illus. 2008. (ENG.). 32p. 16.95 *(978-1-897238-36-3(3))* Namaste Publishing, Inc. CAN. Dist: Publishers Group West (PGW).

Hoban, Julia. Willow. 2010. (ENG.). 336p. (YA). (gr. 9-18). 8.99 *(978-0-14-241666-2(5),* Speak) Penguin Young Readers Group.

Hobbie, Holly. You Are My Sunshine. 2010. (Toot & Puddle Ser.: 3). (ENG., Illus.). 32p. (J). (gr. -1-3). pap. 7.99 *(978-0-316-16703-1(7))* Little, Brown Bks. for Young Readers.

Hoena, Blake A. & Fuentes, Benny. Spotlight Striker, 1 vol. Sandoval, Gerardo, illus. 2010. (Sports Illustrated Kids Graphic Novels Ser.). (ENG.). 56p. (gr. 2-3). 26.65 *(978-1-4342-2128-5(8))*; pap. 7.19 *(978-1-4342-2787-4(1))* Stone Arch Bks.

Hoffman, C. J. Hiss: A Story about Love, Trust & Growing Up. 2008. 24p. pap. 11.49 *(978-1-4389-3842-4(X))* AuthorHouse.

Hoffman, Mary. Stravaganza: City of Swords. 2012. (Stravaganza Ser.). (ENG.). 368p. (YA). (gr. 7-12). 18.99 *(978-1-59990-842-7(5)*, 9781599908427, Bloomsbury USA Childrens) Bloomsbury Publishing USA.

Holtz-Bacha, Christina. Second Chance. 2007. 96p. 8.95 *(978-0-9773082-6-2(X))* LBF Bks., LLC.

Holzwarth, Werner. I Wish I Were A... Jeschke, Stefanie, illus. 2013. (ENG.). 40p. (J). (gr. -1-k). 16.95 *(978-1-62087-993-1(X)*, 620993, Sky Pony Pr.) Skyhorse Publishing Co., Inc.

Hope, Laura Lee. Outdoor Girls in Florida. 2006. 26.95 *(978-1-4218-2982-1(7))*; pap. 11.95 *(978-1-4218-3082-7(5))* 1st World Publishing, Inc.

Hopkins, Ellen. Fallout. 2010. (ENG.). 672p. (YA). (gr. 9-18). 18.99 *(978-1-4169-5009-7(5)*, McElderry, Margaret K. Bks.) McElderry, Margaret K. Bks.

—Identical. (ENG.). (YA). (gr. 9-18). 2010. 592p. pap. 12.99 *(978-1-4169-5006-6(0))* 2008. 576p. 17.99 *(978-1-4169-5005-9(2))* McElderry, Margaret K. Bks. (McElderry, Margaret K. Bks.).

Houston, Debby. Mervous Tames Ocd. 2012. 28p. pap. 21.99 *(978-1-4771-0943-4(9))* Xlibris Corp.

Hrdlitschka, Shelley. Kat's Fall. 2005. 168p. 18.95 *(978-0-7569-6315-6(X))* Perfection Learning Corp.

Huber, Mike. The Amazing Erik. Cowman, Joseph, illus. 2014. (ENG.). 32p. (gr. -1). 15.95 *(978-1-60554-209-6(1))* Redleaf Pr.

—Mama's Gloves. Cowman, Joseph, illus. 2014. (ENG.). 32p. (gr. -1). 15.95 *(978-1-60554-210-2(5))* Redleaf Pr.

Hudson, Wade. Feelings I Love to Share. 2009. 24p. 5.95 *(978-1-60349-011-5(6)*, Marimba Bks.) Hudson Publishing Group, The.

Huebner, Dawn. Sometimes I Worry Too Much: A Book to Help Children Who Worry When They Don't Need To. Schader, Karen, ed. Morris, Robin C., illus. 2003. (J). per. 17.95 *(978-1-58815-060-8(7)*, 63814) Childswork/Childsplay.

Hug Machine. 2014. (ENG., Illus.). 40p. (J). (gr. -1-2). 17.99 *(978-1-4424-5935-9(2)*, Atheneum Bks. for Young Readers) Simon & Schuster Children's Publishing.

Hulslander, Dyan. God's Precious Gift. 2009. 24p. pap. 14.99 *(978-1-4389-6903-9(1))* AuthorHouse.

Hunkins, Liz & Hunkins, P. J. Herbie the Erbie: What Are These Things Called Feelings? 2007. 24p. per. 24.95 *(978-1-4241-8548-1(3))* America Star Bks.

I Am Twee' 2013. (Illus.). 24p. (J). pap. 12.99 *(978-0-9889113-2-1(9))* Coda Grove Publishing.

I Was a Tree Once. 2008. 272p. pap. 17.95 *(978-0-595-52197-5(5))* iUniverse, Inc.

Ibarrola, Begonia. Story of a Can. Amado, Antonio, illus. 2013. (ENG.). 32p. (J). *(978-84-95923-94-3(7))* Primera Persona.

Imes, Jarold. Never Too Much - the Remix. 2007. (YA). per. 10.99 *(978-1-934195-07-9(3))* Tinsley Phelps, LLC.

Impey, Rose & Huws, Emily. Dymuniad Mewn Eiliad. 2005. (WEL., Illus.). 64p. pap. *(978-0-86381-912-4(5))* Gwasg Carreg Gwalch.

Ingalls, Melodi J. Everyone Is Differphant. 2008. 20p. pap. 11.99 *(978-1-4389-1206-6(4))* AuthorHouse.

Ironside, Virgina & Ironside, Virginia. The Huge Bag of Worries. Rodgers, Frank, illus. 2011. (ENG.). 32p. (J). (gr. -1-17). pap. 11.99 *(978-0-340-90317-9(1))* Hodder & Stoughton GBR. Dist: Hachette Bk. Group.

Ives, Penny. Celestine, Drama Queen. 2009. (J). *(978-0-545-08715-5(5))*; pap. *(978-0-545-08714-8(7))* Scholastic, Inc. (Levine, Arthur A. Bks.).

Jackson, Everett E. Kimme Gets a Valentine. 2008. 28p. pap. 16.99 *(978-1-4389-0982-0(9))* AuthorHouse.

Jahn-Clough, Lisa. Me, Penelope. 2009. (ENG.). 208p. (YA). (gr. 9). pap. 12.99 *(978-0-547-07632-4(0))* Houghton Mifflin Harcourt Publishing Co.

Jazwierska, Jennifer & Popiel, Candice Bataille. Discovery of Glow. 2008. (Glowmundo Ser.). (J). (gr. 2-6). pap. 12.95 *(978-0-9814930-0-8(9))* Elora Media, LLC.

Jean-Baptiste, Marie V. Goodnight & Seeyoutomorrow. 2013. 28p. pap. 24.95 *(978-1-4626-9551-5(5))* America Star Bks.

Jeffers, Oliver. The Heart & the Bottle. Jeffers, Oliver, illus. 2010. (ENG., Illus.). 32p. (J). (gr. -1-3). 17.99 *(978-0-399-25452-9(8)*, Philomel Bks.) Penguin Young Readers Group.

Jefferson, Cassandra And Maya. King Martin. 2012. 24p. 24.95 *(978-1-4626-5852-7(0))* America Star Bks.

Jenkins, T. L. On the Bed & off the Bed. 2009. 28p. pap. 12.49 *(978-1-4389-2468-3(0))* AuthorHouse.

Jesset, Aurore. Loopy. Korthues, Barbara, illus. 2008. (ENG.). 32p. (J). (gr. -1-3). 16.95 *(978-0-7358-2175-0(5))* North-South Bks., Inc.

Johnson, Sandra, adapted by. Shoobie, 1 vol. 2009. 15p. pap. 24.95 *(978-1-60813-705-3(8))* America Star Bks.

Johnston, E. K. Exit, Pursued by a Bear. 2016. (ENG.). 256p. (YA). (gr. 9). 17.99 *(978-1-101-99458-0(4)*, Dutton Books for Young Readers) Penguin Young Readers Group.

Johnston, Gayle. The Adventures of Jazzi G: Search for the Missing Peace. 2016. (Adventures of Jazzi G Ser.: 1). (ENG., Illus.). 202p. (J). 32.95 *(978-1-63047-841-4(5))* Morgan James Publishing.

Jones, Patrick. Outburst. 2014. (Alternative Ser.). (ENG.). 104p. (YA). (gr. 6-12). lib. bdg. 27.93 *(978-1-4677-3901-6(4))* Lerner Publishing Group.

—Outburst. 2014. (Alternative Ser.). (ENG.). 104p. (YA). (gr. 6-12). pap. 7.95 *(978-1-4677-4484-3(0)*, Darby Creek) Lerner Publishing Group.

—Returning to Normal. 2015. (Locked Out Ser.). (ENG.). 112p. (J). (gr. 6-12). lib. bdg. 27.99 *(978-1-4677-5799-7(3))* Lerner Publishing Group.

Jonsberg, Barry. Dreamrider. 2009. (ENG.). 256p. (YA). (gr. 9). pap. 8.99 *(978-0-375-84458-4(9)*, Knopf Bks. for Young Readers) Random Hse. Children's Bks.

Joosse, Barbara M. Wally Wants to Hug. Ashdown, Rebecca, illus. 2017. (ENG.). 32p. (J). (gr. -1-3). 16.99 *(978-1-4998-0404-1(0))* Little Bee Books Inc.

Jorgenson, Norman. In Flanders Fields. Harrison-Lever, Brian, illus. 2010. (ENG.). 32p. (J). (gr. -1-3). pap. 9.95 *(978-1-894965-83-5(3))* Simply Read Bks. CAN. Dist: Ingram Publisher Services.

Juback, Wendy L. Sorry about Your Luck, Chuck. 2012. 40p. pap. 20.99 *(978-1-4685-7275-9(X))* AuthorHouse.

Julian, Sean. Sloppy Wants a Hug. 2017. (ENG., Illus.). 32p. (J). (gr. -1-3). 17.95 *(978-0-7358-4273-1(6))* North-South Bks., Inc.

Kadohata, Cynthia. Half a World Away. 2014. 240p. 16.99 *(978-1-4814-1806-5(8))* Simon & Schuster, Inc.

—Half a World Away. 2015. lib. bdg. 18.40 *(978-0-606-37845-1(6))* Turtleback Bks.

Kam, Jennifer Wolf. Devin Rhodes Is Dead. 2014. (ENG.). 240p. (YA). (gr. 7). 16.95 *(978-1-934133-59-0(0)*, Mackinac Island Press, Inc.) Charlesbridge Publishing, Inc.

Karst, Patrice. The Smile That Went Around the World. 2009. (Illus.). 32p. (J). (gr. -1-4). 15.95 *(978-0-87516-827-2(2)*, Devorss Pubns.) DeVorss & Co.

—The Smile That Went Around the World (Revised) New Updated Edition. Christy, Jana, illus. 2014. (ENG.). 22p. (J). 15.95 *(978-0-87516-875-3(2)*, Devorss Pubns.) DeVorss & Co.

Katie, Byron & Wilhelm, Hans. Tiger-Tiger, Is It True? Four Questions to Make You Smile Again. 2009. (ENG., Illus.). 32p. 14.95 *(978-1-4019-2560-4(X)*, 1076) Hay Hse., Inc.

Katz, Karen. How Does Baby Feel? A Karen Katz Lift-The-Flap Book. Katz, Karen, illus. 2013. (ENG., Illus.). 14p. (J). (gr. -1 — 1). bds. 6.99 *(978-1-4424-5204-6(8)*, Little Simon) Little Simon.

—Mommy Hugs. Katz, Karen, illus. 2007. (Classic Board Bks.). (ENG., Illus.). 32p. (J). (gr. -1 — 1). bds. 7.99 *(978-1-4169-4121-7(5)*, Little Simon) Little Simon.

Keplinger, Kody. The DUFF: Designated Ugly Fat Friend. (ENG.). (YA). (gr. 10-17). 2011. 304p. pap., pap. 10.99 *(978-0-316-08424-6(7))* 2015. 320p. pap. 10.00 *(978-0-316-38180-2(2))* Little, Brown Bks. for Young Readers. (Poppy).

Kerz, Anna. The Mealworm Diaries, 1 vol. 2009. (ENG.). 160p. (J). (gr. 4-7). pap. 9.95 *(978-1-55143-982-2(4))* Orca Bk. Pubs. USA.

Kessler, Jackie Morse. Hunger. 2010. (Riders of the Apocalypse Ser.: 1). (ENG.). 192p. (YA). (gr. 7-18). pap. 9.99 *(978-0-547-34124-8(5))* Houghton Mifflin Harcourt Publishing Co.

Keyser, Amber J. & Burkhart, Kiersi. At Top Speed. 2017. (Quartz Creek Ranch Ser.). (ENG.). 240p. (gr. 4-8). 35.99 ***(978-1-5124-2697-7(0)***, Darby Creek) Lerner Publishing Group.

Kim, HoJeong. Kanga & Anger. Kim, SookKyeong, illus. rev. ed. 2014. (MySELF Bookshelf Ser.). (ENG.). 32p. (J). (gr. k-2). lib. bdg. 25.27 *(978-1-59953-643-9(9))* Norwood Hse. Pr.

Kimball, Michael D. Alligator Bay: A Beary Tale. 2009. 132p. pap. 11.95 *(978-1-4401-1804-3(3))* iUniverse, Inc.

Kimmel, Haven. Kaline Klattermaster's Tree House. Brown, Peter, illus. 2010. (ENG.). 160p. (J). (gr. 2-7). pap. 5.99 *(978-0-689-87403-1(0)*, Atheneum Bks. for Young Readers) Simon & Schuster Children's Publishing.

Kingsley, Charles. Ther Water Babies. Johnstone, Anne Grahame, illus. 2012. (ENG.). 32p. 9.95 *(978-1-84135-236-7(5))* Award Pubns. Ltd. GBR. Dist: Parkwest Pubns., Inc.

—Water Babies. 2004. 21.95 *(978-0-8488-2728-1(7))* Amereon Ltd.

Kinsella, Sophie, pseud. Finding Audrey. (ENG.). 304p. (YA). (gr. 7). 2016. pap. 9.99 *(978-0-553-53653-9(2)*, Ember) 2015. 18.99 *(978-0-553-53651-5(6)*, Delacorte Pr.) Random Hse. Children's Bks.

—Finding Audrey. 2016. lib. bdg. 20.85 *(978-0-606-38874-0(5))* Turtleback Bks.

Kletter, Kerry. The First Time She Drowned. 2016. (ENG.). 352p. (YA). (gr. 9). 17.99 *(978-0-399-17103-1(7)*, Philomel Bks.) Penguin Young Readers Group.

Kline, Karen E. The Bell That Wouldn't Ring. Spencer, Monica, illus. 2008. 16p. pap. 24.95 *(978-1-60672-497-2(5))* PublishAmerica, Inc.

Klise, Kate. Why Do You Cry? Not a Sob Story. Klise, M. Sarah, illus. rev. ed. 2006. (ENG.). 32p. (J). (gr. -1-2). 18.99 *(978-0-8050-7319-5(1)*, 9780805073195, Holt, Henry & Co. Bks. For Young Readers) Holt, Henry & Co.

Knowles, Alison. Ollie & His Super Powers. Wiltshire, Sophie, illus. 2016. (Ollie & His Superpowers Ser.). (ENG.). 32p. (J). 15.95 *(978-1-78592-049-3(9)*, 8455) Kingsley, Jessica Pubs. GBR. Dist: Macmillan Distribution Ltd.

Knowles, Jo. Lessons from a Dead Girl. 2009. (ENG., Illus.). 224p. (YA). (gr. 9). pap. 7.99 *(978-0-7636-4485-7(4))* Candlewick Pr.

—Living with Jackie Chan. 2013. (ENG.). 384p. (YA). (gr. 9). 16.99 *(978-0-7636-6280-6(1))* Candlewick Pr.

Kobus, Joanne. Mr Frog's Bad Day. 2009. 40p. pap. 16.99 *(978-1-4389-7513-9(9))* AuthorHouse.

Konigsburg, E. L. Journey to an 800 Number. 2008. (ENG.). 160p. (J). (gr. 4-8). pap. 6.99 *(978-1-4169-5875-8(4)*, Atheneum Bks. for Young Readers) Simon & Schuster Children's Publishing.

Kopple, Deborah, ed. Heads in the Ground: Short Stories by Norwalk High School Honor's English Students. 2008. 188p. pap. 13.95 *(978-0-595-50775-7(1))* iUniverse, Inc.

Kotchman, Susan C. With Love, from Grandma. 2011. 44p. pap. 18.46 *(978-1-4567-4458-8(5))* AuthorHouse.

Krosoczka, Jarrett J. Annie Was Warned. 2013. (ENG., Illus.). 32p. (J). (gr. -1-2). 7.99 *(978-0-385-75341-8(1)*, Dragonfly Bks.) Random Hse. Children's Bks.

Krossing, Karen. Punch Like a Girl, 1 vol. 2015. (ENG.). 240p. (YA). (gr. 8-12). pap. 12.95 *(978-1-4598-0828-7(2))* Orca Bk. Pubs. USA.

Kuhn, Tom B. Little Chick: Learns to Trust in the Lord, 1 vol. Kuhn, Douglas W., illus. 2009. 23p. pap. 24.95 *(978-1-60836-929-4(3))* America Star Bks.

Kulig, Ann & Skulski, Monica Fitch. A Garbage Can Day. 2011. 32p. pap. 16.50 *(978-1-4634-3654-4(8))* AuthorHouse.

Kurkosky, Tina. Bunny Brothers. 2011. 24p. pap. 24.95 *(978-1-4626-3608-2(X))* America Star Bks.

Kuskowski, Alex. Tia: Fitting In. 2012. (Juicy Central Ser.: 1). lib. bdg. 20.80 *(978-0-606-25132-7(4)*, Turtleback) Turtleback Bks.

Lahey, Sandra. Let's Talk. 2016. (ENG., Illus.). 26p. (J). pap. 28.22 ***(978-1-5245-1995-7(2))*** Xlibris Corp.

Lamballe, Jérôme. The Curious Story of Pablo Picasslug. 2010. 28p. 16.95 *(978-1-4452-8949-6(0))* Lulu Pr., Inc.

Lane, Bryan. Stepbrothers. 2010. 16p. 9.00 *(978-1-4520-1305-3(5))* AuthorHouse.

Lannen, Jon Jon. The Giraffe That Taught Me How to Laugh. 2010. 28p. pap. 14.99 *(978-1-4490-5930-9(9))* AuthorHouse.

Lansdowne, Marcella. The Adventures of Patty & Annabel: The Javelinas & Releasing the Cords. 2009. 28p. pap. 15.95 *(978-1-4389-1645-3(0))* AuthorHouse.

LaPoint, Crystal Godfrey. When My Mommy Cries: A Story to Help Families Cope with Sadness. Eldridge, Crystal, illus. 2012. (ENG.). 32p. (gr. k-6). pap. 19.99 *(978-1-4525-4241-6(4)*, 7529fdad-44ef-45a0-9351-f4e3e18c4d7c, Balboa Pr.) Author Solutions, Inc.

LaSala, Paige. Pig Kissing. Gullotti, Pat, illus. 2010. 24p. pap. 12.99 *(978-1-4520-2849-1(4))* AuthorHouse.

Lasser, Jon & Foster-Lasser, Sage. Grow Happy. Lyles, Christopher, illus. 2017. 32p. (J). 15.95 *(978-1-4338-2331-2(4)*, Magination Pr.) American Psychological Assn.

Laubach, Melody. Words & Thoughts. 2008. 28p. pap. 17.95 *(978-1-4327-2596-9(3))* Outskirts Pr., Inc.

Law, Felicia. Feelings. Knight, Paula, illus. 2015. (Patchwork Ser.). (ENG.). 24p. (J). (gr. k-3). lib. bdg. 22.60 *(978-1-59953-712-2(5))* Norwood Hse. Pr.

Lawler, Janet. If Kisses Were Colors. Jay, Alison, illus. 2010. (ENG.). 22p. (J). (gr. -1 — 1). bds. 6.99 *(978-0-8037-3530-9(8)*, Dial Bks) Penguin Young Readers Group.

Lawrence, Diane. The Oblit. 2013. 28p. pap. 13.95 *(978-1-4525-8409-6(5)*, Balboa Pr.) Author Solutions, Inc.

Lay, Kathryn. Book 4: Time under the Sea. 2016. (Time Twisters Ser.). (ENG.). (J). (gr. 2-6). lib. bdg. 27.07 ***(978-1-62402-180-0(8))*** ABDO Publishing Co.

Lemieux, Jean. Toby Laughs Last, 1 vol. Cummins, Sarah, tr. from FRE. Casson, Sophie, illus. 2006. (Formac First Novels Ser.: 59). (ENG.). 64p. (J). (gr. 2-5). 4.95 *(978-0-88780-716-9(X)*, 9780887807169) Formac Publishing Co., Ltd. CAN. Dist: Casemate Pubs. & Bk. Distributors, LLC.

Lester, Helen. Hurty Feelings. Munsinger, Lynn, illus. 2007. (ENG.). 32p. (J). (gr. -1-3). 7.99 *(978-0-618-84062-5(1))* Houghton Mifflin Harcourt Publishing Co.

—Hurty Feelings. Munsinger, Lynn, illus. 2014. (Laugh-Along Lessons Ser.). (ENG.). 32p. (J). (gr. -1-3). 8.99 *(978-0-544-10622-2(9))* Houghton Mifflin Harcourt Publishing Co.

Leveen, Tom. Shackled: The Truth Doesn't Always Set You Free. 2015. (ENG., Illus.). 224p. (YA). (gr. 9). 17.99 *(978-1-4814-2249-9(9)*, Simon Pulse) Simon Pulse.

Levine, Gail Carson. Betsy Red Hoodie. Nash, Scott, illus. 2010. (ENG.). 40p. (J). (gr. -1-3). 16.99 *(978-0-06-146870-4(3))* HarperCollins Pubs.

Levine, Karen R. Daddy's Picture. Stasuyk, Max, illus. 2013. 24p. pap. 14.95 *(978-1-57258-794-6(6)*, Aspect Bk.) TEACH Services, Inc.

Levithan, David. Another Day. 2017. (ENG.). 352p. (YA). (gr. 7). pap. 9.99 *(978-0-385-75623-5(2)*, Ember) Random Hse. Children's Bks.

—Every You, Every Me. Levithan, David & Farmer, Jonathan, photos by. 2012. (ENG., Illus.). 256p. (YA). (gr. 7). pap. 9.99 *(978-0-375-85451-4(7)*, Ember) Random Hse. Children's Bks.

—Every You, Every Me. Farmer, Jonathan, photos by. 2012. (Illus.). lib. bdg. 20.85 *(978-0-606-26816-5(2)*, Turtleback) Turtleback Bks.

Levitt, Tamara. Happiness Doesn't Come from Headstands. 2017. (ENG., Illus.). 38p. (J). 15.95 *(978-1-61429-405-4(4))* Wisdom Pubns.

Liberty, Anita. The Center of the Universe: Yep, That Would Be Me. 2008. (ENG.). 304p. (YA). (gr. 7-18). pap. 9.99 *(978-1-4169-5789-8(8)*, Simon Pulse) Simon Pulse.

Licht, S. Goodbye, Pacifier! Edelstein, Racheli, illus. 2013. 24p. (J). 10.95 *(978-1-60091-284-9(2))* Israel Bookshop Pubns.

Lincoln, Peggy. Oh, Dear! 2013. 16p. pap. 10.00 *(978-1-62516-400-1(9)*, Strategic Bk. Publishing) Strategic Book Publishing & Rights Agency (SBPRA).

Lindsay, Debbie. The Itty-Bitty Icky Committee/Heroes of the Heart. 2013. 76p. pap. 27.97 *(978-1-4525-7329-8(8)*, Balboa Pr.) Author Solutions, Inc.

Littman, Sarah Darer. Purge. 2010. (ENG.). 240p. (J). (gr. 7). 8.99 *(978-0-545-05237-5(8)*, Scholastic Paperbacks) Scholastic, Inc.

Lloyd, Sam. Grumpy Gertie. 2013. (ENG., Illus.). 24p. (J). (gr. -1-k). 12.99 *(978-1-84365-228-1(5)*, Pavilion) Pavilion Bks. GBR. Dist: Independent Pubs. Group.

Lluch, Isabel. The Fabulous Book of Me! The Ultimate Girls' Guide Journal & Keepsake That's All about You! 2009. (ENG.). 100p. (J). (gr. 6-7). spiral bd. 12.95 *(978-1-934386-57-6(X))* WS Publishing.

Logan, Ashley. Laugh Oh My Soul. 2011. 28p. pap. 12.79 *(978-1-4634-2131-1(1))* AuthorHouse.

Loiodice, Lisa M. Through His Eyes. 2009. 32p. pap. 16.99 *(978-1-4389-5132-4(9))* AuthorHouse.

London, Kiara. Kiss Cam. 2016. (ENG.). 272p. (YA). pap. 9.99 *(978-1-250-07096-8(1)*, 9781250070968) Feiwel & Friends.

Long, Michelle. Mckayla, the Girl with the Special Hug, Makes A Friend. 2009. (Illus.). 30p. (J). pap. 13.95 *(978-1-4327-4730-5(4))* Outskirts Pr., Inc.

Lootens, Ann. The Birthday Surprise. Faas, Linde, illus. 2013. (Wild Woods Ser.). (ENG.). 32p. (J). (gr. -1-k). 15.95 *(978-1-60537-147-4(5))* Cobblestone Publishing Co.

Lopez, Barbara J. Pepper's Wish. 2009. 32p. pap. 14.49 *(978-1-4389-4976-5(6))* AuthorHouse.

Louise, Zanni. Too Busy Sleeping. 2015. (Illus.). 32p. (J). (— 1). 18.99 *(978-1-74297-962-5(9))* Little Hare Bks. AUS. Dist: Independent Pubs. Group.

Luedeke, Lisa. Smashed. 2012. (ENG.). 336p. (YA). (gr. 9). 16.99 *(978-1-4424-2779-2(5)*, McElderry, Margaret K. Bks.) McElderry, Margaret K. Bks.

Lukeman, Noah. Everybody Gets Angry. 2015. (ENG., Illus.). 24p. (J). pap. 5.99 *(978-1-63291-360-9(7))* Morgan Rice Bks.

—Everybody Gets Jealous. 2015. (ENG., Illus.). 24p. (J). pap. 5.99 *(978-1-63291-450-7(6))* Morgan Rice Bks.

Luker, Lynne M. Mr Mushroom's Busy Day: Little Forest People. 2009. 32p. pap. 21.95 *(978-1-4389-8971-6(7))* AuthorHouse.

Lyga, Barry. Bang. 2017. (ENG.). 304p. (J). (gr. 7-17). 17.99 *(978-0-316-31550-0(8))* Little, Brown Bks. for Young Readers.

—Boy Toy. 2009. (ENG.). 416p. (YA). (gr. 9). pap. 9.99 *(978-0-547-07634-8(7))* Houghton Mifflin Harcourt Publishing Co.

Lyon, George Ella. No Dessert Forever! Catalanotto, Peter, illus. 2006. (ENG.). 40p. (J). (gr. k-4). 17.99 *(978-1-4169-0385-7(2)*, Atheneum/Richard Jackson Bks.) Simon & Schuster Children's Publishing.

Lyons, I. j. April's Pond. 2009. (Illus.). 80p. pap. 11.49 *(978-1-4490-3066-7(1))* AuthorHouse.

MacDonald, Maryann. How to Hug, 0 vols. Christy, Jana & Mitchell, Jana Christy, illus. 2011. (ENG.). 32p. (J). (gr. -1-3). 16.99 *(978-0-7614-5804-3(2)*, 9780761458043, Amazon Children's Publishing) Amazon Publishing.

Mackall, Dandi Daley. Unhappy Appy. 2003. (Winnie the Horse Gentler Ser.: 5). (ENG., Illus.). 192p. (J). mass mkt. 6.99 *(978-0-8423-5546-9(4))* Tyndale Hse. Pubs.

Mackintosh, David. Lucky. 2014. (ENG., Illus.). 32p. (J). (gr. -1-3). 17.95 *(978-1-4197-0809-1(0)*, Abrams Bks. for Young Readers) Abrams, Inc.

Mackler, Carolyn. Guyaholic. 2007. (ENG., Illus.). 192p. (YA). (gr. 9-18). 16.99 *(978-0-7636-2537-5(X))* Candlewick Pr.

—Tangled. 2009. (ENG.). 320p. (YA). (gr. 9-18). 16.99 *(978-0-06-173104-4(8)*, HarperTeen) HarperCollins Pubs.

MacLean, Kerry Lee. Just Me & My Mind. 2014. (ENG., Illus.). 16p. (J). (gr. -1-1). 18.95 *(978-1-61429-124-4(1))* Wisdom Pubns.

Maddox, Jake. Karate Countdown, 1 vol. Tiffany, Sean, illus. 2009. (Jake Maddox Sports Stories Ser.). (ENG.). 72p. (gr. 2-3). lib. bdg. 25.32 *(978-1-4342-1200-9(9))* Stone Arch Bks.

—Paintball Problems, 1 vol. Aburtov, Jesus Aburto, illus. 2013. (Jake Maddox Sports Stories Ser.). (ENG.). 72p. (gr. 2-3). pap. 5.95 *(978-1-4342-6207-3(3))* Stone Arch Bks.

—Paintball Problems. 2013. (Jake Maddox Sports Stories Ser.). (ENG.). 72p. (gr. 2-3). pap. 35.70 *(978-1-4342-6237-0(5))* Stone Arch Bks.

—Paintball Problems, 1 vol. Aburtov, Jesus Aburto, illus. 2013. (Jake Maddox Sports Stories Ser.). (ENG.). 72p. (gr. 2-3). lib. bdg. 25.32 *(978-1-4342-5974-5(9))* Stone Arch Bks.

—Volleyball Victory. Wood, Katie, illus. 2016. (Jake Maddox Girl Sports Stories Ser.). (ENG.). 72p. (gr. 2-3). lib. bdg. 25.32 *(978-1-4965-2619-9(8))* Stone Arch Bks.

Madill, Emily Elizabeth & Bzymek, Izabela. Grateful Jake. 2012. (Illus.). 30p. *(978-0-9812579-7-6(6))*; pap. *(978-0-9812579-6-9(8))* EM & Joe Bks. Co.

Madison, Ron. Ned & the General: A Lesson about Deployment. Covolo, David, illus. 2004. 24p. (J). 8.95 *(978-1-887206-24-2(8))* Ned's Head Productions.

Maloney, Peter & Zekauskas, Felicia. Thanks for Nothing! 2003. (Illus.). 31p. (J). *(978-0-439-55360-5(1))* Scholastic, Inc.

Maltbie, Priscilla. Bambino & Mr. Twain. 2012. 40p. 29.95 *(978-0-8045-4237-1(6))* Spoken Arts, Inc.

Manchego, Chelo. The Want Monsters. 2017. (ENG.). 32p. (J). (gr. -1-1). 16.95 *(978-1-61180-365-5(9))* Shambhala Pubns., Inc.

Mann, Jennifer K. I Will Never Get a Star on Mrs. Benson's Blackboard. Mann, Jennifer K., illus. 2017. (ENG., Illus.). 40p. (J). (gr. k-3). 6.99 *(978-0-7636-9299-5(9))* Candlewick Pr.

Mannering, Rose. Boo's Beard. Straker, Bethany, illus. 2015. (ENG.). 32p. (J). (gr. -1-k). 16.99 *(978-1-63450-207-8(8)*, Sky Pony Pr.) Skyhorse Publishing Co., Inc.

Manushkin, Fran. Katie Woo, Don't Be Blue, 1 vol. Lyon, Tammie, illus. 2013. (Katie Woo Ser.). (ENG.). 96p. (gr. k-2). pap. 4.95 *(978-1-4048-8101-3(8))* Picture Window Bks.

Marcus, Kimberly. Exposed. 2012. (ENG.). 272p. (YA). (gr. 9). pap. 8.99 *(978-0-375-86591-6(8)*, Ember) Random Hse. Children's Bks.

Martín Anguita, Carmen & Carmen, Martín Anguita. Marta y Su Dragón (Martha & Her Dragon) Cortazar, Alicia Canas, illus. 2008. (SPA.). 32p. (J). 10.99 *(978-84-241-5444-8(4))* Everest Editora ESP. Dist: Lectorum Pubns., Inc.

Martin, Molly. Princess Addison Gets Angry, 1 vol. Florian, Mélanie, illus. 2013. (Princess Heart Ser.). (ENG.). 24p. (gr. -1-1). 6.95 *(978-1-4048-8107-5(7))*; lib. bdg. 22.65 *(978-1-4048-7851-8(3))* Picture Window Bks.

—Princess Harper Gets Happy, 1 vol. Florian, Mélanie, illus. 2013. (Princess Heart Ser.). (ENG.). 24p. (gr. -1-1). 6.95 *(978-1-4048-8108-2(5))*; lib. bdg. 22.65 *(978-1-4048-7852-5(1))* Picture Window Bks.

—Princess Heart. Florian, Mélanie, illus. 2013. (Princess Heart Ser.). (ENG.). 24p. (gr. -1-1). 90.60 *(978-1-4048-8056-6(9))* Picture Window Bks.

—Princess Sophia Gets Scared, 1 vol. Florian, Mélanie, illus. 2013. (Princess Heart Ser.). (ENG.). 24p. (gr. -1-1). 6.95 *(978-1-4048-8110-5(7))*; lib. bdg. 22.65 *(978-1-4048-7854-9(8))* Picture Window Bks.

—Princess Stella Gets Sad, 1 vol. Florian, Mélanie, illus. 2013. (Princess Heart Ser.). (ENG.). 24p. (gr. -1-1). 6.95 *(978-1-4048-8109-9(3))*; lib. bdg. 22.65 *(978-1-4048-7853-2(X))* Picture Window Bks.

Matson, Cheri. Moleys Yacolt Garden. 2007. (Illus.). 32p. (J). *(978-0-9636066-6-2(2))* Gillette, Frances A.

Matson, Morgan. Amy & Roger's Epic Detour. 2010. (ENG.). 352p. (YA). (gr. 7-18). 19.99 *(978-1-4169-9065-9(8)*, Simon & Schuster Bks. For Young Readers) Simon & Schuster Bks. For Young Readers.

Matthews, Caroline. Uncle Orange. 2012. 30p. 24.95 *(978-1-4626-6623-2(X))* America Star Bks.

Maude Spelman, Cornelia & Spelman, Cornelia Maude. When I Feel Worried. Parkinson, Kathy, illus. 2014. (Way I Feel Bks.). (ENG.). 24p. (J). (gr. -1-3). pap. 6.99 *(978-0-8075-8895-6(4))* Whitman, Albert & Co.

Mayer, Mercer. I Was So Mad. 2015. 24p. pap. 4.00 *(978-1-61003-546-0(1))* Center for the Collaborative Classroom.

McAuslan, Fiona & Nicholson, Peter. The Resolving Anger Book. 2010. (Resolving Bks). (ENG., Illus.). 88p. (J). pap. 9.95 *(978-1-84730-222-9(X))* Veritas Pubns. IRL. Dist: Dufour Editions, Inc.

E
F
G

McBratney, Sam. There, There. Bates, Ivan, illus. (ENG.). (J). 2015. 32p. (-k). bds. 7.99 *(978-0-7636-7565-3(2))* 2013. 40p. (gr. -1-2). 15.99 *(978-0-7636-6702-3(1))* Candlewick Pr. (Templar).

McBride, Anthony. Willie the Whiskers. 2013. (Illus.). 24p. pap. 13.77 *(978-1-4907-0670-2(4))* Trafford Publishing.

McCartney, Tania. Smile Cry: Happy or Sad, Wailing or Glad - How Do You Feel Today? Rackyleft, Jess, illus. 2017. (ENG.). 32p. (J). (gr. -1-k). 12.99 *(978-1-925335-37-8(2),* EK Bks.) Exisle Publishing Pty Ltd. AUS. Dist: Hachette Bk. Group.

—Smile/Cry: Happy or Sad, Wailing or Glad - How Do You Feel Today? Rackyleft, Jess, illus. 2016. (ENG.). 32p. (J). (gr. -1-1). 16.95 *(978-1-921966-98-9(X),* EK Bks.) Exisle Publishing Pty Ltd. AUS. Dist: Hachette Bk. Group.

McClure, Brian D. The Sun & the Moon. 2006. (Illus.). 36p. (J). 14.95 *(978-1-933426-09-9(8))* Universal Flag Publishing.

McCumbee, Stephie. Priscilla & the Perfect Storm. De Weerd, Kelsey, illus. 2014. (ENG.). 32p. (J). pap. 10.95 *(978-1-934490-60-0(1))* Boys Town Pr.

McDonald, Megan. The Holly Joliday. Reynolds, Peter H., illus. 2008. (Judy Moody Ser.: No. 1). (ENG.). 96p. (J). (gr. k-3). pap. 7.99 *(978-0-7636-4113-9(8))* Candlewick Pr.

—Judy Moody. 2010. (Judy Moody Ser.: 1). lib. bdg. 16.00 *(978-0-606-12330-3(X),* Turtleback) Turtleback Bks.

—Judy Moody Esta de Mal Humor, de Muy Mal Humor. Mendoza Garcia, Isabel, tr. Reynolds, Peter H., illus. 2004. (SPA.). 160p. (J). (gr. 3-5). pap. 7.95 *(978-1-59437-816-4(9))* Ediciones Alfaguara ESP. Dist: Two Rivers Distribution.

—Mood Martian. Reynolds, Peter H., illus. 2015. (Judy Moody Ser.). (ENG.). 208p. (J). (gr. 1-4). pap. 5.99 *(978-0-7636-8015-2(X))* Candlewick Pr.

—Was in a Mood. Reynolds, Peter H., illus. 2010. (Judy Moody Ser.: 1). (ENG.). 176p. (J). (gr. 1-4). pap. 5.99 *(978-0-7636-4849-7(3))* Candlewick Pr.

—Was in a Mood. Reynolds, Peter H., illus. 2010. (Judy Moody Ser.: 1). (ENG.). 160p. (J). (gr. 1-4). 15.99 *(978-0-7636-4850-3(7))* Candlewick Pr.

McDonnell, Patrick. Shine! 2017. (ENG., Illus.). 40p. (J). (gr. -1-3). 16.99 *(978-0-316-26278-1(1))* Little Brown & Co.

McGee, Krista. Revolutionary, 1 vol. 2014. (Anomaly Ser.: 3). (ENG.). 320p. (YA). pap. 9.99 *(978-1-4016-8876-9(4))* Nelson, Thomas Inc.

McGinty, Sean. The End of FUN. 2016. (ENG.). 416p. (YA). (gr. 9-17). 17.99 *(978-1-4847-2211-4(6))* Hyperion Bks. for Children.

McLeod, Rona. Big Daddy Chinaberry: Love Given - Love Returned. McLeod, Herbert, illus. 2012. 24p. pap. 24.95 *(978-1-4626-7700-9(2))* America Star Bks.

McMann, Lisa. Wake. 2008. (Wake Ser.: Bk. 1). (ENG.). 224p. (YA). (gr. 9). pap. 11.99 *(978-1-4169-7447-5(4));* 17.99 *(978-1-4169-5357-9(4))* Simon Pulse. (Simon Pulse).

McNamee, Kevin. What Is That Thing? Snider, K. C., illus. 2011. 16p. pap. 9.95 *(978-1-61633-141-2(0))* Guardian Angel Publishing, Inc.

McPhail, David. I Hug. 2017. (I Like to Read(r) Ser.). (ENG.). 32p. (J). (gr. -1-3). 6.99 ***(978-0-8234-3847-1(3))***; 14.95 ***(978-0-8234-3854-9(6))*** Holiday Hse., Inc.

Mead, Erni. Ryan Is Moving Away. 2009. 32p. pap. 12.99 *(978-1-4389-7226-8(1))* AuthorHouse.

Mead, Purnima & Kerber, Kathy. Bibia, the Butterfly. 2009. 24p. pap. 18.50 *(978-1-4389-6644-1(X))* AuthorHouse.

Medeiros, Jamie. Perfect Patty. 2012. 16p. pap. 15.99 *(978-1-4685-8767-8(6))* AuthorHouse.

Mehta, Shyam. Stories for Children. 2009. 68p. pap. 8.47 *(978-1-4092-8990-6(7))* Lulu Pr., Inc.

Meister, Cari. Beat Bugs: Penny Lane. 2017. (I Can Read Level 1 Ser.). 32p. (J). (gr. -1-3). pap. 3.99 *(978-0-06-264071-0(2))* HarperCollins Pubs.

—The Grumpy Lobster, 1 vol. Harpster, Steve, illus. 2012. (Ocean Tales Ser.). (ENG.). 32p. (gr. 2-4). pap. 6.25 *(978-1-4342-4230-3(7));* lib. bdg. 22.65 *(978-1-4342-4025-5(8))* Stone Arch Bks.

Mellom, Robin. Hannah Sparkles. Brantley-Newton, Vanessa, illus. 2017. 32p. (J). (gr. -1-3). 17.99 *(978-0-06-232233-3(8))* HarperCollins Pubs.

Menchin, Scott. Taking a Bath with the Dog & Other Things That Make Me Happy. Menchin, Scott, illus. 2013. (ENG., Illus.). 40p. (J). (gr. -1-3). 7.99 *(978-0-7636-6335-3(2))* Candlewick Pr.

Mercer, M. J. O'No It's Henry. 2010. 24p. 12.99 *(978-1-4520-2125-6(2))* AuthorHouse.

Merchant, Peter. Sojourner Truth: Path to Glory. Denos, Julia, illus. 2007. (Ready-To-read SOFA Ser.). (ENG.). 48p. (J). (gr. 1-3). pap. 3.99 *(978-0-689-87207-5(0),* Simon Spotlight) Simon Spotlight.

Mesrobian, Carrie. Just a Girl. 2017. 304p. (YA). (gr. 9). 17.99 *(978-0-06-234991-0(0))* HarperCollins Pubs.

—Sex & Violence. 2013. (ENG.). 304p. (YA). (gr. 9-12). 17.95 *(978-1-4677-0597-4(7),* Carolrhoda Lab™) Lerner Publishing Group.

Metzger, Steve & Antonini, Gabriele, illus. Huggapotamus. 2011. (J). *(978-0-545-34352-7(6))* Scholastic, Inc.

Meyers, Ann Marie. Up in the Air. 2013. 244p. (J). 22.99 *(978-1-939967-03-9(1),* Jolly Fish Pr.) North Star Editions.

Michaels, Rune. Genesis Alpha. 2011. (ENG.). 224p. (YA). (gr. 7). pap. 8.99 *(978-1-4169-6500-8(9),* Atheneum Bks. for Young Readers) Simon & Schuster Children's Publishing.

—Nobel Genes. 2010. (ENG.). 192p. (YA). (gr. 7-18). 16.99 *(978-1-4169-1259-0(2),* Atheneum Bks. for Young Readers) Simon & Schuster Children's Publishing.

Michels, Anna. 26 Kisses. 2016. (ENG.). (YA). (gr. 9). pap. 12.99 *(978-1-4814-8515-9(6))* Simon & Schuster.

Michot, Fabienne. Maki, I Am Happy. braille ed. 2004. (J). (gr. 1). spiral bd., bds. *(978-0-616-07267-7(8))* Canadian National Institute for the Blind/Institut National Canadien pour les Aveugles.

Miles, Brenda & Patterson, Colleen A. Move Your Mood! A Guide for Kids about Mind-Body Connection. Clifton-Brown, Holly, illus. 2016. 32p. (J). *(978-1-4338-2112-7(5),* Magination Pr.) American Psychological Assn.

Milgrim, David. Wild Feelings. 2015. (ENG., Illus.). 40p. (J). (gr. -1-3). 16.99 *(978-0-8050-9587-6(X),* 9780805095876, Holt, Henry & Co. Bks. For Young Readers) Holt, Henry & Co.

Mlawer, Teresa, tr. Feeling Great!/Sentirse Bien! Stockham, Jess, illus. 2013. (Just Like Me! Ser.). (ENG & SPA.). 12p. (J). (gr. -1). bds. *(978-1-84643-561-4(7))* Child's Play International Ltd.

Mlynowski, Sarah. Bras & Broomsticks. 2006. (Magic in Manhattan Ser.: No. 1). (ENG.). 320p. (YA). (gr. 7-12). reprint ed. pap. 8.99 *(978-0-385-73184-3(1),* Delacorte Pr.) Random Hse. Children's Bks.

Mohler, Marie. Swallow the Sun. 2008. 32p. 18.95 *(978-1-4357-1340-6(0))* Lulu Pr., Inc.

Molesworth & Molesworth, Mary Louisa S. Grandmother Dear. 2008. 128p. pap. 10.95 *(978-1-60664-225-2(1))* Aegypan.

Molokie, Tom. Introducing Willy Mcspry. 2011. 36p. pap. 15.65 *(978-1-4634-3697-1(1))* AuthorHouse.

Moncure, Jane Belk. What Do You Do with a Grumpy Kangaroo? A Book about Feelings. Gallagher-Cole, Mernie, illus. 2013. (Magic Castle Readers Ser.). (ENG.). 32p. (J). (gr. -1-2). 25.64 *(978-1-62323-589-5(8),* 206324) Child's World, Inc., The.

Moniz, Madalena. Today I Feel ... An Alphabet of Emotions. 2017. (ENG., Illus.). 64p. (J). (gr. -1-k). 14.95 *(978-1-4197-2324-7(3),* Abrams Appleseed) Abrams, Inc.

Monte, Diane E. Coming Home: Welcome Home at Last. 2012. 24p. pap. 17.99 *(978-1-4772-5713-5(6))* AuthorHouse.

Montgomery-Higham, Amanda. Max & the Doglins. 2007. (Child's Play Library). (ENG., Illus.). 32p. (J). (gr. 2-3). pap. *(978-1-84643-043-5(7))* Child's Play International Ltd.

Mooney, Bel. Mr. Tubs Is Lost. 2006. (Blue Bananas Ser.). (ENG., Illus.). 48p. (J). (gr. -1-3). *(978-0-7787-0904-6(3))* Crabtree Publishing Co.

Moore, Katherine Roberts. Is God Behind the Big Blue Sky? Moore, Kristen L., illus. 2010. 34p. pap. 13.95 *(978-1-60911-705-4(0),* Eloquent Bks.) Strategic Book Publishing & Rights Agency (SBPRA).

Moran, Alex. Six Silly Foxes. Baker, Keith, illus. 2003. (Green Light Readers Level 1 Ser.). (ENG.). 24p. (J). (gr. -1-3). pap. 3.95 *(978-0-15-204863-1(4))* Houghton Mifflin Harcourt Publishing Co.

Morelli, Yamile, tr. Me Robaron a Mi Mejor Amig. 2012. 138p. pap. 5.99 *(978-0-9831557-3-7(9))* WordWorks Publishing.

Moreno Lcsw, Melissa. My Feelings Are Mine to Have: Love, Happy, Sad, Afraid, Anger. 2012. 52p. pap. 20.99 *(978-1-4525-6049-6(8))* Balboa Pr.

Morris, Deborah K. & Morris, Douglas. How Are You? 2011. 20p. pap. 10.95 *(978-1-61204-664-8(9),* Strategic Bk. Publishing) Strategic Book Publishing & Rights Agency (SBPRA).

Mosby, Pamela. I'm So Angry. Brever, Amy, illus. 2013. 28p. pap. 7.99 *(978-0-9886272-4-6(8))* Brothers N Publishing Corp.

Moses, Brian. Anna Angrysaurus. 2014. (Dinosaurs Have Feelings Ser.). (ENG.). 32p. (J). (gr. -1-1). pap. 6.99 *(978-1-4380-0404-4(4))* Barron's Educational Series, Inc.

—Jayden Jealousaurus. 2014. (Dinosaurs Have Feelings Ser.). (ENG.). 32p. (J). (gr. -1-1). pap. 6.99 *(978-1-4380-0402-0(8))* Barron's Educational Series, Inc.

Moss, Marissa. Amelia's Guide to Gossip: The Good, the Bad, & the Ugly. Moss, Marissa, illus. 2006. (Amelia Ser.). (ENG., Illus.). 80p. (J). (gr. 5-8). 9.95 *(978-1-4169-1475-4(7),* Simon & Schuster/Paula Wiseman Bks.) Simon & Schuster/Paula Wiseman Bks.

Munsch, Robert. I'm So Embarrassed! 2007. (J). 12.65 *(978-0-7569-7624-8(3))* Perfection Learning Corp.

—Kiss Me, I'm Perfect! Martchenko, Michael, illus. 2008. (J). (gr. -1-3). 11.65 *(978-0-7569-9007-7(6))* Perfection Learning Corp.

Murphy, Mary. A Kiss Like This. Murphy, Mary, illus. 2012. (ENG., Illus.). 32p. (J). (gr. k-k). 12.99 *(978-0-7636-6182-3(1))* Candlewick Pr.

Murphy, Stuart J. Percy Gets Upset. 2011. (I See I Learn Ser.). (ENG., Illus.). 32p. (J). (gr. -1-k). 14.95 *(978-1-58089-460-9(7));* pap. 6.95 *(978-1-58089-461-6(5))* Charlesbridge Publishing, Inc.

—Percy Se Enoja. 2012. (I See I Learn Ser.). (SPA & ENG., Illus.). 32p. (J). (-k). 14.95 *(978-1-58089-492-0(5));* pap. 6.95 *(978-1-58089-493-7(3))* Charlesbridge Publishing, Inc.

Murrow, Marjorie. The Surprise in Grandma's Eyes. 2009. (Illus.). 16p. pap. 10.98 *(978-1-4389-8104-8(X))* AuthorHouse.

Musgrave, Sugin. Butterfly in the Sky: Daddy's Little Girl. 2008. 32p. 14.00 *(978-1-4389-2218-8(3))* AuthorHouse.

Myers, Nancy. Tad's Story. 2010. 95p. pap. 9.99 *(978-0-557-60737-2(X))* Lulu Pr., Inc.

Myers, Walter Dean. The Dream Bearer. 2004. (ENG.). 192p. (YA). (gr. 5-18). reprint ed. pap. 6.99 *(978-0-06-447289-0(2),* Amistad) HarperCollins Pubs.

—Shooter. 2004. (ENG.). 224p. (J). 15.99 *(978-0-06-029519-6(8),* HarperTeen) HarperCollins Pubs.

Naraynan, Manjula. The Grey Grey Cloud. 2010. (Illus.). 32p. pap. 14.49 *(978-1-4490-8507-0(5))* AuthorHouse.

Nash, Sarah. Scaredy Bear. Everitt-Stewart, Andy, illus. 2009. (Stories to Grow with Ser.). 24p. (J). (gr. -1-2). 22.60 *(978-1-60754-472-2(5))* Windmill Bks.

Natile, Jeffrey Michael. Emily Gets Angry. 2006. (J). 9.95 *(978-0-9779822-0-2(3))* ErieKIDS, Inc.

Naylor, Phyllis Reynolds. Alice in Blunderland. 2005. 200p. (J). (gr. 2-7). 13.65 *(978-0-7569-5075-0(9))* Perfection Learning Corp.

Neal, Christopher Silas. Everyone. Neal, Christopher Silas, illus. 2016. (ENG., Illus.). 32p. (J). (gr. -1-1). 15.99 *(978-0-7636-7683-4(7))* Candlewick Pr.

Nees, Susan. School Play. 2013. (Missy's Super Duper Royal Deluxe Ser.: 3). (ENG., Illus.). 80p. (J). (gr. k-2). pap. 4.99 *(978-0-545-43853-7(5))* Scholastic, Inc.

Nelson, Scott. My Tummy Disaster. 2015. (Embarrassing to the Max Ser.). (ENG., Illus.). 32p. (gr. k-3). pap. 9.95 *(978-1-941437-54-4(0))* Heritage Builders, LLC.

Nettrour, Nelani. The Imagynairs of Jemmidar, Bk. A. l.t. ed. 2006. (Illus.). 73p. (J). pap. 11.95 *(978-1-932657-53-1(3))* Third Millennium Pubns.

Newman, Lesléa. The Boy Who Cried Fabulous. Ferguson, Peter, illus. 2007. (ENG.). 32p. (J). (gr. -1-2). pap. 7.99 *(978-1-58246-224-0(0),* Tricycle Pr.) Random Hse. Children's Bks.

Nichols, Cherrie L. Curtiz Says: I'm Not Blue! 2011. 20p. (gr. 1-2). pap. 10.03 *(978-1-4567-6428-9(4))* AuthorHouse.

Niven, Jennifer. All the Bright Places. 2015. (ENG.). 400p. pap. *(978-0-14-135703-4(7))* Penguin Bks., Ltd.

—All the Bright Places. (ENG.). (YA). (gr. 9). 2016. 416p. pap. 10.99 *(978-0-385-75591-7(0),* Ember) 2015. 400p. lib. bdg. 20.99 *(978-0-385-75589-4(9),* Knopf Bks. for Young Readers) 2015. 400p. 17.99 *(978-0-385-75588-7(0),* Knopf Bks. for Young Readers) Random Hse. Children's Bks.

—All the Bright Places. 2016. lib. bdg. 22.10 *(978-0-606-38876-4(1))* Turtleback Bks.

Noble, Midge. Ice Cube Award: Learning to Be Cool under Pressure. 2011. 48p. pap. 20.45 *(978-1-4525-3767-2(4))* Get Published.

Nolan, Han. When We Were Saints. 2005. (ENG.). 312p. (YA). (gr. 7-12). pap. 15.95 *(978-0-15-205322-2(0))* Houghton Mifflin Harcourt Publishing Co.

Noyes, Kristie Spangler. Mr. Daisy. 2008. 40p. pap. 24.95 *(978-1-60474-276-3(3))* America Star Bks.

Oaks, J. Adams. Why I Fight. (ENG.). 240p. (YA). (gr. 7). 2010. pap. 9.99 *(978-1-4424-0254-6(7),* Atheneum Bks. for Young Readers) 2009. 17.99 *(978-1-4169-1177-7(4),* Atheneum/Richard Jackson Bks.) Simon & Schuster Children's Publishing.

Oates, Joyce Carol. After the Wreck, I Picked Myself Up, Spread My Wings, & Flew Away. 2006. (YA). (gr. 9-12). 304p. 16.99 *(978-0-06-073525-8(2));* 292p. lib. bdg. 17.89 *(978-0-06-073526-5(0))* HarperCollins Pubs. (HarperTeen).

O'Connor, Melisa Bass. The Master's Brick: A Story about Purpose. 2012. 30p. pap. 16.95 *(978-1-4497-5645-1(X),* WestBow Pr.) Author Solutions, Inc.

Odom, Mel. The Secret Explodes. 2013. (Hunter's League Ser.: 3). (ENG.). 240p. (J). (gr. 7). pap. 15.99 *(978-1-4814-0156-2(4),* Simon Pulse) Simon Pulse.

O'Donnell, Kerri. A Giraffe Can Laugh. 2006. (Neighborhood Readers Ser.). (ENG.). 12p. (gr. -1-3). pap. 5.90 *(978-1-4042-5762-7(4),* Rosen Classroom) Rosen Publishing Group, Inc., The.

—When Sue Is Sad. 2006. (Neighborhood Readers Ser.). (ENG.). 8p. (gr. -1-3). pap. 5.15 *(978-1-4042-5653-8(9),* Rosen Classroom) Rosen Publishing Group, Inc., The.

Oelschlager, Vanita. Let Me Bee. Blackwood, Kristin, illus. 2008. (ENG.). 42p. (J). (gr. -1-3). 17.95 *(978-0-9800162-1-5(5))* VanitaBooks.

Ohrt, Kate. The Rainbow Book. 2011. (ENG.). 18p. (J). (gr. -1-1). pap. 9.99 *(978-1-4494-0171-9(6))* Andrews McMeel Publishing.

Okada, Toshihiko. The Balloon. 2008. 48p. pap. 18.50 *(978-1-60693-089-2(3),* Eloquent Bks.) Strategic Book Publishing & Rights Agency (SBPRA).

Oldland, Nicholas. Big Bear Hug. Oldland, Nicholas, illus. 2014. (Life in the Wild Ser.). (ENG., Illus.). 32p. (J). (gr. -1-2). 7.95 *(978-1-77138-151-2(5))* Kids Can Pr., Ltd. CAN. Dist: Hachette Bk. Group.

O'Neill, Rachael. Do You Want a Hug, Honey Bunny? O'Neill, Rachael, illus. 2008. (Tiger Tales Ser.). (Illus.). 12p. (J). (gr. -1-k). 8.95 *(978-1-58925-829-7(0))* Tiger Tales.

Oram, Hiawyn. Ned & the Joybaloo. Kitamura, Satoshi, illus. 2012. (ENG.). 32p. (J). (gr. -1-k). pap. 10.99 *(978-1-84270-605-3(5))* Andersen Pr. GBR. Dist: Independent Pubs. Group.

Orsak, Lane Rockford. Keiko the Fairy, the Kujiki. 2010. 192p. pap. 14.95 *(978-0-557-47206-2(7))* Lulu Pr., Inc.

Ortega, Ingrid. Cuentos Golosos. Welin, Raquel, illus. 2006. (SPA.). 64p. (J). mass mkt. 12.50 *(978-1-59835-012-8(9))* Cambridge BrickHouse, Inc.

Ortner, Alex. Gorilla Thumps & Bear Hugs: A Tapping Solution Children's Story. Mariano, Erin, illus. 2016. (ENG.). 32p. 16.99 ***(978-1-4019-5287-7(9))*** Hay Hse., Inc.

Osborne, Mary Pope. Dragon of the Red Dawn. Murdocca, Sal, illus. 2008. (Magic Tree House Merlin Mission Ser.: 9). (ENG.). 144p. (J). (gr. 2-5). 5.99 *(978-0-375-83728-9(0),* Random Hse. Bks. for Young Readers) Random Hse. Children's Bks.

Osterlund, Anne. Academy 7. 2009. (ENG.). 272p. (YA). (gr. 7-18). pap. 8.99 *(978-0-14-241437-8(9),* Speak) Penguin Young Readers Group.

Ostermann, Riley. So Big. 2009. 24p. pap. 12.00 *(978-1-60693-970-3(X),* Eloquent Bks.) Strategic Book Publishing & Rights Agency (SBPRA).

Owen, Bob. Billy. 2012. 24p. pap. 15.99 *(978-1-4653-9835-2(X))* Xlibris Corp.

Pagel, Beth. What's Wrong with Grandma? 2008. 32p. pap. 11.96 *(978-0-557-00302-0(4))* Lulu Pr., Inc.

Palacio, R. J. We're All Wonders. 2017. (ENG.). 32p. (J). (gr. -1-3). 18.99 ***(978-1-5247-6649-8(6))***; (Illus.). lib. bdg. 21.99 ***(978-1-5247-6650-4(X))*** Random Hse. Children's Bks. (Knopf Bks. for Young Readers).

Pantelides, Sherry. Make A Choice to Rejoice! A Story about Being Cheerful. Perez, Debi, illus. 2007. 32p. (J). 12.99 *(978-0-9771076-2-9(0))* Lacey Productions.

Paris, Jacqueline. Persevere. 2012. 24p. pap. 16.99 *(978-1-4685-8354-0(9))* AuthorHouse.

Park, Barbara. Turkeys We Have Loved & Eaten, No. 28. Brunkus, Denise, illus. 2012. (Junie B. Jones Ser.: 28). (ENG.). 144p. (J). (gr. 1-4). lib. bdg. 14.99 *(978-0-375-97063-4(0),* Random Hse. Bks. for Young Readers) Random Hse. Children's Bks.

—Turkeys We Have Loved & Eaten (and Other Thankful Stuff), No. 28. Brunkus, Denise, illus. 2012. (Junie B. Jones Ser.). (ENG.). 144p. (J). (gr. 1-4). 11.99 *(978-0-375-87063-7(6),* Random Hse. Bks. for Young Readers) Random Hse. Children's Bks.

Parker, Vicki Sue. The Get Well Soon... Balloon. Beebe, Susan, illus. 2005. 16p. (J). 15.00 *(978-1-931117-35-7(7),* BALL) Lash & Assocs. Publishing/Training, Inc.

Parr, Todd. The Feel Good Book. 2009. (ENG., Illus.). 32p. (J). (gr. -1-1). pap. 7.99 *(978-0-316-04345-8(1))* Little Brown & Co.

—The Feelings Book. 2005. (ENG., Illus.). 24p. (J). (gr. -1 — 1). bds. 6.99 *(978-0-316-01249-2(1),* Tingley, Megan Bks.) Little, Brown Bks. for Young Readers.

—Feelings Book. 2009. (ENG., Illus.). 32p. (J). (gr. -1-1). pap. 7.99 *(978-0-316-04346-5(X))* Little Brown & Co.

—The Thankful Book. 2012. (ENG., Illus.). 32p. (J). (gr. -1-1). 11.99 *(978-0-316-18101-3(3),* Tingley, Megan Bks.) Little, Brown Bks. for Young Readers.

Patterson, Colleen A. & Miles, Brenda. 1-2-3 a Calmer Me. Keay, Claire, illus. 2015. (J). *(978-1-4338-1931-5(7))* American Psychological Assn.

Patterson, Horace. Ernie the Ermine. Parker, Jack, illus. 2007. 28p. per. 7.99 *(978-1-58942-374-9(7))* R.H. Boyd Publishing Corp.

Paulsen, Gary. The Crossing. 2006. (Point Ser.). (ENG.). 128p. (J). (gr. 2-5). per. 6.99 *(978-0-439-78661-4(4),* Scholastic Paperbacks) Scholastic, Inc.

Pearce, Philippa. Amy's Three Best Things. Craig, Helen, illus. 2013. (ENG.). 40p. (J). (gr. -1-3). 15.99 *(978-0-7636-6314-8(X))* Candlewick Pr.

Pearson, Mary E. The Miles Between. 2011. (ENG.). 288p. (YA). (gr. 9-12). pap. 15.99 *(978-0-312-65926-4(1))* Square Fish.

Penton-Grayson, Mildred. From A Prayer Warrior's Closet. 2007. 70p. 7.95 *(978-0-9793516-0-0(X),* Writing The Vision) Scribe Publishing & Consulting Services, The.

Perlman, Willa. Pocket Kisses. McDonald, Jill, illus. 2011. (ENG.). 14p. (J). (gr. -1-17). 7.99 *(978-0-316-07787-3(9))* Little, Brown Bks. for Young Readers.

Perry, Tristan. Cinnamon Takes a Vacation: Furry Tails #2, 1 vol. 2009. 122p. pap. 19.95 *(978-1-60836-451-0(8))* America Star Bks.

Peters, Julie Anne. Revenge of the Snob Squad. 2009. (ENG.). 128p. (J). (gr. 3-7). pap. 5.99 *(978-0-316-00812-9(5))* Little, Brown Bks. for Young Readers.

Peterseil, Yaacov. What Can You Do with a Cheshire Smile? 2014. (ENG.). 32p. (J). (gr. k-2). 16.95 *(978-965-7514-09-2(6))* Urim Pubns. ISR. Dist: Independent Pubs. Group.

Peterson, John C. Adam Has No Brothers. 2009. 20p. pap. 10.99 *(978-1-4490-3207-4(9))* AuthorHouse.

Petrucci, Lou. Heart of the Hide. 2008. 320p. 22.95 *(978-1-4401-0102-1(7),* iUniverse Star) iUniverse, Inc.

Petty, Kate. Ha Ha, Baby! Birkett, Georgie, illus. 2008. (ENG.). 32p. (J). (gr. -1-k). 14.95 *(978-1-905417-12-4(8))* Boxer Bks., Ltd. GBR. Dist: Sterling Publishing Co., Inc.

Phillips, Dee. Fight, 1 vol. unabr. ed. 2011. (Right Now! Ser.). (ENG.). 45p. (YA). (gr. 9-12). pap. 8.95 *(978-1-61651-248-4(2))* Saddleback Educational Publishing, Inc.

Pierre, Eileen. It's Not Easy Being Mean. 2010. 56p. pap. 10.00 *(978-1-60860-929-1(4),* Eloquent Bks.) Strategic Book Publishing & Rights Agency (SBPRA).

Piggy Toes Press, creator. Giggles & More! with Abby & Friends. 2010. (Illus.). 95p. (J). pap. 7.95 *(978-1-61524-233-7(3),* Intervisual/Piggy Toes) Bendon, Inc.

Pippin-Mathur, Courtney. Maya Was Grumpy. Pippin-Mathur, Courtney, illus. 2013. (ENG., Illus.). 32p. (J). (gr. k-2). 16.95 *(978-1-936261-13-0(8))* Flashlight Pr.

Pippin-Mathur, Courtney, illus. Maya Was Grumpy. 2013. (J). *(978-0-545-62077-2(5))* Flashlight Pr.

Plum-Ucci, Carol. The Body of Christopher Creed. 2008. (ENG., Illus.). 272p. (YA). (gr. 7). pap. 7.99 *(978-0-15-206386-3(2))* Houghton Mifflin Harcourt Publishing Co.

Poage, Brenda. Ima Nobody Becomes Somebody! Book One in the Ima Nobody Series. 2009. 88p. pap. 10.99 *(978-1-4490-0157-5(2))* AuthorHouse.

Poe, Edgar Allen. The Tell-Tale Heart Package. Calero, Dennis, illus. 2013. (ENG.). 62p. (J). (gr. 5-8). pap. 35.70 *(978-1-4342-4285-3(4))* Stone Arch Bks.

Polak, Monique. Scarred, 1 vol. 2007. (Lorimer SideStreets Ser.). (ENG.). 168p. (YA). (gr. 9-12). 16.95 *(978-1-55028-965-7(9),* 9781550289657) Lorimer, James & Co., Ltd., Pubs. CAN. Dist: Casemate Pubs. & Bk. Distributors, LLC.

Polglase, Pamela. Handy & Dandy. 2008. 182p. 27.76 *(978-1-4357-4588-9(4))* Lulu Pr., Inc.

Pollock, A. K. I Am Joshua: Heart Matters Series. 2013. 214p. (gr. 4-6). pap. 17.95 *(978-1-4497-9726-3(1),* WestBow Pr.) Author Solutions, Inc.

Poole, Susie. Whatever Is Lovely: Based on Philippians 4:4-9. 2006. (ENG., Illus.). 26p. bds. 7.99 *(978-1-904637-26-4(4),* 1904637264, Pupfish) Authentic Media GBR. Dist: EMI CMG Distribution.

The Portal in the Park: By Cricket Casey, songs & audio book performed by Grandmaseter Melle Mel, features Lady Gaga, Included CD in Book. 2010. (Illus.). 132p. (J). mass mkt. 19.95 *(978-0-9786488-0-0(3))* SCOJO ENTERTAINMENT.

Porter, Eleanor H. Pollyanna. 2007. (ENG.). 184p. pap. 19.99 *(978-1-4346-0972-4(3));* 206p. pap. 22.99 *(978-1-4346-1071-3(3))* Creative Media Partners, LLC.

—Pollyanna. 2005. 104p. per. 4.95 *(978-1-4209-2555-5(5))* Digireads.com Publishing.

Porter, Rhonda. Brody Meets a Bully. 2008. 16p. pap. 24.95 *(978-1-60610-311-1(3))* America Star Bks.

Potvin, Amy K. I Miss Daddy. 2009. 28p. pap. 13.99 *(978-1-4259-1705-0(4))* AuthorHouse.

Powers-Fish, Amy Rose. Buddy's Forever Home. l.t. ed. 2006. (Illus.). 41p. (J). (gr. -1-3). per. 11.99 *(978-1-59879-192-1(3))* Lifevest Publishing, Inc.

Pratt, Non. Trouble. 2015. (ENG., Illus.). 400p. (YA). (gr. 9). pap. 10.99 *(978-1-4424-9773-3(4))* Simon & Schuster, Inc.

Prince, Mark E. I'm Happy When. 2009. 20p. pap. 12.99 *(978-1-4389-5523-0(5))* AuthorHouse.

Prochovnic, Dawn Babb. So Many Feelings: Sign Language for Feelings & Emotions, 1 vol. Bauer, Stephanie, illus. 2012. (ENG.). 32p. (J). 28.50 *(978-1-61641-841-0(9),* Looking Glass Library) Magic Wagon.

Profilet, Cynthia. Maggie's Golden Moment. Barron, Ann, illus. 2005. (J). *(978-0-9637735-1-7(8))* Sterling Pr., Inc.

Publications International Ltd. Staff, ed. If You're Happy & You Know It! 2011. 22p. (J). bds. 6.98 *(978-1-4508-1886-5(2))* Phoenix International Publications, Inc.

Rae, Lisa. A Distinguished Old Bentley Drove down to the Sea, 1 vol. Pickersgill, Peter, illus. 2007. (ENG.). 28p. (J). (gr. -1-2). pap. 8.95 *(978-1-897174-05-0(5),* Tuckamore Bks) Creative Bk. Publishing CAN. Dist: Orca Bk. Pubs. USA.

Rainfield, Cheryl. Scars. 2011. 8.67 *(978-0-7848-3439-8(3),* Everbind) Marco Bk. Co.

Randle, Kristen D. The Only Alien on the Planet. 2009. (ENG.). 240p. (YA). (gr. 7-12). pap. 11.99 *(978-1-4022-2669-4(1),* 9781402226694, Sourcebooks Jabberwocky) Sourcebooks, Inc.

Random House Disney Staff. Inside Out Junior Novelization (Disney/Pixar Inside Out) Random House Disney Staff, illus. 2015. (Junior Novel Ser.). (ENG., Illus.). 128p. (J). (gr. 4-7).

5.99 *(978-0-7364-3312-9(0),* Random Hse. Bks. for Young Readers) Random Hse. Children's Bks.
—Journey into the Mind. Random House Disney Staff, illus. 2015. (Step into Reading Ser.). (ENG., Illus.). 32p. (J). (gr. -1-1). 4.99 *(978-0-7364-3316-7(3),* RH/Disney) Random Hse. Children's Bks.
—Welcome to Headquarters. Random House Disney Staff, illus. 2015. (Step into Reading Ser.). (ENG., Illus.). 32p. (J). (gr. -1-1). 4.99 *(978-0-7364-3318-1(X));* lib. bdg. 12.99 *(978-0-7364-8170-0(2))* Random Hse. Children's Bks. (RH/Disney).
Rasheed, Winona. Stories from Grandma's Garden. 2008. 41p. pap. 15.94 *(978-1-4357-5075-3(6))* Lulu Pr., Inc.
Ratchford, Marjorie. A Party in the Sky, 1 vol. 2009. 24p. pap. 24.95 *(978-1-60813-296-6(X))* America Star Bks.
Rayburn, Tricia. Maggie Bean in Love. 2009. (ENG.). 288p. (J). (gr. 4-8). pap. 6.99 *(978-1-4169-8700-0(2),* Aladdin) Simon & Schuster Children's Publishing.
Reade, O. K. The Little Girl & Her Shadow. 2015. (Illus.). (J). 12.99 *(978-1-4621-1618-8(3))* Cedar Fort, Inc./CFI Distribution.
Reed, Amy. Beautiful. 2010. (ENG.). 256p. (YA). (gr. 9). pap. 10.99 *(978-1-4169-7831-2(3),* Simon Pulse) Simon Pulse.
Reed, Amy Lynn. Beautiful. 2009. (ENG.). 240p. (YA). (gr. 9-18). 16.99 *(978-1-4169-7830-5(5),* Simon Pulse) Simon Pulse.
Rees, Celia. This Is Not Forgiveness. 2012. (ENG.). 288p. (YA). (gr. 9-12). 17.99 *(978-1-59990-776-5(3),* 9781599907765, Bloomsbury USA Childrens) Bloomsbury Publishing USA.
Regan, Lisa. No Hitting, Henry: Don't Hurt. 2017. (You Choose Ser.). (Illus.). 32p. (J). (gr. 2-2). lib. bdg. 25.27 ***(978-0-7660-8702-6(6))*** Enslow Pubs., Inc.
Reschke, Kathleen. Grandma, Mommy & Me. 2010. 20p. pap. 12.95 *(978-1-4490-5550-9(8))* AuthorHouse.
Resman, Michael. Lliana Ageiraü. Cayetano, Eldred Roy, tr. Gathigo, Cyrus Ngatia, illus. 2013. 40p. pap. *(978-976-8142-50-4(2))* Producciones de la Hamaca.
Rex, Annmarie. Black's Adventure in the Big, Scary, Hairy World. 2007. (Illus.). 46p. (J). 19.99 *(978-1-59879-365-9(9),* Lifevest) Lifevest Publishing, Inc.
—Black's Adventure in the Big, Scary, Hairy World. Rex, Annmarie, illus. 2007. (Illus.). 46p. (J). (gr. -1-3). per. 15.99 *(978-1-59879-364-2(0),* Lifevest) Lifevest Publishing, Inc.
Rey, H. A. & Rey, Margret, illus. Curious George's Are You Curious? 2003. (J). bds. 9.95 *(978-0-618-27710-0(2))* Houghton Mifflin Harcourt Trade & Reference Pubs.
Reynolds Jr., R. A. Simon's Big Move. Balek, Dayna Courtney, illus. 2008. 19p. pap. 24.95 *(978-1-60672-676-1(5))* America Star Bks.
RH Disney Staff. Inside Out Big Golden Book (Disney/Pixar Inside Out) RH Disney Staff, illus. 2015. (Big Golden Book Ser.). (ENG., Illus.). 64p. (J). (gr. -1-2). 9.99 *(978-0-7364-3313-6(9),* RH/Disney) Random Hse. Children's Bks.
—Rainbow of Emotions. RH Disney Staff, illus. 2015. (Color Plus Rainbow Pencil Ser.). (ENG., Illus.). 128p. (J). (gr. -1-2). pap. 7.99 *(978-0-7364-3287-0(6),* Golden/Disney) Random Hse. Children's Bks.
RH Disney Staff & Glum, Felicity. Simply Sadness/Joy's Greatest Joy, 2 bks. in 1. RH Disney Staff & Tyminski, Lori, illus. 2015. (Pictureback(R) Ser.). (ENG.). 24p. (J). (gr. -1-2). 4.99 *(978-0-7364-3314-3(7),* RH/Disney) Random Hse. Children's Bks.
Ribiero, Nelson & Spotlight Editors. Laugh with Mammoth Madness. Gorelick, Victor, illus. 2007. (Archie Digest Library). (ENG.). 80p. (J). (gr. 3-6). 24.21 *(978-1-59961-281-2(X))* Spotlight.
—Laugh with Snack Swap. Gorelick, Victor, illus. 2007. (Archie Digest Library). (ENG.). 80p. (J). (gr. 3-6). 24.21 *(978-1-59961-282-9(8))* Spotlight.
—Laugh with Stampede. Gorelick, Victor, illus. 2007. (Archie Digest Library). (ENG.). 80p. (J). (gr. 3-6). 24.21 *(978-1-59961-283-6(6))* Spotlight.
Richmond, Marianne. Beautiful Blue Eyes. 2011. (ENG.). 32p. (J). (gr. -1-3). 15.99 *(978-1-4022-5639-4(6),* Sourcebooks Jabberwocky) Sourcebooks, Inc.
Riley, Zach. Quarterback Crisis. Ricci, Andrés, illus. 2012. (Zach Riley Ser.). 80p. (J). (gr. 3-6). lib. bdg. 27.07 *(978-1-61783-534-6(X))* Magic Wagon.
Ripken, Cal, Jr. Hothead. aut. ed. 2011. 16.99 *(978-1-4231-5168-5(2))* Disney Pr.
—Hothead. 2011. (Playaway Children Ser.). (J). (gr. 4-6). 44.99 *(978-1-61707-430-1(6))* Random Hse., Inc.
Ripken, Cal, Jr. & Cowherd, Kevin. Hothead. 2012. (ENG.). 160p. (J). (gr. 3-7). pap. 6.99 *(978-1-4231-4003-0(6))* Hyperion Pr.
Rippin, Sally. The Worry Monsters. Spartels, Stephanie, illus. 2014. (ENG.). 48p. (J). pap. 4.99 *(978-1-61067-126-2(0))* Kane Miller.
Rivett, Rachel. Are You Sad, Little Bear? A Book about Learning to Say Goodbye. Macnaughton, Tina, illus. 2010. (ENG.). 28p. (J). (gr. k-k). 12.99 *(978-0-7459-6137-8(1))* Lion Hudson PLC GBR. Dist: Independent Pubs. Group.
Roberts, Willo Davis. Blood on His Hands. 2014. (ENG., Illus.). 192p. (YA). (gr. 7). pap. 13.99 *(978-1-4814-4461-3(1),* Simon Pulse) Simon Pulse.
Robinson, Nadolyn H. Boo! Hoo! Bluepurdue. 2011. 28p. pap. 15.99 *(978-1-4568-6570-2(6))* Xlibris Corp.
Rolli, Jennifer Hansen. Just One More. 2014. (ENG., Illus.). 40p. (J). (gr. -1-k). 16.99 *(978-0-670-01563-4(6),* Viking Books for Young Readers) Penguin Young Readers Group.
Root, Phyllis. Lilly & the Pirates. Shepperson, Rob, illus. 2010. (ENG.). 116p. (J). (gr. 4-6). 16.95 *(978-1-59078-583-6(5),* Front Street) Boyds Mills Pr.
Rosa-Mendoza, Gladys. When I Am/Cuando Estoy. Regan, Dana, illus. 2004. (English-Spanish Foundations Ser.). (SPA & ENG.). 20p. (J). (gr. -1). bds. 6.95 *(978-1-931398-12-1(7))* Me+Mi Publishing.
Rose, Robin. Reaching for the Stars. 2008. 24p. pap. 11.95 *(978-1-4389-2299-7(X))* AuthorHouse.
Rosen, Michael. Michael Rosen's Sad Book. Blake, Quentin, illus. 2005. (ENG.). 32p. (J). (gr. k-12). 16.99 *(978-0-7636-2597-9(3))* Candlewick Pr.
Rotellar, Carlos. Little Red Monster: Tales of Monica. 2009. 24p. pap. 11.49 *(978-1-4490-2812-1(8))* AuthorHouse.
Roth, Carol. Hold Your Temper, Tiger. Rashin, illus. 2017. (ENG.). 32p. (J). (gr. -1-3). 17.95 *(978-0-7358-4274-8(4))* North-South Bks., Inc.
Roth, Susan L. Mi Amor Por Ti/My Love for You. 2003. (ENG & SPA., Illus.). 26p. (J). (gr. -1 — 1). bds. 6.99 *(978-0-8037-2944-5(8),* Dial Bks) Penguin Young Readers Group.
Roy, James. Miss Understood. 2011. (ENG.). 288p. (J). 12.99 *(978-1-86471-860-7(9))* Random Hse. Australia AUS. Dist: Independent Pubs. Group.
Rudolph, Miriam. A Frozen Dream. 2009. 28p. pap. 12.00 *(978-1-60693-962-8(9),* Eloquent Bks.) Strategic Book Publishing & Rights Agency (SBPRA).
Running Press Staff & Hello Kitty Staff. Hello Kitty: A Little Book of Happiness. 2009. (Miniature Editions Ser.). (ENG.). 96p. 5.95 *(978-0-7624-3594-4(1))* Running Pr. Bk. Pubs.
Sáenz, Benjamin Alire. He Forgot to Say Goodbye. 2008. (ENG.). 336p. (YA). (gr. 7-12). 18.99 *(978-1-4169-4963-3(1),* Simon & Schuster Bks. For Young Readers) Simon & Schuster Bks. For Young Readers.
Sakmar-Sullivan, Eva M. Kangaroo's Out of This World Restaurant, 1 vol. Sakmar-Sullivan, Eva M., illus. 2013. (ENG., Illus.). 32p. (J). 14.99 *(978-0-7643-4519-7(2),* 9780764345197) Schiffer Publishing, Ltd.
Saldaña, Jr. A Good Long Way. 2010. 128p. (J). (gr. 6-18). pap. 10.95 *(978-1-55885-607-3(2),* Piñata Books) Arte Publico Pr.
Saldin, Erin. The Girls of No Return. 2012. (YA). pap. *(978-0-545-31027-7(X));* (ENG.). 352p. (J). (gr. 9-9). 17.99 *(978-0-545-31026-0(1))* Scholastic, Inc. (Levine, Arthur A. Bks.).
Salom, Andree. When the Anger Ogre Visits. Salom, Ivette, illus. 2015. (ENG.). 40p. (J). 18.95 *(978-1-61429-166-4(7))* Wisdom Pubns.
Sammy. 2007. *(978-0-9793490-4-1(4))* Dynasty Publishing, Inc.
Samuel, Josiah C. Mr. Tortoise Funny Life, Bk. 1. 2013. 132p. pap. 45.07 *(978-1-4669-9904-6(7))* Trafford Publishing.
Sanchez, Alex. Bait. (ENG.). 256p. (YA). (gr. 7). 2010. pap. 12.99 *(978-1-4169-3774-6(9))* 2009. 17.99 *(978-1-4169-3772-2(2))* Simon & Schuster Bks. For Young Readers. (Simon & Schuster Bks. For Young Readers).
Sargent, David M. Emma! Huff, Jeane, illus. 2004. (Doggie Tails Ser.). (J). *(978-1-56763-851-6(1));* pap. *(978-1-56763-852-3(X))* Ozark Publishing.
Sam, Amélie & Trouillot, Virgile. Recipe for Happiness. 2009. (Groove High Ser.). (Illus.). 112p. (YA). (gr. 5-8). 31.95 *(978-1-60754-532-3(2));* pap. 15.25 *(978-1-60754-533-0(0))* Windmill Bks.
Samo-Doyle, Christine. Your Inside Shape. 2012. (ENG., Illus.). 32p. (J). 17.95 *(978-0-9824461-0-2(1))* SDP Publishing.
Sartori, Rosanne Sheritz. Tales of Temper: Grades 3-6. Barber, David L., illus. 2005. 128p. per. 21.95 *(978-1-931636-48-3(6))* National Ctr. For Youth Issues.
Saumande, Juliette. In Search of Happiness. Weller, Andrew, tr. from FRE. Puybaret, Eric, illus. 2010. 32p. (J). (gr. -1-2). 14.99 *(978-0-8416-7141-6(9))* Hammond World Atlas Corp.
Schirmer, Jodi L. It Is a Good Day: Clay. 2009. 23p. (J). pap. 11.95 *(978-1-4327-4018-4(0))* Outskirts Pr., Inc.
Schmid, Paul. Hugs from Pearl. Schmid, Paul, illus. 2011. (ENG., Illus.). 40p. (J). (gr. -1-2). 14.99 *(978-0-06-180434-2(7))* HarperCollins Pubs.
Schmidt, Gary D. Orbiting Jupiter. (ENG.). 192p. (gr. 7). 2017. (YA). pap. 9.99 *(978-0-544-93839-7(9),* HMH Books For Young Readers) 2015. (J). 17.99 *(978-0-544-46222-9(X),* Clarion Bks.) Houghton Mifflin Harcourt Publishing Co.
—Orbiting Jupiter. 2017. (ENG.). (YA). (gr. 7). lib. bdg. 20.85 ***(978-0-606-39818-3(X))*** Turtleback Bks.
Schmidt, Tiffany. Bright Before Sunrise. 2015. (ENG.). 304p. (YA). (gr. 7). pap. 9.99 *(978-0-8027-3502-7(9),* 9780802735027, Bloomsbury USA Childrens) Bloomsbury Publishing USA.
Schott, Joanna. Bellows in Hell. 2013. 416p. pap. 18.95 *(978-1-59299-804-3(6))* Inkwater Pr.
Schraff, Anne. To Be a Man. 2011. (Urban Underground — Harriet Tubman High School Ser.). (YA). lib. bdg. 20.80 *(978-0-606-14815-3(9),* Turtleback) Turtleback Bks.
Schulz, Charles M. Be Thankful: Peanuts Wisdom to Carry You Through. 2013. (ENG., Illus.). 72p. (J). (gr. -1-17). 7.95 *(978-0-7624-5045-9(2),* Running Pr. Kids) Running Pr. Bk. Pubs.
Scieszka, Jon. Melvin Might? Gordon, David et al, illus. 2008. (Jon Scieszka's Trucktown Ser.). (ENG.). 44p. (J). (gr. -1-3). 16.99 *(978-1-4169-4134-7(7),* Simon & Schuster Bks. For Young Readers) Simon & Schuster Bks. For Young Readers.
—Melvin's Valentine. Shannon, David et al, illus. 2009. (Jon Scieszka's Trucktown Ser.). (ENG.). 24p. (J). (gr. -1-1). pap. 3.99 *(978-1-4169-4144-6(4));* lib. bdg. 15.99 *(978-1-4169-4155-2(X))* Simon Spotlight. (Simon Spotlight).
Scott, Elizabeth. Living Dead Girl. 2008. (ENG.). 176p. (YA). (gr. 10-18). 17.99 *(978-1-4169-6059-1(7),* Simon Pulse) Simon Pulse.
—Perfect You. 2008. (ENG.). 304p. (YA). (gr. 9-12). pap. 9.99 *(978-1-4169-5355-5(8),* Simon Pulse) Simon Pulse.
Seeger, Laura Vaccaro. Walter Was Worried. Seeger, Laura Vaccaro, illus. 2016. (ENG., Illus.). 40p. (J). 14.99 *(978-1-62672-251-4(X),* 9781626722514) Roaring Brook Pr.
—Walter Was Worried. Seeger, Laura Vaccaro, illus. 2006. (ENG., Illus.). 40p. (J). (gr. -1-3). pap. 8.99 *(978-1-59643-196-6(2),* 9781596431966) Square Fish.
Seibers, Elexis. Zoac Moves to Jugabh. 2011. 36p. pap. 21.99 *(978-1-4568-1585-1(7))* Xlibris Corp.
Sellers, Sandra. Gran's Story IV: Gathering Wild Violets. 2011. 24p. (gr. -1). pap. 15.99 *(978-1-4269-5707-9(6))* Trafford Publishing.
Sesame Street, Sesame. Sesame Street: Happy Like Elmo/Grouchy Like Oscar. 2016. (ENG.). 20p. (J). (gr. -1-k). bds. 10.99 *(978-0-7944-3803-6(2))* Studio Fun International.
Shapiro, Jane. Daddy, What Is Love? Robinson, Don, illus. 2008. (ENG.). 28p. (J). (gr. -1-3). *(978-1-59700-244-8(5))* Island Heritage Publishing.
Shapiro, Lawrence. Ethan Has Too Much Energy: An Emotional Literacy Book. Harpster, Steve, illus. 2005. (Emotional Literacy Ser.). 42p. (J). 14.95 *(978-0-9747789-4-5(X),* 36027) CTC Publishing.
Sharp, Andre L. I Don't Talk Funny, I Stutter: A Children's Motivational Book. 2011. 28p. pap. 15.99 *(978-1-4628-9685-1(5))* Xlibris Corp.
Shaw, Natalie. I'm Feeling Mad. Fruchter, Jason, illus. 2016. (Daniel Tiger's Neighborhood Ser.). (ENG.). 14p. (J). (gr. -1 — 1). bds. 5.99 *(978-1-4814-6176-4(1),* Simon Spotlight) Simon Spotlight.
Shaw, Susan. One of the Survivors. 2009. (ENG.). 208p. (J). (gr. 5-9). 15.99 *(978-1-4169-6129-1(1),* McElderry, Margaret K. Bks.) McElderry, Margaret K. Bks.
Sheinmel, Courtney. Positively. 2010. (ENG.). 240p. (J). (gr. 4-9). pap. 6.99 *(978-1-4424-0622-3(4),* Simon & Schuster Bks. For Young Readers) Simon & Schuster Bks. For Young Readers.
Shore, Diane Z. How to Drive Your Sister Crazy. Rankin, Laura, illus. 2012. (I Can Read Level 2 Ser.). (ENG.). 48p. (J). (gr. k-3). pap. 3.99 *(978-0-06-052764-8(1))* HarperCollins Pubs.
Shulevitz, Uri. Troto & the Trucks. 2015. (ENG., Illus.). 32p. (J). (gr. -1-1). 17.99 *(978-0-374-30080-7(1),* 9780374300807, Farrar, Straus & Giroux (BYR)) Farrar, Straus & Giroux.
Shull, Megan. Amazing Grace. 2005. (ENG., Illus.). 256p. (gr. 6-9). 15.99 *(978-0-7868-5690-9(4))* Hyperion Pr.
Sills, Kathy & Sills, Karen. Feelings, Feelings, Feelings. 2012. 19p. 19.00 *(978-1-4349-8743-3(4),* RoseDog Bks.) Dorrance Publishing Co., Inc.
Silver, Gail. Anh's Anger. Kromer, Christiane, illus. 2011. (J). *(978-1-935209-65-2(5),* Plum Blossom Bks.) Parallax Pr.
—Anh's Anger. Krömer, Christiane, illus. 2009. (ENG.). 40p. (J). (gr. -1-3). 16.95 *(978-1-888375-94-7(9),* Plum Blossom Bks.) Parallax Pr.
—Steps & Stones: An Anh's Anger Story. Krömer, Christiane, illus. 2007. (ENG.). 40p. (J). (gr. -1-3). 16.95 *(978-1-935209-87-4(6),* Plum Blossom Bks.) Parallax Pr.
Silverstein, Shel. The Giving Tree. (Illus.). 95.94 *(978-0-06-056897-9(6))* HarperCollins Pubs.
—The Giving Tree. Silverstein, Shel, illus. anniv. ed. 2014. (ENG., Illus.). 64p. (J). (gr. -1-3). 19.99 *(978-0-06-058675-1(3))* HarperCollins Pubs.
Silvestri, Linda. Clementina & the Hooey-Phooey Circus Troupe. 2007. (ESP., Illus.). (YA). 12.95 *(978-0-9710696-8-8(9))* Jorlan Publishing, Inc.
Skalla, Nancy. Grandma's Telos Boxes of Wishes. 2011. (Illus.). 50p. pap. 22.00 *(978-0-557-77686-3(4))* Lulu Pr., Inc.
Sklaver, Ellen. Aleph Finds Her Voice. 2010. 36p. pap. 13.00 *(978-1-4520-8931-7(0))* AuthorHouse.
Skye Toggles. Bella the Witch & Her Worries. 2010. 36p. pap. 16.99 *(978-1-4490-6803-5(0))* AuthorHouse.
SLAY, Jenette. ABBY, the Easter Chicken. 2008. 29p. 13.96 *(978-1-4357-1062-7(2))* Lulu Pr., Inc.
Smart Kidz Media. Love Bug: Sad. 2012. (How I Feel Ser.). (ENG.). 24p. (J). 10.99 *(978-1-891100-46-8(7))* Smart Kidz Media, Inc.
Smith, Amber. The Way I Used to Be. 2017. (ENG.). 384p. (YA). (gr. 9). pap. 10.99 *(978-1-4814-4936-6(2),* McElderry, Margaret K. Bks.) McElderry, Margaret K. Bks.
—The Way I Used to Be. Twomey, Kevin, photos by. 2016. (ENG., Illus.). 384p. (YA). (gr. 9). 17.99 *(978-1-4814-4935-9(4),* McElderry, Margaret K. Bks.) McElderry, Margaret K. Bks.
Smith, Brian, Brian. Memory. 2014. (ENG.). 216p. (C). pap. 49.95 *(978-1-138-87117-5(6),* Y178984) Routledge.
Smith, Bryan. Mindset Matters. Griffin, Lisa, illus. 2017. (Without Limits Ser.: 2). (ENG.). 32p. (J). (gr. k-5). pap. 10.95 ***(978-1-944882-12-9(X))*** Boys Town Pr.
—Of Course It's a Big Deal. Griffin, Lisa, illus. 2017. (Executive Function Ser.: 3). (ENG.). 32p. (J). (gr. k-5). pap. 10.95 ***(978-1-944882-11-2(1))*** Boys Town Pr.
Smith, Debora Ann Baker. The Magnificent Fairy Party. 2010. (Illus.). 30p. pap. 13.00 *(978-1-60911-404-6(3),* Eloquent Bks.) Strategic Book Publishing & Rights Agency (SBPRA).
Snodgrass, Kimberly J. I Am a Foster Child, & That's Okay with Me. 2008. 39p. pap. 24.95 *(978-1-60813-127-3(0))* America Star Bks.
Snyder, Zilpha Keatley. The Unseen. 2005. 199p. 16.00 *(978-0-7569-5670-7(6))* Perfection Learning Corp.
Solomon, Enid. Toby Visits Mommy: A Book for Children Who See Their Parents Only During Scheduled Visitations. 2010. 32p. pap. 13.25 *(978-1-4490-0683-9(3))* AuthorHouse.
Solomon, Sharon. A Walk With Grandpa/Un Paseo con el Abuelo. Del Risco, Eida, tr. Barcita, Pamela, illus. 2009. (ENG & SPA.). 32p. (J). (gr. -1-3). 16.95 *(978-1-932748-91-8(1),* Raven Tree Pr.,Csi) Continental Sales, Inc.
Solomon, Sharon K. A Walk with Grandpa. Barcita, Pamela, illus. 2009. (ENG.). 32p. (J). (gr. -1-3). 16.95 *(978-1-934960-11-0(X),* Raven Tree Pr.,Csi) Continental Sales, Inc.
Sommer, Carl. Can You Help Me Find My Smile? 2003. (Another Sommer-Time Story Ser.). (Illus.). 48p. (J). (gr. k-4). lib. bdg. 23.95 incl. audio *(978-1-57537-757-5(8))* Advance Publishing, Inc.
—Can You Help Me Find My Smile? Budwine, Greg, illus. 2003. (Another Sommer-Time Story Ser.). (ENG.). 48p. (J). (gr. k-4). lib. bdg. 23.95 incl. audio compact disk *(978-1-57537-707-0(1))* Advance Publishing, Inc.
—Can You Help Me Find My Smile? 2003. (Another Sommer-Time Story Ser.). (Illus.). 48p. (J). (gr. 1-4). 16.95 incl. audio *(978-1-57537-556-4(7))* Advance Publishing, Inc.
—Can You Help Me Find My Smile? Budwine, Greg, illus. 2003. (Another Sommer-Time Story Ser.). (ENG.). 48p. (J). (gr. 1-4). 16.95 incl. audio compact disk *(978-1-57537-507-6(9))* Advance Publishing, Inc.
—Lost & Found(Perdida y Encontrada) Budwine, Greg, illus. 2009. (Quest for Success Bilingual Ser.). (ENG & SPA.). 96p. (YA). lib. bdg. 14.95 *(978-1-57537-229-7(0))* Advance Publishing, Inc.
Sophia Hansen, Hansen & Hansen, Sophia. The Crow & the Raven. 2010. 20p. 9.50 *(978-1-4269-2752-2(5))* Trafford Publishing.
Soprano, Sophie, illus. Laughing All the Way. 2008. (J). *(978-1-59811-642-7(8))* Covenant Communications.
Spelman, Cornelia. When I Feel Angry. Cote, Nancy, illus. 2012. (J). reprint ed. lib. bdg. 32.71 *(978-1-61913-139-2(0))* Weigl Pubs., Inc.
Spencer, Katherine. Saving Grace. 2007. (Saving Grace Ser.). (ENG., Illus.). 256p. (YA). (gr. 7-12). pap. 15.95 *(978-0-15-206096-1(0))* Houghton Mifflin Harcourt Publishing Co.
Spinelli, Eileen. When You Are Happy. Valério, Geraldo, illus. 2006. (ENG.). 40p. (J). (gr. -1-3). 19.99 *(978-0-689-86251-9(2),* Simon & Schuster Bks. For Young Readers) Simon & Schuster Bks. For Young Readers.
Spotlight Editors. Laugh with a Test Case. Gorelick, Victor, illus. 2007. (Archie Digest Library). (ENG.). 80p. (J). (gr. 3-6). 24.21 *(978-1-59961-284-3(4))* Spotlight.
Springstubb, Tricia. Cody & the Fountain of Happiness. Wheeler, Eliza, illus. 2015. (ENG.). 160p. (J). (gr. 2-5). 14.99 *(978-0-7636-5857-1(X))* Candlewick Pr.
Stacy, Heidi. Hoppy Feelings. 2013. 28p. pap. 13.99 *(978-1-4525-8451-5(6),* Balboa Pr.) Author Solutions, Inc.
Stahler, David, Jr. Spinning Out. 2011. (ENG.). 288p. (YA). (gr. 7-17). 16.99 *(978-0-8118-7780-0(9))* Chronicle Bks. LLC.
Stalder, Päivi. My Wish Tonight. Wolferman, Iris, illus. 2010. (ENG.). 32p. (J). (gr. -1-3). 12.95 *(978-0-7358-2331-0(6))* North-South Bks., Inc.
Stan, Andreea. The Cloud Fairy Tales: The Clouds Are Our Feelings. 2011. 48p. pap. 21.99 *(978-1-4568-1563-9(6))* Xlibris Corp.
Stangl, Katrin, illus. Strong As a Bear. 2016. (ENG.). 40p. (J). (gr. -1-3). 16.95 *(978-1-59270-198-8(1))* Enchanted Lion Bks., LLC.
Staub, Leslie. Everybody Gets the Blues. Roth, R G, illus. 2012. (ENG.). 32p. (J). (gr. -1-3). 16.99 *(978-0-15-206300-9(5))* Houghton Mifflin Harcourt Publishing Co.
Staunton, Ted. Super Move, Morgan! Slavin, Bill, illus. 2006. (Formac First Novels Ser.: 35). (ENG.). 64p. (J). (gr. 2-5). 14.95 *(978-0-88780-704-6(6),* 9780887807046); 4.95 *(978-0-88780-702-2(X),* 9780887807022) Formac Publishing Co., Ltd. CAN. Dist: Casemate Pubs. & Bk. Distributors, LLC.
Stevens, Courtney. The Lies about Truth. 2017. 336p. (YA). (gr. 9). pap. 9.99 *(978-0-06-224542-7(2),* HarperTeen) HarperCollins Pubs.
Stevenson, Robin. Out of Order, 1 vol. 2007. (ENG.). 232p. (YA). (gr. 7-12). per. 9.95 *(978-1-55143-693-7(0))* Orca Bk. Pubs. USA.
—The World Without Us. 2014. 240p. pap. *(978-1-4598-0681-8(6))* Orca Bk. Pubs.
Stewart, Maddie. Bertie Rooster. Aggs, Patrice, tr. Aggs, Patrice, illus. 2007. (Panda Cubs Ser.: 02). (ENG.). 48p. (J). pap. 9.95 *(978-0-86278-798-1(X))* O'Brien Pr., Ltd., The IRL. Dist: Dufour Editions, Inc.
Stileman, Kali. Roly Poly Egg. 2011. (ENG.). 26p. (J). (gr. -1-k). 12.95 *(978-1-58925-852-5(5))* Tiger Tales.
Stubbs, Lisa. Grumpy Feet. Stubbs, Lisa, illus. 2017. (Lily & Bear Ser.). (ENG., Illus.). 32p. (J). (gr. -1-3). 17.99 *(978-1-4814-7167-1(8),* Simon & Schuster/Paula Wiseman Bks.) Simon & Schuster/Paula Wiseman Bks.
Studio Mouse Staff. Pooh & Eeyore. 2008. (ENG., Illus.). 36p. (J). (gr. -1). 7.99 *(978-1-59069-418-3(X))* Studio Mouse LLC.
—Sesame Street Share & Care, It's Only Fair. 2009. (ENG.). 60p. (J). (gr. -1). 12.99 *(978-1-59069-739-9(1))* Studio Mouse LLC.
Sullivan, Licsw. Mindfully Me! 2012. 12p. pap. 10.99 *(978-1-105-46639-7(6))* Lulu Pr., Inc.
Summers, Courtney. Cracked up to Be. 2008. (ENG.). 224p. (YA). (gr. 9-18). pap. 12.99 *(978-0-312-38369-5(X),* 9780312383695, St. Martin's Griffin) St. Martin's Pr.
—Some Girls Are. 2010. (ENG.). 256p. (YA). (gr. 9-18). pap. 11.99 *(978-0-312-57380-5(4),* 9780312573805, St. Martin's Griffin) St. Martin's Pr.
—What Goes Around: Two Books in One: Cracked up to Be & Some Girls Are. 2013. (ENG.). 480p. (YA). (gr. 9-12). pap. 9.99 *(978-1-250-03844-9(8),* 9781250038449, St. Martin's Griffin) St. Martin's Pr.
Sunderland, Margot & Hancock, Nicky. A Nifflenoo Called Nevermind. Armstrong, Nicky, tr. Armstrong, Nicky, illus. (ENG.). 32p. pap. *(978-0-86388-496-2(2),* 002-5064, Routledge) Taylor & Francis Group.
Supplee, Kathryn. Choose Happy. 2013. 34p. pap. 11.99 *(978-1-939268-05-1(2))* Pilot Communications Group, Inc.
Sutton, Kelsey. Where Silence Gathers. 2014. (ENG.). 360p. (YA). pap. 9.99 *(978-0-7387-3947-2(2),* Flux) North Star Editions.
Swann, Mary. A Fearsome Day. Swann, Mary, illus. 2007. (Illus.). 56p. (J). (gr. 1-3). 19.95 *(978-0-932616-87-6(9))* BrickHouse Bks., Inc.
Swartz, Elly. Finding Perfect. 2016. (ENG.). 304p. (J). 16.99 *(978-0-374-30312-9(6),* 9780374303129, Farrar, Straus & Giroux (BYR)) Farrar, Straus & Giroux.
Syrstad, Suzi. Timmy the Tiny Troubled Turtle, 1 vol. Maki, Tab, illus. 2009. 13p. pap. 24.95 *(978-1-61546-455-5(7))* PublishAmerica, Inc.
Szish, Jill Henry. TJ & the Good Luck Cricket. Perry, Jennifer A., illus. 2007. 32p. per. 24.95 *(978-1-4241-8502-3(5))* America Star Bks.
Taddonio, Lea. Book 4: First Kiss. 2016. (Head over Heels Ser.). (ENG.). (J). (gr. 2-8). lib. bdg. 28.50 ***(978-1-62402-195-4(6))*** ABDO Publishing Co.
Tagliaferri, Saria & Spada, Alberto. Why That Face, 1 vol. 2011. (ENG.). 20p. pap. 9.95 *(978-90-79761-21-0(4))* Tectum B.V.B.A. BEL. Dist: Innovative Logistics.
Tankard, Jeremy. Grumpy Bird. 2016. (ENG.). 30p. (J). (— 1). bds. 6.99 *(978-0-545-87182-2(4),* Scholastic Pr.) Scholastic, Inc.
Tansil-Mitchell, Angela. Kimmie C Sunshine: When Mommy & Daddy Loses Their Jobs. 2011. 24p. pap. 13.79 *(978-1-4567-5666-6(4))* AuthorHouse.
Tate, Nikki. Fallout, 1 vol. 2011. (Orca Soundings Ser.). (ENG.). 128p. (YA). (gr. 8-12). lib. bdg. 16.95 *(978-1-55469-976-6(2))* Orca Bk. Pubs. USA.
Ten Turtles on Tuesday: A Story for Children about Obsessive-Compulsive Disorder. 2014. (Illus.). 80p. (J). *(978-1-4338-1643-7(1),* Magination Pr.) American Psychological Assn.
Tennant, Linda. Polly & Meril & the Wicked Spell. 2009. (Illus.). 20p. pap. 15.49 *(978-1-4389-7471-2(X))* AuthorHouse.
Tharp, Tim. Badd. 2012. (ENG.). 324p. (YA). (gr. 9). pap. 9.99 *(978-0-375-86401-8(6),* Ember) Random Hse. Children's Bks.
That's When I'm Happy. (Picture Books Ser.). 24p. *(978-1-4054-9538-7(3))* Parragon, Inc.

E
F
G

Theobald, Joseph. Marvin Gets Mad! 2013. pap. *(978-0-545-55294-3(X))* Scholastic, Inc.
Thomas, Louis. Hug It Out! 2017. (ENG., Illus.). 40p. (J). 16.99 *(978-0-374-30314-3(2)*, 9780374303143, Farrar, Straus & Giroux (BYR)) Farrar, Straus & Giroux.
Thompson, Colin. The Short & Incredibly Happy Life of Riley. Lissiat, Amy, illus. 2006. 32p. (J). *(978-0-7344-0806-8(4)*, Lothian Children's Bks.) Hachette Australia.
Thompson, Joan. Lucy Russell: Stardom & Stinkwater. 2003. 129p. (YA). pap. 10.95 *(978-0-595-26867-2(6)*, Writers Club Pr.) iUniverse, Inc.
Thompson, Lauren. The Forgiveness Garden. Hale, Christy & Apostolou, Christine Hale, illus. 2012. (ENG.). 32p. (J). (gr. k-1). 17.99 *(978-0-312-62599-3(5)*, 9780312625993) Feiwel & Friends.
Thurmond, Joey. Nojoe Makes New Friends. 2009. 16p. pap. 10.99 *(978-1-4490-4156-4(6))* AuthorHouse.
Tia, Rocio. Maire & the Monster, 1 vol. 2010. 64p. pap. 19.95 *(978-1-60749-724-0(7))* America Star Bks.
Tims, Laura. The Best Thing about Pain. 2017. 336p. (YA). (gr. 8). 17.99 *(978-0-06-231735-3(0)*, HarperTeen) HarperCollins Pubs.
Toms, Kate. I Udderly Love You! 2007. (Illus.). 25p. (gr. -1). *(978-1-84610-680-4(X))* Make Believe Ideas.
A Touch of Gray: A Great American Story. 2004. (Illus.). (YA). per. *(978-0-9654140-3-6(5))* Upword Pr.
Townsend, Marjorie. Wee's Moving Day. 2008. 24p. pap. 14.95 *(978-1-4327-2828-1(8))* Outskirts Pr., Inc.
Trout, Holly Christian. The Firefly Who Lost Her Way. 2013. 24p. pap. 24.95 *(978-1-62709-594-5(2))* America Star Bks.
Trueman, Terry & Trueman. Stuck in Neutral. 2012. (Stuck in Neutral Ser.: 1). (ENG.). 144p. (YA). (gr. 8-18). pap. 9.99 *(978-0-06-447213-5(2)*, HarperTeen) HarperCollins Pubs.
Tucker, Patricia Wright. The Princess Who Couldn't Laugh. 2012. 24p. pap. 24.95 *(978-1-4626-8133-4(6))* America Star Bks.
Tutu, Desmond. Desmond & the Very Mean Word. Ford, A. G., illus. 2012. (ENG.). 32p. (J). (gr. 1-4). 15.99 *(978-0-7636-5229-6(6))* Candlewick Pr.
Tyree, Omar R. 12 Brown Boys. 2008. 196p. (J). (gr. 3-7). pap. 9.95 *(978-1-933491-12-7(4))* Just Us Bks., Inc.
Urban, Linda. Mouse Was Mad. Cole, Henry, illus. (ENG.). 40p. (J). (gr. -1-3). 2012. pap. 7.99 *(978-0-547-72750-9(X))* 2009. 16.99 *(978-0-15-205337-6(9))* Houghton Mifflin Harcourt Publishing Co.
Urbanovic, Jackie. Prince of a Frog. 2015. (ENG., Illus.). 32p. (J). (gr. -1-k). 17.99 *(978-0-545-63652-0(3)*, Orchard Bks.) Scholastic, Inc.
Ure, Jean. Ice Lolly. 2010. (ENG., Illus.). 208p. (J). (gr. 4-7). 9.99 *(978-0-00-728173-2(0)*, HarperCollins Children's Bks.) HarperCollins Pubs. Ltd. GBR. Dist: HarperCollins Pubs.
Uyeda, Laura. The Bing Bong Book. Tilley, Scott, illus. 2015. (Little Golden Book Ser.). (ENG.). 24p. (J). (-k). 4.99 *(978-0-7364-3321-1(X)*, Golden/Disney) Random Hse. Children's Bks.
Vail, Rachel. School, Drool, & Other Daily Disasters. Cordell, Matthew, illus. 2011. (Justin Case Ser.: 1). (ENG.). 272p. (J). (gr. 2-4). pap. 7.99 *(978-0-312-56357-8(4)*, 9780312563578) Square Fish.
—Sometimes I'm Bombaloo. Heo, Yumi, illus. 2005. (Bookshelf Ser.). (ENG.). 32p. (J). (gr. -1-3). pap. 6.99 *(978-0-439-66941-2(3))* Scholastic, Inc.
Valentine, James. Stuff Happens: Luke. 12th ed. 2016. (Stuff Happens Ser.). (ENG.). 96p. (J). (gr. 2-4). 8.99 ***(978-0-14-330897-3(1))*** Random Hse. Australia AUS. Dist: Independent Pubs. Group.
Vallat, Christelle. Celia. Augusseau, Stphanie, illus. 2014. 36p. pap. 16.99 *(978-1-4413-1536-6(5))* Peter Pauper Pr. Inc.
VanCil, Marybelle. Sadie Fourpaws & the Magic Rocking Chair. 2009. (Illus.), 57p. pap. 26.95 *(978-1-4327-3642-2(6))* Outskirts Pr., Inc.
Vandepeer, Helen. Gifts. 2008. 76p. pap. 35.80 *(978-0-557-03191-7(5))* Lulu Pr., Inc.
Ventura, Marne. Nervous Nellie Fights First-Day Frenzy. Trinidad, Leo, illus. 2016. (Worry Warriors Ser.). (ENG.). 96p. (gr. 2-4). lib. bdg. 25.99 *(978-1-4965-3613-6(4))* Stone Arch Bks.
Vili, Fane. Mano: The Awakening. Frakes, Clint, ed. 2006. (Illus.). (YA). per. 19.95 *(978-0-9774074-0-8(3))* Plankton Pr.
Viorst, Judith. Alexander & the Terrible, Horrible, No Good, Very Bad Day. Cruz, Ray, illus. 2014. (Classic Board Bks.). (ENG.). 34p. (J). (gr. -1 — 1). bds. 7.99 *(978-1-4424-9816-7(1)*, Little Simon) Little Simon.
—Alexander & the Terrible, Horrible, No Good, Very Bad Day: Lap Edition. Cruz, Ray, illus. 2014. (ENG.). 34p. (J). (gr. -1 — 1). bds. 12.99 *(978-1-4814-1412-8(7)*, Little Simon) Little Simon.
Von Chamisso, Adelbert. Peter Schlemihl. Bowring, John, tr. 2011. 98p. pap. 8.95 *(978-1-60664-434-8(3))* Rodgers, Alan Bks.
Voss, Dawn. Avenging Aja. 2007. 50p. pap. 15.00 *(978-0-615-15324-7(0))* Voss, Dawn L.
Vrettos, Adrienne Maria. Burnout. (ENG., 208p. (YA). (gr. 7). 2012. Illus.). pap. 8.99 *(978-1-4169-9470-1(2))* 2011. 16.99 *(978-1-4169-9469-5(6))* McElderry, Margaret K. Bks. (McElderry, Margaret K. Bks.).
Waddell, Martin. The Super Hungry Dinosaur. Lord, Leonie, illus. 2009. (ENG.). 32p. (J). (gr. -1-k). 17.99 *(978-0-8037-3446-3(8)*, Dial Bks) Penguin Young Readers Group.
Wagenbach, Debbie. The Grouchies. Mack, Steve, illus. 2009. 32p. (J). (gr. -1-3). 14.95 *(978-1-4338-0543-1(X))*; pap. 9.95 *(978-1-4338-0553-0(7))* American Psychological Assn. (Magination Pr.).
Walker, B. Mr Peeze, Say Something Else Please! 2011. 28p. pap. 15.99 *(978-1-4568-2937-7(8))* Xlibris Corp.
Walker-Cox, Krysten. Amber's Metal Singlet. 2009. 48p. pap. 12.13 *(978-1-60860-316-9(4)*, Eloquent Bks.) Strategic Book Publishing & Rights Agency (SBPRA).
Wallace, Rich. Game-Day Jitters. Holder, Jimmy, illus. 2012. (Kickers Ser.). (ENG.). 128p. (J). (gr. 2-5). 5.99 *(978-0-375-85095-0(3)*, Yearling) Random Hse. Children's Bks.
Walsh, Ann. Shabash! 2nd ed. 2008. (ENG.). 112p. (J). (gr. 4-8). pap. 11.99 *(978-1-55002-829-4(4)*, Sandcastle Bks.) Dundurn CAN. Dist: Ingram Publisher Services.
Walsh, Joanna. The Perfect Hug. Abbot, Judi, illus. 2012. (ENG.). 32p. (J). (gr. -1-3). 14.99 *(978-1-4424-6606-7(5)*, Simon & Schuster/Paula Wiseman Bks.) Simon & Schuster/Paula Wiseman Bks.
Walton, Amy Catherine. Susan: A Story for Children. 2007. 118p. pap. 18.99 *(978-1-4346-5183-9(5))*; (ENG.). 132p. pap. 19.99 *(978-1-4346-5184-6(3))* Creative Media Partners, LLC.
Wan, Joyce. We Belong Together. Wan, Joyce, illus. 2011. (ENG., Illus.). 14p. (J). (gr. k — 1). bds. 6.99 *(978-0-545-30740-6(6)*, Cartwheel Bks.) Scholastic, Inc.
Warman, Jessica. The Last Good Day of the Year. 2016. (ENG.). 288p. (YA). pap. 9.99 *(978-0-8027-3663-5(7)*, 9780802736635, Bloomsbury USA Childrens) Bloomsbury Publishing USA.
Warner, Tucker. The Breakthrough & Funeral of a Grandfather, 1 vol. 2009. 48p. pap. 16.95 *(978-1-4489-6684-4(1))* PublishAmerica, Inc.
Warnick, Ryan. Gracie. 2007. 48p. (J). pap. 25.90 *(978-0-615-14266-1(4))* Opacity, Inc.
Watson, Philip & Ofiesh, Nicole. The Treasure Chest. 2011. 52p. 20.50 *(978-1-4269-5350-7(X))*; pap. 10.50 *(978-1-4269-5269-2(4))* Trafford Publishing.
Wattenberg, Jane. Mrs. Mustard's Baby Faces. rev. enl. ed. 2007. (Mrs. Mustards Ser.: MRSM). (ENG., Illus.). 14p. (J). (gr. -1 — 1). bds. 6.95 *(978-0-8118-5967-7(3))* Chronicle Bks. LLC.
Watts, Frances. Kisses for Daddy. Legge, David, illus. 2010. (ENG.). 26p. (J). (gr. -1-k). bds. 7.99 *(978-1-4169-8721-5(5)*, Little Simon) Little Simon.
Webber, Katherine. The Heartbeats of Wing Jones. 2017. (ENG.). 336p. (YA). (gr. 7). 17.99 *(978-0-399-55502-2(1)*, Delacorte Pr.) Random Hse. Children's Bks.
Wechterowicz, Przemyslaw & Dziubak, Emilia. Hug Me Please. 2017. (ENG.). 32p. (J). (gr. -1-k). 17.95 ***(978-1-68297-142-0(2)***, Words & Pictures) Quarto Publishing Group UK GBR. Dist: Hachette Bk. Group.
Weidknecht, Lisa. E Is for Emotions. 2009. 56p. pap. 21.99 *(978-1-4343-9260-2(0))* AuthorHouse.
Werlin, Nancy. The Killer's Cousin. 2009. (ENG.). 240p. (YA). (gr. 7-18). 7.99 *(978-0-14-241373-9(9)*, Speak) Penguin Young Readers Group.
West, Kasie. P. S. I Like You. 2016. (ENG.). 336p. (YA). (gr. 7). 17.99 *(978-0-545-85097-1(5))* Scholastic, Inc.
West, Tracey. Forget This! RH Disney Staff, illus. 2015. (Stepping Stone Book Ser.). (ENG.). 128p. (J). (gr. 1-4). 5.99 *(978-0-7364-3430-0(5)*, RH/Disney) Random Hse. Children's Bks.
—Sadness Saves the Day! RH Disney Staff, illus. 2016. (Disney Chapters Ser.). (ENG.). 128p. (J). (gr. 1-4). 5.99 *(978-0-7364-3637-3(5)*, RH/Disney) Random Hse. Children's Bks.
—What Should Riley Do? Random House Disney Staff, illus. 2015. (Stepping Stone Book Ser.). (ENG.). 128p. (J). (gr. 1-4). lib. bdg. 12.99 *(978-0-7364-8242-4(3)*, RH/Disney) Random Hse. Children's Bks.
Weston Woods Staff, creator. Crow Boy. 2011. 18.95 *(978-0-545-23383-5(6))*; 29.95 *(978-0-545-23382-8(8))*; 38.75 *(978-0-545-23384-2(4))* Weston Woods Studios, Inc.
Whitaker, Kenneth. Hood-Hearted Child, Life as a Nobody: Based on a True Story, 1 vol. 2009. 48p. pap. 16.95 *(978-1-61546-369-5(0))* America Star Bks.
Whitfield, Peter. No Presents Please. Bevington, Nancy, illus. 2005. (Zen Tails Ser.). (ENG.). 28p. (J). (gr. -1-3). 15.95 *(978-1-894965-23-1(X))* Simply Read Bks. CAN. Dist: Ingram Publisher Services.
Whittemore, Jo. Vanessa's Design Dilemma. 2017. (Confidentially Yours Ser.: 6). 288p. (J). (gr. 3-7). pap. 6.99 *(978-0-06-235903-2(7))* HarperCollins Pubs.
Wilcut-Bledsoe, Robin. The Imagination of Hollie Mason. 2008. 88p. pap. 19.95 *(978-1-60703-804-7(8))* America Star Bks.
Willems, Mo. My Friend Is Sad. Willems, Mo, illus. 2007. (Elephant & Piggie Book Ser.). (ENG., Illus.). 64p. (J). (gr. -1-k). 9.99 *(978-1-4231-0297-7(5))* Hyperion Pr.
—The Pigeon Has Feelings, Too! Willems, Mo, illus. 2005. (Pigeon Ser.). (ENG., Illus.). 12p. (J). (gr. -1-k). 6.99 *(978-0-7868-3650-5(4))* Hyperion Pr.
Williams, Bonnie. Say Cheese, Teddy Rex! Gordon, John, illus. 2016. (Dino School Ser.). (J). (ENG.). 24p. (gr. -1-1). pap. 3.99 *(978-1-4814-6609-7(7))*; ***(978-1-5182-1896-5(2))*** Simon Spotlight. (Simon Spotlight).
Wilson, Essdale. Growing up on the cul de Sac. 2003. 156p. (YA). pap. 11.95 *(978-0-595-26945-7(1))* iUniverse, Inc.
Wilson, Jacqueline. Kiss. 2010. (ENG., Illus.). 256p. (YA). (gr. 7-12). 32.99 *(978-1-59643-242-0(X)*, 9781596432420) Roaring Brook Pr.
Wilson, John. Adrift in Time. 2005. (ENG., Illus.). 136p. (J). pap. 9.95 *(978-1-55380-007-1(9))* Ronsdale Pr. CAN. Dist: Literary Pr. Group of Canada.
Wilson, Martin. We Now Return to Regular Life. 2017. (ENG.). 384p. (YA). (gr. 9). 17.99 ***(978-0-7352-2782-8(9)***, Dial Bks) Penguin Young Readers Group.
Wilson, Patty Ann. Where Do I Belong? 2010. 20p. 12.49 *(978-1-4520-4339-5(0))* AuthorHouse.
Wilson, Shannan. The Littlest Peanut: A Baby Book for the Teeny Tiny Ones. Cuniff, Joe, illus. 2011. 32p. 16.95 *(978-1-61254-023-8(6))* Brown Books Publishing Group.
Wise, Rachel. Texting 1, 2, 3. 2013. (Dear Know-It-All Ser.: 8). (ENG., Illus.). 160p. (J). (gr. 3-7). 16.99 *(978-1-4424-7520-5(X))*; pap. 6.99 *(978-1-4424-7519-9(6))* Simon Spotlight. (Simon Spotlight).
Witek, Jo. All My Treasures: A Book of Joy. Roussey, Christine, illus. 2016. (Growing Hearts Ser.). (ENG.). 32p. (J). (gr. -1 — 1). bds. 16.95 *(978-1-4197-2204-2(2)*, Abrams Appleseed) Abrams, Inc.
—In My Heart: A Book of Feelings. Roussey, Christine, illus. 2014. (Growing Hearts Ser.). (ENG.). 32p. (J). (gr. -1 — 1). 16.95 *(978-1-4197-1310-1(8)*, Abrams Appleseed) Abrams, Inc.
Withrow, Sarah. The Black Sunshine of Goody Pryne, 1 vol. (ENG.). 184p. pap. 9.95 *(978-0-88899-577-3(6))* Groundwood Bks. CAN. Dist: Publishers Group West (PGW).
Wolford, Margo. The Moinks Collection Presents: Sami's Big Day. 2009. (Illus.). 39p. (J). pap. 18.95 *(978-1-4327-3980-5(8))* Outskirts Pr., Inc.
Wolitzer, Meg. Belzhar. (ENG.). 272p. (YA). (gr. 9). 2015. 10.99 *(978-0-14-242629-6(6)*, Speak) 2014. 17.99 *(978-0-525-42305-8(2)*, Dutton Books for Young Readers) Penguin Young Readers Group.
Wood, Douglas. Where the Sunrise Begins. Popp, K. Wendy, illus. 2010. (ENG.). 32p. (J). (gr. -1-3). 17.99 *(978-0-689-86172-7(9)*, Simon & Schuster Bks. For Young Readers) Simon & Schuster Bks. For Young Readers.
Woodell, Dolly M. Little Old Woman with a Wart on Her Nose. 2013. 16p. pap. 7.95 *(978-1-4908-1015-7(3)*, WestBow Pr.) Author Solutions, Inc.
Woolston, Blythe. The Freak Observer. 2010. (Carolrhoda YA Ser.). (ENG.). 208p. (YA). (gr. 9-12). 16.95 *(978-0-7613-6212-8(6)*, Carolrhoda Lab™) Lerner Publishing Group.
Wray, Patricia. Sasha, the Dreamer, 1 vol. 2009. 192p. pap. 24.95 *(978-1-60672-885-7(7))* PublishAmerica, Inc.
Wyatt, Chris 'Doc'. Bravest Warriors: The Great Core Caper, Vol.1. Howell, Corin, illus. 2014. (ENG.). 112p. (J). pap. 7.99 *(978-1-4215-7539-1(6))* Viz Media.
Wynne-Jones, Tim. Blink & Caution. (ENG., Illus.). 352p. (YA). (gr. 9). 2012. pap. 8.99 *(978-0-7636-5697-3(6))* 2011. 16.99 *(978-0-7636-3983-9(4))* Candlewick Pr.
Yabuki, Akiko. Ishi: Simple Tips from a Solid Friend. 2016. (ENG., Illus.). 40p. (J). (-k). 12.95 *(978-1-57687-816-3(3)*, powerHouse Bks.) powerHouse Cultural Entertainment, Inc.
Yamada, Kobi. What Do You Do with a Problem? Besom, Mae, illus. 2016. (ENG.). 36p. (J). (gr. -1-3). 16.95 *(978-1-943200-00-9(9))* Compendium, Inc., Publishing & Communications.
Yin, Leah. Zona & the Big Buzzzy Secret. Yin, Leah, illus. 2013. (Illus.). 54p. *(978-0-9918396-0-5(9))* Leah Yin Studio.
Yolen, Jane. Como Dicen Estoy Enojado los Dinosaurios? Teague, Mark, illus. 2014. (SPA.). 40p. (J). (gr. -1-k). pap. 6.99 *(978-0-545-62780-1(X)*, Scholastic en Espanol) Scholastic, Inc.
—How Do Dinosaurs Say I'm Mad? Teague, Mark, illus. 2013. (How Do Dinosaurs... ? Ser.). (ENG.). 40p. (J). (gr. -1-k). 16.99 *(978-0-545-14315-8(2)*, Blue Sky Pr., The) Scholastic, Inc.
Young, Judy. The Lucky Star. Ellison, Chris, illus. 2008. (Tales of Young Americans Ser.). (ENG.). 32p. (J). (gr. 3-7). 17.95 *(978-1-58536-348-3(0))* Sleeping Bear Pr.
Young, Samantha. I Can't Wait. 2012. 12p. pap. 15.99 *(978-1-4772-6013-5(7))* AuthorHouse.
Young, Suzanne. The Adjustment. 2017. (Program Ser.: 5). (ENG., Illus.). 416p. (YA). (gr. 9). 17.99 *(978-1-4814-7132-9(5)*, Simon Pulse) Simon Pulse.
—All in Pieces. 2016. (ENG., Illus.). 272p. (YA). (gr. 9). 17.99 *(978-1-4814-1883-6(1)*, Simon Pulse) Simon Pulse.
Yvette, Sylvia. My Silly Imagination. 2012. 24p. (-18). pap. 15.99 *(978-1-4797-2966-1(3))* Xlibris Corp.
Zindel, Paul. The Pigman. 2005. (ENG., Illus.). 224p. (YA). (gr. 9-18). pap. 8.99 *(978-0-06-075735-9(3)*, HarperTeen) HarperCollins Pubs.
—The Pigman. Date not set. (Scholastic Bookfiles Ser.). 64p. (J). pap. 4.99 *(978-0-439-53831-2(9))* Scholastic, Inc.

EMPERORS

see Kings, Queens, Rulers, etc.

EMPLOYEES—TRAINING OF

Henneberg, Susan. Money-Making Opportunities for Teens Who Like Working with Kids. 2013. (Make Money Now! Ser.). (Illus.). 80p. (YA). (gr. 7-12). lib. bdg. 33.25 *(978-1-4488-9385-0(2))* Rosen Publishing Group, Inc., The.

EMPLOYEES AND OFFICIALS

see Civil Service

see also names of countries, cities, etc. and organizations with the subdivision officials and employees, e.g. United States—Officials and Employees

EMPLOYEES' REPRESENTATION IN MANAGEMENT

see Management—Employee Participation

EMPLOYMENT DISCRIMINATION

see Discrimination in Employment

EMPLOYMENT OF WOMEN

see Women—Employment

EMUS

Bastakos, Matina. Emma Emu's Eager Environmental Endeavour: 'E' as in Earth. 2009. (Illus.). 40p. pap. 18.49 *(978-1-4490-3952-3(9))* AuthorHouse.
Murray, Julie. Emus, 1 vol. 2011. (Australian Animals Ser.). (ENG., Illus.). 32p. (J). (gr. 2-5). 28.50 *(978-1-61783-010-5(0))* ABDO Publishing Co.
Silverman, Buffy. Can You Tell an Ostrich from an Emu. 2012. (Animal Look-Alikes Ser.). (Illus.). 32p. (J). (gr. k-2). lib. bdg. 25.26 *(978-0-7613-6741-3(1)*, Lerner Pubns.) Lerner Publishing Group.
—Can You Tell an Ostrich from an Emu? 2012. (Lightning Bolt Books (tm) — Animal Look-Alikes Ser.). 32p. (gr. k-2). (ENG.). pap. 7.95 *(978-0-7613-8555-4(X))*; pap. 45.32 *(978-0-7613-9258-3(0))* Lerner Publishing Group.

ENAMEL AND ENAMELING

Johnston, William R. The Fabergé Menagerie. rev. ed. 2003. (ENG., Illus.). 160p. 58.00 *(978-0-85667-563-8(6))* I. B. Tauris & Co., Ltd. GBR. Dist: Macmillan.

ENCHANTED FOREST (IMAGINARY PLACE: WREDE)—FICTION

Pearson, Kimberly Ann. Mystling Glen Book I: The Tale of A Prince. 2009. 207p. pap. 14.95 *(978-1-4327-4169-3(1))* Outskirts Pr., Inc.
Wrede, Patricia C. Calling on Dragons. unabr. ed. 2004. (Enchanted Forest Chronicles: Bk. 3). 244p. (J). (gr. 6-18). pap. 38.00 incl. audio *(978-0-8072-0792-5(6)*, LYA 347 SP, Listening Library) Random Hse. Audio Publishing Group.
—Talking to Dragons. unabr. ed. 2004. (Enchanted Forest Chronicles: Bk. 4). 255p. (J). (gr. 6-18). pap. 38.00 incl. audio *(978-0-8072-0983-7(X)*, S YA 385 SP, Listening Library) Random Hse. Audio Publishing Group.
Wrede, Patricia C. & Wrede, Patricia. Dealing with Dragons. 2015. (Enchanted Forest Chronicles Ser.: Bk. 1). (gr. 7-12). lib. bdg. 18.40 *(978-0-613-56300-0(X)*, Turtleback) Turtleback Bks.

ENCYCLOPEDIAS AND DICTIONARIES

Anderson, Jennifer Joline. Wikipedia: The Company & Its Founders, 1 vol. 2011. (Technology Pioneers Set 1 Ser.). (ENG., Illus.). 112p. (J). (gr. 6-12). lib. bdg. 35.64 *(978-1-61714-812-5(1))* ABDO Publishing Co.
Anon. The Great Men & Women That Shaped Our World - a Selection of Articles from a Classic Children's Encyclopedi. 2012. 504p. pap. 32.95 *(978-1-4474-6903-2(8))* Audubon Pr. & Christian Bk. Service.
Ash, Russell & Terry, Paul. Top 10 for Boys. 2nd ed. 2013. (ENG., Illus.). 320p. (J). (gr. 4-7). 24.95 *(978-1-77085-223-5(9)*, 9781770852235) Firefly Bks., Ltd.
Ashley, Susan. I Can Use a Dictionary. 2004. (I Can Do It! Ser.). (Illus.). 24p. (gr. k-3). lib. bdg. 21.00 *(978-0-8368-4326-2(6)*, Weekly Reader Leveled Readers) Stevens, Gareth Publishing LLLP.
AZ Books Staff. Discoveries & Inventions. Kazimirova, Karina, ed. 2012. (Encyclopedia with Flaps Ser.). (ENG.). 22p. (J). (gr. 1-3). bds. 13.95 *(978-1-61889-152-5(9))* AZ Bks. LLC.
Barbey, Dorine, et al. Creative Discoveries, 8 vols., Set. (Illus.). 640p. (J). lib. bdg. 191.60 *(978-0-88682-942-1(9))* Creative Co., The.
Basic Dictionary. (J). (gr. 3-6). pap. *(978-0-87548-626-0(6)*, 48-626) Open Court Publishing Co.
Bilingual Picture Dictionary [Capstone Sole Source]. 2010. (Bilingual Picture Dictionaries Ser.). 32p. lib. bdg. 155.94 *(978-1-4296-5847-8(9)*, Aplus Bks.) Capstone Press of Coughlan Cos.
Brooks, Felicity. Children's Encyclopedia. rev. ed. 2011. (First Encyclopedias Ser.). 320p. (J). ring bd. 15.99 *(978-0-7945-3027-3(3)*, Usborne) EDC Publishing.
Brooks, Felicity & Litchfield, J. The Usborne Picture Dictionary: A First Alphabetical Word Book. 2004. (Picture Dictionaries Ser.). (ENG., Illus.). 96p. (J). 16.95 *(978-0-7945-0176-1(1)*, Usborne) EDC Publishing.
Brooks, Felicity & Milbourne, Anna. The Usborne Internet-Linked Children's Encyclopedia. 2004. (First Encyclopedias Ser.). (ENG., Illus.). 320p. (J). 29.95 *(978-0-7945-0368-0(3)*, Usborne) EDC Publishing.
Bunting, Jane. My First Action Word Book: A Picture Dictionary of 1,000 First Words. (Illus.). 48p. (J). pap. 17.99 *(978-0-590-24897-6(9))* Scholastic, Inc.
Cabot, Paloma & Larousse Editors, eds. Larousse Children's Spanish Dictionary. 2005. (SPA & ENG., Illus.). 128p. (J). (gr. 5-7). 12.95 *(978-2-03-542099-2(7))* Larousse, Editions FRA. Dist: Houghton Mifflin Harcourt Publishing Co.
Callery, Sean, et al. Kingfisher Encyclopedia of Everything. 2017. (Kingfisher Encyclopedias Ser.). (ENG.). 320p. (J). pap. 16.99 *(978-0-7534-7355-9(0)*, 9780753473559, Kingfisher) Roaring Brook Pr.
Childrens Ocean Life Encyclopedia. 2008. (1st Encyclopedia Ser.). 224p. *(978-1-4075-1309-6(5))* Parragon, Inc.
Children's Picture Encyclopedia. (Children's Reference Ser.). 224p. *(978-1-4054-9459-5(X))*; 2008. 256p. *(978-1-4075-3205-9(7))* Parragon, Inc.
Children's Planet Earth Encyclopedia. 2008. (1st Encyclopedia Ser.). 224p. *(978-1-4075-1310-2(9))* Parragon, Inc.
Children's Weather Encyclopedia. 2008. (Mini Children's Reference Ser.). 256p. *(978-1-4075-3206-6(5))* Parragon, Inc.
CJ Publishing Co. What Is Child Support? No. 3: 25 Definitions Your Children Want to Know About. 2008. (ENG., Illus.). 25p. (YA). (gr. 4-9). pap. *(978-0-9655777-0-0(8))* CJ Publishing Co.
Collins Dictionaries. Collins First School Dictionary. 2017. (Collins Primary Dictionaries Ser.). (ENG.). 176p. (J). (gr. 3-6). pap. 13.99 ***(978-0-00-820676-5(7))*** HarperCollins Pubs. Ltd. GBR. Dist: Independent Pubs. Group.
—Collins Junior Dictionary. 2017. (Collins Primary Dictionaries Ser.). (ENG.). 576p. (J). pap. 16.99 ***(978-0-00-820675-8(9))*** HarperCollins Pubs. Ltd. GBR. Dist: Independent Pubs. Group.
Collins Dictionaries Staff. Collins Very First Irish Dictionary. 2nd rev. ed. 2016. (GLE & ENG., Illus.). 80p. (J). (gr. 1-3). pap. 9.99 *(978-0-00-815029-7(X))* HarperCollins Pubs. Ltd. GBR. Dist: Independent Pubs. Group.
Collins Easy Learning Staff. ABC Dictionary Ages 3 to 4. 2017. (ENG., Illus.). 64p. (J). (— 1). pap. 9.99 ***(978-0-00-820946-9(4))*** HarperCollins Pubs. Ltd. GBR. Dist: Independent Pubs. Group.
Cultures of the Past, 4 bks., Set, Group 3. (J). (gr. 5-18). lib. bdg. 114.00 *(978-0-7614-0268-8(3)*, Benchmark Bks.) Marshall Cavendish Corp.
Cultures of the Past - Group 4, 4 bks., Set. (Illus.). 80p. (J). (gr. 5-18). lib. bdg. 119.71 *(978-0-7614-0300-5(0)*, Benchmark Bks.) Marshall Cavendish Corp.
Daly, Kathleen N. Greek & Roman Mythology A to Z. 3rd rev. ed. 2009. (Mythology A to Z Ser.). (Illus.). 176p. (gr. 5-8). 45.00 *(978-1-60413-412-4(7)*, Chelsea Hse.) Facts On File, Inc.
—Norse Mythology A to Z, Third Edition. 3rd rev. ed. 2009. (Mythology A to Z Ser.). (Illus.). 144p. (gr. 5-8). 45.00 *(978-1-60413-411-7(9)*, Chelsea Hse.) Facts On File, Inc.
del Pino, Brittany Moya, et al. Awesome 8 Extreme. 2017. (ENG., Illus.). 112p. (J). (gr. 3-7). pap. 12.99 *(978-1-4263-2738-4(2)*, National Geographic Children's Bks.) National Geographic Society.
Diccionario Enciclopedico, 15 vols., Set. (SPA.). (YA). (gr. 7-18). 199.00 *(978-0-8347-5189-7(5))* Encyclopaedia Britannica, Inc.
Diccionario Escolar Infantil.Tr. of Young Student's Dictionary. (SPA., Illus.). 208p. (J). (gr. 3-5). *(978-958-04-0704-1(5)*, NR4073) Norma S.A. COL. Dist: Distribuidora Norma, Inc.
Disney Book Group Staff. Junior Encyclopedia of Animated Characters. Disney Storybook Art Team, illus. 2014. (ENG.). 144p. (J). (gr. 1-3). 12.99 *(978-1-4231-8914-5(0))* Disney Pr.
Dorling Kindersley Publishing Staff. First Children's Dictionary. 2016. (ENG., Illus.). 256p. (J). (gr. 2-5). 16.99 *(978-1-4654-5467-6(5)*, DK Children) Dorling Kindersley Publishing, Inc.
—First Earth Encyclopedia. 2010. (ENG.). 128p. (J). (gr. k-4). 16.99 *(978-0-7566-7139-6(6)*, DK Children) Dorling Kindersley Publishing, Inc.
—First Encyclopedia. 2nd ed. 2015. (ENG., Illus.). 168p. (J). (gr. 2-5). 16.99 *(978-1-4654-3556-9(5)*, DK Children) Dorling Kindersley Publishing, Inc.
—Muppets Character Encyclopedia. 2014. (ENG.). 200p. (J). (gr. 2-5). 16.99 *(978-1-4654-1748-0(6)*, DK Children) Dorling Kindersley Publishing, Inc.

—My First Encyclopedia. 2013. (ENG.). 80p. (J). (gr. k-4). 15.99 *(978-1-4654-1425-0(8)*, DK Children) Dorling Kindersley Publishing, Inc.
—The New Children's Encyclopedia. 2013. (ENG.). 304p. (J). (gr. 1-4). pap. 19.99 *(978-1-4654-1235-5(2)*, DK Children) Dorling Kindersley Publishing, Inc.
—Picturepedia. 2015. (ENG., Illus.). 360p. (J). (gr. 3-7). 29.99 *(978-1-4654-3828-7(9)*, DK Children) Dorling Kindersley Publishing, Inc.
—Super Human Encyclopedia. 2014. (ENG., Illus.). 208p. (J). (gr. 3-7). 24.99 *(978-1-4654-2445-7(8)*, DK Children) Dorling Kindersley Publishing, Inc.
Dorling Kindersley Publishing Staff & Bingham, Caroline. My Encyclopedia of Very Important Things. 2016. (ENG., Illus.). 224p. (J). ***(978-0-241-22493-9(4))*** Dorling Kindersley Publishing, Inc.
Dorling Kindersley Publishing Staff & Wallace, Daniel. Spider-Man Character Encyclopedia. 2014. (ENG.). 208p. (J). (gr. 2-5). 16.99 *(978-1-4654-1574-5(2)*, DK Children) Dorling Kindersley Publishing, Inc.
Elliot, Jane & King, Colin. Children's Encyclopedia. 2004. (Encyclopedias Ser.). (ENG., Illus.). 1p. (J). 7.95 *(978-0-7945-0006-1(4)*, Usborne) EDC Publishing.
Elliot, Jane & King, Colin, eds. Children's Encyclopedia. 2004. (Usborne Encyclopedia Ser.). (Illus.). 135p. (J). (gr. 3-7). pap. 14.95 *(978-0-7460-3922-9(0))* EDC Publishing.
Elliott, Jane & King, Colin. Children's Encyclopedia. 2004. (Encyclopedias Ser.). (Illus.). 135p. (J). (gr. 4-7). lib. bdg. 22.95 *(978-1-58086-258-5(6))* EDC Publishing.
Encyclopaedia Britannica. Britannica Student Encyclopedia 2012, 16 vols. 2012. (Illus.). 2900p. 399.00 *(978-1-61535-519-8(7))* Encyclopaedia Britannica, Inc.
Encyclopaedia Britannica, Inc. Staff, compiled by. Encyclopaedia Britannica Children's Learning Suite 2007. 2007. (gr. 7-14). DVD, cd-rom 29.95 *(978-1-59339-538-4(8))* Encyclopaedia Britannica, Inc.
—My First Britannica, 13 vols. 2008. (gr. 7-11). 299.00 *(978-1-59339-567-4(1))* Encyclopaedia Britannica, Inc.
—My First Britannica: Birds, Insects, Reptiles, & Aquatic Life. 2008. (gr. 7-12). *(978-1-59339-411-0(X))* Encyclopaedia Britannica, Inc.
—My First Britannica: Mammals. 2008. (gr. 7-12). *(978-1-59339-412-7(8))* Encyclopaedia Britannica, Inc.
—My First Britannica: Reference Guide & Index. 2008. (gr. 7-12). *(978-1-59339-413-4(6))* Encyclopaedia Britannica, Inc.
—My First Britannica Set: A Captivating 13-Volume Reference Set for Children 6-11 Years, 13 vols. 2003. (Illus.). 1288p. 299.00 *(978-1-59339-048-8(3))* Encyclopaedia Britannica, Inc.
Encyclopaedia Britannica Publishers. Britannica Student Encyclopedia, 16 vols., Set. 2007. (Illus.). 2900p. (J). (gr. 3-6). *(978-1-59339-300-7(8))* Encyclopaedia Britannica, Inc.
Encyclopaedia Britannica Publishers, Inc. Staff. Britannica Illustrated Science Library, 16 vols., Set. 2008. (Illus.). 1664p. (YA). (gr. 5-8). 425.00 *(978-1-59339-382-3(2))* Encyclopaedia Britannica, Inc.
—My First Britannica. 2008. 1288p. (YA). 299.00 *(978-1-59339-372-4(5))* Encyclopaedia Britannica, Inc.
Encyclopaedia Britannica Publishers, Inc. Staff, contrib. by. My First Britannica: An Engaging 13-Volume Thematic Reference Set for Grades 2-5, 13 vols. 2004. (ENG., Illus.). 1p. (J). (gr. 2-5). 249.00 net. *(978-1-59339-017-4(3)*, 046501-EN-REF) Encyclopaedia Britannica, Inc.
Farndon, John. A History of Civilization Illustrated History Encyclopedia: The Great Landmarks in the Development of Mankind. 2006. (Illus.). 256p. (gr. 7-10). reprint ed. pap. 22.00 *(978-1-4223-5514-5(4))* DIANE Publishing Co.
First Encyclopedia. 2003. (Illus.). 128p. (J). 7.98 *(978-1-4054-0520-1(1))* Parragon, Inc.
First Fun Reference Library, 5 vols. (Illus.). 128p. (J). (gr. 3-18). lib. bdg. *(978-1-59084-553-0(6))* Mason Crest.
Fleming, Denise. The Everything Book. Fleming, Denise, illus. rev. ed. 2004. (ENG., Illus.). 26p. (J). (— 1). bds. 7.95 *(978-0-8050-7709-4(X)*, 9780805077094, Holt, Henry & Co. Bks. For Young Readers) Holt, Henry & Co.
Frost, Adam. The Awesome Book of Awesomeness. Bramall, Dan, illus. 2015. (ENG.). 112p. (J). (gr. 2-4). pap. 9.99 *(978-1-61963-793-1(6)*, 9781619637931, Bloomsbury USA Childrens) Bloomsbury Publishing USA.
Gale Editors & Corporate Contributor Staff, eds. Junior Worldmark Encyclopedia of World Cultures, 9 vols., 9 Volume Set. 2nd ed. 2011. (ENG.). 2000p. lib. bdg. 742.00 *(978-1-4144-8671-0(5)*, UXL) Cengage Gale.
Gall, Susan B., ed. Junior Worldmark Encyclopedia of Physical Geography, 5 vols. 2003. (Illus.). (J). *(978-0-7876-6266-0(6))*; *(978-0-7876-6267-7(4))*; *(978-0-7876-6268-4(2))*; *(978-0-7876-6269-1(0))*; *(978-0-7876-6633-0(5))* Cengage Gale. (UXL).
Gall, Timothy L. & Gall, Susan B. Junior Worldmark Encyclopedia of the States. 5th ed. 2007. (J). *(978-1-4144-1107-1(3))*; *(978-1-4144-1108-8(1))*; *(978-1-4144-1110-1(3))*; *(978-1-4144-1109-5(X))* Cengage Gale.
Gifford, Clive. How the World Works: Know It All, from How the Sun Shines to How the Pyramids Were Built. 2013. (ENG., Illus.). 160p. (J). (gr. 3-7). 18.99 *(978-0-7534-7119-7(1)*, 9780753471197, Kingfisher) Roaring Brook Pr.
Goodman, Marlene. Let's Learn Hebrew Picture Dictionary. 2003. (ENG & HEB., Illus.). 80p. 13.00 *(978-0-07-140825-7(8)*, 0071408258) McGraw-Hill Cos., The.
—Let's Learn Italian Picture Dictionary. 2003. (ENG & ITA., Illus.). 80p. 13.00 *(978-0-07-140826-4(6)*, 0071408266) McGraw-Hill Education.
—Let's Learn Japanese Picture Dictionary. 2003. (JPN & ENG., Illus.). 80p. 13.00 *(978-0-07-140827-1(4)*, 0071408274) McGraw-Hill Cos., The.
Grolier Educational Staff, contrib. by. Grolier Student Encyclopedia, 17 vols. 2003. (Illus.). (J). 269.00 *(978-0-7172-5865-9(3)*, Grolier) Scholastic Library Publishing.
Hasan, Heather. Wikipedia, 3.5 Million Articles & Counting: Using & Assessing the People's Encyclopedia. 2011. (Digital & Information Literacy Ser.). (ENG.). 48p. (YA). (gr. 5-8). pap. 11.75 *(978-1-4488-5620-6(5))*; lib. bdg. 29.25 *(978-1-4488-5557-5(8))* Rosen Publishing Group, Inc., The. (Rosen Reference).
Hicks, Kelli L., ed. Complete History of Our Presidents Encyclopedia, 14 vols., Set. 2014. (ENG., Illus.). 896p. (gr. 3-8). lib. bdg. 570.00 *(978-1-60694-293-2(X))* Rourke Educational Media.
Hippocrene Books Staff. Children's Illustrated Czech Dictionary: English-Czech/Czech-English. 2003. (Hippocrene Children's Illustrated Foreign Language Dictionaries Ser.). (ENG., Illus.). 96p. pap. 11.95 *(978-0-7818-0987-0(8))* Hippocrene Bks., Inc.
Hippocrene Books Staff, ed. Children's Illustrated Korean Dictionary: English-Korean/Korean-English. 2006. (ENG & KOR.). 104p. pap. 14.95 *(978-0-7818-1132-3(5))* Hippocrene Bks., Inc.
Hirsch, E. D., Jr., et al. The New First Dictionary of Cultural Literacy: What Your Child Needs to Know. 3rd rev. ed. 2004. (ENG., Illus.). 320p. pap. 17.99 *(978-0-618-40853-5(3))* Houghton Mifflin Harcourt Publishing Co.
How Do I Use a Dictionary? 2014. (Research Tools You Can Use Ser.). 32p. (J). (gr. 3-6). 23.45 *(978-1-62275-344-4(5))* Rosen Publishing Group, Inc., The.
Illustrated Family Encyclopedia. 2004. (YA). 69.99 *(978-0-9753127-0-4(7))* Family Bks. at Home.
Der Jugend Brockhaus, 3 vols., Set. 3rd rev. ed. (GER., Illus.). (YA). (gr. 5-11). *(978-3-7653-2303-4(9))* Brockhaus, F. A., GmbH DEU. Dist: International Bk. Import Service, Inc.
Junior Worldmark Encyclopedia of Physical Geography, 5 vols. 2003. (ENG., Illus.). 832p. (J). 458.00 *(978-0-7876-6265-3(8)*, UXL) Cengage Gale.
Juventud Staff & Martin, A - Weissmann. Diccionario Portugues - Espanol. (SPA.). 524p. (J). 29.95 *(978-84-261-2888-1(2))* Juventud, Editorial ESP. Dist: AIMS International Bks., Inc.
Kalman, Bobbie. A Visual Dictionary of a Colonial Community. 2007. (Crabtree Visual Dictionaries Ser.). (ENG., Illus.). 32p. (J). (gr. 4-7). lib. bdg. *(978-0-7787-3502-1(8))* Crabtree Publishing Co.
Kamous Janna Il Hawonat.Tr. of Dictionary of the Zoo. (ARA., Illus.). 37p. (J). pap. 5.50 *(978-0-86685-355-2(3)*, LDL2804) Librairie du Liban Pubns. FRA. Dist: International Bk. Ctr., Inc.
Khatib, Ahmed. Al Mousou'a al Ilmiya al Mouysarah: Illustrated Children's Encyclopedia. (ARA., Illus.). 48p. (J). 30.00 *(978-0-86685-351-4(0)*, LDL1333) International Bk. Ctr., Inc.
Kingfisher Editors. Kingfisher First Encyclopedia. 3rd ed. 2011. (Kingfisher Encyclopedias Ser.). (ENG., Illus.). 160p. (J). (gr. k-3). pap. 10.99 *(978-0-7534-6587-5(6)*, 9780753465875, Kingfisher) Roaring Brook Pr.
—The Kingfisher History Encyclopedia. 3rd ed. 2012. (Kingfisher Encyclopedias Ser.). (ENG., Illus.). 496p. (J). (gr. 4-9). 32.99 *(978-0-7534-6875-3(1)*, 9780753468753, Kingfisher) Roaring Brook Pr.
Kralovansky, Susan. What Would You Do with a Dictionary?, 1 vol. 2013. (Library Resources Ser.). (ENG.). 32p. (J). (gr. k-4). lib. bdg. 27.07 *(978-1-61783-604-6(4)*, Super SandCastle) ABDO Publishing Co.
—What Would You Do with a Thesaurus?, 1 vol. 2013. (Library Resources Ser.). (ENG.). 32p. (J). (gr. k-4). lib. bdg. 27.07 *(978-1-61783-605-3(2)*, Super SandCastle) ABDO Publishing Co.
—What Would You Do with an Encyclopedia?, 1 vol. 2013. (Library Resources Ser.). (ENG.). 32p. (J). (gr. k-4). lib. bdg. 27.07 *(978-1-61783-607-7(9)*, Super SandCastle) ABDO Publishing Co.
Kudela, Katy R. My First Book of Korean Words. Translations.com Staff, tr. 2011. (Bilingual Picture Dictionaries Ser.). (MUL.). 32p. (gr. 1-2). pap. 47.70 *(978-1-4296-6166-9(6)*, Aplus Bks.) Capstone Press of Coughlan Cos.
Levy, Joel. Phobiapedia. 2011. (ENG.). 80p. (J). (gr. 3-7). pap. 8.99 *(978-0-545-34929-1(X)*, Scholastic Paperbacks) Scholastic, Inc.
Lisl. Dictionary with a Difference. 2009. 116p. pap. 31.99 *(978-1-4490-0125-4(4))* AuthorHouse.
Mackay, David. What in the World? Date not set. (Whizz Bang Bumper Bk.). (Illus.). 64p. (J). 129.15 *(978-0-582-19329-1(X))* Addison-Wesley Longman, Ltd. GBR. Dist: Trans-Atlantic Pubns., Inc.
Makishi, Cynthia. The Heinle Picture Dictionary for Children - Monkey Puppet. 2007. (ENG.). (C). 19.95 *(978-1-4240-1834-5(X))* Cengage Heinle.
Martin, Robert, Jr. Vietnamese Children's Picture Dictionary: English-Vietnamese/Vietnamese-English. Voltaggio, Nicholas, illus. 2006. (ENG & VIE.). 112p. (J). (gr. 3-7). pap. 14.95 *(978-0-7818-1133-0(3))* Hippocrene Bks., Inc.
Masoff, Joy. Oh, Yikes! History's Grossest, Wackiest Moments. Sirrell, Terry, illus. 2006. (ENG.). 320p. (J). (gr. 3-7). pap. 14.95 *(978-0-7611-3684-2(3)*, 13684) Workman Publishing Co., Inc.
—Oh, Yuck! The Encyclopedia of Everything Nasty. (ENG., Illus.). 1p. (J). pap. 119.60 *(978-0-7611-2529-7(9)*, 22529) Workman Publishing Co., Inc.
McDonald, Megan. Stink-O-Pedia. 2009. (Stink Ser.). lib. bdg. 16.00 *(978-0-606-06752-2(3)*, Turtleback) Turtleback Bks.
—Stink-O-Pedia: Volume 1 Super Stink-Y Stuff from A to Zzzz, 1 vol. Reynolds, Peter H., illus. 2012. (Stink Ser.: No. 2). (ENG.). 144p. (J). (gr. 2-5). 24.21 *(978-1-59961-195-2(3))* Spotlight.
—Stink-O-Pedia: Volume 2 More Stink-Y Stuff from A to Z, 1 vol. Reynolds, Peter H., illus. 2012. (Stink Ser.: No. 2). (ENG.). 144p. (J). (gr. 2-5). 24.21 *(978-1-59961-196-9(1))* Spotlight.
Merriam-Webster, Inc. Staff, ed. Merriam-Webster's Notebook Thesaurus. 2004. (ENG.). 96p. (gr. 5-7). pap. 4.95 *(978-0-87779-671-8(8)*, MER-671) Merriam-Webster, Inc.
Meyer, Susan. Jimmy Wales & Wikipedia. 2012. (Internet Biographies Ser.). (ENG.). 128p. (YA). (gr. 7-12). lib. bdg. 34.60 *(978-1-4488-6912-1(9))* Rosen Publishing Group, Inc., The.
Milet Publishing Staff. Clothes. 2014. (My First Bilingual Book Ser.). (Illus.). 20p. (J). (— 1). (SPA & ENG.). bds. 7.99 *(978-1-84059-870-4(0))*; (ENG & KOR., bds. 7.99 *(978-1-84059-865-0(4))* Milet Publishing.
—Clothes - My First Bilingual Book. 2014. (My First Bilingual Book Ser.). (Illus.). 20p. (J). (— 1). (ENG & ITA.). bds. 7.99 *(978-1-84059-864-3(6))*; (POR & ENG., bds. 7.99 *(978-1-84059-867-4(0))*; (ENG & CHI., bds. 7.99 *(978-1-84059-860-5(3))*; (ENG & VIE., bds. 7.99 *(978-1-84059-873-5(5))* Milet Publishing.
—Colors. 2010. (My First Bilingual Book Ser.). (SPA & ENG., Illus.). 24p. (J). (gr. k — 1). bds. 7.99 *(978-1-84059-539-0(6))* Milet Publishing.
—Colours - My First Bilingual Book. 2010. (My First Bilingual Book Ser.). (ENG & POL., Illus.). 24p. (J). (gr. k — 1). bds. 8.99 *(978-1-84059-538-3(8))*; bds. 8.99 *(978-1-84059-536-9(1))*; bds. 8.99 *(978-1-84059-537-6(X))* Milet Publishing.
—My First Bilingual Book - Clothes. 2014. (My First Bilingual Book Ser.). (Illus.). 20p. (J). (— 1). (ENG & SOM.). bds. 7.99 *(978-1-84059-869-8(7))*; (ENG & GER., bds. 7.99 *(978-1-84059-863-6(8))*; (ENG & RUS., bds. 7.99 *(978-1-84059-868-1(9))*; (FRE & ENG., bds. 7.99 *(978-1-84059-862-9(X))*; (ENG & TUR., bds. 7.99 *(978-1-84059-871-1(9))*; (ENG & URD., bds. 7.99 *(978-1-84059-872-8(7))*; (ENG & ARA., bds. 7.99 *(978-1-84059-858-2(1))*; (ENG, POL & POR., bds. 7.99 *(978-1-84059-866-7(2))*; (ENG & BEN., bds. 7.99 *(978-1-84059-859-9(X))*; (ENG & PER., bds. 7.99 *(978-1-84059-861-2(1))* Milet Publishing.
—My First Bilingual Book - Colours. 2010. (My First Bilingual Book Ser.). (Illus.). 24p. (J). (gr. k — 1). (FRE & ENG.). bds. 8.99 *(978-1-84059-535-2(3))*; (ENG & TUR., bds. 7.99 *(978-1-84059-540-6(X))* Milet Publishing.
—My First Bilingual Book - Numbers. 2010. (My First Bilingual Book Ser.). (Illus.). 24p. (J). (gr. k — 1). (ENG & GER.). bds. 7.99 *(978-1-84059-542-0(6))*; (SPA & ENG., bds. 8.99 *(978-1-84059-545-1(0))*; (ENG & TUR., bds. 7.99 *(978-1-84059-546-8(9))* Milet Publishing.
—My First Bilingual Book - Plants. 2014. (My First Bilingual Book Ser.). (Illus.). 20p. (J). (— 1). (POR & ENG.). bds. 7.99 *(978-1-84059-883-4(2))*; (ENG & TUR., bds. 7.99 *(978-1-84059-887-2(5))*; (ENG & SOM., bds. 7.99 *(978-1-84059-885-8(9))*; (ENG & ARA., bds. 7.99 *(978-1-84059-874-2(3))*; (ENG & CHI., bds. 7.99 *(978-1-84059-876-6(X))* Milet Publishing.
—My First Bilingual Book - Plants (English-Farsi) 2014. (My First Bilingual Book Ser.). (ENG & PER., Illus.). 20p. (J). (— 1). bds. 7.99 *(978-1-84059-877-3(8))* Milet Publishing.
—My First Bilingual Book - Plants (English-Korean) 2014. (My First Bilingual Book Ser.). (ENG & KOR., Illus.). 20p. (J). (— 1). bds. 7.99 *(978-1-84059-881-0(6))* Milet Publishing.
—My First Bilingual Book - School. 2014. (My First Bilingual Book Ser.). (Illus.). 20p. (J). (— 1). (ENG & BEN.). bds. 7.99 *(978-1-84059-891-9(3))*; (POR & ENG., bds. 7.99 *(978-1-84059-899-5(9))*; (FRE & ENG., bds. 7.99 *(978-1-84059-894-0(8))*; (ENG & VIE., bds. 7.99 *(978-1-84059-905-3(7))*; (ENG & TUR., bds. 7.99 *(978-1-84059-903-9(0))*; (ENG & CHI., bds. 7.99 *(978-1-84059-892-6(1))*; (ENG & GER., bds. 7.99 *(978-1-84059-895-7(6))* Milet Publishing.
—My First Bilingual Book - School (English-Korean) 2014. (My First Bilingual Book Ser.). (ENG & KOR., Illus.). 20p. (J). (— 1). bds. 7.99 *(978-1-84059-897-1(2))* Milet Publishing.
—My First Bilingual Book - School (English-Somali) 2014. (My First Bilingual Book Ser.). (ENG & SOM., Illus.). 20p. (J). (— 1). bds. 7.99 *(978-1-84059-901-5(4))* Milet Publishing.
—My First Bilingual Book - Tools. 2014. (My First Bilingual Book Ser.). (Illus.). 20p. (J). (— 1). (ENG & BEN.). bds. 7.99 *(978-1-84059-907-7(3))*; (ENG & URD., bds. 7.99 *(978-1-84059-920-6(0))*; (ENG, POL & POR., bds. 7.99 *(978-1-84059-914-5(6))*; (ENG & GER., bds. 7.99 *(978-1-84059-911-4(1))*; (SPA & ENG., bds. 7.99 *(978-1-84059-918-3(9))*; (ENG & ARA., bds. 7.99 *(978-1-84059-906-0(5))*; (ENG & TUR., bds. 7.99 *(978-1-84059-919-0(7))*; (ENG & RUS., bds. 7.99 *(978-1-84059-916-9(2))* Milet Publishing.
—My First Bilingual Book - Tools - English. 2014. (My First Bilingual Book Ser.). (ENG & VIE., Illus.). 20p. (J). (— 1). bds. 7.99 *(978-1-84059-921-3(9))* Milet Publishing.
—My First Bilingual Book - Tools - Ferramentas. 2014. (My First Bilingual Book Ser.). (POR & ENG., Illus.). 20p. (J). (— 1). bds. 7.99 *(978-1-84059-915-2(4))* Milet Publishing.
—My First Bilingual Book - Tools (English-Somali) 2014. (My First Bilingual Book Ser.). (ENG & SOM., Illus.). 20p. (J). (— 1). bds. 7.99 *(978-1-84059-917-6(0))* Milet Publishing.
—My First Bilingual Book - Vehicles. 2014. (My First Bilingual Book Ser.). (ENG & CHI., Illus.). 20p. (J). (— 1). bds. 7.99 *(978-1-84059-924-4(3))*; bds. 7.99 *(978-1-84059-935-0(9))*; bds. 7.99 *(978-1-84059-925-1(1))*; bds. 7.99 *(978-1-84059-929-9(4))*; bds. 7.99 *(978-1-84059-933-6(2))*; bds. 7.99 *(978-1-84059-937-4(5))* Milet Publishing.
—My First Bilingual Book - Vehicles (English-Russian) 2014. (My First Bilingual Book Ser.). (ENG & RUS., Illus.). 20p. (J). (— 1). bds. 7.99 *(978-1-84059-932-9(4))* Milet Publishing.
—Numbers - My First Bilingual Book. 2010. (My First Bilingual Book Ser.). (Illus.). 24p. (J). (gr. k — 1). (ENG & ITA.). bds. 7.99 *(978-1-84059-543-7(4))*; (FRE & ENG., bds. 7.99 *(978-1-84059-541-3(8))*; (ENG & POL., bds. 8.99 *(978-1-84059-544-4(2))* Milet Publishing.
—Plants - My First Bilingual Book. 2014. (My First Bilingual Book Ser.). (Illus.). 20p. (J). (— 1). (ENG & RUS.). bds. 7.99 *(978-1-84059-884-1(0))*; (FRE & ENG., bds. 7.99 *(978-1-84059-878-0(6))*; (ENG & ITA., bds. 7.99 *(978-1-84059-880-3(8))*; (ENG & BEN., bds. 7.99 *(978-1-84059-875-9(1))*; (ENG & URD., bds. 7.99 *(978-1-84059-888-9(3))*; (ENG, POL & POR., bds. 7.99 *(978-1-84059-882-7(4))*; (ENG & VIE., bds. 7.99 *(978-1-84059-889-6(1))*; (SPA & ENG., bds. 7.99 *(978-1-84059-886-5(7))* Milet Publishing.
—School. 2014. (My First Bilingual Book Ser.). (ENG & ITA., Illus.). 20p. (J). (— 1). bds. 7.99 *(978-1-84059-896-4(4))* Milet Publishing.
—School - My First Bilingual Book. 2014. (My First Bilingual Book Ser.). (Illus.). 20p. (J). (— 1). (ENG & ARA.). bds. 7.99 *(978-1-84059-890-2(5))*; (ENG & URD., bds. 7.99 *(978-1-84059-904-6(9))*; (ENG & RUS., bds. 7.99 *(978-1-84059-900-8(6))*; (SPA & ENG., bds. 7.99 *(978-1-84059-902-2(2))* Milet Publishing.
—School - My First Bilingual Book (Szkola) 2014. (My First Bilingual Book Ser.). (ENG, POL & POR., Illus.). 20p. (J). (— 1). bds. 7.99 *(978-1-84059-898-8(0))* Milet Publishing.
—Tools. 2014. (My First Bilingual Book Ser.). (ENG & ITA., Illus.). 20p. (J). (— 1). bds. 7.99 *(978-1-84059-912-1(X))* Milet Publishing.
—Tools - My First Bilingual Book. 2014. (My First Bilingual Book Ser.). (ENG & CHI., Illus.). 20p. (J). (— 1). bds. 7.99 *(978-1-84059-908-4(1))*; bds. 7.99 *(978-1-84059-909-1(X))*; bds. 7.99 *(978-1-84059-913-8(8))* Milet Publishing.
—Tools (English-French) 2014. (My First Bilingual Book Ser.). (FRE & ENG., Illus.). 20p. (J). (— 1). bds. 7.99 *(978-1-84059-910-7(3))* Milet Publishing.
—Vehicles. 2014. (My First Bilingual Book Ser.). (Illus.). 20p. (J). (— 1). (SPA & ENG.). bds. 7.99 *(978-1-84059-934-3(0))*; (ENG & ITA., bds. 7.99 *(978-1-84059-928-2(6))*; (ENG & ARA., bds. 7.99 *(978-1-84059-922-0(7))* Milet Publishing.
—Vehicles - My First Bilingual Book. 2014. (My First Bilingual Book Ser.). (Illus.). 20p. (J). (— 1). (ENG, POL & POR.). bds. 7.99 *(978-1-84059-930-5(8))*; (ENG & BEN., bds. 7.99 *(978-1-84059-923-7(5))*; (ENG & URD., bds. 7.99 *(978-1-84059-936-7(7))*; (FRE & ENG., bds. 7.99 *(978-1-84059-926-8(X))*; (POR & ENG., bds. 7.99 *(978-1-84059-931-2(6))* Milet Publishing.
—Vehicles (English-German) 2014. (My First Bilingual Book Ser.). (ENG & GER., Illus.). 20p. (J). (— 1). bds. 7.99 *(978-1-84059-927-5(8))* Milet Publishing.
Mini My First Picture Dictiona. 2004. (Early Learning Ser.). 18p. (J). bds. 2.99 *(978-1-85854-832-6(2))* Brimax Books Ltd. GBR. Dist: Byeway Bks.
Mio Primo Dizionario Illustrato de Italia. (ITA., Illus.). pap. 9.95 *(978-88-8148-840-7(X))* European Language Institute ITA. Dist: Distribooks, Inc.
Mio Primo Dizionario Illustrato de Italiano. (ITA., Illus.). pap. 9.95 *(978-88-8148-830-8(2))*; pap. 9.95 *(978-88-8148-835-3(3))*; pap. 9.95 *(978-88-8148-845-2(0))* European Language Institute ITA. Dist: Distribooks, Inc.
Morgan, Nicola. Two-Can First Encyclopedia. 2004. (ENG., Illus.). 64p. (J). (gr. -1-3). 12.95 *(978-1-58728-440-3(5))* Cooper Square Publishing Llc.
My First Encyclopedia. (Mini Children's Reference Ser.). 256p. *(978-1-4054-5898-6(4))*; (Illus.). (J). *(978-1-4054-1706-8(4))* Parragon, Inc.
My First Picture Dictionary: Art & Music. 2009. 40p. 9.99 *(978-1-4231-1877-0(4))* Disney Pr.
My First Picture Dictionary: Let's Explore! 2009. 40p. 9.99 *(978-1-4231-1878-7(2))* Disney Pr.
My First Picture Encyclopedias. 2013. (My First Picture Encyclopedias Ser.). (ENG.). 32p. (gr. 1-2). 41.70 *(978-1-62065-924-3(7))*; 63.60 *(978-1-62065-933-5(6))* Capstone Press of Coughlan Cos. (Aplus Bks.).
O'Sullivan, Jill Korey. Picture Dictionary for Children. 2007. (ENG.). 176p. (C). pap. 32.95 *(978-1-4240-0876-6(X))* Cengage Heinle.
Oxford Analytica Staff & Langley, Andrew, eds. Oxford First Encyclopedia. 2015. (ENG., Illus.). 144p. 16.95 *(978-0-19-911995-0(3))* Oxford Univ. Pr., Inc.
Oxford University Press. Children's Visual Dictionary, French-English. 2014. (Children's Visual Dictionaries Ser.). (ENG.). 128p. (J). (gr. 1-6). pap. 12.99 *(978-1-4380-0451-8(6))* Barron's Educational Series, Inc.
—Children's Visual Dictionary, Spanish-English. 2014. (Children's Visual Dictionaries Ser.). (ENG.). 128p. (J). (gr. 1-6). pap. 12.99 *(978-1-4380-0452-5(4))* Barron's Educational Series, Inc.
Palmer, Douglas. Firefly Encyclopedia of Dinosaurs & Prehistoric Animals. 2014. (ENG., Illus.). 256p. (J). (gr. 4-7). pap. 19.95 *(978-1-77085-460-4(6)*, 9781770854604) Firefly Bks., Ltd.
Peterson, Megan Cooley, et al. My First Picture Encyclopedias. (My First Picture Encyclopedias Ser.). (ENG.). 32p. (gr. 1-2). 2013. lib. bdg. 218.56 *(978-1-62065-061-5(4))* 2013. lib. bdg. 109.28 *(978-1-62065-060-8(6))* 2012. lib. bdg. 109.28 *(978-1-4296-9124-6(7))* Capstone Press of Coughlan Cos. (Aplus Bks.).
Phillips, Sarah. My Picture Encyclopedia. Metcalf, Paula, illus. 2007. 64p. (J). (gr. k-2). *(978-1-84610-445-9(9))* Make Believe Ideas.
Picture Dictionary. 2003. (J). per. *(978-1-884907-28-9(8))* Paradise Pr., Inc.
Pons Juniorwoerterbuch Deutsch. (GER., Illus.). 192p. (YA). (gr. 3-18). 34.95 *(978-3-12-517630-0(1)*, KL517630E) Klett, Ernst, Verlag GmbH DEU. Dist: Continental Bk. Co., Inc.
Priddy, Roger. Palabras Words. 2004. (Happy Baby Ser.). (ENG & SPA., Illus.). 28p. (J). (gr. -1 — 1). bds. 6.99 *(978-0-312-49230-4(8)*, 9780312492304, Priddy Bks.) St. Martin's Pr.
Roberts, Jeremy. Japanese Mythology A to Z, Second Edition. 2nd rev. ed. 2009. (Mythology A to Z Ser.). (Illus.). 168p. (gr. 5-8). 45.00 *(978-1-60413-435-3(6)*, Chelsea Hse.) Facts On File, Inc.
Root, Betty & Langley, Jonathan. My First Dictionary. (Illus.). (J). pap. 23.95 *(978-0-590-74595-6(6))* Scholastic, Inc.
Saunders, Catherine. Character Encyclopedia. 2014. (ENG.). 176p. (J). (gr. k-4). 18.99 *(978-1-4654-2135-7(1)*, DK Children) Dorling Kindersley Publishing, Inc.
—LEGO Friends Character Encyclopedia. 2014. (ENG.). 176p. (J). (gr. k-4). 18.99 *(978-1-4654-1894-4(6)*, DK Children) Dorling Kindersley Publishing, Inc.
Scarry, Richard. Best Picture Dictionary Ever. Scarry, Richard, illus. 2016. (Giant Little Golden Book Ser.). (ENG., Illus.). 128p. (J). (gr. -1-2). 15.99 *(978-0-307-15548-1(X)*, 15548, Golden Bks.) Random Hse. Children's Bks.
Scholastic, Inc. Staff, ed. The Children's Visual Dictionary. (Illus.). 64p. (J). pap. 21.99 *(978-0-590-24522-7(8))* Scholastic, Inc.
—Scholastic First Encyclopedia, 4 vols., Set. (Illus.). (J). (gr. k-3). 60.00 *(978-0-590-24498-5(1))* Scholastic, Inc.
Stileman, Kali, illus. Big Book of My World. 2012. (ENG.). 48p. (J). *(978-1-58925-114-4(8))* Tiger Tales.
Terry, Paul. Top 10 of Everything 2015. 2014. (ENG., Illus.). 320p. (J). (gr. 5-12). 24.95 *(978-1-77085-469-7(X)*, 9781770854697) Firefly Bks., Ltd.
Truesdell, Ann. Find New Words with Dictionaries. 2012. (Explorer Junior Library: Information Explorer Junior Ser.). (ENG., Illus.). 24p. (J). (gr. 1-4). pap. 12.79 *(978-1-61080-393-9(0)*, 201330); lib. bdg. 28.50 *(978-1-61080-368-7(X)*, 201270) Cherry Lake Publishing.
—Find the Facts with Encyclopedias. 2012. (Explorer Junior Library: Information Explorer Junior Ser.). (ENG., Illus.). 24p.

EFG

(J). (gr. 1-4). pap. 12.79 (978-1-61080-392-2(2), 201329) Cherry Lake Publishing.

Turhan, Sedat & Hagin, Sally. Milet Mini Picture Dictionary. 2005. (Milet Mini Picture Dictionary Ser.). (Illus.). 28p. (J). (gr. -1 — 1). (ENG & POL.). pap. 7.99 (978-1-84059-472-0(1)); (ENG & KOR., pap. 7.99 (978-1-84059-470-6(5)); (ENG, PER & FRI., pap. 7.99 (978-1-84059-468-3(3)); (POR & ENG., pap. 7.99 (978-1-84059-473-7(X)); (RUS & ENG., pap. 7.99 (978-1-84059-474-4(8)); (JPN & ENG., pap. 7.99 (978-1-84059-469-0(1)) Milet Publishing.

Wallace, Carlton, ed. The Pocket Book for Schoolboys 1958. 2008. (ENG., Illus.). 160p. (YA). (gr. 7). 9.95 (978-0-237-53494-3(0)) Evans Brothers, Ltd. GBR. Dist: Independent Pubs. Group.

Wallechinsky, David, et al. The Book of Lists: The Original Compendium of Curious Information. 2006. (ENG.). 800p. mass mkt. 10.99 (978-0-7704-3009-2(0), Seal Bks) Knopf Canada CAN. Dist: Penguin Random Hse. LLC.

Weaver, Janice. The A to Z of Everyday Things. Blake, Francis, illus. 2004. (ENG.). 128p. (J). (gr. 5). pap. 8.95 (978-0-88776-671-8(4), Tundra Bks.) Tundra Bks. CAN. Dist: Penguin Random Hse. LLC.

Weinick, Suzanne. How Do I Use an Encyclopedia? 2014. (Research Tools You Can Use Ser.). 32p. (J). (gr. 3-6). pap. 12.90 (978-1-62275-386-4(0)) Rosen Publishing Group, Inc., The.

Whitfield, Philip. Firefly Encyclopedia of Animals. 2014. (ENG., Illus.). 256p. (J). (gr. 4-7). pap. 19.95 (978-1-77085-457-4(6), 9781770854574) Firefly Bks., Ltd.

Wittels, Harriet & Greisman, Joan. A First Dictionary. Biggs, Gene, illus. 2004. 239p. (J). (gr. 4-8). reprint ed. pap. 15.00 (978-0-7567-8422-5(0)) DIANE Publishing Co.

Wooster, Patricia & Dell, Pamela. My First Picture Encyclopedias. 2013. (My First Picture Encyclopedias Ser.). (ENG.). 32p. (gr. 1-2). 31.80 (978-1-4765-3626-2(0)); 95.40 (978-1-4765-3627-9(9)); pap. 31.80 (978-1-4765-3624-8(4)); lib. bdg. 327.84 (978-1-4296-8772-0(X)) Capstone Press of Coughlan Cos. (Aplus Bks.).

World Book, Inc. Staff, contrib. by. Childcraft: The How & Why Library, 15 vols. 2005. (Illus.). (gr. k-5). 349.00 (978-0-7166-2203-1(3)) World Bk., Inc.

World Book, Inc Staff, contrib. by. Childcraft: The How & Why Library, 15 vols. 2006. (Illus.). (J). (978-0-7166-5729-3(5)) World Bk., Inc.

World Book, Inc. Staff, contrib. by. Childcraft - the How & Why Library, 15 vols. 2003. (Illus.). 16&17p. (J). (978-0-7166-6030-9(X)) World Bk., Inc.

—Party Animal, 13 vols. 2005. (Me & My Pet Ser.). (Illus.). 1p. (J). (gr. 1-5). (978-0-7166-7500-6(5), SKU 20174) World Bk., Inc.

—The World Book Student Discovery Encyclopedia, 13 vols. (Illus.). (J). 2004. (978-0-7166-7410-8(6)) 2003. 2,464p. 359.00 (978-0-7166-7409-2(2)) World Bk., Inc.

The World Book Student Discovery Encyclopedia, 13 vols. 2,464p. 369.00 (978-0-7166-7413-9(0), 20176) World Bk., Inc.

Young, Caroline & Brooks, Felicity. The Usborne Very First Dictionary. Litchfield, Jo, illus. 2005. 64p. (J). (gr. -1-3). 11.95 (978-0-7945-1002-2(7), Usborne) EDC Publishing.

END OF THE WORLD

McIntosh, Kenneth. Prophecies & End-Time Speculations: The Shape of Things to Come. 2007. (Religion & Modern Culture Ser.). (Illus.). 112p. (YA). (gr. 7-12). lib. bdg. 22.95 (978-1-59084-979-8(5), 1248068) Mason Crest.

ENDANGERED PLANTS

Bodden, Valerie. Critical Plant Life. 2010. (Earth Issues Ser.). 48p. (YA). (gr. 5-18). 23.95 (978-1-58341-984-7(5), Creative Education) Creative Co., The.

Fandel, Jennifer. Endangered Plants. 2003. (Endangered Plants & Animals of North America Ser.). (J). pap. (978-1-58417-217-8(7)); lib. bdg. (978-1-58417-216-1(9)) Lake Street Pubs.

—Endangered Trees & Shrubs. 2003. (Endangered Plants & Animals of North America Ser.). (J). pap. (978-1-58417-215-4(0)); lib. bdg. (978-1-58417-214-7(2)) Lake Street Pubs.

Haugen, Brenda. Giant Pandas, 1 vol. 2012. (Endangered & Threatened Animals Ser.). (ENG., Illus.). 32p. (gr. 3-4). lib. bdg. 27.99 (978-1-4296-8663-1(4), Snap Bks.) Capstone Press of Coughlan Cos.

Hyde, Natalie. Great Barrier Reef Research Journal. 2017. (Illus.). 32p. (J). (978-0-7787-3470-3(6)); pap. (978-0-7787-3495-6(1)) Crabtree Publishing Co.

—Rocky Mountains Research Journal. 2017. (Illus.). 32p. (J). (978-0-7787-3471-0(4)); pap. (978-0-7787-3496-3(X)) Crabtree Publishing Co.

Lundgren, Julie K. Why Plants Become Extinct. 2012. (ENG.). 24p. (gr. 3-4). pap. 8.95 (978-1-61810-222-5(2)) Rourke Educational Media.

ENDANGERED SPECIES

see also Wildlife Conservation

Africa. 2015. (FAYFT: the World of Endangered Animals Ser.). 64p. (gr. 4-10). lib. bdg. 39.95 (978-1-78121-079-6(9)) Windmill Bks. Ltd. GBR. Dist: Black Rabbit Bks.

Allen, Kathy. Giant Pandas in a Shrinking Forest: A Cause & Effect Investigation, 1 vol. 2010. (Animals on the Edge Ser.). (ENG.). 32p. (gr. 3-4). lib. bdg. 27.32 (978-1-4296-5401-2(5), Fact Finders) Capstone Press of Coughlan Cos.

—Sea Turtles' Race to the Sea: A Cause & Effect Investigation, 1 vol. 2010. (Animals on the Edge Ser.). (ENG.). 32p. (gr. 3-4). lib. bdg. 27.32 (978-1-4296-5402-9(3), Fact Finders) Capstone Press of Coughlan Cos.

Allgor, Marie. Endangered Animals of Africa. 2011. (Save Earth's Animals! Ser.). 24p. (J). (ENG.). pap. 8.25 (978-1-4488-2640-7(3)); (Illus.). (gr. 3-4). lib. bdg. 22.60 (978-1-4488-2528-8(8)) Rosen Publishing Group, Inc., The. (PowerKids Pr.).

—Endangered Animals of Antarctica & the Arctic. 2011. (Save Earth's Animals! Ser.). (Illus.). 24p. (J). pap. 8.25 (978-1-4488-2652-0(7)); (gr. 3-4). lib. bdg. 22.60 (978-1-4488-2534-9(2)) Rosen Publishing Group, Inc., The. (PowerKids Pr.).

—Endangered Animals of Asia. 2011. (Save Earth's Animals! Ser.). 24p. (J). (ENG.). pap. 8.25 (978-1-4488-2642-1(X)); (Illus.). (gr. 3-4). lib. bdg. 22.60 (978-1-4488-2529-5(6)) Rosen Publishing Group, Inc., The. (PowerKids Pr.).

—Endangered Animals of Australia. 2011. (Save Earth's Animals! Ser.). 24p. (J). (ENG.). pap. 8.25 (978-1-4488-2644-5(6)); (Illus.). (gr. 3-4). lib. bdg. 22.60 (978-1-4488-2530-1(X)) Rosen Publishing Group, Inc., The. (PowerKids Pr.).

—Endangered Animals of Europe. 2011. (Save Earth's Animals! Ser.). (Illus.). 24p. (J). pap. 8.25 (978-1-4488-2646-9(2)); (gr. 3-4). 22.60 (978-1-4488-2531-8(8)) Rosen Publishing Group, Inc., The. (PowerKids Pr.).

—Endangered Animals of North America. 2011. (Save Earth's Animals! Ser.). (Illus.). 24p. (J). pap. 8.25 (978-1-4488-2648-3(9)); (gr. 3-4). 22.60 (978-1-4488-2532-5(6)) Rosen Publishing Group, Inc., The. (PowerKids Pr.).

—Endangered Animals of South America. 2011. (Save Earth's Animals! Ser.). 24p. (J). (ENG.). pap. 8.25 (978-1-4488-2650-6(0)); (Illus.). (gr. 3-4). lib. bdg. 22.60 (978-1-4488-2533-2(4)) Rosen Publishing Group, Inc., The. (PowerKids Pr.).

—Endangered Desert Animals. 2012. (Save Earth's Animals! Ser.). (ENG., Illus.). 24p. (J). (gr. k-5). 22.60 (978-1-4488-7423-1(8)); pap. 8.25 (978-1-4488-7496-5(3)) Rosen Publishing Group, Inc., The. (PowerKids Pr.).

—Endangered Forest Animals. 2012. (Save Earth's Animals! Ser.). (ENG., Illus.). 24p. (J). (gr. k-5). pap. 8.25 (978-1-4488-7497-2(1)); lib. bdg. 22.60 (978-1-4488-7424-8(6)) Rosen Publishing Group, Inc., The. (PowerKids Pr.).

—Endangered Grassland Animals. 2012. (Save Earth's Animals! Ser.). (ENG., Illus.). 24p. (J). (gr. k-5). pap. 8.25 (978-1-4488-7498-9(X)); lib. bdg. 22.60 (978-1-4488-7425-5(4)) Rosen Publishing Group, Inc., The. (PowerKids Pr.).

—Endangered Ocean Animals. 2012. (Save Earth's Animals! Ser.). (ENG., Illus.). 24p. (J). (gr. k-5). pap. 8.25 (978-1-4488-7493-4(9)); lib. bdg. 22.60 (978-1-4488-7420-0(3)) Rosen Publishing Group, Inc., The. (PowerKids Pr.).

—Endangered Rain Forest Animals. 2012. (Save Earth's Animals! Ser.). (ENG., Illus.). 24p. (J). (gr. k-5). pap. 8.25 (978-1-4488-7495-8(5)); lib. bdg. 22.60 (978-1-4488-7422-4(X)) Rosen Publishing Group, Inc., The. (PowerKids Pr.).

—Endangered Tundra Animals. 2012. (Save Earth's Animals! Ser.). (ENG., Illus.). 24p. (J). (gr. k-5). pap. 8.25 (978-1-4488-7494-1(7)); lib. bdg. 22.60 (978-1-4488-7421-7(1)) Rosen Publishing Group, Inc., The. (PowerKids Pr.).

Aloian, Molly & Kalman, Bobbie. Endangered Frogs. 2006. (Earth's Endangered Animals Ser.). (ENG., Illus.). 32p. (J). (gr. 4-7). pap. (978-0-7787-1918-2(9)) Crabtree Publishing Co.

—Endangered Monkeys. rev. ed. 2007. (Earth's Endangered Animals Ser.). (ENG., Illus.). 32p. (J). (gr. 1-5). pap. (978-0-7787-1908-3(1)) Crabtree Publishing Co.

—Les Singes. 2010. (FRE., Illus.). 32p. (J). pap. 9.95 (978-2-89579-288-8(7)) Bayard Canada Livres CAN. Dist: Crabtree Publishing Co.

Ames, Lee J. & Budd, Warren. Draw 50 Endangered Animals: The Step-by-Step Way to Draw Humpback Whales, Giant Pandas, Gorillas, & More Friends We May Lose... 2013. (ENG., Illus.). 64p. pap. 9.99 (978-0-8230-8608-5(9), Watson-Guptill) Potter/TenSpeed/Harmony.

Amstutz, L. J. & Cooper, Sharon Katz. E for Endangered. 2016. (E for Endangered Ser.). (ENG.). 32p. (gr. 1-2). 109.28 (978-1-4914-8668-9(6), Aplus Bks.) Capstone Press of Coughlan Cos.

Animals on the Edge, 1 vol. 2010. (Animals on the Edge Ser.). (ENG.). 32p. (gr. 3-4). lib. bdg. 81.96 (978-1-4296-4535-5(0), Fact Finders) Capstone Press of Coughlan Cos.

Austen, Amy. Endangered Animals: Develop Understanding of Fractions & Numbers. 2014. (Rosen Common Core Math Readers Ser.). (ENG.). 24p. (J). (gr. 3-4). pap. 8.25 (978-1-4777-4921-0(7), PowerKids Pr.) Rosen Publishing Group, Inc., The.

Bailey, Diane. Battling Wildlife Poachers: The Fight to Save Elephants, Rhinos, Lions, Tigers, & More. 2017. (J). (978-1-4222-3874-5(1)) Mason Crest.

Baillie, Marilyn, et al. How to Save a Species. 2014. (ENG.). 48p. (J). (gr. 3-7). 17.95 (978-1-77147-063-6(1), Owlkids) Owlkids Bks. Inc. CAN. Dist: Publishers Group West (PGW).

Barker, David. Top 50 Reasons to Care about Great Apes: Animals in Peril. 2010. (Top 50 Reasons to Care about Endangered Animals Ser.). (Illus.). 104p. (J). (gr. 5-9). 33.27 (978-0-7660-3456-3(9)) Enslow Pubs., Inc.

Bath, Louella. Saving Endangered Animals. 2016. (Global Guardians Ser.). 00024p. (J). (gr. 3-3). 23.60 (978-1-4994-2936-7(3)); pap. 8.25 (978-1-4994-2753-0(0)) Rosen Publishing Group, Inc., The. (PowerKids Pr.).

Becker, John. Grizzly Bears. 2003. (Returning Wildlife Ser.). (Illus.). 48p. (J). (gr. 3-5). 23.70 (978-0-7377-1534-7(0), Kidhaven) Cengage Gale.

Becker, John E. The California Condor. 2004. (Returning Wildlife Ser.). (ENG., Illus.). 48p. (J). 27.50 (978-0-7377-2292-5(4), Kidhaven) Cengage Gale.

—Green Sea Turtles. 2003. (Returning Wildlife Ser.). (Illus.). 48p. (J). 26.20 (978-0-7377-1831-7(5), Greenhaven Pr., Inc.) Cengage Gale.

—The Northern Elephant Seal. 2004. (Returning Wildlife Ser.). (ENG., Illus.). 48p. (J). (gr. 4-7). 27.50 (978-0-7377-2291-8(6), Greenhaven Pr., Inc.) Cengage Gale.

Bell, Samantha S. 12 Amphibians Back from the Brink. 2015. (ENG., Illus.). 32p. (J). pap. 9.95 (978-1-63235-060-2(2)) RiverStream Publishing.

—12 Insects Back from the Brink. 2014. (ENG., Illus.). 32p. (J). (978-1-63235-002-2(5)) Pr. Room Editions LLC.

—12 Reptiles Back from the Brink. 2014. (ENG., Illus.). 32p. (J). (978-1-63235-005-3(X)) Pr. Room Editions LLC.

Benchmark Education Company, compiled by. Bringing Back the Whooping Crane & ¡Vamos a Rescatar a la Grulla Blanca! 2005. (J). 62.00 net. (978-1-4108-4494-1(3)) Benchmark Education Co.

Benson, Sonia, et al. Endangered Species, 3 vols. 2nd ed. 2003. (Illus.). xxxviii, 740p. (J). (978-0-7876-7621-6(7)); (978-0-7876-7619-3(5)); (978-0-7876-7620-9(9)) Cengage Gale. (UXL).

Bily, Cynthia A. Endangered Species. 2010. (Issues That Concern You Ser.). (ENG.). 144p. (gr. 7-10). 42.00 (978-0-7377-4953-3(9)) Cengage Gale.

Bily, Cynthia A. & Des Chenes, Elizabeth, eds. Endangered Species. 2007. (Introducing Issues with Opposing Viewpoints Ser.). (ENG., Illus.). 128p. (YA). (gr. 7-12). lib. bdg. 35.75 (978-0-7377-3849-0(9)) Cengage Gale.

Blomquist, Christopher. Desert Tortoises. (Library of Turtles & Tortoises Ser.). 24p. 2009. (gr. 3-3). 42.50 (978-1-60853-946-8(6), PowerKids Pr.) 2004. (Illus.). (YA). (gr. 2-5). lib. bdg. 22.60 (978-0-8239-6739-1(5)) Rosen Publishing Group, Inc., The.

—Green Sea Turtles. (Library of Turtles & Tortoises Ser.). 24p. 2009. (gr. 3-3). 42.50 (978-1-60853-947-5(4)) 2004. (Illus.). (J). lib. bdg. 22.60 (978-0-8239-6738-4(7)) Rosen Publishing Group, Inc., The. (PowerKids Pr.).

Bodden, Valerie. Wildlife in Danger. 2010. (Earth Issues Ser.). (Illus.). 48p. (J). (gr. 5-18). 23.95 (978-1-58341-987-8(X), Creative Education) Creative Co., The.

Bogart, Jon. Animals & Oil Spills. 2013. (Animal 911: Environmental Threats Ser.). 48p. (J). (gr. 3-5). pap. 84.30 (978-1-4339-9712-9(6)); pap. 14.05 (978-1-4339-9711-2(8)); (ENG., Illus.). lib. bdg. 31.95 (978-1-4339-9710-5(X)) Stevens, Gareth Publishing LLLP.

Boothroyd, Jennifer. Endangered & Extinct Birds. 2014. (Lightning Bolt Books Animals in Danger Ser.). (ENG., Illus.). 32p. (gr. k-2). lib. bdg. 26.60 (978-1-4677-1330-6(9), Lerner Pubns.) Lerner Publishing Group.

—Endangered & Extinct Fish. 2014. (Lightning Bolt Books Animals in Danger Ser.). (ENG., Illus.). 32p. (gr. k-2). lib. bdg. 26.60 (978-1-4677-1331-3(7), Lerner Pubns.) Lerner Publishing Group.

—Endangered & Extinct Invertebrates. 2014. (Lightning Bolt Books Animals in Danger Ser.). (ENG., Illus.). 32p. (gr. k-2). lib. bdg. 26.60 (978-1-4677-1333-7(3), Lerner Pubns.) Lerner Publishing Group.

—Endangered & Extinct Mammals. 2014. (Lightning Bolt Books Animals in Danger Ser.). (ENG., Illus.). 32p. (gr. k-2). lib. bdg. 26.60 (978-1-4677-1329-0(5), Lerner Pubns.) Lerner Publishing Group.

—Endangered & Extinct Reptiles. 2014. (Lightning Bolt Books Animals in Danger Ser.). (ENG., Illus.). 32p. (gr. k-2). pap. 7.95 (978-1-4677-2373-2(8)); lib. bdg. 26.60 (978-1-4677-1334-4(1), Lerner Pubns.) Lerner Publishing Group.

Bouncing Back from Extinction. 2017. (Bouncing Back from Extinction Ser.). 32p. (gr. 9-10). 157.50 (978-1-5081-5579-9(8)); pap. 60.00 (978-1-5081-5580-5(1)) Rosen Publishing Group, Inc., The. (PowerKids Pr.).

Bow, James. Saving Endangered Plants & Animals. 2008. (Science Solves It Ser.). (ENG., Illus.). 32p. (J). (gr. 3-7). pap. (978-0-7787-4177-0(X), 1286291) Crabtree Publishing Co.

Bow, Patricia. Chimpanzee Rescue: Changing the Future for Endangered Wildlife. 2004. (Firefly Animal Rescue Ser.). (ENG., Illus.). 64p. (J). (gr. 5-8). 19.95 (978-1-55297-909-9(1), 9781552979099); pap. 9.95 (978-1-55297-908-2(3), 9781552979082) Firefly Bks., Ltd.

Brecke, Nicole & Stockland, Patricia M. Extinct & Endangered Animals You Can Draw. Brecke, Nicole, illus. 2010. (Ready, Set, Draw! Ser.). (ENG., Illus.). 32p. (gr. 2-4). lib. bdg. 25.26 (978-0-7613-4165-9(X), Millbrook Pr.) Lerner Publishing Group.

Bruin, Jessica. The Cube Book. 2011. (ENG., Illus.). 48p. (J). (gr. -1-1). bds. 16.95 (978-1-77049-325-4(5), Tundra Bks.) Tundra Bks. CAN. Dist: Penguin Random Hse. LLC.

Burton, Margie, et al. Endangered Animals & Animales en peligro de Extinción: 6 English, 6 Spanish Adaptations. 2011. (J). spiral bd. 75.00 net. (978-1-4108-5622-7(4)) Benchmark Education Co.

Capstone Press. Animals on the Edge. 2010. (Animals on the Edge Ser.). (ENG.). 32p. lib. bdg. 103.96 (978-1-4296-5923-9(8), Fact Finders) Capstone Press of Coughlan Cos.

Carson, Mary Kay. Emi & the Rhino Scientist. Uhlman, Tom, photos by. 2010. (Scientists in the Field Ser.). (ENG., Illus.). 64p. (J). (gr. 5-7). pap. 9.99 (978-0-547-40850-7(1)) Houghton Mifflin Harcourt Publishing Co.

Catala, Ellen. Animals in Danger. 2005. (Yellow Umbrella Fluent Level Ser.). (ENG.). 16p. (gr. k-1). pap. 35.70 (978-0-7368-5298-2(0), Yellow Umbrella Bks.) Capstone Press of Coughlan Cos.

Charman, Andrew. I Wonder Why the Dinosaurs Died Out: And Other Questions about Extinct & Endangered Animals. 2013. (I Wonder Why Ser.). (ENG., Illus.). 32p. (J). (gr. k-3). 6.99 (978-0-7534-6953-8(7), 9780753469538, Kingfisher) Roaring Brook Pr.

Cherry Lake Publishing Staff, compiled by. Road to Recovery. 2009. 32p. lib. bdg. 319.20 (978-1-60279-106-0(6), 200075) Cherry Lake Publishing.

Christopherson, Sara Cohen. Top 50 Reasons to Care about Marine Turtles: Animals in Peril. 2010. (Top 50 Reasons to Care about Endangered Animals Ser.). (Illus.). 104p. (J). (gr. 5-9). 33.27 (978-0-7660-3455-6(0)) Enslow Pubs., Inc.

—Top 50 Reasons to Care about Whales & Dolphins: Animals in Peril. 2010. (Top 50 Reasons to Care about Endangered Animals Ser.). (Illus.). 104p. (J). (gr. 5-9). 33.27 (978-0-7660-3453-2(4)) Enslow Pubs., Inc.

Cimarusti, Marie Torres & George, Jean Craighead. The Buffalo Are Back. Peterson, Stephanie & Minor, Wendell, illus. 2010. (ENG.). 32p. (J). (gr. k-3). 16.99 (978-0-525-42215-0(3), Dutton Books for Young Readers) Penguin Young Readers Group.

Ciovacco, Justine. Saving the Endangered Grizzly Bear, 01 vols., 1. 2016. (Conservation of Endangered Species Ser.). (ENG., Illus.). 32p. (J). pap. 12.90 (978-1-5081-0054-6(3), Britannica Educational Publishing) Rosen Publishing Group, Inc., The.

Clarke, Ginjer L. & dePaola, Tomie. What's up in the Amazon Rainforest. 2015. (What's Up Ser.). (ENG., Illus.). 144p. (J). (gr. 3-7). bds. 8.99 (978-0-448-48103-6(0), Grosset & Dunlap) Penguin Young Readers Group.

Claus, Matteson. Animals & Deforestation. 2013. (Animal 911: Environmental Threats Ser.). (Illus.). 48p. (J). (gr. 3-5). pap. 14.05 (978-1-4339-9707-5(X), 1358474); pap. 84.30 (978-1-4339-9708-2(8), 1358474); (ENG., lib. bdg. 31.95 (978-1-4339-9706-8(1), 1358474) Stevens, Gareth Publishing LLLP.

Close, Edward. Endangered Animals. 2013. (Discovery Education: Habitats Ser.). 32p. (J). (gr. 3-6). 25.25 (978-1-4777-1325-9(5)); pap. 10.00 (978-1-4777-1485-0(5)); pap. 60.00 (978-1-4777-1486-7(3)) Rosen Publishing Group, Inc., The. (PowerKids Pr.).

Cohn, Jessica. Hand to Paw: Protecting Animals, 1 vol. 2nd rev. ed. 2013. (Nonfiction Readers Ser.). (ENG., Illus.). 48p. (J). (gr. 4-4). pap. 29.96 (978-1-4807-1119-8(5)) Shell Educational Publishing.

—Una Mano a la Pata: Protegiendo Los Animales. 2017. (TIME for Kids en Español - Level 4 Ser.). (SPA., Illus.). 48p. (gr. 4-4). lib. bdg. 31.99 (978-1-5157-5148-9(1)) Time for Kids Inc AUS. Dist: Capstone Pub.

Cooper, Sharon Katz. A Is for Albatross: ABCs of Endangered Birds. 2016. (E for Endangered Ser.). (ENG., Illus.). 32p. (gr. 1-2). lib. bdg. 27.32 (978-1-4914-8032-8(7), Aplus Bks.) Capstone Press of Coughlan Cos.

Coupe, Robert. Cats of the Wild. 2014. (Discovery Education: Animals Ser.). 32p. (J). (gr. 3-6). 26.25 (978-1-4777-6944-7(7)); pap. 10.00 (978-1-4777-6945-4(5)) Rosen Publishing Group, Inc., The. (PowerKids Pr.).

Craats, Rennay. Black-Footed Ferret. 2003. (Endangered Plants & Animals of North America Ser.). (J). pap. (978-1-58417-209-3(6)); lib. bdg. (978-1-58417-208-6(8)) Lake Street Pubs.

—Whooping Cranes. 2003. (Endangered Plants & Animals of the United States Ser.). (J). pap. (978-1-58417-211-6(8)); lib. bdg. (978-1-58417-210-9(X)) Lake Street Pubs.

Crossingham, John & Kalman, Bobbie. Endangered Pandas. 2005. (Earth's Endangered Animals Ser.). (ENG., Illus.). 32p. (J). (gr. 3-5). pap. (978-0-7787-1904-5(9)) Crabtree Publishing Co.

Czech, Jan M. The Rhino: A MyReportLinks. com Book. 2005. (Endangered & Threatened Animals Ser.). (Illus.). 48p. (J). lib. bdg. 25.26 (978-0-7660-5062-4(9), MyReportLinks.com Bks.) Enslow Pubs., Inc.

Davies, Ann & Davies, Gill. The One Tiger. 2008. (Illus.). 32p. (J). pap. 7.99 (978-1-905470-23-5(1)) SeaSquirt Pubns. GBR. Dist: Basic Distribution, Inc.

DeFries, Cheryl L. The Bald Eagle: A MyReportLinks. com Book. 2003. (Endangered & Threatened Animals Ser.). (Illus.). 48p. (J). (gr. 4-10). lib. bdg. 26.60 (978-0-7660-5057-0(2), MyReportLinks.com Bks.) Enslow Pubs., Inc.

deMarin, Layne. Save the Animals, 1 vol. (Wonder Readers: Science Ser.). (ENG.). (gr. -1-2). 2012. 20p. lib. bdg. 22.65 (978-1-4296-9612-8(5)) 2011. 16p. pap. 35.94 (978-1-4296-8144-5(6)) 2011. 32p. pap. 5.99 (978-1-4296-7941-1(7)) Capstone Press of Coughlan Cos. (Wonder Readers).

Dembicki, Matt, ed. Wild Ocean: Sharks, Whales, Rays, & Other Endangered Sea Creatures. 2014. (ENG., Illus.). 156p. (YA). (gr. 7). pap. 19.95 (978-1-938486-38-8(2)) Fulcrum Publishing.

Diamond, Claudia C. Gorilla Families. 2009. (Reading Room Collection 2 Ser.). 24p. (gr. 3-4). 42.50 (978-1-60851-965-1(1), PowerKids Pr.) Rosen Publishing Group, Inc., The.

Dudley, Karen. Giant Pandas with Code. 2012. (Animals on the Brink Ser.). (ENG., Illus.). 48p. (J). (gr. 4-7). pap. 14.95 (978-1-61913-434-8(9)); lib. bdg. 29.99 (978-1-61913-433-1(0)) Weigl Pubs., Inc. (AV2 by Weigl).

Dunne, Abbie. Endangered & Threatened Animals. 2016. (Life Science Ser.). (ENG., Illus.). 24p. (gr. k-1). lib. bdg. 26.65 (978-1-5157-0945-9(0), Pebble Plus) Capstone Press of Coughlan Cos.

Edwards, Roberta. Polar Bears: In Danger. Johnson, Pamela, illus. 2008. (Penguin Young Readers, Level 3 Ser.). (ENG.). 48p. (J). (gr. 1-3). mass mkt. 3.99 (978-0-448-44924-1(2), Penguin Young Readers) Penguin Young Readers Group.

Endangered!, 6 bks., Set. Incl. Bears. Haywood, Karen Diane. lib. bdg. 29.93 (978-0-7614-2987-6(5)); Eagles. Haywood, Karen. lib. bdg. 29.93 (978-0-7614-2991-3(3)); Sharks. Nobleman, Marc Tyler. lib. bdg. 29.93 (978-0-7614-2988-3(3)); Tigers. Nobleman, Marc Tyler. lib. bdg. 29.93 (978-0-7614-2986-9(7)); Whales. Haney, Johannah. lib. bdg. 29.93 (978-0-7614-2990-6(5)); Wolves. Bjorklund, Ruth. lib. bdg. 29.93 (978-0-7614-2993-7(X)); 48p. (gr. 3-18). (Endangered! Ser.). 2008. Set lib. bdg. 179.58 (978-0-7614-2985-2(9), Benchmark Bks.) Marshall Cavendish Corp.

Endangered Animals, 6 vols. (Book2WebTM Ser.). (gr. 4-8). 36.50 (978-0-322-02978-1(3)) Wright Group/McGraw-Hill.

Endangered Mammals - Asia & China: An Educational Coloring Book. (J). (gr. 3-18). pap. 1.99 (978-0-86545-214-5(8)) Spizzirri Pr., Inc.

Endangered Species, 3 vols. 2nd ed. 2003. (ENG., Illus.). 840p. (J). 272.00 (978-0-7876-7618-6(7), UXL) Cengage Gale.

Firestone, Mary. Top 50 Reasons to Care about Elephants: Animals in Peril. 2010. (Top 50 Reasons to Care about Endangered Animals Ser.). (Illus.). 104p. (J). (gr. 5-9). 33.27 (978-0-7660-3454-9(2)) Enslow Pubs., Inc.

—Top 50 Reasons to Care about Giant Pandas: Animals in Peril. 2010. (Top 50 Reasons to Care about Endangered Animals Ser.). (Illus.). 104p. (J). (gr. 5-9). 33.27 (978-0-7660-3451-8(8)) Enslow Pubs., Inc.

—Top 50 Reasons to Care about Rhinos: Animals in Peril. 2010. (Top 50 Reasons to Care about Endangered Animals Ser.). (Illus.). 104p. (J). (gr. 5-9). 33.27 (978-0-7660-3457-0(7)) Enslow Pubs., Inc.

—Top 50 Reasons to Care about Tigers: Animals in Peril. 2010. (Top 50 Reasons to Care about Endangered Animals Ser.). (Illus.). 104p. (J). (gr. 5-9). 33.27 (978-0-7660-3452-5(6)) Enslow Pubs., Inc.

Forier, Elise. We Both Read-Endangered Animals. 2006. (We Both Read Ser.). (Illus.). 40p. (J). (gr. k-4). 7.99 (978-1-891327-71-1(2)) Treasure Bay, Inc.

—We Both Read-Endangered Animals: Level 2. 2006. (We Both Read Ser.). (Illus.). 40p. (J). (gr. k-4). pap. 4.99 (978-1-891327-72-8(0)) Treasure Bay, Inc.

Friedman, Lauri S. Endangered Species. 2007. (Writing the Critical Essay Ser.). (ENG., Illus.). 128p. (J). (gr. 10-12). lib. bdg. 38.30 (978-0-7377-3856-8(1), Greenhaven Pr., Inc.) Cengage Gale.

Friedman, Lauri S., ed. Endangered Species. 2011. (Introducing Issues with Opposing Viewpoints Ser.). (Illus.). 144p. (YA). (gr. 9-12). 36.95 *(978-0-7377-5676-0(4))* Cengage Gale.

Furstinger, Nancy. 12 Birds Back From the Brink. 2015. (ENG., Illus.). 32p. (J). pap. 9.95 *(978-1-63235-061-9(0))* RiverStream Publishing.

—12 Birds Back from the Brink. 2014. (ENG., Illus.). 32p. (J). *(978-1-63235-001-5(7))* Pr. Room Editions LLC.

—12 Mammals Back from the Brink. 2014. (ENG., Illus.). 32p. (J). *(978-1-63235-003-9(3))* Pr. Room Editions LLC.

—12 Marine Animals Back from the Brink. 2014. (ENG., Illus.). 32p. (J). *(978-1-63235-004-6(1))* Pr. Room Editions LLC.

Gagne, Tammy. The Most Endangered Animals in the World. 2015. (All about Animals Ser.). (ENG.). 24p. (gr. 1-2). pap. 6.95 *(978-1-4914-2237-3(8))* Capstone Press of Coughlan Cos.

Gale (Firm) Staff, contrib. by. U X L Endangered Species. 3rd ed. 2016. (Illus.). (J). *(978-1-4103-3298-1(5)*, Blackbirch Pr., Inc.) Cengage Gale.

Ganeri, Anita. Survival in the Jungle. 2011. (ENG.). 24p. (J). pap. *(978-0-7787-7880-6(0))*; (gr. 3-6). *(978-0-7787-7858-5(4))* Crabtree Publishing Co.

George, Jean Craighead. The Eagles Are Back. Minor, Wendell, illus. 2013. (ENG.). 32p. (J). (gr. 1-3). 17.99 *(978-0-8037-3771-6(8)*, Dial Bks) Penguin Young Readers Group.

—The Wolves Are Back. 2008. (J). (gr. 1-4). 28.95 incl. audio compact disk *(978-1-4301-0594-7(1))* Live Oak Media.

—The Wolves Are Back. Minor, Wendell, illus. 2008. (J). (gr. 1-4). 25.95 incl. audio *(978-1-4301-0591-6(7))* Live Oak Media.

Gerdes, Louise. Biodiversity. 2010. (At Issue Ser.). (J). 34.45 *(978-0-7377-4677-8(7))*; pap. 24.45 *(978-0-7377-4678-5(5))* Cengage Gale. (Greenhaven Pr., Inc.).

Gibbons, Gail. Giant Pandas. 2004. (ENG., Illus.). 32p. (J). (gr. k-3). pap. 7.99 *(978-0-8234-1828-2(6))* Holiday Hse., Inc.

—Grizzly Bears. Gibbons, Gail, illus. 2003. (ENG., Illus.). 32p. (J). (gr. k-3). tchr. ed. 17.95 *(978-0-8234-1793-3(X))* Holiday Hse., Inc.

Godkin, Celia. Skydiver: Saving the Fastest Bird in the World. Godkin, Celia, illus. (ENG., Illus.). 32p. (J). (gr. 1-3). 2015. pap. 8.95 *(978-1-927485-89-7(4))* 2014. 17.95 *(978-1-927485-61-3(4))* Pajama Pr. CAN. Dist: Ingram Publisher Services.

Goldish, Meish. Red Wolves: And Then There Were (Almost) None. 2007. (America's Animal Comebacks Ser.). (Illus.). 32p. (YA). (gr. 2-5). lib. bdg. 25.27 *(978-1-59716-742-0(8))* Bearport Publishing Co., Inc.

Goldstein, Natalie & Lockwood, Julie L. Biodiversity. 2nd rev. ed. 2011. (Global Issues Ser.). (Illus.). 362p. (C). (gr. 9). 45.00 *(978-0-8160-8242-1(1))* Facts On File, Inc.

Graham, Amy & Haslam, William. The Woodland Caribou: A MyReportLinks.com Book. 2003. (Endangered & Threatened Animals Ser.). (Illus.). 48p. (J). (gr. 4-10). lib. bdg. 26.60 *(978-0-7660-5054-9(8)*, MyReportLinks.com Bks.) Enslow Pubs., Inc.

Green, Carl R. The Giant Panda: A MyReportLinks. com Book. 2004. (Endangered & Threatened Animals Ser.). (Illus.). 48p. (J). lib. bdg. 26.60 *(978-0-7660-5061-7(0)*, MyReportLinks.com Bks.) Enslow Pubs., Inc.

—The Tiger: A MyReportLinks.com Book. 2003. (Endangered & Threatened Animals Ser.). (Illus.). 48p. (J). (gr. 4-10). lib. bdg. 26.60 *(978-0-7660-5059-4(9)*, MyReportLinks.com Bks.) Enslow Pubs., Inc.

Green, Jen. Wildlife in Danger. 2006. (Illus.). 32p. (YA). (gr. 4-18). lib. bdg. 27.10 *(978-1-59389-117-6(2))* Chrysalis Education.

Gregory, Cam. Why Are Polar Bears in Danger? 2014. (Little Books of Answers: Level e Ser.). (Illus.). 16p. (gr. k-2). pap. 7.95 *(978-1-927136-44-7(X))* Three Crows Media NZL. Dist: RiverStream Publishing.

Grucella, A. J. Prairie Dogs in Danger. 2013. (Animals at Risk Ser.). 24p. (J). (gr. 2-5). pap. 48.90 *(978-1-4339-9166-0(7))*; (ENG., Illus.). lib. bdg. 22.60 *(978-1-4339-9164-6(0))* Stevens, Gareth Publishing LLLP.

Hamilton, Garry. Frog Rescue: Changing the Future for Endangered Wildlife. 2004. (Firefly Animal Rescue Ser.). (ENG., Illus.). 64p. (J). (gr. 5-8). pap. 9.95 *(978-1-55297-596-1(7)*, 9781552975961) Firefly Bks., Ltd.

—Rhino Rescue: Changing the Future for Endangered Wildlife. 2006. (Firefly Animal Rescue Ser.). (ENG., Illus.). 64p. (J). (gr. 5-12). 19.95 *(978-1-55297-912-9(1)*, 9781552979129); pap. 9.95 *(978-1-55297-910-5(5)*, 9781552979105) Firefly Bks., Ltd.

Haney, Johannah. Dolphins. 2010. (Endangered! 2 Ser.). 48p. (gr. 3). lib. bdg. 29.93 *(978-0-7614-4049-9(6))* Marshall Cavendish Corp.

—Whales. 2008. (Endangered! Ser.). 48p. (gr. 3-18). lib. bdg. 29.93 *(978-0-7614-2990-6(5)*, Benchmark Bks.) Marshall Cavendish Corp.

Harasymiw, N. D. Condors in Danger. 2013. (Animals at Risk Ser.). 24p. (J). (gr. 2-5). pap. 48.90 *(978-1-4339-9156-1(X))*; pap. 8.15 *(978-1-4339-9155-4(1))*; (ENG., Illus.). lib. bdg. 22.60 *(978-1-4339-9154-7(3))* Stevens, Gareth Publishing LLLP.

Harkins, Susan Sales & Harkins, William H. Threat to the Whooping Crane. 2008. (On the Verge of Extinction Ser.). (Illus.). 32p. (J). (gr. 2-5). lib. bdg. 25.70 *(978-1-58415-685-7(6))* Mitchell Lane Pubs., Inc.

Harkrader, Lisa. The Cheetah: A MyReportLinks. com Book. 2005. (Endangered & Threatened Animals Ser.). (Illus.). 48p. (J). lib. bdg. 26.26 *(978-0-7660-5065-5(3)*, MyReportLinks.com Bks.) Enslow Pubs., Inc.

Harris, Tim. Australia & South East Asia. 2015. (FAYFT: the World of Endangered Animals Ser.). 64p. (gr. 4-10). lib. bdg. 39.95 *(978-1-78121-078-9(0)*, Brown Bear Bks.) Windmill Bks. Ltd. GBR. Dist: Black Rabbit Bks.

—Europe. 2015. (FAYFT: the World of Endangered Animals Ser.). (Illus.). 64p. (gr. 4-10). lib. bdg. 39.95 *(978-1-78121-076-5(4)*, Brown Bear Bks.) Windmill Bks. Ltd. GBR. Dist: Black Rabbit Bks.

—North & South America. 2015. (FAYFT: the World of Endangered Animals Ser.). (Illus.). 64p. (gr. 4-10). lib. bdg. 39.95 *(978-1-78121-075-8(6)*, Brown Bear Bks.) Windmill Bks. Ltd. GBR. Dist: Black Rabbit Bks.

—South & Central Asia. 2015. (FAYFT: the World of Endangered Animals Ser.). (Illus.). 64p. (gr. 4-10). lib. bdg. 39.95 *(978-1-78121-077-2(2)*, Brown Bear Bks.) Windmill Bks. Ltd. GBR. Dist: Black Rabbit Bks.

Harris, Tim, ed. Birds. 2011. (FAYFT: Endangered Animals Ser.). 64p. (gr. 4-10). lib. bdg. 39.95 *(978-1-936333-31-8(7))* Brown Bear Bks.

—Fish. 2011. (FAYFT: Endangered Animals Ser.). 64p. (gr. 4-10). lib. bdg. 39.95 *(978-1-936333-32-5(5))* Brown Bear Bks.

—Invertebrates. 2011. (FAYFT: Endangered Animals Ser.). 64p. (gr. 4-10). lib. bdg. 39.95 *(978-1-936333-33-2(3))* Brown Bear Bks.

—Mammals of the Northern Hemisphere. 2011. (FAYFT: Endangered Animals Ser.). 64p. (gr. 4-10). lib. bdg. 39.95 *(978-1-936333-34-9(1))* Brown Bear Bks.

Haugen, Brenda. African Elephants, 1 vol. 2012. (Endangered & Threatened Animals Ser.). (ENG., Illus.). 32p. (gr. 3-4). lib. bdg. 27.99 *(978-1-4296-8664-8(2)*, Snap Bks.) Capstone Press of Coughlan Cos.

Hickman, Pamela. Birds of Prey Rescue: Changing the Future for Endangered Wildlife. 2006. (Firefly Animal Rescue Ser.). (ENG., Illus.). 64p. (J). (gr. 5-12). 19.95 *(978-1-55407-145-6(3)*, 9781554071456); pap. 9.95 *(978-1-55407-144-9(5)*, 9781554071449) Firefly Bks., Ltd.

—Turtle Rescue: Changing the Future for Endangered Wildlife. 2005. (Firefly Animal Rescue Ser.). (ENG., Illus.). 64p. (J). (gr. 5-12). 19.95 *(978-1-55297-916-7(4)*, 9781552979167); pap. 9.95 *(978-1-55297-915-0(6)*, 9781552979150) Firefly Bks., Ltd.

Hinman, Bonnie. Threat to the Leatherback Turtle. 2008. (On the Verge of Extinction Ser.). (Illus.). 32p. (YA). (gr. 2-5). lib. bdg. 25.70 *(978-1-58415-690-1(2))* Mitchell Lane Pubs., Inc.

Hirsch, Rebecca. Save the Planet: Helping Endangered Animals. 2010. (Explorer Library: Language Arts Explorer Ser.). (ENG.). 32p. (gr. 4-8). pap. 14.21 *(978-1-60279-667-6(X)*, 200914); lib. bdg. 28.50 *(978-1-60279-658-4(0)*, 200351) Cherry Lake Publishing.

Hirsch, Rebecca E. Top 50 Reasons to Care about Polar Bears: Animals in Peril. 2010. (Top 50 Reasons to Care about Endangered Animals Ser.). (Illus.). 104p. (J). (gr. 5-9). 33.27 *(978-0-7660-3458-7(5))* Enslow Pubs., Inc.

Hoare, Ben. Endangered Animals. 2010. (DK Eyewitness Bks.). (ENG.). 72p. (J). (gr. 3-7). 19.99 *(978-0-7566-6884-6(0))*; 16.99 *(978-0-7566-6883-9(2))* Dorling Kindersley Publishing, Inc. (DK Children).

Holden, Henry M. The American Alligator: A MyReportLinks. Com Book. 2003. (Endangered & Threatened Animals Ser.). (Illus.). 48p. (J). lib. bdg. 26.60 *(978-0-7660-5117-1(X)*, MyReportLinks.com Bks.) Enslow Pubs., Inc.

Hoose, Phillip. The Race to Save the Lord God Bird. rev. ed. 2014. (ENG., Illus.). 224p. (YA). (gr. 7-12). 24.99 *(978-0-374-30035-7(6)*, Farrar, Straus & Giroux (BYR)) Farrar, Straus & Giroux.

Hoyt, Erich. Whale Rescue: Changing the Future for Endangered Wildlife. 2005. (Firefly Animal Rescue Ser.). (ENG., Illus.). 64p. (J). (gr. 5-8). 19.95 *(978-1-55297-601-2(7)*, 9781552976012); pap. 9.95 *(978-1-55297-600-5(9)*, 9781552976005) Firefly Bks., Ltd.

Hunt, Jilly. Saving Endangered Animals. 2017. (Beyond the Headlines! Ser.). (ENG.). 48p. (gr. 4-6). lib. bdg. 33.32 ***(978-1-4846-4140-8(X)***, Heinemann InfoSearch) Heinemann-Raintree.

Imbriaco, Alison. The Otter: A MyReportLinks. com Book. 2005. (Endangered & Threatened Animals Ser.). (Illus.). 48p. (J). lib. bdg. 26.60 *(978-0-7660-5067-9(X)*, MyReportLinks.com Bks.) Enslow Pubs., Inc.

—The Red Wolf: Help Save This Endangered Species! 2007. (Saving Endangered Species Ser.). (Illus.). 128p. (J). (gr. 5-9). lib. bdg. 34.60 *(978-1-59845-038-5(7)*, MyReportLinks.com Bks.) Enslow Pubs., Inc.

Innovative Kids Staff. Baby Animals. 2009. (ENG., Illus.). 20p. (J). (gr. -1-1). 6.99 *(978-1-58476-809-8(6))* Innovative Kids.

Iyer, Rani. Endangered Rain Forests: Investigating Rain Forests in Crisis. 2015. (Endangered Earth Ser.). (ENG.). 32p. (gr. 3-4). lib. bdg. 27.32 *(978-1-4914-2039-3(1))* Capstone Press of Coughlan Cos.

Jackson, Donna M. The Wildlife Detectives: How Forensic Scientists Fight Crimes Against Nature. Shattil, Wendy & Rozinski, Bob, photos by. 2005. (Scientists in the Field Ser.). (Illus.). 47p. (gr. 3-7). 20.00 *(978-0-7569-5191-7(7))* Perfection Learning Corp.

Jenkins, Steve. Almost Gone: The World's Rarest Animals. Jenkins, Steve, illus. 2006. (Let's-Read-And-Find-Out Science 2 Ser.). (ENG., Illus.). 40p. (J). (gr. k-4). 16.99 *(978-0-06-053598-8(9))*; pap. 5.99 *(978-0-06-053600-8(4))* HarperCollins Pubs. (Collins).

Johnson, Robin. Les Manchots. 2012. (FRE.). 32p. (J). pap. 9.95 *(978-2-89579-442-4(1))* Bayard Canada CAN. Dist: Crabtree Publishing Co.

Kainen, Dan & Wollard, Kathy. Wild: A Photicular Book. 2017. (Photicular Ser.). (ENG., Illus.). 24p. 25.95 ***(978-1-5235-0147-2(2))*** Workman Publishing Co., Inc.

Kalman, Bobbi. The ABCs of Endangered Animals. 2014. 32p. pap. 9.00 *(978-1-61003-364-0(7))* Center for the Collaborative Classroom.

Kalman, Bobbie. The ABCs of Endangered Animals. 2009. (ABCs of the Natural World Ser.). (ENG., Illus.). 32p. (J). (gr. 1-5). pap. *(978-0-7787-3435-2(8))*; (gr. 2-4). lib. bdg. *(978-0-7787-3415-4(3))* Crabtree Publishing Co.

—Big Challenges That Animals Face. 2016. (ENG., Illus.). 32p. (J). lib. bdg. *(978-0-7787-2781-1(5))* Crabtree Publishing Co.

—Les Dragons de Komodo. 2010. (Petit Monde Vivant Ser.). (FRE., Illus.). 32p. (J). pap. 9.95 *(978-2-89579-315-1(8))* Bayard Canada Livres CAN. Dist: Crabtree Publishing Co.

—Endangered Baby Animals. 2012. (ENG., Illus.). 24p. (J). *(978-0-7787-4076-6(5))*; pap. *(978-0-7787-4081-0(1))* Crabtree Publishing Co.

—Endangered Elephants. 2005. (Earth's Endangered Animals Ser.). (ENG., Illus.). 32p. (J). (gr. 1-5). pap. *(978-0-7787-1906-9(5))* Crabtree Publishing Co.

—Endangered Komodo Dragons. 2004. (Earth's Endangered Animals Ser.). (ENG., Illus.). 32p. (J). pap. *(978-0-7787-1903-8(0))*; lib. bdg. *(978-0-7787-1857-4(3))* Crabtree Publishing Co.

—Endangered Monk Seals. 2004. (Earth's Endangered Animals Ser.). (ENG., Illus.). 32p. (J). pap. *(978-0-7787-1897-0(2))* Crabtree Publishing Co.

—Endangered Rhinoceros. 2004. (Earth's Endangered Animals Ser.). (ENG., Illus.). 32p. (J). pap. *(978-0-7787-1898-7(0))* Crabtree Publishing Co.

—Endangered Sea Turtles. 2004. (Earth's Endangered Animals Ser.). (ENG., Illus.). 32p. (J). pap. *(978-0-7787-1899-4(9))* Crabtree Publishing Co.

—Endangered Tigers. 2008. (FRE.). 32p. (J). pap. 9.95 *(978-2-89579-204-8(6))* Bayard Canada Livres CAN. Dist: Crabtree Publishing Co.

—Endangered Tigers. 2004. (Earth's Endangered Animals Ser.). (ENG., Illus.). 32p. (J). pap. *(978-0-7787-1896-3(4))* Crabtree Publishing Co.

—Endangered Wolves. 2004. (Earth's Endangered Animals Ser.). (ENG., Illus.). 32p. (J). pap. *(978-0-7787-1900-7(6))* Crabtree Publishing Co.

—Les Gorilles de Montagne. 2009. (Petit Monde Vivant Ser.). (FRE., Illus.). 32p. (J). pap. 9.95 *(978-2-89579-230-7(5))* Bayard Canada Livres CAN. Dist: Crabtree Publishing Co.

—Why & Where Are Animals Endangered? 2015. (ENG., Illus.). 24p. (J). *(978-0-7787-1469-9(1))* Crabtree Publishing Co.

Kalman, Bobbie & Burns, Kylie. Endangered Bears. 2007. (Earth's Endangered Animals Ser.). (ENG., Illus.). 32p. (J). (gr. 1-5). lib. bdg. *(978-0-7787-1861-1(1))*; pap. *(978-0-7787-1907-6(3))* Crabtree Publishing Co.

Kalman, Bobbie & Dyer, Hadley. Les Chimpanzés. Briere, Marie-Josee, tr. from ENG. rev. ed. 2007. (Petit Monde Vivant Ser.). (FRE., Illus.). 32p. (J). (gr. 1-7). pap. 9.95 *(978-2-89579-128-7(7))* Bayard Canada Livres CAN. Dist: Crabtree Publishing Co.

—Endangered Chimpanzees. 2005. (Earth's Endangered Animals Ser.). (ENG., Illus.). 32p. (J). (gr. 1-5). pap. *(978-0-7787-1905-2(7))*; (gr. 3-5). lib. bdg. *(978-0-7787-1859-8(X))* Crabtree Publishing Co.

—Endangered Manatees. 2006. (Earth's Endangered Animals Ser.). (ENG., Illus.). 32p. (J). (gr. 3-7). pap. *(978-0-7787-1914-4(6))*; lib. bdg. *(978-0-7787-1868-0(9))* Crabtree Publishing Co.

—Les Léopards. 2010. (Petit Monde Vivant Ser.). (FRE., Illus.). 32p. (J). pap. 9.95 *(978-2-89579-316-8(6))* Bayard Canada Livres CAN. Dist: Crabtree Publishing Co.

Kalman, Bobbie & Johnson, Robin. Endangered Butterflies. 2006. (Earth's Endangered Animals Ser.). (ENG., Illus.). 32p. (J). (gr. 4-7). pap. *(978-0-7787-1916-8(2))* Crabtree Publishing Co.

—Endangered Penguins. 2007. (Earth's Endangered Animals Ser.). (ENG., Illus.). 32p. (J). (gr. 3-7). lib. bdg. *(978-0-7787-1863-5(8))*; (gr. -1-3). pap. *(978-0-7787-1909-0(X))* Crabtree Publishing Co.

Kalman, Bobbie & Lundblad, Kristina. Endangered Bats. 2006. (Earth's Endangered Animals Ser.). (ENG., Illus.). 32p. (J). (gr. -1-3). pap. *(978-0-7787-1912-0(X))* Crabtree Publishing Co.

—Endangered Mountain Gorillas. 2004. (Earth's Endangered Animals Ser.). (ENG., Illus.). 32p. (J). pap. *(978-0-7787-1901-4(4))*; lib. bdg. *(978-0-7787-1855-0(7))* Crabtree Publishing Co.

Katirgis, Jane & Czech, Jan M. Endangered Rhinos. 2015. (Wildlife at Risk Ser.). (ENG., Illus.). 48p. (J). (gr. 6-6). 27.93 *(978-0-7660-6902-2(8))* Enslow Pubs., Inc.

Katirgis, Jane & Green, Carl R. Endangered Giant Pandas. 2015. (Wildlife at Risk Ser.). (ENG.). 48p. (J). (gr. 6-6). pap. 11.70 *(978-0-7660-6892-6(7))*; (Illus.). 27.93 *(978-0-7660-6894-0(3))* Enslow Pubs., Inc.

—Endangered Gorillas. 2015. (Wildlife at Risk Ser.). (ENG.). 48p. (J). (gr. 6-6). pap. 11.70 *(978-0-7660-6896-4(X))*; (Illus.). 27.93 *(978-0-7660-6898-8(6))* Enslow Pubs., Inc.

—Endangered Tigers. 2015. (Wildlife at Risk Ser.). (ENG.). 48p. (J). (gr. 6-6). pap. 11.70 *(978-0-7660-6904-6(4))*; (Illus.). 27.93 *(978-0-7660-6906-0(0))* Enslow Pubs., Inc.

Katirgis, Jane & Harkrader, Lisa. Endangered Orangutans. 2015. (Wildlife at Risk Ser.). (ENG.). 48p. (J). (gr. 6-6). pap. 11.70 *(978-0-7660-6884-1(6))*; (Illus.). 27.93 *(978-0-7660-6886-5(2))* Enslow Pubs., Inc.

Kenyon, Linda. Rainforest Bird Rescue: Changing the Future for Endangered Wildlife. 2006. (Firefly Animal Rescue Ser.). (ENG., Illus.). 64p. (J). (gr. 5-12). 19.95 *(978-1-55407-153-1(4)*, 9781554071531); pap. 9.95 *(978-1-55407-152-4(6)*, 9781554071524) Firefly Bks., Ltd.

Kinsner, Kathy. Doomed to Disappear? Endangered Species & Condenadas a desaparecer? Especies en peligro de Extinción: 6 English, 6 Spanish Adaptations. 2011. (ENG & SPA.). (J). 97.00 net. *(978-1-4108-5698-2(4))* Benchmark Education Co.

Knowlton, Laurie Lazzaro. African Giants. Tusan, Stan, illus. Prebeg, Rick, photos by. 2005. (J). *(978-1-933248-08-0(4))* World Quest Learning.

Kopp, Megan. Rhinos. 2014. (Illus.). 48p. (J). *(978-1-62127-228-1(1))* Weigl Pubs., Inc.

Kortemeier, Todd. Saving Endangered Species. 2017. (Illus.). 32p. (J). *(978-1-62143-520-4(2))* Pr. Room Editions LLC.

Kortemeier, Todd & Smibert, Angie. Saving Endangered Species. 2016. (Science Frontiers Ser.). (ENG., Illus.). 32p. (J). pap. 9.95 *(978-1-63235-396-2(2))* Pr. Room Editions LLC.

Labella, Susan. Animal Survivors, 6 bks., Set. Incl. Chameleons & Other Animals with Amazing Skin. (Illus.). 24p. (J). (gr. 1-2). 2005. lib. bdg. 22.00 *(978-0-516-24925-4(8))*; (Scholastic News Nonfiction Readers Ser.). 2005. 108.00 o.p. *(978-0-516-25390-9(5)*, Children's Pr.) Scholastic Library Publishing.

Lasky, Kathryn. Interrupted Journey: Saving Endangered Sea Turtles. Knight, Christopher G., photos by. 2006. (ENG., Illus.). 48p. (J). (gr. 1-4). 6.99 *(978-0-7636-2883-3(2))* Candlewick Pr.

Leavitt, Amie. Threat to the Yangtze River Dolphin. 2008. (On the Verge of Extinction Ser.). (Illus.). 32p. (J). (gr. 2-5). lib. bdg. 25.70 *(978-1-58415-684-0(8))* Mitchell Lane Pubs., Inc.

Ledu-Frattini, Stephanie. The Tiger. Uhlig, Elizabeth, tr. from FRE. Sah, Anup, photos by. 2004. (Animal Close-Ups Ser.). (Illus.). 28p. (J). pap. 6.95 *(978-1-57091-373-0(0))* Charlesbridge Publishing, Inc.

Levete, Sarah. Habitats & Wildlife in Danger. 2010. (Protecting Our Planet Ser.). (ENG., Illus.). 32p. (J). (gr. 3-6). *(978-0-7787-5213-4(5))*; pap. *(978-0-7787-5230-1(5))* Crabtree Publishing Co.

Long, Matthew & Long, Thomas. Any Bear Can Wear Glasses: The Spectacled Bear & other Curious Creatures. Long, Sylvia, illus. 2005. 24p. (J). (gr. k-4). reprint ed. 17.00 *(978-0-7567-9763-8(2))* DIANE Publishing Co.

Lourie, Peter. The Manatee Scientists: Saving Vulnerable Species. 2016. (Scientists in the Field Ser.). (ENG., Illus.). 80p. (J). (gr. 5-7). pap. 9.99 *(978-0-544-22529-9(5)*, HMH Books For Young Readers) Houghton Mifflin Harcourt Publishing Co.

MacAulay, Kelley. Les Zebres. 2008. (FRE.). 32p. (J). pap. 9.95 *(978-2-89579-203-1(8))* Bayard Canada Livres CAN. Dist: Crabtree Publishing Co.

MacAulay, Kelley & Kalman, Bobbie. Endangered Zebras. 2007. (Earth's Endangered Animals Ser.). (ENG., Illus.). 32p. (J). (gr. 1-5). lib. bdg. *(978-0-7787-1864-2(6))*; pap. *(978-0-7787-1910-6(3))* Crabtree Publishing Co.

MacMillan, Dianne M. Cheetahs. rev. ed. 2009. (Nature Watch Ser.). (ENG.). 48p. (gr. 4-8). 27.93 *(978-0-8225-9417-8(X))* Lerner Publishing Group.

—Humpback Whales. 2003. (Nature Watch Ser.). (ENG., Illus.). 48p. (J). (gr. 4-8). 27.93 *(978-1-57505-347-9(0))* Lerner Publishing Group.

Maimone, Sofia. Snow Leopards in Danger. 2013. (Animals at Risk Ser.). 24p. (J). (gr. 2-5). pap. 8.15 *(978-1-4339-9175-2(6))*; pap. 48.90 *(978-1-4339-9176-9(4))*; (ENG., Illus.). lib. bdg. 22.60 *(978-1-4339-9174-5(8))* Stevens, Gareth Publishing LLLP.

Malnor, Carol L. & Malnor, Bruce. Earth Heroes, Champions of Wild Animals, 1 vol. Hovemann, Anisa Claire, illus. 2010. (ENG.). 144p. (J). pap. 11.95 *(978-1-58469-123-5(9))* Dawn Pubns.

Marsico, Katie. Bears. 2017. (True Book(tm) — The Most Endangered Ser.). (ENG., Illus.). 48p. (J). lib. bdg. 31.00 *(978-0-531-22725-1(1)*, Children's Pr.) Scholastic Library Publishing.

—Elephants. 2017. (True Book(tm) — The Most Endangered Ser.). (ENG., Illus.). 48p. (J). lib. bdg. 31.00 *(978-0-531-22727-5(8)*, Children's Pr.) Scholastic Library Publishing.

—Gorillas. 2017. (True Book(tm) — The Most Endangered Ser.). (ENG.). 48p. (J). lib. bdg. 31.00 *(978-0-531-22728-2(6)*, Children's Pr.) Scholastic Library Publishing.

Martin, Patricia A. Fink. Gray Wolves. 2003. (True Bks.). (ENG., Illus.). 48p. (J). (gr. 3-5). pap. 6.95 *(978-0-516-27472-0(4)*, Children's Pr.) Scholastic Library Publishing.

—Manatees. 2003. (True Bks.). (ENG., Illus.). 48p. (J). (gr. 3-5). pap. 6.95 *(978-0-516-27473-7(2)*, Children's Pr.) Scholastic Library Publishing.

Martin, Patricia A. Fink & Fink-Martin, Patricia A. California Condors. 2003. (True Bks.). (ENG., Illus.). 48p. (J). (gr. 3-5). pap. 6.95 *(978-0-516-27470-6(8)*, Children's Pr.) Scholastic Library Publishing.

Mcisaac, Gerald. Bird from Hell: Third Edition. 3rd rev. ed. 2012. 184p. (gr. 2-4). 24.50 *(978-1-4669-5026-9(9))*; pap. 14.50 *(978-1-4669-5027-6(7))* Trafford Publishing.

McLimans, David. Gone Wild. McLimans, David, illus. 2016. (ENG., Illus.). 32p. (J). bds. 7.99 *(978-1-61963-954-6(8)*, 9781619639546, Bloomsbury USA Childrens) Bloomsbury Publishing USA.

McNab, Chris. Endangered Reptiles. 2006. (Nature's Monsters Ser.). (Illus.). 32p. (gr. 2-6). lib. bdg. 26.00 *(978-0-8368-6171-6(X)*, Gareth Stevens Learning Library) Stevens, Gareth Publishing LLLP.

Miller-Schroeder, Patricia. Blue Whales. 2013. (Illus.). 48p. (J). *(978-1-61913-423-2(3))* Weigl Pubs., Inc.

—Blue Whales, with Code. 2012. (Animals on the Brink Ser.). (ENG., Illus.). 48p. (J). (gr. 5-9). pap. 14.95 *(978-1-61913-424-9(1)*, AV2 by Weigl) Weigl Pubs., Inc.

Mineo, Ella. Sea Otters in Danger. 2013. (Animals at Risk Ser.). 24p. (J). (gr. 2-5). pap. 48.90 *(978-1-4339-9171-4(3))*; pap. 8.15 *(978-1-4339-9170-7(5))*; (ENG., Illus.). lib. bdg. 22.60 *(978-1-4339-9169-1(1))* Stevens, Gareth Publishing LLLP.

Morgan, Jody. Elephant Rescue: Changing the Future for Endangered Wildlife. 2004. (Firefly Animal Rescue Ser.). (ENG., Illus.). 64p. (J). (gr. 5-8). 19.95 *(978-1-55297-595-4(9)*, 9781552975954); pap. 9.95 *(978-1-55297-594-7(0)*, 9781552975947) Firefly Bks., Ltd.

Murdoch, J. D. The African Wild Dog. 2009. (Library of Wolves & Wild Dogs Ser.). 24p. (gr. 3-3). 42.50 *(978-1-60853-967-3(9)*, PowerKids Pr.) Rosen Publishing Group, Inc., The.

Nagle, Jeanne. Endangered Wildlife: Habitats in Peril. 2009. (Extreme Environmental Threats Ser.). 64p. (gr. 6-6). 58.50 *(978-1-61512-429-9(2))* Rosen Publishing Group, Inc., The.

Nagle, Jeanne M. Endangered Wildlife: Habitats in Peril. 2009. (Extreme Environmental Threats Ser.). (ENG., Illus.). 64p. (J). (gr. 7-12). pap. 12.95 *(978-1-4358-5375-1(X))*; (YA). (gr. 5-9). lib. bdg. 31.95 *(978-1-4358-5019-4(X))* Rosen Publishing Group, Inc., The.

National Geographic Kids & Hogan, Zeb. Monster Fish: True Stories of Adventures with Animals. 2017. (NGK Chapters Ser.). (ENG., Illus.). 112p. (J). (gr. 2-5). pap. 5.99 *(978-1-4263-2703-2(X)*, National Geographic Children's Bks.) National Geographic Society.

National Geographic Learning. National Geographic Explore: Endangered Species. 2016. (ENG., Illus.). 56p. (J). pap. 14.95 *(978-1-305-10677-2(6))* National Geographic School Publishing, Inc.

Newman, Patricia. Zoo Scientists to the Rescue. Crawley, Annie, photos by. 2017. (ENG., Illus.). (J). (gr. 4-8). lib. bdg. 33.32 ***(978-1-5124-1571-1(5)***, Millbrook Pr.) Lerner Publishing Group.

Nobleman, Marc Tyler. Sharks. 2008. (Endangered! Ser.). 48p. (gr. 3-18). lib. bdg. 29.93 *(978-0-7614-2988-3(3)*, Benchmark Bks.) Marshall Cavendish Corp.

—Tigers. 2008. (Endangered! Ser.). 48p. (gr. 3-18). lib. bdg. 29.93 *(978-0-7614-2986-9(7)*, Benchmark Bks.) Marshall Cavendish Corp.

O'Connell, Kim A. The Galapagos Penguin: A MyReportLinks. com Book. 2005. (Endangered & Threatened Animals Ser.). (Illus.). 48p. (J). lib. bdg. 26.60 *(978-0-7660-5063-1(7)*, MyReportLinks.com Bks.) Enslow Pubs., Inc.

E
F
G

—The Wallaby: A MyReportLinks. com Book. 2005. (Endangered & Threatened Animals Ser.). (Illus.). 48p. (J). lib. bdg. 25.26 *(978-0-7660-5064-8(5)*, MyReportLinks.com Bks.) Enslow Pubs., Inc.

O'Connor, Karen. Animals on the Verge of Extinction. 2013. (Animal 911: Environmental Threats Ser.). 48p. (J). (gr. 3-5). pap. 14.05 *(978-1-4339-9715-0(0))*; pap. 84.30 *(978-1-4339-9716-7(9))*; (ENG., Illus.). lib. bdg. 31.95 *(978-1-4339-9714-3(2))* Stevens, Gareth Publishing LLLP.

O'Connor, Rebecca K. Frogs & Toads. 2003. (Endangered Animals & Habitats Ser.). (Illus.). 112p. (J). 29.95 *(978-1-56006-919-5(8))*, Lucent Bks.) Cengage Gale.

O'Neal, Claire. Threat to the Bengal Tiger. 2008. (On the Verge of Extinction Ser.). (Illus.). 32p. (J). (gr. 1-5). lib. bdg. 25.70 *(978-1-58415-688-8(0))* Mitchell Lane Pubs., Inc.

Orme, David. Endangered Animals. 2009. (Fact to Fiction Ser.). (Illus.). 36p. (J). pap. 6.95 *(978-0-7891-7901-2(6))* Perfection Learning Corp.

Orme, David & Orme, David. Endangered Animals. 2008. (Trailblazers Ser.). (ENG., Illus.). 36p. pap. *(978-1-84167-691-3(8))* Ransom Publishing Ltd.

Orr, Tamra B. Battling Extinction. 2014. (Explorer Library: Follow the Clues Ser.). (ENG., Illus.). 32p. (J). (gr. 4-8). 28.50 *(978-1-62431-780-4(4)*, 203316) Cherry Lake Publishing.

Osborne, Mary Pope & Boyce, Natalie Pope. Pandas & Other Endangered Species: A Perfect Time for Pandas. Murdocca, Sal, illus. 2012. (Magic Tree House - Fact Tracker Ser.: 26). (ENG.). 128p. (J). (gr. 2-5). 6.99 *(978-0-375-87025-5(3)*, Random Hse. Bks. for Young Readers) Random Hse. Children's Bks.

—Pandas & Other Endangered Species: A Perfect Time for Pandas. 2012. (Magic Tree House Fact Tracker Ser.: 26). lib. bdg. 16.00 *(978-0-606-26400-6(0)*, Turtleback) Turtleback Bks.

Parker, Russ. Wildlife Crisis. 2009. (Planet in Crisis Ser.). 32p. (gr. 5-8). (ENG., Illus.). (J). pap. 10.00 *(978-1-4358-0685-6(9))*; (YA). lib. bdg. 25.25 *(978-1-4358-5255-6(9))* Rosen Publishing Group, Inc., The. (Rosen Reference).

Parker, Steve. Endangered Animals. 2010. (Discovery of Life Ser.). 48p. (YA). lib. bdg. 19.95 *(978-1-4222-1519-7(9))* Mason Crest.

Pesta, K. My Ferret Dexter. 2008. 20p. per. 24.95 *(978-1-4241-9137-6(8))* America Star Bks.

Podojil, Catherine. Saving Endangered Species. 2005. (ENG., Illus.). 24p. (J). (gr. 5). pap. 5.97 net. *(978-0-328-13528-8(3)*, Scott Foresman) Pearson Schl.

Poitier, Anton. Once I Was a Cardboard Box... But Now I'm a Book about Polar Bears. Evans, Melvyn, illus. 2010. 24p. (J). (gr. k-3). 7.99 *(978-0-8416-7200-0(8))* Hammond World Atlas Corp.

—Once I Was a Comic... But Now I'm a Book about Tigers. Evans, Melvyn, illus. 2010. 24p. (J). (gr. k-3). 7.99 *(978-0-8416-7201-7(6))* Hammond World Atlas Corp.

Portman, Michael. Gorillas in Danger. 2011. (Animals at Risk Ser.). 24p. (J). (gr. 2-5). pap. 8.15 *(978-1-4339-5796-3(5))*; lib. bdg. 22.60 *(978-1-4339-5794-9(9))* Stevens, Gareth Publishing LLLP. (Gareth Stevens Learning Library).

—Pandas in Danger. 2011. (Animals at Risk Ser.). (Illus.). 24p. (J). (gr. 2-5). pap. 8.15 *(978-1-4339-5800-7(7))*; lib. bdg. 22.60 *(978-1-4339-5798-7(1))* Stevens, Gareth Publishing LLLP. (Gareth Stevens Learning Library).

—Tasmanian Devils in Danger. 2011. (Animals at Risk Ser.). (Illus.). 24p. (J). (gr. 2-5). 22.60 *(978-1-4339-5806-9(6))*; pap. 8.15 *(978-1-4339-5808-3(2))* Stevens, Gareth Publishing LLLP. (Gareth Stevens Learning Library).

—Tigers in Danger. 2011. (Animals at Risk Ser.). (Illus.). 24p. (J). (gr. 2-5). pap. 8.15 *(978-1-4339-5812-0(0))*; lib. bdg. 22.60 *(978-1-4339-5810-6(4))* Stevens, Gareth Publishing LLLP. (Gareth Stevens Learning Library).

—Whales in Danger. 2011. (Animals at Risk Ser.). (Illus.). 24p. (J). (gr. 2-5). 22.60 *(978-1-4339-5814-4(7))*; pap. 8.15 *(978-1-4339-5816-8(3))* Stevens, Gareth Publishing LLLP. (Gareth Stevens Learning Library).

Pratt-Serafini, Kristin Joy. A Walk in the Rainforest. Pratt-Serafini, Kristin Joy, illus. 2007. (Simply Nature Book Ser.). (Illus.). 26p. (J). (gr. -1 — 1). bds. 7.95 *(978-1-58469-088-7(7))* Dawn Pubns.

Pyers, Greg. Biodiversity of Coasts. 2010. (Biodiversity Ser.). 32p. (gr. 4-18). 28.50 *(978-1-60870-069-1(0))* Marshall Cavendish Corp.

—Biodiversity of Coral Reefs. 2010. (Biodiversity Ser.). 32p. (gr. 4-18). 28.50 *(978-1-60870-070-7(4))* Marshall Cavendish Corp.

—Biodiversity of Deserts. 2010. (Biodiversity Ser.). 32p. (gr. 4-18). 28.50 *(978-1-60870-071-4(2))* Marshall Cavendish Corp.

QEB Start Reading Together National Book Stores Edition: Animals in Danger. 2006. (J). per. *(978-1-59566-259-0(6))* QEB Publishing Inc.

Radley, Gail. Forests & Jungles. Sherlock, Jean, illus. (Vanishing from Ser.). 32p. 2005. (gr. 6-12). lib. bdg. 22.60 *(978-1-57505-405-6(1))* 2003. (J). (gr. 3-5). 6.95 *(978-1-57505-567-1(8))* Lerner Publishing Group.

—Grasslands & Deserts. Sherlock, Jean, illus. (Vanishing from Ser.). 32p. 2005. (J). (gr. 6-12). lib. bdg. 22.60 *(978-1-57505-406-3(X))* 2003. (YA). (gr. 3-5). 6.95 *(978-1-57505-568-8(6)*, Carolrhoda Bks.) Lerner Publishing Group.

—The Skies. Sherlock, Jean, illus. (Vanishing from Ser.). 32p. 2005. (gr. 6-12). lib. bdg. 22.60 *(978-1-57505-407-0(8))* 2003. (J). (gr. 3-5). pap. 6.95 *(978-1-57505-566-4(X))* Lerner Publishing Group.

—Waterways. Sherlock, Jean, illus. 2003. (Vanishing from Ser.). 32p. (J). (gr. 3-5). 6.95 *(978-1-57505-569-5(4))* Lerner Publishing Group.

Ransom, Candice. Endangered & Extinct Amphibians. 2014. (Lightning Bolt Books Animals in Danger Ser.). (ENG., Illus.). 32p. (gr. k-2). lib. bdg. 26.60 *(978-1-4677-1332-0(5)*, Lerner Pubns.) Lerner Publishing Group.

Reiter, Chris. The Blue Whale: A MyReportLinks.com Book. 2003. (Endangered & Threatened Animals Ser.). (Illus.). 48p. (J). (gr. 4-10). lib. bdg. 26.60 *(978-0-7660-5055-6(6)*, MyReportLinks.com Bks.) Enslow Pubs., Inc.

—The Gray Wolf: A MyReportLinks.com Book. 2003. (Endangered & Threatened Animals Ser.). (Illus.). 48p. (J). (gr. 4-10). lib. bdg. 26.60 *(978-0-7660-5056-3(4)*, MyReportLinks.com Bks.) Enslow Pubs., Inc.

Rhodes, Wendell. Threatened, Endangered, & Extinct Species. 2016. (Spotlight on Ecology & Life Science Ser.). 00024p. (J). (gr. 4-6). pap. 10.00 *(978-1-4994-2600-7(3)*, PowerKids Pr.) Rosen Publishing Group, Inc., The.

Rice, William. Animales Del Desierto en Peligro. 2016. (TIME for Kids en Español - Level 5 Ser.). (SPA.). 64p. (gr. 5-5). lib. bdg. 31.99 *(978-1-5157-2934-1(6))* Time for Kids Inc AUS. Dist: Capstone Pub.

—Animales Del Mar en Peligro. 2016. (TIME for Kids en Español - Level 5 Ser.). (SPA & ENG.). 64p. (gr. 5-5). lib. bdg. 31.99 *(978-1-5157-2935-8(4))* Time for Kids Inc AUS. Dist: Capstone Pub.

Rice, William B. Endangered Animals of the Desert, 1 vol. 2nd rev. ed. 2013. (Nonfiction Readers Ser.). (ENG.). 64p. (J). (gr. 5-5). pap. 10.99 *(978-1-4333-4936-2(1))*; (Illus.). pap. 31.96 *(978-1-4333-7435-7(8))* Teacher Created Materials, Inc.

—Endangered Animals of the Jungle, 1 vol. 2nd rev. ed. 2013. (Nonfiction Readers Ser.). (ENG.). 64p. (J). (gr. 5-5). pap. 10.99 *(978-1-4333-4937-9(X))*; (Illus.). pap. 31.96 *(978-1-4333-7436-4(6))* Teacher Created Materials, Inc.

—Endangered Animals of the Sea, 1 vol. 2nd rev. ed. 2013. (Nonfiction Readers Ser.). (ENG.). 64p. (J). (gr. 5-5). pap. 10.99 *(978-1-4333-4935-5(3))*; (Illus.). pap. 31.96 *(978-1-4333-7434-0(X))* Teacher Created Materials, Inc.

Riehecky, Janet, et al. Endangered & Threatened Animals. 2012. (Endangered & Threatened Animals Ser.). (ENG.). 32p. (gr. 3-4). lib. bdg. 167.94 *(978-1-4296-9179-6(4)*, Snap Bks.) Capstone Press of Coughlan Cos.

Ring, Susan. Project Otter. Kissock, Heather & Marshall, Diana, eds. 2003. (Zoo Life Ser.). (Illus.). 24p. (J). pap. 8.95 *(978-1-59036-059-0(1))* Weigl Pubs., Inc.

Robbins, Ken. Thunder on the Plains: The Story of the American Buffalo. Robbins, Ken, illus. 2009. (ENG., Illus.). 36p. (J). (gr. 2-5). pap. 10.99 *(978-1-4169-9536-4(6)*, Atheneum Bks. for Young Readers) Simon & Schuster Children's Publishing.

Roberts, Russell. Manatees. 2003. (Endangered Plants & Animals of the United States Ser.). (J). pap. *(978-1-58417-207-9(X))*; lib. bdg. *(978-1-58417-206-2(1))* Lake Street Pubs.

Rockett, Paul. Ten Thousand, Eight Hundred & Twenty Endangered Species in the Animal Kingdom. Ruffle, Mark, illus. 2015. (Big Countdown Ser.). (ENG.). 32p. (gr. 3-5). 29.99 *(978-1-4109-6879-1(0)*, Raintree Perspectives) Heinemann-Raintree.

Rosen Publishing Staff. Invaders from Earth, 1 vol. 2015. (Invaders from Earth Ser.). (ENG.). 32p. (J). 157.50 *(978-1-4777-5725-3(2)*, PowerKids Pr.) Rosen Publishing Group, Inc., The.

Roth, Susan L. & Trumbore, Cindy. Parrots over Puerto Rico, 1 vol. Roth, Susan L., illus. 2013. (ENG., Illus.). 48p. (J). 19.95 *(978-1-62014-004-8(7))* Lee & Low Bks., Inc.

Royston, Angela. Disappearing Wildlife. 2016. (Protect Our Planet Ser.). (ENG.). 32p. (gr. 1-3). pap. 8.29 *(978-1-4846-3591-9(4)*, Heinemann First Library) Heinemann-Raintree.

—Save the Giant Panda, 1. 2014. (Animal SOS! Ser.). (ENG.). 32p. (J). (gr. k-5). pap. 10.00 *(978-1-4777-6035-2(0)*, Windmill Bks.) Rosen Publishing Group, Inc., The.

—Save the Gorilla, 1. 2014. (Animal SOS! Ser.). (ENG., Illus.). 32p. (J). (gr. k-5). pap. 10.00 *(978-1-4777-6037-6(7)*, Windmill Bks.) Rosen Publishing Group, Inc., The.

—Save the Tiger, 1. 2014. (Animal SOS! Ser.). (ENG.). 32p. (J). (gr. k-5). 26.25 *(978-1-4777-6029-1(6)*, Windmill Bks.) Rosen Publishing Group, Inc., The.

Salmansohn, Pete & Kress, Stephen W. Saving Birds: Heroes Around the World, 1 vol. 2005. (ENG., Illus.). 40p. (gr. 3-6). 16.95 *(978-0-88448-237-6(5))* Tilbury Hse. Pubs.

Schueler, Donald G. The Gopher Tortoise: A MyReportLinks.com Book. 2003. (Endangered & Threatened Animals Ser.). (Illus.). 48p. (J). (gr. 4-10). lib. bdg. 25.26 *(978-0-7660-5053-2(X)*, MyReportLinks.com Bks.) Enslow Pubs., Inc.

Scott, Karen. Endangered Species & Friends in the U. S. A. Seamans, Amanda, illus. unabr. ed. Date not set. (J). (gr. -1-6). 16.95 *(978-1-889667-00-3(5))* Second Ark Pubns.

Shea, Abigail. Wolves in Danger. 2013. (Animals at Risk Ser.). 24p. (J). (gr. 2-5). pap. 8.15 *(978-1-4339-9179-0(9))* Stevens, Gareth Publishing LLLP.

Shea, Adele. Wolves in Danger. 2013. (Animals at Risk Ser.). (ENG., Illus.). 24p. (J). (gr. 2-5). lib. bdg. 22.60 *(978-1-4339-9178-3(0))* Stevens, Gareth Publishing LLLP.

Shea, Nicole. Poaching & Illegal Trade. 2013. (Animal 911: Environmental Threats Ser.). 48p. (J). (gr. 3-5). pap. 84.30 *(978-1-4339-9720-4(7))*; (ENG., Illus.). lib. bdg. 31.95 *(978-1-4339-9718-1(5))* Stevens, Gareth Publishing LLLP.

Sheehan, Sean. Endangered Species. 2009. (What If We Do Nothing? Ser.). 48p. (YA). (gr. 4-7). lib. bdg. 31.00 *(978-1-4339-0086-0(6))* Stevens, Gareth Publishing LLLP.

Simpson, Phillip. How Can We Save the Cheetah? A Problem & Solution Text, 1 vol. 2014. (Text Structures Ser.). (ENG.). 32p. (gr. 1-3). pap. 7.99 *(978-1-4846-0415-1(6)*, Heinemann First Library) Heinemann-Raintree.

Slade, Suzanne. What Can We Do about Endangered Animals? 2009. (J). 49.50 *(978-1-4358-2478-2(4)*, PowerKids Pr.); (ENG.). 24p. (J). pap. 8.25 *(978-1-4358-2477-5(6)*, PowerKids Pr.); (ENG., Illus.). 24p. (YA). (gr. 2-5). lib. bdg. 22.60 *(978-1-4042-8080-9(4))* Rosen Publishing Group, Inc., The.

Smalley, Carol Parenzan. Threat to the Spotted Owl. 2008. (On the Verge of Extinction Ser.). (Illus.). 32p. (YA). (gr. 2-5). lib. bdg. 25.70 *(978-1-58415-687-1(2))* Mitchell Lane Pubs., Inc.

Snyder, Lydia. Rhinos in Danger. 2013. (Animals at Risk Ser.). 24p. (J). (gr. 2-5). pap. 8.15 *(978-1-4339-9160-8(8))*; pap. 48.90 *(978-1-4339-9161-5(6))*; (ENG., Illus.). lib. bdg. 22.60 *(978-1-4339-9159-2(4))* Stevens, Gareth Publishing LLLP.

Snyder, Trish. Alligator & Crocodile Rescue: Changing the Future for Endangered Wildlife. 2006. (Firefly Animal Rescue Ser.). (ENG., Illus.). 64p. (J). (gr. 5-12). 19.95 *(978-1-55297-920-4(2)*, 9781552979204); pap. 9.95 *(978-1-55297-919-8(9)*, 9781552979198) Firefly Bks., Ltd.

Sobol, Richard, photos by. An Elephant in the Backyard. 2004. (Illus.). (J). *(978-0-525-46970-4(2)*, Dutton Juvenile) Penguin Publishing Group.

Somervill, Barbara A. American Bison. 2007. (21st Century Skills Library: Road to Recovery Ser.). (ENG., Illus.). 32p. (gr. 4-8). lib. bdg. 29.93 *(978-1-60279-031-5(0)*, 200077) Cherry Lake Publishing.

Sovak, Jan. Endangered Animals. 2009. (Dover Nature Coloring Book Ser.). (ENG., Illus.). 32p. (J). (gr. 1-5). pap. 3.99 *(978-0-486-46793-1(7))* Dover Pubns., Inc.

Spilsbury, Louise. Save the Cheetah, 1. 2014. (Animal SOS! Ser.). (ENG.). 32p. (J). (gr. k-5). 26.25 *(978-1-4777-6033-8(4)*, Windmill Bks.) Rosen Publishing Group, Inc., The.

—Save the Chimpanzee, 1. 2014. (Animal SOS! Ser.). (ENG., Illus.). 32p. (J). (gr. k-5). pap. 10.00 *(978-1-4777-6036-9(9)*, Windmill Bks.) Rosen Publishing Group, Inc., The.

—Save the Humpback Whale, 1. 2014. (Animal SOS! Ser.). (ENG.). 32p. (J). (gr. k-5). pap. 10.00 *(978-1-4777-6034-5(2)*, Windmill Bks.) Rosen Publishing Group, Inc., The.

Spilsbury, Richard. Invaders from Earth, 1 vol. 2015. (Invaders from Earth Ser.). (ENG.). 32p. (J). 60.00 *(978-1-4994-0324-4(0)*, PowerKids Pr.) Rosen Publishing Group, Inc., The.

Spilsbury, Richard & Spilsbury, Louise. Animals in Danger. 2013. (Animals in Danger Ser.). (ENG.). 32p. (gr. 1-3). pap. 47.94 *(978-1-4329-7685-9(0))*; lib. bdg. 109.28 *(978-1-4329-7678-1(8))* Heinemann-Raintree. (Heinemann First Library).

—Animals in Danger in Africa, 1 vol. 2013. (Animals in Danger Ser.). (ENG.). 32p. (gr. 1-3). 27.32 *(978-1-4329-7672-9(9))*; pap. 8.95 *(978-1-4329-7679-8(6))* Heinemann-Raintree. (Heinemann First Library).

—Animals in Danger in Asia, 1 vol. 2013. (Animals in Danger Ser.). (ENG.). 32p. (gr. 1-3). 27.32 *(978-1-4329-7673-6(7))*; pap. 8.95 *(978-1-4329-7680-4(X))* Heinemann-Raintree. (Heinemann First Library).

—Animals in Danger in Australia, 1 vol. 2013. (Animals in Danger Ser.). (ENG.). 32p. (gr. 1-3). pap. 8.95 *(978-1-4329-7681-1(8)*, Heinemann First Library) Heinemann-Raintree.

—Animals in Danger in Europe, 1 vol. 2013. (Animals in Danger Ser.). (ENG.). 32p. (gr. 1-3). 27.32 *(978-1-4329-7675-0(3))*; pap. 8.95 *(978-1-4329-7682-8(6))* Heinemann-Raintree. (Heinemann First Library).

—Animals in Danger in North America, 1 vol. 2013. (Animals in Danger Ser.). (ENG.). 32p. (gr. 1-3). 27.32 *(978-1-4329-7676-7(1))*; pap. 8.95 *(978-1-4329-7683-5(4))* Heinemann-Raintree. (Heinemann First Library).

—Animals in Danger in South America, 1 vol. 2013. (Animals in Danger Ser.). (ENG.). 32p. (gr. 1-3). pap. 8.95 *(978-1-4329-7684-2(2)*, Heinemann First Library) Heinemann-Raintree.

Stearns, Precious. Eye to Eye with Endangered Species, 10 vols., Set. Incl. Steller Sea Lions. (Illus.). 24p. (J). (gr. 3-6). 2009. lib. bdg. 27.07 *(978-1-60694-402-8(9))*; 2011. Set lib. bdg. 270.70 o.p. *(978-1-61590-960-5(5))* Rourke Educational Media.

Stille, Darlene R. Protecting Animals. 2011. (Go Green! Ser.). (ENG.). 32p. (J). (gr. 1-4). lib. bdg. 28.50 *(978-1-60973-174-8(3)*, 201153) Child's World, Inc., The.

Stone, Lynn M. Tigers. 2004. (Nature Watch Ser.). (ENG.). 48p. (gr. 4-8). 27.93 *(978-1-57505-578-7(3)*, Carolrhoda Bks.) Lerner Publishing Group.

Stone, Tanya Lee. Gorillas. 2003. (Wild Wild World Ser.). (Illus.). 24p. (J). 24.94 *(978-1-56711-814-8(3)*, Blackbirch Pr., Inc.) Cengage Gale.

Thomas, Keltie. Bear Rescue: Changing the Future for Endangered Wildlife. 2006. (Firefly Animal Rescue Ser.). (ENG., Illus.). 64p. (J). (gr. 5-12). 19.95 *(978-1-55297-922-8(9)*, 9781552979228); pap. 9.95 *(978-1-55297-921-1(0)*, 9781552979211) Firefly Bks., Ltd.

Torres, John. Threat to the Giant Panda. 2008. (On the Verge of Extinction Ser.). (Illus.). 32p. (YA). (gr. 2-5). lib. bdg. 25.70 *(978-1-58415-689-5(9))* Mitchell Lane Pubs., Inc.

Torres, John Albert. The African Elephant: A MyReportLinks. com Book. 2004. (Endangered & Threatened Animals Ser.). (Illus.). 48p. (J). lib. bdg. 25.26 *(978-0-7660-5174-4(9)*, MyReportLinks.com Bks.) Enslow Pubs., Inc.

—The Manatee: A MyReportLinks. com Book. 2004. (Endangered & Threatened Animals Ser.). (Illus.). 48p. (J). lib. bdg. 25.26 *(978-0-7660-5173-7(0)*, MyReportLinks.com Bks.) Enslow Pubs., Inc.

Tracqui, Valérie. The Whale. 2004. (Animal Close-Ups Ser.). (Illus.). 28p. (J). pap. 6.95 *(978-1-57091-625-0(X))* Charlesbridge Publishing, Inc.

Twist, Clint. Endangered Animals Dictionary: An a to Z of Threatened Species. 2004. (Illus.). 64p. (J). *(978-0-439-55094-9(7))* Scholastic, Inc.

Vanishing From. 2004. (Illus.). lib. bdg. 7.95 *(978-0-8225-3344-3(8))* Lerner Publishing Group.

Wade, Mary Dodson. Texas Plants & Animals. 2003. (Heinemann State Studies). (Illus.). 48p. (J). lib. bdg. 27.07 *(978-1-4034-0690-3(1))* Heinemann-Raintree.

Wagner, Viqi. Endangered Species. 2007. (Opposing Viewpoints Ser.). (ENG.). 224p. (gr. 10-12). 48.80 *(978-0-7377-2931-3(7)*, Greenhaven Pr., Inc.) Cengage Gale.

Wagner, Viqi, ed. Endangered Species. 2007. (Opposing Viewpoints Ser.). (ENG.). 230p. (YA). (gr. 7-12). 29.45 *(978-0-7377-2932-0(5)*, Greenhaven Pr., Inc.) Cengage Gale.

Walker, Sally M. Crocodiles. 2003. (Nature Watch Ser.). (ENG., Illus.). 48p. (gr. 4-8). lib. bdg. 27.93 *(978-1-57505-345-5(4))* Lerner Publishing Group.

Watson, Cindy. Unloved & Endangered Animals: What You Can Do. 2010. (Green Issues in Focus Ser.). (Illus.). 128p. (J). (gr. 7-12). 33.27 *(978-0-7660-3345-0(7))* Enslow Pubs., Inc.

Watt, E. Melanie. Leatherback Turtles, with Code. 2012. (Animals on the Brink Ser.). (ENG., Illus.). 48p. (J). (gr. 3-7). pap. 14.95 *(978-1-61913-428-7(4)*, AV2 by Weigl) Weigl Pubs., Inc.

Webb, Barb. Endangered! 2011. (ENG., Illus.). 24p. (gr. k-2). pap. 8.95 *(978-1-61741-974-4(5))* Rourke Educational Media.

Wells, Robert E. Can We Share the World with Tigers? Wells, Robert E., illus. 2012. (Wells of Knowledge Science Ser.). (ENG., Illus.). 32p. (J). (gr. 1-3). 16.99 *(978-0-8075-1055-1(6))* Whitman, Albert & Co.

Williams, Judith. Saving Endangered Animals with a Scientist. 2004. (I Like Science! Ser.). (Illus.). 24p. (J). (gr. 2-4). lib. bdg. 21.26 *(978-0-7660-2276-8(5))* Enslow Pubs., Inc.

Williams, Lily. If Sharks Disappeared. Williams, Lily, illus. 2017. (ENG., Illus.). 40p. (J). 17.99 *(978-1-62672-413-6(X)*, 9781626724136) Roaring Brook Pr.

Winter, Barbara. The 10 Most Endangered Animals. 2008. 14.99 *(978-1-55448-552-9(5))* Scholastic Library Publishing.

Wolves in Danger. 2013. (Animals at Risk Ser.). 24p. (J). (gr. 2-5). pap. 48.90 *(978-1-4339-9180-6(2))* Stevens, Gareth Publishing LLLP.

World Book, Inc Staff, contrib. by. Code Red: Animals in Peril: A Supplement to Childcraft-The How & Why Library. 2011. (Illus.). 206p. (J). *(978-0-7166-0626-0(7))* World Bk., Inc.

—Endangered & Threatened Species of Africa. 2014. (J). *(978-0-7166-5621-0(3))* World Bk., Inc.

—Endangered Animals of Australia, New Zealand, & Pacific Islands. 2014. *(978-0-7166-5623-4(X))* World Bk., Inc.

World Book, Inc. Staff, contrib. by. Endangered Animals of Europe. 2014. (J). *(978-0-7166-5624-1(8))* World Bk., Inc.

World Book, Inc Staff, contrib. by. Endangered Animals of North America. 2014. (J). *(978-0-7166-5625-8(6))* World Bk., Inc.

—Endangered Animals of the Oceans. 2014. (J). *(978-0-7166-5627-2(2))* World Bk., Inc.

—Endangered Animals of the World. 2014. (J). *(978-0-7166-5620-3(5))* World Bk., Inc.

—Wildlife & Climate Change. (Illus.). 44p. (J). 2016. *(978-0-7166-2719-7(1))* 2015. *(978-0-7166-2709-8(4))* World Bk., Inc.

Yomtov, Nelson. Poachers. 2016. (True Book(tm), a — The New Criminals Ser.). (ENG., Illus.). 48p. (J). lib. bdg. 31.00 *(978-0-531-21467-1(2)*, Children's Pr.) Scholastic Library Publishing.

Young, Sarah & Candlewick Press Staff. Endangered Animals: a 3D Pocket Guide. Young, Sarah, illus. 2014. (Panorama Pops Ser.). (ENG., Illus.). 30p. (J). (gr. k-4). 8.99 *(978-0-7636-6985-0(7))* Candlewick Pr.

ENDANGERED SPECIES—FICTION

Bracegirdle, P. J. Fiendish Deeds. 2009. (Joy of Spooking Ser.: 1). (ENG.). 224p. (J). (gr. 3-7). pap. 5.99 *(978-1-4169-3417-2(0)*, McElderry, Margaret K. Bks.) McElderry, Margaret K. Bks.

Child, Lauren. I Am Going to Save a Panda! 2010. (Charlie & Lola Ser.). lib. bdg. 13.55 *(978-0-606-10628-3(6)*, Turtleback) Turtleback Bks.

Cline-Ransome, Lesa. Whale Trails, Before & Now. Karas, G. Brian, illus. 2015. (ENG.). 40p. (J). (gr. k-4). 17.99 *(978-0-8050-9642-2(6)*, 9780805096422, Holt, Henry & Co. Bks. For Young Readers) Holt, Henry & Co.

Cochard, David, illus. The Legend of Honey Hollow. 2008. 46p. (J). 16.99 *(978-0-9799444-0-6(6))* Joey Publishing.

Cowcher, Helen. Jaguar. (CHI, ENG, URD, TUR & VIE., Illus.). 40p. 16.95 *(978-1-84059-009-8(2))* Milet Publishing.

—Jaguar. (J). (gr. 1-2). *(978-0-590-36037-1(X))*; (SPA., Illus.). pap. 3.96 net. *(978-0-590-87599-8(X)*, SO30738, Scholastic Pr.) Scholastic, Inc.

Doerr, Bonnie J. Kenzie's Key. Aberle, Xylena Apotheloz, illus. 2003. 211p. (J). 16.95 *(978-0-9619155-6-8(0))* Laurel & Herbert, Inc.

—Stakeout. Edwards, Laurie J. & Britt, Joanna, illus. 2011. 310p. pap. 12.99 *(978-1-61603-007-0(0))* Leap Bks.

Dowson, Nick. Tracks of a Panda. Rong, Yu, illus. 2007. (ENG.). 32p. (J). (gr. k-3). 16.99 *(978-0-7636-3146-8(9))* Candlewick Pr.

—Tracks of a Panda: Read & Wonder. Rong, Yu, illus. 2010. (Read & Wonder Ser.). (ENG.). 32p. (J). (gr. -1-3). pap. 6.99 *(978-0-7636-4737-7(3))* Candlewick Pr.

Gibbs, Stuart. Big Game. 2015. (FunJungle Ser.). (ENG.). 352p. (J). (gr. 3-7). 17.99 *(978-1-4814-2333-5(9)*, Simon & Schuster Bks. For Young Readers) Simon & Schuster Bks. For Young Readers.

Gill, Shelley. Big Blue. Barrow, Ann, illus. 2005. (ENG.). 32p. (J). (gr. k-3). 7.95 *(978-1-57091-667-0(5))* Charlesbridge Publishing, Inc.

Irwin, Bindi, et al. Surfing with Turtles: Bindi Wildlife Adventures. 2013. (Bindi's Wildlife Adventures Ser.: 8). (ENG.). 112p. (J). (gr. 3-6). pap. 4.99 *(978-1-4022-8094-8(7)*, Sourcebooks Jabberwocky) Sourcebooks, Inc.

Jordan, Rosa. The Last Wild Place, 1 vol. 2008. (ENG.). 256p. (J). (gr. 3-7). 15.95 *(978-1-56145-458-7(3)*, Peachtree Junior) Peachtree Pubs.

Kehret, Peg. Screaming Eagles. 2008. (ENG.). 128p. (J). (gr. 3-7). pap. 7.99 *(978-1-4169-9106-9(9)*, Simon & Schuster/Paula Wiseman Bks.) Simon & Schuster/Paula Wiseman Bks.

Leavitt, Martine. Blue Mountain. 2014. (ENG.). 176p. (J). (gr. 3-7). 15.99 *(978-0-374-37864-6(9)*, 9780374378646, Farrar, Straus & Giroux (BYR)) Farrar, Straus & Giroux.

Lee, Julia Elizabeth. Seahorses Down Under. Weiser, Robert, ed. (Defenders of Wildlife Ser.). (Illus.). 50+p. (J). (gr. k-3). lib. bdg. 9.95 *(978-0-9666857-0-1(9))* Dawn of Day Childrens Publishing Co., Inc.

Lumry, Amanda & Hurwitz, Laura. Project Panda. 2008. (J). *(978-1-60040-009-4(4))*; *(978-1-60040-008-7(6))* Eaglemont Pr.

Martin, Bill, Jr. Oso Panda, Oso Panda, ¿Qué Ves Ahí? Mlawer, Teresa, tr. Carle, Eric, illus. 2008. (Brown Bear & Friends Ser.).Tr. of Brown Bear, Brown Bear, What Do You See? (SPA & ENG.). 32p. (J). (gr. -1-k). 17.95 *(978-0-8050-8348-4(0)*, 9780805083484, Holt, Henry & Co. Bks. For Young Readers) Holt, Henry & Co.

—Oso Panda, Oso Panda, ¿Qué Ves Ahí? Mlawer, Teresa, tr. Carle, Eric, illus. 2009. (Brown Bear & Friends Ser.).Tr. of Brown Bear, Brown Bear, What Do You See? (SPA & ENG.). 26p. (J). (gr. -1-k). 9.99 *(978-0-8050-8756-7(7)*, 9780805087567, Holt, Henry & Co. Bks. For Young Readers) Holt, Henry & Co.

—Panda Bear, Panda Bear, What Do You See? Carle, Eric, illus. (Brown Bear & Friends Ser.). (J). 2014. (ENG.). 28p. (gr. -1-k). bds. 12.99 *(978-0-8050-9950-8(6)*, 9780805099508) 2011. (ENG.). 40p. (gr. -1-2). 8.99 *(978-0-8050-9292-9(7)*, 9780805092929) 2007. 32p. 7.95

(978-0-8050-8799-4(0)) 2007. (ENG.). 32p. (gr. -1-k). pap. 27.99 *(978-0-8050-8102-2(X)*, 9780805081022) 2006. (ENG.). 28p. (gr. -1-k). bds. 7.95 *(978-0-8050-8078-0(3)*, 9780805080780) Holt, Henry & Co. (Holt, Henry & Co. Bks. For Young Readers).

—Panda Bear, Panda Bear, What Do You See?, 1 vol. Carle, Eric, illus. unabr. ed. 2011. (Brown Bear & Friends Ser.). (ENG.). (J). (gr. -1-k). 9.99 *(978-1-4272-1254-2(6)*, 9781427212542) Macmillan Audio.

—Panda Bear, Panda Bear, What Do You See? Carle, Eric, illus. 2013. (Slide & Find Ser.). (ENG.). 22p. (J). (gr. -1 — 1). bds. 12.99 *(978-0-312-51581-2(2)*, 9780312515812, Priddy Bks.) St. Martin's Pr.

—Panda Bear, Panda Bear, What Do You See? 10th Anniversary Edition. Carle, Eric, illus. 2013. (ENG.). 28p. (J). (gr. -1-k). 19.99 *(978-0-8050-9778-8(3)*, 9780805097788, Holt, Henry & Co. Bks. For Young Readers) Holt, Henry & Co.

McClements, George. Dinosaur Woods: Can Seven Clever Critters Save Their Forest Home? McClements, George, illus. 2009. (ENG., Illus.). 40p. (J). (gr. -1-2). 16.99 *(978-1-4169-8626-3(X)*, Beach Lane Bks.) Beach Lane Bks.

Meadows, Daisy. Kitty the Tiger Fairy. 2015. (Baby Animal Rescue Fairies Ser.: 2). (ENG.). 80p. (J). (gr. 2-5). pap. 4.99 *(978-0-545-70846-3(X)*, Scholastic Paperbacks) Scholastic, Inc.

Mitchell, Todd. Species. 2017. (ENG.). 256p. (J). (gr. 3-7). 16.99 *(978-0-399-55558-9(7)*, Delacorte Bks. for Young Readers) Random Hse. Children's Bks.

Osborne, Mary Pope. Tigers at Twilight. unabr. ed. 2004. (Magic Tree House Ser.: No. 19). 72p. (J). (gr. k-3). pap. 17.00 incl. audio *(978-0-8072-0928-8(7)*, S FTR 251 SP, Listening Library) Random Hse. Audio Publishing Group.

Osborne, Mary Pope, et al. Tigres Al Anochecer. Murdocca, Sal, illus. 2008. (Casa del Arbol Ser.: 19).Tr. of Tigers at Twilight. (SPA.). (J). (gr. 2-4). pap. 5.99 *(978-1-933032-49-8(9))* Lectorum Pubns., Inc.

Panda, Jake G. The Case of the Cursed Dodo. 2014. (Illus.). 173p. (J). pap. 8.99 *(978-0-9909391-1-5(1))* Woolley Family Studios.

Phillips, Helen. Here Where the Sunbeams Are Green. (ENG.). 304p. (J). (gr. 5). 2013. 7.99 *(978-0-307-93145-0(5)*, Yearling) 2012. E-Book *(978-0-307-97487-7(1)*, Delacorte Bks. for Young Readers) Random Hse. Children's Bks.

Ruddra, Anshumani. Dorje's Stripes. A-Park, Gwangjo & A-Park, Jung, illus. 2011. (ENG.). 40p. (J). (gr. k-4). 9.99 *(978-1-935279-98-3(X))* Kane Miller.

Skurzynski, Gloria & Ferguson, Alane. Over the Edge. 2008. (Mysteries in Our National Park Ser.). (ENG., Illus.). 160p. (J). (gr. 3-7). per. 4.99 *(978-1-4263-0177-3(4)*, National Geographic Children's Bks.) National Geographic Society.

Smith, Dale. What the Orangutan Told Alice: A Rain Forest Adventure. Smith, Dale & Russon, Anne E., photos by. 2003. (Illus.). 192p. (gr. 6-12). pap. 15.95 *(978-0-9651452-8-2(X))* Deer Creek Publishing.

Steinkraus, Kyla. La Casita Del Arbol. 2012. (SPA & ENG.). 24p. (gr. 2-3). pap. 8.95 *(978-1-61810-539-4(6))* Rourke Educational Media.

Storm, Hannah, frwd. Buddy Booby's Birthmark. 2006. (Illus.). 36p. (J). 21.99 *(978-0-9794413-0-1(7))*; pap. 15.99 *(978-0-9794413-1-8(5))* E & D Bks., Ltd.

Tiitinen, Esko-Pekka. Drops of Life. 2012. (ENG., Illus.). 24p. (J). (gr. k-2). *(978-84-15241-31-7(3))* D P & G Military Pubs.

Van Draanen, Wendelin. Sammy Keyes & the Wild Things. Biggs, Brian, illus. 2008. (Sammy Keyes Ser.: 11). (ENG.). 320p. (J). (gr. 5-7). 7.99 *(978-0-440-42112-2(8)*, Yearling) Random Hse. Children's Bks.

Wall, Suzy. The Dodo's Last Stand. 2005. (J). pap. *(978-1-4108-4221-3(5))* Benchmark Education Co.

ENDURANCE, PHYSICAL

see Physical Fitness

ENERGY

see Force and Energy

ENFORCEMENT OF LAW

see Law Enforcement

ENGINEERING

see also specific forms of engineering, e.g. Chemical Engineering

ABDO Publishing Company Staff. Great Achievements in Engineering. 2014. (Great Achievements in Engineering Ser.: 6). (ENG.). 112p. (J). (gr. 6-12). lib. bdg. 213.84 *(978-1-62403-424-4(1)*, Essential Library) ABDO Publishing Co.

Allen, John. Careers in Environmental & Energy Technology. 2017. (ENG.). 80p. (J). (gr. 5-12). *(978-1-68282-110-7(2))* ReferencePoint Pr., Inc.

Amidon Lusted, Marcia. Solving Real World Problems with Agricultural Engineering, 01 vols., 1. 2016. (Let's Find Out! Ser.). (ENG., Illus.). 32p. (J). 23.45 *(978-1-68048-261-4(0)*, Britannica Educational Publishing) Rosen Publishing Group, Inc., The.

Anderson, Kelli. This Book Is a Planetarium: And Other Extraordinary Pop-Up Contraptions. 2017. (ENG., Illus.). 5p. 40.00 *(978-1-4521-3621-9(1))* Chronicle Bks. LLC.

Bailey, Diane. Biomedical Engineers!, Vol. 10. 2015. (Scientists in Action Ser.). (Illus.). 48p. (J). (gr. 5). 20.95 *(978-1-4222-3420-4(7))* Mason Crest.

Barber, Nicola. Buildings & Structures, 1 vol. 2010. (From Fail to Win! Learning from Bad Ideas Ser.). (ENG.). 56p. (gr. 5-8). 34.65 *(978-1-4109-3907-4(3)*, Raintree Freestyle) Heinemann-Raintree.

Basher, Simon & Jackson, Tom. Engineering: The Riveting World of Buildings & Machines. 2017. (Basher Science Ser.). (ENG.). 128p. 14.99 *(978-0-7534-7310-8(0)*, 9780753473108, Kingfisher) Roaring Brook Pr.

—Engineering Your World: The Riveting World of Buildings & Machines. 2017. (Basher Science Ser.). (ENG.). 128p. pap. 9.99 *(978-0-7534-7311-5(9)*, 9780753473115, Kingfisher) Roaring Brook Pr.

Beaty, Andrea. Rosie Revere's Big Project Book for Bold Engineers. Roberts, David, illus. 2017. (ENG.). 96p. (J). (gr. k-2). pap. 14.95 *(978-1-4197-1910-3(6)*, Abrams Bks. for Young Readers) Abrams, Inc.

Biskup, Agnieszka. The Incredible Work of Engineers with Max Axiom, Super Scientist, 1 vol. Baez, Marcelo, illus. 2013. (Graphic Science & Engineering in Action Ser.). (ENG.). 32p. (gr. 3-4). pap. 8.10 *(978-1-62065-705-8(8))*; lib. bdg. 30.65 *(978-1-4296-9937-2(X))* Capstone Press of Coughlan Cos. (Graphic Library).

Biskup, Agnieszka & Enz, Tammy. Max Axiom Science & Engineering Activities. Baez, Marcelo, illus. 2015. (Max Axiom Science & Engineering Activities Ser.). (ENG.). 32p. (gr. 3-4). pap. 31.80 *(978-1-4914-2536-7(9)*, Graphic Library) Capstone Press of Coughlan Cos.

—Super Cool Science & Engineering Activities. 2015. (ENG., Illus.). 128p. (gr. 3-4). pap. 14.95 *(978-1-62370-232-8(1))* Capstone Young Readers of Coughlan Cos.

Biskup, Agnieszka, et al. Graphic Science & Engineering in Action. Baez, Marcelo, illus. 2013. (Graphic Science & Engineering in Action Ser.). (ENG.). 32p. (gr. 3-4). lib. bdg. 122.60 *(978-1-4296-9938-9(8)*, Graphic Library) Capstone Press of Coughlan Cos.

Bow, James. Energy from Earth's Core: Geothermal Energy. 2015. (Next Generation Energy Ser.). (ENG., Illus.). 32p. (J). *(978-0-7787-1979-3(0))* Crabtree Publishing Co.

Brasch, Nicolas. Triumphs of Engineering. 2012. (Discovery Education: Technology Ser.). (ENG., Illus.). 32p. (J). (gr. 3-6). 25.25 *(978-1-4488-7887-1(X))*; pap. 10.00 *(978-1-4488-7969-4(8))* Rosen Publishing Group, Inc., The. (PowerKids Pr.).

Brennan, Linda Crotta. Geothermal Power. 2013. (J). *(978-1-61080-969-6(6))*; (ENG.). 32p. (gr. 4-8). 28.50 *(978-1-61080-894-1(0)*, 202555); (ENG.). 32p. (gr. 4-8). pap. 14.21 *(978-1-61080-919-1(X)*, 202557) Cherry Lake Publishing.

Britcher, Angela. The Pros & Cons of Geothermal Power. 2016. (Economics of Energy Ser.). (ENG., Illus.). 80p. (J). (gr. 7-7). lib. bdg. 35.64 *(978-1-5026-0956-4(8))* Cavendish Square Publishing.

Conklin, Wendy. STEM Careers: Enhancing Engineering. 2017. (Time for Kids Nonfiction Readers Ser.). lib. bdg. 20.85 ***(978-0-606-40289-7(6))*** Turtleback Bks.

Cook, Eric. Prototyping. 2015. (21st Century Skills Innovation Library: Makers As Innovators Ser.). (ENG.). 32p. (J). (gr. 4-8). 29.93 *(978-1-63188-869-4(2)*, 206056) Cherry Lake Publishing.

Craats, Rennay. Construction Q & A. 2013. (J). *(978-1-62127-412-4(8))*; pap. *(978-1-62127-418-6(7))* Weigl Pubs., Inc.

Designing Engineering Solutions. 2015. (Designing Engineering Solutions Ser.). (ENG.). 144p. (YA). (gr. 8-8). 299.53 *(978-1-5026-0386-9(1))* Cavendish Square Publishing.

Doeden, Matt. Finding Out about Geothermal Energy. 2014. (Searchlight Books — What Are Energy Sources? Ser.). (Illus.). 40p. (gr. 3-4). pap. 8.95 *(978-1-4677-4554-3(5))*; (ENG., (J). lib. bdg. 27.93 *(978-1-4677-3658-9(9)*, Lerner Pubns.) Lerner Publishing Group.

Dorling Kindersley Publishing Staff. DK Findout! Engineering. 2017. (DK Find Out! Ser.). (ENG.). 64p. (J). (gr. 1-4). pap. 10.99 ***(978-1-4654-6234-3(1)***, DK Children) Dorling Kindersley Publishing, Inc.

Duke, Shirley. Enterprise Stem. 2011. (ENG., Illus.). 48p. (gr. 4-6). pap. 10.95 *(978-1-61741-983-6(4))* Rourke Educational Media.

Ebner, Aviva. Engineering Science Experiments. 2011. (Experiments for Future Scientists Ser.). (Illus.). 164p. (J). (gr. 5-8). 35.00 *(978-1-60413-852-8(1))* Facts On File, Inc.

Engineering Eurekas. 2016. (Engineering Eurekas Ser.). 00032p. (J). (gr. 3-4). 157.50 *(978-1-5081-5319-1(1)*, PowerKids Pr.) Rosen Publishing Group, Inc., The.

Enz, Tammy. Build It: Invent New Structures & Contraptions, 1 vol. 2012. (Invent It Ser.). (ENG.). 32p. (gr. 3-4). pap. 8.10 *(978-1-4296-7981-7(6))*; pap. 47.70 *(978-1-4296-8455-2(0))*; lib. bdg. 27.32 *(978-1-4296-7635-9(3))* Capstone Press of Coughlan Cos. (Fact Finders).

—Build Your Own Car, Rocket, & Other Things That Go. 2011. (Build It Yourself Ser.). (ENG.). 32p. (gr. 3-4). pap. 47.70 *(978-1-4296-6428-8(2)*, Edge Bks.) Capstone Press of Coughlan Cos.

—Build Your Own Fort, Igloo, & Other Hangouts. 2011. (Build It Yourself Ser.). (ENG.). 32p. (gr. 3-4). pap. 47.70 *(978-1-4296-6429-5(0)*, Edge Bks.) Capstone Press of Coughlan Cos.

—Build Your Own Fort, Igloo, & Other Hangouts, 1 vol. Haus, Estudio, illus. 2010. (Build It Yourself Ser.). (ENG.). 32p. (gr. 3-4). lib. bdg. 27.99 *(978-1-4296-5436-4(8)*, Edge Bks.) Capstone Press of Coughlan Cos.

—Build Your Own Mini Golf Course, Lemonade Stand, & Other Things to Do. (Build It Yourself Ser.). (ENG.). 32p. (gr. 3-4). 2011. pap. 47.70 *(978-1-4296-6430-1(4))* 2010. lib. bdg. 27.99 *(978-1-4296-5438-8(4))* Capstone Press of Coughlan Cos. (Edge Bks.).

—Build Your Own Periscope, Flashlight, & Other Useful Stuff. 2011. (Build It Yourself Ser.). (ENG.). 32p. (gr. 3-4). pap. 47.70 *(978-1-4296-6431-8(2)*, Edge Bks.) Capstone Press of Coughlan Cos.

—Building Structures & Towers. 2017. (Young Engineers Ser.). (ENG., Illus.). 32p. (gr. 1-2). lib. bdg. 27.32 *(978-1-4846-3746-3(1)*, Heinemann First Library) Heinemann-Raintree.

—Invent It. 2012. (Invent It Ser.). (ENG.). 32p. (gr. 3-4). pap. 190.80 *(978-1-4296-8460-6(7))*; pap. 31.80 *(978-1-4296-8459-0(3))*; lib. bdg. 81.96 *(978-1-4296-8164-3(0))* Capstone Press of Coughlan Cos. (Fact Finders).

—Super Cool Construction Activities with Max Axiom. Baez, Marcelo, illus. 2015. (Max Axiom Science & Engineering Activities Ser.). (ENG.). 32p. (gr. 3-4). lib. bdg. 30.65 *(978-1-4914-2078-2(2)*, Graphic Library) Capstone Press of Coughlan Cos.

—Super Cool Mechanical Activities with Max Axiom. Baez, Marcelo, illus. 2015. (Max Axiom Science & Engineering Activities Ser.). (ENG.). 32p. (gr. 3-4). lib. bdg. 30.65 *(978-1-4914-2080-5(4)*, Graphic Library) Capstone Press of Coughlan Cos.

Enz, Tammy & Biskup, Agnieszka. Max Axiom Science & Engineering Activities. Baez, Marcelo, illus. 2015. (Max Axiom Science & Engineering Activities Ser.). (ENG.). 32p. (gr. 3-4). lib. bdg. 122.60 *(978-1-4914-2535-0(0)*, Graphic Library) Capstone Press of Coughlan Cos.

Enz, Tammy, et al. Graphic Science & Engineering in Action. Baez, Marcelo, illus. 2013. (Graphic Science & Engineering in Action Ser.). (ENG.). 32p. (gr. 3-4). pap. 31.80 *(978-1-62065-707-2(4))*; pap. 190.80 *(978-1-62065-708-9(2))* Capstone Press of Coughlan Cos. (Graphic Library).

Felix, Rebecca. Cool Engineering Projects: Fun & Creative Workshop Activities. 2016. (ENG., Illus.). 32p. (J). *(978-1-68078-127-4(8))* ABDO Publishing Co.

Flynn, Riley. Finding Information & Making Arguments. 2016. (Science & Engineering Practices Ser.). (ENG., Illus.). 24p. (gr. k-1). lib. bdg. 26.65 *(978-1-5157-0948-0(5)*, Pebble Plus) Capstone Press of Coughlan Cos.

—Science & Engineering Practices. 2016. (Science & Engineering Practices Ser.). (ENG.). 24p. (gr. k-1). pap. 27.80 *(978-1-5157-1388-3(1)*, Pebble Plus) Capstone Press of Coughlan Cos.

Ford, Carin T. Henry Ford: The Car Man. 2003. (Famous Inventors Ser.). (Illus.). 32p. (J). (gr. 1-4). lib. bdg. 22.60 *(978-0-7660-2179-2(3))* Enslow Pubs., Inc.

Gardner, Robert & Conklin, Joshua. Experiments for Future Engineers. 2016. (Experiments for Future STEM Professionals Ser.). 128p. (J). (gr. 6-6). 37.27 *(978-0-7660-7853-6(1))* Enslow Pubs., Inc.

Goeken, Brook. My Mom's an Engineer. 2004. (Illus.). 32p. 9.99 *(978-1-881018-93-3(8))* Great Lakes Press, Inc.

Gonzales, Doreen. Seven Wonders of the Modern World: A MyReportLinks. com Book. 2005. (Seven Wonders of the World Ser.). (Illus.). 48p. (J). lib. bdg. 25.26 *(978-0-7660-5292-5(3)*, MyReportLinks.com Bks.) Enslow Pubs., Inc.

—What Are the 7 Wonders of the Modern World? 2013. (What Are the Seven Wonders of the World? Ser.). 48p. (J). (gr. 4-10). pap. 8.95 *(978-1-4644-0231-9(0))*; 25.27 *(978-0-7660-4152-3(2))* Enslow Pubs., Inc.

Good, Keith. Build It! Activities for Setting up Super Structures. 2008. (Design It! Ser.). pap. 6.95 *(978-0-8225-9928-9(7))* Lerner Publishing Group.

Grady, Colin. Geothermal Energy. 2016. (Saving the Planet Through Green Energy Ser.). (Illus.). 24p. (J). pap. 9.35 *(978-0-7660-8280-9(6))* Enslow Pubs., Inc.

Great Engineering. 2015. (Great Engineering Ser.). (ENG.). 32p. (J). (gr. 3-4). 171.00 *(978-1-5026-0378-4(0))*; pap., pap., pap. 63.48 *(978-1-5026-0692-1(5))* Cavendish Square Publishing.

Gregoire, Maryellen. Structures, 1 vol. 2011. (Wonder Readers Early Level Ser.). (ENG.). (gr. -1-1). 32p. pap. 5.99 *(978-1-4296-7835-3(6))*; 16p. pap. 35.94 *(978-1-4296-8160-5(8))* Capstone Press of Coughlan Cos. (Wonder Readers).

Gregory, Josh. From Thistle Burrs to... Velcro. 2012. (21st Century Skills Innovation Library: Innovations from Nature Ser.). (ENG.). 32p. (gr. 4-8). 28.50 *(978-1-61080-494-3(5)*, 202104); pap. 14.21 *(978-1-61080-668-8(9)*, 202278) Cherry Lake Publishing.

Haslam, Andrew, et al. Building. (Make It Work! Ser.). (Illus.). 48p. (J). pap. 15.95 *(978-0-590-24332-2(2))* Scholastic, Inc.

Hearst, Michael. Curious Constructions: A Peculiar Portfolio of Fifty Fascinating Structures. Johnstone, Matt, illus. 2017. (ENG.). 112p. (J). 19.99 *(978-1-4521-4484-9(2))* Chronicle Bks. LLC.

Herrington, Lisa M. Totally Strange Buildings. 2017. (Rookie Amazing America(tm) Ser.). (ENG., Illus.). 32p. (J). pap. 5.95 *(978-0-531-22591-2(7)*, Children's Pr.) Scholastic Library Publishing.

Horn, Geoffrey M. Environmental Engineer. 2009. (Cool Careers: Cutting Edge Ser.). 32p. (J). (gr. 5-8). (ENG.). pap. 10.50 *(978-1-4339-2155-1(3))*; lib. bdg. 26.00 *(978-1-4339-1956-5(7))* Stevens, Gareth Publishing LLLP.

Hunt, Emily M. & Pantoya, Michelle L. Engineering Elephants. 2010. 44p. pap. 16.99 *(978-1-4490-5816-6(7))* AuthorHouse.

Hunt, Shannon. Engineered! Engineering Design at Work. Hancock, James Gulliver, illus. 2017. (ENG.). 48p. (J). (gr. 3-7). 17.99 ***(978-1-77138-560-2(X))*** Kids Can Pr., Ltd. CAN. Dist: Hachette Bk. Group.

Jackson, Tom. Buildings & Structures. 2012. (FAYFT: Invention & Technology Ser.). 64p. (gr. 4-10). lib. bdg. 39.95 *(978-1-936333-38-7(4))* Brown Bear Bks.

Kenah, Katharine. Amazing Creations. 2006. (Extreme Readers: Level 2 Ser.). (Illus.). 32p. (gr. 4-7). 13.95 *(978-0-7569-6844-1(5))* Perfection Learning Corp.

Kenney, Karen Latchana. What Makes Medical Technology Safer? 2015. (ENG., Illus.). 32p. (J). (gr. 4-6). 26.65 *(978-1-4677-7916-6(4)*, Lerner Pubns.) Lerner Publishing Group.

—What Makes Vehicles Safer? 2015. (ENG., Illus.). 32p. (gr. 4-6). (J). 26.65 *(978-1-4677-7913-5(X))*; 26.65 *(978-1-4677-8652-2(7))* Lerner Publishing Group. (Lerner Pubns.).

Koch, Melissa. 3D Printing: The Revolution in Personalized Manufacturing. 2017. (ENG.). 112p. (YA). (gr. 8-12). 34.65 *(978-1-5124-1570-4(7)*, Twenty-First Century Bks.) Lerner Publishing Group.

Kulling, Monica. Sky High: George Ferris's Big Wheel. Barretta, Gene, illus. 2016. (Step into Reading Ser.). (ENG.). 48p. (J). (gr. k-3). pap. 3.99 *(978-1-101-93452-4(2)*, Random Hse. Bks. for Young Readers) Random Hse. Children's Bks.

Lachner, Elizabeth. Bioengineering. 2015. (Biotechnology Revolution Ser.). (ENG., Illus.). 128p. (J). (gr. 10-10). 38.75 *(978-1-62275-580-6(4)*, Britannica Educational Publishing) Rosen Publishing Group, Inc., The.

Law, Felicia. Buildings & Structures. 2015. (Stone Age Science Ser.). (ENG., Illus.). 32p. (J). *(978-0-7787-1887-1(5))* Crabtree Publishing Co.

Leavitt, Amie Jane. Becoming a Software Engineer. 2017. (Tech Track: Building Your Career in IT Ser.). 80p. (J). (gr. 12-12). 35.75 ***(978-1-5081-7554-4(3)***, Rosen Young Adult) Rosen Publishing Group, Inc., The.

Lee, Dora & Palmer, Dora. Biomimicry: Inventions Inspired by Nature. Thompson, Margot, illus. 2011. (ENG.). 40p. (J). (gr. 3-7). 18.95 *(978-1-55453-467-8(4))* Kids Can Pr., Ltd. CAN. Dist: Hachette Bk. Group.

Lew, Kristi. Engineer. 2016. (Careers in Construction Ser.). (ENG., Illus.). 112p. (J). (gr. 7-7). lib. bdg. 42.79 *(978-1-5026-0976-2(2))* Cavendish Square Publishing.

—Solving Real World Problems with Environmental & Green Engineering, 01 vols., 1. 2016. (Let's Find Out! Ser.). (ENG., Illus.). 32p. (J). pap. 12.90 *(978-1-5081-0075-1(6)*, Britannica Educational Publishing) Rosen Publishing Group, Inc., The.

Lüsted, Marcia Amidon. For People Who Love to Fix Things. 2016. (Cool Careers Without College Ser.). 00104p. (J). (gr. 7-7). 38.45 *(978-1-5081-7284-0(6))* Rosen Publishing Group, Inc., The.

Mara, Wil. From Cats' Eyes to... Reflectors. 2012. (21st Century Skills Innovation Library: Innovations from Nature Ser.). (ENG.). 32p. (gr. 4-8). pap. 14.21 *(978-1-61080-674-9(3)*, 202284) Cherry Lake Publishing.

May, Vicki V. Engineering: Cool Women Who Design. Bruce, Allison, illus. 2016. 106p. (J). ***(978-1-4844-8450-0(9)***, 1401403) Nomad Pr.

May, Vicki V. 3-D Engineering: Design & Build Your Own Prototypes. Christensen, Andrew, illus. 2015. (Build It Yourself Ser.). (ENG.). 128p. (gr. 3-7). 22.95 *(978-1-61930-311-9(6))* Open City Bks.

Mercer, Bobby. Junk Drawer Engineering: 25 Construction Challenges That Don't Cost a Thing. 2017. (Junk Drawer Science Ser.). (ENG.). 224p. (J). (gr. 4). pap. 14.99 *(978-1-61373-716-3(5))* Chicago Review Pr., Inc.

Merchant, Raina G. Engineering, 1 vol., 1. 2016. (Study of Science Ser.). (ENG.). 96p. (J). (gr. 8-8). 36.25 *(978-1-68048-238-6(6)*, Britannica Educational Publishing) Rosen Publishing Group, Inc., The.

Merchant, Raina G., ed. Engineering. 2016. (Study of Science Ser.). 96p. (gr. 8-8). 72.50 *(978-1-68048-237-9(8)*, Britannica Educational Publishing) Rosen Publishing Group, Inc., The.

Miller, Reagan. Engineering in Our Everyday Lives. 2013. (ENG., Illus.). 24p. (J). *(978-0-7787-0092-0(5))*; pap. *(978-0-7787-0099-9(2))* Crabtree Publishing Co.

Moore Niver, Heather. Cool Careers Without College for People Who Can Build Things. 2013. (New Cool Careers Without College Ser.). (Illus.). 144p. (J). (gr. 7-12). 35.95 *(978-1-4777-1824-7(9))* Rosen Publishing Group, Inc., The.

Morris, Neil. Transportation, 1 vol. 2010. (From Fail to Win! Learning from Bad Ideas Ser.). (ENG., Illus.). 56p. (gr. 5-8). 34.65 *(978-1-4109-3911-1(1)*, Raintree Freestyle) Heinemann-Raintree.

Nixon, Jonathan. Energy Engineering & Powering the Future. 2016. (Engineering in Action Ser.). (ENG., Illus.). 32p. (J). (gr. 5-8). *(978-0-7787-7539-3(9))* Crabtree Publishing Co.

O'Brien Novak, Patty. Engineering the ABCs. 2009. (ENG.). 32p. pap. 11.95 *(978-1-933916-51-4(6)*, Ferne Pr.) Nelson Publishing & Marketing.

Osier, Dan. Backhoes, 1 vol., 1. 2014. (Construction Site Ser.). (ENG.). 24p. (J). (gr. k-2). 23.60 *(978-1-4777-2860-4(0)*, PowerKids Pr.) Rosen Publishing Group, Inc., The.

Otfinoski, Steven. 3D Printing: Science, Technology, & Engineering. 2016. (Calling All Innovators: a Career for You Ser.). (ENG., Illus.). 64p. (J). lib. bdg. 32.00 *(978-0-531-21865-5(1))*; pap. 8.95 *(978-0-531-21988-1(7))* Scholastic Library Publishing. (Children's Pr.).

Owen, Ruth. Master Blasters: Working with Explosives in Demolition & Construction. 2016. (Get to Work with Science & Technology Ser.). (ENG.). 32p. (J). (gr. 2-7). 19.95 *(978-1-910549-93-3(2))* Bearport Publishing Co., Inc.

Owings, Lisa. What Protects Us During Natural Disasters? 2015. (ENG., Illus.). 32p. (gr. 4-6). (J). 26.65 *(978-1-4677-7914-2(8))*; 26.65 *(978-1-4677-8649-2(7))* Lerner Publishing Group. (Lerner Pubns.).

Paris, Stephanie. Engineering Feats & Failures, 1 vol. 2nd rev. ed. 2013. (Nonfiction Readers Ser.). (ENG., Illus.). 48p. (J). (gr. 4-4). pap. 29.96 *(978-1-4807-1123-5(3))* Shell Educational Publishing.

—Ingeniería: Hazañas y Fracasos. 2017. (TIME for Kids en Español - Level 4 Ser.). (SPA., Illus.). 48p. (gr. 4-4). lib. bdg. 31.99 *(978-1-5157-5152-6(X))* Time for Kids Inc AUS. Dist: Capstone Pub.

Parker, Janice. The Science of Structures. 2003. (Living Science Ser.). (Illus.). 32p. (J). (gr. 1-3). pap. 9.95 *(978-1-930954-26-7(3))* Weigl Pubs., Inc.

Perritano, John. Building Math. 2008. (Math Alive! Ser.). 32p. (gr. 4-18). lib. bdg. 28.50 *(978-0-7614-3210-4(8)*, Benchmark Bks.) Marshall Cavendish Corp.

Petrikowski, Nicki Peter. Getting the Most Out of Makerspaces to Create with 3-D Printers. 2014. (Makerspaces Ser.). 64p. (J). (gr. 6-12). 32.95 *(978-1-4777-8602-4(3))*; pap. 77.70 *(978-1-4777-7814-2(4))*; pap. 12.95 *(978-1-4777-7813-5(6))* Rosen Publishing Group, Inc., The. (Rosen Reference).

Rau, Dana Meachen. Building Snow Forts. 2012. (How-To Library). (ENG., Illus.). 32p. (J). (gr. 3-6). 28.50 *(978-1-61080-469-1(4)*, 202079); pap. 14.21 *(978-1-61080-643-5(3)*, 202253) Cherry Lake Publishing.

Richards, Jon. The Human-Made World. 2016. (Mapographica Ser.). (ENG., Illus.). 32p. (J). (gr. 3-6). *(978-0-7787-2657-9(6))* Crabtree Publishing Co.

Rivera, Alane & Rivera, Raymundo. Rocks, Jeans, & Busy Machines: An Engineering Kids Storybook. 2nd ed. 2010. (ENG.). 32p. 9.95 *(978-0-9801695-0-8(X))* Rivera Engineering.

Rooney, Anne. Agricultural Engineering & Feeding the Future. 2015. (ENG., Illus.). 32p. (J). *(978-0-7787-7504-1(6))* Crabtree Publishing Co.

—Audio Engineering & the Science of Soundwaves. 2013. (ENG., Illus.). 32p. (J). *(978-0-7787-1196-4(X))*; pap. *(978-0-7787-1229-9(X))* Crabtree Publishing Co.

Sally Ride Science Editors, Sally Ride Science. What Do You Want to Be? Explore Engineering. 2005. (J). 6.00 *(978-0-9753920-6-5(9))* Sally Ride Science.

Schwartz, Heather E. Cool Engineering Activities for Girls, 1 vol. 2012. (Girls Science Club Ser.). (ENG., 32p. (gr. 3-4). Illus.). pap. 8.19 *(978-1-4296-8021-9(0))*; pap. 47.70 *(978-1-4296-8519-1(0))*; lib. bdg. 27.99 *(978-1-4296-7677-9(9))* Capstone Press of Coughlan Cos. (Snap Bks.).

Sheen, Barbara. Cutting Edge Transportation Technology. 2016. (ENG.). 80p. (J). (gr. 5-12). lib. bdg. *(978-1-68282-046-9(7))* ReferencePoint Pr., Inc.

Sjonger, Rebecca. Robotics Engineering & Our Automated World. 2016. (Engineering in Action Ser.). (ENG., Illus.). 32p. (J). (gr. 5-8). *(978-0-7787-7537-9(2))* Crabtree Publishing Co.

Smibert, Angie. Exciting Engineering Activities. 2017. (Curious Scientists Ser.). (ENG.). 24p. (gr. 1-2). lib. bdg. 25.32 ***(978-1-5157-6884-5(8)***, First Facts) Capstone Press of Coughlan Cos.

Snedden, Robert. Materials Engineering & Exploring Properties. 2015. (ENG., Illus.). 32p. (J). (978-0-7787-7514-0(3)) Crabtree Publishing Co.

Sohn, Emily & Hansen, Anya. Models & Designs: It's a Roller Coaster Ride! 2011. (IScience Readers Ser.). 48p. (J). (gr. 5-6). lib. bdg. 23.94 (978-1-59953-429-9(0)) Norwood Hse. Pr.

Steffens, Bradley. Biomedical Engineer. 2017. (ENG.). 64p. (YA). (gr. 5-12). (978-1-68282-178-7(1)) ReferencePoint Pr., Inc.

Stefoff, Rebecca & Stanborough, Rebecca. Engineering Wonders. 2016. (Engineering Wonders Ser.). (ENG.). 32p. (gr. 3-4). 109.28 (978-1-4914-8211-7(7), Fact Finders) Capstone Press of Coughlan Cos.

VanCleave, Janice. Engineering for Every Kid: Easy Activities That Make Learning Science Fun. 2007. (Science for Every Kid Ser.: 119). (ENG., Illus.). 220p. (gr. 3-7). pap. 14.95 (978-0-471-47182-0(8), Wiley) Wiley, John & Sons, Inc.

Vescia, Monique. Engineers at Work. 2017. (Scientists at Work Ser.). 32p. (gr. 6-8). pap. 12.90 (978-1-68048-757-2(4), Britannica Educational Publishing) Rosen Publishing Group, Inc., The.

Walker, Sally M. & Feldmann, Roseann. Put Screws to the Test. 2011. (Searchlight Books (tm) — How Do Simple Machines Work? Ser.). (ENG., Illus.). 40p. (gr. 3-5). lib. bdg. 27.93 (978-0-7613-5323-2(2)) Lerner Publishing Group.

Waters, Rosa. Instagram: How Kevin Systrom & Mike Krieger Changed the Way We Take & Share Photos. 2014. (Wizards of Technology Ser.: 10). 64p. (J). (gr. 7-18). 23.95 (978-1-4222-3183-8(6)) Mason Crest.

Williams, Brian. Transport Technology. 2010. (New Technology Ser.). (ENG., Illus.). 48p. (J). 23.99 (978-0-237-53429-5(0)) Evans Brothers, Ltd. GBR. Dist: Independent Pubs. Group.

Worms, Penny. Eco Cars. 2016. (Motormania Ser.). 32p. (gr. 2-7). 31.35 (978-1-59920-994-4(2), Smart Apple Media) Black Rabbit Bks.

Yes Magazine Editors. Fantastic Feats & Failures. Kurisu, Jane, illus. 2004. (ENG.). 52p. (J). (gr. 3-7). 9.95 (978-1-55337-634-7(X)) Kids Can Pr., Ltd. CAN. Dist: Hachette Bk. Group.

Zeiger, Jennifer. Restoring Structures. 2015. (Explorer Library: Science Explorer Ser.). (ENG., Illus.). 32p. (J). (gr. 4-8). lib. bdg. 29.93 (978-1-63362-388-0(2), 206972) Cherry Lake Publishing.

Zoom in on Engineering. 2017. (Zoom in on Engineering Ser.). 24p. (gr. 2-2). pap. 56.10 (978-0-7660-8887-0(1)); lib. bdg. 135.60 (978-0-7660-8602-9(X)) Enslow Pubs., Inc.

ENGINEERING—HISTORY

Hoena, Blake, et al. You Choose: Engineering Marvels, 1 vol. 2014. (You Choose: Engineering Marvels Ser.). (ENG.). 112p. (gr. 3-4). pap. 27.80 (978-1-4914-0411-9(6), You Choose Bks.) Capstone Press of Coughlan Cos.

Paris, Stephanie. Engineering Feats & Failures, 1 vol. 2nd rev. ed. 2012. (Nonfiction Readers Ser.). (ENG., Illus.). 48p. (J). (gr. 4-4). pap. 9.99 (978-1-4333-4871-6(3)) Teacher Created Materials, Inc.

Sandvold, Lynnette Brent. Revolution in Construction. 2009. (It Works! Ser.). 32p. (gr. 3). 28.50 (978-0-7614-4378-0(9)) Marshall Cavendish Corp.

ENGINEERING—VOCATIONAL GUIDANCE

Brezina, Corona. Careers in Nanotechnology. 2007. (Cutting-Edge Careers Ser.). (Illus.). 64p. (J). (gr. 3-7). lib. bdg. 31.95 (978-1-4042-0955-8(7)) Rosen Publishing Group, Inc., The.

Conklin, Wendy. STEM Careers. 2017. (TIME for KIDS(r) Nonfiction Readers Ser.). 48p. (J). (gr. 7-7). pap. 9.99 (978-1-4938-3622-2(6)) Teacher Created Materials, Inc.

Cunningham, Kevin. Roller Coasters: From Concept to Consumer. 2013. (Calling All Innovators). (ENG.). 64p. (J). pap. 8.95 (978-0-531-22009-2(5)); lib. bdg. 30.00 (978-0-531-26521-5(8)) Scholastic Library Publishing. (Children's Pr.).

Duke, Shirley. STEM Jobs in Music. 2014. (ENG., Illus.). 48p. (gr. 4-8). 35.64 (978-1-62717-699-6(3)) Rourke Educational Media.

Ferguson, creator. Engineering. 3rd rev. ed. 2007. (Careers in Focus Ser.). (Illus.). 208p. (gr. 6-12). 32.95 (978-0-8160-6571-4(3), Ferguson Publishing Co.) Facts On File, Inc.

Ferguson Publishing Staff, creator. Engineering. 2nd rev. ed. 2007. (What Can I Do Now? Ser.). (Illus.). 224p. (YA). (gr. 7-12). 32.95 (978-0-8160-6026-9(6)) Facts On File, Inc.

Forbes, Charlotte. Those Amazing Engineers. Pillion, Dean, illus. 2nd rev. ed. 2005. (Those Amazing... Ser.). (ENG.). 30p. (J). pap. 10.95 (978-0-9772799-0-6(1)) Trilogy Pubns. LLC.

Gray, Susan H. Bioengineer. 2011. (21st Century Skills Library: Cool Science Careers Ser.). (ENG.). 32p. (gr. 4-8). lib. bdg. 28.50 (978-1-61080-035-8(4), 200996) Cherry Lake Publishing.

Guillain, Charlotte. Building Things, 1 vol. 2012. (Jobs If You Like... Ser.). (ENG.). 32p. (gr. 1-3). pap. 8.29 (978-1-4329-6816-8(5), Heinemann First Library) Heinemann-Raintree.

Hagler, Gina. Top STEM Careers in Engineering. 2014. (Cutting-Edge STEM Careers Ser.). 128p. (YA). (gr. 9-12). 35.60 (978-1-4777-7672-8(9)); pap. 18.85 (978-1-4777-7674-2(5)) Rosen Publishing Group, Inc., The.

Hamon, Susan E. Engineering, 1 vol. 2011. (Inside the Industry Ser.). (ENG., Illus.). 112p. (J). (gr. 6-12). lib. bdg. 35.64 (978-1-61714-798-2(2), Essential Library) ABDO Publishing Co.

Harmon, Daniel E. A Career As an Electrician. 2010. (Essential Careers Ser.). (Illus.). 80p. (YA). lib. bdg. 33.25 (978-1-4358-9470-9(7)) Rosen Publishing Group, Inc., The.

Hayes, Vicki C. Working in Engineering. 2018. (ENG.). 32p. (gr. 3-6). (978-1-63235-444-0(6), 12-Story Library) Pr. Room Editions LLC.

Hutson, Matt. Totally Amazing Careers in Engineering. 2006. (J). 7.80 (978-1-933798-04-2(1)) Sally Ride Science.

Hynson, Colin. Dream Jobs in Engineering. 2017. (Illus.). 32p. (J). (978-0-7787-2945-7(1)) Crabtree Publishing Co.

Indovino, Shaina. Women in Engineering. Lee-Karlon, Ann, ed. 2013. (Major Women in Science Ser.: 10). 64p. (J). (gr. 7-18). 22.95 (978-1-4222-2926-2(2)) Mason Crest.

Katirgis, Jane. STEM Jobs in Food & Nutrition. 2014. (ENG., Illus.). 48p. (gr. 4-8). 35.64 (978-1-62717-703-0(5)) Rourke Educational Media.

—STEM Jobs with Cars. 2014. (ENG.). 48p. (gr. 4-8). 35.64 (978-1-62717-702-3(7)) Rourke Educational Media.

Kemper, Bitsy. Software Engineer. 2017. (ENG.). 64p. (YA). (gr. 5-12). (978-1-68282-188-6(9)) ReferencePoint Pr., Inc.

La Bella, Laura. Top STEM Careers in Technology. 2014. (Cutting-Edge STEM Careers Ser.). (Illus.). 128p. (J). (gr. 9-12). 35.60 (978-1-4777-7668-1(0)) Rosen Publishing Group, Inc., The.

LeBoutillier, Linda. Unusual & Awesome Jobs Using Technology: Roller Coaster Designer, Space Robotics Engineer, & More. 2015. (You Get Paid for THAT? Ser.). (ENG.). 32p. (gr. 3-4). 27.99 (978-1-4914-2029-4(4)) Capstone Press of Coughlan Cos.

Lüsted, Marcia Amidon. Careers for Tech Girls in Engineering. 2015. (Tech Girls Ser.). (ENG., Illus.). 80p. (J). (gr. 7-8). 34.25 (978-1-4994-6097-1(X), Rosen Young Adult) Rosen Publishing Group, Inc., The.

Mooney, Carla. STEM Jobs in Movies. 2014. (ENG.). 48p. (gr. 4-8). 35.64 (978-1-62717-701-6(9)) Rourke Educational Media.

Mullins, Matt. Remote Systems Control Engineer. 2013. (21st Century Skills Library: Cool STEM Careers Ser.). (ENG.). 32p. (J). (gr. 4-8). 28.50 (978-1-62431-006-5(0), 202475); pap. 14.21 (978-1-62431-030-0(3), 202477) Cherry Lake Publishing.

Paige, Joy. Cool Careers Without College for People Who Love to Build Things. 2009. (Cool Careers Without College Ser.). 144p. (gr. 6-6). 66.50 (978-1-61511-970-7(1)) Rosen Publishing Group, Inc., The.

Raymos, Rick. STEM Jobs in Sports. 2014. (ENG.). 48p. (gr. 4-8). 35.64 (978-1-62717-696-5(9)) Rourke Educational Media.

Reeves, Diane Lindsey. Find Your Future in Technology. 2016. (Bright Futures Press: Find Your Future in STEAM Ser.). (ENG., Illus.). 32p. (J). (gr. 4-6). 29.93 (978-1-63471-899-8(2), 208917) Cherry Lake Publishing.

Ringstad, Arnold. Portable Toilet Cleaner. 2015. (Gross Jobs Ser.). (ENG.). 24p. (J). (gr. 2-5). 27.07 (978-1-63143-689-5(9), 208525) Child's World, Inc., The.

Slade, Suzanne. Cycles in Nature, 6 bks., Set. Incl. Nitrogen Cycle. (J). lib. bdg. 21.25 (978-1-4042-3491-8(8), PowerKids Pr.); Phases of the Moon. (YA). lib. bdg. 22.60 (978-1-4042-3488-8(8)); Rock Cycle. (YA). lib. bdg. 22.60 (978-1-4042-3493-2(4)); Water on the Move. (J). lib. bdg. 21.25 (978-1-4042-3492-5(6), PowerKids Pr.); (Illus.). 24p. (gr. 3-7). 2007. 2007. Set lib. bdg. 127.50 (978-1-4042-3506-9(X), PowerKids Pr.) Rosen Publishing Group, Inc., The.

Suen, Anastasia. Top STEM Careers in Science. 2014. (Cutting-Edge STEM Careers Ser.). (Illus.). 128p. (J). (gr. 9-12). 35.60 (978-1-4777-7664-3(8)) Rosen Publishing Group, Inc., The.

Szumski, Bonnie & Karson, Jill. Careers in Engineering. 2014. (Exploring Careers). (Illus.). 80p. (J). (978-1-60152-676-2(8)) ReferencePoint Pr., Inc.

ENGINEERING DRAWING

see Mechanical Drawing

ENGINEERING MATERIALS

see Materials

ENGINEERS

Alber, Christopher. Casey Jones. 2014. (J). pap. (978-1-62712-284-9(2)) Cavendish Square Publishing.

Aldrich, Lisa J. Nikola Tesla & the Taming of Electricity. 2005. (Profiles in Science Ser.). (Illus.). 160p. (J). (gr. 3-7). lib. bdg. 26.95 (978-1-931798-46-4(X)) Reynolds, Morgan Inc.

Ambrosek, Renee. Shawn Fanning: The Founder of Napster. 2009. (Internet Career Biographies Ser.). 112p. (gr. 8-8). 63.90 (978-1-61513-600-1(2)) Rosen Publishing Group, Inc., The.

Assein, Kristine Carlson. TiVo: The Company & Its Founders, 1 vol. 2012. (Technology Pioneers Set 2 Ser.). (ENG.). 112p. (J). (gr. 6-12). lib. bdg. 35.64 (978-1-61783-336-6(3), Essential Library) ABDO Publishing Co.

Bailey, Diane. Biomedical Engineers!, Vol. 10. 2015. (Scientists in Action Ser.). (Illus.). 48p. (J). (gr. 5). 20.95 (978-1-4222-3420-4(7)) Mason Crest.

Bankston, John. Karl Benz & the Single Cylinder Engine. 2004. (Uncharted, Unexplored, & Unexplained Ser.). (Illus.). 48p. (J). (gr. 4-8). lib. bdg. 29.95 (978-1-58415-244-6(3)) Mitchell Lane Pubs., Inc.

Barnham, Kay. Thomas Edison, 1 vol. 2014. (Science Biographies Ser.). (ENG.). 32p. (gr. 2-4). lib. bdg. 30.65 (978-1-4109-6239-3(3), Raintree Perspectives) Heinemann-Raintree.

Boothroyd, Jennifer. Robert Fulton: A Life of Innovation. 2007. (Pull Ahead Bks.). (Illus.). 32p. (J). (gr. 3-7). lib. bdg. 22.60 (978-0-8225-6458-4(0), Lerner Pubns.) Lerner Publishing Group.

Brackett, Virginia. Steve Jobs: Computer Genius of Apple. 2003. (Internet Biographies Ser.). (Illus.). 48p. (J). (gr. 4-10). lib. bdg. 23.93 (978-0-7660-1970-6(5)) Enslow Pubs., Inc.

Bradley, Michael. Ferrari. 2008. (Cars Ser.). 32p. (gr. 3-18). lib. bdg. 28.50 (978-0-7614-2978-4(6), Benchmark Bks.) Marshall Cavendish Corp.

Braun, Eric. Fatal Faults: The Story of the Challenger Explosion. 2015. (Tangled History Ser.). (ENG., Illus.). 112p. (gr. 3-4). lib. bdg. 31.99 (978-1-4914-7077-0(1)) Capstone Press of Coughlan Cos.

Burgan, Michael. Who Was Henry Ford? Hammond, Ted, illus. 2014. 105p. (J). lib. bdg. (978-1-4844-3671-4(7), Grosset & Dunlap) Penguin Publishing Group.

Burns, Kylie. William Kamkwamba: Powering His Village. 2016. (Remarkable Lives Revealed Ser.). (ENG., Illus.). 32p. (J). (gr. 2-5). (978-0-7787-2690-6(8)) Crabtree Publishing Co.

Callery, Sean. Victor Wouk: The Father of the Hybrid Car. 2009. (Voices for Green Choices Ser.). (ENG., Illus.). 48p. (J). (gr. 5-9). pap. (978-0-7787-4677-5(1)); lib. bdg. (978-0-7787-4664-5(X)) Crabtree Publishing Co.

Carson, Mary Kay. Who Invented Home Video Games? Ralph Baer. 2012. (I Like Inventors! Ser.). (Illus.). 24p. (J). (gr. k-3). pap. 7.95 (978-1-4644-0135-0(7), Enslow Elementary) Enslow Pubs., Inc.

—Who Invented Television? — Philo Farnsworth. 2012. (I Like Inventors! Ser.). 24p. (J). (gr. k-3). 22.60 (978-0-7660-3974-2(9), Enslow Elementary) Enslow Pubs., Inc.

—Who Invented Television? Philo Farnsworth. 2012. (I Like Inventors! Ser.). (Illus.). 24p. (J). (gr. k-3). pap. 7.95 (978-1-4644-0134-3(9), Enslow Elementary) Enslow Pubs., Inc.

Cornell, Kari. Mars Science Lab Engineer Diana Trujillo. 2016. (STEM Trailblazer Bios Ser.). (ENG., Illus.). 32p. (J). (gr. 2-5). pap. 8.99 (978-1-4677-9721-4(9), Lerner Pubns.) Lerner Publishing Group.

Davis, Kathryn Gibbs. Mr. Ferris & His Wheel. Ford, Gilbert, illus. 2014. (ENG.). 40p. (J). (gr. -1-3). 17.99 (978-0-547-95922-1(2), HMH Books For Young Readers) Houghton Mifflin Harcourt Publishing Co.

Davis, Lynn. Henry Ford, 1 vol. 2016. (ENG., Illus.). 24p. (J). (978-1-62403-724-5(0)) ABDO Publishing Co.

—Thomas Edison, 1 vol. 2016. (ENG., Illus.). 24p. (J). 25.65 (978-1-62403-723-8(2)) ABDO Publishing Co.

Delano, Marfe Ferguson. Inventing the Future: A Photobiography of Thomas Alva Edison. 2006. (Photobiographies Ser.). (ENG., Illus.). 64p. (J). (gr. 5-7). per. 7.95 (978-0-7922-5934-3(3), National Geographic Children's Bks.) National Geographic Society.

Demuth, Patricia Brennan. Thomas Edison & His Bright Idea. Tuya, Jez, illus. 2016. (Penguin Young Readers, Level 3 Ser.). (ENG.). 32p. (J). (gr. 1-3). pap. 3.99 (978-0-448-48830-1(2), Penguin Young Readers) Penguin Young Readers Group.

Dykstra, Danell. The Man Who Invented the Ferris Wheel: The Genius of George Ferris. 2013. (Genius Inventors & Their Great Ideas Ser.). (Illus.). 48p. (J). (gr. 3-18). 25.27 (978-0-7660-4136-3(0)) Enslow Pubs., Inc.

Enz, Tammy. Young Engineers. 2017. (Young Engineers Ser.). (ENG.). 32p. (gr. 1-2). 109.28 (978-1-4846-3771-5(2), Heinemann First Library) Heinemann-Raintree.

Feldman, Heather. Dennis Tito: The First Space Tourist. 2009. (Space Firsts Ser.). 24p. (gr. 3-4). 42.50 (978-1-60853-112-7(0), PowerKids Pr.) Rosen Publishing Group, Inc., The.

Frith, Margaret. Who Was Thomas Alva Edison? O'brien, John, illus. 2005. (Who Was... ? Ser.). 106p. (gr. 3-7). 15.00 (978-0-7569-5830-5(X)) Perfection Learning Corp.

Glatzer, Jenna. George Ferris' Grand Idea: The Ferris Wheel. Dominguez, Stephanie, illus. 2015. (Story Behind the Name Ser.). (ENG.). 32p. (gr. 2-3). pap. 7.95 (978-1-4795-7165-9(2)); lib. bdg. 28.65 (978-1-4795-7135-2(0)) Picture Window Bks.

Glenn, John. Civil Engineers!, Vol. 10. 2015. (Scientists in Action Ser.). (Illus.). 48p. (J). (gr. 5). lib. bdg. 20.95 (978-1-4222-3421-1(5)) Mason Crest.

Goldsworthy, Steve. Steve Jobs. 2011. (J). (gr. 4-6). pap. 12.95 (978-1-61690-675-7(8), AV2 by Weigl); (Illus.). 24p. (YA). (gr. 3-6). 27.13 (978-1-61690-670-2(7)) Weigl Pubs., Inc.

Gould, Jane H. Steve Jobs. 2013. (Jr. Graphic American Inventors Ser.). (ENG., Illus.). 24p. (J). (gr. 3-6). pap. 10.60 (978-1-4777-0145-4(1)); lib. bdg. 25.25 (978-1-4777-0080-8(3)) Rosen Publishing Group, Inc., The. (PowerKids Pr.).

Gravenhorst, Edna Campos. Ay, Mijo! Why Do You Want to Be an Engineer? 2007. 155p. (978-0-9745346-3-3(3)) Big River Distribution.

Green, Sara. Steve Jobs. 2014. (Tech Icons Ser.). (ENG., Illus.). 24p. (J). (gr. 3-8). lib. bdg. 25.95 (978-1-60014-994-8(4), Pilot Bks.) Bellwether Media.

Gregory, Josh. Henry Ford: Father of the Auto Industry. 2013. (True Book(tm), a — Great American Business Ser.). (ENG.). 48p. (J). 31.00 (978-0-531-24777-8(5)); pap. 6.95 (978-0-531-28463-6(8)) Scholastic Library Publishing.

—Steve Jobs. 2013. (True Book(tm), A — Biographies Ser.). (ENG., Illus.). (J). 48p. lib. bdg. 31.00 (978-0-531-21907-2(0)); 64p. pap. 8.95 (978-0-531-21964-5(X)); 48p. pap. 6.95 (978-0-531-23878-3(4)); 64p. lib. bdg. 30.00 (978-0-531-23606-2(4)) Scholastic Library Publishing.

Hardyman, Robyn. Nikola Tesla & Thomas Edison. 2014. (Dynamic Duos of Science Ser.). 48p. (YA). (gr. 5-8). pap. 84.30 (978-1-4824-1285-7(3)) Stevens, Gareth Publishing LLLP.

Hartland, Jessie. Steve Jobs: Insanely Great. 2015. (ENG., Illus.). 240p. (YA). (gr. 7). 22.95 (978-0-307-98295-7(5), Schwartz & Wade Bks.) Random Hse. Children's Bks.

Hayes, Amy. Tim Cook: Industrial Engineer & CEO of Apple. 2017. (Breakout Biographies Ser.). 32p. (gr. 9-10). pap. 10.00 (978-1-5081-6074-8(0), PowerKids Pr.) Rosen Publishing Group, Inc., The.

Herweck, Don. Making It Go: The Life & Work of Robert Fulton, 1 vol. 2007. (Science Readers Ser.). (ENG.). 32p. (J). (gr. 3-3). pap. 8.99 (978-0-7439-0578-7(4)) Shell Educational Publishing.

Hinton, Kerry. A Career As an Operating & Stationary Engineer, 01 vols., 1. 2016. (Essential Careers Ser.). (ENG.). 80p. (J). 34.25 (978-1-4994-6223-4(9), Rosen Young Adult) Rosen Publishing Group, Inc., The.

Hirschmann, Kris. Burt Rutan: Aircraft Designer. 2006. (Innovators (Kidhaven) Ser.). (Illus.). 64p. (J). (gr. 3-7). lib. bdg. 28.25 (978-0-7377-3450-8(7), Kidhaven) Cengage Gale.

Honders, Christine. Steve Jobs: Father of the Digital Revolution. 2015. (Britannica Beginner Bios Ser.). (ENG., Illus.). 32p. (J). (gr. 2-3). 23.45 (978-1-62275-921-7(4), Britannica Educational Publishing) Rosen Publishing Group, Inc., The.

Horn, Geoffrey M. Environmental Engineer. 2009. (Cool Careers: Cutting Edge Ser.). 32p. (J). (gr. 5-8). (ENG.). pap. 10.50 (978-1-4339-2155-1(3)); lib. bdg. 26.00 (978-1-4339-1956-5(7)) Stevens, Gareth Publishing LLLP.

—Sewer Inspector. 2010. (Benchmark Rockets: Dirty & Dangerous Jobs Ser.). 32p. (J). (gr. 3-6). 28.50 (978-1-60870-178-0(6)) Marshall Cavendish Corp.

Hulick, Kathryn. Kimberly Bryant: Founder of Black Girls Code. 2017. (J). (978-1-5026-2703-2(5)) Cavendish Square Publishing.

Hunt, Shannon. Engineered! Engineering Design at Work. Hancock, James Gulliver, illus. 2017. (ENG.). 48p. (J). (gr. 3-7). 17.99 (978-1-77138-560-2(X)) Kids Can Pr., Ltd. CAN. Dist: Hachette Bk. Group.

Imbimbo, Anthony. Steve Jobs: The Brilliant Mind Behind Apple. 2009. (Life Portraits Ser.). (Illus.). 112p. (YA). (gr. 7-12). lib. bdg. 36.00 (978-1-4339-0060-0(2)) Stevens, Gareth Publishing LLLP.

Indovino, Shaina. Women in Engineering. Lee-Karlon, Ann, ed. 2013. (Major Women in Science Ser.: 10). 64p. (J). (gr. 7-18). 22.95 (978-1-4222-2926-2(2)) Mason Crest.

Isabella, Jude. Steve Jobs: Visionary Entrepreneur of the Digital Age. 2013. (ENG.). 112p. (J). E-Book (978-1-4271-8936-3(6)); (Illus.). (978-0-7787-1189-6(7)); (Illus.). pap. (978-0-7787-1191-9(9)) Crabtree Publishing Co.

Jackson, Aurelia. Disney's Pixar(r): How Steve Jobs Changed Hollywood. 2014. (Wizards of Technology Ser.: 10). 64p. (J). (gr. 7-18). 23.95 (978-1-4222-3180-7(1)) Mason Crest.

—Google(Tm) How Larry Page & Sergey Brin Changed the Way We Search the Web. 2014. (Illus.). 64p. (J). (978-1-4222-3178-4(X)) Mason Crest.

—Tumblr(r): How David Karp Changed the Way We Blog. 2014. (Wizards of Technology Ser.: 10). (Illus.). 64p. (J). (gr. 7-18). 23.95 (978-1-4222-3186-9(0)) Mason Crest.

Jacobson, Fiona. Nikola Tesla Lights the World. 2013. (InfoMax Readers Ser.). (ENG.). 24p. (J). (gr. 3-4). pap. 8.25 (978-1-4777-2510-8(5)); pap. 49.50 (978-1-4777-2511-5(3)) Rosen Publishing Group, Inc., The. (Rosen Classroom).

James, Emily. Henry Ford. 2017. (Great Scientists & Inventors Ser.). (ENG.). 24p. (gr. k-1). lib. bdg. 26.65 (978-1-5157-3880-0(9), Pebble Plus) Capstone Press of Coughlan Cos.

Johns, Linda. A Rocket Boy Grows Up. 2005. (Illus.). 16p. (J). (978-0-7367-2904-8(6)) Zaner-Bloser, Inc.

Kamkwamba, William. The Boy Who Harnessed the Wind: Creating Currents of Electricity & Hope. 2009. 14.44 (978-0-7848-3872-3(0), Everbind) Marco Bk. Co.

—The Boy Who Harnessed the Wind: Creating Currents of Electricity & Hope. Hymas, Anna, illus. 2015. (ENG.). 304p. (J). (gr. 5). 18.99 (978-0-8037-4080-8(8), Dial Bks) Penguin Young Readers Group.

Kamkwamba, William & Mealer, Bryan. The Boy Who Harnessed the Wind: Young Readers Edition. Zunon, Elizabeth, illus. (ENG.). (J). 2016. 304p. (gr. 5). 8.99 (978-0-14-751042-6(2), Puffin Books) 2012. 32p. (gr. 1-3). 17.99 (978-0-8037-3511-8(1), Dial Bks) Penguin Young Readers Group.

Kraft, Betsy Harvey. The Fantastic Ferris Wheel: The Story of Inventor George Ferris. Salerno, Steven, illus. 2015. (ENG.). 42p. (J). (gr. k-4). 17.99 (978-1-62779-072-7(1), 9781627790727, Holt, Henry & Co. Bks. For Young Readers) Holt, Henry & Co.

Krensky, Stephen. Casey Jones. 2008. pap. 40.95 (978-0-8225-9292-1(4)) Lerner Publishing Group.

—Casey Jones. Schroder, Mark, illus. 2006. (On My Own Folklore Ser.). (ENG.). 48p. (J). (gr. 2-4). lib. bdg. 25.26 (978-1-57505-890-0(1), Millbrook Pr.) Lerner Publishing Group.

—Casey Jones. Schroder, Mark, illus. 2007. (On My Own Folklore Ser.). (ENG.). 48p. (gr. 2-4). per. 6.95 (978-0-8225-6476-8(9), First Avenue Editions) Lerner Publishing Group.

Kulling, Monica. Eat My Dust! Henry Ford's First Race. Walz, Richard, illus. 2004. (Step into Reading Ser.). 48p. (J). (gr. 1-3). 11.65 (978-0-7569-3231-2(9)) Perfection Learning Corp.

—Eat My Dust! Henry Ford's First Race. Walz, Richard, illus. 2004. (Step into Reading Ser.). (ENG.). 48p. (J). (gr. k-3). pap. 3.99 (978-0-375-81510-2(4), Random Hse. Bks. for Young Readers) Random Hse. Children's Bks.

—Spic-and-Span! Lillian Gilbreth's Wonder Kitchen. Parkins, David, illus. 2016. (Great Idea Ser.). (ENG.). 32p. (J). (gr. k-3). pap. 6.99 (978-1-101-91843-2(8), Tundra Bks.) Tundra Bks. CAN. Dist: Penguin Random Hse. LLC.

—Spic-and-Span! Lillian Gilbreth's Wonder Kitchen. 2014. (Great Idea Ser.). (ENG., Illus.). 32p. (J). (gr. k-3). 17.99 (978-1-77049-380-3(8), Tundra Bks.) Tundra Bks. CAN. Dist: Penguin Random Hse. LLC.

Kulling, Monica & Slavin, Bill. Zap! Nikola Tesla Takes Charge. 2016. (Great Idea Ser.). (ENG., Illus.). 32p. (J). (gr. k-3). 17.99 (978-1-77049-522-7(3), Tundra Bks.) Tundra Bks. CAN. Dist: Penguin Random Hse. LLC.

Kupperberg, Paul. Jerry Yang. 2009. (Asian Americans of Achievement Ser.). (Illus.). 128p. (YA). (gr. 7-12). 35.00 (978-1-60413-569-5(7)) Facts On File, Inc.

La Bella, Laura. Hulu & Jason Kilar, 1 vol. 2015. (ENG.). 128p. (YA). 35.60 (978-1-4777-7921-7(3), Rosen Young Adult) Rosen Publishing Group, Inc., The.

Labrecque, Ellen. Yvonne Brill & Satellite Propulsion. 2017. (21st Century Junior Library: Women Innovators Ser.). (ENG., Illus.). 24p. (J). (gr. 2-5). lib. bdg. 27.07 (978-1-63472-184-4(5), 209308) Cherry Lake Publishing.

Latta, Sara L. Microwave Man: Percy Spencer & His Sizzling Invention. 2014. (Inventors at Work! Ser.). 48p. (J). pap. 8.95 (978-1-4644-0345-3(7), Enslow Elementary) Enslow Pubs., Inc.

—Who Invented the Ferris Wheel? George Ferris. 2012. (I Like Inventors! Ser.). (Illus.). 24p. (J). (gr. k-3). pap. 7.95 (978-1-4644-0132-9(2), Enslow Elementary) Enslow Pubs., Inc.

Law, Government, & Public Safety. 2010. (Green Careers Ser.). (Illus.). 176p. (C). (gr. 9-18). 32.95 (978-0-8160-8152-3(2), Ferguson Publishing Co.) Facts On File, Inc.

Leavitt, Amie Jane. The Vo-Tech Track to Success in Architecture & Construction. 2014. (Learning a Trade, Preparing for a Career Ser.). (Illus.). 80p. (J). (gr. 7-12). 34.25 (978-1-4777-7726-8(1)) Rosen Publishing Group, Inc., The.

Lemke, Donald B. Steve Jobs, Steve Wozniak, & the Personal Computer, 1 vol. Smith, Tod G. & Milgrom, Al, illus. 2006. (Inventions & Discovery Ser.). (ENG.). 32p. (gr. 3-4). 30.65 (978-0-7368-6488-6(1), Graphic Library) Capstone Press of Coughlan Cos.

—Steve Jobs, Steve Wozniak, & the Personal Computer, 1 vol. Milgrom, Al & Smith, Tod G., illus. 2006. (Inventions & Discovery Ser.). (ENG.). 32p. (gr. 3-4). pap. 8.10 (978-0-7368-9650-4(3)); pap. 47.70 (978-0-7368-9762-4(3)) Capstone Press of Coughlan Cos. (Graphic Library).

Lew, Kristi. Engineer. 2016. (Careers in Construction Ser.). (ENG., Illus.). 112p. (J). (gr. 7-7). lib. bdg. 42.79 *(978-1-5026-0976-2(2))* Cavendish Square Publishing.

Lewis, Anna M. Women of Steel & Stone: 22 Inspirational Architects, Engineers, & Landscape Designers. 2014. (Women of Action Ser.). (ENG., Illus.). 272p. (YA). (gr. 7). 19.95 *(978-1-61374-508-3(7))* Chicago Review Pr., Inc.

Luz, Oscar. A Day at Work with an Electrical Engineer, 01 vols., 1. 2016. (Super STEM Careers Ser.). (ENG., Illus.). 24p. (J). pap. 8.25 *(978-1-5081-4422-9(2)*, PowerKids Pr.) Rosen Publishing Group, Inc., The.

MacLeod, Elizabeth. Thomas Edison. Krystoforski, Andrej, illus. 2008. (ENG.). 32p. (J). (gr. 1-3). 14.95 *(978-1-55453-057-1(1))*; pap. 3.95 *(978-1-55453-058-8(X))* Kids Can Pr., Ltd. CAN. Dist: Hachette Bk. Group.

Manatt, Kathleen. Robot Scientist. 2007. (21st Century Skills Library: Cool Science Careers Ser.). (ENG.). 32p. (gr. 4-8). pap. 14.21 *(978-1-60279-083-4(3)*, 200644) Cherry Lake Publishing.

Manatt, Kathleen G. Robot Scientist. 2007. (21st Century Skills Library: Cool Science Careers Ser.). (ENG., Illus.). 32p. (gr. 4-8). lib. bdg. 28.50 *(978-1-60279-051-3(5)*, 200016) Cherry Lake Publishing.

Mara, Wil. Henry Ford: Automotive Innovator. 2017. (Rookie Biographies Ser.). (ENG.). 32p. (J). lib. bdg. 25.00 ***(978-0-531-23225-5(5)***, Children's Pr.) Scholastic Library Publishing.

Mara, Wil. Petroleum Engineer. 2015. (21st Century Skills Library: Cool STEAM Careers Ser.). (ENG., Illus.). 32p. (J). (gr. 4-7). pap. 14.21 *(978-1-63362-044-5(1)*, 205933) Cherry Lake Publishing.

Marcovitz, Hal. Larry Page, Sergey Brin, & Google. 2015. (Illus.). 80p. (J). *(978-1-60152-874-2(4))* ReferencePoint Pr., Inc.

Marsico, Katie. Inventor, Engineer, & Physicist Nikola Tesla. 2017. (STEM Trailblazer Bios Ser.). (ENG.). 32p. (J). (gr. 2-5). 26.65 ***(978-1-5124-3448-4(5))*** Lerner Publishing Group.

Mattern, Joanne. Steve Jobs. 2013. (Rookie Biographies(r) Ser.). (ENG.). 32p. (J). pap. 5.95 *(978-0-531-24705-1(8)*, Children's Pr.); lib. bdg. 23.00 *(978-0-531-24739-6(2))* Scholastic Library Publishing.

May, Vicki V. Engineering: Cool Women Who Design. Bruce, Allison, illus. 2016. 106p. (J). ***(978-1-4844-8450-0(9)***, 1401403) Nomad Pr.

—Engineering: Cool Women Who Design. Bruce, Allison, illus. 2016. (Girls in Science Ser.). (ENG.). 112p. (J). (gr. 3-7). 19.95 *(978-1-61930-341-6(8)*, 1401403) Open City Bks.

McPherson, Stephanie Sammartino. Tim Berners-Lee: Inventor of the World Wide Web. 2009. (USA TODAY Lifeline Biographies Ser.). (ENG., Illus.). 112p. (J). (gr. 6-12). lib. bdg. 34.60 *(978-0-8225-7273-2(7))* Lerner Publishing Group.

Miller, Reagan. Engineers Build Models. 2013. (ENG., Illus.). 24p. (J). *(978-0-7787-0093-7(3))*; pap. *(978-0-7787-0100-2(X))* Crabtree Publishing Co.

—Engineers Solve Problems. 2013. (ENG.). 24p. (J). *(978-0-7787-0094-4(1))*; (Illus.). pap. *(978-0-7787-0101-9(8))* Crabtree Publishing Co.

Miller, Reagan & Johnson, Robin. How Engineers Find Solutions. 2013. (ENG., Illus.). 24p. (J). *(978-0-7787-0095-1(X))*; pap. *(978-0-7787-0113-2(1))* Crabtree Publishing Co.

Mortensen, Lori & Picture Window Books Staff. Thomas Edison: Inventor, Scientist, & Genius, 1 vol. Thompson, Jeffrey, illus. 2007. (Biographies Ser.). (ENG.). 24p. (gr. k-3). 26.65 *(978-1-4048-3105-6(3))* Picture Window Bks.

Mullins, Matt. Remote Systems Control Engineer. 2013. (21st Century Skills Library: Cool STEM Careers Ser.). (ENG.). 32p. (J). (gr. 4-8). 28.50 *(978-1-62431-006-5(0)*, 202475); pap. 14.21 *(978-1-62431-030-0(3)*, 202477) Cherry Lake Publishing.

Murphy, Patricia J. Grace Hopper: Computer Pioneer. 2004. (Famous Inventors Ser.). (Illus.). 32p. (J). lib. bdg. 22.60 *(978-0-7660-2273-7(0))* Enslow Pubs., Inc.

Nakaya, Andrea C. Steve Jobs & Apple. 2015. (ENG., Illus.). 80p. (J). lib. bdg. *(978-1-60152-880-3(9))* ReferencePoint Pr., Inc.

O'Brien Novak, Patty. Engineering the ABCs. 2009. (ENG.). 32p. pap. 11.95 *(978-1-933916-51-4(6)*, Ferne Pr.) Nelson Publishing & Marketing.

O'Shei, Tim. Philo T. Farnsworth: Visionary Inventor of Television. 2008. (Inventors Who Changed the World Ser.). (Illus.). 128p. (J). (gr. 6-18). lib. bdg. 34.60 *(978-1-59845-075-0(1)*, MyReportLinks.com Bks.) Enslow Pubs., Inc.

Pederson, Charles E. Thomas Edison, 1 vol. 2007. (Essential Lives Set 1 Ser.). (ENG., Illus.). 112p. (J). (gr. 6-12). lib. bdg. 35.64 *(978-1-59928-845-1(1))* ABDO Publishing Co.

Pelleschi, Andrea. Mathematician & Computer Scientist Grace Hopper. 2016. (STEM Trailblazer Bios Ser.). (ENG., Illus.). 32p. (J). (gr. 2-5). 26.65 *(978-1-5124-0785-3(2))* Lerner Publishing Group.

Pierce, Morris A. Robert Fulton & the Development of the Steamboat. 2009. (Library of American Lives & Times Ser.). 112p. (gr. 5-5). 69.20 *(978-1-60853-502-6(9))* Rosen Publishing Group, Inc., The.

Pollack, Pam, et al. Who Was Steve Jobs? Harrison, Nancy et al, illus. 2012. (Who Was? Ser.). (ENG.). 112p. (J). (gr. 3-7). pap. 5.99 *(978-0-448-46211-0(7)*, Grosset & Dunlap) Penguin Young Readers Group.

Porterfield, Jason. Tim Berners-Lee, 01 vols., 1. 2016. (Tech Pioneers Ser.). (ENG.). 112p. (J). 35.60 *(978-1-4994-6290-6(5)*, Rosen Young Adult) Rosen Publishing Group, Inc., The.

Randolph, Joanne. Dennis Tito: First Space Tourist. 2009. (Reading Room Collection 2 Ser.). 24p. (gr. 3-4). 42.50 *(978-1-60851-962-0(7)*, PowerKids Pr.) Rosen Publishing Group, Inc., The.

Rausch, Monica L. Henry Ford & the Model T Car. 2007. (Inventors & Their Discoveries Ser.). (Illus.). 24p. (gr. 1-4). lib. bdg. 22.00 *(978-0-8368-7500-3(1)*, Weekly Reader Leveled Readers) Stevens, Gareth Publishing LLLP.

—Henry Ford y el Automovil Modelo T. 2007. (Inventores y sus descubrimientos (Inventors & Their Discoveries) Ser.). (ENG & SPA., Illus.). 24p. (gr. 1-4). pap. 8.15 *(978-0-8368-8000-7(5))*; lib. bdg. 22.00 *(978-0-8368-7995-7(3))* Stevens, Gareth Publishing LLLP. (Weekly Reader Leveled Readers).

Reis, Ronald A. Henry Ford for Kids: His Life & Ideas, with 21 Activities. 2016. (For Kids Ser.). (ENG., Illus.). 144p. (J). (gr. 4). pap. 16.95 *(978-1-61373-090-4(X))* Chicago Review Pr., Inc.

Rich, Mari. Engineering, Vol. 10. Gilmore, Malinda & Pouson, Mel, eds. 2016. (Black Achievement in Science Ser.). 64p. (J). (gr. 7). 23.95 *(978-1-4222-3558-4(0))* Mason Crest.

—Technology, Vol. 10. Gilmore, Malinda & Pouson, Mel, eds. 2016. (Black Achievement in Science Ser.). (Illus.). 64p. (J). (gr. 7). 23.95 *(978-1-4222-3564-5(5))* Mason Crest.

Rivera, Alane & Rivera, Raymundo. Rocks, Jeans, & Busy Machines: An Engineering Kids Storybook. 2nd ed. 2010. (ENG.). 32p. 9.95 *(978-0-9801695-0-8(X))* Rivera Engineering.

Roberts, Steven. Robert Fulton. 2013. (Jr. Graphic American Inventors Ser.). (ENG., Illus.). 24p. (J). (gr. 3-6). pap. 10.60 *(978-1-4777-0139-3(7))*; lib. bdg. 25.25 *(978-1-4777-0077-8(3))* Rosen Publishing Group, Inc., The. (PowerKids Pr.).

Rooney, Thomas L. Tobey Boland & the Blackstone Canal. Donovan, Patte, illus. 2005. 30p. (J). *(978-1-929039-30-2(1))* Ambassador Bks., Inc.

Royston, Angela. Robert Fulton & the Steamboat, 01 vols., 1. 2016. (Inventions That Changed the World Ser.). (ENG.). 32p. (J). pap. 10.00 *(978-1-5081-4635-3(7)*, PowerKids Pr.) Rosen Publishing Group, Inc., The.

Rusch, Elizabeth. Electrical Wizard. 2015. (Candlewick Biographies Ser.). lib. bdg. 14.75 *(978-0-606-36873-5(6))* Turtleback Bks.

Scott, Celicia. YouTube: How Steve Chen Changed the Way We Watch Videos. 2014. (Wizards of Technology Ser.: 10). (Illus.). 64p. (J). (gr. 7-18). 23.95 *(978-1-4222-3188-3(7))* Mason Crest.

Shea, Therese. Solving Real World Problems with Mechanical Engineering, 01 vols., 1. 2016. (Let's Find Out! Ser.). (ENG., Illus.). 32p. (J). pap. 12.90 *(978-1-5081-0079-9(9)*, Britannica Educational Publishing) Rosen Publishing Group, Inc., The.

Sheen, Barbara. Steve Jobs. 2009. (People in the News Ser.). (ENG., Illus.). 128p. (YA). (gr. 7-12). 33.95 *(978-1-4205-0160-5(7))* Cengage Gale.

Shoup, Kate. Life As an Engineer on the First Railroads in America. 2016. (Life As... Ser.). (ENG.). 32p. (J). (gr. 3-3). pap. 63.48 *(978-1-5026-1088-1(4))* Cavendish Square Publishing.

Silver, Tony. What's the Big Idea? The Story of Thomas Edison. (Illus.). 16p. *(978-0-7367-2880-5(5))* Zaner-Bloser, Inc.

Skurzynski, Gloria. This Is Rocket Science: True Stories of the Risk-Taking Scientists Who Figure Out Ways to Explore Beyond. 2010. (ENG., Illus.). 80p. (J). (gr. 5-18). lib. bdg. 28.90 *(978-1-4263-0598-6(2)*, National Geographic Children's Bks.) National Geographic Society.

Skurzynski, Gloria & National Geographic Kids Staff. This Is Rocket Science: True Stories of the Risk-Taking Scientists Who Figure Out Ways to Explore Beyond. 2010. (ENG., Illus.). 80p. (J). (gr. 5-18). 18.95 *(978-1-4263-0597-9(4)*, National Geographic Children's Bks.) National Geographic Society.

Smith, Andrea P. Casey Jones. 2012. (Illus.). 24p. (J). 63.60 *(978-1-4488-5229-1(3))*; pap. 10.60 *(978-1-4488-5228-4(5))*; lib. bdg. 25.25 *(978-1-4488-5195-9(5))* Rosen Publishing Group, Inc., The. (PowerKids Pr.).

Sneed, Dani. Ferris Wheel! George Ferris & His Amazing Invention. 2008. (Genius at Work! Great Inventor Biographies Ser.). (Illus.). 32p. (J). (gr. 3-7). lib. bdg. 23.94 *(978-0-7660-2834-0(8)*, Enslow Elementary) Enslow Pubs., Inc.

—The Man Who Invented the Ferris Wheel: The Genius of George Ferris. 2013. (Genius Inventors & Their Great Ideas Ser.). 48p. (J). (gr. 3-4). pap. 8.95 *(978-1-4644-0206-7(X)*, Enslow Elementary) Enslow Pubs., Inc.

Sprunger, Reed. Thomas Edison: Incredible Inventor, 1 vol. 2013. (Beginner Biographies Set 2 Ser.). (ENG.). 32p. (J). (gr. -1-4). lib. bdg. 28.50 *(978-1-61641-936-3(9)*, Looking Glass Library) Magic Wagon.

Technicians. 3rd rev. ed. 2010. (Careers in Focus Ser.). (Illus.). 192p. (gr. 6-12). 32.95 *(978-0-8160-8021-2(6)*, Ferguson Publishing Co.) Facts On File, Inc.

Venezia, Mike. Henry Ford: Big Wheel in the Auto Industry. Venezia, Mike, illus. 2009. (Getting to Know the World's Greatest Inventors & Scientists Ser.). (ENG., Illus.). 32p. (J). (gr. 3-4). pap. 6.95 *(978-0-531-21335-3(8)*, Children's Pr.); (gr. 2-5). 28.00 *(978-0-531-23726-7(5))* Scholastic Library Publishing.

—Steve Jobs & Steve Wozniak: Geek Heroes Who Put the Personal in Computers. 2010. (Getting to Know the World's Greatest Inventors & Scientists Ser.). 32p. (J). pap. 6.95 *(978-0-531-22351-2(5)*, Children's Pr.) Scholastic Library Publishing.

—Thomas Edison: Inventor with a Lot of Bright Ideas. Venezia, Mike, illus. 2008. (Getting to Know the World's Greatest Inventors & Scientists Ser.). (ENG., Illus.). 32p. (J). (gr. 2-5). 28.00 *(978-0-531-14978-2(1))* Scholastic Library Publishing.

Ventura, Marne & Feynman, Drew. The Creators of the iPhone. Glass, Simon, illus. 2017. (Awesome Minds Ser.). (ENG.). 56p. (J). (gr. 1-5). 14.99 *(978-1-938093-77-7(1)*, Duo Pr. Llc (US)) Duo Pr. LLC.

Vescia, Monique. Engineers at Work. 2017. (Scientists at Work Ser.). 32p. (gr. 6-8). pap. 12.90 ***(978-1-68048-757-2(4)***, Britannica Educational Publishing) Rosen Publishing Group, Inc., The.

Wallmark, Laurie. Grace Hopper: Queen of Computer Code. Wu, Katy, illus. 2017. (ENG.). 48p. (J). (gr. k). 16.95 *(978-1-4549-2000-7(9))* Sterling Publishing Co., Inc.

Wargin, Kathy-jo. Alfred Nobel: The Man Behind the Peace Prize. Pullen, Zachary, illus. 2009. (ENG.). 32p. (J). (gr. k-6). 17.95 *(978-1-58536-281-3(6))* Sleeping Bear Pr.

Waters, Rosa. Instagram: How Kevin Systrom & Mike Krieger Changed the Way We Take & Share Photos. 2014. (Wizards of Technology Ser.: 10). 64p. (J). (gr. 7-18). 23.95 *(978-1-4222-3183-8(6))* Mason Crest.

Waxman, Laura Hamilton. Aerospace Engineer Aprille Ericsson. 2015. (STEM Trailblazer Bios Ser.). (ENG., Illus.). 32p. (J). (gr. 2-5). pap. 7.95 *(978-1-4677-6118-5(4))*; lib. bdg. 26.60 *(978-1-4677-5793-5(4))* Lerner Publishing Group. (Lerner Pubns.).

—Computer Engineer Ruchi Sanghvi. 2015. (STEM Trailblazer Bios Ser.). 32p. (J). (gr. 2-5). pap. 7.95 *(978-1-4677-6119-2(2))*; lib. bdg. 26.60 *(978-1-4677-5794-2(2))* Lerner Publishing Group. (Lerner Pubns.).

Weakland, Mark. When Thomas Edison Fed Someone Worms. Radcliffe, Thomas, illus. 2017. (J). *(978-1-5158-0139-9(X))* 2016. (ENG.). 32p. (gr. 2-3). lib. bdg. 27.99 *(978-1-4795-9683-6(3))* Picture Window Bks.

Whiting, Jim. James Watt & the Steam Engine. 2005. (Uncharted, Unexplored, & Unexplained Ser.). (Illus.). 48p. (J). (gr. 4-8). lib. bdg. 29.95 *(978-1-58415-371-9(7))* Mitchell Lane Pubs., Inc.

Woodside, Martin. Thomas Edison: The Man Who Lit up the World. 2007. (Sterling Biographies(r) Ser.). (ENG., Illus.). 128p. (J). (gr. 5-9). pap. 5.95 *(978-1-4027-3229-4(5))* Sterling Publishing Co., Inc.

Wyckoff, Edwin Brit. The Guy Who Invented Home Video Games: Ralph Baer & His Awesome Invention. 2010. (Genius at Work! Great Inventor Biographies Ser.). (Illus.). 32p. (J). (gr. 2-5). 23.94 *(978-0-7660-3450-1(X))* Enslow Pubs., Inc.

—Laser Man: Theodore H. Maiman & His Brilliant Invention. 2007. (Genius at Work! Great Inventor Biographies Ser.). (Illus.). 32p. (J). (gr. 3-7). lib. bdg. 23.94 *(978-0-7660-2848-7(8)*, Enslow Elementary) Enslow Pubs., Inc.

—The Man Who Invented Television: The Genius of Philo T. Farnsworth. 2013. (Genius Inventors & Their Great Ideas Ser.). 48p. (J). (gr. 3-4). pap. 8.95 *(978-1-4644-0209-8(4))*; (Illus.). 25.27 *(978-0-7660-4139-4(5))* Enslow Pubs., Inc. (Enslow Elementary).

—The Teen Who Invented Television: Philo T. Farnsworth & His Awesome Invention. 2007. (Genius at Work! Great Inventor Biographies Ser.). (Illus.). 32p. (J). (gr. 4-7). lib. bdg. 23.94 *(978-0-7660-2845-6(3)*, Enslow Elementary) Enslow Pubs., Inc.

Zuehlke, Jeffrey. Henry Ford. 2007. (History Maker Bios Ser.). (Illus.). 48p. (J). (gr. 3-7). lib. bdg. 26.60 *(978-0-8225-6583-3(8)*, Lerner Pubns.) Lerner Publishing Group.

ENGINEERS—VOCATIONAL GUIDANCE

Coleman, Miriam. Designing Computer Programs: Software Engineers, 01 vols., 1. 2016. (Engineers Rule Ser.). (ENG.). 32p. (J). pap. 11.75 *(978-1-5081-4544-8(X)*, PowerKids Pr.) Rosen Publishing Group, Inc., The.

Gazlay, Suzy. Re-Greening the Environment: Careers in Cleanup, Remediation, & Restoration. 2011. (ENG.). 64p. (J). pap. *(978-0-7787-4869-4(3))* Crabtree Publishing Co.

Mara, Wil. Information Security Analyst. 2013. (21st Century Skills Library: Cool STEM Careers Ser.). (ENG.). 32p. (J). (gr. 4-8). 28.50 *(978-1-62431-005-8(2)*, 202471); pap. 14.21 *(978-1-62431-029-4(X)*, 202473) Cherry Lake Publishing.

—Sound Engineer. 2015. (21st Century Skills Library: Cool STEAM Careers Ser.). (ENG., Illus.). 32p. (J). (gr. 4-7). 29.93 *(978-1-63362-563-1(X)*, 206436) Cherry Lake Publishing.

ENGINES

see also Automobiles—Engines; Fire Engines; Fuel; Steam-Engines

Bridges, Sarah. Rev It Up!, 6 vols., Set. Incl. Muscle Cars. lib. bdg. 26.65 *(978-1-4296-5316-9(7))*; Sports Cars. lib. bdg. 26.65 *(978-1-4296-5318-3(3))*; (gr. k-1). (Rev It Up! Ser.). (ENG.). 24p. 2010. Set lib. bdg. 53.30 *(978-1-4296-5320-6(5)*, Pebble Plus) Capstone Press of Coughlan Cos.

Capstone Press. Full Throttle, 1 vol. 2010. (Full Throttle Ser.). (ENG.). 32p. lib. bdg. 266.50 *(978-1-4296-5938-3(6)*, Edge Bks.) Capstone Press of Coughlan Cos.

Cardenas, Ernesto A. Wheels & Motors. 2009. 19.95 *(978-1-60698-023-1(8))*; pap. 3.95 *(978-1-60698-021-7(1))* Milo Educational Bks. & Resources.

Full Throttle. 2010. (Full Throttle Ser.). (ENG.). 32p. (gr. 3-4). lib. bdg. 111.96 *(978-1-4296-4755-7(8))*; lib. bdg. 279.90 *(978-1-4296-4754-0(X))* Capstone Press of Coughlan Cos. (Edge Bks.).

Higgins, Melissa. Wind Energy, 1 vol. 2013. (Innovative Technologies Ser.). (ENG.). 112p. (J). (gr. 6-12). 35.64 *(978-1-61783-469-1(6))* ABDO Publishing Co.

ENGLAND

Allport, Alan. England. 2nd rev. ed. 2007. (Modern World Nations Ser.). (Illus.). 128p. (YA). (gr. 7-12). lib. bdg. 35.00 *(978-0-7910-9514-0(2))* Facts On File, Inc.

Desmet, Wendy. My Dad Is Different. 2012. (Illus.). 20p. pap. 19.82 *(978-1-4678-9064-9(2))* AuthorHouse.

Dyan, Penelope. The Place of Tales — a Kid's Guide to Canterbury, Kent, England. Weigand, John, photos by. 2011. (Illus.). 40p. pap. 12.95 *(978-1-935630-66-1(0))* Bellissima Publishing, LLC.

—Steam Train! All the Way to Canterbury, England. Weigand, John D., photos by. 2011. (Illus.). 40p. pap. 11.95 *(978-1-935630-75-3(X))* Bellissima Publishing, LLC.

Edward, Herman. Pink Floyd. 2007. (Popular Rock Superstars of Yesterday & Today Ser.). (Illus.). 64p. (YA). (gr. 3-7). pap. 7.95 *(978-1-4222-0313-2(1))* Mason Crest.

Edwards, Roberta. Who Is Jane Goodall? 2012. (Who Is... ? Ser.). lib. bdg. 16.00 *(978-0-606-26651-2(8)*, Turtleback) Turtleback Bks.

Faiella, Graham. England: A Primary Source Cultural Guide. 2005. (Primary Sources of World Cultures Ser.). (Illus.). 128p. (J). (gr. 4-8). lib. bdg. 37.25 *(978-1-4042-2911-2(6))* Rosen Publishing Group, Inc., The.

Faiella, Graham. England: A Primary Source Cultural Guide. 2009. (Primary Sources of World Cultures Ser.). 128p. (gr. 4-5). 79.90 *(978-1-60851-919-4(8))* Rosen Publishing Group, Inc., The.

Harman, Alice. England. 2016. (Fact Cat: United Kingdom Ser.). (ENG., Illus.). 24p. (J). (gr. k-2). pap. 9.99 *(978-0-7502-8927-6(9)*, Wayland) Hachette Children's Group GBR. Dist: Hachette Bk. Group.

Juarez, Christine. England, 1 vol. 2014. (Countries Ser.). (ENG.). 24p. (gr. k-1). lib. bdg. 26.65 *(978-1-4765-4228-7(7)*, Pebble Plus) Capstone Press of Coughlan Cos.

Lin, Yoming S. Charles Darwin & Evolution. 2012. (Eureka! Ser.). (Illus.). 24p. (YA). (gr. 3-6). lib. bdg. 22.60 *(978-1-4488-5031-0(2))* Rosen Publishing Group, Inc., The.

Lynch, Annabelle. Living in England. 2017. (Living in the UK Ser.). (ENG., Illus.). 24p. (J). (gr. k-2). pap. 11.99 *(978-1-4451-4813-7(7)*, Franklin Watts) Hachette Children's Group GBR. Dist: Hachette Bk. Group.

Nikola-lisa, W. Till Year's Good End. Manson, Christopher, illus. 2009. (ENG.). 36p. (J). (gr. 1-4). 12.99 *(978-1-4424-0225-6(3)*, Atheneum Bks. for Young Readers) Simon & Schuster Children's Publishing.

Obregón, José María. England: Inglaterra. 2009. (Great National Soccer Teams / Grandes selecciones del fútbol mundial Ser.). (SPA & ENG.). 24p. pap. 8.25 *(978-1-4358-3235-0(3)*, PowerKids Pr.) Rosen Publishing Group, Inc., The.

—England: Inglaterra. Benson, Megan, tr. 2009. (Great National Soccer Teams / Grandes Selecciones Del Fútbol Mundial Ser.). (SPA & ENG., Illus.). 24p. (J). (gr. 2-5). lib. bdg. 22.60 *(978-1-4042-8089-2(8)*, PowerKids Pr.) Rosen Publishing Group, Inc., The.

Powell, Jillian. Tudor Times. 2017. (Craft Box Ser.). (ENG., Illus.). 32p. (J). (gr. 4-6). pap. 11.99 *(978-0-7502-8405-9(6)*, Wayland) Hachette Children's Group GBR. Dist: Hachette Bk. Group.

Ray, Jane. The Twelve Days of Christmas. 2011. (ENG., Illus.). 32p. (J). (gr. -1-2). 16.99 *(978-0-7636-5735-2(2))* Candlewick Pr.

Rechner, Amy. England. 2017. (Country Profiles Ser.). (ENG., Illus.). 32p. (J). (gr. 3-8). lib. bdg. 26.95 ***(978-1-62617-679-9(5)***, Blastoff! Discovery) Bellwether Media.

Sandler, Martin W. How the Beatles Changed the World. 2014. (ENG., Illus.). 176p. (J). (gr. 5-8). 20.99 *(978-0-8027-3565-2(7)*, 9780802735652, Bloomsbury USA Childrens) Bloomsbury Publishing USA.

Sheen, Barbara, ed. Foods of England. 2011. (Taste of Culture Ser.). (ENG.). 64p. (J). (gr. 3-6). 30.45 *(978-0-7377-5881-8(3)*, Kidhaven) Cengage Gale.

Turner, Patrenia. A Christmas Carol For Keeng Troyius. 2016. (Illus.). pap. *(978-0-578-18261-2(0))* Royalty Patrenia Turner Publications.

Ukoha, Ndubuisi. Dear England. 2008. (Illus.). 60p. pap. 21.99 *(978-1-4389-2337-6(6))* AuthorHouse.

The United Kingdom: England. 2013. (Britannica Guide to Countries of the European Union Ser.). 400p. (YA). (gr. 9-12). 106.00 *(978-1-61530-976-4(4))* Rosen Publishing Group, Inc., The.

Wallenfeldt, Jeff, ed. The United Kingdom: England. 2013. (Britannica Guide to Countries of the European Union Ser.). 400p. (YA). (gr. 9-12). 53.00 *(978-1-61530-963-4(2))* Rosen Publishing Group, Inc., The.

ENGLAND—FICTION

Aiken, Joan. Midwinter Nightingale. 2005. 248p. (J). (gr. 5). 13.65 *(978-0-7569-5684-4(6))* Perfection Learning Corp.

Albright, Emily. The Heir & the Spare. 2016. (ENG.). 287p. (YA). 17.99 *(978-1-4405-9010-8(9)*, Simon Pulse) F&W Media, Inc.

Allen, M. E. Gotta Get Some Bish Bash Bosh. 2005. (Illus.). 208p. (J). 15.99 *(978-0-06-073198-4(2)*, HarperTeen) HarperCollins Pubs.

Allison, Jennifer. The Ghost Sonata. 2008. (Gilda Joyce Ser.). (ENG.). 352p. (J). (gr. 3-7). 8.99 *(978-0-14-241232-9(5)*, Puffin Books) Penguin Young Readers Group.

Almond, David. The Boy Who Climbed into the Moon. Dunbar, Polly, illus. 2010. (ENG.). 128p. (J). (gr. 3-7). 15.99 *(978-0-7636-4217-4(7))* Candlewick Pr.

—Half a Creature from the Sea: A Life in Stories. Taylor, Eleanor, illus. 2015. (ENG.). 240p. (YA). (gr. 7). 16.99 *(978-0-7636-7877-7(5))* Candlewick Pr.

—Kit's Wilderness. unabr. ed. 2004. 240p. (J). (gr. 7-18). pap. 36.00 incl. audio *(978-0-8072-8216-8(2)*, Listening Library) Random Hse. Audio Publishing Group.

—My Dad's a Birdman. Dunbar, Polly, illus. 2008. (ENG.). 128p. (J). (gr. 3-7). 15.99 *(978-0-7636-3667-8(3))* Candlewick Pr.

—My Name Is Mina. (ENG.). 304p. (J). 2012. (gr. 5). 6.99 *(978-0-375-87327-0(9)*, Yearling) 2011. (gr. 3-7). 15.99 *(978-0-385-74073-9(5)*, Delacorte Bks. for Young Readers) Random Hse. Children's Bks.

—Raven Summer. 2011. (ENG.). 208p. (YA). (gr. 7). pap. 7.99 *(978-0-385-73807-1(2)*, Ember) Random Hse. Children's Bks.

—Skellig. 2009. 9.14 *(978-0-7848-2973-8(X)*, Everbind) Marco Bk. Co.

—Slog's Dad. McKean, Dave, illus. 2011. (ENG.). 64p. (J). (gr. 5-18). 15.99 *(978-0-7636-4940-1(6))* Candlewick Pr.

—A Song for Ella Grey. 2015. (ENG.). 272p. (YA). (gr. 7). 16.99 *(978-0-553-53359-0(2)*, Delacorte Pr.) Random Hse. Children's Bks.

—The Tightrope Walkers. (ENG.). 336p. (YA). (gr. 9). 2016. pap. 9.99 *(978-0-7636-9104-2(6))* 2015. 17.99 *(978-0-7636-7310-9(2))* Candlewick Pr.

—The Tightrope Walkers. 2016. (ENG.). 336p. (YA). (gr. 9). 20.85 *(978-0-606-39108-5(8))* Turtleback Bks.

Alton, Steve. The Firehills. 2005. (ENG.). 192p. (YA). (gr. 5-12). 15.95 *(978-1-57505-798-9(0)*, Carolrhoda Bks.) Lerner Publishing Group.

—The Malifex. 2003. (Middle Readers Ser.). (Illus.). 182p. (J). (gr. 3-7). 14.95 *(978-0-8225-0959-2(8))* Lerner Publishing Group.

Andersen, Alan Lance. Wizard Academies - Rumpots, Crackpots, & Pooka-Mazed Halfwits. 2008. 174p. pap. 19.96 *(978-0-615-18594-1(0))* Wizard Academies, LLC.

Anderson, Julian. View Halloo. 2005. (ENG., Illus.). 48p. pap. *(978-1-84401-601-3(3))* Athena Pr.

Anderson, R. J. Wayfarer. 2010. (ENG.). 304p. (J). (gr. 8-18). 16.99 *(978-0-06-155477-3(4)*, HarperTeen) HarperCollins Pubs.

Andrews, Julie. The Little Grey Men: A Story for the Young in Heart. Watkins-Pitchford, Denys, illus. 2004. 304p. (J). 17.89 *(978-0-06-055449-1(5)*, Julie Andrews Collection) HarperCollins Pubs.

Angus, Sam. A Horse Called Hero. 2014. (ENG.). 304p. (J). (gr. 4-7). 16.99 *(978-1-250-04508-9(8)*, 9781250045089) Feiwel & Friends.

EFG

Armstrong, Tony. The Water Troll. 2008. (ENG.). 16p. 8.49 (978-1-4389-1925-6(5)) AuthorHouse.

Arnold, Louise. Golden & Grey: An Unremarkable Boy & a Rather Remarkable Ghost. 2006. (ENG., Illus.). 272p. (J). (gr. 3-7). reprint ed. pap. 6.99 (978-0-689-87585-4(1), McElderry, Margaret K. Bks.) McElderry, Margaret K. Bks.

—Golden & Grey: The Nightmares That Ghosts Have. 2007. (ENG.). 304p. (J). (gr. 3-7). pap. 5.99 (978-0-689-87587-8(8), McElderry, Margaret K. Bks.) McElderry, Margaret K. Bks.

—Golden & Grey - A Good Day for Haunting. 2009. (ENG.). 336p. (J). (gr. 3-7). pap. 6.99 (978-1-4169-0864-7(1), McElderry, Margaret K. Bks.) McElderry, Margaret K. Bks.

Austen, Jane. Pride & Prejudice. Kronheimer, Ann, illus. 2013. (Jane Austen Ser.). (ENG.). 64p. pap. 6.95 (978-1-906230-06-7(4)) Real Reads Ltd. GBR. Dist: Casemate Pubs. & Bk. Distributors, LLC.

—Pride & Prejudice. 2003. (Saddleback Classics Ser.). (Illus.). 48p. (J). stu. ed., per. 17.95 (978-1-56254-530-7(2), SP5302); 80p. (YA). (gr. 8-12). per. 6.95 (978-1-56254-529-1(9), SP5299) Saddleback Educational Publishing, Inc.

—Sense & Sensibility. 2011. (ENG.). 464p. (YA). (gr. 8). pap. 8.99 (978-0-06-201563-1(X), HarperTeen) HarperCollins Pubs.

—Sense & Sensibility. Kronheimer, Ann, illus. 2013. (Jane Austen Ser.). (ENG.). 64p. pap. 6.95 (978-1-906230-11-1(0)) Real Reads Ltd. GBR. Dist: Casemate Pubs. & Bk. Distributors, LLC.

Austen, Jane & Fisher, Eric Scott. Pride & Prejudice, 1 vol. 2012. (Calico Illustrated Classics Ser.: No. 4). (ENG., Illus.). 112p. (J). (gr. 3-6). 27.07 (978-1-61641-619-5(X)) Magic Wagon.

Awdry, Wilbert V. & Awdry, W. Down at the Docks. Courtney, Richard, illus. 2003. (Pictureback Ser.). (ENG.). 24p. (J). (gr. -1-2). pap. 3.99 (978-0-375-82592-7(4), Random Hse. Bks. for Young Readers) Random Hse. Children's Bks.

Bachmann, Stefan. The Peculiar. (Peculiar Ser.: 1). (ENG.). (J). (gr. 4). 2013. 400p. pap. 8.99 (978-0-06-219519-7(0)) 2012. 384p. 16.99 (978-0-06-219518-0(2)) HarperCollins Pubs. (Greenwillow Bks.).

—The Whatnot. 2013. 421p. (J). (978-0-06-228630-7(7), Collins Design) HarperCollins Pubs.

Baglio, Ben M. Colt on Christmas Eve. Baum, Ann & Lasher, Mary Ann, illus. 2005. 142p. (J). pap. (978-0-439-77522-9(1)) Scholastic, Inc.

Bailey, Ethel M. T. Lily Pond Village, 1 vol. 2009. 57p. pap. 16.95 (978-1-60703-379-0(8)) America Star Bks.

Baldwin, May. Sarah's School Friend. 2007. 280p. 28.95 (978-1-4218-4206-6(8)); per. 13.95 (978-1-4218-4304-9(8)) 1st World Publishing, Inc. (1st World Library - Literary Society).

—Sarah's School Friend. 2007. 224p. pap. 20.99 (978-1-4346-3544-0(9)); 248p. pap. 22.99 (978-1-4346-3545-7(7)) Creative Media Partners, LLC.

Ballantyne, R. M. The Battle & the Breeze. 2004. reprint ed. pap. 1.99 (978-1-4192-5365-2(4)); pap. 15.95 (978-1-4191-5365-5(X)) Kessinger Publishing, LLC.

—The Crew of the Water Wagtail. 2011. 146p. pap. 12.95 (978-1-60664-550-5(1)) Rodgers, Alan Bks.

Balliett, Blue. The Calder Game. Helquist, Brett, illus. (ENG.). (J). (gr. 3-7). 2010. 416p. 7.99 (978-0-439-85208-1(0), Scholastic Paperbacks) 2008. 400p. 17.99 (978-0-439-85207-4(2), Scholastic Pr.) Scholastic, Inc.

Ballou, Kathy. The Tracks Out Back. l.t. ed. 2005. (Illus.). 24p. (J). per. 10.00 (978-1-932338-50-8(0)) Lifevest Publishing, Inc.

Banks, Lynne Reid. Uprooted - a Canadian War Story. 2014. (ENG.). 336p. (J). 8.99 (978-0-00-758943-2(3), HarperCollins Children's Bks.) HarperCollins Pubs. Ltd. GBR. Dist: HarperCollins Pubs.

Barklem, Jill. Autumn Story. Barklem, Jill, illus. 2011. (Brambly Hedge Ser.). (ENG., Illus.). 32p. (J). 9.99 (978-0-00-183739-3(7), HarperCollins Children's Bks.) HarperCollins Pubs. Ltd. GBR. Dist: HarperCollins Pubs.

Barr, Lester. Robots Land at Manchester Airport. 2012. (Illus.). 80p. pap. 13.66 (978-1-4772-2248-5(0)) AuthorHouse.

Barradel, Isabel. Toyshop Tales. 2006. 275p. pap. 27.95 (978-1-4241-2798-6(X)) PublishAmerica, Inc.

Barrett, Tracy. The Beast of Blackslope. 2011. (Sherlock Files Ser.: 2). (ENG., Illus.). 192p. (J). (gr. 3-7). pap. 7.99 (978-0-312-65918-9(0), 9780312659189) Square Fish.

—The 100-Year-Old Secret. 2010. (Sherlock Files Ser.: 1). (ENG., Illus.). 176p. (J). (gr. 3-7). pap. 6.99 (978-0-312-60212-3(X), 9780312602123) Square Fish.

Basic, Zdenko, illus. Steampunk Charles Dickens' a Christmas Carol. 2014. (ENG.). 204p. (gr. 7). 18.95 (978-0-7624-5090-9(8), Running Pr. Kids) Running Pr. Bk. Pubs.

Bates, Melinda. Nick Pricer: An American Heir. 2012. 88p. 19.95 (978-1-4697-8478-6(5)); pap. 9.95 (978-1-4697-8476-2(9)) iUniverse, Inc.

Beauvais, Clémentine. Gargoyles Gone AWOL. Horne, Sarah, illus. 2015. (Sesame Seade Mystery Ser.: 2). (ENG.). 208p. (J). (gr. 2-6). 16.95 (978-0-8234-3205-9(X)) Holiday Hse., Inc.

—Scam on the Cam. Horne, Sarah, illus. 2016. (Sesame Seade Mystery Ser.: 3). (ENG.). 192p. (J). 16.95 (978-0-8234-3630-9(6)) Holiday Hse., Inc.

—Sleuth on Skates. Horne, Sarah, illus. 2014. (Sesame Seade Mystery Ser.: 1). (ENG.). 224p. (J). (gr. 2-5). 16.95 (978-0-8234-3197-7(5)) Holiday Hse., Inc.

Becker, Tom. Lifeblood. 2010. (Darkside Ser.: 2). (ENG.). 288p. (J). (gr. 7). 7.99 (978-0-545-03746-4(8), Orchard Bks.) Scholastic, Inc.

Bedford, David. The Team Bind-up. 2007. (Illus.). 227p. (978-1-921272-04-2(X)) Little Hare Bks. AUS. Dist: HarperCollins Pubs. Australia.

Bedford, Martyn. The Flip. 2012. (ENG.). 272p. (YA). (gr. 7). pap. 8.99 (978-0-375-86552-7(7), Ember) Random Hse. Children's Bks.

Bell, Julia. Massive. 2006. (ENG., Illus.). 272p. (YA). (gr. 7-18). pap. 8.99 (978-1-4169-0207-2(4), Simon Pulse) Simon Pulse.

Bellairs, John. The Secret of the Underground Room (A Johnny Dixon Mystery: Book Eight) 2011. 96p. pap. 14.95 (978-1-61756-352-2(8)) Open Road Integrated Media, Inc.

Benjamin, Floella. My Two Grannies. Chamberlain, Margaret, illus. 2009. (ENG.). 32p. (J). (gr. k-3). pap. 7.95 (978-1-84780-034-3(3), Frances Lincoln Children's Bks.) Quarto Publishing Group UK GBR. Dist: Hachette Bk. Group.

Berry, Kit. Solstice at Stonewylde. 2011. (ENG.). 400p. (gr. 13-17). 10.99 (978-0-575-09887-9(2), Gollancz) Orion Publishing Group, Ltd. GBR. Dist: Hachette Bk. Group.

Bingham, J. & Brontë, Emily. Wuthering Heights. 2004. (Paperback Classics Ser.). 144p. (J). pap. 4.95 (978-0-7945-0573-8(2)) EDC Publishing.

Blackford, Cheryl. Lizzie & the Lost Baby. (ENG.). 192p. (J). (gr. 5-7). 2017. pap. 6.99 (978-0-544-93525-9(X)) 2016. 16.99 (978-0-544-57099-3(5)) Houghton Mifflin Harcourt Publishing Co. (HMH Books For Young Readers).

Blair, Eric, et al. Tom Thumb: A Retelling of the Grimm's Fairy Tale, 1 vol. Ouren, Todd, illus. 2010. (My First Classic Story Ser.). (ENG.). 32p. (gr. k-3). lib. bdg. 22.65 (978-1-4048-6071-1(1), My First Classic Story) Picture Window Bks.

Blythe, Daniel. Shadow Breakers. 2013. (J). (978-0-545-47980-6(0)); (ENG.). 256p. (gr. 5-9). 16.99 (978-0-545-47979-0(7)) Scholastic, Inc. (Chicken Hse., The).

Bond, Michael. Paddington. Alley, R. W., illus. 2014. (Paddington Ser.). (ENG.). 32p. (J). (gr. -1-3). 17.99 (978-0-06-231719-3(9)) HarperCollins Pubs.

—Paddington Here & Now. Alley, R. W., illus. 176p. (J). 2009. pap. 5.99 (978-0-06-147366-1(9)) 2008. (ENG.). (gr. 3-7). 15.99 (978-0-06-147364-7(2)) HarperCollins Pubs.

Boston, Lucy M. The Children of Green Knowe Collection. 2013. (ENG., Illus.). 368p. (J). 12.95 (978-0-571-30347-2(1)) Faber & Faber, Inc.

Bowler, Tim. Buried Thunder. 2011. (ENG.). 224p. (J). 16.95 (978-0-8234-2397-2(2)) Holiday Hse., Inc.

—Playing Dead. 2010. (Blade Ser.: 1). (ENG.). 256p. (YA). (gr. 9-18). 7.99 (978-0-14-241600-6(2), Speak) Penguin Young Readers Group.

Boyce, Frank Cottrell. Chitty Chitty Bang Bang over the Moon. Berger, Joe, illus. 2015. (Chitty Chitty Bang Bang Ser.). (ENG.). 304p. (J). (gr. 4-7). pap. 6.99 (978-0-7636-7666-7(7)) Candlewick Pr.

—Millions. 2005. 247p. (gr. 3-7). 19.00 (978-0-7569-5439-0(8)) Perfection Learning Corp.

Brandeis, Madeline. Little Tom of England. 2011. 160p. 41.95 (978-1-258-09313-6(8)) Literary Licensing, LLC.

Bray, Libba. A Great & Terrible Beauty. 2005. (Gemma Doyle Trilogy Ser.: Bk. 1). (ENG.). 432p. (YA). (gr. 7). reprint ed. pap. 9.99 (978-0-385-73231-4(7), Ember) Random Hse. Children's Bks.

—Rebel Angels. 2006. (Gemma Doyle Trilogy Ser.: Bk. 2). (ENG.). 576p. (YA). (gr. 7-12). pap. 10.99 (978-0-385-73341-0(0), Ember) Random Hse. Children's Bks.

—The Sweet Far Thing. 2009. (Gemma Doyle Trilogy Ser.: Bk. 3). (ENG.). 848p. (YA). (gr. 7). pap. 10.99 (978-0-440-23777-8(7), Ember) Random Hse. Children's Bks.

Brege, K. B. Ghost Board Posse London Screaming! 2008. (Ghost Board Posse Ser.: No. 1). (Illus.). 207p. (YA). pap. 6.99 (978-0-9774119-6-2(6)) Team B Creative LLC.

Brennan, Herbie. The Doomsday Box: A Shadow Project Adventure. 2011. (Shadow Project Ser.: 2). (ENG.). 352p. (J). (gr. 5). pap. 6.99 (978-0-06-175650-4(4)) HarperCollins Pubs.

Brennan, Sarah Rees. Unmade. (Lynburn Legacy Ser.: Bk. 3). (ENG.). 384p. (YA). (gr. 7). 2015. pap. 9.99 (978-0-375-87105-4(5), Ember) 2014. (Illus.). 17.99 (978-0-375-87043-9(1), Random Hse. Bks. for Young Readers) Random Hse. Children's Bks.

—Unspoken. (Lynburn Legacy Ser.: Bk. 1). (ENG.). (YA). (gr. 7). 2012. 384p. 18.99 (978-0-375-87041-5(5), Random Hse. Bks. for Young Readers)Bk. 1. 2013. 400p. pap. 8.99 (978-0-375-87103-0(9), Ember) Random Hse. Children's Bks.

—Untold. Fochesato, Giorgio, illus. 2013. (Lynburn Legacy Ser.: Bk. 2). (ENG.). 384p. (YA). (gr. 7). 18.99 (978-0-375-87042-2(3), Random Hse. Bks. for Young Readers) Random Hse. Children's Bks.

Briard, Cheryl. The Bear Pond Ferry. 2011. 142p. pap. 15.95 (978-0-557-77738-9(0)) Lulu Pr., Inc.

Briley, Randy. Mr Underneath. 2013. 134p. pap. 12.99 (978-0-9896269-0-3(3)) Raven Mad Studios.

Brontë, Charlotte. Jane Eyre. 2004. (Fast Track Classics Ser.). (Illus.). 48p. (J). pap. (978-0-237-52687-0(5)) Evans Brothers, Ltd.

—Jane Eyre: From the Story by Charlotte Bronte. Harvey, Bob, illus. rev. ed. 2007. (Usborne Classics Retold Ser.). 176p. (J). (gr. 4). per. 4.99 (978-0-7945-1870-7(2), Usborne) EDC Publishing.

Brontë, Emily. Wuthering Heights. 2004. (Graphic Novels Ser.). (ENG., Illus.). 72p. (J). pap. 7.99 (978-0-237-52581-1(X)) Evans Brothers, Ltd. GBR. Dist: Independent Pubs. Group.

—Wuthering Heights. Bryant, Clive, ed. Burns, John M., illus. 2011. (ENG.). 160p. lib. bdg. 24.95 (978-1-907127-80-9(1)) Classical Comics GBR. Dist: Publishers Group West (PGW).

—Wuthering Heights. (Classics Illustrated Ser.). (Illus.). 52p. (YA). pap. 4.95 (978-1-57209-011-8(1)) Classics International Entertainment, Inc.

—Wuthering Heights. Warner, Darrell, illus. 2004. (Paperback Classics Ser.). 158p. (J). (gr. 5). lib. bdg. 12.95 (978-1-58086-604-0(2)) EDC Publishing.

Brooks, Kevin. Naked '76. 2016. (ENG.). 424p. (gr. 9-12). 18.99 (978-1-5124-0418-0(7), Carolrhoda Bks.); (YA). 38.65 (978-1-5124-0445-6(4), Carolrhoda Lab™) Lerner Publishing Group.

Brown, Carron, ed. Beauty & the Beast & Jack & the Beanstalk: Two Tales & Their Histories. 2009. (World of Fairy Tales Ser.). (Illus.). 32p. (J). (gr. -1-2). pap. 10.55 (978-1-60754-650-4(7)); lib. bdg. 22.60 (978-1-60754-649-8(3)) Windmill Bks.

Brown, Ruth. Gracie, the Lighthouse Cat. Brown, Ruth, illus. 2011. (Andersen Press Picture Bks). (ENG., Illus.). 32p. (J). (gr. -1-3). 16.95 (978-0-7613-7454-1(X)) Lerner Publishing Group.

Brown, Tina. My Haunted Summer Holiday. 2010. 52p. pap. 9.99 (978-1-60911-820-4(0), Eloquent Bks.) Strategic Book Publishing & Rights Agency (SBPRA).

Bryson, Brenda. The Adventures of Roo & Winston - Crop Circles. 2009. 64p. pap. 12.43 (978-0-557-17564-2(X)) Lulu Pr., Inc.

Buckley-Archer, Linda. The Many Lives of John Stone. 2015. (ENG., Illus.). 544p. (YA). (gr. 7). 17.99 (978-1-4814-2637-4(0)) Simon & Schuster Children's Publishing.

Bullock, Rob. Noah Ramsbottom & the Cave Elves. 2009. 48p. pap. 12.25 (978-1-60860-335-0(0), Strategic Bk. Publishing) Strategic Book Publishing & Rights Agency (SBPRA).

Burbridge, Ella. Egg on Their Faces. 2013. (Illus.). 232p. pap. 12.50 (978-1-84426-044-7(5)) Upfront Publishing Ltd. GBR. Dist: Printondemand-worldwide.com.

Burchill, Julie. Sugar Rush. 2005. 288p. (J). lib. bdg. 17.89 (978-0-06-077620-6(X), HarperTeen) HarperCollins Pubs.

Burgess, Barbara. The Magic Manuscript: Voyage to Eve Ilion. 2013. 202p. pap. 9.99 (978-0-9918574-4-9(5)) Sulby Hall Publishing.

Burgess, Melvin. The Hit. 2014. (ENG.). 304p. (J). (gr. 9). 17.99 (978-0-545-55699-6(6), Chicken Hse., The) Scholastic, Inc.

—Lady: My Life as a Bitch. 2003. (Illus.). 272p. (J). pap. 6.99 (978-0-06-054033-3(8)) HarperCollins Pubs.

—Nicholas Dane. 2013. (ENG.). 432p. (YA). (gr. 9-13). pap. 9.99 (978-0-312-55146-9(0), 9780312551469) Square Fish.

—Sara's Face. 2007. (ENG., Illus.). 272p. (YA). (gr. 9-12). 16.99 (978-1-4169-3617-6(3), Simon & Schuster Bks. For Young Readers) Simon & Schuster Bks. For Young Readers.

—Sara's Face. 2007. 272p. 16.99 (978-1-4169-3295-6(X)) Simon & Schuster Children's Publishing.

—Sara's Face. 2008. (ENG.). 288p. (YA). (gr. 9-12). pap. 7.99 (978-1-4169-5815-4(0), Simon Pulse) Simon Pulse.

—Smack. 2010. (ENG.). 352p. (YA). (gr. 9-13). pap. 13.99 (978-0-312-60862-0(4), 9780312608620) Square Fish.

Burgess, Melvyn & Pearson Education Staff. Billy Elliot: 'A Writer of the Hightest Quality with Exceptional Powers of Insight' 2nd ed. 2008. (ENG., Illus.). 64p. pap. 11.99 (978-1-4058-8176-0(3)) Pearson Education.

Burks, David W. Full Circle: The Story of Outlaw-Prince Edwin, High King of England. 2007. 124p. 20.95 (978-0-595-70485-9(9)); per. 10.95 (978-0-595-46753-2(9)) iUniverse, Inc.

Burnett, Frances Hodgson. A Lady of Quality. 2011. 190p. 26.95 (978-1-4638-9631-7(X)) Rodgers, Alan Bks.

—Little Lord Fauntleroy. (J). 21.95 (978-0-8488-0792-4(8)) Amereon Ltd.

—Little Lord Fauntleroy. 2004. (Aladdin Classics Ser.). (ENG.). 288p. (J). (gr. 3-7). pap. 6.99 (978-0-689-86994-5(0), Simon & Schuster/Paula Wiseman Bks.) Simon & Schuster/Paula Wiseman Bks.

—A Little Princess. 2008. 156p. 25.95 (978-1-60664-768-4(7)); pap. 13.95 (978-1-60664-141-5(7)) Aegypan.

—A Little Princess. 2008. 212p. (gr. 2-4). 24.99 (978-0-554-38458-0(2)); 27.99 (978-0-554-29155-0(X)) Creative Media Partners, LLC.

—A Little Princess. Aldous, Kate, illus. 2005. 62p. (J). (gr. 4-7). 8.95 (978-0-7945-1123-4(6), Usborne) EDC Publishing.

—A Little Princess. 2012. (ENG., Illus.). 280p. (978-1-905716-04-3(4), Collector's Library, The) Pan Macmillan.

—A Little Princess. Gill, Margery, illus. 2008. (Puffin Classics Ser.). (ENG.). 320p. (J). (gr. 5-7). 5.99 (978-0-14-132112-7(1), Puffin Books) Penguin Young Readers Group.

—A Little Princess. 188p. 2009. pap. 13.95 (978-1-4385-0876-4(X)) 2008. pap. 13.45 (978-1-4385-0194-9(3)) Standard Pubns., Inc. (Book Jungle).

—A Little Princess. McKowen, Scott, illus. 2004. (Sterling Unabridged Classics Ser.). (ENG.). 208p. (J). (gr. 5). 9.95 (978-1-4027-1454-2(8)) Sterling Publishing Co., Inc.

—A Little Princess. Engelbreit, Mary, illus. 2007. (Mary Engelbreit's Classic Library). (ENG.). 304p. (J). (gr. 3-7). 9.99 (978-0-06-008137-9(6), HarperFestival) HarperCollins Pubs.

—A Little Princess. 2012. (Children's Classics Ser.). (ENG.). 186p. pap. 19.99 (978-1-909438-52-1(9), Sovereign) Bollinger, Max GBR. Dist: Lightning Source UK, Ltd.

—A Little Princess. Kliros, Thea, illus. abr. ed. 2012. (Dover Children's Thrift Classics Ser.). (ENG.). 96p. (J). (gr. 3-8). pap. 3.00 (978-0-486-29171-0(5)) Dover Pubns., Inc.

—A Little Princess: Being the whole story of Sara Crewe now told for T. 2007. 196p. per. 19.99 (978-1-4346-7028-1(7)); (ENG.). 210p. per. 22.99 (978-1-4346-7029-8(5)) Creative Media Partners, LLC.

—A Little Princess: The Story of Sara Crewe. (J). 16.95 (978-0-8488-1253-9(0)) Amereon Ltd.

—A Little Princess: The Story of Sara Crewe. Warren, Eliza, ed. Marcos, Pablo, illus. 2006. 239p. (YA). reprint ed. 10.00 (978-0-7567-9835-2(3)) DIANE Publishing Co.

—A Little Princess: The Story of Sara Crewe. 2005. 112p. per. 4.95 (978-1-4209-2529-6(6)) Digireads.com Publishing.

—A Little Princess: The Story of Sara Crewe. 2006. pap. (978-1-4065-0559-7(5)) Dodo Pr.

—A Little Princess: The Story of Sara Crewe. l.t. ed. 2005. 376p. pap. (978-1-84637-117-2(1)) Echo Library.

—A Little Princess: The Story of Sara Crewe. 2004. reprint ed. pap. 22.95 (978-1-4191-0213-4(3)); pap. 1.99 (978-1-4192-0213-1(8)) Kessinger Publishing, LLC.

—A Little Princess: The Story of Sara Crewe. 2006. 204p. (YA). 19.95 (978-1-934169-20-9(X)); pap. 7.95 (978-1-934169-21-6(8)) Norilana Bks.

—A Little Princess: The Story of Sara Crewe. 2005. (Twelve-Point Ser.). lib. bdg. 25.00 (978-1-58287-320-6(8)); lib. bdg. 26.00 (978-1-58287-814-0(5)) North Bks.

—A Little Princess: The Story of Sara Crewe. Rust, Graham, illus. (J). pap. 22.95 (978-0-590-24079-6(X)) Scholastic, Inc.

—A Little Princess: The Story of Sara Crewe. l.t. ed. 2003. 342p. pap. 10.95 (978-0-7862-6247-2(8)) Thorndike Pr.

—A Little Princess: With a Discussion of Generosity. Gribbon, Sean & Jael, trs. Gribbon, Sean & Jael, illus. 2003. (Values in Action Illustrated Classics Ser.). (J). (978-1-59203-050-7(5)) Learning Challenge, Inc.

—Robin. 2008. 236p. 29.95 (978-1-60664-770-7(9)) Aegypan.

—The Secret Garden. 2012. (Illus.). 304p. (978-1-4351-4212-1(8)) Barnes & Noble, Inc.

—The Secret Garden. Robinson, Charles, illus. 2011. 304p. (J). (978-1-4351-3344-0(7)) Barnes & Noble, Inc.

—The Secret Garden. Moore, Inga, illus. 2008. (ENG.). 272p. (J). (gr. 1-4). 22.99 (978-0-7636-3161-1(2)) Candlewick Pr.

—The Secret Garden. Robinson, Charles, illus. 2014. (ENG.). 336p. (J). (gr. 2-4). 24.99 (978-1-4052-6740-3(2)) Egmont Bks., Ltd. GBR. Dist: Independent Pubs. Group.

—The Secret Garden. 2003. (ENG., Illus.). 288p. (gr. 12-18). mass mkt. 5.95 (978-0-451-52883-4(2), Signet) Penguin Publishing Group.

—The Secret Garden. 2003. (Modern Library Classics Ser.). (ENG.). 288p. (J). (gr. 3-7). pap. 7.95 (978-0-8129-6998-6(7), Modern Library) Random House Publishing Group.

—The Secret Garden. 2013. (ENG.). 384p. (J). (gr. 4-7). pap. 11.99 (978-0-09-957295-4(8)) Random Hse. GBR. Dist: Independent Pubs. Group.

—The Secret Garden. Ingpen, Robert R., illus. 2011. (Sterling Illustrated Classics Ser.). (ENG.). 240p. (J). (gr. 5-18). 19.95 (978-1-4027-7872-8(4)) Sterling Publishing Co., Inc.

—The Secret Garden. Moore, Inga, illus. 2010. (ENG.). 272p. (J). (gr. 1-4). pap. 16.99 (978-0-7636-4732-2(2)) Candlewick Pr.

—The Secret Garden. Corvino, Lucy, illus. 2005. (Classic Starts(tm) Ser.). (ENG.). 160p. (J). (gr. 2-4). 6.95 (978-1-4027-1319-4(3)) Sterling Publishing Co., Inc.

—The Secret Garden: A Young Reader's Edition of the Classic Story. 2004. (Illus.). (J). (gr. 1-4). spiral bd. (978-0-616-14565-4(9)); spiral bd. (978-0-616-14566-1(7)) Canadian National Institute for the Blind/Institut National Canadien pour les Aveugles.

—The Secret Garden: Faber Children's Classics. 2015. (ENG., Illus.). 416p. pap. 8.95 (978-0-571-32339-5(1)) Faber & Faber, Inc.

—The Secret Garden: With a Discussion of Compassion. Lauter, Richard, illus. 2003. (Values in Action Illustrated Classics Ser.). 191p. (J). (978-1-59203-037-8(8)) Learning Challenge, Inc.

—The Secret Garden Book & Charm. Tudor, Tasha, illus. deluxe ed. 2005. (Charming Classics). 368p. (J). 9.99 (978-0-06-075771-7(X), HarperFestival) HarperCollins Pubs.

Bush, Penelope. Alice in Time. 2011. (ENG., Illus.). 208p. (YA). (gr. 7-18). 17.95 (978-0-8234-2329-3(8)) Holiday Hse., Inc.

Byng, Georgia. Molly Moon y el Increible Libro. 2003. (SPA.). 349p. (J). 18.99 (978-84-348-9076-3(3)) SM Ediciones ESP. Dist: Lectorum Pubns., Inc.

—Molly Moon's Incredible Book of Hypnotism. 2003. 135.92 (978-0-06-057217-4(5)) 2003. (Molly Moon Ser.: 1). (Illus.). 384p. (J). (gr. 3-7). 17.99 (978-0-06-051406-8(X)) 2004. (Molly Moon Ser.: 1). (ENG., Illus.). 384p. (J). (gr. 3-7). reprint ed. pap. 7.99 (978-0-06-051409-9(4)) HarperCollins Pubs.

—Molly Moon's Incredible Book of Hypnotism. 2004. (Molly Moon Ser.). 371p. (gr. 3-7). 18.00 (978-0-7569-3484-2(2)) Perfection Learning Corp.

Cain. Tommy Tan & the Bowl of Time. 2011. (ENG.). 150p. (gr. 3-9). pap. 11.95 (978-988-18094-3-8(6)) Haven Bks.

Calcutt, David. Robin Hood. Baker-Smith, Grahame, illus. 2012. (ENG.). 176p. (J). (gr. 4-6). pap. 12.99 (978-1-84686-799-6(1)) Barefoot Bks., Inc.

Cann, Kate. Consumed. (ENG.). 336p. (J). (gr. 9). 2012. pap. 9.99 (978-0-545-26387-0(5)) 2011. 16.99 (978-0-545-26388-7(3)) Scholastic, Inc.

—Possessed. (ENG.). 336p. (J). (gr. 9-9). 2011. pap. 9.99 (978-0-545-12813-1(7)) 2010. 16.99 (978-0-545-12812-4(9)) Scholastic, Inc.

Carney, Larry, adapted by. Jack & the Beanstalk. 2009. (ENG., Illus.). 24p. (J). 6.95 (978-1-60072-115-1(X)) PC Treasures, Inc.

Carpenter, Ann. The Slumber Girls & the Mystical Dollhouse. 2006. (J). per. 8.99 (978-0-9771030-0-3(5)) Kidz By Dezign Pr., Inc.

Carter, Ally. Heist Society. 2011. (Heist Society Novel Ser.). (ENG.). 304p. (J). (gr. 5-9). pap. 9.99 (978-1-4231-1661-5(5)) Hyperion Pr.

—Uncommon Criminals. 2011. (Playaway Children Ser.). (YA). (gr. 7-12). 69.99 (978-1-4558-2483-0(6)) Findaway World, LLC.

—Uncommon Criminals. 2012. (Heist Society Novel Ser.). (ENG.). 304p. (J). (gr. 5-9). pap. 9.99 (978-1-4231-4807-4(X)) Hyperion Pr.

Cassidy, Anne. Butterfly Grave. 2014. (ENG.). 304p. (YA). (gr. 7). pap. 13.99 (978-1-4088-1552-6(4), 9781408815526, Bloomsbury USA Childrens) Bloomsbury Publishing USA.

—Looking for JJ. 2009. (ENG., Illus.). 336p. (J). (gr. 7). pap. 20.95 (978-0-15-206638-3(1)) Houghton Mifflin Harcourt Publishing Co.

Cassidy, Cathy. Indigo Blue. 2006. (ENG.). 240p. (J). (gr. 5-18). 7.99 (978-0-14-240703-5(8), Puffin Books) Penguin Young Readers Group.

Caterer, Claire M. The Key & the Flame. (ENG.). (J). (gr. 3-7). 2015. 496p. pap. 7.99 (978-1-4424-5742-3(2)) 2013. 480p. 17.99 (978-1-4424-5741-6(4)) McElderry, Margaret K. Bks. (McElderry, Margaret K. Bks.).

Caygill, Ronald. Scrope Hall. 2009. 48p. pap. 11.49 (978-1-4490-5078-8(6)) AuthorHouse.

Charles, Valerie. The Dancing Light. 2013. 118p. pap. (978-1-84944-167-4(7)) UKUnpublished.

Chaucer, Geoffrey. The Canterbury Tales - Literary Touchstone Edition. 2005. 128p. (YA). per. 3.99 (978-1-58049-396-3(3), PWH3963) Prestwick Hse., Inc.

Chesterman, Simon. Finding Aracadia. 2017. (ENG.). 200p. (J). (gr. 7-10). pap. 14.99 **(978-981-4751-51-3(0))** Marshall Cavendish International (Asia) Private Ltd. SGP. Dist: National Bk. Network.

Child, Lauren. Utterly Me, Clarice Bean. Child, Lauren, illus. 2005. (Clarice Bean Ser.). (ENG., Illus.). 208p. (J). (gr. 3-7). reprint ed. pap. 5.99 (978-0-7636-2788-1(7)) Candlewick Pr.

—Utterly Me, Clarice Bean. Child, Lauren, illus. 2006. (Clarice Bean Ser.). (Illus.). 16.00 (978-0-7569-6567-9(5)) Perfection Learning Corp.

A Christmas Carol. 2004. (J). cd-rom 7.99 (978-0-9740847-9-4(4)) GiGi Bks.

A Christmas Carol. 2003. (Illus.). 32p. (J). 9.98 (978-1-4054-0997-1(5)); 4.98 (978-1-4054-0980-3(0)) Parragon, Inc.

Clover, Louise. Bullring Kid & Country Cowboy Level 4 Intermediate. 2009. (ENG., Illus.). 96p. pap. 12.75 (978-84-8323-495-2(5)) Cambridge Univ. Pr.

Clover, Peter. Rescue Riders: Ghost Pony. l.t. ed. 2007. 92p. per. (978-1-905665-28-0(8)) Pollinger In Print.

Cockcroft, Jason. Counter Clockwise. 2009. 208p. (J). lib. bdg. 16.89 (978-0-06-125555-7(6), Tegen, Katherine Bks) HarperCollins Pubs.

Colfer, Eoin. The Arctic Incident. 2009. (Artemis Fowl Ser.). (ENG.). 304p. (J). (gr. 5-9). pap. 8.99 (978-1-4231-2454-2(5)) Hyperion Pr.

—The Arctic Incident. 2003. (Artemis Fowl Ser.: 2). 277p. (J). (gr. 5-7). lib. bdg. 19.65 (978-0-613-62927-0(2), Turtleback) Turtleback Bks.

—Artemis Fowl, 3 vols., Set. 2010. (Artemis Fowl Ser.). (ENG.). 944p. (J). (gr. 5-17). pap. 19.99 (978-1-4231-3681-1(0)) Disney Pr.

—Artemis Fowl. (Artemis Fowl Ser.: Bk. 1). (FRE.). pap. 34.95 (978-2-07-054681-7(0)) Gallimard, Editions FRA. Dist: Distribooks, Inc.

—Artemis Fowl. rev. ed. 2009. (Artemis Fowl Ser.). (ENG.). 304p. (J). (gr. 5-9). pap. 8.99 (978-1-4231-2452-8(9)) Hyperion Pr.

—Artemis Fowl. (Artemis Fowl Ser.: Bk. 1). pap. 34.95 (978-88-04-49788-2(2)) Mondadori ITA. Dist: Distribooks, Inc.

—Artemis Fowl. (Artemis Fowl Ser.: 1). (YA). 2007. 1.25 (978-1-4193-6020-6(5)) 2006. 52.75 (978-1-4193-6023-7(X)) 2006. 54.75 (978-1-4193-6021-3(3)) 2006. 54.75 (978-1-4193-6026-8(4)) 2006. 132.75 (978-1-4193-6022-0(1)) 2005. 56.75 (978-1-4193-6024-4(8)) Recorded Bks., Inc.

—Artemis Fowl. 2009. (Artemis Fowl Ser.: 1). (J). (gr. 5-8). lib. bdg. 19.65 (978-0-613-60637-0(X), Turtleback) Turtleback Bks.

—Artemis Fowl. Feldmann, Claudia, tr. (Artemis Fowl Ser.: Bk. 1). (GER.). pap. 24.95 (978-3-548-60320-9(3)) Ullstein-Taschenbuch-Verlag DEU. Dist: Distribooks, Inc.

—Artemis Fowl: El Mundo Subterráneo. 2013. (Vintage Espanol Ser.: Bk. 1). (SPA.). 288p. (YA). (gr. 5). pap. 9.95 (978-0-345-80418-1(X), Vintage Espanol) Knopf Doubleday Publishing Group.

—Encuentro en el Artico. 2013. (Vintage Espanol Ser.).Tr. of Arctic Incident. (SPA.). 320p. (YA). pap. 9.95 (978-0-345-80535-5(6), Vintage Espanol) Knopf Doubleday Publishing Group.

—The Eternity Code. rev. ed. 2009. (Artemis Fowl Ser.). (ENG.). 336p. (J). (gr. 5-9). pap. 8.99 (978-1-4231-2453-5(7)) Hyperion Pr.

—EL MUNDO SUBTERRÁNEO (ARTEMIS FOWL 1) (Artemis Fowl Ser.: Bk. 1). (SPA.). 288p. pap. (978-84-8441-115-4(X), MO31567) Grijalbo Mondadori, S.A.-Montena.

—The Opal Deception. 2006. (Artemis Fowl Ser.: Bk. 4). 17.10 (978-0-7569-6828-1(3)) Disney Pr.

—The Opal Deception. rev. ed. 2009. (Artemis Fowl Ser.). (ENG.). 368p. (J). (gr. 5-9). pap. 8.99 (978-1-4231-2455-9(3)) Hyperion Pr.

—The Opal Deception. (Artemis Fowl Ser.: 4). (J). 2007. 1.25 (978-1-4193-6041-1(8)) 2006. 69.75 (978-1-4193-6047-3(7)) 2006. 72.75 (978-1-4193-6045-9(0)) Recorded Bks., Inc.

Colfer, Eoin & Donkin, Andrew. Artemis Fowl. Rigano, Giovanni & Lamanna, Paolo, illus. 2007. (Artemis Fowl Ser.). (ENG.). 112p. (J). (gr. 5-9). 18.99 (978-0-7868-4881-2(2)); pap. 12.99 (978-0-7868-4882-9(0)) Hyperion Pr.

—The Eternity Code. Rigano, Giovanni & Lamanna, Paolo, illus. 2013. (Artemis Fowl Ser.: 3). (ENG.). 112p. (J). (gr. 5-9). 19.99 (978-1-4231-4527-1(5)) Hyperion Pr.

—Eternity Code. Rigano, Giovanni & Lamanna, Paolo, illus. 2013. (Artemis Fowl Ser.: 3). (ENG.). 112p. (J). (gr. 5-9). pap. 12.99 (978-1-4231-4577-6(1)) Hyperion Pr.

Collingwood, Harry. Across the Spanish Main. 2011. 204p. 26.95 (978-1-4638-9643-0(3)) Rodgers, Alan Bks.

Collins, Tim. Notes from a Hairy-Not-Scary Werewolf. Pinder, Andrew, illus. 2013. (ENG.). 288p. (J). (gr. 5-9). 12.99 (978-1-4424-8207-4(9), Aladdin) Simon & Schuster Children's Publishing.

—Notes from a Totally Lame Vampire: Because the Undead Have Feelings Too! Pinder, Andrew, illus. 2010. (ENG.). 336p. (J). (gr. 5-9). 12.99 (978-1-4424-1183-8(X), Aladdin) Simon & Schuster Children's Publishing.

—Prince of Dorkness: More Notes from a Totally Lame Vampire. Pinder, Andrew, illus. 2011. (ENG.). 336p. (J). (gr. 5-9). 12.99 (978-1-4424-3388-5(4), Aladdin) Simon & Schuster Children's Publishing.

Conness, Steven A. George Huck, the Founding of Huckville: The Huck Family Chronicles, 1 vol. 2010. 78p. pap. 19.95 (978-1-4489-4471-2(6)) PublishAmerica, Inc.

Cooper, Susan. The Dark Is Rising. 2009. 10.36 (978-0-7848-3502-9(0), Everbind) Marco Bk. Co.

—The Dark Is Rising. 2007. (YA). 1.25 (978-1-4193-7923-9(2)) Recorded Bks., Inc.

—The Dark Is Rising Sequence: Over Sea, under Stone - The Dark Is Rising - Greenwitch - The Grey King - Silver on the Tree. 2013. (Dark Is Rising Sequence Ser.). (ENG.). 1088p. (J). (gr. 3-7). pap. 39.99 (978-1-4424-8967-7(7), McElderry, Margaret K. Bks.) McElderry, Margaret K. Bks.

—The Dark Is Rising Sequence Set: Over Sea, under Stone; The Dark Is Rising; Greenwitch; The Grey King; Silver on the Tree. 2013. (Dark Is Rising Sequence Ser.). (ENG.). 1088p. (J). (gr. 3-7). 89.99 (978-1-4424-8968-4(5), McElderry, Margaret K. Bks.) McElderry, Margaret K. Bks.

Corlett, William. The Door in the Tree. 2010. (Magician's House Quartet Ser.: 2). (ENG.). 304p. (YA). (gr. 5-8). pap. 13.99 (978-1-4424-1414-3(6), Simon Pulse) Simon Pulse.

—The Steps up the Chimney. 2011. (Magician's House Quartet Ser.: 1). (ENG.). 288p. (YA). (gr. 7). pap. 13.99 (978-1-4424-2935-2(6), Simon Pulse) Simon Pulse.

Cousins, Dave. Waiting for Gonzo. 2015. (ENG.). 288p. (YA). pap. 9.99 (978-0-7387-4199-4(X), Flux) North Star Editions.

Cressey, Roger. The Talking Giraffe. Cressey, Roger, illus. 2013. (Illus.). 118p. pap. (978-1-78222-143-2(3)) Paragon Publishing, Rothersthorpe.

Crews, Nina. Jack & the Beanstalk. Crews, Nina, illus. 2011. (ENG., Illus.). 32p. (J). (gr. -1-2). 16.99 (978-0-8050-8765-9(6), 9780805087659, Holt, Henry & Co. Bks. For Young Readers) Holt, Henry & Co.

Cronin, Bernie. We're Coming Home. 2004. 56p. pap. (978-1-84401-253-4(0)) Athena Pr.

Culbertson, Jan E. The Legend of Dunsmoor Manor. 2006. 88p. pap. 13.95 (978-1-58909-348-5(8)) Bookstand Publishing.

Cunliffe, John. Postman Pat Has Too Many Parcels, Pt. 8. (Illus.). 32p. (J). (978-0-340-67812-1(7)) Hodder & Stoughton.

Cushman, Karen. Aprendiz de Comadrona. 2003.Tr. of Midwife's Apprentice. (SPA.). 96p. (YA). (gr. 5-8). (978-84-236-4773-6(0), ED3133) Edebé ESP. Dist: Lectorum Pubns., Inc.

—Catherine, Called Birdy. 2012. lib. bdg. 18.40 (978-0-606-24712-2(2), Turtleback) Turtleback Bks.

—Matilda Bone. 2014. (ENG.). 176p. (J). (gr. 5-7). pap. 6.99 (978-0-547-72242-9(7), HMH Books For Young Readers) Houghton Mifflin Harcourt Publishing Co.

—Matilda Bone. unabr. ed. 2004. (Middle Grade Cassette Librariestm Ser.). 176p. (J). (gr. 5-9). pap. 36.00 incl. audio (978-0-8072-1725-2(5), S YA 252 SP, Listening Library) Random Hse. Audio Publishing Group.

Dahl, Roald. The Witches. Blake, Quentin, illus. 2007. (ENG.). 224p. (J). (gr. 3-7). 7.99 (978-0-14-241011-0(X), Puffin Books) Penguin Young Readers Group.

Davidson, Susanna, retold by. Secret Garden (Picture Book) 2008. (Picture Book Classics Ser.). 24p. (J). 9.99 (978-0-7945-2232-2(7), Usborne) EDC Publishing.

Davies, Katie. The Great Cat Conspiracy. Shaw, Hannah, illus. 2012. (Great Critter Capers Ser.). (ENG.). 224p. (J). (gr. 3-7). 12.99 (978-1-4424-4513-0(0), Beach Lane Bks.) Beach Lane Bks.

—The Great Dog Disaster. Shaw, Hannah, illus. 2013. (Great Critter Capers Ser.). (ENG.). 208p. (J). (gr. 3-7). 12.99 (978-1-4424-4517-8(3), Beach Lane Bks.) Beach Lane Bks.

—The Great Hamster Massacre. Shaw, Hannah, illus. 2011. (Great Critter Capers Ser.). (ENG.). 208p. (J). (gr. 3-7). 12.99 (978-1-4424-2062-5(6), Beach Lane Bks.) Beach Lane Bks.

Davies, Nicola. King of the Sky. Carlin, Laura, illus. 2017. (ENG.). 48p. (J). (gr. -1-3). 17.99 (978-0-7636-9568-2(8)) Candlewick Pr.

Davis, Graeme. Re-Read Harry Potter & the Chamber of Secrets Today! an Unauthorized Guide. 2008. 112p. pap. 15.49 (978-1-934840-72-6(6)) Nimble Bks. LLC.

Day, Susie. My Invisible Boyfriend. 2010. (ENG.). 288p. (J). (gr. 7-18). 16.99 (978-0-545-07354-7(5), Scholastic Pr.) Scholastic, Inc.

—Serafina67 - "Urgently Requires Life" 2010. (ENG.). 256p. (J). (gr. 7-12). 8.99 (978-0-545-07352-3(9), Scholastic Paperbacks) Scholastic, Inc.

Deane, Nancy Lou. Meg's Secret. 2011. 148p. (gr. 4-6). pap. 14.69 (978-1-4567-8884-1(1)) AuthorHouse.

Dell, Pamela. Pete's Visit to England. 2016. (Spring Forward Ser.). (J). (gr. 2). (978-1-4900-9415-1(6)) Benchmark Education Co.

DeMasque, Catherine. The Quest of the White Stag. 2011. (ENG.). 346p. per. 16.95 (978-0-9725230-3-5(0)) Wandering Sage Pubns., LLC.

Dennard, Deborah. Hedgehog Haven: The Story of an English Hedgerow Community. Hynes, Robert, illus. 2005. (ENG.). (J). (gr. 1-4). 32p. 19.95 (978-1-56899-989-0(5), BC7020); 36p. 15.95 (978-1-56899-987-6(9), B7020); 36p. pap. 6.95 (978-1-56899-988-3(7), S7020) Soundprints.

Dent, Grace & Dent, Grace. Diva Without a Cause. 2009. (ENG.). 240p. (YA). (gr. 10-17). pap. 18.99 (978-0-316-03482-1(7), Poppy) Little, Brown Bks. for Young Readers.

Dickens, Charles. A Christmas Carol. 2008. (Illus.). 116p. (Orig.). pap. 7.99 (978-1-60450-545-0(1), Serenity Pubs.) Arc Manor.

—A Christmas Carol. 2003. (ENG.). 128p. (Orig.). (C). pap. 16.95 (978-0-7593-9886-3(0), Cengage Learning) CENGAGE Learning.

—A Christmas Carol. Lynch, P. J., illus. 2006. (ENG.). 160p. (Orig.). (J). (gr. 5-6). 19.99 (978-0-7636-3120-8(5)) Candlewick Pr.

—A Christmas Carol. Bryant, Clive, ed. Collins, Mike & Offredi, James, illus. 2012. (ENG.). 160p. (Orig.). (gr. 6). lib. bdg. 24.95 (978-1-907127-40-3(2)) Classical Comics GBR. Dist: Publishers Group West (PGW).

—A Christmas Carol. Howell, Keith, tr. Roach, David & Offredi, James, illus. 2008. (ENG.). 144p. (Orig.). (gr. 4-18). pap. 16.95 (978-1-906332-51-8(7)); pap. 16.95 (978-1-906332-52-5(5)) Classical Comics GBR. (Classical Comics, Ltd.). Dist: Publishers Group West (PGW).

—A Christmas Carol. 2008. 160p. (Orig.). (gr. 5-6). pap. 11.95 (978-1-4341-0214-0(9)) Editorium, The.

—A Christmas Carol. 2006. (Illus.). 61p. (Orig.). (J). lib. bdg. 30.77 (978-1-4242-1016-9(X)) Fitzgerald Bks.

—A Christmas Carol. 2009. 84p. (Orig.). (gr. -1-18). pap. 19.99 (978-1-4432-6003-9(7)) General Bks. LLC.

—A Christmas Carol. Helquist, Brett, illus. 2009. (ENG.). 40p. (Orig.). (J). (gr. k). 17.99 (978-0-06-165099-4(4)) HarperCollins Pubs.

—A Christmas Carol. 2008. (Puffin Classics Ser.). (ENG., Illus.). 160p. (Orig.). (J). (gr. 5-7). 5.99 (978-0-14-132452-4(X), Puffin Books) Penguin Young Readers Group.

—A Christmas Carol. Donnelly, Karen, illus. 2013. (Charles Dickens Ser.). (ENG.). 64p. (Orig.). pap. 6.95 (978-1-906230-02-9(1)) Real Reads Ltd. GBR. Dist: Casemate Pubs. & Bk. Distributors, LLC.

—A Christmas Carol. Andrews, Gary, illus. 2008. (Fast Track Classics Ser.). 46p. (Orig.). (J). (gr. 4-7). pap. 10.00 (978-1-4190-5087-9(7)) Steck-Vaughn.

—A Christmas Carol. McKowen, Scott, illus. 2009. (Sterling Unabridged Classics Ser.). (ENG.). 96p. (Orig.). (J). (gr. 5). 9.95 (978-1-4027-6690-9(4)) Sterling Publishing Co., Inc.

—A Christmas Carol. Sanchez Almara, Dono & Almara, Dono Sanchez, illus. 2015. (Graphic Revolve: Common Core Editions Ser.). (ENG.). 72p. (gr. 2-3). lib. bdg. 27.99 (978-1-4965-0370-1(8)) Stone Arch Bks.

—A Christmas Carol. Blake, Quentin, illus. unabr. ed. 2004. (Chrysalis Childrens Classics Ser.). 190p. (Orig.). (YA). pap. (978-1-84365-063-8(0), Pavilion Children's Books) Pavilion Bks.

—A Christmas Carol, 1 vol. 2010. (Illustrated Classics Ser.). (ENG., Illus.). 64p. (Orig.). (YA). (gr. 9-12). pap. 9.95 (978-1-56254-890-2(5)) Saddleback Educational Publishing, Inc.

—A Christmas Carol: Being a Ghost Story of Christmas. 2013. (Cambridge Library Collection - Fiction & Poetry Ser.). (ENG., Illus.). 186p. pap. 28.99 (978-1-108-05714-1(4)) Cambridge Univ. Pr.

—David Copperfield. 2006. (ENG.). 130p. per. 18.95 (978-1-84002-570-5(0)) Consortium Bk. Sales & Distribution.

—David Copperfield. 2008. (Bring the Classics to Life Ser.). (Illus.). 72p. (gr. 4-12). pap., act. bk. ed. 10.95 (978-1-55576-322-0(7), EDCTR-408B) EDCON Publishing Group.

—David Copperfield. 2009. 186p. pap. 19.99 (978-1-4590-4328-2(6)) General Bks. LLC.

—David Copperfield. 2009. (Foundation Classics Ser.). 56p. (J). (gr. 5-9). lib. bdg. 27.95 (978-1-60754-852-2(6)) Windmill Bks.

—David Copperfield. 2006. (Oxford Progressive English Readers Ser.). (ENG., Illus.). 103p. (J). (gr. 4-7). per. (978-0-19-597140-8(X)) Oxford Univ. Pr.

—Great Expectations. 2004. (Graphic Novels Ser.). (ENG., Illus.). 72p. (J). pap. 7.99 (978-0-237-52315-2(9)) Evans Brothers, Ltd. GBR. Dist: Independent Pubs. Group.

—Great Expectations. Donnelly, Karen, illus. 2013. (Charles Dickens Ser.). (ENG.). 64p. pap. 6.95 (978-1-906230-01-2(3)) Real Reads Ltd. GBR. Dist: Casemate Pubs. & Bk. Distributors, LLC.

—Great Expectations. (Classics Illustrated Ser.). (Illus.). 52p. (YA). pap. 4.95 (978-1-57209-001-9(4)) Classics International Entertainment, Inc.

—Great Expectations. 2011. (Puffin Classics Ser.). (ENG.). 432p. (J). (gr. 5-7). pap. 4.99 (978-0-14-133013-6(9), Puffin Books) Penguin Young Readers Group.

—Great Expectations. 2014. (Differentiated Timeless Classics Ser.). (ENG.). 80p. (YA). (gr. 9-12). 12.95 (978-1-62250-718-4(5)) Saddleback Educational Publishing, Inc.

—Great Expectations: And Related Readings. 2006. (McDougal Littell Literature Connections Ser.). (ENG., Illus.). 704p. (gr. 10-10). lib. bdg. 18.50 (978-0-395-87484-4(X), 2-70843) Great Source Education Group, Inc.

—Hard Times. 2009. (Real Reads Ser.). (Illus.). 64p. (J). (gr. 4-8). lib. bdg. 29.25 (978-1-60754-385-5(0)) Windmill Bks.

—Hard Times. Donnelly, Karen, illus. 2014. (Charles Dickens Ser.). (ENG.). 64p. pap. 6.95 (978-1-906230-05-0(6)) Real Reads Ltd. GBR. Dist: Casemate Pubs. & Bk. Distributors, LLC.

—Oliver Twist. Donnelly, Karen, illus. 2013. (Charles Dickens Ser.). (ENG.). 64p. pap. 6.95 (978-1-906230-00-5(5)) Real Reads Ltd. GBR. Dist: Casemate Pubs. & Bk. Distributors, LLC.

—Quentin Blake's a Christmas Carol. Blake, Quentin, illus. 2012. (ENG.). 150p. (J). (gr. 2-4). 16.99 (978-1-84365-165-9(3), Pavilion Children's Books) Pavilion Bks. GBR. Dist: Independent Pubs. Group.

Dickens, Charles & Dauvillier, Loïc. Oliver Twist. 70th anniv. ed. 2012. (Classics Illustrated Deluxe Graphic Nove Ser.). (ENG., Illus.). 240p. (J). (gr. 3-9). pap. 19.99 (978-1-59707-307-3(5), 9781597073073) Papercutz.

Dickinson, Peter. Chuck & Danielle. 115p. (J). (gr. 3-5). pap. 3.99 (978-0-8072-1504-3(X), Listening Library) Random Hse. Audio Publishing Group.

d'Lacey, Chris. Dark Fire. (Last Dragon Chronicles Ser.: 5). (ENG.). 576p. (J). (gr. 3-7). 2011. pap. 8.99 (978-0-545-10273-5(1)) 2010. 17.99 (978-0-545-10272-8(3), Orchard Bks.) Scholastic, Inc.

—Gauge. 2010. (Dragons of Wayward Crescent Ser.: No. 2). (ENG.). 112p. (J). (gr. 2-5). 9.99 (978-0-545-16831-1(7), Orchard Bks.) Scholastic, Inc.

Doctorow, Cory. Pirate Cinema. 2013. (ENG.). 384p. (YA). (gr. 7). pap. 9.99 (978-0-7653-2909-7(3), 9780765329097, Tor Teen) Doherty, Tom Assocs., LLC.

Doherty, Berlie. Treason. 2012. (ENG.). 352p. (J). (gr. 4-7). pap. 12.99 (978-1-84939-121-4(1)) Andersen Pr. GBR. Dist: Independent Pubs. Group.

Dorfman, Joaquin. The Long Wait for Tomorrow. 2009. (YA). (978-0-375-84696-0(4)) Random Hse., Inc.

Downham, Jenny. Before I Die. 2011. 11.24 (978-0-7848-3377-3(X), Everbind) Marco Bk. Co.

—Before I Die. 2009. (ENG.). 336p. (YA). (gr. 9). pap. 9.99 (978-0-385-75183-4(4), Ember) Random Hse. Children's Bks.

—Unbecoming. (ENG.). 384p. (J). (gr. 9-9). 2017. pap. 9.99 **(978-1-338-16072-7(9))** 2016. 17.99 (978-0-545-90717-0(9)) Scholastic, Inc.

—Unbecoming. 2017. lib. bdg. 20.85 **(978-0-606-40147-0(4))** Turtleback Bks.

Downham, Jenny. You Against Me. 2012. (ENG.). 416p. (YA). (gr. 9). pap. 9.99 (978-0-385-75266-4(0), Ember) Random Hse. Children's Bks.

Doyle, Arthur Conan. The Adventures & the Memoirs of Sherlock Holmes. McKowen, Scott, illus. 2004. (Sterling Unabridged Classics Ser.). (ENG.). 576p. (J). (gr. 5). 14.95 (978-1-4027-1453-5(X)) Sterling Publishing Co., Inc.

—The Hound of the Baskervilles. Harvey, Bob, illus. 2004. (Paperback Classics Ser.). 158p. (J). (gr. 5). lib. bdg. 12.95 (978-1-58086-605-7(0)) EDC Publishing.

Druvert, Hélène. Mary Poppins: Up, up & Away. 2017. (ENG., Illus.). 36p. (gr. k-4). 24.95 (978-0-500-65104-9(3), 565104) Thames & Hudson.

Dumas, Alexandre. The Count of Monte Cristo. 2008. (Bring the Classics to Life Ser.). (ENG., Illus.). 72p. (gr. 5-12). pap., act. bk. ed. 10.95 (978-1-55576-359-6(6), EDCTR-509B) EDCON Publishing Group.

Dunlap, Susanne. In the Shadow of the Lamp. 2012. (ENG., Illus.). 320p. (YA). (gr. 7). pap. 9.99 (978-1-59990-753-6(4), 9781599907536, Bloomsbury USA Childrens) Bloomsbury Publishing USA.

E. S. Townsend. The Secrets of Marsh House. 2013. 208p. pap. (978-1-907011-44-3(7)) Esteemworld Pubns.

Eagland, Jane. Wildthorn. 2012. (ENG.). 352p. (YA). (gr. 9). pap. 8.99 (978-0-547-57736-4(2)) Houghton Mifflin Harcourt Publishing Co.

Earle, Phil. The Bubble Wrap Boy. 2015. (ENG., Illus.). 288p. (J). (gr. 5). 19.99 (978-0-553-51316-5(8)); 16.99 (978-0-553-51315-8(X)) Random Hse. Children's Bks. (Delacorte Bks. for Young Readers).

Easton, T. S. Boys Don't Knit. 2015. (ENG.). 272p. (YA). (gr. 8). 16.99 (978-1-250-05331-2(5), 9781250053312) Feiwel & Friends.

—Boys Don't Knit. 2016. (ENG.). 272p. (YA). pap. 9.99 (978-1-250-07354-9(5), 9781250073549) Square Fish.

Edwards, Julie Andrews. Mandy. Westerman, Johanna, illus. 2nd ed. 2006. (Julie Andrews Collection). (ENG.). 320p. (J). (gr. 3-7). 17.99 (978-0-06-113162-2(8)); pap. 6.99 (978-0-06-120707-5(1)) HarperCollins Pubs.

Eitner-England, Lita. Bullmina the Courageous Bulldog to the Rescue. 2010. 588p. 33.99 (978-1-4490-8225-3(4)); pap. 15.00 (978-1-4490-8224-6(6)) AuthorHouse.

Eliot, George. Silas Marner. 2008. (Bring the Classics to Life Ser.). (ENG., Illus.). 72p. (gr. 2-12). pap., act. bk. ed. 10.95 (978-1-55576-356-5(1), EDCTR-209B) EDCON Publishing Group.

Ellis, Deborah. No Safe Place. 2013. 224p. pap. (978-1-4596-6447-0(7)) ReadHowYouWant.com, Ltd.

Ephron, Amy. The Castle in the Mist. 2017. (ENG.). 192p. (J). (gr. 3-7). 16.99 (978-0-399-54698-3(7), Philomel Bks.) Penguin Young Readers Group.

Eschberger, Beverly. The Elephants Tour England: An Elephant Family Adventure. Gower, Jim, illus. 2009. 86p. (J). per. 3.99 (978-1-932926-29-3(1), Kinkajou Pr.) Artemesia Publishing, LLC.

Everest, D. D. Archie Greene & the Magician's Secret. 2015. (Archie Greene Ser.: 1). (ENG.). 320p. (J). (gr. 3-7). 16.99 (978-0-06-231211-2(1)) HarperCollins Pubs.

Ewing, Juliana Horatia. A Flat Iron for a Farthing. Wheelhouse, M. V., illus. 2007. 212p. per. (978-1-4065-2524-3(3)) Dodo Pr.

—Six To. 2007. 196p. per. (978-1-4065-2535-9(9)) Dodo Pr.

Fafoutakis, Anne. Enchanted Talisman & Other Stories for Children of All Ages. 2004. 132p. pap. 13.50 (978-1-84426-296-0(0)) Upfront Publishing Ltd. GBR. Dist: Printondemand-worldwide.com.

Falkner, John Meade. Moonfleet. 2013. (Oxford Children's Classics Ser.). (ENG.). 304p. 9.95 (978-0-19-273478-5(4)) Oxford Univ. Pr., Inc.

—Moonfleet: A Classic Tale of Smuggling. Marks, Alan, illus. 2007. (Young Reading Series 3 Gift Bks). 63p. (J). (gr. 4-7). 8.99 (978-0-7945-1906-3(7), Usborne) EDC Publishing.

Farley, Donna. The Ravens of Fame: A Tale of Saint Cuthbert. 2010. 32p. pap. 14.95 (978-0-9822770-5-8(9)) Ancient Faith Publishing.

Farrant, Natasha. The Secret Diary of Lydia Bennet. 2016. (ENG.). 336p. (YA). (gr. 7). 17.99 (978-0-545-94031-3(1), Chicken Hse., The) Scholastic, Inc.

Field, C. D. The Peculiar World of Billy Peanut. 2017. (ENG.). 136p. pap. 11.95 **(978-1-78710-324-5(2),** 761715a7-350b-426e-b9ac-f5e11430104d) Austin, Stan AUS. Dist: Bookmasters Distribution.

—Zackery Grimm Investigates: The Ghost of Agapantha Claypole. 2016. (ENG.). 91p. (J). 19.95 (978-1-78612-531-6(5), 189f44f5-9499-4f02-a614-3d6db5444361) Austin, Stan AUS. Dist: Bookmasters Distribution.

—Zackery Grimm Investigates: the Ghost of Agapantha Claypole. 2016. (ENG.). 91p. (J). pap. 10.95 (978-1-78612-530-9(7), bedfa740-2a75-4fd8-8f86-a12279b743bd) Austin, Stan AUS. Dist: Bookmasters Distribution.

Fiona Fox Staff, ed. The Railway Children. 2012. (ENG., Illus.). 64p. (J). 15.00 (978-1-84135-840-6(1)) Award Pubns. Ltd. GBR. Dist: Parkwest Pubns., Inc.

—The Secret Garden. 2012. (ENG., Illus.). 64p. 15.00 (978-1-84135-837-6(1)) Award Pubns. Ltd. GBR. Dist: Parkwest Pubns., Inc.

Fisher, Catherine. Darkwater. 2012. (ENG.). 240p. (YA). (gr. 7). 16.99 (978-0-8037-3818-8(8), Dial Bks) Penguin Young Readers Group.

Five Children & It. 2013. 58p. pap. 5.60 (978-1-236-72792-3(4)) General Bks. LLC.

Five Children & It. 2010. (CAM.). 142p. pap. 10.95 (978-1-4385-3539-5(2), Book Jungle) Standard Pubns., Inc.

Fletcher, Christopher. The Guardian Angel. 2008. 212p. pap. (978-1-84923-031-5(5)) YouWriteOn.

Flood, C. J. Infinite Sky. (ENG., Illus.). 256p. (YA). (gr. 7). 2015. pap. 10.99 (978-1-4814-0659-8(0)) 2014. 17.99 (978-1-4814-0658-1(2), Atheneum Bks. for Young Readers) Simon & Schuster Children's Publishing.

Foreman, Michael. War Game (Special 100th Anniversary of WW1 Ed.) 100th ed. 2014. (ENG., Illus.). 96p. (J). (gr. 3-5). 17.99 (978-1-84365-178-9(5), Pavilion) Pavilion Bks. GBR. Dist: Independent Pubs. Group.

Foster, Jo. Chedworth Roman Villa: Discover Roman Britain. Percival, Tom, illus. 2017. (ENG.). 32p. pap. 9.99 **(978-1-911384-38-0(4))** History Pr. Ltd.,The GBR. Dist: Independent Pubs. Group.

Francis, Pauline, retold by. The Count of Monte Cristo. 2010. (Essential Classics - Adventure Ser.). (Illus.). 48p. pap. (978-0-237-54086-9(X)) Evans Brothers, Ltd.

Francis, Pauline & Burnett, Frances Hodgson. The Secret Garden. 2003. (Fast Track Classics Ser.). (Illus.). 48p. (YA). pap. (978-0-237-52535-4(6)) Evans Brothers, Ltd.

Frederick, Heather Vogel. A Little Women Christmas. Ibatoulline, Bagram, illus. 2014. (ENG.). 32p. (J). (gr. -1-3). 17.99 (978-1-4424-1359-7(X), Simon & Schuster Bks. For Young Readers) Simon & Schuster Bks. For Young Readers.

—Pies & Prejudice. (Mother-Daughter Book Club Ser.). (ENG.). (J). (gr. 4-7). 2011. 400p. pap. 8.99 (978-1-4424-2019-9(7)) 2010. 384p. 15.99 (978-1-4169-7431-4(8)) Simon & Schuster Bks. For Young Readers. (Simon & Schuster Bks. For Young Readers).

Frederick Marryat. The Children of the New Forest. 2007. 412p. per. 17.95 (978-1-4218-4823-5(6)); 33.95 (978-1-4218-4726-9(4)) 1st World Publishing, Inc. (1st World Library - Literary Society).

Funke, Cornelia. Ghost Knight. 2013.Tr. of Geisterritter. (ENG., Illus.). 352p. (J). (gr. 3-7). pap. 7.99 (978-0-316-05616-8(2)) Little, Brown Bks. for Young Readers.

Furniss, Clare. How Not to Disappear. 2017. (ENG., Illus.). 448p. (YA). (gr. 7). 17.99 (978-1-4814-2102-7(6), McElderry, Margaret K. Bks.) McElderry, Margaret K. Bks.

Gadsby, Maggie. Owl Be Home for Christmas. 2012. (J). 14.95 (978-1-62086-064-9(3)) Mascot Bks., Inc.

Gale Editors & Wilson, Sean Michael. The Canterville Ghost: The Graphic Novel. 2011. (Classic Graphic Novel Collection). (ENG.). 160p. (gr. 7-10). lib. bdg. 39.40 (978-1-4205-0629-7(3)) Cengage Gale.

Gale, Emily. Girl Out Loud. 2012. (YA). (978-0-545-30439-9(3)); (ENG.). 288p. (J). (gr. 7-7). 17.99 (978-0-545-30438-2(5)) Scholastic, Inc. (Chicken Hse., The).

Gardam, Jane. Bilgewater. 2016. (ENG.). 208p. pap. 17.00 (978-1-60945-331-2(X)) Europa Editions, Inc.

—The Hollow Land. 2015. (ENG.). 160p. (gr. 12). pap. 15.00 (978-1-60945-246-9(1)) Europa Editions, Inc.

Garner, Alan. Elidor. 192p. (YA). (gr. 5-18). pap. 6.00 (978-0-8072-1545-6(7), Listening Library) Random Hse. Audio Publishing Group.

Gaughen, A. C. Scarlet. 2013. (Scarlet Ser.: 1). (ENG.). 304p. (YA). (gr. 7-12). pap. 9.99 (978-0-8027-3424-2(3), 9780802734242, Bloomsbury USA Childrens) Bloomsbury Publishing USA.

Gensler, Sonia. The Dark Between. 2015. (ENG.). 352p. (YA). (gr. 7). pap. 9.99 (978-0-375-86140-6(8), Ember) Random Hse. Children's Bks.

Geras, Adèle. Pictures of the Night. 2005. (ENG.). 192p. (YA). (gr. 7-12). pap. 11.95 (978-0-15-205543-1(6)) Houghton Mifflin Harcourt Publishing Co.

—Watching the Roses: The Egerton Hall Novels, Volume Two, Vol. 2. 2005. (ENG.). 192p. (YA). (gr. 7-12). pap. 11.95 (978-0-15-205531-8(2)) Houghton Mifflin Harcourt Publishing Co.

Gilbert, D. Hide & Seek: A Mystery Novel for Children. 2005. 187p. pap. 24.95 (978-1-4137-9748-0(2)) PublishAmerica, Inc.

Gilfillan, Ross. Losing It: The Growing Pains of a Teenage Vampire. 2014. (ENG.). 257p. (YA). (gr. 8-17). pap. 12.95 (978-1-78279-366-3(6), Lodestone Bks.) Hunt, John Publishing Ltd. GBR. Dist: National Bk. Network.

Gilman, David. Blood Sun. 2012. (Danger Zone Ser.). (ENG.). 432p. (YA). (gr. 7). pap. 10.99 (978-0-440-42241-9(8), Ember) Random Hse. Children's Bks.

Globe-Fearon Staff, ed. Jane Eyre, Grades 5-12. pap., tchr. ed. 4.95 (978-0-8359-0109-3(2)) Globe Fearon Educational Publishing.

Godley, Marie. The Special Christmas Bear. 2007. (Illus.). 52p. per. (978-1-84748-005-7(5)) Athena Pr.

Goodwin, Vincent. The Adventure of the Blue Carbuncle, 1 vol. Dunn, Ben, illus. 2012. (Graphic Novel Adventures of Sherlock Holmes Set 2 Ser.). (ENG.). 48p. (J). (gr. 3-8). lib. bdg. 29.93 (978-1-61641-891-5(5), Graphic Planet) Magic Wagon.

—The Adventure of the Copper Beeches, 1 vol. Dunn, Ben, illus. 2012. (Graphic Novel Adventures of Sherlock Holmes Set 2 Ser.). (ENG.). 48p. (J). (gr. 3-8). lib. bdg. 29.93 (978-1-61641-892-2(3), Graphic Planet) Magic Wagon.

—The Adventure of the Engineer's Thumb, 1 vol. Dunn, Ben, illus. 2012. (Graphic Novel Adventures of Sherlock Holmes Set 2 Ser.). (ENG.). 48p. (J). (gr. 3-8). lib. bdg. 29.93 (978-1-61641-893-9(1), Graphic Planet) Magic Wagon.

—The Adventure of the Solitary Cyclist, 1 vol. Dunn, Ben, illus. 2012. (Graphic Novel Adventures of Sherlock Holmes Set 2 Ser.). (ENG.). 48p. (J). (gr. 3-8). lib. bdg. 29.93 (978-1-61641-894-6(X), Graphic Planet) Magic Wagon.

—The Adventure of the Three Students, 1 vol. Dunn, Ben, illus. 2012. (Graphic Novel Adventures of Sherlock Holmes Set 2 Ser.). (ENG.). 48p. (J). (gr. 3-8). lib. bdg. 29.93 (978-1-61641-895-3(8), Graphic Planet) Magic Wagon.

—The Adventure of Wisteria Lodge, 1 vol. Dunn, Ben, illus. 2012. (Graphic Novel Adventures of Sherlock Holmes Set 2 Ser.). (ENG.). 48p. (J). (gr. 3-8). lib. bdg. 29.93 (978-1-61641-896-0(6), Graphic Planet) Magic Wagon.

Gordon, Roderick. Spiral, 9 vols. 2012. (Tunnels Ser.: 5). (J). 132.75 (978-1-4618-4519-5(X)); 134.75 (978-1-4618-4517-1(3)); 121.75 (978-1-4618-4516-4(5)); 296.75 (978-1-4618-4515-7(7)) Recorded Bks., Inc.

Goudge, Elizabeth. The Little White Horse. movie tie-in ed. 2008. (ENG., Illus.). 248p. (J). (gr. 4-7). pap. (978-0-7459-6118-7(5)) Lion Hudson PLC GBR. Dist: Independent Pubs. Group.

Grahame, Abby. Wentworth Hall. 2013. (ENG.). 288p. (YA). (gr. 7). pap. 9.99 (978-1-4424-5197-1(1), Simon & Schuster Bks. For Young Readers) Simon & Schuster Bks. For Young Readers.

Grahame, Kenneth. The Gates of Dawn. Johnson, Joe, tr. Plessix, Michel, illus. 2003. (Wind in the Willows Ser.: Vol. 3). (ENG.). 32p. (gr. 4-7). pap. 15.95 (978-1-56163-245-9(7)) NBM Publishing Co.

—The Golden Age. 2006. pap. (978-1-4068-3332-4(0)) Echo Library.

—Mr. Toad, Vol. 2. Johnson, Joe, tr. from FRE. 2003. (Wind in the Willows Ser.: Vol. 2). (ENG., Illus.). 32p. (gr. 4-7). 15.95 (978-1-56163-218-3(X)) NBM Publishing Co.

—El Viento en los Sauces.Tr. of Wind in the Willows. (SPA.). 192p. (J). I. 9.50 (978-84-372-1882-3(9))II. 9.50 (978-84-372-1883-0(7)) Santillana USA Publishing Co., Inc.

—The Wind in the Willows. Shepard, Ernest H., illus. 2007. 259p. (J). (gr. 5-6). reprint ed. lib. bdg. 22.95 (978-0-88411-877-0(0)) Amereon Ltd.

—The Wind in the Willows. Bransom, Paul, illus. 2013. 176p. pap. 35.00 (978-1-927558-25-6(5)) Birch Tree Publishing.

—The Wind in the Willows. Roberts, David, illus. 2013. (ENG.). 256p. (J). (gr. 5). 24.99 (978-0-7636-6526-5(6)) Candlewick Pr.

—The Wind in the Willows. Daily, Don, illus. 2014. (ENG.). 64p. (J). (gr. -1). 18.95 (978-1-60433-478-4(9), Applesauce Pr.) Cider Mill Pr. Bk. Pubs., LLC.

—The Wind in the Willows. l.t. ed. 2007. (ENG.). 174p. pap. 21.99 (978-1-4264-6997-8(7)) Creative Media Partners, LLC.

—The Wind in the Willows. Kliros, Thea, illus. abr. ed. 2011. (Dover Children's Thrift Classics Ser.). (ENG.). 96p. (J). (gr. 3-8). pap. 4.00 (978-0-486-28600-6(2)) Dover Pubns., Inc.

—The Wind in the Willows. Benson, Patrick, illus. 2009. (ENG.). 304p. pap. 11.99 (978-0-00-647926-0(X)) HarperCollins Pubs.

—The Wind in the Willows. 2013. 258p. pap. 12.99 (978-1-60796-643-2(3)) Meirovich, Igal.

—The Wind in the Willows. Taso, Alex, illus. 2006. (ENG.). 240p. (J). (gr. 5-18). 5.95 (978-0-451-53014-1(4), Signet) Penguin Publishing Group.

—The Wind in the Willows. 2005. (ENG.). 240p. (gr. 2-5). 14.00 (978-0-14-303909-9(1), Penguin Classics) Penguin Publishing Group.

—The Wind in the Willows. 2013. (Easy Reader Classics Ser.). (ENG., Illus.). 192p. (J). (gr. 1-3). pap. 9.95 (978-1-4549-0590-5(5)) Sterling Publishing Co., Inc.

—The Wind in the Willows. Ingpen, Robert R., illus. 2012. (Sterling Illustrated Classics Ser.). (ENG.). 224p. (J). (gr. 2-8). 19.95 (978-1-4027-8283-1(7)) Sterling Publishing Co., Inc.

—The Wind in the Willows. Hanft, Joshua, ed. (Great Illustrated Classics Ser.: Vol. 39). (Illus.). 240p. (J). (gr. 3-6). 9.95 (978-0-86611-990-0(6)) Waldman Publishing Corp.

Grahame, Kenneth & Todd, Justin. The Wind in the Willows. 2013. (Calla Editions Ser.). (ENG., Illus.). 208p. (J). (gr. 3). 30.00 (978-1-60660-044-3(3)) Dover Pubns., Inc.

Grainger, A. J. Captive. 2016. (ENG.). 272p. (YA). (gr. 7). pap. 11.99 (978-1-4814-2904-7(3)) Simon & Schuster Children's Publishing.

Gray, Christopher. There Be Goblins in the Wood! 2012. 112p. (gr. 2-4). 23.99 (978-1-4772-6994-7(0)); pap. 14.95 (978-1-4772-6995-4(9)) AuthorHouse.

Gray, Elizabeth Janet. Adam of the Road. Lawson, Robert, illus. 2006. (Puffin Modern Classics Ser.). (ENG.). 320p. (J). (gr. 3-7). 7.99 (978-0-14-240659-5(7), Puffin Books) Penguin Young Readers Group.

Gray, Jennifer. Atticus Claw Breaks the Law. Ecob, Mark, illus. 2016. (Atticus Claw Ser.). (ENG.). 224p. (gr. 1-4). pap. 7.95 (978-0-571-28449-8(3)) Faber & Faber, Inc.

Gray, Keith. Ostrich Boys. 2011. (ENG.). 304p. (YA). (gr. 7). pap. 9.99 (978-0-375-85844-4(X), Random Hse. Bks. for Young Readers) Random Hse. Children's Bks.

Green, Norman, illus. Knights of the Round Table. 2005. (Reader's Workshop Ser.). (ENG.). 112p. (C). pap. 19.95 (978-0-7362-2786-5(5)) CENGAGE Learning.

Green, Roger Lancelyn. The Adventures of Robin Hood. Hall, Arthur, illus. 2010. (Puffin Classics Ser.). (ENG.). 320p. (J). (gr. 5-7). pap. 5.99 (978-0-14-132938-3(6), Puffin Books) Penguin Young Readers Group.

Green, Roger Lancelyn & Green, Richard. Adventures of Robin Hood. Hall, Arthur & Terrazzini, Daniela Jaglenka, illus. 2010. (Puffin Classics Ser.). (ENG.). 320p. (J). (gr. 5-7). 16.99 (978-0-14-133489-9(4), Puffin Books) Penguin Young Readers Group.

Green, Sally. Half Bad. (ENG.). (YA). 2015. (Half Bad Trilogy Ser.: 1). 432p. (gr. 7). pap. 9.99 (978-0-14-751146-1(1), Speak) 2014. (Half Bad Trilogy Ser.: 1). 416p. (gr. 7). 18.99 (978-0-670-01678-5(0), Viking Books for Young Readers)Pack. 2015. pap. 89.91 (978-0-14-751591-9(2), Speak) Penguin Young Readers Group.

—Half Wild. 2015. (Half Bad Trilogy Ser.: 2). (ENG.). 432p. (YA). (gr. 7). 18.99 (978-0-670-01713-3(2), Viking Books for Young Readers) Penguin Young Readers Group.

Griffin, M. A. Lifers. 2017. (ENG.). 288p. (J). (gr. 7). 17.99 (978-1-338-06553-4(X), Chicken Hse., The) Scholastic, Inc.

Grindley, Sally. Bravo, Max! Ross, Tony, illus. 2007. (ENG.). 160p. (J). (gr. 1-4). pap. 8.99 (978-1-4169-3645-9(9), Simon & Schuster/Paula Wiseman Bks.) Simon & Schuster/Paula Wiseman Bks.

Grindley, Sally & Lucas, D J. Dear Max. Ross, Tony, illus. 2007. (ENG.). 144p. (J). (gr. 1-4). pap. 7.99 (978-1-4169-3443-1(X), Simon & Schuster/Paula Wiseman Bks.) Simon & Schuster/Paula Wiseman Bks.

Groethe, Kd. The Virtual Adventures of Megan & Timmy. 2012. 230p. (gr. 4-6). 27.99 (978-1-4685-5050-4(0)); pap. 16.95 (978-1-4685-5049-8(7)) AuthorHouse.

The Guardians. 2014. (ENG., Illus.). 288p. (J). (gr. 4-8). pap. 7.99 (978-1-4814-1834-8(3), Aladdin) Simon & Schuster Children's Publishing.

Guerra, Elisa Puricelli. The City of Lizards. Zeni, Marco, tr. from ITA. Bernstein, Gabriel León, illus. 2015. (Minerva Mint Ser.). (ENG.). 160p. (gr. 2-4). lib. bdg. 25.32 (978-1-4342-9671-9(7)) Stone Arch Bks.

Gutteridge, Alex. No Going Back. 2016. (ENG.). 368p. (YA). (gr. 8). pap. 11.99 (978-1-84877-927-3(5)) Bonnier Publishing GBR. Dist: Independent Pubs. Group.

Haddon, Mark. Boom! 2011. (ENG.). 208p. (J). (gr. 3-7). 7.99 (978-0-385-75224-4(5), Yearling) Random Hse. Children's Bks.

—The Curious Incident of the Dog in the Night-Time. 2007. (ENG., Illus.). 320p. mass mkt. (978-1-4000-2535-0(4), Seal Bks) Doubleday Canada, Ltd. CAN. Dist: Random Hse., Inc.

Haggard, H. Rider. Red Eve. 2007. (ENG.). 266p. pap. 21.99 (978-1-4346-4929-4(6)); 294p. pap. 23.99 (978-1-4346-4930-0(X)) Creative Media Partners, LLC.

Halahmy, Miriam. Hidden. 2016. (ENG.). 224p. (J). 16.95 (978-0-8234-3694-1(2)) Holiday Hse., Inc.

Hall, Duncan. Brambleholme Summer. 2010. 125p. pap. 12.95 (978-1-4461-4462-6(3)) Lulu Pr., Inc.

Hardinge, Frances. Fly by Night. 2017. (ENG.). 432p. (YA). (gr. 7-17). pap. 10.95 (978-1-4197-2485-5(1), Amulet Bks.) Abrams, Inc.

Hardy, Thomas. The Mayor of Casterbridge. Reed, Neil, illus. 2004. (Graphic Novels Ser.). (ENG.). 72p. (J). pap. 7.99 (978-0-237-52314-5(0)) Evans Brothers, Ltd. GBR. Dist: Independent Pubs. Group.

—THE MAYOR OF CASTERBRIDGE LEVEL 5 UPPER-INTERMEDIATE. 2009. (ENG.). 112p. pap. 14.50 (978-84-8323-560-7(9)) Cambridge Univ. Pr.

—THE MAYOR OF CASTERBRIDGE LEVEL 5 UPPER-INTERMEDIATE BOOK WITH CD-ROM AND AUDIO CDS (2) PACK, 1 vol. 2009. (ENG.). 112p. pap. 16.50 incl. cd-rom, audio compact disk (978-84-8323-556-0(0)) Cambridge Univ. Pr.

Harper, Meg. No More School. 2006. 184p. per. (978-1-904529-28-6(3), Back to Front) Solidus.

Harrison, Michelle. 13 Treasures. 2011. (13 Treasures Trilogy Ser.: 1). (ENG.). 384p. (J). (gr. 3-7). pap. 8.99 (978-0-316-04147-8(5)) Little, Brown Bks. for Young Readers.

Hart, Derek. Secret of the Dragon's Eye. 2007. 264p. per. 16.95 (978-0-595-42967-7(X)) iUniverse, Inc.

Hawkins, Rachel. Demonglass. 2012. (ENG.). 384p. (YA). (gr. 6-17). pap. 8.99 (978-1-4231-2844-1(3)) Hyperion Pr.

Hayes, Tracey J. Bartina in Trouble Again. 2009. 64p. pap. 15.99 (978-1-4415-2050-0(3)) Xlibris Corp.

Hearn, Julie. The Minister's Daughter. 2006. (ENG.). 272p. (YA). (gr. 7-12). pap. 7.99 (978-0-689-87691-2(2), Atheneum Bks. for Young Readers) Simon & Schuster Children's Publishing.

Hébert-Collins, Sheila. Jacques et la Canne à Sucre: A Cajun Jack & the Beanstalk, 1 vol. Lyne, Alison Davis, illus. 2004. (FRE & ENG.). 32p. (J). (gr. k-3). pap. 16.99 (978-1-58980-191-2(1)) Pelican Publishing Co., Inc.

Henderson, Lauren. Kiss Me Kill Me. 2009. (ENG.). 272p. (YA). (gr. 9). pap. 8.99 (978-0-385-73488-2(3), Delacorte Pr.) Random Hse. Children's Bks.

Henry, Marguerite. King of the Wind: The Story of the Godolphin Arabian. 2011. 8.32 (978-0-7848-3456-5(3), Everbind) Marco Bk. Co.

—King of the Wind: The Story of the Godolphin Arabian. unabr. ed. 2004. 173p. (J). (gr. 4-7). pap. 38.00 incl. audio (978-0-8072-8697-5(4), YA239SP, Listening Library) Random Hse. Audio Publishing Group.

—King of the Wind: The Story of the Godolphin Arabian. 2015. (ENG., Illus.). 192p. (J). (gr. 3-7). 19.99 (978-1-4814-2133-1(6), Aladdin) Simon & Schuster Children's Publishing.

—King of the Wind: The Story of the Godolphin Arabian. Dennis, Wesley, illus. 2006. (ENG.). 176p. (J). (gr. 3-7). pap. 7.99 (978-1-4169-2786-0(7), Aladdin) Simon & Schuster Children's Publishing.

Hicks, Deron R. Tower of the Five Orders. Geyer, Mark Edward, illus. 2013. (Shakespeare Mysteries Ser.: 2). (ENG.). 320p. (J). (gr. 5-7). 16.99 (978-0-547-83953-0(7)) Houghton Mifflin Harcourt Publishing Co.

—Tower of the Five Orders: The Shakespeare Mysteries, Book 2. Geyer, Mark Edward, illus. 2014. (Shakespeare Mysteries Ser.). (ENG.). 320p. (J). (gr. 5-7). pap. 7.99 (978-0-544-33630-8(5), HMH Books For Young Readers) Houghton Mifflin Harcourt Publishing Co.

Higgins, Jack & Richards, Justin. Death Run. 2009. (Rich & Jade Ser.: Bk. 2). (ENG.). 288p. (YA). (gr. 7-18). 8.99 (978-0-14-241475-0(1), Speak) Penguin Young Readers Group.

Hill, Susan. Lassie Come-Home: An Adaptation of Eric Knight's Classic Story. Ivanov, Aleksey & Olga, illus. 75th ed. 2015. (ENG.). 32p. (J). (gr. -1-3). 17.99 (978-1-62779-294-3(5), 9781627792943, Holt, Henry & Co. Bks. For Young Readers) Holt, Henry & Co.

Hill, Will. Darkest Night (Department 19, Book 5) 2016. (Department 19 Ser.: 5). (ENG.). 736p. (J). pap. 9.99 (978-0-00-815427-1(9), HarperCollins Children's Bks.) HarperCollins Pubs. Ltd. GBR. Dist: HarperCollins Pubs.

—The Rising: A Department 19 Novel. 2013. (Department Nineteen Ser.: 2). (ENG.). 592p. (YA). (gr. 9). pap. 9.99 (978-1-59514-629-8(6), Razorbill) Penguin Young Readers Group.

Hill, William. Department Nineteen. 2012. (Department Nineteen Ser.: 1). (ENG.). 544p. (YA). (gr. 9). 9.99 (978-1-59514-485-0(4), Razorbill) Penguin Young Readers Group.

Hoffman, Mary. Women of Camelot: Queens & Enchantresses at the Court of King Arthur. Balit, Christina, illus. 2006. 69p. (YA). (gr. 5-9). 20.00 (978-1-4223-5260-1(9)) DIANE Publishing Co.

Holeman, Linda. Search of the Moon King's Daughter. 2003. (ENG.). 320p. (J). (gr. 5). pap. 10.95 (978-0-88776-609-1(9), Tundra Bks.) Tundra Bks. CAN. Dist: Penguin Random Hse. LLC.

Hollyer, Belinda & Brontë, Charlotte. Jane Eyre. 2003. (Illus.). 48p. (978-0-7502-3668-3(X), Wayland) Hachette Children's Group.

Holmes, Victoria. Rider in the Dark: An Epic Horse Story. 2004. (Illus.). 320p. (J). (gr. 5-18). (ENG.). 15.99 (978-0-06-052025-0(6)); lib. bdg. 16.89 (978-0-06-052026-7(4)) HarperCollins Pubs.

Hooper, Mary. Poppy. 2016. (ENG.). 288p. (YA). 17.99 (978-1-61963-496-1(1), 9781619634961, Bloomsbury USA Childrens) Bloomsbury Publishing USA.

Hopkins, Cathy. Teen Queens & Has-Beens. 2010. (Truth or Dare Ser.). (ENG.). 192p. (YA). (gr. 7). pap. 9.99 (978-1-4424-1416-7(2), Simon Pulse) Simon Pulse.

Hornby, Nick. Slam. (ENG.). 320p. (gr. 12). 2009. 16.00 (978-1-59448-471-1(6)) 2008. 15.00 (978-1-59448-345-5(0)) Penguin Publishing Group. (Riverhead Bks. (Hardcover)).

Horowitz, Anthony. Point Blanc. 2004. (Alex Rider Ser.: Bk. 2). (SPA.). 264p. pap. 7.95 (978-84-414-1410-5(6)) Editorial Edaf, S.L. ESP. Dist: Spanish Pubs., LLC.

—Point Blank. 2006. (Alex Rider Ser.). (ENG.). 320p. (J). (gr. 5-18). 8.99 (978-0-14-240612-0(0), Puffin Books) Penguin Young Readers Group.

—Raven's Gate. 2006. (Gatekeepers Ser.: 1). (ENG.). 272p. (J). (gr. 3-7). pap. 8.99 (978-0-439-68009-7(3), Scholastic Paperbacks) Scholastic, Inc.

—Raven's Gate. 2005. 288p. pap. (978-1-84428-619-5(3)) Walker Bks., Ltd.

—Return to Groosham Grange: The Unholy Grail. 2010. (ENG.). 224p. (J). (gr. 5-18). 7.99 (978-0-14-241571-9(5), Puffin Books) Penguin Young Readers Group.

—Skeleton Key. Kanako & Yuzuru, illus. 2009. (Alex Rider Ser.: Bk. 3). (ENG.). 176p. (J). (gr. 5-18). pap. 14.99 (978-0-399-25418-5(8), Philomel Bks.) Penguin Young Readers Group.

—Skeleton Key. (Alex Rider Ser.: Bk. 3). (ENG.). (J). (gr. 5-18). 2006. 368p. 8.99 (978-0-14-240614-4(7), Puffin Books) 2003. 240p. 17.99 (978-0-399-23777-5(1), Philomel Bks.) Penguin Young Readers Group.

—Stormbreaker. Damerum, Kanako et al, illus. 2006. (Alex Rider Ser.). (ENG.). 144p. (J). (gr. 5-18). pap. 14.99 (978-0-399-24633-3(9), Philomel Bks.) Penguin Young Readers Group.

—Stormbreaker. 2006. (Alex Rider Ser.: Bk. 1). (ENG.). 304p. (J). (gr. 5-18). 8.99 (978-0-14-240611-3(2), Puffin Books) Penguin Young Readers Group.

—Stormbreaker. 2004. (Alex Rider Ser.: Bk. 1). 208p. (J). (gr. 4-7). pap. 38.00 incl. audio (978-0-8072-2277-5(1), Listening Library) Random Hse. Audio Publishing Group.

—The Switch. 2010. (ENG.). 192p. (J). (gr. 5-18). 7.99 (978-0-14-241547-4(2), Puffin Books) Penguin Young Readers Group.

Horvath, Polly. Lord & Lady Bunny — Almost Royalty! Blackall, Sophie, illus. 2016. (ENG.). 304p. (J). (gr. 3-7). pap. 8.99 (978-0-307-98068-7(5), Yearling) Random Hse. Children's Bks.

Hounslow, Gaynor. Snoop & Sniffly Wiffly - the Tale of Two Hedgehogs: The Children's Book of Wildlife Stories. 2009. (Illus.). 32p. pap. 12.99 (978-1-4389-6069-2(7)) AuthorHouse.

Howard, Ellen. The Gate in the Wall. 2007. (ENG.). 160p. (J). (gr. 3-7). pap. 9.95 (978-1-4169-6796-5(6), Simon & Schuster/Paula Wiseman Bks.) Simon & Schuster/Paula Wiseman Bks.

Howard, Vera. My Gran: Country Stories for Young Children. 2004. 88p. pap. (978-1-84401-331-9(6)) Athena Pr.

Hue, Wendy. Tópé Arrives. 2011. (Illus.). 100p. pap. 12.10 (978-1-4567-7640-4(1)) AuthorHouse.

Hughes, Carol. The Princess & the Unicorn. 2010. (ENG.). 288p. (J). (gr. 3-7). 7.99 (978-0-375-85563-4(7), Bluefire) Random Hse. Children's Bks.

Hughes, Shirley. The Christmas Eve Ghost. Hughes, Shirley, illus. 2010. (ENG., Illus.). 32p. (J). (gr. -1-3). 15.99 (978-0-7636-4472-7(2)) Candlewick Pr.

—An Evening at Alfie's. Hughes, Shirley, illus. 2009. (Alfie Ser.). (ENG., Illus.). 32p. (J). (gr. k-k). pap. 11.99 (978-1-86230-786-5(5), Red Fox) Random House Children's Books GBR. Dist: Independent Pubs. Group.

Hughes, Thomas. Tom Browns Schooldays. 2006. pap. (978-1-4068-1407-1(5)) Echo Library.

Hunter, Scott. The Ley Lines of Lushbury. 2010. 241p. pap. 18.95 (978-1-4461-5713-8(X)) Lulu Pr., Inc.

Hussey, Charmian. The Valley of Secrets. Crump, Christopher, illus. 2006. (ENG.). 400p. (J). (gr. 7-12). per. 17.99 (978-1-4169-0015-3(2), Simon Pulse) Simon Pulse.

Ibbotson, Eva. Dial-a-Ghost. Hawkes, Kevin, illus. 2003. (ENG.). 224p. (J). (gr. 3-7). pap. 6.99 (978-0-14-250018-7(6), Puffin Books) Penguin Young Readers Group.

—The Great Ghost Rescue. Hawkes, Kevin, illus. 2003. (ENG.). 192p. (J). (gr. 3-7). pap. 6.99 (978-0-14-250087-3(9), Puffin Books) Penguin Young Readers Group.

Jacobs, Anna. Salem Street. 2015. (ENG.). 464p. (gr. 13-17). **(978-1-4736-1632-5(8))** Hodder & Stoughton GBR. Dist: Hachette Bk. Group.

Jacobs, Jordan. Samantha Sutton & the Winter of the Warrior Queen. 2014. (Samantha Sutton Ser.: 2). (ENG.). 368p. (J). (gr. 4-7). pap. 6.99 (978-1-4022-7563-0(3), 9781402275630, Sourcebooks Jabberwocky) Sourcebooks, Inc.

Jacobs, Joseph, ed. English Fairy Tales. 2005. (Twelve-Point Ser.). lib. bdg. 24.00 (978-1-58287-370-1(4)); lib. bdg. 25.00 (978-1-58287-862-1(5)) North Bks.

Jarvis, Robin. The Whitby Witches. 2017. (Modern Classics Ser.). (ENG., Illus.). 336p. (YA). (gr. 6). pap. 9.99 **(978-1-4052-8540-7(0))** Egmont Bks., Ltd. GBR. Dist: Independent Pubs. Group.

Johnson, Anne E. Trouble at the Scriptorium. 2012. (ENG., Illus.). 144p. (YA). (gr. 7-13). pap. 9.99 (978-0-88092-392-7(X)) Royal Fireworks Publishing Co.

Johnson, Carol V. Somerset Dreams. 2011. (Illus.). 112p. pap. 32.12 (978-1-4567-9012-7(9)) AuthorHouse.

Johnson, Gillian. Thora. Johnson, Gillian, illus. 2003. (Illus.). 128p. (978-0-207-19815-1(2)) HarperCollins Pubs. Australia.

Johnson, Jane. The Secret Country. Stower, Adam, illus. 2007. (Eidolon Chronicles Ser.: 1). (ENG.). 336p. (J). (gr. 3-7). per. 15.99 (978-1-4169-3815-6(X), Simon & Schuster Bks. For Young Readers) Simon & Schuster Bks. For Young Readers.

Johnson, Vargie. Charles Darwin, the Discoverer: What Made Them Famous? 2006. (Illus.). 152p. (J). per. 15.00 (978-1-931195-91-1(9)) KiwE Publishing, Ltd.

Jones, Diana Wynne. Enchanted Glass. 304p. (J). (gr. 3-7). 2011. pap. 6.99 (978-0-06-186685-2(7)) 2010. 16.99 (978-0-06-186684-5(9)) HarperCollins Pubs. (Greenwillow Bks.).

Jones, Frewin. The Seventh Daughter. 2009. (Faerie Path Ser.: 3). (ENG.). 352p. (YA). (gr. 8). pap. 9.99 (978-0-06-087110-9(5), HarperTeen) HarperCollins Pubs.

Joseph, Curtis M. Max Baxter. 2008. 57p. pap. 16.95 (978-1-60610-206-0(0)) America Star Bks.

Jules. Bubble's World: Book Five Frogs & Fairies. 2011. 40p. pap. 16.59 (978-1-4567-6730-3(5)) AuthorHouse.

—Bubble's World: Book Four Enchanted England. 2010. 40p. 16.99 (978-1-4520-5407-0(X)) AuthorHouse.

Kazerooni, Abbas. The Boy with Two Lives. 2016. (ENG.). 256p. (YA). (gr. 7). 12.99 (978-1-74331-483-8(3)) Allen & Unwin AUS. Dist: Independent Pubs. Group.

Keeble, Helen. Fang Girl. 2012. (ENG.). 352p. (YA). (gr. 8). pap. 9.99 (978-0-06-208225-1(6), HarperTeen) HarperCollins Pubs.

Kelly, Tom. Finn's Going. 2007. 278p. (YA). (gr. 8-12). 16.99 (978-0-06-121453-0(1), Greenwillow Bks.) HarperCollins Pubs.

Kennedy, Emma. The Case of the Fatal Phantom, 3 vols. Marc, Sylvain, illus. 2012. (Wilma Tenderfoot Ser.: 3). (ENG.). 368p. (J). (gr. 3-7). 16.99 (978-0-8037-3542-2(1), Dial Bks) Penguin Young Readers Group.

—The Case of the Frozen Hearts. 2012. (Wilma Tenderfoot Ser.: 1). (ENG.). 368p. (J). (gr. 3-7). 7.99 (978-0-14-242140-6(5), Puffin Books) Penguin Young Readers Group.

—The Case of the Putrid Poison, 2 vols. Marc, Sylvain & Dorman, Brandon, illus. 2011. (Wilma Tenderfoot Ser.: 2). (ENG.). 336p. (J). (gr. 3-7). 16.99 (978-0-8037-3541-5(3), Dial Bks) Penguin Young Readers Group.

—Wilma Tenderfoot - The Case of the Frozen Hearts. Marc, Sylvain et al, illus. 2011. (Wilma Tenderfoot Ser.: 1). (ENG.). 352p. (J). (gr. 3-7). 16.99 (978-0-8037-3540-8(5), Dial Bks) Penguin Young Readers Group.

—Wilma Tenderfoot: the Case of the Fatal Phantom. Marc, Sylvain, illus. 2013. (Wilma Tenderfoot Ser.: 3). (ENG.). 384p. (J). (gr. 3-7). pap. 7.99 (978-0-14-242609-8(1), Puffin Books) Penguin Young Readers Group.

Kerr, Esme. The Girl with the Glass Bird. 2015. (ENG.). 272p. (J). (gr. 3-7). 16.99 (978-0-545-69984-6(3)) Scholastic, Inc.

Kessler, Liz. A Year Without Autumn. (ENG.). 304p. (J). (gr. 4-7). 2012. pap. 7.99 (978-0-7636-6060-4(4)) 2011. (Illus.). 15.99 (978-0-7636-5595-2(3)) Candlewick Pr.

Ketteman, Helen. Waynetta & the Cornstalk: A Texas Fairy Tale. Greenseid, Diane, illus. 2012. (J). (978-1-61913-152-1(8)) Weigl Pubs., Inc.

Kindl, Patrice. Keeping the Castle. (ENG.). (YA). (gr. 7). 2013. 304p. pap. 10.99 *(978-0-14-242655-5(5)*, Speak) 2012. 224p. 16.99 *(978-0-670-01438-5(9)*, Viking Books for Young Readers) Penguin Young Readers Group.

Kindl, Patrice & Wells, Rosemary. A School for Brides. 2015. (ENG.). 272p. (J). (gr. 7). bds. 17.99 *(978-0-670-78608-4(X)*, Viking Books for Young Readers) Penguin Young Readers Group.

King, Carrie. Joni-Pip. Boddy, James & Moon, Paul, illus. 2010. 476p. pap. *(978-0-9555246-9-1(5))* Bothy Bks., Corwall, A Div. of Grace & Patrick Pubs., Ltd.

King-smith, Dick. The Catlady. Eastwood, John, illus. 2007. (ENG.). 80p. (J). (gr. 1-4). 5.99 *(978-0-440-42031-6(8)*, Yearling) Random Hse. Children's Bks.

—Funny Frank. Eastwood, John, illus. 2003. (ENG.). 112p. (J). (gr. 1-4). 5.99 *(978-0-440-41880-1(1)*, Yearling) Random Hse. Children's Bks.

—Titus Rules! Eastwood, John, illus. 2004. (ENG.). 96p. (J). (gr. 1-4). reprint ed. 5.50 *(978-0-440-42000-2(8)*, Yearling) Random Hse. Children's Bks.

Kingsley, Kate. Kiss & Break Up. 2011. (Young, Loaded, & Fabulous Ser.: 3). (ENG.). 320p. (YA). (gr. 9-18). pap. 9.99 *(978-1-4169-9401-5(7)*, Simon Pulse) Simon Pulse.

Kirchel, Karen. Irrepressible Lucie Archer. 2006. 147p. pap. 24.95 *(978-1-4241-3400-7(5))* PublishAmerica, Inc.

Knight, Eric. Lassie Come-Home. Kirmse, Marguerite, illus. 2007. (ENG.). 256p. (J). (gr. 3-7). per. 7.99 *(978-0-312-37131-9(4)*, 9780312371319) Square Fish.

Koponen, Libby. Blow Out the Moon. 2006. (ENG., Illus.). 224p. (gr. 8-17). per. 18.99 *(978-0-316-01480-9(X)*, Tingley, Megan Bks.) Little, Brown Bks. for Young Readers.

Kulling, Monica. Mary Anning's Curiosity, 1 vol. Castrillón, Melissa, illus. 2017. (ENG.). 156p. (J). (gr. 2-7). 14.95 *(978-1-55498-898-3(5))* Groundwood Bks. CAN. Dist: Publishers Group West (PGW).

Kurtagich, Dawn. The Dead House. 2015. (ENG., Illus.). 432p. (J). (gr. 10-17). 18.00 *(978-0-316-29868-1(9))* Little, Brown Bks. for Young Readers.

LaFevers, R. L. The Wyverns' Treasure. Murphy, Kelly, illus. 2012. (Nathanial Fludd, Beastologist Ser.: 3). (ENG.). 160p. (J). (gr. 1-4). pap. 6.99 *(978-0-547-85823-4(X))* Houghton Mifflin Harcourt Publishing Co.

Lancaster, Mike A. The Future We Left Behind. 2012. (ENG.). 384p. (J). (gr. 7). 16.99 *(978-1-60684-410-6(5)*, Carolrhoda Lab™) Lerner Publishing Group.

—Human. 4. 2012. (ENG.). 240p. (J). (gr. 7). pap. 8.99 *(978-1-60684-309-3(5)*, Carolrhoda Lab™) Lerner Publishing Group.

Lawrence, Michael. A Crack in the Line. 2004. (Withern Rise Ser.). (ENG.). 336p. (J). 15.99 *(978-0-06-072477-1(3))* HarperCollins Pubs.

—A Crack in the Line. 2005. (Withern Rise Trilogy). 323p. (YA). (gr. 9). 16.65 *(978-0-7569-5739-1(7))* Perfection Learning Corp.

—Small Eternities. (Withern Rise Ser.). 336p. 2006. (Illus.). (J). (gr. 7). pap. 7.99 *(978-0-06-072482-5(X)*, HarperTeen) 2005. (YA). 16.89 *(978-0-06-072481-8(1))* 2005. (ENG.). (J). (gr. 8). 15.99 *(978-0-06-072480-1(3)*, Greenwillow Bks.) HarperCollins Pubs.

—The Underwood See. 2007. (Withern Rise Ser.). (gr. 9). (ENG.). 384p. (J). pap. 7.99 *(978-0-06-072485-6(4)*, Greenwillow Bks.); 372p. (YA). 16.99 *(978-0-06-072483-2(8))* HarperCollins Pubs.

Lawson, Barbara. Huff the Magicless Dragon, 1 vol. Swope, Brenda, illus. 2009. 35p. pap. 24.95 *(978-1-61546-419-7(0))* PublishAmerica, Inc.

Le Feuvre, Amy. Teddy's Button. 2007. 92p. per. *(978-1-4065-2383-6(6))* Dodo Pr.

—Teddy's Button. 2004. reprint ed. pap. 15.95 *(978-1-4191-5094-4(4))*; pap. 1.99 *(978-1-4192-5094-1(9))* Kessinger Publishing, LLC.

Lean, Sarah. A Hundred Horses. 2015. (ENG.). 240p. (J). (gr. 3-7). pap. 6.99 *(978-0-06-212230-8(4)*, Tegen, Katherine Bks) HarperCollins Pubs.

Lefeuvre, Amy. Probable Sons. 2004. reprint ed. pap. 15.95 *(978-1-4191-4306-9(9))*; pap. 1.99 *(978-1-4192-4306-6(3))* Kessinger Publishing, LLC.

Leslie, Emma. The Captives: Or, Escape from the Druid Council. 2007. 200p. 22.95 *(978-1-934671-02-3(9))*; per. 12.95 *(978-1-934671-03-0(7))* Salem Ridge Press LLC.

—Gytha's Message: A Tale of Saxon England. Staniland, C., illus. 2007. 256p. 22.95 *(978-1-934671-11-5(8))* Salem Ridge Press LLC.

—The Martyr's Victory: A Story of Danish England. Stacey, W., illus. 2007. 300p. 24.95 *(978-1-934671-08-5(8))*; per. 14.95 *(978-1-934671-09-2(6))* Salem Ridge Press LLC.

Lewis, Gill. One White Dolphin. Aparicio, Raquel, illus. 2013. (ENG.). 368p. (J). (gr. 3-7). pap. 8.99 *(978-1-4424-1448-8(0)*, Atheneum Bks. for Young Readers) Simon & Schuster Children's Publishing.

Limke, Jeff. King Arthur: Excalibur Unsheathed. Yeates, Thomas, illus. 2007. (Graphic Myths & Legends Ser.). (ENG.). 48p. (gr. 4-8). per. 8.95 *(978-0-8225-6483-6(1))* Lerner Publishing Group.

—El Rey Arturo: La Espada Excalibur Desenvainada: Una Leyenda Inglesa. Translations.com Staff, tr. from ENG. Yeates, Thomas, illus. 2007. (Mitos y leyendas en viñetas (Graphic Myths & Legends) Ser.).Tr. of King Arthur - Excalibur Unsheathed [An English Legend. (SPA.). 48p. (gr. 4-8). per. 8.95 *(978-0-8225-7968-7(5))* Lerner Publishing Group.

Lindon, David A. The Lost Children of the Namuh & the Chamber of Souls - the First of a Trilogy. 2008. 376p. pap. *(978-1-906210-88-5(8))* Grosvenor Hse. Publishing Ltd.

Linney, Graham F. The Seaside Adventure of Carrot, Pea, & Friends. 2011. 32p. pap. 13.00 *(978-1-61204-435-4(2)*, Strategic Bk. Publishing) Strategic Book Publishing & Rights Agency (SBPRA).

Literature Connections English: Jane Eyre. 2004. (gr. 6-12). *(978-0-395-77557-8(4)*, 2-80126) Holt McDougal.

Lloyd Jones, Rob, retold by. Robin Hood. 2008. (Young Reading Series 2 Gift Bks). 64p. (J). 8.99 *(978-0-7945-2090-8(1)*, Usborne) EDC Publishing.

Lloyd, Saci. The Carbon Diaries 2015. 2008. (ENG., Illus.). 384p. (YA). pap. *(978-0-340-97015-7(4)*, Hodder Children's Books) Hachette Children's Group.

—The Carbon Diaries 2015. 2009. (ENG.). 384p. (YA). (gr. 9-18). 17.95 *(978-0-8234-2190-9(2))* Holiday Hse., Inc.

—Momentum. 2012. (ENG.). 224p. (J). 16.95 *(978-0-8234-2414-6(6))* Holiday Hse., Inc.

Loiske, Jennifer. Black Diamond. 2013. 246p. (J). pap. 13.61 *(978-1-291-30145-8(3))* Lulu Pr., Inc.

Longshore, Katherine. Manor of Secrets. 2014. (ENG.). 336p. (J). (gr. 7). 17.99 *(978-0-545-56758-9(0))* Scholastic, Inc.

Lorenzo, Mike. Allison's Summer Of '53. 2005. 53p. pap. 16.95 *(978-1-4241-1074-2(2))* PublishAmerica, Inc.

Love, D. Anne. The Puppeteer's Apprentice. 2004. (ENG., Illus.). 192p. (J). (gr. 3-7). reprint ed. pap. 9.99 *(978-0-689-84425-6(5)*, McElderry, Margaret K. Bks.) McElderry, Margaret K. Bks.

—The Puppeteer's Apprentice. 2004. (Aladdin Historical Fiction Ser.). 185p. (gr. 3-7). 17.00 *(978-0-7569-4323-3(X))* Perfection Learning Corp.

Macauley, Jo. Secrets & Spies, 1 vol. 2014. (Secrets & Spies Ser.). (ENG.). 224p. (gr. 4-7). 53.30 *(978-1-4342-8770-0(X))* Stone Arch Bks.

MacDonald, Tom. Secret of the Tree: Marcus Speer's Ecosentinel. Stieber, Joel, illus. 2009. 300p. 28.95 *(978-0-595-51985-9(7))* iUniverse, Inc.

Malley, Gemma. The Declaration. 2008. (Declaration Ser.). (ENG., Illus.). 320p. (YA). (gr. 7). 10.99 *(978-1-59990-295-1(8)*, 9781599902951, Bloomsbury USA Childrens) Bloomsbury Publishing USA.

—The Declaration, 7 vols. (YA). 2008. 119.75 *(978-1-4281-7284-5(X))* 2007. 1.25 *(978-1-4281-7275-3(0))* 2007. 121.75 *(978-1-4281-7282-1(3))* 2007. 245.75 *(978-1-4281-7279-1(3))* 2007. 91.75 *(978-1-4281-7278-4(5))* 2007. 89.75 *(978-1-4281-7280-7(7))* Recorded Bks., Inc.

—The Legacy. 2011. (Declaration Ser.). (ENG.). 272p. (YA). (gr. 7-18). 17.99 *(978-1-59990-567-9(1)*, 9781599905679, Bloomsbury USA Childrens) Bloomsbury Publishing USA.

—The Returners. 2010. (Declaration Ser.). (ENG.). 256p. (YA). (gr. 7-18). 16.99 *(978-1-59990-443-6(8)*, 9781599904436, Bloomsbury USA Childrens) Bloomsbury Publishing USA.

Marr, Andrew. Born in the Darkest Time of Year: Stories for the Season of the Christ Child. 2004. 180p. (J). pap. 13.95 *(978-0-595-32633-4(1))* iUniverse, Inc.

Marryat. The Children of the New Forest, Level 2. Bassett, Jennifer, ed. 3rd ed. 2008. (ENG., Illus.). 64p. pap. 10.00 *(978-0-19-479054-3(1))* Oxford Univ. Pr., Inc.

Marryat, Captian. The Children of the New Forest. 2008. 332p. (gr. 8-12). 28.99 *(978-0-554-38541-9(4))*; 29.99 *(978-0-554-29238-0(6))* Creative Media Partners, LLC.

—The Children of the New Forest. 2007. 312p. per. *(978-1-4065-5647-6(5))* Dodo Pr.

—The Children of the New Forest. 2006. 216p. pap. *(978-1-84637-527-9(4))*; pap. *(978-1-84702-355-1(X))* Echo Library.

—The Children of the New Forest. 2004. reprint ed. pap. 28.95 *(978-1-4191-5655-7(1))*; pap. 1.99 *(978-1-4192-5655-4(6))* Kessinger Publishing, LLC.

—The Children of the New Forest. 2008. 292p. pap. 16.95 *(978-1-60597-491-0(9)*, Book Jungle) Standard Pubns., Inc.

Marryat, Frederick. Children of the New Forest (Yesterday's Classics) 2007. (J). pap. 12.95 *(978-1-59915-050-5(6))* Yesterday's Classics.

Masefield, John. The Box of Delights. Masefield, Judith, illus. 2007. (ENG.). 312p. (J). (gr. 4-7). 17.95 *(978-1-59017-251-3(5)*, NYR Children's Collection) New York Review of Bks., Inc., The.

Mason, Caroline. The Blacksmith's Cottage: A Pastoral War. 2009. 150p. pap. 13.95 *(978-1-4327-4969-9(2))*; 120p. pap. 33.95 *(978-1-4327-2987-5(X))* Outskirts Pr., Inc.

Mason, Simon. Running Girl. 2016. (ENG.). 432p. (J). (gr. 9). 18.99 *(978-1-338-03642-8(4))* Scholastic, Inc.

Matchett, Gillian. The Adventures of Weston Super Cat with Activities. 2009. (Illus.). 92p. pap. 30.49 *(978-1-4389-2241-6(8))* AuthorHouse.

Matthews, Steve. Lord Grott of Grott Hall. 2015. (ENG.). 61p. (J). (gr. 2-3). mass mkt. 10.95 *(978-1-78554-268-8(0)*, 4e62726f-2944-495d-b6d7-3f986cb7e57f) Austin, Stan AUS. Dist: Bookmasters Distribution.

May, Chris. A Cricketing Dream. 2012. 64p. pap. 15.99 *(978-1-4797-1498-8(4))* Xlibris Corp.

Mayfield, Sue. Hill of the Angels. 2016. (ENG., Illus.). pap. ***(978-0-281-07641-3(3))*** SPCK Publishing.

McAllister, Margaret. The Octave of Angels. 2004. 128p. (J). pap. 8.00 *(978-0-8028-5240-3(8))* Eerdmans, William B. Publishing Co.

McCartney, Tania. An English Year: Twelve Months in the Life of England's Kids. Snerling, Tina, illus. 2015. (ENG.). 32p. (J). (gr. -1-3). 17.99 *(978-1-921966-86-6(6)*, EK Bks.) Exisle Publishing Pty Ltd. AUS. Dist: Hachette Bk. Group.

McGowan, Anthony. The Knife That Killed Me. 2011. (ENG.). 224p. (YA). (gr. 9). pap. 8.99 *(978-0-375-85516-0(5)*, Ember) Random Hse. Children's Bks.

McKay, Hilary. Caddy Ever After. (ENG.). 224p. (J). 2007. (gr. 4-8). per. 6.99 *(978-1-4169-0931-6(1))* 2006. (gr. 5-9). 16.99 *(978-1-4169-0930-9(3))* McElderry, Margaret K. Bks. (McElderry, Margaret K. Bks.).

—Caddy's World. (ENG.). (J). (gr. 5-9). 2013. 288p. pap. 6.99 *(978-1-4424-4106-4(2))* 2012. 272p. 16.99 *(978-1-4424-4105-7(4))* McElderry, Margaret K. Bks. (McElderry, Margaret K. Bks.).

—The Exiles at Home. 2007. (ENG.). 208p. (J). (gr. 3-7). pap. 12.95 *(978-1-4169-6729-3(X)*, McElderry, Margaret K. Bks.) McElderry, Margaret K. Bks.

—The Exiles in Love. 2007. (ENG.). 176p. (J). (gr. 3-7). pap. 9.95 *(978-1-4169-6797-2(4)*, McElderry, Margaret K. Bks.) McElderry, Margaret K. Bks.

—Forever Rose. (ENG.). 304p. (J). 2009. (gr. 4-9). pap. 6.99 *(978-1-4169-5487-3(2))* 2008. (Illus.). (gr. 5-9). 17.99 *(978-1-4169-5486-6(4))* McElderry, Margaret K. Bks. (McElderry, Margaret K. Bks.).

—Indigo's Star. 2006. (ENG.). 272p. (J). (gr. 3-7). reprint ed. per. 7.99 *(978-1-4169-1403-7(X)*, McElderry, Margaret K. Bks.) McElderry, Margaret K. Bks.

—Permanent Rose. 2006. (ENG.). 256p. (J). (gr. 3-7). reprint ed. per. 7.99 *(978-1-4169-2804-1(9)*, McElderry, Margaret K. Bks.) McElderry, Margaret K. Bks.

—Saffy's Angel. 2003. (ENG., Illus.). 160p. (J). (gr. 3-7). pap. 7.99 *(978-0-689-84934-3(6)*, McElderry, Margaret K. Bks.) McElderry, Margaret K. Bks.

—Saffy's Angel. 2004. (Casson Family Ser.: Bk. 1). 160p. (J). (gr. 4-7). pap. 36.00 incl. audio *(978-0-8072-2098-6(1)*, Listening Library) Random Hse. Audio Publishing Group.

McNish, Cliff. Breathe: A Ghost Story. (Exceptional Reading & Language Arts Titles for Intermediate Grades Ser.). (ENG.). 264p. (J). (gr. 4-8). 2009. pap. 6.95 *(978-0-7613-4962-4(6)*, First Avenue Editions) 2006. lib. bdg. 15.95 *(978-0-8225-6443-0(2)*, Carolrhoda Bks.) Lerner Publishing Group.

Meade, L. T. The Children's Pilgrimage. 2007. (ENG.). 254p. pap. 21.99 *(978-1-4346-4863-1(X))*; 280p. pap. 23.99 *(978-1-4346-4864-8(8))* Creative Media Partners, LLC.

Meister, Cari. King Arthur & the Sword in the Stone, 1 vol. Erkocak, Sahin, illus. 2008. (Read-It! Readers: Legends Ser.). (ENG.). 32p. (gr. k-3). 21.32 *(978-1-4048-4837-5(1)*, Easy Readers) Picture Window Bks.

Meyer, Carolyn. Doomed Queen Anne. 2004. (Young Royals Ser.: 3). (ENG., Illus.). 240p. (YA). (gr. 7-12). pap. 7.99 *(978-0-15-205086-3(8))* Houghton Mifflin Harcourt Publishing Co.

Miller, Gary & Miller, Lynda. The Adventures of Bob & Betty. 2006. (J). spiral bd. *(978-1-933594-92-7(6))* FBC Pubns. & Printing.

Mitchelhill, Barbara. A Twist of Fortune. 2014. (ENG.). 236p. (J). (gr. 4-6). pap. 12.99 *(978-1-84939-562-5(4))* Andersen Pr. GBR. Dist: Independent Pubs. Group.

Mitchen, Scott. Will of the Pirates. 2008. 180p. 22.95 *(978-0-595-70652-5(5))* iUniverse, Inc.

Moiser, Liam. Moore Field School & the Mystery. 2013. 118p. pap. 10.95 *(978-1-62516-787-3(3)*, Strategic Bk. Publishing) Strategic Book Publishing & Rights Agency (SBPRA).

Molesworth & Molesworth, Mary Louisa S. Peterkin. 2009. 128p. 23.95 *(978-1-60664-659-5(1))* Rodgers, Alan Bks.

—Us. 2008. 116p. 22.95 *(978-1-60664-989-3(2))* Aegypan.

Molesworth, Mary Louisa S. Us: An Old Fashioned Story. 2007. (ENG.). 142p. pap. 18.99 *(978-1-4346-0600-6(7))*; 156p. pap. 21.99 *(978-1-4346-0675-4(9))* Creative Media Partners, LLC.

Molesworth, Mary Louisa S. & Molesworth. Peterkin. 2009. 128p. pap. 10.95 *(978-1-60664-287-0(1))* Rodgers, Alan Bks.

—Rosy. 2008. 120p. 22.95 *(978-1-60664-727-1(X))* Rodgers, Alan Bks.

Moloney, James. Black Taxi. 2005. 272p. (J). (gr. 7-18). 15.99 *(978-0-06-055937-3(3))* HarperCollins Pubs.

—Black Taxi. 2003. 288p. *(978-0-207-19989-9(2))* HarperCollins Pubs. Australia.

Montgomery, L. M. Emily Climbs. 2009. (ENG.). 376p. pap. 16.95 *(978-0-7710-9382-1(9)*, New Can Library) McClelland & Stewart CAN. Dist: Random Hse., Inc.

—Emily's Quest. 2009. (ENG.). 272p. pap. 19.95 *(978-0-7710-9383-8(7)*, New Can Library) McClelland & Stewart CAN. Dist: Random Hse., Inc.

Moore, Victor L. The Pentacle of Northumbria. 2013. 432p. pap. *(978-1-78222-073-2(9))* Paragon Publishing, Rothersthorpe.

More Than This. 2014. (ENG.). 480p. (YA). (gr. 9). pap. 10.99 *(978-0-7636-7620-9(9))* Candlewick Pr.

Morgan, Jennifer. A Wind from the Sea. 2003. (ENG.). 192p. pap. 12.95 *(978-1-84323-209-4(X))* Beekman Bks., Inc.

Moriarty, Jaclyn. A Corner of White. 2013. (Colors of Madeleine Ser.: 1). (ENG.). 384p. (J). (gr. 7). 18.99 *(978-0-545-39736-0(7)*, Levine, Arthur A. Bks.) Scholastic, Inc.

—The Cracks in the Kingdom. 2014. (Colors of Madeleine Ser.: 2). (ENG.). 480p. (J). (gr. 7). 18.99 *(978-0-545-39738-4(3)*, Levine, Arthur A. Bks.) Scholastic, Inc.

—A Tangle of Gold. 2016. (Colors of Madeleine Ser.: 3). (ENG.). 480p. (YA). (gr. 7). 18.99 *(978-0-545-39740-7(5)*, Levine, Arthur A. Bks.) Scholastic, Inc.

Morpurgo, Michael. Farm Boy. Foreman, Michael, illus. 2007. (ENG.). 76p. (J). (gr. 4-7). pap. 15.99 *(978-1-84365-090-4(8))* Pavilion Bks. GBR. Dist: Independent Pubs. Group.

—Listen to the Moon. 2015. (ENG.). 352p. (J). (gr. 5-9). 16.99 *(978-1-250-04204-0(6)*, 9781250042040) Feiwel & Friends.

—Out of the Ashes, 1. unabr. ed. 2012. (ENG., Illus.). 128p. (J). (gr. 4-7). pap. 9.95 *(978-1-4472-0733-7(5))* Pan Macmillan GBR. Dist: Independent Pubs. Group.

Morris, Gerald. Parsifal's Page. 2008. (Squire's Tales Ser.: 4). (ENG.). 240p. (J). (gr. 5-7). pap. 7.99 *(978-0-547-01434-0(1))* Houghton Mifflin Harcourt Publishing Co.

—The Savage Damsel & the Dwarf. 2008. (Squire's Tales Ser.: 3). (ENG.). 224p. (J). (gr. 5-7). pap. 7.99 *(978-0-547-01437-1(6))* Houghton Mifflin Harcourt Publishing Co.

—The Squire, His Knight, & His Lady. 2008. (Squire's Tales Ser.: 2). (ENG., Illus.). 240p. (J). (gr. 5-7). pap. 7.99 *(978-0-547-01438-8(4))* Houghton Mifflin Harcourt Publishing Co.

—The Squire's Tale. 2008. (Squire's Tales Ser.: 1). (ENG.). 224p. (J). (gr. 5-7). pap. 7.99 *(978-0-618-73743-7(X))* Houghton Mifflin Harcourt Publishing Co.

Morris, Paula. Dark Souls. 2011. (ENG.). 304p. (J). (gr. 7-7). 17.99 *(978-0-545-25132-7(X))* Scholastic, Inc.

Morton-Shaw, Christine. The Riddles of Epsilon. 384p. 2006. (ENG.). (YA). (gr. 8). per. 7.99 *(978-0-06-072821-2(3)*, Tegen, Katherine Bks) Vol. 1. 2005. (gr. 7-18). 16.99 *(978-0-06-072819-9(1))* HarperCollins Pubs.

Moss, Alexandra. Lara's Leap of Faith. 2005. (Royal Ballet School Diaries). 138p. (J). 12.65 *(978-0-7569-5894-7(6))* Perfection Learning Corp.

Mulligan, Andy. Return to Ribblestrop. 2016. (Ribblestrop Ser.). (ENG., Illus.). 352p. (J). (gr. 3-7). 17.99 *(978-1-4424-9907-2(9)*, Beach Lane Bks.) Beach Lane Bks.

—Ribblestrop. (Ribblestrop Ser.). (ENG., Illus.). (J). (gr. 3-7). 2016. 400p. pap. 7.99 *(978-1-4424-9905-8(2))* 2014. 384p. 16.99 *(978-1-4424-9904-1(4))* Beach Lane Bks. (Beach Lane Bks.).

—Ribblestrop Forever! 2016. (Ribblestrop Ser.). (ENG., Illus.). 320p. (J). (gr. 3-7). 16.99 *(978-1-4424-9910-2(9)*, Beach Lane Bks.) Beach Lane Bks.

Murail, Marie-aude. Sin Azúcar, Gracias. 2003. (la Orilla Del Viento Ser.). (SPA.). 101p. (J). pap. 8.50 *(978-968-16-6725-2(5))* Fondo de Cultura Economica USA.

Mussi, Sarah. The Door of No Return. (ENG.). 400p. (YA). (gr. 7). 2009. pap. 10.99 *(978-1-4169-6825-2(3))* 2008. 17.99 *(978-1-4169-1550-8(8))* McElderry, Margaret K. Bks. (McElderry, Margaret K. Bks.).

My Way Sally: Evaluation Guide. 2006. (J). *(978-1-55942-418-9(4))* Witcher Productions.

Myers, Walter Dean. On a Clear Day. 2014. (ENG.). 256p. (YA). (gr. 7). 17.99 *(978-0-385-38753-8(9)*, Crown Books For Young Readers) Random Hse. Children's Bks.

Nadin, Joanna. Wonderland. 2011. (ENG., Illus.). 224p. (YA). (gr. 9-18). 16.99 *(978-0-7636-4846-6(9))* Candlewick Pr.

Naughton, Bill. The Goalkeeper's Revenge. 2012. (ENG.). 110p. (YA). pap. 12.99 *(978-1-4482-0443-4(7)*, 9781448204434, Bloomsbury Reader) Bloomsbury Publishing Plc GBR. Dist: Macmillan.

Nesbit, E. The Enchanted Castle. 2007. 252p. per. 13.95 *(978-1-4218-3942-4(3))*; (gr. -1-7). 28.95 *(978-1-4218-3842-7(7))* 1st World Publishing, Inc. (1st World Library - Literary Society).

—The Enchanted Castle. (gr. -1-7). 2006. 168p. per. 13.95 *(978-1-59818-831-8(3))* 2005. 256p. 26.95 *(978-1-59818-173-9(4))* Aegypan.

—The Enchanted Castle. 2007. (ENG.). 190p. pap. 19.99 *(978-1-4346-5225-6(4))*; 212p. pap. 22.99 *(978-1-4346-5226-3(2))* Creative Media Partners, LLC.

—The Enchanted Castle. lt. ed. 2005. 388p. pap. *(978-1-84637-202-5(X))* Echo Library.

—Five Children & It. 2007. 192p. per. 12.95 *(978-1-4218-3940-0(7))*; (gr. 4-7). 27.95 *(978-1-4218-3840-3(0))* 1st World Publishing, Inc. (1st World Library - Literary Society).

—Five Children & It. 207p. 20.95 *(978-0-8488-2523-2(3))* Amereon Ltd.

—Five Children & It. 2013. 132p. pap. *(978-1-908388-99-5(4))* Aziloth Bks.

—Five Children & It. (gr. 4-6). 2011. 428p. pap. 35.75 *(978-1-179-45023-0(X))* 2008. 200p. 22.99 *(978-0-554-38716-1(6))* 2008. 200p. 25.99 *(978-0-554-29413-1(3))* Creative Media Partners, LLC.

—Five Children & It. Millar, H. R., illus. 2007. (ENG.). 178p. pap. 19.99 *(978-1-4346-7586-6(6))*; 198p. pap. 21.99 *(978-1-4346-7587-3(4))* Creative Media Partners, LLC.

—Five Children & It. 2005. 96p. per. 4.95 *(978-1-4209-2587-6(3))* Digireads.com Publishing.

—Five Children & It. Millar, H. R., illus. 2007. (ENG.). 204p. per. *(978-1-4065-3077-3(8))* Dodo Pr.

—Five Children & It. 2017. (Dover Children's Evergreen Classics Ser.). (ENG., Illus.). 160p. (J). (gr. 3-8). pap. 4.00 *(978-0-486-42366-1(2))* Dover Pubns., Inc.

—Five Children & It. 2006. pap. *(978-1-4068-3501-4(3))* 2005. 296p. pap. *(978-1-84637-200-1(3))* Echo Library.

—Five Children & It. 2010. 98p. pap. 19.99 *(978-1-153-62213-4(0))* General Bks. LLC.

—Five Children & It. 2010. 144p. pap. *(978-1-4076-4577-3(3))* HardPr.

—Five Children & It. 2010. 152p. pap. 17.56 *(978-1-162-66290-9(5))* 2010. 152p. (gr. 3-7). 29.56 *(978-1-169-26518-9(9))* 2010. 152p. 36.95 *(978-1-161-43155-1(1))* 2004. reprint ed. pap. 21.95 *(978-1-4191-1987-3(7))* 2004. reprint ed. pap. 1.99 *(978-1-4192-1987-0(1))* Kessinger Publishing, LLC.

—Five Children & It. 2013. (Oxford Children's Classics Ser.). (ENG.). 208p. 9.95 *(978-0-19-273343-6(5))* Oxford Univ. Pr., Inc.

—Five Children & It. Hische, Jessica, illus. 2013. (Penguin Drop Caps Ser.). (ENG.). 256p. (J). (gr. 12). 25.00 *(978-0-14-312466-5(8)*, Penguin Books) Penguin Publishing Group.

—Five Children & It. 2008. (Puffin Classics Ser.). (ENG., Illus.). 272p. (J). (gr. 5-7). 5.99 *(978-0-14-132161-5(X)*, Puffin Books) Penguin Young Readers Group.

—Five Children & It. 2013. (ENG., Illus.). 272p. (J). (gr. 4-7). pap. 10.99 *(978-0-09-957298-5(2))* Random Hse. GBR. Dist: Independent Pubs. Group.

—Five Children & It. 2005. (J). 1.25 *(978-1-4025-4084-4(1))* Recorded Bks., Inc.

—Five Children & It. 2013. 160p. *(978-3-8495-1928-5(7))* 2013. 160p. pap. *(978-3-8495-0897-5(8))* 2011. 208p. pap. *(978-3-8424-8390-3(2))* Tredition GmbH.

—Five Children & It. 2009. 128p. (gr. 4-7). pap. 4.95 *(978-1-60459-692-2(9))* Wilder Pubns., Corp.

—Five Children & It. 2005. (ENG.). 29.95 *(978-1-55742-510-2(8))*; pap. 14.95 *(978-1-55742-506-5(X))* Wildside Pr., LLC.

—Jack & the Beanstalk. Tavares, Matt, illus. 2006. (ENG.). 48p. (J). (gr. -1-2). 16.99 *(978-0-7636-2124-7(2))* Candlewick Pr.

—The Railway Children. 2007. 236p. per. 12.95 *(978-1-4218-3945-5(8))*; (ENG.). (gr. 4-7). 27.95 *(978-1-4218-3845-8(1))* 1st World Publishing, Inc. (1st World Library - Literary Society).

—The Railway Children. 2006. (ENG.). 228p. (gr. 4-7). per. 14.95 *(978-1-59818-933-9(6))*; 26.95 *(978-1-59818-179-1(3))* Aegypan.

—The Railway Children. 2013. 140p. pap. *(978-1-908388-94-0(3))* Aziloth Bks.

—The Railway Children. 2008. (J). 8.99 *(978-1-59166-924-1(3))* BJU Pr.

—The Railway Children. Brock, C. E., illus. (YA). 14.95 *(978-0-8118-4933-3(3))* Chronicle Bks. LLC.

—The Railway Children. 2012. (ENG.). 234p. pap. 14.99 *(978-1-4812-4818-1(9))* CreateSpace Independent Publishing Platform.

—The Railway Children. 2008. 204p. (gr. 4-7). 27.99 *(978-0-554-26706-7(3))*; 24.99 *(978-0-554-36009-6(8))* Creative Media Partners, LLC.

—The Railway Children. 2008. (gr. 4-7). pap. 5.99 *(978-1-4209-3105-1(9))* Digireads.com Publishing.

—The Railway Children. Brock, C. E., illus. 2008. (ENG.). 248p. per. *(978-1-4065-9815-5(1))* Dodo Pr.

—The Railway Children. 2007. (ENG.). 204p. per. *(978-1-4065-3083-4(2))* Dodo Pr.

—The Railway Children. 2006. pap. *(978-1-4068-3505-2(6))* 2005. 348p. pap. *(978-1-84637-205-6(4))* Echo Library.

—The Railway Children. Brock, Charles Edmund, illus. 2012. 232p. pap. *(978-1-78201-004-3(1))* Evertype.

E
F
G

—The Railway Children. 2010. (Illus.). 118p. pap. 19.99 *(978-1-153-71841-7(3))* General Bks. LLC.

—The Railway Children. Dryhurst, Dinah, tr. Dryhurst, Dinah, illus. 2004. 184p. 18.95 *(978-1-56792-261-5(9))* Godine, David R. Pub.

—The Railway Children. 2010. 184p. pap. *(978-1-4076-1891-3(1))* HardPr.

—The Railway Children. (J). *(978-0-340-71497-3(2))* Hodder & Stoughton.

—The Railway Children. 2010. 194p. 30.36 *(978-1-169-28328-2(4))* 2010. 194p. pap. 18.36 *(978-1-162-70632-0(5))* 2010. 194p. 37.95 *(978-1-161-47496-1(X))* 2004. reprint ed. pap. 22.95 *(978-1-4191-7972-3(1))* 2004. reprint ed. pap. 1.99 *(978-1-4192-7972-0(6))* Kessinger Publishing, LLC.

—The Railway Children. 2006. (Twelve-Point Ser.). lib. bdg. 25.00 *(978-1-58287-399-2(2))*; lib. bdg. 26.00 *(978-1-58287-890-4(0))* North Bks.

—The Railway Children. 2012. (Oxford Children's Classics Ser.). (ENG.). 240p. 9.95 *(978-0-19-275819-4(5))* Oxford Univ. Pr., Inc.

—The Railway Children. 2nd ed. 2008. (ENG., Illus.). 48p. pap. 11.99 *(978-1-4058-6964-5(X))* Pearson Education.

—The Railway Children. 2nd ed. 2011. (Puffin Classics Ser.). (ENG., Illus.). 304p. (J). (gr. 5-7). pap. 5.99 *(978-0-14-132160-8(1)*, Puffin Books) Penguin Young Readers Group.

—The Railway Children. (ENG.). (J). (gr. 4-7). 2013. 320p. pap. 10.99 *(978-0-09-957299-2(0))* 2012. 290p. 10.99 *(978-0-09-957715-7(1))* Random Hse. GBR. Dist: Independent Pubs. Group.

—The Railway Children. 2010. 146p. (gr. 4-7). pap. 8.95 *(978-1-61104-337-2(9))* ReadaClassic.com.

—The Railway Children. 2004. (ENG.). 580p. *(978-0-9548401-2-9(7))* Shoes & Ships & Sealing Wax Ltd.

—The Railway Children. 2011. 200p. (gr. 4-7). pap. *(978-3-8424-4120-0(7))* Tredition GmbH.

—The Railway Children. 2009. 156p. (gr. 4-7). pap. 6.99 *(978-1-60459-698-4(8))* Wilder Pubns., Corp.

—The Story of the Amulet. 2009. 176p. (gr. -1-7). pap. 4.95 *(978-1-60459-694-6(5))* Wilder Pubns., Corp.

Nesbø, Jo. The Magical Fruit. 2014. (Doctor Proctor's Fart Powder Ser.). (ENG., Illus.). 320p. (J). (gr. 3-7). pap. 7.99 *(978-1-4424-9343-8(7)*, Aladdin) Simon & Schuster Children's Publishing.

—The Magical Fruit. Chace, Tara F., tr. from NOR. Lowery, Mike, illus. 2013. (Doctor Proctor's Fart Powder Ser.). (ENG.). 320p. (J). (gr. 3-7). 17.99 *(978-1-4424-9342-1(9)*, Aladdin) Simon & Schuster Children's Publishing.

Ness, Patrick. A Monster Calls: Inspired by an Idea from Siobhan Dowd. (ENG.). 240p. (YA). (gr. 7). 2016. pap. 9.99 *(978-0-7636-9215-5(8))* 2015. pap. 12.00 *(978-0-7636-8081-7(8))* Candlewick Pr.

—A Monster Calls: Inspired by an Idea from Siobhan Dowd. Kay, Jim, illus. (ENG.). 224p. (YA). (gr. 7). 2013. pap. 12.00 *(978-0-7636-6065-9(5))* 2011. 16.99 *(978-0-7636-5559-4(7))* Candlewick Pr.

—A Monster Calls: Inspired by an Idea from Siobhan Dowd. 2011. (Playaway Children Ser.). (YA). (gr. 7-12). 54.99 *(978-1-4558-4499-9(3))* Findaway World, LLC.

—A Monster Calls: Inspired by an Idea from Siobhan Dowd. 2013. lib. bdg. 23.30 *(978-0-606-31603-3(5)*, Turtleback) Turtleback Bks.

Newman, Gerry. Nellie, the Scarecrow: A Dorset Fable. 2003. (Illus.). 188p. pap. 12.50 *(978-1-84426-184-0(0))* Upfront Publishing Ltd. GBR. Dist: Printondemand-worldwide.com.

Newman, John. Mimi. 2011. (ENG., Illus.). 192p. (J). (gr. 3-7). 15.99 *(978-0-7636-5415-3(9))* Candlewick Pr.

Nicholls, Sally. Season of Secrets. 2011. (J). 225p. pap. *(978-0-545-21826-9(8))*; (ENG.). 240p. (gr. 3-7). 16.99 *(978-0-545-21825-2(X))* Scholastic, Inc. (Levine, Arthur A. Bks.).

Norton, Mary. The Borrowers. Krush, Beth & Krush, Joe, illus. 2003. (Borrowers Ser.: 1). (ENG.). 192p. (J). (gr. 2-5). pap. 7.99 *(978-0-15-204737-5(9))* Houghton Mifflin Harcourt Publishing Co.

—The Borrowers Afield. Krush, Beth & Krush, Joe, illus. 50th anniv. ed. 2003. (Borrowers Ser.: 2). (ENG.). 224p. (J). (gr. 2-5). pap. 7.99 *(978-0-15-204732-0(8))* Houghton Mifflin Harcourt Publishing Co.

—The Borrowers Afloat. Krush, Beth & Krush, Joe, illus. 2003. (Borrowers Ser.: 3). (ENG.). 192p. (J). (gr. 2-5). pap. 7.99 *(978-0-15-204733-7(6))* Houghton Mifflin Harcourt Publishing Co.

—The Borrowers Avenged. Krush, Joe et al, illus. 50th anniv. ed. 2003. (Borrowers Ser.: 5). (ENG.). 304p. (J). (gr. 2-5). pap. 7.99 *(978-0-15-204731-3(X))* Houghton Mifflin Harcourt Publishing Co.

Nosy Crow Staff. Jack & the Beanstalk: a Nosy Crow Fairy Tale. Bryan, Ed, illus. 2017. (ENG.). 32p. (J). (gr. -1-2). 9.99 *(978-0-7636-9332-9(4)*, Nosy Crow) Candlewick Pr.

Noyes, Deborah. Angel & Apostle. 2007. (ENG.). 304p. per. 14.95 *(978-1-932961-29-4(1))* Unbridled Bks.

O'connell, Tyne. A Royal Match. 2011. (Calypso Chronicles Ser.). (ENG.). 512p. (YA). pap. 9.99 *(978-1-59990-751-2(8)*, 9781599907512, Bloomsbury USA Childrens) Bloomsbury Publishing USA.

O'Neill, Katrina & Thompson, Lisa. Hunting down the Grail. 2007. (Illus.). 52p. (J). pap. *(978-1-4207-0722-9(1))* Sundance/Newbridge Educational Publishing.

O'Rourke, Tim. Flashes. 2015. (ENG.). 320p. (J). (gr. 9). 16.99 *(978-0-545-82959-5(3))* Scholastic, Inc.

Oulton, Harry. A Pig Called Heather. 2015. (ENG.). 192p. (J). (gr. 3-7). 16.95 *(978-0-8234-3290-5(4))* Holiday Hse., Inc.

Outram, Evelyn. Sav & Josh O Lucky's Christmas Adventure & Magic Street. 2010. 56p. pap. 17.95 *(978-1-60911-876-1(6)*, Eloquent Bks.) Strategic Book Publishing & Rights Agency (SBPRA).

Packard, Edward. The Forbidden Castle. Willis, Drew, illus. 2013. (U-Ventures Ser.). (ENG.). 192p. (J). (gr. 3-7). pap. 5.99 *(978-1-4424-3428-8(7)*, Simon & Schuster Bks. For Young Readers) Simon & Schuster Bks. For Young Readers.

Page, Chris. Veneficus - Stones of the Chosen. 2008. 252p. 26.50 *(978-1-60693-473-9(2)*, Eloquent Bks.) Strategic Book Publishing & Rights Agency (SBPRA).

Parker, Emma. Jack & the Beanstalk. 2010. (Illus.). 24p. pap. *(978-1-877561-49-8(5))* First Edition Ltd.

Parker, Gilbert. Michel & Angele. 2009. 124p. pap. 10.95 *(978-1-60664-418-8(1))* Rodgers, Alan Bks.

Pass, Emma. Acid. 2014. (ENG.). 384p. (YA). (gr. 9). 17.99 *(978-0-385-74387-7(4)*, Delacorte Pr.) Random Hse. Children's Bks.

Patterson, James. Demons & Druids. 2011. (Daniel X Ser.: 3). (ENG.). 304p. (J). (gr. 3-7). pap., pap. 8.00 *(978-0-316-03830-0(X)*, Jimmy Patterson) Little Brown & Co.

Patterson, James & Sadler, Adam. Demons & Druids. l.t. ed. 2010. (Daniel X Ser.: 3). (ENG.). 320p. 29.99 *(978-0-316-08731-5(9)*, Jimmy Patterson) Little Brown & Co.

Paul, Bette. Nurses: Claire's Conquests & Jan's Journey. 2007. 312p. per. *(978-1-905665-43-3(1))* Pollinger In Print.

Peachey, Ted. The Adventures of Ryan & His Magic Carrot. 2010. 90p. pap. 9.99 *(978-1-60911-222-6(9)*, Eloquent Bks.) Strategic Book Publishing & Rights Agency (SBPRA).

Pedraza, M. Eugenia Rueda. Nico's Voyage. 2013. 32p. pap. *(978-1-4602-2360-4(8))* FriesenPress.

Peet, Mal. Tamar: A Novel of Espionage, Passion, & Betrayal. (ENG., Illus.). 432p. (YA). (gr. 9). 2008. pap. 8.99 *(978-0-7636-4063-7(8))* 2007. 17.99 *(978-0-7636-3488-9(3))* Candlewick Pr.

Perkins, John. Perceval: King Arthur's Knight of the Holy Grail, 1 vol. Spirin, Gennady, illus. 2007. (ENG.). 40p. (J). (gr. 3-7). 16.99 *(978-0-7614-5339-0(3))* Marshall Cavendish Corp.

Peter L. Ward. Freya & the Fenris-Wolf. 2010. 184p. 24.50 *(978-1-4269-2511-5(5))*; pap. 14.50 *(978-1-4269-2510-8(7))* Trafford Publishing.

Peterson, Will. The Gathering. 2010. (Triskellion Ser.: 3). (ENG., Illus.). 384p. (YA). (gr. 9-18). 16.99 *(978-0-7636-4847-3(7))* Candlewick Pr.

Petty, Heather W. Mind Games. 2016. (Lock & Mori Ser.). (ENG., Illus.). 304p. (YA). (gr. 9). 17.99 *(978-1-4814-2306-9(1)*, Simon & Schuster Bks. For Young Readers) Simon & Schuster Bks. For Young Readers.

Picard, Barbara Leonie. One Is One. 2006. (ENG.). 286p. (J). (gr. 3-7). per. 9.95 *(978-1-58988-027-6(7))* Consortium Bk. Sales & Distribution.

Picture Window Books Staff. Robin Hood & the Golden Arrow, 1 vol. Yilmaz, Necdet, illus. 2008. (Read-It! Readers: Legends Ser.). (ENG.). 32p. (gr. k-3). 21.32 *(978-1-4048-4843-6(6)*, Easy Readers) Picture Window Bks.

Pismarov, Vivienne. The Crazy Days of Sam B. 2009. 88p. pap. 10.49 *(978-1-4490-3826-7(3))* AuthorHouse.

Pitcher, Annabel. Ketchup Clouds. 2013. (ENG.). 272p. (YA). (gr. 7-17). 18.00 *(978-0-316-24676-7(X))* Little Brown & Co.

—My Sister Lives on the Mantelpiece. (ENG.). (YA). (gr. 7-17). 2013. 240p. pap. 10.00 *(978-0-316-17689-7(3))* 2012. 224p. 18.00 *(978-0-316-17690-3(7))* Little, Brown Bks. for Young Readers.

—Yours Truly. 2014. (ENG., Illus.). 288p. (YA). (gr. 7-17). pap. 9.99 *(978-0-316-24678-1(6))* Little, Brown Bks. for Young Readers.

Pollock, Hal. Meet the Brittles: In Monstermania. 2009. (ENG.). 32p. (J). (gr. -1-3). 15.95 *(978-1-59687-858-7(4))* IBks., Inc.

Potter, Ellen. The Kneebone Boy. 2011. (ENG.). 304p. (J). (gr. 4-7). pap. 8.99 *(978-0-312-67432-8(5)*, 9780312674328) Square Fish.

Powell, Laura. Witch Fire. 2013. (ENG.). 336p. (YA). (gr. 7). 17.99 *(978-1-61963-006-2(0)*, 9781619630062, Bloomsbury USA Childrens) Bloomsbury Publishing USA.

Pratchett, Terry. Johnny & the Dead. 2006. (Johnny Maxwell Trilogy). 213p. (J). (gr. 3-7). 15.99 *(978-0-06-054188-0(1))*; lib. bdg. 16.89 *(978-0-06-054189-7(X))* HarperCollins Pubs.

Price, David J. Tom & Emily's Incredible Adventure to the World of the Gossamerians. 2013. 130p. pap. *(978-1-909740-41-9(1))* Legend Pr.

Priestley, Chris. Redwulf's Curse. 2005. (ENG., Illus.). 176p. (YA). (gr. 6-10). 16.99 *(978-0-385-60695-0(8)*, Doubleday UK) Transworld Publishers Ltd. GBR. Dist: Trafalgar Square Publishing.

Pritchard, David. Ghost of Spring. 2010. 228p. pap. *(978-1-907652-11-0(6))* Grosvenor Hse. Publishing Ltd.

Pullein-Thompson, Christine. Phantom Horse in Danger. 2012. (ENG., Illus.). 176p. (J). pap. 9.95 *(978-1-84135-824-6(X))* Award Pubns. Ltd. GBR. Dist: Parkwest Pubns., Inc.

Pullman, Philip. Lyra's Oxford. Lawrence, John, illus. 2006. (His Dark Materials Ser.). 49p. (YA). reprint ed. 11.00 *(978-1-4223-5410-0(5))* DIANE Publishing Co.

—Lyra's Oxford. Lawrence, John, illus. 2007. (His Dark Materials Ser.). (ENG.). 64p. (J). (gr. 5-12). per. 6.99 *(978-0-375-84369-3(8)*, Knopf Bks. for Young Readers) Random Hse. Children's Bks.

—Sally y la Sombra del Norte. 2003.Tr. of Shadow in the North. (SPA., Illus.). 352p. (YA). 14.95 *(978-84-95618-43-6(5)*, Umbriel) Ediciones Urano S. A. ESP. Dist: Spanish Pubs., LLC.

Pyle, Howard. The Merry Adventures of Robin Hood, 1 vol. Simon, Ute, illus. 2011. (Calico Illustrated Classics Ser.: No. 3). (ENG.). 112p. (J). (gr. 3-6). 27.07 *(978-1-61641-107-7(4))* Magic Wagon.

—The Story of King Arthur & His Knights. Pyle, Howard, illus. 2006. (ENG., Illus.). 416p. (gr. 12-18). 6.95 *(978-0-451-53024-0(1)*, Signet) Penguin Publishing Group.

Pyle, Howard, illus. The Merry Adventures of Robin Hood. 2015. (J). 13.32 *(978-1-4677-5841-3(8)*, First Avenue Editions) Lerner Publishing Group.

Pyle, Robert. The Merry Adventures of Robin Hood. 2009. 284p. (J). pap. 14.99 *(978-1-934941-61-4(1))* Red & Black Pubs.

Quiller-Couch, Arthur Thomas. The Splendid Spur. 2008. 172p. per. 13.95 *(978-1-60312-436-2(5))* Aegypan.

—The Twelve Dancing Princesses & Other Fairy Tales. Nielsen, Kay, illus. 2012. (Calla Editions Ser.). (ENG.). 208p. (gr. 4). 40.00 *(978-1-60660-025-2(7))* Dover Pubns., Inc.

Ransome, Arthur. Swallowdale. 2014. (ENG., Illus.). 464p. (gr. 4-13). 24.95 *(978-1-4683-0956-0(0)*, 460956) Overlook Pr., The.

—We Didn't Mean to Go to Sea. 2010. (ENG.). 100p. (gr. 2). pap. 22.95 *(978-1-906582-05-0(X))* Aurora Metro Pubns. Ltd. GBR. Dist: Consortium Bk. Sales & Distribution.

Rasheed, Leila. Doughnuts, Dreams & Drama Queens. 2013. (Fantastic Diary of Bathsheba Claric de Trop Ser.). 299p. (J). pap. 5.99 *(978-0-7945-3030-3(3)*, Usborne) EDC Publishing.

Ratcliff, Carol J. Grannie's Secret Garden: (Somewhere in England) 2009. (Illus.). 48p. pap. 19.49 *(978-1-4490-4355-1(0))* AuthorHouse.

Raymond, Patrick. Daniel & Esther. 2007. (ENG.). 176p. (J). (gr. 3-7). pap. 9.95 *(978-1-4169-6798-9(2)*, Simon & Schuster/Paula Wiseman Bks.) Simon & Schuster/Paula Wiseman Bks.

Renninson, Lou. Frontalknutschen. pap. 17.95 *(978-3-570-30008-4(0))* Bertelsman, Verlagsgruppe C. GmbH DEU. Dist: Distribooks, Inc.

Rennison, Louise. Angus, Thongs & Full-Frontal Snogging. 2006. (Confessions of Georgia Nicolson Ser.: 1). (ENG.). 272p. (YA). (gr. 8-18). pap. 9.99 *(978-0-06-447227-2(2)*, HarperTeen) HarperCollins Pubs.

—Angus, Thongs & Full-Frontal Snogging. 2009. (Confessions of Georgia Nicolson Ser.: No. 1). 10.36 *(978-0-7848-1994-4(7)*, Everbind) Marco Bk. Co.

—Angus, Thongs & Full-Frontal Snogging. (Confessions of Georgia Nicolson Ser.: 1). (J). 2008. 70.49 *(978-1-4281-7895-3(3))* 2005. 1.25 *(978-1-4193-4293-6(2))* 2004. 68.75 *(978-1-4025-9087-0(3))* Recorded Bks., Inc.

—Are These My Basoomas I See Before Me? Final Confessions of Georgia Nicolson. 2010. (Confessions of Georgia Nicolson Ser.: 10). (ENG.). 336p. (YA). (gr. 8-9). pap. 8.99 *(978-0-06-145937-5(2)*, HarperTeen) HarperCollins Pubs.

—Dancing in My Nuddy-Pants. 2006. (Confessions of Georgia Nicolson Ser.: 4). (ENG.). 240p. (YA). (gr. 8). reprint ed. pap. 8.99 *(978-0-06-009748-6(5)*, HarperTeen) HarperCollins Pubs.

—Knocked Out by My Nunga-Nungas. 2006. (Confessions of Georgia Nicolson Ser.: No. 3). 183p. (gr. 7-12). 19.00 *(978-0-7569-6729-1(5))* Perfection Learning Corp.

—Love Is a Many Trousered Thing. 2008. (Confessions of Georgia Nicolson Ser.: 8). (ENG.). 304p. (YA). (gr. 8). pap. 9.99 *(978-0-06-085389-1(1)*, HarperTeen) HarperCollins Pubs.

—A Midsummer Tights Dream. 2013. (Misadventures of Tallulah Casey Ser.: 2). (ENG.). 272p. (YA). (gr. 8). pap. 9.99 *(978-0-06-179938-9(6)*, HarperTeen) HarperCollins Pubs.

—On the Bright Side, I'm Now the Girlfriend of a Sex God: Further Confessions of Georgia Nicolson. (Confessions of Georgia Nicolson Ser.: 2). (ENG.). 2006. 272p. (YA). (gr. 8). pap. 8.99 *(978-0-06-447226-5(4)*, HarperTeen) 2003. 256p. (J). pap. 6.99 *(978-0-06-052185-1(6))* HarperCollins Pubs.

—Startled by His Furry Shorts. (Confessions of Georgia Nicolson Ser.: 7). (YA). 2007. (ENG.). 304p. (gr. 8-12). pap. 9.99 *(978-0-06-085386-0(7))* 2006. 288p. (gr. 7-12). 16.99 *(978-0-06-085384-6(0))* 2006. 278p. (gr. 7-12). lib. bdg. 17.89 *(978-0-06-085385-3(9))* HarperCollins Pubs. (HarperTeen).

—Stop in the Name of Pants! (Confessions of Georgia Nicolson Ser.: 9). (YA). 2009. (ENG.). 336p. (gr. 8). pap. 9.99 *(978-0-06-145934-4(8))* 2008. 256p. (gr. 7-18). 16.99 *(978-0-06-145932-0(1))* 2008. 320p. (gr. 7-18). lib. bdg. 17.89 *(978-0-06-145933-7(X))* HarperCollins Pubs. (HarperTeen).

—Stop in the Name of Pants!, 6 vols. 2010. (Confessions of Georgia Nicolson Ser.: 9). (YA). 82.75 *(978-1-4407-7777-6(2))*; 85.75 *(978-1-4407-7775-2(6))*; 172.75 *(978-1-4407-7772-1(1))*; 67.75 *(978-1-4407-7773-8(X))*; 70.75 *(978-1-4407-7771-4(3))*; 1.25 *(978-1-4407-7779-0(9))* Recorded Bks., Inc.

—Then He Ate My Boy Entrancers: More Mad, Marvy Confessions of Georgia Nicolson. (Confessions of Georgia Nicolson Ser.: 6). 2006. (ENG.). 336p. (YA). (gr. 8-12). pap. 9.99 *(978-0-06-058939-4(6))* 2005. 320p. (J). lib. bdg. 16.89 *(978-0-06-058938-7(8))* HarperCollins Pubs. (HarperTeen).

—Withering Tights. (Misadventures of Tallulah Casey Ser.: 1). (ENG.). (YA). (gr. 8). 2012. 304p. pap. 8.99 *(978-0-06-179933-4(5))* 2011. 288p. 16.99 *(978-0-06-179931-0(9))* HarperCollins Pubs. (HarperTeen).

Riding, Will. Ebenezer's Tale. 2008. (Illus.). 188p. pap. 14.49 *(978-1-4343-9694-5(0))* AuthorHouse.

Roberts, Scott A. The Rollicking Adventures of Tam O'Hare. Roberts, Scott A., illus. 2007. (ENG., Illus.). 228p. (J). (gr. 4-7). per. 16.95 *(978-1-60037-289-6(9))* Morgan James Publishing.

Rogger. The Fifty-Fifth Bear & the Awkward Rabbits: An Amazing Thick Blue Wood Bear Adventure. 2009. (Illus.). 60p. pap. 21.99 *(978-1-4389-1672-9(8))* AuthorHouse.

Rosoff, Meg. How I Live Now. (ENG.). (YA). (gr. 7). 2013. 208p. pap. 8.99 *(978-0-449-81960-9(4)*, Ember) 2006. 224p. reprint ed. pap. 8.99 *(978-0-553-37605-0(5)*, Lamb, Wendy Bks.) Random Hse. Children's Bks.

—Just in Case. 2008. (ENG.). 256p. (gr. 12-18). 14.00 *(978-0-452-28937-6(8)*, Penguin Books) Penguin Publishing Group.

Rowling, J. K. Harrius Potter et Camera Secretorum. Needham, Peter, tr. from ENG. 2007. (Harry Potter Ser.).Tr. of Harry Potter & the Chamber of Secrets. (LAT & ENG., Illus.). 288p. (YA). (gr. 5). 23.95 *(978-1-59990-067-4(X)*, 9781599900674, Bloomsbury USA Childrens) Bloomsbury Publishing USA.

—Harrius Potter et Philosophi Lapis. Needham, Peter, tr. from ENG. 2003. (Harry Potter Ser.).Tr. of Harry Potter & the Philosopher's Stone. (LAT & ENG., Illus.). 256p. (YA). (gr. 7). 29.99 *(978-1-58234-825-4(1)*, 9781582348254, Bloomsbury USA Childrens) Bloomsbury Publishing USA.

—Harry Potter à l'École des Sorciers. Menard, Jean-François, tr. from ENG. 2007. (Harry Potter Ser.: Year 1).Tr. of Harry Potter & the Sorcerer's Stone. 311p. (J). per. 14.95 *(978-2-07-061236-9(8))* Gallimard, Editions FRA. Dist: Distribooks, Inc.

—Harry Potter & the Chamber of Secrets. 2009. 9.64 *(978-0-7848-1444-4(9)*, Everbind) Marco Bk. Co.

—Harry Potter & the Chamber of Secrets. unabr. ed. 2004. (Harry Potter Ser.: Year 2). 352p. (J). (gr. 3-18). pap. 46.00 incl. audio *(978-0-8072-8207-6(3)*, S YA 137 SP, Listening Library) Random Hse. Audio Publishing Group.

—Harry Potter & the Chamber of Secrets. (Harry Potter Ser.: 2). (J). 2006. 1.25 *(978-1-4193-8079-2(6))* 2003. 78.75 *(978-1-4025-6698-1(0))* Recorded Bks., Inc.

—Harry Potter & the Chamber of Secrets. (Harry Potter Ser.: Year 2). (RUS., Illus.). 28.95 *(978-5-8451-0947-7(7))* Rosmen-Izdat RUS. Dist: Distribooks, Inc.

—Harry Potter & the Chamber of Secrets. Kay, Jim, illus. 2016. (Harry Potter Ser.: 2). (ENG.). 272p. (J). (gr. 3). 39.99 *(978-0-545-79132-8(4))*; 275.00 *(978-1-338-11986-2(9))* Scholastic, Inc. (Levine, Arthur A. Bks.).

—Harry Potter & the Chamber of Secrets. l.t. ed. 2003. (Harry Potter Ser.: Year 2). (ENG.). 466p. pap. 13.95 *(978-1-59413-001-4(9))* Thorndike Pr.

—Harry Potter & the Chamber of Secrets. 2013. (Harry Potter (Kazu Kibuishi Illustrations) Ser.: 2). lib. bdg. 24.50 *(978-0-606-32346-8(5)*, Turtleback) Turtleback Bks.

—Harry Potter & the Deathly Hallows. (Illus.). 2008. 832p. pap. *(978-0-7475-9586-1(0))* 2007. (ENG., 608p. *(978-0-7475-9106-1(7))* Bloomsbury Publishing Plc.

—Harry Potter & the Deathly Hallows. braille ed. 2007. (Harry Potter Ser.: Year 7). (J). (gr. 4-7). 34.99 *(978-0-939173-57-0(3))* National Braille Pr.

—Harry Potter & the Deathly Hallows. 2010. 25.00 *(978-1-60686-882-9(9))* Perfection Learning Corp.

—Harry Potter & the Deathly Hallows, 17 vols. 2007. (Harry Potter Ser.: 7). (YA). 129.79 *(978-1-4281-6654-7(8))*; 131.75 *(978-1-4281-6652-3(1))* Recorded Bks., Inc.

—Harry Potter & the Deathly Hallows. GrandPré, Mary, illus. (Harry Potter Ser.: 7). (ENG.). (J). 2009. 784p. (gr. 4-7). pap. 14.99 *(978-0-545-13970-0(8)*, Levine, Arthur A. Bks.) 2007. 784p. (gr. 5-9). 34.99 *(978-0-545-01022-1(5))* 2007. 816p. (gr. 4-7). 65.00 *(978-0-545-02937-7(6)*, Levine, Arthur A. Bks.) Scholastic, Inc.

—Harry Potter & the Deathly Hallows. l.t. ed. 2009. (ENG.). 970p. pap. 14.95 *(978-1-59413-355-8(7)*, Large Print Pr.) 2007. (Harry Potter Ser.: Year 7). (Illus.). 969p. (J). (gr. 4-7). 34.95 *(978-0-7862-9665-1(8))* Thorndike Pr.

—Harry Potter & the Deathly Hallows. (Harry Potter (Kazu Kibuishi Illustrations) Ser.: 7). 2013. lib. bdg. 29.40 *(978-0-606-32351-2(1))* 2009. lib. bdg. 26.95 *(978-0-606-00420-6(3))* Turtleback Bks. (Turtleback).

—Harry Potter & the Deathly Hallows. Bar-hillel, Gili, tr. from ENG. 2007. (Harry Potter Ser.: Year 7). (HEB., Illus.). 568p. (J). (gr. 4-7). pap. *(978-965-482-635-8(6))* Yediot Aharonot Bks., Miscal.

—Harry Potter & the Goblet of Fire. 2009. 10.24 *(978-0-7848-1587-8(9)*, Everbind) Marco Bk. Co.

—Harry Potter & the Goblet of Fire. (Harry Potter Ser.: 4). (J). 2006. 1.25 *(978-1-4193-8531-5(3))* 2003. 101.75 *(978-1-4025-6702-5(2))* Recorded Bks., Inc.

—Harry Potter & the Goblet of Fire. GrandPré, Mary, illus. l.t. ed. 2003. (Harry Potter Ser.: Vol. 4). (ENG.). 936p. pap. 11.66 *(978-1-59413-003-8(5))* Thorndike Pr.

—Harry Potter & the Goblet of Fire. 2013. (Harry Potter (Kazu Kibuishi Illustrations) Ser.: 4). lib. bdg. 26.95 *(978-0-606-32348-2(1)*, Turtleback) Turtleback Bks.

—Harry Potter & the Half-Blood Prince. 2005. (ENG.). cd-rom *(978-0-7475-8258-8(0))* Bloomsbury Publishing Plc.

—Harry Potter & the Half-Blood Prince, 9 vols. braille ed. 2005. (Harry Potter Ser.: Year 6). (J). (gr. 4-8). 29.99 *(978-0-939173-39-6(5)*, HALF) National Braille Pr.

—Harry Potter & the Half-Blood Prince. GrandPré, Mary, illus. 2006. (Harry Potter Ser.: Year 6). 652p. (gr. 4-8). 23.00 *(978-0-7569-6765-9(1))* Perfection Learning Corp.

—Harry Potter & the Half-Blood Prince. (Harry Potter Ser.: 6). (J). 2007. 1.25 *(978-1-4193-5430-4(2))* 2006. 110.75 *(978-1-4193-5436-6(1))* 2006. 193.75 *(978-1-4193-5432-8(9))* 2005. 113.75 *(978-1-4193-5434-2(5))* Recorded Bks., Inc.

—Harry Potter & the Half-Blood Prince. GrandPré, Mary, illus. (Harry Potter Ser.: 6). (ENG.). 672p. (J). (gr. 4-8). 2005. 29.99 *(978-0-439-78454-2(9))* 2006. reprint ed. per. 12.99 *(978-0-439-78596-9(0))* Scholastic, Inc. (Levine, Arthur A. Bks.).

—Harry Potter & the Half-Blood Prince. (Illus.). (J). (gr. 4-7). 2007. (ENG.). 832p. per. 14.95 *(978-1-59413-221-6(6))* 2005. (Harry Potter Ser.: Year 6). 831p. 29.95 *(978-0-7862-7745-2(9))* Thorndike Pr. (Large Print Pr.).

—Harry Potter & the Half-Blood Prince. 2013. (Harry Potter (Kazu Kibuishi Illustrations) Ser.: 6). lib. bdg. 26.95 *(978-0-606-32350-5(3)*, Turtleback) Turtleback Bks.

—Harry Potter & the Half Blood Prince - Chinese Language. 2005. (Harry Potter Ser.: Year 6). (CHI.). 496p. (YA). (gr. 4-8). pap. 28.95 *(978-7-02-005323-0(8)*, HAP06) People's Literature Publishing Hse. CHN. Dist: Chinasprout, Inc.

—Harry Potter & the Order of the Phoenix. (ENG.). 768p. (J). (gr. 6-10). pap. *(978-0-7475-6107-1(9))* Bloomsbury Publishing Plc.

—Harry Potter & the Order of the Phoenix. 2008. *(978-977-14-2697-4(4))* Nahdat Misr Bkshop for Printing and Pubs.

—Harry Potter & the Order of the Phoenix, 13 vols. braille ed. 2003. (Harry Potter Ser.: Year 5). (YA). 29.99 *(978-0-939173-38-9(7))* National Braille Pr.

—Harry Potter & the Order of the Phoenix. 2003. (Harry Potter Ser.: Year 5). (CHI.). 575p. (YA). pap. 26.95 *(978-7-02-004327-9(5)*, HAP05) People's Literature Publishing Hse. CHN. Dist: Chinasprout, Inc.

—Harry Potter & the Order of the Phoenix. 2004. (Harry Potter Ser.). 870p. (gr. 4-6). 16.49 *(978-0-7569-4163-5(6))* Perfection Learning Corp.

—Harry Potter & the Order of the Phoenix. 2003. (ENG.). 768p. *(978-1-55192-570-7(2))* Raincoast Bk. Distribution.

—Harry Potter & the Order of the Phoenix. GrandPré, Mary, illus. (Harry Potter Ser.: 5). (ENG.). (J). (gr. 3-7). 2004. 896p. mass mkt. 12.99 *(978-0-439-35807-1(8)*, Scholastic Paperbacks) 2003. 870p. 29.99 *(978-0-439-35806-4(X))* Scholastic, Inc.

—Harry Potter & the Order of the Phoenix. l.t. ed. 2003. (Harry Potter Ser.: Year 5). 1093p. 29.95 *(978-0-7862-5778-2(4)*, Large Print Pr.) Thorndike Pr.

—Harry Potter & the Order of the Phoenix. GrandPré, Mary, illus. l.t. ed. 2003. (Thorndike Young Adult Ser.). (ENG.). 1232p. (J). (gr. 4-7). per. 14.95 *(978-1-59413-112-7(0)*, Large Print Pr.) Thorndike Pr.

—Harry Potter & the Order of the Phoenix. (Harry Potter (Kazu Kibuishi Illustrations) Ser.: 5). 2013. lib. bdg. 26.95 *(978-0-606-32349-9(X))* 2004. lib. bdg. 24.50 *(978-0-613-99916-8(9))* Turtleback Bks. (Turtleback).

—Harry Potter & the Philosopher's Stone. 2014. (ENG., Illus.). 352p. *(978-1-4088-5589-8(5))* Bloomsbury Publishing Plc.

—Harry Potter & the Prisoner of Azkaban. 2009. 9.64 *(978-0-7848-1542-7(9)*, Everbind) Marco Bk. Co.

—Harry Potter & the Prisoner of Azkaban. 2005. (Harry Potter Ser.: Year 3). (CHI.). 260p. (YA). pap. 16.95 *(978-7-02-003345-4(8),* HAP03) People's Literature Publishing Hse. CHN. Dist: Chinasprout, Inc.

—Harry Potter & the Prisoner of Azkaban, 10 vols. 2003. (Harry Potter Ser.: 3). (J). 84.75 *(978-1-4025-6700-1(6))* Recorded Bks., Inc.

—Harry Potter & the Prisoner of Azkaban. l.t. ed. 2003. (Harry Potter Ser.: Year 3). (ENG.). 592p. pap. 13.95 *(978-1-59413-002-1(7),* Large Print Pr.) Thorndike Pr.

—Harry Potter & the Prisoner of Azkaban. 2013. (Harry Potter (Kazu Kibuishi Illustrations) Ser.: 3). lib. bdg. 24.50 *(978-0-606-32347-5(3),* Turtleback) Turtleback Bks.

—Harry Potter & the Sorcerer's Stone. 2014. (ENG.). lthr. 79.00 *(978-1-62715-772-8(7))* Leatherbound Bestsellers.

—Harry Potter & the Sorcerer's Stone. 2009. 8.44 *(978-0-7848-2438-2(X));* 10.84 *(978-0-7848-1357-7(4))* Marco Bk. Co. (Everbind).

—Harry Potter & the Sorcerer's Stone. 2003. (Harry Potter Ser.: Year 1). (CHI.). 191p. (YA). pap. 14.95 *(978-7-02-003343-0(1),* HAP01) People's Literature Publishing Hse. CHN. Dist: Chinasprout, Inc.

—Harry Potter & the Sorcerer's Stone. (Harry Potter Ser.: 1). (J). 2004. 1.25 *(978-1-4025-6757-5(X))* 2003. 80.75 *(978-1-4025-6696-7(4))* Recorded Bks., Inc.

—Harry Potter & the Sorcerer's Stone. Kay, Jim, illus. 2015. (Harry Potter Ser.: 1). (ENG.). 256p. (J). (gr. 3). 39.99 *(978-0-545-79035-2(2),* Levine, Arthur A. Bks.) Scholastic, Inc.

—Harry Potter & the Sorcerer's Stone, Bk. 1. 2013. (Harry Potter Ser.: 1). (ENG., Illus.). 336p. (J). (gr. 4). pap. 12.99 *(978-0-545-58288-9(1))* Scholastic, Inc.

—Harry Potter & the Sorcerer's Stone. 2013. (Harry Potter (Kazu Kibuishi Illustrations) Ser.: 1). lib. bdg. 24.50 *(978-0-606-32345-1(7),* Turtleback) Turtleback Bks.

—Harry Potter e a Camara Secreta. (Harry Potter Ser.: Year 2).Tr. of Harry Potter & the Chamber of Secrets. (POR.). pap. 28.95 *(978-85-325-1166-9(X))* Rocco, Editora, Ltda BRA. Dist: Distribooks, Inc.

—Harry Potter e a Pedra Filosofal. (Harry Potter Ser.: Year 1).Tr. of Harry Potter & the Philospher's Stone. (POR.). pap. 28.95 *(978-85-325-1101-0(5))* Rocco, Editora, Ltda BRA. Dist: Distribooks, Inc.

—Harry Potter e a Prisioneiro de Azkaban. (Harry Potter Ser.: Year 3).Tr. of Harry Potter & the Prisoner of Azkaban. (POR.). pap. 29.95 *(978-85-325-1206-2(2))* Rocco, Editora, Ltda BRA. Dist: Distribooks, Inc.

—Harry Potter e il Prigioniero di Azkaban. (Harry Potter Ser.: Year 3).Tr. of Harry Potter & the Prisoner of Azkaban. (ITA.). pap. 32.95 *(978-88-7782-852-1(8))* Salani ITA. Dist: Distribooks, Inc.

—Harry Potter e o Cálice de Fogo. (Harry Potter Ser.: Year 4).Tr. of Harry Potter & the Goblet of Fire. (POR.). pap. 38.95 *(978-85-325-1252-9(6))* Rocco, Editora, Ltda BRA. Dist: Distribooks, Inc.

—Harry Potter y el Prisionero de Azkaban. 2004. (Harry Potter Ser.: Year 3).Tr. of Harry Potter & the Prisoner of Azkaban. (SPA., Illus.). 360p. (gr. 3-18). 17.95 *(978-84-7888-519-0(6),* SAL1889) Emece Editores ESP. Dist: Lectorum Pubns., Inc.

—Harry Potter y la Camara Secreta. 2004. (Harry Potter Ser.: Year 2).Tr. of Harry Potter & the Chamber of Secrets. (SPA., Illus.). 288p. (YA). (gr. 3-18). 15.95 *(978-84-7888-495-7(5),* SAL4595) Emece Editores ESP. Dist: Lectorum Pubns., Inc.

—Harry Potter y la Piedra Filosofal. 2004. (Harry Potter Ser.: Year 1).Tr. of Harry Potter & the Sorcerer's Stone. (SPA., Illus.). 256p. (YA). (gr. 7-18). 15.95 *(978-84-7888-445-2(9),* SAL2819) Emece Editores ESP. Dist: Lectorum Pubns., Inc.

Rowling, J. K. & Scholastic, Inc. Staff. Harry Potter. 2007. (Harry Potter Ser.: Years 1-7). (ENG.). (J). (gr. 3-7). 205.93 *(978-0-545-04425-7(1),* Levine, Arthur A. Bks.) Scholastic, Inc.

Roy, Oscar. I Was Captured by Pirates. 2013. 110p. pap. 11.00 *(978-1-62212-790-0(0),* Strategic Bk. Publishing) Strategic Book Publishing & Rights Agency (SBPRA).

Rumford, James, illus. & retold by. Beowulf: A Hero's Tale Retold. Rumford, James, retold by. 2006. (J). *(978-0-399-24391-2(7))* Penguin Publishing Group.

Russell, Christopher & Russell, Christine. Warrior Sheep Go Jurassic. 2014. (Warrior Sheep Ser.). (ENG.). 256p. (J). (gr. 2-4). pap. 7.99 *(978-1-4052-6718-2(6))* Egmont Bks., Ltd. GBR. Dist: Independent Pubs. Group.

Sales, Leila. Once Was a Time: An Alliteration Adventure. 2016. (ENG., Illus.). 272p. (J). (gr. 5-17). 16.99 *(978-1-4521-4009-4(X))* Chronicle Bks. LLC.

Salzman, Jeremiah. Mike's Adventure Packs: England. Smith, Stephan, illus. 2010. (Mike's Adventure Packs Ser.). 144p. (J). pap. 16.95 *(978-0-9842632-5-7(X))* Scandora.

Sanderson, Jeanette. Robin Hood Shoots for the Queen: A Legend from England. 2006. (J). pap. *(978-1-4108-7167-1(3))* Benchmark Education Co.

Saunders, Kate. Magicalamity. 2013. (ENG.). 320p. (J). (gr. 4-7). 6.99 *(978-0-385-74078-4(6),* Yearling) Random Hse. Children's Bks.

Schott, Elizabeth, illus. Jake & Sam at the Empty Abbey. 2006. 96p. (J). per. 9.95 *(978-0-9724421-1-4(1))* Fountain Square Publishing.

Schroeder, Lisa. Sealed with a Secret. 2016. (ENG.). 224p. (J). (gr. 3-7). 16.99 *(978-0-545-90734-7(9),* Scholastic Pr.) Scholastic, Inc.

Scott, Michael. The Sorceress. (Secrets of the Immortal Nicholas Flamel Ser.: 3). (ENG.). 512p. (YA). (gr. 7-18). 2010. pap. 10.99 *(978-0-385-73530-8(8),* Ember) 2009. 17.99 *(978-0-385-73529-2(4),* Delacorte Bks. for Young Readers) Random Hse. Children's Bks.

—The Sorceress. 2010. (Secrets of the Immortal Nicholas Flamel Ser.: 3). lib. bdg. 22.10 *(978-0-606-14133-8(2),* Turtleback) Turtleback Bks.

—The Sorceress the Secrets of the Immortal Nicholas Flamel. l.t. ed. 2009. (Secrets of the Immortal Nicholas Flamel Ser.). (ENG.). 614p. (YA). 23.95 *(978-1-4104-2092-3(2))* Thorndike Pr.

Seabag-Montefiore, Mary, retold by. David Copperfield. 2008. (Young Reading Series 3 Gift Books - Famous Lives Ser.). 64p. (J). 8.99 *(978-0-7945-2097-7(9),* Usborne) EDC Publishing.

The Secret Garden. 2016. (Ladybird Classics Ser.). (ENG., Illus.). 72p. (J). (gr. 3-7). 8.99 *(978-1-4093-1126-3(0))* Penguin Bks., Ltd. GBR. Dist: Independent Pubs. Group.

Semionov, Vladimir & Louie, Wes, illus. Forecast from Stonehenge. 2007. (Choose Your Own Adventure Ser.: No. 19). 127p. (J). (gr. 4-7). pap. 6.99 *(978-1-933390-19-2(0))* Chooseco LLC.

Seven, John. The Outlaw of Sherwood Forest, 1 vol. Hans, Stephanie, illus. 2014. (Time-Tripping Faradays Ser.). (ENG.). 192p. (gr. 4-5). lib. bdg. 26.65 *(978-1-4342-9174-5(X))* Stone Arch Bks.

Sewell, Anna. Black Beauty. (J). 21.95 *(978-0-88411-065-1(6))* Amereon Ltd.

—Black Beauty. l.t. ed. 2010. (ENG.). 260p. pap. 22.95 *(978-1-4104-2390-0(5),* Kennebec Large Print) Cengage Gale.

—Black Beauty. (J). reprint ed. lib. bdg. 48.00 *(978-0-7426-1042-2(X))* Classic Bks.

—Black Beauty. 2008. (Bring the Classics to Life Ser.). (Illus.). 72p. (gr. 2-12). pap., act. bk. ed. 10.95 *(978-0-931334-51-1(9),* EDCTR201B) EDCON Publishing Group.

—Black Beauty. deluxe ed. 2005. (Charming Classics). 288p. (J). pap. 9.99 *(978-0-06-075770-0(1),* HarperFestival) HarperCollins Pubs.

—Black Beauty. (Illus.). 192p. (J). 9.95 *(978-1-56156-310-4(2))* Kidsbooks, LLC.

—Black Beauty, 2 vols., Set. l.t. ed. (YA). (gr. 8-18). reprint ed. 10.00 *(978-0-89064-017-3(3))* National Assn. for Visually Handicapped.

—Black Beauty. l.t. ed. 2004. (Large Print Ser.). 268p. 25.00 *(978-1-58287-619-1(3))* North Bks.

—Black Beauty. (J). 8.97 *(978-0-13-052329-7(1))* Prentice Hall PTR.

Shakespeare, William. Henry V: The Graphic Novel. 2010. (Classic Graphic Novel Collection). (ENG.). 160p. (gr. 7-12). 39.40 *(978-1-4205-0371-5(5))* Cengage Gale.

Shan, Darren, pseud. Zom-B, Vol. 8. 2014. (Zom-B Ser.: 8). (ENG., Illus.). 192p. (YA). (gr. 7-17). 15.99 *(978-0-316-21429-2(9))* Little, Brown Bks. for Young Readers.

—The Zom-B Chronicles #2. 2015. (Zom-B Ser.). (ENG., Illus.). 544p. (J). (gr. 7-17). pap. 13.00 *(978-0-316-30073-5(X))* Little, Brown Bks. for Young Readers.

Shaw, Sandy. The Adventures of Dilly Dog: Dilly at the Lakes. 2017. (ENG., Illus.). 16p. (J). pap. 13.95 **(978-1-78693-586-1(4),** 5d695943-b94e-4707-ab27-a18a86393def) Austin, Stan AUS. Dist: Bookmasters Distribution.

Shearer, Alex. Canned. 2008. (J). *(978-0-439-90310-3(6),* Scholastic Pr.) Scholastic, Inc.

Shields, Gillian. Eternal. (Immortal Ser.: 3). (ENG.). (YA). (gr. 8). 2012. 384p. pap. 9.99 *(978-0-06-200040-8(3))* 2011. 368p. 16.99 *(978-0-06-200039-2(X))* HarperCollins Pubs. (Tegen, Katherine Bks).

—Immortal. 2010. (Immortal Ser.: 1). (ENG.). 384p. (YA). (gr. 8). pap. 8.99 *(978-0-06-137583-5(7),* Tegen, Katherine Bks) HarperCollins Pubs.

Singleton, Jennifer. That magnificent Medallion. 2009. 66p. pap. 13.95 *(978-1-4452-0639-4(0))* Lulu Pr., Inc.

Skelton, Matthew. Endymion Spring. 2008. (ENG.). 416p. (YA). (gr. 7). pap. 9.99 *(978-0-385-73456-1(5),* Delacorte Bks. for Young Readers) Random Hse. Children's Bks.

Slahor, Stephenie. Tales from Merrie England I & Tales from Merrie England II, Vol. 2. 119p. (J). (gr. 3-5). 9.99 *(978-0-88092-262-3(1))* Royal Fireworks Publishing Co.

Sloane, Richard. Back to the Dark Ages! 2013. 138p. (gr. 4-6). 22.95 *(978-1-4669-7401-2(X));* pap. 12.95 *(978-1-4669-7399-2(4))* Trafford Publishing.

Smallman, Steve. Santa Is Coming to Birmingham. Dunn, Robert, illus. 2013. (ENG.). 32p. (J). (-3). 9.99 *(978-1-4022-9106-7(X),* Sourcebooks Jabberwocky) Sourcebooks, Inc.

—Santa Is Coming to Manchester. Dunn, Robert, illus. 2013. (ENG.). 32p. (J). (-3). 9.99 *(978-1-4022-9115-9(9),* Sourcebooks Jabberwocky) Sourcebooks, Inc.

Smedley, Frank E. Frank Fairlegh. 2008. 224p. pap. 15.95 *(978-1-60664-179-8(4));* 244p. pap. 15.95 *(978-1-60664-178-1(6))* Aegypan.

—Frank Fairlegh: Scenes from the Life of a Private Pupil. 2007. (ENG.). 570p. per. 30.99 *(978-1-4346-4557-9(6));* 640p. per. 45.75 *(978-1-4346-4558-6(4))* Creative Media Partners, LLC.

Smiley, Diane. Ollie. 2012. (Illus.). 40p. pap. 22.88 *(978-1-4772-1812-9(2))* AuthorHouse.

Snowe, Olivia. A Home in the Sky, 1 vol. Lamoreaux, Michelle, illus. 2013. (Twicetold Tales Ser.). (ENG.). 128p. (gr. 3-4). 8.95 *(978-1-4342-6279-0(0));* lib. bdg. 25.32 *(978-1-4342-5041-4(5))* Stone Arch Bks.

Standish, Burt L. Frank Merriwell in England. Rudman, Jack, ed. 2003. (Frank Merriwell Ser.). 29.95 *(978-0-8373-9344-5(2));* pap. 9.95 *(978-0-8373-9044-4(3))* Merriwell, Frank Inc.

Stanley, Malaika Rose. Dance Dreams. 2013. (ENG., Illus.). 144p. (J). (gr. 3-6). pap. 8.99 *(978-1-84853-055-3(2))* Transworld Publishers Ltd. GBR. Dist: Independent Pubs. Group.

Steel, Flora Annie. English Fairy Tales. 2007. (ENG.). 262p. pap. 21.99 *(978-1-4346-0692-1(9));* 296p. pap. 23.99 *(978-1-4346-0752-2(6))* Creative Media Partners, LLC.

Stein, Evaleen. Our Little Crusader Cousin of Long Ago. Meister, Charles E., illus. 2007. 136p. per. 8.95 *(978-1-59915-243-1(6))* Yesterday's Classics.

—Our Little Frankish Cousin of Long Ago. Landau, Helena Von & Meister, Charles, illus. 2007. 92p. per. 8.95 *(978-1-59915-244-8(4))* Yesterday's Classics.

Stevens, Robin. Murder Is Bad Manners. 2015. (Wells & Wong Mystery Ser.). (ENG., Illus.). 320p. (J). (gr. 5). 17.99 *(978-1-4814-2212-3(X),* Simon & Schuster Bks. For Young Readers) Simon & Schuster Bks. For Young Readers.

—Poison Is Not Polite. 2016. (Wells & Wong Mystery Ser.). (ENG., Illus.). 336p. (J). (gr. 5). 17.99 *(978-1-4814-2215-4(4),* Simon & Schuster Bks. For Young Readers) Simon & Schuster Bks. For Young Readers.

Stoker, Bram. Dracula. Kliros, Thea, illus. abr. ed. 2011. (Dover Children's Thrift Classics Ser.). (ENG.). 96p. (J). (gr. 3-8). reprint ed. pap. 4.00 *(978-0-486-29567-1(2))* Dover Pubns., Inc.

Stone Arch Books Staff. Jack & the Beanstalk: The Graphic Novel, 1 vol. Tercio, Ricardo, illus. 2008. (Graphic Spin Ser.). (ENG.). 40p. (gr. 1-3). pap. 5.95 *(978-1-4342-0862-0(1),* Graphic Revolve) Stone Arch Bks.

Stretton, Hesba. Jessica's First Prayer. 2006. 84p. pap. 9.95 *(978-1-59462-373-8(2),* 409, Book Jungle) Standard Pubns., Inc.

Stroud, Jonathan. Buried Fire. 2004. 332p. (J). pap. *(978-0-7818-5794-9(5))* Hippocrene Bks., Inc.

Sullivan, Laura L. Delusion. 2014. (ENG.). 352p. (YA). (gr. 7). pap. 18.99 *(978-0-544-10478-5(1))* Houghton Mifflin Harcourt Publishing Co.

—Under the Green Hill. 2011. (ENG.). 336p. (J). (gr. 4-8). pap. 17.99 *(978-0-312-55149-0(5),* 9780312551490) Square Fish.

Suzuma, Tabitha. Forbidden. (ENG.). 464p. (YA). (gr. 11). 2012. pap. 11.99 *(978-1-4424-1996-4(2))* 2011. 17.99 *(978-1-4424-1995-7(4))* Simon Pulse. (Simon Pulse).

Sylvester, Kevin. Neil Flambé & the Bard's Banquet. Sylvester, Kevin, illus. 2015. (Neil Flambe Capers Ser.: 5). (ENG., Illus.). 320p. (J). (gr. 3-7). 12.99 *(978-1-4814-1038-0(5),* Simon & Schuster Bks. For Young Readers) Simon & Schuster Bks. For Young Readers.

Syson, Lydia. That Burning Summer. 2017. (ENG.). 336p. (J). (gr. 6). 17.99 *(978-1-5107-1172-3(4),* Sky Pony Pr.) Skyhorse Publishing Co., Inc.

Tarasova, Julia. Daniel's Travels. 2008. 48p. 21.50 *(978-1-4357-1249-2(8))* Lulu Pr., Inc.

Tavner, Gill & Dickens, Charles. David Copperfield. Donnelly, Karen, illus. 2009. (Real Reads Ser.). 64p. (J). (gr. 4-8). pap. 13.55 *(978-1-60754-383-1(4))* Windmill Bks.

—Hard Times. Donnelly, Karen, illus. 2009. (Real Reads Ser.). 64p. (J). (gr. 4-8). pap. 13.55 *(978-1-60754-386-2(9))* Windmill Bks.

Taylor, G. P. The Shadowmancer Returns: The Curse of Salamander Street. 2008. (ENG.). 256p. (gr. 7-12). pap. 17.99 *(978-1-59979-084-8(X),* Realms) Charisma Media.

—The Shadowmancer Returns: The Curse of Salamander Street. 2007. (Shadowmancer; 04 Ser.). 240p. (J). *(978-1-4287-4670-1(6),* Putnam Juvenile) Penguin Publishing Group.

Teacher Created Resources Staff & Collins, Susan. A Guide for Using Time Soldiers in the Classroom. 2009. (ENG.). 48p. pap. 9.99 *(978-1-4206-2003-0(7))* Teacher Created Resources, Inc.

Terango, Christine. Teddy's Surprise Adventure. 2011. 24p. 12.95 *(978-1-4567-4069-6(5))* AuthorHouse.

Terry, Teri. The Book of Lies. 2017. (ENG.). 384p. (YA). (gr. 7). 17.99 **(978-0-544-90048-6(0),** Clarion Bks.) Houghton Mifflin Harcourt Trade & Reference Pubs.

—Fractured. 2014. (Slated Ser.: 2). (ENG.). 352p. (YA). (gr. 7). pap. 9.99 *(978-0-14-242504-6(4),* Speak) Penguin Young Readers Group.

—Shattered. (Slated Ser.: 3). (ENG.). (YA). (gr. 7). 2015. 336p. pap. 9.99 *(978-0-14-242507-7(9),* Speak) 2014. 320p. 17.99 *(978-0-399-16174-2(0),* Nancy Paulsen Books) Penguin Young Readers Group.

—Slated. 2013. (Slated Ser.: 1). (ENG.). 368p. (YA). (gr. 7). pap. 9.99 *(978-0-14-242503-9(6),* Speak) Penguin Young Readers Group.

Thame, Val. Witches in Trouble. l.t. ed. 2006. 104p. per. *(978-1-905665-27-3(X))* Pollinger In Print.

Thompson, Emma. The Christmas Tale of Peter Rabbit. Taylor, Eleanor, illus. 2013. (Peter Rabbit Ser.). (ENG.). 72p. (J). (gr. -1-2). 20.00 *(978-0-7232-7694-4(3),* Warne) Penguin Young Readers Group.

Thompson, Gareth. Sunshine to the Sunless. 2008. (ENG.). 256p. (YA). (gr. 7). pap. 11.99 *(978-1-86230-467-3(X))* Transworld Publishers Ltd. GBR. Dist: Independent Pubs. Group.

Thompson, Kate. La Musica del Tiempo. Delgado, Diana, tr. 2nd ed. 2007. (SPA., Illus.). 317p. (J). (gr. 4-7). 18.95 *(978-84-96544-97-0(4))* Roca Editorial ESP. Dist: Spanish Pubs., LLC.

Toft, Di. The Twilight Circus. 2011. (Wolven Ser.: 2). (ENG.). 384p. (J). (gr. 3-7). 17.99 *(978-0-545-29492-8(4),* Chicken Hse., The) Scholastic, Inc.

—Wolven, Bk. 1. 2011. (Wolven Ser.: 1). (ENG.). 352p. (J). (gr. 3-7). pap. 7.99 *(978-0-545-17110-6(5),* Chicken Hse., The) Scholastic, Inc.

Tracey, Rhian. When Isla Meets Luke Meets Isla. 2003. (ENG.). 224p. (YA). (gr. 7). pap. 12.95 *(978-0-7475-6344-0(6))* Bloomsbury Publishing Plc GBR. Dist: Independent Pubs. Group.

Travers, P. L. Mary Poppins in the Park. Shepard, Mary, illus. 2015. (Mary Poppins Ser.). (ENG.). 272p. (J). (gr. 5-7). pap. 6.99 *(978-0-544-51384-6(3),* HMH Books For Young Readers) Houghton Mifflin Harcourt Publishing Co.

—Mary Poppins Opens the Door. Shepard, Mary & Sims, Agnes, illus. 2015. (Mary Poppins Ser.). (ENG.). 256p. (J). (gr. 5-7). pap. 6.99 *(978-0-544-43958-0(9),* HMH Books For Young Readers) Houghton Mifflin Harcourt Publishing Co.

—Mary Poppins Vintage Boxed Set: Three Enchanting Classics: Mary Poppins, Mary Poppins Comes Back, & Mary Poppins Opens the Door. 2007. (Illus.). (J). 38.85 *(978-0-15-205858-6(3))* Harcourt Children's Bks.

Turnbull, Peter. Aftermath. l.t. ed. 2013. (Hennessey & Yellich Mystery Ser.: 21). (ENG.). 288p. *(978-0-7278-9602-5(4))* Severn Hse. Pubs., Ltd.

Turner, Suzy. The Temporal Stone: A Morgan Sisters Novel. 2013. 288p. pap. *(978-989-98351-0-8(2))* Turner, Suzanne.

Twain, Mark, pseud. The Prince & the Pauper. (J). 19.95 *(978-0-8488-0849-5(5))* Amereon Ltd.

—The Prince & the Pauper. (J). 9.95 *(978-1-56156-311-1(0))* Kidsbooks, LLC.

Unglick, Richard. Sherlock Holmes: the Hound of the Baskervilles. 2016. (Playmobil Ser.). (ENG.). 96p. (J). (gr. 1-7). 19.95 *(978-1-63322-078-2(8),* Walter Foster Jr) Quarto Publishing Group USA.

Vaughan, M. M. The Ability. Bruno, Iacopo, illus. (Ability Ser.). (ENG.). (YA). (gr. 3-7). 2014. 352p. pap. 6.99 *(978-1-4424-5201-5(3))* 2013. 336p. 15.99 *(978-1-4424-5200-8(5))* McElderry, Margaret K. Bks. (McElderry, Margaret K. Bks.).

—Mindscape. Bruno, Iacopo, illus. 2015. (Ability Ser.). (ENG.). 336p. (YA). (gr. 3-7). pap. 7.99 *(978-1-4424-5205-3(6),* McElderry, Margaret K. Bks.) McElderry, Margaret K. Bks.

Vaughan, M. M. & Caletti, Deb. The Last Forever. Bruno, Iacopo, illus. 2016. (ENG.). 352p. (YA). (gr. 7-7). pap. 10.99 *(978-1-4424-5002-8(9),* Simon & Schuster Bks. For Young Readers) Simon & Schuster Bks. For Young Readers.

Vicary, Tim. Grace Darling. Oxford University Press Staff & Bassett, Jennifer, eds. 3rd ed. 2008. (ENG., Illus.). 64p. 10.00 *(978-0-19-479061-1(4))* Oxford Univ. Pr., Inc.

Voorhoeve, Anne C. My Family for the War. Reichel, Tammi, tr. from GER. 2015. (ENG.). 416p. (YA). (gr. 7). pap. 9.99 *(978-0-14-751183-6(6),* Speak) Penguin Young Readers Group.

Wade, Rebecca. The Theft & the Miracle. 2007. 351p. (J). (gr. 4-7). lib. bdg. 17.89 *(978-0-06-077495-0(9))* HarperCollins Pubs.

—The Whispering House. 2012. (ENG.). 272p. (J). (gr. 3-7). 16.99 *(978-0-06-077497-4(5),* Tegen, Katherine Bks) HarperCollins Pubs.

Wakeham, Kate. Pride & Prejudice, 1 vol. Tempest, Annabel, illus. 2017. (ENG.). 30p. (J). 12.99 **(978-1-4236-4783-6(1))** Gibbs Smith, Publisher.

Walton, O. F. Christie's Old Organ or Home, Sweet Home. 2005. reprint ed. pap. 22.95 *(978-0-7661-9430-4(2))* Kessinger Publishing, LLC.

Wang, Holman & Wang, Jack. Charles Dickens's Great Expectations. 2016. (ENG., Illus.). 24p. (J). (gr. -1 — 1). bds. 9.95 *(978-1-4521-5243-1(8))* Chronicle Bks. LLC.

—Jane Austen's Pride & Prejudice. 2016. (ENG., Illus.). 24p. (J). (gr. -1 — 1). bds. 9.95 *(978-1-4521-5244-8(6))* Chronicle Bks. LLC.

Wang, Jack, et al. Jane Austen's Emma. 2016. (ENG., Illus.). 24p. (J). (gr. -1 — 1). bds. 9.95 *(978-1-4521-5255-4(1))* Chronicle Bks. LLC.

Ward, Rachel. Numbers. 2010. (Numbers Ser.: 1). (ENG.). 336p. (J). (gr. 7-12). 17.99 *(978-0-545-14299-1(7),* Chicken Hse., The) Scholastic, Inc.

Watson, Renée. This Side of Home. 2017. (ENG.). 352p. (YA). pap. 9.99 *(978-1-61963-930-0(0),* 9781619639300, Bloomsbury USA Childrens) Bloomsbury Publishing USA.

Weatherly, Lee. Child X. 2004. 211p. 16.00 *(978-0-7569-3211-4(4))* Perfection Learning Corp.

Weitz, Chris. The New Order. 2015. (Young World Ser.: 2). (ENG.). 320p. (YA). (gr. 10-17). 19.00 *(978-0-316-22630-1(0))* Little, Brown Bks. for Young Readers.

—The Revival. 2016. (Young World Ser.: 3). (ENG.). 272p. (YA). (gr. 10-17). 18.99 *(978-0-316-22634-9(3))* Little, Brown Bks. for Young Readers.

Wells, H. G. & Geary, Rick. The Invisible Man. (Classics Illustrated Ser.). (Illus.). 52p. (YA). pap. 4.95 *(978-1-57209-020-0(0))* Classics International Entertainment, Inc.

Westall, Robert. Blitzcat. 2015. (ENG.). 240p. (J). (gr. 4-6). pap. 8.99 *(978-1-4472-8460-4(7))* Pan Macmillan GBR. Dist: Independent Pubs. Group.

Weyn, Suzanne. The Titanic Locket. 2014. (Haunted Museum Ser.: 1). (ENG.). 208p. (J). (gr. 3-7). pap. 6.99 *(978-0-545-58842-3(1),* Scholastic Paperbacks) Scholastic, Inc.

—The Titanic Locket. 2014. (Hauntings: the Haunted Museum Ser.: 1). lib. bdg. 17.20 *(978-0-606-35809-5(9))* Turtleback Bks.

Whitaker, Sue. And Jake Makes Three. Ludlam, Jamie, illus. 2013. 108p. pap. *(978-1-907978-16-6(X))* ETA Publishing Hse.

—And Jake Makes Three & the Secret of Badlands. Ludlam, Jamie, illus. 2013. 92p. pap. *(978-1-907978-26-5(7))* ETA Publishing Hse.

—And Jake Makes Three in the Snow. Ludlam, Jamie, illus. 2013. 104p. pap. *(978-1-907978-21-0(6))* ETA Publishing Hse.

—And Jake Makes Three in the Vampires Den. Thomas-Brown, Cauline, ed. Ludlam, Jamie, illus. 2013. 86p. pap. *(978-1-907978-31-9(3))* ETA Publishing Hse.

Whitby, Adele. Beth's Story 1914. 2014. (Secrets of the Manor Ser.: 1). (ENG., Illus.). 160p. (J). (gr. 3-7). 16.99 *(978-1-4814-0632-1(9),* Simon Spotlight) Simon Spotlight.

Whitehouse, Howard. The Faceless Fiend: Being the Tale of a Criminal Mastermind, His Masked Minions & a Princess with a Butter Knife, Involving Explosives & a Certain Amount of Pushing & Shoving. Slavin, Bill, illus. 2007. (Mad Misadventures of Emmaline & Rubberbones Ser.). (ENG.). 272p. (J). (gr. 4-7). 7.95 *(978-1-55453-180-6(2))* Kids Can Pr., Ltd. CAN. Dist: Hachette Bk. Group.

Whybrow, Ian. The Unvisibles. 2006. 184p. (J). (gr. 4-7). 16.95 *(978-0-8234-1972-2(X))* Holiday Hse., Inc.

Whytock, Cherry. My Cup Runneth Over: The Life of Angelica Cookson Potts. Whytock, Cherry, illus. 2012. (ENG., Illus.). 192p. (YA). (gr. 7). pap. 9.99 *(978-1-4424-6055-3(5),* Simon Pulse) Simon Pulse.

—My Scrumptious Scottish Dumplings: The Life of Angelica Cookson Potts. Whytock, Cherry, illus. 2006. (ENG., Illus.). 192p. (YA). mass mkt. 5.99 *(978-0-689-86552-7(X),* Simon Pulse) Simon Pulse.

Wiggin, Kate Douglas. The Diary of a Goose Girl. 2007. 108p. per. 9.95 *(978-1-60312-330-3(X));* 22.95 *(978-1-60312-748-6(8))* Aegypan.

—The Diary of a Goose Girl. 2004. reprint ed. pap. 1.99 *(978-1-4192-5922-7(9))* Kessinger Publishing, LLC.

—The Diary of a Goose Girl. Shepperson, Claude A., illus. 2004. reprint ed. pap. 20.95 *(978-1-4179-1501-9(3))* Kessinger Publishing, LLC.

—Penelope's English Experiences. 2004. reprint ed. pap. 15.95 *(978-1-4191-4070-9(1));* pap. 1.99 *(978-1-4192-4070-6(6))* Kessinger Publishing, LLC.

Wilde, Oscar. The Canterville Ghost. Date not set. (Nelson Readers Ser.). (J). pap. *(978-0-17-557035-5(3))* Addison-Wesley Longman, Inc.

—The Canterville Ghost. Marks, Alan, illus. 2005. (Young Reading Ser.: Vol. 2). 64p. (J). (gr. 2-18). lib. bdg. 13.95 *(978-1-58086-781-8(2),* Usborne) EDC Publishing.

—The Canterville Ghost: Complete & Unabridged with Extensive Notes. annot. ed. 2013. (ENG.). 96p. pap. 4.99 *(978-93-5036-302-7(X))* Ratna, Sagar Pvt. Ltd. IND. Dist: Midpoint Trade Bks., Inc.

—The Picture of Dorian Gray, 2 vols. l.t. ed. (YA). (gr. 10-18). reprint ed. 10.00 *(978-0-89064-049-4(1))* National Assn. for Visually Handicapped.

Wilson, A. c. & Wilson, A. C. Ambersil - the Legacy of Mr Harrison. 2011. 496p. pap. *(978-1-908105-45-5(3))* Grosvenor Hse. Publishing Ltd.

Wilson, Jacqueline. Best Friends. Sharratt, Nick, illus. 2009. (ENG.). 256p. (J). (gr. 4-7). pap. 8.99 *(978-0-312-58144-2(0),* 9780312581442) Square Fish.

—Candyfloss. Sharratt, Nick, illus. 2008. (ENG.). 352p. (J). (gr. 4-7). pap. 9.99 *(978-0-312-38418-0(1),* 9780312384180) Square Fish.

Wiseman, David. Jeremy Visick. 2005. 176p. (YA). (gr. 5-18). 21.25 *(978-0-8446-7271-7(8),* 3594) Smith, Peter Pub., Inc.

Wodehouse, P. G. Mike at Wrykyn. 2013. 189p. reprint ed. lthr. 69.00 *(978-0-7426-3265-3(2))* Classic Bks.

Wood, Maryrose. The Hidden Gallery. Klassen, Jon, illus. 2011. (Incorrigible Children of Ashton Place Ser.: Bk. 2). (J). (gr. 3-7). 16.89 *(978-0-06-179114-7(8))* HarperCollins Pubs.

—The Incorrigible Children of Ashton Place Bk. 4: The Interrupted Tale. Wheeler, Eliza, illus. 2015. (Incorrigible Children of Ashton Place Ser.: 4). (ENG.). 400p. (J). (gr. 3-7). pap. 6.99 *(978-0-06-179123-9(7))* HarperCollins Pubs.

Wrede, Patricia C. Snow White & Rose Red. 2009. (ENG.). 288p. (YA). (gr. 7-18). 8.99 *(978-0-14-241121-6(3),* Firebird) Penguin Young Readers Group.

Young, Julian. The Daniel Model: Understanding the Pathway to Promotion & Power in the Kingdom of God. 2017. (ENG.). pap. 13.99 ***(978-0-9990279-9-8(9))*** Crown Media Publishing.

—The Peter Model: Understanding the Key That Unlock Maximum Kingdom Impact. 2017. (ENG.). pap. 14.99 ***(978-0-9990279-8-1(0))*** Crown Media Publishing.

Zamorsky, Tania & Burnett, Frances Hodgson. A Little Princess. Corvino, Lucy, illus. 2005. (Classic Starts(tm) Ser.). (ENG.). 160p. (J). (gr. 2-4). 6.95 *(978-1-4027-1275-3(8))* Sterling Publishing Co., Inc.

Zaugg, Sandy. Murdock Mystery #1: A House Called Fernley Manor. 2009. 103p. (J). pap. 10.95 *(978-1-4327-2914-1(4))* Outskirts Pr., Inc.

Zephaniah, Benjamin. Gangsta Rap. 2004. (ENG.). 336p. (YA). (gr. 9-13). pap. 8.99 *(978-1-58234-886-5(3),* 9781582348865, Bloomsbury USA Childrens) Bloomsbury Publishing USA.

ENGLAND—HISTORY

see Great Britain—History

ENGLISH AUTHORS

see Authors, English

ENGLISH COMPOSITION

see English Language—Composition and Exercises

ENGLISH DRAMA

see also Bible Plays

Pullman, Philip. His Dark Materials. rev. ed. 2005. (ENG.). 192p. per. 20.95 *(978-1-85459-831-8(7))* Hern, Nick Bks., Ltd. GBR. Dist: Consortium Bk. Sales & Distribution.

Shakespeare, William & SparkNotes Staff. Twelfth Night. Crowther, John, ed. 2003. (No Fear Shakespeare Ser.). (ENG., Illus.). 256p. pap. 5.95 *(978-1-58663-851-1(3),* Spark Notes) Sterling Publishing Co., Inc.

Umansky, Kaye. Cinderella: Photocopiable Plays. 2nd unabr. ed. 2003. (Curtain Up Ser.: Vol. 5). (ENG., Illus.). 48p. (J). (gr. 1-4). pap. *(978-0-7136-4341-1(2),* A&C Black) Bloomsbury Publishing Plc.

ENGLISH FOR FOREIGNERS

see English Language—Textbooks for Foreign Speakers

ENGLISH HISTORY

see Great Britain—History

ENGLISH LANGUAGE

Ackland, Nick. First Words. Bradley, Jennie, illus. 2016. (Baby Sparkler Ser.). (ENG.). 10p. (J). (gr. -1 — 1). bds. 5.99 *(978-0-7641-6856-7(8))* Barron's Educational Series, Inc.

ACT English Victory Student Textbook. 2nd ed. 2005. per. *(978-1-58894-032-2(2))* Cambridge Educational Services, Inc.

Allen, Kathy. Ancient Egyptian Hieroglyphs, 1 vol. 2012. (Ancient Egyptian Civilization Ser.). (ENG.). 32p. (gr. 3-4). lib. bdg. 27.32 *(978-1-4296-7627-4(2),* Fact Finders) Capstone Press of Coughlan Cos.

American Museum of Natural History Staff. ABC Dinosaurs. Hartman, Scott, illus. 2011. (AMNH ABC Board Bks.). (ENG.). 18p. (J). (gr. -1-k). bds. 7.95 *(978-1-4027-7715-8(9))* Sterling Publishing Co., Inc.

Amery, Heather & Cartwright, Stephen. Céad Focal: The First Hundred Words. 2003. (GLE & IRI., Illus.). 36p. (J). pap. 18.00 *(978-0-7171-3580-6(2))* M.H. Gill & Co. U. C. IRL. Dist: Dufour Editions, Inc.

Analogies & Multiple Meanings (Gr. 4-5) 2004. (J). *(978-1-58232-139-4(6))* ECS Learning Systems, Inc.

Antarctica. (J). pap. 19.39 *(978-0-8136-3619-1(1))* Modern Curriculum Pr.

Aracich, Charles. TIME for Kids: Practicing for Today's Tests Language Arts Level 4. 2015. (Test Preparation for Reading Comp Ser.). (ENG., Illus.). 112p. (gr. 4-4). pap. 24.99 *(978-1-4258-1437-3(9))* Shell Educational Publishing.

Axton-Higgs, Rachel. English Grammar, Punctuation & Spelling Test: Revision & Practice. 2nd rev. ed. 2016. (ENG.). 240p. (J). (gr. 5-6). pap. 155.00 *(978-0-00-817328-9(1))* HarperCollins Pubs. Ltd. GBR. Dist: Independent Pubs. Group.

Ayotte-Irwin, Tracy & Jordan, Sara. Bilingual Songs - English-French, 2 vols., Vol. 2. 2003. (Bilingual Song English-French Ser.: 2). (FRE., Illus.). 48p. (J). 17.95 *(978-1-894262-80-4(8),* 1894262808) Jordan, Sara Publishing.

Bajaj, Varsha. T Is for Taj Mahal: An India Alphabet. Crawford, Robert, illus. 2011. (Discover the World Ser.). (ENG.). 40p. (J). (gr. k-6). 17.95 *(978-1-58536-504-3(1))* Sleeping Bear Pr.

—T Is for Taj Mahal: An India Alphabet. 2016. (Av2 Fiction Readalong 2017 Ser.). (ENG.). (J). (gr. k-6). 34.28 ***(978-1-4896-5227-0(2),*** AV2 by Weigl) Weigl Pubs., Inc.

Barchers, Suzanne. TIME for Kids: Practicing for Today's Tests Language Arts Level 6. 2015. (Test Preparation for Reading Comp Ser.). (ENG., Illus.). 120p. (gr. 6-6). pap. 24.99 *(978-1-4258-1439-7(5))* Shell Educational Publishing.

Barney Malloon's Balloon: 3-in-1 Package. (Sails Literacy Ser.). 24p. (gr. 2-18). 57.00 *(978-0-7578-3212-3(1))* Rigby Education.

Barney Malloon's Balloon: 6 Small Books. (Sails Literacy Ser.). 24p. (gr. 2-18). 25.00 *(978-0-7578-3188-1(5))* Rigby Education.

Battistoni, I. At the Zoo: Learning the Z Sound. 2009. (PowerPhonics Ser.). 24p. (gr. 1-1). 39.90 *(978-1-60851-433-5(1),* PowerKids Pr.) Rosen Publishing Group, Inc., The.

Beck, Ray, et al. Practicing Basic Skills in Language Arts. 2005. (Illus.). 584p. per. 59.95 *(978-1-59318-271-7(6))* Cambium Education, Inc.

Beckwith, Carrie, et al. Editor in Chief A2: Grammar Disasters & Punctuation Faux Pas. 2012. (Editor in Chief Ser.). (Illus.). 72p. (gr. 4-5). pap. 14.99 *(978-0-89455-719-4(X),* MP9704) Critical Thinking Co., The.

Belasco, Susan. Constructing Literacies. pap. 65.95 *(978-0-8384-9227-7(4))* Cengage Heinle.

Berry, Shilo. E-Mails Home. 2008. (Illus.). 24p. (J). pap. 10.95 *(978-1-59646-565-7(4))* Dingles & Co.

Big Book of English & Math. 2003. (Bumper Gold Stars Ser.). (Illus.). 240p. (J). 9.98 *(978-1-4054-1720-4(X));* 9.98 *(978-1-4054-1719-8(6))* Parragon, Inc.

Big Book Package, 6 bks., Set. 2004. (gr. 2-18). 218.30 *(978-0-673-61067-6(5))* Addison-Wesley Educational Pubs., Inc.

Big Books Package 1.2, 6 bks., Set. 2004. (gr. 1-18). 218.30 *(978-0-673-59062-6(3))* Addison-Wesley Educational Pubs., Inc.

Big Books Package 1.3-1.6, 4 bks., Set. 2004. (gr. 1-18). 145.55 *(978-0-673-59063-3(1))* Addison-Wesley Educational Pubs., Inc.

Blachowicz, Camille L. Z. Reading Fluency. 2004. (JT: READING RATE & FLUENCY Ser.). (ENG.). (gr. 6-12). 74p. pap. 17.04 *(978-0-07-861713-3(8),* 0078617138); 36p. pap. 24.64 *(978-0-07-861710-2(3),* 0078617103) McGraw-Hill Cos., The.

Blackstone, Stella. Zoe & Her Zebra. Beaton, Clare, illus. 2011. (ENG.). 32p. (J). (gr. -1-2). pap. 6.99 *(978-1-84686-536-7(0))* Barefoot Bks., Inc.

Blake, Quentin. Quentin Blake's ABC. 2013. (ENG., Illus.). 32p. (J). (-k). pap. 12.99 *(978-1-84941-688-7(5),* Red Fox) Random House Children's Books GBR. Dist: Independent Pubs. Group.

Bleiman, Andrew & Eastland, Chris. ABC ZooBorns! 2013. (ZooBorns Ser.). (ENG., Illus.). 40p. (J). (gr. -1 — 1). bds. 7.99 *(978-1-4424-7376-6(2),* Little Simon) Little Simon.

Body, Wendy. Meebie's Magic Box. 2006. (Qeb Fun with Phonics Ser.). (Illus.). 24p. (J). (gr. -1-3). lib. bdg. 15.95 *(978-1-59566-221-7(9))* QEB Publishing Inc.

Bogard, Jennifer M. Strategies to Integrate the Arts in Language Arts, 1 vol. rev. ed. 2013. (Strategies to Integrate the Arts Ser.). (ENG., Illus.). 256p. (gr. k-12). pap. 45.99 *(978-1-4258-1090-0(X))* Shell Educational Publishing.

Book Company, Popular. Complete English Workout, Volume 1. 2008. 271p. pap. *(978-1-897164-51-8(3))* Popular Bk. Co. (Canada) Ltd.

—Complete English Workout, Volume 4. 2008. 271p. pap. *(978-1-897164-54-9(8))* Popular Bk. Co. (Canada) Ltd.

—Complete English Workout, Volume 5. 2008. 271p. pap. *(978-1-897164-55-6(6))* Popular Bk. Co. (Canada) Ltd.

Boyden, Linda. Giveaways: An ABC Book of Loanwords from the Americas. 2010. (ENG., Illus.). 74p. (J). (gr. 3-6). 19.95 *(978-0-8263-4726-8(6))* Univ. of New Mexico Pr.

Broadbent, Paul, et al. Maths & English, Age 9-10. 2015. (Letts KS2 Success Ser.). (ENG., Illus.). 128p. (J). (gr. 4-5). pap. 12.95 *(978-1-84419-857-3(X))* HarperCollins Pubs. Ltd. GBR. Dist: Independent Pubs. Group.

Brock, Paula. Nudges. 2004. 113p. pap. 12.95 *(978-1-888842-31-9(8))* Absey & Co.

Brooks, Felicity. Goodnight Baby. 2005. (Busy Baby Board Books Ser.). 10p. (J). 8.95 *(978-0-7945-0874-6(X),* Usborne) EDC Publishing.

Brown, Margaret Wise. Goodnight Moon ABC: An Alphabet Book. Hurd, Clement, illus. 2010. (ENG.). (J). (gr. -1-k). 30p. bds. 8.99 *(978-0-06-189490-9(7),* HarperFestival); 32p. 16.99 *(978-0-06-189484-8(2))* HarperCollins Pubs.

BRWL2003. Letterbook 1 10 Pack: Replacement Components. 2003. (Elementary Begin Read, Write & Listen Ser.). (ENG.). (gr. k-k). pap. 43.88 *(978-0-02-190825-7(7),* 0021908257) Macmillan/McGraw-Hill Schl. Div.

—Letterbook 11 10 Pack: Replacement Components. 2003. (Elementary Begin Read, Write & Listen Ser.). (ENG.). (gr. k-k). pap. 43.88 *(978-0-02-190835-6(4),* 0021908354) Macmillan/McGraw-Hill Schl. Div.

—Letterbook 12 10 Pack: Replacement Components. 2003. (Elementary Begin Read, Write & Listen Ser.). (ENG.). (gr. k-k). pap. 43.88 *(978-0-02-190836-3(2),* 0021908362) Macmillan/McGraw-Hill Schl. Div.

—Letterbook 13 10 Pack: Replacement Components. 2003. (Elementary Begin Read, Write & Listen Ser.). (ENG.). (gr. k-k). pap. 43.88 *(978-0-02-190837-0(0),* 0021908370) Macmillan/McGraw-Hill Schl. Div.

—Letterbook 14 10 Pack: Replacement Components. 2003. (Elementary Begin Read, Write & Listen Ser.). (ENG.). (gr. k-k). pap. 43.88 *(978-0-02-190838-7(9),* 0021908389) Macmillan/McGraw-Hill Schl. Div.

—Letterbook 15 10 Pack: Replacement Components. 2003. (Elementary Begin Read, Write & Listen Ser.). (ENG.). (gr. k-k). pap. 43.88 *(978-0-02-190839-4(7),* 0021908397) Macmillan/McGraw-Hill Schl. Div.

—Letterbook 16 10 Pack: Replacement Components. 2003. (Elementary Begin Read, Write & Listen Ser.). (ENG.). (gr. k-k). pap. 43.88 *(978-0-02-190840-0(0),* 0021908400) Macmillan/McGraw-Hill Schl. Div.

—Letterbook 18 10 Pack: Replacement Components. 2003. (Elementary Begin Read, Write & Listen Ser.). (ENG.). (gr. k-k). pap. 43.88 *(978-0-02-190842-4(7),* 0021908427) Macmillan/McGraw-Hill Schl. Div.

—Letterbook 19 10 Pack: Replacement Components. 2003. (Elementary Begin Read, Write & Listen Ser.). (ENG.). (gr. k-k). pap. 43.88 *(978-0-02-190843-1(5),* 0021908435) Macmillan/McGraw-Hill Schl. Div.

—Letterbook 2 10 Pack: Replacement Components. 2003. (Elementary Begin Read, Write & Listen Ser.). (ENG.). (gr. k-k). pap. 43.88 *(978-0-02-190826-4(5),* 0021908265) Macmillan/McGraw-Hill Schl. Div.

—Letterbook 20 10 Pack: Replacement Components. 2003. (Elementary Begin Read, Write & Listen Ser.). (ENG.). (gr. k-k). pap. 43.88 *(978-0-02-190844-8(3),* 0021908443) Macmillan/McGraw-Hill Schl. Div.

—Letterbook 22 10 Pack: Replacement Components. 2003. (Elementary Begin Read, Write & Listen Ser.). (ENG.). (gr. k-k). pap. 43.88 *(978-0-02-190846-2(X),* 002190846X) Macmillan/McGraw-Hill Schl. Div.

—Letterbook 23 10 Pack: Replacement Components. 2003. (Elementary Begin Read, Write & Listen Ser.). (ENG.). (gr. k-k). pap. 43.88 *(978-0-02-190847-9(8),* 0021908478) Macmillan/McGraw-Hill Schl. Div.

—Letterbook 24 10 Pack: Replacement Components. 2003. (Elementary Begin Read, Write & Listen Ser.). (ENG.). (gr. k-k). pap. 43.88 *(978-0-02-190848-6(6),* 0021908486) Macmillan/McGraw-Hill Schl. Div.

—Letterbook 4 10 Pack: Replacement Components. 2003. (Elementary Begin Read, Write & Listen Ser.). (ENG.). (gr. k-k). pap. 43.88 *(978-0-02-190828-8(1),* 0021908281) Macmillan/McGraw-Hill Schl. Div.

—Letterbook 7 10 Pack: Replacement Components. 2003. (Elementary Begin Read, Write & Listen Ser.). (ENG.). (gr. k-k). pap. 43.88 *(978-0-02-190831-8(1),* 0021908311) Macmillan/McGraw-Hill Schl. Div.

—Letterbook 9 10 Pack: Replacement Components. 2003. (Elementary Begin Read, Write & Listen Ser.). (ENG.). (gr. k-k). pap. 43.88 *(978-0-02-190833-2(8),* 0021908338) Macmillan/McGraw-Hill Schl. Div.

Building Dreams, Grade 3: American Readers. (J). tchr. ed., wbk. ed. *(978-0-669-05019-6(9));* wbk. ed. *(978-0-669-05018-9(0))* Houghton Mifflin Harcourt School Pubs.

Bull, Andrea & Bull, Robert J. Animal Appetites: A Book of Unusual ABCs. Bull, Andrea & Bull, Robert J., illus. 2015. (ENG., Illus.). 40p. pap. 10.95 *(978-0-9948622-0-4(2))* Bk.Baby Print.

Bulloch, Ivan & James, Diane. Learn with Me ABC. Pangbourne, Daniel, photos by. 2007. (ENG., Illus.). 45p. (J). (gr. -1-3). pap. 6.95 *(978-1-58728-599-8(1))* Cooper Square Publishing Llc.

Bunches of Sentence Fun - 2. 2004. (YA). ring bd. 59.95 *(978-1-58804-376-4(2))* P C I Education.

Burg, Ann. E Is for Empire: A New York State Alphabet. Brookfield, Maureen, illus. 2003. (Discover America State by State Ser.). (ENG.). 40p. (J). 17.95 *(978-1-58536-113-7(5))* Sleeping Bear Pr.

Burke, David. BEAUTY & the BEAST (Japanese to English - Level 3) Learn ENGLISH Through Fairy Tales. 2007. (JPN & ENG.). (J). per. 14.95 incl. audio compact disk *(978-1-891888-05-2(6))* Slangman Publishing.

—La Bella y la Bestia: Nivel 3: Aprende Ingles con Cuentos de Hadas. Redoles, Marcela, tr. Sandoval, Migs, illus. 2006. (Slangman para Ninos: Nivel 3 Ser.). (SPA & ENG.). 29p. (J). (gr. -1-3). pap. 14.95 incl. audio compact disk *(978-1-891888-97-7(8))* Slangman Publishing.

—La Cenicienta: Nivel 1: Aprende Ingles con Cuentos de Hadas. Bobrick, Julie, ed. Redoles, Marcela, tr. Sandoval, Migs, illus. 2006. (Slangman para Ninos: Nivel 1 Ser.). (SPA & ENG.). 29p. pap. 14.95 incl. cd-rom *(978-1-891888-95-3(1))* Slangman Publishing.

—CINDERELLA (Japanese to English - Level 1) Learn ENGLISH Through Fairy Tales. 2007. (JPN & ENG.). (J). per. 14.95 incl. audio compact disk *(978-1-891888-03-8(X))* Slangman Publishing.

—CINDERELLA (Korean to English - Level 1) Learn ENGLISH Through Fairy Tales. 2007. (KOR & ENG.). (J). per. 14.95 incl. audio compact disk *(978-1-891888-07-6(2))* Slangman Publishing.

Burr, Holly. An a-Bee-Sea Book. Abremski, Kathy, illus. 2012. 28p. pap. 14.95 *(978-1-61493-040-2(6))* Peppertree Pr., The.

Buzz & Bingo in the Monster Maze. 2012. (Collins Big Cat Ser.). (ENG.). 16p. (J). pap., wbk. ed. 4.99 *(978-0-00-747387-8(7))* HarperCollins Pubs. Ltd. GBR. Dist: Independent Pubs. Group.

Callaghan, Melissa. TIME for Kids: Practicing for Today's Tests Language Arts Level 2. 2015. (Test Preparation for Reading Comp Ser.). (ENG., Illus.). 112p. (gr. 2-2). pap. 24.99 *(978-1-4258-1474-8(3))* Shell Educational Publishing.

Carlson, Lavelle. The Fable of Mable with a Ladle at the Table: A Phonemic Awareness Tale. 2003. (Illus.). 32p. (J). per. 16.95 *(978-0-9725803-1-0(X))* Children's Publishing.

Carroll, Joyce Armstrong, et al. Writing & Grammar: Communication in Action, 3 vols. 2003. (ENG.). 952p. (YA). (gr. 6-6). 476.00 *(978-0-13-037483-7(0))* Prentice Hall Pr.

Cars. 2012. (Collins Big Cat Ser.). (ENG.). 64p. (J). pap., wbk. ed. 4.99 *(978-0-00-747497-4(0))* HarperCollins Pubs. Ltd. GBR. Dist: Independent Pubs. Group.

Carson-Dellosa Publishing Staff, compiled by. Early Skills, Grade 1. 2013. (Complete Ser.). (ENG.). 352p. (gr. 1-1). pap. 14.95 *(978-1-62399-096-1(3))* Carson-Dellosa Publishing, LLC.

—Early Skills, Grade K. 2013. (Complete Ser.). (ENG.). 352p. (gr. k-k). pap. 14.95 *(978-1-62399-095-4(5))* Carson-Dellosa Publishing, LLC.

—Early Skills, Grade PK. 2013. (Complete Ser.). (ENG.). 352p. (gr. -1 — 1). pap. 14.95 *(978-1-62399-094-7(7))* Carson-Dellosa Publishing, LLC.

Case, Jessica. TIME for Kids: Practicing for Today's Tests Language Arts Level 5. 2015. (Test Preparation for Reading Comp Ser.). (ENG., Illus.). 112p. (gr. 5-5). pap. 24.99 *(978-1-4258-1438-0(7))* Shell Educational Publishing.

Charlesworth, Liza. Sight Word Songs. 2017. (ENG., Illus.). 26p. (gr. k-2). 26.99 *(978-1-338-11313-6(5))* Scholastic, Inc.

Claire, Elizabeth. Help Your Buddy Learn English, Bk. 1. Nichols, Dave, illus. l.t. ed. 2003. 64p. 15.00 *(978-0-937630-04-4(7))* Eardley Pubns.

Cleary, Brian. Slide & Slurp, Scratch & Burp: More about Verbs. Gable, Brian, illus. 2009. (Words Are CATegorical (r) Ser.). (ENG.). 32p. (gr. 2-5). pap. 6.95 *(978-1-58013-935-9(3),* First Avenue Editions) Lerner Publishing Group.

Cleary, Brian P. Cool! Whoa! Ah & Oh! What Is an Interjection? Gable, Brian, illus. (Words Are CATegorical (r) Ser.). (ENG.). 32p. (gr. 2-5). 2013. pap. 6.95 *(978-1-4677-0900-2(X),* Millbrook Pr.) 2011. 16.95 *(978-1-58013-594-8(3))* Lerner Publishing Group.

—Dearly, Nearly, Insincerely: What Is an Adverb? Gable, Brian, illus. 2003. (Words Are CATegorical (r) Ser.). (ENG.). 32p. (gr. 2-5). 16.95 *(978-0-87614-924-9(7))* Lerner Publishing Group.

—Feet & Puppies, Thieves & Guppies: What Are Irregular Plurals? Gable, Brian, illus. 2014. (Words Are CATegorical (r) Ser.). (ENG.). 32p. (gr. 2-5). pap. 6.95 *(978-1-4677-2627-6(3),* Millbrook Pr.) Lerner Publishing Group.

—I'm & Won't, They're & Don't: What's a Contraction? Gable, Brian, illus. (Words Are CATegorical (r) Ser.). (ENG.). 32p. (gr. 2-5). 2012. pap. 6.95 *(978-0-7613-8504-2(5),* Millbrook Pr.) 2010. (J). lib. bdg. 16.95 *(978-0-8225-9155-9(3))* Lerner Publishing Group.

—Lazily, Crazily, Just a Bit Nasally: More about Adverbs. Gable, Brian, illus. 2010. (Words Are CATegorical (r) Ser.). (ENG.). 32p. (gr. 2-5). pap. 6.95 *(978-1-58013-937-3(X),* First Avenue Editions) Lerner Publishing Group.

—The Peaches on the Beaches. Miskimins, Jason, illus. 2009. (Sounds Like Reading (r) Ser.: 7). (ENG.). (gr. -1-2). pap. 39.62 *(978-0-7613-4706-4(2))* Lerner Publishing Group.

—Pre- & Re-, Mis- & Dis- What Is a Prefix? Goneau, Martin, illus. 2013. (Words Are CATegorical (r) Ser.). (ENG.). 32p. (J). (gr. 2-5). lib. bdg. 16.95 *(978-0-7613-9031-2(6),* Millbrook Pr.) Lerner Publishing Group.

—Slide & Slurp, Scratch & Burp: More about Verbs. Gable, Brian, illus. 2006. (Words Are CATegorical (r) Ser.). (ENG.). (gr. 2-5). pap. 39.62 *(978-0-7613-4815-3(8))* Lerner Publishing Group.

—They're There on Their Vacation. Paillot, Jim, illus. 2015. (ENG.). 32p. (J). (gr. 2-5). 26.65 *(978-1-4677-8847-2(3),* Millbrook Pr.) Lerner Publishing Group.

—Thumbtacks, Earwax, Lipstick, Dipstick: What Is a Compound Word? Gable, Brian, illus. (Words Are CATegorical (r) Ser.). (ENG.). 32p. (gr. 2-5). 2013. pap. 6.95 *(978-1-4677-1379-5(1))* 2011. lib. bdg. 16.95 *(978-0-7613-4917-4(0))* Lerner Publishing Group. (Millbrook Pr.).

Cleary, Brian P. & Maday, Alice M. The Peaches on the Beaches: A Book about Inflectional Endings. Miskimins, Jason, illus. 2009. (Sounds Like Reading (r) Ser.: 7). (ENG.). 32p. (gr. -1-2). lib. bdg. 23.93 *(978-0-8225-7636-5(8))* Lerner Publishing Group.

—Sounds Like Reading, 8 vols., Set. Miskimins, Jason, illus. Incl. Bug in the Jug Wants a Hug: A Short Vowel Sounds Book. lib. bdg. 23.93 *(978-0-7613-9503-4(2));* Clown in the Gown Drives the Car with the Star: A Book about Diphthongs & R-Controlled Vowel. lib. bdg. 23.93 *(978-0-8225-7637-2(6));* Frail Snail on the Trail: Long Vowel Sounds with Consonant Blends. lib. bdg. 23.93 *(978-0-8225-7638-9(4));* Nice Mice in the Rice: A Long Vowel Sound Book. lib. bdg. 23.93 *(978-0-8225-7628-0(7));* Peaches on the Beaches: A Book about Inflectional Endings. lib. bdg. 23.93 *(978-0-8225-7636-5(8));* Stop, Drop, & Flop in the Slop: A Short Vowel Sounds Book with Consonant Blends. lib. bdg. 23.93 *(978-0-8225-7635-8(X));* Thing on the Wing Can Sing: Short Vowel Sounds & Consonant Digraphs. lib. bdg. 23.93 *(978-0-8225-7639-6(2));* Whose Shoes Would You Choose? A Long Vowel Sounds Book with Consonant Digraphs. lib. bdg. 23.93 *(978-0-8225-7640-2(6));* (Illus.). 32p. (gr. -1-2). 2009. lib. bdg. *(978-0-7613-9502-7(4),* Millbrook Pr.) Lerner Publishing Group.

Cline, Mike & Yi-Cline, Nancy. Franky Fox's Fun with English Activity Book, Level A1. Yi-Cline, Nancy, ed. Cline, Mike, illus. 2007. (Illus.). 62p. pap. 7.99 *(978-0-9777419-1-5(5),* SIAB) Lingo Pr. LLC.

—Franky Fox's Fun with English Level A1. Yi-Cline, Nancy, ed. Cline, Mike, illus. 2007. (Illus.). 65p. 14.99 *(978-0-9777419-0-8(7),* SITB) Lingo Pr. LLC.

—Franky Fox's Fun with English Resource Guide Level A1. 2007. (Illus.). 120p. ring bd. 24.99 *(978-0-9777419-4-6(X))* Lingo Pr. LLC.

Clink! Clink! Clink!, 6 vols. 8p. (gr. k-1). 21.50 *(978-0-322-02057-3(3))* Wright Group/McGraw-Hill.

Coirault, Christine. Alphabet. 2008. (Gymboree Play & Music Ser.). (ENG., Illus.). 26p. (gr. -1). bds. *(978-1-55470-031-8(0))* Magma.

Cole, John O. Plugged in to English: English & Language Arts Activities for the Computer Lab. 2003. (ENG., Illus.). 144p. pap. 28.95 *(978-1-877673-60-3(9),* PI-BWK03) Cottonwood Pr., Inc.

Collins Easy Learning Staff, et al. Comprehension, Ages 7-9. 2015. (Collins Easy Learning Ser.). (ENG.). 32p. (J). (gr. 2-4). pap. 6.95 *(978-0-00-813427-3(8))* HarperCollins Pubs. Ltd. GBR. Dist: Independent Pubs. Group.

Collins Publishers Staff. KS3 English. 2014. (ENG.). 216p. (YA). (gr. 6-9). pap. 16.95 *(978-0-00-756281-7(0))* HarperCollins Pubs. Ltd. GBR. Dist: Independent Pubs. Group.

Collins UK Publishing Staff & Collins KS3 Staff. KS3 English. 2014. (ENG., Illus.). 144p. (YA). (gr. 6-9). pap. 12.95 *(978-0-00-756280-0(2))* HarperCollins Pubs. Ltd. GBR. Dist: Independent Pubs. Group.

Collins UK Publishing Staff & Letts KS1 Staff. English Practice Test Papers, Age 5-7. 2016. (ENG.). 96p. (J). (gr. 1-2). pap. 9.95 *(978-1-84419-817-7(0))* HarperCollins Pubs. Ltd. GBR. Dist: Independent Pubs. Group.

—Maths & English Practice Test Papers. 2016. (ENG.). 192p. (J). (gr. 1-2). pap. 15.95 *(978-1-84419-819-1(7))* HarperCollins Pubs. Ltd. GBR. Dist: Independent Pubs. Group.

Collins UK Publishing Staff & Letts KS2 Staff. English Practice Test Papers. 2016. (Letts KS2 Success Ser.). (ENG.). 104p. (J). (gr. 3-6). pap. 9.95 *(978-1-84419-831-3(6))* HarperCollins Pubs. Ltd. GBR. Dist: Independent Pubs. Group.

—Maths & English Practice Test Papers. 2016. (Letts KS2 Success Ser.). (ENG.). 216p. (J). (gr. 3-6). pap. 15.95 *(978-1-84419-835-1(9))* HarperCollins Pubs. Ltd. GBR. Dist: Independent Pubs. Group.

—Maths, English & Science Test Practice Papers. 2016. (Letts KS2 Success Ser.). (ENG.). 280p. (gr. 3-6). pap. 20.95 *(978-1-84419-836-8(7))* HarperCollins Pubs. Ltd. GBR. Dist: Independent Pubs. Group.

Come on, Dot: Short Vowel o: Level A, 6 vols. (Wright Skills Ser.). 12p. (gr. k-3). 17.95 *(978-0-322-03112-8(5))* Wright Group/McGraw-Hill.

Common Core Grade 1. 2013. (ENG.). pap. 950.01 *(978-1-4765-9460-6(0))* Capstone Press of Coughlan Cos.

Common Core Grade 2. 2013. (ENG.). pap. 802.93 *(978-1-4765-9459-0(7))* Capstone Press of Coughlan Cos.

Common Core Grade 4. 2013. (ENG.). pap. 916.07 *(978-1-4765-9457-6(0))* Capstone Press of Coughlan Cos.

Composing Made Easy Videotape: Videotape Packages. 2003. (Share the Music Ser.). (gr. 5-8). *(978-0-02-295493-2(7))* Macmillan/McGraw-Hill Schl. Div.

Concept Books: 1 Each of 8 Student Books. 16p. (gr. k-1). 28.50 *(978-0-7802-3862-6(1))*; Vol. 2. 38.95 *(978-0-7802-6810-4(5))* Wright Group/McGraw-Hill.

Connolly, Techla & Meyers-Herron, Carrie. Test Practice for Common Core. 2015. (Barron's Core Focus Ser.). (ENG.). 216p. pap. 14.99 *(978-1-4380-0706-9(X))* Barron's Educational Series, Inc.

Connors, Kathleen & Stevens, Gareth. Contractions at the Zoo. 2012. (Word Play Ser.). (Illus.). 24p. (J). (gr. 1-3). pap. 8.15 *(978-1-4339-7184-6(4))*; lib. bdg. 22.60 *(978-1-4339-7183-9(6))* Stevens, Gareth Publishing LLLP.

Core Language Skills. 2013. (Core Language Skills Ser.). 24p. (J). (gr. 2-2). 135.60 *(978-1-4777-1148-4(1))*; pap. 297.00 *(978-1-4777-2667-9(5))*; pap. 49.50 *(978-1-4777-2666-2(7))* Rosen Publishing Group, Inc., The. (PowerKids Pr.).

Coyote, Fox, & Wolf Tales: Level M, 6 vols. 128p. (gr. 2-3). 41.95 *(978-0-7699-1022-2(X))* Shortland Pubns. (U. S. A.) Inc.

Creepy Creatures: Level O, 6 vols. (Explorers Ser.). 32p. (gr. 3-6). 44.95 *(978-0-7699-0592-1(7))* Shortland Pubns. (U. S. A.) Inc.

Daily Word Routine Flip Chart. 2004. (gr. 3-18). suppl. ed. 275.00 *(978-0-673-63004-9(8))*; (gr. 4-18). suppl. ed. 275.00 *(978-0-673-63005-6(6))*; (gr. 5-18). suppl. ed. 275.00 *(978-0-673-63006-3(4))*; (gr. 6-18). suppl. ed. 275.00 *(978-0-673-63007-0(2))* Addison-Wesley Educational Pubs., Inc.

Dance My Dance: Level M, 6 vols. (Take-Twostm Ser.). 32p. 36.95 *(978-0-322-03401-3(9))* Wright Group/McGraw-Hill.

Dancin' Down, 6 vols., Set B. 32p. (gr. 1-3). 31.50 *(978-0-7802-8048-9(2))* Wright Group/McGraw-Hill.

de Brunhoff, Laurent. Babar's ABC. 2010. (ENG., Illus.). 40p. (J). (gr. -1-3). pap. 7.95 *(978-0-8109-8922-1(0))* UK Abrams Bks. for Young Readers.

DeBellis, Aaron. A Bee's C's, 1 vol. 2010. 38p. pap. 24.95 *(978-1-4489-6112-2(2))* PublishAmerica, Inc.

Delessert, Etienne. A Was an Apple Pie. Delessert, Etienne, illus. 2005. (Creative Editions Ser.). (Illus.). 28p. (J). (gr. -1-3). 18.95 *(978-1-56846-196-0(8))* Creative Co., The.

Denmark-Allen, Eva. I Was, I Am, i Will Be! - Yo Fui! Yo soy! Yo Sere! 2007. (ENG & SPA., Illus.). 56p. (J). per. 12.00 *(978-0-9792016-8-4(3))* Professional Publishing Hse. LLC.

Diagnostic Tests: Student Testing Kit, Features Tests for Language Arts, Including Reading & Mathematics & Also Includes a Parents Cumulative, Set. 2004. (Illus.). (YA). (gr. 7-12). pap. 19.95 *(978-0-7403-0097-4(0)*, AS9923) Alpha Omega Pubns., Inc.

Dinosaur Rock. 2012. (Collins Big Cat Ser.). (ENG., Illus.). 104p. (J). pap., wbk. ed. 4.99 *(978-0-00-747490-5(3))* HarperCollins Pubs. Ltd. GBR. Dist: Independent Pubs. Group.

Dobson, Jolie. Bang Bang Plink Plink. 2014. (Snappy Sounds Ser.). (ENG., Illus.). 22p. (J). (gr. -1 — 1). bds. 5.95 *(978-1-77085-438-3(X)*, 9781770854383) Firefly Bks., Ltd.

—Beep Beep Choo Choo. 2014. (Snappy Sounds Ser.). (ENG., Illus.). 22p. (J). (gr. -1 — 1). bds. 5.95 *(978-1-77085-436-9(3)*, 9781770854369) Firefly Bks., Ltd.

—Ring Ring Pop Pop. 2014. (Snappy Sounds Ser.). (ENG., Illus.). 22p. (J). (gr. -1 — 1). bds. 5.95 *(978-1-77085-437-6(1)*, 9781770854376) Firefly Bks., Ltd.

—Snap Snap Woof Woof. 2014. (Snappy Sounds Ser.). (ENG., Illus.). 22p. (J). (gr. -1 — 1). bds. 5.95 *(978-1-77085-435-2(5)*, 9781770854352) Firefly Bks., Ltd.

Dolphin, Colleen. It's E!, 1 vol. 2010. (It's the Alphabet! Ser.). (ENG., Illus.). 24p. (gr. k-4). 25.65 *(978-1-60453-592-1(X)*, Super SandCastle) ABDO Publishing Co.

Dorling Kindersley Publishing Staff. ABC. 2012. (Touch & Feel Ser.). (ENG.). 12p. (J). (gr. -1-k). bds. 6.99 *(978-1-4654-0163-2(6)*, DK Children) Dorling Kindersley Publishing, Inc.

Doudna, Kelly. Emma & Eddie, 1 vol. 2005. (First Sounds Ser.). (Illus.). (J). (gr. k-3). (ENG.). 24p. lib. bdg. 24.21 *(978-1-59679-144-2(6)*, SandCastle); 23p. pap. 48.42 *(978-1-59679-145-9(4))* ABDO Publishing Co.

—Eva & Ethan, 1 vol. 2005. (First Sounds Ser.). (Illus.). (J). (gr. k-3). (ENG.). 24p. lib. bdg. 24.21 *(978-1-59679-146-6(2)*, SandCastle); 23p. pap. 48.42 *(978-1-59679-147-3(0))* ABDO Publishing Co.

—Fay & Felix, 1 vol. 2005. (First Sounds Ser.). (ENG., Illus.). 24p. (J). (gr. k-3). lib. bdg. 24.21 *(978-1-59679-148-0(9)*, SandCastle) ABDO Publishing Co.

—Flora & Floyd, 1 vol. 2005. (First Sounds Ser.). (Illus.). (J). (gr. k-3). (ENG.). 24p. lib. bdg. 24.21 *(978-1-59679-150-3(0)*, SandCastle); 23p. pap. 48.42 *(978-1-59679-151-0(9))* ABDO Publishing Co.

—Fran & Fred, 1 vol. 2005. (First Sounds Ser.). (Illus.). (J). (gr. k-3). (ENG.). 24p. lib. bdg. 24.21 *(978-1-59679-152-7(7)*, SandCastle); 23p. pap. 48.42 *(978-1-59679-153-4(5))* ABDO Publishing Co.

—Gail & Gary, 1 vol. 2005. (First Sounds Ser.). (J). (gr. k-3). (ENG.). 24p. lib. bdg. 24.21 *(978-1-59679-154-1(3)*, SandCastle); 23p. pap. 48.42 *(978-1-59679-155-8(1))* ABDO Publishing Co.

—Gina & George, 1 vol. 2005. (First Sounds Ser.). (Illus.). (J). (gr. k-3). (ENG.). 24p. lib. bdg. 24.21 *(978-1-59679-156-5(X)*, SandCastle); 23p. pap. 48.42 *(978-1-59679-157-2(8))* ABDO Publishing Co.

—Gladys & Glen, 1 vol. 2005. (First Sounds Ser.). (Illus.). (J). (gr. k-3). (ENG.). 24p. lib. bdg. 24.21 *(978-1-59679-158-9(6)*, SandCastle); 23p. pap. 48.42 *(978-1-59679-159-6(4))* ABDO Publishing Co.

—Grace & Grant, 1 vol. 2005. (First Sounds Ser.). (Illus.). (J). (gr. k-3). (ENG.). 24p. lib. bdg. 24.21 *(978-1-59679-160-2(8)*, SandCastle); 23p. pap. 48.42 *(978-1-59679-161-9(6))* ABDO Publishing Co.

—Hannah & Henry, 1 vol. 2005. (First Sounds Ser.). (Illus.). (J). (gr. k-3). (ENG.). 24p. lib. bdg. 24.21 *(978-1-59679-162-6(4)*, SandCastle); 23p. pap. 48.42 *(978-1-59679-163-3(2))* ABDO Publishing Co.

—India & Iggy, 1 vol. 2005. (First Sounds Ser.). (Illus.). (J). (gr. k-3). (ENG.). 24p. lib. bdg. 24.21 *(978-1-59679-166-4(7)*, SandCastle); 23p. pap. 48.42 *(978-1-59679-167-1(5))* ABDO Publishing Co.

—Splish Splash, 1 vol. 2004. (Sound Words Ser.). (ENG., Illus.). 24p. (J). (gr. k-3). lib. bdg. 24.21 *(978-1-59197-453-6(4)*, SandCastle) ABDO Publishing Co.

Duyal, Yasar, ed. Paper Clips. 2013. (ENG.). pap. *(978-1-107-61420-8(1))* Cambridge Univ. Pr.

Early Emergent Skills Guide. (Sunshine Skills Guides). 15.50 *(978-0-7802-9809-5(8))* Wright Group/McGraw-Hill.

Eastman, P. D. The Alphabet Book. 2015. (Bright & Early Books(R) Ser.). (ENG., Illus.). 36p. (J). (gr. -1-2). lib. bdg. 13.99 *(978-0-375-97464-9(4)*, Random Hse. Bks. for Young Readers) Random Hse. Children's Bks.

Education.com. Write It Your Way: A Workbook of Reading, Writing, & Literature. 2015. (ENG.). 112p. (J). (gr. 4-4). pap. 7.99 *(978-0-486-80270-1(1))* Dover Pubns., Inc.

—Your World of Words: A Workbook of Books & Words. 2015. (ENG.). 112p. (J). (gr. 5-5). pap. 7.99 *(978-0-486-80272-5(8))* Dover Pubns., Inc.

Eisele. Hip Hip Hooray. 2003. (ENG., Illus.). 112p. (C). pap., stu. ed. 25.93 *(978-0-13-061190-1(5))* Pearson ESL.

Eisele & Hanlon. Hip Hip Hooray. 2003. (ENG.). (C). pap., act. bk. ed. 14.00 *(978-0-13-182614-4(X))* Prentice Hall, ESL Dept.

Emigh, Karen. Herman's Hiding Places: Discovering up, in, under & Behind. 2013. (ENG.). 32p. pap. 9.95 *(978-1-935274-61-2(9))* Future Horizons, Inc.

Encounter: Narrative Nonfiction Picture Books. 2015. (Encounter: Narrative Nonfiction Picture Bks.). (ENG.). 46.85 *(978-1-62370-595-4(9))* Encounter Bks.

English: Grades 3 - 4. (Illus.). (J). pap., wbk. ed. 4.99 *(978-0-88743-844-8(X))* School Zone Publishing Co.

English Ages 3-4. Date not set. (Gold Stars Workbook Ser.). (Illus.). 32p. (J). 2.98 *(978-0-7525-9556-6(3))* Parragon, Inc.

English Ages 4-5. Date not set. (Gold Stars Workbook Ser.). (Illus.). 32p. (J). 2.98 *(978-0-7525-9557-3(1))* Parragon, Inc.

English Ages 5-6. Date not set. (Gold Stars Workbook Ser.). (Illus.). 32p. (J). 2.98 *(978-0-7525-9558-0(X))* Parragon, Inc.

English Ages 6-7. Date not set. (Gold Stars Workbook Ser.). (Illus.). 32p. (J). 2.98 *(978-0-7525-9559-7(8))* Parragon, Inc.

English I: Language Skills, Chapter 1 Activities. 2005. (Illus.). 44p. (YA). pap. 5.00 *(978-1-59476-137-9(X))* Paradigm Accelerated Curriculum.

English I: Language Skills, Chapter 1 Text, 11 vols. 2005. (Illus.). 58p. (YA). pap. 7.00 *(978-1-59476-132-4(9))* Paradigm Accelerated Curriculum.

English I: Language Skills, Chapter 3 Activities. 2005. (Illus.). 54p. (YA). pap. 5.00 *(978-1-59476-139-3(6))* Paradigm Accelerated Curriculum.

English I: Language Skills Full Course Kit, 11 bks. 2005. (Illus.). 852p. (YA). 75.00 *(978-1-59476-093-8(4))* Paradigm Accelerated Curriculum.

English II: Communication Skills, Chapter 2, Text. 2004. Orig. Title: English Communication Skills, Chapter 2, Text. (Illus.). 64p. (YA). pap. *(978-1-59476-002-0(0))* Paradigm Accelerated Curriculum.

English II: Communication Skills, Chapter 3, Text. 2004. Orig. Title: English Communication Skills, Chapter 3, Text. (Illus.). 58p. (YA). pap. *(978-1-59476-003-7(9))* Paradigm Accelerated Curriculum.

English II: Communication Skills, Chapter 4, Text. 2004. Orig. Title: English Communication Skills, Chapter 4, Text. (Illus.). 66p. (YA). pap. *(978-1-59476-004-4(7))* Paradigm Accelerated Curriculum.

English III: Communication Skills, Chapter 5, Activities. 2004. Orig. Title: English Communication Skills, Chapter 5, Text. 72p. (YA). pap. 5.00 *(978-1-59476-020-4(9))* Paradigm Accelerated Curriculum.

English/Math 3-4. 2003. (Illus.). 48p. (J). wbk. ed. 7.98 *(978-1-4054-1264-3(X))* Parragon, Inc.

English/Math 4-5. 2003. (Illus.). 48p. (J). wbk. ed. 7.98 *(978-1-4054-1265-0(8))* Parragon, Inc.

English/Math 5-6. 2003. (Illus.). 48p. (J). wbk. ed. 7.98 *(978-1-4054-1266-7(6))* Parragon, Inc.

English/Math 6-7. 2003. (Illus.). 48p. (YA). wbk. ed. 7.98 *(978-1-4054-1267-4(4))* Parragon, Inc.

Evan-Moor. Daily Paragraph Editing Grade 2. 2004. (Evan-Moor Writing Ser.). (ENG.). 176p. (J). (gr. 2-18). pap. 21.99 *(978-1-55799-956-6(2)*, EMC 2725) Evan-Moor Educational Pubs.

—Daily Paragraph Editing Grade 3. 2004. (ENG.). 176p. (J). (gr. 3-18). pap. 21.99 *(978-1-55799-957-3(0)*, EMC 2726) Evan-Moor Educational Pubs.

—Daily Paragraph Editing Grade 4. 2004. (ENG.). 176p. (J). (gr. 4-18). pap. 21.99 *(978-1-55799-958-0(9)*, EMC 2727) Evan-Moor Educational Pubs.

—Daily Paragraph Editing Grade 5. 2004. (ENG.). 176p. (J). (gr. 5-18). pap. 21.99 *(978-1-55799-959-7(7)*, EMC 2728) Evan-Moor Educational Pubs.

—Daily Paragraph Editing Grade 6+ 2004. (ENG.). 176p. (J). (gr. 6-18). pap. 21.99 *(978-1-55799-960-3(0)*, EMC 2729) Evan-Moor Educational Pubs.

—Literacy Centers, Grades 2-3. 2005. (ENG.). 192p. (J). (gr. 2-3). pap. 24.99 *(978-1-55799-976-4(7)*, EMC 2723) Evan-Moor Educational Pubs.

—Literacy Centers, Grades 4-5. 2005. (ENG.). 192p. (gr. 4-5). pap. 24.99 *(978-1-55799-977-1(5)*, EMC 2724) Evan-Moor Educational Pubs.

—Literacy Centers, Grades 4-6. 2005. (Take It to Your Seat Learning Centers). (ENG., Illus.). 192p. (J). (gr. 4-6). pap., suppl. ed. 24.99 *(978-1-55799-851-4(5)*, EMC 2719) Evan-Moor Educational Pubs.

Falls, C. B. ABC Book. 2015. (ENG., Illus.). 64p. (J). (gr. k-3). pap. 7.99 *(978-0-486-79431-0(8))* Dover Pubns., Inc.

Fatus, Sophie & Couëlle, Jennifer. My Big Barefoot Book of French & English Words. 2016. (FRE & ENG.). (J). pap. *(978-1-78285-303-9(0))* Barefoot Bks., Inc.

Felix, Rebecca. Heavy, Heavier, Heaviest. 2015. (Size It Up Ser.). (Illus.). 16p. (J). 25.65 *(978-1-60753-576-8(9))* Amicus Publishing.

Ferguson, John E. & Allport, Alan. Immigration Policy. 2nd rev. ed. 2009. (Point/Counterpoint Ser.). (Illus.). 152p. (C). (gr. 9-18). 35.00 *(978-1-60413-126-0(8)*, Chelsea Hse.) Facts On File, Inc.

Fern, Tracey. W Is for Webster: Noah Webster & His American Dictionary. Kulikov, Boris, illus. 2015. (ENG.). 40p. (J). 17.99 *(978-0-374-38240-7(9)*, 9780374382407, Farrar, Straus & Giroux (BYR)) Farrar, Straus & Giroux.

Ferne, Catherine. B Sounds. 2012. (First Step Nonfiction - Hard Consonants Ser.). (ENG., Illus.). 8p. (J). (gr. -1-1). pap. 4.95 *(978-1-4677-0506-6(3))* Lerner Publishing Group.

—C Sounds. 2012. (First Step Nonfiction - Hard Consonants Ser.). (ENG., Illus.). 8p. (J). (gr. -1-1). pap. 4.95 *(978-1-4677-0507-3(1))* Lerner Publishing Group.

—D Sounds. 2012. (First Step Nonfiction - Hard Consonants Ser.). (ENG., Illus.). 8p. (J). (gr. -1-1). pap. 4.95 *(978-1-4677-0508-0(X))* Lerner Publishing Group.

—G Sounds. 2012. (First Step Nonfiction - Hard Consonants Ser.). (ENG., Illus.). 8p. (J). (gr. -1-1). pap. 4.95 *(978-1-4677-0509-7(8))* Lerner Publishing Group.

—K Sounds. 2012. (First Step Nonfiction - Hard Consonants Ser.). (ENG., Illus.). 8p. (J). (gr. -1-1). pap. 4.95 *(978-1-4677-0510-3(1))* Lerner Publishing Group.

—P Sounds. 2012. (First Step Nonfiction - Hard Consonants Ser.). (ENG., Illus.). 8p. (J). (gr. -1-1). pap. 4.95 *(978-1-4677-0511-0(X))* Lerner Publishing Group.

—T Sounds. 2012. (First Step Nonfiction - Hard Consonants Ser.). (ENG., Illus.). 8p. (J). (gr. -1-1). pap. 4.95 *(978-1-4677-0512-7(8))* Lerner Publishing Group.

Ferrie, Chris. ABC's of Science. 2017. (Baby University Ser.: 0). (ENG.). 26p. (J). bds. 9.99 ***(978-1-4926-5631-9(3)***, Sourcebooks Jabberwocky) Sourcebooks, Inc.

Fiedler, Heidi. The Know-Nonsense Guide to Grammar: The Awesomely Fun Guide to the Parts of a Sentence, Metaphors, Similes, Idioms & So Much More! Kearney, Brendan, illus. 2017. (Know Nonsense Ser.). (ENG.). 64p. (J). (gr. 3-6). 14.95 *(978-1-63322-296-0(9)*, Walter Foster Jr) Quarto Publishing Group USA.

Find it, Write It, Read It: Paragraphs. 2004. (J). pap. 7.95 *(978-1-56911-180-2(4))* Learning Resources, Inc.

Findley, Violet. Sight Word Wheels: Reproducible Patterns for Hands-On Wheels That Teach the First 25 Sight Words. 2009. (ENG.). 64p. pap. 11.99 *(978-0-545-09441-2(0)*, Teaching Resources) Scholastic, Inc.

Fitzsimmons, Jim & Whiteford, Rhona. English Tests. (Illus.). 32p. (J). pap. 6.99 *(978-0-340-68069-8(5))* Hodder & Stoughton GBR. Dist: Trafalgar Square Publishing.

Flash Kids Editors, Flash Kids, ed. Summer Study, Grade 1. 2016. (Summer Study Ser.). (ENG., Illus.). 160p. (J). (gr. 1-1). pap. 9.95 *(978-1-4114-7857-2(6)*, Spark Publishing Group) Sterling Publishing Co., Inc.

Fletcher, Alan. Anteaters to Zebras. 2012. (ENG., Illus.). 56p. (gr. -1-1). 16.95 *(978-1-84976-004-1(7))* Tate Publishing, Ltd. GBR. Dist: Abrams, Inc.

Flor Ada, Alma & Campoy, F. Isabel, contrib. by. Voices. (Literature Collection of Gateways to the Sun Ser.). 32p. (J). (gr. k-6). pap. 13.95 *(978-1-59437-719-8(7))* Santillana USA Publishing Co., Inc.

Freeman, Maggie, et al. Castles. Moon, Cliff, ed. 2012. (Collins Big Cat Ser.). (ENG.). 16p. (J). pap., wbk. ed. 4.99 *(978-0-00-747373-1(7))* HarperCollins Pubs. Ltd. GBR. Dist: Independent Pubs. Group.

From Heart to Page. 2004. (gr. 4-8). pap. 7.00 *(978-1-886061-31-6(9))* Wordsmiths.

Fuerst, Jeffrey B. A-Hunting We Will Go. Greenhead, Bill, illus. 2010. (Rising Readers Ser.). (J). 3.49 *(978-1-60719-684-6(0))* Newmark Learning LLC.

—Bingo. Greenhead, Bill, illus. 2010. (Rising Readers Ser.). (J). 3.49 *(978-1-60719-687-7(5))* Newmark Learning LLC.

Fujikawa, Gyo. Gyo Fujikawa's A to Z Picture Book. 2010. (ENG., Illus.). 72p. (J). (gr. -1-2). 9.95 *(978-1-4027-6818-7(4)*, 1318769) Sterling Publishing Co., Inc.

Gallardo, Yuri, ed. Houses & Apartments under 1000 Square Feet. 2013. (ENG., Illus.). 256p. pap. 24.95 *(978-1-77085-214-3(X)*, 9781770852143) Firefly Bks., Ltd.

Ganeri, Anita. Joining Words: Conjunctions, 1 vol. 2012. (Getting to Grips with Grammar Ser.). (ENG.). 32p. (gr. 1-3). pap. 8.29 *(978-1-4329-5814-5(3))*; lib. bdg. 27.32 *(978-1-4329-5807-7(0))* Heinemann-Raintree. (Heinemann First Library).

Gates, Valerie. The Other Colors: An ABC Book. Cutting, Ann, photos by. 2013. (ENG., Illus.). 56p. (J). (gr. -1-k). 14.95 *(978-1-62087-537-7(3)*, 620537, Sky Pony Pr.) Skyhorse Publishing Co., Inc.

Geatches, Hazel. Cities, Level 2. 2012. (ENG., Illus.). 40p. pap. 9.38 *(978-0-19-464682-6(3))* Oxford Univ. Pr., Inc.

Geatches, Hazel, ed. At the Beach. 2012. (ENG., Illus.). 32p. 9.38 *(978-0-19-464628-4(9))* Oxford Univ. Pr., Inc.

—Earth. 2012. (ENG., Illus.). 40p. pap., act. bk. ed. 10.00 *(978-0-19-464679-6(3))* Oxford Univ. Pr., Inc.

Get Ready to Print. 2003. 16p. (J). 3.79 *(978-1-58792-046-2(8))* Trend Enterprises, Inc.

Ghigna, Charles. The Alphabet Parade. Jatkowska, Ag, illus. 2014. 24p. (J). pap. *(978-1-4795-1930-9(8))* Picture Window Bks.

Gifford, Myrna. Meet the Lit Kids: A Read-and-Sing Book. Cooper, Frances, illus. 2003. 12p. (J). 9.95 *(978-0-9720763-7-1(9))* Action Factor, Inc.

Glastetter, KC & Hollman, Jeremie, photos by. Yellowstone Natl Park Abc Adv. 2010. (Illus.). 64p. (J). pap. 12.00 *(978-0-87842-572-3(1))* Mountain Pr. Publishing Co., Inc.

Golden Books & Williams, Garth. Bunnies' ABC. Williams, Garth, illus. 2015. (Little Golden Book Ser.). (ENG., Illus.). 24p. (J). (-k). 4.99 *(978-0-385-39128-3(5)*, Golden Bks.) Random Hse. Children's Bks.

Gorrell, Gena K. Say What? The Weird & Mysterious Journey of the English Language. 2009. (ENG.). 152p. (J). (gr. 5-9). pap. 10.95 *(978-0-88776-878-1(4)*, Tundra Bks.) Tundra Bks. CAN. Dist: Penguin Random Hse. LLC.

Gould, Mike, et al. English a - a Concise Revision Course for CSEC(r). 2017. (ENG.). 260p. (YA). (gr. 9). pap. 19.99 ***(978-0-00-820813-4(1))*** HarperCollins Pubs. Ltd. GBR. Dist: Independent Pubs. Group.

Graphic Organizer Flip Chart. 2004. (gr. k-18). suppl. ed. 92.65 *(978-0-673-61440-7(9))* Addison-Wesley Educational Pubs., Inc.

Gregorich, Barbara. Brain Quest, Grade 4: A Whole Year of Curriculum-Based Exercises & Activities in One Fun Book! McGee, Patty, ed. 2008. (ENG., Illus.). 320p. (J). (gr. 4-4). pap., wbk. ed. 12.95 *(978-0-7611-5018-3(8)*, 15018) Workman Publishing Co., Inc.

Gregory, Josh. Nouns. Petelinsek, Kathleen, illus. 2013. (Explorer Junior Library: the Parts of Speech Ser.). (ENG.). 24p. (J). (gr. 1-4). 25.64 *(978-1-62431-177-2(6)*, 203028); pap. 12.79 *(978-1-62431-309-7(4)*, 203030) Cherry Lake Publishing.

Grudzina, Rebecca. Baby Bumblebee. Boyer, Lyn, illus. 2010. (Rising Readers Ser.). (J). 3.49 *(978-1-60719-688-4(3))* Newmark Learning LLC.

Gürth, Per-Henrik. ABC of Toronto. Gürth, Per-Henrik, illus. 2013. (ENG., Illus.). 32p. (J). (gr. -1-k). 15.95 *(978-1-77138-037-9(3))* Kids Can Pr., Ltd. CAN. Dist: Hachette Bk. Group.

Hall, Pamela. Code Blue Calling All Capitals!, 1 vol. Currant, Gary, illus. 2009. (Grammar's Slammin' Ser.). (ENG.). 32p. (J). (gr. -1-3). 28.50 *(978-1-60270-614-9(X))* Magic Wagon.

—The Muscle-Bound Compounds, 1 vol. Currant, Gary, illus. 2009. (Grammar's Slammin' Ser.). (ENG.). 32p. (J). (gr. -1-3). 28.50 *(978-1-60270-616-3(6))* Magic Wagon.

Hamilton, Fran Santoro. Hands-on English. Hamilton, Michael, illus. 2nd l.t. ed. 2004. 192p. per. 14.95 *(978-0-9664867-5-9(7))* Portico Bks.

Hanson, Anders. Jill & John, 1 vol. 2005. (First Sounds Ser.). (Illus.). (J). (gr. k-3). (ENG.). 24p. lib. bdg. 24.21 *(978-1-59679-168-8(3)*, SandCastle); 23p. pap. 48.42 *(978-1-59679-169-5(1))* ABDO Publishing Co.

—Kim & Ken, 1 vol. 2005. (First Sounds Ser.). (Illus.). (J). (gr. k-3). (ENG.). 24p. lib. bdg. 24.21 *(978-1-59679-170-1(5)*, SandCastle); 23p. 48.42 *(978-1-59679-171-8(3))* ABDO Publishing Co.

—Liz & Len, 1 vol. 2005. (First Sounds Ser.). (Illus.). (J). (gr. k-3). (ENG.). 24p. lib. bdg. 24.21 *(978-1-59679-172-5(1)*, SandCastle); 23p. pap. 48.42 *(978-1-59679-173-2(X))* ABDO Publishing Co.

—Meg & Mark, 1 vol. 2005. (First Sounds Ser.). (Illus.). (J). (gr. k-3). (ENG.). 24p. lib. bdg. 24.21 *(978-1-59679-174-9(8)*, SandCastle); 23p. pap. 48.42 *(978-1-59679-175-6(6))* ABDO Publishing Co.

—Nan & Nick, 1 vol. 2005. (First Sounds Ser.). (Illus.). (J). (gr. k-3). (ENG.). 24p. lib. bdg. 24.21 *(978-1-59679-176-3(4)*, SandCastle); 23p. pap. 48.42 *(978-1-59679-177-0(2))* ABDO Publishing Co.

—Olga & Olaf, 1 vol. 2005. (First Sounds Ser.). (Illus.). (gr. k-3). (ENG.). 24p. (J). lib. bdg. 24.21 *(978-1-59679-178-7(0)*, SandCastle); 23p. pap. 48.42 *(978-1-59679-179-4(9))* ABDO Publishing Co.

—Olive & Oscar, 1 vol. 2005. (First Sounds Ser.). (Illus.). (gr. k-3). (ENG.). 24p. (J). lib. bdg. 24.21 *(978-1-59679-180-0(2)*, SandCastle); 23p. pap. 48.42 *(978-1-59679-181-7(0))* ABDO Publishing Co.

—Pam & Pete, 1 vol. 2005. (First Sounds Ser.). (Illus.). (J). (gr. k-3). (ENG.). 24p. lib. bdg. 24.21 *(978-1-59679-182-4(9)*, SandCastle); 23p. pap. 48.42 *(978-1-59679-183-1(7))* ABDO Publishing Co.

—Quinn & Quenton, 1 vol. 2005. (First Sounds Ser.). (Illus.). (J). (gr. k-3). (ENG.). 24p. lib. bdg. 24.21 *(978-1-59679-184-8(5)*, SandCastle); 23p. pap. 48.42 *(978-1-59679-185-5(3))* ABDO Publishing Co.

—Ruth & Rob, 1 vol. 2005. (First Sounds Ser.). (J). (gr. k-3). (ENG.). 24p. lib. bdg. 24.21 *(978-1-59679-186-2(1)*, SandCastle); 23p. pap. 48.42 *(978-1-59679-187-9(X))* ABDO Publishing Co.

—Sara & Sam, 1 vol. 2005. (First Sounds Ser.). (Illus.). (J). (gr. k-3). (ENG.). 24p. lib. bdg. 24.21 *(978-1-59679-188-6(8)*, SandCastle); 23p. pap. 48.42 *(978-1-59679-189-3(6))* ABDO Publishing Co.

—Sharon & Shawn, 1 vol. 2005. (First Sounds Ser.). (Illus.). (J). (gr. k-3). (ENG.). 24p. lib. bdg. 24.21 *(978-1-59679-190-9(X)*, SandCastle); 23p. pap. 48.42 *(978-1-59679-191-6(8))* ABDO Publishing Co.

Harcourt School Publishers Staff. Harcourt Language Arts: Standardized Test Preparation. 2nd ed. 2003. (Harcourt Language Ser.). (Illus.). (gr. 2-18). 7.60 *(978-0-15-321223-9(3))*; (gr. 3-18). 7.60 *(978-0-15-321224-6(1))*; (gr. 4-18). 7.60 *(978-0-15-321225-3(X))*; (gr. 5-18). 7.60 *(978-0-15-321226-0(8))* Harcourt Schl. Pubs.

—Writing Express, Grade 6. 2nd ed. 2003. (Trofeos Ser.). (SPA.). (gr. 6-18). tchr. ed. 10.10 incl. cd-rom *(978-0-15-324609-8(X))* Harcourt Schl. Pubs.

Harper, Charley. ABC's. 2013. (ENG., Illus.). 62p. (J). 16.95 *(978-1-62326-003-3(5))* AMMO Bks., LLC.

Harvey, Stephanie, et al. Living on the Coast. 2014. (Ladders Social Studies). (ENG.). 24p. 8.95 *(978-1-285-34802-5(8))* National Geographic School Publishing, Inc.

Hatanaka, Kellen. Work: An Occupational ABC, 1 vol. 2014. (ENG., Illus.). 40p. (J). (gr. -1-2). 16.95 *(978-1-55498-409-1(2))* Groundwood Bks. CAN. Dist: Publishers Group West (PGW).

Headway Level B Teacher Phonic. (J). (gr. 1). *(978-0-89688-448-9(1)*, 88-448) Open Court Publishing Co.

Headway Level C: Blue Hill Skill. (J). (gr. 1-2). *(978-0-89688-473-1(2)*, 1678) Open Court Publishing Co.

Headway Level J: Close to Sun. (J). (gr. 6). tchr. ed. *(978-0-89688-493-9(7)*, 88-493) Open Court Publishing Co.

Heinrichs, Ann. Prefixes & Suffixes. McGeehan, Dan & Moore, David, Jr., illus. 2010. (Language Rules! Ser.). (ENG.). 24p. (J). (gr. 1-4). lib. bdg. 27.07 *(978-1-60253-430-8(6)*, 200434) Child's World, Inc., The.

Heinrichs, Ann. Similes & Metaphors. 2016. (J). ***(978-1-4896-5998-9(6)***, AV2 by Weigl) Weigl Pubs., Inc.

Helman, Andrea. O Is for Orca. Wolfe, Art, photos by. 2016. (ENG., Illus.). 20p. (J). (— 1). bds. 9.99 *(978-1-63217-033-0(7)*, Little Bigfoot) Sasquatch Bks.

Hernandez, Jose Francisco. Ingles para Ninos-Un Metodo Facil y Efectivo para Sus Hijos.Tr. of English for Your Kids. (SPA.). 7.98 *(978-970-643-104-2(7))* Selector, S.A. de C.V. MEX. Dist: AIMS International Bks., Inc.

Herrera, Mario & Hojel, Barbara. Balloons: Mascot Puppet Funny Froggy. 2005. (J). (gr. 3-18). 17.50 *(978-0-7652-6327-8(0))* Longman Publishing Group.

—Balloons: Mascot Puppet Lucky Ducky. 2005. (J). (gr. 2-18). 17.50 *(978-0-7652-6326-1(2))* Longman Publishing Group.

—Balloons: Mascot Puppet Sunny Bunny. 2005. (J). (gr. 1-18). 17.50 (978-0-7652-6325-4(4)) Longman Publishing Group.

—Balloons: Picture Cards. 2005. (J). (gr. 1-18). 33.95 (978-0-7652-6302-5(5)); (gr. 2-18). 33.95 (978-0-7652-6322-3(X)); (gr. 3-18). 33.95 (978-0-7652-6323-0(8)) Longman Publishing Group.

—Balloons: Storybooks Package. 2005. (J). 66.50 (978-0-7652-6313-1(0)) Longman Publishing Group.

Herrera, Mario & Hojel, Barbara. Big Fun Reading & Writing Workbook. 2014. (ENG., Illus.). 91p. (C). pap. 22.00 **(978-0-13-343756-0(6))** Pearson Education.

Herzog, Joyce. School in a Box: Mini-Book. 2004. 4.00 (978-1-887225-27-4(7)) Herzog, Joyce.

—Todder School in a Box: Mini Book. 2004. 4.00 (978-1-887225-35-9(8)) Herzog, Joyce.

Hey, Kids! (8-lesson edition) Book 1 Student's Book (with CD) English Language Teaching. 2003. (Illus.). 96p. spiral bd. incl. audio compact disk (978-0-7428-0908-6(0)) C C L S Publishing Hse.

Hey, Kids! (8-lesson edition) Book 2 Student's Book (with CD) English Language Teaching. 2003. (Illus.). 96p. spiral bd. incl. audio compact disk (978-0-7428-0909-3(9)) C C L S Publishing Hse.

Hey, Kids! (8-lesson edition) Book 3 Student's Book (with CD) English Language Teaching. 2003. (Illus.). 96p. spiral bd. incl. audio compact disk (978-0-7428-0910-9(2)) C C L S Publishing Hse.

Hey, Kids! (8-lesson edition) Book 4 Student's Book (with CD) English Language Teaching. 2003. (Illus.). 112p. spiral bd. incl. audio compact disk (978-0-7428-0911-6(0)) C C L S Publishing Hse.

Hockett, M. A. & Hockett, Margaret. The Language Mechanic: Tuning up English with Logic. 2013. (The Language Mechanic Ser.). 184p. (gr. 4-7). pap. 24.99 (978-0-89455-761-3(0)) Critical Thinking Co., The.

Hodge, Deborah. West Coast Wild: A Nature Alphabet, 1 vol. Reczuch, Karen, illus. 2015. (ENG.). 48p. (J). (gr. -1-2). 18.95 (978-1-55498-440-4(8)) Groundwood Bks. CAN. Dist: Publishers Group West (PGW).

Hodson, Sarah E. Wh- Questions. 2012. (Illus.). (J). (978-0-7606-1382-5(6)) LinguiSystems, Inc.

Hojel, Barbara & Herrera, Mario. Pockets 3. 2005. (ENG.). (C). pap. 20.33 (978-0-13-124670-6(4)) Pearson ESL.

Holt, Rinehart and Winston Staff. Elements of Literature: Language Handbook Worksheets. 5th ed. 2003. (Elements of Literature Ser.). pap. 31.40 (978-0-03-073918-7(7)); pap. 31.40 (978-0-03-073919-4(5)); pap. 31.40 (978-0-03-073917-0(9)) Holt McDougal.

—Elements of Literature: Language Handbook, Worksheets & Answer Key. 5th ed. 2003. (Illus.). pap. 13.20 (978-0-03-073927-9(6)) Holt McDougal.

—Elements of Literature: Language Handbook Worksheets Answer Key. 5th ed. 2003. pap. 13.20 (978-0-03-073929-3(2)); pap. 13.20 (978-0-03-073928-6(4)) Holt McDougal.

—Florida Preparation & Response in English/Language Arts/FCAT. 3rd ed. 2003. (J). pap. 12.20 (978-0-03-070217-4(8)); pap. 12.20 (978-0-03-070216-7(X)); pap. 12.16 (978-0-03-070214-3(3)); pap. 12.20 (978-0-03-070213-6(5)); pap. 12.20 (978-0-03-070212-9(7)); pap. 12.20 (978-0-03-070211-2(9)) Holt, Rinehart & Winston of Canada, Ltd. CAN. Dist: Harcourt Canada, Ltd.

Howe, Alan, et al. Core English Ks3 - Real Progress in Reading. 2014. 192p. pap. 36.50 (978-1-4441-6895-2(9)) Hodder Education Group GBR. Dist: Trans-Atlantic Pubns., Inc.

Hruby, Patrick. ABC Is for Circus. 2013. (ENG., Illus.). 56p. (J). 16.95 (978-1-62326-006-4(X)) AMMO Bks., LLC.

Hubbard, Frances K. & Spencer, Lauren. Writing to Inform. 2011. (J). 183.60 (978-1-4488-4864-5(4)); (Illus.). 64p. (J). 77.70 (978-1-4488-4745-7(1)); (Illus.). 64p. (J). pap. 12.95 (978-1-4488-4687-0(0)); (Illus.). 64p. (YA). (gr. 5-9). lib. bdg. 31.95 (978-1-4488-4681-8(1)) Rosen Publishing Group, Inc., The.

I'm Learning Spanish, Vol. 3. 2005. (J). 12.99 (978-1-894677-77-6(3)) Kidzup Productions.

Iversen, Sandra. Alphabet Book Aa. 2009. (Quick60 Alphabet Bks.). (ENG., Illus.). 12p. (J). pap. (978-1-77540-000-4(X)) Iversen Publishing Ltd.

—Alphabet Book Bb. 2009. (Quick60 Alphabet Bks.). (ENG., Illus.). 12p. (J). pap. (978-1-77540-001-1(8)) Iversen Publishing Ltd.

—Alphabet Book Cc. 2009. (Quick60 Alphabet Bks.). (ENG., Illus.). 12p. (J). pap. (978-1-77540-002-8(6)) Iversen Publishing Ltd.

—Alphabet Book Dd. 2009. (Quick60 Alphabet Bks.). (ENG., Illus.). 12p. (J). pap. (978-1-77540-003-5(4)) Iversen Publishing Ltd.

—Alphabet Book Ee. 2009. (Quick60 Alphabet Bks.). (ENG., Illus.). 12p. (J). pap. (978-1-77540-004-2(2)) Iversen Publishing Ltd.

—Alphabet Book Ff. 2009. (Quick60 Alphabet Bks.). (ENG., Illus.). 12p. (J). pap. (978-1-77540-005-9(0)) Iversen Publishing Ltd.

—Alphabet Book Gg. 2009. (Quick60 Alphabet Bks.). (ENG., Illus.). 12p. (J). pap. (978-1-77540-006-6(9)) Iversen Publishing Ltd.

—Alphabet Book Hh. 2009. (Quick60 Alphabet Bks.). (ENG., Illus.). 12p. (J). pap. (978-1-77540-007-3(7)) Iversen Publishing Ltd.

—Alphabet Book Ii. 2009. (Quick60 Alphabet Bks.). (ENG., Illus.). 12p. (J). pap. (978-1-77540-008-0(5)) Iversen Publishing Ltd.

—Alphabet Book Jj. 2009. (Quick60 Alphabet Bks.). (ENG., Illus.). 12p. (J). pap. (978-1-77540-009-7(3)) Iversen Publishing Ltd.

—Alphabet Book Kk. 2009. (Quick60 Alphabet Bks.). (ENG., Illus.). 12p. (J). pap. (978-1-77540-010-3(7)) Iversen Publishing Ltd.

—Alphabet Book Ll. 2009. (Quick60 Alphabet Bks.). (ENG., Illus.). 12p. (J). pap. (978-1-77540-011-0(5)) Iversen Publishing Ltd.

—Alphabet Book Mm. 2009. (ENG., Illus.). 12p. (J). pap. (978-1-77540-012-7(3)) Iversen Publishing Ltd.

—Alphabet Book Nn. 2009. (Quick60 Alphabet Bks.). (ENG., Illus.). 12p. (J). pap. (978-1-77540-013-4(1)) Iversen Publishing Ltd.

—Alphabet Book Oo. 2009. (Quick60 Alphabet Bks.). (ENG., Illus.). 12p. (J). pap. (978-1-77540-014-1(X)) Iversen Publishing Ltd.

—Alphabet Book Pp. 2009. (Quick60 Alphabet Bks.). (ENG., Illus.). 12p. (J). pap. (978-1-77540-015-8(8)) Iversen Publishing Ltd.

—Alphabet Book Zz. 2009. (Quick60 Alphabet Bks.). (ENG., Illus.). 12p. (J). pap. (978-1-77540-025-7(5)) Iversen Publishing Ltd.

Jeopardy Langauge Arts Grade 4. 2006. (J). 28.00 (978-1-933178-54-7(X)) Pflaum Publishing Group.

Jeopardy Langauge Arts Grade 5. 2006. (J). 28.00 (978-1-933178-55-4(8)) Pflaum Publishing Group.

Jeopardy Language Arts Grade 3. 2006. (J). 28.00 (978-1-933178-53-0(1)) Pflaum Publishing Group.

Johnson, Michael. Iroquois: People of the Longhouse. 2013. (ENG., Illus.). 160p. 35.00 (978-1-77085-218-1(2), 9781770852181) Firefly Bks., Ltd.

Jordan, Christopher. Hockey ABC. 2010. (My First NHL Bks.). (ENG., Illus.). 30p. (J). (gr. -1). bds. (978-1-55168-365-2(2)) Me to We.

Josiah, Iris. Tiny Bird's Alphabet Book. 2015. (Illus.). 40p. (J). pap. (978-0-9572728-9-7(8)) Tiny Island Pr.

Joubert, Beverly & Joubert, Dereck. African Animal Alphabet. 2011. (ENG., Illus.). 48p. (J). (gr. -1-k). 16.95 (978-1-4263-0781-2(0), National Geographic Children's Bks.) National Geographic Society.

Kalman, Bobbie. The ABCs of Continents. 2009. (ABCs of the Natural World Ser.). (ENG., Illus.). 32p. (J). (gr. 1-5). pap. (978-0-7787-3434-5(X)) Crabtree Publishing Co.

—The ABCs of Insects. 2009. (ABCs of the Natural World Ser.). (ENG., Illus.). 32p. (J). (gr. 1-5). pap. (978-0-7787-3436-9(6)) Crabtree Publishing Co.

Kaufman, Elliott, photos by. Alphabet Everywhere. 2012. (ENG., Illus.). 60p. (J). (gr. -1). 14.95 (978-0-7892-1115-6(7), Abbeville Kids) Abbeville Pr., Inc.

Kidzup Productions Staff. I'm Learning Spanish. 2005. (J). Vol. 1. 12.99 (978-1-894677-75-2(7)) Vol. 2. 12.99 (978-1-894677-76-9(5)) Kidzup Productions.

Kiehm, Eve Begley. B Is for Bagpipes: A Scotland Alphabet. Rutherford, Alexa, illus. 2010. (Discover the World Ser.). (ENG.). 40p. (J). 17.95 (978-1-58536-453-4(3)) Sleeping Bear Pr.

Kindle, Karen. Using Read-Alouds to Teach Vocabulary: Research-Based Strategies & Model Lessons for Using Fiction & Nonfiction Books to Build Children's Vocabulary & Improve Their Reading, Writing, & Speaking Skills. 2011. (ENG.). 128p. (gr. k-2). pap. 18.99 (978-0-545-16513-6(X), Teaching Resources) Scholastic, Inc.

Kirk, Heather. My First Picture Alphabet. 2012. (ENG., Illus.). 18p. (J). 9.95 (978-1-84135-522-1(4)) Award Pubns. Ltd. GBR. Dist: Parkwest Pubns., Inc.

Kirszner, Laurie G. Brief Holt Handbook for UCF. 3rd ed. pap. 48.95 (978-0-8384-7081-7(5)) Cengage Heinle.

Kirszner, Laurie G. & Mandell, Stephen R. Brief Holt Handbook with APA Update Card. 3rd ed. pap. 43.95 (978-0-8384-7817-2(4)); pap. 49.95 (978-0-8384-8227-8(9)) Cengage Heinle.

Klingel, Cynthia Fitterer & Klingel, Cynthia. Go Fly a Kite! (and Other Sayings We Don't Really Mean) Gallagher-Cole, Mernie, illus. 2007. (Sayings & Phrases Ser.). (ENG.). 24p. (J). (gr. 2-5). 28.50 (978-1-59296-904-3(6), 200788) Child's World, Inc., The.

—You Let the Cat Out of the Bag! (and Other Crazy Animal Sayings) Cole, Mernie, illus. 2007. (Sayings & Phrases Ser.). (ENG.). 24p. (J). (gr. 2-5). 28.50 (978-1-59296-903-6(8), 200791) Child's World, Inc., The.

—You're Clean as a Whistle! (And Other Silly Sayings) Cole, Mernie & Gallagher-Cole, Mernie, illus. 2007. (Sayings & Phrases Ser.). (ENG.). 24p. (J). (gr. 2-5). 28.50 (978-1-59296-905-0(4), 200792) Child's World, Inc., The.

Kontis, Alethea. Alpha Oops! The Day Z Went First. Kolar, Bob, illus. 2012. lib. bdg. 17.20 (978-0-606-26928-5(2), Turtleback) Turtleback Bks.

Kossuth, Kornel. English for Common Entrance 13+ Practice Book. 2014. (ENG.). 112p. (gr. 8-10). pap. 39.50 (978-1-4718-0411-3(9)) Hodder Education Group GBR. Dist: Trans-Atlantic Pubns., Inc.

Lagunilla, Cheryl, told to. The ABC's of Tennis. 2003. (Illus.). (J). lib. bdg. 24.95 (978-0-9726419-0-6(4)) GHL Publishing LLC.

Lambert, Deborah. Adjectives. 2009. (Learning to Write Ser.). (Illus.). 24p. (J). (gr. 4-6). 8.95 (978-1-60596-049-4(7)); lib. bdg. 24.45 (978-1-60596-048-7(9)) Weigl Pubs., Inc.

—Adverbs. 2009. (Learning to Write Ser.). 24p. (J). (gr. 4-6). 8.95 (978-1-60596-051-7(9)); (Illus.). lib. bdg. 24.45 (978-1-60596-050-0(0)) Weigl Pubs., Inc.

Lambert, Deborah G. Adjectives. 2016. **(978-1-5105-2273-2(5))** SmartBook Media, Inc.

—Adverbs. 2016. **(978-1-5105-2275-6(1))** SmartBook Media, Inc.

—Nouns. 2016. (J). **(978-1-5105-2283-1(2))** SmartBook Media, Inc.

—Pronouns. 2016. **(978-1-5105-2287-9(5))** SmartBook Media, Inc.

—Verbs. 2016. **(978-1-5105-2289-3(1))** SmartBook Media, Inc.

Langsam, Miriam. Velcro Interactive Phonics Instruction Book. (Illus.). (J). (gr. 2-4). pap. (978-0-9673268-1-8(8)) Learning Fasten-Ations, Inc.

Language Arts. 2004. (Switched on Schoolhouse Ser.).Tr. of Language Arts. (YA). (gr. 7). cd-rom 69.95 (978-0-7403-0588-7(3));Set. (Illus.). (gr. 11). tchr. ed., stu. ed. 66.95 (978-1-58095-706-9(4), LAN1115, Lifepac);Set. (Illus.). (gr. 12). tchr. ed., stu. ed. 51.95 (978-1-58095-709-0(9), LAN1215, Lifepac) Alpha Omega Pubns., Inc.

Language Arts: Student Testing Kit. 2004. (gr. 7-12). pap., stu. ed. 5.00 (978-1-58095-816-5(8), LD002, Lifepac) Alpha Omega Pubns., Inc.

Language Works: Cheese. (J). pap. 16.15 (978-0-8136-3630-6(2)) Modern Curriculum Pr.

Language Works Staff. Early Morning, Vol. 1. 16p. (J). pap. (978-0-8136-3539-2(X)) Modern Curriculum Pr.

—Language Works Vol. I: Crocodile. 8p. (J). pap. (978-0-8136-3531-6(4)) Modern Curriculum Pr.

—Peter & the Wolf. 32p. (J). pap. (978-0-8136-3592-7(6)) Modern Curriculum Pr.

—Red Hen. 24p. (J). pap. (978-0-8136-3577-4(2)) Modern Curriculum Pr.

—Red Jack. 24p. (J). pap. (978-0-8136-3591-0(8)) Modern Curriculum Pr.

—Rhyme Time. 8p. (J). pap. (978-0-8136-3562-0(4)) Modern Curriculum Pr.

—Stone Soup. 8p. (J). pap. (978-0-8136-3556-9(X)) Modern Curriculum Pr.

Lanza, Janet R. & Flahive, Lynn K. Blooming Speech & Language Activities. 2003. (J). spiral bd. 37.95 (978-0-7606-0509-7(2)) LinguiSystems, Inc.

Laurence, Jo. How to Be a Wizard at Nursery Rhymes. Ford, Kate, illus. 48p. (J). (gr. 1-3). pap. (978-1-876367-28-2(8)) Wizard Bks.

LeapFrog Staff. LeapPad Grade 1 Getting Starter Kit. 2003. (Illus.). (J). (gr. 1). spiral bd. 99.00 (978-1-59319-014-9(X), LeapFrog Schl. Hse.) LeapFrog Enterprises, Inc.

—LeapPad Grade 2 Getting Starter Kit. 2003. (Illus.). (J). (gr. 2). spiral bd. 99.00 (978-1-59319-015-6(8), LeapFrog Schl. Hse.) LeapFrog Enterprises, Inc.

—LeapPad Kindergarten Getting Starter Kit. 2003. (Illus.). (J). spiral bd. 99.00 (978-1-59319-013-2(1), LeapFrog Schl. Hse.) LeapFrog Enterprises, Inc.

Lee, David. Ellie's Family Album. 2013. (Rosen Readers Ser.). (ENG.). 24p. (J). (gr. 2-3). pap. 8.25 (978-1-4777-2257-2(2)); pap. 49.50 (978-1-4777-2258-9(0)) Rosen Publishing Group, Inc., The. (Rosen Classroom).

Let's Print (Modern) 2003. 16p. (J). 3.79 (978-1-58792-049-3(2)) Trend Enterprises, Inc.

Let's Print (Zaner-Bloser) 2003. 16p. (J). 3.79 (978-1-58792-048-6(4)) Trend Enterprises, Inc.

Letters & Numbers. (Early Learning Ser.). (J). incl. audio NewSound, LLC.

Letts 11+, Letts. 11+ Practice Test Papers for the CEM Tests. 2017. (Letts 11+ Success Ser.). (ENG.). 312p. (J). (gr. 4-7). pap. 29.99 **(978-1-84419-898-6(7))** HarperCollins Pubs. Ltd. GBR. Dist: Independent Pubs. Group.

Level A. (J). (gr. 1). 6.50 (978-0-669-20678-4(4)) Houghton Mifflin Harcourt School Pubs.

Lewis, Jan, illus. My First Learning Library: 3 Great Books: First Abc First 123 First Words, 3 vols. 2014. (ENG.). 72p. (J). (gr. -1-1). bds., bds., bds. 9.99 (978-1-86147-387-5(7), Armadillo) Anness Publishing GBR. Dist: National Bk. Network.

Lindop, Christine. Where Is It? 2010. (ENG., Illus.). 20p. 4.81 (978-0-19-440084-8(0)) Oxford Univ. Pr., Inc.

LinguiSystems. Preschool Phonology Cards. 2007. (J). 69.95 (978-0-7606-9953-9(4)) LinguiSystems, Inc.

The Lion & the Mouse. 2012. (Collins Big Cat Ser.). (ENG., Illus.). 16p. (J). pap., wbk. ed. 4.99 (978-0-00-747292-5(7)) HarperCollins Pubs. Ltd. GBR. Dist: Independent Pubs. Group.

Literacy & Math Centers. 2005. (J). pap. (978-1-60015-019-7(5)) Steps To Literacy, LLC.

Lluch, Alex A. I Like to Learn Alphabet: Zoo Clues. 2011. (ENG.). 32p. (J). (gr. -1-k). bds. 4.95 (978-1-934386-00-2(6)) WS Publishing.

Loewen, Nancy. The Duckster Ducklings Go to Mars: Understanding Capitalization. 2015. (Language on the Loose Ser.). (ENG., Illus.). 24p. (gr. 2-4). pap. 7.95 (978-1-4795-6970-0(4)) Picture Window Bks.

—She Sells Seashells & Other Tricky Tongue Twisters, 1 vol. Wu, Donald, illus. 2010. (Ways to Say It Ser.). (ENG.). 24p. (gr. 3-5). lib. bdg. 27.99 (978-1-4048-6273-9(0)) Picture Window Bks.

Long, Ethan. Ms. Spell. 2015. (ENG., Illus.). 32p. (J). (gr. 1-4). 15.95 (978-0-8234-3292-9(0)) Holiday Hse., Inc.

Lopez, Andre. Emily's Electricity Experiments. 2013. (Rosen Readers Ser.). (ENG.). 24p. (J). (gr. 3-4). pap. 49.50 (978-1-4777-2459-0(1)); pap. 8.25 (978-1-4777-2458-3(3)) Rosen Publishing Group, Inc., The. (Rosen Classroom).

Lord, Roberta. Reflections: Albanian Version. 2003. 200p. 9.95 net. (978-1-931934-24-4(X)) Back Yard Pub.

Lucia Kemp, Henry. Now I Know My Word Families & Sight Words. 2014. (Now I Know My Ser.). (ENG.). 224p. (gr. -1-1). pap. 8.99 (978-0-545-77683-7(X), Teaching Resources) Scholastic, Inc.

Lundquist, Joegil K. & Lundquist, Jeanne L. English from the Roots up, Volume II: Help for Reading, Writing, Spelling & S. A. T. Scores. 2003. (English from the Roots Up Ser.). (Illus.). 107p. (J). (gr. -1-3). 44.95 (978-1-885942-30-2(3)) Cune Pr., LLC.

—English from the Roots up Volume II: Help for Reading, Writing, Spelling, & S. A. T. Scores, vols. 2, II. 2003. (Illus.). 125p. 29.95 net. (978-1-885942-31-9(1)) Cune Pr., LLC.

MacPhee, K. M. Maths & English: Basics Manual for Young People. 2010. 254p. pap. (978-0-7552-0482-3(4)) Authors OnLine, Ltd.

Magner, Laura. Researching Adventures: Challenging GLYPH-Making Activities. 2004. (J). pap. 12.95 (978-1-931334-43-3(9)) Pieces of Learning.

MagneTalk Match-Up Adventure Kit (with Barrier) Gb181. 2006. (J). 59.99 (978-1-58650-616-2(1)) Super Duper Pubns.

MagneTalk Match-Up Adventure Kit (without Barrier) Gb182. 2006. (J). 59.99 (978-1-58650-653-7(6)) Super Duper Pubns.

Maher, Adele. Franky Fox's Fun with English Readers Level A1. Maher, Adele & Cline, Mike, illus. 2007. 228p. (J). 26.99 (978-0-9777419-5-3(8)) Lingo Pr. LLC.

Main Idea & Details (Gr. 4-5) 2004. (J). (978-1-58232-132-5(9)) ECS Learning Systems, Inc.

Make-a-Story Journal. 2004. (J). pap. 12.95 (978-1-56911-183-3(9)) Learning Resources, Inc.

Martin, Kathy. Animals, Birds & the Alphabets. 2011. 32p. 14.39 (978-1-4567-3302-5(8)) AuthorHouse.

Marzollo, Jean. I Spy Letters. Wick, Walter, illus. 2012. (I Spy Ser.). (ENG.). 32p. (J). (gr. -1-k). pap. 3.99 (978-0-545-41584-2(5)) Scholastic, Inc.

McDonald, Susan. I Like Different Books with Different Looks. 2012. 20p. pap. 16.64 (978-1-4669-9845-2(8)) Trafford Publishing.

McNamara, Margaret. Apple ABC. Parker, Jake, illus. 2012. (J). (978-0-439-72809-6(6)) Scholastic, Inc.

Meador, Karen. Tiered Activities for Learning Centers. 2004. (J). pap. 15.95 (978-1-931334-29-7(3)) Pieces of Learning.

Medcalf, Carol & Hempstock, Becky. Letts Monster Practice e Starting School Age 4-5. 2014. (Letts Monster Practice Ser.). (ENG.). 32p. (J). (gr. -1-k). pap. 6.99 (978-1-84419-773-6(5)) HarperCollins Pubs. Ltd. GBR. Dist: Independent Pubs. Group.

Meister, Cari. When & Why Did the Horse Fly? Knowing & Using Question Words, 1 vol. Jagucki, Marek, illus. 2013. (Language on the Loose Ser.). (ENG.). 24p. (gr. 2-4). pap. 7.95 (978-1-4795-1918-7(9)); lib. bdg. 27.99 (978-1-4048-8319-2(3)) Picture Window Bks.

Meister, Cari & Loewen, Nancy. Language on the Loose, 4 vols. Jagucki, Marek, illus. 2015. (Language on the Loose Ser.). (ENG.). 24p. (gr. 2-4). 111.96 (978-1-4795-8021-7(X)) Picture Window Bks.

Metropolitan Museum of Art Staff. Nyc ABC. 2011. (ENG., Illus.). 60p. (J). (gr. -1-3). 15.95 (978-0-8478-3701-4(7), Skira) Rizzoli International Pubns., Inc.

Meyer, Jan. Brain Quest, Grade 3: A Whole Year of Curriculum-Based Exercises & Activities in One Fun Book! Shults, Anna, ed. 2008. (ENG., Illus.). 320p. (J). (gr. 3-3). wbk. ed. 12.95 (978-0-7611-4916-3(3), 14916) Workman Publishing Co., Inc.

Miles, Liz. Structure of Words: Understanding Roots & Smaller Parts of Words. 2013. (Find Your Way with Words Ser.). (ENG.). 56p. (gr. 6-7). 34.65 (978-1-4329-7656-9(7)) Heinemann-Raintree.

Moak, Allan. A Big City Alphabet. 2009. (ABC Our Country Ser.). (ENG., Illus.). 32p. (J). (gr. -1-3). pap. 7.95 (978-0-88776-939-9(X), Tundra Bks.) Tundra Bks. CAN. Dist: Penguin Random Hse. LLC.

Mocombe, Paul C. Mocombe's Reading Room Series. 2008. 84p. pap. 15.99 (978-1-4363-2467-0(X)) Xlibris Corp.

Molter, Carey. Silent B As in Lamb, 1 vol. 2004. (Silent Letters Ser.). (ENG., Illus.). 24p. (J). (gr. k-3). lib. bdg. 24.21 (978-1-59197-443-7(7), SandCastle) ABDO Publishing Co.

—Silent Gh As in Light, 1 vol. 2004. (Silent Letters Ser.). (ENG., Illus.). 24p. (J). (gr. k-3). lib. bdg. 24.21 (978-1-59197-444-4(5), SandCastle) ABDO Publishing Co.

—Silent H As in Ghost, 1 vol. 2004. (Silent Letters Ser.). (ENG., Illus.). 24p. (J). (gr. k-3). lib. bdg. 24.21 (978-1-59197-445-1(3), SandCastle) ABDO Publishing Co.

—Silent K As in Knot, 1 vol. 2004. (Silent Letters Ser.). (ENG., Illus.). 24p. (J). (gr. k-3). lib. bdg. 24.21 (978-1-59197-446-8(1), SandCastle) ABDO Publishing Co.

—Silent L As in Chalk, 1 vol. 2004. (Silent Letters Ser.). (ENG., Illus.). 24p. (J). (gr. k-3). lib. bdg. 24.21 (978-1-59197-447-5(X), SandCastle) ABDO Publishing Co.

—Silent W As in Wreath, 1 vol. 2004. (Silent Letters Ser.). (ENG., Illus.). 24p. (J). (gr. k-3). lib. bdg. 24.21 (978-1-59197-448-2(8), SandCastle) ABDO Publishing Co.

Montgomary, Beverly. Mommy where Is Heaven. 2004. (J). (978-0-9763093-3-8(5)) Creative Bk. Pubs.

—Mommy Why Don't I Look Good in the Mirror. 2004. (J). (978-0-9763093-4-5(3)) Creative Bk. Pubs.

Moore, Sheila. Abadaba Alphabet: Learning Letter Sounds. Holsinger, Carol, illus. 2006. 31p. (gr. -1-3). 19.95 (978-0-9789473-0-9(4)) Abadaba Reading LLC.

Morning Bath: Big Book: Level M. Group 1. (Sunshine Ser.). 24p. 36.50 (978-0-7802-5795-5(2)) Wright Group/McGraw-Hill.

Myers, R. E. Language Fundamentals. Mitchell, Judith, ed. Smith, Bron, illus. 2005. 96p. (J). Bk. 1. pap. 11.95 (978-1-57310-450-0(7))Bk. 2. pap. 11.95 (978-1-57310-451-7(5)) Teaching & Learning Co.

Nadakavukaren Schefer, Krista. Social Regulation in the WTO: Trade Policy & International Legal Development. 2011. (ENG., Illus.). 336p. pap. 56.00 (978-1-84980-078-5(2)) Elgar, Edward Publishing, Inc.

Nama, Michael D., et al. Stay Tuned Workbook For 6 éme. 2nd rev. ed. 2005. (ENG.). 64p. pap. 3.70 (978-0-521-67579-6(0)) Cambridge Univ. Pr.

Neist, P. M. Barely Behaving Daughters. 2013. (Illus.). (J). (978-1-940413-01-3(X), Blackbirch Pr., Inc.) Mardick Pr.

Nixon, Caroline. Kid's Box, 1 vol. 2nd ed. 2014. (ENG.). 48p. pap., tchr. ed. 202.50 incl. DVD (978-1-107-63114-4(9)) Cambridge Univ. Pr.

—Kid's Box American English Level 1 Student's Book. 2010. (ENG.). 96p. pap. 21.25 (978-0-521-17762-7(6)) Cambridge Univ. Pr.

—Kid's Box, Level 2, 103, Pack. 2nd rev. ed. 2014. (ENG.). 103p. 47.75 (978-1-107-68044-9(1)) Cambridge Univ. Pr.

—Kid's Box Starter Flashcards, 78, Pack. 2nd ed. 2014. (ENG.). 78p. 45.75 (978-1-107-66022-9(X)) Cambridge Univ. Pr.

Nolan, Chris & Spencer, Lauren. Writing to Persuade. 2011. (Illus.). 63p. (J). 77.70 (978-1-4488-4749-5(4), Rosen Reference); (J). pap. 12.95 (978-1-4488-4691-7(9), Rosen Reference); (YA). (gr. 5-9). lib. bdg. 31.95 (978-1-4488-4685-6(4)) Rosen Publishing Group, Inc., The.

Noyed, Bob & Amoroso, Cynthia. Cute! The Sound of Long U. 2015. (Long & Short Vowels Ser.). (ENG.). 24p. (J). (gr. -1-2). 25.64 (978-1-63407-021-8(6), 208856) Child's World, Inc., The.

Nunn, Daniel. ABCs at Home, 1 vol. 2012. (Everyday Alphabet Ser.). (ENG.). 32p. (gr. -1-k). pap. 9.95 (978-1-4109-4736-9(X)); lib. bdg. 25.32 (978-1-4109-4731-4(9)) Heinemann-Raintree.

—ABCs in Nature, 1 vol. 2012. (Everyday Alphabet Ser.). (ENG.). 32p. (gr. -1-k). pap. 9.95 (978-1-4109-4737-6(8)) Heinemann-Raintree.

O'Connor, John. Literacy in Context for AQA A. 2003. (Literacy in Context Ser.). (ENG., Illus.). 208p. pap. 23.00 (978-0-521-53528-1(X)) Cambridge Univ. Pr.

O'Dell. Elements of Language. 2003. (Elements of Language Ser.). (gr. 6-18). pupil's gde. ed. 64.73 (978-0-03-052662-6(0)) Holt McDougal.

Oelschlager, Vanita. Life Is a Bowl Full of Cherries. 2011. (ENG., Illus.). 40p. (J). (gr. -1-3). 15.95 (978-0-9826366-3-3(6)); pap. 8.95 (978-0-9826366-2-6(8)) VanitaBooks.

Ogburn, Jacqueline K. A Dignity of Dragons. Ceccoli, Nicoletta, illus. 2010. (ENG.). 32p. (J). (gr. -1-3). 17.00 (978-0-618-86254-2(4)) Houghton Mifflin Harcourt Publishing Co.

The OH Book. 2007. (Illus.). 12p. (J). 14.99 (978-0-9793506-1-0(1)) Sportime International.

Olien, Rebecca. Kids Write: Fantasy & Sci Fi, Mystery, Autobiography, Adventure & More! Kline, Michael, illus. 2005. (ENG.). 128p. (J). (gr. 4-7). pap. 14.25 (978-0-8249-6771-0(2), Ideal Pubns.) Worthy Publishing.
Olivia's ABC. 2014. (ENG., Illus.). 30p. (J). (gr. -1-k). bds. 7.99 (978-1-4814-2192-8(1), Atheneum Bks. for Young Readers) Simon & Schuster Children's Publishing.
Onish, Liane. Brain Quest, Grade 2: A Whole Year of Curriculum-Based Exercises & Activities in One Fun Book! Swann, Jill, ed. 2008. (ENG., Illus.). 320p. (J). (gr. 2-2). wbk. ed. 12.95 (978-0-7611-4915-6(5), 14915) Workman Publishing Co., Inc.
—Brain Quest, Pre-K: A Whole Year of Curriculum-Based Exercises & Activities in One Fun Book! Fung, Jane, ed. 2008. (ENG., Illus.). 320p. (J). (gr. -1 — 1). wbk. ed. 12.95 (978-0-7611-4961-3(9), 14961) Workman Publishing Co., Inc.
Open Court Staff. Breaking Code Sentence Strips. (J). pap. (978-0-87548-958-2(3), 8513) Open Court Publishing Co.
Orange & Turquoise Levels Certificate Only. (gr. k-5). 89.00 (978-0-7578-6543-5(7)) Rigby Education.
Orange Level Certificate Only. (Sails Literacy Ser.). (gr. 1-6). 89.00 (978-0-7578-6554-1(2)) Rigby Education.
Oshiro, Kim Teresa. A B C in Harmony. 2011. 36p. (gr. -1). 15.49 (978-1-4269-6164-9(2)) Trafford Publishing.
Otfinoski, Steven. F. W. Prep, 8 bks., Set. Incl. Extraordinary Short Story Writing. (Illus.). 128p. (YA). (gr. 8-13). 2005. lib. bdg. 31.00 (978-0-531-16760-1(7), Watts, Franklin); 2005. Set lib. bdg. 244.00 o.p. (978-0-531-16823-3(9), Watts, Franklin) Scholastic Library Publishing.
O'Toole, Patrick & Coloring Books Staff. Alphabetimals Coloring Book. 2012. (Dover Coloring Bks.). (ENG.). 32p. (J). (gr. -1-2). pap. 3.99 (978-0-486-48700-7(8)) Dover Pubns., Inc.
Owings, Lisa. Boom! Zap! Pow! Teaching Onomatopoeia. 2016. (Playing with Words Ser.). (ENG.). 16p. (J). (gr. -1-2). 25.64 (978-1-5038-0832-4(7), 210682) Child's World, Inc., The.
Pallotta, Jerry. The Ocean Alphabet Board Book. Mazzola, Frank, Jr., illus. 2003. (ENG.). 28p. (J). (-k). bds. 7.95 (978-1-57091-524-6(5)) Charlesbridge Publishing, Inc.
Parker, Helen. Trace, Stick Learn Borrar Primeras Palabras/Wipe Clean First Words. 2007. (Trace, Stick & Learn Ser.). (Illus.). 12p. (gr. -1-k). pap. (978-1-84610-645-3(1)) Make Believe Ideas.
Patrizzi, Barbara. O Is for Oystercatcher: A Book of Seaside ABCs. Patrizzi, Barbara, illus. 2003. (Illus.). 55p. 15.95 (978-1-59322-008-2(1)) Down The Shore Publishing Corp.
Pearson, Yvonne. Cows, Horses, & Sheep: Teaching Plural Words. 2016. (Playing with Words Ser.). (ENG.). 16p. (J). (gr. -1-2). 25.64 (978-1-5038-0834-8(3), 210684) Child's World, Inc., The.
Pebble Soup Explorations: Complete Pebble Soup Explorations Package. 1650.00 (978-0-7578-3313-7(6)) Rigby Education.
Pebble Soup Explorations: Pebble Soup Explorations Extra Ingredients. 239.00 (978-0-7578-3341-0(1)) Rigby Education.
Pebble Soup Explorations: SAVE when you purchase the Complete Pebble Soup Exploration/Exploraciones Program! 3100.00 (978-0-7578-5226-8(2)) Rigby Education.
Phillips, Heather. Habitats. Tom, Darcy et al, eds. Tom, Darcy, illus. 2003. (Stepping into Standards Theme Ser.). 64p. (J). (gr. 2-4). pap. 10.99 (978-1-59198-007-0(0), CTP2489) Creative Teaching Pr., Inc.
Phonics Ad Libs: Blends & Digraphs. 2003. (J). pap. 9.95 (978-1-56911-105-5(7)) Learning Resources, Inc.
Piatti, Celestino. Celestino Piatti's Animal ABC. 2015. (ENG., Illus.). 40p. (J). 17.95 (978-0-7358-4206-9(X)) North-South Bks., Inc.
Pickles, Jonathan & Van Ackooy, Maureen. English (ELA) 8 X-treme Review: Concise Training for NYS ELA Intermediate Assessment. Stich, Paul & Gamsey, Wayne, eds. 2007. (Illus.). 112p. per. 13.95 (978-0-935487-88-6(3), X-treme Reviews) N&N Publishing Co., Inc.
Pinestein Press. Abcs of Language & Literacy. Carroll, Raymond, illus. 2007. 180p. per. 19.99 (978-0-9795364-4-1(8)) Chowder Bay Bks.
Pinnell, Gay Su & Fountas, Irene C. Phonics Lessons: Letters, Words, & How They Work - Grade 2. 2003. (Phonics Lessons Ser.). (ENG.). 496p. (J). (gr. 2). pap. 82.00 (978-0-325-00409-9(9), E00409) Heinemann.
Playing with Words, 6 Packs. (Action Packs Ser.). 104p. (gr. 3-5). 44.00 (978-0-7635-2988-8(5)) Rigby Education.
Potter, Beatrix. Peter Rabbit A B C: With Giant Fold-Out Pages. 2013. (Peter Rabbit Ser.). (ENG., Illus.). 16p. (J). (gr. -1-k). bds. 6.99 (978-0-7232-6864-2(9), Warne) Penguin Young Readers Group.
Powell, Marie. What Good Is a U? 2015. (Vowels Ser.). (ENG., Illus.). 16p. (J). (gr. k-2). 17.95 (978-1-60753-712-0(5), Amicus Readers) Amicus Publishing.
—What Good Is a Y? 2015. (Vowels Ser.). (ENG., Illus.). 16p. (gr. k-2). 17.95 (978-1-60753-713-7(3), Amicus Readers) Amicus Publishing.
—What Good Is an E? 2015. (Vowels Ser.). (ENG., Illus.). 16p. (J). (gr. k-2). 17.95 (978-1-60753-709-0(5), Amicus Readers) Amicus Publishing.
—What Good Is an I? 2015. (Vowels Ser.). (ENG., Illus.). 16p. (J). (gr. k-2). 17.95 (978-1-60753-710-6(9), Amicus Readers) Amicus Publishing.
—What Good Is an O? 2015. (Vowels Ser.). (ENG., Illus.). 16p. (J). (gr. k-2). 17.95 (978-1-60753-711-3(7), Amicus Readers) Amicus Publishing.
Practice Power School Bus Book: First Grade Language Arts. 2003. (Illus.). 24p. (J). (gr. k-1). spiral bd. (978-1-930355-43-9(2)) Bright of America.
Preece, Bronwyn & Walton, Alex. Gulf Islands Alphabet. 2012. (ENG., Illus.). 56p. (J). (gr. k). 17.95 (978-1-897476-29-1(9)) Simply Read Bks. CAN. Dist: Ingram Publisher Services.
Priddy, Roger. Little Alphaprints: Words. 2015. (Alphaprints Ser.). (ENG.). 10p. (J). (gr. -1 — 1). bds. 5.99 (978-0-312-51831-8(5), 9780312518318, Priddy Bks.) St. Martin's Pr.
—Sneak-a-Peek Words. 2015. (Sneak-A-Peek Ser.). (ENG.). 12p. (J). (gr. -1 — 1). bds. 7.99 (978-0-312-51801-1(3), 9780312518011, Priddy Bks.) St. Martin's Pr.
Prior, Jennifer. Time for Kids: Practicing for Today's Tests Language Arts Level 3. 2015. (Test Preparation for Reading Comp Ser.). (ENG., Illus.). 112p. (gr. 3-3). pap. 24.99 (978-1-4258-1436-6(0)) Shell Educational Publishing.
Progressive Langauge Staff, prod. Bluw Wolf & Friends, Units 1-4. l.t. ed. 2004. (Illus.). 53p. act. bk. ed. (978-0-9758759-3-3(0)) Progressive Language, Inc.
Proudfit, Benjamin. Writing Letters. 2014. (Write Right! Ser.). 24p. (J). (gr. 2-5). 22.60 (978-1-4824-1132-4(6)) Stevens, Gareth Publishing LLLP.
Publications International Ltd. Staff, ed. Baby's ABC. 2010. 18p. (J). bds. 7.98 (978-1-60553-961-4(9)) Publications International, Ltd.
—My Alphabet Book. 2011. 32p. (J). bds. 5.98 (978-1-4508-1020-3(9)) Publications International, Ltd.
Purslow, Frances. Descriptive Paragraphs. 2016. **(978-1-5105-2277-0(8))** SmartBook Media, Inc.
—Descriptive Paragraphs. 2007. (Learning to Write Ser.). (Illus.). 24p. (J). (gr. 4-7). lib. bdg. 24.45 (978-1-59036-737-7(5)); per. 8.95 (978-1-59036-738-4(3)) Weigl Pubs., Inc.
—Expository Paragraphs. 2016. **(978-1-5105-2279-4(4))** SmartBook Media, Inc.
—Expository Paragraphs. 2007. (Learning to Write Ser.). (Illus.). 24p. (J). (gr. 4-7). lib. bdg. 24.45 (978-1-59036-735-3(9)); per. 8.95 (978-1-59036-736-0(7)) Weigl Pubs., Inc.
—Narrative Paragraphs. 2016. **(978-1-5105-2281-7(6))** SmartBook Media, Inc.
—Narrative Paragraphs. 2007. (Learning to Write Ser.). (Illus.). 24p. (J). (gr. 4-7). lib. bdg. 24.45 (978-1-59036-733-9(2)); per. 8.95 (978-1-59036-734-6(0)) Weigl Pubs., Inc.
Purslow, Frances. Persuasive Paragraphs. 2016. (J). **(978-1-5105-2285-5(9))** SmartBook Media, Inc.
—Persuasive Paragraphs. 2007. (Learning to Write Ser.). (Illus.). 24p. (J). (gr. 4-6). lib. bdg. 24.45 (978-1-59036-731-5(6)); per. 8.95 (978-1-59036-732-2(4)) Weigl Pubs., Inc.
Quinton, Sasha. Go-Go-Goat: A Phonics Reader. 2009. (Illus.). pap. (978-1-936199-09-9(2)) Book Shop, Ltd., The.
—I-Spy: A Phonics Reader. 2009. (Illus.). (978-1-936199-06-8(8)) Book Shop, Ltd., The.
—Peck-A-peck: A Phonics Reader. 2009. (Illus.). pap. (978-1-936199-08-2(4)) Book Shop, Ltd., The.
—Rat-A-Tat: A Phonics Reader. 2009. (Illus.). pap. (978-1-936199-04-4(1)) Book Shop, Ltd., The.
—Ring-A-Ding: A Phonics Reader. 2009. (Illus.). pap. (978-1-936199-00-6(9)) Book Shop, Ltd., The.
—Root-A-Toot: A Phonics Reader. 2009. (Illus.). pap. (978-1-936199-01-3(7)) Book Shop, Ltd., The.
—Rub-A-Dub: A Phonics Reader. 2009. (Illus.). (978-1-936199-03-7(3)) Book Shop, Ltd., The.
—Yay-Hooray: A Phonics Reader. 2009. (Illus.). pap. (978-1-936199-07-5(6)) Book Shop, Ltd., The.
Raby, Charlotte & Jenny, Christine. Seasons Scrapbook. 2012. (Collins Big Cat Ser.). (ENG.). 16p. (J). pap., wbk. ed. 4.99 (978-0-00-747512-4(8)) HarperCollins Pubs. Ltd. GBR. Dist: Independent Pubs. Group.
Rau, Dana Meachen. Ace Your Writing Assignment. 2009. (Ace It! Information Literacy Ser.). (Illus.). 48p. (J). (gr. 2-5). lib. bdg. 25.27 (978-0-7660-3394-8(5)) Enslow Pubs., Inc.
Reeg, Cynthia. Hamster Holidays: Noun & Adjective Adventures. Grady, Kit, illus. 2009. 24p. pap. 10.95 (978-1-935137-62-7(X)) Guardian Angel Publishing, Inc.
Research Masters Staff & Barron's Educational Staff. Barron's Common Core Success Grade 2 ELA Workbook: Preparing Students for a Brilliant Future. 2015. (Barron's Common Core Success Ser.). (ENG., Illus.). 168p. (gr. 2-2). pap. 12.99 (978-1-4380-0671-0(3)) Barron's Educational Series, Inc.
—Barron's Common Core Success Grade 5 ELA Workbook: Preparing Students for a Brilliant Future. 2015. (Barron's Common Core Success Ser.). (ENG.). 184p. (gr. 5-5). pap. 12.99 (978-1-4380-0677-2(2)) Barron's Educational Series, Inc.
—Barron's Common Core Success Grade 6 ELA Workbook: Preparing Students for a Brilliant Future. 2015. (Barron's Common Core Success Ser.). (ENG., Illus.). 208p. (gr. 6-6). pap. 12.99 (978-1-4380-0679-6(9)) Barron's Educational Series, Inc.
Rice, Dona Herweck. Kids Around the World, 1 vol. 2nd rev. ed. 2014. (TIME for KIDS(r) Nonfiction Readers Ser.). (ENG., Illus.). 20p. (J). (gr. 1-1). pap. 19.96 (978-1-4807-1032-0(6)) Shell Educational Publishing.
—Land, 1 vol. 2nd rev. ed. 2013. (Nonfiction Readers Ser.). (ENG., Illus.). 12p. (J). (gr. 1-1). pap. 15.96 (978-1-4807-1013-9(X)) Shell Educational Publishing.
RIGBY. Across the United States: Fourth Grade Class Collection Books. 2003. (Rigby on Our Way to English Ser.). (ENG.). 32p. (gr. 4-4). pap. 50.70 (978-0-7578-4338-9(7)) Rigby Education.
—Hello! I'm Paty: Second Grade Big Books. 2003. (Rigby on Our Way to English Ser.). (ENG.). 24p. (gr. 2-2). pap. 50.70 (978-0-7578-1413-6(1)) Rigby Education.
Riggs, Kate. Adjectives. 2013. (Illus.). 24p. 25.65 (978-1-60818-236-7(3), Creative Education) Creative Co., The.
—Grammar Basics: Adjectives. 2013. (Grammar Basics Ser.). (ENG., Illus.). 24p. (J). (gr. 1-3). pap. 10.99 (978-0-89812-799-7(8), Creative Paperbacks) Creative Co., The.
—Grammar Basics: Nouns. 2013. (Grammar Basics Ser.). (ENG.). 24p. (J). (gr. 1-3). pap. 10.99 (978-0-89812-801-7(3), Creative Paperbacks) Creative Co., The.
—Grammar Basics: Verbs. 2013. (Grammar Basics Ser.). (ENG.). 24p. (J). (gr. 1-3). pap. 10.99 (978-0-89812-802-4(1), Creative Paperbacks) Creative Co., The.
—Nouns. 2013. 25.65 (978-1-60818-238-1(X), Creative Education) Creative Co., The.
—Verbs. 2013. (J). 25.65 (978-1-60818-239-8(8), Creative Education) Creative Co., The.
Rissman, Rebecca. ABCs at the Park, 1 vol. 2012. (Everyday Alphabet Ser.). (ENG.). 32p. (gr. -1-k). pap. 9.95 (978-1-4109-4735-2(1)); lib. bdg. 25.32 (978-1-4109-4730-7(0)) Heinemann-Raintree.
—ABCs at the Store, 1 vol. 2012. (Everyday Alphabet Ser.). (ENG., Illus.). 32p. (gr. -1-k). pap. 9.95 (978-1-4109-4734-5(3)); lib. bdg. 25.32 (978-1-4109-4729-1(7)) Heinemann-Raintree.
Robertson, Carolyn & Salter, Wanda. Phonological Awareness Test 2 Forms. 2007. (J). 41.95 (978-0-7606-9996-6(8)) LinguiSystems, Inc.
Roman, Edward. My Busy Year. 2012. (InfoMax Readers Ser.). (ENG., Illus.). 24p. (J). (gr. 1-2). pap. 8.25 (978-1-4488-9004-0(7), Rosen Classroom) Rosen Publishing Group, Inc., The.
Rondeau, Amanda. Cat + Fish = Catfish, 1 vol. 2004. (Compound Words Ser.). (ENG., Illus.). 24p. (J). (gr. k-3). lib. bdg. 24.21 (978-1-59197-432-1(1), SandCastle) ABDO Publishing Co.
—Rain + Bow = Rainbow, 1 vol. 2004. (Compound Words Ser.). (ENG., Illus.). 24p. (J). (gr. k-3). lib. bdg. 24.21 (978-1-59197-436-9(4), SandCastle) ABDO Publishing Co.
—Rattle + Snake = Rattlesnake, 1 vol. 2004. (Compound Words Ser.). (ENG., Illus.). 24p. (J). (gr. k-3). lib. bdg. 24.21 (978-1-59197-437-6(2), SandCastle) ABDO Publishing Co.
—Skate + Board = Skateboard, 1 vol. 2004. (Compound Words Ser.). (ENG., Illus.). 24p. (J). (gr. k-3). lib. bdg. 24.21 (978-1-59197-438-3(0), SandCastle) ABDO Publishing Co.
—Snow + Shoe = Snowshoe, 1 vol. 2004. (Compound Words Ser.). (ENG., Illus.). 24p. (J). (gr. k-3). lib. bdg. 24.21 (978-1-59197-439-0(9), SandCastle) ABDO Publishing Co.
—Tea + Pot = Teapot, 1 vol. 2004. (Compound Words Ser.). (ENG., Illus.). 24p. (J). (gr. k-3). lib. bdg. 24.21 (978-1-59197-441-3(0), SandCastle) ABDO Publishing Co.
Rosen Publishing Staff. Core Language Skills: Set 2, 1 vol. 2015. (Core Language Skills Ser.). (ENG.). 24p. (J). 141.60 (978-1-4777-7397-0(5), PowerKids Pr.) Rosen Publishing Group, Inc., The.
—Core Skills: Set 2, 1 vol. 2015. (Core Skills Ser.). (ENG.). 32p. (J). 157.50 (978-1-4777-7372-7(X), PowerKids Pr.) Rosen Publishing Group, Inc., The.
Ruscoe, Michael. Kick Ball Capitalization. 2009. (Grammar All-Stars: Writing Tools Ser.). 32p. (J). (gr. 2-5). pap. 10.50 (978-1-4339-2135-3(9)); lib. bdg. 26.00 (978-1-4339-1942-8(7)) Stevens, Gareth Publishing LLLP. (Gareth Stevens Learning Library).
Salas, Laura Purdie. J Is for Jingle Bells: A Christmas Alphabet, 1 vol. 2010. (Alphabet Fun Ser.). (ENG & ABK.). 32p. (gr. 1-2). lib. bdg. 27.32 (978-1-4296-4463-1(X), Aplus Bks.) Capstone Press of Coughlan Cos.
Salzmann, Mary Elizabeth. Alex & Max, 1 vol. 2005. (First Sounds Ser.). (Illus.). (J). (gr. k-3). (ENG.). 24p. lib. bdg. 24.21 (978-1-59679-122-0(5), SandCastle); 23p. pap. 48.42 (978-1-59679-123-7(3)) ABDO Publishing Co.
—Amy & Abe, 1 vol. 2005. (First Sounds Ser.). (Illus.). (J). (gr. k-3). (ENG.). 24p. lib. bdg. 24.21 (978-1-59679-124-4(1), SandCastle); 23p. pap. 48.42 (978-1-59679-125-1(X)) ABDO Publishing Co.
—Ann & Alan. 2005. (First Sounds Ser.). (Illus.). (J). (gr. k-3). (ENG.). 24p. lib. bdg. 24.21 (978-1-59679-126-8(8), SandCastle); 23p. pap. 48.42 (978-1-59679-127-5(6)) ABDO Publishing Co.
—Bess & Bill, 1 vol. 2005. (First Sounds Ser.). (Illus.). (J). (gr. k-3). (ENG.). 24p. lib. bdg. 24.21 (978-1-59679-216-6(7), SandCastle); 23p. pap. 48.42 (978-1-59679-217-3(5)) ABDO Publishing Co.
—Blair & Blaine, 1 vol. 2005. (First Sounds Ser.). (Illus.). (J). (gr. k-3). (ENG.). 24p. lib. bdg. 24.21 (978-1-59679-128-2(4), SandCastle); 23p. pap. 48.42 (978-1-59679-129-9(2)) ABDO Publishing Co.
—Brandi & Brent, 1 vol. 2005. (First Sounds Ser.). (Illus.). (J). (gr. k-3). (ENG.). 24p. lib. bdg. 24.21 (978-1-59679-130-5(6), SandCastle); 23p. pap. 48.42 (978-1-59679-131-2(4)) ABDO Publishing Co.
—Cassie & Carl, 1 vol. 2005. (First Sounds Ser.). (Illus.). (J). (gr. k-3). (ENG.). 24p. lib. bdg. 24.21 (978-1-59679-132-9(2), SandCastle); 23p. pap. 48.42 (978-1-59679-133-6(0)) ABDO Publishing Co.
—Chelsey & Chad, 1 vol. 2005. (First Sounds Ser.). (J). (gr. k-3). (ENG.). 24p. lib. bdg. 24.21 (978-1-59679-134-3(9), SandCastle); 23p. pap. 48.42 (978-1-59679-135-0(7)) ABDO Publishing Co.
—Cindy & Cecil, 1 vol. 2005. (First Sounds Ser.). (Illus.). (J). (gr. k-3). (ENG.). 24p. lib. bdg. 24.21 (978-1-59679-136-7(5), SandCastle); 23p. pap. 48.42 (978-1-59679-137-4(3)) ABDO Publishing Co.
—Cristy & Craig, 1 vol. 2005. (First Sounds Ser.). (Illus.). (J). (gr. k-3). (ENG.). 24p. lib. bdg. 24.21 (978-1-59679-138-1(1), SandCastle); 23p. pap. 48.42 (978-1-59679-139-8(X)) ABDO Publishing Co.
—Deb & Dan, 1 vol. 2005. (First Sounds Ser.). (Illus.). (J). (gr. k-3). (ENG.). 24p. lib. bdg. 24.21 (978-1-59679-140-4(3), SandCastle); 23p. pap. 48.42 (978-1-59679-141-1(1)) ABDO Publishing Co.
—Drew & Drake, 1 vol. 2005. (First Sounds Ser.). (Illus.). (J). (gr. k-3). (ENG.). 24p. lib. bdg. 24.21 (978-1-59679-142-8(X), SandCastle); 23p. pap. 48.42 (978-1-59679-143-5(8)) ABDO Publishing Co.
Sandviks HOP, Inc. Staff. Hooked on Kindergarten. 2007. 39.99 (978-1-60143-788-4(9)) HOP, LLC.
Santillo, LuAnn. Blends & Ends - Level B, 36 vols. Santillo, LuAnn, ed. 2003. (Half-Pint Kids Readers Ser.). (Illus.). 7p. (J). (gr. -1-1). pap. 39.95 (978-1-59256-127-8(6)) Half-Pint Kids, Inc.
—Moving A-Long Level C, 36 vols. Santillo, LuAnn, ed. 2003. (Half-Pint Kids Readers Ser.). (Illus.). 7p. (J). (gr. -1-1). pap. 39.95 (978-1-59256-128-5(4)) Half-Pint Kids, Inc.
Saviola, Ava. Dinosaur ABCs. 2012. (Dinosaur School Ser.). (Illus.). 24p. (J). (gr. -1-1). pap. 8.15 (978-1-4339-7136-5(4)); lib. bdg. 22.60 (978-1-4339-7135-8(6)) Stevens, Gareth Publishing LLLP.
Schaefer, A. Help Me Find Something. 2007. (ENG., Illus.). 16p. (gr. k-2). 28.50 (978-1-60472-108-9(1)) Rourke Educational Media.
Scheunemann, Pam. Cool Stuff for Reading & Writing: Creative Projects for Kids, 1 vol. 2012. (Cool Stuff Ser.). (ENG., Illus.). 32p. (J). (gr. 3-6). 28.50 (978-1-61714-982-5(9)) ABDO Publishing Co.
—Emma Is Cooking! Word Building with Prefixes & Suffixes, 1 vol. 2012. (Word Building Ser.). (ENG.). 24p. (J). (gr. k-4). 25.65 (978-1-61714-966-5(7)) ABDO Publishing Co.
—The Repainted School: Word Building with Prefixes & Suffixes, 1 vol. 2012. (Word Building Ser.). (ENG.). 24p. (J). (gr. k-4). 25.65 (978-1-61714-969-6(1)) ABDO Publishing Co.
—Silky Is the Luckiest Cat! Word Building with Prefixes & Suffixes, 1 vol. 2012. (Word Building Ser.). (ENG.). 24p. (J). (gr. k-4). 25.65 (978-1-61714-970-2(5)) ABDO Publishing Co.
—Skye & Skip, 1 vol. 2005. (First Sounds Ser.). (Illus.). (J). (gr. k-3). (ENG.). 24p. lib. bdg. 24.21 (978-1-59679-192-3(6), SandCastle); 23p. pap. 48.42 (978-1-59679-193-0(4)) ABDO Publishing Co.
—Sloane & Sly, 1 vol. 2005. (First Sounds Ser.). (Illus.). (J). (gr. k-3). (ENG.). 24p. lib. bdg. 24.21 (978-1-59679-194-7(2), SandCastle); 23p. pap. 48.42 (978-1-59679-195-4(0)) ABDO Publishing Co.
—Stacy & Steve, 1 vol. 2005. (First Sounds Ser.). (Illus.). (J). (gr. k-3). (ENG.). 24p. lib. bdg. 24.21 (978-1-59679-196-1(9), SandCastle); 23p. pap. 48.42 (978-1-59679-197-8(7)) ABDO Publishing Co.
—Tam & Tom, 1 vol. 2005. (First Sounds Ser.). (Illus.). (J). (gr. k-3). (ENG.). 24p. lib. bdg. 24.21 (978-1-59679-198-5(5), SandCastle); 23p. pap. 48.42 (978-1-59679-199-2(3)) ABDO Publishing Co.
—Tracy & Treavor, 1 vol. 2005. (First Sounds Ser.). (ENG., Illus.). 24p. (J). (gr. k-3). lib. bdg. 24.21 (978-1-59679-200-5(0), SandCastle) ABDO Publishing Co.
—Tracy & Trevor (6-pack) 2005. (First Sounds Ser.). (Illus.). 23p. (J). pap. 48.42 (978-1-59679-201-2(9)) ABDO Publishing Co.
—Ulma & Umberto, 1 vol. 2005. (First Sounds Ser.). (ENG.). 24p. (J). (gr. k-3). lib. bdg. 24.21 (978-1-59679-202-9(7), SandCastle) ABDO Publishing Co.
—Ulma & Umberto (6-pack) 2005. (First Sounds Ser.). 23p. (J). pap. 48.42 (978-1-59679-203-6(5)) ABDO Publishing Co.
—Unity & Uri, 1 vol. 2005. (First Sounds Ser.). (gr. k-3). (ENG.). 24p. (J). lib. bdg. 24.21 (978-1-59679-204-3(3), SandCastle); 23p. pap. 48.42 (978-1-59679-205-0(1)) ABDO Publishing Co.
—The Unknown Ballplayer: Word Building with Prefixes & Suffixes, 1 vol. 2012. (Word Building Ser.). (ENG.). 24p. (J). (gr. k-4). 25.65 (978-1-61714-971-9(3)) ABDO Publishing Co.
—Val & Vince, 1 vol. 2005. (First Sounds Ser.). (Illus.). (J). (gr. k-3). (ENG.). 24p. lib. bdg. 24.21 (978-1-59679-206-7(X), SandCastle); 23p. pap. 48.42 (978-1-59679-207-4(8)) ABDO Publishing Co.
—Wendy & Wally, 1 vol. 2005. (First Sounds Ser.). (Illus.). (J). (gr. k-3). (ENG.). 24p. lib. bdg. 24.21 (978-1-59679-208-1(6), SandCastle); 23p. pap. 48.42 (978-1-59679-209-8(4)) ABDO Publishing Co.
—Whitney & Wheeler, 1 vol. 2005. (First Sounds Ser.). (Illus.). (J). (gr. k-3). (ENG.). 24p. lib. bdg. 24.21 (978-1-59679-210-4(8), SandCastle); 23p. pap. 48.42 (978-1-59679-211-1(6)) ABDO Publishing Co.
—Yana & Yosef, 1 vol. 2005. (First Sounds Ser.). (Illus.). (J). (gr. k-3). (ENG.). 24p. lib. bdg. 24.21 (978-1-59679-212-8(4), SandCastle); 23p. pap. 48.42 (978-1-59679-213-5(2)) ABDO Publishing Co.
—Zoe & Zach, 1 vol. 2005. (First Sounds Ser.). (Illus.). (J). (gr. k-3). (ENG.). 24p. lib. bdg. 24.21 (978-1-59679-214-2(0), SandCastle); 23p. pap. 48.42 (978-1-59679-215-9(9)) ABDO Publishing Co.
Scholastic, Inc. Staff. Sight Word Tales Interactive E-Storybooks: 25 e-Books with Engaging Interactive Whiteboard Activities That Teach the Top 100 High-Frequency Words. 2014. (ENG., Illus.). 144p. (-2). 129.99 (978-0-545-64707-6(X), Teaching Resources) Scholastic, Inc.
School Readiness Set, No. 1: Oral Language. 2011. (ENG.). (gr. -1-2). pap. 96.46 (978-1-4296-6778-4(8), NA (CAP)) Capstone Press of Coughlan Cos.
School Zone Publishing Company Staff. English: Grades 1 & 2. (Illus.). (J). 19.99 incl. audio compact disk (978-0-88743-971-1(3)) School Zone Publishing Co.
—English: Grades 3 & 4. (Illus.). (J). 19.99 incl. audio compact disk (978-0-88743-943-8(8)) School Zone Publishing Co.
—Language Arts 1. (Illus.). (J). 19.99 incl. audio compact disk (978-0-88743-969-8(1)) School Zone Publishing Co.
—Language Arts 2. (Illus.). (J). 19.99 incl. audio compact disk (978-0-88743-970-4(5)) School Zone Publishing Co.
Schwartz, Joanne. City Alphabet, 1 vol. Beam, Matt, illus. 2009. (ENG.). 60p. (gr. -1-4). 18.95 (978-0-88899-928-3(3)) Groundwood Bks. CAN. Dist: Publishers Group West (PGW).
Schwartz, Linda. Language Arts Quiz Whiz 3-5, Vol. 430. VanBlaricum, Pam, ed. Armstrong, Beverly, illus. 2004. 128p. (J). (gr. 3-5). pap. 14.99 (978-0-88160-373-6(2), LW-430) Creative Teaching Pr., Inc.
Sesame Workshop, ed. ABC Sesame Street Flash Cards. 2009. (ENG.). 30p. 9.95 (978-1-74185-997-3(2), Ideal Pubns.) Worthy Publishing.
—Pets Elmos World Flash Cards. 2009. (ENG.). 30p. 9.95 (978-1-74185-995-9(6), Ideal Pubns.) Worthy Publishing.
—Your Body Elmos World Flash Cards. 2009. (ENG.). 15p. 9.95 (978-1-74185-994-2(8), Ideal Pubns.) Worthy Publishing.
Seuss, Dr. Dr. Seuss's ABC: An Amazing Alphabet Book! 2014. (Big Bright & Early Board Book Ser.). (ENG., Illus.). 24p. (J). (— 1). bds. 6.99 (978-0-385-37516-0(6), Random Hse. Bks. for Young Readers) Random Hse. Children's Bks.
Shaskan, Trisha Speed. If You Were a Capital Letter, 1 vol. Gray, Sara, illus. 2009. (Word Fun Ser.). (ENG.). 24p. (gr. 2-4). pap. 7.95 (978-1-4048-5694-3(3)); lib. bdg. 27.99 (978-1-4048-5515-1(7)) Picture Window Bks.
—If You Were a Compound Word, 1 vol. Gray, Sara, illus. 2008. (Word Fun Ser.). (ENG.). 24p. (gr. 2-4). 27.99 (978-1-4048-4771-2(5)); pap. 7.95 (978-1-4048-4776-7(6)) Picture Window Bks.
—If You Were a Contraction, 1 vol. Gray, Sara, illus. 2008. (Word Fun Ser.). (ENG.). 24p. (gr. 2-4). 27.99 (978-1-4048-4772-9(3)) Picture Window Bks.
—If You Were a Plural Word, 1 vol. Gray, Sara, illus. 2009. (Word Fun Ser.). (ENG.). 24p. (gr. 2-4). pap. 7.95 (978-1-4048-5696-7(X)) Picture Window Bks.

E F G

—If You Were Onomatopoeia. Gray, Sara, illus. 2008. (Word Fun Ser.). (ENG.). 24p. (gr. 2-4). lib. bdg. 27.99 *(978-1-4048-4098-0(2))* Picture Window Bks.

Shyu, Theresa. Bilingual Songs - English-Mandarin-Chinese, 2 vols., Vol. 1. 2009. (Bilingual Songs English Mandarin Ser.: 1). (MAN, ENG & CHI.). 48p. (J). 17.95 *(978-1-55386-107-2(8)*, 1553861078) Jordan, Sara Publishing.

Simpson, Matt, creator. Happy Heart: English Book 1. l.t. ed. 2003. (Illus.). 44p. (J). per. *(978-0-9727660-0-5(6))* Bks. by Matt.

Simpson, Ron. Quick Revision KS3 English. 2007. pap. 9.95 *(978-0-340-94307-6(6)*, Hodder Education) Hodder Education Group GBR. Dist: Trans-Atlantic Pubns., Inc.

Smith, Jodene. Cut & Paste - Language Arts. 2003. (ENG.). 96p. pap. 12.99 *(978-0-7439-3707-8(4))* Teacher Created Resources, Inc.

Solomon, Elena Vestri & Shelley, John. Listening, Note Taking, & Speaking Across the Disciplines Bk. 1, 2 vols. 2005. (Key Concepts: Listening, Note Taking, & Speaking Across the Disciplines Ser.). (ENG., Illus.). 143p. (C). pap. 56.95 *(978-0-618-38240-8(2)*, 357616) Thomson ELT.

—Listening, Note Taking, & Speaking Across the Disciplines Bk. 2. 2005. (Key Concepts: Listening, Note Taking, & Speaking Across the Disciplines Ser.). (ENG.). 160p. (C). pap. 56.95 *(978-0-618-38241-5(0)*, 357617) Thomson ELT.

Spanish/English Desk Cards. 2004. (J). 8.95 *(978-1-56911-177-2(4))* Learning Resources, Inc.

Spectrum, compiled by. Spectrum Math & Language Arts Kit, Grade 3. 2013. (Spectrum Ser.). (ENG.). 12p. (gr. 3-3). 18.99 *(978-1-4838-0199-5(3)*, Spectrum) Carson-Dellosa Publishing, LLC.

—Spectrum Math & Language Arts Kit, Grade 4. 2013. (Spectrum Ser.). (ENG.). 12p. (gr. 4-4). 18.99 *(978-1-4838-0200-8(0)*, Spectrum) Carson-Dellosa Publishing, LLC.

—Spectrum Math & Language Arts Kit, Grade 5. 2013. (Spectrum Ser.). (ENG.). 12p. (gr. 5-5). 18.99 *(978-1-4838-0201-5(9)*, Spectrum) Carson-Dellosa Publishing, LLC.

—Spectrum Math & Language Arts Kit, Grade 6. 2013. (Spectrum Ser.). (ENG.). 12p. (gr. 6-6). 18.99 *(978-1-4838-0202-2(7)*, Spectrum) Carson-Dellosa Publishing, LLC.

Spilsbury, Richard. I'm Good at English... What Job Can I Get? 2012. (What's a Good Job for Me? Ser.). (ENG., Illus.). 32p. (J). (gr. 5-6). *(978-1-4488-6631-1(6)*, PowerKids Pr.) Rosen Publishing Group, Inc., The.

Steel, Abigail & Collins UK Publishing Staff. Composition, Bk. 5. 2015. (Collins Treasure House Ser.). (ENG.). 64p. (J). (gr. 4-5). pap. 14.95 *(978-0-00-813350-4(6))* HarperCollins Pubs. Ltd. GBR. Dist: Independent Pubs. Group.

—Comprehension, Bk. 5. 2015. (Collins Treasure House Ser.). (ENG.). 48p. (J). (gr. 4-5). pap. 14.95 *(978-0-00-813344-3(1))* HarperCollins Pubs. Ltd. GBR. Dist: Independent Pubs. Group.

Steffek, Tracey H. Coloring Fun with Words: Learn to Spell & Remember Difficult Words Through Coloring. 2012. 56p. pap. 12.95 *(978-1-4772-0633-1(7))* AuthorHouse.

Sterling Publishing Co., Inc. First Words. 2012. (Say & Play Ser.). (ENG., Illus.). 28p. (J). (gr. k — 1). bds. 4.95 *(978-1-4027-9893-1(8))* Sterling Publishing Co., Inc.

—First Words/Primeras Palabras. 2013. (Say & Play Ser.). (ENG & SPA., Illus.). 28p. (J). (— 1). bds. 4.95 *(978-1-4549-1039-8(9))* Sterling Publishing Co., Inc.

Strother, Ruth. B Is for Blue Planet: An Earth Science Alphabet. Marstall, Robert, illus. 2011. (Sleeping Bear Alphabets Ser.). (ENG.). 40p. (J). (gr. k-6). lib. bdg. 16.95 *(978-1-58536-454-1(1))* Sleeping Bear Pr.

Sylvan Learning Staff. Kindergarten Page per Day: Reading Skills. 2012. (Sylvan Page per Day Series, Language Arts Ser.). (ENG.). 64p. (J). (gr. -1-2). pap. 6.99 *(978-0-307-94457-3(3)*, Sylvan Learning Publishing) Random Hse. Children's Bks.

Taplin, Sam. Listen & Learn First English Words. 2015. (Listen & Learn First English Words Ser.). (ENG.). 4p. (J). 19.99 *(978-0-7945-3446-2(5)*, Usborne) EDC Publishing.

Taylor, Susan. Blast Off! 2006. (Neighborhood Readers Ser.). (ENG.). 16p. (gr. 1-3). pap. 6.50 *(978-1-4042-6978-1(9)*, Rosen Classroom) Rosen Publishing Group, Inc., The.

The Research Masters Staff & Barron's Educational Staff. Barron's Common Core Success Grade 1: Preparing Students for a Brilliant Future. 2015. (Barron's Common Core Success Ser.). (ENG., Illus.). 144p. (gr. 1-1). pap., wbk. ed. 12.99 *(978-1-4380-0669-7(1))* Barron's Educational Series, Inc.

Theme Packs for ELL: Theme Packs Complete Set. 2995.00 *(978-0-7635-2870-6(6))* Rigby Education.

ThemeMaker Student Tool. 2005. 4.90 *(978-0-9769527-9-4(3))* Mindwing Concepts, Inc.

Thinking Kids & Carson-Dellosa Publishing, compiled by. First Grade Essentials. 2017. (ENG.). 256p. (gr. 1-1). pap. 5.99 ***(978-1-4838-3818-2(8)**, Thinking Kids)* Carson-Dellosa Publishing, LLC.

Thornhill, Jan. The Wildlife ABC: A Nature Alphabet Book. Thornhill, Jan, illus. 2012. (ENG., Illus.). 32p. (J). (gr. -1-2). pap. 7.95 *(978-1-926973-08-1(9)*, Owlkids) Owlkids Bks. Inc. CAN. Dist: Publishers Group West (PGW).

Thurlby, Paul. Paul Thurlby's Alphabet. Thurlby, Paul, illus. 2011. (ENG., Illus.). 64p. (J). (gr. -1-2). 16.99 *(978-0-7636-5565-5(1)*, Templar) Candlewick Pr.

Tiger Tales, ed. 100 First Words. 2016. (My First Ser.). (ENG.). 16p. (J). (gr. -1-k). bds. 8.99 *(978-1-58925-240-0(3))* Tiger Tales.

Tiger Tales Staff, creator. Farm. 2013. (My First Touch & Feel Ser.). (ENG., Illus.). 10p. (gr. -1). bds. 7.99 *(978-1-58925-634-7(4))* Tiger Tales.

Toliver, Marilyn. Marcellus Alphabet Book: One, Two, Three What a Words Do You See? 2012. 32p. pap. 17.25 *(978-1-4669-0035-6(0))* Trafford Publishing.

Trowell, Michelle. Magnetic My First Words Day's Out. 2008. *(978-1-84666-586-8(8))* Top That! Publishing PLC.

—Magnetic My First Words School Days. 2008. *(978-1-84666-585-1(X))* Top That! Publishing PLC.

Tuxworth, Nicola. Puppies. 2013. (ENG.). 12p. (J). (gr. -1-12). bds. 6.99 *(978-0-7548-2210-3(9))* Anness Publishing GBR. Dist: National Bk. Network.

—Splish Splash. 2013. (ENG.). 12p. (J). (gr. -1 — 1). bds. 6.99 *(978-0-7548-2211-0(7))* Anness Publishing GBR. Dist: National Bk. Network.

Usage (Gr. 1-3) 2003. (J). *(978-1-58232-049-6(7))* ECS Learning Systems, Inc.

Viewpoints. 2003. instr.'s gde. ed. *(978-0-618-04260-9(1))* CENGAGE Learning.

Wade, Angela. New York City. 2006. (Illus.). 8p. (J). pap. *(978-0-439-74035-7(5))* Scholastic, Inc.

Walton, Rick. Just Me & 6,000 Rats: A Tale of Conjunctions, 1 vol. Gordon, Carl & Gordon, Mike, illus. 2011. (ENG.). 36p. (J). pap. 7.99 *(978-1-4236-2076-1(3))* Gibbs Smith, Publisher.

Watt, Fiona. Este No Es Mi Tren. rev. ed. 2004. (Titles in Spanish Ser.).Tr. of That's Not My Train. 32p. (J). 12.99 *(978-1-58086-585-2(2))* EDC Publishing.

Watterson, Carol. The Edible Alphabet: 26 Reasons to Love the Farm. Sorrentino, Michela, illus. 2011. (ENG.). 48p. (J). (gr. k-3). 16.99 *(978-1-58246-421-3(9)*, Tricycle Pr.) Random Hse. Children's Bks.

Werner, Sharon, et al. Alphabeasties. Nelson, Sarah, illus. 2010. (ENG.). 26p. (J). (gr. k-12). 15.99 *(978-1-60905-003-0(7))* Blue Apple Bks.

Whelan, Gloria & Nolan, Jenny. K Is for Kabuki: A Japan Alphabet. Han, Oki S., illus. 2009. (Discover the World Ser.). (ENG.). 40p. (J). (gr. 1-3). 17.95 *(978-1-58536-444-2(4)*, 202169) Sleeping Bear Pr.

Whiskeyman, Lauri, et al. Spotlight on Articulation Set (6) 2006. (J). 83.70 *(978-0-7606-9975-1(5))* LinguiSystems, Inc.

White, Jason, et al. Maths & English Ages, 10-11. 2015. (Letts KS2 Success Ser.). (ENG., Illus.). 128p. (J). (gr. 5-6). pap. 12.95 *(978-1-84419-858-0(8))* HarperCollins Pubs. Ltd. GBR. Dist: Independent Pubs. Group.

White, Teagan. Adventures with Barefoot Critters. 2014. (ENG., Illus.). 32p. (J). (gr. -1-3). 16.99 *(978-1-77049-624-8(6)*, Tundra Bks.) Tundra Bks. CAN. Dist: Penguin Random Hse. LLC.

Whitney, Chris & Collins UK Publishing Staff. Composition, Bk. 6. 2015. (Collins Treasure House Ser.). (ENG.). 64p. (J). (gr. 5-6). pap. 15.95 *(978-0-00-813349-8(2))* HarperCollins Pubs. Ltd. GBR. Dist: Independent Pubs. Group.

Wilbur, Helen L. F Is for Friendship: A Quilt Alphabet. van Frankenhuyzen, Gijsbert, illus. 2011. (Sleeping Bear Alphabets Ser.). (ENG.). 32p. (J). (gr. 1-4). lib. bdg. 16.95 *(978-1-58536-532-6(7)*, 202215) Sleeping Bear Pr.

William H. Sadlier Staff. Composition Workshop: Student Text. (Composition Workshop Ser.). (gr. 11-12). stu. ed. 9.00 net. *(978-0-8215-0711-7(7))*; 2005. stu. ed. 9.00 net. *(978-0-8215-0708-7(7))*; 2005. (gr. 7-8). stu. ed. 9.00 net. *(978-0-8215-0707-0(9))* Sadlier, William H. Inc.

Williams-Ashe, Marcella Norton. Granny Says. Williams Jr., Anthony, illus. 2012. 46p. pap. 12.00 *(978-0-9764198-4-6(X))* Allecram Publishing.

Wittrock, Jeni. ABCs. Banks, Timothy, illus. 2013. (Wizard of Oz Ser.). (ENG.). 24p. (gr. 1-2). 27.99 *(978-1-4765-3765-8(8))* Capstone Press of Coughlan Cos.

Wolf, Gita & Ramanathan, Rathna. In the Land of Punctuation. Rao, Sirish, tr. from GER. 2009. (ENG., Illus.). 32p. (gr. 4). 19.95 *(978-81-907546-0-6(2))* Tara Books Agency IND. Dist: Publishers Group West (PGW).

Woop Studios Staff. A Zeal of Zebras: An Alphabet of Collective Nouns. 2011. (ENG.). 64p. (J). (gr. -1-17). 17.99 *(978-1-4521-0492-8(1))* Chronicle Bks. LLC.

Wright, Anna. A Tower of Giraffes: Animal Bunches. Wright, Anna, illus. 2015. (ENG., Illus.). 32p. (J). (gr. -1-2). lib. bdg. 17.95 *(978-1-58089-707-5(X))* Charlesbridge Publishing, Inc.

Wright, Craig, ed. The Tough Task. 2010. (ENG., Illus.). 16p. act. bk. ed. 4.06 *(978-0-19-440168-5(5))* Oxford Univ. Pr., Inc.

Wynne Pechter, Lesley. Alligator, Bear, Crab: A Baby's ABC, 1 vol. 2011. (ENG., Illus.). 24p. (J). (gr. -1-k). bds. 9.95 *(978-1-55469-360-3(8))* Orca Bk. Pubs. USA.

Yellow Umbrella English Big Books [Kaplan]. 2011. (Big Book - English Edition Ser.). 16p. 149.70 *(978-1-4296-6641-1(2)*, Yellow Umbrella Bks.) Capstone Press of Coughlan Cos.

Yoyo Books Staff. ABC: Mini Baby's First Library. 2005. 42p. bds. *(978-90-5843-806-5(6))* YoYo Bks.

Zuckerman, Rory. Alphabetical Sleepy Sheep. Roos, Maryn, illus. 2004. (J). bds. 12.95 *(978-0-9749305-3-4(9))* Castle Pacific Publishing.

The 5W's & H (Gr. 4-5) 2004. (J). *(978-1-58232-130-1(2))* ECS Learning Systems, Inc.

ENGLISH LANGUAGE—AMERICANISMS

see Americanisms

ENGLISH LANGUAGE—BUSINESS ENGLISH

see also Commercial Correspondence

E. Taylor, Marcia. Orientation Business English Lev 1. (J). (gr. 7-12). *(978-0-8325-0684-0(2))* McGraw-Hill/Contemporary.

HelliwellMargaret. BUSINESS PLUS LEVEL 1 STUDENT'S BOOK. 2014. (ENG.). 118p. pap. 62.00 *(978-1-107-64068-9(7))* Cambridge Univ. Pr.

Marsh, Carole. Work Words: Job/Business/Career Words & Terms You Need to Know! 2012. (Carole Marsh's Careers Curriculum Ser.). (ENG., Illus.). 58p. (J). pap. 19.99 *(978-0-635-10556-1(X))* Gallopade International.

ENGLISH LANGUAGE—COMPOSITION AND EXERCISES

Adams, Alison. Changes in the Kitchen. 2017. (Text Connections Guided Close Reading Ser.). (J). (gr. 1). *(978-1-4900-1803-4(4))* Benchmark Education Co.

Arco Staff. High Stakes: Writing. 2003. (ENG.). 288p. pap. 16.95 *(978-0-7689-1073-5(0)*, Arco) Peterson's.

Ashley, Susan. I Can Write a Letter. 2004. (I Can Do It! Ser.). (Illus.). 24p. (J). (gr. k-3). pap. 8.15 *(978-0-8368-4335-4(5))*; lib. bdg. 21.00 *(978-0-8368-4328-6(2))* Stevens, Gareth Publishing LLLP. (Weekly Reader Leveled Readers).

Babsky, Irene. Playing with Words. 2009. (ENG.). 64p. (J). (gr. -1-3). pap. 7.99 *(978-1-84476-621-5(7))* Anness Publishing GBR. Dist: National Bk. Network.

Benchmark Education Company, LLC Staff, compiled by. Comprehension Strategy Poster Set Levels A-E (1-8) Emergent. 2004. (Comprehension Ser.). (J). spiral bd., instr.'s gde. ed. 70.00 *(978-1-4108-1521-7(8))* Benchmark Education Co.

—Comprehension Strategy Poster Set Levels J-M (18-28) Fluent. 2004. (Comprehension Ser.). (J). spiral bd., instr.'s gde. ed. 90.00 *(978-1-4108-1523-1(4))* Benchmark Education Co.

—Comprehension Strategy Posters Set levels F-I (9-16) Early. 2004. (Comprehension Ser.). (J). spiral bd., instr.'s gde. ed. 85.00 *(978-1-4108-1522-4(6))* Benchmark Education Co.

Benke, Karen. Rip the Page! Adventures in Creative Writing. 2010. (ENG., Illus.). 256p. (J). (gr. 4-7). pap. 16.95 *(978-1-59030-812-7(3)*, Roost Books) Shambhala Pubns., Inc.

Benke, Karen, tr. Leap Write In! Adventures in Creative Writing to Stretch & Surprise Your One-Of-a-Kind Mind. 2013. (ENG.). 256p. pap. 18.95 *(978-1-61180-015-9(3)*, Roost Books) Shambhala Pubns., Inc.

Bodden, Valerie. Write & Revise Your Project. 2015. (Info Wise Ser.). (ENG., Illus.). 40p. (J). (gr. 4-6). lib. bdg. 30.65 *(978-1-4677-5225-1(8)*, Lerner Pubns.) Lerner Publishing Group.

Book Company, Popular. Complete English Workout, Volume 2. 2007. 271p. pap. *(978-1-897164-52-5(1))* Popular Bk. Co. (Canada) Ltd.

—Complete English Workout, Volume 3. 2007. 271p. pap. *(978-1-897164-53-2(X))* Popular Bk. Co. (Canada) Ltd.

—Complete English Workout, Volume 6. 2007. 271p. pap. *(978-1-897164-56-3(4))* Popular Bk. Co. (Canada) Ltd.

—Complete English Workout, Volume 7. 2007. 271p. pap. *(978-1-897164-57-0(2))* Popular Bk. Co. (Canada) Ltd.

—Complete English Workout, Volume 8. 2007. 271p. pap. *(978-1-897164-58-7(0))* Popular Bk. Co. (Canada) Ltd.

Burke, Sandra & Flebotte, Morrigan. The Crusading Communicator. Flebotte, Morrigan, ed. 2004. (Illus.). 2p. (J). per. *(978-0-9735303-8-4(3))* Black Castle Industries, Inc.

Calkins, Lucy, et al. Writing Reviews. 2013. (Illus.). x, 145p. pap. *(978-0-325-04726-3(X)*, Firsthand) Heinemann.

Center for Learning Network Staff. Ceremony: Curriculum Unit. 2003. (Novel Ser.). 60p. (YA). tchr. ed., spiral bd. 19.95 *(978-1-56077-731-1(1))* Center for Learning, The.

Cheyney, Arnold. Write Away! 140 Writing Prompts for Grades 4-6. 2006. 154p. (J). (gr. 3-7). per. 19.95 *(978-1-59647-087-3(9))* Good Year Bks.

Collins Easy Learning Staff. English Ages 9-11. 2014. (Collins Easy Learning Ser.). (ENG.). 48p. (J). (gr. 4-6). pap. 7.99 *(978-0-00-755988-6(7))* HarperCollins Pubs. Ltd. GBR. Dist: Independent Pubs. Group.

Collins Easy Learning Staff, et al. Comprehension Ages 5-7. 2015. (Collins Easy Learning Ser.). (ENG.). 32p. (J). (gr. k-2). pap. 6.95 *(978-0-00-813430-3(8))* HarperCollins Pubs. Ltd. GBR. Dist: Independent Pubs. Group.

—Grammar & Punctuation Ages 5-7. 2015. (Collins Easy Learning Ser.). (ENG.). 32p. (J). (gr. 1-2). pap. 6.95 *(978-0-00-813432-7(4))* HarperCollins Pubs. Ltd. GBR. Dist: Independent Pubs. Group.

—Grammar & Punctuation, Ages 7-9. 2015. (Collins Easy Learning Ser.). (ENG.). 32p. (J). (gr. 2-4). pap. 6.95 *(978-0-00-813422-8(7))* HarperCollins Pubs. Ltd. GBR. Dist: Independent Pubs. Group.

Collins UK Publishing Staff & Collins Easy Learning Staff. English Ages 5-7. 2014. (Collins Easy Learning Ser.). (ENG.). 32p. (J). (gr. 1-2). pap. 6.99 *(978-0-00-755984-8(4))* HarperCollins Pubs. Ltd. GBR. Dist: Independent Pubs. Group.

—English Ages 8-10. 2014. (Collins Easy Learning Ser.). (ENG.). 48p. (J). (gr. 3-5). pap. 7.99 *(978-0-00-755987-9(9))* HarperCollins Pubs. Ltd. GBR. Dist: Independent Pubs. Group.

Donegan, Patricia. Haiku: Learn to Express Yourself by Writing Poetry in the Japanese Tradition. 2003. (Asian Arts & Crafts for Creative Kids Ser.). (ENG., Illus.). 64p. (J). (gr. 2-6). 15.95 *(978-0-8048-3501-5(2))* Tuttle Publishing.

Education.com. Adventures in Writing: A Workbook of Imagination & Writing. 2015. (ENG.). 128p. (J). (gr. 1-1). pap. 7.99 *(978-0-486-80261-9(2))* Dover Pubns., Inc.

English II: Composition Skills, Full Course Kit with CD-ROM. 2005. (Illus.). 910p. (YA). pap. 75.00 *(978-1-59476-147-8(7))* Paradigm Accelerated Curriculum.

English III: Writing Skills, Chapter 1, Activities. 2005. (Illus.). 44p. (YA). pap. 7.00 *(978-1-59476-016-7(0))* Paradigm Accelerated Curriculum.

English III: Writing Skills, Chapter 1, Text. 2005. (Illus.). 52p. (YA). 7.00 *(978-1-59476-006-8(3))* Paradigm Accelerated Curriculum.

English III: Writing Skills, Chapter 2, Activities. 2005. (Illus.). 78p. (YA). pap. 5.00 *(978-1-59476-017-4(9))* Paradigm Accelerated Curriculum.

English III: Writing Skills, Chapter 2, Text. 2005. (Illus.). 86p. (YA). pap. 7.00 *(978-1-59476-007-5(1))* Paradigm Accelerated Curriculum.

English III: Writing Skills, Chapter 3, Activities. 2005. (Illus.). 76p. (YA). pap. 5.00 *(978-1-59476-018-1(7))* Paradigm Accelerated Curriculum.

English III: Writing Skills, Chapter 3, Text. 2005. 72p. (YA). pap. 7.00 *(978-1-59476-008-2(X))* Paradigm Accelerated Curriculum.

English III: Writing Skills, Chapter 4, Activities. 2005. (Illus.). 68p. (YA). pap. 5.00 *(978-1-59476-019-8(5))* Paradigm Accelerated Curriculum.

English III: Writing Skills, Chapter 4, Text. 2005. (Illus.). 60p. (YA). pap. 7.00 *(978-1-59476-009-9(8))* Paradigm Accelerated Curriculum.

English III: Writing Skills, Chapter 5, Text. 2005. (Illus.). 96p. (YA). pap. 7.00 *(978-1-59476-010-5(1))* Paradigm Accelerated Curriculum.

English III: Writing Skills, Full Course Kit. 2005. (Illus.). 982p. (YA). 75.00 *(978-1-59476-149-2(3))* Paradigm Accelerated Curriculum.

Felix, Rebecca. Long, Longer, Longest. 2015. (Size It Up Ser.). (Illus.). 16p. (J). 25.65 *(978-1-60753-577-5(7))* Amicus Publishing.

Fields, Jan. You Can Write Great Letters & E-Mails, 1 vol. 2012. (You Can Write Ser.). (ENG.). 24p. (gr. 1-2). pap. 7.29 *(978-1-4296-7963-3(8))*; pap. 41.70 *(978-1-4296-8385-2(6))*; lib. bdg. 25.32 *(978-1-4296-7613-7(2))* Capstone Press of Coughlan Cos. (First Facts).

Flash Kids Editors, ed. Writing Skills: Grade 2 (Flash Skills) 2010. (Flash Skills Ser.). (ENG.). 64p. (J). pap. 3.95 *(978-1-4114-3448-6(X)*, Spark Publishing Group) Sterling Publishing Co., Inc.

—Writing Skills: Grade 3 (Flash Skills) 2010. (Flash Skills Ser.). (ENG.). 64p. (J). pap. 3.95 *(978-1-4114-3447-9(1)*, Spark Publishing Group) Sterling Publishing Co., Inc.

Fletcher, Ralph. Writer's Notebook: Unlocking the Writer Within You. 2003. (ENG.). 144p. (J). (gr. 3-7). pap. 6.99 *(978-0-380-78430-1(0))* HarperCollins Pubs.

Fletcher, Ralph J. & Fletcher, R. Writer's Notebook: Unlocking the Writer Within You. 2003. (J). (gr. 3-6). 16.00 *(978-0-613-65014-4(X)*, Turtleback) Turtleback Bks.

Fontichiaro, Kristin. Review It! Helping Peers Create Their Best Work. Petelinsek, Kathleen, illus. 2015. (Explorer Junior Library: Information Explorer Junior Ser.). (ENG.). 24p. (J). (gr. 1-4). 29.93 *(978-1-63188-865-6(X)*, 206040) Cherry Lake Publishing.

Forest, Christopher. Present What You Know: Sharing Information. 2013. (Research Tool Kit Ser.). (ENG.). 32p. (gr. 3-4). pap. 47.70 *(978-1-62065-789-8(9))*; pap. 8.10 *(978-1-62065-788-1(0))*; lib. bdg. 27.32 *(978-1-4296-9949-5(3))* Capstone Press of Coughlan Cos. (Fact Finders).

Francis, Barbara. Other People's Words: What Plagiarism Is & How to Avoid It. 2005. (Issues in Focus Today Ser.). (Illus.). 112p. (J). (gr. 6-13). lib. bdg. 33.27 *(978-0-7660-2525-7(X))* Enslow Pubs., Inc.

Future Ready Project Skills. 2017. (Future Ready Project Skills Ser.). 48p. (gr. 3-4). pap. 70.20 ***(978-0-7660-8809-2(X))***; lib. bdg. 167.58 ***(978-0-7660-8593-0(7))*** Enslow Pubs., Inc.

Ganeri, Anita. I Can Write Instructions, 1 vol. 2013. (I Can Write Ser.). (ENG., Illus.). 32p. (gr. 1-3). pap. 8.29 *(978-1-4329-6941-7(2))*; lib. bdg. 27.32 *(978-1-4329-6934-9(X))* Heinemann-Raintree. (Heinemann First Library).

—I Can Write Letters & E-Mails, 1 vol. 2013. (I Can Write Ser.). (ENG., Illus.). 32p. (gr. 1-3). pap. 8.29 *(978-1-4329-6942-4(0))*; lib. bdg. 27.32 *(978-1-4329-6935-6(8))* Heinemann-Raintree. (Heinemann First Library).

—I Can Write Reports, 1 vol. 2013. (I Can Write Ser.). (ENG.). 32p. (gr. 1-3). lib. bdg. 27.32 *(978-1-4329-6937-0(4)*, Heinemann First Library) Heinemann-Raintree.

—I Can Write Stories, 1 vol. 2013. (I Can Write Ser.). (ENG., Illus.). 32p. (gr. 1-3). pap. 8.29 *(978-1-4329-6945-5(5))*; lib. bdg. 27.32 *(978-1-4329-6938-7(2))* Heinemann-Raintree. (Heinemann First Library).

—Reports. 2013. (I Can Write Ser.). (ENG.). 32p. (gr. 1-3). pap. 8.29 *(978-1-4329-6944-8(7)*, Heinemann First Library) Heinemann-Raintree.

—Writing Stories. 2013. (Writing Stories Ser.). (ENG.). 32p. (gr. 1-3). pap. 47.94 *(978-1-4329-7542-5(0))*; lib. bdg. 163.92 *(978-1-4329-7535-7(8))* Heinemann-Raintree. (Heinemann First Library).

Glencoe McGraw-Hill Staff, creator. Glencoe Writer's Choice: Grammar & Composition, Grade 6. 2004. (Writer's Choice Ser.). (ENG., Illus.). 736p. (gr. 6-6). stu. ed. 96.88 *(978-0-07-829814-1(8)*, 0078298148) McGraw-Hill Higher Education.

Gould, Mike & Burchell, Julia, eds. Checkpoint English - Stage 8. 2016. (ENG.). 96p. pap., wbk. ed. 14.95 *(978-0-00-814050-2(2))* HarperCollins Pubs. Ltd. GBR. Dist: Independent Pubs. Group.

Greek, Joseph. Writing Term Papers with Cool New Digital Tools. 2013. (Way Beyond PowerPoint: Making 21st Century Presentations Ser.). (Illus.). 48p. (J). (gr. 5-8). 29.95 *(978-1-4777-1835-3(4))*; pap. 11.75 *(978-1-4777-1853-7(2))* Rosen Publishing Group, Inc., The. (Rosen Reference).

Green, Lyric & Meachen Rau, Dana. Future Ready Creative Writing Projects. 2017. (Future Ready Project Skills Ser.). 48p. (J). (gr. 3-4). pap. 11.70 ***(978-0-7660-8767-5(0))***; lib. bdg. 27.93 ***(978-0-7660-8653-1(4))*** Enslow Pubs., Inc.

—Future Ready Writing Assignments. 2017. (Future Ready Project Skills Ser.). 48p. (gr. 3-4). lib. bdg. 27.93 ***(978-0-7660-8719-4(0))*** Enslow Pubs., Inc.

Gutman, Dan. My Weird Writing Tips. Paillot, Jim, illus. 2013. (My Weird School Ser.). (ENG.). 160p. (J). (gr. 3-7). 16.99 *(978-0-06-209107-9(7))*; pap. 6.99 *(978-0-06-209106-2(9))* HarperCollins Pubs.

Hadkins, Helen. Interactive, Level 3, Bk. 3. 2012. (ENG., Illus.). 128p. pap., stu. ed. 36.50 *(978-0-521-71219-4(X))* Cambridge Univ. Pr.

Herman, Gail. Make-a-Splash Writing Rules. 2009. (Grammar All-Stars: Writing Tools Ser.). 32p. (J). (gr. 2-5). (ENG.). pap. 10.50 *(978-1-4339-2136-0(7))*; lib. bdg. 26.00 *(978-1-4339-1943-5(5))* Stevens, Gareth Publishing LLLP. (Gareth Stevens Learning Library).

—Snowboarding Similes & Metaphors. 2009. (Grammar All-Stars: Writing Tools Ser.). 32p. (J). (gr. 2-5). (ENG.). pap. 10.50 *(978-1-4339-2138-4(3))*; lib. bdg. 26.00 *(978-1-4339-1945-9(1))* Stevens, Gareth Publishing LLLP. (Gareth Stevens Learning Library).

Hiatt, Kay & Green, Mary. Pupil Book, Bk. 5. 2008. (Collins Primary Literacy Ser.). (ENG., Illus.). 96p. (J). (gr. 5-5). pap. 15.99 *(978-0-00-722699-3(3))* HarperCollins Pubs. Ltd. GBR. Dist: Independent Pubs. Group.

Howe, Alan, et al. Core English KS3 Real Progress in Writing. 2014. 180p. pap. 36.50 *(978-1-4441-6898-3(3))* Hodder Education Group GBR. Dist: Trans-Atlantic Pubns., Inc.

Howell, Sara. How to Plan, Revise, & Edit Your Text, 1 vol., 1. 2014. (Core Writing Skills Ser.). (ENG.). 24p. (J). (gr. 3-4). 23.60 *(978-1-4777-2910-6(0)*, PowerKids Pr.) Rosen Publishing Group, Inc., The.

—How to Write an Explanatory Text, 1 vol., 1. 2014. (Core Writing Skills Ser.). (ENG.). 24p. (J). (gr. 3-4). 23.60 *(978-1-4777-2907-6(0)*, PowerKids Pr.) Rosen Publishing Group, Inc., The.

Hutchinson, Emily. Descriptive Writing, 1 vol. Saddleback Educational Publishing Staff, ed. 2013. (Writing 4 Ser.). (ENG.). 64p. (gr. 6-12). pap. 32.95 *(978-1-62250-024-6(5))* Saddleback Educational Publishing, Inc.

Hutson-Nechkash, Peg. Help Me Write: Frames & Rubrics for Classroom Writing Success. 2003. (Illus.). (J). 34.95 *(978-1-932054-12-5(X))* Super Duper Pubns.

Jarnow, Jill. Writing to Instruct. 2009. (Write Now: A Kid's Guide to Nonfiction Writing Ser.). 24p. (gr. 3-4). 42.50 *(978-1-60854-896-5(1)*, PowerKids Pr.) Rosen Publishing Group, Inc., The.

Kalman, Bobbie. I Can Write a Book about Butterflies. 2012. (ENG.). 32p. (J). (978-0-7787-7987-2(4)); pap. (978-0-7787-7996-4(3)) Crabtree Publishing Co.
—I Can Write a Book about Countries. 2012. (ENG.). 32p. (J). (978-0-7787-7988-9(2)); pap. (978-0-7787-7997-1(1)) Crabtree Publishing Co.
—I Can Write a Book about Culture. 2012. (ENG.). 32p. (J). (978-0-7787-7989-6(0)); pap. (978-0-7787-7998-8(X)) Crabtree Publishing Co.
—I Can Write a Book about History. 2012. (ENG.). 32p. (J). (978-0-7787-7990-2(4)); pap. (978-0-7787-7999-5(8)) Crabtree Publishing Co.
—I Can Write a Book about Landforms. 2012. (ENG.). 32p. (J). (978-0-7787-7992-6(0)); pap. (978-0-7787-8001-4(5)) Crabtree Publishing Co.
—I Can Write a Book about My Life. 2012. (ENG.). 32p. (J). (978-0-7787-7993-3(9)); pap. (978-0-7787-8002-1(3)) Crabtree Publishing Co.
Langston-George, Rebecca. Telling Tales: Writing Captivating Short Stories. 2015. (Writer's Notebook Ser.). (ENG., Illus.). 64p. (gr. 4-5). pap. 8.95 (978-1-4914-5995-9(6)) Capstone Press of Coughlan Cos.
Langston-George, Rebecca, et al. Inkblot: Ideas, Advice, & Examples to Inspire Young Writers. 2015. (Writer's Notebook Ser.). (ENG., Illus.). 208p. (gr. 4-5). pap. 14.95 (978-1-4914-6000-9(8)) Capstone Press of Coughlan Cos.
Law, Karina. Homework, Bk. 2. 2008. (Collins Primary Literacy Ser.). (ENG.). 96p. (J). (gr. 2-2). pap. 5.99 (978-0-00-722715-0(9)) HarperCollins Pubs. Ltd. GBR. Dist: Independent Pubs. Group.
Learn to Write. (Learning Ser.). 22p. (J). bds. (978-2-7643-0038-1(7)) Phidal Publishing, Inc./Editions Phidal, Inc.
Levy, Meredith. Interactive, 1 vol., Bk. 4. 2012. (ENG., Illus.). 104p. pap., wbk. ed. 26.25 (978-0-521-71225-5(4)) Cambridge Univ. Pr.
—Interactive Level 3 Workbook with Downloadable Audio, 1 vol. 2012. (ENG., Illus.). 103p. pap. 20.75 (978-0-521-71220-0(3)) Cambridge Univ. Pr.
The Library of Writing Skills. 2005. (Illus.). 48p. (gr. 5-8). lib. bdg. 159.00 (978-1-4042-0349-5(4)) Rosen Publishing Group, Inc., The.
Loewen, Nancy. Sincerely Yours: Writing Your Own Letter, 1 vol. Lyles, Christopher, illus. 2009. (Writer's Toolbox Ser.). (ENG.). 32p. (gr. 2-4). pap. 8.95 (978-1-4048-5339-3(1)) Picture Window Bks.
—Writing Powerful Persuasive Pieces. 2015. (ENG., Illus.). 56p. (J). (gr. 6-8). 33.32 (978-1-4677-7906-7(7)) Lerner Publishing Group.
Lynette, Rachel. Leah & Leshawn Build a Letter. Cox, Steve, illus. 2012. (Writing Builders Ser.). 32p. (J). (gr. 2-4). pap. 11.94 (978-1-60357-390-0(9)); lib. bdg. 25.27 (978-1-59953-510-4(6)) Norwood Hse. Pr.
McDougal-Littell Publishing Staff. Language Network. 2006. (McDougal Littell Language Network Ser.). (ENG., Illus.). 736p. (gr. 11-11). stu. ed. 88.05 (978-0-395-96741-6(4), 2-22036) Great Source Education Group, Inc.
McDougal-Littell Publishing Staff, creator. Language Network. 2006. (Illus.). 624p. (gr. 6-18). stu. ed. (978-0-395-96736-2(8), 2-22031) Holt McDougal.
McGraw-Hill Education Staff. Writer's Choice, Grade 9: Grammar & Composition. 2004. (Writer's Choice Ser.). (ENG., Illus.). 1008p. (gr. 9-9). stu. ed. 101.16 (978-0-07-829817-2(2), 0078298172) McGraw-Hill Higher Education.
McKay, Laura Lee. Write Fantasy Fiction in 5 Simple Steps. 2012. (Creative Writing in 5 Simple Steps Ser.). (Illus.). 48p. (J). (gr. 5-9). 25.27 (978-0-7660-3834-9(3)) Enslow Pubs., Inc.
McIlwain, John, et al. The Collins Primary Literacy, Bk. 6. 2007. (Collins Primary Literacy Ser.). (ENG.). 16p. (J). (gr. 6-6). pap., stu. ed. 15.99 (978-0-00-722700-6(0)) HarperCollins Pubs. Ltd. GBR. Dist: Independent Pubs. Group.
Meister, Cari. Sasha Sings: Understanding Parts of a Sentence. Whitehouse, Ben, illus. 2015. (Language on the Loose Ser.). (ENG.). 24p. (gr. 2-4). pap. 7.95 (978-1-4795-6968-7(2)) Picture Window Bks.
Minden, Cecilia & Roth, Kate. How to Write a How To. 2012. (Explorer Junior Library: Language Arts Explorer Junior Ser.). (ENG., Illus.). 24p. (J). (gr. 1-4). lib. bdg. 25.64 (978-1-61080-307-6(8), 201279) Cherry Lake Publishing.
—How to Write a Report. 2011. (Explorer Junior Library: Language Arts Explorer Junior Ser.). (ENG.). 24p. (gr. 1-4). lib. bdg. 25.64 (978-1-61080-105-8(9), 201112) Cherry Lake Publishing.
—How to Write a Thank-You Letter. 2012. (Explorer Junior Library: Language Arts Explorer Junior Ser.). (ENG.). 24p. (gr. 1-4). 25.64 (978-1-61080-489-9(9), 202099); pap. 12.79 (978-1-61080-663-3(8), 202273) Cherry Lake Publishing.
—How to Write about Your Adventure. 2011. (Explorer Junior Library: Language Arts Explorer Junior Ser.). (ENG.). 24p. (gr. 1-4). lib. bdg. 25.64 (978-1-61080-106-5(7), 201114) Cherry Lake Publishing.
—How to Write an Essay. 2012. (Explorer Junior Library: Language Arts Explorer Junior Ser.). (ENG.). 24p. (gr. 1-4). 25.64 (978-1-61080-492-9(9), 202102); pap. 12.79 (978-1-61080-666-4(2), 202276) Cherry Lake Publishing.
Minden, Cecilia, et al. How to Write a How To. 2012. (Explorer Junior Library: Language Arts Explorer Junior Ser.). (ENG., Illus.). 24p. (J). (gr. 1-4). pap. 12.79 (978-1-61080-317-5(5), 201281) Cherry Lake Publishing.
Murray, Kara. Simple & Compound Sentences. 2013. (Core Language Skills Ser.). 24p. (J). (gr. 2-2). 22.60 (978-1-4777-0802-6(2)); (ENG., Illus.). pap. 8.25 (978-1-4777-0977-1(0)) Rosen Publishing Group, Inc., The. (PowerKids Pr.).
Muschla, Gary Robert. Practice Makes Perfect Exploring Writing. 2010. (Practice Makes Perfect Ser.). (ENG., Illus.). 240p. pap. 14.00 (978-0-07-174715-8(X), 007174715X) McGraw-Hill Education.
—Practice Makes Perfect Mastering Writing. 2010. (Practice Makes Perfect Ser.). (ENG.). 256p. pap. 14.00 (978-0-07-174716-5(8), 0071747168) McGraw-Hill Education.
Nash, Kimberley. Essays & Research Reports - Level B: A one year writing Course. 2007. (ENG., Illus.). 247p. spiral bd., wbk. ed. 35.00 (978-0-9710950-2-1(7), 12020) Resurrection Resources LLC.
Nobisso, Josephine. Show; Don't Tell! Secrets of Writing. Montanari, Eva, illus. 2004. (ENG.). 40p. (J). (gr. 2-6). 28.95 (978-0-940112-13-1(2)) Gingerbread Hse.
Orehovec, Barbara & Alley, Marybeth. Revisiting the Writing Workshop: Management, Assessment, & Mini-Lessons. 2007. (ENG., Illus.). 160p. (gr. 17). pap. 20.99 (978-0-439-92643-0(2)) Scholastic, Inc.
Osborn, Anna. Flyers: Three Practice Tests for Cambridge English. 2014. (ENG.). 48p. pap. 20.99 (978-0-00-753598-9(8)) HarperCollins Pubs. Ltd. GBR. Dist: Independent Pubs. Group.
Parkman, Mary Rosetta. Guide Book for Language, Grade Three: Shepherd-Parkman Language Series. Norman, Vera Stone, illus. 2011. 236p. 46.95 (978-1-258-08037-2(0)) Literary Licensing, LLC.
Phillips, Wanda C. Easy Grammar Grade 3 Student Workbook. 2006. pap. 13.95 (978-0-936981-48-2(2)) Isha Enterprises, Inc.
—Easy Grammar Grade 4 Student Test Booklet. 2006. pap. 4.95 (978-0-936981-50-5(4)) Isha Enterprises, Inc.
—Easy Grammar Grade 5 Student Test Booklet. 2006. pap. 4.95 (978-0-936981-51-2(2)) Isha Enterprises, Inc.
—Easy Grammar Grade 5 Student Workbook. 2006. pap. 13.95 (978-0-936981-45-1(8)) Isha Enterprises, Inc.
—Easy Grammar Grade 6 Student Test Booklet. 2006. pap. 4.95 (978-0-936981-52-9(0)) Isha Enterprises, Inc.
—Easy Grammar Grade 6 Student Workbook. 2006. pap. 13.95 (978-0-936981-46-8(6)) Isha Enterprises, Inc.
—Easy Grammar Plus Student Test Booklet. 2006. pap. 4.95 (978-0-936981-53-6(9)) Isha Enterprises, Inc.
Polon, Linda Beth. Storywriting: Grades 1-3. 2004. (Illus.). 88p. (gr. 1-3). pap. 11.95 (978-0-673-57580-7(2)) Good Year Bks.
—Storywriting: Grades 4-6. 2004. (Illus.). 88p. (gr. 4-6). pap. 9.95 (978-0-673-57726-9(0)) Good Year Bks.
Prentice-Hall Staff. PH Grammar & Composition. 3rd ed. (J). (978-0-13-708926-0(0)); (978-0-13-708934-5(1)); (978-0-13-708942-0(2)); (978-0-13-708868-3(X)) Prentice Hall (Schl. Div.).
Prokos, Anna & Voege, Debra. Track Star Sentences. 2009. (Grammar All-Stars: Writing Tools Ser.). 32p. (J). (gr. 2-5). (ENG.). pap. 10.50 (978-1-4339-2139-1(1)); lib. bdg. 26.00 (978-1-4339-1946-6(X)) Stevens, Gareth Publishing LLLP. (Gareth Stevens Learning Library).
Proudfit, Benjamin. Writing Opinion Papers. 2014. (Write Right! Ser.). 24p. (J). (gr. 2-5). 22.60 (978-1-4824-1128-7(8)) Stevens, Gareth Publishing LLLP.
—Writing Research Papers. 2014. (Write Right! Ser.). 24p. (J). (gr. 2-5). 22.60 (978-1-4824-1120-1(2)) Stevens, Gareth Publishing LLLP.
Puchta, Herbert & Gerngross, Günter. More!, Level 3. 2nd ed. 2014. (ENG.). 128p. pap., stu. ed. 42.00 (978-1-107-63737-5(6)) Cambridge Univ. Pr. GBR. Dist: Cambridge Univ. Pr.
—Super Minds. 2012. (ENG.). 114p. pap., stu. ed. 26.75 (978-0-521-14852-8(9)) Cambridge Univ. Pr.
—Super Minds Level 1 Student's Book with DVD-ROM. 2012. (ENG.). 130p. pap. 29.00 (978-0-521-14855-9(3)) Cambridge Univ. Pr.
—Super Minds Level 2 Student's Book with DVD-ROM. 2012. (ENG.). 130p. pap. 29.00 (978-0-521-14859-7(6)) Cambridge Univ. Pr.
—Super Minds Starter Workbook. 2012. (ENG., Illus.). 112p. pap. 21.25 (978-0-521-14853-5(7)) Cambridge Univ. Pr.
Quinley, Elliott. Persuasive Writing, 1 vol. Saddleback Educational Publishing Staff, ed. 2013. (Writing 4 Ser.). (ENG.). 64p. (gr. 6-12). pap. 32.95 (978-1-62250-027-7(X)) Saddleback Educational Publishing, Inc.
Rawlings Miller, Carol & Glasscock, Sarah. Exceptional Essays. 2005. (Overhead Writing Lessons Ser.). (ENG., Illus.). 48p. (gr. 5-18). pap. 13.99 (978-0-439-22258-7(3), Teaching Resources) Scholastic, Inc.
Reed, Susannah. Guess What! American English Level 4 Student's Book. 2015. (ENG., Illus.). 104p. pap. 19.50 (978-1-107-55695-9(3)) Cambridge Univ. Pr.
—Guess What! American English Level 5 Student's Book. 2015. (ENG., Illus.). 104p. pap. 19.50 (978-1-107-55703-1(8)) Cambridge Univ. Pr.
RIGBY. Rigby on Our Way to English: Leveled Reader Grade 2 (Level I) Desert Clowns. 2013. (Rigby on Our Way to English Ser.). (ENG.). 16p. (gr. 2-2). pap. 11.35 (978-0-7578-1365-8(8)) Rigby Education.
Rondeau, Amanda. Base + Ball = Baseball, 1 vol. 2004. (Compound Words Ser.). (ENG., Illus.). 24p. (J). (gr. k-3). lib. bdg. 24.21 (978-1-59197-430-7(5), SandCastle) ABDO Publishing Co.
—Bed + Time = Bedtime, 1 vol. 2004. (Compound Words Ser.). (ENG., Illus.). 24p. (J). (gr. k-3). lib. bdg. 24.21 (978-1-59197-431-4(3), SandCastle) ABDO Publishing Co.
—Key + Board = Keyboard, 1 vol. 2004. (Compound Words Ser.). (ENG., Illus.). 24p. (J). (gr. k-3). lib. bdg. 24.21 (978-1-59197-434-5(8), SandCastle) ABDO Publishing Co.
—Pan + Cake = Pancake, 1 vol. 2004. (Compound Words Ser.). (ENG., Illus.). 24p. (J). (gr. k-3). lib. bdg. 24.21 (978-1-59197-435-2(6), SandCastle) ABDO Publishing Co.
—Sun + Screen = Sunscreen, 1 vol. 2004. (Compound Words Ser.). (ENG., Illus.). 24p. (J). (gr. k-3). lib. bdg. 24.21 (978-1-59197-440-6(2), SandCastle) ABDO Publishing Co.
Roy, Jennifer Rozines. You Can Write Using Good Grammar. 2004. (You Can Write Ser.). (Illus.). 64p. (J). lib. bdg. 23.94 (978-0-7660-2084-9(3)) Enslow Pubs., Inc.
Roy, Jennifer Rozines & Haney, Johannah. Sharpen Your Essay Writing Skills. 2011. (Sharpen Your Writing Skills Ser.). (Illus.). 64p. (J). (gr. 6-18). pap. 8.95 (978-1-59845-342-3(4)); lib. bdg. 29.27 (978-0-7660-3903-2(X)) Enslow Pubs., Inc.
—You Can Write an Essay. 2004. (You Can Write Ser.). (Illus.). 64p. (J). lib. bdg. 23.94 (978-0-7660-2091-7(6)) Enslow Pubs., Inc.
Simple & Compound Sentences. 2013. (Core Language Skills Ser.). 24p. (J). (gr. 2-2). pap. 49.50 (978-1-4777-0979-5(7), PowerKids Pr.) Rosen Publishing Group, Inc., The.
Spilsbury, Louise. Tips for Better Writing, Vol. 1. 2014. (Student's Toolbox Ser.). 32p. (gr. 4-5). (ENG.). pap. 10.50 (978-1-4824-0155-4(X)); (J). 26.60 (978-1-4824-0154-7(1)) Stevens, Gareth Publishing LLLP.
Steck-Vaughn Staff. Language Exercises. 2004. (Steck-Vaughn Language Exercises Ser.). (ENG.). 40p. (gr. 8-8). pap., tchr. ed. 16.65 (978-0-7398-9128-5(6)); (Illus.). 144p. (gr. 8-8). pap., stu. ed. 23.60 (978-0-7398-9120-9(0));Level B. (Illus.). 112p. (gr. 2-2). pap., stu. ed. 22.65 (978-0-7398-9114-8(6)) Houghton Mifflin Harcourt Publishing Co.
—Language Exercises, Grade 3, Level C. 2004. (Steck-Vaughn Language Exercises Ser.). (ENG., Illus.). 112p. (gr. 3-3). pap., tchr. ed. 22.65 (978-0-7398-9115-5(4)) Houghton Mifflin Harcourt Publishing Co.
—Language Exercises, Level D. 2004. (Steck-Vaughn Language Exercises Ser.). (ENG., Illus.). 112p. (gr. 4-4). pap. 23.60 (978-0-7398-9116-2(2)) Houghton Mifflin Harcourt Publishing Co.
Storm, Wilda. Write up A Storm! ¿ Practice for Proficiency: Student Handbook 3rd Grade. 2007. ring bd. (978-0-9772935-8-2(0)) DoveTail Hse., Inc.
—Write up A Storm! ¿ Practice for Proficiency: Student Handbook 4th Grade. 2007. ring bd. (978-0-9772935-9-9(9)) DoveTail Hse., Inc.
—Write up A Storm! ¿ Writing Tools: A Student Guide ¿ Grade 2-3. 2007. ring bd. (978-0-9772935-5-1(6)) DoveTail Hse., Inc.
—Write up A Storm! Take Rewarding Revisions by Storm. 2007. ring bd. (978-0-9772935-2-0(1)) DoveTail Hse., Inc.
Stride, Lottie. Write (or Is It Right?) Every Time: Cool Ways to Improve Your English. 2011. (ENG.). 144p. (YA). (gr. 4-6). 9.99 (978-1-60652-341-4(4)) Reader's Digest Assn., Inc., The.
Tamblyn, Catherine. 40 Fabulous Social Studies Activities: Easy Projects That Work with the Topics You Teach & Help Build Reading, Writing, & Research Skills. 2013. (ENG.). 64p. (gr. 2-3). pap. 11.99 (978-0-545-31505-0(0), Teaching Resources) Scholastic, Inc.
Teacher Created Resources Staff. Learning to Print Grd K-2. 2012. (ENG.). 64p. pap. 8.99 (978-1-4206-2769-5(4)) Teacher Created Resources, Inc.
Thurston, Cheryl Miller & DiPrince, Dawn. Unjournaling: Daily Writing Exercises That Are Not Personal, Not Introspective, Not Boring! 2006. (ENG.). 108p. (YA). (gr. 7-12). pap. 15.95 (978-1-877673-70-2(6), 9781877673702) Prufrock Pr.
Tyler, Jenny & Gee, R. Ready for Writing. 2004. (First Learning Ser.). (ENG., Illus.). 1p. (J). (gr. -1-18). pap., act. bk. ed. 4.99 (978-0-7460-3520-7(9)) EDC Publishing.
Webley, Ann. The Collins Primary Literacy, Bk. 4. 2008. (Collins Primary Literacy Ser.). (ENG.). 96p. (J). (gr. 4-4). pap., stu. ed. 15.99 (978-0-00-722698-6(5)) HarperCollins Pubs. Ltd. GBR. Dist: Independent Pubs. Group.
Willis, Meredith Sue. Blazing Pencils. 2nd ed. 2013. 126p. pap. 14.95 (978-1-932727-14-2(0)) Montemayor Pr.
Write Right! Sets 1-2. 2014. (Write Right! Ser.). 24p. (J). (gr. 2-5). pap. 97.80 (978-1-4824-1597-1(6)) Stevens, Gareth Publishing LLLP.
Writing Term Papers with Cool New Digital Tools. 2013. (Way Beyond PowerPoint: Making 21st Century Presentations Ser.). (Illus.). 48p. (J). (gr. 5-8). pap. 70.50 (978-1-4777-1854-4(0), Rosen Reference) Rosen Publishing Group, Inc., The.
Writing Works with NC Wordcrafter & Joey: Grade 3+ 2004. 28.00 (978-0-9790796-0-3(8)) PJR Assocs., Ltd.
Writing Works with NC Wordcrafter & Joey: Grade 4+ 2004. 28.00 (978-0-9790796-1-0(6)) PJR Assocs., Ltd.
Writing Works with NC Wordcrafter & Joey: Grade 5+ 2004. 28.00 (978-0-9790796-2-7(4)) PJR Assocs., Ltd.

ENGLISH LANGUAGE—CONVERSATION AND PHRASE BOOKS

see English Language—Textbooks for Foreign Speakers

ENGLISH LANGUAGE—DICTIONARIES

Alex, Ioan, illus. My First Words. 2004. 63p. (J). 9.95 (978-1-59496-000-0(3)) Teora USA LLC.
American Heritage Dictionaries, Editors of the. The American Heritage Children's Dictionary. 2015. (ENG., Illus.). 896p. (gr. 3-6). 19.95 (978-0-544-33610-0(0)) Houghton Mifflin Harcourt Publishing Co.
—The American Heritage First Dictionary. 2015. (ENG., Illus.). 416p. (J). (gr. k-2). 17.95 (978-0-544-33663-6(1)) Houghton Mifflin Harcourt Publishing Co.
—The American Heritage Picture Dictionary. 2015. (ENG., Illus.). 144p. (J). (gr. -1-k). 16.95 (978-0-544-33609-4(7)) Houghton Mifflin Harcourt Publishing Co.
—The American Heritage Student Dictionary. 2015. (ENG., Illus.). 1088p. (gr. 6-10). 19.95 (978-0-544-33608-7(9)) Houghton Mifflin Harcourt Publishing Co.
American Heritage Dictionaries, Editors of the, ed. Curious George's Dictionary. 2015. (ENG., Illus.). 128p. (J). (gr. -1-k). 13.95 (978-0-544-33665-0(8)) Houghton Mifflin Harcourt Publishing Co.
American Heritage Publishing Staff. The American Heritage Student Grammar Dictionary. 2011. (ENG., Illus.). 160p. (gr. 5-7). pap. 13.95 (978-0-547-47265-2(X)) Houghton Mifflin Harcourt Publishing Co.
Amery, Heather. First Hundred Words in English II. 2015. (First Hundred Words Ser.). (ENG.). 32p. (J). pap. 6.99 (978-0-7945-3516-2(X), Usborne) EDC Publishing.
Ashley, Susan. I Can Use a Dictionary. 2004. (I Can Do It! Ser.). (Illus.). 24p. (gr. k-3). lib. bdg. 21.00 (978-0-8368-4326-2(6), Weekly Reader Leveled Readers) Stevens, Gareth Publishing LLLP.
Author, Oxford. Oxford Picture Dictionary Content Area for Kids. 2nd ed. 2012. (ENG & SPA., Illus.). 208p. pap. 26.19 (978-0-19-401777-0(X)) Oxford Univ. Pr., Inc.
—Oxford Picture Dictionary Content Areas for Kids Pack: Reproducibles Collection. 2nd ed. 2012. (ENG.). pap. 290.06 (978-0-19-401784-8(2)) Oxford Univ. Pr., Inc.
Award, Anna. English/French. Burton, Terry, illus. 2012. (FRE & ENG.). 96p. (J). 11.50 (978-1-84135-798-0(7)) Award Pubns. Ltd. GBR. Dist: Parkwest Pubns., Inc.
Ballard & Tighe Publishers Staff. IDEA Picture Dictionary: An IDEA Language Development Resource. 2005. (Illus.). 152p. 18.00 (978-1-55501-523-7(9)) Ballard & Tighe Pubs.
Berlitz Publishing Staff. Italian - Berlitz Picture Dictionary. 2nd ed. 2004. (Kids Picture Dictionary Ser.). (ITA & ENG., Illus.). 128p. (J). (gr. -1-4). pap. 12.95 (978-981-246-390-6(9), 463909) APA Publications Services SGP. Dist: Ingram Publisher Services.
Bollard, John. Scholastic Pocket Thesaurus. 2005. (Scholastic Reference Ser.). (ENG.). 272p. (J). (gr. 3-7). pap. 7.99 (978-0-439-62037-6(6), Scholastic Reference) Scholastic, Inc.
Bollard, John K. & Bollard, John. Scholastic Children's Thesaurus. Reed, Mike, illus. rev. ed. 2006. (ENG.). 240p. (J). (gr. 3-7). 17.99 (978-0-439-79831-0(0), Scholastic Reference) Scholastic, Inc.
Brooks, F. & Litchfield, J. Picture Dictionary: A First Alphabetical Word Book. 2004. (Picture Dictionaries Ser.). 96p. (J). lib. bdg. 24.95 (978-1-58086-437-4(6)) EDC Publishing.
Bruzzone, Catherine, et al. French-English Picture Dictionary. Comfort, Louise & Dix, Steph, illus. 2011. (First Bilingual Picture Dictionaries Ser.). (FRE & ENG.). 48p. (J). (gr. -1-3). pap. 7.99 (978-0-7641-4660-2(2)) Barron's Educational Series, Inc.
Buckley, Elizabeth & Keyes, Joan Ross. Oxford Picture Dictionary Content Area for Kids. 2nd ed. 2012. (ENG., Illus.). 184p. pap., wbk. ed. 17.00 (978-0-19-401779-4(6)) Oxford Univ. Pr., Inc.
Burton, Terry & Ward, Anna. English. Burton, Terry, illus. 2012. (ENG., Illus.). 96p. (J). 11.50 (978-1-84135-797-3(9)) Award Pubns. Ltd. GBR. Dist: Parkwest Pubns., Inc.
Carson-Dellosa Publishing Staff. Dictionary, Grades 6-12. 2003. (ENG.). 448p. (gr. 6-12). pap. 2.99 (978-0-7696-3308-4(0)) Carson-Dellosa Publishing, LLC.
Caso, Adolph. The KaSO English to Italian Dictionary: With a Proposed One-to-One Relationship of Italian Graphemes (Letters) & Phonemes (Sounds) 2003. 525p. per. 19.95 (978-0-8283-2082-5(9)) Branden Bks.
Chambers Editors. Chambers Junior Illustrated Dictionary. 2009. (Illus.). 288p. (978-0-550-10477-9(1), Chambers) Hodder & Stoughton.
Cobuild Basic American English Dictionary. 2nd rev. ed. 2016. (ENG., Illus.). 608p. pap. 29.95 (978-0-00-813579-9(7)) HarperCollins Pubs. Ltd. GBR. Dist: Independent Pubs. Group.
Collins Dictionaries. Collins Gem School Dictionary & Thesaurus. 2nd rev. ed. 2015. (ENG.). 840p. (YA). (gr. 7). pap. 9.99 (978-0-00-810286-9(4)) HarperCollins Pubs. Ltd. GBR. Dist: Independent Pubs. Group.
—Collins Irish School Dictionary. 2016. (ENG & GLE.). 640p. (J). (gr. 5-10). pap. 10.99 **(978-0-00-819028-6(3))** HarperCollins Pubs. Ltd. GBR. Dist: Independent Pubs. Group.
Collins Dictionaries. Collins Primary Illustrated Dictionary: Boost Your Word Power. 2nd rev. ed. 2015. (Collins Primary Dictionaries Ser.). (ENG., Illus.). 488p. (J). (gr. 4). pap. 17.99 (978-0-00-757875-7(X)) HarperCollins Pubs. Ltd. GBR. Dist: Independent Pubs. Group.
Collins Dictionaries & Harpercollins Staff. Collins Junior Illustrated Thesaurus. 2nd rev. ed. 2014. (Collins Primary Dictionaries Ser.). (ENG., Illus.). 192p. (J). pap. 16.99 (978-0-00-757873-3(3)) HarperCollins Pubs. Ltd. GBR. Dist: Independent Pubs. Group.
Collins Dictionaries Staff. Collins Cobuild Primary Learnere's Dictionary. 2nd rev. ed. 2014. (Collins Cobuild Ser.). (ENG., Illus.). 528p. (J). 15.99 (978-0-00-755654-0(3)) HarperCollins Pubs. Ltd. GBR. Dist: Independent Pubs. Group.
—Dictionary & Thesaurus in Colour. 2nd ed. 2015. (ENG.). 840p. (YA). (gr. 7). pap. 14.95 (978-0-00-811195-3(2)) HarperCollins Pubs. Ltd. GBR. Dist: Independent Pubs. Group.
—School Dictionary. 5th rev. ed. 2016. (ENG.). 736p. (YA). (gr. 7-9). pap. 8.95 (978-0-00-814646-7(2)) HarperCollins Pubs. Ltd. GBR. Dist: Independent Pubs. Group.
—School Thesaurus. 5th rev. ed. 2016. (ENG.). 736p. (YA). (gr. 7-9). pap. 8.95 (978-0-00-814645-0(4)) HarperCollins Pubs. Ltd. GBR. Dist: Independent Pubs. Group.
Collins Easy Learning, Collins Easy. My First Dictionary, Ages 4-5. 2017. (Collins Easy Learning Ser.). (ENG., Illus.). 80p. (J). (gr. -1-k). pap. 10.99 **(978-0-00-820948-3(0))** HarperCollins Pubs. Ltd. GBR. Dist: Independent Pubs. Group.
Dahl, Roald & Oxford Dictionaries Staff. Oxford Roald Dahl Dictionary: From Aardvark to Zozimus, a Real Dictionary of Everyday & Extra-Usual Words. Blake, Quentin, illus. 2016. (ENG.). 288p. (J). 24.95 (978-0-19-273645-1(0)) Oxford Univ. Pr., Inc.
Davies, H. French Dictionary for Beginners Internet-Referenced. 2010. (Beginners Dictionaries Ser.). 128p. (J). pap. 12.99 (978-0-7945-2633-7(0), Usborne) EDC Publishing.
Dorling Kindersley Publishing Staff. Children's Illustrated Dictionary. 3rd ed. 2014. (ENG., Illus.). 256p. (J). (gr. k-4). 17.99 (978-1-4654-2020-6(7), DK Children) Dorling Kindersley Publishing, Inc.
—Merriam-Webster Children's Dictionary. 2015. (ENG., Illus.). 960p. (J). (gr. 1-4). 22.99 (978-1-4654-2446-4(6), DK Children) Dorling Kindersley Publishing, Inc.
—My First Dictionary. 2012. (ENG.). 96p. (J). (gr. k-4). 15.99 (978-0-7566-9313-8(6), DK Children) Dorling Kindersley Publishing, Inc.
Durrie, Karen. Fun: Arabic-English Bilingual Edition. 2016. (Community Helpers Ser.). (ENG.). (J). (gr. 3-7). 29.99 (978-1-61913-902-2(2)) Weigl Pubs., Inc.
Durrie, Karen. Safety: Arabic-English Bilingual Edition. 2016. (Community Helpers Ser.). (ENG.). (J). (gr. -1-3). 29.99 **(978-1-61913-904-6(9))** Weigl Pubs., Inc.
First Dictionary. 2003. (Illus.). 96p. (J). 7.98 (978-1-4054-0519-5(8)) Parragon, Inc.
First Dictionary. (Foundation Ser.). (gr. k-3). 52p. 22.95 (978-0-322-01559-3(6)); 42p. act. bk. ed. 20.95 (978-0-322-01560-9(X)) Wright Group/McGraw-Hill.
French, Mary. Animal Gazetteer. 2nd ed. 2011. (Illus.). 569p. (J). (978-1-934669-05-1(9)) Dictionary Project, Inc., The.
Giles, Sophie, et al. My First Picture Dictionary. Burton, Terry & Hicks, Angela, illus. 2014. (ENG.). 125p. 17.50 (978-1-84135-873-4(8)) Award Pubns. Ltd. GBR. Dist: Parkwest Pubns., Inc.
Goldsmith, Evelyn, et al. Collins Junior Illustrated Dictionary. 2nd rev. ed. 2014. (Collins Primary Dictionaries Ser.). (ENG., Illus.). 280p. (J). (gr. 2). pap. 16.99 (978-0-00-755305-1(6)) HarperCollins Pubs. Ltd. GBR. Dist: Independent Pubs. Group.

E
F
G

Goodman, Marlene. Let's Learn English Picture Dictionary. 2003. (ENG., Illus.). 80p. 13.00 *(978-0-07-140822-6(3)*, 0071408223) McGraw-Hill Cos., The.
—Let's Learn Italian Picture Dictionary. 2003. (ENG & ITA., Illus.). 80p. 13.00 *(978-0-07-140826-4(6)*, 0071408266) McGraw-Hill Education.
—Let's Learn Japanese Picture Dictionary. 2003. (JPN & ENG., Illus.). 80p. 13.00 *(978-0-07-140827-1(4)*, 0071408274) McGraw-Hill Cos., The.
Gould, Vera Dobson & Hughes, Patricia J. The Dominie Thesaurus for Young Writers. 2003. 393p. (J). 18.95 *(978-0-7685-2298-3(6))* Dominie Pr., Inc.
Grandison, Alice & Chambers Harrap Publishers Staff. Mini School Dictionary. rev. ed. 2005. 768p. pap. *(978-0-550-10147-1(0)*, Chambers) Hodder & Stoughton.
Groner, Judyth. My First Hebrew Word Book. Marzel, Pépi, illus. 2005. (ENG.). 32p. (J). (gr. -1-2). lib. bdg. 17.95 *(978-1-58013-126-1(3)*, Kar-Ben Publishing) Lerner Publishing Group.
HarperCollins Publishers Ltd. Staff. Collins Illustrated Dictionary. 2013. (ENG., Illus.). 512p. (J). pap. 15.95 *(978-0-00-733751-4(5))*; (gr. 2). 19.95 *(978-0-00-733750-7(7))* HarperCollins Pubs. Ltd. GBR. Dist: Independent Pubs. Group.
Harpercollins Staff. Collins First Dictionary. 2014. (ENG., Illus.). 160p. (J). (gr. 3). pap. 14.99 *(978-0-00-757872-6(5))* HarperCollins Pubs. Ltd. GBR. Dist: Independent Pubs. Group.
HarperCollins UK Staff. Cobuild Essential English Dictionary. 2nd rev. ed. 2014. (ENG., Illus.). 520p. (J). 20.99 *(978-0-00-755653-3(5))* HarperCollins Pubs. Ltd. GBR. Dist: Independent Pubs. Group.
Harrap & Chambers Editors. French Student's Dictionary. (ENG & FRE., Illus.). 800p. *(978-0-245-60676-2(9))* Harrap, Larousse Pubs.
Hayward, Linda. The Sesame Street Dictionary. Mathieu, Joe, illus. 2004. (ENG.). 256p. (J). (gr. -1-2). 24.99 *(978-0-375-82810-2(9)*, Random Hse. Bks. for Young Readers) Random Hse. Children's Bks.
Heinle Childrens Picture Dict-Amer English Sing-Along. 2007. (ENG.). (C). cd-rom 71.95 *(978-1-4240-0942-8(1))* Cengage Heinle.
Heil-Höflinger, Philippa. My First Coloring Dictionary from a to Z. 2012. 56p. pap. *(978-3-8482-0712-1(5))* Books on Demand GmbH.
Henggeler, Mary F. Where's Wendy? The Curious Cat. 2009. 44p. pap. 18.99 *(978-1-4389-7577-1(5))* AuthorHouse.
Hippocrene Books Staff. Hippocrene Hindi Children's Picture Dictionary. Martin, Robert Stanly, ed. Voltaggio, Nicholas, illus. 2006. (ENG.). 112p. (J). pap. 14.95 *(978-0-7818-1129-3(5))* Hippocrene Bks., Inc.
Hippocrene Books Staff, ed. Chinese Children's Picture Dictionary: English-Chinese/Chinese-English. 2006. (CHI & ENG., Illus.). 114p. pap. 14.95 *(978-0-7818-1161-3(9))* Hippocrene Bks., Inc.
—Hebrew Children's Picture Dictionary: English-Hebrew/Hebrew-English. 2006. (HEB & ENG., Illus.). 114p. pap. 14.95 *(978-0-7818-1163-7(5))* Hippocrene Bks., Inc.
—Norwegian Children's Picture Dictionary: English-Norwegian/Norwegian-English. 2006. (ENG., Illus.). 114p. pap. 14.95 *(978-0-7818-1164-4(3))* Hippocrene Bks., Inc.
Hochstatter, Daniel J. Just Look 'n Learn English Picture Dictionary. 2003. (ENG., Illus.). 96p. 14.00 *(978-0-07-140833-2(9)*, 0071408339) McGraw-Hill Cos., The.
Hochstatter, Daniel J., contrib. by. Just Look 'n Learn English Picture Dictionary. 2003. (Just Look 'n Learn Picture Dictionary Ser.). (Illus.). 96p. (J). (gr. 4-7). 11.95 *(978-0-8442-5022-9(8)*, 50228, Passport Bks.) McGraw-Hill Trade.
How Do I Use a Dictionary? 2014. (Research Tools You Can Use Ser.). 32p. (J). (gr. 3-6). 23.45 *(978-1-62275-344-4(5))* Rosen Publishing Group, Inc., The.
How Do I Use a Thesaurus? 2014. (Research Tools You Can Use Ser.). 32p. (J). (gr. 3-6). 23.45 *(978-1-62275-369-7(0))* Rosen Publishing Group, Inc., The.
IDEA Picture Dictionary: An IDEA Language Development Resource. 2004. (Illus.). 200p. (J). *(978-1-55501-522-0(0))* Ballard & Tighe Pubs.
Jolivet, Joëlle. Almost Everything. Siegel, Alexis, tr. from FRE. Jolivet, Joëlle, illus. 2005. (ENG., Illus.). 40p. (J). (gr. -1-3). 29.99 *(978-1-59643-090-7(7)*, 9781596430907) Roaring Brook Pr.
Karapetian, Marjam. Bilingual Content Dictionary: English to Armenian. 2004. (ARM & ENG.). 9.95 *(978-0-9767958-4-1(1))*; 4.95 *(978-0-9767958-2-7(5))*; 15.95 *(978-0-9767958-7-2(6))*; 13.95 *(978-0-9767958-6-5(8))*; 4.95 *(978-0-9767958-3-4(3))* WizdomInc.
—Bilingual Content Dictionary: English to Armenian: Social Studies - American History Through 1776. 2004. (ARM & ENG.). 14.95 *(978-0-9767958-5-8(X))* WizdomInc.
—Bilingual Content Dictionary: English to Korean. 2004. (KOR & ENG.). 4.95 *(978-0-9764829-7-0(5))*; 4.95 *(978-0-9764829-6-3(7))*; 13.95 *(978-0-9767958-0-3(9))*; 9.95 *(978-0-9764829-8-7(3))*; 15.95 *(978-0-9767958-1-0(7))* WizdomInc.
—Bilingual Content Dictionary: English to Korean: Social Studies - American History Through 1776. 2004. (KOR & ENG.). 14.95 *(978-0-9764829-9-4(1))* WizdomInc.
—Bilingual Content Dictionary: English to Mandarin Chinese. 2004. (CHI & ENG.). 4.95 *(978-0-9768053-0-4(8))*; 13.95 *(978-0-9768053-4-2(0))*; 9.95 *(978-0-9768053-2-8(4))*; 15.95 *(978-0-9768053-5-9(9))*; 4.95 *(978-0-9768053-1-1(6))* WizdomInc.
—Bilingual Content Dictionary: English to Mandarin Chinese: Social Studies - American History Through 1776. 2004. (CHI & ENG.). 14.95 *(978-0-9768053-3-5(2))* WizdomInc.
Kauffman, Dorothy & Apple, Gary. English Dictionary for the Content Areas, Set, Pack. 2nd ed. 2010. (ENG., Illus.). xiii, 196p. (J). pap. 478.50 *(978-0-19-452526-8(0))* Oxford Univ. Pr. GBR. Dist: Oxford Univ. Pr., Inc.
Kauffman, Dorothy, et al. English Dictionary. 2nd ed. 2010. (Oxford Picture Dictionary for the Content Areas 2e Ser.). (ENG., Illus.). 196p. pap. 26.19 *(978-0-19-452500-8(7))* Oxford Univ. Pr., Inc.
Kingfisher Editors. The Kingfisher Illustrated Pocket Dictionary. 2007. (ENG., Illus.). 231p. (J). (gr. 5-9). pap. 11.99 *(978-0-7534-6116-7(1)*, 9780753461167, Kingfisher) Roaring Brook Pr.
Kudela, Katy R. My First Book of Arabic Words. Translations.com Staff, tr. (Bilingual Picture Dictionaries Ser.). (MUL.). 32p. (gr. 1-2). 2011. pap. 47.70 *(978-1-4296-6162-1(3))* 2010. lib. bdg. 27.32 *(978-1-4296-5266-7(7))* Capstone Press of Coughlan Cos. (Aplus Bks.).
—My First Book of Greek Words. Translations.com Staff, tr. (Bilingual Picture Dictionaries Ser.). (MUL.). 32p. (gr. 1-2). 2011. pap. 47.70 *(978-1-4296-6172-0(0))* 2010. lib. bdg. 27.32 *(978-1-4296-5966-6(1))* Capstone Press of Coughlan Cos. (Aplus Bks.).
—My First Book of Italian Words. Translations.com Staff, tr. 2011. (Bilingual Picture Dictionaries Ser.). (MUL.). 32p. (gr. 1-2). pap. 47.70 *(978-1-4296-6160-7(7)*, Aplus Bks.) Capstone Press of Coughlan Cos.
—My First Book of Japanese Words, 1 vol. Translations.com Staff, tr. 2011. (Bilingual Picture Dictionaries Ser.). 32p. (gr. 1-2). (ENG & MUL.). pap. 8.10 *(978-1-4296-6337-3(5))*; (MUL.). pap. 47.70 *(978-1-4296-6464-6(9))* Capstone Press of Coughlan Cos. (Aplus Bks.).
—My First Book of Korean Words. Translations.com Staff, tr. 2011. (Bilingual Picture Dictionaries Ser.). (MUL.). 32p. (gr. 1-2). pap. 47.70 *(978-1-4296-6166-9(6)*, Aplus Bks.) Capstone Press of Coughlan Cos.
—My First Book of Portuguese Words. Translations.com Staff, tr. (Bilingual Picture Dictionaries Ser.). (MUL.). 32p. (gr. 1-2). 2011. pap. 47.70 *(978-1-4296-6170-6(4))* 2010. lib. bdg. 27.32 *(978-1-4296-5965-9(3))* Capstone Press of Coughlan Cos. (Aplus Bks.).
—My First Book of Russian Words, 1 vol. Translations.com Staff, tr. 2011. (Bilingual Picture Dictionaries Ser.). 32p. (gr. 1-2). (ENG & MUL.). pap. 8.10 *(978-1-4296-6336-6(7))*; (MUL.). pap. 47.70 *(978-1-4296-6463-9(0))* Capstone Press of Coughlan Cos. (Aplus Bks.).
—My First Book of Vietnamese Words. Translations.com Staff, tr. 2011. (Bilingual Picture Dictionaries Ser.). (MUL.). 32p. (gr. 1-2). pap. 47.70 *(978-1-4296-6164-5(X)*, Aplus Bks.) Capstone Press of Coughlan Cos.
Levey, Judith S. Scholastic First Dictionary. rev. ed. 2006. (ENG., Illus.). 256p. (J). (gr. -1-3). 16.99 *(978-0-439-79834-1(5)*, Scholastic Reference) Scholastic, Inc.
Liccioni, Tina. The Clownfish/el Pez Payaso: An English/Spanish Bilingual Book. Vesazquez, Gloria, tr. 2013. (ENG.). 36p. (J). pap. 21.95 *(978-1-4327-9060-8(9))* Outskirts Pr., Inc.
Lisl. Dictionary with a Difference. 2009. 116p. pap. 31.99 *(978-1-4490-0125-4(4))* AuthorHouse.
Magic Spanish Picture Dictionary. 2009. (ENG.). 144p. pap. 9.99 *(978-1-4231-2265-4(8))* Disney Pr.
Makishi, Cynthia. The Heinle Picture Dictionary for Children - Monkey Puppet. 2007. (ENG.). (C). 19.95 *(978-1-4240-1834-5(X))* Cengage Heinle.
Melis, Luisanna Fodde. Noah Webster & the First American Dictionary. 2009. (Library of American Lives & Times Ser.). 112p. (gr. 5-5). 69.20 *(978-1-60853-495-1(2))* Rosen Publishing Group, Inc., The.
Merriam-Webster, creator. Merriam-Webster's Intermediate Dictionary. rev. ed. 2016. (ENG., Illus.). 1024p. (J). 19.95 *(978-0-87779-697-8(1))* Merriam-Webster, Inc.
Merriam-Webster, Inc. Staff. Merriam-Webster's First Dictionary. Heller, Ruth, illus. rev. ed. 2011. (ENG.). 448p. (gr. k-2). 16.95 *(978-0-87779-274-1(7))* Merriam-Webster, Inc.
—Merriam-Webster's School Dictionary. 2015. (ENG., Illus.). 1280p. (J). 19.95 *(978-0-87779-680-0(7)*, Merriam-Webster) Merriam-Webster, Inc.
Merriam-Webster, Inc. Staff, ed. Merriam-Webster's Dictionary for Children. 2010. (ENG., Illus.). 672p. (J). (gr. 3-5). pap. 13.95 *(978-0-87779-730-2(7))* Merriam-Webster, Inc.
—Merriam-Webster's Elementary Dictionary. enl. ed. 2013. (ENG., Illus.). 848p. (J). 18.95 *(978-0-87779-676-3(9)*, Merriam-Webster) Merriam-Webster, Inc.
—Merriam-Webster's Elementary Dictionary. rev. ed. 2010. (gr. 3-6). lib. bdg. 25.70 *(978-0-613-23808-3(7)*, Turtleback) Turtleback Bks.
Milet Publishing Staff. Bilingual Visual Dictionary. (Milet Bilingual Visual Dictionary Ser.). (Illus.). (J). (gr. k-2). 2012. (ENG & ITA.). 148p. 34.95 *(978-1-84059-690-8(2))* 2011. (ENG & PER., 1p. cd-rom 19.95 *(978-1-84059-583-3(3))* 2011. (ENG & SOM., 1p. cd-rom 19.95 *(978-1-84059-591-8(4))* 2011. (ENG & ITA., 1p. cd-rom 19.95 *(978-1-84059-586-4(8))* 2011. (ENG & GER., 1p. cd-rom 19.95 *(978-1-84059-585-7(X))* 2011. (ENG & POR., 1p. cd-rom 19.95 *(978-1-84059-589-5(2))* 2011. (ENG & VIE., 1p. cd-rom 19.95 *(978-1-84059-595-6(7))* 2011. (SPA & ENG., 1p. cd-rom 19.95 *(978-1-84059-592-5(2))* 2011. (BEN & ENG., 1p. cd-rom 19.95 *(978-1-84059-581-9(7))* 2011. (ENG, POL & POR., 1p. cd-rom 19.95 *(978-1-84059-588-8(4))* 2011. (ENG & ARA., 1p. cd-rom 19.95 *(978-1-84059-580-2(9))* 2011. (ENG & RUS., 1p. cd-rom 19.95 *(978-1-84059-590-1(6))* 2011. (ENG & URD., 1p. cd-rom 19.95 *(978-1-84059-594-9(9))* 2011. (ENG & TUR., 1p. cd-rom 19.95 *(978-1-84059-593-2(0))* 2011. (FRE & ENG., 1p. cd-rom 19.95 *(978-1-84059-584-0(1))* 2011. (ENG & CHI., 1p. cd-rom 19.95 *(978-1-84059-582-6(5))* Milet Publishing.
—Bilingual Visual Dictionary CD-ROM (English-Korean) 2011. (Milet Multimedia Ser.). (ENG & KOR., Illus.). 1p. (J). (gr. k-2). cd-rom 19.95 *(978-1-84059-587-1(6))* Milet Publishing.
—Milet Bilingual Visual Dictionary. 2012. (Milet Bilingual Visual Dictionary Ser.). (ENG & TUR., Illus.). 148p. (J). (gr. k-2). 34.95 *(978-1-84059-697-7(X))*; 34.95 *(978-1-84059-694-6(5))* Milet Publishing.
—Milet Bilingual Visual Dictionary (English-Bengali) 2012. (Milet Bilingual Visual Dictionary Ser.). (ENG & BEN., Illus.). 148p. (J). (gr. k-2). 34.95 *(978-1-84059-685-4(6))* Milet Publishing.
—Milet Bilingual Visual Dictionary (English-Portuguese) 2012. (Milet Bilingual Visual Dictionary Ser.). (ENG & POR., Illus.). 148p. (J). (gr. k-2). 34.95 *(978-1-84059-693-9(7))* Milet Publishing.
—My First Bilingual Book - School. 2014. (My First Bilingual Book Ser.). (ENG & PER., Illus.). 20p. (J). (— 1). bds. 7.99 *(978-1-84059-893-3(X))* Milet Publishing.
Miller, Susan A. My First Dictionary. Williams, Ted, illus. 2005. (My First Ser.). 160p. (J). 7.98 *(978-0-7853-8369-7(7)*, 7183800) Phoenix International Publications, Inc.
Modéré, Armelle. My First English/Norwegian Dictionary of Sentences. 2008. (NOR & ENG., Illus.). 128p. (J). *(978-1-57534-048-7(8))* Skandisk, Inc.
Modéré, Armelle & Hokenson, Linda. My First English/Swedish Dictionary of Sentences. 2008. (SWE & ENG.). 128p. *(978-1-57534-049-4(6))* Skandisk, Inc.
Moore, Colista. A Student's Dictionary. 2011. (Illus.). 382p. (J). pap. *(978-1-934669-16-7(4))* Dictionary Project, Inc., The.
—A Student's Dictionary & Gazetteer. (Illus.). 524p. (J). 10th ed. 2006. pap. *(978-0-9771777-2-1(6))* 11th ed. 2006. pap. *(978-0-9771777-5-2(0))* 16th ed. 2009. pap. *(978-1-934669-04-4(0))* 17th ed. 2009. pap. *(978-1-934669-08-2(3))* 19th ed. 2011. pap. *(978-1-934669-21-1(0))* 20th ed. 2012. pap. ***(978-1-934669-24-2(5))*** Dictionary Project, Inc., The.
—A Student's English Dictionary. 2007. (Illus.). 366p. (J). pap. *(978-0-9771777-7-6(7))* Dictionary Project, Inc., The.
Morgan, Nicola. Two-Can First Dictionary. 2005. (ENG., Illus.). 64p. (J). (gr. -1-3). 12.95 *(978-1-58728-439-7(1))* Cooper Square Publishing Llc.
My Second Pictionary. Incl. My Second Picture Dictionary. 448p. (J). (gr. 2-5). 1990. pap. 16.38 *(978-0-673-28453-2(0)*, Scott Foresman); 448p. 15.95 *(978-0-673-12490-6(8))* Addison-Wesley Educational Pubs., Inc.
Oliver, Archie. First Picture Dictionary. 2004. (Illus.). 96p. (J). *(978-1-74121-401-7(7))* Hinkler Bks. Pty. Ltd.
O'Neill, Mary, et al. Primary Dictionary. 2008. (Illus.). 640p. *(978-0-550-10319-2(8)*, Chambers) Hodder & Stoughton.
—Primary Thesaurus. 2008. 400p. *(978-0-550-10320-8(1)*, Chambers) Hodder & Stoughton.
O'Sullivan, Jill Korey. The Heinle Picture Dictionary for Children. 2007. (ENG., Illus.). 160p. (C). (gr. 3-7). pap. 23.95 *(978-1-4240-0849-0(2))* Cengage Heinle.
O'Sullivan, Jill Korey & Makishi, Cynthia. Heinle Picture Dictionary for Children. 2007. (Heinle Picture Dictionary Ser.). (ENG.). 160p. (C). pap. 33.95 *(978-1-4130-2256-8(1))* Cengage Heinle.
Oxford Dictionaries Staff, ed. Oxford Illustrated Children's Dictionary: The Perfect Family Dictionary. 2010. (ENG., Illus.). 288p. (YA). (gr. 3-18). pap. 18.95 *(978-0-19-911993-6(7))* Oxford Univ. Pr., Inc.
Oxford Picture Dictionary Content Area for Kids English Dictionary Student Pack. 2012. pap. 31.80 *(978-0-19-401787-9(7))* Oxford Univ. Pr., Inc.
Oxford Picture Dictionary for Kids 2e Ebook Pack. 2nd ed. 2013. (ENG.). 12.44 *(978-0-19-401795-4(8))* Oxford Univ. Pr., Inc.
Oxford University Press Staff. Oxford American Desk Dictionary & Thesaurus. 3rd ed. 2009. (gr. 7-12). lib. bdg. 19.65 *(978-0-613-36859-9(2)*, Turtleback) Turtleback Bks.
Passport Books Staff, ed. Let's Learn American English. Goodman, Marlene, illus. 2003. (Let's Learn... Picture Dictionary Ser.). 72p. (J). (gr. 4-7). 9.95 *(978-0-8442-5453-1(3)*, 54533, Passport Bks.) McGraw-Hill Trade.
Picture Dictionary/Thematic Dictionary. (Foundation Ser.). 68p. (gr. k-3). 25.50 *(978-0-322-01562-3(6))* Wright Group/McGraw-Hill.
Publications International Ltd. Staff, ed. My First Phonics Dictionary. 2011. (Illus.). 96p. (J). 8.98 *(978-1-4508-1480-5(8))* Phoenix International Publications, Inc.
Santamaria, Jenni Currie & Keyes, Joan Ross. Content Areas for Kids: Accelerates Academic Language Development. 2nd ed. 2012. (ENG., Illus.). 200p. pap. 26.19 *(978-0-19-401775-6(3))* Oxford Univ. Pr., Inc.
Santamaria, Jenni Currie, et al. Oxford Picture Dictionary Content Areas for Kids. 2nd ed. 2012. (ENG., Illus.). 376p. tchr. ed., spiral bd. 64.31 *(978-0-19-401780-0(X))* Oxford Univ. Pr., Inc.
Scholastic, Inc. Staff. Children's Dictionary. 2013. (ENG., Illus.). 864p. (J). (gr. 3-7). 19.99 *(978-0-545-60495-6(8))* Scholastic, Inc.
—Scholastic Pocket Dictionary. 2011. (ENG.). 672p. (J). (gr. 3-7). pap. 9.99 *(978-0-545-38371-4(4))* Scholastic, Inc.
Scholastic, Inc. Staff, contrib. by. Scholastic Pocket Dictionary of Synonyms, Antonyms & Homonyms. 2012. (ENG.). 240p. (J). (gr. 3-7). pap. 6.99 *(978-0-545-42667-1(7)*, Scholastic Reference) Scholastic, Inc.
Scholastic, Inc. Staff & de la Bretesche, Genevieve. Scholastic First Picture Dictionary. rev. ed. 2009. (ENG., Illus.). 96p. (J). (gr. -1-k). 16.99 *(978-0-545-13769-0(1)*, Cartwheel Bks.) Scholastic, Inc.
Shank, Cathy, et al. Collaborations Literacy: Newbury Dictionary. pap., stu. ed. 37.95 *(978-0-8384-9487-5(0))* Cengage Heinle.
Shannon, Rosemarie & Southern, Shelley, adapted by. Franklin's Picture Dictionary. 2004. (Franklin Ser.). (ENG., Illus.). 112p. (J). (gr. k-3). 15.95 *(978-1-55337-711-5(7))* Kids Can Pr., Ltd. CAN. Dist: Hachette Bk. Group.
Simon and Schuster Staff. Macmillan Dictionary for Children. Morris, Christopher G., ed. 2007. (ENG., Illus.). 848p. (J). (gr. 3-7). 19.99 *(978-1-4169-3959-7(8)*, Simon & Schuster Bks. For Young Readers) Simon & Schuster Bks. For Young Readers.
—Macmillan Dictionary for Children: 4th Revised Edition. rev. ed. 2005. 896p. (J). 9.95 *(978-0-689-86656-2(9))* Simon & Schuster Children's Publishing.
—Macmillan First Dictionary. Morris, Christopher G., ed. 2008. (ENG.). 400p. (J). (gr. k-3). 19.99 *(978-1-4169-5043-1(5)*, Simon & Schuster Bks. For Young Readers) Simon & Schuster Bks. For Young Readers.
A Student's Dictionary & Gazetteer. 2011. (Illus.). 429p. (J). pap. *(978-1-934669-19-8(9))* Dictionary Project, Inc., The.
SunshineTM My First Dictionary. 64p. (gr. k-3). 15.50 *(978-0-7802-6168-6(2))* Wright Group/McGraw-Hill.
Sussman, Joni. My First Yiddish Word Book. Marzel, Pepi, illus. 2014. (ENG.). 32p. (J). (gr. -1-2). pap. 12.95 *(978-1-4677-5175-9(8)*, Kar-Ben Publishing) Lerner Publishing Group.
Sussman, Joni Kibort. My First Yiddish Word Book. Marzel, Pepi, illus. 2009. (Israel Ser.). 32p. (J). (gr. -1-3). bds. 17.95 *(978-0-8225-8755-2(6)*, Kar-Ben Publishing) Lerner Publishing Group.
Terban, Marvin. Scholastic Dictionary of Idioms. rev. ed. 2006. (ENG.). 298p. (J). (gr. 3-7). pap. 9.99 *(978-0-439-77083-5(1)*, Scholastic Reference) Scholastic, Inc.
Truesdell, Ann. Find New Words with Dictionaries. 2012. (Explorer Junior Library: Information Explorer Junior Ser.). (ENG., Illus.). 24p. (J). (gr. 1-4). pap. 12.79 *(978-1-61080-393-9(0)*, 201330); lib. bdg. 28.50 *(978-1-61080-368-7(X)*, 201270) Cherry Lake Publishing.
Turhan, Sedat. Milet Picture Dictionary. 2005. (SIT, ENG & HMN., Illus.). 1p. (J). pap. 14.95 *(978-1-84059-465-2(9))* Milet Publishing.
—New Bilingual Visual Dictionary (English-Arabic) 2nd ed. 2017. (New Bilingual Visual Dictionary Ser.). (ENG & ARA., Illus.). 144p. (J). (gr. k-2). 19.95 ***(978-1-78508-881-0(5))*** Milet Publishing.
—New Bilingual Visual Dictionary (English-Bengali) 2nd ed. 2017. (New Bilingual Visual Dictionary Ser.). (ENG & BEN., Illus.). 144p. (J). (gr. k-2). 19.95 ***(978-1-78508-882-7(3))*** Milet Publishing.
—New Bilingual Visual Dictionary (English-Chinese) 2nd ed. 2017. (New Bilingual Visual Dictionary Ser.). (ENG & CHI., Illus.). 144p. (J). (— 1). 19.95 ***(978-1-78508-883-4(1))*** Milet Publishing.
—New Bilingual Visual Dictionary (English-Farsi) 2nd ed. 2017. (New Bilingual Visual Dictionary Ser.). (ENG & PER., Illus.). 144p. (J). (gr. k-2). 19.95 ***(978-1-78508-884-1(X))*** Milet Publishing.
—New Bilingual Visual Dictionary (English-German) 2nd ed. 2017. (New Bilingual Visual Dictionary Ser.). (ENG & GER., Illus.). 144p. (J). (gr. k-2). 19.95 *(978-1-78508-886-5(6))* Milet Publishing.
—New Bilingual Visual Dictionary (English-Korean) 2017. (New Bilingual Visual Dictionary Ser.). (ENG & KOR., Illus.). 144p. (J). (gr. k-2). 19.95 ***(978-1-78508-888-9(2))*** Milet Publishing.
—New Bilingual Visual Dictionary (English-Russian) 2nd ed. 2017. (New Bilingual Visual Dictionary Ser.). (ENG & RUS., Illus.). 144p. (J). (gr. k-2). 19.95 ***(978-1-78508-891-9(2))*** Milet Publishing.
—New Bilingual Visual Dictionary (English-Somali) 2nd ed. 2017. (New Bilingual Visual Dictionary Ser.). (ENG & SOM., Illus.). 144p. (J). (gr. k-2). 19.95 *(978-1-78508-892-6(0))* Milet Publishing.
—New Bilingual Visual Dictionary (English-Turkish) 2nd ed. 2017. (New Bilingual Visual Dictionary Ser.). (ENG & TUR., Illus.). 144p. (J). (gr. k-2). 19.95 *(978-1-78508-894-0(7))* Milet Publishing.
—New Bilingual Visual Dictionary (English-Urdu) 2nd ed. 2017. (New Bilingual Visual Dictionary Ser.). (ENG & URD., Illus.). 144p. (J). (gr. k-2). 19.95 ***(978-1-78508-895-7(5))*** Milet Publishing.
—New Bilingual Visual Dictionary (English-Vietnamese) 2nd ed. 2017. (New Bilingual Visual Dictionary Ser.). (ENG & VIE., Illus.). 144p. (J). (gr. k-2). 19.95 ***(978-1-78508-896-4(3))*** Milet Publishing.
Turhan, Sedat & Hagin, Sally. Milet Mini Picture Dictionary. 2003. (Milet Mini Picture Dictionary Ser.). (ENG., Illus.). 28p. (J). (— 1). bds. 6.99 *(978-1-84059-367-9(9))*; bds. 7.99 *(978-1-84059-369-3(5))*; bds. 7.99 *(978-1-84059-371-6(7))*; bds. 7.99 *(978-1-84059-372-3(5))*; bds. 7.99 *(978-1-84059-385-3(7))*; bds. 7.99 *(978-1-84059-379-2(2))*; bds. 7.99 *(978-1-84059-378-5(4))*; bds. 7.99 *(978-1-84059-377-8(6))*; bds. 7.99 *(978-1-84059-373-0(3))*; bds. 7.99 *(978-1-84059-375-4(X))*; bds. 7.99 *(978-1-84059-376-1(8))* Milet Publishing.
—Milet Picture Dictionary. 2003. (Milet Picture Dictionary Ser.). (Illus.). 48p. (J). (gr. -1). (ENG & FRE.). 14.95 *(978-1-84059-352-5(0))*; (ARA & ENG., 14.95 *(978-1-84059-348-8(2))*; (ENG & GER., 14.95 *(978-1-84059-353-2(9))*; (ENG & ITA., 14.95 *(978-1-84059-354-9(7))*; (KOR & ENG., 14.95 *(978-1-84059-356-3(3))*; (POR & ENG., 14.95 *(978-1-84059-357-0(1))*; (RUS & ENG., 14.95 *(978-1-84059-358-7(X))*; (SOM, ENG, VIE, SPA & PER., 14.95 *(978-1-84059-359-4(8))*; (ENG & SPA., 14.95 *(978-1-84059-360-0(1))*; (URD & ENG., 14.95 *(978-1-84059-362-4(8))*; (ENG & VIE., 14.95 *(978-1-84059-363-1(6))*; (ENG, PER & FAR., 14.95 *(978-1-84059-351-8(2))*; (BEN, ENG, VIE, SPA & PER., 14.95 *(978-1-84059-349-5(0))*; (ENG, TUR, VIE, SPA & PER., 14.95 *(978-1-84059-361-7(X))* Milet Publishing.
—Milet Picture Dictionary. Hagin, Sally, illus. 18th ed. 2003. (Milet Picture Dictionary Ser.). (ENG., Illus.). 48p. (J). (gr. -1). 13.95 *(978-1-84059-346-4(6))* Milet Publishing.
Wardley, R. & Bingham, J. First Dictionary. 2004. (Illus.). 144p. (J). (gr. k-18). 15.95 *(978-0-7945-0145-7(1)*, Usborne); lib. bdg. 23.95 *(978-1-58086-436-7(8))* EDC Publishing.
Webster's New Explorer Student Dictionary, Third Edition. 3rd ed. 2010. (J). 12.98 *(978-1-59695-086-3(2))* Federal Street Pr.
Weinick, Suzanne. How Do I Use an Encyclopedia? 2014. (Research Tools You Can Use Ser.). 32p. (J). (gr. 3-6). pap. 12.90 *(978-1-62275-386-4(0))* Rosen Publishing Group, Inc., The.
Wernham, Sara & Lloyd, Sue. Dictionary. Stephen, Lib, illus. 2003. (Jolly Grammar Ser.: DICTIONARY). (ENG.). 300p. (J). pap. 13.50 *(978-1-84414-001-5(6)*, JL016, Jolly Learning) Jolly Learning, Ltd. GBR. Dist: American International Distribution Corp.
Wilkes, Ian. London Rabbit: A Guide to Cockney Rhyming Slang. 2004. (Illus.). 64p. (YA). (gr. 6-12). pap. *(978-0-86025-538-3(7))* Henry, Ian Pubns.
Williams, Carol. Beth Yw'r Gair Am... 2004.Tr. of What's the World For.... (WEL & ENG., Illus.). 126p. (J). pap. 20.00 *(978-0-7083-1736-5(7))* Gwasg Prifysgol Cymru / Univ. of Wales Pr. GBR. Dist: Chicago Distribution Ctr.
Worcester, Joseph E. (Joseph Emerson). An Elementary Dictionary of the English Language by Joseph E Worcester, LI D. 2006. 404p. per. 26.99 *(978-1-4255-4293-1(X))* Michigan Publishing.
World Book Student Dictionary. 2005. (gr. 2-8). 39.00 *(978-0-7166-1555-2(X))* World Bk., Inc.

Wright, Tony. Collins Picture Dictionary for Young Learners. Date not set. (Illus.). (J). pap. *(978-0-17-556761-4(1))* Addison-Wesley Longman, Inc.

ENGLISH LANGUAGE—DICTIONARIES—FRENCH

Brooks, Felicity. Very First Dictionary in French - Internet Referenced. 2008. (Very First Dictionaries Ser.). 80p. (J). 11.99 *(978-0-7945-2047-2(2)*, Usborne) EDC Publishing.
Collins. Collins French School Dictionary. 3rd rev. ed. 2011. (FRE & ENG.). 640p. (J). pap. 9.95 *(978-0-00-736785-6(6))* HarperCollins Pubs. Ltd. GBR. Dist: Independent Pubs. Group.
Collins Dictionaries. Collins French School Dictionary. 4th rev. ed. 2015. (FRE & ENG.). 640p. (YA). (gr. 6-11). pap. 9.99 *(978-0-00-756931-1(9))*; (Illus.). (gr. 5-11). pap. 10.99 *(978-0-00-756935-9(1))* HarperCollins Pubs. Ltd. GBR. Dist: Independent Pubs. Group.
—Collins Primary French Dictionary. 2014. (FRE & ENG., Illus.). 640p. (J). (gr. 2-6). 14.99 *(978-0-00-757874-0(1))* HarperCollins Pubs. Ltd. GBR. Dist: Independent Pubs. Group.
Crabbé, Raoul & Barwell, Eve. Boats Through the Ages. Marcellin, Jean, illus. 6th ed. 2013. (ENG & FRE.). 25p. ***(978-0-245-50382-5(X))*** Harrap, Larousse Pubs.
Kenny, Chantal Lacourcière. The Kids Can Press French & English Phrase Book. Hendry, Linda, illus. 2004. (ENG.). 40p. (J). 7.95 *(978-1-55337-650-7(1))* Kids Can Pr., Ltd. CAN. Dist: Hachette Bk. Group.
Turhan, Sedat. New Bilingual Visual Dictionary (English-French) 2nd ed. 2017. (New Bilingual Visual Dictionary Ser.). (FRE & ENG., Illus.). 144p. (J). (gr. k-2). 19.95 *(978-1-78508-885-8(8))* Milet Publishing.
York, M. J. Learn French Words. Petelinsek, Kathleen, illus. 2014. (Foreign Language Basics Ser.). (ENG.). 24p. (J). (gr. 2-5). 27.07 *(978-1-62687-374-2(7)*, 207121) Child's World, Inc., The.

ENGLISH LANGUAGE—DICTIONARIES—GERMAN

Collins Dictionaries. German School Dictionary. 2015. (GER & ENG.). 624p. (YA). 2nd rev. ed. (gr. 6-11). pap. 7.99 *(978-0-00-756932-8(7))* 4th rev. ed. (gr. 5-11). pap. 10.99 *(978-0-00-756934-2(3))* HarperCollins Pubs. Ltd. GBR. Dist: Independent Pubs. Group.
Goodman, Marlene. Let's Learn German Picture Dictionary. 2003. (ENG & GER., Illus.). 80p. 13.00 *(978-0-07-140824-0(X)*, 007140824X) McGraw-Hill Cos., The.
Hippocrene Books Staff. Children's Illustrated German Dictionary: English-German, German-English. 2003. (Hippocrene Children's Illustrated Foreign Language Dictionaries Ser.). (ENG & GER., Illus.). 122p. pap. 11.95 *(978-0-7818-0986-3(X))* Hippocrene Bks., Inc.
Kudela, Katy R. My First Book of German Words, 1 vol. 2011. (Bilingual Picture Dictionaries Ser.). 32p. (gr. 1-2). (ENG & MUL.). pap. 8.10 *(978-1-4296-6335-9(9))*; (MUL.). pap. 47.70 *(978-1-4296-6462-2(2))* Capstone Press of Coughlan Cos. (Aplus Bks.).
Milet Publishing Staff. Milet Bilingual Visual Dictionary. 2012. (Milet Bilingual Visual Dictionary Ser.). (ENG & GER., Illus.). 148p. (J). (gr. k-2). 34.95 *(978-1-84059-689-2(9))* Milet Publishing.

ENGLISH LANGUAGE—DICTIONARIES—POLISH

Hippocrene Books Staff, creator. Hippocrene Polish Children's Dictionary: English-Polish/Polish-English. 2006. (ENG & POL., Illus.). 108p. (J). (gr. 3-7). pap. 14.95 *(978-0-7818-1127-9(9))* Hippocrene Bks., Inc.
Kudela, Katy R. My First Book of Polish Words. Translations.com Staff, tr. (Bilingual Picture Dictionaries Ser.). (MUL.). 32p. (gr. 1-2). 2011. pap. 47.70 *(978-1-4296-6168-3(2))* 2010. lib. bdg. 27.32 *(978-1-4296-5964-2(5))* Capstone Press of Coughlan Cos. (Aplus Bks.).
Milet Publishing Staff. Milet Bilingual Visual Dictionary. 2012. (Milet Bilingual Visual Dictionary Ser.). (ENG, POL & POR., Illus.). 148p. (J). (gr. k-2). 34.95 *(978-1-84059-692-2(9))* Milet Publishing.
Turhan, Sedat. New Bilingual Visual Dictionary (English-Polish) 2nd ed. 2017. (New Bilingual Visual Dictionary Ser.). (ENG & POL., Illus.). 144p. (J). (gr. k-2). 19.95 *(978-1-78508-889-6(0))* Milet Publishing.
Turhan, Sedat & Hagin, Sally. Milet Picture Dictionary. 2005. (Milet Picture Dictionary Ser.). (ENG & POL., Illus.). 48p. (J). (gr. -1-3). pap. 14.95 *(978-1-84059-466-9(7))* Milet Publishing.

ENGLISH LANGUAGE—DICTIONARIES—SPANISH

Bennet, Archie & Gutiérrez Bello, Marta. Beginner's English/Spanish Dictionary & Guide to Usage. 2004. (Back to School Basics Ser.).Tr. of Diccionario Espanol/Ingles para principiantes Y Guia de Uso. (ENG & SPA., Illus.). 512p. (J). 12.95 *(978-1-58279-360-3(3))* Standard International Media.
Brooks, Felicity. Very First Dictionary in Spanish - Internet Referenced. 2008. (Very First Dictionaries Ser.). 80p. (J). 11.99 *(978-0-7945-2104-2(5)*, Usborne) EDC Publishing.
Brooks, Felicity & Mackinnon, Mairi. Picture Dictionary in Spanish. 2004. (Picture Dictionaries Ser.). (ENG & SPA., Illus.). 112p. (J). lib. bdg. 24.95 *(978-1-58086-477-0(5))* EDC Publishing.
Bruzzone, Catherine. Spanish-English Picture Dictionary. 2011. (First Bilingual Picture Dictionaries Ser.). (SPA & ENG., Illus.). 48p. (J). (gr. -1-3). pap. 7.99 *(978-0-7641-4661-9(0))* Barron's Educational Series, Inc.
Collins Dictionaries. Collins Spanish School Dictionary. 3rd rev. ed. 2015. (SPA & ENG.). 640p. (J). (gr. 2). pap. 10.99 *(978-0-00-756933-5(5))* HarperCollins Pubs. Ltd. GBR. Dist: Independent Pubs. Group.
—Spanish School Dictionary. 3rd rev. ed. 2015. (SPA & ENG.). 640p. (YA). (gr. 6-11). pap. 7.99 *(978-0-00-756930-4(0))* HarperCollins Pubs. Ltd. GBR. Dist: Independent Pubs. Group.
Collins Dictionaries Staff. Collins Primary Illustrated Spanish Dictionary. 2015. (SPA & ENG., Illus.). 640p. (J). (gr. 3-6). 14.95 *(978-0-00-811196-0(0))* HarperCollins Pubs. Ltd. GBR. Dist: Independent Pubs. Group.
Collins Dictionary Staff. Collins Spanish School Dictionary. 2nd ed. 2011. (SPA & ENG.). 640p. (J). pap. 9.95 *(978-0-00-736784-9(8))* HarperCollins Pubs. Ltd. GBR. Dist: Independent Pubs. Group.
Dorling Kindersley Publishing Staff. Spanish Language Learner. 2011. (ENG.). 160p. (J). (gr. 5-12). 19.99 *(978-0-7566-8256-9(8)*, DK Children) Dorling Kindersley Publishing, Inc.
Hippocrene Books Staff, creator. Children's Picture Dictionary. 2006. (Hippocrene Children's Illustrated Dictionaries Ser.). (ENG & SPA., Illus.). 108p. (J). (gr. 3-7). pap. 14.95 *(978-0-7818-1130-9(9))* Hippocrene Bks., Inc.
Karapetian, Marjam. Bilingual Content Dictionary: English to Spanish. 2004. (SPA & ENG.). 9.95 *(978-0-9764829-2-5(4))* WizdomInc.
Kauffman, Dorothy, et al. Oxford Picture Dictionary for the Content Areas. 2nd ed. 2010. (Oxford Picture Dictionary for the Content Areas 2e Ser.). (SPA & ENG., Illus.). 216p. pap. 27.00 *(978-0-19-452502-2(3))* Oxford Univ. Pr., Inc.
Kudela, Katy R. My First Book of Spanish Words, 1 vol. 2009. (Bilingual Picture Dictionaries Ser.). (SPA, ENG & MUL.). 32p. (gr. 1-2). lib. bdg. 27.32 *(978-1-4296-3298-0(4)*, Aplus Bks.) Capstone Press of Coughlan Cos.
Laud, Valerie. The Picture Book Dictionary: The Essential Source for Bilingual Families, English-Spanish Edition. Latushkin, Valentin, illus. l.t. ed. 2005. (ENG & SPA.). 96p. (J). *(978-0-9747387-0-3(0))* EKADOO Publishing Group.
Lipton, Gladys C. Spanish Beginner's Bilingual Dictionary. 4th rev. ed. 2009. (Barron's Beginner's Bilingual Dictionaries Ser.). (ENG & SPA., Illus.). 456p. pap. 8.99 *(978-0-7641-3968-0(1))* Barron's Educational Series, Inc.
Merriam-Webster. Merriam-Webster's Illustrated Spanish-English Student Dictionary. 2012. (ENG., Illus.). 495p. (gr. 4-8). 21.95 *(978-0-87779-177-5(5))* Merriam-Webster, Inc.
O'Sullivan, Jill Korey. Picture Dictionary for Children. 2007. (ENG.). 176p. (C). pap. 32.95 *(978-1-4240-0876-6(X))* Cengage Heinle.
Oxford Picture Dictionary Content Area for Kids English-Spanish Dictionary Student Pack. 2012. pap. 31.80 *(978-0-19-401788-6(5))* Oxford Univ. Pr., Inc.
Pearson Longman Staff & Pearson Education Staff. Longman Diccionario Pocket, Ingles-Espanol, Espanol-Ingles: Para Estudiantes Mexicanos. 2004. (ENG & SPA., Illus.). 832p. (C). pap. 27.27 *(978-0-582-51157-6(7))* Pearson Education.
Richmond Advanced Dictionary: Spanish/English, English/Spanish. (ENG & SPA.). 720p. (J). (gr. 9-12). 30.95 *(978-84-294-9861-5(3)*, Richmond) Santillana USA Publishing Co., Inc.
Richmond Pocket Dictionary: Spanish-English, English-Spanish. (SPA & ENG.). 806p. (J). (gr. 6-12). pap. 10.95 *(978-84-294-9860-8(5))* Santillana USA Publishing Co., Inc.
Sauri, Trudy. Gift of Yucatan Nouns A-Z. 2008. (ENG & SPA., Illus.). 64p. (J). per. 18.00 *(978-0-9797637-3-1(8))* Your Culture Gifts.
Spanish-English Picture Dictionary. 2003. (SPA & ENG.). (J). per. *(978-1-884907-30-2(X))* Paradise Pr., Inc.
Tallarico, Tony J., Jr. English - Spanish Word Search: Sopa de Letras, Vol. 2. 2011. (Dover Children's Language Activity Bks.). (ENG.). 48p. (J). (gr. 2-5). pap. 4.99 *(978-0-486-48098-5(4))* Dover Pubns., Inc.
—English-Spanish Word Search. 2011. (Dover Children's Language Activity Bks.). (ENG., Illus.). 48p. (J). (gr. 2-5). pap. 4.99 *(978-0-486-48097-8(6))* Dover Pubns., Inc.
York, M. J. Learn Spanish Words. Petelinsek, Kathleen, illus. 2014. (Foreign Language Basics Ser.). (ENG.). 24p. (J). (gr. 2-5). 27.07 *(978-1-62687-379-7(8)*, 207126) Child's World, Inc., The.

ENGLISH LANGUAGE—ETYMOLOGY

Aboff, Marcie. If You Were a Prefix, 1 vol. Gray, Sara, illus. 2008. (Word Fun Ser.). (ENG.). 24p. (gr. 2-4). pap. 7.95 *(978-1-4048-4777-4(4))* Picture Window Bks.
—If You Were a Suffix, 1 vol. Gray, Sara, illus. 2008. (Word Fun Ser.). (ENG.). 24p. (gr. 2-4). pap. 7.95 *(978-1-4048-4778-1(2))* Picture Window Bks.
American Heritage Dictionaries Editors, ed. 100 Words Every 4th Grader Should Know. 2014. (100 Words Ser.). (ENG.). 96p. (J). (gr. 2-5). pap. 6.95 *(978-0-544-10611-6(3))* Houghton Mifflin Harcourt Publishing Co.
Amery, H. & Cartwright, S. Pairs. 2004. (Pairs Ser.). (Illus.). (J). 8.95 *(978-0-7945-0327-7(6)*, Usborne) EDC Publishing.
Baker, Rosalie. In a Word: 750 Words & Their Fascinating Stories & Origins. Lopes, Tom, illus. 2003. (ENG.). 250p. (J). 17.95 *(978-0-8126-2710-7(5))* Cricket Bks.
Doudna, Kelly. Tick Tock, 1 vol. 2004. (Sound Words Ser.). (ENG., Illus.). 24p. (J). (gr. k-3). lib. bdg. 24.21 *(978-1-59197-455-0(0)*, SandCastle) ABDO Publishing Co.
Terban, Marvin. Guppies in Tuxedos: Funny Eponyms. Maestro, Giulio, illus. 2008. (ENG.). 64p. (J). (gr. 5-7). pap. 7.95 *(978-0-547-03188-0(2))* Houghton Mifflin Harcourt Publishing Co.

ENGLISH LANGUAGE—GRAMMAR

Abraham, Philip. Language Development Grammer Usage. 2004. (BrainBuilders Ser.). (ENG.). 48p. (gr. k-4). pap. 5.25 *(978-1-4042-8519-4(9))* Rosen Publishing Group, Inc., The.
—Language Development Writing Process. 2004. (BrainBuilders Ser.). (ENG.). 48p. (gr. k-4). pap. 5.25 *(978-1-4042-8520-0(2))* Rosen Publishing Group, Inc., The.
Abrams, Majella. Reading Pals: Short & Long Vowels Gr. K-1. Taylor, Jennifer, ed. Sexton, Brenda, illus. 2007. (J). per. 6.99 *(978-1-59198-436-8(X))* Creative Teaching Pr., Inc.
Adams, C. Planes Go Places: Learning the PL Sound. 2009. (PowerPhonics Ser.). 24p. (gr. 1-1). 39.90 *(978-1-60851-468-7(4)*, PowerKids Pr.) Rosen Publishing Group, Inc., The.
Adjectives & Adverbs. 2013. (Core Language Skills Ser.). 24p. (J). (gr. 2-2). pap. 49.50 *(978-1-4777-0971-9(1)*, PowerKids Pr.) Rosen Publishing Group, Inc., The.
Alinas, Marv. Boxes for Max: The Sound of X. 2016. (Consonants Ser.). (ENG.). 24p. (J). (gr. -1-2). 25.64 *(978-1-5038-0925-3(0)*, 210745) Child's World, Inc., The.
American Heritage Publishing Staff. The American Heritage Student Grammar Dictionary. 2011. (ENG., Illus.). 160p. (gr. 5-7). pap. 13.95 *(978-0-547-47265-2(X))* Houghton Mifflin Harcourt Publishing Co.
Amoroso, Cynthia. Hot Pot: The Sound of Short O. 2015. (Long & Short Vowels Ser.). (ENG.). 24p. (J). (gr. -1-2). 25.64 *(978-1-63407-023-2(2)*, 208858) Child's World, Inc., The.
—On the Boat: The Sound of Long O. 2015. (Long & Short Vowels Ser.). (ENG.). 24p. (J). (gr. -1-2). 25.64 *(978-1-63407-025-6(9)*, 208860) Child's World, Inc., The.
—Ten Pets: The Sound of Short E. 2015. (Long & Short Vowels Ser.). (ENG.). 24p. (J). (gr. -1-2). 25.64 *(978-1-63407-019-5(4)*, 208854) Child's World, Inc., The.
Amoroso, Cynthia & Noyed, Bob. What a Week: The Sound of Long E. 2015. (Long & Short Vowels Ser.). (ENG.). 24p. (J). (gr. -1-2). 25.64 *(978-1-63407-028-7(3)*, 208863) Child's World, Inc., The.
Analogies 1: Grade 7-8. 2004. (Analogies Ser.). pap. 7.25 *(978-0-8388-2225-8(8))* Educators Publishing Service, Inc.
Analogies 2: Grade 9-10. 2004. (Analogies Ser.). pap. 7.25 *(978-0-8388-2227-2(4))* Educators Publishing Service, Inc.
Analogies 3: Grade 11-12. 2004. (Analogies Ser.). pap. 7.25 *(978-0-8388-2229-6(0))* Educators Publishing Service, Inc.
Analogies 3: Grade11-12 Quiz Book. 2004. (Analogies Ser.). pap. 8.20 *(978-0-8388-2230-2(4))* Educators Publishing Service, Inc.
Arnold, Julie & Wall, Lynda. English in Practice Workbook 1. 2013. (ENG.). pap., stu. ed. *(978-1-107-67236-9(8))* Cambridge Univ. Pr.
—English in Practice Workbook 2. 2013. (ENG.). pap., stu. ed. *(978-1-107-69366-1(7))* Cambridge Univ. Pr.
Ashley, Moana. Wonders of the Worlds. 2008. (Illus.). 24p. (J). pap. 10.95 *(978-1-59646-541-1(7))* Dingles & Co.
Atlee, Nancy. The Absolutely Essential Grammar Guide. 2004. (J). per. 13.95 *(978-1-883055-69-1(5))* Dandy Lion Pubns.
Atwood, Megan. Cailyn & Chloe Learn about Conjunctions. 2014. (Language Builders Ser.). (ENG., Illus.). 32p. (J). (gr. 2-4). lib. bdg. 25.27 *(978-1-59953-671-2(4))* Norwood Hse. Pr.
—Cailyn & Chloe Learn about Conjunctions. Haus, Estudio, illus. 2014. (Language Builders Ser.). (ENG.). 32p. (J). (gr. 2-4). pap. 11.94 *(978-1-60357-706-9(8))* Norwood Hse. Pr.
—Patrick & Paula Learn about Prepositions. Otero, Sole, illus. 2014. (Language Builders Ser.). (ENG.). 32p. (J). (gr. 2-4). pap. 11.94 *(978-1-60357-708-3(4))*; lib. bdg. 25.27 *(978-1-59953-673-6(0))* Norwood Hse. Pr.
Baicker, Karen & Scholastic Canada Ltd. Staff. Quick Cloze Passages for Boosting Comprehension Grades 4-6: 40 Leveled Cloze Passages That Give Students Practice in Using Context Clues to Build Vocabulary & Comprehension. 2012. (ENG.). 48p. (gr. 4-6). pap. 10.99 *(978-0-545-30110-7(6)*, Teaching Resources) Scholastic, Inc.
Baicker, Karen & Scholastic, Inc. Staff. Quick Cloze Passages for Boosting Comprehension: 40 Leveled Cloze Passages That Give Students Practice in Using Context Clues to Build Vocabulary & Comprehension. 2012. (ENG.). 48p. (gr. 2-3). pap. 10.99 *(978-0-545-30108-4(4)*, Teaching Resources) Scholastic, Inc.
Bailer, Darice. Austin & Alex Learn about Adjectives. Girouard, Patrick, illus. 2014. (Language Builders Ser.). (ENG.). 32p. (J). (gr. 2-4). pap. 11.94 *(978-1-60357-703-8(3))*; lib. bdg. 25.27 *(978-1-59953-668-2(4))* Norwood Hse. Pr.
—Iris & Ian Learn about Interjections. Oseid, Kelsey, illus. 2014. (Language Builders Ser.). (ENG.). 32p. (J). (gr. 2-4). pap. 11.94 *(978-1-60357-707-6(6))*; lib. bdg. 25.27 *(978-1-59953-672-9(2))* Norwood Hse. Pr.
Ballard, Peg & Amoroso, Cynthia. Little Bit: The Sound of Short I. 2015. (Long & Short Vowels Ser.). (ENG.). 24p. (J). (gr. -1-2). 25.64 *(978-1-63407-024-9(0)*, 208859) Child's World, Inc., The.
Barchers, Suzanne. 180 Days of Language for Fifth Grade, 1 vol. rev. ed. 2014. (180 Days Ser.). (ENG., Illus.). 208p. (gr. 5-5). pap. 19.99 *(978-1-4258-1170-9(1))* Shell Educational Publishing.
—180 Days of Language for Fourth Grade, 1 vol. rev. ed. 2014. (180 Days Ser.). (ENG., Illus.). 208p. (gr. 4-4). pap. 19.99 *(978-1-4258-1169-3(8))* Shell Educational Publishing.
—180 Days of Language for Sixth Grade, 1 vol. rev. ed. 2014. (180 Days Ser.). (ENG., Illus.). 208p. (gr. 6-6). pap. 19.99 *(978-1-4258-1171-6(X))* Shell Educational Publishing.
Barker, Ray & Moorcroft, Christine. Grammar First, Bk. 3. 2003. (ENG., Illus.). 64p. (J). (gr. 6-9). pap., stu. ed. 13.95 *(978-0-7487-6537-9(9))* Nelson Thornes Ltd. GBR. Dist: Trans-Atlantic Pubns., Inc.
Basher, Simon & Budzik, Mary. Grammar. Basher, Simon, illus. 2011. (Basher Basics Ser.). (ENG., Illus.). 64p. (J). (gr. 3-7). pap. 7.99 *(978-0-7534-6596-7(5)*, 9780753465967, Kingfisher) Roaring Brook Pr.
Battistoni, I. I Fight Fires: Learning the Long I Sound. 2009. (PowerPhonics Ser.). 24p. (gr. 1-1). 39.90 *(978-1-60851-447-2(1)*, PowerKids Pr.) Rosen Publishing Group, Inc., The.
—What a Whale! Learning the WH Sound. 2009. (PowerPhonics Ser.). 24p. (gr. 1-1). 39.90 *(978-1-60851-478-6(1)*, PowerKids Pr.) Rosen Publishing Group, Inc., The.
Becker, Helaine. AlphaBest: The Zany, Zanier, Zaniest Book about Comparatives & Superlatives. Whamond, Dave, illus. 2012. (ENG.). 32p. (J). (gr. -1-3). 16.95 *(978-1-55453-715-0(0))* Kids Can Pr., Ltd. CAN. Dist: Hachette Bk. Group.
Beech, Linda. Comprehension Skills: 40 Short Passages for Close Reading - Grade 1. 2012. (ENG.). 48p. (gr. 1-1). pap. 10.99 *(978-0-545-46052-1(2)*, Teaching Resources) Scholastic, Inc.
Beech, Linda Ward. Comprehension Skills: 40 Short Passages for Close Reading, Grade 2. 2012. (ENG.). 48p. (gr. 2-2). pap. 10.99 *(978-0-545-46053-8(0)*, Teaching Resources) Scholastic, Inc.
—Comprehension Skills: 40 Short Passages for Close Reading, Grade 3. 2012. (ENG.). 48p. (gr. 3-3). pap. 10.99 *(978-0-545-46054-5(9)*, Teaching Resources) Scholastic, Inc.
—Comprehension Skills: 40 Short Passages for Close Reading, Grade 4. 2012. (ENG.). 48p. (gr. 4-4). pap. 10.99 *(978-0-545-46055-2(7)*, Teaching Resources) Scholastic, Inc.
—Comprehension Skills - 40 Short Passages for Close Reading. 2012. (ENG.). 48p. (gr. 5-5). pap. 10.99 *(978-0-545-46056-9(5)*, Teaching Resources) Scholastic, Inc.
—Comprehension Skills - Short Passages for Close Reading. 2012. (ENG.). 48p. (gr. 6-6). pap. 10.99 *(978-0-545-46057-6(3)*, Teaching Resources) Scholastic, Inc.
—Great Grammar Practice: Grade 1. 2015. (Great Grammar Practice Ser.). (ENG.). 64p. (gr. 1-1). pap. 11.99 *(978-0-545-79421-3(8)*, Teaching Resources) Scholastic, Inc.
—Great Grammar Practice: Grade 2. 2015. (Great Grammar Practice Ser.). (ENG.). 64p. (gr. 2-2). pap. 11.99 *(978-0-545-79422-0(6)*, Teaching Resources) Scholastic, Inc.
—Great Grammar Practice: Grade 3. 2015. (Great Grammar Practice Ser.). (ENG.). 64p. (gr. 3-3). pap. 11.99 *(978-0-545-79423-7(4)*, Teaching Resources) Scholastic, Inc.
—Great Grammar Practice: Grade 4. 2015. (Great Grammar Practice Ser.). (ENG.). 64p. (gr. 4-4). pap. 11.99 *(978-0-545-79424-4(2)*, Teaching Resources) Scholastic, Inc.
—Great Grammar Practice: Grade 5. 2015. (Great Grammar Practice Ser.). (ENG.). 64p. (gr. 5-5). pap. 11.99 *(978-0-545-79425-1(0)*, Teaching Resources) Scholastic, Inc.
Beginning Consonant Sounds. (Basic Skills Ser.). 48p. (gr. -1-2). 5.99 *(978-0-513-02334-5(8)*, TSD23348) Denison, T. S. & Co., Inc.
Bentley, Linda M. & Bentley, Linda. The Big Book of Quick & Easy Art Activities: More Than 75 Creative Activities with Curriculum Connections That Keep Kids Creating & Learning All Year Long! 2007. (ENG., Illus.). 208p. pap. 26.99 *(978-0-439-58060-1(9)*, Teaching Resources) Scholastic, Inc.
Bergman, Carol Ann. Heath Grammar & Composition: Level 5. (J). (gr. 11). *(978-0-669-15978-3(6))* Houghton Mifflin Harcourt School Pubs.
Bergman, Mats. Heath Grammar & Composition: Grade 7. (gr. 7). pap., tchr. ed., wbk. ed. *(978-0-669-09771-9(3))*; (YA). pap., wbk. ed. *(978-0-669-06594-7(3))*; (YA). suppl. ed. *(978-0-669-07696-7(1))* Houghton Mifflin Harcourt School Pubs.
BJU Staff. Writing Grammar Tests Ak Grd 8. 2004. pap. 5.50 *(978-1-57924-370-8(3))* BJU Pr.
—Writing Grammar Tests Grd 8. 2004. pap. 9.00 *(978-1-57924-369-2(X))* BJU Pr.
—Writing Grammar Worktext Grd 2. 2004. pap. 13.50 *(978-1-57924-820-8(9))* BJU Pr.
—Writing Grammar Worktext Grd 3. 2004. pap. 13.50 *(978-1-57924-827-7(6))* BJU Pr.
—Writing Grammar Worktext Grd 4. 2004. pap. 13.50 *(978-1-57924-839-0(X))* BJU Pr.
—Writing Grammar Worktext Grd 7. 2004. pap. 15.50 *(978-1-57924-261-9(8))* BJU Pr.
—Writing Grammar Worktext Grd 8. 2004. pap. 15.50 *(978-1-57924-338-8(X))* BJU Pr.
Bladon, Rachel. Improve Your Grammar. 2004. (Better English Ser.). 32p. (YA). (gr. 5-18). lib. bdg. 14.95 *(978-1-58086-325-4(6))* EDC Publishing.
Blaisdell, Bette. A Backpack Full of Verbs, 1 vol. 2014. (Words I Know Ser.). (ENG.). 32p. (gr. 1-2). lib. bdg. 27.32 *(978-1-4765-3936-2(7)*, Aplus Bks.) Capstone Press of Coughlan Cos.
—A Hat Full of Adjectives, 1 vol. 2014. (Words I Know Ser.). (ENG.). 32p. (gr. 1-2). lib. bdg. 27.32 *(978-1-4765-3937-9(5)*, Aplus Bks.) Capstone Press of Coughlan Cos.
—A Pocket Full of Nouns, 1 vol. 2014. (Words I Know Ser.). (ENG.). 32p. (gr. 1-2). lib. bdg. 27.32 *(978-1-4765-3938-6(3)*, Aplus Bks.) Capstone Press of Coughlan Cos.
—Words I Know, 1 vol. 2014. (Words I Know Ser.). (ENG.). 32p. (gr. 1-2). lib. bdg. 109.28 *(978-1-4765-7858-3(3)*, Aplus Bks.) Capstone Press of Coughlan Cos.
Blaise, Kimberly. Reading Response Bookmarks & Graphic Organizers: Reproducible Learning Tools That Prompt Kids to Reflect on Text During & after Reading to Maximize Comprehension. 2012. (ENG.). 48p. (gr. 1-3). pap. 11.99 *(978-0-545-21185-7(9)*, Teaching Resources) Scholastic, Inc.
Boardworks Learning Centers: Sentence Fixer-Uppers. 2006. (J). bds. *(978-0-9755252-7-2(1))* Evergreen Pr. of Brainerd, LLC.
Bones: Long Vowel o, CVCe Pattern: Level B, 6 vols. (Wright Skills Ser.). 16p. (gr. k-3). 17.95 *(978-0-322-01466-4(2))* Wright Group/McGraw-Hill.
Braidich, S. Little Pigs, Big Pigs: Learning the Short I Sound. 2009. (PowerPhonics Ser.). 24p. (gr. 1-1). 39.90 *(978-1-60851-456-4(0)*, PowerKids Pr.) Rosen Publishing Group, Inc., The.
—Meet Me on the Farm: Learning the Long E Sound. 2009. (PowerPhonics Ser.). 24p. (gr. 1-1). 39.90 *(978-1-60851-458-8(7)*, PowerKids Pr.) Rosen Publishing Group, Inc., The.
Brimner, Larry Dane. A Bit Is a Bite. Kono, Erin Eitter, illus. 2007. (Rookie Reader Skill Set Ser.). (ENG.). 32p. (J). (gr. -1-3). pap. 4.95 *(978-0-531-17780-8(7)*, Children's Pr.) Scholastic Library Publishing.
Bromwell, L. Anne. English Grammar Basics. 2005. 42p. spiral bd. 14.95 *(978-1-59196-932-7(8))* Instant Pub.
Can Jo Fly? Open Vowel Words Ending in y with Long i Sound, Ending in o, Ending in e: Level B, 6 vols. (Wright Skills Ser.). 16p. (gr. k-3). 26.50 *(978-0-322-03098-5(6))* Wright Group/McGraw-Hill.
Capitalization & Punctuation (Gr. 1-3) 2003. (J). *(978-1-58232-050-2(0))* ECS Learning Systems, Inc.
Carbo Recorded Books: Easy Primary. 2003. (Illus.). (J). (gr. -1-2). pap. 895.00 incl. audio *(978-1-883186-28-9(5)*, NAPS16) National Reading Styles Institute, Inc.
Carbo Recorded Books: Primary. 2003. (Illus.). (J). (gr. 2-4). pap. 1007.00 incl. audio *(978-1-883186-29-6(3)*, NAPS13) National Reading Styles Institute, Inc.
Carroll, Joyce Armstrong, et al. Writing & Grammar: Communication in Action, 3 vols. 2003. (ENG.). 988p. (YA). (gr. 9-9). 494.00 *(978-0-13-037494-3(6)*, Prentice Hall) Pearson Schl.
—Writing & Grammar: Communication in Action, Bronze Level, 3 vols. 2003. (ENG.). 812p. (YA). (gr. 7-7). 406.00 *(978-0-13-037492-9(X))* Prentice Hall Pr.
—Writing & Grammar: Communication in Action, Platinum Level, 3 vols. 2004. 992p. (YA). (gr. 10-18). 496.00 *(978-0-13-116634-9(4))* Prentice Hall Pr.

E
F
G

Carter, Andrew. Adjectives. Schrey, Sophie, ed. (Grammar Ray: A Graphic Guide to Grammar Ser.). (Illus.). 24p. (J). (gr. 2-5). 2010. pap. 8.15 (978-1-60754-745-7(7)) 2009. 22.60 (978-1-60754-737-2(6)) Windmill Bks.

—Adverbs. Edwards, Nicola, ed. (Grammar Ray: A Graphic Guide to Grammar Ser.). (Illus.). 24p. (J). (gr. 2-5). 2010. pap. 8.15 (978-1-60754-747-1(3)) 2009. 22.60 (978-1-60754-738-9(4)) Windmill Bks.

—Nouns & Pronouns. Schrey, Sophie, ed. 2009. (Grammar Ray: a Graphic Guide to Grammar Ser.). (Illus.). 24p. (J). (gr. 2-5). 22.60 (978-1-60754-735-8(X)); pap. 8.15 (978-1-60754-741-9(4)) Windmill Bks.

—Prepositions. 2008. (Grammar Ray Ser.). (ENG., Illus.). 24p. (J). pap. 10.99 (978-0-237-53851-4(2)) Evans Brothers, Ltd. GBR. Dist: Independent Pubs. Group.

—Prepositions. Schrey, Sophie, ed. 2009. (Grammar Ray: a Graphic Guide to Grammar Ser.). 24p. (J). (gr. 2-5). 22.60 (978-1-60754-739-6(2)); pap. 8.15 (978-1-60754-749-5(X)) Windmill Bks.

—Punctuation & Sentences. 2009. (Grammar Ray Ser.). (ENG., Illus.). 24p. (J). pap. 10.99 (978-0-237-53852-1(0)) Evans Brothers, Ltd. GBR. Dist: Independent Pubs. Group.

—Punctuation & Sentences. Jones, Bryony, ed. 2009. (Grammar Ray: a Graphic Guide to Grammar Ser.). 24p. (J). (gr. 2-5). 22.60 (978-1-60754-740-2(6)); pap. 8.15 (978-1-60754-751-8(1)) Windmill Bks.

—Verbs. Edwards, Nicola, ed. 2009. (Grammar Ray: a Graphic Guide to Grammar Ser.). (Illus.). 24p. (J). (gr. 2-5). 22.60 (978-1-60754-736-5(8)); pap. 8.15 (978-1-60754-743-3(0)) Windmill Bks.

Celia's Gift: Fourth Grade Guided Comprehension Level N. (On Our Way to English Ser.). (gr. 4-18). 34.50 (978-0-7578-7163-4(1)) Rigby Education.

Chambers, Catherine E. DK Adventures: Clash of the Gladiators: Clash of the Gladiators. 2014. (DK Adventures Ser.). (ENG.). 128p. (J). (gr. 3-7). 16.99 (978-1-4654-1976-7(4), DK Children) Dorling Kindersley Publishing, Inc.

Champlin, DeeAnn. Eddie E & the Eggs. Champlin, DeeAnn, illus. Date not set. (Little Lyrics Short Vowel Collection: Vol. 2). (Illus.). (J). (gr. k-2). pap. 12.00 (978-1-893429-26-0(1)) Little Lyrics Pubns.

Chin, Beverly. Grammar for Writing 2007: Level Orange, Consumable. 2007. (Grammar for Writing Ser.). (gr. 10). pap. 17.00 net. (978-0-8215-0220-4(4)) Sadlier, William H. Inc.

Cimochowski, Anna. PassWord Decoder for Prefix, Root Word & Suffix Meanings. 2003. 72p. (gr. 3-5). wbk. ed. (978-1-56762-183-9(X)) Modern Learning Pr.

—PassWord Decoder for Tricky Letter Teams. 2003. 48p. (gr. 2-4). wbk. ed. (978-1-56762-182-2(1)) Modern Learning Pr.

Clark, Cherith & Stokes, Kirstin. Monster Spray. 2008. 36p. per. 12.95 (978-1-59800-325-3(9)) Outskirts Pr., Inc.

Cleary, Brian. Breezier, Cheesier, Newest, & Bluest: What Are Comparatives & Superlatives? Gable, Brian, illus. 2015. (Words Are CATegorical (r) Ser.). (ENG.). 32p. (gr. 2-5). pap. 6.95 (978-1-4677-6078-2(1), Millbrook Pr.) Lerner Publishing Group.

—A Lime, a Mime, a Pool of Slime: More about Nouns. Gable, Brian, illus. (Words Are CATegorical (r) Ser.). (ENG.). 32p. (gr. 2-5). 2008. pap. 6.95 (978-1-58013-934-2(5), First Avenue Editions) 2006. lib. bdg. 16.95 (978-1-57505-937-2(1), Millbrook Pr.) Lerner Publishing Group.

Cleary, Brian P. But & for, yet & Nor: What Is a Conjunction? Gable, Brian, illus. (Words Are CATegorical (r) Ser.). (ENG.). 32p. (gr. 2-5). 2012. pap. 6.95 (978-0-7613-8503-5(7), Millbrook Pr.) 2010. pap. 39.62 (978-0-7613-9205-7(X), Millbrook Pr.) 2010. lib. bdg. 16.95 (978-0-8225-9153-5(7)) Lerner Publishing Group.

—Dearly, Nearly, Insincerely: What Is an Adverb? Gable, Brian, illus. 2005. (Words Are CATegorical (r) Ser.). (ENG.). 32p. (gr. 2-5). per. 6.95 (978-1-57505-919-8(3)) Lerner Publishing Group.

—Dearly, Nearly, Insincerely: What Is an Adverb? Gable, Brian, illus. 2006. (Words Are Categorical Ser.). (gr. k-2). 17.00 (978-0-7569-6881-6(X)) Perfection Learning Corp.

—Feet & Puppies, Thieves & Guppies: What Are Irregular Plurals? Gable, Brian, illus. 2012. (Words Are CATegorical (r) Ser.). (ENG.). 32p. (J). (gr. 2-5). lib. bdg. 16.95 (978-0-7613-4918-1(9), Millbrook Pr.) Lerner Publishing Group.

—Ful & -Less, -Er And -Ness: What Is a Suffix? Goneau, Martin, illus. (Words Are CATegorical (r) Ser.). (ENG.). 32p. (gr. 2-5). 2016. (J). pap. 6.95 (978-1-5124-0088-5(2)) 2014. lib. bdg. 16.95 (978-1-4677-0610-0(8)) Lerner Publishing Group. (Millbrook Pr.).

—Hairy, Scary, Ordinary: What Is an Adjective? Prosmitsky, Jenya, illus. 2006. (Words Are Categorical Ser.). (gr. 2-4). 17.00 (978-0-7569-6882-3(8)) Perfection Learning Corp.

—I & You & Don't Forget Who: What Is a Pronoun? Gable, Brian, illus. 2006. (Words Are Categorical Ser.). (gr. 2-4). 17.00 (978-0-7569-6728-4(7)) Perfection Learning Corp.

—I & You & Don't Forget Who: What Is a Prounoun? Gable, Brian, illus. 2006. (Words Are CATegorical (r) Ser.). (ENG.). 32p. (gr. 2-5). per. 6.95 (978-0-8225-6469-0(6), First Avenue Editions) Lerner Publishing Group.

—Lazily, Crazily, Just a Bit Nasally: More about Adverbs. Gable, Brian, illus. 2008. (Words Are CATegorical (r) Ser.). (ENG.). 32p. (gr. 2-5). lib. bdg. 16.95 (978-0-8225-7848-2(4)) Lerner Publishing Group.

—Quirky, Jerky, Extra Perky: More about Adjectives. Gable, Brian, illus. (Words Are CATegorical (r) Ser.). (ENG.). 32p. (gr. 2-5). 2009. pap. 6.95 (978-1-58013-936-6(1), First Avenue Editions) 2007. (J). lib. bdg. 16.95 (978-0-8225-6709-7(1), Millbrook Pr.) Lerner Publishing Group.

—Slide & Slurp, Scratch & Burp: More about Verbs. Gable, Brian, illus. 2007. (Words Are CATegorical (r) Ser.). (ENG.). 32p. (gr. 2-5). lib. bdg. 16.95 (978-0-8225-6207-8(3), Millbrook Pr.) Lerner Publishing Group.

—To Root, to Toot, to Parachute: What Is a Verb? Prosmitsky, Jenya, illus. 2006. (Words Are Categorical Ser.). (gr. 2-4). 17.00 (978-0-7569-6884-7(4)) Perfection Learning Corp.

—Under, over, by the Clover: What Is a Preposition? Gable, Brian, illus. 2006. (Words Are Categorical Ser.). (gr. 2-4). 16.95 (978-0-7569-6885-4(2)) Perfection Learning Corp.

Cleary, Brian P. & Maday, Alice M. The Bug in the Jug Wants a Hug: A Short Vowel Sounds Book. Miskimins, Jason, illus. 2009. (Sounds Like Reading (r) Ser.: 1). (ENG.). 32p. (gr. -1-2). lib. bdg. 23.93 (978-0-7613-9503-4(2)) Lerner Publishing Group.

—The Clown in the Gown Drives the Car with the Star: A Book about Diphthongs & R-Controlled Vowel. Miskimins, Jason, illus. 2009. (Sounds Like Reading (r) Ser.: 8). (ENG.). 32p. (gr. -1-2). lib. bdg. 23.93 (978-0-8225-7637-2(6)) Lerner Publishing Group.

—The Frail Snail on the Trail: Long Vowel Sounds with Consonant Blends. Miskimins, Jason, illus. 2009. (Sounds Like Reading (r) Ser.: 4). (ENG.). 32p. (gr. -1-2). lib. bdg. 23.93 (978-0-8225-7638-9(4)) Lerner Publishing Group.

—The Nice Mice in the Rice: A Long Vowel Sound Book. Miskimins, Jason, illus. 2009. (Sounds Like Reading (r) Ser.: 3). (ENG.). 32p. (gr. -1-2). lib. bdg. 23.93 (978-0-8225-7628-0(7)) Lerner Publishing Group.

—Stop, Drop, & Flop in the Slop: A Short Vowel Sounds Book with Consonant Blends. Miskimins, Jason, illus. 2009. (Sounds Like Reading (r) Ser.: 2). (ENG.). 32p. (gr. -1-2). lib. bdg. 23.93 (978-0-8225-7635-8(X)) Lerner Publishing Group.

—The Thing on the Wing Can Sing: Short Vowel Sounds & Consonant Digraphs. Miskimins, Jason, illus. 2009. (Sounds Like Reading (r) Ser.: 5). (ENG.). 32p. (gr. -1-2). lib. bdg. 23.93 (978-0-8225-7639-6(2)) Lerner Publishing Group.

—Whose Shoes Would You Choose? A Long Vowel Sounds Book with Consonant Digraphs. Miskimins, Jason, illus. 2009. (Sounds Like Reading (r) Ser.: 6). (ENG.). 32p. (gr. -1-2). lib. bdg. 23.93 (978-0-8225-7640-2(6)) Lerner Publishing Group.

Coffelt, Nancy. Big, Bigger, Biggest! Coffelt, Nancy, illus. 2009. (ENG., Illus.). 32p. (J). (gr. -1-2). 17.99 (978-0-8050-8089-6(9), 9780805080896, Holt, Henry & Co. Bks. For Young Readers) Holt, Henry & Co.

Collins Easy Learning, Collins Easy. Grammar & Punctuation Quick Quizzes Ages 5-7. 2017. (Collins Easy Learning KS1 Ser.). (ENG., Illus.). 32p. (J). (gr. k-2). pap. 6.99 **(978-0-00-821246-9(5))** HarperCollins Pubs. Ltd. GBR. Dist: Independent Pubs. Group.

Collins Easy Learning Staff, et al. Grammar & Punctuation Ages 5-7. 2015. (Collins Easy Learning Ser.). (ENG.). 32p. (J). (gr. 1-2). pap. 6.95 (978-0-00-813432-7(4)) HarperCollins Pubs. Ltd. GBR. Dist: Independent Pubs. Group.

—Grammar & Punctuation, Ages 7-9. 2015. (Collins Easy Learning Ser.). (ENG.). 32p. (J). (gr. 2-4). pap. 6.95 (978-0-00-813422-8(7)) HarperCollins Pubs. Ltd. GBR. Dist: Independent Pubs. Group.

Collins UK Publishing Staff & Letts KS2 Staff. Grammar, Punctuation & Spelling. 2016. (Letts KS2 Success Ser.). (ENG.). 64p. (J). (gr. 3-6). pap. 8.95 (978-1-84419-834-4(0)) HarperCollins Pubs. Ltd. GBR. Dist: Independent Pubs. Group.

Complete Sentences with Your Family. 2013. (Write Right! Ser.). 24p. (J). (gr. 2-5). pap. 48.90 (978-1-4339-9071-7(7)) Stevens, Gareth Publishing LLLP.

Conjunctions with Your Friends. 2013. (Write Right! Ser.). 24p. (J). (gr. 2-5). pap. 48.90 (978-1-4339-9075-5(X)) Stevens, Gareth Publishing LLLP.

Continental Press Staff. Finish Line for ELLs: English Proficiency Practice: Student Book. 2009. pap., stu. ed. 20.95 (978-0-8454-6092-4(7)) 2008. pap., stu. ed. 20.95 (978-0-8454-5840-2(X)) 2008. pap., stu. ed. 20.95 (978-0-8454-5841-9(8)) Continental Pr., Inc.

Correct Writing. (J). 16.00 (978-1-931555-01-2(X)) Our Lady of Victory Schl.

Courtney, Carla. On the Banks of Plum Creek: Reading Comprehension Guide. 2007. (Logos School Literature Ser.). 94p. (J). (gr. 4-18). spiral bd. 15.00 (978-1-930443-21-1(8), C115) Canon Pr.

Dahl, Michael. If You Were a Noun, 1 vol. Gray, Sara, illus. 2006. (Word Fun Ser.). (ENG.). 24p. (gr. 2-4). 7.95 (978-1-4048-1980-1(0)) Picture Window Bks.

—If You Were a Verb, 1 vol. Gray, Sara, illus. 2006. (Word Fun Ser.). (ENG.). 24p. (gr. 2-4). 27.99 (978-1-4048-1354-0(3)) Picture Window Bks.

—If You Were an Adjective, 1 vol. Gray, Sara, illus. 2006. (Word Fun Ser.). (ENG.). 24p. (gr. 2-4). 7.95 (978-1-4048-1982-5(7)) Picture Window Bks.

—If You Were an Adverb, 1 vol. Gray, Sara, illus. 2006. (Word Fun Ser.). (ENG.). 24p. (gr. 2-4). 27.99 (978-1-4048-1357-1(8)); per. 7.95 (978-1-4048-1983-2(5)) Picture Window Bks.

Daily Grams Workbook Grade 5. 2003. 180p. pap. 12.95 (978-0-936981-38-3(5)) Isha Enterprises, Inc.

Daily Grams Workbook Grade 7. 2003. 180p. pap. 12.95 (978-0-936981-37-6(7)) Isha Enterprises, Inc.

Dorling Kindersley Publishing Staff. Visual Guide to Grammar & Punctuation. 2017. (ENG.). 128p. (J). (gr. k-3). 16.99 **(978-1-4654-6258-9(9)**, DK Children) Dorling Kindersley Publishing, Inc.

Dorling Kindersley Publishing Staff & Bray, Adam. What Makes a Monster? 2014. (DK Adventures Ser.). (ENG.). 128p. (J). (gr. 3-7). pap. 5.99 (978-1-4654-1991-0(8), DK Children) Dorling Kindersley Publishing, Inc.

Doudna, Kelly. Ida & Ike, 1 vol. 2005. (First Sounds Ser.). (Illus.). (J). (gr. k-3). (ENG.). 24p. lib. bdg. 24.21 (978-1-59679-164-0(0), SandCastle); 23p. pap. 48.42 (978-1-59679-165-7(9)) ABDO Publishing Co.

Doyle, Sheri. What Is a Noun? 2013. (Parts of Speech Ser.). (ENG.). 24p. (gr. k-1). pap. 35.70 (978-1-62065-830-7(5), Pebble Bks.) Capstone Press of Coughlan Cos.

—What Is a Preposition?, 1 vol. 2013. (Parts of Speech Ser.). (ENG.). 24p. (gr. k-1). pap. 6.29 (978-1-62065-831-4(3), Pebble Bks.); pap. 35.70 (978-1-62065-832-1(1), Pebble Bks.); (Illus.). lib. bdg. 26.65 (978-1-62065-131-5(9), Pebble Plus) Capstone Press of Coughlan Cos.

—What Is a Pronoun? 2013. (Parts of Speech Ser.). (ENG.). 24p. (gr. k-1). pap. 35.70 (978-1-62065-834-5(8), Pebble Bks.); pap. 6.29 (978-1-62065-833-8(X), Pebble Bks.); lib. bdg. 26.65 (978-1-62065-127-8(0), Pebble Plus) Capstone Press of Coughlan Cos.

Doyle, Sheri & Fandel, Jennifer. Parts of Speech. 2013. (Parts of Speech Ser.). (ENG.). 24p. (gr. k-1). lib. bdg. 159.90 (978-1-62065-132-2(7), Pebble Plus) Capstone Press of Coughlan Cos.

Doyle, Sheri & Saunders-Smith, Gail. What Is a Noun?, 1 vol. 2013. (Parts of Speech Ser.). (ENG., Illus.). 24p. (gr. k-1). pap. 6.29 (978-1-62065-829-1(1), Pebble Bks.); lib. bdg. 26.65 (978-1-62065-126-1(2), Pebble Plus) Capstone Press of Coughlan Cos.

Dugan, Christine. 180 Days of Language for First Grade, 1 vol. rev. ed. 2014. (180 Days Ser.). (ENG., Illus.). 208p. (gr. 1-1). pap. 19.99 (978-1-4258-1166-2(3)) Shell Educational Publishing.

—180 Days of Language for Second Grade, 1 vol. rev. ed. 2014. (180 Days Ser.). (ENG., Illus.). 208p. (gr. 2-2). pap. 19.99 (978-1-4258-1167-9(1)) Shell Educational Publishing.

—180 Days of Language for Third Grade, 1 vol. rev. ed. 2014. (180 Days Ser.). (ENG., Illus.). 208p. (gr. 3-3). pap. 19.99 (978-1-4258-1168-6(X)) Shell Educational Publishing.

Dugan, Christine & Shell Education Staff. 180 Days of Language for Kindergarten, 1 vol. rev. ed. 2014. (180 Days Ser.). (ENG., Illus.). 208p. (gr. k-k). pap. 19.99 (978-1-4258-1172-3(8)) Shell Educational Publishing.

Early Fluency Skills Guide. (Sunshine Skills Guides). 25.95 (978-0-7802-9811-8(X)) Wright Group/McGraw-Hill.

Editors of TIME For Kids Magazine. Grammar Rules! 2013. (ENG.). 176p. (J). (gr. 3-17). pap. 11.99 (978-1-60320-954-0(9)) Time Inc. Bks.

Elliott, Karen. Kid's Box Level 3 Language Portfolio. 2nd ed. 2014. (ENG.). 13p. pap. 7.50 (978-1-107-64380-2(5)) Cambridge Univ. Pr.

Elson, William H., et al. The Elson Readers, 9 vols. 2005. (Illus.). (J). pap. (978-1-890623-23-4(7)) Lost Classics Bk. Co.

Emberley, Rebecca. My Room/Mi Cuarto. 2005. (SPA & ENG., Illus.). 10p. (J). (gr. -1 — 1). bds. 6.99 (978-0-316-00052-9(3)) Little, Brown Bks. for Young Readers.

English Grammar Skills, Chapter 1, Activities. 2005. (Illus.). 64p. (YA). pap. 7.00 (978-1-59476-126-3(4)) Paradigm Accelerated Curriculum.

English Grammar Skills, Chapter 1, Text. 2005. (Illus.). 54p. (YA). pap. 7.00 (978-1-59476-121-8(3)) Paradigm Accelerated Curriculum.

English Grammar Skills, Chapter 2, Activities. 2005. (Illus.). 54p. (YA). pap. 5.00 (978-1-59476-127-0(2)) Paradigm Accelerated Curriculum.

English Grammar Skills, Chapter 2, Text. 2005. (Illus.). 46p. (YA). pap. 7.00 (978-1-59476-122-5(1)) Paradigm Accelerated Curriculum.

English Grammar Skills, Chapter 3, Activities. 2005. (Illus.). 50p. (YA). pap. 5.00 (978-1-59476-128-7(0)) Paradigm Accelerated Curriculum.

English Grammar Skills, Chapter 3, Text. 2005. (Illus.). 44p. (YA). pap. 7.00 (978-1-59476-123-2(X)) Paradigm Accelerated Curriculum.

English Grammar Skills, Chapter 4, Activities. 2005. (Illus.). 46p. (YA). pap. 5.00 (978-1-59476-129-4(9)) Paradigm Accelerated Curriculum.

English Grammar Skills, Chapter 4, Text. 2005. (Illus.). 40p. (YA). pap. 7.00 (978-1-59476-124-9(8)) Paradigm Accelerated Curriculum.

English Grammar Skills, Chapter 5, Activities. 2005. (Illus.). 48p. (YA). pap. 5.00 (978-1-59476-130-0(2)) Paradigm Accelerated Curriculum.

English Grammar Skills, Chapter 5, Text. 2005. (Illus.). 46p. (YA). pap. 7.00 (978-1-59476-125-6(6)) Paradigm Accelerated Curriculum.

English Grammar Skills, Full Course Kit. 2005. (Illus.). 736p. (YA). 75.00 (978-1-59476-092-1(6)) Paradigm Accelerated Curriculum.

English I: Language Skills, Chapter 2 Text. 2005. (Illus.). 54p. (YA). pap. 7.00 (978-1-59476-133-1(7)) Paradigm Accelerated Curriculum.

English I: Language Skills, Chapter 3 Text. 2005. (Illus.). 54p. (YA). pap. 7.00 (978-1-59476-134-8(5)) Paradigm Accelerated Curriculum.

English I: Language Skills, Chapter 4 Activities. 2005. (Illus.). 72p. (YA). pap. 5.00 (978-1-59476-140-9(X)) Paradigm Accelerated Curriculum.

English I: Language Skills, Chapter 4 Text. 2005. (Illus.). 62p. (YA). pap. 7.00 (978-1-59476-135-5(3)) Paradigm Accelerated Curriculum.

English I: Language Skills, Chapter 5 Activites. 2005. (Illus.). 66p. (YA). pap. 5.00 (978-1-59476-141-6(8)) Paradigm Accelerated Curriculum.

English I: Language Skills, Chapter 5 Text. 2005. (Illus.). 76p. (YA). pap. 7.00 (978-1-59476-136-2(1)) Paradigm Accelerated Curriculum.

Espanol Activo: Septimo Grado. (SPA & ENG.). (YA). (gr. 7). 14.25 (978-84-499-4721-6(9), CPR82) Prous, J. R. S.A. ESP. Dist: Continental Bk. Co., Inc.

Exercises in English: Grammar for Life; Level C. 2004. (gr. 3-18). tchr. ed. (978-0-8294-2016-6(9)); stu. ed. (978-0-8294-1741-8(9)) Loyola Pr.

Exercises in English: Grammar for Life; Level F. 2004. (gr. 6-18). tchr. ed. (978-0-8294-2019-7(3)); stu. ed. (978-0-8294-1748-7(6)) Loyola Pr.

Exercises in English: Grammar for Life; Level G. 2004. (gr. 7-18). stu. ed. (978-0-8294-1750-0(8)) Loyola Pr.

Exercises in English: Grammar for Life; Level H. 2004. (gr. 8-18). tchr. ed. (978-0-8294-2021-0(5)); stu. ed. (978-0-8294-1752-4(4)) Loyola Pr.

Exercises in English Grammar: Level E. 2004. (Illus.). (gr. 5-18). stu. ed. (978-0-8294-1745-6(1)) Loyola Pr.

Fandel, Jennifer. What Is a Conjunction? 2013. (Parts of Speech Ser.). (ENG.). 24p. (gr. k-1). pap. 35.70 (978-1-62065-828-4(3), Pebble Bks.); (Illus.). lib. bdg. 26.65 (978-1-62065-130-8(0), Pebble Plus) Capstone Press of Coughlan Cos.

—What Is a Verb? 2013. (Parts of Speech Ser.). (ENG.). 24p. (gr. k-1). pap. 35.70 (978-1-62065-836-9(4), Pebble Bks.) Capstone Press of Coughlan Cos.

—What Is an Adjective? 2013. (Parts of Speech Ser.). (ENG.). 24p. (gr. k-1). pap. 35.70 (978-1-62065-838-3(0), Pebble Bks.) Capstone Press of Coughlan Cos.

Fandel, Jennifer & Doyle, Sheri. Parts of Speech. 2013. (Parts of Speech Ser.). (ENG.). 24p. (gr. k-1). pap. 35.70 (978-1-62065-839-0(9)); pap. 214.20 (978-1-62065-840-6(2)) Capstone Press of Coughlan Cos. (Pebble Bks.).

Fandel, Jennifer & Saunders-Smith, Gail. What Is a Conjunction?, 1 vol. 2013. (Parts of Speech Ser.). (ENG., Illus.). 24p. (gr. k-1). pap. 6.29 (978-1-62065-827-7(5), Pebble Bks.) Capstone Press of Coughlan Cos.

—What Is a Verb?, 1 vol. 2013. (Parts of Speech Ser.). (ENG.). 24p. (gr. k-1). pap. 6.29 (978-1-62065-835-2(6), Pebble Bks.); lib. bdg. 26.65 (978-1-62065-128-5(9), Pebble Plus) Capstone Press of Coughlan Cos.

—What Is an Adjective?, 1 vol. 2013. (Parts of Speech Ser.). (ENG.). 24p. (gr. k-1). pap. 6.29 (978-1-62065-837-6(2), Pebble Bks.); lib. bdg. 26.65 (978-1-62065-129-2(7), Pebble Plus) Capstone Press of Coughlan Cos.

Felix, Rebecca. Big, Bigger, Biggest. 2015. (Size It Up Ser.). (Illus.). 16p. (J). 25.65 (978-1-60753-574-4(2)) Amicus Publishing.

—Short, Shorter, Shortest. 2015. (Size It Up Ser.). (Illus.). 16p. (J). 25.65 (978-1-60753-575-1(0)) Amicus Publishing.

—Small, Smaller, Smallest. 2015. (Size It Up Ser.). (Illus.). 16p. (J). 25.65 (978-1-60753-578-2(5)) Amicus Publishing.

—Tall, Taller, Tallest. 2014. (Size It Up Ser.). (Illus.). 16p. 25.65 (978-1-60753-579-9(3)) Amicus Publishing.

Fenner, M. On My Block: Learning the BL Sound. 2009. (PowerPhonics Ser.). 24p. (gr. 1-1). 39.90 (978-1-60851-464-9(1), PowerKids Pr.) Rosen Publishing Group, Inc., The.

Figorito, C. Go Far in the Car: Learning the AR Sound. 2009. (PowerPhonics Ser.). 24p. (gr. 1-1). 39.90 (978-1-60851-444-1(7), PowerKids Pr.) Rosen Publishing Group, Inc., The.

Fisher, Doris & Gibbs, D. L. Bowling Alley Adjectives. Angle, Scott & Chandler, Jeff, illus. 2008. (Grammar All-Stars Ser.). 32p. (J). (gr. 2-5). lib. bdg. 26.00 (978-0-8368-8901-7(0), Gareth Stevens Learning Library) Stevens, Gareth Publishing LLLP.

—Bowling Alley Adjectives, 6 vols. Chandler, Jeff, illus. 2008. (Grammar All-Stars: the Parts of Speech Ser.). 32p. (gr. 2-5). pap. 10.50 (978-0-8368-8908-6(8), Gareth Stevens Learning Library) Stevens, Gareth Publishing LLLP.

—Grammar All-Stars: Parts of Speech, 6 vols. Angle, Scott, illus. 2008. (Grammar All-Stars Ser.). 32p. (gr. 2-5). pap. 10.50 (978-0-8368-8912-3(6)); pap. 10.50 (978-0-8368-8913-0(4)); pap. 10.50 (978-0-8368-8910-9(X)) Stevens, Gareth Publishing LLLP. (Gareth Stevens Learning Library).

—Hole-in-One Adverbs. Chandler, Jeff, illus. 2008. (Grammar All-Stars Ser.). 32p. (J). (gr. 2-5). lib. bdg. 26.00 (978-0-8368-8902-4(9), Gareth Stevens Learning Library) Stevens, Gareth Publishing LLLP.

—Hole-in-One Adverbs. Angle, Scott, illus. 2008. (Grammar All-Stars Ser.). 32p. (gr. 2-5). pap. 10.50 (978-0-8368-8909-3(6), Gareth Stevens Learning Library) Stevens, Gareth Publishing LLLP.

—Home Run Verbs. Angle, Scott & Roper, Robert, illus. 2008. (Grammar All-Stars Ser.). 32p. (J). (gr. 2-5). lib. bdg. 26.00 (978-0-8368-8903-1(7), Gareth Stevens Learning Library) Stevens, Gareth Publishing LLLP.

—Slam Dunk Pronouns. Chandler, Jeff, photos by. 2008. (Grammar All-Stars Ser.). (Illus.). 32p. (J). (gr. 2-5). lib. bdg. 26.00 (978-0-8368-8904-8(5), Gareth Stevens Learning Library) Stevens, Gareth Publishing LLLP.

—Slam dunk Pronouns, 6 vols. Angle, Scott, illus. 2008. (Grammar All-Stars Ser.). 32p. (gr. 2-5). pap. 10.50 (978-0-8368-8911-6(8), Gareth Stevens Learning Library) Stevens, Gareth Publishing LLLP.

—Tennis Court Conjunctions. Rose, Drew, illus. 2008. (Grammar All-Stars Ser.). 32p. (J). (gr. 2-5). lib. bdg. 26.00 (978-0-8368-8905-5(3), Gareth Stevens Learning Library) Stevens, Gareth Publishing LLLP.

—Touchdown Nouns. Angle, Scott, illus. 2008. (Grammar All-Stars Ser.). 32p. (J). (gr. 2-5). lib. bdg. 26.00 (978-0-8368-8906-2(1), Gareth Stevens Learning Library) Stevens, Gareth Publishing LLLP.

Flanagan, Alice K. Play Day: The Sound of Long A. 2015. (Long & Short Vowels Ser.). (ENG.). 24p. (J). (gr. -1-2). 25.64 (978-1-63407-026-3(7), 208861) Child's World, Inc., The.

Food - Set 2: Adjective-Noun. 2004. (J). spiral bd. 23.40 (978-0-9770248-2-7(2)) Sidedoor Publishing LLC.

Francis, Gill. Chambers Language Builder. 2008. (Illus.). 224p. pap. (978-0-550-10340-6(6), Chambers) Hodder & Stoughton.

Ganeri, Anita. Action Words: Verbs, 1 vol. 2012. (Getting to Grips with Grammar Ser.). (ENG.). 32p. (gr. 1-3). lib. bdg. 27.32 (978-1-4329-5810-7(0), Heinemann First Library) Heinemann-Raintree.

—Describing Words: Adjectives, Adverbs, & Prepositions, 1 vol. 2012. (Getting to Grips with Grammar Ser.). (ENG.). 32p. (gr. 1-3). lib. bdg. 27.32 (978-1-4329-5805-3(4), Heinemann First Library) Heinemann-Raintree.

—Getting to Grips with Grammar. 2012. (Getting to Grips with Grammar Ser.). (ENG.). 32p. (gr. 1-3). pap. 16.58 (978-1-4329-5818-3(6), Heinemann First Library) Heinemann-Raintree.

—Grouping Words: Sentences, 1 vol. 2012. (Getting to Grips with Grammar Ser.). (ENG., Illus.). 32p. (gr. 1-3). pap. 8.29 (978-1-4329-5816-9(X), Heinemann First Library) Heinemann-Raintree.

—Naming Words: Nouns & Pronouns, 1 vol. 2012. (Getting to Grips with Grammar Ser.). (ENG.). 32p. (gr. 1-3). lib. bdg. 27.32 (978-1-4329-5806-0(2), Heinemann First Library) Heinemann-Raintree.

Gareth Stevens Publishing, creator. Grammar All-Stars Complete Set. 2009. (J). 288.00 (978-1-4339-0015-0(7)) Stevens, Gareth Publishing LLLP.

Garfield, Tom. Modern US History 1865 - Present. 2007. (Logos School Literature Ser.). (Illus.). 152p. (gr. 4-18). spiral bd. 20.00 (978-1-930443-22-8(6), C116) Canon Pr.

Gifford, Myrna. Name Those Vowels: A Read-and-Sing Book. Cooper, Frances, illus. 2003. 12p. (J). 9.95 (978-0-9720763-4-0(4)) Action Factor, Inc.

—Oh, Do You Know? A Read-and-Sing Book. Cooper, France, illus. 2003. 12p. (J). 9.95 (978-0-9720763-5-7(2)) Action Factor, Inc.

Gillham, Bill, et al. Essential Skills, 4 bks. (Illus.). 128p. (YA). pap. 15.99 (978-0-340-71583-3(9)) Hodder & Stoughton GBR. Dist: Trafalgar Square Publishing.

Glasscock, Sarah. Skill-Building Mini-Lessons, Activities, & Games. 2010. (Grammar Activities That Really Grab 'Em!

Ser.). (ENG.). 64p. (gr. 3-5). pap. 11.99 (978-0-545-11265-9(6), Teaching Resources) Scholastic, Inc.
Glencoe McGraw-Hill Staff, creator. Glencoe Writer's Choice: Grammar & Composition, Grade 6. 2004. (Writer's Choice Ser.). (ENG., Illus.). 736p. (gr. 6-6). stu. ed. 96.88 (978-0-07-829814-1(8), 0078298148) McGraw-Hill Higher Education.
Glendinning, Eric. Technology. 2009. (ENG., Illus.). 136p. 31.19 (978-0-19-456950-7(0)) Oxford Univ. Pr., Inc.
Goldsmith, Rose. Over & Under. 2008. (Discovering & Exploring Science Ser.). (Illus.). 16p. (J). (gr. -1-3). lib. bdg. 12.95 (978-0-7569-8422-9(X)) Perfection Learning Corp.
Grammar Ad Libs. 2003. (J). pap. 9.95 (978-1-56911-106-2(5)) Learning Resources, Inc.
Grammar in Action: Class Pack; 10 of Each Title. 2004. (Grammar Practice Book Ser.). (978-0-8294-1052-5(X)); (978-0-8294-1050-1(3)) Loyola Pr.
Grammar in Action: Parts of Speech. 2004. (Grammar Practice Book Ser.). tchr. ed. (978-0-8294-0952-9(1)) Loyola Pr.
Grammar in Action: Punctuation, Capitalization, & Sentence Structure. 2004. (Grammar Practice Book Ser.). tchr. ed. (978-0-8294-0954-3(8)) Loyola Pr.
Grammar in Action: Student Pack; One of Each Title. 2004. (Grammar Practice Book Ser.). (978-0-8294-1051-8(1)) Loyola Pr.
Grammar Practice Book. 2004. (Scott Foresman Reading Ser.). (gr. 1-18). suppl. ed. 1.95 (978-0-328-01175-9(4)); (gr. 2-18). suppl. ed. 1.95 (978-0-328-01176-6(2)); (gr. 3-18). 1.95 (978-0-328-01177-3(0), Scott Foresman); (gr. 4-18). 1.95 (978-0-328-01178-0(9)); (gr. 5-18). 1.95 (978-0-328-01179-7(7), Scott Foresman); (gr. 6-18). 1.95 (978-0-328-01180-3(0)) Addison-Wesley Educational Pubs., Inc.
Grammar Readers Classroom Library Set. 2004. (J). pap. 249.95 (978-1-56911-185-7(5)) Learning Resources, Inc.
Grammar Readers Foundation Set. 2004. (J). pap. 44.95 (978-1-56911-184-0(7)) Learning Resources, Inc.
Gravois, Michael. Fill-In Flip Books for Grammar, Vocabulary, & More, Grades 3-5: 25 Interactive Study AIDS That Kids Fill Out & Use Again & Again to Reinforce Essential Language Arts Content. 2005. (ENG., Illus.). 80p. (gr. 3-5). per. 12.99 (978-0-439-67682-3(7), Teaching Resources) Scholastic, Inc.
Gregory, Josh. Adjectives. Petelinsek, Kathleen, illus. 2013. (Explorer Junior Library: the Parts of Speech Ser.). (ENG.). 24p. (J). (gr. 1-4). 25.64 (978-1-62431-180-2(6), 203040); pap. 12.79 (978-1-62431-312-7(4), 203042) Cherry Lake Publishing.
—Adverbs. Petelinsek, Kathleen, illus. 2013. (Explorer Junior Library: the Parts of Speech Ser.). (ENG.). 24p. (J). (gr. 1-4). 25.64 (978-1-62431-183-3(0), 203052); pap. 12.79 (978-1-62431-315-8(9), 203054) Cherry Lake Publishing.
—Verbs. Petelinsek, Kathleen, illus. 2013. (Explorer Junior Library: the Parts of Speech Ser.). (ENG.). 24p. (J). (gr. 1-4). 25.64 (978-1-62431-179-6(2), 203036); pap. 12.79 (978-1-62431-311-0(6), 203038) Cherry Lake Publishing.
Hall, Pamela. Find Your Function at Conjunction Junction, 1 vol. Currant, Gary, illus. 2009. (Grammar's Slammin' Ser.). (ENG.). 32p. (J). (gr. -1-3). 28.50 (978-1-60270-615-6(8)) Magic Wagon.
—Stand-in Pronouns Save the Scene!, 1 vol. Currant, Gary, illus. 2009. (Grammar's Slammin' Ser.). (ENG.). 32p. (J). (gr. -1-3). 28.50 (978-1-60270-618-7(2)) Magic Wagon.
—Wheel of Subject-Verb Agreement, 1 vol. Currant, Gary, illus. 2009. (Grammar's Slammin' Ser.). (ENG.). 32p. (J). (gr. -1-3). 28.50 (978-1-60270-619-4(0)) Magic Wagon.
HarperCollins UK Staff & Collins Easy Learning Staff. Grammar & Punctuation Practice. 2012. (Collins Easy Learning Age 7-11 Ser.). (ENG.). 96p. (J). pap. 6.99 (978-0-00-746735-8(4)) HarperCollins Pubs. Ltd. GBR. Dist: Independent Pubs. Group.
Harte, May. ABCs in My House. 2004. (Look-And-Learn Books). (Illus.). (J). lib. bdg. 8.95 (978-1-4042-2824-5(1), PowerKids Pr.) Rosen Publishing Group, Inc., The.
Headway: Level E from Sea to Sea. (J). (gr. 2-3). (978-0-89688-457-1(0), 88-457) Open Court Publishing Co.
Heath Grammar & Composition. (YA). (gr. 10). pap., stu. ed. (978-0-669-06583-1(8)); (YA). (gr. 11). pap., stu. ed. (978-0-669-06584-8(6)); (YA). (gr. 12). pap., stu. ed. (978-0-669-06586-2(2)); (J). (gr. 6). pap., stu. ed. (978-0-669-12993-9(3)); (YA). (gr. 7). pap., stu. ed. (978-0-669-06580-0(3)); (YA). (gr. 8). pap., stu. ed. (978-0-669-06581-7(1)) Houghton Mifflin Harcourt School Pubs.
Heath Grammar & Composition: Grade 10. (gr. 10). pap. (978-0-669-06590-9(0)); (YA). pap., wbk. ed. (978-0-669-06597-8(8)); (YA). suppl. ed. (978-0-669-10107-2(9)); (YA). suppl. ed. (978-0-669-07699-8(6)) Houghton Mifflin Harcourt School Pubs.
Heath Grammar & Composition: Grade 12. (YA). (gr. 12). pap. (978-0-669-15971-4(9)); pap., wbk. ed. (978-0-669-06599-2(4)); suppl. ed. (978-0-669-10114-0(1)); suppl. ed. (978-0-669-07701-8(1)) Houghton Mifflin Harcourt School Pubs.
Heath Grammar & Composition: Grade 7. (YA). (gr. 7). pap., stu. ed. (978-0-669-15965-3(4)); suppl. ed. (978-0-669-12365-4(X)) Houghton Mifflin Harcourt School Pubs.
Heath Grammar & Composition: Grade 8. (YA). (gr. 8). pap., stu. ed. (978-0-669-15967-7(0)); suppl. ed. (978-0-669-07697-4(X)); suppl. ed. (978-0-669-12366-1(8)) Houghton Mifflin Harcourt School Pubs.
Heath Grammar & Composition: Grade 9. (YA). (gr. 9). stu. ed. (978-0-669-15968-4(9)); suppl. ed. (978-0-669-10104-1(4)) Houghton Mifflin Harcourt School Pubs.
Heath Grammar & Comprehension Grade 8. (J). (gr. 8). (978-0-669-15983-7(2)) Houghton Mifflin Harcourt School Pubs.
Heinrichs, Ann. Adjectives. 2016. (J). **(978-1-4896-5980-4(3)**, AV2 by Weigl) Weigl Pubs., Inc.
—Adverbs. 2016. (J). **(978-1-4896-5983-5(8)**, AV2 by Weigl) Weigl Pubs., Inc.
—Conjunctions. McGeehan, Dan & Moore, David, illus. 2010. (Language Rules! Ser.). (ENG.). 24p. (J). (gr. 1-4). lib. bdg. 27.07 (978-1-60253-427-8(6), 200431) Child's World, Inc., The.
—Conjunctions. 2016. (J). **(978-1-4896-5986-6(2)**, AV2 by Weigl) Weigl Pubs., Inc.
—Interjections. McGeehan, Dan & Moore, David, illus. 2010. (Language Rules! Ser.). (ENG.). 24p. (J). (gr. 1-4). lib. bdg. 27.07 (978-1-60253-428-5(4), 200432) Child's World, Inc., The.
—Interjections. 2016. (J). **(978-1-4896-5989-7(7)**, AV2 by Weigl) Weigl Pubs., Inc.
—Nouns. 2016. (J). **(978-1-4896-5992-7(7)**, AV2 by Weigl) Weigl Pubs., Inc.
—Prefixes & Suffixes. 2016. (J). **(978-1-4896-5995-8(1)**, AV2 by Weigl) Weigl Pubs., Inc.
—Pronouns. McGeehan, Dan & Moore, David, illus. 2010. (Language Rules! Ser.). (ENG.). 24p. (J). (gr. 1-4). lib. bdg. 27.07 (978-1-60253-432-2(2), 200436) Child's World, Inc., The.
—Pronouns. 2016. (J). **(978-1-4896-6082-4(8)**, AV2 by Weigl) Weigl Pubs., Inc.
—Verbs. 2016. (J). **(978-1-4896-6001-5(1)**, AV2 by Weigl) Weigl Pubs., Inc.
Herman, Gail & Voege, Debra. Catch-a-Wave Compounds. 2009. (Grammar All-Stars: Kinds of Words Ser.). 32p. (J). (gr. 2-5). pap. 10.50 (978-1-4339-0149-2(8)); (Illus.). lib. bdg. 26.00 (978-1-4339-0008-2(4)) Stevens, Gareth Publishing LLLP. (Gareth Stevens Learning Library).
—Karate Contractions. 2009. (Grammar All-Stars: Kinds of Words Ser.). 32p. (gr. 2-5). pap. 10.50 (978-1-4339-0151-5(X)); (Illus.). (J). lib. bdg. 26.00 (978-1-4339-0009-9(2)) Stevens, Gareth Publishing LLLP. (Gareth Stevens Learning Library).
Herzog, Joyce. Expedition with Vowels: Student Activity Book. Sinclair, Angie & Sinclair, Dan, eds. 2005. (J). spiral bd. 15.00 (978-1-887225-44-1(7)) Herzog, Joyce.
—Expedition with Vowels Reader: Part of the Little Beginner's Book Series. 2005. (J). spiral bd. 15.00 (978-1-887225-34-2(X)) Herzog, Joyce.
Hex, Kathleen. Grammar Minutes: 100 Minutes to Better Basic Skills. Kim, Regina Hurh & Snoddy, Gillian, eds. Grayson, Rick, illus. 2009. 112p. (J). pap. 14.99 (978-1-60689-124-7(3)) Creative Teaching Pr., Inc.
High Point. (High Point Ser.). (gr. 6-12). 57.61 (978-0-7362-0969-4(7)); 7.52 (978-0-7362-0935-9(2)); 7.52 (978-0-7362-0967-0(0)); tchr. ed. 33.37 (978-0-7362-0981-6(6)); tchr. ed. 33.37 (978-0-7362-0949-6(2)); suppl. ed. 57.61 (978-0-7362-0937-3(9)); tchr.'s assessmt. gde. ed. 27.50 (978-0-7362-0950-2(6)); instr.'s hndbk. ed. 27.50 (978-0-7362-0982-3(4)); tchr. ed. 14.19 (978-0-7362-0968-7(9)); tchr. ed. 14.19 (978-0-7362-0936-6(0)) CENGAGE Learning.
Hockett, Margaret. Punctuation Puzzler - Commas & More B1. 2003. (Punctuation Puzzler Ser.). 48p. (gr. 5-6). pap. 8.99 (978-0-89455-815-3(3)) Critical Thinking Co., The.
—Punctuation Puzzler - Run-Ons C1. 2005. (Punctuation Puzzler Ser.). 48p. (gr. 7-8). pap. 8.99 (978-0-89455-819-1(6)) Critical Thinking Co., The.
Holt, Rinehart and Winston Staff. Elements of Language: Developing Language Skills Answer Key. 4th ed. Date not set. (YA). (gr. 10). pap. 12.80 (978-0-03-070072-9(8)); (gr. 11). pap. 12.80 (978-0-03-070073-6(6)); (gr. 12). pap. 12.80 (978-0-03-070074-3(4)); (gr. 9). pap. 12.80 (978-0-03-070071-2(X)) Holt McDougal.
Howell, Jennifer. Tracking down the Parts of Speech Game. 2005. (YA). 49.95 (978-1-58804-387-0(8)) P C I Education.
Hubbard, L. Ron. Grammar & Communication for Children. 2004. (ENG., Illus.). 491p. (gr. 4-7). per. 24.95 (978-1-4031-5890-1(8)) Bridge Pubns., Inc.
Hutchinson, Emily. Descriptive Writing, 1 vol. Saddleback Educational Publishing Staff, ed. 2013. (Writing 4 Ser.). (ENG.). 64p. (gr. 6-12). pap. 32.95 (978-1-62250-024-6(5)) Saddleback Educational Publishing, Inc.
Improving Student Reading Comprehension - Grades 1-2. 2004. (J). pap. 14.95 (978-1-56911-166-6(9)) Learning Resources, Inc.
Improving Student Reading Comprehension - Grades 3-4. 2004. (J). pap. 14.95 (978-1-56911-167-3(7)) Learning Resources, Inc.
Improving Student Reading Comprehension - Grades 5-6. 2004. (J). pap. 14.95 (978-1-56911-168-0(5)) Learning Resources, Inc.
Improving Student Writing: Grammar. 2004. (J). per. 12.95 (978-1-56911-527-5(3)) Learning Resources, Inc.
In the Garden. 2012. (Collins Big Cat Ser.). (ENG., Illus.). 16p. (J). pap., wbk. ed. 4.99 (978-0-00-747489-9(X)) HarperCollins Pubs. Ltd. GBR. Dist: Independent Pubs. Group.
JacKris Publishing, creator. Growing with Grammar Grade 3 Student Manual. 2005. 238p. stu. ed., spiral bd. 17.99 (978-0-9772923-0-1(4)) Davis, Tamela.
—Growing with Grammar Grade 3 Student Workbook & Answer Key. 2005. 234p. spiral bd., wbk. ed. 13.99 (978-0-9772923-1-8(2)) Davis, Tamela.
—Growing with Grammar Grade 4 Student Manual. 2006. 286p. spiral bd. 17.99 (978-0-9772923-2-5(0)) Davis, Tamela.
—Growing with Grammar Grade 4 Student Workbook & Answer Key. 2006. 229p. spiral bd. 13.99 (978-0-9772923-3-2(9)) Davis, Tamela.
Johnson, Robin. The Word Wizard's Book of Adjectives. 2014. (ENG., Illus.). 24p. (J). (978-0-7787-1304-3(0)) Crabtree Publishing Co.
—The Word Wizard's Book of Adverbs. 2014. (ENG., Illus.). 24p. (J). (978-0-7787-1306-7(7)) Crabtree Publishing Co.
—The Word Wizard's Book of Nouns. 2014. (ENG., Illus.). 24p. (J). (978-0-7787-1290-9(7)) Crabtree Publishing Co.
—The Word Wizard's Book of Prefixes & Suffixes. 2015. (ENG., Illus.). 24p. (J). (978-0-7787-1921-2(9)) Crabtree Publishing Co.
—The Word Wizard's Book of Pronouns. 2015. (ENG., Illus.). 24p. (J). (978-0-7787-1922-9(7)) Crabtree Publishing Co.
—The Word Wizard's Book of Verbs. 2014. (ENG., Illus.). 24p. (J). (978-0-7787-1292-3(3)) Crabtree Publishing Co.
Jones, Carmen S. Grammar Minutes: 100 Minutes to Better Basic Skills. Ly, Dorothy, ed. Grayson, Rick, illus. 2009. 112p. (J). pap. 14.99 (978-1-60689-123-0(5)) Creative Teaching Pr., Inc.
Jones, Vernie O. & Jensen, Frode M. A Journey Through Grammar Land, Parts 1 And 2. 2007. (Illus.). 184p. per. 29.00 (978-1-886061-41-5(6)) Wordsmiths.
—A Journey Through Grammar Land, Parts 1 & 2 Tests & Answers. 2007. 40p. 1.00 (978-1-886061-42-2(4)) Wordsmiths.
Journey Through Grammar Land 3. 2004. (gr. 5-7). pap. 30.00 (978-1-886061-32-3(7)) Wordsmiths.
Kemp, Beth. Grammar for GCSE English. 2014. (Aiming for Second Editions Ser.). (ENG.). 16p. (J). pap. 15.99 (978-0-00-754755-5(2)) HarperCollins Pubs. Ltd. GBR. Dist: Independent Pubs. Group.
Konrad, Dee C. Grammar Handbook. 2004. 146p. pap. 12.95 (978-0-673-58662-9(6)) Good Year Bks.
Kumon Publishing, creator. ABC's Write & Wipe! Lowercase Letters. 2007. (Kumon Flash Cards Ser.). 32p. (J). 9.95 (978-1-933241-44-9(6)) Kumon Publishing North America, Inc.
—My Book of Sentences: Ages 6,7, 8. 2007. (Kumon Workbooks Ser.). (Illus.). 80p. per. 7.95 (978-1-933241-38-8(1)) Kumon Publishing North America, Inc.
—My Book of Simple Sentences: Learning about Nouns & Verbs. 2005. (Kumon Workbooks Ser.). (Illus.). 80p. (J). (gr. -1-3). per. 7.95 (978-1-933241-05-0(5)) Kumon Publishing North America, Inc.
—My Book of Writing Words: Learning about Consonants & Vowels. 2005. (Kumon Workbooks Ser.). (Illus.). 80p. (J). (gr. k-2). per. 7.95 (978-1-933241-04-3(7)) Kumon Publishing North America, Inc.
Lakeshore Learning Materials Staff, contrib. by. The Big Surprise: A Homophone Story, Set of 6 Student Books. 2007. (J). pap. 18.95 (978-1-59746-028-6(1)) Lakeshore Learning Materials.
—The Big Surprise: A Homophone Story Big Book. 2007. (J). pap. 19.95 (978-1-59746-024-8(9)) Lakeshore Learning Materials.
—The Game: A Multiple Meaning Story, Set of 6 Student Books. 2007. (J). pap. 18.95 (978-1-59746-029-3(X)) Lakeshore Learning Materials.
—The Game: A Multiple Meaning Story Big Book. 2007. (J). pap. 19.95 (978-1-59746-025-5(7)) Lakeshore Learning Materials.
—The Great Race: A Synonym Story Big Book. 2007. (J). pap. 19.95 (978-1-59746-022-4(2)) Lakeshore Learning Materials.
—Partner Reading Book Set. 2007. (J). pap. 39.95 (978-1-59746-021-7(4)) Lakeshore Learning Materials.
—Reading Comprehension Mystery Readers, Set of 18 Books. 2007. (J). 49.95 (978-1-59746-017-0(6)) Lakeshore Learning Materials.
Lambert, Deborah. Nouns. 2009. (Learning to Write Ser.). 24p. (J). (gr. 4-6). 8.95 (978-1-60596-047-0(0)); (Illus.). lib. bdg. 24.45 (978-1-60596-046-3(2)) Weigl Pubs., Inc.
—Pronouns. 2009. (Learning to Write Ser.). (Illus.). 24p. (J). (gr. 3-5). lib. bdg. 24.45 (978-1-60596-043-2(8)); (gr. 4-6). 8.95 (978-1-60596-619-9(3)) Weigl Pubs., Inc.
—Verbs. 2009. (Learning to Write Ser.). 24p. (J). (gr. 3-5). 8.95 (978-1-60596-045-6(4)); (Illus.). (gr. 4-6). lib. bdg. 24.45 (978-1-60596-044-9(6)) Weigl Pubs., Inc.
Larousse Mexico Staff. Ingles para Todos Gramatica. (SPA & ENG.). 256p. (J). pap. 9.95 (978-970-607-305-1(1), LA3051) Larousse, Ediciones, S. A. de C. V. MEX. Dist: Continental Bk. Co., Inc.
Larson, Randy. Bunches of Grammar Fun - Binder 3. 2004. (YA). ring bd. 79.95 (978-1-58804-320-7(7)) P C I Education.
Law, Karina. Let's Eat Grandma! A Life-Saving Guide to Grammar & Punctuation. Phillips, Mike, illus. 2017. (ENG.). 48p. (J). (gr. 4-7). pap. 12.99 **(978-1-4451-4201-2(5)**, Franklin Watts) Hachette Children's Group GBR. Dist: Hachette Bk. Group.
LD COACH. TEH Learns to Read: Pronouns & Possessive Adjectives, Volume Three. 2004. (Illus.). 40p. (J). 34.95 (978-0-9745938-3-8(4)) LD Coach, LLC.
Learning Company Books Staff, ed. Reader Rabbit: Writing Mechanics. 2003. (Illus.). 32p. (J). pap., wbk. ed. (978-0-7630-7642-9(2)) Magma.
Leigh, A. Giant Giraffes: Learning the Soft G Sound. 2009. (PowerPhonics Ser.). 24p. (gr. 1-1). 39.90 (978-1-60851-443-4(9), PowerKids Pr.) Rosen Publishing Group, Inc., The.
—It Grows in Spring: Learning the GR Sound. 2009. (PowerPhonics Ser.). 24p. (gr. 1-1). 39.90 (978-1-60851-453-3(6), PowerKids Pr.) Rosen Publishing Group, Inc., The.
Lindeen, Mary. Cupcakes for My Birthday: Teaching Compound Words. 2016. (Playing with Words Ser.). (ENG.). 16p. (J). (gr. -1-2). 25.64 (978-1-5038-0835-5(1), 210685) Child's World, Inc., The.
Loewen, Nancy. Frog. Frog? Frog! Understanding Sentence Types, 1 vol. Rainey, Merrill, illus. 2013. (Language on the Loose Ser.). (ENG.). 24p. (gr. 2-4). 27.99 (978-1-4048-8321-5(5)); pap. 7.95 (978-1-4795-1920-0(0)) Picture Window Bks.
—If You Were a Conjunction, 1 vol. Gray, Sara, illus. 2006. (Word Fun Ser.). (ENG.). 24p. (gr. 2-4). per. 7.95 (978-1-4048-2389-1(1)) Picture Window Bks.
—If You Were a Preposition. Gray, Sara, illus. 2006. (Word Fun Ser.). (ENG.). 24p. (gr. 2-4). lib. bdg. 27.99 (978-1-4048-2386-0(7)); per. 7.95 (978-1-4048-2390-7(5)) Picture Window Bks.
—If You Were a Pronoun, 1 vol. Gray, Sara, illus. 2006. (Word Fun Ser.). (ENG.). 24p. (gr. 2-4). per. 7.95 (978-1-4048-2639-7(4)) Picture Window Bks.
—If You Were an Interjection. Gray, Sara, illus. 2006. (Word Fun Ser.). (ENG.). 24p. (gr. 2-4). lib. bdg. 27.99 (978-1-4048-2636-6(X)); per. 7.95 (978-1-4048-2638-0(6)) Picture Window Bks.
Loewen, Nancy, et al. Language on the Loose. 2013. (Language on the Loose Ser.). (ENG.). 24p. (gr. 2-4). 111.96 (978-1-4048-7731-3(2)); pap. 31.80 (978-1-4795-1976-7(6)) Picture Window Bks.
Lubben, Amy & Williams, Rozanne Lanczak. Build-a-Skill Instant Books Word Families-Long Vowels. Shiotsu, Vicky & Faulkner, Stacey, eds. Campbell, Jenny & Tom, Darcy, illus. 2007. (J). 4.99 (978-1-59198-409-2(2)) Creative Teaching Pr., Inc.
—Build-a-Skill Instant Books Word Families-Short Vowels. Shiotsu, Vicky & Faulkner, Stacey, eds. Campbell, Jenny & Tom, Darcy, illus. 2007. (J). 4.99 (978-1-59198-408-5(4)) Creative Teaching Pr., Inc.
Mack, Nancy. Teaching Grammar with Playful Poems: Engaging Lessons with Model Poems by Favorite Poets That Motivate Kids to Learn Grammar. 2005. (ENG., Illus.). 80p. (gr. 3-5). pap. 14.99 (978-0-439-57411-2(0), Teaching Strategies) Scholastic, Inc.
Malaspina, Ann. Nathan & Nicole Learn about Nouns. Hamblin, George, illus. 2014. (Language Builders Ser.). (ENG.). 32p. (J). (gr. 2-4). pap. 11.94 (978-1-60357-701-4(7)); lib. bdg. 25.27 (978-1-59953-666-8(8)) Norwood Hse. Pr.
—Vivian & Victor Learn about Verbs. Prater, Linda, illus. 2014. (Language Builders Ser.). (ENG.). 32p. (J). (gr. 2-4). pap. 11.94 (978-1-60357-702-1(5)); lib. bdg. 25.27 (978-1-59953-667-5(6)) Norwood Hse. Pr.
Marcet, Jane. Mary's Grammar. 2011. 336p. pap. 13.95 (978-1-59915-390-2(4)) Yesterday's Classics.
Marsico, Katie. Conjunctions. Petelinsek, Kathleen, illus. 2013. (Explorer Junior Library: the Parts of Speech Ser.). (ENG.). 24p. (J). (gr. 1-4). 25.64 (978-1-62431-181-9(4), 203044); pap. 12.79 (978-1-62431-313-4(2), 203046) Cherry Lake Publishing.
—Interjections. Petelinsek, Kathleen, illus. 2013. (Explorer Junior Library: the Parts of Speech Ser.). (ENG.). 24p. (J). (gr. 1-4). 25.64 (978-1-62431-184-0(9), 203056); pap. 12.79 (978-1-62431-316-5(7), 203058) Cherry Lake Publishing.
—Prepositions. Petelinsek, Kathleen, illus. 2013. (Explorer Junior Library: the Parts of Speech Ser.). (ENG.). 24p. (J). (gr. 1-4). 25.64 (978-1-62431-182-6(2), 203048); pap. 12.79 (978-1-62431-314-1(0), 203050) Cherry Lake Publishing.
—Pronouns. Petelinsek, Kathleen, illus. 2013. (Explorer Junior Library: the Parts of Speech Ser.). (ENG.). 24p. (J). (gr. 1-4). 25.64 (978-1-62431-178-9(4), 203032); pap. 12.79 (978-1-62431-310-3(8), 203034) Cherry Lake Publishing.
Maslen, Bobby Lynn & Kertell, Lynn Maslen. Sight Words, First Grade, Set. Maslen, John & Hendra, Sue, illus. 2010. (Bob Bks.). (ENG.). 120p. (J). (gr. -1-k). pap. 16.99 (978-0-545-01924-8(9), Cartwheel Bks.) Scholastic, Inc.
—Sight Words Kindergarten, Set. Maslen, John & Hendra, Sue, illus. 2010. (Bob Bks.). (ENG.). 120p. (J). (gr. -1-k). pap. 16.99 (978-0-545-01923-1(0), Cartwheel Bks.) Scholastic, Inc.
Mazzeo, J. L. Aimee's A Book (BL) el libro A de Aimée, 1. 2007. (My Letter Library Ser.: 1). (SPA., Illus.). (J). pap. 10.95 (978-1-59646-420-9(8)); lib. bdg. 23.60 (978-1-59646-419-3(4)) Dingles & Co.
—Cassie's C Book (BL) el libro C de Cassie: S, 3 vols. 2007. (My Letter Library Ser.: 3). (SPA & ENG., Illus.). (J). lib. bdg. 23.60 (978-1-59646-431-5(3)) Dingles & Co.
—Cassie's C Book (BL) el libro C de Cassie (PB), 3 vols. 2007. (My Letter Library Ser.: 3). (SPA & ENG., Illus.). (J). pap. 10.95 (978-1-59646-432-2(1)) Dingles & Co.
—Uri's U Book, 21 vols. 2007. (My Letter Library Ser.: 21). (Illus.). (J). lib. bdg. 23.60 (978-1-59646-536-7(0)) Dingles & Co.
—Uri's U Book (PB), 21 vols. 2007. (My Letter Library Ser.: 21). (Illus.). (J). pap. 10.95 (978-1-59646-537-4(9)) Dingles & Co.
—Yola's Y Book, 25 vols. 2007. (My Letter Library Ser.: 25). (Illus.). (J). lib. bdg. 23.60 (978-1-59646-560-2(3)) Dingles & Co.
—Yola's Y Book (PB), 25 vols. 2007. (My Letter Library Ser.: 25). (Illus.). (J). pap. 10.95 (978-1-59646-561-9(1)) Dingles & Co.
—Zach's Z Book (BL) el libro Z de Zach, 26 vols. 2007. (My Letter Library Ser.: 26). (SPA & ENG., Illus.). (J). lib. bdg. 23.60 (978-1-59646-569-5(7)) Dingles & Co.
—Zach's Z Book (BL) el libro Z de Zach (PB), 26 vols. 2007. (My Letter Library Ser.: 26). (SPA & ENG., Illus.). (J). pap. 10.95 (978-1-59646-570-1(0)) Dingles & Co.
McCarty, Diane Bischoff. Copywork for Children: For Grades 1-3. 2004. (Illus.). 63p. (J). (978-0-9712124-1-1(4)) Angel Heart Children's Pr.
McDougal-Littell Publishing Staff. Language Network. 2006. (McDougal Littell Language Network Ser.). (ENG., Illus.). 736p. (gr. 11-11). stu. ed. 88.05 (978-0-395-96741-6(4), 2-22036) Great Source Education Group, Inc.
McDougal-Littell Publishing Staff, creator. Language Network. 2006. (Illus.). 624p. (gr. 6-18). stu. ed. (978-0-395-96736-2(8), 2-22031) Holt McDougal.
McGraw-Hill Education Staff. Writer's Choice, Grade 9: Grammar & Composition. 2004. (Writer's Choice Ser.). (ENG., Illus.). 1008p. (gr. 9-9). stu. ed. 101.16 (978-0-07-829817-2(2), 0078298172) McGraw-Hill Higher Education.
McNeal, Drema & Teets, Ashley, illus. Jake Learns All 8 Parts of Speech. 2010. (J). (978-0-929915-55-5(0)) Headline Bks., Inc.
Meachen Rau, Dana. Blow Out. 2006. (Bookworms Ser.). (Illus.). 32p. (gr. 1-2). lib. bdg. 15.95 (978-0-7614-2288-4(9), Benchmark Bks.) Marshall Cavendish Corp.
—Bookworms: Verbs in Action, 6 bks., Set. Incl. Dig In. (gr. -1-3). lib. bdg. (978-0-7614-1937-2(3)); Fall Down. (gr. -1-3). lib. bdg. (978-0-7614-1936-5(5)); Grow Up. (gr. -1-3). lib. bdg. (978-0-7614-1932-7(2)); On the Run. (gr. 1-2). lib. bdg. (978-0-7614-1934-1(9)); Spin Around. (gr. -1-3). lib. bdg. (978-0-7614-1933-4(0)); Spring Out. (gr. -1-3). lib. bdg. (978-0-7614-1935-8(7)); (Illus.). 32p. (J). 2005. (978-0-7614-1931-0(4), Benchmark Bks.) Marshall Cavendish Corp.
—Carry On. 2006. (Bookworms Ser.). (Illus.). 32p. (gr. 1-2). lib. bdg. 15.95 (978-0-7614-2289-1(7), Benchmark Bks.) Marshall Cavendish Corp.
—Dig In. (Bookworms: Verbs in Action Ser.). (Illus.). (J). (gr. -1-3). 2007. 31p. pap. 6.99 (978-0-7614-3333-0(3), Cavendish Children's Bks.) 2005. 32p. lib. bdg. (978-0-7614-1937-2(3), Benchmark Bks.) Marshall Cavendish Corp.
—Fall Down. 2005. (Bookworms Ser.). (Illus.). 32p. (J). (gr. -1-3). lib. bdg. (978-0-7614-1936-5(5), Benchmark Bks.) Marshall Cavendish Corp.

EFG

—Grow Up. (Bookworms: Verbs in Action Ser.). (Illus.). (J). (gr. -1-3). 2007. 31p. pap. 6.99 *(978-0-7614-3335-4(X)*, Cavendish Children's Bks.) 2005. 32p. lib. bdg. *(978-0-7614-1932-7(2)*, Benchmark Bks.) Marshall Cavendish Corp.

—Move Along. 2006. (Bookworms Ser.). (Illus.). 32p. (gr. 1-2). lib. bdg. 15.95 *(978-0-7614-2291-4(9)*, Benchmark Bks.) Marshall Cavendish Corp.

—On the Run. 2005. (Bookworms Ser.). (Illus.). 32p. (J). (gr. 1-2). lib. bdg. *(978-0-7614-1934-1(9)*, Benchmark Bks.) Marshall Cavendish Corp.

—Play Ball. 2006. (Bookworms Ser.). (Illus.). 32p. (gr. 1-2). lib. bdg. 15.95 *(978-0-7614-2292-1(7)*, Benchmark Bks.) Marshall Cavendish Corp.

—Spin Around. (Bookworms: Verbs in Action Ser.). (Illus.). (J). (gr. -1-3). 2007. 31p. pap. 6.99 *(978-0-7614-3339-2(2))* 2005. 32p. lib. bdg. *(978-0-7614-1933-4(0))* Marshall Cavendish Corp. (Benchmark Bks.).

—Spring Out. (Bookworms: Verbs in Action Ser.). (Illus.). (J). (gr. -1-3). 2007. 31p. pap. 6.99 *(978-0-7614-3341-5(4)*, Cavendish Children's Bks.) 2005. 32p. lib. bdg. *(978-0-7614-1935-8(7)*, Benchmark Bks.) Marshall Cavendish Corp.

—Turn Into. 2006. (Bookworms Ser.). (Illus.). 32p. (gr. 1-2). lib. bdg. 15.95 *(978-0-7614-2293-8(5)*, Benchmark Bks.) Marshall Cavendish Corp.

—Verbs in Action Group 2, 6 bks., Set. Incl. Blow Out. lib. bdg. 15.95 *(978-0-7614-2288-4(9))*; Carry On. lib. bdg. 15.95 *(978-0-7614-2289-1(7))*; Move Along. lib. bdg. 15.95 *(978-0-7614-2291-4(9))*; Play Ball. lib. bdg. 15.95 *(978-0-7614-2292-1(7))*; Turn Into. lib. bdg. 15.95 *(978-0-7614-2293-8(5))*; Verbs in Action: Make a Face. lib. bdg. 15.95 *(978-0-7614-2290-7(0))*; (Illus.). 32p. (gr. 1-2). (Bookworms: Verbs in Action Ser.). 2006. Set lib. bdg. 95.70 *(978-0-7614-2287-7(0)*, Benchmark Bks.) Marshall Cavendish Corp.

—Verbs in Action: Make a Face. 2006. (Bookworms Ser.). (Illus.). 32p. (gr. 1-2). lib. bdg. 15.95 *(978-0-7614-2290-7(0)*, Benchmark Bks.) Marshall Cavendish Corp.

Meister, Cari. How Big Is It? A Book about Adjectives. Conger, Holli, illus. 2016. (Say What?: Parts of Speech Ser.). (ENG.). 16p. (J). (gr. k-3). 17.95 *(978-1-60753-930-8(6))* Amicus Publishing.

—How Fast Is It? A Book about Adverbs. Conger, Holli, illus. 2016. (Say What?: Parts of Speech Ser.). (ENG.). 16p. (J). (gr. k-3). 17.95 *(978-1-60753-931-5(4))* Amicus Publishing.

—No School Today: A Book about Nouns. Conger, Holli, illus. 2016. (Say What?: Parts of Speech Ser.). (ENG.). 16p. (J). (gr. k-3). 17.95 *(978-1-60753-934-6(9))* Amicus Publishing.

—Ouch! It Bit Me! A Book about Interjections. Conger, Holli, illus. 2016. (Say What?: Parts of Speech Ser.). (ENG.). 16p. (J). (gr. k-3). 17.95 *(978-1-60753-932-2(2))* Amicus Publishing.

—Pepperoni or Sausage? A Book about Conjunctions. Conger, Holli, illus. 2016. (Say What?: Parts of Speech Ser.). (ENG.). 16p. (J). (gr. k-3). 17.95 *(978-1-60753-935-3(7))* Amicus Publishing.

—What Is It Doing? A Book about Verbs. Conger, Holli, illus. 2016. (Say What?: Parts of Speech Ser.). (ENG.). 16p. (J). (gr. k-3). 17.95 *(978-1-60753-933-9(0))* Amicus Publishing.

—Who Ate It? A Book about Pronouns. Conger, Holli, illus. 2016. (Say What?: Parts of Speech Ser.). (ENG.). 16p. (gr. k-3). 17.95 *(978-1-60753-937-7(3))* Amicus Publishing.

—Who Is up There? A Book about Prepositions. Conger, Holli, illus. 2016. (Say What?: Parts of Speech Ser.). (ENG.). 16p. (J). (gr. k-3). 17.95 *(978-1-60753-936-0(5))* Amicus Publishing.

Menken, John. Hands-on English with Linking Blocks Program Handbook. 2006. 31p. spiral bd. 17.00 *(978-0-9797375-1-0(6))* E3 Concepts LLC.

—Hands-on English with Linking Blocks Student Workbook. 2006. 139p. spiral bd. 39.00 *(978-0-9797375-2-7(4))* E3 Concepts LLC.

Metz, L. Every Egg: Learning the Short E Sound. 2009. (PowerPhonics Ser.). 24p. (gr. 1-1). 39.90 *(978-1-60851-440-3(4)*, PowerKids Pr.) Rosen Publishing Group, Inc., The.

Modern Staff. Paco's Pockets: Consonants p, s. (J). (gr. k-1). 38.95 *(978-0-8136-1328-4(0))* Modern Curriculum Pr.

Molter, Carey & ABDO Publishing Company Staff. Silent Letters, 1 vol. 2004. (Silent Letters Ser.: 6). (ENG.). 24p. (J). (gr. k-3). lib. bdg. 145.26 *(978-1-59197-442-0(9)*, SandCastle) ABDO Publishing Co.

Moreau, Maryellen Rooney & Welch, Brian Scott. Talk to Write, Write to Learn Manual: A Teachers' Manual for Differentiated Instruction & Tiered Intervention. 2007. pap. 65.00 *(978-0-9761393-9-3(1))* Mindwing Concepts, Inc.

Murray, Kara. Adjectives & Adverbs. 2013. (Core Language Skills Ser.). 24p. (J). (gr. 2-2). 22.60 *(978-1-4777-0799-9(9))*; (ENG., Illus.). pap. 8.25 *(978-1-4777-0970-2(3))* Rosen Publishing Group, Inc., The. (PowerKids Pr.).

—Contractions & Possessives. 2013. (Core Language Skills Ser.). 24p. (J). (gr. 2-2). pap. 49.50 *(978-1-4777-0983-2(5))*; pap. 8.25 *(978-1-4777-0982-5(7))*; (Illus.). lib. bdg. 22.60 *(978-1-4777-0804-0(9))* Rosen Publishing Group, Inc., The. (PowerKids Pr.).

—Nouns & Pronouns. 2013. (Core Language Skills Ser.). 24p. (J). (gr. 2-2). 22.60 *(978-1-4777-0800-2(6))*; (ENG., Illus.). pap. 8.25 *(978-1-4777-0972-6(X))* Rosen Publishing Group, Inc., The. (PowerKids Pr.).

—Verbs. 2013. (Core Language Skills Ser.). 24p. (J). (gr. 2-2). 22.60 *(978-1-4777-0801-9(4))*; (ENG., Illus.). pap. 8.25 *(978-1-4777-0974-0(6))* Rosen Publishing Group, Inc., The. (PowerKids Pr.).

Muschla, Gary Robert. Exploring Grammar. 2010. (Practice Makes Perfect Ser.). (ENG.). 256p. pap. 14.00 *(978-0-07-174548-2(3)*, 0071745483) McGraw-Hill Education.

—Mastering Grammar. 2010. (Practice Makes Perfect Ser.). (ENG.). 256p. pap. 14.00 *(978-0-07-174547-5(5)*, 0071745475) McGraw-Hill Education.

Nesbitt, M. L. Grammar-Land. Waddy, F., illus. 2009. 124p. pap. 8.95 *(978-1-59915-332-2(7))* Yesterday's Classics.

Nickelodeon Staff, ed. ABC, Dora the Explorer. 2010. (Write, Slide & Learn Ser.). 14p. (J). (gr. -1-1). 9.99 *(978-1-74184-522-8(X)*, Ideal Pubns.) Worthy Publishing.

—Phonics - Spongebob Squarepants. 2010. (Write, Slide & Learn Ser.). 14p. (J). (gr. -1-1). 9.99 *(978-1-74184-520-4(3)*, Ideal Pubns.) Worthy Publishing.

Nixon, Caroline. Kid's Box Level 1 Flashcards (Pack Of 96) 2nd rev. ed. 2014. (ENG.). 96p. 47.75 *(978-1-107-68826-1(4))* Cambridge Univ. Pr.

Nouns & Pronouns. 2013. (Core Language Skills Ser.). 24p. (J). (gr. 2-2). pap. 49.50 *(978-1-4777-0973-3(8)*, PowerKids Pr.) Rosen Publishing Group, Inc., The.

Noyed, Bob & Amoroso, Cynthia. Smiles: The Sound of Long I. 2015. (Long & Short Vowels Ser.). (ENG.). 24p. (J). (gr. -1-2). 25.64 *(978-1-63407-027-0(5)*, 208862) Child's World, Inc., The.

Nunn, Daniel. On or Under: Where's Eddie?, 1 vol. 2012. (Hide & Seek Ser.). (ENG.). 24p. (gr. -1-k). pap. 9.95 *(978-1-4109-4717-8(3))*; lib. bdg. 25.32 *(978-1-4109-4711-6(4))* Heinemann-Raintree.

Owings, Lisa. Chase, Wiggle, Chomp: Teaching Verbs. 2016. (Playing with Words Ser.). (ENG.). 16p. (J). (gr. -1-2). 25.64 *(978-1-5038-0833-1(5)*, 210683) Child's World, Inc., The.

Palazzolo, Fran. Wise Owl's First Sounds & Sight Words. 2009. 248p. pap. 88.50 *(978-0-557-08128-8(9))* Lulu Pr., Inc.

—Wise Owl's Vowels. 2009. 290p. pap. 98.95 *(978-0-557-07812-7(1))* Lulu Pr., Inc.

Parkman, Mary Rosetta. Guide Book for Language, Grade Three: Shepherd-Parkman Language Series. Norman, Vera Stone, illus. 2011. 236p. 46.95 *(978-1-258-08037-2(0))* Literary Licensing, LLC.

Parts of Speech. 2004. (Grammar Pocket Handbook Ser.). *(978-0-8294-0924-6(6))*; stu. ed., wbk. ed. *(978-0-8294-0949-9(1))* Loyola Pr.

Parts of Speech (Gr. 1-3) 2003. (J). *(978-1-58232-048-9(9))* ECS Learning Systems, Inc.

Parts of Speech (Gr. 3+) 2003. (J). *(978-1-58232-054-0(3))* ECS Learning Systems, Inc.

Pearson Education Staff. Spin!, Level C: Grammar, Vocabulary, & Writing. 2003. (ENG.). 112p. (C). pap., stu. ed. 22.80 *(978-0-13-041980-4(X))* Prentice Hall, ESL Dept.

Pearson, Yvonne. A Bird in a Nest in a Tree: Teaching Nouns. 2016. (Playing with Words Ser.). (ENG.). 16p. (J). (gr. -1-2). 25.64 *(978-1-5038-0831-7(9)*, 210681) Child's World, Inc., The.

—In & Out: Teaching Prepositions. 2016. (Playing with Words Ser.). (ENG.). 16p. (J). (gr. -1-2). 25.64 *(978-1-5038-0837-9(8)*, 210688) Child's World, Inc., The.

—Smelly, Stinky Skunk: Teaching Adjectives. 2016. (Playing with Words Ser.). (ENG.). 16p. (J). (gr. -1-2). 25.64 *(978-1-5038-0842-3(4)*, 210692) Child's World, Inc., The.

Phillips, Wanda C. Easy Grammar Grade 3 Student Test Booklet. 2006. pap. 4.95 *(978-0-936981-49-9(0))* Isha Enterprises, Inc.

—Easy Grammar Grade 3 Student Workbook. 2006. pap. 13.95 *(978-0-936981-48-2(2))* Isha Enterprises, Inc.

—Easy Grammar Grade 4 Student Test Booklet. 2006. pap. 4.95 *(978-0-936981-50-5(4))* Isha Enterprises, Inc.

—Easy Grammar Grade 5 Student Test Booklet. 2006. pap. 4.95 *(978-0-936981-51-2(2))* Isha Enterprises, Inc.

—Easy Grammar Grade 5 Student Workbook. 2006. pap. 13.95 *(978-0-936981-45-1(8))* Isha Enterprises, Inc.

—Easy Grammar Grade 6 Student Test Booklet. 2006. pap. 4.95 *(978-0-936981-52-9(0))* Isha Enterprises, Inc.

—Easy Grammar Grade 6 Student Workbook. 2006. pap. 13.95 *(978-0-936981-46-8(6))* Isha Enterprises, Inc.

—Easy Grammar Plus Student Test Booklet. 2006. pap. 4.95 *(978-0-936981-53-6(9))* Isha Enterprises, Inc.

—Easy Grammar Plus Student Workbook. 2006. 347p. (gr. 6-18). pap., wbk. ed. 13.95 *(978-0-936981-14-7(8))* Isha Enterprises, Inc.

—Easy Grammar Plus teacher Edition. 2006. 663p. (gr. 6-18). pap. 32.95 *(978-0-936981-13-0(X))* Isha Enterprises, Inc.

Phonics Ad Libs: Vowels & Consonants. 2003. (J). pap. 9.95 *(978-1-56911-104-8(9))* Learning Resources, Inc.

Pike, Katy. Apples & Ants. Jurevicius, Luke, illus. 2006. (Funny Photo Alphabet Ser.). (J). pap. 3.95 *(978-0-8225-6267-2(7)*, Lerner Pubns.) Lerner Publishing Group.

—Big Bad Bears. Jurevicius, Luke, illus. 2006. (Funny Photo Alphabet Ser.). 11p. (J). pap. 3.95 *(978-0-8225-6268-9(5)*, Lerner Pubns.) Lerner Publishing Group.

—Candles on a Cake. Jurevicius, Luke, illus. 2006. (Funny Photo Alphabet Ser.). 11p. (J). pap. 3.95 *(978-0-8225-6269-6(3)*, Lerner Pubns.) Lerner Publishing Group.

—Dancing Dog. Jurevicius, Luke, illus. 2006. (Funny Photo Alphabet Ser.). 11p. (J). pap. 3.95 *(978-0-8225-6270-2(7)*, Lerner Pubns.) Lerner Publishing Group.

—Eggs & Elephants. Jurevicius, Luke, illus. 2006. (Funny Photo Alphabet Ser.). 11p. (J). pap. 3.95 *(978-0-8225-6271-9(5)*, Lerner Pubns.) Lerner Publishing Group.

—Funny Fish. Jurevicius, Luke, illus. 2006. (Funny Photo Alphabet Ser.). 11p. (J). pap. 3.95 *(978-0-8225-6272-6(3)*, Lerner Pubns.) Lerner Publishing Group.

—Giggly Goat. Jurevicius, Luke, illus. 2006. (Funny Photo Alphabet Ser.). 11p. (J). pap. 3.95 *(978-0-8225-6273-3(1)*, Lerner Pubns.) Lerner Publishing Group.

—Happy Horse. Jurevicius, Luke, illus. 2006. (Funny Photo Alphabet Ser.). 11p. (J). pap. 3.95 *(978-0-8225-6274-0(X)*, Lerner Pubns.) Lerner Publishing Group.

—Icky Insects. Jurevicius, Luke, illus. 2006. (Funny Photo Alphabet Ser.). 11p. (J). pap. 3.95 *(978-0-8225-6275-7(8)*, Lerner Pubns.) Lerner Publishing Group.

—Jolly Jellybeans. Jurevicius, Luke, illus. 2006. (Funny Photo Alphabet Ser.). 11p. (J). pap. 3.95 *(978-0-8225-6276-4(6)*, Lerner Pubns.) Lerner Publishing Group.

—Lots of Lizards. Jurevicius, Luke, illus. 2006. (Funny Photo Alphabet Ser.). 11p. (J). pap. 3.95 *(978-0-8225-6278-8(2)*, Lerner Pubns.) Lerner Publishing Group.

—Mini Mouse. Jurevicius, Luke, illus. 2006. (Funny Photo Alphabet Ser.). 11p. (J). pap. 3.95 *(978-0-8225-6279-5(0)*, Lerner Pubns.) Lerner Publishing Group.

—Nine Nuts. Jurevicius, Luke, illus. 2006. (Funny Photo Alphabet Ser.). 11p. (J). pap. 3.95 *(978-0-8225-6280-1(4)*, Lerner Pubns.) Lerner Publishing Group.

—Orange Octopus. Jurevicius, Luke, illus. 2006. (Funny Photo Alphabet Ser.). 11p. (J). (gr. k-k). pap. 3.95 *(978-0-8225-6281-8(2)*, Lerner Pubns.) Lerner Publishing Group.

—Penguin Pond. Jurevicius, Luke, illus. 2006. (Funny Photo Alphabet Ser.). 11p. (J). pap. 3.95 *(978-0-8225-6282-5(0)*, Lerner Pubns.) Lerner Publishing Group.

—The Queen's Question. Jurevicius, Luke, illus. 2006. (Funny Photo Alphabet Ser.). 11p. (J). pap. 3.95 *(978-0-8225-6283-2(9)*, Lerner Pubns.) Lerner Publishing Group.

—Rabbit on a Raft. Jurevicius, Luke, illus. 2006. (Funny Photo Alphabet Ser.). 11p. (J). pap. 3.95 *(978-0-8225-6284-9(7)*, Lerner Pubns.) Lerner Publishing Group.

—Silly Seagulls. Jurevicius, Luke, illus. 2006. (Funny Photo Alphabet Ser.). 11p. (J). pap. 3.95 *(978-0-8225-6285-6(5)*, Lerner Pubns.) Lerner Publishing Group.

—Talking Tigers. Jurevicius, Luke, illus. 2006. (Funny Photo Alphabet Ser.). 11p. (J). pap. 3.95 *(978-0-8225-6286-3(3)*, Lerner Pubns.) Lerner Publishing Group.

—Under Umbrellas. Jurevicius, Luke, illus. 2006. (Funny Photo Alphabet Ser.). 11p. (J). pap. 3.95 *(978-0-8225-6287-0(1)*, Lerner Pubns.) Lerner Publishing Group.

—Vegetables in a Van. Jurevicius, Luke, illus. 2006. (Funny Photo Alphabet Ser.). 11p. (J). pap. 3.95 *(978-0-8225-6288-7(X)*, Lerner Pubns.) Lerner Publishing Group.

—Wet Whales. Jurevicius, Luke, illus. 2006. (Funny Photo Alphabet Ser.). 11p. (J). pap. 3.95 *(978-0-8225-6289-4(8)*, Lerner Pubns.) Lerner Publishing Group.

—X As in Fox. Jurevicius, Luke, illus. 2006. (Funny Photo Alphabet Ser.). 11p. (J). pap. 3.95 *(978-0-8225-6290-0(1)*, Lerner Pubns.) Lerner Publishing Group.

—Yellow Yo-Yo. Jurevicius, Luke, illus. 2006. (Funny Photo Alphabet Ser.). (J). pap. 3.95 *(978-0-8225-6291-7(X)*, Lerner Pubns.) Lerner Publishing Group.

—Zebras in a Zoo. Jurevicius, Luke, illus. 2006. (Funny Photo Alphabet Ser.). (J). pap. 3.95 *(978-0-8225-6292-4(8)*, Lerner Pubns.) Lerner Publishing Group.

Pike, Katy & Jurevicius, Luke. Kicking Kangaroo: Pictures by Luke Jurevicius. 2006. (Funny Photo Alphabet Ser.). (Illus.). 11p. (J). pap. 3.95 *(978-0-8225-6277-1(4)*, Lerner Pubns.) Lerner Publishing Group.

Pitzer, Marjorie W. My up & down & All Around Book. Pitzer, Marjorie W., photos by. 2008. (ENG., Illus.). 16p. (J). (gr. -1-1). pap. 10.95 *(978-1-890627-90-4(9))* Woodbine Hse.

Plurals & Possessives (Gr. 2-3) 2003. (J). *(978-1-58232-122-6(1))* ECS Learning Systems, Inc.

Porter, Matthew. Calling All Animals. 2010. (ENG., Illus.). 28p. (J). (gr. -1 — 1). bds. 8.95 *(978-1-897476-34-5(5))* Simply Read Bks. CAN. Dist: Ingram Publisher Services.

Preciado, Tony. Super Grammar. Montijo, Rhode, illus. 2012. (ENG.). 176p. (J). (gr. 2-5). pap. 8.99 *(978-0-545-42515-5(8)*, Scholastic Reference) Scholastic, Inc.

Prefixes, Suffixes, & Root Words (Gr. 2-3) 2003. (J). *(978-1-58232-123-3(X))* ECS Learning Systems, Inc.

Prefixes, Suffixes, & Root Words (Gr. 4-5) 2004. (J). *(978-1-58232-137-0(X))* ECS Learning Systems, Inc.

Prentice-Hall Staff. PH Grammar & Composition. 3rd ed. (J). *(978-0-13-708926-0(0))*; *(978-0-13-708934-5(1))*; *(978-0-13-708942-0(2))*; *(978-0-13-708868-3(X))* Prentice Hall (Schl. Div.).

Price, Stern & Mad Libs Staff. Dog Ate My Mad Libs. 2015. (Mad Libs Ser.). (ENG.). 48p. (J). (gr. 3-7). bds. 4.99 *(978-0-8431-8293-4(8)*, Mad Libs) Penguin Young Readers Group.

Prokos, Anna & Voege, Debra. Half-Pipe Homonyms. Angle, Scott, illus. 2009. (Grammar All-Stars Ser.). 32p. (gr. 2-5). (J). lib. bdg. 26.00 *(978-1-4339-0010-5(6))*; pap. 10.50 *(978-1-4339-0150-8(1))* Stevens, Gareth Publishing LLLP. (Gareth Stevens Learning Library).

—Slap Shot Synonyms & Antonyms. 2009. (Grammar All-Stars: Kinds of Words Ser.). 32p. (J). (gr. 2-5). pap. 10.50 *(978-1-4339-0153-9(6))*; (Illus.). lib. bdg. 26.00 *(978-1-4339-0013-6(0))* Stevens, Gareth Publishing LLLP. (Gareth Stevens Learning Library).

—Track Star Sentences. 2009. (Grammar All-Stars: Writing Tools Ser.). 32p. (J). (gr. 2-5). (ENG.). pap. 10.50 *(978-1-4339-2139-1(1))*; lib. bdg. 26.00 *(978-1-4339-1946-6(X))* Stevens, Gareth Publishing LLLP. (Gareth Stevens Learning Library).

Pulse- Fun with Grammar. 2006. cd-rom 4.99 *(978-1-60245-037-0(4))* GDL Multimedia, LLC.

Quinley, Elliott. Persuasive Writing, 1 vol. Saddleback Educational Publishing Staff, ed. 2013. (Writing 4 Ser.). (ENG.). 64p. (gr. 6-12). pap. 32.95 *(978-1-62250-027-7(X))* Saddleback Educational Publishing, Inc.

Rajczak, Kristen. Complete Sentences with Your Family. 2013. (Write Right! Ser.). (Illus.). 24p. (J). (gr. 2-5). pap. 8.15 *(978-1-4339-9070-0(9))*; (ENG., lib. bdg. 22.60 *(978-1-4339-9069-4(5))* Stevens, Gareth Publishing LLLP.

—Conjunctions with Your Friends. 2013. (Write Right! Ser.). (Illus.). 24p. (J). (gr. 2-5). pap. 8.15 *(978-1-4339-9074-8(1))*; (ENG., lib. bdg. 22.60 *(978-1-4339-9073-1(3))* Stevens, Gareth Publishing LLLP.

—Sequential Words with Your Pets. 2013. (Write Right! Ser.). 24p. (J). (gr. 2-5). pap. 8.15 *(978-1-4339-9078-6(4))*; (ENG., Illus.). lib. bdg. 22.60 *(978-1-4339-9077-9(6))* Stevens, Gareth Publishing LLLP.

—Subjects & Verbs with Your Neighbors. 2013. (Write Right! Ser.). (Illus.). 24p. (J). (gr. 2-5). pap. 8.15 *(978-1-4339-9082-3(2))*; (ENG., lib. bdg. 22.60 *(978-1-4339-9081-6(4))* Stevens, Gareth Publishing LLLP.

—Transition Words with Your Team. 2013. (Write Right! Ser.). (Illus.). 24p. (J). (gr. 2-5). pap. 8.15 *(978-1-4339-9086-1(5))*; (ENG., lib. bdg. 22.60 *(978-1-4339-9085-4(7))* Stevens, Gareth Publishing LLLP.

Rasinski, Tim. Practice with Prefixes, 1 vol. rev. ed. 2012. (Professional Resources Ser.). (ENG.). 240p. (gr. 5-8). 24.99 *(978-1-4258-0882-2(4))* Shell Educational Publishing.

Rau, Dana Meachen. Family Photo. Gordon, Mike, illus. 2007. (Rookie Reader Skill Set Ser.). (ENG.). 32p. (J). (gr. k-2). pap. 4.95 *(978-0-531-12492-5(4)*, Children's Pr.) Scholastic Library Publishing.

Read All about It! Fifth Grade Guided Comprehension Level S. (On Our Way to English Ser.). (gr. 5-18). 34.50 *(978-0-7578-6623-4(9))* Rigby Education.

Reading Rods Readers: Advanced Vowel Mastery Set. 2004. (J). per. 44.95 *(978-1-56911-532-9(X))* Learning Resources, Inc.

Reading Rods Readers: Advanced Vowel Mastery Set Classpack. 2004. (J). per. 249.95 *(978-1-56911-574-9(5))* Learning Resources, Inc.

Reading Rods Readers: Long Vowel Mastery Set. 2004. (J). per. 32.95 *(978-1-56911-531-2(1))* Learning Resources, Inc.

Reading Rods Readers: Long Vowel Mastery Set Classpack. 2004. (J). per. 184.95 *(978-1-56911-549-7(4))* Learning Resources, Inc.

Reading Rods Readers: Short Vowel Mastery Set. 2004. (J). per. 32.95 *(978-1-56911-530-5(3))* Learning Resources, Inc.

Ready Reader Staff. The Lucky Duck: Short Vowels, 6 bks., set. Level B. 2003. (J). (gr. -1-3). 24.50 *(978-0-8136-2013-8(9))* Modern Curriculum Pr.

Richter, A. By the Ocean: Learning the Long O Sound. 2009. (PowerPhonics Ser.). 24p. (gr. 1-1). 39.90 *(978-1-60851-436-6(6)*, PowerKids Pr.) Rosen Publishing Group, Inc., The.

Riggs, Kate. Adverbs. 2013. 25.65 *(978-1-60818-237-4(1)*, Creative Education) Creative Co., The.

—Crowds of Creatures. Dogi, Fiammetta, illus. 2017. (ENG.). 14p. (J). (gr. -1 — 1). bds. 7.99 *(978-1-56846-301-8(4)*, Creative Education) Creative Co., The.

—Grammar Basics: Adverbs. 2013. (Grammar Basics Ser.). (ENG.). 24p. (J). (gr. 1-3). pap. 10.99 *(978-0-89812-800-0(5)*, Creative Paperbacks) Creative Co., The.

—Under the Sea. Leonard, Tom, illus. 2017. (ENG.). 14p. (J). (gr. -1 — 1). bds. 7.99 *(978-1-56846-302-5(2)*, Creative Editions) Creative Co., The.

Robinson, Joanna Jarc. Andrew & Allen Learn about Adverbs. Boyer, Robin, illus. 2014. (Language Builders Ser.). (ENG.). 32p. (J). (gr. 2-4). pap. 11.94 *(978-1-60357-704-5(1))*; lib. bdg. 25.27 *(978-1-59953-669-9(2))* Norwood Hse. Pr.

—Phillip & Penny Learn about Pronouns. Hu, Caroline, illus. 2014. (Language Builders Ser.). (ENG.). 32p. (J). (gr. 2-4). pap. 11.94 *(978-1-60357-705-2(X))*; lib. bdg. 25.27 *(978-1-59953-670-5(6))* Norwood Hse. Pr.

Rollins, Brenda. How to Write a Paragraph: 80 Interactive Screen Pages. 2011. (Writing Skills Ser.). (J). (gr. 3-8). pap. 39.95 *(978-1-55319-505-4(1)*, Classroom Complete Pr.) Rainbow Horizons Publishing, Inc.

Rondeau, Amanda & ABDO Publishing Company Staff. Compound Words. 2004. (Compound Words Ser.: 12). (ENG.). 24p. (J). (gr. k-3). lib. bdg. 290.52 *(978-1-59197-429-1(1)*, SandCastle) ABDO Publishing Co.

Rooney Moreau, Maryellen & Welch, Brian Scott. Talk to Write, Write to Learn Kit. 2007. pap. 199.95 *(978-0-9769527-5-6(0))* Mindwing Concepts, Inc.

Rosa-Mendoza, Gladys. Lupe Lupita, Where Are You?/Lupe Lupita Donde Estas? Ochoa, Ana, illus. 2007. (English Spanish Foundations Ser.). 20p. (gr. -1-k). pap. 19.95 *(978-1-931398-82-4(8))* Me+Mi Publishing.

Rosenthal, Betsy R. An Ambush of Tigers: A Wild Gathering of Collective Nouns. Jago, illus. 2015. (ENG.). 32p. (J). (gr. k-3). lib. bdg. 19.99 *(978-1-4677-1464-8(X)*, Millbrook Pr.) Lerner Publishing Group.

Roy, Jennifer Rozines. Sharpen Your Good Grammar Skills. 2011. (Sharpen Your Writing Skills Ser.). (Illus.). 64p. (J). (gr. 6-18). lib. bdg. 29.27 *(978-0-7660-3902-5(1))* Enslow Pubs., Inc.

—You Can Write Using Good Grammar. 2004. (You Can Write Ser.). (Illus.). 64p. (J). lib. bdg. 23.94 *(978-0-7660-2084-9(3))* Enslow Pubs., Inc.

Roza, G. On Flat Land: Learning the FL Sound. 2009. (PowerPhonics Ser.). 24p. (gr. 1-1). 39.90 *(978-1-60851-463-2(3)*, PowerKids Pr.) Rosen Publishing Group, Inc., The.

Rules of the Game. 2004. (Rules of the Game Ser.). Bk. 1. (gr. 5-6). pap., stu. ed. 9.15 *(978-0-8388-2237-1(1))*Bk. 2. (gr. 7-8). pap., stu. ed. 9.15 *(978-0-8388-2239-5(8))*Bk. 3 (gr. 9-10). pap., stu. ed. 9.15 *(978-0-8388-2241-8(X))* Educators Publishing Service, Inc.

Ruscoe, Michael & Voege, Debra. Pit Stop Prefixes. 2009. (Grammar All-Stars: Kinds of Words Ser.). 32p. (J). (gr. 2-5). pap. 10.50 *(978-1-4339-0152-2(8))*; (Illus.). lib. bdg. 26.00 *(978-1-4339-0011-2(4))* Stevens, Gareth Publishing LLLP. (Gareth Stevens Learning Library).

—Soccer Goal Suffixes. 2009. (Grammar All-Stars: Kinds of Words Ser.). 32p. (J). (gr. 2-5). pap. 10.50 *(978-1-4339-0154-6(4))*; (Illus.). lib. bdg. 26.00 *(978-1-4339-0012-9(2))* Stevens, Gareth Publishing LLLP. (Gareth Stevens Learning Library).

Sarris, Eno & Aihara, Masaaki, eds. Long Vowels Write & Wipe. 2008. (J). 9.95 *(978-1-933241-48-7(9))* Kumon Publishing North America, Inc.

Sarris, Eno & Masaaki, Aihara, eds. Short Vowels Write & Wipe. 2008. (J). 9.95 *(978-1-933241-47-0(0))* Kumon Publishing North America, Inc.

Saslow, Joan M. & Collins, Tim. Living & Working in English, 4 vols. 2004. (ENG., Illus.). xii, 148p. (C). pap. 31.33 *(978-0-13-192802-2(3))* Prentice Hall, ESL Dept.

—Workplace Plus 1 with Grammar Booster, 4 vols. 2004. (ENG., Illus.). (C). pap. 31.33 *(978-0-13-192799-5(X))* Prentice Hall, ESL Dept.

—Workplace Plus 2 with Grammar Booster, 4 vols. 2004. (ENG., Illus.). xiii, 148p. (C). pap. 31.33 *(978-0-13-192800-8(7))* Prentice Hall, ESL Dept.

—Workplace Plus 3 with Grammar Booster, 4 vols. 2004. (ENG., Illus.). 162p. (C). pap. 31.33 *(978-0-13-192801-5(5))* Prentice Hall, ESL Dept.

Schmitt, Conrad. ¡Así Se Dice! 2009. (Glencoe Spanish Ser.). (ENG & SPA.). 160p. (gr. 6-12). pap., wbk. ed. 21.84 *(978-0-07-892935-9(0)*, 0078929350) McGraw-Hill Education.

—Asi Se Dice 2009, Level 1A. 2009. (Glencoe Spanish Ser.). (ENG & SPA.). 160p. (gr. 6-12). pap., wbk. ed. 21.84 *(978-0-07-892934-2(2)*, 0078929342) McGraw-Hill Education.

Schneider, Melissa. G. U. M. Drops 1-2. 2005. 128p. pap. 12.95 *(978-1-933407-00-5(X)*, In the Think of Things) Rainbow Resource Ctr., Inc.

—G. U. M. Drops 3. 2005. pap. 12.95 *(978-1-933407-01-2(8)*, In the Think of Things) Rainbow Resource Ctr., Inc.

—G. U. M. Drops 4. 2005. pap. 12.95 *(978-1-933407-02-9(6)*, In the Think of Things) Rainbow Resource Ctr., Inc.

School Zone Staff. Nouns, Verbs & More. 2005. (ENG., Illus.). 56p. (J). 2.99 *(978-1-58947-420-8(1))* School Zone Publishing Co.

Scrambled Sentences (Gr. 1-2) 2003. (J). *(978-1-58232-126-4(4))* ECS Learning Systems, Inc.

Sequential Words with Your Pets. 2013. (Write Right! Ser.). 24p. (J). (gr. 2-5). pap. 48.90 *(978-1-4339-9079-3(2))* Stevens, Gareth Publishing LLLP.

Sevaly, Karen & Scholastic, Inc. Staff. Short Vowels Mats. 2007. (ENG.). (J). (gr. k-2). 14.99 *(978-0-439-91988-3(6))* Scholastic, Inc.

Sewell, James Witt. Classical Grammar. 2011. (Illus.). 195p. (J). *(978-1-892331-92-2(6))* Angelus Pr.

Shaskan, Trisha Speed. If You Were a Plural Word, 1 vol. Gray, Sara, illus. 2009. (Word Fun Ser.). (ENG.). 24p. (gr. 2-4). lib. bdg. 27.99 *(978-1-4048-5516-8(5))* Picture Window Bks.

—If You Were Alliteration. Gray, Sara, illus. 2008. (Word Fun Ser.). (ENG.). 24p. (gr. 2-4). lib. bdg. 27.99 *(978-1-4048-4097-3(4))* Picture Window Bks.

Smith, Daniel. My Grammar & I Activity Book. 2016. (ENG.). 224p. pap. 14.95 ***(978-1-78243-580-8(8))*** O'Mara, Michael Bks., Ltd. GBR. Dist: Independent Pubs. Group.

Snyders, Natalie & Stuckey, Kevin. Articulation Quick Take along Mini-Book: Ta120. 2011. spiral bd. 12.95 net. *(978-1-58650-999-6(3))* Super Duper Pubns.

Sprick, Marilyn, et al. Student Workbook 3 (Plain Text) Unit 19 through Vowel Review Unit. 2003. (Read Well Level K Ser.). (J). *(978-1-59318-168-0(X))* Cambium Education, Inc.

—Student Workbook 3 (Slant Text) Unit 19 through Vowel Review Unit. 2003. (Read Well Level K Ser.). (Illus.). 104p. (J). *(978-1-59318-171-0(X))* Cambium Education, Inc.

Stamper, Judith Bauer. Text-Marking Lessons for Active Nonfiction Reading: Reproducible Nonfiction Passages with Lessons That Guide Students to Read Strategically, Identify Text Structures, & Activate Comprehension. 2012. (ENG., Illus.). 64p. (gr. 2-3). 16.99 *(978-0-545-28817-0(7))*; (gr. 4-8). 16.99 *(978-0-545-28819-4(3))* Scholastic, Inc. (Teaching Resources).

Steck-Vaughn Staff. Access Writing. 2004. (Steck-Vaughn Access Ser.). (ENG.). 32p. (gr. 9-12). pap., tchr. ed. 9.05 *(978-0-7398-8933-6(8))* Houghton Mifflin Harcourt Publishing Co.

—At-Home Workbooks: Vowels. 2004. (Illus.). pap., wbk. ed. *(978-0-7398-8535-2(9))* Steck-Vaughn.

—Head for Home: Consonant Blends. 2004. (Illus.). pap. 5.99 *(978-0-7398-8536-9(7))* Steck-Vaughn.

Steel, Abigail. Vocabulary, Grammar & Punctuation, Bk. 2. 2017. (ENG.). 48p. (J). pap. 9.99 ***(978-0-00-823641-0(0))*** HarperCollins Pubs. Ltd. GBR. Dist: Independent Pubs. Group.

Stefoff, Rebecca. Me, Myself, & I — The More Grammar Changes, the More It Remains Th Same. 2017. (Why Do We Say That? Ser.). (ENG.). 32p. (gr. 3-4). lib. bdg. 27.32 ***(978-1-5157-6387-1(0)***, Fact Finders) Capstone Press of Coughlan Cos.

Stella, Heather. Get Ready for Pre-K: Letters & Sight Words - 245 Fun Exercises for Mastering Basic Skills. 2013. (Get Ready for School Ser.). (ENG.). 128p. (J). (gr. -1-k). pap. 7.99 *(978-1-57912-935-4(8)*, 81935, Black Dog & Leventhal Pubs. Inc.) Hachette Bks.

Stride, Lottie. Write Every Time. 2017. (Buster Reference Ser.). (ENG., Illus.). 128p. (J). (gr. 3-7). pap. 8.99 ***(978-1-78055-469-3(9))*** O'Mara, Michael Bks., Ltd. GBR. Dist: Independent Pubs. Group.

Stride, Lottie. Write (or Is It Right?) Every Time: Cool Ways to Improve Your English. 2011. (ENG.). 144p. (YA). (gr. 4-6). 9.99 *(978-1-60652-341-4(4))* Reader's Digest Assn., Inc., The.

Subjects & Verbs with Your Neighbors. 2013. (Write Right! Ser.). 24p. (J). (gr. 2-5). pap. 48.90 *(978-1-4339-9083-0(0))* Stevens, Gareth Publishing LLLP.

Sutton, Lynn Parrish. Animally. Mitchell, Hazel, illus. 2016. (ENG.). 30p. (J). 11.99 *(978-1-61067-345-7(X))* Kane Miller.

Terban, Marvin. Marvin Terban's Guide to Grammar: Parts of Speech - A Mini-Curriculum with Engaging Lessons, Fun Videos, Interactive Whiteboard Activities, & Reproducible Practice Pages for Teaching the Parts of Speech. 2014. (ENG., Illus.). 72p. (gr. 3-6). pap. 39.99 *(978-0-545-55038-3(6)*, Teaching Resources) Scholastic, Inc.

—Your Foot's on My Feet! And Other Tricky Nouns. Maestro, Giulio, illus. 2008. (ENG.). 64p. (J). (gr. 2-5). pap. 8.99 *(978-0-618-19166-6(6))* Houghton Mifflin Harcourt Publishing Co.

Thomas, M. I Jog Around: Learning the J Sound. 2009. (PowerPhonics Ser.). 24p. (gr. 1-1). 39.90 *(978-1-60851-450-2(1)*, PowerKids Pr.) Rosen Publishing Group, Inc., The.

Transition Words with Your Team. 2013. (Write Right! Ser.). 24p. (J). (gr. 2-5). pap. 48.90 *(978-1-4339-9087-8(3))* Stevens, Gareth Publishing LLLP.

Using Capitalization (Gr. 3+) 2003. (J). *(978-1-58232-051-9(9))* ECS Learning Systems, Inc.

Vale, David. Picture Grammar for Children 1: Topic-Based Grammar Practice. 64p. pap., stu. ed. *(978-0-435-29734-3(1))* Heinemann.

—Picture Grammar for Children 1: Topic-Based Grammar Practice, Answer Key. 34p. pap. *(978-0-435-29735-0(X))* Heinemann.

—Picture Grammar for Children 2: Topic-Based Grammar Practice. 64p. pap., stu. ed. *(978-0-435-29736-7(8))* Heinemann.

—Picture Grammar for Children 2: Topic-Based Grammar Practice, Answer Key. 34p. pap. *(978-0-435-29737-4(6))* Heinemann.

Vastola, P. Huge Animals: Learning the Long U Sound. 2009. (PowerPhonics Ser.). 24p. (gr. 1-1). 39.90 *(978-1-60851-445-8(5)*, PowerKids Pr.) Rosen Publishing Group, Inc., The.

Verbs. 2013. (Core Language Skills Ser.). 24p. (J). (gr. 2-2). pap. 49.50 *(978-1-4777-0975-7(4)*, PowerKids Pr.) Rosen Publishing Group, Inc., The.

Vickers, Rebecca. Punctuation & Spelling: Rules That Make Things Clear, 1 vol. 2013. (Find Your Way with Words Ser.). (ENG.). 56p. (gr. 6-7). 34.65 *(978-1-4329-7655-2(9))* Heinemann-Raintree.

—Types of Words: Unleashing Powerful Parts of Speech, 1 vol. 2013. (Find Your Way with Words Ser.). (ENG.). 56p. (gr. 6-7). 34.65 *(978-1-4329-7657-6(5))* Heinemann-Raintree.

Voyages in English: Writing & Grammar. 2004. (gr. 1-18). tchr. ed. *(978-0-8294-0980-2(7))*; (gr. 1-18). tchr. ed., wbk. ed. *(978-0-8294-1383-0(9))*; (gr. 1-18). stu. ed. *(978-0-8294-0981-9(5))*; (gr. 1-18). stu. ed., wbk. ed. *(978-0-8294-1382-3(0))*; (gr. 2-18). tchr. ed. *(978-0-8294-0982-6(3))*; (gr. 2-18). tchr. ed., wbk. ed. *(978-0-8294-1385-4(5))*; (gr. 2-18). stu. ed. *(978-0-8294-0983-3(1))*; (gr. 2-18). stu. ed., wbk. ed. *(978-0-8294-1384-7(7))*; (gr. 3-18). *(978-0-8294-1303-8(0))*; (gr. 3-18). tchr. ed. *(978-0-8294-0985-7(8))*; (gr. 3-18). tchr. ed., wbk. ed. *(978-0-8294-1319-9(7))*; (gr. 3-18). stu. ed. *(978-0-8294-0986-4(6))*; (gr. 3-18). stu. ed., wbk. ed. *(978-0-8294-1318-2(9))*; (gr. 4-18). tchr. ed., wbk. ed. *(978-0-8294-1321-2(9))*; (gr. 4-18). stu. ed. *(978-0-8294-0988-8(2))* Loyola Pr.

Wallaker, Jillayne Prince. Grammar Rules! High-Interest Activities for Practice & Mastery of Basic Grammar Skills. Walkush, Donna, ed. 2003. (Skills for Success Ser.). (ENG.). 128p. (gr. 5-6). pap. 16.99 *(978-0-88724-977-8(9)*, CD-4339) Carson-Dellosa Publishing, LLC.

—Grammar Rules!, Grades 3-4: High-Interest Activities for Practice & Mastery of Basic Grammar Skills. Walkush, Donna, ed. 2003. (Skills for Success Ser.). (ENG.). 128p. (gr. 3-4). pap. 16.99 *(978-0-88724-976-1(0)*, CD-4338) Carson-Dellosa Publishing, LLC.

—Grammer Rules! High-Interest Activities for Practice & Mastery of Basic Grammar Skills. Walkush, Donna, ed. 2003. (Skills for Success Ser.). (ENG.). 128p. (gr. 1-2). pap. 16.99 *(978-0-88724-975-4(2))* Carson-Dellosa Publishing, LLC.

Walton, Rick. Bullfrog Pops! Adventures in Verbs & Objects, 1 vol. McAllister, Chris, illus. 2011. (ENG.). 36p. (J). (gr. 2-3). pap. 7.99 *(978-1-4236-2079-2(8))* Gibbs Smith, Publisher.

—Herd of Cows! Flock of Sheep! Olson, Julie, illus. 2011. (ENG.). 36p. (gr. 2-3). pap. 7.99 *(978-1-4236-2090-7(9))* Gibbs Smith, Publisher.

—Suddenly Alligator: Adventures in Adverbs, 1 vol. Bradshaw, Jim, illus. 2011. (ENG.). 36p. (J). (gr. 2-3). pap. 7.99 *(978-1-4236-2087-7(9))* Gibbs Smith, Publisher.

Weakland, Mark. Fast, Strong, Fearless: Football Adjectives. 2015. (Football Words Ser.). (ENG., Illus.). 32p. (gr. 2-4). lib. bdg. 27.32 *(978-1-62065-175-9(0))* Capstone Press of Coughlan Cos.

—Pass, Catch, Tackle: Football Verbs. 2015. (Football Words Ser.). (ENG., Illus.). 32p. (gr. 2-4). lib. bdg. 27.32 *(978-1-62065-159-9(9))* Capstone Press of Coughlan Cos.

—Stadium, Jersey, Player: Football Nouns. 2015. (Football Words Ser.). (ENG., Illus.). 32p. (gr. 2-4). lib. bdg. 27.32 *(978-1-62065-174-2(2))* Capstone Press of Coughlan Cos.

Webber, Sharon, et al. Party Pups: The Game of Prepositional Fun! Ink, Bruce, illus. 2011. (J). 39.95 net. *(978-1-60723-002-1(X))* Super Duper Pubns.

Wernham, Sara. Phonic, 6 Bks., Pack. Stephen, Lib, illus. 2003. (Jolly Phonics Readers, Complete Set Level 2 Ser.). (ENG.). 12p. (J). pap. 12.50 *(978-1-903619-86-5(6)*, JL866, Jolly Learning) Jolly Learning, Ltd. GBR. Dist: American International Distribution Corp.

Whiteford, Rhona. Grammar & Punctuation, Age 10-11: Helping You Support Your Child in Year 6. 2003. (Hodder Home Learning Ser.). (ENG., Illus.). 32p. (J). pap. 6.99 *(978-0-340-79185-1(3))* Hodder & Stoughton GBR. Dist: Trafalgar Square Publishing.

Whiteford, Rhona & Hachette Children's Group. Complete English, 3 bks. in 1. (Illus.). 96p. (YA). pap. 15.99 *(978-0-340-71582-6(0))* Hodder & Stoughton GBR. Dist: Trafalgar Square Publishing.

WHS Staff, contrib. by. Vocabulary Workshop, Level Green, Test Booklets Cycle One. 2006. (Vocabulary Workshop 2006 Ser.). (Illus.). 44p. (gr. 3-4). 42.00 net. *(978-0-8215-0430-7(4))* Sadlier, William H. Inc.

—Vocabulary Workshop, Level Green, Test Booklets Cycle Two. 2006. (Vocabulary Workshop 2006 Ser.). (Illus.). 44p. (gr. 3-4). 42.00 net. *(978-0-8215-0440-6(1))* Sadlier, William H. Inc.

Wilson, Nancy. Our Mother Tongue: A Guide to English Grammar. 2003. (ENG.). 184p. pap., stu. ed. 20.00 *(978-1-59128-011-8(7))* Canon Pr.

—Our Mother Tongue - Answer Key. 2004. (ENG.). 54p. pap. 5.00 *(978-1-59128-016-3(8))* Canon Pr.

Windsor, Lucinda. Grammar in Story Vol. 2: The Transparencies, 2 vols. 2004. 410p. pap. 38.50 *(978-1-888842-17-3(2))* Absey & Co.

Wise, Sue. Cómo se Dice... ? Coirault, Christine, illus. 2006. (How I Say That? Ser.). (ENG & SPA.). 32p. (gr. k-4). lib. bdg. 26.00 *(978-0-8368-6259-1(7)*, Gareth Stevens Learning Library) Stevens, Gareth Publishing LLLP.

—How Do I Say That? (¿Cómo se Dice?) Coirault, Christine, illus. 2006. (How Do I Say That?/ Como se dice? Ser.). (ENG & SPA.). 32p. (gr. k-4). pap. 10.50 *(978-0-8368-6583-7(9)*, Gareth Stevens Learning Library) Stevens, Gareth Publishing LLLP.

Wright, Marsha. Sentences & Vowel Pairs - Digraphs, 8 vols. 2003. 48p. (J). per. 7.99 *(978-1-56472-195-2(7))* Edupress, Inc.

—Sentences for Consonant Blends - Digraphs, 8 vols. 2003. 48p. (J). per. 7.99 *(978-1-56472-193-8(0))* Edupress, Inc.

—Sentences for R-Controlled Vowels - Diphthongs, 8 vols. 2003. 48p. (J). per. 7.99 *(978-1-56472-197-6(3))* Edupress, Inc.

—Sentences for Short - Long Vowels, 8 vols. 2003. (Illus.). 48p. (J). per. 7.99 *(978-1-56472-191-4(4))* Edupress, Inc.

—Stories for Consonant Blends - Digraphs, 8 vols. 2003. 48p. (J). per. *(978-1-56472-194-5(9))* Edupress, Inc.

—Stories for R-Controlled Vowels - Diphthongs, 8 vols. 2003. 48p. (J). per. 7.99 *(978-1-56472-198-3(1))* Edupress, Inc.

—Stories for Short - Long Vowels, 8 vols. 2003. 48p. (J). per. 7.99 *(978-1-56472-192-1(2))* Edupress, Inc.

—Stories for Vowel Pairs - Digraphs, 8 vols. 2003. 48p. (J). per. 7.99 *(978-1-56472-196-9(5))* Edupress, Inc.

Writer's Solution Bronze Level: Grammar Practice Book Answer Key. (YA). (gr. 7). 1.97 *(978-0-13-434759-2(5))* Prentice Hall PTR.

Writer's Solution Diamond Level: Grammar Practice Book Answer Key. (YA). (gr. 12). 1.97 *(978-0-13-434766-0(8))* Prentice Hall PTR.

Writer's Solution Gold Level: Grammar Practice Book Answer Key. (YA). (gr. 9). 1.97 *(978-0-13-434761-5(7))* Prentice Hall PTR.

Writer's Solution Platinum Level: Grammar Practice Book Answer Key. (YA). (gr. 10). 1.97 *(978-0-13-434763-9(3))* Prentice Hall PTR.

Writer's Solution Ruby Level: Grammar Practice Book Answer Key. (YA). (gr. 11). 1.97 *(978-0-13-434764-6(1))* Prentice Hall PTR.

Writer's Solution Silver Level: Grammar Practice Book Answer Key. (YA). (gr. 8). 1.97 *(978-0-13-434760-8(9))* Prentice Hall PTR.

Writing Sentences (Gr. 2-3) 2003. (J). *(978-1-58232-127-1(2))* ECS Learning Systems, Inc.

Writing Works with NC Wordcrafter & Joey: Grade 3+ 2004. 28.00 *(978-0-9790796-0-3(8))* PJR Assocs., Ltd.

Writing Works with NC Wordcrafter & Joey: Grade 4+ 2004. 28.00 *(978-0-9790796-1-0(6))* PJR Assocs., Ltd.

Writing Works with NC Wordcrafter & Joey: Grade 5+ 2004. 28.00 *(978-0-9790796-2-7(4))* PJR Assocs., Ltd.

Wyldeck, Kathi. Grammar & Vocabulary Games for Children. 2007. 83p. pap. 12.95 *(978-1-84799-930-6(1))*; 81p. pap. 12.95 *(978-1-84753-579-5(8))* Lulu Pr., Inc.

Yates, Irene. How to Be a Wizard at Grammer. Ford, Kate, illus. 48p. (J). (gr. 3-6). pap. *(978-1-876367-29-9(6))* Wizard Bks.

Zocchi, Judith Mazzeo. Uri's "U" Book. Revutsky, Helen Ross, illus. 2007. (J). *(978-1-59646-538-1(7))* Dingles & Co.

—Will's W Book: El Libro "W" de Will. 2005. (ENG & SPA., Illus.). *(978-1-59646-553-4(0))* Dingles & Co.

—Yola's "Y" Book. Revutsky, Helen Ross, illus. 2007. (J). *(978-1-59646-562-6(X))* Dingles & Co.

Zocchi, Judith Mazzeo, et al. Aimee's a Book: El Libro a de Aimee. Revutsky, Helen Ross, illus. 2005. (J). *(978-1-59646-421-6(6))* Dingles & Co.

—Bebe's "B" Book: El Libro "B" de Bibi. Revutsky, Helen Ross, illus. 2005. (SPA & ENG.). (J). *(978-1-59646-427-8(5))* Dingles & Co.

—Delia's D Book: El Libro D de Delia. Revutsky, Helen Ross, illus. 2005. (SPA.). (J). *(978-1-59646-439-1(9))* Dingles & Co.

—Tad's "T" Book: El Libro "T" de Tad. 2005. (ENG & SPA., Illus.). (J). *(978-1-59646-535-0(2))* Dingles & Co.

—Vera's "V" Book: El Libro "V" de Vera. 2005. (ENG & SPA., Illus.). (J). *(978-1-59646-547-3(6))* Dingles & Co.

—Xavia's "X" Book: El Libro "X" de Xavia. Revutsky, Helen Ross, illus. 2005. (SPA.). *(978-1-59646-559-6(X))* Dingles & Co.

—Zach's "Z" Book: El Libro "Z" de Zach. Revutsky, Helen Ross, illus. 2005. (SPA & ENG.). (J). *(978-1-59646-571-8(9))* Dingles & Co.

Zocchi, Judy. Cassie's "C" Book: El Libro "C" de Cassie. 2005. (SPA & ENG., Illus.). (J). *(978-1-59646-433-9(X))* Dingles & Co.

ENGLISH LANGUAGE—HISTORY

Atkinson, Mary. What Do You Mean? Communication Isn't Easy. 2007. (Illus.). 36p. (J). pap. *(978-0-531-18811-8(6))* Children's Pr., Ltd.

—What Do You Mean? Communication Isn't Easy. 2007. (Shockwave: People & Communities Ser.). (ENG., Illus.). 36p. (J). (gr. 3-5). 25.00 *(978-0-531-17571-2(5)*, Children's Pr.) Scholastic Library Publishing.

ENGLISH LANGUAGE—HOMONYMS

Aiken, Zora & David. Double-Talk: Word Sense & Nonsense, 1 vol. Aiken, David, illus. 2012. (ENG.). 32p. (J). 14.99 *(978-0-7643-3962-2(1)*, 9780764339622) Schiffer Publishing, Ltd.

Alda, Arlene. Did You Say Pears? (ENG., Illus.). 32p. (J). (gr. -1-2). 2011. pap. 7.95 *(978-1-77049-278-3(X))* 2006. 16.95 *(978-0-88776-739-5(7))* Tundra Bks. CAN. (Tundra Bks.). Dist: Penguin Random Hse. LLC.

Cleary, Brian. A Bat Cannot Bat, a Stair Cannot Stare: More about Homonyms & Homophones. Goneau, Martin, illus. 2016. (Words Are CATegorical (r) Ser.). (ENG.). 32p. (J). (gr. 2-5). pap. 6.95 *(978-1-5124-1799-9(8)*, Millbrook Pr.) Lerner Publishing Group.

Cleary, Brian P. A Bat Cannot Bat, a Stair Cannot Stare: More about Homonyms & Homophones. Goneau, Martin, illus. 2014. (Words Are CATegorical (r) Ser.). (ENG.). 32p. (gr. 2-5). lib. bdg. 16.95 *(978-0-7613-9032-9(4)*, Millbrook Pr.) Lerner Publishing Group.

—How Much Can a Bare Bear Bear? Gable, Brian, illus. 2004. (Words Are CATegorical (r) Ser.). (ENG.). (gr. 2-5). pap. 39.62 *(978-0-8225-9899-2(X))* Lerner Publishing Group.

—How Much Can a Bare Bear Bear? What Are Homonyms & Homophones? Gable, Brian, illus. (Words Are CATegorical (r) Ser.). (ENG.). 32p. (gr. 2-5). 2007. per. 6.95 *(978-0-8225-6710-3(5)*, First Avenue Editions) 2005. lib. bdg. 16.95 *(978-1-57505-824-5(3))* Lerner Publishing Group.

—They're There on Their Vacation. Paillot, Jim, illus. 2015. (ENG.). 32p. (J). (gr. 2-5). 26.65 *(978-0-7613-9033-6(2)*, Millbrook Pr.) Lerner Publishing Group.

Coffelt, Nancy. Aunt Ant Leaves Through the Leaves: A Story with Homophones & Homonyms. Coffelt, Nancy, illus. 2012. (ENG., Illus.). 32p. (J). 16.95 *(978-0-8234-2353-8(0))* Holiday Hse., Inc.

Connors, Kathleen. Homophones at Home. 2012. (Word Play Ser.). (Illus.). 24p. (J). (gr. 1-3). pap. 8.15 *(978-1-4339-7188-4(7))*; lib. bdg. 22.60 *(978-1-4339-7187-7(9))* Stevens, Gareth Publishing LLLP.

Felix, Rebecca. Are You a Ewe? 2015. (Hear Homophones Here Ser.). (Illus.). 16p. (J). 25.65 *(978-1-60753-568-3(8))* Amicus Publishing.

—Can You Be a Bee? 2015. (Hear Homophones Here Ser.). (Illus.). 16p. (J). 25.65 *(978-1-60753-569-0(6))* Amicus Publishing.

—The New Gnu Knew. 2015. (Hear Homophones Here Ser.). (Illus.). 16p. (J). 25.65 *(978-1-60753-570-6(X))* Amicus Publishing.

—A Pair of Pears. 2015. (Hear Homophones Here Ser.). (Illus.). 16p. (J). 25.65 *(978-1-60753-571-3(8))* Amicus Publishing.

—Rows of Roses. 2015. (Hear Homophones Here Ser.). (Illus.). 16p. (J). 25.65 *(978-1-60753-572-0(6))* Amicus Publishing.

—They Won One! 2015. (Hear Homophones Here Ser.). 16p. (J). 25.65 *(978-1-60753-573-7(4))* Amicus Publishing.

Fowler, Josefine A. What's the Point? (a book about multiple meaning Words) 2010. 24p. pap. 11.49 *(978-1-4490-5967-5(8))* AuthorHouse.

Hanson, Joan. Still More Homonyms: Night & Knight & Other Words That Sound the Same but Look As Different As Ball & Bawl. Hanson, Joan, illus. (Joan Hanson Word Bks.). (Illus.). (J). (gr. -1-3). lib. bdg. 4.95 *(978-0-8225-1107-6(X)*, Lerner Pubns.) Lerner Publishing Group.

Jocelyn, Marthe & Jocelyn, Nell. Where Do You Look? 2013. (ENG., Illus.). 32p. (J). (-k). 15.95 *(978-1-77049-376-6(X)*, Tundra Bks.) Tundra Bks. CAN. Dist: Penguin Random Hse. LLC.

Johnson, Robin. The Word Wizard's Book of Homonyms. 2015. (ENG., Illus.). 24p. (J). *(978-0-7787-1920-5(0))* Crabtree Publishing Co.

Lindeen, Mary. I See the Sea: Teaching Homophones. 2016. (Playing with Words Ser.). (ENG.). 16p. (J). (gr. -1-2). 25.64 *(978-1-5038-0840-9(8)*, 210687) Child's World, Inc., The.

Lisl. Dictionary with a Difference. 2009. 116p. pap. 31.99 *(978-1-4490-0125-4(4))* AuthorHouse.

Loewen, Nancy. If You Were a Homonym or a Homophone, 1 vol. Gray, Sara, illus. 2007. (Word Fun Ser.). (ENG.). 24p. (gr. 2-4). lib. bdg. 27.99 *(978-1-4048-3161-2(4))*; per. 7.95 *(978-1-4048-3571-9(7)*, 1265671) Picture Window Bks.

Presson, Leslie. What in the World Is a Homophone? Bosson, Jo-Ellen, illus. 192p. (J). 11.95 *(978-0-7641-2698-7(9))* Barron's Educational Series, Inc.

Prokos, Anna & Voege, Debra. Half-Pipe Homonyms. Angle, Scott, illus. 2009. (Grammar All-Stars Ser.). 32p. (gr. 2-5). (J). lib. bdg. 26.00 *(978-1-4339-0010-5(6))*; pap. 10.50 *(978-1-4339-0150-8(1))* Stevens, Gareth Publishing LLLP. (Gareth Stevens Learning Library).

Rayevsky, Kim. Antonyms, Synonyms & Homonyms. Rayevsky, Robert, illus. 2006. (ENG.). 32p. (J). (gr. -1-3). 16.95 *(978-0-8234-1889-3(8))* Holiday Hse., Inc.

Synonyms, Antonyms, & Homonyms (Gr. 4-5) 2004. (J). *(978-1-58232-138-7(8))* ECS Learning Systems, Inc.

Terban, Marvin. The Dove Dove: Funny Homograph Riddles. Huffman, Tom, illus. 2008. (ENG.). 64p. (J). (gr. 5-7). pap. 6.95 *(978-0-547-03186-6(6))* Houghton Mifflin Harcourt Publishing Co.

ENGLISH LANGUAGE—IDIOMS

Amoroso, Cynthia. Hold Your Horses! (And Other Peculiar Sayings) Cole, Mernie & Gallagher-Cole, Mernie, illus. 2011. (Sayings & Phrases Ser.). (ENG.). 24p. (J). (gr. 2-5). lib. bdg. 28.50 *(978-1-60253-681-4(3)*, 200780) Child's World, Inc., The.

—I'm All Thumbs! (and Other Odd Things We Say) Gallagher-Cole, Mernie, illus. 2011. (Sayings & Phrases Ser.). (ENG.). 24p. (J). (gr. 2-5). lib. bdg. 28.50 *(978-1-60253-682-1(1)*, 200781) Child's World, Inc., The.

—It's a Long Shot! (and Other Strange Sayings) Gallagher-Cole, Mernie, illus. 2011. (Sayings & Phrases Ser.). (ENG.). 24p. (J). (gr. 2-5). lib. bdg. 28.50 *(978-1-60253-683-8(X)*, 200782) Child's World, Inc., The.

—That's the Last Straw! (And Other Weird Things We Say) Gallagher-Cole, Mernie, illus. 2011. (Sayings & Phrases Ser.). (ENG.). 24p. (J). (gr. 2-5). lib. bdg. 28.50 *(978-1-60954-230-6(4)*, 200783) Child's World, Inc., The.

Brennan-Nelson, Denise. My Daddy Likes to Say. Donovan, Jane Monroe, illus. 2009. (ENG.). 32p. (J). (gr. k-6). 15.95 *(978-1-58536-432-9(0))* Sleeping Bear Pr.

—My Grandma Likes to Say. Donovan, Jane Monroe, illus. rev. ed. 2007. (ENG.). 32p. (J). (gr. k-6). 16.95 *(978-1-58536-284-4(0))* Sleeping Bear Pr.

—My Momma Likes to Say. Donovan, Jane Monroe, illus. 2003. (ENG.). 32p. (J). (gr. k-6). 15.95 *(978-1-58536-106-9(2))* Sleeping Bear Pr.

—My Teacher Likes to Say. Monroe Donovan, Jane & Donovan, Jane Monroe, illus. rev. ed. 2004. (ENG.). 32p. (J). (gr. k-6). 15.95 *(978-1-58536-212-7(3))* Sleeping Bear Pr.

Doeden, Matt. Put on Your Thinking Cap: And Other Expressions about School. 2012. (It's Just an Expression Ser.). (ENG., Illus.). 32p. (J). (gr. 4-6). lib. bdg. 26.60 *(978-0-7613-7891-4(X)*, Lerner Pubns.) Lerner Publishing Group.

—Stick Out Like a Sore Thumb: And Other Expressions about Body Parts. 2012. (It's Just an Expression Ser.). (ENG., Illus.). 32p. (J). (gr. 4-6). lib. bdg. 26.60 *(978-0-7613-7887-7(1)*, Lerner Pubns.) Lerner Publishing Group.

Donovan, Sandy. Keep Your Eye on the Ball: And Other Expressions about Sports. 2012. (It's Just an Expression Ser.). (ENG., Illus.). 32p. (J). (gr. 4-6). lib. bdg. 26.60 *(978-0-7613-7889-1(8)*, Lerner Pubns.) Lerner Publishing Group.

—Until the Cows Come Home: And Other Expressions about Animals. Blecha, Aaron, illus. 2012. (It's Just an Expression Ser.). (ENG.). 32p. (gr. 4-6). lib. bdg. 26.60 *(978-0-7613-7890-7(1)*, Lerner Pubns.) Lerner Publishing Group.

Edwards, Wallace. The Cat's Pajamas. Edwards, Wallace, illus. 2010. (ENG., Illus.). 32p. (J). (gr. 1-6). 18.95 *(978-1-55453-308-4(2))* Kids Can Pr., Ltd. CAN. Dist: Hachette Bk. Group.

—Monkey Business. Edwards, Wallace, illus. (ENG., Illus.). 32p. (J). (gr. 1-6). 2008. pap. 8.95 *(978-1-55453-228-5(0))* 2004. 18.95 *(978-1-55337-462-6(2))* Kids Can Pr., Ltd. CAN. Dist: Hachette Bk. Group.

Hahn, Jill. A to Z Idioms. 2012. 60p. pap. 24.99 *(978-1-4685-5254-6(6))* AuthorHouse.

Heos, Bridget. At the Eleventh Hour: And Other Expressions about Money & Numbers. 2012. (It's Just an Expression Ser.). (ENG., Illus.). 32p. (J). (gr. 4-6). lib. bdg. 26.60 *(978-0-7613-8164-8(3)*, Lerner Pubns.) Lerner Publishing Group.

—Cool As a Cucumber: And Other Expressions about Food. 2012. (It's Just an Expression Ser.). (ENG., Illus.). 32p. (J). (gr. 4-6). lib. bdg. 26.60 *(978-0-7613-7888-4(X)*, Lerner Pubns.) Lerner Publishing Group.

Larsen, C. S. All Pooped Out: And Other Gross Expressions. Blecha, Aaron, illus. 2012. (It's Just an Expression Ser.). (ENG.). 32p. (J). (gr. 4-6). lib. bdg. 26.60 *(978-0-7613-7892-1(8)*, Lerner Pubns.) Lerner Publishing Group.

E
F
G

Loewen, Nancy. Talking Turkey & Other Clichés We Say, 1 vol. Watkins, Adam, illus. 2010. (Ways to Say It Ser.). (ENG.). 24p. (gr. 3-5). lib. bdg. 27.99 *(978-1-4048-6272-2(2))* Picture Window Bks.

Oelschlager, Vanita. Birds of a Feather. Hegan, Robin, illus. 2011. (ENG.). 32p. (J). (gr. -1-3). pap. 8.95 *(978-0-9826366-1-9(X))* VanitaBooks.

—Birds of a Feather: A Book of Idioms & Silly Pictures. Hegan, Robin, illus. 2009. (ENG.). 32p. (J). (gr. -1-3). 17.95 *(978-0-9800162-8-4(2))* VanitaBooks.

—Out of the Blue: A book of color idioms & silly Pictures. Hegan, Robin, illus. 2012. (ENG.). 40p. (J). (gr. -1-3). 15.95 *(978-0-9832904-2-1(3))*; pap. 8.95 *(978-0-9832904-1-4(5))* VanitaBooks.

Ringstad, Arnold. The Bizarre Origins of Kangaroo Court & Other Idioms. McGeehan, Dan, illus. 2012. (Idioms Ser.). (ENG.). 32p. (J). (gr. 3-6). 29.93 *(978-1-61473-231-0(0)*, 204938) Child's World, Inc., The.

—The Compelling Histories of Long Arm of the Law & Other Idioms. McGeehan, Dan, illus. 2012. (Idioms Ser.). (ENG.). 32p. (J). (gr. 3-6). 29.93 *(978-1-61473-232-7(9)*, 204939) Child's World, Inc., The.

—The Over-the-Top Histories of Chew the Scenery & Other Idioms. McGeehan, Dan, illus. 2012. (Idioms Ser.). (ENG.). 32p. (J). (gr. 3-6). 29.93 *(978-1-61473-234-1(5)*, 204941) Child's World, Inc., The.

—The Shocking Stories Behind Lightning in a Bottle & Other Idioms. McGeehan, Dan, illus. 2012. (Idioms Ser.). (ENG.). 32p. (J). (gr. 3-6). 29.93 *(978-1-61473-236-5(1)*, 204943) Child's World, Inc., The.

—The Thrilling Sources of Push the Envelope & Other Idioms. McGeehan, Dan, illus. 2012. (Idioms Ser.). (ENG.). 32p. (J). (gr. 3-6). 29.93 *(978-1-61473-237-2(X)*, 204944) Child's World, Inc., The.

—The Unbelievable Origins of Snake Oil & Other Idioms. McGeehan, Dan, illus. 2012. (Idioms Ser.). (ENG.). 32p. (J). (gr. 3-6). 29.93 *(978-1-61473-238-9(8)*, 204945) Child's World, Inc., The.

Rondina, Catherine. Don't Touch That Toad & Other Strange Things Adults Tell You. Sylvester, Kevin, illus. (ENG.). 96p. (J). (gr. 2-5). 2014. pap. 8.95 *(978-1-55453-455-5(0))* 2010. 14.95 *(978-1-55453-454-8(2))* Kids Can Pr., Ltd. CAN. Dist: Hachette Bk. Group.

Terban, Marvin. In a Pickle: And Other Funny Idioms. Maestro, Giulio, illus. 2007. (ENG.). 64p. (J). (gr. -1-3). pap. 8.99 *(978-0-618-83001-5(4))* Houghton Mifflin Harcourt Publishing Co.

—Mad As a Wet Hen! And Other Funny Idioms. Maestro, Giulio, illus. 2007. (ENG.). 64p. (J). (gr. -1-3). pap. 8.99 *(978-0-618-83003-9(0))* Houghton Mifflin Harcourt Publishing Co.

—Scholastic Dictionary of Idioms. rev. ed. 2006. (ENG.). 298p. (J). (gr. 3-7). pap. 9.99 *(978-0-439-77083-5(1)*, Scholastic Reference) Scholastic, Inc.

ENGLISH LANGUAGE—ORTHOGRAPHY

see English Language—Spelling

ENGLISH LANGUAGE—PHONETICS

see Phonetics

ENGLISH LANGUAGE—PHRASES AND TERMS

see English Language—Terms and Phrases

ENGLISH LANGUAGE—PUNCTUATION

see Punctuation

ENGLISH LANGUAGE—READERS

see Readers

also subdivision readers for languages other than English, e.g. French Language—Readers

ENGLISH LANGUAGE—RHETORIC

see Rhetoric

ENGLISH LANGUAGE—RHYME

Bodden, Valerie. Write Me a Poem: Finding the Rhyme in a Poem. 2016. (Illus.). 22p. (J). *(978-1-60818-620-4(2)*, Creative Education) Creative Co., The.

Body, Wendy. Blinki's Shopping List. 2006. (Qeb Fun with Phonics Ser.). (Illus.). 24p. (J). (gr. -1-3). lib. bdg. 15.95 *(978-1-59566-224-8(3))* QEB Publishing Inc.

Bulloch, Ivan & James, Diane. Learn with Me 123. Pangbourne, Daniel, illus. Pangbourne, Daniel, photos by. 2007. (ENG.). 46p. (J). (gr. -1 — 1). pap. 6.95 *(978-1-58728-622-3(X))* Cooper Square Publishing Llc.

Cleary, Brian P. Chips & Cheese & Nana's Knees: What Is Alliteration? Goneau, Martin, illus. 2015. (Words Are CATegorical (r) Ser.). (ENG.). 32p. (gr. 2-5). lib. bdg. 17.95 *(978-1-4677-2649-8(4)*, Millbrook Pr.) Lerner Publishing Group.

Coat, Janik. Rhymoceros. 2015. (ENG., Illus.). 36p. (J). (gr. -1 — 1). bds. 15.95 *(978-1-4197-1514-3(3))* Abrams, Inc.

Connors, Kathleen. Rhyming on the Road. 2012. (Word Play Ser.). (Illus.). 24p. (J). (gr. 1-3). 22.60 *(978-1-4339-7199-0(2))*; pap. 8.15 *(978-1-4339-7200-3(X))* Stevens, Gareth Publishing LLLP.

Dompierre, Judith. Rhymes the Size of Dimes, 1 vol. 2010. 42p. pap. 29.95 *(978-1-4489-8841-9(1))* America Star Bks.

Doudna, Kelly. Art from the Mart, 1 vol. (First Rhymes Ser.). (Illus.). (J). (gr. k-3). 2006. (ENG.). 24p. lib. bdg. 24.21 *(978-1-59679-449-8(6)*, SandCastle) 2005. 23p. pap. 48.42 *(978-1-59679-450-4(X))* ABDO Publishing Co.

—Billy Goat Can Float, 1 vol. (First Rhymes Ser.). (Illus.). (J). (gr. k-3). 2006. (ENG.). 24p. lib. bdg. 24.21 *(978-1-59679-453-5(4)*, SandCastle) 2005. 23p. pap. 48.42 *(978-1-59679-454-2(2))* ABDO Publishing Co.

—Bret & His Pet, 1 vol. (First Rhymes Ser.). (Illus.). (J). (gr. k-3). 2006. (ENG.). 24p. lib. bdg. 24.21 *(978-1-59679-489-4(5)*, SandCastle) 2005. 23p. pap. 48.42 *(978-1-59679-490-0(9))* ABDO Publishing Co.

—The Bride & the Slide, 1 vol. (First Rhymes Ser.). (Illus.). (J). (gr. k-3). 2006. (ENG.). 24p. lib. bdg. 24.21 *(978-1-59679-455-9(0)*, SandCastle) 2005. 23p. pap. 48.42 *(978-1-59679-456-6(9))* ABDO Publishing Co.

—The Crook Can Cook!, 1 vol. (First Rhymes Ser.). (Illus.). (J). (gr. k-3). 2006. (ENG.). 24p. lib. bdg. 24.21 *(978-1-59679-467-2(4)*, SandCastle) 2005. 23p. pap. 48.42 *(978-1-59679-468-9(2))* ABDO Publishing Co.

—Dip the Chip, 1 vol. 2006. (First Rhymes Ser.). (ENG., Illus.). 24p. (J). (gr. k-3). lib. bdg. 24.21 *(978-1-59679-469-6(0)*, SandCastle) ABDO Publishing Co.

—Dip the Chip! (6-pack) 2005. (First Rhymes Ser.). (ENG., Illus.). 23p. (J). pap. *(978-1-59679-470-2(4)*, SandCastle) ABDO Publishing Co.

—The Flock on the Dock, 1 vol. (First Rhymes Ser.). (Illus.). (J). (gr. k-3). 2006. (ENG.). 24p. lib. bdg. 24.21 *(978-1-59679-481-8(X)*, SandCastle) 2005. 23p. pap. 48.42 *(978-1-59679-482-5(8))* ABDO Publishing Co.

—Grant's Aunts from France, 1 vol. 2005. (Rhyme Time Ser.). (Illus.). (J). (gr. k-3). (ENG.). 24p. lib. bdg. 24.21 *(978-1-59197-792-6(4)*, SandCastle); 23p. pap. 48.42 *(978-1-59197-898-5(X))* ABDO Publishing Co.

—Gwen the Hen, 1 vol. (First Rhymes Ser.). (Illus.). (J). (gr. k-3). 2006. (ENG.). 24p. lib. bdg. 24.21 *(978-1-59679-487-0(9)*, SandCastle) 2005. 23p. pap. 48.42 *(978-1-59679-488-7(7))* ABDO Publishing Co.

—The Jelly Bean Machine, 1 vol. 2005. (Rhyme Time Ser.). (Illus.). (J). (gr. k-3). (ENG.). 24p. lib. bdg. 24.21 *(978-1-59197-795-7(9)*, SandCastle); 23p. pap. 48.42 *(978-1-59197-901-2(3))* ABDO Publishing Co.

—Jump from the Stump, 1 vol. (First Rhymes Ser.). (Illus.). (J). (gr. k-3). 2006. (ENG.). 24p. lib. bdg. 24.21 *(978-1-59679-485-6(2)*, SandCastle) 2005. 23p. pap. 48.42 *(978-1-59679-486-3(0))* ABDO Publishing Co.

—Knead with Speed, Chef Mead!, 1 vol. 2005. (Rhyme Time Ser.). (Illus.). (J). (gr. k-3). (ENG.). 24p. lib. bdg. 24.21 *(978-1-59197-799-5(1)*, SandCastle); 23p. pap. 48.42 *(978-1-59197-905-0(6))* ABDO Publishing Co.

—The Mermaid Parade, 1 vol. 2005. (Rhyme Time Ser.). (Illus.). (J). (gr. k-3). (ENG.). 24p. lib. bdg. 24.21 *(978-1-59197-804-6(1)*, SandCastle); 23p. pap. 48.42 *(978-1-59197-910-4(2))* ABDO Publishing Co.

—Moe's Toes Froze, 1 vol. 2005. (Rhyme Time Ser.). (Illus.). (J). (gr. k-3). (ENG.). 24p. lib. bdg. 24.21 *(978-1-59197-805-3(X)*, SandCastle); 23p. pap. 48.42 *(978-1-59197-911-1(0))* ABDO Publishing Co.

—The Pin in the Bin, 1 vol. (First Rhymes Ser.). (Illus.). (J). (gr. k-3). 2006. (ENG.). 24p. lib. bdg. 24.21 *(978-1-59679-539-6(5)*, SandCastle) 2005. 23p. pap. 48.42 *(978-1-59679-540-2(9))* ABDO Publishing Co.

—The Sheep Is Asleep, 1 vol. (First Rhymes Ser.). (Illus.). (J). (gr. k-3). 2006. (ENG.). 24p. lib. bdg. 24.21 *(978-1-59679-521-1(2)*, SandCastle) 2005. 23p. pap. 48.42 *(978-1-59679-522-8(0))* ABDO Publishing Co.

—Squeak from My Cheek, 1 vol. 2005. (Rhyme Time Ser.). (Illus.). (J). (gr. k-3). (ENG.). 24p. lib. bdg. 24.21 *(978-1-59197-817-6(3)*, SandCastle); 23p. pap. 48.42 *(978-1-59197-923-4(4))* ABDO Publishing Co.

—The Tweet Fleet, 1 vol. 2006. (First Rhymes Ser.). (ENG., Illus.). 24p. (J). (gr. k-3). lib. bdg. 24.21 *(978-1-59679-523-5(9)*, SandCastle) ABDO Publishing Co.

—The Tweet Fleet (6-pack) 2005. (First Rhymes Ser.). (Illus.). 23p. (J). pap. 48.42 *(978-1-59679-524-2(7))* ABDO Publishing Co.

Hanson, Anders. Adell & the Secret Well. (First Rhymes Ser.). (Illus.). (J). (gr. k-3). 2006. (ENG.). 24p. lib. bdg. 24.21 *(978-1-59679-447-4(X)*, SandCastle) 2005. 23p. pap. 48.42 *(978-1-59679-448-1(8))* ABDO Publishing Co.

—A Career for Mr. Lear, 1 vol. 2005. (Rhyme Time Ser.). (Illus.). (J). (gr. k-3). (ENG.). 24p. lib. bdg. 24.21 *(978-1-59197-779-7(7)*, SandCastle); 23p. pap. 48.42 *(978-1-59197-885-5(8))* ABDO Publishing Co.

—Chuck Has a Big Truck, 1 vol. (First Rhymes Ser.). (J). (gr. k-3). 2006. (ENG.). 24p. lib. bdg. 24.21 *(978-1-59679-463-4(1)*, SandCastle) 2005. 23p. pap. 48.42 *(978-1-59679-464-1(X))* ABDO Publishing Co.

—Claire's Bear Scare, 1 vol. 2005. (Rhyme Time Ser.). (ENG., Illus.). 24p. (J). (gr. k-3). lib. bdg. 24.21 *(978-1-59197-780-3(0)*, SandCastle) ABDO Publishing Co.

—The Cow with a Plow, 1 vol. (First Rhymes Ser.). (Illus.). (J). (gr. k-3). 2006. (ENG.). 24p. lib. bdg. 24.21 *(978-1-59679-465-8(8)*, SandCastle) 2005. 23p. pap. 48.42 *(978-1-59679-466-5(6))* ABDO Publishing Co.

—The Deer on Mount Ranier, 1 vol. 2005. (Rhyme Time Ser.). (ENG., Illus.). 24p. (J). (gr. k-3). lib. bdg. 24.21 *(978-1-59197-784-1(3)*, SandCastle) ABDO Publishing Co.

—Don't Hop with Pop!, 1 vol. (First Rhymes Ser.). (Illus.). (J). (gr. k-3). 2006. (ENG.). 24p. lib. bdg. 24.21 *(978-1-59679-471-9(2)*, SandCastle) 2005. 23p. pap. 48.42 *(978-1-59679-472-6(0))* ABDO Publishing Co.

—Dunk-Tank Frank, 1 vol. (First Rhymes Ser.). (Illus.). (J). (gr. k-3). 2006. (ENG.). 24p. lib. bdg. 24.21 *(978-1-59679-475-7(5)*, SandCastle) 2005. 23p. pap. 48.42 *(978-1-59679-476-4(3))* ABDO Publishing Co.

—Elaine's Rain Cane, 1 vol. 2005. (Rhyme Time Ser.). (Illus.). (J). (gr. k-3). (ENG.). 24p. lib. bdg. 24.21 *(978-1-59197-788-9(6)*, SandCastle); 23p. pap. 48.42 *(978-1-59197-894-7(7))* ABDO Publishing Co.

—Eli & the High Pie, 1 vol. 2005. (Rhyme Time Ser.). (Illus.). (J). (gr. k-3). (ENG.). 24p. lib. bdg. 24.21 *(978-1-59197-789-6(4)*, SandCastle); 23p. pap. 48.42 *(978-1-59197-895-4(5))* ABDO Publishing Co.

—Hun Plays One-on — One, 1 vol. 2005. (Rhyme Time Ser.). (ENG., Illus.). 24p. (J). (gr. k-3). lib. bdg. 24.21 *(978-1-59197-794-0(0)*, SandCastle) ABDO Publishing Co.

—The Hun Plays One-On-One. 2005. (See It, Say It, Hear It, Read It! Ser.). (Illus.). 23p. (J). pap. 48.42 *(978-1-59197-900-5(5))* ABDO Publishing Co.

—Jill & the Giant Spill, 1 vol. (First Rhymes Ser.). (Illus.). (J). (gr. k-3). 2006. (ENG.). 24p. lib. bdg. 24.21 *(978-1-59679-491-7(7)*, SandCastle) 2005. 23p. pap. 48.42 *(978-1-59679-492-4(5))* ABDO Publishing Co.

—Joe Grows Tomatoes, 1 vol. 2005. (Rhyme Time Ser.). (Illus.). (J). (gr. k-3). (ENG.). 24p. lib. bdg. 24.21 *(978-1-59197-796-4(7)*, SandCastle); 23p. pap. 48.42 *(978-1-59197-902-9(1))* ABDO Publishing Co.

—Kay's Maze Phase, 1 vol. 2005. (Rhyme Time Ser.). (Illus.). (J). (gr. k-3). (ENG.). 24p. lib. bdg. 24.21 *(978-1-59197-798-8(3)*, SandCastle); 23p. pap. 48.42 *(978-1-59197-904-3(8))* ABDO Publishing Co.

—Let's Sled Instead, 1 vol. 2005. (Rhyme Time Ser.). (Illus.). (J). (gr. k-3). (ENG.). 24p. lib. bdg. 24.21 *(978-1-59197-802-2(5)*, SandCastle); 23p. pap. 48.42 *(978-1-59197-908-1(0))* ABDO Publishing Co.

—May by the Bay, 1 vol. (First Rhymes Ser.). (Illus.). (J). (gr. k-3). 2006. (ENG.). 24p. lib. bdg. 24.21 *(978-1-59679-495-5(X)*, SandCastle) 2005. 23p. pap. 48.42 *(978-1-59679-496-2(8))* ABDO Publishing Co.

—Nate Is Great. 2005. (Rhyme Time Ser.). (Illus.). (J). (gr. k-3). (ENG.). 24p. lib. bdg. 24.21 *(978-1-59197-807-7(6)*, SandCastle); 23p. pap. 48.42 *(978-1-59197-913-5(7))* ABDO Publishing Co.

—Neil & His Meal Mobile, 1 vol. 2005. (Rhyme Time Ser.). (Illus.). (J). (gr. k-3). (ENG.). 24p. lib. bdg. 24.21 *(978-1-59197-808-4(4)*, SandCastle); 23p. pap. 48.42 *(978-1-59197-914-2(5))* ABDO Publishing Co.

—The Owl Swings a Dowel, 1 vol. 2005. (Rhyme Time Ser.). (Illus.). (J). (gr. k-3). (ENG.). 24p. lib. bdg. 24.21 *(978-1-59197-809-1(2)*, SandCastle); 23p. pap. 48.42 *(978-1-59197-915-9(3))* ABDO Publishing Co.

—The Pest with a Vest, 1 vol. (First Rhymes Ser.). (Illus.). (J). (gr. k-3). 2006. (ENG.). 24p. lib. bdg. 24.21 *(978-1-59679-503-7(4)*, SandCastle) 2005. 23p. pap. 48.42 *(978-1-59679-504-4(2))* ABDO Publishing Co.

—The Pig with a Wig. 2005. (First Rhymes Ser.). (Illus.). 23p. (J). 48.42 *(978-1-59679-508-2(5))* ABDO Publishing Co.

—The Pig with the Wig, 1 vol. 2006. (First Rhymes Ser.). (ENG., Illus.). 24p. (J). (gr. k-3). lib. bdg. 24.21 *(978-1-59679-507-5(7)*, SandCastle) ABDO Publishing Co.

—The Pink Mink, 1 vol. (First Rhymes Ser.). (Illus.). (J). (gr. k-3). 2006. (ENG.). 24p. lib. bdg. 24.21 *(978-1-59679-509-9(3)*, SandCastle) 2005. 23p. pap. 48.42 *(978-1-59679-510-5(7))* ABDO Publishing Co.

—Rob the Blob, 1 vol. 2006. (First Rhymes Ser.). (Illus.). (J). (gr. k-3). (ENG.). 24p. lib. bdg. 24.21 *(978-1-59679-477-1(1)*, SandCastle); 23p. pap. 48.42 *(978-1-59679-478-8(X))* ABDO Publishing Co.

—Simone on the Throne, 1 vol. (First Rhymes Ser.). (Illus.). (J). (gr. k-3). 2006. (ENG.). 24p. lib. bdg. 24.21 *(978-1-59679-505-1(0)*, SandCastle) 2005. 23p. pap. 48.42 *(978-1-59679-506-8(9))* ABDO Publishing Co.

—The Waste Is Traced, 1 vol. 2005. (Rhyme Time Ser.). (Illus.). (J). (gr. k-3). (ENG.). 24p. lib. bdg. 24.21 *(978-1-59197-820-6(3)*, SandCastle); 23p. pap. 48.42 *(978-1-59197-926-5(9))* ABDO Publishing Co.

Hanson, Anders, et al. First Rhymes (set of 47 Titles) 2006. (First Rhymes Ser.: 47). (ENG.). 24p. (J). (gr. k-3). lib. bdg. 1137.87 *(978-1-59679-446-7(1)*, SandCastle) ABDO Publishing Co.

Harris, Trudy. The Royal Treasure Measure. Stevanovic, Ivica, illus. 2012. (Math Is Fun! Ser.). (ENG.). 32p. (gr. k-2). lib. bdg. 16.95 *(978-0-7613-6806-9(X)*, Millbrook Pr.) Lerner Publishing Group.

Kertell, Lynn Maslen. Rhyming Words. Sullivan, Dana, illus. 2013. (Bob Bks.). (ENG.). 16p. (J). (gr. -1-k). pap. 16.99 *(978-0-545-51322-7(7))* Scholastic, Inc.

Kompelien, Tracy. A Calico in the Window, 1 vol. 2005. (Rhyme Time Ser.). (Illus.). (J). (gr. k-3). (ENG.). 24p. lib. bdg. 24.21 *(978-1-59197-778-0(9)*, SandCastle); 23p. pap. 48.42 *(978-1-59197-884-8(X))* ABDO Publishing Co.

—Dwight & the Magic Kite, 1 vol. 2005. (Rhyme Time Ser.). (ENG., Illus.). 24p. (J). (gr. k-3). lib. bdg. 24.21 *(978-1-59197-787-2(8)*, SandCastle) ABDO Publishing Co.

—The Mole with a Goal, 1 vol. 2005. (Rhyme Time Ser.). (Illus.). (J). (gr. k-3). (ENG.). 24p. lib. bdg. 24.21 *(978-1-59197-806-0(8)*, SandCastle); 23p. pap. 48.42 *(978-1-59197-912-8(9))* ABDO Publishing Co.

—Scott the Astronaut, 1 vol. 2005. (Rhyme Time Ser.). (Illus.). (J). (gr. k-3). (ENG.). 24p. lib. bdg. 24.21 *(978-1-59197-815-2(7)*, SandCastle); 23p. pap. 48.42 *(978-1-59197-921-0(8))* ABDO Publishing Co.

—The Thumb & His Chum, 1 vol. 2005. (Rhyme Time Ser.). (ENG., Illus.). 24p. (J). (gr. k-3). lib. bdg. 24.21 *(978-1-59197-819-0(X)*, SandCastle) ABDO Publishing Co.

—The Yaks Relax, 1 vol. 2005. (Rhyme Time Ser.). (Illus.). (J). (gr. k-3). (ENG.). 24p. lib. bdg. 24.21 *(978-1-59197-821-3(1)*, SandCastle); 23p. pap. 48.42 *(978-1-59197-927-2(7))* ABDO Publishing Co.

Rosenthal, Betsy R. An Ambush of Tigers: A Wild Gathering of Collective Nouns. Jago, illus. 2015. (ENG.). 32p. (J). (gr. k-3). lib. bdg. 19.99 *(978-1-4677-1464-8(X)*, Millbrook Pr.) Lerner Publishing Group.

Ryan, Pam Muñoz. Our California. López, Rafael, illus. 2008. (ENG.). 48p. (J). (gr. 1-4). 18.95 *(978-1-58089-116-5(0))*; per. 9.95 *(978-1-58089-117-2(9))* Charlesbridge Publishing, Inc.

Salzmann, Mary Elizabeth. Bee & Flea Go to the Sea, 1 vol. 2005. (Rhyme Time Ser.). (Illus.). (J). (gr. k-3). (ENG.). 24p. lib. bdg. 24.21 *(978-1-59197-776-6(2)*, SandCastle); 23p. pap. 48.42 *(978-1-59197-882-4(3))* ABDO Publishing Co.

—Cash for Trash, 1 vol. (First Rhymes Ser.). (Illus.). (J). (gr. k-3). 2006. (ENG.). 24p. lib. bdg. 24.21 *(978-1-59679-457-3(7)*, SandCastle) 2005. 23p. pap. 48.42 *(978-1-59679-458-0(5))* ABDO Publishing Co.

—The Chap & the Cap, 1 vol. (First Rhymes Ser.). (Illus.). (J). (gr. k-3). 2006. (ENG.). 24p. lib. bdg. 24.21 *(978-1-59679-459-7(3)*, SandCastle) 2005. 23p. pap. 48.42 *(978-1-59679-460-3(7))* ABDO Publishing Co.

—Don't Sneeze on Skis, 1 vol. 2005. (Rhyme Time Ser.). (ENG., Illus.). 24p. (J). (gr. k-3). lib. bdg. 24.21 *(978-1-59197-785-8(1)*, SandCastle) ABDO Publishing Co.

—The Fan in the Can, 1 vol. (First Rhymes Ser.). (Illus.). (J). (gr. k-3). 2006. (ENG.). 24p. lib. bdg. 24.21 *(978-1-59679-479-5(8)*, SandCastle) 2005. 23p. pap. 48.42 *(978-1-59679-480-1(1))* ABDO Publishing Co.

—Fay Loves Ballet, 1 vol. 2005. (Rhyme Time Ser.). (ENG., Illus.). 24p. (J). (gr. k-3). lib. bdg. 24.21 *(978-1-59197-790-2(8)*, SandCastle) ABDO Publishing Co.

—Kangaroo & the Crew, 1 vol. 2005. (Rhyme Time Ser.). (Illus.). (J). (gr. k-3). (ENG.). 24p. lib. bdg. 24.21 *(978-1-59197-797-1(5)*, SandCastle); 23p. pap. 48.42 *(978-1-59197-903-6(X))* ABDO Publishing Co.

—Kyle Wears a Smile, 1 vol. 2005. (Rhyme Time Ser.). (Illus.). (J). (gr. k-3). (ENG.). 24p. lib. bdg. 24.21 *(978-1-59197-800-8(9)*, SandCastle); 23p. pap. 48.42 *(978-1-59197-906-7(4))* ABDO Publishing Co.

—Lady Bauer in the Tower, 1 vol. 2005. (Rhyme Time Ser.). (Illus.). (J). (gr. k-3). (ENG.). 24p. lib. bdg. 24.21 *(978-1-59197-801-5(7)*, SandCastle); 23p. pap. 48.42 *(978-1-59197-907-4(2))* ABDO Publishing Co.

—Nate, Let's Skate, 1 vol. (First Rhymes Ser.). (Illus.). (J). (gr. k-3). 2006. (ENG.). 24p. lib. bdg. 24.21 *(978-1-59679-497-9(6)*, SandCastle) 2005. 23p. pap. 48.42 *(978-1-59679-498-6(4))* ABDO Publishing Co.

—The Paw That Can Draw, 1 vol. (First Rhymes Ser.). (Illus.). (J). (gr. k-3). 2006. (ENG.). 24p. lib. bdg. 24.21 *(978-1-59679-501-3(8)*, SandCastle) 2005. 23p. pap. 48.42 *(978-1-59679-502-0(6))* ABDO Publishing Co.

—Pete the Parakeet, 1 vol. 2005. (Rhyme Time Ser.). (Illus.). (J). (gr. k-3). (ENG.). 24p. lib. bdg. 24.21 *(978-1-59197-811-4(4)*, SandCastle); 23p. pap. 48.42 *(978-1-59197-917-3(X))* ABDO Publishing Co.

—The Race for the Vase, 1 vol. 2005. (Rhyme Time Ser.). (Illus.). (J). (gr. k-3). (ENG.). 24p. lib. bdg. 24.21 *(978-1-59197-813-8(0)*, SandCastle); 23p. pap. 48.42 *(978-1-59197-919-7(6))* ABDO Publishing Co.

—The Ram & the Clam. 2005. (First Rhymes Ser.). (Illus.). 23p. (J). pap. 48.42 *(978-1-59679-518-1(2))* ABDO Publishing Co.

—The RAM & the Clam, 1 vol. 2006. (First Rhymes Ser.). (ENG., Illus.). 24p. (J). (gr. k-3). lib. bdg. 24.21 *(978-1-59679-517-4(4)*, SandCastle) ABDO Publishing Co.

—Scat the Fat Cat, 1 vol. (First Rhymes Ser.). (Illus.). (J). (gr. k-3). 2006. (ENG.). 24p. lib. bdg. 24.21 *(978-1-59679-519-8(0)*, SandCastle) 2005. 23p. pap. 48.42 *(978-1-59679-520-4(4))* ABDO Publishing Co.

—A Snack for Jack, 1 vol. (First Rhymes Ser.). (Illus.). (J). (gr. k-3). 2006. (ENG.). 24p. lib. bdg. 24.21 *(978-1-59679-527-3(1)*, SandCastle) 2005. 23p. pap. 48.42 *(978-1-59679-528-0(X))* ABDO Publishing Co.

—The Snail Tale, 1 vol. 2005. (Rhyme Time Ser.). (Illus.). (J). (gr. k-3). (ENG.). 24p. lib. bdg. 24.21 *(978-1-59197-816-9(5)*, SandCastle); 23p. pap. 48.42 *(978-1-59197-922-7(6))* ABDO Publishing Co.

—The Snake by the Lake, 1 vol. (First Rhymes Ser.). (Illus.). (J). (gr. k-3). 2006. (ENG.). 24p. lib. bdg. 24.21 *(978-1-59679-529-7(8)*, SandCastle) 2005. 23p. pap. 48.42 *(978-1-59679-530-3(1))* ABDO Publishing Co.

—A Stag in the Bag, 1 vol. (First Rhymes Ser.). (Illus.). (J). (gr. k-3). 2006. (ENG.). 24p. lib. bdg. 24.21 *(978-1-59679-531-0(X)*, SandCastle) 2005. 23p. pap. 48.42 *(978-1-59679-532-7(8))* ABDO Publishing Co.

—Thad & His Dad, 1 vol. (First Rhymes Ser.). (Illus.). (J). (gr. k-3). 2006. (ENG.). 24p. lib. bdg. 24.21 *(978-1-59679-537-2(9)*, SandCastle) 2005. 23p. pap. 48.42 *(978-1-59679-538-9(7))* ABDO Publishing Co.

—The Train to Spain, 1 vol. (First Rhymes Ser.). (Illus.). (J). (gr. k-3). 2006. (ENG.). 24p. lib. bdg. 24.21 *(978-1-59679-541-9(7)*, SandCastle) 2005. 23p. pap. 48.42 *(978-1-59679-542-6(5))* ABDO Publishing Co.

Scheunemann, Pam. The Band in the Sand. 2005. (First Rhymes Ser.). (Illus.). 23p. (J). pap. 48.42 *(978-1-59679-452-8(6))* ABDO Publishing Co.

—Band in the Sand, 1 vol. 2006. (First Rhymes Ser.). (ENG., Illus.). 24p. (J). (gr. k-3). lib. bdg. 24.21 *(978-1-59679-451-1(8)*, SandCastle) ABDO Publishing Co.

—The Chick on the Thick Brick, 1 vol. (First Rhymes Ser.). (Illus.). (J). (gr. k-3). 2006. (ENG.). 24p. lib. bdg. 24.21 *(978-1-59679-461-0(5)*, SandCastle) 2005. 23p. pap. 48.42 *(978-1-59679-462-7(3))* ABDO Publishing Co.

—The Crane Loves Grain, 1 vol. 2005. (Rhyme Time Ser.). (ENG., Illus.). 24p. (J). (gr. k-3). lib. bdg. 24.21 *(978-1-59197-781-0(9)*, SandCastle) ABDO Publishing Co.

—Drew & the Crew, 1 vol. (First Rhymes Ser.). (Illus.). (J). (gr. k-3). 2006. (ENG.). 24p. lib. bdg. 24.21 *(978-1-59679-473-3(9)*, SandCastle) 2005. 23p. pap. 48.42 *(978-1-59679-474-0(7))* ABDO Publishing Co.

—Four Soar & Roar, 1 vol. 2005. (Rhyme Time Ser.). (Illus.). (J). (gr. k-3). (ENG.). 24p. lib. bdg. 24.21 *(978-1-59197-791-9(6)*, SandCastle); 23p. pap. 48.42 *(978-1-59197-897-8(1))* ABDO Publishing Co.

—The Frog in the Clog, 1 vol. (First Rhymes Ser.). (Illus.). (J). (gr. k-3). 2006. (ENG.). 24p. lib. bdg. 24.21 *(978-1-59679-483-2(6)*, SandCastle) 2005. 23p. pap. 48.42 *(978-1-59679-484-9(4))* ABDO Publishing Co.

—The King on a Spring, 1 vol. (First Rhymes Ser.). (Illus.). (J). (gr. k-3). 2006. (ENG.). 24p. lib. bdg. 24.21 *(978-1-59679-493-1(3))* 2005. 23p. pap. 48.42 *(978-1-59679-494-8(1))* ABDO Publishing Co.

—Lou Flew Too!, 1 vol. 2005. (Rhyme Time Ser.). (Illus.). (J). (gr. k-3). (ENG.). 24p. lib. bdg. 24.21 *(978-1-59197-803-9(3)*, SandCastle); 23p. pap. 48.42 *(978-1-59197-909-8(9))* ABDO Publishing Co.

—The One-Cent Tent, 1 vol. (First Rhymes Ser.). (Illus.). (J). (gr. k-3). 2006. (ENG.). 24p. lib. bdg. 24.21 *(978-1-59679-499-3(2)*, SandCastle) 2005. 23p. pap. 48.42 *(978-1-59679-500-6(X))* ABDO Publishing Co.

—Peas & Cheese, 1 vol. 2005. (Rhyme Time Ser.). (Illus.). (J). (gr. k-3). (ENG.). 24p. lib. bdg. 24.21 *(978-1-59197-810-7(6)*, SandCastle); 23p. pap. 48.42 *(978-1-59197-916-6(1))* ABDO Publishing Co.

—The Pot with a Dot, 1 vol. (First Rhymes Ser.). (Illus.). (J). (gr. k-3). 2006. (ENG.). 24p. lib. bdg. 24.21 *(978-1-59679-511-2(5)*, SandCastle) 2005. 23p. pap. 48.42 *(978-1-59679-512-9(3))* ABDO Publishing Co.

—The Pug with a Mug, 1 vol. (First Rhymes Ser.). (Illus.). (J). (gr. k-3). 2006. (ENG.). 24p. lib. bdg. 24.21 *(978-1-59679-513-6(1)*, SandCastle) 2005. 23p. pap. 48.42 *(978-1-59679-514-3(X))* ABDO Publishing Co.

—The Raccoon & the Balloon, 1 vol. (First Rhymes Ser.). (Illus.). (J). (gr. k-3). 2006. (ENG.). 24p. lib. bdg. 24.21 *(978-1-59679-515-0(8)*, SandCastle) 2005. 23p. pap. 48.42 *(978-1-59679-516-7(6))* ABDO Publishing Co.

—The Rare Fair, 1 vol. 2005. (Rhyme Time Ser.). (Illus.). (J). (gr. k-3). (ENG.). 24p. lib. bdg. 24.21 *(978-1-59197-814-5(9)*, SandCastle); 23p. pap. 48.42 *(978-1-59197-918-0(8))* ABDO Publishing Co.

—The Skunk & His Junk, 1 vol. (First Rhymes Ser.). (Illus.). (J). (gr. k-3). 2006. (ENG.). 24p. lib. bdg. 24.21 *(978-1-59679-525-9(5)*, SandCastle) 2005. 23p. pap. 48.42 *(978-1-59679-526-6(3))* ABDO Publishing Co.

—The Sub Club, 1 vol. (First Rhymes Ser.). (Illus.). (J). (gr. k-3). 2006. (ENG.). 24p. lib. bdg. 24.21 *(978-1-59679-533-4(6)*, SandCastle) 2005. 23p. pap. 48.42 *(978-1-59679-534-1(4))* ABDO Publishing Co.

—Ted's Red Sled, 1 vol. (First Rhymes Ser.). (Illus.). (J). (gr. k-3). 2006. (ENG.). 24p. lib. bdg. 24.21 *(978-1-59679-535-8(2)*, SandCastle) 2005. 23p. pap. 48.42 *(978-1-59679-536-5(0))* ABDO Publishing Co.

—Tennis in Venice, 1 vol. 2005. (Rhyme Time Ser.). (Illus.). (J). (gr. k-3). (ENG.). 24p. lib. bdg. 24.21 *(978-1-59197-818-3(1)*, SandCastle); 23p. pap. 48.42 *(978-1-59197-924-1(2))* ABDO Publishing Co.

Shaskan, Trisha Speed. If You Were Alliteration. Gray, Sara, illus. 2008. (Word Fun Ser.). (ENG.). 24p. (gr. 2-4). lib. bdg. 27.99 *(978-1-4048-4097-3(4))* Picture Window Bks.

Sprick, Marilyn, et al. Rhyming Fun: Read Well Level K Unit 6 Storybook. Jerde, Susan, illus. 2003. (Read Well Level K Ser.). 20p. (J). *(978-1-57035-678-0(5))* Cambium Education, Inc.

Westberg, Jan. The Athlete with Big Feet, 1 vol. 2005. (Rhyme Time Ser.). (Illus.). (J). (gr. k-3). (ENG.). 24p. lib. bdg. 24.21 *(978-1-59197-774-2(6)*, SandCastle); 23p. pap. 48.42 *(978-1-59197-880-0(7))* ABDO Publishing Co.

—The Bale of Mail, 1 vol. 2005. (Rhyme Time Ser.). (Illus.). (J). (gr. k-3). (ENG.). 24p. lib. bdg. 24.21 *(978-1-59197-775-9(4)*, SandCastle); 23p. pap. 48.42 *(978-1-59197-881-7(5))* ABDO Publishing Co.

—Bo Loves to Row, 1 vol. 2005. (Rhyme Time Ser.). (Illus.). (J). (gr. k-3). (ENG.). 24p. lib. bdg. 24.21 *(978-1-59197-777-3(0)*, SandCastle); 23p. pap. 48.42 *(978-1-59197-883-1(1))* ABDO Publishing Co.

—Curious Miss Muss, 1 vol. 2005. (Rhyme Time Ser.). (ENG., Illus.). 24p. (J). (gr. k-3). lib. bdg. 24.21 *(978-1-59197-782-7(7)*, SandCastle) ABDO Publishing Co.

—The Cute Boot, 1 vol. 2005. (Rhyme Time Ser.). (ENG., Illus.). 24p. (J). (gr. k-3). lib. bdg. 24.21 *(978-1-59197-783-4(5)*, SandCastle) ABDO Publishing Co.

—Door to the Shore, 1 vol. 2005. (Rhyme Time Ser.). (ENG., Illus.). 24p. (J). (gr. k-3). lib. bdg. 24.21 *(978-1-59197-786-5(X)*, SandCastle) ABDO Publishing Co.

—Guy the Shy Fly. 2005. (Rhyme Time Ser.). (Illus.). (J). (gr. k-3). (ENG.). 24p. lib. bdg. 24.21 *(978-1-59197-793-3(2)*, SandCastle); 23p. pap. 48.42 *(978-1-59197-899-2(8))* ABDO Publishing Co.

—The Polite Knight, 1 vol. 2005. (Rhyme Time Ser.). (Illus.). (J). (gr. k-3). (ENG.). 24p. lib. bdg. 24.21 *(978-1-59197-812-1(2)*, SandCastle); 23p. pap. 48.42 *(978-1-59197-920-3(X))* ABDO Publishing Co.

ENGLISH LANGUAGE—RHYME—DICTIONARIES

Dictionary, Oxford, ed. Oxford First Rhyming Dictionary. 2014. (ENG., Illus.). 80p. pap. 12.95 *(978-0-19-273559-1(4))* Oxford Univ. Pr., Inc.

Zephaniah, Benjamin. Chambers Primary Rhyming Dictionary. 2004. (Illus.). 240p. *(978-0-550-10089-4(X)*, Chambers) Hodder & Stoughton.

ENGLISH LANGUAGE—SPELLING

Baniti, Nailah & Bayramoglu, Hatice. Nia's Dream. Bayramoglu, Hatice, illus. 2012. (Illus.). 26p. pap. 7.99 *(978-0-9853574-4-3(4))* Mountan Creek Pubns.

Barker, Ray & Moorcroft, Christine. Spelling First, Bk. 3. 2003. (ENG.). 48p. pap., stu. ed. *(978-0-7487-6816-5(5))* Nelson Thornes Ltd.

BJU Staff. Spelling Worktext Grd 2. 2004. pap. 12.50 *(978-1-57924-322-7(3))* BJU Pr.

—Spelling Worktext Grd 3. 2004. pap. 12.50 *(978-1-57924-340-1(1))* BJU Pr.

—Spelling Worktext Grd 4. 2004. pap. 12.50 *(978-1-57924-373-9(8))* BJU Pr.

—Spelling Worktext Grd 6. 2004. pap. 12.50 *(978-1-57924-410-1(6))* BJU Pr.

Blanchard, Cherie & Plant, Cherie A. Word Roots A2: Learning the Building Blocks of Better Spelling & Vocabulary. 2013. (Word Roots Ser.). 80p. (gr. 5-12). pap. 16.99 *(978-0-89455-865-8(X))* Critical Thinking Co., The.

—Word Roots B2 Bk. 2: Learning the Building Blocks of Better Spelling & Vocabulary. 2005. (Word Roots Ser.). 136p. (gr. 7-12). pap. 16.99 *(978-0-89455-866-5(8))* Critical Thinking Co., The.

Bluedorn, Harvey. Handy English Encoder Decoder: All the Spelling & Phonics Rules You Could Ever Want to Know. 2nd ed. 2004. 104p. per. 9.00 *(978-0-9743616-2-8(3))* Trivium Pursuit.

Buckton, Chris & Corbett, Pie. Searchlights for Spelling Year 2: For Interactive Whole-Class Teaching. 2003. (Searchlights for Spelling Ser.). (ENG., Illus.). cd-rom 108.25 *(978-0-521-75579-5(4))* Cambridge Univ. Pr.

Burr, Holly. If I Get to Be in Charge of Spelling. Abremski, Kathy, illus. 2012. 16p. pap. 10.95 *(978-1-61493-039-6(2))* Peppertree Pr., The.

Burt, A. & Hachette Children's Group. Spelling. (Illus.). 32p. (J). (gr. 4-6). pap. *(978-0-340-72651-8(2))* Hodder & Stoughton.

Cernak, Kim. Build-a-Skill Instant Books R-Controled Vowels & Vowel Digraphs. Shiotsu, Vicky & Faulkner, Stacey, eds. Campbell, Jenny & Tom, Darcy, illus. 2007. (J). 4.99 *(978-1-59198-413-9(0))* Creative Teaching Pr., Inc.

Chambers & Hawker, Gordon T. Chambers Spell It Yourself! 2007. (ENG.). 144p. pap. 8.95 *(978-0-550-10346-8(5)*, Chambers) Hodder & Stoughton GBR. Dist: Hachette Bk. Group.

Cleary, Brian P. Miss Pell Would Never Misspell & Other Painless Tricks for Memorizing How to Spell & Use Wily Words. Sandy, J. P., illus. 2011. (Adventures in Memory Ser.). (ENG.). 48p. (gr. 4-6). lib. bdg. 26.60 *(978-0-8225-7822-2(0))* Lerner Publishing Group.

Collins Dictionaries, Collins. Collins Spell Like a Champion. 2017. (ENG.). 320p. (J). (gr. 2). pap. 11.99 ***(978-0-00-824197-1(X))*** HarperCollins Pubs. Ltd. GBR. Dist: Independent Pubs. Group.

Collins Easy Learning, Collins Easy. Spelling Quick Quizzes Ages 5-7. 2017. (Collins Easy Learning KS1 Ser.). (ENG., Illus.). 32p. (J). (gr. k-2). pap. 6.99 *(978-0-00-821245-2(7))* HarperCollins Pubs. Ltd. GBR. Dist: Independent Pubs. Group.

—Spelling Word Searches Ages 5-7. 2017. (Collins Easy Learning KS1 Ser.). (ENG.). 32p. (J). (gr. k-2). pap. 6.99 ***(978-0-00-821264-3(3))*** HarperCollins Pubs. Ltd. GBR. Dist: Independent Pubs. Group.

—Spelling Word Searches Ages 7-9. 2017. (Collins Easy Learning KS2 Ser.). (ENG.). 32p. (J). (gr. 2-4). pap. 6.99 ***(978-0-00-821265-0(1))*** HarperCollins Pubs. Ltd. GBR. Dist: Independent Pubs. Group.

Collins Easy Learning Staff & Law, Karina. Spelling Ages 5-6. 2015. (Collins Easy Learning Ser.). (ENG.). 32p. (J). (gr. k-1). pap. 6.95 *(978-0-00-813436-5(7))* HarperCollins Pubs. Ltd. GBR. Dist: Independent Pubs. Group.

Collins UK Publishing Staff & Letts KS2 Staff. Grammar, Punctuation & Spelling. 2016. (Letts KS2 Success Ser.). (ENG.). 64p. (J). (gr. 3-6). pap. 8.95 *(978-1-84419-834-4(0))* HarperCollins Pubs. Ltd. GBR. Dist: Independent Pubs. Group.

Cundy, David. Animals Spell Love. 2016. (Illus.). 40p. (J). *(978-1-56792-586-9(3))* Godine, David R. Pub.

Cunningham, Patricia. Making Places. 2005. (Four-Blocks Ser.). (J). per. 24.99 *(978-1-59441-199-1(9)*, CD-104108) Four Blocks.

Curriculum Associates Staff, ed. Spelling Power Book H. 2004. pap., tchr. ed. 26.95 *(978-0-7609-0902-7(4))* Curriculum Assocs., LLC.

Dorling Kindersley Publishing Staff. Spell Check. 2016. (ENG.). 128p. (J). (gr. 2-4). pap. 12.99 *(978-1-4654-5083-8(1)*, DK Children) Dorling Kindersley Publishing, Inc.

—Spelling Games. 2015. (ENG.). 80p. (J). (gr. k-4). pap. 9.99 *(978-1-4654-3438-8(0)*, DK Children) Dorling Kindersley Publishing, Inc.

—10 Minutes a Day - Spelling. 2013. (ENG.). 80p. (J). (gr. 1-3). pap. 9.99 *(978-1-4654-1714-5(1)*, DK Children) Dorling Kindersley Publishing, Inc.

—10 Minutes a Day Spelling, Grade 4. 2013. (ENG.). 80p. (J). (gr. 4-7). pap. 9.99 *(978-1-4654-1715-2(X)*, DK Children) Dorling Kindersley Publishing, Inc.

Evan-Moor. Skill Sharpeners, Spell & Write, Grade 1. 2005. (ENG., Illus.). 144p. (J). pap. 9.99 *(978-1-59673-045-8(5)*, emc 4537) Evan-Moor Educational Pubs.

—Skill Sharpeners Spell & Write, Grade 2. 2005. (ENG.). 144p. (J). pap. 9.99 *(978-1-59673-046-5(3)*, emc 4538) Evan-Moor Educational Pubs.

—Skill Sharpeners, Spell & Write, Grade 3. 2005. (ENG.). 144p. (J). pap. 9.99 *(978-1-59673-047-2(1)*, emc 4539) Evan-Moor Educational Pubs.

—Skill Sharpeners Spell & Write, Grade 4. 2005. (ENG.). 144p. (J). pap. 9.99 *(978-1-59673-048-9(X)*, emc 4540) Evan-Moor Educational Pubs.

—Skill Sharpeners Spell & Write, Grade 5. 2005. (ENG., Illus.). 144p. (J). pap. 9.99 *(978-1-59673-049-6(8)*, emc 4542) Evan-Moor Educational Pubs.

—Skill Sharpeners, Spell & Write, Grade 6. 2005. (ENG., Illus.). 144p. (J). pap. 9.99 *(978-1-59673-050-2(1)*, emc 4542) Evan-Moor Educational Pubs.

—Skill Sharpeners Spell & Write Grade PreK. 2005. (Skill Sharpeners Ser.). (ENG., Illus.). 144p. (J). pap. 9.99 *(978-1-59673-043-4(9)*, emc 4535) Evan-Moor Educational Pubs.

Falletta, Bernadette. We Love to Read Stories Coloring Book & Word Search Puzzles. 2005. 23p. (J). 10.95 *(978-1-4116-6291-9(1))* Lulu Pr., Inc.

Gale, John E. Speedyread: A Phonics-Based Reading & Spelling Program. 2005. 353p. ring bd. 275.00 *(978-0-9777683-0-1(9))* Mirror Pond Publishing.

Gateman, Ryan, creator. Spelling the Number Words: From a Child's View. 2004. (Illus.). 24p. (J). 8.95 *(978-1-932226-23-2(0))* Wizard Academy Pr.

Gifford, Myrna. Spelling Families: A Read-and-Sing Book. Cooper, Frances, illus. 2003. 12p. (J). 9.95 *(978-0-9720763-6-4(0))* Action Factor, Inc.

Gobo, creator. My Magnetic Spelling Book Let's Pretend! 2006. (Illus.). 8p. (J). (gr. -1-3). 9.95 *(978-1-932915-18-1(4))* Sandvik Innovations, LLC.

Grambs, David L. & Levine, Ellen S. So You Think You Can Spell? Killer Quizzes for the Incurably Competitive & Overly Confident. 2009. (ENG.). 288p. (gr. 12-18). 13.95 *(978-0-399-53528-4(4)*, TarcherPerigee) Penguin Publishing Group.

Hall, Nancy. Spellwell B: Grade 3. 2004. (Spellwell Ser.). (J). pap., stu. ed. 6.65 *(978-0-8388-2193-0(6))* Educators Publishing Service, Inc.

Halverson, Jim. Spelling Works. 2013. (ENG.). 122p. (J). (gr. 5). pap. 14.99 *(978-0-9847753-4-7(X))* Better Karma, LLC.

HarperCollins UK. Phonics & Spelling. 2011. (Collins Practice Ser.). (ENG.). 96p. (J). pap. 11.99 *(978-0-00-745235-4(7))* HarperCollins Pubs. Ltd. GBR. Dist: Independent Pubs. Group.

Heembrock, Roberta. Why Kids Can't Spell: A Practical Guide to the Missing Component in Language Proficiency. 2008. (ENG.). 160p. 97.00 *(978-1-57886-844-5(0))*; pap. 37.00 *(978-1-57886-845-2(9))* Rowman & Littlefield Education.

Hinkler Books Staff, ed. Spelling. 2009. (ENG.). 24p. (J). 9.99 *(978-0-8249-1402-8(3)*, Ideal Pubns.) Worthy Publishing.

Hirschmann, Kris. Feed Me Words. Hindle, James K., illus. 2016. (Scripps National Spelling Bee Ser.). (ENG.). 96p. (J). 17.99 *(978-1-62672-173-9(4)*, 9781626721739) Roaring Brook Pr.

How to Spell, Bk. 1. 2004. (How to Teach Spelling Ser.). pap. 7.15 *(978-0-8388-1848-0(X))* Educators Publishing Service, Inc.

How to Spell: Grade 7-12, Bk. 4. 2004. (How to Teach Spelling Ser.). pap. 9.20 *(978-0-8388-1854-1(4))* Educators Publishing Service, Inc.

Hyperion Staff. Finger Spelling Pack. 2007. 16p. (J). (gr. -1-3). 6.99 *(978-1-4231-0249-6(5))* Hyperion Pr.

Kemmerer, Susan. Apples: Daily Spelling Drills for Secondary Students. 2nd ed. 2005. 172p. per. 14.95 *(978-0-9758543-0-3(5))* Schoolhouse Publishing.

Kottmeyer, William A. Basic Goals in Spelling: Grade 5. 8th ed. (J). 148.20 *(978-0-07-036155-3(X))* Macmillan/McGraw-Hill Schl. Div.

Major, Sarah. Easy-For-Me Children's Readers Set C. Major, Sarah, illus. 2012. (Illus.). pap. 52.95 *(978-1-936981-49-6(1))* Child1st Pubns., LLC.

Mancini, Joan. 25 Super Sight Word Songs & Mini-Books: Fun Songs Set to Favorite Tunes with Companion Read & Write Mini-Books That Teach Essential Sight Words. 2009. (ENG.). 112p. (gr. k-2). 20.99 *(978-0-545-10582-8(X)*, Teaching Resources) Scholastic, Inc.

Mayers, Shareen. Spelling & Phonics Age 5-6. 2013. (Letts Monster Practice Ser.). (ENG., Illus.). 48p. (J). (gr. k-1). pap. 6.99 *(978-1-84419-749-1(2))* HarperCollins Pubs. Ltd. GBR. Dist: Independent Pubs. Group.

—Spelling & Phonics Age 6-7. 2013. (Letts Monster Practice Ser.). (ENG., Illus.). 16p. (J). (gr. 1-2). pap. 6.99 *(978-1-84419-750-7(6))* HarperCollins Pubs. Ltd. GBR. Dist: Independent Pubs. Group.

Modern Curriculum Press Staff. MCP Spelling Workout. 3rd ed. (J). Bk. C. (gr. 3). stu. ed. 11.95 net. *(978-0-8136-2817-2(2))*Bk. D. (gr. 4). stu. ed. 11.95 net. *(978-0-8136-2818-9(0))*Bk. E. (gr. 5). stu. ed. 11.95 net. *(978-0-8136-2819-6(9))* Modern Curriculum Pr.

—McP Spelling Workout Student B, Bk. B. 3rd ed. (J). (gr. 2). 11.95 net. *(978-0-8136-2816-5(4))* Modern Curriculum Pr.

Perret, Fany. ABC Word Play. 2016. (ENG., Illus.). 18p. (J). (gr. -1-k). bds. 19.99 *(978-1-4521-4811-3(2))* Chronicle Bks. LLC.

Rasinski, Timothy V. Daily Word Ladders: 80+ Word Study Activities That Target Key Phonics Skills to Boost Young Learners' Reading, Writing & Spelling Confidence. 2012. (ENG.). 64p. (gr. k-1). pap. 14.99 *(978-0-545-22379-9(2)*, Teaching Resources) Scholastic, Inc.

—Daily Word Ladders, Grades 1-2: 150+ Word Study Activities That Help Kids Boost Reading, Vocabulary, Spelling & Phonics Skills. 2012. (ENG., Illus.). 176p. (gr. 1-2). 27.99 *(978-0-545-37486-6(3)*, Teaching Resources) Scholastic, Inc.

—Daily Word Ladders, Grades 4-6: 100 Word Study Activities That Help Kids Boost Reading, Vocabulary, Spelling & Phonics Skills. 2012. (ENG., Illus.). 112p. (gr. 4-6). 27.99 *(978-0-545-37488-0(X)*, Teaching Resources) Scholastic, Inc.

—Daily Word Ladders, Grades K-1: 80+ Word Study Activities That Target Key Phonics Skills to Boost Young Learners' Reading, Writing & Spelling Confidence. 2012. (ENG., Illus.). 96p. (gr. k-1). 27.99 *(978-0-545-37485-9(5)*, Teaching Resources) Scholastic, Inc.

—100 Reproducible Word Study Lessons That Help Kids Boost Reading, Vocabulary, Spelling & Phonics Skills - Independently! 2005. (Daily Word Ladders Ser.). (ENG., Illus.). 112p. (gr. 4-6). pap. 15.99 *(978-0-439-77345-4(8)*, Teaching Resources) Scholastic, Inc.

Read & Spell with Zoo-phonics. 2004. (J). cd-rom 29.95 *(978-1-886441-46-0(4))* Zoo-phonics, Inc.

Read & Spell with Zoo=Phonics Guide for CD-ROM. 2004. (J). 14.95 *(978-1-886441-45-3(6))* Zoo-phonics, Inc.

Ruscoe, Michael. Skating to Spelling Success. 2009. (Grammar All-Stars: Writing Tools Ser.). 32p. (J). (gr. 2-5). pap. 10.50 *(978-1-4339-2137-7(5))*; lib. bdg. 26.00 *(978-1-4339-1944-2(3))* Stevens, Gareth Publishing LLLP. (Gareth Stevens Learning Library).

Say It, Rhyme It, Spell It Game 2. 2005. (J). 49.95 *(978-1-58804-404-4(1))* P C I Education.

Scarborough. Target Spelling 1020. 2004. (Steck-Vaughn Target Spelling Ser.). (ENG., Illus.). 144p. (gr. 5-9). pap., stu. ed. 25.05 *(978-0-7398-9192-6(8))* Houghton Mifflin Harcourt Publishing Co.

—Target Spelling 180. 2004. (Steck-Vaughn Target Spelling Ser.). (ENG.). (gr. 2-5). 192p. pap., tchr. ed. 23.60 *(978-0-7398-9194-0(4))*; (Illus.). 144p. pap., stu. ed. 25.05 *(978-0-7398-9188-9(X))* Houghton Mifflin Harcourt Publishing Co.

—Target Spelling 360. 2004. (Steck-Vaughn Target Spelling Ser.). (ENG.). (gr. 2-6). 144p. pap. 26.05 *(978-0-7398-9189-6(8))*; 192p. pap., tchr. ed. 24.55 *(978-0-7398-9195-7(2))* Houghton Mifflin Harcourt Publishing Co.

—Target Spelling 540. 2004. (Steck-Vaughn Target Spelling Ser.). (ENG.). (gr. 3-7). 192p. pap., tchr. ed. 24.55 *(978-0-7398-9196-4(0))*; (Illus.). 144p. pap. 26.05 *(978-0-7398-9190-2(1))* Houghton Mifflin Harcourt Publishing Co.

—Target Spelling 780. 2004. (Steck-Vaughn Target Spelling Ser.). (ENG.). (gr. 4-8). 144p. pap. 26.05 *(978-0-7398-9191-9(X))*; 192p. pap., tchr. ed. 24.55 *(978-0-7398-9197-1(9))* Houghton Mifflin Harcourt Publishing Co.

School Zone Interactive Staff, et al. Spelling 1-2. 2006. (ENG.). 64p. (J). (gr. 1-3). 15.99 *(978-1-58947-827-5(4))* School Zone Publishing Co.

School Zone Publishing Company Staff. Spelling 2. (Illus.). (J). 19.99 incl. audio compact disk *(978-0-88743-939-1(X))* School Zone Publishing Co.

School Zone Staff, ed. Kindergarten Spelling Bee. 2006. (ENG.). 6p. (J). 5.99 *(978-1-58947-847-3(9))* School Zone Publishing Co.

SIPPS Beginning Package of Little Books. 2004. *(978-1-57621-458-9(3))* Center for the Collaborative Classroom.

SIPPS Beginning Reproducible Book. 2004. *(978-1-57621-459-6(1))* Center for the Collaborative Classroom.

Snashall, Sarah. Spelling Skills. 2017. (ENG.). 92p. (J). pap., tchr. ed. 36.99 ***(978-0-00-822309-0(2))*** HarperCollins Pubs. Ltd. GBR. Dist: Independent Pubs. Group.

Spelling Ad Libs. 2004. (J). pap. 10.95 *(978-1-56911-159-8(6))* Learning Resources, Inc.

SRA Publications Staff & McGraw-Hill Staff. Spelling Mastery. 4th ed. 2006. (Spelling Mastery Ser.). (ENG.). 64p. (gr. 1-1). pap., wbk. ed. 16.80 *(978-0-07-604481-8(5)*, 0076044815) McGraw-Hill Education.

Steck-Vaughn Staff. Language Art & Spelling, 8, Pack. 2004. pap. 68.00 *(978-0-7398-9933-5(3))* Harcourt Schl. Pubs.

—Language Arts & Spelling, 8 Packs. 2004. pap. 68.00 *(978-0-7398-9929-8(5))*; pap. 8.50 *(978-0-7398-9848-2(5))*; pap., tchr. ed. 10.00 *(978-0-7398-9904-5(X))* Harcourt Schl. Pubs.

Stoneman, Sonya. First Aid in Spelling. (Illus.). (J). pap. *(978-1-876367-53-4(9))* Wizard Bks.

Stride, Lottie. Write Every Time. 2017. (Buster Reference Ser.). (ENG., Illus.). 128p. (J). (gr. 3-7). pap. 8.99 ***(978-1-78055-469-3(9))*** O'Mara, Michael Bks., Ltd. GBR. Dist: Independent Pubs. Group.

Traditional Catholic Speller. (J). (gr. 1). wbk. ed. 12.00 *(978-1-931555-33-3(8))*; (J). (gr. 2). wbk. ed. 12.00 *(978-1-931555-34-0(6))*; (J). (gr. 3). wbk. ed. 12.00 *(978-1-931555-35-7(4))*; (J). (gr. 4). wbk. ed. 12.00 *(978-1-931555-36-4(2))*; (J). (gr. 5). wbk. ed. 12.00 *(978-1-931555-37-1(0))*; (J). (gr. 6). wbk. ed. 12.00 *(978-1-931555-38-8(9))*; (YA). (gr. 7). wbk. ed. 12.00 *(978-1-931555-39-5(7))*; (YA). (gr. 8). wbk. ed. 12.00 *(978-1-931555-40-1(0))* Our Lady of Victory Schl.

Traynor, Tracy. Cheese Please, Chimpanzees: Fun with Spelling. Bronfeyn, Lily, illus. 2008. (Milet Wordwise Ser.). (ENG.). 28p. (J). (gr. k-2). pap. 6.95 *(978-1-84059-511-6(6))* Milet Publishing.

Valentino, Catherine. Blue Ribbon Spelling & Vocabulary, Level 1. (J). pap. 7.95 *(978-0-86651-196-4(2))* Seymour, Dale Pubns.

Vickers, Rebecca. Punctuation & Spelling: Rules That Make Things Clear, 1 vol. 2013. (Find Your Way with Words Ser.). (ENG.). 56p. (gr. 6-7). 34.65 *(978-1-4329-7655-2(9))* Heinemann-Raintree.

Wagstaff, Janiel M. 85 Differentiated Word Sorts: One-Page Leveled Word Sorts for Building Decoding & Spelling Skills. 2016. (ENG., Illus.). 96p. (J). (gr. k-3). pap. 14.99 *(978-0-545-90736-1(5))* Scholastic, Inc.

West, Tracey. Lunchbox Words. Hindle, James K., illus. 2017. (Scripps National Spelling Bee Ser.). (ENG.). 144p. (J). pap. 10.99 ***(978-1-62672-718-2(X)***, 9781626727182) Roaring Brook Pr.

Whiteford, Rhona & Hachette Children's Group. Complete English, 3 bks. in 1. (Illus.). 96p. (YA). pap. 15.99 *(978-0-340-71582-6(0))* Hodder & Stoughton GBR. Dist: Trafalgar Square Publishing.

Whiteford, Rhona & Hodder Children's Books Staff. Spelling: Helping You Support Your Child in Year 6. 2003. (Hodder Home Learning Ser.). (ENG., Illus.). 32p. (J). (gr. 4-6). pap. 6.99 *(978-0-340-79184-4(5))* Hodder & Stoughton GBR. Dist: Hachette Bk. Group.

Yates, Irene. How to Be a Wizard at Spelling. 48p. (J). (gr. 2-6). pap. *(978-1-875739-65-3(3))* Wizard Bks.

Zoo-phonics Quick Tests for the Classroom. 2004. cd-rom *(978-1-886441-41-5(3))* Zoo-phonics, Inc.

ENGLISH LANGUAGE—STUDY AND TEACHING

Albright, Thomas B. Universal English: Second Language for All. unabr. l.t. ed. 2003. (Languages: Universal English for All). (ENM.). 128p. pap. 7.00 *(978-1-888264-17-3(9))* Twenty-First Century Co., The.

American Heritage Dictionary Editors. 100 Words Every Middle Schooler Should Know. 2010. (100 Words Ser.). (ENG.). 128p. (gr. 6-8). pap. 6.95 *(978-0-547-33322-9(6))* Houghton Mifflin Harcourt Publishing Co.

Arengo, Sue. Mansour & the Donkey. 2nd ed. 2012. (ENG., Illus.). 16p. pap., act. bk. ed. 6.19 *(978-0-19-423855-7(5))* Oxford Univ. Pr., Inc.

Barker, Chris & Mitchell, Libby. Cambridge Global English Stage 9 Workbook: For Cambridge Secondary 1 English As a Second Language. 2016. (ENG.). 128p. pap. 20.94 *(978-1-107-63520-3(9))* Cambridge Univ. Pr.

Beatty, Ken. Starship English, Student Book 4. 2012. (ENG., Illus.). 72p. (J). (gr. -1-3). pap. 27.75 incl. cd-rom *(978-1-74235-903-8(5))* Houghton Mifflin Harcourt Trade & Reference Pubs.

Big Blue Bedtime Book. 2007. (Illus.). 26p. (J). pap. 17.99 *(978-0-9793506-0-3(3))* Sportime International.

Brooks, Felicity. Easy English Words Sticker Book. 2012. (First Sticker Language Bks). 24p. (J). pap. 6.99 *(978-0-7945-3263-5(2)*, Usborne) EDC Publishing.

Chamberlain, Frances. Smarter Balanced Grade 7 ELA. 2017. (Smarter Balanced Ser.). (ENG.). 208p. (J). (gr. 7-7). pap. 14.99 ***(978-1-4380-1034-2(6))*** Barron's Educational Series, Inc.

Chavez, Sonia, et al. What Will He Wear? 2010. (Reach for Reading Ser.). (ENG., Illus.). 8p. (C). pap. 7.95 *(978-0-7362-7991-8(1))* CENGAGE Learning.

Diagramming. 2004. (Grammar Pocket Handbook Ser.). *(978-0-8294-0926-0(2))*; stu. ed., wbk. ed. *(978-0-8294-0950-5(5))* Loyola Pr.

Education.com. Wonderful Words: A Workbook of Spelling, Bit by Bit. 2015. (ENG.). 128p. (J). (gr. 2-2). pap. 7.99 *(978-0-486-80262-6(0))* Dover Pubns., Inc.

Embacher, Eric. Stowed Away, 1 vol. unabr. ed. 2012. (Astonishing Headlines Ser.). (ENG.). 92p. (YA). (gr. 9-12). 8.95 *(978-1-61651-925-4(8))* Saddleback Educational Publishing, Inc.

Far from the Madding Crowd: Teaching Unit. 2003. 92p. (YA). ring bd. *(978-1-58049-471-7(4)*, TU4714) Prestwick Hse., Inc.

Fare, Dennis & Cacciatore, Mark G. PARCC ELA/Literacy Assessments, Grades 9-12. 2013. (Common Core State Standards Ser.). (ENG.). 416p. (gr. 9-12). pap. 18.95 *(978-0-7386-1167-9(0))* Research & Education Assn.

Frino, Lucy. Kid's Box Level 2 Teacher's Book. 2nd rev. ed. 2014. (ENG.). 225p. pap. 59.00 *(978-1-107-66840-9(9))* Cambridge Univ. Pr.

Garcia, Mario, et al. My Family. 2010. (Reach for Reading Ser.). (ENG., Illus.). 8p. (C). pap. 7.95 *(978-0-7362-7985-7(7))* CENGAGE Learning.

Gonzalez, Tomás, et al. Family Feelings. 2010. (Reach for Reading Ser.). (ENG., Illus.). 8p. (C). pap. 7.95 *(978-0-7362-7986-4(5))* CENGAGE Learning.

Hamilton, Karen, et al. Inside Listening & Speaking, Level 3: The Academic Word List in Context. 2015. (ENG.). stu. ed. 50.50 *(978-0-19-471933-9(2))* Oxford Univ. Pr., Inc.

Hamlin, Daniel, et al. Inside Listening & Speaking, Level 4: The Academic Word List in Context. 2015. (ENG.). pap., stu. ed. 50.50 *(978-0-19-471943-8(X))* Oxford Univ. Pr., Inc.

Hansen, Jane, et al. The Prek-2 Writing Classroom: Growing Confident Writers. 2011. (ENG.). 128p. (gr. -1-2). pap. 18.99 *(978-0-545-20868-0(8)*, Teaching Resources) Scholastic, Inc.

Harcourt School Publishers Staff. Teacher's Edition Package: Texas Edition. 3rd ed. 2003. (gr. 1). tchr. ed. 237.70 *(978-0-15-320185-1(1))*; (gr. 2). 252.30 *(978-0-15-320186-8(X))*; (gr. 3). 252.30 *(978-0-15-320187-5(8))*; (gr. 4). 277.90 *(978-0-15-320188-2(6))* Harcourt Schl. Pubs.

Herman, Gail. Make-a-Splash Writing Rules. 2009. (Grammar All-Stars: Writing Tools Ser.). 32p. (J). (gr. 2-5). (ENG.). pap. 10.50 *(978-1-4339-2136-0(7))*; lib. bdg. 26.00 *(978-1-4339-1943-5(5))* Stevens, Gareth Publishing LLLP. (Gareth Stevens Learning Library).

—Snowboarding Similes & Metaphors. 2009. (Grammar All-Stars: Writing Tools Ser.). 32p. (J). (gr. 2-5). (ENG.). pap. 10.50 *(978-1-4339-2138-4(3))*; lib. bdg. 26.00 *(978-1-4339-1945-9(1))* Stevens, Gareth Publishing LLLP. (Gareth Stevens Learning Library).

Hirschmann, Kris. Spell Across America. Hindle, James K., illus. 2017. (Scripps National Spelling Bee Ser.). (ENG.). 96p. (J). 17.99 *(978-1-62672-175-3(0)*, 9781626721753) Roaring Brook Pr.

E
F
G

Holt, Rinehart and Winston Staff. Middle School Practice for Middle School English Subject Area. 3rd ed. 2003. (YA). (gr. 6-8). pap. 12.16 *(978-0-03-070908-1(3))* Holt McDougal.

Jarnow, Jill. Writing to Instruct. 2006. (Write Now: a Kid's Guide to Nonfiction Writing Ser.). (Illus.). 24p. (YA). (gr. 2-5). lib. bdg. 22.60 *(978-1-4042-2834-4(9))* Rosen Publishing Group, Inc., The.

Jordan, Sara & Gomez, Patricia. Bilingual Beginners: English-Spanish, 2 vols. abr. ed. 2010. (ENG & SPA.). 48p. (J). 17.95 *(978-1-55386-114-0(0)*, 1553861140) Jordan, Sara Publishing.

Kehl, Esther. The Amazing Action Alphabet Activities. Carlson, Andy, illus. 2009. 40p. (J). spiral bd. 12.50 *(978-0-9788089-1-4(6))* SeeHearDo Co., LLC, The.

Ladybird Books Staff. How to Use Ladybird Readers: A Teacher & Parent Guide. 2016. (Ladybird Readers Ser.). (ENG.). 16p. (J). pap. 5.99 *(978-0-241-26230-6(5))* Penguin Bks., Ltd. GBR. Dist: Independent Pubs. Group.

Lang. Arts: Student Testing Kit. 2004. (gr. 1-8). stu. ed. 5.00 *(978-0-86717-287-4(8)*, LD001, Lifepac) Alpha Omega Pubns., Inc.

Larson, Julie, et al. Jobs in Our Community. 2010. (Reach for Reading Ser.). (ENG., Illus.). 8p. (C). pap. 7.95 *(978-0-7362-7995-6(4))* CENGAGE Learning.

—Up in the Sky. 2010. (Reach for Reading Ser.). (ENG., Illus.). 8p. (C). pap. 7.95 *(978-0-7362-7998-7(9))* CENGAGE Learning.

Learning Company Books Staff, ed. Reader Rabbit: Phonics. 2003. (Illus.). 32p. (J). pap., wbk. ed. *(978-0-7630-7580-4(9))*; pap., wbk. ed. *(978-0-7630-7576-7(0))*; pap., wbk. ed. *(978-0-7630-7579-8(5))* Magma.

Lin, Aja, et al. What Do You See? 2010. (ENG., Illus.). 8p. (C). pap. 7.95 *(978-0-7362-7997-0(0))* CENGAGE Learning.

Lindeen, Mary. Mom, Pop, & Tot: Teaching Palindromes. 2016. (Playing with Words Ser.). (ENG.). 16p. (J). (gr. -1-2). 25.64 *(978-1-5038-0839-3(4)*, 210690) Child's World, Inc., The.

Loewen, Nancy. The BIG Problem (and the Squirrel Who Eventually Solved It) Understanding Adjectives & Adverbs. 2015. (Language on the Loose Ser.). (ENG., Illus.). 24p. (gr. 2-4). pap. 7.95 *(978-1-4795-6969-4(0))* Picture Window Bks.

Lopez, Juan, et al. School Tools. 2010. (Reach for Reading Ser.). (ENG., Illus.). 8p. (C). pap. 7.95 *(978-0-7362-7983-3(0))* CENGAGE Learning.

Marie-France, Marcie. Bilingual Beginners Kit: English-French, 2 vols. 2010. (FRE., Illus.). 48p. (J). 17.95 *(978-1-55386-120-1(5)*, 1553861205) Jordan, Sara Publishing.

—Bilingual Kids Beginners - English-French: Ready-to-Use Reproducible Worksheets & Exercises. Content-Based Units Making Language Acquisition Easy Fun. 2010. (FRE.). 64p. (J). 15.95 *(978-1-55386-122-5(1)*, 1553861221) Jordan, Sara Publishing.

Meister, Cari. Sasha Sings: Understanding Parts of a Sentence. Whitehouse, Ben, illus. 2015. (Language on the Loose Ser.). (ENG.). 24p. (gr. 2-4). pap. 7.95 *(978-1-4795-6968-7(2))* Picture Window Bks.

—They're up to Something in There: Understanding There, Their, & They're. Jagucki, Marek, illus. 2015. (Language on the Loose Ser.). (ENG.). 24p. (gr. 2-4). pap. 7.95 *(978-1-4795-6971-7(2))* Picture Window Bks.

Minden, Cecilia & Roth, Kate. How to Write about Your Adventure. 2011. (Explorer Junior Library: Language Arts Explorer Junior Ser.). (ENG.). 24p. (gr. 1-4). lib. bdg. 25.64 *(978-1-61080-106-5(7)*, 201114) Cherry Lake Publishing.

—How to Write an Essay. 2012. (Explorer Junior Library: Language Arts Explorer Junior Ser.). (ENG.). 24p. (gr. 1-4). 25.64 *(978-1-61080-492-9(9)*, 202102); pap. 12.79 *(978-1-61080-666-4(2)*, 202276) Cherry Lake Publishing.

Mocombe, Paul C. Mocombe's Reading Room Series Advance 1: Advance 1. 2008. 76p. 24.99 *(978-1-4363-4904-8(4))*; pap. 15.99 *(978-1-4363-4903-1(6))* Xlibris Corp.

My First 100 Words in French/English. 2003. (First Words & Pictures Book Ser.).Tr. of My First 100 Words. (FRE.). 32p. (J). 11.95 *(978-0-7525-7768-5(9))* Parragon, Inc.

NCPTA Staff, et al. English for the Brighter Child. (Illus.). 24p. pap. 6.99 *(978-0-340-71679-3(7)*, Coronet) Hodder & Stoughton GBR. Dist: Trafalgar Square Publishing.

Newmark Learning, compiled by. Rising Readers Set A Sets Of 6. 2009. (Rising Readers Ser.). (J). (gr. -1-k). 1005.12 net. *(978-1-60719-110-0(5))* Newmark Learning LLC.

Nixon, Caroline. Kid's Box Level 3 Activity Book with Online Resources. 2nd ed. 2014. (ENG.). 88p. pap. 29.50 *(978-1-107-64400-7(3))* Cambridge Univ. Pr.

—Kid's Box Level 3 Pupil's Book. 2nd ed. 2014. (ENG.). 87p. pap. 29.75 *(978-1-107-65450-1(5))* Cambridge Univ. Pr.

Northcott, Richard. In the Mountains. Geatches, Hazel, ed. 2013. (ENG.). 40p. pap. 9.38 *(978-0-19-464687-1(4))* Oxford Univ. Pr., Inc.

O'Keefe, Vivien. Short & Sweet. 2011. pap. *(978-1-74284-091-8(4))* ReadOnTime.

Oxford, ed. First Language English for IGCSERG Evaluation Pack. 2014. (ENG.). 336p. 42.00 *(978-0-19-838904-0(3))* Oxford Univ. Pr., Inc.

Parker, Tyrone, et al. Community Places. 2010. (Reach for Reading Ser.). (ENG., Illus.). 8p. (C). pap. 7.95 *(978-0-7362-7993-2(8))* CENGAGE Learning.

Rasinski, Timothy V. Daily Word Ladders: 80+ Word Study Activities That Target Key Phonics Skills to Boost Young Learners' Reading, Writing & Spelling Confidence. 2012. (ENG.). 64p. (gr. k-1). pap. 14.99 *(978-0-545-22379-9(2)*, Teaching Resources) Scholastic, Inc.

—Daily Word Ladders, Grades 1-2: 150+ Word Study Activities That Help Kids Boost Reading, Vocabulary, Spelling & Phonics Skills. 2012. (ENG., Illus.). 176p. (gr. 1-2). 27.99 *(978-0-545-37486-6(3)*, Teaching Resources) Scholastic, Inc.

—Daily Word Ladders, Grades 4-6: 100 Word Study Activities That Help Kids Boost Reading, Vocabulary, Spelling & Phonics Skills. 2012. (ENG., Illus.). 112p. (gr. 4-6). 27.99 *(978-0-545-37488-0(X)*, Teaching Resources) Scholastic, Inc.

—Daily Word Ladders, Grades K-1: 80+ Word Study Activities That Target Key Phonics Skills to Boost Young Learners' Reading, Writing & Spelling Confidence. 2012. (ENG., Illus.). 96p. (gr. k-1). 27.99 *(978-0-545-37485-9(5)*, Teaching Resources) Scholastic, Inc.

Richardson, Jan. The Guided Reading Teacher's Companion: Prompts, Discussion Starters & Teaching Points. 2016. (ENG.). 26p. (gr. k-8). pap. 19.99 *(978-1-338-11226-9(0)*, Scholastic Professional) Scholastic, Inc.

Roy, Jennifer Rozines & Haney, Johannah. Sharpen Your Essay Writing Skills. 2011. (Sharpen Your Writing Skills Ser.). (Illus.). 64p. (J). (gr. 6-18). pap. 8.95 *(978-1-59845-342-3(4))* Enslow Pubs., Inc.

—You Can Write an Essay. 2004. (You Can Write Ser.). (Illus.). 64p. (J). lib. bdg. 23.94 *(978-0-7660-2091-7(6))* Enslow Pubs., Inc.

Rustad, Martha E. H. Language Arts, 1 vol. 2014. (Language Arts Ser.). (ENG.). 24p. (gr. k-1). 106.60 *(978-1-4914-0679-3(8)*, Pebble Plus) Capstone Press of Coughlan Cos.

Santiano, Carlos, et al. Where Is He? 2010. (Reach for Reading Ser.). (ENG., Illus.). 8p. (C). pap. 7.95 *(978-0-7362-7994-9(6))* CENGAGE Learning.

Saslow, Joan M. & Collins, Tim. Workplace Plus 1 with Grammar Booster, 4 vols. 2004. (ENG., Illus.). (C). pap. 31.33 *(978-0-13-192799-5(X))* Prentice Hall, ESL Dept.

Sweeney, Jacqueline. Perfect Poetry Playlets: Read-Aloud Reproducible Mini Plays That Boost All-Important Speaking & Fluency Skills to Meet the Common Core. 2014. (ENG.). 80p. (gr. 3-5). pap. 12.99 *(978-0-545-47084-1(6)*, Teaching Resources) Scholastic, Inc.

Tears of a Tiger: Teaching Unit. 2003. 88p. (YA). ring bd. *(978-1-58049-429-8(3)*, TU4293) Prestwick Hse., Inc.

Villegas, Corrina, et al. What Will I Be? 2010. (Reach for Reading Ser.). (ENG., Illus.). 8p. (C). pap. 7.95 *(978-0-7362-7996-3(2))* CENGAGE Learning.

Walch Publishing Staff. Humanities. 2007. (Daily Warm-Ups Ser.). 197p. (gr. 5-6). tchr. ed., spiral bd. 24.99 *(978-0-8251-6449-1(4))* Walch Education.

Weisman, Linda Klein. Yes, I Can Read! 2013. (Illus.). 614p. pap. 29.99 *(978-1-4669-8073-0(7))* Trafford Publishing.

West, Tracey. Lunchbox Words. Hindle, James K., illus. 2017. (Scripps National Spelling Bee Ser.). (ENG.). 144p. (J). pap. 10.99 ***(978-1-62672-718-2(X)***, 9781626727182) Roaring Brook Pr.

What Is a Tangaroo. 2007. (Illus.). 32p. (J). pap. 24.99 *(978-0-9793506-2-7(X))* Sportime International.

World Book, Inc. Staff. The Wonderful World of English. Date not set. (Illus.). 35p. (J). (gr. 1-5). *(978-0-7166-5301-1(X)*, 6164) World Bk., Inc.

Yang, Maya, et al. Let's Grow! 2010. (Reach for Reading Ser.). (ENG., Illus.). 8p. (C). pap. 7.95 *(978-0-7362-7990-1(3))* CENGAGE Learning.

Year 1 Impact Intervention. 2017. (ENG.). 96p. (J). (gr. k-1). pap. 43.99 ***(978-0-00-822838-5(8))*** HarperCollins Pubs. Ltd. GBR. Dist: Independent Pubs. Group.

Yee, Soo, et al. School Places. 2010. (Reach for Reading Ser.). (ENG., Illus.). 8p. (C). pap. 7.95 *(978-0-7362-7984-0(9))* CENGAGE Learning.

ENGLISH LANGUAGE—SYNONYMS AND ANTONYMS

ABDO Publishing Company Staff & Kompelien, Tracy. Synonyms, 1 vol. 2007. (Synonyms Ser.: 6). (ENG.). 24p. (J). (gr. k-3). lib. bdg. 145.26 *(978-1-59928-727-0(7)*, SandCastle) ABDO Publishing Co.

ABDO Publishing Company Staff & Salzmann, Mary Elizabeth. Antonyms, 1 vol. 2007. (Antonyms Ser.: 6). (ENG.). 24p. (J). (gr. k-3). lib. bdg. 145.26 *(978-1-59928-713-3(7)*, SandCastle) ABDO Publishing Co.

All about Opposites. 2016. (All about Opposites Ser.). 24p. (J). pap. 56.10 *(978-0-7660-8417-9(5))* Enslow Pubs., Inc.

Arps, Melissa. Opposites. 2006. (Illus.). (J). *(978-0-7364-2382-3(6))* Random Hse. Children's Bks.

Baruzzi, Agnese. Opposites: A Cut-Paper Book. Baruzzi, Agnese, illus. 2013. (ENG., Illus.). 10p. (J). (— 1). 15.99 *(978-1-85707-803-9(9))* Tango Bks. GBR. Dist: Independent Pubs. Group.

Beal, George. Kingfisher First Thesaurus. Chatterton, Martin, illus. 2011. (Kingfisher First Reference Ser.). (ENG.). 144p. (J). (gr. k-3). pap. 10.99 *(978-0-7534-6586-8(8)*, 9780753465868, Kingfisher) Roaring Brook Pr.

Bentley, Joyce. Soft. 2006. (Things Around Us Ser.). (J). *(978-1-59389-278-4(0))* Chrysalis Education.

—Wet. 2006. (Things Around Us Ser.). (J). *(978-1-59389-279-1(9))* Chrysalis Education.

Blackstone, Stella. You & Me. Manna, Giovanni, illus. 2009. (ENG.). 32p. (J). 14.99 *(978-1-84686-336-3(8))* Barefoot Bks., Inc.

Blackstone, Stella & Bauer, Stephanie. Octopus Opposites. Bauer, Stephanie, illus. 2011. (ENG., Illus.). 32p. (J). (gr. -1-k). 8.99 *(978-1-84686-591-6(3))* Barefoot Bks., Inc.

Bollard, John. Scholastic Student Thesaurus. rev. ed. 2007. (ENG.). 208p. (J). (gr. 7). 16.99 *(978-0-439-02588-1(5))* Scholastic, Inc.

Bollard, John K. & Bollard, John. Scholastic Children's Thesaurus. Reed, Mike, illus. rev. ed. 2006. (ENG.). 240p. (J). (gr. 3-7). 17.99 *(978-0-439-79831-0(0)*, Scholastic Reference) Scholastic, Inc.

Brown, Janet Allison. My First Book of Opposites. Endersby, Frank, illus. 2004. (Early Learning Ser.). 18p. (J). bds. 5.99 *(978-1-85854-530-1(7))* Brimax Books Ltd. GBR. Dist: Byeway Bks.

Bryant, Jen. The Right Word: Roget & His Thesaurus. Sweet, Melissa, illus. 2014. (ENG.). 42p. (J). 17.50 *(978-0-8028-5385-1(4)*, Eerdmans Bks For Young Readers) Eerdmans, William B. Publishing Co.

Burg, Ann E. Pirate Pickle & the White Balloon. Janovitz, Marilyn, illus. 2007. (Rookie Reader Skill Set Ser.). (ENG.). 32p. (J). (gr. -1-3). pap. 4.95 *(978-0-531-17778-5(5)*, Children's Pr.) Scholastic Library Publishing.

Butler, Nathalie. Oddball Opposites. 2017. (Learning with Stories Ser.). 24p. (gr. 4-6). pap. 8.25 ***(978-1-5081-6237-7(9)***, PowerKids Pr.) Rosen Publishing Group, Inc., The.

Caiella, Kim & Williams, Rozanne Lanczak. Build-a-SKill Instant Books Synonyms & Antonyms. Faulkner, Stacey, ed. Campbell, Jenny, illus. 2007. (J). 4.99 *(978-1-59198-419-1(X))* Creative Teaching Pr., Inc.

Carle, Eric. Eric Carle's All Around Us. Carle, Eric, illus. 2013. (World of Eric Carle Ser.). (ENG., Illus.). 14p. (J). (gr. -1-k). bds. 7.99 *(978-0-448-47784-8(X)*, Grosset & Dunlap) Penguin Young Readers Group.

—Eric Carle's Opposites. 2007. (World of Eric Carle Ser.). (ENG., Illus.). 16p. (J). (gr. -1-k). 7.99 *(978-0-448-44565-6(4)*, Grosset & Dunlap) Penguin Young Readers Group.

Cleary, Brian P. Pitch & Throw, Grasp & Know: What Is a Synonym? Gable, Brian, illus. (Words Are CATegorical (r) Ser.). (ENG.). 32p. (gr. 2-5). 2007. pap. 6.95 *(978-0-8225-6877-3(2)*, First Avenue Editions) 2005. 16.95 *(978-1-57505-796-5(4))* Lerner Publishing Group.

—Stop & Go, Yes & No. Gable, Brian, illus. 2009. (Words Are CATegorical (r) Ser.). (ENG.). (gr. 2-5). pap. 39.62 *(978-0-8225-9904-3(X))* Lerner Publishing Group.

—Stop & Go, Yes & No: What Is an Antonym? Gable, Brian, illus. (Words Are CATegorical (r) Ser.). (ENG.). 32p. (gr. 2-5). 2008. per. 6.95 *(978-0-8225-9025-5(5)*, First Avenue Editions) 2006. lib. bdg. 16.95 *(978-1-57505-860-3(X)*, Millbrook Pr.) Lerner Publishing Group.

—Straight & Curvy, Meek & Nervy: More about Antonyms. Gable, Brian, illus. (Words Are CATegorical (r) Ser.). (ENG.). 32p. (gr. 2-5). 2011. pap. 6.95 *(978-1-58013-939-7(6)*, Millbrook Pr.) 2009. 16.95 *(978-0-8225-7878-9(6))* 2008. pap. 39.62 *(978-0-7613-7605-7(4)*, Millbrook Pr.) Lerner Publishing Group.

—Stroll & Walk, Babble & Talk. 2011. (Words Are CATegorical (r) Ser.). (ENG., Illus.). (gr. 2-5). pap. 39.62 *(978-0-7613-7000-0(5))* Lerner Publishing Group.

—Stroll & Walk, Babble & Talk: More about Synonyms. Gable, Brian, illus. (Words Are CATegorical (r) Ser.). (ENG.). 32p. (gr. 2-5). 2010. pap. 6.95 *(978-1-58013-938-0(8)*, First Avenue Editions) 2008. 16.95 *(978-0-8225-7850-5(6))* Lerner Publishing Group.

Coat, Janik. Hippopposites. 2012. (ENG., Illus.). 38p. (J). (gr. -1 — 1). bds. 15.95 *(978-1-4197-0151-1(7)*, Abrams Appleseed) Abrams, Inc.

Coffelt, Nancy. Big, Bigger, Biggest! Coffelt, Nancy, illus. 2009. (ENG., Illus.). 32p. (J). 17.99 *(978-0-8050-8089-6(9))*, 9780805080896, Holt, Henry & Co. Bks. For Young Readers) Holt, Henry & Co.

Collins Dictionaries. Collins Gem School Dictionary & Thesaurus. 2nd rev. ed. 2015. (ENG.). 840p. (YA). (gr. 7). pap. 9.99 *(978-0-00-810286-9(4))* HarperCollins Pubs. Ltd. GBR. Dist: Independent Pubs. Group.

Collins Dictionaries & Harpercollins Staff. Collins Junior Illustrated Thesaurus. 2nd rev. ed. 2014. (Collins Primary Dictionaries Ser.). (ENG., Illus.). 192p. (J). pap. 16.99 *(978-0-00-757873-3(3))* HarperCollins Pubs. Ltd. GBR. Dist: Independent Pubs. Group.

Collins Dictionaries Staff. Dictionary & Thesaurus in Colour. 2nd ed. 2015. (ENG.). 840p. (YA). (gr. 7). pap. 14.95 *(978-0-00-811195-3(2))* HarperCollins Pubs. Ltd. GBR. Dist: Independent Pubs. Group.

—School Thesaurus. 5th rev. ed. 2016. (ENG.). 736p. (YA). (gr. 7-9). pap. 8.95 *(978-0-00-814645-0(4))* HarperCollins Pubs. Ltd. GBR. Dist: Independent Pubs. Group.

Connors, Kathleen. Opposites at the Park. 2012. (Word Play Ser.). (Illus.). 24p. (J). (gr. 1-3). 22.60 *(978-1-4339-7191-4(7))*; pap. 8.15 *(978-1-4339-7192-1(5))* Stevens, Gareth Publishing LLLP.

—Synonyms at School. 2012. (Word Play Ser.). (Illus.). 24p. (J). (gr. 1-3). pap. 8.15 *(978-1-4339-7204-1(2))*; lib. bdg. 22.60 *(978-1-4339-7203-4(4))* Stevens, Gareth Publishing LLLP.

Crawford, Andy. Fun with Opposites. Crawford, Andy, photos by. (Illus.). (J). pap. 9.99 *(978-0-590-24640-8(2))* Scholastic, Inc.

Dahl, Michael. If You Were a Synonym, 1 vol. Gray, Sara, illus. 2007. (Word Fun Ser.). (ENG.). 24p. (gr. 2-4). per. 7.95 *(978-1-4048-2391-4(3)*, 1265673) Picture Window Bks.

Dahl, Michael & Picture Window Books Staff. If You Were a Synonym, 1 vol. Gray, Sara, illus. 2007. (Word Fun Ser.). (ENG.). 24p. (gr. 2-4). 27.99 *(978-1-4048-2387-7(5))* Picture Window Bks.

Davis, Caroline. First Opposites. 2012. (ENG., Illus.). 10p. (J). (gr. -1-1). bds. 7.99 *(978-1-84322-844-8(0)*, Armadillo) Anness Publishing GBR. Dist: National Bk. Network.

Davis, Lee. The Lifesize Animal Opposites Book. (Illus.). 32p. (J). pap. 16.95 *(978-0-590-24372-8(1))* Scholastic, Inc.

DeGrie, Eve. Opposites. Rose, Drew, illus. 2008. (ENG.). 12p. (J). bds. 6.95 *(978-0-8249-6559-4(0)*, Ideal Pubns.) Worthy Publishing.

Delahunty, Andrew. Barron's First Thesaurus. 2nd rev. ed. 2014. (ENG.). 128p. (J). (gr. 1-6). pap. 12.99 *(978-1-4380-0450-1(8))* Barron's Educational Series, Inc.

Dicmas, Courtney. Opposites. Dicmas, Courtney, illus. 2017. (Wild! Concepts Ser.: 4). (ENG., Illus.). 14p. (J). bds. ***(978-1-84643-997-1(3))*** Child's Play International Ltd.

Dorling Kindersley Publishing Staff. Children's Illustrated Thesaurus. 2017. (ENG.). 256p. (J). (gr. 4-7). 19.99 ***(978-1-4654-6237-4(6)***, DK Children) Dorling Kindersley Publishing, Inc.

Eck, Kristin. Opposites in My House. 2004. (Look-And-Learn Books). (Illus.). (J). lib. bdg. 8.95 *(978-1-4042-2700-2(8)*, PowerKids Pr.) Rosen Publishing Group, Inc., The.

(Ed.), Chambers. Mini School Thesaurus. rev. ed. 2005. 640p. pap. *(978-0-550-10162-4(4)*, Chambers) Hodder & Stoughton.

Falk, Laine. Let's Talk about Opposites, Morning to Night. Michael, Joan & Larsen, Eric, illus. 2007. (Let's Find Out Early Learning Bks.). (ENG.). 24p. (J). (gr. -1-3). 18.00 *(978-0-531-14872-3(6)*, Children's Pr.) Scholastic Library Publishing.

Fare, Dennis & Cacciatore, Mark G. PARCC ELA/ Literacy Assessments, Grades 6-8. 2013. (Common Core State Standards Ser.). (ENG.). 400p. (gr. 6-8). pap. 18.95 *(978-0-7386-1168-6(9))* Research & Education Assn.

Feldman, Thea. My Magnetic Opposites: Big & Little: Best Friends. Dillard, Sarah, illus. 2007. (Magnix Learning Fun Ser.). 10p. (gr. -1-k). bds. 9.95 *(978-1-932915-39-6(7))* Sandvik Innovations, LLC.

Furgang, Kathy. Building Bridges: Set Of 6. 2011. (Navigators Ser.). (J). 44.00 net. *(978-1-4108-0404-4(6))* Benchmark Education Co.

Gerver, Jane E. Little Sister, Big Mess! Dieterichs, Shelley, illus. 2007. (Rookie Reader Skill Set Ser.). (ENG.). 32p. (J). (gr. -1-3). 19.50 *(978-0-531-17545-3(6)*, Children's Pr.) Scholastic Library Publishing.

Gordon, Sharon. Dirty Clean/Sucio Limpio. 2006. (Bookworms Ser.). (SPA & ENG., Illus.). 24p. (gr. k-1). lib. bdg. 15.95 *(978-0-7614-2446-8(6))* Marshall Cavendish Corp.

—Dirty/Clean. 2007. (J). pap. 6.99 *(978-0-7614-3280-7(9))* Marshall Cavendish Corp.

—Duro Blando. 2006. (Bookworms Ser.). (SPA & ENG., Illus.). 24p. (gr. k-1). lib. bdg. 15.95 *(978-0-7614-2368-3(0))* Marshall Cavendish Corp.

—Fast/Slow/Rapido/Lento. 2006. (Bookworms Ser.). (ENG & SPA., Illus.). 24p. (gr. k-1). lib. bdg. 15.95 *(978-0-7614-2447-5(4))* Marshall Cavendish Corp.

—Hard/Soft. 2007. (J). pap. 6.99 *(978-0-7614-3282-1(5))* Marshall Cavendish Corp.

—Hard/Soft/Duro/Blando. 2006. (Bookworms Ser.). (ENG & SPA., Illus.). 24p. (gr. k-1). lib. bdg. 15.95 *(978-0-7614-2448-2(2))* Marshall Cavendish Corp.

—Mojado Seco. 2006. (Bookworms Ser.). (SPA & ENG., Illus.). 24p. (gr. k-1). lib. bdg. 15.95 *(978-0-7614-2370-6(2))* Marshall Cavendish Corp.

—Rapido Lento. 2006. (Bookworms Ser.). (SPA & ENG., Illus.). 24p. (gr. k-1). lib. bdg. 15.95 *(978-0-7614-2367-6(2))* Marshall Cavendish Corp.

—Up/down. 2007. (J). pap. 6.99 *(978-0-7614-3283-8(3))* Marshall Cavendish Corp.

—Wet/Dry. 2007. (J). pap. 6.99 *(978-0-7614-3285-2(X))* Marshall Cavendish Corp.

—Wet/Dry/Seco/Mojado. 2006. (Bookworms Ser.). (ENG & SPA., Illus.). 24p. (gr. k-1). lib. bdg. 15.95 *(978-0-7614-2450-5(4))* Marshall Cavendish Corp.

Gould, Vera Dobson & Hughes, Patricia J. The Dominie Thesaurus for Young Writers. 2003. 393p. (J). 18.95 *(978-0-7685-2298-3(6))* Dominie Pr., Inc.

Group/McGraw-Hill, Wright. Opposites: Collection 4. (Storyteller Interactive Writing Cards Ser.). (gr. k-3). *(978-0-322-09326-3(0))* Wright Group/McGraw-Hill.

Gunzi, Christiane. Opposites. Murrell, Deborah, ed. 2nd rev. ed. 2015. (ENG., Illus.). 34p. (J). 7.99 *(978-1-906572-21-1(6))* Award Pubns. Ltd. GBR. Dist: Parkwest Pubns., Inc.

Hatanaka, Kellen. Drive, 1 vol. 2015. (ENG., Illus.). 32p. (J). (gr. -1-2). 16.95 *(978-1-55498-731-3(8))* Groundwood Bks. CAN. Dist: Publishers Group West (PGW).

Hellweg, Paul. The American Heritage Children's Thesaurus. 2015. (ENG., Illus.). 288p. (J). (gr. 3-6). 18.95 *(978-0-544-54272-3(X))* Houghton Mifflin Harcourt Publishing Co.

Hierlmaier Nelson, Christine M. Green Yellow Go! Nat Knows Bananas. Hierlmaier, Joy, illus. 2004. 26p. (J). spiral bd. 14.95 *(978-0-9759362-0-7(4))* Expressive Ink.

Hilgendorf, Sarah. Thesaurus of Synonyms & Antonyms: Canadian Edition. 2010. 311p. pap. *(978-1-934669-12-9(1))* Dictionary Project, Inc., The.

Hills, Tad. What's up, Duck? A Book of Opposites. Hills, Tad, illus. 2008. (Duck & Goose Ser.). (ENG., Illus.). 22p. (J). (gr. k — 1). bds. 6.99 *(978-0-375-84738-7(3)*, Schwartz & Wade Bks.) Random Hse. Children's Bks.

Hine, Eileen, illus. Desert Opposites. 2005. (ENG.). 12p. (J). (gr. -1 — 1). bds. 5.95 *(978-0-87358-890-4(8))* Cooper Square Publishing Llc.

Hnatov, Catherine. Up & Down, 1 vol. Hnatov, Catherine, illus. 2014. (ENG., Illus.). 32p. (J). bds. 5.99 *(978-1-59572-340-6(4))* Star Bright Bks., Inc.

Hoffert, Kara & Fribley, Kara. Find the Right Words with Thesauruses. 2012. (Explorer Junior Library: Information Explorer Junior Ser.). (ENG., Illus.). 24p. (J). (gr. 1-4). pap. 12.79 *(978-1-61080-394-6(9)*, 201331); lib. bdg. 28.50 *(978-1-61080-369-4(8)*, 201272) Cherry Lake Publishing.

Hogan, Martina, illus. Dinosaur Big, Dinosaur Small. 2016. (Early Birds Ser.). (ENG.). 12p. (J). (gr. -1 — 1). bds. 6.99 *(978-1-4998-0184-2(X))* Little Bee Books Inc.

Holland, Gini. Alive & Not Alive (Vivo y no Vivo) 2007. (I Know Opposites/Conceptos Contrarios Ser.). (SPA & ENG., Illus.). 16p. (gr. -1-3). lib. bdg. 19.00 *(978-0-8368-8303-9(9)*, Weekly Reader Leveled Readers) Stevens, Gareth Publishing LLLP.

—Alive & Not Alive/Vivo y No Vivo. 2007. (I Know Opposites/Conceptos Contrarios Ser.). (SPA & ENG., Illus.). 16p. (gr. -1-3). pap. 5.30 *(978-0-8368-8308-4(X)*, Weekly Reader Leveled Readers) Stevens, Gareth Publishing LLLP.

—Hot & Cold/Caliente y Frio. 2007. (I Know Opposites/Conceptos Contrarios Ser.). (SPA & ENG.). 16p. (gr. -1-3). lib. bdg. 19.00 *(978-0-8368-8304-6(7)*, Weekly Reader Leveled Readers) Stevens, Gareth Publishing LLLP.

Holmen, Lene. Lift & Learn Opposites. Snaith, Andy, photos by. 2006. (Illus.). 24p. (gr. -1 — 1). per., bds. *(978-1-84610-031-4(3))* Make Believe Ideas.

Hood, Susan. Double Take! A New Look at Opposites. Fleck, Jay, illus. 2017. (ENG.). 32p. (J). (gr. -1-2). 16.99 ***(978-0-7636-7291-1(2))*** Candlewick Pr.

How Do I Use a Thesaurus? 2014. (Research Tools You Can Use Ser.). 32p. (J). (gr. 3-6). 23.45 *(978-1-62275-369-7(0))* Rosen Publishing Group, Inc., The.

Jackaman, Philippa. Fun to Learn Opposites: Kaleidoscope Book. Daniel, Carol, illus. 16p. (J). *(978-1-84322-125-8(X))* Bookmart Ltd.

Johnson, Robin. The Word Wizard's Book of Synonyms & Antonyms. 2015. (ENG., Illus.). 24p. (J). *(978-0-7787-1923-6(5))* Crabtree Publishing Co.

Johnstone, Michael. Sticker & Color-In Playbook: Teddy Bear Opposites. Tulip, Jenny, illus. 2016. (ENG.). 16p. (J). (gr. -1-12). pap. 4.99 *(978-1-86147-721-7(X)*, Armadillo) Anness Publishing GBR. Dist: National Bk. Network.

Jordan, Apple. Empty Full. 2nd rev. ed. 2011. (Bookworms 2nd Edition: Opposites Ser.). 16p. (gr. k-1). 21.36 *(978-1-60870-420-0(3))* Marshall Cavendish Corp.

—Open Shut. 2nd rev. ed. 2011. (Bookworms 2nd Edition: Opposites Ser.). 16p. (gr. k-1). 21.36 *(978-1-60870-423-1(8))* Marshall Cavendish Corp.

Jordan, Christopher. Baseball Opposites. 2014. (Major League Baseball: First Base Bks.). (ENG., Illus.). 32p. (gr. -1-2). 12.99 *(978-1-77049-518-0(5)*, Fenn-Tundra) Tundra Bks. CAN. Dist: Penguin Random Hse. LLC.

—Hockey Opposites. 2011. (My First NHL Book Ser.). (ENG., Illus.). 30p. (J). (-k). bds. 8.99 *(978-1-77049-318-6(2))* Tundra Bks. CAN. Dist: Random Hse., Inc.

Jullien, Jean. Before & After. 2017. (ENG., Illus.). 40p. (gr. -1 — 1). bds. 12.95 ***(978-0-7148-7408-1(6))*** Phaidon Pr., Inc.

Katirgis, Jane. Back & Front. 2011. (All about Opposites Ser.). (Illus.). 24p. (J). (gr. -1-18). pap. 7.95 *(978-1-59845-259-4(2),* Enslow Elementary); (gr. k-3). lib. bdg. 22.60 *(978-0-7660-3916-2(1))* Enslow Pubs., Inc.

Killen, Nicola. Animal Opposites. 2014. (Nicola Killen Animals Ser.). (ENG., Illus.). 10p. (J). (— 1). bds. 9.99 *(978-1-4052-6286-6(9))* Egmont Bks., Ltd. GBR. Dist: Independent Pubs. Group.

Kompelien, Tracy. The Castle Is Cold, Ancient & Old!, 1 vol. 2007. (Synonyms Ser.). (ENG., Illus.). 24p. (J). (gr. k-3). lib. bdg. 24.21 *(978-1-59928-728-7(5),* SandCastle) ABDO Publishing Co.

—Ella Is Right, Smart & Bright!, 1 vol. 2007. (Synonyms Ser.). (ENG., Illus.). 24p. (J). (gr. k-3). lib. bdg. 24.21 *(978-1-59928-729-4(3),* SandCastle) ABDO Publishing Co.

—The Pickle Is Dilly, Cool & Chilly!, 1 vol. 2007. (Synonyms Ser.). (ENG., Illus.). 24p. (J). (gr. k-3). lib. bdg. 24.21 *(978-1-59928-730-0(7),* SandCastle) ABDO Publishing Co.

—Why Are You Sad & Blue?, 1 vol. 2007. (Synonyms Ser.). (ENG., Illus.). 24p. (J). (gr. k-3). lib. bdg. 24.21 *(978-1-59928-731-7(5),* SandCastle) ABDO Publishing Co.

—Why Is Today Cloudy & Gray?, 1 vol. 2007. (Synonyms Ser.). (ENG., Illus.). 24p. (J). (gr. k-3). lib. bdg. 24.21 *(978-1-59928-732-4(3),* SandCastle) ABDO Publishing Co.

—Yell & Scream for Your Team!, 1 vol. 2007. (Synonyms Ser.). (ENG., Illus.). 24p. (J). (gr. k-3). lib. bdg. 24.21 *(978-1-59928-733-1(1),* SandCastle) ABDO Publishing Co.

Lakeshore Learning Materials Staff, contrib. by. The Great Race: A Synonym Story, Set of 6 Student Books. 2007. (J). pap. 19.95 *(978-1-59746-026-2(5))* Lakeshore Learning Materials.

Land of Opposites. (Illus.). 12p. (J). bds. *(978-2-7643-0125-8(1))* Phidal Publishing, Inc./Editions Phidal, Inc.

Larranaga, Ana M. Pull & Play - Opposites. Martín, Ana I., illus. 2013. (Pull & Play Ser.). (ENG.). 10p. (J). (— 1). bds. 7.99 *(978-0-230-75040-1(0))* Pan Macmillan GBR. Dist: Independent Pubs. Group.

LD COACH. TEH Learns to Read: Opposites, Volume Four. 2004. (Illus.). 40p. (J). 34.95 *(978-0-9745938-4-5(2))* LD Coach, LLC.

Lindeen, Mary. Neat, Tidy, & Clean: Teaching Synonyms. 2016. (Playing with Words Ser.). (ENG.). 16p. (J). (gr. -1-2). 25.64 *(978-1-5038-0841-6(6),* 210691) Child's World, Inc., The.

Loewen, Nancy. If You Were an Antonym, 1 vol. Gray, Sara, illus. 2007. (Word Fun Ser.). (ENG.). 24p. (gr. 2-4). lib. bdg. 27.99 *(978-1-4048-2384-6(0))* Picture Window Bks.

Loewen, Nancy & Dahl, Michael. If You Were an Antonym, 1 vol. Gray, Sara, illus. 2007. (Word Fun Ser.). (ENG.). 24p. (gr. 2-4). per. 7.95 *(978-1-4048-2388-4(3),* 1265670) Picture Window Bks.

Mara, Wil. The Frog in the Pond. Mendenhall, Cheryl, illus. 2007. (Rookie Reader Skill Set Ser.). (ENG.). 32p. (J). (gr. -1-3). 19.50 *(978-0-531-17541-5(3),* Children's Pr.) Scholastic Library Publishing.

Matthews, Colin. I Know Opposites. 2017. (What I Know Ser.). 24p. (J). (gr. k-k). pap. 8.15 ***(978-1-4824-6297-5(4))*** Stevens, Gareth Publishing LLLP.

Mckee, David & McKee, David. Elmer's Opposites. McKee, David, illus. 2012. (Andersen Press Board Bks). (ENG., Illus.). 10p. (J). (gr. -1-2). bds. 7.95 *(978-0-7613-8998-9(9))* Lerner Publishing Group.

Meyers. Playground Opposites. 2013. (Steck-Vaughn Pait-It Books Emergent Stage 1 Ser.). (ENG.). 16p. (J). (gr. k-1). pap. 5.65 *(978-0-8172-6415-4(9))* Houghton Mifflin Harcourt Publishing Co.

Michael, Joan, illus. The Five Senses/Opposites & Position Words, 4 bks., Set. Incl. Let's Play a Five Senses Guessing Game. Miller, Amanda. 18.00 *(978-0-531-14871-6(8));* Let's Talk about Opposites, Morning to Night. Falk, Laine. Larsen, Eric, illus. 18.00 *(978-0-531-14872-3(6));* 24p. (J). (gr. -1-3). 2007. (Let's Find Out Early Learning Bks.). 2007. 72.00 o.p. *(978-0-531-17574-3(X),* Children's Pr.) Scholastic Library Publishing.

Milet Publishing Staff. My First Bilingual Book - Opposites. 2012. (My First Bilingual Book Ser.). (ENG & URD., Illus.). 24p. (J). (gr. k — 1). bds. 8.99 *(978-1-84059-746-2(1));* bds. 7.99 *(978-1-84059-732-5(1))* Milet Publishing.

—My First Bilingual Book-Opposites. 2012. (My First Bilingual Book Ser.). (ENG & GER., Illus.). 24p. (J). (gr. k — 1). bds. 7.99 *(978-1-84059-737-0(2));* bds. 7.99 *(978-1-84059-740-0(2));* bds. 7.99 *(978-1-84059-734-9(8))* Milet Publishing.

—My First Bilingual Book-Opposites (English-Bengali) 2012. (My First Bilingual Book Ser.). (ENG & BEN., Illus.). 24p. (J). (gr. k — 1). bds. 7.99 *(978-1-84059-733-2(X))* Milet Publishing.

—My First Bilingual Book-Opposites (English-Korean) 2012. (My First Bilingual Book Ser.). (ENG & KOR., Illus.). 24p. (J). (gr. k — 1). bds. 7.99 *(978-1-84059-739-4(9))* Milet Publishing.

—My First Bilingual Book-Opposites (English-Russian) 2012. (My First Bilingual Book Ser.). (ENG & RUS., Illus.). 24p. (J). (gr. k — 1). bds. 7.99 *(978-1-84059-742-4(9))* Milet Publishing.

—My First Bilingual Book-Opposites (English-Vietnamese) 2012. (My First Bilingual Book Ser.). (ENG & VIE., Illus.). 24p. (J). (gr. k — 1). bds. 7.99 *(978-1-84059-747-9(X))* Milet Publishing.

—Opposites. 2012. (My First Bilingual Book Ser.). (Illus.). 24p. (J). (gr. k — 1). (FRE & ENG.). bds. 7.99 *(978-1-84059-736-3(4));* (ENG & SOM., bds. 7.99 *(978-1-84059-743-1(7));* (ENG & PER., bds. 7.99 *(978-1-84059-735-6(6))* Milet Publishing.

—Opposites - My First Bilingual Book. 2012. (My First Bilingual Book Ser.). (ENG & TUR., Illus.). 24p. (J). (gr. k — 1). bds. 7.99 *(978-1-84059-745-5(3));* bds. 8.99 *(978-1-84059-738-7(0))* Milet Publishing.

Milne, Barbara L. W. Opposites Are Fun. Munoz, Olga M., illus. I.t. ed. 2005. 40p. (J). 19.95 *(978-0-9708796-0-8(1),* TLConcepts, Inc.) Tender Learning Concepts.

MMStudios & Allman, Howard, photos by. Big & Little: A Book about Opposites. 2007. (Usborne Look & Say Ser.). (Illus.). 18p. (J). (gr. -1-3). bds. 14.99 *(978-0-7945-1884-4(2),* Usborne) EDC Publishing.

National Wildlife Federation Staff. My First Book of Animal Opposites. 2016. (ENG., Illus.). 22p. (J). (— 1). bds. 6.95 *(978-1-62354-062-3(3))* Charlesbridge Publishing, Inc.

Nunn, Daniel. Eddie & Ellie's Opposites. 2013. (Eddie & Ellie's Opposites Ser.). (ENG.). 24p. (gr. -1-k). pap. 27.80 *(978-1-4109-5349-0(1));* lib. bdg. 90.60 *(978-1-4109-5344-5(0))* Heinemann-Raintree. (NA-r).

—Eddie & Ellie's Opposites at the Circus, 1 vol. 2013. (Eddie & Ellie's Opposites Ser.). (ENG.). 24p. (gr. -1-k). 22.65 *(978-1-4109-5341-4(6));* pap. 7.95 *(978-1-4109-5346-9(7))* Heinemann-Raintree. (NA-r).

—Eddie & Ellie's Opposites at the Zoo, 1 vol. 2013. (Eddie & Ellie's Opposites Ser.). (ENG., Illus.). 24p. (gr. -1-k). 22.65 *(978-1-4109-5340-7(8));* pap. 7.95 *(978-1-4109-5345-2(9))* Heinemann-Raintree. (NA-r).

Olsen, Jan Z. Mat Man Opposites. Delaney, Molly, illus. 2009. (ENG.). stu. ed. 13.75 *(978-1-891627-94-1(5))* Handwriting Without Tears.

O'Neill, Mary, et al. Primary Thesaurus. 2008. 400p. *(978-0-550-10320-8(1),* Chambers) Hodder & Stoughton.

Opposites. 2004. (Early Days Ser.). (Illus.). 18p. (J). bds. *(978-1-84229-974-6(3))* Top That! Publishing PLC.

Opposites. 2003. 16p. (J). 3.79 *(978-1-58792-053-0(0))* Trend Enterprises, Inc.

Owings, Lisa. Doctor by Day, Ninja by Night: Teaching Antonyms. 2016. (Playing with Words Ser.). (ENG.). 16p. (J). (gr. -1-2). 25.64 *(978-1-5038-0836-2(X),* 210686) Child's World, Inc., The.

Paré, Roger. Les Contraires. 2004. (J). (gr. -1-2). spiral bd. *(978-0-616-01847-7(9))* Canadian National Institute for the Blind/Institut National Canadien pour les Aveugles.

Parker, Ant, illus. Amazing Machines First Concepts: Opposites. 2015. (ENG.). 12p. (J). (gr. -1-1). bds. 5.99 *(978-0-7534-7234-7(1),* 9780753472347, Kingfisher) Roaring Brook Pr.

Patricelli, Leslie. Baby Happy Baby Sad. Patricelli, Leslie, illus. 2008. (Leslie Patricelli Board Bks.). (ENG., Illus.). 24p. (J). (— 1). bds. 6.99 *(978-0-7636-3245-8(7))* Candlewick Pr.

—No No Yes Yes. Patricelli, Leslie, illus. 2008. (Leslie Patricelli Board Bks.). (ENG., Illus.). 24p. (J). (— 1). bds. 6.99 *(978-0-7636-3244-1(9))* Candlewick Pr.

—Quiet Loud. Patricelli, Leslie, illus. 2003. (Leslie Patricelli Board Bks.). (ENG., Illus.). 24p. (J). (gr. k — 1). bds. 6.99 *(978-0-7636-1952-7(3))* Candlewick Pr.

Phillips, Sarah & Wallace, Bruce. Flip Flaps Opposites. 2005. (Flip Flaps (Make Believe Ideas) Ser.). (Illus.). 12p. (gr. -1-k). per., bds. *(978-1-905051-95-3(6))* Make Believe Ideas.

Priddy, Roger. Picture Fit Board Books: a Stampede of Dinosaurs: An Opposites Book. 2017. (Picture Fit Ser.). (ENG., Illus.). 14p. (J). bds. 8.99 *(978-0-312-52298-8(3),* 9780312522988, Priddy Bks.) St. Martin's Pr.

—Picture Fit Board Books: a Stampede of Dinosaurs (Large) An Opposites Book. 2017. (Picture Fit Ser.). (ENG., Illus.). 14p. (J). bds. 12.99 *(978-0-312-52524-8(9),* 9780312525248, Priddy Bks.) St. Martin's Pr.

Rayevsky, Kim. Antonyms, Synonyms & Homonyms. Rayevsky, Robert, illus. 2006. (ENG.). 32p. (J). (gr. -1-3). 16.95 *(978-0-8234-1889-3(8))* Holiday Hse., Inc.

Rebman, Nick. What Goes Together? A Book about Opposites. 2016. (Concept Fun Ser.). (ENG.). 16p. (J). (gr. -1-2). 25.64 *(978-1-5038-0764-8(9),* 210612) Child's World, Inc., The.

Reich, Kass, illus. Up Hamster, down Hamster, 1 vol. 2015. (ENG.). 24p. (J). (gr. -1-k). bds. 9.95 *(978-1-4598-1013-6(9))* Orca Bk. Pubs. USA.

Rigol, Francesc, illus. Dan & Din Learn Opposites. 2009. (Learning with Dan & Din Ser.). 12p. (J). (gr. -1-k). bds. 11.40 *(978-1-60754-403-6(2))* Windmill Bks.

Rissman, Rebecca. Eddie & Ellie's Opposites at the Farm, 1 vol. 2013. (Eddie & Ellie's Opposites Ser.). (ENG.). 24p. (gr. -1-k). 22.65 *(978-1-4109-5343-8(2));* pap. 7.95 *(978-1-4109-5348-3(3))* Heinemann-Raintree. (NA-r).

—Eddie & Ellie's Opposites at the Park, 1 vol. 2013. (Eddie & Ellie's Opposites Ser.). (ENG.). 24p. (gr. -1-k). pap. 7.95 *(978-1-4109-5347-6(5));* (Illus.). 22.65 *(978-1-4109-5342-1(4))* Heinemann-Raintree. (NA-r).

A Rookie Reader Skill Set: Opposites, 5 bks. Incl. Frog in the Pond. Mara, Wil. Mendenhall, Cheryl, illus. 19.50 *(978-0-531-17541-5(3));* Little Sister, Big Mess! Gerver, Jane E. Dieterichs, Shelley, illus. 19.50 *(978-0-531-17545-3(6));* 32p. (J). (gr. -1-3). 2007. 97.50 o.p. *(978-0-531-17735-8(1),* Children's Pr.) Scholastic Library Publishing.

Rosa-Mendoza, Gladys. Opposites/Opuestos. Cifuentes, Carolina, ed. McGeehan, Dan, illus. 2008. (English-Spanish Foundations Ser.). (gr. -1-k). bds. 6.95 *(978-1-931398-04-6(6))* Me+Mi Publishing.

Salzmann, Mary Elizabeth. Can a Giraffe Cry or Laugh?, 1 vol. 2007. (Antonyms Ser.). (ENG., Illus.). 24p. (J). (gr. k-3). lib. bdg. 24.21 *(978-1-59928-714-0(5),* SandCastle) ABDO Publishing Co.

—Can You Go Fast or Slow?, 1 vol. 2007. (Antonyms Ser.). (ENG., Illus.). 24p. (J). (gr. k-3). lib. bdg. 24.21 *(978-1-59928-715-7(3),* SandCastle) ABDO Publishing Co.

—Did I Hear a Hello from above or Below?, 1 vol. 2007. (Antonyms Ser.). (ENG., Illus.). 24p. (J). (gr. k-3). lib. bdg. 24.21 *(978-1-59928-716-4(1),* SandCastle) ABDO Publishing Co.

—Does It Fly Away in the Night or Day?, 1 vol. 2007. (Antonyms Ser.). (ENG., Illus.). 24p. (J). (gr. k-3). lib. bdg. 24.21 *(978-1-59928-717-1(X),* SandCastle) ABDO Publishing Co.

—Is It a Day for Work or Play?, 1 vol. 2007. (Antonyms Ser.). (ENG., Illus.). 24p. (J). (gr. k-3). lib. bdg. 24.21 *(978-1-59928-718-8(8),* SandCastle) ABDO Publishing Co.

—Is the Treat Sour or Sweet?, 1 vol. 2007. (Antonyms Ser.). (ENG., Illus.). 24p. (J). (gr. k-3). lib. bdg. 24.21 *(978-1-59928-719-5(6),* SandCastle) ABDO Publishing Co.

Scholastic, Inc. Staff, contrib. by. Scholastic Pocket Dictionary of Synonyms, Antonyms & Homonyms. 2012. (ENG.). 240p. (J). (gr. 3-7). pap. 6.99 *(978-0-545-42667-1(7),* Scholastic Reference) Scholastic, Inc.

Schumacher, Bev. Which Way? 2005. (ENG., Illus.). 20p. (J). lib. bdg. 9.95 *(978-0-9768706-2-3(2))* Learning Props.

—Which Way? (Chinese-English) 2008. (CHI & ENG.). 20p. (J). lib. bdg. 9.95 *(978-1-935292-03-6(X))* Learning Props.

Seeger, Laura Vaccaro. Black? White! Day? Night! A Book of Opposites. 2016. (ENG., Illus.). 20p. (J). 14.99 *(978-1-62672-254-5(4),* 9781626722545) Roaring Brook Pr.

Sesame's: A Giant Coloring Book that Teaches about Opposites. 2006. (J). 6.99 *(978-1-59949-497-5(3))* Food Marketing Consultants, Inc.

Shepherd, Jodie. The Crayola Opposites Book. 2017. (Crayola (r) Concepts Ser.). (ENG.). 24p. (J). (gr. -1-3). 26.65 ***(978-1-5124-3287-9(3))*** Lerner Publishing Group.

Simon and Schuster Staff. Simon & Schuster Thesaurus for Children: The Ultimate Student Thesaurus. 2005. 272p. (J). 9.95 *(978-0-689-86657-9(7))* Simon & Schuster Children's Publishing.

Smith, Sian. Hard & Soft, 1 vol. 2014. (Opposites Ser.). (ENG.). 24p. (gr. -1-1). pap. 5.99 *(978-1-4846-0333-8(8),* Acorn) Heinemann-Raintree.

Synonyms, Antonyms, & Homonyms (Gr. 2-3) 2003. (J). *(978-1-58232-124-0(8))* ECS Learning Systems, Inc.

Synonyms, Antonyms, & Homonyms (Gr. 4-5) 2004. (J). *(978-1-58232-138-7(8))* ECS Learning Systems, Inc.

Traditional Catholic Speller. (J). (gr. 1). wbk. ed. 12.00 *(978-1-931555-33-3(8));* (J). (gr. 2). wbk. ed. 12.00 *(978-1-931555-34-0(6));* (J). (gr. 3). wbk. ed. 12.00 *(978-1-931555-35-7(4));* (J). (gr. 4). wbk. ed. 12.00 *(978-1-931555-36-4(2));* (J). (gr. 5). wbk. ed. 12.00 *(978-1-931555-37-1(0));* (J). (gr. 6). wbk. ed. 12.00 *(978-1-931555-38-8(9));* (YA). (gr. 7). wbk. ed. 12.00 *(978-1-931555-39-5(7));* (YA). (gr. 8). wbk. ed. 12.00 *(978-1-931555-40-1(0))* Our Lady of Victory Schl.

Turrell, Linda. Synonyms, Antonyms, & Homonyms Student Activities Book: Mastering Language Arts Series. Matthews, Douglas L., ed. 2003. (Illus.). stu. ed., wbk. ed. *(978-1-931680-81-3(7),* Expert Systems for Teachers) Teaching Point, Inc.

Twine, Alice. My Favorite Book of Opposites. 2008. (Board Bks.). (Illus.). 14p. (J). (gr. -1-k). bds. 11.95 *(978-1-4042-4257-9(0),* PowerKids Pr.) Rosen Publishing Group, Inc., The.

Watt, Mélanie. Opposites. Watt, Mélanie, illus. 2005. (Learning with Animals Ser.). (ENG., Illus.). 24p. (J). (gr. -1 — 1). bds. 5.95 *(978-1-55337-832-7(6))* Kids Can Pr., Ltd. CAN. Dist: Hachette Bk. Group.

Weakland, Mark. Football Opposites, 1 vol. 2013. (SI Kids Rookie Bks.). (ENG., Illus.). 20p. (gr. 1-2). bds. 7.95 *(978-1-4296-9967-9(1))* Capstone Press of Coughlan Cos.

Wen, Dref. Fy Llyfr Geiriau Croes Cyntaf. 2005.Tr. of My First Opposites. (WEL., Illus.). 34p. *(978-1-85596-671-0(9))* Dref Wen.

Wilcox, Alison. Descriptosaurus: Supporting Creative Writing for Ages 8-14. 2nd rev. ed. 2013. (ENG., Illus.). 272p. (C). 62.95 *(978-0-415-64086-2(5),* Y140474) Routledge.

Wishinsky, Frieda. What's up, Bear? A Book about Opposites. Moore, Sean L., illus. 2012. (ENG.). 32p. (J). (gr. -1-2). 16.95 *(978-1-926973-41-8(0),* Owlkids) Owlkids Bks. Inc. CAN. Dist: Publishers Group West (PGW).

Yates, Gene. The Dragon Opposites Book. 2005. (Illus.). 14p. (J). *(978-1-58865-283-6(1))* Kidsbooks, LLC.

Yates, Gene, illus. The Dragon Opposites Book. 2006. (J). *(978-1-58865-362-8(5))* Kidsbooks, LLC.

Yoon, Jung-Huyn. Popposites: A Lift, Pull, & Pop Book of Opposites. (Illus.). 14p. (J). pap. 16.99 *(978-0-590-24937-9(1))* Scholastic, Inc.

ENGLISH LANGUAGE—TERMS AND PHRASES

Cleary, Brian P. I & You & Don't Forget Who: What Is a Pronoun? Gable, Brian, illus. 2004. (Words Are CATegorical (r) Ser.). (ENG.). 32p. (gr. 2-5). 16.95 *(978-1-57505-596-1(1))* Lerner Publishing Group.

Herman, Gail. Snowboarding Similes & Metaphors. 2009. (Grammar All-Stars: Writing Tools Ser.). 32p. (J). (gr. 2-5). (ENG.). pap. 10.50 *(978-1-4339-2138-4(3));* lib. bdg. 26.00 *(978-1-4339-1945-9(1))* Stevens, Gareth Publishing LLLP. (Gareth Stevens Learning Library).

Leedy, Loreen & Street, Pat. There's a Frog in My Throat! 440 Animal Sayings a Little Bird Told Me. Leedy, Loreen, illus. 2004. (ENG., Illus.). 48p. (J). (gr. k-3). reprint ed. pap. 8.99 *(978-0-8234-1819-0(7))* Holiday Hse., Inc.

McCowan Nevills, Jennifer. Have You Ever? Part 2. 2008. (Illus.). 31p. (YA). pap. 17.99 *(978-0-9655792-4-7(7))* Don Paul Publishing, LLC.

—Have You Ever? Part 3. 2008. (Illus.). 31p. (YA). pap. 17.99 *(978-0-9655792-5-4(5))* Don Paul Publishing, LLC.

—Have You Ever? Part 4. 2008. (Illus.). 33p. (YA). pap. 17.99 *(978-0-9655792-6-1(3))* Don Paul Publishing, LLC.

Oelschlager, Vanita. Birds of a Feather. Hegan, Robin, illus. 2011. (ENG.). 32p. (J). (gr. -1-3). pap. 8.95 *(978-0-9826366-1-9(X))* VanitaBooks.

Olson, Gillia M. Monsters Can Mosey: Understanding Shades of Meaning, 1 vol. Stevanovic, Ivica, illus. 2013. (Language on the Loose Ser.). (ENG.). 24p. (gr. 2-4). 27.99 *(978-1-4048-8320-8(7));* pap. 7.95 *(978-1-4795-1919-4(7))* Picture Window Bks.

Rajczak, Kristen. Transition Words with Your Team. 2013. (Write Right! Ser.). (Illus.). 24p. (J). (gr. 2-5). pap. 8.15 *(978-1-4339-9086-1(5));* (ENG., lib. bdg. 22.60 *(978-1-4339-9085-4(7))* Stevens, Gareth Publishing LLLP.

Ruscoe, Michael & Voege, Debra. Soccer Goal Suffixes. 2009. (Grammar All-Stars Ser.). (Illus.). 32p. (J). (gr. 2-5). lib. bdg. 26.00 *(978-1-4339-0012-9(2),* Gareth Stevens Learning Library) Stevens, Gareth Publishing LLLP.

Shaskan, Trisha Speed. If You Were a Contraction, 1 vol. Gray, Sara, illus. 2008. (Word Fun Ser.). (ENG.). 24p. (gr. 2-4). pap. 7.95 *(978-1-4048-4775-0(8))* Picture Window Bks.

Street, Pat & Brace, Eric. You're Pulling My Leg! 400 Human-Body Sayings from Head to Toe. Brace, Eric, illus. (ENG., Illus.). 48p. (J). (gr. 1-5). 2017. 8.99 *(978-0-8234-3772-6(8))* 2016. 18.95 *(978-0-8234-2135-0(X))* Holiday Hse., Inc.

Terban, Marvin. In a Pickle: And Other Funny Idioms. Maestro, Giulio, illus. 2007. (ENG.). 64p. (J). (gr. -1-3). pap. 8.99 *(978-0-618-83001-5(4))* Houghton Mifflin Harcourt Publishing Co.

—Mad As a Wet Hen! And Other Funny Idioms. Maestro, Giulio, illus. 2007. (ENG.). 64p. (J). (gr. -1-3). pap. 8.99 *(978-0-618-83003-9(0))* Houghton Mifflin Harcourt Publishing Co.

Transition Words with Your Team. 2013. (Write Right! Ser.). 24p. (J). (gr. 2-5). pap. 48.90 *(978-1-4339-9087-8(3))* Stevens, Gareth Publishing LLLP.

Your Baby Can Learn! Patterns, Vol. 1. 2007. (J). 7.95 *(978-1-931026-15-4(7))* Infant Learning Co., The.

Your Baby Can Learn! Prepositions, Vol. 1. 2007. (J). 7.95 *(978-1-931026-16-1(5))* Infant Learning Co., The.

ENGLISH LANGUAGE—TEXTBOOKS FOR FOREIGN SPEAKERS

Abbs, Brian, et al. Postcards 1. 2nd ed. 2007. (ENG.). 136p. pap. 27.00 *(978-0-13-179131-2(1))* Pearson ESL.

Award, Anna. English/French. Burton, Terry, illus. 2012. (FRE & ENG.). 96p. (J). 11.50 *(978-1-84135-798-0(7))* Award Pubns. Ltd. GBR. Dist: Parkwest Pubns., Inc.

Baker, Ann. Tree or Three? An Elementary Pronunciation Course, 1 vol. 2nd ed. 2006. (ENG., Illus.). 136p. pap., stu. ed. 46.75 incl. audio compact disk *(978-0-521-68527-6(3));* per. 28.50 *(978-0-521-68526-9(5))* Cambridge Univ. Pr.

Baker, Mary E. English - French Counting Book, 1 vol. Mason, Alfonso & Mason, Ruth, illus. 2010. 28p. pap. 24.95 *(978-1-4489-4347-0(7))* PublishAmerica, Inc.

Beaver, Simon. Dangerous & Dirty Jobs Low Intermediate Book with Online Access. 2014. (ENG., Illus.). 28p. pap. 9.50 *(978-1-107-64567-7(0))* Cambridge Univ. Pr.

BeaverSimon. FANTASTIC CREATURES: MONSTERS, MERMAIDS, AND WILD MEN BEGINNING BOOK WITH ONLINE ACCESS. 2014. (ENG.). 24p. (J). pap. 9.50 *(978-1-107-69637-2(2))* Cambridge Univ. Pr.

—A LIGHT IN THE NIGHT: THE MOON BEGINNING BOOK WITH ONLINE ACCESS. 2014. (ENG.). 24p. (J). pap. 9.50 *(978-1-107-64756-5(8))* Cambridge Univ. Pr.

—PARIS: CITY OF LIGHT BEGINNING BOOK WITH ONLINE ACCESS. 2014. (ENG.). 24p. (J). pap. 9.50 *(978-1-107-64577-6(8))* Cambridge Univ. Pr.

—SPORT, GAME OR HOBBY? LOW INTERMEDIATE BOOK WITH ONLINE ACCESS. 2014. (ENG., Illus.). 48p. (J). pap. 9.50 *(978-1-107-68658-8(X))* Cambridge Univ. Pr.

—WILD AUSTRALIA! BEGINNING BOOK WITH ONLINE ACCESS. 2014. (ENG., Illus.). 24p. (J). pap. 9.50 *(978-1-107-62165-7(8))* Cambridge Univ. Pr.

—YOUNG AND AMAZING: TEENS AT THE TOP HIGH BEGINNING BOOK WITH ONLINE ACCESS. 2014. (ENG., Illus.). 24p. pap. 9.50 *(978-1-107-62252-4(2))* Cambridge Univ. Pr.

Big Books for ESL/ELD: Grade 1 Collection. (J). (gr. k-2). 270.93 *(978-0-7362-2989-0(2))* CENGAGE Learning.

Big Books for ESL/ELD: Grade 2 Collection. (J). (gr. k-2). 270.93 *(978-0-7362-2990-6(6))* CENGAGE Learning.

Big Books for ESL/ELD: Kindergarten Collection. (J). (gr. k-2). 317.99 *(978-0-7362-2988-3(4))* CENGAGE Learning.

Bluedorn, Harvey. Handy English Encoder Decoder: All the Spelling & Phonics Rules You Could Ever Want to Know. 2nd ed. 2004. 104p. per. 9.00 *(978-0-9743616-2-8(3))* Trivium Pursuit.

Bouchard, Margaret. Comprehension Strategies for English Language Learners: 30 Research-Based Reading Strategies That Help Students Read, Understand, & Really Learn Content from Their Textbooks & Other Nonfiction Materials. 2005. (ENG., Illus.). 128p. (gr. 4). pap. 18.99 *(978-0-439-55428-2(4),* Teaching Strategies) Scholastic, Inc.

Bourke, Kenna. Deadly Animals High Beginning Book with Online Access. 2014. (ENG., Illus.). 24p. (J). pap. 9.50 *(978-1-107-69371-5(3))* Cambridge Univ. Pr.

BourkeKenna. JEFF CORWIN: WILD MAN BEGINNING BOOK WITH ONLINE ACCESS. 2014. (ENG.). 24p. pap. 9.50 *(978-1-107-68039-5(5))* Cambridge Univ. Pr.

—LOST: THE MYSTERY OF AMELIA EARHART HIGH BEGINNING BOOK WITH ONLINE ACCESS. 2014. (ENG.). 24p. (J). pap. 9.50 *(978-1-107-69335-7(7))* Cambridge Univ. Pr.

Brennan, Frank. Three Tomorrows, Level 1. 2007. (Cambridge English Readers Ser.). (ENG., Illus.). 32p. pap. 9.50 *(978-0-521-69377-6(2))* Cambridge Univ. Pr.

British Broadcasting Corporation Staff. English Pronunciation: Learning the Sounds of American English. unabr. ed. 128p. (YA). pap. 49.50 incl. audio *(978-0-88432-674-8(8),* S32560) Pavilion Pubs.

Brooks, Felicity & MacKinnon, Mairi. Ya Hablo Ingles. 2007. (Como Se Dice? Ser.). (Illus.). 14p. (J). (gr. -1-3). 14.99 *(978-0-7460-8365-9(3),* Usborne) EDC Publishing.

Bruzzone, Catherine & Martinneau, Susan. Hide & Speak English. Comfort, Louise, tr. Comfort, Louise, illus. 2003. (Hide & Speak Ser.). (ENG.). 32p. (J). (gr. 1-4). pap. 9.99 *(978-1-902915-74-6(7))* B Small Publishing GBR. Dist: Independent Pubs. Group.

Collins, Tim & Maples, Mary Jane. Time Zones 1. 2009. (Time Zones: Explore, Discover, Learn Ser.). (ENG.). 144p. (J). pap., stu. ed. 45.95 incl. cd-rom *(978-1-4240-3489-5(2))* Thomson ELT.

Collins UK Publishing Staff & Greenway, Karen. English for Mathematics, Bk. A. 2016. (ENG., Illus.). 80p. (J). pap. 9.95 *(978-0-00-813570-6(3))* HarperCollins Pubs. Ltd. GBR. Dist: Independent Pubs. Group.

Continental Press Staff. Finish Line for ELLs: English Proficiency Practice: Student Book. 2009. pap., stu. ed. 20.95 *(978-0-8454-6092-4(7))* 2008. pap., stu. ed. 20.95 *(978-0-8454-5840-2(X))* 2008. pap., stu. ed. 20.95 *(978-0-8454-5841-9(8))* Continental Pr., Inc.

Cook, Berty Segal. Linking the ESL Student to the Mainstream. (Teaching English Through Total Physical Response Ser.). 58p. (YA). (gr. 3-12). pap. 14.50 *(978-0-938395-39-3(4),* BSC5394) Segal, Berty Inc.

Cox, Marian. Cambridge Checkpoint English Coursebook 8. 2013. (ENG.). 190p. pap. 33.69 *(978-1-107-69099-8(4))* Cambridge Univ. Pr.

—Cambridge Checkpoint English Workbook 8. 2013. (ENG.). 94p. pap. 16.19 *(978-1-107-66315-2(6))* Cambridge Univ. Pr.

Eleanor, Coerr. Sadako & the Thousand Paper Cranes. 2014. (Puffin Modern Classics Ser.). (ENG.). 80p. (J). (gr. 3-7). 10.24 *(978-1-63245-199-6(9))* Lectorum Pubns., Inc.

Elliott, Karen. Kid's Box Level 2 Language Portfolio. 2nd rev. ed. 2014. (ENG.). 13p. pap. 7.50 *(978-1-107-67499-8(9))* Cambridge Univ. Pr.

English At Your Command! Beginning Level: Classroom Set. (J). (gr. k). 273.54 *(978-0-7362-2986-9(8))* CENGAGE Learning.

EFG

English At Your Command! Primary Level: Classroom Set. (J). (gr. 1). 219.03 (978-0-7362-2987-6(6)) CENGAGE Learning.

English, "Living Language Courses" For French Speakers. (YA). pap. 29.95 incl. audio (978-0-88432-930-5(5), SEN605) Pavilion Pubs.

English, "Living Language Courses" For German Speakers. (YA). pap. 29.95 incl. audio (978-0-88432-931-2(3), AFE610) Pavilion Pubs.

English, "Living Language Courses" For Italian Speakers. (YA). pap. 29.95 incl. audio (978-0-88432-932-9(1), SEN615) Pavilion Pubs.

Esol, Cambridge. CAMBRIDGE YOUNG LEARNERS ENGLISH TESTS 7 FLYERS ANSWER BOOKLET. 2011. (ENG., Illus.). 32p. pap. 3.75 (978-0-521-17376-6(0)) Cambridge Univ. Pr.

—Cambridge Young Learners English Tests 7 Flyers Student's Book: Examination Papers from University of Cambridge ESOL Examinations. 2011. (ENG., Illus.). 80p. pap. 20.25 (978-0-521-17375-9(2)) Cambridge Univ. Pr.

—CAMBRIDGE YOUNG LEARNERS ENGLISH TESTS 7 MOVERS ANSWER BOOKLET. 2011. (ENG., Illus.). 31p. pap. 3.75 (978-0-521-17372-8(8)) Cambridge Univ. Pr.

—Cambridge Young Learners English Tests 7 Movers Student's Book: Examination Papers from University of Cambridge ESOL Examinations. 2011. (ENG., Illus.). 75p. pap. 20.25 (978-0-521-17371-1(X)) Cambridge Univ. Pr.

—CAMBRIDGE YOUNG LEARNERS ENGLISH TESTS 7 STARTERS ANSWER BOOKLET. 2011. (ENG., Illus.). 24p. pap. 3.75 (978-0-521-17369-8(8)) Cambridge Univ. Pr.

—CAMBRIDGE YOUNG LEARNERS ENGLISH TESTS 7 STARTERS STUDENT'S BOOK. 2011. (ENG., Illus.). 57p. pap. 10.50 (978-0-521-17367-4(1)) Cambridge Univ. Pr.

EventoSusan. YOUR DREAM VACATION HIGH BEGINNING BOOK WITH ONLINE ACCESS. 2014. (ENG.). 24p. (J). pap. 9.50 (978-1-107-69043-1(9)) Cambridge Univ. Pr.

Fancy, Robin Lyn & Welch, Vala Jeanne. My Filipino Word Book: English - Tagalog - Ilokano. Gasmen, Imelda Fines, ed. Lynn, Ronny, illus. 2007. 28p. (J). (gr. -1-3). 10.95 (978-1-57306-276-3(6)) Bess Pr., Inc.

Frazier. Time Zones, Vol. 1. 2010. (ENG.). 160p. (J). pap., stu. ed. (978-1-4240-6008-5(7)) Thomson ELT.

Frino, Lucy. Kid's Box Level 2 Teacher's Book. 2nd rev. ed. 2014. (ENG.). 225p. pap. 59.00 (978-1-107-66840-9(9)) Cambridge Univ. Pr.

Goodey, Diana & Goodey, Noel. Messages, 3 vols., Bk. 1. 2005. (ENG., Illus.). 144p. pap., stu. ed. 31.75 (978-0-521-54707-9(5)) Cambridge Univ. Pr.

Goodey, Diana, et al. Messages 3 Student's Book, 3 vols. 2005. (ENG., Illus.). 144p. stu. ed., per. 30.50 (978-0-521-61433-7(3)) Cambridge Univ. Pr.

Gould, Jane & Gould, Mike. Cambridge IGCSE English as a Second Language. 2013. (Collins IGCSE English As a Second Langua Ser.). (ENG., Illus.). 104p. (YA). (gr. 9). pap., stu. ed., wbk. ed. 12.99 (978-0-00-745689-5(1)) HarperCollins Pubs. Ltd. GBR. Dist: Independent Pubs. Group.

Greenway, Linda, et al. English for Mathematics, Bk. B. 2016. (ENG., Illus.). 80p. (J). pap. 9.95 (978-0-00-813571-3(1)) HarperCollins Pubs. Ltd. GBR. Dist: Independent Pubs. Group.

Hadkins, Helen. Interactive, Level 2. 2011. (ENG.). 128p. pap., stu. ed. 36.50 (978-0-521-71212-5(2)) Cambridge Univ. Pr.

—Interactive, Level 3, Bk. 3. 2012. (ENG., Illus.). 128p. pap., stu. ed. 36.50 (978-0-521-71219-4(X)) Cambridge Univ. Pr.

Handle with Care. 64p. (YA). (gr. 9-12). pap. 9.95 (978-0-8224-7151-6(5), 7151) Globe Fearon Educational Publishing.

Harcourt School Publishers Staff. Esl Support Book Horizons. 3rd ed. 2003. (gr. 1). pap. 9.50 (978-0-15-338321-2(6)); (gr. 2). pap. 9.50 (978-0-15-338322-9(4)); (gr. 3). pap. 12.70 (978-0-15-338323-6(2)) Harcourt Schl. Pubs.

HarrisNic. EMPIRE: RISE AND FALL LOW INTERMEDIATE BOOK WITH ONLINE ACCESS. 2014. (ENG., Illus.). 24p. (J). pap. 9.50 (978-1-107-62844-1(X)) Cambridge Univ. Pr.

—GROWING UP: FROM BABY TO ADULT HIGH BEGINNING BOOK WITH ONLINE ACCESS. 2014. (ENG.). 24p. (J). pap. 9.50 (978-1-107-68744-8(6)) Cambridge Univ. Pr.

—HOW COOL IS COLD! LOW INTERMEDIATE BOOK WITH ONLINE ACCESS. 2014. (ENG.). 24p. (J). pap. 9.50 (978-1-107-65803-5(9)) Cambridge Univ. Pr.

—MEDICINE: OLD AND NEW LOW INTERMEDIATE BOOK WITH ONLINE ACCESS. 2014. (ENG., Illus.). 24p. (J). pap. 9.50 (978-1-107-65866-0(7)) Cambridge Univ. Pr.

—THE SCIENCE OF HEAT LOW INTERMEDIATE BOOK WITH ONLINE ACCESS. 2014. (ENG., Illus.). 24p. (J). pap. 9.50 (978-1-107-69772-0(7)) Cambridge Univ. Pr.

—WONDERS OF THE WORLD HIGH BEGINNING BOOK WITH ONLINE ACCESS. 2014. (ENG.). 24p. (J). pap. 9.50 (978-1-107-64298-0(1)) Cambridge Univ. Pr.

Harvey, Stephanie, et al. Ladders Social Studies 4: the Pacific Coast (on-Level) 2014. (Ladders Social Studies). (ENG.). 32p. 8.95 (978-1-285-34852-0(4)) National Geographic School Publishing, Inc.

—Ladders Social Studies 5: the Maya (on-Level) 2014. (Ladders Social Studies). (ENG.). 32p. 8.95 (978-1-285-34924-4(5)) National Geographic School Publishing, Inc.

—Living on the Coast. 2014. (Ladders Social Studies). (ENG.). 24p. 8.95 (978-1-285-34803-2(6)) National Geographic School Publishing, Inc.

Interlink Resources International. New Bridges - Book 3: Connecting People Through Language & Culture. 2007. (Illus.). 138p. spiral bd. 14.00 net. (978-0-9796411-4-5(4)) CJR.

Irving, N. Improve Your English. 2004. 96p. (J). lib. bdg. 22.95 (978-1-58086-611-8(5), Usborne) EDC Publishing.

Johnson-Stefanidou, Catherine. Kid's Box Levels 1-2 Monty's Alphabet Book. 2nd rev. ed. 2014. (ENG.). 32p. pap. 18.50 (978-1-107-65840-0(3)) Cambridge Univ. Pr.

Kaleta, Magda & Gerngross, Günter. Join Us for English Level 2 Pupil's Book with CD-ROM Polish Edition. 2008. (Join In Ser.). (Illus.). pap. 19.00 incl. cd-rom (978-0-521-71745-8(0)) Cambridge Univ. Pr.

—Join Us for English Level 3 Pupil's Book with CD-ROM Polish Edition. 2008. (Join In Ser.). (Illus.). pap. 19.00 incl. cd-rom (978-0-521-71746-5(9)) Cambridge Univ. Pr.

Kehe, David & Kehe, Peggy Dustin. Conversation Strategies: Pair & Group Activities for Developing Communicative Competence. 2nd ed. 2004. 150p. (Orig.). (gr. 7-12). pap., stu. ed. 17.00 (978-0-86647-189-3(8)) Pro Lingua Assocs., Inc.

Kellas, Lydia. Our English 3 Student Book: Volume 0, Part 0: Integrated Course for the Caribbean. 2007. pap., stu. ed. (978-0-521-69177-2(X)) Cambridge Univ. Pr.

Kellas, Lydia, et al. Our English, 1 vol. 2007. (ENG., Illus.). 260p. pap., stu. ed. 16.95 incl. audio compact disk (978-0-521-69168-0(0)) Cambridge Univ. Pr.

—Our English 4, 1 vol. 2008. (ENG., Illus.). 254p. pap. 24.00 incl. audio compact disk (978-0-521-69176-5(1)) Cambridge Univ. Pr.

Kocienda, Genevieve. Aliens: Is Anybody Out There? Low Intermediate Book with Online Access. 2014. (ENG.). 24p. (J). pap. 9.50 (978-1-107-66000-7(9)) Cambridge Univ. Pr.

—Do Not Disturb: the Importance of Sleep High Beginning Book with Online Access. 2014. (ENG., Illus.). 24p. pap. 9.50 (978-1-107-64682-7(0)) Cambridge Univ. Pr.

—Madagascar Low Intermediate Book with Online Access. 2014. (ENG., Illus.). 24p. (J). pap. 9.50 (978-1-107-62940-0(3)) Cambridge Univ. Pr.

—Only in America Low Intermediate Book with Online Access. 2014. (ENG.). 28p. (J). pap. 9.50 (978-1-107-63700-9(7)) Cambridge Univ. Pr.

KociendaGenevieve. BLIZZARDS: KILLER SNOWSTORM BEGINNING BOOK WITH ONLINE ACCESS. 2014. (ENG.). 24p. pap. 9.50 (978-1-107-62164-0(X)) Cambridge Univ. Pr.

—FAST: THE NEED FOR SPEED HIGH BEGINNING BOOK WITH ONLINE ACCESS. 2014. (ENG., Illus.). 24p. pap. 9.50 (978-1-107-68068-5(9)) Cambridge Univ. Pr.

—THE MAGIC OF MUSIC LOW INTERMEDIATE BOOK WITH ONLINE ACCESS. 2014. (ENG., Illus.). 24p. (J). pap. 9.50 (978-1-107-66558-3(2)) Cambridge Univ. Pr.

—SUSHI NATION LOW INTERMEDIATE BOOK WITH ONLINE ACCESS. 2014. (ENG., Illus.). 28p. (J). pap. 9.50 (978-1-107-63147-2(5)) Cambridge Univ. Pr.

—THREE IN ONE: THE CHALLENGE OF THE TRIATHLON LOW INTERMEDIATE BOOK WITH ONLINE ACCESS. 2014. (ENG., Illus.). 24p. (J). pap. 9.50 (978-1-107-62255-5(7)) Cambridge Univ. Pr.

—WATER: VITAL FOR LIFE LOW INTERMEDIATE BOOK WITH ONLINE ACCESS. 2014. (ENG., Illus.). 24p. (J). pap. 9.50 (978-1-107-62251-7(4)) Cambridge Univ. Pr.

—WEIRD ANIMALS LOW INTERMEDIATE BOOK WITH ONLINE ACCESS. 2014. (ENG.). 24p. (J). pap. 9.50 (978-1-107-65664-2(8)) Cambridge Univ. Pr.

—WHAT ARE THE ODDS? FROM SHARK ATTACK TO LIGHTNING STRIKE LOW INTERMEDIATE BOOK WITH ONLINE ACCESS. 2014. (ENG.). 24p. pap. 9.50 (978-1-107-66839-3(5)) Cambridge Univ. Pr.

Konda, Cynthia. Okasan & Me: Japanese American Educational Program. 2003. (JPN., Illus.). 26p. (J). (gr. -1-18). spiral bd. 19.99 (978-0-9743613-0-7(5)) Okasan & Me.

Levy, Meredith. Interactive, 1 vol., Bk. 4. 2012. (ENG., Illus.). 104p. pap., wbk. ed. 26.25 (978-0-521-71225-5(4)) Cambridge Univ. Pr.

—Interactive Level 1 Workbook with Downloadable Audio, 1 vol. 2011. (ENG., Illus.). 103p. pap. 20.75 (978-0-521-71209-5(2)) Cambridge Univ. Pr.

—Interactive Level 2 Workbook, 1 vol. 2011. (ENG.). 103p. pap. 20.75 (978-0-521-71215-6(7)) Cambridge Univ. Pr.

—Interactive Level 3 Workbook with Downloadable Audio, 1 vol. 2012. (ENG., Illus.). 103p. pap. 20.75 (978-0-521-71220-0(3)) Cambridge Univ. Pr.

Mackay, Barbara. Starters: Three Practice Tests for Cambridge English. 2014. (Collins English for Exams Ser.). (ENG.). 24p. pap. 20.99 (978-0-00-753596-5(1)) HarperCollins Pubs. Ltd. GBR. Dist: Independent Pubs. Group.

Maggart, Kaye Wiley & Prentice Hall Staff. Shining Star, Introductory Level. 2003. (ENG., Illus.). xiv, 289p. (gr. 6-12). 73.20 (978-0-13-111285-8(6)) Pearson ESL.

Mahoney, Judy. Teach Me Everyday English V1, 2 bks & 2 cd's, Vol 1. Girouard, Patrick, illus. 2008. (ENG.). 32p. (J). (gr. -1). 19.95 (978-1-59972-108-8(2)) Teach Me Tapes, Inc.

Marsh, Carole. Way to Go Amigo!English for Kids! 2007. 32p. pap. 5.95 (978-0-635-06369-4(7)) Gallopade International.

MauleDavid. ARE YOU LISTENING? THE SENSE OF HEARING HIGH BEGINNING BOOK WITH ONLINE ACCESS. 2014. (ENG.). 24p. (J). pap. 9.50 (978-1-107-63251-6(X)) Cambridge Univ. Pr.

—GENIUS BEGINNING BOOK WITH ONLINE ACCESS. 2014. (ENG.). 24p. (J). pap. 9.50 (978-1-107-67865-1(X)) Cambridge Univ. Pr.

Milet Publishing Staff. Animals. 2011. (My First Bilingual Book Ser.). (Illus.). 24p. (J). (gr. k — 1). (FRE & ENG.). bds. 8.99 (978-1-84059-612-0(0)); (ENG & POR., bds. 7.99 (978-1-84059-616-8(3)); (ENG & ITA., bds. 7.99 (978-1-84059-614-4(7)); (ENG., bds. 7.99 (978-1-84059-622-9(8)); (ENG., bds. 8.99 (978-1-84059-617-5(1)); (ENG., bds. 8.99 (978-1-84059-615-1(5)); (ENG., bds. 8.99 (978-1-84059-613-7(9)) Milet Publishing.

—Animals - My First Bilingual Book. 2011. (My First Bilingual Book Ser.). (ENG., Illus.). 24p. (J). (gr. k — 1). bds. 8.99 (978-1-84059-623-6(6)); bds. 7.99 (978-1-84059-608-3(2)); bds. 7.99 (978-1-84059-618-2(X)) Milet Publishing.

—Colors. 2011. (My First Bilingual Book Ser.). (ENG.). 24p. (J). (gr. k — 1). bds. 7.99 (978-1-84059-606-9(6)); bds. 8.99 (978-1-84059-597-0(3)) Milet Publishing.

—Colors - My First Bilingual Book. 2011. (My First Bilingual Book Ser.). (ENG.). 24p. (J). (gr. k — 1). bds. 7.99 (978-1-84059-599-4(X)); bds. 7.99 (978-1-84059-601-4(5)) Milet Publishing.

—Fruit. 2011. (My First Bilingual Book Ser.). (ENG., Illus.). 24p. (J). (gr. k — 1). bds. 7.99 (978-1-84059-625-0(2)) Milet Publishing.

—Fruit - My First Bilingual Book. 2011. (My First Bilingual Book Ser.). (ENG., Illus.). 24p. (J). (gr. k — 1). bds. 7.99 (978-1-84059-634-2(1)); bds. 7.99 (978-1-84059-624-3(4)); bds. 7.99 (978-1-84059-632-8(5)); bds. 8.99 (978-1-84059-630-4(9)); bds. 7.99 (978-1-84059-637-3(6)) Milet Publishing.

—Fruit (English-French) 2011. (My First Bilingual Book Ser.). (FRE & ENG., Illus.). 24p. (J). (gr. k — 1). bds. 7.99 (978-1-84059-628-1(7)) Milet Publishing.

—Home. 2011. (My First Bilingual Book Ser.). (ENG., Illus.). 24p. (J). (gr. k — 1). bds. 7.99 (978-1-84059-642-7(2)); bds. 7.99 (978-1-84059-646-5(5)) Milet Publishing.

—Home - My First Bilingual Book. 2011. (My First Bilingual Book Ser.). (ENG., Illus.). 24p. (J). (gr. k — 1). bds. 7.99 (978-1-84059-653-3(8)); bds. 8.99 (978-1-84059-645-8(7)); bds. 7.99 (978-1-84059-641-0(4)); bds. 7.99 (978-1-84059-654-0(6)) Milet Publishing.

—Home (English-Arabic) 2011. (My First Bilingual Book Ser.). (ENG., Illus.). 24p. (J). (gr. k — 1). bds. 7.99 (978-1-84059-640-3(6)) Milet Publishing.

—Home (English-French) 2011. (My First Bilingual Book Ser.). (FRE & ENG., Illus.). 24p. (J). (gr. k — 1). bds. 8.99 (978-1-84059-644-1(9)) Milet Publishing.

—Home (English-Polish) 2011. (My First Bilingual Book Ser.). (ENG & POR., Illus.). 24p. (J). (gr. k — 1). bds. 7.99 (978-1-84059-648-9(1)) Milet Publishing.

—Home (English-Portuguese) 2011. (My First Bilingual Book Ser.). (ENG., Illus.). 24p. (J). (gr. k — 1). bds. 7.99 (978-1-84059-649-6(X)) Milet Publishing.

—Milet Interactive for Kids - English for French Speakers. 2012. (Milet Interactive for Kids Ser.). (FRE & ENG., Illus.). 1p. (J). (gr. k-2). cd-rom 24.95 (978-1-84059-673-1(2)) Milet Publishing.

—Milet Interactive for Kids - English for Turkish Speakers. 2012. (Milet Interactive for Kids Ser.). (ENG., Illus.). 1p. (J). (gr. k-2). cd-rom 24.95 (978-1-84059-675-5(9)) Milet Publishing.

—My First Bilingual Book - Animals. 2011. (My First Bilingual Book Ser.). (ENG., Illus.). 24p. (J). (gr. k — 1). bds. 8.99 (978-1-84059-610-6(4)); bds. 7.99 (978-1-84059-611-3(2)); bds. 7.99 (978-1-84059-621-2(X)); bds. 7.99 (978-1-84059-609-0(0)) Milet Publishing.

—My First Bilingual Book - Animals (English-Somali) 2011. (My First Bilingual Book Ser.). (ENG., Illus.). 24p. (J). (gr. k — 1). bds. 8.99 (978-1-84059-619-9(8)) Milet Publishing.

—My First Bilingual Book - Colors. 2011. (My First Bilingual Book Ser.). (ENG.). 24p. (J). (gr. k — 1). bds. 7.99 (978-1-84059-603-8(1)); bds. 7.99 (978-1-84059-602-1(3)); bds. 7.99 (978-1-84059-604-5(X)); bds. 7.99 (978-1-84059-598-7(1)); bds. 7.99 (978-1-84059-600-7(7)) Milet Publishing.

—My First Bilingual Book - Colors (English-Urdu) 2011. (My First Bilingual Book Ser.). (ENG.). 24p. (J). (gr. k — 1). bds. 7.99 (978-1-84059-605-2(8)) Milet Publishing.

—My First Bilingual Book - Fruit. 2011. (My First Bilingual Book Ser.). (ENG., Illus.). 24p. (J). (gr. k — 1). bds. 8.99 (978-1-84059-626-7(0)); bds. 7.99 (978-1-84059-627-4(9)); bds. 7.99 (978-1-84059-631-1(7)); bds. 7.99 (978-1-84059-629-8(5)); bds. 8.99 (978-1-84059-633-5(3)) Milet Publishing.

—My First Bilingual Book - Home. 2011. (My First Bilingual Book Ser.). (ENG., Illus.). 24p. (J). (gr. k — 1). bds. 7.99 (978-1-84059-643-4(0)); bds. 7.99 (978-1-84059-647-2(3)) Milet Publishing.

—My First Bilingual Book - Vegetables. 2011. (My First Bilingual Book Ser.). (Illus.). 24p. (J). (gr. k — 1). (FRE & ENG.). bds. 8.99 (978-1-84059-660-1(0)); (ENG., bds. 8.99 (978-1-84059-666-3(X)); (ENG., bds. 7.99 (978-1-84059-658-8(9)); (ENG., bds. 7.99 (978-1-84059-669-4(4)) Milet Publishing.

—My First Bilingual Book-Fruit (English-Somali) 2011. (My First Bilingual Book Ser.). (ENG., Illus.). 24p. (J). (gr. k — 1). bds. 7.99 (978-1-84059-635-9(X)) Milet Publishing.

—My First Bilingual Book-Fruit (English-Urdu) 2011. (My First Bilingual Book Ser.). (ENG., Illus.). 24p. (J). (gr. k — 1). bds. 7.99 (978-1-84059-638-0(4)) Milet Publishing.

—My First Bilingual Book-Home (English-Russian) 2011. (My First Bilingual Book Ser.). (ENG., Illus.). 24p. (J). (gr. k — 1). bds. 7.99 (978-1-84059-650-2(3)) Milet Publishing.

—My First Bilingual Book-Home (English-Somali) 2011. (My First Bilingual Book Ser.). (ENG., Illus.). 24p. (J). (gr. k — 1). bds. 7.99 (978-1-84059-651-9(1)) Milet Publishing.

—My First Bilingual Book-Home (English-Vietnamese) 2011. (My First Bilingual Book Ser.). (ENG., Illus.). 24p. (J). (gr. k — 1). bds. 8.99 (978-1-84059-655-7(4)) Milet Publishing.

—My First Bilingual Book-Vegetables. 2011. (My First Bilingual Book Ser.). (ENG., Illus.). 24p. (J). (gr. k — 1). bds. 7.99 (978-1-84059-663-2(5)) Milet Publishing.

—My First Bilingual Book-Vegetables (English-Arabic) 2011. (My First Bilingual Book Ser.). (ENG., Illus.). 24p. (J). (gr. k — 1). bds. 8.99 (978-1-84059-656-4(2)) Milet Publishing.

—My First Bilingual Book-Vegetables (English-Farsi) 2011. (My First Bilingual Book Ser.). (ENG., Illus.). 24p. (J). (gr. k — 1). bds. 7.99 (978-1-84059-659-5(7)) Milet Publishing.

—My First Bilingual Book-Vegetables (English-Urdu) 2011. (My First Bilingual Book Ser.). (ENG., Illus.). 24p. (J). (gr. k — 1). bds. 7.99 (978-1-84059-670-0(8)) Milet Publishing.

—My First Bilingual Book-Vegetables (English-Vietnamese) 2011. (My First Bilingual Book Ser.). (ENG., Illus.). 24p. (J). (gr. k — 1). bds. 8.99 (978-1-84059-671-7(6)) Milet Publishing.

—Vegetables. 2011. (My First Bilingual Book Ser.). (ENG., Illus.). 24p. (J). (gr. k — 1). bds. 7.99 (978-1-84059-667-0(8)); bds. 7.99 (978-1-84059-657-1(0)); bds. 7.99 (978-1-84059-664-9(3)) Milet Publishing.

—Vegetables - My First Bilingual Book. 2011. (My First Bilingual Book Ser.). (ENG., Illus.). 24p. (J). (gr. k — 1). bds. 7.99 (978-1-84059-665-6(1)); bds. 7.99 (978-1-84059-661-8(9)) Milet Publishing.

—Vegetables (Le Verdure) 2011. (My First Bilingual Book Ser.). (ENG & ITA., Illus.). 24p. (J). (gr. k — 1). bds. 7.99 (978-1-84059-662-5(7)) Milet Publishing.

Monckeberg, Paulina. Artilugia English 2008. 2007. (Pascualina Family of Products Ser.). (ENG.). 114p. (J). spiral bd. 14.99 (978-956-8222-62-8(6)) Pascualina Producciones S.A.

—Pascualina English 2008. 2007. (Pascualina Family of Products Ser.). (ENG.). 274p. spiral bd. 16.99 (978-956-8222-61-1(8)) Pascualina Producciones S.A.

National Geographic, et al. Living on the Plains. 2014. (Ladders Social Studies). (ENG.). 24p. 8.95 (978-1-285-34796-7(X)) National Geographic School Publishing, Inc.

National Geographic Learning, National Geographic Learning. English At Your Command! Beginning Level: Add-on Components. 2005. (Avenues Ser.). (ENG.). (C). (gr. k). pap. 18.95 (978-0-7362-2910-4(8)) CENGAGE Learning.

—English At Your Command! Primary Level: Add-on Components. 2005. (Avenues Ser.). (ENG.). 40p. (C). (gr. 1). pap. 19.95 (978-0-7362-2913-5(2)) CENGAGE Learning.

Naughton, Diane. Bones: And the Stories They Tell. 2014. (ENG.). 28p. (J). pap. 9.50 (978-1-107-67054-9(3)) Cambridge Univ. Pr.

—Venice: The Floating City. 2014. (ENG., Illus.). 28p. (J). pap. 9.50 (978-1-107-62163-3(1)) Cambridge Univ. Pr.

—What Are You Afraid of? Fears & Phobias Intermediate Book with Online Access. 2014. (ENG.). 28p. (J). pap. 9.50 (978-1-107-65051-0(8)) Cambridge Univ. Pr.

Nixon, Caroline. Kid's Box American English Level 1 Student's Book. 2010. (ENG.). 96p. pap. 21.25 (978-0-521-17762-7(6)) Cambridge Univ. Pr.

—Kid's Box Level 1 Pupil's Book. 2nd rev. ed. 2014. (ENG.). 96p. pap. 29.75 (978-1-107-61757-5(X)) Cambridge Univ. Pr.

—Kid's Box Level 2 Pupil's Book. 2nd rev. ed. 2014. (ENG.). 112p. pap. 29.75 (978-1-107-64497-7(6)) Cambridge Univ. Pr.

—Kid's Box Level 3 Activity Book with Online Resources. 2nd ed. 2014. (ENG.). 88p. pap. 29.50 (978-1-107-64400-7(3)) Cambridge Univ. Pr.

—Kid's Box Level 3 Pupil's Book. 2nd ed. 2014. (ENG.). 87p. pap. 29.75 (978-1-107-65450-1(5)) Cambridge Univ. Pr.

Nunn, Daniel. Colors in English, 1 vol. 2012. (World Languages - Colors Ser.). (ENG.). 24p. (gr. 1-3). pap. 6.29 (978-1-4329-6663-8(4)); lib. bdg. 21.99 (978-1-4329-6656-0(1)) Heinemann-Raintree. (Acorn).

—Families in English, 1 vol. 2013. (World Languages - Families Ser.). (ENG., Illus.). 24p. (gr. 1-3). pap. 6.29 (978-1-4329-7184-7(0), Acorn) Heinemann-Raintree.

—Numbers in English. 2012. (World Languages - Numbers Ser.). (ENG.). 24p. (gr. 1-3). pap. 6.29 (978-1-4329-6684-3(7), Acorn) Heinemann-Raintree.

—Numbers in English: One, Two, Three... 2012. (World Languages - Numbers Ser.). (ENG.). 24p. (gr. 1-3). lib. bdg. 22.65 (978-1-4329-6677-5(4), Acorn) Heinemann-Raintree.

O'Dell, Kathryn. Bright Lights on Broadway. 2014. (ENG., Illus.). 28p. (J). pap. 9.50 (978-1-107-65022-0(4)) Cambridge Univ. Pr.

—Life Online: the Digital Age Low Intermediate Book with Online Access. 2014. (ENG.). 28p. (J). pap. 9.50 (978-1-107-65069-5(0)) Cambridge Univ. Pr.

O'DellKathryn. THE SCIENCE OF DARKNESS LOW INTERMEDIATE BOOK WITH ONLINE ACCESS. 2014. (ENG., Illus.). 28p. (J). pap. 9.50 (978-1-107-65493-8(9)) Cambridge Univ. Pr.

—THE SCIENCE OF LIGHT LOW INTERMEDIATE BOOK WITH ONLINE ACCESS. 2014. (ENG., Illus.). 28p. (J). pap. 9.50 (978-1-107-68198-9(7)) Cambridge Univ. Pr.

—SURVIVAL GUIDE: LOST IN THE MOUNTAINS LOW INTERMEDIATE BOOK WITH ONLINE ACCESS. 2014. (ENG.). 28p. (J). pap. 9.50 (978-1-107-64328-4(7)) Cambridge Univ. Pr.

Osborn, Anna. Flyers: Three Practice Tests for Cambridge English. 2014. (ENG.). 48p. pap. 20.99 (978-0-00-753598-9(8)) HarperCollins Pubs. Ltd. GBR. Dist: Independent Pubs. Group.

—Movers: Three Practice Tests for Cambridge English. 2014. (ENG.). 48p. pap. 20.99 (978-0-00-753597-2(X)) HarperCollins Pubs. Ltd. GBR. Dist: Independent Pubs. Group.

Puchta, Herbert. Super Minds Level 4 Workbook. 2012. (ENG., Illus.). 120p. pap. 18.00 (978-0-521-22238-9(9)) Cambridge Univ. Pr.

Puchta, Herbert & Gerngross, Gnter. More! Level 3. 2008. (ENG., Illus.). 80p. pap., wbk. ed. 20.50 incl. audio compact disk (978-0-521-71308-5(0)) Cambridge Univ. Pr.

Puchta, Herbert & Gerngross, Günter. American English, Level 3, Bk. 3. 2012. (ENG., Illus.). 128p. pap., stu. ed. 29.00 (978-1-107-60424-7(9)) Cambridge Univ. Pr.

—More!, Level 3. 2nd ed. 2014. (ENG.). 128p. pap., stu. ed. 42.00 (978-1-107-63737-5(6)) Cambridge Univ. Pr. GBR. Dist: Cambridge Univ. Pr.

—Super Minds. 2012. (ENG.). 114p. pap., stu. ed. 26.75 (978-0-521-14852-8(9));Bk. 3. 128p. pap., stu. ed. 27.75 (978-0-521-22168-9(4));Bk. 4. 128p. pap., stu. ed. 29.00 (978-0-521-22218-1(4)) Cambridge Univ. Pr.

—Super Minds American English Level 4 Student's Book with DVD-ROM. 2012. (ENG., Illus.). 128p. pap. 28.00 (978-1-107-60432-2(X)) Cambridge Univ. Pr.

—SUPER MINDS AMERICAN ENGLISH LEVEL 5 STUDENT'S BOOK WITH DVD-ROM. 2013. (ENG.). 128p. pap. 29.00 (978-1-107-60440-7(0)) Cambridge Univ. Pr.

—Super Minds Flashcards Starter, 1 vol., Pack. 2012. (ENG.). 78p. 45.00 (978-0-521-22163-4(3)) Cambridge Univ. Pr.

—Super Minds Level 1 Student's Book with DVD-ROM. 2012. (ENG.). 130p. pap. 29.00 (978-0-521-14855-9(3)) Cambridge Univ. Pr.

—Super Minds Level 2 Student's Book with DVD-ROM. 2012. (ENG.). 130p. pap. 29.00 (978-0-521-14859-7(6)) Cambridge Univ. Pr.

—Super Minds Starter Workbook. 2012. (ENG., Illus.). 112p. pap. 21.25 (978-0-521-14853-5(7)) Cambridge Univ. Pr.

PuchtaHerbert & Gerngross, Günter. SUPER MINDS AMERICAN ENGLISH LEVEL 6 STUDENT'S BOOK WITH DVD-ROM. 2013. (ENG.). 128p. pap., stu. ed. 29.00 (978-1-107-60446-9(X)) Cambridge Univ. Pr.

Reed, Susannah. Guess What! American English Level 2 Student's Book. 2015. (ENG., Illus.). 104p. pap. 31.00 (978-1-107-55673-7(2)) Cambridge Univ. Pr.

—Guess What! American English Level 4 Student's Book. 2015. (ENG., Illus.). 104p. pap. 19.50 (978-1-107-55695-9(3)) Cambridge Univ. Pr.

—Guess What! American English Level 5 Student's Book. 2015. (ENG., Illus.). 104p. pap. 19.50 (978-1-107-55703-1(8)) Cambridge Univ. Pr.

Rempel, Cherie J., ed. New Bridges - Book 1: Connecting People Through Language & Culture. 2008. (Illus.). 138p. spiral bd. 14.00 net. (978-0-9796411-0-7(1)) CJR.

—New Bridges - Book 2: Connecting People Through Language & Culture. 2007. (Illus.). 138p. spiral bd. 14.00 net. *(978-0-9796411-2-1(8))* CJR.
—New Bridges - Book 4: Connecting People Through Language & Culture. 2007. (Illus.). 138p. spiral bd. 14.00 net. *(978-0-9796411-6-9(0))* CJR.
—New Bridges - Book 5: Connecting People Through Language & Culture. 2008. (Illus.). 138p. spiral bd. 14.00 net. *(978-0-9796411-8-3(7))* CJR.
Richards, Jack C. Connect, 1 vol., No. 3. 2nd ed. 2009. (ENG., Illus.). 148p. pap., stu. ed. 25.00 incl. audio compact disk *(978-0-521-73712-8(5))* Cambridge Univ. Pr.
Rivers, Susan. Touchstone, Bk. 2. 2005. (ENG., Illus.). 104p. pap., stu. ed., wbk. ed. 19.50 *(978-0-521-66604-6(X))* Cambridge Univ. Pr.
Robertson, Lynne Marie. Guess What! American English Level 5 Workbook with Online Resources, 1 vol. 2015. (ENG., Illus.). 96p. pap. 20.25 *(978-1-107-55708-6(9))* Cambridge Univ. Pr.
RobinsonAnne. FUN FOR FLYERS STUDENT'S BOOK WITH AUDIO WITH ONLINE ACTIVITIES 3RD EDITION. 3rd rev. ed. 2015. (ENG.). 143p. pap. 32.50 *(978-1-107-44483-6(7))* Cambridge Univ. Pr.
—FUN FOR MOVERS STUDENT'S BOOK WITH AUDIO WITH ONLINE ACTIVITIES 3RD EDITION. 3rd rev. ed. 2015. (ENG., Illus.). 126p. pap. 32.50 *(978-1-107-44478-2(0))* Cambridge Univ. Pr.
—FUN FOR STARTERS STUDENT'S BOOK WITH AUDIO WITH ONLINE ACTIVITIES 3RD EDITION, 1 vol. 3rd rev. ed. 2015. (ENG., Illus.). 110p. pap. 32.50 *(978-1-107-44470-6(5))* Cambridge Univ. Pr.
The Rosetta Stone Language Library: English Level 1 (British) 2005. (J). (gr. 1-18). cd-rom 209.00 *(978-1-58022-042-2(8))* Rosetta Stone Ltd.
The Rosetta Stone Language Library: English Level 2 (British) 2005. (J). (gr. 1-18). cd-rom 239.00 *(978-1-58022-044-6(4))* Rosetta Stone Ltd.
Sargent, Brian. Altruism: What's in It for Me? 2014. (ENG., Illus.). 32p. (J). pap. 9.50 *(978-1-107-62262-3(X))* Cambridge Univ. Pr.
—Found: Discovery & Recovery Intermediate Book with Online Access. 2014. (ENG., Illus.). 28p. (J). pap. 9.50 *(978-1-107-63212-7(9))* Cambridge Univ. Pr.
—Gold: Greed & Glory Intermediate Book with Online Access. 2014. (ENG., Illus.). 28p. pap. 9.50 *(978-1-107-65260-6(X))* Cambridge Univ. Pr.
—Life on the Edge. 2014. (ENG.). 28p. (J). pap. 9.50 *(978-1-107-63028-4(2))* Cambridge Univ. Pr.
—Losing It: The Meaning of Loss. 2014. (ENG., Illus.). 28p. (J). pap. 9.50 *(978-1-107-68191-0(X))* Cambridge Univ. Pr.
—Mark Your Territory Intermediate Book with Online Access. 2014. (ENG., Illus.). 28p. pap. 9.50 *(978-1-107-65895-0(0))* Cambridge Univ. Pr.
SargentBrian. LIFE IN MUMBAI HIGH BEGINNING BOOK WITH ONLINE ACCESS. 2014. (ENG., Illus.). 24p. pap. 9.50 *(978-1-107-62167-1(4))* Cambridge Univ. Pr.
—THE TRADITIONS OF DEATH INTERMEDIATE BOOK WITH ONLINE ACCESS. 2014. (ENG.). 28p. (J). pap. 9.50 *(978-1-107-63578-4(0))* Cambridge Univ. Pr.
Schreyer, Karmel. Turtles: Ancient Symbol/Modern Survivor Upper Intermediate Book with Online Access. 2014. (ENG.). 28p. (J). pap. 9.50 *(978-1-107-66057-1(2))* Cambridge Univ. Pr.
SchreyerKarmel. BOUNCE! THE WONDERFUL WORLD OF RUBBER UPPER INTERMEDIATE BOOK WITH ONLINE ACCESS. 2014. (ENG., Illus.). 28p. (J). pap. 9.50 *(978-1-107-64154-9(3))* Cambridge Univ. Pr.
—TRAGEDY ON THE SLOPES UPPER INTERMEDIATE BOOK WITH ONLINE ACCESS. 2014. (ENG., Illus.). 28p. pap. 9.50 *(978-1-107-62159-6(3))* Cambridge Univ. Pr.
Shackleton, Caroline. Deep Blue: Discovering the Sea Intermediate Book with Online Access. 2014. (ENG., Illus.). 28p. (J). pap. 9.50 *(978-1-107-69705-8(0))* Cambridge Univ. Pr.
—Down to Earth Intermediate Book with Online Access. 2014. (ENG., Illus.). 28p. pap. 9.50 *(978-1-107-66117-2(X))* Cambridge Univ. Pr.
—Get Smart: Our Amazing Brain Intermediate Book with Online Access. 2014. (ENG., Illus.). 28p. (J). pap. 9.50 *(978-1-107-65063-3(1))* Cambridge Univ. Pr.
ShackletonCaroline. AVALANCHE! HIGH INTERMEDIATE BOOK WITH ONLINE ACCESS, 1 vol. 2014. (ENG., Illus.). 28p. pap. 9.50 *(978-1-107-62157-2(7))* Cambridge Univ. Pr.
—LIFT OFF: EXPLORING THE UNIVERSE HIGH INTERMEDIATE BOOK WITH ONLINE ACCESS. 2014. (ENG., Illus.). 28p. (J). pap. 9.50 *(978-1-107-69249-7(0))* Cambridge Univ. Pr.
—POISON: MEDICINE, MURDER, AND MYSTERY HIGH INTERMEDIATE BOOK WITH ONLINE ACCESS. 2014. (ENG., Illus.). 28p. (J). pap. 9.50 *(978-1-107-62260-9(3))* Cambridge Univ. Pr.
—UP IN THE AIR: OUR FIGHT AGAINST GRAVITY INTERMEDIATE BOOK WITH ONLINE ACCESS. 2014. (ENG.). 28p. (J). pap. 9.50 *(978-1-107-63470-1(9))* Cambridge Univ. Pr.
—THE WHEEL LOW INTERMEDIATE BOOK WITH ONLINE ACCESS. 2014. (ENG.). 28p. (J). pap. 9.50 *(978-1-107-66739-6(9))* Cambridge Univ. Pr.
Smith, Jill & Diller, Howard. Consonant Primer II. 2015. 110p. (J). (gr. k). pap. 24.00 *(978-1-933873-99-2(X))* Read Well Publishing Inc.
Stamper, Judith Bauer & Keyes, Joan Ross. A Sweet Surprise. 2005. (Oxford Picture Dictionary for Kids Ser.). (ENG., Illus.). 16p. 6.94 *(978-0-19-430933-2(9))* Oxford Univ. Pr., Inc.
Steck-Vaughn Staff. ESL: Building English Proficiency. 2003. (ESL: Building English Proficiency Ser.). (ENG.). 128p. (gr. 1-2). pap. 15.99 *(978-0-7398-7096-9(3))* Houghton Mifflin Harcourt Publishing Co.
—ESL - Building English Proficiency, Grades 2-3. 2003. (ESL: Building English Proficiency Ser.). (ENG.). 128p. (gr. 2-3). pap. 15.99 *(978-0-7398-7097-6(1))* Houghton Mifflin Harcourt Publishing Co.
—Esl/Ell. 2003. (ESL: Building English Proficiency Ser.). (ENG.). 128p. (gr. 4-6). pap. 15.99 *(978-0-7398-7098-3(X))* Houghton Mifflin Harcourt Publishing Co.
Stephens, Edna Cucksey. Rock U. S. A. & the American Way! A Freedom Handbook. Herrick, Mark J., illus. 2004. (Connect-It Ser.). 124p. (J). (gr. -1-3). pap. 29.95 *(978-0-9749412-1-9(2))* EDCO Publishing, Inc.
Through the Looking Glass. (Read-Along Ser.). (YA). pap., stu. ed. 34.95 incl. audio *(978-0-88432-971-8(2), S23946)* Pavilion Pubs.
Traynor, Tracy. American English with Abby & Zak. Hambleton, Laura, illus. 2007. (Abby & Zak Ser.). (ENG.). 48p. (J). (gr. k-2). pap. 16.95 *(978-1-84059-491-1(8))* Milet Publishing.
Walker, Robin & Harding, Keith. Tourism 2. 2009. (ENG., Illus.). 144p. stu. ed. 31.19 *(978-0-19-455103-8(2))* Oxford Univ. Pr., Inc.
Walker, Theo. Swing, Slither, Swim Low Intermediate Book with Online Access. 2014. (ENG., Illus.). 24p. pap. 9.50 *(978-1-107-69242-8(3))* Cambridge Univ. Pr.
WalkerTheo. EAT UP! BEGINNING BOOK WITH ONLINE ACCESS. 2014. (ENG.). 24p. (J). pap. 9.50 *(978-1-107-68962-6(7))* Cambridge Univ. Pr.
—FEEDING TIME: THE FEEDING HABITS OF ANIMALS HIGH BEGINNING BOOK WITH ONLINE ACCESS. 2014. (ENG., Illus.). 24p. (J). pap. 9.50 *(978-1-107-67867-5(6))* Cambridge Univ. Pr.
—SUGAR: OUR GUILTY PLEASURE LOW INTERMEDIATE BOOK WITH ONLINE ACCESS. 2014. (ENG., Illus.). 28p. (J). pap. 9.50 *(978-1-107-68146-0(4))* Cambridge Univ. Pr.
Wallwork, Adrian. Business Vision. 2003. (ENG.). audio compact disk 35.95 *(978-0-19-437984-7(1))* Oxford Univ. Pr., Inc.
West, Clare. Recycling Advanced English Student's Book. 4th ed. 2013. (Georgian Press Ser.). (ENG.). 270p. pap. 26.50 *(978-1-107-65751-9(2))* Cambridge Univ. Pr.
Wright, Craig. Double Trouble. 2010. (ENG., Illus.). 14p. act. bk. ed. 4.06 *(978-0-19-440152-4(9))* Oxford Univ. Pr., Inc.
Wright, Craig, ed. Just Like Mine. 2010. (ENG., Illus.). 14p. act. bk. ed. 4.06 *(978-0-19-440164-7(2))* Oxford Univ. Pr., Inc.
—Let's Go to the Rainforest. 2010. (ENG., Illus.). 14p. act. bk. ed. 4.06 *(978-0-19-440167-8(7))* Oxford Univ. Pr., Inc.
—New Girl in School, Level 3. 2010. (ENG., Illus.). 14p. act. bk. ed. 4.06 *(978-0-19-440162-3(6))* Oxford Univ. Pr., Inc.
—Students in Space, Level 3. 2010. (ENG., Illus.). 14p. act. bk. ed. 4.06 *(978-0-19-440160-9(X))* Oxford Univ. Pr., Inc.
—Things That Fly. 2010. (ENG., Illus.). 14p. act. bk. ed. 4.06 *(978-0-19-440166-1(9))* Oxford Univ. Pr., Inc.
—What Did You Do Yesterday? 2010. (ENG., Illus.). 14p. pap., act. bk. ed. 4.06 *(978-0-19-440161-6(8))* Oxford Univ. Pr., Inc.
—Yesterday, Today, & Tomorrow, Level 4. 2010. (ENG., Illus.). 16p. act. bk. ed. 4.06 *(978-0-19-440169-2(3))* Oxford Univ. Pr., Inc.
Wyldeck, Kathi. English for Everyone - Book. 2007. 148p. per. 16.95 *(978-1-84799-927-6(1))* Lulu Pr., Inc.
—English for Everyone - Book 1. 2007. 89p. pap. 10.95 *(978-1-84799-926-9(3))* Lulu Pr., Inc.
Zelman, Nancy Ellen. Conversation Inspirations: Over 2400 Conversation Topics. 3rd ed. 2005. 114p. (gr. 7-12). pap. 19.00 *(978-0-86647-195-4(2))* Pro Lingua Assocs., Inc.

ENGLISH LANGUAGE—TEXTBOOKS FOR FOREIGN SPEAKERS—SPANISH

Beaton, Clare, illus. English-Spanish Bilingual First Books, 6 bks. (J). lib. bdg. 86.70 *(978-1-56674-944-2(1))* Forest Hse. Publishing Co., Inc.
Ferrándiz, Elena, illus. Mis Primeras 1000 Palabras/My First 1,000 Words. 2004. (ENG & SPA.). 72p. (J). (gr. -1-2). 15.95 *(978-1-58394-100-3(2), Frog Children's Bks.)* North Atlantic Bks.
Harvey, William C. Ingles para Ninos: English for Children. 2nd rev. ed. 2012. (SPA.). 216p. (gr. 2-6). pap. 12.99 *(978-1-4380-0001-5(4))* Barron's Educational Series, Inc.
Inglés Básico para niños: Edad 7-12, Basic English for Children: ¡Aprenda las 250 Palabras Más Importantes en Inglés!, Learn the 250 Most Important Words in English! 2005. 30.00 *(978-0-9769266-2-7(8))* Weapons of Mass Instruction.
Mahmout, Ulfet & Thompson, Alan. My Life Story. 2004. (Illus.). 34p. (J). *(978-1-85269-885-0(3))* Mantra Lingua.
Maldonado, Premier. Animales. 2006. (SPA.). 14.99 *(978-0-9727886-5-6(4))* Osmosis, LLC.
—Cuerpo. 2006. (SPA., Illus.). 14.99 *(978-0-9727886-4-9(6))* Osmosis, LLC.
Milet Publishing Staff. Animals - My First Bilingual Book. 2011. (My First Bilingual Book Ser.). (SPA & ENG., Illus.). 24p. (J). (gr. k — 1). bds. 8.99 *(978-1-84059-620-5(1))* Milet Publishing.
—Home - My First Bilingual Book. 2011. (My First Bilingual Book Ser.). (SPA & ENG., Illus.). 24p. (J). (gr. k — 1). bds. 8.99 *(978-1-84059-652-6(X))* Milet Publishing.
—Milet Interactive for Kids - English for Spanish Speakers. 2012. (Milet Interactive for Kids Ser.). (SPA & ENG., Illus.). 1p. (J). (gr. k-2). cd-rom 24.95 *(978-1-84059-674-8(0))* Milet Publishing.
—My First Bilingual Book-Fruit (English-Spanish) 2011. (My First Bilingual Book Ser.). (SPA & ENG., Illus.). 24p. (J). (gr. k — 1). bds. 7.99 *(978-1-84059-636-6(8))* Milet Publishing.
—My First Bilingual Book-Vegetables (English-Spanish) 2011. (My First Bilingual Book Ser.). (SPA & ENG., Illus.). 24p. (J). (gr. k — 1). bds. 8.99 *(978-1-84059-668-7(6))* Milet Publishing.
Ninos Aprenden Ingles Corp. Children Learning English. 2004. (Illus.). 119p. (J). pap. 19.95 *(978-1-934665-03-9(7))* Ninos Aprenden Ingles Corp.
Practice Pal Bilingual Addition/Subtraction Practice Book. 2004. (Illus.). 16p. (J). (gr. k-2). spiral bd. *(978-1-930355-50-7(5))* Bright of America.
Villafane-Leon, Ines. A Story for All Seasons: Un Cuento Para Cada Estacion: Immigration of One. 2004. (ENG & SPA.). xiii, 367p. (YA). pap. 22.95 *(978-1-882897-78-0(1))* Lost Coast Pr.

ENGLISH LANGUAGE—VERSIFICATION

see Versification

ENGLISH LITERATURE

see also Authors, English; English Drama; English Poetry; English Wit and Humor; Parodies; Short Stories

Balsamo, Annelise. VCE Literature Units 3 & 4, 2017-2020. 2016. (Cambridge Checkpoints Ser.). (ENG.). pap. *(978-1-316-78371-9(5))* Cambridge Univ. Pr.
Brown, Robin. Practice Papers: English. 2nd ed. (Illus.). 32p. (YA). pap. 6.99 *(978-0-340-72687-7(3))* Hodder & Stoughton GBR. Dist: Trafalgar Square Publishing.
Collins Publishers Staff. KS3 English. 2014. (ENG.). 216p. (YA). (gr. 6-9). pap. 16.95 *(978-0-00-756281-7(0))* HarperCollins Pubs. Ltd. GBR. Dist: Independent Pubs. Group.
Collins UK Publishing Staff & Collins KS3 Staff. KS3 English. 2014. (ENG., Illus.). 144p. (YA). (gr. 6-9). pap. 12.95 *(978-0-00-756280-0(2))* HarperCollins Pubs. Ltd. GBR. Dist: Independent Pubs. Group.
Doyle, Arthur Conan & Saddleback Educational Publishing Staff, eds. The Hound of the Baskervilles. 2011. (Timeless Classics Ser.). (ENG.). 48p. (YA). (gr. 9-12). pupil's gde. ed. 19.95 incl. cd-rom *(978-1-61651-137-1(0))* Saddleback Educational Publishing, Inc.
Gould, Mike, et al. English a - a Concise Revision Course for CSEC(r). 2017. (ENG.). 260p. (YA). (gr. 9). pap. 19.99 ***(978-0-00-820813-4(1))*** HarperCollins Pubs. Ltd. GBR. Dist: Independent Pubs. Group.
Hackman, Sue. Highlights of English Literature. 2008. 96p. (gr. 12-13). pap. 21.50 *(978-0-340-96632-7(7))* Hodder Education Group GBR. Dist: Trans-Atlantic Pubns., Inc.
Johnson, Claudia, ed. Colonialism in Joseph Conrad's Heart of Darkness. 2012. (Social Issues in Literature Ser.). (ENG., Illus.). 224p. (gr. 10-12). pap. 32.00 *(978-0-7377-5804-7(X))*; lib. bdg. 40.95 *(978-0-7377-5803-0(1))* Cengage Gale. (Greenhaven Pr., Inc.).
Kossuth, Kornel. English for Common Entrance 13+ Practice Book. 2014. (ENG.). 112p. (gr. 8-10). pap. 39.50 *(978-1-4718-0411-3(9))* Hodder Education Group GBR. Dist: Trans-Atlantic Pubns., Inc.
Letts 11+, Letts. 11+ Practice Test Papers for the CEM Tests. 2017. (Letts 11+ Success Ser.). (ENG.). 312p. (J). (gr. 4-7). pap. 29.99 ***(978-1-84419-898-6(7))*** HarperCollins Pubs. Ltd. GBR. Dist: Independent Pubs. Group.
Lord, Roberta. Reflections: French Version. 2003. 200p. 9.95 net. *(978-1-931934-25-1(8))* Back Yard Pub.
Neumann Press Staff. American Cardinal Readers, Bk. 4. McLaughlin, Edith M. & Curtis, T. Adrian, eds. 2014. (American Cardinal Reader Ser.: 4). (ENG., Illus.). 268p. (J). (gr. 2-5). reprint ed. 19.95 *(978-0-911845-39-6(9), Neumann Pr.)* TAN Bks.
O'Connor, John. Literacy in Context for AQA A. 2003. (Literacy in Context Ser.). (ENG., Illus.). 208p. pap. 23.00 *(978-0-521-53528-1(X))* Cambridge Univ. Pr.
Saddleback Educational Publishing Staff, ed. Captains Courageous. 2011. (Timeless Classics Ser.). (ENG.). 48p. (YA). (gr. 9-12). pupil's gde. ed. 19.95 incl. cd-rom *(978-1-61651-129-6(X))* Saddleback Educational Publishing, Inc.
—Christmas Carol. 2011. (Timeless Classics Ser.). (ENG.). 48p. (YA). (gr. 9-12). pupil's gde. ed. 19.95 incl. cd-rom *(978-1-61651-130-2(3))* Saddleback Educational Publishing, Inc.
—Dr. Jekyll & Mr. Hyde. 2011. (Timeless Classics Ser.). (ENG.). 48p. (YA). (gr. 9-12). pupil's gde. ed. 19.95 incl. cd-rom *(978-1-61651-133-3(8))* Saddleback Educational Publishing, Inc.
—Dracula. 2011. (Timeless Classics Ser.). (ENG.). 48p. (YA). (gr. 9-12). pupil's gde. ed. 19.95 incl. cd-rom *(978-1-61651-132-6(X))* Saddleback Educational Publishing, Inc.
—Frankenstein. 2011. (Timeless Classics Ser.). (ENG.). 48p. (YA). (gr. 9-12). pupil's gde. ed. 19.95 incl. cd-rom *(978-1-61651-134-0(6))* Saddleback Educational Publishing, Inc.
—Great Expectations. 2011. (Timeless Classics Ser.). (ENG.). 48p. (YA). (gr. 9-12). pupil's gde. ed. 19.95 incl. cd-rom *(978-1-61651-135-7(4))* Saddleback Educational Publishing, Inc.
—Hamlet. 2011. (Timeless Shakespeare Ser.). (ENG.). 48p. (YA). (gr. 9-12). pupil's gde. ed. 19.95 incl. cd-rom *(978-1-61651-159-3(1))* Saddleback Educational Publishing, Inc.
—Jane Eyre. 2011. (Timeless Classics Ser.). (ENG.). 48p. (YA). (gr. 9-12). pupil's gde. ed. 19.95 incl. cd-rom *(978-1-61651-139-5(7))* Saddleback Educational Publishing, Inc.
—Julius Caesar. 2011. (Timeless Shakespeare Ser.). (ENG.). 48p. (YA). (gr. 9-12). pupil's gde. ed. 19.95 incl. cd-rom *(978-1-61651-160-9(5))* Saddleback Educational Publishing, Inc.
—King Lear. 2011. (Timeless Shakespeare Ser.). (ENG.). 48p. (YA). (gr. 9-12). pupil's gde. ed. 19.95 incl. cd-rom *(978-1-61651-161-6(3))* Saddleback Educational Publishing, Inc.
—Macbeth. 2011. (Timeless Shakespeare Ser.). (ENG.). 48p. (YA). (gr. 9-12). pupil's gde. ed. 19.95 incl. cd-rom *(978-1-61651-162-3(1))* Saddleback Educational Publishing, Inc.
—Merchant of Venice. 2011. (Timeless Shakespeare Ser.). (ENG.). 48p. (YA). (gr. 9-12). pupil's gde. ed. 19.95 incl. cd-rom *(978-1-61651-163-0(X))* Saddleback Educational Publishing, Inc.
—A Midsummer Night's Dream. 2011. (Timeless Shakespeare Ser.). (ENG.). 48p. (YA). (gr. 9-12). pupil's gde. ed. 19.95 incl. cd-rom *(978-1-61651-164-7(8))* Saddleback Educational Publishing, Inc.
—Oliver Twist. 2011. (Timeless Classics Ser.). (ENG.). 48p. (YA). (gr. 9-12). pupil's gde. ed. 19.95 incl. cd-rom *(978-1-61651-145-6(1))* Saddleback Educational Publishing, Inc.
—Othello. 2011. (Timeless Shakespeare Ser.). (ENG.). 48p. (YA). (gr. 9-12). pupil's gde. ed. 19.95 incl. cd-rom *(978-1-61651-165-4(6))* Saddleback Educational Publishing, Inc.
—Pride & Prejudice. 2011. (Timeless Classics Ser.). (ENG.). 48p. (YA). (gr. 9-12). pupil's gde. ed. 19.95 incl. cd-rom *(978-1-61651-146-3(X))* Saddleback Educational Publishing, Inc.
—Robinson Crusoe. 2011. (Timeless Classics Ser.). (ENG.). 48p. (YA). (gr. 9-12). pupil's gde. ed. 19.95 incl. cd-rom *(978-1-61651-149-4(4))* Saddleback Educational Publishing, Inc.
—Romeo & Juliet. 2011. (Timeless Shakespeare Ser.). (ENG.). 48p. (YA). (gr. 9-12). pupil's gde. ed. 19.95 incl. cd-rom *(978-1-61651-166-1(4))* Saddleback Educational Publishing, Inc.
—Tale of Two Cities. 2011. (Timeless Classics Ser.). (ENG.). 48p. (YA). (gr. 9-12). tchr. ed. 19.95 incl. cd-rom *(978-1-61651-152-4(4))* Saddleback Educational Publishing, Inc.
—The Tempest. 2011. (Timeless Shakespeare Ser.). (ENG.). 48p. (YA). (gr. 9-12). pupil's gde. ed. 19.95 incl. cd-rom *(978-1-61651-167-8(2))* Saddleback Educational Publishing, Inc.
Steel, Abigail & Collins UK Publishing Staff. Composition, Bk. 5. 2015. (Collins Treasure House Ser.). (ENG.). 64p. (J). (gr. 4-5). pap. 14.95 *(978-0-00-813350-4(6))* HarperCollins Pubs. Ltd. GBR. Dist: Independent Pubs. Group.
—Comprehension, Bk. 5. 2015. (Collins Treasure House Ser.). (ENG.). 48p. (J). (gr. 4-5). pap. 14.95 *(978-0-00-813344-3(1))* HarperCollins Pubs. Ltd. GBR. Dist: Independent Pubs. Group.
Whitney, Chris & Collins UK Publishing Staff. Composition, Bk. 6. 2015. (Collins Treasure House Ser.). (ENG.). 64p. (J). (gr. 5-6). pap. 15.95 *(978-0-00-813349-8(2))* HarperCollins Pubs. Ltd. GBR. Dist: Independent Pubs. Group.

ENGLISH LITERATURE—COLLECTIONS

Harcourt School Publishers Staff. Trophies: Distant Voyages. 3rd ed. 2003. (Harcourt School Publishers Trophies Ser.). (ENG., Illus.). 768p. (gr. 5-5). stu. ed. 82.50 *(978-0-15-339788-2(8))* Harcourt Schl. Pubs.
—Trophies Level 1-4: Time Together. 3rd ed. 2003. (Harcourt School Publishers Trophies Ser.). (ENG., Illus.). 264p. (gr. 1-1). 40.05 *(978-0-15-339779-0(9))* Harcourt Schl. Pubs.
—Trophies Level 1-5: Gather Around. 3rd ed. 2003. (Harcourt School Publishers Trophies Ser.). (ENG., Illus.). 276p. (gr. 1-1). 40.05 *(978-0-15-339781-3(0))* Harcourt Schl. Pubs.
—Trophies Level 2-1: Just for You. 3rd ed. 2003. (Harcourt School Publishers Trophies Ser.). (ENG., Illus.). 464p. (gr. 2-2). 58.70 *(978-0-15-339782-0(9))* Harcourt Schl. Pubs.
Oliver, Patrick M., ed. Turn the Page & You Don't Stop: Sharing Successful Chapters in Our Lives with Youth. 2006. (Illus.). 156p. pap. 12.00 *(978-0-9779499-0-8(7))* Say It Loud! Readers & Writers Series.
Students of Animo Inglewood Charter High School Staff. Rhythm of the Chain: Young Writers Explore Teamwork. 2006. (ENG.). 182p. per. 12.00 *(978-0-9768467-0-3(5))* 826 Valencia.

ENGLISH LITERATURE—CRITICISM

see English Literature—History and Criticism

ENGLISH LITERATURE—HISTORY AND CRITICISM

Beers. Elements of Literature: Premier Online Edition. 5th ed. 2004. (gr. 9). 82.20 *(978-0-03-073847-0(4))* Holt McDougal.
Bloom, Harold. London. 2005. (Bloom's Literary Places Ser.). (Illus.). 150p. (YA). (gr. 9-13). 40.00 *(978-0-7910-7841-9(8))* Facts On File, Inc.
Bloom, Harold, ed. Frankenstein. 2nd annot. rev. ed. 2006. (Bloom's Modern Critical Interpretations Ser.). (Illus.). 256p. (C). (gr. 9-18). 45.00 *(978-0-7910-9303-0(4))* Facts On File, Inc.
Bloom, Harold & Marson, Janyce, eds. A Midsummer Night's Dream. 2008. (Bloom's Shakespeare Through the Ages Ser.). 260p. (YA). (gr. 9-12). 50.00 *(978-0-7910-9595-9(9))* Facts On File, Inc.
Bodden, Valerie. Poetry Basics - Nursery Rhymes. 2009. (Poetry Basics Ser.). 32p. 19.95 *(978-1-58341-778-2(8), Creative Education)* Creative Co., The.
Borus, Audrey. Reading & Interpreting the Works of George Orwell. 2016. (Lit Crit Guides). (Illus.). 176p. (J). 39.93 *(978-0-7660-8354-7(3))* Enslow Pubs., Inc.
Boshier, Rosa. How to Analyze the Works of Virginia Woolf, 1 vol. 2012. (Essential Critiques Set 3 Ser.). (ENG.). 112p. (J). (gr. 6-12). lib. bdg. 35.64 *(978-1-61783-459-2(9), Essential Library)* ABDO Publishing Co.
British Literature, 6 vols., Set. 2004. (Illus.). (YA). (gr. 9). tchr. ed., stu. ed. 38.95 *(978-0-7403-0203-9(5), ES9515, Lifepac)* Alpha Omega Pubns., Inc.
British Literature. 2004. (gr. 12-18). cd-rom *(978-0-618-30391-5(X), 2-04296)* Holt McDougal.
Brontë, Charlotte. Charlotte Brontë's Jane Eyre. Bloom, Harold, ed. 2nd rev. ed. 2006. (Bloom's Modern Critical Interpretations Ser.). 235p. (C). (gr. 9-18). lib. bdg. 45.00 *(978-0-7910-9304-7(2), Chelsea Hse.)* Facts On File, Inc.
Clinton, Greg. Reading & Interpreting the Works of J.R.R. Tolkien. 2016. (Lit Crit Guides). (Illus.). 176p. (J). 39.93 *(978-0-7660-8362-2(4))* Enslow Pubs., Inc.
Helms, Neil. J. R. R. Tolkien. 2004. (Great Writers Ser.). (Illus.). 128p. (YA). (gr. 9-13). 31.95 *(978-0-7910-7847-1(7), Chelsea Hse.)* Facts On File, Inc.
Johnson, Claudia. Issues of Class in Jane Austen's Pride & Prejudice. 2008. (Social Issues in Literature Ser.). (ENG., Illus.). 178p. (YA). (gr. 10-12). 28.45 *(978-0-7377-4259-6(3), LML02109-243174, Greenhaven Pr., Inc.)* Cengage Gale.
Johnson, Claudia, ed. Issues of Class in Jane Austen's Pride & Prejudice. 2008. (Social Issues in Literature Ser.). (ENG., Illus.). 224p. (gr. 10-12). 46.40 *(978-0-7377-4258-9(5), LML02109-243170, Greenhaven Pr., Inc.)* Cengage Gale.
Jones, Darryl. Jane Austen, 1 vol. 2004. (Critical Issues Ser.). (ENG., Illus.). x, 252p. 110.00 *(978-0-333-72743-0(6), 9780333727430)* Palgrave Macmillan.
Kirk, Connie Ann. A Student's Guide to Jane Austen. 2016. (Lit Crit Guides). (Illus.). 176p. (J). (gr. 6-6). 39.93 *(978-0-7660-7911-3(2))* Enslow Pubs., Inc.
Kirk, E. J. Step into Narnia: A Journey Through the Lion, the Witch & the Wardrobe. 2005. (Chronicles of Narnia Ser.). (Illus.). 64p. (J). lib. bdg. 20.89 *(978-0-06-074234-8(8))* HarperCollins Pubs.
Linking Literature: Using Oral History to Connect Books to the World. 2004. per. *(978-1-932948-07-3(4))* Student Pr. Initiative.
Loos, Pamela. Reading Sounder. 2005. (Engaged Reader Ser.). (Illus.). 80p. (gr. 5-8). lib. bdg. 25.00 *(978-0-7910-8833-3(2), Chelsea Hse.)* Facts On File, Inc.
Mussari, Mark. The Sonnets. 2010. (Shakespeare Explained 3 Ser.). (Illus.). 112p. (gr. 7-18). 42.79 *(978-1-60870-018-9(6))* Marshall Cavendish GBR. Dist: Marshall Cavendish Corp.
Orwell, George. 1984. Orwell, George & Bloom, Harold, eds. 2nd rev. ed. 2006. (Bloom's Modern Critical Interpretations Ser.). 216p. (C). (gr. 9-18). lib. bdg. 45.00 *(978-0-7910-9300-9(X), Chelsea Hse.)* Facts On File, Inc.

Pasachoff, Naomi E. A Student's Guide to the Brontë Sisters. 2009. (Understanding Literature Ser.). (Illus.). 160p. (YA). (gr. 9-12). lib. bdg. 29.27 (978-0-7660-3267-5(1)) Enslow Pubs., Inc.

Peterson-Hilleque, Victoria. How to Analyze the Works of J. K. Rowling, 1 vol. 2011. (Essential Critiques Set 2 Ser.). (ENG., Illus.). 112p. (J). (gr. 6-12). lib. bdg. 35.64 (978-1-61783-093-8(3)) ABDO Publishing Co.

Saddleback Educational Publishing Staff, ed. Twelfth Night. 2011. (Timeless Shakespeare Ser.). (ENG.). 48p. (YA). (gr. 9-12). pupil's gde. ed. 19.95 incl. cd-rom (978-1-61651-168-5(0)) Saddleback Educational Publishing, Inc.

—War of the Worlds. 2011. (Timeless Classics Ser.). (ENG.). 48p. (YA). (gr. 9-12). pupil's gde. ed. 19.95 incl. cd-rom (978-1-61651-157-9(5)) Saddleback Educational Publishing, Inc.

School Zone Publishing Company Staff. Story Problems: Grades 1 & 2. (Illus.). (J). 19.99 incl. audio compact disk (978-0-88743-936-0(5)) School Zone Publishing Co.

Stephenson, William. John Fowles. 2003. (ENG., Illus.). 128p. (C). 80.00 (978-0-7463-1019-9(6)); pap. 19.95 (978-0-7463-0987-2(2)) Northcote Hse. Publishers, Ltd. GBR. Dist: Casemate Academic.

Stobaugh, James. British Literature Student. 2005. (Broadman & Holman Literature Ser.). 288p. stu. ed. 24.99 (978-0-8054-5894-7(8)) B&H Publishing Group.

Streissguth, Thomas & Streissguth, Tom. Legends of Dracula. 2003. (Biography Ser.). (Illus.). 112p. (YA). (gr. 6-18). pap. 7.95 (978-0-8225-9682-0(2), Carolrhoda Bks.) Lerner Publishing Group.

Thomas, Ruth. Emma: Insight Text Guide (Large Print 16pt) 2013. 86p. pap. (978-1-4596-5995-7(3)) ReadHowYouWant.com, Ltd.

Tibbetts, Stacy Glen. Reading Roll of Thunder, Hear My Cry. 2005. (Engaged Reader Ser.). (Illus.). 88p. (gr. 5-8). lib. bdg. 25.00 (978-0-7910-8832-6(4), Chelsea Hse.) Facts On File, Inc.

Walters, Tracey Lorraine. Zadie Smith. 2013. (J). (978-1-60870-507-8(2)) Marshall Cavendish.

ENGLISH PARODIES

see Parodies

ENGLISH POETRY

Berquist, Laura M. The Harp & Laurel Wreath: Poetry & Dictation for the Classical Curriculum. 2011. (Illus.). 493p. pap. (978-1-58617-691-4(9)) Ignatius Pr.

Dahl, Roald. Revolting Rhymes. 2009. (ENG.). 48p. (J). (gr. 1-3). pap. 7.99 (978-0-14-241482-8(4), Puffin Books) Penguin Young Readers Group.

Dunbar, Polly, illus. Here's a Little Poem: A Very First Book of Poetry. 2007. (ENG.). 112p. (J). (gr. k-12). 21.99 (978-0-7636-3141-3(8)) Candlewick Pr.

Esiri, Allie & Kelly, Rachel, eds. IF: A Treasury of Poems for Almost Every Possibility. Lawton, Natasha, illus. 2012. (ENG.). 288p. (J). (gr. 4). 28.00 (978-0-85786-557-1(9)) Canongate Bks. GBR. Dist: Publishers Group West (PGW).

Greenaway, Kate. Kate Greenaway's Birthday Book. unabr. ed. 2012. (Illus.). 269p. 49.99 (978-1-4622-8642-3(9)) Repressed Publishing LLC.

Holden, J. T. Alice in Verse the Lost Rhymes of Wonderland: The Lost Rhymes of Wonderland. Johnson, Andrew, illus. 2011. (ENG.). 112p. (J). 14.99 (978-0-9825089-9-2(9)) Candleshoe Bks.

Keats, John & Prosek, James. Bird, Butterfly, Eel. Prosek, James, illus. 2009. (ENG., Illus.). 32p. (J). (gr. 1-5). 17.99 (978-0-689-86829-0(4), Simon & Schuster Bks. For Young Readers) Simon & Schuster Bks. For Young Readers.

Kennedy, Caroline. Poems to Learn by Heart. Muth, Jon J., illus. 2013. (ENG.). 194p. (J). (gr. 5-9). 21.99 (978-1-4231-0805-4(1)) Hyperion Pr.

Kennedy, Caroline & Sampson, Ana. Poems to Learn by Heart. Muth, Jon J., illus. 2014. (ENG.). 224p. 22.95 (978-1-78243-145-9(4)) O'Mara, Michael Bks., Ltd. GBR. Dist: Independent Pubs. Group.

Lear, Edward. Nonsense Poems. 2011. (Dover Children's Thrift Classics Ser.). (ENG., Illus.). 96p. (Orig.). (J). (gr. 3-8). reprint ed. pap. 4.00 (978-0-486-28031-8(4)) Dover Pubns., Inc.

—Nonsense Song. l.t. ed. 2006. 108p. pap. (978-1-84637-276-6(3)) Echo Library.

Milne, A. A. Now We Are Six. Shepard, Ernest H., illus. deluxe ed. 2008. (Winnie-The-Pooh Ser.). (ENG.). 128p. (J). (gr. 3-7). 19.99 (978-0-525-47929-1(5), Dutton Books for Young Readers) Penguin Young Readers Group.

Mitton, Tony. Plum. GrandPré, Mary, illus. 2003. (J). (978-0-439-36410-2(8), Levine, Arthur A. Bks.) Scholastic, Inc.

Moses, Brian. I'm Telling on You! Poems about Brothers & Sisters. Maddison, Lucy, illus. 2003. (ENG.). 60p. (J). pap. (978-0-330-36867-4(2), Pan) Pan Macmillan.

Moskowitz, Cheryl. Can It Be about Me? Asquith, Ros, illus. 2013. (ENG.). 96p. (J). (gr. 2-5). pap. 8.99 (978-1-84780-340-5(7), Frances Lincoln) Quarto Publishing Group UK GBR. Dist: Hachette Bk. Group.

Stevenson, Robert Louis. A Child's Garden of Verses Shape Book. Peat, Fern Bisel, illus. 2011. (ENG.). 16p. (J). pap. 9.95 (978-1-59583-429-4(X), Darling & Co.) Laughing Elephant.

Temperley, Howard. In the Days of Dinosaurs: A Rhyming Romp Through Dino History. Kline, Michael P., illus. 2004. (J). pap. 9.95 (978-1-885593-81-6(3), Ideal Pubns.) Worthy Publishing.

Tolkien, J. R. R. Bilbo's Last Song. Baynes, Pauline, illus. 2012. (ENG.). 32p. (J). (gr. k-12). 12.99 (978-0-375-82373-2(5), Knopf Bks. for Young Readers) Random Hse. Children's Bks.

ENGLISH POETRY—COLLECTIONS

Hamilton, Meredith, illus. They're Poets & They Know It! A Collection of 30 Timeless Poems. 2007. 31p. (J). pap. (978-0-545-03017-5(X)) Scholastic, Inc.

Ross, Harriet, ed. Great English Story Poems: Collections. 160p. (YA). (gr. 5-12). pap. 8.95 (978-0-87460-364-4(1)) Lion Bks.

Williamson, Melanie, illus. Drift upon a Dream: Poems for Sleepy Babies. 2004. 32p. (J). 16.95 (978-1-57091-577-2(6)) Charlesbridge Publishing, Inc.

ENGLISH POETRY—HISTORY AND CRITICISM

Bloom, Harold & Harley, Alexis, eds. William Blake. 2008. (Bloom's Classic Critical Views Ser.). 232p. (YA). (gr. 9-12). 45.00 (978-1-60413-138-3(1)) Facts On File, Inc.

Duffy, Carol Ann & York Notes Staff. Poems of Duffy. 2005. (ENG.). 160p. pap. 20.00 (978-1-4058-0705-0(9)) Pearson Education, Ltd. GBR. Dist: Trans-Atlantic Pubns., Inc.

Fandel, Jennifer. Keats, Shakespeare, & Other Wordsmiths. 2005. (Understanding Poetry Ser.). (Illus.). 48p. (YA). (gr. 4-7). lib. bdg. 21.95 (978-1-58341-343-2(X)) Creative Co., The.

Houle, Michelle M. Modern British Poetry: "The World Is Never the Same" 2010. (Poetry Rocks! Ser.). (Illus.). 160p. (YA). (gr. 9-12). 35.94 (978-0-7660-3278-1(7)) Enslow Pubs., Inc.

—Modern British Poetry- The World Is Never the Same. 2011. (Poetry Rocks! Ser.). (Illus.). 160p. (YA). (gr. 9-18). pap. 10.95 (978-1-59845-381-2(5)) Enslow Pubs., Inc.

Johanson, Paula. Early British Poetry: "Words That Burn" (Poetry Rocks! Ser.). (Illus.). 160p. (YA). (gr. 9-18). 2011. pap. 10.95 (978-1-59845-383-6(1)) 2009. lib. bdg. 35.94 (978-0-7660-3276-7(0)) Enslow Pubs., Inc.

Sellars, Roy & Allen, Graham, eds. The Salt Companion to Harold Bloom. 2007. (ENG.). 536p. per. (978-1-876857-20-2(X)) Salt Publishing.

Sheppard, Robert, ed. The Salt Companion to Lee Harwood. 2007. (ENG.). 252p. pap. (978-1-84471-077-5(7)) Salt Publishing.

ENGLISH SHORT STORIES

see Short Stories

ENGLISH WIT AND HUMOR

Lear, Edward. Nonsense Songs & Stories 1888. fac. ed. 2009. (ENG., Illus.). 128p. 24.95 (978-0-7123-5043-3(8)) British Library, The GBR. Dist: Independent Pubs. Group.

ENGRAVING

see also Wood-Engraving

Kamberg, Mary-Lane. Fab Lab Creating with Laser Cutters & Engravers. 2016. (Getting Creative with Fab Lab Ser.). 00064p. (J). (gr. 6-6). 34.45 (978-1-4994-6504-4(1)) Rosen Publishing Group, Inc., The.

Tonatiuh, Duncan. Funny Bones: Posada & His Day of the Dead Calaveras. 2015. (ENG., Illus.). 40p. (J). (gr. 1-5). 18.95 (978-1-4197-1647-8(6), Abrams Bks. for Young Readers) Abrams, Inc.

ENGRAVINGS

see Engraving

ENSEMBLES (MATHEMATICS)

see Set Theory

ENSIGNS

see Flags

ENTERTAINERS

see also Actors and Actresses; Clowns; Dancers

Annie Oakley. 2010. (Legends of the Wild West Ser.). (Illus.). 104p. (gr. 6-12). 35.00 (978-1-60413-594-7(8), Chelsea Hse.) Facts On File, Inc.

Annie Oakley. 2009. 48p. pap. 8.95 (978-0-8225-5788-3(6)) Lerner Publishing Group.

Armstrong, Linda J. African-American Stage, Radio, Film, & TV Entertainers. 2012. (978-1-4222-2393-2(0)) Mason Crest.

—African-American Stage, Radio, Film, & TV Entertainers. Hill, Marc Lamont, ed. 2012. (Major Black Contributions from Emancipation to Civil Rights Ser.). 64p. (J). (gr. 5). 22.95 (978-1-4222-2380-2(9)) Mason Crest.

Bill Cosby: Entertainer & Activist. 2nd rev. ed. 2010. (Black Americans of Achievement Legacy Edition Ser.). (Illus.). 104p. (gr. 6-12). 35.00 (978-1-60413-711-8(8)) Facts On File, Inc.

Blair, Eric. Annie Oakley, 1 vol. Silverman, Dianne, illus. 2011. (My First Classic Story Ser.). (ENG.). 32p. (gr. k-3). lib. bdg. 22.65 (978-1-4048-6577-8(2), My First Classic Story) Picture Window Bks.

Bloom, Harold, ed. Maya Angelou's I Know Why the Caged Bird Sings. 2nd rev. ed. 2009. (Bloom's Modern Critical Interpretations Ser.). 141p. (C). (gr. 9-18). 45.00 (978-1-60413-187-1(X), Chelsea Hse.) Facts On File, Inc.

Buffalo Bill Cody. 2010. (Legends of the Wild West Ser.). (Illus.). 136p. (gr. 6-12). 35.00 (978-1-60413-528-2(X), Chelsea Hse.) Facts On File, Inc.

Feinstein, Stephen. Read about Annie Oakley. 2006. (I Like Biographies! Ser.). (Illus.). 24p. (J). (gr. 1-3). lib. bdg. 22.60 (978-0-7660-2583-7(7), Enslow Elementary) Enslow Pubs., Inc.

Finkelstein, Norman H. Jewish Comedy Stars: Classic to Cutting Edge. 2010. (ENG., Illus.). 96p. (J). (gr. 5-12). pap. 9.95 (978-0-8225-9942-5(2), Kar-Ben Publishing) Lerner Publishing Group.

Fleming, Candace. Presenting Buffalo Bill: The Man Who Invented the Wild West. 2016. (ENG., Illus.). 288p. (J). 19.99 (978-1-59643-763-0(4), 9781596437630) Roaring Brook Pr.

Flynn, Jean. Annie Oakley: Sharpshooter & Entertainer. 2015. (J). pap. (978-0-7660-6441-6(7)) Enslow Pubs., Inc.

Forte, Virginia, ed. The 100 Most Influential Entertainers of Stage & Screen, Vol. 1. 2016. (Britannica Guide to the World's Most Influential People Ser.). (ENG.). 224p. (J). (gr. 10-10). 54.00 (978-1-68048-278-2(5), Britannica Educational Publishing) Rosen Publishing Group, Inc., The.

Gilbert, Sara. Annie Oakley. 2005. (Legends of the West (Creative Education) Ser.). (Illus.). 48p. (J). (gr. 5-9). lib. bdg. 21.95 (978-1-58341-334-0(0), Creative Education) Creative Co., The.

Goodman, Michael E. Buffalo Bill. 2005. (Legends of the West (Creative Education) Ser.). (Illus.). 48p. (J). (gr. 5-9). lib. bdg. 21.95 (978-1-58341-336-4(7), Creative Education) Creative Co., The.

Graves, Charles P. Annie Oakley: The Shooting Star. Cary, illus. 2011. 80p. (gr. 4-7). 37.95 (978-1-258-01390-5(8)) Literary Licensing, LLC.

Herringshaw, DeAnn. Lucille Ball: Actress & Comedienne, 1 vol. 2011. (Essential Lives Set 7 Ser.). (ENG., Illus.). 112p. (J). (gr. 6-12). lib. bdg. 35.64 (978-1-61783-002-0(X)) ABDO Publishing Co.

Hiller, Sandra J. Annie Oakley. 2014. (Jr. Graphic American Legends Ser.). 24p. (J). (gr. 3-6). lib. bdg. 26.25 (978-1-4777-7185-3(9), PowerKids Pr.) Rosen Publishing Group, Inc., The.

Hollander, Barbara Gottfried. Ellen DeGeneres: Television's Funniest Host, 1 vol. 2015. (ENG.). 112p. (YA). 35.60 (978-1-4777-7895-1(0), Rosen Young Adult) Rosen Publishing Group, Inc., The.

Holub, Joan. Who Was Jim Henson? Harrison, Nancy, illus. 2010. (Who Was? Ser.). (ENG.). 112p. (J). (gr. 3-7). pap. 5.99 (978-0-448-45406-1(8), Grosset & Dunlap) Penguin Young Readers Group.

Johns, Michael-Anne. Celeb Fact Files! The 411 on All Your Faves. 2006. (Illus.). 48p. (J). pap. (978-0-439-87972-9(8)) Scholastic, Inc.

—Class Acts: Your Favorite Stars in School. 2007. (Illus.). 48p. (J). (978-0-545-00183-0(8)) Scholastic, Inc.

Kimmel, Eric A. A Spotlight for Harry. Madsen, Jim, illus. 2010. (Stepping Stone Book Ser.). (ENG.). 112p. (J). (gr. 2-5). pap. 4.99 (978-0-375-85696-9(X), Random Hse. Bks. for Young Readers) Random Hse. Children's Bks.

Korb, Rena B. Pulling down the Walls: The Struggle of African American Performers. 2005. (ENG., Illus.). 24p. (J). (gr. 6-6). pap. 5.97 net. (978-0-328-13625-4(5), Scott Foresman) Pearson Schl.

Kunstler, James Howard. Annie Oakley, 1 vol. Warter, Fred, illus. 2004. (Rabbit Ears-A Classic Tale Ser.). (ENG.). 36p. (gr. k-5). 25.65 (978-1-59197-759-9(2)) Spotlight.

Landau, Elaine. Annie Oakley: Wild West Sharpshooter. 2004. (Best of the West Biographies Ser.). (Illus.). 48p. (J). lib. bdg. 23.93 (978-0-7660-2205-8(6)) Enslow Pubs., Inc.

Lang, Heather. The Original Cowgirl: The Wild Adventures of Lucille Mulhall. Beaky, Suzanne, illus. 2015. (ENG.). 32p. (J). (gr. -1-3). 16.99 (978-0-8075-2931-7(1)) Whitman, Albert & Co.

Leavitt, Amie Jane. For People Who Love to Entertain. 2016. (Cool Careers Without College Ser.). 00104p. (J). (gr. 7-7). 38.45 (978-1-5081-7274-1(9)) Rosen Publishing Group, Inc., The.

Macy, Sue. Bull's Eye: A Photobiography of Annie Oakley. 2015. (Photobiographies Ser.). (ENG.). 64p. (J). (gr. 5). pap. 7.99 (978-1-4263-2218-1(6), National Geographic Children's Bks.) National Geographic Society.

Marcovitz, Hal. Eddie Murphy. 2nd rev. ed. 2011. (Black Americans of Achievement Legacy Edition Ser.). 112p. (gr. 6-12). 35.00 (978-1-60413-844-3(0)) Facts On File, Inc.

Meltzer, Brad. I Am Lucille Ball. Eliopoulos, Christopher, illus. 2015. (Ordinary People Change the World Ser.). (ENG.). 40p. (J). (gr. k-3). 12.99 (978-0-525-42855-8(0), Dial Bks) Penguin Young Readers Group.

Miller, Dean & Talbot, Jeffrey. Annie Oakley. 2014. (Illus.). 32p. (J). 28.50 (978-1-62712-286-3(9)) Cavendish Square Publishing.

Mitchell Lane Publishers Inc. Staff. Blue Banner Biographies: Pop Entertainers II, 13 vols., Set. 2005. (gr. 3-8). (J). lib. bdg. (978-1-58415-423-5(3)); (Illus.). (YA). lib. bdg. 334.10 (978-1-58415-353-5(9)) Mitchell Lane Pubs., Inc.

Overbey, Theresa. Michael Jackson. l.t. ed. 2003. (Blue Banner Biography Ser.). (Illus.). 32p. (J). (gr. 3-8). lib. bdg. 25.70 (978-1-58415-216-3(8)) Mitchell Lane Pubs., Inc.

Pollack, Pamela D. & Meg Belviso. Who Was Lucille Ball? 2017. (Who Was... ? Ser.). lib. bdg. 16.00 **(978-0-606-39781-0(7))** Turtleback Bks.

Porterfield, Jason. Annie Oakley: Tiradora del Lejano Oeste (Annie Oakley: Wild West Sharpshooter) 2009. (Grandes personajes en la historia de los Estados Unidos (Famous People in American History) Ser.). 32p. (gr. 2-3). 47.90 (978-1-61512-789-4(5), Editorial Buenas Letras) Rosen Publishing Group, Inc., The.

—Annie Oakley: Wild West Sharpshooter. 2009. (Primary Sources of Famous People in American History Ser.). 32p. (gr. 2-3). 47.90 (978-1-60851-651-3(2)) Rosen Publishing Group, Inc., The.

—Annie Oakley: Wild West Sharpshooter / Tiradora del Lejano Oeste. 2009. (Famous People in American History/Grandes personajes en la historia de los Estados Unidos Ser.). 32p. (gr. 2-3). 47.90 (978-1-61512-537-1(X), Editorial Buenas Letras) Rosen Publishing Group, Inc., The.

Randolph, Joanne. African American Musicians & Entertainers. 2017. **(978-0-7660-9250-1(X))** Enslow Pubs., Inc.

Roberts, Christa. Guinness World Records: Awesome Entertainers! 2016. (Guinness World Records Ser.). (Illus.). 112p. (J). (gr. 1-5). pap. 5.99 (978-0-06-234169-3(3)) HarperCollins Pubs.

Rose, Katherine. Annie Oakley. 2014. (Illus.). 32p. (J). pap. (978-1-62712-287-0(7)) Cavendish Square Publishing.

Ruffin, Frances E. Annie Oakley. 2009. (American Legends Ser.). 24p. (gr. 3-3). 42.50 (978-1-61511-378-1(9), PowerKids Pr.) Rosen Publishing Group, Inc., The.

Sanford, William R. & Green, Carl R. Buffalo Bill Cody: Courageous Wild West Showman. 2012. (Courageous Heroes of the American West Ser.). (Illus.). 48p. (J). pap. 8.95 (978-1-4644-0090-2(3)); (gr. 5-18). 22.60 (978-0-7660-4007-6(0)) Enslow Pubs., Inc.

Scheunemann, Pam. Cool Jobs for Young Entertainers: Ways to Make Money Putting on an Event, 1 vol. 2011. (Cool Kid Jobs Ser.). (ENG.). 32p. (gr. 3-6). 28.50 (978-1-61613-199-9(3), Checkerboard Library) ABDO Publishing Co.

Schoell, William. "I Can Do Anything" The Sammy Davis, Jr. Story. 2004. (Avisson Young Adult Ser.). (Illus.). 116p. (J). pap. 19.95 (978-1-888105-61-2(5)) Avisson Pr., Inc.

Shoup, Kate & Spence, Kelly. Ellen DeGeneres: Television Comedian & Gay Rights Activist. 2016. (Leading Women Ser.). 112p. (gr. 7-7). 39.93 (978-1-5026-1989-1(X)) Cavendish Square Publishing.

Silate, Jennifer. Little Sure Shot: Annie Oakley & Buffalo Bill's Wild West Show. 2009. (Great Moments in American History Ser.). 32p. (gr. 3-3). 47.90 (978-1-61513-147-1(7)) Rosen Publishing Group, Inc., The.

Spies, Karen Bornemann. Buffalo Bill Cody: Legend of the Wild West. 2015. (Legendary American Biographies Ser.). 96p. (J). (gr. 6-12). 27.94 (978-0-7660-6450-8(6)); pap. 10.95 (978-0-7660-6451-5(4)) Enslow Pubs., Inc.

Tina Fey. 2010. (Women of Achievement Ser.). (Illus.). 136p. (J). (gr. 6-12). 35.00 (978-1-60413-709-5(6), Chelsea Hse.) Facts On File, Inc.

Wadsworth, Ginger. Annie Oakley. 2005. (History Maker Bios Ser.). (Illus.). 48p. (J). (gr. 3-7). lib. bdg. 26.60 (978-0-8225-2940-8(8), Lerner Pubns.) Lerner Publishing Group.

White, Katherine. The Wayans Brothers. 2009. (Famous Families Ser.). 48p. (gr. 5-5). 53.00 (978-1-61512-512-8(4)) Rosen Publishing Group, Inc., The.

Williams, Brian. Sport & Entertainment: Biggest & Best. 2003. (Biggest & Best Ser.). (Illus.). 40p. (J). pap. 7.95 (978-1-84236-063-7(9)) Miles Kelly Publishing, Ltd. GBR. Dist: Independent Pubs. Group.

Wills, Chuck. Annie Oakley. 2007. (DK Biography Ser.). (ENG., Illus.). 128p. (J). (gr. 5-12). per. 6.99 (978-0-7566-2997-7(7), DK Children) Dorling Kindersley Publishing, Inc.

York, M. J. 12 Entertainers Who Changed the World. 2015. (Change Makers Ser.). (ENG., Illus.). 32p. (J). (gr. 3-5). (978-1-63235-147-0(1), 12-Story Library) Pr. Room Editions LLC.

ENTERTAINING

see also Amusements; Etiquette; Games; Parties

Beery, Barbara. Barbara Beery's Pink Princess Party Cookbook. Williams, Zac, photos by. 2011. (ENG., Illus.). 64p. (J). (gr. 2-7). spiral bd. 15.99 (978-1-4424-1231-6(3), Simon & Schuster Bks. For Young Readers) Simon & Schuster Bks. For Young Readers.

Braun, Eric. Plan an Outdoor Party. 2014. (Party Time! Ser.). (ENG., Illus.). 32p. (gr. 4-8). lib. bdg. 26.60 (978-1-4677-3833-0(6), Lerner Pubns.) Lerner Publishing Group.

Hauser, Mindy Moser. The Vo-Tech Track to Success in Hospitality & Tourism. 2014. (Learning a Trade, Preparing for a Career Ser.). (Illus.). 80p. (J). (gr. 7-12). 34.25 (978-1-4777-7728-2(8)) Rosen Publishing Group, Inc., The.

Lynette, Rachel. Let's Throw a Christmas Party! 2011. (J). 49.50 (978-1-4488-2732-9(9)); pap. 8.25 (978-1-4488-2731-2(0)); lib. bdg. 22.60 (978-1-4488-2571-4(7)) Rosen Publishing Group, Inc., The. (PowerKids Pr.).

—Let's Throw a Valentine's Day Party! 2011. (J). 49.50 (978-1-4488-2730-5(2)); pap. 8.25 (978-1-4488-2729-9(9)); lib. bdg. 22.60 (978-1-4488-2570-7(9)) Rosen Publishing Group, Inc., The. (PowerKids Pr.).

Riley, Rowan. Great Careers with a High School Diploma: Hospitality, Human Services, & Tourism. 2008. (Great Careers with a High School Diploma Ser.). 93p. (C). (gr. 9). 32.95 (978-0-8160-7048-0(2), Ferguson Publishing Co.) Facts On File, Inc.

Segarra, Mercedes. Fun Party Food: Little Chef Recipes. 2013. (Little Chef Ser.). 36p. (J). lib. bdg. 23.94 (978-0-7660-4262-9(6)); pap. 7.95 (978-1-4644-0467-2(4)) Enslow Pubs., Inc. (Enslow Elementary).

Speregen, Debra Newberger. Party Girl: How to Throw a Fab Fest. Tallardy, Laura, illus. 2008. 48p. pap. (978-0-545-04093-8(0)) Scholastic, Inc.

Swain, Gwenyth, et al. Celebrating. 2003. (Avenues Ser.). (ENG., Illus.). 24p. (C). (gr. k-2). pap. 12.95 (978-1-57505-372-1(1)) National Geographic School Publishing, Inc.

ENTERTAINING—FICTION

Aguila, Priscilla. An Unexpected Visitor. 2006. 48p. pap. 17.96 (978-1-4116-5734-2(9)) Lulu Pr., Inc.

DeLand, M. Maitland. Busy Bees on Broadway. Martin, Lyn, illus. 2011. 32p. 15.95 (978-1-60832-063-9(4)) Greenleaf Book Group.

Depisco, Dorothea. Beetle Bugs Party: A Counting Book. Parry, Jo, illus. 2005. 10p. (J). (gr. -1-3). 10.95 (978-1-58117-415-1(2), Intervisual/Piggy Toes) Bendon, Inc.

Dixon, Dallas L. Shelby's Collection Day. Williams, Nancy E., ed. Forrest, Grace Metzger, illus. 2013. 24p. (J). pap. 12.98 (978-1-938526-54-1(6)) Laurus Bks.

Draper, Sharon M. The Silver Secret. 2010. (J). (978-0-545-07157-4(7), Scholastic Pr.) Scholastic, Inc.

Ferguson, Sarah. Tea for Ruby. Glasser, Robin Preiss, illus. 2008. (ENG.). 40p. (J). (gr. -1-3). 16.99 (978-1-4169-5419-4(8), Simon & Schuster/Paula Wiseman Bks.) Simon & Schuster/Paula Wiseman Bks.

Fraser, Mary Ann. Pet Shop Follies. 2010. (ENG.). 32p. (J). (gr. -1-1). 16.95 (978-1-59078-619-2(X)) Boyds Mills Pr.

Hillert, Margaret. Dear Dragon Goes Camping. Schimmell, David, illus. 2010. (BeginningtoRead Ser.). 32p. (J). (gr. k-2). lib. bdg. 22.60 (978-1-59953-345-2(6)) Norwood Hse. Pr.

Hope, Laura Lee. Bunny Brown & his Sister Sue Giving a Show. 2007. (ENG.). 140p. per. 18.99 (978-1-4346-2879-4(5)); 156p. per. 21.99 (978-1-4346-2914-2(7)) Creative Media Partners, LLC.

Kattan, Peter & Kattan, Nicola. More Kindergarten Sudoku: 4x4 Classic Sudoku Puzzles for Kids. 2008. 48p. pap. 7.50 (978-0-615-18718-1(8)) Kattan, Peter I.

Lemke, Donald B. Coldfinger, 1 vol. Holgate, Douglas, illus. 2009. (Zinc Alloy Ser.). (ENG.). 40p. (gr. 1-3). lib. bdg. 23.99 (978-1-4342-1586-4(5), Graphic Sparks) Stone Arch Bks.

Lutz, Nancie Anne. Patsy Ann Back Again. Lutz, Nancie Anne, illus. 2005. (Illus.). 25p. (J). pap. 14.50 (978-0-9760064-0-4(5)) Dollworks.

Malot, Hector & Crewe-Jones, Florence. Nobody's Boy: Companion Story to Nobody's Girl. Gooch, Thelma & Gruelle, Johnny, illus. 2006. 237p. (J). pap. (978-1-894666-75-6(5)) Inheritance Pubns.

Meister, Cari. Moopy the Underground Monster, 1 vol. Messner, Dennis, illus. 2009. (Monster Friends Ser.). (ENG.). 32p. (gr. 2-3). 22.65 (978-1-4342-1630-4(6)); pap. 6.25 (978-1-4342-1745-5(0)) Stone Arch Bks.

Merberg, Julie & Bober, Suzanne. Mini Masters: 4 Board Books Inside! Degas, Matisse, Monet, Van Gogh, 4 vols. 2006. (Mini Masters Ser.: MINI). (ENG., Illus.). (J). (gr. -1 — 1). bds. 19.99 (978-0-8118-5518-1(X)) Chronicle Bks. LLC.

Meyerhoff, Jenny. The Barftastic Life of Louie Burger. 2015. (J). lib. bdg. 17.20 (978-0-606-37585-6(6)) Turtleback Bks.

Park, Barbara. Junie B. Jones Is a Party Animal. unabr. ed. 2004. (Junie B. Jones Ser.: No. 10). 71p. (J). (gr. k-3). pap. 17.00 incl. audio (978-0-8072-0531-0(1), Listening Library) Random Hse. Audio Publishing Group.

Pietsch, Nicole. Sideshow of Merit. 2013. 330p. 22.95 (978-1-60898-163-2(0)); pap. 11.95 (978-1-60898-164-9(9)) namelos llc.

Santillo, LuAnn. The Tune. Santillo, LuAnn, ed. 2003. (Half-Pint Kids Readers Ser.). (Illus.). 7p. (J). (gr. -1-1). pap. 1.00 (978-1-59256-102-5(0)) Half-Pint Kids, Inc.

Schieldt, Corine. Somebody's Gotta Get Rid of That Vacuum. Schieldt, Jodi, illus. 2008. 24p. per. 24.95 *(978-1-4241-9121-5(1))* America Star Bks.

Seuss, Dr. Hooper Humperdink... ? Not Him! Nash, Scott, illus. 2006. (Bright & Early Books(R) Ser.). (ENG.). 48p. (J). (gr. -1-k). 9.99 *(978-0-679-88129-2(8),* Random Hse. Bks. for Young Readers) Random Hse. Children's Bks.

Smith, Alex T. Foxy & Egg: Starring Vivien Vixen As Foxy Dubois - Introducing Edward l'Ouef As Egg. Smith, Alex T., illus. 2011. (Illus.). 32p. (J). (gr. -1-3). 17.95 *(978-0-8234-2330-9(1))* Holiday Hse., Inc.

Sorel, Edward. Johnny on the Spot. 2012. (ENG.). 32p. (J). (gr. 1-4). 16.99 *(978-1-4424-8108-4(0),* McElderry, Margaret K. Bks.) McElderry, Margaret K. Bks.

Thaler, Mike. The Talent Show from the Black Lagoon. Lee, Jared, illus. 2004. (Black Lagoon Adventures Ser.: 2). (ENG.). 64p. (J). (gr. 2-5). 4.99 *(978-0-439-43894-0(2),* Scholastic Paperbacks) Scholastic, Inc.

Wells, Carolyn & E. C. CASWELL. Two Little Women on a Holiday. l.t. ed. 2006. 178p. pap. 21.99 *(978-1-4264-2807-4(3))* Creative Media Partners, LLC.

ENTERTAINMENTS

see Amusements

ENTOMOLOGY

see Insects

ENTOMOLOGY, ECONOMIC

see Insect Pests

ENTOZOA

see Parasites

ENTRANCE REQUIREMENTS FOR COLLEGE AND UNIVERSITIES

see Universities and Colleges—Entrance Requirements

ENVIRONMENT

see Adaptation (Biology); Ecology; Human Beings—Effect of Environment on; Human Geography; Nature—Effect of Human Beings on

ENVIRONMENT AND PESTICIDES

see Pesticides—Environmental Aspects

ENVIRONMENTAL EFFECTS ON HUMAN BEINGS

see Human Beings—Effect of Environment on

ENVIRONMENTAL PROTECTION

see also Conservation of Natural Resources

ABDO Publishing Company Staff. Climate Change. 2010. (ABDO & Daughters Ser.). 32p. 162.42 *(978-1-61613-452-5(6),* Abdo & Daughters) ABDO Publishing Co.

African-American Environmentalists. Date not set. (My Ancestors — My Heroes Ser.: Vol. 32). (J). (gr. 3-4). *(978-1-893091-31-3(7))* Parker-Wallace Publishing Co., LLC.

Ake, Anne. Everglades: An Ecosystem Facing Choices & Challenges. 2008. (ENG., Illus.). 110p. (J). (gr. 6-9). 19.95 *(978-1-56164-410-0(2))* Pineapple Pr., Inc.

Allen, Heather. Earth Day Is Every Day! 2011. (Dover Children's Activity Bks.). (ENG.). 48p. (J). (gr. 1-5). pap. 4.99 *(978-0-486-47765-7(7))* Dover Pubns., Inc.

Allen, John. Careers in Environmental & Energy Technology. 2017. (ENG.). 80p. (J). (gr. 5-12). *(978-1-68282-110-7(2))* ReferencePoint Pr., Inc.

Aloian, Molly. Earth Day. 2009. (Celebrations in My World Ser.). (ENG., Illus.). 32p. (J). (gr. -1-3). pap. *(978-0-7787-4306-4(3))* Crabtree Publishing Co.

Anderson, Dale. Al Gore: A Wake-Up Call to Global Warming. 2009. (Voices for Green Choices Ser.). (ENG., Illus.). 48p. (J). (gr. 5-9). pap. *(978-0-7787-4679-9(8))* Crabtree Publishing Co.

Anderson, Michael. The Politics of Saving the Environment. 2011. (Illus.). 102p. (J). lib. bdg. 31.70 *(978-1-61530-505-6(X))* Rosen Publishing Group, Inc., The.

Antil, Sara. 10 Ways I Can Save the Earth. 2012. (I Can Make a Difference Ser.). (ENG.). 24p. (J). (gr. 2-5). pap. 8.25 *(978-1-4488-6365-5(1));* lib. bdg. 22.60 *(978-1-4488-6203-0(5))* Rosen Publishing Group, Inc., The. (PowerKids Pr.).

Appelt, Kathi. Miss Lady Bird's Wildflowers: How a First Lady Changed America. Hein, Joy Fisher, illus. 2005. 40p. (J). lib. bdg. 17.89 *(978-0-06-001108-6(4));* (ENG.). (gr. 2-5). 17.99 *(978-0-06-001107-9(6))* HarperCollins Pubs.

Appleby, Alex. Happy Earth Day!, Vol. 1. 2014. (Happy Holidays! Ser.). 24p. (J). (gr. k-k). (ENG.). 22.60 *(978-1-4339-9935-2(8));* pap. 8.15 *(978-1-4339-9937-6(4))* Stevens, Gareth Publishing LLLP.

Audouin, Laurent, illus. Keeping It Green! 2009. (Taking Action for My Planet Ser.). 32p. (YA). (gr. 3-6). lib. bdg. 22.60 *(978-1-60754-797-6(X))* Windmill Bks.

Barnham, Kay. Protect Nature. 2007. (Environment Action Ser.). (ENG., Illus.). 32p. (J). (gr. 3-7). pap. *(978-0-7787-3668-4(7))* Crabtree Publishing Co.

Bastakos, Matina. Emma Emu's Eager Environmental Endeavour: 'E' as in Earth. 2009. (Illus.). 40p. pap. 18.49 *(978-1-4490-3952-3(9))* AuthorHouse.

Benchmark Education Co., LLC Staff, et al. Celebrating Earth Day. 2015. (Content Connections Ser.). (J). (gr. k). *(978-1-4900-0482-2(3))* Benchmark Education Co.

—Celebrating Earth Day: Big Book Edition. 2015. (Content Connections Ser.). (J). (gr. k). *(978-1-4900-0476-1(9))* Benchmark Education Co.

Berlatsky, Noah. China. 2010. (Opposing Viewpoints Ser.). (Illus.). 240p. (J). 42.95 *(978-0-7377-4765-2(X),* 1304557); pap. 29.45 *(978-0-7377-4766-9(8),* 1304557) Cengage Gale. (Greenhaven Pr., Inc.).

Bily, Cynthia A. Pollution. 2010. (Issues That Concern You Ser.). (Illus.). 144p. 36.95 *(978-0-7377-4746-1(3))* Cengage Gale.

Bishop, Amanda. Climate Change. 2008. (Saving Our World Ser.). 32p. (gr. 4-18). lib. bdg. 28.50 *(978-0-7614-3219-7(1),* Benchmark Bks.) Marshall Cavendish Corp.

—How to Reduce Your Carbon Footprint. 2008. (Energy Revolution Ser.). (ENG., Illus.). 32p. (J). (gr. 3-8). pap. *(978-0-7787-2932-7(X));* lib. bdg. *(978-0-7787-2918-1(4))* Crabtree Publishing Co.

Bortolotti, Dan. Panda Rescue: Changing the Future for Endangered Wildlife. 2003. (Firefly Animal Rescue Ser.). (ENG., Illus.). 64p. (J). (gr. 5-18). 19.95 *(978-1-55297-598-5(3),* 9781552975985); pap. 9.95 *(978-1-55297-557-2(6),* 9781552975572) Firefly Bks., Ltd.

—Tiger Rescue: Changing the Future for Endangered Wildlife. 2003. (Firefly Animal Rescue Ser.). (ENG., Illus.). 64p. (J). (gr. 5-18). 19.95 *(978-1-55297-599-2(1),* 9781552975992); pap. 9.95 *(978-1-55297-558-9(4),* 9781552975589) Firefly Bks., Ltd.

Braun, Eric. Taking Action to Help the Environment. 2016. (Who's Changing the World? Ser.). (ENG., Illus.). 48p. (J). (gr. 4-6). 33.32 *(978-1-4677-9392-6(2));* 50.65 *(978-1-4677-9667-5(0))* Lerner Publishing Group. (Lerner Pubns.).

Brownjohn, Emma. Help Save Our Planet. Brownjohn, Emma, illus. 2007. (Yes I Can! Ser.). (ENG., Illus.). 18p. (J). (gr. -1-k). 12.99 *(978-1-85707-701-8(6))* Tango Bks. GBR. Dist: Independent Pubs. Group.

Bruchac, Joseph & Locker, Thomas. Rachel Carson: Preserving a Sense of Wonder. 2009. (ENG., Illus.). 32p. (gr. 3-5). pap. 12.95 *(978-1-55591-695-4(3))* Fulcrum Publishing.

Buchanan, Shelly. Shaping Our Environment. rev. ed. 2014. (Primary Source Readers Content & Literacy Ser.). (ENG., Illus.). 32p. (gr. 3-3). pap. 8.99 *(978-1-4333-7368-8(8))* Teacher Created Materials, Inc.

Bullard, Lisa. Earth Day Every Day. Xin, Xiao, illus. 2011. (Planet Protectors Ser.). pap. 39.62 *(978-0-7613-8652-0(1),* Millbrook Pr.) Lerner Publishing Group.

—Earth Day Every Day. Xin, Xiao & Zheng, Xin, illus. 2011. (Cloverleaf Books (tm) — Planet Protectors Ser.). (ENG.). 24p. (gr. k-2). pap. 6.95 *(978-0-7613-8512-7(6),* Millbrook Pr.) Lerner Publishing Group.

—Power up to Fight Pollution. Thomas, Wes, illus. 2011. (Planet Protectors Ser.). pap. 39.62 *(978-0-7613-8655-1(6),* Millbrook Pr.); (ENG.). 24p. (J). lib. bdg. 23.93 *(978-0-7613-6108-4(1))* Lerner Publishing Group.

—Power up to Fight Pollution. Thomas, Wes & Thomas, John, Jr., illus. 2011. (Cloverleaf Books (tm) — Planet Protectors Ser.). (ENG.). 24p. (gr. k-2). pap. 6.95 *(978-0-7613-8515-8(0),* Millbrook Pr.) Lerner Publishing Group.

Burstein, Chaya M. The Kids' Catalog of Animals & the Earth. Burstein, Chaya M., illus. 2005. (Kids' Catalog Ser.). (ENG., Illus.). 200p. (gr. 3). per. 16.95 *(978-0-8276-0785-9(7))* Jewish Pubn. Society.

Business & Construction. 2010. (Green Careers Ser.). (Illus.). 160p. (C). (gr. 9-18). 32.95 *(978-0-8160-8149-3(2),* Ferguson Publishing Co.) Facts On File, Inc.

Byles, Monica. Los Polos. (Coleccion Tierra Viva).Tr. of Polar Lands. (SPA.). 32p. (YA). (gr. 5-8). *(978-84-348-3372-2(7))* SM Ediciones.

Callery, Sean. I Wonder Why There's a Hole in the Sky. 2012. (I Wonder Why Ser.). (ENG., Illus.). 32p. (J). (gr. k-3). 6.99 *(978-0-7534-6799-2(2),* 9780753467992, Kingfisher) Roaring Brook Pr.

Capstone Press. Green Crafts. 2010. (Green Crafts Ser.). (ENG.). 32p. lib. bdg. 159.90 *(978-1-4296-5940-6(8),* Snap Bks.) Capstone Press of Coughlan Cos.

Castaldo, Nancy F. Keeping Our Earth Green. Caputo, Jim, illus. 2008. (ENG.). 128p. (J). (gr. 3-8). pap. 12.99 *(978-0-8249-6825-0(5));* (gr. 8). 16.99 *(978-0-8249-6824-3(7))* Worthy Publishing. (Ideal Pubns.).

Centore, Michael. Environment & Sustainability, Vol. 10. 2016. (Stem in Current Events Ser.). (Illus.). 64p. (J). (gr. 7). 23.95 *(978-1-4222-3591-1(2))* Mason Crest.

Challen, Paul C. Environmental Disaster Alert! 2004. (Disaster Alert! Ser.). (ENG., Illus.). 32p. (J). lib. bdg. *(978-0-7787-1581-8(7))* Crabtree Publishing Co.

Challen, Paul C. & Challen, Paul. Environmental Disaster Alert! 2004. (Disaster Alert! Ser.). (ENG., Illus.). 32p. (J). pap. *(978-0-7787-1613-6(9))* Crabtree Publishing Co.

Chancellor, Deborah. The Changing Environment. 2014. (Kingfisher Readers Ser.). (ENG., Illus.). 48p. (J). (gr. k-3). 12.99 *(978-0-7534-7152-4(3),* 9780753471524, Kingfisher) Roaring Brook Pr.

—The Changing Environment, Level 5. 2014. (Kingfisher Readers Ser.). (ENG., Illus.). 48p. (J). (gr. k-3). pap. 3.99 *(978-0-7534-7153-1(1),* 9780753471531, Kingfisher) Roaring Brook Pr.

Chandler, Gary & Graham, Kevin. Making a Better World, 4 bks. Incl. Guardians of Wildlife. (YA). lib. bdg. 25.90 *(978-0-8050-4626-7(7));* Recycling. lib. bdg. 25.90 *(978-0-8050-4622-9(4));* 64p. (gr. 5-18). 1997. (Illus.). Set lib. bdg. 103.60 *(978-0-7613-3066-0(6),* Twenty-First Century Bks.) Lerner Publishing Group.

Clare, Patricia. Living Green: Saving Our Earth. 2009. (Real Life Readers Ser.). 24p. (gr. 3-4). pap. 8.25 *(978-1-4358-0121-9(0),* Rosen Classroom); 24p. (gr. 3-3). 42.50 *(978-1-61511-216-6(2),* PowerKids Pr.); (J). lib. bdg. 22.60 *(978-1-4358-2968-8(9),* PowerKids Pr.) Rosen Publishing Group, Inc., The.

Claybourne, Anna. Saving the Earth. 2010. (Discovery of Life Ser.). 48p. (YA). lib. bdg. 19.95 *(978-1-4222-1526-5(1))* Mason Crest.

Coach Pedro & Adam-Rita, Susan. 20 Easy Ways to Help Save the Earth. 2008. 48p. pap. 19.49 *(978-1-4343-9392-0(5))* AuthorHouse.

Cohen, Sheila & Terman Cohen, Sheila. Gaylord Nelson: Champion for Our Earth. 2010. (Badger Biographies Ser.). (ENG., Illus.). 120p. (J). pap. 12.95 *(978-0-87020-443-2(2))* Wisconsin Historical Society.

Cohn, Jessica. Hand to Earth: Saving the Environment, 1 vol. 2nd rev. ed. 2013. (Nonfiction Readers Ser.). (ENG., Illus.). 48p. (J). (gr. 4-4). pap. 29.96 *(978-1-4807-1120-4(9))* Shell Educational Publishing.

—Hand to Earth Saving the Environment, 1 vol. 2nd rev. ed. 2012. (Nonfiction Readers Ser.). (ENG.). 48p. (J). (gr. 4-4). pap. 9.99 *(978-1-4333-4868-6(3))* Teacher Created Materials, Inc.

—Una Mano a la Tierra: Salvando el Medio Ambiente. 2017. (TIME for Kids en Español - Level 4 Ser.). (SPA., Illus.). 48p. (gr. 4-4). lib. bdg. 31.99 *(978-1-5157-5149-6(X))* Time for Kids Inc AUS. Dist: Capstone Pub.

Communication, Education, & Travel. 2010. (Green Careers Ser.). (Illus.). 160p. (C). (gr. 9-18). 32.95 *(978-0-8160-8154-7(9),* Ferguson Publishing Co.) Facts On File, Inc.

Connolly, Sean. Greenpeace. 2009. (Global Organizations Ser.). (Illus.). 46p. (J). (gr. 4-7). pap. *(978-1-897563-34-2(5))* Saunders Bk. Co.

Crabtree Publishing, creator. Green Team, Set. 2008. (ENG.). 32p. (J). *(978-0-7787-4094-0(3))* Crabtree Publishing Co.

Cronin, Ali & Sayer, Melissa. Making a Difference: The Changing the World Handbook. 2009. (Really Useful Handbooks Ser.). (ENG., Illus.). 48p. (J). (gr. 5-11). pap. *(978-0-7787-4403-0(5))* Crabtree Publishing Co.

Currie, Stephen. Environmentalism in America. 2010. (American History Ser.). (Illus.). 128p. (J). 34.80 *(978-1-4205-0210-7(7),* Lucent Bks.) Cengage Gale.

Dahlen, Noelle. Gone Green Stickers. 2010. (Dover Little Activity Books Stickers Ser.). (ENG.). 4p. (J). (gr. -1-5). pap. 1.50 *(978-0-486-47555-4(7))* Dover Pubns., Inc.

David, Sarah B. Reducing Your Carbon Footprint at Home. 2009. (Your Carbon Footprint Ser.). 48p. (gr. 5-5). 53.00 *(978-1-60854-910-8(0),* Rosen Reference) Rosen Publishing Group, Inc., The.

Dickmann, Nancy. Leaving Our Mark: Reducing Our Carbon Footprint. 2016. (ENG., Illus.). 32p. (J). *(978-0-7787-2381-3(X))* Crabtree Publishing Co.

Dorion, Christiane. Pollution. 2009. (What If We Do Nothing? Ser.). 48p. (YA). (gr. 4-7). lib. bdg. 31.00 *(978-1-4339-1984-8(2))* Stevens, Gareth Publishing LLLP.

Down, Susan Brophy. Legally Green: Careers in Environmental Law. 2011. (Green-Collar Careers Ser.). (ENG.). 64p. (J). (gr. 5-9). *(978-0-7787-4857-1(X))* Crabtree Publishing Co.

Eboch, Chris. Green Movement, 1 vol. 2013. (Essential Library of Social Change Ser.). (ENG.). 112p. (J). (gr. 6-12). lib. bdg. 35.64 *(978-1-61783-888-0(8),* Essential Library) ABDO Publishing Co.

EcoWorks. 2013. (EcoWorks Ser.). 32p. (J). (gr. 3-5). 159.60 *(978-1-4339-9683-2(9));* pap. 63.00 *(978-1-4339-9802-7(5));* pap. 378.00 *(978-1-4339-9803-4(3))* Stevens, Gareth Publishing LLLP.

Edwards, Tanille. Jordan & Justine's Weekend Adventures Tm: Go Go Green. 2008. 24p. (J). (gr. -1-3). pap. 12.95 *(978-0-9787302-6-0(7))* Fire Flies Entertainment, LLC.

Encyclopaedia Britannica Publishers, Inc. Staff. Earth's Changing Environment. 2008. (Illus.). 128p. (YA). (gr. 8-18). 29.95 *(978-1-59339-429-5(2))* Encyclopaedia Britannica, Inc.

Environment. (YA). (gr. 6-12). 19.47 *(978-0-673-21549-9(0))* Addison-Wesley Educational Pubs., Inc.

Environment at Risk, 5 vols., Set. Incl. Controlling Earth's Pollutants. Petersen, Christine. 39.93 *(978-0-7614-4005-5(4));* Protecting Earth's Food Supply. Petersen, Christine. 39.93 *(978-0-7614-4008-6(9));* Renewing Earth's Waters. Petersen, Christine. 39.93 *(978-0-7614-4004-8(6));* Sustaining Earth's Energy Resources. Heinrichs, Ann. 39.93 *(978-0-7614-4007-9(0));* 112p. (gr. 7-18). (Environment at Risk Ser.). 2010. Set lib. bdg. 199.65 o.p. *(978-0-7614-4002-4(X))* Marshall Cavendish Corp.

Environmental - Saving Our Earth, 6 bks., Set. (J). (gr. k-6). lib. bdg. 111.70 *(978-1-56674-933-6(6))* Forest Hse. Publishing Co., Inc.

Farquhar, Jackie, et al. Try This at Home: Planet-Friendly Projects for Kids. 2008. (ENG., Illus.). 96p. (J). (gr. 3-4). pap. 10.95 *(978-2-89579-192-8(9))* Owlkids Bks. Inc. CAN. Dist: Publishers Group West (PGW).

Farrell, Courtney. Green Jobs, 1 vol. 2011. (Inside the Industry Ser.). (ENG., Illus.). 112p. (J). (gr. 6-12). lib. bdg. 35.64 *(978-1-61714-801-9(6),* Essential Library) ABDO Publishing Co.

Faust, Daniel R. Energy Crisis: The Future of Fossil Fuels. (Jr. Graphic Environmental Dangers Ser.). (ENG., Illus.). 24p. (gr. 3-8). 2009. pap. 10.60 *(978-1-4042-4598-3(7))* 2008. (J). lib. bdg. 25.25 *(978-1-4042-4231-9(7))* Rosen Publishing Group, Inc., The.

Feinstein, Stephen. Drying Up: Running Out of Water. 2016. (End of Life As We Know It Ser.). (ENG., Illus.). 144p. (YA). (gr. 7-8). lib. bdg. 37.27 *(978-0-7660-7286-2(X))* Enslow Pubs., Inc.

Feinstein, Stephen & Library. Conserving & Protecting Water: What You Can Do. 2010. (Green Issues in Focus Ser.). (Illus.). 128p. (J). (gr. 7-12). lib. bdg. 33.27 *(978-0-7660-3346-7(5))* Enslow Pubs., Inc.

Flounders, Anne. Friends in the Wild. 2014. (Our Green Earth Ser.). (Illus.). 32p. (gr. 2-4). pap. 8.95 *(978-1-939656-29-2(X))* Red Chair Pr.

—Healthy Trees, Healthy Planet. 2014. (Our Green Earth Ser.). (Illus.). 32p. (gr. 2-4). pap. 8.95 *(978-1-939656-32-2(X))* Red Chair Pr.

—Reducing Waste. 2014. (Our Green Earth Ser.). (Illus.). 32p. (gr. 2-4). pap. 8.95 *(978-1-939656-34-6(6))* Red Chair Pr.

Gagne, Tammy. Take Care of the Earth Every Day. 2013. (J). pap. *(978-1-60753-551-5(3))* Amicus Publishing.

Gardner, Robert. Air: Green Science Projects for a Sustainable Planet. 2011. (Team Green Science Projects Ser.). (Illus.). 128p. (J). (gr. 5-9). lib. bdg. 33.27 *(978-0-7660-3646-8(4))* Enslow Pubs., Inc.

Garrett, Leslie & Dorling Kindersley Publishing Staff. Earth Smart, Level 2: How to Take Care of the Environment. 2006. (DK Readers Ser.). (ENG., Illus.). 32p. (J). (gr. 1-3). pap. 3.99 *(978-0-7566-1912-1(2),* DK Children) Dorling Kindersley Publishing, Inc.

Gazlay, Suzy. David Suzuki: Doing Battle with Climate Change. 2009. (Voices for Green Choices Ser.). (ENG., Illus.). 48p. (J). (gr. 5-9). pap. *(978-0-7787-4678-2(X))* Crabtree Publishing Co.

—Re-Greening the Environment: Careers in Cleanup, Remediation, & Restoration. 2011. (ENG.). 64p. (J). pap. *(978-0-7787-4869-4(3))* Crabtree Publishing Co.

George, Charles & Currie-McGhee, Leanne. Protecting Ecosystems. 2009. (21st Century Skills Library: Real World Science Ser.). (ENG.). 32p. (gr. 4-8). lib. bdg. 28.50 *(978-1-60279-462-7(6),* 200230) Cherry Lake Publishing.

Gibson, Brylee. Looking after Our World. 2007. (Connectors Ser.). (gr. 2-5). pap. *(978-1-877453-03-8(X))* Global Education Systems Ltd.

Gifford, Peggy. The Great Big Green. Desimini, Lisa, illus. 2014. (ENG.). 32p. (J). (gr. -1-2). 15.95 *(978-1-62091-629-2(0))* Boyds Mills Pr.

Giles, Sophie. The Children's Book of Green Habits. Davies, Kate, illus. 2014. (ENG.). 32p. (J). pap. 10.00 *(978-1-84135-908-3(4))* Award Pubns. Ltd. GBR. Dist: Parkwest Pubns., Inc.

Gleason, Carrie. Environmental Activist. 2009. (Get Involved! Ser.). (ENG.). 32p. (J). (gr. 3-6). pap. *(978-0-7787-4706-2(9));* (Illus.). *(978-0-7787-4694-2(1))* Crabtree Publishing Co.

Globe-Fearon Staff. Working Together Against Destruction of the Environment. 64p. (YA). (gr. 6-12). pap. 15.95 *(978-0-8359-1130-6(6))* Globe Fearon Educational Publishing.

Goodings, Christina. Growing Green: A Young Person's Guide to Taking Care of the Planet. Furukawa, Masumi, illus. 2008. (ENG.). 32p. (J). (gr. k-2). 12.95 *(978-0-7459-6171-2(1))* Lion Hudson PLC GBR. Dist: Independent Pubs. Group.

Grack, Rachel. Earth Day. 2017. (Celebrating Holidays! Ser.). (ENG.). 24p. (J). (gr. k-3). lib. bdg. 25.95 ***(978-1-62617-619-5(1),*** Blastoff! Readers) Bellwether Media.

Grayson, Robert. Ed Begley, Jr. Living Green. 2009. (Voices for Green Choices Ser.). (ENG., Illus.). 48p. (J). (gr. 5-9). pap. *(978-0-7787-4680-5(1))* Crabtree Publishing Co.

Green Careers, 6 vols., Set. 2010. (Green Careers Ser.). (C). (gr. 9). 197.70 *(978-0-8160-8291-9(X),* Ferguson Publishing Co.) Facts On File, Inc.

Green Crafts, 1 vol. 2010. (Green Crafts Ser.). (ENG.). 32p. (gr. 3-4). lib. bdg. 111.96 *(978-1-4296-4768-7(X));* lib. bdg. 55.98 *(978-1-4296-4769-4(8))* Capstone Press of Coughlan Cos. (Snap Bks.).

Greene, Carol. I Love Our Air. 2012. (I Love Our Earth Ser.). (Illus.). 24p. (J). (gr. 3-4). 22.60 *(978-0-7660-4037-3(2),* Enslow Elementary) Enslow Pubs., Inc.

—I Love Our Land. 2012. (I Love Our Earth Ser.). (Illus.). 24p. (J). (gr. 3-4). 22.60 *(978-0-7660-4040-3(2),* Enslow Elementary) Enslow Pubs., Inc.

—I Love Our Water. 2012. (I Love Our Earth Ser.). (Illus.). 24p. (J). pap. 7.95 *(978-1-4644-0138-1(1));* (gr. 3-4). 22.60 *(978-0-7660-4042-7(9))* Enslow Pubs., Inc.

Gresham, Joel. Our Bearable World: Featuring the Imagination Bears. 2005. 19.95 *(978-0-9708446-8-2(9))* Gresham, Joel.

Gunderson, Jessica. The Energy Dilemma. 2010. (Earth Issues Ser.). 48p. (YA). (gr. 5-18). 23.95 *(978-1-58341-980-9(2),* Creative Education) Creative Co., The.

Gutman, Dan. Recycle This Book: 100 Top Children's Book Authors Tell You How to Go Green. 2009. (J). *(978-0-385-90653-1(6),* Yearling) Random Hse. Children's Bks.

Gutman, Dan, ed. Recycle This Book: 100 Top Children's Book Authors Tell You How to Go Green. 2009. (ENG.). 288p. (J). (gr. 3-7). 6.99 *(978-0-385-73721-0(1),* Yearling) Random Hse. Children's Bks.

Hand, Carol. Amazing Feats of Environmental Engineering, 1 vol. 2014. (Great Achievements in Engineering Ser.). (ENG.). 112p. (J). (gr. 6-12). lib. bdg. 35.64 *(978-1-62403-429-9(2),* Essential Library) ABDO Publishing Co.

Hare, Tony. Capa de Ozono. 6th ed.Tr. of Ozone Layer. (SPA., Illus.). 32p. (J). 10.95 *(978-84-348-3260-2(7))* SM Ediciones ESP. Dist: AIMS International Bks., Inc.

Harper, Clay & Ingram, Jas. Are You Sure That Was a Rabbit?, 1 vol. 2012. (ENG., Illus.). 32p. (J). 12.99 *(978-0-7643-4007-9(7),* 9780764340079) Schiffer Publishing, Ltd.

Herzog, Brad. S Is for Save the Planet: A How-to-Be Green Alphabet. Ayriss, Linda Holt, illus. 2009. (Science Ser.). (ENG.). 40p. (J). (gr. 1-5). 17.95 *(978-1-58536-428-2(2),* 1291948) Sleeping Bear Pr.

Hewitt, Sally. Your Food. 2008. (Green Team Ser.). (ENG., Illus.). 32p. (J). (gr. 3-7). pap. *(978-0-7787-4106-0(0))* Crabtree Publishing Co.

—Your Local Enviornment. 2008. (Green Team Ser.). (ENG., Illus.). 32p. (J). (gr. 3-7). pap. *(978-0-7787-4107-7(9))* Crabtree Publishing Co.

—Your Local Environment. 2008. (Green Team Ser.). (ENG., Illus.). 32p. (J). (gr. 3-7). lib. bdg. *(978-0-7787-4100-8(1))* Crabtree Publishing Co.

Hirschmann, Kris. Going Green. 2008. *(978-1-60217-025-4(8))* Erickson Pr.

Hoffman, Mary Y. The Great Big Green Book. Asquith, Ros, illus. 2015. (ENG.). 40p. (J). (gr. -1-3). 18.99 *(978-1-84780-445-7(4),* Frances Lincoln) Quarto Publishing Group UK GBR. Dist: Hachette Bk. Group.

Holden, Pam. Our World. 2015. (ENG., Illus.). 16p. (-1). pap. *(978-1-77654-118-8(9),* Red Rocket Readers) Flying Start Bks.

Hollar, Sherman. Protecting the Environment. 2011. lib. bdg. 31.70 *(978-1-61530-503-2(3))* Rosen Publishing Group, Inc., The.

Holt, Rinehart and Winston Staff. Environmental Science: Assessments. 4th ed. 2004. (SPA.). pap. 16.33 *(978-0-03-068344-2(0))* Holt McDougal.

—Environmental Science 2004. 4th ed. 2004. (SPA.). pap., stu. ed. 11.13 *(978-0-03-068343-5(2))* Holt McDougal.

—Holt Science & Technology Chapter 21: Life Science: Environmental Problems & Solutions. 5th ed. 2004. (Illus.). pap. 12.86 *(978-0-03-030236-7(6))* Holt McDougal.

Hopkins, William G., ed. The Green World, 11 vols., Set. 2007. (Green World Ser.). 136p. (gr. 6-12). 412.50 *(978-0-7910-9454-9(5),* Chelsea Hse.) Facts On File, Inc.

Horn, Geoffrey M. Environmental Engineer. 2009. (Cool Careers: Cutting Edge Ser.). 32p. (J). (gr. 5-8). (ENG.). pap. 10.50 *(978-1-4339-2155-1(3));* lib. bdg. 26.00 *(978-1-4339-1956-5(7))* Stevens, Gareth Publishing LLLP.

How to Be Earth Friendly, 6 vols., Set. Incl. Earth-Friendly Buildings. Coleman, Miriam. lib. bdg. 25.25 *(978-1-4488-2588-2(1));* Earth-Friendly Energy. Gosman, Gillian. lib. bdg. 25.25 *(978-1-4488-2587-5(3));* Earth-Friendly Food. Gosman, Gillian. lib. bdg. 25.25 *(978-1-4488-2589-9(X));* Earth-Friendly Living. Coleman, Miriam. lib. bdg. 25.25 *(978-1-4488-2592-9(X));* Earth-Friendly Shopping. Gosman, Gillian. lib. bdg. 25.25 *(978-1-4488-2591-2(1));* Earth-Friendly Transportation. Coleman, Miriam. lib. bdg. 25.25 *(978-1-4488-2590-5(3));* (YA). (gr. 3-6). (How to Be Earth Friendly Ser.). (Illus.). 32p. 2011. Set lib. bdg. 143.70 *(978-1-4488-2794-7(9),* PowerKids Pr.) Rosen Publishing Group, Inc., The.

Hunt, Jilly. Protecting Our Planet. 2017. (Beyond the Headlines! Ser.). (ENG.). 48p. (gr. 4-6). lib. bdg. 33.32 ***(978-1-4846-4143-9(4),*** Heinemann InfoSearch) Heinemann-Raintree.

E
F
G

Hunter, Nick. How Carbon Footprints Work. 2013. 32p. (J). (gr. 3-5). pap. 10.50 *(978-1-4339-9553-8(0))*; pap. 63.00 *(978-1-4339-9554-5(9))*; (ENG., Illus.). lib. bdg. 26.60 *(978-1-4339-9552-1(2))* Stevens, Gareth Publishing LLLP.

Jakab, Cheryl. Natural Wonders. 2010. (Environment in Focus Ser.). 32p. (gr. 4). 28.50 *(978-1-60870-092-9(5))* Marshall Cavendish Corp.

Jankeliowitch, Anne. Kids Who Are Changing the World. Arthus-Bertrand, Yann, photos by. 2014. (ENG., Illus.). 144p. (J). (gr. 3-6). pap. 14.99 *(978-1-4022-9532-4(4)*, 9781402295324, Sourcebooks Jabberwocky) Sourcebooks, Inc.

Jankéliowitch, Anne. 50 Ways to Save the Earth. Bourseiller, Philippe, photos by. 2008. (ENG., Illus.). 144p. (J). (gr. 3-7). 19.95 *(978-0-8109-7239-1(5)*, Abrams Bks. for Young Readers) Abrams, Inc.

Javna, John, et al. The New 50 Simple Things Kids Can Do to Save the Earth. Montez, Michele & Bodger, Lorraine, illus. 2009. (ENG.). 208p. pap. 14.99 *(978-0-7407-7746-2(7))* Andrews McMeel Publishing.

Jerome, Kate Boehm & National Geographic Learning Staff. Protecting the Planet. 2007. (Reading Expeditions Ser.). (ENG., Illus.). 32p. (J). pap. 17.95 *(978-0-7922-8864-0(5))* CENGAGE Learning.

Kalman, Bobbie. The ABCs of the Environment. 2009. (ABCs of the Natural World Ser.). (ENG., Illus.). 32p. (J). (gr. 1-5). pap. *(978-0-7787-3437-6(4))*; (gr. 2-4). lib. bdg. *(978-0-7787-3417-8(X))* Crabtree Publishing Co.

Kaye, Cathryn Berger, et al. Make a Splash! A Kid's Guide to Protecting Our Oceans, Lakes, Rivers, & Wetlands. 2012. (ENG., Illus.). 128p. (J). (gr. 3-7). pap. 13.99 *(978-1-57542-417-0(7))* Free Spirit Publishing, Inc.

Kelly McGovern Lu. Be Kind to the Earth: A Little Kid's Guide to Reducing your Carbon Footprint. Justin McGovern, illus. 2009. 28p. pap. 14.99 *(978-1-4389-7356-2(X))* AuthorHouse.

Kopp, Megan. Living in a Sustainable Way: Green Communities. 2015. (Next Generation Energy Ser.). (ENG., Illus.). 32p. (J). *(978-0-7787-2000-3(4))* Crabtree Publishing Co.

—Putting Earth First: Eating & Living Green. 2016. (ENG., Illus.). 32p. (J). *(978-0-7787-2382-0(8))* Crabtree Publishing Co.

Kruger, Leanne Flett. Taking Care of Mother Earth. Hamelin, Marie-Micheline, illus. 2005. (ENG.). 20p. (J). pap. 10.95 *(978-1-894778-30-5(8))* Theytus Bks., Ltd. CAN. Dist: Univ. of Toronto Pr.

—Taking Care of Mother Earth. Hamelin, Marie-Micheline, illus. 2009. (Caring for Me Ser.). (ENG.). 20p. pap. 9.95 *(978-1-894778-55-8(3))* Theytus Bks., Ltd. CAN. Dist: Univ. of Toronto Pr.

Landau, Elaine. Celebrating Earth Day. 2012. (Celebrating Holidays Ser.). 48p. (J). (gr. 3-18). 25.27 *(978-0-7660-4034-2(8)*, Enslow Elementary) Enslow Pubs., Inc.

Law, Government, & Public Safety. 2010. (Green Careers Ser.). (Illus.). 176p. (C). (gr. 9-18). 32.95 *(978-0-8160-8152-3(2)*, Ferguson Publishing Co.) Facts On File, Inc.

Levy, Janey. Making Good Choices about Conservation. 2009. (J). 77.70 *(978-1-4358-5611-0(2)*, Rosen Reference); (ENG.). 64p. (YA). pap. 12.95 *(978-1-4358-5610-3(4)*, Rosen Reference); (Illus.). 64p. (YA). (gr. 5-9). lib. bdg. 31.95 *(978-1-4358-5314-0(8))* Rosen Publishing Group, Inc., The.

Linde, Barbara M.. Pollution. 2013. (Habitat Havoc Ser.). 32p. (gr. 3-6). pap. 10.50 *(978-1-4339-9857-7(2))* Stevens, Gareth Publishing LLLP.

Llewellyn, Bridget McGovern. One Child, One Planet: Inspiration for the Young Conservationist. Sams, Carl R., 2nd & Stoick, Jean, photos by. 2009. (Illus.). 48p. (J). 19.95 *(978-0-9841880-0-0(2))* Emerald Shamrock Pr. LLC.

Llewellyn, Claire. Let's Recycle. 2005. (Illus.). 32p. (YA). (gr. 1-18). lib. bdg. 27.10 *(978-1-932333-22-0(3))* Chrysalis Education.

—Protect Natural Habitats. 2005. (Illus.). 32p. (YA). (gr. 1-18). lib. bdg. 27.10 *(978-1-932333-20-6(7))* Chrysalis Education.

Mallory, Kenneth. A Home by the Sea: Protecting Coastal Wildlife. 2003. (Illus.). 64p. (YA). (gr. 4-8). reprint ed. 20.00 *(978-0-7567-6562-0(5))* DIANE Publishing Co.

Maloof, Torrey. People & the Planet, 1 vol. 2015. (Science Readers: Content & Literacy Ser.). (ENG., Illus.). 32p. (gr. 3-3). pap. 8.99 *(978-1-4807-4650-3(9))* Teacher Created Materials, Inc.

Manos, John. It's Earth Day! 2006. (Early Explorers Ser.). (J). pap. *(978-1-4108-6124-5(4))* Benchmark Education Co.

Mara, Wil. Environmental Protection. 2013. (Cornerstones of Freedom™, Third Ser.). (ENG., Illus.). 64p. (J). pap. 8.95 *(978-0-531-21961-4(5))*; lib. bdg. 30.00 *(978-0-531-23603-1(X))* Scholastic Library Publishing.

Marsh, Carole. Environmental Issues Around the World - Common Core Lessons & Activities. 2015. (Common Core Ser.). (ENG.). (J). pap. 4.99 *(978-0-635-11988-9(9))* Gallopade International.

Marsico, Katie. Greenpeace Fund. 2016. (Community Connections: How Do They Help? Ser.). (ENG.). 24p. (J). (gr. 2-5). 27.07 *(978-1-63471-049-7(5)*, 208276) Cherry Lake Publishing.

Martin, Jacqueline Briggs. Creekfinding: A True Story. McGehee, Claudia, illus. 2017. (ENG.). 36p. 16.95 ***(978-0-8166-9802-8(3))*** Univ. of Minnesota Pr.

Mason, Paul. How Big Is Your Shopping Footprint? 2009. (Environmental Footprints Ser.). 32p. (gr. 4). 28.50 *(978-0-7614-4414-5(9))* Marshall Cavendish Corp.

Mckay, Kim & Bonnin, Jenny. True Green Kids: 100 Things You Can Do to Save the Planet. 2008. (True Green Ser.). (ENG., Illus.). 144p. (J). (gr. 5-9). 27.90 *(978-1-4263-0443-9(9)*, National Geographic Children's Bks.) National Geographic Society.

Mckay, Kim, et al. True Green Kids: 100 Things You Can Do to Save the Planet. 2008. (True Green Ser.). (ENG., Illus.). 144p. (J). (gr. 5-9). pap. 15.95 *(978-1-4263-0442-2(0)*, National Geographic Children's Bks.) National Geographic Society.

McKenzie, Precious. Cleaning up the Earth. 2011. (ENG., Illus.). 24p. (gr. k-2). pap. 8.95 *(978-1-61741-970-6(2))* Rourke Educational Media.

Meredith, Sue. Why Should I Bother about the Planet? - Internet Referenced. 2008. (What's Happening? Ser.). 48p. (J). pap. 6.99 *(978-0-7945-2089-2(8)*, Usborne) EDC Publishing.

Meredith, Susan. Going Green. 2009. (Kid Kits Ser.). 48p. (J). 18.99 *(978-1-60130-158-1(8)*, Usborne) EDC Publishing.

Miller, Debra A. Conserving the Environment. 2010. (Current Controversies Ser.). (Illus.). 240p. (J). 40.95 *(978-0-7377-4661-7(0))*; pap. 28.45 *(978-0-7377-4662-4(9))* Cengage Gale. (Greenhaven Pr., Inc.).

Minden, Cecilia. Kids Can Clean up Trash. 2010. (21st Century Basic Skills Library: Kids Can Ser.). (ENG.). 24p. (gr. k-3). lib. bdg. 22.79 *(978-1-60279-870-0(2)*, 200606) Cherry Lake Publishing.

—Kids Can Keep Air Clean. 2010. (21st Century Basic Skills Library: Kids Can Ser.). (ENG.). 24p. (gr. k-3). lib. bdg. 22.79 *(978-1-60279-871-7(0)*, 200608) Cherry Lake Publishing.

—Kids Can Reuse. 2010. (21st Century Basic Skills Library: Kids Can Ser.). (ENG.). 24p. (gr. k-3). lib. bdg. 22.79 *(978-1-60279-868-7(0)*, 200602) Cherry Lake Publishing.

—Kids Can Use Less. 2010. (21st Century Basic Skills Library: Kids Can Ser.). (ENG.). 24p. (gr. k-3). lib. bdg. 22.79 *(978-1-60279-869-4(9)*, 200604) Cherry Lake Publishing.

Mitchell Lane Publishers Inc. Staff. On the Verge of Extinction: Crisis in the Environment, 5 vols., Set. 2007. (J). (gr. 1-4). lib. bdg. 128.50 *(978-1-58415-589-8(2))* Mitchell Lane Pubs., Inc.

Morgan, Anne. The Smallest Carbon Footprint in the Land & Other Eco-Tales. McKinnon, Gay, illus. 2012. 80p. pap. *(978-1-922120-23-6(5)*, IP Kidz) Interactive Pubns. Pty, Ltd.

Nagle, Jeanne. Reducing Your Carbon Footprint at School. 2009. (Your Carbon Footprint Ser.). 48p. (gr. 5-5). 53.00 *(978-1-60854-911-5(9)*, Rosen Reference) Rosen Publishing Group, Inc., The.

—Smart Shopping: Shopping Green. 2009. (Your Carbon Footprint Ser.). 48p. (gr. 5-5). 53.00 *(978-1-60854-914-6(3)*, Rosen Reference) Rosen Publishing Group, Inc., The.

Napoli, Donna Jo. Mama Miti: Wangari Maathai & the Trees of Kenya. Nelson, Kadir, illus. 2010. (ENG.). 40p. (J). (gr. -1-3). 18.99 *(978-1-4169-3505-6(3)*, Simon & Schuster/Paula Wiseman Bks.) Simon & Schuster/Paula Wiseman Bks.

Nelson, Robin. Earth Day. 2003. (First Step Nonfiction Ser.). (Illus.). 24p. (J). (gr. -1-3). pap. 5.95 *(978-0-8225-1320-9(X))*; (gr. k-2). lib. bdg. 18.60 *(978-0-8225-1283-7(1))* Lerner Publishing Group.

—How We Clean up a Park. 2014. (First Step Nonfiction - Responsibility in Action Ser.). (ENG., Illus.). 24p. (gr. k-2). pap. 6.95 *(978-1-4677-3646-6(5))*; lib. bdg. 23.93 *(978-1-4677-3637-4(6)*, Lerner Pubns.) Lerner Publishing Group.

Newman, Mark. Sooper Yooper: Environmental Defender. Heckman, Mark, illus. 2010. 48p. (J). 17.95 *(978-1-933272-26-9(0))* Thunder Bay Pr.

Noblet, Jean-François & Levesque, Catherine, texts. Keeping It Green! 2009. (Taking Action for My Planet Ser.). (Illus.). 32p. (YA). (gr. 3-6). pap. 10.55 *(978-1-60754-791-4(0))* Windmill Bks.

Ollhoff, Jim. Living in a Warmer World, 1 vol. 2010. (ABDO & Daughters Ser.). (ENG.). 32p. 27.07 *(978-1-61613-453-2(4)*, Abdo & Daughters) ABDO Publishing Co.

—Myths & Controversies, 1 vol. 2010. (ABDO & Daughters Ser.). (ENG.). 32p. 27.07 *(978-1-61613-454-9(2)*, Abdo & Daughters) ABDO Publishing Co.

—The Science, 1 vol. 2010. (ABDO & Daughters Ser.). (ENG.). 32p. 27.07 *(978-1-61613-455-6(0)*, Abdo & Daughters) ABDO Publishing Co.

—Social Solutions, 1 vol. 2010. (ABDO & Daughters Ser.). (ENG.). 32p. 27.07 *(978-1-61613-456-3(9)*, Abdo & Daughters) ABDO Publishing Co.

—Technological Solutions, 1 vol. 2010. (ABDO & Daughters Ser.). (ENG.). 32p. 27.07 *(978-1-61613-457-0(7)*, Abdo & Daughters) ABDO Publishing Co.

—Water & Ice, 1 vol. 2010. (ABDO & Daughters Ser.). (ENG.). 32p. 27.07 *(978-1-61613-458-7(5)*, Abdo & Daughters) ABDO Publishing Co.

Omawumi Kola-Lawal, Constance. We Learn about Preserving the Environment. 2013. 36p. pap. *(978-1-909204-30-0(7))* BookPublishingWorld.

Orme, Helen. Living Green. 2008. (Earth in Danger Ser.). (Illus.). 32p. (YA). (gr. 3-6). lib. bdg. 25.27 *(978-1-59716-728-4(2)*, 1284323) Bearport Publishing Co., Inc.

Orr, Tamra. Environmentalist. 2009. (21st Century Skills Library: Cool Careers Ser.). (ENG.). 32p. (gr. 4-8). lib. bdg. 28.50 *(978-1-60279-501-3(0)*, 200311) Cherry Lake Publishing.

Oxlade, Chris. Environment Infographics, 1 vol. 2014. (Infographics Ser.). (ENG.). 32p. (gr. 1-3). lib. bdg. 29.99 *(978-1-4109-6217-1(2)*, Read Me!) Heinemann-Raintree.

—Infographics, 1 vol. 2014. (Infographics Ser.). (ENG.). 32p. (gr. 1-3). lib. bdg. 119.96 *(978-1-4109-6220-1(2)*, Read Me!) Heinemann-Raintree.

Paquet, Laura Byrne. The Environment in Contemporary Africa. 2016. (Focus on Africa Ser.). 128p. (YA). 45.64 *(978-1-5026-2393-5(5))* Cavendish Square Publishing.

Parker, Russ. Planet in Crisis, 6 vols., Set. Incl. Climate Crisis. lib. bdg. 25.25 *(978-1-4358-5254-9(0))*; Energy Supplies in Crisis. lib. bdg. 25.25 *(978-1-4358-5251-8(6))*; Pollution Crisis. lib. bdg. 25.25 *(978-1-4358-5252-5(4))*; Waste Management Crisis. lib. bdg. 25.25 *(978-1-4358-5253-2(2))*; Water Supplies in Crisis. lib. bdg. 25.25 *(978-1-4358-5250-1(8))*; Wildlife Crisis. lib. bdg. 25.25 *(978-1-4358-5255-6(9))*; 32p. (YA). (gr. 5-8)., Rosen Reference 2009. Set lib. bdg. 151.50 *(978-1-4358-5336-2(9))* Rosen Publishing Group, Inc., The.

Parry, Ann. Greenpeace. 2005. (Humanitarian Organizations Ser.). (Illus.). 32p. (gr. 5-8). lib. bdg. 25.00 *(978-0-7910-8815-9(4)*, Chelsea Hse.) Facts On File, Inc.

Pesout, Christine. The Earth, the Alphabet, & Me. Donaldson, Jennifer, illus. 2011. (J). *(978-0-615-47220-1(6))* Pesout, Christine.

Peterson, Cris. Amazing Grazing. Upitis, Alvis, photos by. 2011. (ENG., Illus.). 32p. (J). (gr. k-2). pap. 10.95 *(978-1-59078-868-4(0))* Boyds Mills Pr.

Poitier, Anton. Once I Was a Cardboard Box... But Now I'm a Book about Polar Bears. Evans, Melvyn, illus. 2010. 24p. (J). (gr. k-3). 7.99 *(978-0-8416-7200-0(8))* Hammond World Atlas Corp.

—Once I Was a Comic... But Now I'm a Book about Tigers. Evans, Melvyn, illus. 2010. 24p. (J). (gr. k-3). 7.99 *(978-0-8416-7201-7(6))* Hammond World Atlas Corp.

Ponto, Joanna. Earth Day. 2016. (Story of Our Holidays Ser.). (ENG., Illus.). 32p. (J). (gr. 3-3). 25.27 *(978-0-7660-7457-6(9))* Enslow Pubs., Inc.

Pratt Serafini, Kristin Joy, illus. A Swim Through the Sea, 1 vol. 2006. (Simply Nature Bks.). (ENG.). 26p. (J). (gr. -1). bds. 7.95 *(978-1-58469-080-1(1))* Dawn Pubns.

Queenston, Rory. Rachel Carson: Saving the Environment. 2013. (InfoMax Readers Ser.). (ENG.). 24p. (J). (gr. 3-4). pap. 8.25 *(978-1-4777-2479-8(6))*; pap. 49.50 *(978-1-4777-2481-1(8))* Rosen Publishing Group, Inc., The. (Rosen Classroom).

Radtke, Becky J. BOOST Keep the Scene Green! Earth-Friendly Activities. 2013. (BOOST Educational Ser.). (ENG.). 32p. (J). (gr. 1-2). pap. 4.99 *(978-0-486-49417-3(9))* Dover Pubns., Inc.

Rauf, Don. Protecting the Environment Through Service Learning, 1 vol. 2015. (ENG., Illus.). 80p. (J). 34.60 *(978-1-4777-7961-3(2)*, Rosen Young Adult) Rosen Publishing Group, Inc., The.

Ravilious, Kate. Power: Ethical Debates about Resources & the Environment. 2009. (Dilemmas in Modern Science Ser.). (YA). (gr. 7-12). 34.25 *(978-1-59920-096-5(1))* Black Rabbit Bks.

—Power - Ethical Debates about Resources & the Environment. 2008. (Dilemmas in Modern Science Ser.). (ENG., Illus.). 48p. (J). 23.99 *(978-0-237-53369-4(3))* Evans Brothers, Ltd. GBR. Dist: Independent Pubs. Group.

Rea, Thelma. Taking Care of Our World. 2003. (Rosen Real Readers: Upper Emergent Ser.). (ENG., Illus.). 12p. (gr. 1-2). pap. 5.90 *(978-0-8239-6368-3(3))* Rosen Publishing Group, Inc., The.

Reaume, Christopher J. The 10 Greatest Threats to Earth. 2008. 14.99 *(978-1-55448-501-7(0))* Scholastic Library Publishing.

Reeves, Diane Lindsey. Food & Natural Resources. 2017. (Bright Futures Press: World of Work Ser.). (ENG., Illus.). 32p. (J). (gr. 4-7). lib. bdg. 29.93 *(978-1-63472-622-1(7)*, 209522) Cherry Lake Publishing.

Reilly, Kathleen M. & Takacs-Moore, Mary. Energy: 25 Projects Investigate Why We Need Power & How We Get It. Takacs-Moore, Mary, illus. 2009. (Build It Yourself Ser.). (ENG., Illus.). 128p. (J). (gr. 3-7). pap. 15.95 *(978-1-934670-34-7(0))* Octavio Publishing.

Rettungsaktion Planet Erde. (GER., Illus.). 96p. *(978-3-411-08011-3(6))* Bibliographisches Institut & F. A. Brockhaus AG DEU. Dist: i. b. d., Ltd.

Reynolds, Alison. Let's Use It Again. Hopgood, Andrew, illus. 2009. (Save Our Planet! Ser.). 12p. (J). (gr. -1-3). bds. 11.40 *(978-1-60754-415-9(6))* Windmill Bks.

Riley, Karen. Don't Trash My Planet. 2004. (Illus.). 20p. (J). (gr. k-5). pap. 10.00 *(978-0-9708135-4-1(6)*, "5,000") S.C.R.A.P. Gallery.

Robertson, Joanne. The Water Walker, 1 vol. 2017. (ENG., Illus.). 36p. (J). (gr. 2-6). 16.95 ***(978-1-77260-038-4(5))*** Second Story Pr. CAN. Dist: Orca Bk. Pubs. USA.

Rodger, Ellen. Building a Green Community. 2008. (Energy Revolution Ser.). (ENG., Illus.). 32p. (J). (gr. 3-8). pap. *(978-0-7787-2930-3(3))*; lib. bdg. *(978-0-7787-2916-7(8))* Crabtree Publishing Co.

Rooney, Anne. Feeding the World. 2010. (World at Risk Ser.). (YA). (gr. 5-9). 34.25 *(978-1-59920-377-5(4))* Black Rabbit Bks.

—Reducing the Carbon Footprint. 2010. (World at Risk Ser.). (YA). (gr. 5-9). 34.25 *(978-1-59920-375-1(8))* Black Rabbit Bks.

Rooney, Frances. Exceptional Women Environmentalists, 1 vol. 2007. (Women's Hall of Fame Ser.). (ENG., Illus.). 120p. (J). (gr. 4-8). pap. 10.95 *(978-1-897187-22-7(X))* Second Story Pr. CAN. Dist: Orca Bk. Pubs. USA.

Saving Our Living Earth, 8 vols., Set. Incl. Earth-Friendly Design. Welsbacher, Anne. lib. bdg. 30.60 *(978-0-8225-7564-1(7))*; Earth-Friendly Energy. Fridell, Ron. lib. bdg. 30.60 *(978-0-8225-7563-4(9))*; Earth-Friendly Waste Management. Wilcox, Charlotte. (Illus.). lib. bdg. 30.60 *(978-0-8225-7560-3(4))*; Protecting Earth's Air Quality. Rapp, Val. lib. bdg. 30.60 *(978-0-8225-7558-0(2))*; Protecting Earth's Land. Rapp, Valerie. (Illus.). lib. bdg. 30.60 *(978-0-8225-7559-7(0))*; Protecting Earth's Rain Forests. Welsbacher, Anne. lib. bdg. 30.60 *(978-0-8225-7562-7(0))*; Protecting Earth's Water Supply. Fridell, Ron. lib. bdg. 30.60 *(978-0-8225-7557-3(4))*; Understanding Global Warming. Johnson, Rebecca L. lib. bdg. 30.60 *(978-0-8225-7561-0(2))*; 72p. (YA). (gr. 4-7). 2008. 2008. Set lib. bdg. 244.80 *(978-0-8225-7556-6(6))* Lerner Publishing Group.

Saving Our World, 6 bks., Set. Incl. Air Pollution. Sechrist, Darren. lib. bdg. 28.50 *(978-0-7614-3220-3(5))*; Climate Change. Bishop, Amanda. lib. bdg. 28.50 *(978-0-7614-3219-7(1))*; Energy Conservation. Bishop, Amanda. lib. bdg. 28.50 *(978-0-7614-3224-1(8))*; Habitat Protection. Smith, Natalie. lib. bdg. 28.50 *(978-0-7614-3225-8(6))*; Recycling Waste. Rodger, Ellen. lib. bdg. 28.50 *(978-0-7614-3222-7(1))*; Water Pollution. Price, Sean. lib. bdg. 28.50 *(978-0-7614-3221-0(3))*; 32p. (gr. 4-18). (Saving Our World Ser.). 2008. Set lib. bdg. 171.00 *(978-0-7614-3218-0(3)*, Benchmark Bks.) Marshall Cavendish Corp.

Senker, Cath, et al. Eco Guides. 2013. (Eco Guides). (ENG.). 56p. (gr. 6-8). pap. 37.96 *(978-1-4329-7053-6(4))* Heinemann-Raintree.

Sévigny, Eric, illus. Caillou Plants a Tree. 2012. (Ecology Club Ser.). (ENG.). 24p. (J). (gr. -1-1). pap. 5.99 *(978-2-89450-834-3(4))* Caillouet, Gerry.

Silverstein, Alvin, et al. Smog, Oil Spills, Sewage, & More: The Yucky Pollution Book. Kelley, Gerald, illus. 2010. (Yucky Science Ser.). 48p. (J). (gr. 5-9). 25.27 *(978-0-7660-3313-9(9))* Enslow Pubs., Inc.

Smalley, Carol. Green Changes You Can Make Around the House. 2009. (Tell Your Parents Ser.). (Illus.). 48p. (J). (gr. 4-7). lib. bdg. 29.95 *(978-1-58415-764-9(X))* Mitchell Lane Pubs., Inc.

Smith, Paula. Be the Change for the Environment. 2014. (ENG., Illus.). 24p. (J). *(978-0-7787-0620-5(6))* Crabtree Publishing Co.

—Protecting Earth's Surface. 2015. (Earth's Processes Close-Up Ser.). (ENG., Illus.). 24p. (J). (gr. k-3). *(978-0-7787-1729-4(1))* Crabtree Publishing Co.

Sollinger, Emily. This Is Our World: A Story about Taking Care of the Earth. Brown, Jo, illus. 2010. (Little Green Bks.). (ENG.). 12p. (J). (gr. -1-1). bds. 7.99 *(978-1-4169-7821-3(6)*, Little Simon) Little Simon.

Sonneborn, Liz. The Environmental Movement: Protecting Our Natural Resources. 2007. (Reform Movements in American History Ser.). (Illus.). 128p. (YA). (gr. 7-12). lib. bdg. 32.50 *(978-0-7910-9537-9(1))* Facts On File, Inc.

Stein, Paul. Floods of the Future. 2009. (Library of Future Weather & Climate Ser.). 64p. (gr. 5-5). 58.50 *(978-1-60853-645-0(9))* Rosen Publishing Group, Inc., The.

Stille, Darlene R. Protecting Animals. 2011. (Go Green! Ser.). (ENG.). 32p. (J). (gr. 1-4). lib. bdg. 28.50 *(978-1-60973-174-8(3)*, 201153) Child's World, Inc., The.

Strange, Cordelia. Environmental Science & Protection: Keeping Our Planet Green. 2010. (New Careers for the 21st Century Ser.). 64p. (YA). (gr. 7-18). pap. 9.95 *(978-1-4222-2034-4(6))* Mason Crest.

Sundance/Newbridge LLC Staff. Kids for the Earth. 2007. (Early Science Ser.). (gr. k-3). 18.95 *(978-1-4007-6188-3(3))*; pap. 6.10 *(978-1-4007-6184-5(0))* Sundance/Newbridge Educational Publishing.

Swartz Pepper, Kenda. Well Earth Well Me! 2011. (ENG., Illus.). 32p. (J). 14.99 *(978-1-936172-25-2(9))* Eifrig Publishing.

Tallarico, Tony J., Jr. Eco-Logical Brain Games. 2009. (Dover Children's Activity Bks.). (ENG., Illus.). 48p. (J). (gr. 3-8). pap. 4.99 *(978-0-486-46840-2(2))* Dover Pubns., Inc.

Tanaka, Shelley. A Great Round Wonder: My Book of the World. Perna, Debi, illus. (J). 4.99 *(978-1-55054-213-4(3))* Da Capo Pr., Inc.

La Tierra en Acción (Earth in Action) 2010. (Tierra en Acción/Earth in Action Ser.). (MUL.). 24p. (gr. k-1). 53.30 *(978-1-4296-6657-2(9))* Capstone Press of Coughlan Cos.

Tilmont, Amy. Man vs. Animal: Species at Risk. 2011. (Second Nature Ser.). 48p. (J). (gr. 5-8). lib. bdg. 26.60 *(978-1-59953-460-2(6))* Norwood Hse. Pr.

—Trash Talk: What You Throw Away. 2011. (Second Nature Ser.). 48p. (J). (gr. 5-8). lib. bdg. 26.60 *(978-1-59953-459-6(2))* Norwood Hse. Pr.

Trueit, Trudi Strain. Wildlife Conservationist. 2014. 64p. pap. 34.21 *(978-1-62712-467-6(5))* Cavendish Square Publishing.

Underwood, Deborah. 101 Ways to Save the Planet, 1 vol. 2011. (101 Ser.). (ENG., Illus.). 56p. (gr. 5-9). 34.65 *(978-1-4109-3898-5(0))*; pap. 9.95 *(978-1-4109-4385-9(2))* Heinemann-Raintree. (NA-r).

Urrutia, Cristina. Who Will Save My Planet? 2012. (ENG., Illus.). 32p. (J). (gr. 2-5). 10.95 *(978-1-77049-281-3(X)*, Tundra Bks.) Tundra Bks. CAN. Dist: Penguin Random Hse. LLC.

Vernon, Caitlyn. Nowhere Else on Earth: Standing Tall for the Great Bear Rainforest, 1 vol. 2011. (ENG., Illus.). 136p. (J). (gr. 4-12). pap. 22.95 *(978-1-55469-303-0(9))* Orca Bk. Pubs. USA.

Wadsworth, Ginger. Camping with the President. Dugan, Karen, illus. 2009. (ENG.). 32p. (J). (gr. 4-18). 16.95 *(978-1-59078-497-6(9)*, Calkins Creek) Boyds Mills Pr.

Wall, Suzy. The Earth Day Garden. 2005. (J). pap. *(978-1-4108-4189-6(8))* Benchmark Education Co.

Wang, Andrea. How Can We Reduce Fossil Fuel Pollution? 2016. (Searchlight Books — What Can We Do about Pollution? Ser.). (ENG., Illus.). 40p. (J). (gr. 3-5). 30.65 *(978-1-4677-9513-5(5))* Lerner Publishing Group.

Wearing, Judy. Roberta Bondar: Canada's First Woman in Space. 2010. (Crabtree Groundbreaker Biographies Ser.). (ENG., Illus.). 112p. (J). (gr. 5-8). lib. bdg. *(978-0-7787-2540-4(5))* Crabtree Publishing Co.

West, Krista. Critical Perspectives on Environmental Protection. 2006. (Scientific American Critical Anthologies on Environment & Climate Ser.). (Illus.). 224p. (J). (gr. 3-7). 37.95 *(978-1-4042-0691-5(4))* Rosen Publishing Group, Inc., The.

West, Krista, ed. Critical Perspectives on Environmental Protection. 2009. (Scientific American Critical Anthologies on Environment & Climate Ser.). 224p. (gr. 9-9). 63.90 *(978-1-60853-066-3(3))* Rosen Publishing Group, Inc., The.

Wilcox, Christine. Careers in Environmental Conservation. 2017. (ENG.). 80p. (YA). (gr. 5-12). ***(978-1-68282-203-6(6))*** ReferencePoint Pr., Inc.

Wimmer, Teresa. Environmental Protection Agency. (Agents of Government Ser.). 48p. (J). 2016. (ENG.). (gr. 5-9). pap. 12.00 *(978-1-62832-145-6(8)*, Creative Paperbacks) 2015. (Illus.). *(978-1-60818-544-3(3)*, Creative Education) Creative Co., The.

Wines, Jacquie. You Can Save the Planet: 50 Ways You Can Make a Difference. Horne, Sarah, illus. 2008. (ENG.). 112p. (J). (gr. 3-7). pap. 4.99 *(978-0-545-05332-7(3)*, Scholastic Reference) Scholastic, Inc.

Winters, Adam. Destruction of Earth's Resources: The Need for Sustainable Development. 2009. (Extreme Environmental Threats Ser.). 64p. (gr. 6-6). 58.50 *(978-1-61512-425-1(X))* Rosen Publishing Group, Inc., The.

Wood, Jenny. Los Desiertos. (Coleccion Tierra Viva).Tr. of Deserts. (SPA.). 32p. (YA). (gr. 5-8). *(978-84-348-3266-4(6))* SM Ediciones.

Woodward, John & Skancke, Jennifer. Conserving the Environment. (Current Controversies Ser.). (ENG., Illus.). 248p. (YA). (gr. 10-12). 2006. 27.50 *(978-0-7377-2477-6(3))* 2004. lib. bdg. 39.70 *(978-0-7377-2476-9(5))* Cengage Gale. (Greenhaven Pr., Inc.).

World Book, Inc Staff, contrib. by. Consumable Goods. 2008. (J). *(978-0-7166-1407-4(3))* World Bk., Inc.

—Pollution. 2008. (J). *(978-0-7166-1406-7(5))* World Bk., Inc.

The World's Deadliest, 6 vols. 2010. (World's Deadliest Ser.). (ENG.). 32p. (gr. 1-2). lib. bdg. 133.25 *(978-1-4296-4418-1(4)*, Blazers) Capstone Press of Coughlan Cos.

The World's Deadliest [Capstone Sole Source]. 2010. (World's Deadliest Ser.). 32p. lib. bdg. 151.92 *(978-1-4296-5890-4(8)*, Blazers) Capstone Press of Coughlan Cos.

Yasuda, Anita. Thinking Green. 2016. (J). **(978-1-5105-2217-6(4))** SmartBook Media, Inc.

ENVIRONMENTAL PROTECTION—FICTION

Adler, David A. The Green School Mystery, No. 28. Allen, Joy, illus. 2009. (Cam Jansen Ser.: 28). (ENG.). 64p. (J). (gr. 2-5). 4.99 (978-0-14-241456-9(5), Puffin Books) Penguin Young Readers Group.

Akinyemi, Rowena. Under the Moon, Level 1. Oxford University Press Staff & Bassett, Jennifer, eds. 3rd ed. 2008. (ENG., Illus.). 64p. 9.38 (978-0-19-478922-6(5)) Oxford Univ. Pr., Inc.

Allen, Elaine Ann. Olly the Oyster Cleans the Bay, 1 vol. Nash, Kelli, illus. 2009. (ENG.). 30p. (J). 13.95 (978-0-87033-603-4(7), 9780870336034, Cornell Maritime Pr./Tidewater Pubs.) Schiffer Publishing, Ltd.

Ambrose, Sophie. The Lonely Giant. Ambrose, Sophie, illus. 2016. (ENG., Illus.). 32p. (J). (gr. -1-3). 16.99 (978-0-7636-8225-5(X)) Candlewick Pr.

Baby Lauren & Theodore, Paperback. 2007. (J). pap. 9.95 (978-0-9779643-0-7(2)) Healing Tree Arts.

Ball Sr., Frank J. Bryanna Global Warrior: Attack of the Alaska Aerial Wolf Hunters, 1 vol. Pelton, Bonnie L., illus. 2009. 23p. pap. 24.95 (978-1-61582-587-5(8)) America Star Bks.

—Planet Earth Past, Present, Future: Bryanna Global Warrior Book 3, 1 vol. Pelton, Bonnie L., illus. 2010. 34p. pap. 24.95 (978-1-4489-8321-6(5)) PublishAmerica, Inc.

Baskwill, Jane & National Geographic Learning Staff. Touch the Earth. Fiore, Peter M., illus. 2010. (Rise & Shine Ser.). (ENG.). 32p. (C). (gr. 1-5). pap. 10.95 (978-1-57255-428-3(2)) National Geographic School Publishing, Inc.

Bater, Alison. Another Chance. 2008. 160p. pap. (978-1-84923-071-1(4)) YouWriteOn.

Batts, Laura. Love Your Pony, Love Your Planet: All about Pony Poo & Other Helpful Things We Can Do! 2013. (ENG., Illus.). 16.95 (978-1-62086-303-9(0)) Mascot Bks., Inc.

Beadle, David M. The Day the Trash Came Out to Play. Faust, Laurie A., illus. 2004. 32p. (J). 16.95 (978-0-9727855-0-1(7)) Ezra's Earth Publishing.

Beard, Darleen Bailey & Maione, Heather Harms. Annie Glover Is Not a Tree Lover. Maione, Heather Harms, illus. 2009. (ENG., Illus.). 128p. (J). (gr. 2-5). 15.99 (978-0-374-30351-8(7), 9780374303518, Farrar, Straus & Giroux (BYR)) Farrar, Straus & Giroux.

Beauregard, Lynda. The Yucky Duck Rescue: A Mystery about Pollution. Torres, German, illus. 2013. (Summer Camp Science Mysteries Ser.: 8). (ENG.). 48p. (gr. 3-6). pap. 6.95 (978-1-4677-0736-7(8), Graphic Universe™) Lerner Publishing Group.

Bell, Aaron. Jak's Story. 2010. (ENG., Illus.). 96p. (YA). (gr. 4). pap. 10.99 (978-1-55488-710-1(0)) Dundurn CAN. Dist: Ingram Publisher Services.

Bell, Holly. Ethan Goes Green. Sidwell, Kathy, illus. 2009. 32p. pap. 12.99 (978-1-4389-0115-2(1)) AuthorHouse.

Berenstain, Jan & Berenstain, Mike. The Berenstain Bears Go Green. 2013. (Berenstain Bears Ser.). (Illus.). (J). lib. bdg. 13.55 (978-0-606-27142-4(2), Turtleback) Turtleback Bks.

Beres, Lisa. My body my World. 2008. (Illus.). (J). 16.95 (978-0-9772392-2-1(5)) Green Nest LLC.

Bergen, Lara. Don't Throw That Away! A Lift-the-Flap Book about Recycling & Reusing. Snyder, Betsy E., illus. 2009. (Little Green Bks.). (ENG.). 14p. (J). (gr. -1-1). bds. 7.99 (978-1-4169-7517-5(9), Little Simon) Little Simon.

—Polar Bears' Home: A Story about Global Warming. Nguyen, Vincent, illus. 2008. (Little Green Bks.). (ENG.). 24p. (J). (gr. -1-1). pap. 3.99 (978-1-4169-6787-3(7), Little Simon) Little Simon.

Berger, Carin. Ok Go. Berger, Carin, illus. 2009. (ENG., Illus.). 32p. (J). (gr. -1-k). 17.99 (978-0-06-157666-9(2), Greenwillow Bks.) HarperCollins Pubs.

Bjork, Linda. Salmon Cavern. 2006. 92p. pap. 10.95 (978-1-59800-546-2(4)) Outskirts Pr., Inc.

Blount, Willie And Ebony. Super Duck Goes Green. 2011. 44p. pap. 16.59 (978-1-4634-1909-7(0)) AuthorHouse.

Bottoms, Bud. Davey & the GOM Giant Oil Monster. 2008. (Illus.). 39p. (J). (gr. -1-5). per. 14.95 (978-0-9795444-1-5(6)) Summerland Publishing.

Brown, Marc. Arthur Turns Green. 2014. (ENG.). 32p. (J). (gr. 1-4). 7.00 (978-0-316-12923-7(2)) Little Brown & Co.

—Arthur Turns Green. 2014. (Arthur Adventures Ser.). (J). lib. bdg. 17.20 (978-0-606-34069-4(6), Turtleback) Turtleback Bks.

Cali, Davide. The Bear with the Sword. Foli, Gianluca, illus. 2010. (ENG.). 32p. (J). (gr. -1-3). 15.99 (978-0-9806070-4-8(3)) Wilkins Farago Pty, Ltd. AUS. Dist: Independent Pubs. Group.

Carlson, Melody. Take Charge, 1 vol. 2016. (Faithgirlz / Girls of Harbor View Ser.). (ENG.). 272p. (J). (gr. 3-7). pap. 9.99 (978-0-310-75373-5(2)) Zonderkidz.

Cavanaugh, Nancy J. This Journal Belongs to Ratchet. 2014. (ENG.). 320p. (J). (gr. 3-6). pap. 6.99 (978-1-4926-0109-8(8), 9781492601098, Sourcebooks Jabberwocky) Sourcebooks, Inc.

Childs, Tera Lynn. Just for Fins. 2013. (Forgive My Fins Ser.: 3). (ENG.). 256p. (YA). (gr. 8). pap. 9.99 (978-0-06-219208-0(6), Tegen, Katherine Bks) HarperCollins Pubs.

Cooper, Susan. Green Boy. (ENG., Illus.). 208p. (J). 2013. (gr. 3-7). 17.99 (978-1-4424-8081-0(5)) 2003. (gr. 4-7). pap. 7.99 (978-0-689-84760-8(2)) McElderry, Margaret K. Bks. (McElderry, Margaret K. Bks.).

Cooper, Susan & National Geographic Learning Staff. Green Boy. 2013. (ENG., Illus.). 208p. (J). (gr. 3-7). pap. 7.99 (978-1-4424-8082-7(3), McElderry, Margaret K. Bks.) McElderry, Margaret K. Bks.

Corrick, Dave. Louie the Bee: The Insects Prevail. 2010. 358p. 29.99 (978-1-4500-1603-2(0)); pap. 19.99 (978-1-4500-1602-5(2)) Xlibris Corp.

Corso, Suzanne. Sammy & Sue Go Green Too! 2009. (J). (978-0-615-19785-2(X)) Beaufort Bks.

—Sammy & Sue Go Green Too! 2009. (Sammy & Sue Ser.: 0). (ENG.). 32p. 16.95 (978-0-8253-0517-7(9)) Beaufort Bks., Inc.

Cote, Genevieve & Côté, Geneviève. Mr. King's Machine. Cote, Genevieve & Côté, Geneviève, illus. 2016. (Mr. King Ser.). (ENG., Illus.). 32p. (J). (gr. -1-2). 16.95 (978-1-77138-021-8(7)) Kids Can Pr., Ltd. CAN. Dist: Hachette Bk. Group.

Cowan, Jennifer. Earthgirl, 1 vol. 2009. (ENG.). 192p. (J). (gr. 8-18). 17.95 (978-0-88899-889-7(9)) Groundwood Bks. CAN. Dist: Publishers Group West (PGW).

Cruz De Jesus, Marta. Chosen: By Nature. 2010. 116p. 21.49 (978-1-4520-3479-9(6)); pap. 10.99 (978-1-4520-3480-5(X)) AuthorHouse.

Dahl, Michael & Nickel, Scott. The Green Queen of Mean. Crowther, Jeff, illus. 2010. (Graphic Sparks Ser.). (ENG.). 40p. (gr. 1-3). pap. 5.95 (978-1-4342-2803-1(7), Graphic Sparks) Stone Arch Bks.

Dance, Jennifer. Hawk. 2016. (ENG.). 248p. (YA). pap. 12.99 (978-1-4597-3184-4(0)) Dundurn CAN. Dist: Ingram Publisher Services.

Darling, Pollyanna. Heartwood. Chalmers, Kirsty, illus. 2013. 66p. (J). pap. (978-0-9871164-4-4(4)) Imaginaria.

De felice, Cynthia. Lostman's River. 2008. (ENG.). 160p. (J). (gr. 3-7). pap. 8.99 (978-1-4169-8690-4(1), Simon & Schuster/Paula Wiseman Bks.) Simon & Schuster/Paula Wiseman Bks.

De la Cruz, Melissa & Johnston, Michael. Stolen Bk. 2: Heart of Dread. 2014. (Heart of Dread Ser.: 2). (ENG.). 304p. (YA). (gr. 7). 17.99 (978-0-399-25755-1(1), G.P. Putnam's Sons Books for Young Readers) Penguin Young Readers Group.

deGroat, Diane. Ants in Your Pants, Worms in Your Plants! Gilbert Goes Green. deGroat, Diane, illus. 2011. (Gilbert Ser.). (ENG., Illus.). 32p. (J). (gr. -1-3). 16.99 (978-0-06-176511-7(2)) HarperCollins Pubs.

Delessert, Etienne. Spartacus the Spider. 2010. (ENG., Illus.). 32p. (J). (gr. 1-3). 17.95 (978-1-56846-213-4(1), Creative Editions) Creative Co., The.

Dixon, Bob. Rooty the Tree Troll. 2009. 28p. pap. 13.99 (978-1-4389-9129-0(0)) AuthorHouse.

d'Lacey, Chris. The Fire Eternal. 2008. (Last Dragon Chronicles Ser.: 4). (ENG.). 512p. (J). (gr. 3-7). 17.99 (978-0-545-05163-7(0), Orchard Bks.) Scholastic, Inc.

Ducote, Billie Seaon. The Adventures of Artie Eco Part One: The Problem with Greed, 2 vols, Vol. 1. Ducote, Billie Seaon, illus. 2007. (ENG., Illus.). 26p. (J). 18.95 (978-0-9787597-5-9(3)) PureLight Pubns.

—The Adventures of Artie Eco Part Two: The Problem with Greed Artie Eco Goes to Dirtyville, 2 vols., Vol. 2. Ducote, Billie Seaon, illus. 2007. (Illus.). 26p. (J). act. bk. ed. 18.95 (978-0-9787597-1-1(0)) PureLight Pubns.

Ellis, Leanne Statland. Tree Huggers. 2010. (J). pap. (978-0-88092-521-1(3)) Royal Fireworks Publishing Co.

Foresman, Timothy. The Last Little Polar Bear: A Global Change Adventure Story. Laura Lee, Cundiff, illus. 2007. 60p. (J). per. 19.95 (978-0-9776906-2-6(8)) Blueline Publishing.

Forte, Lauren. Olivia Helps Mother Nature. 2014. (Olivia Ready-To-Read Level 1 Ser.). lib. bdg. 13.55 (978-0-606-35452-3(2)) Turtleback Bks.

French, Lisa S. A Planet Called Home: Eco-Pig's Animal Protection, 1 vol. Gott, Barry, illus. 2009. (Eco-Pig Ser.). (ENG.). 32p. (J). (gr. -1-2). 28.50 (978-1-60270-662-0(X)) ABDO Publishing Co.

—What Does It Mean to Be Green? Eco-Pig Explains Living Green, 1 vol. Gott, Barry, illus. 2009. (Eco-Pig Ser.). (ENG.). 32p. (J). (gr. -1-2). 28.50 (978-1-60270-665-1(4)) ABDO Publishing Co.

Friedman, Laurie. Mallory Goes Green! Kalis, Jennifer, illus. (Mallory Ser.). 160p. (J). 2011. pap. 33.92 (978-0-7613-7606-4(2), Darby Creek) 2011. (ENG.). (gr. 2-5). pap. 5.95 (978-0-7613-3949-6(3)) 2010. (ENG.). (gr. 2-5). 15.95 (978-0-8225-8885-6(4), Carolrhoda Bks.) Lerner Publishing Group.

Fujita, Rima. Save the Himalayas. 2011. (ENG, JPN & TIB., Illus.). 44p. 19.95 (978-1-935548-09-6(3)) One Peace Bks., Inc.

Galliez, Roxane Marie. The Earth Has Caught Cold. Lhomme, Sandrine, illus. 2009. 24p. (J). (gr. -1-3). 9.99 (978-0-8416-7140-9(0)) Hammond World Atlas Corp.

Ganz, Yaffa. Four in One: Four Favorites. Klineman, Harvey, illus. 2008. 24.99 (978-1-59826-183-7(5)) Feldheim Pubs.

George, Jean Craighead. The Last Polar Bear. Minor, Wendell, illus. 2009. (ENG.). 32p. (J). (gr. -1-2). 16.99 (978-0-06-124067-6(2)) HarperCollins Pubs.

Gilbert, Nikki Murphy. Gilbert Green. 2009. 32p. pap. 14.99 (978-1-4490-4377-3(1)) AuthorHouse.

Gilman, David. Blood Sun. 2012. (Danger Zone Ser.). (ENG.). 432p. (YA). (gr. 7). pap. 10.99 (978-0-440-42241-9(8), Ember) Random Hse. Children's Bks.

—The Devil's Breath Bk. 1. 2010. (Danger Zone Ser.). (ENG.). 416p. (YA). (gr. 7). pap. 9.99 (978-0-440-42239-6(6), Ember) Random Hse. Children's Bks.

Giuliano, Kevin. When I Was Young. 2010. 36p. pap. 18.99 (978-1-4520-6314-0(1)) AuthorHouse.

Golding, Julia. The Gorgon's Gaze, 0 vols., Bk. 2. 2010. (Companions Quartet Ser.: 2). (ENG.). 320p. (J). (gr. 4-7). pap. 9.99 (978-0-7614-5653-7(8), 9780761456537, Amazon Children's Publishing) Amazon Publishing.

—Secret of the Sirens, 0 vols. 2009. (Companions Quartet Ser.: 1). (ENG.). 368p. (J). (gr. 4-7). pap. 9.99 (978-0-7614-5617-9(1), 9780761456179, Amazon Children's Publishing) Amazon Publishing.

Golio, Janet & Golio, Mike. Present from the Past. 2nd ed. 2009. (ENG.). 120p. (YA). pap. 14.99 (978-1-59092-145-6(3)) Blue Forge Pr.

Goodman, Larry. Clean up the Glup! 2007. 24p. per. 24.95 (978-1-4241-9141-3(6)) America Star Bks.

Gove, Susan E. Kids Get It: Shrinking Our Carbon Footprint. 2010. 40p. pap. 16.99 (978-1-4520-8391-9(6)) AuthorHouse.

Gutman, Dan. Roberto & Me. 2010. (Baseball Card Adventures Ser.: Bk. 10). (ENG.). 192p. (J). (gr. 5-9). 16.99 (978-0-06-123484-2(2)) HarperCollins Pubs.

Handy, Femida & Carpenter, Carole H. Sandy's Incredible Shrinking Footprint, 1 vol. Steele-Card, Adrianna & Second Story Press Staff, illus. 2010. (ENG.). 24p. (J). (gr. 3 — 1). 15.95 (978-1-897187-69-2(6)) Second Story Pr. CAN. Dist: Orca Bk. Pubs. USA.

Harley, Bill. Night of the Spadefoot Toads, 1 vol. 2008. (ENG.). 192p. (J). (gr. 3-7). 15.95 (978-1-56145-459-4(1)) Peachtree Pubs.

Harrison, Patrick Gb. Who says Kist Can't Fight Global Warming. 2009. pap. 16.97 (978-1-61584-921-5(1)) Independent Pub.

Hart, Deborah. Guarding Eden: Champions of Climate Action. 2015. (ENG., Illus.). 256p. (YA). (gr. 8-12). pap. 14.99 (978-1-76011-235-6(6)) Allen & Unwin AUS. Dist: Independent Pubs. Group.

Hautman, Pete & Logue, Mary. Skullduggery. 2007. (Bloodwater Mysteries Ser.). (ENG.). 192p. (J). (gr. 5-18). 16.99 (978-0-399-24378-3(X), G.P. Putnam's Sons Books for Young Readers) Penguin Young Readers Group.

Hawkins, Denise. The Plight of Sanna, the Polar Bear, 1 vol. 2010. 106p. pap. 19.95 (978-1-60441-672-5(6)) America Star Bks.

Heinrich, Julie. Bob White & Whippoorwill. 2008. 32p. 14.50 (978-1-4357-1074-0(6)) Lulu Pr., Inc.

Helget, Nicole. The End of the Wild. 2017. (ENG., Illus.). 272p. (J). (gr. 3-7). 16.99 (978-0-316-24511-1(9)) Little, Brown Bks. for Young Readers.

Henry, Pam. Cold Call. 2011. 200p. pap. (978-1-84903-065-6(0)) Schiel & Denver Publishing Ltd.

Herndon, Susen A. Janie's World: Walk with Me Through Nature's Door. 2013. 36p. pap. 16.46 (978-1-4669-8057-0(5)) Trafford Publishing.

Hiaasen, Carl. Flush. 2007. 263p. (gr. 5-9). 19.00 (978-0-7569-8192-1(1)) Perfection Learning Corp.

—Flush. (ENG.). 272p. (J). (gr. 5-6). 2010. 6.99 (978-0-375-86125-3(4), Yearling) 2007. pap. 8.99 (978-0-375-84185-9(7), Knopf Bks. for Young Readers) 2005. 16.95 (978-0-375-82182-0(1), Knopf Bks. for Young Readers) Random Hse. Children's Bks.

—Hoot. 2004. (ENG.). 304p. (YA). (gr. 7). reprint ed. pap. 8.99 (978-0-375-82916-1(4), Ember) Random Hse. Children's Bks.

Hiiasen, Carl. Hoot. 2014. 17.00 (978-1-63419-707-6(0)) Perfection Learning Corp.

Hughes, Ann. Kaitlyn & the Moonman. 2008. (Illus.). 56p. pap. (978-1-84748-470-3(0)) Athena Pr.

Hughes, Monica. The Golden Aquarians. 2009. (ENG.). 192p. (YA). (gr. 7-7). pap. 9.99 (978-1-4424-0223-2(7), Simon & Schuster Bks. For Young Readers) Simon & Schuster Bks. For Young Readers.

Inches, Alison. I Can Save the Earth! One Little Monster Learns to Reduce, Reuse, & Recycle. Garofoli, Viviana, illus. 2008. (Little Green Bks.). (ENG.). 24p. (J). (gr. -1-1). pap. 3.99 (978-1-4169-6789-7(3), Little Simon) Little Simon.

James, Martin. William Is Going Green. 2008. 38p. 14.95 (978-0-9799465-1-6(4)) Martin, James Jr.

Janelle, Nicole & Cholette, Daniel. Naby Recycles. 2012. 32p. pap. 14.60 (978-1-105-53454-6(5)) Lulu Pr., Inc.

Johnson, Patricia. Make Your Own Magic Soil: Life's Lessons on Sustainable Living. 2013. 60p. 24.99 (978-1-4797-0525-2(X)); pap. 15.99 (978-1-4797-0524-5(1)) Xlibris Corp.

Jordan-Tegtmeier. Jennifer. The Small Shady Tree. 2008. 16p. pap. 8.49 (978-1-4343-7382-3(7)) AuthorHouse.

Kann, Victoria. Emeraldalicious. Kann, Victoria, illus. 2013. (Illus.). 40p. (J). (gr. -1-3). (ENG.). 17.99 (978-0-06-178126-1(9)); lib. bdg. 18.89 (978-0-06-178127-8(4)) HarperCollins Pubs.

Keene, Carolyn. Earth Day Escapade. Pamintuan, Macky, illus. 2009. (Nancy Drew & the Clue Crew Ser.: 18). (ENG.). 96p. (J). (gr. 1-4). pap. 5.99 (978-1-4169-7218-1(8), Aladdin) Simon & Schuster Children's Publishing.

Kharbanda, Priya. Flumpa & Bosly Learn the Magic Three Rs: Reduce, Reuse & Recycle. 2010. 32p. pap. 23.50 (978-1-4461-3602-7(7)) Lulu Pr., Inc.

Knight, Mary. Saving Wonder. 2016. (ENG.). 288p. (J). (gr. 3-7). 16.99 (978-0-545-82893-2(7), Scholastic Pr.) Scholastic, Inc.

Koss, Amy Goldman. Kailey. Howe, Philip, illus. 2003. (American Girl of Today Ser.). (ENG.). 160p. (J). pap. 6.95 (978-1-58485-591-0(6)) American Girl Publishing, Inc.

Kravitz, Cathy. What We Can Do: A Book about Global Warming. 2008. 44p. pap. 16.95 (978-1-59858-589-6(4)) Dog Ear Publishing, LLC.

Lacaille, Link. Roots, Rock, Rap & Reggae, 1 vol. 2009. 25p. pap. 24.95 (978-1-60836-930-0(7)) America Star Bks.

Lannin, Ann. A Child from Nowhere. 2011. 128p. (gr. 2-4). 21.95 (978-1-4620-2346-2(0)); pap. 11.95 (978-1-4620-2347-9(9)) iUniverse, Inc.

Layton, Neal. The Tree. Layton, Neal, illus. 2017. (ENG., Illus.). 40p. (J). (-k). 16.99 (978-0-7636-8952-0(1)) Candlewick Pr.

Lee, Julia Elizabeth. Seahorses Down Under. Weiser, Robert, ed. (Defenders of Wildlife Ser.). (Illus.). 50+p. (J). (gr. k-3). lib. bdg. 9.95 (978-0-9666857-0-1(9)) Dawn of Day Childrens Publishing Co., Inc.

Lee, WonKyeong. Green River. Yang, HyeWon, illus. 2014. (MySELF Bookshelf Ser.). (ENG.). 32p. (J). (gr. k-2). pap. 11.94 (978-1-60357-695-6(9)); lib. bdg. 25.27 (978-1-59953-660-6(9)) Norwood Hse. Pr.

Lennon, Julian & Davis, Bart. Touch the Earth. Coh, Smiljana, illus. 2017. (ENG.). 40p. (J). (gr. -1-k). 17.99 (978-1-5107-2083-1(9), Sky Pony Pr.) Skyhorse Publishing Co., Inc.

Lewis, Gill. One White Dolphin. Aparicio, Raquel, illus. 2013. (ENG.). 368p. (J). (gr. 3-7). pap. 8.99 (978-1-4424-1448-8(0), Atheneum Bks. for Young Readers) Simon & Schuster Children's Publishing.

Lewis, J. Patrick. Make the Earth Your Companion. Balbusso, Anna & Balbusso, Elena, illus. 2017. (ENG.). 32p. (J). (gr. 1-3). pap. 18.99 (978-1-56846-269-1(7), Creative Education) Creative Co., The.

Little Green Giants. 2008. (Illus.). 28p. (J). 14.95 (978-0-615-21480-1(0)) Allocca, Christine A.

Livingston, Mary A. & Shufelberger, Amanda. Buddy & the Magic Chicken Tree, 2 bks. Livingston, Tim, illus. 2014th ed. 2014. (ENG.). 34p. (J). 19.99 (978-0-9635757-3-9(2)) Red Tail Publishing.

London, Matt. The 8th Continent. 2014. (8th Continent Ser.: 1). (ENG.). 224p. (J). (gr. 3-7). 12.99 (978-1-59514-754-7(3), Razorbill) Penguin Young Readers Group.

—The Lord of Opium. 2014. (ENG., Illus.). 448p. (YA). (gr. 7). pap. 12.99 (978-1-4424-8255-5(9), Atheneum Bks. for Young Readers) Simon & Schuster Children's Publishing.

Lowery, Paul. Do You Know Where Sea Turtles Go? 2007. (J). 15.99 (978-0-9792379-0-4(4)) PBL Stories LLC.

MacGregor, Doug, creator. Ochre the Smoker: A fantastic Fable. 2007. (Illus.). 48p. (J). per. 14.95 (978-0-9654843-2-9(7)) MacGregor, Doug.

Markowitz-Meredith, Susan. Environmentally Friendly World: Set Of 6. checkpt. ed. 2011. (Early Connections Ser.). (J). pap. 38.00 (978-1-4108-1561-3(7)) Benchmark Education Co.

Markowitz, Susan Meredith. The Great Green Forest & el gran bosque Verde: 6 English, 6 Spanish Adaptations. 2011. (ENG & SPA.). (J). 75.00 net. (978-1-4108-5653-1(4)) Benchmark Education Co.

McClements, George. Dinosaur Woods: Can Seven Clever Critters Save Their Forest Home? McClements, George, illus. 2009. (ENG., Illus.). 40p. (J). (gr. -1-2). 16.99 (978-1-4169-8626-3(X), Beach Lane Bks.) Beach Lane Bks.

McCluskey, J. E. The Adventures of Peter the Pleasant Platypus & Friends: First Adventure, Tidy Time. 2004. 48p. pap. 24.95 (978-1-4137-2546-9(5)) PublishAmerica, Inc.

McDonald, Abby. Boys, Bears, & a Serious Pair of Hiking Boots. (ENG., Illus.). 304p. (YA). (gr. 9). 2011. pap. 7.99 (978-0-7636-4994-4(5)) 2010. 16.99 (978-0-7636-4382-9(3)) Candlewick Pr.

McDonald, Megan. Judy Moody Saves the World! Reynolds, Peter H., illus. 2004. (Judy Moody Ser.: Bk. 3). 144p. (J). (gr. 1-5). 13.65 (978-0-7569-2588-8(6)) Perfection Learning Corp.

—Judy Moody Saves the World! Reynolds, Peter H., illus. 2010. (Judy Moody Ser.: 3). (ENG.). 160p. (J). (gr. 1-4). 15.99 (978-0-7636-4860-2(4)) Candlewick Pr.

—Judy Moody Saves the World! 2010. (Judy Moody Ser.: 3). lib. bdg. 16.00 (978-0-606-12340-2(7), Turtleback) Turtleback Bks.

—Judy Moody Saves the World!, Bk. 3. Reynolds, Peter H., illus. 2010. (Judy Moody Ser.: 3). (ENG.). 160p. (J). (gr. 1-4). pap. 5.99 (978-0-7636-4859-6(0)) Candlewick Pr.

McNamara, Margaret. Earth Day. Gordon, Mike, illus. 2009. (Robin Hill School Ser.). (ENG.). 32p. (J). (gr. -1-1). pap. 3.99 (978-1-4169-5535-1(6), Simon Spotlight) Simon Spotlight.

Meadows, Daisy. Coral the Reef Fairy. 2014. (Earth Fairies Ser.: 4). (ENG.). 80p. (J). (gr. 2-5). pap. 4.99 (978-0-545-60527-4(X), Scholastic Paperbacks) Scholastic, Inc.

—Edie the Garden Fairy. 2014. (Earth Fairies Ser.: 3). (ENG.). 80p. (J). (gr. 2-5). pap. 4.99 (978-0-545-60526-7(1), Scholastic Paperbacks) Scholastic, Inc.

Medina, Sylvia M. & Ballock-Dixon, Saige J. Green Springs Junior. Eagle, Joy, illus. 2013. 36p. pap. 11.59 (978-0-9836602-7-9(1)) Green Kids Club, Inc.

Medlicott, Mary. Open Secret. 2004. (ENG.). 152p. pap. 12.95 (978-1-84323-289-6(8)) Beekman Bks., Inc.

Messner, Kate. Marty McGuire Digs Worms! Floca, Brian, illus. 2012. (ENG.). 176p. (J). (gr. 1-3). pap. 5.99 (978-0-545-14247-2(4), Scholastic Pr.) Scholastic, Inc.

Mihaley, James. You Can't Have My Planet: But Take My Brother, Please. 2013. (ENG.). 272p. (J). (gr. 4-7). pap. 8.99 (978-1-250-01667-6(3), 9781250016676) Square Fish.

Montesinos Anzures, Luis. Tecolote. 2009. 176p. pap. 11.99 (978-1-4389-5885-9(4)) AuthorHouse.

Morgan, Beth. Earth's Treasure Green Pearl. 2011. 48p. pap. 24.95 (978-1-4560-0186-5(8)) America Star Bks.

Morgan, Melissa J. Politically Incorrect. 2010. (Camp Confidential Ser.: 23). (ENG.). 176p. (J). (gr. 3-7). pap. 4.99 (978-0-448-45267-8(7), Grosset & Dunlap) Penguin Young Readers Group.

O'Connor, Jane. Every Day Is Earth Day. Ivanov, Aleksey et al, illus. 2010. (I Can Read Level 1 Ser.). (ENG.). 32p. (J). (gr. -1-3). 16.99 (978-0-06-187327-0(6)) HarperCollins Pubs.

—Every Day Is Earth Day. Ivanov, Aleksey et al, illus. 2010. (I Can Read Level 1 Ser.). (ENG.). 32p. (J). (gr. -1-3). pap. 3.99 (978-0-06-187326-3(8)) HarperCollins Pubs.

Ogden, Charles, ed. Edgar & Ellen Graphic Novelty: A Comics Collection. 2009. (Edgar & Ellen Ser.). (ENG.). 112p. (J). (gr. 3-7). pap. 7.99 (978-1-4169-5004-2(4), Simon & Schuster/Paula Wiseman Bks.) Simon & Schuster/Paula Wiseman Bks.

Osterhold, Jared, illus. OLIVIA Helps Mother Nature. 2014. (Olivia TV Tie-In Ser.). (ENG.). 24p. (J). (gr. -1-1). pap. 3.99 (978-1-4424-9664-4(9), Simon Spotlight) Simon Spotlight.

Pakkala, Christine. Last-But-Not-Least Lola Going Green. Hoppe, Paul, illus. 2014. (Last-But-Not-Least Lola Ser.). (ENG.). 192p. (J). (gr. 2-5). pap. 7.95 (978-1-62979-113-5(X)) Boyds Mills Pr.

Patricia Diane Craine, Ma-Lmft. Our Miracle Our Earth. 2009. 56p. pap. 24.49 (978-1-4389-5918-4(4)) AuthorHouse.

Perera, Oleene. Timmy Tangelo Goes Green. 2010. 20p. 12.50 (978-0-557-41286-0(2)) Lulu Pr., Inc.

Perla, Victoria. When Santa Turned Green. 2007. (Illus.). 44p. (J). (978-0-9799454-0-3(2)) Brinsights, LLC.

Postma, Carryl. The Tree That Could Be Green. 2009. 20p. pap. 14.99 (978-1-4389-5842-2(0)) AuthorHouse.

Raffensperger. The Eagle Tree. 2013. 60p. (J). pap. 14.95 (978-0-9896338-6-4(1)) Barringer Publishing.

Reader's Digest Staff. Let's Help the Earth. Brannon, Tom, illus. 2008. (Sesame Street Ser.). (ENG.). 12p. (J). (gr. -1-k). bds. 12.99 (978-0-7944-1696-6(9)) Reader's Digest Assn., Inc., The.

Rentala, Sita Kanaka Valli. Ocean Flows: In Prose: Zcumby's Judo (on Global Warming) 2010. 44p. (J). pap. 19.99 (978-1-4490-8780-7(9)) AuthorHouse.

Rey, H. A. Curious George Plants a Tree. Wilcox, Mary, ed. 2010. (Curious George Ser.). (ENG., Illus.). 24p. (J). (gr. -1-3). pap. 4.99 (978-0-547-29776-7(9)) Houghton Mifflin Harcourt Publishing Co.

—Curious George Plants a Tree. 2009. (Curious George Ser.). (ENG., Illus.). 32p. (J). (gr. -1-3). 14.99 (978-0-547-15087-1(3)) Houghton Mifflin Harcourt Publishing Co.

Reynolds, Paul A. Sydney & Simon: Going Green! Reynolds, Paul A. & Reynolds, Peter H., illus. 2015. (Sydney & Simon Ser.). (ENG.). 48p. (J). (gr. 1-4). lib. bdg. 12.95 (978-1-58089-677-1(4)) Charlesbridge Publishing, Inc.

Ross, Joel. The Fog Diver. 2015. (Fog Diver Ser.: 1). (ENG.). 336p. (J). (gr. 3-7). 16.99 (978-0-06-235293-4(8)) HarperCollins Pubs.

Salisbury, Linda G. Mudd Saves the Earth: Booger Glue, Cow Diapers & Other Good Ideas. 2009. (Illus.). 96p. (J). pap. 8.95 (978-1-881539-47-6(4)) Tabby Hse. Bks.

Santore, Charles, illus. William the Curious: Knight of the Water Lilies. 2012. (J). *(978-1-60464-034-2(0))* Appleseed Pr. Bk. Pub. LLC.

Schwartz, Joel. The Extraordinary Pupfish of Calaveras County. 2008. 216p. 25.95 *(978-1-4401-0892-1(7))* iUniverse, Inc.

Semionov, Vladimir & Louie, Wes, illus. Forecast from Stonehenge. 2007. (Choose Your Own Adventure Ser.: No. 19). 127p. (J). (gr. 4-7). pap. 6.99 *(978-1-933390-19-2(0))* Chooseco LLC.

Sharpe, Susan. Waterman's Boy. 2007. (ENG.). 176p. (J). (gr. 3-7). pap. 11.95 *(978-1-4169-6453-7(3)*, Simon & Schuster/Paula Wiseman Bks.) Simon & Schuster/Paula Wiseman Bks.

Sheldon, Dyan. The Crazy Things Girls Do for Love. (ENG.). 352p. (YA). (gr. 7). 2013. pap. 8.99 *(978-0-7636-6468-8(5))* 2011. (Illus.). 16.99 *(978-0-7636-5018-6(8))* Candlewick Pr.

Sherrell, Deborah. Baby Lauren & Theodore,hardcover. 2007. (Illus.). (J). bds. 17.95 *(978-0-9779643-5-2(3))* Healing Tree Arts.

Sierra, Judy. Ballyhoo Bay. Anderson, Derek, illus. 2009. (ENG.). 40p. (J). (gr. -1-3). 16.99 *(978-1-4169-5888-8(6)*, Simon & Schuster/Paula Wiseman Bks.) Simon & Schuster/Paula Wiseman Bks.

Silver, Shana & Shane, Rachel. Alice in Wonderland High. 2015. (ENG.). 300p. (YA). 17.99 *(978-1-4405-8466-4(4)*, Simon Pulse) Simon Pulse.

Soffe, Caroline Dawn. Billy Barnet & the House of Fern: An Environmental Story. 2011. 222p. pap. 24.95 *(978-1-4560-5201-0(2))* America Star Bks.

Sorrentino, Dawn. I Wish I Were. 2013. 16p. pap. 14.99 *(978-1-4772-3176-0(5))* AuthorHouse.

Spinelli, Eileen. Miss Fox's Class Goes Green. Kennedy, Anne, illus. 2012. (J). 34.28 *(978-1-61913-123-1(4))* Weigl Pubs., Inc.

—Miss Fox's Class Goes Green. Kennedy, Anne, illus. 2011. (Miss Fox's Class Ser.). (ENG.). 32p. (J). (gr. 1-3). 6.99 *(978-0-8075-5167-7(8))* Whitman, Albert & Co.

Sterrett, Nicole. 1-2 Recycling's for You! 2008. 12p. pap. 24.95 *(978-1-60610-223-7(0))* America Star Bks.

Sullivan, Jenny. Nowhere Again. 2004. (ENG.). 230p. pap. 13.95 *(978-1-84323-297-1(9))* Beekman Bks., Inc.

Sullivan, Silvia. Hip Hip Hurray We Found Teddy: A Book Series to Teach Children Practical Life Skills & Eco-Friendly Skills. 2008. 32p. pap. 15.48 *(978-1-4343-5897-4(6))* AuthorHouse.

Taylor, W. Y. I'm Not too Little to Help the Earth. 2009. 14p. 9.95 *(978-1-58117-913-2(8)*, Intervisual/Piggy Toes) Bendon, Inc.

Terry & the Ecological Disaster. pap. *(978-1-56002-792-8(4))* Univ. Editions.

Tidwell, Susan. Little Lotus & the Loving-Kindness Cup. Lee, Wei-Chun, illus. 2012. 77p. (J). 6.95 *(978-1-932293-72-2(8))* Buddha's Light Publications USA Corp.

Tomkins, D. Michael. The World Below. 2006. (YA). 39.95 *(978-0-9774451-2-7(7))* DSA Publishing & Design, Inc.

Trantham, Cary Gordon. The Saving of Sophi: El Rescate de Sofia. 2012. 28p. pap. 19.99 *(978-1-4772-0799-4(6))* AuthorHouse.

Van Allsburg, Chris. Just a Dream. Van Allsburg, Chris, illus. 2014. (Illus.). 48p. pap. 9.00 *(978-1-61003-182-0(2))* Center for the Collaborative Classroom.

—Just a Dream 25th Anniversary Edition. 2015. (ENG., Illus.). 48p. (J). (gr. -1-3). 18.99 *(978-0-544-42283-4(X)*, HMH Books For Young Readers) Houghton Mifflin Harcourt Publishing Co.

Violet Mackerel's Pocket Protest. 2014. (Violet Mackerel Ser.). (ENG., Illus.). 128p. (J). (gr. 1-5). 17.99 *(978-1-4424-9458-9(1)*, Atheneum Bks. for Young Readers) Simon & Schuster Children's Publishing.

Ward, Kaitlin. Bleeding Earth. 2016. (ENG.). 256p. (YA). 17.99 *(978-0-9864484-8-5(6))* Adaptive Studios.

Waters, Summer. River Rescue, 10. 2010. (Silver Dolphins Ser.: 10). (ENG.). 176p. (J). (gr. 2-4). pap. 7.99 *(978-0-00-736750-4(3)*, HarperCollins Children's Bks.) HarperCollins Pubs. Ltd. GBR. Dist: HarperCollins Pubs.

Weiss, Dylan. Sebastian's Tale: A Skunk Tales Trilogy Book. 2016. (J). *(978-1-943267-16-3(2))* Red Engine Pr.

Weyn, Suzanne. Empty. 2010. (ENG.). 192p. (J). (gr. 7-18). 17.99 *(978-0-545-17278-3(0)*, Scholastic Pr.) Scholastic, Inc.

White, J. Scratch & Sniff: The Case of the Stuck Seagull. 2013. 32p. pap. *(978-1-4602-0552-5(9))* FriesenPress.

Wiley, Thom. Big Earth, Little Me. Endle, Kate, illus. 2009. 16p. (J). pap. *(978-0-545-22335-5(0))* Scholastic, Inc.

Wright, Maureen. Earth Day, Birthday!, 0 vols. Kim, Violet, illus. 2012. (ENG.). 32p. (J). (gr. k-3). 17.99 *(978-0-7614-6109-8(4)*, 9780761461098, Amazon Children's Publishing) Amazon Publishing.

Wylie, Peter. Chem Cloud. 2011. 16p. pap. 10.00 *(978-1-60976-980-2(5)*, Eloquent Bks.) Strategic Book Publishing & Rights Agency (SBPRA).

Yellowknife, Jessica. Spring Break Adventure. 2011. 84p. pap. 11.11 *(978-1-4269-6952-2(X))* Trafford Publishing.

Yolen, Jane. Where Have the Unicorns Gone? Sanderson, Ruth, illus. 2003. (ENG.). 32p. (J). (gr. -1-3). 9.99 *(978-0-689-86359-2(4)*, Simon & Schuster/Paula Wiseman Bks.) Simon & Schuster Bks. For Young Readers.

EOLITHIC PERIOD

see Stone Age

EPILEPSY

Allyn, Daisy. What Happens When I Hiccup? 2013. (My Body Does Strange Stuff! Ser.). (ENG., Illus.). 24p. (J). (gr. 1-3). pap. 8.15 *(978-1-4339-9339-8(2))*; lib. bdg. 22.60 *(978-1-4339-9338-1(4))* Stevens, Gareth Publishing LLLP.

Bender, Lionel. Explaining Epilepsy. 2009. (Explaining... Ser.). 48p. (gr. 7-12). 37.10 *(978-1-59920-309-6(X))* Black Rabbit Bks.

Bjorklund, Ruth. Epilepsy. 2006. (Health Alert Ser.). (Illus.). 64p. (YA). (gr. 4-7). lib. bdg. 32.79 *(978-0-7614-2206-8(4))* Marshall Cavendish Corp.

Chillemi, Stacey. My Mommy Has Epilepsy. 2008. 60p. pap. 31.95 *(978-1-4357-2910-0(2))* 2005. 63p. (J). pap. 15.96 *(978-1-4116-2019-3(4))* Lulu Pr., Inc.

Chilman-Blair, Kim, et al. Medikidz Explain Epilepsy: What's up with Wendy? 2009. (Illus.). 32p. (J). pap. *(978-1-906935-00-9(9))* Medikidz Ltd.

Christopherson, Sara Cohen. Living with Epilepsy, 1 vol. 2012. (Living with Health Challenges Set 1 Ser.). (ENG.). 112p. (J). (gr. 6-12). lib. bdg. 35.64 *(978-1-61783-127-0(1)*, Essential Library) ABDO Publishing Co.

Dougherty, Terri & Gale Editors. Epilepsy. 2009. (Diseases & Disorders Ser.) (Illus.). 128p. (J). 34.95 *(978-1-4205-0218-3(2)*, Lucent Bks.) Cengage Gale.

Emanuele, Patricia. Everything You Need to Know about Epilepsy. 2005. (Need to Know Library). (Illus.). 64p. (YA). (gr. 7-12). 31.95 *(978-0-8239-3161-3(7)*, NTEPIL) Rosen Publishing Group, Inc., The.

Gay, Kathlyn. Epilepsy: The Ultimate Teen Guide, Vol. 2nd ed. 2017. (It Happened to Me Ser.: 52). (ENG., Illus.). 158p. (J). (gr. 8-14). 45.00 *(978-1-4422-7171-5(X))* Rowman & Littlefield Publishers, Inc.

Gay, Kathlyn & McGarrahan, Sean. Epilepsy: The Ultimate Teen Guide. 2007. (It Happened to Me Ser.: 2). (ENG., Illus.). 112p. (gr. 8-12). per. 20.00 *(978-0-8108-5835-0(5))* Scarecrow Pr., Inc.

Goodfellow, Greg. Epilepsy. 2005. (Diseases & Disorders Ser.). (ENG., Illus.). 120p. (YA). (gr. 6-9). 32.45 *(978-1-56006-701-6(2)*, GML12001-178053, Lucent Bks.) Cengage Gale.

Karia, Roopal. The Why & What of Epilepsy: A Book for Children & Teens. Mittal, Shiekha, illus. 2008. 17p. pap. 24.95 *(978-1-60610-951-9(0))* America Star Bks.

Kolpin, Molly. Why Do I Hiccup? 2015. (My Silly Body Ser.). (ENG.). 24p. (gr. k-1). lib. bdg. 26.65 *(978-1-4914-2106-2(1)*, Pebble Plus) Capstone Press of Coughlan Cos.

Lambert, Kate. Can I Tell You about Epilepsy? A Guide for Friends, Family & Professionals. Hellier, Scott, illus. 2012. (Can I Tell You About...? Ser.). (ENG.). 48p. pap. 13.95 *(978-1-84905-309-9(X)*, 5847) Kingsley, Jessica Pubs. GBR. Dist: Macmillan Distribution Ltd.

Parker, Vic. I Know Someone with Epilepsy, 1 vol. 2011. (Understanding Health Issues Ser.). (ENG.). 32p. (gr. 1-3). 27.32 *(978-1-4329-4561-9(0)*, Heinemann First Library) Heinemann-Raintree.

Parks, Peggy J. Epilepsy. 2010. (Compact Research Ser.). 96p. (YA). (gr. 7-12). lib. bdg. 25.95 *(978-1-60152-094-4(8))* ReferencePoint Pr., Inc.

Passudetti, Christopher. Being Sara. 2013. (Av2 Audio Chapter Bks.). (ENG., Illus.). 81p. (J). (gr. 4-7). lib. bdg. 27.13 *(978-1-62127-970-9(7)*, AV2 by Weigl) Weigl Pubs., Inc.

Sévigny, Eric, illus. Caillou Gets the Hiccups! 2013. (Clubhouse Ser.). (ENG.). 24p. (J). (gr. -1-1). 3.99 *(978-2-89718-063-8(3))* Caillouet, Gerry.

Sherman, Rebecca. Migraines & Seizures. 2017. (Living with Diseases & Disorders Ser.: Vol. 11). (ENG.). (YA). (gr. 7-12). 23.95 ***(978-1-4222-3757-1(5))*** Mason Crest.

What Happens When I Hiccup? 2013. (My Body Does Strange Stuff! Ser.). 24p. (J). (gr. 1-3). pap. 48.90 *(978-1-4339-9340-4(6))* Stevens, Gareth Publishing LLLP.

What Happens When I Sneeze? 2013. (My Body Does Strange Stuff! Ser.). 24p. (J). (gr. 1-3). pap. 48.90 *(978-1-4339-9344-2(9))* Stevens, Gareth Publishing LLLP.

Zelenka, Yvonne. Aprendamos con Tito sobre la Epilepsia. Zelenka, Yvonne, illus. 2007. (SPA., Illus.). 24p. (J). 6.95 *(978-0-9787727-1-0(7))* Medicus Pr., Inc.

EPILEPSY—FICTION

Benedis-Grab, Daphne. Clementine for Christmas. 2015. (ENG.). 256p. (J). (gr. 3-7). 16.99 *(978-0-545-83951-8(3)*, Scholastic Pr.) Scholastic, Inc.

DeLand, Maitland. The Great Katie Kate Explains Epilepsy. 2014. (ENG., Illus.). 32p. (J). 14.95 *(978-1-62634-007-7(2)*, Greenleaf Book Group Pr.) Greenleaf Book Group.

Fabian, Cynthia. Orchestra in Our Brain: The Story of a Child with Epilepsy. Stevens, Daniel, illus. 2011. 20p. pap. 10.95 *(978-1-60976-783-9(7)*, Eloquent Bks.) Strategic Book Publishing & Rights Agency (SBPRA).

Howard, Ellen. Edith Herself. 2007. (ENG.). 144p. (J). (gr. 3-7). pap. 10.95 *(978-1-4169-6454-4(1)*, Simon & Schuster/Paula Wiseman Bks.) Simon & Schuster/Paula Wiseman Bks.

Oakes, Stephanie. The Arsonist. 2017. (ENG.). 496p. (YA). (gr. 7). 17.99 ***(978-0-8037-4071-6(9)***, Dial Bks) Penguin Young Readers Group.

Pohlmann-Eden, Bernd. The Secret of the Bounce-Back Mom. Hofer, Klaus C., tr. Erker, Robert, illus. 2013. 34p. pap. *(978-1-897462-27-0(1))* Glen Margaret Publishing.

Saldivar, Jose A. The Adventures of Oskar: Oskar's New School. Nilsson, Janet Busbey, ed. Jasnoch, Dorothy, illus. 2013. 32p. pap. 13.99 *(978-1-937752-14-9(3))*; (ENG.). pap. 13.99 *(978-1-937752-07-1(0))* Owl About Bks. Pub., Inc.

Skead, Robert & Simmel, Mike. Mighty Mike Bounces Back: A Boy's Life with Epilepsy. 2011. 64p. (J). 14.95 *(978-1-4338-1043-5(3))*; pap. 9.95 *(978-1-4338-1042-8(5))* American Psychological Assn. (Magination Pr.).

Smith, Andrew. 100 Sideways Miles. 2014. (ENG., Illus.). 288p. (YA). (gr. 9). 17.99 *(978-1-4424-4495-9(9)*, Simon & Schuster Bks. For Young Readers) Simon & Schuster Bks. For Young Readers.

Thomas, Leah. Because You'll Never Meet Me. (ENG.). (YA). 2017. 368p. pap. 9.99 *(978-1-68119-021-1(4)*, 9781681190211) 2015. 352p. (gr. 9-12). 17.99 *(978-1-61963-590-6(9)*, 9781619635906) Bloomsbury Publishing USA. (Bloomsbury USA Childrens).

—Because You'll Never Meet Me. 2017. (YA). lib. bdg. 20.85 ***(978-0-606-40347-4(7))*** Turtleback Bks.

Thomas, Leah. Nowhere near You. 2017. (ENG.). 400p. (YA). 17.99 *(978-1-68119-178-2(4)*, 9781681191782, Bloomsbury USA Childrens) Bloomsbury Publishing USA.

Woodworth, Adam. Monsters under My Bed. 2006. (J). per. 12.00 *(978-0-9769132-7-6(5))* Capri Publishing.

EPISTEMOLOGY

see Knowledge, Theory of

EPIZOA

see Parasites

EQUALITY

see also Aristocracy (Social Class); Democracy; Social Classes; Socialism

Benchmark Education Company, LLC Staff, compiled by. Fairness & Equality: Theme Set. 2006. (J). 136.00 *(978-1-4108-7068-1(5))* Benchmark Education Co.

Engdahl, Sylvia. Amendment XIV: Equal Protection. 2009. (Constitutional Amendments Ser.). (ENG., Illus.). 144p. (YA). (gr. 9-12). lib. bdg. 37.90 *(978-0-7377-4126-1(0)*, LML02109-243015) Cengage Gale.

Hanson, Anders. Everyone Is Equal: The Kids' Book of Tolerance, 1 vol. 2014. (What We Stand For Ser.). (ENG.). 24p. (gr. 5-10). lib. bdg. 25.65 *(978-1-62403-293-6(1)*, Super SandCastle) ABDO Publishing Co.

Harrison, Geoffrey C. & Scott, Thomas F. The Fight for Freedom. Stewart, Mark & Kennedy, Mike, eds. 2014. (Great Debates Ser.). (ENG.). 48p. (J). (gr. 5-8). lib. bdg. 29.27 *(978-1-59953-588-3(2))* Norwood Hse. Pr.

Hermann, Spring. The Struggle for Equality: Women & Minorities in America. 2006. (American Saga Ser.). (Illus.). 128p. (J). (gr. 5-9). lib. bdg. 33.27 *(978-0-7660-2573-8(X))* Enslow Pubs., Inc.

January, Brendan. Globalize It! The Stories of the IMF, the World Bank, the WTO - And Those Who Protest. 2003. (Single Titles Ser.). (Illus.). 144p. (gr. 7-18). 26.90 *(978-0-7613-2417-1(8)*, Twenty-First Century Bks.) Lerner Publishing Group.

Kallen, Stuart A. Does Equality Exist in America? 2006. (At Issue Ser.). (ENG., Illus.). 106p. (YA). (gr. 9-12). pap. 34.45 *(978-0-7377-3433-1(7))* Cengage Gale.

Lankford, Ronnie D. Are America's Wealthy Too Powerful? 2010. (At Issue Ser.). (ENG.). 128p. pap. 24.45 *(978-0-7377-5088-1(X)*, Greenhaven Pr., Inc.); (gr. 10-12). 39.40 *(978-0-7377-5087-4(1))* Cengage Gale.

Ogden, Charlie. Equality & Diversity. 2017. 32p. (J). ***(978-0-7787-3265-5(7))*** Crabtree Publishing Co.

Pegis, Jessica. Why Does Democracy Matter? 2016. (Citizenship in Action Ser.). (ENG.). 24p. (J). (gr. 1-4). *(978-0-7787-2597-8(9))* Crabtree Publishing Co.

Rodger, Ellen & Field, Jon Eben. Social Justice Activist. 2009. (Get Involved! Ser.). (ENG., Illus.). 32p. (J). (gr. 3-6). *(978-0-7787-4696-6(8))*; pap. *(978-0-7787-4708-6(5))* Crabtree Publishing Co.

Rossi, Anna Maria. The Struggle for Equality. 2007. (Rise & Shine Ser.). (ENG., Illus.). 40p. (J). pap. 19.95 *(978-0-7922-4559-9(8))* CENGAGE Learning.

EQUESTRIANISM

see Horsemanship

ERICSON, LEIF, -APPROXIMATELY 1020

see Leiv Eiriksson, -approximately 1020

ERICSSON, JOHN, 1803-1889

Wooldridge, Connie N. & Wooldridge, Connie Nordhielm. Thank You Very Much, Captain Ericsson! Glass, Andrew, photos by. 2004. (ENG., Illus.). 32p. (J). (gr. k-3). tchr. ed. 16.95 *(978-0-8234-1626-4(7))* Holiday Hse., Inc.

ERIKSSON, LEIF, -APPROXIMATELY 1020

see Leiv Eiriksson, -approximately 1020

ERIE, LAKE—FICTION

Winfield, Arthur M. The Rover Boys on the Great Lakes. 2004. reprint ed. pap. 22.95 *(978-1-4191-8119-1(X))* Kessinger Publishing, LLC.

Winfield, Arthur M. The Rover Boys on the Great Lakes. 2004. reprint ed. pap. 1.99 *(978-1-4192-8119-8(4))* Kessinger Publishing, LLC.

ERIE CANAL (N.Y.)

Aller, Susan Bivin. What Difference Could a Waterway Make? And Other Questions about the Erie Canal. 2010. (Six Questions of American History Ser.). (ENG.). (gr. 4-6). pap. 56.72 *(978-0-7613-6947-9(3))*; 48p. pap. 9.95 *(978-0-7613-6124-4(3))*; 48p. lib. bdg. 30.60 *(978-1-58013-667-9(2))* Lerner Publishing Group.

Bullard, Lisa. The Erie Canal. 2009. (Lightning Bolt Books (tm) — Famous Places Ser.). (ENG.). 32p. (gr. k-2). 26.60 *(978-0-8225-9405-5(6)*, Lerner Pubns.) Lerner Publishing Group.

Coleman, Wim & Perrin, Pat. The Amazing Erie Canal & How a Big Ditch Opened up the West. 2006. (Wild History of the American West Ser.). (Illus.). 128p. (J). (gr. 5-9). lib. bdg. 34.60 *(978-1-59845-017-0(4)*, MyReportLinks.com Bks.) Enslow Pubs., Inc.

Kampff, Joseph. The Erie Canal: Joining the Hudson River & Lake Erie. 2012. (Spotlight on New York Ser.). (ENG.). 24p. (J). (gr. 4-7). lib. bdg. 99.95 *(978-1-4488-9209-9(0)*, Rosen Classroom) Rosen Publishing Group, Inc., The.

Kendall, Martha E. The Erie Canal. 2008. (ENG., Illus.). 128p. (J). (gr. 5-9). 18.95 *(978-1-4263-0022-6(0))*; lib. bdg. 28.90 *(978-1-4263-0023-3(9))* National Geographic Society. (National Geographic Children's Bks.).

Kleinmartin, Hex. The Erie Canal. 2016. (Expanding America Ser.). (ENG., Illus.). 96p. (J). (gr. 8-8). lib. bdg. 42.79 *(978-1-5026-0966-3(5))* Cavendish Square Publishing.

LaPlante, Walter. The Erie Canal. 2016. (Road Trip Ser.). (Illus.). 24p. (J). (gr. 3-2). pap. 8.15 *(978-1-4824-4674-6(X))* Stevens, Gareth Publishing LLLP.

Levy, Janey. A Journey along the Erie Canal: Dividing Multidigit Numbers by a One-Digit Number Without Remainders. 2009. (PowerMath Ser.). (ENG., Illus.). 32p. (gr. 4-5). pap. 10.00 *(978-0-8239-8904-1(6))* Rosen Publishing Group, Inc., The.

Murray, Julie. Erie Canal, 1 vol. 2005. (All Aboard America Ser.). (ENG., Illus.). 24p. (gr. k-4). 25.65 *(978-1-59197-504-5(2)*, Buddy Bks.) ABDO Publishing Co.

Nagle, Jeanne. The Erie Canal. 2017. (J). ***(978-1-5383-0012-1(5)***, Britannica Educational Publishing) Rosen Publishing Group, Inc., The.

Newswanger, Rebecca. This Is the Erie Canal. Wine, Rosene, illus. 2016. 47p. (J). ***(978-0-7399-2526-3(1))*** Rod & Staff Pubs., Inc.

Sahgal, Lara & Levy, Janey. Primary Source Investigation of the Erie Canal. 2015. (Uncovering American History Ser.). (ENG.). 64p. (J). (gr. 5-6). 32.95 *(978-1-4994-3509-2(6)*, Rosen Central) Rosen Publishing Group, Inc., The.

ERIE CANAL (N.Y.)—FICTION

Meadowcroft, Enid Lamonte & Vigilante, Sylvester. We Were There at the Opening of the Erie Canal. McCann, Gerald, illus. 2011. 192p. 42.95 *(978-1-258-09742-4(7))* Literary Licensing, LLC.

Stafford, Gerry. Young Canaller. Wanecski, Erica Joan, illus. 2012. 60p. (J). pap. *(978-0-9667989-7-5(X))* Carlisle Pr.- Walnut Creek.

Thomas, Peggy. Joshua the Giant Frog, 1 vol. Smith, Cat Bowman, illus. 2005. (ENG.). 32p. (J). (gr. k-3). 16.99 *(978-1-58980-267-4(5))* Pelican Publishing Co., Inc.

EROSION

see also Soil Conservation

Bailey, Jacqui. Cracking Up: A Story about Erosion. Lilly, Matthew, illus. 2006. (Science Works). (ENG.). 32p. (gr. 3-6). per. 7.95 *(978-1-4048-1996-2(7))* Picture Window Bks.

Benchmark Education Company. Weathering & Erosion (Teacher Guide) 2005. *(978-1-4108-4648-8(2))* Benchmark Education Co.

Brannon, Barbara. Discover Erosion. 2005. (J). pap. *(978-1-4108-5133-8(8))* Benchmark Education Co.

Brannon, Cecelia H. A Look at Erosion & Weathering. 2016. (Rock Cycle Ser.). (ENG.). 32p. (J). (gr. 3-4). pap. 10.52 *(978-0-7660-7278-7(9))*; (Illus.). 25.27 *(978-0-7660-7280-0(0))* Enslow Pubs., Inc.

Dee, Willa. Erosion & Weathering, 1 vol., 1. 2014. (Rocks: the Hard Facts Ser.). (ENG.). 24p. (J). (gr. 3-6). 23.60 *(978-1-4777-2904-5(6)*, PowerKids Pr.) Rosen Publishing Group, Inc., The.

Duke, Shirley. Erosion. 2014. (ENG.). 48p. (gr. 4-6). 35.64 *(978-1-62717-751-1(5))* Rourke Educational Media.

Estigarribia, Diana. Learning about Rocks, Weathering, & Erosion with Graphic Organizers. 2009. (Graphic Organizers in Science Ser.). 24p. (gr. 3-4). 42.50 *(978-1-61513-044-3(6)*, PowerKids Pr.) Rosen Publishing Group, Inc., The.

Geiger, Beth & National Geographic Learning (Firm) Staff. Earth's Changing Land. 2007. (Avenues Ser.). (ENG., Illus.). 36p. (J). pap. 18.95 *(978-0-7922-5427-0(9))* CENGAGE Learning.

Hoffman, Steven M. Weathering & Erosion: Wearing down Rocks. 2011. (Rock It! Ser.). (Illus.). 24p. (J). pap. 8.25 *(978-1-4488-2711-4(6))*; lib. bdg. 22.60 *(978-1-4488-2710-7(8))* Rosen Publishing Group, Inc., The. (PowerKids Pr.).

Hyde, Natalie. Soil Erosion & How to Prevent It. 2010. (Everybody Digs Soil Ser.). (ENG., Illus.). 32p. (J). (gr. 3-6). pap. *(978-0-7787-5416-9(2))* Crabtree Publishing Co.

Kazunas, Ariel & Simon, Charnan. Super Cool Science Experiments: Erosion. 2009. (Explorer Library: Science Explorer Ser.). (ENG., Illus.). 32p. (gr. 4-8). lib. bdg. 28.50 *(978-1-60279-525-9(8)*, 200284) Cherry Lake Publishing.

Koontz, Robin Michal. Erosion: Changing Earth's Surface, 1 vol. Harrad, Matthew, illus. 2006. (Amazing Science Ser.). (ENG.). 24p. (gr. k-4). per. 8.95 *(978-1-4048-2201-6(1))* Picture Window Bks.

Maloof, Torrey. Weathering & Erosion, 1 vol. rev. ed. 2014. (Science Readers: Content & Literacy Ser.). (ENG.). 32p. (gr. 2-2). pap. 8.99 *(978-1-4807-4611-4(8))* Teacher Created Materials, Inc.

Mattern, Joanne. Weathering & Erosion & the Rock Cycle. 2006. (Shaping & Reshaping of Earth's Surface Ser.). (ENG., Illus.). 24p. (J). lib. bdg. 22.60 *(978-1-4042-3198-6(6)*, PowerKids Pr.) Rosen Publishing Group, Inc., The.

Maurer, Daniel D. Do You Really Want to Create a Mudslide? A Book about Erosion. Alberini, Teresa, illus. 2016. (Adventures in Science Ser.). (ENG.). 24p. (J). (gr. k-3). 20.95 *(978-1-60753-957-5(8))* Amicus Publishing.

McAneney, Caitie. Weathering & Erosion. 2017. (J). ***(978-1-5383-0026-8(5))*** Rosen Publishing Group, Inc., The.

Nagle, Frances. What Is Erosion? 2017. (Look at Earth's Rocks Ser.). 32p. (gr. 2-2). pap. 10.50 ***(978-1-4824-6015-5(7))*** Stevens, Gareth Publishing LLLP.

Nelson, Maria. Weathering & Erosion. 2013. (That Rocks! Ser.). (Illus.). 24p. (J). (gr. 2-5). pap. 8.15 *(978-1-4339-8330-6(3))*; lib. bdg. 22.60 *(978-1-4339-8329-0(X))* Stevens, Gareth Publishing LLLP.

Reader dsm-3 erosion Ea. 2004. (J). *(978-1-59242-523-5(2))* Delta Education, LLC.

Redlin, Janice L., ed. Land Abuse & Soil Erosion. 2006. (Understanding Global Issues Ser.). (Illus.). 56p. (J). (gr. 3-7). lib. bdg. 28.50 *(978-1-59036-237-2(3))* Weigl Pubs., Inc.

Riley, Joelle. Erosion. (Illus.). 48p. (J). 2007. pap. 8.95 *(978-0-8225-6619-9(2))* 2006. (gr. 3-7). lib. bdg. 25.26 *(978-0-8225-5949-8(8)*, Lerner Pubns.) Lerner Publishing Group.

—Examining Erosion. 2013. (Searchlight Books (tm) — Do You Dig Earth Science? Ser.). (ENG., Illus.). 40p. (gr. 3-5). pap. 8.95 *(978-1-4677-0790-9(2))*; lib. bdg. 27.93 *(978-1-4677-0021-4(5))* Lerner Publishing Group.

Ripley, Ellen. Erosion. 2009. (Real Life Readers Ser.). 16p. (gr. 2-3). pap. 7.05 *(978-1-4358-0101-1(6)*, Rosen Classroom) Rosen Publishing Group, Inc., The.

Robertson, Charmaine. All about Erosion. 2016. (Rosen REAL Readers: STEM & STEAM Collection). 12p. (gr. 1-k). pap. 6.33 *(978-1-5081-2461-0(2)*, Rosen Classroom) Rosen Publishing Group, Inc., The.

Smith, Paula. How Do Wind & Water Change Earth? 2015. (Earth's Processes Close-Up Ser.). (ENG., Illus.). 24p. (J). (gr. k-3). *(978-0-7787-1727-0(5))* Crabtree Publishing Co.

Spickert, Diane Nelson. Earthsteps: A Rock's Journey Through Time. Wallace, Marianne D., illus. 2010. (ENG.). 32p. (J). (gr. -1-3). pap. 9.95 *(978-1-55591-730-2(5))* Fulcrum Publishing.

Stradling, Jan. Erosion & Weathering: Level K, 6 vols., Vol. 2. (First Explorers Ser.). 24p. (gr. 1-2). 34.95 *(978-0-7699-1457-2(8))* Shortland Pubns. (U. S. A.) Inc.

Trumbauer, Lisa. Weathering & Erosion. 2005. (J). pap. *(978-1-4108-4600-6(8))* Benchmark Education Co.

Weathering & Erosion. 2013. (That Rocks! Ser.). 24p. (J). (gr. 2-5). pap. 48.90 *(978-1-4339-8331-3(1))* Stevens, Gareth Publishing LLLP.

Wilson, Steve. Erosion & Sediments. 2016. (Spotlight on Earth Science Ser.). 00024p. (J). (gr. 4-6). pap. 10.00 *(978-1-4994-2509-3(0)*, PowerKids Pr.) Rosen Publishing Group, Inc., The.

Zappa, Marcia. Erosion, 1 vol. 2010. (Big Buddy Bks.). (ENG.). 32p. (J). (gr. 2-5). 28.50 *(978-1-61613-491-4(7))* ABDO Publishing Co.

ERUPTIONS

see Volcanoes

ESCAPES

Altman, Linda Jacobs. Escape-Teens on the Run: Primary Sources from the Holocaust. 2010. (True Stories of Teens in the Holocaust Ser.). (Illus.). 128p. (YA). (gr. 9-12). 33.27 *(978-0-7660-3270-5(1))* Enslow Pubs., Inc.

Braun, Eric. Escape from Alcatraz: The Mystery of the Three Men Who Escaped from the Rock. 2017. (Encounter:

Narrative Nonfiction Stories Ser.). (ENG.). 112p. (gr. 3-4). lib. bdg. 29.99 (978-1-5157-4551-8(1)) Encounter Bks.

—Trapped Behind Enemy Lines: The Story of the U. S. Army Air Force 807th Medical Evacuation Squadron. 2016. (Encounter: Narrative Nonfiction Stories Ser.). (ENG., Illus.). 224p. (gr. 4-6). lib. bdg. 32.65 (978-1-4914-8042-7(4), 1400082) Encounter Bks.

Chandler, Matt. Outrunning the Nazis: The Brave Escape of Resistance Fighter Sven Somme. Sirois, Douglas A., illus. 2017. (Great Escapes of World War II Ser.). (ENG.). 32p. (gr. 3-4). lib. bdg. 30.65 (978-1-5157-3529-8(X), Graphic Library) Capstone Press of Coughlan Cos.

Derby, Katy. The 10 Most Daring Escapes. 2008. 14.99 (978-1-55448-487-4(1)) Scholastic Library Publishing.

Dowswell, Paul. Escape. 2008. (True Stories Ser.). (Illus.). 140p. (YA). (gr. 8-12). per. 4.99 (978-0-7945-1982-7(2), Usborne) EDC Publishing.

—True Escape Stories. Tyler, Jenny, ed. 2004. (True Adventure Stories Ser.). (Illus.). 144p. (J). pap. 4.95 (978-0-7945-0087-0(0), Usborne) EDC Publishing.

—True Escape Stories. 2004. (True Adventure Stories Ser.). (Illus.). 140p. (J). (gr. 5). lib. bdg. 12.95 (978-1-58086-680-4(8), Usborne) EDC Publishing.

Fradin, Dennis Brindell & Fradin, Judith Bloom. The Irish Potato Famine. 2011. (Great Escapes Ser.). (Illus.). 80p. (J). (gr. 6). 34.21 (978-1-60870-473-6(4)) Marshall Cavendish Corp.

Guillain, Charlotte. Great Escapes, 1 vol. 2011. (War Stories Ser.). (ENG.). 32p. (gr. 3-6). 30.65 (978-1-4329-4835-1(0), NA-h) Heinemann-Raintree.

Lewis, Simon. Desperate Escapes. 2009. (Difficult & Dangerous Ser.). (J). 28.50 (978-1-59920-158-0(5)) Black Rabbit Bks.

Schanzer, Rosalyn. John Smith Escapes Again! 2006. (ENG., Illus.). 64p. (J). (gr. 4-7). 16.95 (978-0-7922-5930-5(0)); lib. bdg. 25.90 (978-0-7922-5931-2(9)) National Geographic Society. (National Geographic Children's Bks.).

Walsh, Alison. Hugh O'Flaherty: His Wartime Adventures. 2011. (ENG., Illus.). 114p. (J). pap. 4.99 (978-1-84889-058-9(3)) Collins Pr., The IRL. Dist: Vearsa.

Watson, Stephanie. The Escape from Alcatraz, 1 vol. 2012. (Unsolved Mysteries (el) Ser.). (ENG.). 112p. (J). (gr. 6-12). lib. bdg. 35.64 (978-1-61783-303-8(7), Essential Library) ABDO Publishing Co.

Yomtov, Nel. Death Camp Uprising: The Escape from Sobibor Concentration Camp. Tortosa, Wilson & Bartolo, Michael, illus. 2017. (Great Escapes of World War II Ser.). (ENG.). 32p. (gr. 3-4). lib. bdg. 30.65 (978-1-5157-3532-8(X), Graphic Library) Capstone Press of Coughlan Cos.

—Great Escapes of World War II. 2017. (Great Escapes of World War II Ser.). (ENG.). 32p. (gr. 3-4). 122.60 (978-1-5157-3533-5(8), Graphic Library) Capstone Press of Coughlan Cos.

ESCAPES—FICTION

Bailey, Linda. Stanleys Wild Ride. Slavin, Bill, illus. 2008. (ENG.). 32p. (J). (gr. -1-2). pap. 7.95 (978-1-55453-254-4(X)) Kids Can Pr., Ltd. CAN. Dist: Hachette Bk. Group.

Baldacci, David. The Keeper. 2016. (Vega Jane Ser.: 2). (ENG.). 448p. (J). (gr. 4-7). pap. 9.99 (978-0-545-83195-6(4), Scholastic Pr.) Scholastic, Inc.

Beadling, Marilyn. The Apple Pie Pickle. 2008. 52p. pap. 9.95 (978-1-4327-2302-6(2)) Outskirts Pr., Inc.

Beasley, Linda L. Meltdowns First Adventure. 2010. 28p. 16.95 (978-1-4490-9725-7(1)) AuthorHouse.

Borden, Louise & Daly, Niki. The Greatest Skating Race: A World War II Story from the Netherlands. Daly, Niki, illus. 2004. (ENG., Illus.). 48p. (J). (gr. 4-7). 19.99 (978-0-689-84502-4(2), McElderry, Margaret K. Bks.) McElderry, Margaret K. Bks.

Brady, S. Lamar. The Littlest Snowflake. Hegerhorst, Bethany Brady, illus. 2013. 36p. pap. 24.95 (978-1-63000-850-5(8)) America Star Bks.

Brown, Judy. Petbots: The Great Escape. 2014. (Petbots Ser.: 1). (ENG., Illus.). 192p. (J). (gr. k-3). pap. 9.99 (978-1-84812-348-9(5)) Bonnier Publishing GBR. Dist: Independent Pubs. Group.

Choyce, Lesley. Breaking Point, 1 vol. 2012. (Orca Soundings Ser.). (ENG.). 128p. (YA). (gr. 8-12). 16.95 (978-1-4598-0129-5(6)); pap. 9.95 (978-1-4598-0128-8(8)) Orca Bk. Pubs. USA.

Dahl, Michael. Monster Hunter, 1 vol. Aime, Luigi, illus. 2012. (Dragonborn Ser.). (ENG.). 72p. (gr. 1-3). pap. 7.10 (978-1-4342-4256-3(0)); lib. bdg. 23.99 (978-1-4342-4040-8(1)) Stone Arch Bks.

Dharma Publishing. The Hunter & the Quail: The Story about the Power of Cooperation. 2010. (ENG.). 36p. (gr. -1-7). pap. 8.95 (978-0-89800-602-5(3)) Dharma Publishing.

Eustache, Harold. Shuswap Journey. 2004. (Shuswap Journey Ser.). (ENG.). 176p. pap. 15.95 (978-1-894778-15-2(4)) Theytus Bks., Ltd. CAN. Dist: Univ. of Toronto Pr.

Fisher, Catherine. Incarceron. 2010. (Playaway Children Ser.). (J). 64.99 (978-1-61637-331-3(8)) Findaway World, LLC.

—Incarceron. 2010. (Incarceron Ser.). (FRE.). 498p. (YA). (gr. 7-12). pap. (978-2-266-17793-1(1)) Le Robert.

—Incarceron. November, S., ed. Yuen, Sammy, illus. 2011. (ENG.). 464p. (YA). (gr. 7-18). pap. 10.99 (978-0-14-241852-9(8), Firebird) Penguin Young Readers Group.

—Incarceron. 2011. (Incarceron Ser.). (ENG.). 442p. (gr. 7-12). 20.00 (978-1-61383-117-5(X)) Perfection Learning Corp.

—INCARCERON. 2010. (SPA.). 512p. (J). (gr. 8-12). pap. 19.99 (978-84-272-0047-0(1)) RBA Libros, S.A. ESP. Dist: Lectorum Pubns., Inc.

—Incarceron. l.t. ed. 2010. (Incarceron Ser.). (ENG.). 526p. 23.99 (978-1-4104-2991-9(1)) Thorndike Pr.

—Incarceron. 2011. lib. bdg. 22.10 (978-0-606-22590-8(0), Turtleback) Turtleback Bks.

Garland, Michael. Last Night at the Zoo. Garland, Michael, illus. 2003. (ENG., Illus.). 32p. (J). (gr. k-2). pap. 10.95 (978-1-59078-167-8(8)) Boyds Mills Pr.

Grifalconi, Ann. The Village That Vanished. Nelson, Kadir, illus. 2004. (ENG.). 40p. (J). (gr. k-3). reprint ed. pap. 7.99 (978-0-14-240190-3(0), Puffin Books) Penguin Young Readers Group.

Hirsch, Jeff. The Darkest Path. 2013. (YA). pap. (978-0-545-51224-4(7), Scholastic Pr.) Scholastic, Inc.

—Magisterium. 2012. (ENG.). 320p. (J). (gr. 7). 17.99 (978-0-545-29018-0(X), Scholastic Pr.) Scholastic, Inc.

Holman, Felice. Slake's Limbo. unabr. ed. 2004. 117p. (J). (gr. 7-18). pap. 29.00 incl. audio (978-0-8072-8744-6(X), YA254SP, Listening Library) Random Hse. Audio Publishing Group.

Johnson, Mary Victoria. Boundary: The Other Horizons Trilogy - Book One. 2015. (ENG.). 296p. (J). (gr. -1-12). pap. 12.95 (978-1-78279-918-4(4), Lodestone Bks.) Hunt, John Publishing Ltd. GBR. Dist: National Bk. Network.

Jordan, Sophie. Reign of Shadows. 2016. (Reign of Shadows Ser.: 1). 304p. (YA). (gr. 8). 17.99 (978-0-06-237764-7(7), HarperTeen) HarperCollins Pubs.

Langlois, Annie. L' Evasion d'Alfred le Dindon. Beaulieu, Jimméy, illus. 2004. (Roman Jeunesse Ser.). (FRE.). 96p. (J). (gr. 4-7). pap. (978-2-89021-687-7(X)) Diffusion du livre Mirabel (DLM).

Leaver, Trisha & Currie, Lindsay. Creed. 2014. (ENG.). 264p. (YA). pap. 9.99 (978-0-7387-4080-5(2), Flux) North Star Editions.

Mason, Albert. Ooshu the Monkey Escapes from the Zoo. 2009. 40p. pap. 16.99 (978-1-4389-0974-5(8)) AuthorHouse.

Matas, Carol. Far. 2008. (Freak Ser.). (ENG.). 152p. (J). (gr. 5-18). pap. (978-1-55470-094-3(9)) Me to We.

McDonnell, Vincent. The Catalpa Adventure: Escape to Freedom. 2010. (ENG.). 128p. (J). pap. 12.95 (978-1-84889-038-1(9)) Collins Pr., The IRL. Dist: Dufour Editions, Inc.

—The Knock Airport Mystery. 2006. (ENG., Illus.). 203p. (J). pap. 11.95 (978-1-903464-87-8(0)) Collins Pr., The IRL. Dist: Dufour Editions, Inc.

Murphy, Shirley Rousseau & Murphy, Pat J. J. The Cat, the Devil, the Last Escape: A Novel. 2015. (ENG., Illus.). 320p. 24.99 (978-0-06-226910-2(0), Morrow, William & Co.) HarperCollins Pubs.

Nöstlinger, Christine. Por Favor, Vuelve a Casa (Please, Come Back Home) (SPA.). 176p. (YA). (gr. 7-9). 9.95 (978-958-04-2379-9(2), 10266266) Norma S.A. COL. Dist: Distribuidora Norma, Inc.

Nussbaum, Ben & Studio Mouse Editorial. Snow White: A New Beginning. 2008. (ENG., Illus.). 36p. (J). (gr. -1). 7.99 (978-1-59069-437-4(6)) Studio Mouse LLC.

Olson, Jennifer Lynn. Chef Charlie & the Great Escape, 1 vol. 2010. 18p. 24.95 (978-1-4489-5638-8(2)) PublishAmerica, Inc.

Pefferly, Lawrence. Larry Tyler & the Planet Buksdahud. 2007. 312p. pap. 16.95 (978-0-9789969-2-5(5)); 24.95 (978-0-9789969-1-8(7)) Tradition Publishing.

Poblocki, Dan. No Way Out. 2017. (Shadow House Ser.: 3). (ENG.). 224p. (J). (gr. 3-7). lib. bdg. 16.99 **(978-1-338-14859-6(1))**; (Illus.). 12.99 **(978-0-545-92552-5(5))** Scholastic, Inc.

Pocha, Michael J. Thomas James & the Ringmaster. 2011. 180p. pap. 24.95 (978-1-4560-6904-9(7)) America Star Bks.

Riggs, Ransom. Hollow City. 2015. (Miss Peregrine's Peculiar Children Ser.: Bk. 2). (ENG., Illus.). 416p. (YA). pap. 10.99 (978-1-59474-735-9(0)) Quirk Bks.

—Hollow City. Riggs, Ransom, illus. 2014. (ENG., Illus.). 352p. (YA). (gr. 9). 18.99 (978-1-59474-612-3(5)) Quirk Bks.

—Hollow City. Riggs, Ransom, illus. 2015. (Miss Peregrine's Peculiar Children Ser.: 2). (Illus.). lib. bdg. 22.10 (978-0-606-36394-5(7)) Turtleback Bks.

Riggs, Ransom & Jean, Cassandra. Hollow City: the Graphic Novel. 2016. (Miss Peregrine's Peculiar Children: the Graphic Novel Ser.: 2). (ENG., Illus.). 272p. (J). (gr. 8-17). 20.00 (978-0-316-30679-9(7), Yen Pr.) Orbit.

Robison, Dan, Jr. Kimo's Escape: The Story of a Hawaiian Boy Who Learns to Believe in Himself. 2005. 100p. (J). per. 19.95 (978-0-922993-28-4(9)) Marquette Bks., LLC.

Simmons, Kristen. The Glass Arrow. 2015. (ENG.). 336p. (YA). (gr. 8-12). 17.99 (978-0-7653-3661-3(8), 9780765336613, Tor Teen) Doherty, Tom Assocs., LLC.

Simmons, Ted. Sandstorm. 2006. (Illus.). 140p. (YA). pap. 13.95 (978-0-9776958-4-3(0)) CyPress Pubns.

Smith, Alexander Gordon. Lockdown. 2009. (Escape from Furnace Ser.: 1). (ENG.). 288p. (YA). (gr. 7-11). 17.99 (978-0-374-32491-9(3), 9780374324919, Farrar, Straus & Giroux (BYR)) Farrar, Straus & Giroux.

—Lockdown. 2010. (Escape from Furnace Ser.: 1). (ENG.). 304p. (YA). (gr. 7-11). pap. 10.99 (978-0-312-61193-4(5), 9780312611934) Square Fish.

Smith, Roland. Jack's Run. 2007. (ENG.). 256p. (J). (gr. 5-17). pap. 6.99 (978-1-4231-0407-0(2)) Hyperion Pr.

Soderberg, Erin. Catnapped! 2016. (Puppy Pirates Ser.). (ENG., Illus.). 96p. (J). (gr. 1-4). lib. bdg. 12.99 (978-0-553-51174-1(2), Random Hse. Bks. for Young Readers) Random Hse. Children's Bks.

Spaht-Gill, Janie. Gator's Out, Said the Trout. Reese, Bob, illus. (J). (gr. k-2). 5.95 (978-0-89868-305-9(X)) ARO Publishing Co.

Tal, Eve. Double Crossing. 2007. (ENG.). 262p. (J). (gr. 7-9). pap. 9.95 (978-1-933693-15-6(0)) Cinco Puntos Pr.

Terrell, Brandon. Recharged, Vol. 12. Tortosa, Wilson, illus. 2013. (Tony Hawk's 900 Revolution Ser.). (ENG.). 128p. (gr. 3-4). lib. bdg. 26.65 (978-1-4342-3843-6(1)) Stone Arch Bks.

—Recharged: Volume Twelve, 1 vol. Tortosa, Wilson, illus. 2013. (Tony Hawk's 900 Revolution Ser.). (ENG.). 128p. (gr. 3-4). pap. 7.19 (978-1-4342-4896-1(8), Tony Hawk's 900 Revolution) Stone Arch Bks.

Van Tol, Alex. Knifepoint, 1 vol. 2010. (Orca Soundings Ser.). (ENG.). 128p. (YA). (gr. 8-12). pap. 9.95 (978-1-55469-305-4(5)) Orca Bk. Pubs. USA.

—A Punta de Cuchillo, 1 vol. 2011. (Spanish Soundings Ser.). (SPA & ENG.). 136p. (YA). (gr. 8-12). pap. 9.95 (978-1-55469-863-9(4)) Orca Bk. Pubs. USA.

Wilkinson, Kerry. Renegade. 2015. (Silver Blackthorn Trilogy Ser.: 2). (ENG.). 368p. (YA). (gr. 8-12). 18.99 (978-1-250-06133-1(4), 9781250061331, St. Martin's Griffin) St. Martin's Pr.

Willis, S. J. The Wishwasher. 2011. 128p. (gr. 4-6). pap. 13.32 (978-1-4567-8751-6(9)) AuthorHouse.

Yolen, Jane. Stone Angel. Green, Katie May, illus. 2015. (ENG.). 40p. (J). (gr. k-3). 16.99 (978-0-399-16741-6(2), Philomel Bks.) Penguin Young Readers Group.

ESKIMOS

Bial, Raymond. The People & Culture of the Inuit. 2016. (First Peoples of North America Ser.). (ENG., Illus.). 128p. (J). (gr. 6-6). 45.70 (978-1-5026-1006-5(X)) Cavendish Square Publishing.

Corriveau, Danielle. The Inuit of Canada. 2005. (First Peoples Ser.). (Illus.). 48p. (gr. 4-8). lib. bdg. 23.95 (978-0-8225-4850-8(X)) Lerner Publishing Group.

Cunningham, Kevin & Benoit, Peter. The Inuit. 2011. (True Bk Ser.). 48p. (J). (ENG.). pap. 6.95 (978-0-531-29302-7(5)); (gr. 3-5). 29.00 (978-0-531-20760-4(9)) Scholastic Library Publishing. (Children's Pr.).

Doak, Robin S. Arctic Peoples, 1 vol. 2011. (First Nations of North America Ser.). (ENG.). 48p. (gr. 3-3). pap. 9.95 (978-1-4329-4956-3(X), Heinemann InfoSearch) Heinemann-Raintree.

Hands-On History! Eskimo: Inuit, Saami & Arctic Peoples. 2014. (ENG., Illus.). 64p. (J). (gr. 3-7). 12.99 (978-1-84322-994-0(3), Armadillo) Anness Publishing GBR. Dist: National Bk. Network.

Kalman, Bobbie & Sjonger, Rebecca. Life in the Far North. 2003. (Native Nations of North America Ser.). (ENG., Illus.). 32p. (J). (gr. 5). pap. (978-0-7787-0469-0(6)); lib. bdg. (978-0-7787-0377-8(0)) Crabtree Publishing Co.

Meachen Rau, Dana. Igloo. 2006. (Bookworms Ser.). (Illus.). 32p. (gr. k-2). lib. bdg. 15.95 (978-0-7614-2273-0(0), Benchmark Bks.) Marshall Cavendish Corp.

Rasmussen, Knud. The Eagle's Gift: Alaska Eskimo Tales. Hutchinson, Isabel, tr. Hansen, Ernest, illus. 2011. 258p. 47.95 (978-1-258-10170-1(X)) Literary Licensing, LLC.

Rau, Dana Meachen. Igloo. 2007. (J). pap. 6.99 (978-0-7614-3299-9(X)) Marshall Cavendish Corp.

Steltzer, Ulli. Building an Igloo. Steltzer, Ulli, photos by. (ENG., Illus.). 100p. (J). (gr. -1-2). (978-0-88899-118-8(5)) Groundwood Bks.

Strudwick, Leslie. Inuit. 2003. (Indigenous Peoples Ser.). (J). pap. 9.95 (978-1-59036-157-3(1)); (Illus.). 32p. lib. bdg. 26.00 (978-1-59036-122-1(9)) Weigl Pubs., Inc.

Titus, David. Native Alaskan String Figures. 2007. (Illus.). 32p. (J). 5.99 (978-0-9744562-7-0(6)) WRDSMTH Productions.

ESKIMOS—FICTION

Amundson, Susan. Free to Be Me: The Eskimo Way. Geiken, Brenda, illus. 2003. 56p. lib. bdg. 16.95 (978-1-883477-65-3(4), Lone Oak Pr., Ltd.) Finney Co., Inc.

Andrews, Jan. Very Last First Time, 1 vol. Wallace, Ian, illus. 2003. (ENG.). 32p. (J). 18.95 (978-0-88899-043-3(X)) Groundwood Bks. CAN. Dist: Publishers Group West (PGW).

Ballantyne, R. M. Red Rooney: Or, the Last of the Crew. 2007. (R. M. Ballantyne Collection). (Illus.). 408p. 22.00 (978-1-934554-08-1(1)) Vision Forum, Inc., The.

—The Walrus Hunters. 2007. 268p. per. (978-1-4065-2066-8(7)) Dodo Pr.

—The Walrus Hunters. 2004. reprint ed. pap. 1.99 (978-1-4192-8706-0(0)); pap. 26.95 (978-1-4191-8706-3(6)) Kessinger Publishing, LLC.

—The Walrus Hunters. 2009. 212p. 26.95 (978-1-60664-594-9(3)); pap. 14.95 (978-1-60664-323-5(1)) Rodgers, Alan Bks.

Ballantyne, Robert Michael. Red Rooney: The Last of the Crew. 2007. (ENG.). 270p. pap. 21.99 (978-1-4346-3693-5(3)); 302p. pap. 24.99 (978-1-4346-3741-3(7)) Creative Media Partners, LLC.

—The Walrus Hunters: A Romance of the Realms of Ice. 2007. 258p. pap. 21.99 (978-1-4346-3699-7(2)); (ENG.). 286p. pap. 23.99 (978-1-4346-3747-5(6)) Creative Media Partners, LLC.

Brown, Tricia. Charlie & the Blanket Toss. Martinsen, Sarah, illus. 2015. (ENG.). 32p. (J). pap. 10.99 (978-1-941821-66-4(9), Alaska Northwest Bks.) Graphic Arts Ctr. Publishing Co.

Burgess, Thornton W. The Christmas Reindeer. Chase, Rhoda, illus. 2013. (Dover Children's Classics Ser.). (ENG.). 160p. (J). (gr. k-3). pap. 5.99 (978-0-486-49153-0(6)) Dover Pubns., Inc.

Conway, Diana Cohen. Northern Lights: A Hanukkah Story. Haas, Shelly O., illus. 2004. (J). 16.95 (978-0-929371-79-5(8), Kar-Ben Publishing) Lerner Publishing Group.

Edwardson, Debby Dahl. Whale Snow. Patterson, Annie, illus. 2004. (ENG.). 32p. (J). (gr. -1-3). pap. 7.95 (978-1-57091-394-5(3)) Charlesbridge Publishing, Inc.

George, Jean Craighead. Ice Whale. Hendrix, John, illus. 2015. (ENG.). 224p. (J). (gr. 4-7). 7.99 (978-0-14-242741-5(1), Puffin Books) Penguin Young Readers Group.

—Julie of the Wolves. Schoenherr, John, illus. (Julie of the Wolves Ser.: 1). (ENG.). (J). (gr. 8-18). 2016. 224p. pap. 6.99 (978-0-06-440058-9(1)) 2003. 208p. pap. 8.99 (978-0-06-054095-1(8), HarperTeen) HarperCollins Pubs.

—Julie of the Wolves. l.t. ed. 2004. (Beeler Mystery Ser.). 32.95 (978-1-58118-121-0(3)) LRS.

Green, Scooter. Ituke's First Hunt. 2012. 32p. 24.95 (978-1-4626-6903-5(4)) America Star Bks.

Grill-Merrill, Karen. The Muk & Tuk Tales. 2006. 65p. 20.00 (978-1-4257-0795-8(5)); pap. 10.00 (978-1-4257-0794-1(7)) Xlibris Corp.

Hader, Berta & Hader, Elmer. Reindeer Trail: A Long Journey from Lapland to Alaska. 2011. 50p. 35.95 (978-1-258-08322-9(1)) Literary Licensing, LLC.

He Who Listens: Individual Title Six-Packs. (Literatura 2000 Ser.). (gr. 2-3). 33.00 (978-0-7635-0171-6(9)) Rigby Education.

Heinz, Brian J. Kayuktuk: An Arctic Quest. Van Zyle, Jon, illus. 2004. (J). pap. 6.95 (978-0-936335-09-4(2)) Ballyhoo BookWorks, Inc.

Hill, Kirkpatrick. Bo at Ballard Creek. Pham, LeUyen, illus. 2013. (ENG.). 288p. (J). (gr. 3-7). 16.99 (978-0-8050-9351-3(6), 9780805093513, Holt, Henry & Co. Bks. For Young Readers) Holt, Henry & Co.

Hobbs, Will. Never Say Die. 224p. (J). (gr. 3-7). 2014. (ENG.). pap. 6.99 (978-0-06-170880-0(1)) 2013. (ENG.). 16.99 (978-0-06-170878-7(X)) 2013. lib. bdg. 17.89 (978-0-06-170879-4(8)) HarperCollins Pubs.

Kirkpatrick, Katherine. Between Two Worlds. (ENG.). 304p. (YA). (gr. 9). 2015. pap. 9.99 (978-0-375-87221-1(3), Ember) 2014. 16.99 (978-0-385-74047-0(6), Lamb, Wendy Bks.) Random Hse. Children's Bks.

Kittredge, Frances. Neeluk: An Eskimo Boy in the Days of the Whaling Ships. Rock, Howard, illus. 2005. 88p. (J). (gr. 3-7). 18.95 (978-0-88240-545-2(4)) Graphic Arts Ctr. Publishing Co.

London, Jonathan. Desolation Canyon. London, Sean, illus. 2015. (Aaron's Wilderness Ser.: 1). (ENG.). 168p. (YA). 23.99 (978-1-941821-60-2(X), West Winds Pr.) Graphic Arts Ctr. Publishing Co.

O'Dell, Scott. Black Star, Bright Dawn. 2011. 8.30 (978-0-7848-3471-8(7), Everbind) Marco Bk. Co.

Orenstein, Denise Gosliner. Unseen Companion. 2003. 368p. (J). 15.99 (978-0-06-052056-4(6)); lib. bdg. 16.89 (978-0-06-052057-1(4)) HarperCollins Pubs.

Paulsen, Gary. Dogsong. 2007. (ENG.). 192p. (J). (gr. 5-9). pap. 7.99 (978-1-4169-3962-7(8), Simon & Schuster Bks. For Young Readers) Simon & Schuster Bks. For Young Readers.

—Dogsong. 2007. (ENG.). 192p. (YA). (gr. 7). mass mkt. 7.99 (978-1-4169-3919-1(9), Simon Pulse) Simon Pulse.

Perkins, Lucy Fitch. The Eskimo Twins. 2004. reprint ed. pap. 1.99 (978-1-4192-6126-8(6)); pap. 15.95 (978-1-4191-6126-1(1)) Kessinger Publishing, LLC.

—The Eskimo Twins (Yesterday's Classics) 2006. (J). per. 9.95 (978-1-59915-059-8(X)) Yesterday's Classics.

Price, Susan. Cân Yr Ysbrydion. 2005. (WEL.). 172p. pap. (978-1-85596-217-0(9)) Dref Wen.

Prins, Piet. Stefan Derksen's Polar Adventure. 2004. (Illus.). 237p. (J). pap. (978-1-894666-67-1(4)) Inheritance Pubns.

Riel, Jörn & Chodzin, Sherab. The Raiders Vol. 2: The Inuk Quartet. Cann, Helen, illus. 2013. (ENG.). 128p. (J). (gr. 4-6). pap. 9.99 (978-1-84686-744-6(4)) Barefoot Bks., Inc.

Riel, Jørn, et al. The Snowstorm. Cann, Helen, illus. 2012. (ENG.). 128p. (J). (gr. 4-6). pap. 9.99 (978-1-84686-797-2(5)) Barefoot Bks., Inc.

Shield, Sophie. Pupitukaar. Smart, George, illus. 2004. (J). pap. 10.00 (978-1-58084-220-4(8)) Lower Kuskokwim Schl. District.

Sís, Peter. A Small Tall Tale from the Far Far North. (Illus.). (J). pap. 7.95 (978-0-88899-431-8(1)) Groundwood Bks. CAN. Dist: Publishers Group West (PGW).

Stafford, Liliana. Snow Bear. Davis, Lambert, illus. 32p. (J). pap. (978-0-88899-441-7(9)) Groundwood Bks.

Stefansson, Vilhjalmur & Irwin, Violet. The Shaman's Revenge: Based on the Arctic Diaries of Vilhjalmur Stefansson. Grier, Geoffrey, illus. 2011. 306p. 48.95 (978-1-258-05790-9(5)) Literary Licensing, LLC.

Taylor, Theodore & Taylor, Theodore. Ice Drift. 2006. (ENG., Illus.). 240p. (J). (gr. 2-5). pap. 7.99 (978-0-15-205550-9(9)) Houghton Mifflin Harcourt Publishing Co.

Vanasse, Deb. Lucy's Dance. 2011. (ENG., Illus.). 29p. 16.95 (978-1-60223-127-6(3)); 32p. pap. 10.95 (978-1-60223-126-9(5)) Univ. of Alaska Pr.

Winslow, Barbara. Dance on a Sealskin. Sloat, Teri, illus. 2015. (ENG.). 32p. (J). pap. 10.99 (978-1-941821-80-0(4), Alaska Northwest Bks.) Graphic Arts Ctr. Publishing Co.

ESKIMOS—FOLKLORE

Millman, Lawrence. A Kayak Full of Ghosts. White, Timothy, illus. 2004. (International Folk Tales Ser.). (ENG.). 208p. pap. 13.95 (978-1-56656-525-7(1)) Interlink Publishing Group, Inc.

ESKIMOS—LEGENDS

see Eskimos—Folklore

ESP

see Extrasensory Perception

ESQUIMAUX

see Eskimos

ESSEX (WHALESHIP)

Philbrick, Nathaniel. In the Heart of the Sea (Young Readers Edition) 2015. (ENG., Illus.). 208p. (J). (gr. 3-7). 8.99 (978-1-101-99776-5(1), Puffin Books) Penguin Young Readers Group.

ESTHER, QUEEN OF PERSIA

Balsley, Tilda & Blalsey, Tilda. The Queen Who Saved Her People. Richard, Ilene, illus. 2011. (ENG.). 32p. (J). (gr. 3-5). pap. 7.95 (978-0-7613-5093-4(4), Kar-Ben Publishing) Lerner Publishing Group.

Brodsky, Irene. Queen Esther's New Coloring Book. Steyert, Bill, illus. 2011. 39p. pap. 17.95 (978-1-4327-6771-6(2)) Outskirts Pr., Inc.

Burkum, Rachel. Matthew's Bible Stories: Esther Is Brave. Keller, Matt, illus. 2011. 52p. (J). 10.00 (978-1-59799-083-7(3)) Deaf Missions.

Gamblin, Rose Tooley & Hernández, Oscar. Esther, the Brave Queen. 2008. (SPA & ENG.). (J). (978-0-8127-0479-2(7)) Autumn Hse. Publishing Co.

—Joash, the Boy King. 2008. (SPA & ENG.). (J). (978-0-8127-0474-7(6)) Autumn Hse. Publishing Co.

Holder, Jennifer. Brave & Beautiful Queen Esther. Julien, Terry, illus. 2014. (Happy Day Ser.). (ENG.). 16p. (J). pap. 2.49 (978-1-4143-9474-9(8)) Tyndale Hse. Pubs.

Johnson, Alice W. Believe & You're There: When Esther Saved, Vol. 8. 2010. (Illus.). 96p. (J). pap. 6.99 (978-1-60641-815-4(7)) Deseret Bk. Co.

Kimmel, Eric A. The Story of Esther. Weber, Jill, illus. 2011. (ENG.). 32p. (J). (gr. -1-3). 16.95 (978-0-8234-2223-4(2)) Holiday Hse., Inc.

Koralek, Jenny. The Story of Queen Esther. Holderness, Grizelda, illus. 2009. (ENG.). 28p. (J). (gr. -1-3). 17.50 (978-0-8028-5348-6(X), Eerdmans Bks For Young Readers) Eerdmans, William B. Publishing Co.

Mackenzie, Carine. Esther: The Brave Queen. McLaren, Duncan, illus. 2008. (Bible Time Ser.). (ENG.). 32p. (J). (gr. -1-2). pap. 3.99 (978-1-84550-195-2(0), 85e88a8d-6aac-445d-8bc7-8399039eafa5) Christian Focus Pubns. GBR. Dist: Bookmasters Distribution.

Miles, David, illus. Brave Queen Esther, 1 vol. 2015. (I Can Read! / Adventure Bible Ser.). (ENG.). 32p. (J). pap. 3.99 (978-0-310-74666-9(3)) Zonderkidz.

Simhoni, S. Legends of Queen Esther. Lask, I. M., tr. Luizada, A., illus. 2011. 62p. 36.95 (978-1-258-09389-1(8)) Literary Licensing, LLC.

Warner Press Kids, creator. Queen Esther. 2008. (Illus.). 16p. (J). (gr. -1-2). pap. 11.34 (978-1-59317-220-6(6)) Warner Pr., Inc.

Woodruff, Stephen B. Esther. (Money at its Best: Millionaires of the Old Testament Ser.). 112p. (YA). (gr. 7-12). 2009. 24.95 (978-1-4222-0469-6(3)) 2007. pap. 14.95 (978-1-4222-0844-1(3)) Mason Crest.

Zondervan Staff. Queen Esther Helps God's People, 1 vol. Pulley, Kelly, illus. 2008. (I Can Read! / the Beginner's Bible Ser.). (ENG.). 32p. (J). pap. 3.99 (978-0-310-71815-4(5)) Zonderkidz.

ESTHER, QUEEN OF PERSIA—FICTION

Booth, Bradley. Esther: A Star Is Born. 2009. (J). pap. 12.99 (978-0-8163-2359-3(3)) Pacific Pr. Publishing Assn.

Morgan-Cole, Trudy J. Esther: Courage to Stand. 2010. 144p. (J). pap. 12.99 (978-0-8280-2430-3(8)) Review & Herald Publishing Assn.

Moscowitz, Moshe & Resnick, Yael. The Queen of Persia. Sokoloff, David, illus. 2004. 107p. (978-1-930925-09-0(3), Shazak Productions) Torah Excel.

ESTONIA

Dyan, Penelope. Cabbages & Kings — A Kid's Guide to Tallinn, Estoni. Weigand, John D., photos by. 2011. (Illus.). 36p. pap. 11.95 (978-1-61477-002-2(6)) Bellissima Publishing, LLC.

Hiisjärv, Piret & Hiiepuu, Ene. Estonia. Bultje, Jan Willem, photos by. 2006. (Looking at Europe Ser.). (Illus.). 48p. (YA). (gr. 5-8). 22.95 (978-1-881508-32-8(3)) Oliver Pr., Inc.

Libal, Autumn & Indovino, Shaina Carmel. Estonia. 2012. (J). (978-1-4222-2239-3(X)) Mason Crest.

Spilling, Michael. Estonia. 2nd rev. ed. 2009. (Cultures of the World 18 Ser.). 144p. (gr. 6). 42.79 (978-0-7614-4846-4(2)) Marshall Cavendish GBR. Dist: Marshall Cavendish Corp.

Spilsbury, Richard & Spilsbury, Louise. Estonia, 1 vol. 2011. (Countries Around the World Ser.). (ENG.). 48p. (gr. 3-6). pap. 9.95 (978-1-4329-5227-3(7)); 33.32 (978-1-4329-5202-0(1)) Heinemann-Raintree. (NA-h).

ESTONIA—FICTION

Adair, Tammi. The Heart of a Christmas Tree. Rudd, Benton, illus. 2013. 32p. 16.99 (978-0-9886409-1-7(0)) Mindstir Media.

Tamberg, Urve. The Darkest Corner of the World, 1 vol. 2016. (ENG.). 208p. (YA). (gr. 7-10). pap. 14.95 (978-1-77086-214-2(5), Dancing Cat Bks.) Cormorant Bks. Inc. CAN. Dist: Orca Bk. Pubs. USA.

Uncle Markie. Pigletté & Bobo Have Visitors. 2003. (YA). ring bd. 9.95 (978-1-933129-12-9(3)) Studio 403.

—Piglettè & Bobo in Estonia. 2003. (YA). ring bd. 9.95 (978-1-933129-13-6(1)) Studio 403.

ETERNAL LIFE

see Future Life

ETHICAL EDUCATION

see Religious Education

ETHICS

see also Good and Evil; Values

Ahmad, Tazeen. Ali's Special Cure. 2010. 36p. 15.99 (978-1-4520-5199-4(2)) AuthorHouse.

All about Character. 2015. (All about Character Ser.). (ENG.). 24p. (J). (gr. -1-1). 135.60 (978-0-7660-7132-2(4)); pap., pap., pap. 336.60 (978-0-7660-6691-5(6)) Enslow Pubs., Inc.

Altman, Linda Jacobs. Bioethics: Who Lives, Who Dies, & Who Decides? 2006. (Issues in Focus Today Ser.). (Illus.). 112p. (J). (gr. 7-12). lib. bdg. 33.27 (978-0-7660-2546-2(2)) Enslow Pubs., Inc.

Amar, Elisheva. One Word Too Many: Stories for Kids about the Life Changing Impact of Words. 2008. 119p. 26.99 (978-1-59826-210-0(6)) Feldheim Pubs.

Amoroso, Cynthia. Responsibility. 2013. (Values to Live By Ser.). (ENG.). 24p. (J). (gr. -1-2). 25.64 (978-1-62323-525-3(1), 206296) Child's World, Inc., The.

—Thankfulness. 2013. (Values to Live By Ser.). (ENG.). 24p. (J). (gr. -1-2). 25.64 (978-1-62323-526-0(X), 206297) Child's World, Inc., The.

Anderson, Judith. Celebrity & Fame. 2010. (Media Power Ser.). 48p. (YA). (gr. 5-9). 35.65 (978-1-60753-112-8(7)) Amicus Publishing.

—Celebrity & Fame. 2011. (Inside Crime Ser.). 48p. (YA). (gr. 5-9). lib. bdg. 34.25 (978-1-59920-398-0(7)) Black Rabbit Bks.

Antill, Sara. Grit. 2013. (Character Strength Ser.). 24p. (J). (gr. 3-6). pap. 8.25 (978-1-4488-9814-5(5)); pap. 49.50 (978-1-4488-9815-2(3)); lib. bdg. 22.60 (978-1-4488-9678-3(9)) Rosen Publishing Group, Inc., The. (PowerKids Pr.).

Baker, Michael O. What Would You Do? Bk. 1: Moral Dilemmas, 2 vols. 2012. (What Would You Do? Ser.). 32p. (gr. 2-5). pap. 10.99 (978-0-89455-348-6(8), 66.01) Critical Thinking Co., The.

Barnabas Fund. Brothers & Sisters: Loving Our Persecuted Family. 2012. (ENG., Illus.). 38p. pap. 10.00 (978-0-9853109-7-4(9)) Isaac Publishing.

Bergstrom, Amy, et al. The Seventh Generation: Native Students Speak about Finding the Good Path. 2003. 300p. (YA). (gr. 7-12). pap. 25.00 (978-1-880785-25-6(0)) ERIC Clearinghouse on Rural Education & Small Schls.

Bhimji, Saleem, tr. from PER. The Islamic Moral System: A Commentary of Surah Al-Hujurat. 2003.Tr. of Nizaam-e-Akhlaaqi-e-Islaam. 313p. per. (978-1-894701-16-7(X), Spotlight Poets) Islamic Humanitarian Service.

Bishop, Jennie & Henson, Susan. Life Lessons from the Princess & the Kiss: Planting Seeds of Purity in Young Hearts. 2004. (Revive Our Hearts Ser.). (ENG., Illus.). 56p. pap. 9.99 (978-0-940110-52-6(0)) Life Action Inc.

Blumenthal, Scott. A Kid's Mensch Handbook: Step by Step to a Lifetime of Jewish Values. 2004. (J). (978-0-87441-700-5(7)) Behrman Hse., Inc.

Boatman, Marva. A Children's Book of Morals. 2003. 16p. pap. 7.00 (978-0-8059-5767-9(7)) Dorrance Publishing Co., Inc.

Bottoms, James "Bud". Kid Ethics 2: From A to Z. 2006. (J). per. 12.95 (978-0-9772078-7-9(0)) Journey Pubns., LLC.

Boyce, P. M. Mom Taught Values with Quotes & Proverbs - a Memoir of Short Stories by P. M. Boyce. 2013. 248p. (978-1-77097-659-7(0)) FriesenPress.

Boyd, Kenneth. A Right to Life - & Death? (Illus.). 64p. (J). (978-0-237-51877-6(5)) Evans Brothers, Ltd.

Brewer, Marie. For Smart Girls Only. 2010. pap. 12.95 (978-0-7414-6184-1(6)) Infinity Publishing.

Burch, Regina G. & Donovan Guntly, Jenette. I Can Be Responsible. Burris, Priscilla, illus. 2004. (Doing the Right Thing Ser.). 16p. (gr. -1-2). lib. bdg. 20.00 (978-0-8368-4245-6(6), Gareth Stevens Learning Library) Stevens, Gareth Publishing LLLP.

—I Can Share with Others. Jarrett, Michael, photos by. 2004. (Doing the Right Thing Ser.). (Illus.). 16p. (gr. -1-2). lib. bdg. 20.00 (978-0-8368-4246-3(4), Gareth Stevens Learning Library) Stevens, Gareth Publishing LLLP.

Carmichael, Tricia & MacDonald, Allison, eds. Deal with It Series Bullying & Conflict Resource Guide, 1 vol. Charette, Geraldine et al, illus. 2011. (Lorimer Deal with It Ser.). (ENG.). 104p. (J). (gr. 4-6). 24.95 (978-1-55277-693-3(X), 9781552776933) Lorimer, James & Co., Ltd., Pubs. CAN. Dist: Casemate Pubs. & Bk. Distributors, LLC.

Cavell-Clarke, Steffi. Respecting Others. 2017. (Illus.). 24p. (J). **(978-0-7787-3263-1(0))** Crabtree Publishing Co.

Cerebellum Academic Team. Lesson Booster 8 Series Set. 2010. (Lesson Booster Ser.). cd-rom 574.98 (978-1-58565-363-8(2)) Cerebellum Corp.

—Lesson Booster Middle School Series. 2010. (Lesson Booster Ser.). cd-rom 454.95 (978-1-58565-365-2(9)) Cerebellum Corp.

Concord, Juliet. I Am Kind / Soy Amable. 2011. (Kids of Character / Chicos con carácter Ser.). (ENG & SPA., Illus.). 24p. (J). (gr. -1-2). 22.60 (978-1-4339-4872-5(9)) Stevens, Gareth Publishing LLLP.

Conner, Kate. Enough: 10 Things We Should Tell Teenage Girls. 2014. (ENG.). 224p. (J). pap. 15.99 (978-1-4336-8293-3(1), B&H Bks.) B&H Publishing Group.

—10 Things for Teen Girls. 2014. (ENG.). 208p. (J). (gr. 8-12). pap. 14.99 (978-1-4336-8291-9(5), B&H Kids) B&H Publishing Group.

Dages, Juliette Garesche. Learning about Virtues: A Guide to Making Good Choices. Dages, Juliette Garesche, illus. 2009. (Illus.). (J). pap. 7.95 (978-0-87029-420-4(2)) Abbey Pr.

Dahl, Regina. When Butterflies Fly. 2013. 24p. pap. 10.95 (978-1-4497-8095-1(4), WestBow Pr.) Author Solutions, Inc.

Deen, Marilyn. Share & Be Fair. 2011. (Wonder Readers Fluent Level Ser.). (ENG.). 16p. (gr. -1-2). pap. 35.94 (978-1-4296-8149-0(7), Wonder Readers) Capstone Press of Coughlan Cos.

Doeden, Matt. Whistle-Blowers: Exposing Crime & Corruption. 2015. (Illus.). 96p. (J). (978-1-4677-6312-7(8)) Twenty First Century Bks.

—Whistleblowers. 2015. (ENG., Illus.). 96p. (J). (gr. 8-12). lib. bdg. 33.32 (978-1-4677-4209-2(0), Twenty-First Century Bks.) Lerner Publishing Group.

Duignan, Brian, ed. Thinkers & Theories in Ethics. 2011. (Britannica Guide to Ethics Ser.). (Illus.). 208p. (YA). 70.00 (978-1-61530-416-5(9)) Rosen Publishing Group, Inc., The.

Dyan, Penelope. Dear God, Thank-You! Dyan, Penelope, illus. 2013. (Illus.). 34p. pap. 11.95 (978-1-61477-072-5(7)) Bellissima Publishing, LLC.

Espejo, Roman. What Is Humanity's Greatest Challenge? 2010. (At Issue Ser.). (Illus.). 128p. (J). 34.45 (978-0-7377-4314-2(X)); pap. 24.45 (978-0-7377-4313-5(1)) Cengage Gale.

Ferguson, John E. & Ferguson, John E., Jr. The Right to Die. 2007. (Point/Counterpoint Ser.). (Illus.). 109p. (YA). (gr. 9-12). lib. bdg. 35.00 (978-0-7910-9287-3(9)) Facts On File, Inc.

Fernandez, Mayte. Secrets of Your Guardian Angels. 2013. 68p. pap. 24.45 (978-1-4525-6765-5(4)) Balboa Pr.

Finn, Carrie. Comportamiento y Modales en el Patio de Juegos. Lensch, Chris, illus. 2011. (¡Así Debemos Ser!: Buenos Modales, Buen Comportamiento/Way to Be!: Manners Ser.).Tr. of Manners on the Playground. (ENG, SPA & MUL.). 24p. (gr. -1-2). lib. bdg. 26.65 (978-1-4048-6699-7(X)) Picture Window Bks.

—Comportamiento y Modales en la Biblioteca. Lensch, Chris, illus. 2011. (¡Así Debemos Ser!: Buenos Modales, Buen Comportamiento/Way to Be!: Manners Ser.).Tr. of Manners in the Library. (ENG, SPA & MUL.). 24p. (gr. -1-2). lib. bdg. 26.65 (978-1-4048-6697-3(3)) Picture Window Bks.

Fisanick, Christina. Is Selling Body Parts Ethical? 2009. (At Issue Ser.). (ENG.). 128p. (gr. 10-12). pap. 24.45 (978-0-7377-4305-0(0)); pap. 34.45 (978-0-7377-4306-7(9)) Cengage Gale. (Greenhaven Pr., Inc.).

Fletcher, Carrie Hope. All I Know Now: Wonderings & Reflections on Growing up Gracefully. 2015. (ENG., Illus.). 352p. (YA). (gr. 8-12). pap. 15.95 (978-1-61519-294-6(8)) Experiment LLC, The.

Gallagher, Debbie. Family Responsibilities. 2008. (Families Ser.). 32p. (gr. 1-2). lib. bdg. 18.56 (978-0-7614-3141-1(1), Benchmark Bks.) Marshall Cavendish Corp.

George, Liz. Thankfulness: A Gratitude Attitude! 2015. (Rookie Talk about It(tm) Ser.). (ENG., Illus.). 32p. (J). pap. 5.95 (978-0-531-21382-7(X), Children's Pr.) Scholastic Library Publishing.

Ginsburg, Sara. Look What My Parents Give Me. David, Racheli, illus. 2014. 29p. (J). (978-1-4226-1489-1(1)) Mesorah Pubns., Ltd.

Glassman, Bruce S. Respect. 2008. (Illus.). 48p. (J). pap. 9.95 (978-1-60108-507-8(9)); (YA). (gr. 3-6). lib. bdg. 29.25 (978-1-60108-506-1(0)) Red Cygnet Pr. (Bearing Bks.).

Graham, Janice Barrett. Me Tarzan, You Jane. Graham, Andrew S. & Ribeira, Lili, illus. 2011. 25p. (J). (gr. 1-4). pap. 6.95 (978-0-9724770-8-6(X)) Tidal Wave Bks.

Graves, Sue. I Want to Win! A Book about Being a Good Sport. Carletti, Emanuela & Guicciardini, Desideria, illus. 2017. (Our Emotions & Behavior Ser.). (ENG.). 28p. (J). (gr. k-4). 12.99 **(978-1-63198-131-9(5))** Free Spirit Publishing, Inc.

Greenhaven Press Editors & Zott, Lynn, eds. Congressional Ethics. 2013. (Opposing Viewpoints Ser.). (ENG., Illus.). 240p. (gr. 10-12). pap. 29.45 (978-0-7377-6047-7(8), Greenhaven Pr., Inc.) Cengage Gale.

Greenwald, Zee. Loving Kindness: Stories of Chessed from Our Sages. 2008. 48p. 17.99 (978-1-59826-267-4(X)) Feldheim Pubs.

Herzog, Brad. Powerful Stories of Perseverance in Sports. 2014. (Count on Me: Sports Ser.). (ENG., Illus.). 96p. (J). (gr. 4-7). pap. 9.99 (978-1-57542-456-9(8)) Free Spirit Publishing, Inc.

Hubbard, Diane. Remembering Rachel. 2010. 52p. pap. 22.49 (978-1-4520-6527-4(6)) AuthorHouse.

Humphrey, Sandra McLeod & Barker, Dan. More-If You Had to Choose, What Would You Do? Strassburg, Brian, illus. 2003. (ENG.). 132p. (J). (gr. 4-7). pap. 14.99 (978-1-59102-077-6(8)) Prometheus Bks., Pubs.

Infante, Marisol. The Adventures of the Smilees: Understanding Our Friends. 2012. 28p. pap. 19.99 (978-1-4772-5821-7(3)) AuthorHouse.

Jamiolkowski, Raymond M. A Baby Doesn't Make the Man: Alternative Sources of Power & Manhood for Young Men. rev. ed. 2005. (Teen Pregnancy Prevention Library). (Illus.). 64p. (YA). (gr. 7-12). lib. bdg. 31.95 (978-0-8239-3470-6(5)) Rosen Publishing Group, Inc., The.

Kavanaugh, Beatrice. Medical Discoveries. 2017. (Illus.). 80p. (J). **(978-1-4222-3710-6(9))** Mason Crest.

Kiesbye, Stefan. Cheating. 2010. (Social Issues Firsthand Ser.). (ENG.). 192p. (gr. 10-12). 38.30 (978-0-7377-5009-6(X), Greenhaven Pr., Inc.) Cengage Gale.

Lennon, Liz. My Behaviour - I Am Kind. 2017. (Little Stars,Sea-To-Sea Ser.). (ENG., Illus.). 24p. (J). (gr. -1-k). pap. 6.99 (978-1-4451-4762-8(9), Franklin Watts) Hachette Children's Group GBR. Dist: Hachette Bk. Group.

Lepetit, Angie. Three Cheers for Trees! A Book about Our Carbon Footprint. 2013. (Earth Matters Ser.). (ENG.). 32p. (gr. 1-2). pap. 47.70 (978-1-62065-742-3(2)); pap. 8.10 (978-1-62065-741-6(4)); lib. bdg. 27.32 (978-1-62065-048-6(7)) Capstone Press of Coughlan Cos. (Aplus Bks.).

Lewis, Barbara A. What Do You Stand For? For Teens: A Guide to Building Character. Espeland, Pamela, ed. 2005. (ENG., Illus.). 288p. (YA). (gr. 5-9). pap. 19.99 (978-1-57542-029-5(5)) Free Spirit Publishing, Inc.

Lewis, Darlene. Don't Be Stupid, Advice for Young People & a Few Old Fools. 2010. 58p. pap. 20.40 (978-0-557-26221-2(6)) Lulu Pr., Inc.

Lishinski, Ann King. Let Your Light Shine. Morello, Charles, ed. Lishinski, Jamie, illus. 2003. (J). pap. 9.95 (978-0-9709575-0-4(5)) Singing River Pubns.

Lo Bosco, Maryellen. David Hume & a Treatise of Human Nature. 2016. (J). lib. bdg. (978-1-68048-547-9(4)) Windmill Bks.

Lovegrove, Ray. Health - Ethical Debates in Modern Medicine. 2008. (Dilemmas in Modern Science Ser.). (ENG., Illus.). 48p. (J). 23.99 (978-0-237-53368-7(5)) Evans Brothers, Ltd. GBR. Dist: Independent Pubs. Group.

MacGregor, Cynthia. Think for Yourself: A Kid's Guide to Solving Life's Dilemmas & Other Sticky Problems. Farias, Susan Norberg, illus. 2004. (ENG.). 96p. (J). (gr. 4-7). pap. 7.95 (978-1-894222-73-0(3)) Lobster Pr. CAN. Dist: Univ. of Toronto Pr.

Marcotte, Arline Seibert. Obeying Rules Brings Happiness. 2010. 16p. 9.49 (978-1-4520-1076-2(5)) AuthorHouse.

Marcovitz, Hal. Teens, Religion, & Values. 2008. (Gallup Youth Survey, Major Issues & Trends Ser.). (Illus.). 112,128p. (YA). (gr. 7-9). lib. bdg. 22.95 (978-1-59084-726-8(1)) Mason Crest.

Marie, Tina. Isabella Learns Responsibility. 2010. 24p. 12.99 (978-1-4520-8841-9(1)) AuthorHouse.

—Isabella Learns to Be Thankful. 2010. 24p. pap. 12.99 (978-1-4520-1380-0(2)) AuthorHouse.

Marshall, Shelley. Molly the Great's Messy Bed: A Book about Responsibility. Mahan, Ben, illus. 2010. (Character Education with Super Ben & Molly the Great Ser.). 24p. (J). pap. 7.95 (978-0-7660-3742-7(8), Enslow Elementary) Enslow Pubs., Inc.

Mayer, Cassie. Being Fair, 1 vol. Beech, Mark, illus. 2007. (Citizenship Ser.). (ENG.). 24p. (gr. -1-3). pap. 6.29 (978-1-4034-9491-7(6), Acorn) Heinemann-Raintree.

—Being Responsible, 1 vol. Beech, Mark, illus. 2007. (Citizenship Ser.). (ENG.). 24p. (gr. -1-3). pap. 6.29 (978-1-4034-9497-9(5), Acorn) Heinemann-Raintree.

—Ser Responsable, 1 vol. 2007. (Civismo Ser.). (SPA., Illus.). 24p. (gr. -1-1). pap. 6.29 (978-1-4329-0409-8(4), Bellota) Heinemann-Raintree.

Mayled, Jon & Ahluwalia, Libby. Philosophy & Ethics. 2003. (ENG., Illus.). 208p. pap. (978-0-7487-7157-8(3)) Nelson Thomes Ltd.

McCumbee, Stephie. The Garden in My Mind: Growing Through Positive Choices. Griffin, Lisa M., illus. 2014. (ENG.). 40p. (J). pap. 12.95 (978-1-934490-54-9(7)) Boys Town Pr.

—The Garden in My Mind Activity Guide: Lessons for Social Skill & Common Core Development. Griffin, Lisa M., illus. 2014. (ENG.). 48p. pap. 20.95 (978-1-934490-55-6(5)) Boys Town Pr.

Merino, Noël. Ethics. Greenhaven Press Staff, ed. 2015. (Opposing Viewpoints Ser.). (ENG.). 224p. (gr. 10-12). pap. 33.80 (978-0-7377-7261-6(1), Greenhaven Pr., Inc.) Cengage Gale.

Merino, Noel. Media Ethics. 2012. (Current Controversies Ser.). (ENG.). 224p. (gr. 10-12). pap. 32.00 (978-0-7377-6238-9(1), Greenhaven Pr., Inc.) Cengage Gale.

Merino, No'l, ed. Media Ethics. 2012. (Current Controversies Ser.). (ENG.). 240p. (gr. 10-12). lib. bdg. 40.95 (978-0-7377-6237-2(3), Greenhaven Pr., Inc.) Cengage Gale.

Metz, Lorijo. What Can We Do about Global Warming? 2009. (Protecting Our Planet Ser.). (Illus.). 24p. (ENG.). (J). pap. 8.25 (978-1-4358-2479-9(2)); (YA). (gr. 2-5). lib. bdg. 22.60 (978-1-4042-8079-3(0)) Rosen Publishing Group, Inc., The.

Mooney, Carla & Currie-McGhee, Leanne K. Bioethics. 2009. (Hot Topics Ser.). (ENG., Illus.). 128p. (gr. 7-10). lib. bdg. 39.40 (978-1-4205-0117-9(8), LML02109-245428, Lucent Bks.) Cengage Gale.

nakaya, andrea. Biomedical Ethics. 2011. (Compact Research Ser.). 96p. (YA). (gr. 7-12). lib. bdg. 27.95 (978-1-60152-157-6(X)) ReferencePoint Pr., Inc.

National, Walt. I Am Responsible. 2011. (Kids of Character Ser.). (Illus.). 24p. (J). (gr. 1-3). lib. bdg. 22.60 (978-1-4339-4879-4(6)) Stevens, Gareth Publishing LLLP.

—I Am Responsible / Soy Responsable. 2011. (Kids of Character / Chicos con carácter Ser.). (ENG & SPA., Illus.). 24p. (J). (gr. -1-2). 22.60 (978-1-4339-4883-1(4)) Stevens, Gareth Publishing LLLP.

Newell, Karmel H. Come Follow Me: A Child's Guide to Faith, Hope, & Charity. Smith, Mary Ann Free, illus. 2003. (J). 16.95 (978-1-57008-809-4(8), Bookcraft, Inc.) Deseret Bk. Co.

Parker, David. I Accept You As You Are! Fiammenghi, Gioia, illus. 2004. (J). (978-0-439-62811-2(3)) Scholastic, Inc.

—I Can Cooperate! Dubin, Jill, illus. 2004. (J). (978-0-439-62812-9(1)) Scholastic, Inc.

Payne, Timothy R. Payne Man. 2007. 52p. per. 7.95 (978-1-4327-0582-4(2)) Outskirts Pr., Inc.

Pezzi, Bryan. Craig Kielburger. 2010. (Illus.). 24p. (978-1-77071-597-4(5)); pap. (978-1-77071-603-2(3)) Weigl Educational Pubs. Ltd.

Pryor, Kimberley Jane. Doing Your Best. 2010. (Values 2 Ser.). 32p. (gr. 1). 18.56 (978-1-60870-142-1(5)) Marshall Cavendish Corp.

—Kindness. 2008. (Values Ser.). 32p. (gr. 1-2). lib. bdg. 18.56 (978-0-7614-3126-8(8), Benchmark Bks.) Marshall Cavendish Corp.

—Respect. 2008. (Values Ser.). 32p. (J). (gr. 1-3). lib. bdg. 18.56 (978-0-7614-3128-2(4)) Marshall Cavendish Corp.

—Responsibility. 2010. (Values 2 Ser.). 32p. (gr. 1). 18.56 (978-1-60870-146-9(8)) Marshall Cavendish Corp.

Raatma, Lucia. Fairness. 2013. (21st Century Junior Library: Character Education Ser.). (ENG., Illus.). 24p. (J). (gr. 1-4). 25.64 (978-1-62431-155-0(5), 202940); pap. 12.79 (978-1-62431-287-8(X), 202942) Cherry Lake Publishing.

—Responsibility. (21st Century Junior Library: Character Education Ser.). (ENG.). 24p. 2013. (J). (gr. 1-4). 25.64 (978-1-62431-157-4(1), 202948) 2013. (J). (gr. 1-4). pap. 12.79 (978-1-62431-289-2(6), 202950) 2009. (gr. 2-5). lib. bdg. 25.64 (978-1-60279-321-7(2), 200217) Cherry Lake Publishing.

Ravilious, Kate. Power - Ethical Debates about Resources & the Environment. 2008. (Dilemmas in Modern Science Ser.). (ENG., Illus.). 48p. (J). 23.99 (978-0-237-53369-4(3)) Evans Brothers, Ltd. GBR. Dist: Independent Pubs. Group.

Reynolds, Luke, ed. Break These Rules: 35 YA Authors on Speaking up, Standing Out, & Being Yourself. 2013. (ENG.). 224p. (YA). (gr. 7). pap. 12.95 (978-1-61374-784-1(5)) Chicago Review Pr., Inc.

Rosenberg, concept. Reach Your Goal. 2011. (YID.). 198p. (YA). 21.00 (978-0-9832102-1-4(7)) Roth Pubs.

Rosenberg, Moshe. Morality for Muggles: Ethics in the Bible & the World of Harry Potter. 2011. (J). (978-1-60280-183-7(5)) Ktav Publishing Hse., Inc.

Salzmann, Mary Elizabeth. I Am Fair. 2003. (Building Character Ser.). (ENG., Illus.). 24p. (J). (gr. k-3). lib. bdg. 24.21 (978-1-57765-826-9(4), SandCastle) ABDO Publishing Co.

Scientific American Staff. Endangered Earth. 2009. (Scientific American Cutting-Edge Science Ser.). 136p. (gr. 9-9). 63.90 (978-1-60853-074-8(4)) Rosen Publishing Group, Inc., The.

Sévigny, Eric, illus. Caillou Borrows a Book. 2014. (Clubhouse Ser.). (ENG.). 24p. (J). (gr. -1 — 1). pap. 3.99 (978-2-89718-141-3(9)) Caillouet, Gerry.

Shepherd, Jodie. Perseverance: I Have Grit! 2015. (Rookie Talk about It(tm) Ser.). (ENG., Illus.). 32p. (J). pap. 5.95 (978-0-531-21379-7(X), Children's Pr.) Scholastic Library Publishing.

Siddoway, Ramona. Grit. 2013. (7 Character Strengths of Highly Successful Students Ser.). 64p. (J). (gr. 5-8). 31.95 (978-1-4488-9540-3(5)); pap. 12.95 (978-1-4488-9559-5(6)); pap. 77.70 (978-1-4488-9560-1(X)) Rosen Publishing Group, Inc., The.

Spero, Yechiel. Touched by a Story: For Children. Schonfeld, Shaya, illus. 2004. (ArtScroll Youth Ser.). 48p. (J). (978-1-57819-436-0(9)) Mesorah Pubns., Ltd.

Stearman, Kaye, et al. Ethical Debates. 2007. (J). 159.00 (978-1-4042-1106-3(3), Rosen Reference) Rosen Publishing Group, Inc., The.

Stefoff, Rebecca. The Right to Die. 2008. (Open for Debate Ser.). 128p. (gr. 7-18). lib. bdg. 42.79 (978-0-7614-2948-7(4), Benchmark Bks.) Marshall Cavendish Corp.

Strazzabosco, Jeanne M. Learning about Responsibility from the Life of Colin Powell. 2009. (Character Building Book Ser.). 24p. (gr. 2-3). 42.50 (978-1-61511-003-2(8), PowerKids Pr.) Rosen Publishing Group, Inc., The.

Strempke, Maria Elena. What's a Hafta? 2011. 24p. 14.95 (978-1-4269-5733-8(5)) Trafford Publishing.

Su, Tami. Sword to Words. Hills, Laila, illus. 2010. 36p. pap. 14.99 (978-1-60844-524-0(0)) Dog Ear Publishing, LLC.

Tardiff, Joe. Congressional Ethics. Greenhaven Press Editors & Zott, Lynn, eds. 2013. (Opposing Viewpoints Ser.). (ENG., Illus.). 224p. (gr. 10-12). lib. bdg. 48.80 (978-0-7377-6046-0(X), Greenhaven Pr., Inc.) Cengage Gale.

Teen Issues, 26 bks., Set. (Illus.). (YA). (gr. 6-12). lib. bdg. 344.10 (978-0-89490-887-3(1)) Enslow Pubs., Inc.

Telias, Ari. Tales of the Chocolate River: How to Make Your Dreams Come True. 2011. 48p. (J). pap. 10.00 (978-0-692-00612-2(5)) Justice Link Publishing.

Thomas, Isabel. Dealing with Feeling... Caring. 2013. (Dealing with Feeling... Ser.). (ENG.). 24p. (gr. 1-2). pap. 6.79 (978-1-4329-7113-7(1)); lib. bdg. 23.32 (978-1-4329-7104-5(2)) Heinemann-Raintree. (Heinemann Read & Learn).

Thompson, Tamara. The Right to Die. Gale, G., ed. 2014. (At Issue Ser.). (ENG.). 128p. (gr. 10-12). lib. bdg. 39.40 (978-0-7377-6850-3(9), Greenhaven Pr., Inc.) Cengage Gale.

Thompson, Tamara, ed. The Ethics of Medical Testing. 2011. (At Issue Ser.). 128p. (J). (gr. 9-12). 34.45 (978-0-7377-5902-0(X)) Cengage Gale.

Tourville, Amanda Doering. Comportamiento y Modales en la Cafetería. Lensch, Chris, illus. 2011. (¡Así Debemos Ser!: Buenos Modales, Buen Comportamiento/Way to Be!: Manners Ser.).Tr. of Manners in the Lunchroom. (ENG, SPA & MUL.). 24p. (gr. -1-2). lib. bdg. 26.65 (978-1-4048-6695-9(7)) Picture Window Bks.

—Manners on the School Bus (Comportamiento y Modales en el Autobús Escolar) Lensch, Chris, illus. 2011. (¡Así Debemos Ser!: Buenos Modales, Buen Comportamiento/Way to Be!: Manners Ser.). (ENG, SPA & MUL.). 24p. (gr. -1-2). lib. bdg. 26.65 (978-1-4048-6696-6(5)) Picture Window Bks.

Turner, Dale. Free to Be. Summer, Angel, ed. Smart, Ross, illus. 2003. 112p. (J). (gr. k-5). 16.95 *(978-1-892696-28-1(2))* High Tide Pr.
Yankee, Kris & Nelson, Marian. Are You Respectful Today? 2014. (ENG., Illus.). 32p. (J). pap. 9.95 *(978-1-938326-25-7(3)*, Ferne Pr.) Nelson Publishing & Marketing.

ETHICS, CHRISTIAN
see Christian Ethics

ETHICS, SEXUAL
see Sexual Ethics

ETHIOPIA
Bankston, John. We Visit Ethiopia. 2012. (J). lib. bdg. 33.95 *(978-1-61228-302-9(0))* Mitchell Lane Pubs., Inc.
Bellward, Stacy. Ethiopian Voices: Tsion's Life. Berge, Erlend, illus. 2008. 32p. (J). (gr. 4-7). 19.99 *(978-0-9797481-1-0(9))* Amharic Kids.
Campbell, Andrew. Ethiopia. 2007. (Countries in the News/Watts Ser.). (Illus.). 32p. (YA). (gr. 4-7). lib. bdg. 28.50 *(978-1-59920-016-3(3))* Black Rabbit Bks.
Corrigan, Jim. Ethiopia. Rotberg, Robert I., ed. 2012. (Evolution of Africa's Major Nations Ser.). (Illus.). 80p. (J). (gr. 7). 22.95 *(978-1-4222-2179-2(2))* Mason Crest.
—Ethiopia. 2011. (J). pap. *(978-1-4222-2207-2(1))* Mason Crest.
Frazel, Ellen. Ethiopia. 2013. (Exploring Countries Ser.). (ENG., Illus.). 32p. (J). (gr. 3-7). lib. bdg. 26.95 *(978-1-60014-859-0(X)*, Blastoff! Readers) Bellwether Media.
Gish, Steven, et al. Ethiopia. 3rd enl. ed. 2016. (Cultures of the World (Third Edition) (r) Ser.). 144p. (J). 47.07 *(978-1-5026-2209-9(2))* Cavendish Square Publishing.
Heinemann Staff. Ethiopia. (World Focus Ser.). (Illus.). 31p. (J). (gr. 3-7). pap. 3.99 *(978-0-431-07262-3(0))* Oxfam Publishing GBR. Dist: Stylus Publishing, LLC.
Heinrichs, Ann & Heinrichs, Anne. Ethiopia. 2005. (Enchantment of the World Ser.). (ENG., Illus.). 144p. (YA). (gr. 5-9). 39.00 *(978-0-516-23680-3(6))* Scholastic Library Publishing.
Pohl, Kathleen. Descubramos Etiopía. 2008. (Descubramos países del mundo (Looking at Countries) Ser.). (SPA.). 32p. (gr. 1-5). (J). lib. bdg. 26.00 *(978-0-8368-9064-8(7))*; pap. 10.50 *(978-0-8368-9065-5(5))* Stevens, Gareth Publishing LLLP. (Gareth Stevens Learning Library).
—Looking at Ethiopia. 2008. (Looking at Countries Ser.). 32p. (gr. 1-5). (J). lib. bdg. 26.00 *(978-0-8368-9062-4(0))*; pap. 10.50 *(978-0-8368-9063-1(9))* Stevens, Gareth Publishing LLLP. (Gareth Stevens Learning Library).
Somervill, Barbara. Ethiopia. 2011. (Explorer Library: Social Studies Explorer Ser.). (ENG.). 48p. (gr. 4-8). lib. bdg. 31.36 *(978-1-61080-099-0(0)*, 201092) Cherry Lake Publishing.

ETHIOPIA—FICTION
Abebe, Elsi. Grandma's Humongous Suitcase: A Tale of Ethiopian History & Culture in A Child Voice... 2011. 20p. (gr. -1). pap. 11.99 *(978-1-4567-6141-7(2))* AuthorHouse.
Ambau, Getty. Desta & the Winds of Washaa Umera: The Winds of Washaa Umera, vols. 7, vol. 2. 2nd ed. 2013. (ENG., Illus.). 454p. (YA). pap. 15.95 *(978-1-884459-03-0(X))* Falcon Pr. International.
Falcon Press International. Desta & King Solomon's Coin of Magic & Fortune: And king solomon's coinof of magic & Fortune, nos. 7, no. 2. 2nd ed. 2010. (ENG., Illus.). 430p. (YA). pap. 15.95 *(978-1-884459-01-6(3))* Falcon Pr. International.
Guillain, Adam. Bella Balistica & the African Safari. 2007. (Bella Balistica Ser.). (ENG., Illus.). 250p. (J). (gr. 4-7). per. 9.95 *(978-1-84059-482-9(9))* Milet Publishing.
Ieronimo, Christine. A Thirst for Home: A Story of Water Across the World. Velasquez, Eric, illus. 2014. (ENG.). 32p. (J). (gr. 1-4). 17.99 *(978-0-8027-2307-9(1)*, 9780802723079, Bloomsbury USA Childrens) Bloomsbury Publishing USA.
Kessler, Cristina. The Best Beekeeper of Lalibela: A Tale from Africa. Jenkins, Leonard, illus. 2006. (ENG.). 32p. (J). (gr. -1-3). 16.95 *(978-0-8234-1858-9(8))* Holiday Hse., Inc.
Laird, Elizabeth. The Garbage King. 2016. (ENG., Illus.). 336p. (J). (gr. 4-7). pap. 9.99 *(978-1-5098-0295-1(9))* Pan Macmillan GBR. Dist: Independent Pubs. Group.
Mohamed, Sultan, tr. & illus. The Story of Coffee. Mohamed, Sultan, illus. 2003. (ENG & AMH.). 24p. (J). (gr. 4-5). 15.99 *(978-0-9605670-9-6(7))* Ananse Pr.
Morgan, Anna. Daughters of the Ark, 1 vol. 2005. (ENG., Illus.). 200p. (J). (gr. 5-12). pap. 9.95 *(978-1-896764-92-4(4))* Second Story Pr. CAN. Dist: Orca Bk. Pubs. USA.
Onyefulu, Ifeoma. New Shoes for Helen. Onyefulu, Ifeoma, photos by. 2011. (First Experiences Ser.). (ENG., Illus.). 32p. (J). (gr. -1-2). 17.95 *(978-1-84780-128-9(5)*, Frances Lincoln) Quarto Publishing Group UK GBR. Dist: Hachette Bk. Group.
Ripken, Cal. Wild Pitch. Cowherd, Kevin, illus. 2014. (Cal Ripken, Jr. 's All Stars Ser.). (ENG.). 224p. (J). (gr. 3-7). pap. 6.99 *(978-1-4231-4005-4(2))* Hyperion Bks. for Children.
Rouss, Sylvia A. Jaekob, the Dreamer. 2015. (Illus.). (J). *(978-1-68115-506-7(0))* Behrman Hse., Inc.
Simpson, Lesley. Yuvi's Candy Tree. Porter, Janice Lee, illus. 2011. (ENG.). 32p. (J). (gr. k-3). pap. 7.95 *(978-0-7613-5652-3(5))*; lib. bdg. 17.95 *(978-0-7613-5651-6(7))* Lerner Publishing Group. (Kar-Ben Publishing).
Wein, Elizabeth. Black Dove, White Raven. (ENG.). (YA). (gr. 7-12). 2016. 384p. pap. 9.99 *(978-1-4231-8523-9(4))* 2015. 368p. 17.99 *(978-1-4231-8310-5(X))* Hyperion Bks. for Children.
Williams, David Morgan. The Crystal Fountain. Jenkins, Laura, illus. 2017. (ENG.). 48p. (J). 11.00 ***(978-1-78461-348-8(7))*** Y Lolfa GBR. Dist: Dufour Editions, Inc.
Yohalem, Eve. Escape under the Forever Sky. (ENG.). 2011. 219p. (YA). (gr. 4-7). pap. 7.99 *(978-0-8118-7874-6(0))* 2009. 224p. (J). (gr. 5-17). 16.99 *(978-0-8118-6653-8(X))* Chronicle Bks. LLC.

ETHNIC GROUPS
see Ethnic Relations; Minorities; Racially Mixed People

ETHNIC RELATIONS
DeSimone, Corkey Hay. The Planet Hue. DeSimone, Corkey Hay, illus. 2003. (Illus.). (J). 14.95 *(978-0-9747921-0-1(1))* Gentle Giraffe Pr.
Hanes, Richard Clay, et al. Prejudice in the Modern World. 2007. (J). *(978-1-4144-0206-2(6))*; *(978-1-4144-0205-5(8))* Cengage Gale.
King, Dr. Dorothy. What Is Ethnophobia? 2005. 64p. pap. 22.13 *(978-1-4116-4348-2(8))* Lulu Pr., Inc.
Malaspina, Ann. The Ethnic & Group Identity Movements: Earning Recognition. 2007. (Reform Movements in American History Ser.). (Illus.). 176p. (YA). (gr. 7-12). lib. bdg. 32.50 *(978-0-7910-9571-3(1))* Facts On File, Inc.
Obadina, Elizabeth. Ethnic Groups in Africa. Ojakorotu, Victor & Rotberg, Robert I., eds. 2013. (Africa: Progress & Problems Ser.: 13). (Illus.). 112p. (J). (gr. 7-18). 24.95 *(978-1-4222-2939-2(4))* Mason Crest.
Palmer, Bill. Gallup Guides for Youth Facing Persistent Prejudice. 2012. (Gallup Guides for Youth Facing Persistent Prejudice Ser.). 64p. (J). (gr. 7-8). 22.95 *(978-1-4222-2466-3(X))* Mason Crest.
Russo, Marisabina. Always Remember Me: How One Family Survived World War II. Russo, Marisabina, illus. 2005. (ENG., Illus.). 48p. (J). (gr. 1-5). 19.99 *(978-0-689-86920-4(7)*, Atheneum Bks. for Young Readers) Simon & Schuster Children's Publishing.
Takaki, Ronald. A Different Mirror for Young People: A History of Multicultural America. 2012. (For Young People Ser.). (ENG., Illus.). 378p. (J). (gr. 5). pap. 18.95 *(978-1-60980-416-9(3)*, Triangle Square) Seven Stories Pr.
Thomson Gale Staff. Prejudice in the Modern World. Hanes, Sharon M., ed. rev. ed. 2007. (Prejudice in the Modern World Reference Library). (ENG.). 256p. (YA). 106.00 *(978-1-4144-0208-6(2)*, UXL) Cengage Gale.
—Prejudice in the Modern World - Almanac, 2.0. Hanes, Richard C. et al, eds. rev. ed. 2007. (Prejudice in the Modern World Reference Library). (ENG.). 462p. (YA). 191.00 *(978-1-4144-0204-8(X)*, UXL) Cengage Gale.
Thomson Gale Staff & Hermsen, Sarah. Prejudice in the Modern World: Biographies. Hanes, Richard C. & Rudd, Kelly, eds. rev. ed. 2007. (Prejudice in the Modern World Reference Library). (ENG.). 288p. (YA). 106.00 *(978-1-4144-0207-9(4)*, UXL) Cengage Gale.
—Prejudice in the Modern World: Cumulative Index. rev. ed. 2007. (Prejudice in the Modern World Reference Library). (ENG.). 34p. (YA). 5.00 *(978-1-4144-0209-3(0)*, UXL) Cengage Gale.
Zermeno C., Francisco. Caft Chronicles. 2007. 96p. per. 17.95 *(978-0-915745-98-2(4))* Floricanto Pr.

ETHNOGRAPHY
see Ethnology

ETHNOLOGY
see also Anthropology; Anthropometry; Archaeology; Civilization; Costume; Ethnic Relations; Folklore; Human Geography; Human Skin Color; Language and Languages; Manners and Customs; Prehistoric Peoples; Race; Race Relations; Totems and Totemism
Alexander, Linda B. & Kwon, Nahyun, eds. Multicultural Programs for Tweens & Teens. 2010. 216p. pap. 50.00 *(978-0-8389-3582-8(6))* American Library Assn.
All about Us Interactive Packages: Here I Am. (Pebble Soup Explorations Ser.). (gr. -1-18). 52.00 *(978-0-7578-5227-5(0))* Rigby Education.
All about Us Interactive Packages: Making Friends. (Pebble Soup Explorations Ser.). (gr. -1-18). 52.00 *(978-0-7578-5228-2(9))* Rigby Education.
Anderson, Joanna. The Many People of America. 2012. (I'm an American Citizen Ser.). (ENG., Illus.). 24p. (J). (gr. 1-3). 22.60 *(978-1-4488-8591-6(4)*, PowerKids Pr.) Rosen Publishing Group, Inc., The.
Barrington, Richard. Bands, Tribes & First Peoples & Nations. Wolff, Ariana, ed. 2014. (Political & Economic Systems Ser.). 312p. (YA). (gr. 9-12). 45.00 *(978-1-62275-362-8(3))* Rosen Publishing Group, Inc., The.
Bernard, Shane K. Cajuns & Their Acadian Ancestors: A Young Reader's History. 2008. (ENG., Illus.). 104p. (gr. 7-12). 18.00 *(978-1-934110-78-2(7))* Univ. Pr. of Mississippi.
Books, Golson. The African Americans, 7 vols. 2011. (Multicultural America Ser.). (Illus.). 256p. (gr. 6-12). 55.00 *(978-0-8160-7813-4(0))* Facts On File, Inc.
—The Arab Americans, 7 vols. 2011. (Multicultural America Ser.). (Illus.). 208p. (gr. 6-12). 55.00 *(978-0-8160-7812-7(2))* Facts On File, Inc.
—The Asian Americans, 7 vols. 2011. (Multicultural America Ser.). (Illus.). 272p. (gr. 6-12). 55.00 *(978-0-8160-7814-1(9))* Facts On File, Inc.
—The European Americans, 7 vols. 2011. (Multicultural America Ser.). (Illus.). 256p. (gr. 6-12). 55.00 *(978-0-8160-7816-5(5))* Facts On File, Inc.
—The Hispanic Americans, 7 vols. 2011. (Multicultural America Ser.). (Illus.). 256p. (gr. 6-12). 55.00 *(978-0-8160-7811-0(4))* Facts On File, Inc.
—The Jewish Americans, 7 vols. 2011. (Multicultural America Ser.). (Illus.). 256p. (gr. 6-12). 55.00 *(978-0-8160-7815-8(7))* Facts On File, Inc.
—The Native Americans, 7 vols. 2011. (Multicultural America Ser.). (Illus.). 256p. (gr. 6-12). 55.00 *(978-0-8160-7817-2(3))* Facts On File, Inc.
Bradshaw, Cody. Cultures in My Class: Represent & Interpret Data. 2014. (Rosen Common Core Math Readers Ser.). (ENG., Illus.). 24p. (J). (gr. 2-3). pap. 8.25 *(978-1-4777-4831-2(8)*, Rosen Classroom) Rosen Publishing Group, Inc., The.
Clarke, Ann. People Are So Different! Smith, Duncan, illus. 2008. 24p. 16.95 *(978-0-9787235-0-7(3))* Precious Little Bks.
Claybourne, Anna & Doherty, Gillian. Peoples of the World. rev. ed. 2005. 96p. (J). pap. 14.95 *(978-0-7945-1025-1(6)*, Usborne) EDC Publishing.
Cole, Sonja. Booktalking Around the World: Great Global Reads for Ages 9-14. 2010. (ENG.). 178p. E-Book *(978-1-59884-614-0(0)*, Libraries Unlimited) ABC-CLIO, LLC.
Cultures of the World - Group 14. 2nd rev. ed. Incl. Algeria. Kagda, Falaq & Latif, Zawiah Abdul. lib. bdg. 42.79 *(978-0-7614-2085-9(1)*, Benchmark Bks.); Armenia. Dhilawala, Sakina. (Illus.). lib. bdg. 42.79 *(978-0-7614-2029-3(0))*; Lithuania. Kagda, Sakina & Latif, Zawiah Abdul. lib. bdg. 42.79 *(978-0-7614-2087-3(8)*, Benchmark Bks.); Luxembourg. Sheehan, Patricia & Dhilawala, Sakina. lib. bdg. 42.79 *(978-0-7614-2088-0(6)*, Benchmark Bks.); Tahiti. NgCheong-Lum, Roseline. lib. bdg. 42.79 *(978-0-7614-2089-7(4)*, Benchmark Bks.); Ukraine. Bassis, Volodymyr & Dhilawala, Sakina. lib. bdg. 42.79 *(978-0-7614-2090-3(8)*, Benchmark Bks.); 144p. (gr. 6). (Cultures of the World 14 Ser.). 2007. Set lib. bdg. 256.74 *(978-0-7614-2084-2(3)*, Benchmark Bks.) Marshall Cavendish Corp.
Cultures of the World - Group 17, 6 vols. Incl. Bangladesh. Whyte, Mariam. (gr. 5-12). 1999. lib. bdg. 37.07 *(978-0-7614-0869-7(X))*; Czech Republic. Sioras, Efstathia. (gr. 5-12). 1999. lib. bdg. 37.07 *(978-0-7614-0870-3(3))*; Democratic Republic of the Congo. Heale, Jay. (gr. 5-12). 1999. lib. bdg. 37.07 *(978-0-7614-0874-1(6))*; Kuwait. O'Shea, Maria. (gr. 5-12). 1999. lib. bdg. 37.07 *(978-0-7614-0871-0(1))*; Senegal. Berg, Elizabeth. (gr. 5-12). 1999. lib. bdg. 37.07 *(978-0-7614-0872-7(X))*; Uruguay. Jermyn, Leslie. (J). (gr. k-17). 1998. lib. bdg. 37.07 *(978-0-7614-0873-4(8))*; 128p. (Illus.). 222.43 *(978-0-7614-0868-0(1)*, Benchmark Bks.) Marshall Cavendish Corp.
Cultures of the World - Group 20, 6 vols. Incl. Fiji. NgCheong-Lum, Roseline. lib. bdg. 37.07 *(978-0-7614-0996-0(3))*; Guyana. Jermyn, Leslie. lib. bdg. 37.07 *(978-0-7614-0994-6(7))*; 128p. (gr. 5-12). 2000. (Illus.). 222.43 *(978-0-7614-0991-5(2)*, Benchmark Bks.) Marshall Cavendish Corp.
Descola, Philippe. Diversité des Natures, Diversité des Cultures. 2010. (FRE.). 84p. *(978-2-227-48207-4(9))* Bayard Editions.
Doherty, Gillian & Claybourne, Anna. Peoples of the World. rev. ed. 2012. (World Cultures Ser.). 96p. (J). pap. 14.99 *(978-0-7945-3280-2(2)*, Usborne) EDC Publishing.
Donovan, Sandra. The Middle Eastern American Experience. 2010. (USA TODAY Cultural Mosaic Ser.). (ENG., Illus.). 80p. (gr. 6-8). lib. bdg. 33.26 *(978-0-7613-4087-4(4))* Lerner Publishing Group.
Fox, Mem. Whoever You Are (Quienquiera Que Seas) Flor Ada, Alma & Campoy, F. Isabel, trs. Staub, Leslie, illus. 2007. (ENG & SPA.). 28p. (J). (gr. k — 1). bds. 6.95 *(978-0-15-205891-3(5))* Houghton Mifflin Harcourt Publishing Co.
Gale Editors & Corporate Contributor Staff, eds. Junior Worldmark Encyclopedia of World Cultures, 9 vols., 9 Volume Set. 2nd ed. 2011. (ENG.). 2000p. lib. bdg. 742.00 *(978-1-4144-8671-0(5)*, UXL) Cengage Gale.
Gall, Timothy L. & Gall, Susan B. Junior Worldmark Encyclopedia of World Cultures. 2nd ed. 2011. (J). *(978-1-4144-8676-5(6))*; *(978-1-4144-8672-7(3))*; *(978-1-4144-8673-4(1))*; *(978-1-4144-8674-1(X))*; *(978-1-4144-8675-8(8))*; *(978-1-4144-8678-9(2))*; *(978-1-4144-8679-6(0))*; *(978-1-4144-8680-2(4))*; *(978-1-4144-8677-2(4))* Cengage Gale. (UXL).
Gayle-Evans, Guda. An Annotated Bibliography of Multi-Cultural Literature for Children Three to Ten Years. 2004. (Mellen Studies in Children's Literature: Vol. 6). (Illus.). 204p. 109.95 *(978-0-7734-6474-2(3))* Mellen, Edwin Pr., The.
Gelletly, LeeAnne. The Kurds. 2010. (Major Muslim Nations Ser.). (Illus.). 120p. (J). (gr. 5-18). lib. bdg. 25.95 *(978-1-4222-1407-7(9))* Mason Crest.
Gustafson, Angela. Imagine a House: A Journey to Fascinating Houses Around the World. 2003. (What a World We Live in Ser.). (Illus.). 32p. (J). (gr. k-6). lib. bdg. 16.95 *(978-0-9726849-0-3(5))* Out of the Box.
Hasday, Judy & Hasday, Judy L. Americans of Eastern European Heritage. 2007. (Successful Americans Ser.). (Illus.). 64p. (YA). (gr. 5-18). pap. 9.95 *(978-1-4222-0860-1(5))* Mason Crest.
Hasday, Judy L. Americans of Eastern European Heritage. 2009. (Successful Americans Ser.). (Illus.). 64p. (YA). (gr. 9-12). 22.95 *(978-1-4222-0528-0(2))* Mason Crest.
Hinds, Kathryn. Goths. 2009. (Barbarians! Ser.). 80p. (gr. 6-8). 35.64 *(978-0-7614-4065-9(8))* Marshall Cavendish Corp.
—Scythians & Sarmatians. 2009. (Barbarians! Ser.). 80p. (gr. 6). 35.64 *(978-0-7614-4072-7(0))* Marshall Cavendish GBR. Dist: Marshall Cavendish Corp.
Horn, Geoffrey M. Margaret Mead. 2004. (Trailblazers of the Modern World Ser.). (Illus.). 48p. (gr. 5-12). pap. 14.05 *(978-0-8368-5259-2(1))*; lib. bdg. 31.00 *(978-0-8368-5099-4(8))* Stevens, Gareth Publishing LLLP. (Gareth Stevens Secondary Library).
McManus, Lori. Mexican Culture, 1 vol. 2012. (Global Cultures Ser.). (ENG.). 48p. (gr. 4-6). pap. 9.95 *(978-1-4329-6792-5(4))*; 32.65 *(978-1-4329-6783-3(5))* Heinemann-Raintree. (NA-h).
Mills, Nathan & Anderson, Joanna. The Many People of America. 2012. (Rosen Readers Ser.). (ENG., Illus.). 24p. (J). (gr. 1-2). pap. 8.25 *(978-1-4488-8866-5(2)*, Rosen Classroom) Rosen Publishing Group, Inc., The.
Minahan, James. The Former Soviet Union's Diverse Peoples: A Reference Sourcebook, 1 vol. Barkan, Elliott Robert, ed. 2004. (Ethnic Diversity Within Nations Ser.). (Illus.). 389p. (C). 75.00 *(978-1-57607-823-5(X)*, SVDPLEC) ABC-CLIO, LLC.
Nagle, Jeanne. Top 5 Reasons Why People Get Tattoos & Other Body Art. 2011. (J). 77.70 *(978-1-4488-4741-9(9))*; (Illus.). 64p. pap. 12.95 *(978-1-4488-4620-7(X))*; (Illus.). 64p. lib. bdg. 31.95 *(978-1-4488-4617-7(X))* Rosen Publishing Group, Inc., The.
Owens, Sharon. Immigration & Migration in Texas. 2014. (Spotlight on Texas Ser.). (ENG.). 32p. (J). (gr. 3-4). 26.25 *(978-1-4777-4522-9(X)*, Rosen Classroom) Rosen Publishing Group, Inc., The.
Peacock, Thomas Love & Wisuri, Marlene. To Be Free: Understanding & eliminating Racism. 2010. (ENG., Illus.). 104p. (J). 24.00 *(978-1-890434-80-9(9))* Afton Historical Society Pr.
Perritano, John. Spanish Missions. 2010. (True Book(tm), a — Spanish Missions Ser.). (Illus.). 48p. (J). (gr. 2-5). 31.00 *(978-0-531-20575-4(4))*; pap. 6.95 *(978-0-531-21238-7(6))* Scholastic Library Publishing.
Ray, Deborah Kogan. The Impossible Voyage of Kon-Tiki. Ray, Deborah Kogan, illus. 2015. (ENG., Illus.). 40p. (J). (gr. 2-5). lib. bdg. 16.95 *(978-1-58089-620-7(0))* Charlesbridge Publishing, Inc.
Santos, Edward J. Everything You Need to Know If You & Your Parents are New Americans. 2009. (Need to Know Library). 64p. (gr. 5-5). 58.50 *(978-1-60854-099-0(5))* Rosen Publishing Group, Inc., The.
Sargent, Brian. Mark Your Territory Intermediate Book with Online Access. 2014. (ENG., Illus.). 28p. pap. 9.50 *(978-1-107-65895-0(0))* Cambridge Univ. Pr.
Sirvaitis, Karen. The European American Experience. 2010. (USA TODAY Cultural Mosaic Ser.). (ENG.). 80p. (gr. 6-8). lib. bdg. 33.26 *(978-0-7613-4088-1(2))* Lerner Publishing Group.
Smith, Daniel. World Cultures Explained, 1 vol. 2015. (ENG.). 136p. (J). 38.25 *(978-1-4777-8130-2(7)*, Rosen Young Adult) Rosen Publishing Group, Inc., The.
Tabor, Nancy Maria Grande. Somos un Arco Iris (We Are a Rainbow) Tabor, Nancy Maria Grande, illus. 2006. (ENG & SPA., Illus.). 28p. (gr. -1-3). 17.95 *(978-0-7569-7027-7(X))* Perfection Learning Corp.
Thorold, David, et al. Roman Invaders & Settlers. 2013. (Step up History Ser.). (ENG., Illus.). 32p. (J). pap. 12.99 *(978-0-237-54378-5(8))* Evans Brothers, Ltd. GBR. Dist: Independent Pubs. Group.
Toufexis, George. Extreme Lions & Tigers Tattoos. 2011. (Dover Tattoos Ser.). (ENG.). 4p. (J). (gr. 1-4). pap. 1.50 *(978-0-486-48184-5(0))* Dover Pubns., Inc.
Webster, Christine. Polynesians. 2012. (J). 28.55 *(978-1-61913-172-9(2))*; pap. 29.99 *(978-1-61913-439-3(X))* Weigl Pubs., Inc.
Whelan, Gloria. Waiting for the Owl's Call. Milelli, Pascal, illus. 2009. (Tales of the World Ser.). (ENG.). 32p. (J). (gr. 1-5). 17.95 *(978-1-58536-418-3(5))* Sleeping Bear Pr.
World Book, Inc Staff, contrib. by. The Polynesians. 2009. (J). *(978-0-7166-2140-9(1))* World Bk., Inc.
World Book, Inc. Staff, contrib. by. The World Book of America's Multicultural Heritage, 2 vols. 2003. (Illus.). 384p. (gr. 4-12). 86.99 *(978-0-7166-7303-3(7))* World Bk., Inc.

ETHNOLOGY—AFRICA
see also Masai (African People); Zulu (African People)
Barghoom, Linda. A Refugee's Journey from Somalia. 2017. 32p. (J). ***(978-0-7787-3675-2(X))*** Crabtree Publishing Co.
Conrad, David C. Empires of Medieval West Africa, Revised Edition. 2nd rev. ed. 2009. (Great Empires of the Past Ser.). (Illus.). 152p. (gr. 6-12). 35.00 *(978-1-60413-164-2(0)*, Chelsea Hse.) Facts On File, Inc.
Craats, Rennay. Maasai with Code. 2012. (World Cultures Ser.). (ENG., Illus.). 32p. (J). (gr. 3-7). pap. 13.95 *(978-1-61913-531-4(0)*, AV2 by Weigl) Weigl Pubs., Inc.
La Bella, Laura. Discovering the Songhay Empire. 2013. (Exploring African Civilizations Ser.). (Illus.). 64p. (J). (gr. 5-8). 31.95 *(978-1-4777-1885-8(0)*, Rosen Reference) Rosen Publishing Group, Inc., The.
Low, Robert. Peoples of the Savanna. 2009. (Peoples & Their Environments Ser.). 24p. (gr. 2-3). 42.50 *(978-1-60851-162-4(6)*, PowerKids Pr.) Rosen Publishing Group, Inc., The.
Schomp, Virginia. The Ancient Africans. 2008. (Myths of the World Ser.). 96p. (gr. 6-18). lib. bdg. 34.21 *(978-0-7614-3099-5(7)*, Benchmark Bks.) Marshall Cavendish Corp.

ETHNOLOGY—AUSTRALIA
World Book, Inc Staff, contrib. by. Australian Aborigines. 2009. (J). *(978-0-7166-2128-7(2))* World Bk., Inc.

ETIQUETTE
see also Courtesy; Dance; Dating (Social Customs); Entertaining; Letter Writing; Manners and Customs
also names of countries with the subdivision Social life and customs
ABDO Publishing Company Staff. Good Manners in Relationships. 2014. (Good Manners in Relationships Ser.: 4). 32p. (J). (gr. -1-4). lib. bdg. 114.00 *(978-1-62402-024-7(0)*, Looking Glass Library) Magic Wagon.
Aikins, Anne Marie. Misconduct: Deal with It Without Bending the Rules, 1 vol. Murray, Steven, illus. 2005. (Lorimer Deal with It Ser.). (ENG.). 32p. (J). (gr. 4-6). 12.95 *(978-1-55028-871-1(7)*, 9781550288711) Lorimer, James & Co., Ltd., Pubs. CAN. Dist: Casemate Pubs. & Bk. Distributors, LLC.
Amos, Janine. After You. 2009. (Best Behavior Ser.). (Illus.). 32p. (J). (gr. -1-2). pap. 10.55 *(978-1-60754-032-8(0))*; lib. bdg. 22.60 *(978-1-60754-020-5(7))* Windmill Bks.
—Courteous Kids, 18 bks. Spenceley, Annabel, illus. Incl. Don't Do That! lib. bdg. 26.00 *(978-0-8368-3605-9(7))*; Don't Say That! lib. bdg. 26.00 *(978-0-8368-3606-6(5))*; Go Away! lib. bdg. 26.00 *(978-0-8368-3607-3(3))*; It Won't Work! lib. bdg. 26.00 *(978-0-8368-3608-0(1))*; It's Mine! lib. bdg. 26.00 *(978-0-8368-3609-7(X))*; Move Over! lib. bdg. 26.00 *(978-0-8368-3610-3(3))*; (gr. -1-2). 2002., Gareth Stevens Learning Library (Courteous Kids Ser.). (Illus.). 32p. 287.16 o.p. *(978-0-8368-3644-8(8))* Stevens, Gareth Publishing LLLP.
—Don't Do That! How Not to Act. 2009. (Best Behavior Ser.). (Illus.). 32p. (J). (gr. -1-2). pap. 10.55 *(978-1-60754-052-6(5))* Windmill Bks.
—Hello! 2009. (Best Behavior Ser.). (Illus.). 32p. (J). (gr. -1-2). pap. 10.55 *(978-1-60754-034-2(7))*; lib. bdg. 22.60 *(978-1-60754-021-2(5))* Windmill Bks.
—I'm Sorry. 2009. (Best Behavior Ser.). (Illus.). 32p. (J). (gr. -1-2). pap. 10.55 *(978-1-60754-040-3(1))*; lib. bdg. 22.60 *(978-1-60754-024-3(X))* Windmill Bks.
—No, Thank You. 2009. (Best Behavior Ser.). (Illus.). 32p. (J). (gr. -1-2). pap. 10.55 *(978-1-60754-036-6(3))*; lib. bdg. 22.60 *(978-1-60754-022-9(3))* Windmill Bks.
—Please. 2009. (Best Behavior Ser.). (Illus.). 32p. (J). (gr. -1-2). pap. 10.55 *(978-1-60754-038-0(X))*; lib. bdg. 22.60 *(978-1-60754-023-6(1))* Windmill Bks.
—Thank You. 2009. (Best Behavior Ser.). (Illus.). 32p. (J). (gr. -1-2). pap. 10.55 *(978-1-60754-042-7(8))*; lib. bdg. 22.60 *(978-1-60754-025-0(8))* Windmill Bks.
Amos, Janine & Spenceley, Annabel. Don't Do That! How Not to Act. 2009. (Best Behavior Ser.). (Illus.). 32p. (J). (gr. -1-2). lib. bdg. 22.60 *(978-1-60754-030-4(4))* Windmill Bks.
—Don't Say That! Let's Talk Nicely. 2009. (Best Behavior Ser.). (Illus.). 32p. (J). (gr. -1-2). pap. 10.55 *(978-1-60754-054-0(1))*; lib. bdg. 22.60 *(978-1-60754-031-1(2))* Windmill Bks.

—It's Mine! Let's Try to Share. 2009. (Best Behavior Ser.). (Illus.). 32p. (J). (gr. -1-2). pap. 10.55 (978-1-60754-048-9(7)); lib. bdg. 22.60 (978-1-60754-028-1(2)) Windmill Bks.

—Let's Take Turns. 2009. (Best Behavior Ser.). (Illus.). 32p. (J). (gr. -1-2). 22.60 (978-1-60754-512-5(8)); pap. 10.55 (978-1-60754-513-2(6)) Windmill Bks.

—Move Over! Learning to Share Our Space. 2009. (Best Behavior Ser.). (Illus.). 32p. (J). (gr. -1-2). pap. 10.55 (978-1-60754-050-2(9)); lib. bdg. 22.60 (978-1-60754-029-8(0)) Windmill Bks.

Bailey, Diane. Cyber Ethics. 2009. (Cyber Citizenship & Cyber Safety Ser.). 48p. (gr. 5-5). 53.00 (978-1-61512-102-1(1), Rosen Reference) Rosen Publishing Group, Inc., The.

Barsocchini, Peter, creator. High School Musical 2 Party Planner. 2010. (Illus.). (J). pap. 4.99 (978-0-7666-2846-5(9)) Modern Publishing.

Baughman, Glenda. Root Rooster Goes to School. 2011. 32p. pap. 24.95 (978-1-4512-8619-9(8)) America Star Bks.

Beker, Jeanne. The Big Night Out. Dion, Nathalie, illus. 2005. (ENG.). 80p. (J). (gr. 4-7). pap. 15.95 (978-0-88776-719-7(2), Tundra Bks.) Tundra Bks. CAN. Dist: Penguin Random Hse. LLC.

Berlatsky, Noah. Netiquette & Online Ethics. 2013. (Opposing Viewpoints Ser.). (ENG., Illus.). 224p. (gr. 10-12). pap. 33.80 (978-0-7377-6429-1(5)); lib. bdg. 48.80 (978-0-7377-6428-4(7)) Cengage Gale. (Greenhaven Pr., Inc.).

Berry, Joy. Help Me Be Good Being Rude. Bartholomew, illus. 2010. (Help Me Be Good Ser.). (ENG.). 32p. (J). (gr. -1-2). pap. 4.99 (978-1-60577-138-0(4)) Berry, Joy Enterprises.

—Teach Me about Mealtime. 2009. (ENG.). 40p. (J). (gr. k — 1). bds. 7.95 (978-1-60577-007-9(8)) Berry, Joy Enterprises.

Björkman, Steve, illus. Dinosaurs Don't, Dinosaurs Do. 2011. (I Like to Read(r) Ser.). (ENG.). 24p. (J). (gr. -1-2). 14.95 (978-0-8234-2355-2(7)) Holiday Hse., Inc.

Bloch, Lyudmila & Civitano, Tom. The Golden Rules of Etiquette at the Plaza Carroll, Rosemary, illus. 2004. 48p. (J). lib. bdg. 16.95 (978-0-9755390-0-2(0)) Fifth Ave Pr.

Bloom, Paul. Rules at Lunch. 2015. (School Rules Ser.). (ENG.). 24p. (J). (gr. k-k). pap. 8.15 (978-1-4824-2637-3(4)) Stevens, Gareth Publishing LLLP.

Burgess, Gelett. Goops - 1900: And How to Be Them. 2006. 100p. pap. 10.45 (978-1-59462-233-5(7), 266, Book Jungle) Standard Pubns., Inc.

Burstein, John. Manners, Please! Why It Pays to Be Polite. 2010. (ENG., Illus.). 32p. (J). pap. (978-0-7787-4811-3(1), 1317438); lib. bdg. (978-0-7787-4795-6(6), 1317438) Crabtree Publishing Co.

Camille, Diana, illus. A Treasury of Goops: Timeless Manners for Every Generation. 2005. Orig. Title: Goops & How to Be Them. (ENG.). 45p. (J). 19.95 (978-0-9712368-5-1(2), 8006811891) Goops Unlimited.

Candell, Arianna. Mind Your Manners: In School. Curto, Rosa M., illus. 2005. (Mind Your Manners Ser.). (ENG.). 36p. (J). pap. 6.99 (978-0-7641-3166-0(4)) Barron's Educational Series, Inc.

Carbone, Courtney. How to Be a Princess (Disney Princess) RH Disney Staff, illus. 2015. (Ultimate Handbook Ser.). (ENG.). 64p. (J). (gr. 1-4). 9.99 (978-0-7364-3415-7(1), RH/Disney) Random Hse. Children's Bks.

Carlson, Amie. Manners Matter! 2016. (Lift-The-Flap Ser.). (ENG., Illus.). 16p. (J). pap. 7.99 (978-1-4964-1580-6(9), Tyndale Kids) Tyndale Hse. Pubs.

Chancellor, Deborah. Good Manners. 2009. (Now We Know About... Ser.). (ENG., Illus.). 24p. (J). (gr. k-3). pap. (978-0-7787-4736-9(0)); lib. bdg. (978-0-7787-4719-2(0)) Crabtree Publishing Co.

A Child's Book of Manners. 2014. (Happy Day Ser.). (ENG., Illus.). 16p. (J). pap. 2.49 (978-1-4143-9462-6(4)) Tyndale Hse. Pubs.

Ciovacco, Justine. Etiquette As a Guest & at Parties. 2016. (Etiquette Rules! Ser.). 00048p. (J). (gr. 6-6). pap. 11.75 (978-1-4994-6484-9(3), Rosen Central); lib. bdg. 31.75 (978-1-4994-6486-3(X)) Rosen Publishing Group, Inc., The.

Coan, Sharon. Using Good Manners (Foundations) 2015. (TIME for KIDS(r) Nonfiction Readers Ser.). (ENG., Illus.). 12p. (gr. k-k). 4.99 (978-1-4938-2064-1(8)) Teacher Created Materials, Inc.

Cornwall, Phyllis. Mind Your Manners Online. 2012. (Explorer Junior Library: Information Explorer Junior Ser.). (ENG., Illus.). 24p. (J). (gr. 1-4). pap. 12.79 (978-1-61080-388-5(4), 201325); lib. bdg. 28.50 (978-1-61080-363-2(9), 201260) Cherry Lake Publishing.

—Super Smart Information Strategies: Online Etiquette & Safety. 2010. (Explorer Library: Information Explorer Ser.). (ENG.). 32p. (gr. 4-8). lib. bdg. 28.50 (978-1-60279-956-1(3), 200637) Cherry Lake Publishing.

David C. Cook Publishing Company Staff. Manners. 2003. (My Jesus Pocket Bks.). (Illus.). 32p. (J). pap., pap. 8.90 (978-1-55513-128-9(X), 155513128X) Cook, David C.

DiCicco, Sue, illus. Totally Monster: Manners. 2013. (Totally Monsters Ser.). (ENG.). 14p. (J). (gr. -1). 12.95 (978-1-60710-645-6(0), Silver Dolphin Bks.) Readerlink Distribution Services, LLC.

Doering Tourville, Amanda. Manners in the Lunchroom. Lensch, Chris, illus. 2009. (Way to Be!: Manners Ser.). 24p. (gr. -1-2). pap. 2.76 (978-1-4048-6051-3(7), Nonfiction Picture Bks.) Picture Window Bks.

—Manners on the School Bus, 1 vol. Lensch, Chris, illus. 2009. (Way to Be!: Manners Ser.). 24p. (gr. -1-2). (ENG.). pap. 7.95 (978-1-4048-5312-6(X)); pap. 2.76 (978-1-4048-6052-0(5), Nonfiction Picture Bks.) Picture Window Bks.

—Manners with a Library Book, 1 vol. Lensch, Chris, illus. 2009. (Way to Be!: Manners Ser.). (ENG.). 24p. (gr. -1-2). pap. 7.95 (978-1-4048-5315-7(4)) Picture Window Bks.

Dunlop, Cliff. Flights of Fancy: An Anthology. 2009. 224p. pap. (978-1-932252-56-9(8)) Creative Continuum, Inc.

Etiquette Rules! 2016. (Etiquette Rules! Ser.). 00048p. (J). (gr. 6-6). 190.50 (978-1-5081-7365-6(6), Rosen Central) Rosen Publishing Group, Inc., The.

Evans, Lezlie. Can You Greet the Whole Wide World? 12 Common Phrases in 12 Different Languages. Roche, Denis, illus. 2010. 32p. (J). (gr. k-3). pap. (978-0-618-81519-7(8)) Houghton Mifflin Harcourt Trade & Reference Pubs.

Excuse Me! (Book of Manners... Ser.). 32p. (978-1-4054-9479-3(4)) Parragon, Inc.

Felix, Rebecca. Good Manners with Your Friends, 1 vol. 2014. (Good Manners in Relationships Ser.). (ENG., Illus.). 32p. (J). (gr. -1-4). lib. bdg. 28.50 (978-1-62402-025-4(9), Looking Glass Library) Magic Wagon.

—Good Manners with Your Parents, 1 vol. 2014. (Good Manners in Relationships Ser.). (ENG., Illus.). 32p. (J). (gr. -1-4). lib. bdg. 28.50 (978-1-62402-026-1(7), Looking Glass Library) Magic Wagon.

—Good Manners with Your Siblings, 1 vol. 2014. (Good Manners in Relationships Ser.). (ENG., Illus.). 32p. (J). (gr. -1-4). lib. bdg. 28.50 (978-1-62402-027-8(5), Looking Glass Library) Magic Wagon.

—Good Manners with Your Teachers, 1 vol. 2014. (Good Manners in Relationships Ser.). (ENG., Illus.). 32p. (YA). (gr. -1-4). lib. bdg. 28.50 (978-1-62402-028-5(3), Looking Glass Library) Magic Wagon.

Finn, Carrie. Manners at School, 1 vol. Lensch, Chris, illus. (Way to Be!: Manners Ser.). 2010. (ENG.). 32p. 8.99 (978-1-4048-6511-2(X)) 2009. 24p. (gr. -1-2). pap. 0.63 (978-1-4048-5991-3(8)) 2009. 24p. (gr. -1-2). pap. 2.76 (978-1-4048-6050-6(9)) Picture Window Bks. (Nonfiction Picture Bks.).

—Manners at School [Scholastic]. Lensch, Chris, illus. 2010. (Way to Be!: Manners Ser.). 24p. pap. 0.55 (978-1-4048-6584-6(5), Nonfiction Picture Bks.) Picture Window Bks.

—Manners at the Table. Lensch, Chris, illus. (Way to Be!: Manners Ser.). 24p. (gr. -1-2). 2009. pap. 0.63 (978-1-4048-5992-0(6), Nonfiction Picture Bks.) 2007. (ENG.). per. 7.95 (978-1-4048-3553-5(9)) Picture Window Bks.

—Manners in Public. Lensch, Chris, illus. (Way to Be!: Manners Ser.). 24p. (gr. -1-2). 2009. pap. 0.63 (978-1-4048-5993-7(4), Nonfiction Picture Bks.) 2007. (ENG.). per. 7.95 (978-1-4048-3555-9(5)) Picture Window Bks.

—Manners in the Library. Lensch, Chris, illus. (Way to Be!: Manners Ser.). 24p. (gr. -1-2). 2009. pap. 0.63 (978-1-4048-5994-4(2), Nonfiction Picture Bks.) 2007. (ENG.). lib. bdg. 26.65 (978-1-4048-3152-0(5), 1265722) 2007. (ENG.). per. 7.95 (978-1-4048-3557-3(1), 1265722) Picture Window Bks.

—Manners on the Playground. Lensch, Chris, illus. 2009. (Way to Be!: Manners Ser.). 24p. (gr. -1-2). pap. 2.76 (978-1-4048-6053-7(3)); pap. 0.63 (978-1-4048-5995-1(0)) Picture Window Bks. (Nonfiction Picture Bks.).

—Manners on the Telephone. Lensch, Chris, illus. (Way to Be!: Manners Ser.). 24p. (gr. -1-2). 2009. pap. 0.63 (978-1-4048-5996-8(9), Nonfiction Picture Bks.) 2007. (ENG.). per. 7.95 (978-1-4048-3561-0(X)) Picture Window Bks.

Finn, Carrie & Picture Window Books Staff. Manners on the Playground, 1 vol. Lensch, Chris, illus. 2007. (Way to Be!: Manners Ser.). (ENG.). 24p. (gr. -1-2). 26.65 (978-1-4048-3154-4(1)) Picture Window Bks.

First Graphics: Manners Matter. 2011. (First Graphics: Manners Matter Ser.). (ENG.). 24p. (gr. 1-2). pap. 142.80 (978-1-4296-6396-0(0)) Capstone Press of Coughlan Cos.

First Graphics: Manners Matter. 2010. (First Graphics: Manners Matter Ser.). (ENG.). 24p. (gr. 1-2). lib. bdg. 95.96 (978-1-4296-5334-3(5)) Capstone Press of Coughlan Cos.

Fontes, Justine. Rude Ralph: A Rookie Reader. Jordan, Charles, illus. 2011. (Rookie Ready to Learn Ser.). 40p. (J). pap. 5.95 (978-0-531-26711-0(3)); (gr. -1-k). lib. bdg. 23.00 (978-0-531-26529-1(3)) Scholastic Library Publishing. (Children's Pr.).

Fulcher, Roz. Mind Your Manners! 2013. (Dover Coloring Bks.). (ENG.). 48p. (J). (gr. 1-5). pap. 4.99 (978-0-486-49883-6(2)) Dover Pubns., Inc.

Furgang, Kathy. Netiquette: A Student's Guide to Digital Etiquette. 2010. (Digital & Information Literacy Ser.). (ENG.). 48p. (YA). pap. 11.75 (978-1-4488-0597-6(X)); lib. bdg. 29.25 (978-1-4358-9429-7(4)) Rosen Publishing Group, Inc., The. (Rosen Reference).

Gray, Carolyn. All about M. E. Manners & Etiquette for TWEENS & TEENS. 2007. 28p. (J). pap. 12.95 (978-1-60131-010-1(2)) Big Tent Bks.

Grisinger Reilly, Teresa Kathryn. Etiquette Lessons Part I,Part II: Girls & Boys at the Table, Teens at the Table, Table Manners, American Cotillion. 2004. 146p. (YA). pap. 13.95 (978-0-595-33198-7(X)) iUniverse, Inc.

—Etiquette Lessons Vol. 2: Modern Manners. 2007. 132p. (gr. 4-7). per. 13.95 (978-0-595-44020-7(7)) iUniverse, Inc.

Hallinan, P. K. Let's Be Patient. 2008. (ENG., Illus.). 28p. (J). bds. 7.95 (978-0-8249-6586-0(8), Ideal Pubns.) Worthy Publishing.

—Let's Be Thankful. Hallinan, P. K., illus. 2008. (ENG., Illus.). 24p. (J). (gr. -1-2). 8.99 (978-0-8249-5604-2(4), Ideal Pubns.) Worthy Publishing.

—Let's Be Thankful. 2005. (ENG., Illus.). 28p. (J). bds. 7.95 (978-0-8249-6585-3(X), Ideal Pubns.) Worthy Publishing.

Heos, Bridget. Manners at a Friend's House. Longhi, Katya, illus. 2015. (Monstrous Manners Ser.). (ENG.). 24p. (J). (gr. 1-3). 19.95 (978-1-60753-743-4(5)) Amicus Publishing.

—Manners at a Restaurant. Longhi, Katya, illus. 2015. (Monstrous Manners Ser.). (ENG.). 24p. (J). (gr. 1-3). 19.95 (978-1-60753-744-1(3)) Amicus Publishing.

—Manners at School. Longhi, Katya, illus. 2015. (Monstrous Manners Ser.). (ENG.). 24p. (J). (gr. 1-3). 19.95 (978-1-60753-745-8(1)) Amicus Publishing.

—Manners at the Store. Longhi, Katya, illus. 2015. (Monstrous Manners Ser.). (ENG.). 24p. (J). (gr. 1-3). 19.95 (978-1-60753-746-5(X)) Amicus Publishing.

—Manners on Vacation. Longhi, Katya, illus. 2015. (Monstrous Manners Ser.). (ENG.). 24p. (J). (gr. 1-3). 19.95 (978-1-60753-747-2(8)) Amicus Publishing.

—Manners with Technology. Longhi, Katya, illus. 2015. (Monstrous Manners Ser.). (ENG.). 24p. (J). (gr. 1-3). 19.95 (978-1-60753-748-9(6)) Amicus Publishing.

Hillings, Phyllis & Hillings, Pamela. A Web of Good Manners - Grown-up Manners for Young People. Mumper-Drumm, Heidrun, illus. (J). 19.95 (978-0-9725364-1-7(8)) Perrin & Kabel Publishing.

Holyoke, Nancy. Manners. 2013. (Smart Girl's Guide Ser.). lib. bdg. 24.50 (978-0-606-34733-4(X), Turtleback) Turtleback Bks.

—A Smart Girl's Guide to Manners: The Secrets to Grace, Confidence, & Being Your Best. Watkins, Michelle, ed. Mingus, Cathi, illus. 2005. (ENG.). 120p. (J). (gr. 3). per. 9.95 (978-1-58485-983-3(0), American Girl) American Girl Publishing, Inc.

Hurt, Avery. Cross-Cultural Etiquette. 2016. (Etiquette Rules! Ser.). 00048p. (J). (gr. 6-6). pap. 11.75 (978-1-4994-6496-2(7)) Rosen Publishing Group, Inc., The.

Ingalls, Ann. Being a Good Guest. Rooney, Ronnie, illus. 2012. (Good Manners Ser.). (ENG.). 24p. (J). (gr. -1-2). 27.07 (978-1-61473-224-2(8), 204919) Child's World, Inc., The.

—Good Manners During Special Occasions. Rooney, Ronnie, illus. 2012. (Good Manners Ser.). (ENG.). 24p. (J). (gr. -1-2). 27.07 (978-1-61473-229-7(9), 204921) Child's World, Inc., The.

—Good Manners in Public. Rooney, Ronnie, illus. 2012. (Good Manners Ser.). (ENG.). 24p. (J). (gr. -1-2). 27.07 (978-1-61473-226-6(4), 204922) Child's World, Inc., The.

—Good Manners on the Phone. Rooney, Ronnie, illus. 2012. (Good Manners Ser.). (ENG.). 24p. (J). (gr. -1-2). 27.07 (978-1-61473-228-0(0), 204923) Child's World, Inc., The.

—Good Manners with Family. Rooney, Ronnie, illus. 2012. (Good Manners Ser.). (ENG.). 24p. (J). (gr. -1-2). 27.07 (978-1-61473-227-3(2), 204924) Child's World, Inc., The.

—Good Table Manners. Rooney, Ronnie, illus. 2012. (Good Manners Ser.). (ENG.). 24p. (J). (gr. -1-2). 27.07 (978-1-61473-230-3(2), 204925) Child's World, Inc., The.

Jean Marie. Me, My Peeps & My Manners. 2012. 48p. pap. 21.95 (978-1-4685-0604-4(8)) AuthorHouse.

Jeffrie, Sally. A Guide to Being a Goddess. 2009. (Best at Everything Ser.). (ENG.). 128p. (J). (gr. 3-7). 9.99 (978-0-545-08537-3(3)) Scholastic, Inc.

Johnson, Dorothea, et al. Children's Tea & Etiquette: Brewing Good Manners in Young Minds. Peterson, Dawn, illus. 2014. (ENG.). 40p. (J). (gr. 2-5). 19.95 (978-0-9663478-9-0(7)) Benjamin Pr.

Jones, Grace. My Manners. 2017. (Illus.). 24p. (J). **(978-0-7787-3260-0(6))** Crabtree Publishing Co.

Joslin, Sesyle. What Do You Say, Dear? Sendak, Maurice, illus. (J). (gr. k-2). 14.45 incl. audio (978-0-8045-6525-7(2), SAC 6525) Spoken Arts, Inc.

Keller, Irene. Thingamajig Book of Manners. Keller, Dick, illus. 2005. (ENG.). 30p. (J). bds. 7.95 (978-0-8249-6590-7(6), Ideal Pubns.) Worthy Publishing.

Kelley, Michelle. Rules, Rules, Rules. 2007. (ENG., Illus.). 16p. (gr. k-2). 28.50 (978-1-60472-111-9(1)) Rourke Educational Media.

Klein, Rebecca T. Frequently Asked Questions about Texting, Sexting, & Flaming. 2012. (FAQ: Teen Life Ser.). (ENG., Illus.). 64p. (J). (gr. 7-12). lib. bdg. 31.95 (978-1-4488-8331-8(8)) Rosen Publishing Group, Inc., The.

Larsen, Carolyn. Being Nice to Others: A Book about Rudeness. O'Connor, Tim, illus. 2016. (Growing God's Kids Ser.). (ENG.). 32p. (J). pap. 4.99 (978-0-8010-0957-0(X)) Baker Bks.

Leaf, Munro. How to Be: How to Grow up to Be Healthy, Wealthy, & Wise. 2015. (Rizzoli Classics Ser.). (ENG., Illus.). 104p. (J). (-k). 19.95 (978-0-7893-3109-0(8)) Universe Publishing.

—Manners Can Be Fun. 2004. (ENG., Illus.). 48p. (J). (gr. -1-3). 14.95 (978-0-7893-1061-3(9)) Universe Publishing.

Leigh, Susan K. God, I Need to Talk to You About Bad Manners. 2005. (J). 1.19 (978-0-7586-0813-0(6)) Concordia Publishing Hse.

Lester, Brian. R U In? Using Technology Responsibly, 1 vol. 2010. (Essential Health: a Guy's Guide Ser.). (ENG.). 112p. (J). (gr. 6-12). lib. bdg. 35.64 (978-1-61613-543-0(3)) ABDO Publishing Co.

Lindeen, Mary. Playing Together. 2015. (BeginningtoRead Ser.). (ENG., Illus.). 32p. (J). (gr. k-2). pap. 11.94 (978-1-60357-762-5(9)) Norwood Hse. Pr.

Lindeen, Mary & Peggy, Nille. Playing Together. 2015. (BeginningtoRead Ser.). (ENG., Illus.). 32p. (J). (gr. k-2). lib. bdg. 22.60 (978-1-59953-702-3(8)) Norwood Hse. Pr.

Loria, Laura. Etiquette among Friends. 2016. (Etiquette Rules! Ser.). 00048p. (J). (gr. 6-6). pap. 11.75 (978-1-4994-6488-7(6)) Rosen Publishing Group, Inc., The.

Maggiore, Evana. FASHION FENG SHUI the Power of Dressing with Intention: Transform Your Look & Your Life! 2007. (Illus.). 204p. 24.95 (978-0-9675941-9-4(7)) Mansion Publishing, Ltd.

Marlowe, Christie. Presenting Yourself: Business Manners, Personality, & Etiquette. 2013. (Earning $50,000 - $100,000 with a High School Diploma or Less Ser.: 14). 64p. (J). (gr. 7-18). 22.95 (978-1-4222-2898-2(3)) Mason Crest.

Marsico, Katie. Good Manners at Home, 1 vol. Haslam, John, illus. 2009. (Good Manners Matter! Ser.). (ENG.). 32p. (J). (gr. -1-2). 28.50 (978-1-60270-607-1(7)) Magic Wagon.

—Good Manners at School, 1 vol. Haslam, John, illus. 2009. (Good Manners Matter! Ser.). (ENG.). 32p. (J). (gr. -1-2). 28.50 (978-1-60270-608-8(5)) Magic Wagon.

—Good Manners in a Restaurant, 1 vol. Haslam, John, illus. 2009. (Good Manners Matter! Ser.). (ENG.). 32p. (J). (gr. -1-2). 28.50 (978-1-60270-609-5(3)) Magic Wagon.

—Good Manners in Public, 1 vol. Haslam, John, illus. 2009. (Good Manners Matter! Ser.). (ENG.). 32p. (J). (gr. -1-2). 28.50 (978-1-60270-610-1(7)) Magic Wagon.

—Good Manners on the Phone, 1 vol. Haslam, John, illus. 2009. (Good Manners Matter! Ser.). (ENG.). 32p. (J). (gr. -1-2). 28.50 (978-1-60270-611-8(5)) Magic Wagon.

—Good Manners on the Playground, 1 vol. Haslam, John, illus. 2009. (Good Manners Matter! Ser.). (ENG.). 32p. (J). (gr. -1-2). 28.50 (978-1-60270-612-5(3)) Magic Wagon.

—Plan Ahead! 2012. (21st Century Basic Skills Library: Kids Can Make Manners Count Ser.). (ENG.). 24p. (gr. k-3). 22.79 (978-1-61080-436-3(8), 202046); pap. 12.79 (978-1-61080-610-7(7), 202220) Cherry Lake Publishing.

—Play Fair! 2012. (21st Century Basic Skills Library: Kids Can Make Manners Count Ser.). (ENG.). 24p. (gr. k-3). 22.79 (978-1-61080-438-7(4), 202048); pap. 12.79 (978-1-61080-612-1(3), 202222) Cherry Lake Publishing.

—Please & Thank You! 2012. (21st Century Basic Skills Library: Kids Can Make Manners Count Ser.). (ENG.). 24p. (gr. k-3). 22.79 (978-1-61080-433-2(3), 202043); pap. 12.79 (978-1-61080-607-7(7), 202217) Cherry Lake Publishing.

—Put Your Stuff Away! 2012. (21st Century Basic Skills Library: Kids Can Make Manners Count Ser.). (ENG.). 24p. (gr. k-3). 22.79 (978-1-61080-439-4(2), 202049); pap. 12.79 (978-1-61080-613-8(1), 202223) Cherry Lake Publishing.

Martin, Melissa. Tessie Tames Her Tongue: A Book about Learning When to Talk & When to Listen. Lehman, Charles, illus. 2017. (ENG.). 48p. (J). (gr. k-4). 14.99 **(978-1-63198-133-3(1))** Free Spirit Publishing, Inc.

Meiners, Cheri J. Respect & Take Care of Things. Johnson, Meredith, illus. 2004. (Learning to Get Along(r) Ser.). (ENG.). 40p. (J). (gr. -1-3). pap. 10.95 (978-1-57542-160-5(7)) Free Spirit Publishing, Inc.

Miller, Connie Colwell. Monster Knows Excuse Me, 1 vol. Chiodi, Maira, illus. 2014. (Monster Knows Manners Ser.). (ENG.). 24p. (gr. -1-2). pap. 6.95 (978-1-4795-2953-7(2)); lib. bdg. 24.65 (978-1-4795-2202-6(3)) Picture Window Bks.

Miller, Shannon. Be Nice Online. 2013. (Internet DOs & DON'ts Ser.). (Illus.). 24p. (J). (gr. k-2). 22.60 (978-1-4777-0756-2(5)); pap. 49.50 (978-1-4777-1567-3(3)); (ENG., pap. 8.25 (978-1-4777-1566-6(5)) Rosen Publishing Group, Inc., The. (PowerKids Pr.).

—Don't Share Your Address Online. 2013. (Internet DOs & DON'ts Ser.). (Illus.). 24p. (J). (gr. k-2). 22.60 (978-1-4777-1536-9(3)); pap. 49.50 (978-1-4777-1559-8(2)); (ENG., pap. 8.25 (978-1-4777-1558-1(4)) Rosen Publishing Group, Inc., The. (PowerKids Pr.).

Mortensen, Lori. Manners Matter in the Classroom. Hunt, Lisa, illus. (First Graphics: Manners Matter Ser.). (ENG.). 24p. (gr. 1-2). 2011. pap. 35.70 (978-1-4296-6392-2(8)) 2010. lib. bdg. 23.99 (978-1-4296-5333-6(7)) Capstone Press of Coughlan Cos.

—Manners Matter in the Library. Hunt, Lisa, illus. 2011. (First Graphics: Manners Matter Ser.). (ENG.). 24p. (gr. 1-2). pap. 35.70 (978-1-4296-6393-9(6)) Capstone Press of Coughlan Cos.

—Manners Matter on a Field Trip. Hunt, Lisa, illus. (First Graphics: Manners Matter Ser.). (ENG.). 24p. (gr. 1-2). 2011. pap. 35.70 (978-1-4296-6394-6(4)) 2010. lib. bdg. 23.99 (978-1-4296-5331-2(0)) Capstone Press of Coughlan Cos.

—Manners Matter on the Playground. Hunt, Lisa, illus. (First Graphics: Manners Matter Ser.). (ENG.). 24p. (gr. 1-2). 2011. pap. 35.70 (978-1-4296-6395-3(2)) 2010. lib. bdg. 23.99 (978-1-4296-5332-9(9)) Capstone Press of Coughlan Cos.

Nagle, Jeanne. Etiquette at Home. 2016. (Etiquette Rules! Ser.). 00048p. (J). (gr. 6-6). pap. 11.75 (978-1-4994-6480-1(0), Rosen Central) Rosen Publishing Group, Inc., The.

Napier, Tanya. Mini Manners: Hello & Goodbye! Saying Sorry! Please & Thank You!: 3 Books Teach 3 New Skills. Anderson, Airlie, illus. 2005. (J). **(978-0-316-74064-7(0))** Little Brown & Co.

National Geographic Learning Staff. Families Share, Vol. 3932. 2012. (ENG., Illus.). 16p. (C). (gr. -1-2). pap. 5.95 (978-1-57471-137-0(7), 3932) National Geographic School Publishing, Inc.

—Helping Mom & Dad, Vol. 4419. 2012. (ENG., Illus.). 16p. (C). (gr. -1-2). pap. 5.95 (978-1-57471-342-8(6), 4419) National Geographic School Publishing, Inc.

Nelson, Maria. I Am Polite. 2013. (Kids of Character Ser.). 24p. (J). (gr. 1-3). 22.60 (978-1-4339-9025-0(3)); pap. 48.90 (978-1-4339-9027-4(X)) Stevens, Gareth Publishing LLLP.

—Saying Please & Thank You. 2015. (J). (978-1-4824-1728-9(6)) Stevens, Gareth Publishing LLLP.

Nunn, Daniel & Smith, Sian. Manners at Home, 1 vol. 2012. (Oh, Behave! Ser.). (ENG.). 24p. (gr. -1-1). lib. bdg. 22.65 (978-1-4329-6636-2(7), Acorn) Heinemann-Raintree.

—Manners at School, 1 vol. 2012. (Oh, Behave! Ser.). (ENG.). 24p. (gr. -1-1). lib. bdg. 22.65 (978-1-4329-6637-9(5), Acorn) Heinemann-Raintree.

—Manners at the Table, 1 vol. 2012. (Oh, Behave! Ser.). (ENG.). 24p. (gr. -1-1). lib. bdg. 22.65 (978-1-4329-6638-6(3), Acorn) Heinemann-Raintree.

Orr, Tamra. I Have Been Shamed on the Internet, Now What? 2016. (Teen Life 411 Ser.). 00112p. (J). (gr. 7-7). 37.10 (978-1-5081-7202-4(1)) Rosen Publishing Group, Inc., The.

Packer, Alex J. How Rude! The Teen Guide to Good Manners, Proper Behavior, & Not Grossing People Out. 2nd rev. ed. 2014. (ENG., Illus.). 480p. (YA). pap. 23.99 (978-1-57542-454-5(1)) Free Spirit Publishing, Inc.

Plattner, Josh. Body Manners, 1 vol. 2016. (ENG., Illus.). 24p. (J). (978-1-62403-714-6(3)) ABDO Publishing Co.

—Manners at Mealtime, 1 vol. 2016. (ENG., Illus.). 24p. (J). (978-1-62403-715-3(1)) ABDO Publishing Co.

—Manners Out & About, 1 vol. 2016. (ENG., Illus.). 24p. (J). (978-1-62403-717-7(8)) ABDO Publishing Co.

—Manners with Family, 1 vol. 2016. (ENG., Illus.). 24p. (J). (978-1-62403-718-4(6)) ABDO Publishing Co.

—Manners with Friends, 1 vol. 2016. (ENG., Illus.). 24p. (J). (978-1-62403-719-1(4)) ABDO Publishing Co.

Post, Peggy & Senning, Cindy Post. Emily's Everyday Manners. Björkman, Steve, illus. 2006. 32p. (J). (gr. -1-2). (ENG.). 16.99 (978-0-06-076174-5(1)); lib. bdg. 17.89 (978-0-06-076177-6(6)) HarperCollins Pubs. (Collins).

—The Guide to Good Manners for Kids. Björkman, Steve, illus. 2006. 144p. (J). (gr. 4-8). reprint ed. 16.00 (978-1-4223-5621-0(3)) DIANE Publishing Co.

—Teen Manners: From Malls to Meals to Messaging & Beyond. 2007. (Illus.). 134p. (YA). (gr. 8-12). lib. bdg. 16.89 (978-0-06-088199-3(2)) HarperCollins Pubs.

—Teen Manners: From Malls to Meals to Messaging & Beyond. Watts, Sharon, illus. 2007. (ENG.). 144p. (YA). (gr. 8-12). 17.99 (978-0-06-088198-6(4), HarperTeen) HarperCollins Pubs.

Post, Peggy, et al. Emily's Magic Words: Please, Thank You, & More. Landry, Leo, illus. 2007. (ENG.). 32p. (J). (gr. -1-1). 15.99 (978-0-06-111680-3(7), Collins) HarperCollins Pubs.

Raatma, Lucia. Good Manners. 2013. (True Book(tm), a — Guides to Life Ser.). (ENG.). 48p. (J). 31.00 (978-0-531-25523-0(9)); pap. 6.95 (978-0-531-23923-0(3)) Scholastic Library Publishing. (Children's Pr.).

Richey, Lisa. Manners to Go. 2003. (J). 22.95 (978-0-9743210-0-4(1)) Eat Your Peas Publishing.

Rondina, Catherine. Rudeness: Deal with It If You Please, 1 vol. Workman, Dan, illus. 2005. (Lorimer Deal with It Ser.). (ENG.). 32p. (J). (gr. 4-6). 12.95 (978-1-55028-870-4(9),

The check digit for ISBN-10 appears in parentheses after the full ISBN-13

9781550288704) Lorimer, James & Co., Ltd., Pubs. CAN. Dist: Casemate Pubs. & Bk. Distributors, LLC.

Rosenthal, Amy Krouse. Cookies: Bite-Size Life Lessons. Dyer, Jane, illus. 2006. (ENG.). 40p. (J). (gr. -1-1). 12.99 (978-0-06-058081-0(X)) HarperCollins Pubs.

Rosson, Denise & Tumblacer, Margaret. Tadpole Dreams Etiquette & Good Manners Program Handbook. 2005. 25p. (J). 12.95 (978-0-9769320-1-7(6), ss0002) Smith, S. Pubns.

Santorum, Karen. Everyday Graces: Child's Book of Good Manners. Torode, Sam, illus. 2003. (Foundations Ser.). 407p. (J). 25.00 (978-1-932236-09-5(0)) ISI Bks.

Senning, Cindy Post & Post, Emily. Emily Post's the Guide to Good Manners for Kids. Björkman, Steve, illus. 2004. (ENG.). 144p. (J). (gr. 3-7). 16.99 (978-0-06-057196-2(9)) HarperCollins Pubs.

Sesame Street Staff, creator. Sesame Street: My First Manners Boxed Set. 2011. 72p. (J). bds. 12.99 (978-1-60745-238-6(3)) Flying Frog Pubs.

Snow, Todd. Manners Are Important. Hartman, Carrie, illus. 2007. (ENG.). 24p. (J). (gr. -1-3). bds. 7.99 (978-1-934277-05-8(3)) Marn Green Publishing, Inc.

—Manners Are Important for You & Me. Hartman, Carrie, illus. 2007. (ENG.). 32p. (J). pap. 10.99 (978-1-934277-04-1(5)) Marn Green Publishing, Inc.

Steinkraus, Kyla. May I Please? 2012. (ENG.). 24p. (gr. k-2). pap. 8.95 (978-1-61810-271-3(0)) Rourke Educational Media.

Tadpole Dreams Etiquette & Good Manners Curriculum. 2005. (YA). ring bd. 249.95 (978-0-9769320-0-0(8), ss0001) Smith, S. Pubns.

Teen Etiquette: Lessons in Gracious Living. 2004. (YA). tchr. ed., spiral bd. (978-0-9758940-0-2(5)) Whitaker, Thurston Information Services, LLC.

Teen Etiquette: Lessons in Gracious Living Student Workbook. 2004. (YA). (978-0-9758940-1-9(3)) Whitaker, Thurston Information Services, LLC.

Thornborough, Kathy. Greetings & Phrases. Petelinsek, Kathleen, illus. 2014. (Talking Hands Ser.). (ENG.). 24p. (J). (gr. k-3). 25.64 (978-1-62687-320-9(8), 207160) Child's World, Inc., The.

Truesdell, Ann. Being Respectful Online. Petelinsek, Kathleen, illus. 2013. (Explorer Junior Library: Information Explorer Junior Ser.). (ENG.). 24p. (J). (gr. 1-4). 28.50 (978-1-62431-131-4(8), 202844); pap. 12.79 (978-1-62431-263-2(2), 202846) Cherry Lake Publishing.

Unstead, Sue. Say Hello. 2004. (J). (978-1-84301-151-4(4), Two-Can Publishing) T&N Children's Publishing.

Verdick, Elizabeth. Don't Behave Like You Live in a Cave. Mark, Steve, illus. 2010. (Laugh & Learn Ser.). (ENG.). 128p. (J). (gr. 3-7). pap. 8.95 (978-1-57542-353-1(7)) Free Spirit Publishing, Inc.

—Listening Time. Heinlen, Marieka, illus. 2008. (Toddler Tools Ser.). (ENG.). 24p. (J). (gr. k — 1). bds. 7.95 (978-1-57542-301-2(4)) Free Spirit Publishing, Inc.

—Manners Time. Heinlen, Marieka, illus. 2009. (Toddler Tools Ser.). (ENG.). 24p. (J). (gr. -1). 7.95 (978-1-57542-313-5(8), 1301012) Free Spirit Publishing, Inc.

—Manners Time / Los Buenos Modales. Heinlen, Marieka, illus. 2016. (Toddler Tools Ser.). (ENG & SPA.). 24p. (J). bds. 7.95 (978-1-63198-120-3(X)) Free Spirit Publishing, Inc.

—Mealtime. Heinlen, Marieka, illus. 2011. (Toddler Tools Ser.). (ENG.). 24p. (J). (gr. k — 1). 7.95 (978-1-57542-366-1(9)) Free Spirit Publishing, Inc.

—Noses Are Not for Picking. Heinlen, Marieka, illus. 2014. (Best Behavior Ser.). (ENG.). 24p. (J). bds. 7.95 (978-1-57542-471-2(1)) Free Spirit Publishing, Inc.

—Words Are Not for Hurting. Heinlen, Marieka, illus. (Best Behavior Ser.). 40p. (J). (gr. -1-2). 2009. (SPA & ENG.). pap. 11.95 (978-1-57542-312-8(X)) 2004. (ENG.). pap. 11.95 (978-1-57542-156-8(9)) Free Spirit Publishing, Inc.

Verdick, Elizabeth & Agassi, Martine. Words Are Not for Hurting (Las Palabras No Son para Lastimar) Heinlen, Marieka, illus. 2009. (Best Behavior Ser.). (SPA, ENG & MUL.). 24p. (J). (gr. -1). 7.95 (978-1-57542-311-1(1)) Free Spirit Publishing, Inc.

Vestergaard, Hope. Potty Animals: What to Know When You've Gotta Go! Petrone, Valeria, illus. 2010. (ENG.). 32p. (J). (gr. -1-1). 14.95 (978-1-4027-5996-3(7)) Sterling Publishing Co., Inc.

Washington, George. George Washington's Rules to Live By: How to Sit, Stand, Smile, & Be Cool! a Good Manners Guide from the Father of Our Country. Harper, Fred, illus. 2014. (ENG.). 128p. (J). (gr. 3-7). 14.99 (978-1-4263-1500-8(7), National Geographic Children's Bks.) National Geographic Society.

Whitaker, Ginger. Teen Etiquette. 2004. (YA). stu. ed., spiral bd., wbk. ed. (978-0-9758940-3-3(X)) Whitaker, Thurston Information Services, LLC.

Willems, Mo. Time to Say Please! Willems, Mo, illus. 2005. (ENG., Illus.). 40p. (J). (gr. -1-k). 16.99 (978-0-7868-5293-2(3)) Hyperion Pr.

Yaun, Katherine. Etiquette at School. 2016. (Etiquette Rules! Ser.). 00048p. (J). (gr. 6-6). 31.75 (978-1-4994-6478-8(9)); pap. 11.75 (978-1-4994-6476-4(2), Rosen Central) Rosen Publishing Group, Inc., The.

Yearling, Tricia. How Do I Use Social Networking? 2015. (Online Smarts Ser.). (ENG.). 32p. (J). (gr. 3-4). pap. 10.52 (978-0-7660-6856-8(0)) Enslow Pubs., Inc.

Young, Mariabelle & Buchwald, Ann. White Gloves & Party Manners. Christiane, illus. 2012. (ENG.). 65p. (J). (gr. 4-7). pap. 14.95 (978-0-88331-000-7(7)) Luce, Robert B. Pubs.

ETIQUETTE—FICTION

Antony, Steve. Please, Mr. Panda. 2014. (ENG.). 32p. (J). (gr. -1-k). 16.99 (978-0-545-78892-2(7), Scholastic Pr.) Scholastic, Inc.

Arps, Melissa & Lagonegro, Melissa. Polite as a Princess. Harding, Niall & Harchy, Atelier Philippe, illus. 2006. (Pictureback(R) Ser.). (ENG.). 24p. (J). (gr. -1-2). pap. 3.99 (978-0-7364-2367-0(2), RH/Disney) Random Hse. Children's Bks.

Bailey, Catherine. Mind Your Monsters. Vidal, Oriol, illus. 2015. (ENG.). 40p. (J). (gr. -1-2). 14.95 (978-1-4549-1103-6(4)) Sterling Publishing Co., Inc.

Banks, Jane Whelen. Loveable Liam: Affirmations for a Perfectly Imperfect Child. 2008. (ENG., Illus.). 32p. 12.95 (978-1-84310-899-3(2), 7171) Kingsley, Jessica Pubs. GBR. Dist: Macmillan Distribution Ltd.

Banks, Jane Whelen & Whelen-Banks, Jane. Liam Says "Sorry" Repairing an Encounter Gone Sour. 2008. (ENG., Illus.). 32p. 12.95 (978-1-84310-903-7(4), 5373) Kingsley, Jessica Pubs. GBR. Dist: Macmillan Distribution Ltd.

Bauer, Marion Dane. Thank You for Me! Sweet, Melissa & Stephenson, Kristina, illus. 2010. (ENG.). 32p. (J). (gr. -1-3). 17.99 (978-0-689-85788-1(8), Simon & Schuster Bks. For Young Readers) Simon & Schuster Bks. For Young Readers.

Bell, Juliet Clare & Chapman, Laura Kate. The Kite Princess. 2012. (ENG., Illus.). (J). 16.99 (978-1-84686-803-0(3)) Barefoot Bks., Inc.

Benenfeld, Rikki. I Go Visiting. 2007. (Toddler Experience Ser.). (Illus.). 32p. (J). (gr. -1-k). 10.95 (978-1-929628-33-9(1)) Hachai Publishing.

Berenstain, Jan & Berenstain, Mike. The Berenstain Bears Say Please & Thank You. Berenstain, Jan & Berenstain, Mike, illus. 2011. (Berenstain Bears Ser.). (ENG., Illus.). 32p. (J). (gr. -1-3). 12.99 (978-0-06-057437-6(2)) HarperCollins Pubs.

Berenstain, Mike, illus. The Berenstain Bears' Please & Thank You Book. 2015. (J). (978-0-8249-1945-0(9), Ideal Pubns.) Worthy Publishing.

Bracken, Beth. Terrible, Awful, Horrible Manners!, 1 vol. Watson, Richard, illus. 2011. (Little Boost Ser.). (ENG.). 32p. (gr. k-3). lib. bdg. 23.99 (978-1-4048-6653-9(1), Little Boost) Picture Window Bks.

—Terrible, Awful, Horrible Manners, 1 vol. Watson, Richard, illus. 2012. (Little Boost Ser.). (ENG.). 32p. (gr. k-3). 7.95 (978-1-4048-7419-0(4), Little Boost) Picture Window Bks.

Bradman, Tony. Snow White & the Magic Mirror, 1 vol. Warburton, Sarah, illus. 2014. (After Happily Ever After Ser.). (ENG.). 56p. (gr. 2-3). lib. bdg. 25.32 (978-1-4342-7950-7(2), After Happily Ever After) Stone Arch Bks.

Bridwell, Norman. Clifford's Manners. 2011. (Clifford's Big Ideas Ser.). (ENG., Illus.). (gr. -1). 14.00 (978-1-60686-963-5(9)) Perfection Learning Corp.

—Clifford's Manners. 2010. (Clifford 8x8 Ser.). (ENG., Illus.). 32p. (J). (gr. -1-3). pap. 3.99 (978-0-545-21586-2(2), Cartwheel Bks.) Scholastic, Inc.

Brooks, Noel. Sometimes I Hear Bad Words. 2011. 28p. pap. 15.99 (978-1-4568-1225-6(4)) Xlibris Corp.

Brown, Margaret Wise. Margaret Wise Brown's Manners. 2017. (Little Golden Book Ser.). (ENG., Illus.). 24p. (J). (-k). 4.99 (978-1-101-93973-4(7), Golden Bks.) Random Hse. Children's Bks.

Brown, Peter. Mr. Tiger Goes Wild. 2013. (ENG.). 48p. (J). 126.00 (978-0-316-25551-6(3)); (Illus.). (gr. -1-1). 18.00 (978-0-316-20063-9(8)) Little, Brown Bks. for Young Readers.

Buzzeo, Toni. One Cool Friend. 2014. (KOR.). 32p. (J). (gr. k-3). (978-89-7938-087-3(9)) Dasan Publishing Hse.

—One Cool Friend. Small, David, illus. 2012. (ENG.). 32p. (J). (gr. k-3). 17.99 (978-0-8037-3413-5(1), Dial Bks) Penguin Young Readers Group.

—One Cool Friend. Small, David, illus. 2015. DVD 59.95 (978-0-545-67553-6(7)) Scholastic, Inc.

Carriger, Gail. Curtsies & Conspiracies. (Finishing School Ser.: 2). (ENG.). (YA). (gr. 7-17). 2014. 336p. pap. 10.00 (978-0-316-19020-6(9)) 2013. 320p. 18.00 (978-0-316-19011-4(X)) Little, Brown Bks. for Young Readers.

—Etiquette & Espionage. 2013. (Finishing School Ser.: 1). (ENG.). 320p. (YA). (gr. 7-17). 18.99 (978-0-316-19008-4(X)) Little Brown & Co.

—Etiquette & Espionage. 2013. (Finishing School Ser.: 1). (ENG.). 336p. (YA). (gr. 7-17). pap. 10.99 (978-0-316-19010-7(1)) Little, Brown Bks. for Young Readers.

—Manners & Mutiny. 2015. (Finishing School Ser.: 4). (ENG., Illus.). 336p. (YA). (gr. 7-17). 18.00 (978-0-316-19028-2(4)) Little, Brown Bks. for Young Readers.

—Manners & Mutiny. 2016. (Finishing School Ser.: 4). (ENG., Illus.). 352p. (YA). (gr. 7-17). pap. 10.99 (978-0-316-19029-9(2)) Little, Brown Bks. for Young Readers.

—Waistcoats & Weaponry. 2014. (Finishing School Ser.: 3). (ENG.). 304p. (YA). (gr. 7-17). 18.00 (978-0-316-19027-5(6)) Little Brown & Co.

—Waistcoats & Weaponry. 2015. (Finishing School Ser.: 3). (ENG.). 320p. (YA). (gr. 7-17). pap. 10.00 (978-0-316-19025-1(X)) Little, Brown Bks. for Young Readers.

Cashman, Mary & Whipple, Cynthia. Merrilee Mannerly & Her Magnificent Manners. Johnson, Meredith, illus. 2010. (J). 16.99 (978-0-615-36448-3(9)) Pink&Brown Publishing, LLP.

Cazet, Denys. Elvis the Rooster & the Magic Words. Cazet, Denys, illus. 2004. (I Can Read Bks.). (ENG., Illus.). 48p. (J). (gr. k-3). 15.99 (978-0-06-000509-2(2)) HarperCollins Pubs.

—Elvis the Rooster & the Magic Words, 4 bks., Set. unabr. ed. 2006. (Readalongs for Beginning Readers Ser.). (J). (gr. -1-3). pap. 31.95 incl. audio compact disk (978-1-59519-693-4(5)); (Illus.). pap. 29.95 incl. audio (978-1-59519-692-7(7)) Live Oak Media.

Chapman, Cheryl. Pass the Fritters, Critters. Roth, Susan L., illus. 2007. (ENG.). 40p. (J). (gr. -1-2). 11.99 (978-1-4169-6160-4(7), Simon & Schuster/Paula Wiseman Bks.) Simon & Schuster/Paula Wiseman Bks.

Cole, Babette. El Libro de Etiqueta de Lady Lupina. 2003. (Babette Cole Ser.).Tr. of Lady Lupin's Book of Etiquett. (SPA.). (J). 18.95 (978-84-233-3337-0(X)) Ediciones Destino ESP. Dist: Planeta Publishing Corp.

Cook, Julia. Decibella & Her 6-Inch Voice. DuFalla, Anita, illus. 2014. (ENG.). 32p. (J). pap. 10.95 (978-1-934490-58-7(X)) Boys Town Pr.

—Personal Space Camp. Hartman, Carrie, illus. 2009. 32p. (J). 15.95 (978-1-931636-89-6(3)) National Ctr. For Youth Issues.

—Table Talk: A Book about Table Manners. DuFalla, Anita, illus. 2016. (Building Relationships Ser.: Vol. 7). (ENG.). 32p. (J). pap. 10.95 (978-1-934490-97-6(0)) Boys Town Pr.

Cook, Julia. Technology Tail: A Digital Footprint Story. DuFalla, Anita, illus. 2017. (ENG.). 32p. (J). (gr. 1-6). pap. 10.95 (978-1-944882-13-6(8)) Boys Town Pr.

Cooney, Doug. I Know Who Likes You. Bernardin, James, illus. 2005. (ENG.). 224p. (J). (gr. 3-7). pap. 10.99 (978-1-4169-0261-4(9), Simon & Schuster Bks. For Young Readers) Simon & Schuster Bks. For Young Readers.

Cosgrove, Stephen. The Grumpling. James, Robin, illus. 2003. (Serendipity Bks.). (Orig.). (J). (gr. k-4). 12.65 (978-0-7569-5259-4(X)) Perfection Learning Corp.

Cullen, Lynn. Dear Mr. Washington. Carpenter, Nancy, illus. 2015. (ENG.). 32p. (J). (gr. k-3). 16.99 (978-0-8037-3038-0(1), Dial Bks) Penguin Young Readers Group.

Cuyler, Margery. Please Say Please! Penguin's Guide to Manners. Hillenbrand, Will, illus. 2005. (J). (978-0-439-67874-2(9)) Scholastic, Inc.

Dahl, Michael. Bear Says Thank You, 1 vol. Vidal, Oriol, illus. 2011. (Hello Genius Ser.). (ENG.). 20p. (gr. 1-2). bds. 7.99 (978-1-4048-6786-4(4)) Picture Window Bks.

—Hello Genius, 1 vol. 2014. (Hello Genius Ser.). (ENG.). 20p. (gr. 1-2). bds. 31.96 (978-1-4795-5809-4(5)) Picture Window Bks.

—Hippo Says "Excuse Me" Vidal, Oriol, illus. 2011. (Hello Genius Ser.). (ENG.). 20p. (gr. 1-2). bds. 7.99 (978-1-4048-6787-1(2)) Picture Window Bks.

—Mouse Says Sorry, 1 vol. Vidal, Oriol, illus. 2011. (Hello Genius Ser.). (ENG.). 20p. (gr. 1-2). bds. 7.99 (978-1-4048-6789-5(9)) Picture Window Bks.

—Penguin Says Please, 1 vol. Vidal, Oriol, illus. 2011. (Hello Genius Ser.). (ENG.). 20p. (gr. 1-2). bds. 7.99 (978-1-4048-6788-8(0)) Picture Window Bks.

—Playdate for Panda. Vidal, Oriol, illus. 2016. (Hello Genius Ser.). (ENG.). 20p. (gr. 1-2). bds. 7.99 (978-1-4795-8741-4(9)) Picture Window Bks.

Davick, Linda. Say Hello! Davick, Linda, illus. 2015. (ENG., Illus.). 40p. (J). (gr. -1-3). 17.99 (978-1-4814-2867-5(5), Beach Lane Bks.) Beach Lane Bks.

Davidson, Susanna. Princess Handbook. Gordon, Mike, illus. 2006. 80p. (J). (gr. 3-7). 12.99 (978-0-7945-1329-0(8), Usborne) EDC Publishing.

Demas, Corinne & Roehrig, Artemis. Are Pirates Polite? Catrow, David, illus. 2016. (ENG.). 40p. (J). (gr. -1-k). 16.99 (978-0-545-62874-7(1)) Scholastic, Inc.

Dewdney, Anna. Nobunny's Perfect. (ENG.). 32p. (J). (gr. -1-k). 2012. bds. 6.99 (978-0-670-01408-8(7), Viking Books for Young Readers) 2010. pap. 6.99 (978-0-14-241533-7(2), Puffin Books) Penguin Young Readers Group.

Disney Sofia the First, Disney Sofia. Disney Sofia the First: Please & Thank You: Your Guide to Becoming the Perfect Princess! 2015. (ENG.). 32p. (J). (gr. -1-1). 10.99 (978-0-7944-3279-9(4), Reader's Digest Children's Bks.) Studio Fun International.

Donaldson, Julia. Chocolate Mousse for Greedy Goose. Sharratt, Nick, illus. (ENG.). (J). 2015. 18p. (-k). bds. 9.99 (978-1-4472-8788-9(6))2. 2006. 24p. (gr. -1-k). pap. 8.99 (978-1-4050-2190-6(X)) Pan Macmillan GBR. Dist: Independent Pubs. Group.

Dowd, Tara. No More Boogers Book. 2009. 16p. 11.50 (978-0-615-26122-5(1)) Pick It Publishing.

Dube, Pierrette. How to Become a Perfect Princess in Five Days. Melanson, Luc, illus. 2009. (Rainy Day Readers Ser.). 32p. (J). (gr. -1-3). 22.60 (978-1-60754-376-3(1)) Windmill Bks.

Dyan, Penelope. When Touching Is Bad. Dyan, Penelope, illus. 2013. (Illus.). 34p. pap. 11.95 (978-1-61477-088-6(3)) Bellissima Publishing, LLC.

Dyckman, Ame. Tea Party Rules. Campbell, K. G., illus. 2013. (ENG.). 36p. (J). (gr. -1-k). 16.99 (978-0-670-78501-8(6), Viking Books for Young Readers) Penguin Young Readers Group.

Evans, Cordelia. OLIVIA & the Fancy Party. Johnson, Shane L., illus. 2014. (Olivia TV Tie-In Ser.). (ENG.). 24p. (J). (gr. -1-2). pap. 3.99 (978-1-4814-0364-1(8), Simon Spotlight) Simon Spotlight.

—Olivia & the Fancy Party. 2014. (Olivia 8x8 Ser.). lib. bdg. 13.55 (978-0-606-35762-3(9)) Turtleback Bks.

Fenske, Jonathan. Plankton Is Pushy. Fenske, Jonathan, illus. 2017. (ENG., Illus.). 40p. (J). (gr. -1-k). 14.99 (978-1-338-09896-9(9), Scholastic Pr.) Scholastic, Inc.

Ferguson, Sarah. Tea for Ruby. Glasser, Robin Preiss, illus. 2008. (ENG.). 40p. (J). (gr. -1-3). 16.99 (978-1-4169-5419-4(8), Simon & Schuster/Paula Wiseman Bks.) Simon & Schuster/Paula Wiseman Bks.

Ferguson, The Duchess of York, Sarah, The Duchess of York. Tea for Ruby. Glasser, Robin Preiss, illus. 2012. (ENG.). 40p. (J). (gr. -1-3). pap. 7.99 (978-1-4169-5420-0(1), Simon & Schuster/Paula Wiseman Bks.) Simon & Schuster/Paula Wiseman Bks.

Finley, Ucal P. A Proper Place for Boogers. Stroud, Brenda D., illus. 2011. 54p. pap. 12.95 (978-0-9834307-0-4(5)) G Publishing LLC.

Fontes, Justine. Henry's Turn. Hefferan, Rob, illus. 2004. (J). (978-1-59336-004-7(5)); pap. (978-1-59336-005-4(3)) Mondo Publishing.

—Please Say Please, Grumpy Bunny! McQueen, Lucinda, illus. 2007. (J). (978-0-439-02012-1(3)) Scholastic, Inc.

Fontes, Justine & Jordan, Charles. Daniel el Descortés. Jordan, Charles, illus. 2011. (Rookie Ready to Learn Español Ser.). (SPA., Illus.). 40p. (J). pap. 5.95 (978-0-531-26790-5(3)); lib. bdg. 23.00 (978-0-531-26122-4(0)) Scholastic Library Publishing. (Children's Pr.).

Friedman, Laurie. Back-to-School Rules. Murfin, Teresa, illus. 2011. (Carolrhoda Picture Books Ser.). (ENG.). 32p. (J). (gr. k-3). lib. bdg. 16.95 (978-0-7613-6070-4(0)) Lerner Publishing Group.

Galan, Ana. iQué Cosas Dice Mi Abuela! 2013. (SPA.). 32p. (J). (gr. -1-3). 3.99 (978-0-545-32863-0(2), Scholastic en Espanol) Scholastic, Inc.

Gallo, Tina, adapted by. Master of Manners. 2016. (Kung Fu Panda TV Ser.). (ENG., Illus.). 24p. (J). (gr. -1-2). pap. 3.99 (978-1-4814-6183-2(4), Simon Spotlight) Simon Spotlight.

Gassman, Julie. Do Not Take Your Dragon to Dinner. Elkerton, Andy, illus. 2017. (Fiction Picture Bks.). (ENG.). 32p. (gr. -1-2). lib. bdg. 21.32 (978-1-4795-9888-5(7)) Picture Window Bks.

Geis, Patricia. Let's Eat! Folch, Sergio, illus. 2009. (Good Habits with Coco & Tula Ser.). 16p. (J). (gr. -1-k). bds. 11.40 (978-1-60754-411-1(3)) Windmill Bks.

Gillis, Jennifer Blizin. What Do You Say? Losa, Ann, illus. 2006. (Reader's Clubhouse Level 2 Reader Ser.). (ENG.). 24p. (J). (gr. 1-4). pap. 3.99 (978-0-7641-3298-8(9)) Barron's Educational Series, Inc.

Gilson, Jamie. My Teacher Is an Idiom. Tilley, Debbie, illus. 2015. (ENG.). 144p. (J). (gr. 1-4). 16.99 (978-0-544-05680-0(9)) Houghton Mifflin Harcourt Publishing Co.

Goldberg, Malky. What Else Do I Say? A Lift the Flap Book. Argoff, Patti, illus. 2007. (J). (gr. -1-k). bds. 9.95 (978-1-929628-34-6(X)) Hachai Publishing.

Gramma Debbie. The Poop Book. 2012. 32p. pap. 19.99 (978-1-4772-5287-1(8)) AuthorHouse.

Gribble, Julie. Bubblegum Princess. Hanson, Lori, illus. 2013. 32p. (J). 16.99 (978-0-9890914-0-4(6)) NY Media Works, LLC.

Hallinan, P. K. I'm Thankful Each Day!/Doy Gracias Cada Dia! 2008. (ENG., Illus.). 32p. (J). (gr. -1-3). per. 4.99 (978-0-8249-5583-0(8), Ideal Pubns.) Worthy Publishing.

—Let's Be Polite. (ENG., Illus.). (J). 2008. 24p. (gr. -1-3). lib. bdg. 8.99 (978-0-8249-5579-3(X)) 2004. 26p. bds. 8.75 (978-0-8249-6562-4(0)) Worthy Publishing. (Ideal Pubns.).

Harcrow, Melissa. Where're Your Manners, William? 2008. 26p. pap. 24.95 (978-1-60563-470-8(0)) America Star Bks.

Hargreaves, Roger. Little Miss Scary. 2009. (Mr. Men & Little Miss Ser.). (ENG.). 32p. (J). (gr. -1-2). mass mkt. 4.99 (978-0-8431-3568-8(9), Price Stern Sloan) Penguin Young Readers Group.

—Mr. Rude. 2009. (Mr. Men & Little Miss Ser.). (ENG.). 32p. (J). (gr. -1-2). mass mkt. 4.99 (978-0-8431-3569-5(7), Price Stern Sloan) Penguin Young Readers Group.

Harvey, Keith & Beard, Lauren. Say Please, Louise! A Story of a Little Girl With Monstrous Manners. 2015. (ENG., Illus.). 24p. pap. 8.99 (978-1-84135-921-2(1)) Award Pubns. Ltd. GBR. Dist: Parkwest Pubns., Inc.

Heim, Alastair. No Tooting at Tea. Not, Sara, illus. 2017. (ENG.). 40p. (J). (gr. -1-3). 16.99 (978-0-544-77474-2(4), Clarion Bks.) Houghton Mifflin Harcourt Trade & Reference Pubs.

Heneghan, Judith. Brandon's So Bossy! Hughes, Jack, illus. 2016. (Dragon School Ser.). (ENG.). 32p. (J). (gr. -1-k). pap. (978-0-7502-8357-1(2), Wayland) Hachette Children's Group GBR. Dist: Hachette Bk. Group.

—Ruby's So Rude! Hughes, Jack, illus. 2016. (Dragon School Ser.). (ENG.). 32p. (J). (gr. -1-k). pap. (978-0-7502-8356-4(4), Wayland) Hachette Children's Group GBR. Dist: Hachette Bk. Group.

Hill, Terri-Sue. I'm Thankful. 2012. 26p. pap. 13.95 (978-1-4525-4739-8(4)) Balboa Pr.

Hoban, Russell. The Little Brute Family. Hoban, Lillian, illus. 2011. (My Readers Ser.). (ENG.). 40p. (J). (gr. k-2). pap. 3.99 (978-0-312-56373-8(6), 9780312563738) Square Fish.

Holm, Jennifer L. An Adventure. 2010. (Boston Jane Ser.: No. 1). (ENG.). 272p. (J). (gr. 3-7). 7.99 (978-0-375-86204-5(8), Yearling) Random Hse. Children's Bks.

—Wilderness Days. 2004. (Boston Jane Ser.: No. 2). 256p. (J). (gr. 5-18). pap. 5.99 (978-0-06-440881-3(7), Harper Trophy) HarperCollins Pubs.

—Wilderness Days. unabr. ed. 2004. (Boston Jane Ser.: No. 2). 288p. (J). (gr. 5-9). pap. 38.00 incl. audio (978-0-8072-0787-1(X), S YA 307 SP, Listening Library) Random Hse. Audio Publishing Group.

—Wilderness Days. 2010. (Boston Jane Ser.: No. 2). (ENG.). 256p. (J). (gr. 3-7). pap. 7.99 (978-0-375-86205-2(6), Yearling) Random Hse. Children's Bks.

Holt, Kimberly Willis. Dinner with the Highbrows. Brooker, Kyrsten, illus. 2014. (ENG.). 36p. (J). (gr. -1-2). 17.99 (978-0-8050-8088-9(0), 9780805080889, Holt, Henry & Co. Bks. For Young Readers) Holt, Henry & Co.

Idle, Molly. Tea Rex. 2013. (ENG., Illus.). 36p. (J). (gr. -1-k). 16.99 (978-0-670-01430-9(3), Viking Books for Young Readers) Penguin Young Readers Group.

InSeon, Chae. Handy Mr. Hippo. YouDae, Kim, illus. rev. ed. 2014. (MySELF Bookshelf Ser.). (ENG.). 32p. (J). (gr. k-2). pap. 11.94 (978-1-60357-661-1(4)); lib. bdg. 25.27 (978-1-59953-652-1(8)) Norwood Hse. Pr.

Isadora, Rachel. Say Hello! Isadora, Rachel, illus. 2010. (ENG., Illus.). 32p. (J). (gr. -1-k). 16.99 (978-0-399-25230-3(4), G.P. Putnam's Sons Books for Young Readers) Penguin Young Readers Group.

Jones, Christianne C. Lacey Walker, Nonstop Talker, 1 vol. Watson, Richard, illus. 2012. (Little Boost Ser.). (ENG.). 32p. (gr. k-3). lib. bdg. 23.99 (978-1-4048-6796-3(1), Little Boost) Picture Window Bks.

Joosse, Barbara M. Please Is a Good Word to Say. Plecas, Jennifer, illus. 2007. (J). (978-1-4287-4649-7(8), Philomel) Penguin Publishing Group.

Katz, Alan. Don't Say That Word! Catrow, David, illus. 2007. (ENG.). 32p. (J). (gr. -1-3). 17.99 (978-0-689-86971-6(1), McElderry, Margaret K. Bks.) McElderry, Margaret K. Bks.

Katz, Karen. No Biting! 2011. (ENG.). 24p. (J). (gr. -1-k). mass mkt. 4.99 (978-0-448-45581-5(1), Grosset & Dunlap) Penguin Young Readers Group.

Kimmelman, Leslie. Everybody Bonjours! McMenemy, Sarah, illus. 2008. (ENG.). 40p. (J). (gr. -1-2). 16.99 (978-0-375-84443-0(0), Knopf Bks. for Young Readers) Random Hse. Children's Bks.

Kipling, Rudyard. How the Rhinoceros Got His Skin: The Graphic Novel, 1 vol. Rodriguez, Pedro, illus. 2012. (Graphic Spin Ser.). (ENG.). 40p. (gr. 1-3). pap. 5.95 (978-1-4342-3882-5(2), Graphic Revolve) Stone Arch Bks.

—How the Rhinoceros Got His Skin: The Graphic Novel, 1 vol. Rodríguez, Pedro, illus. 2012. (Graphic Spin Ser.). (ENG.). 40p. (gr. 1-3). lib. bdg. 23.99 (978-1-4342-3025-6(2), Graphic Revolve) Stone Arch Bks.

Knowlton, Laurie Lazzaro. Pirates Don't Say Please!, 1 vol. Tans, Adrian, illus. 2012. (ENG.). 32p. (J). (gr. k-3). 16.99 (978-1-58980-982-6(3)) Pelican Publishing Co., Inc.

Koffsky, Ann D., illus. Shabbat Shalom, Hey! 2015. (ENG.). 24p. (J). (gr. -1-k). lib. bdg. 16.95 (978-1-4677-4917-6(6), Kar-Ben Publishing) Lerner Publishing Group.

LeCron, Helen Cowles. The Animal Etiquette Book of Rhymes. Day, Maurice, illus. 2014. (ENG.). 64p. (J). (gr. 1-5). pap. 4.99 (978-0-486-78234-8(4)) Dover Pubns., Inc.

little bee books, little bee & Powell, Richard. If You See a Cow. Martin Larranaga, Ana, illus. 2015. (ENG.). 12p. (J). (gr. -1-k). 4.99 (978-1-4998-0112-5(2)) Little Bee Books Inc.

Livermore, Edward. Phebe the Blackberry Girl. 2004. reprint ed. pap. 15.95 (978-1-4191-4126-3(0)); pap. 1.99

(978-1-4192-4126-0(5)); pap. 15.95 (978-1-4191-4126-3(0)) Kessinger Publishing, LLC.

Long, Ethan. Hi! 2015. (Animal Sounds Ser.). (ENG., Illus.). 20p. (J). (gr. -1 — 1). bds. 7.95 (978-1-4197-1365-1(5)) Abrams, Inc.

—Thank You! 2016. (Animal Sounds Ser.). (ENG., Illus.). 20p. (J). (gr. -1 — 1). bds. 7.95 (978-1-4197-1364-4(7)) Abrams, Inc.

Lorraine, Loria. Wild about Manners. Spino, Bonnie, illus. 2013. 36p. pap. 11.95 (978-0-9881889-0-7(2)) Piccolo Tales.

MacDonald, Alan. Worms!, 1 vol. Roberts, David, illus. 2013. (Dirty Bertie Ser.). (ENG.). 112p. (gr. 1-3). pap. 4.95 (978-1-4342-4823-7(2)); lib. bdg. 25.32 (978-1-4342-4619-6(1)) Stone Arch Bks.

Manushkin, Fran & Lyon, Tammie. La Jefa Del Mundo, 1 vol. Lyon, Tammie, illus. 2012. (Katie Woo en Español Ser.). (SPA., Illus.). 32p. (gr. k-2). pap. 6.95 (978-1-4048-7679-8(0)); lib. bdg. 21.32 (978-1-4048-7523-4(9)) Picture Window Bks.

McConduit, Denise Walter. D. J. & the Debutante Ball, 1 vol. Henriquez, Emile F., illus. 2004. (D. J. Ser.). (ENG.). 32p. (J). (gr. k-3). 16.99 (978-1-58980-173-8(3)) Pelican Publishing Co., Inc.

McElligott, Matthew. The Lion's Share. McElligott, Matthew, illus. 2012. (ENG., Illus.). 40p. (J). (gr. k-8). pap. 8.99 (978-0-8027-2360-4(8), 9780802723604, Bloomsbury USA Childrens) Bloomsbury Publishing USA.

—The Lion's Share: A Tale of Halving Cake & Eating It, Too. McElligott, Matthew, illus. 2009. (ENG., Illus.). 32p. (J). (gr. k-3). 16.99 (978-0-8027-9768-1(7), 9780802797681, Bloomsbury USA Childrens) Bloomsbury Publishing USA.

Modan, Rutu. Maya Makes a Mess. Modan, Rutu, illus. 2012. (ENG., Illus.). 32p. (J). (gr. -1-3). 12.95 (978-1-935179-17-7(9)) TOON Books / RAW Junior, LLC.

Morgan, Michaela. Never Shake a Rattlesnake. Sharratt, Nick, illus. 2016. (ENG.). 32p. (J). (gr. -1-k). pap. 8.99 (978-1-5098-1704-7(2)) Pan Macmillan GBR. Dist: Independent Pubs. Group.

Morris, Jennifer E. May I Please Have a Cookie? Morris, Jennifer E., illus. (ENG., Illus.). (J). 2015. 30p. (— 1). bds. 6.99 (978-0-545-81502-4(9)) 2005. 32p. (gr. -1-3). per. 4.99 (978-0-439-73819-4(9)) Scholastic, Inc. (Cartwheel Bks.).

Mountbatten-Windsor, Sarah & York, Sarah. Tea for Ruby. 2012. lib. bdg. 18.40 (978-0-606-26884-4(7), Turtleback) Turtleback Bks.

Mullarkey, Lisa. TJ Zaps the One-Upper: Stopping One-Upping & Cell Phone Bullying #2, 1 vol. LaCoste, Gary, illus. 2012. (TJ Trapper, Bully Zapper Ser.). (ENG.). 80p. (J). (gr. 2-5). lib. bdg. 27.07 (978-1-61641-906-6(7), Calico Chapter Bks) Magic Wagon.

Murphy, Mary. Say Hello Like This. Murphy, Mary, illus. 2014. (ENG., Illus.). 32p. (J). (-k). 12.99 (978-0-7636-6951-5(2)) Candlewick Pr.

Murphy, Stuart J. Freda Says Please. Jones, Tim, illus. 2013. (I See I Learn Ser.). (ENG.). 32p. (J). (-k). pap. 6.95 (978-1-58089-475-3(5)) Charlesbridge Publishing, Inc.

—Freda Says Please. Jones, Tim, illus. 2013. (I See I Learn Ser.). (ENG.). 32p. (J). (-k). lib. bdg. 14.95 (978-1-58089-474-6(7)) Charlesbridge Publishing, Inc.

Ohanesian, Diane. The ABCs of Thanks & Please. Chamberlain, Margaret, illus. 2011. (J). (978-0-545-37962-5(8)) Scholastic, Inc.

One Cool Friend. 2014. pap. 16.99 (978-0-545-67554-3(5)) Scholastic, Inc.

O'Reilly, Bill & Patterson, James. Give Please a Chance. 2016. (ENG., Illus.). 56p. (J). (gr. -1-1). 17.99 (978-0-316-27688-7(X), Jimmy Patterson) Little Brown & Co.

Parker, David. I Show Respect! Fiammenghi, Gioia, illus. 2004. (J). pap. (978-0-439-62809-9(1)) Scholastic, Inc.

Parker, Emma & Renaud, Marguerite. Chatterbox Caz. 2010. (Illus.). 16p. pap. (978-1-877561-77-1(0)) First Edition Ltd.

Pearson, Peter. How to Eat an Airplane. Catusanu, Mircea, illus. 2016. (Bad Idea Book Club Ser.). 40p. (J). (gr. -1-3). 17.99 (978-0-06-232062-9(9)) HarperCollins Pubs.

Please! Thank You! (Book of Manners... Ser.). 32p. (978-1-4054-9481-6(6)) Parragon, Inc.

Primavera, Elise. Louise the Big Cheese & the Ooh-la-La Charm School. Goode, Diane, illus. 2012. (ENG.). 40p. (J). (gr. k-3). 16.99 (978-1-4424-0599-6(6), Simon & Schuster/Paula Wiseman Bks.) Simon & Schuster/Paula Wiseman Bks.

Prom Etiquette Scrapbook. 2011. 128p. 8.99 (978-1-4231-4566-0(6)) Disney Pr.

Publications International Ltd. Staff, ed. Disney Princess: Please & Thank You. 2011. 12p. (J). bds. (978-1-4508-0399-1(7)) Phoenix International Publications, Inc.

—Please & Thank You. 2010. 20p. (J). bds. 10.98 (978-1-60553-439-8(0), PIL Kids) Publications International, Ltd.

Rao, Lisa & Gallo, Tina. It's Nice to Be Nice! Giles, Mike, illus. 2009. (Yo Gabba Gabba! Ser.). (ENG.). 24p. (J). (gr. -1-2). pap. 3.99 (978-1-4169-7866-4(6), Simon Spotlight) Simon Spotlight.

Rosenberg, Madelyn. How to Behave at a Tea Party. Ross, Heather, illus. 2014. (ENG.). 32p. (J). (gr. -1-3). 17.99 (978-0-06-227926-2(2), Tegen, Katherine Bks) HarperCollins Pubs.

Rovetch, L. Bob & Whitman, Emily. Sir Henry, the Polite Knight. Barnard, Bryn, illus. 2006. (J). (978-1-58987-204-2(5)) Kindermusik International.

Roxbee Cox, Phil. Say Please, Louise! Tyler, Jenny, ed. McCafferty, Jan, illus. 2007. (Cautionary Tales Ser.). 23p. (J). (gr. -1-3). per. 7.99 (978-0-7945-1726-7(9), Usborne) EDC Publishing.

Samoun, Abigail. How Hippo Says Hello! Watts, Sarah, illus. 2014. (Little Traveler Ser.). (ENG.). 22p. (J). (gr. -1-k). bds. 6.95 (978-1-4549-0820-3(3)) Sterling Publishing Co., Inc.

Sandra De Mos. Cleo's Playground Adventure. 2009. 40p. pap. 16.99 (978-1-4389-2049-8(0)) AuthorHouse.

Scarry, Richard. Richard Scarry's Polite Elephant. Scarry, Richard, illus. 2016. (Little Golden Book Ser.). (ENG., Illus.). 24p. (J). (-k). 4.99 (978-1-101-93090-8(X), Golden Bks.) Random Hse. Children's Bks.

—School Bus Box Set. 2014. (Illus.). (J). (978-0-7641-6690-7(5)) Barron's Educational Series, Inc.

Sierra, Judy. Mind Your Manners, B. B. Wolf. Seibold, J. Otto, illus. 2012. (ENG.). 40p. (J). (gr. -1-2). pap. 7.99 (978-0-307-93101-6(3), Dragonfly Bks.) Random Hse. Children's Bks.

—Mind Your Manners, B. B. Wolf. 2012. lib. bdg. 18.40 (978-0-606-26784-7(0), Turtleback) Turtleback Bks.

Sparklington, Madame & Gurney, Stella. Princess: A Glittering Guide for Young Ladies. Allsop, Sophie et al, illus. 2006. (Genuine & Moste Authentic Guide Ser.: 2). (ENG.). 26p. (J). (gr. 1-4). 15.99 (978-0-7636-3430-8(1)) Candlewick Pr.

Spurr, Elizabeth. Monsters, Mind Your Manners! Scales, Simon, illus. 2012. (J). 34.28 (978-1-61913-124-8(2)) Weigl Pubs., Inc.

Stein, David Ezra. The Nice Book. Stein, David Ezra, illus. 2013. (ENG., Illus.). 32p. (J). (gr. -1 — 1). bds. 6.99 (978-0-399-16534-4(7), Nancy Paulsen Books) Penguin Young Readers Group.

Stepanian, Isabel H. Cat Paws Through History: Ko-Ko the Cat Meets Napoleon Bonaparte. 2011. 292p. (gr. -1). 28.00 (978-1-4389-5811-8(0)); pap. 18.00 (978-1-4389-5810-1(2)) AuthorHouse.

Sutton, Joe. Wanda & the Oblahlahs. 2011. (ENG., Illus.). 24p. (J). 19.95 (978-1-936474-11-0(5), 9f8eb10d-b421-4222-af62-15e42efdae23) Bright Sky Pr.

Tayleur, Karen. Manners! Staying Out of Trouble with David Mortimore Baxter. Garvey, Brann, illus. 2007. (David Mortimore Baxter Ser.). (ENG.). 88p. (gr. 2-3). per. 6.05 (978-1-59889-207-9(X), David Mortimore Baxter) Stone Arch Bks.

Tekavec, Heather. Manners Are Not for Monkeys. Huyck, David, illus. 2016. (ENG.). 32p. (J). (gr. -1-2). 16.95 (978-1-77138-051-5(9)) Kids Can Pr., Ltd. CAN. Dist: Hachette Bk. Group.

Tiger Tales, ed. Hello Baby! Ward, Sarah, illus. 2016. (To Baby with Love Ser.). (ENG.). 10p. (J). (gr. -1 — 1). bds. 9.99 (978-1-58925-210-3(1)) Tiger Tales.

Tym, Kate. Be Nice. 2008. (Manners Ser.). (Illus.). 24p. (J). (gr. -1-1). lib. bdg. 16.95 (978-1-59566-590-4(0)) QEB Publishing Inc.

Watkins, Rowboat. Rude Cakes. 2015. (ENG., Illus.). 40p. (J). (gr. -1-k). 16.99 (978-1-4521-3851-0(6)) Chronicle Bks. LLC.

Watt, Mélanie. You're Finally Here! Watt, Mélanie, illus. 2011. (Illus.). 40p. (J). (gr. -1-1). 15.99 (978-1-4231-3486-2(9)) Hyperion Pr.

Wax, Wendy. What Do You Say? Please & Thank You. Dillard, Sarah, illus. 2005. (J). (978-1-58987-108-3(1)) Kindermusik International.

Webster, Kyle T. Please Say Please! Webster, Kyle T., illus. 2016. (ENG., Illus.). 32p. (J). (gr. -1-k). 17.99 (978-0-545-84485-7(1), Scholastic Pr.) Scholastic, Inc.

Wells, Rosemary. Say Hello, Sophie! 2017. (ENG., Illus.). 32p. (J). (— 1). 17.99 (978-1-101-99925-7(X), Viking Books for Young Readers) Penguin Young Readers Group.

Weston Woods Staff, creator. How Do Dinosaurs Eat Their Food? 2011. 38.75 (978-0-439-02740-3(3)); 18.95 (978-0-439-02748-9(9)) Weston Woods Studios, Inc.

Whelen-Banks, Jane. Liam Says "Hi" Learning to Greet a Friend. 2008. (ENG., Illus.). 32p. 12.95 (978-1-84310-901-3(8), 5372) Kingsley, Jessica Pubs. GBR. Dist: Macmillan Distribution Ltd.

Willems, Mo. The Duckling Gets a Cookie!? Willems, Mo, illus. 2012. (ENG., Illus.). 40p. (J). (gr. -1-k). 16.99 (978-1-4231-5128-9(3)) Hyperion Pr.

Wisk, Dar. Grandma Always Says... 2012. 36p. pap. 14.99 (978-1-4575-1539-2(3)) Dog Ear Publishing, LLC.

Wood, Maryrose. The Hidden Gallery, Bk. 2. Klassen, Jon, illus. 2012. (Incorrigible Children of Ashton Place Ser.: Bk. 2). (ENG.). 320p. (J). (gr. 3-7). pap. 6.99 (978-0-06-179113-0(X)) HarperCollins Pubs.

—The Mysterious Howling. Klassen, Jon, illus. 2011. (Incorrigible Children of Ashton Place Ser.: Bk. 1). (ENG.). 288p. (J). (gr. 3-7). pap. 6.99 (978-0-06-179110-9(5)) HarperCollins Pubs.

Yolen, Jane. How Do Dinosaurs Eat Their Food? Teague, Mark, illus. 2005. (How Do Dinosaurs...? Ser.). (ENG.). 40p. (J). (gr. -1-k). 16.99 (978-0-439-24102-1(2), Blue Sky Pr., The) Scholastic, Inc.

Yolen, Jane, narrated by. How Do Dinosaurs Eat Their Food? 2011. (J). (gr. -1-2). 29.95 (978-0-439-02746-5(2)) Weston Woods Studios, Inc.

ETIQUETTE—POETRY

Burgess, Gelett. Goops & How to Be Them: A Manual of Manners for Polite Infants. 2005. (ENG., Illus.). 108p. 17.95 (978-1-55709-392-9(X)) Applewood Bks.

Greenberg, David. Don't Forget Your Etiquette! The Essential Guide to Misbehavior. Westcott, Nadine Bernard, illus. 2006. (ENG.). 40p. (J). (gr. 1-4). 17.99 (978-0-374-34990-5(8), 9780374349905, Farrar, Straus & Giroux (BYR)) Farrar, Straus & Giroux.

Hazen, Barbara Shook. The Please & Thank You Book. Chollat, Emilie, illus. 2009. (Little Golden Book Ser.). (ENG.). 24p. (J). (gr. -1-2). 4.99 (978-0-375-84758-5(8), Golden Bks.) Random Hse. Children's Bks.

Ross, Barbara, ed. Goops & How to Be Them: A Manual of Manners for Polite Children. 2nd ed. 2007. (ENG., Illus.). 96p. (J). (gr. 1-8). reprint ed. 14.95 (978-0-9712368-0-6(1)) Goops Unlimited.

EUCLID

Campbell, Josette & Hayhurst, Chris. Euclid: The Father of Geometry. 2015. (Greatest Greek Philosophers Ser.). (ENG., Illus.). 112p. (J). (gr. 7-8). 35.60 (978-1-4994-6128-2(3), Rosen Young Adult) Rosen Publishing Group, Inc., The.

Hayhurst, Chris. Euclid: The Great Geometer. 2009. (Library of Greek Philosophers Ser.). 112p. (gr. 6-6). 66.50 (978-1-60853-659-7(9), Rosen Reference) Rosen Publishing Group, Inc., The.

Hightower, Paul. The Father of Geometry: Euclid & His 3-D World. 2010. (Great Minds of Ancient Science & Math Ser.). 112p. (J). 33.27 (978-0-7660-3409-9(7)) Enslow Pubs., Inc.

EUPHRATES RIVER

Miller, Gary G. & Miller, Gary. The Tigris & Euphrates: Rivers of the Fertile Crescent. 2010. (Rivers Around the World Ser.). (ENG., Illus.). 32p. (J). (gr. 5-8). pap. (978-0-7787-7471-6(6)); lib. bdg. (978-0-7787-7448-8(1)) Crabtree Publishing Co.

Mountjoy, Shane. The Tigris & Euphrates Rivers. 2004. (Rivers in World History Ser.). (Illus.). 120p. (C). (gr. 9-13). 32.50 (978-0-7910-8246-1(6), Chelsea Hse.) Facts On File, Inc.

Rice Jr., Earle. The Tigris/Euphrates River. 2012. (Illus.). 47p. (J). lib. bdg. 29.95 (978-1-61228-298-5(9)) Mitchell Lane Pubs., Inc.

EURASIA

Layne, Adriana. To be the First One. 2011. 33p. (J). pap. 29.95 (978-1-4327-6828-7(X)) Outskirts Pr., Inc.

EUROPE

Allen, Kathy. The Horrible, Miserable Middle Ages: The Disgusting Details about Life During Medieval Times. 2010. (Disgusting History Ser.). (ENG.). 32p. (gr. 3-4). lib. bdg. 27.32 (978-1-4296-3958-3(X), Fact Finders) Capstone Press of Coughlan Cos.

Allgor, Marie. Endangered Animals of Europe. 2011. (Save Earth's Animals! Ser.). (Illus.). 24p. (J). pap. 8.25 (978-1-4488-2646-9(2)); (gr. 3-4). 22.60 (978-1-4488-2531-8(8)) Rosen Publishing Group, Inc., The. (PowerKids Pr.).

Aloian, Molly & Kalman, Bobbie. Explore Europe. 2007. (Explore the Continents Ser.). (ENG., Illus.). 32p. (J). (gr. 3-7). lib. bdg. (978-0-7787-3074-3(3)); (gr. 1-5). pap. (978-0-7787-3088-0(3)) Crabtree Publishing Co.

Batt, Tanya Robyn & Barefoot Books. Barefoot Book of Faeries. Newey, Gail, illus. 2015. 64p. (J). (gr. k-5). 16.99 (978-1-78285-225-4(5)) Barefoot Bks., Inc.

Benchmark Education Co., LLC. The Geography of Europe. 2014. (PRIME Ser.). (J). (gr. 6-8). pap. (978-1-4509-9506-1(3)) Benchmark Education Co.

Bliss, John. Jewish Migration, 1 vol. 2011. (Children's True Stories: Migration Ser.). (ENG., Illus.). 32p. (gr. 3-3). 30.65 (978-1-4109-4075-9(6), Raintree Perspectives) Heinemann-Raintree.

Burgan, Michael. United Kingdom in Our World. 2011. (Countries in Our World Ser.). 32p. (YA). (gr. 4-7). lib. bdg. 28.50 (978-1-59920-435-2(5)) Black Rabbit Bks.

CultureGrams 2005 World Edition - Europe. 2004. (YA). per. 39.99 (978-1-931694-90-2(7)) ProQuest LLC.

Donaldson, Madeline. Europe. 2005. (Pull Ahead Bks.). (Illus.). 32p. (gr. k-3). (J). lib. bdg. 22.60 (978-0-8225-4719-8(8)); (ENG., pap. 7.95 (978-0-8225-2493-9(7)) Lerner Publishing Group.

Encyclopaedia Britannica Publishers, Inc. Staff. Views of Europe. 2003. (Britannica Learning Library). (Illus.). 14.95 (978-1-59339-009-9(2)) Encyclopaedia Britannica, Inc.

Gibson, Karen Bush. Spotlight on Europe, 1 vol. 2010. (Spotlight on the Continents Ser.). (ENG.). 24p. (gr. 1-2). lib. bdg. 25.32 (978-1-4296-6625-1(0), First Facts) Capstone Press of Coughlan Cos.

Glencoe McGraw-Hill Staff. Exploring Our World: People, Places & Cultures. 2007. (WORLD & ITS PEOPLE EASTERN Ser.). (ENG., Illus.). 108p. (gr. 6-9). pap. 11.32 (978-0-07-878170-4(1), 0078781701) McGraw-Hill Higher Education.

—Exploring Our World - People, Places, & Cultures: Western Hemisphere, Europe, & Russia. 2007. (WORLD & ITS PEOPLE EASTERN Ser.). (ENG., Illus.). 59p. (gr. 6-9). per. 6.48 (978-0-07-877728-8(3), 0078777283) McGraw-Hill Higher Education.

Glencoe McGraw-Hill Staff, creator. Exploring Our World - Eastern Hemisphere: People, Places, & Cultures. 2nd ed. 2007. (WORLD & ITS PEOPLE EASTERN Ser.). (ENG., Illus.). 766p. (gr. 6-8). lib. bdg., stu. ed. 98.00 (978-0-07-874578-2(0), 0078745780) McGraw-Hill Education.

Green, Jen. Ancient Celts: Archaeology Unlocks the Secrets of the Celts' Past. 2008. (National Geographic Investigates Ser.). (ENG., Illus.). 64p. (J). (gr. 5). lib. bdg. 27.90 (978-1-4263-0226-8(6), National Geographic Children's Bks.) National Geographic Society.

Green, Jen & National Geographic Kids Staff. Ancient Celts: Archaeology Unlocks the Secrets of the Celts' Past. 2008. (National Geographic Investigates Ser.). (ENG., Illus.). 64p. (J). (gr. 5). 17.95 (978-1-4263-0225-1(8), National Geographic Children's Bks.) National Geographic Society.

Hovanec, Erin M. An Online Visit to Europe. 2009. (Internet Field Trips Ser.). 24p. (gr. 3-3). 45.00 (978-1-61513-605-6(3), PowerKids Pr.) Rosen Publishing Group, Inc., The.

Hunkins, Boehm Armstrong & McGraw-Hill Education Editors. Exploring Our World: People, Places, & Cultures. 2007. (WORLD & ITS PEOPLE EASTERN Ser.). (ENG., Illus.). 95p. (gr. 6-9). pap. 6.48 (978-0-07-877743-1(7), 0078777437) McGraw-Hill Higher Education.

Life in Medieval Europe. 2016. (Life in Medieval Europe Ser.). 80p. (gr. 6-6). lib. bdg. 142.56 (978-1-5026-1822-1(2)) Cavendish Square Publishing.

Maynard, Charles W. The Alps. 2009. (Great Mountain Ranges of the World Ser.). 24p. (gr. 3-3). 42.50 (978-1-61513-167-9(1), PowerKids Pr.) Rosen Publishing Group, Inc., The.

McGraw-Hill Education Editors. Exploring Our World: People, Places, & Culture. 2007. (WORLD & ITS PEOPLE EASTERN Ser.). (ENG & SPA., Illus.). 108p. (gr. 6-9). per. 12.04 (978-0-07-878172-8(8), 0078781728) McGraw-Hill Education.

—Exploring Our World: People, Places, & Cultures - Eastern Hemisphere. 2007. (WORLD & ITS PEOPLE EASTERN Ser.). (ENG., Illus.). 192p. (gr. 6-8). per. 23.20 (978-0-07-878166-7(3), 0078781663) McGraw-Hill Education.

McGraw-Hill-Glencoe Staff & McGraw-Hill Education Staff. Exploring Our World, Western Hemisphere with Europe & Russia, Student Edition. 2nd ed. 2007. (WORLD & ITS PEOPLE EASTERN Ser.). (ENG.). (gr. 6-9). 98.00 (978-0-07-874580-5(2), 0078745802) McGraw-Hill Education.

McGraw-Hill Staff. Exploring Our World, Eastern Hemisphere, Interactive Tutor Self Assessment. 2007. (WORLD & ITS PEOPLE EASTERN Ser.). (ENG.). (gr. 6-8). cd-rom 104.00 (978-0-07-879098-0(0), 0078790980) McGraw-Hill Education.

—Exploring Our World, Western Hemisphere with Europe & Russia. 2007. (WORLD & ITS PEOPLE EASTERN Ser.). (ENG.). (gr. 6-9). cd-rom 104.00 (978-0-07-879088-1(3), 0078790883) McGraw-Hill Education.

Newman, Sandra. Europe. (True Bks.). (ENG., Illus.). 48p. (J). 2009. pap. 6.95 (978-0-531-21829-7(5), Children's Pr.) 2008. (gr. 2-5). 29.00 (978-0-531-16867-7(0)) Scholastic Library Publishing.

Oachs, Emily Rose. Europe. 2016. (Discover the Continents Ser.). (ENG., Illus.). 24p. (J). (gr. k-3). lib. bdg. 25.95 (978-1-62617-327-9(3), Blastoff! Readers) Bellwether Media.

Reynolds, Jan. Far North. 2007. (Vanishing Cultures Ser.). (ENG., Illus.). 32p. (J). (gr. 4-7). 8.95 (978-1-60060-127-9(8)); 16.95 (978-1-60060-142-2(1)) Lee & Low Bks., Inc.

Ross, Simon. Exploring Geography in a Changing World, Vol. 2. 2009. 152p. pap. 39.50 (978-0-340-94605-3(9)) Hodder Education Group GBR. Dist: Trans-Atlantic Pubns., Inc.

Sayre, April Pulley. Hello Europe! 2003. (Illus.). 32p. (J). (gr. 2-5). pap. 7.95 (978-0-7613-1990-0(5), Millbrook Pr.) Lerner Publishing Group.

Watson, Galadriel Findlay. Europe. 2005. (Continents Ser.). (Illus.). 32p. (J). (gr. 4-6). lib. bdg. 26.00 (978-1-59036-320-1(5)) Weigl Pubs., Inc.

Weintraub, Aileen. Discovering Europe's Land, People, & Wildlife: A MyReportLinks. com Book. 2004. (Continents of the World Ser.). (Illus.). 48p. (J). lib. bdg. 26.60 (978-0-7660-5203-1(6), MyReportLinks.com Bks.) Enslow Pubs., Inc.

Wimmer, Teresa. Causes. 2011. (War on Terror Ser.). (Illus.). 48p. (J). (gr. 5-9). 34.25 (978-1-60818-097-4(2)) Creative Co., The.

Wolny, Philip. Muslims Around the World Today. 2009. (Understanding Islam Ser.). 64p. (gr. 6-6). 58.50 (978-1-60854-626-8(8)) Rosen Publishing Group, Inc., The.

EUROPE, CENTRAL

Bultje, Jan Willem. The Czech Republic. 2006. (Looking at Europe Ser.). (Illus.). 48p. (J). (gr. 4-7). 22.95 (978-1-881508-29-8(3)) Oliver Pr., Inc.

Kollár, Daniel. Slovakia. 2006. (Looking at Europe Ser.). (Illus.). 48p. (J). (gr. 4-7). 22.95 (978-1-881508-49-6(8)) Oliver Pr., Inc.

Roux, Lindy. Czech Republic. 2004. (Countries of the World Ser.). (Illus.). 96p. (gr. 5-12). lib. bdg. 31.00 (978-0-8368-3109-2(8)) Stevens, Gareth Publishing LLLP.

Veceric, Danica. Slovenia. 2006. (Looking at Europe Ser.). (Illus.). 48p. (J). (gr. 4-7). 22.95 (978-1-881508-74-8(9)) Oliver Pr., Inc.

EUROPE—CIVILIZATION—HISTORY

Benchmark Education Company, LLC Staff, compiled by. Historical Communities: Theme Set. 2006. (J). 121.00 (978-1-4108-7097-1(9)) Benchmark Education Co.

Eastwood, Kay. Medieval Society. 2003. (Medieval World Ser.). (ENG., Illus.). 32p. (J). (gr. 5). pap. (978-0-7787-1377-7(6)) Crabtree Publishing Co.

Elliott, Lynne. The Renaissance in Europe. 2009. (Renaissance World Ser.). (ENG., Illus.). 32p. (J). (gr. 5-8). pap. (978-0-7787-4611-9(9)); lib. bdg. (978-0-7787-4591-4(0)) Crabtree Publishing Co.

Flatt, Lizann. Cities & Statecraft in the Renaissance. 2009. (Renaissance World Ser.). (ENG.). 32p. (J). (gr. 6-9). pap. (978-0-7787-4615-7(1)); (Illus.). (gr. 5-7). (978-0-7787-4595-2(3)) Crabtree Publishing Co.

Flint, David. Europe. 2005. (Continents of the World Ser.). (Illus.). 64p. (gr. 5-12). pap. 14.05 (978-0-8368-5920-1(0)); lib. bdg. 34.00 (978-0-8368-5913-3(8)) Stevens, Gareth Publishing LLLP. (Gareth Stevens Secondary Library).

Hinds, Kathryn. Everyday Life in Medieval Europe. 2008. (Everyday Life in... Ser.). 288p. (gr. 6-18). lib. bdg. 42.79 (978-0-7614-3927-1(7), Benchmark Bks.) Marshall Cavendish Corp.

—Everyday Life in the Renaissance. 2009. (Everyday Life in... Ser.). 336p. (gr. 6-18). 42.79 (978-0-7614-4483-1(1)) Marshall Cavendish Corp.

Huff, Toby E. An Age of Science & Revolutions, 1600-1800. (Illus.). 2006. 173p. (J). 32.95 (978-0-19-522269-2(5)) 2005. (ENG., 176p. (YA). (gr. 7-18). lib. bdg. 32.95 (978-0-19-517724-4(X)) Oxford Univ. Pr., Inc.

Kops, Deborah. Discover Ancient Rome. 2014. (Discover Ancient Civilizations Ser.). (Illus.). 112p. (J). (gr. 5-18). 33.27 (978-0-7660-4199-8(9)) Enslow Pubs., Inc.

Kuskowski, Alex. Super Simple European Art: Fun & Easy Art from Around the World, 1 vol. 2014. (Super Simple Cultural Art Set 2 Ser.). (ENG.). 32p. (gr. 5-10). lib. bdg. 27.07 (978-1-62403-279-0(6), Super SandCastle) ABDO Publishing Co.

Nardo, Don. The Vikings. 2010. (World History Ser.). (ENG.). 96-128p. 34.95 (978-1-4205-0316-6(2), Lucent Bks.) Cengage Gale.

Romanek, Trudee. Great Ideas of the Renaissance. 2009. (Renaissance World Ser.). (ENG., Illus.). 32p. (J). (gr. 5-7). (978-0-7787-4596-9(1)); (gr. 6-9). pap. (978-0-7787-4616-4(X)) Crabtree Publishing Co.

Weintraub, Aileen. Discovering Europe's Land, People, & Wildlife: A MyReportLinks. com Book. 2004. (Continents of the World Ser.). (Illus.). 48p. (J). lib. bdg. 26.60 (978-0-7660-5203-1(6), MyReportLinks.com Bks.) Enslow Pubs., Inc.

EUROPE—DESCRIPTION AND TRAVEL

The Britannica Guide to Countries of the European Union. 2013. (Britannica Guide to Countries of the European Union Ser.). (YA). (gr. 9-12). 1378.00 (978-1-62275-064-1(0)) Rosen Publishing Group, Inc., The.

Chanek, Sherilin & National Geographic Learning Staff. Europe & Russia: Geography & Environments. 2007. (Reading Expeditions Ser.). (ENG., Illus.). 64p. pap. 25.95 (978-0-7922-4374-8(9)) CENGAGE Learning.

—Europe & Russia - People & Places. 2007. (Reading Expeditions Ser.). (ENG., Illus.). 64p. (J). pap. 25.95 (978-0-7922-4375-5(7)) CENGAGE Learning.

Haughwout, Pixie & Folsom, Ralph. Canal Cruising in the South of France: The Romantic Canal Du Midi. 5th ed. 2004. 162p. stu. ed., spiral bd. 39.95 (978-0-9676620-9-1(5)) Kalmia Publishing.

Jackson, Ellen, ed. My Tour of Europe: By Teddy Roosevelt, Age 10. Brighton, Catherine, illus. 2003. 40p. 14.95 (978-0-7613-1998-6(0), Millbrook Pr.) Lerner Publishing Group.

Kat, Kika & Chickena, Hib. Off the Map. Maul, Paul F., ed. 2003. (ENG., Illus.). 144p. pap. 6.95 *(978-0-9709101-3-4(4))* CrimethInc. Workers' Collective.

Kingsley, M. t., et al. The Best Worst Summer Ever. 2010. 254p. pap. 14.95 *(978-1-59330-654-0(7))* Aventine Pr.

Linde, Barbara. Mapping Europe. 2013. (Mapping the World Ser.). 24p. (J). (gr. 2-5). pap. 48.90 *(978-1-4339-9111-0(X))*; (ENG., Illus.). pap. 8.15 *(978-1-4339-9110-3(1))* Stevens, Gareth Publishing LLLP.

Linde, Barbara & Linde, Barbara M. Mapping Europe. 2013. 24p. (J). (gr. 2-5). 22.60 *(978-1-4339-9109-7(8))* Stevens, Gareth Publishing LLLP.

Litten, Kristyna. Rome: a 3D Keepsake Cityscape. Litten, Kristyna, illus. 2013. (Panorama Pops Ser.). (ENG., Illus.). 15p. (J). (gr. k-12). 8.99 *(978-0-7636-6415-2(4))* Candlewick Pr.

Lonely Planet Publications Staff. Europe: Everything You Ever Wanted to Know, 1 vol. 2013. (Lonely Planet Kids Ser.). (ENG., Illus.). 96p. (J). pap. 12.99 *(978-1-74321-914-0(8)*, 4632) Lonely Planet Pubns.

Putumayo Kids Staff, creator. Europe Sticker Collection. 2011. (J). 11.95 *(978-1-58759-289-8(4))* Putumayo World Music & Crafts.

Rockett, Paul. Mapping Europe. 2016. (Mapping the Continents Ser.). (ENG., Illus.). 32p. (J). (gr. 3-6). *(978-0-7787-2615-9(0))* Crabtree Publishing Co.

Streissguth, Thomas. Albania in Pictures. 2010. (Visual Geography Series, Second Ser.). (ENG.). 80p. (gr. 5-12). lib. bdg. 31.93 *(978-0-7613-4629-6(5))* Lerner Publishing Group.

Vierow, Wendy. Europe. (Atlas of the Seven Continents Ser.). 24p. 2009. (gr. 3-3). 42.50 *(978-1-61511-480-1(7))* 2004. (Illus.). (J). lib. bdg. 22.60 *(978-0-8239-6691-2(7))* Rosen Publishing Group, Inc., The. (PowerKids Pr.).

Walker, Ida. Belgium. 2007. (European Union Ser.). (Illus.). 88p. (YA). (gr. 3-7). lib. bdg. 21.95 *(978-1-4222-0040-7(X)*, 1247982) Mason Crest.

Walker, Ida & Indovino, Shaina C. Germany. Bruton, John, ed. 2012. (Major European Union Nations Ser.). 64p. (J). (gr. 7). 22.95 *(978-1-4222-2243-0(8))* Mason Crest.

Walker, Ida & Indovino, Shaina Carmel. Germany. 2012. (J). pap. *(978-1-4222-2274-4(8))* Mason Crest.

Woods, Michael & Woods, Mary B. Seven Natural Wonders of Europe. 2009. (Seven Wonders Ser.). (ENG., Illus.). 80p. (gr. 5-8). 33.26 *(978-0-8225-9072-9(7))* Lerner Publishing Group.

Yanofsky, Tsivia. Take Me to Europe: Jewish Life in England, Spain, France, & Italy. 2013. (Illus.). 85p. (J). *(978-1-4226-1349-8(6))* Mesorah Pubns., Ltd.

EUROPE, EASTERN

DiPiazza, Francesca. Slovakia in Pictures. 2010. (Visual Geography Series, Second Ser.). (ENG.). 80p. (gr. 5-12). lib. bdg. 31.93 *(978-0-7613-4627-2(9))* Lerner Publishing Group.

Levy, Patricia & Spilling, Michael. Belarus. 2nd rev. ed. 2008. (Cultures of the World Ser.). 144p. (gr. 6-18). lib. bdg. 42.79 *(978-0-7614-3411-5(9)*, Benchmark Bks.) Marshall Cavendish Corp.

Rauf, Don. Eurasia, Vol. 10. 2016. (Social Progress & Sustainability Ser.). (Illus.). 80p. (J). (gr. 7). 24.95 *(978-1-4222-3495-2(9))* Mason Crest.

EUROPE—FICTION

Anderson, Nancy. Jeff's Trip to Holland. 2016. (Rosen REAL Readers: STEM & STEAM Collection). 12p. (gr. 1-k). pap. 6.33 *(978-1-5081-2679-9(8)*, Rosen Classroom) Rosen Publishing Group, Inc., The.

Bakshi, Kelly. Myth-Busting Columbus. 2012. 24p. 18.95 *(978-1-61633-316-4(2))*; pap. 10.95 *(978-1-61633-317-1(0))* Guardian Angel Publishing, Inc.

Banks, Kate. City Cat. Castillo, Lauren, illus. 2013. (ENG.). 48p. (J). (gr. -1-2). 17.99 *(978-0-374-31321-0(0)*, 9780374313210, Farrar, Straus & Giroux (BYR)) Farrar, Straus & Giroux.

Barnhouse, Rebecca. Ring-Giver. 2013. (J). *(978-0-307-98178-3(9))* Random Hse., Inc.

Bowlby, Linda S. Nentuck's New Family. Helms, Dana, illus. 2008. 30p. (J). (gr. -1-3). pap. 9.95 *(978-0-9779993-8-5(6))* Red Earth Publishing.

Burnett, Eric. Gymnastics Jenny Stands on Her Own. 2003. 108p. pap. 9.95 *(978-0-595-27919-7(8))* iUniverse, Inc.

Burnham, Niki & Saidens, Amy. Royally Jacked. 2003. (Romantic Comedies Ser.). (ENG.). 208p. (YA). mass mkt. 6.99 *(978-0-689-86668-5(2)*, Simon Pulse) Simon Pulse.

Carter, Ally. Heist Society. 2011. (Heist Society Novel Ser.). (ENG.). 304p. (J). (gr. 5-9). pap. 9.99 *(978-1-4231-1661-5(5))* Hyperion Pr.

—Uncommon Criminals. 2011. (Playaway Children Ser.). (YA). (gr. 7-12). 69.99 *(978-1-4558-2483-0(6))* Findaway World, LLC.

—Uncommon Criminals. 2012. (Heist Society Novel Ser.). (ENG.). 304p. (J). (gr. 5-9). pap. 9.99 *(978-1-4231-4807-4(X))* Hyperion Pr.

Cokal, Susann. The Kingdom of Little Wounds. 2016. (ENG.). 576p. (YA). (gr. 11). pap. 12.99 *(978-0-7636-8757-1(X))* Candlewick Pr.

Colfer, Eoin. The Hangman's Revolution. 2015. (W. A. R. P. Ser.: 2). (YA). lib. bdg. 20.85 *(978-0-606-36896-4(5))* Turtleback Bks.

Connelly, Peggy. My Quirky, Oddball, Eccentric, Unpredictable Grandma. 2006. (ENG.). 112p. per. 19.95 *(978-1-4241-4486-0(8))* PublishAmerica, Inc.

Cooper, Michelle. A Brief History of Montmaray. 2011. (Montmaray Journals). (ENG.). 324p. (YA). (gr. 7). pap. 8.99 *(978-0-375-85154-4(2)*, Knopf Bks. for Young Readers) Random Hse. Children's Bks.

Court, Georgia. Traitor of Bled. 2005. 108p. pap. 19.95 *(978-1-4137-9595-0(1))* PublishAmerica, Inc.

Culbertson, Kim. The Wonder of Us. 2017. (ENG.). 336p. (J). (gr. 7). 17.99 ***(978-0-545-73151-5(8))*** Scholastic, Inc.

Cutchin, Marcia, illus. Feathers: A Jewish Tale from Eastern Europe. 2005. (ENG.). 32p. (J). (gr. k-3). 16.95 *(978-0-87483-755-1(3)*, 1249133) August Hse. Pubs., Inc.

De Fombelle, Timothee. Vango: Between Sky & Earth. 2016. (Vango Ser.: 1). lib. bdg. 20.85 *(978-0-606-37948-9(7))* Turtleback Bks.

D'Elia, Amy & Clerman, Lisa. Dreams Come True: A story about the blessing of Adoption. 2007. *(978-0-9777744-1-8(4))* Finneran, Lisa.

Dickman, Jacqueline Rosett. Rebecca & Mom: Friends Forever, 1 vol. 2010. 116p. pap. 19.95 *(978-1-4489-4088-2(5))* America Star Bks.

Falkner, Brian. Battlesaurus: Rampage at Waterloo. 2016. (Battlesaurus Ser.: 2). (ENG.). 352p. (YA). 17.99 *(978-0-374-30077-7(1)*, 9780374300777, Farrar, Straus & Giroux (BYR)) Farrar, Straus & Giroux.

Farnol, Jeffery. Money Moon. 2006. pap. 13.95 *(978-1-4218-3066-7(3))* 1st World Publishing, Inc.

Forman, Gayle. Just One Day. 2013. (ENG.). (YA). (gr. 9). 416p. pap. 10.99 *(978-0-14-242295-3(9)*, Speak); 384p. 17.99 *(978-0-525-42591-5(8)*, Dutton Books for Young Readers) Penguin Young Readers Group.

—Just One Day. 2013. lib. bdg. 22.10 *(978-0-606-34405-0(5)*, Turtleback) Turtleback Bks.

—Just One Year. 2013. (ENG.). 336p. (YA). (gr. 9). 17.99 *(978-0-525-42592-2(6)*, Dutton Books for Young Readers) Penguin Young Readers Group.

Fuqua, Jonathon. Medusa's Daughter. 2012. (ENG., Illus.). 144p. (YA). lib. bdg. 19.95 *(978-0-9848808-2-9(8)*, Red Giant Entertainment) Active Media Publishing, LLC.

Fuqua, Jonathon Scott. Medusa's Daughter. Parke, Steven, illus. 2012. (YA). *(978-0-9745645-8-6(3))* Active Media Publishing, LLC.

Gay, Marie-Louise & Homel, David. The Traveling Circus, 1 vol. 2015. (ENG., Illus.). 144p. (J). (gr. 1-5). 15.95 *(978-1-55498-420-6(3))* Groundwood Bks. CAN. Dist: Publishers Group West (PGW).

Haas, Jessie & Wedekind, Annie. Mercury's Flight: The Story of a Lipizzaner Stallion. 2011. (Breyer Horse Collection: 4). (ENG.). 128p. (J). (gr. 4-7). pap. 9.99 *(978-0-312-64451-2(5)*, 9780312644512) Feiwel & Friends.

Hall, Maggie. The Conspiracy of Us, 9 vols., Pack. 2015. (ENG.). (YA). 161.91 *(978-0-399-17404-9(4)*, G.P. Putnam's Sons Books for Young Readers) Penguin Young Readers Group.

Hathorn, Sarah Alexandra. Teenagents: World Challenge. 2012. 240p. pap. 12.99 *(978-2-9700738-2-6(X))* Simon & Schuster, Inc.

Hawthorne, Rachel. A Year in Europe. 2007. (ENG.). 544p. (YA). (gr. 7-11). per. 7.99 *(978-0-375-84073-9(7)*, Laurel Leaf) Random Hse. Children's Bks.

Hicks, Clifford B. Alvin Fernald, Foreign Trader. Schluenderfritz, Theodore, illus. 2007. (Alvin Fernald Mysteries Ser.). 181p. (J). (gr. 4). per. 11.95 *(978-1-883937-74-4(4))* Bethlehem Bks.

Hill, Kevin Kelvin. The Supreme Sorcerer Ollie Tooth Pick & His Two Henchmen versus the Magical Dragons. 2011. 40p. 20.76 *(978-1-4567-3254-7(4))* AuthorHouse.

Hull, Norman. Joyce's Holiday in France. 2011. 96p. (gr. -1). pap. 9.99 *(978-1-4634-3694-0(7))* AuthorHouse.

Johnson, Maureen. 13 Little Blue Envelopes. (13 Little Blue Envelopes Ser.: 1). (ENG., Illus.). (YA). (gr. 8-18). 2005. 336p. 17.99 *(978-0-06-054141-5(5))* 2010. 368p. reprint ed. pap. 9.99 *(978-0-06-054143-9(1))* HarperCollins Pubs. (HarperTeen).

—13 Little Blue Envelopes. 2007. 317p. 20.00 *(978-0-7569-7830-3(0))* Perfection Learning Corp.

Kincaid, Tracy. The Adventures of Casey the Lost Suitcase. 2007. (Illus.). 32p. (J). (gr. -1-3). 16.95 *(978-0-929915-67-8(4))* Headline Bks., Inc.

Kindt, Matt. Super Spy. 2007. (Super Spy Ser.). (ENG., Illus.). 304p. pap. 19.95 *(978-1-891830-96-9(1)*, 9781891830969) Top Shelf Productions.

Konigsburg, E. L. The Second Mrs. Gioconda. 2005. (ENG.). 160p. (YA). (gr. 7). pap. 9.99 *(978-1-4169-0342-0(9)*, Atheneum Bks. for Young Readers) Simon & Schuster Children's Publishing.

Lang, Andrew. The Olive Fairy Book. Lang, Andrew, ed. 2011. 216p. (gr. 3-7). pap. 15.95 *(978-1-4638-0030-7(4))* Rodgers, Alan Bks.

Lang, Andrew, ed. The Olive Fairy Book. 2011. 216p. (gr. 3-7). 26.95 *(978-1-4638-9787-1(1))* Rodgers, Alan Bks.

Leppard, Lois Gladys. The Mandie Collection, Bks. 16-20, Vol. 4. 2009. (ENG.). 608p. (J). pap. 16.99 *(978-0-7642-0663-4(X))* Bethany Hse. Pubs.

Malone, Jen. Wanderlost. 2016. 352p. (YA). (gr. 9). pap. 9.99 *(978-0-06-238015-9(X)*, HarperTeen) HarperCollins Pubs.

McNamara, Joan. Borya & the Burps: An Eastern European Adoption Story. Majewski, Dawn, illus. 2005. 30p. (J). (gr. -1 — 1). 18.00 *(978-0-944934-31-9(5))* Perspectives Pr., Inc.

Meyer, L. A. Viva Jacquelina! Being an Account of the Further Adventures of Jacky Faber, over the Hills & Far Away. 2012. (Bloody Jack Adventures Ser.: 10). (ENG.). 368p. (YA). (gr. 9). 16.99 *(978-0-547-76350-7(6))* Houghton Mifflin Harcourt Publishing Co.

Meyers, Terri. Shih Tzu Achoo!! 2009. 24p. pap. 12.99 *(978-1-4389-5696-1(7))* AuthorHouse.

Mindel, Nissan. Eight Chanukah Tales. Toron, Eli & Graybar, Shmuel, illus. 2007. 78p. (J). 10.95 *(978-0-8266-0039-4(5))* Kehot Pubn. Society.

Molesworth & Molesworth, Mary Louisa S. The Tapestry Room. 2008. 116p. 22.95 *(978-1-60664-990-9(6))*; per. 9.95 *(978-1-60312-540-6(X))* Aegypan.

Nayeri, Daniel and Dina. Another Faust. 2010. (ENG., Illus.). 400p. (YA). (gr. 9). pap. 8.99 *(978-0-7636-4834-3(5))* Candlewick Pr.

Nislick, June Levitt. Zayda Was a Cowboy. 2005. (ENG.). 88p. pap. 11.95 *(978-0-8276-0817-7(9))* Jewish Pubn. Society.

Nuri, Alya & Nuri, Alya. Amr's Adventure in Europe. 2013. 68p. pap. *(978-1-935948-29-2(6))* Roxby Media Ltd.

O'Porter, Dawn. Paper Airplanes. 2014. (ENG.). 272p. (YA). (gr. 9-17). 16.95 *(978-1-4197-1184-8(9)*, Amulet Bks.) Abrams, Inc.

Oxford University Press Staff & Bassett, Jennifer, eds. Omega Files - Short Stories. 3rd ed. 2008. (ENG., Illus.). 64p. 10.00 *(978-0-19-478913-4(6))* Oxford Univ. Pr., Inc.

Paterson, Katherine. The Day of the Pelican. 2010. (ENG.). 160p. (J). (gr. 5-7). pap. 7.99 *(978-0-547-40627-5(4))* Houghton Mifflin Harcourt Publishing Co.

Peart, Hendry. Red Falcons of Tremoine. Brevannes, Maurice, illus. 2007. (Living History Library (Bethlehem Books) Ser.). 239p. (YA). (gr. 8-12). pap. 12.95 *(978-1-932350-15-9(2))* Bethlehem Bks.

Pierce, Nicola. Kings of the Boyne. 2017. (ENG.). 336p. (J). pap. 13.00 ***(978-1-84717-627-1(5))*** O'Brien Pr., Ltd., The IRL. Dist: Dufour Editions, Inc.

Pullman, Philip. The Tin Princess. 2008. (Sally Lockhart Ser.). (ENG.). 304p. (YA). (gr. 7). pap. 7.99 *(978-0-375-84514-7(3)*, Knopf Bks. for Young Readers) Random Hse. Children's Bks.

Rennie, Cliff. Goal Behind the Curtain. 2011. (Freestyle Fiction 12+ Ser.). (ENG.). 176p. (J). mass mkt. 8.99 *(978-1-871676-47-1(9)*, df3a7515-5c5f-4709-ab1d-e32b03bb9c87) Christian Focus Pubns. GBR. Dist: Bookmasters Distribution.

Rosenberg, Michael. The Story of Bendalot. 2008. 40p. pap. 16.99 *(978-1-4343-9932-8(X))* AuthorHouse.

Roy, Lillian Elizabeth. Polly in Egypt: The Polly Brewster Series. Barbour, H. S., illus. 2011. 226p. 44.95 *(978-1-258-09808-7(3))* Literary Licensing, LLC.

Runholt, Susan. The Mystery of the Third Lucretia. 2009. (Kari & Lucas Mystery Ser.). (ENG.). 304p. (J). (gr. 5-18). pap. 6.99 *(978-0-14-241338-8(0)*, Puffin Books) Penguin Young Readers Group.

Schreiber, Joe. Perry's Killer Playlist. (ENG.). 224p. (YA). (gr. 9). 2013. pap. 8.99 *(978-0-544-10489-1(7))* 2012. 16.99 *(978-0-547-60117-5(4))* Houghton Mifflin Harcourt Publishing Co.

Sealed with a Lie. 2014. (ENG., Illus.). 256p. (YA). (gr. 9). 17.99 *(978-1-4814-0052-7(5)*, Simon & Schuster Bks. For Young Readers) Simon & Schuster Bks. For Young Readers.

Sedgwick, Marcus. Midwinterblood. 2014. (YA). lib. bdg. 20.85 *(978-0-606-35221-5(X))* Turtleback Bks.

Sellers, Sandra. Gran's Story V: Roxanne in Europe. 2011. 24p. (gr. -1). pap. 12.99 *(978-1-4269-6290-5(8))* Trafford Publishing.

Sidney, Margaret. Five Little Peppers Abroad. 2008. 212p. (gr. 4-7). 26.95 *(978-1-60664-996-1(5))*; per. 14.95 *(978-1-60312-546-8(9))* Aegypan.

Slade, Arthur. Island of Doom: Hunchback Assignments 4. 2013. (Hunchback Assignments Ser.). (ENG.). 320p. (YA). (gr. 7). pap. 9.99 *(978-0-375-85406-4(1)*, Ember) Random Hse. Children's Bks.

Standish, Burt L. Frank Merriwell in Europe. Rudman, Jack, ed. (Frank Merriwell Ser.). (YA). (gr. 9-18). 29.95 *(978-0-8373-9308-7(6))*; pap. 9.95 *(978-0-8373-9008-6(7)*, FM-008) Merriwell, Frank Inc.

Stansberry, Don. Inky & the Missing Gold. 2007. (Illus.). 128p. (YA). per. 15.95 *(978-0-929915-10-4(0)*, Publisher Page) Headline Bks., Inc.

Stanton, Angie. Royally Lost. 2014. (ENG.). 336p. (YA). (gr. 8). pap. 9.99 *(978-0-06-227258-4(6)*, HarperTeen) HarperCollins Pubs.

Steedman, Amy. Our Island Saints (Yesterday's Classics) 2006. (J). per. 9.95 *(978-1-59915-031-4(X))* Yesterday's Classics.

Stein, Tammar. High Dive. 2011. (ENG.). 208p. (YA). (gr. 7). pap. 7.99 *(978-0-440-23903-1(6)*, Knopf Bks. for Young Readers) Random Hse. Children's Bks.

Stephenson, Norman E. God's Blood: The Fate of the Lost Templar Treasure. 2007. 176p. per. 13.95 *(978-0-595-47539-1(6))* iUniverse, Inc.

Stevermer, Caroline & Wrede, Patricia C. The Grand Tour: Being a Revelation of Matters of High Confidentiality & Greatest Importance, Including Extracts from the Intimate Diary of a Noblewoman & the Sworn Testimony of a Lady of Quality. 2006. (ENG., Illus.). 480p. (YA). (gr. 7-12). pap. 21.95 *(978-0-15-205556-1(8))* Houghton Mifflin Harcourt Publishing Co.

StJohn, Amanda. Frog Went A-Traveling: A Russian Folktale. Wenzel, David, illus. 2011. (Folktales from Around the World Ser.). (ENG.). 24p. (J). (gr. k-3). 28.50 *(978-1-60973-136-6(0)*, 201142) Child's World, Inc., The.

Strauss, Linda Leopold. The Elijah Door. Natchev, Alexi, illus. 2012. (ENG.). 32p. (J). 16.95 *(978-0-8234-1911-1(8))* Holiday Hse., Inc.

Toro, Sandra. Dona Gracia: Beacon of Hope. 2016. 292p. (YA). pap. *(978-1-935604-75-4(9))* Gaon Bks.

Touring Europe on a Magic Carpet. 2004. (J). ring bd. 4.50 *(978-0-9762740-9-4(4))* Smart Smiles Co., The.

Toybox Innovations, creator. Pixar's Ratatouille. 2007. (Ratatouille Ser.). (ENG.). (J). (gr. -1-3). pap. *(978-0-7634-2185-4(5))* Walt Disney Records.

Van Dyne, Edith. Aunt Jane's Nieces at Work. 2005. 27.95 *(978-1-4218-1423-0(4)*, 1st World Library - Literary Society) 1st World Publishing, Inc.

—Aunt Jane's Nieces at Work. 2006. (ENG.). 154p. pap. 19.99 *(978-1-4264-6763-9(X))* Creative Media Partners, LLC.

Walker, Landry. Secrets & Lies. Takara, Marcio, illus. 2010. (Incredibles Ser.). 112p. (J). (gr. 3-8). pap. 9.99 *(978-1-60886-583-3(5))* Boom! Studios.

Ward, John. Le Secret de l'Alchimiste. Guitard, Agnes & Pineau, Severine, trs. from ENG. 2004. (FRE., Illus.). 336p. (J). pap. *(978-2-89021-672-3(1))* Diffusion du livre Mirabel (DLM).

Whitney, Barbara I. Barbara's Quest to Find a Messenger: Journeys I & II. 2009. 40p. pap. 19.49 *(978-1-4415-0159-2(2))* Xlibris Corp.

Wiggin, Kate Douglas. Penelope Travels Abroad. 2008. 460p. 34.95 *(978-1-60664-818-6(7))* Aegypan.

—Penelope's Postscripts. 2008. 96p. (gr. 4-7). pap. 8.95 *(978-1-60664-193-4(X))* Aegypan.

Wrede, Patricia C. & Stevermer, Caroline. The Mislaid Magician or Ten Years After: Being the Private Correspondence Between Two Prominent Families Regarding a Scandal Touching the Highest Levels of Government & Thesecurity of the Realm. 2009. (ENG., Illus.). 336p. (J). (gr. 7). pap. 18.95 *(978-0-15-206209-5(2))* Houghton Mifflin Harcourt Publishing Co.

EUROPE—HISTORY

Allen, Kathy. The Horrible, Miserable Middle Ages: The Disgusting Details about Life During Medieval. 2011. (Disgusting History Ser.). (ENG.). 32p. (gr. 3-4). pap. 47.70 *(978-1-4296-6479-0(7)*, Fact Finders) Capstone Press of Coughlan Cos.

—The Horrible, Miserable Middle Ages: The Disgusting Details about Life During Medieval Times. 2011. (Disgusting History Ser.). (ENG.). 32p. (gr. 3-4). pap. 8.10 *(978-1-4296-6350-2(2)*, Fact Finders) Capstone Press of Coughlan Cos.

Allman, Toney. Medieval Medicine & Disease. 2014. (The Library of Medieval Times Ser). (ENG., Illus.). 80p. (J). lib. bdg. *(978-1-60152-656-4(3))* ReferencePoint Pr., Inc.

Aloian, Molly & Kalman, Bobbie. Explora Europa. 2007. (Explora Los Continentes Ser.). (SPA., Illus.). 32p. (J). (gr. 3-7). pap. *(978-0-7787-8299-5(9))* Crabtree Publishing Co.

Altman, Linda Jacobs. Trade & Commerce. 2007. (ENG., Illus.). 98p. (C). (gr. 6-18). lib. bdg. 175.00 *(978-0-7656-8111-9(0)*, Y184849) Routledge.

Anderson, Dale. Churches & Religion in the Middle Ages. 2005. (World Almanac Library of the Middle Ages). (Illus.). 48p. (gr. 5-12). lib. bdg. 31.00 *(978-0-8368-5892-1(1)*, Gareth Stevens Secondary Library) Stevens, Gareth Publishing LLLP.

Austria, Croatia, & Slovenia. 2013. (Britannica Guide to Countries of the European Union Ser.). 240p. (YA). (gr. 9-12). 106.00 *(978-1-61530-978-8(0))* Rosen Publishing Group, Inc., The.

Bauer, Susan Wise & Weiss, Jim. Early Modern Times Vol. 3: From Elizabeth the First to the Forty-Niners. 2nd unabr. ed. 2008. (Story of the World Ser.: 0). (ENG.). 1p. cd-rom 49.95 *(978-1-933339-17-7(9)*, 333917) Well-Trained Mind Pr.

Baxter, Roberta. Learning about Europe. 2015. (ENG., Illus.). 40p. (J). (gr. 3-5). 29.32 *(978-1-4677-8019-3(7)*, Lerner Pubns.) Lerner Publishing Group.

Bodden, Valerie. Barbarians. 2013. 24p. pap. *(978-1-60818-466-8(8))* Creative Co., The.

—Great Warriors: Barbarians. 2014. (Great Warriors Ser.). (ENG.). 24p. (J). (gr. 1-3). pap. 9.99 *(978-1-62832-066-4(4)*, Creative Paperbacks) Creative Co., The.

Bordessa, Kris. Great Medieval Projects. Braley, Shawn, illus. 2008. (Build It Yourself Ser.). (ENG.). 128p. (J). (gr. 3-7). 21.95 *(978-1-934670-26-2(X))* Octavio Publishing.

—Great Medieval Projects: You Can Build Yourself. Braley, Shawn, illus. 2008. (Build It Yourself Ser.). (ENG.). 128p. (J). (gr. 3-7). pap. 15.95 *(978-0-9792268-0-9(5))* Octavio Publishing.

Bredeson, Carmen. Don't Let the Barber Pull Your Teeth: Could You Survive Medieval Medicine? Kelley, Gerald, illus. 2011. (Ye Yucky Middle Ages Ser.). 48p. (J). (gr. 7-12). lib. bdg. 25.27 *(978-0-7660-3693-2(6))* Enslow Pubs., Inc.

The Britannica Guide to Countries of the European Union. 2013. (Britannica Guide to Countries of the European Union Ser.). (YA). (gr. 9-12). 689.00 *(978-1-61530-974-0(8))* Rosen Publishing Group, Inc., The.

Broida, Marian. Projects about Nineteenth-Century European Immigrants. 2005. (Hands-On History Ser.). (Illus.). 48p. (J). (gr. 3-7). lib. bdg. *(978-0-7614-1980-8(2)*, Benchmark Bks.) Marshall Cavendish Corp.

Brooks, Susie. Croatia. (Unpacked Ser.). (ENG., Illus.). 32p. (J). (gr. 4-6). 2017. pap. 11.99 *(978-0-7502-9165-1(6))* 2016. 17.99 *(978-0-7502-9163-7(X))* Hachette Children's Group GBR. (Wayland). Dist: Hachette Bk. Group.

Burgan, Michael. The European Industrial Revolution. 2013. (ENG.). 64p. (J). 30.00 *(978-0-531-28202-1(3))*; pap. 8.95 *(978-0-531-27667-9(8))* Scholastic Library Publishing.

Byers, Ann. Saving Children from the Holocaust: The Kindertransport. 2011. (Holocaust Through Primary Sources Ser.). (Illus.). 128p. (J). (gr. 9-12). lib. bdg. 33.27 *(978-0-7660-3323-8(6))* Enslow Pubs., Inc.

Chambers, Catherine. Why Why Why... Did Knights Wear Heavy Armor? 2010. (Why Why Why Ser.). (Illus.). 32p. (J). (gr. 1-3). lib. bdg. 18.95 *(978-1-4222-1575-3(X))* Mason Crest.

Chandler, Julia. The Colonial & Postcolonial Experience in East & Southeast Asia. 2016. (Colonial & Postcolonial Experience Ser.). 00128p. (J). (gr. 10-10). 54.00 *(978-1-5081-0438-4(7))* Rosen Publishing Group, Inc., The.

Cohen, Robert Z. Transylvania: Birthplace of Vampires. 2011. (J). 77.70 *(978-1-4488-2234-8(3)*, Rosen Reference); (J). pap. 12.95 *(978-1-4488-2231-7(9)*, Rosen Reference); (YA). (gr. 5-9). lib. bdg. 31.95 *(978-1-4488-1228-8(3))* Rosen Publishing Group, Inc., The.

Coletti, Sharon. Everything You Need to Teach Europe. 2005. (YA). ring bd. 149.95 *(978-1-933558-02-8(4))* InspirEd Educators.

The Colonial & Postcolonial Experience. 2016. (Colonial & Postcolonial Experience Ser.). 00128p. (J). (gr. 10-10). 270.00 *(978-1-5081-0441-4(7)*, Britannica Educational Publishing) Rosen Publishing Group, Inc., The.

Cooper, R., et al. Croatia. 2nd rev. ed. 2010. (Cultures of the World 21 Ser.). 144p. (gr. 6). lib. bdg. 42.79 *(978-1-60870-215-2(4))* Marshall Cavendish Corp.

Cristina, Henriqueta. Three Balls of Wool. Kono, Yara, illus. 2017. (ENG.). 32p. (J). (gr. -1-4). 16.95 *(978-1-59270-220-6(1))* Enchanted Lion Bks., LLC.

The Crusades from Medieval European & Muslim Perspectives. (YA). (gr. 6-9). spiral bd., tchr.'s planning gde. ed. 12.00 *(978-0-382-44469-2(8))* Cobblestone Publishing Co.

Cunningham, Kevin. The Bubonic Plague, 1 vol. 2011. (Essential Events Set 6 Ser.). (ENG., Illus.). 112p. (J). (gr. 6-12). lib. bdg. 35.64 *(978-1-61714-762-3(1))* ABDO Publishing Co.

Cuthbert, Megan. Europe. 2014. (J). *(978-1-4896-0950-2(4))* Weigl Pubs., Inc.

Davey, Frances. A Brief Political & Geographic History of Europe: Where Are... Prussia, Gaul, & the Holy Roman Empire. 2007. (Places in Time Ser.). (Illus.). 112p. (YA). (gr. 5-9). lib. bdg. 37.10 *(978-1-58415-625-3(2))* Mitchell Lane Pubs., Inc.

Day, Nancy. Your Travel Guide to Renaissance Europe. 2005. (Passport to History Ser.). (Illus.). 96p. (gr. 5-8). lib. bdg. 26.50 *(978-0-8225-3080-0(5))* Lerner Publishing Group.

DBQ Practice: European History. 2003. spiral bd. 19.95 *(978-1-56004-146-7(3))* Social Studies Schl. Service.

Deem, James M. Auschwitz: Voices from the Death Camp. 2011. (Holocaust Through Primary Sources Ser.). (Illus.). 128p. (J). (gr. 6-18). pap. 10.95 *(978-1-59845-346-1(7))* Enslow Pubs., Inc.

Docalavich, Heather & Indovino, Shaina C. Denmark. Bruton, John, ed. 2012. (Major European Union Nations Ser.). 64p. (J). (gr. 7). 22.95 *(978-1-4222-2238-6(1))* Mason Crest.

Docalavich, Heather & Indovino, Shaina Carmel. Croatia. 2012. (J). *(978-1-4222-2235-5(7))*; pap. *(978-1-4222-2266-9(7))* Mason Crest.

E
F
G

—Denmark. 2012. (J). pap. (978-1-4222-2269-0(1)) Mason Crest.

—Hungary. 2012. (J). (978-1-4222-2245-4(4)); pap. (978-1-4222-2276-8(4)) Mason Crest.

—Slovakia. 2012. (J). (978-1-4222-2257-7(8)); pap. (978-1-4222-2288-1(8)) Mason Crest.

—Slovenia. 2012. (J). (978-1-4222-2258-4(6)); pap. (978-1-4222-2289-8(6)) Mason Crest.

Encyclopaedia Britannica, Inc. Staff, compiled by. Views of Europe. 2003. (Illus.). 64p. 14.95 (978-1-59339-040-2(8)) Encyclopaedia Britannica, Inc.

Europe: Regions of the World. 2003. spiral bd. 16.95 (978-1-56004-157-3(9)) Social Studies Schl. Service.

European Dance: Ireland, Poland, Spain, & Greece. 2nd rev. ed. 2010. (World of Dance Ser.). (Illus.). 128p. (C). (gr. 9-18). 35.00 (978-1-60413-480-3(1), Chelsea Hse.) Facts On File, Inc.

Fischell, Emma. Northern Europe. 2004. (Cultures & Costumes Ser.). (Illus.). 64p. (YA). (gr. 7-18). lib. bdg. 19.95 (978-1-59084-439-7(4)) Mason Crest.

Francis, Suzanne. Europe, 1 vol. 2013. (Continents Ser.). (ENG.). 48p. (J). (gr. 3-6). lib. bdg. 32.79 (978-1-61783-932-0(9)) ABDO Publishing Co.

Glynne, Andy. Rachel's Story: A Real-Life Account of Her Journey from Eurasia. 2017. (Seeking Refuge Ser.). (ENG.). 32p. (gr. 3-4). 27.32 **(978-1-5158-1416-0(5))** Picture Window Bks.

Hall, Derek. Europe. 2008. (Facts at Your Fingertips Ser.). (Illus.). 64p. (YA). (gr. 7-12). lib. bdg. 34.25 (978-1-933834-09-2(9)) Brown Bear Bks.

Helget, Nicole Lea. Barbarians. 2012. (Fearsome Fighters Ser.). 48p. (gr. 5-12). 23.95 (978-1-60818-182-7(0), Creative Education) Creative Co., The.

Hirsch, E. D., Jr., ed. Europe in the Middle Ages, Level 4. 2003. stu. ed. 49.95 (978-0-7690-2847-7(0)) Pearson Learning.

Hirsch, Rebecca E. Europe. 2012. (ENG.). 32p. (J). lib. bdg. 23.00 (978-0-531-28979-2(6)); (gr. -1-3). pap. 5.95 (978-0-531-29279-2(7)) Scholastic Library Publishing.

Hull, Robert. Merchant. 2009. (Medieval Lives Ser.). (J). 32.80 (978-1-59920-170-2(4)) Black Rabbit Bks.

Hunt, Norman Bancroft. Living in the Middle Ages. 2008. (Living in the Ancient World Ser.). (Illus.). 96p. (YA). (gr. 7-12). 35.00 (978-0-8160-6341-3(9)) Facts On File, Inc.

Indovino, Shaina Carmel. Bulgaria. 2012. (J). (978-1-4222-2234-8(9)) Mason Crest.

Johnson, Robert. European History 1870-1918: The Rise of Nationalism. 2003. (Studymates Ser.). (ENG., Illus.). 164p. (C). pap. 27.50 (978-1-84285-031-2(8)) GLMP Ltd. GBR. Dist: Chicago Distribution Ctr.

Johnson, Robin. Pompeii. 2012. (ENG.). 48p. (J). (978-0-7787-7927-8(0)); pap. (978-0-7787-7936-0(X)) Crabtree Publishing Co.

Jovinelly, Joann. The Crafts & Culture of a Medieval Cathedral. 2009. (Crafts & Cultures of the Middle Ages Ser.). 48p. (gr. 5-5). 58.50 (978-1-61512-054-3(8), Rosen Reference) Rosen Publishing Group, Inc., The.

—The Crafts & Culture of a Medieval Guild. 2009. (Crafts & Cultures of the Middle Ages Ser.). 48p. (gr. 5-5). 58.50 (978-1-61512-055-0(6), Rosen Reference) Rosen Publishing Group, Inc., The.

—The Crafts & Culture of a Medieval Manor. 2009. (Crafts & Cultures of the Middle Ages Ser.). 48p. (gr. 5-5). 58.50 (978-1-61512-053-6(X), Rosen Reference) Rosen Publishing Group, Inc., The.

—The Crafts & Culture of a Medieval Monastery. 2009. (Crafts & Cultures of the Middle Ages Ser.). 48p. (gr. 5-5). 58.50 (978-1-61512-056-7(4), Rosen Reference) Rosen Publishing Group, Inc., The.

Jovinelly, Joann & Netelkos, Jason. The Crafts & Culture of a Medieval Cathedral. 2006. (Crafts & Cultures of the Middle Ages Ser.). (Illus.). 48p. (J). (gr. 3-7). lib. bdg. 29.25 (978-1-4042-0758-5(9)) Rosen Publishing Group, Inc., The.

—The Crafts & Culture of a Medieval Guild. 2006. (Crafts & Cultures of the Middle Ages Ser.). (Illus.). 48p. (J). (gr. 3-7). lib. bdg. 29.25 (978-1-4042-0757-8(0)) Rosen Publishing Group, Inc., The.

—The Crafts & Culture of a Medieval Manor. 2006. (Crafts & Cultures of the Middle Ages Ser.). (Illus.). 48p. (J). (gr. 3-7). lib. bdg. 29.25 (978-1-4042-0756-1(2)) Rosen Publishing Group, Inc., The.

—The Crafts & Culture of a Medieval Monastery. 2006. (Crafts & Cultures of the Middle Ages Ser.). (Illus.). 48p. (J). (gr. 4-8). lib. bdg. 29.25 (978-1-4042-0759-2(7)) Rosen Publishing Group, Inc., The.

Kallen, Stuart. The Chunnel. 2014. (Great Idea Ser.). (ENG., Illus.). 48p. (J). (gr. 4-6). pap. 13.26 (978-1-60357-576-8(6)) Norwood Hse. Pr.

Kallen, Stuart A. Medieval Food & Customs. 2014. (The Library of Medieval Times Ser). (ENG., Illus.). 80p. (J). lib. bdg. (978-1-60152-718-9(7)) ReferencePoint Pr., Inc.

Kalman, Bobbie. L'Europe. 2012. (FRE.). 32p. (J). pap. 10.95 (978-2-89579-459-2(6)) Bayard Canada CAN. Dist: Crabtree Publishing Co.

Kennedy, Mike & Stewart, Mark. Soccer in Eastern Europe. 2011. (Smart about Soccer Ser.). 24p. (J). (gr. k-3). lib. bdg. 22.60 (978-1-59953-445-9(2)) Norwood Hse. Pr.

—Soccer in Western Europe. 2011. (Smart about Soccer Ser.). 24p. (J). (gr. k-3). lib. bdg. 22.60 (978-1-59953-447-3(9)) Norwood Hse. Pr.

Kings Curriculum Binder: Absolute Monarchs Curriculum with Audio CD. 2006. 208p. (YA). ring bd. 135.00 (978-0-9791118-0-8(3)) History Jukebox, LLC.

Kopka, Deborah. Norway. 2010. (Country Explorers Ser.). (ENG.). 48p. (gr. 2-4). pap. 9.95 (978-0-7613-5557-1(X)) Lerner Publishing Group.

Kopka, Deborah L. Norway. 2010. (Country Explorers Ser.). (ENG.). 48p. (gr. 2-4). lib. bdg. 29.27 (978-1-58013-603-7(6)) Lerner Publishing Group.

Lee, Adrienne. Knights, 1 vol. Martin, Cynthia, illus. 2013. (Legendary Warriors Ser.). (ENG.). 32p. (gr. 1-2). 26.65 (978-1-4765-3115-1(3), Blazers) Capstone Press of Coughlan Cos.

Libal, Autumn & Indovino, Shaina Carmel. Estonia. 2012. (J). (978-1-4222-2239-3(X)) Mason Crest.

Llimós, Anna. Medieval Castle Adventure Crafts. 2010. (Fun Adventure Crafts Ser.). (Illus.). 32p. (J). pap. 7.95 (978-0-7660-3735-9(5), Enslow Elementary) Enslow Pubs., Inc.

Llimós, Anna & Library Association Staff. Medieval Castle Adventure Crafts. 2010. (Fun Adventure Crafts Ser.). (Illus.). 32p. (J). 23.94 (978-0-7660-3734-2(7), Enslow Elementary) Enslow Pubs., Inc.

MacDonald, Fiona. How to Be a Medieval Knight. Bergin, Mark, illus. 2005. (How to Be Ser.). (ENG.). 32p. (J). (gr. 3-7). 21.90 (978-0-7922-3634-4(3), National Geographic Children's Bks.) National Geographic Society.

Macdonald, Fiona. The Medieval Chronicles: Vikings, Knights, & Castles. Antram, David, illus. 2013. 92p. (J). (978-1-4351-5067-6(8)) Barnes & Noble, Inc.

—Warfare in the Middle Ages. 2015. (Warriors Ser.). (Illus.). 48p. (gr. 4-7). 37.10 (978-1-62588-356-8(0)) Black Rabbit Bks.

—You Wouldn't Want to Be in a Medieval Dungeon! Prisoners You'd Rather Not Meet. Antram, David, illus. 2013. (You Wouldn't Want to... Ser.). (ENG.). (J). 40p. pap. 9.95 (978-0-531-24504-0(7)); 32p. 29.00 (978-0-531-25948-1(X)) Scholastic Library Publishing. (Watts, Franklin).

—You Wouldn't Want to Be in a Medieval Dungeon! Prisoners You'd Rather Not Meet. 2013. (You Wouldn't Want To... Ser.). lib. bdg. 20.80 (978-0-606-31629-3(9), Turtleback) Turtleback Bks.

MacDonald, Fiona & Bergin, Mark. How to Be a Medieval Knight. 2005. (How to Be Ser.). (ENG., Illus.). 32p. (J). (gr. 3-7). 14.95 (978-0-7922-3619-1(X), National Geographic Children's Bks.) National Geographic Society.

Madison, Amelia. Predators of Europe & Africa. 2015. (J). lib. bdg. (978-1-62713-553-5(7)) Cavendish Square Publishing.

McAdam, Claudia Cangilla. Kristoph & the First Christmas Tree: A Legend of St. Boniface. Hill, David, illus. 2015. (ENG.). 32p. (J). 16.99 (978-1-61261-630-8(5)) Paraclete Pr., Inc.

McIntosh, Jane R. Handbook to Life in Prehistoric Europe. 2006. (Handbook to Life Ser.). (Illus.). 404p. (C). (gr. 9-18). 70.00 (978-0-8160-5779-5(6)) Facts On File, Inc.

McKenna, Amy, ed. Estonia, Latvia, Lithuania, & Poland. 2013. (Britannica Guide to Countries of the European Union Ser.). (ENG., Illus.). 240p. (YA). (gr. 9-12). lib. bdg. 53.00 (978-1-61530-971-9(3)) Rosen Publishing Group, Inc., The.

Medieval Europe: PowerPoint Presentations in World History. 2005. cd-rom 49.95 net. (978-1-56004-231-0(1)) Social Studies Schl. Service.

Middle Ages Europe: Mr Donn & Maxie's World History Series. 2006. spiral bd. 29.95 net. (978-1-56004-243-3(5)) Social Studies Schl. Service.

Morris, Neil. Everyday Life in Medieval Europe. 2008. (Uncovering History Ser.). (ENG., Illus.). 48p. (J). (gr. 2-7). 19.95 (978-88-89272-57-2(0)) McRae Bks. Srl ITA. Dist: Independent Pubs. Group.

Murray, Lorraine, ed. Austria, Croatia, & Slovenia. 2013. (Britannica Guide to Countries of the European Union Ser.). (ENG., Illus.). 240p. (YA). (gr. 9-12). lib. bdg. 53.00 (978-1-61530-970-2(5)) Rosen Publishing Group, Inc., The.

Nardo, Don. The Age of Colonialism. 2006. (World History Ser.). (ENG., Illus.). 104p. (YA). (gr. 7-10). lib. bdg. 33.45 (978-1-59018-833-0(0), Lucent Bks.) Cengage Gale.

—The European Colonization of Africa. 2011. (World History Ser.). (Illus.). 112p. 28.95 (978-1-59935-142-1(0)) Reynolds, Morgan Inc.

Oachs, Emily Rose. Croatia. 2016. (Exploring Countries Ser.). (ENG., Illus.). 32p. (J). (gr. 3-7). 26.95 (978-1-62617-403-0(2), Blastoff! Readers) Bellwether Media.

Oachs, Emily Rose. Europe. 2017. (Europe Ser.). 24p. (J). (gr. k-3). pap. 6.99 **(978-1-61891-258-9(5)**, Blastoff! Readers) Bellwether Media.

O'Brian, Pliny. Feudalism in Medieval Europe. 2015. (Exploring the Ancient & Medieval Worlds Ser.). (ENG., Illus.). 160p. (J). (gr. 8-8). lib. bdg. 45.64 (978-1-5026-0681-5(X)) Cavendish Square Publishing.

Oxlade, Chris. Introducing Europe, 1 vol. 2013. (Introducing Continents Ser.). (ENG.). 32p. (gr. 1-3). 27.32 (978-1-4329-8042-9(4)); pap. 8.95 (978-1-4329-8050-4(5)) Heinemann-Raintree. (Heinemann First Library).

Platt, Richard. In the Renaissance. Lawrence, David, illus. 2011. (How They Made Things Work! Ser.). 32p. (YA). (gr. 2-5). lib. bdg. 28.50 (978-1-59771-289-7(2)) Sea-To-Sea Pubns.

Power & Religion in Medieval & Renaissance Times. 2017. (Power & Religion in Medieval & Renaissance Times Ser.). 112p. (gr. 14-15). 145.00 **(978-1-5081-0554-1(5)**, Britannica Educational Publishing) Rosen Publishing Group, Inc., The.

Randall, Jesseca. Christopher Columbus: Navigated by God - A Historical Children's Novel about One of the Most Important Figures of the Age of Exploration. 2009. 124p. pap. 11.99 (978-1-60791-926-1(5)) Salem Author Services.

Randolph, Joanne. Number Crunch Your Way Around Europe. 2015. (Math Exploration: Using Math to Learn about the Continents Ser.). (ENG., Illus.). 32p. (J). (gr. 3-4). pap. 10.00 (978-1-4994-1245-1(2), PowerKids Pr.) Rosen Publishing Group, Inc., The.

Rauf, Don. Europe, Vol. 10. 2016. (Social Progress & Sustainability Ser.). (Illus.). 80p. (J). (gr. 7). 24.95 (978-1-4222-3496-9(7)) Mason Crest.

Riggs, Kate. Knights. 2011. (Great Warriors Ser.). 24p. (J). (ENG.). (gr. 1-3). pap. 9.99 (978-0-89812-572-6(3), Creative Paperbacks); (Illus.). (gr. k-2). 16.95 (978-1-60818-001-1(8), Creative Education) Creative Co., The.

Roscoe, Kelly. The Italian & Northern Renaissance. 2017. (Power & Religion in Medieval & Renaissance Times Ser.). 112p. (gr. 14-15). 36.25 **(978-1-68048-627-8(6)**, Britannica Educational Publishing) Rosen Publishing Group, Inc., The.

Rosinski & Van Hamme, Jean. Chlid of the Stars. Rosinski, Adolf, illus. 2007. (Thorgal Ser.: 1). (ENG.). 96p. per. 19.95 (978-1-905460-23-6(6)) CineBook GBR. Dist: National Bk. Network.

Roumanis, Alexis. Europe. 2014. (Illus.). 24p. (J). (978-1-4896-3038-4(4)) Weigl Pubs., Inc.

—Exploring Continents: Europe. 2015. 24p. pap. 12.95 (978-1-4896-3041-4(4)) Weigl Pubs., Inc.

Sanna, Jeanine & Indovino, Shaina C. Austria. Bruton, John, ed. 2012. (Major European Union Nations Ser.). 64p. (J). (gr. 7). 22.95 (978-1-4222-2232-4(2)) Mason Crest.

Sanna, Jeanine & Indovino, Shaina Carmel. Austria. 2012. (J). pap. (978-1-4222-2263-8(2)) Mason Crest.

Sayre, April Pulley. Hello Europe! 2003. (Exploring Our Continents Ser.: 4). (Illus.). 32p. lib. bdg. 21.90 (978-0-7613-2151-4(9), Millbrook Pr.) Lerner Publishing Group.

Schley, Michael. The Heart of Prague. 2004. (Illus.). 96p. 45.00 (978-0-9759645-0-7(X)) Schley, Michael.

Sebastian, Emily. The Colonial & Postcolonial Experience in Latin America & the Caribbean. 2016. (Colonial & Postcolonial Experience Ser.). 00128p. (J). (gr. 10-10). 54.00 (978-1-5081-0439-1(5)) Rosen Publishing Group, Inc., The.

Shea, John M. Vlad the Impaler. 2016. (History's Most Murderous Villains Ser.). (Illus.). 32p. (J). (gr. 5-4). pap. 10.50 (978-1-4824-4804-7(1)) Stevens, Gareth Publishing LLLP.

Sheehan, Patricia & Quek, Lynette. Moldova. 2nd rev. ed. 2010. (Cultures of the World 20 Ser.). 144p. (gr. 6). 42.79 (978-1-60870-025-7(9)) Marshall Cavendish Corp.

Shukin, Barbara. Renaissance History Portfolio: A History of Europe & the Americas from the 14th -18th Centuries. 2004. (J). ring bd. 29.95 (978-0-9762918-2-4(7)) Homeschool Journey.

Sia, Nicole & Indovino, Shaina Carmel. Finland. 2012. (J). (978-1-4222-2241-6(1)); pap. (978-1-4222-2272-0(1)) Mason Crest.

Snyder, Elaine. Anna & Solomon. Bliss, Harry, illus. 2014. (ENG.). 32p. (J). (gr. -1-3). 17.99 (978-0-374-30362-4(2), 9780374303624, Farrar, Straus & Giroux (BYR)) Farrar, Straus & Giroux.

Spilsbury, Richard & Spilsbury, Louise. Animals in Danger in Europe, 1 vol. 2013. (Animals in Danger Ser.). (ENG.). 32p. (gr. 1-3). 27.32 (978-1-4329-7675-0(3)); pap. 8.95 (978-1-4329-7682-8(6)) Heinemann-Raintree. (Heinemann First Library).

Stanley, George Edward. The European Settlement of North America (1492-1754) 2005. (Primary Source History of the United States Ser.). (Illus.). 48p. (gr. 5-12). pap. 14.05 (978-0-8368-5833-4(6)); lib. bdg. 31.00 (978-0-8368-5824-2(7)) Stevens, Gareth Publishing LLLP. (Gareth Stevens Secondary Library).

Stewart, David. You Wouldn't Want to Be in a Medieval Dungeon! Antram, David, illus. rev. ed. 2013. (You Wouldn't Want to... Ser.). (ENG.). 32p. (J). 29.00 (978-0-531-25949-8(8), Watts, Franklin) Scholastic Library Publishing.

Stiefel, Chana. Sweaty Suits of Armor: Could You Survive Being a Knight? Kelley, Gerald, illus. 2011. (Ye Yucky Middle Ages Ser.). 48p. (J). (gr. 7-12). lib. bdg. 25.27 (978-0-7660-3784-7(3)) Enslow Pubs., Inc.

—There's a Rat in My Soup: Could You Survive Medieval Food? Kelley, Gerald, illus. 2011. (Ye Yucky Middle Ages Ser.). 48p. (J). (gr. 7-12). lib. bdg. 25.27 (978-0-7660-3785-4(1)) Enslow Pubs., Inc.

—Ye Castle Stinketh: Could You Survive Living in a Castle? Kelley, Gerald, illus. 2011. (Ye Yucky Middle Ages Ser.). 48p. (J). (gr. 7-12). lib. bdg. 25.27 (978-0-7660-3786-1(X)) Enslow Pubs., Inc.

Synge, M. B. The Awakening of Europe (Yesterday's Classics) Synge, E. M., illus. l.t. ed. 2006. 268p. (J). per. 11.95 (978-1-59915-015-4(8)) Yesterday's Classics.

Toler, Pamela D. Transatlantic Slave Networks. 2017. (J). **(978-1-5026-2696-7(9))** Cavendish Square Publishing.

Walker, Ida. Belgium. 2007. (European Union Ser.). (Illus.). 88p. (YA). (gr. 3-7). lib. bdg. 21.95 (978-1-4222-0040-7(X), 1247982) Mason Crest.

Walker, Ida & Indovino, Shaina C. Belgium. Bruton, John, ed. 2012. (Major European Union Nations Ser.). 64p. (J). (gr. 7). 22.95 (978-1-4222-2233-1(0)) Mason Crest.

Walker, Ida & Indovino, Shaina Carmel. Belgium. 2012. (J). pap. (978-1-4222-2264-5(0)) Mason Crest.

Watson, Danielle. The Castle in Medieval Europe. 2016. (Life in Medieval Europe Ser.). (Illus.). 80p. (J). (gr. 6-6). 35.64 (978-1-5026-1878-8(8)) Cavendish Square Publishing.

—The Countryside in Medieval Europe. 2016. (Life in Medieval Europe Ser.). (Illus.). 80p. (J). (gr. 6-6). 35.64 (978-1-5026-1882-5(6)) Cavendish Square Publishing.

Watson, Galadriel Findlay. Europe. (J). 2016. **(978-1-4896-5731-2(2))** 2012. (978-1-61913-447-8(0)) 2012. pap. (978-1-61913-448-5(9)) Weigl Pubs., Inc.

Wells, Donald. The Silk Road. 2004. (Great Journeys Ser.). (Illus.). 32p. (J). lib. bdg. 26.00 (978-1-59036-207-5(1)) Weigl Pubs., Inc.

Wilkinson, Carole. How to Live in the Dark Ages. 2007. 96p. (J). pap. (978-1-4207-0725-0(6)) Sundance/Newbridge Educational Publishing.

Wolfe, James. The Industrial Revolution: Steam & Steel. 2015. (Age of Revolution Ser.). (ENG., Illus.). 128p. (J). (gr. 9-10). 35.25 (978-1-68048-026-9(X), Britannica Educational Publishing) Rosen Publishing Group, Inc., The.

Woog, Adam. The Early Middle Ages. 2011. (Understanding World History Ser.). (ENG., Illus.). 96p. (YA). (gr. 7-12). lib. bdg. 27.95 (978-1-60152-151-4(0)) ReferencePoint Pr., Inc.

World Book, Inc Staff, contrib. by. The Age of Knights & Castles. 2011. (J). (978-0-7166-1787-7(0)) World Bk., Inc.

World Book, Inc. Staff, contrib. by. Endangered Animals of Europe. 2014. (J). (978-0-7166-5624-1(8)) World Bk., Inc.

Zocchi, Judy. In Sweden. Brodie, Neale, illus. 2005. (Global Adventures II Ser.). 32p. (J). pap. 10.95 (978-1-59646-176-5(4)) Dingles & Co.

—In Sweden/en Suecia. Brodie, Neale, illus. 2005. (Global Adventures I Ser.).Tr. of En Japón. (ENG & SPA.). 32p. (J). pap. 10.95 (978-1-59646-178-9(0)) Dingles & Co.

—In Switzerland. Brodie, Neale, illus. 2005. (Global Adventures I Ser.). 32p. (J). pap. 10.95 (978-1-59646-156-7(X)); lib. bdg. 21.65 (978-1-59646-006-5(7)) Dingles & Co.

—In Switzerland/en Suiza. Brodie, Neale, illus. 2005. (Global Adventures I Ser.).Tr. of En Suiza. (ENG & SPA.). 32p. (J). pap. 10.95 (978-1-59646-158-1(6)); lib. bdg. 21.65 (978-1-59646-007-2(5)) Dingles & Co.

EUROPE—HISTORY—FICTION

Baldwin, Kathleen. A School for Unusual Girls. 2015. (Stranje House Ser.: 1). (ENG.). 352p. (YA). (gr. 8-12). 17.99 (978-0-7653-7600-8(8), 9780765376008, Tor Teen) Doherty, Tom Assocs., LLC.

Bondoux, Anne-Laure. A Time of Miracles. Maudet, Y., tr. from FRE. 2012. (ENG., Illus.). 192p. (YA). (gr. 7). pap. 7.99 (978-0-375-86036-2(3), Ember) Random Hse. Children's Bks.

Brown, Teri. Born of Deception. 2014. (Born of Illusion Ser.: 2). (ENG.). 336p. (YA). (gr. 8). 17.99 (978-0-06-218757-4(0)) HarperCollins Pubs.

Carlon, Mick. Riding on Duke's Train. 2011. (LeapKids Ser.). (ENG.). 160p. (J). (gr. k-7). pap. 9.95 (978-1-935248-06-4(5)) Leapfrog Pr.

Comrie, Margaret S. The Heroes of Castle Bretten. 2003. (Illus.). 229p. (J). (978-1-894666-65-7(8)) Inheritance Pubns.

de Fombelle, Timothée. Vango: Between Sky & Earth. Ardizzone, Sarah, tr. 2016. (ENG.). 432p. (YA). (gr. 7). pap. 9.99 (978-0-7636-8781-6(2)) Candlewick Pr.

Flusfeder, David. John the Pupil. 2015. 240p. 24.99 (978-0-06-233918-8(4)) HarperCollins Pubs.

Gregory, Philippa. Stormbringers. van Deelen, Fred, illus. 2013. (Order of Darkness Ser.: 2). (ENG.). 336p. (YA). (gr. 9). pap. 9.99 (978-1-4424-7688-2(5)); 17.99 (978-1-4424-7687-5(7)) Simon Pulse. (Simon Pulse).

Haddix, Margaret Peterson. Caught. 2013. (Missing Ser.: 5). lib. bdg. 18.40 (978-0-606-27045-8(0), Turtleback) Turtleback Bks.

Henty, A. G. With Frederick the Great. 2007. 324p. 98.99 (978-1-4280-7565-8(8)); per. 92.99 (978-1-4280-7566-5(6)) IndyPublish.com.

Hill, Will. The Rising: A Department 19 Novel. 2013. (Department Nineteen Ser.: 2). (ENG.). 592p. (YA). (gr. 9). pap. 9.99 (978-1-59514-629-8(6), Razorbill) Penguin Young Readers Group.

Hill, William. Department Nineteen. 2012. (Department Nineteen Ser.: 1). (ENG.). 544p. (YA). (gr. 9). 9.99 (978-1-59514-485-0(4), Razorbill) Penguin Young Readers Group.

Ibbotson, Eva. The Dragonfly Pool. 2009. (ENG.). 384p. (J). (gr. 3-7). 7.99 (978-0-14-241486-6(7), Puffin Books) Penguin Young Readers Group.

—The Dragonfly Pool, 9 vols. 2008. (YA). 120.75 (978-1-4361-5211-2(9)); 90.75 (978-1-4361-5207-5(0)); 92.75 (978-1-4361-5205-1(4)); 256.75 (978-1-4361-5206-8(2)); 122.75 (978-1-4361-5209-9(7)); 1.25 (978-1-4361-5202-0(X)) Recorded Bks., Inc.

Keun, Irmgard. Child of All Nations. Hofmann, Michael, tr. from GER. 2008. (ENG.). 208p. (gr. 4-13). 23.95 (978-1-59020-099-5(3), 902099) Overlook Pr., The.

Lake, A. J. The Book of the Sword. 2007. (Darkest Age Ser.). (ENG.). 240p. (YA). (gr. 4-7). 16.95 (978-1-59990-039-1(4), 9781599900391, Bloomsbury USA Childrens) Bloomsbury Publishing USA.

Lee, Mackenzi. The Gentleman's Guide to Vice & Virtue. 2017. 528p. (YA). (gr. 8). 18.99 (978-0-06-238280-1(2), Tegen, Katherine Bks) HarperCollins Pubs.

Marsh, Katherine. Jepp, Who Defied the Stars. 2013. (ENG.). 400p. (J). (gr. 5-9). pap. 9.99 (978-1-4231-3786-3(8)) Hyperion Pr.

Meyer, L. A. Viva Jacquelina! Being an Account of the Further Adventures of Jacky Faber, over the Hills & Far Away. 2014. (Bloody Jack Adventures Ser.: 10). (ENG.). 384p. (YA). (gr. 9). pap. 9.99 (978-0-544-23439-0(1), HMH Books For Young Readers) Houghton Mifflin Harcourt Publishing Co.

Montgomery, R. A. Return to Haunted House. 2010. (Illus.). 80p. (J). pap. 7.99 (978-1-933390-40-6(9)) Chooseco LLC.

O'Brien, Johnny. Day of the Assassins. Hardcastle, Nick, illus. 2010. (Jack Christie Adventure Ser.: 1). (ENG.). 224p. (J). (gr. 4-7). pap. 6.99 (978-0-7636-4995-1(3), Templar) Candlewick Pr.

—Day of the Assassins: A Jack Christie Novel. Hardcastle, Nick, illus. 2009. (Jack Christie Adventure Ser.: 1). (ENG.). 224p. (J). (gr. 4-7). 15.99 (978-0-7636-4595-3(8), Templar) Candlewick Pr.

Peyton, K. M. Wild Lily. 2017. (ENG.). 336p. (J). (gr. 7). 18.99 (978-1-338-08160-2(8)) Scholastic, Inc.

Ruiz Zafón, Carlos. The Prince of Mist. 2011. (ENG.). 256p. (YA). (gr. 7-17). pap., pap. 10.99 (978-0-316-04480-6(6)) Little, Brown Bks. for Young Readers.

Scott, Elaine. The Spanish Web: An Encounter with Picasso. 2004. (Art Encounters Ser.). (J). 15.95 (978-0-8230-0410-2(4)); pap. 6.99 (978-0-8230-0413-3(9)) Watson-Guptill Pubns., Inc.

Sedgwick, Marcus. Midwinterblood. 2013. (ENG.). 272p. (YA). (gr. 7). 17.99 (978-1-59643-800-2(2), 9781596438002) Roaring Brook Pr.

—Midwinterblood. 2014. (ENG., Illus.). 288p. (YA). (gr. 7). pap. 9.99 (978-1-250-04007-7(8), 9781250040077) Square Fish.

Sepetys, Ruta. Between Shades of Gray. 2009. 10.36 (978-0-7848-3779-5(1), Everbind) Marco Bk. Co.

—Between Shades of Gray. (ENG., (YA). (gr. 7-18). 2012. Illus.). 384p. pap. 9.99 (978-0-14-242059-1(X), Speak) 2011. 352p. 17.99 (978-0-399-25412-3(9), Philomel Bks.) Penguin Young Readers Group.

—Between Shades of Gray. l.t. ed. 2011. (ENG.). 420p. (YA). 23.99 (978-1-4104-4083-9(4)) Thorndike Pr.

—Between Shades of Gray. 2012. lib. bdg. 20.85 (978-0-606-26089-3(7), Turtleback) Turtleback Bks.

Spradlin, Michael. Orphan of Destiny: Book 3, 3 vols. 2011. (Youngest Templar Ser.: 3). (ENG.). 272p. (J). (gr. 5-18). 7.99 (978-0-14-241959-5(1), Puffin Books) Penguin Young Readers Group.

Storrie, Paul D. William Tell: A Swiss Legend. Yeates, Thomas, illus. 2008. (Graphic Myths & Legends Ser.). (ENG.). 48p. (gr. 4-8). 27.93 (978-0-8225-7175-9(7), Graphic Universe™) Lerner Publishing Group.

Synge, M. B. The Struggle for Sea Power. 2008. 152p. pap. 9.99 (978-1-60459-496-6(9)) Wilder Pubns., Corp.

Van Halsema, Thea B. This Was John Calvin. 2011. 184p. (gr. 3-7). 42.95 (978-1-258-05962-0(2)) Literary Licensing, LLC.

Van Ryk, Laverne. A Garland of Emeralds. 2006. (Illus.). 305p. 31.50 (978-1-4122-0156-8(X)) Trafford Publishing.

Whitcomb, Laura. The Fetch. 2010. (ENG.). 384p. (YA). (gr. 7). pap. 20.99 (978-0-547-41163-7(4)) Houghton Mifflin Harcourt Publishing Co.

Wisniewski, David. Golem. Wisniewski, David, illus. 2007. (ENG., Illus.). 32p. (J). (gr. 5-7). 7.99 (978-0-618-89424-6(1)) Houghton Mifflin Harcourt Publishing Co.

Wolf, Joan M. Someone Named Eva. 2009. (ENG., Illus.). 208p. (J). (gr. 5-7). pap. 7.99 (978-0-547-23766-4(9)) Houghton Mifflin Harcourt Publishing Co.

EUROPE—HISTORY—TO 476

Hinds, Kathryn. Huns. 2009. (Barbarians! Ser.). 80p. (gr. 6). 35.64 (978-0-7614-4066-6(6)) Marshall Cavendish GBR. Dist: Marshall Cavendish Corp.

Kroll, Steven. Barbarians! Byrd, Robert, illus. 2009. (ENG.). 48p. (J). (gr. 3-7). 20.99 (978-0-525-47958-1(9), Dutton Books for Young Readers) Penguin Young Readers Group.

Rice, Earle. The Life & Times of Attila the Hun. 2009. (Biography from Ancient Civilizations Ser.). 48p. (J). (gr. 4-8). 29.95 (978-1-58415-741-0(0)) Mitchell Lane Pubs., Inc.

EUROPE—HISTORY—476-1492

see also Holy Roman Empire; Hundred Years' War, 1339-1453

Bredeson, Carmen. Don't Let the Barber Pull Your Teeth: Could You Survive Medieval Medicine? Kelley, Gerald, illus. 2011. (Ye Yucky Middle Ages Ser.). 48p. (J). (gr. 5-18). pap. 8.95 (978-1-59845-373-7(4)) Enslow Pubs., Inc.

Currie, Stephen. Medieval Punishment & Torture. 2014. (The Library of Medieval Times Ser). (ENG., Illus.). 80p. (J). lib. bdg. (978-1-60152-658-8(X)) ReferencePoint Pr., Inc.

Dwyer, Helen. The Middle Ages, 600 to 1492. 2010. (CC: Atlas of World History Ser.). 112p. (gr. 6-12). 42.80 (978-1-933834-67-2(6)) Brown Bear Bks.

Hanawalt, Barbara. The European World, 400-1450. 2006. (Illus.). 189p. 32.95 (978-0-19-522267-8(9)) Oxford Univ. Pr., Inc.

Hanawalt, Barbara A. The European World, 400-1450. 2005. (Medieval & Early Modern World Ser.). (ENG., Illus.). 192p. (YA). 36.95 (978-0-19-517844-9(0)) Oxford Univ. Pr., Inc.

Hardyman, Robyn. Horrible Jobs in Medieval Times, Vol. 1. 2014. (History's Most Horrible Jobs Ser.). 48p. (J). (gr. 5-6). (ENG.). 31.95 (978-1-4824-0337-4(4)); pap. 14.05 (978-1-4824-0339-8(0)) Stevens, Gareth Publishing LLLP.

Hattstein, Markus & Udelhoven, Hermann-Josef. The Middle Ages & the Early Modern Period: From the 5th Century to the 18th Century. 2012. (Witness to History: A Visual Chronicle of the World Ser.). (ENG., Illus.). 200p. (J). (gr. 7-12). 46.50 (978-1-4488-7223-7(5)) Rosen Publishing Group, Inc., The.

Hull, Robert. Stonemason. 2009. (J). 32.80 (978-1-59920-173-3(9)) Black Rabbit Bks.

Kenney, Karen Latchana. Harsh or Heroic? The Middle Ages. 2007. (Shockwave: History & Politics Ser.). (ENG., Illus.). 36p. (J). (gr. 3-5). 25.00 (978-0-531-17754-9(8), Children's Pr.) Scholastic Library Publishing.

Kems, Ann. Did Castles Have Bathrooms? And Other Questions about the Middle Ages. 2010. (Is That a Fact? Ser.). (ENG.). 40p. (gr. 4-6). lib. bdg. 26.60 (978-0-7613-4915-0(4)) Lerner Publishing Group.

Kroll, Steven. Barbarians! Byrd, Robert, illus. 2009. (ENG.). 48p. (J). (gr. 3-7). 20.99 (978-0-525-47958-1(9), Dutton Books for Young Readers) Penguin Young Readers Group.

MacDonald, Fiona. Monarchs in the Middle Ages. 2005. (World Almanac Library of the Middle Ages). (Illus.). 48p. (gr. 5-12). pap. 14.05 (978-0-8368-5905-8(7), Gareth Stevens Secondary Library) Stevens, Gareth Publishing LLLP.

—Monarchs in the Middle Ages. 2005. (World Almanac Library of the Middle Ages). (Illus.). 48p. (gr. 5-12). lib. bdg. 31.00 (978-0-8368-5896-9(4), Gareth Stevens Secondary Library) Stevens, Gareth Publishing LLLP.

Nardo, Don. Medeival Europe: Medieval Europe. 2011. (World History Ser.). (gr. 7-12). 28.95 (978-1-59935-172-8(2)) Reynolds, Morgan Inc.

Park, Louise. Life in the Middle Ages. 2013. (Discovery Education: Ancient Civilizations Ser.). (ENG., Illus.). 32p. (J). (gr. 3-6). pap. 10.00 (978-1-4777-0095-2(1)); lib. bdg. 25.25 (978-1-4777-0055-6(2)) Rosen Publishing Group, Inc., The. (PowerKids Pr.).

Powell, Jillian & Buckingham, Matt. The Middle Ages. 2010. (Gruesome Truth about Ser.). (ENG.). 32p. (J). (gr. 4-6). lib. bdg. 22.60 (978-1-61533-219-9(7)) Windmill Bks.

Ross, Stewart. Medieval Europe, 1 vol. 2010. (Research It! Ser.). (ENG., Illus.). 56p. (gr. 6-9). lib. bdg. 34.65 (978-1-4329-3498-9(8), NA-h) Heinemann-Raintree.

Samuels, Charlie. Timeline of the Middle Ages. 2010. (History Highlights: A Gareth Stevens Timeline Ser.). (Illus.). 48p. (gr. 6-8). (J). pap. 14.05 (978-1-4339-3484-1(1)); (YA). lib. bdg. 31.95 (978-1-4339-3483-4(3)) Stevens, Gareth Publishing LLLP. (Gareth Stevens Secondary Library).

Watson, Danielle. The City in Medieval Europe. 2016. (Life in Medieval Europe Ser.). (Illus.). 80p. (J). (gr. 6-6). 35.64 (978-1-5026-1880-1(X)) Cavendish Square Publishing.

EUROPE—HISTORY—1492-1789

see also Thirty Years' War, 1618-1648

Hattstein, Markus & Udelhoven, Hermann-Josef. The Middle Ages & the Early Modern Period: From the 5th Century to the 18th Century. 2012. (Witness to History: A Visual Chronicle of the World Ser.). (ENG., Illus.). 200p. (J). (gr. 7-12). 46.50 (978-1-4488-7223-7(5)) Rosen Publishing Group, Inc., The.

Hinds, Kathryn. The Countryside. 2004. (Life in the Roman Empire Ser.). (Illus.). 80p. (gr. 6). 34.21 (978-0-7614-1656-2(0), Benchmark Bks.) Marshall Cavendish Corp.

Roscoe, Kelly, ed. The Emergence of Modern Europe. 2017. (Power & Religion in Medieval & Renaissance Times Ser.). 112p. (gr. 14-15). 36.25 **(978-1-68048-621-6(7)**, Britannica Educational Publishing) Rosen Publishing Group, Inc., The.

EUROPE—HISTORY—18TH CENTURY

Allman, Toney. The Enlightenment. 2014. (Understanding World History Ser.). (Illus.). 96p. (J). lib. bdg. (978-1-60152-740-0(3)) ReferencePoint Pr., Inc.

EUROPE—HISTORY—1789-1900

Arnold, James R. The Aftermath of the French Revolution. 2008. (Aftermath of History Ser.). (ENG.). 160p. (gr. 9-12). lib. bdg. 38.60 (978-0-8225-7598-6(1)) Lerner Publishing Group.

Maybury, Richard J. World War I: The Rest of the Story & How It Affects You Today, 1870 To 1935. Williams, Jane A., ed. rev. ed. 2003. ("Uncle Eric" Bk.: 10). (ENG., Illus.). 253p. pap. 17.95 (978-0-942617-42-9(8)) Bluestocking Pr.

EUROPE—HISTORY—20TH CENTURY

Fremon, David K. Schindler, Wallenberg, Miep Gies: The Holocaust Heroes. 2014. (Remembering the Holocaust Ser.). 96p. (J). (gr. 6-12). 27.94 (978-0-7660-6217-7(1)) Enslow Pubs., Inc.

Gunderson, Cory. Great Depression, 1 vol. 2004. (American Moments Ser.). (ENG.). 48p. (gr. 4-8). 27.07 (978-1-59197-286-0(8), Abdo & Daughters) ABDO Publishing Co.

Prentzas, G. S. The Marshall Plan. 2011. (Milestones in Modern World History Ser.). 128p. (C). (gr. 9). 35.00 (978-1-60413-460-5(7), Chelsea Hse.) Facts On File, Inc.

Smith, William Herbert Cecil. Twentieth Century Europe. 2004. (Twentieth Century History Ser.). (Illus.). 127p. (978-0-298-76285-9(4), Weidenfeld & Nicolson) Orion Publishing Group, Ltd.

Undset, Sigrid. Happy Times in Norway. 2013. (ENG., Illus.). 240p. pap. 16.95 (978-0-8166-7827-3(8)) Univ. of Minnesota Pr.

Yeatts, Tabatha. Wiesel, Wiesenthal, Klarsfeld: The Holocaust Survivors. 2014. (Remembering the Holocaust Ser.). 96p. (J). (gr. 6-12). pap. 10.95 (978-0-7660-6203-0(1)) Enslow Pubs., Inc.

EUROPE—HISTORY—1914-1945

see also World War, 1939-1945

Jeffrey, Gary. The Western Front. 2012. (ENG., Illus.). 48p. (J). (978-0-7787-4196-1(6)); pap. (978-0-7787-4203-6(2)) Crabtree Publishing Co.

EUROPE—HISTORY—1945-

European Commission Staff, contrib. by. May Day: Young Literature from the Ten New Member States of the European Union. 2005. (ENG & MUL., Illus.). 152p. (978-92-894-9358-1(5)) Office for Official Pubns. of the European Communities.

Mason, Antony. New Europe. 2009. (J). 32.80 (978-1-59604-208-7(7)) Black Rabbit Bks.

Seidlitz, Lauri. The Legacy of World War II. 2015. (ENG., Illus.). 48p. (J). (978-0-7787-2117-8(5)) Crabtree Publishing Co.

EUROPE—KINGS AND RULERS

Chambers, Catherine. A King's Guide. Pentney, Ryan, illus. 2017. (How-To Guides for Fiendish Rulers Ser.). (ENG.). 32p. (J). (gr. 3-6). lib. bdg. 26.65 (978-1-5124-1550-6(2)); 7.99 **(978-1-5124-3624-2(0))**; 39.99 **(978-1-5124-2706-6(3))**; 39.99 **(978-1-5124-3623-5(2))** Lerner Publishing Group.

Flatt, Lizann. Cities & Statecraft in the Renaissance. 2009. (Renaissance World Ser.). (ENG.). 32p. (J). (gr. 6-9). pap. (978-0-7787-4615-7(1)); (Illus.). (gr. 5-7). (978-0-7787-4595-2(3)) Crabtree Publishing Co.

Heos, Bridget. Who Wants to Be a Princess? What It Was Really Like to Be a Medieval Princess. Migy, illus. 2017. (ENG.). 32p. (J). 16.99 (978-0-8050-9769-6(4), 9780805097696, Holt, Henry & Co. Bks. For Young Readers) Holt, Henry & Co.

EUROPE—POLITICS AND GOVERNMENT

Adams, Simon. Britain & the European Union. 2017. (ENG., Illus.). 64p. (J). (gr. 4-6). 17.99 (978-1-4451-5062-8(X), Franklin Watts) Hachette Children's Group GBR. Dist: Hachette Bk. Group.

Allport, Alan. The Congress of Vienna. 2011. (Milestones in Modern World History Ser.). (Illus.). 126p. (J). (gr. 9). 35.00 (978-1-60413-497-1(6), Chelsea Hse.) Facts On File, Inc.

Baker, Brynn. Life in America: Comparing Immigrant Experiences. 2015. (U. S. Immigration in The 1900s Ser.). (ENG., Illus.). 48p. (gr. 3-4). pap. 8.95 (978-1-4914-4174-9(7)) Capstone Press of Coughlan Cos.

Colligan, Louise H. Government. 2014. (Life in Colonial America Ser.). 80p. (YA). (gr. 6-8). lib. bdg. 35.64 (978-1-62712-891-9(3)) Cavendish Square Publishing.

Greene, Meg. The Transcontinental Treaty 1819: A Primary Source Examination of the Treaty Between the United States & Spain over the American West. 2009. (Primary Sources of American Treaties Ser.). 64p. (gr. 5-8). 58.50 (978-1-60851-514-1(1)) Rosen Publishing Group, Inc., The.

Heing, Bridey. Trade Routes to India. 2017. (J). **(978-1-5026-2694-3(2))** Cavendish Square Publishing.

Heuston, Kimberley. Otto von Bismarck: Iron Chancellor of Germany. 2009. (Wicked History Ser.). (ENG., Illus.). 128p. (YA). (gr. 5-9). 31.00 (978-0-531-21278-3(5)) Scholastic Library Publishing.

Indovino, Shaina Carmel. The European Union: Facts & Figures. 2012. (J). (978-1-4222-2240-9(3)); (978-1-4222-2231-7(4)); pap. (978-1-4222-2271-3(3)) Mason Crest.

Kelly, Martin & Kelly, Melissa. Government. 2007. (ENG., Illus.). 96p. (C). (gr. 6-18). lib. bdg. 158.00 (978-0-7656-8112-6(9), Y182476) Routledge.

Kravitz, Danny. Journey to America: A Chronology of Immigration in the 1900s. 2015. (U. S. Immigration in The 1900s Ser.). (ENG., Illus.). 48p. (gr. 3-4). pap. 8.95 (978-1-4914-4172-5(0)) Capstone Press of Coughlan Cos.

MacDonald, Fiona. Monarchs in the Middle Ages. 2005. (World Almanac Library of the Middle Ages). (Illus.). 48p. (gr. 5-12). pap. 14.05 (978-0-8368-5905-8(7), Gareth Stevens Secondary Library) Stevens, Gareth Publishing LLLP.

—Monarchs in the Middle Ages. 2005. (World Almanac Library of the Middle Ages). (Illus.). 48p. (gr. 5-12). lib. bdg. 31.00 (978-0-8368-5896-9(4), Gareth Stevens Secondary Library) Stevens, Gareth Publishing LLLP.

Marriott, Emma. Did Anything Good Come Out of the Great Depression?, 01 vols., 1. 2016. (Innovation Through Adversity Ser.). (ENG.). 48p. (J). 30.25 (978-1-5081-7072-3(X), Rosen Young Adult) Rosen Publishing Group, Inc., The.

Paul, Michael. Pan Am 103 & State-Sponsored Terrorism. 2006. (Terrorism in Today's World Ser.). (Illus.). 48p. (gr. 5-12). pap. 14.05 (978-0-8368-6566-0(9)); lib. bdg. 31.00 (978-0-8368-6559-2(6)) Stevens, Gareth Publishing LLLP. (Gareth Stevens Secondary Library).

Whiting, Jim. The Life & Times of Pericles. 2005. (Biography from Ancient Civilizations Ser.). (Illus.). 48p. (J). (gr. -1-7). lib. bdg. 29.95 (978-1-58415-339-9(3)) Mitchell Lane Pubs., Inc.

EUROPEAN COMMON MARKET

see European Economic Community

EUROPEAN ECONOMIC COMMUNITY

Docalavich, Heather. Sweden. 2007. (European Union Ser.). (Illus.). 88p. (YA). (gr. 3-7). lib. bdg. 21.95 (978-1-4222-0063-6(9)) Mason Crest.

Etingoff, Kim. Portugal. 2007. (European Union Ser.). (Illus.). 88p. (YA). (gr. 3-7). lib. bdg. 21.95 (978-1-4222-0059-9(0)) Mason Crest.

Simons, Rae. Luxembourg. 2007. (European Union Ser.). (Illus.). 88p. (YA). (gr. 3-7). lib. bdg. 21.95 (978-1-4222-0055-1(8)) Mason Crest.

Stafford, James. Malta. 2007. (European Union Ser.). (Illus.). 88p. (YA). (gr. 3-7). lib. bdg. 21.95 (978-1-4222-0056-8(6)) Mason Crest.

EUROPEAN WAR, 1914-1918

see World War, 1914-1918

EUROPEAN WAR, 1939-1945

see World War, 1939-1945

EUTHANASIA

see also Assisted Suicide; Right to Die

Coster, Patience. Euthanasia. 2012. (Both Sides of the Story Ser.). (ENG., Illus.). 48p. (YA). (gr. 5-8). 29.25 (978-1-4488-7186-5(7), Rosen Reference) Rosen Publishing Group, Inc., The.

Ferguson, John E. & Ferguson, John E., Jr. The Right to Die. 2007. (Point/Counterpoint Ser.). (Illus.). 109p. (YA). (gr. 9-12). lib. bdg. 35.00 (978-0-7910-9287-3(9)) Facts On File, Inc.

Forman, Lillian. Assisted Suicide, 1 vol. 2008. (Essential Viewpoints Set 2 Ser.). (ENG., Illus.). 112p. (J). (gr. 6-12). lib. bdg. 35.64 (978-1-60453-056-8(1)) ABDO Publishing Co.

Harris, Nancy. The Right to Die. annot. ed. 2005. (At Issue Ser.). (ENG.). 94p. (YA). (gr. 10-12). pap. 31.80 (978-0-7377-3439-3(6), Greenhaven Pr., Inc.) Cengage Gale.

Medina, Loreta M., ed. Euthanasia. 2004. (History of Issues Ser.). (ENG.). 235p. (YA). (gr. 10-13). lib. bdg. 42.15 (978-0-7377-2005-1(0), Greenhaven Pr., Inc.) Cengage Gale.

Nakaya, Andrea C., ed. Terminal Illness. 2005. (Opposing Viewpoints Ser.). (ENG., Illus.). 204p. (YA). (gr. 10-13). pap. 39.70 (978-0-7377-2963-4(5), Greenhaven Pr., Inc.) Cengage Gale.

Stearman, Kaye. The Debate about Euthanasia. 2010. (Ethical Debates Ser.). (ENG.). 48p. (YA). lib. bdg. 29.25 (978-1-4358-9652-9(1), Rosen Reference) Rosen Publishing Group, Inc., The.

Stefoff, Rebecca. The Right to Die. 2008. (Open for Debate Ser.). 128p. (gr. 7-18). lib. bdg. 42.79 (978-0-7614-2948-7(4), Benchmark Bks.) Marshall Cavendish Corp.

Wise, Steve. Critical World Issues: Euthanasia, Vol. 16. 2016. (Critical World Issues Ser.: Vol. 16). (ENG., Illus.). 112p. (J). (gr. 7-12). 25.95 (978-1-4222-3653-6(6)) Mason Crest.

Woodward, John. The Right to Die. annot. ed. 2004. (At Issue Ser.). (ENG.). 94p. (YA). (gr. 10-12). 22.50 (978-0-7377-3440-9(X), Greenhaven Pr., Inc.) Cengage Gale.

Woolf, Alex. Euthanasia. 2004. (World Issues Ser.). (J). lib. bdg. (978-1-59389-156-5(3)) Chrysalis Education.

Yount, Lisa. Right to Die & Euthanasia. 2nd rev. ed. 2007. (Library in a Book). (Illus.). 320p. (C). (gr. 9-18). 45.00 (978-0-8160-6275-1(7)) Facts On File, Inc.

EVALUATION OF LITERATURE

see Books and Reading; Criticism; Literature—History and Criticism

EVANGELICALISM

Donahue, Laurie. God's Plan My Response. Rittenhouse, Ralph, ed. 2003. (Illus.). 100p. pap. 10.99 (978-0-9718306-0-8(6)) LifeSong Pubs.

Donahue, Laurie & Rittenhouse, Ralph. God... Should I Be Baptized? 2003. (Illus.). 96p. (gr. 4-6). pap. 11.99 (978-0-9718306-1-5(4)) LifeSong Pubs.

EVANGELISTS

Benge, Janet & Benge, Geoff. D. L. Moody: Bringing Souls to Christ. 2011. (ENG.). (YA). pap. 9.99 (978-1-57658-552-8(2)) YWAM Publishing.

Davis, Rebecca. George Mueller: A Father to the Fatherless. 2004. (Illus.). 135p. (J). pap. 7.49 (978-1-59166-255-6(9)) BJU Pr.

Dredge, Kath. Living 4 God: Learning from the Lives of William Tyndale, John Newton, David Brainerd, Eric Liddell. 2007. (Illus.). 80p. 7.00 (978-1-84625-034-7(X)) DayOne Pubns. GBR. Dist: Send The Light Distribution LLC.

Liardon, Roberts & Goldenberg, Olly. God's Generals for Kids, Volume 2: Smith Wigglesworth. 2013. (ENG., Illus.). 160p. (J). (gr. 4-7). pap. 11.99 (978-1-61036-115-6(6)) Bridge-Logos, Inc.

Martin, William C. Prophet with Honor: The Billy Graham Story, 1 vol. 2013. (ZonderKidz Biography Ser.). (ENG., Illus.). 144p. (J). pap. 6.99 (978-0-310-71935-9(6)) Zonderkidz.

Sheafer, Silvia Anne. Aimee Semple McPherson. 2004. (Spiritual Leaders & Thinkers Ser.). (Illus.). 120p. (C). (gr. 9-13). 30.00 (978-0-7910-7867-9(1), Chelsea Hse.) Facts On File, Inc.

EVANGELISTS—FICTION

Paulsen, Gary. The Tent: A Parable in One Sitting. 2006. (ENG., Illus.). 96p. (YA). (gr. 7-12). pap. 7.95 (978-0-15-205833-3(8)) Houghton Mifflin Harcourt Publishing Co.

—The Tent: A Parable in One Sitting. 2006. 86p. (gr. 7-12). 15.95 (978-0-7569-6891-5(7)) Perfection Learning Corp.

Walters, Helen B. When John Wesley Was a Boy. 2011. 98p. 38.95 (978-1-258-06562-1(2)) Literary Licensing, LLC.

EVANS, ARTHUR, SIR, 1851-1941

Evans, Arthur. The Palace of Minos 4 Volume Set in 7 Pieces: A Comparative Account of the Successive Stages of the Early Cretan Civilization As Illustrated by the Discoveries at Knossos. 2013. (Cambridge Library Collection - Archaeology Ser.). (ENG.). 3734p. pap., pap., pap. 417.00 (978-1-108-06107-0(9)) Cambridge Univ. Pr.

EVEREST, MOUNT (CHINA AND NEPAL)

Alcraft, Rob. Everest Ice Climbers. 2017. (ENG.). 48p. (J). pap. 8.99 **(978-0-00-820887-5(5))** HarperCollins Pubs. Ltd. GBR. Dist: Independent Pubs. Group.

Bodden, Valerie. Mount Eeverest. 2010. (Big Outdoors Ser.). 24p. (J). (gr. k-3). 16.95 (978-1-58341-817-8(2)) Creative Co., The.

—To the Top of Mount Everest. (Great Expeditions Ser.). (Illus.). 48p. (J). 2012. (ENG.). (gr. 4-7). pap. 12.00 (978-0-89812-668-6(1)) 2011. (gr. 5-8). lib. bdg. 34.25 (978-1-60818-070-7(0)) Creative Co., The. (Creative Education).

Burleigh, Robert. Tiger of the Snows: Tenzing Norgay: the Boy Whose Dream Was Everest. Young, Ed, illus. 2010. (ENG.). 40p. (J). (gr. 2-5). 16.99 (978-1-4424-2192-9(4), Atheneum Bks. for Young Readers) Simon & Schuster Children's Publishing.

Coburn, Broughton. Triumph on Everest: A Photobiography of Sir Edmund Hillary. 2003. (Photographies Ser.). (ENG., Illus.). 64p. (J). (gr. 5). pap. 7.95 (978-0-7922-7932-7(8), National Geographic Children's Bks.) National Geographic Society.

Crompton, Samuel Willard. Sir Edmund Hillary. 2009. (Great Explorers Ser.). (Illus.). 112p. (J). (gr. 6-12). 30.00 (978-1-60413-420-9(8), Chelsea Hse.) Facts On File, Inc.

Dickmann, Nancy. Mount Everest, 1 vol. 2012. (Explorer Tales Ser.). (ENG.). 32p. (gr. 1-3). 29.99 (978-1-4109-4783-3(1), Read Me!) Heinemann-Raintree.

Dowswell, Paul. True Everest Adventures. Woodcock, John, illus. 2004. (True Adventure Stories Ser.). 144p. (J). pap. 4.95 (978-0-7945-0373-4(X), Usborne) EDC Publishing.

Glassman, Jackie. La conquista del Monte Everest. 2011. (SPA.). 32p. (J). pap. 49.00 net. (978-1-4108-2343-4(1), A23431) Benchmark Education Co.

Graham, Ian. You Wouldn't Want to Climb Mount Everest! A Deadly Journey to the Top of the World. 2010. (You Wouldn't Want to... Ser.). 32p. (J). 29.00 (978-0-531-20505-1(3)); (ENG., Illus.). (gr. 3-18). pap. 9.95 (978-0-531-13785-7(6)) Scholastic Library Publishing. (Watts, Franklin).

Heinrichs, Ann. Mount Everest. 2009. (Nature's Wonders 2 Ser.). 96p. (gr. 6). 35.64 (978-0-7614-3933-2(1)) Marshall Cavendish Corp.

Helfand, Lewis. Conquering Everest: The Lives of Edmund Hillary & Tenzing Norgay. Tayal, Amit, illus. 2011. (Campfire Graphic Novels Ser.). (ENG.). 96p. (YA). (gr. 5-12). pap. 12.99 (978-93-80741-24-6(3), Campfire) Steerforth Pr.

Hinman, Bonnie. Mount Everest. 2014. (ENG., Illus.). 47p. (J). lib. bdg. 29.95 (978-1-62469-002-0(5)) Purple Toad Publishing, Inc.

Hyde, Natalie. Conquering Everest. 2013. (ENG., Illus.). 48p. (J). pap. (978-0-7787-1175-9(7)) Crabtree Publishing Co.

Jankowski, Emily. Reaching Everest's Summit. 2015. (Incredible True Adventures Ser.). (ENG., Illus.). 32p. (J). (gr. 3-4). pap. 10.50 (978-1-4824-2046-3(5)) Stevens, Gareth Publishing LLLP.

Johnson, Robin. Conquering Everest. 2013. (ENG., Illus.). 48p. (J). (978-0-7787-1167-4(6)) Crabtree Publishing Co.

Jones, Brenn. Learning about Teamwork from the Lives of Sir Edmund Hillary & Tenzing Norgay. 2009. (Character Building Book Ser.). 24p. (gr. 2-3). 42.50 (978-1-60854-968-9(2), PowerKids Pr.) Rosen Publishing Group, Inc., The.

Kalz, Jill. Mount Everest. 2004. (Natural Wonders of the World Ser.). (Illus.). 32p. (J). lib. bdg. (978-1-58341-325-8(1), Creative Education) Creative Co., The.

Lappi, Megan. Mount Everest. (J). 2012. (978-1-61913-527-7(2)) 2004. lib. bdg. 26.00 (978-1-59036-271-6(3)) Weigl Pubs., Inc.

—Mount Everest: The Highest Mountain in the World. 2006. (Natural Wonders Ser.). (Illus.). 32p. (J). (gr. 3-7). lib. bdg. 26.00 (978-1-59036-450-5(3)); (gr. 5-6). pap. 9.95 (978-1-59036-456-7(2), 1266425) Weigl Pubs., Inc.

Marsico, Katie. The Highest & the Lowest. 2015. (True Book(tm), a — Extreme Places Ser.). (ENG., Illus.). 48p. (J). lib. bdg. 31.00 (978-0-531-21723-8(X), Children's Pr.) Scholastic Library Publishing.

Medina, Nico. Where Is Mount Everest? Hinderliter, John & Groff, David, illus. 2015. (Where Is? Ser.). (ENG.). 112p. (J). (gr. 3-7). 5.99 (978-0-448-48408-2(0), Grosset & Dunlap) Penguin Young Readers Group.

—Where Is Mount Everest? 2015. (Where Is... ? Ser.). lib. bdg. 16.00 (978-0-606-36759-2(4)) Turtleback Bks.

Megan, Lappi. Mount Everest: The Highest Mountain in the World. 2006. (Natural Wonders Ser.). (Illus.). 32p. (gr. 3-7). 17.95 (978-0-7569-6995-0(6)) Perfection Learning Corp.

Salkeld, Audrey. Climbing Everest: Tales of Triumph & Tragedy on the World's Highest Mountain. 2003. (ENG., Illus.). 128p. (J). (gr. 5). 21.00 (978-0-7922-5105-7(9), National Geographic Children's Bks.) National Geographic Society.

Sandler, Michael. Mountains: Surviving on Mt. Everest. 2005. (X-treme Places Ser.). (Illus.). 32p. (J). (gr. 2-5). lib. bdg. 25.27 (978-1-59716-086-5(5)) Bearport Publishing Co., Inc.

Shea, Therese. Climbing Mount Everest: Understanding Commutative, Associative, & Distributive Properties. (PowerMath Ser.). (Illus.). 32p. (gr. 5-6). 2009. (ENG.). pap. 10.00 (978-1-4042-5142-7(1), PowerKids Pr.) 2005. (YA). lib. bdg. 25.25 (978-1-4042-2939-6(6)) Rosen Publishing Group, Inc., The.

—Climbing Mount Everest: Understanding Commutative, Associative & Distributive Properties. 2009. (PowerMath: Proficiency Plus Ser.). 32p. (gr. 4-5). 47.90 (978-1-60851-408-3(0), PowerKids Pr.) Rosen Publishing Group, Inc., The.

Sheehan, Robert. Conquering Mount Everest. 2013. (Discovery Education: Sensational True Stories Ser.). (ENG., Illus.). 32p. (J). (gr. 3-6). pap. 10.00 (978-1-4777-0109-6(5)); lib. bdg. 25.25 (978-1-4777-0062-4(5)) Rosen Publishing Group, Inc., The. (PowerKids Pr.).

Skreslet, Laurie & MacLeod, Elizabeth. To the Top of Everest. 2003. (ENG., Illus.). 56p. (J). (gr. 3-6). 9.95 (978-1-55074-814-7(9)) Kids Can Pr., Ltd. CAN. Dist: Hachette Bk. Group.

Taylor-Butler, Christine. Sacred Mountain: Everest. 2009. (ENG., Illus.). 48p. (J). (gr. 2-7). 19.95 (978-1-60060-255-9(X)) Lee & Low Bks., Inc.

—Sacred Mountain - Everest. 2014. (ENG., Illus.). 48p. (J). pap. 10.95 (978-1-62014-161-8(2)) Lee & Low Bks., Inc.

Trussell-Cullen, Alan. Edmund Hillary. 2009. pap. 13.25 (978-1-60559-058-5(4)) Hameray Publishing Group, Inc.

Weintraub, Aileen. Mount Everest: The Highest Mountain. 2009. (Great Record Breakers in Nature Ser.). 24p. (gr. 3-4). 42.50 (978-1-61513-181-5(7), PowerKids Pr.) Rosen Publishing Group, Inc., The.

World Book, Inc Staff, contrib. by. Nature's Skyscrapers. 2017. (J). **(978-0-7166-3368-6(X))** World Bk., Inc.

Yomtov, Nel. Amelia Earhart Flies Across the Atlantic. 2015. (Extraordinary Explorers Ser.). (ENG., Illus.). 24p. (J). (gr. 3-7). lib. bdg. 29.95 (978-1-62617-290-6(0), Black Sheep) Bellwether Media.

—Edmund Hillary Reaches the Top of Everest. 2015. (Extraordinary Explorers Ser.). (ENG., Illus.). 24p. (J). (gr. 3-7). lib. bdg. 29.95 *(978-1-62617-291-3(9)*, Black Sheep) Bellwether Media.

EVERGLADES (FLA.)

Adams, Colleen. The Everglades: Analyzing Graphs, Tables, & Charts. (PowerMath Ser.). 32p. 2009. (ENG.). (gr. 5-6). pap. 10.00 *(978-1-4042-5127-4(8))* 2009. (gr. 4-5). 47.90 *(978-1-60851-420-5(X))* 2005. (Illus.). (J). (gr. 3-6). lib. bdg. 25.25 *(978-1-4042-2933-4(7))* Rosen Publishing Group, Inc., The. (PowerKids Pr.).

Ake, Anne. Everglades: An Ecosystem Facing Choices & Challenges. 2008. (ENG., Illus.). 110p. (J). (gr. 6-9). 19.95 *(978-1-56164-410-0(2))* Pineapple Pr., Inc.

Benjamin, Lisa. People of the Wetlands. 2005. (Voices Reading Ser.). (Illus.). 32p. (J). *(978-0-7367-2947-5(X))* Zaner-Bloser, Inc.

Bullard, Lisa. The Everglades. 2010. (Lightning Bolt Books (tm) — Famous Places Ser.). (ENG.). 32p. (gr. k-2). lib. bdg. 26.60 *(978-0-7613-4453-7(5)*, Lerner Pubns.) Lerner Publishing Group.

Franchino, Vicky. Florida Wetlands. 2016. (Community Connections: Getting to Know Our Planet Ser.). (ENG., Illus.). 24p. (J). (gr. 2-5). 27.07 *(978-1-63470-516-5(5)*, 207795) Cherry Lake Publishing.

Furstinger, Nancy. The Everglades. 2004. (Natural Wonders of the U. S. A. Ser.). (Illus.). 32p. (J). (gr. 4-7). per. 9.95 *(978-1-59036-160-3(1))* Weigl Pubs., Inc.

—The Everglades: The Largest Marsh in the United States. 2003. (Natural Wonders of the U. S. A. Ser.). (Illus.). 32p. (J). (gr. 3-7). lib. bdg. 26.00 *(978-1-59036-039-2(7))* Weigl Pubs., Inc.

George, Jean Craighead. Autumn Moon. 2003. (J). (gr. 3-7). 20.75 *(978-0-8446-7241-0(6))* Smith, Peter Pub., Inc.

Jankowski, Susan. Everglades National Park: Adventure, Explore, Discover. 2008. (America's National Parks Ser.). (Illus.). 128p. (J). (gr. 5-9). lib. bdg. 34.60 *(978-1-59845-091-0(3))* Enslow Pubs., Inc.

Johnson, Robin. Everglades Research Journal. 2017. (Illus.). 32p. (J). ***(978-0-7787-3469-7(2))***; pap. ***(978-0-7787-3494-9(3))*** Crabtree Publishing Co.

Kinser, Kathy. The Everglades: Set Of 6. 2011. (Early Connections Ser.). (J). pap. 39.00 net. *(978-1-4108-1543-9(9))* Benchmark Education Co.

Kinsner, Kathy. The Everglades. 2011. (Early Connections Ser.). (J). *(978-1-61672-675-1(X))* Benchmark Education Co.

Leotti-Bachem, Janice. The Everglades. 2005. (Rookie Read-About Geography Ser.). (ENG., Illus.). 32p. (J). (gr. 1-2). 20.50 *(978-0-516-22750-4(5)*, Children's Pr.) Scholastic Library Publishing.

Lerner Classroom Staff & Bullard, Lisa. The Everglades. 2010. (Lightning Bolt Books (tm) — Famous Places Ser.). (ENG., Illus.). 32p. (gr. k-2). pap. 7.95 *(978-0-7613-5569-4(3))* Lerner Publishing Group.

Marsico, Katie. The Everglades. 2013. (Explorer Library: Social Studies Explorer Ser.). (ENG.). 32p. (gr. 4-8). pap. 14.21 *(978-1-62431-041-6(9)*, 202521); lib. bdg. 28.50 *(978-1-62431-017-1(6)*, 202519) Cherry Lake Publishing.

Marx, Trish. Everglades Forever: Restoring America's Great Wetland, 1 vol. Karp, Cindy, illus. Karp, Cindy, photos by. 2004. (ENG.). 40p. (J). 17.95 *(978-1-58430-164-6(3))* Lee & Low Bks., Inc.

Repko, Marya. The Story of Everglades City: A History for Younger Readers. 2004. (Illus.). 48p. (YA). pap. 5.00 *(978-0-9716006-1-4(9)*, ECity Publishing) ECity Publishing.

EVERGLADES (FLA.)—FICTION

Ashley-Hollinger, Mika. Precious Bones. 2013. (ENG.). 352p. (J). (gr. 4-7). 8.99 *(978-0-307-93070-5(X)*, Yearling) Random Hse. Children's Bks.

Berkes, Marianne. The Swamp Where Gator Hides, 1 vol. Baird, Roberta, illus. 2014. (ENG.). 32p. (J). (gr. k-4). 16.95 *(978-1-58469-470-0(X))*; pap. 8.95 *(978-1-58469-471-7(8))* Dawn Pubns.

Brezenoff, Steve. The Everglades Poacher Who Pretended, 1 vol. Calo, Marcos, illus. 2012. (Field Trip Mysteries Ser.). (ENG.). 88p. (gr. 2-3). pap. 6.10 *(978-1-4342-4197-9(1))*; lib. bdg. 25.32 *(978-1-4342-3790-3(7))* Stone Arch Bks.

Coman, Carolyn. Sneaking Suspicions. Shepperson, Rob, illus. 2007. (ENG.). 204p. (J). (gr. 4-6). 16.95 *(978-1-59078-491-4(X)*, Front Street) Boyds Mills Pr.

Creghan, Brian C. Pauly: The alligator who wore tennis Shoes. 2010. 48p. pap. 24.00 *(978-1-4269-3614-2(1))* Trafford Publishing.

De felice, Cynthia. Lostman's River. 2008. (ENG.). 160p. (J). (gr. 3-7). pap. 8.99 *(978-1-4169-8690-4(1)*, Simon & Schuster/Paula Wiseman Bks.) Simon & Schuster/Paula Wiseman Bks.

Douglas, Marjory Stoneman & Milkweed Editions Staff. Alligator Crossing. Nicholson, Trudy, illus. 2003. (ENG.). 192p. (J). (gr. 3-8). pap. 7.95 *(978-1-57131-644-8(2))* Milkweed Editions.

Hanson, Ed. The Swamp. 2003. (Barclay Family Adventure Ser.: Bk. 10). (Illus.). 64p. (J). (gr. k-6). per. 3.95 *(978-1-56254-558-1(2))* Saddleback Educational Publishing, Inc.

Messner, Kate. Wake up Missing. 2014. (ENG.). 288p. (YA). (gr. 5-8). pap. 7.99 *(978-0-8027-3748-9(X)*, 9780802737489, Bloomsbury USA Childrens) Bloomsbury Publishing USA.

Raffa, Edwina & Rigsby, Annelle. Escape to the Everglades. 2013. (Florida Historical Fiction for Youth Ser.). (ENG.). 112p. (J). pap. 9.95 *(978-1-56164-619-7(9))* Pineapple Pr., Inc.

—Escape to the Everglades Teacher's Activity Guide. 2006. (ENG., Illus.). 31p. pap., tchr. ed., act. bk. ed. 6.00 *(978-1-56164-362-2(9))* Pineapple Pr., Inc.

Rorby, Ginny. Lost in the River of Grass. (Carolrhoda YA Ser.). (ENG.). 264p. (YA). (gr. 7-12). 2012. pap. 9.95 *(978-0-7613-8498-4(7))* 2011. 17.95 *(978-0-7613-5685-1(1))* Lerner Publishing Group. (Carolrhoda Lab™).

Saddleback Educational Publishing Staff, ed. Swamp, 1 vol. unabr. ed. 2011. (Heights Ser.). (ENG.). 49p. (gr. 5-8). 7.95 *(978-1-61651-625-3(9))* Saddleback Educational Publishing, Inc.

Spradlin, Michael P. Feeding Frenzy. 2013. (Illus.). 167p. (J). *(978-0-545-62200-4(X))* Scholastic, Inc.

—Killer Species #3: Out for Blood. 2014. (Killer Species Ser.: 3). (ENG.). 192p. (J). (gr. 3-7). pap. 5.99 *(978-0-545-50676-2(X)*, Scholastic Paperbacks) Scholastic, Inc.

—Menace from the Deep. 2013. (Illus.). 225p. (J). *(978-0-545-56366-6(6))* Scholastic, Inc.

—Out for Blood. 2014. 168p. (J). pap. *(978-0-545-67523-9(5))* Scholastic, Inc.

—Out for Blood. 2014. (Killer Species Ser.: 3). lib. bdg. 16.00 *(978-0-606-35398-4(4))* Turtleback Bks.

—Ultimate Attack. 2014. (Killer Species Ser.: 4). lib. bdg. 16.00 *(978-0-606-35853-8(6))* Turtleback Bks.

EVERGLADES NATIONAL PARK (FLA.)

Bullard, Lisa. The Everglades. 2010. (Lightning Bolt Books (tm) — Famous Places Ser.). (ENG.). 32p. (gr. k-2). lib. bdg. 26.60 *(978-0-7613-4453-7(5)*, Lerner Pubns.) Lerner Publishing Group.

Connors, Kathleen. Everglades National Park. 2015. (Road Trip Ser.). (ENG., Illus.). 24p. (J). (gr. 2-3). lib. bdg. 22.60 *(978-1-4824-1678-7(6))* Stevens, Gareth Publishing LLLP.

Frisch, Nate. Everglades National Park. 2013. (Illus.). 48p. (J). 35.65 *(978-1-60818-195-7(2)*, Creative Education) Creative Co., The.

—Preserving America: Everglades National Park. 2014. (Preserving America Ser.). (ENG.). 48p. (J). (gr. 4-7). pap. 12.00 *(978-0-89812-878-9(1)*, Creative Paperbacks) Creative Co., The.

Furstinger, Nancy. The Everglades. 2013. (J). *(978-1-62127-473-5(X))*; pap. *(978-1-62127-479-7(9))* Weigl Pubs., Inc.

Gilbert, Sara. Everglades. 2016. (Illus.). 22p. (J). *(978-1-60818-631-0(8)*, Creative Education) Creative Co., The.

Jankowski, Susan. Everglades National Park: Adventure, Explore, Discover. 2008. (America's National Parks Ser.). (Illus.). 128p. (J). (gr. 5-9). lib. bdg. 34.60 *(978-1-59845-091-0(3))* Enslow Pubs., Inc.

Kalman, Bobbie. Everglades National Park. 2009. (Introducing Habitats Ser.). (ENG., Illus.). 32p. (J). (gr. k-3). pap. *(978-0-7787-2988-4(5))*; (gr. 1-3). lib. bdg. *(978-0-7787-2960-0(5))* Crabtree Publishing Co.

Kras, Sara Louise. The Everglades. 2009. (Nature's Wonders 2 Ser.). 96p. (gr. 6). 35.64 *(978-0-7614-3931-8(5))* Marshall Cavendish Corp.

Leotti-Bachem, Janice. The Everglades. 2005. (Rookie Read-About Geography Ser.). (ENG., Illus.). 32p. (J). (gr. 1-2). 20.50 *(978-0-516-22750-4(5)*, Children's Pr.) Scholastic Library Publishing.

Lerner Classroom Staff & Bullard, Lisa. The Everglades. 2010. (Lightning Bolt Books (tm) — Famous Places Ser.). (ENG., Illus.). 32p. (gr. k-2). pap. 7.95 *(978-0-7613-5569-4(3))* Lerner Publishing Group.

Stewart, Melissa. Life in a Wetland. Maka, Stephen, photos by. 2003. (Ecosystems in Action Ser.). (ENG., Illus.). 72p. (gr. 5-9). lib. bdg. 26.60 *(978-0-8225-4687-0(6))* Lerner Publishing Group.

Wade, Linda R. Everglades National Park, 1 vol. 2005. (National Parks Ser.). (ENG., Illus.). 32p. (gr. 3-8). 27.07 *(978-1-59197-424-6(0)*, Abdo & Daughters) ABDO Publishing Co.

EVOLUTION

see also Adaptation (Biology); Anatomy, Comparative; Biology; Creation; Embryology; Human Beings—Effect of Environment on; Human Beings—Origin; Human Skin Color; Mendel's Law; Natural Selection; Religion and Science; Social Change

Adamson, Heather. Charles Darwin & the Theory of Evolution, 1 vol. Purcell, Gordon & Milgrom, Al, illus. 2007. (Inventions & Discovery Ser.). (ENG.). 32p. (gr. 3-4). 30.65 *(978-1-4296-0145-0(0)*, Graphic Library) Capstone Press of Coughlan Cos.

Anderson, Dale. How Do We Know the Nature of Humankind. 2005. (Great Scientific Questions & the Scientists Who Answered Them Ser.). (Illus.). 112p. (J). (gr. 7-12). lib. bdg. 34.60 *(978-1-4042-0077-7(0))* Rosen Publishing Group, Inc., The.

Anderson, Margaret J. Charles Darwin: Genius of a Revolutionary Theory. 2015. (Genius Scientists & Their Genius Ideas Ser.). 96p. (J). (gr. 5-12). 27.94 *(978-0-7660-6545-1(6))*; pap. 10.95 *(978-0-7660-6546-8(4))* Enslow Pubs., Inc.

The Answer Book for Kids: 25 Questions on Dinosaurs & the Flood of Noah. 2008. 60p. (J). pap. 7.99 *(978-0-89051-527-3(1))* Master Bks.

Answers to Evolution Wall Chart. 2004. *(978-1-890947-87-3(3))* Rose Publishing.

Ardia, Dan & Rice, Elizabeth. Evolution. 2012. (J). 32.79 *(978-0-7614-4970-6(1))* Marshall Cavendish Corp.

Barr, Catherine & Williams, Steve. The Story of Life: A First Book about Evolution. Husband, Amy, illus. 2015. (ENG.). 40p. (J). (gr. k-3). 18.99 *(978-1-84780-485-3(3)*, Frances Lincoln) Quarto Publishing Group UK GBR. Dist: Hachette Bk. Group.

Bowler, Peter J. An Interview with Charles Darwin. 2014. (Meet the Masters Ser.). 112p. (YA). (gr. 9-12). lib. bdg. 42.79 *(978-1-62712-909-1(X))* Cavendish Square Publishing.

Bradley, James V. How Species Change. 2006. (Nature Walk Ser.). (Illus.). 80p. (J). (gr. 4-6). lib. bdg. 28.00 *(978-0-7910-9118-0(X)*, Chelsea Hse.) Facts On File, Inc.

Byrne, Eugene. Darwin: A Graphic Biography. Gurr, Simon, illus. 2013. (ENG.). 100p. (J). (gr. 7). pap. 9.95 *(978-1-58834-352-9(9)*, Smithsonian Bks.) Smithsonian Institution Scholarly Pr.

Clingan, B. V. The Great Geese Migration: The Science of Evolution Series for Kids. 2011. 32p. pap. 12.99 *(978-1-4634-3416-8(2))* AuthorHouse.

Creator & Creation. 3rd rev. ed. 2008. (Illus.). 118p. (YA). pap. 15.00 *(978-0-9723239-8-7(8))* Ye Hedge Schl.

Crewe, Sabrina & Uschan, Michael V. The Scopes "Monkey" Trial. 2005. (Events That Shaped America Ser.). (Illus.). 32p. (gr. 3-6). lib. bdg. 26.00 *(978-0-8368-3415-4(1)*, Gareth Stevens Learning Library) Stevens, Gareth Publishing LLLP.

Currie, Stephen. The Importance of Evolution Theory. 2015. (ENG., Illus.). 80p. (J). lib. bdg. *(978-1-60152-896-4(5))* ReferencePoint Pr., Inc.

Darwin, Charles. The Riverbank. Negrin, Fabian, illus. 2010. (ENG.). 32p. (J). (gr. 1-3). 17.95 *(978-1-56846-207-3(7)*, Creative Editions) Creative Co., The.

Dlugos, Jenn & Hatton, Charlie. Mystifying Mutants. 2016. (Things That Make You Go Yuck! Ser.: 0). (ENG., Illus.). 88p. (J). (gr. 4-7). pap. 7.95 *(978-1-61821-564-2(7)*, 9781618215642) Prufrock Pr.

Eason, Sarah, ed. Evolution. 2011. (FAYFT: Introducing Biology Ser.). 64p. (gr. 4-10). lib. bdg. 39.95 *(978-1-936333-01-1(5))* Brown Bear Bks.

Encyclopaedia Britannica, Inc. Staff, compiled by. Britannica Illustrated Science Library: Evolution & Genetics, 16 vols. 2008. (Illus.). (J). 29.95 *(978-1-59339-388-5(1))* Encyclopaedia Britannica, Inc.

Engdahl, Sharon & Engdahl, Terry. The Evolution of Creation: A Children's Primer on the Evolution of God's Creation, 1 vol. 2010. 30p. 24.95 *(978-1-4489-4228-2(4))* PublishAmerica, Inc.

Evolution. 2010. (Science Foundations Ser.). (Illus.). 128p. (gr. 6-12). 35.00 *(978-1-60413-338-7(4)*, Chelsea Hse.) Facts On File, Inc.

Fleisher, Paul. Evolution. 2005. (Great Ideas of Science Ser.). (ENG., Illus.). 80p. (gr. 8-12). lib. bdg. 27.93 *(978-0-8225-2134-1(2))* Lerner Publishing Group.

Gardner, Robert. Genetics & Evolution Science Fair Projects: Using Skeletons, Cereal, Earthworms, & More. 2005. (Biology! Best Science Projects Ser.). (Illus.). 128p. (J). (gr. 6-13). lib. bdg. 27.94 *(978-0-7660-1175-5(5))* Enslow Pubs., Inc.

—Genetics & Evolution Science Fair Projects, Revised & Expanded Using the Scientific Method. LaBaff, Stephanie, illus. 2010. (Biology Science Projects Using the Scientific Method Ser.). 160p. (J). (gr. 5-18). 35.94 *(978-0-7660-3422-8(4))* Enslow Pubs., Inc.

Garside, Jeff. Extreme Environments: Living on the Edge. 2011. (Second Nature Ser.). 48p. (J). (gr. 5-8). lib. bdg. 26.60 *(978-1-59953-458-9(4))* Norwood Hse. Pr.

Gladstone, James. When Planet Earth Was New. Diemert, Katherine, illus. 2017. (ENG.). 40p. (J). (gr. -1-5). 18.95 ***(978-1-77147-203-6(0))*** Owlkids Bks. Inc. CAN. Dist: Publishers Group West (PGW).

Gordon, Sherri Mabry. The Evolution Debate: Darwinism vs. Intelligent Design. 2009. (Issues in Focus Today Ser.). (Illus.). 128p. (J). (gr. 6). lib. bdg. 33.27 *(978-0-7660-2911-8(5))* Enslow Pubs., Inc.

Granström, Brita. What Mr Darwin Saw. Manning, Mick, illus. 2014. (ENG.). 48p. (J). (gr. 1-4). pap. 9.95 *(978-1-84780-107-4(2)*, Frances Lincoln) Quarto Publishing Group UK GBR. Dist: Hachette Bk. Group.

Graves, Renee. The Scopes Trial. 2003. (Cornerstones of Freedom Ser.). (ENG., Illus.). 48p. (YA). (gr. 4-7). 26.00 *(978-0-516-24221-7(0))* Scholastic Library Publishing.

Green, Jen. Evolution. 2004. (Routes of Science Ser.). (Illus.). 40p. (J). (gr. 4-7). 24.95 *(978-1-4103-0303-5(9)*, Blackbirch Pr., Inc.) Cengage Gale.

—Evolution: Investigating the Origin & Development of the Species. 2012. (Scientific Pathways Ser.). (ENG., Illus.). 48p. (J). (gr. 5-8). lib. bdg. 27.95 *(978-1-4488-7198-8(0))* Rosen Publishing Group, Inc., The.

Heiligman, Deborah. Charles & Emma: The Darwins' Leap of Faith. 2009. (ENG.). 272p. (YA). (gr. 8-12). 18.95 *(978-0-8050-8721-5(4)*, 9780805087215, Holt, Henry & Co. Bks. For Young Readers) Holt, Henry & Co.

Heos, Bridget. Shell, Beak, Tusk: Shared Traits & the Wonders of Convergent Evolution. 2017. (ENG., Illus.). 32p. (J). (gr. 1-4). 16.99 *(978-0-544-81166-9(6)*, HMH Books For Young Readers) Houghton Mifflin Harcourt Publishing Co.

Higgins, Nadia. Life Science Through Infographics. Waananen, Lisa, illus. 2013. (Super Science Infographics Ser.). (ENG.). 32p. (J). (gr. 3-5). pap. 8.95 *(978-1-4677-1592-8(1))*; lib. bdg. 26.60 *(978-1-4677-1288-0(4)*, Lerner Pubns.) Lerner Publishing Group.

Hodge, Russ. Genetics & Evolution, 6 vols., Set. 2010. (Genetics & Evolution Ser.). (C). (gr. 9). 237.00 *(978-0-8160-8300-8(2))* Facts On File, Inc.

Hooper, Meredith. Pebble in My Pocket: A History of Our Earth. Coady, Chris, illus. rev. ed. 2015. (ENG.). 40p. (J). (gr. 2-5). pap. 9.99 *(978-1-84780-768-7(2)*, Frances Lincoln Children's Bks.) Quarto Publishing Group UK GBR. Dist: Hachette Bk. Group.

Howell, Izzi. Charles Darwin's Voyages of Discovery. 2016. (Why Do We Remember? Ser.). (ENG., Illus.). 32p. (J). (gr. 1-3). 17.99 *(978-1-4451-4853-3(6)*, Franklin Watts) Hachette Children's Group GBR. Dist: Hachette Bk. Group.

Human, Katy, ed. Biological Evolution: An Anthology of Current Thought. (Contemporary Discourse in the Field of Biology Ser.). 2009. 224p. (gr. 10-12). 63.90 *(978-1-61511-909-7(4))* 2005. (Illus.). 187p. (YA). (gr. 7-12). lib. bdg. 35.95 *(978-1-4042-0403-4(2))* Rosen Publishing Group, Inc., The.

Hunter, Nick. Charles Darwin, 1 vol. 2014. (Science Biographies Ser.). (ENG.). 32p. (gr. 2-4). pap. 8.95 *(978-1-4109-6602-5(X)*, Raintree Perspectives) Heinemann-Raintree.

Hynes, Margaret & White, Mike. The Best Book of Early People. 2003. (Best Book Of Ser.). (ENG., Illus.). 32p. (J). (gr. k-3). tchr. ed. 12.99 *(978-0-7534-5577-7(3)*, 9780753455777, Kingfisher) Roaring Brook Pr.

Jackson, Ellen B. The Tree of Life: The Wonders of Evolution. Wiley, Judeanne Winter, illus. 2004. (ENG.). 41p. (J). (gr. -1-3). pap. 14.99 *(978-1-59102-240-4(1))* Prometheus Bks., Pubs.

Johnson, Anne Janette. The Scopes Monkey Trial. 2006. (Defining Moments Ser.). (Illus.). 246p. (gr. 9-18). 55.00 *(978-0-7808-0955-0(6))* Omnigraphics, Inc.

Johnson, Sylvia A. Shaking the Foundation: Charles Darwin & the Theory of Evolution. 2013. (ENG.). 88p. (gr. 6-12). lib. bdg. 33.27 *(978-0-7613-5486-4(7)*, Twenty-First Century Bks.) Lerner Publishing Group.

Keranen, Rachel. Evolution. 2016. (Great Discoveries in Science Ser.). (Illus.). 128p. (J). (gr. 9-9). 45.64 *(978-1-5026-1951-8(2))* Cavendish Square Publishing.

Kowalski, Kathiann M. Evolution on Trial: From the Scopes Monkey Case to Inherit the Wind. 2009. (Famous Court Cases That Became Movies Ser.). (Illus.). 112p. (J). (gr. 7-12). lib. bdg. 33.27 *(978-0-7660-3056-5(3))* Enslow Pubs., Inc.

Krull, Kathleen. Charles Darwin. Kulikov, Boris, illus. 2015. (Giants of Science Ser.). (ENG.). 144p. (J). (gr. 3-7). 7.99 *(978-0-14-751463-9(0)*, Puffin Books) Penguin Young Readers Group.

Larson, Kirsten W. Mutants in Nature. 2015. (Freaky Nature Ser.). (ENG., Illus.). 32p. (J). (gr. 2-4). 19.95 *(978-1-60753-780-9(X))* Amicus Publishing.

Lew, Kristi. Evolution: The Adaptation & Survival of Species. 2010. (Understanding Genetics Ser.). (ENG.). 80p. (YA). lib. bdg. 33.25 *(978-1-4358-9534-8(7))* Rosen Publishing Group, Inc., The.

Lin, Yoming S. Charles Darwin & Evolution. 2012. (Eureka! Ser.). (Illus.). 24p. (YA). (gr. 3-6). lib. bdg. 22.60 *(978-1-4488-5031-0(2))* Rosen Publishing Group, Inc., The.

Lindsay, William. Prehistoric Life. 2012. (DK Eyewitness Bks.). (ENG.). 72p. (J). (gr. 3-7). 19.99 *(978-0-7566-9078-6(1))*; 16.99 *(978-0-7566-9077-9(3))* Dorling Kindersley Publishing, Inc. (DK Children).

Loxton, Daniel. Evolution. Loxton, Daniel, illus. 2010. (ENG., Illus.). 56p. (J). (gr. 3-8). 18.95 *(978-1-55453-430-2(5))* Kids Can Pr., Ltd. CAN. Dist: Hachette Bk. Group.

Murphy, Glenn. Evolution: The Whole Life on Earth Story. unabr. ed. 2014. (Science Sorted Ser.). (ENG., Illus.). 176p. (J). (gr. 4-6). pap. 7.99 *(978-1-4472-5460-7(0))* Pan Macmillan GBR. Dist: Independent Pubs. Group.

Nicolson, Cynthia Pratt. Totally Human: Why We Look & Act the Way We Do. Eastman, Dianne, illus. 2011. (ENG.). 40p. (J). (gr. 4-8). 16.95 *(978-1-55453-569-9(7))* Kids Can Pr., Ltd. CAN. Dist: Hachette Bk. Group.

Norton, James R. Looking at the Mechanisms & Patterns of Evolution with Graphic Organizers. 2009. (Using Graphic Organizers to Study the Living Environment Ser.). 48p. (gr. 6-6). 53.00 *(978-1-60854-716-6(7)*, Rosen Reference) Rosen Publishing Group, Inc., The.

O'Donnell, Kerri. Aves: Dinosaurios de nuestros días (Birds: Modern-Day Dinosaurs) 2009. (Reading Room Collection: Spanish Ser.). (SPA.). 24p. (gr. 3-4). 42.50 *(978-1-60854-176-8(2)*, Editorial Buenas Letras) Rosen Publishing Group, Inc., The.

—Birds: Modern-Day Dinosaurs. 2009. (Reading Room Collection 2 Ser.). 24p. (gr. 3-4). 42.50 *(978-1-60851-960-6(0)*, PowerKids Pr.) Rosen Publishing Group, Inc., The.

Parker, Steve. A Brief Illustrated History of Life on Earth. 2017. (Brief Illustrated History Ser.). (ENG.). 32p. (gr. 3-5). lib. bdg. 27.32 *(978-1-5157-2521-3(9)*, Fact Finders) Capstone Press of Coughlan Cos.

Patkau, Karen. Creatures Yesterday & Today. Patkau, Karen, illus. 2012. (ENG., Illus.). 32p. (J). (gr. 1-4). pap. 8.95 *(978-1-77049-310-0(7)*, Tundra Bks.) Tundra Bks. CAN. Dist: Penguin Random Hse. LLC.

Peters, Lisa Westberg. Our Family Tree: An Evolution Story. Stringer, Lauren, illus. 2003. (ENG.). 48p. (J). (gr. -1-3). 17.99 *(978-0-15-201772-9(0))* Houghton Mifflin Harcourt Publishing Co.

PH Inc. Staff. PH Science Evolution. 2nd ed. (J). pap., act. bk. ed. *(978-0-13-225541-7(3))* Prentice Hall (Schl. Div.).

Pringle, Laurence. Billions of Years, Amazing Changes: The Story of Evolution. Jenkins, Steve, illus. 2011. (ENG.). 112p. (J). (gr. 3). 17.95 *(978-1-59078-723-6(4))* Boyds Mills Pr.

Rafferty, John P. Biomes & Ecosystems. 2011. (Living Earth Ser.). (Illus.). 240p. (YA). (gr. 9-12). lib. bdg. 51.70 *(978-1-61530-302-1(2))* Rosen Publishing Group, Inc., The.

Rieger, Linda. Dinosaur Party. Bianchi, John, illus. 2007. 20p. (J). *(978-0-9779427-2-5(4))* Pathways into Science.

Rubino, Michael. Bang! How We Came to Be. 2011. (ENG.). 69p. (J). (gr. 4-7). pap. 17.00 *(978-1-61614-472-2(6))* Prometheus Bks., Pubs.

Schutten, Jan Paul. The Mystery of Life: How Nothing Became Everything. Watkinson, Laura, tr. from DUT. Rieder, Floor, illus. 2015. (ENG.). 240p. (YA). (gr. 5-9). 15.99 *(978-1-58270-525-5(9)*, Simon & Schuster/Paula Wiseman Bks.) Simon & Schuster/Paula Wiseman Bks.

The Science of Life. 2016. (Illus.). 48p. (J). *(978-1-4222-3514-0(9))* Mason Crest.

The Scopes Monkey Trial: Debate over Evolution. 2010. (Milestones in American History Ser.). (Illus.). 128p. (J). (gr. 6-12). 35.00 *(978-1-60413-679-1(0)*, Chelsea Hse.) Facts On File, Inc.

Suzuki, David. From Naked Ape to Superspecies. abr. ed. 2005. (gr. 9-12). *(978-0-660-17795-3(1))* Canadian Broadcasting Corp./Societe Radio-Canada.

Swanson, Jennifer A. How Have Animals Evolved & Adapted? 2015. (Let's Find Out! Animal Life Ser.). (ENG., Illus.). 32p. (J). (gr. 2-3). 23.45 *(978-1-62275-996-5(6)*, Britannica Educational Publishing) Rosen Publishing Group, Inc., The.

Tweet, Jonathan. Grandmother Fish: A Child's First Book of Evolution. Lewis, Karen, illus. 2016. (ENG.). 40p. (J). 17.99 *(978-1-250-11323-8(7)*, 9781250113238) Feiwel & Friends.

Uschan, Michael V. The Scopes "Monkey" Trial. 2004. (Landmark Events in American History Ser.). (Illus.). 48p. (gr. 5-12). pap. 14.05 *(978-0-8368-5424-4(1))*; lib. bdg. 31.00 *(978-0-8368-5396-4(2))* Stevens, Gareth Publishing LLLP. (Gareth Stevens Secondary Library).

Walker, Robert. What Is the Theory of Evolution? 2010. (Shaping Modern Science Ser.). (ENG.). 64p. (J). (gr. 5-8). pap. *(978-0-7787-7205-7(5))*; lib. bdg. *(978-0-7787-7198-2(9))* Crabtree Publishing Co.

Wanjie, Anne, ed. The Basics of Evolution. 2013. (Core Concepts Ser.). (ENG., Illus.). 96p. (YA). (gr. 7-12). lib. bdg. 34.60 *(978-1-4777-0557-5(0))* Rosen Publishing Group, Inc., The.

Webster, Stephen. Charles Darwin. 2016. (History Makers Ser.). (ENG., Illus.). 144p. (J). (gr. 9-9). 45.64 *(978-1-5026-1916-7(4))* Cavendish Square Publishing.

Whiting, Jim. The Scopes Monkey Trial. 2006. (Monumental Milestones Ser.). (Illus.). 48p. (YA). (gr. 4-7). lib. bdg. 29.95 *(978-1-58415-468-6(3))* Mitchell Lane Pubs., Inc.

Winston, Robert M. L. Evolution Revolution. 2016. (Illus.). 96p. (J). *(978-1-4844-8141-7(0))* Dorling Kindersley Publishing, Inc.

EXCAVATION

Gordon, Nick. Monster Diggers. 2013. (Monster Machines Ser.). (ENG., Illus.). 24p. (J). (gr. k-3). lib. bdg. 25.95 *(978-1-60014-937-5(5)*, Blastoff! Readers) Bellwether Media.

Litchfield, Jo & Brooks, Felicity. Diggers. 2004. (Chunky Board Bks.). (ENG., Illus.). 6p. (J). bds. 4.95 *(978-0-7945-0350-5(0)*, Usborne) EDC Publishing.

National Geographic Kids Staff. Dig. 2015. (Look & Learn Ser.). (ENG., Illus.). 24p. (J). (-k). bds. 6.99 *(978-1-4263-2062-0(0)*, National Geographic Children's Bks.) National Geographic Society.

Tractors & Diggers. 2003. (Illus.). 32p. 12.98 *(978-1-4054-2005-1(7))* Parragon, Inc.

EXCAVATIONS (ARCHAEOLOGY)

see also Mounds and Mound Builders

Aksomitis, Gerard. Solving the Mysteries of the Past. 2008. (Science Solves It Ser.). (ENG., Illus.). 32p. (J). (gr. 3-7). lib. bdg. *(978-0-7787-4171-8(0))* Crabtree Publishing Co.

Alexander, Suzanna M., et al. Prehistoric People of Moccasin Bend, Chattanooga, Tennessee: An Educational Coloring Book. 2006. (J). *(978-0-9779189-3-5(9))* Waldenhouse Pubs., Inc.

Aronovsky, Ilona & Gopinath, Sujata. The Indus Valley. 2016. (Excavating the Past Ser.). (ENG.). 48p. (gr. 4-6). pap. 8.99 *(978-1-4846-3644-2(9)*, NA-h) Heinemann-Raintree.

Askomitis, Gerard & Aksomitis, Gerard. Solving the Mysteries of the Past. 2008. (Science Solves It Ser.). (ENG., Illus.). 32p. (J). (gr. 3-7). pap. *(978-0-7787-4178-7(8))* Crabtree Publishing Co.

Burnham, Brad. Qumran Caves: Hiding Place for the Dead Sea Scrolls. (Famous Caves of the World Ser.). 24p. 2009. (gr. 3-4). 42.50 *(978-1-61512-499-2(3))* 2003. (Illus.). (J). lib. bdg. 22.60 *(978-0-8239-6259-4(8))* Rosen Publishing Group, Inc., The. (PowerKids Pr.).

Capek, Michael. Secrets of the Terracotta Army: Tomb of an Ancient Chinese Emperor, 1 vol. 2014. (Archaeological Mysteries Ser.). (ENG.). 32p. (gr. 3-4). lib. bdg. 27.99 *(978-1-4765-9917-5(3))* Capstone Press of Coughlan Cos.

—Unsolved Archaeological Mysteries. 2015. (Unsolved Mystery Files Ser.). (ENG., Illus.). 32p. (gr. 3-4). pap. 7.95 *(978-1-4914-4338-5(3))* Capstone Press of Coughlan Cos.

Chrisp, Peter. Explore 360° the Tomb of Tutankhamen: Be Transported Back in Time with a Breathtaking 3D Tour. 2016. (ENG., Illus.). 48p. (J). (gr. 3-9). 18.99 *(978-0-7641-6821-5(5))* Barron's Educational Series, Inc.

Cline, Eric H. & Rubalcaba, Jill. Digging for Troy: From Homer to Hisarlik. Brannen, Sarah S., illus. 2011. (ENG.). 80p. (J). (gr. 4-7). 17.95 *(978-1-58089-326-8(0))*; pap. 9.95 *(978-1-58089-327-5(9))* Charlesbridge Publishing, Inc.

Cottman, Michael & National Geographic Kids Staff. Shackles from the Deep: Tracing the Path of a Sunken Slave Ship, a Bitter Past, & a Rich Legacy. 2017. (ENG.). 128p. (J). (gr. 5-7). 17.99 *(978-1-4263-2663-9(7)*, National Geographic Children's Bks.) National Geographic Society.

Croy, Anita. Solving the Mysteries of Aztec Cities. 2008. (Digging into History Ser.). 32p. (gr. 4-18). lib. bdg. 29.93 *(978-0-7614-3102-2(0)*, Benchmark Bks.) Marshall Cavendish Corp.

Deem, James M. Bodies from the Ash: Life & Death in Ancient Pompeii. 2005. (ENG., Illus.). 64p. (J). (gr. 5-7). 17.99 *(978-0-618-47308-3(4))* Houghton Mifflin Harcourt Publishing Co.

Digging up the Dead. 2014. (Digging up the Dead Ser.). 32p. (J). (gr. 4-6). 159.60 *(978-1-4824-1174-4(1))* Stevens, Gareth Publishing LLLP.

Evans, Arthur. The Palace of Minos 4 Volume Set in 7 Pieces: A Comparative Account of the Successive Stages of the Early Cretan Civilization As Illustrated by the Discoveries at Knossos. 2013. (Cambridge Library Collection - Archaeology Ser.). (ENG.). 3734p. pap., pap., pap. 417.00 *(978-1-108-06107-0(9))* Cambridge Univ. Pr.

Gimpel, Diane Marczely. Pompeii, 1 vol. 2014. (Digging up the Past Ser.). (ENG.). 112p. (J). (gr. 6-12). lib. bdg. 35.64 *(978-1-62403-236-3(2)*, Essential Library) ABDO Publishing Co.

Graphic Expeditions. 2010. (Graphic Expeditions Ser.). 32p. lib. bdg. 293.20 *(978-1-4296-5860-7(6)*, Graphic Library) Capstone Press of Coughlan Cos.

Green, Jen. Ancient Celts: Archaeology Unlocks the Secrets of the Celts' Past. 2008. (National Geographic Investigates Ser.). (ENG., Illus.). 64p. (J). (gr. 5). lib. bdg. 27.90 *(978-1-4263-0226-8(6)*, National Geographic Children's Bks.) National Geographic Society.

Green, Jen & National Geographic Kids Staff. Ancient Celts: Archaeology Unlocks the Secrets of the Celts' Past. 2008. (National Geographic Investigates Ser.). (ENG., Illus.). 64p. (J). (gr. 5). 17.95 *(978-1-4263-0225-1(8)*, National Geographic Children's Bks.) National Geographic Society.

Hanbury-Murphy, Trudy. Solving the Mysteries of Ancient Rome. 2008. (Digging into History Ser.). 32p. (gr. 4-18). lib. bdg. 29.93 *(978-0-7614-3101-5(2)*, Benchmark Bks.) Marshall Cavendish Corp.

Hanson, Anders. Archaeologist's Tools, 1 vol. 2011. (Professional Tools Ser.). (ENG., Illus.). 24p. (J). (gr. 3-5). lib. bdg. 25.65 *(978-1-61613-577-5(8)*, Super SandCastle) ABDO Publishing Co.

Haze, Xaviant. Ancient America's Lost Giants. 2017. (Discovering Ancient America Ser.). 200p. (J). (gr. 12-14). 39.75 ***(978-1-4994-6676-8(5)***, Rosen Young Adult) Rosen Publishing Group, Inc., The.

Heitkamp, Kristina Lyn. The Rift Valley & the Archaeological Evidence of the First Humans. 2016. (First Humans & Early Civilizations Ser.). 64p. (J). (gr. 6-6). pap. 12.95 *(978-1-4994-6318-7(9))* Rosen Publishing Group, Inc., The.

Holliday, Diane & Malone, Bobbie. Digging & Discovery, Teachers Guide & Student Materials, 2nd Edition, on CD: Wisconsin Archaeology. 2011. (New Badger History Ser.). (ENG.). (J). cd-rom 49.95 *(978-0-87020-480-7(7))* Wisconsin Historical Society.

Holliday, Diane Young & Malone, Bobbie. Digging & Discovery: Wisconsin Archaeology. 2nd ed. 2006. (New Badger History Ser.). (Illus.). 120p. (gr. 2-7). pap. 15.95 *(978-0-87020-376-3(2))* Wisconsin Historical Society.

Huey, Lois Miner. American Archaeology Uncovers the Earliest English Colonies. 2009. (American Archaeology Ser.). 64p. (gr. 5-6). 31.36 *(978-0-7614-4264-6(2))* Marshall Cavendish Corp.

—American Archaeology Uncovers the Underground Railroad. 2009. (American Archaeology Ser.). 64p. (gr. 5-6). 31.36 *(978-0-7614-4267-7(7))* Marshall Cavendish Corp.

—American Archaeology Uncovers the Westward Movement. 2009. (American Archaeology Ser.). (Illus.). 64p. (J). (gr. 5-6). 31.36 *(978-0-7614-4265-3(0))* Marshall Cavendish Corp.

Jango-Cohen, Judith. Dump Trucks on the Move. 2011. (Lightning Bolt Books Vroom-Vroom Ser.). 32p. pap. 45.32 *(978-0-7613-7616-3(X))*; (ENG.). pap. 7.95 *(978-0-7613-7108-3(7))* Lerner Publishing Group.

Kaplan, Sarah Pitt. Pompeii: City of Ashes. 2005. (High Interest Bks.). (ENG., Illus.). 48p. (J). (gr. 3-7). per. 6.95 *(978-0-516-25091-5(4)*, Children's Pr.) Scholastic Library Publishing.

Kerns, Ann. Troy. 2008. (Unearthing Ancient Worlds Ser.). (ENG.). 80p. (gr. 5-8). lib. bdg. 30.60 *(978-0-8225-7582-5(5))* Lerner Publishing Group.

Kops, Deborah. Palenque. 2008. (Unearthing Ancient Worlds Ser.). (ENG., Illus.). 80p. (J). (gr. 5-8). lib. bdg. 30.60 *(978-0-8225-7504-7(3))* Lerner Publishing Group.

Lanser, Amanda. Ötzi the Iceman, 1 vol. 2014. (Digging up the Past Ser.). (ENG., Illus.). 112p. (J). (gr. 6-12). lib. bdg. 35.64 *(978-1-62403-235-6(4)*, Essential Library) ABDO Publishing Co.

Lindeen, Mary. Ashes to Ashes: Uncovering Pompeii. 2008. (Illus.). 36p. (J). pap. *(978-0-531-15544-8(7))* Children's Pr., Ltd.

—Ashes to Ashes: Uncovering Pompeii. 2007. (Shockwave: People & Communities Ser.). (ENG., Illus.). 36p. (J). (gr. 3-5). 25.00 *(978-0-531-17745-7(9)*, Children's Pr.) Scholastic Library Publishing.

Liu-Perkins, Christine. At Home in Her Tomb: Lady Dai & the Ancient Chinese Treasures of Mawangdui. Brannen, Sarah S., illus. 2014. (ENG.). 80p. (J). (gr. 4-7). lib. bdg. 19.95 *(978-1-58089-370-1(8))* Charlesbridge Publishing, Inc.

—At Home in Her Tomb: Lady Dai & the Ancient Chinese Treasures of Mawangdui. 2014. 80p. pap. 19.95 *(978-1-60734-615-9(X))* Charlesbridge Publishing, Inc.

Macdonald, Fiona. Amazing Archaeologists: True Stories of Astounding Archaeological Discoveries, 1 vol. 2014. (Ultimate Adventurers Ser.). (ENG.). 48p. (gr. 6-6). lib. bdg. 29.99 *(978-1-4109-5419-0(6))* Heinemann-Raintree.

Malam, John. Burial Places: Discover Stone, Bronze & Iron Age Britain. 2017. (Prehistoric Adventures Ser.). (ENG., Illus.). 32p. (J). (gr. 2-4). 17.99 *(978-0-7502-9594-9(5)*, Wayland) Hachette Children's Group GBR. Dist: Hachette Bk. Group.

—Hill Forts: Discover Stone, Bronze & Iron Age Britain. 2017. (Prehistoric Adventures Ser.). (ENG., Illus.). 32p. (J). (gr. 2-4). 17.99 *(978-0-7502-9593-2(7)*, Wayland) Hachette Children's Group GBR. Dist: Hachette Bk. Group.

Morris, Neil. Lost Cities. 2009. (Amazing History Ser.). (Illus.). 32p. (J). (gr. 4-7). pap. 7.95 *(978-1-59920-209-9(3))* Black Rabbit Bks.

Parker, Steve. Fossils. 2010. (Unpredictable Nature Ser.). (Illus.). 48p. (J). (gr. 3-18). lib. bdg. 19.95 *(978-1-4222-2000-9(1))* Mason Crest.

Peterson, Judy Monroe. Digging up History: Archaeologists. 2009. (Extreme Scientists Ser.). 24p. (gr. 2-3). 42.50 *(978-1-61512-450-3(0)*, PowerKids Pr.); (Illus.). (YA). lib. bdg. 22.60 *(978-1-4042-4523-5(5))* Rosen Publishing Group, Inc., The.

Reinke, Beth. Backhoes Dig! 2017. (Bumba Books (tm) — Construction Zone Ser.). (ENG.). (J). (gr. -1-1). pap. 6.99 ***(978-1-5124-5539-7(3))***; (Illus.). lib. bdg. 25.32 ***(978-1-5124-3355-5(1))*** Lerner Publishing Group.

Rinaldo, Denise. Cities of the Dead: Finding Lost Civilizations. 2008. (24/7: Science Behind the Scenes Ser.). (ENG., Illus.). 64p. (J). (gr. 9-12). 29.00 *(978-0-531-12079-8(1))*; pap. 7.95 *(978-0-531-18739-5(X))* Scholastic Library Publishing. (Watts, Franklin).

—Lost City Spotted from Space! Is There a Hidden Land under the Sand? 2011. (J). pap. *(978-0-545-32929-3(9))* Scholastic, Inc.

Rosebrough, Amy & Malone, Bobbie. Water Panthers, Bears, & Thunderbirds: Exploring Wisconsin's Effigy Mounds. 2003. (New Badger History Ser.). (ENG., Illus.). 48p. (J). (gr. 4-7). pap. 9.95 *(978-0-87020-357-2(6))* Wisconsin Historical Society.

Rubalcaba, Jill & Robertshaw, Peter. Every Bone Tells a Story: Hominin Discoveries, Deductions, & Debates. 2010. (ENG., Illus.). 192p. (J). (gr. 5-8). 18.95 *(978-1-58089-164-6(0))* Charlesbridge Publishing, Inc.

Samuel, Charlie. Solving the Mysteries of Pompeii. 2008. (Digging into History Ser.). 32p. (gr. 4-18). lib. bdg. 29.93 *(978-0-7614-3105-3(5)*, Benchmark Bks.) Marshall Cavendish Corp.

Samuels, Charlie. Forgotten Cities. 2012. (ENG.). 32p. (J). pap. *(978-0-7787-8012-0(0))* Crabtree Publishing Co.

Schlitz, Laura Amy. The Hero Schliemann: The Dreamer Who Dug up Troy. Byrd, Robert, illus. 2006. (ENG.). 80p. (J). (gr. 4-7). lib. bdg. 17.99 *(978-0-7636-2283-1(4))* Candlewick Pr.

Shea, Therese. The African Burial Ground. 2016. (Hidden History Ser.). 00032p. (J). pap. 10.50 *(978-1-4824-5787-2(3))* Stevens, Gareth Publishing LLLP.

Shone, Rob. Ancient Treasures. 2009. (Graphic Discoveries Ser.). (ENG.). 48p. (YA). (gr. 5-5). 58.50 *(978-1-61512-923-2(5)*, Rosen Reference) Rosen Publishing Group, Inc., The.

—Ancient Treasures. Spender, Nick, illus. 2008. (Graphic Nonfiction Ser.). (ENG.). 48p. (gr. 3-8). pap. 14.05 *(978-1-4042-9593-3(3))*; (YA). (gr. 5-9). lib. bdg. 31.95 *(978-1-4042-1089-9(X))* Rosen Publishing Group, Inc., The.

Shuter, Jane. Ancient China. 2016. (Excavating the Past Ser.). (ENG.). 48p. (gr. 4-6). pap. 8.99 *(978-1-4846-3645-9(7)*, NA-h) Heinemann-Raintree.

Smith, Tod G., contrib. by. Graphic Expeditions, 10 vols., Set. Incl. Getting to the Bottom of Global Warming: An Isabel Soto Investigation. Collins, Terry. Schulz, Barbara, illus. lib. bdg. 30.65 *(978-1-4296-3972-9(5))*; Mesa Verde Cliff Dwellers: An Isabel Soto Archaeology Adventure. Collins, Terry. Anderson, Bill, illus. lib. bdg. 30.65 *(978-1-4296-3971-2(7))*; Searching for UFOs: An Isabel Soto Investigation. Sautter, Aaron. lib. bdg. 30.65 *(978-1-4296-3974-3(1))*; Secrets of Martial Arts: An Isabel Soto History Adventure. Harbo, Christopher L. lib. bdg. 30.65 *(978-1-4296-3973-6(3))*; (gr. 3-4). (Graphic Expeditions Ser.). (ENG.). 32p. 2010. Set lib. bdg. 306.50 o.p. *(978-1-4296-4449-5(4)*, Graphic Library) Capstone Press of Coughlan Cos.

Sonneborn, Liz. Pompeii. 2008. (Unearthing Ancient Worlds Ser.). (ENG., Illus.). 80p. (gr. 5-8). lib. bdg. 30.60 *(978-0-8225-7505-4(1))* Lerner Publishing Group.

Soriano, Joan & Malizia, Diana. A Visual History of Archaeological Discoveries Around the World. 2016. (Visual History of the World Ser.). 00096p. (J). (gr. 8-8). 37.10 *(978-1-4994-6576-1(9))* Rosen Publishing Group, Inc., The.

Stern, Steven L. Wretched Ruins. 2010. (Scary Places Ser.). (Illus.). 32p. (YA). (gr. 4-7). lib. bdg. 25.27 *(978-1-936087-55-6(3))* Bearport Publishing Co., Inc.

Sturm, Jeanne. Filling the Earth with Trash. 2010. (ENG., Illus.). 24p. (J). (gr. k-2). pap. 8.95 *(978-1-61590-542-3(1))* Rourke Educational Media.

Waxman, Laura Hamilton. Mysteries of Pompeii. 2017. (Ancient Mysteries Ser.). (ENG.). 32p. (J). (gr. 3-6). 27.99 ***(978-1-5124-4017-1(5))*** Lerner Publishing Group.

Woods, Michael & Woods, Mary B. The Tomb of King Tutankhamen. 2008. (Unearthing Ancient Worlds Ser.). (ENG., Illus.). 80p. (gr. 5-8). lib. bdg. 30.60 *(978-0-8225-7506-1(X))* Lerner Publishing Group.

World Book, Inc Staff, contrib. by. The Secrets of Ancient Tombs. 2014. (J). *(978-0-7166-2661-9(6))* World Bk., Inc.

York, M. J. 12 Ancient Mysteries. 2017. (Scary & Spooky Ser.). (ENG., Illus.). 32p. (J). (gr. 3-6). 21.95 *(978-1-63235-291-0(5))* Pr. Room Editions LLC.

EXCAVATIONS (ARCHAEOLOGY)—FICTION

Adlington, L. J. Glittering Eye. 2009. (ENG.). 320p. (J). (gr. 4-6). pap. 8.99 *(978-0-340-95681-6(X))* Hodder & Stoughton GBR. Dist: Hachette Bk. Group.

Herr, Melody & Darnell, Regna. Edward Sapir: Linguist, Anthropologist, Humanist. 2010. (ENG., Illus.). 520p. pap. 35.00 *(978-0-8032-2437-7(0))* Univ. of Nebraska Pr.

Hunt, Elizabeth Singer. The Secret of the Sacred Temple. Williamson, Brian, illus. 2008. (Secret Agent Jack Stalwart Ser.: 5). (ENG.). 128p. (J). (gr. 1-4). per. 5.99 *(978-1-60286-003-2(3)*, Weinstein Bks.) Perseus Bks. Group.

Jacobs, Jordan. Samantha Sutton & the Winter of the Warrior Queen. 2014. (Samantha Sutton Ser.: 2). (ENG.). 368p. (J). (gr. 4-7). pap. 6.99 *(978-1-4022-7563-0(3)*, 9781402275630, Sourcebooks Jabberwocky) Sourcebooks, Inc.

Jones, Allan Frewin. The Wreckers. 2003. (ENG.). 163p. (J). mass mkt. *(978-0-330-36810-0(9)*, Pan) Pan Macmillan.

Moss, Marissa. The All-New Amelia. Moss, Marissa, illus. (ENG., Illus.). (J). 2013. 5.99 *(978-1-4169-1289-7(4))* 2007. 40p. (gr. 2-5). 12.99 *(978-1-4169-0908-8(7))* Simon & Schuster/Paula Wiseman Bks. (Simon & Schuster/Paula Wiseman Bks.).

Priestley, Chris. Redwulf's Curse. 2005. (ENG., Illus.). 176p. (YA). (gr. 6-10). 16.99 *(978-0-385-60695-0(8)*, Doubleday UK) Transworld Publishers Ltd. GBR. Dist: Trafalgar Square Publishing.

Stilton, Geronimo & Stilton, Thea. Thea Stilton & the Blue Scarab Hunt. 2012. (Thea Stilton Ser.: 11). (ENG.). 176p. (J). (gr. 2-5). pap. 8.99 *(978-0-545-34104-2(3)*, Scholastic Paperbacks) Scholastic, Inc.

Sutton, Laurie S. Legend of the Gator Man. Neely, Scott, illus. 2016. (Scooby-Doo Comic Chapter Bks.). (ENG.). 88p. (gr. 3-7). pap. 5.95 *(978-1-4965-3588-7(X))* Capstone Press of Coughlan Cos.

Travis, Alva. Secret of the Hidden Chamber. 2006. pap. 16.95 *(978-1-4241-2071-0(3))* PublishAmerica, Inc.

EXECUTIONS

see Capital Punishment

EXECUTIVE POWER

Berlatsky, Noah. Presidential Powers. 2010. (Opposing Viewpoints Ser.). (ENG.). 240p. 42.95 *(978-0-7377-4982-3(2))*; 238p. pap. 29.45 *(978-0-7377-4983-0(0))* Cengage Gale. (Greenhaven Pr., Inc.).

Bow, James. What Is the Executive Branch? 2013. (ENG.). 32p. (J). *(978-0-7787-0902-2(7))*; pap. *(978-0-7787-0907-7(8))* Crabtree Publishing Co.

Hinman, Bonnie. The Executive Branch. 2011. (My Guide to the Constitution Ser.). 48p. (J). (gr. 3-6). pap. 16.50 *(978-1-61228-185-8(0))*; (Illus.). lib. bdg. 29.95 *(978-1-58415-943-8(X))* Mitchell Lane Pubs., Inc.

Miller, Amanda. What Does the President Do? 2009. (Scholastic News Nonfiction Readers Ser.). 24p. (J). (gr. 1-2). (ENG.). pap. 6.95 *(978-0-531-22425-0(2))*; (Illus.). 22.00 *(978-0-531-21088-8(X))* Scholastic Library Publishing.

Sévigny, Eric, illus. Caillou: Accidents Happen. 2014. (ENG.). 24p. (J). (gr. -1-1). pap. 3.99 *(978-2-89718-120-8(6))* Caillouet, Gerry.

Thorburn, Mark. The President & the Executive Branch: How Our Nation Is Governed. 2012. (Constitution & the United States Government Ser.). (Illus.). 104p. (J). (gr. 5-18). 33.27 *(978-0-7660-4063-2(1))* Enslow Pubs., Inc.

Wittekind, Erika & Gerhardt, Michael J. The United States v. Nixon: The Watergate Scandal & Limits to Us Presidential Power, 1 vol. 2012. (Landmark Supreme Court Cases Ser.). (ENG., Illus.). 160p. (J). (gr. 6-12). 37.07 *(978-1-61783-478-3(5))* ABDO Publishing Co.

EXECUTIVES

Aller, Susan Bivin. Madam C. J. Walker. 2007. (History Maker Biographies Ser.). (ENG., Illus.). 48p. (gr. 3-6). lib. bdg. 27.93 *(978-0-8225-6582-6(X)*, Lerner Pubns.) Lerner Publishing Group.

Bryant, Jill. Phenomenal Female Entrepreneurs, 1 vol. 2013. (Women's Hall of Fame Ser.). (ENG.). 128p. (J). (gr. 6-8). pap. 10.95 *(978-1-927583-12-8(8))* Second Story Pr. CAN. Dist: Orca Bk. Pubs. USA.

Eason, Sarah. Alex Ferguson: A Football Legend! 2017. (Real-Life Stories Ser.). (ENG., Illus.). 32p. (J). (gr. 4-6). pap. 11.99 *(978-0-7502-9475-1(2)*, Wayland) Hachette Children's Group GBR. Dist: Hachette Bk. Group.

Faulkner, Nicholas. 101 Entrepreneurs & Business Leaders. 2016. (J). lib. bdg. *(978-1-68048-507-3(5))* Windmill Bks.

Ferguson. Business Managers. 2nd rev. ed. 2009. (Careers in Focus Ser.). 204p. (gr. 6-12). 32.95 *(978-0-8160-7296-5(5)*, Ferguson Publishing Co.) Facts On File, Inc.

Gitlin, Martin. EBay: The Company & Its Founder, 1 vol. 2011. (Technology Pioneers Set 1 Ser.). (ENG., Illus.). 112p. (J). (gr. 6-12). lib. bdg. 35.64 *(978-1-61714-807-1(5))* ABDO Publishing Co.

Harbo, Christopher L., et al. Business Leaders, 1 vol. 2014. (Business Leaders Ser.). (ENG.). 24p. (gr. k-1). pap. 23.80 *(978-1-4765-9656-3(5)*, Pebble Bks.) Capstone Press of Coughlan Cos.

Krohn, Katherine E. Madam C. J. Walker & New Cosmetics, 1 vol. Dominquez, Richard et al, illus. 2006. (Inventions & Discovery Ser.). (ENG.). 32p. (gr. 3-4). 8.10 *(978-0-7368-9647-4(3)*, Graphic Library) Capstone Press of Coughlan Cos.

Lasky, Kathryn. Vision of Beauty: The Story of Sarah Breedlove Walker. Bennett, Nneka, illus. 2012. (Candlewick Biographies Ser.). (ENG.). 56p. (J). (gr. 3-7). 14.99 *(978-0-7636-6428-2(6))*; pap. 4.99 *(978-0-7636-6092-5(2))* Candlewick Pr.

Leavitt, Amie Jane. Becoming a Project Manager. 2017. (Tech Track: Building Your Career in IT Ser.). 80p. (J). (gr. 12-12). 35.75 ***(978-1-5081-7560-5(8)***, Rosen Young Adult) Rosen Publishing Group, Inc., The.

Porterfield, Jason. What Is the Executive Branch? 2015. (Let's Find Out! Government Ser.). (ENG., Illus.). 32p. (J). (gr. 2-3). 23.45 *(978-1-62275-922-4(2)*, Britannica Educational Publishing) Rosen Publishing Group, Inc., The.

Rajczak, Kristen. Women in Business. 2015. (Women Groundbreakers Ser.). (ENG.). 32p. (J). (gr. 4-5). pap. 10.00 *(978-1-4994-1040-2(9)*, PowerKids Pr.) Rosen Publishing Group, Inc., The.

Rosenthal, Beth. Are Executives Paid Too Much? Greenhaven Press Editors, ed. 2011. (At Issue Ser.). (ENG.). 128p. (gr. 10-12). 39.40 *(978-0-7377-5888-7(0))*; pap. 27.80 *(978-0-7377-5889-4(9)*, Greenhaven Pr., Inc.) Cengage Gale.

Shores, Erika L., et al. Business Leaders, 1 vol. 2014. (Business Leaders Ser.). (ENG.). 24p. (gr. k-1). lib. bdg. 87.96 *(978-1-4765-9655-6(7)*, Pebble Bks.) Capstone Press of Coughlan Cos.

Strom, Laura Layton. Racing on the Wind: Steve Fossett. 2008. (Illus.). 36p. (J). pap. *(978-0-531-15541-7(2))* Children's Pr., Ltd.

Tougas, Shelley. Girls Rule! Amazing Tales of Female Leaders, 1 vol. 2013. (Girls Rock! Ser.). (ENG.). 64p. (gr. 4-5). 34.65 *(978-1-4765-0235-9(8))* Capstone Press of Coughlan Cos.

Viegas, Jennifer. Pierre Omidyar: The Founder of EBay. 2009. (Internet Career Biographies Ser.). 112p. (gr. 8-8). 63.90 *(978-1-61513-596-7(0))* Rosen Publishing Group, Inc., The.

Vitale, Ann. Manager. Riggs, Ernestine G. & Gholar, Cheryl, eds. 2013. (Careers with Character Ser.: 18). 96p. (J). (gr. 7-18). 22.95 *(978-1-4222-2759-6(6))* Mason Crest.

Woog, Adam. Pierre M. Omidyar: Creator of Ebay. 2007. (Innovators Ser.). (ENG., Illus.). 64p. (J). (gr. 4-8). lib. bdg. 29.95 *(978-0-7377-3864-3(2)*, LML02109-234925, Kidhaven) Cengage Gale.

EXERCISE

see also Gymnastics; Physical Education and Training; Physical Fitness

also names of special kinds of exercises, e.g. Rowing, etc.

ABDO Publishing Company Staff. Super Simple Exercise, 1 vol. 2011. (Super Simple Exercise Ser.). (ENG., Illus.). 32p. 162.42 *(978-1-61714-958-0(6)*, Super SandCastle) ABDO Publishing Co.

Adams, Michelle. Zumba Fitness. 2014. 48p. (gr. 4-8). 29.95 *(978-1-61228-554-2(6))* Mitchell Lane Pubs., Inc.

Aliotti, Johnny. Johnny's Simple Dumbbell Workout. 2004. spiral bd. 14.95 *(978-0-9740600-1-9(1))*; (Illus.). 102p. per. 13.95 *(978-0-9740600-0-2(3))* ProTips(TM) Media.

Antill, Sara. 10 Ways I Can Live A Healthy Life. 2012. (I Can Make a Difference Ser.). (ENG., Illus.). 24p. (J). (gr. 2-5). 22.60 *(978-1-4488-6207-8(8))*; pap. 8.25 *(978-1-4488-6373-0(2))* Rosen Publishing Group, Inc., The. (PowerKids Pr.).

April, Elyse. We Like to Move - Spanish / English Edition: Exercise Is Fun. 2012. (We Like To Ser.). (SPA & ENG., Illus.). 32p. pap. 10.95 *(978-1-935826-08-8(5))* Kalindi Pr.

April, Elyse & Ryan, Regina Sara. We Like to Move: Exercise Is Fun. 2011. (We Like To Ser.). (ENG.). 32p. pap. 9.95 *(978-1-935826-02-6(6))* Kalindi Pr.

April, Elyse, et al. Nos Gusta Movernos: El Ejercicio Es Divertido = We Like to Move: Exercise Is Fun. Iverson, Diane, illus. 2009. (SPA & ENG.). (J). pap. *(978-1-890772-95-6(X))* Hohm Pr.

Bellisario, Gina. Move Your Body! My Exercise Tips. Kurilla, Renee, illus. 2014. (Cloverleaf Books — My Healthy Habits Ser.). (ENG.). 24p. (gr. k-2). lib. bdg. 23.93 *(978-1-4677-1349-8(X)*, Millbrook Pr.) Lerner Publishing Group.

Benchmark Education Company, LLC Staff, compiled by. Nutrition & Exercise. 2006. (J). 91.00 *(978-1-4108-7036-0(7))* Benchmark Education Co.

Berger, Melvin & Berger, Gilda. Kicking, Running, & Stretching. 2007. (Illus.). 32p. (J). pap. *(978-0-439-02449-5(8))* Scholastic, Inc.

Bersma, Danielle & Visscher, Marjoke. Yoga Games for Children: Fun & Fitness with Postures, Movements & Breath. Evans, Amina Marix, tr. from DUT. Kooistra, Alex, illus. 2003. (SmartFun Activity Bks.). (ENG.). 160p. (J). pap. 14.95 *(978-0-89793-389-6(3)*, Hunter Hse.) Turner Publishing Co.

Brezina, Corona. What Happens to Your Body When You Are Weight Training. 2009. (How & Why of Exercise Ser.). (Illus.). 48p. (YA). (gr. 5-9). 29.25 *(978-1-4358-5307-2(5))* Rosen Publishing Group, Inc., The.

Buckley, Annie. The Breathing Bridge. (Illus.). 2012. *(978-1-927004-14-2(4))* 2011. pap. *(978-1-927004-13-5(6))* Brighter Bks. Publishing Hse.

Capucilli, Alyssa Satin. My First Yoga Class. Wachter, Jill, photos by. 2017. (My First Ser.). (ENG., Illus.). 32p. (J). (gr. -1-k). 16.99 ***(978-1-5344-0485-4(6))***; pap. 3.99 ***(978-1-5344-0484-7(8))*** Simon Spotlight. (Simon Spotlight).

Carle, Eric. De la Cabeza a los Pies, 1 vol. Carle, Eric, illus. 2007.Tr. of From Head to Toe. (SPA., Illus.). 32p. (J). (gr. -1-3). pap. 6.99 *(978-0-06-051313-9(6))* HarperCollins Pubs.

Carleton, Kate. What Happens to Your Body When You Cycle. 2009. (How & Why of Exercise Ser.). (Illus.). 48p. (YA). (gr. 5-9). 29.25 *(978-1-4358-5308-9(3))* Rosen Publishing Group, Inc., The.

Clarkson, Stephanie. Let's Get Moving with Wenlock & Mandeville! 2012. (London 2012 Ser.). (ENG., Illus.). 32p. (J). (gr. -1-k). pap. 10.99 *(978-1-84732-645-4(5))* Carlton Bks., Ltd. GBR. Dist: Independent Pubs. Group.

Cleary, Brian P. Run & Hike, Play & Bike: What Is Physical Activity? Goneau, Martin, illus. 2011. (Food Is CATegorical

Ser.). (ENG.). 32p. (gr. k-3). pap. 7.95 (978-0-7613-6390-3(4)) Lerner Publishing Group.

—Run & Hike, Play & Bike: What Is Physical Activity? Goneau, Martin & Gable, Brian, illus. 2010. (Food Is CATegorical Ser.). (ENG.). 32p. (gr. k-3). lib. bdg. 25.26 (978-1-58013-593-1(5)) Lerner Publishing Group.

Cleary, Brian P. & Goneau, Martin. Run & Hike, Play & Bike: What Is Physical Activity? 2011. (Food Is CATegorical Ser.). pap. 45.32 (978-0-7613-8353-6(0), Millbrook Pr.) Lerner Publishing Group.

Cleland, Jo. Get Moving. 2012. (ENG., Illus.). 24p. (gr. k-2). pap. 8.95 (978-1-61810-216-4(8)) Rourke Educational Media.

Coan, Sharon. Good for Me: Play & Exercise. 2015. (TIME for KIDS(r) Nonfiction Readers Ser.). (ENG., Illus.). 12p. (gr. k-k). 4.99 (978-1-4938-2152-5(0)) Teacher Created Materials, Inc.

Conklin, Wendy. Safe & Sound: Our Health. 2017. (J). pap. 9.99 **(978-1-4938-3629-1(3))** Teacher Created Materials, Inc.

Currie-McGhee, Leanne K. Exercise Addiction. 2011. (Diseases & Disorders Ser.). 128p. lib. bdg. 34.95 (978-1-4205-0551-1(3), Lucent Bks.) Cengage Gale.

de Brunhoff, Laurent. Babar's Yoga for Elephants. 2006. (ENG., Illus.). 48p. (gr. -1-3). 10.95 (978-0-8109-3076-6(5), Abrams Image) Abrams, Inc.

deMarin, Layne. Everybody Moves, 1 vol. 2012. (Wonder Readers: Science Ser.). (ENG.). 20p. (gr. -1-2). lib. bdg. 22.65 (978-1-4296-9611-1(7), Wonder Readers) Capstone Press of Coughlan Cos.

DiPrimio, Pete. The World of CrossFit. 2014. 48p. (gr. 4-8). 29.95 (978-1-61228-552-8(X)) Mitchell Lane Pubs., Inc.

Doeden, Matt. Stay Fit! How You Can Get in Shape. 2009. pap. 52.95 (978-0-7613-4687-6(2)) Lerner Publishing Group.

—Stay Fit! How You Can Get in Shape. Desrocher, Jack, illus. 2008. (Health Zone Ser.). 64p. (YA). (gr. 4-7). lib. bdg. 30.60 (978-0-8225-7553-5(1)) Lerner Publishing Group.

Dolphin, Colleen. Cool Exercise: Healthy & Fun Ways to Get Your Body Moving, 1 vol. 2012. (Cool Health & Fitness Ser.). (ENG.). 32p. (J). (gr. 3-6). lib. bdg. 27.07 (978-1-61783-427-1(0), Checkerboard Library) ABDO Publishing Co.

Dru Tecco, Betsy. Food for Fuel: The Connection Between Food & Physical Activity. 2008. (Library of Nutrition Ser.). (Illus.). 48p. (YA). (gr. 8-12). lib. bdg. 29.25 (978-1-4042-1871-0(8), Rosen Reference) Rosen Publishing Group, Inc., The.

Editors of Time Magazine. TIME Your Body. 2013. (ENG., Illus.). 112p. (gr. 11-17). 29.95 (978-1-61893-083-5(4), Time Bks.) Time Inc. Bks.

Evans, Lynette. Move Your Bones. 2007. (Shockwave: the Human Experience Ser.). (ENG., Illus.). 36p. (J). (gr. 3-5). 25.00 (978-0-531-17761-7(0), Children's Pr.) Scholastic Library Publishing.

Feeney, Rik. Cheerleading Conditioning for Back Hands. 2007. (Illus.). 96p. per. 17.95 (978-0-9637991-8-0(5)) Richardson Publishing, Inc.

Gardner, Robert, et al. Ace Your Exercise & Nutrition Science Project: Great Science Fair Ideas. 2009. (Ace Your Biology Science Project Ser.). (Illus.). 128p. (J). (gr. 5-9). lib. bdg. 33.27 (978-0-7660-3218-7(3)) Enslow Pubs., Inc.

Gillen, Jim & Gillen, Lynea. Yoga Calm for Children: Educating Heart, Mind, & Body. 2008. (ENG., Illus.). 181p. (J). per. 29.95 (978-0-9799289-0-1(7)) Three Pebble Pr., LLC.

Gogerly, Liz. Exercise. Gordon, Mike, illus. 2008. (Looking after Me Ser.). (ENG.). 32p. (J). (gr. -1-3). pap. (978-0-7787-4118-3(4)) Crabtree Publishing Co.

Goodbody, Slim. Exercising. McGinnis, Ben, illus. Pinchbeck, Chris, photos by. 2007. (Slim Goodbody Good Health Guides). 32p. (J). (gr. 2-6). lib. bdg. 26.00 (978-0-8368-7741-0(1), Gareth Stevens Learning Library) Stevens, Gareth Publishing LLLP.

Goodbody, Slim & Burstein, John. A Million Moves: Keeping Fit. 2008. (Slim Goodbody's Lighten Up! Ser.). (ENG., Illus.). 32p. (J). (gr. 3-7). pap. (978-0-7787-3930-2(9)); lib. bdg. (978-0-7787-3912-8(0)) Crabtree Publishing Co.

Goodrow, Carol. Happy Feet, Healthy Food: Your Child's First Journal of Exercise & Healthy Eating. Goodrow, Carol, illus. 2004. (ENG., Illus.). 112p. (J). 14.00 (978-1-891369-46-9(6)) Breakaway Bks.

Gordon, Sharon. Exercise. 2003. (Rookie Read-About Health Ser.). (ENG., Illus.). 32p. (J). (gr. k-2). pap. 5.95 (978-0-516-26950-4(X), Children's Pr.) Scholastic Library Publishing.

Greathouse, Lisa. Get Moving, 1 vol. 2011. (Science Readers: a Closer Look Ser.). (ENG.). 32p. (J). (gr. 3-3). pap. 8.99 (978-1-4333-3089-6(X)) Teacher Created Materials, Inc.

Green, Emily K. Keeping Fit. 2006. (Blastoff! Readers Ser.). (ENG., Illus.). 24p. (J). (gr. k-3). lib. bdg. 24.95 (978-1-60014-006-8(8)) Bellwether Media.

—Keeping Fit. 2011. (Blastoff! Readers: New Food Guide Pyramid Ser.). (Illus.). 24p. (J). pap. 5.95 (978-0-531-25853-8(X), Children's Pr.) Scholastic Library Publishing.

Hallinan, P. K. Let's Be Fit. 2007. (ENG., Illus.). 32p. (J). (gr. 3-7). 8.99 (978-0-8249-5528-1(5), Ideal Pubns.) Worthy Publishing.

Hardyman, Robyn. Healthy Bodies. 2012. (Healthy & Happy Ser.). (Illus.). 32p. (J). (gr. 1-4). lib. bdg. 26.50 (978-1-4488-5274-1(9)) Rosen Publishing Group, Inc., The.

Hawes, Alison. My Exercise Diary: Band 02B/Red B. 2006. (Collins Big Cat Ser.). (ENG., Illus.). 16p. (J). (gr. -1-k). pap. 5.99 (978-0-00-718669-3(X)) HarperCollins Pubs. Ltd. GBR. Dist: Independent Pubs. Group.

Head, Honor. Keeping Fit. 2013. (Let's Read & Talk about Ser.). (Illus.). 32p. (J). (gr. 2-5). 28.50 (978-1-59771-396-2(1)) Sea-To-Sea Pubns.

Herrington, Lisa M. I Like to Exercise. 2015. (Rookie Read-About(tm) Health Ser.). (ENG., 32p. (J). Illus.). lib. bdg. 25.00 (978-0-531-21011-6(1)); pap. 5.95 (978-0-531-21068-0(5)) Scholastic Library Publishing.

Hill, Z. B. Core Workouts. Hart, Diane H., ed. 2014. (Integrated Life of Fitness Ser.). 64p. (J). (gr. 7-18). pap. 11.95 (978-1-4222-3195-1(X)); 23.95 (978-1-4222-3157-9(7)) Mason Crest.

Hopper, Karina. Mouth & Tongue Let's Have Some Fun! Macdonald, Lisa, illus. 2010. (ENG.). 48p. pap. 9.95 (978-1-84905-161-3(5), 3101) Kingsley, Jessica Pubs. GBR. Dist: Macmillan Distribution Ltd.

Hunt, Jamie. Getting Stronger, Getting Fit: The Importance of Exercise. 2010. (Kids & Obesity Ser.). (Illus.). 48p. (YA). lib. bdg. 19.95 (978-1-4222-1709-2(4)) Mason Crest.

James, Sara. Step Aerobics & Aerobic Dance. Hart, Diane H., ed. 2014. (Integrated Life of Fitness Ser.: 10). 64p. (J). (gr. 7-18). 23.95 (978-1-4222-3164-7(X)) Mason Crest.

—Yoga & Pilates. Hart, Diane H., ed. 2014. (Integrated Life of Fitness Ser.). (Illus.). 64p. (J). (gr. 7-18). pap. 11.95 (978-1-4222-3204-0(2)); 23.95 (978-1-4222-3166-1(6)) Mason Crest.

Jennings, Madeleine & Drewe, James. Tai Chi Step-By-Step. 2010. (Skills in Motion Ser.). (Illus.). 96p. (YA). (gr. 9-18). lib. bdg. 33.25 (978-1-4488-1551-7(7), Rosen Reference) Rosen Publishing Group, Inc., The.

Johnson, Marlys. Understanding Exercise Addiction. 2005. (Teen Eating Disorder Prevention Book Ser.). (Illus.). 192p. (YA). (gr. 7-12). lib. bdg. 34.60 (978-0-8239-2990-0(6), E2EXAD) Rosen Publishing Group, Inc., The.

Kay, Jill. Fernando Exercises! 2013. (Core Math Skills: Measurement & Geometry Ser.). 24p. (J). (gr. 1-2). 22.60 (978-1-4777-2228-2(9)); (ENG.). pap. 8.25 (978-1-4777-2106-3(1)) Rosen Publishing Group, Inc., The. (Rosen Classroom).

—Fernando Exercises! Tell & Write Time. 2013. (Rosen Math Readers Ser.). (ENG.). 24p. (J). (gr. 1-2). pap. 49.50 (978-1-4777-2107-0(X), Rosen Classroom) Rosen Publishing Group, Inc., The.

Kreisman, Rachelle. Start Sweating! A Kids' Guide to Being Active. Haggerty, Tim, illus. 2014. (Start Smart: Health Ser.). 32p. (J). (gr. 1-3). pap. 7.95 (978-1-937529-64-2(9)) Red Chair Pr.

Labrecque, Ellen. Speed: Get Quick!, 1 vol. 2012. (Exercise! Ser.). (ENG.). 32p. (gr. 1-3). 27.32 (978-1-4329-6732-1(0)); pap. 8.29 (978-1-4329-6739-0(8)) Heinemann-Raintree. (Heinemann First Library).

—Stamina: Get Stronger & Play Longer!, 1 vol. 2012. (Exercise! Ser.). (ENG.). 32p. (gr. 1-3). 27.32 (978-1-4329-6733-8(9), Heinemann First Library) Heinemann-Raintree.

—Strength: Build Muscles & Climb High!, 1 vol. 2012. (Exercise! Ser.). (ENG.). 32p. (gr. 1-3). 27.32 (978-1-4329-6735-2(5), Heinemann First Library) Heinemann-Raintree.

Lark, Liz. Yoga for Kids. Park, Clare, photos by. 2005. (Illus.). 127p. (J). reprint ed. pap. 20.00 (978-0-7567-9410-1(2)) DIANE Publishing Co.

Leavitt, Amy. Yoga Fitness. 2014. (ENG.). 48p. (gr. 4-8). 29.95 (978-1-61228-551-1(1)) Mitchell Lane Pubs., Inc.

Lee, Ilchi. Meridian Exercise for Self-Healing Book 1: Classfied by Common Symptoms, 2 vols. 2003. (Dahnhak, the Way to Perfect Health Ser.: Vol. 1). (Illus.). 151p. per. 17.95 (978-0-9720282-7-1(7)) Healing Society, Inc.

—Meridian Exercise for Self-Healing Book 2: Classified by Common Symptoms, 2 vols., Vol. 2. 2003. (Dahnhak, the Way to Perfect Health Ser.: 2). (Illus.). 193p. per. 17.95 (978-0-9720282-8-8(5)) Healing Society, Inc.

Libal, Autumn. Exercise for Fitness & Weight Loss. Garcia, Victor, ed. 2014. (Understanding Obesity Ser.: 10). (Illus.). 104p. (J). (gr. 7-18). lib. bdg. 24.95 (978-1-4222-3060-2(0)) Mason Crest.

Liebman, Hollis Lance. Core Fitness, 1 vol. 2015. (ENG.). 192p. (YA). 38.25 (978-1-4777-8168-5(4), Rosen Young Adult) Rosen Publishing Group, Inc., The.

Llewellyn, Claire. Estoy Sano? Aprender Sobre Alimentacion y Actividad Fisica. Gordon, Mike, illus. (SPA.). (J). (gr. k-2). pap. (978-950-24-0945-0(0)) Albatros ARG. Dist: Lectorum Pubns., Inc.

Llewelyn, Claire. Exercise. 2006. (QEB Looking After Me Ser.). (Illus.). 24p. (J). (gr. -1-3). lib. bdg. 16.95 (978-1-59566-193-7(X)) QEB Publishing Inc.

—Healthy Eating. 2006. (QEB Looking After Me Ser.). (Illus.). 24p. (J). (gr. -1-3). lib. bdg. 19.95 (978-1-59566-192-0(1)) QEB Publishing Inc.

Lloyd, Rachel. Connor the Conker & the Breezy Day: An Interactive Pilates Adventure. 2015. (ENG., Illus.). 40p. (J). 17.95 (978-1-84819-294-2(0), 8183) Kingsley, Jessica Pubs. GBR. Dist: Macmillan Distribution Ltd.

Loh-Hagan, Virginia. Training Course. 2016. (D. I. Y. Make It Happen Ser.). (ENG., Illus.). 32p. (J). (gr. 4-8). 29.93 (978-1-63471-104-3(1), 208527, 45th Parallel Press) Cherry Lake Publishing.

Marsico, Katie. Exercise! 2015. (21st Century Junior Library: Your Healthy Body Ser.). (ENG.). 24p. (J). (gr. 2-5). 27.07 (978-1-63188-984-4(2), 205848) Cherry Lake Publishing.

Mills, Nathan & Faraday, Daniel. Walk, Run, Skip, & Jump! 2012. (Rosen Readers Ser.). (ENG., Illus.). 16p. (J). (gr. k-1). pap. 7.00 (978-1-4488-8680-7(5), Rosen Classroom) Rosen Publishing Group, Inc., The.

Minden, Cecilia. Exercise by the Numbers. 2007. (21st Century Skills Library: Real World Math Ser.). (ENG., Illus.). 32p. (gr. 4-8). lib. bdg. 28.50 (978-1-60279-010-0(8), 200063) Cherry Lake Publishing.

Nagle, Jeanne. What Happens to Your Body When You Swim. 2009. (How & Why of Exercise Ser.). (Illus.). 48p. (YA). (gr. 5-9). 29.25 (978-1-4358-5309-6(1)) Rosen Publishing Group, Inc., The.

Nelson, Robin. Exercising. 2006. (Pull Ahead Books: Health Ser.). (ENG., Illus.). 32p. (gr. k-3). 22.60 (978-0-8225-3489-1(4)) Lerner Publishing Group.

Pappas, Diane H., et al. Why I Need Exercise. Estrada, Ric, illus. 2007. (J). pap. (978-0-545-01428-1(X)) Scholastic, Inc.

Parker, Steve. How Do My Muscles Get Strong? Muscles & Exercise, 1 vol. 2011. (Inside My Body Ser.). (ENG.). 32p. (gr. 3-5). pap. 7.99 (978-1-4109-4028-5(4)); lib. bdg. 30.65 (978-1-4109-4017-9(9)) Heinemann-Raintree. (NA-r).

Payment, Simone. What Happens to Your Body When You Run. 2009. (How & Why of Exercise Ser.). (Illus.). 48p. (YA). (gr. 5-9). 29.25 (978-1-4358-5306-5(7)) Rosen Publishing Group, Inc., The.

Peters, Celeste A. Health Q & A. 2013. (J). (978-1-62127-414-8(4)); pap. (978-1-62127-420-9(9)) Weigl Pubs., Inc.

Power, Teresa. The ABCs of Yoga for Kids. Rietz, Kathleen, illus. 2009. (ENG.). 32p. (J). (gr. -1-3). 19.95 (978-0-9822587-0-5(4), 4e17cd6f-1cd3-4995-a291-23f8e9041df7) Stafford House.

Power, Teresa Anne. The ABCs of Yoga for Kids 56 Learning Cards. Rietz, Kathleen, illus. 2011. (ENG.). 57p. (J). 19.95 (978-0-9822587-3-6(9)) Stafford House.

Reese, Brandon. Draw Me Healthy! Reese, Brandon, illus. 2012. (Illus.). 32p. (J). 7.99 (978-0-8280-2680-2(7)) Review & Herald Publishing Assn.

Rissman, Rebecca & Smith, Sian. Getting Exercise, 1 vol. 2012. (Take Care of Yourself! Ser.). (ENG.). 24p. (gr. -1-1). 22.65 (978-1-4329-6710-9(X)); pap. 6.29 (978-1-4329-6717-8(7)) Heinemann-Raintree. (Acorn).

Rockwell, Lizzy. The Busy Body Book: A Kid's Guide to Fitness. Rockwell, Lizzy, illus. (ENG., Illus.). 40p. (J). (gr. -1-2). 2008. pap. 7.99 (978-0-553-11374-7(7), Dragonfly Bks.) 2004. 15.95 (978-0-375-82203-2(8), Crown Books For Young Readers) Random Hse. Children's Bks.

—Busy Body Book: A Kid's Guide to Fitness. 2014. 17.00 (978-1-63419-689-5(9)) Perfection Learning Corp.

Royston, Angela. Why Do I Run? 2012. (My Body Ser.). (ENG., Illus.). 24p. (gr. k-4). pap. 7.95 (978-1-77092-000-2(5)) Saunders Bk. Co. CAN. Dist: RiverStream Publishing.

Rustad, Martha E. H. I Stay Active. 2017. (Healthy Me Ser.). (ENG., Illus.). 24p. (gr. k-1). lib. bdg. 21.99 (978-1-5157-3982-1(1)) Capstone Press of Coughlan Cos.

Salzmann, Mary Elizabeth. Run! Jump! Play! Healthy Active Habits, 1 vol. 2014. (Healthy Habits Ser.). (ENG.). 24p. (J). (gr. -1-3). 24.21 (978-1-62403-530-2(2)) ABDO Publishing Co.

Schaefer, Adam. Ejercicio, 1 vol. 2010. (Salud y el Estado Fisico Ser.). (SPA.). 32p. (gr. 1-3). 27.32 (978-1-4329-4443-8(6)); pap. 8.29 (978-1-4329-4448-3(7)) Heinemann-Raintree.

Schuh, Mari. Get Moving!, 1 vol. 2012. (What's on Myplate? Ser.). (ENG., 24p. (gr. k-1). Illus.). pap. 7.29 (978-1-4296-9414-8(9)); pap. 41.70 (978-1-4296-9415-5(7)) Capstone Press of Coughlan Cos. (Pebble Plus).

Schuh, Mari C. Get Moving!, 1 vol. 2012. (What's on Myplate? Ser.). (ENG., Illus.). 24p. (gr. k-1). lib. bdg. 26.65 (978-1-4296-8747-8(9), Pebble Plus) Capstone Press of Coughlan Cos.

—¡Muévete! Strictly Spanish LLC. Staff, tr. from ENG. 2013. (¿Qué Hay en Miplato?/What's on My Plate? Ser.).Tr. of Get Moving! (SPA, ENG & MUL.). 24p. (gr. k-1). lib. bdg. 26.65 (978-1-62065-944-1(1)) Capstone Press of Coughlan Cos.

Senker, Cath. Exercise & Play. 2008. (Healthy Choices Ser.). (Illus.). 24p. (J). (gr. 3-7). lib. bdg. 22.60 (978-1-4042-4305-7(4), PowerKids Pr.) Rosen Publishing Group, Inc., The.

Sjonger, Rebecca. Do Your Bit to Be Physically Fit! 2015. (ENG., Illus.). 24p. (J). (978-0-7787-1879-6(4)) Crabtree Publishing Co.

—Hop, Throw, & Play: Build Your Skills Every Day! 2016. (ENG., Illus.). 24p. (J). (978-0-7787-2349-3(6)) Crabtree Publishing Co.

Smithyman, Kathryn & Kalman, Bobbie. Active Kids: Fun Ways to Be Active. 2003. (Kid Power Ser.). (ENG., Illus.). 32p. (J). (gr. 3). pap. (978-0-7787-1275-6(3)); lib. bdg. (978-0-7787-1253-4(2)) Crabtree Publishing Co.

Spilsbury, Louise. Get Active! 2010. (Crabtree Connections Ser.). (ENG.). 24p. (J). (gr. 3-6). (978-0-7787-9941-2(7)); pap. (978-0-7787-9963-4(8)) Crabtree Publishing Co.

Spilsbury, Richard, et al. Your Body for Life. 2013. (Your Body for Life Ser.). (ENG.). 64p. (gr. 7-8). pap. 59.94 (978-1-4329-7095-6(X)) Heinemann-Raintree.

Strauss, Greg. Eleven Minute Workout: Total Fitness in 11 Minutes a Day. 2003. (Illus.). 124p. per. 11.00 (978-0-9744568-0-5(2), EMW:0974456802) Motion Fitness LLC.

Tecco, Betsy Dru. Food for Fuel: The Connection Between Food & Physical Activity. (Library of Nutrition Ser.). 48p. (gr. 5-8). 2009. 53.00 (978-1-60853-766-2(8), Rosen Reference) 2008. (ENG., Illus.). per. 11.75 (978-1-4042-1635-8(9)) Rosen Publishing Group, Inc., The.

Thomas, Isabel. Number Fun: Making Numbers with Your Body, 1 vol. 2014. (ENG., Illus.). 24p. (gr. -1-1). 25.99 (978-1-4846-0409-0(1)) Heinemann-Raintree.

Tieck, Sarah. Stay Fit, 1 vol. 2012. (ENG.). 32p. 27.07 (978-1-61783-236-9(7), Buddy Bks.) ABDO Publishing Co.

Torrisi, Cathy. Get up & Go! 2011. pap. 39.95 (978-0-7664-3746-3(9)) Abrams & Co. Pubs., Inc.

Tourville, Amanda Doering. Get up & Go: Being Active, 1 vol. Rooney, Ronnie, illus. 2008. (How to Be Healthy! Ser.). (ENG.). 24p. (gr. k-2). 26.65 (978-1-4048-4811-5(8)) Picture Window Bks.

Troupe, Thomas Kingsley. Kitanai & Lazy Lizard Get Fit. Christoph, Jamey, illus. 2015. (Kitanai's Healthy Habits Ser.). (ENG.). 24p. (gr. k-2). lib. bdg. 26.65 (978-1-4795-6083-7(9)) Picture Window Bks.

Vogel, Elizabeth. ¡A hacer ejercicio! (Let's Exercise) 2009. (Limpieza y salud todo el día (Clean & Healthy All Day Long) Ser.). (SPA.). 24p. (gr. 1-1). 37.50 (978-1-61514-291-0(6), Editorial Buenas Letras) Rosen Publishing Group, Inc., The.

—Let's Exercise / ¡A hacer Ejercicio! 2009. (Clean & Healthy All Day Long / Limpieza y salud todo el día Ser.). (SPA.). 24p. (gr. 1-1). 37.50 (978-1-61511-871-7(3), Editorial Buenas Letras) Rosen Publishing Group, Inc., The.

Wechsler, Kimberly. 303 Kid-Approved Exercises & Active Games. Sleva, Michael, illus. 2013. (SmartFun Activity Bks.). (ENG.). (gr. k-3). 144p. pap. 14.95 (978-0-89793-619-4(1)); 168p. spiral bd. 19.95 (978-0-89793-624-8(8)) Turner Publishing Co. (Hunter Hse.).

—303 Preschooler-Approved Exercises & Active Games. Sleva, Michael, illus. 2013. (SmartFun Activity Bks.). (ENG.). 168p. (gr. k-k). pap. 14.95 (978-0-89793-618-7(3)); spiral bd. 19.95 (978-0-89793-623-1(X)) Turner Publishing Co. (Hunter Hse.).

—303 Tween-Approved Exercises & Active Games. Sleva, Michael, illus. 2013. (SmartFun Activity Bks.). (ENG.). 168p. (gr. 3-6). pap. 14.95 (978-0-89793-620-0(5)); spiral bd. 19.95 (978-0-89793-625-5(6)) Turner Publishing Co. (Hunter Hse.).

Willett, Edward. Frequently Asked Questions about Exercise Addiction. 2008. (FAQ: Teen Life Ser.). (Illus.). 64p. (YA). (gr. 7-12). lib. bdg. 31.95 (978-1-4042-1806-2(8)) Rosen Publishing Group, Inc., The.

Willis, Laurie. Exercise & Fitness. 2013. (Issues That Concern You Ser.). (ENG., Illus.). 144p. (gr. 7-10). lib. bdg. 42.00 (978-0-7377-6293-8(4)) Cengage Gale.

Wilson, Michael R. Living a Heart-Healthy Life. 2010. (Healthy Habits Ser.). 64p. (YA). (ENG.). pap. 12.95 (978-1-4488-0608-9(9)); (Illus.). (gr. 5-8). lib. bdg. 31.95 (978-1-4358-9438-9(3)) Rosen Publishing Group, Inc., The. (Rosen Reference).

Winkler, Peter, et al. Keeping Fit. 2006. (Nonfiction Reading & Writing Workshops Ser.). (ENG., Illus.). 32p. (J). pap. 17.95 (978-0-7922-8863-3(7)) CENGAGE Learning.

Wollering, Loretta. Tai Chi, 1 vol. 2015. (ENG.). 192p. (J). 38.25 (978-1-4777-8166-1(8), Rosen Young Adult) Rosen Publishing Group, Inc., The.

Zuravicky, Orli. The Skipping Book. 2009. (Let's Get Moving Ser.). 24p. (gr. k-k). 42.50 (978-1-61514-231-6(2), PowerKids Pr.) Rosen Publishing Group, Inc., The.

—The Skipping Book / Avanzar a Saltitos. 2009. (Let's Get Moving / Diviértete en movimiento Ser.). (ENG & SPA.). 24p. (gr. k-1). 42.50 (978-1-61514-237-8(1), Editorial Buenas Letras) Rosen Publishing Group, Inc., The.

EXHIBITIONS

Hamilton, John. Roping. 2013. (Xtreme Rodeo Ser.). (Illus.). 32p. (J). (gr. 3-9). lib. bdg. 27.07 (978-1-61783-982-5(5), Abdo & Daughters) ABDO Publishing Co.

Jackson, Robert. Meet Me in St. Louis: A Trip to the 1904 World's Fair. 2004. (ENG., Illus.). 144p. (J). (gr. 3-18). 17.99 (978-0-06-009267-2(X)) HarperCollins Pubs.

Radtke, Becky. At the State Fair Coloring Book. 2004. (Dover Coloring Bks.). (ENG., Illus.). 32p. (J). (gr. -1-2). pap. 2.95 (978-0-486-43339-4(0)) Dover Pubns., Inc.

Roslund, Samantha & Fontichiaro, Kristin. Maker Faire. 2013. (21st Century Skills Innovation Library: Makers As Innovators Ser.). (ENG., Illus.). 32p. (J). (gr. 4-8). 28.50 (978-1-62431-136-9(9), 202864) Cherry Lake Publishing.

EXILES

see Refugees

EXORCISM

see Witchcraft

EXPEDITIONS, ANTARCTIC AND ARCTIC

see Antarctica; Arctic Regions

EXPEDITIONS, SCIENTIFIC

see Scientific Expeditions

EXPERIMENTS, SCIENTIFIC

see Science—Experiments

EXPLORATION, SUBMARINE

see Underwater Exploration

EXPLORATION AND DISCOVERY

see Discoveries in Geography

EXPLORATION, UNDERWATER

see Underwater Exploration

EXPLORERS

see also America—Discovery and Exploration; Discoveries in Geography; Travelers; Voyages and Travels

also names of countries with the subdivision Description and Travel and Exploring Expeditions, e.g. United States—Description and Travel; United States—Exploring Expeditions, etc.; and names of individual explorers

ABDO Publishing Company. Great Explorers: Set Of 6. 2013. (Great Explorers Ser.: 6). 32p. (J). (gr. 5-9). lib. bdg. 162.42 (978-1-61783-962-7(0), Abdo & Daughters) ABDO Publishing Co.

Abnett, Dan. Christopher Columbus & the Voyage of 1492. Q2A Staff, illus. 2007. (Jr. Graphic Biographies Ser.). (ENG.). 24p. (gr. 3-8). pap. 10.60 (978-1-4042-2143-7(3), PowerKids Pr.) Rosen Publishing Group, Inc., The.

—Christopher Columbus & the Voyage Of 1492. (Jr. Graphic Biographies Ser.). (ENG.). 24p. (J). (gr. 2-3). 2009. 47.90 (978-1-61513-810-4(2), PowerKids Pr.) 2007. (Illus.). lib. bdg. 25.25 (978-1-4042-3390-4(3)) Rosen Publishing Group, Inc., The.

—Cristóbal Colón y el Viaje de 1942. 2009. (Historietas Juveniles: Biografías (Jr. Graphic Biographies) Ser.). (SPA & ENG., Illus.). 24p. (J). (gr. 2-5). 25.25 (978-1-4358-8559-2(7)); (gr. 3-8). pap. 10.60 (978-1-4358-3312-8(0)) Rosen Publishing Group, Inc., The.

Adams, Simon. Encyclopedia of Great Explorers: Discover the World in the Footsteps of Famous Explorers. 2012. (Illus.). 224p. (J). (978-1-4351-4350-0(7)) Barnes & Noble, Inc.

Adler, David A. A Picture Book of Lewis & Clark. Himler, Ronald, illus. 2003. (ENG.). 32p. (J). (gr. k-3). tchr. ed. 17.95 (978-0-8234-1735-3(2)) Holiday Hse., Inc.

Adler, David A. & Adler, Michael S. A Picture Book of Daniel Boone. Collins, Matt, illus. 2013. (ENG.). 32p. (J). (gr. -1-3). 17.95 (978-0-8234-2748-2(X)) Holiday Hse., Inc.

Allen, Nancy Kelly. Daniel Boone: Trailblazer, 1 vol. Waites, Joan C., illus. 2005. (ENG.). 32p. (J). (gr. k-3). 16.99 (978-1-58980-212-4(8)) Pelican Publishing Co., Inc.

Aller, Susan Bivin. Christopher Columbus. 2003. (History Maker Bios Ser.). (Illus.). 48p. (J). (gr. 3-5). lib. bdg. 26.60 (978-0-8225-0398-9(0)) Lerner Publishing Group.

Anderson, Michael. Biographies of the New World: From Leif Eriksson to Charles Darwin. 2012. (Impact on America: Collective Biographies Ser.). (ENG., Illus.). 136p. (J). (gr. 7-12). lib. bdg. 32.90 (978-1-61530-672-5(2)) Rosen Publishing Group, Inc., The.

Anderson, Michael, ed. Biographies of the New World: Leif Eriksson, Henry Hudson, Charles Darwin, & More. 2012. (Impact on America: Collective Biographies Ser.). (ENG., Illus.). 112p. (YA). (gr. 7-12). 65.80 (978-1-61530-803-3(2)) Rosen Publishing Group, Inc., The.

Anderson, Wendy. Expeditions. 2007. (Action Numeracy Middle Primary Ser.). 32p. pap. 9.95 (978-0-86431-646-2(1)) ACER Pr. AUS. Dist: ISBS Publisher Services.

Anderson, Zachary. John Cabot: Searching for a Westward Passage to Asia. 2015. (Incredible Explorers Ser.). (ENG., Illus.). 64p. (J). (gr. 7-7). 34.21 (978-1-5026-0173-5(7)) Cavendish Square Publishing.

—Samuel de Champlain: Exploring the Great Lakes. 2015. (J). lib. bdg. (978-1-62713-423-1(9)); (ENG., Illus.). 64p. (gr. 7-7). 34.21 (978-1-5026-0138-4(9)) Cavendish Square Publishing.

Anema, Durlynn. Louise Arner Boyd: Arctic Explorer. 2004. (Women Adventurers Ser.). (Illus.). 112p. (gr. 5-18). 21.95 *(978-1-883846-42-8(0))* Reynolds, Morgan Inc.

Angelis, Gina De. Hernando Cortes & the Conquest of Mexico. 2007. (Illus.). 63p. (J). 25.00 *(978-1-4223-6717-9(7))* DIANE Publishing Co.

Ariganello, Lisa. Henry the Navigator: Prince of Portuguese Exploration. 2006. (In the Footsteps of Explorers Ser.). (ENG., Illus.). 32p. (J). (gr. 4-7). pap. *(978-0-7787-2469-8(7))*; lib. bdg. *(978-0-7787-2433-9(6))* Crabtree Publishing Co.

Arlon, Penelope. Explorers. 2014. (Scholastic Discover More Ser.). (ENG.). 80p. (J). (gr. 2-5). 12.99 *(978-0-545-79122-9(7))* Scholastic, Inc.

Aronson, Marc, et al. The World Made New: Why the Age of Exploration Happened & How It Changed the World. 2007. (Timelines of American History Ser.). (ENG., Illus.). 64p. (J). (gr. 5-9). 17.95 *(978-0-7922-6454-5(1)*, National Geographic Children's Bks.) National Geographic Society.

Asselin, Kristine Carlson. Who Really Discovered America? 2011. (Race for History Ser.). (ENG.). 32p. (gr. 3-4). pap. 47.70 *(978-1-4296-6415-8(0)*, Fact Finders) Capstone Press of Coughlan Cos.

Bach, Nancy. Cristoforo Colombo e la Pasta Al Pomodoro - Christopher Columbus & the Pasta with Tomato Sauce: A Bilingual Picture Book (Italian-English Text) Lätti, Leo, illus. 2013. 30p. pap. *(978-1-938712-06-7(4))* Roxby Media Ltd.

Bader, Bonnie. Who Was Christopher Columbus? Harrison, Nancy, illus. 2013. (Who Was? Ser.). (ENG.). 112p. (J). (gr. 3-7). pap. 5.99 *(978-0-448-46333-9(4)*, Grosset & Dunlap) Penguin Young Readers Group.

—Who Was Christopher Columbus? 2013. (Who Was... ? Ser.). lib. bdg. 16.00 *(978-0-606-31684-2(1)*, Turtleback) Turtleback Bks.

Baicker, Karen. Conquistador: Francisco Pizarro Ravages the Inca Empire. 2011. (J). pap. *(978-0-545-32940-8(X))* Scholastic, Inc.

Bailey, Gerry & Foster, Karen. Columbus's Chart. Radford, Karen & Noyes, Leighton, illus. 2008. (Stories of Great People Ser.). (ENG.). 40p. (J). (gr. 3-8). pap. *(978-0-7787-3708-7(X))*; lib. bdg. *(978-0-7787-3686-8(5))* Crabtree Publishing Co.

—Marco Polo's Silk Purse. Radford, Karen & Noyes, Leighton, illus. 2008. (Stories of Great People Ser.). (ENG.). 40p. (J). (gr. 3-8). pap. *(978-0-7787-3710-0(1))*; lib. bdg. *(978-0-7787-3688-2(1))* Crabtree Publishing Co.

Bailey, Katharine. Ferdinand Magellan: Circumnavigating the World. 2005. (In the Footsteps of Explorers Ser.). (ENG., Illus.). 32p. (J). (gr. 4-7). pap. *(978-0-7787-2452-0(2))* Crabtree Publishing Co.

—Radisson & des Groseilliers: Fur Traders of the North. 2006. (In the Footsteps of Explorers Ser.). (ENG., Illus.). 32p. (J). (gr. 3-7). lib. bdg. *(978-0-7787-2422-3(0)*, 1253444); (gr. 4-7). pap. *(978-0-7787-2458-2(1)*, 1253444) Crabtree Publishing Co.

—Vasco Da Gama: Quest for the Spice Trade. 2007. (In the Footsteps of Explorers Ser.). (ENG., Illus.). 32p. (J). (gr. 3-7). lib. bdg. *(978-0-7787-2421-6(2))*; pap. *(978-0-7787-2457-5(3))* Crabtree Publishing Co.

Barile, Mary. Alphonso Wetmore: Soldier, Adventurer, & Writer. 2015. (ENG., Illus.). 48p. (J). 24.00 *(978-1-61248-147-0(7))* Truman State Univ. Pr.

Bauman, Amy & Durman, Laura. Personalities & Places. 2010. (CC: Native North Americans Ser.). 112p. (gr. 6-12). 42.80 *(978-1-933834-81-8(1))* Brown Bear Bks.

Beales, R. A. James Cook: The Pacific Coast & Beyond. 2005. (In the Footsteps of Explorers Ser.). (ENG., Illus.). 32p. (J). (gr. 4-5). pap. *(978-0-7787-2451-3(4))*; lib. bdg. *(978-0-7787-2415-5(8))* Crabtree Publishing Co.

Bedesky, Baron. Peary & Henson: The Race to the North Pole. 2006. (In the Footsteps of Explorers Ser.). (ENG., Illus.). 32p. (J). (gr. 4-7). lib. bdg. *(978-0-7787-2426-1(3))* Crabtree Publishing Co.

Benchmark Education Company. England Explores the Americas (Teacher Guide) 2005. *(978-1-4108-4659-4(8))* Benchmark Education Co.

—France Explores the Americas (Teacher Guide) 2005. *(978-1-4108-4652-5(0))* Benchmark Education Co.

—Spain Explores the Americas (Teacher Guide) 2005. *(978-1-4108-4645-7(8))* Benchmark Education Co.

Benchmark Education Company, LLC Staff, compiled by. Early Explorers. 2006. spiral bd. 330.00 *(978-1-4108-7009-4(X))* 2005. (J). spiral bd. 265.00 *(978-1-4108-5770-5(0))* Benchmark Education Co.

—Early Explorers: Theme Set. 2006. (J). 131.00 *(978-1-4108-7124-4(X))* Benchmark Education Co.

—Social Studies Theme: Early Explorers. 2005. spiral bd. 115.00 *(978-1-4108-5324-0(1))* Benchmark Education Co.

Benge, Janet & Benge, Geoff. Heroes of History - Christopher Columbus: Across the Ocean Sea. 2005. (Heroes of History Ser.). (ENG.). 191p. (YA). (gr. 5). pap. 9.99 *(978-1-932096-23-1(X))* Emerald Bks.

—Heroes of History - Daniel Boone: Frontiersman. 2004. (ENG.). 224p. (YA). pap. 9.99 *(978-1-932096-09-5(4))* Emerald Bks.

—Heroes of History - John Smith: A Foothold in the New World. 2006. (Heroes of History Ser.). (ENG., Illus.). 224p. (YA). (gr. 3-7). pap. 9.99 *(978-1-932096-36-1(1))* Emerald Bks.

Bergreen, Laurence. Over the Edge of the World. 2017. (ENG., Illus.). 224p. (J). (gr. 5-9). 19.99 *(978-1-62672-120-3(3)*, 9781626721203) Roaring Brook Pr.

Berne, Emma Carlson. Did Christopher Columbus Really Discover America? And Other Questions about the New World. 2015. (Good Question! Ser.). (ENG., Illus.). 40p. (J). (gr. 2). 12.95 *(978-1-4549-1258-3(8))* Sterling Publishing Co., Inc.

Bertozzi, Nick. Shackleton: Antarctic Odyssey. Bertozzi, Nick, illus. 2014. (ENG., Illus.). 128p. (YA). (gr. 7-12). pap. 16.99 *(978-1-59643-451-6(1)*, First Second Bks.) Roaring Brook Pr.

Bingham, Jane. Adventurers. 2011. (20th Century Lives Ser.). (ENG.). 32p. (YA). (gr. 3-6). lib. bdg. 26.50 *(978-1-4488-3291-0(8))* Rosen Publishing Group, Inc., The.

Bodden, Valerie. To the Heart of Africa. 2011. (Illus.). 48p. (J). 35.65 *(978-1-60818-066-0(2)*, Creative Education) Creative Co., The.

—To the Ocean Deep. (Great Expeditions Ser.). 48p. (J). 2012. (ENG.). (gr. 4-7). pap. 12.00 *(978-0-89812-665-5(7)*, Creative Paperbacks) 2011. (Illus.). 35.65 *(978-1-60818-067-7(0)*, Creative Education) Creative Co., The.

—To the South Pole. (Great Expeditions Ser.). 48p. (J). 2012. (ENG.). (gr. 4-7). pap. 12.00 *(978-0-89812-667-9(3)*, Creative Paperbacks) 2011. (Illus.). 35.65 *(978-1-60818-069-1(7)*, Creative Education) Creative Co., The.

Bone, Emily. See Inside Exploration & Discovery IR. 2015. (See Inside Board Bks.). (ENG.). 16p. (J). (gr. k-5). 14.99 *(978-0-7945-3499-8(6)*, Usborne) EDC Publishing.

Bowen, Richard. Captain James Cook: British Explorer. 2013. (People of Importance Ser.: 21). (Illus.). 32p. (J). (gr. 4-18). 19.95 *(978-1-4222-2843-2(6))* Mason Crest.

Brannon, Barbara. Discover English Explorers. 2005. (J). pap. *(978-1-4108-5155-0(9))* Benchmark Education Co.

—Discover French Explorers. 2005. (J). pap. *(978-1-4108-5154-3(0))* Benchmark Education Co.

—Discover Spanish Explorers. 2005. (J). pap. *(978-1-4108-5153-6(2))* Benchmark Education Co.

Brasch, Nicolas. Ernest Shackleton's Antarctic Expedition. 2013. (Discovery Education: Sensational True Stories Ser.). (ENG., Illus.). 32p. (J). (gr. 3-6). pap. 10.00 *(978-1-4777-0111-9(7))*; lib. bdg. 25.25 *(978-1-4777-0063-1(3))* Rosen Publishing Group, Inc., The. (PowerKids Pr.).

Brezina, Corona. Jacques Cartier. 2016. (Spotlight on Explorers & Colonization Ser.). 00048p. (J). (gr. 6-6). pap. 11.75 *(978-1-5081-7206-2(4))* Rosen Publishing Group, Inc., The.

Bridy, Dan & Solomon, Sharon K. Christopher Newport: Jamestown Explorer, 1 vol. 2013. (ENG., Illus.). 32p. (J). (gr. k-3). 16.99 *(978-1-4556-1752-4(0))* Pelican Publishing Co., Inc.

The Britannica Guide to Explorers & Adventurers. 2013. (Britannica Guide to Explorers & Adventurers Ser.). (YA). (gr. 9-12). 352.50 *(978-1-62275-065-8(9))*; 176.25 *(978-1-62275-033-7(0))* Rosen Publishing Group, Inc., The.

Brown, Janet Hubbard. Hernando de Soto & His Expeditions Across the Americas. Goetzmann, William H., ed. 2005. (Explorers of New Lands Ser.). (Illus.). 100p. (gr. 5-8). lib. bdg. 30.00 *(978-0-7910-8610-0(0))* Facts On File, Inc.

Buckley, James, Jr. Who Was Ernest Shackleton? Hergenrother, Max, illus. 2013. (Who Was? Ser.). (ENG.). 112p. (J). (gr. 3-7). 5.99 *(978-0-448-47931-6(1)*, Grosset & Dunlap) Penguin Young Readers Group.

Buckley, James. Who Was Ernest Shackleton? 2013. (Who Was... ? Ser.). lib. bdg. 16.00 *(978-0-606-34162-2(5)*, Turtleback) Turtleback Bks.

Burgan, Michael. The Story of North America's First Explorers. 2016. (Discovering the New World Ser.). (ENG., Illus.). 48p. (gr. 3-4). lib. bdg. 29.32 *(978-1-5157-1868-0(9))* Capstone Press of Coughlan Cos.

Burger, James P. Mountain Men of the West. 2009. (Library of the Westward Expansion Ser.). 24p. (gr. 3-4). 42.50 *(978-1-60853-937-6(7)*, PowerKids Pr.) Rosen Publishing Group, Inc., The.

Burleigh, Robert. Black Whiteness: Admiral Byrd Alone in the Antarctic. Krudop, Walter Lyon, illus. 2011. (ENG.). 40p. (J). (gr. 2-5). pap. 19.99 *(978-1-4424-5334-0(6)*, Atheneum Bks. for Young Readers) Simon & Schuster Children's Publishing.

Burnett, Betty. Ferdinand Magellan: The First Voyage Around the World. 2009. (Library of Explorers & Exploration Ser.). 112p. (gr. 5-8). 66.50 *(978-1-60853-602-3(5)*, Rosen Reference) Rosen Publishing Group, Inc., The.

Byers, Ann. Pedro Álvares Cabral. 2016. (Spotlight on Explorers & Colonization Ser.). 48p. (J). (gr. 6-6). pap. 11.75 *(978-1-4777-8821-9(2))* Rosen Publishing Group, Inc., The.

Cado, Herman. Early Explorers & Fur Traders in Colorado, 01 vols., 1. 2016. (Spotlight on Colorado Ser.). (ENG.). 48p. (J). (gr. 4-5). pap. 11.75 *(978-1-4994-1450-9(1)*, PowerKids Pr.) Rosen Publishing Group, Inc., The.

Calvert, Patricia. Vasco Da Gama: So Strong a Spirit. 2004. (Great Explorations Ser.). (Illus.). 80p. (gr. 6). 22.95 *(978-0-7614-1611-1(0)*, Benchmark Bks.) Marshall Cavendish Corp.

Caravantes, Peggy. Marooned in the Arctic: The True Story of Ada Blackjack, the Female Robinson Crusoe. 2016. (Women of Action Ser.). (ENG., Illus.). 208p. (YA). (gr. 7). 19.95 *(978-1-61373-098-0(5))* Chicago Review Pr., Inc.

Carr, Roger Vaughan & Knapsey, Kath. How to Discover the World. 2007. 96p. (J). pap. *(978-1-4207-0729-8(9))* Sundance/Newbridge Educational Publishing.

Childrens Great Explorers Encyclopedia. 2008. (1st Encyclopedia Ser.). 224p. *(978-1-4075-1645-5(0))* Parragon, Inc.

Clarke, Penny. The Story of Explorers & Exploration. 2013. (Illus.). 64p. (J). *(978-1-4351-5031-7(7))* Barnes & Noble, Inc.

Claybourne, Anna. The Story of Exploration. McNee, Ian, illus. 2010. (Science Stories Ser.). 103p. (YA). (gr. 3-18). pap. 10.99 *(978-0-7945-2400-5(1)*, Usborne) EDC Publishing.

Clifton, Chuck & Clifton, Joyce. A Daily Walk with Lewis & Clark - 1804. 2003. 308p. (J). spiral bd. 14.95 *(978-0-9669760-3-8(7))* Maple Canyon Co.

—A Daily Walk with Lewis & Clark - 1805. 2003. 390p. (J). spiral bd. 14.95 *(978-0-9669760-4-5(5))* Maple Canyon Co.

—A Daily Walk with Lewis & Clark - 1806. 2003. 292p. (J). spiral bd. 14.95 *(978-0-9669760-5-2(3))* Maple Canyon Co.

Cohen, Robert Z. Hernando de Soto. 2016. (Spotlight on Explorers & Colonization Ser.). 00048p. (J). (gr. 6-6). pap. 11.75 *(978-1-5081-7210-9(2))* Rosen Publishing Group, Inc., The.

Collier, James Lincoln. Christopher Columbus: To the New World. 2006. (Great Explorations Ser.). (Illus.). 80p. (J). (gr. 3-7). lib. bdg. 32.79 *(978-0-7614-2221-1(8)*, Benchmark Bks.) Marshall Cavendish Corp.

Collins. Collins Fascinating Facts - Explorers. 2016. (Collins Fascinating Facts Ser.). (ENG., Illus.). 72p. (J). (gr. 1-3). pap. 10.99 *(978-0-00-816926-8(8))* HarperCollins Pubs. Ltd. GBR. Dist: Independent Pubs. Group.

Como Funcionan Algunas Cosas, 6 vols., Vol. 3. (Explorers. Exploradores Nonfiction Sets Ser.). (SPA.). (gr. 3-6). *(978-0-7699-0656-0(7))* Shortland Pubns. (U. S. A.) Inc.

Conklin, Wendy. Exploring the New World, 1 vol. 2004. (Primary Source Readers Ser.). (ENG.). 24p. (J). (gr. 5-5). 8.99 *(978-0-7439-8740-0(3))* Shell Educational Publishing.

Connelly, Jack. Christopher Columbus: Discovering the Americas. 2015. (Incredible Explorers Ser.). (ENG., Illus.). 64p. (J). (gr. 7-7). 34.21 *(978-1-5026-0171-1(0))* Cavendish Square Publishing.

—Ferdinand Magellan: Circumnavigating the Globe. 2015. (Incredible Explorers Ser.). (ENG., Illus.). 64p. (J). (gr. 7-7). 34.21 *(978-1-5026-0132-2(X))* Cavendish Square Publishing.

La Conquista de Las Alturas, 6 vols., Vol. 3. (Explorers. Exploradores Nonfiction Sets Ser.). (SPA.). (gr. 3-6). *(978-0-7699-0655-3(9))* Shortland Pubns. (U. S. A.) Inc.

Cooke, Tim. The Exploration of Africa. 2013. (Explorers Discovering the World Ser.). (Illus.). 48p. (J). (gr. 4-6). pap. 14.05 *(978-1-4339-8612-3(4))*; lib. bdg. 31.95 *(978-1-4339-8611-6(6))* Stevens, Gareth Publishing LLLP.

—The Exploration of Arabia & Asia. 2013. (Explorers Discovering the World Ser.). (Illus.). 48p. (gr. 4-6). 31.95 *(978-1-4339-8615-4(9))*; pap. 14.05 *(978-1-4339-8616-1(7))* Stevens, Gareth Publishing LLLP. (Gareth Stevens Learning Library).

—The Exploration of North America. 2013. (Explorers Discovering the World Ser.). (Illus.). 48p. (J). (gr. 4-6). pap. 14.05 *(978-1-4339-8624-6(8))* Stevens, Gareth Publishing LLLP.

—The Exploration of North America. 2013. (Explorers Discovering the World Ser.). (Illus.). 48p. (J). (gr. 4-6). lib. bdg. 31.95 *(978-1-4339-8623-9(X))* Stevens, Gareth Publishing LLLP.

—The Exploration of South America. 2013. (Explorers Discovering the World Ser.). (Illus.). 48p. (gr. 4-6). 31.95 *(978-1-4339-8627-7(2))*; pap. 14.05 *(978-1-4339-8628-4(0))* Stevens, Gareth Publishing LLLP. (Gareth Stevens Learning Library).

—Explore with Francisco Vazquez de Coronado. 2016. (Travel with the Great Explorers Ser.). (ENG., Illus.). 32p. (J). (gr. 3-6). *(978-0-7787-2847-4(1))* Crabtree Publishing Co.

—Explore with Henry Hudson. 2014. (ENG., Illus.). 32p. (J). *(978-0-7787-1246-6(X))*; pap. *(978-0-7787-1258-9(3))* Crabtree Publishing Co.

—Maps & Exploration. 2010. (Understanding Maps of Our World Ser.). 48p. (YA). (gr. 4-7). lib. bdg. 31.00 *(978-1-4339-3512-1(0))*; (Illus.). (gr. 6-8). pap. 14.05 *(978-1-4339-3513-8(9)*, Gareth Stevens Secondary Library) Stevens, Gareth Publishing LLLP.

Craats, Rennay. Exploration of North America. 2005. (Great Journeys Ser.). (Illus.). 32p. (J). (gr. 3-7). per. 9.95 *(978-1-59036-258-7(6))* Weigl Pubs., Inc.

Crompton, Samuel Willard. Ferdinand Magellan & the Quest to Circle the Globe. Goetzmann, William H., ed. 2005. (Explorers of New Lands Ser.). (Illus.). 110p. (J). (gr. 5-8). lib. bdg. 30.00 *(978-0-7910-8608-7(9))* Facts On File, Inc.

—Francis Drake & the Oceans of the World. Goetzmann, William H., ed. 2005. (Explorers of New Worlds Ser.). (Illus.). 160p. (J). (gr. 5-8). lib. bdg. 30.00 *(978-0-7910-8615-5(1))* Facts On File, Inc.

—Lewis & Clark. 2009. (Great Explorers Ser.). (Illus.). 120p. (J). (gr. 6-12). 30.00 *(978-1-60413-418-6(6)*, Chelsea Hse.) Facts On File, Inc.

—Marco Polo: Epic Traveler Throughout Asia. 2017. (Spotlight on Explorers & Colonization Ser.). 48p. (gr. 10-11). 70.50 ***(978-1-5081-7504-9(7)**,* Rosen Young Adult) Rosen Publishing Group, Inc., The.

Crompton, Samuel Willard. Robert de la Salle. 2009. (Great Explorers Ser.). (Illus.). 112p. (J). (gr. 6-12). 30.00 *(978-1-60413-419-3(4)*, Chelsea Hse.) Facts On File, Inc.

Cummins, Julie. Women Explorers. Harness, Cheryl, illus. 2015. (ENG.). 48p. (J). (gr. 2-5). 8.99 *(978-0-14-751736-4(2)*, Puffin Books) Penguin Young Readers Group.

Curley, Robert, contrib. by. Explorers of the Renaissance. 2012. (Renaissance Ser.). (ENG.). 168p. (gr. 9-12). (J). lib. bdg. 38.75 *(978-1-61530-879-8(2))*; (Illus.). (YA). 77.50 *(978-1-61530-885-9(7))* Rosen Publishing Group, Inc., The.

Currie, Stephen & National Geographic Learning Staff. Travels to Distant Lands, 1000-1400. 2007. (Nonfiction Reading & Writing Workshops Ser.). (ENG., Illus.). 32p. (J). pap. 17.95 *(978-0-7922-4542-1(3))* CENGAGE Learning.

Curtis, Suzanne. John Wesley Powell: American Hero. 2013. (ENG & SPA., Illus.). 78p. (J). pap. 8.95 *(978-0-86541-176-4(6))* Filter Pr., LLC.

Dalrymple, Lisa. Explore with James Cook. 2015. (Travel with the Great Explorers Ser.). (ENG., Illus.). 32p. (J). (gr. 3-6). *(978-0-7787-1701-0(1))* Crabtree Publishing Co.

Dalrymple, Lisa & O'Brien, Cynthia. Explore with John Cabot. 2015. (Travel with the Great Explorers Ser.). (ENG., Illus.). 32p. (J). (gr. 3-6). *(978-0-7787-1702-7(X))* Crabtree Publishing Co.

Daly, Ruth. French Explorers. 2016. (J). ***(978-1-5105-1873-5(8))*** SmartBook Media, Inc.

D'Aulaire, Ingri & D'Aulaire, Edgar Parin. Leif the Lucky. 2014. (ENG., Illus.). 60p. 16.95 *(978-0-8166-9545-4(8))* Univ. of Minnesota Pr.

Davenport, John. Juan Ponce de Leon & His Lands of Discovery. Goetzmann, William H., ed. 2005. (Explorers of New Lands Ser.). (Illus.). 110p. (gr. 5-8). lib. bdg. 30.00 *(978-0-7910-8607-0(0))* Facts On File, Inc.

Davis, Linda. Sir Ernest Shackleton. 2009. (Great Explorers Ser.). (Illus.). 144p. (gr. 6-12). 30.00 *(978-1-60413-421-6(6)*, Chelsea Hse.) Facts On File, Inc.

DeFries, Cheryl L. Leif Eriksson: Viking Explorer of the New World. 2010. (Great Explorers of the World Ser.). (Illus.). 112p. (J). (gr. 7-12). lib. bdg. 33.27 *(978-1-59845-126-9(X))* Enslow Pubs., Inc.

Demi. Columbus, 0 vols. Demi, illus. 2012. (ENG., Illus.). 64p. (J). (gr. 3-7). 19.99 *(978-0-7614-6167-8(1)*, 9780761461678, Amazon Children's Publishing) Amazon Publishing.

—The Great Voyages of Zheng He. 2012. (Illus.). (J). 21.95 *(978-1-885008-45-9(7)*, Shen's Bks.) Lee & Low Bks., Inc.

Dickmann, Nancy. The South Pole, 1 vol. 2012. (Explorer Tales Ser.). (ENG.). 32p. (gr. 1-3). 29.99 *(978-1-4109-4785-7(8))*; pap. 8.29 *(978-1-4109-4792-5(0))* Heinemann-Raintree. (Read Me!).

DiConsiglio, John. Francisco Pizarro: Destroyer of the Inca Empire. 2008. (Wicked History Ser.). (ENG., Illus.). 128p. (J). 31.00 *(978-0-531-18551-3(6)*, Watts, Franklin) Scholastic Library Publishing.

Ditchfield, Christin. The Lewis & Clark Expedition. 2006. (True Bks.). (ENG., Illus.). 48p. (J). (gr. 3-7). pap. 6.95 *(978-0-516-25222-3(4)*, Children's Pr.) Scholastic Library Publishing.

Donaldson-Forbes, Jeff. Jacques Cartier. 2009. (Primary Source Library of Famous Explorers Ser.). 24p. (gr. 4-4). 42.50 *(978-1-60854-126-3(6)*, PowerKids Pr.) Rosen Publishing Group, Inc., The.

—Jacques Marquette & Louis Jolliet. 2009. (Primary Source Library of Famous Explorers Ser.). 24p. (gr. 4-4). 42.50 *(978-1-60854-127-0(4)*, PowerKids Pr.) Rosen Publishing Group, Inc., The.

—La Salle. 2009. (Primary Source Library of Famous Explorers Ser.). 24p. (gr. 4-4). 42.50 *(978-1-60854-129-4(0)*, PowerKids Pr.) Rosen Publishing Group, Inc., The.

Donohue, Moira Rose. Christopher Columbus. 2013. (Illus.). 24p. (J). *(978-1-938813-04-7(9))*; pap. *(978-1-938813-08-5(1))* State Standards Publishing, LLC.

—Christopher Newport. 2013. (Illus.). 24p. (J). *(978-1-938813-05-4(7))*; pap. *(978-1-938813-09-2(X))* State Standards Publishing, LLC.

—Henry Hudson. 2014. (Illus.). 24p. (J). *(978-1-938813-16-0(2))* State Standards Publishing, LLC.

—Hernando de Soto. 2015. (Illus.). 24p. (J). *(978-1-938813-20-7(0))* State Standards Publishing, LLC.

—Jacques Cartier. 2013. (Illus.). 24p. (J). *(978-1-938813-03-0(0))* State Standards Publishing, LLC.

—John Cabot. 2014. (Illus.). 24p. (J). *(978-1-938813-15-3(4))* State Standards Publishing, LLC.

—Juan Ponce de León. 2013. (Illus.). 24p. (J). *(978-1-938813-06-1(5))* State Standards Publishing, LLC.

Dowling, Lucy. Why Why Why... Do People Want to Explore? 2010. (Why Why Why Ser.). (Illus.). 32p. (J). (gr. 1-3). lib. bdg. 18.95 *(978-1-4222-1584-5(9))* Mason Crest.

Draper, Allison Stark. Vasco da Gama: The Portuguese Quest for a Sea Route from Europe to India. rev. ed. (Library of Explorers & Explorationtm Ser.). (Illus.). 112p. (YA). (gr. 5-8). lib. bdg. 31.95 *(978-1-4042-0637-3(X)*, Rosen Reference) Rosen Publishing Group, Inc., The.

Eagen, Rachel. Ponce de Leon: Exploring Florida & Puerto Rico. 2005. (In the Footsteps of Explorers Ser.). (ENG., Illus.). 32p. (J). (gr. 4-5). pap. *(978-0-7787-2448-3(4))* Crabtree Publishing Co.

Editors of Kingfisher. Epic Explorers. 2017. (It's All About... Ser.). (ENG.). 32p. pap. 5.99 *(978-0-7534-7280-4(5)*, 9780753472804, Kingfisher) Roaring Brook Pr.

Espinosa, Rod. Lewis & Clark, 1 vol. Espinosa, Rod, illus. 2007. (Bio-Graphics Ser.). (ENG., Illus.). 32p. (J). (gr. 3-6). 28.50 *(978-1-60270-069-7(9)*, Graphic Planet- Nonfiction) ABDO Publishing Co.

Evan-Moor & McFarren, Kathleen. History Pockets: Explorers of North America, Grades 4-6. 2003. (History Pockets Ser.). (ENG., Illus.). 96p. (J). (gr. 4-6). 96p. pap., suppl. ed. 14.99 *(978-1-55799-905-4(8)*, EMC 3708) Evan-Moor Educational Pubs.

Everett, Felicity & Reid, Struan. The Usborne Book of Explorers. Dennis, Peter & Draper, Richard, illus. rev. ed. 2007. (Famous Lives Ser.). 47p. (J). (gr. 4-7). pap. 8.99 *(978-0-7945-1533-1(9)*, Usborne) EDC Publishing.

Exploradores. 2003. (Megabites Ser.). (SPA., Illus.). (J). pap. 8.95 *(978-0-9715256-8-9(4))* Planeta Publishing Corp.

Explorers of New Worlds. 2005. (Explorers of New Worlds Ser.). (gr. 5-8). 225.00 *(978-0-7910-9154-8(6)*, Chelsea Hse.) Facts On File, Inc.

Exploring North America, 1800-1900, Revised Edition. 2nd rev. ed. 2009. (Discovery & Exploration Ser.). (Illus.). 152p. (YA). (gr. 7-12). 35.00 *(978-1-60413-194-9(2))* Facts On File, Inc.

Exploring the Pacific, Revised Edition. 2nd rev. ed. 2009. (Discovery & Exploration Ser.). (Illus.). 120p. (YA). (gr. 7-12). 35.00 *(978-1-60413-197-0(7))* Facts On File, Inc.

Famous Explorers of the American West. (Illus.). (J). (gr. k-5). 112.50 *(978-0-8239-7265-4(8))* Rosen Publishing Group, Inc., The.

Feeney, Kathy. Marco Polo: Explorer of China. 2004. (Explorers! Ser.). (Illus.). 48p. (J). lib. bdg. 23.93 *(978-0-7660-2145-7(9))* Enslow Pubs., Inc.

Feinstein, Stephen. Marco Polo: Amazing Adventures in China. 2013. (Great Explorers of the World Ser.). 112p. (gr. 6-12). pap. 10.95 *(978-0-7660-5430-1(6))* Enslow Pubs., Inc.

Feinstein, Stephen. Captain Cook: Great Explorer of the Pacific. 2010. (Great Explorers of the World Ser.). (Illus.). 112p. (J). (gr. 7-12). 33.27 *(978-1-59845-102-3(2))* Enslow Pubs., Inc.

—Columbus: Opening up the New World. 2009. (Great Explorers of the World Ser.). (Illus.). 112p. (J). (gr. 7-12). lib. bdg. 33.27 *(978-1-59845-101-6(4))* Enslow Pubs., Inc.

—Marco Polo: Amazing Adventures in China. 2009. (Great Explorers of the World Ser.). (Illus.). 112p. (J). (gr. 7-12). lib. bdg. 33.27 *(978-1-59845-103-0(0))* Enslow Pubs., Inc.

Fertig, Dennis. Sylvia Earle: Ocean Explorer, 1 vol. 2014. (Women in Conservation Ser.). (ENG., Illus.). 48p. (J). (gr. 3-6). pap. 8.99 *(978-1-4846-0475-5(X)*, Heinemann InfoSearch) Heinemann-Raintree.

Fisher, Ann Richmond. Explorers of the New World Time Line. Mitchell, Judy & Lindeen, Mary, eds. Smith, Bron, illus. 2007. 112p. (J). pap. 12.95 *(978-1-57310-523-1(6))* Teaching & Learning Co.

Fox, Suzanne G. Meriwether Lewis & William Clark: The Corp of Discovery & the Exploration of the American Frontier. 2009. (Library of American Lives & Times Ser.). 112p. (gr. 5-5). 69.20 *(978-1-60853-493-7(6))* Rosen Publishing Group, Inc., The.

Freedman, Russell. Who Was First? Discovering the Americas. 2007. (ENG., Illus.). 96p. (J). (gr. 5-7). 19.00 *(978-0-618-66391-0(6))* Houghton Mifflin Harcourt Publishing Co.

Fryer, Mary Beacock. Champlain: Peacemaker & Explorer. 2011. (ENG., Illus.). 152p. (YA). (gr. 6). pap. 19.99 *(978-1-55488-940-2(5))* Dundurn CAN. Dist: Ingram Publisher Services.

Fuhr, Ute & Sautai, Raoul. Life below the City. 2012. (ENG., Illus.). 36p. (J). (gr. -1-k). spiral bd. 12.99 *(978-1-85103-410-9(2))* Moonlight Publishing, Ltd. GBR. Dist: Independent Pubs. Group.

E
F
G

Gallagher, Aileen. Prince Henry the Navigator: Pioneer of Modern Exploration. rev. ed. (Library of Explorers & Explorationtm Ser.). (Illus.). 112p. (YA). (gr. 5-8). lib. bdg. 31.95 *(978-1-4042-0636-6(1),* Rosen Reference) Rosen Publishing Group, Inc., The.

Ganeri, Anita. On Expedition with Lewis & Clark. 2010. (ENG.). 32p. (J). (gr. 3-5). *(978-0-7787-9896-5(8));* (Crabtree Connections Ser.: No. 2). pap. *(978-0-7787-9917-7(4))* Crabtree Publishing Co.

—The Top Ten Explorers That Changed the World. 2009. (J). 60.00 *(978-1-4358-9169-2(4),* PowerKids Pr.); (ENG.). 32p. (J). pap. 10.00 *(978-1-4358-9168-5(6),* PowerKids Pr.); (ENG., Illus.). 32p. (YA). (gr. 3-6). 26.50 *(978-1-4358-9167-8(8))* Rosen Publishing Group, Inc., The.

George, Lynn. What Do You Know about the Age of Exploration? (20 Questions: History Ser.). 24p. (gr. 2-3). 2009. 42.50 *(978-1-60854-956-6(9),* PowerKids Pr.) 2008. (Illus.). (J). lib. bdg. 22.60 *(978-1-4042-4190-9(6))* Rosen Publishing Group, Inc., The.

Gitlin, Martin. Vikings, 1 vol. 2013. (Great Warriors Ser.). (ENG.). 48p. (J). (gr. 3-6). lib. bdg. 32.79 *(978-1-61783-729-6(6));* (Illus.). pap. 15.64 *(978-1-61783-779-1(2),* Core Library) ABDO Publishing Co.

Gitlin, Marty & Koran, Maria. Italian Explorers. 2016. (J). ***(978-1-5105-1869-8(X))*** SmartBook Media, Inc.

—Portuguese Explorers. 2016. (J). ***(978-1-5105-1875-9(4))*** SmartBook Media, Inc.

Gleason, Carrie. Henry Hudson: Seeking the Northwest Passage. 2005. (In the Footsteps of Explorers Ser.). (ENG., Illus.). 32p. (J). (gr. -1-9). pap. *(978-0-7787-2444-5(1))* Crabtree Publishing Co.

Goldberg, Jan. Hernando de Soto: Trailblazer of the American Southeast. (Library of Explorers & Exploration Ser.). 112p. (gr. 5-8). 2009. 66.50 *(978-1-60853-607-8(6))* 2003. (Illus.). lib. bdg. 34.60 *(978-0-8239-3623-6(6))* Rosen Publishing Group, Inc., The. (Rosen Reference).

Gondosch, Linda. Where Did Sacagawea Join the Corps of Discovery? And Other Questions about the Lewis & Clark Expedition. 2011. (Six Questions of American History Ser.). (ENG.). 48p. (gr. 4-6). pap. 56.72 *(978-0-7613-7644-6(5));* pap. 9.95 *(978-0-7613-7131-1(1));* lib. bdg. 30.60 *(978-0-7613-5226-6(0))* Lerner Publishing Group.

Gould, Jane H. Ferdinand Magellan. 2013. (Jr. Graphic Famous Explorers Ser.). (ENG., Illus.). 24p. (J). (gr. 3-6). pap. 10.60 *(978-1-4777-0123-2(0));* lib. bdg. 25.25 *(978-1-4777-0069-3(2))* Rosen Publishing Group, Inc., The. (PowerKids Pr.).

—Henry Hudson. 2013. (Jr. Graphic Famous Explorers Ser.). (ENG., Illus.). 24p. (J). (gr. 3-6). pap. 10.60 *(978-1-4777-0127-0(3));* lib. bdg. 25.25 *(978-1-4777-0071-6(4))* Rosen Publishing Group, Inc., The. (PowerKids Pr.).

Great Explorations - Group 3, 6 Bks, Set. 2004. (J). 179.57 *(978-0-7614-1606-7(4))* Marshall Cavendish Corp.

Great Explorations Group 4, 6 bks., Set. Incl. Christopher Columbus: To the New World. Collier, James Lincoln. 80p. (J). (gr. 3-7). lib. bdg. 32.79 *(978-0-7614-2221-1(8));* David Livingstone: Deep in the Heart of Africa. Otfinoski, Steven. 79p. (J). (gr. 3-7). lib. bdg. 32.79 *(978-0-7614-2226-6(9));* Edmund Hillary: First to the Top. Elish, Dan. 80p. (J). (gr. 3-7). lib. bdg. 32.79 *(978-0-7614-2224-2(2));* Henry Hudson: In Search of the Northwest Passage. Otfinoski, Steven. 80p. (J). (gr. 3-7). lib. bdg. 32.79 *(978-0-7614-2225-9(0));* Kit Carson: He Led the Way. Calvert, Patricia. 80p. (gr. 6-7). lib. bdg. 22.95 *(978-0-7614-2223-5(4));* Richard Francis Burton: Explorer, Scholar, Spy. Young, Serinity. 80p. (gr. 6-7). lib. bdg. 22.95 *(978-0-7614-2222-8(6));* (Illus.). 2006. 2007. Set lib. bdg. 196.71 *(978-0-7614-2219-8(6),* Benchmark Bks.) Marshall Cavendish Corp.

Green, Jen. The Story of the Race to the Moon. Mark Bergin, illus. 2017. (Explorers Ser.). 32p. (gr. 3-6). 31.35 ***(978-1-910706-92-3(2))*** Book Hse. GBR. Dist: Black Rabbit Bks.

Green, Jen. You Wouldn't Want to Be a Polar Explorer! (Revised Edition) Antram, David, illus. 2017. (You Wouldn't Want to... Adventurers & Explorers Ser.). (ENG.). 40p. (J). pap. 9.95 *(978-0-531-23154-8(2),* Children's Pr.) Scholastic Library Publishing.

Greenberger, Robert. Juan Ponce de Leon: The Exploration of Florida & the Search for the Fountain of Youth. rev. ed. (Library of Explorers & Explorationtm Ser.). (Illus.). 112p. (YA). (gr. 5-8). lib. bdg. 31.95 *(978-1-4042-0635-9(3),* Rosen Reference) Rosen Publishing Group, Inc., The.

Greenway, Shirley. Exploration of North America. 2010. (History of Exploration Ser.). 48p. 32.80 *(978-1-84898-301-4(8))* Black Rabbit Bks.

Greenway, Shirley, et al. Great Explorers. 2009. (ENG.). 128p. (J). (gr. 4-7). pap. 12.95 *(978-1-84696-208-0(0),* TickTock Books) Octopus Publishing Group GBR. Dist: Independent Pubs. Group.

Greenwood, Rosie. I Wonder Why Columbus Crossed the Ocean: And Other Questions about Explorers. 2013. (I Wonder Why Ser.). (ENG., Illus.). 32p. (J). (gr. k-3). 15.99 *(978-0-7534-6967-5(7),* 9780753469675, Kingfisher) Roaring Brook Pr.

Group/McGraw-Hill, Wright. First Explorers: Student Book Set - 1 Each of 12 Titles. (First Explorers. Primeros Exploradores Nonfiction Sets Ser.). (gr. 1-2). 59.95 *(978-0-7699-1363-6(6))* Shortland Pubns. (U. S. A.) Inc.

—Twentieth-Century Explorers, 6 vols. (Book2WebTM Ser.). (gr. 4-8). 36.50 *(978-0-322-04468-5(5))* Wright Group/McGraw-Hill.

Guillain, Charlotte. Great Explorers. 2015. (Collins Big Cat Ser.). (ENG.). 24p. (J). (gr. 2-2). pap. 7.95 *(978-0-00-759119-0(5))* HarperCollins Pubs. Ltd. GBR. Dist: Independent Pubs. Group.

Gunderson, Jessica. Christopher Columbus: New World Explorer or Fortune Hunter?, 1 vol. 2013. (Perspectives on History Ser.). (ENG.). 32p. (gr. 3-4). 27.32 *(978-1-4765-0242-7(0));* pap. 7.95 *(978-1-4765-3406-0(3))* Capstone Press of Coughlan Cos. (Fact Finders).

Guy, John. Drake & the Elizabethan Explorers. 2010. (History of Exploration Ser.). 48p. 32.80 *(978-1-84898-304-5(2))* Black Rabbit Bks.

Hammond World Atlas Corporation Staff. Explorer Atlas. 2006. (Atlas Ser.). (Illus.). 32p. (J). 10.95 *(978-0-8437-0919-3(7),* 709197) Langenscheidt Publishing Group.

Harris, Laurie Lanzen, ed. Biography for Beginners: World Explorers. 2003. (Illus.). 598p. (J). (gr. 3-6). lib. bdg. 55.00 *(978-1-931360-20-3(0))* Favorable Impressions.

Harvey, Gill. True Desert Adventures. 2004. (True Adventure Stories Ser.). (Illus.). 144p. (J). (gr. 5). lib. bdg. 12.95 *(978-1-58086-679-8(4),* Usborne) EDC Publishing.

Hazelton, Amie. Henry Hudson: An Explorer of the Northwest Passage. 2017. (World Explorers Ser.). (ENG., Illus.). 32p. (gr. 3-4). lib. bdg. 27.32 *(978-1-5157-4205-0(9))* Capstone Press of Coughlan Cos.

—Hernando de Soto: An Explorer of the Southeast. 2017. (World Explorers Ser.). (ENG., Illus.). 32p. (gr. 3-4). lib. bdg. 27.32 *(978-1-5157-4204-3(0))* Capstone Press of Coughlan Cos.

Hazleton, Amie. Francisco Vasquez de Coronado: An Explorer of the Southwest. 2017. (World Explorers Ser.). (ENG., Illus.). 32p. (gr. 3-4). lib. bdg. 27.32 *(978-1-5157-4203-6(2))* Capstone Press of Coughlan Cos.

—Sieur de la Salle: An Explorer of the Great West. 2017. (World Explorers Ser.). (ENG., Illus.). 32p. (gr. 3-4). lib. bdg. 27.32 *(978-1-5157-4206-7(7))* Capstone Press of Coughlan Cos.

—World Explorers. 2017. (World Explorers Ser.). (ENG.). 32p. (gr. 3-4). 109.28 *(978-1-5157-4253-1(9),* Fact Finders) Capstone Press of Coughlan Cos.

Heckschler, Melissa & Shulman, Mark. The Explorer's Gazette: Amazing Stories of 30 Real-Life Journeys. 2004. (Illus.). (J). pap. *(978-0-439-67653-3(3))* Scholastic, Inc.

Henry Stanley & the Quest for the Source of the Nile. 2014. (ENG.). 176p. (J). (gr. 3-7). pap. 13.95 *(978-1-59077-348-2(9))* Evans, M. & Co., Inc.

Henson, Heather. Lift Your Light a Little Higher: The Story of Stephen Bishop: Slave-Explorer. Collier, Bryan, illus. 2016. (ENG.). 32p. (J). (gr. -1-3). 17.99 *(978-1-4814-2095-2(X),* Atheneum/Caitlyn Dlouhy Books) Simon & Schuster Children's Publishing.

Hernández, Roger E. Early Explorations: The 1500s. 2008. (Hispanic America Ser.). 80p. (gr. 5-18). lib. bdg. 34.21 *(978-0-7614-2937-1(9),* Benchmark Bks.) Marshall Cavendish Corp.

Hiram Bingham & the Dream of Gold. 2014. (ENG.). 192p. (J). (gr. 3-7). pap. 13.95 *(978-1-59077-350-5(0))* Evans, M. & Co., Inc.

Holub, Joan. This Little Explorer: A Pioneer Primer. Roode, Daniel, illus. 2016. (This Little Ser.). (ENG.). 26p. (J). (gr. -1-k). bds. 7.99 *(978-1-4814-7175-6(9),* Little Simon) Little Simon.

—Who Was Marco Polo? O'brien, John et al, illus. 2007. (Who Was? Ser.). (ENG.). 112p. (J). (gr. 3-7). pap. 5.99 *(978-0-448-44540-3(9),* Grosset & Dunlap) Penguin Young Readers Group.

—Who Was Marco Polo? O'brien, John, illus. 2007. (Who Was... ? Ser.). 105p. (gr. 4-7). 15.00 *(978-0-7569-8165-5(4))* Perfection Learning Corp.

Hoogenboom, Lynn. Amerigo Vespucci. 2009. (Primary Source Library of Famous Explorers Ser.). 24p. (gr. 4-4). 42.50 *(978-1-60854-118-8(5),* PowerKids Pr.) Rosen Publishing Group, Inc., The.

—Amerigo Vespucci: A Primary Source Biography. 2005. (Primary Source Library of Famous Explorers Ser.). (Illus.). 24p. (J). (gr. 3-7). lib. bdg. 21.25 *(978-1-4042-3037-8(8),* PowerKids Pr.) Rosen Publishing Group, Inc., The.

—Christopher Columbus. 2009. (Primary Source Library of Famous Explorers Ser.). 24p. (gr. 4-4). 42.50 *(978-1-60854-119-5(3),* PowerKids Pr.) Rosen Publishing Group, Inc., The.

—Christopher Columbus: A Primary Source Biography. 2006. (Primary Source Library of Famous Explorers Ser.). (Illus.). 24p. (YA). (gr. 2-5). lib. bdg. 22.60 *(978-1-4042-3036-1(X))* Rosen Publishing Group, Inc., The.

—Ferdinand Magellan. 2009. (Primary Source Library of Famous Explorers Ser.). 24p. (gr. 4-4). 42.50 *(978-1-60854-120-1(7),* PowerKids Pr.) Rosen Publishing Group, Inc., The.

—Ferdinand Magellan: A Primary Source Biography. 2006. (Primary Source Library of Famous Explorers Ser.). (Illus.). 24p. (YA). (gr. 2-5). lib. bdg. 22.60 *(978-1-4042-3039-2(4))* Rosen Publishing Group, Inc., The.

—Francisco Pizarro. 2009. (Primary Source Library of Famous Explorers Ser.). 24p. (gr. 4-4). 42.50 *(978-1-60854-121-8(5),* PowerKids Pr.) Rosen Publishing Group, Inc., The.

—Francisco Pizarro: A Primary Source Biography. 2006. (Primary Source Library of Famous Explorers Ser.). (Illus.). 24p. (YA). (gr. 2-5). lib. bdg. 22.60 *(978-1-4042-3038-5(6))* Rosen Publishing Group, Inc., The.

—Juan Ponce de Leon. 2009. (Primary Source Library of Famous Explorers Ser.). 24p. (gr. 4-4). 42.50 *(978-1-60854-128-7(2),* PowerKids Pr.) Rosen Publishing Group, Inc., The.

—Juan Ponce de Leon: A Primary Source Biography. 2006. (Primary Source Library of Famous Explorers Ser.). (Illus.). 24p. (YA). (gr. 2-5). lib. bdg. 22.60 *(978-1-4042-3040-8(8))* Rosen Publishing Group, Inc., The.

—Sir Francis Drake. 2009. (Primary Source Library of Famous Explorers Ser.). 24p. (gr. 4-4). 42.50 *(978-1-60854-131-7(2),* PowerKids Pr.) Rosen Publishing Group, Inc., The.

—Sir Francis Drake: A Primary Source Biography. 2006. (Primary Source Library of Famous Explorers Ser.). (Illus.). 24p. (YA). (gr. 2-5). lib. bdg. 22.60 *(978-1-4042-3035-4(1))* Rosen Publishing Group, Inc., The.

Hopkinson, Deborah. Keep On! The Story of Matthew Henson, Co-Discoverer of the North Pole, 1 vol. Alcorn, Stephen, illus. (ENG.). 36p. (J). (gr. 1-5). 2015. pap. 7.95 *(978-1-56145-886-8(4))* 2009. 17.95 *(978-1-56145-473-0(7))* Peachtree Pubs.

Howell, Izzi. An Intrepid History of Explorers. 2017. (Blast Through the Past Ser.). (ENG., Illus.). 32p. (J). (gr. 2-4). 16.99 ***(978-1-4451-4931-8(1),*** Franklin Watts) Hachette Children's Group GBR. Dist: Hachette Bk. Group.

Howse, Jennifer. English Explorers. 2016. (J). ***(978-1-5105-1867-4(3))*** SmartBook Media, Inc.

Hulick, Kathryn. Bad Days in Exploration. 2017. (Whoops! a History of Bad Days Ser.). (ENG., Illus.). 48p. (gr. 5-8). lib. bdg. 33.32 *(978-1-4109-8561-3(X))* Heinemann-Raintree.

Hunter, Nick. Christopher Columbus & Neil Armstrong. 2015. (Comparing People from the Past Ser.). (ENG., Illus.). 32p. (gr. 3-3). pap. 6.49 *(978-1-4846-0920-0(4),* Heinemann First Library) Heinemann-Raintree.

—New Worlds, 1 vol. 2012. (Explorer Tales Ser.). (ENG.). 32p. (gr. 1-3). pap. 8.29 *(978-1-4109-4788-8(2),* Read Me!) Heinemann-Raintree.

Hurwicz, Claude. Henry the Navigator. 2009. (Primary Source Library of Famous Explorers Ser.). 24p. (gr. 4-4). 42.50 *(978-1-60854-124-9(X),* PowerKids Pr.) Rosen Publishing Group, Inc., The.

Hyde, Natalie. Explore with Leif Eriksson. 2014. (ENG., Illus.). 32p. (J). *(978-0-7787-1427-9(6))* Crabtree Publishing Co.

Hynson, Colin. Exploration of Africa. 2010. (History of Exploration Ser.). 48p. 32.80 *(978-1-84898-300-7(X))* Black Rabbit Bks.

Incredible Explorers. 2015. (Incredible Explorers Ser.). (ENG.). 64p. (J). (gr. 7-7). 205.26 *(978-1-5026-0298-5(9))* Cavendish Square Publishing.

Isaacs, Sally. Helen Thayer's Arctic Adventure: A Woman & a Dog Walk to the North Pole. Sasheva, Iva, illus. 2016. (Encounter: Narrative Nonfiction Picture Bks.). (ENG.). 32p. (gr. 4-5). lib. bdg. 28.65 *(978-1-4914-8044-1(0))* Encounter Bks.

Isaacs, Sally Senzell. Helen Thayer's Arctic Adventure: A Woman & a Dog Walk to the North Pole. Sasheva, Iva, illus. 2017. (Encounter: Narrative Nonfiction Picture Bks.). (ENG.). 32p. (gr. 4-5). pap. 7.95 *(978-1-4914-8045-8(9))* Capstone Press of Coughlan Cos.

Jackson, Donna M. Extreme Scientists: Exploring Nature's Mysteries from Perilous Places. 2014. (Scientists in the Field Ser.). (ENG., Illus.). 80p. (J). (gr. 5-7). pap. 9.99 *(978-0-544-25003-1(6),* HMH Books For Young Readers) Houghton Mifflin Harcourt Publishing Co.

—Extreme Scientists: Exploring Nature's Mysteries from Perilous Places. 2014. (Scientists in the Field Ser.). lib. bdg. 20.85 *(978-0-606-35330-4(5))* Turtleback Bks.

James, Michaela. Women Explorers. 2016. (Uncommon Women Ser.). (ENG., Illus.). 48p. (gr. 3-8). 27.99 *(978-1-62920-587-8(7))* Scobre Pr. Corp.

Johnson, Dolores. Onward: A Photobiography of African-American Polar Explorer Matthew Henson. 2005. (Photobiographies Ser.). (ENG., Illus.). 64p. (gr. k-3). 27.90 *(978-0-7922-7915-0(8));* 17.95 *(978-0-7922-7914-3(X))* National Geographic Society. (National Geographic Children's Bks.).

Johnson, Rebecca L. Ernest Shackleton: Gripped by the Antarctic. 2003. (Trailblazer Biographies Ser.). (ENG., Illus.). 112p. (gr. 5-9). 31.93 *(978-0-87614-920-1(4))* Lerner Publishing Group.

Johnston, Charles H. Famous Discoverers & Explorers of Amer. 2006. pap. 38.95 *(978-1-4254-9677-7(6))* Kessinger Publishing, LLC.

Jones, Charlotte Foltz. Westward Ho! Eleven Explorers of the American West. 2005. (ENG., Illus.). 240p. (J). (gr. 4-6). tchr. ed. 22.95 *(978-0-8234-1586-1(4))* Holiday Hse., Inc.

Jones, Rebecca C. Captain John Smith's Big & Beautiful Bay, 1 vol. Shute, Linda, illus. 2011. (ENG.). 32p. (J). 14.99 *(978-0-7643-3869-4(2),* 9780764338694, Schiffer Publishing Ltd) Schiffer Publishing, Ltd.

Kachurek, Sandra J. Francisco Pizarro: Explorer of South America. 2004. (Explorers! Ser.). (Illus.). 48p. (J). lib. bdg. 23.93 *(978-0-7660-2178-5(5))* Enslow Pubs., Inc.

Kallen, Stuart A. A Journey with Christopher Columbus. 2017. (Primary Source Explorers Ser.). (ENG.). 40p. (J). (gr. 3-5). lib. bdg. 30.65 *(978-1-5124-0772-3(0))* Lerner Publishing Group.

—A Journey with Francisco Vázquez de Coronado. 2017. (Primary Source Explorers Ser.). (ENG.). 40p. (J). (gr. 3-5). 30.65 *(978-1-5124-0773-0(9))* Lerner Publishing Group.

Kamer, Julie. Roald Amundsen: The Conquest of the South Pole. 2006. (In the Footsteps of Explorers Ser.). (ENG., Illus.). 32p. (J). (gr. 3-7). pap. *(978-0-7787-2468-1(9))* Crabtree Publishing Co.

Keller, Susanna. The True Story of Lewis & Clark. 2013. (What Really Happened? Ser.). (ENG., Illus.). 24p. (J). (gr. 3-6). pap. 8.25 *(978-1-4488-9846-6(3));* lib. bdg. 22.60 *(978-1-4488-9694-3(0))* Rosen Publishing Group, Inc., The. (PowerKids Pr.).

Kennedy, Emily. Daniel Boone. 2014. (Illus.). 31p. (J). lib. bdg. *(978-1-62712-280-1(X))* Cavendish Square Publishing.

Kespert, Deborah. Explore! The Most Dangerous Journeys of All Time. 2016. (ENG., Illus.). 96p. (J). (gr. 4-6). pap. 13.95 *(978-0-500-29230-3(2),* 529230) Thames & Hudson.

Kling, Andrew A., ed. Age of Exploration. 2013. (World History Ser.). (ENG., Illus.). 128p. (J). (gr. 7-10). lib. bdg. 34.95 *(978-1-4205-0930-4(6),* Lucent Bks.) Cengage Gale.

Kneib, Martha. Christopher Columbus: Master Italian Navigator in the Court of Spain. 2009. (Library of Explorers & Exploration Ser.). 112p. (gr. 5-8). 66.50 *(978-1-60853-601-6(7),* Rosen Reference) Rosen Publishing Group, Inc., The.

Knudsen, Anders. Antoine de la Mothe Cadillac: French Settlements at Detroit & Louisiana. 2006. (In the Footsteps of Explorers Ser.). (ENG., Illus.). 32p. (J). (gr. 3-9). lib. bdg. *(978-0-7787-2429-2(8));* (gr. 4-7). pap. *(978-0-7787-2465-0(4))* Crabtree Publishing Co.

—Sir John Franklin: The Search for the Northwest Passage. 2007. (In the Footsteps of Explorers Ser.). (ENG., Illus.). 32p. (J). (gr. 4-7). lib. bdg. *(978-0-7787-2420-9(4));* pap. *(978-0-7787-2456-8(5))* Crabtree Publishing Co.

Knudsen, Shannon. Leif Eriksson. Oldroyd, Mark, illus. 2005. (On My Own Biography Ser.). (ENG.). 48p. (gr. 2-4). pap. 6.95 *(978-1-57505-828-3(6));* lib. bdg. 25.26 *(978-1-57505-649-4(6),* Carolrhoda Bks.) Lerner Publishing Group.

Koestler-Grack, Rachel A. Ferdinand Magellan. 2009. (Great Explorers Ser.). (Illus.). 112p. (gr. 6-12). 30.00 *(978-1-60413-422-3(4),* Chelsea Hse.) Facts On File, Inc.

—Hernando Cortes & the Fall of the Aztecs. Goetzmann, William H., ed. 2005. (Explorers of New Lands Ser.). (Illus.). 176p. (gr. 5-8). lib. bdg. 30.00 *(978-0-7910-8609-4(7))* Facts On File, Inc.

—Vasco Da Gama & the Sea Route to India. Goetzmann, William H., ed. 2005. (Explorers of New Lands Ser.). (Illus.). 168p. (gr. 5-8). lib. bdg. 30.00 *(978-0-7910-8611-7(9))* Facts On File, Inc.

Kostyal, K. M. Trial by Ice: A Photobiography of Sir Ernest Shackleton. 2006. (Illus.). 64p. pap. 7.99 *(978-0-15-356619-6(1))* Houghton Mifflin Harcourt School Pubs.

Kramer, Alan. The Ogs Discover Fire & Other Stuff. 2011. (Navigators Ser.). (J). pap. *(978-1-61672-970-7(8))* Benchmark Education Co.

Kramer, Sydelle. Who Was Daniel Boone? Ulrich, George, illus. 2006. (Who Was? Ser.). (ENG.). 112p. (J). (gr. 3-7). pap. 5.99 *(978-0-448-43902-0(6),* Grosset & Dunlap) Penguin Young Readers Group.

—Who Was Daniel Boone? Ulrich, George, illus. 2006. (Who Was... ? Ser.). 108p. (gr. 2-6). 15.00 *(978-0-7569-6951-6(4))* Perfection Learning Corp.

—Who Was Daniel Boone? 2006. (Who Was... ? Ser.). 16.00 *(978-1-4177-8317-5(6),* Turtleback) Turtleback Bks.

—Who Was Ferdinand Magellan? Wolf, Elizabeth & Harrison, Nancy, illus. 2004. (Who Was? Ser.). (ENG.). 112p. (J). (gr. 3-7). pap. 5.99 *(978-0-448-43105-5(X),* Grosset & Dunlap) Penguin Young Readers Group.

—Who Was Ferdinand Magellan? Wolf, Elizabeth, illus. 2004. (Who Was... ? Ser.). 105p. (J). (gr. 3-7). 12.65 *(978-0-7569-4615-9(8))* Perfection Learning Corp.

Krasner, Barbara. Sir Francis Drake. 2016. (Spotlight on Explorers & Colonization Ser.). 00048p. (J). (gr. 6-6). pap. 11.75 *(978-1-5081-7218-5(8))* Rosen Publishing Group, Inc., The.

Krull, Kathleen. Lives of the Explorers: Discoveries, Disasters (and What the Neighbors Thought) Hewitt, Kathryn, illus. 2014. (ENG.). 96p. (J). (gr. 5-7). 20.99 *(978-0-15-205910-1(5),* HMH Books For Young Readers) Houghton Mifflin Harcourt Publishing Co.

Kudlinski, Kathleen. Christopher Columbus: Young Explorer. 2005. 199p. (J). lib. bdg. 18.46 *(978-1-4242-1727-4(X))* Fitzgerald Bks.

Kuligowski, Stephanie. La Salle: Uno de los Primeros Exploradores de Texas. 2013. (Primary Source Readers Ser.). (SPA.). lib. bdg. 19.65 *(978-0-606-31863-1(1),* Turtleback) Turtleback Bks.

Lace, William W. Captain James Cook. 2009. (Great Explorers Ser.). (Illus.). 112p. (gr. 6-12). 30.00 *(978-1-60413-416-2(X),* Chelsea Hse.) Facts On File, Inc.

—Sir Francis Drake. 2009. (Great Explorers Ser.). (Illus.). 112p. (gr. 6-12). 30.00 *(978-1-60413-417-9(8),* Chelsea Hse.) Facts On File, Inc.

Lackey, Jennifer. Jacques Cartier: Exploring the St. Lawrence River. 2006. (In the Footsteps of Explorers Ser.). (ENG., Illus.). 32p. (J). (gr. 4-7). pap. *(978-0-7787-2466-7(2))* Crabtree Publishing Co.

Landau, Elaine. Ferdinand Magellan. 2005. (History Maker Bios Ser.). (Illus.). 48p. (J). (gr. 3-7). lib. bdg. 26.60 *(978-0-8225-2942-2(4),* Lerner Pubns.) Lerner Publishing Group.

Landau, Jennifer. Vasco Da Gama. 2016. (Spotlight on Explorers & Colonization Ser.). 48p. (J). (gr. 6-6). pap. 11.75 *(978-1-4777-8825-7(5))* Rosen Publishing Group, Inc., The.

Larkin, Tanya. Jacques Marquette & Louis Jolliet: Explorers of the Mississippi. 2009. (Library of Explorers & Exploration Ser.). 112p. (gr. 5-8). 66.50 *(978-1-60853-608-5(4),* Rosen Reference) Rosen Publishing Group, Inc., The.

Leavitt, Amie Jane. Christopher Columbus. 2007. (What's So Great About... ? Ser.). (Illus.). 32p. (J). (gr. 2-4). lib. bdg. 25.70 *(978-1-58415-578-2(7))* Mitchell Lane Pubs., Inc.

LernerClassroom Editors, ed. Country Explorers: Complete Set. 2008. pap. 634.95 *(978-0-8225-9179-5(0))* Lerner Publishing Group.

Levene, Rebecca. Captain Cook. Cuzik, David, illus. 2005. (Usborne Famous Lives Gift Bks.). 61p. (J). (gr. -1-3). 8.95 *(978-0-7945-1051-0(5),* Usborne) EDC Publishing.

Levy, Janey. Lewis & Clark in Their Own Words, Vol. 1. 2014. (Eyewitness to History Ser.). 32p. (J). (gr. 4-5). (ENG.). pap. 10.50 *(978-1-4339-9930-7(7));* 26.60 *(978-1-4339-9929-1(3))* Stevens, Gareth Publishing LLLP.

—Spanish Explorers of North America. 2009. (Real Life Readers Ser.). 32p. (gr. 4-5). pap. 10.00 *(978-1-4358-0171-4(7),* Rosen Classroom) Rosen Publishing Group, Inc., The.

Loker, Aleck. Fearless Captain: The Adventures of John Smith. 2006. (Founders of the Republic Ser.). (Illus.). 176p. (J). (gr. 6-12). lib. bdg. 26.95 *(978-1-931798-83-9(4))* Reynolds, Morgan Inc.

Lonely Planet Publications Staff. How to Be a World Explorer, 1 vol. 2012. (Lonely Planet Kids Ser.). (ENG., Illus.). 160p. (J). 17.99 *(978-1-74321-425-1(1),* 4356) Lonely Planet Pubns.

Lynette, Rachel. Meriwether Lewis & William Clark. 2013. (Pioneer Spirit: the Westward Expansion Ser.). 24p. (J). (gr. 3-6). 22.60 *(978-1-4777-0783-8(2));* pap. 49.50 *(978-1-4777-0900-9(2));* (ENG., Illus.). pap. 8.25 *(978-1-4777-0899-6(5))* Rosen Publishing Group, Inc., The. (PowerKids Pr.).

MacLeod, Elizabeth. Samuel de Champlain. Mantha, John, illus. 2008. (Kids Can Read Ser.). (ENG.). 32p. (J). (gr. 1-3). 14.95 *(978-1-55453-049-6(0));* pap. 3.95 *(978-1-55453-050-2(4))* Kids Can Pr., Ltd. CAN. Dist: Hachette Bk. Group.

Magoon, Kekla. The Zebulon Pike Expedition, 1 vol. 2009. (Essential Events Set 3 Ser.). (ENG., Illus.). 112p. (J). (gr. 6-12). lib. bdg. 35.64 *(978-1-60453-518-1(0))* ABDO Publishing Co.

Malam, John. Extreme Exploration. 2009. (Difficult & Dangerous Ser.). (Illus.). 32p. (J). (gr. 4-7). pap. *(978-1-897563-24-3(8))* Saunders Bk. Co.

Marsh, Carole. Alvar Nunez Cabeza de Vaca:Explorer & Survivor: Explorer & Survivor. 2003. 12p. (gr. k-4). 2.95 *(978-0-635-02135-9(8))* Gallopade International.

—Father Junipero Serra: California Missions Founder: California Missions Founder. 2003. 12p. (gr. k-4). 2.95 *(978-0-635-02136-6(6))* Gallopade International.

—Ferdinand Magellan, World Voyager. 2004. 12p. (gr. k-4). 2.95 *(978-0-635-02373-5(3))* Gallopade International.

—Henry Hudson. 2004. 12p. (gr. k-4). 2.95 *(978-0-635-02379-7(2))* Gallopade International.

—Hernando de Soto: First Discovered the Mississippi River: First Discovered the Mississippi River. 2003. 12p. (gr. k-4). 2.95 *(978-0-635-02134-2(X))* Gallopade International.

—John C. Fremont. 2004. 12p. (gr. k-4). 2.95 *(978-0-635-02380-3(6))* Gallopade International.

—Lewis & Clark Go on a Hike. 2003. 32p. (J). (gr. 3-8). pap. 5.95 *(978-0-635-02122-9(6))* Gallopade International.

—Marco Polo. 2004. 12p. (gr. k-4). 2.95 *(978-0-635-02376-6(8))* Gallopade International.

—Meriwether Lewis & William Clark: Explorers of the Uncharted West: Explorers of the Uncharted West. 2003. 12p. (gr. k-4). 2.95 *(978-0-635-02133-5(1))* Gallopade International.

Mass, Wendy. John Cabot: Early Explorer. 2004. (Explorers! Ser.). (Illus.). 48p. (J). lib. bdg. 25.27 *(978-0-7660-2144-0(0))* Enslow Pubs., Inc.

Mattern, Joanne. Leif Eriksson: Viking Explorer. 2004. (Explorers! Ser.). (Illus.). 48p. (J). lib. bdg. 25.27 *(978-0-7660-2146-4(7))* Enslow Pubs., Inc.

—Will Steger, 1 vol. 2014. (Conservationists Ser.). (ENG., Illus.). 32p. (gr. 3-6). lib. bdg. 27.07 *(978-1-62403-096-3(3),* Checkerboard Library) ABDO Publishing Co.

Matthews, Rupert. Explorer. 2012. (DK Eyewitness Bks.). (ENG.). 72p. (J). (gr. 3-7). 16.99 *(978-0-7566-9825-6(1),* DK Children) Dorling Kindersley Publishing, Inc.

Maynard, Charles W. Jedediah Smith: Mountain Man of the American West. (Famous Explorers of the American West Ser.). 24p. 2009. (gr. 3-4). 42.50 *(978-1-61512-501-2(9))* 2003. (Illus.). (J). lib. bdg. 22.60 *(978-0-8239-6287-7(3))* Rosen Publishing Group, Inc., The. (PowerKids Pr.).

—John Charles Fremont: The Pathfinder. 2009. (Famous Explorers of the American West Ser.). 24p. (gr. 3-4). 42.50 *(978-1-61512-503-6(5),* PowerKids Pr.) Rosen Publishing Group, Inc., The.

—John Wesley Powell: Soldier, Scientist, & Explorer. (Famous Explorers of the American West Ser.). 24p. 2009. (gr. 3-4). 42.50 *(978-1-61512-505-0(1),* PowerKids Pr.) 2003. (Illus.). (YA). (gr. 1-4). lib. bdg. 22.60 *(978-0-8239-6290-7(3))* Rosen Publishing Group, Inc., The.

—Zebulon Pike: Soldier-Explorer of the American Southwest. 2009. (Famous Explorers of the American West Ser.). 24p. (gr. 3-4). 42.50 *(978-1-61512-506-7(X),* PowerKids Pr.) Rosen Publishing Group, Inc., The.

McCormick, Lisa Wade. Christopher Columbus. 2005. (Scholastic News Nonfiction Readers Ser.). (ENG., Illus.). 24p. (J). (gr. 1-2). lib. bdg. 22.00 *(978-0-516-24938-4(X))* Scholastic Library Publishing.

McNeese, Tim. Christopher Columbus & the Discovery of the Americas, Explorers of New Lands. Goetzmann, William H., ed. 2005. (Explorers of New Lands Ser.). (Illus.). 100p. (gr. 5-8). lib. bdg. 30.00 *(978-0-7910-8613-1(5))* Facts On File, Inc.

—John Smith. 2010. (Leaders of the Colonial Era Ser.). 128p. (gr. 5-8). 35.00 *(978-1-60413-742-2(8),* Chelsea Hse.) Facts On File, Inc.

—Marco Polo & the Realm of Kublai Khan. Goetzmann, William H., ed. 2005. (Explorers of New Lands Ser.). (Illus.). 100p. (gr. 5-8). lib. bdg. 30.00 *(978-0-7910-8612-4(7))* Facts On File, Inc.

McPherson, Stephanie Sammartino. Sir Walter Raleigh. 2005. (History Maker Bios Ser.). (Illus.). 48p. (J). (gr. 3-7). lib. bdg. 26.60 *(978-0-8225-2945-3(9),* Lerner Pubns.) Lerner Publishing Group.

Meyer, Susan. Ferdinand Magellan. 2016. (Spotlight on Explorers & Colonization Ser.). 48p. (J). (gr. 6-6). pap. 11.75 *(978-1-4777-8800-4(X))* Rosen Publishing Group, Inc., The.

—James Cook. 2016. (Spotlight on Explorers & Colonization Ser.). 00048p. (J). (gr. 6-6). pap. 11.75 *(978-1-5081-7232-1(3))* Rosen Publishing Group, Inc., The.

Miles, Justin. Ultimate Explorer Guide for Kids. 2015. (ENG., Illus.). 96p. (J). (gr. 5-8). pap. 9.95 *(978-1-77085-618-9(8),* 9781770856189) Firefly Bks., Ltd.

Mitchell, Mark. Raising la Belle. Mitchell, Mark, illus. (Professor Wigglestix & the Weather Ser.). (Illus.). 112p. 10.95 *(978-1-57168-703-6(3))* Eakin Pr.

Molzahn, Arlene Bourgeois. Ferdinand Magellan: First Explorer Around the World. 2003. (Illus.). 48p. (J). (gr. 1-4). lib. bdg. 23.93 *(978-0-7660-2068-9(1))* Enslow Pubs., Inc.

—Henry Hudson: Explorer of the Hudson River. 2003. (Explorers! Ser.). (Illus.). 48p. (J). lib. bdg. 25.27 *(978-0-7660-2070-2(3))* Enslow Pubs., Inc.

—Lewis & Clark: American Explorers. 2003. (Explorers! Ser.). (Illus.). 48p. (J). (gr. 1-4). lib. bdg. 25.27 *(978-0-7660-2067-2(3))* Enslow Pubs., Inc.

—Ponce de Leon: Explorer of Florida. 2003. (Explorers! Ser.). (Illus.). 48p. (J). lib. bdg. 23.93 *(978-0-7660-2071-9(1))* Enslow Pubs., Inc.

—Vasco Nunez de Balboa: Explorer to the Pacific Ocean. 2004. (Explorers! Ser.). (Illus.). 48p. (J). lib. bdg. 25.27 *(978-0-7660-2142-6(4))* Enslow Pubs., Inc.

Morganelli, Adrianna. Christopher Columbus: Sailing to a New World. 2005. (In the Footsteps of Explorers Ser.). (ENG., Illus.). 32p. (J). (gr. -1-9). pap. *(978-0-7787-2445-2(X));* lib. bdg. *(978-0-7787-2409-4(3))* Crabtree Publishing Co.

—Samuel de Champlain: From New France to Cape Cod. 2005. (In the Footsteps of Explorers Ser.). (ENG., Illus.). 32p. (J). (gr. 4-5). pap. *(978-0-7787-2450-6(6))* Crabtree Publishing Co.

Morley, Jacqueline. You Wouldn't Want to Explore with Marco Polo! A Really Long Trip You'd Rather Not Take. Antram, David, illus. 2009. (You Wouldn't Want to Ser.). (ENG.). 32p. (J). (gr. 3-12). 29.00 *(978-0-531-21327-8(7));* pap. 9.95 *(978-0-531-20518-1(5))* Scholastic Library Publishing.

Morriss, Roger. Captain Cook & His Exploration of the Pacific. 2010. (History of Exploration Ser.). 48p. 32.80 *(978-1-84898-303-8(4))* Black Rabbit Bks.

Mountjoy, Shane. Francisco Coronado & the Seven Cities of Gold. Goetzmann, William H., ed. 2005. (Explorers of New Lands Ser.). (Illus.). 160p. (gr. 5-8). lib. bdg. 30.00 *(978-0-7910-8631-5(3))* Facts On File, Inc.

—Francisco Pizarro & the Conquest of the Inca. Goetzmann, William H., ed. 2005. (Explorers of New Lands Ser.). (Illus.). 100p. (gr. 5-8). 30.00 *(978-0-7910-8614-8(3),* Chelsea Hse.) Facts On File, Inc.

Mulhall, Jill K. Lewis & Clark. 2017. (Primary Source Readers Ser.). (Illus.). 32p. (J). (gr. 4-5). pap. 8.99 *(978-1-4938-3886-8(5))* Teacher Created Materials, Inc.

Un Mundo Oculto, 6 vols., Vol. 3. (Explorers. Exploradores Nonfiction Sets Ser.). (SPA.). (gr. 3-6). *(978-0-7699-0652-2(4))* Shortland Pubns. (U. S. A.) Inc.

Nagelhout, Ryan. Vasco Núñez de Balboa. 2016. (Spotlight on Explorers & Colonization Ser.). 48p. (J). (gr. 6-6). pap. 11.75 *(978-1-4777-8828-8(X))* Rosen Publishing Group, Inc., The.

Napoli, Tony. Vasco Da Gama: Discovering the Sea Route to India. 2010. (Great Explorers of the World Ser.). (Illus.). 112p. (J). (gr. 7-12). 33.27 *(978-1-59845-127-6(8))* Enslow Pubs., Inc.

Nardo, Don. The Spanish Conquistadors. 2009. (World History Ser.). (ENG.). 128p. (J). (gr. 7-10). 34.95 *(978-1-4205-0133-9(X),* Lucent Bks.) Cengage Gale.

Nemerson, Roy. Daniel Boone. 2005. (Heroes of America Ser.). 239p. (gr. 3-8). 27.07 *(978-1-59679-256-2(6),* Abdo & Daughters) ABDO Publishing Co.

Nichols, Catherine. Polar Adventures. 2003. (True Tales Ser.). (ENG., Illus.). 48p. (J). 22.50 *(978-0-516-22920-1(6),* Children's Pr.) Scholastic Library Publishing.

Nick, Charles. Sir Francis Drake: Slave Trader & Pirate. 2010. (ENG., Illus.). 128p. (C). (gr. 6-12). pap. 9.95 *(978-0-531-20740-6(4))* National Geographic School Publishing, Inc.

—Sir Francis Drake: Slave Trader & Pirate. 2009. (Wicked History Ser.). (ENG., Illus.). 128p. (J). (gr. 6-12). 31.00 *(978-0-531-21800-6(7),* Watts, Franklin) Scholastic Library Publishing.

Nivola, Claire A. Life in the Ocean: The Story of Oceanographer Sylvia Earle, 1 vol. Nivola, Claire A., illus. 2012. (ENG., Illus.). 32p. (J). (gr. -1-3). 18.99 *(978-0-374-38068-7(6),* 9780374380687, Farrar, Straus & Giroux (BYR)) Farrar, Straus & Giroux.

—Life in the Ocean: The Story of Oceanographer Sylvia Earle. 2012. (J). 38.75 *(978-1-4703-0113-2(X))* Recorded Bks., Inc.

Nussbaum, Ben. Junipero Serra: A Spanish Missionary. 2017. (Primary Source Readers Ser.). (Illus.). 32p. (gr. 4-4). 9.99 ***(978-1-4258-3235-3(0))*** Teacher Created Materials, Inc.

O'Brien, Cynthia. Explore with Christopher Columbus. 2014. (ENG., Illus.). 32p. (J). *(978-0-7787-1245-9(1));* pap. *(978-0-7787-1257-2(5))* Crabtree Publishing Co.

—Explore with Francisco Pizarro. 2015. (Travel with the Great Explorers Ser.). (ENG., Illus.). 32p. (J). (gr. 3-6). *(978-0-7787-1700-3(3))* Crabtree Publishing Co.

—Explore with John Franklin. 2015. (Travel with the Great Explorers Ser.). (ENG., Illus.). 32p. (J). (gr. 3-6). *(978-0-7787-1703-4(8))* Crabtree Publishing Co.

—Explore with Marquette & Jolliet. 2016. (Travel with the Great Explorers Ser.). (ENG., Illus.). 32p. (J). (gr. 3-6). *(978-0-7787-2850-4(1))* Crabtree Publishing Co.

—Explore with Ponce de León. 2014. (ENG., Illus.). 32p. (J). *(978-0-7787-1429-3(2))* Crabtree Publishing Co.

—Explore with Samuel de Champlain. 2014. (ENG., Illus.). 32p. (J). *(978-0-7787-1256-5(7));* pap. *(978-0-7787-1260-2(5))* Crabtree Publishing Co.

—Explore with Sieur de la Salle. 2014. (ENG., Illus.). 32p. (J). *(978-0-7787-1430-9(6))* Crabtree Publishing Co.

Ollhoff, Jim. Captain Cook. 2013. (Great Explorers Ser.). 32p. (gr. 5-9). lib. bdg. 27.07 *(978-1-61783-965-8(5),* Abdo & Daughters) ABDO Publishing Co.

—Christopher Columbus. 2013. (Great Explorers Ser.). 32p. (J). (gr. 5-9). lib. bdg. 27.07 *(978-1-61783-964-1(7),* Abdo & Daughters) ABDO Publishing Co.

—The Conquistadors, 1 vol. 2011. (Hispanic American History Ser.). (ENG., Illus.). 32p. (YA). (gr. 5-9). 27.07 *(978-1-61783-055-6(0))* ABDO Publishing Co.

—Ferdinand Magellan. 2013. (Great Explorers Ser.). 32p. (J). (gr. 5-9). lib. bdg. 27.07 *(978-1-61783-967-2(1),* Abdo & Daughters) ABDO Publishing Co.

—Marco Polo. 2013. (Great Explorers Ser.). 32p. (J). (gr. 5-9). lib. bdg. 27.07 *(978-1-61783-968-9(X),* Abdo & Daughters) ABDO Publishing Co.

Olson, Steven P. Sir Walter Raleigh: Explorer for the Court of Queen Elizabeth. 2009. (Library of Explorers & Exploration Ser.). 112p. (gr. 5-8). 66.50 *(978-1-60853-612-2(2),* Rosen Reference) Rosen Publishing Group, Inc., The.

Opening up North America, 1497-1800, Revised Edition. 2nd rev. ed. 2009. (Discovery & Exploration Ser.). (Illus.). 144p. (gr. 5-8). 35.00 *(978-1-60413-196-3(9),* Chelsea Hse.) Facts On File, Inc.

Otfinoski, Steven. David Livingstone: Deep in the Heart of Africa. 2006. (Great Explorations Ser.). (Illus.). 79p. (J). (gr. 3-7). lib. bdg. 32.79 *(978-0-7614-2226-6(9),* Benchmark Bks.) Marshall Cavendish Corp.

—Henry Hudson: In Search of the Northwest Passage. 2006. (Great Explorations Ser.). (Illus.). 80p. (J). (gr. 3-7). lib. bdg. 32.79 *(978-0-7614-2225-9(0),* Benchmark Bks.) Marshall Cavendish Corp.

—Juan Ponce de Leon: Discoverer of Florida. 2004. (Great Explorations Ser.). 80p. (gr. 6). 22.95 *(978-0-7614-1610-4(2),* Benchmark Bks.) Marshall Cavendish Corp.

—Native Americans at the Time of the Explorers: Text Pairs. 2008. (Bridges/Navigators Ser.). (J). (gr. 5). 89.00 *(978-1-4108-8420-6(1))* Benchmark Education Co.

Owens, Ann-Maureen & Yealland, Jane. Canadian Exploration. Mantha, John, illus. 2008. (Kids Book Of Ser.). (ENG.). 56p. (J). (gr. 3-7). pap. 14.95 *(978-1-55453-257-5(4))* Kids Can Pr., Ltd. CAN. Dist: Hachette Bk. Group.

Owens, L. L. A Journey with Hernán Cortés. 2017. (Primary Source Explorers Ser.). (ENG.). 40p. (J). (gr. 3-5). 30.65 *(978-1-5124-0777-8(1))* Lerner Publishing Group.

—A Journey with Sieur de la Salle. 2017. (Primary Source Explorers Ser.). (ENG.). 40p. (J). (gr. 3-5). 30.65 *(978-1-5124-0775-4(5))* Lerner Publishing Group.

Oxlade, Chris. Be an Explorer. Sassin, Eva, illus. 2015. (Go Wild Ser.). (ENG.). 32p. (gr. 3-6). (J). lib. bdg. 26.65 *(978-1-4677-6358-5(6));* 26.65 *(978-1-4677-7223-5(2))* Lerner Publishing Group.

—Kingfisher Readers L5: Explorers. 2014. (Kingfisher Readers Ser.). (ENG., Illus.). 48p. (J). (gr. k-3). 12.99 *(978-0-7534-7126-5(4),* 9780753471265, Kingfisher) Roaring Brook Pr.

Parker, Lewis K. Spanish Colonies in the Americas. (European Colonies in the Americas Ser.). 24p. 2009. (gr. 2-2). 42.50 *(978-1-61512-320-9(2))* 2003. (Illus.). (J). lib. bdg. 22.60 *(978-0-8239-6471-0(X))* Rosen Publishing Group, Inc., The. (PowerKids Pr.).

Payment, Simone. La Salle: Claiming the Mississippi River for France. (Library of Explorers & Exploration Ser.). 112p. (gr. 5-8). 2009. 66.50 *(978-1-60853-610-8(6))* 2004. (Illus.). lib. bdg. 34.60 *(978-0-8239-3628-1(7))* Rosen Publishing Group, Inc., The. (Rosen Reference).

Pelleschi, Andrea. Juan Ponce de Leon. 2013. (Jr. Graphic Famous Explorers Ser.). (ENG., Illus.). 24p. (J). (gr. 3-6). pap. 10.60 *(978-1-4777-0131-7(1));* lib. bdg. 25.25 *(978-1-4777-0073-0(0))* Rosen Publishing Group, Inc., The. (PowerKids Pr.).

—Samuel de Champlain. 2013. (Jr. Graphic Famous Explorers Ser.). (ENG., Illus.). 24p. (J). (gr. 3-6). pap. 10.60 *(978-1-4777-0133-1(8));* lib. bdg. 25.25 *(978-1-4777-0074-7(9))* Rosen Publishing Group, Inc., The. (PowerKids Pr.).

Peppas, Lynn. Why Sieur de La Salle Matters to Texas. 2014. (Illus.). 32p. (J). lib. bdg. 26.25 *(978-1-4777-0917-7(7))* Rosen Publishing Group, Inc., The.

Perritano, John. The Lewis & Clark Expedition. 2010. (True Book Ser.). (ENG.). 48p. (J). (gr. 3-5). pap. 6.95 *(978-0-531-21245-5(9),* Children's Pr.); (Illus.). (gr. 2-5). 29.00 *(978-0-531-20582-2(7))* Scholastic Library Publishing.

Peterson, Cris. Birchbark Brigade: A Fur Trade History. 2009. (ENG.). 136p. (J). (gr. 4-18). 18.95 *(978-1-59078-426-6(X),* Calkins Creek) Boyds Mills Pr.

Petrie, Kristin. Christopher Columbus, 1 vol. 2004. (Explorers Set 1 Ser.). (ENG., Illus.). 32p. (gr. k-6). 27.07 *(978-1-59197-595-3(6),* Checkerboard Library) ABDO Publishing Co.

—Daniel Boone, 1 vol. 2004. (Explorers Set 1 Ser.). (ENG.). 32p. (gr. k-6). 27.07 *(978-1-59197-592-2(1),* Checkerboard Library) ABDO Publishing Co.

—Ferdinand Magellan, 1 vol. 2007. (Explorers Set 2 Ser.). (ENG., Illus.). 32p. (gr. 4-7). 27.07 *(978-1-59679-744-4(4),* Checkerboard Library) ABDO Publishing Co.

—Francisco Vasquez de Coronado, 1 vol. 2004. (Explorers Set 1 Ser.). (ENG.). 32p. (gr. k-6). 27.07 *(978-1-59197-597-7(2),* Checkerboard Library) ABDO Publishing Co.

—Henry Hudson, 1 vol. 2007. (Explorers Set 2 Ser.). (ENG., Illus.). 32p. (gr. 4-7). 27.07 *(978-1-59679-741-3(X),* Checkerboard Library) ABDO Publishing Co.

—Hernan Cortes, 1 vol. 2004. (Explorers Set 1 Ser.). (ENG., Illus.). 32p. (gr. k-6). 27.07 *(978-1-59197-598-4(0),* Checkerboard Library) ABDO Publishing Co.

—Hernando de Soto, 1 vol. 2004. (Explorers Set 1 Ser.). (ENG.). 32p. (gr. k-6). 27.07 *(978-1-59197-600-4(6),* Checkerboard Library) ABDO Publishing Co.

—Jacques Cartier, 1 vol. 2004. (Explorers Set 1 Ser.). (ENG., Illus.). 32p. (gr. k-6). 27.07 *(978-1-59197-594-6(8),* Checkerboard Library) ABDO Publishing Co.

—James Cook, 1 vol. 2004. (Explorers Set 1 Ser.). (ENG., Illus.). 32p. (gr. k-6). 27.07 *(978-1-59197-596-0(4),* Checkerboard Library) ABDO Publishing Co.

—John C. Fremont, 1 vol. 2004. (Explorers Set 1 Ser.). (ENG., Illus.). 32p. (gr. k-6). 27.07 *(978-1-59197-602-8(2),* Checkerboard Library) ABDO Publishing Co.

—John Cabot, 1 vol. 2004. (Explorers Set 1 Ser.). (ENG.). 32p. (gr. k-6). 27.07 *(978-1-59197-593-9(X),* Checkerboard Library) ABDO Publishing Co.

—John Smith, 1 vol. 2007. (Explorers Set 2 Ser.). (ENG., Illus.). 32p. (gr. 4-7). 27.07 *(978-1-59679-751-2(7),* Checkerboard Library) ABDO Publishing Co.

—Juan Ponce de Leon, 1 vol. 2007. (Explorers Set 2 Ser.). (ENG., Illus.). 32p. (gr. 4-7). 27.07 *(978-1-59679-742-0(8),* Checkerboard Library) ABDO Publishing Co.

—Lewis & Clark, 1 vol. 2007. (Explorers Set 2 Ser.). (ENG., Illus.). 32p. (gr. 4-7). 27.07 *(978-1-59679-743-7(6),* Checkerboard Library) ABDO Publishing Co.

—Marco Polo, 1 vol. 2007. (Explorers Set 2 Ser.). (ENG., Illus.). 32p. (gr. 4-5). 27.07 *(978-1-59679-747-5(9),* Checkerboard Library) ABDO Publishing Co.

—Marquette & Jolliet, 1 vol. 2007. (Explorers Set 2 Ser.). (ENG., Illus.). 32p. (gr. 4-7). 27.07 *(978-1-59679-745-1(2),* Checkerboard Library) ABDO Publishing Co.

—Robert Peary, 1 vol. 2007. (Explorers Set 2 Ser.). (ENG., Illus.). 32p. (gr. 4-5). 27.07 *(978-1-59679-746-8(0),* Checkerboard Library) ABDO Publishing Co.

—La Salle, 1 vol. 2007. (Explorers Set 2 Ser.). (ENG., Illus.). 32p. (gr. 4-7). 27.07 *(978-1-59679-750-5(9),* Checkerboard Library) ABDO Publishing Co.

—Sir Walter Raleigh, 1 vol. 2007. (Explorers Set 2 Ser.). (ENG., Illus.). 32p. (gr. 4-7). 27.07 *(978-1-59679-748-2(7),* Checkerboard Library) ABDO Publishing Co.

—Vasco Da Gama, 1 vol. 2004. (Explorers Set 1 Ser.). (ENG., Illus.). 32p. (gr. k-6). 27.07 *(978-1-59197-603-5(0),* Checkerboard Library) ABDO Publishing Co.

—Vasco Núñez de Balboa, 1 vol. 2007. (Explorers Set 2 Ser.). (ENG., Illus.). 32p. (gr. 4-7). 27.07 *(978-1-59679-740-6(1),* Checkerboard Library) ABDO Publishing Co.

Pletcher, Kenneth, ed. Explorers in the 20th & 21st Centuries. 2013. (Britannica Guide to Explorers & Adventurers Ser.). 232p. (YA). (gr. 9-12). 35.25 *(978-1-62275-022-1(5))* Rosen Publishing Group, Inc., The.

—Nineteenth-Century Explorers. 2013. (Britannica Guide to Explorers & Adventurers Ser.). 216p. (YA). (gr. 9-12). 35.25 *(978-1-62275-021-4(7))* Rosen Publishing Group, Inc., The.

Powell, Marie. Explore with Ferdinand Magellan. 2014. (ENG., Illus.). 32p. (J). *(978-0-7787-1425-5(X))* Crabtree Publishing Co.

—Explore with Jacques Cartier. 2014. (ENG., Illus.). 32p. (J). pap. *(978-0-7787-1432-3(2))* Crabtree Publishing Co.

Putnam, Jeff. Explorers of the Land. 2004. (Trio Bks). (Illus.). 90p. (gr. 4-6). pap. 5.00 *(978-0-7367-1797-7(8))* Zaner-Bloser, Inc.

Que Pasa Alla Afuera?, 6 vols., Vol. 2. (Explorers. Exploradores Nonfiction Sets Ser.). (SPA.). 32p. (gr. 3-6). 44.95 *(978-0-7699-0644-7(3))* Shortland Pubns. (U. S. A.) Inc.

Ramen, Fred. Francisco Pizarro: The Exploration of Peru & the Conquest of the Inca. (Library of Explorers & Exploration Ser.). 112p. (gr. 5-8). 2009. 66.50 *(978-1-60853-603-0(3))* 2004. (Illus.). lib. bdg. 34.60 *(978-0-8239-3618-2(X))* Rosen Publishing Group, Inc., The. (Rosen Reference).

—Hernán Cortés: The Conquest of Mexico & the Aztec Empire. 2015. (Incredible Explorers Ser.). (ENG., Illus.). 64p. (J). (gr. 7-7). 34.21 *(978-1-5026-0129-2(X))* Cavendish Square Publishing.

—Hernán Cortés: The Conquest of Mexico & the Aztec Empire. 2009. (Library of Explorers & Exploration Ser.). 112p. (gr. 5-8). 66.50 *(978-1-60853-606-1(8),* Rosen Reference) Rosen Publishing Group, Inc., The.

Randall, Jesseca. Christopher Columbus: Navigated by God - A Historical Children's Novel about One of the Most Important Figures of the Age of Exploration. 2009. 124p. pap. 11.99 *(978-1-60791-926-1(5))* Salem Author Services.

Randolph, Joanne. African American Explorers. 2017. (J). ***(978-0-7660-9249-5(6))*** Enslow Pubs., Inc.

Ransom, Candice. Daniel Boone. 2005. (History Maker Biographies Ser.). (ENG., Illus.). 48p. (gr. 3-6). lib. bdg. 27.93 *(978-0-8225-2941-5(6),* Lerner Pubns.) Lerner Publishing Group.

—Lewis & Clark. 2003. (History Maker Bios Ser.). (Illus.). 48p. (J). (gr. 2-4). 26.60 *(978-0-8225-0394-1(8),* Lerner Pubns.) Lerner Publishing Group.

Redmond, Shirley Raye. Lewis & Clark: A Prairie Dog for the President. Manders, John, illus. 2003. (Step into Reading Ser.). 48p. 14.00 *(978-0-7569-1697-8(6))* Perfection Learning Corp.

Reid, Struan & Champion, Neil. Explorers, 8 bks., Set. (Illus.). (J). (gr. 4-6). lib. bdg. 204.22 *(978-1-58810-182-2(7))* Heinemann-Raintree.

Reis, Ronald A. Christopher Columbus & the Age of Exploration for Kids: With 21 Activities. 2013. (For Kids Ser.). (ENG., Illus.). 160p. (J). (gr. 4). pap. 16.95 *(978-1-61374-674-5(1))* Chicago Review Pr., Inc.

Rengel, Marian. John Cabot: The Ongoing Search for a Westward Passage to Asia. 2003. (Library of Explorers & Exploration Ser.). (Illus.). 112p. (J). (gr. 5-8). lib. bdg. 34.60 *(978-0-8239-3626-7(0),* Rosen Reference) Rosen Publishing Group, Inc., The.

Rice, Earle. The Life & Times of Erik the Red. 2008. (Biography from Ancient Civilizations Ser.). (Illus.). 48p. (J). (gr. 4-8). lib. bdg. 29.95 *(978-1-58415-701-4(1))* Mitchell Lane Pubs., Inc.

—The Life & Times of Leif Eriksson. 2008. (Biography from Ancient Civilizations Ser.). (Illus.). 48p. (J). (gr. 4-8). lib. bdg. 29.95 *(978-1-58415-702-1(X))* Mitchell Lane Pubs., Inc.

Riddle, John. Marco Polo: 13th Century Italian Trader. 2013. (People of Importance Ser.: 21). (Illus.). 32p. (J). (gr. 4-18). 19.95 *(978-1-4222-2850-0(9))* Mason Crest.

—Robert F. Scott: British Explorer of the South Pole. 2013. (People of Importance Ser.: 21). (Illus.). 32p. (J). (gr. 4-18). 19.95 *(978-1-4222-2855-5(X))* Mason Crest.

Roberts, Steven. Francisco Vasquez de Coronado. 2013. (Jr. Graphic Famous Explorers Ser.). (ENG., Illus.). 24p. (J). (gr. 3-6). pap. 10.60 *(978-1-4777-0125-6(7));* lib. bdg. 25.25 *(978-1-4777-0070-9(6))* Rosen Publishing Group, Inc., The. (PowerKids Pr.).

—John Cabot. 2013. (Jr. Graphic Famous Explorers Ser.). (ENG., Illus.). 24p. (J). (gr. 3-6). pap. 10.60 *(978-1-4777-0129-4(X));* lib. bdg. 25.25 *(978-1-4777-0072-3(2))* Rosen Publishing Group, Inc., The. (PowerKids Pr.).

Robinson, Kate. Lewis & Clark: Exploring the American West. 2010. (Great Explorers of the World Ser.). (Illus.). 112p. (J). (gr. 7-12). 33.27 *(978-1-59845-124-5(3))* Enslow Pubs., Inc.

Rodger, Ellen. Lewis & Clark: Opening the American West. 2005. (In the Footsteps of Explorers Ser.). (ENG., Illus.). 32p. (J). (gr. -1-9). pap. *(978-0-7787-2446-9(8))* Crabtree Publishing Co.

Rooney, Frances. Extraordinary Women Explorers, 1 vol. 2005. (Women's Hall of Fame Ser.). (ENG., Illus.). 110p. (J). (gr. 4-8). pap. 10.95 *(978-1-896764-98-6(3))* Second Story Pr. CAN. Dist: Orca Bk. Pubs. USA.

Rosen, Michael J. Place Hacking: Venturing off Limits. 2015. (Illus.). 72p. (J). *(978-1-4677-6311-0(X))* Twenty First Century Bks.

—Urban Exploration. 2015. (ENG., Illus.). 72p. (J). (gr. 8-12). lib. bdg. 33.32 *(978-1-4677-2515-6(3),* Twenty-First Century Bks.) Lerner Publishing Group.

Ross, Michael Elsohn. Exploring the Earth with John Wesley Powell. Smith, Wendy, illus. 2005. (Naturalist's Apprentice Biographies Ser.). 48p. (gr. 3-6). lib. bdg. 19.93 *(978-1-57505-254-0(7))* Lerner Publishing Group.

Ross, Stewart. Into the Unknown: How Great Explorers Found Their Way by Land, Sea, & Air. Biesty, Stephen, illus. (ENG.). 96p. (J). (gr. 3-7). 2014. pap. 9.99 *(978-0-7636-6992-8(X))* 2011. 19.99 *(978-0-7636-4948-7(1))* Candlewick Pr.

Roxburgh, Ellis. Robert Peary vs. Frederick Cook: Race to the North Pole. 2016. (History's Greatest Rivals Ser.). (ENG., Illus.). 48p. (J). (gr. 6-8). pap. 14.05 *(978-1-4824-4231-1(0))* Stevens, Gareth Publishing LLLP.

Roza, Greg. Early Explorers of Texas. 2010. (Spotlight on Texas Ser.). (Illus.). 32p. (J). (gr. 3-4). (ENG.). pap. 11.75 *(978-1-61532-454-5(2));* lib. bdg. 25.25 *(978-1-61532-489-7(5))* Rosen Publishing Group, Inc., The.

Saddleback Educational Publishing Staff, ed. Daniel Boone, 1 vol. unabr. ed. 2008. (Graphic Biographies Ser.). (ENG., Illus.). 25p. (YA). (gr. 9-12). pap. 7.95 *(978-1-59905-219-9(9))* Saddleback Educational Publishing, Inc.

Sammons, Sandra Wallus. Ponce de Leon & the Discovery of Florida. 2013. (ENG., Illus.). 72p. (J). (gr. 4-6). 12.95 *(978-1-56164-592-3(3));* pap. 9.95 *(978-1-56164-593-0(1))* Pineapple Pr., Inc.

Sanders, Walter. England Explores the Americas. 2005. (J). pap. *(978-1-4108-4611-2(3))* Benchmark Education Co.

—France Explores the Americas. 2005. (J). pap. *(978-1-4108-4604-4(0))* Benchmark Education Co.

—Spain Explores the Americas. 2005. (J). pap. *(978-1-4108-4597-9(4))* Benchmark Education Co.

Sandler, Michael. Explorers of the Americas: Set Of 6. 2010. (Navigators Ser.). (J). pap. 48.00 net. *(978-1-4108-5107-9(9))* Benchmark Education Co.

—Explorers of the Americas: Text Pairs. 2008. (Bridges/Navigators Ser.). (J). (gr. 5). 94.00 *(978-1-4108-8416-9(3))* Benchmark Education Co.

Sanford, William R. & Green, Carl R. John C. Frémont: Courageous Pathfinder of the Wild West. 2012. (Courageous Heroes of the American West Ser.). (Illus.). 48p. (J). pap. 8.95 *(978-1-4644-0091-9(1));* (gr. 5-18). 22.60 *(978-0-7660-4008-3(9))* Enslow Pubs., Inc.

—Zebulon Pike: Courageous Rocky Mountain Explorer. 2012. (Courageous Heroes of the American West Ser.). (Illus.).

E
F
G

48p. (J). (gr. 5-18). lib. bdg. 22.60 *(978-0-7660-4012-0(7))* Enslow Pubs., Inc.

Sansevere-Dreher, Diane. Explorers Who Got Lost. Renfro, Ed, illus. 2016. (ENG.). 176p. (J). pap. 14.99 *(978-0-7653-8151-4(6)*, 9780765381514, Starscape) Doherty, Tom Assocs., LLC.

Sapp, Richard. Lewis & Clark on Their Journey to the Pacific. 2006. (In the Footsteps of American Heroes Ser.). (Illus.). 64p. (gr. 5-12). lib. bdg. 34.00 *(978-0-8368-6429-8(8)*, Gareth Stevens Secondary Library) Stevens, Gareth Publishing LLLP.

Schanzer, Rosalyn. John Smith Escapes Again! 2006. (ENG., Illus.). 64p. (J). (gr. 4-7). 16.95 *(978-0-7922-5930-5(0))*; lib. bdg. 25.90 *(978-0-7922-5931-2(9))* National Geographic Society. (National Geographic Children's Bks.).

Schraff, Anne. Daredevil American Heroes of Exploration & Flight. 2013. (Inspiring Collective Biographies Ser.). 112p. (J). (gr. 5-12). pap. 10.95 *(978-1-4644-0247-0(7))* Enslow Pubs., Inc.

Schraff, Anne E. Daredevil American Heroes of Exploration & Flight. 2013. (Inspiring Collective Biographies Ser.). (Illus.). 112p. (J). (gr. 5-18). 33.27 *(978-0-7660-4163-9(8))* Enslow Pubs., Inc.

Schwartz, Simon. First Man: Reimagining Matthew Henson. Watkinson, Laura, tr. 2015. (ENG., Illus.). 160p. (YA). (gr. 8-12). 31.99 *(978-1-4677-8856-4(2)*, Graphic Universe™) Lerner Publishing Group.

—First Man: The Voyages of Matthew Henson. Watkinson, Laura, tr. from GER. 2015. (ENG., Illus.). 160p. (J). (gr. 8-12). 31.99 *(978-1-4677-5842-0(6)*, Graphic Universe™) Lerner Publishing Group.

Scraper, Katherine. Matthew Henson. 2011. (Early Connections Ser.). (J). *(978-1-61672-563-1(X))* Benchmark Education Co.

Seiple, Samantha. Byrd & Igloo: A Polar Adventure. 2013. (J). (ENG.). 192p. (gr. 3-7). 18.99 *(978-0-545-56276-8(7))*; (Illus.). 186p. *(978-0-545-61642-3(5))* Scholastic, Inc. (Scholastic Pr.).

Seres Extranos, 6 vols. (Explorers. Exploradores Nonfiction Sets Ser.). (SPA.). 32p. (gr. 3-6). 44.95 *(978-0-7699-0628-7(1))* Shortland Pubns. (U. S. A.) Inc.

Shafer, Susan. Ponce de Leon & the Fountain of Youth. 2005. (J). pap. *(978-1-4108-4231-2(2))* Benchmark Education Co.

Sheehan, Robert. Francis Drake: Patriot or Pirate? 2013. (Discovery Education: Sensational True Stories Ser.). (ENG., Illus.). 32p. (J). (gr. 3-6). pap. 10.00 *(978-1-4777-0105-8(2))*; lib. bdg. 25.25 *(978-1-4777-0060-0(9))* Rosen Publishing Group, Inc., The. (PowerKids Pr.).

Sherman, Josepha. Henry Hudson: English Explorer of the Northwest Passage. 2009. (Library of Explorers & Exploration Ser.). 112p. (gr. 5-8). 66.50 *(978-1-60853-605-4(X)*, Rosen Reference) Rosen Publishing Group, Inc., The.

—Henry Hudson: Exploring the Northwest Passage. 2015. (Incredible Explorers Ser.). (ENG., Illus.). 64p. (J). (gr. 7-7). 34.21 *(978-1-5026-0127-8(3))* Cavendish Square Publishing.

—Samuel de Champlain: Explorer of the Great Lakes Region & Founder of Quebec. (Library of Explorers & Exploration Ser.). 112p. (gr. 5-8). 2009. 66.50 *(978-1-60853-611-5(4))* 2003. (Illus.). (J). lib. bdg. 34.60 *(978-0-8239-3629-8(5))* Rosen Publishing Group, Inc., The. (Rosen Reference).

Slavicek, Louise Chipley. Juan Ponce de Leon. 2003. (Great Hispanic Heritage Ser.). (Illus.). 112p. (gr. 6-12). 35.00 *(978-0-7910-7255-4(X)*, Chelsea Hse.) Facts On File, Inc.

Smalley, Carol Parenzan. Lewis & Clark. 2008. (What's So Great About...? Ser.). (Illus.). 32p. (YA). (gr. 2-4). lib. bdg. 25.70 *(978-1-58415-725-0(9))* Mitchell Lane Pubs., Inc.

Smalley, Roger. The Adventures of Marco Polo, 1 vol. Carter, Greg & Bascle, Brian, illus. 2005. (Graphic History Ser.). (ENG.). 32p. (gr. 3-4). 30.65 *(978-0-7368-3830-6(9)*, Graphic Library) Capstone Press of Coughlan Cos.

Smith, Andrea P. Daniel Boone. 2012. (Illus.). 24p. (J). 63.60 *(978-1-4488-5227-7(7))*; pap. 10.60 *(978-1-4488-5226-0(9))*; lib. bdg. 25.25 *(978-1-4488-5194-2(7))* Rosen Publishing Group, Inc., The. (PowerKids Pr.).

Smith, Michael. Shackleton - the Boss: The Remarkable Adventures of Ernest Shackleton. Brady, Annie, illus. 2nd rev. ed. 2010. (ENG.). 128p. (J). pap. 15.95 *(978-1-905172-27-6(3))* Collins Pr., The IRL. Dist: Dufour Editions, Inc.

Smith, Tom. Discovery of the Americas, 1492-1800. 2nd rev. ed. 2009. (Discovery & Exploration Ser.). (Illus.). 136p. (gr. 5-8). 35.00 *(978-1-60413-195-6(0)*, Chelsea Hse.) Facts On File, Inc.

Snowden, Maxine. Polar Explorers for Kids: Historic Expeditions to the Arctic & Antarctic with 21 Activities. 2003. (For Kids Ser.). (ENG.). 160p. (J). (gr. 4). pap. 16.95 *(978-1-55652-500-1(1))* Chicago Review Pr., Inc.

Somervill, Barbara A. Francisco Pizarro: Conqueror of the Incas, 1 vol. 2005. (Signature Lives: Renaissance Era Ser.). (ENG., Illus.). 112p. (gr. 6-7). 35.32 *(978-0-7565-0815-9(0)*, 1240121, Signature Lives) Compass Point Bks.

Sonneborn, Liz. Pizarro: Conqueror of the Mighty Incas. 2010. (Great Explorers of the World Ser.). (Illus.). 112p. (J). (gr. 7-12). 33.27 *(978-1-59845-128-3(6))* Enslow Pubs., Inc.

Souza, D. M. John C. Fremont. 2004. (Watts Library). (ENG., Illus.). 64p. (J). (gr. 5-7). pap. 8.95 *(978-0-531-16652-9(X)*, Watts, Franklin) Scholastic Library Publishing.

Souza, Dorothy M. John Wesley Powell. 2004. (Watts Library). (ENG., Illus.). 64p. (J). (gr. 5-7). pap. 8.95 *(978-0-531-16653-6(8)*, Watts, Franklin) Scholastic Library Publishing.

Spangenburg, Ray, et al. Robert Ballard. 2009. (Makers of Modern Science Ser.). (Illus.). 176p. (gr. 6-12). 35.00 *(978-0-8160-6173-0(4)*, Chelsea Hse.) Facts On File, Inc.

Spotlight on Explorers & Colonization: Set 3. 2017. (Spotlight on Explorers & Colonization Ser.). 48p. (gr. 10-11). 127.00 ***(978-1-4994-6646-1(3))***; pap. 47.00 ***(978-1-4994-6648-5(X))*** Rosen Publishing Group, Inc., The. (Rosen Young Adult).

Stathis, Roberta & Blanch, Gregory. Daring Explorers Who Sailed the Oceans. 2005. (Illus.). 79p. 17.00 *(978-1-55501-548-0(4))* Ballard & Tighe Pubs.

Staunton, Ted. The Northwest Passage. 2007. (Dreadful Truth Ser.). (ENG., Illus.). 96p. (J). (gr. 3-8). *(978-0-88780-735-0(6))* Formac Publishing Co., Ltd.

Steele, Philip. Explorers. 2016. (Epic! Ser.). (ENG., Illus.). 32p. (J). (gr. 4-6). pap. 11.99 *(978-0-7502-9733-2(6)*, Wayland) Hachette Children's Group GBR. Dist: Hachette Bk. Group.

Stille, Darlene R. The Journals of Lewis & Clark, 1 vol. 2012. (Documenting U. S. History Ser.). (ENG.). 48p. (gr. 3-6). pap. 9.95 *(978-1-4329-6763-5(0))*; lib. bdg. 32.65 *(978-1-4329-6754-3(1))* Heinemann-Raintree. (NA-h).

Stuckey, Rachel. Explore with Hernando de Soto. 2016. (Travel with the Great Explorers Ser.). (ENG., Illus.). 32p. (J). (gr. 3-6). *(978-0-7787-2849-8(8))* Crabtree Publishing Co.

—Explore with Lewis & Clark. 2014. (ENG., Illus.). 32p. (J). *(978-0-7787-1247-3(8))*; pap. *(978-0-7787-1259-6(1))* Crabtree Publishing Co.

—Go West with Famous Trailblazers. 2016. (ENG.). 32p. (J). *(978-0-7787-2324-0(0))* Crabtree Publishing Co.

Sutcliffe, Jane. Juan Ponce de Leon. 2005. (History Maker Bios Ser.). (Illus.). 48p. (J). (gr. 3-7). lib. bdg. 26.60 *(978-0-8225-2944-6(0)*, Lerner Pubns.) Lerner Publishing Group.

Sutherland, Katrice. Spanish Explorers. 2016. (J). ***(978-1-5105-1872-8(X))***; ***(978-1-5105-1871-1(1))*** SmartBook Media, Inc.

Swanson, Jennifer. Bartolomeu Dias: First European Sailor to Reach the Indian Ocean. 2017. (Spotlight on Explorers & Colonization Ser.). 48p. (gr. 10-11). pap. 11.75 ***(978-1-5081-7495-0(4)***, Rosen Young Adult) Rosen Publishing Group, Inc., The.

Swanson, Jennifer. Lewis & Clark. 2016. (Spotlight on Explorers & Colonization Ser.). 00048p. (J). (gr. 6-6). pap. 11.75 *(978-1-5081-7237-6(4))* Rosen Publishing Group, Inc., The.

Tabilio, Marco & Schwandt, Kerstin. Marco Polo: The Silk Road. Tabilio, Marco, illus. 2017. (ENG., Illus.). 208p. (J). (gr. 9-12). 29.32 *(978-1-5124-1182-9(5)*, Graphic Universe™) Lerner Publishing Group.

Tan, Richard. The Famous Explorers of New York City. 2011. (My Community Ser.). (ENG., Illus.). 12p. (gr. 2-2). pap. 6.95 *(978-1-4488-5725-8(2)*, Rosen Classroom) Rosen Publishing Group, Inc., The.

Taylor-Butler, Christine. Explorers of North America. (True Bks.). (ENG., Illus.). 48p. (J). (gr. 3-5). 2008. pap. 6.95 *(978-0-531-14782-5(7))* 2007. lib. bdg. 29.00 *(978-0-531-12632-5(3))* Scholastic Library Publishing. (Children's Pr.).

Throp, Claire. The Nile River, 1 vol. 2012. (Explorer Tales Ser.). (ENG.). 32p. (gr. 1-3). 29.99 *(978-1-4109-4784-0(X)*, Read Me!) Heinemann-Raintree.

Todd, Margaret. Explorers. 2004. (Illus.). (J). (gr. 4-7). 48.00 *(978-1-57336-399-0(5)*, 15003) Interaction Pubs., Inc.

Toth, Henrietta. Henry Hudson. 2016. (Spotlight on Explorers & Colonization Ser.). 00048p. (J). (gr. 6-6). pap. 11.75 *(978-1-5081-7222-2(6))* Rosen Publishing Group, Inc., The.

Toufexis, George. Great Explorers Activity Book. 2012. (Dover Children's Activity Bks.). (ENG.). 48p. (J). (gr. 2-6). pap. 4.99 *(978-0-486-48367-2(3))* Dover Pubns., Inc.

Trussell-Cullen, Alan. Edmund Hillary. 2009. pap. 13.25 *(978-1-60559-058-5(4))* Hameray Publishing Group, Inc.

Turner, Tracey. Hard As Nails Travelers & Explorers. 2015. (Hard As Nails in History Ser.). (ENG., Illus.). 64p. (J). (gr. 3-6). *(978-0-7787-1521-4(3))* Crabtree Publishing Co.

U. S. National Geographic Society Staff. Beginner's United States Atlas. 2009. (ENG., Illus.). 128p. (J). (gr. 1-4). 27.90 *(978-1-4263-0558-0(3)*, National Geographic Children's Bks.) National Geographic Society.

U. S. National Geographic Society Staff & National Geographic Learning Staff. Beginner's United States: It's Your Country. Be a Part of It! 3rd ed. 2009. (ENG., Illus.). 128p. (J). (gr. 1-4). 18.95 *(978-1-4263-0512-2(5)*, National Geographic Children's Bks.) National Geographic Society.

Uhl, Xina M. Francisco de Vasquez Coronado. 2016. (Spotlight on Explorers & Colonization Ser.). 00048p. (J). (gr. 6-6). pap. 11.75 *(978-1-5081-7214-7(5))* Rosen Publishing Group, Inc., The.

Vietze, Andrew. Zheng He: China's Greatest Navigator. 2017. (Spotlight on Explorers & Colonization Ser.). 48p. (gr. 10-11). pap. 11.75 ***(978-1-5081-7507-0(1)***, Rosen Young Adult) Rosen Publishing Group, Inc., The.

Wade, Mary Dodson. Amazing Arctic Explorer Matthew Henson. (Amazing Americans Ser.). (Illus.). 24p. (J). 2013. (gr. k-3). pap. 7.95 *(978-0-7660-5974-0(X)*, Enslow Elementary) 2009. (gr. 1-3). lib. bdg. 22.60 *(978-0-7660-3286-6(8))* Enslow Pubs., Inc.

—Christopher Columbus. 2014. (Rookie Biographies(r) Ser.). (ENG., Illus.). 32p. (J). lib. bdg. *(978-0-531-20559-4(2))*; pap. 5.95 *(978-0-531-21202-8(5))* Scholastic Library Publishing.

—Christopher Columbus: Famous Explorer, 1 vol. Whigham, Rod & Barnett, Charles, III, illus. 2007. (Graphic Biographies Ser.). (ENG.). 32p. (gr. 3-4). per. 8.10 *(978-0-7368-7905-7(6)*, 1264941, Graphic Library) Capstone Press of Coughlan Cos.

Wade, Mary Dodson & Capstone Press Staff. Christopher Columbus: Famous Explorer, 1 vol. Whigham, Rod & Barnett, Charles, III, illus. 2007. (Graphic Biographies Ser.). (ENG.). 32p. (gr. 3-4). 30.65 *(978-0-7368-6853-2(4)*, 1264941, Graphic Library) Capstone Press of Coughlan Cos.

Wagner, Heather Lehr. Hernan Cortes. 2009. (Great Explorers Ser.). (Illus.). 120p. (gr. 6-12). 30.00 *(978-1-60413-424-7(0)*, Chelsea Hse.) Facts On File, Inc.

Waldman, Stuart. The Last River: John Wesley Powell & the Colorado River Exploring Expedition. Manchess, Gregory, illus. 2015. (ENG.). 48p. (J). (gr. 4-8). pap. 12.95 *(978-1-931414-58-6(0)*, 9781931414586) Mikaya Pr.

—Magellan's World. Manchess, Gregory, illus. 2007. (Great Explorers Ser.). (ENG.). 48p. (J). (gr. 4-8). 22.95 *(978-1-931414-19-7(X)*, 9781931414197) Mikaya Pr.

—We Asked for Nothing. McNally, Tom, illus. 2014. (ENG.). 208p. (J). (gr. 5-7). pap. 8.95 *(978-1-931414-50-0(5)*, 9781931414500) Mikaya Pr.

Walsh, Steve. Zebulon Montgomery Pike: Explorer & Military Officer. 2011. (ENG & SPA., Illus.). 54p. (J). pap. 8.95 *(978-0-86541-123-4(9))* Filter Pr., LLC.

Ward, Nancy. Sir Walter Raleigh: Founding the Virginia Colony. 2006. (In the Footsteps of Explorers Ser.). (ENG., Illus.). 32p. (J). (gr. 4-7). lib. bdg. *(978-0-7787-2424-7(7)*, 1253445) Crabtree Publishing Co.

Warrick, Karen Clemens. The Perilous Search for the Fabled Northwest Passage in American History. 2004. (In American History Ser.). (Illus.). 128p. (J). lib. bdg. 26.60 *(978-0-7660-2148-8(3))* Enslow Pubs., Inc.

—The Race for the North Pole & Robert Peary in World History. 2003. (In World History Ser.). (Illus.). 128p. (J). (gr. 5-12). lib. bdg. 27.94 *(978-0-7660-1933-1(0))* Enslow Pubs., Inc.

Waxman, Laura Hamilton. A Journey with Henry Hudson. 2017. (Primary Source Explorers Ser.). (ENG.). 40p. (J). (gr. 3-5). 30.65 *(978-1-5124-0774-7(7))* Lerner Publishing Group.

—A Journey with Juan Ponce de León. 2017. (Primary Source Explorers Ser.). (ENG.). 40p. (J). (gr. 3-5). 30.65 *(978-1-5124-0776-1(3))* Lerner Publishing Group.

Weaver, Janice. Hudson. Craig, David, illus. 2010. (ENG.). 48p. (J). (gr. 3-7). 22.95 *(978-0-88776-814-9(8)*, Tundra Bks.) Tundra Bks. CAN. Dist: Penguin Random Hse. LLC.

Webb, Sarah Powers. When They Came: A Chronology of North American Exploration. 2016. (Discovering the New World Ser.). (ENG., Illus.). 48p. (gr. 3-4). lib. bdg. 29.32 *(978-1-5157-1867-3(0)*, Connect) Stone Arch Bks.

Weidt, Maryann N. Matthew Henson. 2003. (History Maker Bios Ser.). (Illus.). 48p. (J). (gr. 2-4). 26.60 *(978-0-8225-0397-2(2)*, Lerner Pubns.) Lerner Publishing Group.

West, David. Christopher Columbus: The Life of a Master Navigator & Explorer. 2009. (Graphic Nonfiction Biographies Ser.). (ENG.). 48p. (YA). (gr. 4-5). 58.50 *(978-1-61513-014-6(4)*, Rosen Reference) Rosen Publishing Group, Inc., The.

—Ten of the Best Adventures in Frozen Landscapes. 2015. (Ten of the Best: Stories of Exploration & Adventure Ser.). (ENG., Illus.). 24p. (J). (gr. 3-6). *(978-0-7787-1834-5(4))* Crabtree Publishing Co.

—Ten of the Best Adventures in New Worlds. 2015. (Ten of the Best: Stories of Exploration & Adventure Ser.). (ENG., Illus.). 24p. (J). (gr. 3-6). *(978-0-7787-1835-2(2))* Crabtree Publishing Co.

—Ten of the Best Adventures in the Jungle. 2015. (Ten of the Best: Stories of Exploration & Adventure Ser.). (ENG., Illus.). 24p. (J). (gr. 3-6). *(978-0-7787-1837-6(9))* Crabtree Publishing Co.

West, David & Gaff, Jackie. Christopher Columbus: The Life of a Master Navigator & Explorer. 2005. (Graphic Nonfiction Biographies Ser.). (ENG., Illus.). 48p. (J). (gr. 4-7). lib. bdg. 31.95 *(978-1-4042-0243-6(9))* Rosen Publishing Group, Inc., The.

Whiting, Jim. The Life & Times of Hernando Cortes. 2006. (Profiles in American History Ser.). (Illus.). 48p. (J). (gr. 3-7). lib. bdg. 29.95 *(978-1-58415-449-5(7))* Mitchell Lane Pubs., Inc.

Wilkinson, Philip. Explorers. 2007. (Illus.). 63p. (J). reprint ed. 17.00 *(978-1-4223-6727-8(4))* DIANE Publishing Co.

Women Explorers. (J). pap. 4.95 *(978-0-88388-203-0(5))* Bellerophon Bks.

Woog, Adam. Jacques Cartier. 2009. (Great Explorers Ser.). (Illus.). 112p. (gr. 6-12). 30.00 *(978-1-60413-430-8(5)*, Chelsea Hse.) Facts On File, Inc.

World Book, Inc Staff, contrib. by. Icy Worlds. 2011. (J). *(978-0-7166-1788-4(9))* World Bk., Inc.

Worth, Richard. Ponce de Leon & the Age of Spanish Exploration in World History. 2003. (In World History Ser.). (Illus.). 112p. (J). (gr. 5-12). lib. bdg. 26.60 *(978-0-7660-1940-9(3))* Enslow Pubs., Inc.

—Vasco da Gama. 2009. (Great Explorers Ser.). (Illus.). 104p. (gr. 6-12). 30.00 *(978-1-60413-423-0(2)*, Chelsea Hse.) Facts On File, Inc.

Yomtov, Nel. Ferdinand Magellan Sails Around the World. 2015. (Extraordinary Explorers Ser.). (ENG., Illus.). 24p. (J). (gr. 3-7). lib. bdg. 29.95 *(978-1-62617-292-0(7)*, Black Sheep) Bellwether Media.

—Roald Amundsen Explores the South Pole. 2015. (Extraordinary Explorers Ser.). (ENG., Illus.). 24p. (J). (gr. 3-7). lib. bdg. 29.95 *(978-1-62617-295-1(1)*, Black Sheep) Bellwether Media.

Young, Ian. Amazing Journeys: Following in History's Footsteps. 2003. (High Five Reading - Green Ser.). (ENG., Illus.). 48p. (gr. 3-4). per. 9.00 *(978-0-7368-2831-4(1)*, High Five Reading (RBL)) Capstone Press of Coughlan Cos.

Young, Jeff C. Henry Hudson: Discoverer of the Hudson River. 2009. (Great Explorers of the World Ser.). (Illus.). 112p. (J). (gr. 7-12). lib. bdg. 33.27 *(978-1-59845-123-8(5))* Enslow Pubs., Inc.

Young, Serinity. Richard Francis Burton: Explorer, Scholar, Spy. 2006. (Great Explorations Ser.). (Illus.). 80p. (gr. 6-7). lib. bdg. 22.95 *(978-0-7614-2222-8(6)*, Benchmark Bks.) Marshall Cavendish Corp.

Zannos, Susan. The Life & Times of Marco Polo. 2004. (Biography from Ancient Civilizations Ser.). (Illus.). 48p. (J). (gr. 4-8). lib. bdg. 29.95 *(978-1-58415-264-4(8))* Mitchell Lane Pubs., Inc.

Zelenyi, Alexander & Zelenyj, Alexander. Marquette & Jolliet: Quest for the Mississippi. 2006. (In the Footsteps of Explorers Ser.). (ENG., Illus.). 32p. (J). (gr. 4-7). pap. *(978-0-7787-2467-4(0))*; lib. bdg. *(978-0-7787-2431-5(X))* Crabtree Publishing Co.

Zelenyj, Alexander. Marco Polo: Overland to China. 2005. (In the Footsteps of Explorers Ser.). (ENG., Illus.). 32p. (J). (gr. 4-5). pap. *(978-0-7787-2453-7(0))* Crabtree Publishing Co.

Zronik, John Paul. Sieur de la Salle: New World Adventurer. 2005. (In the Footsteps of Explorers Ser.). (ENG., Illus.). 32p. (J). (gr. 4-5). pap. *(978-0-7787-2449-0(2))* Crabtree Publishing Co.

Zronik, John Paul & Zronik, John. Daniel Boone: Woodsman of Kentucky. 2006. (In the Footsteps of Explorers Ser.). (ENG., Illus.). 32p. (J). (gr. 4-7). pap. *(978-0-7787-2464-3(6)*, 1253442); lib. bdg. *(978-0-7787-2428-5(X)*, 1253442) Crabtree Publishing Co.

—Francisco Pizarro: Journeys Through Peru & South America. 2005. (In the Footsteps of Explorers Ser.). (ENG., Illus.). 32p. (J). (gr. -1-9). pap. *(978-0-7787-2447-6(6))* Crabtree Publishing Co.

EXPLORERS—FICTION

Appleton, Victor. Tom Swift & His Undersea Search. 2007. 228p. 29.95 *(978-1-4344-8363-8(0))*; per. 17.95 *(978-1-4344-8362-1(2))* Wildside Pr., LLC.

Atkinson, Cale. Explorers of the Wild. Atkinson, Cale, illus. 2016. (ENG., Illus.). 40p. (J). (gr. -1-k). 16.99 *(978-1-4847-2340-1(6))* Disney Pr.

Barell, John. Surviving Erebus: An Antarctic Adventure Onboard Her Majesty's Ships Erebus & Terror. 2008. (YA). pap. *(978-0-88092-703-1(8))*; lib. bdg. *(978-0-88092-702-4(X))* Royal Fireworks Publishing Co.

Beinstein, Phoebe. Dora & the Stuck Truck. Roper, Robert, illus. 2008. (Dora the Explorer Ser.: 25). (ENG.). 24p. (J). (gr. -1-2). pap. 3.99 *(978-1-4169-4799-8(X)*, Simon Spotlight/Nickelodeon) Simon Spotlight/Nickelodeon.

—Los Deseos de Dora. Ziegler, Argentina Palacios, tr. from ENG. Roper, Robert, illus. 2008. (Dora la Exploradora Ser.).Tr. of Dora's Bedtime Wishes. (ENG.). 14p. (J). (gr. -1). bds. 4.99 *(978-1-4169-5036-3(2)*, Libros Para Ninos) Libros Para Ninos.

Berkeley, Jon. Between the Light. Dorman, Brandon, illus. 2008. (Julie Andrews Collection). (J). lib. bdg. 17.89 *(978-0-06-075514-0(8))* HarperCollins Pubs.

Biskup, Agnieszka. Graphic Expeditions. Stewart, Roger, illus. 2012. (Graphic Expeditions Ser.). (ENG.). 32p. (gr. 3-4). pap. 667.80 *(978-1-4296-8474-3(7))*; lib. bdg. 61.30 *(978-1-4296-8174-2(8))* Capstone Press of Coughlan Cos. (Graphic Library).

Burroughs, Edgar Rice. The Land That Time Forgot: Graphic Novel. Jones, K. L., illus. 2011. (Campfire Graphic Novels Ser.). (ENG.). 72p. (YA). (gr. 5-12). pap. 9.99 *(978-93-80028-38-5(5)*, Campfire) Steerforth Pr.

Cohen-Spence, Susan. An Amazing Adventure Back in Time. Scott, Susan, illus. 2013. 32p. pap. 14.99 *(978-0-9886360-4-0(2))* Kids At Heart Publishing, LLC.

Connor, Naomi. Big Brown Eyes. 2010. 24p. pap. 12.99 *(978-1-4490-7331-2(X))* AuthorHouse.

Day, Jan. The World's Greatest Explorer, 1 vol. Mason, Janeen, illus. 2009. (ENG.). 32p. (J). (gr. k-3). 16.99 *(978-1-58980-603-0(4))* Pelican Publishing Co., Inc.

Domínguez, Adriana, tr. Dora y la Aventura de Cumpleaños. Roper, Robert, illus. 2010. (Dora la Exploradora Ser.). (SPA.). 24p. (J). 6.99 *(978-1-4424-0286-7(5)*, Libros Para Ninos) Libros Para Ninos.

Duble, Kathleen Benner. Quest. 2008. (ENG.). 256p. (J). (gr. 5-9). 17.99 *(978-1-4169-3386-1(7)*, McElderry, Margaret K. Bks.) McElderry, Margaret K. Bks.

Earp-Bridgmon, Krista D. The Adventures of Jim-Bob: A Bearography. 2013. 24p. pap. 10.99 *(978-1-4582-1005-0(7)*, Abbott Pr.) Author Solutions, Inc.

The Explorer: Individual Title Six-Packs. (gr. -1-2). 27.00 *(978-0-7635-9448-0(2))* Rigby Education.

Explorer Guide: Leader's Handbook. 2004. (Caravan Ser.). 272p. pap. 12.99 *(978-0-8341-2120-1(4))* Beacon Hill Pr. of Kansas City.

Explorer Scout. 2004. (Caravan Ser.). 128p. pap., stu. ed. 9.50 *(978-0-8341-2122-5(0))* Beacon Hill Pr. of Kansas City.

Explorer Sentry. 2004. (Caravan Ser.). 128p. pap., stu. ed. 9.50 *(978-0-8341-2121-8(2))* Beacon Hill Pr. of Kansas City.

Gannon, Nicholas. The Doldrums. 368p. (J). (gr. 3-7). 2017. pap. 7.99 ***(978-0-06-232095-7(5))*** 2015. (ENG., Illus.). 17.99 *(978-0-06-232094-0(7))* HarperCollins Pubs. (Greenwillow Bks.).

Garfield, Henry. The Lost Voyage of John Cabot. 2007. (ENG., Illus.). 320p. (YA). (gr. 7). pap. 16.95 *(978-1-4169-5460-6(0)*, Simon Pulse) Simon Pulse.

Glasgow, Yvonne M. Frankie the Firefly Belongs. 2008. 20p. per. 24.95 *(978-1-4241-9424-7(5))* America Star Bks.

Hammill, Matt. Sir Reginald's Logbook. Hammill, Matt, illus. 2008. (ENG., Illus.). 32p. (J). (gr. k-4). 17.95 *(978-1-55453-202-5(7))* Kids Can Pr., Ltd. CAN. Dist: Hachette Bk. Group.

Hardcastle, Henry. Explorer: A Daring Guide for Young Adventurers. Steer, Dugald A., ed. 2007. (Genuine & Moste Authentic Guide Ser.). (ENG., Illus.). 32p. (J). (gr. 1-4). 15.99 *(978-0-7636-3648-7(7))* Candlewick Pr.

Hart, Alison. Leo, Dog of the Sea, 1 vol. Montgomery, Michael G., illus. 2017. (Dog Chronicles Ser.: 5). (ENG.). 176p. (J). (gr. 2-5). 12.95 *(978-1-56145-964-3(X))* Peachtree Pubs.

Hierl, Christine Gormican. Wyatt Walker Turbo Talker. Thompson, Michelle Gormican & Thompson, Janet M., illus. 2004. 28p. *(978-0-9760680-0-6(1))* Cedar Shamrock Publishing.

Histories presents Christopher Cowlumbus. 2006. (J). bds. 14.99 *(978-0-9763233-3-4(8))* Little Germ That Could...Creations, Inc., The.

Horse, Harry. The Last Polar Bears. Horse, Harry, illus. 2007. (ENG., Illus.). 128p. (J). (gr. 1-5). 12.95 *(978-1-56145-379-5(X)*, Peachtree Junior) Peachtree Pubs.

Inches, Alison. Just Like Dora! Aikins, Dave, illus. 2005. (Dora the Explorer Ser.: Vol. 8). (ENG.). 24p. (J). pap. 3.99 *(978-0-689-87675-2(0)*, Simon Spotlight/Nickelodeon) Simon Spotlight/Nickelodeon.

—La Quinceañera. Aikins, Dave, illus. 2006. (Dora la Exploradora Ser.). (SPA.). 24p. (J). (gr. -1-3). pap. 3.99 *(978-1-4169-2462-3(0)*, Libros Para Ninos) Libros Para Ninos.

—Súper Bebés! Miller, Victoria, illus. 2006. (Dora la Exploradora Ser.). (SPA.). 24p. (J). (gr. -1-3). pap. 3.99 *(978-1-4169-2461-6(2)*, Libros Para Ninos) Libros Para Ninos.

Jendresen, Erik & Villoldo, Alberto. The First Story Ever Told. Yoshi, illus. 2008. (ENG.). 36p. (J). (gr. -1-2). 12.99 *(978-1-4169-8961-5(7)*, Simon & Schuster Bks. For Young Readers) Simon & Schuster Bks. For Young Readers.

Johnson, Vargie. Eric the Red the Fearless: What Made Them Famous? 2006. (J). per. 15.00 *(978-1-931195-94-2(3))* KiwE Publishing, Ltd.

Karr, Kathleen. Born for Adventure, 0 vols. unabr. ed. 2013. (ENG.). 208p. (YA). (gr. 7-10). pap. 9.99 *(978-1-4778-1701-8(8)*, 9781477817018, Amazon Children's Publishing) Amazon Publishing.

Karwoski, Gail Langer. SeaMan: The Dog Who Explored the West with Lewis & Clark, 1 vol. Watling, James, illus. 2003. (Peachtree Junior Publication Ser.). (ENG.). 192p. (J). (gr. 3-7). 16.95 *(978-1-56145-276-7(9)*, Q20194) Peachtree Pubs.

Kibuishi, Kazu. The Lost Islands. 2013. (Explorer Ser.: 1). (J). lib. bdg. 22.05 *(978-0-606-33456-3(4)*, Turtleback) Turtleback Bks.

Kiesling, Ralph W. The Exploration, 1 vol. 2009. 253p. pap. 27.95 *(978-1-61546-668-9(1))* America Star Bks.

Kirk, Daniel. Library Mouse: A World to Explore. 2010. (ENG., Illus.). 32p. (J). (gr. 1-4). 17.95 *(978-0-8109-8968-9(9))*, Abrams Bks. for Young Readers) Abrams, Inc.

Kittredge, James M. The Three Little Explorers, 1 vol. Reyes, Glendalys, illus. 2010. 16p. pap. 24.95 *(978-1-4489-8973-7(6))* PublishAmerica, Inc.

Kramer, Candice. Matthew Henson en el Polo Norte & Matthew Henson at the North Pole. 2005. spiral bd. 76.00 *(978-1-4108-5790-3(5))* Benchmark Education Co.

Kuefler, Joseph. Beyond the Pond. Kuefler, Joseph, illus. 2015. (ENG., Illus.). 40p. (J). (gr. -1-3). 17.99 *(978-0-06-236427-2(8))* HarperCollins Pubs.

Lawrence, Iain. The Winter Pony. 2012. (ENG., Illus.). 256p. (J). (gr. 4-7). 7.99 *(978-0-440-23972-7(9))*, Yearling) Random Hse. Children's Bks.

London, C. Alexander. We Are Not Eaten by Yaks. (Accidental Adventure Ser.: 1). (ENG.). (J). (gr. 3-7). 2013. 384p. pap. 7.99 *(978-0-14-242056-0(5))*, Puffin Books) 2011. 224p. 12.99 *(978-0-399-25487-1(0))*, Philomel Bks.) Penguin Young Readers Group.

—We Dine with Cannibals. 2013. (Accidental Adventure Ser.: 2). (ENG.). 384p. (J). (gr. 3-7). pap. 7.99 *(978-0-14-242474-2(9))*, Puffin Books) Penguin Young Readers Group.

—We Give a Squid a Wedgie. Duddle, Jonny, illus. 2013. (Accidental Adventure Ser.: 3). (ENG.). 400p. (J). (gr. 3-7). pap. 7.99 *(978-0-14-242475-9(7))*, Puffin Books) Penguin Young Readers Group.

Luna, Rachel Nickerson. The Haunting of Captain Snow. 2005. (Eel Grass Girls Mystery Ser.: No. 2). (Illus.). 332p. pap. 11.95 *(978-1-886551-08-4(1))* Howard, Emma Bks.

Marsh, Carole. The Breathtaking Mystery on Mt. Everest. 2009. (Around the World in 80 Mysteries Ser.). 144p. (J). 18.99 *(978-0-635-06836-1(2))*, Marsh, Carole Bks.) Gallopade International.

Newbery, Linda. Polly's March. 2009. (Historical House Ser.). 192p. (YA). (gr. 5-18). pap. 5.99 *(978-0-7945-2336-7(6))*, Usborne) EDC Publishing.

Nick Barry. Revenge of Poseidon's Trident: An Ethan Sparks Adventure. 2010. 176p. 23.95 *(978-1-4502-1090-4(2))*; pap. 13.95 *(978-1-4502-1088-1(0))* iUniverse, Inc.

O'Ryan, Ray. Journey to Juno. Jack, Colin, illus. 2013. (Galaxy Zack Ser.: 2). (ENG.). 128p. (J). (gr. k-4). 17.99 *(978-1-4424-5391-3(5))*; pap. 5.99 *(978-1-4424-5390-6(7))* Little Simon. (Little Simon).

—Journey to Juno. 2013. (Galaxy Zack Ser.: 2). lib. bdg. 16.00 *(978-0-606-32443-4(7))*, Turtleback) Turtleback Bks.

Parton, Paula. Room 17 'Where History Comes Alive!' Book Ii, Explorers. 2008. 120p. pap. 8.95 *(978-0-9794815-3-6(8))* Bellissima Publishing, LLC.

Pennington, Stacey & Pennington, J. C. D. Let's Go Aquarium: A Magnetic Storybook. Allen, Marie, illus. 2008. 6p. (J). (gr. -1-1). bds. 10.99 *(978-2-7641-2184-9(9))* Gardner Pubns.

Publications International Ltd. Staff, ed. Dora Explorer Write & Erase Look & Find. 2012. 28p. (J). bds. 9.98 *(978-1-4508-4081-1(7))*, 360fbb38-07f6-4512-9772-3e56d91517aa) Phoenix International Publications, Inc.

Rao, Lisa. Dora's Magic Watering Can. Miller, Victoria, illus. 2008. (Dora the Explorer Ser.). (ENG.). 16p. (J). (gr. -1-1). pap. 4.99 *(978-1-4169-4772-1(8))*, Simon Spotlight/Nickelodeon) Simon Spotlight/Nickelodeon.

Reeve, Philip. Oliver & the Sea Monkeys. Mcintyre, Sarah, illus. 2016. (Not-So-Impossible Tale Ser.). (ENG.). 224p. (J). (gr. 2-5). pap. 6.99 *(978-0-385-38789-7(X))*, Yearling) Random Hse. Children's Bks.

—Oliver & the Seawigs. Mcintyre, Sarah, illus. 2014. (Not-So-Impossible Tale Ser.). (ENG.). 208p. (J). (gr. 2-5). 12.99 *(978-0-385-38788-0(1))*, Random Hse. Bks. for Young Readers) Random Hse. Children's Bks.

Reid, James. Edward the Explorer, 1 vol. rev. ed. 2013. (Fiction Readers Ser.). (ENG., Illus.). 12p. (J). (gr. 1-1). 4.99 *(978-1-4333-5455-7(1))*; pap. 12.96 *(978-1-4807-1134-1(9))* Shell Educational Publishing.

Reisner, Molly. Halloween Hoedown! (Dora the Explorer) Aikins, David, illus. 2013. (Pictureback(R) Ser.). (ENG.). 24p. (J). (gr. -1-2). 3.99 *(978-0-449-81762-9(8))*, Random Hse. Bks. for Young Readers) Random Hse. Children's Bks.

Rider, Cynthia. The Explorers. Aguilar, Sandra, illus. 2013. (Start Reading Ser.). (ENG.). 24p. (gr. k-1). pap. 7.95 *(978-1-4765-4097-9(7))* Capstone Press of Coughlan Cos.

Rosen, Michael J. Sailing the Unknown: Around the World with Captain Cook. Pritelli, Maria Cristina, illus. 2012. (ENG.). 40p. (J). (gr. 1-3). 19.99 *(978-1-56846-216-5(6))*, Creative Editions) Creative Co., The.

Shapiro, David R. Terra Tempo: The Four Corners of Time. Herndon, Christopher, illus. 2013. (Terra Tempo Ser.). (ENG.). 264p. (J). pap. 17.99 *(978-0-9844422-6-3(X))* Craigmore Creations.

Smith, Roland. The Captain's Dog: My Journey with the Lewis & Clark Tribe. 2008. (ENG., Illus.). 304p. (J). (gr. 5-7). pap. 7.99 *(978-0-15-202696-7(7))* Houghton Mifflin Harcourt Publishing Co.

Snell, Gordon. The King of Quizzical Island. McKee, David, illus. 2009. (ENG.). 40p. (J). (gr. -1-3). 16.99 *(978-0-7636-3857-3(9))* Candlewick Pr.

Stilton, Geronimo & Wolf, Matt. All Because of a Cup of Coffee. 2004. (Geronimo Stilton Ser.: No. 10). (Illus.). 112p. (J). lib. bdg. 10.00 *(978-1-4242-0279-9(5))* Fitzgerald Bks.

Taylor, Mark. Henry the Castaway. Booth, Graham, illus. 2010. 48p. (J). (gr. -1-3). 18.95 *(978-1-930900-47-9(3))* Purple Hse. Pr.

Verne, Jules. Journey to the Center of the Earth. Freeberg, Eric, illus. 2011. (Classic Starts(tm) Ser.). (ENG.). 160p. (J). (gr. 2-4). 6.95 *(978-1-4027-7313-6(7))* Sterling Publishing Co., Inc.

—A Journey to the Center of the Earth, 1 vol. Fisher, Eric Scott, illus. 2011. (Calico Illustrated Classics Ser.: No. 3). (ENG.). 112p. (J). (gr. 3-6). 27.07 *(978-1-61641-104-6(X))* Magic Wagon.

—A Journey to the Interior of the Earth. 2006. 196p. per. 13.95 *(978-1-59818-461-7(X))* Aegypan.

—Journey to the Interior of the Earth. 2006. 196p. 26.95 *(978-1-59818-557-7(8))* Aegypan.

Younger, David. Spanky, the Brave Space Mouse, 1 vol. 2010. 18p. 24.95 *(978-1-4489-4661-7(1))* PublishAmerica, Inc.

EXPLORING EXPEDITIONS

see names of countries with the subdivision Exploring Expeditions (e.g. United States—Exploring Expeditions; etc.) and names of Expeditions, e.g. Lewis and Clark Expedition; etc.

ABDO Publishing Company. Explore the Countries: Set Of 16. 2013. (Explore the Countries Ser.: 16). (ENG.). 40p. (J). (gr. 2-5). lib. bdg. 478.88 *(978-1-61783-803-3(9))*, Big Buddy Bks.) ABDO Publishing Co.

EXPLOSIVES

Albright, Rosie. Detection Rats. 2012. (Animal Detectives Ser.). (ENG., Illus.). 24p. (J). (gr. k-3). pap. 8.25 *(978-1-4488-6256-6(6))*; lib. bdg. 22.60 *(978-1-4488-6149-1(7))* Rosen Publishing Group, Inc., The. (PowerKids Pr.).

—Detection Rats: Ratas Detectoras. Alamán, Eduardo, tr. from ENG. 2012. (Animal Detectives / Detectives Del Reino Animal Ser.). (SPA & ENG.). 24p. (J). (gr. k-3). lib. bdg. 22.60 *(978-1-4488-6715-8(0))*, PowerKids Pr.) Rosen Publishing Group, Inc., The.

Bearce, Stephanie. Explosive Experiments. 2017. (Twisted True Tales from Science Ser.: 0). (ENG., Illus.). 125p. (J). (gr. 4-7). pap. 8.95 *(978-1-61821-576-5(0))* Prufrock Pr.

Beyer, Mark. Demolition Experts: Life Blowing Things Up. 2009. (Extreme Careers Ser.). 64p. (gr. 5-5). 58.50 *(978-1-61512-389-6(X))*, Rosen Reference) Rosen Publishing Group, Inc., The.

Cobb, Vicki. Fireworks. 2008. pap. 52.95 *(978-0-8225-9449-9(8))* Lerner Publishing Group.

—Fireworks. Gold, Michael, photos by. 2005. (Where's the Science Here? Ser.). (Illus.). 48p. (J). (gr. 3-7). lib. bdg. 23.93 *(978-0-7613-2771-4(1))*, Millbrook Pr.) Lerner Publishing Group.

Discovery Channel (Firm) Staff, contrib. by. Mythbusters. 2013. (Illus.). 48p. (J). *(978-1-935442-24-0(4))*, Beckon Bks.) Southwestern Publishing Group, Inc.

Gordon, Nick. Bomb Squad Technician. 2012. (Dangerous Jobs Ser.). (ENG., Illus.). 24p. (J). (gr. 3-7). lib. bdg. 25.95 *(978-1-60014-777-7(1))*, Torque Bks.) Bellwether Media.

Harmon, Daniel E. Careers in Explosives & Arson Investigation. 2009. (Careers in Forensics Ser.). 64p. (gr. 5-5). 58.50 *(978-1-61511-803-8(9))*, Rosen Reference) Rosen Publishing Group, Inc., The.

Loveless, Antony. Bomb & Mine Disposal Officers. 2009. (World's Most Dangerous Jobs Ser.). (ENG., Illus.). 32p. (J). (gr. 3-6). pap. *(978-0-7787-5109-0(0))*; lib. bdg. *(978-0-7787-5095-6(7))* Crabtree Publishing Co.

Perritano, John. Bomb Squad Technician, Vol. 12. 2015. (On a Mission Ser.). (Illus.). 48p. (J). (gr. 5). 20.95 *(978-1-4222-3392-4(8))* Mason Crest.

Rosen Central, creator. Careers in Forensics. 2008. (J). 175.50 *(978-1-4042-1476-7(3))*, Rosen Reference) Rosen Publishing Group, Inc., The.

Trueit, Trudi Strain. Gunpowder. 2006. (Inventions That Shaped the World Ser.). (Illus.). 80p. (gr. 5-8). 19.95 *(978-0-7569-6857-1(7))* Perfection Learning Corp.

Weil, Ann. Bomb-Sniffing Dogs. 2013. (Animals with Jobs Ser.). (ENG.). 32p. (gr. 1-4). 28.50 *(978-1-60753-378-8(2))* Amicus Publishing.

Wood, Alix. Bombs, Mines, & IEDs, 01 vols., 1. 2016. (Today's High-Tech Weapons Ser.). (ENG.). 32p. (J). pap. 10.00 *(978-1-5081-4675-9(6))*, PowerKids Pr.) Rosen Publishing Group, Inc., The.

—Explosives Expert, 1 vol., 1. 2014. (World's Coolest Jobs Ser.). (ENG.). 32p. (J). (gr. 3-6). pap. 10.00 *(978-1-4777-6012-3(1))*; lib. bdg. 26.25 *(978-1-4777-6011-6(3))* Rosen Publishing Group, Inc., The. (PowerKids Pr.).

EXTINCT ANIMALS

see also names of extinct animals, e.g. Mastodon, etc.

Batten, Mary. Extinct! Creatures of the Past. Doyle, Beverly, illus. 2004. (J). pap. *(978-0-375-82554-5(1))*; lib. bdg. *(978-0-375-92554-2(6))* Random Hse. Children's Bks. (Random Hse. Bks. for Young Readers).

Brecke, Nicole & Stockland, Patricia M. Extinct & Endangered Animals You Can Draw. Brecke, Nicole, illus. 2010. (Ready, Set, Draw! Ser.). (ENG., Illus.). 32p. (gr. 2-4). lib. bdg. 25.26 *(978-0-7613-4165-9(X))*, Millbrook Pr.) Lerner Publishing Group.

Charman, Andrew. I Wonder Why the Dinosaurs Died Out: And Other Questions about Extinct & Endangered Animals. 2013. (I Wonder Why Ser.). (ENG., Illus.). 32p. (J). (gr. k-3). 6.99 *(978-0-7534-6953-8(7))*, 9780753469538, Kingfisher) Roaring Brook Pr.

Frisch, Joy. Ground Sloths. 2015. (Ice Age Animals Ser.). (ENG.). 24p. (gr. k-1). pap. 6.95 *(978-1-4914-2319-6(6))*, Pebble Plus) Capstone Press of Coughlan Cos.

Green, Tamara. The Dodo: Extinct Species. Gibbons, Tony, illus. 2007. 24p. (J). reprint ed. 15.00 *(978-1-4223-6677-6(4))* DIANE Publishing Co.

Gunby, Shirley & Laman, Judi-Lynn. Extinct & Endangered: Big Animals Small World - Painting for Peanuts. 2007. (Steck-Vaughn BOLDPRINT Anthologies Ser.). (ENG., Illus.). 48p. (gr. 4-8). pap. 16.90 *(978-1-4190-4023-8(5))* Houghton Mifflin Harcourt Publishing Co.

Higgins, Melissa. Sabertooth Cats. 2015. (Ice Age Animals Ser.). (ENG.). 24p. (gr. k-1). pap. 6.95 *(978-1-4914-2321-9(8))*, Pebble Plus) Capstone Press of Coughlan Cos.

Hirsch, Rebecca E. De-Extinction: The Science of Bringing Lost Species Back to Life. 2017. (Nonfiction — Young Adult Ser.). (ENG.). 120p. (gr. 8-12). (YA). 19.99 ***(978-1-5124-3902-1(9)***, Twenty-First Century Bks.); (YA). 53.32 ***(978-1-5124-3903-8(7)***, Twenty-First Century Bks.); (YA). 53.32 ***(978-1-5124-2848-3(5)***, Twenty-First Century Bks.); (Illus.). (J). lib. bdg. 35.99 *(978-1-4677-9490-9(2))* Lerner Publishing Group.

Kalman, Bobbie. Why Do Animals Become Extinct? 2012. (ENG.). 32p. (J). *(978-0-7787-2774-3(2))*; pap. *(978-0-7787-2779-8(3))* Crabtree Publishing Co.

Laverdunt, Damien. Small & Tall Tales of Extinct Animals. Rajcak, Hélène, illus. 2012. (Gecko Press Titles Ser.). (ENG.). 80p. (gr. -1). 22.95 *(978-1-877579-06-6(8))* Gecko Pr. NZL. Dist: Lerner Publishing Group.

McDaniel, Melissa. Mysterious Nature: A Chapter Book. 2005. (True Tales Ser.). (ENG., Illus.). 48p. (J). (gr. 2-4). lib. bdg. 22.50 *(978-0-516-25183-7(X))*, Children's Pr.) Scholastic Library Publishing.

Pobst, Sandra. Animals on the Edge: Science Races to Save Species Threatened with Extinction. 2008. (National Geographic Investigates Science Ser.). (ENG., Illus.). 64p. (J). (gr. 5). 17.95 *(978-1-4263-0358-6(0))*; lib. bdg. 27.90 *(978-1-4263-0265-7(7))* National Geographic Society. (National Geographic Children's Bks.).

Reinhart, Matthew & Sabuda, Robert. Encyclopedia Prehistorica Sharks & Other Sea Monsters. Reinhart, Matthew & Sabuda, Robert, illus. 2006. (Encyclopedia Prehistorica Ser.: 2). (ENG., Illus.). 12p. (J). (gr. k-4). 34.99 *(978-0-7636-2229-9(X))* Candlewick Pr.

Rhodes, Wendell. Threatened, Endangered, & Extinct Species. 2016. (Spotlight on Ecology & Life Science Ser.). 00024p. (J). (gr. 4-6). pap. 10.00 *(978-1-4994-2600-7(3))*, PowerKids Pr.) Rosen Publishing Group, Inc., The.

Säfström, Maja. Animals of a Bygone Era: An Illustrated Compendium. 2017. (ENG., Illus.). 112p. 14.99 *(978-0-399-57852-6(8))*, Ten Speed Pr.) Potter/TenSpeed/Harmony.

Thornhill, Jan. The Tragic Tale of the Great Auk, 1 vol. 2016. (ENG., Illus.). 44p. (J). (gr. 2-6). 18.95 *(978-1-55498-865-5(9))* Groundwood Bks. CAN. Dist: Publishers Group West (PGW).

West, David. Giant Sloth: Graphic Prehistoric Animals. Poluzzi, Alessandro, illus. 2017. (Graphic Prehistoric Animals Ser.). 32p. (gr. 3-7). lib. bdg. 31.35 *(978-1-62588-409-1(5))* Black Rabbit Bks.

Wittrock, Jeni. Ancient Armadillos. 2015. (Ice Age Animals Ser.). (ENG.). 24p. (gr. k-1). pap. 6.95 *(978-1-4914-2322-6(6))*, Pebble Plus) Capstone Press of Coughlan Cos.

World Book, Inc. Staff, contrib. by. Extinct! 2014. (J). *(978-0-7166-5628-9(0))* World Bk., Inc.

Young, Judy. The Hidden Bestiary of Marvelous, Mysterious, & (Maybe Even) Magical Creatures. Filippucci, Laura Francesca, illus. 2009. (ENG.). 32p. (J). (gr. 1-4). 16.95 *(978-1-58536-433-6(9))*, 1299753) Sleeping Bear Pr.

Zeiger, Jennifer. Mammoth & Mastodon. 2015. (21st Century Junior Library: Dinosaurs & Prehistoric Creatures Ser.). (ENG., Illus.). 24p. (J). (gr. 2-5). lib. bdg. 27.07 *(978-1-63362-383-5(1))*, 206952) Cherry Lake Publishing.

—Saber-Toothed Cat. 2015. (21st Century Junior Library: Dinosaurs & Prehistoric Creatures Ser.). (ENG., Illus.). 24p. (J). (gr. 2-5). lib. bdg. 27.07 *(978-1-63362-386-6(6))*, 206964) Cherry Lake Publishing.

EXTINCT CITIES

see also Excavations (Archaeology)

Abbott, Jacob. Hannibal. 2009. (J). pap. 12.00 *(978-1-59128-059-0(1))* Canon Pr.

Barber, Nicola. Lost Cities, 1 vol. 2013. (Treasure Hunters Ser.). (ENG., Illus.). 48p. (gr. 5-8). pap. 9.25 *(978-1-4109-4959-2(1))*; lib. bdg. 29.99 *(978-1-4109-4952-3(4))* Heinemann-Raintree.

Blake, Kevin. Salton Sea Resort: Death in the Desert. 2015. (Abandoned: Towns Without People Ser.). (ENG.). 32p. (J). (gr. 2-7). lib. bdg. 26.60 *(978-1-62724-523-4(5))* Bearport Publishing Co., Inc.

Bodden, Valerie. Ghost Towns. 2017. (J). *(978-1-60818-807-9(8))*, Creative Education) Creative Co., The.

Brooks, Philip. Hannibal. rev. ed. 2015. (Wicked History Ser.). (ENG., Illus.). 144p. (J). lib. bdg. 33.00 *(978-0-531-22122-8(9))*, Children's Pr.) Scholastic Library Publishing.

Burns, Kylie. Sparta! 2013. (ENG.). 48p. (J). *(978-0-7787-1099-8(8))*; pap. *(978-0-7787-1105-6(6))* Crabtree Publishing Co.

Evans, Arthur. The Palace of Minos 4 Volume Set in 7 Pieces: A Comparative Account of the Successive Stages of the Early Cretan Civilization As Illustrated by the Discoveries at Knossos. 2013. (Cambridge Library Collection - Archaeology Ser.). (ENG.). 3734p. pap., pap., pap. 417.00 *(978-1-108-06107-0(9))* Cambridge Univ. Pr.

Lunis, Natalie & Johnston, Paul F. Lost Cities. 2012. (Scary Places Ser.). 32p. (J). (gr. 4-8). lib. bdg. 25.27 *(978-1-61772-567-8(6))* Bearport Publishing Co., Inc.

Markovics, Joyce L. Ghostly Towns. 2017. (Tiptoe into Scary Places Ser.). (ENG., Illus.). 24p. (J). (gr. k-3). 18.95 *(978-1-68402-051-5(4))* Bearport Publishing Co., Inc.

McEwan, Rebecca. Lost Cities & Ciudades Perdidas: 6 English, 6 Spanish Adaptations. 2011. (ENG & SPA.). (J). 97.00 net. *(978-1-4108-5691-3(7))* Benchmark Education Co.

Morris, Neil. Lost Cities. 2009. (Amazing History Ser.). (Illus.). 32p. (J). (gr. 4-7). pap. 7.95 *(978-1-59920-209-9(3))* Black Rabbit Bks.

Otfinoski, Steven. Spartans. 2013. (Great Warriors EBook Ser.:). (ENG., Illus.). 48p. (J). pap. 15.64 *(978-1-61783-778-4(4))*, Core Library) ABDO Publishing Co.

Owings, Lisa. Battleship Island: The Deserted Island. 2017. (Abandoned Places Ser.). (ENG., Illus.). 24p. (J). (gr. 3-7). lib. bdg. 25.95 ***(978-1-62617-693-5(0)***, Torque Bks.) Bellwether Media.

Price, Sean. Hannibal of Carthage, 1 vol. 2013. (Hero Journals). (ENG., Illus.). 48p. (gr. 4-6). 33.32 *(978-1-4109-5359-9(9))*; pap. 9.95 *(978-1-4109-5366-7(1))* Heinemann-Raintree. (NA-r).

Price, Sean Stewart. The Kids' Guide to Lost Cities, 1 vol. 2011. (Kids' Guides). (ENG.). 32p. (gr. 3-4). 27.99 *(978-1-4296-6009-9(0))*, Edge Bks.) Capstone Press of Coughlan Cos.

Rinaldo, Denise. Cities of the Dead: Finding Lost Civilizations. 2008. (24/7: Science Behind the Scenes Ser.). (ENG., Illus.). 64p. (J). (gr. 9-12). 29.00 *(978-0-531-12079-8(1))*; pap. 7.95 *(978-0-531-18739-5(X))* Scholastic Library Publishing. (Watts, Franklin).

Samuels, Charlie. Forgotten Cities. 2012. (ENG.). 32p. (J). pap. *(978-0-7787-8012-0(0))* Crabtree Publishing Co.

Schuetz, Kari. Bodie: The Gold-Mining Ghost Town. 2017. (Abandoned Places Ser.). (ENG., Illus.). 24p. (J). (gr. 3-7). lib. bdg. 25.95 ***(978-1-62617-694-2(9)***, Torque Bks.) Bellwether Media.

Weil, Ann. The World's Most Amazing Lost Cities, 1 vol. 2011. (Landmark Top Tens Ser.). (ENG.). 32p. (gr. 3-5). pap. 8.29 *(978-1-4109-4250-0(3))*; 30.65 *(978-1-4109-4239-5(2))* Heinemann-Raintree. (Raintree Perspectives).

Wolny, Philip. Investigating Atlantis & Other Lost Cities, 1 vol. 2015. (ENG.). 48p. (J). 25.85 *(978-1-62275-857-9(9))*, Britannica Educational Publishing) Rosen Publishing Group, Inc., The.

World Book, Inc Staff, contrib. by. The Mysteries of the Amazon Rain Forest. 2015. (Illus.). 48p. (J). *(978-0-7166-2671-8(3))* World Bk., Inc.

EXTINCT CITIES—FICTION

Larson, Kirsten. The Ghost Town Mystery. 2008. pap. 34.95 *(978-1-58013-773-7(3))* Kane Press, Inc.

Timothy, Ering. Frog Belly Rat F & G. 2003. (J). bds. 16.99 *(978-0-7636-2248-0(6))* Candlewick Pr.

Voelkel, J. P. The Lost City. 2015. (Jaguar Stones Ser.: 4). (ENG., Illus.). 368p. (J). (gr. 5-12). 16.99 *(978-1-5124-0184-4(6))*, Darby Creek) Lerner Publishing Group.

EXTINCT PLANTS

see Plants, Fossil

EXTINCTION (BIOLOGY)

Andryszewski, Tricia. Mass Extinction: Examining the Current Crisis. 2008. (Discovery! Ser.). (ENG., Illus.). 112p. (gr. 6-12). lib. bdg. 31.93 *(978-0-8225-7523-8(X))* Lerner Publishing Group.

Batten, Mary. Extinct! Creatures of the Past. Doyle, Beverly, illus. 2004. (J). pap. *(978-0-375-82554-5(1))*; lib. bdg. *(978-0-375-92554-2(6))* Random Hse. Children's Bks. (Random Hse. Bks. for Young Readers).

Hecht, Jeff. Vanishing Life: The Mystery of Mass Extinctions. 2009. (ENG.). 160p. (YA). (gr. 7). pap. 8.99 *(978-1-4169-9422-0(X))*, Atheneum Bks. for Young Readers) Simon & Schuster Children's Publishing.

Hunter, Nick. Science vs. Animal Extinction. 2013. (Science Fights Back Ser.). (Illus.). 48p. (gr. 4-6). 31.95 *(978-1-4339-8675-8(2))*; pap. 14.05 *(978-1-4339-8676-5(0))* Stevens, Gareth Publishing LLLP. (Gareth Stevens Learning Library).

Jenkins, Martin. Can We Save the Tiger? White, Vicky, illus. 2014. (ENG.). 56p. (J). (gr. k-3). 9.99 *(978-0-7636-7378-9(1))* Candlewick Pr.

Kalman, Bobbie. Why Do Animals Become Extinct? 2012. (ENG.). 32p. (J). *(978-0-7787-2774-3(2))*; pap. *(978-0-7787-2779-8(3))* Crabtree Publishing Co.

Kinsner, Kathy. Doomed to Disappear? Endangered Species & Condenadas a desaparecer? Especies en peligro de Extinción: 6 English, 6 Spanish Adaptations. 2011. (ENG & SPA.). (J). 97.00 net. *(978-1-4108-5698-2(4))* Benchmark Education Co.

Orr, Tamra B. Battling Extinction. 2014. (Explorer Library: Follow the Clues Ser.). (ENG., Illus.). 32p. (J). (gr. 4-8). 28.50 *(978-1-62431-780-4(4))*, 203316) Cherry Lake Publishing.

Parker, Steve. Extinction. 2010. (Unpredictable Nature Ser.). (Illus.). 48p. (J). (gr. 3-18). lib. bdg. 19.95 *(978-1-4222-1998-0(4))* Mason Crest.

Pipe, Jim & Newland, Sonya. Extinction! 2012. (ENG.). 48p. (J). *(978-0-7787-7925-4(4))*; pap. *(978-0-7787-7934-6(3))* Crabtree Publishing Co.

Spilsbury, Louise. Ice Age Animals. 2010. (Big Picture: Climate Ser.). (ENG.). 24p. (gr. 1-2). pap. 41.70 *(978-1-4296-5823-2(1))*, First Facts) Capstone Press of Coughlan Cos.

World Book, Inc. Staff, contrib. by. Endangered Animals of Europe. 2014. (J). *(978-0-7166-5624-1(8))* World Bk., Inc.

—Extinct! 2014. (J). *(978-0-7166-5628-9(0))* World Bk., Inc.

EXTRACURRICULAR ACTIVITIES

see Student Activities

EXTRASENSORY PERCEPTION

Brunke, Dawn Baumann. Animal Voices, Animal Guides: Discover Your Deeper Self Through Communication with Animals. 2nd ed. 2009. (ENG.). 256p. pap. 16.00 *(978-1-59143-098-8(4))* Bear & Co.

Green, Carl R. & Sanford, William R. Astonishing Mind Powers. Kelley, Gerald, illus. 2011. (Investigating the Unknown Ser.). 48p. (J). (gr. 5-18). pap. 8.95 *(978-1-59845-305-8(X))*; lib. bdg. 25.27 *(978-0-7660-3820-2(3))* Enslow Pubs., Inc.

Herbst, Judith. Esp. 2004. (Unexplained Ser.). (Illus.). 48p. (J). pap. 8.95 *(978-0-8225-2405-2(8))* Lerner Publishing Group.

—ESP. 2005. (Unexplained Ser.). (Illus.). 48p. (J). (gr. 5-12). lib. bdg. 26.60 *(978-0-8225-1628-6(4))* Lerner Publishing Group.

Johnson, Julie Tallard. Teen Psychic: Exploring Your Intuitive Spiritual Powers. 2003. (ENG., Illus.). 256p. (YA). (gr. 7-12). pap. 14.95 *(978-0-89281-094-9(7))* Inner Traditions International, Ltd.

Maurer, Tracy. Eerie ESP. 2017. (Searchlight Books (tm) — Fear Fest Ser.). (ENG.). (J). (gr. 3-5). pap. 9.99 ***(978-1-5124-5604-2(7))***; (Illus.). lib. bdg. 30.65 ***(978-1-5124-3404-0(3))*** Lerner Publishing Group.

Noll, Elizabeth. ESP. 2017. (Strange ... but True? Ser.). (ENG.). 32p. (gr. 3-7). 31.35 ***(978-1-68072-022-8(8))*** Black Rabbit Bks.

Owings, Lisa. Esp. 2015. (Unexplained Mysteries Ser.). (ENG., Illus.). 24p. (J). (gr. 3-7). lib. bdg. 25.95 *(978-1-62617-201-2(3))*, Epic Bks.) Bellwether Media.

Stone, Adam. Esp. 2010. (Unexplained Ser.). (ENG., Illus.). 24p. (J). (gr. 3-7). lib. bdg. 25.95 *(978-1-60014-499-8(3))*, Torque Bks.) Bellwether Media.

Walker, Kathryn. Mysteries of the Mind. 2009. (Unsolved! Ser.). (ENG., Illus.). 32p. (J). (gr. 3-5). pap. *(978-0-7787-4162-6(1))*; (gr. 4-6). *(978-0-7787-4149-7(4))* Crabtree Publishing Co.

EXTRASENSORY PERCEPTION—FICTION

Bo, Ben. Skullcrack. 2003. (ENG.). 168p. (YA). (gr. 5-12). pap. 6.95 *(978-0-8225-3311-5(1))* Lerner Publishing Group.

Bowe, Kristine. Seers. 2013. (ENG.). 216p. (YA). (gr. 7). 16.95 *(978-1-934133-55-2(8))*; pap. 8.95 *(978-1-934133-56-9(6))* Charlesbridge Publishing, Inc.

Bray, Libba. Lair of Dreams. 2015. (Diviners Ser.: 2). (ENG.). 624p. (YA). (gr. 10-17). 19.00 *(978-0-316-12604-5(7))*; (gr. 7-17). E-Book *(978-0-316-36488-1(6))* Little, Brown Bks. for Young Readers.

Brennan, Herbie. The Doomsday Box: A Shadow Project Adventure. 2011. (Shadow Project Ser.: 2). (ENG.). 352p. (J). (gr. 5). pap. 6.99 *(978-0-06-175650-4(4))* HarperCollins Pubs.

Bruchac, Joseph. Killer of Enemies. (Killer of Enemies Ser.). (ENG.). 400p. (YA). 2016. pap. 11.99 *(978-1-62014-276-9(7))* 2013. 19.95 *(978-1-62014-143-4(4))* Lee & Low Bks., Inc. (Tu Bks.).

Carmody, Isobelle. The Farseekers. 2003. (Obernewtyn Chronicles: Bk. 2). (Illus.). 316p. (J). 13.65 *(978-0-7569-4608-1(5))* Perfection Learning Corp.

Cashore, Kristin. Fire. November, S., ed. 2011. (ENG.). 528p. (YA). (gr. 7-18). pap. 10.99 *(978-0-14-241591-7(X)*, Firebird) Penguin Young Readers Group.

—Fire. 2011. (Graceling Realm Ser.: 2). lib. bdg. 22.10 *(978-0-606-23085-8(8)*, Turtleback) Turtleback Bks.

Christopher, Matt. The Dog That Called the Pitch. Vasconcellos, Dan, illus. 2010. (Matt Christopher Sports Readers Ser.). 48p. (J). (gr. 1-3). lib. bdg. 23.93 *(978-1-59953-353-7(7))* Norwood Hse. Pr.

—The Dog That Pitched a No-Hitter. 2013. (Passport to Reading Level 3 Ser.). (ENG., Illus.). 48p. (J). (gr. 1-4). 4.99 *(978-0-316-21848-1(0))* Little, Brown Bks. for Young Readers.

—The Dog That Stole Football Plays. Vasconcellos, Daniel et al, illus. 2013. (Passport to Reading Level 3 Ser.). (ENG.). 32p. (J). (gr. 1-4). pap. 4.99 *(978-0-316-21849-8(9))* Little, Brown Bks. for Young Readers.

—The Dog That Stole Home. Vasconcellos, Dan, illus. 2010. (Matt Christopher Sports Readers Ser.). 48p. (J). (gr. 1-3). lib. bdg. 23.93 *(978-1-59953-352-0(9))* Norwood Hse. Pr.

—The Dog That Stole the Football Plays. Ogden, Bill, illus. 2010. (Matt Christopher Sports Readers Ser.). 48p. (J). (gr. 1-3). lib. bdg. 23.93 *(978-1-59953-350-6(2))* Norwood Hse. Pr.

—The Great Quarterback Switch. 2008. (New Matt Christopher Sports Library). 144p. (J). (gr. 4-6). lib. bdg. 26.60 *(978-1-59953-216-5(6))* Norwood Hse. Pr.

Cooper, Abby. Bubbles. 2017. (ENG.). 272p. (J). 16.99 *(978-0-374-30290-0(1)*, 9780374302900, Farrar, Straus & Giroux (BYR)) Farrar, Straus & Giroux.

Cusick, Richie Tankersley. It Begins - Rest in Peace, Vol. 1. 2012. (Unseen Ser.: 1). (ENG.). 576p. (YA). (gr. 7). pap. 7.99 *(978-0-14-242336-3(X)*, Speak) Penguin Young Readers Group.

—The Unseen Volume 2: Blood Brothers/Sin & Salvation. 2012. (Unseen Ser.: 2). (ENG.). 640p. (YA). (gr. 7). pap. 7.99 *(978-0-14-242337-0(8)*, Speak) Penguin Young Readers Group.

De felice, Cynthia. The Strange Night Writing of Jessamine Colter. 2008. (ENG.). 56p. (J). (gr. 5-9). pap. 5.99 *(978-1-4169-7908-1(5)*, Atheneum Bks. for Young Readers) Simon & Schuster Children's Publishing.

Duncan, Lois. A Gift of Magic. 2012. (ENG., Illus.). 208p. (YA). (gr. 7-17). pap. 17.99 *(978-0-316-09894-6(9))* Little, Brown Bks. for Young Readers.

—The Third Eye. 2012. (ENG.). 288p. (YA). (gr. 7-17). pap. 10.99 *(978-0-316-09908-0(2))* Little, Brown Bks. for Young Readers.

Epstein, Robin. Hear. 2015. (ENG., Illus.). 272p. (YA). (gr. 9). 18.99 *(978-1-61695-581-6(3)*, Soho Teen) Soho Pr., Inc.

Garcia, Kami & Stohl, Margaret. Beautiful Creatures. 2009. (Beautiful Creatures Ser.: 1). (ENG.). 576p. (YA). (gr. 7-17). 17.99 *(978-0-316-04267-3(6))* Little Brown & Co.

—Beautiful Creatures. (Beautiful Creatures Ser.: 1). (ENG.). 592p. (YA). (gr. 7-17). 2010. pap. 12.99 *(978-0-316-07703-3(8))* 2012. mass mkt. 7.99 *(978-0-316-23165-7(7))* 2012. pap. 10.99 *(978-0-316-23167-1(3))* Little, Brown Bks. for Young Readers.

—Beautiful Creatures. 2013. (ENG., Illus.). 240p. (gr. 8-17). 20.00 *(978-0-316-18271-3(0)*, Yen Pr.) Orbit.

—Beautiful Creatures. 2010. (Beautiful Creatures Ser.: 1). (YA). lib. bdg. 23.30 *(978-0-606-26699-4(2)*, Turtleback) Turtleback Bks.

—Beautiful Redemption. 2012. (Beautiful Creatures Ser.: 4). (ENG.). (YA). (gr. 7-17). 464p. 18.99 *(978-0-316-12353-2(6))*; 576p. pap. 9.99 *(978-0-316-22519-9(3))* Little, Brown Bks. for Young Readers.

George, Elisabeth. The Edge of the Shadows. 2015. (Edge of Nowhere Ser.). (ENG.). 464p. (YA). (gr. 7). 18.99 *(978-0-670-01298-5(X)*, Viking Books for Young Readers) Penguin Young Readers Group.

Gibbs, Stuart. Spaced Out. (Moon Base Alpha Ser.). (ENG.). (J). (gr. 3-7). 2017. 368p. pap. 7.99 *(978-1-4814-2337-3(1))* 2016. (Illus.). 352p. 17.99 *(978-1-4814-2336-6(3))* Simon & Schuster Bks. For Young Readers. (Simon & Schuster Bks. For Young Readers).

—Spaced Out. 2017. (Moon Base Alpha Ser.: 2). lib. bdg. 18.40 ***(978-0-606-39762-9(0))*** Turtleback Bks.

Grunwell, Jeanne Marie. Mind Games. 2006. (ENG., Illus.). 144p. (J). (gr. 5-7). pap. 10.95 *(978-0-618-68947-7(8))* Houghton Mifflin Harcourt Publishing Co.

Haddix, Margaret Peterson. Claim to Fame. 2010. (ENG.). 272p. (YA). (gr. 7). pap. 9.99 *(978-1-4169-3918-4(0)*, Simon & Schuster Bks. For Young Readers) Simon & Schuster Bks. For Young Readers.

Hale, Shannon. The Forgotten Sisters. 2015. (Princess Academy Ser.: 3). (ENG.). 336p. (YA). (gr. 5-8). 17.99 *(978-1-61963-485-5(6)*, 9781619634855, Bloomsbury USA Childrens) Bloomsbury Publishing USA.

—Palace of Stone. (Princess Academy Ser.: 2). (ENG.). (YA). (gr. 5-8). 2015. 352p. pap. 7.99 *(978-1-61963-257-8(8)*, 9781619632578) 2012. 336p. 17.99 *(978-1-59990-873-1(5)*, 9781599908731) Bloomsbury Publishing USA. (Bloomsbury USA Childrens).

—Palace of Stone. 2015. (Princess Academy Ser.: 2). (YA). lib. bdg. 18.40 *(978-0-606-36439-3(0))* Turtleback Bks.

—Princess Academy. (Princess Academy Ser.: 1). (ENG.). (YA). (gr. 5-8). 2005. 320p. 17.99 *(978-1-58234-993-0(2)*, 9781582349930) 2nd ed. 2015. 336p. pap. 7.99 *(978-1-61963-613-2(1)*, 9781619636132) Bloomsbury Publishing USA. (Bloomsbury USA Childrens).

—Princess Academy. 2009. (Princess Academy Ser.: No. 1). 8.86 *(978-0-7848-2867-0(9)*, Everbind) Marco Bk. Co.

—Princess Academy. 2007. (Princess Academy Ser.: No. 1). 314p. (gr. 5-9). 18.00 *(978-0-7569-8180-8(8))* Perfection Learning Corp.

—Princess Academy. (Princess Academy Ser.: No. 1). *(978-0-439-88811-0(5)*, Scholastic) Scholastic, Inc.

—Princess Academy. l.t. ed. 2006. (Princess Academy Ser.: No. 1). 339p. (J). (gr. 5-9). 23.95 *(978-0-7862-8733-8(0))* Thorndike Pr.

—Princess Academy. 2015. (Princess Academy Ser.: 1). (YA). lib. bdg. 18.40 *(978-0-606-36438-6(2))* Turtleback Bks.

Hamburg, Jennifer. Hazy Bloom & the Tomorrow Power. Mourning, Tuesday & Hamie, Jenn, illus. 2017. (Hazy Bloom Ser.). (ENG.). 176p. (J). 15.99 *(978-0-374-30494-2(7)*, 9780374304942, Farrar, Straus & Giroux (BYR)) Farrar, Straus & Giroux.

Higgins, Wendy. Sweet Evil. 2012. (Sweet Evil Ser.: 1). (ENG.). 464p. (YA). (gr. 8). pap. 9.99 *(978-0-06-208561-0(1)*, HarperTeen) HarperCollins Pubs.

King, A. S. Glory O'Brien's History of the Future. 2014. (ENG.). 320p. (YA). (gr. 10-17). 18.00 *(978-0-316-22272-3(0))* Little, Brown Bks. for Young Readers.

Lasky, Kathryn. Double Trouble Squared. 2008. (ENG., Illus.). 240p. (J). (gr. 2-5). pap. 14.99 *(978-0-15-205878-4(8))* Houghton Mifflin Harcourt Publishing Co.

—Shadows in the Water. 2008. (ENG., Illus.). 224p. (J). (gr. 2-5). pap. 14.95 *(978-0-15-205874-6(5))* Houghton Mifflin Harcourt Publishing Co.

—A Voice in the Wind. 2008. (ENG., Illus.). 272p. (J). (gr. 2-5). pap. 15.95 *(978-0-15-205875-3(3))* Houghton Mifflin Harcourt Publishing Co.

McNish, Cliff. Breathe: A Ghost Story. (Exceptional Reading & Language Arts Titles for Intermediate Grades Ser.). (ENG.). 264p. (J). (gr. 4-8). 2009. pap. 6.95 *(978-0-7613-4962-4(6)*, First Avenue Editions) 2006. lib. bdg. 15.95 *(978-0-8225-6443-0(2)*, Carolrhoda Bks.) Lerner Publishing Group.

Miller, Sarah. The Other Girl. 2010. (ENG.). 304p. (YA). (gr. 8). pap. 20.99 *(978-0-312-33416-1(8)*, 9780312334161, St. Martin's Griffin) St. Martin's Pr.

Nelson, N. A. Bringing the Boy Home. 2008. (ENG.). 224p. (J). (gr. 3-7). 16.99 *(978-0-06-088698-1(6))* HarperCollins Pubs.

Oliver, Lin & Baker, Theo. The Shadow Mask, No. 2. 2013. (Sound Bender Ser.: 2). (ENG.). 368p. (J). (gr. 5-9). 16.99 *(978-0-545-19694-9(9)*, Scholastic Pr.) Scholastic, Inc.

—Sound Bender. 2011. (ENG.). 272p. (J). (gr. 5-9). 16.99 *(978-0-545-19692-5(2)*, Scholastic Pr.) Scholastic, Inc.

Pearson, Ridley. The Syndrome. 2015. (Kingdom Keepers Ser.). (ENG., Illus.). 300p. (J). (gr. 5-9). 12.99 *(978-1-4847-2408-8(9))* Hyperion Bks. for Children.

Peyton, Veronica. Silo & the Rebel Raiders. 2016. (ENG.). 304p. (J). (gr. 3-7). 16.99 *(978-0-399-55241-0(3)*, Delacorte Bks. for Young Readers) Random Hse. Children's Bks.

Plum, Amy. Until the Beginning. 2015. (After the End Ser.: 2). (ENG.). 336p. (YA). (gr. 8). 17.99 *(978-0-06-222563-4(4)*, HarperTeen) HarperCollins Pubs.

Ritter, William. Jackaby. (Jackaby Ser.: 1). (ENG.). 304p. (YA). (gr. 9-12). 2015. pap. 9.95 *(978-1-61620-546-1(6))* 2014. 16.95 *(978-1-61620-353-5(6)*, 73353) Algonquin Bks. of Chapel Hill.

Stiefvater, Maggie. The Raven Boys. 2015. 50.87 *(978-1-320-56337-6(6))* Blurb, Inc.

—The Raven Boys. 2013. (Raven Cycle Ser.: 1). 20.00 *(978-1-62765-119-6(5))* Perfection Learning Corp.

—The Raven Boys. (Raven Cycle Ser.: 1). (ENG.). 416p. (J). (gr. 9). 2013. pap. 10.99 *(978-0-545-42493-6(3)*, Scholastic Paperbacks) 2012. 18.99 *(978-0-545-42492-9(5)*, Scholastic Pr.) 2012. E-Book *(978-0-545-46979-1(1))* Scholastic, Inc.

—The Raven Boys. 2016. (CHI.). 448p. (YA). (gr. 7). pap. *(978-986-361-180-6(8))* Sitak Group Holding, Ltd.

—The Raven Boys. 2013. (Raven Cycle Ser.: 1). lib. bdg. 20.85 *(978-0-606-32028-3(8)*, Turtleback) Turtleback Bks.

Stolarz, Laurie Faria. Red Is for Remembrance. l.t. ed. 2008. (Blue Is for Nightmares Ser.: Bk. 4). 385p. (YA). (gr. 7). 22.95 *(978-1-4104-0339-1(4))* Thorndike Pr.

—Silver Is for Secrets. 2005. (Stolarz Ser.: 3). (ENG.). 288p. (YA). pap. 11.99 *(978-0-7387-0631-3(0)*, Flux) North Star Editions.

Talbot, Sophie. Fabulous Terrible: The Adventures of You. 2011. 280p. (YA). (gr. 7-18). pap. 12.99 *(978-1-933390-76-5(X))* Chooseco LLC.

Watts, Julia. Free Spirits. 2009. (ENG.). 176p. (J). (gr. 1). pap. 8.95 *(978-0-9667359-2-5(7)*, BeanPole Bks.) Harren Communications, LLC.

Yansky, Brian. Alien Invasion & Other Inconveniences. 2010. (ENG., Illus.). 240p. (YA). (gr. 9-18). 15.99 *(978-0-7636-4384-3(X))* Candlewick Pr.

—Homicidal Aliens & Other Disappointments. 2013. (ENG.). 336p. (YA). (gr. 9). 16.99 *(978-0-7636-5962-2(2))* Candlewick Pr.

EXTRATERRESTRIAL BEINGS

Biskup, Agnieszka. Aliens & Energy, 1 vol. Aón, Carlos, illus. 2011. (Monster Science Ser.). (ENG.). 32p. (gr. 3-4). pap. 8.10 *(978-1-4296-7325-9(7))*; pap. 47.70 *(978-1-4296-7326-6(5))*; lib. bdg. 30.65 *(978-1-4296-6580-3(7))* Capstone Press of Coughlan Cos. (Graphic Library).

Bullard, Lisa. I'm from Outer Space! Meet an Alien. Moran, Mike, illus. 2014. (Monster Buddies Ser.). (ENG.). 24p. (gr. k-2). pap. 6.95 *(978-1-4677-4999-2(0))*; lib. bdg. 23.93 *(978-0-7613-9193-7(2))* Lerner Publishing Group. (Millbrook Pr.).

Coddington, Andrew. Aliens. 2016. (Creatures of Fantasy Ser.). 64p. (J). (gr. 6-6). 34.21 *(978-1-5026-1862-7(1))* Cavendish Square Publishing.

Coddington, Andrew. Aliens, UFOs, & Unexplained Encounters. 2017. (J). ***(978-1-5026-2845-9(7))*** Cavendish Square Publishing.

Dailey, Kirsten. Encounters with Ufos & Extraterrestrial Life. Pye, Michael, ed. 2012. (Mysteries Uncovered, Secrets Declassified Ser.). (ENG., Illus.). 224 –p. (YA). (gr. 7-12). 37.25 *(978-1-4488-9252-5(X))* Rosen Publishing Group, Inc., The.

Dicker, Katie. Visitors from Space. 2015. (Mystery! Ser.). (Illus.). 24p. (gr. 3-6). 28.50 *(978-1-62588-206-6(8)*, 1381015) Black Rabbit Bks.

Diker, Katie. Visitors from Space. 2015. (ENG., Illus.). 24p. (J). pap. 8.95 *(978-1-77092-237-2(7))* RiverStream Publishing.

Gribbin-Lindemon, Sharon. Do Martians Recycle? 2009. (Illus.). 36p. pap. 16.99 *(978-1-4490-3749-9(6))* AuthorHouse.

Halls, Kelly Milner. Alien Investigation: Searching for the Truth about UFOs & Aliens. Spears, Rick. C., illus. 2015. (ENG.). 64p. (gr. 5-12). 34.65 *(978-1-4677-5987-8(2)*, Lerner Digital) Lerner Publishing Group.

—Alien Investigation: Searching for the Truth about UFOs & Aliens. Spears, Rick, illus. 2012. (Single Titles Ser.). (ENG.). 64p. (gr. 5-12). lib. bdg. 20.95 *(978-0-7613-6204-3(5)*, Millbrook Pr.) Lerner Publishing Group.

Herbst, Judith. Aliens. 2004. (Unexplained Ser.). (Illus.). 48p. (J). pap. 8.95 *(978-0-8225-2402-1(3)*, Lerner Pubns.); (ENG., (gr. 5-12). lib. bdg. 26.60 *(978-0-8225-0960-8(1))* Lerner Publishing Group.

Hile, Lori. Aliens & UFOs. King, Chris, illus. 2013. (Solving Mysteries with Science Ser.). (ENG.). 48p. (gr. 3-6). pap. 9.95 *(978-1-4109-5504-3(4))* Heinemann-Raintree.

—Aliens & UFOs. 2013. (Solving Mysteries with Science Ser.). (ENG.). 48p. (gr. 3-6). 29.99 *(978-1-4109-5498-5(6))* Heinemann-Raintree.

History Channel, History & Steinberg, Don. Ancient Aliens. 2015. (ENG., Illus.). 112p. (J). (gr. 3-7). 19.99 *(978-1-62672-064-0(9)*, 9781626720640) Roaring Brook Pr.

—The Young Investigator's Guide to Ancient Aliens. 2015. (ENG., Illus.). 112p. (J). (gr. 3-7). pap. 14.99 *(978-1-62672-063-3(0)*, 9781626720633) Roaring Brook Pr.

Hodge, Susie & Mason, Paul. Investigating UFOs & Aliens. 2010. (Extreme! Ser.). (ENG.). 32p. (gr. 3-4). pap. 47.70 *(978-1-4296-5115-8(6)*, Fact Finders) Capstone Press of Coughlan Cos.

Hunter, Nick. Have Aliens Visited Earth? 2016. (Top Secret! Ser.). (ENG., Illus.). 48p. (gr. 4-6). lib. bdg. 33.32 *(978-1-4109-8159-2(2))* Heinemann-Raintree.

Kallen, Stuart K. The search for extraterrestrial Life. 2011. (Extraterrestrial Life Ser.). (Illus.). 80p. (YA). (gr. 7-12). lib. bdg. 27.95 *(978-1-60152-171-2(5))* ReferencePoint Pr., Inc.

Kallio, Jamie. Aliens. 2015. (Unsolved Mysteries Ser.). (ENG.). 24p. (J). (gr. 1-4). 28.50 *(978-1-63407-068-3(2)*, 208903) Child's World, Inc., The.

Lynette, Rachel. Area 51. 2009. (Mysterious Encounters Ser.). (ENG., Illus.). 48p. (J). (gr. 4-8). lib. bdg. 29.00 *(978-0-7377-4410-1(3)*, LML02109-245411, Kidhaven) Cengage Gale.

Marcovitz, Hal. Aliens in Pop Culture. 2011. (Extraterrestrial Life Ser.). (ENG.). 80p. (YA). (gr. 7-12). lib. bdg. 27.95 *(978-1-60152-154-5(5))* ReferencePoint Pr., Inc.

McCollum, Sean. Handbook to UFOs, Crop Circles, & Alien Encounters. 2016. (Paranormal Handbooks Ser.). (ENG., Illus.). 32p. (gr. 3-4). lib. bdg. 27.99 *(978-1-5157-1309-8(1)*, Edge Bks.) Capstone Press of Coughlan Cos.

Miller, Joshua. The Extraterrestrial Compendium. 2011. (Illus.). 200p. (YA). 29.95 *(978-0-9828186-8-8(8))* Sea Lion Bks.

Murray, Laura K. Aliens. 2017. (Illus.). 24p. (J). *(978-1-60818-759-1(4)*, Creative Education) Creative Co., The.

Murray, Laura K. Are They Real?: Aliens. 2017. (Are They Real? Ser.). (ENG., Illus.). 24p. (J). (gr. 1-3). pap. 8.99 ***(978-1-62832-367-2(1)***, Creative Paperbacks) Creative Co., The.

Owen, Ruth. Aliens & Other Visitors. 2013. (Not near Normal: the Paranormal Ser.). 32p. (J). (gr. 3-8). lib. bdg. 26.60 *(978-1-61772-723-8(7))* Bearport Publishing Co., Inc.

Parks, Peggy J. Aliens. 2006. (Mysterious Encounters Ser.). (ENG., Illus.). 48p. (J). (gr. 3-7). lib. bdg. 27.50 *(978-0-7377-3518-5(X)*, Kidhaven) Cengage Gale.

Pipe, Jim. Aliens. 2013. (Twilight Realm Ser.). (Illus.). 32p. (J). (gr. 4-6). 26.60 *(978-1-4339-8747-2(3))*; pap. 10.50 *(978-1-4339-8748-9(1))* Stevens, Gareth Publishing LLLP. (Gareth Stevens Learning Library).

Pye, Michael & Dalley, Kirsten, eds. Ancient Secret Societies & Lost Knowledge, 01 vols., 1. 2016. (Ancient Secrets & Alien Gods Ser.). (ENG.). 224p. (YA). 38.25 *(978-1-5081-7100-3(9)*, Rosen Young Adult) Rosen Publishing Group, Inc., The.

Rooney, Anne. Alien Abduction. 2008. (Crabtree Contact Ser.). (ENG., Illus.). 32p. (J). (gr. 3-7). lib. bdg. *(978-0-7787-3762-9(4))* Crabtree Publishing Co.

—UFOs & Aliens. 2010. (Amazing Mysteries Ser.). (YA). (gr. 3-6). 28.50 *(978-1-59920-368-3(5))* Black Rabbit Bks.

Shaw-Russell, Susan. Create Your Own Aliens Sticker Activity Book. 2011. (Dover Little Activity Books Stickers Ser.). (ENG., Illus.). 4p. (J). (gr. k-3). 1.99 *(978-0-486-47225-6(6))* Dover Pubns., Inc.

Silverstein, Janna. Close Encounters with Aliens. (Unsolved Mysteries: the Secret Files Ser.). 48p. 2009. (gr. 5-8). 53.00 *(978-1-60854-693-0(4)*, Rosen Reference) 2005. (Illus.). (YA). (gr. 4-7). lib. bdg. 29.25 *(978-0-8239-3562-8(0))* Rosen Publishing Group, Inc., The.

Summers, Portia & Rau, Dana Meachen. Are Aliens Real? 2016. (I Want to Know Ser.). 32p. (J). pap. 10.52 *(978-0-7660-8228-1(8))* Enslow Pubs., Inc.

Tieck, Sarah. Aliens, 1 vol. 2015. (ENG., Illus.). 32p. (J). *(978-1-62403-763-4(1))* ABDO Publishing Co.

Walker, Kathryn. Mysteries of Alien Visitors & Abductions. 2008. (ENG., Illus.). 32p. (J). (gr. 3-7). pap. *(978-0-7787-4154-1(0))* Crabtree Publishing Co.

Whelon, Chuck. Alien Invasion! Mazes. 2010. (Dover Children's Activity Bks.). (ENG., Illus.). 48p. (J). (gr. k-3). pap. 4.99 *(978-0-486-47233-1(7))* Dover Pubns., Inc.

EXTRATERRESTRIAL BEINGS—FICTION

The Alien, 6 vols., Pack. (gr. 1-2). 25.00 *(978-0-7635-9192-2(0))* Rigby Education.

Alien at the Zoo, 6 vols. (Sunshinetm Ser.). 16p. (gr. k-18). 29.50 *(978-0-7802-5429-9(5))* Wright Group/McGraw-Hill.

Alien in Space. Date not set. (Illus.). (J). bds. 1.98 *(978-0-7525-9838-3(4))* Parragon, Inc.

The Alien Next Door. 2005. (J). audio, cd-rom 24.95 *(978-0-9771381-8-0(6))* Williams, Geoffrey T.

Alien Nine: Ultimate Collection, Vol. 3. 2003. (Illus.). 224p. pap. 15.95 *(978-1-58664-893-0(4)*, CMX 64203G, CPM Manga) Central Park Media Corp.

Aliens & Space. Date not set. (Illus.). 64p. (J). 2.98 *(978-1-4054-0446-4(9))* Parragon, Inc.

Aliens on the Lawn, 6 vols., Pack. (gr. 1-2). 25.00 *(978-0-7635-9126-7(2))* Rigby Education.

Allen, Cassandra R. Morty the Alien: The Beginnings... 2009. 16p. pap. 12.50 *(978-1-4389-7283-1(0))* AuthorHouse.

Allen, Elise & Conners, Daryle. Gabby Duran, Book 2 Gabby Duran: Troll Control. (Gabby Duran Ser.). (ENG.). (J). (gr. 3-7). 2017. 256p. pap. 7.99 ***(978-1-4847-2540-5(9))*** 2016. (Illus.). 240p. 16.99 *(978-1-4847-0936-8(5))* Hyperion Bks. for Children.

—Gabby Duran, Book 3 Gabby Duran: Multiple Mayhem. 2017. (Gabby Duran Ser.). (ENG.). 224p. (J). (gr. 3-7). 16.99 ***(978-1-4847-0937-5(3))*** Hyperion Bks. for Children.

—Troll Control. 2017. (Gabby Duran Ser.: 2). (J). lib. bdg. 18.40 ***(978-0-606-39970-8(4))*** Turtleback Bks.

Allen, Elise & Daryle Connors. Gabby Duran & the Unsittables. 2016. (Gabby Duran Ser.: 1). (J). lib. bdg. 18.40 *(978-0-606-39443-7(5))* Turtleback Bks.

Ambassador. 2014. (ENG., Illus.). 240p. (J). (gr. 3-7). 16.99 *(978-1-4424-9764-1(5)*, McElderry, Margaret K. Bks.) McElderry, Margaret K. Bks.

Anaya, Rudolfo. ChupaCabra & the Roswell UFO. 2008. (ENG.). 144p. (YA). (gr. 9-18). 9.95 *(978-0-8263-4469-4(0))* Univ. of New Mexico Pr.

Anderson, Dwayne. Partially Human. 2006. (YA). per. 12.00 *(978-0-9788612-0-9(5))* Capri Publishing.

Anderson, M. T. He Laughed with His Other Mouths. Cyrus, Kurt, illus. 2014. (Pals in Peril Tale Ser.). (ENG.). 304p. (J). (gr. 5-9). 17.99 *(978-1-4424-5110-0(6)*, Beach Lane Bks.) Beach Lane Bks.

Anderson, Matt & Hutchins, Eric. White Picket Fences: Red Scare TP: Red Scare TP. 2011. (Illus.). 104p. (J). pap. 12.99 *(978-1-934944-30-1(0))* Ape Entertainment.

Anderson, R. J. Quicksilver. 2013. (ENG.). 328p. (YA). (gr. 7-12). 17.95 *(978-0-7613-8799-2(4)*, Carolrhoda Lab™) Lerner Publishing Group.

—Ultraviolet. (ENG.). 312p. (YA). (gr. 7-12). 2013. pap. 9.95 *(978-1-4677-0914-9(X))* 2011. 17.95 *(978-0-7613-7408-4(6))* Lerner Publishing Group. (Carolrhoda Lab™).

Angleberger, Tom. Star Wars - Return of the Jedi: Beware the Power of the Dark Side! McCaig, Iain, illus. 2015. (ENG.). 432p. (J). (gr. 3-7). 17.99 *(978-1-4847-0913-9(6)*, Disney Lucasfilm Press) Disney Publishing Worldwide.

Anthony, David & David, Charles. Heroes A2Z #1: (Heroes a to Z): Alien Ice Cream. Blakeslee, Lys, illus. 2007. 128p. (J). pap. 4.99 *(978-0-9728461-8-9(2))* Sigil Publishing.

Apelian, Virginia. Aliens Celebrating CHRISTMAS. 2012. 30p. pap. 19.99 *(978-1-62419-384-2(6))* Salem Author Services.

Applegate, Katherine. The Capture. 2012. (Animorphs Ser.: 6). lib. bdg. 17.20 *(978-0-606-26194-4(X)*, Turtleback) Turtleback Bks.

Appleton, Victor. Tom Swift & the Visitor from Planet X. 2006. pap. *(978-1-4065-0913-7(2))* Dodo Pr.

Armentrout, Jennifer L. Lux - Beginnings. 2014. (Lux Novel Ser.: Bks. 1-2). (ENG.). 800p. (YA). (gr. 7-12). pap. 12.99 *(978-1-62266-448-1(5)*, 9781622664481); 19.99 *(978-1-62266-481-8(7)*, 9781622664818); pap. 12.99 *(978-1-62266-449-8(3)*, 9781622664498) Entangled Publishing, LLC.

—Obsidian. 2012. (Lux Novel Ser.: 1). (ENG.). 400p. (YA). pap. 9.99 *(978-1-62061-007-7(8)*, 9781620610077) Entangled Publishing, LLC.

—Onyx. 2012. (Lux Novel Ser.: 2). (ENG.). 416p. (YA). pap. 9.99 *(978-1-62061-011-4(6)*, 9781620610114) Entangled Publishing, LLC.

—Opal. 2012. (Lux Novel Ser.: 3). (ENG.). 452p. (YA). (gr. 9). pap. 9.99 *(978-1-62061-009-1(4)*, 9781620610091) Entangled Publishing, LLC.

—Opposition. (ENG.). 2013. (Lux Ser.: Bk. 5). (J). pap. 9.99 *(978-1-62266-026-1(9)*, Entangled Teen) 2014. (Lux Novel Ser.: 5). 500p. (YA). 19.99 *(978-1-62266-733-8(6)*, 9781622667338) 2014. (Lux Novel Ser.: 5). 500p. (YA). (gr. 7-12). pap. 11.99 *(978-1-62266-264-7(4)*, 9781622662647) Entangled Publishing, LLC.

—Origin. 2013. (ENG.). (Lux Ser.: Bk. 4). (J). pap. 9.99 *(978-1-62061-280-4(1))*; (Lux Novel Ser.: 4). 400p. (YA). (gr. 7-12). pap. 9.99 *(978-1-62266-075-9(7)*, 9781622660759) Entangled Publishing, LLC.

Arnold, Tedd. Green Wilma, Frog in Space. Arnold, Tedd, illus. 2009. (ENG., Illus.). 32p. (J). (gr. -1-3). 16.99 *(978-0-8037-2698-7(8)*, Dial Bks) Penguin Young Readers Group.

Aronson, Deborah. Dragons from Mars. Jack, Colin, illus. 2016. 32p. (J). (gr. -1-3). 17.99 *(978-0-06-236850-8(8))* HarperCollins Pubs.

Ashley, Elana. Splunkunio Splunkey Detective & Peacemaker: Case One: The Missing Friendship Bracelet. 2003. (ENG & SPA., Illus.). 32p. (J). 17.95 *(978-0-9744812-0-3(3))* Dream Image Pr., LLC.

—Splunkunio Splunkey Detective & Peacemaker Detective y Pacificador: Case One: The Missing Friendship Bracelet Caso Primero: El Brazalete de la Amistad Desaparecido. Nikolov, Stefan V., tr. Ashley, Elana, photos by. 2005. (SPA & ENG., Illus.). 32p. (J). (gr. k-3). 17.95 *(978-0-9744812-1-0(1))* Dream Image Pr., LLC.

Aslan, Austin. The Islands at the End of the World. 2015. (ENG., Illus.). 384p. (YA). (gr. 7). pap. 9.99 *(978-0-385-74403-4(X)*, Ember) Random Hse. Children's Bks.

Asquith, Ros. Letters from an Alien Schoolboy. 2013. (ENG., Illus.). 192p. (J). (gr. 1-5). 12.95 *(978-1-62087-536-0(5)*, 620536, Sky Pony Pr.) Skyhorse Publishing Co., Inc.

Bader, Bonnie. Go to Bed, Blue. Robertson, Michael, illus. 2014. (Penguin Young Readers, Level 1 Ser.). (ENG.). 32p. (J). (gr. k-1). pap. 3.99 *(978-0-448-48219-4(3)*, Penguin Young Readers) Penguin Young Readers Group.

—Play with Blue. Robertson, Michael, illus. 2013. (Penguin Young Readers, Level 1 Ser.). (ENG.). 32p. (J). (gr. k-1). mass mkt. 3.99 *(978-0-448-46254-7(0)*, Penguin Young Readers) Penguin Young Readers Group.

Balawajder, Thomas, et al. The Ultimate Homework Survival Guide: A Reality Horror Production. Wise, Noreen, ed. 2nd ed. 2003. (Illus.). 64p. (J). per. 6.95 *(978-1-58584-559-0(0))* Huckleberry Pr.

Ball, Nate. Alien in My Pocket: Radio Active. Pamintuan, Macky, illus. 2014. (Alien in My Pocket Ser.: 3). (ENG.). 144p. (J). (gr. 1-5). 15.99 *(978-0-06-231493-2(9))* HarperCollins Pubs.

—Alien in My Pocket - Blast Off! Pamintuan, Macky, illus. 2014. (Alien in My Pocket Ser.: 1). (ENG.). 160p. (J). (gr. 1-5). pap. 4.99 *(978-0-06-221623-6(6))* HarperCollins Pubs.

—Alien in My Pocket - The Science Unfair. Pamintuan, Macky, illus. 2014. (Alien in My Pocket Ser.: 2). (ENG.). 144p. (J). (gr. 1-5). pap. 4.99 *(978-0-06-221625-0(2))* HarperCollins Pubs.

—Alien in My Pocket #5: Ohm vs. Amp. Pamintuan, Macky, illus. 2015. (Alien in My Pocket Ser.: 5). (ENG.). 144p. (J). (gr. 1-5). 15.99 *(978-0-06-231489-5(0))* HarperCollins Pubs.

—Alien in My Pocket #6: Forces of Nature. Pamintuan, Macky, illus. 2015. (Alien in My Pocket Ser.: 6). (ENG.). 144p. (J). (gr. 1-5). pap. 4.99 *(978-0-06-221633-5(3))* HarperCollins Pubs.

—Alien in My Pocket #8: Space Invaders. Pamintuan, Macky, illus. 2016. (Alien in My Pocket Ser.: 8). 144p. (J). (gr. 1-5). pap. 4.99 *(978-0-06-237091-4(X))* HarperCollins Pubs.

—Alien in My Pocket: on Impact! Pamintuan, Macky, illus. 2014. (Alien in My Pocket Ser.: 4). (ENG.). 128p. (J). (gr. 1-5). pap. 4.99 *(978-0-06-221629-8(5))* HarperCollins Pubs.

—Blast Off! 2014. (Alien in My Pocket Ser.: 1). (J). lib. bdg. 14.75 *(978-0-606-35181-2(7))* Turtleback Bks.

—Forces of Nature. 2015. (Alien in My Pocket Ser.: 6). (J). lib. bdg. 14.75 *(978-0-606-37611-2(9))* Turtleback Bks.

—On Impact! 2014. (Alien in My Pocket Ser.: 4). (J). lib. bdg. 14.75 *(978-0-606-35952-8(4))* Turtleback Bks.

—Radio Active. 2014. (Alien in My Pocket Ser.: 3). (J). lib. bdg. 14.75 *(978-0-606-35349-6(6))* Turtleback Bks.

—The Science Unfair. Pamintuan, Macky, illus. 2014. (Alien in My Pocket Ser.: 2). (ENG.). 144p. (J). (gr. 1-5). 15.99 *(978-0-06-231494-9(7))* HarperCollins Pubs.

—The Science Unfair. 2014. (Alien in My Pocket Ser.: 2). (J). lib. bdg. 14.75 *(978-0-606-35182-9(5))* Turtleback Bks.

—Telescope Troubles. Pamintuan, Macky, illus. 2016. (Alien in My Pocket Ser.: 7). 144p. (J). (gr. 1-5). pap. 4.99 *(978-0-06-237088-4(X))* HarperCollins Pubs.

Baltazar, Art & Aureliani, Franco. The Mysterious Alien Menace!, 1 vol. 2014. (Superman Family Adventures Ser.). (ENG., Illus.). 32p. (gr. 1-2). 22.60 *(978-1-4342-6477-0(7))* Stone Arch Bks.

Baltazar, Art, et al. Hal Versus Atrocitus, 1 vol. Brizuela, Dario, illus. 2014. (Green Lantern: the Animated Ser.). (ENG.). 32p. (gr. 2-3). 22.60 *(978-1-4342-6481-7(5))* Stone Arch Bks.

—True Colors, 1 vol. Brizuela, Dario, illus. 2013. (Green Lantern: the Animated Ser.). (ENG.). 32p. (gr. 2-3). 22.60 *(978-1-4342-4795-7(3))* Stone Arch Bks.

Beaty, Andrea. Attack of the Fluffy Bunnies. 2012. (Fluffy Bunnies Ser.). (ENG.). 192p. (YA). (gr. 2-8). pap. 7.95 *(978-1-4197-0519-9(9)*, Amulet Bks.) Abrams, Inc.

—Fluffy Bunnies 2: The Schnoz of Doom. Santat, Dan, illus. (Fluffy Bunnies Ser.). (ENG.). (J). (gr. 3-7). 2016. 208p. pap. 7.95 *(978-1-4197-1942-4(4))* 2015. 192p. 12.95 *(978-1-4197-1051-3(6))* Abrams, Inc. (Amulet Bks.).

Beechen, Adam. Small Time, 1 vol. Barberi, Carlo & Wong, Walden, illus. 2013. (Justice League Unlimited Ser.). (ENG.). 32p. (gr. 2-3). 22.60 *(978-1-4342-4715-5(5))* Stone Arch Bks.

Benton, Jim. Howard Hubbins Half Hour Hero. 2008. (J). pap. 4.99 *(978-0-06-059774-0(7))* HarperCollins Pubs.

Bergens, Teri. Xerplek's Schmizzle. 2012. 44p. pap. 10.99 *(978-1-4575-1226-1(2))* Dog Ear Publishing, LLC.

Berry, Julie. The Amaranth Enchantment. (ENG.). (YA). (gr. 5-8). 2010. 336p. pap. 7.99 *(978-1-59990-449-8(7)*, 9781599904498) 2009. 320p. 16.99 *(978-1-59990-334-7(2)*, 9781599903347) Bloomsbury Publishing USA. (Bloomsbury USA Childrens).

Biro, Val. Gumdrop & the Martians. (Illus.). 32p. (J). *(978-0-340-71485-0(9))* Hodder & Stoughton.

Bissett, Josie. Boogie Monster. Atteberry, Kevan J., illus. 2011. 36p. (J). (gr. -1-3). 16.95 *(978-1-935414-10-0(0))* Compendium, Inc., Publishing & Communications.

Blacker, Terence. The Angel Factory. 2012. (ENG., Illus.). 224p. (J). (gr. 5-9). pap. 10.99 *(978-0-689-86413-1(2)*, Simon & Schuster/Paula Wiseman Bks.) Simon & Schuster/Paula Wiseman Bks.

Blackman, Haden & Caldwell, Ben. Star Wars: Clone Wars Adventures, 1 vol. 2012. (Star Wars Digests Ser.). (ENG., Illus.). 96p. (J). (gr. 4-7). 27.07 *(978-1-59961-904-0(0))* Spotlight.

Blackman, Haden & The Fillbach Brothers. Star Wars: Clone Wars Adventures, 1 vol. 2012. (Star Wars Digests Ser.). (ENG., Illus.). 96p. (J). (gr. 4-7). 27.07 *(978-1-59961-905-7(9))*; 27.07 *(978-1-59961-906-4(7))* Spotlight.

Bodeen, S. A. Found. 2017. (Shipwreck Island Ser.: 4). (ENG.). 160p. (J). 16.99 *(978-1-250-02783-2(7)*, 9781250027832) Feiwel & Friends.

Bradman, Tony. Alien. 2012. (Stoke Books Titles Ser.). 64p. (J). (gr. 5-8). pap. 7.95 *(978-1-78112-026-2(9))*; lib. bdg. 22.60 *(978-1-78112-025-5(0))* Stoke Bks.

Breathed, Berkeley. Mars Needs Moms! Breathed, Berkeley, illus. 2007. (ENG., Illus.). 40p. (J). (gr. k-3). 17.99 *(978-0-399-24736-1(X)*, Philomel Bks.) Penguin Young Readers Group.

Brennan, Herbie. Zartog's Remote. Layton, Neal, illus. 2003. (Middle Grade Fiction Ser.). 96p. (J). (gr. 3-6). 14.95 *(978-1-57505-507-7(4)*, Carolrhoda Bks.) Lerner Publishing Group.

Brezenoff, Steve. The Outlaw from Outer Space: An Interactive Mystery Adventure. Calo, Marcos, illus. 2017. (You Choose Stories: Field Trip Mysteries Ser.). (ENG.). 112p. (gr. 3-7). lib. bdg. 32.65 *(978-1-4965-2644-1(9))* Stone Arch Bks.

—The Sleeper, 1 vol. Percival, Tom, illus. 2012. (Ravens Pass Ser.). (ENG.). 96p. (gr. 2-3). pap. 6.15 *(978-1-4342-4211-2(0))*; lib. bdg. 25.32 *(978-1-4342-3792-7(3))* Stone Arch Bks.

British Broadcasting Corporation Children's Books Staff & Richards, Justin. The American Adventures. 2016. (ENG.). 192p. (J). 14.99 *(978-1-4059-2872-4(7)*, 9781405928724) Penguin Bks., Ltd. GBR. Dist: Diamond Comic Distributors, Inc.

Brown, Billowby. A Wibble Named Wally. 2012. 28p. pap. 19.99 *(978-1-4772-6694-6(1))* AuthorHouse.

Brown, Jennifer. Life on Mars. 2014. (ENG.). 240p. (YA). (gr. 3-6). 16.99 *(978-1-61963-252-3(7)*, 9781619632523, Bloomsbury USA Childrens) Bloomsbury Publishing USA.

Budhos, Marina. Ask Me No Questions. 2007. (ENG.). 192p. (YA). (gr. 7-12). pap. 10.99 *(978-1-4169-4920-6(8)*, Atheneum Bks. for Young Readers) Simon & Schuster Children's Publishing.

Bunker, Lisa. Felix Yz. 2017. (ENG.). 288p. (J). (gr. 5-9). 16.99 *(978-0-425-28850-4(1)*, Viking Books for Young Readers) Penguin Young Readers Group.

Butterworth, Nick. Q Pootle 5. Butterworth, Nick, illus. 2009. (ENG., Illus.). 32p. (J). (gr. -1-k). pap. 11.95 *(978-0-00-717235-1(4)*, HarperCollins Children's Bks.) HarperCollins Pubs. Ltd. GBR. Dist: HarperCollins Pubs.

Caldwell, Denise. Our Alien Friends. 2004. 35p. pap. 24.95 *(978-1-4137-1066-3(2))* PublishAmerica, Inc.

Carney, John & Carney, Veta. Teddy's Journey. 2009. 37p. pap. 15.98 *(978-0-557-15269-8(0))* Lulu Pr., Inc.

Carter, Darlene. Little Spit-N-Gasser Finds New Friends. 2009. 16p. pap. 8.90 *(978-1-4389-5168-3(X))* AuthorHouse.

Cazet, Denys. Minnie & Moo & the Potato from Planet X, 4 bks. 2004. (Readalongs for Beginning Readers Ser.). (Illus.). 46p. (J). (gr. -1-2). pap. 31.95 incl. audio compact disk *(978-1-59112-881-6(1))* Live Oak Media.

Cazet, Denys, reader. Minnie & Moo & the Potato from Planet X. 2004. (Readalongs for Beginning Readers Ser.). (Illus.). (J). (gr. -1-3). 28.95 incl. audio compact disk *(978-1-59112-880-9(3))*; 25.95 incl. audio *(978-1-59112-258-6(9))*; pap. 29.95 incl. audio *(978-1-59112-259-3(7))* Live Oak Media.

Chaban, Liz. Jules of the World: The California Caper. 2012. 42p. pap. 18.99 *(978-1-105-92248-0(0))* Lulu Pr., Inc.

Chartrand, Kenneth. A Martian's Dream of Christmas. 2006. 48p. pap. 16.95 *(978-1-4241-4123-4(0))* PublishAmerica, Inc.

Chase, Jeffrey Scott. Andy the Alien. 2006. (J). pap. 16.00 *(978-0-8059-7081-4(9))* Dorrance Publishing Co., Inc.

Childress, Jamie. Galactic Treasure Hunt: Lost City of Atlantis. Braun, Chris, illus. 2015. (ENG.). 100p. (J). pap. 4.99 *(978-1-931882-62-0(2))* Adventures Unlimited Pr.

—Galactic Treasure Hunt: Lost City of the Moon. Braun, Chris, illus. 2015. (ENG.). 100p. (J). (gr. -1-7). per. 4.99 *(978-1-931882-45-3(2))* Adventures Unlimited Pr.

Chiodo, Stephen & Strain, Jim. Chiodo Bros. ' Alien Xmas. Chiodo, Charles, illus. 2015. (ENG.). 100p. (J). (gr. -1). pap. 17.95 *(978-0-9729388-4-6(2))* Baby Tattoo Bks.

Clarke, Carol Page. The Cuddly Mogs. 2006. (Illus.). 72p. pap. *(978-1-84401-620-4(X))* Athena Pr.

Clevenger, Lee. IncrediBoy: Be Careful What You Wish. 2004. 267p. (J). pap. 12.95 *(978-0-9764052-0-7(2))* Thomas Max Publishing.

Connely, Chris L. & Vaughan, Mark. An Alien from Earth. 2003. 175p. per. 9.95 *(978-0-9745544-0-2(5))* Lewis Lynn Bks.

Coville, Bruce. Aliens Ate My Homework. Coville, Katherine, illus. 2008. (Rod Allbright & the Galactic Patrol Ser.). 179p. (gr. 3-7). 17.00 *(978-0-7569-8466-3(1))* Perfection Learning Corp.

—Aliens Ate My Homework: Rod Allbright & the Galactic Patrol. Coville, Katherine, illus. 2007. (Rod Allbright & the Galactic Patrol Ser.). (ENG.). 192p. (J). (gr. 3-7). pap. 7.99 *(978-1-4169-3883-5(4)*, Aladdin) Simon & Schuster Children's Publishing.

—Aliens Stole My Body. Coville, Katherine, illus. 2008. (Rod Allbright & the Galactic Patrol Ser.). (ENG.). 240p. (J). (gr. 3-7). pap. 7.99 *(978-1-4169-5359-3(0)*, Simon & Schuster/Paula Wiseman Bks.) Simon & Schuster/Paula Wiseman Bks.

—I Left My Sneakers in Dimension X. Coville, Katherine, illus. 2007. (Rod Allbright & the Galactic Patrol Ser.). (ENG.). 192p. (J). (gr. 3-7). pap. 7.99 *(978-1-4169-3882-8(6)*, Simon & Schuster/Paula Wiseman Bks.) Simon & Schuster/Paula Wiseman Bks.

—I Lost My Grandfather's Brain. unabr. ed. 2004. (I Was a Sixth Grade Alien Ser.: Vol. 3). 160p. (J). (gr. 3-6). pap. 29.00 incl. audio *(978-0-8072-8385-1(1)*, YA180SP, Listening Library) Random Hse. Audio Publishing Group.

—I Was a Sixth Grade Alien. (I Was a Sixth Grade Alien Ser.: Vol. 1). 170p. (J). (gr. 4-6). pap. 3.99 *(978-0-8072-8202-1(2))*; 2004. (gr. 3-6). pap. 29.00 incl. audio *(978-0-8072-8201-4(4)*, S YA 138 SP) Random Hse. Audio Publishing Group. (Listening Library).

—The Monsters of Morley Manor. 2003. (Madcap Adventures Ser.). 223p. (gr. 3-7). 17.00 *(978-0-7569-1627-5(5))* Perfection Learning Corp.

—The Monsters of Morley Manor: A Madcap Adventure. 2003. (ENG.). 240p. (J). (gr. 2-5). pap. 7.99 *(978-0-15-204705-4(0))* Houghton Mifflin Harcourt Publishing Co.

—My Teacher Fried My Brains. Pierard, John, illus. 2014. (My Teacher Bks.: 2). (ENG.). 176p. (J). (gr. 3-7). 17.99 *(978-1-4814-0431-0(8)*, Aladdin) Simon & Schuster Children's Publishing.

—My Teacher Is an Alien. unabr. ed. 2004. (My Teacher Is an Alien Ser.: Bk. 1). 123p. (J). (gr. 3-6). pap. 29.00 incl. audio *(978-0-8072-8029-4(1)*, S YA 971 SP, Listening Library) Random Hse. Audio Publishing Group.

—My Teacher Is an Alien. Wimmer, Mike, illus. 2005. (My Teacher Bks.: 1). (ENG.). 160p. (J). (gr. 3-7). pap. 6.99 *(978-1-4169-0334-5(8)*, Aladdin) Simon & Schuster Children's Publishing.

—My Teacher Is an Alien. Wimmer, Mike, illus. 2014. (My Teacher Bks.: 1). (ENG.). 160p. (J). (gr. 3-7). 17.99 *(978-1-4814-0430-3(X)*, Simon & Schuster/Paula Wiseman Bks.) Simon & Schuster/Paula Wiseman Bks.

—The Search for Snout. Coville, Katherine, illus. 2007. (Rod Allbright & the Galactic Patrol Ser.). (ENG.). 224p. (J). (gr. 3-7). pap. 7.99 *(978-1-4169-4980-0(1)*, Simon & Schuster/Paula Wiseman Bks.) Simon & Schuster/Paula Wiseman Bks.

—There's an Alien in My Classroom! (Illus.). 201p. (J). pap. 8.95 *(978-0-340-73634-0(8))* Hodder & Stoughton GBR. Dist: Trafalgar Square Publishing.

Crewe, Megan. A Sky Unbroken, 0 vols. 2015. (Earth & Sky Trilogy Ser.: 3). (ENG., Illus.). 347p. (J). (gr. 7-12). pap. 9.99 *(978-1-5039-4657-6(6)*, 9781503946576, Skyscape) Amazon Publishing.

Crider. Mike Gonzo & the Sewer Monster. 2012. (ENG., Illus.). 144p. (J). (gr. 3-7). pap. 8.99 *(978-1-4424-8127-5(7)*, Simon & Schuster/Paula Wiseman Bks.) Simon & Schuster/Paula Wiseman Bks.

—Mike Gonzo & the UFO Terror. 2012. (ENG., Illus.). 128p. (J). (gr. 3-7). pap. 7.99 *(978-1-4424-8129-9(3)*, Simon & Schuster/Paula Wiseman Bks.) Simon & Schuster/Paula Wiseman Bks.

Crisp, Dan, illus. Five Little Men in a Flying Saucer. 2005. (Classic Books with Holes Board Book Ser.). (ENG.). 14p. (J). bds. *(978-1-904550-58-7(4))* Child's Play International Ltd.

Cullimore, Stan. Alien Swap. Schon, Nick, illus. 2005. (ENG.). 24p. (J). lib. bdg. 23.65 *(978-1-59646-744-6(4))* Dingles & Co.

Czerneda, Julie E. This Gulf of Time & Stars: Reunification #1. 2015. (Reunification Ser.: 1). (ENG.). 464p. (gr. 12). 25.95 *(978-0-7564-0869-5(5)*, DAW) DAW.

Dahl, Michael. Alien Snow, 1 vol. Glass House Graphics Staff, illus. 2011. (Good vs Evil Ser.). (ENG.). 48p. (gr. 1-2). pap. 6.29 *(978-1-4342-3444-5(4)*, Good vs Evil) Stone Arch Bks.

—Brain Invaders. Catling, Andy, illus. 2016. (Igor's Lab of Fear Ser.). (ENG.). 40p. (gr. 1-3). lib. bdg. 23.99 *(978-1-4965-3526-9(X))* Stone Arch Bks.

Denman, K. L. Destination Human, 1 vol. 2013. (Orca Currents Ser.). (ENG.). 136p. (J). (gr. 5-9). pap. 9.95 *(978-1-4598-0371-8(X))*; lib. bdg. 16.95 *(978-1-4598-0372-5(8))* Orca Bk. Pubs. USA.

Depken, Kristen L. Chase's Space Case. 2016. (Step into Reading Level 1 Ser.). lib. bdg. 14.75 *(978-0-606-38480-3(4))* Turtleback Bks.

—Chase's Space Case (Paw Patrol) Jackson, Mike, illus. 2016. (Step into Reading Ser.). (ENG.). 24p. (J). (gr. -1-1). 4.99 *(978-0-553-53886-1(1)*, Random Hse. Bks. for Young Readers) Random Hse. Children's Bks.

Diggs, Dylan. Palladium: Second Contact. 2006. (J). mass mkt. 3.80 *(978-1-886366-13-8(6)*, 5,000) Sights Productions.

Disney Book Group. World of Reading Star Wars Chaos at the Castle. 2016. (ENG.). 32p. (J). (gr. 1-3). pap. 3.99 *(978-1-4847-7410-6(8)*, Disney Lucasfilm Press) Disney Publishing Worldwide.

Disney Book Group & LucasFilm Press Staff. Finn & Rey Escape! Rood, Brian, illus. 2015. (ENG.). 24p. (J). (gr. 1-3). pap. 4.99 *(978-1-4847-0479-0(7))* Disney Pr.

Disney Book Group Staff. Star Wars: Ewoks Join the Fight, Level 1. 2015. (ENG.). 32p. (J). (gr. 1-3). pap. 3.99 *(978-1-4847-0548-3(3)*, Disney Lucasfilm Press) Disney Publishing Worldwide.

—Star Wars: Return of the Jedi Read-Along Storybook & CD. 2015. (Read-Along Storybook & CD Ser.). (ENG.). 32p. (J). (gr. 1-3). pap. 6.99 *(978-1-4847-0685-5(4)*, Disney Lucasfilm Press) Disney Publishing Worldwide.

Disney Book Group Staff & Schaefer, Elizabeth A. Hera's Phantom Flight, Level 2. 2015. (World of Reading Ser.). (ENG.). 32p. (J). (gr. 1-3). pap. 3.99 *(978-1-4847-0465-3(7)*, Disney Lucasfilm Press) Disney Publishing Worldwide.

Disney Book Group Staff & Siglain, Michael. Star Wars - Use the Force, Level 2. Disney Book Group Staff et al, illus. 2015. (World of Reading Ser.). (ENG.). 32p. (J). (gr. 1-3). pap. 3.99 *(978-1-4847-0464-6(9))* Disney Pr.

Disney Book Group Staff & Thornton, Randy. Star Wars: a New Hope Read-Along Storybook & CD. Rood, Brian, illus. 2015. (Read-Along Storybook & CD Ser.). (ENG.). 32p. (J). (gr. 1-3). pap. 6.99 *(978-1-4847-0667-1(6)*, Disney Lucasfilm Press) Disney Publishing Worldwide.

Disney Book Group Staff, et al. Star Wars Rebels Always Bet on Chopper: Level 1. 2015. (World of Reading Ser.). (ENG., Illus.). 32p. (J). (gr. 1-3). pap. 3.99 *(978-1-4847-0560-5(2)*, Disney Lucasfilm Press) Disney Publishing Worldwide.

Disney Press Editors. Star Wars: Escape from Darth Vader. 2014. (Star Wars: World of Reading Ser.). (J). lib. bdg. 13.55 *(978-0-606-35924-5(9))* Turtleback Bks.

Disney Storybook Artists Staff, ed. Disney Lilo & Stitch Drawing Book & Kit. 2008. 32p. pap. 10.95 *(978-1-60058-103-8(X))* Quarto Publishing Group USA.

DiTerlizzi, Tony. A Hero for WondLa, 13 vols. 2012. (Search for Wondra Ser.: 2). (J). 110.75 *(978-1-4640-3934-8(8))* Recorded Bks., Inc.

—A Hero for WondLa. DiTerlizzi, Tony, illus. (Search for WondLa Ser.: 2). (ENG., Illus.). (J). (gr. 5). 2013. 480p. pap. 8.99 *(978-1-4169-8313-2(9))* 2012. 464p. 17.99 *(978-1-4169-8312-5(0))* Simon & Schuster Bks. For Young Readers. (Simon & Schuster Bks. For Young Readers).

—The Search for WondLa. DiTerlizzi, Tony, illus. (Search for WondLa Ser.: 1). (ENG., Illus.). (J). (gr. 5). 2012. 512p. pap. 12.99 *(978-1-4169-8311-8(2))* 2010. 496p. 17.99 *(978-1-4169-8310-1(4))* Simon & Schuster Bks. For Young Readers. (Simon & Schuster Bks. For Young Readers).

DiTerlizzi, Tony & DiTerlizzi, Angela. Big Fun! DiTerlizzi, Tony, illus. 2009. (Adventure of Meno Ser.: 1). (ENG., Illus.). 48p. (J). (gr. -1-k). 9.99 *(978-1-4169-7148-1(3)*, Simon & Schuster Bks. For Young Readers) Simon & Schuster Bks. For Young Readers.

—Uh-Oh Sick! DiTerlizzi, Tony, illus. 2010. (Adventure of Meno Ser.: 4). (ENG., Illus.). 52p. (J). (gr. -1-k). 9.99 *(978-1-4169-7153-5(X)*, Simon & Schuster Bks. For Young Readers) Simon & Schuster Bks. For Young Readers.

—Wet Friend! DiTerlizzi, Tony, illus. 2009. (Adventure of Meno Ser.: 2). (ENG., Illus.). 48p. (J). (gr. -1-k). 9.99 *(978-1-4169-7149-8(1)*, Simon & Schuster Bks. For Young Readers) Simon & Schuster Bks. For Young Readers.

—Yummy Trip! DiTerlizzi, Tony, illus. 2010. (Adventure of Meno Ser.: 3). (ENG., Illus.). 48p. (J). (gr. -1-k). 9.99 *(978-1-4169-7150-4(5)*, Simon & Schuster Bks. For Young Readers) Simon & Schuster Bks. For Young Readers.

Divine, Miss Jill. The alien who came to Tea. 2009. (Illus.). 88p. pap. 10.50 *(978-1-4092-8010-1(1))* Lulu Pr., Inc.

Dixon, Andy. Star Quest. Brooks, Felicity, ed. Harris, Nick, illus. 2006. (Usborne Fantasy Puzzle Bks.). 32p. (YA). (gr. 7). lib. bdg. 15.99 *(978-1-58086-906-5(8)*, Usborne) EDC Publishing.

Dolan, Elys. Nuts in Space. Dolan, Elys, illus. 2015. (ENG., Illus.). 32p. (J). (gr. k-3). 17.99 *(978-0-7636-7609-4(8)*, Nosy Crow) Candlewick Pr.

Dorling Kindersley Publishing Staff & Fentiman, David. Fight the Empire. 2015. (DK Readers Ser.). (ENG.). 64p. (J). (gr. 2-4). 14.99 *(978-1-4654-1988-0(8)*, DK Children) Dorling Kindersley Publishing, Inc.

Dorman, Brandon. Hoolie & the Hooligans, Book 1: The Alien That Ate My Socks. Dorman, Brandon, illus. 2016. (Hoolie & the Hooligans Ser.: 1). (ENG., Illus.). 224p. (J). (gr. 2-7). 13.99 *(978-1-62972-222-1(7)*, Shadow Mountain) Shadow Mountain Publishing.

Douglas, Atom. Mathew's Space Ship. Douglas, Atom, . 2007. (Illus.). 32p. (J). 6.50 *(978-0-9798316-0-7(1))* JaxPublishing.net.

Durk, Jim, illus. Rabbid of the Sea. 2015. (Rabbids Invasion Ser.). (ENG.). 40p. (J). (gr. 1-3). pap. 3.99 *(978-1-4814-3545-1(0)*, Simon Spotlight) Simon Spotlight.

Eason, Alethea. Hungry. 2007. 197p. (J). (gr. 5-18). lib. bdg. 16.89 *(978-0-06-082555-3(3)*, Eos) HarperCollins Pubs.

Edwards, Jean Pearce. Little Jean's War. 2008. (Illus.). 208p. pap. 14.49 *(978-1-4343-9133-9(7))* AuthorHouse.

Elish, Dan. The Attack of the Frozen Woodchucks. Call, Greg, illus. 2008. (ENG.). 256p. (J). (gr. 3-7). 16.99 *(978-0-06-113870-6(3)*, Geringer, Laura Book) HarperCollins Pubs.

Elliott, David. Wuv Bunnies from Outers Pace. Long, Ethan, illus. 2008. (ENG.). (J). 108p. (gr. 4-7). pap. 6.95 *(978-0-8234-2183-1(X))*; 112p. (gr. 2-4). 16.95 *(978-0-8234-1902-9(9))* Holiday Hse., Inc.

ELLIS, B. J. Mrs. Morgan's Adventures with Aliens. 2008. 249p. 29.50 *(978-0-557-00095-1(5))* Lulu Pr., Inc.

Emerson, Kevin. The Fellowship for Alien Detection. 2013. (ENG.). 432p. (J). (gr. 3-7). 16.99 *(978-0-06-207185-9(8)*, Waldon Pond Pr.) HarperCollins Pubs.

England, Paul. Knights of Bonalla. 2010. (Illus.). 260p. pap. 14.49 *(978-1-4490-9444-7(9))* AuthorHouse.

Epstein, Adam Jay & Jacobson, Andrew. Starbounders. McClellan, David, illus. 2013. (Starbounders Ser.: 1). (ENG.). 320p. (J). (gr. 3-7). 16.99 *(978-0-06-212022-9(0))* HarperCollins Pubs.

—Starbounders Vol. 2: Rebellion. 2014. (Starbounders Ser.: 2). (ENG.). 304p. (J). (gr. 3-7). 16.99 *(978-0-06-212027-4(1))* HarperCollins Pubs.

Falkner, Brian. The Assault (Recon Team Angel #1) 2013. (Recon Team Angel Ser.: 1). (ENG.). 304p. (YA). (gr. 7). pap. 9.99 *(978-0-375-87190-0(X)*, Ember) Random Hse. Children's Bks.

—Task Force. 2013. (Recon Team Angel Ser.). (ENG., Illus.). 288p. (YA). (gr. 7). 17.99 *(978-0-449-81299-0(5)*, Random Hse. Bks. for Young Readers) Random Hse. Children's Bks.

—Task Force (Recon Team Angel #2) 2014. (Recon Team Angel Ser.). (ENG.). 416p. (YA). (gr. 7). pap. 9.99 *(978-0-449-81302-7(9)*, Ember) Random Hse. Children's Bks.

Farrell, Robert E., Jr. Alien Log. 2004. 250p. per. 12.95 *(978-1-59196-523-7(3))* Instant Pub.

Fearing, Mark & Rummel, Tim. Earthling! 2012. (ENG., Illus.). 248p. (J). (gr. 3-7). 22.99 *(978-0-8118-7106-8(1))* Chronicle Bks. LLC.

—Earthling. 2012. (ENG., Illus.). 248p. (J). (gr. 3-7). pap. 12.99 *(978-1-4521-0906-0(0))* Chronicle Bks. LLC.

Fentiman, David. Finn's Mission. 2016. (Star Wars DK Readers Level 3 Ser.). lib. bdg. 13.55 *(978-0-606-38710-1(2))* Turtleback Bks.

Fields, Bryan W. Lunchbox & the Aliens. Atteberry, Kevan, illus. 2009. (Froonga Ser.). (ENG.). 208p. (J). (gr. 4-7). pap. 11.99 *(978-0-312-56115-4(6)*, 9780312561154) Square Fish.

Fillbach Brothers. Star Wars: Clone Wars Adventures, 1 vol. 2013. (Star Wars Digests Set 2 Ser.). (ENG.). 80p. (J). (gr. 4-8). lib. bdg. 27.07 *(978-1-61479-059-4(0))*; lib. bdg. 27.07 *(978-1-61479-058-7(2))* ABDO Publishing Co. (Essential Library).

Fillbach, Brothers & The Fillbach Brothers. Star Wars: Clone Wars Adventures, 1 vol. 2012. (Star Wars Digests Ser.). (ENG., Illus.). (J). (gr. 4-7). 88p. 27.07 *(978-1-59961-909-5(1))*; 96p. 27.07 *(978-1-59961-907-1(5))* Spotlight.

Fontes, Justine & Fontes, Ron. Casebook: UFOs and/or Alien Encounter. 2009. (Top Secret Graphica Mysteries Ser.). (Illus.). 48p. (YA). (gr. 2-6). 29.25 *(978-1-60754-603-0(5))*; pap. 11.75 *(978-1-60754-604-7(3))* Windmill Bks.

Fosgitt, Jay P. Little Green Men. 2010. (ENG., Illus.). 100p. (YA). pap. 9.95 *(978-1-936340-01-9(1)*, 9781936340019) Ape Entertainment.

—Little Green Men: Small Package, Big Fun! GN: Small Package, Big Fun! GN. 2012. (ENG., Illus.). 48p. pap. 6.95 *(978-1-936340-63-7(1)*, 9781936340637) Ape Entertainment.

Freedman, Claire. Aliens in Underpants Save the World. Cort, Ben, illus. 2012. (Underpants Bks.). (ENG.). 32p. (J). (gr. -1-2). 17.99 *(978-1-4424-2768-6(X)*, Simon & Schuster/Paula Wiseman Bks.) Simon & Schuster/Paula Wiseman Bks.

—Aliens Love Dinopants. Cort, Ben, illus. 2016. (Underpants Bks.). (ENG.). 32p. (J). (gr. -1-2). 17.99 *(978-1-4814-6736-0(0)*, Aladdin) Simon & Schuster Children's Publishing.

—Aliens Love Panta Claus. Cort, Ben, illus. 2011. (Underpants Bks.). (ENG.). 32p. (J). (gr. -1-2). 16.99 *(978-1-4424-2830-0(9)*, Simon & Schuster/Paula Wiseman Bks.) Simon & Schuster/Paula Wiseman Bks.

French, Vivian. If I Were an Alien. Williams, Lisa, illus. 2009. (Get Set Readers Ser.). 32p. (J). (gr. -1-2). lib. bdg. 22.60 *(978-1-60754-267-4(6))* Windmill Bks.

Ghislain, Gary. How I Stole Johnny Depp's Alien Girlfriend. 2011. (ENG., Illus.). 208p. (YA). (gr. 7-17). 16.99 *(978-0-8118-7460-1(5))* Chronicle Bks. LLC.

Gibbs, Stuart. Space Case. 2015. (Moon Base Alpha Ser.). (ENG., Illus.). 368p. (J). (gr. 3-7). pap. 7.99 *(978-1-4424-9487-9(5)*, Simon & Schuster Bks. For Young Readers) Simon & Schuster Bks. For Young Readers.

—Space Case. 2015. (Moon Base Alpha Ser.: 1). lib. bdg. 18.40 *(978-0-606-37883-3(9))* Turtleback Bks.

—Spaced Out. (Moon Base Alpha Ser.). (ENG.). (J). (gr. 3-7). 2017. 368p. pap. 7.99 *(978-1-4814-2337-3(1))* 2016. (Illus.). 352p. 17.99 *(978-1-4814-2336-6(3))* Simon & Schuster Bks. For Young Readers. (Simon & Schuster Bks. For Young Readers).

—Spaced Out. 2017. (Moon Base Alpha Ser.: 2). lib. bdg. 18.40 ***(978-0-606-39762-9(0))*** Turtleback Bks.

Glanville, K. L. 2108: Eyes Open. 2012. (ENG.). 280p. (YA). pap. 12.99 *(978-1-61222-210-3(2))* Luminations Media Group, Inc.

Golden Books Staff. Sponge in Space! (SpongeBob SquarePants) Martinez, Heather, illus. 2012. (Little Golden Book Ser.). (ENG.). 24p. (J). (gr. k-k). 4.99

(978-0-307-92990-7(6), Golden Bks.) Random Hse. Children's Bks.

Goodman, Alison. Singing the Dogstar Blues. 2008. 240p. (YA). *(978-0-7322-8863-1(0))* HarperCollins Pubs. Australia.

Greenburg, Dan. Just Add Water... & Scream! Davis, Jack E., illus. 2004. (Zack Files Ser.). 56p. lib. bdg. 15.00 *(978-0-7569-2239-9(9))* Perfection Learning Corp.

Greenburg, Dan & National Geographic Learning Staff. Just Add Water... & Scream!, 29 vols. Davis, Jack E., illus. 2003. (Zack Files Ser.: 29). (ENG.). 64p. (J). (gr. 2-5). mass mkt. 4.99 *(978-0-448-42887-1(3),* Grosset & Dunlap) Penguin Young Readers Group.

Gregar, Steve. Al the Alien. 2004. 23p. pap. 14.98 *(978-1-4116-1149-8(7))* Lulu Pr., Inc.

Grey, Allan. Alienology. Steer, Dugald A., ed. Carrell, Douglas, illus. 2010. (Ologies Ser.: 10). (ENG.). 32p. (J). (gr. 3-7). 21.99 *(978-0-7636-4565-6(6))* Candlewick Pr.

Gudeon, Adam. Peep & Zeep. 2017. (I Like to Read(r) Ser.). (ENG.). 24p. (J). (gr. -1-3). 14.95 *(978-0-8234-3674-3(8))* Holiday Hse., Inc.

—Peeper & Zeep. 2017. (I Like to Read(r) Ser.). (ENG.). 24p. (J). (gr. -1-3). 6.99 *(978-0-8234-3779-5(5))* Holiday Hse., Inc.

Gutman, Dan. Funny Boy Meets the Airsick Alien from Andromeda. Dykes, John S., illus. 2012. (Funny Boy Ser.). (ENG.). 136p. (J). (gr. 2-5). pap. 10.99 *(978-1-4532-9527-4(5))* Open Road Integrated Media, Inc.

—Funny Boy Versus the Bubble-Brained Barbers from the Big Bang. Dietz, Mike, illus. 2012. (Funny Boy Ser.). (ENG.). 144p. (J). (gr. 2-5). pap. 6.99 *(978-1-4532-9532-8(1))* Open Road Integrated Media, Inc.

—Mr. Cooper Is Super! Paillot, Jim, illus. 2015. (My Weirdest School Ser.: 1). (ENG.). 112p. (J). (gr. 1-5). pap. 4.99 *(978-0-06-228421-1(5))* HarperCollins Pubs.

—Mr. Cooper Is Super! Paillot, Jim, illus. 2015. (My Weirdest School Ser.: 1). (J). lib. bdg. 14.75 *(978-0-606-36482-9(X))* Turtleback Bks.

Haber, Karen. Crossing Infinity. 2011. (ENG.). 256p. (J). (gr. -1-12). pap. 9.95 *(978-1-59687-411-4(2))* IBks., Inc.

Haddix, Margaret Peterson. Children of Refuge. 2017. (Children of Exile Ser.: 2). (ENG., Illus.). 272p. (J). (gr. 5). 17.99 ***(978-1-4424-5006-6(1)***, Simon & Schuster Bks. For Young Readers) Simon & Schuster Bks. For Young Readers.

Haddon, Mark. Boom! 2011. (ENG.). 208p. (J). (gr. 3-7). 7.99 *(978-0-385-75224-4(5),* Yearling) Random Hse. Children's Bks.

Hadland, W. Into the Night. 2010. 312p. (gr. 4-6). pap. 19.13 *(978-1-4251-4187-5(0))* Trafford Publishing.

Haladay, Max. Max Gets Mad. 2006. (Neighborhood Readers Ser.). (ENG.). 8p. (gr. 1-3). pap. 5.15 *(978-1-4042-6811-1(1),* Rosen Classroom) Rosen Publishing Group, Inc., The.

Hale, Nathan. One Trick Pony. 2017. (ENG., Illus.). 128p. (J). (gr. 3-7). 14.95 *(978-1-4197-2128-1(3),* Amulet Bks.) Abrams, Inc.

Hansen, Lynne. Reckless Revolution. 2007. (YA). *(978-1-4114-9672-9(8),* Spark Publishing Group) Sterling Publishing Co., Inc.

—Shades of Blue & Gray. 2007. (YA). pap. *(978-1-4114-9674-3(4),* Spark Publishing Group) Sterling Publishing Co., Inc.

—A Time for Witches. 2007. (YA). *(978-1-4114-9671-2(X),* Spark Publishing Group) Sterling Publishing Co., Inc.

Harkrader, Lisa. No Place Like Space: Kindness. Warrick, Jessica, illus. 2017. (How to Be an Earthling (r) Ser.: 5). (ENG.). 64p. (J). (gr. 1-3). lib. bdg. 22.65 *(978-1-57565-843-8(7))* Kane Press, Inc.

Harper, Charise Mericle. Alien Encounter. Harper, Charise Mericle, illus. 2014. (Sasquatch & Aliens Ser.: 1). (ENG., Illus.). 208p. (J). (gr. 2-5). 12.99 *(978-0-8050-9621-7(3),* 9780805096217, Holt, Henry & Co. Bks. For Young Readers) Holt, Henry & Co.

—Super Sasquatch Showdown. Harper, Charise Mericle, illus. 2015. (Sasquatch & Aliens Ser.: 2). (ENG., Illus.). 176p. (J). (gr. 2-5). 13.99 *(978-0-8050-9622-4(1),* 9780805096224, Holt, Henry & Co. Bks. For Young Readers) Holt, Henry & Co.

HarperCollins Publishers Ltd. Staff, et al. James Cameron's Avatar. movie tie-in ed. 2009. (James Cameron's Avatar Ser.). (ENG., Illus.). 48p. (J). (gr. -1-2). pap. 7.99 *(978-0-06-180124-2(0),* HarperFestival) HarperCollins Pubs.

Harrison, Zac. Crash Landing, 1 vol. 2013. (Hyperspace High Ser.). (ENG.). 288p. (gr. 4-8). 27.32 *(978-1-4342-6306-3(1))* Stone Arch Bks.

—Frozen Enemies, 1 vol. 2013. (Hyperspace High Ser.). (ENG.). 288p. (gr. 4-8). 27.32 *(978-1-4342-6307-0(X))* Stone Arch Bks.

—Galactic Battle, 1 vol. 2014. (Hyperspace High Ser.). (ENG., Illus.). 288p. (gr. 4-8). 27.32 *(978-1-4342-6569-2(2))* Stone Arch Bks.

—Hyperspace High, 1 vol. (Hyperspace High Ser.). (ENG.). 288p. (gr. 4-8). 2014. 54.64 *(978-1-4342-8935-3(4))* 2013. 109.28 *(978-1-4342-6314-8(2))* 2013. pap. 35.80 *(978-1-4342-9039-7(5))* Stone Arch Bks.

—Robot Warriors, 1 vol. 2013. (Hyperspace High Ser.). (ENG.). 288p. (gr. 4-8). pap. 8.95 *(978-1-4342-6312-4(6));* 27.32 *(978-1-4342-6308-7(8))* Stone Arch Bks.

—Space Plague, 1 vol. 2014. (Hyperspace High Ser.). (ENG., Illus.). 288p. (gr. 4-8). 27.32 *(978-1-4342-6568-5(4))* Stone Arch Bks.

—Warlord's Revenge, 1 vol. 2013. (Hyperspace High Ser.). (ENG.). 288p. (gr. 4-8). pap. 8.95 *(978-1-4342-6313-1(4));* 27.32 *(978-1-4342-6309-4(6))* Stone Arch Bks.

Hatton, L. J. Sing down the Stars, 0 vols. 2015. (Sing down the Stars Ser.: 1). (ENG.). 380p. (YA). (gr. 8-13). pap. 9.99 *(978-1-5039-4656-9(8),* 9781503946569, Skyscape) Amazon Publishing.

Hawking, Lucy & Hawking, Stephen W. George's Cosmic Treasure Hunt. Parsons, Garry, illus. 2011. (George's Secret Key Ser.). (ENG.). 352p. (J). (gr. 3-7). pap. 11.99 *(978-1-4424-2175-2(4),* Simon & Schuster Bks. For Young Readers) Simon & Schuster Bks. For Young Readers.

Hawking, Stephen W. & Hawking, Lucy. George's Cosmic Treasure Hunt. Parsons, Garry, illus. 2009. (George's Secret Key Ser.). (ENG.). 320p. (J). (gr. 3-7). 19.99 *(978-1-4169-8671-3(5),* Simon & Schuster Bks. For Young Readers) Simon & Schuster Bks. For Young Readers.

Hayes, Malcolm. The Dreamcatchers. 2006. 282p. pap. 20.14 *(978-1-4120-8320-1(6))* Trafford Publishing.

Hayes, Vicki C. Out of Gas, 1 vol. 2015. (Red Rhino Ser.). (ENG.). 68p. (J). (gr. 4-6). pap. 7.95 *(978-1-62250-917-1(X))* Saddleback Educational Publishing, Inc.

Hill, Nick. Carlton Casey: Alien Incident. 2007. 100p. per. 9.95 *(978-1-59800-310-9(0))* Outskirts Pr., Inc.

Hoena, Blake A. Ack's New Pet, 1 vol. Harpster, Steve, illus. 2014. (Eek & Ack Early Chapter Bks.). (ENG.). 32p. (gr. k-2). lib. bdg. 22.65 *(978-1-4342-6406-0(8))* Stone Arch Bks.

—The Big Mistake, 1 vol. Harpster, Steve, illus. 2014. (Eek & Ack Early Chapter Bks.). (ENG.). 32p. (gr. k-2). lib. bdg. 22.65 *(978-1-4342-6408-4(4))* Stone Arch Bks.

—The Black Hole Report, 1 vol. Harpster, Steve, illus. 2014. (Eek & Ack Early Chapter Bks.). (ENG.). 32p. (gr. k-2). lib. bdg. 22.65 *(978-1-4342-6409-1(2))* Stone Arch Bks.

—Eek & Ack vs the Wolfman, 1 vol. Harpster, Steve, illus. 2009. (Eek & Ack Ser.). (ENG.). 40p. (gr. 1-3). lib. bdg. 23.99 *(978-1-4342-1189-7(4),* Graphic Sparks) Stone Arch Bks.

—Eek Discovers Earth, 1 vol. Harpster, Steve, illus. 2014. (Eek & Ack Early Chapter Bks.). (ENG.). 32p. (gr. k-2). lib. bdg. 22.65 *(978-1-4342-6407-7(6))* Stone Arch Bks.

—The Puzzling Pluto Plot: Eek & Ack, 1 vol. Harpster, Steve, illus. 2008. (Graphic Sparks Ser.). (ENG.). 40p. (gr. 1-3). pap. 5.95 *(978-1-4342-0502-5(9),* Graphic Sparks) Stone Arch Bks.

Hoes, Holly. When Aliens Took over the World. 2012. 44p. pap. 21.99 *(978-1-4797-4870-9(6))* Xlibris Corp.

Hoffman, Nina Kiriki. Meeting. 2011. (Magic Next Door Ser.). (ENG.). 336p. (J). (gr. 5). E-Book *(978-1-101-52934-8(2),* Viking Books for Young Readers) Penguin Young Readers Group.

Homer, Elizabeth. Peter Wolfe & the Scepter of Myleah. 2008. 212p. pap. 13.95 *(978-1-60693-197-4(0),* Eloquent Bks.) Strategic Book Publishing & Rights Agency (SBPRA).

Hopper, Ada. The Sky Is Falling. Ricks, Sam, illus. 2016. (DATA Set Ser.: bk.3). (ENG.). 128p. (J). (gr. k-4). pap. 5.99 *(978-1-4814-6309-6(8),* Little Simon) Little Simon.

Horvath, Joshua W. Slinky My Alien Friend. 2011. 16p. pap. 8.32 *(978-1-4634-3540-0(1))* AuthorHouse.

Houran, Lori Haskins. Alien in the Outfield: Perseverance. Warrick, Jessica, illus. 2017. (How to Be an Earthling (r) Ser.: 6). (ENG.). 64p. (gr. 1-3). 34.65 ***(978-1-57565-852-0(6))*** Kane Press, Inc.

—Earth's Got Talent! Warrick, Jessica, illus. 2016. (How to Be an Earthling (r) Ser.: 4). (ENG.). 64p. (gr. 1-3). lib. bdg. 22.65 *(978-1-57565-827-8(5))* Kane Press, Inc.

—Earth's Got Talent! Courage. Warrick, Jessica, illus. 2016. (How to Be an Earthling (r) Ser.: 4). (ENG.). 64p. (gr. 1-3). 34.65 *(978-1-57565-829-2(1))* Kane Press, Inc.

—Greetings, Sharkling! Warrick, Jessica, illus. 2016. (How to Be an Earthling (r) Ser.: 2). (ENG.). 64p. (gr. 1-3). 22.65 *(978-1-57565-821-6(6))* Kane Press, Inc.

—Greetings, Sharkling! Honesty. Warrick, Jessica, illus. 2016. (How to Be an Earthling (r) Ser.: 2). (ENG.). 64p. (gr. 1-3). 34.65 *(978-1-57565-823-0(2))* Kane Press, Inc.

—Money Doesn't Grow on Mars: Self-Control. Warrick, Jessica, illus. 2017. (How to Be an Earthling (r) Ser.: 8). (ENG.). 64p. (gr. 1-3). 34.65 ***(978-1-57565-854-4(2))***; (J). lib. bdg. 22.65 *(978-1-57565-846-9(1))* Kane Press, Inc.

Houran, Lori Haskins. Money Doesn't Grow on Mars: Self-Control. Warrick, Jessica, illus. 2017. (How to Be an Earthling (r) Ser.: 8). (ENG.). 64p. (J). (gr. 1-3). 6.99 *(978-1-57565-850-6(X))* Kane Press, Inc.

Howe, James. Invasion of the Mind Swappers from Asteroid 6! 2004. (Tales from the House of Bunnicula Ser.). 112p. (J). (gr. 3-6). pap. 17.00 incl. audio *(978-1-4000-8633-7(7),* Listening Library) Random Hse. Audio Publishing Group.

—Invasion of the Mind Swappers from Asteroid 6! Helquist, Brett, illus. 2003. (Tales from the House of Bunnicula Ser.). 89p. (J). (gr. 2-5). 11.65 *(978-0-7569-2814-8(1))* Perfection Learning Corp.

—Invasion of the Mind Swappers from Asteroid 6! Helquist, Brett, illus. 2003. (Tales from the House of Bunnicula Ser.: 2). (ENG.). 112p. (J). (gr. 2-5). pap. 5.99 *(978-0-689-83950-4(2),* Simon & Schuster/Paula Wiseman Bks.) Simon & Schuster/Paula Wiseman Bks.

Huggins-Cooper, Lynn. Alien Invaders (Invasores Extraterrestres) de La Vega, Eida, tr. Leick, Bonnie, illus. 2005. (SPA & ENG.). 32p. (J). (gr. 4-7). 7.95 *(978-0-9741992-7-6(3),* 626999, Raven Tree Pr.,Csi) Continental Sales, Inc.

—Alien Invaders/Invasores Extraterrestres. de la Vega, Eida, tr. from ENG. Leick, Bonnie, illus. 2005.Tr. of Invasores Extraterrestres. (SPA & ENG.). 32p. (J). (gr. 4-7). 16.95 *(978-0-9724973-9-8(0),* 626999, Raven Tree Pr.,Csi) Continental Sales, Inc.

Hughes, Monica. The Golden Aquarians. 2009. (ENG.). 192p. (YA). (gr. 7-7). pap. 9.99 *(978-1-4424-0223-2(7),* Simon & Schuster Bks. For Young Readers) Simon & Schuster Bks. For Young Readers.

Hughes, Suz. The Night the Stars Went Out. 2016. (Fiction Picture Bks.). (ENG.). 32p. (gr. 1-2). lib. bdg. 23.32 *(978-1-5158-0214-3(0),* Fiction Picture Bks.) Picture Window Bks.

I Thought This Was a Bear Book. 2015. (ENG., Illus.). 32p. (J). (gr. -1-2). 17.99 *(978-1-4424-6307-3(4),* Aladdin) Simon & Schuster Children's Publishing.

Iacobucci, Vincent. The Little Book All about Fluguls. 2006. (Illus.). (J). *(978-0-9779390-0-8(6))* Flugul Pubng.

James, Hollis. Alien Attack! Random House Staff & Spaziante, Patrick, illus. 2015. (Step into Reading Ser.). (ENG.). 24p. (J). (gr. -1-1). 4.99 *(978-0-553-52286-0(8),* Random Hse. Bks. for Young Readers) Random Hse. Children's Bks.

Jansen, Patty. The Far Horizon. 2012. 176p. pap. *(978-0-9872009-4-5(1))* Capricornica Pubns.

Jeffers, Oliver. The Way Back Home. Jeffers, Oliver, illus. 2008. (ENG., Illus.). 32p. (J). (gr. -1-3). 17.99 *(978-0-399-25074-3(3),* Philomel Bks.) Penguin Young Readers Group.

Johnson, Shane L., illus. Attack of the Zombie Rabbids. 2016. (Rabbids Invasion Ser.). (ENG.). 40p. (J). (gr. 1-3). pap. 3.99 *(978-1-4814-6066-8(8),* Simon Spotlight) Simon Spotlight.

—The Chickens & the Eggs. 2014. (Rabbids Invasion Ser.). (ENG.). 40p. (J). (gr. 1-3). pap. 3.99 *(978-1-4814-0042-8(8),* Simon Spotlight) Simon Spotlight.

Johnson, Shane L. & Mawhinney, Art, illus. The Deep Freeze. 2014. (Rabbids Invasion Ser.). (ENG.). 40p. (J). (gr. 1-3). pap. 3.99 *(978-1-4814-0045-9(2),* Simon Spotlight) Simon Spotlight.

Johnston, Tony. Hanging Out. DiTerlizzi, Tony, illus. 2003. (Alien & Possum Ser.). 48p. (J). 11.65 *(978-0-7569-1544-5(9))* Perfection Learning Corp.

Jolley, Dan. Alien Adventure on Planet J. Wendt, Matt, illus. 2008. (Twisted Journeys (r) Ser.: 8). (ENG.). 112p. (J). (gr. 4-7). 27.93 *(978-0-8225-6998-5(1),* Graphic Universe™) Lerner Publishing Group.

—Attack of the Mutant Meteors. Witt, David, illus. 2010. (Twisted Journeys (r) Ser.: 14). (ENG.). 112p. (J). (gr. 4-7). pap. 7.95 *(978-0-8225-9255-6(X),* Graphic Universe™); lib. bdg. 27.93 *(978-0-8225-9249-5(5))* Lerner Publishing Group.

Jones, Carrie. Flying. 2016. (Flying Ser.: 1). (ENG.). 256p. (YA). 17.99 *(978-0-7653-3657-6(X),* 9780765336576, Tor Teen) Doherty, Tom Assocs., LLC.

Judge, Malcolm. Jonny Jakes Investigates the Hamburgers of Doom. Brown, Alan, illus. 2016. (Middle-Grade Novels Ser.). (ENG.). 240p. (gr. 4-7). lib. bdg. 26.65 *(978-1-4965-2678-6(3))* Stone Arch Bks.

Jung, Mike. Unidentified Suburban Object. (ENG.). 272p. (J). (gr. 3-7). 2017. pap. 6.99 ***(978-0-545-78227-2(9))*** 2016. 16.99 *(978-0-545-78226-5(0),* Levine, Arthur A. Bks.) Scholastic, Inc.

Jury, Walter & Fine, Sarah. Burn. 2015. (ENG.). 352p. (YA). (gr. 7). bds. 17.99 *(978-0-399-16068-4(X),* G.P. Putnam's Sons Books for Young Readers) Penguin Young Readers Group.

Kade, Stacey. Project Paper Doll the Trials. 2016. (Project Paper Doll Ser.). (ENG.). 336p. (YA). (gr. 7-12). pap. 9.99 *(978-1-4231-9474-3(8))* Hyperion Bks. for Children.

—The Trials. 2015. (Project Paper Doll Ser.). (ENG., Illus.). 336p. (YA). (gr. 7-12). 17.99 *(978-1-4231-8463-8(7))* Hyperion Bks. for Children.

Kann, Victoria. Pinkalicious & Planet Pink. Kann, Victoria, illus. 2016. (I Can Read Level 1 Ser.). (Illus.). 32p. (J). (gr. -1-3). pap. 3.99 *(978-0-06-241068-9(7))* HarperCollins Pubs.

Kaplan, Arie. The New Kid from Planet Glorf, 1 vol. Bradley, Jessica, illus. 2013. (Comics Land Ser.). (ENG.). 32p. (gr. k-2). 7.95 *(978-1-4342-4272-3(2));* lib. bdg. 25.32 *(978-1-4342-4032-3(0))* Stone Arch Bks.

Keats, Israel. Alien Invasion. 2017. (Level Up Ser.). (ENG.). (J). (gr. 6-12). 120p. pap. 7.99 ***(978-1-5124-5356-0(0))***; lib. bdg. 26.65 ***(978-1-5124-3984-7(3))*** Lerner Publishing Group. (Darby Creek).

Kennedy, Mike. Thrill of the Hunt. 2004. (ENG., Illus.). 96p. pap. 6.95 *(978-1-59307-257-5(0))* Dark Horse Comics.

Kennedy Tosten, S. Troy's Amazing Universe: A for Aliens. 2005. 124p. pap. 13.95 *(978-1-59113-672-9(5))* Booklocker.com, Inc.

Khanlu, Nancy Yousefian. A Trip into Space. 2012. 16p. pap. 7.95 *(978-1-4525-0399-8(0))* Get Published.

Kirby, Matthew J. The Arctic Code. 2015. (Dark Gravity Sequence Ser.: 1). (ENG.). 336p. (J). (gr. 3-7). 16.99 *(978-0-06-222487-3(5))* HarperCollins Pubs.

Klein, Joel & Klein, Abby. The Night I Saved the Universe: From the Files of the Galactic Police Department. 2009. 126p. (J). *(978-0-545-12933-6(8))* Scholastic, Inc.

Kline, Trish. Earth Academy 7, Purple Book One: Journey to Earth. 2003. (J). per. 7.50 *(978-0-9717234-7-4(8))* Ghost Hunter Productions.

—Earth Academy 7, Red Book One: The Aliens Are Coming! 2003. (J). per. 7.50 *(978-0-9717234-4-3(3))* Ghost Hunter Productions.

Kloepfer, John. Galaxy's Most Wanted. Edwards, Nick, illus. 2014. (Galaxy's Most Wanted Ser.: 1). (ENG.). 224p. (J). (gr. 3-7). 12.99 *(978-0-06-223101-7(4))* HarperCollins Pubs.

—Galaxy's Most Wanted #2: into the Dorkness. Edwards, Nick, illus. 2016. (Galaxy's Most Wanted Ser.: 2). 272p. (J). (gr. 3-7). pap. 6.99 *(978-0-06-223109-3(X))* HarperCollins Pubs.

—Galaxy's Most Wanted #3: Starship Bloopers. Edwards, Nick, illus. 2016. (Galaxy's Most Wanted Ser.: 3). 240p. (J). (gr. 3-7). 12.99 *(978-0-06-223106-2(5))* HarperCollins Pubs.

—Into the Dorkness. Edwards, Nick, illus. 2015. (Galaxy's Most Wanted Ser.: 2). (ENG.). 256p. (J). (gr. 3-7). 12.99 *(978-0-06-223104-8(9))* HarperCollins Pubs.

Knox, Regina. The Clintonville Abduction. 2007. 108p. per. 19.95 *(978-1-4241-2996-6(6))* PublishAmerica, Inc.

Kochalka, James. The Glorkian Warrior & the Mustache of Destiny. 2016. (Glorkian Warrior Ser.: 3). (ENG., Illus.). 128p. (J). pap. 14.99 *(978-1-62672-022-0(3),* 9781626720220, First Second Bks.) Roaring Brook Pr.

—The Glorkian Warrior Delivers a Pizza. Kochalka, James, illus. 2014. (Glorkian Warrior Ser.: 1). (ENG., Illus.). 112p. (J). (gr. k-4). pap. 12.99 *(978-1-59643-917-7(3),* 9781596439177, First Second Bks.) Roaring Brook Pr.

Kogge, Michael. Star Wars Rebels: Battle to the End. 2015. (Star Wars Saga Chapter Book Ser.). (ENG.). 144p. (J). (gr. 1-3). pap. 5.99 *(978-1-4847-0487-5(8),* Disney Lucasfilm Press) Disney Publishing Worldwide.

Kooi, Jason. Hunter's Legacy: Cause. 2008. 256p. pap. 16.95 *(978-0-595-52910-0(0))* iUniverse, Inc.

Korba, Joanna & Benchmark Education Co., LLC. Who Are You? Fabbri, Daniele, illus. 2014. (Text Connections Ser.). (J). (gr. 3). *(978-1-4509-9664-8(7))* Benchmark Education Co.

Krokos, Dan. The Black Stars. 2015. (ENG., Illus.). 304p. (J). (gr. 3-8). pap. 21.99 *(978-0-7653-7668-8(7),* 9780765376688, Starscape) Doherty, Tom Assocs., LLC.

Krulik, Nancy. Don't Sneeze! 2017. (Kid from Planet Z Ser.: 2). lib. bdg. 16.00 ***(978-0-606-40108-1(3))*** Turtleback Bks.

Krull, Kathleen. How to Trick or Treat in Outer Space. Brewer, Paul, illus. 2004. (ENG.). 32p. (J). (gr. k-3). tchr. ed. 16.95 *(978-0-8234-1844-2(8))* Holiday Hse., Inc.

Landers, Melissa. Invaded. 2015. (Alienated Ser.). (ENG.). 368p. (YA). (gr. 7-12). 17.99 *(978-1-4231-6949-9(2))* Hyperion Bks. for Children.

Lee, Fonda. Exo. 2017. (ENG.). 384p. (J). (gr. 7). 17.99 *(978-0-545-93343-8(9),* Scholastic Pr.) Scholastic, Inc.

Leicht, Martin & Neal, Isla. Mothership. 2012. (Ever-Expanding Universe Ser.: 1). (ENG., Illus.). 320p. (YA). (gr. 9). 16.99 *(978-1-4424-2960-4(7),* Simon & Schuster Bks. For Young Readers) Simon & Schuster Bks. For Young Readers.

Levine, Caroline Anne. Jay Grows an Alien. 2007. 73p. (J). (gr. 5-13). pap. 13.95 *(978-1-931282-29-1(3))* Autism Asperger Publishing Co.

Lewman, David. Case File #1 First Contact. Spaziante, Patrick, illus. 2014. (Rabbids Invasion Ser.). (ENG.). 96p. (J). (gr. 2-5). pap. 4.99 *(978-1-4814-0037-4(1),* Simon Spotlight) Simon Spotlight.

—Case File #4 Rabbids Go Viral. Spaziante, Patrick, illus. 2015. (Rabbids Invasion Ser.). (ENG.). 96p. (J). (gr. 2-5). 16.99 *(978-1-4814-2766-1(0),* Simon Spotlight) Simon Spotlight.

—Case File #7 Red Carpet Rabbids. Johnson, Shane L., illus. 2016. (Rabbids Invasion Ser.). (ENG.). 96p. (J). (gr. 2-5). 16.99 *(978-1-4814-5253-3(3),* Simon Spotlight) Simon Spotlight.

—New Developments, No. 2. Spaziante, Patrick, illus. 2014. (Rabbids Invasion Ser.). (ENG.). 96p. (J). (gr. 2-5). pap. 4.99 *(978-1-4814-0204-0(8),* Simon Spotlight) Simon Spotlight.

—Red Carpet Rabbids. Johnson, Shane L., illus. 2016. (Rabbids Invasion Ser.). (ENG.). 96p. (J). (gr. 2-5). pap. 5.99 *(978-1-4814-5252-6(5),* Simon Spotlight) Simon Spotlight.

Lipsyte, Robert. The Twin Powers. 2014. (ENG.). 256p. (J). (gr. 5-7). 16.99 *(978-0-547-97335-7(7))* Houghton Mifflin Harcourt Publishing Co.

Lo, Malinda. Adaptation. 2013. (ENG.). 416p. (YA). (gr. 10-17). pap. 10.00 *(978-0-316-19798-4(X))* Little, Brown Bks. for Young Readers.

—Inheritance. 2014. (ENG.). 480p. (YA). (gr. 10-17). pap. 25.99 *(978-0-316-19799-1(8))* Little, Brown Bks. for Young Readers.

Locke, Terry. Spencer Hurley & the Aliens: Book One: the Abduction. Hucks, Robin, ed. 2008. (Spencer Hurley & the Aliens Ser.: 1). (ENG., Illus.). 256p. (J). 12.95 *(978-0-9786940-0-5(7),* SHAB1V1E1CB) Dream Workshop Publishing Co., LLC, The.

—Spencer Hurley & the Aliens: Book One: the Abduction, Vol. 1. Hucks, Robin, ed. Locke, Terry, illus. 2008. (Spencer Hurley & the Aliens Ser.: 1). (Illus.). 256p. (J). per. 8.99 *(978-0-9786940-1-2(5))* Dream Workshop Publishing Co., LLC, The.

Lofficier, Randy & Lofficier, Jean-Marc. Robonocchio. Pijuán Aragón, Miren, tr. Martiniere, Stephan, illus. 2004. (SPA.). 128p. (YA). per. 14.95 *(978-1-932983-25-8(2),* Black Coat Pr.) HollywoodComics.com, LLC.

—Robonocchio. Martiniere, Stephan, illus. 2004. (FRE.). 128p. (YA). per. 14.95 *(978-1-932983-04-3(X),* Black Coat Pr.) HollywoodComics.com, LLC.

Lore, Pittacus. The Fate of Ten. 2015. 399p. (YA). *(978-0-06-242751-9(2)); (978-0-06-242452-5(1))* Harper & Row Ltd.

—The Fate of Ten. (Lorien Legacies Ser.: 6). (YA). (gr. 9). 2016. 432p. pap. 10.99 *(978-0-06-219476-3(3))* 2015. (ENG.). 416p. 18.99 *(978-0-06-219475-6(5))* HarperCollins Pubs.

—The Fate of Ten. 2016. (Lorien Legacies Ser.: 6). (YA). lib. bdg. 20.85 *(978-0-606-38760-6(9))* Turtleback Bks.

—I Am Number Four. (YA). (gr. 9). 2016. (Lorien Legacies: the Lost Files Ser.). 416p. pap. 9.99 *(978-0-06-238771-4(5))* 2011. (Lorien Legacies Ser.: 1). (ENG.). 496p. pap. 9.99 *(978-0-06-196957-7(5))* 2010. (Lorien Legacies Ser.: 1). (ENG.). 448p. 17.99 *(978-0-06-196955-3(9))* 2011. (Lorien Legacies Ser.: 1). (ENG.). 496p. pap. 9.99 *(978-0-06-211655-0(X))* 2011. (Lorien Legacies Ser.: 1). (ENG.). 480p. 17.99 *(978-0-06-202624-8(0))* HarperCollins Pubs.

—I Am Number Four. 2009. (Lorien Legacies Ser.: Bk. 1). 11.04 *(978-0-7848-3715-3(5),* Everbind) Marco Bk. Co.

—I Am Number Four. 2011. (I Am Number Four Ser.: Vol. 1). (ENG.). 440p. (gr. 9-12). 20.00 *(978-1-61383-207-3(9))* Perfection Learning Corp.

—I Am Number Four. 2011. (Lorien Legacies Ser.: 1). (YA). lib. bdg. 20.85 *(978-0-606-23545-7(0),* Turtleback) Turtleback Bks.

—I Am Number Four: The Lost Files: Rebel Allies. 2015. (Lorien Legacies: the Lost Files Ser.). (ENG.). 416p. (YA). (gr. 9). pap. 9.99 *(978-0-06-236404-3(9))* HarperCollins Pubs.

—I Am Number Four: The Lost Files: Secret Histories. 2013. (Lorien Legacies: the Lost Files Ser.). (ENG.). 416p. (YA). (gr. 9). pap. 9.99 *(978-0-06-222367-8(4))* HarperCollins Pubs.

—The Legacies. 2012. (Lorien Legacies: the Lost Files Ser.). (YA). lib. bdg. 20.85 *(978-0-606-26874-5(X),* Turtleback) Turtleback Bks.

—The Power of Six. (Lorien Legacies Ser.: 2). (ENG.). (YA). (gr. 9). 2012. 448p. pap. 9.99 *(978-0-06-197457-1(9))* 2011. 416p. 17.99 *(978-0-06-197455-7(2))* HarperCollins Pubs.

—The Power of Six. 2012. (Lorien Legacies Ser.: 2). (YA). lib. bdg. 20.85 *(978-0-606-26289-7(X),* Turtleback) Turtleback Bks.

—The Revenge of Seven. 2014. 371p. (J). *(978-0-06-236719-8(6))* Harper & Row Ltd.

—The Revenge of Seven. (Lorien Legacies Ser.: Bk. 5). (ENG.). 416p. 2015. (YA). (gr. 9). pap. 9.99 *(978-0-06-219473-2(9))* 2014. (J). 17.99 *(978-0-06-219472-5(0))* HarperCollins Pubs.

—The Revenge of Seven. 2015. (Lorien Legacies Ser.: 5). 415p. lib. bdg. 20.85 *(978-0-606-36981-7(3))* Turtleback Bks.

—The Rise of Nine. (Lorien Legacies Ser.: 3). (ENG.). 416p. (YA). (gr. 9). 2013. pap. 9.99 *(978-0-06-197460-1(9))* 2012. 17.99 *(978-0-06-197458-8(7))* HarperCollins Pubs.

—The Rise of Nine. 2013. (Lorien Legacies Ser.: 3). (YA). lib. bdg. 20.85 *(978-0-606-31830-3(5),* Turtleback) Turtleback Bks.

—Secret Histories. 2013. (Lorien Legacies: the Lost Files Ser.). (YA). lib. bdg. 20.85 *(978-0-606-31823-5(2),* Turtleback) Turtleback Bks.

Lore, Pittacus. United As One. 2017. (Lorien Legacies Ser.: 7). (ENG.). (YA). (gr. 9). lib. bdg. 20.85 ***(978-0-606-40055-8(9))*** Turtleback Bks.

Lucas Film Book Group & Simonson, Louise. A New Hope: The Rise of a Hero. Simonson, Walter, illus. 2017. (ENG.). 48p. (J). (gr. 1-3). 10.99 *(978-1-4847-9933-8(X),* Disney Lucasfilm Press) Disney Publishing Worldwide.

Luthardt, Kevin. When Edgar Met Cecil, 1 vol. Luthardt, Kevin, illus. 2013. (ENG., Illus.). 32p. (J). (gr. -1-3). 15.95 *(978-1-56145-706-9(X))* Peachtree Pubs.

Luzzatto, Caroline. Interplanetary Avenger. 2005. (ENG., Illus.). 128p. (J). (gr. 3-7). 16.95 *(978-0-8234-1933-3(9))* Holiday Hse., Inc.

Lyga, Barry. Archvillain. 2010. (Archvillain Ser.: 1). (ENG.). 192p. (J). (gr. 3-7). 16.99 *(978-0-545-19649-9(3)*, Scholastic Pr.) Scholastic, Inc.

Ma, Jyoti & Devi, Chandra. Sparkling Together: Starbright & His Earthling Friends. 2004. (ENG., Illus.). 96p. (J). pap. 19.95 *(978-0-932040-54-1(3)*, 9780932040541) Integral Yoga Pubns.

Maberry, Jonathan. The Orphan Army. 2015. (Nightsiders Ser.: 1). (ENG., Illus.). 400p. (J). (gr. 3-7). 16.99 *(978-1-4814-1575-0(1)*, Simon & Schuster Bks. For Young Readers) Simon & Schuster Bks. For Young Readers.

—The Orphan Army. 2016. (Nightsiders Ser.: 1). lib. bdg. 18.40 *(978-0-606-38959-4(8))* Turtleback Bks.

—Vault of Shadows. (Nightsiders Ser.: 2). (ENG.). 464p. (J). (gr. 3-7). 2017. pap. 8.99 *(978-1-4814-1579-8(4))* 2016. (Illus.). 16.99 *(978-1-4814-1578-1(6))* Simon & Schuster Bks. For Young Readers. (Simon & Schuster Bks. For Young Readers).

Marr, Andrew. Born in the Darkest Time of Year: Stories for the Season of the Christ Child. 2004. 180p. (J). pap. 13.95 *(978-0-595-32633-4(1))* iUniverse, Inc.

Marrero Laurano, Edward A. Aliens & Angels: Secrets & Mysteries. 2011. 48p. pap. 8.95 *(978-1-4620-6122-8(2))* iUniverse, Inc.

Marsh, Carole. Dear Alien: The Little Green Man Mystery. 2007. (Postcard Mysteries Ser.). (Illus.). 115p. (J). (gr. 2-9). 14.95 *(978-0-635-06397-7(2))*; per. 5.99 *(978-0-635-06341-0(7))* Gallopade International. (Marsh, Carole Family CD-Rom).

Martin, Justin McCory. The Planet Without Pronouns. Lee, Jared, illus. 2004. (Grammar Tales Ser.). (ENG.). 16p. (J). (gr. 3-7). pap. 3.25 *(978-0-439-45820-7(X))* Scholastic, Inc.

Martin, K. F. Qwuedeviv Crew 52: We Come with Peas. 2013. 132p. (J). pap. 8.95 *(978-1-4787-0612-0(0))* Outskirts Pr., Inc.

Marvel & McCann, Jim. Guardians of the Galaxy, Vol. 2. 2017. (ENG.). 176p. (J). (gr. 3-7). pap. 6.99 *(978-0-316-27165-3(9))* Little, Brown Bks. for Young Readers.

Mather, Daniel, illus. Case File #3 the Accidental Accomplice. 2014. (Rabbids Invasion Ser.: 3). (ENG.). 96p. (J). (gr. 2-5). pap. 4.99 *(978-1-4814-1720-4(7)*, Simon Spotlight) Simon Spotlight.

Matson, Erik. Robobattlepets - Home Invasion. 2012. 144p. pap. 7.99 *(978-0-9841187-6-2(4))* Asteroid Publishing.

McBroom, Jill D. Here Comes Bobtyblob! 2008. 16p. pap. 7.76 *(978-1-4251-7174-2(5))* Trafford Publishing.

McElligott, Matthew. Even Aliens Need Snacks. McElligott, Matthew, illus. 2014. (ENG., Illus.). 40p. (J). (gr. k-3). pap. 7.99 *(978-0-8027-3652-9(1)*, 9780802736529, Bloomsbury USA Childrens) Bloomsbury Publishing USA.

McGeddon, R. Aliens! McGeddon, R. & Littler, Jamie, illus. 2016. (Disaster Diaries). (ENG.). 208p. (J). 9.99 *(978-1-250-09088-1(1)*, 9781250090881) Imprint IND. Dist: Macmillan.

McGee, Joe. Peanut Butter & Aliens: A Zombie Culinary Tale. Santoso, Charles, illus. 2017. (ENG.). 32p. (J). (gr. -1-2). 16.95 ***(978-1-4197-2530-2(0)***, Abrams Bks. for Young Readers) Abrams, Inc.

McGrath, Raymond, illus. My Alien: Individual Title Six-Packs. (Sails Literacy Ser.). 16p. (gr. k-18). 27.00 *(978-0-7635-4394-5(2))* Rigby Education.

McNamara, Margaret. The Three Little Aliens & the Big Bad Robot. Fearing, Mark, illus. 2011. (ENG.). 40p. (J). (gr. -1-3). 16.99 *(978-0-375-86689-0(2)*, Schwartz & Wade Bks.) Random Hse. Children's Bks.

McNamee, Kevin. What Is That Thing? Snider, K. C., illus. 2011. 16p. pap. 9.95 *(978-1-61633-141-2(0))* Guardian Angel Publishing, Inc.

McNichol, John. The Tripods Attack! 2008. (Young Chesterton Chronicles Ser.). 367p. (YA). (gr. 8-12). pap. 17.95 *(978-1-933184-26-5(4))* Sophia Institute Pr.

Metzger, Joanna. The Space Program. Elizalde, Marcelo, illus. 2006. 142p. (J). *(978-1-59336-695-7(7))* Mondo Publishing.

Meyer, Marissa. Cinder. 2012. (Lunar Chronicles Ser.: 1). (ENG.). 400p. (YA). (gr. 7-12). 19.99 *(978-0-312-64189-4(3)*, 9780312641894) Feiwel & Friends.

—Cinder. 2013. (Lunar Chronicles Ser.: 1). (ENG.). 448p. (YA). (gr. 7-12). pap. 9.99 *(978-1-250-00720-9(8)*, 9781250007209) Square Fish.

—Cinder. l.t. ed. 2012. (Lunar Chronicles: Bk. 1). (ENG.). 496p. (J). (gr. 7-12). 23.99 *(978-1-4104-4607-7(7))* Thorndike Pr.

—Cinder. 2013. (Lunar Chronicles Ser.: 1). (YA). lib. bdg. 20.85 *(978-0-606-28633-6(0)*, Turtleback) Turtleback Bks.

—Cinder. 2015. (Cinder Ser.: 1). (SPA.). 416p. (YA). (gr. 9-12). pap. 20.99 *(978-987-612-927-5(9))* V&R Editoras.

—Cress. 2014. (YA). (Lunar Chronicles: Bk. 3). (ENG.). 560p. (gr. 7-12). 19.99 *(978-0-312-64297-6(0)*, 9780312642976); 552p. *(978-1-250-05632-0(2))* Feiwel & Friends.

—Fairest: Levana's Story. 2016. (Lunar Chronicles Ser.: 0). (YA). lib. bdg. 20.85 *(978-0-606-38438-4(3))* Turtleback Bks.

—Fairest: The Lunar Chronicles: Levana's Story. 2015. (YA). 222p. *(978-1-250-06959-7(9))*; (ENG.). 272p. (gr. 7-12). 17.99 *(978-1-250-06055-6(9)*, 9781250060556) Feiwel & Friends.

—Fairest: The Lunar Chronicles: Levana's Story. Barcellona, Christine, ed. 2016. (Lunar Chronicles Ser.). (ENG.). 288p. (YA). pap. 10.99 *(978-1-250-07355-6(3)*, 9781250073556) Square Fish.

—Scarlet. 2013. (Lunar Chronicles: Bk. 2). (ENG.). 464p. (YA). (gr. 7). 19.99 *(978-0-312-64296-9(2)*, 9780312642969) Feiwel & Friends.

—Scarlet. 2014. (Lunar Chronicles Ser.: 2). (ENG.). 512p. (YA). (gr. 7-12). pap. 9.99 *(978-1-250-00721-6(6)*, 9781250007216) Square Fish.

—Scarlet. l.t. ed. 2013. (Lunar Chronicles: Bk. 2). (ENG.). 572p. 23.99 *(978-1-4104-5623-6(4))* Thorndike Pr.

—Scarlet. 2014. (Lunar Chronicles Ser.: 2). (YA). lib. bdg. 20.85 *(978-0-606-35097-6(7)*, Turtleback) Turtleback Bks.

—Scarlet. 2016. (SPA.). 430p. (YA). (gr. 9-12). pap. 20.99 *(978-987-612-990-9(2))* V&R Editoras.

—Stars Above: A Lunar Chronicles Collection. 2016. (Lunar Chronicles Ser.). (ENG.). 400p. (YA). (gr. 7-12). 17.99 *(978-1-250-09184-0(5)*, 9781250091840) Feiwel & Friends.

—Winter. 2015. (Lunar Chronicles Ser.: 4). (ENG.). 832p. (YA). (gr. 7-12). 22.99 *(978-0-312-64298-3(9)*, 9780312642983) Feiwel & Friends.

Mihaley, James. You Can't Have My Planet: But Take My Brother, Please. 2013. (ENG.). 272p. (J). (gr. 4-7). pap. 8.99 *(978-1-250-01667-6(3)*, 9781250016676) Square Fish.

Miller, Lee. Ete: (Extraterrestrial Elements) 2006. 80p. pap. 16.95 *(978-1-4241-3498-4(6))* PublishAmerica, Inc.

Milway, Alex. Alien Moon. Milway, Alex, illus. 2014. (ENG., Illus.). 240p. (J). pap. 5.99 *(978-1-61067-164-4(3))* Kane Miller.

Mitchell, Lakeya Geneene. King of Mud! 2009. 32p. pap. 15.28 *(978-0-557-04313-2(1))* Lulu Pr., Inc.

Molengraf, Jonathan Eric. Take Me to Your Leader. 2012. 20p. pap. 24.95 *(978-1-4626-8208-9(1))* America Star Bks.

Molloy, Tom. Everything but the Beach: A Slice of Manchester Life. 2012. (Illus.). 192p. (J). pap. 9.60 *(978-1-291-15817-5(0))* Lulu Pr., Inc.

Montgomery, R. A. Prisoner of the Ant People. 2007. 144p. (J). pap. *(978-1-86504-932-8(8))* Chooseco LLC.

—Prisoner of the Ant People. 2005. (Illus.). 115p. (J). pap. *(978-0-7608-9698-3(4))* Sundance/Newbridge Educational Publishing.

—Punishment: Earth. 2010. 144p. pap. 6.99 *(978-1-933390-36-9(0))* Chooseco LLC.

Montgomery, Ross. Perijee & Me. 2016. (ENG.). 224p. (J). (gr. 3-7). 16.99 *(978-0-399-55397-4(5)*, Lamb, Wendy Bks.) Random Hse. Children's Bks.

Moon, Jonny. The Dog's Dinner. 2009. (GUNK Aliens Ser.: 3). (ENG., Illus.). 112p. (J). (gr. 2-4). pap. 7.99 *(978-0-00-731096-8(X))* HarperCollins Pubs. Ltd. GBR. Dist: HarperCollins Pubs.

—The Elephant's Trump. 2009. (GUNK Aliens Ser.: 2). (ENG., Illus.). 112p. (J). (gr. 2-4). pap. 7.99 *(978-0-00-731095-1(1))* HarperCollins Pubs. Ltd. GBR. Dist: HarperCollins Pubs.

—The Nit Picker. 2011. (GUNK Aliens Ser.). (ENG., Illus.). 112p. (J). (gr. 2-4). 7.99 *(978-0-00-732617-4(3))* HarperCollins Pubs. Ltd. GBR. Dist: Independent Pubs. Group.

—The Sewers Crisis. 2010. (GUNK Aliens Ser.). (ENG., Illus.). 112p. (J). (gr. 2-4). pap. 7.99 *(978-0-00-731097-5(8))* HarperCollins Pubs. Ltd. GBR. Dist: Independent Pubs. Group.

—The Verruca Bazooka. 2009. (GUNK Aliens Ser.: 1). (ENG., Illus.). 112p. (J). (gr. 2-4). pap. 7.99 *(978-0-00-731094-4(3))* HarperCollins Pubs. Ltd. GBR. Dist: HarperCollins Pubs.

Morris, Kimberly. Take Me to Your Weeder. Warrick, Jessica, illus. 2016. (How to Be an Earthling (r) Ser.: 3). (ENG.). 64p. (gr. 1-3). lib. bdg. 22.65 *(978-1-57565-824-7(0))* Kane Press, Inc.

—Take Me to Your Weeder: Responsibility. Warrick, Jessica, illus. 2016. (How to Be an Earthling (r) Ser.: 3). (ENG.). 64p. (gr. 1-3). 34.65 *(978-1-57565-826-1(7))* Kane Press, Inc.

Moss, Marissa. Alien Eraser to the Rescue. Moss, Marissa, illus. 2009. (Max Disaster Ser.: No. 1). (ENG., Illus.). 56p. (J). (gr. 3-7). pap. 6.99 *(978-0-7636-4407-9(2))* Candlewick Pr.

My Teacher Is an Alien Collection. 2014. (My Teacher Bks.). (ENG., Illus.). 736p. (J). (gr. 3-7). pap. 27.99 *(978-1-4814-1594-1(8)*, Aladdin) Simon & Schuster Children's Publishing.

Myers, Bill. Invisible Terror Collection, 1 vol., Vol. 2. 2011. (Forbidden Doors Ser.). (ENG.). 368p. (YA). pap. 12.99 *(978-0-310-72904-4(1))* Zondervan.

—My Life As a Prickly Porcupine from the Planet Pluto, 1 vol. 2004. (Incredible Worlds of Wally Mcdoogle Ser.: 23). (ENG.). 128p. pap. 6.99 *(978-0-8499-5994-3(2))* Nelson, Thomas Inc.

Natl Children's Book & Literacy Alliance. The Exquisite Corpse Adventure. 2011. (ENG., Illus.). 288p. (J). (gr. 4-7). pap. 7.99 *(978-0-7636-5773-4(5))* Candlewick Pr.

Neilson, G. E. F. Cosmic Aviators - Book 1 - Flight Edition. 2013. 288p. pap. *(978-0-9576132-5-6(3))* Buzzword Pr.

Nelson, Peter. Herbert's Wormhole. Rao, Rohitash, illus. 2010. (Herbert's Wormhole Ser.: 1). (ENG.). 304p. (J). (gr. 3-7). pap. 6.99 *(978-0-06-168870-6(3))* HarperCollins Pubs.

—Herbert's Wormhole: The Rise & Fall of el Solo Libre. Rao, Rohitash, illus. 2014. (Herbert's Wormhole Ser.: 2). (ENG.). 336p. (J). (gr. 3-7). pap. 6.99 *(978-0-06-201219-7(3))* HarperCollins Pubs.

—The Rise & Fall of el Solo Libre. Rao, Rohitash, illus. 2012. (Herbert's Wormhole Ser.: 2). (ENG.). 320p. (J). (gr. 3-7). 12.99 *(978-0-06-201218-0(5))* HarperCollins Pubs.

Nesbø, Jo. Who Cut the Cheese? Chace, Tara F., tr. Lowery, Mike, illus. 2012. (Doctor Proctor's Fart Powder Ser.). (ENG.). 464p. (J). (gr. 3-7). pap. 7.99 *(978-1-4424-3308-3(6)*, Aladdin) Simon & Schuster Children's Publishing.

—Who Cut the Cheese? Chace, Tara, tr. from NOR. Lowery, Mike, illus. 2012. (Doctor Proctor's Fart Powder Ser.). (ENG.). 464p. (J). (gr. 3-7). 17.99 *(978-1-4424-3307-6(8)*, Aladdin) Simon & Schuster Children's Publishing.

Nguyen, Tao. Mighty Mite: A New Beginning. Nguyen, Tao, illus. 2006. (Illus.). (J). 14.95 *(978-0-9776282-1-6(3))* Amazing Factory, The.

Nickel, Scott. Blastoff to the Secret Side of the Moon!, 1 vol. Bradley, Jessica, illus. 2013. (Comics Land Ser.). (ENG.). 32p. (gr. k-2). 7.95 *(978-1-4342-4273-0(0))*; lib. bdg. 25.32 *(978-1-4342-4031-6(2))* Stone Arch Bks.

Nix, Garth. One Beastly Beast: Two Aliens, Three Inventors, Four Fantastic Tales. Biggs, Brian, illus. 2007. 176p. (J). (gr. 2-6). lib. bdg. 16.89 *(978-0-06-084320-5(9)*, Eos) HarperCollins Pubs.

Nylund, Eric. The Resisters. 2011. (Resisters Ser.). (ENG.). 224p. (J). (gr. 3-7). 16.99 *(978-0-375-86856-6(9)*, Random Hse. Bks. for Young Readers) Random Hse. Children's Bks.

—The Resisters #1: the Resisters. 2012. (Resisters Ser.). (ENG.). 240p. (J). (gr. 5-9). 7.99 *(978-0-375-87224-2(8)*, Yearling) Random Hse. Children's Bks.

—The Resisters #2: Sterling Squadron. 2012. (Resisters Ser.: 2). (ENG.). 320p. (J). (gr. 5-9). 7.99 *(978-0-375-87225-9(6)*, Yearling) Random Hse. Children's Bks.

—The Resisters #3: Titan Base. 2013. (Resisters Ser.: 3). (ENG.). 288p. (J). (gr. 5-9). 7.99 *(978-0-307-97854-7(0)*, Yearling) Random Hse. Children's Bks.

—The Resisters #4: Operation Inferno. 2013. (Resisters Ser.). (ENG.). 288p. (J). (gr. 5-9). 6.99 *(978-0-307-97855-4(9)*, Yearling) Random Hse. Children's Bks.

Nylund, Eric S. The Sterling Squadron. 2012. (Resisters Ser.: 2). (ENG.). 320p. (J). (gr. 5-9). 16.99 *(978-0-375-86857-3(7)*, Random Hse. Bks. for Young Readers) Random Hse. Children's Bks.

Oakes, Cory Putman. Dinosaur Boy. 2015. (Dinosaur Boy Ser.: 1). (ENG.). 224p. (J). (gr. 3-7). 12.99 *(978-1-4926-0537-9(9)*, 9781492605379, Sourcebooks Jabberwocky) Sourcebooks, Inc.

—Dinosaur Boy Saves Mars. 2016. (Dinosaur Boy Ser.: 2). (ENG., Illus.). 224p. (J). (gr. 3-7). 12.99 *(978-1-4926-0540-9(9)*, 9781492605409, Sourcebooks Jabberwocky) Sourcebooks, Inc.

—Dinosaur Boy Saves Mars. 2016. (Dinosaur Boy Ser.: 2). (ENG.). 224p. (J). (gr. 3-7). 18.40 *(978-0-606-39306-5(4))* Turtleback Bks.

Oberne, Sharon. Kelsey. 2006. 88p. (YA). pap. 13.95 *(978-1-58909-340-9(2))* Bookstand Publishing.

Olander, Johan. A Field Guide to Aliens: Intergalactic Worrywarts, Bubblonauts, Sliver-Slurpers, & Other Extraterrestrials, 0 vols. 2010. (ENG.). 64p. (J). (gr. 3-7). 15.99 *(978-0-7614-5594-3(9)*, 9780761455943, Amazon Children's Publishing) Amazon Publishing.

Palacios, Tomas. Guardians of the Galaxy: The Story of the Guardians. 2014. (World of Reading Ser.). (ENG.). 32p. (J). (gr. 1-3). pap. 3.99 *(978-1-4847-0065-5(1)*, Marvel Pr.) Disney Publishing Worldwide.

—Guardians of the Galaxy Hallo-Scream Spook-Tacular!!! 2016. (J). lib. bdg. 16.00 *(978-0-606-38338-7(7))* Turtleback Bks.

—These Are the Guardians of the Galaxy. 2014. (Marvel World of Reading Level 1 Ser.). (J). lib. bdg. 13.55 *(978-0-606-35280-2(5))* Turtleback Bks.

Palacios, Tomas & Hosten, Colin. Guardians of the Galaxy Hallo-Scream Spook-tacular!!! 2016. (ENG.). 24p. (J). (gr. 1-3). pap. 5.99 *(978-1-4847-3214-4(6)*, Marvel Pr.) Disney Publishing Worldwide.

Parker, Emma & Renaud, Marguerite. Aliens from Zen. 2010. (Illus.). 16p. pap. *(978-1-877561-79-5(7))* First Edition Ltd.

Parry, Jo. Blast Off! 2009. (Wow! Bks.). (Illus.). (J). bds. 12.99 *(978-1-934650-26-4(9))* Just For Kids Pr., LLC.

Parsons, Garry. Krong! Parsons, Garry, illus. 2006. (Illus.). 32p. (J). (gr. -1-3). 15.95 *(978-1-58925-061-1(3))* Tiger Tales.

Patterson, Eric. Carl Nose the Truth. Wright, Christopher, illus. 2007. 104p. (J). pap. 6.95 *(978-0-9797106-6-7(9))* Avid Readers Publishing Group.

Patterson, James. Armageddon. 2012. (Daniel X Ser.: 5). (ENG.). 304p. (J). (gr. 3-7). 16.99 *(978-0-316-10179-0(6)*, Jimmy Patterson) Little Brown & Co.

—The Dangerous Days of Daniel X. 2014. lthr. 79.00 *(978-1-62715-506-9(6))* Leatherbound Bestsellers.

—The Dangerous Days of Daniel X. (Daniel X Ser.: 1). (ENG.). 2010. 272p. (J). (gr. 3-7). pap. 8.00 *(978-0-316-11970-2(9)*, Jimmy Patterson) 2008. 304p. pap. 20.99 *(978-0-316-03025-0(2))* Little Brown & Co.

—The Dangerous Days of Daniel X. 2010. (Daniel X Ser.: 1). (J). lib. bdg. 18.45 *(978-0-606-14720-0(9)*, Turtleback) Turtleback Bks.

—Demons & Druids. 2011. (Daniel X Ser.: 3). (ENG.). 304p. (J). (gr. 3-7). pap., pap. 8.00 *(978-0-316-03830-0(X)*, Jimmy Patterson) Little Brown & Co.

—The Manga. 2012. (Daniel X: the Manga Ser.: 3). lib. bdg. 24.55 *(978-0-606-26463-1(9)*, Turtleback) Turtleback Bks.

—Watch the Skies. 2014. lthr. 79.00 *(978-1-62715-571-7(6))* Leatherbound Bestsellers.

—Watch the Skies. l.t. ed. 2009. (Daniel X Ser.: 2). (ENG.). 352p. pap. 21.99 *(978-0-316-04363-2(X))* Little Brown & Co.

—Watch the Skies. 2010. (Daniel X Ser.: 2). (J). lib. bdg. 18.45 *(978-0-606-10550-7(6)*, Turtleback) Turtleback Bks.

Patterson, James & Grabenstein, Chris. Armageddon. 2013. (Daniel X Ser.: 5). (ENG.). 320p. (J). (gr. 3-7). pap. 8.00 *(978-0-316-10177-6(X)*, Jimmy Patterson) Little Brown & Co.

—Armageddon. 2013. (Daniel X Ser.: 5). (J). lib. bdg. 18.45 *(978-0-606-31747-4(3)*, Turtleback) Turtleback Bks.

—Daniel X: Lights Out. 2015. (Daniel X Ser.: 6). (ENG.). 272p. (J). (gr. 3-7). 17.00 *(978-0-316-20745-4(4)*, Jimmy Patterson) Little Brown & Co.

Patterson, James & Ledwidge, Michael. The Dangerous Days of Daniel X. 2009. (Daniel X Ser.: 1). (ENG.). 288p. mass mkt. 7.99 *(978-0-446-50913-8(2)*, Jimmy Patterson) Little Brown & Co.

Patterson, James & Rust, Ned. Daniel X. Kye, SeungHui, illus. 2011. (Daniel X: the Manga Ser.: 2). (ENG.). 208p. (gr. 7-17). pap. 12.99 *(978-0-316-07765-1(8)*, Yen Pr.) Orbit.

—Game Over. 2012. (Daniel X Ser.: 4). (J). lib. bdg. 18.45 *(978-0-606-26165-4(6)*, Turtleback) Turtleback Bks.

—Watch the Skies. 2010. (Daniel X Ser.: 2). (ENG.). 288p. (J). (gr. 3-7). pap. 8.00 *(978-0-316-11969-6(5)*, Jimmy Patterson) Little Brown & Co.

Patterson, James & Sadler, Adam. Demons & Druids. l.t. ed. 2010. (Daniel X Ser.: 3). (ENG.). 320p. 29.99 *(978-0-316-08731-5(9)*, Jimmy Patterson) Little Brown & Co.

Pearson, Maggie. Alien Draw. 214p. (J). pap. *(978-0-340-68077-3(6))* Hodder & Stoughton.

Pellerin, Mona. Peetie & the Marsh Aliens, 1 vol. 2010. 58p. pap. 16.95 *(978-1-4489-7017-9(2))* America Star Bks.

Perisic, Zoran. An Alien Called Freddy. 2012. 152p. pap. 9.95 *(978-1-60594-907-9(8)*, Lumina Pr.) Aeon Publishing Inc.

Picayo, Mario & Picayo, Pablo, illus. Four Wishes for Robbie. 2012. (J). *(978-1-934370-19-3(3)*, Campanita Bks.) Editorial Campana.

Pike, Christopher, pseud. Aliens in the Sky. 2014. (Spooksville Ser.: 4). (ENG., Illus.). 128p. (J). (gr. 3-7). pap. 6.99 *(978-1-4814-1058-8(X)*, Aladdin) Simon & Schuster Children's Publishing.

Pinkwater, Daniel M. Adventures of a Cat-Whiskered Girl. 2011. (ENG., Illus.). 288p. (J). (gr. 5-7). pap. 16.95 *(978-0-547-55002-2(2))* Houghton Mifflin Harcourt Publishing Co.

Pinkwater, Daniel M. Lizard Music. Pinkwater, Daniel M., illus. 2017. (ENG., Illus.). 160p. (J). (gr. 4-7). pap. 9.99 ***(978-1-68137-184-9(7)***, NYRB Kids) New York Review of Bks., Inc., The.

—Lizard Music. 2011. (ENG., Illus.). 160p. (J). (gr. 4-7). 15.95 *(978-1-59017-387-9(2)*, NYR Children's Collection) New York Review of Bks., Inc., The.

Piper, Henry Beam. Little Fuzzy. 2007. (ENG.). 172p. per. 19.99 *(978-1-4346-2928-9(7))*; 188p. per. 21.99 *(978-1-4346-2952-4(X))* Creative Media Partners, LLC.

Pittman, Eddie. Red's Planet. 2016. (Red's Planet Ser.). (ENG., Illus.). 192p. (J). (gr. 3-7). 19.95 *(978-1-4197-1907-3(6)*, Amulet Bks.) Abrams, Inc.

Portis, Antoinette. Best Frints in the Whole Universe. 2016. (ENG., Illus.). 40p. (J). 16.99 *(978-1-62672-136-4(X)*, 9781626721364) Roaring Brook Pr.

Posner-Sanchez, Andrea. Miles from Tomorrowland (Disney Junior: Miles from Tomorrowland) RH Disney, illus. 2016. (Big Golden Book Ser.). (ENG.). 32p. (J). (-k). 9.99 *(978-0-7364-3494-2(1)*, Golden/Disney) Random Hse. Children's Bks.

Preller, James. Jigsaw Jones: the Case from Outer Space. 2017. (Jigsaw Jones Mysteries Ser.). (ENG., Illus.). 96p. (J). pap. 4.99 *(978-1-250-11017-6(3)*, 9781250110176) Feiwel & Friends.

Prendergast, G. S. Zero Repeat Forever. 2017. (Nahx Invasions Ser.: 1). (ENG., Illus.). 496p. (YA). (gr. 9). 17.99 ***(978-1-4814-8184-7(3)***, Simon & Schuster Bks. For Young Readers) Simon & Schuster Bks. For Young Readers.

Prendergast, Gabrielle. Zero Repeat Forever. 2017. (YA). pap. ***(978-1-4814-8185-4(1)***, Simon & Schuster Bks. For Young Readers) Simon & Schuster Bks. For Young Readers.

Publications International Ltd. Staff, ed. Gross (Look & Find) 2010. 24p. (J). 7.98 *(978-1-60553-899-0(X))* Publications International, Ltd.

Random House. Red Alert! (Teenage Mutant Ninja Turtles) Spaziante, Patrick, illus. 2015. (Pictureback(R) Ser.). (ENG.). 16p. (J). (gr. -1-2). 4.99 *(978-0-553-50901-4(2)*, Random Hse. Bks. for Young Readers) Random Hse. Children's Bks.

Ray, Joanna Z. 'elaran! Isithan!' 2007. (ENG.). 92p. (YA). per. 15.95 *(978-1-4116-9393-7(0))* Lulu Pr., Inc.

Reisman, Michael. Simon Bloom, the Gravity Keeper. 2009. (ENG.). 320p. (J). (gr. 3-7). 8.99 *(978-0-14-241368-5(2)*, Puffin Books) Penguin Young Readers Group.

Rex, Adam. Smek for President! Rex, Adam, illus. (Smek Smeries Ser.). (ENG., Illus.). 272p. (J). (gr. 3-7). 2016. pap. 7.99 *(978-1-4847-0969-6(1))* 2015. 16.99 *(978-1-4847-0951-1(9))* Hyperion Bks. for Children.

—The True Meaning of Smekday. Rex, Adam, illus. 2015. (ENG., Illus.). 432p. (J). (gr. 3-7). pap. 7.99 *(978-1-4847-2946-5(3))* Hyperion Bks. for Children.

—The True Meaning of Smekday. Rex, Adam, illus. 2009. (Smek Smeries Ser.). (ENG., Illus.). 432p. (J). (gr. 3-7). pap. 7.99 *(978-0-7868-4901-7(0))* Hyperion Pr.

—The True Meaning of Smekday. 2009. (Illus.). 423p. 18.00 *(978-1-60686-525-5(0))* Perfection Learning Corp.

Rex, Michael. The Egg of Misery. Rex, Michael, illus. 2012. (Fangbone! Third Grade Barbarian Ser.). (ENG., Illus.). 128p. (J). (gr. 2-4). E-Book *(978-1-101-55043-4(0)*, G.P. Putnam's Sons Books for Young Readers) Penguin Young Readers Group.

—The Egg of Misery. 2012. (Fangbone Ser.: 2). lib. bdg. 16.00 *(978-0-606-23635-5(X)*, Turtleback) Turtleback Bks.

—The Egg of Misery: Fangbone, Third Grade Barbarian. Rex, Michael, illus. 2012. (Fangbone! Third Grade Barbarian Ser.: 2). (ENG., Illus.). 128p. (J). (gr. 2-4). 7.99 *(978-0-399-25522-9(2)*, G.P. Putnam's Sons Books for Young Readers) Penguin Young Readers Group.

—Fangbone! Third-Grade Barbarian. 2012. (Illus.). 120p. (J). *(978-0-545-44042-4(4)*, Putnam Juvenile) Penguin Publishing Group.

—Third-Grade Barbarian. 2012. (Fangbone Ser.: 1). lib. bdg. 18.40 *(978-0-606-23634-8(1)*, Turtleback) Turtleback Bks.

Richards, Kitty. Meet the Sparkplugs, Level 3. Simard, Remy, illus. 2006. (ENG.). 24p. (J). (gr. 1-17). per. 3.99 *(978-1-58476-419-9(8)*, IKIDS) Innovative Kids.

Riseman, Daniel. They Return. 2012. 48p. pap. 21.99 *(978-1-4771-3649-2(5))* Xlibris Corp.

Robbins, Trina. The Bark in Space. Page, Tyler, illus. 2013. (Chicagoland Detective Agency Ser.: 5). (ENG.). 64p. (gr. 4-8). (J). lib. bdg. 29.27 *(978-0-7613-8166-2(X))*; pap. 6.95 *(978-1-4677-0725-1(2))* Lerner Publishing Group. (Graphic Universe™).

Rodriguez, Antonio Orlando. Que Extranos Son Los Terricolas/Earthlings, How Weird They Are! Cuellar, Olga, illus. 2006. (Bilingual Collection). (SPA.). 51p. (J). (gr. k-2). *(978-958-30-1737-7(X))* Panamericana Editorial.

Rosen, Lucy. Justice League: Meet the Justice League. Gordon, Eric A. & Gordon, Steven E., illus. 2013. (I Can Read Level 2 Ser.). (ENG.). 32p. (J). (gr. -1-3). pap. 3.99 *(978-0-06-221002-9(5))* HarperCollins Pubs.

Ross, Tony & Camp, Lindsay. Why? 2008. (ENG., Illus.). 32p. (J). (gr. -1-k). pap. 12.99 *(978-1-84270-607-7(1))* Andersen Pr. GBR. Dist: Independent Pubs. Group.

Routley, Becky. Moon Golf. 2009. (Illus.). 28p. pap. 12.49 *(978-1-4490-4713-9(0))* AuthorHouse.

Rovetch, L. Bob. Hot Dog & Bob: And the Dangerously Dizzy Attack of the Hypno Hamsters. Whamond, Dave, illus. 2007. (Hot Dog & Bob Ser.: HOTD). (ENG.). 96p. (J). (gr. 1-5). per. 4.95 *(978-0-8118-5602-7(X))* Chronicle Bks. LLC.

Roy, Ron. January Joker. Gurney, John Steven, illus. 2009. (Calendar Mysteries Ser.: 1). (ENG.). 96p. (J). (gr. 1-4). 4.99 *(978-0-375-85661-7(7)*, Random Hse. Bks. for Young Readers) Random Hse. Children's Bks.

Runberg, Sylvain. Orbital Vol. 5: Justice. Pelle, Serge, illus. 2014. (Orbital Ser.: 5). (ENG.). 56p. pap. 13.95 *(978-1-84918-172-3(1))* CineBook GBR. Dist: National Bk. Network.

Russell, David O. & Auseon, Andrew. Alienated. 2010. (ENG.). 352p. (J). (gr. 3-7). pap. 5.99 *(978-1-4169-8299-9(X)*, Aladdin) Simon & Schuster Children's Publishing.

Sachar, Louis. Marvin Redpost #6: a Flying Birthday Cake? Record, Adam, illus. 2015. (Marvin Redpost Ser.: 6). (ENG.). 96p. (J). (gr. 1-4). lib. bdg. 12.99 *(978-0-553-53544-0(7)*, Random Hse. Bks. for Young Readers) Random Hse. Children's Bks.

Said, S. F. Phoenix. McKean, Dave, illus. 2016. (ENG.). 496p. (J). (gr. 5). 19.99 *(978-0-7636-8850-9(9))* Candlewick Pr.

Sasaki, Chris & Wells, H. G. The War of the Worlds. Akib, Jamel, illus. 2007. (Classic Starts Ser.). 151p. (J). *(978-1-4287-4208-6(5))* Sterling Publishing Co., Inc.

E
F
G

Sauer, Tammi. Your Alien. Fujita, Goro, illus. 2015. (ENG.). 32p. (J). (gr. -1). 14.95 *(978-1-4549-1129-6(8))* Sterling Publishing Co., Inc.

—Your Alien Returns. Fujita, Goro, illus. 2016. (ENG.). 40p. (J). (gr. -1). 14.95 *(978-1-4549-1130-2(1))* Sterling Publishing Co., Inc.

Sava, Scott Christian. Ed's Terrestrials. 2006. 84p. 19.95 *(978-0-9789168-1-7(6))* Blue Dream Studios.

Scarborough, R. A. Starblade: The Beginning, 1 vol. 2010. 128p. pap. 19.95 *(978-1-4489-3906-0(2))* America Star Bks.

Schanback, Mindy. Princess from Another Planet. 2005. (ENG.). 254p. (J). (gr. 5-9). 16.95 *(978-0-8234-1847-3(2))* Holiday Hse., Inc.

Schindler, Roslyn. Zeon. Schindler, Roslyn, illus. 2013. (Illus.). 28p. pap. 13.95 *(978-1-61493-192-8(5))* Peppertree Pr., The.

Schneider, John Lee. Extinction: Dragons of Earth: A Novel. 2005. 173p. (YA). pap. *(978-1-890109-79-0(7)*, Cross Time) Crossquarter Publishing Group.

Schories, Pat. When Jack Goes Out. 2010. (Jacks Ser.). (ENG., Illus.). 32p. (J). (gr. -1-1). 14.95 *(978-1-59078-652-9(1)*, Front Street) Boyds Mills Pr.

Scieszka, Jon. Spaceheadz. Prigmore, Shane, illus. (Spaceheadz Ser.: 3). (ENG.). (J). (gr. 2-5). 2012. 224p. pap. 7.99 *(978-1-4169-7956-2(5))* 2011. 224p. 15.99 *(978-1-4169-7955-5(7))* 2010. 176p. 14.99 *(978-1-4169-7951-7(4))*Set. 2013. 864p. pap. 23.99 *(978-1-4424-9858-7(7))* Simon & Schuster Bks. For Young Readers. (Simon & Schuster Bks. For Young Readers).

—SPHDZ 4 Life! Prigmore, Shane, illus. 2013. (Spaceheadz Ser.: 4). (ENG.). 192p. (J). (gr. 2-5). pap. 5.99 *(978-1-4169-7958-6(1))*;Bk. 4. 16.99 *(978-1-4169-7957-9(3))* Simon & Schuster Bks. For Young Readers. (Simon & Schuster Bks. For Young Readers).

—SPHDZ Book #1! Prigmore, Shane, illus. 2011. (Spaceheadz Ser.: 1). (ENG.). 192p. (J). (gr. 2-5). pap. 7.99 *(978-1-4424-1986-5(5)*, Simon & Schuster Bks. For Young Readers) Simon & Schuster Bks. For Young Readers.

—SPHDZ Book #2! Prigmore, Shane, illus. (Spaceheadz Ser.: 2). (ENG.). (J). (gr. 2-5). 2011. 256p. pap. 7.99 *(978-1-4169-7954-8(9))* 2010. 240p. 14.99 *(978-1-4169-7953-1(0))* Simon & Schuster Bks. For Young Readers. (Simon & Schuster Bks. For Young Readers).

Seigel, Jonathan & Rother, Beverly S. Myrtle the Turtle & Popeye the Mouse: Learning about Our Solar System. 2012. 40p. pap. 24.95 *(978-1-4626-6587-7(X))* America Star Bks.

Service, Pamela F. Alien Contact. Gorman, Mike, illus. (Alien Agent Ser.: 5). (ENG.). 144p. (J). (gr. 4-6). 2010. lib. bdg. 16.95 *(978-0-7613-5363-8(1)*, Carolrhoda Bks.)No. 5. 2011. pap. 5.95 *(978-0-7613-7297-4(0)*, Darby Creek) Lerner Publishing Group.

—Alien Encounter. Gorman, Mike, illus. (Alien Agent Ser.: 4). (ENG.). 152p. (J). (gr. 4-6). 2011. pap. 5.95 *(978-0-7613-5248-8(1))* 2010. 16.95 *(978-0-8225-8873-3(0)*, Carolrhoda Bks.) Lerner Publishing Group.

—Alien Envoy. Gorman, Mike, illus. (Alien Agent Ser.). 176p. (J). (gr. 4-6). 2012. pap. 33.92 *(978-0-7613-9208-8(4)*, Darby Creek) 2012. (ENG.). pap. 5.95 *(978-0-7613-7298-1(9)*, Darby Creek) 2011. (ENG.). 16.95 *(978-0-7613-5364-5(X))* Lerner Publishing Group.

—Alien Expedition. 2010. pap. 33.92 *(978-0-7613-6958-5(9))* Lerner Publishing Group.

—Alien Expedition. Gorman, Mike, illus. (Alien Agent Ser.: 3). (ENG.). 160p. (J). (gr. 4-6). 2009. 16.95 *(978-0-8225-8870-2(6))*No. 3. 2010. pap. 5.95 *(978-0-7613-5249-5(X))* Lerner Publishing Group. (Carolrhoda Bks.).

—Camp Alien. 2010. pap. 33.92 *(978-0-7613-6955-4(4))* Lerner Publishing Group.

—Camp Alien. Gorman, Mike, illus. (Alien Agent Ser.: 2). (ENG.). 160p. (J). (gr. 4-6). 2010. pap. 5.95 *(978-0-7613-5247-1(3))* 2009. 16.95 *(978-0-8225-8656-2(8)*, Carolrhoda Bks.) Lerner Publishing Group.

—Escape from Planet Yastol. Gorman, Mike, illus. (Way-Too-Real Aliens Ser.: 1). (ENG.). 112p. (J). (gr. 4-6). 2015. 34.65 *(978-1-4677-5960-1(0)*, Lerner Digital)No. 1. 2011. 15.95 *(978-0-7613-7918-8(5)*, Darby Creek)No. 1. 2011. pap. 5.95 *(978-0-7613-7921-8(5)*, Darby Creek) Lerner Publishing Group.

—My Cousin, the Alien. 2010. pap. 33.92 *(978-0-7613-6952-3(X))* Lerner Publishing Group.

—My Cousin, the Alien. Gorman, Mike, illus. (Alien Agent Ser.: 1). (ENG.). 160p. (J). (gr. 4-6). 2009. pap. 5.95 *(978-0-7613-4964-8(2)*, First Avenue Editions) 2008. 16.95 *(978-0-8225-7627-3(9)*, Carolrhoda Bks.) Lerner Publishing Group.

—The Not-So-Perfect Planet. Gorman, Mike, illus. (Way-Too-Real Aliens Ser.: 2). (ENG.). 120p. (J). (gr. 4-6). 2015. 34.65 *(978-1-4677-5961-8(9)*, Lerner Digital) 2012. 15.95 *(978-0-7613-7919-5(3)*, Darby Creek) 2012. pap. 6.95 *(978-0-7613-7923-2(1)*, Darby Creek) Lerner Publishing Group.

—The Wizards of Wyrd World. Gorman, Mike, illus. (Way-Too-Real Aliens Ser.: 3). (ENG.). 112p. (J). (gr. 4-6). 2015. 34.65 *(978-1-4677-5962-5(7)*, Lerner Digital) 2013. pap. 6.95 *(978-0-7613-7922-5(3)*, Darby Creek) 2012. 15.95 *(978-0-7613-7920-1(7))* Lerner Publishing Group.

—#4 Alien Encounter. Gorman, Mike, illus. 2011. (Alien Agent Ser.). 152p. (J). pap. 33.92 *(978-0-7613-7608-8(9)*, Darby Creek) Lerner Publishing Group.

—#5 Alien Contact. Gorman, Mike, illus. 2011. (Alien Agent Ser.). pap. 33.92 *(978-0-7613-8347-5(6)*, Darby Creek) Lerner Publishing Group.

Shepherd, Megan. The Cage. (Cage Ser.: 1). (YA). (gr. 8). 2016. 416p. pap. 9.99 *(978-0-06-224306-5(3))* 2015. (ENG.). 400p. 17.99 *(978-0-06-224305-8(5))* HarperCollins Pubs.

Shipton, Paul. The Games Player of Zob. McCafferty, Jan, illus. 2007. (Collins Big Cat Ser.). (ENG.). 1p. (J). (gr. 3-4). pap. 8.99 *(978-0-00-723094-5(X))* HarperCollins Pubs. Ltd. GBR. Dist: Independent Pubs. Group.

Shusterman, Neal. The Dark Side of Nowhere. 2012. (ENG.). (YA). (gr. 7). 240p. 17.99 *(978-1-4424-5812-3(7))*; 256p. pap. 9.99 *(978-1-4424-2281-0(5))* Simon & Schuster Bks. For Young Readers. (Simon & Schuster Bks. For Young Readers).

Siglain, Michael, adapted by. Zeb to the Rescue. 2014. (Illus.). 32p. (J). *(978-1-4844-3445-1(5))* Disney Publishing Worldwide.

Signorino, John. Billy & the Aliens of Alpha-C, 1 vol. 2008. (ENG.). 36p. pap. 24.95 *(978-1-60474-882-6(6))* America Star Bks.

Silver, Eve. Crash. 2015. (Game Ser.: 3). (ENG.). 368p. (YA). (gr. 9). 17.99 *(978-0-06-219219-6(1)*, Tegen, Katherine Bks) HarperCollins Pubs.

—Rush. (Game Ser.: 1). (ENG.). (YA). (gr. 9). 2014. 384p. pap. 9.99 *(978-0-06-219214-1(0)*, Tegen, Katherine Bks) 2013. 368p. 17.99 *(978-0-06-219213-4(2))* HarperCollins Pubs.

Simonson, Bill. Itt 'N' Ott's Pizza Journey. 2013. 32p. 16.99 *(978-0-9892711-6-5(1))* Mindstir Media.

Slack, Michael. Wazdot? 2014. (ENG., Illus.). 48p. (J). (gr. -1 — 1). 16.99 *(978-1-4231-8347-1(9))* Hyperion Bks. for Children.

Small, Wylie J. The Great Prune Caper. 2009. 94p. pap. 9.98 *(978-1-84728-350-4(0))* Lulu Pr., Inc.

Smillie, Bryan. A Time for Evron. Rooth, Mike, illus. 2004. 190p. 11.95 *(978-0-9689516-0-6(0))* Shabrya Publishing CAN. Dist: Hushion Hse. Publishing, Ltd.

Smith, Clete Barrett. Alien on a Rampage. 2013. (Intergalactic Bed & Breakfast Ser.). (ENG.). 320p. (J). (gr. 3-7). pap. 6.99 *(978-1-4231-5525-6(4))* Hyperion Pr.

—Aliens in Disguise. Slade, Christian, illus. 2013. (Intergalactic Bed & Breakfast Ser.). (ENG.). 240p. (J). (gr. 3-7). 16.99 *(978-1-4231-6598-9(5))* Disney Pr.

—Aliens in Disguise. 2014. (Intergalactic Bed & Breakfast Ser.). (ENG.). 256p. (J). (gr. 3-7). pap. 6.99 *(978-1-4231-6638-2(8))* Hyperion Bks. for Children.

—Aliens on Vacation. Slade, Christian, illus. 2012. (Intergalactic Bed & Breakfast Ser.). (ENG.). 272p. (J). (gr. 3-7). pap. 6.99 *(978-1-4231-5723-6(0))* Hyperion Pr.

Solomons, David. My Gym Teacher Is an Alien Overlord. Ferguson, Laura Ellen, illus. 2016. (ENG.). 288p. (J). (gr. 3-7). 16.99 *(978-0-451-47494-0(5)*, Viking Books for Young Readers) Penguin Young Readers Group.

Solomons, David. My Gym Teacher Is an Alien Overlord. 2017. lib. bdg. 18.40 ***(978-0-606-40090-9(7))*** Turtleback Bks.

Soo, Kean. Monster in the City. 2014. (Jellaby Ser.). (ENG., Illus.). 184p. (gr. 4-8). pap. 12.95 *(978-1-4342-6421-3(1))* Stone Arch Bks.

Space Case. 2014. (Moon Base Alpha Ser.). (ENG., Illus.). 352p. (J). (gr. 3-7). 17.99 *(978-1-4424-9486-2(7)*, Simon & Schuster Bks. For Young Readers) Simon & Schuster Bks. For Young Readers.

Spaziante, Patrick, illus. OLIVIA & Her Alien Brother. 2014. (Olivia TV Tie-In Ser.). (ENG.). 24p. (J). (gr. -1-2). pap. 3.99 *(978-1-4424-9749-8(1)*, Simon Spotlight) Simon Spotlight.

Spendlove, Joanna. The Adventures of Gooky & Spinnet: The Universe, Our Wonderland. 2011. 24p. 14.99 *(978-1-4567-1066-8(4))* AuthorHouse.

Spiegelman, Nadja. Zig & Wikki in Something Ate My Homework. Loeffler, Trade, illus. 2013. (ENG.). 40p. (J). (gr. -1-3). pap. 6.99 *(978-1-935179-38-2(1))* TOON Books / RAW Junior, LLC.

—Zig & Wikki in the Cow. Loeffler, Trade, illus. 2012. (ENG.). 40p. (J). (gr. -1-3). 12.95 *(978-1-935179-15-3(2))* TOON Books / RAW Junior, LLC.

Spiegelman, Nadja & Loeffler, Trade. Zig & Wikki in Something Ate My Homework. 2013. (Toon Books Level 3 Ser.). lib. bdg. 14.75 *(978-0-606-32252-2(3)*, Turtleback) Turtleback Bks.

St. Mark Kindergarten. Kindergarten Goes to Outer Space for the Day. 2009. 28p. pap. 12.49 *(978-1-4490-0587-0(X))* AuthorHouse.

Stadler, Alexander. Invasion of the Relatives. 2009. (Julian Rodriguez Ser.: 2). (ENG.). 144p. (J). (gr. 2-5). pap. 5.99 *(978-0-439-91971-5(1)*, Scholastic Pr.) Scholastic, Inc.

—Trash Crisis on Earth, No. 1. 2009. (Julian Rodriguez Ser.: 1). (ENG.). 128p. (J). (gr. 2-5). 5.99 *(978-0-439-91970-8(3)*, Scholastic Paperbacks) Scholastic, Inc.

Stanchfield, Justin. Timewalker. 2011. (Fiction Ser.). 330p. (J). pap. 5.99 *(978-0-7945-3032-7(X)*, Usborne) EDC Publishing.

Stephens, Sarah Hines. Backward Bowwow, 1 vol. Baltazar, Art, illus. 2011. (DC Super-Pets Ser.). (ENG.). 56p. (gr. 2-2). pap. 4.95 *(978-1-4048-6845-8(3))*; lib. bdg. 23.99 *(978-1-4048-6480-1(6))* Picture Window Bks. (DC Super-Pets).

Steve Chering. There's Something in Granny's Garden! 2013. 48p. pap. *(978-3-85040-854-7(X))* Chytra-Verlag Vindobona.

Stilton, Geronimo. Alien Escape. 2014. (Geronimo Stilton Spacemice Ser.: 1). (ENG., Illus.). 128p. (J). (gr. 2-5). pap. 6.99 *(978-0-545-64650-5(2)*, Scholastic Paperbacks) Scholastic, Inc.

—Beware! Space Junk! 2016. (Geronimo Stilton Spacemice Ser.: 7). (ENG.). 128p. (J). (gr. 2-5). pap. 7.99 *(978-0-545-87245-4(6)*, Scholastic Paperbacks) Scholastic, Inc.

—The Galactic Goal. 2015. (Geronimo Stilton Spacemice Ser.: 4). (ENG., Illus.). 128p. (J). (gr. 2-5). pap. 7.99 *(978-0-545-74620-5(5)*, Scholastic Paperbacks) Scholastic, Inc.

—Rescue Rebellion. 2015. (Geronimo Stilton Spacemice Ser.: 5). lib. bdg. 17.20 *(978-0-606-37775-1(1))* Turtleback Bks.

—The Underwater Planet. 2016. (Geronimo Stilton Spacemice Ser.: 6). (ENG., Illus.). 128p. (J). (gr. 2-5). pap. 7.99 *(978-0-545-87243-0(X)*, Scholastic Paperbacks) Scholastic, Inc.

—You're Mine, Captain! 2014. (Geronimo Stilton Spacemice Ser.: 2). lib. bdg. 18.40 *(978-0-606-35845-3(5))* Turtleback Bks.

Stilton, Geronimo & Pizzelli, Anna. The Underwater Planet. Facciotto, Giuseppe & Verzini, Daniele, illus. 2016. 113p. (J). ***(978-1-5182-0303-9(5))*** Scholastic, Inc.

Stine, R. L. The Creatures from Beyond Beyond, 0 vols. unabr. ed. 2012. (ENG.). 144p. (J). (gr. 2-4). pap. 4.99 *(978-1-61218-327-5(1)*, 9781612183275, Amazon Children's Publishing) Amazon Publishing.

—My Alien Parents, 0 vols. unabr. ed. 2012. (ENG.). 60p. (J). (gr. 3-7). pap. 4.99 *(978-1-61218-325-1(5)*, 9781612183251, Amazon Children's Publishing) Amazon Publishing.

—Weirdo Halloween. 2010. 240p. (J). (Goosebumps HorrorLand Ser.: No. 16). pap. *(978-1-4071-1637-2(1))*; (Goosebumps Horrorland Ser.: 16). (ENG.). (gr. 3-7). 7.99 *(978-0-545-16197-8(5)*, Scholastic Paperbacks) Scholastic, Inc.

Stohl, Margaret. Icons. (ENG.). (YA). (gr. 7-17). 2014. (Icons Ser.: 1). 464p. pap. 24.99 *(978-0-316-20519-1(2))* 2013. 448p. 18.00 *(978-0-316-20518-4(4))* Little, Brown Bks. for Young Readers.

Streblow, Mary. A Martian for Christmas. 2007. (ENG.). 32p. per. 23.95 *(978-1-4303-0794-5(3))* Lulu Pr., Inc.

Teague, Mark & Scholastic, Inc. Staff. The Doom Machine. Teague, Mark, illus. 2009. (ENG., Illus.). 384p. (J). (gr. 3-7). 17.99 *(978-0-545-15142-9(2)*, Blue Sky Pr., The) Scholastic, Inc.

Tennapel, Doug. Cardboard. 2012. (ENG., Illus.). 288p. (J). (gr. 4-7). 24.99 *(978-0-545-41872-0(0))*; pap. 12.99 *(978-0-545-41873-7(9))* Scholastic, Inc. (Graphix).

Testa, Maggie. Olivia & Her Alien Brother. 2014. (Olivia 8x8 Ser.). lib. bdg. 13.55 *(978-0-606-35199-7(X))* Turtleback Bks.

Thomas, Nigel. Tom Travis: The Lost People of Orion. 2006. 193p. pap. 24.95 *(978-1-4241-0382-9(7))* PublishAmerica, Inc.

Thomson, Rachel Starr. Theodore Pharris Saves the Universe. 2013. 176p. pap. *(978-1-927658-18-5(7))* Little Dozen Press.

Thorne MBE, Tony. The junior philosophical Society. 2007. 114p. pap. 12.95 *(978-1-4116-9623-5(9))* Lulu Pr., Inc.

Tomizawa, Hitoshi. Alien Nine: Emulators. Pannone, Frank, ed. Jackson, Laura & Kobayashi, Yoko, trs. from JPN. Tomizawa, Hitoshi, illus. 2004. (Illus.). 248p. pap. 9.99 *(978-1-58664-924-1(8)*, CMX 65004G, CPM Manga) Central Park Media Corp.

—Alien Nine 2, Vol. 2. Pannone, Frank, ed. Jackson, Laura & Kobayashi, Yoko, trs. from JPN. Tomizawa, Hitoshi, illus. 2003. (Illus.). 224p. (gr. 11-18). pap. 15.95 *(978-1-58664-892-3(6)*, CMX 64202G, CPM Manga) Central Park Media Corp.

Toriyama, Akira. Dragon Ball Full Color Freeza Arc, Volume 1. 2016. (Dragon Ball Freeza Ser.: 1). lib. bdg. 33.05 *(978-0-606-38706-4(4))* Turtleback Bks.

—Dragon Ball Full Color Freeza Arc, Volume 2. 2016. (Dragon Ball Freeza Ser.: 2). lib. bdg. 33.05 *(978-0-606-38934-1(2))* Turtleback Bks.

Toufexis, George. MONSTER MASH-Up — Aliens Meet Their Match. 2012. (Dover Coloring Bks.). (ENG.). 48p. (J). (gr. 3-8). pap. 4.99 *(978-0-486-48949-0(3))* Dover Pubns., Inc.

Tran, Hensley. Agatha's Stolen Curve. 2013. 80p. (gr. 4-6). 18.95 *(978-1-4759-7312-9(8))* iUniverse, Inc.

Trine, Greg. Invasion from Planet Dork. Montijo, Rhode, illus. 2010. (Melvin Beederman, Superhero Ser.: 8). (ENG.). 144p. (J). (gr. 2-7). pap. 8.99 *(978-0-8050-8167-1(4)*, 9780805081671) Square Fish.

Turner, Paul. ULYSSES: the Pegasi Incident. 2007. 216p. pap. 15.95 *(978-1-84753-642-6(5))* Lulu Pr., Inc.

Vaughn, C. L. I See Aliens. 2007. 15p. 10.95 *(978-1-4357-0117-5(8))* Lulu Pr., Inc.

Walden, Mark. Earthfall. 2013. (Earthfall Trilogy Ser.: 1). (ENG., Illus.). 272p. (J). (gr. 3-7). 16.99 *(978-1-4424-9415-2(8)*, Simon & Schuster Bks. For Young Readers) Simon & Schuster Bks. For Young Readers.

—Retribution. 2015. (Earthfall Trilogy Ser.: 2). (ENG., Illus.). 272p. (J). (gr. 3-7). 17.99 *(978-1-4424-9418-3(2)*, Simon & Schuster Bks. For Young Readers) Simon & Schuster Bks. For Young Readers.

Walker, Nan. Spork Out of Orbit. Warrick, Jessica, illus. 2016. (How to Be an Earthling (r) Ser.: 1). (ENG.). 64p. (gr. 1-3). 22.65 *(978-1-57565-818-6(6))* Kane Press, Inc.

—Spork Out of Orbit: Respect. Warrick, Jessica, illus. 2016. (How to Be an Earthling (r) Ser.: 1). (ENG.). 64p. (gr. 1-3). 34.65 *(978-1-57565-820-9(8))* Kane Press, Inc.

Watson, Jude. Death on Naboo. 2006. (Star Wars Ser.: No. 4). 135p. (J). lib. bdg. 13.00 *(978-1-4242-0777-0(0))* Fitzgerald Bks.

—Underworld. 2005. (Star Wars Ser.: No. 3). 137p. (J). lib. bdg. 20.00 *(978-1-4242-0776-3(2))* Fitzgerald Bks.

Watson, Vicki. Bob & the Alien Escapade. 2013. 226p. pap. *(978-0-9574062-2-3(3))* Green, Callisto.

Watts, Julia. Free Spirits. 2009. (ENG.). 176p. (J). (gr. 1). pap. 8.95 *(978-0-9667359-2-5(7)*, BeanPole Bks.) Harren Communications, LLC.

Webb, Philip. Where the Rock Splits the Sky. 2014. (ENG.). 272p. (J). (gr. 9). 17.99 *(978-0-545-55701-6(1)*, Chicken Hse., The) Scholastic, Inc.

Weisner, David. Mr. Wuffles! Weisner, David, illus. 2013. (Illus.). 49.99 *(978-0-9777098-7-8(6))*; 14.99 *(978-0-9777098-8-5(4))* Dreamscape Media, LLC.

Wells, H. G. The War of the Worlds. 2008. (Bring the Classics to Life Ser.). (ENG., Illus.). 72p. (gr. 3-12). pap., act. bk. ed. 10.95 *(978-1-55576-097-7(X)*, EDCTR-306B) EDCON Publishing Group.

—The War of the Worlds, 1 vol. Fisher, Eric Scott, illus. 2011. (Calico Illustrated Classics Ser.: No. 3). (ENG.). 112p. (YA). (gr. 3-6). 27.07 *(978-1-61641-111-4(2))* Magic Wagon.

Wells, Robison. Dark Energy. 2016. 288p. (YA). (gr. 8). 17.99 *(978-0-06-227505-9(4)*, HarperTeen) HarperCollins Pubs.

West, Melissa. Hover. 2013. (Taking Ser.: 2). (ENG.). 352p. (YA). (gr. 7-12). pap. 9.99 *(978-1-62266-008-7(0)*, 9781622660087) Entangled Publishing, LLC.

White, Ruth. You'll Like It Here (Everybody Does) 2012. (ENG.). 272p. (J). (gr. 4-7). 7.99 *(978-0-375-86596-1(9)*, Yearling) Random Hse. Children's Bks.

Wiesner, David. Mr. Wuffles! 2013. (CHI.). 40p. (J). *(978-986-189-418-8(7))* Grimm Culltural Ent., Co., Ltd.

—Mr. Wuffles! 2013. (ENG., Illus.). 32p. (J). (gr. -1-3). 17.99 *(978-0-618-75661-2(2)*, Clarion Bks.) Houghton Mifflin Harcourt Publishing Co.

Williams, Suzanne. Human or Alien? Carter, Abby, illus. 2004. (Marvelous Mind of Matthew Mcghee Age 8 Ser.). 57p. (J). (gr. 1-4). 11.65 *(978-0-7569-5529-8(7))* Perfection Learning Corp.

Windham, Ryder. Journey Through Space. rev. ed. 2015. (DK Readers Ser.). (ENG.). 48p. (J). (gr. 1-3). pap. 3.99 *(978-1-4654-3390-9(2)*, DK Children) Dorling Kindersley Publishing, Inc.

Winick, Judd. The Boy Who Crashed to Earth. 2015. (Hilo Ser.: 1). (ENG., Illus.). 208p. (J). (gr. 3-7). 16.99 *(978-0-385-38618-0(4)*, Random Hse. Bks. for Young Readers) Random Hse. Children's Bks.

—Saving the Whole Wide World. 2016. (Hilo Ser.: 2). (ENG., Illus.). 208p. (J). (gr. 3-7). 16.99 *(978-0-385-38624-1(9))*;Bk. 2. 13.99 *(978-0-385-38623-4(0))* Random Hse. Children's Bks. (Random Hse. Bks. for Young Readers).

Winterfeld, Henry. Star Girl. Schabert, Kyrill, tr. from GER. Wegner, Fritz, illus. 2015. (ENG.). 192p. (J). (gr. 3-8). pap. 7.99 *(978-0-486-79468-6(7))* Dover Pubns., Inc.

Wong, Clarissa S. The Story of the Guardians of the Galaxy. 2014. (Marvel World of Reading Level 2 Ser.). (J). lib. bdg. 13.55 *(978-0-606-35279-6(1))* Turtleback Bks.

Wronski, Gareth. Holly Farb & the Princess of the Galaxy. 2017. (ENG., Illus.). 320p. (J). (gr. 3-7). 16.99 ***(978-1-4814-7177-0(5)***, Aladdin) Simon & Schuster Children's Publishing.

Wyatt, Chris. Knowhere to Run: Starring Star-Lord. Lim, Ronald & Troy, Andy, illus. 2014. 117p. (J). ***(978-1-4844-4394-1(2)***, Marvel Pr.) Disney Publishing Worldwide.

Wyatt, Chris 'Doc'. Bravest Warriors: The Great Core Caper, Vol.1. Howell, Corin, illus. 2014. (ENG.). 112p. (J). pap. 7.99 *(978-1-4215-7539-1(6))* Viz Media.

Yaccarino, Dan. New Pet. Yaccarino, Dan, illus. 2003. (ENG., Illus.). 40p. (gr. -1-2). pap. 4.99 *(978-0-7868-1429-9(2))* Hyperion Pr.

—Zorgoochi Intergalactic Pizza: Delivery of Doom. Yaccarino, Dan, illus. 2014. (ENG., Illus.). 336p. (J). (gr. 3-7). 16.99 *(978-1-250-00844-2(1)*, 9781250008442) Feiwel & Friends.

Yager, Fred. Sound from a Star: A Novel. 2011. 150p. (YA). 31.95 *(978-1-889262-90-1(0))* Hannacroix Creek Bks., Inc.

Yancey, Rick. The Infinite Sea. (5th Wave Ser.: 2). (ENG.). (YA). (gr. 9-12). 2015. 336p. pap. 10.99 *(978-1-101-99698-0(6)*, Speak) 2014. 320p. 18.99 *(978-0-399-16242-8(9)*, G.P. Putnam's Sons Books for Young Readers) Penguin Publishing Group.

—The Infinite Sea. 2015. (5th Wave Ser.: 2). lib. bdg. 22.10 *(978-0-606-38204-5(6))* Turtleback Bks.

—The Last Star. 2016. (5th Wave Ser.: 3). (ENG.). 352p. (YA). (gr. 9). 18.99 *(978-0-399-16243-5(7)*, G.P. Putnam's Sons Books for Young Readers) Penguin Young Readers Group.

—The Last Star. 2017. (5th Wave Ser.: 3). lib. bdg. 22.10 ***(978-0-606-40098-5(2))*** Turtleback Bks.

Yancey, Rick. The 5th Wave. (5th Wave Ser.: Bk. 1). (ENG.). (YA). (gr. 9). 2015. 512p. pap. 10.99 *(978-0-14-242583-1(4)*, Speak) 2013. 480p. 18.99 *(978-0-399-16241-1(0)*, G.P. Putnam's Sons Books for Young Readers) Penguin Publishing Group.

—The 5th Wave. movie tie-in ed. 2015. (ENG.). (YA). (gr. 9-12). (5th Wave Ser.: 1). 512p. pap. 10.99 *(978-0-14-751908-5(X)*, Speak); (5th Wave Ser.: Bk. 1). 480p. 18.99 *(978-1-101-99651-5(X)*, G.P. Putnam's Sons Books for Young Readers);Set. pap., pap., pap. 21.98 *(978-1-101-99998-1(5)*, Speak) Penguin Young Readers Group.

—The 5th Wave. 2015. (5th Wave Ser.: Vol. 1). (ENG.). (YA). (gr. 9). lib. bdg. 21.60 ***(978-1-62765-623-8(5))*** Perfection Learning Corp.

—The 5th Wave. 2015. (5th Wave Ser.: 1). lib. bdg. 22.10 *(978-0-606-36640-3(7))*; lib. bdg. 22.10 *(978-0-606-37680-8(1))* Turtleback Bks.

Yansky, Brian. Alien Invasion & Other Inconveniences. 2010. (ENG., Illus.). 240p. (YA). (gr. 9-18). 15.99 *(978-0-7636-4384-3(X))* Candlewick Pr.

—Homicidal Aliens & Other Disappointments. 2013. (ENG.). 336p. (YA). (gr. 9). 16.99 *(978-0-7636-5962-2(2))* Candlewick Pr.

Yorinks, Arthur. Company's Going. (J). pap. 14.99 *(978-0-06-205125-7(3))* HarperCollins Pubs.

Yorinks, Arthur, et al. Company's Going. Date not set. (J). lib. bdg. 15.89 *(978-0-06-205126-4(1))* HarperCollins Pubs.

Young, J. E. Horror in Space. Huddleston, Courtney, illus. 2011. (Twisted Journeys Ser.: 18). (ENG.). 112p. (J). (gr. 4-7). pap. 45.32 *(978-0-7613-7614-9(3))*; lib. bdg. 27.93 *(978-0-8225-9265-5(7))* Lerner Publishing Group. (Graphic Universe™).

Young, Jennifer Hayman. Aliens, Eh ! 2011. 248p. (gr. 4-6). pap. 16.95 *(978-1-4620-0588-8(8))* iUniverse, Inc.

Young, Ned. Zoomer's Out-of-This-World Christmas. Young, Ned, illus. 2013. (ENG., Illus.). 32p. (J). (gr. -1-3). 17.99 *(978-0-06-199959-8(8))* HarperCollins Pubs.

Zoomer's Out-Of-This-World Christmas. 2013. (Illus.). (J). *(978-0-06-199960-4(1))* Harper & Row Ltd.

EXTRATERRESTRIAL LIFE

see Extraterrestrial Beings; Life on Other Planets

EXTREME SPORTS

ABDO Publishing Company. Action Sports. 2014. (Action Sports Ser.: 6). (ENG.). 32p. (J). (gr. 8-15). lib. bdg. 162.42 *(978-1-62403-438-1(1)*, A&D Xtreme) ABDO Publishing Co.

ABDO Publishing Company Staff. Extreme Sports Stars. 2014. (Extreme Sports Stars Ser.: 6). (ENG.). 32p. (gr. 8-15). lib. bdg. 162.42 *(978-1-62403-452-7(7)*, SportsZone) ABDO Publishing Co.

—Xtreme Adventure. 2014. (Xtreme Adventure Ser.: 6). (ENG.). 32p. (gr. 3-9). lib. bdg. 162.42 *(978-1-62403-209-7(5)*, Abdo & Daughters) ABDO Publishing Co.

Abraham, Philip. Extreme Sports Stars. 2007. (Sports Stars Ser.). (ENG., Illus.). 48p. (J). (gr. 4-7). pap. 6.95 *(978-0-531-18702-9(0))* Scholastic Library Publishing.

Adamson, Thomas K. Big Air Skateboarding. 2015. (Extreme Sports Ser.). (ENG., Illus.). 24p. (J). (gr. 3-7). lib. bdg. 25.95 *(978-1-62617-272-2(2)*, Epic Bks.) Bellwether Media.

—Big Air Snowboarding. 2016. (Extreme Sports Ser.). (ENG., Illus.). 24p. (J). (gr. 3-7). lib. bdg. 25.95 *(978-1-62617-351-4(6)*, Epic Bks.) Bellwether Media.

—BMX Freestyle. 2015. (Extreme Sports Ser.). (ENG., Illus.). 24p. (J). (gr. 3-7). lib. bdg. 25.95 *(978-1-62617-273-9(0)*, Epic Bks.) Bellwether Media.

—BMX Racing. 2015. (Extreme Sports Ser.). (ENG., Illus.). 24p. (J). (gr. 3-7). lib. bdg. 25.95 *(978-1-62617-274-6(9)*, Epic Bks.) Bellwether Media.

—Motocross Racing. 2015. (Extreme Sports Ser.). (ENG., Illus.). 24p. (J). (gr. 3-7). lib. bdg. 25.95 *(978-1-62617-276-0(5)*, Epic Bks.) Bellwether Media.

—Skateboarding Street Style. 2015. (Extreme Sports Ser.). (ENG., Illus.). 24p. (J). (gr. 3-7). lib. bdg. 25.95 *(978-1-62617-277-7(3)*, Epic Bks.) Bellwether Media.

Antram, David. Extreme Sports. 2012. (How to Draw Ser.). (ENG.). 32p. (J). (gr. 4-6). pap. 11.75 *(978-1-4488-6465-2(8))*; lib. bdg. 26.50

(978-1-4488-6459-1(3)) Rosen Publishing Group, Inc., The. (PowerKids Pr.).
Bach, Rachel. The Bike Race. 2017. (Let's Race Ser.). (ENG., Illus.). 16p. (J). (gr. -1-1). pap. 7.99 *(978-1-68152-129-9(6))* Amicus.
—The Bike Race. 2016. (Let's Race Ser.). (ENG., Illus.). 16p. (gr. k-3). 17.95 *(978-1-60753-910-0(1))* Amicus Publishing.
Bass, Scott. Surf! Your Guide to Longboarding, Shortboarding, Tubing, Aerials, Hanging Ten & More. 2003. (Extreme Sports Ser.). (ENG., Illus.). 64p. (J). (gr. 4-7). pap. 8.95 *(978-0-7922-5108-8(3),* National Geographic Children's Bks.) National Geographic Society.
Benjamin, Daniel. Extreme Rock Climbing. 2013. (Sports on the Edge 2 Ser.). 48p. (J). (gr. 4-8). pap. 12.93 *(978-1-62712-133-0(1));* (Illus.). 29.93 *(978-1-60870-223-7(5))* Cavendish Square Publishing.
Blomquist, Christopher. BMX in the X Games. 2009. (Kid's Guide to the X Games Ser.). 24p. (gr. 3-3). 42.50 *(978-1-61511-207-4(3),* PowerKids Pr.) Rosen Publishing Group, Inc., The.
—Skateboarding in the X Games. 2009. (Kid's Guide to the X Games Ser.). 24p. (gr. 3-3). 42.50 *(978-1-61511-210-4(3),* PowerKids Pr.) Rosen Publishing Group, Inc., The.
Bloomquist, Christopher. BMX in the X Games. 2003. (Kid's Guide to the X Games Ser.). (Illus.). 24p. (J). lib. bdg. 22.60 *(978-0-8239-6298-3(9),* PowerKids Pr.) Rosen Publishing Group, Inc., The.
Bowman, Chris. Vert Skateboarding. 2016. (Extreme Sports Ser.). (ENG., Illus.). 24p. (J). (gr. 3-7). lib. bdg. 25.95 *(978-1-62617-354-5(0),* Epic Bks.) Bellwether Media.
Butler, Erin K. Extreme Air Sports. 2017. (Sports to the Extreme Ser.). (ENG.). 32p. (gr. 3-4). lib. bdg. 27.99 ***(978-1-5157-7861-5(4),*** Edge Bks.) Capstone Press of Coughlan Cos.
—Extreme Land Sports. 2017. (Sports to the Extreme Ser.). (ENG.). 32p. (gr. 3-4). lib. bdg. 27.99 ***(978-1-5157-7860-8(6),*** Edge Bks.) Capstone Press of Coughlan Cos.
—Extreme Snow & Ice Sports. 2017. (Sports to the Extreme Ser.). (ENG.). 32p. (gr. 3-4). lib. bdg. 27.99 ***(978-1-5157-7859-2(2),*** Edge Bks.) Capstone Press of Coughlan Cos.
—Extreme Water Sports. 2017. (Sports to the Extreme Ser.). (ENG.). 32p. (gr. 3-4). lib. bdg. 27.99 ***(978-1-5157-7862-2(2),*** Edge Bks.) Capstone Press of Coughlan Cos.
Chambers, Jo. That's Extreme. 2007. (Trackers-Math Ser.). (gr. 2-5). pap. 5.00 *(978-1-59055-936-9(3))* Pacific Learning, Inc.
Cohn, Jessica. BASE Jumping. 2013. (Incredibly Insane Sports Ser.). (Illus.). 48p. (J). (gr. 4-6). 31.95 *(978-1-4339-8818-9(6));* pap. 14.05 *(978-1-4339-8819-6(4))* Stevens, Gareth Publishing LLLP. (Gareth Stevens Learning Library).
Coy, John. For Extreme-Sports Crazy Boys Only. 2015. (ENG., Illus.). 160p. (J). (gr. 2-7). 15.99 *(978-1-250-04944-5(X),* 9781250049445) Feiwel & Friends.
Crossingham, John. Extreme Skateboarding. 2003. (Extreme Sports - No Limits Ser.). (ENG., Illus.). 32p. (J). (gr. 3). pap. *(978-0-7787-1714-0(3))* Crabtree Publishing Co.
—Extreme Sports - No Limits, 4 bks. Incl. Extreme BMX. Bishop, Amanda. pap. *(978-0-7787-1712-6(7));* Extreme in-Line Skating. Kalman, Bobbie. pap. *(978-0-7787-1713-3(5));* Extreme Skateboarding. pap. *(978-0-7787-1714-0(3));* Extreme Surfing. Kalman, Bobbie. pap. *(978-0-7787-1715-7(1));* 32p. (J). (gr. 3). 2003. (Illus.). 2003. Set pap. *(978-0-7787-1711-9(9));* Set lib. bdg. *(978-0-7787-1665-5(1))* Crabtree Publishing Co.
Crossingham, John & Bishop, Amanda. Extreme BMX. 2003. (Extreme Sports - No Limits Ser.). (ENG., Illus.). 32p. (J). (gr. 3). pap. *(978-0-7787-1712-6(7));* lib. bdg. *(978-0-7787-1666-2(X));* lib. bdg. *(978-0-7787-1666-2(X))* Crabtree Publishing Co.
Crossingham, John & Kalman, Bobbie. Extreme in-Line Skating. 2003. (Extreme Sports - No Limits Ser.). (ENG., Illus.). 32p. (J). (gr. 3). pap. *(978-0-7787-1713-3(5))* Crabtree Publishing Co.
—Extreme Surfing. 2003. (Extreme Sports - No Limits Ser.). (ENG., Illus.). 32p. (J). (gr. 3). pap. *(978-0-7787-1715-7(1));* lib. bdg. *(978-0-7787-1669-3(4))* Crabtree Publishing Co.
—La Planche à Roulettes Extrême. Briere, Marie-Josee, tr. from ENG. rev. ed. 2007. (Sans Limites Ser.). (FRE., Illus.). 32p. (J). (gr. 1-7). pap. 9.95 *(978-2-89579-123-2(6))* Bayard Canada Livres CAN. Dist: Crabtree Publishing Co.
Daredevil Sports. 2015. (Daredevil Sports Ser.). (ENG.), 32p. (J). (gr. 1-1). 151.50 *(978-1-4824-2555-0(6));* pap., pap., pap. 378.00 *(978-1-4824-3450-7(4))* Stevens, Gareth Publishing LLLP.
Domnauer, Teresa & Kenah, Katharine. Ultimate Sports. 2006. (Extreme Readers: Level 3 Ser.). (Illus.). 32p. (gr. 1-2). 14.45 *(978-0-7569-6850-2(X))* Perfection Learning Corp.
Douglas, Peter. Extreme Sports: Pointers for Pushing the Limits. 2017. (Preparing for Game Day Ser.: Vol. 10). (ENG.). (YA). (gr. 7-12). 24.95 ***(978-1-4222-3916-2(0))*** Mason Crest.
Edwardes, Dan. Parkour. 2009. (ENG., Illus.). 32p. (J). (gr. 6-8). lib. bdg. *(978-0-7787-3821-3(3))* Crabtree Publishing Co.
Elish, Dan. Extreme Mountain Biking. 2011. (Sports on the Edge Ser.). (Illus.). 48p. (J). (gr. 6). 29.93 *(978-1-60870-228-2(6))* Marshall Cavendish Corp.
Evans, Lynette. Camp Extreme. 2008. (Illus.). 36p. pap. *(978-0-531-15492-2(0))* Children's Pr., Ltd.
—Camp Extreme. 2007. (Shockwave: the Human Experience Ser.). (ENG., Illus.). 36p. (J). (gr. 3-5). 25.00 *(978-0-531-17758-7(0),* Children's Pr.) Scholastic Library Publishing.
—Extreme Sports. 2008. (Illus.). 36p. (J). pap. *(978-0-531-15493-9(9))* Children's Pr., Ltd.
—Extreme Sports. 2007. (Shockwave: the Human Experience Ser.). (ENG., Illus.). 36p. (J). (gr. 4-6). lib. bdg. 25.00 *(978-0-531-17759-4(9),* Children's Pr.) Scholastic Library Publishing.
Extreme Sports, 6 vols. (Wildcats Ser.). 32p. (gr. 2-8). *(978-0-322-00605-8(8))* Wright Group/McGraw-Hill.
Extreme Sports Coloring Book. 2004. (J). mass mkt. 5.99 *(978-0-9763757-0-8(2))* Cypress Knees Publishing.
Gitlin, Martin. Extreme Sports & Their Greatest Competitors, 1 vol. 2015. (ENG.). 80p. (YA). 31.70 *(978-1-62275-596-7(0),* Britannica Educational Publishing) Rosen Publishing Group, Inc., The.
Gitlin, Marty. Brutal Games: History's Most Dangerous Sports. 2013. (Dangerous History Ser.). (ENG.). 32p. (gr. 3-4). 27.99 *(978-1-4765-0125-3(4),* Edge Bks.) Capstone Press of Coughlan Cos.
Glidewell, Steve. Inline Skating. 2003. (Extreme Sports Ser.). (ENG., Illus.). 32p. (gr. 3-6). lib. bdg. 22.60 *(978-0-8225-1244-8(0))* Lerner Publishing Group.
Greek, Joe. Parkour. 2015. (Sports to the Extreme Ser.). (ENG., Illus.). 48p. (J). (gr. 5-6). 30.25 *(978-1-4994-3553-5(3),* Rosen Central) Rosen Publishing Group, Inc., The.
Hamilton, John. Bmx. 2014. (Action Sports Ser.). (ENG.). 32p. (gr. 8-15). lib. bdg. 27.07 *(978-1-62403-439-8(X),* A&D Xtreme) ABDO Publishing Co.
—Go-Kart Racing. 2014. (Action Sports Ser.). (ENG., Illus.). 32p. (J). (gr. 8-15). lib. bdg. 27.07 *(978-1-62403-440-4(3),* A&D Xtreme) ABDO Publishing Co.
—Inline Skating. 2014. (Action Sports Ser.). (ENG., Illus.). 32p. (J). (gr. 8-15). lib. bdg. 27.07 *(978-1-62403-441-1(1),* Abdo & Daughters) ABDO Publishing Co.
Hamilton, S. L. White Water. 2010. (Xtreme Sports Ser.). 32p. (gr. 3-9). 27.07 *(978-1-61613-006-0(7),* A&D Xtreme) ABDO Publishing Co.
Heinrichs, Ann. Storm Chaser. 2009. (21st Century Skills Library: Cool Science Careers Ser.). (ENG.). 32p. (gr. 4-8). lib. bdg. 28.50 *(978-1-60279-308-8(5),* 200204) Cherry Lake Publishing.
Herzog, Brad. E Is for Extreme: An Extreme Sports Alphabet. Rose, Melanie, illus. rev. ed. 2007. (Sports Ser.). (ENG.). 40p. (J). (gr. -1-3). 17.95 *(978-1-58536-310-0(3))* Sleeping Bear Pr.
—E Is for Extreme: An Extreme Sports Alphabet. Rose, Melanie, illus. 2015. (Av2 Fiction Readalong 2016 Ser.). (ENG.). (J). (gr. 1-4). lib. bdg. 34.28 *(978-1-4896-3735-2(4),* AV2 by Weigl) Weigl Pubs., Inc.
Jackson, Demi. Parkour. 2015. (Daredevil Sports Ser.). (ENG., Illus.). 32p. (J). (gr. 1-1). pap. 10.50 *(978-1-4824-2993-0(4))* Stevens, Gareth Publishing LLLP.
Job, Chris. BMX. 2003. (Extreme Sports Ser.). (ENG., Illus.). 32p. (gr. 3-6). lib. bdg. 22.60 *(978-0-8225-1243-1(2))* Lerner Publishing Group.
Kalman, Bobbie. Extreme Wakeboarding. 2006. (Extreme Sports No Limits! Ser.). (ENG., Illus.). 32p. (J). (gr. 3-7). pap. *(978-0-7787-1726-3(7));* lib. bdg. *(978-0-7787-1680-8(5))* Crabtree Publishing Co.
Kalman, Bobbie & Crossingham, John. Extreme Climbing. 2003. (Extreme Sports No Limits! Ser.). (ENG., Illus.). 32p. (J). pap. *(978-0-7787-1717-1(8));* lib. bdg. *(978-0-7787-1671-6(6))* Crabtree Publishing Co.
—Extreme Motocross. 2003. (Extreme Sports - No Limits Ser.). (ENG., Illus.). 32p. (J). pap. *(978-0-7787-1716-4(X));* lib. bdg. *(978-0-7787-1670-9(8))* Crabtree Publishing Co.
—Extreme Skydiving. 2006. (Extreme Sports No Limits! Ser.). (ENG., Illus.). 32p. (J). (gr. 3-7). pap. *(978-0-7787-1730-0(5));* lib. bdg. *(978-0-7787-1684-6(8))* Crabtree Publishing Co.
—Extreme Sports. 2003. (Extreme Sports - No Limits Ser.). (ENG., Illus.). 32p. (J). pap. *(978-0-7787-1719-5(4))* Crabtree Publishing Co.
Kalman, Bobbie & MacAulay, Kelley. Extreme Snowboarding. 2003. (Extreme Sports - No Limits Ser.). (ENG., Illus.). 32p. (J). pap. *(978-0-7787-1718-8(6));* lib. bdg. *(978-0-7787-1672-3(4))* Crabtree Publishing Co.
Kelley, K. C. BASE Jumping. 2011. (Extreme Sports Ser.). (ENG., Illus.). 32p. (J). (gr. 2-5). lib. bdg. 28.50 *(978-1-60973-205-9(7),* 201121) Child's World, Inc., The.
—Gliding. 2012. (Extreme Sports Ser.). (ENG., Illus.). 32p. (J). (gr. 2-5). lib. bdg. 28.50 *(978-1-60973-207-3(3),* 201125) Child's World, Inc., The.
—Hang Gliding. 2011. (Extreme Sports Ser.). (ENG., Illus.). 32p. (J). (gr. 2-5). lib. bdg. 28.50 *(978-1-60973-208-0(1),* 201126) Child's World, Inc., The.
—Stand-up Paddleboarding. 2011. (Extreme Sports Ser.). (ENG., Illus.). 32p. (J). (gr. 2-5). lib. bdg. 28.50 *(978-1-60973-179-3(4),* 201134) Child's World, Inc., The.
Kennedy, Robert C. Would You Dare Be an MMA Fighter? 2016. (Would You Dare? Ser.). 00032p. (J). pap. 10.50 *(978-1-4824-5814-5(4))* Stevens, Gareth Publishing LLLP.
Kidder, Jeffrey L. Parkour & the City: Risk, Masculinity, & Meaning in a Postmodern Sport. 2017. (Critical Issues in Sport & Society Ser.). (ENG., Illus.). 256p. (gr. 11). pap. 29.95 *(978-0-8135-7195-9(2))* Rutgers Univ. Pr.
A Kid's Guide to the X Games. (Illus.). (J). (gr. k-5). *(978-0-8239-7258-6(5))* Rosen Publishing Group, Inc., The.
Kissock, Heather. Extreme Sports. 2012. (J). *(978-1-61913-239-9(7));* pap. *(978-1-61913-244-3(3))* Weigl Pubs., Inc.
Koll, Hilary & Mills, Steve. A Math Journey Through Extreme Sports. 2016. (ENG., Illus.). 32p. (J). *(978-0-7787-2313-4(5))* Crabtree Publishing Co.
Labrecque, Ellen. Cliff Diving. 2012. (Extreme Sports Ser.). (ENG., Illus.). 32p. (J). (gr. 2-5). lib. bdg. 28.50 *(978-1-60973-178-6(6),* 201123) Child's World, Inc., The.
—Rope Sports, 1 vol. 2011. (Extreme Sports Ser.). (ENG., Illus.). 32p. (gr. 1-2). 29.99 *(978-1-4109-4218-0(X),* Read Me!) Heinemann-Raintree.
—Whitewater Kayaking. 2011. (Extreme Sports Ser.). (ENG., Illus.). 32p. (J). (gr. 2-5). lib. bdg. 28.50 *(978-1-60973-187-8(5),* 201138) Child's World, Inc., The.
Laurendeau, Jason. BASE Jumping: The Ultimate Guide, 1 vol. 2012. (Greenwood Guides to Extreme Sports Ser.). (Illus.). 131p. (C). 41.00 *(978-0-313-38397-7(9),* A2881C, Greenwood) ABC-CLIO, LLC.
Li, Wenfang. Extreme Sports. 2010. (Getting the Edge Ser.). 96p. (YA). lib. bdg. 24.95 *(978-1-4222-1729-0(9))* Mason Crest.
Loh-Hagan, Virginia. Extreme Base Jumping. 2015. (Nailed It! Ser.). (ENG., Illus.). 32p. (J). (gr. 4-8). 29.93 *(978-1-63470-022-1(8),* 206716); pap. 14.21 *(978-1-63470-049-8(X),* 206717) Cherry Lake Publishing.
—Extreme BMX Freestyle. 2015. (Illus.). 32p. *(978-1-63470-016-0(3))* Cherry Lake Publishing.
—Extreme Flyboarding. 2016. (Nailed It! Ser.). (ENG., Illus.). 32p. (J). (gr. 4-8). 29.93 *(978-1-63471-090-9(8),* 208471, 45th Parallel Press) Cherry Lake Publishing.
—Extreme Ice Cross Downhill. 2016. (Illus.). 32p. (J). *(978-1-63470-486-1(X))* Cherry Lake Publishing.
—Extreme Kite Surfing. 2015. (J). *(978-1-63470-019-1(8))* Cherry Lake Publishing.
—Extreme Mountain Climbing. 2016. (Nailed It! Ser.). (ENG., Illus.). 32p. (J). (gr. 4-8). 29.93 *(978-1-63470-491-5(6),* 207695) Cherry Lake Publishing.
—Extreme Parkour. 2016. (Illus.). 32p. (J). *(978-1-63470-487-8(8))* Cherry Lake Publishing.
—Extreme Skateboarding. 2015. (Illus.). 32p. (J). *(978-1-63470-015-3(5))* Cherry Lake Publishing.
—Extreme Sky Diving. 2015. (Illus.). 32p. *(978-1-63470-021-4(X))* Cherry Lake Publishing.
—Extreme Snow Skiing. 2015. (Illus.). 32p. (J). *(978-1-63470-017-7(1))* Cherry Lake Publishing.
—Extreme Snowboarding. 2015. (Illus.). 32p. (J). *(978-1-63470-018-4(X))* Cherry Lake Publishing.
—Extreme Street Luging. 2016. (Illus.). 32p. (J). *(978-1-63470-488-5(6))* Cherry Lake Publishing.
—Extreme Tightrope. 2016. (Illus.). 32p. (J). *(978-1-63470-489-2(4))* Cherry Lake Publishing.
—Extreme Trials Biking. 2016. (Illus.). 32p. (J). *(978-1-63470-485-4(1))* Cherry Lake Publishing.
—Extreme Ultra Running. 2016. (Illus.). 32p. *(978-1-63470-484-7(3))* Cherry Lake Publishing.
MacAulay, Kelley & Kalman, Bobbie. Extreme Mountain Biking. 2006. (Extreme Sports No Limits! Ser.). (ENG., Illus.). 32p. (J). (gr. 3-7). pap. *(978-0-7787-1724-9(0));* lib. bdg. *(978-0-7787-1678-5(3))* Crabtree Publishing Co.
—Extreme Skiing. 2006. (Extreme Sports No Limits! Ser.). (ENG., Illus.). 32p. (J). (gr. 3-7). pap. *(978-0-7787-1728-7(3),* 1253447); lib. bdg. *(978-0-7787-1682-2(1),* 1253447) Crabtree Publishing Co.
—Le Vélo de Montagne Extrême. 2008. (FRE.). 32p. (J). pap. 9.95 *(978-2-89579-185-0(6))* Bayard Canada Livres CAN. Dist: Crabtree Publishing Co.
Mahaney, Ian F. Taig Khris: In-Line Skate Champion. 2005. (Extreme Sports Biographies Ser.). (Illus.). 24p. (J). 22.60 *(978-1-4042-2746-0(6),* PowerKids Pr.) Rosen Publishing Group, Inc., The.
—Taig Khris: In-Line Skating Champion. 2009. (Extreme Sports Biographies Ser.). 24p. (gr. 3-4). 42.50 *(978-1-61512-471-8(3),* PowerKids Pr.) Rosen Publishing Group, Inc., The.
Mara, Wil. Extreme BMX. 2011. (Sports on the Edge Ser.). (Illus.). 48p. (J). (gr. 6). 29.93 *(978-1-60870-227-5(8))* Marshall Cavendish GBR. Dist: Marshall Cavendish Corp.
—Extreme Motocross. 2013. (Sports on the Edge 2 Ser.). 48p. (J). (gr. 4-8). pap. 12.93 *(978-1-62712-132-3(3));* (Illus.). 29.93 *(978-1-60870-222-0(7))* Cavendish Square Publishing.
Mason, Paul. Extreme Sports Stars. 2012. (Celebrity Secrets Ser.). (ENG., Illus.). 24p. (J). (gr. 5-8). pap. 8.25 *(978-1-4488-7080-6(1));* lib. bdg. 22.60 *(978-1-4488-7035-6(6))* Rosen Publishing Group, Inc., The. (PowerKids Pr.).
McClellan, Ray. Downhill BMX. 2008. (Action Sports Ser.). (ENG., Illus.). 24p. (J). (gr. 3-7). lib. bdg. 25.95 *(978-1-60014-139-3(0))* Bellwether Media.
McNab, Chris. Extreme Sports. 2005. (Sports Injuries Ser.). (Illus.). 64p. (YA). lib. bdg. 19.95 *(978-1-59084-630-8(3))* Mason Crest.
Mitchell Lane Publishers Inc. Staff. A Robbie Reader-Extreme Sports, 5 vols. 2007. (J). lib. bdg. 128.50 *(978-1-58415-599-7(X))* Mitchell Lane Pubs., Inc.
Murdico, Suzanne J. Street Luge & Dirtboarding. (World of Skateboarding Ser.). 48p. (gr. 5-8). 2009. 53.00 *(978-1-60854-316-8(1),* Rosen Reference) 2005. (Illus.). (YA). lib. bdg. 29.25 *(978-0-8239-3647-2(3))* Rosen Publishing Group, Inc., The.
Murdico, Suzanne J. & Michalski, Peter. Street Luge & Dirtboarding. 2016. (Skateboarding Tips & Tricks Ser.). 48p. (J). (gr. 5-5). pap. 11.75 *(978-1-4777-8870-7(0),* Rosen Reference) Rosen Publishing Group, Inc., The.
Orme, David. Extreme Sports. 2011. (Fact to Fiction Grafx Ser.). (ENG., Illus.). 36p. (J). (gr. 4-7). lib. bdg. 17.45 *(978-1-61384-019-1(5))* Perfection Learning Corp.
Orr, Tamara B. Extreme Skysurfing. 2013. (Sports on the Edge 2 Ser.). 48p. (J). (gr. 4-8). pap. 12.93 *(978-1-62712-136-1(6))* Cavendish Square Publishing.
—Extreme Wakeboarding. 2013. (Sports on the Edge 2 Ser.). (Illus.). 48p. (J). (gr. 4-8). pap. 12.93 *(978-1-62712-134-7(X))* Cavendish Square Publishing.
Orr, Tamra. Extreme In-Line Skating. 2011. (Sports on the Edge Ser.). (Illus.). 48p. (J). (gr. 6). 29.93 *(978-1-60870-225-1(1))* Marshall Cavendish Corp.
—Extreme Street Luge. 2011. (Sports on the Edge Ser.). (Illus.). 48p. (J). (gr. 6). 29.93 *(978-1-60870-230-5(8))* Marshall Cavendish Corp.
Orr, Tamra B. Extreme Skysurfing. 2013. 48p. (J). (gr. 4-8). 29.93 *(978-1-60870-232-9(4))* Cavendish Square Publishing.
Osborne, Ian. Mountain Biking. (Extreme Sports Ser.). (Illus.). 32p. (J). (gr. 3-6). 2004. lib. bdg. 22.60 *(978-0-8225-1245-5(9))* 2003. pap. 6.95 *(978-0-8225-1195-3(9))* Lerner Publishing Group.
Osborne, Mary Pope & Boyce, Natalie Pope. Dogsledding & Extreme Sports. 2016. (Magic Tree House Fact Tracker Ser.: 34). lib. bdg. 16.00 *(978-0-606-38450-6(2))* Turtleback Bks.
—Dogsledding & Extreme Sports: A Nonfiction Companion to Magic Tree House #54: Balto of the Blue Dawn. Molinari, Carlo, illus. 2016. (Magic Tree House - Fact Tracker Ser.: 34). (ENG.). 128p. (J). (gr. 2-5). 6.99 *(978-0-385-38644-9(3),* Random Hse. Bks. for Young Readers) Random Hse. Children's Bks.
Otfinoski, Steven. Extreme Paintball. 2013. (Sports on the Edge 2 Ser.). (Illus.). 48p. (J). (gr. 4-8). pap. 12.93 *(978-1-62712-135-4(8))* Cavendish Square Publishing.
—Extreme Skateboarding. 2013. (Sports on the Edge 2 Ser.). 48p. (J). (gr. 4-8). pap. 12.93 *(978-1-62712-131-6(5));* (Illus.). 29.93 *(978-1-60870-221-3(9))* Cavendish Square Publishing.
—Extreme Surfing. 2011. (Sports on the Edge Ser.). (Illus.). 48p. (J). (gr. 6). 29.93 *(978-1-60870-231-2(6))* Marshall Cavendish GBR. Dist: Marshall Cavendish Corp.
Poolos, Jamie. Surfing & Wind Surfing. 2015. (Sports to the Extreme Ser.). (ENG., Illus.). 48p. (J). (gr. 5-6). 30.25 *(978-1-4994-3573-3(8),* Rosen Central) Rosen Publishing Group, Inc., The.
Rosenberg, Aaron. Taig Khris: In-Line Skating Superstar. 2009. (Extreme Sports Biographies Ser.). 64p. (gr. 3-4). 58.50 *(978-1-61512-470-1(5),* Rosen Reference) Rosen Publishing Group, Inc., The.
—Taig Khris:In-Line Skating. 2005. (Extreme Sports Biographies Ser.). (Illus.). 64p. (J). (gr. 5-8). lib. bdg. 31.95 *(978-1-4042-0069-2(X))* Rosen Publishing Group, Inc., The.
Roytman, Arkady, illus. Extreme Sports. 2008. (Dover Coloring Bks.). (ENG.). 32p. (J). (gr. k-5). pap. 3.99 *(978-0-486-46688-0(4))* Dover Pubns., Inc.
Scheff, Matt. Best Extreme Sports Stars of All Time, 1 vol. 2014. (Sports' Best Ever Ser.). (ENG.). 64p. (gr. 3-6). lib. bdg. 32.79 *(978-1-62403-618-7(X),* SportsZone) ABDO Publishing Co.
—Jamie Bestwick, 1 vol. 2014. (Extreme Sports Stars Ser.). (ENG.). 32p. (gr. 8-15). lib. bdg. 27.07 *(978-1-62403-456-5(X),* SportsZone) ABDO Publishing Co.
—Kelly Slater, 1 vol. 2014. (Extreme Sports Stars Ser.). (ENG.). 32p. (gr. 8-15). lib. bdg. 27.07 *(978-1-62403-458-9(6),* SportsZone) ABDO Publishing Co.
—Lyn-Z Adams Hawkins Pastrana, 1 vol. 2014. (Extreme Sports Stars Ser.). (ENG., Illus.). 32p. (J). (gr. 8-15). lib. bdg. 27.07 *(978-1-62403-454-1(3),* SportsZone) ABDO Publishing Co.
—Shaun White, 1 vol. 2014. (Extreme Sports Stars Ser.). (ENG.). 32p. (gr. 8-15). lib. bdg. 27.07 *(978-1-62403-455-8(1),* SportsZone) ABDO Publishing Co.
—Tony Hawk, 1 vol. 2014. (Extreme Sports Stars Ser.). (ENG.). 32p. (gr. 8-15). lib. bdg. 27.07 *(978-1-62403-453-4(5),* SportsZone) ABDO Publishing Co.
—Torah Bright, 1 vol. 2014. (Extreme Sports Stars Ser.). (ENG.). 32p. (gr. 8-15). lib. bdg. 27.07 *(978-1-62403-457-2(8),* SportsZone) ABDO Publishing Co.
Schuh, Mari C. The Motorcycle Race. 2017. (Let's Race Ser.). (ENG., Illus.). 16p. (J). (gr. -1-1). pap. 7.99 *(978-1-68152-135-0(0))* Amicus.
—The Motorcycle Race. 2016. (Let's Race Ser.). (ENG., Illus.). 16p. (J). (gr. k-3). 17.95 *(978-1-60753-915-5(2))* Amicus Publishing.
Shafran, Michael. Skate! Your Guide to Inline, Aggressive, Vert, Street, Roller Hockey, Speed Skating, Dance, Fitness Training, & More. 2003. (Extreme Sports Ser.). (ENG., Illus.). 64p. (J). (gr. 4-7). pap. 8.95 *(978-0-7922-5107-1(5),* National Geographic Children's Bks.) National Geographic Society.
Sports to the Extreme. 2015. (Sports to the Extreme Ser.). (ENG.). 48p. (J). (gr. 5-6). pap., pap., pap. 564.00 *(978-1-4777-8625-3(2),* Rosen Central) Rosen Publishing Group, Inc., The.
Teitelbaum, Michael. Sailing. 2012. (Extreme Sports Ser.). (ENG., Illus.). 32p. (J). (gr. 2-5). lib. bdg. 28.50 *(978-1-60973-184-7(0),* 201130) Child's World, Inc., The.
Thomas, Isabel. Board Sports. 2011. (On the Radar: Sports Ser.). (ENG., Illus.). 32p. (gr. 4-8). lib. bdg. 26.60 *(978-0-7613-7763-4(8))* Lerner Publishing Group.
Top That Publishing Staff. Extreme Sports. 2006. (Illus.). 48p. *(978-1-84510-101-5(4))* Top That! Publishing PLC.
Wacky World of Sports. 2014. (Wacky World of Sports Ser.). 32p. (J). (gr. 3-6). pap. 63.00 *(978-1-4824-1590-2(9))* Stevens, Gareth Publishing LLLP.
Weigl Publishers Staff & Craats, Rennay. For the Love of Skateboarding. Nault, Jennifer & Turner, Kara, eds. 2003. (For the Love of Sports Ser.). (Illus.). 24p. (J). pap. 8.95 *(978-1-59036-070-5(2))* Weigl Pubs., Inc.
Wood, Alix. Wacky & Dangerous. 2014. (Wacky World of Sports Ser.). 32p. (J). (gr. 3-6). pap. 63.00 *(978-1-4824-1239-0(X))* Stevens, Gareth Publishing LLLP.
—Wacky in the Water. 2014. (Wacky World of Sports Ser.). (Illus.). 32p. (J). (gr. 3-6). pap. 63.00 *(978-1-4824-1240-6(3))* Stevens, Gareth Publishing LLLP.
Woods, Mark. Xtreme! Owen, Ruth, illus. 2010. (Top Score Maths Ser.). 32p. pap. *(978-0-237-54282-5(X))* Evans Brothers, Ltd.
Woods, Mark & Owen, Ruth. Xtreme! Extreme Sports Facts & Stats. 2011. (Top Score Math Ser.). (Illus.). 32p. (J). (gr. 3-6). lib. bdg. 26.60 *(978-1-4339-5020-9(0))* Stevens, Gareth Publishing LLLP.

EXTREME SPORTS—FICTION

Extreme Danger. 2007. 15.00 *(978-0-7569-7603-3(0))* Perfection Learning Corp.
Gattis, Ryan. Air. 2016. (ENG.). 320p. (YA). 17.99 *(978-0-9864484-2-3(7))* Adaptive Studios.
Wheeler, Lisa. Dino-Boarding. Gott, Barry, illus. 2014. (ENG.). 32p. (J). (gr. k-3). lib. bdg. 16.95 *(978-1-4677-0213-3(7),* Carolrhoda Bks.) Lerner Publishing Group.
Withers, Pam. First Descent. 2014. (ENG., Illus.). 266p. (YA). (gr. 7). pap. 9.99 *(978-1-77049-412-1(X),* Tundra Bks.) Tundra Bks. CAN. Dist: Penguin Random Hse. LLC.

EXTREMISM (POLITICAL SCIENCE)

see Right and Left (Political Science)

EYE

see also Optometry; Vision

Acampora, Courtney. Eyes & Ears. Kushnir, Hilli, illus. 2016. (ENG.). 22p. (J). (gr. -1). bds. 12.99 *(978-1-62686-749-9(6),* Silver Dolphin Bks.) Readerlink Distribution Services, LLC.
Aguirre Cox, Maria Victoria & Aguirre Cox, Ernest. The Patch. 2005. (Illus.). 50p. (J). *(978-0-9767994-0-5(5))* Aguirre Cox, Vicki & Ernest.
All Kinds of Eyes, 6 vols., Pack. (Discovery World Ser.). 16p. (gr. 1-2). 28.00 *(978-0-7635-8456-6(8))* Rigby Education.
Ballard, Carol. Why Do I Need Glasses? Vision, 1 vol. 2011. (Inside My Body Ser.). (ENG.). 32p. (gr. 3-5). 30.65 *(978-1-4109-4010-0(1),* NA-r) Heinemann-Raintree.
Baumbusch, Brigitte. Eyes in Art. 2005. (What Makes a Masterpiece? Ser.). (Illus.). 32p. (gr. 1-4). lib. bdg. 23.00 *(978-0-8368-4445-0(9),* Gareth Stevens Learning Library) Stevens, Gareth Publishing LLLP.
Beckering, Analise. Sight. 2009. (World of Wonder Ser.). (Illus.). 24p. (J). (gr. 2-4). pap. 8.95 *(978-1-60596-053-1(5))* Weigl Pubs., Inc.
Bekkering, Annalise. Sight. 2009. (World of Wonder Ser.). (Illus.). 24p. (J). (gr. 2-4). lib. bdg. 24.45 *(978-1-60596-052-4(7))* Weigl Pubs., Inc.

E
F
G

Bellamy, Adam. What's That I See? 2017. (All about My Senses Ser.). 24p. (J). (gr. k-1). lib. bdg. 22.60 (978-0-7660-8605-0(4)) Enslow Pubs., Inc.

Biskup, Agnieszka. The Science Behind Superman's Sight. 2017. (Science Behind Superman Ser.). (ENG.). 24p. (gr. 1-2). lib. bdg. 25.32 (978-1-5157-5098-7(1), DC Super Heroes) Stone Arch Bks.

—Seeing Through Walls: Superman & the Science of Sight. 2016. (Superman Science Ser.). (ENG., Illus.). 32p. (gr. 3-4). lib. bdg. 27.32 (978-1-5157-0912-1(4), DC Super Heroes) Stone Arch Bks.

Biskup, Agnieszka & Enz, Tammy. Science Behind Superman. 2017. (Science Behind Superman Ser.). (ENG.). 24p. (gr. 1-2). 101.28 (978-1-5157-5116-8(3), DC Super Heroes) Stone Arch Bks.

Boothroyd, Jennifer. Eye Color: Brown, Blue, Green, & Other Hues. 2012. (Lightning Bolt Books (tm) — What Traits Are in Your Genes? Ser.). (Illus.). 32p. (gr. k-2). (SPA & ENG.). pap. 7.95 (978-1-58013-954-0(X)); (ENG., lib. bdg. 26.60 (978-0-7613-8938-5(5)) Lerner Publishing Group.

Burton, Margie, et al. Animals' Eyes & Ears. 2011. (Early Connections Ser.). (J). (978-1-61672-479-5(X)) Benchmark Education Co.

Canetti, Yanitzia. La Adaptación, ¡qué Sensación! 2010. (SPA.). (J). (978-1-59835-172-9(9)) Cambridge BrickHouse, Inc.

—Amazing Adaptations! 2010. (J). (978-1-59835-196-5(6)) Cambridge BrickHouse, Inc.

Carr, Aaron. Vista. 2014. (SPA., Illus.). 24p. (J). (978-1-62127-577-0(9)) Weigl Pubs., Inc.

Caster, Shannon. Eyes. 2010. (Body Works Ser.). (Illus.). 24p. (J). pap. 8.25 (978-1-4358-9826-4(5), PowerKids Pr.) Rosen Publishing Group, Inc., The.

Colby, Jennifer. I Need Glasses. 2015. (Tell Me Why Library). (ENG., Illus.). 24p. (J). (gr. 2-5). 27.07 (978-1-63362-613-3(X), 206636) Cherry Lake Publishing.

Curry, Don L. Take Care of Your Eyes. 2005. (Rookie Read-About Health Ser.). (ENG., Illus.). 32p. (J). (gr. k-2). 20.50 (978-0-516-25874-4(5), Children's Pr.) Scholastic Library Publishing.

Dickmann, Nancy. What You Need to Know about Pink Eye. 2016. (Focus on Health Ser.). (ENG., Illus.). 32p. (gr. 3-4). lib. bdg. 27.32 (978-1-4914-8241-4(9)) Capstone Press of Coughlan Cos.

Douglas, Lloyd G. My Eyes. 2004. (Wel-My Body Ser.). (J). 19.00 (978-0-516-24060-2(9), Children's Pr.) Scholastic Library Publishing.

Enslow, Brian. My Eyes. 2010. (All about My Body Ser.). (Illus.). 24p. (J). 22.60 (978-0-7660-3813-4(0)); pap. 7.95 (978-1-59845-169-6(3)) Enslow Pubs., Inc. (Enslow Elementary).

Eyes. (Amazing Animals Ser.). 32p. (J). (gr. 1). pap. (978-1-882210-76-3(X)) Action Publishing, Inc.

Eyes: Level C, 6 vols. (Wonder Worldtm Ser.). 16p. 24.95 (978-0-7802-1992-2(9)) Wright Group/McGraw-Hill.

Eyes & Ears Sets: 1 Each of 3 Big Books. (Sunshinetm Science Ser.). (gr. 1-2). 111.50 (978-0-7802-1445-3(5)) Wright Group/McGraw-Hill.

Eyes & Ears Sets: 1 Each of 3 Student Books. (Sunshinetm Science Ser.). (gr. 1-2). 20.95 (978-0-7802-1747-8(0)) Wright Group/McGraw-Hill.

Fernandez, A. & Fernandez, Q. Hooray for My Eyes. (Hooray for My Senses Ser.). (Illus.). (J). 19.27 (978-1-58952-374-6(1)) Rourke Educational Media.

Furgang, Kathy. My Eyes. 2009. (My Body Ser.). 24p. (gr. 3-3). 42.50 (978-1-61514-688-8(1), PowerKids Pr.) Rosen Publishing Group, Inc., The.

Ganeri, Anita. Sight. 2013. (Senses Ser.). 24p. (gr. k-3). 28.50 (978-1-59920-852-7(0)) Black Rabbit Bks.

Gordon, Sharon. Pinkeye. 2003. (Rookie Read-About Health Ser.). (ENG., Illus.). 32p. (J). (gr. k-2). pap. 5.95 (978-0-516-27396-9(5)); 20.50 (978-0-516-22583-8(9)) Scholastic Library Publishing. (Children's Pr.).

Halvorson, Karin. Inside the Eyes, 1 vol. 2013. (Super Simple Your Body Ser.). (ENG.). 32p. (J). (gr. k-4). 27.07 (978-1-61783-611-4(7)) ABDO Publishing Co.

Hengel, Katherine. Eyes Are for Winking: The Sense of Sight, 1 vol. 2012. (All about Your Senses Ser.). (ENG.). 24p. (J). (gr. k-3). lib. bdg. 24.21 (978-1-61783-197-3(2), SandCastle) ABDO Publishing Co.

Hidalgo, Maria. Sight. 2003. 24p. (J). lib. bdg. 21.35 (978-1-58340-303-7(5)) Black Rabbit Bks.

Honders, Christine. How Cats & Other Animals See at Night. 2015. (Superior Animal Senses Ser.). (ENG., Illus.). 24p. (J). (gr. 3-4). pap. 8.25 (978-1-4994-0989-5(3), PowerKids Pr.) Rosen Publishing Group, Inc., The.

Huddle, Rusty & Viegas, Jennifer. The Eye in 3D. 2015. (Human Body In 3D Ser.). (ENG., Illus.). 64p. (J). (gr. 5-6). 32.95 (978-1-4994-3589-4(4), Rosen Central) Rosen Publishing Group, Inc., The.

Klingel, Cynthia & Noyed, Robert B. Eyes. 2010. (Let's Read about Our Bodies Ser.). (Illus.). 24p. (gr. k-3). pap. 8.15 (978-1-4339-3357-8(8)); (J). lib. bdg. 22.00 (978-1-4339-3356-1(X)) Stevens, Gareth Publishing LLLP.

—Eyes / Los Ojos. 2010. (Let's Read about Our Bodies / Hablemos del cuerpo humano Ser.). (SPA., Illus.). 24p. (gr. k-3). pap. 8.15 (978-1-4339-3733-0(6)) Stevens, Gareth Publishing LLLP.

—Eyes/Los Ojos. 2010. (Let's Read about Our Bodies / Hablemos del cuerpo humano Ser.). (SPA., Illus.). 24p. (J). (gr. k-3). lib. bdg. 22.00 (978-1-4339-3732-3(8)) Stevens, Gareth Publishing LLLP.

Klosterman, Lorrie. Vision Disorders. 2009. (Health Alert 6 Ser.). 64p. (gr. 4). 32.79 (978-0-7614-3982-0(X)) Marshall Cavendish Corp.

Labrecque, Ellen. Patricia Bath & Laser Surgery. 2017. (21st Century Junior Library: Women Innovators Ser.). (ENG., Illus.). 24p. (J). (gr. 2-5). lib. bdg. 27.07 (978-1-63472-180-6(2), 209292) Cherry Lake Publishing.

Loria, Laura. The Eyes in Your Body, 1 vol. 2015. (ENG.). 32p. (J). 23.45 (978-1-62275-648-3(7), Britannica Educational Publishing) Rosen Publishing Group, Inc., The.

Macaulay, David & Keenan, Sheila. Eye: How It Works. 2015. (ENG., Illus.). 32p. (J). (gr. 1-4). 17.99 (978-1-62672-212-5(9), 9781626722125, Macaulay, David Studio) Roaring Brook Pr.

Markle, Sandra. Lost Sight. 2010. (Powerful Medicine Ser.). (ENG., Illus.). 48p. (gr. 5-8). lib. bdg. 27.93 (978-0-8225-8701-9(7)) Lerner Publishing Group.

Markle, Sandra. What If You Had Animal Eyes? McWilliam, Howard, illus. 2017. (ENG.). 32p. (J). (gr. -1-3). pap. 4.99 **(978-1-338-10108-9(0))**; lib. bdg. 19.99 **(978-1-338-20645-6(1))** Scholastic, Inc.

Marsico, Katie. I Cry. 2014. (Tell Me Why Library). (ENG., Illus.). 24p. (J). (gr. 2-5). 25.64 (978-1-63188-004-9(7), 205423) Cherry Lake Publishing.

Meachen Rau, Dana. Look! [Scholastic]: A Book about Sight. Peterson, Rick, illus. 2010. (Amazing Body: the Five Senses Ser.). 24p. pap. 0.56 (978-1-4048-4390-5(6), Nonfiction Picture Bks.) Picture Window Bks.

Miller, Sara Swan. All Kinds of Eyes. 2007. (All Kinds Of Ser.). (Illus.). 48p. (gr. 3-3). lib. bdg. 29.93 (978-0-7614-2519-9(5)) Marshall Cavendish Corp.

Mitchell, Melanie S. Eyes. 2004. (First Step Nonfiction - Animal Traits Ser.). (ENG.). 8p. (gr. -1-1). pap. 4.95 (978-0-8225-3911-7(X), Lerner Pubns.) Lerner Publishing Group.

Nelson, Robin. Seeing & Hearing Well. 2006. (Pull Ahead Bks.). (Illus.). 32p. (J). (gr. -1-3). lib. bdg. 22.60 (978-0-8225-3488-4(6), Lerner Pubns.) Lerner Publishing Group.

Olson, Karen W. Eyes, Ears, Nose & Mouth. George, Leonard, Jr., illus. (ENG.). 20p. 2005. (J). pap. 10.95 (978-1-894778-34-3(0)) 2009. pap. 9.95 (978-1-894778-52-7(9)) Theytus Bks., Ltd. CAN. Dist: Univ. of Toronto Pr.

Our Eyes. (Sunshinetm Science Ser.). 24p. (gr. 1-2). 37.50 (978-0-7802-1420-0(X)) Wright Group/McGraw-Hill.

Our Eyes: 6 Each of 1 Student Book, 6 vols. (Sunshinetm Science Ser.). 24p. (gr. 1-2). 41.95 (978-0-7802-1419-4(6)) Wright Group/McGraw-Hill.

Parker, Steve & Parker, Vic. Having an Eye Test, 1 vol. 2011. (Growing Up Ser.). (ENG.). 24p. (gr. k-2). 23.32 (978-1-4329-4798-9(2), Heinemann Read & Learn) Heinemann-Raintree.

Pastor Fernández, Andrea. La Vista. (Coleccion Mundo Maravilloso). (SPA., Illus.). 48p. (J). (gr. 2-4). (978-84-348-4318-9(8), SM0099) SM Ediciones.

Phillips, Carey R. & Johannen, Kevin C. Physiology of the Eye. Doggett, W. Kirk, illus. 2nd ed. 2005. (C). cd-rom 95.00 (978-0-9759464-1-1(2), Interactive Eye, L.L.C.) Interactive Knowledge, Inc.

Phillips, Jillian. The World Around Us! Seeing. 2010. (Dover Coloring Bks.). (ENG., Illus.). 32p. (J). (gr. k-3). pap. 4.99 (978-0-486-47731-2(2)) Dover Pubns., Inc.

Pruessen, Linda. Saving Eyesight: Adventures of Seva Around the World. 2015. (ENG., Illus.). 64p. (J). (gr. 4-8). 19.95 (978-1-77085-616-5(1), 9781770856165); pap. 9.95 (978-1-77085-615-8(3), 9781770856158) Firefly Bks., Ltd.

Pryor, Kimberley Jane. Seeing. 2003. (Senses Ser.). (Illus.). 32p. (gr. 2-4). 23.00 (978-0-7910-7555-5(9), Chelsea Hse.) Facts On File, Inc.

Randolph, Joanne. Whose Eyes Are These? 2009. (Animal Clues Ser.). 24p. (gr. 1-1). 42.50 (978-1-61511-432-0(7)); (Illus.). (J). lib. bdg. 22.60 (978-1-4042-4453-5(0)) Rosen Publishing Group, Inc., The. (PowerKids Pr.).

—Whose Eyes Are These? De Quién Son Estos Ojos? 2009. (Animal Clues / ¿Adivina de Quién Es? Ser.). (SPA & ENG., Illus.). 24p. (J). lib. bdg. 22.60 (978-1-4358-2530-7(6)) Rosen Publishing Group, Inc., The.

—Whose Eyes Are These? / ¿de quién son estos Ojos? 2009. (Animal Clues / ¿Adivina de Quién Es? Ser.). (ENG & SPA.). 24p. (gr. 1-1). 42.50 (978-1-61511-438-2(6), Editorial Buenas Letras) Rosen Publishing Group, Inc., The.

Rice, Dona Herweck. Animal Eyes, 1 vol. 2nd rev. ed. 2011. (TIME for KIDS(r) Nonfiction Readers Ser.). (ENG.). 12p. (J). (gr. 1-1). 4.99 (978-1-4333-3578-5(6)) Teacher Created Materials, Inc.

—Ojos de Animales, 1 vol. 2nd rev. ed. 2011. (Nonfiction Readers Ser.). (SPA.). 12p. (J). (gr. 1-1). pap. 4.99 (978-1-4333-4417-6(3)) Teacher Created Materials, Inc.

Rotner, Shelley. Whose Eye Am I? Rotner, Shelley, photos by. 2016. (ENG., Illus.). 32p. (J). 16.95 (978-0-8234-3558-6(X)) Holiday Hse., Inc.

Rustad, Martha E. H. Seeing. 2014. (Illus.). 24p. (J). lib. bdg. 25.65 (978-1-62031-116-5(X), Bullfrog Bks.) Jump! Inc.

Samson, Tess. Look & See. 2010. (Sight Word Readers Ser.). (J). 3.49 (978-1-60719-614-3(X)) Newmark Learning LLC.

Sheen, Barbara. Artificial Eyes. 2016. (Tech Bytes Ser.). (ENG., Illus.). 48p. (J). (gr. 4-6). lib. bdg. 26.60 (978-1-59953-761-0(3)) Norwood Hse. Pr.

Sideri, Simona. Let's Look at Eyes. Noble, Sheilagh, illus. 2003. (Let's Look at Ser.). 24p. (J). (978-1-84089-146-1(7)) Zero to Ten, Ltd.

Silverstein, Virginia. Handy Health Guide to Your Eyes. 2013. (Handy Health Guides). 48p. (J). (gr. 5-12). pap. 8.95 (978-1-4644-0489-4(5)) Enslow Pubs., Inc.

Silverstein, Virginia & Nunn, Laura Silverstein. Handy Health Guide to Your Eyes. 2013. (Handy Health Guides). 48p. (J). lib. bdg. 25.27 (978-0-7660-4273-5(1)) Enslow Pubs., Inc.

Simon, Seymour. Eyes & Ears. (ENG., Illus.). 32p. (J). (gr. k-5). 2005. pap. 6.99 (978-0-06-073302-5(0)) 2003. 15.99 (978-0-688-15303-8(8)) HarperCollins Pubs.

—Eyes & Ears. 2005. (Illus.). (gr. k-3). 17.00 (978-0-7569-5398-0(7)) Perfection Learning Corp.

Slike, Janet. Take a Closer Look at Your Eyes. 2013. (Take a Closer Look Ser.). (ENG.). 24p. (J). (gr. 2-5). 28.50 (978-1-62323-544-4(8), 206351) Child's World, Inc., The.

Souder, Patricia. Blindness & Vision Impairment. Albers, Lisa et al, eds. 2014. (Living with a Special Need Ser.: 16). 128p. (J). (gr. 7-18). 25.95 (978-1-4222-3030-5(9)) Mason Crest.

Souder, Patti. A Different Way of Seeing: Youth with Visual Impairments & Blindness. 2003. (Youth with Special Needs Ser.). (Illus.). 127p. (YA). (gr. 7). pap. 14.95 (978-1-4222-0418-4(9)) Mason Crest.

Stanley, Debbie. Coping with Vision Disorders. 2005. (Coping Ser.). (Illus.). 192p. (YA). (gr. 7-12). lib. bdg. 34.60 (978-0-8239-3198-9(6)) Rosen Publishing Group, Inc., The.

—Everything You Need to Know about Vision Disorders. (Need to Know Library). 64p. 2009. (gr. 5-5). 58.50 (978-1-60854-096-9(0)) 2005. (Illus.). (YA). (gr. 7-12). 31.95 (978-0-8239-3225-2(7)) Rosen Publishing Group, Inc., The.

Stewart, Melissa. Amazing Eyes up Close. 2012. (Animal Bodies up Close Ser.). 24p. (J). (gr. k-3). (Illus.). pap. 7.95 (978-1-4644-0080-3(6)); 22.60 (978-0-7660-3889-9(0)) Enslow Pubs., Inc. (Enslow Elementary).

—The Eyes Have It: The Secrets of Eyes & Seeing. Hamlin, Janet, illus. 2009. (Gross & Goofy Body Ser.). 48p. (gr. 3-4). 29.93 (978-0-7614-4167-0(0)) Marshall Cavendish Corp.

Tekiela, Stan. Peepers & Peekers, 1 vol. 2013. (Adventure Boardbook Ser.). (ENG.). 22p. (J). (gr. -1-k). bds. 6.95 (978-1-59193-423-3(0)) Adventure Pubns.

Tildes, Phyllis Limbacher. Eye Guess: A Foldout Guessing Game. Tildes, Phyllis Limbacher, illus. 2005. (ENG., Illus.). 36p. (J). (gr. -1-2). 11.95 (978-1-57091-650-2(0)) Charlesbridge Publishing, Inc.

Viegas, Jennifer. The Eye: Learning How We See. 2009. (3-D Library of the Human Body Ser.). 48p. (gr. 5-8). 55.90 (978-1-60853-321-3(2), Rosen Reference) Rosen Publishing Group, Inc., The.

Vogel, Julie. Your Sensational Sense of Sight. Squier, Robert, illus. 2011. (Sensational Senses Ser.). (ENG.). 32p. (J). (gr. k-3). lib. bdg. 27.07 (978-1-60954-287-0(8), 200816) Child's World, Inc., The.

Wheeler-Toppen, Jodi Lyn. Our Eyes Can See. 2017. (Our Amazing Senses Ser.). (ENG.). 24p. (gr. k-1). lib. bdg. 21.99 **(978-1-5157-6714-5(0)**, Pebble Bks.) Capstone Press of Coughlan Cos.

EYEGLASSES

see also Lenses

Ballard, Carol. Why Do I Need Glasses? Vision, 1 vol. 2011. (Inside My Body Ser.). (ENG.). 32p. (gr. 3-5). 30.65 (978-1-4109-4010-0(1), NA-r) Heinemann-Raintree.

Colby, Jennifer. I Need Glasses. 2015. (Tell Me Why Library). (ENG., Illus.). 24p. (J). (gr. 2-5). 27.07 (978-1-63362-613-3(X), 206636) Cherry Lake Publishing.

Fejtö, Raphaël. Glasses. 2016. (Little Inventions Ser.). (ENG., Illus.). 32p. (J). (gr. 3-5). 9.95 (978-1-77085-747-6(8), 9781770857476) Firefly Bks., Ltd.

Klosterman, Lorrie. Vision Disorders. 2009. (Health Alert 6 Ser.). 64p. (gr. 4). 32.79 (978-0-7614-3982-0(X)) Marshall Cavendish Corp.

Santos, D. My New Glasses: Learning the GL Sound. 2009. (PowerPhonics Ser.). 24p. (gr. 1-1). 39.90 (978-1-60851-461-8(7), PowerKids Pr.) Rosen Publishing Group, Inc., The.

Williams, Brian. The Science of a Pair of Glasses: The Science of Light. 2009. (Science of... Ser.). (Illus.). 32p. (YA). (gr. 3-6). lib. bdg. 26.00 (978-1-4339-0044-0(0)) Stevens, Gareth Publishing LLLP.

EYEGLASSES—FICTION

Adamson, Ged. Douglas, You Need Glasses! 2016. (ENG., Illus.). 40p. (J). (gr. -1-2). 16.99 (978-0-553-52243-3(4), Schwartz & Wade Bks.) Random Hse. Children's Bks.

Barclay, Eric. I Can See Just Fine. 2013. (ENG., Illus.). 32p. (J). (gr. -1-k). 15.95 (978-1-4197-0801-5(5), Abrams Appleseed) Abrams, Inc.

Baum, Lonna. Monty the Menace: Understanding Differences. Messing, Dave, illus. 2012. (ENG.). 32p. (J). 16.95 (978-0-9839373-0-2(3)) Baum & Baum, LLC.

Berne, Jennifer. Calvin, Look Out! A Bookworm Birdie Gets Glasses. Bendis, Keith, illus. 2014. (ENG.). 32p. (J). (gr. -1-2). 14.95 (978-1-4549-0910-1(2)) Sterling Publishing Co., Inc.

Braunstein, M. & Braunstein, J. Don't I Look Smart. 2009. (978-1-61584-845-4(2)) Independent Pub.

—Don't Look Smart?! 2009. (J). pap. (978-1-61623-138-5(6)) Independent Pub.

Brezinova, Ivona. Dorothy & the Glasses. Llapashtica, Mentor, illus. 2007. 32p. (J). (POL & ENG.). pap. 12.95 (978-1-60195-099-4(3)); (ARA & ENG.). pap. 12.95 (978-1-60195-088-8(8)) International Step by Step Assn.

Bright, Rachel. Benjamin & the Super Spectacles (the Wonderful World of Walter & Winnie) 2015. (Wonderful World of Walter & Winnie Ser.). (ENG.). 32p. (J). 17.99 (978-0-00-758595-3(0), HarperCollins Children's Bks.) HarperCollins Pubs. Ltd. GBR. Dist: HarperCollins Pubs.

Carmona, Adela. The Boy Who Could See. Chapman, Robert E., illus. 2008. 32p. pap. 24.95 (978-1-60672-697-6(8)) PublishAmerica, Inc.

Cohen, Peter. Boris's Glasses. Sandin, Joan, tr. from SWE. Landstrom, Olof, illus. 2003. 28p. (J). (gr. k-3). 15.00 (978-91-29-65942-9(6)) R & S Bks. SWE. Dist: Macmillan.

Cole, Hana. Hooray! I'm Catholic. Steege, Joanna, illus. 2010. 32p. (J). 14.95 (978-0-8091-6746-3(8), Ambassador Bks.) Paulist Pr.

Coulton, Mia. Carla's New Glasses. Totire, Valerie, illus. 2005. (ENG.). 16p. (gr. k-2). pap. 7.95 (978-1-57874-092-5(4), Kaeden Bks.) Kaeden Corp.

Coven, Wanda. Heidi Heckelbeck Gets Glasses. Burris, Priscilla, illus. 2012. (Heidi Heckelbeck Ser.: 5). (ENG.). 128p. (J). (gr. k-2). pap. 5.99 (978-1-4424-4171-2(2)); 15.99 (978-1-4424-4172-9(0)) Little Simon. (Little Simon).

Dacquino, Vin. Max's Glasses. 2011. (Navigators Ser.). (J). pap. (978-1-61672-959-2(7)) Benchmark Education Co.

Day, Shirley. Luna & the Big Blur: A Story for Children Who Wear Glasses. Morris, Don, illus. 2008. 32p. (J). (gr. -1-3). 14.95 (978-1-4338-0398-7(4)); pap. 9.95 (978-1-4338-0399-4(2)) American Psychological Assn. (Magination Pr.).

Dean, James & Dean, Kimberly. Pete the Cat & His Magic Sunglasses. Dean, James, illus. 2013. (Pete the Cat Ser.). (Illus.). 40p. (J). (gr. -1-3). lib. bdg. 18.89 (978-0-06-227557-8(7)) HarperCollins Pubs.

Driscoll, Laura. Super Specs. Gott, Barry, illus. 2005. (Math Matters Ser.). (ENG.). 32p. (J). (gr. -1-3). pap. 5.95 (978-1-57565-145-3(9)) Kane Press, Inc.

Dyan, Penelope. To See or Not to See — -the Story of Kourtney's Glasses. Dyan, Penelope, illus. 2008. (Illus.). 44p. pap. 11.95 (978-1-935118-38-1(2)) Bellissima Publishing, LLC.

Guiffre, William. Gramma's Glasses. Pippin, Barbara, illus. 2008. 32p. (J). (gr. -1-3). pap. 9.95 (978-1-931650-35-9(7)) Bks. for Children Publishing.

Guiffre, William A. Gramma's Glasses. Pippin, Barbara, illus. 2008. 32p. (J). (gr. -1-7). lib. bdg. 17.95 (978-1-931650-19-9(5)) Bks. for Children Publishing.

Hay, Sam. Knit-Knotters. Tran, Turine, illus. 2016. (Stella & the Night Sprites Ser.: 1). (ENG.). 96p. (J). (gr. 1-3). pap. 4.99 (978-0-545-81998-5(9)) Scholastic, Inc.

—Tooth Bandits. Manuzak, Lisa, illus. 2016. (Stella & the Night Sprites Ser.: 2). (ENG.). 96p. (J). (gr. 1-3). 15.99 (978-0-545-82001-1(4)) Scholastic, Inc.

Headley, Justina Chen. The Patch. Vane, Mitch, illus. 2007. (ENG.). 32p. (J). (gr. k-3). pap. 7.95 (978-1-58089-170-7(5)) Charlesbridge Publishing, Inc.

Heling, Kathryn & Hembrook, Deborah. I Wish I Had Glasses Like Rosa. Adamson, Bonnie, illus. (I Wish Ser.). (ENG.). 32p. (J). (gr. 4-7). 2010. pap. 7.95 (978-1-934960-49-3(7)) 2009. 16.95 (978-1-934960-48-6(9)) Continental Sales, Inc. (Raven Tree Pr.,Csi).

Hughes, Jack. Rex's Specs. 2014. (Dinosaur Friends Ser.). (Illus.). 32p. (J). (gr. k-3). lib. bdg. 26.25 (978-1-4777-9226-1(0)) Windmill Bks.

Ismail, Yasmeen. Specs for Rex. 2015. (ENG., Illus.). 32p. (J). (gr. -1-3). 16.99 (978-1-61963-710-8(3), 9781619637108, Bloomsbury USA Childrens) Bloomsbury Publishing USA.

Jacobs, Lana. A Brand-New Look. 2013. (Penguin Young Readers Level 2 Ser.). lib. bdg. 13.55 (978-0-606-29293-1(4), Turtleback) Turtleback Bks.

Kennedy, Kim. Misty Gordon & the Mystery of the Ghost Pirates. 2010. (ENG., Illus.). 240p. (YA). (gr. 3-7). 15.95 (978-0-8109-9357-0(0), Amulet Bks.) Abrams, Inc.

Lathan, Edward. My Glasses Are a Friend to Me. 2012. 24p. pap. 15.99 (978-1-4771-4903-4(1)) Xlibris Corp.

Lundquist, Jenny. Seeing Cinderella. 2012. (Mix Ser.). (ENG.). 240p. (J). (gr. 4-8). pap. 6.99 (978-1-4424-2926-0(7), Aladdin) Simon & Schuster Children's Publishing.

—Seeing Cinderella. 2012. (ENG.). 240p. (J). (gr. 4-8). 16.99 (978-1-4424-4550-5(5), Simon & Schuster/Paula Wiseman Bks.) Simon & Schuster/Paula Wiseman Bks.

Machon, Daphne E. Charlee's New Glasses. 2013. (Illus.). 16p. pap. 8.50 (978-1-78035-736-2(2), Fastprint Publishing) Upfront Publishing Ltd. GBR. Dist: Printondemand-worldwide.com.

Manson, Sheri. Bumpy & Boo Visits the Eye Doctor: Guess Who Needs Glasses? Cabrera, Marcela, illus. 2006. 32p. (J). 15.95 (978-0-9744307-3-7(0)) Merry Lane Pr.

Manushkin, Fran. Who Needs Glasses?, 1 vol. Lyon, Tammie, illus. 2013. (Katie Woo Ser.). (ENG.). 32p. (gr. k-2). pap. 5.95 (978-1-4048-8049-8(6)); lib. bdg. 21.32 (978-1-4048-7655-2(3)) Picture Window Bks.

Meister, Cari. The Lucky Manatee, 1 vol. Harpster, Steve, illus. 2012. (Ocean Tales Ser.). (ENG.). 32p. (gr. 2-4). pap. 6.25 (978-1-4342-4231-0(5)); lib. bdg. 22.65 (978-1-4342-4028-6(2)) Stone Arch Bks.

Nanette. Oinky the Yellow Pig. 2004. (Life on Granny's Farm Ser.). (J). 12.95 (978-0-9741269-4-4(2)) St. Bernard Publishing, LLC.

O'Connor, Jane. Spectacular Spectacles. Glasser, Robin Preiss & Enik, Ted, illus. 2010. (I Can Read Level 1 Ser.). (ENG.). 32p. (J). (gr. -1-3). 16.99 (978-0-06-188263-0(1)) HarperCollins Pubs.

—Spectacular Spectacles, Level 1. Glasser, Robin Preiss & Enik, Ted, illus. 2010. (I Can Read Level 1 Ser.). (ENG.). 32p. (J). (gr. -1-3). pap. 3.99 (978-0-06-188264-7(X)) HarperCollins Pubs.

Park, Barbara. Toothless Wonder. Brunkus, Denise, illus. 2003. (Junie B. Jones Ser.: Bk. 3). 80p. (gr. 1-4). 15.00 (978-0-7569-1621-3(6)) Perfection Learning Corp.

Payne, Yadira V. Brown Eyes: Ojos Marrones. Payne, Yadira V., ed. Payne, Emerald M., illus. 2004. (MUL.). (J). pap. 12.50 (978-0-9747350-1-6(9)) Payne, Yadira V. Publishing.

Saltzberg, Barney. Arlo Needs Glasses. 2012. (ENG., Illus.). 24p. (gr. k-1). 17.95 (978-0-7611-6879-9(6), 16879) Workman Publishing Co., Inc.

Santa Gets New Glasses. 2005. (J). 5.95 (978-0-9769321-2-3(1)) Steingart, Nathan Publishing.

Sena, Keiko. Gracie Meets a Ghost. 2016. (Gracie Wears Glasses Book Ser.). (ENG.). 32p. (J). (gr. -1-k). 16.99 (978-1-940842-13-4(1)) Museyon.

Shusterman, Neal. The Eyes of Kid Midas. 2009. (ENG.). 176p. (YA). (gr. 7). pap. 10.99 (978-1-4169-9750-4(4), Simon & Schuster Bks. For Young Readers) Simon & Schuster Bks. For Young Readers.

Simon, Coco. Mia: A Matter of Taste. 2013. (Cupcake Diaries: 14). lib. bdg. 16.00 (978-0-606-32042-9(3), Turtleback) Turtleback Bks.

—Mia a Matter of Taste. 2013. (Cupcake Diaries: 14). (ENG., Illus.). 160p. (J). (gr. 3-7). 15.99 (978-1-4424-7480-2(7)); pap. 6.99 (978-1-4424-7435-2(1)) Simon Spotlight. (Simon Spotlight).

Stair, Karen Smith. Glasses, Glasses Oh What Do I See. 2004. (Illus.). 32p. 14.95 (978-0-9755407-1-8(8)) Book Pubs. Network.

Stemke, Kathy. Sh Sh Sh Let the Baby Sleep. Foster, Jack, illus. 2011. 20p. pap. 10.95 (978-1-61633-156-6(9)) Guardian Angel Publishing, Inc.

Thomas, Charlie. I Need Glasses. Goldfinger, Jennifer P., illus. 2005. (Rookie Readers Ser.). (ENG.). 32p. (J). (gr. k-2). lib. bdg. 19.50 (978-0-516-24863-9(4), Children's Pr.) Scholastic Library Publishing.

Wilson, Sarah. Hocus Focus. Wummer, Amy, tr. Wummer, Amy, illus. 2004. (Science Solves It! Ser.). 32p. (J). pap. 5.95 (978-1-57565-136-1(X)) Kane Press, Inc.

F

FABLES

see also Animals—Fiction; Folklore; Parables

Aaron. Aesop's Fables. Date not set. 88p. (J). 7.98 (978-0-7525-9844-4(9)) Parragon, Inc.

Aesop. Aesop's Fables. Jones, V. S. Vernon, tr. from GEC. Rackham, Arthur, illus. 2003. (Barnes & Noble Classics Ser.). (ENG.). 304p. pap. 8.95 (978-1-59308-062-4(X)) Barnes & Noble, Inc.

—Animal Fables from Aesop. McClintock, Barbara, illus. 2012. (ENG.). 48p. (J). 17.95 *(978-0-87923-913-8(1))* Godine, David R. Pub.

—Animal Fables from Aesop. 2012. (ENG., Illus.). 48p. (J). (gr. 1-18). reprint ed. pap. 9.95 *(978-1-56792-144-1(2))* Godine, David R. Pub.

—The Fables of Aesop. 2013. (ENG., Illus.). 252p. pap. 17.95 *(978-1-4290-9807-6(4))* New-York Historical Society.

—Fabulas de Esopo.Tr. of Aesop's Fables. (SPA., Illus.). 28p. (J). 18.50 *(978-84-233-1922-0(9))* Ediciones Destino ESP. Dist: AIMS International Bks., Inc.

—The Lion & the Mouse. 2016. (ENG.). 79.82 **(978-1-367-86708-6(8))** Blurb, Inc.

—The Lion & the Mouse. 2017. (Let's Learn Aesop's Fables Ser.). 24p. (gr. 6-7). 24.60 **(978-1-4994-8369-7(4))**; pap. 8.25 **(978-1-4994-8374-1(0))** Rosen Publishing Group, Inc., The. (Windmill Bks.).

—The Miller & the Donkey: A Tale about Thinking for Yourself. Branch, Beverly, illus. 2006. (J). *(978-1-59939-087-1(6)*, Reader's Digest Young Families, Inc.) Studio Fun International.

—The Wolf in Sheep's Clothing: A Tale about Appearances. 2006. (J). *(978-1-59939-086-4(8)*, Reader's Digest Young Families, Inc.) Studio Fun International.

Aesop, illus. Aesop's Fables. 2006. (ENG.). 32p. (J). (gr. -1-3). 16.95 *(978-0-7358-2068-5(6))* North-South Bks., Inc.

Aesop Enterprise Inc. Staff. The Lion & the Mouse. Watts, Bernadette, illus. 2007. (ENG.). 32p. (J). (gr. -1-3). pap. 8.95 *(978-0-7358-2129-3(1))* North-South Bks., Inc.

Aesop Enterprise Inc. Staff & Baruzzi, Agnese. Aesop's Fables. Baruzzi, Agnese, illus. 2012. (ENG., Illus.). 16p. (J). (gr. k-2). 18.99 *(978-1-85707-895-4(0))* Tango Bks. GBR. Dist: Independent Pubs. Group.

Andersen, Hans Christian & White, Mus. For Sure! for Sure! Czernecki, Stefan, illus. 2005. (ENG.). 32p. (J). (gr. k-3). 16.95 *(978-0-87483-742-1(1))* August Hse. Pubs., Inc.

Avalon, Dawn. Bubbels. Een Vochtig Draakje. 2006. 60p. pap. 8.23 *(978-1-4116-1193-1(4))* Lulu Pr., Inc.

—Bubbles. A Wet Dragon. 2006. 59p. pap. 8.21 *(978-1-4116-1177-1(2))* Lulu Pr., Inc.

Bellamy, Marian Meredith. Goldie & Androcles — A Fable for the 21st Century. Bellamy, Marian Meredith, illus. 2005. (Illus.). 91p. (YA). per. 20.00 *(978-0-9765341-0-5(X))* Meredith Group Ltd., The.

Boyd, Roland. The Fisherman & His Wife. Wright, Carol, ed. Zarvatski, Derek, illus. rev. ed. 20p. (J). (gr. 1-2). pap. 6.95 *(978-0-9701573-0-0(4))* Chameleon Designs.

Brett, Jan. Town Mouse Country Mouse. Brett, Jan, illus. 2003. (ENG., Illus.). 32p. (J). (gr. -1-3). pap. 6.99 *(978-0-698-11986-4(X)*, Puffin Books) Penguin Young Readers Group.

—Town Mouse Country Mouse. 2003. (gr. -1-2). 17.20 *(978-0-613-59140-9(2)*, Turtleback) Turtleback Bks.

Cleveland, Rob. The Bear, the Bat & the Dove: Three Stories from Aesop. Hoffmire, Baird, illus. 2006. (Story Cove Ser.). (ENG.). 32p. (J). (gr. -1-3). pap. 3.95 *(978-0-87483-810-7(X))* August Hse. Pubs., Inc.

Clynes, Kate. Little Red Hen & Wheat. 2004. (Illus.). 32p. (J). *(978-1-84444-058-0(3))* Mantra Lingua.

Dominie Press Staff. Aesop's Fables. (J). pap., tchr.'s training gde. ed. 15.50 *(978-0-7685-0177-3(6))* Dominie Pr., Inc.

Doman, Rae. Sunbuddy Fables. 2013. 108p. pap. 9.99 *(978-0-9896218-3-0(9))* Sunraehealing.

Emberley, Rebecca. The Crocodile & the Scorpion. Emberley, Ed, illus. 2013. (ENG.). 32p. (J). (gr. -1-2). 17.99 *(978-1-59643-494-3(5)*, 9781596434943) Roaring Brook Pr.

Enderle, Dotti. Aesop's Opposites: Interactive Aesop Fables. Mitchell, Judy, ed. Shalansky, Len, illus. 2004. 64p. (J). pap. 9.95 *(978-1-57310-424-1(8))* Teaching & Learning Co.

Fabulas. (Coleccion Estrella).Tr. of Fables. (SPA., Illus.). 64p. (J). 14.95 *(978-950-11-0006-8(5)*, SGM006) Sigmar ARG. Dist: Continental Bk. Co., Inc.

Fabulas de la Fontaine. (SPA., Illus.). (YA). 11.95 *(978-84-201-0304-4(7)*, AF1100) Auriga, Ediciones S.A. ESP. Dist: Continental Bk. Co., Inc.

Feathery Fables: Individual Title Six-Packs. (Action Packs Ser.). 128p. (gr. 3-5). 44.00 *(978-0-7635-3312-0(2))* Rigby Education.

Floyd, Lucy. Rabbit & Turtle Go to School. Denise, Christopher, illus. 2003. (Green Light Readers Level 1 Ser.). (ENG.). 24p. (J). (gr. -1-3). pap. 3.95 *(978-0-15-204851-8(0))* Houghton Mifflin Harcourt Publishing Co.

—Rabbit & Turtle Go to School. 2003. (Green Light Readers — Level 1 Ser.). (gr. k-3). lib. bdg. 13.50 *(978-0-613-63339-0(3)*, Turtleback) Turtleback Bks.

Forest, Heather. Ancient & Epic Tales: From Around the World. 2016. (ENG.). 175p. (J). (gr. 3-5). pap. 17.95 *(978-1-939160-87-4(1))* August Hse. Pubs., Inc.

Franco, Betsy. Why the Frog Has Big Eyes. 2003. (Green Light Readers — Level 2 Ser.). (gr. -1-2). lib. bdg. 13.50 *(978-0-613-64618-5(5)*, Turtleback) Turtleback Bks.

Franco, Betsy & Franco-Feeney, Betsy. Why the Frog Has Big Eyes. Kim, Joung Un, illus. 2003. (Green Light Readers Level 2 Ser.). (ENG.). 24p. (J). (gr. -1-3). pap. 3.95 *(978-0-15-204834-1(0))* Houghton Mifflin Harcourt Publishing Co.

Fujikawa, Gyo, illus. Fairy Tales & Fables. 2008. (ENG.). 128p. (J). (gr. -1-2). 9.95 *(978-1-4027-5698-6(4))* Sterling Publishing Co., Inc.

Gavin, Jamila & Quarto Generic Staff. School for Princes: Stories from the Panchatantra. Willey, Bee, illus. 2012. (ENG.). 64p. (J). (gr. 2-5). 19.99 *(978-1-84507-990-1(6)*, Frances Lincoln) Quarto Publishing Group UK GBR. Dist: Hachette Bk. Group.

Griffin, Sandi Z. Yea Us Series (Tails with a Moral), 3 bks., Set. Griffin, Sandi Z., illus. Incl. Becca Bumbum Bunny. 14.00 *(978-1-883838-03-4(7))*; Curly Pig. 14.00 *(978-1-883838-02-7(9))*; Lumpa Lou Elephant. 14.00 *(978-1-883838-01-0(0))*; (Illus.). 28p. (J). (gr. -1-2). 1993. *(978-1-883838-00-3(2))* Griffin, Sandi Zambarano.

Handford, S. A. Aesop's Fables. Winter, Nilo, illus. l.t. ed. Date not set. (J). (gr. 1-12). lib. bdg. 22.95 *(978-0-88411-991-3(2))* Amereon Ltd.

—Aesop's Fables. Salter, Safaya, illus. 2003. (Chrysalis Childrens Classics Ser.). 111p. (YA). pap. *(978-1-84365-035-5(5)*, Pavilion Children's Books) Pavilion Bks.

Handford, S. A. & Lawrence, Jacob. Aesop's Fables. 2003. (ENG., Illus.). 56p. (C). 24.95 *(978-0-295-97641-9(1))* Univ. of Washington Pr.

Hardyman, Robyn. What Is a Fable?, 1 vol., 1. 2014. (Britannica Common Core Library). (ENG.). 32p. (gr. 2-5). 23.45 *(978-1-62275-200-3(7))* Rosen Publishing Group, Inc., The.

Harris, John. Pop-Up Aesop. Brown, Calef, illus. 2005. (ENG.). 10p. (gr. -1-7). 19.95 *(978-0-89236-814-3(4))* Oxford Univ. Pr., Inc.

Hennessy, B. G. The Boy Who Cried Wolf. Kulikov, Boris, illus. 2006. (ENG.). 40p. (J). (gr. -1-3). 17.99 *(978-0-689-87433-8(2)*, Simon & Schuster Bks. For Young Readers) Simon & Schuster Bks. For Young Readers.

Hoberman, Mary Ann. You Read to Me, I'll Read to You: Very Short Fables to Read Together. Emberley, Michael, illus. 2013. (You Read to Me, I'll Read to You Ser.). (ENG.). 32p. (J). (gr. -1-3). 7.00 *(978-0-316-21847-4(2))* Little, Brown Bks. for Young Readers.

Jaekel, Susan, illus. The Tortoise & the Hare: A Tale about Determination. 2006. (J). 6.99 *(978-1-59939-015-4(9))* Cornerstone Pr.

Jaekel, Susan M., illus. Tug of War: A Tale about Being Resourceful. 2006. (J). *(978-1-59939-091-8(4)*, Reader's Digest Young Families, Inc.) Studio Fun International.

Jian, Li. The Snake Goddess Colors the World: A Chinese Tale Told in English & Chinese. 2013. (ENG & CHI., Illus.). 42p. (J). (gr. -1-3). 16.95 *(978-1-60220-982-4(0))* BetterLink Pr., Inc.

Johnson, Richard. Little Red Hen & the Grains of Wheat: Big Book English Only. 2004. (Illus.). (J). *(978-1-84444-298-0(5))* Mantra Lingua.

L. A. Goal Members, contrib. by. Disabled Fables: Aesop's Fables Retold & Illustrated by Artists with Developmental Disabilities, 1 vol. 2005. (ENG., Illus.). 32p. (J). (gr. 1-18). 19.95 *(978-1-932065-97-8(0))* Star Bright Bks., Inc.

Lang, Andrew. The Hut in the Forest: A Tale about Being Kind to Animals. Johnson, Meredith, illus. 2006. (J). *(978-1-59939-083-3(3)*, Reader's Digest Young Families, Inc.) Studio Fun International.

Lasky, Kathryn. The Hatchling. 2005. (Guardians of Ga'hoole Ser.: 7). (ENG.). 240p. (J). (gr. 3-7). pap. 6.99 *(978-0-439-73950-4(0)*, Scholastic Paperbacks) Scholastic, Inc.

Leray, Marjolaine & Ardizzone, Sarah. Little Red Hood. Ardizzone, Sarah, tr. from FRE. Leray, Marjolaine, illus. 2013. (ENG., Illus.). 40p. (J). (gr. -1). 12.99 *(978-1-907912-00-9(2))* Phoenix Yard Bks. GBR. Dist: Independent Pubs. Group.

Leyendas, Fábulas y Cuentos. 2003. (SPA., Illus.). 112p. (YA). (gr. 3-18). 9.95 *(978-968-6966-14-5(5))* EDITER'S Publishing Hse. MEX. Dist: EDITER'S Publishing Hse.

Little Red Hen & the Grains of Wheat. 2004. (J). (ENG & VIE.). *(978-1-84444-620-9(4))*; (ENG & URD.). *(978-1-84444-619-3(0))*; (ENG & TUR.). *(978-1-84444-618-6(2))*; (ENG & TAM.). *(978-1-84444-617-9(4))*; (ENG & TAG.). *(978-1-84444-616-2(6))*; (ENG & SPA.). *(978-1-84444-615-5(8))*; (ENG & SOM.). *(978-1-84444-614-8(X))*; (ENG & RUS.). *(978-1-84444-613-1(1))*; (ENG & POR.). *(978-1-84444-612-4(3))*; (ENG & POL.). *(978-1-84444-610-0(7))*; (ENG & PAN.). *(978-1-84444-609-4(3))*; (ENG & KUR.). *(978-1-84444-608-7(5))*; (ENG & KOR.). *(978-1-84444-607-0(7))*; (ENG & JPN.). *(978-1-84444-606-3(9))*; (ENG & ITA.). *(978-1-84444-605-6(0))*; (ENG & HIN.). *(978-1-84444-604-9(2))*; (ENG & GUJ.). *(978-1-84444-603-2(4))*; (ENG & GRE.). *(978-1-84444-602-5(6))*; (ENG & FRE.). *(978-1-84444-601-8(8))*; (ENG & PER.). *(978-1-84444-600-1(X))*; (CRO & ENG.). *(978-1-84444-599-8(2))*; (CHI & ENG.). *(978-1-84444-598-1(4))*; (CHI & ENG.). *(978-1-84444-597-4(6))*; (BEN & ENG.). *(978-1-84444-596-7(8))*; (ARA & ENG.). *(978-1-84444-595-0(X))*; (ALB & ENG.). *(978-1-84444-594-3(1))* Mantra Lingua.

Little Red HenGrains. 2004. (J). cd-rom *(978-1-84444-462-5(7))* Mantra Lingua.

MacLaren, Dorothy H. Esopus Hodie, Aesop Today, Vol. 1. (ENG & LAT.). 64p. (YA). (gr. 9-12). 9.75 *(978-0-939507-06-1(4)*, B20) American Classical League, The.

Masson, J. Moussaieff. The Cat Who Came in from the Cold: A Fable. 2004. 107p. *(978-0-345-47867-2(3)*, Ballantine Bks.) Random House Publishing Group.

McNamee, Gregory. The North Wind & the Sun: And Other Fables of Aesop. 2004. (ENG.). 107p. pap. 26.00 *(978-3-85630-636-6(6)*, 9783856306366) Daimon Verlag CHE. Dist: Bookmasters Distribution.

Mejuto, Eva. Run Pumpkin, Run. 2007. (ENG., Illus.). 36p. (J). 17.95 *(978-84-96788-88-6(1))* OQO, Editora ESP. Dist: Baker & Taylor Bks.

Mhlophe, Gcina. African Tales: A Barefoot Collection. Griffin, Rachel, illus. 2015. 96p. (J). (gr. 3-6). 14.99 *(978-1-84686-590-9(5))* Barefoot Bks., Inc.

Miller, Reagan & Rosen, Suri. How to Tell a Fable. Crabtree Publishing Staff, ed. 2011. (Text Styles Ser.: No. 1). (ENG.). 32p. (J). (gr. 3-6). pap. *(978-0-7787-1635-8(X))* Crabtree Publishing Co.

—How to Tell a Fable. 2011. (Text Styles Ser.). (ENG.). 32p. (J). (gr. 3-6). lib. bdg. *(978-0-7787-1630-3(9))* Crabtree Publishing Co.

Morpurgo, Michael & Aesop. The McElderry Book of Aesop's Fables. Chichester Clark, Emma, illus. 2005. (ENG.). 96p. (J). (gr. 1-5). 24.99 *(978-1-4169-0290-4(2)*, McElderry, Margaret K. Bks.) McElderry, Margaret K. Bks.

Nunes, Shiho S. Chinese Fables: The Dragon Slayer & Other Timeless Tales of Wisdom. Tay-Audouard, Lak-Khee, illus. 2013. (ENG.). 64p. (J). (gr. 3-6). 16.95 *(978-0-8048-4152-8(7))* Tuttle Publishing.

Osborne, M. D. The Rescue of Mr. Goldsmith. l.t. ed. 2005. (Illus.). 40p. (J). 12.95 *(978-0-9762852-1-2(5))* Wooden Shoe Pr.

Osei, Leah. The Boy Who Cried Wolf & Other Aesop Fables, 1 vol. rev. ed. 2013. (Fiction Readers Ser.). (ENG., Illus.). 32p. (J). (gr. 3-3). pap. 8.99 *(978-1-4333-5648-3(1))* Shell Educational Publishing.

Palmer, Judd. The Giant Killer Vol. 5, No. 5: Preposterous Fables for Unusual Children. 2004. (Prepost Fable Unusual Children Ser.: 5). (ENG., Illus.). 128p. (J). 6.95 *(978-1-896209-47-0(5))* Bayeux Arts, Inc. CAN. Dist: Chicago Distribution Ctr.

Parable Venture Partners Staff. Ethan's Parables: Ethan & the Good Samantha. 2005. 16p. cd-rom 12.95 *(978-0-9728501-1-7(2))* Parable Venture Partners, LLC.

Parker, Emma & Aesop. The Lion & the Mouse. 2010. (Illus.). pap. *(978-1-877547-45-4(X))* First Edition Ltd.

Patacrœa. BABY WHISKERS. 2007. (ENG., Illus.). 36p. (J). 17.95 *(978-84-96788-90-9(3))* OQO, Editora ESP. Dist: Baker & Taylor Bks.

Percy, Graham. The Fox & the Stork. 2009. (Aesop's Fables Ser.). (ENG., Illus.). 32p. (J). (gr. k-3). 28.50 *(978-1-60253-200-7(1)*, 200036) Child's World, Inc., The.

Pinkney, Jerry. The Grasshopper & the Ants. 2015. (ENG., Illus.). 40p. (J). (gr. -1-3). 18.00 *(978-0-316-40081-7(5))* Little, Brown Bks. for Young Readers.

—The Lion & the Mouse. 2009. (ENG., Illus.). 40p. (J). (gr. -1-3). 18.00 *(978-0-316-01356-7(0))* Little, Brown Bks. for Young Readers.

—The Lion & the Mouse. 2011. 29.95 *(978-0-545-29677-9(3))* Weston Woods Studios, Inc.

Price, Nick, illus. Aesop's Fables. 2004. (Young Reading Series Two Ser.). 64p. (J). (gr. 2-18). pap. 5.95 *(978-0-7945-0409-0(4)*, Usborne) EDC Publishing.

Le Rat de Ville et le Rat des Champs: Opposites, Means of Transport, Utensils, Prepositions. (FRE & ENG., Illus.). 24p. (J). (gr. -1-5). pap., stu. ed. 5.95 *(978-88-8148-242-9(8))* EMC/Paradigm Publishing.

El Raton de Ciudad y el Raton de Campo. (SPA & ENG., Illus.). (J). (gr. -1-5). pap. 5.95 incl. audio compact disk *(978-88-8148-252-8(5))* EMC/Paradigm Publishing.

Rojas, Emilio. Mitos, Leyendas, Cuentos, Fábulas, Apólogos y Parábolas. 2003. (SPA., Illus.). 224p. (YA). (gr. 5-18). Vol. I. 15.95 *(978-968-6966-03-9(X))* Vol. II. 15.95 *(978-968-6966-11-4(0))* Vol. III. 15.95 *(978-968-6966-17-6(X))* EDITER'S Publishing Hse. MEX. Dist: EDITER'S Publishing Hse.

Rushdie, Salman. Luka & the Fire of Life. 2009. 14.75 *(978-0-7848-3731-3(7)*, Everbind) Marco Bk. Co.

—Luka & the Fire of Life. 2011. (ENG.). 240p. (J). (gr. 7). pap. 17.00 *(978-0-679-78347-3(4)*, Random Hse. Trade Paperbacks) Random House Publishing Group.

Scieszka, Jon. Squids Will Be Squids: Fresh Morals, Beastly Fables. Smith, Lane, illus. 2003. (ENG.). 48p. (J). (gr. 3-7). pap. 7.99 *(978-0-14-250040-8(2)*, Puffin Books) Penguin Young Readers Group.

Seton, Ernest Thompson. Woodmyth & Fable. 2005. pap. 22.95 *(978-1-885529-83-1(X))* Stevens Publishing.

Silver, Jago, illus. Mr. Aesop's Story Shop. 2011. (ENG.). 48p. (J). (gr. 1-4). 14.99 *(978-0-7459-6915-2(1))* Lion Hudson PLC GBR. Dist: Independent Pubs. Group.

Silverstein, Shel & Silverstein. The Missing Piece. Silverstein, Shel, illus. 30th anniv. ed. 2006. (Ursula Nordstrom Bk.). (ENG., Illus.). 112p. (J). (gr. -1-3). 17.99 *(978-0-06-025671-5(0))* HarperCollins Pubs.

Sommer, Carl. The Ant & the Grasshopper. Noé, Ignacio, illus. 2016. (ENG.). 32p. (J). (gr. k-4). lib. bdg. 16.95 *(978-1-57537-925-8(2)*, Another Sommer-Time Story) Advance Publishing, Inc.

—The Lion & the Mouse. Mercado, Jorge, illus. 2014. (Sommer-Time Story Classics Ser.). (ENG.). 32p. (J). (gr. k-4). 16.95 *(978-1-57537-082-8(4))* Advance Publishing, Inc.

Sommer, Carl & Aesop. Divide to Conquer(Divide y Venceras) Mercado, Jorge, illus. 2009. (Quest for Success Bilingual Ser.). (ENG & SPA.). 72p. (YA). lib. bdg. 14.95 *(978-1-57537-225-9(8))* Advance Publishing, Inc.

The Talking Beasts. l.t. ed. 2007. (ENG.). 288p. pap. 23.99 *(978-1-4264-7504-7(7))* Creative Media Partners, LLC.

Testa, Fulvio, et al. Aesop's Fables. Waters, Fiona, ed. Testa, Fulvio, illus. 2015. (ENG., Illus.). 128p. (J). (gr. 2-4). pap. 18.99 *(978-1-84939-247-1(1))* Andersen Pr. GBR. Dist: Independent Pubs. Group.

Thistle, Louise. Dramatizando la Gallinita Roja: Un Cuento para Contar y Actuar. Packer, Emily, illus. l.t. ed. 2003.Tr. of Dramatizing the Little Red Hen. (SPA.). 32p. (J). (gr. k-2). pap. 10.00 *(978-0-9644186-4-6(9))* Literature Dramatization Pr.

—Dramatizing the Little Red Hen. Landes, William-Alan, ed. Packer, Emily, illus. l.t. ed. 2003. 32p. (J). (gr. k-2). pap. 10.00 *(978-0-9644186-5-3(7))* Literature Dramatization Pr.

Van Gorder, Vivian Ezeife. Master Kofi & Friskey the Dog. 2012. 20p. pap. 17.99 *(978-1-4772-6817-9(0))* AuthorHouse.

Walbesser, Henry H. Imagination. 2003. 96p. pap. 8.95 *(978-0-595-27851-0(5))* iUniverse, Inc.

Ward, Helen. Hare & Tortoise. 2005. (Illus.). 32p. (J). (RUS & ENG.). pap. *(978-1-84444-797-8(9))*; (ENG & RUM., pap. *(978-1-84444-796-1(0))*; (POL & ENG., pap. *(978-1-84444-794-7(4))*; pap. *(978-1-84444-793-0(6))*; pap. *(978-1-84444-790-9(1))*; pap. *(978-1-84444-789-3(8))*; (FRE & ENG., pap. *(978-1-84444-787-9(1))*; pap. *(978-1-84444-786-2(3))*; pap. *(978-1-84444-783-1(9))*; pap. *(978-1-84444-781-7(2))*; pap. *(978-1-84444-780-0(4))*; (SOM & ENG., pap. *(978-1-84444-799-2(5))*; (SPA & ENG., pap. *(978-1-84444-800-5(2))*; (ENG., pap. *(978-1-84444-801-2(0))*; (TUR & ENG., pap. *(978-1-84444-803-6(7))*; pap. *(978-1-84444-805-0(3))*; (VIE & ENG., pap. *(978-1-84444-806-7(1))*; (POR., pap. *(978-1-84444-795-4(2))* Mantra Lingua.

Ward, Helen & Aesop. Hare & Tortoise. 2005. (Illus.). 32p. (J). (SWA & ENG.). pap. *(978-1-84444-798-5(7))*; pap. *(978-1-84444-791-6(X))*; pap. *(978-1-84444-788-6(X))* Mantra Lingua.

Weale, David. Three Tall Trees. McNevin, Dale, illus. 2004. (ENG.). 24p. pap. 6.95 *(978-1-894838-13-9(0))* Acorn Pr., The CAN. Dist: Univ. of Toronto Pr.

Whatley, Bruce & Beatrice, Chris, illus. Aesop's Fables: A Pop-Up Book of Classic Tales. 2011. (ENG.). 14p. (J). (gr. -1-3). 27.99 *(978-1-4169-7146-7(7)*, Little Simon) Little Simon.

White, Mark & Aesop Enterprise Inc. Staff. The Lion & the Mouse: A Retelling of Aesop's Fable, 1 vol. Pérez, Sara Rojo, illus. 2010. (My First Classic Story Ser.). (ENG.). 24p. (gr. k-3). lib. bdg. 22.65 *(978-1-4048-6525-9(X)*, My First Classic Story) Picture Window Bks.

Wildish, Lee, illus. The Boy Who Cried Wolf. 2008. (I'm Going to Read(r) Ser.). (ENG.). 32p. (J). (gr. 1-2). pap. 3.95 *(978-1-4027-5546-0(5))* Sterling Publishing Co., Inc.

Winter, Milo, illus. Aesops Fables for Children. 2012. 294p. pap. *(978-1-907256-72-1(5))* Abela Publishing.

Wormell, Christopher. Mice, Morals, & Monkey Business: Lively Lessons from Aesop's Fables. 2005. (Illus.). 64p. 18.95 *(978-0-7624-2611-9(X))* Running Pr. Bk. Pubs.

Yogananda, Paramahansa. Due Rane Nel Guai. 2011. 30p. 22.00 *(978-0-87612-125-2(3))* Self-Realization Fellowship Pubs.

Young, Ed. Seven Blind Mice. Young, Ed, illus. 2007. (Illus.). pap. 14.95 incl. audio *(978-0-439-02784-7(5))*; (J). 24.95 incl. audio *(978-0-439-02782-3(9))* Scholastic, Inc.

—Seven Blind Mice. Young, Ed, illus. 2011. (Illus.). 18.95 *(978-0-439-02785-4(3))*; (J). 29.95 *(978-0-439-02783-0(7))* Weston Woods Studios, Inc.

Young, Ed & Adams, Tracey. The Lost Horse: A Chinese Folktale. 2004. (ENG., Illus.). 32p. (J). (gr. -1-3). pap. 7.00 *(978-0-15-205023-8(X))* Houghton Mifflin Harcourt Publishing Co.

Zwerger, Lisbeth & Aesop, illus. Aesop's Fables. 2006. (ENG.). 32p. (J). (gr. -1-3). pap. 6.95 *(978-0-7358-2069-2(4))* North-South Bks., Inc.

FABRIC PICTURES

see Collage

FABRICS

see Textile Industry

FACE PAINTING

Boase, Petra & Graham, Bettina. Dressing Up! 50 Step-By-Step Amazing Outfits to Make & Faces to Paint. 2014. (ENG., Illus.). 96p. (J). (gr. 3-8). 13.99 *(978-1-84322-914-8(5)*, Armadillo) Anness Publishing GBR. Dist: National Bk. Network.

Caudron, Chris & Childs, Caro. Face Painting. 2004. (How to Make Ser.). (Illus.). 32p. (J). pap. 7.95 *(978-0-7945-0236-2(9)*, Usborne); lthr. 15.95 *(978-1-58086-460-2(0))* EDC Publishing.

—The Usborne Book of Face Painting. Knighton, Kate, ed. Chaisty, Chris & Lyle, Kevin, illus. Moller, Ray, photos by. 2007. (Activity Bks). 47p. (J). (gr. -1-3). 12.99 *(978-0-7945-1783-0(8)*, Usborne) EDC Publishing.

Cool Cats Face Painting. 2004. (Fun Kits Ser.). (Illus.). 48p. (J). *(978-1-84229-731-5(7))* Top That! Publishing PLC.

Emberley, Edward R. Ed Emberley's Drawing Book of Faces. Emberley, Edward R., illus. 2006. (ENG., Illus.). 32p. (J). (gr. 2-17). pap. 7.99 *(978-0-316-78970-7(4))* Little, Brown Bks. for Young Readers.

Face Painting. 2004. (Whizz Kits Ser.). (Illus.). 48p. (J). *(978-1-84229-944-9(1))* Top That! Publishing PLC.

Funtastic Face Painting. 2004. (How 2 Kits Ser.). (Illus.). 48p. (J). *(978-1-84229-933-3(6))* Top That! Publishing PLC.

Key Porter Books, creator. Face Painting: Enchanting Designs for Faces & Bodies. rev. ed. 2007. (Gymboree Play & Music Ser.). (ENG., Illus.). 36p. (J). (gr. -1-2). bds. *(978-1-55263-962-7(2))* Magma.

Thomas, Isabel. Masks & Face Painting, 1 vol. 2011. (Start with Art Ser.). (ENG.). 24p. (gr. k-2). 23.32 *(978-1-4329-5190-0(4)*, Heinemann Read & Learn) Heinemann-Raintree.

Top That. Fun Kits Cool Cat's Face Painting. 2008. *(978-1-84666-591-2(4))* Top That! Publishing PLC.

Walters Schermerhorn, Lilly. Face Painting Tips & Designs: A Face Painters Guide to Go from Amateur to Professional. 2009. 60p. (YA). 20.00 *(978-0-9824987-3-6(X))* Schermerhorn, Walters Co.

Wild Things Face Painting. 2004. (Fun Kits Ser.). (Illus.). 48p. (J). *(978-1-84229-858-9(5))* Top That! Publishing PLC.

Wolfe, Brian & Wolfe, Nick. Fun Face Painting Ideas for Kids: 40 Step-By-Step Demos. 2013. (ENG., Illus.). 128p. (J). pap. 24.99 *(978-1-4403-2706-3(8)*, Impact) F&W Media, Inc.

FACETIAE

see Wit and Humor

FACTORIES

Bailey, Rachel A. The Triangle Shirtwaist Factory Fire. 2014. (Perspectives Library). (ENG., Illus.). 32p. (J). (gr. 4-8). 28.50 *(978-1-63137-620-7(9)*, 205263) Cherry Lake Publishing.

Broyles, Janell. The Triangle Shirtwaist Factory Fire of 1911. 2004. (Tragic Fires Throughout History Ser.). (Illus.). 48p. (gr. 5-8). lib. bdg. 29.25 *(978-0-8239-4489-7(1)*, Rosen Reference) Rosen Publishing Group, Inc., The.

—The Triangle Shirtwaist Factory Fire Of 1911. 2009. (Tragic Fires Throughout History Ser.). 48p. (gr. 5-8). 53.00 *(978-1-60854-584-1(9)*, Rosen Reference) Rosen Publishing Group, Inc., The.

Crewe, Sabrina & Schaefer, Adam. The Triangle Shirtwaist Factory Fire. 2004. (Events That Shaped America Ser.). (Illus.). 32p. (gr. 3-6). lib. bdg. 26.00 *(978-0-8368-3402-4(X)*, Gareth Stevens Learning Library) Stevens, Gareth Publishing LLLP.

Greene, Jacqueline Dembar. The Triangle Shirtwaist Factory Fire. 2007. (Code Red Ser.). (Illus.). 32p. (YA). (gr. 2-5). lib. bdg. 25.27 *(978-1-59716-359-0(7))* Bearport Publishing Co., Inc.

Lieurance, Suzanne. The Triangle Shirtwaist Fire & Sweatshop Reform in American History. 2003. (In American History Ser.). (Illus.). 128p. (J). (gr. 5-12). lib. bdg. 27.94 *(978-0-7660-1839-6(3))* Enslow Pubs., Inc.

Marrin, Albert. Flesh & Blood So Cheap: The Triangle Fire & Its Legacy. 2015. (ENG.). 192p. (J). (gr. 5). pap. 15.99 *(978-0-553-49935-3(1)*, Yearling) Random Hse. Children's Bks.

Marsico, Katie. The Triangle Shirtwaist Factory Fire: Its Legacy of Labor Rights. 2009. (Perspectives Ser.). 112p. (gr. 7-18). 39.93 *(978-0-7614-4027-7(5))* Marshall Cavendish Corp.

—Working at a Factory. 2008. (21st Century Junior Library: Careers Ser.). (ENG., Illus.). 24p. (gr. 2-5). lib. bdg. 25.64 *(978-1-60279-268-5(2)*, 200173) Cherry Lake Publishing.

Roslund, Samantha & Rodgers, Emily Puckett. Makerspaces. 2013. (21st Century Skills Innovation Library: Makers As Innovators Ser.). (ENG.). 32p. (J). (gr. 4-8). pap. 14.21

E
F
G

(978-1-62431-273-1(X), 202886); (Illus.). 28.50 (978-1-62431-141-3(5), 202884) Cherry Lake Publishing.
Spilsbury, Richard. Hi-Tech Clothes, 1 vol. 2013. (Design & Engineering for STEM Ser.). (ENG., Illus.). 56p. (gr. 6-8). pap. 9.99 (978-1-4329-7037-6(2), NA-h); lib. bdg. 34.65 (978-1-4329-7032-1(1)) Heinemann-Raintree.
Zemlicka, Shannon. From Iron to Car. 2013. (Start to Finish, Second Series: Everyday Products Ser.). (ENG., Illus.). 24p. (gr. k-3). pap. 6.95 (978-1-4677-0795-4(3)) Lerner Publishing Group.

FACTORIES—TRAINING DEPARTMENTS
see Employees—Training of

FACTORY SCHOOLS
see Employees—Training of

FACULTY (EDUCATION)
see Educators; Teachers

FAIENCE
see Pottery

FAIR EMPLOYMENT PRACTICE
see Discrimination in Employment

FAIRIES
see also Fairy Tales
Abbott, Simon, illus. Learn to Draw: Fairies. 2011. (Learn to Draw Ser.). (ENG.). 24p. (J). (gr. k-2). pap. 6.95 (978-1-84898-203-1(8), TickTock Books) Octopus Publishing Group GBR. Dist: Independent Pubs. Group.
Adams, Adrienne. Shoemaker & the Elves. 2017. (ENG.). 32p. (J). (gr. -1-3). 13.99 (978-1-5344-1241-5(7), Atheneum Bks. for Young Readers) Simon & Schuster Children's Publishing.
Adams, Georgie & ADAMS, GEORGIE. Historias de Hadas Contadas Por Hadas. Gardner, Sally, tr. 2004. (SPA., Illus.). 42p. (J). 18.99 (978-84-8488-072-1(9)) Serres, Ediciones, S. L. ESP. Dist: Lectorum Pubns., Inc.
Altmann, Scott, illus. Fairy Fashion. 2008. (Dover Coloring Bks.). (ENG.). 32p. (gr. k-5). pap. 3.99 (978-0-486-46684-2(1)) Dover Pubns., Inc.
Barker, Cicely Mary. Flower Fairies Alphabet Coloring Book. 2010. (Flower Fairies Ser.). (ENG.). 24p. (J). (gr. -1-2). 4.99 (978-0-7232-6496-5(1), Warne) Penguin Young Readers Group.
—How to Host a Flower Fairy Tea Party. 2004. (Flower Fairies Ser.). (ENG., Illus.). 48p. (J). (gr. -1-2). pap. 7.99 (978-0-7232-5360-0(9), Warne) Penguin Young Readers Group.
Batt, Tanya Robyn. The Barefoot Book of Faeries. Newey, Gail, illus. 2009. (ENG.). 64p. (J). 19.99 (978-1-84686-317-2(1)) Barefoot Bks., Inc.
Batt, Tanya Robyn & Barefoot Books. Barefoot Book of Faeries. Newey, Gail, illus. 2015. 64p. (J). (gr. k-5). 16.99 (978-1-78285-225-4(5)) Barefoot Bks., Inc.
Beaumont, Steve. How to Draw Orcs, Elves, & Dwarves. 2007. (Drawing Fantasy Art Ser.: Vol. 2). (Illus.). 32p. (J). (gr. 4-7). lib. bdg. 26.50 (978-1-4042-3859-6(X)) Rosen Publishing Group, Inc., The.
—How to Draw Wizards, Warriors, Orcs & Elves. 2007. (Illus.). 143p. pap. 7.99 (978-0-7858-2345-2(X), Chartwell) Book Sales, Inc.
Berk, Ari. The Secret History of Hobgoblins. 2012. (ENG., Illus.). 48p. (J). (gr. 3-7). 16.99 (978-0-7636-5223-4(7)) Candlewick Pr.
Broutin, Christian & Delafosse, Claude. Let's Look at Fairies, Witches, Giants & Dragons. 2012. (ENG., Illus.). 38p. (J). (gr. k-3). pap. 11.99 (978-1-85103-358-4(0)) Moonlight Publishing, Ltd. GBR. Dist: Independent Pubs. Group.
Burns, Jan. Fairies. 2007. (Mysterious Encounters Ser.). (ENG., Illus.). 48p. (gr. 3-5). lib. bdg. 33.60 (978-0-7377-3635-9(6), Kidhaven) Cengage Gale.
Chambers, Catherine. The Tooth Fairy. Billiau, Loic, illus. 2015. (Autobiographies You Never Thought You'd Read! Ser.). (ENG.). 32p. (gr. 1-3). pap. 7.99 (978-1-4109-7969-8(5), Read Me!) Heinemann-Raintree.
Clibbon, Meg. The Fairyspotters Guide. Loveheart, Lucy, ed. Clibbon, Lucy, illus. Loveheart, Lucy, photos by. 2006. (Gift Bks.). (ENG.). 32p. (J). pap. 9.99 (978-1-84089-465-3(2)) Meg and Lucy Bks. GBR. Dist: Independent Pubs. Group.
Clinton, Greg. Fairies. 2015. (Creatures of Fantasy Ser.). (ENG., Illus.). 64p. (J). (gr. 5-5). 34.21 (978-1-5026-0508-5(2)) Cavendish Square Publishing.
D'Aulaire, Ingri & D'Aulaire, Edgar Parin. D' Aulaires' Book of Trolls. 2006. (New York Review Children's Collection Ser.). (ENG., Illus.). 76p. (J). (gr. k-4). 19.95 (978-1-59017-217-9(5), NYR Children's Collection) New York Review of Bks., Inc., The.
Davidson, Susanna & Stowell, Louie. My First Fairyland Book. Raffaella, Ligi, illus. 2012. (My First Book Ser.). 16p. (J). ring bd. 6.99 (978-0-7945-3227-7(6), Usborne) EDC Publishing.
Dieterichs, Shelley, et al. Fabulous Fairies Coloring Book. 2011. (Dover Coloring Bks.). (ENG.). 32p. (J). (gr. -1-3). pap. 3.99 (978-0-486-48267-5(7)) Dover Pubns., Inc.
Disney Storybook Artists Staff. Favorite Fairies: Learn to Draw the Magical World of Tinker Bell, Silver Mist, Rosetta, & All of Your Favorite Disney Fairies! 2012. (Licensed Learn to Draw Ser.). (ENG., Illus.). 64p. (J). (gr. 1-3). pap. 9.95 (978-1-60058-298-1(2), 1600582982) Quarto Publishing Group USA.
Doherty, Gillian. 1001 Cosas Que Buscar en el Psia de las Hadas. Gower, Teri, illus. 2007. (Titles in Spanish Ser.). 32p. (J). 9.99 (978-0-7460-8346-8(7), Usborne) EDC Publishing.
DuBose, Judy. Santa's Count down 'Til Christmas. 2011. 36p. (gr. -1). pap. 16.00 (978-1-4269-6545-6(1)) Trafford Publishing.
Fairies. 2009. (Mysteries, Legends, & Unexplained Phenomena Ser.). (Illus.). 128p. (YA). (gr. 7-12). 29.95 (978-1-60413-630-2(8)) Facts On File, Inc.
Fairy-Tale Superstars, 4 vols., Set. Incl. Truth about Fairies. Johnson, J. Angelique. Farías, Carolina, illus. lib. bdg. 27.32 (978-1-4048-5746-9(X)); Truth about Princesses. Allen, Nancy Kelly. Kim, Youngsun, illus. lib. bdg. 27.32 (978-1-4048-5747-6(8)); Truth about Trolls. Troupe, Thomas Kingsley. Taylor, Bridget Starr, illus. lib. bdg. 27.32 (978-1-4048-5984-5(5)); (gr. 1-3). (Fairy-Tale Superstars Ser.). (ENG.). 32p. 2010. Set lib. bdg. 81.96 (978-1-4048-6008-7(8)) Picture Window Bks.
Frevert, Darshell. Myst. 2010. 48p. pap. 15.99 (978-1-4535-3661-2(2)) Xlibris Corp.
Gilpin, Rebecca. Christmas fairy things to make & Do. Fearn, Katrina, illus. 2004. 34p. (J). pap. 6.95 (978-0-7945-0835-7(9), Usborne) EDC Publishing.
Goldsack, Gaby. Fairies Die Cut. (Die-Cut Kids Ser.). 10p. bds. (978-1-4054-6966-1(8)) Parragon, Inc.
Greenwell, Jessica. Fairies Sticker Coloring Book. 2012. (First Sticker Coloring Bks). 16p. (J). pap. 5.99 (978-0-7945-3129-4(6), Usborne) EDC Publishing.
Guiley, Rosemary. Fairies. 2010. (Mysteries, Legends, & Unexplained Phenomena Ser.). (Illus.). 128p. (gr. 6-12). pap. 10.95 (978-1-60413-916-7(1)) Facts On File, Inc.
Guillain, Charlotte. Fairies, 1 vol. 2010. (Mythical Creatures Ser.). (ENG.). 32p. (gr. 1-2). 29.99 (978-1-4109-3802-2(6), Read Me!) Heinemann-Raintree.
Hamilton, John. Elves & Fairies, 1 vol. 2004. (Fantasy & Folklore Ser.). (ENG., Illus.). 32p. (gr. 4-8). 27.07 (978-1-59197-712-4(6), Abdo & Daughters) ABDO Publishing Co.
—Goblins & Trolls, 1 vol. 2004. (Fantasy & Folklore Ser.). (ENG., Illus.). 32p. (gr. 4-8). 27.07 (978-1-59197-713-1(4), Abdo & Daughters) ABDO Publishing Co.
Hamilton, Sue. Ghosts & Goblins, 1 vol. 2007. (World of Horror Ser.). (ENG., Illus.). 32p. (gr. 4-8). 27.07 (978-1-59928-767-6(6), Abdo & Daughters) ABDO Publishing Co.
Hyman, Trina Schart, illus. Hershel & the Hanukkah Goblins. 25th anniv. ed. 2014. (ENG.). 32p. (J). (gr. -1-3). 17.95 (978-0-8234-3164-9(9)) Holiday Hse., Inc.
Jeffrey, Gary. Goblins. Verma, Dheeraj, illus. 2012. (Graphic Mythical Creatures Ser.). (ENG.). 24p. (J). (gr. 3-5). pap. 8.15 (978-1-4339-6761-0(8)); lib. bdg. 23.95 (978-1-4339-6759-7(6)) Stevens, Gareth Publishing LLLP. (Gareth Stevens Learning Library).
Johnson, J. Angelique. The Truth about Fairies, 1 vol. Farías, Carolina, illus. 2010. (Fairy-Tale Superstars Ser.). (ENG.). 32p. (gr. 1-3). lib. bdg. 27.32 (978-1-4048-5746-9(X)) Picture Window Bks.
Johnson, Sheri A. The Girls' Guide to Fairies: Everything Irresistible about the Fair Folk. 2011. (Girls' Guides to Everything Unexplained Ser.). (ENG.). 32p. (gr. 3-4). lib. bdg. 27.99 (978-1-4296-6556-8(4), Snap Bks.) Capstone Press of Coughlan Cos.
Kane, Barry & Kane, Tracy. Fairy Houses ... Everywhere! 2006. (Fairy Houses Ser.). (ENG., Illus.). 56p. (J). (gr. -1-k). 14.95 (978-0-9708104-4-1(X)) Light-Beams Publishing.
Kerven, Rosalind & Quarto Generic Staff. The Fairy-Spotter's Handbook. Anderson, Wayne, illus. 2004. (ENG.). 48p. (J). (gr. k-3). 14.95 (978-1-84507-152-3(2), Frances Lincoln) Quarto Publishing Group UK GBR. Dist: Hachette Bk. Group.
Klepeis, Alicia. Goblins. 2016. (Creatures of Fantasy Ser.). (ENG., Illus.). 64p. (J). (gr. 6-6). 34.21 (978-1-5026-0934-2(7)) Cavendish Square Publishing.
—Trolls. 2016. (Creatures of Fantasy Ser.). (Illus.). 64p. (J). (gr. 6-6). 34.21 (978-1-5026-1858-0(3)) Cavendish Square Publishing.
Knudsen, Shannon. Fairies & Elves. 2009. (Fantasy Chronicles Ser.). (ENG.). 48p. (gr. 4-7). lib. bdg. 27.93 (978-0-8225-9979-1(1)) Lerner Publishing Group.
—Giants, Trolls, & Ogres. 2009. (Fantasy Chronicles Ser.). (ENG., Illus.). 48p. (gr. 4-7). lib. bdg. 27.93 (978-0-8225-9985-2(6)) Lerner Publishing Group.
Krensky, Stephen. Watchers in the Woods. 2008. pap. 52.95 (978-0-8225-9892-3(2)) 2007. (ENG., Illus.). 48p. (gr. 4-7). lib. bdg. 26.60 (978-0-8225-6763-9(6), Lerner Pubns.) Lerner Publishing Group.
Kronheimer, Ann. The Fairy Colouring Book. Kronheimer, Ann, illus. 2014. (ENG., Illus.). 64p. (J). (gr. 1). pap. 8.99 (978-1-78055-343-6(9)) O'Mara, Michael Bks., Ltd. GBR. Dist: Independent Pubs. Group.
Lacey, Minna, ed. 50 Fairy Things to Make & Do. 2009. (Fairies Ser.). 104p. (J). (gr. 1). spiral bd. 9.99 (978-0-7945-2392-3(7), Usborne) EDC Publishing.
Loh-Hagan, Virginia. Fairies. 2017. (Magic, Myth, & Mystery Ser.). (ENG., Illus.). 32p. (J). (gr. 4-8). lib. bdg. 29.93 (978-1-63472-147-9(0), 209160, 45th Parallel Press) Cherry Lake Publishing.
—Trolls. 2017. (Magic, Myth, & Mystery Ser.). (ENG., Illus.). 32p. (J). (gr. 4-8). lib. bdg. 29.93 (978-1-63472-150-9(0), 209172, 45th Parallel Press) Cherry Lake Publishing.
Losure, Mary. The Fairy Ring: Or Elsie & Frances Fool the World. (ENG.). 192p. (J). (gr. 5). 2014. pap. 8.99 (978-0-7636-7495-3(8)) 2012. (Illus.). 16.99 (978-0-7636-5670-6(4)) Candlewick Pr.
Lynette, Rachel. Trolls. 2009. (Monsters Ser.). (ENG., Illus.). 48p. (gr. 4-8). lib. bdg. 35.20 (978-0-7377-4408-8(1), LML02109-245409, Kidhaven) Cengage Gale.
Marsico, Katie. Magic Monsters: From Witches to Goblins. 2017. (Monster Mania Ser.). (ENG.). 32p. (J). (gr. 2-5). 12.99 (978-1-5124-3821-5(9), Lerner Pubns.); 39.99 (978-1-5124-3822-2(7), Lerner Pubns.); 39.99 (978-1-5124-2815-5(9), Lerner Pubns.); (Illus.). 26.65 (978-1-5124-2595-6(8)) Lerner Publishing Group.
May, Darcy. Fairies to Paint or Color. 2008. (Dover Art Coloring Book Ser.). (ENG., Illus.). 48p. (gr. 3-5). pap. 5.99 (978-0-486-46544-9(6)) Dover Pubns., Inc.
McGrath, Barbara Barbieri. The Little Red Elf. Bonnet, Rosalinde, illus. 2010. (ENG.). 32p. (J). (gr. -1-2). pap. 7.95 (978-1-58089-237-7(X)) Charlesbridge Publishing, Inc.
Meg, Magic. The Fairyspotters Guide. Loveheart, Lucy & Clibbon, Lucy, illus. 2007. (ENG.). 24p. (J). (gr. 2-4). (978-1-84089-297-0(8)) Zero to Ten, Ltd.
Mortensen, Lori. Leprechauns. 2007. (Mysterious Encounters Ser.). (ENG., Illus.). 48p. (J). (gr. 3-5). 29.00 (978-0-7377-3663-2(1), Kidhaven) Cengage Gale.
Murray, Laura K. Are They Real?: Fairies. 2017. (Are They Real? Ser.). (ENG., Illus.). 24p. (J). (gr. 1-3). pap. 8.99 (978-1-62832-371-9(X), Creative Paperbacks) Creative Co., The.
Murray, Laura K. Fairies: Are They Real? 2017. (Illus.). 24p. (J). (978-1-60818-763-8(2), Creative Education) Creative Co., The.
Nathan, Helen. Flossie Crums & the Enchanted Cookie Tree: A Flossie Crums Baking Adventure. Stevenson, Daryl, illus. 2012. (Flossie Crums Ser.). (ENG.). 56p. (J). (gr. k-2). pap. 8.99 (978-1-84365-197-0(1), Pavilion Children's Books) Pavilion Bks. GBR. Dist: Independent Pubs. Group.
Newsome, Joel. Elves. 2016. (Creatures of Fantasy Ser.). 64p. (J). (gr. 6-6). 34.21 (978-1-5026-1852-8(4)) Cavendish Square Publishing.
Osborne, Mary Pope & Boyce, Natalie Pope. Leprechauns & Irish Folklore: A Nonfiction Companion to Leprechaun in Late Winter. Murdocca, Sal, illus. 2010. (Magic Tree House - Fact Tracker Ser.: 21). (ENG.). 128p. (J). (gr. 2-5). 6.99 (978-0-375-86009-6(6), Random Hse. Bks. for Young Readers) Random Hse. Children's Bks.
—Leprechauns & Irish Folklore: A Nonfiction Companion to Leprechaun in Late Winter. 2010. (Magic Tree House Fact Tracker Ser.: 21). lib. bdg. 17.20 (978-0-606-07030-0(3), Turtleback) Turtleback Bks.
Pereira, Diego Jourdan. FLIP OUTS — Fairy Fun: Color Your Own Cartoon! 2015. (ENG., Illus.). 64p. (J). (gr. k-3). pap. 1.99 (978-0-486-79487-7(3)) Dover Pubns., Inc.
Peter Pauper Press Staff, creator. Garden Fairies: Scratch & Sketch: an Art Activity Book. 2007. (Activity Book Ser.). (Illus.). 64p. (J). (gr. 3-7). 12.99 (978-1-59359-870-9(X)) Peter Pauper Pr. Inc.
Pratt, Leonie & Atkinson, Catherine. Christmas Fairy Cooking. Sage, Molly, illus. Allman, Howard, photos by. 2006. (Usborne Activities Ser.). (ENG.). 32p. (J). (gr. -1-3). pap. 8.99 (978-0-7945-1118-0(X), Usborne) EDC Publishing.
Renison, J. The Secret History of Fairies. 2008. (Illus.). 96p. (978-1-904756-98-9(0)) Kandour Ltd.
Repchuk, Caroline. Fairy Colors. O'Neill, Rachael, illus. 2007. (ENG.). 5p. (J). (gr. k — 1). bds. 5.99 (978-0-439-88704-5(6), Cartwheel Bks.) Scholastic, Inc.
Ross, Kathy. Fairy World Crafts. Bosch, Nicole in den, illus. 2008. (Girl Crafts Ser.). (ENG.). 48p. (gr. 2-5). lib. bdg. 26.60 (978-0-8225-7509-2(4), Millbrook Pr.) Lerner Publishing Group.
Ryland Peters and Small Staff, creator. Now I Am a Fairy. 2007. (ENG., Illus.). 48p. (978-1-84597-498-5(0)) Ryland Peters & Small.
Sautter, A. J. A Field Guide to Dragons, Trolls, & Other Dangerous Monsters, 1 vol. Ashcroft, Colin Michael et al, illus. 2014. (Fantasy Field Guides). (ENG.). 32p. (gr. 3-4). lib. bdg. 27.99 (978-1-4914-0691-5(7)) Capstone Press of Coughlan Cos.
—A Field Guide to Elves, Dwarves, & Other Magical Folk, 1 vol. Ashcroft, Colin Michael et al, illus. 2014. (Fantasy Field Guides). (ENG.). 32p. (gr. 3-4). lib. bdg. 27.99 (978-1-4914-0692-2(5)) Capstone Press of Coughlan Cos.
Savery, Annabel. Fairies. 2012. (It's Amazing Ser.). 32p. (gr. 3-6). 31.35 (978-1-59920-688-2(9)) Black Rabbit Bks.
Shirley, Rebekah Joy. I Want to Be a Fairy. 2011. (Let's Play Dress up Ser.). (ENG., Illus.). 24p. (J). (gr. k-3). lib. bdg. 25.25 (978-1-61533-358-5(4)) Windmill Bks.
Silver Dolphin en Español Editors. Serie Aprendizaje: Drawing with Fairies. 2006. (SPA., Illus.). 22p. (J). bds. 16.95 (978-970-718-331-5(4)) Readerlink Distribution Services, LLC.
Starrenburg, Hasko. The Queen's Orb. 2012. (Illus.). 144p. pap. 8.00 (978-1-4349-8782-2(5), RoseDog Bks.) Dorrance Publishing Co., Inc.
stewart, gail. Trolls. 2011. (Monsters & Mythical Creatures Ser.). (Illus.). 80p. (YA). (gr. 7-12). lib. bdg. 27.95 (978-1-60152-183-5(9)) ReferencePoint Pr., Inc.
Storey, Rita. Fairies. 2013. (Have Fun with Arts & Crafts Ser.). 48p. (gr. 2-5). 28.50 (978-1-59920-898-5(9)) Black Rabbit Bks.
Streit, Jakob. Liputto: Stories of Gnomes & Trolls. Mitchell, David, ed. Kuettel, Nina J., tr. Mitchell, Susanne, illus. 2nd rev. ed. 2016. (ENG.). 60p. (J). reprint ed. pap. 16.00 (978-1-888365-26-9(9)) Waldorf Publications.
Susaeta, Equipo. Leo y Veo, los Gnomos.Tr. of I Read & See, the Elves. (SPA.). 24p. (J). 3.48 (978-84-305-9407-8(8)) Susaeta Ediciones, S.A. ESP. Dist: AIMS International Bks., Inc.
Troupe, Thomas Kingsley. The Truth about Elves, 1 vol. Squier, Robert, illus. 2010. (Fairy-Tale Superstars Ser.). (ENG.). 32p. (gr. 1-3). lib. bdg. 27.32 (978-1-4048-6047-6(9)) Picture Window Bks.
—The Truth about Trolls, 1 vol. Taylor, Bridget Starr, illus. 2010. (Fairy-Tale Superstars Ser.). (ENG.). 32p. (gr. 1-3). lib. bdg. 27.32 (978-1-4048-5984-5(5)) Picture Window Bks.
Vodicka-Paredes, Lenka & Curte, Asia. Forest Fairy Crafts: Enchanting Fairies & Felt Friends from Simple Supplies. 2013. (ENG., Illus.). 144p. (J). (gr. k-3). pap. 19.95 (978-1-60705-690-4(9)) C & T Publishing.
Watt, Fiona. Fairies. Cartwright, Stephen & Bird, Glen, illus. 2004. 10p. (J). (gr. -1 — 1). per. 15.95 (978-0-7945-0811-1(1), Usborne) EDC Publishing.
—Fairy Things to Stitch & Sew. Fearn, Katrina & Hussain, Nelupa, illus. 2006. (Usborne Activities Ser.). 32p. (J). (gr. 1-4). pap. 6.99 (978-0-7945-1235-4(6), Usborne) EDC Publishing.
Watt, Fiona & Gilpin, Rebecca. Big Bk of Fairy Things to Make & Do. 2006. 96p. (J). pap. 14.99 (978-0-7945-1437-2(5), Usborne) EDC Publishing.
Wood, Anita. Fairy Doodles, 1 vol. Kalis, Jennifer, illus. 2014. (ENG.). 240p. (J). pap. 9.99 (978-1-4236-3606-9(6)) Gibbs Smith, Publisher.

FAIRIES—FICTION
Aaron, Taylor. Pumpkin Goblin Makes Friends. 2008. 36p. (J). 16.95 (978-1-934572-00-9(4)) Emerald Bk. Co.
ABDO Publishing Company Staff. Fairy Realm - 10 Titles. 2007. (Fairy Realm Ser.). (ENG., Illus.). 110p. 256.50 (978-1-59961-322-2(0)) Spotlight.
Abedi, C. J. Fae. 2013. (Fae Ser.: 1). (ENG.). 348p. pap. 16.99 (978-1-62681-161-4(X)) Diversion Publishing Corp.
Adams, Alison. Jack & the Beanstalk: Classic Tales Edition. Magnuson, Diana, illus. 2011. (Classic Tales Ser.). (J). (978-1-936258-68-0(4)) Benchmark Education Co.
Adam's Creations Publishing. Enchanted Fairyland: A Sphinx & Trevi Adventure. Bishop, Christina, illus. 2007. (ENG.). 30p. (J). 19.95 (978-0-9785695-0-1(4)) Adam's Creations Publishing, LLC.
Adams, Ea "Beth". A Tiny Wish Granted: A tiny fairy meets a tiny Troll. 2010. 28p. pap. 13.59 (978-1-4490-7565-1(7)) AuthorHouse.
Adams, Jennifer. A Midsummer Night's Dream: A Babylit Fairies Primer, 1 vol. Oliver, Alison, illus. 2016. (ENG.). 22p. (J). bds. 9.99 (978-1-4236-4181-0(7)) Gibbs Smith, Publisher.
Adams, Jennifer Lynn. For I Am Always with You: Valerie's True Fairy Tale. 2012. 46p. pap. 20.95 (978-1-4497-4910-1(0), WestBow Pr.) Author Solutions, Inc.
Adams, Leon. Dragon Pearls. 2008. 176p. pap. 13.95 (978-1-4357-0395-7(2)) Lulu Pr., Inc.
Adams, "Little John". Legend of the Mono Gnome: A Story from Gnome Hollow. 2013. 32p. pap. 16.95 (978-1-4497-9816-1(0), WestBow Pr.) Author Solutions, Inc.
Adkins, Laura. Ordinary Oscar. Hearn, Sam, illus. 2010. (ENG.). 32p. (J). (gr. -1-2). 15.95 (978-1-58925-085-7(0)); (gr. k-2). pap. 7.95 (978-1-58925-418-3(X)) Tiger Tales.
Aebersold, Carol V. & Bell, Chanda. The Elf on the Shelf - a Christmas Tradition: Girl Dark. Steinwart, Coe, illus. 2012. (J). lib. bdg. 29.95 (978-0-9843651-5-9(X)) CCA & B, LLC.
Aebersold, Carol V. & Chanda, Bell. The Elf on the Shelf: Spanish Girl Dark Elf. Steinwart, Coe, illus. 2012. (J). lib. bdg. 29.95 (978-0-9843651-6-6(8)) CCA & B, LLC.
Aesop. Aesop's Fables. abr. ed. 2013. (Puffin Classics Ser.). lib. bdg. 14.75 (978-0-606-31697-2(3), Turtleback) Turtleback Bks.
Aine, Mhari. The Little Children & the Fairies. 2008. 56p. pap. (978-1-84748-375-1(5)) Athena Pr.
Akchurin, Sergo. Blackie & the Magic Stone. 2011. 16p. 12.99 (978-1-4269-6337-7(8)) Trafford Publishing.
—Canadian Story. 2011. 16p. 12.99 (978-1-4269-5215-9(5)) Trafford Publishing.
Albam, Jessica. The Boy in the Oak. 2010. (ENG., Illus.). 40p. (J). (gr. k-4). 17.95 (978-1-897476-52-9(3)) Simply Read Bks. CAN. Dist: Ingram Publisher Services.
Aldrick, Shirley H. F. Tobias & the Pale, Pale Leprechaun. 2009. 52p. pap. 19.50 (978-1-60693-959-8(9), Strategic Bk. Publishing) Strategic Book Publishing & Rights Agency (SBPRA).
Allen, Elise. Barbie: A Fashion Fairytale. 2010. (Illus.). (J). (978-0-7944-2167-0(9), Reader's Digest Children's Bks.) Studio Fun International.
Allen, Elise & Conners, Daryle. Gabby Duran, Book 2 Gabby Duran: Troll Control. (Gabby Duran Ser.). (ENG.). (J). (gr. 3-7). 2017. 256p. pap. 7.99 (978-1-4847-2540-5(9)) 2016. (Illus.). 240p. 16.99 (978-1-4847-0936-8(5)) Hyperion Bks. for Children.
—Troll Control. 2017. (Gabby Duran Ser.: 2). (J). lib. bdg. 18.40 (978-0-606-39970-8(4)) Turtleback Bks.
Alton, Steve. The Firehills. 2005. (ENG.). 192p. (YA). (gr. 5-12). 15.95 (978-1-57505-798-9(0), Carolrhoda Bks.) Lerner Publishing Group.
Andersen, Hans Christian. The Snow Queen. Dulac, Edmund, illus. 2012.Tr. of ??????? ????????. (J). (978-1-59583-459-1(1)) Laughing Elephant.
Anderson, Jodi Lynn. Tiger Lily. (ENG.). 304p. (YA). (gr. 9). 2013. pap. 9.99 (978-0-06-200326-3(7)) 2012. 17.99 (978-0-06-200325-6(9)) HarperCollins Pubs. (HarperTeen).
Anderson, P. The Secret World of Fairies. 2010. 116p. pap. 39.99 (978-0-557-44401-4(2)) Lulu Pr., Inc.
Anderson, R. J. Spell Hunter. 2009. (Faery Rebels Ser.). (ENG.). 336p. (J). (gr. 8-18). 16.99 (978-0-06-155474-2(X)) HarperCollins Pubs.
—Wayfarer. 2010. (ENG.). 304p. (J). (gr. 8-18). 16.99 (978-0-06-155477-3(4), HarperTeen) HarperCollins Pubs.
Andrew-Kollmann, Marcia. Blinky the Magical Elf. Dittus, Jade Moon, illus. 2012. 28p. pap. 24.95 (978-1-4626-5345-4(6)) America Star Bks.
Andrew Lang, ed. The Orange Fairy Book. H. J. Ford, illus. 2010. 260p. pap. 6.89 (978-1-60386-308-7(7), Merchant Bks.) Rough Draft Printing.
—The Pink Fairy Book. H. J. Ford, illus. 2010. 276p. pap. 6.89 (978-1-60386-291-2(9), Merchant Bks.) Rough Draft Printing.
Andrews, Julie & Hamilton, Emma Walton. A Fairy Merry Christmas. Davenier, Christine, illus. 2012. (Passport to Reading Level 1 Ser.). (ENG.). 32p. (J). (gr. -1-3). pap. 4.99 (978-0-316-21962-4(2)) Little, Brown Bks. for Young Readers.
—The Very Fairy Princess: A Winter Wonderland Surprise. 2015. (Very Fairy Princess Ser.). (J). lib. bdg. 16.00 (978-0-606-37465-1(5)) Turtleback Bks.
—The Very Fairy Princess: Teacher's Pet. 2013. (Passport to Reading Level 1 Ser.). (J). lib. bdg. 14.75 (978-0-606-31741-2(4), Turtleback) Turtleback Bks.
Anstee, Ashlyn. No, No, Gnome! Anstee, Ashlyn, illus. 2016. (ENG., Illus.). 40p. (J). (gr. -1-3). 17.99 (978-1-4814-3091-3(2), Simon & Schuster Bks. For Young Readers) Simon & Schuster Bks. For Young Readers.
Apted, Violet. Jasmin & the Nature Fairies. Hollinrake, Chriss, illus. 2012. 16p. pap. 10.00 (978-1-61897-806-6(3), Strategic Bk. Publishing) Strategic Book Publishing & Rights Agency (SBPRA).
Arengo, Sue. Little Red Hen. 2nd ed. 2012. (ENG.). 16p. pap., act. bk. ed. 6.19 (978-0-19-423871-7(7)) Oxford Univ. Pr., Inc.
—The Shoemaker & the Elves, Pack. 2nd ed. 2012. (ENG.). 12.81 (978-0-19-423885-4(7)) Oxford Univ. Pr., Inc.
Arias De Cordoba, Heather & Arias de Cordoba, Kaiya. A Year Full of Fairies. 2011. (Illus.). 28p. pap. 19.99 (978-1-257-74775-7(4)) Lulu Pr., Inc.
Aronson, Sarah. The Worst Fairy Godmother Ever! 2017. (Wish List Ser.: 1). (ENG.). 176p. (J). (gr. 3-7). 14.99 (978-0-545-94151-8(2), Scholastic Pr.) Scholastic, Inc.
Asbjørnsen, Peter Christen. The Three Billy Goats Gruff. Scott, Gavin, illus. 2014. (J). (978-1-4723-5209-5(2)) Parragon Bk. Service Ltd.
Ashley, John A. The Gathering of the Fairy Horses Series. 2008. 64p. 44.58 (978-1-4092-2152-4(0)) Lulu Pr., Inc.
Attia, Stephan. Other Christmas Stories. 2009. 42p. pap. 19.68 (978-0-557-11189-3(7)) Lulu Pr., Inc.
Augenstein, Marianne R. The Quest for Kair, 1 vol. 2009. 152p. pap. 24.95 (978-1-60813-899-9(2)) America Star Bks.
August, Elaine. Fira Gani: An Earthly Fable. 2012. 40p. pap. 24.95 (978-1-4626-7589-0(1)) America Star Bks.
Auxier, Bryan. Where Have All the Fairies Gone? Ramey, Cindy, illus. l.t. ed. 2005. 24p. (J). pap. 7.95 (978-0-9719144-3-8(5)) Where? Pr., Inc.
Avanti, Michele. GreeHee the Journey of Five: Tales of Tamoor Book One. 2008. (Illus.). 304p. (J). per. 14.99 (978-0-9779590-4-4(X)) GreeHee Publishing.
Ayaz, Huda. Freeze-Land: A New Beginning. 2013. 110p. pap. 11.99 (978-1-4808-0267-4(0)) Archway Publishing.

Bachmann, Stefan. The Peculiar. (Peculiar Ser.: 1). (ENG.). (J). (gr. 4). 2013. 400p. pap. 8.99 (978-0-06-219519-7(0)) 2012. 384p. 16.99 (978-0-06-219518-0(2)) HarperCollins Pubs. (Greenwillow Bks.).

—The Whatnot. 2013. (J). (Peculiar Ser.: 2). (ENG.). 432p. (gr. 3-7). 16.99 (978-0-06-219521-0(2), Greenwillow Bks.); 421p. (978-0-06-228630-7(7), Collins Design) HarperCollins Pubs.

Badger, Meredith. Fairy School Dropout Undercover. 2011. (Fairy School Ser.: 2). (ENG., Illus.). 160p. (J). (gr. 2-4). pap. 14.99 (978-0-312-61951-0(0), 9780312619510) Square Fish.

Baia, Edward. Barau Barau. Witnes, Vitus, illus. 2013. 24p. pap. (978-9980-86-491-8(5)) University of Papua New Guinea Press.

Bailer, Darice & Domínguez, Madelca. La Bella Durmiente. Vila Delclòs, Jordi, illus. 2007. (SPA & ENG.). 28p. (J). (978-0-545-03030-4(7)) Scholastic, Inc.

Bailer, Darice, et al. Pulgarcita. Andrada, Javier, illus. 2007. (SPA & ENG.). 28p. (J). (978-0-545-02099-2(9)) Scholastic, Inc.

Bailey, Kristin. Average Joe. 2006. 56p. per. (978-1-84667-004-6(7)) Derwent Pr., The.

Bajpai, Sneha. Grant Me a Wish: Sometimes... you do get exactly what you wish For. 2010. 28p. pap. 12.49 (978-1-4490-9780-6(4)) AuthorHouse.

Baker, E. D. Fairy Lies. (ENG., (YA). 2013. Illus.). 272p. (gr. 1-8). pap. 7.99 (978-1-61963-035-2(4), 9781619630352) 2012. 256p. (gr. 5-8). 16.99 (978-1-59990-550-1(7), 9781599905501) Bloomsbury Publishing USA. (Bloomsbury USA Childrens).

—The Fairy-Tale Matchmaker. (Fairy-Tale Matchmaker Ser.: 1). (ENG.). (YA). (gr. 3-6). 2015. 368p. pap. 8.99 (978-1-61963-800-6(2), 9781619638006) 2014. 352p. 16.99 (978-1-61963-140-3(7), 9781619631403) Bloomsbury Publishing USA. (Bloomsbury USA Childrens).

—Fairy Wings: A Fairy Tale. 2012. (ENG.). 336p. (YA). (gr. 5-14). pap. 8.99 (978-1-59990-756-7(9), 9781599907567, Bloomsbury USA Childrens) Bloomsbury Publishing USA.

—The Perfect Match. (Fairy-Tale Matchmaker Ser.). (ENG.). 2016. 304p. (J). pap. 8.99 (978-1-68119-147-8(4), 9781681191478) 2015. 288p. (YA). (gr. 3-6). 16.99 (978-1-61963-588-3(7), 9781619635883) Bloomsbury Publishing USA. (Bloomsbury USA Childrens).

—The Truest Heart. 2016. (Fairy-Tale Matchmaker Ser.). (ENG.). 272p. (J). 16.99 (978-1-61963-849-5(5), 9781619638495, Bloomsbury USA Childrens) Bloomsbury Publishing USA.

Baker, E. D. & Baker, E. No Place for Magic, Bk. 4. 2006. (Tales of the Frog Princess Ser.: 4). (ENG.). 256p. (YA). (gr. 4-6). 16.99 (978-1-58234-654-0(2), 9781582346540, Bloomsbury USA Childrens) Bloomsbury Publishing USA.

—Wings: A Fairy Tale. 2008. (ENG.). 320p. (YA). (gr. 5-9). 16.99 (978-1-59990-193-0(5), 9781599901930, Bloomsbury USA Childrens) Bloomsbury Publishing USA.

Baker, Mary. Christmas Annie. 2009. 70p. pap. 7.96 (978-0-557-17289-4(6)) Lulu Pr., Inc.

Bangs, Jude Hatcher. The Elf King, 2 vols. 2005. (978-0-9724979-8-5(6)); (978-0-9724979-7-8(8)) A Cappela Publishing. (Advocate Hse.).

Banks, Lynne Reid. The Fairy Rebel. 2004. (ENG., Illus.). 128p. (J). (gr. 3-7). 5.99 (978-0-440-41925-9(5), Yearling) Random Hse. Children's Bks.

Banks, Melanee R. Bryana's Biggest Wish: Believe. Give. Imagine. Create. Hope. Love. 2012. 48p. pap. 21.99 (978-1-4772-4472-2(7)) AuthorHouse.

Banks, Rosie. Enchanted Palace. 2014. (Secret Kingdom Ser.: 1). lib. bdg. 14.75 (978-0-606-35390-8(9)) Turtleback Bks.

—Glitter Beach. 2015. (Secret Kingdom Ser.: 6). lib. bdg. 14.75 (978-0-606-36349-5(1)) Turtleback Bks.

—Mermaid Reef. 2014. (Secret Kingdom Ser.: 4). lib. bdg. 14.75 (978-0-606-35842-2(0)) Turtleback Bks.

—Secret Kingdom #4: Mermaid Reef. 2014. (Secret Kingdom Ser.: 4). (ENG.). 128p. (J). (gr. 2-5). pap. 4.99 (978-0-545-53556-4(5), Scholastic Paperbacks) Scholastic, Inc.

—Secret Kingdom #6: Glitter Beach. 2015. (Secret Kingdom Ser.: 6). (ENG., Illus.). 128p. (J). (gr. 2-5). pap. 4.99 (978-0-545-53558-8(1), Scholastic Paperbacks) Scholastic, Inc.

Banks, Rosie. Starlight Adventure. 2017. (Secret Kingdom Ser.). (ENG., Illus.). 208p. (J). (gr. k-2). pap. 5.99 **(978-1-4083-2918-4(2)**, Orchard Bks.) Hachette Children's Group GBR. Dist: Hachette Bk. Group.

Banks, Steven. Lemonade with a Twist. Miller, Victoria, illus. 2004. (Fairly Oddparents Ser.). 32p. (J). (gr. k-2). 11.65 (978-0-7569-1990-0(8)) Perfection Learning Corp.

Barber, Shirley. Spellbound & the Fairy Book: Packed with 3-D Pictures. Barber, Shirley, illus. 2005. (Illus.). 64p. (J). incl. audio compact disk (978-1-74124-486-1(2)) Bonnier Publishing Australia.

Barker, Cicely Mary. Fairyopolis. 2005. (Flower Fairies Ser.). (ENG., Illus.). 32p. (J). (gr. k-4). 19.99 (978-0-7232-5724-0(8), Warne) Penguin Young Readers Group.

—Flower Fairies Sparkly Sticker Book. 2005. (Flower Fairies Ser.). (ENG., Illus.). 16p. (J). (gr. -1-2). 5.99 (978-0-7232-5377-8(3), Warne) Penguin Young Readers Group.

—The Girls' Book of Flower Fairies. 2008. (Flower Fairies Ser.). (ENG., Illus.). 208p. (J). (gr. -1-2). 20.00 (978-0-7232-6273-2(X), Warne) Penguin Young Readers Group.

—How to Find Flower Fairies. 2007. 24p. (J). (gr. 2-18). 19.99 (978-0-7232-5962-6(3), Warne) Penguin Publishing Group.

—How to Find Flower Fairies. 2007. (Flower Fairies Ser.). (ENG., Illus.). 24p. (J). (gr. k-4). 22.99 (978-0-7232-5890-2(2), Warne) Penguin Young Readers Group.

—Magical Doors: Discover the Doors to Fairyopolis. 2009. (Flower Fairies Ser.). (ENG.). 16p. (J). (gr. k-4). 22.99 (978-0-7232-6351-7(5), Warne) Penguin Young Readers Group.

Barnard, Bobbie. The Fairies of the Big Forest. 2013. 16p. pap. 24.95 (978-1-63004-359-9(1)) America Star Bks.

Barnett, Brandi. Glamour. 2008. 231p. 19.95 (978-1-930709-68-3(4)) HAWK Publishing Group.

Barnholdt, Lauren. Hailey Twitch & the Campground Itch. Beaky, Suzanne, illus. 2011. (Hailey Twitch Ser.: 3). (ENG.). 144p. (J). (gr. 2-4). pap. 8.99 (978-1-4022-2446-1(X), Sourcebooks Jabberwocky) Sourcebooks, Inc.

—Hailey Twitch & the Great Teacher Switch. Beaky, Suzanne, illus. 2010. (Hailey Twitch Ser.: 2). (ENG.). 176p. (J). (gr. 2-4). pap. 6.99 (978-1-4022-2445-4(1), Sourcebooks Jabberwocky) Sourcebooks, Inc.

—Hailey Twitch Is Not a Snitch. Beaky, Suzanne, illus. 2010. (Hailey Twitch Ser.: 1). (ENG.). 160p. (J). (gr. 2-4). pap. 6.99 (978-1-4022-2444-7(3), Sourcebooks Jabberwocky) Sourcebooks, Inc.

Baron Cohen, H. V. The Story of Joe & His Magic Snout: An Operetta of Nursery Fairytales for 2 to 10 years Olds. 2009. 106p. pap. 19.27 (978-1-4251-3582-9(X)) Trafford Publishing.

Barrera, F. M. Tales of the Blue Wizard: The Children of Jamomere. 2005. (Illus.). 180p. (YA). (gr. 4-9). per. 10.99 (978-0-9670848-1-7(4)) Talisman Pr.

Barrie, J. M. Peter Pan. 2013. (Puffin Chalk Ser.). (ENG.). 224p. (J). (gr. 3-7). pap. 7.99 (978-0-14-750865-2(7), Puffin Books) Penguin Young Readers Group.

—Peter Pan. 2013. (ENG., Illus.). 256p. (J). (gr. 4-7). pap. 10.99 (978-0-09-957304-3(0)) Random Hse. GBR. Dist: Independent Pubs. Group.

Barrie, J. M. & Random House Disney Staff. Peter Pan. Walt Disney Studios Staff & Dempster, Al, illus. 2007. (Little Golden Book Ser.). (ENG.). 24p. (J). (gr. -1-2). 4.99 (978-0-7364-0238-5(1), Golden/Disney) Random Hse. Children's Bks.

Barron, Liz. Salcombe Seaside Fairies: Kevin the Crabshell Fairy. 2010. (Illus.). 24p. pap. 11.49 (978-1-4490-6142-5(7)) AuthorHouse.

—Salcombe Seaside Fairies: Louise the Lobster Pot Fairy. 2009. (Illus.). 24p. pap. 11.49 (978-1-4389-8525-1(8)) AuthorHouse.

—Salcombe Seaside Fairies: Michael the Mussel Fairy. 2010. (Illus.). 24p. pap. 11.49 (978-1-4490-5904-0(X)) AuthorHouse.

Bartha, Alysa. Petal's Wish. 2010. 32p. 14.99 (978-1-4490-7417-3(0)) AuthorHouse.

Barton, Zoe. Always Neverland. 2011. (ENG.). 320p. (J). (gr. 3-7). 16.99 (978-0-06-196325-4(9)) HarperCollins Pubs.

Bateman, Teresa. Leprechaun under the Bed. Meisel, Paul, illus. 2012. (ENG.). 32p. (J). 17.95 (978-0-8234-2221-0(6)) Holiday Hse., Inc.

Bateson, Maggie. My Fairy Fashion Show: A Pop-up & Play Book. Comfort, Louise, illus. 2008. (ENG.). 20p. (J). (gr. 4-8). 23.95 (978-0-230-53035-5(4), Macmillan) Pan Macmillan GBR. Dist: Trans-Atlantic Pubns., Inc.

Batt, Tanya Robyn. The Barefoot Book of Faeries. Newey, Gail, illus. 2008. (ENG.). 64p. (J). (gr. -1-3). 15.99 (978-1-84686-163-5(2)) Barefoot Bks., Inc.

Batt Tanya Robyn. Faeries Gift. Ceccoli Nicoletta, illus. 2006. 0032p. pap. 6.99 (978-1-905236-73-2(5)) Barefoot Bks., Inc.

Batt, Tanya Robyn & Barefoot Books. Faery's Gift. Ceccoli, Nicoletta, illus. 2015. 32p. (J). (gr. -1-2). 10.99 (978-1-78285-145-5(3)) Barefoot Bks., Inc.

Bauer, A. C. E. & Shakespeare, William. Come Fall. 2011. (ENG.). 240p. (J). (gr. 3-7). pap. 6.99 (978-0-375-85826-0(1), Yearling) Random Hse. Children's Bks.

Baum, L. Frank. Enchanted Island of Yew. 2006. 268p. pap. 11.45 (978-1-59462-396-7(1), Book Jungle) Standard Pubns., Inc.

—The Sea Fairies. 2007. 112p. per. 9.95 (978-1-60312-375-4(X)) Aegypan.

Baxter, Nicola. Classic Fairy Tales from Hans Christian Andersen. Shuttleworth, Cathie, illus. 2012. (ENG.). 96p. (J). (gr. 2-7). pap. 9.99 (978-1-84322-875-2(0)) Anness Publishing GBR. Dist: National Bk. Network.

—Classic Fairy Tales from the Brothers Grimm. Shuttleworth, Cathie, illus. 2012. (ENG.). 96p. (J). (gr. 2-7). pap. 9.99 (978-1-84322-874-5(2)) Anness Publishing GBR. Dist: National Bk. Network.

—Dreamland Fairies: Magical Bedtime Stories from Fairyland. Manson, Beverlie, illus. 2012. (ENG.). 80p. (J). (gr. k-4). pap. 9.99 (978-1-84322-806-6(8)) Anness Publishing GBR. Dist: National Bk. Network.

—My Treasury of Fairies & Elves: A Collection of 20 Magical Stories. Manson, Beverlie, illus. 2012. (ENG.). 240p. (J). (gr. k-4). 18.99 (978-1-84322-835-6(1)) Anness Publishing GBR. Dist: National Bk. Network.

—A Visit from the Tooth Fairy: Magical Stories & a Special Message from the Little Friend Who Collects Your Baby Teeth. Manson, Beverlie, illus. 2013. (ENG.). 40p. (J). (gr. k-4). 14.99 (978-1-84322-987-2(0), Armadillo) Anness Publishing GBR. Dist: National Bk. Network.

Baxter, Nicola, compiled by. The Wonderful World of Fairies: Eight Enchanted Tales from Fairyland. 2013. (ENG., Illus.). 80p. (J). (gr. 3-7). pap. 9.99 (978-1-84322-968-1(4)) Anness Publishing GBR. Dist: National Bk. Network.

Baxter, Nicola & Jones, Deborah. Rainbow Fairies. (Illus.). 16p. (J). (978-1-84322-052-7(0), Armadillo) Anness Publishing.

Baxter, Nicola & Manson, Beverly. Storybook of Fairy Princesses: Six Tales from an Enchanted Secret World. 2013. (ENG., Illus.). 80p. (J). (gr. 2-8). pap. 9.99 (978-1-84322-898-1(X)) Anness Publishing GBR. Dist: National Bk. Network.

Beausoleil, Dana. The Elf in the Oak Tree. 2010. 32p. pap. 17.99 (978-1-4251-1572-2(1)) Trafford Publishing.

Bell, Hilari. The Goblin Gate. 2010. (ENG.). 384p. (YA). (gr. 8-18). 16.99 (978-0-06-165102-1(8), HarperTeen) HarperCollins Pubs.

—The Goblin Wood. 2004. (Illus.). 371p. (J). (gr. 5-9). 14.65 (978-0-7569-3253-4(X)) Perfection Learning Corp.

Bell, Nick. Mary the Tooth Fairy. Bell, Nick, illus. (Illus.). 32p. (J). 2008. pap. 6.95 (978-1-60108-025-7(5)) 2007. (gr. -1-2). 15.95 (978-1-60108-015-8(8)) Red Cygnet Pr.

Bell-Rehwoldt, Sheri. You Think It's Easy Being the Tooth Fairy? Slonim, David, illus. 2007. (ENG.). 32p. (J). (gr. -1-3). 15.99 (978-0-8118-5460-3(4)) Chronicle Bks. LLC.

Bell, Taj. The Little Night Fairy: Written & illustrated by Taj Bell graphic design & co-illustration by Lisa. 2008. 40p. pap. 20.99 (978-1-4389-2602-5(2)) AuthorHouse.

Bennett, Holly. The Bonemender, 1 vol. 2005. (Bonemender Ser.: 1). (ENG., Illus.). 208p. (YA). (gr. 8-12). per. 9.95 (978-1-55143-336-3(2)) Orca Bk. Pubs. USA.

Bently, Peter. Royal Visit. 2017. (Tooth Fairy Ser.). (ENG., Illus.). 32p. (J). (gr. -1-k). 17.99 (978-1-4449-2853-2(8)) Hachette Children's Group GBR. Dist: Hachette Bk. Group.

—The Tooth Fairy's Christmas. Parsons, Garry, illus. 2014. (J). (978-1-4351-5739-2(7)) Barnes & Noble, Inc.

Benz, Derek & Lewis, J. S. The Revenge of the Shadow King. 2006. (Grey Griffins Ser.: 1). (ENG.). (J). (gr. 3-7). audio compact disk 84.95 (978-0-439-87913-2(2)); (Illus.). audio compact disk 39.95 (978-0-439-87592-9(7), Scholastic) Scholastic, Inc.

Berenstain, Jan, et al. The Big Bedtime Book. Berenstain, Jan & Berenstain, Stan, illus. 2008. (Berenstain Bears Ser.). (ENG.). 48p. (J). (gr. -1-3). 12.99 (978-0-06-057434-5(8), HarperFestival) HarperCollins Pubs.

Berenstain, Stan, et al. The Berenstain Bears' Big Bedtime Book. Berenstain, Stan & Berenstain, Jan, illus. 2011. (Berenstain Bears Ser.). (ENG.). 48p. (J). (gr. -1-3). pap. 6.99 (978-0-06-057436-9(4)) HarperCollins Pubs.

—The Berenstain Bears' Big Bedtime Book. Berenstain, Jan & Berenstain, Mike, illus. 2008. (Berenstain Bears Ser.). 48p. (J). (gr. -1-3). 13.89 (978-0-06-057435-2(6)) HarperCollins Pubs.

Bergstrom, William. The Magic Telescope. 2006. 9.95 (978-0-9787648-0-7(3)) Bergstrom Bks.

Bernadine, Joyce. The Teeth Keepers. 2008. 73p. pap. 19.95 (978-1-60563-848-5(X)) America Star Bks.

Bib, Betty. Betty Bib's Fairy Handbook: A Field Guide to Fairies & Their Habitats. 2005. (Illus.). 72p. (J). (gr. 2-6). (978-1-84483-194-4(9), Duncan Baird Pubs.) Watkins Media Limited.

Biederman, Ashley. Eyes Opened. 2012. 140p. 25.99 (978-1-105-52166-9(4)) Lulu Pr., Inc.

—Eyes Opened #2. 2012. 120p. 25.99 (978-1-105-52168-3(0)) Lulu Pr., Inc.

Biedrzycki, David. Santa's New Jet. Biedrzycki, David & Bonnet, Rosalinde, illus. 2011. (ENG.). 32p. (J). (gr. -1-2). 16.95 (978-1-58089-291-9(4)); pap. 7.95 (978-1-58089-292-6(2)) Charlesbridge Publishing, Inc.

Bigalow, Stephen W. Who Is Santa? And How Did He Get to the North Pole? Megenhardt, Bill, illus. 2013. (ENG.). 144p. (J). (gr. 4-7). 19.95 (978-0-9773757-3-8(0)) Profit Publishing.

Billingsley, Franny. The Folk Keeper. unabr. ed. 2004. 176p. (J). (gr. 5-9). pap. 36.00 incl. audio (978-0-8072-0662-1(8), Listening Library) Random Hse. Audio Publishing Group.

Bingham, Laura. Alvor. 2009. pap. 17.99 (978-1-59955-272-9(8)) Cedar Fort, Inc./CFI Distribution.

—Wings of Light. 2011. 240p. pap. 15.99 (978-1-59955-492-1(5), Sweetwater Bks.) Cedar Fort, Inc./CFI Distribution.

Binns, Paul J. Paul & the Porch Gnome. 2011. 24p. pap. 12.99 (978-1-4634-3226-3(7)) AuthorHouse.

Bird, Helen. Party Time. 2008. (Siti's Sisters Ser.). (ENG.). 36p. (978-1-84167-726-2(4)) Ransom Publishing Ltd.

Biro, Val. Cinderella: See the Picture & Say the Word. 2012. (ENG.). 24p. (J). pap. 9.95 (978-1-84135-516-0(X)) Award Pubns. Ltd. GBR. Dist: Parkwest Pubns., Inc.

Bishop, Debbie. The Fairies of Bladderwhack Pond. Park, Andy, illus. 2003. (Fairies of Bladderwhack Pond Ser.: Vol. 1). (ENG.). 152p. (J). (gr. 4-9). 19.99 (978-1-932431-01-8(2)) Left Field,Angel Gate.

—MYST of the Lost Shadow Boys. 2008. (ENG.). 228p. (J). (gr. 4-9). pap. 6.99 (978-1-932431-79-7(9)) Left Field,Angel Gate.

Bishop, Helena Edwards. Lucille Tinderbox. 2012. (Illus.). 40p. pap. 18.95 (978-1-4710-6053-3(5)) Lulu Pr., Inc.

Bizzarro, Grace. Christmas on the Internet. Bohart, Lisa, illus. 2013. 20p. pap. 12.95 (978-1-61493-197-3(6)) Peppertree Pr., The.

Black, Holly. The Darkest Part of the Forest. 2015. (ENG.). 336p. (YA). (gr. 7-17). 18.00 (978-0-316-21307-3(1)) Little Brown & Co.

—The Darkest Part of the Forest. 2016. (ENG.). 352p. (YA). (gr. 10-17). pap. 10.99 (978-0-316-21308-0(X)) Little, Brown Bks. for Young Readers.

—The Darkest Part of the Forest. 2016. (YA). lib. bdg. 22.10 (978-0-606-37533-7(3)) Turtleback Bks.

—Ironside: A Modern Faery's Tale. (ENG.). 336p. (YA). (gr. 9). 2008. pap. 10.99 (978-0-689-86821-4(9)) 2007. 17.99 (978-0-689-86820-7(0)) McElderry, Margaret K. Bks. (McElderry, Margaret K. Bks.).

—Kin. Naifeh, Ted, illus. (Good Neighbors Ser.: 1). (ENG.). 144p. (J). (gr. 7). 2009. pap. 12.99 (978-0-439-85565-5(9)) 2008. 16.99 (978-0-439-85562-4(4)) Scholastic, Inc. (Graphix).

—Kind. Naifeh, Ted, illus. 2010. (Good Neighbors Ser.: 3). (ENG.). 128p. (J). (gr. 3-7). 16.99 (978-0-439-85564-8(0), Graphix) Scholastic, Inc.

—Kith. Naifeh, Ted, illus. 2010. (Good Neighbors Ser.: 2). (ENG.). 128p. (J). (gr. 3-7). pap. 12.99 (978-0-439-85566-2(7), Graphix) Scholastic, Inc.

—Modern Faerie Tales: Tithe; Valiant; Ironside. 2010. (ENG.). 1040p. (YA). (gr. 9). pap. 24.99 (978-1-4424-2020-5(0), McElderry, Margaret K. Bks.) McElderry, Margaret K. Bks.

—Tithe: A Modern Faerie Tale. 2004. (ENG.). 336p. (YA). (gr. 8). reprint ed. pap. 10.99 (978-0-689-86704-0(2), McElderry, Margaret K. Bks.) McElderry, Margaret K. Bks.

Black, Holly & DiTerlizzi, Tony. Arthur Spiderwick's Field Guide to the Fantastical World Around You. Black, Holly & DiTerlizzi, Tony, illus. 2005. (Spiderwick Chronicles Ser.). (ENG., Illus.). 142p. (J). (gr. 3). 24.99 (978-0-689-85941-0(4), Simon & Schuster Bks. For Young Readers) Simon & Schuster Bks. For Young Readers.

—Arthur Spiderwick's Field Guide to the Fantastical World Around You. DiTerlizzi, Tony, illus. movie tie-in ed. 2008. (Spiderwick Chronicles Ser.). (ENG., Illus.). 142p. (J). (gr. 3-7). 24.99 (978-1-4169-6095-9(3), Simon & Schuster Bks. For Young Readers) Simon & Schuster Bks. For Young Readers.

—The Field Guide. DiTerlizzi, Tony, illus. (Spiderwick Chronicles Ser.: 1). (ENG., Illus.). (J). 2013. 128p. (gr. 1-5). 17.99 (978-1-4424-8693-5(7)) 2013. 144p. (gr. 1-5). pap. 7.99 (978-1-4424-8692-8(9)) 2008. 128p. (gr. 2-5). 10.99 (978-1-4169-5017-2(6)) Simon & Schuster Bks. For Young Readers. (Simon & Schuster Bks. For Young Readers).

—The Ironwood Tree. DiTerlizzi, Tony, illus. 2013. (Spiderwick Chronicles Ser.: 4). (ENG., Illus.). (J). (gr. 1-5). 128p. 15.99 (978-1-4424-8702-4(X)); 144p. pap. 7.99 (978-1-4424-8701-7(1)) Simon & Schuster Bks. For Young Readers. (Simon & Schuster Bks. For Young Readers).

—The Seeing Stone. DiTerlizzi, Tony, illus. (Spiderwick Chronicles Ser.: 2). (ENG., Illus.). (J). (gr. 1-5). 2013. 128p. 15.99 (978-1-4424-8695-9(3)) 2013. 144p. pap. 7.99 (978-1-4424-8694-2(5))Bk. 2. 2nd ed. 2003. 128p. 11.99 (978-0-689-85937-3(6), 53409541) Simon & Schuster Bks. For Young Readers. (Simon & Schuster Bks. For Young Readers).

—The Spiderwick. DiTerlizzi, Tony, illus. 2009. (Spiderwick Chronicles Ser.). (ENG., Illus.). 608p. (J). (gr. 3-7). 29.99 (978-1-4169-8685-0(5), Simon & Schuster Bks. For Young Readers) Simon & Schuster Bks. For Young Readers.

—The Spiderwick Chronicles Set: The Field Guide - The Seeing Stone - Lucinda's Secret - The Ironwood Tree - The Wrath of Mulgrath. DiTerlizzi, Tony, illus. 2013. (Spiderwick Chronicles Ser.). (ENG., Illus.). (J). (gr. 1-5). 752p. pap. 39.99 (978-1-4424-8798-7(4)); 672p. 79.99 (978-1-4424-8797-0(6)) Simon & Schuster Bks. For Young Readers. (Simon & Schuster Bks. For Young Readers).

—The Wrath of Mulgarath. DiTerlizzi, Tony, illus. 2013. (Spiderwick Chronicles Ser.: 5). (ENG., Illus.). (J). (gr. 1-5). 160p. 15.99 (978-1-4424-8704-8(6)); 176p. pap. 7.99 (978-1-4424-8703-1(8)) Simon & Schuster Bks. For Young Readers. (Simon & Schuster Bks. For Young Readers).

—The Wrath of Mulgarath. l.t. ed. 2006. (Spiderwick Chronicles: Bk. 5). (Illus.). 183p. (J). (gr. 3-7). 23.95 (978-0-7862-8579-2(6)) Thorndike Pr.

—The Wyrm King. DiTerlizzi, Tony, illus. 2009. (Beyond the Spiderwick Chronicles Ser.: 3). (ENG., Illus.). 224p. (J). (gr. 2-7). 11.99 (978-0-689-87133-7(3), Simon & Schuster Bks. For Young Readers) Simon & Schuster Bks. For Young Readers.

Blackford, Ami. Quest for the Elfin Elixir: A Duncan Family Adventure Book 2. Blackford, Ami, illus. 2007. (Illus.). 79p. (J). (gr. 3-7). 16.95 (978-1-60108-021-9(2)) Red Cygnet Pr.

Blair, Eric. The Brave Little Tailor: A Retelling of the Grimm's Fairy Tale, 1 vol. Shaw, David, illus. 2011. (My First Classic Story Ser.). (ENG.). 32p. (gr. k-3). pap. 7.10 (978-1-4048-7357-5(0), My First Classic Story) Picture Window Bks.

—Puss in Boots: A Retelling of the Grimm's Fairy Tale, 1 vol. Ouren, Todd, illus. 2011. (My First Classic Story Ser.). (ENG.). 32p. (gr. k-3). pap. 7.10 (978-1-4048-7359-9(7), My First Classic Story) Picture Window Bks.

—Sleeping Beauty: A Retelling of the Grimm's Fairy Tale, 1 vol. Ouren, Todd, illus. 2011. (My First Classic Story Ser.). (ENG.). 32p. (gr. k-3). pap. 7.10 (978-1-4048-7360-5(0), My First Classic Story) Picture Window Bks.

Blair, Eric, et al. The Brave Little Tailor: A Retelling of the Grimm's Fairy Tale, 1 vol. Shaw, David, illus. 2010. (My First Classic Story Ser.). (ENG.). 32p. (gr. k-3). lib. bdg. 22.65 (978-1-4048-6074-2(6), My First Classic Story) Picture Window Bks.

—Sleeping Beauty: A Retelling of the Grimm's Fairy Tale, 1 vol. Ouren, Todd, illus. 2010. (My First Classic Story Ser.). (ENG.). 32p. (gr. k-3). lib. bdg. 22.65 (978-1-4048-6080-3(0), My First Classic Story) Picture Window Bks.

—Tom Thumb: A Retelling of the Grimm's Fairy Tale, 1 vol. Ouren, Todd, illus. 2010. (My First Classic Story Ser.). (ENG.). 32p. (gr. k-3). lib. bdg. 22.65 (978-1-4048-6071-1(1), My First Classic Story) Picture Window Bks.

Blair, Rachael. Maya's Gossamer: A Gentle Guide on How to Manifest Virtues in Children. 2014. 80p. pap. 27.99 (978-1-4525-8684-7(5), Balboa Pr.) Author Solutions, Inc.

Blaylock, Kathy. Adventures of Buddy Fairy & Friends. 2007. 48p. 16.95 (978-1-4137-9195-2(6)) America Star Bks.

Blevins, Wiley. Snow White & the Seven Trolls. Cox, Steve, illus. 2016. (Scary Tales Retold Ser.). (ENG.). 24p. (gr. k-3). lib. bdg. 23.99 (978-1-63440-105-0(0)) Red Chair Pr.

Bliss, Bob, illus. The Hardest Lessons: The Lost Babies Series #3. 2007. 118p. (J). per. 5.99 (978-0-9792499-2-1(9)) Eagle Tree Pr.

—The Ruby Hind: The Lost Babies Series #1. 2007. 116p. (J). per. 5.99 (978-0-9792499-0-7(2)) Eagle Tree Pr.

—Too Many Parents: The Lost Babies Series #2. 2007. 109p. (J). per. 5.99 (978-0-9792499-1-4(0)) Eagle Tree Pr.

Block, Francesca Lia. The Waters & the Wild. 2009. (ENG.). 128p. (YA). (gr. 9-18). 16.99 (978-0-06-145244-4(0), HarperTeen) HarperCollins Pubs.

Bloomsbury. Lift-The-Flap Friends: Fairy. 2016. (ENG.). 14p. (J). bds. 9.99 (978-1-68119-098-3(2), 9781681190983, Bloomsbury Activity Bks.) Bloomsbury Publishing USA.

Blount, Jill Rutland. Tara's Gift. 2010. 24p. pap. 11.99 (978-1-4520-0507-2(9)) AuthorHouse.

Blubaugh, Penny. Blood & Flowers. 2011. (ENG.). 352p. (YA). (gr. 8-18). 16.99 (978-0-06-172862-4(4), HarperTeen) HarperCollins Pubs.

Blume, Lesley M. M. Modern Fairies, Dwarves, Goblins, & Other Nasties: A Practical Guide by Miss Edythe McFate. Foote, David, illus. 2010. (ENG.). 256p. (J). (gr. 3-7). 16.99 (978-0-375-86203-8(X), Knopf Bks. for Young Readers) Random Hse. Children's Bks.

Blyton, Enid. Mister Meddle's Muddles. (ENG., Illus.). 111p. (J). pap. 6.95 (978-0-7475-3860-8(3)) Bloomsbury Publishing Plc GBR. Dist: Trafalgar Square Publishing.

Blyton, Enid, et al. The Fairies' Shoemaker & Other Stories. 2013. (ENG., Illus.). 192p. (J). 9.99 (978-1-84135-458-3(9)) Award Pubns. Ltd. GBR. Dist: Parkwest Pubns., Inc.

Boelts, Maribeth. The Fairy Dogmother. 2017. (Step into Reading Ser.). (ENG.). 48p. (J). (gr. k-3). 3.99 (978-1-101-93446-3(8), Random Hse. Bks. for Young Readers) Random Hse. Children's Bks.

Bohn, Kendall. Fantasy Adventure. 2008. (Kaleidoscopia Coloring Book Ser.). (Illus.). 56p. (J). (gr. -1-7). 8.95 (978-0-929636-83-2(X)) Syren Bk. Co.

Bonner, Sally. Millie's Daydream. 2010. 32p. 12.99 (978-1-4520-8101-4(8)) AuthorHouse.

Booraem, Ellen. Small Persons with Wings. 2012. (ENG.). 304p. (J). (gr. 5-18). 7.99 (978-0-14-242054-6(9), Puffin Books) Penguin Young Readers Group.

Booth, Anne. The Fairiest Fairy. Beardshaw, Rosalind, illus. 2016. (ENG.). 32p. (J). (gr. -1-2). 15.99 (978-0-7636-8659-8(X), Nosy Crow) Candlewick Pr.

Botha, Si. Goosala Goop. 2009. 48p. pap. 16.50 *(978-1-60860-124-0(2)*, Strategic Bk. Publishing) Strategic Book Publishing & Rights Agency (SBPRA).

Bottner, Barbara & Kruglik, Gerald. Pish & Posh. Bottner, Barbara, illus. 2004. (I Can Read Bks.). (Illus.). 48p. (J). (gr. k-3). pap. 15.99 *(978-0-06-051416-7(7))* HarperCollins Pubs.

—Pish & Posh Wish for Fairy Wings. Bottner, Barbara, illus. (I Can Read Level 2 Ser.). (Illus.). 48p. (J). 2007. (ENG.). (gr. k-3). pap. 3.99 *(978-0-06-051421-1(3)*, Tegen, Katherine Bks) 2006. (gr. -1-3). lib. bdg. 16.89 *(978-0-06-051420-4(5))* HarperCollins Pubs.

Bow, James. Fathom Five: The Unwritten Books. 2007. (Unwritten Bks.: 2). (ENG.). 232p. (YA). (gr. 7). pap. 12.99 *(978-1-55002-692-4(5))* Dundurn CAN. Dist: Ingram Publisher Services.

Bow, Patricia. The Bone Flute, 1 vol. 2004. (ENG.). 144p. (J). (gr. 5-12). pap. 6.95 *(978-1-55143-301-1(X))* Orca Bk. Pubs. USA.

Bowers, Mary. The Faerie Box. 2012. 36p. pap. 17.95 *(978-1-105-11387-1(6))* Lulu Pr., Inc.

Boyd, William T. The Pumpkin Fairy. Roberts, Mary Jo, illus. 2003. 32p. (J). (gr. k-1). 14.95 *(978-0-9718161-0-7(7))* Wyatt Pr.

Bozarth, Jan. The Fairy Godmother Academy #6: Trinity's Book. 2013. (Fairy Godmother Academy Ser.). (ENG., Illus.). 240p. (J). (gr. 3-7). 6.99 *(978-0-375-86576-3(4)*, Yearling) Random Hse. Children's Bks.

—Kerka's Book. Burden, Andrea, illus. 2010. (Fairy Godmother Academy Ser.: No. 2). (ENG.). 224p. (J). (gr. 3-7). pap. 6.99 *(978-0-375-85183-4(6)*, Yearling) Random Hse. Children's Bks.

—Lilu's Book. 2011. (Fairy Godmother Academy Ser.: No. 4). (ENG., Illus.). 192p. (J). (gr. 3-7). 6.99 *(978-0-375-85187-2(9)*, Yearling) Random Hse. Children's Bks.

—Zally's Book. Burden, Andrea, illus. 2010. (Fairy Godmother Academy Ser.: No. 3). (ENG.). 208p. (J). (gr. 3-7). pap. 6.99 *(978-0-375-85185-8(2)*, Yearling) Random Hse. Children's Bks.

Bracken, Beth & Fraser, Kay. At the Edge of the Woods, 1 vol. Sawyer, Odessa, illus. 2013. (Faerieground Ser.). (ENG.). 96p. (gr. 1-3). lib. bdg. 23.99 *(978-1-4342-4489-5(X))* Stone Arch Bks.

—Believe, 1 vol. Sawyer, Odessa, illus. 2014. (Faerieground Ser.). (ENG.). 288p. (gr. 4-8). 12.95 *(978-1-62370-113-0(9))* Capstone Young Readers of Coughlan Cos.

—Bloodfate, 1 vol. Sawyer, Odessa, illus. 2012. (Faerieground Ser.). (ENG.). 96p. (gr. 1-3). lib. bdg. 23.99 *(978-1-4342-3305-9(7)*, Faerieground) Stone Arch Bks.

—Faerieground, 1 vol. Sawyer, Odessa, illus. 2014. (Faerieground Ser.). (ENG.). 96p. (gr. 1-3). 95.96 *(978-1-4342-9465-4(X)*, Faerieground) Stone Arch Bks.

—Fate of the Willow Queen. Sawyer, Odessa, illus. 2013. (Faerieground Ser.). (ENG.). 96p. (gr. 1-3). 23.99 *(978-1-4342-4492-5(X)*, Faerieground) Stone Arch Bks.

—The Hidden Things, 1 vol. Sawyer, Odessa, illus. 2014. (Faerieground Ser.). (ENG.). 96p. (gr. 1-3). 23.99 *(978-1-4342-9185-1(5)*, Faerieground) Stone Arch Bks.

—A Murder of Crows, 1 vol. Sawyer, Odessa, illus. 2013. (Faerieground Ser.). (ENG.). 96p. (gr. 1-3). lib. bdg. 23.99 *(978-1-4342-4491-8(1))* Stone Arch Bks.

—The Seventh Kingdom, 1 vol. Sawyer, Odessa, illus. 2014. (Faerieground Ser.). (ENG.). 96p. (gr. 1-3). 23.99 *(978-1-4342-9186-8(3)*, Faerieground) Stone Arch Bks.

—The Shadows, 1 vol. Sawyer, Odessa, illus. 2012. (Faerieground Ser.). (ENG.). 96p. (gr. 1-3). lib. bdg. 23.99 *(978-1-4342-3306-6(5)*, Faerieground) Stone Arch Bks.

—Two Mothers. Sawyer, Odessa, illus. 2013. (Faerieground Ser.). (ENG.). 96p. (gr. 1-3). 23.99 *(978-1-4342-4490-1(3)*, Faerieground) Stone Arch Bks.

—The Willow Queen's Gate, 1 vol. Sawyer, Odessa, illus. 2012. (Faerieground Ser.). (ENG.). 96p. (gr. 1-3). lib. bdg. 23.99 *(978-1-4342-3304-2(9)*, Faerieground) Stone Arch Bks.

—Wish, 1 vol. Sawyer, Odessa, illus. 2013. (Faerieground Ser.). (ENG.). 304p. (gr. 4-8). 12.95 *(978-1-62370-003-4(5))* Stone Arch Bks.

—A Wish in the Woods, 1 vol. Sawyer, Odessa, illus. 2012. (Faerieground Ser.). (ENG.). 96p. (gr. 1-3). lib. bdg. 23.99 *(978-1-4342-3303-5(0)*, Faerieground) Stone Arch Bks.

Bradley, Adrian. The Faraway Kingdom of Oop Loop la Pink. Laurente, Lourdes, illus. 2013. 36p. pap. 10.95 *(978-0-9910180-0-0(1))* Someday Ranch.

Bradman, Tony. The Fairy Godmother Takes a Break. Warburton, Sarah, illus. 2009. (After Happily Ever After Ser.). (ENG.). 56p. (gr. 2-3). 25.32 *(978-1-4342-1302-0(1)*, After Happily Ever After) Stone Arch Bks.

—Flora the Fairy. Carlow, Emma, illus. 2nd ed. 2016. (Reading Ladder Ser.). (ENG.). 48p. (J). (gr. k-2). pap. 7.99 *(978-1-4052-8225-3(8))* Egmont Bks., Ltd. GBR. Dist: Independent Pubs. Group.

—Flora the Fairy's Magic Spells. Carlow, Emma, illus. 2nd ed. 2016. (Reading Ladder Ser.). (ENG.). 48p. (J). (gr. k-2). 7.99 *(978-1-4052-8227-7(4))* Egmont Bks., Ltd. GBR. Dist: Independent Pubs. Group.

Brandon, Wendy. Cinderbear: Board Book & Puppet Theater. Winter, Janet, illus. 2004. (J). *(978-1-883043-47-6(6))* Straight Edge Pr., The.

Braun, Eric. Trust Me, Jack's Beanstalk Stinks! The Story of Jack & the Beanstalk as Told by the Giant. Bernardini, Cristian, illus. 2011. (Other Side of the Story Ser.). (ENG.). 24p. (gr. 2-3). pap. 6.95 *(978-1-4048-7050-5(4))*; lib. bdg. 27.32 *(978-1-4048-6675-1(2))* Picture Window Bks.

Brauner, Barbara & Mattson, James Iver. The Glitter Trap. Halpin, Abigail, illus. 2014. (Oh My Godmother Ser.). (ENG.). 256p. (J). (gr. 3-7). pap. 6.99 *(978-1-4231-6474-6(1))* Hyperion Bks. for Children.

Bravo, Emile. Goldilocks & the Seven Squat Bears. 2010. (Squat Bears Ser.). (ENG., Illus.). 32p. (J). (gr. k-17). 14.99 *(978-0-316-08358-4(5)*, Yen Pr.) Orbit.

Brennan, Herbie. The Faeman Quest. (Faerie Wars Chronicles Ser.). (ENG.). 368p. (YA). (gr. 7). 2012. pap. 9.99 *(978-1-59990-833-5(6)*, 9781599908335) 2011. 18.99 *(978-1-59990-476-4(4)*, 9781599904764) Bloomsbury Publishing USA. (Bloomsbury USA Childrens).

—Faerie Lord. (Faerie Wars Chronicles Ser.). (ENG.). 432p. (YA). (gr. 7). 2009. pap. 8.99 *(978-1-59990-330-9(X)*, 9781599903309) 2008. 18.95 *(978-1-59990-120-6(X)*, 9781599901206) Bloomsbury Publishing USA. (Bloomsbury USA Childrens).

—Faerie Lord. 2009. 1.00 *(978-1-4074-4311-9(9))* Recorded Bks., Inc.

—Faerie Wars. 2003. (Faerie Wars Chronicles Ser.). (ENG., Illus.). 368p. (YA). (gr. 7). 17.95 *(978-1-58234-810-0(3)*, 9781582348100, Bloomsbury USA Childrens) Bloomsbury Publishing USA.

—Faerie Wars. 2007. (ENG.). 384p. (gr. 7-12). per. 6.99 *(978-0-7653-5674-1(0)*, 9780765356741, Tor Bks.) Doherty, Tom Assocs., LLC.

—Faerie Wars. 1.00 *(978-1-4074-5906-6(6))* Recorded Bks., Inc.

—Ruler of the Realm. (Faerie Wars Chronicles Ser.). (ENG.). (YA). (gr. 7). 2007. 448p. pap. 9.99 *(978-1-59990-149-7(8)*, 9781599901497) 2006. (Illus.). 432p. 18.95 *(978-1-58234-881-0(2)*, 9781582348810) Bloomsbury Publishing USA. (Bloomsbury USA Childrens).

Brett, Jan. Beauty & the Beast. Brett, Jan, illus. 2011. (ENG., Illus.). 32p. (J). (gr. k-3). 17.99 *(978-0-399-25731-5(4)*, G.P. Putnam's Sons Books for Young Readers) Penguin Young Readers Group.

Brightwood, Laura. The Banana Fairy Fuss. Pifer, Kimberly, ed. Brightwood, Laura, illus. 2012. (Illus.). (J). *(978-1-934409-34-3(0))* 3-C Institute for Social Development.

Brinson, Julie L. Princess Olivia & the Leap Frog, 1 vol. Brinson, Connor J., illus. 2009. 22p. pap. 24.95 *(978-1-60813-802-9(X))* America Star Bks.

Brisebois, Ro. Sherlock & Elf: The Mystery of the Thicket Behind the Shed. 2008. 100p. pap. 12.99 *(978-1-4343-9987-8(7))* AuthorHouse.

Brock, H. M., illus. Beauty & the Beast. 2012. (ENG.). 48p. (J). 12.95 *(978-1-59583-460-7(5)*, 9781595834607, Green Tiger Pr.) Laughing Elephant.

Broderick, Marian. The Lost Fairy. Caffrey, Aileen, illus. 2nd rev. ed. 2015. (ENG.). 64p. (J). 9.00 *(978-1-84717-739-1(5))* O'Brien Pr., Ltd., The IRL. Dist: Dufour Editions, Inc.

Brown. The Wondrous Worlds of the Wishing Well, 1 vol. 2009. 46p. pap. 24.95 *(978-1-60749-779-0(4))* America Star Bks.

Brown, Carron, ed. Sleeping Beauty & Snow White & the Seven Dwarfs: Two Tales & Their Histories. 2009. (World of Fairy Tales Ser.). (Illus.). 32p. (J). (gr. -1-2). pap. 10.55 *(978-1-60754-635-1(3))*; lib. bdg. 22.60 *(978-1-60754-634-4(5))* Windmill Bks.

Brown, E.A. Gossamer. 2012. 24p. pap. 24.95 *(978-1-4626-5043-9(0))* America Star Bks.

Brown, Rachael. Faerie Wings. 2008. 58p. pap. 10.50 *(978-1-4092-0908-9(3))* Lulu Pr., Inc.

Buck, Angela R. Lily Elf. 2008. 73p. pap. 16.95 *(978-1-60672-881-9(4))* PublishAmerica, Inc.

Bugbird, Tim. Molly the Muffin Fairy. 2015. (ENG.). 32p. (J). 15.99 *(978-1-78393-466-9(2))* Make Believe Ideas GBR. Dist: Nelson, Thomas Inc.

Bunting, Eve. That's What Leprechauns Do. McCully, Emily Arnold, illus. 2006. (ENG.). 32p. (J). (gr. -1-3). 17.99 *(978-0-618-35410-8(7))* Houghton Mifflin Harcourt Publishing Co.

—That's What Leprechauns Do. McCully, Emily Arnold, illus. 2009. (ENG.). 32p. (J). (gr. -1-3). pap. 7.99 *(978-0-547-07673-7(8))* Houghton Mifflin Harcourt Publishing Co.

Burbridge, Ella. Egg on Their Faces. 2013. (Illus.). 232p. pap. 12.50 *(978-1-84426-044-7(5))* Upfront Publishing Ltd. GBR. Dist: Printondemand-worldwide.com.

Burghall, Johan. The Vale of the Faeries. 2012. 274p. (-18). pap. *(978-0-9571863-3-0(9))* Burghall, Johan.

Burke, David. Cinderella: Level 1: Learn Italian Through Fairy Tales. Bobrick, Julie, ed. Filippi, Alessio, tr. Sandoval, Migs, illus. 2006. (Learn Italian Through Fairy Tales Ser.). (ENG & ITA.). 29p. pap. 14.95 incl. audio compact disk *(978-1-891888-77-9(3))* Slangman Publishing.

—Cinderella: Level 1: Learn Spanish Through Fairy Tales. Bobrick, Julie, ed. Redoles, Marcela, tr. Sandoval, Migs, illus. 2006. (Learn Spanish Through Fairy Tales Ser.). (ENG & SPA.). 29p. pap. 14.95 incl. audio compact disk *(978-1-891888-74-8(9))* Slangman Publishing.

—Goldilocks & the 3 Bears: Level 2: Learn Spanish Through Fairy Tales. Sandoval, Migs, illus. 2006. (Learn Spanish Through Fairy Tales Ser.). (ENG & SPA.). 29p. (J). (gr. -1-3). pap. 14.95 incl. audio compact disk *(978-1-891888-80-9(3))* Slangman Publishing.

Burnett, Frances Hodgson. The Racketty-Packetty House. Halperin, Wendy Anderson, illus. 100th anniv. ed. 2006. (ENG.). 96p. (J). (gr. 4-7). 21.99 *(978-0-689-86974-7(6)*, Simon & Schuster Bks. For Young Readers) Simon & Schuster Bks. For Young Readers.

—The Racketty-Packetty House. 2006. 128p. per. 12.45 *(978-1-59462-419-3(4)*, 455, Book Jungle) Standard Pubns., Inc.

—RackettyPacketty House. l.t. ed. 2006. 52p. pap. *(978-1-84637-262-9(3))* Echo Library.

Burton, Martin Nelson. Fooling the Tooth Fairy. Hansen, Clint, illus. 2005. (J). pap. *(978-0-9666490-3-1(6))* London Town Pr.

Busch, Jean. Colleen & the Willow Fairy. 2008. 48p. pap. 16.95 *(978-1-60672-212-1(3))* America Star Bks.

Button, Kevin. The Giving Gnome. Guritz, Linda F., illus. 2010. 28p. pap. 12.95 *(978-1-936343-22-5(3))* Peppertree Pr., The.

Caldwell, Stella. Fairy World: Beautiful Maidens & Mischievous Sprites. Forshaw, Ryan, illus. 2016. (ENG.). 80p. (J). (gr. 4-8). 18.99 *(978-0-7641-6820-8(7))* Barron's Educational Series, Inc.

Cali, Davide. Snow White & the 77 Dwarfs. Barbanegre, Raphaelle, illus. 2015. (ENG.). 36p. (J). (gr. -1-2). 17.99 *(978-1-77049-763-4(3)*, Tundra Bks.) Tundra Bks. CAN. Dist: Penguin Random Hse. LLC.

Caliri, Matt. The Gnome Exchange Program: North Pole Rescue. 2017. (ENG.). (J). (gr. 3-7). pap. 17.99 ***(978-1-4621-2012-3(1)***, Sweetwater Bks.) Cedar Fort, Inc./CFI Distribution.

Callahan, Sean. The Leprechaun Who Lost His Rainbow, 1 vol. Cote, Nancy, illus. 2010. (ENG.). 32p. (J). (gr. 1-3). pap. 6.99 *(978-0-8075-4455-6(8))* Whitman, Albert & Co.

Campana, Augustine. The Last Fairy. 2008. 204p. (gr. -1— 1). 24.95 *(978-0-595-50892-1(8))*; pap. 14.95 *(978-0-595-52086-2(3))* iUniverse, Inc.

Campbell, Jennifer. Edwin the Wee Elf. 2017. (ENG., Illus.). 31p. (J). pap. 16.95 ***(978-1-78554-247-3(8)***, be52f0fd-66b7-441b-8fac-bc9a1e42226e) Austin, Stan AUS. Dist: Bookmasters Distribution.

Capone, Deb. Tooth Fairy Tales. 2005. (J). 14.95 *(978-0-9728666-7-5(1))* As Simple As That Publishing.

Capone, Deb & compiled by. Tooth Fairy Tales Learning & Activity Guide. Capone, Deb, compiled by. 2007. (Illus.). 20p. (J). 9.95 *(978-0-9728666-8-2(X))* As Simple As That Publishing.

Carey, Janet Lee. Dragonswood. 2013. (ENG.). 416p. (YA). (gr. 7). pap. 9.99 *(978-0-14-242432-2(3)*, Firebird) Penguin Young Readers Group.

—In the Time of Dragon Moon. 2015. (ENG.). 480p. (YA). (gr. 7). 17.99 *(978-0-8037-3810-2(2)*, Kathy Dawson Books) Penguin Young Readers Group.

Carlow, Emma & Bradman, Tony. Flora the Fairy. Carlow, Emma, illus. 2005. (Green Bananas Ser.). (ENG., Illus.). 48p. (J). lib. bdg. *(978-0-7787-1022-6(X))* Crabtree Publishing Co.

Carmody, Isobelle. A Fox Called Sorrow. 2008. (Little Fur Ser.: Bk. 2). (ENG., Illus.). 272p. (J). (gr. 3-7). 5.99 *(978-0-375-83857-6(0)*, Yearling) Random Hse. Children's Bks.

—A Mystery of Wolves. 2009. (Little Fur Ser.: Bk. 3). (ENG., Illus.). 256p. (J). (gr. 3-7). 6.99 *(978-0-375-83859-0(7)*, Yearling) Random Hse. Children's Bks.

—A Riddle of Green. 2009. (Little Fur Ser.: Bk. 4). (J). *(978-0-375-83860-6(0))* Random House Children's Books.

Carretero, Mónica. Fairy Handbook. 2011. (Handbooks Ser.). (ENG., Illus.). 32p. (J). (gr. k-2). *(978-84-937814-9-1(5))* D P & G Military Pubs.

Carroll, Emma. In Darkling Wood. 2017. (ENG.). 240p. (J). (gr. 5). 16.99 *(978-0-399-55601-2(X)*, Delacorte Bks. for Young Readers) Random Hse. Children's Bks.

Carroll, Lewis, pseud. Alice's Adventures in Wonderland. Evangelista, Mauro, illus. 2006. 63p. (J). (gr. 2). 8.99 *(978-0-7945-1239-2(9)*, Usborne) EDC Publishing.

Carroll, Yvonne. Great Irish Legends for Children, 1 vol. Lawrie, Robin, illus. 2005. (ENG.). 64p. (J). (gr. k-3). 18.99 *(978-1-58980-345-9(0))* Pelican Publishing Co., Inc.

Carville, Declan. The Fairy Glen. (Illus.). 36p. pap. 7.95 *(978-0-9538222-3-2(0))* Discovery Pubns. GBR. Dist: Irish Bks. & Media, Inc.

Casilio, L. J. Fairy Tales. 2011. 28p. pap. 15.99 *(978-1-4568-5342-6(2))* Xlibris Corp.

Castle, Amber. Evie the Swan Sister. Hall, Mary, illus. 2012. (ENG.). 160p. (J). (gr. 2-4). pap. 7.99 *(978-0-85707-252-8(8)*, Simon & Schuster Children's) Simon & Schuster, Ltd. GBR. Dist: Simon & Schuster, Inc.

—Grace the Sea Sister. Hall, Mary, illus. 2012. (ENG.). 160p. (J). (gr. 2-4). pap. 5.99 *(978-0-85707-251-1(X)*, Simon & Schuster Children's) Simon & Schuster, Ltd. GBR. Dist: Simon & Schuster, Inc.

—Isabella: The Butterfly Sister. Hall, Mary, illus. 2012. (ENG.). 160p. (J). (gr. 2-4). pap. 7.99 *(978-0-85707-249-8(8)*, Simon & Schuster Children's) Simon & Schuster, Ltd. GBR. Dist: Simon & Schuster, Inc.

—The Silver Sister. Hall, Mary, illus. 2012. (ENG.). 160p. (J). (gr. 2-4). pap. 7.99 *(978-0-85707-250-4(1)*, Simon & Schuster Children's) Simon & Schuster, Ltd. GBR. Dist: Simon & Schuster, Inc.

—Sophia: The Flame Sister. Hall, Mary, illus. 2012. (ENG.). 160p. (J). (gr. 2-4). pap. 7.99 *(978-0-85707-247-4(1)*, Simon & Schuster Children's) Simon & Schuster, Ltd. GBR. Dist: Simon & Schuster, Inc.

Catmull, Katherine. The Radiant Road. 2016. (ENG.). 368p. (YA). (gr. 7). 17.99 *(978-0-525-95347-0(7)*, Dutton Books for Young Readers) Penguin Young Readers Group.

Caviezel, Giovanni. Fairy. Mesturini, Cristina, illus. 2009. (Mini People Shape Bks.). (ENG.). 12p. (J). (gr. -1-2). bds. 5.99 *(978-0-7641-6218-3(7))* Barron's Educational Series, Inc.

Cech, John. The Elves & the Shoemaker. Chelushkin, Kirill, illus. 2015. (Classic Fairy Tale Collection). (ENG.). 32p. (J). (gr. -1-2). pap. 6.95 *(978-1-4549-1676-5(1))* Sterling Publishing Co., Inc.

Cecil, Lauren. Lalaloopsy: Lala-Oopsies: Meet the Lala-Oopsies. 2013. (ENG.). 24p. (J). (gr. -1-3). pap. 3.99 *(978-0-545-57224-8(X))* Scholastic, Inc.

Cefalo, Maria Raffaella. If Dreams Could Talk. 2012. (ENG.). 25p. (J). pap. 17.95 *(978-1-4327-9623-5(2))*; pap. 27.95 *(978-1-4327-9708-9(5))* Outskirts Pr., Inc.

Chance, C. The Trepets Book Three Rabbit Race Day. Champion, Vanessa, illus. 2007. 112p. per. *(978-0-9551289-2-9(7)*, Bumble Bks.) Dragonfly Bks. & Arts.

Chance, Megan. The Veil, 0 vols. 2015. (Fianna Trilogy Ser.: 3). (ENG.). 366p. (YA). (gr. 7-12). 16.99 *(978-1-5039-4571-5(5)*, 9781503945715, Skyscape) Amazon Publishing.

Chapman, Linda. Mr Monkey & the Fairy Tea Party. Hearn, Sam, illus. 2016. (Early Reader Ser.). (ENG.). 64p. (J). (gr. k-2). 6.99 *(978-1-4440-1552-2(4)*, Orion Children's Bks.) Hachette Children's Group GBR. Dist: Hachette Bk. Group.

Charley, Grace. The Trouble with Benny Bubble. 2007. (Illus.). 72p. per. 9.76 *(978-1-4251-0147-3(X))* Trafford Publishing.

Christen, Dennis H. Lundon's Bridge & the Three Keys. 2008. 221p. (J). pap. 12.95 *(978-0-9718151-5-5(1))* C-It Entertainment Group, LLC.

Christensen, Gerda. Troll Peter Discovers the Bog-Woman's Secret & Other Stories. 2010. 40p. pap. 18.27 *(978-1-4251-8822-1(2))* Trafford Publishing.

—Troll Peter Finds A Treasure at the End of the Rainbow & Other Stories: Troll Peter's Adventures, Book 2. 2010. 36p. pap. 18.41 *(978-1-4269-3697-5(4))* Trafford Publishing.

Christensen, Margaret Kate. The Hollyhock Fairies. 2004. 48p. per. *(978-1-932077-85-8(5))* Athena Pr.

Ciccone, Tiziana. Tooth Fairy Trouble. 2013. 36p. pap. 13.95 *(978-1-62857-176-9(4)*, Strategic Bk. Publishing) Strategic Book Publishing & Rights Agency (SBPRA).

Claflin, Willy. Rapunzel & the Seven Dwarfs: A Maynard Moose Tale. Stimson, James, illus. 2011. (ENG.). 33p. (J). (gr. -1-3). 18.95 *(978-0-87483-914-2(9))* August Hse. Pubs., Inc.

Clark, CoraMarie. Emily's Magical Journey with Toothena the Tooth Fairy. Lawton, Val, illus. 2007. (ENG.). 32p. (J). *(978-0-9783779-0-8(7))* Strategix Ltd.

Clarke, E. J. Oakwing: A Fairy's Tale. 2017. (Oakwing Ser.: 1). (ENG., Illus.). 192p. (J). (gr. 2-6). 16.99 ***(978-1-4814-8191-5(6)***, Aladdin) Simon & Schuster Children's Publishing.

—Oakwing: A Fairy's Tale. 2017. (J). pap. ***(978-1-4814-8190-8(8)***, Simon & Schuster/Paula Wiseman Bks.) Simon & Schuster/Paula Wiseman Bks.

Clibbon, Meg, et al. The Fairyland Olympics. Clibbon, Lucy, illus. 2008. (ENG.). 32p. (J). (gr. k-2). *(978-1-84089-504-9(7))* Zero to Ten, Ltd.

Cloke, Rene, illus. Cinderella. 2012. (ENG.). 24p. pap. 6.50 *(978-1-84135-535-1(6))* Award Pubns. Ltd. GBR. Dist: Parkwest Pubns., Inc.

Coiner, Tea Railene. Hear the Song of the Fairies. 2009. 74p. pap. 19.95 *(978-1-61582-833-3(8))* America Star Bks.

Colandro, Lucille. There Was an Old Lady Who Swallowed a Clover! 2012. (There Was an Old Lady Ser.). lib. bdg. 17.20 *(978-0-606-23937-0(5)*, Turtleback) Turtleback Bks.

Colfer, Chris. Trollbella Throws a Party: A Tale from the Land of Stories. Dorman, Brandon, illus. 2017. (ENG.). 32p. (J). (gr. -1-3). 17.99 *(978-0-316-38340-0(6))* Little Brown & Co.

Colfer, Eoin. The Arctic Incident. 2009. (Artemis Fowl Ser.). (ENG.). 304p. (J). (gr. 5-9). pap. 8.99 *(978-1-4231-2454-2(5))* Hyperion Pr.

—The Arctic Incident. 2003. (Artemis Fowl Ser.: 2). 277p. (J). (gr. 5-7). lib. bdg. 19.65 *(978-0-613-62927-0(2)*, Turtleback) Turtleback Bks.

—Artemis Fowl, 3 vols., Set. 2010. (Artemis Fowl Ser.). (ENG.). 944p. (J). (gr. 5-17). pap. 19.99 *(978-1-4231-3681-1(0))* Disney Pr.

—Artemis Fowl. (Artemis Fowl Ser.: Bk. 1). (FRE.). pap. 34.95 *(978-2-07-054681-7(0))* Gallimard, Editions FRA. Dist: Distribooks, Inc.

—Artemis Fowl. rev. ed. 2009. (Artemis Fowl Ser.). (ENG.). 304p. (J). (gr. 5-9). pap. 8.99 *(978-1-4231-2452-8(9))* Hyperion Pr.

—Artemis Fowl. (Artemis Fowl Ser.: Bk. 1). pap. 34.95 *(978-88-04-49788-2(2))* Mondadori ITA. Dist: Distribooks, Inc.

—Artemis Fowl. (Artemis Fowl Ser.: 1). (YA). 2007. 1.25 *(978-1-4193-6020-6(5))* 2006. 52.75 *(978-1-4193-6023-7(X))* 2006. 54.75 *(978-1-4193-6021-3(3))* 2006. 54.75 *(978-1-4193-6026-8(4))* 2006. 132.75 *(978-1-4193-6022-0(1))* 2005. 56.75 *(978-1-4193-6024-4(8))* Recorded Bks., Inc.

—Artemis Fowl. 2009. (Artemis Fowl Ser.: 1). (J). (gr. 5-8). lib. bdg. 19.65 *(978-0-613-60637-0(X)*, Turtleback) Turtleback Bks.

—Artemis Fowl. Feldmann, Claudia, tr. (Artemis Fowl Ser.: Bk. 1). (GER.). pap. 24.95 *(978-3-548-60320-9(3))* Ullstein-Taschenbuch-Verlag DEU. Dist: Distribooks, Inc.

—Artemis Fowl: El Mundo Subterráneo. 2013. (Vintage Espanol Ser.: Bk. 1). (SPA.). 288p. (YA). (gr. 5). pap. 9.95 *(978-0-345-80418-1(X)*, Vintage Espanol) Knopf Doubleday Publishing Group.

—Artemis Fowl & the Atlantis Complex. 2012. (ENG.). 384p. (J). (gr. 5-9). pap. 8.99 *(978-1-4231-2972-1(5))* Hyperion Pr.

—The Atlantis Complex. 2010. (Artemis Fowl Ser.: 7). (ENG.). 368p. (J). (gr. 5-9). 17.99 *(978-1-4231-2819-9(2))* Hyperion Pr.

—The Atlantis Complex. 2012. (Artemis Fowl Ser.: 7). (J). lib. bdg. 19.65 *(978-0-606-23614-0(7)*, Turtleback) Turtleback Bks.

—Encuentro en el Artico. 2013. (Vintage Espanol Ser.).Tr. of Arctic Incident. (SPA.). 320p. (YA). pap. 9.95 *(978-0-345-80535-5(6)*, Vintage Espanol) Knopf Doubleday Publishing Group.

—The Eternity Code. rev. ed. 2009. (Artemis Fowl Ser.). (ENG.). 336p. (J). (gr. 5-9). pap. 8.99 *(978-1-4231-2453-5(7))* Hyperion Pr.

—The Last Guardian. 2012. (Artemis Fowl Ser.). (ENG.). 336p. (J). (gr. 5-9). 18.99 *(978-1-4231-6161-5(0))* Hyperion Pr.

—The Last Guardian. 2014. (Artemis Fowl Ser.: 8). (J). lib. bdg. 19.65 *(978-0-606-32288-1(4)*, Turtleback) Turtleback Bks.

—The Lost Colony. rev. ed. 2009. (Artemis Fowl Ser.). (ENG.). 432p. (J). (gr. 5-9). pap. 8.99 *(978-1-4231-2494-8(4))* Hyperion Pr.

—EL MUNDO SUBTERRÁNEO (ARTEMIS FOWL 1) (Artemis Fowl Ser.: Bk. 1). (SPA.). 288p. pap. *(978-84-8441-115-4(X)*, MO31567) Grijalbo Mondadori, S.A.-Montena.

—The Opal Deception. 2006. (Artemis Fowl Ser.: Bk. 4). 17.10 *(978-0-7569-6828-1(3))* Disney Pr.

—The Opal Deception. rev. ed. 2009. (Artemis Fowl Ser.). (ENG.). 368p. (J). (gr. 5-9). pap. 8.99 *(978-1-4231-2455-9(3))* Hyperion Pr.

—The Opal Deception. (Artemis Fowl Ser.: 4). (J). 2007. 1.25 *(978-1-4193-6041-1(8))* 2006. 69.75 *(978-1-4193-6047-3(7))* 2006. 72.75 *(978-1-4193-6045-9(0))* Recorded Bks., Inc.

—The Time Paradox. 2009. (Artemis Fowl Ser.). (ENG.). 448p. (J). (gr. 5-9). pap. 8.99 *(978-1-4231-0837-5(X))* Hyperion Pr.

—The Time Paradox. 2009. (Artemis Fowl Ser.: 6). (J). lib. bdg. 19.65 *(978-0-606-10579-8(4)*, Turtleback) Turtleback Bks.

Colfer, Eoin & Donkin, Andrew. Artemis Fowl. Rigano, Giovanni & Lamanna, Paolo, illus. 2007. (Artemis Fowl Ser.). (ENG.). 112p. (J). (gr. 5-9). 18.99 *(978-0-7868-4881-2(2))*; pap. 12.99 *(978-0-7868-4882-9(0))* Hyperion Pr.

—Artemis Fowl the Opal Deception Graphic Novel. Rigano, Giovanni & Lamanna, Paolo, illus. 2014. (Artemis Fowl Ser.: 4). (ENG.). 112p. (J). (gr. 5-9). pap. 12.99 *(978-1-4231-4549-3(6))* Hyperion Bks. for Children.

—Eternity Code. Rigano, Giovanni & Lamanna, Paolo, illus. 2013. (Artemis Fowl Ser.: 3). (ENG.). 112p. (J). (gr. 5-9). pap. 12.99 *(978-1-4231-4577-6(1))* Hyperion Pr.

Colum, Padraic. The King of Ireland's Son. Pogány, Willy, illus. 2009. 308p. pap. 12.95 *(978-1-59915-083-3(2))* Yesterday's Classics.

Cone, Carl. There's a Season for All. Cone, Carl, illus. 2008. (ENG., Illus.). pap. 14.95 *(978-0-9801555-6-3(8))* Argus Enterprises International, Inc.

Connick, Harry, Jr. The Happy Elf. Andreasen, Dan, illus. 2011. (ENG.). 32p. (J). (gr. -1-3). 17.99 *(978-0-06-128879-1(9))* HarperCollins Pubs.

Cook, Eileen. Fourth Grade Fairy. 2011. (Fourth Grade Fairy Ser.: 1). (ENG.). 176p. (J). (gr. 3-7). pap. 7.99 (978-1-4169-9811-2(X), Aladdin) Simon & Schuster Children's Publishing.

—Gnome Invasion. 2011. (Fourth Grade Fairy Ser.: 3). (ENG.). 160p. (J). (gr. 3-7). pap. 6.99 (978-1-4169-9813-6(6), Aladdin) Simon & Schuster Children's Publishing.

—Wishes for Beginners. 2011. (Fourth Grade Fairy Ser.: 2). (ENG.). 160p. (J). (gr. 3-7). pap. 6.99 (978-1-4169-9812-9(8), Aladdin) Simon & Schuster Children's Publishing.

Cook, Philip. Erden: Flame of the Creator. 2014. xiii, 259p. (YA). (978-1-4908-2033-0(7), WestBow Pr.) Author Solutions, Inc.

Coombs, Kate. The Tooth Fairy Wars. Parker, Jake, illus. 2014. (ENG.). 40p. (J). (gr. -1-3). 17.99 (978-1-4169-7915-9(8)) Simon & Schuster Children's Publishing.

Cooper, Diana. Tara & the Talking Kitten Meet a Unicorn. Shannon, Kate, illus. 2011. (Tara & Ash-ting Ser.). (ENG.). 80p. (J). (gr. k-4). 8.95 (978-1-84409-557-5(6)) Innovation Pr., The.

—Tara & the Talking Kitten Meet Angels & Fairies. Shannon, Kate, illus. 2011. (Tara & Ash-ting Ser.). (ENG.). 80p. (J). (gr. k-4). 8.95 (978-1-84409-551-3(7)) Innovation Pr., The.

Corby, Linda. The girl who believed in Fairies. 2005. 36p. (J). pap. 7.25 (978-1-4116-5135-7(9)) Lulu Pr., Inc.

Corderoy, Tracey. Beastly Feast!, 1 vol. Artful Doodlers Limited Staff, illus. 2012. (Grunt & the Grouch Ser.). (ENG.). 112p. (gr. 1-3). pap. 5.19 (978-1-4342-4269-3(2)); 25.32 (978-1-4342-4603-5(5)) Stone Arch Bks.

—Big Splash!, 1 vol. Artful Doodlers Limited Staff, illus. 2012. (Grunt & the Grouch Ser.). (ENG.). 112p. (gr. 1-3). pap. 5.19 (978-1-4342-4268-6(4)); 25.32 (978-1-4342-4602-8(7)) Stone Arch Bks.

—Freaky Funfair, 1 vol. 2013. (Grunt & the Grouch Ser.). (ENG.). 112p. (gr. 1-3). pap. 5.19 (978-1-4342-4828-2(3)); lib. bdg. 25.32 (978-1-4342-4620-2(5)) Stone Arch Bks.

—Pick 'n' Mix, 1 vol. 2013. (Grunt & the Grouch Ser.). (ENG.). 112p. (gr. 1-3). pap. 5.19 (978-1-4342-4829-9(1)); lib. bdg. 25.32 (978-1-4342-4621-9(3)) Stone Arch Bks.

Cordwell, Mary Hebert. The Dirty-Foot Fairy. 2010. 28p. 13.99 (978-1-4490-9153-8(9)) AuthorHouse.

Cosgrove, Stephen. Gnome from Nome. James, Robin, illus. 2012. (Paws IV Ser.). (ENG.). 32p. (J). (gr. -1-2). pap. 10.99 (978-1-57061-777-5(5), Little Bigfoot) Sasquatch Bks.

Coville, Bruce. The Evil Elves. Coville, Katherine, illus. 2006. (Moongobble & Me Ser.: Bk. 3). (ENG.). 80p. (J). (gr. 1-5). pap. 6.99 (978-0-689-85759-1(4), Simon & Schuster/Paula Wiseman Bks.) Simon & Schuster/Paula Wiseman Bks.

—Goblins in the Castle. Coville, Katherine, illus. 2015. (ENG.). 208p. (J). (gr. 3-7). 17.99 (978-1-4814-3900-8(6), Aladdin) Simon & Schuster Children's Publishing.

—Goblins on the Prowl. 2015. (ENG., Illus.). 272p. (J). (gr. 3-7). 17.99 (978-1-4169-1440-2(4), Aladdin) Simon & Schuster Children's Publishing.

Coville, Bruce. Trolled. Kidby, Paul, illus. 2017. (Enchanted Files Ser.: 3). (ENG.). 288p. (J). (gr. 3-7). 16.99 **(978-0-385-39259-4(1)**, Random Hse. Bks. for Young Readers) Random Hse. Children's Bks.

Cowen-Fletcher, Jane. Nell's Elf. Cowen-Fletcher, Jane, illus. 2006. (ENG., Illus.). 32p. (J). (gr. -1-3). 14.99 (978-0-7636-2391-3(1)) Candlewick Pr.

Cowsert, Sandra. The Continuing Adventures of Tammi & Her Dragon. 2007. 48p. per. 16.95 (978-1-4241-8313-5(8)) America Star Bks.

Cox, Karen. Gwyneira, the Crystal Fairy. 2005. 35p. 14.84 (978-1-4116-4777-0(7)) Lulu Pr., Inc.

COX, Margaret. The Emerald-fire. 2010. 166p. pap. 11.50 (978-1-4461-3379-8(6)) Lulu Pr., Inc.

Craig, Carol. Floral Fairies Coloring Book. 2015. (ENG.). 32p. (J). (gr. 3-8). pap. 3.99 (978-0-486-78327-7(8)) Dover Pubns., Inc.

Crawford, Susan. The Sea Sprites. 2011. 12p. 12.68 (978-1-4269-5009-4(8)) Trafford Publishing.

Creese, Sarah. Sparkle Town Fairies Esme the Emerald Fairy. 2017. (ENG.). (J). (gr. -1-7). **(978-1-78598-948-3(0))** Make Believe Ideas.

Cregan, Mairin. Old John. Sewell, Helen, illus. 2012. 198p. 44.95 (978-1-258-23306-8(1)); pap. 29.95 (978-1-258-24727-0(5)) Literary Licensing, LLC.

Croall, Marie P. My Boyfriend Is a Monster - Under His Spell. Park, Hyeondo, illus. 2011. (My Boyfriend Is a Monster Ser.: 4). (ENG.). 128p. (YA). (gr. 7-12). pap. 9.95 (978-0-7613-7076-5(5), Graphic Universe™) Lerner Publishing Group.

—Under His Spell, 4 vols., No. 4. Park, Hyeondo, illus. 2011. (My Boyfriend Is a Monster Ser.: 4). (ENG.). 128p. (YA). (gr. 7-12). 29.27 (978-0-7613-5602-8(9)) Lerner Publishing Group.

Crompton, Anne Eliot. Percival's Angel. 2011. (ENG.). 240p. (YA). (gr. 8-12). pap. 7.99 (978-1-4022-3784-3(7)) Sourcebooks, Inc.

Cronin, Doreen. Bloom. Small, David, illus. 2016. (ENG.). 40p. (J). (gr. -1-3). 17.99 (978-1-4424-0620-9(8)) Simon & Schuster Children's Publishing.

Cronshaw, Joseph. Podge & Dodge. 2009. 32p. pap. 13.50 (978-1-60693-868-3(1), Strategic Bk. Publishing) Strategic Book Publishing & Rights Agency (SBPRA).

Cross, Frances. The Mystery of the Green Elephant. 2007. (Blobber Ser.). (ENG.). 84p. (J). per. (978-1-84167-559-6(8)) Ransom Publishing Ltd.

Curtis, Christopher Paul. Mr. Chickee's Messy Mission. 2008. (ENG., Illus.). 240p. (J). (gr. 3-7). 6.99 (978-0-440-22922-3(7), Yearling) Random Hse. Children's Bks.

Curtis, Jillian M. The Little Prince & His Magic Wand. 2005. (Illus.). 28p. (J). 24.95 (978-1-59858-015-0(9)); pap. 16.95 (978-1-59858-010-5(8)) Dog Ear Publishing, LLC.

Curtis, Tony. The Gnomes of Genom. 2009. 196p. pap. 15.99 (978-1-4389-5789-0(0)) AuthorHouse.

Cynthia, A. Sears. A World Divided: The Fairy Princess Chronicles - Book 1. 2012. 656p. (978-1-4602-0516-7(2)); pap. (978-1-4602-0514-3(6)) FriesenPress.

Daffney. The Birthday Fairy. 2009. 16p. pap. 8.49 (978-1-4490-0095-0(9)) AuthorHouse.

Dahl, Michael. Dark Tower Rising, 1 vol. Kovar, Ben, illus. 2012. (Troll Hunters Ser.). (ENG.). 112p. (gr. 2-3). lib. bdg. 25.32 (978-1-4342-3308-0(1), Troll Hunters) Stone Arch Bks.

—The Goblin in the Grass: And Other Scary Tales. Bonet, Xavier, illus. 2016. (Michael Dahl's Really Scary Stories Ser.). (ENG.). 72p. (gr. 2-3). lib. bdg. 25.32 (978-1-4965-3773-7(4)) Stone Arch Bks.

—The Lava Crown, 1 vol. Kovar, Ben, illus. 2012. (Troll Hunters Ser.). (ENG.). 112p. (gr. 2-3). lib. bdg. 25.32 (978-1-4342-3309-7(X), Troll Hunters) Stone Arch Bks.

—Skyfall, 1 vol. Kovar, Ben, illus. 2012. (Troll Hunters Ser.). (ENG.). 112p. (gr. 2-3). lib. bdg. 25.32 (978-1-4342-3307-3(3), Troll Hunters) Stone Arch Bks.

Dakin, Margaret. Secrets of the Flower Fairies. 2004. (Fairy Dust Tales: Bk. 1). (Illus.). 77p. (J). (gr. 1-6). pap. 16.95 (978-1-930002-60-9(2)) I & L Publishing.

Dale, Jay. What Is the Matter, Mrs. Long?, 1 vol. Diggory, Nick, illus. 2012. (Engage Literacy Green Ser.). (ENG.). 32p. (gr. k-2). pap. 5.99 (978-1-4296-9030-0(5), Engage Literacy) Capstone Press of Coughlan Cos.

Daley, Pj. Roger & the Xmas Elf. 2012. 16p. pap. 12.69 (978-1-4669-7211-7(4)) Trafford Publishing.

Dalton, Andrew & Boatfield, Jonny. The New Empire of Malplaquet. 2009. (ENG., Illus.). 192p. (gr. 4-7). 35.00 (978-0-7188-3096-0(2)); pap. 17.50 (978-0-7188-3093-9(8)) Lutherworth Pr., The GBR. Dist: Casemate Academic.

Daughtrey, Patricia & Benson, Gary. Shanaya & Friends: Litter Bugs Turn Eco H. E. R. O. S. Balkovek, Jim, illus. 2011. 40p. pap. 14.95 (978-1-60911-475-6(2), Eloquent Bks.) Strategic Book Publishing & Rights Agency (SBPRA).

D'Aulaire, Ingri, et al. The Terrible Troll-Bird. 2007. (ENG., Illus.). 52p. (J). (gr. k-4). 15.95 (978-1-59017-252-0(3), NYR Children's Collection) New York Review of Bks., Inc., The.

Davidsen, Keith & Hayes, Drew. Hyena, 2 vols., Vol. 1. 2006. (Poison Elves Ser.). (Illus.). 128p. pap. 14.95 (978-1-57989-084-1(9)) Sirius Entertainment, Inc.

Davidson, Susanna. See Inside Fairyland. Ligi, Raffaella, illus. 2007. (See Inside Board Bks). 14p. (J). (gr. -1-k). bds. 12.99 (978-0-7945-1570-6(3), Usborne) EDC Publishing.

—Usborne Stories of Dolls & Fairies. Wanert, Amandine, illus. 2007. (Usborne Ser.). 96p. (J). 9.99 (978-0-7945-1779-3(X), Usborne) EDC Publishing.

Davies, Lewis. Tai & the Tremorfa Troll. Acreman, Hayley, illus. 2007. (ENG.). 20p. (J). pap. 7.95 (978-1-905762-48-4(8)) Parthian Bks. GBR. Dist: Independent Pubs. Group.

Davis, Brandon. Mary the Glary Tree Fairy. 2013. 28p. pap. 15.99 (978-1-4797-7398-5(0)) Xlibris Corp.

Davis, Daniel N. Affair's Apology: The Tooth Fairy Speaks. 2012. 24p. pap. 15.99 (978-1-4691-5250-9(9)) Xlibris Corp.

Davis, Elena. Where Do the Balloons Go? Jurinich, Anna, illus. 2006. (ENG.). 32p. (J). (gr. -1-3). 16.95 (978-0-9714372-3-4(8)) Red Rock Pr., Inc.

Davis, Harold. The Starrigans of Little Brook Bottom, 1 vol. Carter, Dana, illus. 2007. (ENG.). 150p. (J). (gr. 3-7). per. 8.95 (978-1-894294-85-0(8), Tuckamore Bks) Creative Bk. Publishing CAN. Dist: Orca Bk. Pubs. USA.

Dawley, Linda. The Tooth Fairy's Mistake. 2nd ed. 2014. (ENG.). 114p. (J). pap. (978-0-9941011-6-7(3), The Little Red Hen Community Pr.) CCB Publishing.

Day, Nancy Raines. Fairy Childs Busy Week. 2006. (978-0-06-052751-8(X)); lib. bdg. (978-0-06-052752-5(8)) HarperCollins Canada, Ltd.

de Brun, Kieran Christopher. The Talking Llama: la Llama Que Habla. de Brun, Brendan Joseph, illus. 2005. (J). pap. 16.00 (978-0-8059-6910-8(1)) Dorrance Publishing Co., Inc.

De Castro, Ines E. The Teddy Bear Faeries. De Castro, Ines E., illus. 2011. (Illus.). 24p. (J). (gr. -1-3). 16.95 (978-1-935359-72-2(X)) Book Pubs. Network.

de Lint, Charles. The Blue Girl. 2006. (ENG.). 384p. (YA). (gr. 7-18). reprint ed. 7.99 (978-0-14-240545-1(0), Firebird) Penguin Young Readers Group.

Dean Wafstet, Cindi. Wings of Light. 2005. 31p. 15.00 (978-1-4116-5567-6(2)) Lulu Pr., Inc.

DEE and AMA, The Toybox Grannies. Katie & Savannah - Special Edition. 2009. 216p. pap. 21.89 (978-0-557-04568-6(1)) Lulu Pr., Inc.

DeGoede, Jeannette. Tulip Fairy's Holiday. 2006. (J). 5.00 (978-0-9778374-0-3(8)) grafixCORP.

DeHart, Leslie Marie. Paloma: The Lilly Fairy, 1 vol. 2010. 50p. pap. 16.95 (978-1-4489-6818-3(6)) America Star Bks.

Deluca, Laura. Flora & the Silver Coins. Manni, Mia (Maio), illus. 2011. 40p. pap. 24.95 (978-1-4560-7752-5(X)) America Star Bks.

Demeritt, Mary Anne. The Twilight Ride of the Pink Fairy. Daniel, Ellen, illus. 2006. 36p. (J). pap. 17.95 (978-1-58597-410-8(2)) Leathers Publishing.

Demers, Dominique. Old Thomas & the Little Fairy. 2004. (Illus.). (J). (gr. -1-18). spiral bd. (978-0-616-07229-5(5)) Canadian National Institute for the Blind/Institut National Canadien pour les Aveugles.

Depken, Kristen L. Castle Caper. Cartobaleno, illus. 2015. (Pictureback(R) Ser.). (ENG.). 24p. (J). (gr. -1-2). 5.99 (978-0-553-52313-3(9), Random Hse. Bks. for Young Readers) Random Hse. Children's Bks.

Dergachov, Oleg. The Yellow Elves. Andryczyk, Mark, tr. from UKR. 2004. (Illus.). 14p. (J). pap. (978-0-9735003-0-1(1)) StudioNib Publishing.

Deutsch, Stacia. Disney Fairies - Legend of the Neverbeast: The Chapter Book. 2015. (ENG.). 96p. (J). (gr. 3-7). pap. 4.99 (978-0-316-28353-3(3)) Little, Brown Bks. for Young Readers.

—The Dragon Queen. 2016. (LEGO Elves Ser.: 2). (ENG.). 128p. (J). (gr. 2-5). pap. 5.99 (978-0-545-85281-4(1)) Scholastic, Inc.

—Dragon Queen. 2016. (LEGO Elves Chapter Book Ser.: 2). (ENG.). 128p. (J). (gr. 2-5). lib. bdg. 16.00 (978-0-606-38108-6(2)) Turtleback Bks.

—Quest for the Keys. 2015. (LEGO Elves Chapter Book Ser.: 1). lib. bdg. 16.00 (978-0-606-37769-0(7)) Turtleback Bks.

Deutsch, Stacia, adapted by. The Pirate Fairy: The Chapter Book. 2014. 117p. (978-0-316-33346-7(8)) Little Brown & Co.

Deutsch, Stacia & Scholastic, Inc. Staff. Quest for the Keys. Scholastic, Inc. Staff, illus. 2015. (LEGO Elves Ser.: 1). (ENG., Illus.). 128p. (J). (gr. 2-5). pap. 5.99 (978-0-545-85280-7(3)) Scholastic, Inc.

D'Ghent, Laurie. Dryer Sheet Fairy. 2013. 20p. pap. 24.95 (978-1-63000-960-1(1)) America Star Bks.

DiBattista, Mary Ann & Finn, Sandra J. The Puddinhead Story. Bresnahan, Patrick, illus. 2010. (ENG.). 34p. 19.95 (978-0-615-24552-2(8), 9780615245522) Puddinhead LLC.

DiCerto, Jospeh J. The Wall People: In Search of a Home. 2014. (Illus.). 128p. (J). pap. 14.00 (978-0-87842-633-1(7)) Mountain Pr. Publishing Co., Inc.

Disney. Disney Fairies: Pixie Hollow Reading Adventures. 2014. (Passport to Reading Level 1 Ser.). (ENG., Illus.). 160p. (J). (gr. -1-3). 7.99 (978-0-316-28329-8(0)) Little, Brown Bks. for Young Readers.

—Disney Fairies: Rosetta's Magical Reading Journey. 2016. (ENG.). 160p. (J). (gr. 3-7). pap. 5.99 (978-0-316-31170-0(7)) Little, Brown Bks. for Young Readers.

—Disney Fairies: Tinker Bell's Fairytastic Reading Adventure. 2016. (ENG.). 160p. (J). (gr. 3-7). pap. 5.99 (978-0-316-31167-0(7)) Little, Brown Bks. for Young Readers.

Disney & Fox, Jennifer. Meet Nyx the Scout Fairy. 2015. (Passport to Reading Level 1 Ser.). (ENG., Illus.). 32p. (J). (gr. -1-1). pap. 3.99 (978-0-316-28352-6(5)) Little, Brown Bks. for Young Readers.

Disney & Sisler, Celeste. Disney Fairies: Meet Tinker Bell. 2014. (Passport to Reading Level 1 Ser.). (ENG., Illus.). 32p. (J). (gr. -1-3). 3.99 (978-0-316-28327-4(4)) Little, Brown Bks. for Young Readers.

—Disney Fairies: Pixie Hollow Bake Off. 2014. (ENG., Illus.). 24p. (J). (gr. -1-3). 4.99 (978-0-316-28332-8(0)) Little, Brown Bks. for Young Readers.

Disney Book Group. Sofia the First Let the Good Times Troll: Book with DVD. Disney Storybook Art Team, illus. 2015. (ENG.). 32p. (J). (gr. -1-k). 9.99 (978-1-4847-0696-1(X)) Disney Pr.

Disney Book Group Staff. Cinderella. Disney Storybook Artists Staff, illus. 2nd ed. 2012. (Read-Along Storybook & CD Ser.). (ENG.). 32p. (J). (gr. -1 — 1). pap. 6.99 (978-1-4231-6321-3(4)) Disney Pr.

—Tinker Bell & the Pirate Fairy. Disney Storybook Art Team, illus. 2014. (Read-Along Storybook & CD Ser.). (ENG.). 32p. (J). (gr. -1-k). pap. 6.99 (978-1-4231-7407-3(0)) Disney Pr.

Disney Book Group Staff, et al. The Curse of Maleficent: The Tale of a Sleeping Beauty. Disney Storybook Artists Staff & Kole, Nicholas, illus. 2014. (ENG.). 240p. (J). (gr. 3-7). 9.99 (978-1-4231-9751-5(8)) Disney Pr.

Disney Storybook Art Team, illus. Legend of the Neverbeast. 2015. (Read-Along Storybook & CD Ser.). (ENG.). 32p. (J). (gr. 1-3). pap. 6.99 (978-1-4847-1075-3(4)) Disney Pr.

DiTerlizzi, Tony & Black, Holly. The Field Guide. DiTerlizzi, Tony, illus. 2003. (Spiderwick Chronicles Ser.: 1). (ENG., Illus.). 128p. (J). (gr. 1-5). 12.99 (978-0-689-85936-6(8), 53409542, Simon & Schuster Bks. For Young Readers) Simon & Schuster Bks. For Young Readers.

—The Ironwood Tree. l.t. ed. 2006. (Spiderwick Chronicles: Bk. 4). 90p. (YA). (gr. 2-18). 23.95 (978-0-7862-8583-9(4)) Thorndike Pr.

—The Nixies Song - A Giant Problem - The Wyrm King Set, Set. DiTerlizzi, Tony, illus. 2009. (Beyond the Spiderwick Chronicles Ser.: Nos. 1-3). (ENG., Illus.). 528p. (J). (gr. 2-5). 33.99 (978-1-4169-9011-6(9), Simon & Schuster Bks. For Young Readers) Simon & Schuster Bks. For Young Readers.

Doerrfeld, Cori. Little Bunny Foo Foo: The Real Story. (ENG., Illus.). 32p. (J). 2016. (-k). pap. 8.99 (978-1-101-99774-1(5), Puffin Books) 2012. (gr. -1-k). 16.99 (978-0-8037-3470-8(0), Dial Bks) Penguin Young Readers Group.

—A Perfect View. Doerrfeld, Cori & Page, Tyler, illus. 2017. (Cici: a Fairy's Tale Ser.: 3). (ENG.). 48p. (J). (gr. 2-5). 26.65 (978-1-4677-6154-3(0)); pap. 7.99 (978-1-5124-3068-4(4)); E-Book 19.99 **(978-1-5124-2700-4(4)**, 9781512427004) Lerner Publishing Group. (Graphic Universe™).

—Truth in Sight. Doerrfeld, Cori & Page, Tyler, illus. 2016. (Cici: a Fairy's Tale Ser.: 2). (ENG.). 48p. (J). (gr. 2-5). lib. bdg. 26.65 (978-1-4677-6153-6(2), Graphic Universe™) Lerner Publishing Group.

Dokey, Cameron. Once: Before Midnight; Golden; Wild Orchid. 2012. (ENG.). 640p. (YA). (gr. 7). pap. 11.99 (978-1-4424-2283-4(1), Simon Pulse) Simon Pulse.

Dolamore, Jaclyn. Magic under Glass. (Magic under Glass Ser.). (ENG.). (YA). (gr. 7). 2011. 256p. pap. 8.99 (978-1-59990-587-7(6), 9781599905877) 2010. 240p. 16.99 (978-1-59990-430-6(6), 9781599904306) Bloomsbury Publishing USA. (Bloomsbury USA Childrens).

—Magic under Stone. 2012. (Magic under Glass Ser.). (ENG.). 304p. (YA). 16.99 (978-1-59990-643-0(0), 9781599906430, Bloomsbury USA Childrens) Bloomsbury Publishing USA.

Donald, George Mac. Cross Purposes. 2012. 104p. pap. 25.95 (978-1-4474-5057-3(4)) Borah Pr.

Donaldson, Julia. Freddie & the Fairy, 7. George, Karen, illus. 4th ed. 2012. (ENG.). 32p. (J). (gr. -1-k). 9.99 (978-0-330-51118-6(1)) Pan Macmillan GBR. Dist: Independent Pubs. Group.

—The Troll, 2. Roberts, David, illus. 3rd ed. 2010. (ENG.). 32p. (J). (gr. -1-k). pap. 11.99 (978-0-230-01794-8(0)) Pan Macmillan GBR. Dist: Independent Pubs. Group.

Donbavand, Tommy. Rampage of the Goblins. Donbavand, Tommy, illus. 2015. (Scream Street Ser.: 10). (ENG., Illus.). 128p. (J). (gr. 3-7). pap. 5.99 (978-0-7636-5762-8(X)) Candlewick Pr.

Dongweck, James. The Goblin's Story. Bixby, Sean, illus. 2013. (J). (978-0-9719632-2-1(3)) Golden Monkey Publishing, LLC.

Donnell, Frances. Goblins Will Be Seen: When It's Time for Halloween. Hebert, Catherine, ed. Merchant, Donna, illus. 2005. 38p. (J). 16.95 (978-0-9770893-0-7(4)) 2 Donn Bks.

Dor, George Vincent. Sit. 2012. (Illus.). 112p. 27.45 (978-1-4678-9732-7(9)); pap. 15.18 (978-1-4678-9731-0(0)) AuthorHouse.

Dorling Kindersley Publishing Staff, ed. Princess: The Essential Guide. 2012. (ENG.). 96p. (J). (gr. 2-5). 12.99 (978-0-7566-9798-3(0), DK Children) Dorling Kindersley Publishing, Inc.

Dorman, Brandon. Santa's Stowaway. Dorman, Brandon, illus. 2009. (ENG., Illus.). 40p. (J). (gr. -1-3). 16.99 (978-0-06-135188-4(1), Greenwillow Bks.) HarperCollins Pubs.

Dorset, Skylar. The Boy with the Hidden Name. 2014. (Otherworld Ser.: 2). (ENG.). 320p. (YA). (gr. 7-12). pap. 9.99 (978-1-4022-9256-9(2), 9781402292569) Sourcebooks, Inc.

Dougherty, Brandi. The Littlest Elf. Richards, Kirsten, illus. 2012. (ENG.). 24p. (J). (gr. -1-k). pap. 4.99 (978-0-545-43654-0(0)) Scholastic, Inc.

—The Littlest Elf. Richards, Kristen, illus. 2012. (J). pap. (978-0-545-48978-2(4), WestBow Pr.) Scholastic, Inc.

Dougherty, John. Bansi O'Hara & the Edges of Halloween. 2011. (Bansi O'Hara Ser.: 2). (ENG.). 416p. (J). (gr. 4-7). pap. 8.99 (978-0-440-86792-0(4)) Transworld Publishers Ltd. GBR. Dist: Independent Pubs. Group.

Down, Reg. The Magic Knot: And other Tangles. 2007. (Illus.). 100p. (J). per. 14.95 (978-0-9794452-0-0(5)) Lightly Pr.

Doyle, Malachy & Jones, Jac. The Changeling. 2003. (ENG., Illus.). 36p. pap. 12.95 (978-1-85902-691-5(5)) Beekman Bks., Inc.

Dozier, Kim. The Confused Tooth Fairy. Dozier, Ashlyn & Dozier, Makenna Joy, illus. 2005. (ENG.). 28p. (J). 10.00 (978-0-9745839-3-8(6), Fun to Read Bks. with Royally Good Morals) MKADesigns.

The Dragon Queen. 2016. 126p. (J). **(978-1-5182-0562-0(3))** Scholastic, Inc.

DreamWorks. DreamWorks Trolls. 2016. (Book with Microphone Ser.: 1). (ENG.). 32p. (J). (gr. -1-1). 19.99 (978-0-7944-3796-1(6), Reader's Digest Children's Bks.) Studio Fun International.

Drescher, Daniela. The Elves' Big Adventure, 1 vol. 2007. (ENG., Illus.). 24p. (J). (978-0-86315-594-9(4)) Floris Bks.

—In the Land of Elves, 1 vol. Orig. Title: Im Zwergenland. (ENG., Illus.). 24p. 14.95 (978-0-86315-484-3(0)) Floris Bks. GBR. Dist: SteinerBooks, Inc.

—In the Land of Fairies, 1 vol. 2004. (ENG., Illus.). 24p. (J). 16.99 (978-0-86315-450-8(6)) Floris Bks. GBR. Dist: SteinerBooks, Inc.

—Little Fairy's Christmas, 1 vol. 2010. (ENG., Illus.). 24p. (J). (gr. -1-1). 16.95 (978-0-86315-773-8(4)) Floris Bks. GBR. Dist: SteinerBooks, Inc.

—What's Hiding in There? 2008. Orig. Title: Was Raschelt Denn Da? (ENG., Illus.). 16p. (J). (978-0-86315-634-2(7)) Floris Bks.

Duey, Kathleen. Following Magic. Tang, Sandara, illus. 2010. (Faeries' Promise Ser.: 2). (ENG.). 128p. (J). (gr. 2-5). pap. 6.99 (978-1-4169-8459-7(3), Aladdin) Simon & Schuster Children's Publishing.

—Following Magic. Tang, Sandara, illus. 2010. (Faeries' Promise Ser.: 2). (ENG.). 128p. (J). (gr. 2-5). 15.99 (978-1-4169-8458-0(5), Simon & Schuster/Paula Wiseman Bks.) Simon & Schuster/Paula Wiseman Bks.

—The Full Moon. Tang, Sandara, illus. 2011. (Faeries' Promise Ser.: 4). (ENG.). 128p. (J). (gr. 2-5). pap. 4.99 (978-1-4169-8463-4(1), Aladdin) Simon & Schuster Children's Publishing.

—The Full Moon. Tang, Sandara, illus. 2011. (Faeries' Promise Ser.: 4). (ENG.). 128p. (J). (gr. 2-5). lib. bdg. 15.99 (978-1-4169-8462-7(3), Simon & Schuster/Paula Wiseman Bks.) Simon & Schuster/Paula Wiseman Bks.

—Silence & Stone. Tang, Sandara, illus. 2010. (Faeries' Promise Ser.: 1). (ENG.). 128p. (J). (gr. 2-5). pap. 6.99 (978-1-4169-8457-3(7), Aladdin) Simon & Schuster Children's Publishing.

—Silence & Stone. Tang, Sandara, illus. 2010. (Faeries' Promise Ser.: 1). (ENG.). 128p. (J). (gr. 2-5). 15.99 (978-1-4169-8456-6(9), Simon & Schuster/Paula Wiseman Bks.) Simon & Schuster/Paula Wiseman Bks.

—Wishes & Wings. Tang, Sandara, illus. 2011. (Faeries' Promise Ser.: 3). (ENG.). 128p. (J). (gr. 2-5). pap. 4.99 (978-1-4169-8461-0(5), Aladdin) Simon & Schuster Children's Publishing.

—Wishes & Wings. Tang, Sandara, illus. 2011. (Faeries' Promise Ser.: 3). (ENG.). 128p. (J). (gr. 2-5). 15.99 (978-1-4169-8460-3(7), Simon & Schuster/Paula Wiseman Bks.) Simon & Schuster/Paula Wiseman Bks.

Duffy, Carol Ann. The Tear Thief. Ceccoli, Nicoletta, illus. 2007. (ENG.). 32p. (J). (gr. -1-3). 16.99 (978-1-84686-045-4(8)) Barefoot Bks., Inc.

Duffy, Carol Ann & Stevenson, Juliet. The Tear Thief. Ceccoli, Nicoletta, illus. 2011. (ENG.). 32p. (J). (gr. k-4). 9.99 (978-1-84686-622-7(7)) Barefoot Bks., Inc.

Duncan, Jodi. Happy Flowers. 2009. 24p. pap. 14.50 (978-1-60693-519-4(4), Eloquent Bks.) Strategic Book Publishing & Rights Agency (SBPRA).

Dunphy, Lorraine F. An Australian Fairy Tale. 2008. 32p. pap. 14.95 (978-1-59858-553-7(3)) Dog Ear Publishing, LLC.

Durand, Delphine. Terrible Trolls. Durand, Delphine, illus. 2011. (ENG., Illus.). 14p. (J). (gr. -1). pap. 10.99 (978-0-230-73932-1(6)) Macmillan Pubs., Ltd. GBR. Dist: Independent Pubs. Group.

Dyan, Penelope. The Story of Snagatooth — -Who Is Commonly Known As the Tooth Fairy. Dyan, Penelope, illus. 2008. (Illus.). 44p. pap. 11.95 (978-1-935118-42-8(0)) Bellissima Publishing, LLC.

—The Warrior Mouse of Forest Hollow. Quinn, Courtney, illus. 2008. 108p. 17.95 (978-1-935118-00-8(5)) Bellissima Publishing, LLC.

Dzidrums, Christine. Fair Youth: Emylee of Forest Springs. Lopez, Lyle & Dzidrums, Joseph, illus. 2012. 120p. pap. 9.99 (978-1-938438-05-9(1)) Creative Media Publishing.

Eaves, Victor Caleb. Vee's the Chapters of Expudict: Book One. 2008. 128p. pap. 12.00 (978-1-4389-3385-6(1)) AuthorHouse.

Eberhard, Phyllis Lunde Brees. Little Miss Neat-As-A-Pin. Jacoby, Nickolina Dye, illus. 2007. (J). (978-0-9722741-7-3(0)) Publishing Factory, The.

Eberhart, Nancy. Anabelle's Wish. Pyers, Kelsey, illus. 2007. (J). 22p. per. 9.99 (978-1-59879-370-3(5)); (gr. -1-3). 13.99 (978-1-59879-371-0(3)) Lifevest Publishing, Inc.

EDCON Publishing Group Staff. Jack & the Beanstalk - The Stubborn Witch - Rapunzel - Betsy - The Magic Bus. l.t. ed. 2008. (Classic Children's Tales Ser.). 32p. (gr. k-4). pap. 8.95 (978-1-55576-551-4(3)) EDCON Publishing Group.

—Little Toot - The Story of White Satin - Five Peas in a Pod - Rumpelstiltskin - The Little Magic Pot. l.t. ed. 2008. (Classic Children's Tales Ser.). 32p. (gr. k-4). pap. 8.95 (978-1-55576-552-1(1)) EDCON Publishing Group.

—Surprise Pies - Snow White & Rose Red - The Emperor's New Clothes - The Three Bears - The Mixed up Family - A

Valentine Story. l.t. ed. 2008. (Classic Children's Tales Ser.). 32p. (gr. k-4). pap. 8.95 (978-1-55576-554-5(8)) EDCON Publishing Group.

Ede, Lara. Press-Out & Play Fairy Land. 2013. (ENG.). 18p. (J). pap. 4.99 (978-1-78235-567-0(7)) Make Believe Ideas GBR. Dist: Nelson, Thomas Inc.

Edgson, Alison, illus. The Elves & the Shoemaker. 2007. (Flip-Up Fairy Tales Ser.). (ENG.). 24p. (J). audio compact disk (978-1-84643-142-5(5)); (gr. 2-2). (978-1-84643-076-3(3)) Child's Play International Ltd.

Edwards, Christine. The Charmed Enchanted Book. 2010. 24p. pap. 16.49 (978-1-4490-7091-5(4)) AuthorHouse.

Edwards, Elizabeth Marshall. How the Fairies Came to Live at Allie's House. 2012. 24p. 24.95 (978-1-4137-7466-5(0)) America Star Bks.

Edwards, Marnie. Magical Mix-Ups: Birthdays & Bridesmaids. Hodgkinson, Leigh, illus. 2012. (Magical Mix-Ups Ser.). (ENG.). 96p. (J). (gr. 2-5). pap. 6.99 (978-0-7636-6272-1(0), Nosy Crow) Candlewick Pr.

Eldridge, Jim. The Final Showdown: Match Six. 2016. (Wrestling Trolls Ser.: 6). (ENG., Illus.). 176p. (J). (gr. k-3). pap. 9.99 (978-1-4714-0269-2(X)) Bonnier Publishing GBR. Dist: Independent Pubs. Group.

—Jack Versus Veto. Bielecki, Jan, illus. 2016. (Wrestling Trolls Ser.: 5). (ENG.). 176p. (YA). (gr. k-3). pap. 9.99 (978-1-4714-0267-8(3)) Bonnier Publishing GBR. Dist: Independent Pubs. Group.

Eliot, Ethel. The Little House in the Fairy Wood. 2006. 108p. per. 9.95 (978-1-59818-097-8(5)); 22.95 (978-1-59818-343-6(5)) Aegypan.

Eliot, Ethel Cook. The Little House in the Fairy Wood. 2004. reprint ed. pap. 1.99 (978-1-4192-7023-9(0)) Kessinger Publishing, LLC.

Ellsworth, Nick. Twinkle the Tooth Fairy. White, Michelle, illus. 32p. (J). 5.98 (978-0-7525-7628-2(3)) Parragon, Inc.

Elves & the Shoemaker. Date not set. (J). 4.99 (978-0-7214-5407-8(0)) Nickel Pr.

The Elves & the Shoemaker. 2016. (Well-Loved Tales Ser.). (ENG., Illus.). 56p. (J). (gr. 3-7). 9.99 (978-0-7232-9756-7(8)) Penguin Bks., Ltd. GBR. Dist: Independent Pubs. Group.

The Elves & the Shoemaker, Level 3. 2016. (Ladybird Readers Ser.). (ENG.). 64p. (J). (gr. 2-4). pap. 9.99 (978-0-241-25385-4(3)) Penguin Bks., Ltd. GBR. Dist: Independent Pubs. Group.

Enersen, Adele. When My Baby Dreams of Fairy Tales. Enersen, Adele, illus. 2013. (ENG., Illus.). 48p. (J). (gr. -1-k). 15.99 (978-0-06-207177-4(7)) HarperCollins Pubs.

England, Brooke. Guardian Fairies. 2006. 17p. 12.00 (978-1-4116-7923-8(7)) Lulu Pr., Inc.

Erickson, Melissa. When the Tooth Fairy Comes... Erickson, Melissa, illus. 2007. (Illus.). 15p. (J). (gr. -1-3). 10.99 (978-1-59879-369-7(1)) Lifevest Publishing, Inc.

Eschler, Linda. The Strawberry Fairies & the Secret of Mystery Island. 2008. 57p. pap. 16.95 (978-1-60610-960-1(X)) America Star Bks.

—The Strawberry Fairies Save Sandcastle Island. 2007. 52p. per. 16.95 (978-1-4241-9175-8(0)) America Star Bks.

Eubank, Patricia Reeder. The Princess & the Snarls. Eubank, Patricia Reeder, illus. 2006. (ENG., Illus.). 32p. (J). (gr. k-3). 16.95 (978-0-8249-5536-6(6), Ideal Pubns.) Worthy Publishing.

Evans, C. S. Sleeping Beauty. Rackham, Arthur, illus. 2012. (ENG.). 104p. (J). 12.95 (978-1-59583-457-7(5), Green Tiger Pr.) Laughing Elephant.

Evans, Cordelia. Olivia Helps the Tooth Fairy. 2015. (Olivia 8x8 Ser.). lib. bdg. 13.55 (978-0-606-37145-2(1)) Turtleback Bks.

Everblaze. 2014. (Keeper of the Lost Cities Ser.: 3). (ENG., Illus.). 624p. (J). (gr. 3-7). 18.99 (978-1-4424-4599-4(8), Aladdin) Simon & Schuster Children's Publishing.

Eze-Offormezie, Ngozika. An Invitation from the Fairy. 2008. 64p. pap. 23.49 (978-1-4343-9784-3(X)) AuthorHouse.

Fairy Gardens Magic Painting Book. 2017. (Magic Painting Bks.). (ENG.). (J). pap. 9.99 **(978-0-7945-3798-2(7)**, Usborne) EDC Publishing.

Fairy Palaces Magic Painting Book. 2017. (Magic Painting Bks.). (ENG.). (J). pap. 9.99 **(978-0-7945-3876-7(2)**, Usborne) EDC Publishing.

Fairy talse s/s - CInderella. 2005. (J). bds. (978-1-4194-0066-7(5)) Paradise Pr., Inc.

The Fairy Who Lost His Wings. 2004. (J). 10.00 (978-0-9760076-0-9(6)) Juniper Berry Pr.

Faraway, Lara. Fleur & the Sunset Chorus. McCathery, Jan, illus. 2013. (Fairythorn Tales Ser.). (ENG.). 124p. (J). (gr. k-3). pap. 8.99 (978-1-84877-972-3(0)) Bonnier Publishing GBR. Dist: Independent Pubs. Group.

—Honeysuckle & the Bees. McCatherty, Jan, illus. 2013. (Fairythorn Tales Ser.). (ENG.). 124p. (J). (gr. k-3). pap. 8.99 (978-1-84877-969-3(0)) Bonnier Publishing GBR. Dist: Independent Pubs. Group.

—Posy & the Trouble with Draglings. McCatherty, Jan, illus. 2013. (Fairythorn Tales Ser.). (ENG.). 124p. (J). (gr. k-3). pap. 8.99 (978-1-84877-970-9(4)) Bonnier Publishing GBR. Dist: Independent Pubs. Group.

—Rose & the Friendship Wish. McCatherty, Jan, illus. 2013. (Fairythorn Tales Ser.). (ENG.). 124p. (J). (gr. k-3). pap. 8.99 (978-1-84877-968-6(2)) Bonnier Publishing GBR. Dist: Independent Pubs. Group.

Farmer, Nancy. The Land of the Silver Apples. 2009. (ENG., Illus.). 528p. (YA). (gr. 7). pap. 11.99 (978-1-4169-0736-7(X), Atheneum Bks. for Young Readers) Simon & Schuster Children's Publishing.

—The Land of the Silver Apples. Sardinha, Rick, illus. 2007. (ENG.). 512p. (J). (gr. 5-9). 18.99 (978-1-4169-0735-0(1), Atheneum/Richard Jackson Bks.) Simon & Schuster Children's Publishing.

—The Sea of Trolls. 2006. (ENG., Illus.). 480p. (YA). (gr. 9-8). reprint ed. pap. 11.99 (978-0-689-86746-0(8), Atheneum Bks. for Young Readers) Simon & Schuster Children's Publishing.

—The Sea of Trolls Trilogy: The Sea of Trolls; the Land of the Silver Apples; the Islands of the Blessed. 2016. (ENG., Illus.). 1504p. (YA). (gr. 7). pap. 32.99 (978-1-4814-9835-7(5), Atheneum Bks. for Young Readers) Simon & Schuster Children's Publishing.

Farnsworth-Simpson., Patricia Ann. The Twinkles Fairy Story. 2008. 115p. pap. 12.50 (978-1-4092-4951-1(4)) Lulu Pr., Inc.

Farnsworth-Simpson, Patricia Ann. The Wonderful Butterbee Angel's. 2010. 125p. pap. 14.50 (978-1-4092-8762-9(9)) Lulu Pr., Inc.

Farrow, G. & Farrow, George. The Mysterious Shin Shira. 2007. 116p. per. 10.95 (978-1-60312-225-2(7)) Aegypan.

Fashion Pixiez Sticker Scene. (Bratz Sticker Scene Books Ser.). 12p. pap. (978-1-4054-8734-4(8)) Parragon, Inc.

Faulkner, Georgene. The Flying Ship: Fairy Tales from the World Over. Richardson, Frederick & Becker, Charlotte, illus. 2011. 100p. 39.95 (978-1-258-10171-8(8)) Literary Licensing, LLC.

The Fearful Fairy. 2007. (ENG., Illus.). 39p. (J). 16.95 (978-0-9793823-0-7(0)) StonesThrow Publishing, LLC.

Ferguson, C.S. A Tale of Two Fairies: The Secret of the Spider's Web. 2013. 268p. pap. 17.95 (978-0-578-11204-6(3)) Boothroyd & Allnut.

Ferri, Giuliano, illus. Illustrated Stories from Aesop. 2014. (ENG.). 272p. (J). 19.99 (978-0-7945-2917-8(8), Usborne) EDC Publishing.

Fields, Frever. Frumpy McDoogle: And the Legend of the Ruby Toad. 2003. 40p. 16.95 (978-0-9632675-1-1(5)) Kimberlite Publishing Co.

Finneron, Karyn A. Susu of the Frufru. Provencher, Annematie, illus. 2012. 32p. (-18). pap. 9.99 (978-0-9857362-0-0(8)) Nana's Stories.

Fishburne, Melody. Three Little Faeries in the Baby Lady Bug Adventure, 1 vol. 2009. 48p. pap. 16.95 (978-1-4489-8897-6(7)) America Star Bks.

Fitzgerald, Gyleen Xavier. The Dream: A Magical Journey in Colourful Stitches. 2005. (ENG., Illus.). 90p. (J). (gr. 4-7). 29.95 (978-0-9768215-1-9(6)) FPI Publishing.

Five Children & It. 2013. 58p. pap. 5.60 (978-1-236-72792-3(4)) General Bks. LLC.

Five Children & It. 2010. (CAM.). 142p. pap. 10.95 (978-1-4385-3539-5(2), Book Jungle) Standard Pubns., Inc.

Fleming, David. Charlie Blue Berry Fipple Berry. 2012. 88p. 19.95 (978-1-4759-1945-5(X)); pap. 9.95 (978-1-4759-1944-8(1)) iUniverse, Inc.

Fleming, Geronda. Among the Fairies. 2008. 149p. pap. 14.00 (978-0-615-16737-4(3)) Faye Bks.

Fleming, Matthew. The Nukie Fairy. 2011. 16p. pap. 13.25 (978-1-4567-4556-1(5)) AuthorHouse.

Fliess, Sue. A Fairy Friend. Keane, Claire, illus. 2016. (ENG.). 32p. (J). 16.99 (978-1-62779-081-9(0), 9781627790819, Holt, Henry & Co. Bks. For Young Readers) Holt, Henry & Co.

Floca, Brian, illus. The Hinky-Pink: An Old Tale. 2008. (ENG.). 48p. (J). (gr. -1-3). 16.99 (978-0-689-87588-5(6), Atheneum/Richard Jackson Bks.) Simon & Schuster Children's Publishing.

Folk Tale Staff. Gingerbread Man. Rodriguez, Beatrix, illus. 2012. (ENG.). 32p. (J). (gr. -1-3). 17.95 (978-0-7358-4086-7(5)) North-South Bks., Inc.

Forest, Heather. The Woman Who Flummoxed the Fairies. Gaber, Susan, illus. 2013. (ENG.). 32p. (J). (gr. -1-3). 8.95 (978-1-939160-71-3(5)) August Hse. Pubs., Inc.

Forrester, Emma. Uncle Arthur's Art Studio. Nunn, Paul E., illus. 2008. (Spiderwick Chronicles). (ENG.). 48p. (J). (gr. 2-7). 10.99 (978-1-4169-4955-8(0), Simon Scribbles) Simon Scribbles.

Foster, Evelyn. The Elves & the Trendy Shoes. Venturini, Claudia, illus. 2015. (ENG.). 32p. (J). (978-0-7787-1932-8(4)) Crabtree Publishing Co.

Fower, C. A. The Bramblefrost Fairies. 2013. 116p. (978-1-909740-40-2(3)); pap. (978-1-909593-96-1(6)) Legend Pr.

Fowler, Susi Gregg. Arctic Aesop's Fables: Twelve Retold Tales. Fowler, Jim, illus. 2013. (Paws IV Ser.). (ENG.). 32p. (J). (gr. 1-4). pap. 10.99 (978-1-57061-861-1(5), Little Bigfoot) Sasquatch Bks.

Fox, Jennifer. Meet the Boxtrolls. 2014. (Passport to Reading Level 2 Ser.). (J). lib. bdg. 13.55 (978-0-606-36529-1(X)) Turtleback Bks.

Francesca, Sieglinde De. A Donsy of Gnomes. 2009. pap. (978-1-61623-243-6(9)) Independent Pub.

Francis, Mamie, et al. Green Isles of the Ocean. Evans, Fran et al, illus. 2005. (ENG.). 32p. pap. 12.95 (978-1-84323-421-0(1)) Beekman Bks., Inc.

Franklin, Teii L. Ameelia's Adventures: Ameelia's First Play. 2010. 32p. pap. 16.49 (978-1-4520-3613-7(6)) AuthorHouse.

Franks, Pam. The Magic Gingerbread House. 2015. (ENG.). 32p. (J). 19.95 (978-1-931721-10-3(6), 9781931721103) Bright Sky Pr.

Frederick, Heather Vogel. Once upon a Toad. 2012. (ENG., Illus.). 272p. (J). (gr. 5-9). 16.99 (978-1-4169-8478-8(X), Simon & Schuster Bks. For Young Readers) Simon & Schuster Bks. For Young Readers.

Freeman, Faith L. Beyond the Magic Waterfall. 2006. 79p. pap. 26.38 (978-1-4116-8202-3(5)) Lulu Pr., Inc.

Freeman, R. Gregory. A Carpenter's Tale: The Mystery of Kidron Valley. 2006. (Illus.). 34p. per. 10.95 (978-1-60002-118-3(2), 3901) Mountain Valley Publishing, LLC.

Frost, Lulu. The Moonlight Tooth Fairy. Brown, Loma, illus. 2013. (J). (978-1-4351-4919-9(X)) Barnes & Noble, Inc.

Froud, Brian, illus. Chelsea Morning. 2004. 32p. (J). (978-0-689-03593-7(4), Milk & Cookies) ibooks, Inc.

Gabriel Jr., Carl L. Jester's Quest: Book One. 2007. (ENG.). 52p. per. 16.95 (978-1-4241-7364-8(7)) America Star Bks.

Gabriel, Thora. Chessie Bligh & the Scroll of Andelthor. 2006. 284p. (J). 27.95 (978-0-595-83579-9(1)) iUniverse, Inc.

Gaia, Kerry-Anne. Fairy Love Heart Story Time & Songs: Love Fairies & the Talking Tree. 2013. 24p. pap. 12.99 (978-1-4525-6838-6(3)) Balboa Pr.

Galdone, Paul. The Elves & the Shoemaker. 2015. (Folk Tale Classics Ser.). (ENG., Illus.). 40p. (J). (gr. -1-3). 8.99 (978-0-544-53099-7(3), HMH Books For Young Readers) Houghton Mifflin Harcourt Publishing Co.

—The Gingerbread Boy. 2011. (Folk Tale Classics Ser.). (ENG., Illus.). 48p. (J). (gr. -1-3). 8.99 (978-0-547-59940-3(4)) Houghton Mifflin Harcourt Publishing Co.

Gale, Audra. The Adventures of Buddy & Me. 2007. 32p. (YA). pap. 8.00 (978-0-8059-7277-1(3)) Dorrance Publishing Co., Inc.

Gale, Eric Kahn. The Wizard's Dog. 2017. (ENG., Illus.). 288p. (J). (gr. 3-7). 16.99 (978-0-553-53736-9(9), Crown Books For Young Readers) Random Hse. Children's Bks.

Galvin, Laura Gates & Studio Mouse Editorial. Cinderella: Dreams Do Come True. 2008. (Illus.). 36p. (J). (gr. -1). 7.99 (978-1-59069-436-7(8)) Studio Mouse LLC.

Gardner, Sally. Cinderella. 2011. (ENG., Illus.). 80p. (J). (gr. -1-k). 7.99 (978-1-4440-0241-6(4), Orion Children's Bks.) Hachette Children's Group GBR. Dist: Hachette Bk. Group.

—The Frog Prince. 2011. (ENG., Illus.). 64p. (J). (gr. -1-k). 7.99 (978-1-4440-0244-7(9), Orion Children's Bks.) Hachette Children's Group GBR. Dist: Hachette Bk. Group.

—I, Coriander. 2007. (ENG., Illus.). 288p. (J). (gr. 5-18). 7.99 (978-0-14-240763-9(1), Puffin Books) Penguin Young Readers Group.

—Operation Bunny. Roberts, David, illus. 2014. (Wings & Co Ser.: 1). (ENG.). 192p. (J). (gr. 2-5). 12.99 (978-0-8050-9892-1(5), 9780805098921, Holt, Henry & Co. Bks. For Young Readers) Holt, Henry & Co.

—Operation Bunny. Roberts, David, illus. 2014. (Wings & Co Ser.: 1). (ENG.). 208p. (J). (gr. 2-5). pap. 6.99 (978-1-250-05053-3(7), 9781250050533) Square Fish.

—The Princess & the Pea. 2011. (ENG., Illus.). 64p. (J). (gr. -1-k). 7.99 (978-1-4440-0245-4(7), Orion Children's Bks.) Hachette Children's Group GBR. Dist: Hachette Bk. Group.

—Sleeping Beauty. 2011. (ENG., Illus.). 64p. (J). (gr. -1-k). 7.99 (978-1-4440-0242-3(2), Orion Children's Bks.) Hachette Children's Group GBR. Dist: Hachette Bk. Group.

—The Vanishing of Billy Buckle. Roberts, David, illus. 2015. (Wings & Co Ser.: 3). (ENG.). 240p. (J). (gr. 2-5). 13.99 (978-0-8050-9915-7(8), 9780805099157, Holt, Henry & Co. Bks. For Young Readers) Holt, Henry & Co.

Garner, Ellen. Santa's Elves & the Tickets. Street, James, illus. 2012. 56p. pap. 12.99 (978-0-615-55920-9(4)) EG Bks.

Gatty, Alfred. The Fairy Godmothers & Other Tales. 2007. 120p. per. (978-1-4065-2815-2(3)) Dodo Pr.

—The Fairy Godmothers & Other Tales. 2007. 104p. (gr. 4-7). per. (978-1-4068-0918-3(7)) Echo Library.

Gay, Marie-Louise. Stella - Fairy of the Forest, 1 vol. 2010. (Stella & Sam Ser.). (ENG., Illus.). 32p. (J). (gr. k-k). pap. 7.95 (978-0-88899-993-1(3)) Groundwood Bks. CAN. Dist: Publishers Group West (PGW).

George, Jessica Day. Princess of the Midnight Ball. 2010. (Twelve Dancing Princesses Ser.). (ENG.). 304p. (YA). (gr. 7-9). pap. 9.99 (978-1-59990-455-9(1), 9781599904559, Bloomsbury USA Childrens) Bloomsbury Publishing USA.

Geronimo Stilton Staff. The Wizard's Wand. 2016. (ENG.). 320p. (J). (gr. 2-5). 14.99 (978-1-338-03291-8(7), Scholastic Paperbacks) Scholastic, Inc.

Ghani, Samna. The Tooth Fairy Goes to School. Williams, Nancy E., ed. Cappoen, Jennifer Tipton, illus. 2013. 44p. (J). pap. 10.98 (978-1-938526-31-2(7)) Laurus Bks.

Gianatti, Silvia, et al. Tinker Bell & Her Magical Arrival. Melaranci, Elisabetta & Urbano, Emilio, illus. 2012. (Disney Fairies Ser.: 9). (ENG.). 64p. (J). (gr. 1-6). 11.99 (978-1-59707-324-0(5), 9781597073240); pap. 7.99 (978-1-59707-323-3(7), 9781597073233) Papercutz.

Gil, Carmen. Story of a Cockroach. 2012. (Mini-Animalist Ser.). (ENG., Illus.). 32p. (J). (gr. -1-2). (978-84-15241-22-5(4)) D P & G Military Pubs.

Giles, Chauncey. The Magic Spectacles: A Fairy Story. 2004. reprint ed. pap. 22.95 (978-0-7661-8731-3(4)) Kessinger Publishing, LLC.

Gili, Phillida. Cinderella: A Pop-up Book. Gili, Phillida, illus. 2007. (Illus.). 12p. (J). 25.00 (978-1-4223-9031-3(4)) DIANE Publishing Co.

Gillingham, Sara. My Little Stocking. 2011. (ENG.). 12p. (J). (gr. -1 — 1). 9.99 (978-1-4521-0225-2(2)) Chronicle Bks. LLC.

Ginoschio De Osceola, Ibrahim. Enter the Corn Bunny, Vol. 1. 2007. 56p. per. 8.95 (978-0-595-45273-6(6)) iUniverse, Inc.

Godden, Rumer. The Fairy Doll. Blythe, Gary, illus. 2016. (ENG.). 80p. (J). (gr. 2-4). pap. 9.99 (978-1-5098-0507-5(9)) Pan Macmillan GBR. Dist: Independent Pubs. Group.

Gold, Carolyn J. Dragonfly Secret. 2014. (ENG., Illus.). 144p. (J). (gr. 3-7). pap. 13.99 (978-1-4814-3755-4(0), Atheneum Bks. for Young Readers) Simon & Schuster Children's Publishing.

Golden Books. One Sparkly Christmas (Shimmer & Shine) Golden Books, illus. 2016. (Hologramatic Sticker Book Ser.). (ENG., Illus.). 64p. (J). (gr. -1-2). pap. 4.99 (978-0-399-55298-4(7), Golden Bks.) Random Hse. Children's Bks.

—Troll Time! Golden Books, illus. 2015. (Color Plus Crayons & Sticker Ser.). (ENG., Illus.). 48p. (J). (gr. -1-2). pap. 4.99 (978-0-385-38769-9(5), Golden Bks.) Random Hse. Children's Bks.

Golden Books Staff. Rainbow Party! Golden Books Staff & Laguna, Fabio, illus. 2016. (Color Plus Rainbow Pencil Ser.). (ENG.). 128p. (J). (gr. -1-2). pap. 7.99 (978-0-399-55902-0(7), Golden Bks.) Random Hse. Children's Bks.

—Save the Unicorn King! Miller, Victoria, illus. 2011. (Paint Box Book Ser.). (ENG.). 48p. (J). (gr. -1-2). pap. 3.99 (978-0-375-87391-1(0), Golden Bks.) Random Hse. Children's Bks.

—Trolls Big Golden Book (DreamWorks Trolls) Golden Books Staff et al, illus. 2016. (Big Golden Book Ser.). (ENG.). 48p. (J). (gr. -1-2). 9.99 (978-0-399-55895-5(0), Golden Bks.) Random Hse. Children's Bks.

—Welcome to Wally's World! VanTuyle, David, illus. 2015. (Pictureback(R) Ser.). (ENG.). 16p. (J). (gr. -1-2). 3.99 (978-0-385-38764-4(4), Golden Bks.) Random Hse. Children's Bks.

Goldstone, Bruce & Poortvliet, Rien. A Gnome's Christmas. 2004. (ENG., Illus.). 48p. (gr. 8-17). 14.95 (978-0-8109-5017-7(0)) Abrams, Inc.

Gomez, Rebecca. Graduation Day at Elf School. 2005. (J). pap. (978-1-4108-4208-4(8)) Benchmark Education Co.

Gooderham, Chris. Even More Wicked Rhymes. 2008. 68p. pap. 13.95 (978-1-4092-1753-4(1)) Lulu Pr., Inc.

Goodman, Carol & Wells, Rosemary. Hawthorn. 2015. (Blythewood Novel Ser.). (ENG.). 416p. (YA). (gr. 7). bds. 17.99 (978-0-670-78478-3(8), Viking Books for Young Readers) Penguin Young Readers Group.

Goodnight, Lora. Ivy Tales: The First Irish Fairy. Goins, Heather Lea, illus. 2012. 28p. pap. 24.95 (978-1-4626-9484-6(5)) America Star Bks.

Gouveia, Keith. The Goblin Pricess. 2008. 208p. (978-1-897370-49-0(0)) Lachesis Publishing.

Graham, Bob. April & Esme Tooth Fairies. Graham, Bob, illus. (ENG., Illus.). 40p. (J). (gr. k-4). 2013. 6.99 (978-0-7636-6347-6(6)) 2010. 16.99 (978-0-7636-4683-7(0)) Candlewick Pr.

Graham, Oakley. In My Little Elf Bed. Gulliver, Amanda, illus. 2015. (In My Little Bed Counting Bks.). (ENG.). 24p. (J). (gr. -1). 8.99 (978-1-78445-381-7(1)) Top That! Publishing PLC GBR. Dist: Independent Pubs. Group.

Grandoit, Jean. In the Quest for Inshalla: Simbies of the Caribbean at the World Under. 2010. 68p. pap. 25.49 (978-1-4520-3900-8(3)) AuthorHouse.

Graudin, Ryan. All That Burns. 2015. (ENG.). 464p. (YA). (gr. 8). pap. 9.99 (978-0-06-218743-7(0), HarperTeen) HarperCollins Pubs.

—All That Glows. 2014. (ENG.). 480p. (YA). (gr. 8). pap. 9.99 (978-0-06-218741-3(4), HarperTeen) HarperCollins Pubs.

Gray, Christopher. There Be Goblins in the Wood! 2012. 112p. (gr. 2-4). 23.99 (978-1-4772-6994-7(0)); pap. 14.95 (978-1-4772-6995-4(9)) AuthorHouse.

Greenham, Caz. The Adventures of Eric Seagull 'Story-Teller' Book 2 a Fairy's Wish. Homfray, Nick, illus. 2013. 48p. pap. (978-1-78132-110-2(8)) SilverWood Bks.

Greenwall, Jessica. First Sticker Book Fairies. 2012. (First Sticker Bks). 24p. (J). pap. 6.99 (978-0-7945-3200-0(4), Usborne) EDC Publishing.

Grethe, James. Weird & Wondrous Tales of Woodland Wyre. 2009. 60p. pap. 11.00 (978-1-4269-1527-7(6)) Trafford Publishing.

Griffiths, Georgina. Granny Carstairs: The Wrinkled Fairy. 2010. (Illus.). 64p. pap. 23.49 (978-1-4490-7479-1(0)) AuthorHouse.

Grimm, Jacob. Cinderella/Cenicienta. 2004. (Illus.). (J). (978-1-933530-13-0(8)) Bingo Bks., Inc.

—Cinderella/Cenicienta Take Home Version. 2004. (Illus.). (J). cd-rom (978-1-933530-39-0(1)) Bingo Bks., Inc.

Grimm, Jacob & Grimm, Wilhelm. Grimm's Household Tales. Peake, Mervyn, illus. 2012. (ENG.). 320p. (J). (gr. 7). 24.99 (978-0-7123-5858-3(7)) British Library, The GBR. Dist: Independent Pubs. Group.

Grimm, Jacob & Grimm, Wilhelm K. Grimm's Fairy Tales, 1 vol. Canga, C. B, illus. 2011. (Calico Illustrated Classics Ser.: No. 3). (ENG.). 112p. (YA). (gr. 3-6). 27.07 (978-1-61641-102-2(3)) Magic Wagon.

Grimm, Jakob & Grimm, Wilhelm K. Grimm's Fairy Tales. Freeberg, Eric, illus. 2011. (Classic Starts(tm) Ser.). (ENG.). 160p. (J). (gr. 2-4). 6.95 (978-1-4027-7311-2(0)) Sterling Publishing Co., Inc.

Grimm, The Brothers, et al. The Complete Grimm's Fairy Tales. 2011. 262p. pap. 8.69 (978-1-936041-79-4(0)) Simon & Brown.

Grimm, W. C. & Grimm, J. L. C. Grimm's Fairy Tales. 2009. (ENG., Illus.). 392p. (978-1-904633-70-9(6), Collector's Library, The) Pan Macmillan.

Grimm, Wilhelm K., et al. Elves & Shoemaker. 2004. 48p. (J). (gr. 2-18). pap. 5.95 (978-0-7945-0758-9(1), Usborne) EDC Publishing.

Grinti, Mike & Grinti, Rachel. Claws. 2012. (J). (978-0-545-43314-3(2)); (ENG.). 256p. (gr. 5-9). 16.99 (978-0-545-43313-6(4)) Scholastic, Inc. (Chicken Hse., The).

Griswold, Elaine. The Fairy Walk: A True Story of Imagination. 2013. 34p. pap. 14.95 (978-1-4575-2394-6(9)) Dog Ear Publishing, LLC.

Grove, Malachai. Malachai Grove Plunt Solinatry: The Song of Malachai. 2010. 24p. 14.99 (978-1-4520-6441-3(5)) AuthorHouse.

—The Return of Malachai. 2011. 24p. pap. 14.99 (978-1-4567-6257-5(5)) AuthorHouse.

Gruelle, Johnny. Raggedy Ann in Cookie Land: (Classic) Gruelle, Johnny, illus. 2010. (Raggedy Ann Ser.). (ENG., Illus.). 96p. (J). (gr. k-5). 21.99 (978-1-4424-2199-8(1), Simon & Schuster Bks. For Young Readers) Simon & Schuster Bks. For Young Readers.

Guillain, Adam & Guillain, Charlotte. The Three Frilly Goats Fluff. Littler, Phil, illus. 2015. (ENG.). 32p. (J). (978-0-7787-1935-9(9)) Crabtree Publishing Co.

Gutierrez-Haley, Lisa. The Wiggly Tooth: Adventures of Hayden & Jace. 2011. 16p. pap. 24.95 (978-1-4626-1874-3(X)) America Star Bks.

Hague, Michael. The Book of Fairies. Hague, Michael, illus. 2006. (ENG., Illus.). 128p. (J). (gr. 2-7). pap., pap. 9.99 (978-0-06-089187-9(4), Harper Trophy) HarperCollins Pubs.

Hahn, Mary Downing. Witch Catcher. (ENG.). 240p. (J). (gr. 5-7). 2011. pap. 7.99 (978-0-547-57714-2(1)) 2006. (Illus.). 16.00 (978-0-618-50457-2(5)) Houghton Mifflin Harcourt Publishing Co.

Haile, Carol J. The Princess Tree: A Tale of Fairies, Elves & Magic. l.t. ed. 2005. (ESK., Illus.). 32p. (J). 19.95 (978-0-9711236-1-8(6)) Firenze Pr.

Hajj, Sharon. Zula Blackburn & the Rising Sun Festival. 2012. 146p. 34.94 (978-1-105-79464-3(4)) Lulu.com GBR. Dist: Lulu Pr., Inc.

Hall, Kirsten. Revamp Your Room. 2005. (Illus.). 48p. pap. (978-0-439-80296-3(2)) Scholastic, Inc.

—The Tooth Fairy. Apperley, Dawn, illus. 2004. (My First Reader Ser.). (ENG.). 32p. (J). (gr. k-1). pap. 3.95 (978-0-516-24640-6(2), Children's Pr.) Scholastic Library Publishing.

Hall, Shirley. A Fairy Tale. 2012. 20p. pap. 15.99 (978-1-4685-5242-3(2)) AuthorHouse.

Hall, Susan Liberty. Scented Adventures of the Bouquet Sisters in Fairyland. Josephine, Wall, illus. 2011. 85p. (YA). pap. 21.50 (978-0-9833247-6-8(X)) Inkwell Books LLC.

Hamilton, C. After Ever Happily. 2006. 80p. pap. 16.95 (978-1-4241-3190-7(1)) PublishAmerica, Inc.

Hamilton, Kersten. Tyger Tyger. 2011. (ENG.). 336p. (YA). (gr. 7). pap. 18.99 (978-0-547-57732-6(X)) Houghton Mifflin Harcourt Publishing Co.

—When the Stars Threw down Their Spears. 2014. (ENG.). 400p. (YA). (gr. 7). pap. 8.99 (978-0-544-22771-2(9), HMH Books For Young Readers) Houghton Mifflin Harcourt Publishing Co.

Hamilton, Peter F. The Secret Throne. Eason, Rohan, illus. 2015. (Queen of Dreams Ser.: 1). (ENG.). 288p. (J). (gr. 4-7). pap. 11.99 *(978-1-4472-8865-7(3))* Pan Macmillan GBR. Dist: Independent Pubs. Group.

Hampton, Brooke. Enchanted Cedar: The Journey Home. 2013. 38p. pap. 16.99 *(978-1-4525-6896-6(0))* Balboa Pr.

Hanson-Roberts, Mary, illus. Cinderella: A Tale of Kindness. 2006. (J). 6.99 *(978-1-59939-001-7(9))* Cornerstone Pr.

Hargreaves, Adam & Hargreaves, Roger. Little Miss Naughty & the Good Fairy. Hargreaves, Adam, illus. 2007. (Mr. Men & Little Miss Ser.). (ENG., Illus.). 32p. (J). (gr. -1-2). mass mkt. 4.99 *(978-0-8431-2122-3(X)*, Price Stern Sloan) Penguin Young Readers Group.

Haris, Martha & Haris, Kimberli. The Adventures of Fairyella the Tooth Fairy & Dragonfly Floyd. 2012. 24p. pap. 14.95 *(978-1-4575-1039-7(1))* Dog Ear Publishing, LLC.

Harmer, Wendy. Pearlie & Sapphire. Taylor, Gypsy, illus. 2014. (Pearlie Ser.: 8). (ENG.). 48p. (J). (gr. 2-4). pap. 7.99 *(978-1-74166-137-8(4))* Random Hse. Australia AUS. Dist: Independent Pubs. Group.

—Pearlie & the Imperial Princess. 2016. (Pearlie Ser.). (ENG., Illus.). 48p. (J). (gr. 2-4). pap. 8.99 *(978-0-85798-628-3(7))* Random Hse. Australia AUS. Dist: Independent Pubs. Group.

Harper, Suzanne. A Gaggle of Goblins. 2012. (Unseen World of Poppy Malone Ser.: 1). (ENG.). 320p. (J). (gr. 3-7). pap. 6.99 *(978-0-06-199609-2(2)*, Greenwillow Bks.) HarperCollins Pubs.

Harrell, Rob. Life of Zarf: The Trouble with Weasels. 2016. (Life of Zarf Ser.: 3). (ENG., Illus.). 272p. (J). (gr. 3-7). 15.99 *(978-0-8037-4105-8(7)*, Dial Bks) Penguin Young Readers Group.

—The Troll Who Cried Wolf. 2015. (Life of Zarf Ser.: 2). (ENG., Illus.). 272p. (J). (gr. 3-7). 14.99 *(978-0-8037-4104-1(9)*, Dial Bks) Penguin Young Readers Group.

Harrington, James. The Last Laugh. 2009. (Illus.). 24p. pap. 11.50 *(978-1-60860-187-5(0)*, Strategic Bk. Publishing) Strategic Book Publishing & Rights Agency (SBPRA).

Harris, Donna. Lucie & the Garden Fairies. 2008. (Illus.). 40p. pap. 18.49 *(978-1-4389-1312-4(5))* AuthorHouse.

Harris, Patricia. Rosalina Becomes a Flower Fairy. 2017. (Rosalina's Flower Garden Ser.). (gr. 4-6). pap. 8.25 ***(978-1-5383-2109-6(2)***, PowerKids Pr.) Rosen Publishing Group, Inc., The.

Harrison, Francesca. Obus the Eucalyptus Tree Fairy. 2012. 26p. pap. *(978-1-909381-03-2(9))* Foote, Douglas.

Harrison, Jo. The Jewellery Box Fairies. 2013. (Illus.). 24p. pap. 19.82 *(978-1-4772-5112-6(X))* AuthorHouse.

Harrison, Mette Ivie. The Princess & the Hound. 2008. (ENG.). 432p. (YA). (gr. 8). pap. 8.99 *(978-0-06-113189-9(X)*, HarperTeen) HarperCollins Pubs.

Harrison, Michelle. One Wish. 2016. (13 Treasures Trilogy Ser.: Prequel). (ENG.). 384p. (J). (gr. 3-7). 17.00 *(978-0-316-33529-4(0))* Little Brown & Co.

—The Thirteen Curses. 2014. (ENG., Illus.). 464p. (YA). pap. 8.99 *(978-1-4711-2168-5(2)*, Simon & Schuster Children's) Simon & Schuster, Ltd. GBR. Dist: Simon & Schuster, Inc.

—The Thirteen Secrets. 2014. (ENG.). 400p. (YA). pap. 8.99 *(978-1-4711-2169-2(0)*, Simon & Schuster Children's) Simon & Schuster, Ltd. GBR. Dist: Simon & Schuster, Inc.

—The Thirteen Treasures. 2014. (ENG., Illus.). 352p. pap. 8.99 *(978-1-4711-2167-8(4)*, Simon & Schuster Children's) Simon & Schuster, Ltd. GBR. Dist: Simon & Schuster, Inc.

—13 Curses. 2011. (13 Treasures Trilogy Ser.: 2). (ENG.). 496p. (J). (gr. 5-9). 15.99 *(978-0-316-04150-8(5))* Little Brown & Co.

—13 Curses. 2012. (13 Treasures Trilogy Ser.: 2). (ENG.). 512p. (J). (gr. 5-9). pap. 8.99 *(978-0-316-04149-2(1))* Little, Brown Bks. for Young Readers.

—13 Curses. 2012. (13 Treasures Ser.: 2). (J). lib. bdg. 19.65 *(978-0-606-26160-9(5)*, Turtleback) Turtleback Bks.

—13 Secrets. 2013. (13 Treasures Trilogy Ser.: 3). (ENG.). 432p. (J). (gr. 5-9). pap. 8.99 *(978-0-316-18562-2(0))* Little, Brown Bks. for Young Readers.

—13 Secrets. 2013. (13 Treasures Ser.: 3). (J). lib. bdg. 19.65 *(978-0-606-31745-0(7)*, Turtleback) Turtleback Bks.

—13 Treasures. 2011. (13 Treasures Trilogy Ser.: 1). (ENG.). 384p. (J). (gr. 3-7). pap. 8.99 *(978-0-316-04147-8(5))* Little, Brown Bks. for Young Readers.

Harrison, Paul. The Elves Help Puss in Boots. Sutcliffe, Tim, illus. 2016. (Fairy Tale Mix-Ups Ser.). (ENG.). 24p. (gr. k-2). lib. bdg. 23.32 *(978-1-4109-8303-9(X))* Heinemann-Raintree.

Harvey, Paul E., Jr. The Adventures of Shamus the Leprechaun. 2009. 48p. pap. 15.50 *(978-1-60693-924-6(6)*, Strategic Bk. Publishing) Strategic Book Publishing & Rights Agency (SBPRA).

Hatke, Ben. Nobody Likes a Goblin. 2016. (ENG., Illus.). 40p. (J). 17.99 *(978-1-62672-081-7(9)*, 9781626720817, First Second Bks.) Roaring Brook Pr.

Hatton, Laura. The Fairy's Garden. 2012. 64p. pap. 26.52 *(978-1-4669-3961-5(3))* Trafford Publishing.

Hauser, Michele. The, Crystal Palace Iii: The Fairy War. 2011. (ENG.). 219p. pap. 12.95 *(978-1-4327-8138-5(3))* Outskirts Pr., Inc.

Hay, Sam. Knit-Knotters. Tran, Turine, illus. 2016. (Stella & the Night Sprites Ser.: 1). (ENG.). 96p. (J). (gr. 1-3). pap. 4.99 *(978-0-545-81998-5(9))* Scholastic, Inc.

—Tooth Bandits. Manuzak, Lisa, illus. 2016. (Stella & the Night Sprites Ser.: 2). (ENG.). 96p. (J). (gr. 1-3). 15.99 *(978-0-545-82001-1(4))* Scholastic, Inc.

Hayes, Celeste. Enchanted Fairyland: A Sphinx & Trevi Adventure. 2011. (Illus.). 30p. (J). pap. 19.95 *(978-0-9785695-4-9(7))* Adam's Creations Publishing, LLC.

Hayes, Kathryn. The Balloon Fairy. 2009. 30p. pap. 13.99 *(978-1-4389-6857-5(4))* AuthorHouse.

Hayes, Vicki C. The Garden Troll, 1 vol. 2015. (Red Rhino Ser.). (ENG.). 68p. (J). (gr. 4-6). pap. 7.95 *(978-1-62250-916-4(1))* Saddleback Educational Publishing, Inc.

Haynes, Georgia. Trixie, the Treat Fairy: A Halloween Fable. 2009. 28p. pap. 13.99 *(978-1-4389-7658-7(5))* AuthorHouse.

Hays, Helen Ashe. The Adventures of Prince Lazybones: And Other Stories. 2007. 152p. pap. 19.99 *(978-1-4264-8474-2(7))*; 168p. pap. 21.99 *(978-1-4264-8532-9(8))* Creative Media Partners, LLC.

Heap, Sue. A Fabulous Fairy Feast. Heap, Sue, illus. 2009. (ENG., Illus.). 32p. (J). (gr. -1-k). pap. 8.99 *(978-1-4052-3644-7(2))* Egmont Bks., Ltd. GBR. Dist: Independent Pubs. Group.

Hearn, Julie. The Minister's Daughter. 2006. (ENG.). 272p. (YA). (gr. 7-12). pap. 7.99 *(978-0-689-87691-2(2)*, Atheneum Bks. for Young Readers) Simon & Schuster Children's Publishing.

Hegarty, Patricia. Five Busy Elves. Woolf, Julia, illus. 2014. (ENG.). 22p. (J). (gr. -1-k). bds. 8.99 *(978-1-58925-561-6(5))* Tiger Tales.

Heible, Beverly. A Christmas Party on River Row. 2012. 98p. pap. 17.95 *(978-1-4626-9575-1(2))* America Star Bks.

Helen, Grace. Santa's Way. 2012. 32p. pap. 24.95 *(978-1-4626-7356-8(2))* America Star Bks.

Heling, Kathryn & Hembrook, Deborah. Ten Lucky Leprechauns. 2013. lib. bdg. 13.55 *(978-0-606-31493-0(8)*, Turtleback) Turtleback Bks.

Heller, Sarah. Tinker Bell My Music MP3 Player: Storybook & Personal Music Player. 2008. (RD Innovative Book & Player Format Ser.). (ENG.). 36p. (YA). bds. 24.99 *(978-0-7944-1673-7(X))* Reader's Digest Assn., Inc., The.

Heller, Sarah & Reader's Digest Staff. Disney Fairies Music Player. 2008. (RD Innovative Book & Player Format Ser.). (ENG.). 36p. (J). 24.99 *(978-0-7944-1300-2(5))* Reader's Digest Assn., Inc., The.

Helliwell, Sheila. Hoonraki Moon: The Murphy Stories. 2006. (J). pap. 9.00 *(978-0-8059-7027-2(4))* Dorrance Publishing Co., Inc.

Henderson, Jeanine. Ever after High - A Wonderlandiful Doodle Book. 2014. (ENG., Illus.). 128p. (J). (gr. 1-17). pap. 12.99 *(978-0-316-37630-3(2))* Little, Brown Bks. for Young Readers.

Henkel, Donald G. Painted Treasures or the Original 288 Tree Gnomes. Henkel, D. B., VIII, illus. 2006. (J). mass mkt. 20.50 *(978-0-9673504-1-7(7))* Quillpen.

Hicks, Hannah. Jessica's Fairies: The Lost Wand. 2013. (Illus.). 24p. pap. 19.82 *(978-1-4772-5152-2(9))* AuthorHouse.

Higgins, Lawrence. Demons & Dragons: Time, Space & Magic. 2010. (ENG., Illus.). 93p. pap. 20.99 *(978-1-906791-68-1(6))* Arena Bks. GBR. Dist: Lightning Source UK, Ltd.

Higgins, Nadia. Goldilocks & the Breakfast Bunch, 1 vol. Johnson, Meredith, illus. 2009. (Fiona & Frieda's Fairy-Tale Adventures Ser.). (ENG.). 80p. (J). (gr. 2-5). 27.07 *(978-1-60270-573-9(9))* Magic Wagon.

Hilgenberg, Bob & Muir, Roberto. Tinker Bell & the Great Fairy Rescue. Storino, Sara & Zanotta, Roberta, illus. movie tie-in ed. 2010. (Disney Fairies Ser.). (ENG.). 56p. (J). (gr. 1-6). 9.99 *(978-1-59707-232-8(X)*, 9781597072328) Papercutz.

Hindmarsh, Ted C. The Elf & the Magic Windows: A Christmas Fairy Tale. 2008. pap. 2.99 *(978-1-59955-179-1(9))* Cedar Fort, Inc./CFI Distribution.

Hinkler Studios Staff., ed. Little Red Riding Hood. 2011. (Fairytale Pop-Ups Ser.). 12p. (J). 12.99 *(978-1-74185-088-6(8))* Hinkler Bks. Pty, Ltd. AUS. Dist: Ideals Pubns.

Hinkler Studios Staff, ed. Snow White. 2011. (Fairytale Pop-Ups Ser.). 12p. (J). 12.99 *(978-1-74185-089-5(4))* Hinkler Bks. Pty, Ltd. AUS. Dist: Ideals Pubns.

Hinman, Bobbie. The Belly Button Fairy. Adams, Mark Wayne, illus. 2009. (ENG.). 32p. (J). (gr. -1-1). 16.95 *(978-0-9786791-3-2(X))* Best Fairy Bks.

—The Fart Fairy. Adams, Mark Wayne, illus. 2010. (ENG.). 32p. (J). (gr. -1-1). 16.95 *(978-0-9786791-4-9(8))* Best Fairy Bks.

—The Knot Fairy. Bridgeman, Kristi, illus. 2010. (ENG.). 32p. (J). (gr. -1-1). 16.95 *(978-0-9786791-0-1(5))* Best Fairy Bks.

—The Sock Fairy. Bridgeman, Kristi, illus. 2008. (ENG.). 32p. (J). (gr. -1-1). 16.95 *(978-0-9786791-1-8(3))* Best Fairy Bks.

Hippie Bob. Tab-Boo & the Witches of Candy Land. 2009. 28p. pap. 13.99 *(978-1-4389-7297-8(0))* AuthorHouse.

Hoberman, Mary Ann. You Read to Me, I'll Read to You: Very Short Fairy Tales to Read Together. 2012. (You Read to Me, I'll Read to You Ser.). (ENG., Illus.). 32p. (J). (gr. -1-3). pap. 6.99 *(978-0-316-20744-7(6))* Little, Brown Bks. for Young Readers.

Hodgkinson, Leigh. Troll Swap. Hodgkinson, Leigh, illus. 2014. (ENG., Illus.). 32p. (J). (gr. -1-2). 15.99 *(978-0-7636-7101-3(0)*, Nosy Crow) Candlewick Pr.

Hodgson, Karen J. The Teeny-Weeny Walking Stick. Lambert, Sally Anne, illus. 2010. (ENG.). 32p. (J). (gr. -1-2). pap. 9.99 *(978-1-907432-02-6(7))* Hogs Back Bks. GBR. Dist: Independent Pubs. Group.

Hodgson, Sandra. The Toof Fairies. 2011. (Illus.). 44p. (gr. -1). pap. 16.76 *(978-1-4567-7978-8(8))* AuthorHouse.

Hoel, Charlotte. The Magical Mischief Maker. 2004. (J). spiral bd. *(978-0-9754004-0-1(1))* Magical Mischief Maker.

Hoffer, Rod. The Strange Christmas Dream. 2012. 64p. pap. 24.99 *(978-1-4772-5949-8(X))* AuthorHouse.

Hoffmann, E. T. A. The Nutcracker. Neugroschel, Joachim, tr. from GER. 2014. (Penguin Christmas Classics Ser.: 4). (ENG., Illus.). 128p. (gr. 12). 16.00 *(978-0-14-312250-0(9)*, Penguin Classics) Penguin Publishing Group.

Hoffmann, E. T. A. & Ventura, Paola Fratalocchi. The Nutcracker. 2010. (ENG., Illus.). 32p. (J). 14.99 *(978-0-7944-2044-4(3))* Reader's Digest Assn., Inc., The.

Holabird, Katherine. Twinkle. Warburton, Sarah, illus. 2014. (J). *(978-1-4351-5628-9(5))* Barnes & Noble, Inc.

Holm, H. R. Forever Santa. 2009. 14p. (J). pap. 2.99 *(978-1-59955-345-0(7))* Cedar Fort, Inc./CFI Distribution.

Holmes-Merritt, Angela. LINK Fairflies & Fairies. 2008. 36p. 17.50 *(978-0-615-17415-0(9))* AngiesInk.

Holt, Jessica. A Night in the Life of a Tooth Fairy. 2008. 16p. pap. 10.00 *(978-1-60693-396-1(5)*, Strategic Bk. Publishing) Strategic Book Publishing & Rights Agency (SBPRA).

Holt, K. A. Gnome-A-geddon. Jack, Colin, illus. 2017. (ENG.). 304p. (J). (gr. 3-7). 16.99 ***(978-1-4814-7845-8(1)***, McElderry, Margaret K. Bks.) McElderry, Margaret K. Bks.

—Gnomeageddon. 2017. (Illus.). 285p. (J). pap. ***(978-1-4814-7846-5(X)***, McElderry, Margaret K. Bks.) McElderry, Margaret K. Bks.

Holub, Joan & Williams, Suzanne. Aphrodite the Fair. 2014. (Goddess Girls Ser.: 15). lib. bdg. 17.20 *(978-0-606-36101-9(4))* Turtleback Bks.

—Snow White Lucks Out. 2014. (Grimmtastic Girls Ser.: 3). (ENG.). 192p. (J). (gr. 3-7). pap. 5.99 *(978-0-545-51985-4(3))* Scholastic, Inc.

Hopkins, Jackie Mims. Joe Bright & the Seven Genre Dudes. Manders, John, illus. 2010. (J). 36p. (gr. 1-5). 17.95 *(978-1-60213-051-7(5))*; *(978-1-60213-049-4(3))* Highsmith Inc. (Upstart Bks.).

Horwitz, Sarah Jean. The Wingsnatchers. 2017. (Carmer & Grit Ser.: 1). (ENG.). 368p. (J). (gr. 5-9). 17.95 *(978-1-61620-663-5(2))* Algonquin Bks. of Chapel Hill.

Houts, Michelle. Winterfrost. 2016. (ENG.). 272p. (J). (gr. 3-7). pap. 7.99 *(978-0-7636-9101-1(1))* Candlewick Pr.

Howell, Ruth. Fairy Friends. Bachmann, B. L., illus. 2013. 28p. 12.95 *(978-0-9899275-2-9(0))* Ravenwood Publishing.

Hoyt, Charlene. Where the Leprechauns Hide. Fischer, Sandi, illus. 2007. (ENG.). 40p. per. 12.99 *(978-0-9792258-9-5(2))* Bezalel Bks.

Hsia, Pei Chen. The Little Dumpling. 2012. 82p. pap. 19.95 *(978-1-4626-8041-2(0))* America Star Bks.

Huang, Yu-Hsuan, illus. Let's Play Fairy Homes. 2016. (Let's Play Ser.). (ENG.). 12p. (J). (gr. -1-k). bds. 16.99 *(978-1-4472-7723-1(6))* Pan Macmillan GBR. Dist: Independent Pubs. Group.

Hughes, Carol. The Princess & the Unicorn. 2010. (ENG.). 288p. (J). (gr. 3-7). 7.99 *(978-0-375-85563-4(7)*, Bluefire) Random Hse. Children's Bks.

Hughes, John H. B. Jiminy Tish - the Animal's Christmas. 2009. 61p. pap. 39.95 *(978-1-4092-9279-1(7))* Lulu Pr., Inc.

Humphrey, Eleanor Cairns. Building Santa's Work Shop from Tales of the Crystal Cave. 2012. 268p. pap. 27.95 *(978-1-4626-7820-4(3))* America Star Bks.

Hyman, Trina Schart, illus. Hershel & the Hanukkah Goblins. 25th anniv. ed. 2014. (ENG.). 32p. (J). (gr. -1-3). 7.99 *(978-0-8234-3194-6(0))* Holiday Hse., Inc.

Impey, Rose. The Most Annoying Fairy. McEwen, Katharine, illus. 2017. (Sir Lance-A-Little Ser.). (ENG.). 32p. (J). (gr. k-2). pap. 9.99 ***(978-1-4083-2528-5(4))***; 9.99 *(978-1-4083-2522-3(5))* Hachette Children's Group GBR. (Orchard Bks.). Dist: Hachette Bk. Group.

Ingelow, Jean. Mopsa the Fairy. 2004. reprint ed. pap. 1.99 *(978-1-4192-3510-8(9))* Kessinger Publishing, LLC.

Iosue, Marilyn. Santa's Busy Day. 2007. pap. 17.00 *(978-0-8059-8761-4(4))* Dorrance Publishing Co., Inc.

Jackson, John. Tales for Great Grandchildren: Folk Tales from India & Nepal. Terrazzini, Daniela Jaglenka, illus. 2014. (ENG.). 142p. 30.00 *(978-0-9569212-3-9(X))* JJ Bks. GBR. Dist: Casemate Pubs. & Bk. Distributors, LLC.

Jackson, Kate. Santa's Special Helper: A Spot-the-Difference Christmas Adventure! 2016. (ENG.). 18p. (J). bds. 7.99 *(978-1-4926-4175-9(8))*, 9781492641759, Sourcebooks Jabberwocky) Sourcebooks, Inc.

Jacob, Violet. The Golden Heart, & Other Fairy Stories. Sandheim, May, illus. 2011. 168p. pap. *(978-1-84921-098-0(5))* Kennedy & Boyd.

Jacobsen, Annie. Ivar, the Short, but Brave Viking. Hanson, Susan Jo, illus. 2007. (J). lib. bdg. 16.95 *(978-0-9778276-1-9(5))* Pickled Herring Pr.

James, Caleb. Haffling. 2nd ed. 2016. (ENG., Illus.). 250p. pap. 14.99 *(978-1-63476-795-8(0)*, DSP Pubns.) Dreamspinner Pr.

James, Hollis. Santa's Christmas Genies (Shimmer & Shine) Laviosa, Mattia Francesco, illus. 2016. (Big Golden Book Ser.). (ENG.). 32p. (J). (gr. -1-2). 9.99 *(978-0-399-55121-5(2)*, Golden Bks.) Random Hse. Children's Bks.

James, M. R. The Five Jars. 2008. 96p. pap. *(978-1-84830-112-2(X)*, Widhem Pr.) Echo Library.

Jensen, Danielle L. Stolen Songbird. 2014. (Malediction Trilogy Ser.: 1). (ENG.). 480p. (YA). (gr. 9). pap. 9.99 *(978-1-908844-96-5(5)*, Angry Robot, Limited) Watkins Media Limited GBR. Dist: Penguin Random Hse. LLC.

Jensen, Kimberly. Always the Elf. Harmon, Glenn, illus. 2007. 38p. (J). (gr. -1-3). 15.99 *(978-1-59955-086-2(5))* Cedar Fort, Inc./CFI Distribution.

Jesrani, Asha. Shirley the Poppy Fairy & the Little Girl Lucky. 2012. (Illus.). 28p. pap. 21.35 *(978-1-4772-1939-3(0))* AuthorHouse.

Jesus, Opal De. The Golden Apple Kingdom, 1 vol. 2009. 48p. pap. 16.95 *(978-1-60749-414-0(0))* America Star Bks.

Jewl, Terry. The Pixies in Home Sweet Home. 2012. 24p. pap. 24.95 *(978-1-4626-5585-4(8))* America Star Bks.

A Job for Little Elf. 2006. (Little Elf Set 1 Ser.). (ENG., Illus.). (J). pap. 7.33 *(978-1-932570-72-4(1))* Pioneer Valley Bks.

Johnson, Alaya. The Goblin King. Gandy, Meg, illus. 2009. (Twisted Journeys (r) Ser.: 10). (ENG.). 112p. (J). (gr. 4-7). pap. 7.95 *(978-0-8225-9259-4(2))* Lerner Publishing Group.

Johnson, Alaya Dawn. The Goblin King, No. 10. Gandy, Meg & Olson, Meagan, illus. 2009. (Twisted Journeys (r) Ser.: 10). (ENG.). 112p. (J). (gr. 4-7). 27.93 *(978-0-8225-9253-2(3)*, Graphic Universe™) Lerner Publishing Group.

Johnson, Lisa. All Hallows' Eve: The Story of the Halloween Fairy. Johnson, Tucker, illus. l.t. ed. 2005. 32p. (J). 12.95 *(978-0-9773096-0-3(6))* Positive Spin Pr.

Johnson, Margaret. Seven Magical Tooth Fairies. 2005. 88p. per. 9.95 *(978-0-595-37420-5(4))* iUniverse, Inc.

Johnson, Melinda & Johnson, Mindy. Tinker Bell: An Evolution. 2013. (Disney Editions Deluxe (Film) Ser.). (ENG., Illus.). 192p. (YA). (gr. 13-17). 40.00 *(978-1-4231-7201-7(9)*, Disney Editions) Disney Pr.

Jones, Christianne C. The Elf Boogie. Randall, Emma, illus. 2015. (Holiday Jingles Ser.). (ENG.). 20p. (gr. -1 — 1). bds. 5.99 *(978-1-4795-6493-4(1))* Picture Window Bks.

Jones, Frewin. The Charmed Return. 2011. (Faerie Path Ser.: 6). (ENG.). 368p. (YA). (gr. 8-18). 17.99 *(978-0-06-087161-1(X)*, HarperTeen) HarperCollins Pubs.

—The Enchanted Quest. (Faerie Path Ser.: 5). (ENG.). 368p. (YA). (gr. 8). 2011. pap. 9.99 *(978-0-06-087160-4(1))* 2010. 16.99 *(978-0-06-087158-1(X))* HarperCollins Pubs. (HarperTeen).

—The Faerie Path. 2008. (Faerie Path Ser.: 1). (ENG., Illus.). 336p. (YA). (gr. 8-12). pap. 8.99 *(978-0-06-087104-8(0)*, HarperTeen) HarperCollins Pubs.

—The Faerie Path Bk. 4: The Immortal Realm. 2010. (Faerie Path Ser.: 4). (ENG.). 368p. (YA). (gr. 8). pap. 9.99 *(978-0-06-087157-4(1)*, HarperTeen) HarperCollins Pubs.

—The Lost Queen. (Faerie Path Ser.: 2). (YA). 2008. (ENG.). 352p. (gr. 8). pap. 8.99 *(978-0-06-087107-9(5)*, HarperTeen) 2007. 335p. (gr. 7). lib. bdg. 17.89 *(978-0-06-087106-2(7)*, Eos) 2007. (ENG.). 352p. (gr. 7-12). 16.99 *(978-0-06-087105-5(9)*, Eos) HarperCollins Pubs.

—The Seventh Daughter. 2009. (Faerie Path Ser.: 3). (ENG.). 352p. (YA). (gr. 8). pap. 9.99 *(978-0-06-087110-9(5)*, HarperTeen) HarperCollins Pubs.

Jones, Heulwen. O'Grady's Well. 2005. (Illus.). 96p. pap. *(978-1-84401-578-8(5))* Athena Pr.

Jones, Janey Louise. Basil the Bear Cub. Poh, Jennie, illus. 2016. (Superfairies Ser.). (ENG.). 56p. (gr. k-3). lib. bdg. 23.99 *(978-1-4795-8641-7(2))* Picture Window Bks.

—Dancer the Wild Pony. Poh, Jennie, illus. 2016. (Superfairies Ser.). (ENG.). 56p. (gr. k-3). lib. bdg. 23.99 *(978-1-4795-8642-4(0))* Picture Window Bks.

—Farrah the Shy Fawn. Poh, Jennie, illus. 2016. (Superfairies Ser.). (ENG.). 56p. (gr. k-3). lib. bdg. 23.99 *(978-1-5158-0432-1(1))* Picture Window Bks.

—Martha the Little Mouse. Poh, Jennie, illus. 2016. (Superfairies Ser.). (ENG.). 56p. (gr. k-3). lib. bdg. 23.99 *(978-1-4795-8643-1(9))* Picture Window Bks.

—Sonny the Daring Squirrel. Poh, Jennie, illus. 2016. (Superfairies Ser.). (ENG.). 56p. (gr. k-3). lib. bdg. 23.99 *(978-1-5158-0433-8(X))* Picture Window Bks.

—Superfairies. Poh, Jennie, illus. 2016. (Superfairies Ser.). (ENG.). 56p. (gr. k-3). 95.96 *(978-1-4795-8657-8(9))* Picture Window Bks.

—Superfairies: Adventures in Peaseblossom Woods. Poh, Jennie, illus. 2017. (ENG.). 192p. (gr. 1-3). pap. 6.95 *(978-1-62370-819-1(2))* Capstone Young Readers of Coughlan Cos.

—Violet the Velvet Rabbit. Poh, Jennie, illus. 2016. (Superfairies Ser.). (ENG.). 56p. (gr. k-3). lib. bdg. 23.99 *(978-1-4795-8644-8(7))* Picture Window Bks.

Jones, Margaret. Nat. 2004. (ENG., Illus.). 112p. pap. 13.95 *(978-1-84323-327-5(4))* Beekman Bks., Inc.

Jones, Wendy & Blackwell, Su. The Fairy-Tale Princess: Seven Classic Stories from the Enchanted Forest. 2012. (ENG., Illus.). 96p. (J). 19.95 *(978-0-500-65006-6(3)*, 565006) Thames & Hudson.

Jordan, Claire. Fanakapan & the Fairies - a Children's Fairy Story. Skou, Nick, illus. 2013. 52p. pap. *(978-1-78148-648-1(4))* Grosvenor Hse. Publishing Ltd.

Joseph, Curtis. Fairy Tales of the Forbidden & Untold. 2011. 24p. pap. 24.95 *(978-1-4626-3485-9(0))* America Star Bks.

Joseph, Lila. The Boy Who Could Talk to Animals. 2008. 36p. pap. 18.95 *(978-1-4327-2873-1(3))* Outskirts Pr., Inc.

Joyce, Melanie. Cinderella. 2009. (Fairydust Fairytales Ser.). (ENG.). 5p. (J). (gr. -1-k). bds. 6.95 *(978-1-84696-964-5(6)*, TickTock Books) Octopus Publishing Group GBR. Dist: Independent Pubs. Group.

Joyce, William. Toothiana Bk. 3: Queen of the Tooth Fairy Armies. Joyce, William, illus. 2012. (Guardians Ser.: 3). (ENG., Illus.). 240p. (J). (gr. 2-6). 15.99 *(978-1-4424-3052-5(4)*, Atheneum Bks. for Young Readers) Simon & Schuster Children's Publishing.

Jules. Bubble's World: Book Five Frogs & Fairies. 2011. 40p. pap. 16.59 *(978-1-4567-6730-3(5))* AuthorHouse.

—Bubble's World: Isabella's Magic Dream. 2012. 58p. pap. 24.99 *(978-1-4772-6956-5(8))* AuthorHouse.

Kagawa, Julie. The Iron Knight. 2011. (Iron Fey Ser.: 4). lib. bdg. 20.85 *(978-0-606-23259-3(1)*, Turtleback) Turtleback Bks.

—The Iron Legends. 2012. (Iron Fey Ser.: 5). lib. bdg. 20.85 *(978-0-606-26516-4(3)*, Turtleback) Turtleback Bks.

—The Iron Queen. 2011. (Iron Fey Ser.: 3). lib. bdg. 20.85 *(978-0-606-23258-6(3)*, Turtleback) Turtleback Bks.

—The Iron Traitor. 2013. (Iron Fey Ser.: 6). lib. bdg. 20.85 *(978-0-606-35037-2(3)*, Turtleback) Turtleback Bks.

—The Lost Prince. 2012. (Iron Fey Ser.: 5). lib. bdg. 20.85 *(978-0-606-26946-9(0)*, Turtleback) Turtleback Bks.

Kalvoda, Mike. The Piper. Gregory, Raven & Kolasinski, Ken, eds. 2008. (ENG., Illus.). 168p. (YA). pap. 15.99 *(978-0-9817550-1-4(1)*, 9780981755014) Zenescope Entertainment.

Kananen, Barbara L. Fairies in My Garden. 2007. 106p. (YA). (gr. 2-2). per. 10.95 *(978-0-595-45082-4(2))* iUniverse, Inc.

—Fairies in My Garden. 2007. 106p. (YA). (gr. 2-2). 20.95 *(978-0-595-91014-4(9))* iUniverse, Inc.

Kane, Tracy. The Fairy Houses Trilogy. 2012. (Fairy Houses Series#174; Ser.). (ENG.). 130p. (J). (gr. -1-k). pap. 24.95 *(978-0-9708104-3-4(1))* Light-Beams Publishing.

Kann, Victoria. Fairy House. Kann, Victoria, illus. 2013. (I Can Read Level 1 Ser.). (ENG., Illus.). 32p. (J). (gr. -1-3). 16.99 *(978-0-06-218783-3(X))* HarperCollins Pubs.

—Fairy House. 2013. (Pinkalicious I Can Read Ser.). (J). lib. bdg. 13.55 *(978-0-606-27134-9(1)*, Turtleback) Turtleback Bks.

—Silverlicious. Kann, Victoria, illus. 2011. (Illus.). 40p. (J). (gr. k-3). (ENG.). 17.99 *(978-0-06-178123-0(1))*; lib. bdg. 18.89 *(978-0-06-178124-7(X))* HarperCollins Pubs.

Kate, Alejandria. How the Strawberry Got Its Seeds. 2012. 32p. pap. 14.99 *(978-1-300-04107-8(2))* Lulu Pr., Inc.

Kato, Haruhi. Vidia & the Fairy Crown. 2017. (ENG.). 208p. (J). pap. 10.99 ***(978-1-4278-5698-2(2)***, 9781427856982) TOKYOPOP, Inc.

Kearney, Rena. Mimi Fairy's Purple Hair. 2009. 32p. pap. 15.99 *(978-1-4490-1554-1(9))* AuthorHouse.

Keegan, Shannon. Legend of the Sea Fairies. 2006. (Illus.). (J). per. 14.99 *(978-0-9773433-0-0(8))* Bixie Gate Publishing.

Keenan, Sheila. Looking for Leprechauns. Meisel, Paul, illus. 2005. (J). *(978-0-439-68057-8(3))* Scholastic, Inc.

Kellie, Kerrie. Benjamin's Journey. 2011. 24p. pap. 24.95 *(978-1-4560-6040-4(6))* America Star Bks.

—The Sleep over Adventure. 2011. 20p. pap. 24.95 *(978-1-4560-6884-4(9))* America Star Bks.

Kelly, Diana. Tamla Bear & the Magic Goblin. Walker, Jack, illus. 2013. 30p. pap. *(978-1-78148-182-0(2))* Grosvenor Hse. Publishing Ltd.

Kennedy, Hugh J. The Flowers & the Fairies. 2009. 32p. pap. 18.97 *(978-1-4490-0265-7(X))* AuthorHouse.

Kerwin, Betsy. The Adventures of Floret the Woodland Fairy: The Adventures Begin. 2008. 44p. pap. 18.49 *(978-1-4343-9426-2(3))* AuthorHouse.

Kessler, Liz. Philippa Fisher & the Dream-Maker's Daughter. (Philippa Fisher Ser.: 2). (ENG.). 288p. (J). (gr. 3-7). 2015. pap. 6.99 *(978-0-7636-7460-1(5))* 2009. (Illus.). 15.99 *(978-0-7636-4202-0(9))* Candlewick Pr.

—Philippa Fisher & the Fairy Godsister. 2015. (Philippa Fisher Ser.: 1). (ENG.). 288p. (J). (gr. 3-7). pap. 6.99 *(978-0-7636-7462-5(1))* Candlewick Pr.

—Philippa Fisher & the Fairy's Promise. (Philippa Fisher Ser.: 3). (ENG.). (J). (gr. 3-7). 2015. 288p. pap. 6.99 *(978-0-7636-7461-8(3))* 2010. (Illus.). 274p. 15.99 *(978-0-7636-5031-5(5))* Candlewick Pr.

Kibbie, George Anthon. Bilwok: Dawn of the Trolls. 2015. 183p. (YA). pap. 13.99 *(978-1-4621-1663-8(9))* Cedar Fort, Inc./CFI Distribution.

Kibuishi, Kazu. Escape from Lucien. 2015. (Amulet Ser.: 6). (ENG., Illus.). 224p. (J). (gr. 3-7). 24.99 *(978-0-545-84899-2(7),* Graphix) Scholastic, Inc.

—Prince of the Elves. 2015. (Amulet Ser.: 5). (ENG.). 208p. (J). (gr. 3-7). 24.99 *(978-0-545-20888-8(2),* Graphix) Scholastic, Inc.

Kibuishi, Kazu, illus. Firelight. 2016. 197p. (J). *(978-1-4806-9909-0(8))* Baker & Taylor, CATS.

Kiendl, Maly M. At the Door: Adapted & Illustrated by Maly M. Kiendle, Based on a Children's Story Book by Katherine M. Yates. 2007. pap. 9.00 *(978-0-8059-8996-0(X))* Dorrance Publishing Co., Inc.

Kilpin, Veronica Paula Marie. Fairy Play. 2012. 36p. pap. 32.70 *(978-1-4771-4071-0(9))* Xlibris Corp.

Kingsley, Charles. The Water Babies: A Fairy Tale for a Land-Baby. Goble, Warwick, illus. 2006. (Dover Children's Classics Ser.). (ENG.). 160p. (J). (gr. 3-6). per. 14.95 *(978-0-486-45000-1(7))* Dover Pubns., Inc.

Kirk, Daniel. Elf Realm: The High Road. (ENG., Illus.). 576p. (YA). (gr. 7-17). 2010. pap. 8.95 *(978-0-8109-8979-5(4))* 2009. 19.95 *(978-0-8109-4075-8(2))* Abrams, Inc. (Amulet Bks.).

—Elf Realm: The Road's End. 2011. (Elf Realm Ser.). (ENG., Illus.). 496p. (YA). (gr. 7-17). 18.95 *(978-0-8109-8978-8(6),* Amulet Bks.) Abrams, Inc.

Kisinger, E. Jean. Firebug & the Mind Spark. Marta, Diana M., illus. 2012. 42p. pap. 12.50 *(978-0-615-58954-1(5))* Firebug Fairy Tales.

Kissock, Heather, ed. The Lion, the Bear, & the Fox: Is It Better to Cooperate or Compete? 2013. (AV2 Animated Storytime Ser.). (ENG., Illus.). 32p. (J). (gr. -1-3). 29.99 *(978-1-62127-920-4(0),* AV2 by Weigl) Weigl Pubs., Inc.

Kisson, Nisha. Leah - the Fairy of the Lime Tree. KecskTs, Anna, illus. 2008. 36p. pap. *(978-1-904312-39-0(X))* MX Publishing, Ltd.

Klein, Zoë. The Goblins of Knottingham: A History of Challah. Bogert, Beth, illus. 2017. (J). ***(978-1-68115-526-5(5))*** Behrman Hse., Inc.

Kondor, Karen. How to Trap a Leprechaun. 2012. 24p. pap. 15.99 *(978-1-4691-5079-6(4))* Xlibris Corp.

Konopka, Annie. The Tale of A Parkie Princess. 2008. 20p. 12.50 *(978-0-615-18598-9(3))* Konopka, Ann Marie.

Koontz, Robin. Los Tres Carneros y el Ogro / the Three Billy Goats & Gruff. 2012. (SPA & ENG.). 24p. (gr. 2-3). pap. 8.95 *(978-1-61810-540-0(X))* Rourke Educational Media.

—Zelda la Cenicienta. 2012. (SPA & ENG.). 24p. (gr. 2-3). pap. 8.95 *(978-1-61810-544-8(2))* Rourke Educational Media.

Kova, Elise. Water's Wrath (Air Awakens Series Book 4) 2016. (ENG., Illus.). 378p. pap. 14.99 *(978-1-61984-425-4(7))* Price World Publishing.

Kovalkova-McKenna, Svetlana. Vasilisa & the Queen of Asps. 2009. 63p. pap. 8.02 *(978-0-557-05710-8(8))* Lulu Pr., Inc.

Kovalkova-McKenna, Svetlana & McKenna, Alexandra. The Fairy Book. 2009. 52p. pap. 7.58 *(978-0-557-06160-0(1))* Lulu Pr., Inc.

Kowen, Dorothy. The Gift of Gold. Mathew, Gillian, illus. 2011. (ENG.). 24p. 13.95 *(978-1-77009-796-4(1))* Jacana Media ZAF. Dist: Independent Pubs. Group.

Krensky, Stephen. Too Many Leprechauns: Or How That Pot O' Gold Got to the End of the Rainbow. Andreasen, Dan, illus. 2007. (ENG.). 32p. (J). (gr. -1-1). 12.99 *(978-0-689-85112-4(X),* Simon & Schuster Bks. For Young Readers) Simon & Schuster Bks. For Young Readers.

Krishnaswami, Uma. The Big Party. 2006. (Early Explorers Ser.). (J). pap. *(978-1-4108-6133-7(3))* Benchmark Education Co.

Kumar, Pradyumna. How the Firefly Got Its Light. 2012. (ENG.). 32p. (J). (gr. -1-12). pap. 9.50 *(978-1-935677-25-3(X))* Mapin Publishing Pvt. Ltd IND. Dist: National Bk. Network.

Kyrja. Rupert's Tales: The Wheel of the Year - Samhain, Yule, Imbolc, & Ostara, 1 vol. Osborn, Tonia Bennington, illus. 2012. (ENG.). 64p. (J). 19.99 *(978-0-7643-3987-5(7),* 9780764339875) Schiffer Publishing, Ltd.

—Rupert's Tales: The Wheel of the Year Activity Book, 1 vol. Osborn, Tonia Bennington, illus. 2012. (ENG.). 40p. (J). pap. 9.99 *(978-0-7643-4020-8(4),* 9780764340208) Schiffer Publishing, Ltd.

Kyrja, et al. Rupert's Tales: The Wheel of the Year Beltane, Litha, Lammas, & Mabon, 1 vol. 2011. (ENG., Illus.). 64p. (J). 19.99 *(978-0-7643-3689-8(4),* 9780764336898, Schiffer Publishing Ltd) Schiffer Publishing, Ltd.

Lamb, Charles & Lamb, Mary. Tales from Shakespeare: "A Midsummer Night's Dream" Strang, Kay, ed. Andrews, Gary, illus. rev. ed. 2005. 39p. pap. 4.95 *(978-0-9542905-3-5(4))* Capercaillie Bks., Ltd GBR. Dist: Wilson & Assocs.

Lambert, Nat. Magnetic Dressing up Fairies. 2014. (ENG.). 10p. (J). (gr. -1-k). 9.99 *(978-1-78244-798-6(9))* Top That! Publishing PLC GBR. Dist: Independent Pubs. Group.

Lampman, Annette. Nicole's Wish. 2006. 23.00 *(978-0-8059-9146-8(8))* Dorrance Publishing Co., Inc.

Landolf, Diane Wright. Thumbelina. Ulkutay Design Group & Choi, Allan, illus. 2009. (Barbie Step into Reading Level 2 Ser.). 29p. lib. bdg. 13.55 *(978-1-4364-5096-6(9),* Turtleback) Turtleback Bks.

Lang, Andrew. The Green Fairy Book. 2007. 228p. per. *(978-1-4068-6082-5(4))* 2005. 636p. pap. *(978-1-84637-147-9(3))* Echo Library.

—The Lilac Fairy Book. l.t. ed. 2005. 508p. pap. *(978-1-84637-149-3(X))* Echo Library.

—The Pink Fairy Book. 2005. 31.95 *(978-1-4218-0004-2(7),* 1st World Library - Literary Society) 1st World Publishing, Inc.

—The Yellow Fairy Book. 2007. 396p. per. 15.95 *(978-1-4218-4502-9(4));* 31.95 *(978-1-4218-4418-3(4))* 1st World Publishing, Inc. (1st World Library - Literary Society).

—The Yellow Fairy Book. 2011. 260p. 29.95 *(978-1-4638-9521-1(6))* Rodgers, Alan Bks.

Langrish, Katherine. Troll Blood. 2011. (ENG., Illus.). 416p. (J). pap. 14.99 *(978-0-00-721488-4(X),* HarperCollins Children's Bks.) HarperCollins Pubs. Ltd. GBR. Dist: HarperCollins Pubs.

—Troll Fell. 2004. (ENG., Illus.). 272p. (J). (gr. 5-18). 16.99 *(978-0-06-058304-0(5))* HarperCollins Pubs.

—Troll Mill. 2008. (ENG., Illus.). 336p. (YA). (gr. 7). pap. 7.99 *(978-0-06-058309-5(6),* Eos) HarperCollins Pubs.

Lapucci, Carlo. Fiabe toscane di maghi, fate, animali, diavoli e Giganti: Edizione economica. Volume I. 2nd ed. 2011. (ITA., Illus.). 228p. (J). pap. 20.00 *(978-88-563-0058-1(3))* Polistampa ITA. Dist: Casemate Academic.

Larbalestier, Justine. How to Ditch Your Fairy. 2009. (ENG.). 336p. (YA). (gr. 7). pap. 8.99 *(978-1-59990-379-8(2),* 9781599903798, Bloomsbury USA Childrens) Bloomsbury Publishing USA.

Larousse Mexico Staff, ed. Historias de Princesas y Hadas. 2008.Tr. of Princess & Fairy Stories. (SPA & ENG., Illus.). 35p. 9.95 *(978-970-22-1449-6(1))* Larousse, Ediciones, S. A. de C. V. MEX. Dist: Houghton Mifflin Harcourt Publishing Co.

Larrypoet. Green, the Fairy: Cici & the Fairy. 2011. (Illus.). 48p. pap. 12.10 *(978-1-4670-0090-1(6))* AuthorHouse.

Larsen, Angela Sage. Petalwink Learns to Fly. Larsen, Angela Sage, illus. 2010. (Illus.). 32p. (J). lib. bdg. 12.95 *(978-1-936086-20-7(4))* Rising Star Studios, LLC.

Laudati, Joe. Faela: A Fairy's Tale. 2008. 190p. pap. 14.50 *(978-0-615-20324-9(8))* Laudati, Joe.

Laura & the Leprechauns. 2007. (J). 19.95 *(978-0-9795933-0-7(1))* Chrysalis Pr.

Lazear, Suzanne. Fragile Destiny. 2014. (Aether Chronicles Ser.: 3). (ENG.). 432p. (YA). pap. 9.99 *(978-0-7387-3986-1(3),* Flux) North Star Editions.

—Innocent Darkness. 2012. (Aether Chronicles Ser.: 1). (ENG.). 408p. (YA). pap. 9.95 *(978-0-7387-3248-0(6),* Flux) North Star Editions.

Leaf, Munro. Noodle. Bemelmans, Ludwig, illus. 2006. 56p. (J). 15.99 *(978-0-590-04310-6(2),* Levine, Arthur A. Bks.) Scholastic, Inc.

Leavell, Tracy. Lily. 2012. 118p. pap. 19.95 *(978-1-4626-9353-5(9))* America Star Bks.

Leavy, Una. The O'Brien Book of Irish Fairy Tales & Legends. Field, Susan, illus. 2012. (ENG.). 96p. (J). pap. 18.95 *(978-1-84717-313-3(6))* O'Brien Pr., Ltd., The IRL. Dist: Dufour Editions, Inc.

Lee, Deborah Baptiste & Atcheson-Melton, Patty. In the Shade of the Spade: This Tale in a Poetry Format Takes Us on a Journey the Illustrations Are Bright & Whimsical. You Can Almost Hear Music. Baptiste, Annette Green, illus. 2013. 48p. pap. 14.95 *(978-0-9858839-1-1(X))* Lee, Deborah I.

Leigh, Anita L. Willow's Gift, 1 vol. 2009. 48p. pap. 16.95 *(978-1-4489-9202-7(8))* America Star Bks.

Lemos, Lauren M. Tooth Fairy Troubles. 2007. (Illus.). 44p. (J). pap. 9.95 *(978-0-9798343-0-1(9))* Animal Crackers Publishing, LLC.

Leprechaun, Seamus T. The o'Shea Chronicles. 2013. 312p. pap. *(978-1-78407-190-5(0))* FeedARead.com.

Lessnick, Jaden. Kira's Dream. 2012. 32p. pap. 17.99 *(978-1-4685-4487-9(X))* AuthorHouse.

Lester, Anna. Stories of Fairies. Gower, Teri, illus. 2006. (Young Reading Series 1 Gift Bks.). 47p. (J). (gr. 2-5). 8.99 *(978-0-7945-1326-9(3),* Usborne) EDC Publishing.

—Stories of Fairytale Castles. Lo Cascio, Maria Cristina, illus. 2007. (Young Reading Series 1 Gift Bks). 48p. (J). (gr. 4-7). 8.99 *(978-0-7945-1679-6(3),* Usborne) EDC Publishing.

Levine, Arthur A. The Very Beary Tooth Fairy. Brannen, Sarah S., illus. 2013. (J). *(978-0-439-47404-7(3),* Scholastic Pr.) Scholastic, Inc.

Levine, Gail Carson. Fairy Haven & the Quest for the Wand. Christiana, David, illus. 2007. 191p. (J). *(978-1-4287-6391-3(0))* Disney Pr.

—The Lost Kingdom of Bamarre. 2017. 400p. (J). (gr. 3-7). 16.99 *(978-0-06-207466-9(0))* HarperCollins Pubs.

Levinthal, David. Who Pushed Humpty Dumpty? And Other Notorious Nursery Tale Mysteries. Nickle, John, illus. 2012. (ENG.). 40p. (J). (gr. -1-3). 20.99 *(978-0-375-94595-3(4));* 17.99 *(978-0-375-84195-8(4))* Random Hse. Children's Bks. (Schwartz & Wade Bks.).

Lewis, Cindy (Didas). The Sugar Spigot. 2011. 34p. pap. 16.95 *(978-1-4560-7012-0(6))* America Star Bks.

Lewis, Jill. Don't Read This Book! Allwright, Deborah, illus. 2010. (ENG.). 32p. (J). (gr. -1-2). 15.95 *(978-1-58925-094-9(X))* Tiger Tales.

Lewis, Kurt. The Improbable Barnsy & the Pocket Full of Teeth. 2009. 152p. pap. 12.96 *(978-0-557-11956-1(1))* Lulu Pr., Inc.

Lewis, Regina N. The Smallest Schoolhouse. Moore, P. M., illus. 2007. 56p. (J). pap. 12.95 *(978-0-9776958-3-6(2))* CyPress Pubns.

Lewman, David. Poppy & the Mane Mania (DreamWorks Trolls Chapter Book #1) Random House, illus. 2017. (ENG.). 128p. (J). (gr. 1-4). 6.99 ***(978-1-5247-1705-6(3));*** lib. bdg. 12.99 ***(978-1-5247-1706-3(1))*** Random Hse. Children's Bks. (Random Hse. Bks. for Young Readers).

Liddiard, Merrilee. Fairy Friends: an Opposites Primer, 1 vol. 2016. (ENG., Illus.). 22p. (J). bds. 9.99 *(978-1-4236-4537-5(5))* Gibbs Smith, Publisher.

—Seasons, 1 vol. 2016. (ENG., Illus.). 22p. (J). bds. 9.99 *(978-1-4236-4540-5(5))* Gibbs Smith, Publisher.

Light, Steve. The Christmas Giant. Light, Steve, illus. 2010. (ENG., Illus.). 32p. (J). (gr. -1-2). 15.99 *(978-0-7636-4692-9(X))* Candlewick Pr.

Lin, Grace. The Red Thread: An Adoption Fairy Tale. Lin, Grace, illus. 2007. (ENG., Illus.). 32p. (J). (gr. -1-3). 16.99 *(978-0-8075-6922-1(4))* Whitman, Albert & Co.

Lindsay, Elizabeth. Bugs & Butterflies. 2012. (Silverlake Fairy School Ser.). 100p. (J). pap. 4.99 *(978-0-7945-3066-2(4),* Usborne) EDC Publishing.

—Dancing Magic. 2012. (Silverlake Fairy School Ser.). 100p. (J). pap. 4.99 *(978-0-7945-3067-9(2),* Usborne) EDC Publishing.

—Ready to Fly. 2011. (Silverlake Fairy School Ser.). 123p. (J). pap. 7.99 *(978-0-7945-3064-8(8),* Usborne) EDC Publishing.

—Stardust Surprise. 2012. (Silverlake Fairy School Ser.). 100p. (J). pap. 4.99 *(978-0-7945-3065-5(6),* Usborne) EDC Publishing.

—Wands & Charms (Book 2) 2011. (Silverlake Fairy School Ser.). 117p. (J). pap. 4.99 *(978-0-7945-3063-1(X),* Usborne) EDC Publishing.

Little Elf Set 1. 2006. (J). *(978-1-932570-70-0(5))* Pioneer Valley Bks.

Livingston, Lesley. Tempestuous. 2012. (Wondrous Strange Trilogy Ser.: 3). (ENG.). 384p. (YA). (gr. 8). pap. 8.99 *(978-0-06-174002-2(0),* HarperTeen) HarperCollins Pubs.

—Wondrous Strange. 2009. (Wondrous Strange Trilogy Ser.: 1). (ENG.). 352p. (YA). (gr. 8). pap. 9.99 *(978-0-06-157539-6(9),* HarperTeen) HarperCollins Pubs.

Lo, Malinda. Ash. 2010. (ENG.). 272p. (gr. 10-17). pap. 10.99 *(978-0-316-04010-5(X))* Little, Brown Bks. for Young Readers.

—Huntress. 2012. (ENG.). 416p. (YA). (gr. 10-17). pap. 11.99 *(978-0-316-03999-4(3))* Little, Brown Bks. for Young Readers.

Lockwood, Vicki. The Magnificent Lizzie Brown & the Fairy Child. Hans, Stephanie, illus. 2015. (Magnificent Lizzie Brown Ser.). (ENG.). 200p. (gr. 5-9). 10.95 *(978-1-62370-210-6(0))* Stone Arch Bks.

Loewen, Nancy. Believe Me, Goldilocks Rocks! The Story of the Three Bears As Told by Baby Bear. Avakyan, Tatevik, illus. 2011. (Other Side of the Story Ser.). (ENG.). 24p. (gr. 2-3). pap. 6.95 *(978-1-4048-7044-4(X))* Picture Window Bks.

—Believe Me, Goldilocks Rocks! The Story of the Three Bears as Told by Baby Bear. Avakyan, Tatevik, illus. 2011. (Other Side of the Story Ser.). (ENG.). 24p. (gr. 2-3). lib. bdg. 27.32 *(978-1-4048-6672-0(8))* Picture Window Bks.

Loggia, Wendy. Aurora: The Perfect Party, 1 vol. Studio IBOIX, illus. 2012. (Disney Princesses Set 2 Ser.). (ENG.). 96p. (J). (gr. 2-6). lib. bdg. 24.21 *(978-1-59961-181-5(3))* Spotlight.

Logue, C. Robert & Logue, Michael. From the Top of the Mountain. 2013. (ENG.). 50p. (J). pap. 12.99 *(978-1-936172-74-0(7))* Elfrig Publishing.

London, Olivia. Welcome to the Crystal Empire! 2013. (My Little Pony 8X8 Picture Bks.). (J). lib. bdg. 14.75 *(978-0-606-32275-1(2),* Turtleback) Turtleback Bks.

Long, Ruth Frances. The Treachery of Beautiful Things. 2013. (ENG.). 384p. (YA). (gr. 7). pap. 9.99 *(978-0-14-242606-7(7),* Speak) Penguin Young Readers Group.

Longo, Kaitlin. The Secret in Olivia's Garden. 2012. 36p. pap. 20.99 *(978-1-4685-5222-5(8))* AuthorHouse.

Longstaff, Abie. And How Rapunzel Got Her Prince! Beard, Lauren, illus. 2014. (Fairytale Hairdresser Ser.: 1). (ENG.). 32p. (J). (-k). pap. 9.99 *(978-0-552-56186-0(X))* Transworld Publishers Ltd. GBR. Dist: Independent Pubs. Group.

—The Fairytale Hairdresser & Cinderella. Beard, Lauren, illus. 2014. (Fairytale Hairdresser Ser.: 2). (ENG.). 32p. (J). (-k). pap. 13.99 *(978-0-552-56535-6(0))* Transworld Publishers Ltd. GBR. Dist: Independent Pubs. Group.

Lord, Jennifer Fallin. Pipersville: And the troll that lost his big Toe. 2011. 32p. pap. 14.50 *(978-1-4670-3820-1(2))* AuthorHouse.

Love, D. Anne. The Secret Prince. 2012. (ENG.). 240p. (J). (gr. 3-7). pap. 11.99 *(978-1-4424-5931-1(X),* McElderry, Margaret K. Bks.) McElderry, Margaret K. Bks.

Loveridge, Pamela. Mr Foo. 2012. 24p. pap. 28.03 *(978-1-4797-5367-5(X))* Xlibris Corp.

—The Tooth Fairy Who Lost a Tooth. 2012. 24p. pap. 28.03 *(978-1-4797-4928-7(1))* Xlibris Corp.

Luberto, Bradley. Clide & Druce: A Repulsive Tale of Trolls & Tax Money. 2006. (ENG.). 48p. per. 16.95 *(978-1-4241-5012-0(4))* PublishAmerica, Inc.

Luna, James & Villarroel, Carolina. The Runaway Piggy/El Cochinito Fugitivo. Lacámara, Laura, illus. 2010. (SPA.). 32p. (J). (gr. -1-3). 16.95 *(978-1-55885-586-1(6),* Piñata Books) Arte Publico Pr.

Lynn, Shannon. Tooth Fairy Trouble Hits Tinsel Tooth Town. 2011. 24p. pap. 12.45 *(978-1-4525-3787-0(9))* Get Published.

Lyons, Sarah. Fairy stories about sally & Mignonette. 2007. pap. 9.99 *(978-1-60034-860-0(2))* Salem Author Services.

Maas, Sarah J. A Court of Mist & Fury. (Court of Thorns & Roses Ser.: 2). (ENG.). (YA). 2017. 656p. pap. 10.99 *(978-1-61963-519-7(4),* 9781619635197) 2016. (Illus.). 640p. (gr. 9). 18.99 *(978-1-61963-446-6(5),* 9781619634466) Bloomsbury Publishing USA. (Bloomsbury USA Childrens).

—A Court of Mist & Fury. 2017. (Court of Thorns & Roses Ser.: 2). (YA). lib. bdg. 22.10 ***(978-0-606-40562-1(3))*** Turtleback Bks.

—A Court of Thorns & Roses. (Court of Thorns & Roses Ser.). (ENG.). (YA). 2017. 56.97 ***(978-1-68119-774-6(X),*** 9781681197746) 2016. 448p. (gr. 9). pap. 10.99 *(978-1-61963-518-0(6),* 9781619635180) 2015. 432p. (gr. 9). 18.99 *(978-1-61963-444-2(9),* 9781619634442) Bloomsbury Publishing USA. (Bloomsbury USA Childrens).

—A Court of Thorns & Roses. 2016. lib. bdg. 22.10 *(978-0-606-38548-0(7))* Turtleback Bks.

—A Court of Wings & Ruin. 2017. (Court of Thorns & Roses Ser.: bk.3). (ENG.). 720p. (YA). 18.99 *(978-1-61963-448-0(1),* 9781619634480, Bloomsbury USA Childrens) Bloomsbury Publishing USA.

Mabie, Hamilton Wright. Fairy Tales Every Child Should Know. 2011. 290p. (gr. -1-3). pap. 17.99 *(978-1-61279-105-0(0));* pap. 18.99 *(978-1-61279-082-4(8))* Publishing in Motion.

MacDonald, George. At the Back of the North Wind. l.t. ed. 2007. (ENG.). 288p. pap. 23.99 *(978-1-4264-6832-2(6))* Creative Media Partners, LLC.

—The Carasoyn. 2008. 108p. 22.95 *(978-1-60664-921-3(3));* pap. 9.95 *(978-1-60664-041-8(0))* Aegypan.

—Cross Purposes & Shadows. 2008. 188p. 26.95 *(978-1-60664-984-8(1))* Aegypan.

—The Golden Key: Classic fairy Tales. McCabe, Steve, illus. 2008. 104p. (J). pap. *(978-0-88835-045-9(7))* Meany, P. D. Pubs.

—The Light Princess. 2006. pap. *(978-1-4068-2160-4(8))* Echo Library.

—The Princess & Curdie. l.t. ed. 2005. 320p. pap. *(978-1-84637-020-5(5))* Echo Library.

—The Princess & the Goblin. 2003. (Illus.). 160p. (J). 19.95 *(978-1-81514-970-2(1))* Antique Collectors' Club.

—The Princess & the Goblin. 2011. 174p. pap. 4.95 *(978-1-61427-173-4(9))* Martino Fine Bks.

—The Princess & the Goblin. Hughes, Arthur, illus. 2003. 136p. pap. 12.99 *(978-1-57646-633-9(7))* Quiet Vision Publishing.

—Princess & the Goblin. Hughes, Arthur, illus. 2nd ed. 2011. (Puffin Classics Ser.). (ENG.). 256p. (J). (gr. 5-7). 5.99 *(978-0-14-133248-2(4),* Puffin Books) Penguin Young Readers Group.

Mace, Aubrey. My Fairy Grandmother. 2009. 270p. pap. 16.99 *(978-1-59955-217-0(5))* Cedar Fort, Inc./CFI Distribution.

Machetto, Augusto, et al. A Present for Tinker Bell. Urbano, Emilio et al, illus. 2011. (Disney Fairies Ser.: 6). (ENG.). 64p. (J). (gr. 1-6). pap. 7.99 *(978-1-59707-256-4(7),* 9781597072564) Papercutz.

—Tinker Bell & the Lucky Rainbow. Dalena, Antonello et al, illus. 2012. (Disney Fairies Ser.: 10). (ENG.). 64p. (J). (gr. 1-6). 11.99 *(978-1-59707-368-4(7),* 9781597073684) Papercutz.

Macinnis, Katherine. Kelsar. 2006. pap. 12.95 *(978-1-58939-876-4(9))* Virtualbookworm.com Publishing, Inc.

MacInnis, Katherine Grace. Kelsar. 2006. 140p. 19.95 *(978-1-58939-877-1(7))* Virtualbookworm.com Publishing, Inc.

Mack, Tracy, et al. Cinderella: Les Petits Fairytales. Lake, Oliver, illus. 2012. (Petits Fairytales Ser.). (ENG.). 24p. (J). (gr. -1 — 1). bds. 7.99 *(978-0-8050-9624-8(8),* 9780805096248, Holt, Henry & Co. Bks. For Young Readers) Holt, Henry & Co.

—Snow White: Les Petits Fairytales. Lake, Oliver, illus. 2012. (Petits Fairytales Ser.). (ENG.). 26p. (J). (gr. -1 — 1). bds. 7.99 *(978-0-8050-9623-1(X),* 9780805096231, Holt, Henry & Co. Bks. For Young Readers) Holt, Henry & Co.

MacLean, Heather. The Moonicorn Fairies. 2011. 40p. pap. *(978-1-77067-687-9(2))* FriesenPress.

Maese, Fares & Shakespeare, William. A Midsummer Night's Dream, 1 vol. Esparza, Andres et al, illus. 2011. (Shakespeare Graphics Ser.). (ENG.). 88p. (gr. 2-3). pap. 7.15 *(978-1-4342-3449-0(5),* Shakespeare Graphics) Stone Arch Bks.

Maguire, Gregory. What-the-Dickens: The Story of a Rogue Tooth Fairy. (ENG., Illus.). 2009. 336p. mass mkt. 6.99 *(978-0-7636-4307-2(6))* 2007. 304p. (J). (gr. 4-7). 15.99 *(978-0-7636-2961-8(8))* Candlewick Pr.

—What-the-Dickens: The Story of a Rogue Tooth Fairy. 2007. (ENG.). 304p. (J). (gr. 4-8). 24.80 *(978-1-4287-6555-9(7),* Follettbound) Follett School Solutions.

Maher, Liam. The Plumber & the Wishing Well. May, Gin, illus. 2012. 24p. (gr. k-3). 19.95 *(978-1-61633-269-3(7));* pap. 10.95 *(978-1-61633-268-6(9))* Guardian Angel Publishing, Inc.

Mahoney, Karen. The Stone Demon. 2013. (Iron Witch Ser.: 3). (ENG.). 336p. (YA). pap. 9.99 *(978-0-7387-3340-1(7),* Flux) North Star Editions.

Maiden, Cecil. The Molliwumps. Price, Christine, illus. 2004. 160p. 12.95 *(978-0-9714612-9-1(5))* Green Mansion Pr. LLC.

Make Believe Ideas. Annie the Apple Pie Fairy. 2013. (ENG.). 32p. (J). pap. 6.99 *(978-1-78235-588-5(X))* Make Believe Ideas GBR. Dist: Nelson, Thomas Inc.

—Clara the Cookie Fairy Sticker Activity Book. 2015. (ENG.). 56p. (J). pap. 6.99 *(978-1-78393-446-1(8))* Make Believe Ideas GBR. Dist: Nelson, Thomas Inc.

—Fairies Scratch & Sniff Camilla the Cupcake Fairy. 2014. (ENG.). 12p. (J). bds. 6.99 *(978-1-78393-041-8(1))* Make Believe Ideas GBR. Dist: Nelson, Thomas Inc.

—Fairies Scratch & Sniff Lola the Lollipop Fairy. 2014. (ENG.). 12p. (J). bds. 6.99 *(978-1-78393-040-1(3))* Make Believe Ideas GBR. Dist: Nelson, Thomas Inc.

—Flower Friends Poppy's Shapes. 2013. (ENG.). 10p. (J). bds. 6.99 *(978-1-78235-603-5(7))* Make Believe Ideas GBR. Dist: Nelson, Thomas Inc.

—Flower Friends Primrose's Counting. 2013. (ENG.). 10p. (J). bds. 6.99 *(978-1-78235-602-8(9))* Make Believe Ideas GBR. Dist: Nelson, Thomas Inc.

—Flower Friends Rosie's Colors. 2013. (ENG.). 10p. (J). bds. 6.99 *(978-1-78235-605-9(3))* Make Believe Ideas GBR. Dist: Nelson, Thomas Inc.

—Katie the Candy Cane Fairy Storybook. 2013. (ENG.). 32p. (J). 15.99 *(978-1-78235-526-7(X))* Make Believe Ideas GBR. Dist: Nelson, Thomas Inc.

—Molly the Muffin Fairy. 2015. (ENG.). 32p. (J). pap. 6.99 *(978-1-78393-441-6(7))* Make Believe Ideas GBR. Dist: Nelson, Thomas Inc.

Man-Kong, Mary. Barbie -Fairy Secret. Random House Staff, illus. 2011. (Pictureback(R) Ser.). (ENG.). 16p. (J). (gr. -1-2). pap. 3.99 *(978-0-375-86555-8(1),* Random Hse. Bks. for Young Readers) Random Hse. Children's Bks.

—Barbie & the Diamond Castle. Rainmaker Entertainment Staff & Rainmaker Entertainment, illus. 2008. (Little Golden Book Ser.). (ENG.). 24p. (J). (gr. -1-2). 3.99 *(978-0-375-87508-3(5),* Golden Bks.) Random Hse. Children's Bks.

—Barbie & the Diamond Castle: A Storybook. Golden Books Staff, illus. 2008. (Pictureback(R) Ser.). (ENG.). 24p. (J). (gr. -1-2). pap. 3.99 *(978-0-375-87505-2(0),* Golden Bks.) Random Hse. Children's Bks.

—Fairy Dreams. Random House Staff, illus. 2013. (Step into Reading Ser.). (ENG.). 32p. (J). (gr. -1-1). 3.99 *(978-0-449-81628-8(1),* Random Hse. Bks. for Young Readers) Random Hse. Children's Bks.

—Fairy Dreams. 2013. (Barbie Step into Reading Level 2 Ser.). lib. bdg. 13.55 *(978-0-606-32193-8(4),* Turtleback) Turtleback Bks.

—Magic of the Rainbow. 2007. (Pictureback(R) Ser.). (ENG., Illus.). 16p. (J). (gr. -1-2). pap. 3.99 *(978-0-375-83985-6(2),* Golden Bks.) Random Hse. Children's Bks.

Man-Kong, Mary, et al. Glimmer, Shimmer, & Shine! Golden Books Staff, illus. 2010. (Hologramatic Sticker Book Ser.). (ENG.). 48p. (J). (gr. -1-2). pap. 3.99 *(978-0-375-86032-4(0),* Golden Bks.) Random Hse. Children's Bks.

Mancil, Arlene. The Garden Fairy. 2008. 32p. pap. 24.95 *(978-1-60441-735-7(8))* PublishAmerica, Inc.

Mandy, Stanley. Bella: The Fairy Ball. Mandy, Stanley, illus. 2010. (ENG., Illus.). 32p. (J). (gr. -1-k). 9.95 *(978-1-58925-851-8(7))* Tiger Tales.

Mangum, James A. & Spires, Sidney. The Fairy the Chupacabra & Those Marfa Lights: A West Texas Fable.

Mangum, James A., illus. 2008. (Illus.). 32p. (J). 17.95 *(978-0-9798391-5-3(7))* Hardy, John M. Publishing Co.
Mantchev, Lisa. Perchance to Dream. 2011. (Theatre Illuminata Ser.: 2). (ENG.). 368p. (YA). (gr. 7-12). pap. 9.99 *(978-0-312-67510-3(0),* 9780312675103) Square Fish.
Mark, Jan. Eyes Wide Open. 2003. (ENG., Illus.). 105p. *(978-0-7136-7648-8(5),* A&C Black) Bloomsbury Publishing Plc.
Markowitz-Meredith, Susan. Frances & the Fairy Dressmaker: Set Of 6. 2011. (Early Connections Ser.). (J). pap. 39.00 net. *(978-1-4108-1557-6(9))* Benchmark Education Co.
Marr, Melissa. Darkest Mercy. 2012. (Wicked Lovely Ser.: 5). (ENG.). 336p. (YA). (gr. 8). pap. 9.99 *(978-0-06-165927-0(4))* HarperCollins Pubs.
—Darkest Mercy, 7 vols. (Wicked Lovely Ser.: 5). (YA). 78.75 *(978-1-4498-6206-0(3));* 1.25 *(978-1-4498-6214-5(4));* 235.75 *(978-1-4498-6205-3(5));* 2011. 99.75 *(978-1-4498-6210-7(1));* 2011. 101.75 *(978-1-4498-6208-4(X))* Recorded Bks., Inc.
—Desert Tales. 2013. (Wicked Lovely Ser.). (ENG.). 272p. (YA). (gr. 8). pap. 9.99 *(978-0-06-228756-4(7))* HarperCollins Pubs.
—Faery Tales & Nightmares. 2013. (ENG.). 432p. (YA). (gr. 8). pap. 9.99 *(978-0-06-185273-2(2))* HarperCollins Pubs.
—Fragile Eternity. 2010. (Wicked Lovely Ser.: 3). (ENG.). 448p. (YA). (gr. 8). pap. 8.99 *(978-0-06-121473-8(6))* HarperCollins Pubs.
—Fragile Eternity, 9 vols. 2009. (Wicked Lovely Ser.: 3). (YA). 110.75 *(978-1-4407-3038-2(5));* 132.75 *(978-1-4407-3040-5(7));* 265.75 *(978-1-4407-3037-5(7));* 112.75 *(978-1-4407-3036-8(9));* 1.25 *(978-1-4407-3044-3(X));* 130.75 *(978-1-4407-3042-9(3))* Recorded Bks., Inc.
—Ink Exchange. (Wicked Lovely Ser.: 2). (ENG.). (YA). (gr. 8). 2009. 352p. pap. 9.99 *(978-0-06-121470-7(1))* 2008. 336p. 17.99 *(978-0-06-121468-4(X))* HarperCollins Pubs.
—Radiant Shadows. 2011. (Wicked Lovely Ser.: 4). (ENG.). 368p. (YA). (gr. 8). pap. 9.99 *(978-0-06-165924-9(X))* HarperCollins Pubs.
—Resolve. Xian Nu Studio, illus. 2011. (Wicked Lovely: Desert Tales Ser.: 3). (ENG.). 176p. (YA). (gr. 8-18). pap. 9.99 *(978-0-06-149350-8(3))* HarperCollins Pubs.
—Seven Black Diamonds. 2016. (ENG.). 400p. (YA). (gr. 8). 17.99 *(978-0-06-201117-6(0))* HarperCollins Pubs.
—Wicked Lovely. (Wicked Lovely Ser.: 1). 2008. (ENG.). 352p. (YA). (gr. 8-12). pap. 9.99 *(978-0-06-121467-7(1))* 2007. 336p. (J). (gr. 7-12). lib. bdg. 17.89 *(978-0-06-121466-0(3),* HarperTeen) HarperCollins Pubs.
Marshall, Ken. The Adventures of Maya & Grampa. 2005. 64p. pap. 9.95 *(978-0-7414-2472-3(X))* Infinity Publishing.
Martin-Fluet, Marie T. The Fairies' Century Celebration. 2011. 40p. pap. 18.62 *(978-1-4567-2477-1(0))* AuthorHouse.
Mass, Wendy. Beauty & the Beast: The Only One Who Didn't Run Away. 2012. (Twice upon a Time Ser.: 3). (ENG.). 288p. (J). (gr. 3-7). 16.99 *(978-0-545-31018-5(0),* Scholastic Pr.) Scholastic, Inc.
May, Elizabeth. The Fallen Kingdom: Book Three of the Falconer Trilogy. 2017. (Falconer Ser.: 3). (ENG.). 400p. (YA). 18.99 ***(978-1-4521-2883-2(9))*** Chronicle Bks. LLC.
—The Vanishing Throne. 2016. (Falconer Ser.: 2). (ENG., Illus.). 458p. (YA). (gr. 7-12). 17.99 *(978-1-4521-2882-5(0))* Chronicle Bks. LLC.
—The Vanishing Throne: Book Two of the Falconer Trilogy. 2017. (Falconer Ser.: 2). (ENG.). 480p. (YA). pap. 10.99 *(978-1-4521-6140-2(2))* Chronicle Bks. LLC.
Mayer, Kirsten. Disney Fairies: the Pirate Fairy: Adventure at Skull Rock. 2014. (ENG., Illus.). 24p. (J). (gr. -1-3). 3.99 *(978-0-316-28331-1(2))* Little, Brown Bks. for Young Readers.
—Disney Fairies: the Pirate Fairy: Reusable Sticker Book. 2014. (ENG., Illus.). 12p. (J). (gr. -1-3). pap. 6.99 *(978-0-316-28334-2(7))* Little, Brown Bks. for Young Readers.
—Go BIG or Go Gnome! Horton, Laura K., illus. 2017. (ENG.). 40p. (J). 16.99 *(978-1-250-11127-2(7),* 9781250111272) Imprint IND. Dist: Macmillan.
Mc Shane, Mary. Karena the Fairy. 2011. 112p. pap. 10.95 *(978-1-4502-9297-9(6))* iUniverse, Inc.
—Karena the Fairy & the Bat Colony. 2011. 344p. (gr. 4-6). pap. 19.95 *(978-1-4620-5295-0(9))* iUniverse, Inc.
McCaughrean, Geraldine & Hoffmann, E. T. A. The Nutcracker: A Magic Theater Book. Swarner, Kristina, illus. 2012. (ENG.). 24p. (J). (gr. 1-17). 19.99 *(978-1-4521-0669-4(X))* Handprint Bks.
McCreadie, Sandi. Thistle Fables. 2013. 64p. pap. 23.99 *(978-1-4808-0313-8(8))* Archway Publishing.
McCullough, Jerletha. Fairies of the Lilies. 2009. 20p. pap. 16.49 *(978-1-4389-2286-7(8))* AuthorHouse.
McDonald, Ann-Eve. The Bad Day. 2004. (J). *(978-0-9770158-1-8(5))* BeachWalk Bks. Inc.
McFadden, Deanna. Rapunzel. Mims, Ashley, illus. 2012. (Silver Penny Stories Ser.). (ENG.). 48p. (J). (gr. -1-1). 4.95 *(978-1-4027-8338-8(8))* Sterling Publishing Co., Inc.
—Snow White & the Seven Dwarfs. Woo Kim, Jin, illus. 2012. (Silver Penny Stories Ser.). (ENG.). 48p. (J). (gr. -1-1). 4.95 *(978-1-4027-8342-5(6))* Sterling Publishing Co., Inc.
McGrath, Barbara Barbieri. The Little Red Elf. Bonnet, Rosalinde, illus. 2010. (ENG.). 32p. (J). (gr. -1-2). pap. 7.95 *(978-1-58089-237-7(X))* Charlesbridge Publishing, Inc.
McGraw, Eloise. The Moorchild. 2006. 241p. (gr. 4-7). 17.00 *(978-0-7569-6823-6(2))* Perfection Learning Corp.
—The Moorchild. 2006. (ENG.). 256p. (J). (gr. 4-7). pap. 8.99 *(978-1-4169-2768-6(9),* Aladdin) Simon & Schuster Children's Publishing.
McGregor, Suzy. The Garden Fairy & Mrs. Mouse. 2013. 58p. pap. 14.95 *(978-0-9824926-6-6(9))* Lollipop Media Productions, LP.
McLean, Wendy & Book Company Staff. Follow an Elf. Worthington, Leonie, illus. 2003. (Sparkle Bks.). 10p. (J). bds. 8.95 *(978-1-74047-314-9(0))* Book Co. Publishing Pty, Ltd., The AUS. Dist: Penton Overseas, Inc.
McNamara, Margaret. Clara & the Magical Charms. Denos, Julia, illus. 2013. (Fairy Bell Sisters Ser.: 4). (ENG.). 128p. (J). (gr. 1-5). 15.99 *(978-0-06-222811-6(0));* pap. 4.99 *(978-0-06-222810-9(2))* HarperCollins Pubs.
—The Fairy Bell Sisters No. 3: Golden at the Fancy-Dress Party. Denos, Julia, illus. 2013. (Fairy Bell Sisters Ser.: 3). (ENG.). 144p. (J). (gr. 1-5). pap. 4.99 *(978-0-06-222807-9(2))* HarperCollins Pubs.
—The Fairy Bell Sisters Vol. 5: Sylva & the Lost Treasure. Denos, Julia, illus. 2014. (Fairy Bell Sisters Ser.: 5). (ENG.). 144p. (J). (gr. 1-5). 15.99 *(978-0-06-226721-4(3))* HarperCollins Pubs.
—The Fairy Bell Sisters - Christmas Fairy Magic. 2014. (Fairy Bell Sisters Ser.: 6). (ENG.). 144p. (J). (gr. 1-5). pap. 4.99 *(978-0-06-226723-8(X))* HarperCollins Pubs.
—The Fairy Bell Sisters #3: Golden at the Fancy-Dress Party. Denos, Julia, illus. 2013. (Fairy Bell Sisters Ser.: 3). (ENG.). 144p. (J). (gr. 1-5). 15.99 *(978-0-06-222808-6(0))* HarperCollins Pubs.
—Golden at the Fancy-Dress Party. 2013. (Fairy Bell Sisters Ser.: 3). (J). lib. bdg. 14.75 *(978-0-606-32154-9(3),* Turtleback) Turtleback Bks.
—Rosy & the Secret Friend. Denos, Julia, illus. 2013. (Fairy Bell Sisters Ser.: 2). (ENG.). 128p. (J). (gr. 1-5). 15.99 *(978-0-06-222805-5(6));* pap. 4.99 *(978-0-06-222804-8(8))* HarperCollins Pubs.
—Rosy & the Secret Friend. 2013. (Fairy Bell Sisters Ser.: 2). (J). lib. bdg. 14.75 *(978-0-606-31797-9(X),* Turtleback) Turtleback Bks.
—Sylva & the Fairy Ball. Denos, Julia, illus. 2013. (Fairy Bell Sisters Ser.: 1). (ENG.). 128p. (J). (gr. 1-5). 15.99 *(978-0-06-222802-4(1));* pap. 4.99 *(978-0-06-222801-7(3))* HarperCollins Pubs.
—Sylva & the Fairy Ball. 2013. (Fairy Bell Sisters Ser.: 1). (J). lib. bdg. 14.75 *(978-0-606-31796-2(1),* Turtleback) Turtleback Bks.
—Sylva & the Lost Treasure. Denos, Julia, illus. 2014. (Fairy Bell Sisters Ser.: 5). (ENG.). 144p. (J). (gr. 1-5). pap. 4.99 *(978-0-06-226720-7(5))* HarperCollins Pubs.
McQuerry, Maureen Doyle. The Peculiars. 2014. (ENG.). 384p. (YA). (gr. 7-17). pap. 8.95 *(978-1-4197-1206-7(3),* Amulet Bks.) Abrams, Inc.
McQuestion, Karen. Celia & the Fairies, 0 vols. unabr. ed. 2010. (ENG.). 142p. (gr. 4-6). pap. 7.95 *(978-1-935597-28-5(0),* 9781935597285, Two Lions) Amazon Publishing.
—Secrets of the Magic Ring, 0 vols. unabr. ed. 2011. (ENG., Illus.). 156p. (J). (gr. 4-6). pap. 8.95 *(978-1-61218-142-4(2),* 9781612181424, Amazon Children's Publishing) Amazon Publishing.
Meacham, Margaret. A Fairy's Guide to Understanding Humans. 2007. (ENG.). 160p. (J). (gr. 5-18). 16.95 *(978-0-8234-2078-0(7))* Holiday Hse., Inc.
—A Mid-Semester Night's Dream. 2004. (ENG.). 144p. (J). (gr. 4-6). tchr. ed. 16.95 *(978-0-8234-1815-2(4))* Holiday Hse., Inc.
Meadown, Daisy. Ellie the Guitar Fairy #2. 2010. (ENG.). 80p. (J). lib. bdg. 15.39 *(978-1-4242-4730-1(6))* Fitzgerald Bks.
Meadows, Daisy. Abigail the Breeze Fairy. Ripper, Georgie, illus. 2006. (Weather Fairies Ser.: 2). (ENG.). 80p. (J). (gr. -1-3). 4.99 *(978-0-439-81386-0(7),* Scholastic Paperbacks) Scholastic, Inc.
—Addison the April Fool's Day Fairy. 2014. (Rainbow Magic — Special Edition Ser.). lib. bdg. 17.20 *(978-0-606-35378-6(X))* Turtleback Bks.
—Adele the Voice Fairy. 2013. (Rainbow Magic — the Superstar Fairies Ser.: 2). lib. bdg. 14.75 *(978-0-606-31514-2(4),* Turtleback) Turtleback Bks.
—Aisha the Princess & the Pea Fairy. 2016. (Illus.). (J). (Fairy Tale Fairies Ser.: 6). (ENG.). 80p. (gr. 2-5). pap. 4.99 *(978-0-545-85199-2(8),* Scholastic Paperbacks); 62p. ***(978-0-545-88741-0(0))*** Scholastic, Inc.
—Alexa the Fashion Editor Fairy. 2013. (Rainbow Magic — the Fashion Fairies Ser.: 4). lib. bdg. 14.75 *(978-0-606-31994-2(8),* Turtleback) Turtleback Bks.
—Alice the Tennis Fairy. 2010. (Sports Fairies Ser.: 6). (ENG.). 80p. (J). (gr. 2-5). 4.99 *(978-0-545-20257-2(4),* Scholastic Paperbacks) Scholastic, Inc.
—Alicia the Snow Queen Fairy. 2016. (Rainbow Magic — Special Edition Ser.). lib. bdg. 17.20 ***(978-0-606-39728-5(0))*** Turtleback Bks.
—Alison the Art Fairy. 2016. (School Day Fairies Ser.: 2). (ENG.). 80p. (J). (gr. 2-5). pap. 4.99 *(978-0-545-85206-7(4),* Scholastic Paperbacks) Scholastic, Inc.
—Alyssa the Snow Queen Fairy. 2016. (Rainbow Magic Special Edition Ser.). (ENG.). 176p. (J). (gr. 2-5). pap. 6.99 *(978-0-545-85201-2(3),* Scholastic Paperbacks) Scholastic, Inc.
—Alyssa the Star-Spotter Fairy. 2013. (Rainbow Magic — the Superstar Fairies Ser.: 6). lib. bdg. 14.75 *(978-0-606-31518-0(7),* Turtleback) Turtleback Bks.
—Amber the Orange Fairy. Ripper, Georgie, illus. 2005. (Rainbow Magic Ser.: 2). (ENG.). 80p. (J). (gr. -1-3). pap. 4.99 *(978-0-439-74465-2(2))* Scholastic, Inc.
—Angelica the Angel Fairy. 2015. (Rainbow Magic — Special Edition Ser.). lib. bdg. 17.20 *(978-0-606-37782-9(4))* Turtleback Bks.
—Angelica the Angel Fairy (Rainbow Magic: Special Edition) 2015. (Rainbow Magic Special Edition Ser.). (ENG., Illus.). 176p. (J). (gr. 2-5). pap. 6.99 *(978-0-545-70828-9(1),* Scholastic Paperbacks) Scholastic, Inc.
—Ashley the Dragon Fairy. 2012. (Illus.). (J). (Magical Animal Fairies Ser.: 1). (ENG.). 80p. (gr. 2-5). pap. 4.99 *(978-0-545-38417-9(6),* Scholastic Paperbacks); 65p. *(978-0-545-42595-7(6))* Scholastic, Inc.
—Autumn the Falling Leaves Fairy. 2013. (Rainbow Magic — Special Edition Ser.). lib. bdg. 17.20 *(978-0-606-32370-3(8),* Turtleback) Turtleback Bks.
—Ava the Sunset Fairy. 2011. (Illus.). 63p. (J). *(978-0-545-38040-9(5))* Scholastic, Inc.
—Bella the Bunny Fairy. Ripper, Georgie, illus. 2008. (Pet Fairies Ser.: 2). (ENG.). 80p. (J). (gr. -1-3). 4.99 *(978-0-545-04185-0(6),* Scholastic Paperbacks) Scholastic, Inc.
—Bella the Bunny Fairy. Ripper, Georgie, illus. 2008. (Rainbow Magic — the Pet Fairies Ser.). 65p. (gr. 7). lib. bdg. 14.75 *(978-1-4178-2996-5(6),* Turtleback) Turtleback Bks.
—Belle the Birthday Fairy. 2012. (Rainbow Magic Ser.). (ENG., Illus.). 176p. (J). (gr. 2-5). pap. 6.99 *(978-0-545-27054-0(5),* Scholastic Paperbacks) Scholastic, Inc.
—Belle the Birthday Fairy. 2012. (Rainbow Magic — Special Edition Ser.). lib. bdg. 17.20 *(978-0-606-23726-0(7),* Turtleback) Turtleback Bks.
—Best Friends in Fairyland. 2010. (Scholastic Reader Level 2 Ser.). (ENG.). 32p. (J). (gr. 1-3). pap. 3.99 *(978-0-545-22293-8(1),* Cartwheel Bks.) Scholastic, Inc.
—Blossom the Flower Girl Fairy. 2016. (Rainbow Magic: Special Edition Ser.). (ENG.). 176p. (J). (gr. 2-5). pap. 6.99 *(978-0-545-85202-9(1),* Scholastic Paperbacks) Scholastic, Inc.
—Brianna the Tooth Fairy. 2013. (Rainbow Magic — Special Edition Ser.). lib. bdg. 17.20 *(978-0-606-31990-4(5),* Turtleback) Turtleback Bks.
—Brittany the Basketball Fairy. 2010. (Sports Fairies Ser.: 4). (ENG.). 80p. (J). (gr. 2-5). 4.99 *(978-0-545-20255-8(8),* Scholastic Paperbacks) Scholastic, Inc.
—Caitlin the Ice Bear Fairy. 2012. (Illus.). 65p. (J). *(978-0-545-42602-2(2))* Scholastic, Inc.
—Cara the Camp Fairy. 2011. (Rainbow Magic Ser.). (Illus.). (J). (ENG.). 176p. (gr. 2-5). pap. 6.99 *(978-0-545-30877-9(1),* Scholastic Paperbacks); 165p. *(978-0-545-31656-9(1))* Scholastic, Inc.
—Carly the School Fairy. 2015. (Rainbow Magic Special Edition Ser.). (Illus.). (J). (ENG.). 176p. (gr. 2-5). pap. 6.99 *(978-0-545-70827-2(3),* Scholastic Paperbacks); 155p. ***(978-1-4806-8807-0(X))*** Scholastic, Inc.
—Carly the School Fairy. 2015. (Rainbow Magic — Special Edition Ser.). lib. bdg. 17.20 *(978-0-606-37774-4(3))* Turtleback Bks.
—Carmen the Cheerleading Fairy. 2017. (Rainbow Magic: Special Edition Ser.). (ENG.). 176p. (J). (gr. 2-5). pap. 6.99 ***(978-1-338-05484-2(8),*** Scholastic Paperbacks) Scholastic, Inc.
—Carmen the Cheerleading Fairy. 2017. (Rainbow Magic — Special Edition Ser.). lib. bdg. 17.20 ***(978-0-606-40166-1(0))*** Turtleback Bks.
—Carrie the Snow Cap Fairy. 2014. (Rainbow Magic — the Earth Fairies Ser.). lib. bdg. 14.75 *(978-0-606-35836-1(6))* Turtleback Bks.
—Cassidy the Costume Fairy. 2012. (Rainbow Magic — the Princess Fairies Ser.: 2). lib. bdg. 14.75 *(978-0-606-26170-8(2),* Turtleback) Turtleback Bks.
—Chelsea the Congratulations Fairy. 2015. (Rainbow Magic — Special Edition Ser.). lib. bdg. 17.20 *(978-0-606-37056-1(0))* Turtleback Bks.
—Clara the Chocolate Fairy. 2014. (Sugar & Spice Fairies Ser.: 4). (ENG.). 80p. (J). (gr. 2-5). pap. 4.99 *(978-0-545-60534-2(2),* Scholastic Paperbacks) Scholastic, Inc.
—Clare the Caring Fairy. 2017. (Friendship Fairies Ser.: 4). (ENG.). 80p. (J). (gr. 2-5). pap. 4.99 ***(978-1-338-15770-3(1),*** Scholastic Paperbacks) Scholastic, Inc.
—Clare the Caring Fairy. 2017. (Rainbow Magic — Friendship Fairies Ser.: 4). lib. bdg. 14.75 ***(978-0-606-40178-4(4))*** Turtleback Bks.
—Coco the Cupcake Fairy. 2014. (Sugar & Spice Fairies Ser.: 3). (ENG.). 80p. (J). (gr. 2-5). pap. 4.99 *(978-0-545-60533-5(4),* Scholastic Paperbacks) Scholastic, Inc.
—The Complete Book of Fairies. 2014. (Rainbow Magic Ser.). (ENG.). 128p. (J). (gr. 2-5). 9.99 *(978-0-545-62217-2(4),* Scholastic Paperbacks) Scholastic, Inc.
—Coral the Reef Fairy. 2014. (Earth Fairies Ser.: 4). (ENG.). 80p. (J). (gr. 2-5). pap. 4.99 *(978-0-545-60527-4(X),* Scholastic Paperbacks) Scholastic, Inc.
—Coral the Reef Fairy. 2014. (Rainbow Magic — the Earth Fairies Ser.). lib. bdg. 14.75 *(978-0-606-35833-0(1))* Turtleback Bks.
—Courtney the Clownfish Fairy. 2011. (Illus.). 62p. (J). *(978-0-545-28877-4(0))* Scholastic, Inc.
—Crystal the Snow Fairy. Ripper, Georgie, illus. 2006. (Weather Fairies Ser.: 1). (ENG.). 80p. (Orig.). (J). (gr. -1-3). mass mkt. 4.99 *(978-0-439-81387-7(5),* Scholastic Paperbacks) Scholastic, Inc.
—Danni the Drum Fairy #4. 2010. (ENG.). 80p. (J). lib. bdg. 15.39 *(978-1-4242-4729-5(2))* Fitzgerald Bks.
—Destiny the Rock Star Fairy. 2011. (Rainbow Magic Ser.). (ENG., Illus.). 176p. (J). (gr. 2-5). pap. 6.99 *(978-0-545-27056-4(1),* Scholastic Paperbacks) Scholastic, Inc.
—The Earth Fairies #1: Nicole the Beach Fairy. 2014. (Earth Fairies Ser.: 1). (ENG.). 80p. (J). (gr. 2-5). pap. 4.99 *(978-0-545-60524-3(5),* Scholastic Paperbacks) Scholastic, Inc.
—The Earth Fairies #2: Isabella the Air Fairy. 2014. (Earth Fairies Ser.: 2). (ENG.). 80p. (J). (gr. 2-5). pap. 4.99 *(978-0-545-60525-0(3),* Scholastic Paperbacks) Scholastic, Inc.
—The Earth Fairies #5: Lily the Rain Forest Fairy. 2014. (Earth Fairies Ser.: 5). (ENG.). 80p. (J). (gr. 2-5). pap. 4.99 *(978-0-545-60528-1(8),* Scholastic Paperbacks) Scholastic, Inc.
—The Earth Fairies #6: Milly the River Fairy. 2014. (Earth Fairies Ser.: 6). (ENG.). 80p. (J). (gr. 2-5). pap. 4.99 *(978-0-545-60529-8(6),* Scholastic Paperbacks) Scholastic, Inc.
—The Earth Fairies #7: Carrie the Snow Cap Fairy. 2014. (Earth Fairies Ser.: 7). (ENG.). 80p. (J). (gr. 2-5). pap. 4.99 *(978-0-545-60530-4(X),* Scholastic Paperbacks) Scholastic, Inc.
—Edie the Garden Fairy. 2014. (Earth Fairies Ser.: 3). (ENG.). 80p. (J). (gr. 2-5). pap. 4.99 *(978-0-545-60526-7(1),* Scholastic Paperbacks) Scholastic, Inc.
—Edie the Garden Fairy. 2014. (Rainbow Magic — the Earth Fairies Ser.). lib. bdg. 14.75 *(978-0-606-35832-3(3))* Turtleback Bks.
—Eleanor the Snow White Fairy. 2016. (Fairy Tale Fairies Ser.: 2). (ENG., Illus.). 80p. (J). (gr. 2-5). pap. 4.99 *(978-0-545-85190-9(4),* Scholastic Paperbacks) Scholastic, Inc.
—Elisa the Royal Adventure Fairy. 2012. (Rainbow Magic — the Princess Fairies Ser.: 4). lib. bdg. 14.75 *(978-0-606-26172-2(9),* Turtleback) Turtleback Bks.
—Elle the Thumbelina Fairy. 2017. (Storybook Fairies Ser.: 1). (ENG.). 80p. (J). (gr. 2-5). pap. 4.99 *(978-1-338-05495-8(3),* Scholastic Paperbacks) Scholastic, Inc.
—Elle the Thumbelina Fairy. 2017. (Rainbow Magic — Storybook Fairies Ser.: 1). lib. bdg. 14.75 ***(978-0-606-39717-9(5))*** Turtleback Bks.
—Ellie the Guitar Fairy. 2010. (Rainbow Magic — the Music Fairies Ser.: 02). lib. bdg. 14.75 *(978-0-606-07089-8(3),* Turtleback) Turtleback Bks.
—Emily, the Emerald Fairy. Ripper, Georgie, illus. 2005. 65p. (J). pap. *(978-0-545-01190-7(6))* Scholastic, Inc.
—Emma the Easter Fairy. 2011. (Rainbow Magic Ser.). (ENG.). 192p. (J). (gr. 2-5). pap. 6.99 *(978-0-545-27051-9(0),* Scholastic Paperbacks) Scholastic, Inc.
—Erin the Phoenix Fairy. 2012. (Illus.). 64p. (J). *(978-0-545-42597-1(2))* Scholastic, Inc.
—Esme the Ice Cream Fairy. 2014. (Sugar & Spice Fairies Ser.: 2). (ENG.). 80p. (J). (gr. 2-5). pap. 4.99 *(978-0-545-60532-8(6),* Scholastic Paperbacks) Scholastic, Inc.
—Esther the Kindness Fairy. 2017. (Rainbow Magic — Friendship Fairies Ser.: 1). lib. bdg. 14.75 ***(978-0-606-40175-3(X))*** Turtleback Bks.
—Esther the Kindness Fairy (Friendship Fairies #1) 2017. (Friendship Fairies Ser.: 1). (ENG.). 80p. (J). (gr. 2-5). pap. 4.99 ***(978-1-338-15767-3(1),*** Scholastic Paperbacks) Scholastic, Inc.
—Eva the Enchanted Ball Fairy. 2012. (Rainbow Magic — the Princess Fairies Ser.: 7). lib. bdg. 14.75 *(978-0-606-26175-3(3),* Turtleback) Turtleback Bks.
—Evie the Mist Fairy. Ripper, Georgie, illus. 2006. (Weather Fairies Ser.: 5). (ENG.). 80p. (Orig.). (J). (gr. -1-3). 4.99 *(978-0-439-81390-7(5),* Scholastic Paperbacks) Scholastic, Inc.
—The Fairies' Birthday Surprise. 2010. (Scholastic Reader Level 2 Ser.). (ENG.). 32p. (J). (gr. 1-3). pap. 3.99 *(978-0-545-22292-1(3),* Cartwheel Bks.) Scholastic, Inc.
—A Fairy Ballet. 2011. (Scholastic Reader, Level 2 Ser.). (ENG.). 32p. (J). (gr. 1-3). pap. 3.99 *(978-0-545-22294-5(X),* Cartwheel Bks.) Scholastic, Inc.
—The Fairy Treasure Hunt. 2012. (Rainbow Magic — Scholastic Reader Ser.). lib. bdg. 13.55 *(978-0-606-23912-7(X),* Turtleback) Turtleback Bks.
—A Fairyland Costume Ball. 2012. (Scholastic Reader Level 2 Ser.). (ENG., Illus.). 32p. (J). (gr. 2-5). pap. 3.99 *(978-0-545-43389-1(4),* Scholastic Paperbacks) Scholastic, Inc.
—A Fairyland Costume Ball. 2012. (Rainbow Magic — Scholastic Reader Ser.). lib. bdg. 13.55 *(978-0-606-26235-4(0),* Turtleback) Turtleback Bks.
—Faith the Cinderella Fairy. 2016. (Illus.). (J). (Fairy Tale Fairies Ser.: 3). (ENG.). 80p. (gr. 2-5). pap. 4.99 *(978-0-545-85195-4(5),* Scholastic Paperbacks); 65p. ***(978-0-545-88744-1(5))*** Scholastic, Inc.
—Fern the Green Fairy. Ripper, Georgie, illus. 2005. (Rainbow Magic Ser.: 4). (ENG.). 80p. (Orig.). (J). (gr. 2-5). 4.99 *(978-0-439-74467-6(9),* Scholastic Paperbacks) Scholastic, Inc.
—Fiona the Flute Fairy #3. 2010. (ENG.). 80p. (J). lib. bdg. 15.39 *(978-1-4242-4731-8(4))* Fitzgerald Bks.
—Florence the Friendship Fairy. 2012. (Rainbow Magic Ser.). (ENG., Illus.). 176p. (J). (gr. 2-5). pap. 6.99 *(978-0-545-45572-5(3),* Scholastic Paperbacks) Scholastic, Inc.
—Florence the Friendship Fairy. 2012. (Rainbow Magic — Special Edition Ser.). lib. bdg. 17.20 *(978-0-606-26754-0(9),* Turtleback) Turtleback Bks.
—Frankie the Makeup Fairy. 2013. (Rainbow Magic — the Superstar Fairies Ser.: 5). lib. bdg. 14.75 *(978-0-606-31517-3(9),* Turtleback) Turtleback Bks.
—Gabriella the Snow Kingdom Fairy. 2009. (Rainbow Magic Ser.). (ENG.). 176p. (J). (gr. 2-5). 6.99 *(978-0-545-10614-6(1),* Scholastic Paperbacks) Scholastic, Inc.
—Gemma the Gymnastics Fairy. 2010. (Sports Fairies Ser.: 7). (ENG.). 80p. (J). (gr. 2-5). 4.99 *(978-0-545-20258-9(2),* Scholastic Paperbacks) Scholastic, Inc.
—Georgia the Guinea Pig Fairy. Ripper, Georgie, illus. 2008. (Pet Fairies Ser.: 3). (ENG.). 80p. (J). (gr. -1-3). 4.99 *(978-0-545-04186-7(4),* Scholastic Paperbacks) Scholastic, Inc.
—Georgia the Guinea Pig Fairy. Ripper, Georgie, illus. 2008. (Rainbow Magic — the Pet Fairies Ser.). 65p. (gr. 3). lib. bdg. 14.75 *(978-1-4178-2997-2(4),* Turtleback) Turtleback Bks.
—Giselle the Christmas Ballet Fairy. 2016. (Rainbow Magic Special Edition Ser.). (ENG.). 176p. (J). (gr. 2-5). pap. 6.99 *(978-0-545-85203-6(X),* Scholastic Paperbacks) Scholastic, Inc.
—Giselle the Christmas Ballet Fairy. 2016. (Rainbow Magic — Special Edition Ser.). (ENG.). 176p. (J). (gr. 2-5). 17.20 *(978-0-606-39141-2(X))* Turtleback Bks.
—Goldie the Sunshine Fairy. Ripper, Georgie, illus. 2006. (Weather Fairies Ser.: 4). (ENG.). 80p. (Orig.). (J). (gr. -1-3). 4.99 *(978-0-439-81389-1(1),* Scholastic Paperbacks) Scholastic, Inc.
—Goldie the Sunshine Fairy. 2004. (Rainbow Magic Ser.). (Illus.). 63p. (Orig.). *(978-0-439-79615-6(6))* Scholastic, Inc.
—Gwen the Beauty & the Beast Fairy. 2016. (Illus.). (J). (Fairy Tale Fairies Ser.: 5). (ENG.). 80p. (gr. 2-5). pap. 4.99 *(978-0-545-85198-5(X),* Scholastic Paperbacks); 67p. ***(978-1-5182-1018-1(X))*** Scholastic, Inc.
—Harriet the Hamster Fairy. Ripper, Georgie, illus. 2008. (Rainbow Magic — the Pet Fairies Ser.). 67p. (gr. -1-3). lib. bdg. 14.75 *(978-1-4178-3007-7(7),* Turtleback) Turtleback Bks.
—Hayley the Rain Fairy. Ripper, Georgie, illus. 2007. (Weather Fairies Ser.: 7). (ENG.). 80p. (Orig.). (J). (gr. -1-3). pap. 4.99 *(978-0-439-81392-1(1),* Scholastic Paperbacks) Scholastic, Inc.
—Hayley the Rain Fairy. 2007. (Rainbow Magic — the Weather Fairies Ser.: 7). (Orig.). lib. bdg. 14.75 *(978-1-4177-7082-3(1),* Turtleback) Turtleback Bks.
—Heather the Violet Fairy. Ripper, Georgie, illus. 2006. (Rainbow Magic Ser.: 7). (ENG.). 80p. (J). (gr. -1-3). 4.99 *(978-0-439-74686-1(8),* Scholastic Paperbacks) Scholastic, Inc.
—Heather the Violet Fairy. 2005. (Rainbow Magic Ser.). 71p. (J). *(978-0-439-69192-5(3))* Scholastic, Inc.
—Helena the Horse-Riding Fairy. 2010. (Sports Fairies Ser.: 1). (ENG.). 80p. (J). (gr. 2-5). 4.99 *(978-0-545-20252-7(3),* Scholastic Paperbacks) Scholastic, Inc.

EFG

—Holly the Christmas Fairy. Ripper, Georgie, illus. 2007. (Rainbow Magic Ser.). (ENG.). 176p. (Orig.). (J). (gr. -1-3). pap. 6.99 (978-0-439-92880-9(X), Scholastic Paperbacks) Scholastic, Inc.

—Holly the Christmas Fairy. Ripper, Georgie, illus. 2007. (Rainbow Magic — Special Edition Ser.). 159p. (Orig.). (gr. -1-3). lib. bdg. 17.20 (978-1-4178-1771-9(2), Turtleback) Turtleback Bks.

—Inky the Indigo Fairy. Ripper, Georgie, illus. 2006. (Rainbow Magic Ser.: 6). (ENG.). 80p. (J). (gr. -1-3). per. 4.99 (978-0-439-74685-4(X), Scholastic Paperbacks) Scholastic, Inc.

—Isabella the Air Fairy. 2014. (Rainbow Magic — the Earth Fairies Ser.). lib. bdg. 14.75 (978-0-606-35831-6(5)) Turtleback Bks.

—Jade the Disco Fairy. 2009. (Rainbow Magic — the Dance Fairies Ser.). lib. bdg. 14.75 (978-0-606-05380-8(8), Turtleback) Turtleback Bks.

—Jessica the Jazz Fairy. 2009. (Rainbow Magic — the Dance Fairies Ser.). lib. bdg. 14.75 (978-0-606-05439-3(1), Turtleback) Turtleback Bks.

—Jessie the Lyrics Fairy. 2013. (Rainbow Magic — the Superstar Fairies Ser.: 1). lib. bdg. 14.75 (978-0-606-31513-5(6), Turtleback) Turtleback Bks.

—Josie the Jewelry Fairy. 2015. (Magical Crafts Fairies Ser.: 4). (ENG., Illus.). 80p. (J). (gr. 2-5). pap. 4.99 (978-0-545-70832-6(X), Scholastic Paperbacks) Scholastic, Inc.

—Joy the Summer Vacation Fairy. Ripper, Georgie, illus. 2007. (Rainbow Magic Ser.). (ENG.). 192p. (J). (gr. -1-3). 6.99 (978-0-439-93442-8(7), Scholastic Paperbacks) Scholastic, Inc.

—Joy the Summer Vacation Fairy. Ripper, Georgie, illus. 2007. (Rainbow Magic — Special Edition Ser.). 177p. (gr. -1-3). lib. bdg. 17.20 (978-1-4177-7081-6(3), Turtleback) Turtleback Bks.

—Julia the Sleeping Beauty Fairy. 2016. (Illus.). 65p. (J). **(978-0-545-88737-3(2))** Scholastic, Inc.

—Juliet the Valentine Fairy. 2009. (Rainbow Magic Ser.). (ENG., Illus.). 192p. (J). (gr. 2-5). pap. 6.99 (978-0-545-14886-3(3), Scholastic Paperbacks) Scholastic, Inc.

—Kathryn the Gym Fairy. 2016. (School Day Fairies Ser.: 4). (ENG.). 80p. (J). (gr. 2-5). pap. 4.99 (978-0-545-85208-1(0), Scholastic Paperbacks) Scholastic, Inc.

—Kathryn the Gym Fairy. 2016. (Rainbow Magic — the School Day Fairies Ser.: 4). lib. bdg. 14.75 (978-0-606-38792-7(7)) Turtleback Bks.

—Katie the Kitten Fairy. Ripper, Georgie, illus. 2008. (J). (Pet Fairies Ser.: 1). (ENG.). 80p. (J). (gr. -1-3). pap. 4.99 (978-0-545-02816-5(7), Scholastic Paperbacks); 65p. pap. (978-0-545-13320-3(3)) Scholastic, Inc.

—Katie the Kitten Fairy. Ripper, Georgie, illus. 2008. (Rainbow Magic — the Pet Fairies Ser.). 65p. (gr. 1-4). lib. bdg. 14.75 (978-1-4178-2999-6(0), Turtleback) Turtleback Bks.

—Kayla the Pottery Fairy. 2015. (Magical Crafts Fairies Ser.: 1). (ENG., Illus.). 80p. (J). (gr. 2-5). pap. 4.99 (978-0-545-70829-6(X), Scholastic Paperbacks) Scholastic, Inc.

—Keira the Movie Star Fairy. 2013. (Rainbow Magic — Special Edition Ser.). lib. bdg. 17.20 (978-0-606-32371-0(6), Turtleback) Turtleback Bks.

—Kimberly the Koala Fairy. 2015. (Baby Animal Rescue Fairies Ser.: 5). (ENG.). 80p. (J). (gr. 2-5). pap. 4.99 (978-0-545-70854-8(0), Scholastic Paperbacks) Scholastic, Inc.

—Kimberly the Koala Fairy. 2015. (Rainbow Magic — Baby Animal Rescue Fairies Ser.: 5). lib. bdg. 14.75 (978-0-606-37053-0(6)) Turtleback Bks.

—Kitty the Tiger Fairy. 2015. (Baby Animal Rescue Fairies Ser.: 2). (ENG.). 80p. (J). (gr. 2-5). pap. 4.99 (978-0-545-70846-3(X), Scholastic Paperbacks) Scholastic, Inc.

—Kitty the Tiger Fairy. 2015. (Rainbow Magic — Baby Animal Rescue Fairies Ser.: 2). lib. bdg. 14.75 (978-0-606-37050-9(1)) Turtleback Bks.

—Kylie the Carnival Fairy. Ripper, Georgie, illus. 2008. (Rainbow Magic Ser.). (ENG.). 192p. (J). (gr. -1-3). pap. 6.99 (978-0-545-05475-1(3), Scholastic Paperbacks) Scholastic, Inc.

—Lacey the Little Mermaid Fairy. 2016. (Illus.). (J). (Fairy Tale Fairies Ser.: 7). (ENG.). 80p. (gr. 2-5). pap. 4.99 (978-0-545-85196-1(3), Scholastic Paperbacks); 65p. **(978-0-545-88742-7(9))** Scholastic, Inc.

—Lara the Black Cat Fairy. 2012. (Illus.). 65p. (J). (978-0-545-42596-4(4)) Scholastic, Inc.

—Lauren the Puppy Fairy. Ripper, Georgie, illus. 2008. (Pet Fairies Ser.: 4). (ENG.). 80p. (J). (gr. -1-3). pap. 4.99 (978-0-545-04187-4(2), Scholastic Paperbacks) Scholastic, Inc.

—Layla the Cotton Candy Fairy. 2014. (Sugar & Spice Fairies Ser.: 6). (ENG.). 80p. (J). (gr. 2-5). pap. 4.99 (978-0-545-60536-6(9), Scholastic Paperbacks) Scholastic, Inc.

—Leona the Unicorn Fairy. 2012. (Illus.). 65p. (J). (978-0-545-42601-5(4)) Scholastic, Inc.

—Libby the Writing Fairy. (Illus.). (J). 2015. (Magical Crafts Fairies Ser.: 6). (ENG.). 80p. (gr. 2-5). pap. 4.99 (978-0-545-70834-0(6), Scholastic Paperbacks) 2014. 65p. (978-0-545-72414-2(7)) Scholastic, Inc.

—Lila & Myla, the Twins Fairies. 2015. (Rainbow Magic — Special Edition Ser.). lib. bdg. 17.20 (978-0-606-36341-9(6)) Turtleback Bks.

—Lily the Rain Forest Fairy. 2014. (Rainbow Magic — the Earth Fairies Ser.). lib. bdg. 14.75 (978-0-606-35834-7(X)) Turtleback Bks.

—Lindsay the Luck Fairy. 2013. (Rainbow Magic — Special Edition Ser.). lib. bdg. 17.20 (978-0-606-31512-8(8), Turtleback) Turtleback Bks.

—Lisa the Lollipop Fairy. 2014. (Sugar & Spice Fairies Ser.: 1). (ENG.). 80p. (J). (gr. 2-5). pap. 4.99 (978-0-545-60531-1(8), Scholastic Paperbacks) Scholastic, Inc.

—Lizzie the Sweet Treats Fairy. 2012. (Rainbow Magic — the Princess Fairies Ser.: 5). lib. bdg. 14.75 (978-0-606-26173-9(7), Turtleback) Turtleback Bks.

—Lola the Fashion Show Fairy. 2013. (Rainbow Magic — the Fashion Fairies Ser.: 7). lib. bdg. 14.75 (978-0-606-31997-3(2), Turtleback) Turtleback Bks.

—Lydia the Reading Fairy. 2016. (School Day Fairies Ser.: 3). (ENG.). 80p. (J). (gr. 2-5). pap. 4.99 (978-0-545-85207-4(2), Scholastic Paperbacks) Scholastic, Inc.

—Lydia the Reading Fairy. 2016. (Rainbow Magic — the School Day Fairies Ser.: 3). lib. bdg. 14.75 (978-0-606-38791-0(9)) Turtleback Bks.

—Madeline the Cookie Fairy. 2014. (Sugar & Spice Fairies Ser.: 5). (ENG.). 80p. (J). (gr. 2-5). pap. 4.99 (978-0-545-60535-9(0), Scholastic Paperbacks) Scholastic, Inc.

—Mae the Panda Fairy. 2015. (Baby Animal Rescue Fairies Ser.: 1). (ENG.). 80p. (J). (gr. 2-5). pap. 4.99 (978-0-545-70844-9(3), Scholastic Paperbacks) Scholastic, Inc.

—Mae the Panda Fairy. 2015. (Rainbow Magic — Baby Animal Rescue Fairies Ser.: 1). lib. bdg. 14.75 (978-0-606-37049-3(8)) Turtleback Bks.

—Mara the Meerkat Fairy. 2015. (Rainbow Magic — Baby Animal Rescue Fairies Ser.: 3). lib. bdg. 14.75 (978-0-606-37051-6(X)) Turtleback Bks.

—Mara the Meerkat Fairy: A Rainbow Magic Book. 2015. (Baby Animal Rescue Fairies Ser.: 3). (ENG.). 80p. (J). (gr. 2-5). pap. 4.99 (978-0-545-70850-0(8), Scholastic Paperbacks) Scholastic, Inc.

—Mariana the Goldilocks Fairy. 2017. (Rainbow Magic — Storybook Fairies Ser.: 2). lib. bdg. 14.75 **(978-0-606-39718-6(3))** Turtleback Bks.

—Marissa the Science Fairy. 2016. (School Day Fairies Ser.: 1). (ENG.). 80p. (J). (gr. 2-5). pap. 4.99 (978-0-545-85205-0(6), Scholastic Paperbacks) Scholastic, Inc.

—Marissa the Science Fairy. 2016. (Rainbow Magic — the School Day Fairies Ser.: 1). lib. bdg. 14.75 (978-0-606-38789-7(7)) Turtleback Bks.

—Mary the Sharing Fairy. 2017. (Friendship Fairies Ser.: 2). (ENG.). 80p. (J). (gr. 2-5). pap. 4.99 **(978-1-338-15768-0(X)**, Scholastic Paperbacks) Scholastic, Inc.

—Mary the Sharing Fairy. 2017. (Rainbow Magic — Friendship Fairies Ser.: 2). lib. bdg. 14.75 **(978-0-606-40176-0(8))** Turtleback Bks.

—Maya the Harp Fairy #5. 2010. (ENG.). 80p. (J). lib. bdg. 15.39 (978-1-4242-4732-5(2)) Fitzgerald Bks.

—Miley the Stylist Fairy. 2013. (Rainbow Magic — the Superstar Fairies Ser.: 4). lib. bdg. 14.75 (978-0-606-31516-6(0), Turtleback) Turtleback Bks.

—Milly the River Fairy. 2014. (Rainbow Magic — the Earth Fairies Ser.). lib. bdg. 14.75 (978-0-606-35835-4(8)) Turtleback Bks.

—Mimi the Laughter Fairy. 2017. (Rainbow Magic — Friendship Fairies Ser.: 3). lib. bdg. 14.75 **(978-0-606-40177-7(6))** Turtleback Bks.

—Mimi the Laughter Fairy (Friendship Fairies #3) 2017. (Friendship Fairies Ser.: 3). (ENG.). 80p. (J). (gr. 2-5). pap. 4.99 **(978-1-338-15769-7(8)**, Scholastic Paperbacks) Scholastic, Inc.

—Molly the Goldfish Fairy. Ripper, Georgie, illus. 2008. (Pet Fairies Ser.: 6). (ENG.). 80p. (J). (gr. -1-3). pap. 4.99 (978-0-545-04189-8(9), Scholastic Paperbacks) Scholastic, Inc.

—Molly the Goldfish Fairy. Ripper, Georgie, illus. 2008. (Rainbow Magic — the Pet Fairies Ser.). 68p. (gr. -1-3). lib. bdg. 14.75 (978-1-4178-3001-5(8), Turtleback) Turtleback Bks.

—Natalie the Christmas Stocking Fairy. 2014. (Rainbow Magic — Special Edition Ser.). lib. bdg. 17.20 (978-0-606-36055-5(7)) Turtleback Bks.

—Nicole the Beach Fairy. 2014. (Rainbow Magic — the Earth Fairies Ser.). lib. bdg. 14.75 (978-0-606-35830-9(7)) Turtleback Bks.

—Nina the Birthday Cake Fairy. 2014. (Sugar & Spice Fairies Ser.: 7). (ENG.). 80p. (J). (gr. 2-5). pap. 4.99 (978-0-545-60537-3(7), Scholastic Paperbacks) Scholastic, Inc.

—Nora the Arctic Fox Fairy. 2015. (Baby Animal Rescue Fairies Ser.: 7). (ENG.). 80p. (J). (gr. 2-5). pap. 4.99 (978-0-545-70856-2(7), Scholastic Paperbacks) Scholastic, Inc.

—Nora the Arctic Fox Fairy. 2015. (Rainbow Magic — Baby Animal Rescue Fairies Ser.: 7). lib. bdg. 14.75 (978-0-606-37055-4(2)) Turtleback Bks.

—Olympia the Games Fairy. 2012. (Rainbow Magic — Special Edition Ser.). lib. bdg. 17.20 (978-0-606-26541-6(4), Turtleback) Turtleback Bks.

—Paige the Christmas Play Fairy. 2010. (Rainbow Magic Ser.). (ENG.). 192p. (J). (gr. 2-5). pap. 6.99 (978-0-545-22177-1(3), Scholastic Paperbacks) Scholastic, Inc.

—Pearl the Cloud Fairy. Ripper, Georgie, illus. 2006. (Weather Fairies Ser.: 3). (ENG.). 80p. (Orig.). (J). (gr. -1-3). 4.99 (978-0-439-81388-4(3), Scholastic Paperbacks) Scholastic, Inc.

—Penny the Pony Fairy. 2008. (Rainbow Magic — the Pet Fairies Ser.). lib. bdg. 14.75 (978-1-4178-3008-4(5), Turtleback) Turtleback Bks.

—Pet Fairies to the Rescue! 2013. (Rainbow Magic — Scholastic Reader Ser.). lib. bdg. 13.55 (978-0-606-31510-4(1), Turtleback) Turtleback Bks.

—Pet Parade. 2013. (Rainbow Magic — Scholastic Reader Ser.). lib. bdg. 13.55 (978-0-606-31973-7(5), Turtleback) Turtleback Bks.

—Pia the Penguin Fairy. 2011. (Illus.). 63p. (J). (978-0-545-28873-6(8)) Scholastic, Inc.

—Poppy the Piano Fairy #1. 2010. (ENG.). 80p. (J). lib. bdg. 15.39 (978-1-4242-4733-2(0)) Fitzgerald Bks.

—The Rainbow Fairies. 2010. (Scholastic Reader Level 2 Ser.). (ENG.). 32p. (J). (gr. 1-3). pap. 3.99 (978-0-545-22291-4(5), Cartwheel Bks.) Scholastic, Inc.

—Rainbow Magic Special Edition: Addison the April Fool's Day Fairy. 2014. (Rainbow Magic Special Edition Ser.). (ENG.). 176p. (J). (gr. 2-5). pap. 6.99 (978-0-545-60538-0(5), Scholastic Paperbacks) Scholastic, Inc.

—Rainbow Magic Special Edition: Autumn the Falling Leaves Fairy. 2013. (Rainbow Magic Special Edition Ser.). (ENG.). 176p. (J). (gr. 2-5). pap. 6.99 (978-0-545-48495-4(2), Scholastic Paperbacks) Scholastic, Inc.

—Rainbow Magic Special Edition: Bailey the Babysitter Fairy. 2014. (Rainbow Magic Special Edition Ser.). (ENG.). 176p. (J). (gr. 2-5). pap. 6.99 (978-0-545-60539-7(3), Scholastic Paperbacks) Scholastic, Inc.

—Rainbow Magic Special Edition: Brianna the Tooth Fairy. 2013. (Rainbow Magic Special Edition Ser.). (ENG.). 176p. (J). (gr. 2-5). pap. 6.99 (978-0-545-48494-7(4), Scholastic Paperbacks) Scholastic, Inc.

—Rainbow Magic Special Edition: Chelsea the Congratulations Fairy. 2015. (Rainbow Magic Special Edition Ser.). (ENG.). 176p. (J). (gr. 2-5). pap. 6.99 (978-0-545-70826-5(5), Scholastic Paperbacks) Scholastic, Inc.

—Rainbow Magic Special Edition: Cheryl the Christmas Tree Fairy. 2012. (Rainbow Magic Special Edition Ser.). (ENG.). 176p. (J). (gr. 2-5). pap. 6.99 (978-0-545-45571-8(5), Scholastic Paperbacks) Scholastic, Inc.

—Rainbow Magic Special Edition: Keira the Movie Star Fairy. 2013. (Rainbow Magic Special Edition Ser.). (ENG.). 192p. (J). (gr. 2-5). pap. 6.99 (978-0-545-48496-1(0), Scholastic Paperbacks) Scholastic, Inc.

—Rainbow Magic Special Edition: Lila & Myla the Twins Fairies. 2015. (Rainbow Magic Special Edition Ser.). (ENG., Illus.). 176p. (J). (gr. 2-5). pap. 6.99 (978-0-545-70825-8(7), Scholastic Paperbacks) Scholastic, Inc.

—Rainbow Magic Special Edition: Lindsay the Luck Fairy. Dynamo Limited Staff, illus. 2013. (Rainbow Magic Special Edition Ser.). (ENG.). 192p. (J). (gr. 2-5). pap. 6.99 (978-0-545-48492-3(8), Scholastic Paperbacks) Scholastic, Inc.

—Rainbow Magic Special Edition: Natalie the Christmas Stocking Fairy. 2014. (Rainbow Magic Special Edition Ser.). (ENG.). 176p. (J). (gr. 2-5). pap. 6.99 (978-0-545-60540-3(7), Scholastic Paperbacks) Scholastic, Inc.

—Rainbow Magic Special Edition: Olympia the Games Fairy. 2012. (Rainbow Magic Ser.). (ENG., Illus.). 176p. (J). (gr. 2-5). pap. 6.99 (978-0-545-45703-3(3)) Scholastic, Inc.

—Rihanna the Seahorse Fairy. 2012. (Illus.). 65p. (J). (978-0-545-42599-5(9)) Scholastic, Inc.

—Rita the Frog Princess Fairy. 2016. (Illus.). (J). (Fairy Tale Fairies Ser.: 4). (ENG.). 80p. (gr. 2-5). pap. 4.99 (978-0-545-85197-8(1), Scholastic Paperbacks); 58p. **(978-0-545-88739-7(9))** Scholastic, Inc.

—Rosalie the Rapunzel Fairy. 2017. (Rainbow Magic — Storybook Fairies Ser.: 3). lib. bdg. 14.75 **(978-0-606-39719-3(1))** Turtleback Bks.

—Rosie the Honey Bear Fairy. 2015. (Baby Animal Rescue Fairies Ser.: 6). (ENG.). 80p. (J). (gr. 2-5). pap. 4.99 (978-0-545-70855-5(9), Scholastic Paperbacks) Scholastic, Inc.

—Rosie the Honey Bear Fairy. 2015. (Rainbow Magic — Baby Animal Rescue Fairies Ser.: 6). lib. bdg. 14.75 (978-0-606-37054-7(4)) Turtleback Bks.

—Roxie the Baking Fairy. 2015. (Magical Crafts Fairies Ser.: 7). (ENG., Illus.). 80p. (J). (gr. 2-5). pap. 4.99 (978-0-545-70835-7(4), Scholastic Paperbacks) Scholastic, Inc.

—Ruby the Red Fairy. Ripper, Georgie, illus. 2005. (Rainbow Magic Ser.: 1). (ENG.). 80p. (Orig.). (J). (gr. -1-3). pap. 4.99 (978-0-439-73861-3(X)) Scholastic, Inc.

—Ruth the Red Riding Hood Fairy. 2017. (Rainbow Magic — Storybook Fairies Ser.: 4). lib. bdg. 14.75 **(978-0-606-39727-8(2))** Turtleback Bks.

—Sadie the Saxophone Fairy #7. 2010. (ENG.). 80p. (J). lib. bdg. 15.39 (978-1-4242-4734-9(9)) Fitzgerald Bks.

—Saffron the Yellow Fairy. Ripper, Georgie, illus. 2004. (Rainbow Magic Ser.). 69p. (Orig.). (J). (978-0-439-69195-6(8)) Scholastic, Inc.

—Samantha the Swimming Fairy. 2010. (Sports Fairies Ser.: 5). (ENG.). 80p. (J). (gr. 2-5). 4.99 (978-0-545-20256-5(6), Scholastic Paperbacks) Scholastic, Inc.

—Savannah the Zebra Fairy. 2015. (Baby Animal Rescue Fairies Ser.: 4). (ENG.). 80p. (J). (gr. 2-5). pap. 4.99 (978-0-545-70853-1(2), Scholastic Paperbacks) Scholastic, Inc.

—Savannah the Zebra Fairy. 2015. (Rainbow Magic — Baby Animal Rescue Fairies Ser.: 4). lib. bdg. 14.75 (978-0-606-37052-3(8)) Turtleback Bks.

—Scholastic Reader Level 2: Rainbow Magic: Pet Fairies to the Rescue! Artful Doodlers Ltd Staff, illus. 2013. (Scholastic Reader Level 2 Ser.). (ENG.). 32p. (J). (gr. -1-3). pap. 3.99 (978-0-545-46295-2(9), Scholastic Paperbacks) Scholastic, Inc.

—Selena the Sleepover Fairy. 2012. (Rainbow Magic — Special Edition Ser.). lib. bdg. 17.20 (978-0-606-26176-0(1), Turtleback) Turtleback Bks.

—Shannon the Ocean Fairy. 2009. (Rainbow Magic Ser.). (ENG.). 176p. (J). (gr. 2-5). 6.99 (978-0-545-10576-7(5), Scholastic Paperbacks) Scholastic, Inc.

—Sky the Blue Fairy. Ripper, Georgie, illus. 2005. (Rainbow Magic Ser.: 5). (ENG.). 80p. (Orig.). (J). (gr. -1-3). per. 4.99 (978-0-439-74684-7(1), Scholastic Paperbacks) Scholastic, Inc.

—Skyler the Fireworks Fairy. 2016. (Rainbow Magic — Special Edition Ser.). lib. bdg. 17.20 (978-0-606-38793-4(5)) Turtleback Bks.

—Skyler the Fireworks Fairy (Rainbow Magic: Special Edition) 2016. (Rainbow Magic Ser.). (ENG., Illus.). 192p. (J). (gr. 2-5). pap. 6.99 (978-0-545-85204-3(8), Scholastic Paperbacks) Scholastic, Inc.

—Sophia the Snow Swan Fairy. 2012. (Illus.). 65p. (J). (978-0-545-42600-8(6)) Scholastic, Inc.

—Stephanie the Starfish Fairy. 2011. (Illus.). 65p. (J). (978-0-545-28875-0(4)) Scholastic, Inc.

—Storm the Lightning Fairy. Ripper, Georgie, illus. 2007. (Weather Fairies Ser.: 6). (ENG.). 80p. (Orig.). (J). (gr. -1-3). pap. 4.99 (978-0-439-81391-4(3), Scholastic Paperbacks) Scholastic, Inc.

—Sunny the Yellow Fairy. Ripper, Georgie, illus. 2005. (Rainbow Magic Ser.: 3). (ENG.). 80p. (J). (gr. 2-5). pap. 4.99 (978-0-439-74466-9(0), Little Apple Bks) Scholastic Canada, Ltd. CAN. Dist: Scholastic, Inc.

—Tess the Sea Turtle Fairy. 2011. (Illus.). 65p. (J). (978-0-545-28874-3(6)) Scholastic, Inc.

—Trixie the Halloween Fairy. 2009. (Rainbow Magic Ser.). (ENG., Illus.). 176p. (J). (gr. 2-5). 6.99 (978-0-545-10613-9(3), Scholastic Paperbacks) Scholastic, Inc.

—Vanessa the Choreography Fairy. 2013. (Rainbow Magic — the Superstar Fairies Ser.: 3). lib. bdg. 14.75 (978-0-606-31515-9(2), Turtleback) Turtleback Bks.

—Victoria the Violin Fairy #6. 2010. (ENG.). 80p. (J). lib. bdg. 15.39 (978-1-4242-4735-6(7)) Fitzgerald Bks.

—Violet the Painting Fairy. 2015. (Illus.). (J). (Magical Crafts Fairies Ser.: 5). (ENG.). 80p. (gr. 2-5). pap. 4.99 (978-0-545-70833-3(8), Scholastic Paperbacks); 65p. (978-0-545-72413-5(9)) Scholastic, Inc.

—Whitney the Whale Fairy. 2011. (Illus.). 64p. (J). (978-0-545-28876-7(2)) Scholastic, Inc.

—Zadie the Sewing Fairy. 2015. (Illus.). (J). (Magical Crafts Fairies Ser.: 3). (ENG.). 80p. (gr. 2-5). pap. 4.99 (978-0-545-70831-9(1), Scholastic Paperbacks); 65p. (978-0-545-72411-1(2)) Scholastic, Inc.

—Zoe the Skating Fairy. 2010. (Sports Fairies Ser.: 3). (ENG.). 80p. (J). (gr. 2-5). 4.99 (978-0-545-20254-1(X), Scholastic Paperbacks) Scholastic, Inc.

Meadows, Daisy & Scholastic, Inc. Staff. The Jewel Fairies Collection, Vol. 1. 2008. (Jewel Fairies Ser.: Bks. 1-4). (ENG., Illus.). 288p. (J). (gr. -1-3). pap. 6.99 (978-0-545-08838-1(0), Scholastic Paperbacks) Scholastic, Inc.

Medders, James. The Tooth Fairy's Quest. Hardin, Teresa, illus. 2008. 32p. pap. 24.95 (978-1-60672-549-8(1)) America Star Bks.

Melling, O. R. The Book of Dreams. 2009. (Chronicles of Faerie Ser.). (ENG.). 720p. (J). (gr. 2-8). 19.95 (978-0-8109-8346-5(X), Amulet Bks.) Abrams, Inc.

—The Chronicles of Faerie: The Book of Dreams. 2010. (Chronicles of Faerie Ser.). (ENG.). 720p. (YA). (gr. 2-8). pap. 12.95 (978-0-8109-8418-9(0), Amulet Bks.) Abrams, Inc.

—The Light-Bearer's Daughter. 2008. (ENG.). 368p. (YA). (gr. 2-8). pap. 9.95 (978-0-8109-7123-3(2), Amulet Bks.) Abrams, Inc.

—The Summer King. 2006. (ENG., Illus.). 380p. (YA). (gr. 5-10). 16.95 (978-0-8109-5969-9(0)) Abrams, Inc.

Melodie. The Arabian Nights, 7 vols. Collective Work Staff, illus. 2012. (ENG.). 32p. (J). (gr. 1). 19.95 (978-2-7338-2150-3(4)) Auzou, Philippe Editions FRA. Dist: Consortium Bk. Sales & Distribution.

Messenger, Lois. Fairy Magic & the Healing Rainbow Colours. 2013. 36p. pap. 15.95 (978-1-4525-7663-3(7), Balboa Pr.) Author Solutions, Inc.

Messenger, Shannon. Exile. (Keeper of the Lost Cities Ser.: 2). (ENG., Illus.). (J). (gr. 3-7). 2014. 592p. pap. 9.99 (978-1-4424-4597-0(1)) 2013. 576p. 19.99 (978-1-4424-4596-3(3)) Simon & Schuster Children's Publishing. (Aladdin).

—Keeper of the Lost Cities. (Keeper of the Lost Cities Ser.: 1). (ENG., Illus.). (J). (gr. 3-7). 2013. 512p. pap. 8.99 (978-1-4424-4594-9(7)) 2012. 496p. 16.99 (978-1-4424-4593-2(9)) 2015. 1744p. pap. 26.99 (978-1-4814-5112-3(X)) Simon & Schuster Children's Publishing. (Aladdin).

—Lodestar. 2016. (Keeper of the Lost Cities Ser.: 5). (ENG., Illus.). 688p. (J). (gr. 3-7). 18.99 (978-1-4814-7495-5(2), Aladdin) Simon & Schuster Children's Publishing.

—Neverseen. (Keeper of the Lost Cities Ser.: 4). (ENG., Illus.). 688p. (J). (gr. 3-7). 2016. pap. 9.99 (978-1-4814-3230-6(3)) 2015. 19.99 (978-1-4814-3229-0(X)) Simon & Schuster Children's Publishing. (Aladdin).

Mifae. 2013. 200p. (978-1-4602-2049-8(8)) FriesenPress.

Miles, Brenda & Sweet, Susan D. Cinderstella: A Tale of Planets Not Princes. Docampo, Valeria, illus. 2016. (J). (978-1-4338-2270-4(9), Magination Pr.) American Psychological Assn.

Miller, Jules. Ellie & the Truth about the Tooth Fairy. Miller, Jules, illus. 2014. (ENG., Illus.). 36p. (J). (gr. -1-k). 16.95 (978-1-62873-590-1(2), Sky Pony Pr.) Skyhorse Publishing Co., Inc.

Miller, Mona. Poppy & Branch's Big Adventure. 2017. (Illus.). 32p. (J). **(978-1-5182-3647-1(2))** Random Hse., Inc.

Mitchell, Hazel. Do Fairies Bring the Spring? 2017. (ENG., Illus.). 32p. (J). (gr. -1-12). 16.95 (978-1-60893-633-5(3)) Down East Bks.

Mitchell, N. J. W. Saraly & the Dragons. 2003. 124p. pap. 10.95 (978-0-595-30264-2(5)) iUniverse, Inc.

Mlynowski, Sarah. Dream On. 2013. (Whatever After Ser.: 4). (ENG.). 176p. (J). (gr. 3-7). 14.99 (978-0-545-41571-2(3), Scholastic Pr.) Scholastic, Inc.

—Fairest of All. 2012. (Whatever After Ser.: 1). (ENG.). 176p. (J). (gr. 3-7). 14.99 (978-0-545-40330-6(8), Scholastic Pr.) Scholastic, Inc.

—If the Shoe Fits. 2013. (Whatever After Ser.: 2). (ENG.). 176p. (J). (gr. 3-7). pap. 5.99 (978-0-545-41568-2(3), Scholastic Pr.) Scholastic, Inc.

Montijo, Rhode. The Halloween Kid. Montijo, Rhode, illus. 2010. (ENG., Illus.). 40p. (J). (gr. -1-3). 14.99 (978-1-4169-3575-9(4), Simon & Schuster Bks. For Young Readers) Simon & Schuster Bks. For Young Readers.

Moore, Daniel. Abdallah Jones & the DisappearingDust. 2006. 168p. pap. 17.00 (978-0-615-13570-0(6)) Ecstatic Exchange, The.

Morozumi, Atsuko. The Elves' First Christmas. 2009. (Illus.). 32p. (J). (gr. -1-1). 16.95 (978-1-935021-61-2(3)) Price, Mathew Ltd.

Morpurgo, Michael. The Pied Piper of Hamelin. Chichester Clark, Emma, illus. 2011. (ENG.). 64p. (J). (gr. k-4). 16.99 (978-0-7636-4824-4(8)) Candlewick Pr.

Morris, Kim. Tinker Bell & the Great Fairy Rescue. 2010. (ENG.). 32p. 12.99 (978-1-4231-2925-7(3)) Disney Pr.

Morrison, Megan. Grounded: The Tale of Rapunzel. 2015. (Illus.). 374p. (J). (978-0-545-75468-2(2)) Scholastic, Inc.

Moseley, Keith. Where's the Fairy? 2014. (Where's The ... ? Ser.). (ENG., Illus.). 26p. (J). (gr. -1-2). 14.95 (978-1-4549-1363-4(0)) Sterling Publishing Co., Inc.

Moseley, Sophia. The Adventures of Charlie. Delderfield, Angela, illus. 2012. 106p. pap. (978-1-78148-757-0(X)) Grosvenor Hse. Publishing Ltd.

Moskowitz, Hannah. A History of Glitter & Blood. 2015. (ENG., Illus.). 280p. (YA). (gr. 9-17). 18.99 *(978-1-4521-2942-6(8))* Chronicle Bks. LLC.

Moss, J. P. The Kind Fairy Adventures: 3 Loving Fairy Tales from the Land of the Faye. 2010. (Illus.). 52p. pap. 22.99 *(978-1-4520-3868-1(6))* AuthorHouse.

Muell, Jason. Descendants. 2017. (ENG.). 80p. (J). pap. 10.99 ***(978-1-4278-5687-6(7)***, 9781427856876) TOKYOPOP, Inc.

Mulazzi, Paola, et al. Disney Fairies Graphic Novel #4: Tinker Bell to the Rescue. Urbano, Emilio et al, illus. 2010. (Disney Fairies Ser.: 4). (ENG.). 80p. (J). (gr. 1-6). 12.99 *(978-1-59707-230-4(3))*; pap. 7.99 *(978-1-59707-200-7(1)*, 9781597072007) Papercutz.

—Tinker Bell & the Pirate Adventure, Vol. 5. Urbano, Emilio et al, illus. 2011. (Disney Fairies Ser.: 5). (ENG.). 64p. (J). (gr. 1-6). pap. 7.99 *(978-1-59707-240-3(0)*, 9781597072403) Papercutz.

—Tinker Bell the Perfect Fairy. Urbano, Emilio et al, illus. 2012. (Disney Fairies Ser.: 7). (ENG.). 64p. (J). (gr. 1-6). 11.99 *(978-1-59707-282-3(6)*, 9781597072823) Papercutz.

Mulock, Dinah Maria. The Fairy Book: The Best Popular Stories Selected & Rendered Anew. 2007. (ENG.). 326p. pap. 23.99 *(978-1-4346-4529-6(0))*; 358p. pap. 26.99 *(978-1-4346-4530-2(4))* Creative Media Partners, LLC.

Muncaster, Harriet. Isadora Moon Goes Camping. 2017. (Isadora Moon Ser.: 2). (ENG.). 128p. (J). (gr. 1-4). 5.99 ***(978-0-399-55827-6(6))***; 14.99 ***(978-0-399-55825-2(X))***; lib. bdg. 17.99 ***(978-0-399-55826-9(8))*** Random Hse. Children's Bks. (Random Hse. Bks. for Young Readers).

—Isadora Moon Goes to School. 2017. (Isadora Moon Ser.: 1). (ENG.). 128p. (J). (gr. 1-4). 5.99 ***(978-0-399-55823-8(3))***; 14.99 ***(978-0-399-55821-4(7))***; lib. bdg. 17.99 ***(978-0-399-55822-1(5))*** Random Hse. Children's Bks. (Random Hse. Bks. for Young Readers).

Muneefa. My Tales for Children. 2006. 90p. (J). pap. 13.95 *(978-1-58909-339-3(9))* Bookstand Publishing.

Murray, Alison. Fairy Felicity's Moonlight Adventure. Murray, Alison, illus. 2016. (ENG., Illus.). 24p. (J). (gr. -1-2). 15.99 *(978-0-7636-8945-2(9))*, Nosy Crow) Candlewick Pr.

Murray, Cecile. Fairies at Play:Tell a Story book About..., 1 vol. 2010. 44p. pap. 24.95 *(978-1-4489-5208-3(5))* PublishAmerica, Inc.

Musgrove, Marianne. Forget-Me-Not Fairy Treasury. MacCarthy, Patricia, illus. 2013. (ENG.). 192p. (J). (gr. -1-3). *(978-1-74308-536-3(2))* Hinkler Bks. Pty. Ltd.

Namm, Diane. Puss in Boots. Zilber, Denis, illus. 2012. (Silver Penny Stories Ser.). (ENG.). 48p. (J). (gr. -1-1). 4.95 *(978-1-4027-8435-4(X))* Sterling Publishing Co., Inc.

Napoli, Donna Jo. Lights on the Nile. 2011. (ENG.). 288p. (J). (gr. 3-7). 16.99 *(978-0-06-166793-0(5))* HarperCollins Pubs.

Natale, Christine. Fairy Tales. 2010. 63p. pap. 32.95 *(978-0-557-59131-2(7))* Lulu Pr., Inc.

Nathan, Helen. Flossie Crums & the Fairies' Cupcake Ball. Stevenson, Daryl, illus. 2012. (Flossie Crums Ser.). (ENG.). 56p. (J). (gr. k-2). pap. 8.99 *(978-1-84365-196-3(3)*, Pavilion Children's Books) Pavilion Bks. GBR. Dist: Independent Pubs. Group.

Nelson, Brett Alan. The Magical Forest. Ueda, Kumiko, illus. 2003. 42p. (J). *(978-0-9655078-7-5(4))* Windsong Publishing Co.

Nena L. Kircher & Julie A. Kircher. The Laid Back Legend of the Three Billy Goats Gruff. 2009. 24p. pap. 13.50 *(978-1-4389-6650-2(4))* AuthorHouse.

Nesbit, E. Five Children & It. 2007. 192p. per. 12.95 *(978-1-4218-3940-0(7))*; (gr. 4-7). 27.95 *(978-1-4218-3840-3(0))* 1st World Publishing, Inc. (1st World Library - Literary Society).

—Five Children & It. 207p. 20.95 *(978-0-8488-2523-2(3))* Amereon Ltd.

—Five Children & It. 2013. 132p. pap. *(978-1-908388-99-5(4))* Aziloth Bks.

—Five Children & It. (gr. 4-6). 2011. 428p. pap. 35.75 *(978-1-179-45023-0(X))* 2008. 200p. 22.99 *(978-0-554-38716-1(6))* 2008. 200p. 25.99 *(978-0-554-29413-1(3))* Creative Media Partners, LLC.

—Five Children & It. Millar, H. R., illus. 2007. (ENG.). 178p. pap. 19.99 *(978-1-4346-7586-6(6))*; 198p. pap. 21.99 *(978-1-4346-7587-3(4))* Creative Media Partners, LLC.

—Five Children & It. 2005. 96p. per. 4.95 *(978-1-4209-2587-6(3))* Digireads.com Publishing.

—Five Children & It. Millar, H. R., illus. 2007. (ENG.). 204p. per. *(978-1-4065-3077-3(8))* Dodo Pr.

—Five Children & It. 2017. (Dover Children's Evergreen Classics Ser.). (ENG., Illus.). 160p. (J). (gr. 3-8). pap. 4.00 *(978-0-486-42366-1(2))* Dover Pubns., Inc.

—Five Children & It. 2006. pap. *(978-1-4068-3501-4(3))* 2005. 296p. pap. *(978-1-84637-200-1(3))* Echo Library.

—Five Children & It. 2010. 98p. pap. 19.99 *(978-1-153-62213-4(0))* General Bks. LLC.

—Five Children & It. 2010. 144p. pap. *(978-1-4076-4577-3(3))* HardPr.

—Five Children & It. 2010. 152p. pap. 17.56 *(978-1-162-66290-9(5))* 2010. 152p. (gr. 3-7). 29.56 *(978-1-169-26518-9(9))* 2010. 152p. 36.95 *(978-1-161-43155-1(1))* 2004. reprint ed. pap. 1.99 *(978-1-4192-1987-0(1))* 2004. reprint ed. pap. 21.95 *(978-1-4191-1987-3(7))* Kessinger Publishing, LLC.

—Five Children & It. 2013. (Oxford Children's Classics Ser.). (ENG.). 208p. 9.95 *(978-0-19-273343-6(5))* Oxford Univ. Pr., Inc.

—Five Children & It. Hische, Jessica, illus. 2013. (Penguin Drop Caps Ser.). (ENG.). 256p. (gr. 12). 25.00 *(978-0-14-312466-5(8)*, Penguin Books) Penguin Publishing Group.

—Five Children & It. Nesbit, E. & Millar, H. R., illus. 2004. (ENG.). 240p. (gr. 12-18). 14.00 *(978-0-14-303915-0(6)*, Penguin Classics) Penguin Publishing Group.

—Five Children & It. 2008. (Puffin Classics Ser.). (ENG., Illus.). 272p. (J). (gr. 5-7). 5.99 *(978-0-14-132161-5(X)*, Puffin Books) Penguin Young Readers Group.

—Five Children & It. 2013. (ENG., Illus.). 272p. (J). (gr. 4-7). pap. 10.99 *(978-0-09-957298-5(2))* Random Hse. GBR. Dist: Independent Pubs. Group.

—Five Children & It. 2005. (J). 1.25 *(978-1-4025-4084-4(1))* Recorded Bks., Inc.

—Five Children & It. 2013. 160p. *(978-3-8495-1928-5(7))* 2013. 160p. pap. *(978-3-8495-0897-5(8))* 2011. 208p. pap. *(978-3-8424-8390-3(2))* Tredition GmbH.

—Five Children & It. 2009. 128p. (gr. 4-7). pap. 4.95 *(978-1-60459-692-2(9))* Wilder Pubns., Corp.

—Five Children & It. 2005. (ENG.). 29.95 *(978-1-55742-510-2(8))*; pap. 14.95 *(978-1-55742-506-5(X))* Wildside Pr., LLC.

Nguy, Hoa X. The Bamboo Girl. 2007. 84p. (J). pap. 20.00 *(978-0-8059-7562-8(4))* Dorrance Publishing Co., Inc.

Niddrie, June. Pom, the Pomegranate Pixie. 2010. 32p. pap. 16.10 *(978-0-557-31875-9(0))* Lulu Pr., Inc.

Nielsen, Amy. Victor & the Sun Orb. 2008. 144p. 21.95 *(978-0-595-50307-0(1))*; pap. 11.95 *(978-0-595-51212-6(7))* iUniverse, Inc.

Nielsen, Jennifer A. Elliot & the Last Underworld War. Kendall, Gideon, illus. 2012. (ENG.). 208p. (J). (gr. 3-8). 12.99 *(978-1-4022-4021-8(X)*, Sourcebooks Jabberwocky) Sourcebooks, Inc.

Nilsen, Anna. Bella's Butterfly Ball. Partis, Joanne, illus. 2012. (ENG.). 20p. (J). (gr. -1-1). pap. 9.99 *(978-1-84365-194-9(7)*, Pavilion Children's Books) Pavilion Bks. GBR. Dist: Independent Pubs. Group.

—Bella's Midsummer Secret. Partis, Joanne, illus. 2005. (ENG.). 18p. (J). (gr. -1-1). pap. 9.99 *(978-1-84458-338-6(4)*, Pavilion Children's Books) Pavilion Bks. GBR. Dist: Independent Pubs. Group.

Nomura, Mizuki. Book Girl & the Suicidal Mime. 2010. (Book Girl Ser.: 1). (ENG., Illus.). 192p. (YA). (gr. 8-17). pap. 13.00 *(978-0-316-07690-6(2)*, Yen Pr.) Orbit.

Norman, Claire. At the End of the Lane. 2012. (Illus.). 48p. (gr. 1-2). pap. 13.66 *(978-1-4685-8237-6(2))* AuthorHouse.

Norris, Christine. Talisman of Zandria, 1. Nagy, Robert, illus. 2005. 187p. (YA). pap. 14.95 *(978-1-885093-44-8(6)*, LBF/Hadrosaur) Hadrosaur Pr.

North, Laura. Cinderella's Big Foot. 2014. (ENG., Illus.). 32p. (J). *(978-0-7787-0440-9(8))*; pap. *(978-0-7787-0448-5(3))* Crabtree Publishing Co.

Norton, Tamra. Shayla Witherwood: A Half-Faerie Tale. 2012. pap. 16.99 *(978-1-59955-963-6(3))* Cedar Fort, Inc./CFI Distribution.

Numeroff, Laura Joffe & Evans, Nate. Ponyella. Munsinger, Lynn, illus. 2011. (ENG.). 32p. (J). (gr. -1-k). 16.99 *(978-1-4231-0259-5(2))* Hyperion Pr.

O'Connor, Edwin. Benjy: A Ferocious Fairy Tale. O'Neill, Catharine, illus. 2006. 96p. (J). reprint ed. pap. 12.00 *(978-1-4223-5421-6(0))* DIANE Publishing Co.

O'Dea, Kendra J. Polar Bear Pond. 2007. (Illus.). 62p. (J). per. 11.95 *(978-0-9799162-0-5(8))* Shortbread Hill Bk. Co.

O'Donnell, Liam. Tank & Fizz: the Case of the Battling Bots, 1 vol. Deas, Mike, illus. 2016. (Tank & Fizz Ser.: 2). (ENG.). 176p. (J). (gr. 3-6). pap. 9.95 *(978-1-4598-0813-3(4))* Orca Bk. Pubs. USA.

O'Guilin, Peadar. The Call. 2016. (ENG.). 320p. (YA). (gr. 9). 18.99 *(978-1-338-04561-1(X))* Scholastic, Inc.

Once upon a Time Spanish Version-the Elves & the Shoemaker. 2005. (J). *(978-1-57022-559-8(1))* ECS Learning Systems, Inc.

Ondrias, Rachel. Cindy Lou Ella: A Country Fairy Tale. Scarborough, Casey, illus. 2007. (ENG.). 56p. (J). 18.95 *(978-1-933660-28-8(7)*, Tadpole Pr. 4 Kids) Smooth Sailing Pr., LLC.

Orchard, Eric. Bera the One-Headed Troll. 2016. (ENG., Illus.). 128p. (J). 17.99 *(978-1-62672-106-7(8)*, 9781626721067, First Second Bks.) Roaring Brook Pr.

O'Reilly, Avril. A Fairy in the Family. 2009. 32p. pap. 22.50 *(978-1-4092-8061-3(6))* Lulu Pr., Inc.

Orsi, Tea. Tinker Bell & Her Magical Friends. 2016. (Disney Fairies Graphic Novels Ser.: 18). (J). lib. bdg. 18.40 *(978-0-606-38371-4(9))* Turtleback Bks.

—Tinker Bell & the Legend of the NeverBeast. 2015. (Disney Fairies Graphic Novels Ser.: 17). (J). lib. bdg. 18.40 *(978-0-606-37295-4(4))* Turtleback Bks.

—Tinker Bell & the Pirate Fairy. 2015. (Disney Fairies Graphic Novels Ser.: 16). (J). lib. bdg. 18.40 *(978-0-606-37294-7(6))* Turtleback Bks.

—Tinker Bell & the Secret of the Wings. 2014. (Disney Fairies Graphic Novels Ser.: 15). (J). lib. bdg. 18.40 *(978-0-606-35533-9(2))* Turtleback Bks.

Orsi, Tea & Panaro, Carlo. Tinker Bell & the Lost Treasure. Razzi, Manuela et al, illus. 2013. (Disney Fairies Ser.: 12). (ENG.). 64p. (J). (gr. 1-6). 11.99 *(978-1-59707-429-2(2)*, 9781597074292); pap. 7.99 *(978-1-59707-428-5(4)*, 9781597074285) Papercutz.

Osborn, Linda. Giant Mike & the Four Fairies. Friesen, Ray, illus. 2013. 24p. (J). mass mkt. 12.95 *(978-0-9887329-5-7(5))* Don't Eat Any Bugs Prodns.

O'Sullivan, Tom & Bacon, Paul, illus. Shirley Temple's Fairyland: The Wild Swans; Beauty & the Beast; Rumpelstiltskin; the Sleeping Beauty. 2011. 62p. 36.95 *(978-1-258-04207-3(X))* Literary Licensing, LLC.

Outside Your Back Door. 2004. (J). bds. 12.00 net. *(978-0-9747081-0-2(0))* Cohen, Deanna Moreau.

Owen, Sarah. Sarah the Fairy Princess's Birthday Party. 2009. 32p. pap. 41.50 *(978-1-4452-5921-5(4))* Lulu Pr., Inc.

Page, Nick & Page, Claire. Giant Sticker Activity Story Book. Baker, Sara, illus. 2006. (Giant Sticker Bks.). 144p. (J). (gr. -1-k). pap. *(978-1-84610-303-2(7))* Make Believe Ideas.

—Read with Me the Elves & the Shoemaker: Sticker Activity Book. Baker, Sara, illus. 2006. (Read with Me (Make Believe Ideas) Ser.). 12p. (J). (gr. k-2). pap. *(978-1-84610-177-9(8))* Make Believe Ideas.

—Ready to Read Jack & the Beanstalk Sticker Activity Workbook. Goodberry, Jo, illus. 2006. (Ready-to-Read Sticker Ser.). 12p. (J). (gr. -1-3). pap., wbk. ed., act. bk. ed. *(978-1-84610-127-4(1))* Make Believe Ideas.

Paiva, Teresa & Pinto, Helena Rebelo. Mein Freund, der Schlaf. 2011. (FRE.). 60p. (gr. 1-2). pap. 14.95 *(978-1-4567-8991-6(0))* AuthorHouse.

Palacios, Laura. Ten Hardworking Elves. 2009. 40p. pap. 17.95 *(978-0-557-22319-0(9))* Lulu Pr., Inc.

Palatini, Margie & Davis, Jack E. Sweet Tooth. Davis, Jack E., illus. 2004. (ENG., Illus.). 40p. (J). (gr. -1-3). 18.99 *(978-0-689-85159-9(6)*, Simon & Schuster Bks. For Young Readers) Simon & Schuster Bks. For Young Readers.

Paquette, Ammi-Joan. The Tiptoe Guide to Tracking Fairies. Unzner, Christa, illus. 2009. (ENG.). 32p. (J). (gr. -1-3). 15.95 *(978-1-933718-20-0(X))* Tanglewood Pr.

Paquette, Ammi-Joan & Unzner, Christa. The Tiptoe Guide to Tracking Fairies. 2010. (ENG., Illus.). 32p. (J). (gr. -1-3). pap. 8.95 *(978-1-933718-50-7(1))* Tanglewood Pr.

Park, Barbara. Toothless Wonder. Brunkus, Denise, illus. 2003. (Junie B. Jones Ser.: No. 3). (ENG.). 96p. (J). (gr. 1-4). pap. 4.99 *(978-0-375-82223-0(2)*, Random Hse. Bks. for Young Readers) Random Hse. Children's Bks.

—Toothless Wonder. 2003. (Junie B. Jones Ser.: 20). (gr. k-3). lib. bdg. 14.75 *(978-0-613-71014-5(2)*, Turtleback) Turtleback Bks.

Parker, Emma. Jack & the Beanstalk. 2010. (Illus.). 24p. pap. *(978-1-877561-49-8(5))* First Edition Ltd.

—Little Red Riding Hood. 2010. (Illus.). pap. *(978-1-877561-01-6(0))* First Edition Ltd.

Parker-Quayle, Eric. Eric Quayle's Tiny Tales. 2015. (ENG., Illus.). 60p. (J). (gr. 2-3). pap. 13.95 *(978-1-78455-867-3(2)*, f25c391c-ecc9-472d-a9fd-362a8bf7e971) Austin, Stan AUS. Dist: Bookmasters Distribution.

Parragon Staff. Pinocchio: The Magical Story. 2010. (Disney Padded Magical Storybks.). (Illus.). 32p. (J). (gr. -1-1). *(978-1-4075-8451-5(0))* Parragon, Inc.

Parry, Jo. Rainbow Fairies. 2009. (Wow! Bks.). (Illus.). (J). bds. 12.99 *(978-1-934650-25-7(0))* Just For Kids Pr., LLC.

Passaniti, Connie. The Fairy Garden Zodiac Adventure. 2012. 38p. pap. 25.49 *(978-1-4478-7060-9(3))* Lulu Pr., Inc.

Paterson, Katherine & Paterson, John B. The Flint Heart. Rocco, John, illus. 2012. (ENG.). 304p. (J). (gr. 2-5). pap. 9.99 *(978-0-7636-6243-1(7))* Candlewick Pr.

Paulitz, Kevin. A Letter from the Tooth Fairy. 2011. 28p. pap. 12.95 *(978-1-4490-6671-0(2))* AuthorHouse.

Paulk, William. The Creatures of Vision City: Pokie's Party, Book One. 2009. 48p. pap. 10.99 *(978-1-4389-5659-6(2))* AuthorHouse.

Pearson, Luke, illus. Hilda & the Troll. 2013. (Hildafolk Ser.). (ENG.). 40p. (J). (gr. k). 18.95 *(978-1-909263-14-7(1))* Flying Eye Bks. GBR. Dist: Consortium Bk. Sales & Distribution.

Pearson, Paul M. Fun Folk & Fairy Tales. 2011. 160p. 41.95 *(978-1-258-02739-1(9))* Literary Licensing, LLC.

Perelman, Helen. Bubble Gum Rescue. Waters, Erica-Jane, illus. 2012. (Candy Fairies Ser.: 8). (ENG.). 128p. (J). (gr. 2-5). pap. 5.99 *(978-1-4424-2217-9(3)*, Aladdin) Simon & Schuster Children's Publishing.

—Bubble Gum Rescue. Waters, Erica-Jane, illus. 2014. (Candy Fairies Ser.: 8). (ENG.). 128p. (J). (gr. 2-5). 15.99 *(978-1-4424-6496-4(8)*, Simon & Schuster/Paula Wiseman Bks.) Simon & Schuster/Paula Wiseman Bks.

—A Candy Fairies Sweet Collection: Chocolate Dreams; Rainbow Swirl; Caramel Moon; Cool Mint. Waters, Erica-Jane, illus. 2013. (Candy Fairies Ser.). (ENG.). 512p. (J). (gr. 2-5). pap. 23.99 *(978-1-4424-9390-2(9)*, Aladdin) Simon & Schuster Children's Publishing.

—Caramel Moon. Waters, Erica-Jane, illus. 2010. (Candy Fairies Ser.: 3). (ENG.). 128p. (J). (gr. 2-5). pap. 5.99 *(978-1-4169-9456-5(4)*, Aladdin) Simon & Schuster Children's Publishing.

—Caramel Moon. Waters, Erica-Jane, illus. 2013. (Candy Fairies Ser.: 3). (ENG.). 128p. (J). (gr. 2-5). 15.99 *(978-1-4424-5922-9(0)*, Simon & Schuster/Paula Wiseman Bks.) Simon & Schuster/Paula Wiseman Bks.

—Chocolate Dreams. Waters, Erica-Jane, illus. 2010. (Candy Fairies Ser.: 1). (ENG.). 128p. (J). (gr. 2-5). pap. 5.99 *(978-1-4169-9454-1(8)*, Aladdin) Simon & Schuster Children's Publishing.

—Chocolate Dreams. Waters, Erica-Jane, illus. 2012. (Candy Fairies Ser.: 1). (ENG.). 128p. (J). (gr. 2-5). 15.99 *(978-1-4424-5775-1(9)*, Simon & Schuster/Paula Wiseman Bks.) Simon & Schuster/Paula Wiseman Bks.

—The Chocolate Rose. Waters, Erica-Jane, illus. 2013. (Candy Fairies Ser.: 11). (ENG.). 128p. (J). (gr. 2-5). pap. 5.99 *(978-1-4424-5299-2(4)*, Aladdin) Simon & Schuster Children's Publishing.

—The Chocolate Rose. Waters, Erica-Jane, illus. 2013. (Candy Fairies Ser.: 11). (ENG.). 128p. (J). (gr. 2-5). 15.99 *(978-1-4424-6499-5(2)*, Simon & Schuster/Paula Wiseman Bks.) Simon & Schuster/Paula Wiseman Bks.

—The Coconut Clue. Waters, Erica-Jane, illus. 2015. (Candy Fairies Ser.: 17). (ENG.). 128p. (J). (gr. 2-5). pap. 5.99 *(978-1-4814-0616-1(7)*, Aladdin) Simon & Schuster Children's Publishing.

—Cool Mint. Waters, Erica-Jane, illus. 2010. (Candy Fairies Ser.: 4). (ENG.). 128p. (J). (gr. 2-5). pap. 5.99 *(978-1-4169-9457-2(2)*, Aladdin) Simon & Schuster Children's Publishing.

—Cool Mint. Waters, Erica-Jane, illus. 2013. (Candy Fairies Ser.: 4). (ENG.). 128p. (J). (gr. 2-5). 15.99 *(978-1-4424-5923-6(9)*, Simon & Schuster/Paula Wiseman Bks.) Simon & Schuster/Paula Wiseman Bks.

—Double Dip. Waters, Erica-Jane, illus. 2012. (Candy Fairies Ser.: 9). (ENG.). 128p. (J). (gr. 2-5). pap. 5.99 *(978-1-4424-2219-3(X)*, Aladdin) Simon & Schuster Children's Publishing.

—Double Dip. Waters, Erica-Jane, illus. 2012. (Candy Fairies Ser.: 9). (ENG.). 128p. (J). (gr. 2-5). 15.99 *(978-1-4424-5972-4(7)*, Simon & Schuster/Paula Wiseman Bks.) Simon & Schuster/Paula Wiseman Bks.

—Frozen Treats. Waters, Erica-Jane, illus. 2014. (Candy Fairies Ser.: 13). (ENG.). 128p. (J). (gr. 2-5). pap. 5.99 *(978-1-4424-5303-6(6)*, Aladdin) Simon & Schuster Children's Publishing.

—Gooey Goblins: Halloween Special. Waters, Erica-Jane, illus. 2011. (Candy Fairies Ser.). (ENG.). 176p. (J). (gr. 2-5). pap. 5.99 *(978-1-4424-2213-1(0)*, Aladdin) Simon & Schuster Children's Publishing.

—Gooey Goblins: Halloween Special. Waters, Erica-Jane, illus. 2013. (Candy Fairies Ser.). (ENG.). 176p. (J). (gr. 2-5). 15.99 *(978-1-4424-6495-7(X)*, Simon & Schuster/Paula Wiseman Bks.) Simon & Schuster/Paula Wiseman Bks.

—Jelly Bean Jumble. Waters, Erica-Jane, illus. 2013. (Candy Fairies Ser.: 10). (ENG.). 128p. (J). (gr. 2-5). pap. 5.99 *(978-1-4424-5297-8(8)*, Aladdin) Simon & Schuster Children's Publishing.

—Jelly Bean Jumble. Waters, Erica-Jane, illus. 2013. (Candy Fairies Ser.: 10). (ENG.). 128p. (J). (gr. 2-5). 15.99 *(978-1-4424-6000-3(8)*, Simon & Schuster/Paula Wiseman Bks.) Simon & Schuster/Paula Wiseman Bks.

—Magic Hearts. Waters, Erica-Jane, illus. 2011. (Candy Fairies Ser.: 5). (ENG.). 128p. (J). (gr. 2-5). pap. 5.99 *(978-1-4424-0823-4(5)*, Aladdin) Simon & Schuster Children's Publishing.

—Magic Hearts. Waters, Erica-Jane, illus. 2013. (Candy Fairies Ser.: 5). (ENG.). 128p. (J). (gr. 2-5). 15.99 *(978-1-4424-6494-0(1)*, Simon & Schuster/Paula Wiseman Bks.) Simon & Schuster/Paula Wiseman Bks.

—Marshmallow Mystery. Waters, Erica-Jane, illus. 2014. (Candy Fairies Ser.: 12). (ENG.). 128p. (J). (gr. 2-5). 15.99 *(978-1-4424-6500-8(X))*; pap. 5.99 *(978-1-4424-5301-2(X))* Simon & Schuster Children's Publishing. (Aladdin).

—A Minty Mess. Waters, Erica-Jane, illus. 2016. (Candy Fairies Ser.: 19). (ENG.). 128p. (J). (gr. 2-5). pap. 5.99 *(978-1-4814-4680-8(0)*, Aladdin) Simon & Schuster Children's Publishing.

—A Minty Mess. Waters, Erica-Jane, illus. 2016. (Candy Fairies Ser.: 19). (ENG.). 128p. (J). (gr. 2-5). 16.99 *(978-1-4814-4681-5(9)*, Simon & Schuster/Paula Wiseman Bks.) Simon & Schuster/Paula Wiseman Bks.

—The Peppermint Princess: Super Special. Waters, Erica-Jane, illus. 2016. (Candy Fairies Ser.). (ENG.). 176p. (J). (gr. 2-5). pap. 5.99 *(978-1-4814-4686-0(X)*, Aladdin) Simon & Schuster Children's Publishing.

—Rainbow Swirl. Waters, Erica-Jane, illus. 2010. (Candy Fairies Ser.: 2). (ENG.). 128p. (J). (gr. 2-5). pap. 5.99 *(978-1-4169-9455-8(6)*, Aladdin) Simon & Schuster Children's Publishing.

—Rainbow Swirl. Waters, Erica-Jane, illus. 2012. (Candy Fairies Ser.: 2). (ENG.). 128p. (J). (gr. 2-5). 15.99 *(978-1-4424-5776-8(7)*, cwc, Simon & Schuster/Paula Wiseman Bks.) Simon & Schuster/Paula Wiseman Bks.

—Rock Candy Treasure. Waters, Erica-Jane, illus. 2016. (Candy Fairies Ser.: 18). (ENG.). 128p. (J). (gr. 2-5). pap. 5.99 *(978-1-4814-4677-8(0)*, Aladdin) Simon & Schuster Children's Publishing.

—A Royal Wedding: Super Special. Waters, Erica-Jane, illus. 2013. (Candy Fairies Ser.). (ENG.). 208p. (J). (gr. 2-5). pap. 5.99 *(978-1-4424-8898-4(0)*, Aladdin) Simon & Schuster Children's Publishing.

—A Royal Wedding: Super Special. Waters, Erica-Jane, illus. 2013. (Candy Fairies Ser.). (ENG.). 208p. (J). (gr. 2-5). 15.99 *(978-1-4424-8899-1(9)*, Simon & Schuster/Paula Wiseman Bks.) Simon & Schuster/Paula Wiseman Bks.

—The Sugar Ball. Waters, Erica-Jane, illus. 2011. (Candy Fairies Ser.: 6). (ENG.). 128p. (J). (gr. 2-5). pap. 5.99 *(978-1-4424-0825-8(1)*, Aladdin) Simon & Schuster Children's Publishing.

—The Sugar Ball. Waters, Erica-Jane, illus. 2013. (Candy Fairies Ser.: 6). (ENG.). 128p. (J). (gr. 2-5). 15.99 *(978-1-4424-6498-8(4)*, Simon & Schuster/Paula Wiseman Bks.) Simon & Schuster/Paula Wiseman Bks.

—Sweet Secrets. Waters, Erica-Jane, illus. 2015. (Candy Fairies Ser.: 15). (ENG.). 128p. (J). (gr. 2-5). pap. 5.99 *(978-1-4814-0610-9(8)*, Aladdin) Simon & Schuster Children's Publishing.

—Taffy Trouble. Waters, Erica-Jane, illus. 2015. (Candy Fairies Ser.: 16). (ENG.). 128p. (J). (gr. -1-5). pap. 5.99 *(978-1-4814-0613-0(2)*, Aladdin) Simon & Schuster Children's Publishing.

Perkins, Kevin. The Little Blue Gnome. 2013. 210p. pap. *(978-1-78148-649-8(2))* Grosvenor Hse. Publishing Ltd.

Perrault, Charles. Cinderella. Innocenti, Roberto, illus. 2013. (ENG.). 32p. (J). (gr. 1-17). pap. 7.99 *(978-0-89812-828-4(5)*, Creative Paperbacks) Creative Co., The.

—The Fairies. 2005. (SPA.). 12p. (J). pap. *(978-958-30-1779-7(5))* Panamericana Editorial.

—Puss in Boots. Arthur, Malcolm, tr. Marcellino, Fred, illus. 2011. (ENG.). 32p. (J). (gr. -1-3). pap. 8.99 *(978-0-312-65945-5(8)*, 9780312659455) Square Fish.

Petalwink Learns to Fly. 2006. (J). 15.95 *(978-0-9789426-0-1(4))* Three Trees, Inc.

Peterson, Janie & Peterson, Macy. The Sleep Fairy. Newlun, Shawn, illus. 2003. (ENG.). 32p. (J). (gr. -1-5). 16.95 *(978-0-9714405-0-0(6))* Behave'n Kids Pr.

Petit, Cheryl. Fairy Princess Melina, 1 vol. 2010. 26p. pap. 24.95 *(978-1-4489-7915-8(3))* PublishAmerica, Inc.

Petrucha, Stefan. Prilla's Talent. Magic Eye Studios Staff et al, illus. 2010. (Disney Fairies Ser.: 1). (ENG.). 80p. (J). (gr. 1-6). pap. 7.99 *(978-1-59707-186-4(2)*, 9781597071864);No. 1. 12.99 *(978-1-59707-187-1(0))* Papercutz.

Petty, J. T. Fairy Killer. Davis, Will, illus. 2011. (ENG.). 128p. (J). (gr. 3-7). pap. 7.99 *(978-1-4424-3097-6(4)*, Simon & Schuster Bks. For Young Readers) Simon & Schuster Bks. For Young Readers.

Phillips, Beth Ann. Crystal Kingdom, 1 vol. 2009. 63p. pap. 19.95 *(978-1-60813-003-0(7))* America Star Bks.

Phillipson, Fiona. Fairy Princesses: Over 1000 Reusable Stickers! 2014. (Little Hands Creative Sticker Play Ser.). (ENG.). 64p. (J). (gr. -1-2). pap. 9.99 *(978-1-4380-0396-2(X))* Barron's Educational Series, Inc.

Phillpotts, Eden. The Flint Heart; a Fairy Story. 2010. 376p. pap. 33.75 *(978-1-171-85836-2(1))* Creative Media Partners, LLC.

—The Flint Heart; a Fairy Story. 2010. (Illus.). 98p. pap. 20.00 *(978-1-154-70758-8(X))* 2009. 134p. pap. 19.99 *(978-1-150-78588-7(8))* General Bks. LLC.

Picouly, Daniel. Thumbelina of Toulaba. Bedrick, Claudia Z., tr. from FRE. Tallec, Olivier & Sorman, Joy, illus. 2007. (ENG.). 36p. (J). (gr. -1-3). 16.95 *(978-1-59270-069-1(1))* Enchanted Lion Bks., LLC.

Pike, Aprilynne. Destined. (Wings Ser.: 4). (ENG.). (YA). (gr. 8). 2013. 336p. pap. 9.99 *(978-0-06-166814-2(1))* 2012. 320p. 17.99 *(978-0-06-166812-8(5))* HarperCollins Pubs. (HarperTeen).

—Hechizos. 2012.Tr. of Spells. (UND & SPA.). 352p. (YA). pap. 18.95 *(978-84-96886-27-8(1))* Ediciones Urano S. A. ESP. Dist: Spanish Pubs., LLC.

—Illusions. 2012. (Wings Ser.: 3). (ENG.). 400p. (YA). (gr. 8). pap. 8.99 *(978-0-06-166811-1(7)*, HarperTeen) HarperCollins Pubs.

—Spells. (Wings Ser.: 2). (ENG.). (YA). (gr. 8). 2011. 384p. pap. 9.99 *(978-0-06-166808-1(7))* 2010. 368p. 16.99 *(978-0-06-166806-7(0))* HarperCollins Pubs. (HarperTeen).

E
F
G

—Spells, 7 vols. 2010. (YA). 78.75 (978-1-4407-8375-3(6)) Recorded Bks., Inc.

—Wings. 2011. (Wings Ser.: 1). (ENG.). 320p. (YA). (gr. 8). pap. 8.99 (978-0-06-166805-0(2), HarperTeen) HarperCollins Pubs.

Pikey, Mikey. The Diamond Tree. 2007. 378p. pap. 31.95 (978-1-84728-234-7(2)) Lulu Pr., Inc.

Pipera, Lady. The Enchanted Meadow. 2009. 52p. pap. 17.50 (978-1-60860-100-4(5), Eloquent Bks.) Strategic Book Publishing & Rights Agency (SBPRA).

Pisella, Donna. The Blue Goblin. 2013. (ENG.). 30p. (J). 22.95 (978-1-4787-1269-5(4)) Outskirts Pr., Inc.

Pitcher, Chelsea. The Last Changeling. 2014. (ENG.). 360p. (YA). pap. 11.99 (978-0-7387-4084-3(5), Flux) North Star Editions.

Plumier, Lea. The Story of Rhu the Fairy. Rambo, Angela, illus. 2012. 208p. pap. 11.95 (978-1-61477-039-8(5)) Bellissima Publishing, LLC.

Polette, Keith. Paco & the Giant Chile Plant/Paco y la Planta de Chile Gigante. de la Vega, Eida, tr. Dulemba, Elizabeth, illus. 2008. (SPA & ENG.). 32p. (J). (gr. -1-3). lib. bdg. 16.95 (978-0-9770906-2-4(0), Raven Tree Pr.,Csi) Continental Sales, Inc.

Pongetti, Freda, illus. & adapted by. Why the Chimes Rang. Pongetti, Freda, adapted by. 2007. 18p. (J). 21.00 net. (978-0-9796625-0-8(8)) GDG Publishing.

Poole, Josephine. BLANCANIEVES. 2007. (SPA., Illus.). 30p. (J). (gr. -1-5). 24.95 (978-84-96629-17-2(1)) S.A. Kokinos ESP. Dist: Lectorum Pubns., Inc.

Pope, Lee Green. The Cinderella Diary: A Not-So-Grimm Faerie Tale. 2008. 44p. pap. 18.49 (978-1-4389-1895-2(X)) AuthorHouse.

Posner-Sanchez, Andrea. Pixie Puzzles, Games, & More! Christy, Jana, illus. 2014. (Never Girls Ser.). (ENG.). 256p. (J). (gr. 1-4). 6.99 (978-0-7364-3152-1(7), Golden/Disney) Random Hse. Children's Bks.

—Sofia's Royal World (Disney Junior: Sofia the First) Lee, Grace & Disney Storybook Artists Staff, illus. 2014. (Big Golden Book Ser.). (ENG.). 64p. (J). (gr. -1-2). 9.99 (978-0-7364-3262-7(0), Golden/Disney) Random Hse. Children's Bks.

Potter, Kay. I Hate Fairies! the Adventures of Katie James. 2013. 140p. pap. 13.97 (978-1-62212-127-4(9), Strategic Bk. Publishing) Strategic Book Publishing & Rights Agency (SBPRA).

Pounder, Sibéal. Witch Switch. Anderson, Laura Ellen, illus. 2017. (Witch Wars Ser.). (ENG.). 272p. (J). 16.99 (978-1-61963-984-3(X), 9781619639843, Bloomsbury USA Childrens) Bloomsbury Publishing USA.

—Witch Wars. Anderson, Laura Ellen, illus. 2016. (Witch Wars Ser.). (ENG.). 272p. (J). 16.99 (978-1-61963-925-6(4), 9781619639256, Bloomsbury USA Childrens) Bloomsbury Publishing USA.

Powell, Angela. Alicia's Blended Family. Gillen, Rosemarie, illus. 2013. 24p. pap. 9.99 (978-1-61286-153-1(9)) Avid Readers Publishing Group.

Prasadam, Smriti. My Fairy Glade. Finn, Rebecca, illus. 2008. (Peep Through Play Bks.). (ENG.). 12p. (J). (gr. k-k). bds. 7.95 (978-0-7475-8809-2(0)) Bloomsbury Publishing Plc GBR. Dist: Independent Pubs. Group.

Pratchett, Terry. A Hat Full of Sky. (Tiffany Aching Ser.: 2). (YA). (gr. 8). 2015. (ENG.). 400p. pap. 9.99 (978-0-06-243527-9(2)) 2004. 288p. 17.99 (978-0-06-058660-7(5)) HarperCollins Pubs.

—A Hat Full of Sky. 2005. 407p. (gr. 7). 19.00 (978-0-7569-5126-9(7)) Perfection Learning Corp.

—A Hat Full of Sky. 2005. (Discworld Ser.: 32). 407p. (YA). 19.65 (978-1-4177-2658-5(X), Turtleback) Turtleback Bks.

—I Shall Wear Midnight. (Tiffany Aching Ser.: 4). (YA). (gr. 8). 2015. (ENG.). 464p. pap. 9.99 (978-0-06-243529-3(9)) 2011. 368p. pap. 9.99 (978-0-06-143306-1(3)) 2010. 368p. 16.99 (978-0-06-143304-7(7)) HarperCollins Pubs.

—The Wee Free Men. (Tiffany Aching Ser.). (YA). (gr. 8). 2010. 576p. pap. 9.99 (978-0-06-201217-3(7)) 2006. 400p. reprint ed. pap. 8.99 (978-0-06-001238-0(2)) HarperCollins Pubs.

—The Wee Free Men. 2004. 19.00 (978-0-7569-3252-7(1)) Perfection Learning Corp.

—The Wee Free Men. 2006. (Discworld Ser.: 28). (YA). 19.65 (978-1-4176-2764-6(6), Turtleback) Turtleback Bks.

—Wintersmith. (YA). 2015. (Tiffany Aching Ser.: 3). (ENG.). 416p. (gr. 8). pap. 9.99 (978-0-06-243528-6(0)) 2007. (Tiffany Aching Ser.: 3). 464p. (gr. 8-12). per. 8.99 (978-0-06-089033-9(9)) 2006. (Discworld Novels Ser.). 323p. (gr. 7-12). 16.99 (978-0-06-089031-5(2), HarperTeen) 2006. (Discworld Novels Ser.). 323p. (gr. 7-12). lib. bdg. 17.89 (978-0-06-089032-2(0), HarperTeen) HarperCollins Pubs.

—Wintersmith. 2007. 450p. (gr. 7). 19.00 (978-0-7569-8091-7(7)) Perfection Learning Corp.

Price, Margaret Evans, illus. The Betty Fairy Book. 2006. (Shape Bks.). (ENG.). 16p. (J). pap. 9.95 (978-1-59583-092-0(8), Green Tiger Pr.) Laughing Elephant.

Promise, 1 vol. 2014. (Faerieground Ser.). (ENG., Illus.). 96p. (gr. 1-3). lib. bdg. 23.99 (978-1-4342-9188-2(X)) Stone Arch Bks.

Public Domain Staff. Five Little Elves. Yaccarino, Dan, illus. 2016. 16p. (J). (gr. -1 — 1). bds. 6.99 (978-0-06-225338-5(7), HarperFestival) HarperCollins Pubs.

Publications International Ltd. Staff. Storybook Paperdoll Play House Disney Fairies. 2008. (J). spiral bd. 15.98 (978-1-4127-5951-9(X), PIL Kids) Publications International, Ltd.

Publications International Ltd. Staff, ed. Disney Fairies: Bienvenuda Tinker Bell! 2011. 12p. (J). bds. 10.98 (978-1-4508-1402-7(6)) Publications International, Ltd.

—Disney Fairies: Tinker Bell (Little Look & Find) 2010. 24p. (J). 2.98 (978-1-4127-6529-9(3)) Publications International, Ltd.

—Disney Fairies: Wellcome Tinker Bell: (Lenticular Play-a-Sound Book) 2010. 14p. (J). bds. 17.98 (978-1-60553-606-4(7)) Phoenix International Publications, Inc.

—First Look & Find Little Elf. 2013. 18p. (J). bds. (978-1-4508-7093-1(7), 1450870937) Phoenix International Publications, Inc.

—My 1st Libraries Disney Classics. 2011. 10p. (J). bds. 13.98 (978-1-4508-1029-6(2)) Phoenix International Publications, Inc.

—Record Story Little Red Riding Hood. 2011. 18p. 17.98 (978-1-4508-1910-7(9)) Phoenix International Publications, Inc.

—Tinker Bell. 2009. 24p. (J). 7.98 (978-1-4127-7144-3(7), PIL Kids) Publications International, Ltd.

—Tinker Bell -Tink's Magical Day. 2011. 8p. (J). bds. (978-1-4508-0910-8(3)) Publications International, Ltd.

—Tinkerbell. 2010. 18p. (J). bds. 7.98 (978-1-60553-697-2(0)) Phoenix International Publications, Inc.

Pyykkonen, Carrie & Washington, Linda. Secrets of the Wee Free Men & Discworld: The Myths & Legends of Terry Pratchett's Multiverse. 2008. (ENG., Illus.). 288p. (YA). (gr. 8-13). pap. 21.99 (978-0-312-37243-9(4), 9780312372439, St. Martin's Griffin) St. Martin's Pr.

Quinn, Jordan. The False Fairy. McPhillips, Robert, illus. 2016. (Kingdom of Wrenly Ser.: 11). (ENG.). 128p. (J). (gr. k-4). pap. 5.99 (978-1-4814-8586-9(5), Little Simon) Little Simon.

—The False Fairy. 2016. (Kingdom of Wrenly Ser.: 11). lib. bdg. 16.00 **(978-0-606-39740-7(X))** Turtleback Bks.

Radford, Ruby Lorraine. Rose Colored Glasses. White, Iris Weddell, illus. 2011. 46p. 35.95 (978-1-258-03586-0(3)) Literary Licensing, LLC.

Radice, Teresa, et al. Tinker Bell & the Wings of Rani. Vetro, Daniela et al, illus. 2010. (Disney Fairies Ser.: 2). (ENG.). 80p. (J). (gr. 1-6). pap. 7.99 (978-1-59707-226-7(5), 9781597072267) Papercutz.

The Rainbow's End. 2003. 14.95 (978-1-929489-75-6(7)) Platinum Medallion Children's Bks.

Rakos, Lynnda, et al. Princesses, Mermaids & Fairies Coloring Book. 2012. (Dover Coloring Bks.). (ENG.). 32p. (J). (gr. -1-2). pap. 3.99 (978-0-486-48664-2(8)) Dover Pubns., Inc.

Raley, Hugh W. Erin the Excellent Elf. 2013. 20p. pap. 12.95 (978-1-4908-0533-7(8), WestBow Pr.) Author Solutions, Inc.

Ralph, Grampa. How Santa Knows. 2007. 56p. pap. 16.95 (978-1-4241-2284-4(8)) America Star Bks.

Ramirez, Ken. You, Me, Naideen & a Bee. 2009. 278p. (YA). pap. 19.95 (978-1-60619-208-5(6)) Twilight Times Bks.

Random House. Everything That Glitters Is Guy! Laguna, Fabio, illus. 2017. (Pictureback(R) Ser.). (ENG.). 16p. (J). (gr. -1-2). pap. 5.99 **(978-1-5247-1732-2(0)**, Random Hse. Bks. for Young Readers) Random Hse. Children's Bks.

—Trolls: the Deluxe Junior Novelization (DreamWorks Trolls) Random House, illus. 2016. (Junior Novel Ser.). (ENG., Illus.). 144p. (J). (gr. 2-5). 9.99 (978-0-399-55909-9(4), Random Hse. Bks. for Young Readers) Random Hse. Children's Bks.

—Trolls: the Junior Novelization (DreamWorks Trolls) Random House, illus. 2016. (Junior Novel Ser.). (ENG., Illus.). 144p. (J). (gr. 2-5). 6.99 (978-0-399-55910-5(8), Random Hse. Bks. for Young Readers) Random Hse. Children's Bks.

Random House Australia Staff & Malone, Jen. Follow Your Art. Random House Australia Staff, illus. 2016. (Stepping Stone Book(TM) Ser.). (ENG., Illus.). 208p. (J). (gr. 3-7). 12.99 (978-0-399-55747-7(4), Random Hse. Bks. for Young Readers) Random Hse. Children's Bks.

Random House Disney Staff. Peter Pan Step into Reading (Disney Peter Pan) Random House Disney Staff, illus. 2013. (Step into Reading Ser.). (ENG., Illus.). 32p. (J). (gr. -1-1). 3.99 (978-0-7364-3114-9(4), RH/Disney) Random Hse. Children's Bks.

Random House Disney Staff & Peymani, Christine. Tangled. Disney Storybook Artists Staff & Orpinas, Jean-Paul, illus. 2010. (Read-Aloud Storybook Ser.). (ENG.). 72p. (J). (gr. -1-2). 9.99 (978-0-7364-2718-0(X), RH/Disney) Random Hse. Children's Bks.

Random House Disney Staff & Smiley, Ben. Tangled. Disney Storybook Artists Staff & Ying, Victoria, illus. 2010. (Little Golden Book Ser.). (ENG.). 24p. (J). (gr. -1-2). 4.99 (978-0-7364-2684-8(1), Golden/Disney) Random Hse. Children's Bks.

Random House Editors. Disney Peter Pan. 2013. (Step into Reading Level 1 Ser.). lib. bdg. 13.55 (978-0-606-26973-5(8), Turtleback) Turtleback Bks.

—Trolls: The Junior Novelization. 2016. (Junior Novel Ser.). (ENG., Illus.). 144p. (J). (gr. 2-5). 17.20 (978-0-606-39355-3(2)) Turtleback Bks.

Random House Staff, illus. Barbie Fairytale Collection. 2011. (Step into Reading Ser.). (ENG.). 160p. (J). (gr. -1-1). pap. 7.99 (978-0-375-87255-6(8), Random Hse. Bks. for Young Readers) Random Hse. Children's Bks.

Rankine-Van Wassenhoven, Jacqueline. A Frog Named Waldor. Zhang, Annie, illus. 2008. 20p. per. 24.95 (978-1-4241-9926-6(3)) America Star Bks.

Ransom, Candice. Tooth Fairy's Night. 2017. (Step into Reading Ser.). (ENG., Illus.). 32p. (J). (gr. -1-1). 3.99 (978-0-399-55364-6(9), Random Hse. Bks. for Young Readers) Random Hse. Children's Bks.

Ranson, Erin. Woodland Fairies. Top That Publishing Staff, ed. Richards, Kirsten, illus. 2008. (Magnetic Story & Play Scene Ser.). 9p. (J). (gr. -1). bds. (978-1-84666-440-3(3), Tide Mill Pr.) Top That! Publishing PLC.

Rasheed, Winona. Sugar & Spice Fairy Tales for Girls. 2008. 69p. pap. 20.51 (978-1-4357-4619-0(8)) Lulu Pr., Inc.

Rauscher, C D. The Fairies of the Clouds. 2008. 68p. pap. 25.49 (978-1-4343-5153-1(X)) AuthorHouse.

—Matchmaking Fairies. 2011. (ENG.). 61p. pap. 20.95 (978-1-4327-6149-3(8)) Outskirts Pr., Inc.

Ray, Jane. The Dollhouse Fairy. Ray, Jane, illus. 2010. (ENG., Illus.). 32p. (J). (gr. -1-2). 16.99 (978-0-7636-4411-6(0)) Candlewick Pr.

Ray, Rebecca E. Amethyst Lily. 2012. 28p. pap. 24.95 (978-1-4626-9563-8(9)) America Star Bks.

Reader's Digest Editors & Miller, Sara. Cinderella: A Royal Wish. Disney Animators Staff, illus. 2012. (Musical Toy Ser.). (ENG.). 32p. (J). (gr. -1-2). 19.99 (978-0-7944-2701-6(4)) Reader's Digest Assn., Inc., The.

Reasoner, Charles. Peek-a-Boo Fairies. Le Ray, Marina, illus. 2013. (Charles Reasoner Peek-A-Boo Bks.). (ENG.). 10p. (gr. -1 — 1). bds. 9.99 (978-1-4795-2173-9(6)) Picture Window Bks.

Red Fox Picture Books Staff & Transworld Publishing Staff. Better Play Times. 2006. (ENG., Illus.). 24p. (J). (gr. k-k). pap. 7.95 (978-1-86230-164-1(6), Red Fox) Random House Children's Books GBR. Dist: Independent Pubs. Group.

Redinger, Robert. The Sylvan Horn: Book One of the Sylvan Chord. 2009. 220p. 25.95 (978-0-595-50536-4(8)); pap. 15.95 (978-0-595-48489-8(1)) iUniverse, Inc.

Redman, Kati. Kate & the Fairy. 2010. 32p. pap. 7.50 (978-0-557-60891-1(0)) Lulu Pr., Inc.

Rees, Gwyneth. Fairy Dreams. 2016. (Fairy Ser.: 3). (ENG., Illus.). 224p. (J). (gr. 2-4). pap. 9.99 (978-1-5098-1866-2(9)) Pan Macmillan GBR. Dist: Independent Pubs. Group.

—Fairy Gold, 1. 2nd unabr. ed. 2006. (Fairy Dust Ser.: 4). (ENG., Illus.). 208p. (J). (gr. 2-4). pap. 8.99 (978-0-330-43938-1(3)) Pan Macmillan GBR. Dist: Independent Pubs. Group.

—Fairy Rescue, 1. 2nd unabr. ed. 2007. (Fairy Dust Ser.: 5). (ENG., Illus.). 240p. (J). (gr. 2-4). pap. 8.99 (978-0-330-43971-8(5)) Pan Macmillan GBR. Dist: Independent Pubs. Group.

—Fairy Treasure. Bannister, Emily, illus. 2016. (Fairy Ser.: 2). (ENG.). 240p. (J). (gr. 2-4). pap. 9.99 (978-1-5098-1868-6(5)) Pan Macmillan GBR. Dist: Independent Pubs. Group.

—Fairy Treasure Vol. 1: A Fairy Who Needs a Friend. Bannister, Emily, illus. 2nd unabr. ed. 2004. (Fairy Dust Ser.: 2). (ENG.). 160p. (J). (gr. 2-4). pap. 9.99 (978-0-330-43730-1(5)) Pan Macmillan GBR. Dist: Independent Pubs. Group.

Reeve, Philip. Goblins. 2013. (ENG.). 352p. (J). (gr. 3-7). 17.99 (978-0-545-22220-4(6), Scholastic Pr.) Scholastic, Inc.

Reinhart, Matthew. Ever after High: an Enchanted Pop-Up Scrapbook. 2016. (ENG., Illus.). 10p. (J). (gr. 1-17). 19.99 (978-0-316-37718-8(X)) Little, Brown Bks. for Young Readers.

Reintjes, Susan B. Through the Fairy Door. Sparling, Bren M., illus. 2012. 128p. (J). pap. 16.95 (978-1-59715-085-9(1)) Chapel Hill Press, Inc.

Renee, Lindsey. What Kind of Fairy Is Merry Berry? 2010. (ENG., Illus.). 36p. (J). (gr. -1-1). 12.99 (978-0-8118-7685-8(3)) Chronicle Bks. LLC.

The Return of the Brownies. 2004. (Illus.). 260p. (J). bds. 22.50 (978-0-9749382-0-2(3)) Celestine Pr.

Return to the Crows, 1 vol. 2014. (Faerieground Ser.). (ENG., Illus.). 96p. (gr. 1-3). lib. bdg. 23.99 (978-1-4342-9187-5(1)) Stone Arch Bks.

Rex, Adam. Champions of Breakfast. 2014. (Cold Cereal Saga Ser.: 3). (ENG., Illus.). 368p. (J). (gr. 3-7). 16.99 (978-0-06-206008-2(2)) HarperCollins Pubs.

Reyes, Yazmin. Fairies vs. Wizards: The Last Battle, 1 vol. 2009. 48p. pap. 16.95 (978-1-4489-9527-1(2)) America Star Bks.

Reynolds, Mariem. The World in Between. 2008. 87p. pap. 16.95 (978-1-60672-144-5(5)) PublishAmerica, Inc.

RH Disney. Cinderella's Best Creations/Snow White & the Three Giants (Disney Princess) RH Disney, illus. 2016. (Pictureback(R) Ser.). (ENG., Illus.). 48p. (J). (gr. -1-2). pap. 5.99 (978-0-7364-3734-9(7), RH/Disney) Random Hse. Children's Bks.

— Fairy's Fire. RH Disney, illus. 2016. (Never Girls Ser.). (ENG., Illus.). 224p. (J). (gr. 1-4). 14.99 (978-0-7364-3556-7(5), RH/Disney) Random Hse. Children's Bks.

RH Disney Staff. Never Girls - In a Blink, 2 bks. in 1. Christy, Jana, illus. 2015. (Never Girls Ser.). (ENG.). 256p. (J). (gr. 1-4). 9.99 (978-0-7364-3432-4(1), RH/Disney) Random Hse. Children's Bks.

RH Disney Staff, illus. The Never Girls Collection, 4 vols. 2013. (ENG.). 128p. (J). (gr. 1-4). 23.96 (978-0-7364-3141-5(1), RH/Disney) Random Hse. Children's Bks.

Rideau, Nicole. What Is a Pookalaka? 2009. 28p. pap. 13.99 (978-1-4389-2275-1(2)) AuthorHouse.

Rigo, L. & Pagnoni, Roberta, illus. Little Elf. 2010. (ENG.). 10p. (J). (gr. -1-2). bds. 7.99 (978-0-7641-6380-7(9)) Barron's Educational Series, Inc.

Riley, Christine. Saving the Tooth Fairy. Warren, Mnetha, illus. 2005. (J). per. 16.00 (978-0-9754298-4-6(1), Ithaca Pr.) Authors & Artists Publishers of New York, Inc.

Riley, James. Half upon a Time. (Half upon a Time Ser.: 1). (ENG.). (J). (gr. 3-7). 2011. 432p. pap. 7.99 (978-1-4169-9594-4(3)) 2010. 400p. 17.99 (978-1-4169-9593-7(5)) Simon & Schuster Children's Publishing. (Aladdin).

Rininger, Alyce. Ka-Boom. Lucas, Diane, illus. 2012. 46p. pap. 13.95 (978-1-61244-069-9(X)) Halo Publishing International.

Risso, Eduardo. Mysteries of the Red Moon, Vol. 3. 2006. (SPA.). 48p. pap. 16.95 (978-1-59497-163-1(3)) Public Square Bks.

Risso, Eduardo & Trillo, Carlos. Los Misterios de la Luna Roja Vol. 2: El Ataque del Circo. 2006. (SPA., Illus.). 72p. (J). (gr. 1). per. 16.95 (978-1-59497-162-4(5)) Public Square Bks.

Rizzo, Cynthia Marie. No No, Coco. 2008. 49p. pap. 16.95 (978-1-60563-819-5(6)) America Star Bks.

Roberts, Esyllt Nest & Owen, Carys Eurwen. Elidir A'r Tylwyth Teg. 2005. (WEL., Illus.). 36p. pap. (978-0-86381-530-0(8)) Gwasg Carreg Gwalch.

Roberts, Laura Peyton. Green. 2011. (ENG.). 272p. (J). (gr. 3-7). 7.99 (978-0-440-42235-8(3), Yearling) Random Hse. Children's Bks.

Roberts, Scott A. The Rollicking Adventures of Tam O'Hare. Roberts, Scott A., illus. 2007. (ENG., Illus.). 228p. (J). (gr. 4-7). per. 16.95 (978-1-60037-289-6(9)) Morgan James Publishing.

Robinson, George. Elmer the Elf & the Magical Jingle Bells, 1 vol. Foster, Janet, illus. 2008. (ENG.). 33p. 24.95 (978-1-60610-606-8(6)) America Star Bks.

Rochelle, Warren. The Called. 2010. (ENG.). 367p. 24.95 (978-1-930846-63-0(0)) Golden Gryphon Pr.

Rodda, Emily. The Charm Bracelet. Vitale, Raoul, illus. 2003. (Fairy Realm Ser.). 128p. (J). (gr. 2-5). 8.99 (978-0-06-009583-3(0)) HarperCollins Pubs.

—The Charm Bracelet Bk. 1. Vitale, Raoul, illus. 2009. (Fairy Realm Ser.: No. 1). (ENG.). 128p. (J). (gr. 2-5). pap. 4.99 (978-0-06-009585-7(7)) HarperCollins Pubs.

—The Flower Fairies. Vitale, Raoul, illus. (Fairy Realm Ser.: No. 2). 128p. (J). 2009. (ENG.). (gr. 2-5). pap. 4.99 (978-0-06-009588-8(1)) 2003. 8.99 (978-0-06-009586-4(5)) HarperCollins Pubs.

—The Rainbow Wand. Vitale, Raoul, illus. 2007. (Fairy Realm Ser.). 116p. (gr. 3-7). 25.65 (978-1-59961-332-1(8)) Spotlight.

—The Star Cloak. Vitale, Raoul, illus. 2007. (Fairy Realm Ser.). (ENG.). 112p. (gr. 3-7). 25.65 (978-1-59961-329-1(8)) Spotlight.

—The Unicorn. Vitale, Raoul, illus. 2007. (Fairy Realm Ser.). 106p. (gr. 3-7). 25.65 (978-1-59961-328-4(X)) Spotlight.

—The Water Sprites. Vitale, Raoul, illus. 2007. (Fairy Realm Ser.). 104p. (gr. 3-7). 25.65 (978-1-59961-330-7(1)) Spotlight.

Rode, Linda & Moodie, Fiona. In the Never-Ever Wood. 2011. (Illus.). 240p. (978-0-624-04768-1(7)) NB Pubs. Ltd.

Rodriguez, AJ. Theodore Da Baer Ii: A New Beginning. 2006. 207p. pap. 24.95 (978-1-4241-1125-1(0)) America Star Bks.

Rose, Tammy Marie. Majik the Black Unicorn, 1 vol. 2009. 74p. pap. 19.95 (978-1-60749-824-7(3)) America Star Bks.

Rosen, Lucy. Disney Fairies: the Pirate Fairy: Meet Zarina the Pirate Fairy. 2014. (Passport to Reading Level 1 Ser.). (ENG., Illus.). 32p. (J). (gr. -1-3). 3.99 (978-0-316-28330-4(4)) Little, Brown Bks. for Young Readers.

Rosen, Michael. Aesop's Fables, 1 vol. Hacikyan, Talleen, illus. 2013. (ENG.). 32p. (J). (gr. -1-2). 16.95 (978-1-896580-81-4(5)) Tradewind Bks. CAN. Dist: Orca Bk. Pubs. USA.

Ross, Joel. Beast & Crown. 2017. 384p. (J). (gr. 3-7). 16.99 **(978-0-06-248459-8(1))** HarperCollins Pubs.

Ross, Tony. My Favourite Fairy Tales. Ross, Tony, illus. 2012. (ENG., Illus.). 96p. (J). (gr. -1-k). pap. 16.99 (978-1-84939-211-2(0)) Andersen Pr. GBR. Dist: Independent Pubs. Group.

Rutledge, Mary. The Toothless Tooth Fairy. 2011. 24p. pap. 12.74 (978-1-4634-6005-1(8)) AuthorHouse.

Ryan, Margaret. Magic Mistakes! Murfin, Teresa, illus. 2010. (Airy Fairy Ser.). (ENG.). 80p. (gr. 2-4). lib. bdg. 24.21 (978-1-59961-499-1(5)) Spotlight.

Safran, Sheri. The Magic Carousel: A Book & Removable 3-D Play Carousel. Safran, Sheri, illus. 2011. (ENG., Illus.). 6p. (J). (gr. -1-k). 24.99 (978-1-85707-800-8(4)) Tango Bks. GBR. Dist: Independent Pubs. Group.

Sagar, Marie. Princess Samantha? 2009. 20p. pap. 12.49 (978-1-4389-5297-0(X)) AuthorHouse.

Sandburg, Carl. Rootabaga Stories. 2011. 126p. (gr. 3-18). 24.95 (978-1-4638-9902-8(5)) Rodgers, Alan Bks.

Sandoval, Migs, illus. Goldilocks & the 3 Bears: Level 2: Learn French Through Fairy Tales. 2006. (Learn French Through Fairy Tales Ser.). (ENG & FRE.). 29p. (J). (gr. -1-3). pap. 14.95 incl. audio compact disk (978-1-891888-81-6(1)) Slangman Publishing.

Santos, Martha. The Littlest Fairy. 2013. pap. 11.95 (978-0-7414-8019-4(0)) Infinity Publishing.

Sargent-Barker, Erika. Casey Moore, the Littlest Leprechaun, 1 vol. 2010. 16p. pap. 24.95 (978-1-4489-5419-3(3)) PublishAmerica, Inc.

Saunders, George P. The Last Elf. 2007. 180p. per. 13.95 (978-0-595-40843-6(5)) iUniverse, Inc.

Saunders, Kate. Magicalamity. 2013. (ENG.). 320p. (J). (gr. 4-7). 6.99 (978-0-385-74078-4(6), Yearling) Random Hse. Children's Bks.

Saunders, Kate & Nesbit, E. Five Children on the Western Front. 2016. (J). (978-0-553-49785-4(5), Delacorte Pr) Random House Publishing Group.

Sawyer, J. Scott. The Broccoli Bush. Bozeman, Gary, illus. 2012. 36p. pap. 24.95 (978-1-4626-2501-7(0)) America Star Bks.

Saxton, Patricia. A Book of Fairies. Saxton, Patricia, illus. 2009. (ENG., Illus.). 32p. (J). (gr. 1-5). 14.95 (978-1-934860-01-4(8)) Shenanigan Bks.

Sayre, Jill K. The Fairies of Turtle Creek. 2013. 322p. 22.17 (978-0-9885066-4-0(5)); pap. 15.70 (978-0-9885066-6-4(1)) Infinity Oak Bks.

Schachner, Judy. Up, up, & Away! 2009. (Skippyjon Jones Ser.). (ENG.). 16p. (J). (gr. -1-k). pap. 5.99 (978-0-448-45082-7(8), Grosset & Dunlap) Penguin Young Readers Group.

Scheid, Petra Maria. Fairy Tales, Elves & Magicans. 2009. 82p. pap. (978-3-8391-1065-2(3)) Books on Demand GmbH.

Schlitz, Laura Amy. The Night Fairy. Barrett, Angela, illus. (ENG.). 128p. (J). (gr. 2-5). 2011. pap. 6.99 (978-0-7636-5295-1(4)) 2010. 16.99 (978-0-7636-3674-6(6)) Candlewick Pr.

—The Night Fairy, 2 vols. unabr. ed. 2010. (J). (gr. 1-4). 54.75 (978-1-4407-6983-2(4)) Recorded Bks., Inc.

Schmid, Susan Maupin. Ghost of a Chance. Marlin, Lissy, illus. 2017. (100 Dresses Ser.: 2). (ENG.). 320p. (J). (gr. 3-7). 16.99 (978-0-553-53373-6(8), Random Hse. Bks. for Young Readers) Random Hse. Children's Bks.

Scholastic, Inc. Staff. Ever after High: Yearbook. 2014. (ENG.). 96p. (J). (gr. 3-7). pap. 8.99 (978-0-545-72368-8(X)) Scholastic, Inc.

—Plan Your Destiny: A Spellbinding School Planner. 2014. (ENG.). 188p. (J). (gr. 3-7). 9.99 (978-0-545-72365-7(5)) Scholastic, Inc.

Schomp, Virginia. Brer Rabbit & the Goober Patch. 2013. (American Legends & Folktales 2 Ser.). (Illus.). 32p. (J). (gr. 6-9). pap. 10.58 (978-1-62712-014-2(9)) Cavendish Square Publishing.

Schweizer, Chris. The Trolls Will Feast! 2016. (Creeps Ser.). (ENG., Illus.). 128p. (J). (gr. 3-7). 17.95 (978-1-4197-1882-3(7), Amulet Bks.) Abrams, Inc.

Scollen, Chris. Busy Kids Sticker Storybook Gingerbread Fred. 2008. (Illus.). 12p. (J). (gr. -1-3). pap. (978-1-84610-809-9(8)) Make Believe Ideas.

—Busy Kids Sticker Storybook Goldilocks. 2008. (Illus.). 12p. (J). (gr. -1-3). pap. (978-1-84610-641-5(9)) Make Believe Ideas.

—Busy Kids Sticker Storybook Little Mermaid. 2008. (Illus.). 12p. (J). (gr. -1-3). pap. (978-1-84610-805-1(5)) Make Believe Ideas.

—Busy Kids Sticker Storybook Sleeping Beauty. 2008. (Illus.). 12p. (J). (gr. -1-3). pap. (978-1-84610-807-5(1)) Make Believe Ideas.

—Busy Kids Sticker Storybook Three Billy Goats. 2008. (Illus.). 12p. (J). (gr. -1-3). pap. (978-1-84610-803-7(9)) Make Believe Ideas.

—Busy Kids Sticker Storybook Three Little Pigs. 2008. (Illus.). 12p. (J). (gr. -1-3). pap. (978-1-84610-639-2(7)) Make Believe Ideas.

Scott, Luke. Through a Crystal Doorknob. 2012. 88p. pap. 19.95 (978-1-4626-7361-2(9)) America Star Bks.

Seaman, Kathleen. Annycole, 1 vol. 2009. 49p. pap. 16.95 (978-1-4489-1970-3(3)) America Star Bks.
Segur, Sophie. Old French Fairy Tales. Sterrett, Virginia Frances, illus. 2010. (ENG.). 296p. (gr. -1-3). pap. 19.95 (978-1-4290-1186-0(6)) Applewood Bks.
Selfors, Suzanne. The Fairy Swarm. Santat, Dan, illus. 2016. (Imaginary Veterinary Ser.: 6). (ENG.). 240p. (J). (gr. 2-7). pap. 7.99 (978-0-316-28692-3(3)) Little, Brown Bks. for Young Readers.
Seltzer, Jerry Joe. There Are Fairies in My Tub. Seltzer, Jerry Joe, illus. 2013. (Illus.). 20p. (J). 12.95 (978-1-60131-175-7(3), Castlebridge Bks.) Big Tent Bks.
Senior, Patricia. Pip & the Magic Flute. 2008. (Illus.). 40p. pap. 18.49 (978-1-4389-0023-0(6)) AuthorHouse.
Seo & So, Chong-O. The Toad Bridegroom & Other Fantastic Tales Retold. Kim, Sung-Min, illus. 2008. 125p. (J). (978-0-9768086-7-1(6)) Rienner, Lynne Pubs.
Sesame Street Staff. Fairly Furry Fairy Tales 3 bk Pack. 2007. 19.99 (978-1-59069-623-1(9)) Studio Mouse LLC.
Sexton, Shirley. Fairy with an Attitude. 2009. 142p. 22.50 (978-1-60860-616-0(3), Strategic Bk. Publishing) Strategic Book Publishing & Rights Agency (SBPRA).
Shanddaramon. Pagan Stories for Children: A Fairy's First Year in the Forest of Songs. 2011. (Illus.). 111p. (J). pap. 12.99 (978-1-257-75438-0(6)) Astor Pr.
Shannon, David. Alice the Fairy. Shannon, David, illus. (ENG., Illus.). (J). (gr. -1-k). 2009. pap. 9.95 incl. audio compact disk (978-0-545-11758-6(5)) 2004. 40p. 17.99 (978-0-439-49025-2(1), Blue Sky Pr., The) Scholastic, Inc.
—Alice the Fairy. 2004. (J). pap. (978-0-439-79165-6(0)) Scholastic, Inc.
Shannon, L. L. On Fairy Wings: Tselina. 2008. 80p. pap. 19.95 (978-1-60672-155-1(0)) America Star Bks.
Shaskan, Trisha Speed. Honestly, Red Riding Hood Was Rotten! The Story of Little Red Riding Hood as Told by the Wolf. Guerlais, Gérald, illus. 2011. (Other Side of the Story Ser.). (ENG.). 24p. (gr. 2-3). pap. 6.95 (978-1-4048-7046-8(6)); lib. bdg. 27.32 (978-1-4048-6673-7(6)) Picture Window Bks.
—Seriously, Cinderella Is So Annoying! The Story of Cinderella as Told by the Wicked Stepmother. Guerlais, Gérald, illus. 2011. (Other Side of the Story Ser.). (ENG.). 24p. (gr. 2-3). pap. 6.95 (978-1-4048-7048-2(2)); lib. bdg. 27.32 (978-1-4048-6674-4(4)) Picture Window Bks.
Shaw, Irene. Cosy Cottage. 2006. (Illus.). 48p. pap. (978-1-84401-792-8(3)) Athena Pr.
Shaw-Lott, Karen. The Binky Fairy. Marquez, Erick, illus. 2009. 12p. pap. 11.00 (978-1-60844-271-3(3)) Dog Ear Publishing, LLC.
Shepard, Aaron. The Princess Mouse: A Tale of Finland. Gore, Leonid, illus. 2008. (ENG.). 40p. (J). (gr. -1-3). 13.99 (978-1-4169-8969-1(2), Atheneum Bks. for Young Readers) Simon & Schuster Children's Publishing.
Sheryl the pearl productions, Sheryl Clayton. Teeny the Magic Genie. 2007. (Illus.). 170p. (J). per. 12.95 (978-0-9795862-0-0(8)) STR8*UP Productions.
Shirley Temple's Favorite Tales of Long Ago. 2011. 66p. 36.95 (978-1-258-04171-7(5)) Literary Licensing, LLC.
Shu, Sammy. There's a Season for All. Cone, Carl, illus. 2006. 54p. (J). (gr. -1-3). 16.95 (978-0-9778211-0-5(2), Raynestorm Bks.) Silver Rose Publishing.
Shubin, Masha. The Fairytale Fracas: A Shubin Cousins Adventure. Shubin, Jon, illus. 2012. 200p. pap. 7.95 (978-0-9792145-8-5(0)) Anno Domini.
Siems, Dorthy R. A Fairy's Wings: Set 1. 2007. (Illus.). 50p. (J). spiral bd. 15.00 net. (978-0-9794483-3-1(6)) Siems, D.R.
Silver Dolphin en Español Editors. Fairies Forever Imanes Magicos. 2006. (Illus.). 8p. (J). (gr. -1). bds. (978-970-718-370-4(5), Silver Dolphin en Español) Advanced Marketing, S. de R. L. de C. V.
Simms, Albert Clint. My Values & Morales Treasury. 2011. 114p. 32.50 (978-1-257-16162-1(8)) Lulu Pr., Inc.
Simner, Janni Lee. Bones of Faerie. (Bones of Faerie Trilogy Ser.). (YA). 2010. (ENG.). 256p. (gr. 7-11). pap. 9.99 (978-0-375-84565-9(8), Random Hse. Bks. for Young Readers) 2009. 247p. (978-0-375-84564-2(X)) Random Hse. Children's Bks.
—Faerie After. 2013. 264p. (YA). pap. (978-0-375-87118-4(7)) Random Hse., Inc.
Simon, Nadine. Flickers of True Destiny. 2010. 58p. pap. 11.95 (978-1-60860-948-2(0), Eloquent Bks.) Strategic Book Publishing & Rights Agency (SBPRA).
Simplicity, Barberella. Uh-Oh, My Foogle Flopped! 2008. 20p. pap. 18.50 (978-1-60693-088-5(5), Eloquent Bks.) Strategic Book Publishing & Rights Agency (SBPRA).
Sims, Anthony. Princess Zoe. 2012. (Illus.). 44p. pap. 24.40 (978-1-4772-2365-9(7)) AuthorHouse.
Sisler, Celeste. Disney Fairies: Meet Rosetta. 2015. (Passport to Reading Level 1 Ser.). (J). lib. bdg. 13.55 (978-0-606-37212-1(1)) Turtleback Bks.
—Disney Fairies: Bedtime Fairy Stories: a Treasury. 2014. (ENG., Illus.). 272p. (J). (gr. -1-3). 11.99 (978-0-316-28339-7(8)) Little, Brown Bks. for Young Readers.
—Disney Fairies: Love, Tinker Bell. 2014. (ENG., Illus.). 10p. (J). (gr. -1 — 1). bds. 6.99 (978-0-316-28347-2(9)) Little, Brown Bks. for Young Readers.
—Disney Fairies: Meet the Fairies: A Collection of Reading Adventures. 2015. (Passport to Reading Level 1 Ser.). (ENG., Illus.). 160p. (J). (gr. -1-3). 9.99 (978-0-316-33739-7(0)) Little, Brown Bks. for Young Readers.
—Disney Fairies: the Perfect Pumpkin. 2015. (ENG., Illus.). 10p. (J). (gr. -1 — 1). bds. 6.99 (978-0-316-37854-3(2)) Little, Brown Bks. for Young Readers.
—Disney Fairies: Tink & Friends Story Collection. 2014. (ENG., Illus.). 160p. (J). (gr. -1-3). 11.99 (978-0-316-28336-6(3)) Little, Brown Bks. for Young Readers.
Sisler, Celeste & Fox, Jennifer. Meet Fawn. 2015. (Passport to Reading Level 1 Ser.). (ENG., Illus.). 32p. (J). (gr. -1-3). pap. 3.99 (978-0-316-28350-2(9)) Little, Brown Bks. for Young Readers.
Skead, Robert. Elves Can't Kick. 2005. 84p. per. 7.99 (978-1-929478-66-8(6)) Cross Training Publishing.
Slater, Teddy. The Luckiest St. Patrick's Day Ever! Long, Ethan, illus. (J). 2008. (ENG.). 32p. (gr. -1-3). pap. 5.99 (978-0-545-03943-7(6), Cartwheel Bks.) 2007. (978-0-439-86648-4(0)) Scholastic, Inc.
Sloper, Gilly. The Fairies of Jenny's Field. 2017. (ENG.). 82p. (J). pap. 10.95 **(978-1-78554-802-4(6)**, 5163a57c-1291-40be-a1f1-b331dccdee8a) Austin, Stan AUS. Dist: Bookmasters Distribution.
Small, Lily. Bella the Bunny. 2015. (Fairy Animals of Misty Wood Ser.: 2). (ENG., Illus.). 144p. (J). (gr. k-3). pap. 5.99 (978-1-62779-142-7(6), 9781627791427, Holt, Henry & Co. Bks. For Young Readers) Holt, Henry & Co.
—Chloe the Kitten. 2015. (Fairy Animals of Misty Wood Ser.: 1). (ENG., Illus.). 144p. (J). (gr. k-3). pap. 5.99 (978-1-62779-141-0(8), 9781627791410, Holt, Henry & Co. Bks. For Young Readers) Holt, Henry & Co.
—Chloe the Kitten, Bella the Bunny, & Paddy the Puppy Bindup. Small, Lily, illus. 2016. (Fairy Animals of Misty Wood Ser.). (ENG., Illus.). 416p. (J). pap. 10.99 (978-1-250-11397-9(0), 9781250113979, Holt, Henry & Co. Bks. For Young Readers) Holt, Henry & Co.
—Daisy the Deer. 2017. (Fairy Animals of Misty Wood Ser.). (ENG., Illus.). 144p. (J). pap. 5.99 (978-1-62779-738-2(6), 9781627797382, Holt, Henry & Co. Bks. For Young Readers) Holt, Henry & Co.
—Hailey the Hedgehog. 2016. (Fairy Animals of Misty Wood Ser.). (ENG., Illus.). 144p. (J). pap. 5.99 (978-1-62779-735-1(1), 9781627797351, Holt, Henry & Co. Bks. For Young Readers) Holt, Henry & Co.
—Kylie the Kitten. 2017. (Fairy Animals of Misty Wood Ser.). (ENG., Illus.). 144p. (J). pap. 5.99 **(978-1-250-12698-6(3)**, 9781250126986, Holt, Henry & Co. Bks. For Young Readers) Holt, Henry & Co.
—Mia the Mouse. 2015. (Fairy Animals of Misty Wood Ser.: 4). (ENG., Illus.). 144p. (J). (gr. k-3). pap. 5.99 (978-1-62779-144-1(2), 9781627791441, Holt, Henry & Co. Bks. For Young Readers) Holt, Henry & Co.
—Paddy the Puppy. 2015. (Fairy Animals of Misty Wood Ser.: 3). (ENG., Illus.). 144p. (J). (gr. k-3). pap. 5.99 (978-1-62779-143-4(4), 9781627791434, Holt, Henry & Co. Bks. For Young Readers) Holt, Henry & Co.
—Penelope the Pony. 2017. (Fairy Animals of Misty Wood Ser.). (ENG., Illus.). 144p. (J). pap. 5.99 **(978-1-250-12700-6(9)**, 9781250127006, Holt, Henry & Co. Bks. For Young Readers) Holt, Henry & Co.
—Poppy the Pony. 2016. (Fairy Animals of Misty Wood Ser.). (ENG., Illus.). 144p. (J). pap. 5.99 (978-1-62779-734-4(3), 9781627797344, Holt, Henry & Co. Bks. For Young Readers) Holt, Henry & Co.
—Poppy the Pony: Fairy Animals of Misty Wood. 2016. (Fairy Animals of Misty Wood Ser.: 5). (ENG.). 144p. (J). (gr. 1-3). 16.00 (978-0-606-39295-2(5)) Turtleback Bks.
Smallman, Steve. Troll Two — Three — Four. Temairik, Jaime, illus. 2014. (J). (978-1-4723-2925-7(2)) Parragon Bk. Service Ltd.
Smith, C. E. Giants of Anglesey. 2011. 176p. (gr. 4-6). 23.95 (978-1-4620-3361-4(X)) iUniverse, Inc.
Smith, Carrie. Little Red Riding Hood: Classic Tales Edition. Kelley, Gerald, illus. 2011. (Classic Tales Ser.). (J). (978-1-936258-75-8(7)) Benchmark Education Co.
Smith, David. Nature's Garden. 2009. 132p. 22.50 (978-1-60693-169-1(5), Eloquent Bks.) Strategic Book Publishing & Rights Agency (SBPRA).
Smith, Debora Ann Baker. The Magnificent Fairy Party. 2010. (Illus.). 30p. pap. 13.00 (978-1-60911-404-6(3), Eloquent Bks.) Strategic Book Publishing & Rights Agency (SBPRA).
Smith, Gloria. Annie Elf & Bo Bo Robin. 2012. 24p. 24.95 (978-1-62709-650-8(7)); pap. 24.95 (978-1-4626-9087-9(4)) America Star Bks.
—Annie Elf Meets Mitty Mouse. Smith, Claire, illus. 2012. 24p. 29.95 (978-1-62709-398-9(2)) America Star Bks.
Smith, Jane Denitz. Fairy Dust. Date not set. (J). (gr. 3-7). mass mkt. 4.99 (978-0-06-440961-2(9)) HarperCollins Pubs.
Smith, Laura Rountree. The Fairy Babies. Dulin, Dorothy, illus. 2011. 126p. 40.95 (978-1-258-09063-0(5)) Literary Licensing, LLC.
Smith, Tiffany Nicole. Bex Carter: Middle School Disaster (and Reluctant Fairy Protector) 2013. 148p. pap. 6.99 (978-0-9893075-8-1(1)) Twisted Spice.
Smyth, Jimmy. The Fairy Princess. 2013. 34p. pap. (978-0-9569314-5-0(6)) Smith, Jimmy.
—The Lost Fairy. 2013. 34p. pap. (978-0-9569314-3-6(X)) Smith, Jimmy.
Snedeker, Erin. The Littlest Elf: Marvin Mcgee & the Candle of Fate. Drotleff, David J., illus. 2010. 44p. pap. 15.50 (978-1-60911-194-6(X), Eloquent Bks.) Strategic Book Publishing & Rights Agency (SBPRA).
Snell, Gordon. Tina & the Tooth Fairy. Blodau, Peter, illus. 2005. (Pandas Ser.: 31). (ENG.). 64p. (J). pap. 9.95 (978-0-86278-601-4(0)) O'Brien Pr., Ltd., The IRL. Dist: Dufour Editions, Inc.
Snyder, Laurel. Up & down the Scratchy Mountains. Dorman, Brandon & Call, Greg, illus. 2010. (ENG.). 272p. (J). (gr. 3-7). 7.99 (978-0-375-84720-2(0), Yearling) Random Hse. Children's Bks.
Soenen, Chantal. Sally: And the Wheel of the Year. 2012. (Illus.). 124p. (gr. 4-6). 27.45 (978-1-4772-3038-1(6)); pap. 15.18 (978-1-4772-3037-4(8)) AuthorHouse.
Sommer, Carl. Androcles & the Lion. Martinez, Jorge, illus. 2014. (Sommer-Time Story Classics Ser.). (ENG.). 32p. (J). (gr. k-4). 16.95 (978-1-57537-075-0(1)) Advance Publishing, Inc.
Sonneborn, Scott. The Computer Meltdown. Lozano, Omar, illus. 2015. (North Police Ser.). (ENG.). 32p. (gr. k-2). lib. bdg. 21.32 (978-1-4795-6485-9(0)) Picture Window Bks.
—Meet the South Police. Lozano, Omar, illus. 2015. (North Police Ser.). (ENG.). 32p. (gr. k-2). lib. bdg. 21.32 (978-1-4795-6486-6(9)) Picture Window Bks.
—The Mystery of Santa's Sleigh. Lozano, Omar, illus. 2015. (North Police Ser.). (ENG.). 32p. (gr. k-2). lib. bdg. 21.32 (978-1-4795-6484-2(2)) Picture Window Bks.
—The North Police. Lozano, Omar, illus. 2015. (North Police Ser.). (ENG.). 32p. (gr. k-2). 85.28 (978-1-4795-7929-7(7)) Picture Window Bks.
—The Reindeer Games. Lozano, Omar, illus. 2015. (North Police Ser.). (ENG.). 32p. (gr. k-2). lib. bdg. 21.32 (978-1-4795-6487-3(7)) Picture Window Bks.
Sowerby, Githa & Sowerby, Millicent, illus. Cinderella. 2012. (J). (978-1-59583-458-4(3)) Laughing Elephant.
Sperring, Mark. The Sunflower Sword. Latimer, Miriam, illus. 2011. (Andersen Press Picture Bks). (ENG.). 32p. (J). (gr. -1-3). 16.95 (978-0-7613-7486-2(8)) Lerner Publishing Group.
Spinner, Stephanie. The Nutcracker. Malone, Peter, illus. 2008. (ENG.). 40p. (J). (gr. -1-2). 17.99 (978-0-375-84464-5(3), Knopf Bks. for Young Readers) Random Hse. Children's Bks.
Spitzer, Linda & Myers, Sarah. Tales of the Paper Bag Fairies/Color Version. 2005. 54p. (J). pap. 14.95 (978-1-4116-4095-5(0)) Lulu Pr., Inc.
Squillace, Elisa, illus. Three Wishes. 2009. (First Reading Level 1 Ser.). 32p. (J). (gr. 2). 6.99 (978-0-7945-2278-0(5), Usborne) EDC Publishing.
St-Onge, Donna Na-Tasa Katherine. The Eye of Isis, 1 vol. 2009. 155p. pap. 24.95 (978-1-60836-986-7(2)) America Star Bks.
Stanek, Robert, pseud. Have a Sleepover. 2008. (ENG., Illus.). 28p. (J). pap. 5.29 (978-1-57545-189-3(1)) RP Media.
—Illustrated Encyclopedia of Ruin Mist. 2008. pap. 15.00 (978-1-57545-157-2(3), Ruin Mist Pubns.) RP Media.
—The Kingdoms & the Elves of the Reaches Ii (Reader's Choice Edition, Keeper Martin's Tales Book 2) 2008. (Illus.). 244p. pap. 15.95 (978-1-57545-197-8(2)) RP Media.
—The Kingdoms & the Elves of the Reaches IV. 2009. (Keeper Martin's Tales Ser.: Bk. 4). (Illus.). 188p. (YA). per. 18.95 (978-1-57545-508-2(0), Reagent Pr. Signature Editions) RP Media.
Stanford, K. B. Sixteen Wishes (paperback) 2008. 188p. pap. 15.47 (978-1-4357-1773-2(2)) Lulu Pr., Inc.
Staniszewski, Anna. My Sort of Fairy Tale Ending. 2013. (My Very Unfairy Tale Life Ser.: 3). (ENG.). 224p. (J). (gr. 4-7). pap. 6.99 (978-1-4022-7933-1(7), Sourcebooks Jabberwocky) Sourcebooks, Inc.
—My Very Unfairy Tale Life. 2011. (My Very Unfairy Tale Life Ser.: 1). (ENG.). 208p. (J). (gr. 4-7). pap. 7.99 (978-1-4022-5946-3(8), Sourcebooks Jabberwocky) Sourcebooks, Inc.
Stanley, Mandy. The Fairy Ball. Stanley, Mandy, illus. 2010. (Lettice Ser.). (ENG., Illus.). 32p. (J). (gr. -1-k). pap. 9.95 (978-0-00-720195-2(8), HarperCollins Children's Bks.) HarperCollins Pubs. Ltd. GBR. Dist: HarperCollins Pubs.
Stanton, Andy. Mr. Gum & the Biscuit Billionaire. Tazzyman, David, illus. 2013. (Mr Gum Ser.: 2). (ENG.). 144p. (J). (gr. 2-5). pap. 7.99 (978-1-4052-2815-2(6)) Egmont Bks., Ltd. GBR. Dist: Independent Pubs. Group.
Star the Tooth Fairy from Treasure Cloud Shares Secrets with You! 2006. (J). per. 9.99 (978-0-9792992-0-9(9)) Twinkle Bks.
Star the Tooth Fairy Is Checking on You! 2004. (J). per. 9.99 (978-0-9792992-2-3(5)) Twinkle Bks.
Star the Tooth Fairy Wants to Know if You Need Braces? 2006. (J). per. 9.99 (978-0-9792992-1-6(7)) Twinkle Bks.
Starwolf. The Dance of the Fire Fairies: Book 1-Just Beginning. 2013. 140p. pap. 47.39 (978-1-4907-1009-9(4)) Trafford Publishing.
Stegman-Bourgeois, Karen M. Trollerella. Long, Ethan, illus. 2006. (ENG.). 32p. (J). (gr. -1-3). 14.95 (978-0-8234-1918-0(5)) Holiday Hse., Inc.
Stephanie K. McMahan. Sylvan Tales: The Secret of Elfenore. 2009. 152p. 22.95 (978-1-4401-5507-9(0)); pap. 12.95 (978-1-4401-5505-5(4)) iUniverse, Inc.
Stepp, Shirley. Santa Lost His Cell Phone. 2012. 24p. 24.95 (978-1-4626-5479-6(7)) America Star Bks.
Stever, Susan. When Fairies Die. 2010. 28p. pap. 13.99 (978-1-4520-0912-4(0)) AuthorHouse.
Stewart-Goodair, Madonna. Key to the Golden Gates: The Mystic Soldier, Book 1, 1 vol. 2009. 48p. pap. 16.95 (978-1-61582-625-4(4)) PublishAmerica, Inc.
—The Mystic Soldier: Warlock of Fire, 1 vol. 2009. 57p. pap. 16.95 (978-1-61546-840-9(4)) PublishAmerica, Inc.
Stiefvater, Maggie. Lament: The Faerie Queen's Deception. 2008. (Lament Novel Ser.: 1). (ENG., Illus.). 336p. (YA). (gr. 8-18). pap. 9.95 (978-0-7387-1370-0(8), 1286181, Flux) North Star Editions.
Stilton, Geronimo. The Amazing Voyage. Barozzi, Danilo, illus. 2011. (Geronimo Stilton & the Kingdom of Fantasy Ser.: 3). (ENG.). 320p. (J). (gr. 2-5). 14.99 (978-0-545-30771-0(6)) Scholastic, Inc.
—The Dragon of Fortune: An Epic Kingdom of Fantasy Adventure. 2017. (Geronimo Stilton & the Kingdom of Fantasy Ser.: 2). (ENG.). 592p. (J). (gr. 2-5). 19.99 **(978-1-338-15939-4(9)**, Scholastic Paperbacks) Scholastic, Inc.
—The Hour of Magic. 2016. (ENG.). 320p. (J). (gr. 2-5). 14.99 (978-0-545-82336-4(6)) Scholastic, Inc.
—The Quest for Paradise. 2010. (Geronimo Stilton & the Kingdom of Fantasy Ser.: 2). (ENG.). 320p. (J). (gr. 2-5). 14.99 (978-0-545-25307-9(1)) Scholastic, Inc.
—The Ship of Secrets (Geronimo Stilton & the Kingdom of Fantasy #10) 2017. (Geronimo Stilton & the Kingdom of Fantasy Ser.: 10). (ENG.). 320p. (J). (gr. 2-5). 14.99 **(978-1-338-08880-9(7)**, Scholastic Paperbacks) Scholastic, Inc.
Stilton, Geronimo. The Volcano of Fire. 2013. (Geronimo Stilton & the Kingdom of Fantasy Ser.: Bk. 5). (ENG., Illus.). 320p. (J). (gr. 2-5). 14.99 (978-0-545-55625-5(2), Scholastic Paperbacks) Scholastic, Inc.
Stilton, Geronimo & Dami, Elisabetta. The Phoenix of Destiny. 2015. (Geronimo Stilton & the Kingdom of Fantasy: Special Edition Ser.). (ENG.). 592p. (J). (gr. 2-5). 19.99 (978-0-545-82907-6(0)) Scholastic, Inc.
Stilton, Thea. The Secret of the Fairies. 2013. (Thea Stilton Ser.). (ENG., Illus.). 320p. (J). (gr. 2-5). 14.99 (978-0-545-55624-8(4), Scholastic Paperbacks) Scholastic, Inc.
Stimson, James, illus. The Bully Goat Grim: A Maynard Moose Tale. 2012. (ENG.). 32p. (J). (gr. 2-6). 18.95 (978-0-87483-952-4(1)) August Hse. Pubs., Inc.
Stine, R. L. Planet of the Lawn Gnomes. 2012. (Goosebumps Most Wanted Ser.: 1). (ENG.). 160p. (J). (gr. 3-7). pap. 6.99 (978-0-545-41798-3(8), Scholastic Paperbacks) Scholastic, Inc.
—Planet of the Lawn Gnomes. 2012. (Goosebumps Most Wanted Ser.: 1). lib. bdg. 17.20 (978-0-606-26761-8(1), Turtleback) Turtleback Bks.
Stinson, Jennifer. Even Fairies Fart. Ashdown, Rebecca, illus. 2017. 32p. (J). (gr. -1-3). 17.99 **(978-0-06-243623-8(6))** HarperCollins Pubs.
Stites, Theresa. The Orange Peel. 2007. 20p. per. 24.95 (978-1-4241-8580-1(7)) America Star Bks.
Stockham, Jess, illus. The Steadfast Tin Soldier. 2012. (Flip-Up Fairy Tales Ser.). (ENG.). 24p. (J). audio compact disk (978-1-84643-516-4(1)) Child's Play International Ltd.
Stockton, Frank Richard. Ting-A-Ling. 2011. 88p. 20.95 (978-1-4638-9581-5(X)) Rodgers, Alan Bks.
—Ting-a-Ling Tales. 2008. 88p. pap. 8.95 (978-1-60664-056-2(9)) Aegypan.
—What Might Have Been Expected. 2006. 304p. per. 23.99 (978-1-4255-3050-1(8)) Michigan Publishing.
Storer, June. Kip, Brenda & Emong's Adventure. 2013. 164p. pap. (978-0-9923603-1-3(5)) BWM Bks.
Stower, Adam. Troll & the Oliver. Stower, Adam, illus. 2015. (ENG., Illus.). 40p. (J). (gr. -1-2). 16.99 (978-0-7636-7956-9(9), Templar) Candlewick Pr.
Straffi, Iginio. Winx Club: Magic Collection. 2014. (ENG.). 832p. (J). pap. 19.99 (978-1-4215-7729-6(1)) Viz Media.
Strangway, Melissa. Finding Hope. 2012. 82p. pap. 11.65 (978-1-61933-676-6(6)) FastPrncil, Inc.
Strasser, Todd. Is That an Unlucky Leprechaun in Your Lunch? Swearingen, Greg, illus. 2009. 184p. (J). (978-0-545-11034-1(3)) Scholastic, Inc.
Streit, Jakob. Puck Trhe Gnome. Mitchell, David S., ed. Kuettel, Nina, tr. from GER. 2004. Orig. Title: Puck der Zwerg. (ENG., Illus.). 100p. (J). per. 15.00 (978-1-888365-54-2(4)) Waldorf Publications.
Stringer. Fairies of Spencer Meadow: Fairy Tales. 2004. (Illus.). 60p. 19.95 (978-1-4120-1667-4(3)) Trafford Publishing.
Studio Mouse Staff. Tinkerbell's Magic Story Writer. rev. ed. 2008. (ENG.). 30p. (J). 14.99 (978-1-59069-616-3(6)) Studio Mouse LLC.
Suen, Anastasia. The Tooth Fairy. Myer, Ed, illus. 2012. (ENG.). 24p. (gr. k-1). pap. 8.95 (978-1-61810-307-9(5)) Rourke Educational Media.
The Sugar Cup. 2014. (Candy Fairies Ser.: 14). (ENG., Illus.). 128p. (J). (gr. 2-5). pap. 5.99 (978-1-4814-0607-9(8), Aladdin) Simon & Schuster Children's Publishing.
The Sugar Cup. 2014. (Candy Fairies Ser.: 14). (ENG., Illus.). 128p. (J). (gr. 2-5). 16.99 (978-1-4814-0608-6(6), Simon & Schuster/Paula Wiseman Bks.) Simon & Schuster/Paula Wiseman Bks.
Sullivan, E. J. How Santa Got His Elves. Eldredge, Ernie, illus. 2006. (J). (gr. -1-3). 9.95 (978-1-58173-308-2(9)) Sweetwater Pr.
Sullivan, Laura L. Under the Green Hill. 2011. (ENG.). 336p. (J). (gr. 4-8). pap. 17.99 (978-0-312-55149-0(5), 9780312551490) Square Fish.
Summers, Gillian. The Goblin's Curse: The Scions of Shadow Trilogy, Book 3. 2012. (Faire Folk Saga Ser.: 6). (ENG.). 312p. (YA). pap. 9.95 (978-0-7387-1572-8(7), Flux) North Star Editions.
—The Quicksilver Faire: The Scions of Shadow Trilogy, Book 2. 2011. (Faire Folk Saga Ser.: 5). (ENG.). 336p. (YA). pap. 9.95 (978-0-7387-1571-1(9), Flux) North Star Editions.
—Shadows of the Redwood Bk. 1, Bk. 1. 2010. (Faire Folk Saga Ser.: 4). (ENG.). 336p. (YA). (gr. 7-18). pap. 9.95 (978-0-7387-1552-0(2), Flux) North Star Editions.
Sutliff, Jamie. The Land of Nen-Us-Yok. Blumberg, Christine A., ed. Evans, Kevin C., illus. 2007. 256p. pap. 10.95 (978-0-9712867-4-0(4)) Cold River Pubns.
Swain, Heather. Selfish Elf Wish. 2010. (ENG.). 208p. (YA). (gr. 7-18). 8.99 (978-0-14-241674-7(6), Speak) Penguin Young Readers Group.
Tao, Teri. Cowherd Boy & Weaver Girl. 2008. (ENG.). 48p. pap. 5.99 (978-1-930655-05-8(3)) Golden Peach Publishing.
Taylor, C. J. Spirits, Fairies, & Merpeople: Native Stories of Other Worlds. 2009. (ENG., Illus.). 40p. (J). (gr. 2-4). 19.95 (978-0-88776-872-9(5), Tundra Bks.) Tundra Bks. CAN. Dist: Penguin Random Hse. LLC.
Taylor, Dereen. The Fairy Midnight Surprise Party. Stone, Lyn, illus. 2012. (ENG.). 12p. (J). (gr. 1-6). 16.99 (978-1-84322-763-2(0)) Anness Publishing GBR. Dist: National Bk. Network.
Taylor, Laini. Blackbringer. 2009. (Dreamdark Ser.: 1). (ENG., Illus.). 368p. (YA). (gr. 7-18). 9.99 (978-0-14-241168-1(X), Firebird) Penguin Young Readers Group.
Taylor, Lillian Webb. Santa's Musical Elves. 2009. 28p. pap. 12.25 (978-1-60860-146-2(3), Strategic Bk. Publishing) Strategic Book Publishing & Rights Agency (SBPRA).
Taylor, Roy. Matilda's Magic Wand: Dreamland Adventure. 2008. 36p. (J). pap. 9.00 (978-0-8059-7716-5(3)) Dorrance Publishing Co., Inc.
Tegen, Katherine Brown. The Story of the Leprechaun. Lambert, Sally Anne, illus. 2011. (J). lib. bdg. 14.89 (978-0-06-143085-5(4)); (ENG.). 40p. (gr. -1-3). 12.99 (978-0-06-143086-2(2)) HarperCollins Pubs.
Thaler, Mike. St. Patrick's Day from the Black Lagoon. Lee, Jared, illus. 2011. 61p. (J). (978-0-545-27328-2(5)) Scholastic, Inc.
Theule, Larissa. Fat & Bones. Doyle, Adam S., illus. 2014. (ENG.). 112p. (J). (gr. 4-12). lib. bdg. 16.95 (978-1-4677-0825-8(9), Carolrhoda Bks.) Lerner Publishing Group.
Thimble The Fairy. Thimble the Fairy's Acorns & Tea. Patch, Sebastion, illus. 2011. (ENG.). 48p. (J). 8.99 (978-0-9827304-0-9(3)) Eleve Publishing.
Thomas Nelson. Sparkle Town Fairies Daphne the Diamond Fairy Sticker Activity Book. 2016. (ENG.). 48p. (J). (gr. -1-7). pap. (978-1-78598-679-6(1)) Make Believe Ideas.
—Sparkle Town Fairies Rosie the Ruby Fairy. 2016. (ENG.). 32p. (J). (gr. -1-7). pap. (978-1-78598-439-6(X)) Make Believe Ideas.
—Sparkle Town Fairies Susie the Sapphire Fairy. 2016. (ENG.). 32p. (J). (gr. -1-7). pap. (978-1-78598-656-7(2)) Make Believe Ideas.
Thomas, Novene. The Enchanted Opera: Supernaturally Enchanting & Spiritually Enlightening. 2013. 192p. pap. 13.95 (978-1-62212-986-7(5), Strategic Bk. Publishing) Strategic Book Publishing & Rights Agency (SBPRA).
Thompson, Gabrielle. Daphne the Diamond Fairy. 2016. (ENG., Illus.). 32p. (J). (gr. -1-2). pap. (978-1-78598-140-1(4)) Make Believe Ideas.

Thompson, Kate. The Last of the High Kings. (YA). 2010. (New Policeman Trilogy Ser.: 2). (ENG.). 336p. (gr. 8). pap. 8.99 *(978-0-06-117597-8(8)*, Greenwillow Bks.) 2008. 323p. (gr. 7-18). lib. bdg. 17.89 *(978-0-06-117596-1(X)*, HarperTeen) HarperCollins Pubs.

—The New Policeman. (Illus.). 2008. (New Policeman Trilogy Ser.: 1). (ENG.). 464p. (YA). (gr. 8-12). pap. 9.99 *(978-0-06-117429-2(7))* 2007. 448p. (J). (gr. 7-12). 16.99 *(978-0-06-117427-8(0))* HarperCollins Pubs. (Greenwillow Bks.).

—The New Policeman. pap. 1.00 *(978-1-4074-4550-2(2))* Recorded Bks., Inc.

Thomson, Sarah L. Cinderella, 0 vols. Ceccoli, Nicoletta, illus. 2012. (ENG.). 32p. (J). (gr. k-3). 17.99 *(978-0-7614-6170-8(1)*, 9780761461708, Amazon Children's Publishing) Amazon Publishing.

Thorogood, Keith. Milli Meets the Tooth Fairies. 2009. (Illus.). 48p. pap. *(978-1-84748-456-7(5))* Athena Pr.

Thorpe, Kiki. Before the Bell. RH Disney Staff & Christy, Jana, illus. 2015. (Never Girls Ser.: 9). (ENG.). 128p. (J). (gr. 1-4). lib. bdg. 12.99 *(978-0-7364-8167-0(2)*, RH/Disney) Random Hse. Children's Bks.

—Before the Bell. RH Disney Staff, illus. 2015. (Never Girls Ser.: No. 9). (ENG.). 128p. (J). (gr. 1-4). 5.99 *(978-0-7364-3304-4(X)*, RH/Disney) Random Hse. Children's Bks.

—A Dandelion Wish. Christy, Jana, illus. 2013. (Stepping Stone Book Series: No. 3). (ENG.). 128p. (J). (gr. 1-4). 5.99 *(978-0-7364-2796-8(1)*, RH/Disney) Random Hse. Children's Bks.

—A Dandelion Wish. Christy, Jana, illus. 2013. (Never Girls Ser.: 3). lib. bdg. 16.00 *(978-0-606-32199-0(3)*, Turtleback) Turtleback Bks.

—A Fairy's Gift (Disney: the Never Girls) Christy, Jana, illus. 2017. (Never Girls Ser.). (ENG.). 224p. (J). (gr. 1-4). 7.99 ***(978-0-7364-3773-8(8)***, RH/Disney) Random Hse. Children's Bks.

—A Fairy's Gift (Disney: the Never Girls) RH Disney Staff, illus. 2015. (Never Girls Ser.). (ENG.). 224p. (J). (gr. 1-4). 14.99 *(978-0-7364-3278-8(7)*, RH/Disney) Random Hse. Children's Bks.

—Far from Shore. RH Disney Staff & Christy, Jana, illus. 2015. (Never Girls Ser.: 8). (ENG.). 128p. (J). (gr. 1-4). lib. bdg. 12.99 *(978-0-7364-8166-3(4)*, RH/Disney) Random Hse. Children's Bks.

—Far from Shore. 2015. (Never Girls Ser.: 8). lib. bdg. 16.00 *(978-0-606-36384-6(X))* Turtleback Bks.

—From the Mist. Christy, Jana, illus. 2013. (Stepping Stone Book Series: No. 4). (ENG.). 128p. (J). (gr. 1-4). 5.99 *(978-0-7364-2797-5(X)*, RH/Disney) Random Hse. Children's Bks.

—In a Blink. Christy, Jana & Random House Disney Staff, illus. 2013. (Never Girls Ser.: 1). (ENG.). 128p. (J). (gr. 1-4). 5.99 *(978-0-7364-2794-4(5)*, RH/Disney) Random Hse. Children's Bks.

—In a Blink. Christy, Jana, illus. 2013. (Never Girls Ser.: 1). lib. bdg. 16.00 *(978-0-606-26977-3(0)*, Turtleback) Turtleback Bks.

—In the Game. 2016. (Never Girls Ser.: 12). lib. bdg. 16.00 *(978-0-606-38468-1(5))* Turtleback Bks.

—Into the Waves. Christy, Jana, illus. 2016. (Never Girls Ser.: 11). (ENG.). 128p. (J). (gr. 1-4). 5.99 *(978-0-7364-3525-3(5)*, RH/Disney) Random Hse. Children's Bks.

—Into the Waves. 2016. (Never Girls Ser.: 11). lib. bdg. 16.00 *(978-0-606-38467-4(7))* Turtleback Bks.

—Never Girls #12: in the Game (Disney: the Never Girls) Christy, Jana, illus. 2016. (Never Girls Ser.: 12). (ENG.). 128p. (J). (gr. 1-4). 5.99 *(978-0-7364-3527-7(1)*, RH/Disney) Random Hse. Children's Bks.

—Never Girls: Books 1-3 (Disney: the Never Girls) Christy, Jana, illus. 2016. (Never Girls Ser.). (ENG.). 384p. (J). (gr. 1-4). 15.99 *(978-0-7364-3580-2(8)*, RH/Disney) Random Hse. Children's Bks.

—Never Girls: Books 4-6 (Disney: the Never Girls) Christy, Jana, illus. 2016. (Never Girls Ser.). (ENG.). 384p. (J). (gr. 1-4). 15.99 *(978-0-7364-3581-9(6)*, RH/Disney) Random Hse. Children's Bks.

—The Never Girls Collection, 4 vols. Christy, Jana & RH Disney Staff, illus. 2014. (ENG.). 640p. (J). (gr. 1-4). 24.96 *(978-0-7364-3184-2(5)*, RH/Disney) Random Hse. Children's Bks.

—The Never Girls Volume 3: Books 7-9 (Disney: the Never Girls) Christy, Jana, illus. 2017. (Never Girls Ser.). (ENG.). 384p. (J). (gr. 1-4). 15.99 ***(978-0-7364-3819-3(X)***, RH/Disney) Random Hse. Children's Bks.

—On the Trail. Christy, Jana, illus. 2015. (Never Girls Ser.: No. 10). (ENG.). 128p. (J). (gr. 1-4). 5.99 *(978-0-7364-3306-8(6)*, RH/Disney) Random Hse. Children's Bks.

—A Pinch of Magic. Christy, Jana, illus. 2014. (Never Girls Ser.: No. 7). (ENG.). 128p. (J). (gr. 1-4). 5.99 *(978-0-7364-3097-5(0)*, RH/Disney) Random Hse. Children's Bks.

—A Pinch of Magic. 2014. (Never Girls Ser.: 7). lib. bdg. 16.00 *(978-0-606-36008-1(5))* Turtleback Bks.

—The Space Between. Christy, Jana & Random House Disney Staff, illus. 2013. (Never Girls Ser.: 2). (ENG.). 128p. (J). (gr. 1-4). 5.99 *(978-0-7364-2795-1(3)*, RH/Disney) Random Hse. Children's Bks.

—The Space Between. Christy, Jana, illus. 2013. (Never Girls Ser.: 2). lib. bdg. 16.00 *(978-0-606-26974-2(6)*, Turtleback) Turtleback Bks.

—Under the Lagoon. Christy, Jana, illus. 2016. (Never Girls Ser.). (ENG.). 128p. (J). (gr. 1-4). 5.99 *(978-0-7364-3529-1(8)*, RH/Disney) Random Hse. Children's Bks.

—Wedding Wings. Christy, Jana, illus. 2014. (Stepping Stone Book Series: No. 5). (ENG.). 128p. (J). (gr. 1-4). 5.99 *(978-0-7364-3077-7(6)*, RH/Disney) Random Hse. Children's Bks.

—Wedding Wings. 2014. (Never Girls Ser.: 5). lib. bdg. 16.00 *(978-0-606-35544-5(8))* Turtleback Bks.

—The Woods Beyond. Christy, Jana, illus. 2014. (ENG.). 128p. (J). (gr. 1-4). (Never Girls Ser.: 6). lib. bdg. 12.99 *(978-0-7364-8148-9(6))*; (Stepping Stone Book Ser.: No. 6). 5.99 *(978-0-7364-3096-8(2))* Random Hse. Children's Bks. (RH/Disney).

—The Woods Beyond. Christy, Jana, illus. 2014. (Never Girls Ser.: 6). lib. bdg. 16.00 *(978-0-606-35545-2(6))* Turtleback Bks.

Thrasher, Amanda M. Mischief in the Mushroom Patch. 2013. (ENG., Illus.). 146p. (J). (gr. 2-4). pap. 7.99 *(978-0-9888568-0-6(8))* Rising Phoenix Pr.

—Mischief in the Mushroom Patch. 174p. 2010. pap. 10.50 *(978-1-60911-165-6(6))* 2009. 23.75 *(978-1-60860-722-8(4))* Strategic Book Publishing & Rights Agency (SBPRA). (Strategic Bk. Publishing).

Tillworth, Mary. A Fairytale Adventure. 2014. (Dora the Explorer 8X8 Ser.). lib. bdg. 13.55 *(978-0-606-36010-4(7))* Turtleback Bks.

—Mariposa & the Fairy Princess (Barbie) Golden Books, illus. 2013. (Little Golden Book Ser.). (ENG.). 24p. (J). (-k). 3.99 *(978-0-449-81633-2(8)*, Golden Bks.) Random Hse. Children's Bks.

—Welcome to Fairy World! (Dora & Friends) Aikins, David, illus. 2015. (Glitter Picturebook Ser.). (ENG.). 16p. (J). (gr. -1-2). 5.99 *(978-0-553-52119-1(5)*, Random Hse. Bks. for Young Readers) Random Hse. Children's Bks.

Timmo. The Magic Christmas Fairy. 2008. 32p. pap. 17.95 *(978-1-4092-3707-5(9))* Lulu Pr., Inc.

Tinker Bell Theater Book. 2008. 32p. 14.95 *(978-1-4231-1727-8(1))* Disney Pr.

Tolley, Diane Stringham & Tolley, Diane Stringam. Carving Angels. 2011. 121p. (J). 12.99 *(978-1-59955-944-5(7)*, Bonneville Bks.) Cedar Fort, Inc./CFI Distribution.

Tomlinson, Heather. Aurelie: A Faerie Tale. 2010. (ENG.). 208p. (YA). (gr. 7-12). pap. 18.99 *(978-0-312-60275-8(8)*, 9780312602758) Square Fish.

Tompert, Ann. Grandfather Tang's Story. Parker, Robert A., illus. 2015. (ENG.). 32p. (J). (gr. -1-2). 16.99 *(978-0-517-57487-4(X)*, Knopf Bks. for Young Readers) Random Hse. Children's Bks.

Tooth, Lucy. Star the Tooth Fairy Haunted by Mr. Jack-O-Lantern in Pumpkinland! 2009. 36p. 16.95 *(978-0-557-10300-3(2))* Lulu Pr., Inc.

—Star the Tooth Fairy Is Checking on You! 2009. 36p. 16.95 *(978-0-557-07500-3(9))* Lulu Pr., Inc.

—Star the Tooth Fairy Wants to Know If You Need Braces? 2009. 36p. 16.95 *(978-0-557-07542-3(4))* Lulu Pr., Inc.

Top That Publishing Staff, ed. Goldilocks & Three Bears. 2006. (Illus.). 10p. bds. *(978-1-905359-93-6(4))* Top That! Publishing PLC.

—The Midnight Fairies. Atkins, Alison, illus. 2007. (Sparkling Jigsaw Book Ser.). 10p. (J). (gr. -1). bds. *(978-1-84666-278-2(8)*, Tide Mill Pr.) Top That! Publishing PLC.

Torribio, Penelope. The Magic in You: From vacant lot to community Garden. 2011. 40p. pap. 16.46 *(978-1-4269-5723-9(8))* Trafford Publishing.

Trabert, John. Gnome Chronicles. 2007. 172p. pap. 4.99 *(978-1-4343-1950-0(4))* AuthorHouse.

Treadwell, Harriette Taylor & Free, Margaret. The Primer. 2009. (Illus.). 118p. pap. *(978-1-904808-26-8(3))* Evertype.

Tripp, Ben. The Accidental Highwayman: Being the Tale of Kit Bristol, His Horse Midnight, a Mysterious Princess, & Sundry Magical Persons Besides. 2014. (ENG., Illus.). 304p. (YA). (gr. 6). 17.99 *(978-0-7653-3549-4(2)*, Tor Teen) Doherty, Tom Assocs., LLC.

Trondheim, Lewis & Robin, Theirry. Happy Halloween, Li'l Santa. Robin, Thierry, illus. 2003. (ENG.). 51p. 14.95 *(978-1-56163-361-6(5))* NBM Publishing Co.

Troupe, Thomas Kingsley. The Problems with Goblins, 1 vol. Gilpin, Stephen, illus. 2013. (Furry & Flo Ser.). (ENG.). 128p. (gr. 2-3). 8.95 *(978-1-62370-034-8(5))*; lib. bdg. 25.32 *(978-1-4342-5042-1(3))* Stone Arch Bks.

Tulien, Sean. Super Billy Goats Gruff. Cano, Fernando, illus. 2015. (Far Out Fairy Tales Ser.). (ENG.). 40p. (gr. 3-4). lib. bdg. 25.32 *(978-1-4342-9649-8(0))* Stone Arch Bks.

Turin, Adela. La Herencia del Hada. Bosnia, Nella, illus. (SPA.). 40p. (J). (gr. 3-5). *(978-84-264-3556-9(4))* Editorial Lumen ESP. Dist: Lectorum Pubns., Inc.

Twinkle the Tooth Fairy. 2008. (Deluxe Charm Book Ser.). 12p. *(978-1-4075-3332-2(0))* Parragon, Inc.

Twinkle Toes. 2011. (ENG., Illus.). 36p. (J). 15.95 *(978-1-935268-57-4(0))* Halo Publishing International.

Tyler, Joe, et al. Grimm Fairy Tales Volume 4, Vol. 4. Tedesco, Ralph & Gregory, Raven, eds. 2012. (ENG., Illus.). 168p. (YA). pap. 12.99 *(978-0-9817550-0-7(3)*, 9780981755007) Zenescope Entertainment.

Uglow, Lorna. The Fairy in the Potting Shed. 2008. (Illus.). 100p. pap. 28.99 *(978-1-4389-0858-8(X))* AuthorHouse.

Ullman, Barb Bentler. Whistle Bright Magic: A Nutfolk Tale. 2010. 224p. (J). (gr. 3-7). 16.99 *(978-0-06-188286-9(0))* HarperCollins Pubs.

Umansky, Kaye. Pongwiffy. Smedley, Chris, illus. 2007. (ENG.). 192p. (J). (gr. 3-7). pap. 10.95 *(978-1-4169-6832-0(6)*, Simon & Schuster/Paula Wiseman Bks.) Simon & Schuster/Paula Wiseman Bks.

Uncle Henry. How the Tooth Fairy, of All People, Saved the Day Uncle Henry, illus. 100th ed. 2004. (Illus.). 64p. pap. 5.99 *(978-1-932568-00-4(X)*, UHB001) Uncle Henry Bks.

Uribe, Veronica & Espopo. El Libro de Oro de las Fabulas. Bravo, Constanza, illus. 2004. (SPA.). 126p. (J). (gr. -1-3). 9.99 *(978-980-257-209-0(8))* Ekare, Ediciones VEN. Dist: Lectorum Pubns., Inc.

Vaitonis, Steven. Edison the Christmas Elf & the Imperfect Perfect Toy. Blue, Melissa, illus. 2014. 32p. (J). (gr. -1-1). pap. 12.95 *(978-1-939930-33-0(2)*, Belle Isle Bks.) Brandylane Pubs., Inc.

Valente, Catherynne M. The Boy Who Lost Fairyland. Juan, Ana, illus. 2015. (Fairyland Ser.: 4). (ENG.). 240p. (YA). (gr. 5-9). 16.99 *(978-1-250-02349-0(1)*, 9781250023490) Feiwel & Friends.

—The Girl Who Circumnavigated Fairyland in a Ship of Her Own Making. Juan, Ana, illus. 2011. (Fairyland Ser.: 1). (ENG.). 256p. (YA). (gr. 5-9). 16.99 *(978-0-312-64961-6(4)*, 9780312649616) Feiwel & Friends.

—The Girl Who Circumnavigated Fairyland in a Ship of Her Own Making. 2012. (CHI & ENG., Illus.). 304p. (J). (gr. 5-8). pap. *(978-986-6026-24-9(8))* Muses Publishing Hse.

—The Girl Who Circumnavigated Fairyland in a Ship of Her Own Making. Juan, Ana, illus. 2012. (Fairyland Ser.: 1). (ENG.). 288p. (YA). (gr. 5-9). pap. 7.99 *(978-1-250-01019-3(5)*, 9781250010193) Square Fish.

—The Girl Who Fell Beneath Fairyland & Led the Revels There. Juan, Ana, illus. 2013. (Fairyland Ser.: 2). (ENG.). 304p. (YA). (gr. 5-9). pap. 7.99 *(978-1-250-03412-0(4)*, 9781250034120) Square Fish.

Valenzuela, Kristine. A Secret Sydney. Green, Matthew, illus. 2013. 44p. (J). pap. *(978-0-9872061-6-9(8))* DoctorZed Publishing.

Van Fleet, Mara. Little Color Fairies. Van Fleet, Mara, illus. 2012. (ENG., Illus.). 16p. (J). (gr. -1-1). 14.99 *(978-1-4424-3434-9(1)*, Simon & Schuster/Paula Wiseman Bks.) Simon & Schuster/Paula Wiseman Bks.

Van King, L. The Dwarf in the Drawer: A Mischievous Parody. Gonzales, Chuck, illus. 2013. (ENG.). 32p. (J). 19.99 *(978-1-250-04143-2(0)*, 9781250041432) Square Fish.

Vance, L. K. Jennadi. 2006. 73p. pap. 16.95 *(978-1-4241-1574-7(4))* PublishAmerica, Inc.

VanDervleuten, Robin M. Keepers of the Fairy Moon. 2013. 200p. *(978-1-4602-1429-9(3))*; pap. *(978-1-4602-1430-5(7))* FriesenPress.

Vanek, Karen & Schmidt, Sharon Vanek. Santa Claus Meets the Tooth Fairy. 2012. 44p. pap. 21.99 *(978-1-4772-4535-4(9))* AuthorHouse.

Vasquez, Natalie, illus. The Pied Piper of Hamelin. 2012. (Flip-Up Fairy Tales Ser.). (ENG.). 24p. (J). audio compact disk *(978-1-84643-519-5(6))* Child's Play International Ltd.

Vernon, Ursula. When Fairies Go Bad, No. 7. 7th ed. 2012. (Dragonbreath Ser.: 7). (ENG.). 208p. (J). (gr. 3-7). 12.99 *(978-0-8037-3678-8(9)*, Dial Bks) Penguin Young Readers Group.

Victoria's Tooth Fairy Adventure. 2007. (Illus.). 40p. (J). 19.95 *(978-0-615-17773-1(5))* Created For You.

Vine, Joshua M. Gnomey & Froggie. 2012. 46p. pap. 21.99 *(978-1-4772-7529-0(0))* AuthorHouse.

Vitale, Mary Ann. The Water Lily Fairy. 2011. 28p. (gr. 2-4). pap. 16.95 *(978-1-4567-6639-9(2))* AuthorHouse.

Viz Media. Fairy Dreams. 2013. (Winx Club Ser.: 5). lib. bdg. 17.20 *(978-0-606-26987-2(8)*, Turtleback) Turtleback Bks.

VIZ Media, . & Straffi, Iginio. WINX Club, Vol. 7. 2013. (ENG.). 96p. (J). pap. 6.99 *(978-1-4215-4204-1(8))* Viz Media.

—WINX Club, Vol. 8. 2013. (ENG.). 96p. (J). pap. 6.99 *(978-1-4215-4205-8(6))* Viz Media.

VIZ Media Staff. WINX Club, Vol. 1. 2012. (ENG.). 96p. (J). pap. 6.99 *(978-1-4215-4159-4(9))* Viz Media.

VIZ Media Staff & Staffi, Iginio. WINX Club, Vol. 5. 2013. (ENG.). 96p. (J). pap. 6.99 *(978-1-4215-4163-1(7))* Viz Media.

VIZ Media Staff & Straffi, Iginio. WINX Club, Vol. 2. 2012. (ENG.). 96p. (J). pap. 6.99 *(978-1-4215-4160-0(2))* Viz Media.

—WINX Club, Vol. 6. 2013. (ENG.). 96p. (J). pap. 6.99 *(978-1-4215-4203-4(X))* Viz Media.

Vornholt, John. The Troll Treasure. 2003. (Troll King Trilogy). 185p. (J). (gr. 5-9). 12.65 *(978-0-7569-3954-0(2))* Perfection Learning Corp.

Wagman, Diana. Extraordinary October. 2016. (ENG.). 264p. (YA). (gr. 6). 18.95 *(978-1-63246-036-3(X))* Ig Publishing, Inc.

Wahl, Jan. Elf Night. Weevers, Peter, illus. 2005. (Picture Bks.). 32p. (gr. k-2). 15.25 *(978-1-57505-512-1(0))* Lerner Publishing Group.

Wakeman, Lars. Prince Harry the Hairy Prince: A hairy fairy Tale. 2011. 24p. (gr. -1). pap. 12.56 *(978-1-4269-6304-9(1))* Trafford Publishing.

Wallace, Adam. How to Catch a Leprechaun. Elkerton, Andy, illus. 2016. (ENG.). 32p. (J). (-6). 10.99 *(978-1-4926-3291-7(0)*, 9781492632917, Sourcebooks Jabberwocky) Sourcebooks, Inc.

—How to Catch the Tooth Fairy. Elkerton, Andy, illus. 2016. (ENG.). 32p. (J). (-6). 10.99 *(978-1-4926-3733-2(5)*, 9781492637332, Sourcebooks Jabberwocky) Sourcebooks, Inc.

Wallace, Adam. Only YOU Can Save Christmas! A Help-The-Elf Adventure. Bruner, Garth, illus. 2017. (ENG.). 40p. (J). (gr. 1-5). 16.99 ***(978-1-4926-4136-0(7)***, Sourcebooks Jabberwocky) Sourcebooks, Inc.

Walsh, Stephen & O'Donovan, Marita. Brendan & the Blarney Stone. Le Feyer, Diane, illus. 2017. (ENG.). 32p. (J). pap. 13.00 ***(978-1-84717-723-0(9))*** O'Brien Pr., Ltd., The IRL. Dist: Dufour Editions, Inc.

Walter, Wendy D. & Walter, Wendy D. Return of the Dullaith: Ambril's Tale. 2012. (Illus.). 318p. (J). pap. 15.99 *(978-0-9857147-1-0(9)*, Angry Bicycle) Walter, Wendy D.

Walters, Adam. Little Red Riding Hood. 2012. 29.95 *(978-0-7414-7325-7(9))* Infinity Publishing.

Walters, Eric. Tagged, 1 vol. 2013. (Orca Soundings Ser.). (ENG.). 136p. (YA). (gr. 8-12). 16.95 *(978-1-4598-0168-4(7))*; pap. 9.95 *(978-1-4598-0167-7(9))* Orca Bk. Pubs. USA.

Walther, William. A Collection of Fairy Tales: Volume One. 2007. (YA). per. 12.95 *(978-0-9795087-0-7(3))* Ctr. Stage Puppets.

Wampol, Pam & Woodard, Heather. Oscar's Dreamzz: The Story of Santa's First Elf. 2013. 40p. pap. *(978-1-4602-0414-6(X))* FriesenPress.

Ward, Helen. Moon Dog. 2005. (Illus.). 40p. (J). *(978-1-84011-864-3(4))* Templar Publishing.

Ward, Nick. The Naughty Fairy's Naughty Surprise! 2008. 24p. (J). 15.99 *(978-1-60010-269-1(7))* Diamond Bk. Distributors.

Webb, Carla. The Magic in Believing: The Tooth Fairies. Lee, Kim, illus. (Magic in Believing Ser.). 36p. (J). (gr. k-5). *(978-0-9705726-0-8(3))* Ageless Treasures.

Weber, Jen Funk. Thimbletack's Activity Book. 2008. (Spiderwick Chronicles). (ENG., Illus.). 64p. (J). (gr. 2-7). pap. 4.99 *(978-1-4169-4954-1(2)*, Simon Scribbles) Simon Scribbles.

Webster, Wendy. Magicus Perfecticum. 2009. (Illus.). 60p. pap. 11.49 *(978-1-4490-0765-2(1))* AuthorHouse.

Weigl Publishers, creator. The Crow & the Raven: Why Should You Be Yourself? 2013. (AV2 Animated Storytime Ser.: Vol. 12). (ENG., Illus.). 32p. (J). (gr. -1-3). lib. bdg. 29.99 *(978-1-62127-916-7(2)*, AV2 by Weigl) Weigl Pubs., Inc.

—The Farmer & His Sons: Why Should You Work Hard? 2013. (AV2 Animated Storytime Ser.: Vol. 13). (ENG., Illus.). 32p. (J). (gr. -1-3). lib. bdg. 29.99 *(978-1-62127-917-4(0)*, AV2 by Weigl) Weigl Pubs., Inc.

—The Shoemaker & His Medicine: Why Should You Tell the Truth? 2013. (AV2 Animated Storytime Ser.: Vol. 18). (ENG., Illus.). 32p. (J). (gr. -1-3). lib. bdg. 29.99 *(978-1-62127-922-8(7)*, AV2 by Weigl) Weigl Pubs., Inc.

—The Snake & His Tail: How Can You Support Your Team? 2013. (AV2 Animated Storytime Ser.: Vol. 19). (ENG., Illus.). 32p. (J). (gr. -1-3). lib. bdg. 29.99 *(978-1-62127-923-5(5)*, AV2 by Weigl) Weigl Pubs., Inc.

—The Wild Donkey & the Tame Donkey: Why Should You Not Judge Others by Their Appearance? 2013. (AV2 Animated Storytime Ser.: Vol. 20). (ENG., Illus.). 32p. (J). (gr. -1-3). lib. bdg. 29.99 *(978-1-62127-924-2(3)*, AV2 by Weigl) Weigl Pubs., Inc.

Weinberg, Jennifer. Surprise for a Princess. 2003. (Disney Princess Step into Reading Ser.). (gr. -1-2). 13.55 *(978-0-613-73686-2(9)*, Turtleback) Turtleback Bks.

Weinshall Liberman, Judith. The Little Fairy. 2013. 32p. 21.99 *(978-1-4575-2351-9(5))* Dog Ear Publishing, LLC.

Weiser, Joey. The Ride Home. 2007. (ENG., Illus.). 168p. pap. 8.95 *(978-0-9770304-4-6(X)*, 9780977030446) AdHouse Bks.

Welch, Lance. Counting with the Fairies of Willow Garden. Welch, Mark, illus. 2012. 16p. pap. 24.95 *(978-1-62709-544-0(6))* America Star Bks.

Werlin, Nancy. Extraordinary. 2011. (ENG.). 416p. (YA). (gr. 7-18). 9.99 *(978-0-14-241974-8(5)*, Speak) Penguin Young Readers Group.

—Impossible. 2011. 11.04 *(978-0-7848-3488-6(1)*, Everbind) Marco Bk. Co.

—Impossible. 2009. (ENG.). 384p. (YA). (gr. 7-18). 9.99 *(978-0-14-241491-0(3)*, Speak) Penguin Young Readers Group.

—Unthinkable. 2014. (ENG.). 416p. (YA). (gr. 7). pap. 9.99 *(978-0-14-242620-3(2)*, Speak) Penguin Young Readers Group.

West, Robert. Escape from the Drooling Octopod!, 1 vol. 2008. (Star-Fighters of Murphy Street Ser.). (ENG., Illus.). 144p. (J). (gr. 4-7). pap. 6.99 *(978-0-310-71427-9(3))* Zonderkidz.

Weston Woods Staff, creator. Harold's Fairy Tale. 2011. 38.75 *(978-0-439-72706-8(5))*; 18.95 *(978-0-439-72704-4(9))* Weston Woods Studios, Inc.

—James Marshall's Cinderella. 2011. 38.75 *(978-0-439-84886-2(5))* Weston Woods Studios, Inc.

—Ready, Freddy! #1: Tooth Trouble. 2011. 20.95 *(978-0-545-05008-1(1))* Weston Woods Studios, Inc.

—A Story-A Story. 2011. 29.95 *(978-0-439-73521-6(1))*; 18.95 *(978-0-439-72891-1(6))* Weston Woods Studios, Inc.

—A Story-Astory. 2011. 38.75 *(978-0-439-72892-8(4))* Weston Woods Studios, Inc.

Wexler, Django. The Forbidden Library. 2015. (ENG., Illus.). 400p. (J). (gr. 5). 8.99 *(978-0-14-242681-4(4)*, Puffin Books) Penguin Young Readers Group.

—The Mad Apprentice. Jansson, Alexander, illus. 2015. (Forbidden Library). (ENG.). 352p. (J). (gr. 5). 16.99 *(978-0-8037-3976-5(1)*, Kathy Dawson Books) Penguin Young Readers Group.

Whelan, Susan & Merritt, Susanne. The Great Sock Secret. Jones, Gwynneth, illus. 2016. (ENG.). 32p. (J). (gr. -1-3). 17.99 *(978-1-925335-24-8(0)*, EK Bks.) Exisle Publishing Pty Ltd. AUS. Dist: Hachette Bk. Group.

Whelan, Susan, et al. The Sugar & Spice Collection. 2016. (ENG., Illus.). 32p. (J). (gr. -1-3). 34.99 *(978-1-925335-20-0(8)*, EK Bks.) Exisle Publishing Pty Ltd. AUS. Dist: Hachette Bk. Group.

White, Kiersten. Endlessly. (Paranormalcy Ser.: 3). (ENG.). (YA). (gr. 8). 2013. 416p. pap. 9.99 *(978-0-06-198589-8(9))* 2012. 400p. 17.99 *(978-0-06-198588-1(0))* HarperCollins Pubs. (HarperTeen).

—Paranormalcy. (Paranormalcy Ser.: 1). (ENG.). (YA). (gr. 8). 2011. 368p. pap. 9.99 *(978-0-06-198585-0(6))* 2010. 352p. 16.99 *(978-0-06-198584-3(8))* HarperCollins Pubs. (HarperTeen).

—Supernaturally. (Paranormalcy Ser.: 2). (ENG.). (YA). (gr. 8). 2012. 368p. pap. 9.99 *(978-0-06-198587-4(2))* 2011. 352p. 17.99 *(978-0-06-198586-7(4))* HarperCollins Pubs. (HarperTeen).

Whitney, A. D. T. Patience Strong's Outings by Mrs a D T Whitney. 2006. 236p. per. 20.99 *(978-1-4255-2007-6(3))* Michigan Publishing.

Whitney, Gary & Whitney, Molly. Thistle Downe. 2016. (ENG., Illus.). 128p. (J). 22.95 *(978-1-942945-14-7(0)*, 9781942945147) Bright Sky Pr.

Wicke, Ed. Wicked Tales. 2006. (ENG., Illus.). 156p. (J). per. 9.99 *(978-0-9677652-7-3(7)*, BlacknBlue Pr. UK) Blacknblue Pr.

Wilcox, Leah. Waking Beauty. Monks, Lydia, illus. 2011. (ENG.). 32p. (J). (gr. -1-k). pap. 6.99 *(978-0-14-241538-2(3)*, Puffin Books) Penguin Young Readers Group.

Wilde, Oscar. The Happy Prince. Russell, P. Craig, illus. 5th ed. 2012. (Fairy Tales of Oscar Wilde Ser.: 5). (ENG.). 32p. (J). (gr. 4-7). 16.99 *(978-1-56163-626-6(6))* NBM Publishing Co.

Wilhelm, Richard, ed. The Chinese Fairy Book. Martens, Frederick H., tr. from CHI. Hood, George W., illus. 2008. (Dover Children's Classics Ser.). (ENG.). 224p. (J). (gr. 4-7). pap. 10.95 *(978-0-486-45435-1(5))* Dover Pubns., Inc.

Wilkinson, James H. Yang the Dragon Tells His Story, Halloween Train. Blake, Carol, illus. 2013. 32p. pap. 15.99 *(978-0-9886360-0-2(X))* Kids At Heart Publishing, LLC.

Williams, Hap. Henry the Elf. Graves, Michelle, illus. 2012. 28p. pap. 24.95 *(978-1-4626-8999-6(X))* America Star Bks.

Williams, Sean J. Fashion Fairies. 2012. 52p. pap. 37.37 *(978-1-4691-7600-0(9))* Xlibris Corp.

Wilson, Barbara-Ann. The Faerie Hill. 2008. 124p. pap. 20.95 *(978-1-4092-1845-6(7))* Lulu Pr., Inc.

Wilson, David Cramb. The Day that the Fairies stole Badger! 2008. 40p. pap. 9.95 *(978-0-557-00247-4(8))* Lulu Pr., Inc.

Wilson, N. D. The Chestnut King. 2011. (100 Cupboards Ser.: 3). (ENG., Illus.). 512p. (J). (gr. 3-7). 8.99 *(978-0-375-83886-6(4)*, Yearling) Random Hse. Children's Bks.

Winslow, Tim, illus. The Kingdom of Avalon. 2005. 48p. (J). *(978-0-9748505-0-4(0))* Winslow's Art.

Winterspell. 2014. (ENG., Illus.). 464p. (YA). (gr. 9). 17.99 *(978-1-4424-6598-5(0)*, Simon & Schuster Bks. For Young Readers) Simon & Schuster Bks. For Young Readers.

Wolfe, Bradley W. Upside Downside Up. 2009. 144p. 27.99 *(978-0-557-11670-6(8))* Lulu Pr., Inc.

Wolfe, Greg. Shmelf the Hanukkah Elf. McWilliam, Howard, illus. 2016. (ENG.). 32p. (J). 16.99 *(978-1-61963-521-0(6)*,

9781619635210, Bloomsbury USA Childrens) Bloomsbury Publishing USA.

Wolfe, Robert Hewitt. The Goblin Crown: Billy Smith & the Goblins, Book 1. 2016. (Billy Smith & the Goblins Ser.: 1). (ENG.). 336p. (J). 31.95 *(978-1-68162-613-0(6))* Turner Publishing Co.

Wood, Kate. Twinkle. 2013. (Illus.). 60p. (J). pap. 20.00 *(978-0-9837334-9-2(X))* Digi-Tall Media.

Wood, Maryrose. How I Found the Perfect Dress. 2008. (ENG.). 240p. (YA). (gr. 9-18). 11.00 *(978-0-425-21939-3(9),* Berkley) Penguin Publishing Group.

Wooding, Chris. Poison. 2006. 1.00 *(978-1-4237-9048-8(0))* Recorded Bks., Inc.

Woods, Titania. Fairy Dust. 2011. (ENG., Illus.). 128p. (J). (gr. 2-4). pap. 11.99 *(978-1-4088-2023-0(4),* 9781408820230, Bloomsbury USA Childrens) Bloomsbury Publishing USA.

—Friends Forever. 2011. (ENG., Illus.). 128p. (J). (gr. 2-4). pap. 11.99 *(978-1-4088-2022-3(6),* 9781408820223, Bloomsbury USA Childrens) Bloomsbury Publishing USA.

Yolen, Jane. Come to the Fairies' Ball. Lippincott, Gary, illus. 2009. (ENG.). 32p. (J). (gr. 2-4). 17.95 *(978-1-59078-464-8(2),* Wordsong) Boyds Mills Pr.

—Curse of the Thirteenth Fey: The True Tale of Sleeping Beauty. 2013. (ENG.). 320p. (J). (gr. 5). pap. 7.99 *(978-0-14-242761-3(6),* Puffin Books) Penguin Young Readers Group.

Young, Amy. The Mud Fairy. Young, Amy, illus. 2010. (ENG., Illus.). 40p. (J). (gr. -1-1). 16.99 *(978-1-59990-104-6(8),* 9781599901046, Bloomsbury USA Childrens) Bloomsbury Publishing USA.

Younger, David. The Mysterious Moat Maiden: A Wandering Firefly Fairy Adventure, 1 vol. 2009. 15p. pap. 24.95 *(978-1-61546-213-1(9))* America Star Bks.

Zahler, Diane. A True Princess. 2012. (ENG.). 208p. (J). (gr. 3-7). pap. 6.99 *(978-0-06-182503-3(4))* HarperCollins Pubs.

Zalesny, Michele. The Elves' Surprise. 2008. (ENG., Illus.). 20p. (J). pap. 9.25 *(978-1-935125-06-8(0))* Robertson Publishing.

Zettel, Sarah. Bad Luck Girl. 2014. (American Fairy Trilogy Ser.: Bk. 3). (ENG.). 368p. (YA). (gr. 7). 17.99 *(978-0-375-86940-2(9),* Random Hse. Bks. for Young Readers) Random Hse. Children's Bks.

—Dust Girl. (American Fairy Trilogy Ser.: Bk. 1). (ENG.). (YA). (gr. 7). 2013. 320p. pap. 9.99 *(978-0-375-87381-2(3),* Bluefire) 2012. 304p. 17.99 *(978-0-375-86938-9(7),* Random Hse. Bks. for Young Readers) Random Hse. Children's Bks.

—Golden Girl. 2013. (American Fairy Trilogy Ser.: Bk. 2). (ENG.). 320p. (YA). (gr. 7). 17.99 *(978-0-375-86939-6(5),* Random Hse. Bks. for Young Readers) Random Hse. Children's Bks.

Zimmerman, Diana S. Kandide & the Secret of the Mists. Gadd, Maxine, illus. 2008. (Calabiyau Chronicles Ser.: Bk. 1). 296p. (YA). (gr. 5-18). 17.99 *(978-0-9794328-3-5(9))*;Bk. 1. 289p. (J). (gr. 4-7). pap. 9.99 *(978-0-9794328-2-8(0))* Noesis Publishing.

FAIRIES—POETRY

Alexander-Heaton, Susanne & Gabriell, Chantal T. The ABC Field Guide to Faeries: Inspiring Reminders of Respect for Ourselves, Each Other & the Environment. 2nd ed. 2009. *(978-0-9813048-0-9(X))* Alexander-Heaton, Susanne.

Barker, Cecily M. Flower Fairies Box Set. 2007. pap. 16.99 *(978-0-7232-5976-3(3))* Penguin Publishing Group.

Barker, Cicely Mary. Flower Fairies of the Autumn. 2008. (Flower Fairies Ser.). (ENG.). 56p. (J). (gr. -1-2). 7.99 *(978-0-7232-6317-3(5),* Warne) Penguin Young Readers Group.

Gordon, Elizabeth. Flower Children: The Little Cousins of the Field & Garden. Ross, M. T., illus. 2008. (ENG.). 96p. (J). (gr. -1-3). pap. 14.95 *(978-1-55709-086-7(6))* Applewood Bks.

FAIRS

see also Exhibitions; Markets

Allan, Delores. Magical Moments with Roy & Toni: Fun at the Fair. 2011. 28p. pap. 13.59 *(978-1-4634-1546-4(X))* AuthorHouse.

Cartogna, Eileen. Fun at the Fair: Learning Subtraction Facts To 10. 2009. (Math for the REAL World Ser.). 12p. (gr. 1-2). pap. 5.90 *(978-0-8239-8846-4(5),* Rosen Classroom) Rosen Publishing Group, Inc., The.

Color All About: A Giant Coloring Book about the County Fair: the County Fair. 2004. (SPA & ENG., Illus.). 36p. (J). *(978-1-59949-004-5(8))* Food Marketing Consultants, Inc.

Color All About: The County Fair: A Giant Coloring Book about Having Fun When the Fair Comes to Town. 2004. (Illus.). (J). *(978-0-9763307-6-9(8))* Food Marketing Consultants, Inc.

Cooling, Wendy. The Camel Fair. 2005. (Collins Big Cat Ser.). (ENG.). 48p. (J). (gr. 2-3). pap. 7.99 *(978-0-00-718634-1(7))* HarperCollins Pubs. Ltd. GBR. Dist: Independent Pubs. Group.

Jackson, Robert. Meet Me in St. Louis: A Trip to the 1904 World's Fair. 2004. (ENG., Illus.). 144p. (J). (gr. 3-18). 17.99 *(978-0-06-009267-2(X))* HarperCollins Pubs.

Justice, Lee S. & Benchmark Education Co., LLC. The Chicago World's Fair Of 1893: Bigger, Brighter, & Better! 2014. (Text Connections Ser.). (J). (gr. 3). *(978-1-4509-9654-9(X))* Benchmark Education Co.

Libal, Joyce. Getting Ready for the Fair: Crafts, Projects, & Prize-Winning Animals. 2009. (Youth in Rural North America Ser.). (Illus.). 96p. (YA). (gr. 3-7). lib. bdg. 22.95 *(978-1-4222-0019-3(1))* Mason Crest.

FAIRS—FICTION

Anastasio, Dina. Math Fun at the Fair & Matemáticas divertidas en la Feria: 6 English, 6 Spanish Adaptations. 2011. (ENG & SPA.). (J). 75.00 net. *(978-1-4108-5639-5(9))* Benchmark Education Co.

Anderson, Jane. Inspector Insector. 2005. (J). pap. *(978-1-4108-4196-4(0))* Benchmark Education Co.

Axelrod, Amy & McGinley-Nally, Sharon. Pigs at Odds: Fun with Math & Games. McGinley-Nally, Sharon, illus. 2003. (ENG., Illus.). 40p. (J). (gr. -1-4). 7.99 *(978-0-689-86144-4(3),* Aladdin) Simon & Schuster Children's Publishing.

Ball, Georgia & Mebberson, Amy. Strawberry Shortcake, Vol. 1. 2013. (ENG., Illus.). 104p. (J). (gr. 4-8). pap. 14.99 *(978-1-937676-61-2(7),* 9781937676612) Ape Entertainment.

Ball, Nate. The Science Unfair. 2014. (Alien in My Pocket Ser.: 2). (J). lib. bdg. 14.75 *(978-0-606-35182-9(5))* Turtleback Bks.

Barrows, Annie & Blackall, Sophie. Ivy + Bean What's the Big Idea?, 1 vol. 2011. (Ivy & Bean Ser.). (ENG., Illus.). 132p. (J). (gr. 1-4). 24.21 *(978-1-59961-934-7(2))* Spotlight.

Birney, Betty G. Humphrey's School Fair Surprise. Burris, Priscilla, illus. 2016. (Humphrey's Tiny Tales Ser.: 4). (ENG.). 112p. (J). (gr. k-3). 14.99 *(978-0-399-17229-8(7),* G.P. Putnam's Sons Books for Young Readers) Penguin Young Readers Group.

—Humphrey's School Fair Surprise. 2016. (Humphrey's Tiny Tales Ser.: 04). lib. bdg. 14.75 *(978-0-606-38423-0(5))* Turtleback Bks.

Chabert, Jack. The Science Fair Is Freaky! Ricks, Sam, illus. 2016. (Eerie Elementary — Branches Ser.: bk.4). (ENG.). 96p. (J). (gr. 1-3). pap. 4.99 *(978-0-545-87368-0(1))* Scholastic, Inc.

—The Science Fair Is Freaky! 2016. (Eerie Elementary — Branches Ser.: bk.4). (ENG.). (J). lib. bdg. 14.75 *(978-0-606-38806-1(0))* Turtleback Bks.

Chaconas, Dori. Hurry down to Derry Fair. Tyler, Gillian, illus. 2011. (ENG.). 36p. (J). (gr. -1-2). 16.99 *(978-0-7636-3208-3(2))* Candlewick Pr.

Clarissa - Evaluation Guide: Evaluation Guide. 2006. (J). *(978-1-55942-402-8(8))* Witcher Productions.

Clark, Sherryl. Kim's Fake Cake Bake. McKenzie, Heath, illus. 2015. (J). pap. *(978-1-4966-0256-5(0))* Capstone Classroom.

—Kim's Super Science Day. McKenzie, Heath, illus. 2015. (J). pap. *(978-1-4966-0250-3(1))* Capstone Classroom.

Cowley, Joy. Mrs. WishyWashy & the Big Farm Fair. 2009. pap. 8.25 *(978-1-60559-231-2(5))* Hameray Publishing Group, Inc.

Crimi-Trent, Ellen & Priddy, Roger. School Fair. 2014. (Schoolies Ser.). (ENG.). 28p. (J). (gr. -1-1). 4.99 *(978-0-312-51663-5(0),* 9780312516635, Priddy Bks.) St. Martin's Pr.

Danziger, Paula. Es Dia de Feria, Amber Dorado. Ross, Tony, illus. 2007. (de Ámbar / a Is for Amber Easy-To-Read Ser.).Tr. of It's a Fair Day, Amber Brown. (SPA.). 48p. (gr. k-3). pap. 8.95 *(978-1-59820-596-1(X))* Santillana USA Publishing Co., Inc.

—It's a Fair Day, Amber Brown. Ross, Tony, illus. 2003. pap. 31.95 incl. audio compact disk *(978-1-59112-564-8(2))*; (J). (gr. -1-2). audio compact disk 28.95 *(978-1-59112-565-5(0))*; (J). (gr. -1-2). audio compact disk 28.95 *(978-1-59112-565-5(0))* Live Oak Media.

—It's a Fair Day, Amber Brown. Ross, Tony, illus. 2003. (Is for Amber Ser.). (ENG.). 48p. (J). (gr. 1-3). pap. 3.99 *(978-0-698-11982-6(7),* Penguin Young Readers) Penguin Young Readers Group.

—It's a Fair Day, Amber Brown. 2003. (Young Amber Brown Easy-To-Read Ser.: 4). (gr. k-3). lib. bdg. 13.55 *(978-0-613-61635-5(9),* Turtleback) Turtleback Bks.

Derrick, Patricia. Farley the Ferret of Farkleberry Farm. Martinez, J-P Loppo, illus. 2007. 32p. (J). (gr. -1-3). 18.95 incl. audio compact disk *(978-1-933818-12-2(3))* Animalations.

Destiny, A. & Helms, Rhonda. Never Too Late. 2015. (Flirt Ser.). (ENG., Illus.). 224p. (YA). (gr. 7). pap. 9.99 *(978-1-4814-5188-8(X),* Simon Pulse) Simon Pulse.

DiCamillo, Kate & Mcghee, Alison. Two for One. Fucile, Tony, illus. (Bink & Gollie Ser.). (ENG.). 96p. (J). (gr. 1-4). 2013. pap. 6.99 *(978-0-7636-6445-9(6))* 2012. 15.99 *(978-0-7636-3361-5(5))* Candlewick Pr.

—Two for One. 2013. (Bink & Gollie Ser.: 2). lib. bdg. 17.20 *(978-0-606-31607-1(8),* Turtleback) Turtleback Bks.

Disney Book Group Staff. Gravity Falls Once upon a Swine. Disney Storybook Artists Staff & No New Art Needed, illus. 2014. (Gravity Falls Chapter Book Ser.: 2). (ENG.). 112p. (J). (gr. 1-3). pap. 4.99 *(978-1-4847-1140-8(8))* Disney Pr.

Disney Book Group Staff & Hapka, Catherine. Sofia the First the Enchanted Science Fair. Disney Storybook Artists Staff, illus. 2014. (ENG.). 24p. (J). (gr. -1-k). pap. 4.99 *(978-1-4847-1309-9(5))* Disney Pr.

Disney Press Staff. Once upon a Swine. 2014. (Gravity Falls Ser.: 2). (J). lib. bdg. 14.75 *(978-0-606-35916-0(8))* Turtleback Bks.

Dowding, Philippa. Carter & the Curious Maze. 2016. (Weird Stories Gone Wrong Ser.: 3). (ENG., Illus.). 136p. (J). pap. 9.99 *(978-1-4597-3249-0(9))* Dundurn CAN. Dist: Ingram Publisher Services.

Ellsberry, Sharon. The Spaniel Family Goes to the State Fair. Espinosa, Chris, illus. 2004. 24p. (J). 9.00 *(978-0-9724637-2-0(0))* Sky Rocket Pr.

Enderle, Dotti & Galey, Chuck. The Cotton Candy Catastrophe at the Texas State Fair, 1 vol. 2004. (ENG., Illus.). 32p. (J). (gr. k-3). 16.99 *(978-1-58980-189-9(X))* Pelican Publishing Co., Inc.

Evans, Gwen & Collins, Darluniau Mike. Delyth A'r Ffair Haf. 2005. (WEL., Illus.). 12p. pap. 2.99 *(978-1-85644-758-4(8))* CAA.

Ferguson, Gloria. Fair Money. 2012. 62p. 19.95 *(978-1-4626-3037-0(5))* America Star Bks.

Finley, Martha. Elsie at the World's Fair. 2007. (ENG.). 156p. pap. 19.99 *(978-1-4346-2508-3(7))* Creative Media Partners, LLC.

—Elsie at the Worlds Fair. 2006. 27.95 *(978-1-4218-2991-3(6))*; pap. 12.95 *(978-1-4218-3091-9(4))* 1st World Publishing, Inc.

—Elsie at the World's Fair. l.t. ed. 2007. 172p. pap. 21.99 *(978-1-4346-2550-2(8))* Creative Media Partners, LLC.

Frasier, Debra. A Fabulous Fair Alphabet. Frasier, Debra, illus. 2010. (ENG., Illus.). 40p. (J). (gr. k-6). 16.99 *(978-1-4169-9817-4(9),* Beach Lane Bks.) Beach Lane Bks.

Fuerst, Jeffrey B. Simple Simon. Ledger, Bill, illus. 2010. (Rising Readers Ser.). (J). 3.49 *(978-1-60719-706-5(5))* Newmark Learning LLC.

Grant, Vicki. Hold the Pickles, 1 vol. 2012. (Orca Currents Ser.). (ENG.). 112p. (J). (gr. 5-9). 16.95 *(978-1-55469-921-6(5))*; pap. 9.95 *(978-1-55469-920-9(7))* Orca Bk. Pubs. USA.

Graves, Sue. Harry & the Horse. 2011. (Tadpoles Ser.). (ENG., Illus.). 24p. (J). (gr. k-2). *(978-0-7787-0579-6(X))*; pap. *(978-0-7787-0590-1(0))* Crabtree Publishing Co.

Greene, Stephanie. Pig Pickin', 0 vols. Mathieu, Joe, illus. 2013. (Moose & Hildy Ser.). (ENG.). 68p. (J). (gr. -1-3). pap. 9.99 *(978-1-4778-1684-4(4),* 9781477816844, Amazon Children's Publishing) Amazon Publishing.

Hankins, Larry. Stickboy at the Fair. 2011. 32p. pap. 24.95 *(978-1-4512-2206-7(8))* America Star Bks.

Harper, Charise Mericle. Just Grace & the Trouble with Cupcakes. (Just Grace Ser.: 10). (ENG., Illus.). 208p. (J). (gr. 1-4). 2014. pap. 5.99 *(978-0-544-33910-1(X),* HMH Books For Young Readers) 2013. 15.99 *(978-0-547-87744-0(7))* Houghton Mifflin Harcourt Publishing Co.

Hensley, Sarah M. Cailloo Goes to the Fair. Coray, Stacy A., illus. l.t. ed. 2005. (HRL Board Book Ser.). (J). (gr. k-18). pap. 10.95 *(978-1-57332-328-4(4),* HighReach Learning, Incorporated) Carson-Dellosa Publishing, LLC.

Hollar, Cheryl Faye. Billy the Bunny Goes to the State Fair. 2005. (J). pap. 7.97 *(978-0-9763826-0-7(1))* Hollar, Cheryl Public Relations.

Holley, Marietta. Samantha at the St. Louis Exposition. 2007. 188p. pap. 19.99 *(978-1-4264-6038-8(4))* Creative Media Partners, LLC.

—Samantha at the World's Fair. 2007. (ENG.). 428p. pap. 26.99 *(978-1-4264-5101-0(6))* Creative Media Partners, LLC.

Hope, Laura Lee. The Bobbsey Twins at the County Fair. 2007. (ENG.). 120p. pap. 18.99 *(978-1-4346-0547-4(7))*; 132p. pap. 19.99 *(978-1-4346-0622-8(8))* Creative Media Partners, LLC.

Houts, Michelle. The Beef Princess of Practical County. 2010. (ENG.). 240p. (J). (gr. 3-7). 7.99 *(978-0-440-42270-9(1),* Yearling) Random Hse. Children's Bks.

James, Lincoln. The Street Fair. 2006. (Neighborhood Readers Ser.). (ENG.). 16p. (gr. 1-3). pap. 6.50 *(978-1-4042-7228-6(3),* Rosen Classroom) Rosen Publishing Group, Inc., The.

Jeanne Marie at the Fair. 2004. (Illus.). 34p. (J). mass mkt. *(978-0-9740599-4-5(3))* Omnibus Publishing.

Jerry, Spinelli. Blue Ribbon Blues. 2014. (Stepping Stone Book Ser. Vol. 2 Ser.). (ENG.). 80p. (J). (gr. 7-12). 8.24 *(978-1-63245-269-6(3))* Lectorum Pubns., Inc.

Jones, Doris McKinney. Introducing Banana Anna & Friends. 2009. 24p. pap. 24.95 *(978-1-60749-852-0(9))* America Star Bks.

Keene, Carolyn. Unicorn Uproar. Pamintuan, Macky, illus. 2009. (Nancy Drew & the Clue Crew Ser.: 22). (ENG.). 96p. (J). (gr. 1-4). pap. 4.99 *(978-1-4169-7810-7(0),* Aladdin) Simon & Schuster Children's Publishing.

Kent, Renee Holmes. Cassie, You're a Winner! 2004. (Adventures in Misty Falls Ser.: Vol. 1). (Illus.). 100p. (gr. 4-7). pap. 2.99 *(978-1-56309-735-5(4),* N007116) New Hope Pubs.

Kinney, Jessica. The Pig Scramble, 1 vol. Brannen, Sarah S., illus. 2011. (ENG.). 36p. (J). 17.95 *(978-1-934031-61-2(5),* bd7fa2f2-9ea3-439a-9713-9f7979711a16) Islandport Pr., Inc.

Krulik, Nancy. All's Fair. John and Wendy Staff, illus. 2013. (Katie Kazoo, Switcheroo Ser.). (ENG.). 144p. (J). (gr. 2-4). pap. 5.99 *(978-0-448-45682-9(6),* Grosset & Dunlap) Penguin Young Readers Group.

Laínez, René Colato. Playing Lotería Mexicana: El Juego de la Lotería Mexicana. Arena, Jillayne, illus. 2005. (ENG., SPA & MUL.). 32p. (J). (gr. -1-3). 15.95 *(978-0-87358-881-2(9))* Cooper Square Publishing Llc.

Lao, Samantha. The Scared Panda. 2009. 20p. pap. 10.49 *(978-1-4389-9226-6(2))* AuthorHouse.

Lawson, Robert. The Great Wheel. Lawson, Robert, illus. 2004. (ENG., Illus.). 192p. (YA). (gr. 5). pap. 9.99 *(978-0-8027-7705-8(8),* 9780802777058, Bloomsbury USA Childrens) Bloomsbury Publishing USA.

Lemke, Donald. Poison Ivy's Scare Fair. 2017. (Batman 8X8 Storybooks Ser.). (J). lib. bdg. 13.55 ***(978-0-606-39619-6(5))*** Turtleback Bks.

Marsh, Carole. Dear Granny: The Spooky State Fair Fiasco. 2007. (Postcard Mysteries Ser.). 128p. (J). (gr. 2-9). 14.95 *(978-0-635-06399-1(9),* Marsh, Carole Family CD-Rom) Gallopade International.

—Dear Pirate, the Buried Treasure Mystery. 2007. (Postcard Mysteries Ser.). (Illus.). 114p. (J). (gr. 2-9). per. 5.99 *(978-0-635-06343-4(3),* Marsh, Carole Family CD-Rom) Gallopade International.

Martinez, G. O. Count Von Ice Dela Cream & the Golden Ice Cream. 2011. 56p. pap. 27.99 *(978-1-4568-6522-1(6))* Xlibris Corp.

May, Eleanor. Albert Doubles the Fun. Melmon, Deborah, illus. 2017. (Mouse Math (r) Ser.). (ENG.). 32p. (gr. -1-1). 22.65 *(978-1-57565-834-6(8))* Kane Press, Inc.

May, Eleanor. Albert Doubles the Fun: Adding Doubles. Melmon, Deborah, illus. 2017. (Mouse Math (r) Ser.). (ENG.). 32p. (gr. -1-1). 34.65 ***(978-1-57565-836-0(4))*** Kane Press, Inc.

Mayer, Mercer. Little Critter: Just Pick Us, Please! Mayer, Mercer, illus. 2017. (My First I Can Read Ser.). (Illus.). 32p. (J). (gr. -1-3). pap. 3.99 ***(978-0-06-243142-4(0))*** HarperCollins Pubs.

McOmber, Rachel B., ed. McOmber Phonics Storybooks: At the Fair. rev. ed. (Illus.). (J). *(978-0-944991-60-2(2))* Swift Learning Resources.

Meachen Rau, Dana. At a Fair. 2007. (Fun Time Ser.). (SPA., Illus.). 24p. (gr. k-1). lib. bdg. 15.95 *(978-0-7614-2606-6(X),* Benchmark Bks.) Marshall Cavendish Corp.

—En el Parque de Atracciones. 2007. (¡A Divertimos! Ser.). (SPA., Illus.). 24p. (gr. k-1). lib. bdg. 15.95 *(978-0-7614-2749-0(X),* Benchmark Bks.) Marshall Cavendish Corp.

Miller, Sibley. Merry-Go-Horses. Chang, Tara Larsen & Gershman, Jo, illus. 2011. (Wind Dancers Ser.: 10). (ENG.). 80p. (J). (gr. 1-4). pap. 5.99 *(978-0-312-60543-8(9),* 9780312605438) Feiwel & Friends.

Mills, Claudia. The Nora Notebooks, Book 2: the Trouble with Babies. Kath, Katie, illus. 2016. (Nora Notebooks Ser.). (ENG.). 192p. (J). (gr. 2-5). 12.99 *(978-0-385-39165-8(X),* Knopf Bks. for Young Readers) Random Hse. Children's Bks.

Montgomery, Lewis B. The Case of the July 4th Jinx. Wummer, Amy, illus. 2010. (Milo & Jazz Mysteries Ser.). 96p. (J). (gr. 2-6). (ENG.). pap. 6.95 *(978-1-57565-308-2(7))*; lib. bdg. 22.60 *(978-1-57565-315-0(X))* Kane Press, Inc.

—The Case of the July 4th Jinx. 5th rev. ed. 2010. pap. 39.62 *(978-0-7613-6520-4(6))* Kane Press, Inc.

Moore, Jordan. The Marshmallow Man, 1 vol. rev. ed. 2013. (Fiction Readers Ser.). (ENG., Illus.). 32p. (J). (gr. 3-3). pap. 8.99 *(978-1-4333-5643-8(0))* Shell Educational Publishing.

—The Mystery of the Grand Bazaar, 1 vol. rev. ed. 2013. (Fiction Readers Ser.). (ENG., Illus.). 32p. (J). (gr. 3-3). pap. 8.99 *(978-1-4333-5645-2(7))* Shell Educational Publishing.

Moore, Nancy Delano. Kiernan's Jam. Peck, Bill, illus. 2006. (J). 10.00 *(978-0-9785775-0-6(7))* Moore, Hullihen.

Mooring, John L. Cricket's Chronicles: The Third Grade Science Fair. 2010. 24p. pap. 12.99 *(978-1-4490-3278-4(8))* AuthorHouse.

Morgan, Melissa J. A Fair to Remember. 2007. (Camp Confidential Ser.: 13). (ENG.). 160p. (J). (gr. 3-7). pap. 4.99 *(978-0-448-44451-2(8),* Grosset & Dunlap) Penguin Young Readers Group.

Nelid, Piper. World's Fair Day, 01 vols., 1. 2016. (Rosen REAL Readers: Social Studies Nonfiction / Fiction: Family, Community, & the World Ser.). (ENG.). 12p. (J). pap. 6.33 *(978-1-5081-1976-0(7),* Rosen Classroom) Rosen Publishing Group, Inc., The.

Neuschwander, Cindy. Sir Cumference & the Fracton Faire. 2017. (Sir Cumference Ser.). lib. bdg. 18.40 ***(978-0-606-39807-7(4))*** Turtleback Bks.

O'Reilly, Sean. The Scare Fair, 1 vol. 2011. (Mighty Mighty Monsters Ser.). (ENG.). 48p. (gr. 2-3). lib. bdg. 23.99 *(978-1-4342-3220-5(4))* Stone Arch Bks.

—The Scare Fair, 1 vol. Arcana Studio Staff, illus. 2012. (Mighty Mighty Monsters Ser.). (ENG.). 48p. (gr. 2-3). pap. 6.10 *(978-1-4342-4611-0(6))* Stone Arch Bks.

Papp, Robert, illus. The Sword of the Silver Knight. 2005. (Boxcar Children Mysteries Ser.: 103). (ENG.). 128p. (J). (gr. 1-5). per. 6.99 *(978-0-8075-0876-3(4))* Whitman, Albert & Co.

Schorr, Titus. The Food Fair, 01 vols., 1. 2016. (Rosen REAL Readers: Social Studies Nonfiction / Fiction: Family, Community, & the World Ser.). (ENG.). 8p. (J). pap. 5.46 *(978-1-5081-1857-2(4),* Rosen Classroom) Rosen Publishing Group, Inc., The.

Shava, Ryder. The Country Fair, 01 vols., 1. 2016. (Rosen REAL Readers: Social Studies Nonfiction / Fiction: Family, Community, & the World Ser.). (ENG.). 12p. (J). pap. 6.33 *(978-1-5081-1904-3(X),* Rosen Classroom) Rosen Publishing Group, Inc., The.

Simon, Coco. Alexis Cupcake Crush. 2016. (Cupcake Diaries: 28). lib. bdg. 17.20 *(978-0-606-38968-6(7))* Turtleback Bks.

Speck, Katie. Maybelle Goes to School. Tagyos, Paul Rátz de, illus. 2015. (Maybelle Ser.). (ENG.). 64p. (J). (gr. 2-5). 16.99 *(978-0-8050-9158-8(0),* 9780805091588, Holt, Henry & Co. Bks. For Young Readers) Holt, Henry & Co.

Steers, Billy. Tractor Mac You're a Winner. (Tractor Mac Ser.). (ENG., Illus.). (J). 2016. 24p. pap. 4.99 *(978-0-374-30538-3(2),* 9780374305383) 2015. 32p. (gr. -1-k). 8.99 *(978-0-374-30104-0(2),* 9780374301040) Farrar, Straus & Giroux. (Farrar, Straus & Giroux (BYR)).

—You're a Winner. 2016. (Tractor Mac Ser.). (ENG.). 24p. (J). (gr. -1-k). 14.75 *(978-0-606-39283-9(1))* Turtleback Bks.

Stephenson, Norman E. God's Blood: The Fate of the Lost Templar Treasure. 2007. 176p. per. 13.95 *(978-0-595-47539-1(6))* iUniverse, Inc.

Stevens, Charles McCellan. The Adventures of Uncle Jeremiah & Family at the Great Fair: Their Observations & Triumphs. 2007. (ENG.). 186p. pap. 19.99 *(978-1-4346-5343-7(9))*; 212p. pap. 22.99 *(978-1-4346-5344-4(7))* Creative Media Partners, LLC.

Stilton, Geronimo. Ride for Your Life! 2014. (Geronimo Stilton — Creepella Von Cacklefur Ser.: 6). lib. bdg. 18.40 *(978-0-606-35847-7(1))* Turtleback Bks.

Swanson, A. M. Momma's Biscuits. 2010. 19p. (J). pap. 14.95 *(978-1-4327-4699-5(5))* Outskirts Pr., Inc.

Train, Mary. Time for the Fair. Hayes, Karel, illus. 2005. (ENG.). 28p. (J). (gr. k-17). 15.95 *(978-0-89272-694-3(6))* Down East Bks.

Tucker, Jasmin. Robot School. 2010. 28p. 12.49 *(978-1-4520-5011-9(2))* AuthorHouse.

Umansky, Kaye. Sophie in Charge. Currey, Anna, illus. 2005. 30p. (J). 9.95 *(978-1-56148-478-2(4),* Good Bks.) Skyhorse Publishing Co., Inc.

Wallace, G. Ira. Bunny Tales: The Journey Begins. 2009. 24p. pap. 12.00 *(978-1-60860-869-0(7),* Strategic Bk. Publishing) Strategic Book Publishing & Rights Agency (SBPRA).

Waszak, Madonna. Mason's Mashed Potato Tree. Johnston, Lisa Harp, illus. 2011. 34p. pap. 14.95 *(978-1-4575-0159-3(7))* Dog Ear Publishing, LLC.

Wilder, Laura Ingalls. County Fair. Wheeler, Jody, illus. 2003. (My First Little House Bks.). 17.00 *(978-0-7569-1727-2(1))* Perfection Learning Corp.

Wilsdon, Christina. A Wild Ride in Texas. Jaekel, Susan, illus. 2006. 26p. (J). 7.99 *(978-1-59939-011-6(6))* Cornerstone Pr.

Zondervan Staff & Poth, Karen. Yuletide Ice Cube Fair, 1 vol. 2014. (Big Idea Books / VeggieTales Ser.). (ENG.). 24p. (J). pap. 3.99 *(978-0-310-74623-2(X))* Zonderkidz.

FAIRY PLAYS

Coville, Bruce. William Shakespeare's a Midsummer Night's Dream. Nolan, Dennis, illus. 2003. (ENG.). 48p. (J). (gr. k-3). pap. 7.99 *(978-0-14-250168-9(9),* Puffin Books) Penguin Young Readers Group.

Walter, Kristin. The Selfish Giant. 2011. (ENG.). 32p. pap. 7.00 *(978-0-87440-244-5(1))* Baker's Plays.

FAIRY TALES

see also Folklore

A and J Studios Staff. Dora's Three Little Fairy Tales. 2005. (Dora the Explorer Ser.). (ENG., Illus.). 36p. (J). bds. 10.99 *(978-1-4169-0640-7(1),* Simon Spotlight/Nickelodeon) Simon Spotlight/Nickelodeon.

Abassi, Ines. My Beautiful Hair. Kala, Sabah, illus. 2016. (Stories & Fables from Around the World Ser.). (ENG.). 24p. (J). (gr. 2-1). lib. bdg. 24.60 *(978-1-4777-5695-9(7),* Windmill Bks.) Rosen Publishing Group, Inc., The.

Abbrederis, Christoph & McLellen, Christoph Elizabeth, illus. Sleeping Beauty. 2003. (Bilingual Fairy Tales Ser.: BILI).Tr. of Bella Durmiente. (ENG & SPA.). 32p. (J). (gr. -1-7). pap. 6.99 *(978-0-8118-3913-6(3))* Chronicle Bks. LLC.

Abela, Donna. The Princess & the Pea Vol. 9: Band 15/Emerald. Stewart, Chantal, illus. 2007. (Collins Big Cat Ser.). (ENG.). 32p. (J). pap. 8.99 *(978-0-00-722866-9(X))* HarperCollins Pubs. Ltd. GBR. Dist: Independent Pubs. Group.

E
F
G

Ackland, Rachel. Nick the Knight & the Dragon! 2017. (ENG.). 22p. (J). (gr. -1-2). pap. 5.99 *(978-1-4380-0983-4(6))* Barron's Educational Series, Inc.

Adams, H. J. Twice Six Tales All Told. 2003. 86p. 22.50 *(978-0-923687-63-2(7))* Celo Valley Bks.

Adams, Jennifer. Arabian Nights Aladdin & the Wonderful Lamp, 1 vol. Oliver, Alison, illus. 2017. (ENG.). 22p. (J). bds. 9.99 *(978-1-4236-4592-4(8))* Gibbs Smith, Publisher.

Aesop. Aesop's Fables. Townsend, George Fyler, tr. 2013. 130p. *(978-1-926606-97-2(3))*; pap. *(978-1-926606-11-8(6))* Engage Bks.

Afanasyev, Alexander. Russian Fairy Tales. Bilibin, Ivan, illus. 2013. 80p. *(978-1-909115-59-0(2))* 2012. 90p. pap. *(978-1-908478-68-9(3))* Planet, The.

—The Tale of Tsarevich Ivan, the Firebird, & the Grey Wolf. Bilibin, Ivan, illus. 2013. 28p. pap. *(978-1-909115-50-7(9))* Planet, The.

Agnew, Leoni & Collins UK Publishing Staff. The Battle of Kupe & Te Wheke. Bianchi, Fausto, illus. 2016. (ENG.). 32p. (J). pap. 8.95 *(978-0-00-814716-7(7))* HarperCollins Pubs. Ltd. GBR. Dist: Independent Pubs. Group.

Aguirre, Jorge. Dragons Beware! 2015. (Chronicles of Claudette Ser.). (ENG., Illus.). 160p. (J). (gr. 2-5). pap. 14.99 *(978-1-59643-878-1(9)*, 9781596438781, First Second Bks.) Roaring Brook Pr.

—Giants Beware! Rosado, Rafael, illus. 2012. (Chronicles of Claudette Ser.). (ENG.). 208p. (J). (gr. 2-5). pap. 15.99 *(978-1-59643-582-7(8)*, 9781596435827, First Second Bks.) Roaring Brook Pr.

Ahdieh, Renée. The Wrath & the Dawn. 2016. (Wrath & the Dawn Ser.). (ENG.). 432p. (YA). (gr. 7). pap. 10.99 *(978-0-14-751385-4(5)*, Speak) Penguin Young Readers Group.

—The Wrath & the Dawn. 2016. lib. bdg. 22.10 *(978-0-606-38849-8(4))* Turtleback Bks.

Ahdieh, Renée & McPike, Elizabeth. The Wrath & the Dawn. 2015. (Wrath & the Dawn Ser.). (ENG., Illus.). 416p. (YA). (gr. 7). 17.99 *(978-0-399-17161-1(4)*, G.P. Putnam's Sons Books for Young Readers) Penguin Young Readers Group.

Ahlberg, Allan. Previously. Ingman, Bruce, illus. 2011. (ENG.). 32p. (J). (gr. -1-3). pap. 6.99 *(978-0-7636-5304-0(7))* Candlewick Pr.

Ahlberg, Jessica. Fairy Tales for Mr. Barker: A Peek-Through Story. Ahlberg, Jessica, illus. 2016. (ENG., Illus.). 32p. (J). (-k). 15.99 *(978-0-7636-8124-1(5))* Candlewick Pr.

Ahmdt, Paula D. Toof Fairy Tales. 2011. 24p. (gr. 1-2). pap. 12.74 *(978-1-4567-6028-1(9))* AuthorHouse.

Ajhar, Brian, illus. Pinocchio. 2005. (Rabbit Ears Ser.). 36p. (J). (gr. k-5). 25.65 *(978-1-59679-228-9(0))* Spotlight.

Alam, Sarah H. Enchanting Fables. 2008. 48p. pap. 16.95 *(978-1-60441-768-5(4))* America Star Bks.

Albam, Jessica. The Boy in the Oak. 2010. (ENG., Illus.). 40p. (J). (gr. k-4). 17.95 *(978-1-897476-52-9(3))* Simply Read Bks. CAN. Dist: Ingram Publisher Services.

Alexander, Lloyd. The High King. 2006. (Chronicles of Prydain: Bk. 5). (Illus.). 253p. (gr. 3-7). 17.00 *(978-0-7569-6816-8(X))* Perfection Learning Corp.

Ali Baba & the Forty Thieves. 2004. (J). (ENG & SPA.). *(978-1-84444-542-4(9))*; (ENG & SOM.). *(978-1-84444-541-7(0))*; (ENG & POL.). *(978-1-84444-538-7(0))*; (ENG & PAN.). *(978-1-84444-537-0(2))*; (ENG & ITA.). *(978-1-84444-535-6(6))*; (ENG & GUJ.). *(978-1-84444-646-9(8))*; (ARA & ENG.). *(978-1-84444-527-1(5))* Mantra Lingua.

Ali BabaForty Thieves. 2004. (J). cd-rom *(978-1-84444-452-6(X))* Mantra Lingua.

Allchin, Rosalind. The Frog Princess. 2004. (Illus.). (J). (gr. k-3). spiral bd. *(978-0-616-14557-9(8))* Canadian National Institute for the Blind/Institut National Canadien pour les Aveugles.

—The Frog Princess. Allchin, Rosalind, illus. 2003. (ENG., Illus.). 32p. (J). (gr. k-3). pap. 5.95 *(978-1-55337-526-5(2))* Kids Can Pr., Ltd. CAN. Dist: Hachette Bk. Group.

Allen, Francesca, illus. First Picture Fairytales. 2008. (Usborne First Book Ser.). 14p. (J). (gr. -1). bds. 18.99 incl. audio compact disk *(978-0-7945-1832-5(X)*, Usborne) EDC Publishing.

Alley, Zoe. There's a Wolf at the Door. Alley, R. W. & Alley, R., illus. 2008. (ENG.). 40p. (J). (gr. -1-3). 21.99 *(978-1-59643-275-8(6)*, 9781596432758) Roaring Brook Pr.

Alrawi, Karim. The Mouse Who Saved Egypt. Willey, Bee, illus. 2011. 32p. (J). (gr. -1-3). 16.95 *(978-1-56656-856-2(0)*, Crocodile Bks.) Interlink Publishing Group, Inc.

Altman, Linda Jacobs. African Mythology Rocks! Bock, William Sauts, illus. 2011. (Mythology Rocks! Ser.). 112p. (J). (gr. 6-18). lib. bdg. 33.27 *(978-0-7660-3896-7(3))* Enslow Pubs., Inc.

Amery, H. & Cartwright, S. Cinderella. 2004. (First Stories Ser.). 16p. (J). pap. 4.99 *(978-0-7945-0605-6(4))* EDC Publishing.

—Little Red Riding Hood. rev. ed. 2004. (First Stories Ser.). 16p. (J). pap. 4.99 *(978-0-7945-0607-0(0))* EDC Publishing.

—Sleeping Beauty. 2004. (First Stories Ser.). 16p. (J). pap. 4.95 *(978-0-7945-0604-9(6))* EDC Publishing.

Amery, Heather. Little Red Riding Hood. Tyler, Jenny, ed. Cartwright, Stephen, illus. 2004. (First Stories Ser.). 16p. (J). (gr. -1). lib. bdg. 12.95 *(978-1-58086-620-0(4)*, Usborne) EDC Publishing.

—Princess Stories. 2005. (First Stories Ser.). 64p. (J). 12.95 *(978-0-7945-0898-2(7)*, Usborne) EDC Publishing.

—Stories from Around the World. 2010. (Stories for young Children Ser.). 127p. (J). 14.99 *(978-0-7945-2683-2(7)*, Usborne) EDC Publishing.

—Traditional Fairy Tales. 2005. (First Stories Ser.). 96p. (J). 13.95 *(978-0-7945-0865-4(0)*, Usborne) EDC Publishing.

Amico, Erin. Viol. 2012. 52p. (-18). pap. 31.99 *(978-1-4653-9534-4(2))* Xlibris Corp.

Andersen, Hans Christian. Andersen's Fairy Tales. 2005. pap. *(978-1-905432-22-6(4))* Dodo Pr.

—The Elf of the Rose & Other Tales. 2012. (Fairy Tales of Hans Christian Andersen Ser.). (ENG., Illus.). 152p. pap. 19.99 *(978-1-909438-15-6(4)*, Sovereign) Bollinger, Max GBR. Dist: Lightning Source UK, Ltd.

—The Emperor & the Nightingale, 1 vol. Van Nutt, Robert, illus. 2007. (Rabbit Ears: A Classic Tale Ser.).Tr. of Nattergalen. (ENG.). 40p. (gr. -1-3). 25.65 *(978-1-59961-307-9(7))* Spotlight.

—The Emperor's New Clothes. 2005. (SPA.). 12p. (J). pap. *(978-958-30-1782-7(5))* Panamericana Editorial.

—The Emperor's New Clothes, 1 vol. Van Nutt, Robert, illus. 2005. (Rabbit Ears-A Classic Tale Set 2 Ser.). (ENG.). 28p. (gr. k-5). 25.65 *(978-1-59197-746-9(0))* Spotlight.

—The Emperor's New Clothes: An All-Star Illustrated Retelling of the Classic Fairy Tale. 2004. (Illus.). 85p. (J). (gr. k-4). reprint ed. *(978-0-7567-7720-3(8))* DIANE Publishing Co.

—The Emperor's New Clothes: The Graphic Novel, 1 vol. Timmins, Jeffrey Stewart, illus. 2009. (Graphic Spin Ser.). (ENG.). 40p. (gr. 1-3). pap. 5.95 *(978-1-4342-1744-8(2)*, Graphic Revolve) Stone Arch Bks.

—The Fairy Tales & Stories of Hans Christian Andersen. Tegner, Hans, illus. 2016. (Knickerbocker Classics Ser.). (ENG.). 600p. 35.00 *(978-1-63106-205-6(0)*, Race Point Publishing) Quarto Publishing Group USA.

—Fairy Tales from Many Lands. Rackham, Arthur, illus. 2014. (ENG.). 164p. (J). (gr. k-3). 22.99 *(978-1-4052-6741-0(0))* Egmont Bks., Ltd. GBR. Dist: Independent Pubs. Group.

—Fairy Tales of Hans Christian Andersen. 2011. 892p. pap. 19.99 *(978-1-61382-020-9(8))* Simon & Brown.

—The Fairy Tales of Hans Christian Andersen. Daniel, Noel & Kobler, Florian, eds. Hersholt, Jean, tr. 2013. (ENG., Illus.). 320p. 39.99 *(978-3-8365-2675-3(1))* TASCHEN DEU. Dist: Ingram Publisher Services.

—For Sure! for Sure! White, Mus, tr. from DAN. Czernecki, Stefan, illus. 2006. 29p. (J). (gr. k-4). reprint ed. 17.00 *(978-1-4223-5208-3(0))* DIANE Publishing Co.

—Hans Andersen's Fairy Tales. Lewis, Naomi, tr. from DAN. 2nd ed. 2010. (Puffin Classics Ser.). (ENG., Illus.). 176p. (J). (gr. 5-7). pap. 5.99 *(978-0-14-132901-7(7)*, Puffin Books) Penguin Young Readers Group.

—Hans Andersen's Fairy Tales: A Selection. Kingsland, L. W., tr. from DAN. Fröhlich, Lorenz & Pedersen, Vilhelm, illus. 2009. (Oxford World's Classics Ser.). (ENG.). 384p. pap. 10.95 *(978-0-19-955585-7(0))* Oxford Univ. Pr., Inc.

—Hans Christian Andersen: Illustrated Fairy Tales, Vol. 2. 2004. (ENG., Illus.). 416p. (J). (gr. -1-3). *(978-87-7247-271-3(5))* Scandinavia Publishing Hse.

—Hans Christian Andersen: The Complete Fairy Tales. Hersholt, Jean P., tr. from DAN. 2014. (Leather-Bound Classics Ser.). (ENG., Illus.). 784p. lthr. 24.99 *(978-1-62686-099-5(8)*, Thunder Bay Pr.) Readerlink Distribution Services, LLC.

—Hans Christian Andersen Illustrated Fairytales. 2004. (Hans Christian Andersen Illustrated Fairytales Ser.). (ENG., Illus.). 144p. (J). (gr. -1-3). *(978-87-7247-264-5(2))* Scandinavia Publishing Hse.

—Hans Christian Andersen Illustrated Fairytales Vol. 1: The Snow Queen; The Little Match Girl; The Little Mermaid; She Was Good for Nothing. 2004. (ENG., Illus.). 144p. (J). (gr. -1-3). *(978-87-7247-256-0(1))* Scandinavia Publishing Hse.

—Hans Christian Andersen Illustrated Fairytales Vol. II: It's Absolutely True; The Pigkeeper; Little Claus & Big Claus; The Racers; The Buckwheat. 2004. (ENG., Illus.). 144p. (J). (gr. -1-3). *(978-87-7247-258-4(8))* Scandinavia Publishing Hse.

—Hans Christian Andersen Illustrated Fairytales Vol. IV: The Snowdrop; There Is a Difference; The Emperor's New Clothes; Thumbelina; What the Old Man Does. 2005. 144p. *(978-87-7247-265-2(0))* Scandinavia Publishing Hse.

—Hans Christian Andersen Illustrated Fairytales Vol. V: The Brave Tin Soldier; Clod Hans; A Gift for Hans; The Ugly Duckling. 2005. 144p. *(978-87-7247-270-6(7))* Scandinavia Publishing Hse.

—Hans Christian Andersen Illustrated Fairytales Vol. VI: The Wild Swans; The Traveling Companion; The Jewish Maiden; The Toad. 2005. 144p. *(978-87-7247-278-2(2))* Scandinavia Publishing Hse.

—Hans Christian Andersen Tales. 2014. (Word Cloud Classics Ser.). (ENG., Illus.). 464p. pap. 14.99 *(978-1-62686-259-3(1)*, Thunder Bay Pr.) Readerlink Distribution Services, LLC.

—Hans Christian Andersen's Fairy Tales: An Illustrated Classic. Rackham, Arthur et al, illus. 2017. (Illustrated Classic Ser.). (ENG.). 260p. 12.99 ***(978-1-68412-031-4(4))*** Readerlink Distribution Services, LLC.

—Hans Christian Andersen's Fairy Tales: The Ugly Duckling, Thumbelina, & Other Stories. Hart, Edna F., illus. 2017. (First Avenue Classics Ser.). (ENG.). 422p. (gr. 3-8). 19.99 ***(978-1-5124-2611-3(3)***, First Avenue Editions) Lerner Publishing Group.

—The Ice-Maiden & Other Tales. Fuller, Fanny, tr. 2007. 128p. per. 10.95 *(978-1-60312-043-2(2))* Aegypan.

—IceMaiden & Other Tales. 2006. pap. *(978-1-4068-0421-8(5))* Echo Library.

—The Little Match Seller. 2005. (SPA.). 12p. (J). pap. *(978-958-30-1509-0(1))* Panamericana Editorial.

—The Little Mermaid & Other Fairy Tales. Kliros, Thea, illus. 2011. (Dover Children's Thrift Classics Ser.). (ENG.). 96p. (J). (gr. 3-8). reprint ed. pap. 3.50 *(978-0-486-27816-2(6))* Dover Pubns., Inc.

—The Little Mermaid & Other Fairy Tales. unabr. ed. 2003. (Dover Children's Evergreen Classics Ser.). (ENG., Illus.). 144p. (J). (gr. 3-8). pap. 3.50 *(978-0-486-42365-4(4))* Dover Pubns., Inc.

—The Little Mermaid & Other Tales. 2012. (Fairy Tales of Hans Christian Andersen Ser.). (ENG.). 152p. pap. 19.99 *(978-1-909438-75-0(8)*, Sovereign) Bollinger, Max GBR. Dist: Lightning Source UK, Ltd.

—The Little Mermaid & the Princess & the Pea: Two Tales & Their Histories. Brown, Carron, ed. 2009. (World of Fairy Tales Ser.). (Illus.). 32p. (J). (gr. -1-2). pap. 10.55 *(978-1-60754-638-2(8))*; lib. bdg. 22.60 *(978-1-60754-637-5(X))* Windmill Bks.

—The Little Mermaid Retold. Charlotte, J. M., illus. 2013. 48p. 18.00 *(978-0-9895422-0-3(3))* MHC Ministries.

—El Patito Feo. 2004. (Caballo Alado Clásico Series-Al Paso Ser.). (SPA & ENG., Illus.). 24p. (J). (gr. -1-k). 7.95 *(978-84-7864-764-4(3))* Combel Editorial, S.A. ESP. Dist: Independent Pubs. Group.

—El Patito Feo. (Mi Primeros Cuentos Ser.). (SPA & ENG., Illus.). (J). (gr. -1-3). pap. 5.95 incl. audio compact disk *(978-88-8148-251-1(7))*; pap. 5.95 incl. audio compact disk *(978-88-8148-251-1(7))* EMC/Paradigm Publishing.

—El Patito Feo. (SPA., Illus.). 48p. (J). (gr. 3-5). *(978-84-241-5525-4(4)*, EV0572) Everest Editora ESP. Dist: Lectorum Pubns., Inc.

—Pictures of Sweden. 2006. pap. *(978-1-4065-0860-4(8))* Dodo Pr.

—The Princess & the Pea. (Fairy Tale Fun Ser.).Tr. of Prindsessen Paa Aerten. (J). 3.95 *(978-0-7214-5433-7(X)*, Dutton Juvenile) Penguin Publishing Group.

—The Princess & the Pea. Kolanovic, Dubravka, illus. 2014. (J). *(978-1-4723-5207-1(6))* Parragon Bk. Service Ltd.

—The Princess & the Pea: The Graphic Novel, 1 vol. Lamoreaux, M. A., illus. 2009. (Graphic Spin Ser.). (ENG.). 40p. (gr. 1-3). pap. 5.95 *(978-1-4342-1743-1(4)*, Graphic Revolve) Stone Arch Bks.

—The Princess & the Pea: The Graphic Novel, 1 vol. Lamoreaux, M. A. & Lamoreaux, Michelle, illus. 2009. (Graphic Spin Ser.). (ENG.). 40p. (gr. 1-3). lib. bdg. 25.32 *(978-1-4342-1594-9(6)*, Graphic Revolve) Stone Arch Bks.

—Princess & the Pea (La Princesa y el Guisante) Estrada, Pau, illus. 2013. (Bilingual Fairy Tales Ser.). (SPA & ENG.). 32p. (J). (gr. 1-4). lib. bdg. 28.50 *(978-1-60753-357-3(X))* Amicus Publishing.

—El Ruisenor. 2004. (Troquelados Clasicos Ser.).Tr. of Nightingale. (SPA.). 16p. (J). pap. 2.95 *(978-84-7864-733-0(3))* Combel Editorial, S.A. ESP. Dist: Independent Pubs. Group.

—Snezhnaya Koroleva - the Snow Queen. Pym, T., illus. 2013. 56p. *(978-1-909115-60-6(6))* Planet, The.

—The Snow Queen. Tatarnikov, Pavel, illus. 2006.Tr. of ??????? ???????? (ENG.). 48p. (J). (gr. 1). 15.95 *(978-1-933327-22-8(7))*; lib. bdg. 16.50 *(978-1-933327-23-5(5))* Purple Bear Bks., Inc.

—The Snow Queen. Lynch, P. J., illus. 2014. Orig. Title: Snedronningen. (ENG.). 48p. (J). (gr. k-2). pap. 10.99 *(978-1-84270-901-6(1))* Andersen Pr. GBR. Dist: Independent Pubs. Group.

—Snow Queen. 2006. (Illus.). 48p. (J). (gr. -1-3). *(978-1-84732-001-8(5))* Carlton Bks., Ltd.

—The Snow Queen. Ibatoulline, Bagram, illus. 2013. (ENG.). 40p. (J). (gr. -1-3). 17.99 *(978-0-06-220950-4(7))* HarperCollins Pubs.

—The Snow Queen. 2007.Tr. of ??????? ???????? (ENG., Illus.). 34p. *(978-1-890568-12-2(0)*, A-BA-BA-HA-LA-MA-HA Pubs.) Windy Press International Publishing Hse., LLC.

—The Snow Queen. Bogdanovic, Toma, illus. adapted ed. 32p. (J). (gr. -1-5). 16.95 *(978-0-87592-048-1(9))* Scroll Pr., Inc.

—The Snow Queen & Other Tales. 2012. (Fairy Tales of Hans Christian Andersen Ser.). (ENG.). 144p. pap. 19.99 *(978-1-909438-77-4(4)*, Sovereign) Bollinger, Max GBR. Dist: Lightning Source UK, Ltd.

—The Steadfast Tin Soldier, 1 vol. Jorgensen, David, illus. 2005. (Rabbit Ears: A Classic Tale Ser.).Tr. of Standhaftige Tinsoldat. (ENG.). 40p. (gr. -1-3). 25.65 *(978-1-59679-346-0(5))* Spotlight.

—Stories from Hans Andersen. 2007. (ENG.). 122p. per. 18.99 *(978-1-4346-2876-3(0))* Creative Media Partners, LLC.

—The Swineherd. (Illus.). 28p. 15.95 *(978-0-86315-129-3(9)*, 1297) Floris Bks. GBR. Dist: SteinerBooks, Inc.

—Tales of Hans Christian Andersen. Stewart, Joel, illus. 2010. (Candlewick Illustrated Classics Ser.). (ENG.). 208p. (J). (gr. 3-7). pap. 12.99 *(978-0-7636-4892-3(2))* Candlewick Pr.

—Thumbelina. Vivanco, Kelly, illus. 2017.Tr. of Tommelise. (ENG.). 48p. (J). (gr. k-4). 17.95 *(978-1-927018-73-6(0))* Simply Read Bks. CAN. Dist: Ingram Publisher Services.

—Thumbelina. Pinkney, Brian, illus. 2003. 40p. (J). 17.89 *(978-0-688-17477-4(9))* HarperCollins Pubs.

—Thumbelina, 1 vol. Johnson, David, illus. 2005. (Rabbit Ears-A Classic Tale Set 2 Ser.). (ENG.). 28p. (gr. k-5). 25.65 *(978-1-59197-756-8(8))* Spotlight.

—The Ugly Duckling, 1 vol. Van Nutt, Robert, illus. 2005. (Rabbit Ears: A Classic Tale Ser.). (ENG.). 40p. (gr. -1-3). 25.65 *(978-1-59679-348-4(1))* Spotlight.

—The Ugly Duckling: The Graphic Novel, 1 vol. Blecha, Aaron, illus. 2009. (Graphic Spin Ser.). (ENG.). 40p. (gr. 1-3). pap. 5.95 *(978-1-4342-1742-4(6)*, Graphic Revolve) Stone Arch Bks.

—The Ugly Duckling & Other Fairy Tales. Golden, Harriet, illus. 2012. (Dover Children's Thrift Classics Ser.). (ENG.). 96p. (Orig.). (J). (gr. 3-8). pap. 3.00 *(978-0-486-27081-4(5))* Dover Pubns., Inc.

—The Ugly Duckling & Other Tales. 2012. (Fairy Tales of Hans Christian Andersen Ser.). (ENG.). 152p. pap. 19.99 *(978-1-909438-73-6(1)*, Sovereign) Bollinger, Max GBR. Dist: Lightning Source UK, Ltd.

—We Both Read-The Emperor's New Clothes. 2014. (Illus.). 44p. (J). 9.95 *(978-1-60115-269-5(8))* Treasure Bay, Inc.

—We Both Read-Thumbelina (Picture Book) Bell, Elizabeth, tr. from FRE. Greban, Quentin, illus. 2007. (We Both Read Ser.).Tr. of Tommelise. 32p. (J). (gr. -1-3). 14.95 *(978-1-60115-007-3(5))* Treasure Bay, Inc.

—What the Moon Saw & Other Tales. 2012. (Fairy Tales of Hans Christian Andersen Ser.). (ENG.). 152p. pap. 19.99 *(978-1-909438-71-2(5)*, Sovereign) Bollinger, Max GBR. Dist: Lightning Source UK, Ltd.

—The Wild Swans. Lewis, Naomi, tr. from DAN. Gilbert, Yvonne, illus. 2005. 48p. (J). 17.99 *(978-1-84148-164-7(5))* Barefoot Bks., Inc.

—The Wild Swans: A Tale of Persistence. Lohmann, Renate, illus. 2006. (J). *(978-1-59939-093-2(0)*, Reader's Digest Young Families, Inc.) Studio Fun International.

—The Wild Swans & Other Tales. 2012. (Fairy Tales of Hans Christian Andersen Ser.). (ENG.). 152p. pap. 19.99 *(978-1-909438-12-5(X)*, Sovereign) Bollinger, Max GBR. Dist: Lightning Source UK, Ltd.

Andersen, Hans Christian, tr. Andersen's Fairy Tales. 2004. 220p. pap. 12.95 *(978-1-59540-305-6(1)*, 1st World Library - Literary Society) 1st World Publishing, Inc.

—Andersen's Fairy Tales. l.t. ed. 2004. (Large Print Ser.). 266p. 25.00 *(978-1-58287-629-0(0))* North Bks.

—Andersen's Fairy Tales. 2004. (ENG.). 172p. 28.95 *(978-0-8095-9507-5(9))* Wildside Pr., LLC.

Andersen, Hans Christian & Andersen. Cuentos de Andersen. Rackham, Arthur, illus. 2003. (SPA.). 240p. 24.95 *(978-84-261-0273-7(5)*, JV30115) Juventud, Editorial ESP. Dist: Lectorum Pubns., Inc., Distribooks, Inc.

Andersen, Hans Christian & Capstone Press Editors. La Bella y la Bestia: La Novela Grafica. Feldman, Luke, illus. 2010. (Graphic Spin en Español Ser.). (SPA.). 40p. (gr. 1-3). lib. bdg. 25.32 *(978-1-4342-1899-5(6)*, Graphic Spin en Español) Stone Arch Bks.

Andersen, Hans Christian & Capstone Press Staff. Caperucita Roja. Rivas, Victor, illus. 2010. (Graphic Spin en Español Ser.). (SPA.). 40p. (gr. 1-3). lib. bdg. 25.32 *(978-1-4342-1903-9(8)*, Graphic Spin en Español) Stone Arch Bks.

—Cenicienta. Feely, Maria Luisa, tr. Timmins, Jeffrey Stewart, illus. 2010. (Graphic Spin en Español Ser.). (SPA.). 40p. (gr. 1-3). lib. bdg. 25.32 *(978-1-4342-1900-8(3)*, Graphic Spin en Español) Stone Arch Bks.

—Hansel y Gretel: La Novela Grafica. Dietrich, Sean, illus. 2010. (Graphic Spin en Español Ser.). (SPA.). 40p. (gr. 1-3). lib. bdg. 25.32 *(978-1-4342-1901-5(1)*, Graphic Spin en Español) Stone Arch Bks.

—Jack y los Frijoles Magicos. Tercio, Ricardo, illus. 2010. (Graphic Spin en Español Ser.). (SPA.). 40p. (gr. 1-3). lib. bdg. 25.32 *(978-1-4342-1902-2(X)*, Graphic Spin en Español) Stone Arch Bks.

—Rumpelstiltskin: La Novela Grafica. Valdez Y Alanis, Erik, illus. 2010. (Graphic Spin en Español Ser.). (SPA.). 40p. (gr. 1-3). lib. bdg. 25.32 *(978-1-4342-1904-6(6)*, Graphic Spin en Español) Stone Arch Bks.

Andersen, Hans Christian & Falloon, Jane. Thumbelina. Chichester Clark, Emma, illus. 2006.Tr. of Tommelise. 38p. (J). (gr. k-4). reprint ed. 16.00 *(978-1-4223-5373-8(7))* DIANE Publishing Co.

Andersen, Hans Christian & Hoekstra, Misha. The Snow Queen. Amoux, Lucie, illus. 2016.Tr. of ??????? ???????? (ENG.). 96p. (J). (gr. 3-7). pap. 9.99 *(978-1-78269-103-7(0)*, Pushkin Press) Steerforth Pr.

Andersen, Hans Christian & Kurt, Robert. Ugly Duckling. Watts, Bernadette, illus. 2008. (ENG.). 32p. (J). (gr. -1-3). pap. 7.95 *(978-0-7358-2146-0(1))* North-South Bks., Inc.

Andersen, Hans Christian & Lewis, Naomi. The Steadfast Tin Soldier. Lynch, P. J., illus. 2005.Tr. of Standhaftige Tinsoldat. (ENG.). 32p. (J). (gr. -1-4). pap. 11.99 *(978-1-84270-443-1(5))* Andersen Pr. GBR. Dist: Independent Pubs. Group.

Andersen, Hans Christian & Sandoval, Gerardo. Thumbelina: The Graphic Novel, 1 vol. Horne, Sarah, illus. 2009. (Graphic Spin Ser.). (ENG.). 40p. (gr. 1-3). pap. 5.95 *(978-1-4342-1741-7(8)*, Graphic Revolve) Stone Arch Bks.

Andersen, Hans Christian & Starbright Foundation Staff. The Emperor's New Clothes. Burton, Virginia Lee, illus. 2014. (Folk Tale Classics Ser.). (ENG.). 48p. (J). (gr. -1-3). 8.99 *(978-0-544-15952-5(7)*, HMH Books For Young Readers) Houghton Mifflin Harcourt Publishing Co.

Andersen, Hans Christian & Stone Arch Books Staff. La Bella y la Bestia: La Novela Grafica, 1 vol. Feldman, Luke, illus. 2010. (Graphic Spin en Español Ser.). (SPA & ENG.). 40p. (gr. 1-3). pap. 5.95 *(978-1-4342-2269-5(1)*, Graphic Spin en Español) Stone Arch Bks.

—Caperucita Roja. Rivas, Victor, illus. 2010. (Graphic Spin en Español Ser.). (SPA & ENG.). 40p. (gr. 1-3). pap. 5.95 *(978-1-4342-2315-9(9)*, Graphic Spin en Español) Stone Arch Bks.

—Cenicienta: La Novela Grafica. Timmins, Jeffrey Stewart, illus. 2010. (Graphic Spin en Español Ser.). (SPA & ENG.). 40p. (gr. 1-3). pap. 5.95 *(978-1-4342-2270-1(5)*, Graphic Spin en Español) Stone Arch Bks.

—Hansel y Gretel: La Novela Grafica. Dietrich, Sean, illus. 2010. (Graphic Spin en Español Ser.). (SPA & ENG.). 40p. (gr. 1-3). pap. 5.95 *(978-1-4342-2271-8(3)*, Graphic Spin en Español) Stone Arch Bks.

—Jack y los Frijoles Magicos. Tercio, Ricardo, illus. 2010. (Graphic Spin en Español Ser.). (SPA & ENG.). 40p. (gr. 1-3). pap. 5.95 *(978-1-4342-2272-5(1)*, Graphic Spin en Español) Stone Arch Bks.

—Rumpelstiltskin: La Novela Grafica, 1 vol. Alanis, Erik Valdez Y., illus. 2010. (Graphic Spin en Español Ser.). (ENG & SPA.). 40p. (gr. 1-3). pap. 5.95 *(978-1-4342-2273-2(X)*, Graphic Spin en Español) Stone Arch Bks.

Andersen, Hans Christian & Tatar, Maria. Hans Christian Andersen. Allen, Julie K., tr. from DAN. 2007. (ENG., Illus.). 496p. 39.95 *(978-0-393-06081-2(0)*, 6081) Norton, W. W. & Co., Inc.

Andrews, Jackie. Gingerbread Man. Burton, Terry, illus. 2012. (ENG.). 32p. pap. 6.50 *(978-1-84135-193-3(8))* Award Pubns. Ltd. GBR. Dist: Parkwest Pubns., Inc.

—Goldilocks & the Three Bears. Taylor, Lawrie, illus. 2012. (ENG.). 32p. (J). pap. 6.50 *(978-1-84135-191-9(1))* Award Pubns. Ltd. GBR. Dist: Parkwest Pubns., Inc.

—Three Billy-Goat Gruff. Bennett, John, illus. 2012. (ENG.). 32p. pap. 6.50 *(978-1-84135-196-4(2))* Award Pubns. Ltd. GBR. Dist: Parkwest Pubns., Inc.

Andrews, Jackie, retold by. Favourite Tales for Young Readers. 2012. (ENG., Illus.). 192p. (J). 19.95 *(978-1-84135-876-5(2))* Award Pubns. Ltd. GBR. Dist: Parkwest Pubns., Inc.

Angeletti, Roberta, illus. The Golden Goose. 2010. (Flip-Up Fairy Tales Ser.). (ENG.). 24p. (J). (gr. -1-2). audio compact disk *(978-1-84643-330-6(4))* Child's Play International Ltd.

Ankhnu Feaster, Teraab & Campbell, Rochelle. The Magic Seeds. 2009. 42p. pap. 19.25 *(978-1-4490-0784-3(8))* AuthorHouse.

Anness, P. L. My Treasury of Traditional Princess Fairytales. Manson, Beverlie, illus. 2015. (ENG.). 160p. 16.99 *(978-1-86147-370-7(2)*, Armadillo) Anness Publishing GBR. Dist: National Bk. Network.

árabe, Cuento popular. ALÍ BABÁ Y LOS CUARENTA LADRONES. 2004. (Troquelados Clásicos Ser.). (SPA & ENG., Illus.). 16p. (J). (gr. -1-k). pap. 3.95 *(978-84-7864-736-1(8))* Combel Editorial, S.A. ESP. Dist: Independent Pubs. Group.

Arengo, Sue. Cinderella, Level 4. 2nd ed. 2011. (ENG., Illus.). 24p. pap. 7.94 *(978-0-19-423942-4(X))* Oxford Univ. Pr., Inc.

—Jack & the Beanstalk. 2012. (ENG., Illus.). 24p. (J). pap. 4.95 *(978-1-84135-772-0(3))* Award Pubns. Ltd. GBR. Dist: Parkwest Pubns., Inc.

—Jack & the Beanstalk. Ratto, Cinzia, illus. 2006. (ENG.). 24p. 5.50 *(978-0-19-422538-0(0))* Oxford Univ. Pr. GBR. Dist: Oxford Univ. Pr., Inc.

—The Shoemaker & the Elves. 2nd ed. 2011. (ENG., Illus.). 24p. pap. 7.94 *(978-0-19-423882-3(2))* Oxford Univ. Pr., Inc.

Argueta, Jorge. El Zipitio, 1 vol. Calderon, Gloria, illus. 2003. (SPA.). 32p. (J). 16.95 (978-0-88899-539-1(3)) Groundwood Bks. CAN. Dist: Publishers Group West (PGW).

Arndt, Rhonda. Mac's Adventure. 2006. 48p. pap. 16.95 (978-1-4241-1321-7(0)) PublishAmerica, Inc.

Arnold, Tedd. Prince Fly Guy. 2015. (Fly Guy Ser.: 15). (ENG., Illus.). 32p. (J). (gr. -1-3). 6.99 (978-0-545-66275-8(3), Cartwheel Bks.) Scholastic, Inc.

—Prince Fly Guy. 2015. (Fly Guy Ser.: 15). lib. bdg. 17.20 (978-0-606-37831-4(6)) Turtleback Bks.

Arnoux, Lucie, illus. In Their Shoes: Fairy Tales & Folktales. 2016. (ENG.). 128p. (J). (gr. 4-7). pap. 9.99 (978-1-78269-101-3(4), Pushkin Children's Bks.) Steerforth Pr.

Arps, Melissa & Lagonegro, Melissa. Belle's Story. RH Disney, illus. 2017. (Pictureback(R) Ser.). (ENG.). 24p. (J). (gr. -1-1). pap. 4.99 (978-0-7364-3592-5(1), RH/Disney) Random Hse. Children's Bks.

Artell, Mike. Jacques & de Beanstalk. Harris, Jim, illus. 2010. (ENG.). 32p. (J). (gr. k-3). 18.99 (978-0-8037-2816-5(6), Dial Bks) Penguin Young Readers Group.

—Petite Rouge. 2004. (J). 27.75 (978-1-4193-1631-9(1)) Recorded Bks., Inc.

Artful Doodlers Limited Staff, illus. It's Absolutely True. 2006. (Famous Fables Ser.). (J). 6.99 (978-1-59939-029-1(9)) Cornerstone Pr.

Asbjørnsen, Peter Christen. The Three Billy Goats Gruff. Vohra, Sibi, illus. 2010. (J). (978-1-60617-149-3(6)) Teaching Strategies, LLC.

—The Three Billy Goats Gruff. Scott, Gavin, illus. 2014. (J). (978-1-4723-5209-5(2)) Parragon Bk. Service Ltd.

Ash, Jutta. Rapunzel. 2012. (ENG., Illus.). 28p. (J). (gr. k-2). pap. 10.99 (978-1-84939-372-0(9)) Andersen Pr. GBR. Dist: Independent Pubs. Group.

Ashley, John A. The Gathering of the Fairy Horses Series. 2009. 59p. pap. 16.84 (978-1-4092-0638-5(6)) 2008. 64p. 44.58 (978-1-4092-2152-4(0)) Lulu Pr., Inc.

Assorted. Once upon a Time ... 2014. (Storytale Treasuries Ser.). (ENG., Illus.). 144p. (J). (gr. -1-k). 14.99 **(978-1-78445-159-2(2))** Top That! Publishing PLC GBR. Dist: Independent Pubs. Group.

Attard, Ebenor. Ali Baba & the Forty Thieves. 2004. (J). (BEN & ENG.). pap. 15.24 (978-1-84444-528-8(3)); (CHI & ENG.). pap. 16.95 (978-1-84444-529-5(1)); (ENG & URD.). pap. 15.24 (978-1-84444-546-2(1)); (ENG & VIE.). pap. 16.95 (978-1-84444-547-9(X)) Mantra Lingua GBR. Dist: Chinasprout, Inc.

Attard, Enebor. Ali Baba & the Forty Thieves. Holland, Richard, illus. 32p. (J). 2005. pap. (978-1-84444-526-4(7)) 2004. (CHI & ENG.). bds. (978-1-84444-530-1(5)) Mantra Lingua.

Auch, Mary Jane. The Princess & the Pizza. Auch, Herm, illus. 2003. (ENG.). 32p. (J). (gr. k-3). 7.99 (978-0-8234-1798-8(0)) Holiday Hse., Inc.

Auerbach, Annie. Cindy Big Hair: A Twisted (and Teased & Braided) Cinderella Story. Maxey, David, illus. 2005. 16p. (J). 12.95 (978-1-58117-387-1(3), Intervisual/Piggy Toes) Bendon, Inc.

Auerbach, Annie & PopCap Games Staff. The Three Little Pigs Fight Back. Grosvenor, Charles & Roberts, Jeremy, illus. 2013. (Plants vs. Zombies Ser.). (ENG.). 24p. (J). (gr. -1-3). pap. 4.99 (978-0-06-222838-3(2), HarperFestival) HarperCollins Pubs.

Austin, Patrick. The Brave Little Tailor. Imodraj, illus. 2014. (ENG.). 16p. (J). (gr. -1-3). 7.99 (978-1-4867-0016-5(0)) Flowerpot Children's Pr. Inc. CAN. Dist: Cardinal Pubs. Group.

Avventure Di Pinocchio. pap. 19.95 (978-88-451-2911-7(X)) Fabbri Editori - RCS Libri ITA. Dist: Distribooks, Inc.

Award, Anna. Cinderella. 2012. (ENG., Illus.). 24p. (J). pap. 4.95 (978-1-84135-768-3(5)) Award Pubns. Ltd. GBR. Dist: Parkwest Pubns., Inc.

—Dally Duck. 2012. (ENG., Illus.). 24p. (J). pap. 4.95 (978-1-84135-769-0(3)) Award Pubns. Ltd. GBR. Dist: Parkwest Pubns., Inc.

—Hansel & Gretel. 2012. (ENG., Illus.). 24p. (J). pap. 4.95 (978-1-84135-771-3(5)) Award Pubns. Ltd. GBR. Dist: Parkwest Pubns., Inc.

—Little Red Riding Hood. 2012. (ENG., Illus.). 24p. (J). pap. 4.95 (978-1-84135-773-7(1)) Award Pubns. Ltd. GBR. Dist: Parkwest Pubns., Inc.

—Puss in Boots. 2012. (ENG., Illus.). 24p. (J). pap. 4.95 (978-1-84135-774-4(X)) Award Pubns. Ltd. GBR. Dist: Parkwest Pubns., Inc.

—The Story of Puss in Boots: See the Picture & Say the Word. 2012. (ENG.). 24p. (J). pap. 9.95 (978-1-84135-512-2(7)) Award Pubns. Ltd. GBR. Dist: Parkwest Pubns., Inc.

—Thumbelina. 2012. (ENG.). 24p. (J). pap. 9.95 (978-1-84135-519-1(4)); (Illus.). pap. 4.95 (978-1-84135-775-1(8)) Award Pubns. Ltd. GBR. Dist: Parkwest Pubns., Inc.

Award, Anna, creator. Hansel & Gretel. 2005. (J). 18.95 (978-0-439-80423-3(X)) Weston Woods Studios, Inc.

Award, Anna, et al. Hansel & Gretel. 2003. (SPA & CAT.). (978-84-246-2535-1(8), GL7967) La Galera, S.A. Editorial ESP. Dist: Lectorum Pubns., Inc.

Award Publications Staff. Jack & the Beanstalk. 2012. (ENG., Illus.). 24p. pap. 6.50 (978-1-84135-537-5(2)) Award Pubns. Ltd. GBR. Dist: Parkwest Pubns., Inc.

Axel, Brett. Goblinheart: A Fairy Tale. Biddlespacher, Tara, illus. 2012. (J). 15.00 (978-0-9769771-2-4(5)) Eastwaterfront Pr.

Aylesworth, Jim. The Gingerbread Man. McClintock, Barbara, illus. 2010. (ENG.). 32p. (J). (gr. k — 1). bds. 6.99 (978-0-545-23514-3(6), Cartwheel Bks.) Scholastic, Inc.

—Goldilocks & the Three Bears. McClintock, Barbara, illus. 2003. (ENG.). 32p. (J). (gr. -1-3). 17.99 (978-0-439-39545-8(3), Scholastic Pr.) Scholastic, Inc.

AZ Books, creator. Cinderella. 2012. (Musical Fairy Tales Ser.). (ENG., Illus.). 12p. (J). (gr. -1-3). bds. 15.95 (978-1-61889-067-2(0)) AZ Bks. LLC.

—French Fairy Tales. 2012. (Fairy Tales from Around the World Ser.). (ENG., Illus.). 16p. (J). (gr. -1-3). bds. 11.95 (978-1-61889-288-1(6)) AZ Bks. LLC.

—Italian Fairy Tales. 2012. (Fairy Tales from Around the World Ser.). (ENG., Illus.). 16p. (J). (gr. -1-3). bds. 11.95 (978-1-61889-289-8(4)) AZ Bks. LLC.

AZ Books Staff. Asian Fairy Tales. 2012. (Fairy Tales from Around the World Ser.). (ENG., Illus.). 16p. (J). (gr. -1-3). bds. 11.95 (978-1-61889-290-4(8)) AZ Bks. LLC.

—British Fairy Tales. 2012. (Fairy Tales from Around the World Ser.). (ENG., Illus.). 16p. (J). (gr. -1-3). bds. 11.95 (978-1-61889-291-1(6)) AZ Bks. LLC.

—Cinderella. Zyl, Olga, ed. 2012. (Classic Fairy Tales Ser.). (ENG.). 10p. (J). (gr. -1-k). bds. 9.95 (978-1-61889-007-8(7)) AZ Bks. LLC.

—Little Thumb. Zyl, Olga, ed. 2012. (Classic Fairy Tales Ser.). (ENG.). 10p. (J). (gr. -1-k). bds. 9.95 (978-1-61889-008-5(5)) AZ Bks. LLC.

Babbitt, Natalie. Elsie Times Eight. Babbitt, Natalie, illus. 2005. (Illus.). 26p. (J). (gr. k-4). reprint ed. 16.00 (978-0-7567-9640-2(7)) DIANE Publishing Co.

—Kneeknock Rise. 2003. (J). (gr. 3-7). 20.75 (978-0-8446-7236-6(X)) Smith, Peter Pub., Inc.

—Ouch! Marcellino, Fred, illus. pap. 18.95 incl. audio compact disk (978-1-59112-350-7(X)); pap. incl. audio compact disk (978-1-59112-558-7(8)) Live Oak Media.

Bach, Shelby. Of Giants & Ice. Loftis, Cory, illus. 2013. (Ever Afters Ser.: 1). (ENG.). 368p. (J). (gr. 3-7). pap. 7.99 (978-1-4424-3147-8(4), Simon & Schuster Bks. For Young Readers) Simon & Schuster Bks. For Young Readers.

—Of Giants & Ice. 2012. (Ever Afters Ser.: 1). (ENG., Illus.). 352p. (J). (gr. 3-7). 15.99 (978-1-4424-3146-1(6), Simon & Schuster Bks. For Young Readers) Simon & Schuster Bks. For Young Readers.

—Of Sorcery & Snow. 2015. (Ever Afters Ser.: 3). (ENG., Illus.). 352p. (J). (gr. 3-7). pap. 8.99 (978-1-4424-9785-6(8), Simon & Schuster Bks. For Young Readers) Simon & Schuster Bks. For Young Readers.

—Of Witches & Wind. 2013. (Ever Afters Ser.: 2). (ENG., Illus.). 400p. (J). (gr. 3-7). 15.99 (978-1-4424-3149-2(0), Simon & Schuster Bks. For Young Readers) Simon & Schuster Bks. For Young Readers.

Baggott, Stella, illus. Lots of Things to Find & Color in Fairyland. 2015. (Lots of Things to Find & Color Ser.). (ENG.). 96p. (J). (gr. k-5). pap. 12.99 (978-0-7945-3329-8(9), Usborne) EDC Publishing.

Bailer, Darice & Domínguez, Madelca. El Lobo y Los Siete Cabritos. Montañà, Marta, illus. 2007. (SPA & ENG.). 28p. (J). (978-0-545-02962-9(7)) Scholastic, Inc.

Bailer, Darice, et al. El Ruiseñor. Max, illus. 2007. (SPA & ENG.). 28p. (J). (978-0-545-03029-8(3)) Scholastic, Inc.

Bajaj, Subash, illus. The Three Little Pigs. 2010. (J). (978-1-60617-135-6(6)) Teaching Strategies, LLC.

Baker, E. D. The Bravest Princess. 2014. (Wide-Awake Princess Ser.: 3). (ENG., Illus.). 272p. (YA). (gr. 5-8). 16.99 (978-1-61963-136-6(9), 9781619631366, Bloomsbury USA Childrens) Bloomsbury Publishing USA.

—Dragon Kiss. 2nd ed. (Tales of the Frog Princess Ser.). (ENG.). (YA). 2009. 288p. (gr. 5-8). 16.99 (978-1-59990-348-4(2), 9781599903484) 2015. 304p. (gr. 3-6). pap. 8.99 (978-1-61963-623-1(9), 9781619636231) Bloomsbury Publishing USA. (Bloomsbury USA Childrens).

—The Dragon Princess. 2010. (Tales of the Frog Princess Ser.). (ENG.). 240p. (YA). (gr. 5-8). pap. 7.99 (978-1-59990-448-1(9), 9781599904481, Bloomsbury USA Childrens) Bloomsbury Publishing USA.

—Dragon's Breath: Read-Along/Homework Pack, 6 vols. unabr. ed. 2005. (Frog Princess Ser.: 2). (SPA.). (J). (gr. 5-8). 78.75 (978-1-4193-3563-1(4), 42041) Recorded Bks., Inc.

—The Frog Princess Returns. 2017. (Tales of the Frog Princess Ser.). (ENG.). 208p. (J). 16.99 (978-1-68119-137-9(7), 9781681191379, Bloomsbury USA Childrens) Bloomsbury Publishing USA.

—The Princess & the Pearl. 2017. (Wide-Awake Princess Ser.). (ENG.). 240p. (J). 16.99 (978-1-68119-135-5(0), 9781681191355, Bloomsbury USA Childrens) Bloomsbury Publishing USA.

—Princess Between Worlds: A Tale of the Wide-Awake Princess. 2016. (Wide-Awake Princess Ser.: 5). (ENG., Illus.). 224p. (J). 16.99 (978-1-61963-847-1(9), 9781619638471, Bloomsbury USA Childrens) Bloomsbury Publishing USA.

—Princess in Disguise. 2015. (Wide-Awake Princess Ser.: 4). (ENG.). 224p. (YA). (gr. 3-6). 16.99 (978-1-61963-573-9(9), 9781619635739, Bloomsbury USA Childrens) Bloomsbury Publishing USA.

—A Question of Magic. 2015. (ENG.). 288p. (YA). (gr. 3-6). pap. 8.99 (978-1-61963-437-4(6), 9781619634374, Bloomsbury USA Childrens) Bloomsbury Publishing USA.

—Unlocking the Spell: A Tale of the Wide-Awake Princess. (Wide-Awake Princess Ser.: 2). (ENG.). (YA). 2014. 288p. (gr. 5-6). pap. 8.99 (978-1-61963-194-6(6), 9781619631946) 2012. 272p. (gr. 3-12). 16.99 (978-1-59990-841-0(7), 9781599908410) Bloomsbury Publishing USA. (Bloomsbury USA Childrens).

—The Wide-Awake Princess. (Wide-Awake Princess Ser.: 1). (ENG.). (YA). (gr. 5-14). 2012. 288p. pap. 8.99 (978-1-59990-658-4(9), 9781599906584) 2010. 272p. 16.99 (978-1-59990-487-0(X), 9781599904870) Bloomsbury Publishing USA. (Bloomsbury USA Childrens).

Baker, Sara, illus. Ready to Read Sleeping Beauty. 2007. (Ready to Read Ser.). 31p. (J). (gr. k-2). (978-1-84610-441-1(6)) Make Believe Ideas.

Balaskovits, A. A. Magic for Unlucky Girls: Stories. 2017. (SFWP Literary Awards Ser.). (ENG.). 230p. pap. 14.95 (978-1-939650-66-5(6)) Santa Fe Writers Project.

Balázs, Béla. The Cloak of Dreams: Chinese Fairy Tales. Lydes, Mariette, illus. 2010. (Oddly Modern Fairy Tales Ser.). (ENG.). 208p. 24.95 (978-0-691-14711-6(6)) Princeton Univ. Pr.

Balducci, Rita. The Nutcracker. Beckett, Sheilah, illus. 2014. (Little Golden Book Ser.). (ENG.). 24p. (J). (-k). 4.99 (978-0-385-36993-0(X), Golden Bks.) Random Hse. Children's Bks.

Baldwin, James. Fifty Famous Stories Retold. 2009. 160p. 32.99 (978-1-59547-545-9(1)) NuVision Pubns., LLC.

Bania, Michael. Kumak's River: A Tall Tale from the Far North. 2012. (ENG., Illus.). 32p. (J). (gr. -1-2). pap. 9.99 (978-0-88240-887-3(9), Alaska Northwest Bks.) Graphic Arts Ctr. Publishing Co.

Bannerman, Helen. Little Black Sambo. 2006. (Illus.). pap. (978-1-4065-0769-0(5)) Dodo Pr.

Barella, Laura, illus. The Brave Little Tailor. 2014. (Flip-Up Fairy Tales Ser.). (ENG.). 24p. (J). (978-1-84643-654-3(0)) Child's Play International Ltd.

—Donkey Skin. 2011. (Flip-Up Fairy Tales Ser.). (ENG.). 24p. (J). audio compact disk (978-1-84643-410-5(6)); (gr. 2-2). (978-1-84643-371-9(1)) Child's Play International Ltd.

—The Little Mermaid. 2010. (Flip-Up Fairy Tales Ser.). (ENG.). 24p. (J). (gr. -1-2). audio compact disk (978-1-84643-331-3(2)) Child's Play International Ltd.

—Sleeping Beauty. 2009. (Flip-Up Fairy Tales Ser.). (ENG.). 24p. (J). (gr. -1-2). pap. (978-1-84643-252-1(9)); audio compact disk (978-1-84643-295-8(2)) Child's Play International Ltd.

—The Stonecutter. 2012. (Flip-Up Fairy Tales Ser.). (ENG.). 24p. (J). audio compact disk (978-1-84643-517-1(X)); (978-1-84643-478-5(5)) Child's Play International Ltd.

Baring-Gould, Sabine. The Crock of Gold: Twelve Fairy Tales, O. 2006. pap. 27.95 (978-1-4254-9842-9(6)) Kessinger Publishing, LLC.

Barkow, Henriette. Ali Baba & the Forty Thieves. Brazell, Derek, illus. 2004. 28p. (J). (POL & ENG.). pap. (978-1-84444-545-5(3)); (ENG & SWE.). pap. (978-1-84444-539-4(9)); (ENG, RUS, SWE & SOM.). pap. (978-1-84444-540-0(2)) Mantra Lingua.

—Buri & the Marrow: Buri Dhe Kungulli. Finlay, Lizzie, illus. 2004. (ENG & ALB.). 24p. (J). pap. (978-1-85269-578-1(1)) Mantra Lingua.

—The Buskers of Bremen. Reed, Nathan, illus. 2004. (ENG & PAN.). 24p. (J). pap. (978-1-85269-772-3(5)) Mantra Lingua.

—Don't Cry, Sly! Johnson, Richard, illus. 2004. (ENG & VIE.). 32p. (J). pap. (978-1-85269-672-6(9)) Mantra Lingua.

—Three Billy Goats Gruff. Johnson, Richard, illus. 2004. (ITA & ENG.). 32p. (J). pap. (978-1-85269-786-0(5)) Mantra Lingua.

Barkow, Henriette & Johnson, Richard, illus. Don't Cry, Sly! Mos Qaj Dhelperush! 2004. (ENG & ALB.). 32p. (J). pap. (978-1-85269-648-1(6)) Mantra Lingua.

Barkow, Henriette & Reed, Nathan, illus. The Buskers of Bremen: Kengetaret Endacak Te Bremenit. 2004. (ALB & ENG.). 24p. (J). pap. (978-1-85269-764-8(4)) Mantra Lingua.

Barna, Beverly. The Daughter of Dreams, a Fable of Destiny. White, David, illus. 2009. 28p. pap. 14.95 (978-1-936051-09-0(5)) Peppertree Pr., The.

Barnhill, Kelly. Iron Hearted Violet. Bruno, Iacopo, illus. 2014. (ENG.). 448p. (J). (gr. 3-7). pap. 7.00 (978-0-316-05675-5(8)) Little, Brown Bks. for Young Readers.

Baron, Lindamichelle. The Lion & the Man: A Fable. Huggins, Carl, illus. 2009. 72p. pap. 15.95 (978-0-940938-25-0(1)) Harlin Jacque Pubns.

Barron, T. A. Merlin's Dragon. 2008. (Merlin Saga Ser.: 6). (ENG.). 336p. (J). (gr. 5-18). 19.99 (978-0-399-24750-7(5), Philomel Bks.) Penguin Young Readers Group.

Bartles, Veronica. The Princess & the Frogs. Palacios, Sara, illus. 2016. 40p. (J). (gr. -1-3). 17.99 (978-0-06-236591-0(6)) HarperCollins Pubs.

Baruzzi, Agnese. Aladdin: A Cut-Paper Book. 2014. (ENG., Illus.). 14p. (J). (gr. k-2). 19.99 (978-1-85707-873-2(X)) Tango Bks. GBR. Dist: Independent Pubs. Group.

Bas, Mercè Escardó I & Boada, Francesc. The Ugly Duckling. Capdevila, Francesc, illus. 2004. (Bilingual Fairy Tales Ser.: BILI). (ENG.). 32p. (J). (gr. -1-7). 6.99 (978-0-8118-4455-0(2)) Chronicle Bks. LLC.

Bateman, Teresa. Traveling Tom & the Leprechaun. Potter, Melisande, illus. 2007. (ENG.). 32p. (J). (gr. -1-3). 16.95 (978-0-8234-1976-0(2)) Holiday Hse., Inc.

Batt, Tanya Robyn. The Fabrics of Fairytale: Stories Spun from Far & Wide. Griffin, Rachel, illus. 2007. (ENG.). 80p. (J). (gr. -1-3). pap. 16.99 (978-1-84686-089-8(X)) Barefoot Bks., Inc.

—The Faerie's Gift. Ceccoli, Nicoletta, illus. 2008. (ENG.). 32p. (J). (gr. -1-3). 17.99 (978-1-84686-230-4(2)) Barefoot Bks., Inc.

Batt Tanya Robyn. Faeries Gift. Ceccoli Nicoletta, illus. 2006. 0032p. pap. 6.99 (978-1-905236-73-2(5)) Barefoot Bks., Inc.

Batt, Tanya Robyn. The Princess & the White Bear King. Ceccoli, Nicoletta, illus. 2004. 40p. (J). 16.99 (978-1-84148-339-9(7)) Barefoot Bks., Inc.

—The Princess & White Bear. Ceccoli, Nicoletta, illus. 2008. (ENG.). 40p. (J). (gr. -1-3). 17.99 (978-1-84686-228-1(0)) Barefoot Bks., Inc.

Baum, L. Frank. American Fairy Tales. 2007. 112p. per. 9.95 (978-1-60312-100-2(5)); 22.95 (978-1-60312-899-5(9)) Aegypan.

—The Discontented Gopher: A Prairie Tale. Conahan, Carolyn Digby, illus. 2006. (Prairie Tales Ser.). 40p. (J). (gr. 3-7). 14.95 (978-0-9749195-9-1(4), South Dakota State Historical Society Pr.) South Dakota State Historical Society Pr.

—The Enchanted Buffalo. Montileaux, Donald F., illus. 2010. 31p. (J). (gr. 2-5). 14.95 (978-0-9822749-3-4(9), South Dakota State Historical Society Pr.) South Dakota State Historical Society Pr.

—Tales of Mother Goose. 2009. 174p. (J). pap. (978-1-934941-68-3(9)) Red & Black Pubs.

Bawden, Deborah & Collins UK Publishing Staff. The Honey-Guide Bird. Auriemma, Monica, illus. 2016. (ENG.). 32p. (J). pap. 8.95 (978-0-00-814710-5(8)) HarperCollins Pubs. Ltd. GBR. Dist: Independent Pubs. Group.

Baxter, Nicola. Favourite Fairy Tales: Picture Fairy Tales for Little Ones. Parry, Jo, illus. 2016. (ENG.). 16p. (J). (gr. -1-12). bds. 10.99 (978-1-84322-625-3(1), Armadillo) Anness Publishing GBR. Dist: National Bk. Network.

—My First Fairy Tales: Eight Exciting Picture Stories for Little Ones. Parry, Jo, illus. 2013. (ENG.). 16p. (J). (gr. -1-2). bds. 13.99 (978-1-84322-991-9(9), Armadillo) Anness Publishing GBR. Dist: National Bk. Network.

—Party at the Fairy Palace: Peek Inside the 3D Windows. Chaffey, Samantha, illus. 2013. (ENG.). 12p. 16.99 (978-1-84322-725-0(8)) Anness Publishing GBR. Dist: National Bk. Network.

—Traditional Fairy Tales from Hans Christian Andersen & the Brothers Grimm. Shuttleworth, Cathie, illus. 2013. (ENG.). 192p. (J). (gr. 1-7). pap. 14.99 (978-1-84322-971-1(4)) Anness Publishing GBR. Dist: National Bk. Network.

Baxter, Nicola & Francis, Jan. Traditional Fairy Tales: Eight Exciting Picture Stories for Little Ones. Parry, Jo, illus. 2013. (ENG.). 16p. (J). (gr. -1-2). 13.99 (978-1-84322-992-6(7), Armadillo) Anness Publishing GBR. Dist: National Bk. Network.

Baxter, Nicola & Ladybird Books Staff. Goldilocks & the Three Bears. 2015. (First Favourite Tales Ser.). (ENG., Illus.). 32p. (J). (-k). 7.99 (978-1-4093-0629-0(1)) Penguin Bks., Ltd. GBR. Dist: Independent Pubs. Group.

—The Three Little Pigs. 2015. (First Favourite Tales Ser.). (ENG., Illus.). 32p. (J). (-k). 7.99 (978-1-4093-0632-0(1)) Penguin Bks., Ltd. GBR. Dist: Independent Pubs. Group.

Baxter, Nicola & Morton, Ken. A Storybook of Ugly Ogres & Terrible Trolls: Ten Fantastic Tales of Frightful Fun. 2013. (ENG., Illus.). 80p. (J). (gr. -1-12). pap. 9.99 (978-1-84322-938-4(2), Armadillo) Anness Publishing GBR. Dist: National Bk. Network.

Beardshaw, Rosalind, illus. Kiss the Frog. 2013. (J). (978-1-4351-4925-0(4)) Barnes & Noble, Inc.

Beaumont, Jeanne Marie Le Prince De. Beauty & the Beast. Crane, Walter, illus. 2013. 28p. pap. (978-1-909115-62-0(2)) Planet, The.

Beauty & the Beast. unabr. ed. (Read-Along Ser.). (J). 7.99 incl. audio (978-1-55723-252-6(0)) Walt Disney Records.

Beauty & the Beast...Getting to Know You. 2008. (Disney 8*8 Ser.). 24p. pap. (978-1-4075-1622-6(1)) Parragon, Inc.

Bechstein, Ludwig. The Rabbit Catcher & Other Fairy Tales. Jarrell, Randall, tr. Fontana, Ugo, illus. 2011. 42p. 35.95 (978-1-258-08375-5(2)) Literary Licensing, LLC.

Beck, Ian. Tom Trueheart & the Land of Dark Stories. 2008. (Illus.). 384p. (J). (gr. 3-7). lib. bdg. 17.89 (978-0-06-115214-6(5), Greenwillow Bks.) HarperCollins Pubs.

Beckford, Avril. The Tooth Fairy. 2010. 28p. (J). pap. 12.49 (978-1-4490-9060-9(5)) AuthorHouse.

Becq, Cecile. Once upon a Timeless Tale: Cinderella. 2016. (Once upon a Timeless Tale Ser.). (ENG.). 32p. (J). (gr. k-2). 9.99 (978-1-74297-403-3(1)) Little Hare Bks. AUS. Dist: Independent Pubs. Group.

Beer, Barbara Vagnozzi. Jack & the Beanstalk. Vagnozzi, Barbara, illus. 2005. (Flip-Up Fairy Tales Ser.). (ENG.). 24p. (J). pap. (978-1-904550-20-4(7)) Child's Play International Ltd.

Bella Addormentata Nel. pap. 14.95 (978-88-04-46595-9(6)) Mondadori ITA. Dist: Distribooks, Inc.

La Belle au Bois Dormant. (FRE.). 48p. pap. 12.95 incl. audio compact disk (978-2-89558-067-6(7)) Coffragants CAN. Dist: Penton Overseas, Inc.

Belle, Trixie & Caruso-Scott, Melissa. Beauty & the Beast: Les Petits Fairytales. Lake, Oliver, illus. 2013. (Petits Fairytales Ser.). (ENG.). 26p. (J). (gr. -1 — 1). bds. 7.99 (978-0-8050-9788-7(0), 9780805097887, Holt, Henry & Co. Bks. For Young Readers) Holt, Henry & Co.

—Goldilocks & the Three Bears: Les Petits Fairytales. Lake, Oliver, illus. 2014. (Petits Fairytales Ser.). (ENG.). 26p. (J). (gr. -1 — 1). bds. 7.99 (978-0-8050-9912-6(3), 9780805099126, Holt, Henry & Co. Bks. For Young Readers) Holt, Henry & Co.

—The Little Mermaid: Les Petits Fairytales. Lake, Oliver, illus. 2013. (Petits Fairytales Ser.). (ENG.). 26p. (J). (gr. -1 — 1). bds. 7.99 (978-0-8050-9789-4(9), 9780805097894, Holt, Henry & Co. Bks. For Young Readers) Holt, Henry & Co.

—Little Red Riding Hood: Les Petits Fairytales. Lake, Oliver, illus. 2014. (Petits Fairytales Ser.). (ENG.). 26p. (J). (gr. -1 — 1). bds. 7.99 (978-0-8050-9905-8(0), 9780805099058, Holt, Henry & Co. Bks. For Young Readers) Holt, Henry & Co.

—Rapunzel. Lake, Oliver, illus. 2013. (Petits Fairytales Ser.). (ENG.). 26p. (J). (gr. -1 — 1). bds. 7.99 (978-0-8050-9790-0(2), 9780805097900, Holt, Henry & Co. Bks. For Young Readers) Holt, Henry & Co.

—Sleeping Beauty: Les Petits Fairytales. Lake, Oliver, illus. 2013. (Petits Fairytales Ser.). (ENG.). 26p. (J). (gr. -1 — 1). bds. 7.99 (978-0-8050-9791-7(0), 9780805097917, Holt, Henry & Co. Bks. For Young Readers) Holt, Henry & Co.

Benedetti, Martha J. Fantasy Fairytale: 7 short Stories. 2009. 108p. pap. 44.99 (978-1-4389-1096-3(7)) AuthorHouse.

Benjamin, Sigalit. Garland of Stars. 2009. 26p. pap. 14.50 (978-1-60860-345-9(8), Eloquent Bks.) Strategic Book Publishing & Rights Agency (SBPRA).

Benthre. Do Not Enter. 2003. (Illus.). 106p. pap. 12.95 (978-0-9721640-7-8(3)) Whispering Wind Publishing Inc.

Bentley, Jonathan, illus. Hansel & Gretel. 2016. (Once upon a Timeless Tale Ser.). (ENG.). 32p. (J). (gr. k-2). 9.99 (978-1-921894-89-3(X)) Little Hare Bks. AUS. Dist: Independent Pubs. Group.

Berk, Ari. The Secret History of Mermaids & Creatures of the Deep. Anderson, Wayne, illus. 2009. (ENG.). 48p. (J). (gr. 3-7). 17.99 (978-0-7636-4515-1(X)) Candlewick Pr.

Bernadine, Joyce. The Teeth Keepers. 2008. 73p. pap. 19.95 (978-1-60563-848-5(X)) America Star Bks.

Berrios, Frank & RH Disney Staff. Snow White & the Seven Dwarfs. Disney Storybook Artists Staff, illus. 2006. (Read-Aloud Board Book Ser.). (ENG.). 24p. (J). (gr. k — 1). bds. 4.99 (978-0-7364-2426-4(1), RH/Disney) Random Hse. Children's Bks.

Beskow, Elsa. The Land of Long Ago. 2010. (ENG., Illus.). 32p. (J). (gr. -1-1). 17.95 (978-0-86315-771-4(8)) Floris Bks. GBR. Dist: SteinerBooks, Inc.

Beston, Henry. The Firelight Fairy Book. 2008. 116p. 22.95 (978-1-60664-890-2(X)); pap. 10.95 (978-1-60664-009-8(7)) Aegypan.

Bevan, Sharon L. Bella Blue Fairy Finds a New Friend. 2009. (Illus.). 48p. pap. (978-1-84748-632-5(0)) Athena Pr.

Bib, Betty. Betty Bib's Fairy Handbook: A Field Guide to Fairies & Their Habitats. 2005. (Illus.). 72p. (J). (gr. 2-6). (978-1-84483-194-4(9), Duncan Baird Pubs.) Watkins Media Limited.

Bilan, J. Jack & the Beanstalk. 2007. 6p. 16.95 (978-1-58117-595-0(7), Intervisual/Piggy Toes) Bendon, Inc.

Bills, Taylor, illus. Jack & the Beanstalk. 2009. 24p. 12.95 (978-0-9776845-3-3(9)) 3D Alley, Inc.

—The Ugly Duckling. 2009. 24p. 12.95 (978-0-9776845-1-9(2)) 3D Alley, Inc.

Bindrim, Hans-Wolfgang. Wilhelm Hauffs die Errettung Fatmes: Textanalyse und Interpretation. 2012. (Europaeische Hochschulschriften / European University Studies / Publications Universitaires Européennes Ser.: 2028). (GER.). 130p. pap. 32.95 (978-3-631-63429-5(3), 263429) Lang, Peter GmbH, Internationaler Verlag der Wissenschaften DEU. Dist: Lang, Peter.

Biro, Val. Little Red Riding Hood: See the Picture & Say the Word. 2012. (ENG.). 24p. (J). pap. 9.95

(978-1-84135-515-3(1)) Award Pubns. Ltd. GBR. Dist: Parkwest Pubns., Inc.

Bishop, Jennie. The Squire & the Scroll: A Tale of the Rewards of a Pure Heart. McDaniels, Preston, illus. 2009. (ENG.). 32p. (J). 15.99 *(978-1-59317-382-1(2))* Warner Pr., Inc.

Black, Holly & DiTerlizzi, Tony. The Wrath of Mulgarath. 5th ed. 2004. (Spiderwick Chronicles Ser.: 5). (ENG., Illus.). 160p. (J). (gr. 2-6). 10.99 *(978-0-689-85940-3(6))*, Simon & Schuster Bks. For Young Readers) Simon & Schuster Bks. For Young Readers.

Blackaby, Susan. El Patito Feo. Ruiz, Carlos, tr. from ENG. Delage, Charlene, illus. 2006. (Read-It! Readers en Español: Cuentos de Hadas Ser.). (SPA.). 32p. (gr. k-3). 21.32 *(978-1-4048-1644-2(5))*, Easy Readers) Picture Window Bks.

—La Princesa Del Guisante: Versión Del Cuento de Hans Christian Anderson. Abello, Patricia, tr. from ENG. Delage, Charlene, illus. 2006. (Read-It! Readers en Español: Cuentos de Hadas Ser.).Tr. of Princess & the Pea - A Retelling of the Grimm's Fairy Tale. (SPA.). 32p. (gr. k-3). 21.32 *(978-1-4048-1634-3(8))*, Easy Readers) Picture Window Bks.

—El Traje Nuevo Del Emperador. Abello, Patricia, tr. from ENG. Delage, Charlene, illus. 2006. (Read-It! Readers en Español: Cuentos de Hadas Ser.). (SPA.). 32p. (gr. k-3). 21.32 *(978-1-4048-1629-9(1))*, Easy Readers) Picture Window Bks.

Blackstone, Stella. Storytime: First Tales for Sharing. Wilson, Anne, illus. 2005. (ENG.). 96p. (J). (gr. -1-3). 19.99 *(978-1-84148-345-0(1))* Barefoot Bks., Inc.

Blair, Eric. Belling the Cat: A Retelling of Aesop's Fable, 1 vol. Silverman, Dianne, illus. 2013. (My First Classic Story Ser.). (ENG.). 24p. (gr. k-3). pap. 7.10 *(978-1-4795-1854-8(9))*, My First Classic Story) Picture Window Bks.

—The Bremen Town Musicians: A Retelling of the Grimm's Fairy Tale, 1 vol. Dickson, Bill, illus. 2013. (My First Classic Story Ser.). (ENG.). 32p. (gr. k-3). pap. 7.10 *(978-1-4795-1848-7(4))*, My First Classic Story) Picture Window Bks.

—The Frog Prince: A Retelling of the Grimm's Fairy Tale, 1 vol. Ouren, Todd, illus. 2013. (My First Classic Story Ser.). (ENG.). 32p. (gr. k-3). pap. 7.10 *(978-1-4795-1853-1(0))*, My First Classic Story) Picture Window Bks.

—El Lobo y los Siete Cabritos. Abello, Patricia, tr. from ENG. Petrusek, Brett, illus. 2006. (Read-It! Readers en Español: Cuentos de Hadas Ser.). (SPA.). 32p. (gr. k-3). 21.32 *(978-1-4048-1645-9(3))*, Easy Readers) Picture Window Bks.

—El Ninito de Jengibre, 1 vol. Abello, Patricia, tr. from ENG. Peterson, Ben, illus. 2006. (Read-It! Readers en Español: Cuentos Folclóricos Ser.).Tr. of Gingerbread Man. (SPA.). 32p. (gr. k-3). 21.32 *(978-1-4048-1647-3(X))*, Easy Readers) Picture Window Bks.

—El Principe Encantado. Abello, Patricia, tr. from ENG. Ouren, Todd, illus. 2006. (Read-It! Readers en Español: Cuentos de Hadas Ser.).Tr. of Frog Prince. (SPA.). 32p. (gr. k-3). 21.32 *(978-1-4048-1631-2(3))*, Easy Readers) Picture Window Bks.

—Rumpelstiltskin: A Retelling of the Grimm's Fairy Tale, 1 vol. Shaw, David, illus. 2013. (My First Classic Story Ser.). (ENG.). 32p. (gr. k-3). pap. 7.10 *(978-1-4795-1850-0(6))*, My First Classic Story) Picture Window Bks.

—The Shoemaker & His Elves: A Retelling of the Grimm's Fairy Tale, 1 vol. Dickson, Bill, illus. 2013. (My First Classic Story Ser.). (ENG.). 32p. (gr. k-3). pap. 7.10 *(978-1-4795-1849-4(2))*, My First Classic Story) Picture Window Bks.

Blakeslee, S. E. Once upon a Blue Moon: The Chronicles of the Blue Moon. Blakeslee, S. E., illus. 2007. (ENG., Illus.). 32p. (J). 17.95 *(978-0-9789031-0-7(2))* Blaumond Pr.

Blanca Nieves - (Estrella de Mar) 2003. (SPA., Illus.). 16p. 2.95 *(978-968-855-185-1(6))* Suromex, Ediciones, S.A. MEX. Dist: Giron Bks.

Blaylock, Kathy. Adventures of Buddy Fairy & Friends. 2007. 48p. 16.95 *(978-1-4137-9195-2(6))* America Star Bks.

Blevins, Wiley. Cinderella & the Vampire Prince. Cox, Steve, illus. 2016. (Scary Tales Retold Ser.). (ENG.). 24p. (gr. k-3). lib. bdg. 23.99 *(978-1-63440-090-9(9))* Red Chair Pr.

Bloch, Carole. The Hyena & the Seven Little Kids. Morris, Hannah, illus. 2012. (Best Loved Tales for Africa Ser.). (ENG.). 32p. (J). (gr. k-2). pap. 9.95 *(978-1-77009-820-6(8))* Jacana Media ZAF. Dist: Independent Pubs. Group.

Block, Francesca Lia. Roses & Bones: Myths, Tales, & Secrets. 2010. (ENG.). 400p. (YA). (gr. 9). pap. 8.99 *(978-0-06-201954-7(6))*, HarperTeen) HarperCollins Pubs.

Blubaugh, Penny. Serendipity Market. 2011. (ENG.). 304p. (YA). (gr. 8). pap. 8.99 *(978-0-06-146877-3(0))*, HarperTeen) HarperCollins Pubs.

Blythe, Gary, illus. A Treasury of Princess Stories. 2009. (ENG.). 80p. (J). (gr. 2-5). 19.99 *(978-0-7636-4478-9(1))* Candlewick Pr.

Blyton, Enid. Beauty & the Beast. 2012. (ENG., Illus.). 24p. pap. 9.95 *(978-1-84135-606-8(9))* Award Pubns. Ltd. GBR. Dist: Parkwest Pubns., Inc.

—Sleeping Beauty. 2012. (ENG., Illus.). 24p. (J). pap. *(978-1-84135-613-6(1))* Award Pubns. Ltd. GBR. Dist: Parkwest Pubns., Inc.

—Tower in Ho-Ho Wood: And Other Stories. 2013. (ENG., Illus.). 192p. (J). 9.95 *(978-1-84135-463-7(5))* Award Pubns. Ltd. GBR. Dist: Parkwest Pubns., Inc.

—Twelve Dancing Princesses. 2012. (ENG., Illus.). 24p. (J). pap. 9.95 *(978-1-84135-610-5(7))* Award Pubns. Ltd. GBR. Dist: Parkwest Pubns., Inc.

Boada, Francesc. Princess & the Pea (la Princesa y el Guisante) A Bilingual Book! Estrada, Pau, illus. 2004. (Bilingual Fairy Tales Ser.: BILI). (ENG.). 32p. (J). (gr. -1-7). pap. 6.99 *(978-0-8118-4452-9(8))* Chronicle Bks. LLC.

Bobrick, Julie, ed. Cinderella: Level 1: Learn Mandarin Chinese Through Fairy Tales. Peters, Li Li & Tao, Ming, trs. Sandoval, Migs, illus. 2006. (Learn Chinese Through Fairy Tales Ser.). (ENG & CHI.). 29p. pap. 14.95 incl. audio compact disk *(978-1-891888-79-3(X))* Slangman Publishing.

Boelts, Maribeth. Dogerella. Wu, Donald, illus. 2008. (Step into Reading Ser.). (ENG.). 48p. (J). (gr. k-3). pap. 3.99 *(978-0-375-83393-9(5))*, Random Hse. Bks. for Young Readers) Random Hse. Children's Bks.

—Pupunzel. 2016. (Step into Reading Ser.). (ENG., Illus.). 48p. (J). (gr. k-3). lib. bdg. 12.99 *(978-1-101-93447-0(6))*, Random Hse. Bks. for Young Readers) Random Hse. Children's Bks.

—Sleeping Bootsie. Cantor, Patricia, illus. 2011. (Step into Reading Ser.). (ENG.). 48p. (J). (gr. k-3). pap. 3.99 *(978-0-375-86678-4(7))*, Random Hse. Bks. for Young Readers) Random Hse. Children's Bks.

Bofill, Francesc. Rapunzel/Rapunzel. Joma, illus. 2006. (Bilingual Fairy Tales Ser.: BILI). (CAT & ENG.). 32p. (J). (gr. -1-7). per. 6.99 *(978-0-8118-5060-5(9))* Chronicle Bks. LLC.

Boldi, Florina, illus. Pug in Boots. 2013. 42p. pap. 9.99 *(978-0-9829132-6-0(5))* Left Paw Pr.

Book Company Staff. Lift-A-Flap Guess Who. 2005. (J). bds. 10.95 *(978-1-74047-620-1(4))* Book Co. Publishing Pty, Ltd., The AUS. Dist: Penton Overseas, Inc.

Borsten, Joan & Vidov, Oleg, eds. Mikhail Baryshnikov's Stories from My Childhood: Beloved Fairy Tales from the Snow Queen to Ivan & His Magicpony to Cinderella. 2005. (Illus.). 128p. (J). (gr. 4-8). reprint ed. 25.00 *(978-0-7567-8941-1(9))* DIANE Publishing Co.

Bouchard, David. The Great Race - The Legend of the Chinese Zodiac. 2004. (J). (gr. k-3). spiral bd. *(978-0-616-01430-1(9))* Canadian National Institute for the Blind/Institut National Canadien pour les Aveugles.

Boucher, Sarah E. Becoming Beauty: A Retelling of Beauty & the Beast. 2014. 249p. (YA). pap. 15.99 *(978-1-4621-1455-9(5))* Cedar Fort, Inc./CFI Distribution.

Boulton, M. T. Megan Button & the Brim-Tree. 2012. 106p. pap. *(978-1-909039-06-3(3))* Legend Pr.

Bowen, Anne. Tooth Fairy's First Night. Berkeley, Jon, illus. 2005. (Carolrhoda Picture Bks.). 32p. (J). (gr. -1-3). 15.95 *(978-1-57505-753-8(0))* Lerner Publishing Group.

Bowen, Betsy, illus. Dhegdheer: A Scary Somali Folktale. 2007. (SOM & ENG.). *(978-1-931016-18-6(6))*; *(978-1-931016-19-3(4))* Minnesota Humanities Ctr.

Bowen, Carl. Jak & the Magic Nano-Beans: a Graphic Novel. Lozano, Omar, illus. 2016. (Far Out Fairy Tales Ser.). (ENG.). 40p. (gr. 3-4). lib. bdg. 25.32 *(978-1-4965-2510-9(8))*, Far Out Fairy Tales) Stone Arch Bks.

Boyle, Eleanor Vere. Beauty & the Beast. 2017. (Calla Editions Ser.). (ENG.). 112p. 25.00 *(978-1-60660-103-7(2))* Dover Pubns., Inc.

Bradman, Tony. After Happily Ever After, 1 vol. Warburton, Sarah, illus. 2014. (After Happily Ever After Ser.). (ENG.). 56p. (gr. 2-3). lib. bdg. 151.92 *(978-1-4342-8929-2(X))*, After Happily Ever After) Stone Arch Bks.

—Fairy Godmother Takes a Break. Warburton, Sarah, illus. 2014. (After Happily Ever After Ser.). (ENG.). 56p. (gr. 2-3). pap. 5.05 *(978-1-4342-7961-3(8))*, After Happily Ever After) Stone Arch Bks.

—Who Will Marry Prince Harry? Bitskoff, Aleksei, illus. 2016. (Reading Ladder Ser.). (ENG.). 48p. (J). (gr. k-2). pap. 7.99 *(978-1-4052-7824-9(2))* Egmont Bks., Ltd. GBR. Dist: Independent Pubs. Group.

Branch, Beverly, illus. Thumbelina: A Tale about Being Nice. 2006. (J). 6.99 *(978-1-59939-024-6(8))* Cornerstone Pr.

Braun, Eric. Little Red Riding Hood: An Interactive Fairy Tale Adventure. Epelbaum, Mariano, illus. 2015. (You Choose: Fractured Fairy Tales Ser.). (ENG.). 112p. (gr. 3-4). pap. 6.95 *(978-1-4914-5929-4(8))*, You Choose Bks.) Capstone Press of Coughlan Cos.

Braun, Eric & Gunderson, Jessica. Cinderella: An Interactive Fairy Tale Adventure. Lopez, Ayesha, illus. 2015. (You Choose: Fractured Fairy Tales Ser.). (ENG.). 112p. (gr. 3-4). lib. bdg. 31.99 *(978-1-4914-5854-9(2))*, You Choose Bks.) Capstone Press of Coughlan Cos.

Bredin, Henrietta & McEwen, Priscilla. The Prince & the Goosegirl: A Story with Activities Based on the Opera by Humperdinck. 2006. (Illus.). 30p. (J). (gr. k-4). reprint ed. pap. 17.00 *(978-1-4223-5538-1(1))* DIANE Publishing Co.

Breslin, Theresa, et al. The Firebird: A Russian Folk Tale. Oliver, Juanbjuan, illus. 2016. (ENG.). 48p. (J). pap. 9.95 *(978-0-00-814718-1(3))* HarperCollins Pubs. Ltd. GBR. Dist: Independent Pubs. Group.

Brett, Jan. Beauty & the Beast. 2014. 16.95 *(978-1-63419-648-2(1))* Perfection Learning Corp.

—Cinders: A Chicken Cinderella. Brett, Jan, illus. 2013. (ENG., Illus.). 32p. (J). (gr. k). 17.99 *(978-0-399-25783-4(7))*, G.P. Putnam's Sons Books for Young Readers) Penguin Publishing Group.

—The Mitten: Oversized Board Book. Brett, Jan, illus. 2014. (ENG., Illus.). 32p. (J). (gr. -1 — 1). bds. 14.99 *(978-0-399-16981-6(4))*, G.P. Putnam's Sons Books for Young Readers) Penguin Young Readers Group.

Brocklehurst, Ruth & Doherty, Gillian. Illustrated Grimm's Fairy Tales. 2011. (Illustrated Stories Ser.). 303p. (J). ring bd. 19.99 *(978-0-7945-2409-8(5))*, Usborne) EDC Publishing.

Brooke, Jasmine. Jack & the Beanstalk: Chart Your Magic Bean's Life Cycle! 2017. (Fairy Tale Fixers: Fixing Fairy Tale Problems with STEM Ser.). 32p. (gr. 3-4). pap. 63.00 ***(978-1-5382-0666-9(8))*** Stevens, Gareth Publishing LLLP.

—The Princess & the Pea: Pass the Pea Pressure Test! 2017. (Fairy Tale Fixers: Fixing Fairy Tale Problems with STEM Ser.). 32p. (gr. 3-4). pap. 63.00 ***(978-1-5382-0667-6(6))*** Stevens, Gareth Publishing LLLP.

—Rapunzel: Let down Your Zip Wire! 2017. (Fairy Tale Fixers: Fixing Fairy Tale Problems with STEM Ser.). 32p. (gr. 3-4). pap. 63.00 ***(978-1-5382-0668-3(4))*** Stevens, Gareth Publishing LLLP.

Brothers Grimm. Snow White & Rose Red. Vivanco, Kelly, illus. 2014. (ENG.). 40p. (J). (gr. -1-4). 17.95 *(978-1-927018-34-7(X))* Simply Read Bks. CAN. Dist: Ingram Publisher Services.

—Tales from the Brothers Grimm. Zwerger, Lisbeth, illus. 2013. (ENG.). 96p. (J). (gr. k-2). 29.99 *(978-988-8240-53-1(6))* Neugebauer, Michael (Publishing) Limited HKG. Dist: Independent Pubs. Group.

—The Twelve Dancing Princesses. Duntze, Dorothee, illus. 2013. (ENG.). 32p. (J). (gr. -1-2). 17.95 *(978-0-7358-4121-5(7))* North-South Bks., Inc.

Brothers Grimm & Andersen, Hans Christian. Little Golden Book Fairy Tale Favorites. 2015. (Little Golden Book Favorites Ser.). (ENG., Illus.). 80p. (J). (-k). 7.99 *(978-0-385-37914-4(5))*, Golden Bks.) Random Hse. Children's Bks.

Brothers Grimm & Grimm Brothers Staff. Hansel & Gretel. Cowley, Joy, ed. Jo, Hyeon-suk, illus. 2015. (World Classics Ser.). (ENG.). 32p. (J). (gr. k-4). pap. 7.99 *(978-1-925186-60-4(1))* Lerner Publishing Group.

Brothers Grimm & Isadora, Rachel. The Fisherman & His Wife. Isadora, Rachel, illus. 2008. (ENG., Illus.). 32p. (J). (gr. -1-3). 16.99 *(978-0-399-24771-2(8))*, G.P. Putnam's Sons Books for Young Readers) Penguin Young Readers Group.

Brothers Grimm, et al. Fairy Tales from the Brothers Grimm: Deluxe Hardcover Classic. Funke, Cornelia, tr. Cruikshank, George, illus. 2013. (Puffin Classics Ser.). (ENG.). 384p. (J). (gr. 3-7). 25.00 *(978-0-14-750949-9(1))*, Puffin Books) Penguin Young Readers Group.

—Little Red Riding Hood. 2011. (ENG., Illus.). 80p. 14.99 *(978-0-06-202051-2(X))*, Collins Design) HarperCollins Pubs.

Brown, Calef. Polkabats & Octopus Slacks: 14 Stories. 2005. (ENG., Illus.). 32p. (J). (gr. -1-3). 7.99 *(978-0-618-11129-9(8))* Houghton Mifflin Harcourt Publishing Co.

Brown, Carron, ed. Beauty & the Beast & Jack & the Beanstalk: Two Tales & Their Histories. 2009. (World of Fairy Tales Ser.). (Illus.). 32p. (J). (gr. -1-2). pap. 10.55 *(978-1-60754-650-4(7))*; lib. bdg. 22.60 *(978-1-60754-649-8(3))* Windmill Bks.

—Cinderella & Aladdin: Two Tales & Their Histories. 2009. (World of Fairy Tales Ser.). (Illus.). 32p. (J). (gr. -1-2). pap. 10.55 *(978-1-60754-644-3(2))*; lib. bdg. 22.60 *(978-1-60754-643-6(4))* Windmill Bks.

—Hansel & Gretel & the Pied Piper of Hamelin: Two Tales & Their Histories. 2009. (World of Fairy Tales Ser.). (Illus.). 32p. (J). (gr. -1-2). pap. 10.55 *(978-1-60754-647-4(7))*; lib. bdg. 22.60 *(978-1-60754-646-7(9))* Windmill Bks.

—The Three Little Pigs & Little Red Riding Hood: Two Tales & Their Histories. 2009. (World of Fairy Tales Ser.). (Illus.). 32p. (J). (gr. -1-2). pap. 10.55 *(978-1-60754-641-2(8))*; lib. bdg. 22.60 *(978-1-60754-640-5(X))* Windmill Bks.

Brown, Janet. Hansel & Gretel: My First Reading Book. Morton, Ken, illus. 2013. (ENG.). 24p. (J). (gr. -1-4). 5.99 *(978-1-84322-737-3(1))*, Armadillo) Anness Publishing GBR. Dist: National Bk. Network.

—Jack & the Beanstalk: My First Reading Book. Morton, Ken, illus. (ENG.). 24p. 2015. pap. 6.99 *(978-1-86147-474-2(1))* 2013. (J). (gr. -1-4). 5.99 *(978-1-84322-738-0(X))* Anness Publishing GBR. (Armadillo). Dist: National Bk. Network.

—Puss in Boots. Morton, Ken, illus. 2012. (ENG.). 24p. (J). (gr. -1-12). 5.99 *(978-1-84322-848-6(3))* Anness Publishing GBR. Dist: National Bk. Network.

—Puss in Boots (Floor Book) My First Reading Book. Morton, Ken, illus. 2013. (ENG.). 24p. (J). (gr. -1-2). pap. 6.99 *(978-1-84322-902-5(1))*, Armadillo) Anness Publishing GBR. Dist: National Bk. Network.

—Snow White & the Seven Dwarves. Morton, Ken, illus. 2012. (ENG.). 24p. (J). (gr. -1-12). 5.99 *(978-1-84322-850-9(5))* Anness Publishing GBR. Dist: National Bk. Network.

—Snow White & the Seven Dwarves (Floor Book) My First Reading Book. Morton, Ken, illus. 2013. (ENG.). 30p. (J). (gr. -1-2). pap. 6.99 *(978-1-84322-903-2(X))*, Armadillo) Anness Publishing GBR. Dist: National Bk. Network.

—The Ugly Duckling. Morton, Ken, illus. 2012. (ENG.). 24p. (J). (gr. -1-12). 5.99 *(978-1-84322-851-6(3))* Anness Publishing GBR. Dist: National Bk. Network.

—The Ugly Duckling (Floor Book) My First Reading Book. Morton, Ken, illus. 2015. (ENG.). 24p. (J). (gr. -1-1). pap. 6.99 *(978-1-86147-398-1(2))*, Armadillo) Anness Publishing GBR. Dist: National Bk. Network.

Brown, Tara. First Kiss. 2013. 264p. pap. *(978-1-927866-05-4(7))* Brown, Tara Publishing.

—White Girl Problems. 2013. 266p. pap. *(978-1-927866-06-1(5))* Brown, Tara Publishing.

Bruchac, Joseph. Dragon Castle. 2011. (ENG.). 352p. (J). (gr. 5-18). 16.99 *(978-0-8037-3376-3(3))*, Dial Bks) Penguin Young Readers Group.

Brundage, Frances, illus. Cinderella: A Fairy Story. 2004. reprint ed. pap. 15.95 *(978-1-4179-8713-9(8))* Kessinger Publishing, LLC.

Bryant, Megan. Merida: The Legend of the Emeralds. 2014. (Disney Princess Early Chapter Bks.). (J). lib. bdg. 14.75 *(978-0-606-31755-9(4))*, Turtleback) Turtleback Bks.

Bryant, Megan & Disney Book Group Staff. Merida: Legend of the Emeralds. Disney Storybook Art Team, illus. 2014. (ENG.). 96p. (J). (gr. 1-3). pap. 4.99 *(978-1-4231-6890-4(9))* Disney Pr.

Bryant, Megan E. Rapunzel. Huxtable, Tonja & Huxtable, John, illus. 2007. (Berry Fairy Tales Ser.). (J). *(978-1-4287-4159-1(3))*, Grosset & Dunlap) Penguin Publishing Group.

Bucay, Jorge. The King & the Magician. Gusti, illus. 2014. (ENG.). 52p. (J). (gr. -1). 14.95 *(978-0-7892-1204-7(8))*, Abbeville Kids) Abbeville Pr., Inc.

Buchan, John. The Magic Walking Stick & Stories from the Arabian Nights. Soper, Vernon, illus. 2007. 136p. per. 19.95 *(978-0-9791702-8-7(1))* Capricorn Hse. Publishing.

Buckler, Carol. Feathered Tales from the Barnyard. l.t. ed. 2004. (J). per. 5.95 *(978-1-932496-20-8(3))* Penman Publishing, Inc.

Buckley, Michael. The Fairy-Tale Detectives. 2017. (Sisters Grimm Ser.: 1). (J). lib. bdg. 19.60 ***(978-0-606-39685-1(3))*** Turtleback Bks.

Buckley, Michael. The Unusual Suspects. Ferguson, Peter, illus. 2005. (ENG.). 290p. (J). (gr. 3-7). 16.95 *(978-0-8109-5926-2(7))*, Abrams Bks. for Young Readers) Abrams, Inc.

Buckmaster, Heath L. Box of Hair: A Fairy Tale, 3 bks., Bk. 1. (Illus.). (YA). 2007. 102p. pap. 12.99 *(978-0-9771802-5-7(5))* 2008. 108p. lib. bdg. 25.00 *(978-0-9771802-4-0(7))* Transaltar Publishing.

—Box of Hair: A Fairy Tale. 2008. 104p. pap. 12.50 *(978-1-4357-2690-1(1))* Lulu Pr., Inc.

—The Venus Diary. 2008. 136p. pap. 13.50 *(978-0-615-20678-3(6))*;Bk. 2. 132p. (YA). lib. bdg. 19.95 *(978-0-9771802-6-4(3))* Transaltar Publishing.

Bunanta, Murti. The Tiny Boy & Other Tales from Indonesia, 1 vol. Hardiyono, illus. 2013. (ENG.). 80p. (J). (gr. 3). 24.95 *(978-1-55498-193-9(X))* Groundwood Bks. CAN. Dist: Publishers Group West (PGW).

Bunton, M. Catherine. The Fairy Tale Keeper. 2012. 134p. pap. 8.95 *(978-1-60594-783-9(0))* Aeon Publishing Inc.

Burke, Arlene Avery & Hamilton, Phyllis McAllister. Grandma's Fairy Tale Museum. 2009. 40p. pap. 21.99 *(978-1-4415-0607-8(1))* Xlibris Corp.

Burke, David. Beauty & the Beast: Level 3: Learn French Through Fairy Tales. Sandoval, Migs, illus. 2006. (Learn French Through Fairy Tales Ser.). (ENG & FRE.). 29p. (J). (gr. -1-3). pap. 14.95 incl. audio compact disk *(978-1-891888-87-8(0))* Slangman Publishing.

—Beauty & the Beast: Level 3: Learn German Through Fairy Tales. Sandoval, Migs, illus. 2006. (Learn German Through Fairy Tales Ser.). (ENG & GER.). 29p. (J). (gr. -1-3). pap. 14.95 incl. audio compact disk *(978-1-891888-88-5(9))* Slangman Publishing.

—Beauty & the Beast: Level 3: Learn Spanish Through Fairy Tales. Sandoval, Migs, illus. 2006. (Learn Spanish Through Fairy Tales Ser.). (ENG & SPA.). 29p. (J). (gr. -1-3). pap. 14.95 incl. audio compact disk *(978-1-891888-86-1(2))* Slangman Publishing.

—Beauty & the Beast (English to Italian - Level 3) Learn ITALIAN Through Fairy Tales. 2007. (Learn Italian Through Fairy Tales Ser.). (ENG & ITA., Illus.). (J). per. 14.95 incl. audio compact disk *(978-1-891888-89-2(7))* Slangman Publishing.

—Cinderella: Level 1: Learn German Through Fairy Tales. Bobrick, Julie, ed. Deese, Teut & Wirth, Petra, trs. Sandoval, Migs, illus. 2006. (Learn German Through Fairy Tales Ser.). (ENG & GER.). 29p. pap. 14.95 incl. audio compact disk *(978-1-891888-76-2(5))* Slangman Publishing.

—Cinderella: Level 1: Learn Italian Through Fairy Tales. Bobrick, Julie, ed. Filippi, Alessio, tr. Sandoval, Migs, illus. 2006. (Learn Italian Through Fairy Tales Ser.). (ENG & ITA.). 29p. pap. 14.95 incl. audio compact disk *(978-1-891888-77-9(3))* Slangman Publishing.

—Cinderella: Level 1: Learn Spanish Through Fairy Tales. Bobrick, Julie, ed. Redoles, Marcela, tr. Sandoval, Migs, illus. 2006. (Learn Spanish Through Fairy Tales Ser.). (ENG & SPA.). 29p. pap. 14.95 incl. audio compact disk *(978-1-891888-74-8(9))* Slangman Publishing.

—Goldilocks (English to German - Level 2) Learn GERMAN Through Fairy Tales. 2007. (Learn German Through Fairy Tales Ser.). (ENG & GER., Illus.). 29p. (J). per. 14.95 incl. audio compact disk *(978-1-891888-83-0(8))* Slangman Publishing.

—Goldilocks (English to Italian - Level 2) Learn ITALIAN Through Fairy Tales. 2007. (Learn Italian Through Fairy Tales Ser.). (ENG & ITA., Illus.). (J). per. 14.95 incl. audio compact disk *(978-1-891888-82-3(X))* Slangman Publishing.

Burke, David, adapted by. GOLDILOCKS (English to Chinese - Level 2) Learn MANDARIN CHINESE Through Fairy Tales. 2007. (Learn Chinese Through Fairy Tales Ser.). (ENG & CHI., Illus.). (J). per. 14.95 incl. audio compact disk *(978-1-891888-85-4(4))* Slangman Publishing.

Burns, A. M. Witches. 2016. (ENG., Illus.). (J). 24.99 ***(978-1-63477-996-8(7))***, Harmony Ink Pr.) Dreamspinner Pr.

Busch, Jean. Aiden & the Frog Prince, 1 vol. 2009. 48p. pap. 16.95 *(978-1-60836-892-1(0))* America Star Bks.

Button, Kevin. The Giving Gnome. Guritz, Linda F., illus. 2010. 28p. pap. 12.95 *(978-1-936343-22-5(3))* Peppertree Pr., The.

Bwesigye, Brian. Fables Out of Nyanj. 2012. (Illus.). 58p. pap. *(978-0-9571420-0-8(5))* Kushinda.

C. Collodi. The Adventures of Pinocchio. 2007. 104p. per. *(978-1-4068-6037-5(9))* Echo Library.

Cabal, Graciela Beatriz. Azul. (SPA.). 32p. pap. 8.95 *(978-950-07-2052-6(3))* Editorial Sudamericana S.A. ARG. Dist: Distribooks, Inc.

Caldwell, J. Lynn. The Tooth Fairy's Guide to Lost Teeth: A Fortune for Every Day a Tooth Is Lost. Jepson, Beth, illus. 2005. (J). per. 11.95 *(978-0-9774463-0-8(1))* Caldwell, Judy.

Call of the Mynah. 2014. 176p. (gr. -1). pap. 8.50 *(978-1-4828-1526-9(5))*, PartridgeIndia) Author Solutions, Inc.

Calonita, Jen. Tricked. 2017. (Fairy Tale Reform School Ser.: 3). (ENG.). 272p. (J). (gr. 5-8). 15.99 *(978-1-4926-3795-0(5))*, 9781492637950, Sourcebooks Jabberwocky) Sourcebooks, Inc.

Campos, Paula. The Turtle's Shell. Ortega, Macarena, illus. 2008.Tr. of tortuga Golosa. (J). pap. 14.95 *(978-0-9801147-5-1(6))* Jorge Pinto Bks.

A Candy Fairies Sugar-Tastic Collection, Bks. 5-8. 2014. (Candy Fairies Ser.). (ENG., Illus.). 512p. (J). (gr. 3-5). pap. 23.99 *(978-1-4814-1659-7(6))*, Aladdin) Simon & Schuster Children's Publishing.

Caperucita Roja: Clothing, Food, Nature, the Human Body. (SPA & ENG., Illus.). (J). (gr. -1-5). pap. 5.95 *(978-88-8148-249-8(5))* EMC/Paradigm Publishing.

Capstone Press Staff. Rapunzel. Timmins, Jeffrey Stewart, illus. 2009. (Graphic Spin Ser.). (ENG.). 40p. (gr. 1-3). pap. 5.95 *(978-1-4342-1392-1(7))*, Graphic Revolve) Stone Arch Bks.

—Sleeping Beauty. Dietrich, Sean, illus. 2009. (Graphic Spin Ser.). (ENG.). 40p. (gr. 1-3). pap. 5.95 *(978-1-4342-1393-8(5))*, Graphic Revolve) Stone Arch Bks.

—Snow White. Valdez Y Alanis, Erik, illus. 2009. (Graphic Spin Ser.). (ENG.). 40p. (gr. 1-3). pap. 5.95 *(978-1-4342-1394-5(3))*, Graphic Revolve) Stone Arch Bks.

—The Three Little Pigs. Blecha, Aaron, illus. 2010. (Graphic Spin Ser.). (ENG.). 40p. (gr. 1-3). pap. 5.95 *(978-1-4342-1395-2(1))*, Graphic Revolve) Stone Arch Bks.

Carey, Bill. Fairy Tales for the 21st Century. 2009. 35p. pap. 17.00 *(978-0-557-03660-8(7))* Lulu Pr., Inc.

Carey, Lorraine. Cinderella's Stepsister & the Big Bad Wolf. Blanco, Migy, illus. 2015. (ENG.). 32p. (J). (gr. -1-2). 15.99 *(978-0-7636-8005-3(2))*, Nosy Crow) Candlewick Pr.

Carroll, Lewis, pseud. Alice au Pays des Merveilles.Tr. of Alice in Wonderland. (FRE.). (J). (gr. 3-8). 7.95 *(978-0-8288-6095-6(5))*, M5497) French & European Pubns., Inc.

—Alice in Wonderland. Steadman, Ralph, illus. 2010. (ENG.). 128p. pap. 19.95 *(978-1-55407-203-3(4))*, 9781554072033) Firefly Bks., Ltd.

—Alice's Adventures in Wonderland. Tenniel, John, illus. 2013. (Cambridge Library Collection - Fiction & Poetry Ser.). (ENG.). 210p. 57.00 *(978-1-108-06037-0(4))*; pap. 29.99 *(978-1-108-05958-9(9))* Cambridge Univ. Pr.

Carroll, Yvonne. Great Irish Legends for Children, 1 vol. Lawrie, Robin, illus. 2005. (ENG.). 64p. (J). (gr. k-3). 18.99 *(978-1-58980-345-9(0))* Pelican Publishing Co., Inc.

Carsey, Alice, illus. Pinocchio, the Tale of a Puppet. 2011. 140p. pap. 12.99 *(978-1-61203-095-1(5))* Bottom of the Hill Publishing.

Cartwright, Stephen, illus. Cinderella. 2006. (First Stories Sticker Bks.). 16p. (J). (gr. -1-3). pap. 6.99 (978-0-7945-1311-5(5), Usborne) EDC Publishing.

—Fairytale Jigsaw Book. 2004. (Jigsaw Books Ser.). 20p. (J). 14.95 (978-0-7945-0771-8(9), Usborne) EDC Publishing.

—Sleeping Beauty. 2006. (First Stories Sticker Bks.). 16p. (J). (gr. -1-3). pap. 6.99 (978-0-7945-1313-9(1), Usborne) EDC Publishing.

—Three Little Pigs. 2006. (First Stories Sticker Bks.). 16p. (J). (gr. -1-3). pap. 6.99 (978-0-7945-1386-3(7), Usborne) EDC Publishing.

Casey, Dawn. The Barefoot Book of Earth Tales. Wilson, Ann, illus. 2013. (ENG.). 96p. (J). (gr. k-5). pap. 14.99 (978-1-84686-941-9(2)) Barefoot Bks., Inc.

—The Barefoot Book of Earth Tales. Wilson, Anne, illus. 2009. (ENG.). 96p. (J). (gr. 1-5). 19.99 (978-1-84686-224-3(8)) Barefoot Bks., Inc.

—The Great Race: The Story of the Chinese Zodiac. Wilson, Anne, illus. 2008. (ENG.). 32p. (J). (gr. -1-2). 8.99 (978-1-84686-202-1(7)) Barefoot Bks., Inc.

Casey, Dawn & Collins UK Publishing Staff. The White Mouse. Masukawa, Masako, illus. 2016. (ENG.). 32p. (J). pap. 9.95 (978-0-00-814721-1(3)) HarperCollins Pubs. Ltd. GBR. Dist: Independent Pubs. Group.

Casey, Dawn, et al. The Barefoot Book of Ballet Stories. Wilson, Anne & Guay, Rebecca, illus. 2009. (ENG.). 80p. (J). (gr. 2-6). 23.99 (978-1-84686-262-5(0)) Barefoot Bks., Inc.

Cassidy, Anne. Puss in Boots. Fereday, Roger, illus. 2016. (Must Know Stories: Level 2 Ser.). (ENG.). 32p. (J). (gr. 1-4). 12.99 (978-1-4451-4669-0(X), Franklin Watts) Hachette Children's Group GBR. Dist: Hachette Bk. Group.

Castor, Harriet. Cinderella. Coh, Smilijana, illus. 2016. (ENG.). 24p. (J). (gr. -1-k). 19.99 (978-1-4052-7175-2(2)) Egmont Bks., Ltd. GBR. Dist: Independent Pubs. Group.

catalán, Cuento popular. LA CASTAÑERA. 2005. (Caballo Alado Clásicos-Al Trote Ser.). (SPA & ENG., Illus.). 24p. (J). (gr. -1-k). 7.95 (978-84-7864-868-9(2)) Combel Editorial, S.A. ESP. Dist: Independent Pubs. Group.

—EL CONEJITO. 2005. (Troquelados Clásicos Ser.). (SPA & ENG., Illus.). 16p. (J). (gr. -1-k). pap. 3.95 (978-84-7864-898-6(4)) Combel Editorial, S.A. ESP. Dist: Independent Pubs. Group.

—LAS FRESAS. 2005. (Caballo Alado Clásicos-Al Trote Ser.). (SPA & ENG., Illus.). 24p. (J). (gr. -1-k). 7.95 (978-84-7864-870-2(4)) Combel Editorial, S.A. ESP. Dist: Independent Pubs. Group.

—LA RATITA PRESUMIDA. 2004. (Caballo Alado Clásico Series-Al Paso Ser.). (SPA & ENG., Illus.). 24p. (J). (gr. -1-k). 7.95 (978-84-7864-763-7(5)) Combel Editorial, S.A. ESP. Dist: Independent Pubs. Group.

Catanese, P. W. Happenstance Found. 2009. (Books of Umber Ser.: 1). (ENG.). 352p. (J). (gr. 3-7). 16.99 (978-1-4169-7519-9(5), Simon & Schuster/Paula Wiseman Bks.) Simon & Schuster/Paula Wiseman Bks.

Cattie, Ray. Ard Righ: The Sword on the Stone. 2005. (ENG., Illus.). 280p. (978-0-9748765-2-8(6)) DNA Pr.

Ceccoli, Nicoletta, illus. Little Red Riding Hood. 2004. 32p. (J). 16.99 (978-1-84148-621-5(3)) Barefoot Bks., Inc.

Ceccoli, Nicoletta & Batt, Tanya Robyn. The Princess & the White Bear King. 2007. (Illus.). 40p. (J). (gr. k-5). 10.99 (978-1-84686-094-2(6)) Barefoot Bks., Inc.

Cech, John. The Nutcracker. Puybaret, Eric, illus. 2016. (ENG.). 40p. (J). (gr. -1-2). pap. 6.95 (978-1-4549-2116-5(1)) Sterling Publishing Co., Inc.

—The Princess & the Pea. Oberdieck, Bernhard, illus. 2015. (Classic Fairy Tale Collection). (ENG.). 32p. (J). (gr. -1-2). pap. 6.95 (978-1-4549-1678-9(8)) Sterling Publishing Co., Inc.

—Rapunzel. Sansom, Fiona, illus. 2015. (Classic Fairy Tale Collection). (ENG.). 32p. (J). (gr. -1-2). pap. 6.95 (978-1-4549-1679-6(6)) Sterling Publishing Co., Inc.

—Rumpelstiltskin. Hargreaves, Martin, illus. 2016. (Classic Fairy Tale Collection). (ENG.). 32p. (J). (gr. -1-2). pap. 6.95 (978-1-4549-1908-7(6)) Sterling Publishing Co., Inc.

—The Twelve Dancing Princesses. Corvino, Lucy, illus. 2016. (Classic Fairy Tale Collection). (ENG.). 32p. (J). (gr. -1-2). pap. 6.95 (978-1-4549-1909-4(4)) Sterling Publishing Co., Inc.

Celtic Folklore 10 Book Set. 2013. (978-1-909302-98-3(8)) Abela Publishing.

Cendrars, Blaise. Petits Contes Negres pour les Enfants. (FRE.). (J). pap. 19.95 (978-2-07-051787-9(X)) Gallimard, Editions FRA. Dist: Distribooks, Inc.

Cendrillon.Tr. of Cinderella. (FRE.). 48p. pap. 12.95 incl. audio compact disk (978-2-89558-065-2(0)) Coffragants CAN. Dist: Penton Overseas, Inc.

Chainani, Soman. The Last Ever After. (School for Good & Evil Ser.: 3). (J). (gr. 3-7). 2016. 704p. pap. 7.99 (978-0-06-210496-0(9)) 2015. 672p. pap. 9.99 (978-0-06-239625-9(0)) HarperCollins Pubs.

Chambers, Bev R. Bouncer & Friends. 2012. (ENG., Illus.). 40p. (J). 14.99 (978-1-937008-14-7(2)) Heart to Heart Publishing, Inc.

Chapman, Frederica. She Greened the Land: A Fairy Tale for the Earth. 2009. 80p. pap. 26.95 (978-1-4389-2953-8(6)) AuthorHouse.

Chapman, Steven Curtis. Cinderella: The Love of a Daddy & His Princess, 1 vol. 2008. (ENG., Illus.). 64p. 14.99 (978-1-4041-0522-5(0)) Nelson, Thomas Inc.

Chardi, Hannah. Oriental Fairy Tales. 2011. 52p. pap. 22.26 (978-1-4490-0467-5(9)) AuthorHouse.

Charles, Veronika Martenova. It's Not about the Apple! Parkins, David, illus. 2010. (Easy-To-Read Wonder Tales Ser.). (ENG.). 64p. (J). (gr. k-3). pap. 5.95 (978-0-88776-955-9(1), Tundra Bks.) Tundra Bks. CAN. Dist: Penguin Random Hse. LLC.

—It's Not about the Ball! Parkins, David, illus. 2013. (Easy-To-Read Wonder Tales Ser.). (ENG.). 64p. (J). (gr. k-3). pap. 5.95 (978-1-77049-330-8(1), Tundra Bks.) Tundra Bks. CAN. Dist: Penguin Random Hse. LLC.

—It's Not about the Beanstalk! Parkins, David, illus. 2013. (Easy-To-Read Wonder Tales Ser.). (ENG.). 64p. (J). (gr. k-3). pap. 5.95 (978-1-77049-327-8(1), Tundra Bks.) Tundra Bks. CAN. Dist: Penguin Random Hse. LLC.

—It's Not about the Crumbs! Parkins, David, illus. 2010. (Easy-To-Read Wonder Tales Ser.). (ENG.). 64p. (J). (gr. k-3). pap. 5.95 (978-0-88776-953-5(5), Tundra Bks.) Tundra Bks. CAN. Dist: Penguin Random Hse. LLC.

—It's Not about the Diamonds! Parkins, David, illus. 2013. (Easy-To-Read Wonder Tales Ser.). (ENG.). 64p. (J). (gr. k-3). pap. 5.95 (978-1-77049-328-5(X), Tundra Bks.) Tundra Bks. CAN. Dist: Penguin Random Hse. LLC.

—It's Not about the Hunter! Parkins, David, illus. 2010. (Easy-To-Read Wonder Tales Ser.). (ENG.). 56p. (J). (gr. k-3). pap. 5.95 (978-0-88776-948-1(9), Tundra Bks.) Tundra Bks. CAN. Dist: Penguin Random Hse. LLC.

—It's Not about the Pumpkin! Parkins, David, illus. 2010. (Easy-To-Read Wonder Tales Ser.). (ENG.). 64p. (J). (gr. k-3). pap. 5.95 (978-0-88776-949-8(7), Tundra Bks.) Tundra Bks. CAN. Dist: Penguin Random Hse. LLC.

—It's Not about the Rose! Parkins, David, illus. 2010. (Easy-To-Read Wonder Tales Ser.). (ENG.). 64p. (J). (gr. k-3). pap. 5.95 (978-0-88776-954-2(3), Tundra Bks.) Tundra Bks. CAN. Dist: Penguin Random Hse. LLC.

—It's Not about the Straw! Parkins, David, illus. 2013. (Easy-To-Read Wonder Tales Ser.). (ENG.). 64p. (J). (gr. k-3). pap. 5.95 (978-1-77049-326-1(3), Tundra Bks.) Tundra Bks. CAN. Dist: Penguin Random Hse. LLC.

—It's Not about the Tiny Girl! Parkins, David, illus. 2013. (Easy-To-Read Wonder Tales Ser.). (ENG.). 64p. (J). (gr. k-3). pap. 5.95 (978-1-77049-329-2(8), Tundra Bks.) Tundra Bks. CAN. Dist: Penguin Random Hse. LLC.

Chase, Mary. Loretta Mason Potts. Berson, Harold, illus. 2014. (ENG.). 224p. (J). (gr. 3-7). 16.95 (978-1-59017-757-0(6), NYR Children's Collection) New York Review of Bks., Inc., The.

Chester, Laura. Hiding Glory. Lippincott, Gary A., illus. 2007. (ENG.). 160p. (J). (gr. 3-7). 18.95 (978-1-59543-616-0(2)) Willow Creek Pr., Inc.

Chichester Clark, Emma, illus. The McElderry Book of Grimms' Fairy Tales. 2006. (ENG.). 128p. (J). (gr. 1-5). 22.99 (978-1-4169-1798-4(5), McElderry, Margaret K. Bks.) McElderry, Margaret K. Bks.

Chinchinian, Harry. The Princess & the Beggar II: Continuing Adventures. Chinchinian, Harry, illus. 2005. (Illus.). 176p. (J). lib. bdg. 18.95 (978-1-892476-11-1(8)) Plum Tree Pr.

Choi, Sooyun. Janie & the Breakfast Fairy. 2012. (ENG.). (J). pap. (978-1-4675-2026-3(8)) Independent Pub.

Chronicle Books Staff. Thumbelina. Capdevila, Francesc, illus. 2004. (Bilingual Fairy Tales Ser.: BILI). (ENG & SPA.). 32p. (J). (gr. -1-7). pap. 6.99 (978-0-8118-3928-0(1)) Chronicle Bks. LLC.

Cinderella. 2009. (Disney Glitter Board Book Ser.). 5p. (978-1-4054-9824-1(2)) Parragon, Inc.

Cinderella. unabr. ed. (Read-Along Ser.). (J). 7.99 incl. audio (978-1-55723-007-2(2)) Walt Disney Records.

Cinderella: 6 Small Books. (gr. k-2). 23.00 (978-0-7635-8514-3(9)) Rigby Education.

Cinderella: Treasures from the Library of Congress. 2004. (Shape Bks.). (Illus.). 20p. (J). reprint ed. 3.95 (978-1-55709-166-6(8)) Applewood Bks.

Cinderella, Level 1. 2016. (Ladybird Readers Ser.). (ENG., Illus.). 48p. (J). (gr. 2-4). pap. 9.99 (978-0-241-25407-3(8)) Penguin Bks., Ltd. GBR. Dist: Independent Pubs. Group.

Cinderfella's Big Night: Individual Title Six-Packs. (Action Packs Ser.). 104p. (gr. 3-5). 44.00 (978-0-7635-2984-0(2)) Rigby Education.

Claflin, Willy. Maynard Moose Tales. 2007. (J). 34.99 (978-1-59895-864-5(X)) Findaway World, LLC.

Clark, Gloria. The Little Candy Breathing Dragons. 2008. 36p. per. 12.95 (978-1-4327-1510-6(0)) Outskirts Pr., Inc.

Clark, Marc. The Princess Fables. Hosford, Eric, illus. 2013. 114p. pap. 5.99 (978-0-9910345-0-5(3)) Seven C's Productions, Inc.

Clarke, E. J. Oakwing: A Fairy's Tale. 2017. (Oakwing Ser.: 1). (ENG., Illus.). 192p. (J). (gr. 2-6). 16.99 (978-1-4814-8191-5(6), Aladdin) Simon & Schuster Children's Publishing.

—Oakwing: A Fairy's Tale. 2017. (J). pap. (978-1-4814-8190-8(8), Simon & Schuster/Paula Wiseman Bks.) Simon & Schuster/Paula Wiseman Bks.

Clarke, Harry & Perrault, Charles, illus. Classic Fairy Tales of Charles Perrault. 2013. (ENG.). 224p. (J). 34.00 (978-0-7171-5408-1(4)) M.H. Gill & Co. U. C. IRL. Dist: Dufour Editions, Inc.

Clement-Davies, David. Fell. 2009. (ENG.). 544p. (YA). (gr. 7-11). pap. 10.95 (978-0-8109-7266-7(2), Amulet Bks.) Abrams, Inc.

Cloke, Rene. Treasury of Traditional Tales. 2012. (ENG., Illus.). 240p. (J). (gr. -1-3). 24.95 (978-1-84135-939-7(4)) Award Pubns. Ltd. GBR. Dist: Parkwest Pubns., Inc.

Cloke, Rene, illus. The Adventures of Tom Thumb. 2012. (ENG.). 24p. (J). pap. 6.50 (978-1-84135-545-0(3)) Award Pubns. Ltd. GBR. Dist: Parkwest Pubns., Inc.

—Aladdin & His Magical Lamp. 2012. (ENG.). 24p. pap. 6.50 (978-1-84135-534-4(8)) Award Pubns. Ltd. GBR. Dist: Parkwest Pubns., Inc.

—Little Red Riding Hood. 2012. (ENG.). 24p. pap. 6.50 (978-1-84135-540-5(2)) Award Pubns. Ltd. GBR. Dist: Parkwest Pubns., Inc.

—The Little Tin Soldier. 2012. (ENG.). 24p. (J). pap. 6.50 (978-1-84135-542-9(9)) Award Pubns. Ltd. GBR. Dist: Parkwest Pubns., Inc.

—Pinocchio. 2012. (ENG.). 24p. pap. 6.50 (978-1-84135-538-2(0)) Award Pubns. Ltd. GBR. Dist: Parkwest Pubns., Inc.

—Puss in Boots. 2012. (ENG.). 24p. (J). pap. 6.50 (978-1-84135-539-9(9)) Award Pubns. Ltd. GBR. Dist: Parkwest Pubns., Inc.

—Snow White & the Seven Dwarfs. 2012. (ENG.). 24p. pap. 6.50 (978-1-84135-541-2(0)) Award Pubns. Ltd. GBR. Dist: Parkwest Pubns., Inc.

—Storytime Classics. 2012. (ENG.). 144p. (J). 12.50 (978-1-84135-521-4(6)) Award Pubns. Ltd. GBR. Dist: Parkwest Pubns., Inc.

—The Ugly Duckling. 2012. (ENG.). 24p. (J). pap. 6.50 (978-1-84135-543-6(7)) Award Pubns. Ltd. GBR. Dist: Parkwest Pubns., Inc.

Cloke, Renee. Storyland Classics. 2012. (ENG.). 144p. 12.50 (978-1-84135-520-7(8)) Award Pubns. Ltd. GBR. Dist: Parkwest Pubns., Inc.

Cloyne, Rachel. The Fairy Tale Colouring Book. Cloyne, Rachel, illus. 2014. (ENG., Illus.). 32p. (J). (gr. 1-4). pap. 8.99 (978-1-78055-252-1(1)) O'Mara, Michael Bks., Ltd. GBR. Dist: Independent Pubs. Group.

Clum, James. Koji's Ninja Secrets. 2011. 36p. pap. 15.96 (978-0-557-60314-5(5)) Lulu Pr., Inc.

Clynes, Kate. Goldilocks & the Three Bears. Daykin, Louise, illus. 32p. (J). 2004. (ENG & ARA.). pap. (978-1-84444-036-8(2)) 2004. (FRE & ENG.). pap. (978-1-84444-040-5(0)) 2004. (ENG & PAN.). pap. (978-1-84444-043-6(5)) 2004. (ENG & POR.). pap. (978-1-84444-044-3(3)) 2004. (ENG & URD.). pap. (978-1-84444-048-1(6)) 2004. (ENG & POL.). pap. (978-1-84444-051-1(6)) 2004. (ENG & HIN.). pap. (978-1-84444-059-7(1)) 2003. (BEN & ENG.). pap. (978-1-84444-037-5(0)) 2003. (CHI & ENG.). pap. (978-1-84444-038-2(9)) 2003. (RUS & ENG.). pap. (978-1-84444-052-8(4)) Mantra Lingua.

—Goldilocks & the Three Bears. Daykin, Louise, tr. Daykin, Louise, illus. 2003. (VIE & ENG.). 32p. (J). pap. 12.95 (978-1-84444-055-9(9)) Mantra Lingua GBR. Dist: Chinasprout, Inc.

Clynes, Kate & Anstey, David. Ali Baba & the Forty Thieves. 2005. (Illus.). 32p. (J). (ALB & ENG.). pap. (978-1-84444-400-7(7)); (ENG & SPA., pap. (978-1-84444-420-5(1)); (SOM & ENG., pap. (978-1-84444-419-9(8)); (ENG & SHO., pap. (978-1-84444-418-2(X)); (ENG & TAM., pap. (978-1-84444-421-2(X)); (TUR & ENG., pap. (978-1-84444-422-9(8)); pap. (978-1-84444-425-0(2)); (RUM & ENG., pap. (978-1-84444-427-4(9)); (RUS & ENG., pap. (978-1-84444-417-5(1)); (POR & ENG., pap. (978-1-84444-416-8(3)); pap. (978-1-84444-413-7(9)); pap. (978-1-84444-401-4(5)); pap. (978-1-84444-403-8(1)); pap. (978-1-84444-404-5(X)); (CHI & ENG., pap. (978-1-84444-405-2(8)); (SER & ENG., pap. (978-1-84444-406-9(6)); pap. (978-1-84444-407-6(4)); (ITA & ENG., pap. (978-1-84444-412-0(0)); pap. (978-1-84444-410-6(4)); pap. (978-1-84444-409-0(0)); (ENG & FRE., pap. (978-1-84444-408-3(2)) Mantra Lingua.

Clynes, Kate, et al. Ali Baba & the Forty Thieves. Holland, Richard, illus. 2005. (ENG & PAN.). 32p. (J). pap. (978-1-84444-414-4(7)); pap. (978-1-84444-411-3(2)); pap. (978-1-84444-402-1(3)); pap. (978-1-84444-415-1(5)); pap. (978-1-84444-424-3(4)) Mantra Lingua.

Coburn, Jewell Reinhart. Angkat: The Cambodian Cinderella. Flotte, Eddie, illus. 2014. (ENG.). 32p. (J). pap. 9.95 (978-1-885008-42-8(2), Shen's Bks.) Lee & Low Bks., Inc.

Coburn, Jewell Reinhart & Lee, Tzexa Cherta. Jouanah: A Hmong Cinderella. O'Brien, Anne Sibley, illus. 2014. (ENG.). 32p. (J). pap. 9.95 (978-1-885008-41-1(4), Shen's Bks.) Lee & Low Bks., Inc.

Codell, Esmé Raji. Fairly Fairy Tales. Chavarri, Elisa, illus. 2011. (ENG.). 32p. (J). (gr. -1-3). 18.99 (978-1-4169-9086-4(0), Aladdin) Simon & Schuster Children's Publishing.

Cole, Babette. Princess Smartypants. Cole, Babette, illus. 2005. (ENG., Illus.). 32p. (J). (gr. -1-3). 16.99 (978-0-399-24398-1(4), G.P. Putnam's Sons Books for Young Readers) Penguin Young Readers Group.

Colfer, Chris. Beyond the Kingdoms. Dorman, Brandon, illus. 2015. (Land of Stories Ser.: Bk. 4). (ENG.). 432p. (J). (gr. 3-7). 19.99 (978-0-316-40689-5(9)) Little, Brown Bks. for Young Readers.

—Beyond the Kingdoms. l.t. ed. 2015. (Land of Stories Ser.: No. 4). (ENG.). 624p. (J). (gr. 3-7). 28.99 (978-0-316-33938-4(5)) Little, Brown Bks. for Young Readers.

—The Curvy Tree. Dorman, Brandon, illus. 2015. (ENG.). 32p. (J). (gr. -1-3). 17.00 (978-0-316-40685-7(6)) Little Brown & Co.

—The Enchantress Returns. (Land of Stories Ser.: 2). (ENG.). (J). (gr. 3-7). 2014. 544p. pap. 9.99 (978-0-316-20155-1(3)) 2013. (Illus.). 528p. 19.99 (978-0-316-20154-4(5)) 2013. 832p. 43.99 (978-0-316-24235-6(7)) Little, Brown Bks. for Young Readers.

—The Enchantress Returns. 2014. (Land of Stories Ser.: 2). (J). lib. bdg. 20.85 (978-0-606-37229-9(6)) Turtleback Bks.

—A Grimm Warning. 2014. (Land of Stories Ser.: Bk. 3). (ENG.). (J). (gr. 3-7). 480p. 19.99 (978-0-316-40681-9(3)); 768p. 32.99 (978-0-316-40964-3(2)) Little, Brown Bks. for Young Readers.

—A Grimm Warning. 2015. (Land of Stories Ser.: 3). (J). lib. bdg. 20.85 (978-0-606-37230-5(X)) Turtleback Bks.

—The Land of Stories: A Treasury of Classic Fairy Tales. Dorman, Brandon, illus. 2016. 323p. (J). (978-0-316-55193-9(7)) Little Brown & Co.

—The Land of Stories: Queen Red Riding Hood's Guide to Royalty. 2017. (ENG.). 128p. (J). (gr. 3-7). 10.99 (978-0-316-38336-3(8)) Little Brown & Co.

—The Land of Stories: a Treasury of Classic Fairy Tales. 2016. (ENG., Illus.). 336p. (J). (gr. 3-7). 25.99 (978-0-316-35591-9(7)) Little, Brown Bks. for Young Readers.

—The Land of Stories: an Author's Odyssey. 2017. (Land of Stories Ser.: 5). (ENG., Illus.). 464p. (J). (gr. 3-7). pap. 9.99 (978-0-316-38321-9(X)) Little, Brown Bks. for Young Readers.

—The Mother Goose Diaries. 2017. (ENG.). 128p. (J). (gr. 3-7). 10.99 (978-0-316-38334-9(1)) Little Brown & Co.

—Queen Red Riding Hood's Guide to Royalty. Dorman, Brandon, illus. 2015. 118p. (J). (978-0-316-38339-4(2)) Little Brown & Co.

—The Wishing Spell. 2013. (Land of Stories Ser.: Bk. 1). (ENG.). 464p. (J). (gr. 3-7). pap. 9.99 (978-0-316-20156-8(1)) Little, Brown Bks. for Young Readers.

—The Wishing Spell. Dorman, Brandon, illus. 2012. (Land of Stories Ser.: 1). (ENG.). 448p. (J). (gr. 3-7). 19.99 (978-0-316-20157-5(X)) Little, Brown Bks. for Young Readers.

—The Wishing Spell. l.t. ed. 2013. (Land of Stories Ser.: 1). (ENG.). 672p. (J). (gr. 3-7). pap. 10.00 (978-0-316-24236-3(5)) Little, Brown Bks. for Young Readers.

—The Wishing Spell. 2013. (Land of Stories Ser.: 1). (J). lib. bdg. 20.85 (978-0-606-31746-7(5), Turtleback) Turtleback Bks.

Colfer, Chris & Dorman, Brandon. The Land of Stories the Wishing Spell. 2013. pap. (978-0-545-64793-9(2)) Scholastic, Inc.

Coll-Seck, Jayden. Fairy Tale Food, 01 vols., 1. 2016. (Rosen REAL Readers: Social Studies Nonfiction / Fiction: Family, Community, & the World Ser.). (ENG.). 12p. (J). pap. 6.33 (978-1-5081-1955-5(4), Rosen Classroom) Rosen Publishing Group, Inc., The.

Collins, Fiona. North Wales Folk Tales for Children. 2016. (Folk Tales for Children Ser.). (ENG., Illus.). 160p. (J). (gr. 3-7). pap. 16.99 (978-0-7509-6427-2(8)) History Pr. Ltd.,The GBR. Dist: Independent Pubs. Group.

Collodi, C. The Adventures of Pinocchio. 2005. 216p. 27.95 (978-1-4218-0608-2(8), 1st World Library - Literary Society) 1st World Publishing, Inc.

—The Adventures of Pinocchio. Della Chiesa, Carol, tr. 2007. (ENG.). 160p. per. (978-1-4065-1463-6(2)) Dodo Pr.

—The Adventures of Pinocchio. 2007. 108p. (gr. 4-7). per. 7.99 (978-1-60459-012-8(2)) Wilder Pubns., Corp.

—Pinocchio: the Tale of a Puppet. Carsey, Alice, illus. 2007. (ENG.). 196p. per. (978-1-4065-1462-9(4)) Dodo Pr.

Collodi, Carlo. Adventures of Pinocchio. Lucas, Ann Lawson, tr. from ITA. 2009. (Oxford World's Classics Ser.). (ENG., Illus.). 256p. pap. 10.95 (978-0-19-955398-3(X)) Oxford Univ. Pr., Inc.

—Pinocchio. 2017. (ENG., Illus.). (J). pap. 9.99 (978-1-366-49758-1(9)) Blurb, Inc.

—Pinocchio. Cowley, Joy, ed. Han, Joon-ho, illus. 2015. (World Classics Ser.). (ENG.). 32p. (gr. k-4). 7.99 (978-1-925246-69-8(8)); 26.65 (978-1-925246-43-8(4)); 26.65 (978-1-925246-17-9(5)) ChoiceMaker Pty. Ltd., The AUS. (Big and SMALL). Dist: Lerner Publishing Group.

—Pinocchio. 2017. (ENG., Illus.). 288p. 12.99 (978-1-5098-4290-2(X), 9781509842902, Collector's Library, The) Pan Macmillan GBR. Dist: Macmillan.

—Pinocchio. McKowen, Scott, illus. 2014. (Sterling Unabridged Classics Ser.). (ENG.). 184p. (J). (gr. 5). 9.95 (978-1-4549-1220-0(0)) Sterling Publishing Co., Inc.

—Pinocchio. Brock, Geoffrey, tr. from ITA. Testa, Fulvio, illus. 2012.Tr. of Avventure di Pinocchio. (ENG.). 184p. (J). (gr. k-4). 24.95 (978-1-59017-588-0(3), NYR Children's Collection) New York Review of Bks., Inc., The.

—Pinocchio: Candlewick Illustrated Classic. Rose, Emma, tr. from ITA. Fanelli, Sara, illus. 2010. (Candlewick Illustrated Classics Ser.). (ENG.). 192p. (J). (gr. 2-5). pap. 12.99 (978-0-7636-4731-5(4)) Candlewick Pr.

Comeau, Joey, et al. Far Out Fairy Tales. Frampton, Otis et al, illus. 2015. (Far Out Fairy Tales Ser.). (ENG.). 40p. (gr. 3-4). 101.28 (978-1-4965-0283-4(3), Far Out Fairy Tales) Stone Arch Bks.

Como te Portas. (SPA.). pap. 9.95 (978-84-272-8327-5(X)) Molino, Editorial ESP. Dist: Distribooks, Inc.

Comotto, Agustin. La Selva Azul. 2005. (SPA.). (J). (gr. k-1). 8.99 (978-980-257-298-4(5)) Ekare, Ediciones VEN. Dist: Iaconi, Mariuccia Bk. Imports.

Compo-Pratt, Paula. BooBoo & the Land of Mists & Dreams. 2012. (J). (gr. k-1). 14.95 (978-1-57197-513-3(6), Ivy House Publishing Group) Pentland Pr., Inc.

Comyns, Barbara. Juniper Tree. 2011. (ENG.). 197p. pap. 14.95 (978-1-907429-19-4(0), Capuchin Classics) Stacey Publishing GBR. Dist: Casemate Pubs. & Bk. Distributors, LLC.

Conejito Azul: Es un Valiente Socorrista.Tr. of Little Blue Bunny: Fairy Tale Story of Bunny Rabbit to the Rescue. (SPA.). (J). 2.98 (978-970-22-0018-5(0)) Larousse, Ediciones, S. A. de C. V. MEX. Dist: Continental Bk. Co., Inc.

Confederated Salish and Kootenai Tribes Staff. Beaver Steals Fire: A Salish Coyote Story. Sandoval, Sam, illus. 2008. (ENG.). 64p. (YA). (gr. k-3). pap. 14.95 (978-0-8032-1640-2(8), Bison Bks.) Univ. of Nebraska Pr.

Connelly, Erin. Watch Out for Wolves! 2017. (Text Connections Guided Close Reading Ser.). (J). (gr. 1). (978-1-4900-1820-1(4)) Benchmark Education Co.

Connolly, MarcyKate. Monstrous. Young, Skottie, illus. (J). (gr. 3-7). 2016. 448p. pap. 7.99 (978-0-06-227272-0(1)) 2015. (ENG.). 432p. 16.99 (978-0-06-227271-3(3)) HarperCollins Pubs.

—Monstrous. 2016. (J). lib. bdg. 18.40 (978-0-606-38136-9(8)) Turtleback Bks.

Constans, Gabriel. Skin of Lions. 2009. 63p. pap. 13.75 (978-1-60695-014-2(2)) Callanish Pr.

Conway, David. The Great Fairy Tale Disaster. Williamson, Melanie, illus. 2012. (ENG.). 32p. (J). (978-1-58925-111-3(3)) Tiger Tales.

Conyers, Miranda Parbhoo. Daddy Please Don't Cry. 2009. (J). (978-1-61623-310-5(9)) Independent Pub.

Coombs, Kate. The Runaway Princess. l.t. ed. 2007. (Literacy Bridge Middle Reader Ser.). 325p. (J). (gr. 3-7). 22.95 (978-0-7862-9633-0(X)) Thorndike Pr.

Cooper, Gem & Martin, Louise. Fairy Tale Theater — Cinderella. 2014. (ENG.). 16p. (J). (gr. -1-3). 6.99 (978-0-486-77985-0(8)) Dover Pubns., Inc.

—Fairy Tale Theater — Little Red Riding Hood. 2014. (ENG.). 16p. (J). (gr. -1-3). 6.99 (978-0-486-77986-7(6)) Dover Pubns., Inc.

Cooper, Janet Evins. Three Proud Princesses. 2006. (Illus.). 50p. (J). (gr. -1-3). 19.95 (978-0-913720-86-8(0)) Beil, Frederic C. Pub., Inc.

Cooper, Susan. The Magician's Boy. Riglietti, Serena, illus. 2006. (ENG.). 112p. (J). (gr. 3-7). pap. 9.99 (978-1-4169-1555-3(9), McElderry, Margaret K. Bks.) McElderry, Margaret K. Bks.

Corazza, Joe, illus. The Frog Prince: A Story about Keeping Your Word. 2006. (J). 6.99 (978-1-59939-008-6(6)) Cornerstone Pr.

Corke, Estelle, illus. The Gingerbread Man. 2007. (Flip-Up Fairy Tales Ser.). (ENG.). 24p. (J). audio compact disk (978-1-84643-144-9(1)); (gr. -1-2). (978-1-84643-078-7(X)) Child's Play International Ltd.

—Goldilocks & the Three Bears. (Flip-Up Fairy Tales Ser.). (ENG.). 24p. (J). 2007. (gr. -1-2). audio compact disk (978-1-84643-085-5(2)) 2005. (gr. 1-2). pap. (978-1-904550-19-8(3)) Child's Play International Ltd.

Cornwell, Betsy. Mechanica. (ENG.). 320p. (gr. 7). 2016. (YA). pap. 8.99 (978-0-544-66868-3(5), HMH Books For Young Readers) 2015. (J). 17.99 (978-0-547-92771-8(1), Clarion Bks.) Houghton Mifflin Harcourt Publishing Co.

E F G

—Venturess. 2017. (ENG.). 320p. (J). (gr. 7). 17.99 (978-0-544-31927-1(3), Clarion Bks.) Houghton Mifflin Harcourt Trade & Reference Pubs.

Corp, Carey & Langdon, Lorie. Destined for Doon, 1 vol. (Doon Novel Ser.). (ENG.). (YA). 2015. 368p. pap. 12.99 (978-0-310-74240-1(4)) 2014. 352p. 17.99 (978-0-310-74233-3(1)) Blink.

—Doon, 1 vol. 2014. (Doon Novel Ser.). (ENG.). 416p. (YA). pap. 12.99 (978-0-310-74239-5(0)) Blink.

Corvino, Lucy, illus. Arabian Nights. 2008. (Classic Starts(tm) Ser.). (ENG.). 160p. (J). (gr. 2-4). 6.95 (978-1-4027-4573-7(7)) Sterling Publishing Co., Inc.

Cosmic Debris Etc., Inc. Staff & Chronicle Books Staff. Thumbelina. Max, illus. 2004. (Bilingual Fairy Tales Ser.: BILI). (ENG & SPA.). 32p. (J). (gr. -1-7). 14.99 (978-0-8118-3927-3(3)) Chronicle Bks. LLC.

Cousins, Lucy. Yummy: Eight Favorite Fairy Tales. Cousins, Lucy, illus. 2009. (ENG., Illus.). 128p. (J). (gr. -1-2). 18.99 (978-0-7636-4474-1(9)) Candlewick Pr.

Coussens, Penrhyn W. A Child's Book of Stories. Smith, Jessie Willcox, illus. 2008. 608p. pap. 19.95 (978-1-59915-248-6(7)) Yesterday's Classics.

Coville, Bruce. The Dragon of Doom. Coville, Katherine, illus. 2005. (Moongobble & Me Ser.: Bk. 1). (ENG.). 80p. (J). (gr. 1-5). pap. 5.99 (978-0-689-85757-7(8), Aladdin) Simon & Schuster Children's Publishing.

—The Dragonslayers. unabr. ed. 2004. (Words Take Wingtm Ser.). 119p. (J). (gr. 3-6). pap. 29.00 incl. audio (978-0-8072-7988-5(9), S YA 958 SP, Listening Library) Random Hse. Audio Publishing Group.

—The Evil Elves. Coville, Katherine, illus. 2006. (Moongobble & Me Ser.: Bk. 3). (ENG.). 80p. (J). (gr. 1-5). pap. 6.99 (978-0-689-85759-1(4), Simon & Schuster/Paula Wiseman Bks.) Simon & Schuster/Paula Wiseman Bks.

—The Mischief Monster. Coville, Katherine, illus. 2008. (Moongobble & Me Ser.: Bk. 4). (ENG.). 80p. (J). (gr. 1-5). pap. 5.99 (978-1-4169-0808-1(0), Aladdin) Simon & Schuster Children's Publishing.

—The Weeping Werewolf. Coville, Katherine, illus. 2006. (Moongobble & Me Ser.). 68p. (gr. 1-5). 16.00 (978-0-7569-6582-2(9)) Perfection Learning Corp.

—The Weeping Werewolf. Coville, Katherine, illus. 2005. (Moongobble & Me Ser.: Bk. 2). (ENG.). 80p. (J). (gr. 1-5). pap. 5.99 (978-0-689-85758-4(6), Aladdin) Simon & Schuster Children's Publishing.

COX, Margaret. The Kiss-diamond. 2009. 173p. pap. 14.50 (978-1-4452-3347-5(9)) Lulu Pr., Inc.

Craft, Mahlon F. Beauty & the Beast. Craft, Kinuko Y., illus. 2016. 32p. (J). (gr. -1-3). 17.99 (978-0-06-053919-1(4)) HarperCollins Pubs.

Craig, Helen. Bedtime Fairy Tales. Craig, Helen, illus. 2016. (ENG., Illus.). 96p. (J). (gr. -1-2). 11.99 (978-1-4083-3840-7(8), Orchard Bks.) Hachette Children's Group GBR. Dist: Hachette Bk. Group.

Craik, Maria Dinah. The Little Lame Prince. 2008. 120p. 24.99 (978-0-554-21709-3(0)) 2006. 124p. pap. 18.99 (978-1-4264-0755-0(6)) 2006. 118p. pap. 19.99 (978-1-4264-0739-0(4)) Creative Media Partners, LLC.

—The Little Lame Prince. 2007. 128p. pap. 9.95 (978-1-60424-390-1(2), Book Jungle) Standard Pubns., Inc.

Crane, Walter. Beauty & the Beast, & Other Tales. (Illus.). [47] p.:p. (978-0-87099-303-9(8)) Bow Historical Bks.

Creanga, Ion. The Old Man's Daughter & the Old Woman's Daughter / Fata Babei Si Fata Mosneagului. Todd Kaplan, Delia Angelescu, tr. Gimlin, Mihaela, illus. 2013. 42p. pap. 17.95 (978-1-936629-30-5(5)) Reflection Publishing.

Cresswell, Helen. A Treasury of Fairy Tales. Bailey, Sian, illus. 2013. (ENG.). 96p. (J). (978-0-00-754651-0(3), HarperCollins Children's Bks.) HarperCollins Pubs. Ltd. GBR. Dist: HarperCollins Pubs.

Croall, Marie. Ali Baba: Fooling the Forty Thieves [an Arabian Tale]. Hilinski, Clint, illus. 2009. (Graphic Myths & Legends Ser.). (ENG.). 48p. (gr. 4-8). pap. 8.95 (978-1-58013-887-1(X)) Lerner Publishing Group.

Croall, Marie P. Ali Baba: Fooling the Forty Thieves: an Arabian Tale. 2008. (Graphic Myths & Legends Ser.). (Illus.). 48p. (J). (gr. 3-7). lib. bdg. 26.60 (978-0-8225-7525-2(6), Graphic Universe™) Lerner Publishing Group.

—Sinbad: Sailing into Peril. Hilinski, Clint, illus. 2008. (Graphic Myths & Legends Ser.). (ENG.). 48p. (gr. 4-8). pap. 8.95 (978-0-8225-8516-9(2)) Lerner Publishing Group.

Crosby, Jeff & Asbjørnsen, Peter Christen. The Rockabilly Goats Gruff. 2014. (ENG., Illus.). 32p. (J). (gr. -1-3). 15.95 (978-0-8234-2666-9(1)) Holiday Hse., Inc.

Cross, Mandy & Ross, Mandy. The Sly Fox & the Little Red Hen. 2015. (First Favourite Tales Ser.). (ENG., Illus.). 32p. (J). (-k). 7.99 (978-1-4093-0955-0(X)) Penguin Bks., Ltd. GBR. Dist: Independent Pubs. Group.

Cross, Ruth Belov. Hansel y Cretel. Pels, Winslow Pinney, illus. 2003. (SPA.). pap. (978-0-439-19894-3(1), SO30113) Scholastic GBR. Dist: Lectorum Pubns., Inc.

Cross, Sarah. Kill Me Softly. 2013. (ENG.). 336p. (J). (gr. 9). pap. 9.99 (978-1-60684-495-3(4), Carolrhoda Lab™) Lerner Publishing Group.

—Tear You Apart. (ENG.). 384p. (gr. 9-12). 2016. pap. 9.99 (978-1-5124-2628-1(8), Carolrhoda Bks.) 2015. 17.99 (978-1-60684-591-2(8), Carolrhoda Lab™) Lerner Publishing Group.

Crossley-Holland, Kevin. Enchantment: Fairy Tales, Ghost Stories & Tales of Wonder. Chichester Clark, Emma, illus. 2003. 128p. (YA). reprint ed. 22.00 (978-0-7567-6961-1(2)) DIANE Publishing Co.

Crowson, Andrew. Flip Flap Fairytale. 2003. (Illus.). 12p. bds. (978-1-85602-444-0(X), Pavilion Children's Books) Pavilion Bks.

Crump Jr., Fred. The Three Little Brown Piggies. 2007. (Illus.). 32p. (J). pap. 9.95 (978-1-932715-83-5(5)) UMI (Urban Ministries, Inc.).

Crystian, Carol Payne. Ebony Black & The 7. 2012. 26p. 24.95 (978-1-62709-469-6(5)); 28p. pap. 24.95 (978-1-4626-9728-1(3)) America Star Bks.

Cuentos de Andersen. (Coleccion Estrella).Tr. of Tales of Andersen. (SPA., Illus.). 64p. (J). 14.95 (978-950-11-0011-2(1), SGM011) Sigmar ARG. Dist: Continental Bk. Co., Inc.

Dahl, Roald. James und der Riesenpfirsich: (Das Buch zum Film)Tr. of James & the Giant Peach. (GER.). (J). pap. 12.50 (978-3-499-20433-3(9)) Rowohlt Taschenbuch Verlag GmbH DEU. Dist: Distribooks, Inc.

Daily, Don. Grimms' Fairy Tales. 2014. (ENG., Illus.). 64p. (J). 18.95 (978-1-60433-498-2(3), Applesauce Pr.) Cider Mill Pr. Bk. Pubs., LLC.

Daly, Niki. Pretty Salma: A Little Red Riding Hood Story from Africa. Daly, Niki, illus. 2007. (ENG., Illus.). 32p. (J). (gr. -1-3). 17.99 (978-0-618-72345-4(5)) Houghton Mifflin Harcourt Publishing Co.

Danson, Lesley, illus. Snow White. (Flip-Up Fairy Tales Ser.). (ENG.). 24p. (J). 2007. (gr. -1-2). audio compact disk (978-1-84643-096-1(8)) 2006. (gr. 1-2). (978-1-84643-023-7(2)) Child's Play International Ltd.

Datlow, Ellen. A Wolf at the Door. Windling, Terri, ed. Elwell, Tristan, illus. 2013. (ENG.). 192p. (J). (gr. 4-9). pap. 13.99 (978-1-4814-0167-8(X), Simon & Schuster Bks. For Young Readers) Simon & Schuster Bks. For Young Readers.

Datlow, Ellen & Windling, Terri, eds. Swan Sister: Fairy Tales Retold. 2013. (ENG., Illus.). 176p. (J). (gr. 3-7). pap. 13.99 (978-1-4814-0166-1(1), Simon & Schuster Bks. For Young Readers) Simon & Schuster Bks. For Young Readers.

Daubenspeck, Julie & Daubenspeck, Vince. May I See the King? Pendergrass, Mark D., illus. 2009. (ENG.). 32p. (gr. k). 14.95 (978-1-59700-797-9(8)) Island Heritage Publishing.

D'Aulaire, Edgar Parin & D'Aulaire, Ingri. D'Aulaires' Book of Norse Myths. 2005. (New York Review Children's Collection). (ENG., Illus.). 160p. (J). (gr. k-4). 29.95 (978-1-59017-125-7(X), NYR Children's Collection) New York Review of Bks., Inc., The.

D'Aulaire, Ingri & D'Aulaire, Edgar Parin, illus. D'Aulaires' Book of Norwegian Folktales. 2016. (ENG.). 192p. (J). 24.95 (978-0-8166-9932-2(1)) Univ. of Minnesota Pr.

D'Aulaire, Ingri, et al. The Terrible Troll-Bird. 2007. (ENG., Illus.). 52p. (J). (gr. k-4). 15.95 (978-1-59017-252-0(3), NYR Children's Collection) New York Review of Bks., Inc., The.

Dauterman, Mary & Antosh, Peter. Dirty Library: Twisted Children's Classics & Folked-Up Fairy Tales. 2014. (ENG., Illus.). 128p. 12.95 (978-0-7624-5440-2(7), Running Pr.) Running Pr. Bk. Pubs.

Davidson, Susanna. Cinderella Picture Book. 2015. (Picture Bks.). (ENG.). 24p. (J). 9.99 (978-0-7945-3423-3(6), Usborne) EDC Publishing.

—Nutcracker with Music. 2012. (Picture Books with Music Ser.). 24p. (J). bds. 18.99 (978-0-7945-2646-7(2), Usborne) EDC Publishing.

—Thumbelina. 2009. (First Reading Level 4 Ser.). 48p. (J). (gr. 2). 6.99 (978-0-7945-2280-3(7), Usborne) EDC Publishing.

Davidson, Susanna, retold by. East of the Sun, West of the Moon. 2009. (Young Reading Ser.). 64p. (J). 6.99 (978-0-7945-2274-2(2), Usborne) EDC Publishing.

—Goldilocks & the Three Bears (Picture Book) 2008. (Picture Book Classics Ser.). 24p. (J). 9.99 (978-0-7945-2251-3(3), Usborne) EDC Publishing.

Davidson, Susanna & Daynes, Katie. Little Princess Treasury. McNicholas, Shelagh & Cascio, Maria Cristina Lo, illus. 2006. (English Heritage Ser.). 96p. (J). 7.99 (978-0-7945-1442-6(1), Usborne) EDC Publishing.

Davidson, Susannah, retold by. Cinderella. 2005. (Young Reading Gift Books Ser.). 48p. (J). (gr. 2-18). 8.99 (978-0-7945-0920-0(7), Usborne) EDC Publishing.

Davies, Kate, illus. Princess Tales. 2012. (ENG.). 96p. 15.00 (978-1-84135-523-8(2)) Award Pubns. Ltd. GBR. Dist: Parkwest Pubns., Inc.

Davis, Aubrey. Kishka for Koppel, 1 vol. Cohen, Sheldon, illus. 2011. (ENG.). 32p. (J). (gr. -1-3). 19.95 (978-1-55469-299-6(7)) Orca Bk. Pubs. USA.

Davis, Yvonne LeBrun, illus. The Girl Who Wore Too Much: A Folktale from Thailand. 2015. (ENG.). 32p. (J). (gr. k-3). pap. 8.95 (978-1-939160-93-5(6)) August Hse. Pubs., Inc.

Daykin, Louise, illus. Goldilocks & the Three Bears. 2004. 32p. (J). (978-1-84444-054-2(0)); (GER & ENG.). (978-1-84444-041-2(9)); (ENG & SPA.). (978-1-84444-046-7(X)); (SOM & ENG.). (978-1-84444-045-0(1)); (978-1-84444-042-9(7)); (TUR & ENG.). (978-1-84444-047-4(8)); (978-1-84444-039-9(7)); (ALB & ENG.). (978-1-84444-035-1(4)); (SER & ENG.). (978-1-84444-053-5(2)); (ITA & ENG.). (978-1-84444-050-4(8)); (CZE & ENG.). (978-1-84444-049-8(4)) Mantra Lingua.

Daykin, Louise, tr. & illus. Goldilocks & the Three Bears. Daykin, Louise, illus. 2004. 31p. (J). (978-1-84444-057-3(5)) Mantra Lingua.

De Graaf, Anne. Best of the Classics: Retold for Today's Children. 2003. (Illus.). 370p. (978-87-7247-182-2(4)) Scandinavia Publishing Hse.

De La Paz, Myrna J. Abadeha: The Philippine Cinderella. Tang, Youshan, illus. 2014. (ENG.). 32p. (J). (gr. 3-7). 16.95 (978-1-885008-17-6(1), Shen's Bks.) Lee & Low Bks., Inc.

de la Paz, Myrna J. Abadeha: The Philippine Cinderella. Tang, Youshan, illus. 2014. (ENG.). 32p. (J). pap. 8.95 (978-1-885008-44-2(9), Shen's Bks.) Lee & Low Bks., Inc.

de Las Casas, Dianne. The Cajun Cornbread Boy & the Buttermilk Biscuit Girl, 1 vol. Gentry, Marita, illus. 2017. 32p. (J). (gr. k-3). 16.99 (978-1-4556-2311-2(3)) Pelican Publishing Co., Inc.

—Cinderellaphant, 1 vol. Jolet, Stefan, illus. 2014. (ENG.). 32p. (J). (gr. k-3). 16.99 (978-1-4556-1900-9(0)) Pelican Publishing Co., Inc.

de Lint, Charles. Seven Wild Sisters: A Modern Fairy Tale. Vess, Charles, illus. 2015. (ENG.). 272p. (J). (gr. 3-7). pap. 9.99 (978-0-316-05352-5(X)) Little, Brown Bks. for Young Readers.

De Los Santos, Elizabeth G. The Secret House. 2011. 18p. pap. 16.95 (978-1-4626-4409-4(0)) America Star Bks.

De Matos, Isabel Freire. El Pececito Magico. Torres, Walter, illus. 2004. (SPA.). 22p. (J). pap. 6.95 (978-1-57581-578-7(8)) Santillana USA Publishing Co., Inc.

De Saint-Exupéry, Antoine. Friends of the Little Prince. 2003. (Illus.). (J). bds. (978-0-15-204729-0(8)) Harcourt Trade Pubs.

—The Little Prince. 2015.Tr. of Petit Prince. (HEB.). (J). (978-965-13-1323-3(4)) Am Oved Pubs., Ltd.

—The Little Prince.Tr. of Petit Prince. 17.95 (978-0-89190-331-4(3)) Amereon Ltd.

—The Little Prince. deluxe ed. 2015. (Little Prince Ser.).Tr. of Petit Prince. (ENG., Illus.). 72p. (J). (gr. 5-7). 35.00 (978-0-544-65649-9(0), HMH Books For Young Readers) Houghton Mifflin Harcourt Publishing Co.

—The Little Prince. Kahler, Evan & Woods, Katherine, trs. 2016.Tr. of Petit Prince. (ENG., Illus.). (J). (gr. 3-7). (978-1-77323-014-6(X)) Rehak, David.

—The Little Prince. l.t. ed. 2005.Tr. of Petit Prince. (ENG.). 168p. pap. 10.95 (978-0-7862-7539-7(1)) Thorndike Pr.

—The Little Prince. Hill, Rowland, tr. Gormand, Caroline, illus. 2016.Tr. of Petit Prince. (ENG.). (J). (gr. 3-6). pap. (978-2-89687-592-4(1)) chouetteditions.com.

—The Little Prince 70th Anniversary Gift Set (Book/CD/Downloadable Audio) Howard, Richard, tr. 2013. (Little Prince Ser.). (ENG., Illus.). 96p. (YA). (gr. 7). audio compact disk 24.99 (978-0-547-97048-6(X)) Houghton Mifflin Harcourt Publishing Co.

—The Little Prince Coloring Book: Beautiful Images for You to Color & Enjoy... 2015. (Little Prince Ser.). (ENG., Illus.). 96p. (gr. 6). 12.99 (978-0-544-79258-6(0), HMH Books For Young Readers) Houghton Mifflin Harcourt Publishing Co.

—The Little Prince Graphic Novel. Sfar, Joann, illus. 2013. (Little Prince Ser.). (ENG.). 112p. (J). (gr. 5-7). 12.99 (978-0-547-33800-2(7)) Houghton Mifflin Harcourt Publishing Co.

—The Little Prince Read-Aloud Storybook: Abridged Original Text. Tamm, Vali, tr. 2015. (Little Prince Ser.). (ENG., Illus.). 40p. (J). (gr. 1-4). 9.99 (978-0-544-79255-5(6), HMH Books For Young Readers) Houghton Mifflin Harcourt Publishing Co.

—Le Petit Prince. 2016. (FRE., Illus.). (J). pap. (978-5-521-00151-4(4)) Books on Demand.

—Le Petit Prince. 2010. (CHI.). 132p. (J). (gr. 5-8). pap. (978-986-189-225-2(7)) Grimm Cultural Ent., Co., Ltd.

—Le Petit Prince. Gormand, Caroline, illus. 2016. (FRE.). (J). (gr. 3-6). pap. (978-2-89687-593-1(X)) chouetteditions.com.

De Saint-Exupéry, Antoine. Il Piccolo Principe.Tr. of Little Prince. (ITA.). 2014. 106p. pap. 6.50 (978-1-4992-7698-5(2)) 2013. 96p. pap. 12.00 (978-1-4948-5566-6(6)) 2013. 106p. pap. 6.50 (978-1-4948-4773-9(6)) CreateSpace Independent Publishing Platform.

—Il Piccolo Principe.Tr. of Little Prince. (ITA.). pap. 17.95 (978-88-452-4741-5(4)) Fabbri Editori - RCS Libri ITA. Dist: Distribooks, Inc.

De Saint-Exupéry, Antoine & Hemerman, Ilana. The Little Prince. 2013.Tr. of Petit Prince. (HEB.). (J). (978-965-13-0883-3(4)); 90p. (978-965-13-2376-8(0)) Am Oved Pubs., Ltd.

de Valera, Sinead. The Enchanted Lake. 2016. (ENG., Illus.). 136p. 17.00 (978-1-85607-979-2(1)) Columba Pr. IRL. Dist: Dufour Editions, Inc.

De Valera, Sinead. The Magic Gifts: Classic Irish Fairytales. (Illus.). 224p. 16.95 (978-0-86327-822-8(1)) Wolfhound Pr. IRL. Dist: Irish Bks. & Media, Inc.

Dean Wafstet, Cindi. Wings of Light. 2005. 31p. 15.00 (978-1-4116-5567-6(2)) Lulu Pr., Inc.

DeFelice, Cynthia C. Nelly May Has Her Say. Cole, Henry, illus. 2013. (ENG.). 32p. (J). (gr. -1-3). 16.99 (978-0-374-39899-6(2), 9780374398996, Farrar, Straus & Giroux (BYR)) Farrar, Straus & Giroux.

—One Potato, Two Potato. U'Ren, Andrea, illus. 2006. (ENG.). 32p. (J). (gr. -1-3). 18.99 (978-0-374-35640-8(8), 9780374356408, Farrar, Straus & Giroux (BYR)) Farrar, Straus & Giroux.

Del George, Dana. The Queen of Fire & the King of Ice. 2009. 24p. 12.50 (978-0-578-00730-4(4)) Del George, Dana.

Delcourt, Denyse, ed. French Fairy Tales: Essays on a Major Literary Tradition. 2016. (ENG.). (C). pap. 0.00 (978-1-5165-1175-4(1), Cognella Academic Publishing) Cognella, Inc.

Denslow, W. W., illus. & adapted by. Humpty Dumpty. Denslow, W. W., adapted by. 2007. (Rare Book Collections). (ENG.). 16p. (J). (gr. -1-3). 9.95 (978-1-55709-077-5(7)) Applewood Bks.

dePaola, Tomie. Adelita: A Mexican Cinderella Story. dePaola, Tomie, illus. 2004. (SPA & ENG., Illus.). 40p. (J). (gr. -1-3). pap. 6.99 (978-0-14-240187-3(0), Puffin Books) Penguin Young Readers Group.

Depken, Kristen L. Fairytale Magic (Dora the Explorer) Random House & Miller, Victoria, illus. 2014. (Step into Reading Ser.). (ENG.). 24p. (J). (gr. -1-1). 3.99 (978-0-385-37503-0(4), Random Hse. Bks. for Young Readers) Random Hse. Children's Bks.

Depken, Kristen L. Sing Your Song! (Nella the Princess Knight) Myers, Nneka, illus. 2017. (Step into Reading Ser.). (ENG.). 24p. (J). (gr. -1-1). pap. 4.99 (978-1-5247-6505-7(8)); lib. bdg. 12.99 (978-1-5247-6506-4(6)) Random Hse. Children's Bks. (Random Hse. Bks. for Young Readers).

Descoteaux, Chad. Once upon A Crime Syndicate: A mafia fairy Tale. 2006. 151p. pap. 24.95 (978-1-4241-0893-0(4)) PublishAmerica, Inc.

DeSpain, Pleasant. Tales of Heroes. 2016. (ENG., Illus.). 80p. (J). (gr. 3-4). pap. 9.95 (978-1-941460-38-2(0)) August Hse. Pubs., Inc.

Deutsch, Stacia. Before Ever after (Disney Tangled: the Series) RH Disney, illus. 2017. (Junior Novel Ser.). (ENG.). 144p. (J). (gr. 3-7). 9.99 (978-0-7364-3824-7(6), RH/Disney) Random Hse. Children's Bks.

Devine, Ginger. The Missing Pencils: A Sam the Lamb Mystery. 2009. 36p. pap. 17.99 (978-1-4389-5313-7(5)) AuthorHouse.

Diaz-Pimienta, Alexis. Cuentos Clasicos en Verso.Tr. of Classic Stories in Verse. (SPA.). (J). (gr. 2-4). pap. 7.98 (978-970-643-142-4(X)) Selector, S.A. de C.V. MEX. Dist: Lectorum Pubns., Inc.

DiCamillo, Kate. The Tale of Despereaux: Being the Story of a Mouse, a Princess, Some Soup & a Spool of Thread. Ering, Timothy Basil, illus. (J). 2015. (ENG.). 272p. (gr. 2-5). pap. 8.99 (978-0-7636-8089-3(3)) 2013. 296p. (978-0-7636-7205-8(X)) 2003. (ENG.). 272p. (gr. 2-5). 17.99 (978-0-7636-1722-6(9)) 2008. (ENG.). 272p. (gr. 2-5). 29.99 (978-0-7636-2928-1(6)) Candlewick Pr.

—The Tale of Despereaux: Being the Story of a Mouse, a Princess, Some Soup & a Spool of Thread. 2008. (J). 34.99 (978-0-7393-7105-3(3)) Findaway World, LLC.

—The Tale of Despereaux: Being the Story of a Mouse, a Princess, Some Soup & a Spool of Thread. 2009. 9.84 (978-0-7848-3043-7(6), Everbind) Marco Bk. Co.

—The Tale of Despereaux: Being the Story of a Mouse, a Princess, Some Soup & a Spool of Thread. 2006. 272p. (gr. 4-6). 18.00 (978-0-7569-6580-8(2)) Perfection Learning Corp.

—The Tale of Despereaux: Being the Story of a Mouse, a Princess, Some Soup & a Spool of Thread, 3 vols. 2006. 42.75 (978-1-4193-7734-1(5)) Recorded Bks., Inc.

—The Tale of Despereaux: Being the Story of a Mouse, a Princess, Some Soup & a Spool of Thread. Ering, Timothy Basil, illus. 2003. pap. (978-0-439-70167-9(8), Scholastic) Scholastic, Inc.

—The Tale of Despereaux: Being the Story of a Mouse, a Princess, Some Soup & a Spool of Thread. Ering, Timothy Basil, illus. l.t. ed. 2004. (Thorndike Literacy Bridge Ser.). (ENG.). 247p. (J). pap. 11.95 (978-1-4104-1527-1(9)) Thorndike Pr.

—The Tale of Despereaux: Being the Story of a Mouse, a Princess, Some Soup & a Spool of Thread. 2015. lib. bdg. 18.40 (978-0-606-37888-8(X)) Turtleback Bks.

—The Tale of Despereaux Student Packet. 2004. (J). (gr. 3-4). stu. ed. 12.99 (978-1-58130-524-1(9)) Novel Units, Inc.

DiCamillo, Kate & Candlewick Press Staff. The Tale of Despereaux: Glow-in-the-Dark Sticker Book. movie tie-in ed. 2008. (Tale of Despereaux Ser.). (ENG., Illus.). 8p. (J). (gr. -1-3). pap. 6.99 (978-0-7636-4079-8(4)) Candlewick Pr.

DiCamillo, Kate & Ering, Timothy Basil. The Tale of Despereaux: Being the Story of a Mouse, a Princess, Some Soup & a Spool of Thread. 2005. (CHI.). (J). pap. 12.95 (978-7-5307-3545-9(4)) New Buds Publishing Hse. CHN. Dist: Chinasprout, Inc.

Dickens, Charles. The Cricket on the Hearth. 2004. reprint ed. pap. 1.99 (978-1-4192-5807-7(9)); pap. 15.95 (978-1-4191-5807-0(4)) Kessinger Publishing, LLC.

—The Cricket on the Hearth. l.t. ed. 2005. 128p. pap. 17.95 (978-1-59688-048-1(1), 1-59688-048-1) Large Print Bk. Co., The.

Dickens, Charles & De Graaf, Anne. The Best of Charles Dickens' Classics. Montero, Jose Perez, illus. 2003. 240p. (978-87-7247-184-6(0)) Scandinavia Publishing Hse.

Diego, Rapi. El Sapo Hechizado. (SPA.). (J). pap. (978-968-7791-20-3(9)) SM Ediciones ESP. Dist: Lectorum Pubns., Inc.

Disney Book Group. Beauty & the Beast Read-Along Storybook & CD. Disney Storybook Art Team, illus. 2017. (Read-Along Storybook & CD Ser.). (ENG.). 32p. (J). (gr. 1-3). pap. 6.99 (978-1-4847-7606-3(2)) Disney Pr.

—Cinderella: The Story of Cinderella. Disney Storybook Art Team, illus. 2016. (ENG.). 112p. (J). (gr. -1-k). 12.99 (978-1-4847-6722-1(5)) Disney Pr.

—Finding Dory Hide-and-Seek with Dory. Disney Storybook Art Team, illus. 2016. (Disney First Tales Ser.). (ENG.). 64p. (J). (gr. 1-3). 10.99 (978-1-4847-9029-8(4)) Disney Pr.

—Snow White & the Seven Dwarfs: The Story of Snow White. Disney Storybook Art Team, illus. 2016. (ENG.). 112p. (J). (gr. -1-k). 12.99 (978-1-4847-6726-9(8)) Disney Pr.

—Whisker Haven Tales with the Palace Pets: Sultan's Triumphs (Storybook Plus Collectible Toy) Disney Storybook Art Team, illus. 2016. (ENG.). 128p. (J). (gr. 1-3). 14.99 (978-1-4847-5245-6(7)) Disney Pr.

Disney Book Group & Geron, Eric. Beauty & the Beast: The Enchantment. Disney Book Group, illus. 2017. (ENG., Illus.). 24p. (J). (gr. -1-k). pap. 5.99 (978-1-4847-8283-5(6)) Disney Pr.

—Beauty & the Beast, Level 2: Something More. Disney Book Group, illus. 2017. (World of Reading Ser.). (ENG., Illus.). 32p. (J). (gr. 1-3). pap. 4.99 (978-1-4847-8284-2(4)) Disney Pr.

Disney Book Group Staff. Disney 5-Minute Fairy Tales. Disney Storybook Artists Staff, illus. 2013. (5-Minute Stories Ser.). (ENG.). 192p. (J). (gr. -1 — 1). 12.99 (978-1-4231-6766-2(X)) Disney Pr.

—Disney Junior Storybook Collection. Disney Storybook Art Team, illus. 2014. (Storybook Collection). (ENG.). 304p. (J). (gr. -1-k). 16.99 (978-1-4231-7875-0(0)) Disney Pr.

—Enchanting Tale. 2010. (ENG.). 128p. (J). (gr. -1-2). 14.99 (978-1-4231-1938-8(X)) Disney Pr.

—The Little Mermaid Read-Along Storybook & CD. Disney Storybook Artists Staff, illus. 2013. (Read-Along Storybook & CD Ser.). (ENG.). 32p. (J). (gr. -1-k). pap. 6.99 (978-1-4231-6889-8(5)) Disney Pr.

—Palace Pets: Teacup the Pup for Belle. 2014. (ENG., Illus.). 10p. (J). (gr. -1-k). bds. 9.99 (978-1-4847-1183-5(1)) Disney Pr.

—Princess Adventure Stories. Disney Storybook Artists Staff, illus. 2013. (Storybook Collection). (ENG.). 304p. (J). (gr. -1 — 1). 15.99 (978-1-4231-4691-9(3)) Disney Pr.

—Tangled. Disney Storybook Art Team, illus. 2010. (Read-Along Storybook & CD Ser.). (ENG.). 32p. (J). (gr. -1 — 1). pap. 6.99 (978-1-4231-3742-9(6)) Disney Pr.

Disney Book Group Staff & Green, Rico. Cinderella Kindness & Courage, Level 2. 2015. (World of Reading Ser.). (ENG.). 32p. (J). (gr. 1-3). pap. 3.99 (978-1-4847-1112-5(2)) Disney Pr.

Disney Book Group Staff & Scollon, William. Mickey Mouse Clubhouse a Goofy Fairy Tale. Disney Storybook Art Team, illus. 2014. (ENG.). 24p. (J). (gr. -1-k). pap. 4.99 (978-1-4231-8900-8(0)) Disney Pr.

Disney Editors. Secrets Unlocked. 2017. (Tales of Rapunzel Ser.: 1). lib. bdg. 16.00 (978-0-606-40247-7(0)) Turtleback Bks.

Disney Staff. Aladdin. (FRE.). 96p. (J). (gr. k-5). pap. 9.95 (978-0-7859-8852-6(1)) French & European Pubns., Inc.

—Beauty & the Beast. 2004. (J). (gr. -1-2). spiral bd. (978-0-616-01631-2(X)) Canadian National Institute for the Blind/Institut National Canadien pour les Aveugles.

—Little Mermaid. (FRE.). 96p. (J). (gr. k-5). pap. 9.95 (978-0-7859-8846-5(7)) French & European Pubns., Inc.

—The Sleeping Beauty. (FRE.). 96p. (J). (gr. k-5). pap. 9.95 (978-0-7859-8854-0(8)) French & European Pubns., Inc.

—Snow White & the Seven Dwarfs. 2004. (J). (gr. -1-2). spiral bd. (978-0-616-01632-9(8)); spiral bd. (978-0-616-01633-6(6)) Canadian National Institute for the Blind/Institut National Canadien pour les Aveugles.

—Snow White & the Seven Dwarfs. (FRE.). 96p. (J). (gr. k-5). pap. 9.95 (978-0-7859-8853-3(X)) French & European Pubns., Inc.

Disney Storybook Art Team, illus. Snow White & the Seven Dwarfs (Read-Along Storybook & CD) 2016. (Read-Along Storybook & CD Ser.). (ENG.). 32p. (J). (gr. 1-3). pap. 6.99 *(978-1-4847-3049-2(6))* Disney Pr.

Disney Writers & Rudnick, Elizabeth. Beauty & the Beast POB Novelization. 2017. (ENG.). 288p. (J). (gr. 3-7). pap. 8.99 *(978-1-4847-8100-5(7))* Disney Pr.

Disney's Beauty & the Beast in Touch-a-Vision Dimensional Technology. (J). *(978-1-878444-02-8(6))* Minardi Photography.

Disney's Read to Me Treasury - Bedtime. 2011. 400p. *(978-1-4231-2394-1(8))* Disney Pr.

DiTerlizzi, Tony & Black, Holly. Notebook for Fantastical Observations. DiTerlizzi, Tony, illus. 2005. (Spiderwick Chronicles Ser.). (ENG., Illus.). 240p. (J). (gr. 2-6). 14.99 *(978-1-4169-0345-1(3),* Simon & Schuster Bks. For Young Readers) Simon & Schuster Bks. For Young Readers.

d'Lacey, Chris. The Fire Eternal. 2010. (Last Dragon Chronicles Ser.: 4). (ENG.). 512p. (J). (gr. 3-7). 8.99 *(978-0-545-05164-4(9),* Orchard Bks.) Scholastic, Inc.

Dockrey Young, Richard & Young, Judy Dockrey. 1492, New World Tales. 2013. (ENG., Illus.). 267p. (J). (gr. 3-5). pap. 16.95 *(978-1-939160-73-7(1))* August Hse. Pubs., Inc.

Dodd, Emma. Cinderelephant. Dodd, Emma, illus. 2013. (ENG., Illus.). 32p. (J). (gr. -1-3). 16.99 *(978-0-545-53285-3(X),* Levine, Arthur A. Bks.) Scholastic, Inc.

Doherty, Berlie & Varios Autores. Cuentos Magicos. 2003. (SPA.). 126p. *(978-84-348-6710-9(9),* NR30568) SM Ediciones ESP. Dist: Lectorum Pubns., Inc.

Dokey, Cameron. Belle: A Retelling of Beauty & the Beast. 2008. (Once upon a Time Ser.). (ENG.). 224p. (YA). (gr. 7-18). mass mkt. 6.99 *(978-1-4169-6131-4(3),* Simon Pulse) Simon Pulse.

—Kissed: Belle; Sunlight & Shadow; Winter's Child. 2013. (ENG.). 624p. (YA). (gr. 7). pap. 9.99 *(978-1-4424-7220-4(0),* Simon Pulse) Simon Pulse.

—Sunlight & Shadow: Her Love Is Trapped Between Night & Day.... 2004. (ENG., Illus.). 192p. (YA). (gr. 9). pap. 6.99 *(978-0-689-86999-0(1),* Simon Pulse) Simon Pulse.

—The Wild Orchid: A Retelling of the Ballad of Mulan. 2009. (Once upon a Time Ser.). (ENG.). 224p. (YA). (gr. 7-18). mass mkt. 7.99 *(978-1-4169-7168-9(8),* Simon Pulse) Simon Pulse.

—The World Above. 2010. (Once upon a Time Ser.). (ENG.). 208p. (YA). (gr. 7-18). pap. 6.99 *(978-1-4424-0337-6(3),* Simon Pulse) Simon Pulse.

Dolan, Penny. The Pied Piper of Hamelin. Impey, Martin, illus. 2016. (Must Know Stories: Level 2 Ser.). (ENG.). 32p. (J). (gr. 1-4). 12.99 *(978-1-4451-4661-4(4),* Franklin Watts) Hachette Children's Group GBR. Dist: Hachette Bk. Group.

Dolye, Brittlyn. Waking Beauty. 2017. (ENG.). pap. 15.99 ***(978-1-4621-2053-6(9),*** Sweetwater Bks.) Cedar Fort, Inc./CFI Distribution.

Domain Public Staff. Three Billy Goats Gruff. Kliros, Thea, illus. 2003. (Once upon a Time Ser.). (ENG.). 20p. (J). (gr. -1-3). bds. 6.99 *(978-0-06-008237-6(2),* HarperFestival) HarperCollins Pubs.

—Three Little Pigs. Kliros, Thea, illus. 2003. (Once upon a Time Ser.). (ENG.). 20p. (J). (gr. -1-1). bds. 6.99 *(978-0-06-008236-9(4),* HarperFestival) HarperCollins Pubs.

Don, Lari, et al. Little Red Riding Hood. Chauffrey, Celia, illus. 2012. (ENG.). 32p. (J). (gr. -1-3). 16.99 *(978-1-84686-766-8(5));* 9.99 *(978-1-84686-768-2(1))* Barefoot Bks., Inc.

Donald, George Mac. Cross Purposes. 2012. 104p. pap. 25.95 *(978-1-4474-5057-3(4))* Borah Pr.

Donfrancesco, Anna. Keepers of the Dream. 2007. (Illus.). 92p. per. *(978-1-84549-238-0(2))* arima publishing.

Donnelly, Jennifer. Beauty & the Beast: Lost in a Book. 2017. (ENG., Illus.). 352p. (J). (gr. 5-9). 16.99 *(978-1-4847-8098-5(1))* Disney Pr.

—Humble Pie. Gammell, Stephen, illus. 2007. (ENG.). 32p. (J). (gr. -1-2). 13.99 *(978-1-4169-6751-4(6),* Aladdin) Simon & Schuster Children's Publishing.

Donofrio, Antonio R. & Donofrio, Beatrice Batnag. G-String Cordilleran Revelries: Fairy Tales Retold for Centuries to Teach Life's Family Values & Basic Reading Skills with Simple Magic Tricks & I. 2009. 176p. pap. 17.99 *(978-1-4490-0181-0(5))* AuthorHouse.

Doolittle, Eva M. Old Fairy Tales Anew. Telielska, M. Magdalena, illus. 2008. 88p. (J). *(978-0-9791065-0-7(8))* Vesta Bks., LLC.

Dopson, Jennifer. Life Goes On. 2008. 202p. pap. 12.96 *(978-0-557-01741-6(6))* Lulu Pr., Inc.

Doyle, Malachy. Long Gray Norris. 2006. (Yellow Bananas Ser.). (ENG., Illus.). 48p. (J). (gr. -1-3). lib. bdg. *(978-0-7787-0956-5(6))* Crabtree Publishing Co.

—Tales from Old Ireland. Sharkey, Niamh, illus. 2008. (ENG.). 96p. (J). 21.99 *(978-1-84686-241-0(8))* Barefoot Bks., Inc.

Doyle, Malachy & Jones, Jac. The Changeling. 2003. (ENG., Illus.). 36p. pap. 12.95 *(978-1-85902-691-5(5))* Beekman Bks., Inc.

Doyle, Malachy & Philpot, Graham. Jack the Giant-Killer. 2009. (Hopscotch Adventures Ser.). (Illus.). 31p. (J). (gr. 1). lib. bdg. 25.65 *(978-1-59771-184-5(5))* Sea-To-Sea Pubns.

Doyle, Malachy & Sharkey, Niamh. Tales from Old Ireland. 2006. (ENG., Illus.). 96p. (J). (gr. 2-6). 16.99 *(978-1-905236-32-9(8))* Barefoot Bks., Inc.

Doyle, Malacy. The Barefoot Book of Fairy Tales. Ceccoli, Nicoletta, illus. 2005. (ENG.). 160p. (J). (gr. k-5). 19.99 *(978-1-84148-798-4(8))* Barefoot Bks., Inc.

Doyle, Richard. Jack the Giant Killer. Doyle, Richard, illus. 2004. (Illus.). 96p. (J). reprint ed. 19.00 *(978-0-7567-7478-3(0))* DIANE Publishing Co.

The Dragon & the Knight. 2014. (ENG., Illus.). 22p. (J). (gr. k). 29.99 *(978-1-4169-6081-2(3),* Little Simon) Little Simon.

Dudek, Mike. The Fairytale of the Morley Dog. 2007. (Illus.). 40p. (YA). spiral bd. 2.49 *(978-0-9740380-1-8(6))* Dudek, Mike.

Dudley, Maywill. The Story of Little Red Riding Hood. 2005. reprint ed. pap. 15.95 *(978-1-4191-5430-0(3))* Kessinger Publishing, LLC.

Duffy, Carol Ann. The Princess's Blankets. Hyde, Catherine Ryan, illus. 2009. (ENG.). 40p. (J). (gr. k-3). 18.99 *(978-0-7636-4547-2(8),* Templar) Candlewick Pr.

Dulac, Edmund, illus. The Sleeping Beauty & Other Fairy Tales. 2011. (Calla Editions Ser.). (ENG.). 208p. 35.00 *(978-1-60660-019-1(2))* Dover Pubns., Inc.

Durst, Sarah Beth. Ice. (ENG.). (YA). (gr. 7). 2010. 336p. pap. 8.99 *(978-1-4169-8644-7(8))* 2009. 320p. 16.99 *(978-1-4169-8643-0(X))* McElderry, Margaret K. Bks. (McElderry, Margaret K. Bks.).

Dwyer, Mindy. Alaska's Sleeping Beauty. Dwyer, Mindy, illus. 2014. (Paws IV Ser.). (ENG., Illus.). 32p. (J). (gr. k-3). pap. 10.99 *(978-1-57061-872-7(0),* Little Bigfoot) Sasquatch Bks.

—Alaska's Snow White & Her Seven Sled Dogs. 2015. (Paws IV Ser.). (ENG., Illus.). 32p. (J). (gr. -1-3). pap. 10.99 *(978-1-57061-975-5(1),* Little Bigfoot) Sasquatch Bks.

East, Jacqueline, illus. Beauty & the Beast. 2015. (J). *(978-1-4723-3133-5(8))* Parragon Bk. Service Ltd.

Ebbitt, Carolyn Q. The Extra-Ordinary Princess. 2010. (ENG.). 336p. (YA). (gr. 3-6). pap. 7.99 *(978-1-59990-484-9(5),* 9781599904849, Bloomsbury USA Childrens) Bloomsbury Publishing USA.

EDCON Publishing Group Staff. Classic Children's Tales. I.t. ed. 2008. (Classic Children's Tales Ser.). 32p. (gr. k-4). pap. 8.95 *(978-1-55576-550-7(5))* EDCON Publishing Group.

Edgson, Alison, illus. The Elves & the Shoemaker. 2007. (Flip-Up Fairy Tales Ser.). (ENG.). 24p. (J). audio compact disk *(978-1-84643-142-5(5));* (gr. 2-2). *(978-1-84643-076-3(3))* Child's Play International Ltd.

—The Emperor's New Clothes. 2006. (Flip-Up Fairy Tales Ser.). (ENG.). 24p. (J). (gr. 2-2). *(978-1-84643-020-6(8))* Child's Play International Ltd.

—The Magician's Apprentice. 2011. (Flip-Up Fairy Tales Ser.). (ENG.). 24p. (J). audio compact disk *(978-1-84643-409-9(2))* Child's Play International Ltd.

—Three Billy Goats Gruff. (Flip-Up Fairy Tales Ser.). (ENG.). 24p. (J). 2007. (gr. -1-2). audio compact disk *(978-1-84643-089-3(5))* 2006. (gr. 1-2). *(978-1-904550-72-3(X))* Child's Play International Ltd.

Edgson, Alison & Stockham, Jessica. Hansel & Gretel. Petrlik, Andrea, illus. 2006. (Flip-Up Fairy Tales Ser.). (ENG.). 24p. (J). (gr. 1-2). *(978-1-904550-73-0(8))* Child's Play International Ltd.

Eisner, Will. The Princess & the Frog. Eisner, Will, illus. 2003. (ENG., Illus.). 30p. (J). (gr. k-4). 15.95 *(978-1-56163-244-2(9))* NBM Publishing Co.

Eliot, Ethel Cook. The House on the Edge of Things. 2007. (J). per. 10.00 *(978-0-9615961-9-4(8))* Raven Rocks Pr.

—The Little House in the Fairy Wood. 2004. reprint ed. pap. 15.95 *(978-1-4191-7023-2(6))* Kessinger Publishing, LLC.

Elliott, Ruth. The Night Princess, 1 disc. Elliott, Ruth, illus. 2007. (SPA., Illus.). (J). per. 12.99 incl. DVD *(978-0-9795017-1-5(7))* Edu Designs.

Elya, Susan Middleton. Little Roja Riding Hood. Guevara, Susan, illus. 2014. (ENG.). 32p. (J). (gr. k-3). 16.99 *(978-0-399-24767-5(X),* G.P. Putnam's Sons Books for Young Readers) Penguin Young Readers Group.

Elya, Susan Middleton. La Princesa & the Pea. Martinez-Neal, Juana, illus. 2017. (ENG.). 32p. (J). (gr. -1-3). 16.99 ***(978-0-399-25156-6(1),*** G.P. Putnam's Sons Books for Young Readers) Penguin Young Readers Group.

Emberley, Rebecca & Emberley, Ed. Chicken Little. 2011. (Illus.). (J). (gr. -1-2). 29.95 *(978-0-545-29673-1(0))* Weston Woods Studios, Inc.

Emmett, Jonathan. Prince Ribbit, 1 vol. Bernatene, Poly, illus. 2017. (ENG.). 32p. (J). (gr. -1-2). 16.95 *(978-1-56145-761-8(2))* Peachtree Pubs.

En el Mundo de los Cuentos. (Coleccion Estrella). (SPA., Illus.). 64p. (J). 14.95 *(978-950-11-0000-6(6),* SGM000) Sigmar ARG. Dist: Continental Bk. Co., Inc.

Encyclopaedia Britannica, Inc. Staff, compiled by. Cinderella. 2008. 49.95 *(978-1-59339-683-1(X))* Encyclopaedia Britannica, Inc.

—Familiar Tales Around the World. 2008. 49.95 *(978-1-59339-676-3(7))* Encyclopaedia Britannica, Inc.

—Hansel & Gretel. 2008. 49.95 *(978-1-59339-687-9(2))* Encyclopaedia Britannica, Inc.

—Legends, Myths & Folktales. 2003. (Illus.). 64p. 14.95 *(978-1-59339-037-2(8))* Encyclopaedia Britannica, Inc.

—Rapunzel. 2008. 49.95 *(978-1-59339-688-6(0))* Encyclopaedia Britannica, Inc.

—Rumpelstiltskin. 2008. 49.95 *(978-1-59339-686-2(4))* Encyclopaedia Britannica, Inc.

—Sleeping Beauty. 2008. 49.95 *(978-1-59339-684-8(8))* Encyclopaedia Britannica, Inc.

—Tales Around the World. 2008. 49.95 *(978-1-59339-682-4(1))* Encyclopaedia Britannica, Inc.

Engelbreit, Mary. Mary Engelbreit's Nursery & Fairy Tales Collection. Engelbreit, Mary, illus. 2014. (ENG., Illus.). 192p. (J). (gr. -1-3). 11.99 *(978-0-06-228707-6(9))* HarperCollins Pubs.

—Mary Engelbreit's Nutcracker. Engelbreit, Mary, illus. 2011. (ENG., Illus.). 40p. (J). (gr. -1-3). 17.99 *(978-0-06-088579-3(3))* HarperCollins Pubs.

—Nursery Tales: A Treasury of Children's Classics. Engelbreit, Mary, illus. 2008. (ENG., Illus.). 136p. (J). (gr. 4-7). 19.99 *(978-0-06-073168-7(0))* HarperCollins Pubs.

—Twelve Timeless Treasures. Engelbreit, Mary, illus. 2010. (ENG., Illus.). 128p. (J). 19.99 *(978-0-06-088583-0(1))* HarperCollins Pubs.

Ensor, Barbara. Cinderella (As If You Didn't Already Know the Story) Ensor, Barbara, illus. 2011. (ENG., Illus.). 128p. (J). (gr. 2-5). 5.99 *(978-0-375-87387-4(2),* Yearling) Random Hse. Children's Bks.

Epelbaum, Mariano & Harrison, Paul. Fairy Tale Mix-Ups. Widdowson, Dan et al, illus. 2016. (Fairy Tale Mix-Ups Ser.). (ENG.). 24p. (gr. k-2). 93.28 *(978-1-4109-8325-1(0))* Heinemann-Raintree.

Equipo Staff. Blanca Nieves.Tr. of Snow White. (SPA.). 24p. (J). 9.98 *(978-84-305-9089-6(7))* Susaeta Ediciones, S.A. ESP. Dist: AIMS International Bks., Inc.

Escobar, Melba. Los Siete Mejores Cuentos Rabes. Neira, Muyi, illus. 2004. (SPA.). (J). (gr. 3-5). *(978-958-04-7212-4(2))* Norma S.A.

Escott, Jamison. The Clockmaker of Mullen. Escott, Esther, illus. 2004. 24p. (J). pap. 8.95 *(978-1-57733-127-8(3),* Papillon Publishing) Blue Dolphin Publishing, Inc.

Eubank, Patricia Reeder. The Princess & the Snarls. Eubank, Patricia Reeder, illus. 2006. (ENG., Illus.). 32p. (J). (gr. k-3). 16.95 *(978-0-8249-5536-6(6),* Ideal Pubns.) Worthy Publishing.

Evans, Latonya, adapted by. Jack & the Beanstalk. I.t. ed. 2005. (Fairy Tales of Special Children Ser.: Book 1). (Illus.). 25p. (J). *(978-0-9767258-0-0(0))* Diversity Ink Publishing.

Evetts-Secker, Josephine. The Barefoot Book of Father & Daughter Tales. Cann, Helen, illus. 2012. (ENG.). 96p. (J). 23.99 *(978-1-84686-761-3(4))* Barefoot Bks., Inc.

Evslin, Bernard. The Trojan War. 2012. (ENG.). 192p. (gr. 3-6). pap. 13.99 *(978-1-4532-7413-2(8),* Open Road Young Readers) Open Road Integrated Media, Inc.

Ewing, Juliana Horatia. Old-Fashioned Fairy Tales. I.t. ed. 2007. 118p. pap. 19.99 *(978-1-4346-1085-0(3))* Creative Media Partners, LLC.

—Old-Fashioned Fairy Tales. 2007. 112p. per. *(978-1-4065-2533-5(2))* Dodo Pr.

Fafoutakis, Anne. Enchanted Talisman & Other Stories for Children of All Ages. 2004. 132p. pap. 13.50 *(978-1-84426-296-0(0))* Upfront Publishing Ltd. GBR. Dist: Printondemand-worldwide.com.

Fairley, Melissa. Ding! Dong! Harland, Jackie, illus. 2011. (ENG.). 12p. (J). (gr. -1-k). 15.95 *(978-1-84898-362-5(X),* TickTock Books) Octopus Publishing Group GBR. Dist: Independent Pubs. Group.

Fairy Tale- Aladdin. 2005. (J). bds. *(978-1-4194-0037-7(1))* Paradise Pr., Inc.

Fairy Tale- Beauty & the Beast. 2005. (J). bds. *(978-1-4194-0038-4(X))* Paradise Pr., Inc.

Fairy Tale- Cinderella. 2005. (J). bds. *(978-1-4194-0039-1(8))* Paradise Pr., Inc.

Fairy Tale Fixers: Fixing Fairy Tale Problems with STEM. 2017. (Fairy Tale Fixers: Fixing Fairy Tale Problems with STEM Ser.). 32p. (gr. 3-4). pap. 42.00 ***(978-1-5382-0614-0(5));*** lib. bdg. 106.40 ***(978-1-5382-0616-4(1))*** Stevens, Gareth Publishing LLLP.

Fairy Tales. (J). 2.29 *(978-1-59445-060-0(9))* Dogs in Hats Children's Publishing Co.

Fairy Tales. 2003. (J). per. *(978-1-57657-913-8(1));* per. *(978-1-57657-912-1(3))* Paradise Pr., Inc.

Fairy Tales - Beauty & the Beast. 2005. (J). bds. *(978-1-4194-0099-5(1))* Paradise Pr., Inc.

Fairy tales - Cinderella. 2005. (J). bds. *(978-1-4194-0100-8(9))* Paradise Pr., Inc.

Fairy Tales - Pinocchio. 2005. (J). bds. *(978-1-4194-0101-5(7))* Paradise Pr., Inc.

Fairy Tales - Snow White. 2005. (J). bds. *(978-1-4194-0102-2(5))* Paradise Pr., Inc.

Fairy Tales- Jack & the Beanstalk. 2005. (J). bds. *(978-1-4194-0040-7(1))* Paradise Pr., Inc.

Fairy Tales- Pinocchio. 2005. (J). bds. *(978-1-4194-0041-4(X))* Paradise Pr., Inc.

Fairy Tales- Sleeping Beauty. 2005. (J). bds. *(978-1-4194-0042-1(8))* Paradise Pr., Inc.

Fairy Tales- Three little Pigs. 2005. (J). bds. *(978-1-4194-0044-5(4))* Paradise Pr., Inc.

Fairy Tales, Fables, & Folktales (Gr. PreK-5) 2003. (J). *(978-1-58232-020-5(9))* ECS Learning Systems, Inc.

Fairy Tales (Gr. 2-3) 2003. (J). *(978-1-58232-071-7(3))* ECS Learning Systems, Inc.

Fairy Tales s/s - Pinocchio. 2005. (J). bds. *(978-1-4194-0067-4(3))* Paradise Pr., Inc.

Fairy tales s/s - SNow White. 2005. (J). bds. *(978-1-4194-0068-1(1))* Paradise Pr., Inc.

Fairy Tales s/s Beauty & the Beast. 2005. (J). bds. *(978-1-4194-0065-0(7))* Paradise Pr., Inc.

Fairy Tales Today. 2015. (Fairy Tales Today Ser.). (ENG.). 24p. (gr. 1-2). 95.96 *(978-1-4795-8618-9(8))* Picture Window Bks.

Fambro, Sonja Grimsley. When Santa Goes to Church. 2011. 84p. pap. 32.26 *(978-1-4634-5983-3(1))* AuthorHouse.

Farjeon, Eleanor. Elsie Piddock Skips in Her Sleep. Voake, Charlotte, illus. 2017. (ENG.). 96p. (J). (gr. 2-5). 12.00 *(978-0-7636-9055-7(4))* Candlewick Pr.

Farrey, Brian. The Secret of Dreadwillow Carse. 2016. (ENG.). 256p. (J). (gr. 3-7). 16.95 *(978-1-61620-505-8(9))* Algonquin Bks. of Chapel Hill.

Faulkner, Georgene. The Little Red Hen & the Fox: Fairy Tales from the World Over. Winter, Milo & Becker, Charlotte, illus. 2011. 98p. 38.95 *(978-1-258-10173-2(4))* Literary Licensing, LLC.

—The Snow Maiden: Fairy Tales from the World Over. Richardson, Frederick & Becker, Charlotte, illus. 2011. 104p. 39.95 *(978-1-258-10524-2(1))* Literary Licensing, LLC.

—Squeaky & the Scare Box: Fairy Tales from the World Over. Richardson, Frederick & Becker, Charlotte, illus. 2011. 96p. 38.95 *(978-1-258-10158-9(0))* Literary Licensing, LLC.

Favorite Fairy Tales Series, 6 bks. (Illus.). (J). (gr. 2-4). lib. bdg. 71.70 *(978-1-56674-924-4(7))* Forest Hse. Publishing Co., Inc.

Fear, Sharon, retold by. Sleeping Beauty. 2004. (Treasure Tree Ser.). (Illus.). 32p. (J). *(978-0-7166-1605-4(X))* World Bk., Inc.

Feldman, Thea, ed. Secrets of Auradon Prep. 2015. (ENG.). 96p. (J). (gr. 3-7). 9.99 *(978-0-7944-3497-7(5),* Reader's Digest Children's Bks.) Studio Fun International.

Felix, Rebecca. The Fisherman & His Wife. Petelinsek, Kathleen, illus. 2013. (Fairy Tale Collection). (ENG.). 24p. (J). (gr. k-3). 28.50 *(978-1-62323-611-3(8),* 206378) Child's World, Inc., The.

Ferchaud, Steve, illus. Glen Robbie: A Scottish Fairy Tale. 2006. (J). 22.95 *(978-1-58478-013-7(4),* Highland Children's Pr.) Heather & Highlands Publishing.

Fernandez, Eugenia. Astria & the Missing Prince. 2009. (Illus.). 39p. (J). 31.99 *(978-1-4363-7543-6(6))* Xlibris Corp.

Ferrier, Charlotte. Little Red Riding Hood. 2016. (Fairytale Cottages Ser.). (ENG.). 12p. (J). (gr. -1-k). bds. 8.99 *(978-0-7641-6818-5(5))* Barron's Educational Series, Inc.

Ferris, Jean. Once upon a Marigold. 2004. 275p. (gr. 5). 17.00 *(978-0-7569-3613-6(6))* Perfection Learning Corp.

—Once upon a Marigold: Part Comedy, Part Love Story, Part Everything-but-the-kitchen-Sink. 2013. (ENG.). 288p. (J). (gr. 2-5). pap. 7.99 *(978-0-544-05400-4(8))* Houghton Mifflin Harcourt Publishing Co.

—The Tales of Marigold Three Books in One! Once upon a Marigold, Twice upon a Marigold, Thrice upon a Marigold. 2016. (ENG.). 832p. (J). (gr. 2-5). 15.99 *(978-0-544-85592-2(2),* HMH Books For Young Readers) Houghton Mifflin Harcourt Publishing Co.

—Thrice upon a Marigold: A Royal Kidnapping Caper. 2014. (ENG.). 256p. (J). (gr. 2-5). pap. 6.99 *(978-0-544-30262-4(1),* HMH Books For Young Readers) Houghton Mifflin Harcourt Publishing Co.

—Twice upon a Marigold. 2013. (ENG.). 304p. (J). (gr. 2-5). pap. 7.99 *(978-0-544-05098-3(3))* Houghton Mifflin Harcourt Publishing Co.

Filipek, Nina. Cinderella. O'Toole, Jeanette, illus. 2009. (Fairy Tale Firsts Ser.). 12p. (J). (gr. -1-k). bds. 11.40 *(978-1-60754-691-7(4))* Windmill Bks.

—The Gingerbread Man. O'Toole, Jeanette, illus. 2009. (Fairy Tale Firsts Ser.). 12p. (J). (gr. -1-k). bds. 11.40 *(978-1-60754-694-8(9))* Windmill Bks.

—The Three Little Pigs. O'Toole, Jeanette, illus. 2009. (Fairy Tale Firsts Ser.). 12p. (J). (gr. -1-k). bds. 11.40 *(978-1-60754-693-1(0))* Windmill Bks.

Filipek, Nina & Andersen, Hans Christian. The Ugly Duckling. O'Toole, Jeanette, illus. 2009. (Fairy Tale Firsts Ser.). 12p. (J). (gr. -1-k). bds. 11.40 *(978-1-60754-692-4(2))* Windmill Bks.

Finch, Mary. Three Billy Goats Gruff PB W CD. 2016. (ENG., Illus.). 32p. (J). (gr. -1-1). 9.99 *(978-1-78285-305-3(7))* Barefoot Bks., Inc.

—Los Tres Chivitos Gruff. Arenson, Roberta, illus. 2003.Tr. of Three Billy Goats Gruff. (SPA.). 32p. (J). pap. 7.99 *(978-1-84148-145-6(9))* Barefoot Bks., Inc.

Findlay, Lisa. Puss in Boots. Bowers, Tim, illus. 2008. (Step into Reading Ser.). (ENG.). 48p. (J). (gr. k-3). pap. 3.99 *(978-0-375-84671-7(9),* Random Hse. Bks. for Young Readers) Random Hse. Children's Bks.

Finn McCool The Magic Leprechaun Cat. Irish Holiday Fairy Tales: Volume 1. 2012. 44p. pap. 19.95 *(978-1-4772-1331-5(7))* AuthorHouse.

Fiona Fox Staff, ed. Tales from the Arabian Nights. 2012. (ENG., Illus.). 304p. (J). 15.00 *(978-1-84135-838-3(X))* Award Pubns. Ltd. GBR. Dist: Parkwest Pubns., Inc.

First Fairy Tales Staff. Tres Chivos Testarudos. (Primeros Cuentos Ser.). (SPA., Illus.). 28p. (J). (gr. k-3). pap. 7.95 *(978-1-56014-457-1(2))* Santillana USA Publishing Co., Inc.

Fischman, Sheila, tr. from FRE. The Flying Canoe. Oberman, Sheldon & Cohen, Sheldon, illus. 2004. (ENG.). 24p. (J). (gr. 3-7). 15.95 *(978-0-88776-636-7(6),* Tundra Bks.) Tundra Bks. CAN. Dist: Penguin Random Hse. LLC.

Flanagan, John. The Burning Bridge, 2 vols., Bk. 2. 2006. (Ranger's Apprentice Ser.: 2). (ENG.). 272p. (J). (gr. 5-18). 18.99 *(978-0-399-24455-1(7),* Philomel Bks.) Penguin Young Readers Group.

Flannigan, Liz. Cara & the Wizard, 2 vols. Docampo, Valeria, illus. 2013. (Magic Stories Ser.). (ENG.). 48p. (J). (gr. 1-4). pap. 8.99 *(978-1-84686-780-4(0))* Barefoot Bks., Inc.

—Starlight Grey. Docampo, Valeria, illus. 2013. (Magic Stories Ser.). (ENG.). 48p. (J). (gr. 1-4). pap. 8.99 *(978-1-84686-778-1(9))* Barefoot Bks., Inc.

Flaxman, Andrew. Little Red Riding Hood: The Classic Grimm's Fairy Tale. Delisa, Patricia, illus. 2006. 32p. (J). (gr. -1-3). 14.95 *(978-0-88010-571-2(2),* Bell Pond Bks.) SteinerBooks, Inc.

Fleming, Candace. Clever Jack Takes the Cake. Karas, G. Brian, illus. 2010. (ENG.). 40p. (J). (gr. -1-3). 17.99 *(978-0-375-84979-4(3),* Schwartz & Wade Bks.) Random Hse. Children's Bks.

Flinn, Alex. Towering. 2013. (YA). (Kendra Chronicles Ser.: 3). (ENG.). 304p. (gr. 9). 17.99 *(978-0-06-202417-6(5),* HarperTeen); (Kendra Chronicles Ser.: 3). 304p. (gr. 9). lib. bdg. 18.89 *(978-0-06-202418-3(3),* HarperTeen); 296p. *(978-0-06-227632-2(8))* HarperCollins Pubs.

Floca, Brian, illus. The Hinky-Pink: An Old Tale. 2008. (ENG.). 48p. (J). (gr. -1-3). 16.99 *(978-0-689-87588-5(6),* Atheneum/Richard Jackson Bks.) Simon & Schuster Children's Publishing.

Flor Ada, Alma. Dear Peter Rabbit. Tryon, Leslie, illus. 2006. (Stories to Go! Ser.). (J). (gr. k-3). 12.65 *(978-0-7569-7322-3(8))* Perfection Learning Corp.

—The Three Golden Oranges. Cartwright, Reg, illus. 2012. (ENG.). 32p. (J). (gr. -1-3). 16.99 *(978-1-4424-7496-3(3),* Atheneum Bks. for Young Readers) Simon & Schuster Children's Publishing.

Foglio, Kaja & Foglio, Phil. Agatha Heterodyne & the Clockwork Princess: A Gaslamp Fantasy with Adventure, Romance & Mad Science. Foglio, Kaja & Foglio, Phil, eds. 2013. (ENG., Illus.). 112p. (YA). pap. 25.00 *(978-1-890856-39-7(8),* 9781890856397) Studio Foglio, LLC.

Fontes, Justine & Fontes, Ron. Sunjata: Warrior King of Mali [A West African Legend]. Carruthers, Sandy, illus. 2009. (Graphic Myths & Legends Ser.). (ENG.). 48p. (gr. 4-8). pap. 8.95 *(978-1-58013-891-8(8))* Lerner Publishing Group.

Ford, Adam B. The Six Sisters & Their Flying Carpets. Abbott, Kristin, illus. 2012. 34p. (-18). 20.95 *(978-0-9794104-6-8(0))* H Bar Pr.

Ford, Ford Madox. The Queen Who Flew. 2013. 425p. reprint ed. lthr. 69.00 *(978-0-7426-3057-4(9))* Classic Bks.

Foreman, Michael, illus. & retold by. Classic Fairy Tales. Foreman, Michael, retold by. 2005. (ENG.). 176p. (J). (gr. 2-5). 12.95 *(978-1-4027-2865-5(4))* Sterling Publishing Co., Inc.

Forest, Heather. The Baker's Dozen. Gaber, Susan, illus. 2013. (ENG.). 32p. (J). (gr. -1-3). 8.95 *(978-1-939160-70-6(7))* August Hse. Pubs., Inc.

—The Contest Between the Sun & the Wind: An Aesop's Fable. Gaber, Susan, illus. 2013. (ENG.). 32p. (J). (gr. -1-3). pap. 8.95 *(978-1-939160-66-9(9))* August Hse. Pubs., Inc.

Foster, Evelyn. The Elves & the Trendy Shoes. Venturini, Claudia, illus. 2015. (ENG.). 32p. (J). *(978-0-7787-1932-8(4))* Crabtree Publishing Co.

Fox, Diane. The Cat, the Dog, Little Red, the Exploding Eggs, the Wolf, & Grandma. Fox, Christyan, illus. 2014. (ENG.). 32p. (J). (gr. -1-3). 16.99 *(978-0-545-69481-0(7),* Scholastic Pr.) Scholastic, Inc.

Fox, Janet. The Charmed Children of Rookskill Castle. 2017. lib. bdg. 19.65 ***(978-0-606-39785-8(X))*** Turtleback Bks.

Frampton, Otis. Red Riding Hood, Superhero. Frampton, Otis, illus. 2015. (Far Out Fairy Tales Ser.). (ENG., Illus.). 40p. (gr. 3-4). lib. bdg. 25.32 *(978-1-4342-9650-4(4))* Stone Arch Bks.

Francis, Suzanne & Marsham, Liz. Ariel Is Fearless/Jasmine Is Helpful (Disney Princess) Disney Storybook Art Team Staff & Thomas, Jeffrey, illus. 2017. (Step into Reading Ser.).

E F G

(ENG.). 48p. (J). (gr. -1-1). lib. bdg. 12.99 **(978-0-7364-9018-4(3)**, RH/Disney) Random Hse. Children's Bks.

Frederick, Heather Vogel. Once upon a Toad. (ENG., Illus.). (J). (gr. 5-9). 2013. 288p. pap. 6.99 (978-1-4169-8479-5(8)) 2012. 272p. 16.99 (978-1-4169-8478-8(X)) Simon & Schuster Bks. For Young Readers. (Simon & Schuster Bks. For Young Readers).

Freeberg, Eric, illus. Animal Stories. 2010. (Classic Starts(tm) Ser.). (ENG.). 160p. (J). (gr. 2-4). 6.95 (978-1-4027-6646-6(7)) Sterling Publishing Co., Inc.

—Ballet Stories. 2010. (Classic Starts(tm) Ser.). (ENG.). 160p. (J). (gr. 2-4). 6.95 (978-1-4027-6663-3(7)) Sterling Publishing Co., Inc.

French, Fiona. Anancy & Mr Dry-Bone. French, Fiona, illus. 2005. (ENG., Illus.). 32p. (J). (gr. -1-2). pap. 7.95 (978-1-84507-164-6(6), Frances Lincoln Children's Bks.) Quarto Publishing Group UK GBR. Dist: Hachette Bk. Group.

French, Vivian. The Bag of Bones: The Second Tale from the Five Kingdoms. Collins, Ross, illus. 2009. (Tales from the Five Kingdoms Ser.: 2). (ENG.). 256p. (J). (gr. 3-7). 14.99 (978-0-7636-4255-6(X)) Candlewick Pr.

—The Flight of Dragons: The Fourth Tale from the Five Kingdoms. Collins, Ross, illus. 2011. (Tales from the Five Kingdoms Ser.: 4). (ENG.). 208p. (J). (gr. 3-7). 15.99 (978-0-7636-5083-4(8)) Candlewick Pr.

—The Flight of Dragons: The Fourth Tale from the Five Kingdoms. Collins, Ross, illus. 2012. (Tales from the Five Kingdoms Ser.: 4). (ENG.). 256p. (J). (gr. 3-7). pap. 5.99 (978-0-7636-5133-6(8)) Candlewick Pr.

—The Heart of Glass: The Third Tale from the Five Kingdoms. Collins, Ross, illus. 2010. (Tales from the Five Kingdoms Ser.: 3). (ENG.). 256p. (J). (gr. 3-7). 14.99 (978-0-7636-4814-5(0)) Candlewick Pr.

—The Music of Zombies. Collins, Ross, illus. 2013. (Tales from the Five Kingdoms Ser.). (ENG.). 304p. (J). (gr. 3-7). 15.99 (978-0-7636-5930-1(4)) Candlewick Pr.

Friedericy Dolls, illus. Into the Woods: Favorite Fairy Tales from the World of Friedericy Dolls. Greer, Rob, photos by. 2009. 74p. (J). (978-0-9824812-0-2(9)) POCEE Publishing.

Fujikawa, Gyo, illus. Fairy Tales & Fables. 2008. (ENG.). 128p. (J). (gr. -1-2). 9.95 (978-1-4027-5698-6(4)) Sterling Publishing Co., Inc.

Furukawa, Masumi, illus. The Ugly Duckling. (Flip-Up Fairy Tales Ser.). (ENG.). 24p. (J). 2007. (gr. -1-2). audio compact disk (978-1-84643-095-4(X)) 2006. (gr. 2-2). pap. (978-1-84643-022-0(4)) Child's Play International Ltd.

Fusek Peters, Andrew. The Talkative Tortoise. 2016. (Traditional Tales with a Twist Ser.). (ENG., Illus.). 32p. (J). pap. incl. audio compact disk (978-1-84643-613-0(3)) Child's Play International Ltd.

Fyne, Olga. My Shadow Is a Copycat. 2009. 56p. pap. 21.99 (978-1-4389-3671-0(0)) AuthorHouse.

Gág, Wanda, et al. More Tales from Grimm. Gág, Wanda, illus. 2006. (Fesler-Lampert Minnesota Heritage Ser.). (ENG., Illus.). 272p. (gr. 4-7). per. 16.95 (978-0-8166-4938-9(3)) Univ. of Minnesota Pr.

Gaiman, NEil. The Sleeper & the Spindle. Riddell, Chris, illus. 2015. (ENG.). 64p. (YA). (gr. 8). 19.99 (978-0-06-239824-6(5)) HarperCollins Pubs.

Gaiman, NEil. The Sleeper & the Spindle Deluxe Edition. Riddell, Chris, illus. 2017. 72p. (YA). (gr. 8). 30.00 **(978-0-06-269792-9(7))** HarperCollins Pubs.

Galdone, Paul. Cinderella. 2013. (Folk Tale Classics Ser.). (ENG., Illus.). 48p. (J). (gr. -1-3). 8.99 (978-0-547-98867-2(2)) Houghton Mifflin Harcourt Publishing Co.

—The Folk Tale Classics Treasury. 2013. (Folk Tale Classics Ser.). (ENG., Illus.). 240p. (J). (gr. -1-3). 18.99 (978-0-544-05247-5(1)) Houghton Mifflin Harcourt Publishing Co.

—The Gingerbread Boy, 1 vol. Galdone, Paul, illus. 2008. (Paul Galdone Classics Ser.). (ENG., Illus.). 40p. (J). (gr. -1-3). audio compact disk 10.99 (978-0-618-89498-7(5)) Houghton Mifflin Harcourt Publishing Co.

—Jack & the Beanstalk. 2013. (Folk Tale Classics Ser.). (ENG., Illus.). 40p. (J). (gr. -1-3). 8.99 (978-0-544-06665-6(0)) Houghton Mifflin Harcourt Publishing Co.

—Rumpelstiltskin. (Folk Tale Classics Ser.). (ENG., Illus.). (J). (gr. -1-3). 2013. 40p. 8.99 (978-0-544-06692-2(8)) 2008. 32p. audio compact disk 10.99 (978-0-547-18181-3(7)) Houghton Mifflin Harcourt Publishing Co.

—The Three Billy Goats Gruff, 1 vol. Galdone, Paul, illus. 2008. (Paul Galdone Classics Ser.). (ENG., Illus.). 32p. (J). (gr. -1-3). audio compact disk 10.99 (978-0-618-89499-4(3)) Houghton Mifflin Harcourt Publishing Co.

Galdone, Paul & Galdone, Joanna C. Puss in Boots. 2016. (Folk Tale Classics Ser.). (ENG., Illus.). 40p. (J). (gr. -1-3). 8.99 (978-0-544-77252-6(0), HMH Books For Young Readers) Houghton Mifflin Harcourt Publishing Co.

Galliez, Roxane Marie. Give Me Moon. Delanssay, Cathy, illus. 2009. 44p. (J). (gr. -1-3). 14.99 (978-0-8416-7138-6(9)) Hammond World Atlas Corp.

Gallo, Tina. The Three Little Pigs: A Wheel-Y Silly Fairy Tale. Bryne, Kelly, illus. 2011. (Little Simon Sillies Ser.). (ENG.). 14p. (J). (gr. -1-1). 5.99 (978-1-4424-2107-3(X), Little Simon) Little Simon.

Gannon, Gretchen. Rince: The Fairytale of Irish Dance. 2012. (ENG.). 32p. (J). pap. 20.95 (978-1-4327-8237-5(1)); pap. 12.95 (978-1-4327-8235-1(5)) Outskirts Pr., Inc.

Garcia, Jose Enrique. Un Pueblo Llamado Pan y Otros Cuentos Infantiles. 2003. (SPA.). 10.36 net. (978-0-9710710-1-8(2), SLT30784) Spanish Language Texts, Inc.

Gardner, Sally. Book of Princesses. (Illus.). 96p. (J). 19.95 (978-1-85881-350-9(6), Orion) Orion Publishing Group, Ltd. GBR. Dist: Trafalgar Square Publishing.

Garey, Barbara J. The Adventures of Princess Naomia, 1 vol. 2009. 32p. pap. 24.95 (978-1-61546-090-8(X)) America Star Bks.

Garland, Michael. King Puck. Garland, Michael, illus. 2009. (ENG., Illus.). 32p. (J). (gr. -1-3). pap. 6.99 (978-0-06-084811-8(1)) HarperCollins Pubs.

Gatty, Alfred. The Fairy Godmothers & Other Tales. 2007. 120p. per. (978-1-4065-2815-2(3)) Dodo Pr.

—The Fairy Godmothers & Other Tales. 2004. reprint ed. pap. 1.99 (978-1-4192-6178-7(9)); pap. 15.95 (978-1-4191-6178-0(4)) Kessinger Publishing, LLC.

Gavin, Jamila. Blackberry Blue & Other Fairy Tales. Collingridge, Richard, illus. 2015. (ENG.). 240p. (J). (gr. 4-6). 10.99 (978-1-84853-107-9(9)) Transworld Publishers Ltd. GBR. Dist: Independent Pubs. Group.

—Three Indian Princesses: The Stories of Savitri, Damayanti & Sita. 2004. (Illus.). 112p. (Orig.). (J). pap. 7.50 (978-0-7497-4613-1(0)) Egmont Bks., Ltd. GBR. Dist: Trafalgar Square Publishing.

Gay, Marie-Louise. Rumplestinskin. (Buenas Noches Ser.). (SPA.). (J). (gr. k-3). pap. 7.95 (978-958-04-5091-7(9)) Norma S.A. COL. Dist: Distribuidora Norma, Inc.

Gentry, Victory. Grandpa's Fairy Tales: Horatio the Hawk. 2010. pap. 9.95 (978-0-7414-5691-5(5)) Infinity Publishing.

Geok, Wee Bee & Collins UK Publishing Staff. The Story of Nian: A Folk Tale from China. Tran, Turine, illus. 2016. (ENG.). 32p. (J). pap. 8.95 (978-0-00-814711-2(6)) HarperCollins Pubs. Ltd. GBR. Dist: Independent Pubs. Group.

George, Jessica Day. Fridays with the Wizards. 2016. (Tuesdays at the Castle Ser.: 4). (ENG.). 240p. (YA). 16.99 (978-1-61963-429-9(5), 9781619634299, Bloomsbury USA Childrens) Bloomsbury Publishing USA.

—Princess of Glass. 2011. (Twelve Dancing Princesses Ser.). (ENG.). 272p. (YA). (gr. 7). pap. 9.99 (978-1-59990-659-1(7), 9781599906591, Bloomsbury USA Childrens) Bloomsbury Publishing USA.

—Princess of the Silver Woods. (Twelve Dancing Princesses Ser.). (ENG.). (YA). (gr. 7). 2013. 352p. pap. 9.99 (978-1-61963-126-7(1), 9781619631267) 2012. 336p. 16.99 (978-1-59990-646-1(5), 9781599906461) Bloomsbury Publishing USA. (Bloomsbury USA Childrens).

—Saturdays at Sea. 2017. (Tuesdays at the Castle Ser.). (ENG.). 272p. (J). 16.99 (978-1-61963-957-7(2), 9781619639577, Bloomsbury USA Childrens) Bloomsbury Publishing USA.

—Sun & Moon, Ice & Snow. 2013. (ENG.). 352p. (YA). (gr. 7). pap. 9.99 (978-1-61963-184-7(9), 9781619631847, Bloomsbury USA Childrens) Bloomsbury Publishing USA.

—Thursdays with the Crown. 2014. (Tuesdays at the Castle Ser.: 3). (ENG.). 224p. (YA). (gr. 3-6). 16.99 (978-1-61963-299-8(3), 9781619632998, Bloomsbury USA Childrens) Bloomsbury Publishing USA.

—Tuesdays at the Castle. 2011. (Tuesdays at the Castle Ser.: 1). (ENG.). 240p. (YA). (gr. 3-12). 16.99 (978-1-59990-644-7(9), 9781599906447, Bloomsbury USA Childrens) Bloomsbury Publishing USA.

—Wednesdays in the Tower. 2017. (Tuesdays at the Castle Ser.). (ENG.). 256p. (J). pap. 7.99 (978-1-68119-219-2(5), 9781681192192, Bloomsbury USA Childrens) 2014. (Tuesdays at the Castle Ser.: 2). (ENG.). 256p. (YA). (gr. 3-6). pap. 7.99 (978-1-61963-265-3(9), 9781619632653, Bloomsbury USA Childrens) 2013. 240p. E-Book 16.99 (978-1-61963-051-2(6)) 2013. (Tuesdays at the Castle Ser.: 2). (ENG.). 240p. (YA). (gr. 3-6). 16.99 (978-1-59990-645-4(7), 9781599906454, Bloomsbury USA Childrens) Bloomsbury Publishing USA.

Gibb, Sarah. Sleeping Beauty: Based on the Original Story by the Brothers Grimm. Gibb, Sarah, illus. 2015. (ENG., Illus.). 32p. (J). (gr. -1-3). 16.99 (978-0-8075-7351-8(5)) Whitman, Albert & Co.

Gibson, James E. & Gibson, Sylvia Scott. Treetoe the Space Monster, 1 vol. Gibson, Gregory V., illus. 2010. 28p. 24.95 (978-1-4489-4896-3(7)) PublishAmerica, Inc.

Gidwitz, Adam. The Grimm Conclusion. Santat, Dan, illus. 2014. (ENG.). 384p. (J). (gr. 5). pap. 7.99 (978-0-14-242736-1(5), Puffin Books) Penguin Young Readers Group.

—The Grimm Conclusion. D'Andrade, Hugh, illus. 2013. (ENG.). 368p. (J). (gr. 5). 16.99 (978-0-525-42615-8(9), Dutton Books for Young Readers) Penguin Young Readers Group.

—The Grimm Conclusion. 2014. (Grimm Ser.: 3). lib. bdg. 18.40 (978-0-606-36187-3(1)) Turtleback Bks.

—In a Glass Grimmly. Santat, Dan, illus. 2013. (ENG.). 352p. (J). (gr. 5). pap. 7.99 (978-0-14-242506-0(0), Puffin Books) Penguin Young Readers Group.

—In a Glass Grimmly. D'Andrade, Hugh, illus. 2012. (ENG.). 336p. (J). (gr. 5). 16.99 (978-0-525-42581-6(0), Dutton Books for Young Readers) Penguin Young Readers Group.

—In a Glass Grimmly. 2013. (Grimm Ser.: 2). lib. bdg. 18.40 (978-0-606-32135-8(7), Turtleback) Turtleback Bks.

—A Tale Dark & Grimm. D'Andrade, Hugh & Santat, Dan, illus. 2011. (ENG.). 288p. (J). (gr. 5-18). 7.99 (978-0-14-241967-0(2), Puffin Books) Penguin Young Readers Group.

—A Tale Dark & Grimm, 4 vols. (J). 55.75 (978-1-4498-6835-2(5)) Recorded Bks., Inc.

—A Tale Dark & Grimm. 2011. (Grimm Ser.: 1). lib. bdg. 18.40 (978-0-606-23144-2(7), Turtleback) Turtleback Bks.

Gidwitz, Adam, et al. A Tale Dark & Grimm. D'Andrade, Hugh, illus. 2010. (ENG.). 272p. (J). (gr. 5-18). 16.99 (978-0-525-42334-8(6), Dutton Books for Young Readers) Penguin Young Readers Group.

Gieselmann, Reinhard. The Happy Prince & Other Tales. 2007. (ENG., Illus.). 87p. 39.00 (978-3-936681-13-0(9)) Edition Axel Menges GmbH DEU. Dist: National Bk. Network.

Gifford, Clare. Dick Whittington. Cerisier, Emmanuel, illus. 2013. (ENG.). 64p. (YA). (gr. 2-4). 21.00 (978-1-4081-8761-6(2), 9781408187616, Bloomsbury USA Childrens) Bloomsbury Publishing USA.

Gilani, Fawzia. Cinderella: An Islamic Tale. 2011. (ENG., Illus.). 44p. (J). (gr. k-5). 14.00 (978-0-86037-473-2(4)) Kube Publishing Ltd. GBR. Dist: Consortium Bk. Sales & Distribution.

Gili, Phillida. Cinderella: A Pop-up Book. Gili, Phillida, illus. 2007. (Illus.). 12p. (J). 25.00 (978-1-4223-9031-3(4)) DIANE Publishing Co.

Gill, Vince. The Emperor's New Clothes: A Country Storybook. Newsom, Carol, illus. 2006. 30p. (J). (gr. 4-8). reprint ed. 17.00 (978-1-4223-5729-3(5)) DIANE Publishing Co.

Gilmore, Rachna. The Flute, 1 vol. Biswas, Pulak, illus. 2012. (ENG.). 32p. (J). (gr. -1-2). 16.95 (978-1-896580-57-9(2)) Tradewind Bks. CAN. Dist: Orca Bk. Pubs. USA.

The Gingerbread Man, Level 2. 2016. (Ladybird Readers Ser.). (ENG.). 48p. (J). pap. 9.99 (978-0-241-25442-4(6)) Penguin Bks., Ltd. GBR. Dist: Independent Pubs. Group.

Giorgio, Marg. Maxi's Magical Dream. 2011. 24p. pap. 12.79 (978-1-4634-4491-4(5)) AuthorHouse.

Gleeson, Brian. Anansi, 1 vol. Guarnaccia, Steven, illus. 2005. (Rabbit Ears: A Classic Tale Ser.). (ENG.). 36p. (gr. -1-3). 25.65 (978-1-59679-342-2(2)) Spotlight.

—Koi & the Kola Nuts, 1 vol. Ruffins, Reynold, illus. 2007. (Rabbit Ears: A Classic Tale Ser.). (ENG.). 36p. (gr. k-3). 25.65 (978-1-59961-310-9(7)) Spotlight.

Gloria North. Dragon Dreams: Tales of Fun & Fantasy. 2005. 77p. pap. 10.00 (978-1-59926-471-4(4)) Xlibris Corp.

Gmeyner, Elizabeth. The Key of the Kingdom: A Book of Stories & Poems for Children. Russell, Joyce, illus. 2004. 100p. (J). pap. 15.00 (978-0-88010-549-1(6), Bell Pond Bks.) SteinerBooks, Inc.

Goble, Paul. The Girl Who Loved Wild Horses. 2015. 32p. pap. 8.00 (978-1-61003-619-1(0)) Center for the Collaborative Classroom.

God's Little Angel Twins, Maryknoll Coloring & Activity Book, Grades Pre-K & K: Rhyming Tales of Mary & Knoll from Maryknoll Land. 2005. (J). 2.00 (978-0-941395-12-0(X)) Maryknoll Missioners.

Goethes Fairy Tale Staff. The Green Snake & the Beautiful Lily. Allen, Joan deRis, ed. Heuscher, Julius E., tr. from GER. Linde, Hermann, illus. 2006. 53p. (J). (gr. 3-7). 25.00 (978-0-88010-570-5(4)) SteinerBooks, Inc.

Golden Books. The Blue Book of Fairy Tales. 2013. (Little Golden Book Ser.). (ENG., Illus.). 24p. (J). (-k). 4.99 (978-0-449-80996-9(X), Golden Bks.) Random Hse. Children's Bks.

—The Little Red Hen. Miller, J. P., illus. 2015. (ENG.). 26p. (J). (-k). bds. 7.99 (978-0-385-39094-1(7), Golden Bks.) Random Hse. Children's Bks.

—The Princess & the Pea. Christy, Jana, illus. 2013. (Little Golden Book Ser.). (ENG.). 24p. (J). (-k). 4.99 (978-0-307-97951-3(2), Golden Bks.) Random Hse. Children's Bks.

—Purpleberry Surprise! (Nella the Princess Knight) Cespedes-Alicea, Marcela, illus. 2017. (Deluxe Paint Box Book Ser.). (ENG.). 128p. (J). (gr. -1-2). pap. 7.99 **(978-1-5247-1673-8(1)**, Golden Bks.) Random Hse. Children's Bks.

—Rainbow Rescue! (Dora the Explorer) Miller, Victoria, illus. 2014. (Color Plus Chunky Crayons Ser.). (ENG.). 48p. (J). (gr. -1-2). pap. 3.99 (978-0-385-37436-1(4), Golden Bks.) Random Hse. Children's Bks.

Golden Books. Shrek Little Golden Book. Nedelcu, Ovi, illus. 2017. (Little Golden Book Ser.). (ENG.). 24p. (J). (-k). 4.99 **(978-1-5247-6770-9(0)**, Golden Bks.) Random Hse. Children's Bks.

Golden Books, illus. Barbie 9 Favorite Fairy Tales (Barbie) 2013. (Little Golden Book Treasury Ser.). (ENG.). 224p. (J). (-k). 10.99 (978-0-449-81861-9(6), Golden Bks.) Random Hse. Children's Bks.

Golden Books Staff. Beautiful Barbie. Golden Books Staff, illus. 2009. (Super Stickerific Ser.). (ENG., Illus.). 64p. (J). (gr. -1-2). pap. 12.99 (978-0-375-85553-5(X), Golden Bks.) Random Hse. Children's Bks.

—Fairy Magic (Dora the Explorer) Fruchter, Jason, illus. 2012. (Color Plus Chunky Crayons Ser.). (ENG.). 48p. (J). (gr. -1-2). pap. 3.99 (978-0-307-93030-9(0), Golden Bks.) Random Hse. Children's Bks.

—The House That Jack Built. Miller, J. P., illus. 2008. (Little Golden Book Ser.). (ENG.). 24p. (J). (gr. -1-2). 4.99 (978-0-375-83530-8(X), Golden Bks.) Random Hse. Children's Bks.

Golden, Christopher. When Rose Wakes. 2010. (ENG.). 320p. pap. 19.99 (978-1-4391-4823-5(6), MTV Bks.) MTV Books.

Goldenburg, Dorothea & Killian, Bette. Treasury of Fairy Tales. LoFaro, Jerry et al, illus. 2004. 320p. (J). 15.98 (978-0-7853-7771-9(9), 3049205) Phoenix International Publications, Inc.

Goldilocks & the Three Bears. 2004. (My First Fairy Tales Ser.). (Illus.). 24p. (J). pap. 3.99 (978-1-85854-686-5(9)) Brimax Books Ltd. GBR. Dist: Byeway Bks.

Goldilocks & the Three Bears. (Ladybird Bks.). (ARA., Illus.). 52p. (J). 12.95 incl. audio (978-0-86685-254-8(9), LDL109C) International Bk. Ctr., Inc.

GoldilocksThree Bears. 2004. (J). E-Book incl. cd-rom (978-1-84444-460-1(0)) Mantra Lingua.

Goldsack, Gaby & Kolanovic, Dubravka, illus. Little Red Riding Hood. 2015. (J). (978-1-4723-3139-7(7)) Parragon Bk. Service Ltd.

Gonzalez, Jorge & Collodi, Carlo. Pinocchio, 1 vol. Ruiz, Alfonso, illus. 2009. (Classic Fiction Ser.).Tr. of Avventure di Pinocchio. (ENG.). 72p. (gr. 2-3). lib. bdg. 27.99 (978-1-4342-1583-3(0), Graphic Revolve) Stone Arch Bks.

Gooderham, Chris. More Wicked Rhymes. 2008. 68p. pap. 13.95 (978-1-4092-1663-6(2)) Lulu Pr., Inc.

—Wicked Rhymes. 2008. 68p. pap. 13.95 (978-1-4092-1662-9(4)) Lulu Pr., Inc.

Goodman, Judith. A Fairy's Tale about Honesty. 2005. (J). 15.00 (978-0-9663144-3-4(3)) Women & Addiction Counseling & Educational Services.

Gopigian, Susan Kadian. Gadoo the Cat: An Armenian Folktale. Bolt, Susan Collier, illus. 2008. 39p. 16.95 (978-0-9801453-0-4(9)) Wayne State Univ. Pr.

Gorbachev, Valeri, illus. Goldilocks & the Three Bears. 2015. (ENG.). 40p. (J). 15.95 (978-0-7358-4211-3(6)) North-South Bks., Inc.

Gordon, Mike, illus. The Emperor's New Clothes. 2006. 24p. (J). (gr. -1-3). 9.99 (978-0-7945-1350-4(6), Usborne) EDC Publishing.

—The Frog Prince. rev. ed. 2007. (Young Reading CD Packs Ser.). 48p. (J). (gr. -1-3). 9.99 incl. audio compact disk (978-0-7945-1868-4(0), Usborne) EDC Publishing.

—The Princess & the Pea. rev. ed. 2007. (Young Reading CD Packs Ser.). 48p. (J). (gr. -1-3). 9.99 incl. audio compact disk (978-0-7945-1875-2(3), Usborne) EDC Publishing.

—Stories of Princesses. 2006. 144p. (J). (gr. 4-7). 14.99 (978-0-7945-1385-6(9), Usborne) EDC Publishing.

Gorey, Edward & Donnelly, James. Three Classic Children's Stories. 2010. (Illus.). 112p. (J). 17.95 (978-0-7649-5546-4(2)) Pomegranate Communications, Inc.

Gorman, Karyn. Rapunzel & the Prince of Pop. Anderson, Laura Ellen, illus. 2015. (ENG.). 32p. (J). (978-0-7787-1929-8(4)) Crabtree Publishing Co.

Gormley, Greg. Fairy Tale Frankie & the Tricky Witch. Lenton, Steven, illus. 2016. (ENG.). 32p. (J). (gr. -1-1). 17.99 (978-1-4814-6625-7(9), Aladdin) Simon & Schuster Children's Publishing.

Gould, Robert. Father & Son Read-Aloud Stories. Gurin, Lara, illus. 2006. (ENG.). 56p. (J). (gr. -1-k). 12.95 (978-1-929945-67-2(1)) Big Guy Bks., Inc.

Graham- Biehl, Anne. The Mists of Afar. 2015. (ENG.). 196p. (J). (gr. 1-2). 11.95 (978-1-84963-673-5(7), d2dbd777-f166-4591-be1c-ecf9c310e448) Austin, Stan AUS. Dist: Bookmasters Distribution.

Grau, Sheila. The Boy with Seventeen Senses. 2016. (ENG.). 256p. (J). (gr. 3-7). 16.95 (978-1-4197-2119-9(4), Amulet Bks.) Abrams, Inc.

Graves, Alfred Perceval. The Irish Fairy Book. 2007. 376p. per. 33.95 (978-0-548-65710-2(6)) Kessinger Publishing, LLC.

Greaves, Margaret. Tattercoats. Chamberlain, Margaret, illus. 32p. (J). (gr. -1-2). pap. (978-0-7112-0649-6(X)) ReiseArt Buchhandlung GmbH.

Green, Roger Lancelyn. Tales of Ancient Egypt. 2011. (Puffin Classics Ser.). (ENG., Illus.). 256p. (J). (gr. 5-7). 4.99 (978-0-14-133259-8(X), Puffin Books) Penguin Young Readers Group.

Green, Roger Lancelyn, ed. Once upon a Time: Folk & Fairy Tales of the World. Kubasta, Vojtech, illus. 2011. 140p. 40.95 (978-1-258-03324-8(0)) Literary Licensing, LLC.

Greene, Joshua M. Kaliya, Serpent King. Wire, Patrick, illus. rev. ed. 2012. (ENG.). 24p. (gr. -1). 14.99 (978-1-60887-148-3(7)) Mandala Publishing.

—Krishna & the Mystery of the Stolen Calves. Amendola, Dominique, illus. 2013. (ENG.). 24p. (gr. -1). 14.99 (978-1-60887-173-5(8)) Mandala Publishing.

Greenway, Betty, ed. Twice-Told Children's Tales Vol. 35: The Influence of Childhood Reading on Writers for Adults. 2005. (Children's Literature & Culture Ser.: Vol. 35). (ENG.). 274p. (C). 150.00 (978-0-415-97205-5(1), RT2051) Routledge.

Greenwood, R. L. A Visit to the Kingdom of Camelot. 2013. 62p. (gr. 2-2). pap. 8.95 (978-1-4759-8097-4(3)) iUniverse, Inc.

Gregory, Manju. Ali Baba & the Forty Thieves. Jago, illus. 2004. (J). (978-1-84444-544-8(5)) Mantra Lingua.

Gresham, Xanthe. The Princess & the Pea. Clara, Miss, illus. 2013. (ENG.). 40p. (J). 17.99 (978-1-84686-905-1(6)) Barefoot Bks., Inc.

—Princess & the Pea. 2017. (ENG., Illus.). 40p. (J). (gr. -1-3). 12.99 **(978-1-78285-355-8(3))** Barefoot Bks., Inc.

Gresham, Xanthe. Thumbelina. Gastaut, Charlotte, illus. 2016. 48p. (J). (gr. 1-5). pap. 9.99 (978-1-78285-276-6(X)) Barefoot Bks., Inc.

Gribben, Valerie. The Fairytale Trilogy: Fairytale, the Emperor's Realm, & the Three Crowns. 2010. (ENG.). 320p. (YA). (gr. 5-10). 24.95 (978-1-58838-251-1(6), NewSouth Bks.) NewSouth, Inc.

griego, Mito. EL REY MIDAS. 2005. (Troquelados Clásicos Ser.). (SPA & ENG., Illus.). 16p. (J). (gr. -1-k). pap. 3.95 (978-84-7864-895-5(X)) Combel Editorial, S.A. ESP. Dist: Independent Pubs. Group.

Griffis, William. Dutch Fairy Tales for Young Folks. 2005. pap. 15.95 (978-1-59605-348-9(8), Cosimo Classics) Cosimo, Inc.

Griffis, William Elliot. Dutch Fairy Tales for Young Folks. 2004. reprint ed. pap. 1.99 (978-1-4192-1705-0(4)) Kessinger Publishing, LLC.

Griffiths, Neil & Nash, Doug. Florence Was No Ordinary Fairy. 2015. (ENG., Illus.). 28p. (J). pap. 13.50 (978-1-905434-03-9(0)) Award Pubns. Ltd. GBR. Dist: Parkwest Pubns., Inc.

Grim, Wilhelm. Grimm: The Illustrated Fairy Tales of the Brothers Grimm. 2017. (ENG., Illus.). 192p. (J). (gr. 1-4). 24.95 **(978-3-89955-788-6(3))** Die Gestalten Verlag DEU. Dist: Penguin Random Hse. LLC.

Grimm. Repunzel. 2005. 24p. incl. cd-rom (978-84-494-2900-2(5)) Oceano Grupo Editoria, S.A.

—Die Schoensten Kinder und Hausmaerchen. (GER.). cd-rom (978-3-15-120018-5(4)) Reclam, Philip jun., Verlag GmbH DEU. Dist: International Bk. Import Service, Inc.

—Tales from the Brothers Grimm. Leupin, Herbert, illus. 2015. (ENG.). 160p. (J). (gr. -1-3). 29.95 (978-0-7358-4228-1(0)) North-South Bks., Inc.

Grimm, Brothers. Hans in Luck: Seven Stories by the Brothers Grimm. Hoffmann, Felix, illus. 2017. (ENG.). 256p. (J). (gr. -1-3). 30.00 **(978-0-7358-4281-6(7))** North-South Bks., Inc.

Grimm Brothers Staff. Hansel & Gretel. Cowley, Joy, ed. Jo, Hyeon-suk, illus. 2015. (World Classics Ser.). (ENG.). 32p. (J). (gr. k-4). 26.65 (978-1-925186-66-6(0)) Lerner Publishing Group.

Grimm Brothers Staff, et al. Grimms' Fairy Tales. Cruikshank, George, illus. 2011. (Puffin Classics Ser.). (ENG.). 400p. (J). (gr. 3-7). 5.99 (978-0-14-133120-1(8), Puffin Books) Penguin Young Readers Group.

Grimm, Jacob. The Elves & the Shoemaker. 2004. (Treasure Tree Ser.). (Illus.). 32p. (J). (978-0-7166-1600-9(9)) World Bk., Inc.

—Grimm's Fairy Stories. 2005. 144p. per. 11.95 (978-1-59818-708-3(2)) Aegypan.

Grimm, Jacob & Grimm, Wilhelm. Grimm's Fairy Tales. McKowen, Scott, illus. 2009. (Sterling Unabridged Classics Ser.). (ENG.). 288p. (J). (gr. 5). 9.95 (978-1-4027-6702-9(1)) Sterling Publishing Co., Inc.

—Hansel & Gretel, 1 vol. Archipova, Anastasiya, illus. 2008. (ENG.). 32p. (J). (gr. -1-3). (978-0-86315-623-6(1)) Floris Bks.

—The Juniper Tree & Other Tales. 2012. (Pushkin Collection). (ENG.). 272p. pap. 16.00 (978-1-906548-68-1(4), Pushkin Press) Steerforth Pr.

—Little Red Riding Hood. Sourdais, Clèmentine, illus. 2014. (ENG.). 28p. (J). (gr. -1-3). 16.95 (978-3-89955-723-7(9)) Die Gestalten Verlag DEU. Dist: Penguin Random Hse. LLC.

—Sleeping Beauty & Other Fairy Tales. 2011. (Dover Children's Thrift Classics Ser.). (ENG., Illus.). 96p. (Orig.). (J). (gr. 3-6). pap. 4.00 (978-0-486-27084-5(X)) Dover Pubns., Inc.

—Snow White. Greban, Quentin, illus. 2013. (ENG.). 32p. (J). (gr. -1-3). pap. 7.95 *(978-0-7358-4116-1(0))* North-South Bks., Inc.

—The Story of Little Red Riding Hood. Bing, Christopher H., illus. 2010. (ENG.). 40p. (J). (gr. k-17). 18.99 *(978-0-8118-6986-7(5))* Chronicle Bks. LLC.

Grimm, Jacob & Grimm, Wilhelm K. The Bremen Town Musicians: A Tale about Working Together. Catalano, Dominic, illus. 2006. (Famous Fables Ser.). (J). *(978-1-59939-039-0(6),* Reader's Digest Young Families, Inc.) Studio Fun International.

—Cinderella & Other Tales. 2005. (Charming Classics). (Illus.). 224p. (J). 6.99 *(978-0-06-059602-6(3),* HarperFestival) HarperCollins Pubs.

—The Complete Fairy Tales of the Brothers Grimm. Zipes, Jack D., tr. from GER. Gruelle, Johnny, illus. 3rd ed. 2003. (Bantam Classics Ser.). (ENG.). 800p. (J). reprint ed. pap. 23.00 *(978-0-553-38216-7(0),* Bantam) Random House Publishing Group.

—Fairy Tales, 14 bks., Set. Incl. Three Feathers. Schmid, Eleanor, illus. (gr. -1-3). lib. bdg. 13.95 *(978-0-87191-941-0(9),* 1178-8); Three Languages. Chermayeff, Ivan, illus. (gr. 5-18). lib. bdg. 13.95 *(978-0-87191-940-3(0),* 1178-9); 32p. (YA). 1984. 195.30 o.p. *(978-0-87191-933-5(8),* Creative Education) Creative Co., The.

—The Fisherman & His Wife, 1 vol. Bryan, Diana, illus. 2005. (Rabbit Ears-A Classic Tale Set 2 Ser.). (ENG.). 32p. (gr. k-5). 25.65 *(978-1-59197-747-6(9))* Spotlight.

—The Fisherman & His Wife: A Tale about Being Happy & Satisfied. Ebert, Len, illus. 2006. (J). *(978-1-59939-097-0(3),* Reader's Digest Young Families, Inc.) Studio Fun International.

—Grandpa Mouse & Little Mouse: A Tale about Respect for Elders. Lonaytis, Olga, illus. 2006. (J). *(978-1-59939-088-8(4),* Reader's Digest Young Families, Inc.) Studio Fun International.

—Grimm's Fairy Stories. 2007. (ENG.). 166p. pap. 19.99 *(978-1-4264-2691-9(7));* 178p. pap. 21.99 *(978-1-4264-2748-0(4))* Creative Media Partners, LLC.

—Grimm's Fairy Tales. Hunt, Margaret, tr. from GER. 2007. (Dover Thrift Editions Ser.). (ENG., Illus.). 208p. per. 5.00 *(978-0-486-45656-0(0))* Dover Pubns., Inc.

—Grimms Fairy Tales. 2006. pap. *(978-1-4068-2141-3(1))* Echo Library.

—Grimm's Fairy Tales. l.t. ed. 2004. (Large Print Ser.). 477p. 26.00 *(978-1-58287-627-6(4))* North Bks.

—Hans My Hedgehog: A Tale from the Brothers Grimm. Nickle, John, illus. 2012. (ENG.). 40p. (J). (gr. k-3). 16.99 *(978-1-4169-1533-1(8),* Atheneum Bks. for Young Readers) Simon & Schuster Children's Publishing.

—Hansel & Gretel. Duntze, Dorothee, illus. 2006. 24p. (J). (gr. k-4). reprint ed. 17.00 *(978-1-4223-5008-9(8))* DIANE Publishing Co.

—Hansel & Gretel. Price, Margaret Evans, illus. 2005. (Shape Bks.). (ENG.). 16p. (J). (gr. -1-3). 9.95 *(978-1-59583-012-8(X),* 9781595830128, Green Tiger Pr.) Laughing Elephant.

—Hut in the Forest, 1 vol. Lawson, Polly, tr. from GER. Stietencron, Bettina, illus. 2007. (Grimm's Fairy Tales Ser.). (ENG.). 28p. (J). *(978-0-86315-615-1(0))* Floris Bks.

—Sleeping Beauty / La Bella Durmiente. 2004. (Illus.). (J). *(978-1-933530-18-5(9))* Bingo Bks., Inc.

—Snow White & Other Fairy Tales. unabr. ed. 2012. (Dover Children's Thrift Classics Ser.). (ENG., Illus.). 96p. (J). (gr. 3-8). pap. 2.50 *(978-0-486-28327-2(5))* Dover Pubns., Inc.

Grimm, Jacob, et al. Animal Fables, 4 bks., Set. Roederer, Charlotte, illus. 2007. (Abbeville Classic Fairy Tales Ser.). (ENG.). 112p. (J). (gr. 1-2). 19.95 *(978-0-7892-0951-1(9))* Abbeville Pr., Inc.

—The Classic Collection of Fairy Tales. Shuttleworth, Cathy, illus. 2011. (ENG.). 192p. (J). (gr. -1-12). pap. 9.99 *(978-1-84322-787-8(8))* Anness Publishing GBR. Dist: National Bk. Network.

—The Elves & the Shoemaker: A Grimm Graphic Novel, 1 vol. Rodriquez, Pedro, illus. 2011. (Graphic Spin Ser.). (ENG.). 40p. (gr. 1-3). lib. bdg. 25.32 *(978-1-4342-2553-5(4),* Graphic Revolve) Stone Arch Bks.

—Family Favorites, 4 bks., Set. Thibault, Dominique & Durual, Christophe, illus. 2007. (Abbeville Classic Fairy Tales Ser.). (ENG.). 112p. (J). (gr. -1-3). 19.95 *(978-0-7892-0952-8(7))* Abbeville Pr., Inc.

—Gris Grimly's Tales from the Brothers Grimm: Being a Selection from the Household Stories Collected by Jacob & Wilhelm Grimm. Hunt, Alfred William & Grimly, Gris, illus. 2016. 288p. (J). (gr. 3-7). 17.99 *(978-0-06-235233-0(4))* HarperCollins Pubs.

—Hansel & Gretel. 2005. 48p. (J). (gr. 2-18). 8.95 *(978-0-7945-1053-4(1),* Usborne) EDC Publishing.

—Hansel & Gretel. Rowe, Louise, illus. 2nd ed. 2014. (Fairytale Pop-Ups Ser.). (ENG.). 16p. (J). (gr. k-2). 27.99 *(978-1-85707-858-9(6))* Tango Bks. GBR. Dist: Independent Pubs. Group.

—Princess Tales, 4 bks., Set. Deru, Myriam et al, illus. 2007. (Abbeville Classic Fairy Tales Ser.). (ENG.). 112p. (J). (gr. -1-3). 19.95 *(978-0-7892-0950-4(0))* Abbeville Pr., Inc.

—The Queen Bee. Ghiuselev, Iassen & James, Elizabeth, illus. 2003. (ENG.). 24p. (J). 16.95 *(978-0-9688768-4-8(6))* Simply Read Bks. CAN. Dist: Ingram Publisher Services.

Grimm, Jacob i Wilhelm (Germans Grimm). CAPERUCITA ROJA. (Coleccion Fabulas y Cuentos Populares). (SPA.). 24p. (J). (gr. 2-4). *(978-84-246-1921-3(8),* GL0132) La Galera, S.A. Editorial ESP. Dist: Lectorum Pubns., Inc.

Grimm, Wilhelm i Jacob. CAPERUCITA ROJA. 2005. (Caballo Alado Clásico Series-Al Paso Ser.). (SPA & ENG., Illus.). 24p. (J). (gr. -1-k). 7.95 *(978-84-7864-851-1(8))* Combel Editorial, S.A. ESP. Dist: Independent Pubs. Group.

—GARBANCITO. 2005. (Caballo Alado Clásico Series-Al Paso Ser.). (SPA & ENG., Illus.). 24p. (J). (gr. -1-k). 7.95 *(978-84-7864-853-5(4))* Combel Editorial, S.A. ESP. Dist: Independent Pubs. Group.

Grimm, Wilhelm K. & Grimm, Jacob. Grimms Complete Fairy Tales. (Illus.). 643p. pap. *(978-0-88029-519-2(8))* Barnes & Noble, Inc.

—Grimm's Fairy Tales Volume 2. 2011. (Illus.). 200p. (YA). 16.99 *(978-1-61377-048-1(0))* Idea & Design Works, LLC.

—Little Red Riding-Hood: A Grimm's Fairy Tale. Lawson, Polly, tr. from GER. Van Zeyl, Marjan, illus. 2008. (ENG.). 20p. (J). (gr. -1-3). *(978-0-86315-622-9(3))* Floris Bks.

—Tales from Grimm. Gág, Wanda, tr. Gág, Wanda, illus. 2006. (Fesler-Lampert Minnesota Heritage Ser.). (ENG.). 256p. (gr. 4-7). per. 16.95 *(978-0-8166-4936-5(7))* Univ. of Minnesota Pr.

Grimm, Wilhelm K., et al. Elves & Shoemaker. 2004. 48p. (J). (gr. 2-18). pap. 5.95 *(978-0-7945-0758-9(1),* Usborne) EDC Publishing.

—Grimm's Fairy Tales. 2005. (Great Illustrated Classics Ser.). (ENG., Illus.). 237p. (gr. 3-8). 21.35 *(978-1-59679-241-8(8))* Spotlight.

—The Twelve Dancing Princesses. Barrager, Brigette, illus. 2011. (ENG.). 40p. (J). (gr. -1-3). 16.99 *(978-0-8118-7696-4(9))* Chronicle Bks. LLC.

Grimm's & Anderson Cinderella. (Grimm's & Andersen Ser.). *(978-1-4054-4782-9(6))* Parragon, Inc.

Gruber, Daveda. Castle of Ice. 2008. 51p. pap. 10.94 *(978-1-4357-3251-3(0))* Lulu Pr., Inc.

Guarnaccia, Steven. Cinderella: A Fashionable Tale. 2013. (ENG., Illus.). 32p. (J). (gr. k-2). 19.95 *(978-1-4197-0986-9(0),* Abrams Bks. for Young Readers) Abrams, Inc.

Guillain, Adam & Guillain, Charlotte. The Three Frilly Goats Fluff. Littler, Phil, illus. 2015. (ENG.). 32p. (J). *(978-0-7787-1935-9(9))* Crabtree Publishing Co.

Guillain, Charlotte. Animal Fairy Tales, 1 vol. Beacon, Dawn, illus. (Animal Fairy Tales Ser.). (ENG.). 24p. 2014. (gr. 1-2). lib. bdg. 119.95 *(978-1-4109-6116-7(8))* 2013. (gr. -1-2). pap. 162.45 *(978-1-4109-5526-5(5))* 2013. (gr. -1-2). pap. 32.45 *(978-1-4109-5033-8(6))* 2013. (gr. -1-2). pap. 324.70 *(978-1-4109-5527-2(3))* 2013. (gr. -1-2). lib. bdg. 119.95 *(978-1-4109-5027-7(1))* Heinemann-Raintree. (NA-r).

—Animal Fairy Tales Big Book Collection. Beacon, Dawn, illus. 2013. (Animal Fairy Tales Ser.). (ENG.). 24p. (gr. -1-2). 130.00 *(978-1-4109-5045-1(X),* NA-r) Heinemann-Raintree.

—Animal Fairy Tales Bind Up 1. 2014. (Animal Fairy Tales Ser.). (ENG.). 120p. (J). (gr. -1-2). spiral bd. 4.75 *(978-1-4109-6783-1(2),* NA-r) Heinemann-Raintree.

—Animal Fairy Tales Bind Up 2. 2014. (Animal Fairy Tales Ser.). (ENG.). 120p. (J). (gr. -1-2). spiral bd. 4.75 *(978-1-4109-6784-8(0),* NA-r) Heinemann-Raintree.

—Cat & the Beanstalk, 1 vol. Beacon, Dawn, illus. 2014. (Animal Fairy Tales Ser.). (ENG.). 24p. (gr. 1-2). lib. bdg. 23.99 *(978-1-4109-6113-6(3),* NA-r) Heinemann-Raintree.

—The Emperor Penguin's New Clothes, 1 vol. Beacon, Dawn, illus. 2014. (Animal Fairy Tales Ser.). (ENG.). 24p. (gr. 1-2). pap. 6.49 *(978-1-4109-6121-1(4));* 26.00 *(978-1-4109-6134-1(6));* lib. bdg. 23.99 *(978-1-4109-6114-3(1))* Heinemann-Raintree. (NA-r).

—The Frog Prince Saves Sleeping Beauty. Widdowson, Dan, illus. 2016. (Fairy Tale Mix-Ups Ser.). (ENG.). 24p. (gr. k-2). lib. bdg. 23.32 *(978-1-4109-8302-2(1))* Heinemann-Raintree.

—Little Red Riding Duck, 1 vol. Beacon, Dawn, illus. 2013. (Animal Fairy Tales Ser.). (ENG.). 24p. (gr. -1-2). pap. 6.49 *(978-1-4109-5030-7(1));* 26.00 *(978-1-4109-5042-0(5));* lib. bdg. 23.99 *(978-1-4109-5024-6(7))* Heinemann-Raintree. (NA-r).

—Pandarella, 1 vol. Beacon, Dawn, illus. 2013. (Animal Fairy Tales Ser.). (ENG.). 24p. (gr. -1-2). pap. 6.49 *(978-1-4109-5031-4(X));* lib. bdg. 23.99 *(978-1-4109-5025-3(5))* Heinemann-Raintree. (NA-r).

—The Poodle & the Pea, 1 vol. Beacon, Dawn, illus. 2013. (Animal Fairy Tales Ser.). (ENG.). 24p. (gr. -1-2). pap. 6.49 *(978-1-4109-5032-1(8));* lib. bdg. 23.99 *(978-1-4109-5026-0(3))* Heinemann-Raintree. (NA-r).

—Ratpunzel, 1 vol. Beacon, Dawn, illus. 2014. (Animal Fairy Tales Ser.). (ENG.). 24p. (gr. 1-2). lib. bdg. 23.99 *(978-1-4109-6112-9(5),* NA-r) Heinemann-Raintree.

—Red Riding Hood Meets the Three Bears. West, Karl, illus. 2016. (Fairy Tale Mix-Ups Ser.). (ENG.). 24p. (gr. k-2). lib. bdg. 23.32 *(978-1-4109-8304-6(8))* Heinemann-Raintree.

—Rumplesnakeskin, 1 vol. Beacon, Dawn, illus. 2014. (Animal Fairy Tales Ser.). (ENG.). 24p. (gr. 1-2). lib. bdg. 23.99 *(978-1-4109-6111-2(7),* NA-r) Heinemann-Raintree.

—Sleeping Badger, 1 vol. Beacon, Dawn, illus. 2014. (Animal Fairy Tales Ser.). (ENG.). 24p. (gr. 1-2). lib. bdg. 23.99 *(978-1-4109-6115-0(X),* NA-r) Heinemann-Raintree.

Guillain, Charlotte & Andersen, Hans Christian. The Poodle & the Pea. Beacon, Dawn, illus. 2013. (Animal Fairy Tales Ser.). (ENG.). 24p. (gr. -1-2). 26.00 *(978-1-4109-5044-4(1),* NA-r) Heinemann-Raintree.

Guillain, Charlotte & Perrault, Charles. Pandarella. Beacon, Dawn, illus. 2013. (Animal Fairy Tales Ser.). (ENG.). 24p. (gr. -1-2). 26.00 *(978-1-4109-5043-7(3),* NA-r) Heinemann-Raintree.

Guin, Anatoly. Smart Tales from Brainy the Cat. 2010. 84p. pap. 29.95 *(978-1-4327-6147-9(1))* Outskirts Pr., Inc.

Gulla, Rosemarie. On the Wings of the Swan. Undercuffler, Gary, illus. 2008. (Treasury of the Lost Scrolls Ser.). (ENG.). 32p. (J). (gr. 1-4). 17.99 *(978-0-9793000-0-4(2),* Alazar Pr.) Royal Swan Enterprises, Inc.

Gunderson, Jessica. Frankly, I'd Rather Spin Myself a New Name! The Story of Rumpelstiltskin As Told by Rumpelstiltskin. Bock, Janna, illus. 2016. (Other Side of the Story Ser.). (ENG.). 24p. (gr. 2-3). lib. bdg. 27.32 *(978-1-4795-8624-0(2))* Picture Window Bks.

—Little Red Riding Hood Stories Around the World: 3 Beloved Tales, 1 vol. Madden, Colleen et al, illus. 2014. (Multicultural Fairy Tales Ser.). (ENG.). 32p. (gr. k-2). lib. bdg. 27.32 *(978-1-4795-5435-5(9))* Picture Window Bks.

—No Lie, Pigs (and Their Houses) CAN Fly! The Story of the Three Little Pigs As Told by the Wolf. Bernardini, Cristian, illus. 2016. (Other Side of the Story Ser.). (ENG.). 24p. (gr. 2-3). lib. bdg. 27.32 *(978-1-4795-8621-9(8))* Picture Window Bks.

—Really, Rapunzel Needed a Haircut! The Story of Rapunzel, as Told by Dame Gothel. Alonso, Denis, illus. 2013. (Other Side of the Story Ser.). (ENG.). 24p. (gr. 2-3). 27.32 *(978-1-4048-7941-6(2))* Picture Window Bks.

—Really, Rapunzel Needed a Haircut! The Story of Rapunzel As Told by Dame Gothel. Alonso, Denis, illus. 2013. (Other Side of the Story Ser.). (ENG.). 24p. (gr. 2-3). 9.95 *(978-1-4795-1946-0(4))* Picture Window Bks.

—Snow White Stories Around the World: 4 Beloved Tales, 1 vol. Belloni, Valentina et al, illus. 2014. (Multicultural Fairy Tales Ser.). (ENG.). 32p. (gr. k-2). lib. bdg. 27.32 *(978-1-4795-5434-8(0))* Picture Window Bks.

Gunderson, Jessica & Loewen, Nancy. Really, Rapunzel Needed a Haircut! The Story of Rapunzel As Told by Dame Gothel. Alonso, Denis & Tayal, Amit, illus. 2013. (Other Side of the Story Ser.). (ENG.). 24p. (gr. 2-3). pap. 6.95 *(978-1-4795-1950-7(2))* Picture Window Bks.

Gunderson, Jessica & Meister, Cari. Multicultural Fairy Tales, 1 vol. Madden, Colleen et al, illus. 2014. (Multicultural Fairy Tales Ser.). (ENG.). 32p. (gr. k-2). 109.28 *(978-1-4795-5547-5(9))* Picture Window Bks.

Gunderson, Jessica, et al. You Choose: Fractured Fairy Tales. 2015. (You Choose: Fractured Fairy Tales Ser.). (ENG.). 112p. (gr. 3-4). 127.96 *(978-1-4914-6969-9(2),* You Choose Bks.) Capstone Press of Coughlan Cos.

Gustafson, Scott. Classic Storybook Fables. 2017. (ENG., Illus.). 84p. (J). 19.95 ***(978-1-57965-704-8(4))*** Artisan.

Hacklfander, F. W. (Friedrich Wilhelm). Enchanting & Enchanted; from the German of Hacklfander by Mrs a L Wister. 2006. 252p. per. 23.99 *(978-1-4255-2209-4(2))* Michigan Publishing.

Hague, Michael. Michael Hague's Read-To-Me Book of Fairy Tales. Hague, Michael, illus. 2013. (ENG., Illus.). 128p. (J). (gr. -1-3). 19.99 *(978-0-688-14010-6(6))* HarperCollins Pubs.

Hahm, Ji-seul. Prokofiev's Peter & the Wolf. Lupton, David, illus. 2016. (Music Storybooks Ser.). (ENG.). 44p. (gr. 3-6). 26.65 *(978-1-925247-39-8(2),* Big and SMALL) ChoiceMaker Pty. Ltd., The AUS. Dist: Lerner Publishing Group.

Hahner, Aaron. The Magic of Midnight. 2004. per. 8.95 *(978-1-932560-58-9(0))* Aeon Publishing Inc.

Hale, Bruce. Snoring Beauty. Fine, Howard, illus. 2008. (ENG.). 44p. (J). (gr. -1-3). 17.99 *(978-0-15-216314-3(X))* Houghton Mifflin Harcourt Publishing Co.

Hale, Shannon. Enna Burning. 2004. (Books of Bayern Ser.: No. 2). (ENG., Illus.). 300p. (YA). 18.99 *(978-1-58234-889-6(8),* 9781582348896, Bloomsbury USA Childrens) Bloomsbury Publishing USA.

—Ever after High: Once upon a Time: A Story Collection. 2014. (ENG.). 272p. (J). (gr. 3-7). 12.99 *(978-0-316-25821-0(0))* Little, Brown Bks. for Young Readers.

—Ever after High: the Storybox of Legends Boxed Set. 2014. (ENG.). 900p. (J). (gr. 3-7). 45.00 *(978-0-316-28720-3(2))* Little, Brown Bks. for Young Readers.

—Forest Born. (Books of Bayern Ser.). (ENG.). (YA). 2017. 400p. pap. 9.99 *(978-1-68119-319-9(1),* 9781681193199) 2011. 400p. (gr. 7). pap. 9.99 *(978-1-59990-692-8(9),* 9781599906928) 2009. (Illus.). 400p. (gr. 7-18). 18.99 *(978-1-59990-167-1(6),* 9781599901671) 2011. 416p. (gr. 7-12). 19.99 *(978-1-59990-691-1(0),* 9781599906911) Bloomsbury Publishing USA. (Bloomsbury USA Childrens).

—The Goose Girl. (Books of Bayern Ser.: No. 2). (ENG., (YA). 2003. Illus.). 400p. (gr. 5-18). 18.99 *(978-1-58234-843-8(X),* 9781582348438) 2005. 432p. (gr. 7-17). reprint ed. pap. 9.99 *(978-1-58234-990-9(8),* 9781582349909) Bloomsbury Publishing USA. (Bloomsbury USA Childrens).

—River Secrets. (Books of Bayern Ser.). (ENG., Illus.). (YA). (gr. 7). 2008. 320p. 9.99 *(978-1-59990-293-7(1),* 9781599902937) 2006. 304p. 18.99 *(978-1-58234-901-5(0),* 9781582349015) Bloomsbury Publishing USA. (Bloomsbury USA Childrens).

—The Storybook of Legends. 2013. (Ever after High Ser.). (ENG., Illus.). 320p. (J). (gr. 3-7). 14.99 *(978-0-316-40122-7(6))* Little, Brown Bks. for Young Readers.

—The Storybook of Legends. 2017. (Ever after High Ser.: 1). (J). lib. bdg. 18.40 ***(978-0-606-40630-7(1))*** Turtleback Bks.

—The Unfairest of Them All. 2014. (Ever after High Ser.). (ENG.). 336p. (J). (gr. 3-7). 14.99 *(978-0-316-28201-7(4))* Little, Brown Bks. for Young Readers.

—A Wonderlandiful World. 2014. (Ever after High Ser.: 3). (ENG.). 336p. (J). (gr. 3-7). 14.99 *(978-0-316-28209-3(X))* Little, Brown Bks. for Young Readers.

Hall, Amanda. Giant Tales from Around the World. Waters, Fiona, illus. 2004. 96p. (J). 17.95 *(978-1-84458-143-6(8))* Avalon Publishing Group.

Hall, Francois, illus. The Emperor's New Clothes. 2007. (First Fairy Tales Ser.). 32p. (J). (gr. -1-3). lib. bdg. 28.50 *(978-1-59771-071-8(7),* 1262700) Sea-To-Sea Pubns.

Hall, Frank. The Prince Who Did Not Want to be King. 2011. 132p. 28.95 *(978-1-4497-1440-6(4));* (J). pap. 11.95 *(978-1-4497-1438-3(2))* Author Solutions, Inc. (WestBow Pr.).

Hall, Gladys, illus. Red Riding Hood. 2007. (Shape Bks.). (ENG.). (J). (gr. -1-3). pap. 9.95 *(978-1-59583-133-0(9),* 9781595831330, Green Tiger Pr.) Laughing Elephant.

Hallworth, Grace. Sing Me a Story: Song-And-Dance Tales from the Caribbean. Clementson, John, illus. 2013. (ENG.). 48p. (J). (gr. 1-4). 9.99 *(978-1-84780-426-6(8),* Frances Lincoln) Quarto Publishing Group UK GBR. Dist: Hachette Bk. Group.

Halsted, John D., ed. & compiled by. Peachy Princesses & Impetuous Princes - for Girls Only! Halsted, John D., compiled by. 2013. 386p. pap. *(978-1-909302-40-2(6))* Abela Publishing.

Hamilton, Libby. The Fairy Tale Handbook. Tomic, Tomislav, illus. 2014. (ENG.). 20p. (J). (gr. k-4). 22.99 *(978-0-7636-7130-3(4),* Templar) Candlewick Pr.

Hamilton, Martha & Weiss, Mitch, retold by. Forty Fun Fables: Tales That Trick, Tickle & Teach. 2015. (ENG., Illus.). 98p. pap. 8.95 *(978-1-939160-77-5(4))* August Hse. Pubs., Inc.

Han, Xuemei. Brave Little Mongolian Sisters. Han, Xuemei, illus. 2007. (Illus.). (J). pap. 12.99 *(978-0-9763168-7-9(0))* DigitalKu.

—The Radish & the Girl with Long Hair. Han, Xuemei, illus. 2008. (Illus.). (J). per. *(978-0-9763168-6-2(2))* DigitalKu.

Hansel & Gretel. (Ladybird Bks.). (ARA., Illus.). 14.95 incl. audio *(978-0-86685-637-9(4),* LDL102C) Librairie du Liban Pubns. FRA. Dist: International Bk. Ctr., Inc.

Hansel e Gretel. pap. 7.95 *(978-88-8148-547-5(8))* European Language Institute ITA. Dist: Distribooks, Inc.

Hansel et Gretel.Tr. of Hansel & Gretel. pap. 5.95 *(978-88-8148-544-4(3))* EMC/Paradigm Publishing.

Hansel und Gretel. pap. 7.95 *(978-88-8148-545-1(1))* European Language Institute ITA. Dist: Distribooks, Inc.

Hanson, Faye. Cinderella's Secret Diary. Hanson, Faye, illus. 2013. (ENG., Illus.). 24p. (J). (gr. 1-3). 19.99 *(978-0-230-74204-8(1))* Pan Macmillan GBR. Dist: Independent Pubs. Group.

Hanson, Mary. How to Save Your Tail: If You Are a Rat Nabbed by Cats Who Really Like Stories about Magic Spoons, Wolves with Snout-Warts, Big, Hairy Chimney Trolls ... & Cookies, Too. 2008. (ENG., Illus.). 112p. (J). (gr. 1-4). 5.99 *(978-0-440-42228-0(0),* Yearling) Random Hse. Children's Bks.

Hanson-Roberts, Mary, illus. Cinderella: A Tale of Kindness. 2006. (J). 6.99 *(978-1-59939-001-7(9))* Cornerstone Pr.

Hardwell, Gary D. A Boo Bears' Story: Stormy Night. 2007. (Illus.). 36p. per. 10.00 *(978-0-9792016-9-1(1))* Professional Publishing Hse. LLC.

Hardyman, Robyn. What Is a Fairy Tale?, 1 vol., 1. 2014. (Britannica Common Core Library). (ENG.). 32p. (gr. 2-5). 23.45 *(978-1-62275-215-7(5))* Rosen Publishing Group, Inc., The.

Harper, Benjamin. Far Out Fairy Tales. Cano, Fern, illus. 2016. (Far Out Fairy Tales Ser.). (ENG.). 40p. (gr. 3-4). pap. 11.90 *(978-1-4965-3135-3(3),* Far Out Fairy Tales) Stone Arch Bks.

—Hansel & Gretel & Zombies: a Graphic Novel. Cano, Fern, illus. 2016. (Far Out Fairy Tales Ser.). (ENG.). 40p. (gr. 3-4). lib. bdg. 25.32 *(978-1-4965-2509-3(4),* Far Out Fairy Tales) Stone Arch Bks.

Harper, Charise Mericle & Mericle Harper, Charise. Princess Patty Finds Her Prince. 2014. (ENG., Illus.). 48p. (J). (gr. -1-k). 16.99 *(978-1-4231-0804-7(3))* Hyperion Bks. for Children.

Harper, Lee. The Emperor's Cool Clothes, 0 vols. 2011. (ENG.). 32p. (J). (gr. -1-2). 16.99 *(978-0-7614-5948-4(0),* 9780761459484, Amazon Children's Publishing) Amazon Publishing.

Harrington, James. The Last Laugh. 2009. (Illus.). 24p. pap. 11.50 *(978-1-60860-187-5(0),* Strategic Bk. Publishing) Strategic Book Publishing & Rights Agency (SBPRA).

Harris, Annmarie. The Nutcracker. Jay, Alison, illus. 2010. (ENG.). 40p. (J). (gr. -1-k). 16.99 *(978-0-8037-3285-8(6),* Dial Bks) Penguin Young Readers Group.

Harris, Joel Chandler. Uncle Remus & Brer Rabbit the Complete Tales. 2013. 74p. pap. 25.00 *(978-1-927558-33-1(6))* Birch Tree Publishing.

Harris, L. Little Girl in Paris. 2004. (Madame Juliette & the Inchanded Crate Ser.: Vol. 1). (Illus.). 330p. (J). pap. 19.95 *(978-0-9749950-2-1(9))* Granny's Pub Co.

Harris, Tricia. Fairy Tales for Fashionistas. 2010. 57p. pap. 12.95 *(978-1-4457-2353-2(0))* Lulu Pr., Inc.

Harrison, David L. Paul Bunyan: My Story. Kanzler, John, illus. 2008. (Step into Reading Ser.). (ENG.). 48p. (J). (gr. k-3). 4.99 *(978-0-375-84688-5(3),* Random Hse. Bks. for Young Readers) Random Hse. Children's Bks.

Harrison, Mette Ivie. The Princess & the Bear. 2010. (ENG.). 352p. (YA). (gr. 8). pap. 8.99 *(978-0-06-155316-5(6),* HarperTeen) HarperCollins Pubs.

—The Princess & the Hound. (YA). 2008. (ENG.). 432p. (gr. 8). pap. 8.99 *(978-0-06-113189-9(X),* HarperTeen) 2007. 410p. (gr. 7-18). lib. bdg. 18.89 *(978-0-06-113188-2(1),* Eos) HarperCollins Pubs.

Harrison, Paula. The Baby Firebird. Williams, Sophy, illus. 2017. (Secret Rescuers Ser.: 3). (ENG.). 128p. (J). (gr. 2-5). pap. 5.99 ***(978-1-4814-7613-3(0),*** Aladdin) Simon & Schuster Children's Publishing.

Hart, Melissa. A Guide for Using the Tale of Despereaux in the Classroom. 2005. (ENG.). 48p. pap. 9.99 *(978-1-4206-3164-7(0))* Teacher Created Resources, Inc.

Hartnett, Edith E. Once upon a Time. 2013. 168p. pap. 22.50 *(978-1-882260-22-5(6))* Calm Unity Pr.

Harvey-Fitzhenry, Alyxandra. Waking, 1 vol. 2006. (ENG.). 128p. (YA). (gr. 8-12). per. 8.95 *(978-1-55143-489-6(X))* Orca Bk. Pubs. USA.

Haselhurst, Maureen. The Emperor's New Uniform. Kennedy, Kelly, illus. 2015. (ENG.). 32p. (J). *(978-0-7787-1933-5(2))* Crabtree Publishing Co.

Haskell, Merrie. The Castle Behind Thorns. 2014. (J). (ENG.). 336p. (gr. 3-7). 16.99 *(978-0-06-200819-0(6),* Tegen, Katherine Bks); 327p. *(978-0-06-200820-6(X))* HarperCollins Pubs.

—Handbook for Dragon Slayers. 2013. (ENG.). 336p. (J). (gr. 3-7). 16.99 *(978-0-06-200816-9(1))* HarperCollins Pubs.

—The Princess Curse. (ENG.). (J). (gr. 3-7). 2013. 352p. pap. 6.99 *(978-0-06-200815-2(3))* 2011. 336p. 16.99 *(978-0-06-200813-8(7))* HarperCollins Pubs.

Hauff, Wilhelm & Pak, Boris. Little Mook & Dwarf Longnose. 2004. (ENG., Illus.). 124p. 19.95 *(978-1-56792-222-6(8))* Godine, David R. Pub.

Hawes, Carlin. Abigail's Bunny. 2012. 16p. pap. 12.68 *(978-1-4669-5601-8(1))* Trafford Publishing.

Hawthorn, P. Little Book of Fairy Stories. 2004. (Mini Storybooks Ser.). (ENG., Illus.). 128p. (J). 7.95 *(978-0-7945-0297-3(0),* Usborne) EDC Publishing.

Hawthorne, Grace. Healthy Air: Book C of Healthy Me, 3 books. Blyth, Eileen, illus. 2004. 48p. (J). pap. 73.75 *(978-0-944235-49-2(2))* American Cancer Society, Inc.

—Healthy Bodies: Book A of Healthy Me, 3 books. Blyth, Eileen, illus. 2004. 48p. (J). pap. 73.75 *(978-0-944235-47-8(6))* American Cancer Society, Inc.

—Healthy Food: Book B of Healthy Me, 3 bks. Blyth, Eileen, illus. 2004. 48p. (J). pap. 73.75 *(978-0-944235-48-5(4))* American Cancer Society, Inc.

—Healthy Me. Blyth, Eileen C., illus. 2004. (ENG.). 144p. (J). (gr. -1-3). pap., act. bk. ed. 6.95 *(978-0-944235-46-1(8),* 9780944235461) American Cancer Society, Inc.

Hay, Sam. Beauty & the Beast. Jackson, Katy, illus. 2017. (3D Colouring & Activity Ser.). (ENG.). 24p. (J). (gr. 1-4). pap. 11.99 ***(978-1-4052-8160-7(X))*** Egmont Bks., Ltd. GBR. Dist: Independent Pubs. Group.

Hayes, Joe. Baila, Nana, Baila: Cuban Folktales in English & Spanish. Trenard Sayago, Mauricio, illus. 2008.Tr. of Dance, Nana, Dance. (SPA & ENG.). 96p. (J). (gr. 3-6). 20.95 *(978-1-933693-17-0(7))* Cinco Puntos Pr.

—The Coyote under the Table (El Coyote Debajo de la Mesa) Castro L., Antonio, illus. 2011. (ENG & SPA.). 144p. (J). (gr. 1-7). pap. 12.95 *(978-1-935955-06-1(3))* Cinco Puntos Pr.

Haynes, Georgia. Trixie, the Treat Fairy: A Halloween Fable. 2009. 28p. pap. 13.99 *(978-1-4389-7658-7(5))* AuthorHouse.

E
F
G

Healy, Christopher. The Hero's Guide to Saving Your Kingdom. Harris, Todd, illus. (Hero's Guide Ser.: 1). (ENG.). (J). (gr. 3-7). 2013. 480p. pap. 7.99 (978-0-06-211745-8(9)) 2012. 448p. 16.99 (978-0-06-211743-4(2)) HarperCollins Pubs. (Waldon Pond Pr.).

—The Hero's Guide to Storming the Castle. Harris, Todd, illus. 2013. (Hero's Guide Ser.: 2). (ENG.). 496p. (J). (gr. 3-7). 16.99 (978-0-06-211845-5(5), Waldon Pond Pr.) HarperCollins Pubs.

Heapy, Teresa. Very Little Cinderella. Heap, Sue, illus. 2015. (Very Little Ser.). (ENG.). 32p. (J). (gr. -1-3). 16.99 (978-0-544-28223-0(X), HMH Books For Young Readers) Houghton Mifflin Harcourt Publishing Co.

Hearn, Lafcadio, et al. The Boy Who Drew Cats & Other Japanese Fairy Tales. Green, Yuko, illus. 2012. (Dover Children's Thrift Classics Ser.). (ENG.). 64p. (J). (gr. 3-8). pap. 3.00 (978-0-486-40348-9(3)) Dover Pubns., Inc.

Hébert-Collins, Sheila. Jacques et la Canne à Sucre: A Cajun Jack & the Beanstalk, 1 vol. Lyne, Alison Davis, illus. 2004. (FRE & ENG.). 32p. (J). (gr. k-3). pap. 16.99 (978-1-58980-191-2(1)) Pelican Publishing Co., Inc.

—Petite Rouge: A Cajun Twist to an Old Tale, 1 vol. Lyne, Alison, illus. 2015. (ENG.). 32p. (J). (gr. k-3). 16.99 (978-1-58980-602-3(6)) Pelican Publishing Co., Inc.

Helbrough, Emma, retold by. Nutcracker. 2005. (Young Reading Gift Books Ser.). 48p. (J). (gr. 2-18). 8.99 (978-0-7945-0921-7(5), Usborne) EDC Publishing.

Helldorfer, M. C. Cabbage Rose. Downing, Julie, illus. 2013. (ENG.). 32p. (J). (gr. -1-3). 16.99 (978-1-4814-2156-0(5), Atheneum Bks. for Young Readers) Simon & Schuster Children's Publishing.

Henkel, Julie Anne. Jungle Seek in the Rainforest: An Enchanted Fairy Tale. 2004. (Illus.). 66p. (J). per. (978-1-932077-09-4(X)) Athena Pr.

Hennessy, Barbara G. The Once upon a Time Map Book: Take a Tour of Six Enchanted Lands. Joyce, Peter, illus. 2013. (ENG.). 16p. (J). (gr. 1-4). 24.99 (978-0-7636-6475-6(8)) Candlewick Pr.

Heurtelou, Maude. Sandra: Cinderalla in Haiti. 2004. (CRP & ENG., Illus.). 24p. (J). 8.50 (978-1-58432-176-7(8)) Educa Vision Inc.

Heyman, Alissa. Twelve Dancing Unicorns. Gerard, Justin, illus. 2014. (ENG.). 32p. (J). (gr. -1-2). 14.95 (978-1-4027-8732-4(4)) Sterling Publishing Co., Inc.

Hicks, Angie, illus. The Fairy Horse. 2012. (ENG.). 24p. (J). 9.95 (978-1-84135-834-5(7)) Award Pubns. Ltd. GBR. Dist: Parkwest Pubns., Inc.

Higgins, Nadia. Beauty & the Beast. Petelinsek, Kathleen, illus. 2013. (Fairy Tale Collection). (ENG.). 24p. (J). (gr. k-3). 28.50 (978-1-62323-607-6(X), 206374) Child's World, Inc., The.

—Cinderella. Petelinsek, Kathleen, illus. 2013. (Fairy Tale Collection). (ENG.). 24p. (J). (gr. k-3). 28.50 (978-1-62323-608-3(8), 206375) Child's World, Inc., The.

—Cinderella & the Bowling Slipper, 1 vol. 2009. (Fiona & Frieda's Fairy-Tale Adventures Ser.). (ENG., Illus.). 80p. (J). (gr. 2-5). 27.07 (978-1-60270-572-2(0)) Magic Wagon.

—Hansel & Gretel. Petelinsek, Kathleen, illus. 2013. (Fairy Tale Collection). (ENG.). 24p. (J). (gr. k-3). 28.50 (978-1-62323-609-0(6), 206376) Child's World, Inc., The.

—Hansel & Gretel & the Cheddar Trail, 1 vol. Johnson, Meredith, illus. 2009. (Fiona & Frieda's Fairy-Tale Adventures Ser.). (ENG.). 80p. (J). (gr. 2-5). 27.07 (978-1-60270-574-6(7)) Magic Wagon.

—Little Red Riding Hood. Petelinsek, Kathleen, illus. 2013. (Fairy Tale Collection). (ENG.). 24p. (J). (gr. k-3). 28.50 (978-1-62323-610-6(X), 206377) Child's World, Inc., The.

—Rapunzel & the Drop of Doom, 1 vol. Johnson, Meredith, illus. 2009. (Fiona & Frieda's Fairy-Tale Adventures Ser.). (ENG.). 80p. (J). (gr. 2-5). 27.07 (978-1-60270-575-3(5)) Magic Wagon.

—Sleeping Beauty & the Snapdragons, 1 vol. Johnson, Meredith, illus. 2009. (Fiona & Frieda's Fairy-Tale Adventures Ser.). (ENG.). 80p. (J). (gr. 2-5). 27.07 (978-1-60270-576-0(3)) Magic Wagon.

—Snow White & the Candy Apple, 1 vol. Johnson, Meredith, illus. 2009. (Fiona & Frieda's Fairy-Tale Adventures Ser.). (ENG.). 80p. (J). (gr. 2-5). 27.07 (978-1-60270-577-7(1)) Magic Wagon.

Higgins, Wendy. The Great Hunt. (YA). (gr. 8). 2017. 448p. pap. 9.99 (978-0-06-238134-7(2)) 2016. 432p. 17.99 (978-0-06-238133-0(4)) HarperCollins Pubs. (HarperTeen).

Highlights for Children Editorial Staff, creator. Fairy Tales. 2016. (Highlights(tm) Find & Color Hidden Pictures(r) Ser.). (ENG.). 32p. (J). (gr. -1-k). pap. 5.99 (978-1-62979-714-4(6), Highlights) Boyds Mills Pr.

Hildahl, Violetta R. Peacock of Taj Mahal. 2011. 28p. (gr. -1). pap. 13.59 (978-1-4520-0259-0(2)) AuthorHouse.

Hill, Tony. The Curse of the Crooked Spire & Other Fairy Tales. 2013. (Illus.). 230p. pap. (978-0-9568409-3-6(0)) Northern Lights Lit.

Hillenbrand, Will, illus. Look Out, Jack! the Giant Is Back! 2003. (ENG.). 32p. (J). (gr. -1-3). 6.95 (978-0-8234-1776-6(X)) Holiday Hse., Inc.

Hillert, Margaret. El Bebé Raro. Jack Pullan & Wendland, Paula, illus. 2017. (BeginningtoRead Ser.).Tr. of Funny Baby. (ENG & SPA.). 32p. (J). (-2). 22.60 **(978-1-59953-844-0(X))** Norwood Hse. Pr.

—Caperucita Roja. Jack Pullan & Barnum-Newman, Winifred, illus. 2017. (BeginningtoRead Ser.).Tr. of Little Red Riding Hood. (ENG & SPA.). 32p. (J). (-2). 22.60 **(978-1-59953-846-4(6))** Norwood Hse. Pr.

—La Casa de Galletitas. Jack Pullan & Utomo, Gabhor, illus. 2017. (BeginningtoRead Ser.).Tr. of Cookie House. (ENG & SPA.). 32p. (J). (-2). 22.60 **(978-1-59953-842-6(3))** Norwood Hse. Pr.

—Cenicienta en el Baile. Jack Pullan & Caminador, Juan, illus. 2017. (BeginningtoRead Ser.).Tr. of Cinderella at the Ball. (ENG & SPA.). 32p. (J). (-2). 22.60 **(978-1-59953-841-9(5))** Norwood Hse. Pr.

—Cinderella at the Ball. Caminador, Juan, illus. 2016. (BeginningtoRead Ser.). (ENG.). 32p. (J). (-2). lib. bdg. 22.60 (978-1-59953-778-8(8)) Norwood Hse. Pr.

—The Cookie House. Utomo, Gabhor, illus. 2016. (BeginningtoRead Ser.). (ENG.). 32p. (J). (-2). lib. bdg. 22.60 (978-1-59953-779-5(6)); (gr. -1-2). pap. 11.94 (978-1-60357-905-6(2)) Norwood Hse. Pr.

—Cuatro Buenos Amigos. Jack Pullan & Collier-Morales, Roberta, illus. 2017. (BeginningtoRead Ser.).Tr. of Four Good Friends. (ENG & SPA.). 32p. (J). (-2). 22.60 **(978-1-59953-843-3(1))** Norwood Hse. Pr.

—Four Good Friends. Collier-Morales, Roberta, illus. 2016. (BeginningtoRead Ser.). (ENG.). 32p. (J). (-2). lib. bdg. 22.60 (978-1-59953-780-1(X)) Norwood Hse. Pr.

—Los Frijoles Mágicos. Jack Pullan & Zaman, Farida, illus. 2017. (BeginningtoRead Ser.).Tr. of Magic Beans. (ENG & SPA.). 32p. (J). (-2). 22.60 **(978-1-59953-847-1(4))** Norwood Hse. Pr.

—The Funny Baby. Wendland, Paula, illus. 2016. (BeginningtoRead Ser.). (ENG.). 32p. (J). (gr. -1-2). pap. 11.94 (978-1-60357-907-0(9)) Norwood Hse. Pr.

—The Little Cookie. Petruccio, Steven James, illus. 2016. (BeginningtoRead Ser.). (ENG.). 32p. (J). (gr. -1-2). pap. 11.94 (978-1-60357-908-7(7)) Norwood Hse. Pr.

—Little Red Riding Hood. Barnum-Newman, Winifred, illus. 2016. (BeginningtoRead Ser.). (ENG.). 32p. (J). (-2). pap. 11.94 (978-1-60357-909-4(5)); lib. bdg. 22.60 (978-1-59953-783-2(4)) Norwood Hse. Pr.

—The Magic Beans. Jamana, Pharida & Zaman, Farida, illus. 2016. (BeginningtoRead Ser.). (ENG.). 32p. (J). (-2). lib. bdg. 22.60 (978-1-59953-784-9(2)) Norwood Hse. Pr.

—The Magic Nutcracker. Osterhold, Jared, illus. 2016. (BeginningtoRead Ser.). (ENG.). 32p. (J). (gr. -1-2). pap. 11.94 (978-1-60357-943-8(5)); (gr. 1-2). 22.60 (978-1-59953-802-0(4)) Norwood Hse. Pr.

—Magic Nutcracker. (Illus.). (J). 4.95 (978-0-87895-667-8(0)) Modern Curriculum Pr.

—Pinocchio. Schwartz, Carol & Regan, Dana, illus. 2016. (BeginningtoRead Ser.). (ENG.). 32p. (J). (gr. -1-2). pap. 11.94 (978-1-60357-912-4(5)) Norwood Hse. Pr.

—Pinocho. Jack Pullan & Regan, Dana, illus. 2017. (BeginningtoRead Ser.).Tr. of Pinocchio. (ENG & SPA.). 32p. (J). (-2). 22.60 **(978-1-59953-849-5(0))**; pap. 11.94 **(978-1-68404-048-3(5))** Norwood Hse. Pr.

—Pulgarcito. Jack Pullan & Han, Yu-Mei, illus. 2017. (BeginningtoRead Ser.).Tr. of Tom Thumb. (ENG & SPA.). 32p. (J). (-2). 22.60 **(978-1-59953-853-2(9))** Norwood Hse. Pr.

—Tom Thumb. Beam, Burgandy & Han, Yu-Mei, illus. 2016. (BeginningtoRead Ser.). (ENG.). 32p. (J). (-2). lib. bdg. 22.60 (978-1-59953-790-0(7)) Norwood Hse. Pr.

Hillert, Margaret. Los Tres Chivos. Jack Pullan & Banks, Timothy, illus. 2017. (BeginningtoRead Ser.).Tr. of Three Goats. (ENG & SPA.). 32p. (J). (-2). 22.60 **(978-1-59953-851-8(2))** Norwood Hse. Pr.

Hillert, Margaret & Andersen, Hans Christian. The Funny Baby. Wendland, Paula Zinngrabe, illus. 2016. (BeginningtoRead Ser.). (ENG.). 32p. (J). (-2). lib. bdg. 22.60 (978-1-59953-781-8(8)) Norwood Hse. Pr.

Hillert, Margaret & Asbjørnsen, Peter Christen. The Three Goats. Banks, Timothy, illus. 2016. (BeginningtoRead Ser.). (ENG.). 32p. (J). (-2). lib. bdg. 22.60 (978-1-59953-788-7(5)) Norwood Hse. Pr.

Hillert, Margaret & Collodi, Carlo. Pinocchio. Schwartz, Carol & Regan, Dana, illus. 2016. (BeginningtoRead Ser.). (ENG.). 32p. (J). (-2). lib. bdg. 22.60 (978-1-59953-786-3(9)) Norwood Hse. Pr.

Hinkler Books, ed. My Treasury of Princess Tales. 2012. 192p. (J). 12.99 (978-1-74308-000-9(X)) Hinkler Bks. Pty. Ltd. AUS. Dist: Ideals Pubns.

Hobbie, Holly & Hobbie, Douglas. Hansel & Gretel. 2015. (ENG., Illus.). 32p. (J). (gr. -1-3). 17.00 (978-0-316-07017-1(3)) Little, Brown Bks. for Young Readers.

Hoberman, Mary Ann. You Read to Me, I'll Read to You: Very Short Fairy Tales to Read Together. Emberley, Michael, illus. 2004. (ENG.). 32p. (J). (gr. -1-3). 16.99 (978-0-316-14611-1(0)) Little, Brown Bks. for Young Readers.

Hodder, Bridget. The Rat Prince. 2016. (ENG.). 272p. (J). 16.99 (978-0-374-30213-9(8), 9780374302139, Farrar, Straus & Giroux (BYR)) Farrar, Straus & Giroux.

Hoena, B. A. Jack & the Beanstalk: An Interactive Fairy Tale Adventure. Tayal, Amit, illus. 2015. (You Choose: Fractured Fairy Tales Ser.). (ENG.). 112p. (gr. 3-4). pap. 6.95 (978-1-4914-5930-0(1), You Choose Bks.) Capstone Press of Coughlan Cos.

Hoffman, Mary. Clever Katya: A Fairy Tale from Old Russia. Cameron, Marie, illus. 2005. 32p. (J). (gr. k-3). pap., pap. 6.99 (978-1-905236-05-3(0)) Barefoot Bks., Inc.

—First Book of Fairy Tales. Downing, Julie, illus. 2006. (ENG.). 80p. (J). (gr. 3-7). pap. 9.99 (978-0-7566-2107-0(0), DK Children) Dorling Kindersley Publishing, Inc.

—The Twelve Dancing Princesses. Clara, Miss, illus. 2012. (ENG.). 64p. (J). (gr. 2-6). pap. 9.99 (978-1-84686-838-2(6)) Barefoot Bks., Inc.

Hoffmann, E. T. A. The Nutcracker. Julian, Alison, illus. 2005. (J). (978-0-7607-6690-3(8)) Barnes & Noble, Inc.

—The Nutcracker. Innocenti, Roberto, illus. 2017. (ENG.). 136p. (J). (gr. 3-5). 29.99 **(978-1-56846-313-1(8)**, Creative Editions) Creative Co., The.

—The Nutcracker. Manheim, Ralph, tr. from GER. Sendak, Maurice, illus. 2012. (ENG.). 120p. (gr. 5). 24.99 (978-0-385-34864-5(9), Crown) Crown/Archetype.

—The Nutcracker. Zwerger, Lisbeth, illus. 2016. (ENG.). 40p. 19.95 (978-0-7358-4270-0(1)) North-South Bks., Inc.

Holden, Pam. The Big Bad Wolf, 6 pack. Hawley, Kelvin, illus. 2009. (Red Rocket Readers Ser.). (ENG.). 16p. (gr. 2-2). pap. (978-1-877363-56-6(1), Red Rocket Readers) Flying Start Bks.

—The Hungry Boy. 2015. (ENG., Illus.). 16p. (-1). pap. (978-1-77654-069-3(7), Red Rocket Readers) Flying Start Bks.

—Naughty Goldilocks, 6 pack. Hoit, Richard, illus. 2009. (Red Rocket Readers Ser.). (ENG.). 16p. (gr. -1-1). pap. (978-1-877363-08-5(1), Red Rocket Readers) Flying Start Bks.

—Red Riding Hood, 6 pack. Hawley, Kelvin, illus. 2009. (Red Rocket Readers Ser.). (ENG.). 16p. (gr. -1-1). pap. (978-1-877363-09-2(X), Red Rocket Readers) Flying Start Bks.

—Three Billy Goats Gruff, 6 pack. Hawley, Kelvin, illus. 2009. (Red Rocket Readers Ser.). (ENG.). 16p. (gr. -1-1). pap. (978-1-877363-10-8(3), Red Rocket Readers) Flying Start Bks.

—Three Little Pigs, 6 pack. Storey, Jim, illus. 2009. (Red Rocket Readers Ser.). (ENG.). 16p. (gr. -1-1). pap. (978-1-877363-11-5(1), Red Rocket Readers) Flying Start Bks.

—Trip, Trap!, 6 pack. Hawley, Kelvin, illus. 2009. (Red Rocket Readers Ser.). (ENG.). 16p. (gr. 2-2). pap. (978-1-877363-62-7(6), Red Rocket Readers) Flying Start Bks.

Holden, Pam. The Ugly Troll. Hawley, Kelvin, illus. 2017. 16p. (J). pap. **(978-1-77654-191-1(X)**, Red Rocket Readers) Flying Start Bks.

Holder, Nancy. Spirited. 2004. (Once upon a Time Ser.). (ENG.). 272p. (YA). (gr. 9). pap. 13.95 (978-0-689-87063-7(9), Simon Pulse) Simon Pulse.

Holmes, Sara Lewis. Letters from Rapunzel. 2007. 184p. (J). (gr. 3-7). lib. bdg. 16.89 (978-0-06-078074-6(6)) HarperCollins Pubs.

Holub, Joan & Williams, Suzanne. Rapunzel Cuts Loose. 2014. (Grimmtastic Girls Ser.: 4). lib. bdg. 16.00 (978-0-606-36064-7(6)) Turtleback Bks.

—Red Riding Hood Gets Lost. 2014. (Grimmtastic Girls Ser.: 2). (ENG.). 192p. (J). (gr. 3-7). pap. 5.99 (978-0-545-51984-7(5)) Scholastic, Inc.

—Snowflake Freezes Up. 2016. (Grimmtastic Girls Ser.: 7). (ENG.). 192p. (J). (gr. 3-7). pap. 5.99 (978-0-545-94534-9(8), Scholastic Paperbacks) Scholastic, Inc.

Hone, Sallie. Phoenix. 2011. (Illus.). 48p. 20.36 (978-1-4567-0074-4(X)) AuthorHouse.

Hong, Lily Toy. Two of Everything. Hong, Lily Toy, illus. 2017. (ENG., Illus.). 32p. (J). (gr. -1-3). pap. 7.99 **(978-0-8075-8158-2(5))** Whitman, Albert & Co.

Hood, Karen Jean Matsko. Jesus Loves the Little Children: Activity & Coloring Book, Vol. 8. Whispering Pine Press International, ed. Artistic Design Service Staff, illus. 2016. (Educational Activity & Coloring Book Ser.). (ENG & SPA.). (J). spiral bd. 21.95 (978-1-59434-087-1(0)) Whispering Pine Pr. International, Inc.

Hopkins, Jackie Mims. Prairie Chicken Little, 1 vol. Cole, Henry, illus. 2013. (ENG.). 32p. (J). (gr. -1-3). 15.95 (978-1-56145-694-9(2)) Peachtree Pubs.

—Three Armadillies Tuff, 1 vol. Brooks, S. G., illus. 2011. (ENG.). 32p. pap. 7.95 (978-1-56145-598-0(9), Peachtree Junior) Peachtree Pubs.

Housman, Laurence. The Field of Clover. 2007. 108p. per. 9.95 (978-1-60312-129-3(3)); 22.95 (978-1-60312-928-2(6)) Aegypan.

Housman, Laurence, ed. Moonshine & Clover. Housman, Clemence, illus. 2013. 236p. (J). pap. (978-1-909302-25-9(2)) Abela Publishing.

Howell, Gill. Snow King. Cann, Helen, illus. 2005. (ENG.). 24p. (J). lib. bdg. 23.65 (978-1-59646-742-2(8)) Dingles & Co.

Howell, Laura. Princess & the Pea. 2009. (Young Reading 1 Ser.). 48p. (J). 6.99 (978-0-7945-2587-3(3), Usborne) EDC Publishing.

Howland, Naomi. Latkes, Latkes, Good to Eat: A Chanukah Story. 2004. (ENG., Illus.). 32p. (J). (gr. -1-3). pap. 6.99 (978-0-618-49295-4(X)) Houghton Mifflin Harcourt Publishing Co.

Hoyos, Hector. Los Siete Mejores Cuentos Chinos. Cuellar, Olga, illus. 2004. (SPA.). (J). (gr. 3-5). (978-958-04-7210-0(6)) Norma S.A.

—Los Siete Mejores Cuentos Indios. Cuellar, Olga, illus. 2004. (SPA.). 55p. (J). (gr. 3-5). (978-958-04-7213-1(0)) Norma S.A.

Hu, Vicky. Titans & Cyclops/ Titanes y Cíclopes. 2013. 56p. pap. (978-1-77097-395-4(8)) FriesenPress.

Huang, Yu-Hsuan. Fairy Friends. 2017. (ENG., Illus.). 10p. (J). (gr. -1-k). bds. 7.99 **(978-1-5098-3578-2(4))** Pan Macmillan GBR. Dist: Independent Pubs. Group.

Huling, Jan. Ol Bloo's Boogie-Woogie Band & Blues Ensemble, 1 vol. Sørensen, Henri, illus. 2010. (ENG.). 32p. (J). (gr. 1-5). 16.95 (978-1-56145-436-5(2)) Peachtree Pubs.

—Puss in Cowboy Boots. Huling, Phil, illus. 2007. (ENG.). 40p. (J). (gr. 1-4). 11.99 (978-1-4169-6749-1(4), Simon & Schuster/Paula Wiseman Bks.) Simon & Schuster/Paula Wiseman Bks.

Humphreys, Audrey. The Dragon Princess. 2012. 24p. pap. 24.99 (978-1-4691-6554-7(6)) Xlibris Corp.

Hunt, Meg, illus. Interstellar Cinderella. 2015. (ENG.). 40p. (J). (gr. -1-k). 16.99 (978-1-4521-2532-9(5)) Chronicle Bks. LLC.

Husain, Shahrukh. The Wise Fool. Archer, Micha, illus. 2012. (ENG.). 64p. (J). (gr. 2-6). pap. 12.99 (978-1-84686-938-9(2)) Barefoot Bks., Inc.

Husain, Shahrukh & Barefoot Books. Wise Fool: Fables from the Islamic World. Archer, Micha, illus. 2015. 64p. (J). (gr. 1-5). 14.99 (978-1-78285-255-1(7)) Barefoot Bks., Inc.

I Thought This Was a Bear Book. 2015. (ENG., Illus.). 32p. (J). (gr. -1-2). 17.99 (978-1-4424-6307-3(4), Aladdin) Simon & Schuster Children's Publishing.

Ice Water Press Staff. Fairytales for Girls. 2010. (978-0-85734-149-5(9)) Igloo Bks.

Ifans, Rhiannon. Magic of the Mabinogion. Holmes, Helen, illus. 2006. (ENG.). 112p. (J). pap. 9.95 (978-0-86243-174-7(3)) Y Lolfa GBR. Dist: Dufour Editions, Inc.

—Tales from Wales. Holmes, Helen, illus. 2009. (ENG.). 112p. (J). pap. 8.95 (978-0-86243-182-2(4)) Y Lolfa GBR. Dist: Dufour Editions, Inc.

Imperato, Teresa. This Little Piggy. Haskamp, Steve, illus. 2006. (ENG.). 22p. (J). 9.95 (978-1-58117-281-2(8), Intervisual/Piggy Toes) Bendon, Inc.

Impey, Martin, illus. Rapunzel. 2006. (First Fairy Tales Ser.). 31p. (J). (gr. -1-3). lib. bdg. 28.50 (978-1-59771-076-3(8)) Sea-To-Sea Pubns.

Impey, Rose. The Big Bad Wolf. McEwen, Katharine, illus. 2016. (Sir Lance-A-Little Ser.). (ENG.). 32p. (J). (gr. k-2). 9.99 (978-1-4083-2520-9(9), Orchard Bks.) Hachette Children's Group GBR. Dist: Hachette Bk. Group.

—The Terribly Ugly Troll. McEwen, Katharine, illus. 2017. (Sir Lance-A-Little Ser.). (ENG.). 32p. (J). (gr. k-2). 9.99 (978-1-4083-2523-0(3), Orchard Bks.) Hachette Children's Group GBR. Dist: Hachette Bk. Group.

Ingelow, Jean. Mopsa the Fairy. 2006. pap. 19.95 (978-1-4304-4177-9(1)) Kessinger Publishing, LLC.

inglés, Cuento popular. LOS TRES CERDITOS. 2004. (Caballo Alado Clásico Series-Al Paso Ser.). (SPA & ENG., Illus.). 24p. (J). (gr. -1-k). 7.95 (978-84-7864-765-1(1)) Combel Editorial, S.A. ESP. Dist: Independent Pubs. Group.

Irvine, Patricia McCune. Beyond the Greenest Hill: A Fairy Tale. 2003. 136p. (YA). pap. 11.95 (978-0-595-26941-9(9)) iUniverse, Inc.

Isadora, Rachel. Hansel & Gretel. Isadora, Rachel, illus. 2009. (ENG., Illus.). 32p. (J). (gr. 1-3). 16.99 (978-0-399-25028-6(X), G.P. Putnam's Sons Books for Young Readers) Penguin Young Readers Group.

—The Princess & the Pea. 2009. (ENG., Illus.). 32p. (J). (gr. -1-3). pap. 6.99 (978-0-14-241393-7(3), Puffin Books) Penguin Young Readers Group.

—The Twelve Dancing Princesses. Isadora, Rachel, illus. 2009. (ENG., Illus.). 32p. (J). (gr. k-3). pap. 6.99 (978-0-14-241450-7(6), Puffin Books) Penguin Young Readers Group.

Itoïz, Mayana. Search & Find: Fairy Tales as Children Have Never Seen Them Before! 2012. (ENG., Illus.). 24p. (J). (gr. k). 12.95 (978-2-7338-1983-8(6)) Auzou, Philippe Editions FRA. Dist: Consortium Bk. Sales & Distribution.

Jack & The Beanstalk. 2008. (Read & Learn Sticker Books Ser.). 48p. pap. (978-1-4075-3195-3(6)) Parragon, Inc.

Jack & the Beanstalk. 2005. (J). bds. 3.99 (978-1-933200-10-1(3)) Family Bks. at Home.

Jackson, Ellen. Cinder Edna. 2014. 16.00 (978-1-63419-691-8(0)) Perfection Learning Corp.

Jackson, Ellen B. Cinnamon Brown & the Seven Dwarfs. Brown, Elbrite, illus. 2006. (J). (978-0-670-06106-8(9), Viking Adult) Penguin Publishing Group.

Jacobs, Joseph. Indian Fairy Tales. Batten, John D., illus. 2011. (Dover Children's Classics Ser.). (ENG.). 255p. (J). (gr. 2-5). reprint ed. pap. 19.95 (978-0-486-21828-1(7)) Dover Pubns., Inc.

—Jack & the Beanstalk. Crane, Walter, illus. 2013. 20p. pap. (978-1-909115-63-7(0)) Planet, The.

Jacobs, Joseph, ed. English Fairy Tales. 2005. (Twelve-Point Ser.). lib. bdg. 24.00 (978-1-58287-370-1(4)); lib. bdg. 25.00 (978-1-58287-862-1(5)) North Bks.

—Europa's Fairy Book. Batten, John D., illus. 2013. 330p. pap. (978-1-909302-35-8(X)) Abela Publishing.

Jacobs, Kim, illus. & retold by. Princess Sophie & the Six Swans: A Tale from the Brothers Grimm. Jacobs, Kim, retold by. 2017. (ENG.). 40p. (J). (gr. k-3). 16.95 (978-1-937786-67-0(6), Wisdom Tales) World Wisdom, Inc.

Jago, illus. Ali Baba & the Forty Thieves. 2004. (ITA & ENG.). 31p. (J). (978-1-84444-543-1(7)) Mantra Lingua.

Jahanforuz, Rita. The Girl with a Brave Heart. Mintzi, Vali, illus. 2013. (ENG.). 40p. (J). (gr. k-5). 16.99 (978-1-84686-929-7(3)) Barefoot Bks., Inc.

James, Hartwell. The Enchanted Castle. 2011. 44p. 13.95 (978-1-4638-9769-7(3)); pap. 8.95 (978-1-4638-0103-8(3)) Rodgers, Alan Bks.

James, Ian. The Gingerbread Boy Uptown. 2006. (J). pap. (978-1-4108-7169-5(X)) Benchmark Education Co.

Janik, Dan. Sourdough Scott's Bedtime Fairy Tales from Alaska. 2005. (Illus.). (J). 12.95 (978-1-59433-031-5(X)) Publication Consultants.

Japan Broadcasting Corporation Staff. Once upon a Time in Japan. Carpenter, Juliet Winters & Pulvers, Roger, trs. 2015. (ENG., Illus.). 120p. (J). (gr. 3-6). 16.95 (978-4-8053-1359-6(5)) Tuttle Publishing.

Jarvie, Gordon, ed. Irish Folk & Fairy Tales. 2nd rev. ed. 2009. (ENG.). 224p. pap. 16.95 (978-0-85640-836-6(0)) Blackstaff Pr., Ltd. GBR. Dist: Dufour Editions, Inc.

Jay, Alison, illus. Twelve Dancing Princesses. 2016. (ENG.). 32p. (J). (gr. -1-3). 16.99 (978-1-4998-0329-7(X)) Little Bee Books Inc.

Jeffers, Susan. Hansel & Gretel. 2011. (ENG.). 32p. (J). (gr. -1-k). 18.99 (978-0-525-42221-1(8), Dutton Books for Young Readers) Penguin Young Readers Group.

—The Nutcracker. Jeffers, Susan, illus. 2007. (Illus.). 40p. (J). (gr. -1-3). 17.89 (978-0-06-074387-1(5)); (ENG., 17.99 (978-0-06-074386-4(7)) HarperCollins Pubs.

Jeffers, Susan & Ehrlich, Amy. Cinderella. Battcock, Gregory, ed. Jeffers, Susan, illus. 2004. (ENG., Illus.). 32p. (J). (gr. -1-3). 18.99 (978-0-525-47345-9(9), Dutton Books for Young Readers) Penguin Young Readers Group.

Jenny Press Staff, illus. Sleeping Beauty. 2016. (ENG.). 24p. pap. 7.99 (978-1-86147-816-0(X), Armadillo) Anness Publishing GBR. Dist: National Bk. Network.

Johnson, David. The Bremen Town Musicians, 1 vol. 2005. (Rabbit Ears Ser.). (ENG., Illus.). 32p. (gr. k-5). 25.65 (978-1-59679-222-7(1)) Spotlight.

Johnson, Jane. Very Pretty Story. 2005. (Illus.). 78p. pap. 25.00 (978-1-85124-065-4(9)) Bodleian Library GBR. Dist: Chicago Distribution Ctr.

Johnson, Paul Brett, illus. & adapted by. Jack Outwits the Giants. Johnson, Paul Brett, adapted by. 2008. (ENG.). 36p. (J). (gr. -1-3). 11.99 (978-1-4169-7861-9(5), Simon & Schuster/Paula Wiseman Bks.) Simon & Schuster/Paula Wiseman Bks.

Johnson, Richard. Little Red Hen & the Grains of Wheat. 2005. (Illus.). 32p. (J). (ITA & ENG.). pap. (978-1-84444-209-6(8)); (SOM & ENG., pap. (978-1-84444-213-3(6)); (ENG & SPA., pap. (978-1-84444-214-0(4)); (TAM & ENG., pap. (978-1-84444-215-7(2)); (TUR & ENG., pap. (978-1-84444-216-4(0)); (YOR & ENG., pap. (978-1-84444-219-5(5)); (BUL & ENG., pap. (978-1-84444-393-2(0)); pap. (978-1-84444-396-3(5)); (RUM & ENG., pap. (978-1-84444-397-0(3)); (SWA & ENG., pap. (978-1-84444-399-4(X)); (GRE & ENG., pap. (978-1-84444-445-8(7)); (JPN & ENG., pap. (978-1-84444-446-5(5)); (KUR & ENG., pap. (978-1-84444-447-2(3)); (ENG., pap. (978-1-84444-448-9(1)); (ALB & ENG., pap. (978-1-84444-198-3(9)); (ENG & ARA., pap. (978-1-84444-199-0(7)); (ENG & CHI., pap. (978-1-84444-202-7(0)); (SER & ENG., pap. (978-1-84444-203-4(9)); (PER & ENG., pap. (978-1-84444-204-1(7)); (GER & ENG., pap. (978-1-84444-206-5(3)); (GUJ & ENG., pap. (978-1-84444-207-2(1)); (VIE & ENG., pap. (978-1-84444-218-8(7)) Mantra Lingua.

Johnson, Richard, illus. Three Little Pigs. (Flip-Up Fairy Tales Ser.). (ENG.). 24p. (J). 2007. (gr. -1-2). audio compact disk

(978-1-84643-087-9(9)) 2005. pap. (978-1-904550-21-1(5)) Child's Play International Ltd.

Johnson, Richard, tr. & illus. Jack & the Beanstalk. Johnson, Richard, illus. 2004. 31p. (J). (978-1-84444-108-2(3)) Mantra Lingua.

Johnson, Richard & Barkow, Henriette. Little Red Hen & the Grains of Wheat. Jago, illus. 2005. 32p. (J). (PAN & ENG.). pap. (978-1-84444-211-9(X)); (ENG & POR.). pap. (978-1-84444-212-6(8)); (ENG & URD.). pap. (978-1-84444-217-1(9)); (POL & ENG.). pap. (978-1-84444-394-9(9)); (ENG & HIN.). pap. (978-1-84444-208-9(X)); (FRE & ENG.). pap. (978-1-84444-205-8(5)); (ENG & CHI.). pap. (978-1-84444-201-0(2)); (ENG & BEN.). pap. (978-1-84444-200-3(4)); (ENG & TGL.). pap. (978-1-84444-395-6(7)); (ENG & RUS.). pap. (978-1-84444-398-7(1)); (KOR & ENG.). pap. (978-1-84444-210-2(1)) Mantra Lingua.

Johnson, Tony. How Bobo Became King. 2010. 16p. (J). pap. 15.95 (978-1-4327-4046-7(6)) Outskirts Pr., Inc.

Johnston, Annie Fellows. The Gate of the Giant Scissors. 2007. (Illus.). 104p. per. (978-1-4065-3512-9(5)) Dodo Pr.

Johnston, E. K. Spindle. 2016. (ENG.). 368p. (YA). (gr. 9-17). 18.99 (978-1-4847-2228-2(0)) Hyperion Bks. for Children.

Johnston, Emily Kate. A Thousand Nights. 2015. (ENG.). 336p. (YA). (gr. 9-17). 18.99 (978-1-4847-2227-5(2)) Hyperion Bks. for Children.

Jolley, Dan. Pigling: A Cinderella Story [A Korean Tale]. Timmons, Anne, illus. 2009. (Graphic Myths & Legends Ser.). (ENG.). 48p. (gr. 4-8). pap. 8.95 (978-1-58013-825-3(X)) Lerner Publishing Group.

Jones, Christine A. Mother Goose Refigured: A Critical Translation of Charles Perrault's Fairy Tales. 2016. (Series in Fairy-Tale Studies). (ENG., Illus.). 228p. pap. 31.99 (978-0-8143-3892-6(5), 2844) Wayne State Univ. Pr.

Jones, Noah Z. Jack & the Snackstalk. Jones, Noah Z., illus. 2016. (ENG., Illus.). 80p. (J). (gr. k-2). 15.99 (978-0-545-84862-6(8)) Scholastic, Inc.

—Little Red Quacking Hood. 2014. (Princess Pink & the Land of Fake-Believe Ser.: 2). (ENG.). 80p. (J). (gr. k-2). 15.99 (978-0-545-63842-5(9)) Scholastic, Inc.

—Little Red Quacking Hood. Jones, Noah Z., illus. 2014. (Princess Pink & the Land of Fake-Believe Ser.: 2). (ENG., Illus.). 80p. (J). (gr. k-2). pap. 4.99 (978-0-545-63841-8(0)) Scholastic, Inc.

—Little Red Quacking Hood. 2014. (Princess Pink & the Land of Fake-Believe Ser.: 2). lib. bdg. 14.75 (978-0-606-36048-7(4)) Turtleback Bks.

—Moldylocks & the Three Beards. Jones, Noah Z., illus. 2014. (Princess Pink & the Land of Fake-Believe Ser.: 1). (ENG., Illus.). 80p. (J). (gr. k-2). pap. 4.99 (978-0-545-63839-5(9)) Scholastic, Inc.

—The Three Little Pugs. 2015. (ENG., Illus.). 80p. (J). (gr. k-2). pap. 4.99 (978-0-545-84857-2(1)) Scholastic, Inc.

Jones, Terry & Foreman, Michael, trs. Fairy Tales & Fantastic Stories. Jones, Terry & Foreman, Michael, illus. 10th anniv. ed. 2003. (Illus.). 256p. (YA). (978-1-84365-055-3(X), Pavilion Children's Books) Pavilion Bks.

Jones, Ursula. Beauty & the Beast. Gibb, Sarah, illus. 2014. (ENG.). 32p. (J). (gr. -1-3). 16.99 (978-0-8075-0600-4(1)) Whitman, Albert & Co.

—The Princess Who Had No Kingdom. 2015. (Illus.). 32p. (J). (978-1-4896-3882-3(2)) Weigl Pubs., Inc.

—The Princess Who Had No Kingdom. Gibb, Sarah, illus. 2014. (ENG.). 32p. (J). (gr. -1-3). 16.99 (978-0-8075-6630-5(6)) Whitman, Albert & Co.

Jones, Wendy Lou. Last Knight of Golden Downs. 2013. 176p. pap. 9.95 (978-0-9777110-4-8(8)) Royal Knight Inc.

Jordan, Apple. Frozen Big Golden Book. RH Disney, illus. 2016. (Big Golden Book Ser.). (ENG.). 32p. (J). (gr. -1-2). 9.99 (978-0-7364-3562-8(X), Golden Bks.) Random Hse. Children's Bks.

Joyce, Melaine. Snow White. 2009. (Fairydust Fairytales Ser.). (ENG.). 5p. (J). (gr. -1-k). bds. 6.95 (978-1-84696-965-2(4), TickTock Books) Octopus Publishing Group GBR. Dist: Independent Pubs. Group.

Joyce, Melanie. Goldilocks. 2009. (Fairydust Fairytales Ser.). (ENG.). 5p. (J). (gr. -1-k). bds. 6.95 (978-1-84696-962-1(X), TickTock Books) Octopus Publishing Group GBR. Dist: Independent Pubs. Group.

Joyce, William. A Bean, a Stalk, & a Boy Named Jack. Joyce, William & Callicutt, Kenny, illus. 2014. (ENG.). 56p. (J). (gr. -1-1). 17.99 (978-1-4424-7349-2(5), Atheneum Bks. for Young Readers) Simon & Schuster Children's Publishing.

Juster, Norton. Alberic the Wise & Other Journeys. Gnoli, Domenico, illus. 2010. (ENG.). 96p. (J). (gr. 3-7). 5.99 (978-0-375-86699-9(X), Yearling) Random Hse. Children's Bks.

Kaesshaefer, Charles. The Lost Princess. 2004. (J). mass mkt. 10.00 (978-0-9744407-0-5(1)) Shelbykay Publishing Co.

Kain, Karen. The Nutcracker. Kupesic, Rajka, illus. 2005. (ENG.). 32p. (J). (gr. k-12). 18.95 (978-0-88776-696-1(X), Tundra Bks.) Tundra Bks. CAN. Dist: Penguin Random Hse. LLC.

Kajikawa, Kimiko. Tsunami! Young, Ed, illus. 2010. (Rise & Shine Ser.). (ENG.). 32p. (C). (gr. -1-k). 27.95 (978-0-399-25006-4(9)) National Geographic School Publishing, Inc.

Kale, Ann Stephanian. Marco & Princess Gina. Kale, Ann Stephanian, illus. 2003. (Illus.). 24p. (J). (gr. k-3). pap. 10.00 (978-0-9704131-5-4(7)) Abril BookStore & Publishing.

Kalvoda, Mike. The Piper. Gregory, Raven & Kolasinski, Ken, eds. 2008. (ENG., Illus.). 168p. (YA). pap. 15.99 (978-0-9817550-1-4(1), 9780981755014) Zenescope Entertainment.

Kaplon, Pat Allen. Betsy's Choice. 2012. 28p. pap. 15.99 (978-1-4771-5949-1(5)) Xlibris Corp.

Karandeev, Oleg. Dmitri II: The Kind Storyteller Book Two of Five. Ciesinska, Izabela, illus. 2007. 76p. (YA). per. 15.95 (978-0-9793944-3-0(0)) Digi-Tall Media.

Karlin, Barbara. Cinderella. Marshall, James, illus. unabr. ed. 2006. (J). (gr. -1-4). 29.95 (978-0-439-84888-6(1), WHCD671); 18.95 (978-0-439-84890-9(3), WPCD671) Weston Woods Studios, Inc.

Kasony_O'Malley, Michael R. An Irish Tale: Tom Moore & the Seal Woman. Rowland, Michael J., illus. 2007. (J). lib. bdg. 19.95 incl. audio compact disk (978-0-9776170-3-6(3)) Green Igric Pr.

Kats, Jewel. Cinderella's Magical Wheelchair: An Empowering Fairy Tale. Kinra, Richa, illus. 2012. (J). 24p. 29.95 (978-1-61599-113-6(1)); 20p. pap. 16.95 (978-1-61599-112-9(3)) Loving Healing Pr., Inc.

Kay, Kimberly. Courage to Face an Ogre. 2012. 28p. pap. 21.99 (978-1-4691-5436-7(6)) Xlibris Corp.

Kaye, Danny. Danny Kaye's Stories from Many Lands. 2011. 32p. pap. 35.95 (978-1-258-00179-7(9)) Literary Licensing, LLC.

Kearney, G. M. The Apple Trees of Tschlin. 2008. (J). 15.99 (978-1-59955-098-5(9)) Cedar Fort, Inc./CFI Distribution.

Kellogg, Steven. The Pied Piper's Magic. Kellogg, Steven, illus. 2009. (ENG., Illus.). 40p. (J). (gr. -1-3). 16.99 (978-0-8037-2818-9(2), Dial Bks) Penguin Young Readers Group.

Kennedy, Richard. Porcelain Man. Date not set. 32p. (J). (gr. -1-3). 15.89 (978-0-06-027216-6(3)); 14.99 (978-0-06-027215-9(5)) HarperCollins Pubs.

Kessler, Brad. The Firebird, 1 vol. Van Nutt, Robert, illus. 2005. (Rabbit Ears Ser.). (ENG.). 36p. (gr. k-5). 25.65 (978-1-59679-224-1(8)) Spotlight.

Ketchedjian, Armen G. & Ketch. Golden Apples. 2007. 12.95 (978-0-9778274-0-4(2)) Parental Interventional Tools, Inc.

Ketteman, Helen. Senorita Gordita. Terry, Will, illus. 2012. (ENG.). 32p. (J). (gr. -1-3). 16.99 (978-0-8075-7302-0(7)) Whitman, Albert & Co.

—Waynetta & the Cornstalk: A Texas Fairy Tale. Greenseid, Diane, illus. 2012. (ENG.). 32p. (J). (gr. -1-3). pap. 7.99 (978-0-8075-8688-4(9)) Whitman, Albert & Co.

Killebrew, Joyce Louise. Triumphant Queen Leah - the Ultimate African American Fairy Tale Picture Book. 2013. 68p. pap. (978-0-9840720-6-4(3)) Roxby Media Ltd.

Killion, Bette. Princess Rosie's Rainbows. Jacobs, Kim, illus. 2015. (ENG.). 36p. (J). (gr. k-3). 16.95 (978-1-937786-44-1(7), Wisdom Tales) World Wisdom, Inc.

Killion, Kathleen. The Glass Heart. Lang, Gary, illus. 2005. 19.95 (978-0-9723067-2-0(2)) Imagine That Enterprises.

Kimmel, Eric. The Runaway Tortilla. Brooks, Erik, illus. (ENG.). 32p. (J). 2017. 26.99 **(978-1-5132-6079-2(0))** 2016. pap. 10.99 (978-1-943328-70-3(6)) Graphic Arts Ctr. Publishing Co. (West Winds Pr.).

Kimmel, Eric A. Anansi & the Magic Stick. Stevens, Janet, illus. 2003. (J). 25.95 incl. audio (978-1-59112-482-5(4)); pap. 39.95 incl. audio compact disk (978-1-59112-519-8(7)); pap. 37.95 incl. audio (978-1-59112-483-2(2)) Live Oak Media.

—The Castle of Cats: A Story from Ukraine. Krenina, Katya, illus. 2004. (ENG.). 32p. (J). (gr. k-3). tchr. ed. 16.95 (978-0-8234-1565-6(1)) Holiday Hse., Inc.

—Los Tres Cabritos, 0 vols. Gilpin, Stephen, illus. 2012. (SPA & ENG.). 32p. (J). (gr. k-3). pap. 9.99 (978-0-7614-5961-3(8), 9780761459613, Amazon Children's Publishing) Amazon Publishing.

—The Mysterious Guests: A Sukkot Story. Krenina, Katya, illus. 2008. (ENG.). 32p. (J). (gr. 1-5). 16.95 (978-0-8234-1893-0(6)) Holiday Hse., Inc.

—Rattlestiltskin. Camarca, Erin, illus. 2016. (ENG.). 32p. (J). 16.99 (978-1-943328-38-3(2), West Winds Pr.) Graphic Arts Ctr. Publishing Co.

—The Three Cabritos, 0 vols. Gilpin, Stephen, illus. 2012. (ENG.). 32p. (J). (gr. -1-3). pap. 7.99 (978-0-7614-6309-2(7), 9780761463092, Amazon Children's Publishing) Amazon Publishing.

Kincaid, C. A. Deccan Nursery Tales: Or, Fairy Tales from the South. 2007. 76p. per. (978-1-4065-1926-6(X)) Dodo Pr.

Kindl, Patrice. Goose Chase. 2010. (ENG.). 240p. (J). (gr. 5-7). pap. 6.99 (978-0-547-33164-5(9)) Houghton Mifflin Harcourt Publishing Co.

King, Karen. Unicorn Magic. Hicks, Angie, illus. 2012. (ENG.). 24p. 9.95 (978-1-84135-832-1(0)) Award Pubns. Ltd. GBR. Dist: Parkwest Pubns., Inc.

KING, R. O. N. S. The Kiss-diamond. 2009. 173p. pap. 14.50 (978-1-4452-4736-6(4)) Lulu Pr., Inc.

Kingfisher Editors, ed. The Kingfisher Book of Classic Boy Stories. 2005. (J). (gr. 3-5). pap. 9.95 (978-0-7534-5843-3(8), Kingfisher) Roaring Brook Pr.

—The Kingfisher Book of Classic Girl Stories. 2005. (J). (gr. 3-5). pap. 9.95 (978-0-7534-5844-0(6), Kingfisher) Roaring Brook Pr.

Kingsley, Charles. The Water-Babies: A Fairy Tale for a Land-Baby. 2008. (ENG., Illus.). 224p. (gr. 12-18). 14.00 (978-0-14-310509-1(4), Penguin Classics) Penguin Publishing Group.

Kirkwood, Ian. Rob & the Black Mill. 2004. (Illus.). 32p. pap. 9.95 (978-0-9545206-7-0(X)) Capercaillie Bks., Ltd GBR. Dist: Wilson & Assocs.

Kline, Suzy & Remkiewicz, Frank. Horrible Harry Bugs the Three Bears. Remkiewicz, Frank & Remkiewicz, illus. 2009. (Horrible Harry Ser.). (ENG.). 80p. (J). (gr. 2-4). 4.99 (978-0-14-241295-4(3), Puffin Books) Penguin Young Readers Group.

Knight, Tom, illus. Little Red Riding Hood. 2013. (Story House Book Ser.). (ENG.). 32p. (J). (gr. -1-k). 16.95 (978-1-907967-38-2(9)) Boxer Bks., Ltd. GBR. Dist: Sterling Publishing Co., Inc.

Koertge, Ron. Lies, Knives, & Girls in Red Dresses. Dezsö, Andrea, illus. 2012. (ENG.). 96p. (YA). (gr. 9). 17.99 (978-0-7636-4406-2(4)) Candlewick Pr.

Konnikova, Svetlana. Grapette, the Runaway Who Rolled Away: A Timeless Tale of Love & Family: A Child Discovering the World. Smishliaev, Anatoli, illus. 2007. (Grapette's Adventures Ser.). (ENG.). 32p. (J). (gr. k-2). 15.95 (978-0-9791758-0-0(1)) Aurora Pubs., Inc.

Kontis, Alethea. Dearest. (Woodcutter Sisters Ser.: 3). (ENG.). 288p. (YA). (gr. 7). 2016. pap. 8.99 (978-0-544-54119-1(7))Bk. 3. 2015. 17.99 (978-0-544-07407-1(6)) Houghton Mifflin Harcourt Publishing Co. (HMH Books For Young Readers).

—Enchanted. (Woodcutter Sisters Ser.: 1). (ENG.). (YA). (gr. 7). 2012. 320p. 17.99 (978-0-547-64570-4(8))Bk. 1. 2013. 352p. pap. 8.99 (978-0-544-02218-8(1)) Houghton Mifflin Harcourt Publishing Co.

—Hero. (Woodcutter Sisters Ser.: 2). (ENG.). (YA). (gr. 7). 2015. 320p. pap. 8.99 (978-0-544-33616-2(X), HMH Books For Young Readers) 2013. 304p. 17.99 (978-0-544-05677-0(9)) Houghton Mifflin Harcourt Publishing Co.

Koontz, Robin Michal. The King's New Clothes. Koontz, Robin Michal, illus. 2011. (ENG., Illus.). 24p. (gr. 2-3). pap. 8.95 (978-1-61236-028-7(9)) Rourke Educational Media.

Korba, Joanna. Sleepless Beauty. 2006. (J). pap. (978-1-4108-7171-8(1)) Benchmark Education Co.

—Yeh-shen: A Cinderella Tale from China. 2006. (J). pap. (978-1-4108-6162-7(7)) Benchmark Education Co.

Kovalski, Maryann. Pizza for Breakfast. 2004. (J). (gr. k-3). spiral bd. (978-0-616-01692-3(1)) Canadian National Institute for the Blind/Institut National Canadien pour les Aveugles.

Krensky, Stephen. Bokuden & the Bully: [A Japanese Folktale]. Noll, Cheryl, illus. 2009. (On My Own Folklore Ser.). (ENG.). 48p. (gr. 2-4). pap. 6.95 (978-1-58013-847-5(0), First Avenue Editions) Lerner Publishing Group.

—The Dragon Emperor: A Chinese Folktale. 2009. pap. 40.95 (978-0-7613-4817-7(4)) Lerner Publishing Group.

—How Coyote Stole the Summer: [A Native American Folktale]. Dupre, Kelly, illus. 2009. (On My Own Folklore Ser.). (ENG.). 48p. (gr. 2-4). pap. 6.95 (978-1-58013-848-2(9), First Avenue Editions) Lerner Publishing Group.

—The Magic Pomegranate: A Jewish Folktale. 2009. pap. 40.95 (978-0-7613-4818-4(2)) Lerner Publishing Group.

—The Tale of la Llorona: A Mexican Folktale. 2009. pap. 40.95 (978-0-7613-4819-1(0)) Lerner Publishing Group.

Kubler, Annie. The Wheels on the Bus, 15 vols. Kubler, Annie, illus. (Illus.). 14p. (J). 2005. (ENG, PER & MUL.). bds. (978-1-84444-532-5(1)) 2005. (SWA, ENG & MUL., bds. (978-1-84444-533-2(X)) 2004. (ENG, TGL & MUL., bds. (978-1-84444-534-9(8)) Mantra Lingua.

Kunhardt, Dorothy, ed. Pinocchio. (FRE.). 96p. (J). (gr. k-5). pap. 9.95 (978-0-7859-8845-8(9)) French & European Pubns., Inc.

Kunstler, James Howard. Aladdin & the Magic Lamp, 1 vol. Couch, Greg, illus. 2005. (Rabbit Ears Ser.). (ENG.). 36p. (gr. k-5). 25.65 (978-1-59679-221-0(3)) Spotlight.

Kurlander, Keith. Tommy the Fishboy. Belomlinsky, Alex, illus. 2012. 34p. 24.95 (978-1-4626-4527-5(5)) America Star Bks.

Kurtz, John. A Fairy Tale Treasury. 2015. (ENG.). 144p. (J). (gr. k-5). pap. 14.99 (978-0-486-79681-9(7)) Dover Pubns., Inc.

—JATS Fairytale Classics - Jack & the Beanstalk. Kurtz, John, illus. 2004. (Illus.). 24p. (J). lib. bdg. 8.00 (978-1-4242-0636-0(7)) Fitzgerald Bks.

Kurtz, John, illus. Disney Princess: Look & Find. 2004. (Disney Princess Ser.). 24p. (J). 7.98 (978-0-7853-7918-8(5), 7179200) Phoenix International Publications, Inc.

Kusama, Yayoi & Andersen, Hans Christian. The Little Mermaid. 2016. (ENG., Illus.). 96p. 45.00 (978-87-92877-59-8(1)) Louisana DNK. Dist: D.A.P./Distributed Art Pubs.

Kushner, Sam. Cinderell. 2012. 34p. 25.99 (978-1-4582-0684-8(X)); pap. 16.99 (978-1-4582-0685-5(8)) Author Solutions, Inc. (Abbott Pr.).

Kyber, Manfred. Mantao the Jester King: A Fairytale from Tibet. Fairall, Barbara, tr. 2010. (Illus.). 66p. pap. (978-1-84748-817-6(X)) Athena Pr.

L. Prince Cloud & Princess Evergreen, 1 vol. 2010. 26p. pap. 24.95 (978-1-4512-9016-5(0)) America Star Bks.

Ladybird Books Staff. Cinderella. (First Fairy Tales Ser.: No. S852-1). (Illus.). (J). (gr. -1-2). pap. 3.95 (978-0-7214-5058-2(X), Dutton Juvenile) Penguin Publishing Group.

Ladybird Tales: Classic Stories to Share. 2016. (Ladybird Tales Ser.). (ENG., Illus.). 224p. (J). (gr. k-3). 19.99 (978-0-7232-9906-6(4)) Penguin Bks., Ltd. GBR. Dist: Independent Pubs. Group.

Lagonegro, Melissa. Beauty & the Beast Deluxe Step into Reading (Disney Beauty & the Beast) RH Disney, illus. 2017. (Step into Reading Ser.). (ENG.). 24p. (J). (gr. -1-1). pap. 4.99 (978-0-7364-3594-9(8), RH/Disney) Random Hse. Children's Bks.

—A Dream for a Princess (Disney Princess) Saichann, Alberto & Estudio, Pulsar, illus. 2016. (Step into Reading Ser.). (ENG.). 24p. (J). (gr. -1-1). pap. 4.99 (978-0-7364-3668-7(5), RH/Disney) Random Hse. Children's Bks.

Lairamore, Dawn. Ivy & the Meanstalk. 2011. (ENG.). 192p. (J). 16.95 (978-0-8234-2392-7(1)) Holiday Hse., Inc.

—Ivy's Ever After. (ENG.). 192p. (J). 2013. (gr. 2-7). pap. 7.99 (978-0-8234-2937-0(7)) 2010. (gr. 3-7). 16.95 (978-0-8234-2261-6(5)) Holiday Hse., Inc.

Laird, Elizabeth & Quarto Generic Staff. The Ogress & the Snake: And Other Stories from Somalia. Fowles, Shelley, illus. 2009. (ENG.). 96p. (J). (gr. 3-6). pap. 7.95 (978-1-84507-870-6(5), Frances Lincoln) Quarto Publishing Group UK GBR. Dist: Hachette Bk. Group.

Laky, Esther. Just Fairy Tales. 2010. 95p. pap. 11.80 (978-0-557-01926-7(5)) Lulu Pr., Inc.

Lambert, Nat. Little Red Riding Hood. Butcher, Rosie, illus. 2016. (Press Out & Build Fairy-Tale Scenes Ser.). (ENG.). 24p. (J). (gr. -1-1). 14.99 (978-1-78244-898-3(5)) Top That! Publishing PLC GBR. Dist: Independent Pubs. Group.

Lance, John & Narvarro. Priscilla Holmes & the Case of the Glass Slipper. 2011. 24p. pap. 14.99 (978-0-9826594-9-6(0)) 4RV Publishing, LLC.

Lang, Andrew. Andrew Lang's Blue, Red, Green & Yellow Fairy Books. 2009. 800p. pap. (978-1-905921-19-5(5)); 756p. pap. (978-1-905921-13-3(6)) Shoes & Ships & Sealing Wax Ltd.

—Andrew Lang's Brown, Orange, Olive & Lilac Fairy Books. 2009. 608p. pap. (978-1-905921-15-7(2)); 644p. pap. (978-1-905921-21-8(7)) Shoes & Ships & Sealing Wax Ltd.

—Andrew Lang's Complete Fairy Book Series: Traditional Folk Tales & Fairy Stories from Around the World. 2006. 825p. per. (978-0-9548401-5-0(1)) Shoes & Ships & Sealing Wax Ltd.

—Andrew Lang's Pink, Grey, Violet & Crimson Fairy Books. 2009. 636p. pap. (978-1-905921-14-0(4)); 676p. pap. (978-1-905921-20-1(9)) Shoes & Ships & Sealing Wax Ltd.

—The Blue Fairy Book. l.t. ed. 2005. 720p. pap. (978-1-84637-144-8(9)) Echo Library.

—The Blue Fairy Book. Lang, Andrew, ed. 2011. 286p. pap. 16.99 (978-1-61279-084-8(4)) Publishing in Motion.

—The Crimson Fairy Book. 2005. 364p. pap. 15.95 (978-1-4218-0106-3(X), 1st World Library - Literary Society) 1st World Publishing, Inc.

—The Crimson Fairy Book. 2007. 384p. 29.95 (978-1-4344-9149-7(8)); per. 19.95 (978-1-4344-9055-1(6)) Wildside Pr., LLC.

—The Green Fairy Book. 2007. 384p. 31.95 (978-1-4218-3823-6(0)); per. 15.95 (978-1-4218-3923-3(7)) 1st World Publishing, Inc. (1st World Library - Literary Society).

—The Green Fairy Book. 2007. 228p. per. (978-1-4068-6082-5(4)) 2005. 636p. pap. (978-1-84637-147-9(3)) Echo Library.

—The Green Fairy Book. 2004. reprint ed. pap. 28.95 (978-1-4191-6492-7(9)); pap. 1.99 (978-1-4192-6492-4(3)) Kessinger Publishing, LLC.

—The Grey Fairy Book. 2007. 332p. per. 14.95 (978-1-4218-3924-0(5), 1st World Library - Literary Society) 1st World Publishing, Inc.

—The Grey Fairy Book. 2007. (ENG.). 264p. pap. 21.99 (978-1-4264-4988-8(7)); 294p. pap. 23.99 (978-1-4264-5289-5(6)) Creative Media Partners, LLC.

—The Lilac Fairy Book. 2005. 384p. pap. 15.95 (978-1-4218-0105-6(1), 1st World Library - Literary Society) 1st World Publishing, Inc.

—The Lilac Fairy Book. 2004. reprint ed. pap. 1.99 (978-1-4192-7006-2(0)); pap. 27.95 (978-1-4191-7006-5(6)) Kessinger Publishing, LLC.

—The Olive Fairy Book. Lang, Andrew, ed. 2011. 216p. (gr. 3-7). pap. 15.95 (978-1-4638-0030-7(4)) Rodgers, Alan Bks.

—The Pink Fairy Book. 2005. 388p. pap. 15.95 (978-1-4218-0104-9(3), 1st World Library - Literary Society) 1st World Publishing, Inc.

—The Pink Fairy Book. 2008. (Dover Children's Classics Ser.). (ENG.). 360p. (J). (gr. 3-8). pap. 14.95 (978-0-486-46966-9(2)) Dover Pubns., Inc.

—The Pink Fairy Book. 2004. reprint ed. pap. 27.95 (978-1-4191-7753-8(2)); pap. 1.99 (978-1-4192-7753-5(7)) Kessinger Publishing, LLC.

—Prince Prigio. 2004. reprint ed. pap. 19.95 (978-1-4179-0522-5(0)) Kessinger Publishing, LLC.

—Prince Ricardo of Pantouflia. 2006. (Illus.). pap. 24.95 (978-1-4286-0645-6(9)) Kessinger Publishing, LLC.

—The Queen & the Mouse: A Story about Friendship. Lohmann, Renate, illus. 2006. (J). (978-1-59939-081-9(7), Reader's Digest Young Families, Inc.) Studio Fun International.

—The Red Fairy Book. 2007. 444p. per. 18.95 (978-1-4218-3926-4(1), 1st World Library - Literary Society) 1st World Publishing, Inc.

—The Red Fairy Book. Lang, Andrew, ed. 2011. 322p. pap. 16.99 (978-1-61279-092-3(5)) Publishing in Motion.

—The Red Romance Book; Tales of Knights. 2006. 396p. per. (978-1-84664-477-1(1), Obscure Pr.) Read Bks.

—The Violet Fairy Book. 2005. 404p. pap. 16.95 (978-1-4218-0107-0(8), 1st World Library - Literary Society) 1st World Publishing, Inc.

—The Violet Fairy Book. 2006. pap. 14.95 (978-1-59605-994-8(X), Cosimo Classics) Cosimo, Inc.

Lang, Andrew, ed. The Brown Fairy Book. 2004. (Twelve-Point Ser.). lib. bdg. 25.00 (978-1-58287-282-7(1)) North Bks.

—The Chronicles of Pantouflia: Prince Prigio; Prince Ricardo of Pantouflia. (J). 20.95 (978-0-89190-088-7(8)) Amereon Ltd.

—The Green Fairy Book. 2007. 316p. per. (978-1-4065-2615-8(0)) Dodo Pr.

—The Green Fairy Book. 2004. (Twelve-Point Ser.). lib. bdg. 25.00 (978-1-58287-283-4(X)) North Bks.

—The Grey Fairy Book. 2006. (Twelve-Point Ser.). lib. bdg. 25.00 (978-1-58287-393-0(3)); lib. bdg. 26.00 (978-1-58287-884-3(6)) North Bks.

—The Lilac Fairy Book. (J). 26.95 (978-0-89190-084-9(5)) Amereon Ltd.

—The Lilac Fairy Book. 2004. (Twelve-Point Ser.). lib. bdg. 25.00 (978-1-58287-284-1(8)); lib. bdg. 26.00 (978-1-58287-778-5(5)) North Bks.

—The Lilac Fairy Book. 2011. 238p. 26.95 (978-1-4638-9786-4(3)); pap. 16.95 (978-1-4638-0112-0(2)) Rodgers, Alan Bks.

—The Olive Fairy Book. 2011. 216p. (gr. 3-7). 26.95 (978-1-4638-9787-1(1)) Rodgers, Alan Bks.

—The Orange Fairy Book. (J). 26.95 (978-0-89190-083-2(7)) Amereon Ltd.

—The Pink Fairy Book. 2004. (Twelve-Point Ser.). lib. bdg. 25.00 (978-1-58287-287-2(2)); lib. bdg. 26.00 (978-1-58287-781-5(5)) North Bks.

—The Yellow Fairy Book. (Twelve-Point Ser.). 2003. lib. bdg. 25.00 (978-1-58287-206-3(6)) 2004. 529p. 26.00 (978-1-58287-690-0(8)) North Bks.

Lang, Andrew & Ford, H. J. The Tale of the Cid: And Other Stories of Knights & Chivalry. Ford, H. J., illus. 2007. (Dover Children's Classics Ser.). (ENG., Illus.). 208p. (J). (gr. 4-7). per. 9.95 (978-0-486-45470-2(3)) Dover Pubns., Inc.

Lanza, Barbara. Time to Fly: A Fairy Lane Book. Lanza, Barbara, illus. 2005. (ENG., Illus.). 32p. (J). (gr. 4-7). 19.95 (978-0-9724853-7-1(6)) Keene Publishing.

Lapucci, Carlo. Fiabe toscane di maghi, fate, animali, diavoli e Giganti: Volume 2. 2011. (ENG.). 204p. (C). pap. 19.50 (978-88-563-0067-3(2)) Polistampa ITA. Dist: Casemate Academic.

Larkin, Rochelle, ed. Beauty & the Beast & Other Stories. (Illus.). 339p. (J). 21.35 (978-0-86611-674-9(5)) Waldman Publishing Corp.

—The Little Mermaid & Other Stories. (Illus.). 239p. (J). 9.95 (978-0-86611-676-3(1)) Waldman Publishing Corp.

LaRochelle, David. The End. Egielski, Richard, illus. 2006. (J). 16.99 (978-0-439-64012-1(1), Levine, Arthur A. Bks.) Scholastic, Inc.

Larson, M. A. The Warrior Princess of Pennyroyal Academy. 2017. (Pennyroyal Academy Ser.). (ENG.). 368p. (J). (gr. 5). 16.99 (978-0-399-54571-9(9), G.P. Putnam's Sons Books for Young Readers) Penguin Young Readers Group.

Lauture, Mireille B. Konpè Kochon Pran Nan Mer: Mancy's Haitian Folktale Collection. 2012. 28p. pap. 16.99 (978-1-4685-6032-9(8)) AuthorHouse.

E
F
G

Lavarello, Jose Maria, illus. Cuentame un Cuento, No. 2. (SPA.). 366p. (J). (gr. k-3). *(978-84-480-1124-6(4)*, TM2346) Timun Mas, Editorial S.A. ESP. Dist: Lectorum Pubns., Inc.

LeapFrog Staff. Disney Princess Stories - France. 2003. (Illus.). spiral bd. 14.99 *(978-1-59319-005-7(0))* LeapFrog Enterprises, Inc.

—Disney Princess Stories - Latin America. 2003. (Illus.). (J). spiral bd. 14.99 *(978-1-59319-001-9(8))* LeapFrog Enterprises, Inc.

Lecis, Alessandro & Shirtliffe, Leanne. I Am Not Little Red Riding Hood. Wolfsgruber, Linda, illus. 2013. (ENG.). 32p. (J). (gr. -1-1). 16.95 *(978-1-62087-985-6(9)*, 620985, Sky Pony Pr.) Skyhorse Publishing Co., Inc.

Lee, Ji-yeong. Tchaikovsky's Swan Lake. Pacheco, Gabriel, illus. 2016. (Music Storybooks Ser.). (ENG.). 44p. (gr. 3-6). pap. 9.99 *(978-1-925247-11-4(2)*, Big and SMALL) ChoiceMaker Pty. Ltd., The AUS. Dist: Lerner Publishing Group.

Lefèvre, A. M. Hugan Fach Goch. 2005. (WEL., Illus.). 10p. *(978-0-86381-645-1(2))* Gwasg Carreg Gwalch.

—Pws Esgid Uchel. 2005. (WEL., Illus.). 10p. *(978-0-86381-647-5(9))* Gwasg Carreg Gwalch.

Legrandi, Francesco. Cinderella. 2015. (J). lib. bdg. 13.55 *(978-0-606-35917-7(6))* Turtleback Bks.

Legrand, Claire. The Cavendish Home for Boys & Girls. Watts, Sarah, illus. (ENG.). (J). (gr. 5). 2013. 368p. pap. 7.99 *(978-1-4424-4292-4(1))* 2012. 352p. 16.99 *(978-1-4424-4291-7(3))* Simon & Schuster Bks. For Young Readers. (Simon & Schuster Bks. For Young Readers).

Lemaître, Pascal, illus. Pinocchio. 2014. (Cartoon Classics Ser.). (ENG.). 144p. (J). (gr. 2-5). 12.99 *(978-0-8050-9699-6(X)*, 9780805096996, Holt, Henry & Co. Bks. For Young Readers) Holt, Henry & Co.

Lemley, Ronald W. The Wee Bannock: A Scottish Fairy Tale. 2008. 43p. pap. 24.95 *(978-1-60610-122-3(6))* America Star Bks.

Lendler, Ian. An Undone Fairy Tale. Martin, Whitney, illus. 2005. (ENG.). 32p. (J). (gr. 1-5). 18.99 *(978-0-689-86677-7(1)*, Simon & Schuster Bks. For Young Readers) Simon & Schuster Bks. For Young Readers.

Lenihan, Eddie. Fionn Mac Cumhail's Amazing Stories, Bk. 3. Clarke, Alan, illus. 2015. (Irish Mystery & Magic Ser.: 3). (ENG.). 64p. (J). 8.00 *(978-1-78117-359-6(1))* Mercier Pr., Ltd., The IRL. Dist: Dufour Editions, Inc.

—Fionn Mac Cumhail's Tales from Ireland, Bk. 1. Clarke, Alan, illus. 2015. (Irish Mystery & Magic Ser.: 1). (ENG.). 64p. (J). 8.00 *(978-1-78117-357-2(5))* Mercier Pr., Ltd., The IRL. Dist: Dufour Editions, Inc.

Lenihan, Edmund. Fionn MacCumhail's Epic Adventures, Bk. 2. Clarke, Alan, illus. 2015. (Irish Mystery & Magic Ser.: 2). (ENG.). 64p. (J). 8.00 *(978-1-78117-358-9(3))* Mercier Pr., Ltd., The IRL. Dist: Dufour Editions, Inc.

Leonard, Barry, ed. Alice in Wonderland. 2003. (Illus.). 12p. (J). (gr. k-4). reprint ed. 17.00 *(978-0-7567-6864-5(0))* DIANE Publishing Co.

—The Little Tin Soldier. 2003. (Illus.). 12p. (J). (gr. k-4). reprint ed. 17.00 *(978-0-7567-6867-6(5))* DIANE Publishing Co.

—Sleeping Beauty. 2003. (Illus.). 12p. (J). (gr. k-4). reprint ed. 17.00 *(978-0-7567-6865-2(9))* DIANE Publishing Co.

—The Three Little Pigs. 2003. (Illus.). 12p. (J). (gr. k-4). reprint ed. 17.00 *(978-0-7567-6860-7(8))* DIANE Publishing Co.

—The Ugly Duckling. 2003. (Illus.). 12p. (J). (gr. k-4). reprint ed. 17.00 *(978-0-7567-6858-4(6))* DIANE Publishing Co.

Leprince de Beaumont, Jeanne-Marie. Beauty & the Beast. Pignataro, Anna, illus. 2016. (Once upon a Timeless Tale Ser.). (ENG.). 32p. (J). (gr. k-2). 9.99 *(978-1-921894-88-6(1))* Little Hare Bks. AUS. Dist: Independent Pubs. Group.

Leprince de Beaumont, Marie. La Bella y la Bestia.Tr. of Beauty & the Beast. (SPA.). 72p. (J). (gr. 3). 7.95 *(978-84-372-1851-9(9))* Santillana USA Publishing Co., Inc.

Leprince de Beaumont, Marie & Perrault, Charles. Beauty & the Beast & Other Fairy Tales. 2011. (Dover Children's Thrift Classics Ser.). (ENG., Illus.). 96p. (Orig.). (J). (gr. 3-8). pap. 3.00 *(978-0-486-28032-5(2))* Dover Pubns., Inc.

Leschnikoff, Nancy & Wood, Helen, des. Illustrated Fairy Tales. 2007. (Illustrated Stories Ser.). (Illus.). 352p. (J). (gr. -1-3). 19.99 *(978-0-7945-1717-5(X)*, Usborne) EDC Publishing.

Levine, Gail Carson. Fairest. 2006. 326p. (J). (gr. 3-7). lib. bdg. 18.89 *(978-0-06-073409-1(4))* HarperCollins Pubs.

—Fairest. l.t. rev. ed. 2007. (Literacy Bridge Young Adult Ser.). 349p. (J). (gr. 3-7). 23.95 *(978-0-7862-9270-7(9))* Thorndike Pr.

—The Princess Tales, No. 2. Elliott, Mark, illus. 2004. (Princess Tales Ser.). (ENG.). 256p. (J). (gr. 2-7). pap. 7.99 *(978-0-06-056043-0(6))* HarperCollins Pubs.

Levine, Gail Carson & Levine, Gail C. Fairest. 2012. (ENG.). 352p. (J). (gr. 3-7). pap. 6.99 *(978-0-06-073410-7(8))* HarperCollins Pubs.

—The Fairy's Return & Other Princess Tales. 2009. (ENG.). 400p. (J). (gr. 3-7). pap. 7.99 *(978-0-06-176898-9(7))* HarperCollins Pubs.

Lewis, C. Robbie. Rapunzel. 2004. 228p. 23.95 *(978-1-4184-8779-9(1))* AuthorHouse.

Lewis, Jan. Princess Fairy Tales: Cinderella, the Princess & the Pea, Sleeping Beauty, the Little Mermaid. Lewis, Jan, illus. 2015. (ENG., Illus.). 48p. bds. 9.99 *(978-1-86147-423-0(7)*, Armadillo) Anness Publishing GBR. Dist: National Bk. Network.

Lewis, Jan, illus. First Fairy Tales: Cinderella. 2013. (ENG.). 24p. (J). (gr. -1-k). bds. 6.99 *(978-1-86147-334-9(6)*, Armadillo) Anness Publishing GBR. Dist: National Bk. Network.

—First Fairy Tales: Sleeping Beauty. 2013. (ENG.). 24p. (J). (gr. -1-k). bds. 6.99 *(978-1-86147-338-7(9)*, Armadillo) Anness Publishing GBR. Dist: National Bk. Network.

—First Fairy Tales: The Ugly Duckling. 2013. (ENG.). 24p. (J). (gr. -1-k). bds. 6.99 *(978-1-86147-333-2(8)*, Armadillo) Anness Publishing GBR. Dist: National Bk. Network.

—First Fairy Tales: Three Little Pigs. 2013. (ENG.). 24p. (J). (gr. -1-k). bds. 6.99 *(978-1-86147-331-8(1)*, Armadillo) Anness Publishing GBR. Dist: National Bk. Network.

—Magical Fairy Tales: Aladdin & the Lamp; the Ugly Duckling; the Emperor's New Clothes; Puss in Boots. 2016. (ENG.). 48p. bds. 9.99 *(978-1-86147-700-2(7)*, Armadillo) Anness Publishing GBR. Dist: National Bk. Network.

—The Pied Piper of Hamelin. 2006. (First Fairy Tales Ser.). 30p. (J). (gr. -1-3). lib. bdg. 28.50 *(978-1-59771-072-5(5))* Sea-To-Sea Pubns.

—The Princess & the Pea. 2015. (ENG.). 24p. bds. 6.99 *(978-1-86147-467-4(9)*, Armadillo) Anness Publishing GBR. Dist: National Bk. Network.

Lin, Grace. Starry River of the Sky. (ENG., Illus.). (J). (gr. 3-7). 2014. 320p. pap. 10.99 *(978-0-316-12597-0(0))* 2012. 304p. 17.99 *(978-0-316-12595-6(4))* Little, Brown Bks. for Young Readers.

—Starry River of the Sky. 2014. (J). lib. bdg. 20.85 *(978-0-606-32277-5(9)*, Turtleback) Turtleback Bks.

—When the Sea Turned to Silver. (ENG.). (J). (gr. 3-7). 2017. 400p. pap. 9.99 ***(978-0-316-12594-9(6))*** 2016. (Illus.). 384p. 18.99 *(978-0-316-12592-5(X))* Little, Brown Bks. for Young Readers.

—When the Sea Turned to Silver. 2017. (J). lib. bdg. 20.85 ***(978-0-606-40629-1(8))*** Turtleback Bks.

Lin, Grace. Where the Mountain Meets the Moon. 2009. (ENG., Illus.). 288p. (J). (gr. 3-7). 18.99 *(978-0-316-11427-1(8))* Little Brown & Co.

—Where the Mountain Meets the Moon. 2011. (ENG., Illus.). 320p. (J). (gr. 3-7). pap., pap. 10.99 *(978-0-316-03863-8(6))* Little, Brown Bks. for Young Readers.

—Where the Mountain Meets the Moon. 2011. (ENG., Illus.). 278p. (gr. 4-7). 19.00 *(978-1-61383-087-1(4))* Perfection Learning Corp.

—Where the Mountain Meets the Moon. 2011. (J). lib. bdg. 22.10 *(978-0-606-16233-3(X)*, Turtleback) Turtleback Bks.

Lindskoog, Kathryn & Hunsicker, Ranelda Mack, eds. Faerie Gold: Treasures from the Lands of Enchantment. 2005. (Classics for Young Readers Ser.). 304p. (J). per. 11.99 *(978-0-87552-738-3(8))* P & R Publishing.

Linn, Susie. Cinderella. Butcher, Rosie, illus. 2016. (Press Out & Build Fairy-Tale Scenes Ser.). (ENG.). 24p. (J). (gr. -1-1). 14.99 *(978-1-78244-897-6(7))* Top That! Publishing PLC GBR. Dist: Independent Pubs. Group.

Lionni, Leo. Tico & the Golden Wings. 2007. (ENG., Illus.). 32p. (J). (gr. -1-2). 16.99 *(978-0-394-81749-1(4)*, Knopf Bks. for Young Readers) Random Hse. Children's Bks.

Lisansky, Sue, illus. Cinderella. 2011. (First Fairy Tales Ser.). (ENG.). 20p. (J). (gr. -1-3). pap. 4.99 *(978-1-934004-19-7(7))* Byeway Bks.

Litchfield, Jo, contrib. by. Goldilocks & the Three Bears. 2008. (Usborne First Fairytales Ser.). (Illus.). 10p. (J). bds. 9.99 *(978-0-7945-1962-9(8)*, Usborne) EDC Publishing.

Litchfield, Jo & Allen, Francesca, illus. First Picture Fairytales. MMStudios, photos by. 2007. (First Picture Board Bks.). 16p. (J). (gr. -1-k). bds. 11.99 *(978-0-7945-1460-0(X)*, Usborne) EDC Publishing.

little bee books, little bee. A Day with Cinderella. 2015. (ENG., Illus.). 16p. (J). (gr. -1-1). 8.99 *(978-1-4998-0061-6(4))* Little Bee Books Inc.

Little Mermaid. 2009. (Disney Glitter Board Book Ser.). 5p. *(978-1-4054-9825-8(0))* Parragon, Inc.

Little Reader Digital Storybook: Cinderella. 2005. (J). cd-rom 8.99 *(978-0-9767657-7-6(2))* Mullings Media.

Little Red Riding Hood. 2017. (Picture Bks.). (ENG.). (J). 9.99 ***(978-0-7945-3723-4(5)***, Usborne) EDC Publishing.

Little Red Riding Hood. 2005. (J). bds. 3.99 *(978-1-933200-15-6(4))* Family Bks. at Home.

Little Red Riding Hood. Date not set. (J). 4.99 *(978-0-7214-5405-4(4))* Nickel Pr.

Little Red Riding Hood. 2005. (J). per. 8.95 *(978-1-59566-147-0(6))* QEB Publishing Inc.

Little Red Riding Hood. 2004. (Folk Tales Set 1 Ser.). (J). 4.00 *(978-1-58453-272-9(6))* Pioneer Valley Bks.

Little Red Riding Hood. 2003. reprint ed. pap. 9.95 *(978-1-891419-27-0(7))* State Historical Society of North Dakota.

Little Red Riding Hood, Level 2. 2016. (Ladybird Readers Ser.). (ENG.). 48p. (J). (gr. 2-4). pap. 9.99 *(978-0-241-25446-2(9))* Penguin Bks., Ltd. GBR. Dist: Independent Pubs. Group.

Little Red Riding Pooh: A Fairy Tale Friend a Board Book & Plush Figure. 2004. (Pooh's Fairy Tale Theater Ser.). 12p. (J). 6.99 *(978-0-7364-2239-0(0)*, RH/Disney) Random Hse. Children's Bks.

Littman, Sarah Darer. Charmed, I'm Sure. 2016. (ENG., Illus.). 208p. (J). (gr. 3-7). 17.99 *(978-1-4814-5127-7(8)*, Aladdin) Simon & Schuster Children's Publishing.

Littman, Sarah Darer. Fairest of Them All. 2017. (ENG., Illus.). 224p. (J). (gr. 3-7). pap. 7.99 ***(978-1-4814-5129-1(4)***, Aladdin) Simon & Schuster Children's Publishing.

Liv‡n, Paco. WHAT A SNOUT! 2007. (ENG., Illus.). 48p. (J). 18.95 *(978-84-96788-87-9(3))* OQO, Editora ESP. Dist: Baker & Taylor Bks.

Lo, Malinda. Huntress. 2012. (ENG.). 416p. (YA). (gr. 10-17). pap. 11.99 *(978-0-316-03999-4(3))* Little, Brown Bks. for Young Readers.

Lodge, Jo. Ali Baba & the Forty Thieves. 2004. (Illus.). 10p. (J). *(978-1-84444-531-8(3))* Mantra Lingua.

Lodico, Cheryl Madeleine. The Ice Princess Trilogy. 2007. pap. 20.00 *(978-0-8059-8967-0(6))* Dorrance Publishing Co., Inc.

Loewen, Nancy. Believe Me, I Never Felt a Pea! The Story of the Princess & the Pea As Told by the Princess. Bernardini, Cristian, illus. 2016. (Other Side of the Story Ser.). (ENG.). 24p. (gr. 2-3). lib. bdg. 27.32 *(978-1-4795-8622-6(6))* Picture Window Bks.

—Frankly, I Never Wanted to Kiss Anybody! The Story of the Frog Prince As Told by the Frog. Alonso, Denis, illus. 2013. (Other Side of the Story Ser.). (ENG.). 24p. (gr. 2-3). 27.32 *(978-1-4048-8304-8(5))* Picture Window Bks.

—Frankly, I Never Wanted to Kiss Anybody! The Story of the Frog Prince As Told by the Frog. Alonso, Denis, illus. 2013. (Other Side of the Story Ser.). (ENG.). 24p. (gr. 2-3). 9.95 *(978-1-4795-1948-4(0))* Picture Window Bks.

—No Kidding, Mermaids Are a Joke! The Story of the Little Mermaid As Told by the Prince. Tayal, Amit, illus. 2013. (Other Side of the Story Ser.). (ENG.). 24p. (gr. 2-3). 9.95 *(978-1-4795-1947-7(2))* Picture Window Bks.

—No Kidding, Mermaids Are a Joke! The Story of the Little Mermaid as Told by the Prince. Tayal, Amit, illus. 2013. (Other Side of the Story Ser.). (ENG.). 24p. (gr. 2-3). 27.32 *(978-1-4048-8303-1(7))* Picture Window Bks.

—No Lie, I Acted Like a Beast: The Story of Beauty & the Beast as Told by the Beast. Bernardini, Cristian, illus. 2013. (Other Side of the Story Ser.). (ENG.). 24p. (gr. 2-3). 9.95 *(978-1-4795-1944-6(8))* Picture Window Bks.

—Once upon a Time: Writing Your Own Fairy Tale, 1 vol. Lyles, Christopher, illus. 2009. (Writer's Toolbox Ser.). (ENG.). 32p. (gr. 2-4). pap. 8.95 *(978-1-4048-5336-2(7))*; lib. bdg. 27.32 *(978-1-4048-5335-5(9))* Picture Window Bks.

—Trust Me, Hansel & Gretel Are SWEET! The Story of Hansel & Gretel As Told by the Witch. Bock, Janna, illus. 2016. (Other Side of the Story Ser.). (ENG.). 24p. (gr. 2-3). lib. bdg. 27.32 *(978-1-4795-8623-3(4))* Picture Window Bks.

Lohmann, Renate, illus. The Lucky Boots. 2006. (Famous Fables Ser.). (J). 6.99 *(978-1-59939-027-7(2))* Cornerstone Pr.

Long, Robert. New Aesop Fables for Children Volume I. 2009. 84p. pap. 29.98 *(978-0-557-00953-4(7))* Lulu Pr., Inc.

—New Aesop Fables for Children Volume II. 2009. 77p. pap. 29.15 *(978-0-557-00952-7(9))* Lulu Pr., Inc.

Long, Susan Hill. The Magic Mirror: Concerning a Lonely Princess, a Foundling Girl, a Scheming King & a Pickpocket Squirrel. 2016. (ENG., Illus.). 320p. (J). (gr. 3-7). 16.99 *(978-0-553-51134-5(3)*, Knopf Bks. for Young Readers) Random Hse. Children's Bks.

Long, Sylvia, illus. Sylvia Long's Thumbelina. 2010. (ENG.). 58p. (J). (gr. k-5). 17.99 *(978-0-8118-5522-8(8))* Chronicle Bks. LLC.

Long, Trishia. How I Met Bigfoot. 2012. 40p. pap. 20.99 *(978-1-4685-9425-6(7))* AuthorHouse.

Longoria, Madelin G. Verdeazul. 2009. (J). *(978-1-59835-132-3(X))* Cambridge BrickHouse, Inc.

Longstaff, Abie. The Fairytale Hairdresser & Sleeping Beauty. Beard, Lauren, illus. 2014. (Fairytale Hairdresser Ser.: 3). (ENG.). 32p. (J). (-k). pap. 12.99 *(978-0-552-56755-8(8))* Transworld Publishers Ltd. GBR. Dist: Independent Pubs. Group.

—The Fairytale Hairdresser & Snow White. Beard, Lauren, illus. 2015. (Fairytale Hairdresser Ser.: 4). (ENG.). 32p. (J). (-k). pap. 9.99 *(978-0-552-56777-0(9))* Transworld Publishers Ltd. GBR. Dist: Independent Pubs. Group.

Lopez, Khrystle M. & Lopez, Yolanda C. Princess Khrystle & the Monster Cancer: An informative fairytale version about brain cancer in Children. 2005. (ENG., Illus.). 63p. (gr. -1-3). 24.95 *(978-0-9772565-0-1(2))* Princess Khrystle & Prince Michael, Inc.

Losantos, Cristina, illus. Beauty & the Beast: La Bella y la Bestia. 2007. (Bilingual Fairy Tales Ser.: BILI). (ENG & SPA.). 32p. (J). (gr. -1-3). pap. 6.95 *(978-0-8118-5970-7(3))* Chronicle Bks. LLC.

—Beauty & the Beast (La Bella y la Bestia) 2013. (Bilingual Fairy Tales Ser.). (SPA & ENG.). 32p. (J). (gr. 1-4). lib. bdg. 28.50 *(978-1-60753-355-9(3))* Amicus Publishing.

—Bella y la Bestia. 2007. (Bilingual Fairy Tales Ser.: BILI).Tr. of Beauty & the Beast. (ENG & SPA.). 32p. (J). (gr. -1-3). 14.95 *(978-0-8118-5969-1(X))* Chronicle Bks. LLC.

Lovejoy, Robert. The Golden Dog Book of Fairy Tales & Animal Stories. 2005. (ENG.). 140p. pap. 13.99 *(978-0-919614-66-6(3))* Dundurn CAN. Dist: Ingram Publisher Services.

Lowell, Susan. Los Tres Pequenos Jabalies: The Three Little Javelinas. Harris, Jim, illus. 2004. (SPA, ENG & MUL.). 32p. (J). (gr. -1-3). 15.95 *(978-0-87358-661-0(1)*, NP611) Rowman & Littlefield Publishers, Inc.

Lowes, Sarah. The Snow Queen. Clara, Miss, illus. (ENG.). 64p. (J). 2013. 17.99 *(978-1-84686-964-8(1))* 2011. (gr. 1-5). 9.99 *(978-1-84686-662-3(6))* Barefoot Bks., Inc.

Lucas, David. The Lying Carpet. Lucas, David, illus. 2011. (ENG., Illus.). 78p. (J). (gr. 4-7). 15.99 *(978-1-84270-441-7(9))* Andersen Pr. GBR. Dist: Independent Pubs. Group.

Lupton, Hugh. Tales of Mystery & Magic. Baruzzi, Agnese, illus. 2010. (ENG.). 64p. (J). (gr. 3-18). 19.99 *(978-1-84686-258-8(2))* Barefoot Bks., Inc.

—Tales of Wisdom & Wonder. Sharkey, Niamh, illus. 2008. (ENG.). 64p. (J). 19.99 *(978-1-84686-243-4(4))* Barefoot Bks., Inc.

Lyall, Maureen. Magus & the Blue Fairy. 2012. 20p. pap. 17.99 *(978-1-4772-6562-8(7))* AuthorHouse.

Mabie, Hamilton Wright. Fairy Tales Every Child Should Know. 2007. (ENG.). 278p. pap. 21.99 *(978-1-4346-2509-0(5))*; 304p. pap. 24.99 *(978-1-4346-2551-9(6))* Creative Media Partners, LLC.

—Fairy Tales Every Child Should Know a Selection of the Best Fairy Tales of All Time & of All Authors. unabr. ed. 2012. (Illus.). 387p. 49.99 *(978-1-4622-9459-6(6))* Repressed Publishing LLC.

Mabie, Hamilton Wright, ed. Fairy Tales Every Child Should Know. 2007. 268p. (gr. -1-3). per. *(978-1-4065-2957-9(5))* Dodo Pr.

Maccarone, Grace. The Nutcracker. Chauffrey, Célia, illus. 2016. (ENG.). 40p. (J). (gr. -1-3). 17.99 *(978-1-4998-0281-8(1))* Little Bee Books Inc.

—Princess Tales: Once upon a Time in Rhyme with Seek-and-Find Pictures. de Marcken, Gail, illus. 2013. (ENG.). 32p. (J). (gr. -1-1). 16.99 *(978-0-312-67958-3(0)*, 9780312679583) Feiwel & Friends.

—Princess Tales Around the World: Once upon a Time in Rhyme with Seek-And-Find Pictures. de Marcken, Gail, illus. 2017. (ENG.). 32p. (J). 16.99 *(978-1-250-06103-4(2)*, 9781250061034) Feiwel & Friends.

MacDonald, Alan. The Magic Porridge Pot. 2015. (First Favourite Tales Ser.). (ENG., Illus.). 32p. (J). (-k). 7.99 *(978-1-4093-0954-3(1))* Penguin Bks., Ltd. GBR. Dist: Independent Pubs. Group.

MacDonald, Alan & Ladybird Books Staff. The Gingerbread Man. 2015. (First Favourite Tales Ser.). (ENG., Illus.). 32p. (J). (-k). 7.99 *(978-1-4093-0630-6(5))* Penguin Bks., Ltd. GBR. Dist: Independent Pubs. Group.

MacDonald, George. The Day Boy & the Night Girl. 2008. 128p. 23.95 *(978-1-60664-922-0(1))*; pap. 10.95 *(978-1-60664-042-5(9))* Aegypan.

—The Light Princess. 2008. 48p. pap. 5.99 *(978-1-4209-3096-2(6))* Digireads.com Publishing.

—Light Princess. l.t. ed. 2006. pap. *(978-1-84702-350-6(9))* Echo Library.

—The Light Princess. 2004. reprint ed. pap. 15.95 *(978-1-4191-7001-0(5))*; pap. 1.99 *(978-1-4192-7001-7(X))* Kessinger Publishing, LLC.

—Light Princess & Other Fairy Stories. 2006. 132p. per. 10.95 *(978-1-59818-618-5(3))*; 24.95 *(978-1-59818-236-1(6))* Aegypan.

—The Light Princess & Other Fairy Stories. 2007. 102p. pap. 18.99 *(978-1-4346-1408-7(5))* Creative Media Partners, LLC.

—The Princess & Curdie. Stratton, Helen, illus. 2003. 162p. pap. 12.99 *(978-1-57646-634-6(5))* Quiet Vision Publishing.

—Princess & Curdie. 2006. 136p. per. 10.95 *(978-1-59818-617-8(5))*; 24.95 *(978-1-59818-235-4(8))* Aegypan.

—The Princess & Curdie. l.t. ed. 2005. 320p. pap. *(978-1-84637-020-5(5))* Echo Library.

—The Princess & Curdie. 2004. reprint ed. pap. 1.99 *(978-1-4192-7867-9(3))* Kessinger Publishing, LLC.

—Princess & the Goblin. 2006. 128p. per. 10.95 *(978-1-59818-653-6(1))*; 23.95 *(978-1-59818-234-7(X))* Aegypan.

—The Princess & the Goblin. abr. ed. 2007. 191p. (J). (gr. 4-7). per. 8.99 *(978-1-59166-799-5(2))* BJU Pr.

—The Princess & the Goblin. 2008. 176p. 25.99 *(978-0-554-28047-9(7))* 2008. 176p. 22.99 *(978-0-554-37350-8(5))* 2007. 162p. pap. 19.99 *(978-1-4346-4583-8(5))* 2007. 174p. pap. 21.99 *(978-1-4346-4584-5(3))* Creative Media Partners, LLC.

—The Princess & the Goblin. 2005. 108p. per. 5.99 *(978-1-4209-2557-9(1))* Digireads.com Publishing.

—The Princess & the Goblin. 2007. 152p. per. *(978-1-4065-3015-5(8))* Dodo Pr.

—The Princess & the Goblin. 2011. (Dover Children's Evergreen Classics Ser.). (ENG., Illus.). 176p. (J). (gr. 3-8). pap. 5.00 *(978-0-486-40787-6(X))* Dover Pubns., Inc.

—The Princess & the Goblin. l.t. ed. 2005. 292p. pap. *(978-1-84637-021-2(3))* Echo Library.

—The Princess & the Goblin. 2008. 188p. pap. 12.95 *(978-1-60096-531-9(8))*; pap. 12.95 *(978-1-60096-825-9(2))* Editorium, The.

—The Princess & the Goblin. 2007. pap. 5.99 *(978-1-59986-657-4(9)*, FQ Classics) Filiquarian Publishing, LLC.

—The Princess & the Goblin. 2004. reprint ed. pap. 1.99 *(978-1-4192-7868-6(1))* Kessinger Publishing, LLC.

—The Princess & the Goblin. 2008. 132p. pap. 4.99 *(978-1-60459-454-6(3))* Wilder Pubns., Corp.

—The Wise Woman. 2009. 128p. 23.95 *(978-1-60664-614-4(1))*; pap. 10.95 *(978-1-60664-352-5(5))* Rodgers, Alan Bks.

MacDonald, George, ed. The Princess & the Goblin. 2004. reprint ed. pap. 20.95 *(978-1-4191-7868-9(7))* Kessinger Publishing, LLC.

MacDonald, Margaret Read. The Farmyard Jamboree. Fatus, Sophie, illus. 2009. (ENG.). (J). 16.99 *(978-1-84686-290-8(6))* Barefoot Bks., Inc.

—The Old Woman Who Lived in a Vinegar Bottle. 2005. (ENG., Illus.). 32p. (J). (gr. -1-3). pap. 8.95 *(978-0-87483-723-0(5))* August Hse. Pubs., Inc.

—Party Croc! A Folktale from Zimbabwe. Sullivan, Derek, illus. 2015. (ENG.). 32p. (J). (gr. -1-3). 16.99 *(978-0-8075-6320-5(X))* Whitman, Albert & Co.

—Too Many Fairies: A Celtic Tale, 0 vols. Mitchell, Susan, illus. 2010. (ENG.). 32p. (J). (gr. -1-3). 17.99 *(978-0-7614-5604-9(X)*, 9780761456049, Amazon Children's Publishing) Amazon Publishing.

Mace, Aubrey. My Fairy Grandmother. 2009. 270p. pap. 16.99 *(978-1-59955-217-0(5))* Cedar Fort, Inc./CFI Distribution.

MacHale, D. J. East of the Sun, West of the Moon, 1 vol. Flesher, Vivienne, illus. 2007. (Rabbit Ears: A Classic Tale Ser.). (ENG.). 36p. (gr. -1-3). 25.65 *(978-1-59961-306-2(9))* Spotlight.

MacKenzie, Donald A. Scottish Fairy Tales. Green, John, illus. 2011. (Dover Children's Thrift Classics Ser.). (ENG.). 96p. (J). (gr. 3-8). pap. 4.50 *(978-0-486-29900-6(7))* Dover Pubns., Inc.

MacKenzie, Robert, illus. Jack & the Beanstalk. 2008. (Classic Fairy Tale Collection). (ENG.). 32p. (J). (gr. -1-2). 14.95 *(978-1-4027-3064-1(0))* Sterling Publishing Co., Inc.

MacManus, Seumas. Donegal Fairy Stories. Verbeck, Frank, illus. 2012. (Dover Children's Classics Ser.). (ENG.). 256p. (J). (gr. 3-8). pap. 8.95 *(978-0-486-21971-4(2))* Dover Pubns., Inc.

The Magic Porridge Pot, Level 1. 2016. (Ladybird Readers Ser.). (ENG.). 48p. (J). pap. 9.99 *(978-0-241-25406-6(X))* Penguin Bks., Ltd. GBR. Dist: Independent Pubs. Group.

The Magical Horses Vol. 2000: A Fairy Tale for the Young & the Young at Heart. l.t. ed. 2005. (Illus.). 127p. (J). per. *(978-0-9738625-0-8(5))* Blue Cat Publishing.

Magpie, Lance White, reader. The Girl Who Loved Wild Horses. 2003. (Richard Jackson Books (Atheneum Hardcover) Ser.). (Illus.). (J). (gr. -1-2). 28.95 incl. audio compact disk *(978-1-59112-752-9(1))* Live Oak Media.

Maguire, Gregory. Leaping Beauty: And Other Animal Fairy Tales. Demarest, Chris L., illus. 2006. (ENG.). 224p. (J). (gr. 3-7). reprint ed. pap. 7.99 *(978-0-06-056419-3(9))* HarperCollins Pubs.

—Matchless: An Illumination of Hans Christian Andersen's Classic the Little Match Girl. 2010. (ENG., Illus.). 112p. pap. 12.99 *(978-0-06-200482-6(4)*, Harper Paperbacks) HarperCollins Pubs.

Mahoney, Jerry. My Stupid Stepbrother Ruined Beauty & the Beast. 2017. (J). lib. bdg. ***(978-1-4965-4465-0(X))*** Stone Arch Bks.

Mahoney, Jerry. My Stupid Stepbrother Ruined Cinderella. 2017. (J). lib. bdg. *(978-1-4965-4466-7(8))* Stone Arch Bks.

Make Believe Ideas. Izzy the Ice Cream Fairy Sticker Dolly Dress Up. 2015. (ENG.). 40p. (J). pap. 6.99 *(978-1-78393-445-4(X))* Make Believe Ideas GBR. Dist: Nelson, Thomas Inc.

—Treasuries Five-Minute Fairy Tales. 2014. (ENG.). 192p. (J). 19.99 *(978-1-78235-874-9(9))* Make Believe Ideas GBR. Dist: Nelson, Thomas Inc.

Malak, Annabel, illus. Cinderella. (Classic Stories Ser.). 48p. (J). (gr. -1-2). incl. audio *(978-2-921997-75-1(4))* Coffragants.

Malaspina, Ann. Jack & the Beanstalk: An English Folktale. Manning, Mary, illus. 2013. (Folktales from Around the World Ser.). (ENG.). 24p. (J). (gr. k-3). 28.50 *(978-1-62323-615-1(0)*, 206382) Child's World, Inc., The.

Man-Kong, Mary. Barbie: A Fairy Secret. Golden Books Staff, illus. 2011. (Little Golden Book Ser.). (ENG.). 24p. (J). (gr. -1-2). 3.99 *(978-0-375-86540-4(3),* Golden Bks.) Random Hse. Children's Bks.

—Barbie - Fashion Fairytale. Random House Value Publishing Staff, illus. 2010. (Step into Reading Ser.). (ENG.). 32p. (J). (gr. -1-1). pap. 3.99 *(978-0-375-86697-5(3),* Random Hse. Bks. for Young Readers) Random Hse. Children's Bks.

—Sleeping Beauty. 2014. (Disney Princess Step into Reading Ser.). lib. bdg. 13.55 *(978-0-606-36001-2(8))* Turtleback Bks.

Manjula Padmanabhan, illus. Unprincess! 2005. 98p. (J). *(978-0-14-333495-8(6),* Puffin) Penguin Publishing Group.

Manna, Anthony & Mitakidou, Christodoula. The Orphan: A Cinderella Story from Greece. Potter, Giselle, illus. 2011. (ENG.). 40p. (J). (gr. -1-3). 17.99 *(978-0-375-86691-3(4),* Schwartz & Wade Bks.) Random Hse. Children's Bks.

Manna, Anthony L. & Mitakidou, Christodoula. Mr. Semolina-Semolinus. Potter, Giselle, illus. 2004. (ENG.). 40p. (J). (gr. -1-3). 19.99 *(978-0-689-86698-2(4),* Simon & Schuster/Paula Wiseman Bks.) Simon & Schuster/Paula Wiseman Bks.

Manson, Beverlie, illus. The Little Mermaid. 2017. (ENG.). 24p. (J). (gr. -1-12). pap. 7.99 ***(978-1-86147-828-3(3),*** Armadillo) Anness Publishing GBR. Dist: National Bk. Network.

—Stories to Share: The Twelve Dancing Princesses. 2017. (ENG.). 24p. (J). (gr. -1-12). pap. 7.99 ***(978-1-86147-829-0(1),*** Armadillo) Anness Publishing GBR. Dist: National Bk. Network.

Marcantonio, Patricia Santos, et al. Red Ridin' in the Hood: And Other Cuentos. Alarcão, Renato, illus. 2005. (ENG.). 192p. (J). (gr. 2-5). 17.99 *(978-0-374-36241-6(6),* 9780374362416, Farrar, Straus & Giroux (BYR)) Farrar, Straus & Giroux.

Marcellino, Fred, illus. The Steadfast Tin Soldier. 2017.Tr. of Standhaftige Tinsoldat. (ENG.). 32p. (J). (gr. -1-3). 17.99 ***(978-1-4814-7662-1(9),*** Atheneum/Caitlyn Dlouhy Books) Simon & Schuster Children's Publishing.

Marlow, Patricia. What Fairy Tales Are All About: Grandma's Stories. 2007. 94p. pap. 19.95 *(978-1-4241-6580-3(6))* America Star Bks.

Marr, Melissa & Pratt, Tim, eds. Rags & Bones: New Twists on Timeless Tales. 2015. (ENG.). 368p. (YA). (gr. 10-17). pap. 12.99 *(978-0-316-21293-9(8))* Little, Brown Bks. for Young Readers.

Marshall, Logan. Favorite Fairy Tales. 2008. 112p. per. 9.95 *(978-1-60312-538-3(8))* Aegypan.

Marshall, Logan, compiled by. Favorite Fairy Tales. 2008. 112p. 22.95 *(978-1-60664-988-6(4))* Aegypan.

Marshall, Rita & Chronicle Books Staff. The Illustrated Treasury of Fairy Tales. Chronicle Books Staff, illus. 2003. (ENG., Illus.). 352p. (J). (gr. 1-3). 29.95 *(978-1-56846-144-1(5))* Creative Co., The.

Martin, George W. The Battle of the Frogs & the Mice. Gwynne, Fred, illus. 2013. (ENG.). 64p. (gr. k-12). pap. 18.95 *(978-0-399-16285-5(2),* TarcherPerigee) Penguin Publishing Group.

Martin, Lynn & Hogg, Glenda. Funky Fairy Tales. (J). (gr. 5-6). pap. *(978-1-875739-81-3(5))* Wizard Bks.

Martin, Rafe. Birdwing. 2007. (ENG.). 384p. (J). (gr. 7-12). pap. 7.99 *(978-0-439-21168-0(9),* Levine, Arthur A. Bks.) Scholastic, Inc.

Martinez, Rocio & Martínez, Rocío. Matias Pierde Su Lapiz. 2005.Tr. of Matthew Loses His Pencil. (SPA.). (J). (gr. k-18). 8.95 *(978-980-257-299-1(3))* Ekare, Ediciones VEN. Dist: Iaconi, Mariuccia Bk. Imports.

Mass, Wendy. Beauty & the Beast: The Only One Who Didn't Run Away. (J). 2013. (Twice upon a Time Ser.: 3). (ENG.). 288p. (gr. 3-7). pap. 6.99 *(978-0-545-31019-2(9),* Scholastic Paperbacks) 2012. 282p. pap. *(978-0-545-50451-5(1))* Scholastic, Inc.

—Beauty & the Beast: The Only One Who Didn't Run Away. 2013. (Twice upon a Time Ser.: 3). lib. bdg. 17.20 *(978-0-606-31956-0(5),* Turtleback) Turtleback Bks.

—Rapunzel: The One with All the Hair. (J). 2012. (Twice upon a Time Ser.: 1). (ENG.). 208p. (gr. 3-7). pap. 6.99 *(978-0-439-79659-0(8),* Scholastic Pr.) 2005. (Illus.). 205p. *(978-0-439-80014-3(5))* Scholastic, Inc.

—Rapunzel: The One with All the Hair. 2012. (Twice upon a Time Ser.: 1). lib. bdg. 17.20 *(978-0-606-26531-7(7),* Turtleback) Turtleback Bks.

—Sleeping Beauty: The One Who Took the Really Long Nap. 2012. (Twice upon a Time Ser.: 2). lib. bdg. 17.20 *(978-0-606-26530-0(9),* Turtleback) Turtleback Bks.

Masters, Phil. Sinbad the Sailor. 2015. (Heroes & Legends Ser.). (ENG., Illus.). 80p. (J). (gr. 7-8). 35.60 *(978-1-4994-6174-9(7),* Rosen Young Adult) Rosen Publishing Group, Inc., The.

Matheis, Mickie. Sparkle Fest Showdown! (Nella the Princess Knight) Lew, Steph, illus. 2017. (Pictureback(R) Ser.). (ENG.). 24p. (J). (gr. -1-2). pap. 5.99 ***(978-1-5247-1723-0(1),*** Random Hse. Bks. for Young Readers) Random Hse. Children's Bks.

Mathis, Tabitha. The Princess & the Tyger. 2012. 28p. pap. 24.95 *(978-1-4626-8265-2(0))* America Star Bks.

Matsumoto, Reiko Odate. The Princess with the Magic Bowl: As retold from the Japanese folk tale By. 2008. 48p. pap. 22.49 *(978-1-4389-1225-7(0))* AuthorHouse.

Matthews, Caitlín, et al. Tales from Celtic Lands. Whelan, Olwyn, illus. 2008. (ENG.). 80p. (J). (gr. -1-3). 21.99 *(978-1-84686-213-7(2))* Barefoot Bks., Inc.

Matthews, John. The Barefoot Book of Knights. Manna, Giovanni, illus. 2009. (ENG.). 80p. (J). 19.99 *(978-1-84686-307-3(4))* Barefoot Bks., Inc.

Maugham, W. Somerset. A Siamese Fairy Tale. 2006. (ENG., Illus.). 30p. 19.95 *(978-974-8304-26-7(4))* Orchid Pr. THA. Dist: National Bk. Network.

Mayer, Marianna. The Adventures of Tom Thumb. Craft, Kinuko Y., illus. 2005. 28p. (J). (gr. k-4). reprint ed. 16.00 *(978-0-7567-9642-6(3))* DIANE Publishing Co.

Mbairamadji, Koffi. African Savannah Stories: Volume 2 Of 2. 2009. (Illus.). 48p. pap. 19.49 *(978-1-4389-2375-8(9))* AuthorHouse.

McAdam, Claudia Cangilla. The Mermaid's Gift, 1 vol. Van Wagoner, Traci, illus. 2015. (ENG.). 32p. (J). (gr. k-3). 16.99 *(978-1-4556-2108-8(0))* Pelican Publishing Co., Inc.

McBride, Angus, tr. & illus. Puss in Boots. McBride, Angus, illus. 2004. (ENG.). 26p. (J). (gr. 1-3). pap. 6.47 net. *(978-0-7685-0327-2(2),* Dominie Elementary) Pearson Schl.

McCafferty, Catherine. Rapunzel. Spong, Clive, illus. 2008. (Keepsake Stories Ser.). (ENG & SPA.). 32p. (gr. -1-3). pap. 3.99 *(978-0-7696-5418-8(5),* Brighter Child) Carson-Dellosa Publishing, LLC.

McCandless Iii, Bruce. Beatrice & the Basilisk. 2012. 66p. pap. 5.99 *(978-0-615-60901-0(5))* Ninth Planet Pr.

McCaughrean, Geraldine. Beauty & the Beast. Blythe, Gary, illus. 2003. (Picture Bks.). 32p. (J). (gr. -1-3). 15.95 *(978-1-57505-491-9(4),* Carolrhoda Bks.) Lerner Publishing Group.

McClinton, Theresa. The Stone Guardian. 2013. 300p. pap. 11.99 *(978-1-939194-78-7(4))* Etopia Pr.

McCombie, Karen & Collins UK Publishing Staff. The Black Bull. Dünzinger, Eva, illus. 2016. (ENG.). 48p. (J). pap. 8.95 *(978-0-00-814717-4(5))* HarperCollins Pubs. Ltd. GBR. Dist: Independent Pubs. Group.

McCullough, Kathy. Opposites Attract. 2017. (Stepping Stone Book(TM) Ser.: 2). (ENG., Illus.). 128p. (J). (gr. 1-4). 5.99 ***(978-0-7364-3828-5(9));*** lib. bdg. 12.99 ***(978-0-7364-3829-2(7))*** Random Hse. Children's Bks. (RH/Disney).

—Secrets Unlocked. 2017. (Stepping Stone Book(TM) Ser.: 1). (ENG., Illus.). 128p. (J). (gr. 1-4). 5.99 ***(978-0-7364-3826-1(2));*** lib. bdg. 12.99 ***(978-0-7364-3827-8(0))*** Random Hse. Children's Bks. (RH/Disney).

McDaniels, Preston, illus. The Prince of Ireland & the Three Magic Stallions. 2003. (ENG.). 32p. (J). (gr. k-3). tchr. ed. 16.95 *(978-0-8234-1573-1(2))* Holiday Hse., Inc.

McFadden, Deanna. Cinderella. Sokolava, Valerie, illus. 2013. (Silver Penny Stories Ser.). (ENG.). 48p. (J). (gr. -1-1). 4.95 *(978-1-4027-8333-3(7))* Sterling Publishing Co., Inc.

—The Elves & the Shoemaker. Calo, Marcos, illus. 2012. (Silver Penny Stories Ser.). (ENG.). 48p. (J). (gr. -1-1). 4.95 *(978-1-4027-8334-0(5))* Sterling Publishing Co., Inc.

—Hansel & Gretel. Graegin, Stephanie, illus. 2012. (Silver Penny Stories Ser.). (ENG.). 48p. (J). (gr. -1-1). 4.95 *(978-1-4027-8335-7(3))* Sterling Publishing Co., Inc.

—Little Red Riding Hood. Wakefield, Scott J., illus. 2013. (Silver Penny Stories Ser.). (ENG.). 48p. (J). (gr. -1-1). 4.95 *(978-1-4027-8337-1(X))* Sterling Publishing Co., Inc.

—Rumpelstiltskin. Quarello, Maurizio A. C., illus. 2014. (Silver Penny Stories Ser.). (ENG.). 48p. (J). (gr. -1-1). 4.95 *(978-1-4027-8340-1(X))* Sterling Publishing Co., Inc.

McFadden, Deanna & Andersen, Hans Christian. The Little Mermaid. Mims, Ashley, illus. 2013. (Silver Penny Stories Ser.). (ENG.). 48p. (J). (gr. -1-1). 4.95 *(978-1-4027-8336-4(1))* Sterling Publishing Co., Inc.

McFadden, Deanna, et al. Sleeping Beauty. Graegin, Stephanie, illus. 2013. (Silver Penny Stories Ser.). (ENG.). 48p. (J). (gr. -1-1). 4.95 *(978-1-4027-8341-8(8))* Sterling Publishing Co., Inc.

McGowan, Maureen. Cinderella: Ninja Warrior. 2010. 320p. pap. 8.95 *(978-1-60747-778-5(5),* Pickwick Pr.) Phoenix Bks., Inc.

McGuire, Sarah. Valiant. 2015. (ENG.). 384p. (gr. 5). 16.99 *(978-1-60684-552-3(7));* (J). 16.99 *(978-1-5124-0198-1(6))* Lerner Publishing Group. (Carolrhoda Bks.).

McHugh, Maura. Twisted Fairy Tales. Laurie, Jane, illus. 2013. (ENG.). 144p. (J). (gr. 6-11). 19.99 *(978-0-7641-6588-7(7))* Barron's Educational Series, Inc.

McKinley, Robin. Beauty: A Retelling of the Story of Beauty & the Beast. 2005. (ENG.). 336p. (YA). (gr. 3-7). pap. 8.99 *(978-0-06-075310-8(2),* HarperTeen) HarperCollins Pubs.

—Beauty: A Retelling of the Story of Beauty & the Beast. 325p. (YA). (gr. 3-18). 23.25 *(978-0-8446-7317-2(X))* Smith, Peter Pub., Inc.

—Spindle's End. 2010. (ENG.). 384p. (YA). (gr. 7). pap. 15.00 *(978-0-441-01767-6(3),* Ace Bks.) Penguin Publishing Group.

McLean, Michael & McLean, Scott. Fairy Tale Christmas. 2014. (ENG., Illus.). 176p. (J). (gr. 3-9). 15.99 *(978-1-60907-930-7(2),* Shadow Mountain) Shadow Mountain Publishing.

McLennan, Connie, illus. Domítila: A Cinderella Tale from the Mexican Tradition. 2014. (ENG.). 32p. (J). pap. 9.95 *(978-1-885008-43-5(0),* Shen's Bks.) Lee & Low Bks., Inc.

McNaughton, Janet. Brave Jack & the Unicorn. Tooke, Susan, illus. 2005. (ENG.). 32p. (J). (gr. k-3). 15.95 *(978-0-88776-677-0(3),* Tundra Bks.) Tundra Bks. CAN. Dist: Penguin Random Hse. LLC.

Meadows, Daisy. Eleanor the Snow White Fairy. 2016. (Illus.). 65p. (J). ***(978-0-545-88738-0(0))*** Scholastic, Inc.

—Elle the Thumbelina Fairy. 2017. (Storybook Fairies Ser.: 1). (ENG.). 80p. (J). (gr. 2-5). pap. 4.99 *(978-1-338-05495-8(3),* Scholastic Paperbacks) Scholastic, Inc.

—Flora the Dress-Up Fairy. 2010. (Rainbow Magic Ser.). (ENG., Illus.). 192p. (J). (gr. 2-5). 6.99 *(978-0-545-22176-4(5),* Scholastic Paperbacks) Scholastic, Inc.

—Julia the Sleeping Beauty Fairy. 2016. (Fairy Tale Fairies Ser.: 1). (ENG., Illus.). 80p. (J). (gr. 2-5). pap. 4.99 *(978-0-545-85189-3(0),* Scholastic Paperbacks) Scholastic, Inc.

—Mariana the Goldilocks Fairy. 2017. (Storybook Fairies Ser.: 2). (ENG.). 80p. (J). (gr. 2-5). pap. 4.99 *(978-1-338-05499-6(6),* Scholastic Paperbacks) Scholastic, Inc.

—Ruth the Red Riding Hood Fairy. 2017. (Storybook Fairies Ser.: 4). (ENG.). 80p. (J). (gr. 2-5). pap. 4.99 *(978-1-338-05505-4(4),* Scholastic Paperbacks) Scholastic, Inc.

Mehta, Lila. Anklet for a Princess: A Cinderella Story from India. Tang, Youshan, illus. 2014. (ENG.). 32p. (J). pap. 9.95 *(978-1-885008-46-6(5),* Shen's Bks.) Lee & Low Bks., Inc.

Meister, Cari. Beauty & the Beast Stories Around the World: 3 Beloved Tales. Madden, Colleen & Sasheva, Iva, illus. 2016. (Multicultural Fairy Tales Ser.). (ENG.). 32p. (gr. k-2). pap. 6.95 *(978-1-5158-0414-7(3))* Capstone Press of Coughlan Cos.

—Cinderella Stories Around the World: 4 Beloved Tales, 1 vol. Belloni, Valentina et al, illus. 2014. (Multicultural Fairy Tales Ser.). (ENG.). 32p. (gr. k-2). lib. bdg. 27.32 *(978-1-4795-5433-1(2))* Picture Window Bks.

—Hansel & Gretel Stories Around the World: 4 Beloved Tales. Chano, Teresa Ramos et al, illus. 2016. (Multicultural Fairy Tales Ser.). (ENG.). 32p. (gr. k-2). lib. bdg. 27.32 *(978-1-4795-9706-2(6))* Capstone Press of Coughlan Cos.

—Multicultural Fairy Tales. Chano, Teresa Ramos & Madden, Colleen, illus. 2016. (Multicultural Fairy Tales Ser.). (ENG.). 32p. (gr. k-2). 163.92 *(978-1-4795-9707-9(4))* Picture Window Bks.

—Rapunzel Stories Around the World: 3 Beloved Tales, 1 vol. Belloni, Valentina et al, illus. 2014. (Multicultural Fairy Tales Ser.). (ENG.). 32p. (gr. k-2). lib. bdg. 27.32 *(978-1-4795-5436-2(7))* Picture Window Bks.

—Scholastic Reader Level 2: Flash Forward Fairy Tales: Snow White & the Seven Dogs. Waters, Erica-Jane, illus. 2014. (Scholastic Reader Level 2 Ser.). (ENG.). 32p. (J). (gr. 1-2). pap. 3.99 *(978-0-545-56569-1(3))* Scholastic, Inc.

Menchú, Rigoberta & Liano, Dante. El Vaso de Miel. Tebalan, Helman, illus. 2003. (SPA.). 96p. (J). (gr. 5-8). pap. 13.95 *(978-970-29-0985-9(6))* Santillana USA Publishing Co., Inc.

Menotti, Gian Carlo. AMAHAL Y LOS TRES REYES. 2004. (Troquelados Clásicos Ser.). (SPA & ENG., Illus.). 16p. (J). (gr. -1-k). pap. 3.95 *(978-84-7864-735-4(X))* Combel Editorial, S.A. ESP. Dist: Independent Pubs. Group.

Metaxas, Eric. The Fool & the Flying Ship, 1 vol. Drescher, Henrick, illus. 2007. (Rabbit Ears: A Classic Tale Ser.). (ENG.). 36p. (gr. -1-3). 25.65 *(978-1-59961-308-6(5))* Spotlight.

—Jack & the Beanstalk, 1 vol. Sorel, Edward, illus. 2005. (Rabbit Ears: A Classic Tale Ser.). (ENG.). 36p. (gr. 2-7). 25.65 *(978-1-59679-345-3(7))* Spotlight.

—Puss in Boots, 1 vol. Le-Tan, Pierre, illus. 2007. (Rabbit Ears: A Classic Tale Ser.). (ENG.). 36p. (gr. -1-3). 25.65 *(978-1-59961-311-6(5))* Spotlight.

Meyer, Marissa. Cress. 2015. (Lunar Chronicles Ser.: 3). (YA). lib. bdg. 22.10 *(978-0-606-36450-8(1))* Turtleback Bks.

Mi-Leing. Chrystal's Castle. 2007. 40p. 18.50 *(978-1-4303-2242-9(X))* Lulu Pr., Inc.

Mihai, Adriana. The Inner of the Diamond Shoes. 2011. 28p. pap. 24.95 *(978-1-4560-0979-3(6))* America Star Bks.

Milbourne, Anna. Illustrated Hans Christian Andersen's Fairy Tales IR. 2015. (Illustrated Stories Ser.). (ENG.). 280p. (J). (gr. k-5). 19.99 *(978-0-7945-3201-7(2),* Usborne) EDC Publishing.

Miles, Linda, et al. Amanda Salamander & the Secret of Happily Ever After. 2005. (J). cd-rom 7.99 *(978-0-9778623-4-4(8))* Miles & Assocs.

Miles, Robin, reader. Mufaro's Beautiful Daughters: An African Tale. 2003. (Illus.). (J). (gr. -1-2). pap. 35.95 incl. audio compact disk *(978-1-59112-541-9(3))* Live Oak Media.

Miller, Bobbi. One Fine Trade. Hillenbrand, Will, illus. 2009. (ENG.). 32p. (J). (gr. -1-3). 16.95 *(978-0-8234-1836-7(7))* Holiday Hse., Inc.

Miller, Connie Colwell. Mary, Anna, & the Little Brother: The Lion, the Bear, & the Fox Remixed. Assanelli, Victoria, illus. 2016. (Aesop's Fables Remixed Ser.). (ENG.). 24p. (J). (gr. k-3). 20.95 *(978-1-60753-955-1(1),* Amicus Illustrated) Amicus Publishing.

—Rosie's Special Gift: The Goose Who Laid the Golden Eggs Remixed. Assanelli, Victoria, illus. 2016. (Aesop's Fables Remixed Ser.). (ENG.). 24p. (J). (gr. k-3). 20.95 *(978-1-60753-953-7(5),* Amicus Illustrated) Amicus Publishing.

Miller, Connie Colwell & Aesop. Abby Visits the Big City: The City Mouse & the Country Mouse Remixed. Assanelli, Victoria, illus. 2016. (Aesop's Fables Remixed Ser.). (ENG.). 24p. (J). (gr. k-3). 20.95 *(978-1-60753-952-0(7))* Amicus Publishing.

—Andrew & the Birthday Surprise: The Boy Who Cried Wolf Remixed. Assanelli, Victoria, illus. 2016. (Aesop's Fables Remixed Ser.). (ENG.). 24p. (J). (gr. k-3). 20.95 *(978-1-60753-951-3(9))* Amicus Publishing.

—Henry's Track & Field Day: The Tortoise & the Hare Remixed. Assanelli, Victoria, illus. 2016. (Aesop's Fables Remixed Ser.). (ENG.). 24p. (J). (gr. k-3). 20.95 *(978-1-60753-950-6(0))* Amicus Publishing.

—James & the Kindergartener: The Lion & the Mouse Remixed. Assanelli, Victoria, illus. 2016. (Aesop's Fables Remixed Ser.). (ENG.). 24p. (J). (gr. k-3). 20.95 *(978-1-60753-954-4(3))* Amicus Publishing.

Miller, Eileen Rudisill. Fairy Tale Princesses Paper Dolls. 2012. (Dover Paper Dolls Ser.). (ENG.). 32p. (J). (gr. k-3). pap. 7.99 *(978-0-486-48990-2(6))* Dover Pubns., Inc.

Millman, Selena. More Than a Hero. 2006. 92p. (YA). per. 11.37 *(978-1-4243-2351-7(7))* Independent Publisher Services.

Minden, Cecilia & Roth, Kate. How to Write a Fairy Tale. 2012. (Explorer Junior Library: Language Arts Explorer Junior Ser.). (ENG.). 24p. (gr. 1-4). lib. bdg. 25.64 *(978-1-61080-309-0(4),* 201282) Cherry Lake Publishing.

Minden, Cecilia, et al. How to Write a Fairy Tale. 2012. (Explorer Junior Library: Language Arts Explorer Junior Ser.). (ENG.). 24p. (gr. 1-4). pap. 12.79 *(978-1-61080-319-9(1),* 201284) Cherry Lake Publishing.

Minh Quoc. Tam & Cam/Tam Cam: The Ancient Vietnamese Cinderella Story. Smith, William, tr. from VIE. Mai Long, illus. 2006. (ENG & VIE.). 32p. (J). (gr. 1-4). 16.95 *(978-0-9701654-4-2(7))* East West Discovery Pr.

Mini Cuentos: Atletas se Entrenan, Zorro y la Cigüena.Tr. of Mini Fairy Tales: Fox & the Swan. (SPA.). (J). (gr. k-4). 4.98 *(978-970-607-621-2(2))* Larousse, Ediciones, S. A. de C. V. MEX. Dist: Continental Bk. Co., Inc.

Mini Cuentos: Hazanas de Baltazar, Pipo, el Perro Fiel.Tr. of Mini Faiy Tales: Pipo, the Loyal Dog. (SPA.). (J). (gr. k-4). 4.98 *(978-970-607-622-9(0))* Larousse, Ediciones, S. A. de C. V. MEX. Dist: Continental Bk. Co., Inc.

Mini Cuentos: Relampago, Caballo Salvaje, Pelirrojo y Tania.Tr. of Mini Faiy Tales: Lightning the Wild Horse. (SPA.). (J). (gr. k-4). 4.98 *(978-970-607-620-5(4))* Larousse, Ediciones, S. A. de C. V. MEX. Dist: Continental Bk. Co., Inc.

Mini Cuentos: Rey de los Sapos, Sapatillas Rojas.Tr. of Mini Fairy Tales: King & His Shoes. (SPA.). (J). (gr. k-4). 4.98 *(978-970-607-619-9(0))* Larousse, Ediciones, S. A. de C. V. MEX. Dist: Continental Bk. Co., Inc.

Mitchell, Denise K. Starbyte the Computer Fairy Collection. 2009. 67p. pap. 10.68 *(978-1-4452-2435-0(6))* Lulu Pr., Inc.

Mitchell, N. J. W. The Search. 2003. 110p. pap. 9.95 *(978-0-595-27251-8(7),* Writers Club Pr.) iUniverse, Inc.

Mlynowski, Sarah. Bad Hair Day. 2014. (Whatever After Ser.: No. 5). (ENG.). 176p. (J). (gr. 3-7). 14.99 *(978-0-545-62728-3(1),* Scholastic Pr.) Scholastic, Inc.

—Beauty Queen. (Whatever After Ser.: 7). (ENG.). 176p. (J). (gr. 3-7). 2016. pap. 5.99 *(978-0-545-74657-1(4))* 2015. 14.99 *(978-0-545-74654-0(X))* Scholastic, Inc. (Scholastic Pr.).

—Cold As Ice. 2015. (Whatever After Ser.: 6). (ENG.). 176p. (J). (gr. 3-7). pap. 5.99 *(978-0-545-62736-8(2),* Scholastic Pr.) Scholastic, Inc.

—Cold as Ice. 2014. (Whatever After Ser.: 6). (ENG.). 176p. (J). (gr. 3-7). 14.99 *(978-0-545-62734-4(6),* Scholastic Pr.) Scholastic, Inc.

—Genie in a Bottle (Whatever After #9) 2016. (Whatever After Ser.: 9). (ENG.). 176p. (J). (gr. 3-7). 14.99 *(978-0-545-85102-2(5),* Scholastic Pr.) Scholastic, Inc.

—If the Shoe Fits. 2013. (Whatever After Ser.: 2). (ENG.). 176p. (J). (gr. 3-7). 14.99 *(978-0-545-41567-5(5),* Scholastic Pr.) Scholastic, Inc.

—Once upon a Frog. 2015. (Whatever After Ser.: 8). (ENG., Illus.). 176p. (J). (gr. 3-7). 14.99 *(978-0-545-74660-1(4),* Scholastic Pr.) Scholastic, Inc.

—Sink or Swim. (Whatever After Ser.: 3). (J). 2014. (ENG.). 176p. (gr. 3-7). pap. 5.99 *(978-0-545-41570-5(5))* 2013. 165p. *(978-0-545-53316-4(3))*Bk. 3. 2013. (ENG.). 176p. (gr. 3-7). 14.99 *(978-0-545-41569-9(1))* Scholastic, Inc. (Scholastic Pr.).

—Sugar & Spice. 2016. (Whatever After Ser.: 10). (ENG.). 176p. (J). (gr. 3-7). 14.99 *(978-0-545-85106-0(8),* Scholastic Pr.) Scholastic, Inc.

—Whatever After Boxset, Bks. 1-6. 2015. (Whatever After Ser.). (ENG.). (J). (gr. 3-7). pap., pap., pap. 35.94 *(978-0-545-85576-1(4))* Scholastic, Inc.

—Whatever after Collection, Bks. 1-3. 2016. (Whatever After Ser.). (ENG.). 528p. (J). (gr. 3-7). pap. 9.99 *(978-1-338-10175-1(7))* Scholastic, Inc.

Moerbeck, Kees, illus. & des. Cinderella. Moerbeck, Kees, des. 2006. (Roly Poly Box Bks.). (ENG.). 24p. (J). *(978-1-84643-019-0(4))* Child's Play International Ltd.

Moerbeek, Kees. Cinderella. 2011. (My Secret Scrapbook Diary Ser.). (ENG., Illus.). 10p. (J). *(978-1-84643-450-1(5))* Child's Play International Ltd.

—Jack's & the Beanstalk. 2011. (My Secret Scrapbook Diary Ser.). (ENG., Illus.). 10p. (J). *(978-1-84643-449-5(1))* Child's Play International Ltd.

—Little Red Riding Hood. 2011. (My Secret Scrapbook Diary Ser.). (ENG., Illus.). 10p. (J). *(978-1-84643-447-1(5))* Child's Play International Ltd.

—Puss in Boots. 2014. (My Secret Scrapbook Diary Ser.). (ENG., Illus.). 10p. (J). *(978-1-84643-592-8(7))* Child's Play International Ltd.

—The Three Little Pigs. 2011. (My Secret Scrapbook Diary Ser.). (ENG., Illus.). 10p. (J). *(978-1-84643-448-8(3))* Child's Play International Ltd.

—The Ugly Duckling. 2014. (My Secret Scrapbook Diary Ser.). (ENG., Illus.). 10p. (J). *(978-1-84643-593-5(5))* Child's Play International Ltd.

El Mono Azul. (Fantasmas de Fear Street Coleccion). (SPA.). (YA). (gr. 5-8). pap. 7.95 *(978-950-04-2022-8(8),* EM10965) Emecé Editores S.A. ARG. Dist: Planeta Publishing Corp., Lectorum Pubns., Inc.

Monroe, George. The Secret Cave on the Hill. 2012. 50p. pap. 21.99 *(978-1-4772-8840-5(6))* AuthorHouse.

Moore, Billy. Cracker's Mule. 2003. (ENG.). 256p. (J). pap. 12.95 *(978-1-58838-105-7(6),* NewSouth Bks.) NewSouth, Inc.

Moore, Raina. A Charming Princess. 2005. (Charming Classics). 256p. (J). pap. 6.99 *(978-0-06-059604-0(X),* HarperFestival) HarperCollins Pubs.

Mora, Pat. Doña Flor: Un Cuento de una Mujer Gigante con un Gran Corazon. Colón, Raúl, illus. 2005. (SPA.). 40p. (J). (gr. -1-2). per. 7.99 *(978-0-440-41768-2(6),* Dragonfly Bks.) Random Hse. Children's Bks.

Morgan, Winter. Attack of the Goblin Army: Tales of a Terrarian Warrior, Book One. 2016. (ENG.). 112p. (J). (gr. 1-7). pap. 7.99 *(978-1-5107-1682-7(3),* Sky Pony Pr.) Skyhorse Publishing Co., Inc.

Moriarty, Kathleen M. Wiil Waal: A Somali Folktale. Adam, Jamal, tr. Amir, Amin Abd al-Fattah Mahmud, illus. 2007. (SOM & ENG.). 32p. (J). (gr. -1-3). 15.95 *(978-1-931016-16-2(X))* Minnesota Humanities Ctr.

Morlock, Theresa. Fairy & Leprechaun Legends. 2017. (Famous Legends Ser.). 32p. (J). (gr. 2-3). pap. 10.50 ***(978-1-5382-0353-8(7))*** Stevens, Gareth Publishing LLLP.

Morpurgo, Michael. Beauty & the Beast. 2017. (Collins Big Cat Tales Ser.). (ENG., Illus.). 32p. (J). (gr. 2-3). pap. 8.99 *(978-0-00-817933-5(6))* HarperCollins Pubs. Ltd. GBR. Dist: Independent Pubs. Group.

Morris, Jackie. The Wild Swans. 2015. (ENG., Illus.). 176p. (J). (gr. 6-9). 18.99 *(978-1-84780-536-2(1),* Frances Lincoln) Quarto Publishing Group UK GBR. Dist: Hachette Bk. Group.

Morrison, Megan. Disenchanted: The Trials of Cinderella. 2016. (Tyme Ser.: 2). (ENG., Illus.). 416p. (J). (gr. 3-7). 17.99 *(978-0-545-64271-2(X),* Levine, Arthur A. Bks.) Scholastic, Inc.

—Grounded: The Tale of Rapunzel. 2015. (Illus.). 374p. (J). *(978-0-545-75468-2(2))* Scholastic, Inc.

Morrison, Toni & Morrison, Slade. The Lion or the Mouse? Lemaître, Pascal, illus. 2014. (Who's Got Game? Ser.: 2). (ENG.). 36p. pap. 13.99 *(978-1-4767-9268-2(2),* Scribner) Scribner.

—The Tortoise or the Hare. Cepeda, Joe, illus. 2014. (ENG.). 32p. (J). (gr. -1-3). 7.99 *(978-1-4169-8335-4(X),* Simon & Schuster/Paula Wiseman Bks.) Simon & Schuster/Paula Wiseman Bks.

Morrissey, Donna. What Beautiful Mistake Did You Make Today? 2012. 24p. pap. 13.95 *(978-1-4772-5669-5(5))* AuthorHouse.

Mortimer, Rachael. Red Riding Hood & the Sweet Little Wolf. Pichon, Liz, illus. 2013. (ENG.). 32p. 12.95 *(978-1-58925-117-5(2))* Tiger Tales.

—The Three Billy Goats Fluff. Pichon, Liz, illus. 2013. (ENG.). 32p. (J). (gr. -1-2). pap. 7.95 *(978-1-58925-439-8(2))* Tiger Tales.

—Three Billy Goats Fluff. Pichon, Liz, illus. 2011. (ENG.). 36p. 15.95 *(978-1-58925-101-4(6))* Tiger Tales.

EFG

Moses, Will & Wells, Rosemary. Fairy Tales for Little Folks. 2015. (ENG., Illus.). 48p. (J). (gr. -1-2). bds. 17.99 (978-0-451-47283-0(7), Viking Books for Young Readers) Penguin Young Readers Group.

Moss, Jenny. Shadow. 2010. (ENG.). 384p. (J). (gr. 7-18). 17.99 (978-0-545-03641-2(0), Scholastic Pr.) Scholastic, Inc.

Mounter, Paddy, retold by. Ali Baba & the Forty Thieves. 2004. (Young Reading Series One Ser.). (Illus.). 48p. (J). (gr. 2-18). pap. 5.95 (978-0-7945-0667-4(4), Usborne) EDC Publishing.

Mouse Works Staff. Snow White Classic. rev. ed. 7.99 (978-1-57082-977-2(2)) Mouse Works.

Mukthavaram, Vasantha. Aesop's Fables: Eternal Leaf Art. Mukthavaram, Vasantha, illus. 2011. (ENG., Illus.). (J). 19.99 (978-0-615-46456-5(4)) Vikasam.

Muloch, Miss. The Little Lame Prince & Other Tales. 2007. 304p. 24.95 (978-1-4344-9379-8(2)); per. 16.95 (978-1-4344-9378-1(4)) Wildside Pr., LLC.

Mulock, Dinah Maria. The Little Lame Prince & the Adventures of a Brownie. Date not set. lib. bdg. 25.95 (978-0-8488-2095-4(9)) Amereon Ltd.

Mulrain, Sabrina. A Prince's Happy Ever After. 2011. 40p. pap. 24.95 (978-1-4560-3251-7(8)) America Star Bks.

Murdock, Catherine Gilbert. Princess Ben. 2009. (ENG.). 352p. (YA). (gr. 7). pap. 9.99 (978-0-547-22325-4(0)) Houghton Mifflin Harcourt Publishing Co.

Murphy, Breena. The Fairy Seekers - the Sand Fairy. Waid, Sara Joyce & Waid, Antoinette M., illus. l.t. ed. 2006. 284p. (J). 24.95 (978-0-9788010-1-4(6)) Edes Publishing Co.

—The Fairy Seekers - the Sand Fairy, 1. Waid, Sara J. & Waid, Antoinette M., illus. l.t. ed. 2006. 284p. (J). per. 14.95 (978-0-9788010-0-7(8)) Edes Publishing Co.

Murphy, Shirley Rousseau. Silver Woven in My Hair. 2015. (ENG., Illus.). 128p. (J). (gr. 3-7). pap. 13.99 (978-1-4814-5865-8(5), Atheneum Bks. for Young Readers) Simon & Schuster Children's Publishing.

Murray, M. A., tr. Pinocchio, As First Translated into English by M a Murray & Illustrated by Charles Folkard. Folkard, Charles, illus. 2009. 280p. pap. 11.95 (978-1-59915-177-9(4)) Yesterday's Classics.

Nadin, Joanna. Snow White & Rose Red: Band 12/Copper. 2017. (Collins Big Cat Tales Ser.). (ENG., Illus.). 32p. (J). (gr. 2-8). pap. 7.99 **(978-0-00-817929-8(8))** HarperCollins Pubs. Ltd. GBR. Dist: Independent Pubs. Group.

Namm, Diane. The Emperor's New Clothes. Mims, Ashley, illus. 2014. (Silver Penny Stories Ser.). (ENG.). 48p. (J). (gr. -1-1). 4.95 (978-1-4027-8428-6(7)) Sterling Publishing Co., Inc.

—The Frog Prince. Quarello, Maurizio A. C., illus. 2013. (Silver Penny Stories Ser.). (ENG.). 48p. (J). (gr. -1-1). 4.95 (978-1-4027-8429-3(5)) Sterling Publishing Co., Inc.

—Jack & the Beanstalk. Quarello, Maurizio A. C., illus. 2012. (Silver Penny Stories Ser.). (ENG.). 48p. (J). (gr. -1-1). 4.95 (978-1-4027-8433-0(3)) Sterling Publishing Co., Inc.

—The Ugly Duckling. Brannen, Sarah, illus. 2012. (Silver Penny Stories Ser.). (ENG.). 48p. (J). (gr. -1-1). 4.95 (978-1-4027-8437-8(6)) Sterling Publishing Co., Inc.

Namm, Diane & Andersen, Hans Christian. The Princess & the Pea. Zilber, Denis & Olafsdottir, Linda, illus. 2013. (Silver Penny Stories Ser.). (ENG.). 48p. (J). (gr. -1-1). 4.95 (978-1-4027-8436-1(8)) Sterling Publishing Co., Inc.

Naomi, Aunt. Jewish Fairy Tales & Legends. 2006. pap. 28.95 (978-1-4254-9788-0(8)) Kessinger Publishing, LLC.

Napoli, Donna Jo. Beast. 2004. (ENG., Illus.). 272p. (YA). (gr. 7). mass mkt. 8.99 (978-0-689-87005-7(1), Simon Pulse) Simon Pulse.

—Zel. 2005. 240p. (J). (gr. 5-9). 21.00 (978-0-8446-7278-6(5), 3593) Smith, Peter Pub., Inc.

Nash, Linda. The Legend of the Lilies. 2013. (ENG.). 64p. (J). 17.95 (978-1-4497-8378-5(3), WestBow Pr.) Author Solutions, Inc.

Nazran, Govinder, illus. Aladdin. (ENG.). 2017. 24p. pap. 7.99 (978-1-86147-819-1(4)) 2014. 48p. (J). (gr. 2-5). pap. 7.99 (978-1-84322-790-8(8)) Anness Publishing GBR. (Armadillo). Dist: National Bk. Network.

Negrin, Fabian, illus. Wizard Tales. 2003. 96p. 19.95 (978-1-55285-558-4(9)) Whitecap Bks., Ltd. CAN. Dist: Graphic Arts Ctr. Publishing Co.

Nelson, Amanda. The Buttermilk Biscuit Boy, 1 vol. Klein, Laurie, illus. 2014. (ENG.). 32p. (J). (gr. k-3). 16.99 (978-1-4556-1970-2(1)) Pelican Publishing Co., Inc.

Neru, Enna. An African Tale. 2009. 159p. (YA). pap. 13.95 (978-1-4327-2348-4(0)) Outskirts Pr., Inc.

Nesbit, E. Jack & the Beanstalk. Tavares, Matt, illus. 2006. (ENG.). 48p. (J). (gr. -1-2). 16.99 (978-0-7636-2124-7(2)) Candlewick Pr.

—Story of the Amulet. 2006. pap. (978-1-4068-3506-9(4)) Echo Library.

—The Story of the Amulet. 2007. 264p. per. 13.95 (978-1-4218-3946-2(6), 1st World Library - Literary Society) 1st World Publishing, Inc.

—The Story of the Amulet. l.t. ed. 2005. 396p. pap. (978-1-84637-206-3(2)) Echo Library.

—The Story of the Amulet. 2010. (CHI.). 270p. (YA). pap. (978-986-146-634-7(7)) Storm & Stress Publishing Co, Ltd.

New York City Ballet, New York. George Balanchine's the Nutcracker. Docampo, Valeria, illus. 2016. (ENG.). 40p. (J). (gr. -1-3). 17.99 (978-1-4814-5829-0(9), Little Simon) Little Simon.

Niland, Kilmeny. The Gingerbread Man. 2006. (Illus.). 16p. (978-1-921049-49-1(9)) Little Hare Bks. AUS. Dist: HarperCollins Pubs. Australia.

Nobacon, Danbert. 3 Dead Princes: An Anarchist Fairy Tale. Cox, Alex, illus. 2010. (ENG.). 208p. (gr. 8-18). pap. 13.00 (978-1-935259-06-0(7)) Exterminating Angel Pr.

Nolte, Nancy. Richard Scarry's the Gingerbread Man. Scarry, Richard, illus. 2015. (Little Golden Book Ser.). (ENG.). 24p. (J). (-k). 4.99 (978-0-385-37619-8(7), Golden Bks.) Random Hse. Children's Bks.

North, Laura. Cinderella: The Terrible Truth. Dreidemy, Joëlle, illus. 2014. (ENG.). 32p. (J). (978-0-7787-1326-5(1)) Crabtree Publishing Co.

—Hansel & Gretel & the Green Witch. Jevons, Chris, illus. 2015. (ENG.). 32p. (J). (978-0-7787-1928-1(6)) Crabtree Publishing Co.

—The Pied Piper & the Wrong Song. Anderson, Scoular, illus. 2015. (ENG.). 32p. (J). (978-0-7787-1934-2(0)) Crabtree Publishing Co.

Nosy Crow Staff. Cinderella: A Nosy Crow Fairy Tale. Bryan, Ed, illus. 2016. (ENG.). (J). (gr. -1-2). 9.99 (978-0-7636-8654-3(9), Nosy Crow) Candlewick Pr.

—Jack & the Beanstalk: a Nosy Crow Fairy Tale. Bryan, Ed, illus. 2017. (ENG.). 32p. (J). (gr. -1-2). 9.99 (978-0-7636-9332-9(4), Nosy Crow) Candlewick Pr.

—Little Red Riding Hood: a Nosy Crow Fairy Tale. Bryan, Ed, illus. 2017. (ENG.). 32p. (J). (gr. -1-2). 9.99 (978-0-7636-9331-2(6), Nosy Crow) Candlewick Pr.

—The Three Little Pigs: A Nosy Crow Fairy Tale. Bryan, Ed, illus. 2016. (ENG.). (J). (gr. -1-2). 9.99 (978-0-7636-8655-0(7), Nosy Crow) Candlewick Pr.

Not Again Red Riding Hood. 2004. (J). E-Book incl. cd-rom (978-1-84444-464-9(3)) Mantra Lingua.

Nowell, Daphne A. Juana Meets Gabriel, the Small Business Angel: What if you Don't Want to Wait Around for a Prince Charming? 2008. (Illus.). 24p. (J). 17.95 (978-0-9798909-1-8(8)) Business Angel Pr.

O'Leary-Coggins, Annette. The Rescueteers' Christmas Mission: Book 2. 2010. 168p. 22.95 (978-1-4502-3085-8(7)); pap. 12.95 (978-1-4502-3087-2(3)) iUniverse, Inc.

O'Leary, John. Goldilocks: A Pop-Up Book. O'Leary, John, illus. 2015. (ENG., Illus.). 16p. (J). (gr. -1-k). 19.99 (978-1-85707-888-6(8)) Tango Bks. GBR. Dist: Independent Pubs. Group.

Oliver, Jana. Briar Rose, 1. unabr. ed. 2015. (ENG.). 480p. (YA). (gr. 8). pap. 9.99 (978-1-4472-4109-6(6)) Pan Macmillan GBR. Dist: Independent Pubs. Group.

Oliver, Juanbjuan, illus. The Prince & the Three Oranges a Fairy Tale from Mexico. 2017. (Text Connections Guided Close Reading Ser.). (J). (gr. 1). (978-1-4900-1822-5(0)) Benchmark Education Co.

Olmstead, Kathleen. The Pied Piper of Hamelin. Brannen, Sarah S., illus. 2014. (Silver Penny Stories Ser.). (ENG.). 48p. (J). (gr. -1-1). 4.95 (978-1-4027-8349-4(3)) Sterling Publishing Co., Inc.

—The Sorcerer's Apprentice. Olafsdottir, Linda, illus. 2015. (J). (978-1-4027-8350-0(7)) Sterling Publishing Co., Inc.

Olmstead, Kathleen & Andersen, Hans Christian. The Little Match Girl. Kim, Jin-Woo, illus. 2014. (J). (978-1-4027-8348-7(5)) Sterling Publishing Co., Inc.

—The Steadfast Tin Soldier. Calo, Marcos, illus. 2013. (Silver Penny Stories Ser.). (ENG.). 48p. (J). (gr. -1-1). 4.95 (978-1-4027-8351-7(5)) Sterling Publishing Co., Inc.

Olmstead, Kathleen & Olafsdottir, Linda. Beauty & the Beast. 2014. (Silver Penny Stories Ser.). (ENG., Illus.). 48p. (J). (gr. -1-1). 4.95 (978-1-4027-8343-2(4)) Sterling Publishing Co., Inc.

Olmstead, Kathleen, et al. Thumbelina. Sokolava, Valerie, illus. 2013. (Silver Penny Stories Ser.). (ENG.). 48p. (J). (gr. -1-1). 4.95 (978-1-4027-8352-4(3)) Sterling Publishing Co., Inc.

O'Malley, Kevin. Once upon a Cool Motorcycle Dude. O'Malley, Kevin et al, illus. 2005. (ENG.). 32p. (J). (gr. 1-5). 16.99 (978-0-8027-8947-1(1), 9780802789471, Bloomsbury USA Childrens) Bloomsbury Publishing USA.

Once upon a Time Spanish Version-Jack & the Beanstalk. 2005. (J). (978-1-57022-560-4(5)) ECS Learning Systems, Inc.

Once upon a Time Spanish Version-Little Red Riding Hood. 2005. (J). (978-1-57022-562-8(1)) ECS Learning Systems, Inc.

Once upon a Time Spanish Version-the Gingerbread Man. 2005. (J). (978-1-57022-556-7(7)) ECS Learning Systems, Inc.

O'Neill, Tom. Old Friends. 2010. (ENG.). 436p. (J). (gr. 3-7). pap. 12.99 (978-1-84840-941-5(9)) Little Island IRL. Dist: Independent Pubs. Group.

The Ooshes A Wish Comes True. 2005. (J). (978-1-932233-05-6(9)) Aurora Libris Corp.

The Ooshes the Night Before Christmas. 2004. (J). mass mkt. (978-1-932233-03-2(2)) Aurora Libris Corp.

Orford, Margie. The Magic Fish. Littlewort, Lizza, illus. 2012. (Best Loved Tales for Africa Ser.). (ENG.). 32p. (J). (gr. k-2). pap. 9.95 (978-1-77009-822-0(4)) Jacana Media ZAF. Dist: Independent Pubs. Group.

Orsi, Tea & Panaro, Carlo. Disney Fairies Graphic Novel #13: Tinker Bell & the Pixie Hollow Games. Razzi, Manuela et al, illus. 2013. (Disney Fairies Ser.: 13). (ENG.). 64p. (J). (gr. 1-6). 11.99 (978-1-59707-447-6(0), 9781597074476); pap. 7.99 (978-1-59707-446-9(2), 9781597074469) Papercutz.

Ortiz, Zirzeria. The Queen in Me & My Bumblebee. 2008. 48p. pap. 24.95 (978-1-60441-045-7(0)) America Star Bks.

Osborne, Mary Pope. The Brave Little Seamstress. Potter, Giselle, illus. 2006. 32p. (gr. -1-3). 17.00 (978-0-7569-6613-3(2)) Perfection Learning Corp.

Osborne, Mary Pope & Osborne, Will. Sleeping Bobby. Potter, Giselle, illus. 2005. (ENG.). 40p. (J). (gr. -1-3). 19.99 (978-0-689-87668-4(8), Atheneum Bks. for Young Readers) Simon & Schuster Children's Publishing.

Osei, Leah. The Bremen Town Musicians: A Retelling of the Story by the Brother's Grimm. rev. ed. 2013. (Fiction Readers Ser.). (ENG., Illus.). 28p. (gr. 3-3). pap. 19.96 (978-1-4807-1723-7(1)) Teacher Created Materials, Inc.

—The Bremen Town Musicians: A Retelling of the Story by the Brothers Grimm, 1 vol. rev. ed. 2013. (Fiction Readers Ser.). (ENG., Illus.). 28p. (J). (gr. 3-3). pap. 8.99 (978-1-4333-5601-8(5)) Shell Educational Publishing.

Ottolenghi, Carol. La Bella Durmiente. 2009. (Keepsake Stories Ser.).Tr. of Sleeping Beauty. (SPA & ENG.). 32p. (gr. -1-2). pap. 3.99 (978-0-7696-5862-9(8), Brighter Child) Carson-Dellosa Publishing, LLC.

—Juan y los Frijoles Magicos (Jack & the Beanstalk), Grades PK-3. Porfirio, Guy, illus. 2005. (Keepsake Stories Ser.). (SPA & ENG.). 32p. (gr. -1-3). pap. 3.99 (978-0-7696-3816-4(3), Brighter Child) Carson-Dellosa Publishing, LLC.

—The Princess & the Pea. 2009. (Keepsake Stories Ser.). (ENG.). 32p. (gr. -1-3). pap. 3.99 (978-0-7696-5869-8(5), Brighter Child) Carson-Dellosa Publishing, LLC.

—The Princess & the Pea (La Princesa y el Guisante) 2009. (Keepsake Stories Ser.). (ENG & SPA.). 32p. (gr. -1-2). pap. 3.99 (978-0-7696-5865-0(2), Brighter Child) Carson-Dellosa Publishing, LLC.

—Puss in Boots. 2009. (Keepsake Stories Ser.). (ENG.). 32p. (gr. -1-3). pap. 3.99 (978-0-7696-5867-4(9), Brighter Child) Carson-Dellosa Publishing, LLC.

—Puss in Boots (El Gato con Botas) 2009. (Keepsake Stories Ser.). (ENG & SPA.). 32p. (gr. -1-2). pap. 3.99 (978-0-7696-5863-6(6), Brighter Child) Carson-Dellosa Publishing, LLC.

—Sleeping Beauty. 2009. (Keepsake Stories Ser.). (ENG.). 32p. (gr. -1-3). pap. 3.99 (978-0-7696-5866-7(0), Brighter Child) Carson-Dellosa Publishing, LLC.

—The Three Billy Goats Gruff. 2009. (Keepsake Stories Ser.). (ENG.). 32p. (gr. -1-3). pap. 3.99 (978-0-7696-5868-1(7), Brighter Child) Carson-Dellosa Publishing, LLC.

—The Three Billy Goats Gruff (Los Tres Chivitos) 2009. (Keepsake Stories Ser.). (ENG & SPA.). 32p. (gr. -1-2). pap. 3.99 (978-0-7696-5864-3(4), Brighter Child) Carson-Dellosa Publishing, LLC.

Owen, Sarah. The Enchanted Tales. 2009. 39p. pap. 26.50 (978-1-4452-5948-2(6)) Lulu Pr., Inc.

Owings, Lisa. What Are Legends, Folktales, & Other Classic Stories? 2014. (Name That Text Type! Ser.). (Illus.). 32p. (gr. 2-4). pap. 7.95 (978-1-4677-4518-5(9)) Lerner Publishing Group.

Oxenbury, Helen. The Helen Oxenbury Nursery Collection. Oxenbury, Helen, illus. 2014. (ENG., Illus.). 96p. (J). (gr. -1-1). 22.99 (978-1-4052-6742-7(9)) Egmont Bks., Ltd. GBR. Dist: Independent Pubs. Group.

Ozaki, Yei Theodora. Japanese Fairy Tales. 2005. 28.95 (978-1-4218-0697-6(5)) 2004. 280p. pap. 13.95 (978-1-59540-147-2(4)) 1st World Publishing, Inc. (1st World Library - Literary Society).

—Japanese Fairy Tales. 2004. reprint ed. pap. 1.99 (978-1-4192-2730-1(0)); pap. 22.95 (978-1-4191-2730-4(6)) Kessinger Publishing, LLC.

Ozaki, Yei Theodora, compiled by. Japanese Fairy Tales. 2007. (Tuttle Classics Ser.). (ENG., Illus.). 256p. (J). (gr. 3-8). pap. 16.95 (978-4-8053-0881-3(8)) Tuttle Publishing.

Ozaki, Yei Theodora, ed. Japanese Fairy Tales. (Twelve-Point Ser.). 2003. lib. bdg. 25.00 (978-1-58287-266-7(X)) 2004. 335p. 26.00 (978-1-58287-750-1(5)) North Bks.

Page, Nick & Page, Claire. The King of Spring. Robert, Yannick, illus. 2006. (Read with Me (Make Believe Ideas) Ser.). 31p. (J). (gr. k-2). (978-1-84610-169-4(7)) Make Believe Ideas.

—Read with Me Rumpelstiltskin: Sticker Activity Book. Baker, Sara, illus. 2006. (Read with Me (Make Believe Ideas) Ser.). 12p. (J). (gr. k-2). pap. (978-1-84610-182-3(4)) Make Believe Ideas.

—Read with Me Three Billy Goats Gruff: Sticker Activity Book. Saunders, Katie, illus. 2006. (Read with Me (Make Believe Ideas) Ser.). 12p. (J). (gr. k-2). pap. (978-1-84610-181-6(6)) Make Believe Ideas.

—Ready to Read Jack & the Beanstalk Sticker Activity Workbook. Goodberry, Jo, illus. 2006. (Ready-to-Read Sticker Ser.). 12p. (J). (gr. -1-3). pap., wbk. ed., act. bk. ed. (978-1-84610-127-4(1)) Make Believe Ideas.

—Three Billy Goats Gruff. 2006. (Read with Me (Make Believe Ideas) Ser.). (Illus.). 32p. (J). (gr. k-2). (978-1-84610-165-6(4)) Make Believe Ideas.

—The Winter Prince. Shimmen, Cathy, illus. 2006. (Read with Me (Make Believe Ideas) Ser.). 31p. (J). (gr. k-2). (978-1-84610-172-4(7)) Make Believe Ideas.

Page, Nick & Claire. The Autumn Princess. 2006. (Read with Me (Make Believe Ideas) Ser.). (Illus.). 32p. (J). (gr. k-2). (978-1-84610-171-7(9)) Make Believe Ideas.

—Elves & the Shoemaker. 2006. (Read with Me (Make Believe Ideas) Ser.). (Illus.). 32p. (J). (gr. k-2). (978-1-84610-161-8(1)) Make Believe Ideas.

Page, P. K. The Sky Tree. Bridgeman, Kristi, illus. 2009. (ENG.). 112p. (J). 19.95 (978-0-88982-258-0(1)) Oolichan Bks. CAN. Dist: Univ. of Toronto Pr.

Palatini, Margie. Lousy Rotten Stinkin' Grapes. Moser, Barry, illus. 2009. (ENG.). 32p. (J). (gr. -1-3). 17.99 (978-0-689-80246-1(3), Simon & Schuster Bks. For Young Readers) Simon & Schuster Bks. For Young Readers.

Pankhurst, Kate, illus. The Three Billy Goats Gruff. adapted ed. 2015. (My First Fairy Tales Ser.). (ENG.). 32p. (J). 7.99 (978-1-58925-459-6(7)) Tiger Tales.

Pantages, Joanna. Fairytale Fitness: Holygrain. 2009. 24p. pap. 12.49 (978-1-4389-4494-4(2)) AuthorHouse.

—Fairytale Fitness: The Goobyland Race. 2009. 20p. pap. 11.95 (978-1-4389-5480-6(8)) AuthorHouse.

Parker, Vic, compiled by. Down the Rabbit Hole & Other Silly Stories. 2016. (Silly Stories Ser.). (ENG.). 40p. (J). (gr. 2-3). pap. 14.05 (978-1-4824-4179-6(9)) Stevens, Gareth Publishing LLLP.

—50 Scary Fairy Tales. 2013. (Illus.). 512p. (J). (978-1-4351-4984-7(X)) Barnes & Noble, Inc.

Parker, Vic, ed. The Boy Who Cried Wolf & Other Fables. 2014. (Aesop's Fables Ser.). 40p. (J). (gr. 2-5). pap. 84.95 (978-1-4824-1254-3(3)) Stevens, Gareth Publishing LLLP.

—The Dog in the Manger & Other Fables. 2014. (Aesop's Fables Ser.). 40p. (J). (gr. 2-5). pap. 84.95 (978-1-4824-0817-1(1)) Stevens, Gareth Publishing LLLP.

—The Fox & the Stork & Other Fables. 2014. (Aesop's Fables Ser.). 40p. (J). (gr. 2-5). pap. 84.95 (978-1-4824-1255-0(1)) Stevens, Gareth Publishing LLLP.

—The Frog & the Ox & Other Fables. 2014. (Aesop's Fables Ser.). 40p. (J). (gr. 2-5). pap. 84.95 (978-1-4824-1256-7(X)) Stevens, Gareth Publishing LLLP.

—The Lion & the Bull & Other Fables. 2014. (Aesop's Fables Ser.). 40p. (J). (gr. 2-5). pap. 84.95 (978-1-4824-1258-1(6)) Stevens, Gareth Publishing LLLP.

—The Mice & the Weasels & Other Fables. 2014. (Aesop's Fables Ser.). 40p. (J). (gr. 2-5). pap. 84.95 (978-1-4824-1259-8(4)) Stevens, Gareth Publishing LLLP.

—The Town Mouse & the Country Mouse & Other Fables. 2014. (Aesop's Fables Ser.). 40p. (J). (gr. 2-5). pap. 84.95 (978-1-4824-1260-4(8)) Stevens, Gareth Publishing LLLP.

—The Wolf & His Shadow & Other Fables. 2014. (Aesop's Fables Ser.). 40p. (J). (gr. 2-5). pap. 84.95 (978-1-4824-0793-8(0)) Stevens, Gareth Publishing LLLP.

Parragon. Jack & the Beanstalk. 2014. (Fairytale Boards Ser.). (ENG., Illus.). 10p. (J). bds. (978-1-4723-5206-4(8)) Parragon Bk. Service Ltd.

Paterson, Katherine. Igual Al Rey. Vagin, Vladimir, illus. (Buenas Noches Ser.).Tr. of King's Equal. (SPA.). (J). (gr. 3-5). pap. 7.16 (978-958-04-4167-0(7)) Norma S.A. COL. Dist: Lectorum Pubns., Inc.

—The Tale of the Mandarin Ducks. Dillon, Leo & Dillon, Diane, illus. 2004. 32p. (J). (gr. k-4). reprint ed. 15.00 (978-0-7567-7698-5(8)) DIANE Publishing Co.

Paterson, Katherine & Paterson, John. The Flint Heart. Rocco, John, illus. 2011. (ENG.). 304p. (J). (gr. 2-5). 19.99 (978-0-7636-4712-4(8)) Candlewick Pr.

Pattou, Edith. East. 2005. (ENG.). 528p. (YA). (gr. 7-12). pap. 8.95 (978-0-15-205221-8(6)) Houghton Mifflin Harcourt Publishing Co.

—East. 2005. 507p. (YA). (gr. 7-12). 16.60 (978-0-7569-5054-5(6)) Perfection Learning Corp.

Paul, Ann Whitford. Manana, Iguana. Long, Ethan, illus. 2005. (ENG.). 32p. (J). (gr. -1-3). 7.99 (978-0-8234-1980-7(0)) Holiday Hse., Inc.

Paulson, Elizabeth. Dead upon a Time. 2015. (ENG.). 224p. (J). (gr. 7). 17.99 (978-0-545-64046-6(6), Scholastic Pr.) Scholastic, Inc.

PC Treasures Staff, prod. Cinderella. 2007. (J). (978-1-60072-032-1(3)) PC Treasures, Inc.

—The Gingerbread Man. 2007. (J). (978-1-60072-015-4(3)) PC Treasures, Inc.

—Hansel & Gretel. 2007. (J). (978-1-60072-030-7(7)) PC Treasures, Inc.

—The Little Mermaid. 2007. (J). (978-1-60072-020-8(X)) PC Treasures, Inc.

—The Ugly Duckling. 2007. (J). (978-1-60072-018-5(8)) PC Treasures, Inc.

Pearce, Suzannah, ed. Five-Mintue Stories for Boys. 2014. (ENG., Illus.). 96p. (J). (978-1-74352-049-9(2)) Hinkler Bks. Pty, Ltd.

—Five-Minute Stories for Girls. 2014. (ENG., Illus.). 96p. (J). (978-1-74352-048-2(4)) Hinkler Bks. Pty, Ltd.

Pearson, Maggie. Magic & Misery: Traditional Tales from Around the World. Greenwood, Francesca, illus. 2016. (World of Stories Ser.). (ENG.). 176p. (J). (gr. 2-6). 26.65 (978-1-5124-1319-9(4)) Lerner Publishing Group.

Peaslee, Jessilyn Stewart. Ella. 2015. 232p. (YA). pap. 15.99 (978-1-4621-1745-1(7)) Cedar Fort, Inc./CFI Distribution.

Peattie, Cindy. A Cinderella Atlas. Mountford, Karl, illus. 2017. (Text Connections Guided Close Reading Ser.). (J). (gr. 1). (978-1-4900-1819-5(0)) Benchmark Education Co.

Peek Inside a Fairy Tale Beauty & the Beast. 2017. (Peek Inside a Fairy Tale BDs* Ser.). (ENG.). (J). bds. 14.99 **(978-0-7945-3947-4(5)**, Usborne) EDC Publishing.

Peek Inside a Fairy Tale Cinderella. 2017. (Peek Inside a Fairy Tale BDs* Ser.). (ENG.). (J). bds. 14.99 **(978-0-7945-3871-2(1)**, Usborne) EDC Publishing.

Penn, M. W. Square Bear Meets Round Hound: A Fairytale of Shapes. Firos, Daphne, illus. 2012. (ENG.). 38p. (J). pap. 11.95 (978-0-9840425-8-6(X)) MathWord Pr., LLC.

Percival, J. M., ed. Romanian Fairy Tales. 2008. 160p. 25.95 (978-1-60664-929-9(9)); pap. 14.95 (978-1-60664-049-4(6)) Aegypan.

Perelman, Helen. Rapunzel: A Day to Remember, 1 vol. Studio IBOIX, illus. 2012. (Disney Princesses Set 2 Ser.). (ENG.). 96p. (J). (gr. 2-6). lib. bdg. 24.21 (978-1-59961-183-9(X)) Spotlight.

Perrault. Bella Durmiente (Caracola) 2003. (SPA.). 3.48 (978-968-855-183-7(X)) Suromex, Ediciones, S.A. MEX. Dist: Giron Bks.

Perrault, Charles. Cenicienta. Porras, Javier Fernando, illus. 2003. (Coleccion Letras Pegadas Ser.). (SPA.). 70p. (J). (gr. -1-7). pap. (978-958-30-0547-3(9)) Panamericana Editorial.

—La Cenicienta.Tr. of Cinderella. (SPA.). (J). 12.95 (978-84-7183-326-6(3), EV6475) El Hogar y La Moda, S.A. ESP. Dist: AIMS International Bks., Inc., Lectorum Pubns., Inc.

—Cinderella. Innocenti, Roberto, illus. 2013. (ENG.). 32p. (J). (gr. 1-17). pap. 7.99 (978-0-89812-828-4(5), Creative Paperbacks) Creative Co., The.

—Cinderella (Cenicienta) Fransoy, Monse, illus. 2013. (Bilingual Fairy Tales Ser.). (ENG & SPA.). 32p. (gr. 1-4). lib. bdg. 28.50 (978-1-60753-356-6(1)) Amicus Publishing.

—The Fairies. 2005. (SPA.). 12p. (J). pap. (978-958-30-1779-7(5)) Panamericana Editorial.

—OXFORD WORLD'S CLASSICS: THE COMPLETE FAIRY TALES. 2010. (Oxford World's Classics Ser.). (ENG., Illus.). 256p. pap. 13.95 (978-0-19-958580-9(6)) Oxford Univ. Pr., Inc.

—Perrault's Fairy Tales. Johnson, A. E., tr. 2004. (ENG.). 144p. pap. 4.99 (978-1-84022-482-5(7)) Wordsworth Editions, Ltd. GBR. Dist: May, L. B. & Assocs.

—Puss in Boots. Adams, Frank & Lawrence, C. H., illus. 2009. (ENG.). 16p. (J). (gr. -1-3). pap. 9.95 (978-1-59583-361-7(7), 9781595833617) Laughing Elephant.

—Puss in Boots (El Gato Con Botas) Merino, Jose Luis, illus. 2004. (Bilingual Fairy Tales Ser.: BILI). (ENG & SPA.). 32p. (J). (gr. -1-7). pap. 6.99 (978-0-8118-3924-2(9)) Chronicle Bks. LLC.

—RICITOS DE ORO. 2005. (Caballo Alado Clásico Series-Al Paso Ser.). (SPA & ENG., Illus.). 24p. (J). (gr. -1-k). 7.95 (978-84-7864-854-2(2)) Combel Editorial, S.A. ESP. Dist: Independent Pubs. Group.

—A Storyteller Book: Cinderella. Spenceley, Annabel, illus. 2014. (ENG.). 48p. (J). (gr. k-5). pap. 7.99 (978-1-84322-883-7(1)) Anness Publishing GBR. Dist: National Bk. Network.

—Tales of Mother Goose. 2006. pap. (978-1-84702-444-2(0)) Echo Library.

Perrault, Charles, contrib. by. The Little Mermaid. 2012. (Musical Fairy Tales Ser.). (ENG., Illus.). 12p. (J). (gr. -1-3). bds. 15.95 (978-1-61889-066-5(2)) AZ Bks. LLC.

Perrotti, P. J. Jason & the Enchanted Forest. 2004. 48p. pap. 16.95 (978-1-4137-4593-1(8)) America Star Bks.

Perry, Dave, et al. Thwacked! A Fractured Fable of Frogs, Folks & Falling Skies. 2011. (ENG.). 260p. pap. 19.99 (978-1-4234-9857-5(7), 1423498577); 72p. pap. 19.99 (978-1-4234-9856-8(9), 1423498569) Shawnee Pr., Inc.

Perry, Pete. The Secret of Bedside Manor. 2009. (Illus.). 140p. pap. 36.49 (978-1-4389-6668-7(7)) AuthorHouse.

Pertile, Paula, illus. The Gingerbread Man. 2010. (J). (978-1-60617-141-7(0)) Teaching Strategies, LLC.

Le Petit Chaperon Rouge: Clothing, Food, Nature, The Human Body. (FRE & ENG., Illus.). 24p. (J). (gr. -1-5). pap., stu. ed. 5.95 (978-88-8148-239-9(8)) EMC/Paradigm Publishing.

La Petite Fille Aux Allumettes.Tr. of Little Match Girl. (FRE.). 48p. pap. 12.95 incl. audio compact disk

(978-2-89558-068-3(5)) Coffragants CAN. Dist: Penton Overseas, Inc.

Petrlik, Andrea, illus. Hansel & Gretel. 2007. (Flip-Up Fairy Tales Ser.). (ENG.). 24p. (J). (gr. -1-2). audio compact disk *(978-1-84643-090-9(9))* Child's Play International Ltd.

Petty, J. T. Fairy Killer. Davis, Will, illus. 2011. (ENG.). 128p. (J). (gr. 3-7). pap. 7.99 *(978-1-4424-3097-6(4),* Simon & Schuster Bks. For Young Readers) Simon & Schuster Bks. For Young Readers.

Phelps, Karen. The Grass Is Always Greener & Let Sleeping Dogs Lie: Two Original Fables. 2006. (J). pap. *(978-1-4108-7155-8(X))* Benchmark Education Co.

Philip, Neil, ed. American Fairy Tales: From Rip Van Winkle to the Rootabaga Stories. McCurry, Michael, illus. 2004. 160p. (J). (gr. k-4). reprint ed. pap. 13.00 *(978-0-7567-8068-5(3))* DIANE Publishing Co.

Phillips, Elizabeth. The Blueberry Princess. Phillips, Elizabeth & Phillips, Andrea, illus. 2008. 25p. pap. 24.95 *(978-1-60672-097-4(X))* America Star Bks.

Phillips, Michael. The Sword, the Garden, & the King. 2013. 248p. pap. 12.99 *(978-0-940652-70-5(6))* Sunrise Bks.

Philpot, Graham, illus. Hansel & Gretel. 2007. (First Fairy Tales Ser.). 32p. (J). (gr. -1-3). lib. bdg. 28.50 *(978-1-59771-075-6(X))* Sea-To-Sea Pubns.

Picayo, Mario, et al. The Shark & the Parrotfish & Other Caribbean Fables. Ward, Cherise, illus. 2014. 31p. (J). pap. *(978-1-934370-36-0(3))* Editorial Campana.

Picture-Book People, 6 Packs. (Story Steps Ser.). (gr. k-2). 32.00 *(978-0-7635-9819-8(4))* Rigby Education.

Pienkowski, Jan & Walser, David. The Glass Mountain: Tales from Poland. Pienkowski, Jan, illus. 2014. (ENG., Illus.). 104p. (J). (gr. 2-4). 17.99 *(978-0-7636-7320-8(X))* Candlewick Pr.

Pinkney, Jerry. Little Red Riding Hood. 2007. (ENG., Illus.). 40p. (J). (gr. -1-3). 18.99 *(978-0-316-01355-0(2))* Little, Brown Bks. for Young Readers.

—The Three Billy Goats Gruff. 2017. (ENG., Illus.). 40p. (J). (gr. -1-3). 17.99 *(978-0-316-34157-8(6))* Little Brown & Co.

Pinocchio: The Human Body, Sea Life, The Bedroom. (FRE & ENG., Illus.). 24p. (J). (gr. -1-5). pap., stu. ed. 5.95 *(978-88-8148-243-6(6))* EMC/Paradigm Publishing.

Playmore Publishers. Blanca Nieves: Cuento Plegable. 2011. pap. 4.95 *(978-0-86611-656-5(7))* Waldman Publishing Corp.

—Cenicienta. 2011. pap. 4.95 *(978-0-86611-654-1(0))* Waldman Publishing Corp.

Playmore Publishers Staff. Sirenita. 2011. pap. 4.95 *(978-0-86611-653-4(2))* Waldman Publishing Corp.

Pleasant, Charles. The Story of Rapunzelresha's First Date. 2010. 6p. 7.95 *(978-0-557-57810-8(8))* Lulu Pr., Inc.

Poer, Nancy Jewel. Mia's Apple Tree. Poer, Nancy Jewel, illus. 2004. (Illus.). 34p. (J). 21.95 *(978-0-9740413-1-5(9))* White Feather Publishing.

Pogany, Elaine. The Golden Cockerel: From the Original Russian Fairy Tale of Alexander Pushkin. Pogány, Willy, illus. 2013. (Dover Children's Classics Ser.). (ENG.). 48p. (J). (gr. 5-8). pap. 14.95 *(978-0-486-49115-8(3))* Dover Pubns., Inc.

Pohrte, Kathysue, et al. In the Land of Liviaann. Pohrte, Kathysue, ed. Pohrte, Olivia & Pohrte, Juliann, illus. I.t. ed. 2003. 36p. (J). pap. 17.95 *(978-0-9722296-0-9(4),* 872493); (gr. -1-6). 12.95 *(978-0-9722296-1-6(2),* 872493) Pohrte, Dorey Publishing, Inc.

Polette, Keith. Paco & the Giant Chile Plant/Paco y la Planta de Chile Gigante. Dulemba, Elizabeth, illus. 2008. (ENG & SPA.). 32p. (J). (gr. -1-3). pap. 7.95 *(978-0-9794462-3-8(6),* Raven Tree Pr.,Csi) Continental Sales, Inc.

Poole, Amy Lowry & Andersen, Hans Christian. The Pea Blossom. 2005. (ENG., Illus.). 32p. (J). (gr. -1-3). 16.95 *(978-0-8234-1864-0(2))* Holiday Hse., Inc.

Popek, Penelope & Mitchell, Toni. Darby Downswallow & His Bumblebee. 2010. 40p. pap. 18.49 *(978-1-4389-7331-9(4))* AuthorHouse.

Posener, Alan. Marchenland. (GER.). (YA). pap. 7.95 *(978-0-8219-1852-4(4),* 45316) EMC/Paradigm Publishing.

—Olli Aus Ossiland. (GER.). (YA). pap. 7.95 *(978-0-8219-1463-2(4),* 45315) EMC/Paradigm Publishing.

Posner-Sanchez, Andrea. Cinderella's Fairy Merry Christmas. Marrucchi, Elisa, illus. 2009. (Pictureback(R) Ser.). (ENG.). 24p. (J). (gr. -1-2). pap. 3.99 *(978-0-7364-2622-0(1),* RH/Disney) Random Hse. Children's Bks.

Postgate, Daniel, illus. Rumpled Stilton Skin. 2015. (ENG.). 32p. (J). *(978-0-7787-1930-4(8))* Crabtree Publishing Co.

—The Ugly Duckling. 2006. (First Reading Level 4 Ser.). 48p. (J). (gr. 1-4). 8.99 *(978-0-7945-1274-3(7),* Usborne) EDC Publishing.

Potter, Beatrix. Selected Tales from Beatrix Potter. 2007. (Peter Rabbit Ser.). (ENG., Illus.). 128p. (J). (gr. -1-2). 9.99 *(978-0-7232-5859-9(7),* Warne) Penguin Young Readers Group.

Potter, Beatrix & Aesop. The Tale of Johnny Town-Mouse. Rasmussen, Wendy, illus. 2009. (Classic Tales by Beatrix Potter Ser.). (ENG.). 24p. (J). (gr. k-3). 28.50 *(978-1-60253-293-9(1),* 200119) Child's World, Inc., The.

Pouzadoux, Claude. Cuentos y Leyendas de la Mitologia Griega. 2003. (Fables & Legends Ser.). (SPA., Illus.). 160p. (J). 9.95 *(978-84-239-9056-6(7))* Espasa Calpe, S.A. ESP. Dist: Planeta Publishing Corp.

Power, Laura. Air-Born. 2013. 322p. pap. 16.99 *(978-0-9894792-4-0(2))* Winter Goose Publishing.

Press Out Sticker: Camilla the Cupcake Fairy. 2015. (ENG.). 36p. (J). (gr. -1-7). pap. *(978-1-78393-779-0(3))* Make Believe Ideas.

Price, Margaret Evans, illus. The Betty Fairy Book. 2006. (Shape Bks.). (ENG.). 16p. (J). pap. 9.95 *(978-1-59583-092-0(8),* Green Tiger Pr.) Laughing Elephant.

Price, Margaret Evans & Wadsworth, Wallace C. Once upon a Time Tales: With Read & Listen MP3 Download. Bates, Katharine Lee, ed. 2012. (Dover Children's Classics Ser.). (ENG., Illus.). 112p. (J). (gr. 2-5). pap. 14.99 *(978-0-486-49840-9(9))* Dover Pubns., Inc.

Priddy, Roger. Lift the Flap - Fairy Tales. 2016. (Can You Find Me? Ser.). (ENG.). 16p. (J). bds. 9.99 *(978-0-312-52059-5(X),* 9780312520595, Priddy Bks.) St. Martin's Pr.

Princesa Stephanie. 2005. (SPA.). (YA). per. 9.95 *(978-0-9764982-8-5(6))* Legacy Publishing Services, Inc.

Princesses. 2009. (FACT ATLAS Ser.). 72p. (J). 15.99 *(978-0-8416-1101-6(7))* Hammond World Atlas Corp.

Prineas, Sarah. Ash & Bramble. 2015. (ENG.). 464p. (YA). (gr. 8). 17.99 *(978-0-06-233794-8(7))* HarperCollins Pubs.

—Rose & Thorn. 2016. 416p. (YA). (gr. 8). 17.99 *(978-0-06-233797-9(1),* HarperTeen) HarperCollins Pubs.

Prokofiev, Sergei. The Love for Three Oranges. Gaudasinska, Elzbieta, illus. 2006. (Musical Stories Ser.: Vol. 1). (ENG.). 40p. (J). (gr. 2-4). 16.95 *(978-0-9646010-3-1(6))* Pumpkin Hse., Ltd.

—Peter & the Wolf. Raschka, Chris, illus. 2008. (ENG.). 40p. (J). (gr. -1-2). 19.99 *(978-0-689-85652-5(0),* Atheneum/Richard Jackson Bks.) Simon & Schuster Children's Publishing.

Protasov, Alexander. Fairy-Tales & Fantasies. 2010. (Illus.). 52p. pap. 22.49 *(978-1-4490-7847-8(8))* AuthorHouse.

Proulx-Willis, Dana. Cinderella vs. the Stepfamily: A Fairy Tale Courtroom Event. 2007. 28p. pap. 7.00 *(978-0-88734-696-5(0))* Players Pr., Inc.

Provantini, Silvia, illus. The Runaway Pancake. 2006. (First Reading Level 4 Ser.). 48p. (J). (gr. 1-4). 8.99 *(978-0-7945-1276-7(3),* Usborne) EDC Publishing.

Publications International Ltd. Staff. Disney Princess Songs. 2013. 12p. (J). (gr. k-4). bds. 21.99 *(978-1-4127-8016-2(0),* fdc578c6-8169-40c1-acde-e3e9449607c7) Phoenix International Publications, Inc.

—Little Sound Barbie Fairytopia. 2007. 12p. (J). 10.98 *(978-1-4127-6770-5(9),* PIL Kids) Publications International, Ltd.

—Mother Goose Treasury. 2007. (ENG., Illus.). 320p. (J). (gr. -1-3). bds. *(978-1-4127-6334-9(7),* 1412763347) Phoenix International Publications, Inc.

—Mother Goose Treasury. 2007. (Illus.). 316p. 15.98 *(978-1-4127-8734-5(3))* Publications International, Ltd.

Publications International Ltd. Staff, creator. Disney Best Friends. 2007. (My First Look & Find Ser.). (Illus.). 12p. (gr. -1-k). 7.98 *(978-1-4127-8738-3(6))* Publications International, Ltd.

—Fairy Tales: Keepsake Collection. 2007. (Illus.). 96p. 12.98 *(978-1-4127-7453-6(5))* Publications International, Ltd.

—Once upon a Time: A Treasury of Fairy Tales. 2007. (Illus.). 318p. 15.98 *(978-1-4127-8732-1(7))* Publications International, Ltd.

—Treasury of Bedtime Stories. 2007. (Padded Treasuries 6x6 Ser.). (Illus.). 318p. (J). (gr. -1-3). 9.98 *(978-1-4127-7433-8(0))* Publications International, Ltd.

—Treasury of Fairy Tales. 2007. (Padded Treasuries 6x6 Ser.). (Illus.). 318p. (J). (gr. -1-3). 9.98 *(978-1-4127-7435-2(7))* Publications International, Ltd.

Publications International Ltd. Staff, ed. Disney Tales of Virtue 5 Book Set. 2008. (J). pap. 4.98 *(978-1-4127-9392-6(0))* Phoenix International Publications, Inc.

—Fairy Tales. Goodell, Jon & Clar, David Austin, illus. 2010. 10p. (J). bds. 12.98 *(978-0-7853-7394-0(2))* Phoenix International Publications, Inc.

—Fairy Tales Red a Long Treaury. 2005. 40p. (J). 12.98 *(978-1-4127-3530-8(0),* 7248200) Publications International, Ltd.

—Read to Me Grandma (Keepsake Story Collection) 2010. 96p. (J). 13.98 *(978-1-60553-792-4(6))* Publications International, Ltd.

—Tangled (Look & Find) 2010. 24p. (J). 7.98 *(978-1-60553-765-8(9))* Publications International, Ltd.

—El Tesoro de Los Cuentos de Hadas. LoFaro, Jerry, illus. 2004. (SPA & ESP.). 384p. (J). 15.98 *(978-1-4127-0165-5(1),* 3995001) Phoenix International Publications, Inc.

Pushkin, Alexander. Skazki Pushkina - Fairy Tales. Bilibin, Ivan, illus. 2013. 48p. *(978-1-909115-58-3(4))* Planet, The.

Pyle, Howard. Pepper & Salt & the Wonder Clock, Set. Pyle, Howard, illus. 2006. (Foundations Ser.). (Illus.). 385p. (J). 45.00 *(978-1-933859-14-9(8))* ISI Bks.

—Pepper & Salt or Seasoning for Young Folk. 2007. 92p. per. *(978-1-4068-2421-6(6))* Echo Library.

—Twilight Land. 2006. (ENG.). 192p. pap. 19.99 *(978-1-4264-0425-2(5))* Creative Media Partners, LLC.

—Twilight Land. 2006. (ENG.). pap. *(978-1-4068-3431-4(9))* Echo Library.

—Twilight Land. 2004. reprint ed. pap. 22.95 *(978-1-4191-9142-8(X))* Kessinger Publishing, LLC.

—The Wonder Clock Or, Four & Twenty Marvelous Tales. 2012. (Dover Children's Classics Ser.). (ENG., Illus.). 319p. (J). (gr. 3-8). per. 12.95 *(978-0-486-21446-7(X))* Dover Pubns., Inc.

Pyle, Robert. The Merry Adventures of Robin Hood. 2009. 284p. (J). pap. 14.99 *(978-1-934941-61-4(1))* Red & Black Pubs.

Qu, Zhi. Little Sima & the Giant Bowl. Wang, Lin, illus. 2009. (On My Own Folklore Ser.). (ENG.). 48p. (gr. 2-4). pap. 6.95 *(978-1-58013-850-5(0),* First Avenue Editions) Lerner Publishing Group.

Quiller-Couch, Arthur. Beauty & the Beast. Domínguez, Ángel, illus. 2017. (ENG.). 96p. (J). (gr. 2-7). 12.99 *(978-1-63158-115-1(5),* Racehorse Publishing) Skyhorse Publishing Co., Inc.

Quiller-Couch, Arthur Thomas. The Twelve Dancing Princesses & Other Fairy Tales. Nielsen, Kay, illus. 2012. (Calla Editions Ser.). (ENG.). 208p. (gr. 4). 40.00 *(978-1-60660-025-2(7))* Dover Pubns., Inc.

Rackham, Arthur. A Fairy Book 1923. 2004. reprint ed. pap. 20.95 *(978-1-4179-7656-0(X))* Kessinger Publishing, LLC.

Randall, Ronne. The Little Red Hen. 2015. (First Favourite Tales Ser.). (ENG., Illus.). 32p. (J). (-k). 7.99 *(978-1-4093-0958-1(4))* Penguin Bks., Ltd. GBR. Dist: Independent Pubs. Group.

Randazzo, Dottie. The Blue Girl. 2008. 81p. pap. 10.95 *(978-0-615-18340-4(9))* Creative Dreaming Ltd.

Random House. Barbie Dreamtopia Pictureback (Barbie) 2017. (Pictureback(R) Ser.). (ENG., Illus.). 24p. (J). (gr. -1-2). pap. 4.99 ***(978-1-5247-1646-2(4),*** Random Hse. Bks. for Young Readers) Random Hse. Children's Bks.

Random House Disney Staff. Princess Story Collection. 2007. (Step into Reading Ser.). (ENG., Illus.). 160p. (J). (gr. k-3). pap. 7.99 *(978-0-7364-2486-8(5),* RH/Disney) Random Hse. Children's Bks.

Ransom, Candice & Lyon, Tammie. Little Red Riding Hood, Grades PK - 3: Caperucita Roja. 2005. (Keepsake Stories Ser.). (ENG & SPA., Illus.). 32p. (gr. -1-3). pap. 3.99 *(978-0-7696-3817-1(1),* Brighter Child) Carson-Dellosa Publishing, LLC.

Ransome, Arthur. Favorite Russian Fairy Tales. Galkin, Simon, illus. 2011. (Dover Children's Thrift Classics Ser.). (ENG.). 96p. (J). (gr. 3-8). pap. 4.00 *(978-0-486-28632-7(0))* Dover Pubns., Inc.

—The Firebird & Other Russian Fairy Tales. 2004. (Dover Children's Classics Ser.). (ENG., Illus.). 128p. (J). (gr. 3-8). pap. 5.95 *(978-0-486-43893-1(7))* Dover Pubns., Inc.

—Old Peter's Russian Tales. 2007. 180p. per. 12.95 *(978-1-60312-321-1(0));* 24.95 *(978-1-60312-739-4(9))* Aegypan.

—Old Peter's Russian Tales. 2007. (ENG.). 200p. pap. 19.99 *(978-1-4346-0606-8(6));* 222p. pap. 22.99 *(978-1-4346-0681-5(3))* Creative Media Partners, LLC.

—Old Peter's Russian Tales. 2007. 140p. per. *(978-1-4068-3744-5(X))* Echo Library.

—Old Peter's Russian Tales. 2005. 35.00 *(978-1-55742-465-5(9));* pap. 15.95 *(978-1-55742-456-3(X))* Wildside Pr., LLC.

La Ratita Presumida. (Coleccion Fabulas y Cuentos Populares). (SPA.). (J). (gr. 2-4). *(978-84-246-1603-8(0),* GL1026) La Galera, S.A. Editorial ESP. Dist: Lectorum Pubns., Inc.

Ray, Jane. Cinderella. Ray, Jane, illus. 2012. (ENG., Illus.). 12p. (J). (gr. k-4). 19.99 *(978-0-7636-6175-5(9))* Candlewick Pr.

Ray, Jane, illus. Classic Fairy Tales: Candlewick Illustrated Classic. 2009. (Candlewick Illustrated Classics Ser.). (ENG.). 224p. (J). (gr. 5-4). pap. 12.99 *(978-0-7636-4212-9(6))* Candlewick Pr.

Read, Lorna & Ladybird Books Staff. The Elves & the Shoemaker. Lewis, Jan, illus. 2015. (First Favourite Tales Ser.). (ENG.). 32p. (J). (-k). 7.99 *(978-1-4093-0628-3(3))* Penguin Bks., Ltd. GBR. Dist: Independent Pubs. Group.

Redbank, Tennant. A Midsummer Night's Dreamy (Disney Palace Pets: Whisker Haven Tales) RH Disney, illus. 2017. (Stepping Stone Book(TM) Ser.). (ENG.). 64p. (J). (gr. 1-4). 5.99 *(978-0-7364-3598-7(0),* RH/Disney) Random Hse. Children's Bks.

Redbank, Tennant, et al. Disney Princess Little Golden Book Favorites: Volume 3 (Disney Princess) Tyminski, Lori & Ying, Victoria, illus. 2014. (Little Golden Book Favorites Ser.). (ENG.). 80p. (J). (-k). 6.99 *(978-0-7364-3098-2(9),* Golden/Disney) Random Hse. Children's Bks.

Reece, Bernadette. Nervy the Ghost. 2004. 21p. pap. 9.95 *(978-1-4137-2021-1(8))* PublishAmerica, Inc.

Reed, Emily. Fairy Tales for Modern Queers. (ENG., Illus.). (J). 2016. 24.99 ***(978-1-63533-012-0(2))*** 2015. 180p. pap. 14.99 *(978-1-63216-720-0(4))* Dreamspinner Pr. (Harmony Ink Pr.).

Reed, Emily. Fairy Tales for Modern Queers [Library Edition]. 2015. (ENG., Illus.). 180p. (J). pap. 14.99 *(978-1-63216-721-7(2),* Harmony Ink Pr.) Dreamspinner Pr.

Reed, Nathan, illus. The Buskers of Bremen. 2004. 24p. (J). (POL & ENG.). *(978-1-85269-800-3(4));* pap. *(978-1-85269-225-4(1));* pap. *(978-1-85269-765-5(2));* (ENG & CHI.). pap. *(978-1-85269-767-9(9));* (ENG & SPA.). pap. *(978-1-85269-778-5(4));* (GER & ENG.). pap. *(978-1-85269-770-9(9));* pap. *(978-1-85269-768-6(7));* (ITA & ENG.). pap. *(978-1-85269-777-8(6));* pap. *(978-1-85269-776-1(8));* (ENG.). pap. *(978-1-85269-775-4(X));* pap. *(978-1-85269-774-7(1));* (CZE & ENG.). pap. *(978-1-85269-773-0(3));* pap. *(978-1-85269-771-6(7));* (TUR & ENG.). pap. *(978-1-85269-780-8(6));* pap. *(978-1-85269-779-2(2))* Mantra Lingua.

Rees, Gwyneth. Fairy Dreams Vol. 1: A Magical Journey to Fairyland. 3rd unabr. ed. 2005. (Fairy Dust Ser.: 3). (ENG., Illus.). 224p. (J). (gr. 2-4). pap. 8.99 *(978-0-330-43476-8(4))* Pan Macmillan GBR. Dist: Independent Pubs. Group.

Regenold, Theresa. Not Your Average Princess: A Real-Life Fairy Tale. 2005. 117p. pap. 19.95 *(978-1-4137-9308-6(8))* PublishAmerica, Inc.

Reinhart, Matthew. Cinderella: A Pop-Up Fairy Tale. Reinhart, Matthew, illus. 2005. (ENG., Illus.). 12p. (J). (gr. -1-3). 34.99 *(978-1-4169-0501-1(4),* Little Simon) Little Simon.

RH Disney. Cinderella - Beginnings. RH Disney, illus. 2017. (Stepping Stone Book(TM) Ser.). (ENG., Illus.). 128p. (J). (gr. 1-4). 6.99 *(978-0-7364-3578-9(6));* lib. bdg. 12.99 *(978-0-7364-8176-2(1))* Random Hse. Children's Bks. (RH/Disney).

—The Critterzen Clue Contest (Disney Palace Pets: Whisker Haven Tales) RH Disney, illus. 2017. (Pictureback Ser.). (ENG., Illus.). 24p. (J). (gr. -1-1). pap. 4.99 *(978-0-7364-3593-2(X),* RH/Disney) Random Hse. Children's Bks.

—A Fairy's Fire. RH Disney, illus. 2016. (Never Girls Ser.). (ENG., Illus.). 224p. (J). (gr. 1-4). lib. bdg. 17.99 *(978-0-7364-8175-5(3),* RH/Disney) Random Hse. Children's Bks.

RH Disney Staff. Cinderella. Dias, Ron & Lorencz, Bill, illus. 2005. (Little Golden Book Ser.). (ENG.). 24p. (J). (gr. -1-2). lib. bdg. 4.99 *(978-0-7364-2362-5(1),* Golden/Disney) Random Hse. Children's Bks.

—Cinderella. RH Disney Staff, tr. (FRE.). 96p. (J). (gr. k-5). pap. 9.95 *(978-0-7859-8855-7(6))* French & European Pubns., Inc.

—Furry, Fluffy & Fabulous! (Disney Princess: Palace Pets) Disney Storybook Artists Staff, illus. 2014. (Big Golden Book Ser.). (ENG.). 64p. (J). (gr. -1-2). 9.99 *(978-0-7364-3263-4(9),* Golden/Disney) Random Hse. Children's Bks.

RH Disney Staff & Depken, Kristen L. My Never Land Journal (Disney: the Never Girls) Christy, Jana, illus. 2014. (Never Girls Ser.). (ENG.). 128p. (J). (gr. 1-4). 12.99 *(978-0-553-49685-7(9),* RH/Disney) Random Hse. Children's Bks.

Richards, Kitty. Cinderella: The Lost Tiara. 2012. (Disney Princess Early Chapter Bks.). (J). lib. bdg. 14.75 *(978-0-606-26572-0(4),* Turtleback) Turtleback Bks.

Richemont, Enid. Brownilocks & the Three Bowls of Cornflakes. 2016. (ENG., Illus.). 32p. (J). *(978-0-7787-2459-9(X))* Crabtree Publishing Co.

Ricitos de Oro. (SPA.). (J). 12.00 *(978-958-02-1237-9(6))* Editorial Voluntad S.A. COL. Dist: Distribuidora Norma, Inc.

Rigby Education Staff. Cinderella: Jumbled Tumble. (gr. k-2). 26.00 *(978-0-7635-2420-3(4))* Rigby Education.

Riggs, Kate. Enchanted Castles. 2013. (Illus.). 24p. (J). 25.65 *(978-1-60818-240-4(1),* Creative Education) Creative Co., The.

—Fairy Godmothers. 2013. (Illus.). 24p. (J). 25.65 *(978-1-60818-241-1(X),* Creative Education) Creative Co., The.

—Princes & Princesses. 2013. (Illus.). 24p. (J). 25.65 *(978-1-60818-243-5(6),* Creative Education) Creative Co., The.

Riggs, Ransom. Tales of the Peculiar. Davidson, Andrew, illus. 2016. (ENG.). 192p. (YA). (gr. 7). 24.99 *(978-0-399-53853-7(4),* Dutton Books for Young Readers) Penguin Young Readers Group.

Riley, James. Once upon the End. 2014. (Half upon a Time Ser.: 3). (ENG., Illus.). 400p. (J). (gr. 3-7). pap. 7.99 *(978-1-4424-7421-5(1),* Aladdin) Simon & Schuster Children's Publishing.

—Once upon the End. 2013. (Half upon a Time Ser.: 3). (ENG.). 384p. (J). (gr. 3-7). 17.99 *(978-1-4424-7422-2(X),* Simon & Schuster/Paula Wiseman Bks.) Simon & Schuster/Paula Wiseman Bks.

—Once upon the End. 2014. (Half upon a Time Ser.: 3). lib. bdg. 18.40 *(978-0-606-35427-1(1))* Turtleback Bks.

—Twice upon a Time. (Half upon a Time Ser.: 2). (ENG.). (J). (gr. 3-7). 2013. 384p. pap. 8.99 *(978-1-4169-9597-5(8))* 2012. 352p. 17.99 *(978-1-4169-9596-8(X))* Simon & Schuster Children's Publishing. (Aladdin).

—Twice upon a Time. 2013. (Half upon a Time Ser.: 2). lib. bdg. 18.40 *(978-0-606-35426-4(3))* Turtleback Bks.

Rimmington, Natasha, illus. The Wolf & the Seven Little Kids. 2014. (Flip-Up Fairy Tales Ser.). (ENG.). 24p. (J). *(978-1-84643-656-7(7))* Child's Play International Ltd.

Ritz, Lee F. The Sun & the Wind. Hale, Randy, illus. 2013. 62p. 23.99 *(978-1-940840-00-0(7))* Ritz, Lee Pubns.

Roberts, Lynn. Cinderella: an Art Deco Fairy Tale. 2017. (ENG., Illus.). 40p. (J). (gr. -1-3). pap. 9.99 ***(978-1-84365-319-6(2),*** Pavilion) Pavilion Bks. GBR. Dist: Independent Pubs. Group.

—Rapunzel: a Groovy 1970's Fairy Tale. 2017. (ENG., Illus.). 40p. (J). (gr. k-2). pap. 9.99 ***(978-1-84365-318-9(4),*** Pavilion) Pavilion Bks. GBR. Dist: Independent Pubs. Group.

Roberts, Lynn & Roberts, David. Sleeping Beauty. 2017. (ENG., Illus.). 32p. (J). (gr. -1-1). 17.99 *(978-1-84365-291-5(9),* Pavilion) Pavilion Bks. GBR. Dist: Independent Pubs. Group.

Roberts, Tom. Red Riding Hood, 1 vol. Kubinyi, Laszlo, illus. 2005. (Rabbit Ears: A Classic Tale Ser.). (ENG.). 28p. (gr. 2-7). 25.65 *(978-1-59197-752-0(5))* Spotlight.

Roberts, Tom & Asbjørnsen, Peter Christen. The Three Billy Goats Gruff, 1 vol. Jorgensen, David, illus. 2005. (Rabbit Ears-A Classic Tale Set 2 Ser.). (ENG.). 28p. (gr. k-5). 25.65 *(978-1-59197-754-4(1))* Spotlight.

Robin, Ink & Rivard, Joanna. A Real Prince Is Hard to Find: A Modern Fairy Tale. 2013. (ENG., Illus.). 32p. (J). (gr. -1-3). 16.99 *(978-1-61963-215-8(2),* 9781619632158); 17.89 *(978-1-61963-216-5(0),* 9781619632165) Bloomsbury Publishing USA. (Bloomsbury USA Childrens).

Robinson, Hilary. Beauty & the Pea. Sanfilippo, Simona, illus. 2013. (ENG.). 32p. (J). pap. *(978-0-7787-1159-9(5))* Crabtree Publishing Co.

—Cinderella & the Beanstalk. Sanfilippo, Simona, illus. 2013. (ENG.). 32p. (J). *(978-0-7787-1156-8(0))* Crabtree Publishing Co.

—The Frog Prince. Abbott, Jane, illus. 2016. (Must Know Stories: Level 2 Ser.). (ENG.). 32p. (J). (gr. 1-4). 12.99 *(978-1-4451-4665-2(7),* Franklin Watts) Hachette Children's Group GBR. Dist: Hachette Bk. Group.

—Hansel, Gretel, & the Ugly Duckling. Sanfilippo, Simona, illus. 2013. (ENG.). 32p. (J). *(978-0-7787-1157-5(9));* pap. *(978-0-7787-1166-7(8))* Crabtree Publishing Co.

—Mixed up Fairy Tales. Sharratt, Nick, illus. 2005. (ENG.). 32p. (J). (gr. -1-k). pap. 11.95 *(978-0-340-87558-2(5))* Hachette Children's Group GBR. Dist: Hachette Bk. Group.

—Rapunzel & the Billy Goats. Sanfilippo, Simona, illus. 2013. (ENG.). 32p. (J). pap. *(978-0-7787-1158-2(7))* Crabtree Publishing Co.

Roderick, Timothy. Briar Blackwood's Grimmest of Fairytales. 2015. (ENG.). 279p. pap. 12.95 *(978-1-78279-922-1(2),* Lodestone Bks.) Hunt, John Publishing Ltd. GBR. Dist: National Bk. Network.

Rodgers, Greg, as told by. Chukfi Rabbit's Big, Bad Bellyache: A Trickster Tale. 2014. (ENG., Illus.). 40p. (J). pap. 7.95 *(978-1-935955-27-6(6))* Cinco Puntos Pr.

Roldan, Gustavo. Cuentos del Zorro. (Cuentamerica Ser.). (SPA.). 64p. (J). (gr. 4-6). *(978-950-07-1557-7(0),* SA30061) Editorial Sudamericana S.A. ARG. Dist: Lectorum Pubns., Inc.

Ross, Mandy. Chicken Licken. 2015. (First Favourite Tales Ser.). (ENG., Illus.). 32p. (J). (-k). 7.99 *(978-1-4093-0956-7(8))* Penguin Bks., Ltd. GBR. Dist: Independent Pubs. Group.

Ross, Mandy & Ladybird Books Staff. Little Red Riding Hood. 2015. (First Favourite Tales Ser.). (ENG., Illus.). 32p. (J). (-k). 7.99 *(978-1-4093-0631-3(3))* Penguin Bks., Ltd. GBR. Dist: Independent Pubs. Group.

Ross, Tony. Goldilocks & the Three Bears. 2016. (ENG., Illus.). 10p. (J). (-k). ring bd. 9.99 *(978-1-78344-409-0(6))* Andersen Pr. GBR. Dist: Independent Pubs. Group.

—Jack & the Beanstalk. 2016. (ENG., Illus.). 10p. (J). (-k). ring bd. 9.99 *(978-1-78344-410-6(X))* Andersen Pr. GBR. Dist: Independent Pubs. Group.

Ross, Tony & Ross, Tony. Goldilocks & the Three Bears. 40th ed. 2017. (ENG., Illus.). 32p. (J). (-k). 14.99 ***(978-1-78344-469-4(X))*** Andersen Pr. GBR. Dist: Independent Pubs. Group.

Rossi, Francesca, illus. Beauty & the Beast. 2015. (Fairy Tale Adventures Ser.). (ENG.). 64p. (J). (gr. 2-6). 7.95 *(978-1-4549-1507-2(2))* Sterling Publishing Co., Inc.

—Cinderella. 2015. (Fairy Tale Adventures Ser.). (ENG.). 64p. (J). (gr. 2-6). 7.95 *(978-1-4549-1508-9(0))* Sterling Publishing Co., Inc.

—The Little Mermaid. 2015. (Fairy Tale Adventures Ser.). (ENG.). 64p. (J). (gr. 2-6). 7.95 *(978-1-4549-1509-6(9))* Sterling Publishing Co., Inc.

EFG

—Little Red Riding Hood. 2015. (Fairy Tale Adventures Ser.). (ENG.). 64p. (J). (gr. 2-6). 7.95 *(978-1-4549-1510-2(2))* Sterling Publishing Co., Inc.

—Rapunzel. 2015. (Fairy Tale Adventures Ser.). (ENG.). 64p. (J). (gr. 2-6). 7.95 *(978-1-4549-1511-9(0))* Sterling Publishing Co., Inc.

—Snow White. 2015. (Fairy Tale Adventures Ser.). (ENG.). 64p. (J). (gr. 2-6). 7.95 *(978-1-4549-1513-3(7))* Sterling Publishing Co., Inc.

Roszel, Karen, illus. The Diamond Button. I.t. ed. 2005. 32p. (J). bds. 14.95 *(978-0-9709630-7-9(6))* Coal Hole Productions.

Rowe, Eric, illus. The Musicians of Bremen. 2004. (ENG.). 19p. (J). (gr. 1-3). pap. 6.47 net. *(978-0-7685-0332-6(9),* Dominie Elementary) Pearson Schl.

Rowling, J. K. Harrys Zauerbox: Books 1 - 4. (GER.). 119.00 *(978-3-551-55300-3(9))* Carlsen Verlag DEU. Dist: Distribooks, Inc.

—The Tales of Beedle the Bard. GrandPré, Mary, illus. 2008. (ENG.). 128p. *(978-0-7475-9987-6(4))* Bloomsbury Publishing Plc.

—The Tales of Beedle the Bard. GrandPré, Mary, illus. collector's ed. 2008. 184p. *(978-0-9560109-0-2(3))* Children's High Level Group.

—The Tales of Beedle the Bard. 2017. (Harry Potter Ser.). (ENG.). 128p. (J). (gr. 3-3). 12.99 *(978-1-338-12568-9(0),* Levine, Arthur A. Bks.) Scholastic, Inc.

—The Tales of Beedle the Bard. 2017. (ENG.). (J). (gr. 3). lib. bdg. 24.50 ***(978-0-606-39695-0(0))*** Turtleback Bks.

Royde-Smith, N. G. Una and the Red Cross Knight & Other T. 2006. (Illus.). pap. 28.95 *(978-1-4254-8407-1(7))* Kessinger Publishing, LLC.

Rudnick, Elizabeth. Cinderella: Junior Novel. 2015. (J). lib. bdg. 16.00 *(978-0-606-35919-1(2))* Turtleback Bks.

Ruiz Abello, Margarita, illus. PEDRITO Y EL REY GLOTÓN. 2004. (Troquelados Clásicos Ser.). (SPA & ENG.). 16p. (J). (gr. -1-k). pap. 3.95 *(978-84-7864-738-5(4))* Combel Editorial, S.A. ESP. Dist: Independent Pubs. Group.

—EL PEZ DE ORO. 2005. (Troquelados Clásicos Ser.). (SPA & ENG.). 16p. (J). (gr. -1-k). pap. 3.95 *(978-84-7864-897-9(6))* Combel Editorial, S.A. ESP. Dist: Independent Pubs. Group.

—UNA PRINCESA DE VERDAD. 2003. (Troquelados Clásicos Ser.). (SPA & ENG.). 16p. (J). (gr. -1-k). pap. 3.95 *(978-84-7864-677-7(9))* Combel Editorial, S.A. ESP. Dist: Independent Pubs. Group.

—EL RUISEÑOR. 2004. (Troquelados Clásicos Ser.). (SPA & ENG.). 16p. (J). (gr. -1-k). pap. 3.95 *(978-84-7864-737-8(6))* Combel Editorial, S.A. ESP. Dist: Independent Pubs. Group.

—EL SASTRECILLO VALIENTE. 2005. (Troquelados Clásicos Ser.). (SPA & ENG.). 16p. (J). (gr. -1-k). pap. 3.95 *(978-84-7864-896-2(8))* Combel Editorial, S.A. ESP. Dist: Independent Pubs. Group.

—LA VENDEDORA DE FÓSFOROS. 2003. (Troquelados Clásicos Ser.). (ENG & SPA.). 16p. (J). (gr. -1-k). pap. 3.95 *(978-84-7864-675-3(2))* Combel Editorial, S.A. ESP. Dist: Independent Pubs. Group.

—ZAPATOS BAILARINES. 2003. (Troquelados Clásicos Ser.). (SPA & ENG.). 16p. (J). (gr. -1-k). pap. 3.95 *(978-84-7864-678-4(7))* Combel Editorial, S.A. ESP. Dist: Independent Pubs. Group.

Rumford, James, illus. & retold by. Beowulf: A Hero's Tale Retold. Rumford, James, retold by. 2006. (J). *(978-0-399-24391-2(7))* Penguin Publishing Group.

Rumpelstiltskin. (Ladybird Bks.). (ARA., Illus.). 52p. (J). 4.95 *(978-0-86685-222-7(0))* International Bk. Ctr., Inc.

Rumpelstiltskin. 2016. (Well-Loved Tales Ser.). (ENG., Illus.). 56p. (J). (gr. 3-7). 9.99 *(978-0-7232-9757-4(6))* Penguin Bks., Ltd. GBR. Dist: Independent Pubs. Group.

Russell, Katherine. Imagine the Butterfly Within Me. 2008. 52p. pap. 26.95 *(978-1-4327-2642-3(0))* Outskirts Pr., Inc.

Russell, Kitty, compiled by. Fairy Hearts & Charms: Stories of Yesteryear. 2012. (ENG.). 434p. 29.95 *(978-1-937922-03-0(0))* Kittyco Pr.

—Fairy Lovely: Stories of Yesteryear. 2012. (ENG.). 416p. 29.95 *(978-1-937922-04-7(9))* Kittyco Pr.

Russell, Rachel Renée. Tales from a Not-So-Happily Ever After. 2014. (Dork Diaries: 8). lib. bdg. 25.75 *(978-0-606-36241-2(X))* Turtleback Bks.

Ryan, Brittney. The Legend of Holly Claus. Long, Laurel, illus. 2004. (Julie Andrews Collection). 544p. (J). (gr. 4-18). 16.99 *(978-0-06-058511-2(0));* lib. bdg. 17.89 *(978-0-06-058514-3(5))* HarperCollins Pubs. (Julie Andrews Collection).

Rylant, Cynthia. Beauty & the Beast. Park, Meg, illus. 2017. (ENG.). 40p. (J). (gr. -1-k). 16.99 *(978-1-4231-1981-4(9))* Disney Pr.

—Sleeping Beauty. McGuire, Erin, illus. 2017. (ENG.). 40p. (J). (gr. -1-k). 16.99 *(978-1-4231-2108-4(2))* Disney Pr.

—Walt Disney's Cinderella. Blair, Mary, illus. 2015. (Walt Disney's Classic Fairytale Ser.). (ENG.). 64p. (J). (gr. -1-k). 16.99 *(978-1-4847-1247-4(1))* Disney Pr.

Rylant, Cynthia & Andersen, Hans Christian. The Steadfast Tin Soldier. Corace, Jen, illus. 2013. (ENG.). 32p. (J). (gr. k-2). 18.95 *(978-1-4197-0432-1(X),* Abrams Bks. for Young Readers) Abrams, Inc.

Rymer, Alta M. Up from Uzam. Rymer, Alta M., illus. (Tharma Lo Fairyland Ser.: Story 1). (Illus.). 28p. (Orig.). (J). (gr. 2-4). pap. 20.00 *(978-0-9600792-8-5(9))* Rymer Bks.

Sabuda, Robert. Beauty & the Beast: A Pop-Up Adaptation of the Classic Tale. Sabuda, Robert, illus. 2010. (ENG., Illus.). 12p. (J). (gr. -1-2). 34.99 *(978-1-4169-6079-9(1),* Little Simon) Little Simon.

—The Little Mermaid. Sabuda, Robert, illus. 2013. (ENG., Illus.). 12p. (J). (gr. 1). 34.99 *(978-1-4169-6080-5(5),* Little Simon) Little Simon.

Sachs, Harley L. A Troll for Christmas & Other Stories. 2009. (ENG., Illus.). 240p. (J). pap. 14.99 *(978-1-934841-80-8(3),* Zumaya Thresholds) Zumaya Pubns. LLC.

Said. The Seven Voyages of Sinbad the Sailor. Rashin, illus. 2015. (ENG.). 64p. (J). 19.95 *(978-0-7358-4240-3(X))* North-South Bks., Inc.

Sakade, Florence & Hayashi, Yoshio. Kintaro's Adventures & Other Japanese Children's Favorite Stories. rev. ed. 2008. (ENG., Illus.). 48p. (J). (gr. -1-3). 12.95 *(978-4-8053-0994-0(6))* Tuttle Publishing.

—Urashima Taro & Other Japanese Children's Favorite Stories. Kurosaki, Yoshisuke, illus. 2008. (ENG.). 48p. (J). (gr. -1-3). 12.95 *(978-4-8053-0997-1(0))* Tuttle Publishing.

Sakade, Florence & Kurosaki, Yoshisuke. Peach Boy & Other Japanese Children's Favorite Stories. 2008. (ENG., Illus.). 48p. (J). (gr. k-3). 12.95 *(978-4-8053-0996-4(2))* Tuttle Publishing.

Salan, Felipe Lopez, illus. Jack & the Beanstalk. 2006. (ENG.). 32p. (J). (gr. -1). 15.95 *(978-1-933327-11-2(1))* Purple Bear Bks., Inc.

The Salt Mountain. 2004. (Illus.). 32p. 3.99 *(978-1-894998-06-2(5))* Lake, Jack Productions, Inc. CAN. Dist: Hushion Hse. Publishing, Ltd.

Samaniego, Félix María. EL CUENTO DE LA LECHERA. 2003. (Troquelados Clásicos Ser.). (SPA & ENG., Illus.). 16p. (J). (gr. -1-k). pap. 3.95 *(978-84-7864-676-0(0))* Combel Editorial, S.A. ESP. Dist: Independent Pubs. Group.

—LA LECHERA. 2005. (Caballo Alado Clásico Series-Al Paso Ser.). (SPA & ENG., Illus.). 24p. (J). (gr. -1-k). 7.95 *(978-84-7864-852-8(6))* Combel Editorial, S.A. ESP. Dist: Independent Pubs. Group.

San Souci, Robert D. Cendrillon: A Caribbean Cinderella. 2014. 19.00 *(978-1-63419-651-2(1))* Perfection Learning Corp.

—Cinderella Skeleton. Catrow, David, illus. 2004. (ENG.). 32p. (J). (gr. -1-3). reprint ed. pap. 6.99 *(978-0-15-205069-6(8))* Houghton Mifflin Harcourt Publishing Co.

Sand, George. What Flowers Say: And Other Stories. Erskine Hirko, Holly, tr. from FRE. Crabapple, Molly, illus. 2014. (ENG.). 224p. (J). (gr. 2-7). pap. 15.95 *(978-1-55861-857-2(0))* Feminist Pr. at The City Univ. of New York.

Sandburg, Carl. Rootabaga Stories. Petersham, Maud & Petersham, Miska, illus. 2003. (ENG.). 192p. (J). (gr. 2-5). pap. 6.95 *(978-0-15-204714-6(X))* Houghton Mifflin Harcourt Publishing Co.

—Rootabaga Stories. 2009. 128p. (gr. 3-18). pap. 10.95 *(978-1-60664-425-6(4))* Rodgers, Alan Bks.

—Rootabaga Stories. 2015. (ENG., Illus.). (J). (gr. 3). 24.95 ***(978-1-297-54480-4(3));*** 24.95 ***(978-1-298-53677-8(4))*** Creative Media Partners, LLC.

—Rootabaga Stories. 2017. (ENG., Illus.). 192p. (J). pap. 5.95 *(978-0-486-81560-2(9))* Dover Pubns., Inc.

Sanderson, Ruth. Papa Gatto: An Italian Fairy Tale. 2015. (ENG., Illus.). 32p. (J). 17.95 *(978-1-56656-090-0(X))* Interlink Publishing Group, Inc.

—Snow Princess. 2014. (ENG., Illus.). 32p. (J). pap. 17.95 *(978-1-56656-985-9(0),* Crocodile Bks.) Interlink Publishing Group, Inc.

Sandoval, Migs, illus. Beauty & the Beast: Level 3: Learn Chinese Mandarin Through Fairy Tales. 2006. (Learn Chinese Through Fairy Tales Ser.). (ENG & CHI.). 29p. (J). (gr. -1-3). pap. 14.95 incl. audio compact disk *(978-1-891888-91-5(9))* Slangman Publishing.

—Cinderella: Level 1: Learn French Through Fairy Tales. 2006. (Learn French Through Fairy Tales Ser.). (ENG & FRE.). 29p. (J). (gr. -1-3). pap. 14.95 incl. audio compact disk *(978-1-891888-75-5(7))* Slangman Publishing.

—Goldilocks & the 3 Bears: Level 2: Learn French Through Fairy Tales. 2006. (Learn French Through Fairy Tales Ser.). (ENG & FRE.). 29p. (J). (gr. -1-3). pap. 14.95 incl. audio compact disk *(978-1-891888-81-6(1))* Slangman Publishing.

Sanfilippo, Simona, illus. Rapunzel. 2009. (Flip-Up Fairy Tales Ser.). (ENG.). 24p. (J). (gr. -1-2). pap. *(978-1-84643-249-1(9));* audio compact disk *(978-1-84643-292-7(8))* Child's Play International Ltd.

Sanrio Company, LTD. Hello Kitty Presents the Storybook Collection: Alice's Adventures in Wonderland. 2016. (Hello Kitty Storybook Ser.). (ENG., Illus.). 32p. (J). (gr. -1-k). 10.95 *(978-1-4197-2032-1(5),* Abrams Appleseed) Abrams, Inc.

Santillo, LuAnn. Jack. Santillo, LuAnn, ed. 2003. (Half-Pint Kids Readers Ser.). (Illus.). 7p. (J). (gr. -1-1). pap. 1.00 *(978-1-59256-062-2(8))* Half-Pint Kids, Inc.

Santoro Licensing. Once upon a Gorjuss Time: Six Classic Tales to Dream By. Santoro, illus. 2016. (Gorjuss Ser.). (ENG.). 112p. (J). (gr. 3-7). 19.99 *(978-0-7636-7742-8(6),* Candlewick Entertainment) Candlewick Pr.

Saxon, Victoria & Posner-Sanchez, Andrea. Belle Is My Babysitter (Disney Princess) Laguna, Fabio & Andreu, Meritxell, illus. 2016. (Little Golden Book Ser.). (ENG.). 24p. (J). (-k). 4.99 *(978-0-7364-3502-4(6),* Golden/Disney) Random Hse. Children's Bks.

Scary Fairy Tales. 2015. (Scary Fairy Tales Ser.). (ENG.). 40p. (J). (gr. 3-4). 319.50 *(978-1-4824-2559-8(9));* pap., pap., pap. 843.00 *(978-1-4824-3489-7(X));* pap., pap., pap. 140.50 *(978-1-4824-3490-3(3))* Stevens, Gareth Publishing LLLP.

Scheid, Petra Maria. Fairy Tales, Elves & Magicans. 2009. 82p. pap. *(978-3-8391-1065-2(3))* Books on Demand GmbH.

Schmid, Susan Maupin. If the Magic Fits. (100 Dresses Ser.: 1). (ENG.). (J). (gr. 3-7). 2017. 320p. 7.99 ***(978-0-553-53369-9(X),*** Yearling) 2016. (Illus.). 304p. 16.99 *(978-0-553-53366-8(5),* Random Hse. Bks. for Young Readers) Random Hse. Children's Bks.

Schmidt, Gary D. Straw into Gold. 2009. (ENG.). 176p. (J). (gr. 2-5). pap. 7.99 *(978-0-547-23776-3(6))* Houghton Mifflin Harcourt Publishing Co.

Schmidt, Karen. The Gingerbread Man. 2007. (ENG., Illus.). (J). (gr. -1-3). 9.99 *(978-0-545-01485-4(9))* Scholastic, Inc.

Schmidt, Karen, retold by. The Gingerbread Man. 2007. (J). (gr. -1-2). pap. 9.95 incl. audio compact disk *(978-0-545-01773-2(4))* Scholastic, Inc.

Schmidt, Karen Lee & Schmidt, Karen. The Gingerbread Man. 2007. (ENG., Illus.). 31p. (J). (gr. -1-3). 18.95 *(978-0-545-01781-7(5))* Scholastic, Inc.

Schow, Betsy. Spelled. 2015. (Storymakers Ser.: 0). (ENG.). 352p. (YA). (gr. 6-12). pap. 9.99 *(978-1-4926-0871-4(8),* 9781492608714) Sourcebooks, Inc.

Schram, Peninnah. The Magic Pomegranate. Hall, Melanie, illus. (On My Own Folklore Ser.). 48p. 2008. (ENG.). (gr. 2-4). pap. 6.95 *(978-0-8225-6746-2(6),* First Avenue Editions) 2007. (J). lib. bdg. 17.95 *(978-0-8225-8856-6(0),* Kar-Ben Publishing) Lerner Publishing Group.

Schroeder, Lisa. The Girl in the Tower. Ceccoli, Nicoletta, illus. 2016. (ENG.). 256p. (J). (gr. 1). 16.99 *(978-0-8050-9513-5(6),* 9780805095135, Holt, Henry & Co. Bks. For Young Readers) Holt, Henry & Co.

Schuette, Sarah L. Princesses & Fairy Tales: A Spot-It Challenge, 1 vol. 2011. (Spot It Ser.). (ENG.). 32p. (gr. 1-2). lib. bdg. 27.32 *(978-1-4296-5987-1(4),* Aplus Bks.) Capstone Press of Coughlan Cos.

Schulman, Janet. The Nutcracker: The Untold Story. Graef, Renee, illus. 2005. 40p. (J). pap. 6.99 *(978-0-06-443790-5(6),* Harper Trophy) HarperCollins Pubs.

Schwartz, Alvin. Scary Stories to Tell in the Dark. Helquist, Brett, illus. 2010. (Scary Stories Ser.). (ENG.). 128p. (J). (gr. 4-18). 16.99 *(978-0-06-083519-4(2));* pap. 5.99 *(978-0-06-083520-0(6))* HarperCollins Pubs.

Schwartz, Alvin. Scary Stories to Tell in the Dark. Gammell, Stephen, illus. 2017. (Scary Stories Ser.: 1). 128p. (J). (gr. 3-7). pap. 6.99 ***(978-0-06-268282-6(2))*** HarperCollins Pubs.

Schwartz, Corey Rosen. Twinderella, a Fractioned Fairy Tale. Marcero, Deborah, illus. 2017. (ENG.). 32p. (J). (gr. -1-3). 17.99 ***(978-0-399-17633-3(0),*** G.P. Putnam's Sons Books for Young Readers) Penguin Young Readers Group.

Scieszka, Jon. The Frog Prince, Continued. 2003. (Live Oak Readalong Ser.). (Illus.). (J). 28.95 incl. audio compact disk *(978-1-59112-515-0(4));* 25.95 incl. audio *(978-1-59112-229-6(5))* Live Oak Media.

—The Frog Prince, Continued. Johnson, Steve, illus. 2003. pap. 39.95 incl. audio compact disk *(978-1-59112-522-8(7))* Live Oak Media.

—The Frog Prince, Continued, 4 bks. 2003. (Live Oak Readalong Ser.). (J). pap. 37.95 incl. audio *(978-1-59112-230-2(9))* Live Oak Media.

—The True Story of the 3 Little Pigs! Smith, Lane, illus. 25th anniv. ed. 2014. (ENG.). 32p. (J). (gr. k-3). 17.99 *(978-0-451-47195-6(4),* Viking Books for Young Readers) Penguin Young Readers Group.

Scollen, C. My Giant Sticker Stencil. 2010. 72p. pap. *(978-1-84610-965-2(5))* Make Believe Ideas.

Scott, Goeffrey. Fairy Tales for Adults. 2007. 116p. per. 19.95 *(978-1-4241-6532-2(6))* America Star Bks.

Scretching, Dorothy/Janis. Story Time with Princess Dorothy. Walters, Steve, ed. Brunot, Katerina, illus. 2012. 32p. (J). 20.00 *(978-0-9719767-4-0(0),* Crowned Warrior Publishing) Walters, Steve Ministries.

Seal, Julia. Three Little Pigs. 2013. (Classic Fairy Tale Pop-Ups Ser.). (ENG.). 12p. (J). (gr. -1-1). 12.99 *(978-0-7641-6599-3(2))* Barron's Educational Series, Inc.

Sedgwick, Marcus. Blood Red, Snow White. 2016. (ENG.). 320p. (YA). 17.99 *(978-1-62672-547-8(0),* 9781626725478) Roaring Brook Pr.

Segovia, Gertrudis. The Spanish Fairy Book. 2012. (Dover Children's Classics Ser.). (AVE, SPA & ENG., Illus.). 321p. (J). (gr. 6-8). pap. 12.95 *(978-0-486-40782-1(9))* Dover Pubns., Inc.

Segur, Sophie. Old French Fairy Tales. Sterrett, Virginia Frances, illus. 2010. (ENG.). 296p. (gr. -1-3). pap. 19.95 *(978-1-4290-1186-0(6))* Applewood Bks.

Seleccion de Oro: Libro Azul.Tr. of Golden Selection of Tales - Blue Book. (SPA.). (J). 13.48 *(978-84-8426-241-1(3))* Susaeta Ediciones, S.A. ESP. Dist: AIMS International Bks., Inc.

Seleccion de Oro: Libro Morado.Tr. of Golden Selection: Purple Book. (SPA.). (J). 13.48 *(978-84-8426-240-4(5))* Susaeta Ediciones, S.A. ESP. Dist: AIMS International Bks., Inc.

Seleccion de Oro: Libro Rojo.Tr. of Golden Selection: Red Book. (SPA.). (J). 13.48 *(978-84-8426-243-5(X))* Susaeta Ediciones, S.A. ESP. Dist: AIMS International Bks., Inc.

Seleccion de Oro: Libro Verde.Tr. of Golden Selection - Green Book. (SPA.). (J). 13.48 *(978-84-8426-242-8(1))* Susaeta Ediciones, S.A. ESP. Dist: AIMS International Bks., Inc.

Selected Classic Fairy Tales Series, 2 bks. (Illus.). (J). (gr. k-6). lib. bdg. 27.90 *(978-1-56674-945-9(X))* Forest Hse. Publishing Co., Inc.

Selfors, Suzanne. Ever after High: Hero Training: A Destiny Do-Over Diary. 2015. (ENG., Illus.). 160p. (J). (gr. 3-7). 9.99 *(978-0-316-40139-5(0))* Little, Brown Bks. for Young Readers.

—Ever after High: Science & Sorcery: a Destiny Do-Over Diary. 2015. (ENG., Illus.). 160p. (J). (gr. 3-7). 9.99 *(978-0-316-40133-3(1))* Little, Brown Bks. for Young Readers.

—Kiss & Spell. 2015. (Ever after High Ser.: Bk. 2). (ENG., Illus.). 224p. (J). (gr. 3-7). 13.99 *(978-0-316-40131-9(5))* Little, Brown Bks. for Young Readers.

—Next Top Villain. 2015. (School Story Ser.). (ENG., Illus.). 224p. (J). (gr. 3-7). 13.99 *(978-0-316-40128-9(5))* Little Brown & Co.

—A Semi-Charming Kind of Life. 2015. (Ever after High Ser.: Bk. 3). 213p. (J). *(978-0-316-40135-7(8))* Little Brown & Co.

—A Semi-Charming Kind of Life. 2015. (Ever after High Ser.: Bk. 3). (ENG., Illus.). 224p. (J). (gr. 3-7). 13.99 *(978-0-316-40136-4(6))* Little, Brown Bks. for Young Readers.

Sesame Street Staff. Fairly Furry 2 bk Big Red Riding Hood 3 Little Grouches. 2007. 15.99 *(978-1-59069-625-5(5))* Studio Mouse LLC.

—Fairly Furry 2 bk Rhyming Rapunzel Rosita & Beanstalk. 2007. 15.99 *(978-1-59069-624-8(7))* Studio Mouse LLC.

—Fairly Furry Fairy Tales 3 bk Pack. 2007. 19.99 *(978-1-59069-623-1(9))* Studio Mouse LLC.

Sewell, Anna. Black Beauty: Faber Children's Classics. 2015. (ENG.). 336p. (J). pap. 8.95 *(978-0-571-32337-1(5))* Faber & Faber, Inc.

Shadow, Stone. Faithful John. 2010. 34p. pap. 21.99 *(978-1-4500-0787-0(2))* Xlibris Corp.

Shapiro, Brigette. The Tale of the Tooth Fairy. 2004. 21p. pap. 24.95 *(978-1-4137-3479-9(0))* PublishAmerica, Inc.

Sharkey, Niamh & Walker, Richard. Jack & the Beanstalk. Sharkey, Niamh, illus. 2006. (ENG., Illus.). 40p. (J). (gr. -1-2). 10.99 *(978-1-905236-69-5(7))* Barefoot Bks., Inc.

Sharpe, Leah Marinsky. The Goat-Faced Girl: A Classic Italian Folktale. Marinsky, Jane, illus. 2009. 32p. (J). (gr. 1-4). 16.95 *(978-1-56792-393-3(3))* Godine, David R. Pub.

Sharratt, Nick & Tucker, Stephen. The Three Little Pigs, 2 vols. Sharratt, Nick, illus. 2016. (Lift-The-Flap Fairy Tales Ser.). (ENG., Illus.). 24p. (J). (gr. -1-k). bds. 11.99 *(978-1-5098-1713-9(1))* Pan Macmillan GBR. Dist: Independent Pubs. Group.

Shaskan, Stephen. The Three Triceratops Tuff. Shaskan, Stephen, illus. 2013. (ENG., Illus.). 32p. (J). (gr. -1-2). 16.99 *(978-1-4424-4397-6(9),* Beach Lane Bks.) Beach Lane Bks.

Shaskan, Trisha Speed. Honestly, Red Riding Hood Was Rotten! The Story of Little Red Riding Hood As Told by the Wolf, 1 vol. Guerlais, Gérald, illus. 2013. (Other Side of the Story Ser.). (ENG.). 24p. (gr. 2-3). 9.95 *(978-1-4795-1940-8(5))* Picture Window Bks.

—Truly, We Both Loved Beauty Dearly! The Story of Sleeping Beauty as Told by the Good & Bad Fairies. Tayal, Amit, illus. 2013. (Other Side of the Story Ser.). (ENG.). 24p. (gr. 2-3). 27.32 *(978-1-4048-7940-9(4))* Picture Window Bks.

—Truly, We Both Loved Beauty Dearly! The Story of Sleeping Beauty As Told by the Good & Bad Fairies. Tayal, Amit, illus. 2013. (Other Side of the Story Ser.). (ENG.). 24p. (gr. 2-3). 9.95 *(978-1-4795-1945-3(6))* Picture Window Bks.

Shaskan, Trisha Speed & Loewen, Nancy. Truly, We Both Loved Beauty Dearly! The Story of Sleeping Beauty, As Told by the Good & Bad Fairies. Tayal, Amit & Alsonso, Denis, illus. 2013. (Other Side of the Story Ser.). (ENG.). 24p. (gr. 2-3). pap. 6.95 *(978-1-4795-1949-1(9))* Picture Window Bks.

Sheldon, Dyan. The Moon Dragons. Blythe, Gary, illus. 2015. (J). 17.32 *(978-1-4677-6318-9(7))* Lerner Publishing Group.

—Moon Dragons. Blythe, Gary, illus. 2015. (ENG.). 32p. (J). (gr. -1-3). 16.95 *(978-1-4677-6314-1(4))* Lerner Publishing Group.

Shepard, Aaron. La Hija del Rey de los Mares. Spirin, Gennady, illus. (SPA.). 32p. (J). (gr. 3-5). *(978-84-264-3725-9(7),* LM5051) Editorial Lumen ESP. Dist: Lectorum Pubns., Inc.

—King o' the Cats. Sorra, Kristin, illus. 2010. (ENG.). 32p. (J). (gr. -1-3). 11.99 *(978-1-4424-1256-9(9),* Atheneum Bks. for Young Readers) Simon & Schuster Children's Publishing.

—One-Eye! Two-Eyes! Three-Eyes! A Very Grimm Fairy Tale. Clement, Gary, illus. 2006. (ENG.). 32p. (J). (gr. k-2). 17.99 *(978-0-689-86740-8(9),* Atheneum Bks. for Young Readers) Simon & Schuster Children's Publishing.

Shepherd, Donna J. Ava's Secret Tea Party. Sinclair, Bella, illus. 2012. 24p. 19.95 *(978-1-61633-285-3(9));* pap. 11.95 *(978-1-61633-286-0(7))* Guardian Angel Publishing, Inc.

Shirley Temple's Favorite Tales of Long Ago. 2011. 66p. 36.95 *(978-1-258-04171-7(5))* Literary Licensing, LLC.

Sholl, Anna. The Faery Tales of Weir. 2006. 116p. per. 9.95 *(978-1-59818-475-4(X))* Aegypan.

—Faery Tales of Weir. 2006. 116p. 22.95 *(978-1-59818-405-1(9))* Aegypan.

Shrestha, Sophie & Shrestha, Romio. In Search of the Thunder Dragon. Shrestha, Sophie & Shrestha, Romio, illus. 2007. (ENG., Illus.). 32p. (J). (gr. 3). 16.95 *(978-1-60109-100-0(1))* Mandala Publishing.

Shulman, Lisa. The Matzo Ball Boy. Litzinger, Rosanne, illus. 2007. (ENG.). 32p. (J). (gr. -1-2). pap. 6.99 *(978-0-14-240769-1(0),* Puffin Books) Penguin Young Readers Group.

Shulman, Polly. The Grimm Legacy. 2011. (ENG.). 352p. (J). (gr. 5-18). 8.99 *(978-0-14-241904-5(4),* Puffin Books) Penguin Young Readers Group.

Shurtliff, Liesl. Jack: The True Story of Jack & the Beanstalk. 2015. (ENG.). 304p. (J). (gr. 3-7). 16.99 *(978-0-385-75579-5(1),* Knopf Bks. for Young Readers) Random Hse. Children's Bks.

—Red: the True Story of Red Riding Hood. (ENG.). 256p. (J). (gr. 3-7). 2017. 7.99 *(978-0-385-75586-3(4),* Yearling) 2016. 16.99 *(978-0-385-75583-2(X),* Knopf Bks. for Young Readers) Random Hse. Children's Bks.

—Rump: The True Story of Rumpelstiltskin. (ENG.). 272p. (J). (gr. 3-7). 2014. pap. 7.99 *(978-0-307-97796-0(X),* Yearling) 2013. 16.99 *(978-0-307-97793-9(5),* Knopf Bks. for Young Readers) 2013. lib. bdg. 19.99 *(978-0-307-97794-6(3),* Knopf Bks. for Young Readers) Random Hse. Children's Bks.

Shuttleworth, Cathie, illus. Classic Collection of Fairy Tales & Poems, 2 vols. 2014. (ENG.). 192p. (J). (gr. 2-12). 19.99 *(978-1-84322-972-8(2),* Armadillo) Anness Publishing GBR. Dist: National Bk. Network.

Siks, Geraldine B. Ali Baba & the Forty Thieves. (Illus.). (YA). (gr. 6-12). 6.00 *(978-0-87602-103-3(8))* Family Plays.

Silver Dolphin. First Stories: Cinderella. 2017. (First Stories Ser.). (ENG., Illus.). 10p. (J). bds. 8.99 *(978-1-62686-898-4(0),* Silver Dolphin Bks.) Readerlink Distribution Services, LLC.

Silver Dolphin Books, Editors of. My Fabulous Fairy Tale Collection. 2017. (ENG., Illus.). 192p. (J). (gr. -1). 14.99 *(978-1-62686-976-9(6),* Silver Dolphin Bks.) Readerlink Distribution Services, LLC.

Silver Dolphin en Español Editors. Disney Princesa Cine en Casa. 2003. (Cine en casa Disney Ser.). (SPA.). 46p. (J). *(978-970-718-111-3(7),* Silver Dolphin en Español) Advanced Marketing, S. de R. L. de C. V.

—Llegs la hora del baile: Time for the Ball, Spanish-Language Edition. 2005. (SPA., Illus.). 22p. (J). *(978-970-718-287-5(3),* Silver Dolphin en Español) Advanced Marketing, S. de R. L. de C. V.

Silver Dolphin en Español Staff, creator. Caritas Felices. 2007. (Disney Princesa (Silver Dolphin) Ser.). (Illus.). 10p. (J). (gr. -1). bds. *(978-970-718-390-2(X),* Silver Dolphin en Español) Advanced Marketing, S. de R. L. de C. V.

Simon and Schuster UK Staff. Sleeping Beauty: A Silhouette Theatre. 2017. (ENG., Illus.). 16p. (J). 24.99 *(978-1-4711-4620-6(0),* Simon & Schuster Children's) Simon & Schuster, Ltd. GBR. Dist: Simon & Schuster, Inc.

Simonson, Louise. Snow White & the Seven Robots. Sanchez, Jimena, illus. 2015. (Far Out Fairy Tales Ser.). (ENG.). 40p. (gr. 3-4). lib. bdg. 25.32 *(978-1-4342-9648-1(2))* Stone Arch Bks.

Simonson, Louise, et al. Far Out Fairy Tales. Frampton, Otis et al, illus. 2016. (Far Out Fairy Tales Ser.). (ENG.). 176p. (gr. 3-4). pap. 12.95 *(978-1-4965-2511-6(6),* Far Out Fairy Tales) Stone Arch Bks.

Sims, Lesley. How Zebras Got Their Stripes. 2009. (Young Reading Ser.). 64p. (J). 6.99 *(978-0-7945-2525-5(3),* Usborne) EDC Publishing.

Sims, Lesley & Sims, Lesley. Stories from Around the World for Children. 2013. (Picture Bks). 128p. (J). ring bd. 18.99 *(978-0-7945-3210-9(1),* Usborne) EDC Publishing.

Singer, Marilyn. Miss Muffet, or What Came After. Litchfield, David, illus. 2016. (ENG.). 40p. (J). (gr. 1-4). 16.99

(978-0-547-90566-2(1)) Houghton Mifflin Harcourt Publishing Co.

Sisler, Celeste. Disney Fairies: Fairy Tales: a Treasury. 2015. (ENG., Illus.). 272p. (J). (gr. -1-3). 11.99 (978-0-316-37856-7(9)) Little, Brown Bks. for Young Readers.

—Disney Fairies: Very Short Fairy Stories: a Treasury. 2015. (ENG., Illus.). 272p. (J). (gr. -1-3). 11.99 (978-0-316-28348-9(7)) Little, Brown Bks. for Young Readers.

Skidmore, Lauren. The Fairest Poison. 2016. (YA). pap. 16.99 (978-1-4621-1792-5(9)) Cedar Fort, Inc./CFI Distribution.

Sky Koster, Amy & Patrick, Ella. Ariel & the Big Baby/Rapunzel Finds a Friend (Disney Princess) Thomas, Jeffrey, illus. 2017. (Pictureback(R) Ser.). (ENG.). 48p. (J). (gr. -1-2). pap. 5.99 **(978-0-7364-3747-9(9)**, RH/Disney) Random Hse. Children's Bks.

Sleeping Beauty. 2008. (Read & Learn Sticker Books Ser.). 48p. pap. (978-1-4075-3196-0(4)) Parragon, Inc.

Sleeping Beauty. (Read-Along Ser.). (J). 7.99 incl. audio (978-1-55723-010-2(2)) Walt Disney Records.

Smallfield, Jane. The Bedtime Treasury of Real Fairy Tales. Smallfield, Graeme, illus. 2005. 96p. 17.95 (978-0-689-03923-2(9), Milk & Cookies) ibooks, Inc.

Smith, Alex T. Little Red & the Very Hungry Lion. 2016. (ENG., Illus.). 32p. (J). (gr. -1-k). 17.99 (978-0-545-91438-3(8), Scholastic Pr.) Scholastic, Inc.

Smith, Jane. Fairytale Mix-up. Raynor, Jackie, illus. 2005. 12p. (J). (gr. -1-3). per. 10.95 (978-1-58117-419-9(5), Intervisual/Piggy Toes) Bendon, Inc.

Smith, Robert Kimmel. Jelly Belly. 155p. (J). (gr. 3-5). pap. 4.50 (978-0-8072-1406-0(X), Listening Library) Random Hse. Audio Publishing Group.

Smith, Sherri L. The Toymaker's Apprentice. 2015. (ENG., Illus.). 400p. (J). (gr. 5). 16.99 (978-0-399-25295-2(9), G.P. Putnam's Sons Books for Young Readers) Penguin Young Readers Group.

—The Toymaker's Apprentice. 2016. (ENG.). 400p. (J). (gr. 5). 19.65 (978-0-606-39322-5(6)) Turtleback Bks.

Snedeker, Gus. Heroes, Fools, & Ghosts: Folk Tales & Legends. 2013. (Illus.). 48p. (J). pap. (978-1-4222-2505-9(4)) Mason Crest.

—Heroes, Fools, & Ghosts: Folk Tales & Legends. Jabbour, Alan, ed. 2012. (North American Folklore for Youth Ser.). (Illus.). 48p. (J). (gr. 4). 19.95 (978-1-4222-2494-6(5)) Mason Crest.

Sneed, Brad & Andersen, Hans Christian. Thumbelina. Sneed, Brad, illus. 2004. (ENG., Illus.). 40p. (J). (gr. -1-3). 17.99 (978-0-8037-2812-7(3), Dial Bks) Penguin Young Readers Group.

Snow White. (Read-Along Ser.). (J). 7.99 incl. audio (978-1-55723-387-5(X)) Walt Disney Records.

Snow White & Rose Red. (Ladybird Bks.). (ARA., Illus.). 52p. (J). 4.95 (978-0-86685-225-8(5), LDL181) International Bk. Ctr., Inc.

Snow White & the Seven Dwarfs. 2008. (Read & Learn Sticker Books Ser.). 48p. pap. (978-1-4075-3197-7(2)) Parragon, Inc.

Snowe, Olivia. Beauty & the Basement, 1 vol. Lamoreaux, Michelle, illus. 2014. (Twicetold Tales Ser.). (ENG.). 128p. (gr. 3-4). 8.95 (978-1-4342-9830-0(2)) Stone Arch Bks.

—Cassie & the Woolf, 1 vol. Lamoreaux, Michelle, illus. 2013. (Twicetold Tales Ser.). (ENG.). 128p. (gr. 3-4). lib. bdg. 25.32 (978-1-4342-3786-6(9)) Stone Arch Bks.

—Dandelion & the Witch, 1 vol. Lamoreaux, Michelle, illus. 2014. (Twicetold Tales Ser.). (ENG.). 128p. (gr. 3-4). 25.32 (978-1-4342-9147-9(2)) Stone Arch Bks.

—The Girl & the Seven Thieves, 1 vol. Lamoreaux, Michelle, illus. 2013. (Twicetold Tales Ser.). (ENG.). 128p. (gr. 3-4). 8.95 (978-1-4342-6280-6(4)); lib. bdg. 25.32 (978-1-4342-6018-5(6)) Stone Arch Bks.

—The Glass Voice, 1 vol. Lamoreaux, Michelle, illus. 2014. (Twicetold Tales Ser.). (ENG.). 128p. (gr. 3-4). 25.32 (978-1-4342-9148-6(0)) Stone Arch Bks.

—Hansen & Gracie, 1 vol. Lamoreaux, Michelle, illus. 2014. (Twicetold Tales Ser.). (ENG.). 128p. (gr. 3-4). pap. 5.95 (978-1-4342-9150-9(2)) Stone Arch Bks.

—A Home in the Sky, 1 vol. Lamoreaux, Michelle, illus. (Twicetold Tales Ser.). (ENG.). 128p. (gr. 3-4). 2014. pap. 5.95 (978-1-4342-9554-5(0)) 2013. 8.95 (978-1-4342-6279-0(0)) 2013. lib. bdg. 25.32 (978-1-4342-5041-4(5)) Stone Arch Bks.

—The Sealed-Up House, 1 vol. Lamoreaux, Michelle, illus. (Twicetold Tales Ser.). (ENG.). 128p. (gr. 3-4). 2014. pap. 5.95 (978-1-4342-9556-9(7)) 2013. 8.95 (978-1-4342-6281-3(2)) 2013. lib. bdg. 25.32 (978-1-4342-6019-2(4)) Stone Arch Bks.

—Twicetold Tales. Lamoreaux, Michelle, illus. 2013. (Twicetold Tales Ser.). (ENG.). 128p. (gr. 3-4). 101.28 (978-1-4342-6355-1(X)) Stone Arch Bks.

So, Meilo & cummings, e. e. Fairy Tales. Firmage, George James, ed. 2004. (ENG., Illus.). 64p. 17.95 (978-0-87140-658-3(6), 40658) Liveright Publishing Corp.

Sohrabi, Behzad. The Legend of Sigh: A Collection of Fairy Tales. 2012. 76p. pap. 41.99 (978-1-4771-1969-3(8)) Xlibris Corp.

Soling, Cevin. Boris the Dog. Kille, Steve, illus. 2015. (ENG.). 44p. 14.95 (978-0-9767771-6-8(9)) Spectacle Films, Inc.

Sommer, Carl. The Boy Who Cried Wolf. Bogdan, Enache, illus. 2014. (Sommer-Time Story Classics Ser.). (ENG.). 32p. (J). (gr. k-4). 16.95 (978-1-57537-079-8(4)) Advance Publishing, Inc.

—Chicken Little. Mercado, Jorge, illus. 2014. (Sommer-Time Story Classics Ser.). (ENG.). 32p. (J). (gr. k-4). 16.95 (978-1-57537-076-7(X)) Advance Publishing, Inc.

—The Country Mouse & the City Mouse. Noe, Ignacio, illus. 2014. (Sommer-Time Story Classics Ser.). (ENG.). 32p. (J). (gr. k-4). 16.95 (978-1-57537-080-4(8)) Advance Publishing, Inc.

—The Emperor & the Seed. Martinez, Jorge, illus. 2016. (J). (978-1-57537-946-3(5)) Advance Publishing, Inc.

—The Emperor's New Clothes. Noe, Ignacio, illus. 2014. (Sommer-Time Story Classics Ser.). (ENG.). 32p. (J). (gr. k-4). 16.95 (978-1-57537-081-1(6)) Advance Publishing, Inc.

—The Great Deception. Noé, illus. 2009. (Quest for Success Ser.). (ENG.). 40p. (YA). pap. 4.95 (978-1-57537-279-2(7)); lib. bdg. 12.95 (978-1-57537-254-9(1)) Advance Publishing, Inc.

—The Great Deception(El Gran Engaño) Noé, illus. 2009. (Quest for Success Bilingual Ser.). (ENG & SPA.). 72p. (YA). lib. bdg. 14.95 (978-1-57537-228-0(2)) Advance Publishing, Inc.

—The Lion & the Three Bulls. Mercado, Jorge, illus. 2014. (Sommer-Time Story Classics Ser.). (ENG.). 32p. (J). (gr. k-4). 16.95 (978-1-57537-083-5(2)) Advance Publishing, Inc.

—The Little Red Hen. Noe, Ignacio, illus. 2014. (Sommer-Time Story Classics Ser.). (ENG.). 32p. (J). (gr. k-4). 16.95 (978-1-57537-084-2(0)) Advance Publishing, Inc.

—Little Red Riding Hood. Noe, Ignacio, illus. 2014. (Sommer-Time Story Classics Ser.). (ENG.). 32p. (J). (gr. k-4). 16.95 (978-1-57537-077-4(8)) Advance Publishing, Inc.

—The Miller, His Son & Their Donkey. Denman, Michael, illus. 2014. (Sommer-Time Story Classics Ser.). (ENG.). 32p. (J). (gr. k-4). 16.95 (978-1-57537-085-9(9)) Advance Publishing, Inc.

—The Tortoise & the Hare. Vignolo, Enrique, illus. 2014. (Sommer-Time Story Classics Ser.). (ENG.). 32p. (J). (gr. k-4). 16.95 (978-1-57537-086-6(7)) Advance Publishing, Inc.

—The Town Musicians of Bremen. Denman, Michael L., illus. 2016. (J). (978-1-57537-947-0(3)) Advance Publishing, Inc.

Sommer, Carl & Aesop. The Tiny Giant. Mercado, Jorge, illus. 2009. (Quest for Success Ser.). (ENG.). 40p. (YA). pap. 4.95 (978-1-57537-286-0(X)); lib. bdg. 12.95 (978-1-57537-261-7(4)) Advance Publishing, Inc.

Soni, Parwinder Singh, illus. Little Red Riding Hood. 2010. (J). (978-1-60617-132-5(1)) Teaching Strategies, LLC.

Soto, Maritza. The Mystery of Fairy Tales. 2013. 84p. pap. 8.95 (978-1-937829-83-4(9), Total Publishing & Media) Yorkshire Publishing Group.

Souhami, Jessica, illus. No Dinner! The Story of the Old Woman & the Pumpkin. 2012. (ENG.). 32p. (J). (gr. -1-2). pap. 8.99 (978-1-84507-818-8(7), Frances Lincoln) Quarto Publishing Group UK GBR. Dist: Hachette Bk. Group.

Soundprints Staff. Fairy Tales. 2005. (Studio Mouse Ser.). (Illus.). 256p. (J). (gr. -1-2). 14.95 (978-1-59069-229-5(2)) Studio Mouse LLC.

—My Princess Treasury. (Kindness Counts Ser.). (ENG., Illus.). 24p. (J). 14.99 (978-1-59069-373-5(6), 1A200); 14.99 (978-1-59069-381-0(7), 1A201) Studio Mouse LLC.

Southgate, Vera. The Three Little Pigs. 2016. (Well-Loved Tales Ser.). (ENG., Illus.). 56p. (J). (gr. 3-7). 9.99 (978-0-7232-9758-1(4)) Penguin Bks., Ltd. GBR. Dist: Independent Pubs. Group.

Souvestre, Emile. Peronnik: A French Fairy Tale of the Grail Quest. 2003. (ENG., Illus.). 1p. (gr. 1-5). 9.95 (978-0-89281-061-1(0), Healing Arts Pr.) Inner Traditions International, Ltd.

Sowers, Sherry. Tallulah & the Three Cowgirls. 2004. 23p. pap. 10.00 (978-1-4116-0771-2(6)) Lulu Pr., Inc.

Spanish Graphic Novels, 6 vols., Set. 2010. (Graphic Spin Ser.). (SPA., Illus.). 40p. 151.92 (978-1-4342-2100-1(8)) Capstone Press of Coughlan Cos.

Spenceley, Annabel, illus. Beauty & the Beast. (ENG.). 2017. 24p. pap. 7.99 (978-1-86147-817-7(8)) 2013. 48p. (J). (gr. -1-4). pap. 7.99 (978-1-84322-789-2(4)) Anness Publishing GBR. (Armadillo). Dist: National Bk. Network.

—Cinderella. 2016. (ENG.). 24p. pap. 7.99 (978-1-86147-813-9(5), Armadillo) Anness Publishing GBR. Dist: National Bk. Network.

Sperling, Thomas, illus. Little Red Riding Hood. 2005. (J). (978-0-7664-1055-8(2)) Abrams, Inc.

Sperling, Vatsala. Ram the Demon Slayer. Weltevrede, Pieter, illus. 2006. (ENG.). 32p. (J). (gr. -1-6). 15.95 (978-1-59143-057-5(7), Bear Cub Bks.) Bear & Co.

Spooner, Meagan. Hunted. 2017. 384p. (YA). (gr. 8). 17.99 (978-0-06-242228-6(6), HarperTeen) HarperCollins Pubs.

Squillace, Elisa, illus. Aladdin. 2007. (Flip-Up Fairy Tales Ser.). (ENG.). 24p. (J). (gr. 2-2). (978-1-84643-113-5(1)) Child's Play International Ltd.

Squires, Janet. The Gingerbread Cowboy. Berry, Holly, illus. 2006. 32p. (J). (gr. -1-3). (ENG.). 17.99 (978-0-06-077863-7(6)); lib. bdg. 18.89 (978-0-06-077864-4(4)) HarperCollins Pubs.

Stanek, Robert, pseud. The Kingdoms & the Elves of the Reaches (Reader's Choice Edition, Keeper Martin's Tales Book 1) 2008. (Illus.). 240p. pap. 15.95 (978-1-57545-196-1(4)) RP Media.

Staniszewski, Anna. My Epic Fairy Tale Fail. 2013. (My Very Unfairy Tale Life Ser.: 2). (ENG.). 224p. (J). (gr. 4-7). pap. 6.99 (978-1-4022-7930-0(2), 9781402279300, Sourcebooks Jabberwocky) Sourcebooks, Inc.

—Once upon a Cruise: a Wish Novel. 2016. (ENG.). 256p. (J). (gr. 3-7). pap. 6.99 (978-0-545-87986-6(8), Scholastic Paperbacks) Scholastic, Inc.

Stanley, Diane. The Cup & the Crown. 2012. (Silver Bowl Ser.: 2). (ENG.). 352p. (J). (gr. 3-7). 16.99 (978-0-06-196321-6(6)) HarperCollins Pubs.

Stanley, P. "Olivia". The Dreadful Noises of Landoshar. 2008. 44p. pap. 12.26 (978-0-557-02381-3(5)) Lulu Pr., Inc.

Steel, Flora Annie. English Fairy Tales. 2007. (ENG.). 262p. pap. 21.99 (978-1-4346-0692-1(9)); 296p. pap. 23.99 (978-1-4346-0752-2(6)) Creative Media Partners, LLC.

—English Fairy Tales. 2005. pap. (978-1-4065-0287-9(1)) Dodo Pr.

Steere, Marcia. Tales from My Coloring Book. 2012. (ENG.). (J). pap. (978-1-4675-2531-2(6)) Independent Pub.

Stegman-Bourgeois, Karen M. Trollerella. Long, Ethan, illus. 2006. (ENG.). 32p. (J). (gr. -1-3). 14.95 (978-0-8234-1918-0(5)) Holiday Hse., Inc.

Steig, Jeanne. A Handful of Beans. Steig, William, illus. 2016. (ENG.). 128p. (YA). (gr. 7). 17.99 (978-1-4814-3961-9(8), Atheneum/Caitlyn Dlouhy Books) Simon & Schuster Children's Publishing.

Steiner, Rudolf. Cinderella at the Ball. (Illus.). (J). lib. bdg. 6.00 (978-0-87895-625-8(5)) Modern Curriculum Pr.

—Three Grimms' Fairy Tales. Wagner, Gerard, illus. 2010. 88p. (J). 25.00 (978-0-88010-716-7(2)) SteinerBooks, Inc.

Stewart, Pat. Invisible Fairy Tales Magic Picture Book. 2003. (Dover Little Activity Bks.). (ENG., Illus.). 16p. (J). (gr. -1-2). pap. 1.50 (978-0-486-43022-5(7)) Dover Pubns., Inc.

Stewig, John Warren. Nobody Asked the Pea. Van Wright, Cornelius, illus. 2013. (ENG.). 32p. (J). (gr. 1-5). 16.95 (978-0-8234-2224-1(0)) Holiday Hse., Inc.

Stickler, John C. & Han, Soma. Maya & the Turtle: A Korean Fairy Tale. 2012. (ENG., Illus.). 32p. (J). (gr. -1-3). 14.95 (978-0-8048-4277-8(9)) Tuttle Publishing.

Stockham, Jess. Cinderella. 2006. (Flip-Up Fairy Tales Ser.). (ENG., Illus.). 24p. (J). (gr. 2-2). (978-1-904550-74-7(6)) Child's Play International Ltd.

Stockham, Jess, illus. Beauty & the Beast. 2007. (Flip-Up Fairy Tales Ser.). (ENG.). 24p. (J). (gr. -1-2). audio compact disk (978-1-84643-155-5(7)); (gr. 2-2). (978-1-84643-114-2(X)) Child's Play International Ltd.

—The Boy Who Cried Wolf. 2011. (Flip-Up Fairy Tales Ser.). (ENG.). 24p. (J). audio compact disk (978-1-84643-407-5(6)) Child's Play International Ltd.

—Cinderella. 2007. (Flip-Up Fairy Tales Ser.). (ENG.). 24p. (J). (gr. -1-2). audio compact disk (978-1-84643-091-6(7)) Child's Play International Ltd.

—The Cockerel, the Mouse & the Little Red Hen. (Flip-Up Fairy Tales Ser.). (ENG.). 24p. (J). 2007. (gr. -1-2). audio compact disk (978-1-84643-092-3(5)) 2006. (gr. 2-2). (978-1-904550-75-4(4)) Child's Play International Ltd.

—The Frog Prince. 2007. (Flip-Up Fairy Tales Ser.). (ENG.). 24p. (J). audio compact disk (978-1-84643-143-2(3)) Child's Play International Ltd.

Stockham, Jess, et al, illus. The Frog Prince. 2007. (Flip-Up Fairy Tales Ser.). (ENG.). 24p. (J). (gr. 2-2). pap. (978-1-84643-077-0(1)) Child's Play International Ltd.

Stockham, Jess, illus. Little Red Riding Hood. (Classic Fairy Tales Ser.). (ENG.). 24p. (J). 2011. audio compact disk (978-1-84643-458-7(0)) 2007. (gr. -1-2). audio compact disk (978-1-84643-088-6(7)) Child's Play International Ltd.

—The Princess & the Pea. 2010. (Flip-Up Fairy Tales Ser.). (ENG.). 24p. (J). (gr. -1-2). audio compact disk (978-1-84643-332-0(0)) Child's Play International Ltd.

—Puss in Boots. 2012. (Classic Fairy Tales Ser.). (ENG.). 24p. (J). (978-1-84643-441-9(6)) Child's Play International Ltd.

—The Steadfast Tin Soldier. 2012. (Flip-Up Fairy Tales Ser.). (ENG.). 24p. (J). (978-1-84643-477-8(7)) Child's Play International Ltd.

—Stone Soup. (Flip-Up Fairy Tales Ser.). (ENG.). 24p. (J). 2007. (gr. -1-2). audio compact disk (978-1-84643-094-7(1)) 2006. (gr. 2-2). pap. (978-1-84643-021-3(6)) Child's Play International Ltd.

Stockham, Jessica, illus. Little Red Riding Hood. 2005. (Flip-Up Fairy Tales Ser.). (ENG.). 24p. (J). pap. (978-1-904550-22-8(3)) Child's Play International Ltd.

Stockton, Frank Richard. The Bee-Man of Orn. 2013. (Notable American Authors Ser.). reprint ed. lthr. 79.00 (978-0-7812-8927-6(0)) Reprint Services Corp.

—The Bee-Man of Orn & Other Fanciful Tales. 2005. 124p. per. 10.95 (978-1-59818-695-6(7)) Aegypan.

—The Bee-Man of Orn & Other Fanciful Tales. 2004. reprint ed. pap. 1.99 (978-1-4192-5383-6(2)); pap. 20.95 (978-1-4191-5383-9(8)) Kessinger Publishing, LLC.

—Ting-a-Ling Tales. 2008. 88p. pap. 8.95 (978-1-60664-056-2(9)) Aegypan.

Stone Arch Books Staff. Beauty & the Beast: The Graphic Novel, 1 vol. Feldman, Luke, illus. 2008. (Graphic Spin Ser.). (ENG.). 40p. (gr. 1-3). pap. 5.95 (978-1-4342-0861-3(3), Graphic Revolve) Stone Arch Bks.

—Cinderella: The Graphic Novel, 1 vol. Timmins, Jeffrey Stewart, illus. 2008. (Graphic Spin Ser.). (ENG.). 40p. (gr. 1-3). pap. 5.95 (978-1-4342-0860-6(5), Graphic Revolve) Stone Arch Bks.

—Jack & the Beanstalk: The Graphic Novel, 1 vol. Tercio, Ricardo, illus. 2008. (Graphic Spin Ser.). (ENG.). 40p. (gr. 1-3). pap. 5.95 (978-1-4342-0862-0(1), Graphic Revolve) Stone Arch Bks.

—Red Riding Hood: The Graphic Novel, 1 vol. Rivas, Victor, illus. 2008. (Graphic Spin Ser.). (ENG.). 40p. (gr. 1-3). pap. 5.95 (978-1-4342-0865-1(6), Graphic Revolve) Stone Arch Bks.

—Rumpelstiltskin: The Graphic Novel, 1 vol. Alanis, Erik Valdez Y., illus. 2008. (Graphic Spin Ser.). (ENG.). 40p. (gr. 1-3). pap. 5.95 (978-1-4342-0864-4(8), Graphic Revolve) Stone Arch Bks.

Stone, Julia. The Lion Book of Fairy Tales. Jatkowska, Ag, illus. 2015. (ENG.). 128p. (J). (gr. -1-k). 17.99 (978-0-7459-6468-3(0)) Lion Hudson PLC GBR. Dist: Independent Pubs. Group.

Storrie, Paul. Perseus: The Hunt for Medusa's Head [A Greek Myth]. Yeates, Thomas, illus. 2009. (Graphic Myths & Legends Ser.). (ENG.). 48p. (gr. 4-8). pap. 8.95 (978-1-58013-888-8(8)) Lerner Publishing Group.

Strom, Laura Layton, et al. Opinions about Two Fairy Tales: Baba Yaga & Hansel & Gretel. Czernichowska, Joanna, illus. 2014. (Text Connections Ser.). (J). (gr. 3). (978-1-4509-9649-5(3)) Benchmark Education Co.

Studio Mouse, ed. Disney Preincess Best Friends: Flat Learn & Carry 4 Board Books & CD. rev. ed. 2008. 80p. (J). 12.99 (978-1-59069-553-1(4)) Studio Mouse LLC.

Studio Mouse Editorial. Belle: The Power of Love. 2008. (ENG., Illus.). 36p. (gr. -1-k). 7.99 (978-1-59069-435-0(X)) Studio Mouse LLC.

Studio Mouse Staff. Disney Princess - Happy Endings. 2005. (ENG., Illus.). 36p. (J). (gr. -1-3). 19.99 (978-1-59069-438-1(4), 1A305) Studio Mouse LLC.

Sunami, Kitoba & Sunami, Christopher. How the Fisherman Tricked the Genie. Hirao, Amiko, illus. 2007. (ENG.). 40p. (J). (gr. k-3). 14.99 (978-1-4169-6137-6(2), Simon & Schuster/Paula Wiseman Bks.) Simon & Schuster/Paula Wiseman Bks.

Susaeta, Equipo. La Bella Durmiente -Sleeping Beauty. Susaeta Publishing, Inc., Staff, ed. 2011. (Cuentos Bilingües Ser.). (SPA & ENG.). 34p. (J). (gr. k-2). 6.95 (978-84-305-2453-2(3)) Susaeta Ediciones, S.A. ESP. Dist: Independent Pubs. Group.

Susaeta Publishing, Inc., Staff, ed. BLANCANIEVES/SNOW WHITE. 2011. (Cuentos Bilingües Ser.). (SPA & ENG.). 34p. (J). (gr. k-2). 6.95 (978-84-305-2454-9(1)) Susaeta Ediciones, S.A. ESP. Dist: Independent Pubs. Group.

Sussman, Elissa. Burn. 2016. (Stray Ser.: 2). 272p. (YA). (gr. 8). 17.99 (978-0-06-227459-5(7), Greenwillow Bks.) HarperCollins Pubs.

—Stray. 2014. (Stray Ser.: 1). (ENG., Illus.). 384p. (YA). (gr. 8). 17.99 (978-0-06-227455-7(4), Greenwillow Bks.) HarperCollins Pubs.

Sutherland, Dianne, illus. Rashiecoat: A Story in Scots for Young Readers. 16p. pap. 6.95 (978-1-899827-19-0(6)) Scottish Children's Pr. GBR. Dist: Wilson & Assocs.

Sutton, Laurie S. & Peters, Stephanie True. Far Out Fairy Tales. Jennings, C. S. & Lopez, Alex, illus. 2016. (Far Out Fairy Tales Ser.). (ENG.). 40p. (gr. 3-4). 202.56 (978-1-4965-3793-5(9), Far Out Fairy Tales) Stone Arch Bks.

—Far Out Fairy Tales: Fall 16. Jennings, C. S. & Lopez, Alex, illus. 2016. (Far Out Fairy Tales Ser.). (ENG.). 40p. (gr. 3-4). pap. 11.90 (978-1-4965-3796-6(3), Far Out Fairy Tales) Stone Arch Bks.

Swan. Rumpelstiltskin. Date not set. (Illus.). 31p. pap. 25.95 (978-0-582-02567-7(2)) Addison-Wesley Longman, Ltd. GBR. Dist: Trans-Atlantic Pubns., Inc.

—Sleeping Beauty. Date not set. (Illus.). 32p. pap. 25.95 (978-0-582-02568-4(0)) Addison-Wesley Longman, Ltd. GBR. Dist: Trans-Atlantic Pubns., Inc.

Swedeen, Staci. Phoebe & the Flame-Bellied Toad: An Original Fairy Tale. 2006. (J). pap. (978-1-4108-7153-4(3)) Benchmark Education Co.

—The Toad Bridegroom: A Fairy Tale from Korea. 2006. (J). pap. (978-1-4108-7152-7(5)) Benchmark Education Co.

—Tombi-Ende & the Frog: A Fairy Tale from Southern Africa. 2006. (J). pap. (978-1-4108-7151-0(7)) Benchmark Education Co.

Swiderska, Barbara. The Fisherman's Bride. Swiderska, Barbara, illus. (Illus.). 32p. (J). (gr. -1-3). 12.95 (978-0-87592-018-4(7)) Scroll Pr., Inc.

Tagg, Christine. Cinderlily: A Floral Fairy Tale. Ellwand, David, ed. Ellwand, David, photos by. 2006. (Illus.). 26p. (J). (gr. k-4). reprint ed. 17.00 (978-1-4223-5558-9(6)) DIANE Publishing Co.

Tait, Elena. The Twisted Fairy Tale. 2009. 36p. pap. 16.99 (978-1-4389-2774-9(6)) AuthorHouse.

Talbott, Hudson & Lapine, James. Into the Woods. Talbott, Hudson, ed. 2006. (Illus.). 91p. (J). (gr. 4-8). pap. 20.00 (978-1-4223-5331-8(1)) DIANE Publishing Co.

Tan, Shaun. The Singing Bones. Tan, Shaun, illus. 2016. (ENG., Illus.). 192p. (J). (gr. 7). 24.99 (978-0-545-94612-4(3), Levine, Arthur A. Bks.) Scholastic, Inc.

Tao, Teri. Cowherd Boy & Weaver Girl. 2008. (ENG.). 48p. pap. 5.99 (978-1-930655-05-8(3)) Golden Peach Publishing.

Taplin, Sam. Little Red Riding Hood. 2008. (First Fairytales Look & Say Ser.). 12p. (J). (gr. -1). bds. 9.99 (978-0-7945-2199-8(1), Usborne) EDC Publishing.

—Sleeping Beauty. 2008. (First Fairytales Look & Say Ser.). 12p. (J). (gr. -1). bds. 9.99 (978-0-7945-2200-1(9), Usborne) EDC Publishing.

Tarico, Valerie. Deas & Other Imaginings: Ten Spiritual Folktales for Children. Troy, Tony, illus. 2011. (ENG.). 132p. (J). 25.95 (978-0-9773929-4-0(5)) Oracle Institute Pr., LLC, The.

Tarnowska, Wafa'. The Arabian Nights. Henaff, Carole, illus. 2010. (ENG.). 128p. (J). (gr. 3-18). 24.99 (978-1-84686-122-2(5)) Barefoot Bks., Inc.

—The Arabian Nights Chapter. Hénaff, Carole, illus. 2011. (ENG.). 160p. (J). (gr. 4-6). pap. 12.99 (978-1-84686-568-8(9)) Barefoot Bks., Inc.

—The Seven Wise Princesses: A Medieval Persian Epic. Nilesh, Misty, illus. 2008. (ENG.). 96p. (J). (gr. 5-9). 19.99 (978-1-84686-250-2(7)) Barefoot Bks., Inc.

TASCHEN. The Fairy Tales of Hans Christian Andersen. 2017. (ENG., Illus.). 224p. 15.00 (978-3-8365-4839-7(9)) TASCHEN DEU. Dist: Ingram Publisher Services.

Tavares, Victor, illus. Beauty & the Beast. 2007. (Picture Book Classics Ser.). (J). 24p. (gr. -1-3). 9.99 (978-0-7945-1855-4(9)); 63p. 8.99 (978-0-7945-1456-3(1)) EDC Publishing. (Usborne).

Tay-Audouard, L. K. Monkey King: A Classic Chinese Tale for Children. 2017. (ENG., Illus.). 32p. (J). (gr. -1-3). 9.95 (978-0-8048-4840-4(8)) Tuttle Publishing.

Taylor, Dan. First Stories: Rapunzel. 2017. (First Stories Ser.). (ENG., Illus.). 10p. (J). bds. 8.99 (978-1-62686-900-4(6), Silver Dolphin Bks.) Readerlink Distribution Services, LLC.

Taylor, Dan, illus. First Stories: Beauty & the Beast. 2017. (First Stories Ser.). (ENG.). 10p. (J). bds. 8.99 (978-1-62686-897-7(2), Silver Dolphin Bks.) Readerlink Distribution Services, LLC.

Tedder, Elizabeth, illus. The Three Bears. 2011. 20p. 35.95 (978-1-258-10100-8(9)) Literary Licensing, LLC.

Tegen, Katherine Brown. The Story of the Jack O'Lantern. Dorman, Brandon, illus. 2010. (ENG.). 32p. (J). (gr. -1-3). 12.99 (978-0-06-143088-6(9)) HarperCollins Pubs.

Teis, Kyra, adapted by. The Magic Flute: An Opera by Mozart, 1 vol. 2008. (ENG., Illus.). 32p. (J). (gr. k-9). 17.95 (978-1-59572-058-0(8)) Star Bright Bks., Inc.

Teitelbaum, Michael. Disney Princess Little Golden Book Favorites, Vol. 2. Williams, Don et al, illus. 2010. (Little Golden Book Favorites Ser.). (ENG.). 80p. (J). (gr. -1-2). 6.99 (978-0-7364-2656-5(6), Golden/Disney) Random Hse. Children's Bks.

Teitelbaum, Michael, et al. Disney Princess. Random House Disney Staff, illus. 2009. (Little Golden Book Favorites Ser.). (ENG.). 80p. (J). (gr. -1-2). 7.99 (978-0-7364-2567-4(5), Golden/Disney) Random Hse. Children's Bks.

Tercio, Ricardo, illus. Jack & the Beanstalk: The Graphic Novel. 2008. (Graphic Spin Ser.). (ENG.). 40p. (gr. 1-3). 25.32 (978-1-4342-0766-1(8), Graphic Revolve) Stone Arch Bks.

Tharp, Shari. Gertrude & Toby's Friday Adventure, bks. 3. Heath, Jim, illus. l.t. ed. 2016. 1. (ENG.). (J). (gr. -1-3). bk. 3. 48p. 16.99 (978-0-9969679-0-7(7))Bk.1. 46p. pap. 7.99 (978-0-9969679-1-4(5)) Atlas Publishing LLC. (Atlas Publishing).

Thom, Marie & Walton, Elizabeth. Make Fairy Tales: Ten Very Easy Crafts for Toddlers. 2005. (Little Fingers Ser.). (ENG., Illus.). 32p. (J). (gr. -1-k). pap. 5.99 **(978-1-85714-334-8(5))** Ragged Bears USA.

Thomas Nelson. Fairy Tales. 2015. (ENG.). 192p. (J). (gr. -1-3). (978-1-78393-832-2(3)) Make Believe Ideas.

—Look & Tell Fairytales. 2016. (ENG.). 24p. (gr. -1). bds. (978-1-78598-472-3(1)) Make Believe Ideas.

—Rapunzel. 2015. (ENG., Illus.). 32p. (J). (gr. 1-3). pap. (978-1-78393-577-2(4)) Make Believe Ideas.

—Rumpelstiltskin. 2015. (ENG., Illus.). 32p. (J). (gr. 1-3). pap. (978-1-78393-582-6(0)) Make Believe Ideas.

EFG

Thomas-Ngabe, T-Imani. Once upon a Frog: From the Chronicles Of. 2012. 44p. pap. 20.72 *(978-1-4669-5974-3(6))* Trafford Publishing.

Thomas, Rhiannon. Kingdom of Ashes. 2016. 368p. (YA). (gr. 9). 17.99 *(978-0-06-230356-1(2)*, HarperTeen) HarperCollins Pubs.

—A Wicked Thing. (YA). (gr. 9). 2016. 368p. pap. 9.99 *(978-0-06-230354-7(6))* 2015. (ENG.). 352p. 17.99 *(978-0-06-230353-0(8))* HarperCollins Pubs. (HarperTeen).

Thompson, Carol, illus. The Emperor's New Clothes. 2016. (Once upon a Timeless Tale Ser.). (ENG.). 32p. (J). (gr. k-2). 9.99 *(978-1-921894-99-2(7))* Little Hare Bks. AUS. Dist: Independent Pubs. Group.

Thorne-Thomsen, Gudrun. East O' the Sun & West O' the Moon. Richardson, Frederick, illus. 2009. 148p. pap. 8.95 *(978-1-59915-337-7(8))* Yesterday's Classics.

—East O' the Sun & West O' the Moon: With Other Norwegian Folk Tales. 2007. (ENG.). 104p. pap. 18.99 *(978-1-4346-0058-5(0))*; 114p. pap. 19.99 *(978-1-4346-0062-2(9))* Creative Media Partners, LLC.

Thorogood, Keith. Milli Meets the Tooth Fairies. 2009. (Illus.). 48p. pap. *(978-1-84748-456-7(5))* Athena Pr.

Three Billy Goat's Gruff. 2004. (J). E-Book incl. cd-rom *(978-1-84444-467-0(8))* Mantra Lingua.

Three Little Pigs. 2004. (My First Fairy Tales Ser.). (Illus.). 24p. (J). pap. 3.99 *(978-1-85854-687-2(7))* Brimax Books Ltd. GBR. Dist: Byeway Bks.

Three Minute Stories: Best-Loved Tales. 2003. (Illus.). 160p. (J). 9.98 *(978-0-7853-6877-9(9)*, 7167900) Publications International, Ltd.

Thrum, Thomas G., compiled by. Hawaiian Folk Tales. 2013. 348p. pap. *(978-1-909302-36-5(8))* Abela Publishing.

Thurber, James. The Wonderful O. Simont, Marc, illus. 2017. (Penguin Classics Deluxe Edition Ser.). (ENG.). 96p. pap. 17.00 ***(978-0-14-313042-0(0)***, Penguin Classics) Penguin Publishing Group.

Tiger Tales, ed. Chicken Little. East, Nick, illus. 2016. (My First Fairy Tales Ser.). (ENG.). 32p. (J). (gr. -1-2). pap. 7.99 *(978-1-58925-476-3(7))* Tiger Tales.

—Rumpelstiltskin. Schauer, Loretta, illus. 2016. (My First Fairy Tales Ser.). (ENG.). 32p. (J). (gr. -1-2). pap. 7.99 *(978-1-58925-478-7(3))* Tiger Tales.

—Three Little Pigs. Jatkowska, Ag, illus. 2016. (My First Fairy Tales Ser.). (ENG.). 32p. (J). (gr. -1-2). pap. 7.99 *(978-1-58925-479-4(1))* Tiger Tales.

Tiger Tales, Tiger, ed. The Elves & the Shoemaker. Waters, Erica-Jane, illus. 2017. (My First Fairy Tales Ser.). (ENG.). 32p. (J). (gr. -1-2). pap. 7.99 ***(978-1-58925-496-1(1))*** Tiger Tales.

—The Ugly Duckling. Eastland, Sue, illus. 2017. (My First Fairy Tales Ser.). (ENG.). 32p. (J). (gr. -1-2). pap. 7.99 ***(978-1-58925-497-8(X))*** Tiger Tales.

Tildes, Phyllis Limbacher. The Magic Babushka. Tildes, Phyllis Limbacher, illus. 2009. (ENG., Illus.). 32p. (J). (gr. k-3). pap. 7.95 *(978-1-58089-225-4(6))* Charlesbridge Publishing, Inc.

Tillworth, Mary. A Fairytale Adventure (Dora the Explorer) Jackson, Mike, illus. 2014. (Pictureback(R) Ser.). (ENG.). 24p. (J). (gr. -1-2). 3.99 *(978-0-385-37443-9(7)*, Random Hse. Bks. for Young Readers) Random Hse. Children's Bks.

Timmins, Jeffrey Stewart, illus. Cinderella: The Graphic Novel, 1 vol. 2008. (Graphic Spin Ser.). (ENG.). 40p. (gr. 1-3). 25.32 *(978-1-4342-0764-7(1)*, Graphic Revolve) Stone Arch Bks.

Tobin, Irene. The Tidy Bunch. 2010. (Illus.). 58p. pap. *(978-1-84748-666-0(5))* Athena Pr.

Todolibro, equipo & Todolibro, Equipo. Fabulas Doradas.Tr. of Golden Fables. (SPA.). (J). 22.48 *(978-84-8426-215-2(4))* Susaeta Ediciones, S.A. ESP. Dist: AIMS International Bks., Inc.

—Historias Doradas.Tr. of Golden Stories for Children. (SPA.). (J). 22.98 *(978-84-8426-214-5(6))* Susaeta Ediciones, S.A. ESP. Dist: AIMS International Bks., Inc.

Tolstoy, Alexei. Enormous Turnip. 2003. (Green Light Readers — Level 2 Ser.). (gr. k-3). lib. bdg. 13.50 *(978-0-613-64495-2(6)*, Turtleback) Turtleback Bks.

Tomlinson, Heather. Aurelie: A Faerie Tale. 2010. (ENG.). 208p. (YA). (gr. 7-12). pap. 18.99 *(978-0-312-60275-8(8)*, 9780312602758) Square Fish.

—The Swan Maiden. 2008. (ENG.). 320p. (YA). (gr. 7-12). pap. 22.99 *(978-0-312-38447-0(5)*, 9780312384470) Square Fish.

Torseter, Øyvind. The Heartless Troll. Torseter, Øyvind, illus. 2016. (ENG., Illus.). 120p. (J). (gr. 1-9). 19.95 *(978-1-59270-193-3(0))* Enchanted Lion Bks., LLC.

Townley, Roderick. The Great Good Thing. 2003. (Richard Jackson Books (Econo-Clad) Ser.). 216p. (gr. 5). 16.00 *(978-0-7569-1435-6(3))* Perfection Learning Corp.

ToyBox Innovations, creator. Disney Princess: Cinderella/Snow White/Sleeping Beauty. unabr. abr. ed. 2005. (Disney Princess Ser.). (J). pap. *(978-0-7634-1150-3(7))* Walt Disney Records.

Trafton, Jennifer. The Rise & Fall of Mount Majestic. Helquist, Brett, illus. 2011. (ENG.). 352p. (J). (gr. 3-7). 6.99 *(978-0-14-241934-2(6)*, Puffin Books) Penguin Young Readers Group.

Treahy, Iona & Ladybird Books Staff. Jack & the Beanstalk. 2015. (First Favourite Tales Ser.). (ENG., Illus.). 32p. (J). (-k). 7.99 *(978-1-4093-0959-8(2))* Penguin Bks., Ltd. GBR. Dist: Independent Pubs. Group.

Treasury of Classic Stories. 2008. (Treasuries Ser.). 192p. *(978-1-4075-1209-9(9))* Parragon, Inc.

Treasury of Virtues for Children. 2012. (Illus.). 159p. (J). *(978-1-4508-3590-9(2))* Publications International, Ltd.

Los Tres Cerditos: The Family, the House, Verbs. (SPA., Illus.). (J). (gr. -1-5). pap. 5.95 incl. audio compact disk *(978-88-8148-250-4(9))* EMC/Paradigm Publishing.

Trevayne, Emma. Flights & Chimes & Mysterious Times. Thomas, Glenn, illus. 2014. (ENG.). 320p. (J). (gr. 3-7). 16.99 *(978-1-4424-9877-8(3)*, Simon & Schuster Bks. For Young Readers) Simon & Schuster Bks. For Young Readers.

—Flights & Chimes & Mysterious Times. 2014. 320p. pap. 16.99 *(978-1-4814-0480-8(6))* Simon & Schuster, Inc.

Trivizas, Eugene. The Three Little Wolves & the Big Bad Pig. Oxenbury, Helen, illus. 2015. 32p. pap. 8.00 *(978-1-61003-621-4(2))* Center for the Collaborative Classroom.

Les Trois Petits Cochons: The Family, The House, Verbs. (FRE., Illus.). 24p. (J). (gr. -1-5). pap., stu. ed. 5.95 *(978-88-8148-240-5(1))* EMC/Paradigm Publishing.

Tucker, Kathy & Hong, Lily Toy. The Seven Chinese Sisters. Bk. 2. Hong, Lily Toy & Lin, Grace, illus. 2010. (Book & DVD Packages with Nutmeg Media Ser.). (ENG.). 4p. (J). (gr. -1-3). 69.95 *(978-0-8075-9984-6(0))* Whitman, Albert & Co.

Tucker Slingsby Ltd., Staff. My Big Book of Fairy Tales in Rhyme! Lewis, Jan, illus. 2004. 224p. (J). *(978-1-902272-31-3(5))* Tucker Slingsby, Ltd.

Tucker, Stephen. Cinderella, 2 vols. Sharratt, Nick, illus. 2017. (Lift-The-Flap Fairy Tales Ser.). (ENG.). 24p. (J). (gr. -1-1). 10.99 ***(978-1-5098-2974-3(1))*** Pan Macmillan GBR. Dist: Independent Pubs. Group.

Tucker, Stephen. Jack & the Beanstalk, 2 vols. Sharratt, Nick, illus. 2016. (Lift-The-Flap Fairy Tales Ser.). (ENG.). 24p. (J). (gr. -1-k). bds. 12.99 *(978-1-5098-1714-6(X))* Pan Macmillan GBR. Dist: Independent Pubs. Group.

Tulien, Sean. Super Billy Goats Gruff. Cano, Fernando, illus. 2015. (Far Out Fairy Tales Ser.). (ENG.). 40p. (gr. 3-4). lib. bdg. 25.32 *(978-1-4342-9649-8(0))* Stone Arch Bks.

Tulien, Sean & Simonson, Louise. Far Out Fairy Tales. Cano, Fern & Sanchez S., Jimena, illus. 2016. (Far Out Fairy Tales Ser.). (ENG.). 40p. (gr. 3-4). 151.92 *(978-1-4965-2515-4(9)*, Far Out Fairy Tales) Stone Arch Bks.

Turnbull, Victoria. Pandora. 2016. (ENG., Illus.). 32p. (J). 18.99 *(978-1-84780-749-6(6)*, Frances Lincoln Children's Bks.) Quarto Publishing Group UK GBR. Dist: Littlehampton Bk Services, Ltd.

Turner, Max. End of Days. 2010. (Night Runner Novels Ser.: 2). (ENG.). 304p. (YA). (gr. 8-12). pap. 20.99 *(978-0-312-59252-3(3)*, 9780312592523, St. Martin's Griffin) St. Martin's Pr.

Turner, Patrenia. Barbie In The Queen Patrenialla Fairy - Tale. Turner, Keeng Troyius, ed. 2014. (Illus.). 31p. pap. *(978-0-578-14812-0(9))* Patrenialla Turner, Queen.

Twin Sister Produtions & Shepherd, Jodie. Sesame Street Big Red Riding Hood. 2010. (J). 14.99 *(978-1-59922-635-4(9))* Twin Sisters IP, LLC.

—Sesame Street Rosita & the Beanstalk. 2010. (J). (gr. k-2). 14.99 *(978-1-59922-634-7(0))* Twin Sisters IP, LLC.

Twin Sister Produtions Staff & Shepherd, Jodie. Sesame Street Big Red Riding Hood. 2010. (J). (gr. k-2). 14.99 *(978-1-59922-526-5(3))* Twin Sisters IP, LLC.

—Sesame Street Rosita & the Beanstalk. 2010. (J). (gr. k-2). 14.99 *(978-1-59922-525-8(5))* Twin Sisters IP, LLC.

Tyler, Jenny & Doherty, Gillian, eds. Usborne Stories for Little Boys. 2008. (Picture Books Ser.). (Illus.). 135p. (J). (gr. -1-3). 18.99 *(978-0-7945-1973-5(3)*, Usborne) EDC Publishing.

—Usborne Stories for Little Girls. 2008. (Picture Books Ser.). (Illus.). 135p. (J). (gr. -1-3). 18.99 *(978-0-7945-1974-2(1)*, Usborne) EDC Publishing.

Tyler, Joe, et al. Grimm Fairy Tales Volume 4, Vol. 4. Tedesco, Ralph & Gregory, Raven, eds. 2012. (ENG., Illus.). 168p. (YA). pap. 12.99 *(978-0-9817550-0-7(3)*, 9780981755007) Zenescope Entertainment.

Tyrrell, Melissa. Beauty & the Beast. McMullen, Nigel, illus. 2005. (Fairytale Friends Ser.). 12p. (J). bds. 5.95 *(978-1-58117-153-2(6)*, Intervisual/Piggy Toes) Bendon, Inc.

—The Gingerbread Man. McMullen, Nigel, illus. 2005. (Fairytale Friends Ser.: Vol. 8). 12p. (J). (gr. -1-k). bds. 5.95 *(978-1-58117-154-9(4)*, Intervisual/Piggy Toes) Bendon, Inc.

—Hansel & Gretel. McMullen, Nigel, illus. 2005. (Fairytale Friends Ser.). 12p. (J). bds. 5.95 *(978-1-58117-152-5(8)*, Intervisual/Piggy Toes) Bendon, Inc.

—Pinocchio. McMullen, Nigel, illus. 2005. (Fairytale Friends Ser.: Vol. 7). 12p. (J). (gr. -1-k). bds. 5.95 *(978-1-58117-151-8(X)*, Intervisual/Piggy Toes) Bendon, Inc.

Uberoi, Meera. Myths & Legends: From Around the World. 2013. (ENG.). 88p. pap. 7.95 *(978-93-5036-247-1(3))* Ratna, Sagar Pvt. Ltd. IND. Dist: Midpoint Trade Bks., Inc.

Underwood, Deborah. Good Night, Baddies. Kangas, Juli, illus. 2016. (ENG.). 32p. (J). (gr. -1-3). 17.99 *(978-1-4814-0984-1(0)*, Beach Lane Bks.) Beach Lane Bks.

Unknown. Where in Tinga Tinga Is Tickbird? 2011. 16p. (J). 6.99 *(978-0-448-45601-0(X)*, Grosset & Dunlap) Penguin Publishing Group.

Vaello, Elda G. The Magical Goat. 2011. 24p. pap. 12.98 *(978-1-4634-1759-8(4))* AuthorHouse.

Vagnozzi, Barbara. The Musicians of Bremen. 2007. (Flip-Up Fairy Tales Ser.). (ENG., Illus.). 24p. (J). (gr. 1-2). *(978-1-84643-115-9(8))* Child's Play International Ltd.

Vagnozzi, Barbara, illus. Jack & the Beanstalk. (Classic Fairy Tales Ser.). (ENG.). 24p. (J). 2011. audio compact disk *(978-1-84643-456-3(4))* 2007. (gr. -1-2). audio compact disk *(978-1-84643-086-2(0))* Child's Play International Ltd.

—Sleeping Beauty. 2007. (First Fairy Tales Ser.). 32p. (J). (gr. -1-3). lib. bdg. 28.50 *(978-1-59771-073-2(3))* Sea-To-Sea Pubns.

Valdez Y Alanis, Erik, illus. Rumpelstiltskin: The Graphic Novel. 2008. (Graphic Spin Ser.). (ENG.). 40p. (gr. 1-3). 25.32 *(978-1-4342-0768-5(4)*, Graphic Revolve) Stone Arch Bks.

Valdejuly, Frances Bragan. Keka en el Museo de Arte de Ponce. Rabenau, Francesca von, illus. 2004. (SPA.). 60p. 21.95 *(978-1-56328-269-0(0))* Editorial Plaza Mayor, Inc.

Van De Leijgraaf, Deborah, illus. Fairies. 2015. (First Sticker Story Fun Ser.). (ENG.). 30p. (J). (gr. -1-k). pap. 9.99 ***(978-1-4472-8656-1(1))*** Pan Macmillan GBR. Dist: Independent Pubs. Group.

Van Nutt, Robert. The Ugly Duckling. Van Nutt, Robert & Bogdanovic, Toma, illus. 32p. (J). (gr. -1-3). 16.95 *(978-0-87592-055-9(1))* Scroll Pr., Inc.

Van Sise, George W. Wonderfultales from the Land of the Seven Kingdoms. 2010. 437p. pap. 22.95 *(978-1-4327-6200-1(1))* Outskirts Pr., Inc.

Van Stockum, Hilda. King Oberon's Forest. 2012. 164p. pap. 11.95 *(978-0-7414-6693-8(7))* Infinity Publishing.

Vande Velde, Vivian. Frogged. 2013. (ENG., Illus.). 208p. (J). (gr. 5-7). 16.99 *(978-0-547-94215-5(X))* Houghton Mifflin Harcourt Publishing Co.

—The Rumpelstiltskin Problem. 2013. (ENG.). 128p. (J). (gr. 5-7). pap. 5.99 *(978-0-544-10486-0(2))* Houghton Mifflin Harcourt Publishing Co.

—Tales from the Brothers Grimm & the Sisters Weird. Weinman, Brad, illus. 2005. (ENG.). 144p. (J). (gr. 5-7). reprint ed. pap. 6.99 *(978-0-15-205572-1(X))* Houghton Mifflin Harcourt Publishing Co.

Various Authors Staff. Fairy Tale Comics: Classic Tales Told by Extraordinary Cartoonists. Duffy, Chris, ed. Hernandez, Gilbert & Mazzucchelli, David, illus. 2013. (ENG.). 128p. (J). (gr. 1-7). 21.99 *(978-1-59643-823-1(1)*, 9781596438231, First Second Bks.) Roaring Brook Pr.

Vasquez, Natalia, illus. The Pied Piper of Hamelin. 2012. (Flip-Up Fairy Tales Ser.). (ENG.). 24p. (J). *(978-1-84643-480-8(7))* Child's Play International Ltd.

Venturini, Claudia. Tom Thumb. 2014. 18.00 *(978-1-63419-745-8(3))* Perfection Learning Corp.

Venturini, Claudia, illus. Ali Baba & the Forty Thieves. 2009. (Flip-Up Fairy Tales Ser.). (ENG.). 24p. (J). (gr. -1-2). audio compact disk *(978-1-84643-294-1(4))* Child's Play International Ltd.

Vera, Luisa, illus. Ali Baba & the Forty Thieves. 2004. 63p. (J). *(978-1-84444-536-3(4))* Mantra Lingua.

Vernon, Ursula. Giant Trouble. 2017. (Hamster Princess Ser.). (ENG., Illus.). 224p. (J). (gr. 3-7). 12.99 *(978-0-399-18652-3(2)*, Dial Bks) Penguin Young Readers Group.

Very, Lydia L. Little Red Riding Hood: Treasures from the Library of Congress. 2004. (Shape Bks.). (ENG., Illus.). 20p. (J). reprint ed. 23.70 *(978-1-55709-167-3(6))* Applewood Bks.

Victoria, Marie Alexandra. A Christmas Tale. 2013. 40p. pap. *(978-3-944704-09-8(6))* Nothnagle, Alan. Edition Graugans.

Vila Delclòs, Jordi, illus. LA BELLA DURMIENTE. 2004. (Caballo Alado Clásicos-Al Trote Ser.). (SPA & ENG.). 24p. (J). (gr. -1-k). 7.95 *(978-84-7864-775-0(9))* Combel Editorial, S.A. ESP. Dist: Independent Pubs. Group.

Le Vilain Petit Canard.Tr. of Ugly Duckling. (FRE.). 48p. (J). pap. 12.95 incl. audio compact disk *(978-2-89558-063-8(4))* Coffragants CAN. Dist: Penton Overseas, Inc.

Le Vilain Petit Canard: Farm Animals, The Farm, Seasons, The Weather. (FRE & ENG., Illus.). 24p. (J). (gr. -1-5). pap., stu. ed. 5.95 *(978-88-8148-241-2(X))* EMC/Paradigm Publishing.

Vincent, Eric. Aesop's Fables. 2013. (Classics Illustrated Graphic Novels Ser.). (ENG., Illus.). 56p. (J). (gr. 5-9). 9.99 *(978-1-59707-441-4(1)*, 9781597074414) Papercutz.

Vohra, Subhash, illus. The Little Red Hen. 2010. (J). *(978-1-60617-129-5(1))* Teaching Strategies, LLC.

von Bassewitz, Gerdt. Peter & Anneli's Journey to the Moon. Baluschek, Hans, illus. 2007. 110p. (J). (gr. 3-7). *(978-0-88010-584-2(4)*, Bell Pond Bks.) SteinerBooks, Inc.

von Olfers, Sibylle. Mother Earth & Her Children: A Quilted Fairy Tale. Zipes, Jack, tr. from GER. Schoen-Smith, Sieglinde, illus. 2007. (ENG.). 32p. (J). (gr. -1-2). 17.95 *(978-1-933308-18-0(4))* Breckling Pr.

Waddell, Martin & Andersen, Hans Christian. Hans Christian Andersen's Fairy Tales. Chichester Clark, Emma, illus. 2014. 127p. (J). *(978-1-4351-5626-5(9))* Barnes & Noble, Inc.

Wade, Barrie. The Emperor's New Clothes. O'kif, A., illus. 2016. (Must Know Stories: Level 2 Ser.). (ENG.). 32p. (J). (gr. 1-4). 12.99 *(978-1-4451-4657-7(6)*, Franklin Watts) Hachette Children's Group GBR. Dist: Hachette Bk. Group.

Wahl, Jan. Cobweb Castle. 2014. (ENG., Illus.). 32p. (J). 14.95 *(978-0-7649-6801-3(7))* Pomegranate Communications, Inc.

Walker, Richard. Jack & the Beanstalk. 2009. (ENG., Illus.). (J). 16.99 *(978-1-84686-297-7(3))* Barefoot Bks., Inc.

—Juan y los Frijoles Magicos. 2008. (ENG & SPA., Illus.). 40p. (J). (gr. -1-1). 10.99 *(978-1-84686-216-8(7))* Barefoot Bks., Inc.

Wallace, Karen. Snow White Sees the Light. Rowland, Andrew, illus. 2015. (ENG.). 32p. (J). *(978-0-7787-1931-1(6))* Crabtree Publishing Co.

Wallner, S. J. Hans & the Golden Stirrup. (Illus.). 48p. (J). (gr. 2-3). lib. bdg. 10.95 *(978-0-87783-016-0(9))*; pap. 3.94 *(978-0-87783-093-1(2))* Oddo Publishing, Inc.

Walser, David. The Thousand Nights & One Night. Pienkowski, Jan, illus. 2011. (Calla Editions Ser.). (ENG.). 160p. (J). (gr. 5). 25.00 *(978-1-60660-020-7(6))* Dover Pubns., Inc.

Walter, Jackie. The Princess & the Pea. Cope, Jane, illus. 2016. (Must Know Stories: Level 2 Ser.). (ENG.). 32p. (J). (gr. 1-4). 12.99 *(978-1-4451-4653-9(3)*, Franklin Watts) Hachette Children's Group GBR. Dist: Hachette Bk. Group.

Wang, Jack, et al. E.T.A. Hoffman's the Nutcracker. 2016. (ENG., Illus.). 24p. (J). (gr. -1 — 1). bds. 9.95 *(978-1-4521-5248-6(9))* Chronicle Bks. LLC.

Wang, Shaoli, illus. Chinese Fairy Tale Feasts: A Literary Cookbook. 2014. 160p. (J). 25.00 *(978-1-56656-993-4(1)*, Crocodile Bks.) Interlink Publishing Group, Inc.

Wanner, Zukiswa. Refilwe: Best Loved Tales for Africa. Hinrichsen, Tamsin, illus. 2015. (ENG.). 32p. (J). (gr. -1-k). pap. 9.95 *(978-1-4314-0098-0(X))* Jacana Media ZAF. Dist: Independent Pubs. Group.

Waters, Fiona, retold by. Faithful Sister. (ENG., Illus.). 94p. (J). pap. 10.99 *(978-0-7475-4704-4(1))* Bloomsbury Publishing Plc GBR. Dist: Trafalgar Square Publishing.

Watson, M. C. V. Fairy Tales & Pixie Trails: From the Series. 2012. 48p. pap. 21.99 *(978-1-4771-5249-2(0))* Xlibris Corp.

WATTS, Bernadette. Mother Holly. 2016. (ENG., Illus.). 32p. 17.95 *(978-0-7358-4267-0(1))* North-South Bks., Inc.

Watts, Bernadette, illus. The Bernadette Watts Collection: Stories & Fairy Tales. 2015. (ENG.). 300p. (J). 34.95 *(978-0-7358-4212-0(4))* North-South Bks., Inc.

Watts, Bernadette, et al. Little Red Riding Hood. Watts, Edith M B., illus. 2011. (ENG.). 32p. (J). pap. 7.95 *(978-0-7358-4008-9(3))* North-South Bks., Inc.

Wax, Wendy A. Musica en Casa: Libro de Cuentos. de Alba, Arlette, tr. 2005. (Disney Princess Ser.). (SPA., Illus.). 38p. (J). (gr. -1-7). incl. audio compact disk *(978-970-718-289-9(X)*, Silver Dolphin en Español) Advanced Marketing, S. de R. L. de C. V.

Webb, Mack Henry, Jr. Webb's Wondrous Tales Book 1. Webb, Celia, illus. 2006. 184p. (YA). per. 14.95 *(978-0-9779576-1-3(6))* Pilinut Pr., Inc.

Webster, Christy. Barbie: A Fairy Secret. Random House Staff, illus. 2011. (Step into Reading Ser.). (ENG.). 32p. (J). (gr. -1-1). pap. 3.99 *(978-0-375-86775-0(9)*, Random Hse. Bks. for Young Readers) Random Hse. Children's Bks.

Werner, Janet. The Giant Golden Book of Elves & Fairies. Williams, Garth, illus. 2008. (Golden Classic Ser.). (ENG.). 80p. (J). (gr. -1-2). 16.99 *(978-0-375-84426-3(0)*, Golden Bks.) Random Hse. Children's Bks.

West, David. Ten of the Best Animal Myths. 2014. (ENG., Illus.). 24p. (J). pap. *(978-0-7787-0807-0(1))* Crabtree Publishing Co.

—Ten of the Best God & Goddess Stories. 2014. (ENG., Illus.). 24p. (J). pap. *(978-0-7787-0823-0(3))* Crabtree Publishing Co.

—Ten of the Best Mythical Hero Stories. 2014. (ENG., Illus.). 24p. (J). *(978-0-7787-0785-1(7))* Crabtree Publishing Co.

—Ten of the Best Prince & Princess Stories. 2014. (ENG., Illus.). 24p. (J). *(978-0-7787-0787-5(3))* Crabtree Publishing Co.

—Ten of the Best Witch & Sorcerer Stories. 2014. (ENG., Illus.). 24p. (J). *(978-0-7787-0797-4(0))* Crabtree Publishing Co.

Weston Woods Staff, creator. Drummer Hoff. 2004. (J). 18.95 *(978-1-55592-405-8(0))* Weston Woods Studios, Inc.

—Hansel & Gretel. 2011. 38.75 *(978-0-439-80425-7(6))* Weston Woods Studios, Inc.

—Mufaro's Beautiful Daughters. 2011. 29.95 *(978-0-439-73504-9(1))* Weston Woods Studios, Inc.

—Rainbabies. 2004. 29.95 *(978-1-55592-112-5(4))* Weston Woods Studios, Inc.

—Red Riding Hood. 2011. 38.75 *(978-0-439-72863-6(5))*; 29.95 *(978-0-439-73518-6(1))*; 18.95 *(978-0-439-72882-9(7))* Weston Woods Studios, Inc.

Weyn, Suzanne. The Crimson Thread: A Retelling of Rumpelstiltskin. 2008. (Once upon a Time Ser.). (ENG.). 240p. (YA). (gr. 7-18). mass mkt. 7.99 *(978-1-4169-5943-4(2)*, Simon Pulse) Simon Pulse.

Whelon, Chuck. Where's the Princess? And Other Fairy Tale Searches. Whelon, Chuck, illus. 2016. (ENG., Illus.). 32p. (J). (gr. k-3). 12.99 *(978-1-4814-4633-4(9)*, Aladdin) Simon & Schuster Children's Publishing.

White, Claudia. Aesop's Secret. 2013. (ENG.). 128p. (J). (gr. 4-6). 11.99 *(978-1-84982-230-5(1))* MP Publishing Ltd. GBR. Dist: Midpoint Trade Bks., Inc.

White, Mark. The Fox & the Grapes: A Retelling of Aesop's Fable, 1 vol. Pérez, Sara Rojo, illus. 2013. (My First Classic Story Ser.). (ENG.). 24p. (gr. k-3). pap. 7.10 *(978-1-4795-1856-2(5)*, My First Classic Story) Picture Window Bks.

—The Wolf in Sheep's Clothing: A Retelling of Aesop's Fable, 1 vol. Pérez, Sara Rojo, illus. 2013. (My First Classic Story Ser.). (ENG.). 24p. (gr. k-3). pap. 7.10 *(978-1-4795-1857-9(3)*, My First Classic Story) Picture Window Bks.

Widener, Leslie Stall, illus. Chukfi Rabbit's Big, Bad Bellyache: A Trickster Tale. 2014. (ENG.). 40p. (J). (gr. k-5). 16.95 *(978-1-935955-26-9(8))* Cinco Puntos Pr.

Wiggin, Kate Douglas & Smith, Archibald Nora. Tales of Wonder Every Child Should Know. 2007. (ENG.). 350p. pap. 23.99 *(978-1-4346-3190-9(7))*; 382p. pap. 26.99 *(978-1-4346-3191-6(5))* Creative Media Partners, LLC.

Wiggin, Kate Douglas & Smith, Nora Archibald. The Fairy Ring. MacKinstry, Elizabeth, illus. 2008. 680p. pap. 20.95 *(978-1-59915-298-1(3))* Yesterday's Classics.

Wilcox, Leah. Falling for Rapunzel. Monks, Lydia, illus. 2005. (ENG.). 32p. (J). (gr. -1-3). pap. 6.99 *(978-0-14-240399-0(7)*, Puffin Books) Penguin Young Readers Group.

Wilde, Oscar. Classic Tales of Oscar Wilde. Robinson, Charles, illus. 2014. (ENG.). 96p. (J). (gr. k-3). 19.99 *(978-1-4052-6423-5(3))* Egmont Bks., Ltd. GBR. Dist: Independent Pubs. Group.

—Fairy Tales of Oscar Wilde: the Complete Hardcover Set 1-5. Russell, P. Craig, illus. 2014. (Fairy Tales of Oscar Wilde Ser.). (ENG.). 192p. (J). (gr. 4-7). 79.99 *(978-1-56163-890-1(0))* NBM Publishing Co.

—The Fairy Tales of Oscar Wilde: the Happy Prince Signed & Numbered. Russell, P. Craig, illus. 2012. (Fairy Tales of Oscar Wilde Ser.). (ENG.). 32p. (J). (gr. 4-7). 49.99 *(978-1-56163-687-7(8))*; 50.00 *(978-1-56163-629-7(0))* NBM Publishing Co.

—El Gigante Egoista. Zwerger, Lisbeth, illus. 2nd ed. (SPA.). 48p. (J). *(978-84-392-8674-5(0))* Gaviota Ediciones ESP. Dist: Lectorum Pubns., Inc.

—The Happy Prince. Delessert, Etienne, illus. 2008. (Creative Short Stories Ser.). 32p. (YA). (gr. 9-18). lib. bdg. 28.50 *(978-1-58341-582-5(3)*, Creative Education) Creative Co., The.

—The Happy Prince. 2005. (SPA.). 12p. (J). pap. *(978-958-30-1510-6(5))* Panamericana Editorial.

—The Happy Prince & Other Stories. 2005. pap. *(978-1-4065-0241-1(3))* Dodo Pr.

—The Happy Prince & Other Stories. 2013. (ENG., Illus.). 304p. *(978-1-905716-62-3(1)*, Collector's Library, The) Pan Macmillan.

—The Happy Prince & Other Stories. Bo, Lars, illus. 2009. (Puffin Classics Ser.). (ENG.). 224p. (J). (gr. 5-7). pap. 5.99 *(978-0-14-132779-2(0)*, Puffin Books) Penguin Young Readers Group.

—The Happy Prince & Other Tales. 2009. 68p. pap. 7.99 *(978-1-60450-658-7(X)*, Serenity Pubs.) Arc Manor.

—The Happy Prince & Other Tales. 2013. 425p. reprint ed. lthr. 69.00 *(978-0-7426-2947-9(3))* Classic Bks.

—The Happy Prince & Other Tales. 2006. 56p. per. 4.99 *(978-1-4209-2736-8(1))* Digireads.com Publishing.

—The Happy Prince & Other Tales. l.t. ed. 2006. 92p. pap. *(978-1-84637-306-0(9))* Echo Library.

—The Happy Prince & Other Tales. 2008. 64p. pap. 8.95 *(978-1-60096-417-6(6))*; (Illus.). 72p. pap. 8.95 *(978-1-4341-0075-7(8))* Editorium, The.

—The Happy Prince & Other Tales. 2004. reprint ed. pap. 15.95 *(978-1-4191-6538-2(0))*; pap. 1.99 *(978-1-4192-6538-9(5))* Kessinger Publishing, LLC.

—The Happy Prince & Other Tales. 2006. per. 4.95 *(978-1-57646-987-3(5))* Quiet Vision Publishing.

—The Happy Prince & Other Tales. 2005. 24.95 *(978-1-59818-275-0(7))* Rodgers, Alan Bks.

—The Happy Prince & Other Tales. 2005. pap. 10.95 *(978-1-59818-412-9(1))*; pap. 9.95 *(978-1-55742-431-0(4))* Wildside Pr., LLC.

—A House of Pomegranates. King, Jessie Marion, illus. 2011. (Calla Editions Ser.). (ENG.). 208p. (J). (gr. 5). 35.00 *(978-1-60660-021-4(4))* Dover Pubns., Inc.

—El Principe Feliz y Otros Cuentos. 2003. (SPA., Illus.). 180p. *(978-84-392-8015-6(7)*, EV0874) Gaviota Ediciones ESP. Dist: Lectorum Pubns., Inc.

—The Selfish Giant: A Tale about Being Unselfish. Ebert, Len, illus. 2006. (J). *(978-1-59939-085-7(X)*, Reader's Digest Young Families, Inc.) Studio Fun International.

Wilde, Oscar & Grodin, Elissa. The Happy Prince. Stutzman, Laura, illus. rev. ed. 2006. (ENG.). 48p. (J). (gr. k-6). 17.95 *(978-1-58536-264-6(6))* Sleeping Bear Pr.

Wilde, Oscar & Hollingsworth, Mary. The Selfish Giant. Bell, Bill, illus. 2013. (ENG.). 40p. (J). (gr. -1-1). 14.95 *(978-1-62087-540-7(3)*, 620540, Sky Pony Pr.) Skyhorse Publishing Co., Inc.

Wilhelm, Hans, retold by. Los Musicos de Bremen. (SPA.). (J). pap. 4.80 net. *(978-0-439-17707-8(3)*, SO30111) Scholastic, Inc.

Wilhelm, Richard, ed. The Chinese Fairy Book. Martens, Frederick H., tr. from CHI. Hood, George W., illus. 2008. (Dover Children's Classics Ser.). (ENG.). 224p. (J). (gr. 4-7). pap. 10.95 *(978-0-486-45435-1(5))* Dover Pubns., Inc.

William Elliot, Griffis. Dutch Fairy Tales for Young Folks. 2007. (ENG.). 140p. pap. 18.99 *(978-1-4264-3924-7(5))* Creative Media Partners, LLC.

Williams, Brenda. The Real Princess. Fatus, Sophie, illus. 2008. (ENG.). 40p. (J). (gr. -1-3). 16.99 *(978-1-905236-88-6(3))* Barefoot Bks., Inc.

Williams, Brenda & Barefoot Books Staff. Una Princesa Real: Un Cuento Matemagico. Fatus, Sophie, illus. 2014. (SPA.). 40p. (J). (gr. k-4). pap. 8.99 *(978-1-78285-078-6(3))* Barefoot Bks., Inc.

Williams, Garth & Brown, Margaret Wise. 75 Years of Little Golden Books: 1942-2017: A Commemorative Set of 12 Best-Loved Books. Gergely, Tibor & Wilkin, Eloise, illus. 2017. (Little Golden Book Ser.). (ENG.). 24p. (J). (-k). 59.88 ***(978-0-399-55951-8(5)***, Golden Bks.) Random Hse. Children's Bks.

Wilson, Anna & Collins UK Publishing Staff. Puss in Boots. Martynets, Denis, illus. 2016. (ENG.). 32p. (J). pap. 8.95 *(978-0-00-814713-6(2))* HarperCollins Pubs. Ltd. GBR. Dist: Independent Pubs. Group.

Wilson, Barbara-Ann. The Faerie Hill. 2008. 124p. pap. 20.95 *(978-1-4092-1845-6(7))* Lulu Pr., Inc.

Wilson Hills, Atheen. Little Crane: A Fairy Tale for All Ages. 2008. (J). pap. 10.00 *(978-0-9792371-5-7(7)*, Moo Pr.) Keene Publishing.

Wilson, Jacqueline. Beauty & the Beast. 2003. (Curtain Up Ser.: Vol. 1). (ENG., Illus.). 48p. (J). (gr. 1-4). pap. *(978-0-7136-4390-9(0)*, A&C Black) Bloomsbury Publishing Plc.

Wilson, Mary & Berrios, Frank. Disney Tales of Magic, 4 vols. 2004. (Illus.). (J). *(978-0-7364-2250-5(1))*; *(978-0-7364-2252-9(8))*; *(978-0-7364-2251-2(X))*; *(978-0-7364-2253-6(6))* Random Hse., Inc.

Wilson-Timmons, Karen & Dubois, Marie Thérèse. Agha the Eight-Mile Monster. rev. ed. 2012. (ENG., Illus.). 32p. (J). (gr. -1). 16.99 *(978-1-60887-124-7(X))* Mandala Publishing.

Windling, Terri & Datlow, Ellen, eds. Troll's-Eye View: A Book of Villainous Tales. 2010. (ENG.). 208p. (J). (gr. 5-18). 7.99 *(978-0-14-241673-0(8)*, Firebird) Penguin Young Readers Group.

Winter, Milo, illus. Aesop's Fables. 2013. (ENG.). 112p. (J). (gr. -1-2). 16.95 *(978-1-4549-0981-1(1)*, Fall River) Sterling Publishing Co., Inc.

—The Three Little Pigs. 2008. (Shape Bks.). (ENG.). 16p. (J). (gr. -1-3). per. 9.95 *(978-1-59583-265-8(3)*, 9781595832658, Green Tiger Pr.) Laughing Elephant.

Wisnewski, Andrea. Little Red Riding Hood. 2006. (ENG., Illus.). 32p. (J). (gr. 3-7). 18.95 *(978-1-56792-303-2(8))* Godine, David R. Pub.

Wong, Carmen L. F. Written By... 2013. 252p. (gr. 4-6). 33.25 *(978-1-4669-3179-4(5))*; pap. 18.85 *(978-1-4669-3178-7(7))* Trafford Publishing.

Wonlah, Ivis. King Ola's Pepper Jar. 2012. 28p. pap. 16.09 *(978-1-4669-1600-5(1))* Trafford Publishing.

Woodbridge, Nancy Garfield. A Bouquet of Fairy Tales. 2012. 108p. 24.99 *(978-1-4771-4493-0(5))*; pap. 15.99 *(978-1-4771-4492-3(7))* Xlibris Corp.

Woollvin, Bethan. Little Red, 1 vol. Woollvin, Bethan, illus. 2016. (ENG., Illus.). 32p. (J). (gr. k-4). 16.95 *(978-1-56145-917-9(8))* Peachtree Pubs.

Woollvin, Bethan. Rapunzel, 1 vol. Woollvin, Bethan, illus. 2017. (ENG., Illus.). 32p. (J). (gr. k-4). 16.95 ***(978-1-68263-003-7(X))*** Peachtree Pubs.

World of Fairy Tales. unabr. ed. 2004. (Chrysalis Childrens Classics Ser.). (Illus.). (YA). pap. *(978-1-84365-064-5(9)*, Pavilion Children's Books) Pavilion Bks.

Worrall, Linda, illus. Snow White & the Seven Dwarfs: A Story about Vanity. 2006. (J). 6.99 *(978-1-59939-025-3(6))* Cornerstone Pr.

Woyiwada, Allison. The Little Fir Tree: A Musical for Primary Children Based on a Story by Hans Christian Andersen. 2003. (Musicals for Young Audiences Ser.). 16p. (J). (gr. k-6). pap. 5.00 *(978-0-88734-428-2(3))* Players Pr., Inc.

Wright, Rebecca Hu-Van & Asbjørnsen, Peter Christen. The Three Billy Goats Gruff, 1 vol. Hu, Ying-Hwa, illus. 2014. (ENG.). 32p. (J). *(978-1-59572-666-7(7))*; pap. 6.99 *(978-1-59572-667-4(5))* Star Bright Bks., Inc.

Yanez-Arellano, Katherine. The Gunny Wolf Story. 2009. 28p. pap. 12.95 *(978-1-4269-1594-9(2))* Trafford Publishing.

Yaroslavskaya, Lyudmila. The Great Lakes Legends & Fairy Tales. 2006. (ENG & RUS., Illus.). (J). per. *(978-0-9791248-0-8(8))* Yaroslavskaya, Lyudmila.

Yasuda, Yuri & Yasuda, Yuri Old tales of Japan. A Treasury of Japanese Folktales. Matsunari, Yumi & Yamaguchi, Yumi, trs. Sakakura, Yoshinobu & Mitsui, Eiichi, illus. 2010. (ENG & JPN.). 112p. (J). (gr. k-8). 19.95 *(978-4-8053-1079-3(0))* Tuttle Publishing.

Yates, Irene. The Enormous Turnip. 2015. (First Favourite Tales Ser.). (ENG., Illus.). 32p. (J). (-k). 9.99 *(978-1-4093-0957-4(6))* Penguin Bks., Ltd. GBR. Dist: Independent Pubs. Group.

Yates, Irene & Ladybird Books Staff. The Three Billy Goats Gruff. 2015. (First Favourite Tales Ser.). (ENG., Illus.). 32p. (J). (-k). 7.99 *(978-1-4093-0633-7(X))* Penguin Bks., Ltd. GBR. Dist: Independent Pubs. Group.

Yep, Laurence. Dragon Prince: A Chinese Beauty & the Beast Tale. 2014. 17.00 *(978-1-63419-696-3(1))* Perfection Learning Corp.

Yeretskaya, Yevgeniya, illus. The Snow Queen: A Pop-Up Adaption of a Classic Fairytale. 2013. (ENG.). 7p. 29.95 *(978-1-60580-955-7(1)*, 9781605809557) Jumping Jack Pr.

Yolen, Jane. Baba Yaga. Date not set. 32p. (J). (gr. -1-1). pap. 5.99 *(978-0-06-443599-4(7))* HarperCollins Pubs.

—Curse of the Thirteenth Fey: The True Tale of Sleeping Beauty. 2013. (ENG.). 320p. (J). (gr. 5). pap. 7.99 *(978-0-14-242761-3(6)*, Puffin Books) Penguin Young Readers Group.

—The Flying Witch. Vagin, Vladimir, illus. 2003. 40p. (J). (gr. -1-1). 15.99 *(978-0-06-028536-4(2))* HarperCollins Pubs.

—Snow in Summer. 2013. (ENG.). 272p. (J). (gr. 5). pap. 7.99 *(978-0-14-242197-0(9)*, Puffin Books) Penguin Young Readers Group.

Yolen, Jane & Stemple, Heidi E. Y. Fairy Tale Feasts: A Literary Cookbook for Young Readers & Eaters. Beha, Philippe, illus. (ENG.). 264p. (J). 2009. (gr. -1-3). pap. 20.00 *(978-1-56656-751-0(3)*, Crocodile Bks.) 2006. (gr. 4-7). 24.95 *(978-1-56656-643-8(6))* Interlink Publishing Group, Inc.

—Jewish Fairy Tale Feasts: A Literary Cookbook. Shefrin, Sima Elizabeth, illus. 2013. (ENG.). 200p. (J). 25.00 *(978-1-56656-909-5(5)*, Crocodile Bks.) Interlink Publishing Group, Inc.

Yorinks, Arthur. The Witch's Child. Smith, Jos. A., illus. 2007. (ENG.). 34p. (J). (gr. 1-4). 17.95 *(978-0-8109-9349-5(X)*, Abrams Bks. for Young Readers) Abrams, Inc.

Young, Billy. Teddy the Bear. 2007. 27p. 19.95 *(978-1-84799-068-6(1))* Lulu Pr., Inc.

Young, Ella. Celtic Wonder-Tales. Gonne, Maud, illus. 2014. (J). *(978-0-486-78065-8(1))* Dover Pubns., Inc.

Young, Lesley. A Storyteller Book - Red Riding Hood. Williams, Jenny, illus. 2013. (ENG.). 48p. (J). (gr. -1-12). pap. 7.99 *(978-1-84322-909-4(9)*, Armadillo) Anness Publishing GBR. Dist: National Bk. Network.

—A Storyteller Book Sleeping Beauty. Press, Jenny, illus. 2013. (ENG.). 48p. (J). (gr. -1-12). pap. 7.99 *(978-1-84322-910-0(2)*, Armadillo) Anness Publishing GBR. Dist: National Bk. Network.

Young, Lesley, retold by. The Children's Treasury of Tales. 2014. (ENG., Illus.). 256p. (J). (gr. k-2). 16.99 *(978-1-84322-976-6(5)*, Armadillo) Anness Publishing GBR. Dist: National Bk. Network.

Yu, Melissa. Ever after High: Thronecoming Reusable Sticker Book. 2014. (ENG., Illus.). 12p. (J). (gr. -1-3). pap. 6.99 *(978-0-316-28285-7(5))* Little, Brown Bks. for Young Readers.

Zahler, Diane. Sleeping Beauty's Daughters. 2013. 216p. (J). lib. bdg. *(978-0-06-200497-0(2))* Harper & Row Ltd.

—Sleeping Beauty's Daughters. 2013. (ENG.). 224p. (J). (gr. 3-7). 16.99 *(978-0-06-200496-3(4))* HarperCollins Pubs.

—The Thirteenth Princess. 2011. (ENG.). 272p. (J). (gr. 3-7). pap. 6.99 *(978-0-06-182500-2(X))* HarperCollins Pubs.

—A True Princess. 2011. (ENG.). 192p. (J). (gr. 3-7). 15.99 *(978-0-06-182501-9(8))* HarperCollins Pubs.

Zakarin, Debra Mostow. First Fairytales. Fiore, Rob, illus. 2010. 10p. 9.95 *(978-1-60747-746-4(7)*, Pickwick Pr.) Phoenix Bks., Inc.

Zavrel, Stepan. Vodnik. Zavrel, Stepan, illus. (Illus.). 32p. (J). (gr. -1-3). 14.95 *(978-0-87592-058-0(6))* Scroll Pr., Inc.

Zeman, Ludmila. Gilgamesh the King. 2014. 18.95 *(978-1-63419-701-4(1))* Perfection Learning Corp.

Zem, Linda L. The Pocket Fairies of Middleburg. Day, Linda S., illus. 2004. (J). per. 9.95 *(978-0-9753098-0-3(3))* Linwood Hse. Publishing.

Ziegler, Rini. Danielle & the Strawberry Fairies. 2013. (ENG., Illus.). 34p. (J). 24.95 *(978-1-939055-14-9(8)*, ab3f8ce4-625b-4480-8b9c-dbc1d4326abe) Bright Sky Pr.

Zipes, Jack, ed. & tr. Beauties, Beasts & Enchantment: Classic French Fairy Tales. Zipes, Jack, tr. 3rd ed. 2013. 610p. pap. *(978-1-86171-432-9(7))*; *(978-1-86171-319-3(3))* Crescent Moon Publishing.

365 Historias Lectura a Partir de 3 Anos.Tr. of 365 Fairy Tales. (SPA.). (J). 14.98 *(978-970-22-0042-0(3))* Larousse, Ediciones, S. A. de C. V. MEX. Dist: Continental Bk. Co., Inc.

FAIRY TALES—INDEXES

Tyler, Jenny & Doherty, Gillian, eds. Usborne Stories for Little Girls. 2008. (Picture Books Ser.). (Illus.). 135p. (J). (gr. -1-3). 18.99 *(978-0-7945-1974-2(1)*, Usborne) EDC Publishing.

FAITH

Adams, Michelle Medlock. God Is Always with You. Siewert, Pauline, illus. 2014. (Peek-A-Boo Promises Ser.). 16p. (J). bds. 8.99 *(978-0-8249-1907-8(6)*, Ideal Pubns.) Worthy Publishing.

—Why I Trust You, God. Munger, Nancy, illus. 2006. 20p. (J). (gr. -1). bds. 5.49 *(978-0-7586-0913-7(2))* Concordia Publishing Hse.

Anderson, George William, ed. Achieving Success with Faith in God: The Concept of Faith - Based Perseverance. 2007. 128p. 15.95 *(978-0-9786565-0-8(4))* Naypree Enterprises, LLC.

Arrington, French L. Exploring the Declaration of Faith. 2003. 112p. spiral bd. 7.99 *(978-0-87148-396-6(3))* Pathway Pr.

Askew, Shirley. Jean's Magical Moments: Faith of a Child. 2010. 56p. pap. 14.95 *(978-1-4327-5168-5(9))* Outskirts Pr., Inc.

Balfour, R. C., III. Fishing for the Abundant Life 2 Journey to Faith. 2004. (gr. 9-18). 26.00 *(978-1-889574-21-9(X))* Sentry Pr., Inc.

Barnholdt, Lauren. One Moment in Time. 2015. (Moment of Truth Ser.: 2). (ENG.). 304p. (YA). (gr. 8). pap. 9.99 *(978-0-06-232141-1(2)*, HarperTeen) HarperCollins Pubs.

Becoming a Girl of Faith: According to God's Word. l.t. ed. 2004. 90p. (YA). 12.95 *(978-0-9764304-2-1(8))* Girls of Faith.

Blake, D M. Achieving Success with Faith in God: The Concept of Faith-Based Perserverance. 2007. 128p. per. 13.95 *(978-0-9786565-1-5(2))* Naypree Enterprises, LLC.

Bradshaw, Frances C. F-A-i-t-h: Do You Have It ?? 2012. 28p. pap. 19.99 *(978-1-4772-9848-0(7))* AuthorHouse.

Buller, Laura & Dorling Kindersley Publishing Staff. A Faith Like Mine: A Celebration of the World's Religions — Seen Through the Eyes of Children. 2005. (ENG., Illus.). 80p. (J). (gr. 5-12). 19.99 *(978-0-7566-1177-4(6)*, DK Children) Dorling Kindersley Publishing, Inc.

Carson Sr., Johnny Lee. Cookies & Dreams. 2013. 40p. pap. 24.95 *(978-1-62709-682-9(5))* America Star Bks.

DiMarco, Hayley. The God Girl Journey: A 30-Day Guide to a Deeper Faith. 2013. (ENG.). 176p. (YA). 14.99 *(978-0-8007-2067-4(9))* Revell.

Donaghy, Thomas J. Celebrating Mass. 2009. (St. Joseph Board Bks.). (Illus.). 12p. bds. 5.95 *(978-0-89942-662-4(X))* Catholic Bk. Publishing Corp.

Dotterweich, Kass P. 25 Stories for Sharing Faith with Teens: Making Connections. Cannizzo, Karen A., ed. 2004. (Youth Ministry Resource Library). 96p. pap. 19.95 *(978-0-937997-58-1(7)*, 702) Pflaum Publishing Group.

Elkins, Stephen. First Steps in Faith: Beginning Lessons of God's Love. Colton, Ellie, illus. 2006. (First Steps in Faith Ser.). 25p. (J). (gr. -1-k). bds. 9.99 incl. audio compact disk *(978-0-8054-2662-5(0))* B&H Publishing Group.

—Tell Me about Faith. 2014. (Train 'Em Up Ser.). (ENG.). 24p. (J). pap. 4.99 *(978-1-4143-9675-0(9))* Tyndale Hse. Pubs.

Fischer, Carl. Days of Faith Assignment Book & Student Planner. Homberg, Ansgar, illus. 2003. 108p. (J). spiral bd. 4.99 *(978-0-89837-232-8(1)*, 9804) Pflaum Publishing Group.

Gaskins, Pearl Fuyo. I Believe In... Christian, Jewish, & Muslim Young People Speak about Their Faiths. 2004. (ENG., Illus.). 160p. (J). 18.95 *(978-0-8126-2713-8(X))* Cricket Bks.

Glassman, Bruce S. Trustworthiness. 2008. (Illus.). 48p. (J). pap. 9.95 *(978-1-60108-511-5(7)*, Bearing Bks.); (YA). (gr. 3-6). lib. bdg. 29.25 *(978-1-60108-510-8(9))* Red Cygnet Pr.

Group Publishing Staff, creator. Grapple - Spring: Preteens' Toughest Questions. the Bible's Smartest Answers, 7 vols. 2013. (ENG.). 112p. (J). (gr. 4-6). pap. 69.99 *(978-1-4707-0469-8(2))* Group Publishing, Inc.

Guzman, Maria Del C. Sheep of Many Colors: Coloring Book. Lovell, Edith, illus. 2013. 26p. pap. 5.99 *(978-0-9855639-4-3(X))* Guzman, Maria del C.

Hall, Mark, et al. Thrive Student Edition: Digging Deep, Reaching Out, 1 vol. 2014. (ENG.). 240p. (YA). pap. 12.99 *(978-0-310-74757-4(0))* Zondervan.

Hudson, Lauriece. Prayers for the Smallest Hands. 2008. (Illus.). 24p. (J). (gr. -1-3). 6.95 *(978-1-60349-003-0(5)*, Marimba Bks.) Hudson Publishing Group, The.

Johnson, Nevlynn L., Sr. Faith, Courage & Wisdom: A Journey to Manhood. 3rd rev. l.t. ed. 2003. Orig. Title: Finding My Way: a Journey to Manhood. 240p. per. 14.95 *(978-0-9741413-0-5(5))* Lone Cypress Pubs.

Labosh, Kathy. The Child with Autism Learns the Faith: The Sunday School Guide. 2007. per. 14.00 *(978-0-9744341-4-8(0))* Labosh Publishing.

MacArthur, John. My Faith & Prayer Journal. 2004. 64p. (J). pap. 4.99 *(978-1-4003-0441-7(5))* Nelson, Thomas Inc.

Monge, Marlyn. Mary & the Little Shepherds of Fatima. Lopez, Maria Joao, illus. 2017. (ENG.). (J). 14.95 ***(978-0-8198-4959-5(6))*** Pauline Bks. & Media.

Mueller, Virginia. What Is Faith? Kolding, Richard Max, illus. 2013. (Happy Day Ser.). (ENG.). 16p. (J). pap. 2.49 *(978-1-4143-9293-6(1))* Tyndale Hse. Pubs.

Nelson, Robin. Am I a Good Friend? A Book about Trustworthiness. 2014. (Show Your Character Ser.). (ENG., Illus.). 32p. (gr. 1-3). lib. bdg. 26.60 *(978-1-4677-1361-0(9)*, Lerner Pubns.) Lerner Publishing Group.

Nielson, Mark S. I Believe in Jesus Too. Stapley, Craig, illus. 2011. (J). 17.99 *(978-1-60908-741-8(0))* Deseret Bk. Co.

Noble, Alan R. Foundations of the Christian Faith. 2008. 160p. pap. 13.99 *(978-1-60477-694-2(3))* Salem Author Services.

Palmer, Alison. Walking the Path of Faith: More Fun Character-Building Activities for LDS Children - a Companion Volume to Planting Seeds of Faith. 2004. (J). per. 9.99 *(978-0-88290-764-2(6)*, Horizon Pubs.) Cedar Fort, Inc./CFI Distribution.

Parker, Amy. How Far Is Faith? (padded Board Book) 2016. (Faith, Hope, Love Ser.). (ENG.). 24p. (J). (gr. -1-k). bds. 9.99 *(978-1-4336-9040-2(3)*, B&H Kids) B&H Publishing Group.

Peckham, Lori. Guide's Greatest Faith Stories. 2015. 159p. (J). *(978-0-8163-5825-0(7))* Pacific Pr. Publishing Assn.

Piepgrass, Arlene. Faith Volume 02: Old Testament Volume 2 Genesis Part 2. Henkel, Vern, illus. 2014. 36p. (J). pap. *(978-1-932381-67-2(8)*, 2002) Bible Visuals International, Inc.

Riley, Jim. Spiritual Grit: Pass It on to Kids 2004. (ENG., Illus.). 125p. per. 8.95 *(978-1-57166-315-3(0))* Quixote Pr.

Risser, Terry. Sports Fun: Guide to Faith & God. 2012. (ENG.). pap. *(978-1-4675-2707-1(6))* Independent Pub.

Rock Solid Tween FaithZine Winter 2009-2010. 2009. (Efs Ser.). 5.20 *(978-0-687-65839-8(X)*, Cokesbury) Abingdon Pr.

Schulz, Charles. Seguridad es un Pulgar y una Manta. (SPA.). (J). 7.00 *(978-84-7655-664-1(0)*, PI3929) Plaza Joven, S.A. ESP. Dist: Lectorum Pubns., Inc.

Sisters of Notre Dame, Chardon, Ohio. We Believe: Grade 3. 2008. (Christ Our Life 2009 Ser.). (ENG.). 252p. (gr. 1-8). pap., stu. ed. 15.20 *(978-0-8294-2410-2(5))* Loyola Pr.

Small, Mary. Ser Digno de Confianza. Previn, Stacey, illus. 2011. (¡Así Debemos Ser!/Way to Be! Ser.).Tr. of Being Trustworthy. (ENG, SPA & MUL.). 24p. (gr. -1-2). lib. bdg. 26.65 *(978-1-4048-6691-1(4))* Picture Window Bks.

Strobel, Lee. The Case for Faith: A Journalist Investigates the Toughest Objections to Christianity, 1 vol. 2014. (Case for ... Series for Students Ser.). (ENG.). 112p. (YA). pap., stu. ed. 9.99 *(978-0-310-74542-6(X))* Zondervan.

—The Case for the Real Jesus: A Journalist Investigates Current Challenges to Christianity, 1 vol. 2014. (Case for ... Series for Students Ser.). (ENG.). 208p. (YA). pap., stu. ed. 9.99 *(978-0-310-74567-9(5))* Zondervan.

Sublett, Kit. After Camp: Beginning the Christian Adventure. 2003. (YA). pap. 3.95 *(978-0-9758577-0-0(3))* Whitecaps Media.

Thomas Nelson Publishing Staff. Faith Journal, 1 vol. 2013. (ENG.). 96p. (J). 9.99 *(978-1-4003-2386-9(X))* Nelson, Thomas Inc.

Torrisi, Cathy. Tell Someone You Trust. 2011. pap. 39.95 *(978-0-7664-3754-8(X))* Abrams & Co. Pubs., Inc.

Walker, Joe. Belief & Science. 2009. (Illus.). 208p. pap., tchr. ed. 43.50 *(978-0-340-97302-8(1))* Hodder Education Group GBR. Dist: Trans-Atlantic Pubns., Inc.

Walker, Joyce MacKichan. Faithful Questions Student Book. 2nd ed. 2004. (YA). spiral bd. 14.99 *(978-0-9752605-7-9(X))* LOGOS System Assocs.

What Is Faith? 2006. (Faith Discovery Ser.). (Illus.). 24p. (J). bds. 6.99 *(978-0-7847-1396-9(0)*, 04056) Standard Publishing.

Windle, Margaret. Assorted Saints & the Virtues. 2006. (Illus.). 64p. (J). 11.99 *(978-0-9798889-1-5(3))* Growing with the Saints, Inc.

FAITH-CURE

see Spiritual Healing

FALCONRY

Brezina, Corona. Falconry & Game Hawking. 2012. (Hunting: Pursuing Wild Game! Ser.). (ENG., Illus.). 64p. (YA). (gr. 5-8). pap. 12.95 *(978-1-4488-8285-4(0))*; lib. bdg. 31.95 *(978-1-4488-8279-3(6))* Rosen Publishing Group, Inc., The. (Rosen Reference).

FALCONRY—FICTION

Brunner, Kym. Flip the Bird. 2016. (ENG.). 368p. (YA). (gr. 7). 17.99 *(978-0-544-80085-4(0)*, HMH Books For Young Readers) Houghton Mifflin Harcourt Publishing Co.

Golding, Julia. The Glass Swallow, 0 vols. 2011. (ENG.). 320p. (gr. 7-12). 17.99 *(978-0-7614-5979-8(0)*, 9780761459798, Amazon Children's Publishing) Amazon Publishing.

Smith, Danna. The Hawk of the Castle: A Story of Medieval Falconry. Ibatoulline, Bagram, illus. 2017. (ENG.). 40p. (J). (gr. -1-3). 16.99 *(978-0-7636-7992-7(5))* Candlewick Pr.

FALCONS

Earley, Chris. Falcons in the City: The Story of a Peregrine Family. Massey, Luke, photos by. 2016. (ENG., Illus.). 48p. (J). (gr. 4-8). pap. 9.95 *(978-1-77085-803-9(2)*, 9781770858039) Firefly Bks., Ltd.

Gish, Melissa. Falcons. 2015. (Illus.). 46p. (J). *(978-1-60818-566-5(4)*, Creative Education) Creative Co., The.

—Falcons: Living Wild. 2016. (Living Wild Ser.). (ENG.). 48p. (J). (gr. 5-9). pap. 12.00 *(978-1-62832-167-8(9)*, Creative Paperbacks) Creative Co., The.

Gove-Berg, Christie. Maggie the One-Eyed Peregrine Falcon: A True Story of Rescue & Rehabilitation, 1 vol. 2016. (Wildlife Rescue Stories Ser.). (ENG., Illus.). 32p. (J). (gr. -1-3). 12.95 *(978-1-59193-516-2(4))* Adventure Pubns.

Haywood, Karen. Hawks & Falcons. 2010. (Endangered! 2 Ser.). 48p. (gr. 3). lib. bdg. 29.93 *(978-0-7614-4051-2(8))* Marshall Cavendish Corp.

Hill, Melissa. Peregrine Falcons. 2015. (Birds of Prey Ser.). (ENG., Illus.). 24p. (gr. k-1). pap. 6.95 *(978-1-4914-2310-3(2)*, Pebble Plus) Capstone Press of Coughlan Cos.

Lunis, Natalie. Peregrine Falcon: Dive, Dive, Dive! 2010. (Blink of an Eye: Superfast Animals Ser.). 24p. (J). (gr. k-3). lib. bdg. 22.61 *(978-1-936087-93-8(6))* Bearport Publishing Co., Inc.

Lynch, Wayne. Falcons. Neidigh, Sherry, illus. 2005. (Our Wild World Ser.). (ENG.). 48p. (J). (gr. 2-5). 10.95 *(978-1-55971-911-7(7))* Cooper Square Publishing Llc.

—Falcons. Neidigh, Sherry, illus. Lynch, Wayne, photos by. 2005. (Our Wild World Ser.). (ENG.). 48p. (J). (gr. 2-5). pap. 7.95 *(978-1-55971-912-4(5))* Cooper Square Publishing Llc.

Marsico, Katie. Falcons. 2015. (ENG.). 48p. (J). pap. 6.95 *(978-0-531-21187-8(8)*, Orchard Bks.) Scholastic Library Publishing.

Norris, Ashley P. Watson. Falcons, 1 vol. 2012. (Birds Ser.). (ENG.). 24p. (gr. 1-2). lib. bdg. 25.32 *(978-1-4296-8606-8(5))* Capstone Press of Coughlan Cos.

Plattner, Josh. Peregrine Falcon: Master of Speed, 1 vol. 2016. (ENG., Illus.). 24p. (J). *(978-1-62403-738-2(0))* ABDO Publishing Co.

Powell, Consie. Peregrine's Sky. Powell, Consie, illus. 2009. (ENG., Illus.). 32p. (J). pap. 7.95 *(978-1-58369-129-8(4))* Western National Parks Assn.

Priebe, Mac. FalconQuest CD-ROM + the Peregrine Falcon Book. 2003. (J). 29.95 *(978-0-9669551-5-6(3))* Mindfull Publishing.

Riggs, Kate. Amazing Animals: Falcons. 2017. (Amazing Animals Ser.). (ENG., Illus.). 24p. (J). (gr. 1-3). pap. 8.99 ***(978-1-62832-361-0(2)***, Creative Paperbacks) Creative Co., The.

Riggs, Kate. Falcons. 2017. (Illus.). 24p. (J). *(978-1-60818-753-9(5)*, Creative Education) Creative Co., The.

Warhol, Tom. Hawks. 2005. (Animalways Ser.). (Illus.). 104p. (gr. 6-7). lib. bdg. 24.95 *(978-0-7614-1744-6(3)*, Benchmark Bks.) Marshall Cavendish Corp.

Wechsler, Doug. Peregrine Falcons. 2009. (Really Wild Life of Animals Ser.). 24p. (gr. 3-4). 42.50 *(978-1-60854-204-8(1)*, PowerKids Pr.) Rosen Publishing Group, Inc., The.

Wilson, Emily. Falcons, 01 vols., 1. 2016. (Raptors! Ser.). (ENG., Illus.). 24p. (J). 23.60 *(978-1-5081-4245-4(9)*, PowerKids Pr.) Rosen Publishing Group, Inc., The.

FALCONS—FICTION

Atwater-Rhodes, Amelia. Falcondance. 2007. (Kiesha'ra Ser.: Bk. 3). (ENG.). 208p. (YA). (gr. 7-12). per. 7.99 *(978-0-440-23885-0(4)*, Delacorte Pr.) Random Hse. Children's Bks.

—Snakecharm. 2006. (Kiesha'ra Ser.: Bk. 2). (ENG.). 176p. (YA). (gr. 7-11). per. 6.99 *(978-0-440-23804-1(8)*, Laurel Leaf) Random Hse. Children's Bks.

Books, Eric Stephen. Wing over Wendover. 2012. 86p. pap. 12.95 *(978-1-4685-6179-1(0))* AuthorHouse.

Daher, Anita. Poachers in the Pingos, 1 vol. 2008. (Orca Young Readers Ser.). (ENG.). 128p. (J). (gr. 3-6). pap. 7.95 *(978-1-55469-011-4(0))* Orca Bk. Pubs. USA.

Dans, Peter E. Perry's Baltimore Adventure: A Bird's-Eye View of Charm City. Harrell, Kim, illus. 2007. (ENG.). 32p. (J). (gr. -1-1). 14.95 *(978-1-933822-08-2(2))* Camino Bks., Inc.

Douglas, Babette. Falcon Eddie. Johnson, John, illus. 2006. (Kiss a Me Teacher Creature Stories Ser.). (J). (gr. -1-3). 9.99 *(978-1-890343-21-7(8))* Kiss A Me Productions, Inc.

Dunphy, Madeleine. The Peregrine's Journey: A Story of Migration. Kest, Kristin, illus. 2008. (ENG.). 32p. (J). (gr. k-4). 16.95 *(978-0-9777539-3-2(X))*; per. 9.95 *(978-0-9777539-2-5(1))* Web of Life Children's Bks.

George, Jean Craighead. Frightful's Mountain. 2014. (ENG.). 272p. (J). (gr. 4-8). 11.24 *(978-1-63245-351-8(7))* Lectorum Pubns., Inc.

Gordon, Amy. Twenty Gold Falcons. (ENG.). 240p. (J). (gr. 3-7). 2012. pap. 8.99 *(978-0-8234-2656-0(4))* 2010. 16.95 *(978-0-8234-2252-4(6))* Holiday Hse., Inc.

E F G

Gutman, Dan. Miss Suki Is Kooky! Paillot, Jim, illus. 2007. (My Weird School Ser.: 17). (J). 14.75 *(978-1-4177-7430-2(4),* Turtleback) Turtleback Bks.

La Fontaine, Jean De. The Falcon & the Little Dog. 2004. reprint ed. pap. 15.95 *(978-1-4191-6181-0(4))* Kessinger Publishing, LLC.

Lambert, Nancy R. World of Reading:Falcon Fear of Flying (Level 2 Early Reader) Level 2. Rosenberg, Rachelle & Lim, Ron, illus. 2016. (ENG.). 32p. (J). (gr. 1-3). pap. 3.99 *(978-1-4847-3200-7(6),* Marvel Pr.) Disney Publishing Worldwide.

Manning, Lisa C. Falcons in the City. Manning, Lisa C., illus. 2013. (ENG., Illus.). 40p. (J). pap. 14.95 *(978-1-59299-886-9(0))* Inkwater Pr.

Whitman, Emily. Wildwing. 2010. (ENG.). 368p. (YA). (gr. 8-18). 16.99 *(978-0-06-172452-7(1),* Greenwillow Bks.) HarperCollins Pubs.

Yelchin, Eugene. The Haunting of Falcon House. Yelchin, Eugene, illus. 2016. (ENG., Illus.). 320p. (J). 15.99 *(978-0-8050-9845-7(3),* 9780805098457, Holt, Henry & Co. Bks. For Young Readers) Holt, Henry & Co.

—The Haunting of Falcon House. 2017. (J). lib. bdg. 18.40 ***(978-0-606-39938-8(0))*** Turtleback Bks.

FALL

see Autumn

FALLACIES

see Logic

FALLING STARS

see Meteors

FALSEHOOD

see Truthfulness and Falsehood

FAMILY

see also Divorce; Domestic Relations; Marriage; Parent and Child; Single-Parent Families; Stepfamilies

also names of members of the family, e.g., Fathers; Mothers; etc.

Adams, Pamela L. Once upon a Family: A Son's Journey of Love, Loss, & Hope. Henderson, Ken, illus. l.t. ed. 2003. 116p. per. *(978-1-891029-35-6(5))* Henderson Publishing.

Adamson, Heather. Families in Many Cultures. 2016. (Life Around the World Ser.). (ENG.). 24p. (gr. k-1). pap. 7.29 *(978-1-5157-3695-0(4),* Pebble Plus) Capstone Press of Coughlan Cos.

Ajmera, Maya, et al. Our Grandparents: A Global Album. 2010. (ENG.). 32p. (J). (gr. -1-3). 16.95 *(978-1-57091-458-4(3))* Charlesbridge Publishing, Inc.

Alcott, Louisa May. Under the Lilacs. l.t. ed. 2005. 444p. pap. *(978-1-84637-059-5(0))* Echo Library.

Anderson, Nancy. Timeline of My Family History. 2016. (Rosen REAL Readers: Social Studies Nonfiction / Fiction: Family, Community, & the World Ser.). 12p. (gr. 1-k). pap. 6.33 *(978-1-5081-2344-6(6),* Rosen Classroom) Rosen Publishing Group, Inc., The.

Antill, Sara. 10 Ways I Can Help My Family. 2012. (I Can Make a Difference Ser.). (ENG.). 24p. (J). (gr. 2-5). pap. 8.25 *(978-1-4488-6367-9(8));* lib. bdg. 22.60 *(978-1-4488-6204-7(3))* Rosen Publishing Group, Inc., The. (PowerKids Pr.).

Apel, Melanie Ann. Home Life in Ancient Greece. 2004. (Primary Sources of Ancient Civilizations Ser.). (ENG., Illus.). 24p. (gr. 4-8). pap. 8.25 *(978-0-8239-8940-9(2),* PowerKids Pr.) Rosen Publishing Group, Inc., The.

Auld, Mary. Meet the Family, 6 bks. Incl. My Aunt & Uncle. lib. bdg. 22.00 *(978-0-8368-3923-4(4));* My Brother. (J). 22.00 *(978-0-8368-3924-1(2));* My Dad. lib. bdg. 22.00 *(978-0-8368-3925-8(0));* My Grandparents. lib. bdg. 22.00 *(978-0-8368-3926-5(9));* My Mom. lib. bdg. 22.00 *(978-0-8368-3927-2(7));* My Sister. lib. bdg. 22.00 *(978-0-8368-3928-9(5));* (gr. k-3)., Gareth Stevens Learning Library (Meet the Family Ser.). (Illus.). 24p. 2004. 127.62 o.p. *(978-0-8368-3922-7(6))* Stevens, Gareth Publishing LLLP.

—Mi Hermana. Coffey, Colleen & Carrillo, Consuelo, trs. from ENG. 2004. (Conoce la Familia Ser.). (SPA., Illus.). 24p. (gr. k-3). lib. bdg. 22.00 *(978-0-8368-3930-2(7),* Gareth Stevens Learning Library) Stevens, Gareth Publishing LLLP.

—Mi hermano (My Brother) Coffey, Colleen & Carrillo, Consuelo, trs. from ENG. 2004. (Conoce la Familia Ser.). (SPA., Illus.). 24p. (gr. k-3). lib. bdg. 22.00 *(978-0-8368-3931-9(5),* Gareth Stevens Learning Library) Stevens, Gareth Publishing LLLP.

—Mi Mama. Coffey, Colleen & Carrillo, Consuelo, trs. from ENG. 2004. (Conoce la Familia Ser.). (SPA., Illus.). 24p. (gr. k-3). lib. bdg. 22.00 *(978-0-8368-3932-6(3),* Gareth Stevens Learning Library) Stevens, Gareth Publishing LLLP.

—Mi Papa. Carrillo, Consuelo & Coffey, Colleen, trs. from ENG. 2004. (Conoce la Familia Ser.). (SPA., Illus.). 24p. (gr. k-3). lib. bdg. 22.00 *(978-0-8368-3933-3(1),* Gareth Stevens Learning Library) Stevens, Gareth Publishing LLLP.

—Mis Abuelos. Carrillo, Consuelo & Coffey, Colleen, trs. from ENG. 2004. (Conoce la Familia Ser.). (SPA., Illus.). 24p. (gr. k-3). lib. bdg. 22.00 *(978-0-8368-3934-0(X),* Gareth Stevens Learning Library) Stevens, Gareth Publishing LLLP.

—Mis Tios. Carrillo, Consuelo & Coffey, Colleen, trs. from ENG. 2004. (Conoce la Familia Ser.). (SPA., Illus.). 24p. (gr. k-3). lib. bdg. 22.00 *(978-0-8368-3935-7(8),* Gareth Stevens Learning Library) Stevens, Gareth Publishing LLLP.

—My Aunt & Uncle. 2004. (Meet the Family Ser.). (Illus.). 24p. (gr. k-3). lib. bdg. 22.00 *(978-0-8368-3923-4(4),* Gareth Stevens Learning Library) Stevens, Gareth Publishing LLLP.

—My Dad. 2004. (Meet the Family Ser.). (Illus.). 24p. (gr. k-3). lib. bdg. 22.00 *(978-0-8368-3925-8(0),* Gareth Stevens Learning Library) Stevens, Gareth Publishing LLLP.

—My Grandparents. 2004. (Meet the Family Ser.). (Illus.). 24p. (gr. k-3). lib. bdg. 22.00 *(978-0-8368-3926-5(9),* Gareth Stevens Learning Library) Stevens, Gareth Publishing LLLP.

—My Mom. 2004. (Meet the Family Ser.). (Illus.). 24p. (gr. k-3). lib. bdg. 22.00 *(978-0-8368-3927-2(7),* Gareth Stevens Learning Library) Stevens, Gareth Publishing LLLP.

—My Sister. 2004. (Meet the Family Ser.). (Illus.). 24p. (gr. k-3). lib. bdg. 22.00 *(978-0-8368-3928-9(5),* Gareth Stevens Learning Library) Stevens, Gareth Publishing LLLP.

—Sharing a Meal. 2011. (My Family & Me Ser.). (Illus.). 24p. (J). lib. bdg. 24.25 *(978-1-59771-231-6(0))* Sea-To-Sea Pubns.

—Welcoming a New Baby. 2011. (My Family & Me Ser.). (Illus.). 24p. (J). lib. bdg. 24.25 *(978-1-59771-232-3(9))* Sea-To-Sea Pubns.

Banks, Delilah & Giacobello, John. Surviving Family Violence, 01 vols., 1. 2016. (Family Issues & You Ser.). (ENG.). 48p. (J). pap. 11.75 *(978-1-4994-3705-8(6),* Rosen Central) Rosen Publishing Group, Inc., The.

Barber, Nicola. A New Baby Arrives. 2009. (Big Day! Ser.). 24p. (J). (gr. k-2). (ENG., Illus.). pap. 8.25 *(978-1-4358-2898-8(4),* 1291898); lib. bdg. 22.60 *(978-1-4358-2842-1(9))* Rosen Publishing Group, Inc., The. (PowerKids Pr.).

Bateman, Vernon. Mommy I Want 2 Fly. 2012. 48p. pap. 21.99 *(978-1-4685-6599-7(0))* AuthorHouse.

Bauman, Carey. God Controls the Storm. Bauman, Carey, tr. 2007. (Little Jewel Book Ser.). (Illus.). 24p. (J). (gr. 2). pap. 2.70 *(978-0-7399-2396-2(X))* Rod & Staff Pubs., Inc.

Benchmark Education Co., LLC. Families Together Big Book. 2014. (Shared Reading Foundations Ser.). (J). (gr. -1). *(978-1-4509-9422-4(9))* Benchmark Education Co.

Benchmark Education Company, LLC Staff, compiled by. Families & Friends: Theme Set. 2006. (J). 274.00 *(978-1-4108-7069-8(3))* Benchmark Education Co.

Beren, Norris L. When Disaster Strikes Home! 101+ Ways to Protect Your Family from Unthinkable Emergencies. 2003. (Illus.). 240p. per. 17.95 *(978-0-9729065-0-0(9))* EPEI Pr.

Bolchazy, Marie Carducci. Quis Me Amat?/Who Loves Me? 2003. (I Am Reading Latin Ser.). (ENG & LAT., Illus.). 64p. (J). (gr. k-3). 10.00 *(978-0-86516-541-0(6))* Bolchazy-Carducci Pubs.

Bradex, Melissa A. Little Gregory. Crane, Eddie, illus. 2009. 32p. pap. 14.99 *(978-1-4490-3549-5(3))* AuthorHouse.

Brieske, Joel. Being Different Is Being Normal. 2005. 32p. (J). pap. 12.95 *(978-1-4116-3378-0(4))* Lulu Pr., Inc.

Broqueville, Paulette-Renee. Unraveling Your Past Relationships. 2003. 288p. per. 20.00 *(978-0-9719413-2-8(7))* Broqueville Publishing, Inc.

Brown, Isobel. Domestic Crime, Vol. 20. Gomez, Manny, ed. 2016. (Crime & Detection Ser.). (Illus.). 96p. (J). (gr. 7). 24.95 *(978-1-4222-3474-7(6))* Mason Crest.

Brun-Cosme, Nadine, et al. Hoy lo Hace Papa! 2004. (SPA., Illus.). 32p. (J). (gr. -1-k). 13.99 *(978-84-8470-116-3(6))* Corimbo, Editorial S.L. ESP. Dist: Lectorum Pubns., Inc.

Bullard, Lisa. My Family, Your Family. 2015. (Cloverleaf Books (tm) — Alike & Different Ser.). (ENG., Illus.). 24p. (J). (gr. k-2). pap. 6.99 *(978-1-4677-6029-4(3));* lib. bdg. 23.99 *(978-1-4677-4901-5(X))* Lerner Publishing Group. (Millbrook Pr.).

Burton, Margie, et al. Doing Jobs Together. 2011. (Early Connections Ser.). (J). *(978-1-61672-288-3(6))* Benchmark Education Co.

Cain, Susan, et al. Quiet Power: The Secret Strengths of Introverts. Snider, Grant, illus. (ENG.). 288p. (J). (gr. 5). 2017. 9.99 *(978-0-14-750992-5(0),* Puffin Books) 2016. 17.99 *(978-0-8037-4060-0(3),* Dial Bks) 2016. lib. bdg. 20.99 *(978-0-399-18672-1(7),* Dial Bks) Penguin Young Readers Group.

Cameron, Amanda-Jane. The Body Armour. 2012. (Illus.). 36p. pap. 22.88 *(978-1-4685-8157-7(0))* AuthorHouse.

Canetti, Yanitzia. En Tiempos Difíciles. Willy, Romont, illus. 2010. (SPA & ENG.). 32p. (J). (gr. k-2). pap. 8.99 *(978-1-59835-102-6(8),* BrickHouse Education) Cambridge BrickHouse, Inc.

—When Times Are Tough. Keating, Alison, tr. Willy, Romont, illus. 2009. 32p. (J). (gr. k-2). 8.99 *(978-1-59835-103-3(6))* Cambridge BrickHouse, Inc.

Canizzaro, Angelina Joyce. Daddy's Magic Lunchbox. 2012. 20p. pap. 12.97 *(978-1-61897-577-5(3),* Strategic Bk. Publishing) Strategic Book Publishing & Rights Agency (SBPRA).

Carr, Jennifer. Be Who You Are. 2010. 40p. pap. 20.99 *(978-1-4520-8725-2(3))* AuthorHouse.

Casselman, Grace. A Hole in the Hedge. 2003. (ENG.). 224p. (YA). (gr. 6-18). pap. 8.95 *(978-0-929141-99-2(7),* Napoleon & Co.) Dundurn CAN. Dist: Ingram Publisher Services.

Catching People in the Love Net. 2005. (YA). 9.75 *(978-1-58942-261-2(9))* R.H. Boyd Publishing Corp.

Catt, Thessaly. My Uncles & Aunts. 2010. (My Family Ser.). (ENG.). 24p. (J). pap. 8.25 *(978-1-4488-1494-7(4));* lib. bdg. 22.60 *(978-1-4488-1464-0(2))* Rosen Publishing Group, Inc., The. (PowerKids Pr.).

—My Uncles & Aunts: MIS Tíos y Tías. 2010. (My Family / Mi Familia Ser.). (SPA & ENG.). 24p. lib. bdg. 22.60 *(978-1-4488-0719-2(0),* PowerKids Pr.) Rosen Publishing Group, Inc., The.

Chen, D. M. & Sun, Michelle. Tie a Wish with Bracelets: Easy & Fun Chinese Knotting. 2012. (ENG., Illus.). 71p. (J). (gr. 4). pap. 10.95 *(978-1-937489-01-4(9))* StoryRobin Co.

Cifuentes, Carolina. My Family. Snider, Jackie, illus. 2010. (My World Ser.). (ENG.). 24p. (J). (gr. -1-1). lib. bdg. 22.60 *(978-1-60754-946-8(8))* Windmill Bks.

Cifuentes, Carolina, ed. My Family. Snider, Jackie, illus. 2010. (My World Ser.). (ENG.). 24p. (J). (gr. -1-1). pap. 8.15 *(978-1-61533-025-6(9))* Windmill Bks.

Cobb, Carlene. Coping with an Abusive Relationship. 2009. (Coping Ser.). 192p. (gr. 7-12). 63.90 *(978-1-61511-990-5(6))* Rosen Publishing Group, Inc., The.

Covey, Sean. Just the Way I Am: Habit 1. Curtis, Stacy, illus. 2009. (7 Habits of Happy Kids Ser.: 1). (ENG.). 32p. (J). (gr. -1-1). 7.99 *(978-1-4169-9423-7(6),* Simon & Schuster Bks. For Young Readers) Simon & Schuster Bks. For Young Readers.

Crist, James J. & Verdick, Elizabeth. Siblings: You're Stuck with Each Other, So Stick Together. 2010. (Laugh & Learn(r) Ser.). (ENG., Illus.). 112p. (J). (gr. 3-7). pap. 8.95 *(978-1-57542-336-4(7),* 1301018) Free Spirit Publishing, Inc.

Crompton, Samuel Willard. The Family Values Movement: Promoting Faith Through Action. 2007. (Reform Movements in American History Ser.). (Illus.). 120p. (J). (gr. 7-12). lib. bdg. 32.50 *(978-0-7910-9608-6(4))* Facts On File, Inc.

Daddy, The Bigg. Bed Time Stories to Grandchildren. 2011. 236p. pap. 19.99 *(978-1-4568-4333-5(8))* Xlibris Corp.

Daronco, Mickey & Ohanesian, Diane. Home with Mom & Dad. 2003. (BuildUp Ser.). (J). pap. 22.00 *(978-1-4108-0753-3(3))* Benchmark Education Co.

Davis, James (Jim) W. Out-takes of 55 Years of Camping 2004. (Illus.). 168p. (YA). per. 5.95 *(978-0-9760960-0-9(5))* Davis, James (Jim).

Dwight, Laura. Brothers & Sisters, 1 vol. (ENG., Illus.). 32p. (J). 2012. pap. 7.95 *(978-1-59572-364-2(1))* 2005. (gr. -1-3). 15.95 *(978-1-887734-80-6(5))* Star Bright Bks., Inc.

Dyan, Penelope. Why Lie? the Truth Is Easier to Remember! 2011. 34p. pap. 11.95 *(978-1-935630-79-1(2))* Bellissima Publishing, LLC.

E Llamas, Melissa Ann. I Came from Your Tummy, Too! Right Mom? 2012. (ENG.). 35p. (J). pap. 15.95 *(978-1-4327-8422-5(6))* Outskirts Pr., Inc.

Easterling, Doris. The Family Vacation. 2011. 32p. pap. 14.99 *(978-1-4567-6906-2(5))* AuthorHouse.

Elasky, Kathy Sue. What Is a Family? 2009. 28p. pap. 12.69 *(978-1-4389-5248-2(1))* AuthorHouse.

English, Carolyn B. Grandpa & the Orange Bowl. 2010. 32p. pap. 12.99 *(978-1-4490-4741-2(6))* AuthorHouse.

Epstein, Brad M. Cornell University 101: My First Text-Board-Book. l.t. ed. 2004. (101 — My First Text-Board Books). (Illus.). 20p. (J). bds. *(978-1-932530-00-1(2))* Michaelson Entertainment.

—Penn State University 101: My First Text-Board-Book. l.t. ed. 2004. (101 — My First Text-Board Books). (Illus.). 20p. (J). bds. *(978-1-932530-04-9(5),* 101 Bk.) Michaelson Entertainment.

Especially for Dads: Introducing Dads with Young Children to Literacy, Language & Learning Through Great Children's Literature. 2004. (J). *(978-0-9753985-4-8(7))* Mother Goose Programs.

Fallon, Michael. Who Are These People? Coping with Family Dynamics, 1 vol. 2010. (Essential Health: a Guy's Guide Ser.). (ENG., Illus.). 112p. (J). (gr. 6-12). lib. bdg. 35.64 *(978-1-61613-545-4(X))* ABDO Publishing Co.

Family. (YA). tchr. ed. 41.95 *(978-0-382-40668-3(0))* Cobblestone Publishing Co.

Family. (Ministry to Adolescent's Program Ser.). (Illus.). (J). (gr. 5-9). 64p. 12.00 *(978-0-85910-794-5(9),* 23-0794); 48p. 8.75 *(978-0-85910-795-2(7),* 23-0795) Concordia Publishing Hse.

Family, Vol. II. 2nd fac. ed. 723p. (YA). reprint ed. pap. 99.00 *(978-0-7404-0383-5(4))* Higginson Bk. Co.

Family Matters, 6 bks. Incl. You & an Illness in Your Family. Wainwright, Tabitha. (YA). lib. bdg. 29.25 *(978-0-8239-3352-5(0));* You & the Rules in Your Family. MacAdam, Lea. (YA). lib. bdg. 29.25 *(978-0-8239-3350-1(4));* You & Violence in Your Family. Giacobello, John. (J). lib. bdg. 29.25 *(978-0-8239-3353-2(9));* You & Your Parents' Divorce. Krohn, Katherine E. (YA). lib. bdg. 29.25 *(978-0-8239-3354-9(7));* (gr. 5-8). (Illus.). 48p. 2005. Set lib. bdg. 143.70 *(978-0-8239-9313-0(2))* Rosen Publishing Group, Inc., The.

Famous Families, 8 Bks., Set. 2005. (YA). 202.00 *(978-1-4042-0376-1(1))* Rosen Publishing Group, Inc., The.

Fannoun, Kathy. Our Loving Grandparents. Date not set. 20p. (J). 4.50 *(978-1-884187-30-8(7))* AMICA Publishing Hse.

Fields, Julianna. First-Generation Immigrant Families. 2010. (Changing Face of Modern Families Ser.). (Illus.). 64p. (YA). (gr. 6-18). lib. bdg. 22.95 *(978-1-4222-1499-2(0))* Mason Crest.

—Gay & Lesbian Parents. 2010. (Changing Face of Modern Families Ser.). (Illus.). 64p. (YA). (gr. 5-18). lib. bdg. 22.95 *(978-1-4222-1495-4(8))* Mason Crest.

—Kids Growing up Without a Home. 2010. (Changing Face of Modern Families Ser.). (Illus.). 64p. (YA). (gr. 5-18). lib. bdg. 22.95 *(978-1-4222-1498-5(2))* Mason Crest.

Flor Ada, Alma. Island Treasures: Growing up in Cuba: Includes Where the Flame Trees Bloom, under the Royal Palms, & Five Brand New Stories. Martorell, Antonio & Rodriguez, Edel, illus. 2015. (ENG.). 240p. (J). (gr. 3-7). pap. 7.99 *(978-1-4814-2900-9(0))* Simon & Schuster Children's Publishing.

Foran, Jill. La Vie de Famille: Le Début de la Colonie. Karvonen, Tanjah, tr. from ENG. 2011. (FRE., Illus.). 24p. (gr. 3-6). *(978-1-77071-419-9(7))* Weigl Educational Pubs. Ltd.

Fox-Lee, Kyme & Fox-Lee, Susan. What Are Parents? Jennings, Randy, illus. 2007. 32p. (J). 15.95 *(978-0-9753699-1-3(1))* StoryTyme Publishing.

Fox-Lee, Susan & Fox-Lee, Kyme. "What Are Parents?" Jennings, Randy, illus. 2005. 32p. (J). 15.95 *(978-0-9753699-0-6(3))* StoryTyme Publishing.

Gallagher, Debbie. Families, 6 bks., Set. Incl. Family Celebrations. lib. bdg. 18.56 *(978-0-7614-3133-6(0));* Family Homes. lib. bdg. 18.56 *(978-0-7614-3136-7(5));* Family Meals. lib. bdg. 18.56 *(978-0-7614-3138-1(1));* Family Members. lib. bdg. 18.56 *(978-0-7614-3139-8(X));* Family Responsibilities. lib. bdg. 18.56 *(978-0-7614-3141-1(1));* Family Stories. lib. bdg. 18.56 *(978-0-7614-3142-8(X));* 32p. (gr. 1-2). (Families Ser.). 2008. Set lib. bdg. 111.36 *(978-0-7614-3132-9(2),* Benchmark Bks.) Marshall Cavendish Corp.

—Family Celebrations. 2008. (Families Ser.). 32p. (gr. 1-2). lib. bdg. 18.56 *(978-0-7614-3133-6(0),* Benchmark Bks.) Marshall Cavendish Corp.

—Family Homes. 2008. (Families Ser.). 32p. (gr. 1-2). lib. bdg. 18.56 *(978-0-7614-3136-7(5),* Benchmark Bks.) Marshall Cavendish Corp.

—Family Meals. 2008. (Families Ser.). 32p. (gr. 1-2). lib. bdg. 18.56 *(978-0-7614-3138-1(1),* Benchmark Bks.) Marshall Cavendish Corp.

—Family Members. 2008. (Families Ser.). 32p. (gr. 1-2). lib. bdg. 18.56 *(978-0-7614-3139-8(X),* Benchmark Bks.) Marshall Cavendish Corp.

—Family Responsibilities. 2008. (Families Ser.). 32p. (gr. 1-2). lib. bdg. 18.56 *(978-0-7614-3141-1(1),* Benchmark Bks.) Marshall Cavendish Corp.

—Family Stories. 2008. (Families Ser.). 32p. (gr. 1-2). lib. bdg. 18.56 *(978-0-7614-3142-8(X),* Benchmark Bks.) Marshall Cavendish Corp.

Gemwitch, Ruby. A Family of Silly Words: Mamma Words, Baby Words, & Other Words... 2012. 24p. 24.95 *(978-1-4626-7209-7(4))* America Star Bks.

The Good, the Bad, & Everything Else: Individual Title Six-Packs. (Action Packs Ser.). 104p. (gr. 3-5). 44.00 *(978-0-7635-2994-9(X))* Rigby Education.

Greene, Carol. Why Boys & Girls Are Different. 2008. pap. 12.99 *(978-0-7586-1415-5(2))* Concordia Publishing Hse.

—Why Boys & Girls Are Different. Dorankamp, Michelle, illus. 2008. pap. 12.99 *(978-0-7586-1409-4(8))* Concordia Publishing Hse.

Greene, Judybeth, illus. Mommy, Open up the Secrets of the World. 2005. (J). pap. 9.95 *(978-1-932672-76-3(1))* Outskirts Pr., Inc.

Greenhaven Press Staff. Single-Parent Families. Greenhaven Press, ed. 2016. (Opposing Viewpoints Ser.). (ENG.). 224p. (J). (gr. 10-12). 48.80 *(978-0-7377-7528-0(9),* Greenhaven Pr., Inc.) Cengage Gale.

Gregoire, Maryellen. My Family. 2012. (Wonder Readers Emergent Level Ser.). (ENG.). (gr. -1-1). 16p. pap. 35.94 *(978-1-4296-9199-4(9));* 32p. pap. 5.99 *(978-1-4296-9189-5(1))* Capstone Press of Coughlan Cos. (Wonder Readers).

Hairston-Piggee, Tameko. My Daddy Lives with God. 2011. 24p. pap. 12.99 *(978-1-4389-1376-6(1))* AuthorHouse.

Hall, Francie. Appalachian Christmas ABCs. Oehm, Kent, illus. 2010. (ENG.). 53p. (J). 16.95 *(978-1-57072-328-5(1))* Overmountain Pr.

Hartley, Susan. A Family Celebration. 2011. (Early Connections Ser.). (J). *(978-1-61672-566-2(4))* Benchmark Education Co.

Heyman, Carly. My Extra Special Brother: How to Love, Understand, & Celebrate Your Sibling with Special Needs. Conley, Stephanie, illus. l.t. ed. 2003. 112p. pap. 12.95 *(978-0-9727865-0-8(3),* 1003894) Fragile X Assn. of Georgia.

Higgins, Melissa. We All Have Different Families, 1 vol. 2012. (Celebrating Differences Ser.). (ENG.). 24p. (gr. k-1). pap. 7.29 *(978-1-4296-7889-6(5));* pap. 41.70 *(978-1-4296-8322-7(8))* Capstone Press of Coughlan Cos. (Pebble Plus).

Holland, Trish. A World of Families. 2010. (J). *(978-1-60617-142-4(9))* Teaching Strategies, LLC.

Hulstedt, Linda. My Brother's Secret: Opening Communication Lines for Families. 2013. 16p. pap. 7.95 *(978-1-4908-0447-7(1),* WestBow Pr.) Author Solutions, Inc.

Hurt, Avery Elizabeth. I Am a Teen Caregiver. Now What? 2016. (Teen Life 411 Ser.). 00112p. (J). (gr. 7-7). 37.10 *(978-1-5081-7204-8(8),* Rosen Young Adult) Rosen Publishing Group, Inc., The.

Hutchison, G. F. How to Handle Your Parents: A Guide for Teens. 2003. 160p. (YA). per. 13.99 *(978-1-885631-78-7(2),* Family Of Man Pr., The) Hutchison, G.F. Pr.

I Love My Family: Big Book: Level C. Group 1. (Sunshine Ser.). 8p. 20.95 *(978-0-7802-5723-8(5))* Wright Group/McGraw-Hill.

I Need a Rest! Individual Title, 6 Packs. (gr. -1-2). 23.00 *(978-0-7635-8818-2(0))* Rigby Education.

Isaacs, Ronald H. & Rostoker-Gruber, Karen. The Family (and Frog!) Haggadah. Urbanovic, Jackie, illus. 2017. (J). *(978-0-87441-937-5(9))* Behrman Hse., Inc.

Jablonski, Carrie. Spot the Duck: A Real Story. 2012. 24p. 24.95 *(978-1-4626-7464-0(X));* pap. 24.95 *(978-1-4626-8328-4(2))* America Star Bks.

Jarvie, Gordon. The Clans. 2011. (ENG., Illus.). 48p. pap. 9.95 *(978-1-905267-44-6(4))* NMS Enterprises Ltd. - Publishing GBR. Dist: National Bk. Network.

Jenner, Caryn. My Brother. 2017. (Family World Ser.). (ENG., Illus.). 24p. (J). (gr. 1-3). pap. 9.99 ***(978-1-4451-5220-2(7),*** Franklin Watts) Hachette Children's Group GBR. Dist: Hachette Bk. Group.

Johnson, Jennifer Hunt & Hansen, Holly T. Family Folklore, 715 vols. 2003. (Illus.). 27p. 9.95 *(978-0-9729610-8-0(9),* CMB7) Tapis & Assocs., Inc.

Johnson, Nevlynn L., Sr. Faith, Courage & Wisdom: A Journey to Manhood. 3rd rev. l.t. ed. 2003. Orig. Title: Finding My Way: a Journey to Manhood. 240p. per. 14.95 *(978-0-9741413-0-5(5))* Lone Cypress Pubs.

Jones, Grace. My Family. 2017. 24p. (J). ***(978-0-7787-3245-7(2))*** Crabtree Publishing Co.

Jones, Tammy. My Family. 2009. (Sight Word Readers Set A Ser.). (J). 3.49 net. *(978-1-60719-148-3(2))* Newmark Learning LLC.

Jones, Viola & Wainwright, Tabitha. Living with an Illness in the Family, 01 vols., 1. 2016. (Family Issues & You Ser.). (ENG.). 48p. (J). 30.25 *(978-1-4994-3693-8(9),* Rosen Central) Rosen Publishing Group, Inc., The.

Jude, T. B's Story. 2011. 62p. 24.99 *(978-1-4535-9563-3(5));* pap. 15.99 *(978-1-4535-9562-6(7))* Xlibris Corp.

Kalar, Bonnie. Jack. Spreen, Kathe, illus. Date not set. 12p. (J). (gr. -1-2). pap. *(978-1-891619-13-7(6))* Corona Pr.

Kalman, Bobbie. Esta Es Mi Familia. 2010. (SPA.). 16p. (J). pap. *(978-0-7787-8585-9(8));* lib. bdg. *(978-0-7787-8559-0(9))* Crabtree Publishing Co.

—My Family Community. 2010. (My World Ser.). (ENG., Illus.). 24p. (J). (gr. k-2). *(978-0-7787-9441-7(5));* pap. *(978-0-7787-9485-1(7))* Crabtree Publishing Co.

—This Is My Family. (My World Ser.). (ENG., 16p. (J). (gr. k-2). 2010. Illus.). *(978-0-7787-9432-5(6))* 2010. (Illus.). pap. *(978-0-7787-9476-9(8))*Pack. 2011. *(978-1-4271-1047-3(6))* Crabtree Publishing Co.

—Who Am I? 2010. (ENG., Illus.). 16p. (J). (gr. k-2). pap. *(978-0-7787-9458-5(X))* Crabtree Publishing Co.

Kaplan, Leslie C. Home Life in Ancient Egypt. 2004. (Primary Sources of Ancient Civilizations Ser.). (ENG., Illus.). 24p. (gr. 4-8). pap. 8.25 *(978-0-8239-8935-5(6),* PowerKids Pr.) Rosen Publishing Group, Inc., The.

Kawasaki, Shauna Mooney, illus. My Family Can Be Forever: Sharing Time Activities. 2003. 62p. (J). pap. *(978-1-59038-232-5(3))* Deseret Bk. Co.

Kiesbye, Stefan. Is Parenthood a Right or a Privilege? 2009. (At Issue Ser.). (ENG., Illus.). 128p. (gr. 10-12). (J). 34.45 *(978-0-7377-4430-9(8));* pap. 27.80 *(978-0-7377-4431-6(6))* Cengage Gale. (Greenhaven Pr., Inc.).

King Sproots, Wendy. Brothers Are Forever. 2011. 24p. pap. 7.99 *(978-0-88144-122-2(8))* Yorkshire Publishing Group.

Kingsley, M. t., et al. The Best Worst Summer Ever. 2010. 254p. pap. 14.95 *(978-1-59330-654-0(7))* Aventine Pr.

Kinkade, Sheila. My Family. Little, Elaine, photos by. 2006. (ENG., Illus.). 32p. (J). (gr. -1-3). 7.95 *(978-1-57091-691-5(8))* Charlesbridge Publishing, Inc.

Kirchmeier, Jenn-Ann, illus. The Tails of Brinkley the Berner: The Beginning. 2008. 32p. (J). 16.95 *(978-0-9793288-0-0(2))* Brinkley Bks., Inc.

Landau, Jennifer. Teens Talk about Family Issues. 2017. (J). ***(978-1-5081-7633-6(7))*** Rosen Publishing Group, Inc., The.

Lawrence, Kenneth. Korah's Travels: The Saga of an Israelite Family. l.t. ed. 2012. (Illus.). 256p. (Orig.). (YA). per. 19.95 *(978-0-910653-14-5(3)*, 8404143, Red River Pr.) Red River Pr.

Lee, David. Ellie's Family Album. 2013. (Rosen Readers Ser.). (ENG.). 24p. (J). (gr. 2-3). pap. 49.50 *(978-1-4777-2258-9(0))*; pap. 8.25 *(978-1-4777-2257-2(2))* Rosen Publishing Group, Inc., The. (Rosen Classroom).

Levete, Sarah. Taking Action Against Family Breakups. 2010. (Taking Action Ser.). (ENG.). 48p. (YA). pap. 11.75 *(978-1-61532-311-1(2)*, Rosen Reference); (gr. 5-9). lib. bdg. 29.25 *(978-1-61532-310-4(4))* Rosen Publishing Group, Inc., The.

Lewis, Clare. Families Around the World, 1 vol. 2014. (Around the World Ser.). (ENG., Illus.). 24p. (gr. -1-1). 22.65 *(978-1-4846-0372-7(9)*, Acorn) Heinemann-Raintree.

Litchfield, Jo. At Home. rev. ed. 2013. (First Words Board Bks). 12p. (J). ring bd. 6.99 *(978-0-7945-2617-7(9)*, Usborne) EDC Publishing.

Loewen, Nancy & Skelley, Paula. Siblings, Curfews, & How to Deal: Questions & Answers about Family Life. Mora, Julissa, illus. 2015. (Girl Talk Ser.). (ENG.). 32p. (gr. 3-4). lib. bdg. 27.99 *(978-1-4914-1858-1(3)*, Snap Bks.) Capstone Press of Coughlan Cos.

Lorenzo, Rose, et al. Families. 2007. (Windows on Literacy Ser.). (ENG., Illus.). 16p. pap. 11.95 *(978-0-7922-8462-8(3))* National Geographic School Publishing, Inc.

Lotorto - Soroka, Mary. Catiana Makes a Family. 2009. 30p. pap. 13.99 *(978-1-4490-0126-1(2))* AuthorHouse.

Lynch, Amy. A Smart Girl's Guide to Understanding Her Family: Feelings, Fighting & Figuring It Out. Scheuer, Lauren, illus. 2009. (ENG.). 64p. (J). (gr. 3-18). pap. 9.95 *(978-1-59369-617-7(5))* American Girl Publishing, Inc.

Lynette, Rachel. Let's Work It Out: What to Do When Your Family Has to Cut Costs. 2010. (Let's Work It Out Ser.). (ENG.). 24p. (J). pap. 8.25 *(978-1-4358-9768-7(4)*, PowerKids Pr.) Rosen Publishing Group, Inc., The.

—What to Do When Your Family Has to Cut Costs. 2010. (Let's Work It Out Ser.). (Illus.). 24p. (J). (gr. 2-5). lib. bdg. 22.60 *(978-1-4358-9340-5(9))* Rosen Publishing Group, Inc., The.

Lynn, Vicki, concept. Hilda Is Here. 2003. per. 14.95 *(978-0-9715737-1-0(9))* Aradiance Publishing.

MacGregor, Kim. Yummy Yummy Nummy Nummy, Should I Put This in My Tummy? 2004. 24p. pap. *(978-0-9731301-2-6(1))* Beautiful Beginnings Youth, Inc.

Marcovitz, Hal. Teens & Family Issues. 2008. (Gallup Youth Survey, Major Issues & Trends Ser.). (Illus.). 112,128p. (YA). (gr. 7-9). lib. bdg. 22.95 *(978-1-59084-725-1(3))* Mason Crest.

Margot. The Best Good Night Present Ever. 2010. 32p. pap. 12.99 *(978-1-4389-9168-9(1))* AuthorHouse.

Marsico, Katie. Good Manners at Home, 1 vol. Haslam, John, illus. 2009. (Good Manners Matter! Ser.). (ENG.). 32p. (J). (gr. -1-2). 28.50 *(978-1-60270-607-1(7))* Magic Wagon.

Mathis, Rev. Catherine. It's Your Big Day. 2013. 16p. pap. 10.70 *(978-1-4669-6573-7(8))* Trafford Publishing.

McDonald, Stacy. Raising Maidens of Virtue: A Study of Feminine Loveliness for Mothers & Daughters. 2004. (Illus.). 226p. (YA). 18.00 *(978-0-9743390-1-6(6))* Bks. on the Path.

Michaels, Gregory. Our Families Help. 2011. (Early Connections Ser.). (J). *(978-1-61672-368-2(8))* Benchmark Education Co.

Michaels, Vanessa Lynn & Harrow, Jeremy. Frequently Asked Questions about Family Violence. 2011. (FAQ: Teen Life Ser.). lib. bdg. 31.95 *(978-1-4488-4628-3(5))* Rosen Publishing Group, Inc., The.

Millennium Male: Separating the Men from the Boys. 2003. 88p. pap. 7.50 *(978-0-9712585-6-3(2))* JuDe Publishing.

Miller, Amanda. This Is the Way We Help at Home. 2009. (Scholastic News Nonfiction Readers Ser.). (ENG.). 24p. (J). (gr. 1-2). pap. 6.95 *(978-0-531-21441-1(9)*, Children's Pr.); lib. bdg. 22.00 *(978-0-531-21340-7(4))* Scholastic Library Publishing.

Miller, Jay. American Indian Families. 2006. (True Bks). (Illus.). 47p. (gr. 3-5). 16.95 *(978-0-7569-7130-4(6))* Perfection Learning Corp.

Miller, Reagan. Mother's Day & Other Family Days. 2010. (Celebrations in My World Ser.). (ENG.). 32p. (J). (gr. k-3). pap. *(978-0-7787-4937-0(1))*; lib. bdg. *(978-0-7787-4930-1(4))* Crabtree Publishing Co.

Miller, Vivian. Grandma's Mercedes. 2010. 36p. pap. 15.49 *(978-1-4520-1710-5(7))* AuthorHouse.

Millerm, April. The Holy Book. 2011. 74p. pap. 19.95 *(978-1-4560-9856-8(X))* America Star Bks.

Minden, Cecilia. Dinner by the Numbers. 2007. (21st Century Skills Library: Real World Math Ser.). (ENG., Illus.). 32p. (gr. 4-8). lib. bdg. 28.50 *(978-1-60279-013-1(2)*, 200062) Cherry Lake Publishing.

Mizell, Sandra. The Biggest & Best Trip Ever: A Trip to Heaven. 2010. 32p. 12.99 *(978-1-4490-7368-8(9))* AuthorHouse.

Molnar, Haya Leah. Under a Red Sky: Memoir of a Childhood in Communist Romania. 2010. (ENG., Illus.). 320p. (J). (gr. 7-12). 24.99 *(978-0-374-31840-6(9)*, Farrar, Straus & Giroux (BYR)) Farrar, Straus & Giroux.

Moore-Malinos, Jennifer & Fabrega, Marta. When My Parents Forgot How to Be Friends. 2005. (Let's Talk about It! Ser.). (ENG., Illus.). 32p. (J). (gr. -1-3). pap. 7.99 *(978-0-7641-3172-1(9))* Barron's Educational Series, Inc.

Morris, Alison. I Love My Family. 2004. (Look at Me... I Love Ser.). (Illus.). 10p. (J). bds. 4.99 *(978-1-85854-342-0(8))* Brimax Books Ltd. GBR. Dist: Byeway Bks.

Moss, Wendy L. & Moses, Donald A. The Tween Book: A Growing-Up Guide for the Changing You. 2015. (Illus.). 125p. (J). *(978-1-4338-1924-7(4)*, Magination Pr.) American Psychological Assn.

My Family. 2010. (My Family Ser.). (ENG.). 24p. (gr. k-1). pap. 25.16 *(978-1-4296-4984-1(4))*; pap. 25.16 *(978-1-4296-5753-2(7))* Capstone Press of Coughlan Cos. (Pebble Bks.).

My Family [Capstone Sole Source]. 2010. (My Family Ser.). 24p. lib. bdg. 82.60 *(978-1-4296-5872-0(X)*, Pebble Bks.) Capstone Press of Coughlan Cos.

My Family Collection. 2010. (My Family Ser.). (ENG.). 24p. (gr. k-1). pap. 25.16 *(978-1-4296-5162-2(8)*, Pebble Bks.) Capstone Press of Coughlan Cos.

My Family Tree 6 Packs. Individual Title. (Story Steps Ser.). (gr. k-2). 29.00 *(978-0-7635-9599-9(3))* Rigby Education.

My Granddad Is Great. 2008. (My Great Relatives... Ser.). 32p. *(978-1-4075-0942-6(X))* Parragon, Inc.

My Grandma Is Great. 2008. (My Great Relatives... Ser.). 32p. *(978-1-4075-0859-7(8))* Parragon, Inc.

Nakaya, Andrea C. Growin up in Japan. 2017. (ENG.). 80p. (YA). (gr. 5-12). ***(978-1-68282-219-7(2))*** ReferencePoint Pr., Inc.

Nana's Sweet Potato Pie, 6 vols. (Multicultural Programs Ser.). 16p. (gr. 1-3). 24.95 *(978-0-7802-9211-6(1))* Wright Group/McGraw-Hill.

Nixon, James. The 1980s. 2016. (My Family Remembers Ser.). (ENG., Illus.). 32p. (J). (gr. 2-17). pap. 11.99 *(978-1-4451-4356-9(9)*, Franklin Watts) Hachette Children's Group GBR. Dist: Hachette Bk. Group.

—The 1990s. 2016. (My Family Remembers Ser.). (ENG., Illus.). 32p. (J). (gr. 2-17). pap. 11.99 *(978-1-4451-4357-6(7)*, Franklin Watts) Hachette Children's Group GBR. Dist: Hachette Bk. Group.

—The 2000s. 2016. (My Family Remembers Ser.). (ENG., Illus.). 32p. (J). (gr. 2-17). pap. 11.99 *(978-1-4451-4358-3(5)*, Franklin Watts) Hachette Children's Group GBR. Dist: Hachette Bk. Group.

Norac, Carl & Dubois, Claude K. Las Palabras Dulces. 2003. (SPA.). 32p. *(978-84-95150-18-9(2))* Corimbo, Editorial S.L.

Nunn, Daniel. Families in English, 1 vol. 2013. (World Languages - Families Ser.). (ENG., Illus.). 24p. (gr. 1-3). pap. 6.29 *(978-1-4329-7184-7(0)*, Acorn) Heinemann-Raintree.

—Families in French: Les Familles. 2013. (World Languages - Families Ser.). (ENG, MUL & FRE., Illus.). 24p. (gr. 1-3). pap. 6.29 *(978-1-4329-7179-3(4)*, Acorn) Heinemann-Raintree.

—Families in French - Les Familles. 2013. (World Languages - Families Ser.). (ENG, MUL & FRE., Illus.). 24p. (gr. 1-3). lib. bdg. 22.65 *(978-1-4329-7172-4(7)*, Acorn) Heinemann-Raintree.

—Families in German: Die Familien, 1 vol. 2013. (World Languages - Families Ser.). (ENG, MUL & GER.). 24p. (gr. 1-3). pap. 6.29 *(978-1-4329-7181-6(6))*; lib. bdg. 22.65 *(978-1-4329-7174-8(3))* Heinemann-Raintree. (Acorn).

—Families in Italian: le Famiglie, 1 vol. 2013. (World Languages - Families Ser.). (ENG, MUL & ITA.). 24p. (gr. 1-3). pap. 6.29 *(978-1-4329-7183-0(2))*; lib. bdg. 22.65 *(978-1-4329-7176-2(X))* Heinemann-Raintree. (Acorn).

—Families in Polish - Rodziny. 2013. (World Languages - Families Ser.). (ENG, MUL & POL., Illus.). 24p. (gr. 1-3). pap. 6.29 *(978-1-4329-7182-3(4))*; lib. bdg. 22.65 *(978-1-4329-7175-5(1))* Heinemann-Raintree. (Acorn).

—Families in Spanish: Las Familias, 1 vol. 2013. (World Languages - Families Ser.). (ENG, MUL & SPA., Illus.). 24p. (gr. 1-3). pap. 6.29 *(978-1-4329-7180-9(8))*; lib. bdg. 22.65 *(978-1-4329-7173-1(5))* Heinemann-Raintree. (Acorn).

—World Languages - Families. 2013. (World Languages - Families Ser.). 24p. (gr. 1-3). (ENG & MUL.). pap. 35.94 *(978-1-4329-7185-4(9))*; (MUL.). lib. bdg. 113.25 *(978-1-4329-7178-6(6))* Heinemann-Raintree. (Acorn).

Oaks, Kristen M. My Home Can Be a Holy Place. Burr, Dan, illus. 2015. (J). 18.99 *(978-1-62972-099-9(2))* Deseret Bk. Co.

Otfinoski, Steve. All in the Family: A Look-It-Up Guide to the In-Laws, Outlaws, & Offspring of Mythology. 2009. (Mythlopedia Ser.). (ENG.). 128p. (J). (gr. 5-9). pap. 13.95 *(978-1-60631-057-1(7)*, Watts, Franklin) Scholastic Library Publishing.

Owens, L. L. Family Gatherings, 1 vol. Davidson, Chris, illus. 2010. (Let's Be Social Ser.). (ENG.). 32p. 28.50 *(978-1-60270-798-6(7)*, Looking Glass Library- Nonfiction) Magic Wagon.

Palmore, Julie. Big Brothers & Big Sisters Are VIP's (Very Important Persons) A Color Me Book. Engle, Jenny, illus. III, 56p. (J). (gr. -1-1). spiral bd. 9.95 *(978-0-9722653-0-0(9))* Palmore, Julie.

Parr, Todd. We Belong Together: A Book about Adoption & Families. 2007. (ENG., Illus.). 32p. (J). (gr. -1-1). 17.99 *(978-0-316-01668-1(3))* Little, Brown Bks. for Young Readers.

Passey, Marion. My Tiny Book of Family. 2004. (Illus.). (J). 5.95 *(978-1-59038-242-4(0))* Deseret Bk. Co.

Peavler, Amy & Peavler, Jan. The King the Queen & the Princess. Peavler, Amy & Peavler, Jan, illus. 2006. (Illus.). 40p. (J). per. *(978-0-9787672-2-8(5))* Lotus Petal Publishing.

Pendleton, Claudette M. I'm Mommy's Little Helper. Scott, Christopher L., illus. 2012. 48p. pap. 24.95 *(978-1-4626-7427-5(5))* America Star Bks.

Perlowitz, Rebecca & Becky, Morah. In My Family. Katz, Avi, illus. 2014. (ENG.). 32p. (J). (gr. k-2). pap. 10.95 *(978-965-7514-10-8(X))* Urim Pubns. ISR. Dist: Independent Pubs. Group.

Picone, Emma Lee. My Blended Family. Harrel, Tina, illus. 2012. 32p. pap. 12.95 *(978-0-9829803-9-2(6))* Joshua Tree Publishing.

Plattner, Josh. Manners with Family, 1 vol. 2016. (ENG., Illus.). 24p. (J). *(978-1-62403-718-4(6))* ABDO Publishing Co.

Plummer, Barbara. Kids in the Backyard. 2007. 60p. per. 16.95 *(978-1-4241-9064-5(9))* America Star Bks.

Poole, H. W. Disability & Families, Vol. 12. 2016. (Families Today Ser.). (Illus.). 48p. (J). (gr. 5). 20.95 *(978-1-4222-3614-7(5))* Mason Crest.

—Foster Families, Vol. 12. 2016. (Families Today Ser.). (Illus.). 48p. (J). (gr. 5). 20.95 *(978-1-4222-3615-4(3))* Mason Crest.

—Homelessness & Families, Vol. 12. 2016. (Families Today Ser.). (Illus.). 48p. (J). (gr. 5). 20.95 *(978-1-4222-3616-1(1))* Mason Crest.

—Immigrant Families, Vol. 12. 2016. (Families Today Ser.). (Illus.). 48p. (J). (gr. 5). 20.95 *(978-1-4222-3617-8(X))* Mason Crest.

—Incarceration & Families, Vol. 12. 2016. (Families Today Ser.). (Illus.). 48p. (J). (gr. 5). 20.95 *(978-1-4222-3618-5(8))* Mason Crest.

—Multigenerational Families, Vol. 12. 2016. (Families Today Ser.). (Illus.). 48p. (J). (gr. 5). 20.95 *(978-1-4222-3621-5(8))* Mason Crest.

Poole, Hilary W. Family Fears. 2017. (J). ***(978-1-4222-3725-0(7))*** Mason Crest.

Poulin, Andrée. The Magic Clothesline. Arbona, Marion, illus. 2012. 32p. (J). pap. 9.95 *(978-1-4338-1195-1(2)*, Magination Pr.) American Psychological Assn.

Powell, Jillian & Samanich, John G. Family Crises. 2008. (Emotional Health Issues Ser.). (Illus.). 48p. (YA). (gr. 7-12). lib. bdg. 31.00 *(978-0-8368-9201-7(1))* Stevens, Gareth Publishing LLLP.

Priddy, Roger. We Are a Family. 2015. (ENG.). 20p. (J). bds. 7.99 *(978-0-312-52033-5(6)*, 9780312520335, Priddy Bks.) St. Martin's Pr.

Quateman, Bill & Quateman, India. Daddy Daughter Dinner Dance: A Father's Steps to a Blended Family That Really Works. Quateman, India, illus. 2003. (Illus.). 96p. 17.95 *(978-0-9729866-0-1(X))* Angel Mind.

Raatma, Lucia. Brothers Are Part of a Family. 2017. (Our Families Ser.). (ENG.). 24p. (gr. k-1). lib. bdg. 21.99 ***(978-1-5157-7461-7(9)***, Pebble Bks.) Capstone Press of Coughlan Cos.

—Fathers Are Part of a Family. 2017. (Our Families Ser.). (ENG.). 24p. (gr. k-1). lib. bdg. 21.99 ***(978-1-5157-7463-1(5)***, Pebble Bks.) Capstone Press of Coughlan Cos.

—Mothers Are Part of a Family. 2017. (Our Families Ser.). (ENG.). 24p. (gr. k-1). lib. bdg. 21.99 ***(978-1-5157-7465-5(1)***, Pebble Bks.) Capstone Press of Coughlan Cos.

—Sisters Are Part of a Family. 2017. (Our Families Ser.). (ENG.). 24p. (gr. k-1). lib. bdg. 21.99 ***(978-1-5157-7460-0(0)***, Pebble Bks.) Capstone Press of Coughlan Cos.

Ragan, Jewel Coochie. Lost & Found. Ragan, Jewel Coochie, illus. 2012. (Illus.). 46p. pap. 11.11 *(978-0-9853809-1-5(8))* Ragan, Jewel.

Rhodes, Corey L. Keep Your Head Up! 2010. 24p. 16.99 *(978-1-4490-7580-4(0))* AuthorHouse.

Rice, Dona Herweck. Mi Gran Familia, 1 vol. 2nd rev. ed. 2011. (Nonfiction Readers Ser.). (SPA.). 12p. (J). (gr. 1-1). pap. 4.99 *(978-1-4333-4409-1(2))* Teacher Created Materials, Inc.

—My Big Family, 1 vol. 2nd rev. ed. 2013. (Nonfiction Readers Ser.). (ENG., Illus.). 12p. (J). (gr. 1-1). pap. 15.96 *(978-1-4807-1009-2(1))* Shell Educational Publishing.

—My Big Family, 1 vol. 2nd rev. ed. 2011. (Nonfiction Readers Ser.). (ENG.). 12p. (J). (gr. 1-1). pap. 4.99 *(978-1-4333-3570-9(0))* Teacher Created Materials, Inc.

Ridley, Sarah. Family. 2017. (Tell Me What You Remember Ser.). (ENG., Illus.). 24p. (J). (gr. k-2). 17.99 *(978-1-4451-3985-2(5)*, Franklin Watts) Hachette Children's Group GBR. Dist: Hachette Bk. Group.

Riordan, Rick & Scholastic, Inc. Staff. The Black Book of Buried Secrets. 2010. (39 Clues Ser.). (ENG.). 192p. (J). (gr. 3-7). 12.99 *(978-0-545-28504-9(6))* Scholastic, Inc.

Rissman, Rebecca. Aunts & Uncles, 1 vol. 2011. (Families Ser.). (ENG., Illus.). 24p. (gr. -1-1). pap. 6.29 *(978-1-4329-4669-2(2))*; lib. bdg. 22.65 *(978-1-4329-4661-6(7))* Heinemann-Raintree. (Acorn).

—Brothers & Sisters, 1 vol. 2011. (Families Ser.). (ENG., Illus.). 24p. (gr. -1-1). pap. 6.29 *(978-1-4329-4663-0(3))*; lib. bdg. 22.65 *(978-1-4329-4655-5(2))* Heinemann-Raintree. (Acorn).

—Cousins, 1 vol. 2011. (Families Ser.). (ENG.). 24p. (gr. -1-1). 22.65 *(978-1-4329-4656-2(0))*; pap. 6.29 *(978-1-4329-4664-7(1))* Heinemann-Raintree. (Acorn).

—Families, 7 vols., Set. Incl. Aunts & Uncles. (Illus.). pap. 6.29 *(978-1-4329-4669-2(2))*; Brothers & Sisters. (Illus.). pap. 6.29 *(978-1-4329-4663-0(3))*; Cousins. pap. 6.29 *(978-1-4329-4664-7(1))*; Foster Parents. (Illus.). pap. 6.29 *(978-1-4329-4665-4(X))*; Grandparents. pap. 6.29 *(978-1-4329-4666-1(8))*; Parents. (Illus.). pap. 6.29 *(978-1-4329-4667-8(6))*; Role Models. (Illus.). pap. 6.29 *(978-1-4329-4668-5(4))*; (gr. -1-1). (Families Ser.). (ENG.). 24p. 2011. Set pap. 44.03 *(978-1-4329-4670-8(8))*; Set lib. bdg. 135.90 *(978-1-4329-4662-3(5))* Heinemann-Raintree. (Acorn).

—Family, 1 vol. 2013. (Say What You See Ser.). (ENG.). 24p. (gr. -1-1). 22.65 *(978-1-4109-5048-2(4))*; pap. 7.10 *(978-1-4109-5053-6(0))* Heinemann-Raintree.

—Foster Parents, 1 vol. 2011. (Families Ser.). (ENG., Illus.). 24p. (gr. -1-1). 22.65 *(978-1-4329-4657-9(9))*; pap. 6.29 *(978-1-4329-4665-4(X))* Heinemann-Raintree. (Acorn).

—Grandparents, 1 vol. 2011. (Families Ser.). (ENG.). 24p. (gr. -1-1). 22.65 *(978-1-4329-4658-6(7))*; pap. 6.29 *(978-1-4329-4666-1(8))* Heinemann-Raintree. (Acorn).

—Parents, 1 vol. 2011. (Families Ser.). (ENG., Illus.). 24p. (gr. -1-1). pap. 6.29 *(978-1-4329-4667-8(6)*, Acorn) Heinemann-Raintree.

—Role Models, 1 vol. 2011. (Families Ser.). (ENG., Illus.). 24p. (gr. -1-1). 22.65 *(978-1-4329-4660-9(9))*; pap. 6.29 *(978-1-4329-4668-5(4))* Heinemann-Raintree. (Acorn).

—What Is a Family?, 1 vol. 2011. (ENG.). 24p. (gr. -1-1). pap. 9.95 *(978-1-4329-5503-8(9))*; 25.99 *(978-1-4329-5358-4(3))* Heinemann-Raintree. (Acorn Read-Aloud).

Roland, James. Growing up in Russia. 2017. (ENG.). 80p. (YA). (gr. 5-12). ***(978-1-68282-223-4(0))*** ReferencePoint Pr., Inc.

Rosa-Mendoza, Gladys. My Family & I. Cifuentes, Carolina, ed. Snider, Jackie, illus. 2004. (English-Spanish Foundations Ser.: Vol. 4).Tr. of Mi Familia y Yo. (ENG & SPA.). 20p. (J). (gr. -1-4). bds. 6.95 *(978-0-9679748-4-2(4))* Me+Mi Publishing.

Ross, Allison J. Coping When a Parent Is Mentally Ill. (Coping Ser.). 192p. (gr. 7-12). 2009. 63.90 *(978-1-61511-987-5(6))* 2005. (Illus.). (YA). lib. bdg. 34.60 *(978-0-8239-3359-4(8))* Rosen Publishing Group, Inc., The.

Rotner, Shelley & Kelly, Sheila M. De Muchas Maneras: Como las Familias Practican Sus Creencias y Religiones. Rotner, Shelley, photos by. 2006. (Spanish Picture Bks.). (SPA., Illus.). 32p. (J). (gr. k-3). lib. bdg. 15.95 *(978-0-8225-6506-2(4)*, Ediciones Lerner) Lerner Publishing Group.

—Families. Rotner, Shelley, photos by. (ENG., Illus.). 32p. (J). 2016. 7.99 *(978-0-8234-3570-8(9))* 2015. (gr. -1-1). 17.95 *(978-0-8234-3053-6(7))* Holiday Hse., Inc.

Rusch, Elizabeth. Ready, Set ... Baby! Leng, Qin, illus. 2017. (ENG.). 32p. (J). (gr. -1-3). 17.99 *(978-0-544-47272-3(1)*, HMH Books For Young Readers) Houghton Mifflin Harcourt Publishing Co.

Ruurs, Margriet. Families Around the World. Gordon, Jessica Rae, illus. 2017. (Around the World Ser.). (ENG.). 40p. (J). (gr. -1-2). pap. 8.95 *(978-1-77138-807-8(2))* Kids Can Pr., Ltd. CAN. Dist: Hachette Bk. Group.

Sasse, Connie R. & McGraw-Hill Education Staff. Families Today, 2 vols. 4th ed. 2003. (Families Today Ser.). (ENG., Illus.). 704p. (gr. 10-12). stu. ed. 85.60 *(978-0-07-829840-0(7)*, 0078298407) McGraw-Hill Education.

Schaefer, Lola M. Aunts. rev. ed. 2008. (Families Ser.). (ENG., Illus.). 24p. (gr. k-1). 21.99 *(978-1-4296-1220-3(7)*, Pebble Bks.) Capstone Press of Coughlan Cos.

—Aunts. Saunders-Smith, Gail, ed. rev. ed. 2008. (Families Ser.). (ENG., Illus.). 24p. (gr. k-1). per. 6.29 *(978-1-4296-1749-9(7)*, Pebble Bks.) Capstone Press of Coughlan Cos.

—Cousins. rev. ed. 2008. (Families Ser.). (ENG., Illus.). 24p. (gr. k-1). 21.99 *(978-1-4296-1222-7(3)*, Pebble Bks.) Capstone Press of Coughlan Cos.

—Uncles. Saunders-Smith, Gail, ed. rev. ed. 2008. (Families Ser.). (ENG., Illus.). 24p. (gr. k-1). 21.99 *(978-1-4296-1229-6(0))*; per. 6.29 *(978-1-4296-1758-1(6))* Capstone Press of Coughlan Cos. (Pebble Bks.).

Schaefer, Lola M. & National Geographic Learning Staff. Cousins. Saunders-Smith, Gail, ed. rev. ed. 2008. (Families Ser.). (ENG., Illus.). 24p. (gr. k-1). per. 6.29 *(978-1-4296-1751-2(9)*, Pebble Bks.) Capstone Press of Coughlan Cos.

Scholastic, Inc. Staff, contrib. by. Who Is in Your Family? 2014. (Rookie Toddler(r) Ser.). (ENG., Illus.). 12p. (J). bds. 6.95 *(978-0-531-20490-0(1))* Scholastic Library Publishing.

Schorr, Titus. My New Family, 01 vols., 1. 2016. (Rosen REAL Readers: Social Studies Nonfiction / Fiction: Family, Community, & the World Ser.). (ENG.). 8p. (J). pap. 5.46 *(978-1-5081-2034-6(X)*, Rosen Classroom) Rosen Publishing Group, Inc., The.

Schuette, Sarah L. Families, 1 vol. rev. ed. 2009. (People Ser.). (ENG.). 24p. (gr. k-1). pap. 6.29 *(978-1-4296-3462-5(6))*; lib. bdg. 21.99 *(978-1-4296-2239-4(3))* Capstone Press of Coughlan Cos. (Pebble Bks.).

—Foster Families, 1 vol. 2010. (My Family Ser.). (ENG.). 24p. (gr. k-1). pap. 6.29 *(978-1-4296-4837-0(6))*; pap. 35.70 *(978-1-4296-5159-2(8))*; lib. bdg. 21.99 *(978-1-4296-3979-8(2))* Capstone Press of Coughlan Cos. (Pebble Bks.).

—My Family, 4 vols., Set. Incl. Adoptive Families. lib. bdg. 21.99 *(978-1-4296-3977-4(6))*; Foster Families. lib. bdg. 21.99 *(978-1-4296-3979-8(2))*; Single-Parent Families. lib. bdg. 21.99 *(978-1-4296-3980-4(6))*; (gr. k-1). (My Family Ser.). (ENG.). 24p. 2010. Set lib. bdg. 65.97 *(978-1-4296-4411-2(7)*, Pebble Bks.) Capstone Press of Coughlan Cos.

Sebastian, Emily. My Cousins. 2010. (My Family Ser.). (ENG.). 24p. (J). pap. 8.25 *(978-1-4488-1496-1(0)*, PowerKids Pr.) Rosen Publishing Group, Inc., The.

—My Cousins: MIS Primos. 2010. (My Family / Mi Familia Ser.). (SPA & ENG.). 24p. lib. bdg. 22.60 *(978-1-4488-0720-8(4)*, Editorial Buenas Letras) Rosen Publishing Group, Inc., The.

Shannon, Terry Miller. Families Have Stories to Tell. 2016. (Spring Forward Ser.). (J). (gr. 2). *(978-1-4900-9413-7(X))* Benchmark Education Co.

Sheldon, Tamia. What Is a Family? Sheldon, Tamia, illus. 2013. (Illus.). 36p. pap. 9.99 *(978-1-62395-527-4(0))* Xist Publishing.

Sherry. Always & Forever: Angel's Ladybugs. 2009. 16p. pap. 10.95 *(978-1-4389-0137-4(2))* AuthorHouse.

Simon, Norma. All Kinds of Families: 40th Anniversary Edition. Brannen, Sarah S., illus. 40th ed. 2016. (ENG.). 32p. (J). (gr. -1-3). 16.99 *(978-0-8075-0286-0(3))* Whitman, Albert & Co.

Slamp, Kathy. Little House in the Arctic: An Adventure Story. l.t. ed. 2004. Orig. Title: Our Little House in the Arctic. (Illus.). 228p. pap. 17.95 *(978-0-9713345-3-3(6))* Vessel Ministries.

Smith, Carrie. Our Family Stories. 2004. (Shared Connections Ser.). (J). instr.'s gde. ed. 34.00 net. *(978-1-4108-1616-0(8))* Benchmark Education Co.

—Our Family Stories: Small Book. 2004. (Shared Connections Ser.). (J). pap. *(978-1-4108-1640-5(0))* Benchmark Education Co.

Snedeker, Gus. Tell Me a Story: Family Folklore. 2013. (Illus.). 48p. (J). pap. *(978-1-4222-2499-1(6))* Mason Crest.

—Tell Me a Story: Family Folklore. Jabbour, Alan, ed. 2012. (North American Folklore for Youth Ser.). (Illus.). 48p. (J). (gr. 4). 19.95 *(978-1-4222-2488-5(0))* Mason Crest.

Snyder, Gail. Growing up in Canada. 2017. (Growing up Around the World Ser.). (ENG.). 80p. (YA). (gr. 5-12). ***(978-1-68282-207-4(9))*** ReferencePoint Pr., Inc.

Snyder, Gail. Marriage & Family Issues. 2008. (Gallup Major Trends & Events Ser.). (Illus.). 118p. (YA). (gr. 7-18). lib. bdg. 22.95 *(978-1-59084-966-8(3)*, 1260831) Mason Crest.

Spilsbury, Louise. Family & Friends. 2012. (Healthy & Happy Ser.). (Illus.). 32p. (J). (gr. 1-4). lib. bdg. 26.50 *(978-1-4488-5275-8(7))* Rosen Publishing Group, Inc., The.

Stewart, Sheila. What Is a Family? 2010. (Changing Face of Modern Families Ser.). (Illus.). 64p. (YA). (gr. 6-18). lib. bdg. 22.95 *(978-1-4222-1528-9(8))* Mason Crest.

—When Daddy Hit Mommy. (Kids Have Troubles Too Ser.). 48p. (YA). (gr. 5-18). 2010. lib. bdg. 19.95 *(978-1-4222-1696-5(9))* 2009. pap. 7.95 *(978-1-4222-1909-6(7))* Mason Crest.

Swain, Cynthia. Families Have Rules. 2006. (Early Explorers Ser.). (J). pap. *(978-1-4108-6028-6(0))* Benchmark Education Co.

Tanious, Karen Wagdy Aldy. My Life, My Favorites, My Dreams. 2012. 32p. pap. 17.25 *(978-1-4669-6732-8(3))* Trafford Publishing.

Telgemeier, Raina. Sisters. 2014. (ENG., Illus.). 208p. (J). (gr. 3-7). 24.99 *(978-0-545-54059-9(3))*; pap. 10.99 *(978-0-545-54060-5(7))* Scholastic, Inc. (Graphix).

—Sisters. 2014. lib. bdg. 22.10 *(978-0-606-36038-8(7))* Turtleback Bks.

Thomas, Kimberly. The Greatest Flag in the World: The Universal Family Flag. 2012. 24p. pap. 16.00 *(978-1-4685-5659-9(2))* AuthorHouse.

Thompson, Aron. Grammy & Me: The Family Tree. 2012. 32p. pap. 21.99 *(978-1-4691-3933-3(2))* Xlibris Corp.

Thornborough, Kathy. Family & Friends. Petelinsek, Kathleen, illus. 2014. (Talking Hands Ser.). (ENG.). 24p. (J). (gr. k-3). 25.64 *(978-1-62687-317-9(8)*, 207157) Child's World, Inc., The.

Towne, Isobel & MacAdam, Lea. Dealing with Family Rules, 01 vols., 1. 2016. (Family Issues & You Ser.). (ENG.). 48p. (J). pap. 11.75 *(978-1-4994-3697-6(1)*, Rosen Central) Rosen Publishing Group, Inc., The.

Unruh, Cindy. What to Expect When Your Family Becomes a Foster Family. 2012. 28p. 24.95 *(978-1-4626-4572-5(0))* America Star Bks.

Vaugelade, Anais. Una Sopa de Piedra. 2005.Tr. of Stone Soup. (SPA.). (J). 9.95 *(978-84-8470-137-8(9))* Corimbo, Editorial S.L. ESP. Dist: Iaconi, Mariuccia Bk. Imports.

Walker, Kathryn. The 1950s. 2017. (My Family Remembers Ser.). (ENG., Illus.). 32p. (J). (gr. 2-17). pap. 11.99 *(978-1-4451-4353-8(4)*, Franklin Watts) Hachette Children's Group GBR. Dist: Hachette Bk. Group.

—The 1960s. 2017. (My Family Remembers Ser.). (ENG., Illus.). 32p. (J). (gr. 2-6). pap. 11.99 *(978-1-4451-4354-5(2)*, Franklin Watts) Hachette Children's Group GBR. Dist: Hachette Bk. Group.

—The 1970s. 2017. (My Family Remembers Ser.). (ENG., Illus.). 32p. (J). (gr. 2-17). pap. 11.99 *(978-1-4451-4355-2(0)*, Franklin Watts) Hachette Children's Group GBR. Dist: Hachette Bk. Group.

Weston, Carol. Girltalk: All the Stuff Your Sister Never Told You. 4th ed. 2004. (ENG.). 448p. pap. 14.99 *(978-0-06-058575-4(7)*, Harper Perennial) HarperCollins Pubs.

What Did I Get?, 6 vols. 8p. (gr. k-1). 21.50 *(978-0-322-02077-1(8))* Wright Group/McGraw-Hill.

White, Benjamin. Defenders of the Family. 2016. (ENG.). (J). (gr. k-3). 14.99 *(978-1-4621-1821-2(6))* Cedar Fort, Inc./CFI Distribution.

Wilcox, Christine. Understanding Family & Personal Relationships. 2017. (Understanding Psychology Ser.). (ENG.). 80p. (YA). (gr. 5-12). ***(978-1-68282-273-9(7))*** ReferencePoint Pr., Inc.

Williams, Colleen. Native American Family Life. Johnson, Troy, ed. 2013. (Native American Life Ser.: 15). 64p. (J). (gr. 5-18). 19.95 *(978-1-4222-2969-9(6))* Mason Crest.

Yacoubou, Jeanne. What's My Heritage? Coloring-Story Book. Stebakova, Elena, illus. 2006. 24p. (J). *(978-0-9788737-2-1(6))* Alaafia Kids Co.

Ytreeide, Arnold. Ishtar's Odyssey: A Storybook for Advent, 1 vol. 2015. 176p. (J). pap. 15.99 *(978-0-8254-4393-0(8))* Kregel Pubns.

Zable, Stacey. Our Families. 2011. (Early Connections Ser.). (J). *(978-1-61672-592-1(3))* Benchmark Education Co.

Zable, Stacy. Our Families: Set Of 6. 2011. (Early Connections Ser.). (J). pap. 37.00 net. *(978-1-4108-1066-3(6))* Benchmark Education Co.

Zoldak, Joyce. When Danger Hits Home: Survivors of Domestic Violence. (Survivors Ser.). 2010. 128p. (YA). (gr. 7-12). 24.95 *(978-1-4222-0460-3(X))* 2009. (J). pap. 24.95 *(978-1-4222-1473-2(7))* Mason Crest.

FAMILY—FICTION

Abbott, Jacob. Stories Told to Rollo's Cousin Lucy. 2005. pap. 22.95 *(978-1-4179-5651-7(8))* Kessinger Publishing, LLC.

Abbruzzi, Danielle. Penelope's Piggies. Sampson, Kathleen, illus. 2012. 42p. 24.95 *(978-1-4626-6264-7(1))* America Star Bks.

Abdel-Fattah, Randa. The Lines We Cross. 2017. (ENG.). 400p. (J). (gr. 7-7). 18.99 ***(978-1-338-11866-7(8)***, Scholastic Pr.) Scholastic, Inc.

Abdulaya, Lina. Once upon a Time in Oromiy: Sheekko Sheekoo. 2011. 52p. pap. 22.28 *(978-1-4567-6540-8(X))* AuthorHouse.

Abolade, Caroline, told to. I'm Going to Be a Big Brother. 2003. 14p. 9.44 *(978-1-4116-0123-9(8))* Lulu Pr., Inc.

Abrams, Penny. The Calabash Tales. Mikki, illus. 2011. 66p. 28.00 *(978-1-4349-1169-8(1))* Dorrance Publishing Co., Inc.

Acampora, Paul. How to Avoid Extinction. 2016. (ENG.). 208p. (J). (gr. 3-7). 16.99 *(978-0-545-89906-2(0)*, Scholastic Pr.) Scholastic, Inc.

Ad Break, 6, Pack. (Bookweb Ser.). 32p. (gr. 4-18). 34.00 *(978-0-7635-3722-7(5))* Rigby Education.

Adahan, Miriam. Torah Tigers. 2009. 48p. 17.99 *(978-1-59826-308-4(0))* Feldheim Pubs.

Adams, Michelle. Sarah Boone: A Lowcountry Girl, 1 vol. Brewster, Jane, illus. 2009. (ENG.). 152p. (J). (gr. 3-6). 15.95 *(978-1-58980-657-3(3))* Pelican Publishing Co., Inc.

Adams, Misty Pedersen. Grandma Goes Home, 1 vol. 2010. 48p. pap. 16.95 *(978-1-4512-9673-0(8))* America Star Bks.

Adamson, Ged, illus. Meet the Mckaws. 2015. (ENG.). 32p. (J). (gr. -1-k). 16.95 *(978-1-62914-618-8(8)*, Sky Pony Pr.) Skyhorse Publishing Co., Inc.

Adderson, Caroline. Jasper John Dooley: Star of the Week. Clanton, Ben, illus. 2014. (Jasper John Dooley Ser.). (ENG.). 128p. (J). (gr. 2-5). pap. 7.95 *(978-1-77138-119-2(1))* Kids Can Pr., Ltd. CAN. Dist: Hachette Bk. Group.

Adina Bates, Shelley. A Lady of Spirit: A Steampunk Adventure Novel. 2014. (ENG.). pap. 13.99 *(978-1-939087-15-7(5)*, Moonshell Bks., Inc.) Shelley Adina.

Adkins, Jan. A Storm Without Rain. 2004. (ENG., Illus.). 179p. (YA). (gr. 7). 14.95 *(978-0-937822-80-7(9))* WoodenBoat Pubns.

Adler, David A. The Babe & I. Widener, Terry, illus. 2006. 28p. (gr. 1-4). 18.00 *(978-0-7569-6560-0(8))* Perfection Learning Corp.

Ahlberg, Allan. Master Track's Train. Amstutz, Andre, illus. (ENG.). 24p. (J). pap. 6.95 *(978-0-14-037881-8(2))* Penguin Bks., Ltd. GBR. Dist: Trafalgar Square Publishing.

Ahlberg, Allan. Mr Tick the Teacher. 2016. (Happy Families Ser.). (ENG., Illus.). 24p. (J). (gr. k-2). pap. 12.99 ***(978-0-14-136996-9(5))*** Penguin Bks., Ltd. GBR. Dist: Independent Pubs. Group.

Ain, Beth. Starring Jules (Third Grade Debut) 2015. (Starring Jules Ser.: 4). (ENG.). 176p. (J). (gr. 2-5). pap. 5.99 *(978-0-545-44359-3(8)*, Scholastic Pr.) Scholastic, Inc.

Airgood, Ellen. Prairie Evers. 2014. (ENG.). 224p. (J). (gr. 3-7). pap. 7.99 *(978-0-14-242668-5(7)*, Puffin Books) Penguin Young Readers Group.

Albin, Gennifer. Crewel - Chapters 1-5. 2012. (Crewel World Ser.: 1). (ENG.). 368p. (YA). (gr. 7). 17.99 *(978-0-374-31641-9(4)*, 9780374316419, Farrar, Straus & Giroux (BYR)) Farrar, Straus & Giroux.

Alborozo. And Then... Alborozo, illus. 2016. (Child's Play Library). (ENG., Illus.). 32p. (J). *(978-1-84643-696-3(6))* Child's Play International Ltd.

Alcock, Deborah. The King's Service: A Story of the Thirty Years' War. 2008. (YA). *(978-1-894666-06-0(2))* Inheritance Pubns.

Alcott, Louisa May. The Annotated Little Women. Matteson, John, ed. 2015. (Annotated Bks.: 0). (ENG., Illus.). 736p. (gr. 11-17). 39.95 *(978-0-393-07219-8(3)*, 7219) Norton, W. W. & Co., Inc.

—Jo's Boys. l.t. ed. 2005. 424p. pap. *(978-1-84637-067-0(1))* Echo Library.

—Spinning-Wheel Stories. 2011. 202p. 27.95 *(978-1-4638-9494-8(5))* Rodgers, Alan Bks.

—Under the Lilacs. 2011. 226p. (gr. 4-7). pap. 15.95 *(978-1-60664-504-8(8))* Rodgers, Alan Bks.

Alegria, Malin. Sofi Mendoza's Guide to Getting Lost in Mexico. 2008. (ENG.). 304p. (YA). (gr. 7). pap. 10.99 *(978-0-689-87812-1(5)*, Simon & Schuster Bks. For Young Readers) Simon & Schuster Bks. For Young Readers.

Alender, Katie. The Dead Girls of Hysteria Hall. (ENG.). 336p. (J). (gr. 7). 2016. pap. 9.99 *(978-1-338-03239-0(9))* 2015. 18.99 *(978-0-545-63999-6(9))* Scholastic, Inc.

—The Dead Girls of Hysteria Hall. 2016. (ENG.). 329p. (YA). (gr. 7). 20.85 *(978-0-606-39121-4(5))* Turtleback Bks.

Alexandria, Shalayne. Nyville High No. 2: Mother May I. 2007. 130p. (YA). pap. 10.00 *(978-0-9786180-4-9(1))* 5 Muses Publishing.

Alfau, Georgette. Alfred & Alex & the Toy Eating Monster. 2009. 16p. 18.95 *(978-0-557-15276-6(3))* Lulu Pr., Inc.

Alger Jr. Horatio Staff. Andy Grants Pluck. rev. ed. 2006. 312p. 29.95 *(978-1-4218-1762-0(4))*; pap. 14.95 *(978-1-4218-1862-7(0))* 1st World Publishing, Inc. (1st World Library - Literary Society).

Ali, Saleena. Behind My Eyes & Truly in Love Stories of Friendship & Love: Book Two. 2012. 76p. pap. 10.84 *(978-1-4669-2217-4(6))* Trafford Publishing.

Allbright, Lauren. Exit Strategy. 2017. (Max Ser.). (ENG., Illus.). 176p. (J). (gr. 4-8). 16.99 ***(978-1-4814-7912-7(1)***, Aladdin) Simon & Schuster Children's Publishing.

Allen, Crystal. The Magnificent Mya Tibbs: the Wall of Fame Game. Kaban, Eda, illus. 2017. 272p. (J). (gr. 3-7). 16.99 *(978-0-06-234236-2(3))* HarperCollins Pubs.

Alma, Ann. Skateway to Freedom. 2nd ed. 2008. (ENG.). 136p. (YA). (gr. 5-8). pap. 11.99 *(978-1-55002-719-8(0))* Dundurn CAN. Dist: Ingram Publisher Services.

Alonso, Fernando & Fernando, Alonso. La Historia de un Hombrecillo de Papel. (Leer Es Vivir Serie Teatro). (SPA.). 96p. (J). (gr. 3-5). 6.36 *(978-84-241-7711-9(8))* Everest Editora ESP. Dist: Lectorum Pubns., Inc.

Alphen, Nick Van. One Day. 2012. 20p. pap. 24.95 *(978-1-4626-5524-3(6))* America Star Bks.

Alvarez, Julia. Antes de Ser Libres. Valenzuela, Liliana, tr. 2004.Tr. of Before We Were Free. (SPA.). 192p. (YA). (gr. 7). mass mkt. 6.99 *(978-0-375-81545-4(7)*, Laurel Leaf) Random Hse. Children's Bks.

Amateau, Gigi. Two for Joy. Marble, Abigail, illus. 2015. (ENG.). 96p. (J). (gr. 2-5). 14.99 *(978-0-7636-3010-2(1))* Candlewick Pr.

Amato, Mary. Get Happy. 2014. (ENG.). 244p. (J). (gr. 7). 16.99 *(978-1-60684-522-6(5)*, Carolrhoda Lab™) Lerner Publishing Group.

Amerel. The Summer Holidays: A Story for Childre. 2006. pap. *(978-1-4065-0808-6(X))* Dodo Pr.

Amestoy, Jennifer. Junkyard Junction: The Story of the Magic Microwave. 2008. 32p. pap. 14.75 *(978-1-4389-1755-9(4))* AuthorHouse.

Amico, Sal. Come Back, Zack! 2006. (Neighborhood Readers Ser.). (ENG., Illus.). 16p. (gr. 1-3). pap. 6.50 *(978-1-4042-7256-9(9)*, Rosen Classroom) Rosen Publishing Group, Inc., The.

Amore, Sandra. The Princess Who Lived on the 174th Floor. 2011. 58p. pap. 18.68 *(978-1-4653-5854-7(4))* Xlibris Corp.

Amoss, Berthe. Mischief & Malice. 2015. (ENG.). 208p. (J). (gr. 3). 18.95 *(978-1-939601-44-5(4))* Ig Publishing, Inc.

Anders, Bill. Becoming Noah. 2004. 114p. (J). pap. 7.95 *(978-0-9762059-0-6(4))* Leaping Antelope Productions.

Andersen, Hans Christian. Little Match Girl. 2008. (ENG.). 31p. (J). 17.00 *(978-1-4379-5327-5(1))* DIANE Publishing Co.

Anderson, Bre. Teaching Joey. 2011. (ENG.). 23p. (J). pap. 11.95 *(978-1-4327-6505-7(1))*; pap. 19.95 *(978-1-4327-7685-5(1))* Outskirts Pr., Inc.

Anderson, Doug. Hadley & the Bean. 2004. (Illus.). (J). 16.95 *(978-1-59404-038-2(9))* Peanut Butter Publishing.

Anderson, Jennifer. Spider. 2013. 174p. pap. 10.99 *(978-1-62237-146-4(1))* Turquoise Morning Pr.

Anderson, Jodi Lynn. Midnight at the Electric. 2017. 272p. (YA). (gr. 9). 17.99 *(978-0-06-239354-8(5)*, HarperTeen) HarperCollins Pubs.

Anderson, Peggy Perry. Joe on the Go. 2012. (Green Light Readers — Level 1 Ser.: 1). lib. bdg. 13.55 *(978-0-606-24018-5(7)*, Turtleback) Turtleback Bks.

Anderson, Salem. Salem Anderson & Her Private Diary. 2011. 24p. pap. 11.32 *(978-1-4490-7115-8(5))* AuthorHouse.

Anderson, S.N. Desperate for a Family. 2005. 57p. pap. 8.98 *(978-1-4116-6162-2(1))* Lulu Pr., Inc.

Andrews, Jan. The Auction, 1 vol. Reczuch, Karen, illus. 2nd ed. 2007. (ENG.). 32p. (J). (gr. k-2). pap. 6.95 *(978-0-88899-842-2(2))* Groundwood Bks. CAN. Dist: Publishers Group West (PGW).

Andrews, Joan. A Best Friend for Thurston. 2010. 20p. 13.77 *(978-1-4269-2976-2(5))* Trafford Publishing.

Andrisano, Micheal. Harold the High Knight & Princess Megan: Harold & Megan. 2013. (ENG.). 221p. (YA). pap. 16.95 *(978-1-4327-9451-4(5))* Outskirts Pr., Inc.

Anholt, Laurence. Bendy Ben. Ross, Tony, illus. 2015. (My Freaky Family Ser.: 5). (ENG.). 48p. (J). (gr. k-2). pap. 8.99 *(978-1-4083-3758-5(4))* Hodder & Stoughton GBR. Dist: Hachette Bk. Group.

—Hairy Harold. Ross, Tony, illus. 2015. (Seriously Scary Ser.: 8). (ENG.). 48p. (J). (gr. k-2). pap. 8.99 *(978-1-4083-3752-3(5))* Hodder & Stoughton GBR. Dist: Hachette Bk. Group.

—Mucky Micky. Ross, Tony, illus. 2015. (My Freaky Family Ser.: 2). (ENG.). 48p. (J). (gr. k-2). pap. 8.99 *(978-1-4083-3764-6(9))* Hodder & Stoughton GBR. Dist: Hachette Bk. Group.

—Poetic Polly. Ross, Tony, illus. 2015. (My Freaky Family Ser.: 3). (ENG.). 48p. (J). (gr. k-2). pap. 8.99 *(978-1-4083-3754-7(1))* Hodder & Stoughton GBR. Dist: Hachette Bk. Group.

—Tiny Tina. Ross, Tony, illus. 2015. (My Freaky Family Ser.: 6). (ENG.). 48p. (J). (gr. k-2). pap. 8.99 *(978-1-4083-3760-8(6))* Hodder & Stoughton GBR. Dist: Hachette Bk. Group.

Ankhnu Feaster, Teraab & Campbell, Rochelle. The Magic Seeds. 2009. 42p. pap. 19.25 *(978-1-4490-0784-3(8))* AuthorHouse.

Anna, Jennifer. Yen Shei & the American Bonsai. 2009. (ENG., Illus.). 88p. (YA). pap. 14.99 *(978-1-59092-153-1(4))* Blue Forge Pr.

Anne, Margo. Lily Rose. 2008. 194p. pap. 24.95 *(978-1-60703-847-4(1))* America Star Bks.

Anns, Lynn. Tent City Princess. 2013. 224p. pap. 9.99 *(978-1-939403-05-6(7))* PageSpring Publishing.

Applegate, Katherine. Crenshaw. 2015. (ENG.). 256p. (J). (gr. 5-9). 16.99 *(978-1-250-04323-8(9)*, 9781250043238) Feiwel & Friends.

—Crenshaw. 2017. (ENG.). 272p. (J). pap. 7.99 ***(978-1-250-09166-6(7)***, 9781250091666) Square Fish.

—Crenshaw. 2017. (J). lib. bdg. 18.40 ***(978-0-606-40539-3(9))*** Turtleback Bks.

—Crenshaw. 2016. (SPA.). 192p. (J). (gr. 5-8). pap. 13.99 *(978-987-747-067-3(5))* V&R Editoras.

—Never Swim in Applesauce. Biggs, Brian, illus. 2008. (Roscoe Riley Rules Ser.: 4). (ENG.). 96p. (J). (gr. 1-5). 15.99 *(978-0-06-114888-0(1))*; pap. 4.99 *(978-0-06-114887-3(3))* HarperCollins Pubs.

Arbuthnott, Gill. The Keepers' Tattoo. 2010. (ENG.). 432p. (J). (gr. 3-7). 17.99 *(978-0-545-17166-3(0)*, Chicken Hse., The) Scholastic, Inc.

Archer, Nick & McDonald, Megan. Rule of Three. 2010. (Sisters Club Ser.: 2). (ENG., Illus.). 240p. (J). (gr. 3-7). pap. 5.99 *(978-0-7636-4830-5(2))* Candlewick Pr.

Arden, Lynne. Guess What Happened to Me, Auntie Kate! Marino, Natalie, illus. 2008. 52p. pap. 18.95 *(978-1-59858-733-3(1))* Dog Ear Publishing, LLC.

Arnold, Elana K. Far from Fair. 2016. (ENG.). 240p. (J). (gr. 5-7). 16.99 *(978-0-544-60227-4(7)*, HMH Books For Young Readers) Houghton Mifflin Harcourt Publishing Co.

Arnold, Ginger Fudge. Two Tipsy Tots, 1 vol. Crème, Aurora C., illus. 2009. 32p. pap. 24.95 *(978-1-4489-1891-1(X))* America Star Bks.

Arnold, Tedd. Big Family. Arnold, Tedd, illus. 2017. (Fly Guy Ser.: 17). (ENG., Illus.). 32p. (J). (gr. -1-3). 6.99 ***(978-0-545-66316-8(4))*** Scholastic, Inc.

Arroyo, Raymond. The Relic of Perilous Falls. 2016. (Will Wilder Ser.). (ENG.). 336p. (J). (gr. 3-7). lib. bdg. 19.99 *(978-0-553-53960-8(4))*; 16.99 *(978-0-553-53959-2(0))* Random Hse. Children's Bks. (Crown Books For Young Readers).

As Told by Milo: My Very Own Family. 2005. (J). 14.95 *(978-0-9772000-0-9(0))* Andrus, Ashley.

Asch, Frank. Star Jumper: Journal of a Cardboard Genius. Asch, Frank, illus. 2006. (Journals of a Cardboard Genius Ser.). (ENG., Illus.). 128p. (J). (gr. 2-5). pap. 7.95 *(978-1-55337-887-7(3))* Kids Can Pr., Ltd. CAN. Dist: Hachette Bk. Group.

Asch, Sheila. Katy's Time. 2007. 184p. pap. 16.95 *(978-1-84753-333-3(7))* Lulu Pr., Inc.

Ashkenas, Bruce. Auntie's Ghost. 2007. 108p. 34.50 *(978-1-4303-1929-0(1))* Lulu Pr., Inc.

Ashman, Linda. The Twelve Days of Christmas in Colorado. 2011. (Twelve Days of Christmas in America Ser.). (ENG., Illus.). 40p. (J). (gr. k-3). 12.95 *(978-1-4027-7463-8(X))* Sterling Publishing Co., Inc.

Asphyxia. The Grimstones Collection. Asphyxia, illus. 2015. (Grimstones Ser.). (ENG., Illus.). 488p. (J). (gr. 3-7). pap. 17.99 *(978-1-76011-391-9(3))* Allen & Unwin AUS. Dist: Independent Pubs. Group.

Athens, Sandra & Colarik, Kim. The Adventures of Foxy: The Lonely Lost Dog. 2009. 44p. pap. 18.50 *(978-1-4490-0506-1(3))* AuthorHouse.

Auborn, Jodi. Secrets of the North Country: The Hobo's Story. 2012. 210p. pap. 24.95 *(978-1-4626-7898-3(X))* America Star Bks.

Aulbach, Kathy. Meet the Flowers. 2009. 31p. 15.95 *(978-0-615-21179-4(8))* Flower Sprouts.

Aumann, Jane & Ladage, Cindy. The Christmas Tractor. Freitag, Charles, illus. 2003. 30p. (J). (gr. k-4). pap. 8.95 *(978-0-9703319-2-2(4))* Roots & Wings.

Austin, Karen D. Jay Jay & the Broken Picture Frame. 2009. 20p. pap. 10.49 *(978-1-4389-9003-3(0))* AuthorHouse.

Auth, Jeannine. Emmy's Question. 2007. 151p. (J). (gr. 4-7). 16.99 *(978-0-9790395-2-2(5))* Morningtide Pr.

Averette, Sonya M. Aunt Ruby's Kisses, 1 vol. Proulx, Denis, illus. 2009. 35p. pap. 24.95 *(978-1-60749-045-6(5))* America Star Bks.

Avery, Tom. Not As We Know It. 2016. (ENG.). 176p. (J). (gr. 4-7). 16.99 *(978-0-553-53509-9(9)*, Schwartz & Wade Bks.) Random Hse. Children's Bks.

Avi. Catch You Later, Traitor. (ENG.). 304p. (J). (gr. 3-7). 2016. pap. 7.95 *(978-1-61620-587-4(3))* 2015. 16.95 *(978-1-61620-359-7(5))* Algonquin Bks. of Chapel Hill.

—The End of Time, No. 3. 2010. (ENG.). 240p. (J). (gr. 5-18). 16.99 *(978-0-06-174080-0(2))* HarperCollins Pubs.

—The Traitors' Gate. Raude, Karina, illus. 2010. (ENG.). 368p. (J). (gr. 5-8). pap. 7.99 *(978-0-689-85336-4(X)*, Atheneum Bks. for Young Readers) Simon & Schuster Children's Publishing.

Aviation Publications Staff & National Geographic Learning Staff. Hard Gold: The Colorado Gold Rush of 1859. 2010. (Rise & Shine Ser.). (ENG.). 240p. (C). (gr. 3-7). pap. 10.95 *(978-1-4231-0520-6(6))* National Geographic School Publishing, Inc.

Ayres, Katherine. Family Tree. 2012. 116p. pap. 7.99 *(978-1-936495-21-4(X))* BookPartners, LLC.

Azore, Barbara. Wanda & the Wild Hair. Graham, Georgia, illus. 2005. (ENG.). 32p. (J). (gr. -1-2). 15.95 *(978-0-88776-717-3(6)*, Tundra Bks.) Tundra Bks. CAN. Dist: Penguin Random Hse. LLC.

Babbitt, Kelli. You Grew in My Heart Instead. 2008. 36p. pap. 24.95 *(978-1-60474-981-6(4))* America Star Bks.

Babbitt, Natalie. The Moon over High Street. 2012. 148p. (J). pap. *(978-0-545-46740-7(3))* Scholastic, Inc.

Baez, Debra. Fly, Fly, Little Fly. 2008. 15p. pap. 24.95 *(978-1-60474-600-6(9))* America Star Bks.

Baghdasaryan, Rouzanna. Moush Wants to Get Lost. Yulia, Lushnikova, illus. 2010. (ARA.). 32p. (J). pap. 16.95 *(978-1-60195-091-8(8))* International Step by Step Assn.

Bagnoli, Christine. Miguel's Family Picnic. 2006. (Neighborhood Readers Ser.). (ENG.). 16p. (gr. 1-3). pap. 6.50 *(978-1-4042-7006-0(X)*, Rosen Classroom) Rosen Publishing Group, Inc., The.

Bailey, Mary R. Vhan Zeely & the Time Prevaricators. 2009. 188p. pap. 12.95 *(978-1-60911-003-1(X)*, Eloquent Bks.) Strategic Book Publishing & Rights Agency (SBPRA).

Bain, Tracie. Peanuts & Life. 2004. 84p. (YA). pap. 8.95 *(978-0-595-33239-7(0))* iUniverse, Inc.

Baker, Ryan. How I Would Paint the World? 2006. (ENG.). 48p. per. 15.95 *(978-1-59800-969-9(9))* Outskirts Pr., Inc.

Baldini-Chavez, Cecilia. The Silver-Golden Feather Secreted at el Dorado, 1 vol. 2009. 92p. pap. 19.95 *(978-1-60813-664-3(7))* America Star Bks.

Baldwin, May. Sarah's School Friend. 2007. 280p. 28.95 *(978-1-4218-4206-6(8))*; per. 13.95 *(978-1-4218-4304-9(8))* 1st World Publishing, Inc. (1st World Library - Literary Society).

—Sarah's School Friend. 2007. 224p. pap. 20.99 *(978-1-4346-3544-0(9))*; 248p. pap. 22.99 *(978-1-4346-3545-7(7))* Creative Media Partners, LLC.

Ballantyne, R. M. Red Rooney: Or, the Last of the Crew. 2007. (R. M. Ballantyne Collection). (Illus.). 408p. 22.00 *(978-1-934554-08-1(1))* Vision Forum, Inc., The.

Banks, Erma. Fruit Cocktail. 2011. 28p. (gr. -1). pap. 13.00 *(978-1-4567-6222-3(2))* AuthorHouse.

Banks, Kate. Dillon Dillon. 2005. 149p. (gr. 3-7). 18.00 *(978-0-7569-5767-4(2))* Perfection Learning Corp.

Bannatyne-Cugnet, Jo. The Day I Became a Canadian: A Citizenship Scrapbook. Zhang, Song Nan, illus. 2008. (ENG.). 24p. (J). (gr. 2-4). pap. 10.95 *(978-0-88776-892-7(X)*, Tundra Bks.) Tundra Bks. CAN. Dist: Penguin Random Hse. LLC.

Banting, Celia. I only said I couldn't Cope. 2006. (Illus.). 240p. (YA). per. 14.99 *(978-0-9786648-2-4(5))* Wighita Pr.

Baraou, Anne & Sardon, Vincent. The Skeleton Family: The Neighbors from Elsewhere. 2005. (Illus.). 64p. *(978-1-59687-825-9(8)*, ipicturebooks) ibooks, Inc.

Baratz-Logsted, Lauren. Petal's Problems. 2010. (Sisters Eight Ser.: 6). (ENG., Illus.). 144p. (J). (gr. 1-4). pap. 5.99 *(978-0-547-33403-5(6))* Houghton Mifflin Harcourt Publishing Co.

—The Twin's Daughter. 2010. (ENG.). 400p. (YA). (gr. 9-12). 16.99 *(978-1-59990-513-6(2)*, 9781599905136, Bloomsbury USA Childrens) Bloomsbury Publishing USA.

Barber, Tiki & Barber, Ronde. Red Zone. 2010. (Barber Game Time Bks.). (ENG.). 176p. (J). (gr. 3-7). 15.99 *(978-1-4169-6860-3(1)*, Simon & Schuster/Paula Wiseman Bks.) Simon & Schuster/Paula Wiseman Bks.

Barensfeld, Debrae. Fox: Lost & Found. 2006. 12.95 *(978-0-9776617-0-1(9))* CreoXimius Publishing Company.

Barickman, Traci. Cooper's Adventures: Facing Our Fears. 2010. 24p. 11.49 *(978-1-4520-0326-9(2))* AuthorHouse.

Barna, Beverly. The Daughter of Dreams, a Fable of Destiny. White, David, illus. 2009. 28p. pap. 14.95 *(978-1-936051-09-0(5))* Peppertree Pr., The.

The Barnabys' New House, 6 Packs. (Literatura 2000 Ser.). (gr. 1-2). 28.00 *(978-0-7635-0458-8(0))* Rigby Education.

Barnes, Derrick. Brand New School, Brave New Ruby. Newton, Vanessa Brantley, illus. 2008. (Ruby & the Booker Boys Ser.: 1). (ENG.). 144p. (J). (gr. 2-5). pap. 5.99 *(978-0-545-01760-2(2)*, Scholastic Paperbacks) Scholastic, Inc.

Barnes, Jennifer Lynn. The Long Game: A Fixer Novel. 2016. (ENG.). 368p. (YA). 17.99 *(978-1-61963-596-8(8)*, 9781619635968, Bloomsbury USA Childrens) Bloomsbury Publishing USA.

Baron, Kathi. Shattered. 2009. 262p. (J). (gr. 9-12). 16.95 *(978-1-934813-08-9(7))* Westside Bks.

Barron Dc, Philip. Daddy Can't Play Now: A bedtime story of understanding & an introduction to Chiropractic Care. 2009. (Illus.). 20p. pap. 10.99 *(978-1-4490-1818-4(1))* AuthorHouse.

Barron, Liz. Salcombe Seaside Fairies: Louise the Lobster Pot Fairy. 2009. (Illus.). 24p. pap. 11.49 *(978-1-4389-8525-1(8))* AuthorHouse.

Barry, Cotter. The Adventures of Morgan Morgan the Rhymester. 2010. 16p. 12.99 *(978-1-4520-0116-6(2))* AuthorHouse.

—The Morgan's Family Circle. 2010. 16p. 12.99 *(978-1-4520-0114-2(6))* AuthorHouse.

Barshaw, Ruth McNally. Best Friends Fur-Ever. Barshaw, Ruth McNally, illus. 2013. (Ellie Mcdoodle Diaries). (ENG., Illus.). 192p. (YA). (gr. 3-6). 12.99 *(978-1-61963-175-5(X)*, 9781619631755, Bloomsbury USA Childrens) Bloomsbury Publishing USA.

—Ellie McDoodle: Best Friends Fur-Ever. Barshaw, Ruth McNally, illus. 2011. (Ellie Mcdoodle Ser.). (ENG., Illus.). 192p. (YA). (gr. 3-6). pap. 7.99 *(978-1-59990-657-7(0)*, 9781599906577, Bloomsbury USA Childrens) Bloomsbury Publishing USA.

—The Ellie McDoodle Diaries: Most Valuable Player. Barshaw, Ruth McNally, illus. 2013. (Ellie Mcdoodle Diaries). (ENG., Illus.). 192p. (YA). (gr. 3-6). 12.99 *(978-1-61963-176-2(8)*, 9781619631762, Bloomsbury USA Childrens) Bloomsbury Publishing USA.

Bartek, Mary. Funerals & Fly Fishing. 2009. (ENG.). 160p. (J). (gr. 3-7). pap. 16.99 *(978-0-312-56124-6(5)*, 9780312561246) Square Fish.

Basham, Tom. Accidental Evie. Calvert, Lissa, illus. 2012. 120p. *(978-1-77097-373-2(7))*; pap. *(978-1-77097-374-9(5))* FriesenPress.

Bashe, Kayla. Kitty Cadawell & the Shadowslayers of Fym. 2008. 290p. pap. 16.50 *(978-0-557-01916-8(8))* Lulu Pr., Inc.

Baskerville, Elliott. Nig Peas & Thweebies. 2012. 34p. pap. *(978-1-84903-159-2(2))* Schiel & Denver Publishing Ltd.

Bassett, Jennifer, ed. Long White Cloud: Stories from New Zealand. 3rd ed. 2008. (ENG., Illus.). 80p. 10.00 *(978-0-19-479139-7(4))* Oxford Univ. Pr., Inc.

Bastianich, Lidia Matticchio. Lidia's Family Kitchen: Nonna's Birthday Surprise. Graef, Renee, illus. 2013. (ENG.). 60p.

(J). (gr. -1-17). 16.95 *(978-0-7624-4655-1(2),* Running Pr. Kids) Running Pr. Bk. Pubs.

Bateman, Marinna. The Toogles' Big Move, 1 vol. 2009. 24p. pap. 24.95 *(978-1-61546-537-8(5))* America Star Bks.

Bates, Melinda. Nick Pricer: An American Heir. 2012. 88p. 19.95 *(978-1-4697-8478-6(5));* pap. 9.95 *(978-1-4697-8476-2(9))* iUniverse, Inc.

Bates, Susan Welch. The Rag Picker's Christmas. 2008. 17p. pap. 24.95 *(978-1-60672-967-0(5))* America Star Bks.

Bateson, Catherine. Millie & the Night Heron. 2005. 160p. (YA). pap. *(978-0-7022-3526-9(1))* Univ. of Queensland Pr.

Batt, Tanya Robyn. The Faerie's Gift. Ceccoli, Nicoletta, illus. 2008. (ENG.). 32p. (J). (gr. -1-3). 17.99 *(978-1-84686-230-4(2))* Barefoot Bks., Inc.

Battle, Cleaton D. A Saturday Surprise. Cooper, Emmanuel, illus. 2006. 68p. (J). pap. 11.95 *(978-1-59663-504-3(5),* Castle Keep Pr.) Rock, James A. & Co. Pubs.

Bauer, Joan. Rules of the Road. 2005. (ENG.). 208p. (YA). (gr. 7-7). pap. 8.99 *(978-0-14-240425-6(X),* Speak) Penguin Young Readers Group.

Baum, L. Frank & van Dyne, Edith. Aunt Jane's Nieces. 2009. 136p. pap. 11.95 *(978-1-60664-272-6(3))* Rodgers, Alan Bks.

Baum, L. Frank & Van Dyne, Edith. Aunt Jane's Nieces. 2003. 25.00 *(978-1-930764-08-8(1))* International Wizard of Oz Club, The.

Baum, L. Frank & van Dyne, Edith. Aunt Jane's Nieces. 2009. 136p. 24.95 *(978-1-60664-647-2(8))* Rodgers, Alan Bks.

Beal, Tracy Lynn. The Puzzle. Cunningham, Charles E., illus. 2008. 17p. pap. 24.95 *(978-1-60610-078-3(5))* America Star Bks.

Bean, Raymond. First Family in Space. 2016. (Out of This World Ser.). (ENG., Illus.). 112p. (gr. 2-5). lib. bdg. 32.65 *(978-1-4965-3617-4(7))* Out of this World GBR. Dist: Capstone Pub.

—Journey to the Moon. 2016. (Out of This World Ser.). (ENG., Illus.). 112p. (gr. 2-5). lib. bdg. 32.65 *(978-1-4965-3616-7(9))* Out of this World GBR. Dist: Capstone Pub.

Beck, Bev. The Birthday Present. DeWeese, Susan, illus. 2011. 40p. pap. 24.95 *(978-1-4560-8398-4(8))* America Star Bks.

Beedham, Edward. The Barking Family Christmas. 2015. (ENG.). 421p. (J). (gr. 4-6). mass mkt. 14.95 *(978-1-78554-793-5(3),* 170d87d7-898e-455e-98ef-fe5b792b577a) Austin, Stan AUS. Dist: Bookmasters Distribution.

Beheler, Rhonda. They Chose Me: A Story of Grandparent Adoption. 2008. 32p. per. 24.95 *(978-1-4241-8616-7(1))* America Star Bks.

Beil, Michael D. Summer at Forsaken Lake. Kneen, Maggie, illus. 2013. (ENG.). 336p. (J). (gr. 5). pap. 8.99 *(978-0-375-86496-4(2),* Yearling) Random Hse. Children's Bks.

Bell, Michele Ashman. Dragon's Jaw: A Heart-Pounding Adventure. 2005. 241p. (J). *(978-1-59156-880-3(3))* Covenant Communications.

Bell, William. The Blue Helmet. 2009. (ENG.). 224p. mass mkt. 6.99 *(978-0-7704-3002-3(3),* Seal Bks) Random Hse. of Canada CAN. Dist: Random Hse., Inc.

Bellisario, Gina. An Extra-Ordinary Girl. Von Innerebner, Jessika, illus. 2016. (Ellie Ultra Ser.). (ENG.). 128p. (gr. 2-3). lib. bdg. 25.99 *(978-1-4965-3139-1(6))* Stone Arch Bks.

—The Twelve Days of Christmas in Illinois. Ebbeler, Jeffrey, illus. 2012. (Twelve Days of Christmas in America Ser.). (ENG.). 40p. (J). (gr. k-3). 12.95 *(978-1-4027-9733-0(8))* Sterling Publishing Co., Inc.

Belshe, Judy. The Fry Family Goes to Hollywood. 2007. (Illus.). 50p. (J). spiral bd. 10.00 *(978-0-9655530-4-9(3))* Snuggle Up Bks.

Benedis-Grab, Daphne. Clementine for Christmas. 2015. (ENG.). 256p. (J). (gr. 3-7). 16.99 *(978-0-545-83951-8(3),* Scholastic Pr.) Scholastic, Inc.

Bennett, Holly. Redwing, 1 vol. 2012. (ENG.). 208p. (YA). (gr. 8-12). pap. 12.95 *(978-1-4598-0038-0(9))* Orca Bk. Pubs. USA.

Bennion, Jay B. From Here to There. 2013. 136p. pap. 9.99 *(978-0-9826175-0-2(X))* Pearl Publishing, LLC.

Benson, Don. Harry 'High-Pockets', 1 vol. 2010. 48p. pap. 16.95 *(978-1-4489-4272-5(1))* America Star Bks.

Benson, Patty. The Nameless Child. 2012. 36p. pap. 24.95 *(978-1-4626-7559-3(X))* America Star Bks.

—Pretty Little Gipsy. 2013. 24p. pap. 24.95 *(978-1-62709-505-1(5))* America Star Bks.

Bentley, Sue. Double Trouble, 4 vols. Farley, Andrew & Swan, Angela, illus. 2009. (Magic Kitten Ser.: 4). (ENG.). 128p. (J). (gr. 1-3). pap. 5.99 *(978-0-448-45060-5(7),* Grosset & Dunlap) Penguin Young Readers Group.

—Double Trouble. 2009. (Magic Kitten Ser.: 4). lib. bdg. 16.00 *(978-0-606-06004-2(9),* Turtleback) Turtleback Bks.

—A Forest Charm, 6 vols. Farley, Andrew & Swan, Angela, illus. 2010. (Magic Puppy Ser.: 6). (ENG.). 128p. (J). (gr. 1-3). pap. 5.99 *(978-0-448-45065-0(8),* Grosset & Dunlap) Penguin Young Readers Group.

—Muddy Paws. 2009. (Magic Puppy Ser.: 2). lib. bdg. 14.75 *(978-0-606-06021-9(9),* Turtleback) Turtleback Bks.

—A Shimmering Splash #11. Swan, Angela & Farley, Andrew, illus. 2014. (Magic Kitten Ser.: 11). (ENG.). 128p. (J). (gr. 1-3). 4.99 *(978-0-448-46789-4(5),* Grosset & Dunlap) Penguin Young Readers Group.

Benton, Jim. Dumbness Is a Dish Best Served Cold. Benton, Jim, illus. 2016. (Dear Dumb Diary Ser.). (ENG., Illus.). 224p. (J). (gr. 3-7). 12.99 *(978-0-545-93228-8(9),* Scholastic Pr.) Scholastic, Inc.

Benway, Robin. Emmy & Oliver. 2017. 368p. (YA). (gr. 8). pap. 9.99 ***(978-0-06-233060-4(8),*** HarperTeen) HarperCollins Pubs.

—Far from the Tree. 2017. 384p. (YA). (gr. 8). 17.99 ***(978-0-06-233062-8(4),*** HarperTeen) HarperCollins Pubs.

Bercun, Brenda. I'm Going to Be a Big Brother! Gross, Sue, illus. 2007. (ENG.). 33p. (J). (gr. -1-k). 15.95 *(978-0-9767198-7-8(8))* Nurturing Your Children Pr.

Berenstain, Jan & Berenstain, Mike. The Berenstain Bears & Mama for Mayor! Berenstain, Jan & Berenstain, Mike, illus. 2012. (I Can Read Level 1 Ser.). (ENG., Illus.). 32p. (J). (gr. k-3). pap. 3.99 *(978-0-06-207527-7(6))* HarperCollins Pubs.

—The Berenstain Bears at the Aquarium. 2012. (Berenstain Bears: I Can Read! Ser.). (J). lib. bdg. 13.55 *(978-0-606-23594-5(9),* Turtleback) Turtleback Bks.

—The Berenstain Bears' Really Big Pet Show. Berenstain, Jan & Berenstain, Mike, illus. 2008. (Berenstain Bears Ser.). (Illus.). 32p. (J). (gr. -1-2). 8.99 *(978-0-06-057406-2(2));* (ENG., pap. 3.99 *(978-0-06-057390-4(2))* HarperCollins Pubs. (HarperFestival).

—The Berenstain Bears' Valentine Party. 2008. (Berenstain Bears Ser.). (ENG., Illus.). 16p. (J). (gr. -1-3). pap. 6.99 *(978-0-06-057425-3(9),* HarperFestival) HarperCollins Pubs.

Berenstain, Jan, et al. Berenstain Bears. 2009. (I Can Read Level 1 Ser.). (J). (gr. k-3). pap. 9.99 *(978-0-06-171904-2(8))* HarperCollins Pubs.

—The Berenstain Bears' Family Reunion. Berenstain, Jan & Berenstain, Mike, illus. 2009. (I Can Read Level 1 Ser.). (ENG.). 32p. (J). (gr. k-3). pap. 3.99 *(978-0-06-058360-6(6))* HarperCollins Pubs.

Berenstain, Mike. We Love Soccer! 2016. (Berenstain Bears: I Can Read! Ser.). (J). lib. bdg. 13.55 *(978-0-606-38123-9(6))* Turtleback Bks.

Berenstain, Stan & Berenstain, Jan. The Berenstain Bears' Family Reunion. 2009. (Berenstain Bears — I Can Read Ser.). (J). lib. bdg. 13.55 *(978-0-606-04776-0(X),* Turtleback) Turtleback Bks.

—Berenstain Bears' Home Sweet Tree. 2013. (ENG.). 32p. (J). (-3). 9.99 *(978-1-4022-9085-5(3),* Sourcebooks Jabberwocky) Sourcebooks, Inc.

—The Berenstain Bears' Sleepover, 7 vols., Date not set. (Early Childhood First Bks.). (Illus.). (J). (gr. -1-2). lib. bdg. 97.65 *(978-1-56674-942-8(5))* Forest Hse. Publishing Co., Inc.

Berenstain, Stan, et al. The Berenstain Bears & the Bad Influence. Berenstain, Stan et al, illus. 2008. (Berenstain Bears Ser.). 32p. (J). (gr. -1-2). 8.99 *(978-0-06-057404-8(6));* (ENG.). pap. 3.99 *(978-0-06-057388-1(0))* HarperCollins Pubs. (HarperFestival).

Berg, Jean Horton. Pierre, the Young Watchmaker. D'Adamo, Anthony, illus. 2011. 190p. 42.95 *(978-1-258-08171-3(7))* Literary Licensing, LLC.

Berg-Seuffert, Barbara. Good Heaven - Eleven! A Tail of Many Cats. 2009. 28p. pap. 12.99 *(978-1-4490-3044-5(0))* AuthorHouse.

Bergren, Lisa T. God Gave Us So Much: A Limited-Edition Three-Book Treasury. Bryant, Laura J., illus. 2010. (ENG.). 112p. 19.99 *(978-0-307-44629-9(8),* WaterBrook Pr.) Crown Publishing Group.

Berk, Ari. Lych Way. 2014. (Undertaken Trilogy Ser.: 3). (ENG., Illus.). 336p. (YA). (gr. 7). 17.99 *(978-1-4169-9119-9(0),* Simon & Schuster Bks. For Young Readers) Simon & Schuster Bks. For Young Readers.

—Mistle Child. 2014. (Undertaken Trilogy Ser.: 2). (ENG., Illus.). 368p. (YA). (gr. 7). pap. 9.99 *(978-1-4169-9118-2(2),* Simon & Schuster Bks. For Young Readers) Simon & Schuster Bks. For Young Readers.

Bernard, Norah S. CLIVE & BRIE. 2006. (YA). per. 8.95 *(978-0-615-15932-4(X))* HELORO Publishing Group.

Bernard, Romily. Trust Me. 2016. (Find Me Ser.: 3). 336p. (YA). (gr. 8). 17.99 *(978-0-06-222909-0(5),* HarperTeen) HarperCollins Pubs.

Bernardo, Anilu. Un Dia con Mis Tias: A Day with My Aunts. Rodriguez, Christina, illus. 2006. (ENG & SPA.). 32p. (J). (gr. -1-2). 16.95 *(978-1-55885-374-4(X),* Piñata Books) Arte Publico Pr.

Bernstein, Jonathan. Bridget Wilder: Spy-In-Training. 2016. (Bridget Wilder Ser.: 1). (J). lib. bdg. 17.20 *(978-0-606-38746-0(3))* Turtleback Bks.

Berrios, Frank. Soccer with Mom. Golden, Jess, illus. 2016. (Little Golden Book Ser.). (ENG.). 24p. (J). (-k). 4.99 *(978-0-553-53854-0(3),* Golden Bks.) Random Hse. Children's Bks.

Berryman, Chelsea. Missing Pages. 2007. 77p. pap. 19.95 *(978-1-60441-747-0(1))* America Star Bks.

Berton, Suzanne. A Special Family. 2008. (Illus.). 44p. pap. 22.95 *(978-0-557-02863-4(9))* Lulu Pr., Inc.

Bertrand, Diane Gonzales. We Are Cousins/Somos Primos. Rodriguez, Christina E., illus. 2007. (SPA & ENG.). 32p. (J). (gr. -1-k). 16.95 *(978-1-55885-486-4(X),* Piñata Books) Arte Publico Pr.

Bessler, edward. A Smile for Billy. 2008. 175p. pap. 13.95 *(978-1-4357-4439-4(X))* Lulu Pr., Inc.

Best, Cari. When We Go Walking, 0 vols. Brooker, Kyrsten, illus. 2013. (ENG.). 32p. (J). (gr. -1-3). 17.99 *(978-1-4778-1648-6(8),* 9781477816486, Amazon Children's Publishing) Amazon Publishing.

Bilovsky, Stephanie. Great Grandpa Is Weird. Bishop, Tracy, illus. 2016. (Family Snaps Ser.). (ENG.). 32p. (gr. k-2). lib. bdg. 16.99 *(978-1-63440-042-8(9))* Red Chair Pr.

Birch, Vanessa Giancamilli. Seagull by the Shore: The Story of a Herring Gull. Langford, Alton, illus. 2010. (Smithsonian Oceanic Collection). (ENG.). 32p. (J). (gr. -1-3). pap. 6.95 *(978-1-60727-090-4(0))* Soundprints.

Bird, Shelia May. My Auntie Susan. Postgate, Daniel, illus. 2008. (Tadpoles Ser.). (ENG.). 24p. (J). (gr. -1-3). pap. *(978-0-7787-3889-3(2));* lib. bdg. *(978-0-7787-3858-9(2))* Crabtree Publishing Co.

Birdseye, Tom. A Tough Nut to Crack. 2006. (ENG.). 128p. (J). (gr. 3-7). 16.95 *(978-0-8234-1967-8(3))* Holiday Hse., Inc.

Biren, Sara. The Last Thing You Said. 2017. (ENG.). 320p. (YA). 17.95 *(978-1-4197-2304-9(9),* Amulet Bks.) Abrams, Inc.

Birtles, Andrew. Chinese Whispers. 2013. (Illus.). 52p. pap. *(978-1-908878-09-0(6))* Cornovia Pr., The.

Bishop, Desmond. The Wizard of Zee. 2012. 194p. pap. 14.95 *(978-1-61897-447-1(5),* Strategic Bk. Publishing) Strategic Book Publishing & Rights Agency (SBPRA).

Bishop, Helena Edwards & Bishop, Franklin, illus. The Wayward Haggis. 2012. 40p. pap. 18.95 *(978-1-4477-6514-1(1))* Lulu Pr., Inc.

Bjornson, Nancy. Llamas, Ponies & Pyrite. 2007. (J). *(978-1-930596-82-5(0))* Amherst Pr.

—Mustangs, Fires & Snakes. 2007. (J). *(978-1-930596-84-9(7))* Amherst Pr.

—Sleds, Skins & Snow. 2007. (J). *(978-1-930596-83-2(9))* Amherst Pr.

Black, Angie. Adopting Jake. Lucas, Diane, illus. 2010. 32p. pap. 12.95 *(978-1-935268-47-5(3))* Halo Publishing International.

Black, Judith. Adult Children of ... Parents. (J). 12.00 *(978-0-9701073-2-9(3))* Black, Judith Storyteller.

Black, Robert A. Lunar Pioneers. 2008. 280p. (YA). pap. 14.99 *(978-1-59092-397-9(9))* Blue Forge Pr.

Blackington, Debbie. Mama's Wish/Daughter's Wish. Sommer, Xiaolan, tr. from CHI. 2004. (Illus.). 48p. (J). 17.95 *(978-0-9760011-0-2(1))* Pebbleton Pr.

Blackstone, Stella. La Familia Activa de Oso. Sarfatti, Esther, tr. Harter, Debbie, illus. 2003. (Bear Ser.). (SPA.). 24p. (J). pap. 6.99 *(978-1-84148-777-9(5))* Barefoot Bks., Inc.

Blake, Ashley Herring. Suffer Love. 2017. (ENG.). (YA). (gr. 9). lib. bdg. 20.85 ***(978-0-606-39817-6(1))*** Turtleback Bks.

Blakemore, Megan Frazer. The Water Castle. 2014. (ENG.). 368p. (YA). (gr. 3-8). pap. 7.99 *(978-0-8027-3593-5(2),* 9780802735935, Bloomsbury USA Childrens) Bloomsbury Publishing USA.

Blaskovic, Eva A. Beyond the Precipice. 2013. 406p. (YA). pap. *(978-0-9881638-1-2(0))* Ashby-BP Publishing.

Blevins, Wiley. Rice & Beans. Cerato, Mattia, illus. 2014. (Family Snaps Ser.). (ENG.). 32p. (J). (gr. k-2). pap. 6.95 *(978-1-939656-63-6(X))* Red Chair Pr.

Blossom, J. I Should Have Been a Long Distance Truck. 2006. 71p. pap. 16.95 *(978-1-4241-3720-6(9))* PublishAmerica, Inc.

Blowers, Norman. Christmas with Carly. 2008. 16p. pap. 11.50 *(978-1-60693-337-4(X),* Strategic Bk. Publishing) Strategic Book Publishing & Rights Agency (SBPRA).

Blue, Darcy. Families Rock. 2011. 52p. pap. 20.49 *(978-1-4490-9901-5(7))* AuthorHouse.

Blume, Judy. Double Fudge. 2013. pap. *(978-0-439-58549-1(X),* Scholastic) Scholastic, Inc.

—Tiger Eyes. 2014. (ENG., Illus.). 256p. (YA). (gr. 7). pap. 10.99 *(978-1-4814-1387-9(2),* Atheneum Bks. for Young Readers) Simon & Schuster Children's Publishing.

Blumenthal, Deborah. Aunt Claire's Yellow Beehive Hair, 1 vol. GrandPré, Mary, illus. 2007. (ENG.). 32p. (J). (gr. k-3). 16.99 *(978-1-58980-491-3(0))* Pelican Publishing Co., Inc.

—Mafia Girl. 2014. (ENG.). 272p. (YA). (gr. 8-12). 16.99 *(978-0-8075-4911-7(8))* Whitman, Albert & Co.

Blundell, Judy. What I Saw & How I Lied. (ENG.). 288p. (J). (gr. 7-12). 2010. 9.99 *(978-0-439-90348-6(3),* Scholastic Paperbacks) 2008. 16.99 *(978-0-439-90346-2(7),* Scholastic Pr.) Scholastic, Inc.

Blunt, Julia & Gilbert, Dawn. How Donkey Became GREAT. 2007. 48p. pap. 22.85 *(978-0-615-16220-1(7))* Runamuck Publishing.

Blyton, Enid. Four in a Family. (Illus.). 87p. (J). pap. 5.95 *(978-0-09-935680-6(5))* Random Hse. GBR. Dist: Trafalgar Square Publishing.

Bochynek, Halina. A Beagle's Tale. 2008. 152p. pap. 14.99 *(978-1-4389-1960-7(3))* AuthorHouse.

Boeve, Eunice. The Summer of the Crow. 2013. 306p. pap. 14.95 *(978-1-939054-06-7(0))* Rowe Publishing and Design.

Boie, Kirsten. Todo Cambio con Jakob. Raúl, III, illus. 2003. (SPA.). 166p. (J). (gr. 3-5). pap. 8.95 *(978-84-204-4764-3(1))* Santillana USA Publishing Co., Inc.

Boie, Kristen. The Little Bitty Story of Austin Q. Peapot, 1 vol. Gentile, Christopher, illus. 2009. 20p. pap. 24.95 *(978-1-60749-548-2(1))* America Star Bks.

Bolden, Tonya. Finding Family. (ENG., Illus.). 192p. (YA). (gr. 3-12). 2012. pap. 7.99 *(978-1-59990-830-4(1),* 9781599908304) 2010. 15.99 *(978-1-59990-318-7(0),* 9781599903187) Bloomsbury Publishing USA. (Bloomsbury USA Childrens).

Bollinger, Georgia G. The Penguins' Perilous Picnic. 2011. 32p. pap. 14.50 *(978-1-4634-2200-4(8))* AuthorHouse.

Bolo the Balloon. Bolo the Balloon. 2007. (Illus.). 22p. (J). per. 10.00 *(978-0-9797549-0-6(9))* DeKruyff, Ruth.

Bond, Gwenda. Strange Alchemy. 2017. (ENG.). 336p. (gr. 9-12). 17.95 ***(978-1-63079-076-9(1))*** Switch Pr.

Bond, Juliet C. Sam's Sister. Majewski, Dawn, illus. 2004. (J). 18.00 *(978-0-944934-30-2(7))* Perspectives Pr., Inc.

Bonilla, Barbara Ann. The Wacky World of Wendy White! A Whopper of a Tale. 2013. (ENG.). 47p. (J). pap. 12.95 *(978-1-4787-1543-6(X))* Outskirts Pr., Inc.

Bonneval, Gwen de & Smith, Owen. William & the Lost Spirit. Smith, Anne Collins, tr. from FRE. Bonhomme, Matthieu, illus. 2013. (ENG.). 160p. (J). (gr. 8-12). lib. bdg. 30.60 *(978-0-7613-8567-7(3),* Graphic Universe™) Lerner Publishing Group.

Bonnie, Compton-Hanson. Holly Jean & the Secret of Razorback Ridge, 5 vols., Vol. 1. 2011. (ENG.). 164p. (J). pap. 7.99 *(978-1-59317-431-6(4))* Warner Pr., Inc.

Boone, Martina. Illusion. 2016. (Heirs of Watson Island Ser.). (ENG., Illus.). 480p. (YA). (gr. 9). 17.99 *(978-1-4814-1128-8(4),* Simon Pulse) Simon Pulse.

—Persuasion. 2015. (Heirs of Watson Island Ser.). (ENG., Illus.). 464p. (YA). (gr. 9). 17.99 *(978-1-4814-1125-7(X),* Simon Pulse) Simon Pulse.

Booth, Coe. Bronxwood. 2011. (ENG.). 336p. (J). (gr. 9). 17.99 *(978-0-439-92534-1(7),* PUSH) Scholastic, Inc.

Bordons, Paloma. La Tierra de las Papas. 5th ed. 2005. (SPA., Illus.). 144p. (J). (gr. 6-8). 7.95 *(978-84-348-5053-8(2))* SM Ediciones ESP. Dist: Iaconi, Mariuccia Bk. Imports, Lectorum Pubns., Inc.

Bosak, Susan V. Something to Remember Me By: A Story about Love & Legacies. McGaw, Laurie, illus. 2003. 32p. (gr. 1-6). *(978-1-896232-01-0(9),* TCP Pr.) Communication Project, The.

Boscarelli, Bonnie & Dani. The Garden of Weeden: Hector the Hedgehog. 2009. 40p. pap. 16.99 *(978-1-4490-0606-8(X))* AuthorHouse.

Bottner, Barbara. Flower Girl, 0 vols. Grier, Laura, illus. Grier, Laura, photos by. 2012. (ENG.). 32p. (J). (gr. k-3). 16.99 *(978-0-7614-6119-7(1),* 9780761461197, Amazon Children's Publishing) Amazon Publishing.

Boussarhane, Ericka. Sam & the Boogie Man. 2009. 28p. pap. 14.99 *(978-1-4389-3107-4(7))* AuthorHouse.

Bowlby, Linda S. Nasaria's Family/la Familia de Nasaria. Helms, Dana, illus. 2008. 45p. (J). (gr. -1-3). pap. 10.95 *(978-0-9779993-9-2(4))* Red Earth Publishing.

—Nentuck's New Family. Helms, Dana, illus. 2008. 30p. (J). (gr. -1-3). pap. 9.95 *(978-0-9779993-8-5(6))* Red Earth Publishing.

—The Rock Garden. Helms, Dana, illus. 2008. 29p. (J). (gr. -1-3). pap. 9.95 *(978-0-9779993-4-7(3))* Red Earth Publishing.

Bowman, Andy. Indian Slim. Travis, Stephanie, illus. 29p. (J). (gr. 1-6). pap. 6.95 *(978-1-931650-06-9(3));* lib. bdg. 14.95 *(978-1-931650-07-6(1))* Coastal Publishing Carolina, Inc.

Bowman, Chaliece. Sarah's Camping Trip. 2012. 20p. pap. 17.99 *(978-1-4772-5531-5(1))* AuthorHouse.

Bowman, Silas. The Daudyhouse. Horst, Melisa, illus. 2012. 51p. (J). *(978-0-7399-2450-1(8))* Rod & Staff Pubs., Inc.

Boyce, Frank Cottrell. Chitty Chitty Bang Bang & the Race Against Time. Berger, Joe, illus. (Chitty Chitty Bang Bang Ser.). (ENG.). 240p. (J). (gr. 4-7). 2014. pap. 6.99 *(978-0-7636-6931-7(8))* 2013. 15.99 *(978-0-7636-5982-0(7))* Candlewick Pr.

—Chitty Chitty Bang Bang Flies Again. Berger, Joe, illus. 2013. (Chitty Chitty Bang Bang Ser.). (ENG.). 224p. (J). (gr. 4-7). pap. 6.99 *(978-0-7636-6353-7(0))* Candlewick Pr.

—Chitty Chitty Bang Bang over the Moon. Berger, Joe, illus. 2015. (Chitty Chitty Bang Bang Ser.). (ENG.). 304p. (J). (gr. 4-7). pap. 6.99 *(978-0-7636-7666-7(7))* Candlewick Pr.

—Framed. Lenton, Steven, illus. unabr. ed. 2006. (ENG.). 320p. pap. 15.95 *(978-0-330-43425-6(X))* Macmillan Pubs., Ltd. GBR. Dist: Trans-Atlantic Pubns., Inc.

Boyd, David. Closer to Hamlet. 2003. 120p. (YA). (gr. 6-9). pap. *(978-0-921156-93-2(6))* Rubicon Publishing, Inc.

Boyne, John. The Terrible Thing That Happened to Barnaby Brocket. Jeffers, Oliver, illus. 2014. (ENG.). 288p. (J). (gr. 3-7). 6.99 *(978-0-307-97765-6(X),* Yearling) Random Hse. Children's Bks.

Brasch, Nicolas. Hot Springs & Brown Bears, 1 vol. rev. ed. 2013. (Fiction Readers Ser.). (ENG., Illus.). 32p. (J). (gr. 3-3). pap. 8.99 *(978-1-4333-5637-7(6))* Shell Educational Publishing.

Braun, Sebastien. I Love My Daddy Board Book. Braun, Sebastien, illus. 2017. (Illus.). 32p. (J). (gr. -1 — 1). bds. 7.99 *(978-0-06-256425-2(0),* Tegen, Katherine Bks) HarperCollins Pubs.

Bray, Diane E. B. First Generation: The Story of Annie. 2008. 53p. pap. 16.95 *(978-1-60563-516-3(2))* America Star Bks.

Brennan, Sarah Rees. Unmade. 2015. (Lynburn Legacy Ser.: Bk. 3). (ENG.). 384p. (YA). (gr. 7). pap. 9.99 *(978-0-375-87105-4(5),* Ember) Random Hse. Children's Bks.

Brewer, Michelle. Sunrise in My Cup. 2011. 28p. (gr. -1). pap. 13.99 *(978-1-4567-3995-9(6))* AuthorHouse.

Brezinova, Ivona. Dorothy & the Glasses. Llapashtica, Mentor, illus. 2007. 32p. (J). (ARA & ENG.). pap. 12.95 *(978-1-60195-088-8(8));* (POL & ENG.). pap. 12.95 *(978-1-60195-099-4(3))* International Step by Step Assn.

Bridwell, Norman. Clifford's Family. Bridwell, Norman, illus. 2010. (Clifford 8x8 Ser.). (ENG., Illus.). 32p. (J). (gr. -1-3). pap. 3.99 *(978-0-545-21585-5(4),* Cartwheel Bks.) Scholastic, Inc.

Briggs, Jay. Giants Child. 2006. 105p. pap. *(978-1-905665-07-5(5))* Pollinger In Print.

Brignaud, Pierre, illus. Caillou Asks Nicely. 2015. (Step by Step Ser.). (ENG.). 24p. (J). (gr. k-k). bds. 5.99 *(978-2-89718-175-8(3))* Caillouet, Gerry.

Brignole, Giancarla, tr. El Pueblo de los Silencios. Bersanetti, Sandra, illus. (Fabulas De Familia Ser.). (SPA.). 32p. *(978-970-20-0271-0(0))* Castillo, Ediciones, S. A. de C. V.

Brindle, I. J. Balthazar Fabuloso in the Lair of the Humbugs. Walker, Sholto, illus. 2016. (ENG.). 240p. (J). 16.95 *(978-0-8234-3577-7(6))* Holiday Hse., Inc.

Bringsvaerd, Tor Age. Ruffen: The Escape to Loch Ness. Hansen, Thore, illus. 2009. (Ruffen Ser.). 72p. (J). (gr. 1-4). 16.95 *(978-0-9815761-2-1(5))* Mackenzie Smiles, LLC.

Brisson, Pat. Star Blanket. Magnus, Erica, illus. 2003. (ENG.). 32p. (J). (gr. k-2). 15.95 *(978-1-56397-889-0(X))* Boyds Mills Pr.

Bristow, Catherine. My Strange & Terrible Malady. 2008. (YA). pap. 15.95 *(978-1-934575-19-2(4))* Autism Asperger Publishing Co.

Broach, Elise. Gumption! Egielski, Richard, illus. 2010. (ENG.). 40p. (J). (gr. k-3). 18.99 *(978-1-4169-1628-4(8),* Atheneum Bks. for Young Readers) Simon & Schuster Children's Publishing.

—Masterpiece. 2010. 18.00 *(978-1-60686-888-1(8))* Perfection Learning Corp.

—Masterpiece. Murphy, Kelly, illus. 2010. (ENG.). 320p. (J). (gr. 4-7). pap. 7.99 *(978-0-312-60870-5(5),* 9780312608705) Square Fish.

—Masterpiece. 2010. (J). lib. bdg. 18.40 *(978-0-606-14604-3(0),* Turtleback) Turtleback Bks.

Brodine, Linda. Gramma Please Tell Us a Story. 2012. (ENG.). (J). pap. 12.99 *(978-1-4675-1215-2(X))* Independent Pub.

The Broken Plant. 2007. pap. 8.00 *(978-0-9769152-2-5(7))* Feed My Sheep Bks.

Bronstein, Christine. Princess Penelope: The Case of the Eweey, Gooey, Gross & Very Stinky Experiment: Young, Karen L., illus. 2016. (Stewie BOOM! Ser.). (ENG.). 58p. (J). (gr. -1-3). 17.99 *(978-0-9963074-8-2(6))* Nothing But The Truth, LLC.

—Princess Penelope: The Case of the Eweey, Gooey, Gross & Very Stinky Experiment. Young, Karen L., illus. 2016. (Stewie BOOM! Ser.). (ENG.). 58p. (J). (gr. -1-3). pap. 9.99 *(978-0-9963074-9-9(4))* Nothing But The Truth, LLC.

—Stewie BOOM! Boss of the Big Boy Bed: Boss of the Big Boy Bed. Young, Karen L., illus. 2015. (Stewie BOOM! Ser.). (ENG.). 60p. (gr. -1-2). 17.99 *(978-0-9904652-9-4(2));* pap. 11.99 *(978-0-9963074-0-6(0))* Nothing But The Truth, LLC.

Bronzan, William M., Sr. A Time to Dream. 2006. 41p. (J). pap. 8.95 *(978-0-7414-3158-5(0))* Infinity Publishing.

Brooks, Heather. Hercules: A Matter of Trust. 2009. (Running Horse Ridge Ser.: 2). (ENG.). 224p. (J). (gr. 5-18). pap. 6.99 *(978-0-06-142981-1(3))* HarperCollins Pubs.

Brooks, Kevin. Dawn. 2009. (ENG.). 256p. (J). (gr. 9-18). 17.99 *(978-0-545-06090-5(7),* Chicken Hse., The) Scholastic, Inc.

Brooks, Linda Sue. Meet Toado & Friends. Mills, Lori, illus. l.t. ed. 2008. (Toado & Friends Ser.). (ENG.). 30p. (J). (gr. -1-3). per. 11.99 *(978-1-59879-314-7(4),* Lifevest) Lifevest Publishing, Inc.

Brooks, Tyrice M. Only the Truth Will Tell. 2012. 64p. pap. 17.95 *(978-1-62709-155-8(6))* America Star Bks.

Brost, April. Luckyduck Luckyduck. 2013. 24p. pap. 24.95 *(978-1-63004-104-5(1))* America Star Bks.

Brouwer, Sigmund. Maverick Mania, 1 vol. 2008. (Orca Sports Ser.). (ENG.). 176p. (YA). (gr. 6-10). pap. 9.95 *(978-1-55469-047-3(1))* Orca Bk. Pubs. USA.

—Timberwolf Prey, 1 vol. Ross, Graham, illus. 2010. (Orca Echoes Ser.). (ENG.). 64p. (J). (gr. 2-3). pap. 6.95 *(978-1-55469-109-8(5))* Orca Bk. Pubs. USA.

Brower, Zoe & the Cocoa-Brown Tutu. Steele, Andrea M., illus. 2nd ed. 2013. 56p. pap. 10.95 *(978-1-936688-79-1(4))* AKA:yoLa.

Brown, Gavin. Josh Baxter Levels Up. 2016. (ENG., Illus.). 192p. (J). (gr. 3-7). 12.99 *(978-0-545-77294-5(X)*, Scholastic Pr.) Scholastic, Inc.

Brown, Gladys M. Home Away from Home. 2005. 36p. pap. 6.95 *(978-1-4116-3026-0(2))* Lulu Pr., Inc.

Brown, Jahla. Nathan Is Nathan. 2009. (ENG., Illus.). 20p. (J). pap. 19.95 *(978-0-9778083-8-0(6))* Everlasting Publishing.

Brown, Jeffrey. Sulk. 2009. (Sulk Ser.: 3). (ENG., Illus.). 64p. pap. 6.00 *(978-1-60309-055-1(X)*, 9781603090551) Top Shelf Productions.

Brown, Margaret Wise. Goodnight Moon 123: A Counting Book. Hurd, Clement, illus. 2013. (ENG.). 30p. (J). (gr. -1-k). bds. 9.99 *(978-0-06-224405-5(1)*, HarperFestival) HarperCollins Pubs.

—Mon Petit Monde (French edition of My World) 2004. 40p. 29.95 *(978-0-320-06689-4(4))* French & European Pubns., Inc.

Brown, Monica. Drama Queen. 2016. (Lola Levine Ser.: 2). (J). lib. bdg. 16.00 *(978-0-606-38329-5(8))* Turtleback Bks.

—Lola Levine, Drama Queen. 2016. (Lola Levine Ser.: 2). (ENG., Illus.). 112p. (J). (gr. 1-5). pap. 5.99 *(978-0-316-25842-5(3))* Little, Brown Bks. for Young Readers.

Brown, Sharon. Nana, Tell Me a Story. 2009. 58p. pap. 15.99 *(978-1-4415-4478-0(X))* Xlibris Corp.

Brown, Stacia Bradley. A Family of His Own. DeKnight, Cathy, illus. 2004. (J). 14.95 *(978-1-58597-283-8(5))* Leathers Publishing.

Brownlee, Sophia Grace & McClelland, Rosie. Tea Time with Sophia Grace & Rosie. McNicholas, Shelagh, illus. 2013. (J). (ENG.). 40p. (gr. -1-k). 17.99 *(978-0-545-50214-6(4))*; pap. *(978-0-545-58534-7(1))* Scholastic, Inc. (Orchard Bks.).

Brozman, Dave. The Littlest Smoke Detector. Roguez, Jesus, illus. 2006. (ENG.). 32p. per. 21.99 *(978-1-4259-6096-4(0))* AuthorHouse.

Bruce Clarke, Margaret. Hunter's Marjory. 2007. 244p. 27.95 *(978-1-4218-4203-5(3))*; per. 12.95 *(978-1-4218-4301-8(3))* 1st World Publishing, Inc. (1st World Library - Literary Society).

Bruce, Relly. Meet My Family: From the Meekus & Myron Collection (Book 4) 2011. 16p. pap. 24.95 *(978-1-4489-9175-4(7))* America Star Bks.

Bruchac, Joseph. Whisper in the Dark. Comport, Sally Wern, illus. 2009. (ENG.). 192p. (J). (gr. 5). pap. 6.99 *(978-0-06-058089-6(5))* HarperCollins Pubs.

Bruel, Nick. Bad Kitty vs. Uncle Murray. Bruel, Nick, illus. 2011. (Bad Kitty Ser.). (ENG., Illus.). 176p. (J). (gr. 2-5). pap. 6.99 *(978-0-312-67483-0(X)*, 9780312674830) Square Fish.

—Bad Kitty vs. Uncle Murray. 2011. (Bad Kitty Chapter Bks.). (J). lib. bdg. 17.20 *(978-0-606-23753-6(4)*, Turtleback) Turtleback Bks.

—Bad Kitty vs. Uncle Murray: The Uproar at the Front Door. Bruel, Nick, illus. 2010. (Bad Kitty Ser.). (ENG., Illus.). 160p. (J). (gr. 2-5). 14.99 *(978-1-59643-596-4(8)*, 9781596435964) Roaring Brook Pr.

Brundige, Patricia. Traveling with Aunt Patty: Aunt Patty Visits London. Wright, Cindy, ed. Hanlon, Leslie, illus. Date not set. (J). (gr. 1-4). 12.95 *(978-0-9659668-0-1(1))* Aunt Patty's Travels-London.

Brunel, Aude. Let's Go to Work. Mancek, Marjan, illus. 2007. 32p. (J). (ARA & ENG.). pap. 16.95 *(978-1-60195-089-5(6))*; (POL & ENG.). pap. 16.95 *(978-1-60195-101-4(9))* International Step by Step Assn.

Brunson, Jodi. A Year Without Dad. Cramer, illus. 2003. (J). per. 10.00 *(978-0-9740683-1-2(4))* Authors & Artists Publishers of New York, Inc.

Bryant, Annie. Katani's Jamaican Holiday. 2008. (Beacon Street Girls Ser.: No. 4). (ENG., Illus.). 192p. (J). (gr. 4-8). pap. 6.99 *(978-1-4169-6443-8(6)*, Aladdin) Simon & Schuster Children's Publishing.

Bryant, G. E. Nirvana's Sunshine Babies. 2009. 28p. pap. 12.95 *(978-1-59858-903-0(2))* Dog Ear Publishing, LLC.

Buchanan, Selena. Sunday Chimes, 1 vol. 2009. 51p. pap. 16.95 *(978-1-4489-2208-6(9))* America Star Bks.

Buckner, Andrew. Grand Poppa's Favorite Chair: No One Is As Special As You. Welker, Matthew S., illus. 2011. 48p. pap. 24.95 *(978-1-4560-8294-9(9))* America Star Bks.

Budhos, Marina. Tell Us We're Home. 2010. (ENG.). 304p. (YA). (gr. 7-18). 17.99 *(978-1-4169-0352-9(6)*, Atheneum Bks. for Young Readers) Simon & Schuster Children's Publishing.

Buehner, Caralyn. Goldilocks & the Three Bears. Buehner, Mark, illus. 2009. (ENG.). 32p. (J). (gr. -1-k). pap. 6.99 *(978-0-14-241275-6(9)*, Puffin Books) Penguin Young Readers Group.

Buggs, Michael A. Tabard. Buggs, Michael A., illus. (Illus.). 64p. (Orig.). (J). (gr. 2-6). pap. 15.00 *(978-0-9657723-0-3(6))* Mogul Comics.

Buhlig Meister, Victoria. Tell Me a Story, Please, Mi-Mi! 2009. 36p. pap. 16.99 *(978-1-4389-2430-4(5))* AuthorHouse.

Bullard, Lisa. Trick-or-Treat on Milton Street. Oeltjenbruns, Joni, illus. 2004. (Carolrhoda Picture Books Ser.). (ENG.). 32p. (J). (gr. k-4). pap. 6.95 *(978-1-57505-793-4(X))* Lerner Publishing Group.

—Turn Left at the Cow. 2015. (ENG.). 304p. (J). (gr. 5-7). pap. 7.99 *(978-0-544-43918-4(X)*, HMH Books For Young Readers) Houghton Mifflin Harcourt Publishing Co.

Buller, Ginny. Happy Misunderstanding: How Folly Gets his Name. Chettle, Julie, illus. 2012. (ENG.). 29p. (J). pap. 16.95 *(978-1-4327-8234-4(7))* Outskirts Pr., Inc.

Bunce, Elizabeth C. A Curse Dark as Gold. 2010. (ENG.). 400p. (J). (gr. 7). 9.99 *(978-0-439-89577-4(4)*, Scholastic Paperbacks) Scholastic, Inc.

Bunting, Eve. I Have an Olive Tree. 2003. (J). stu. ed. 183.75 *(978-0-7887-3674-2(4)*, 46977) Recorded Bks., Inc.

—A Picnic in October. Carpenter, Nancy, illus. 2010. (Rise & Shine Ser.). (ENG.). 32p. (C). (gr. -1-3). reprint ed. pap. 12.95 *(978-0-15-205065-8(5))* National Geographic School Publishing, Inc.

Burch, Genny. My Name Is Bobby Claus: A fictional Christmas story for Children. 2009. 36p. pap. 15.99 *(978-1-4490-4233-2(3))* AuthorHouse.

Burch, Robert. Queenie Peavey. l.t. ed. 2003. (LRS Large Print Cornerstone Ser.). 166p. (J). lib. bdg. 29.95 *(978-1-58118-115-9(9))* LRS.

Burchett, Claudette. Time for Fun. 2009. 20p. pap. 10.49 *(978-1-4490-2798-8(9))* AuthorHouse.

Burchett, Loni. Bear & Katie in A Riverboat Ride, 4 vols., Vol. 4. 2006. (Illus.). 104p. (J). per. 12.95 *(978-0-9742815-3-7(0))* Black Lab Publishing LLC.

Burd, Nick. The Vast Fields of Ordinary. 2009. (ENG.). 320p. (YA). (gr. 9-18). 16.99 *(978-0-8037-3340-4(2)*, Dial Bks) Penguin Young Readers Group.

Burg, Ann E. Serafina's Promise. 2015. (ENG.). 304p. (J). (gr. 3-7). pap. 7.99 *(978-0-545-53567-0(0)*, Scholastic Pr.) Scholastic, Inc.

—Unbound. 2016. (ENG.). 352p. (J). (gr. 4-6). 16.99 *(978-0-545-93427-5(3)*, Scholastic Pr.) Scholastic, Inc.

Burnham, Molly B. Teddy Mars: Almost a World Record Breaker. Spencer, Trevor, illus. 2016. (Teddy Mars Ser.: 1). 240p. (J). (gr. 3-7). pap. 6.99 *(978-0-06-227811-1(8)*, Tegen, Katherine Bks) HarperCollins Pubs.

Burroughs, Scott, illus. Trouble at the Arcade. 2010. (Hardy Boys: the Secret Files Ser.: 1). (ENG.). 96p. (J). (gr. 1-4). pap. 5.99 *(978-1-4169-9164-9(6)*, Aladdin) Simon & Schuster Children's Publishing.

Burshek, Edward & Burshek, Tonja. Explorers of the Word: Episode 1: the Creation. Peterson, Melanie, illus. 2007. (ENG.). 76p. per. 19.95 *(978-1-4241-6691-6(8))* America Star Bks.

Bush, Laura & Hager, Jenna Bush. Our Great Big Backyard. Rogers, Jacqueline, illus. 40p. (J). (gr. -1-3). 2018. pap. 7.99 **(978-0-06-246841-3(3))** 2016. (ENG.). 18.99 *(978-0-06-246835-2(9))* 2016. lib. bdg. 19.89 *(978-0-06-246836-9(7))* HarperCollins Pubs.

Butcher, Kristin. Alibi, 1 vol. 2014. (Orca Currents Ser.). (ENG.). 120p. (J). (gr. 5-9). pap. 9.95 *(978-1-4598-0767-9(7))* Orca Bk. Pubs. USA.

—Zach & Zoe: Bully & the Beagle, 1 vol. 2009. (Lorimer Streetlights Ser.). (ENG.). 120p. (J). (gr. 2-4). 8.95 *(978-1-55277-427-4(9)*, 9781552774274) Lorimer, James & Co., Ltd., Pubs. CAN. Dist: Casemate Pubs. & Bk. Distributors, LLC.

Butler, Dori Hillestad. Do You Know the Monkey Man?, 1 vol. 2005. (ENG.). 195p. (YA). (gr. 5-9). 15.95 *(978-1-56145-340-5(4))* Peachtree Pubs.

—Yes, I Know Monkey Man, 1 vol. 2009. (ENG.). 224p. (YA). (gr. 5-9). 16.95 *(978-1-56145-479-2(6))* Peachtree Pubs.

Buzzy. One Sunny Day. Martin, John, ed. Simpkins, Iravis, illus. 2003. 52p. (J). (gr. -1-2). pap. 7.99 *(978-0-9719054-1-2(X))* Buzzy's Bks.

Byars, Betsy. The Not-Just-Anybody Family. (Blossom Family Ser.: Bk. 1). 149p. (J). (gr. 4-6). pap. 4.50 *(978-0-8072-1429-9(9)*, Listening Library) Random Hse. Audio Publishing Group.

Caban, Connie. Don't Be Afraid of the Storm. Page, illus. 2011. 32p. pap. 12.95 *(978-1-936343-97-3(5))* Peppertree Pr., The.

Cabot, Meg. Being Nikki. (Airhead Ser.: 2). (ENG.). 352p. (J). 2010. (gr. 3-7). pap. 9.99 *(978-0-545-04058-7(2))* 2009. (gr. 7-18). 16.99 *(978-0-545-04056-3(6))* Scholastic, Inc.

—Moving Day. 2009. (Allie Finkle's Rules for Girls Ser.: Bk. 1). (ENG.). 256p. (J). (gr. 3-7). 6.99 *(978-0-545-04041-9(8)*, Scholastic Paperbacks) Scholastic, Inc.

Cabot, Meg & Cabot, Frank. From the Notebooks of a Middle School Princess. 2015. (From the Notebooks of a Middle School Princess Ser.). (ENG., Illus.). 192p. (J). (gr. 3-7). 16.99 *(978-1-250-06602-2(6)*, 9781250066022) Feiwel & Friends.

Cagan, Kayla. Piper Perish. 2017. (ENG., Illus.). 416p. (YA). 17.99 *(978-1-4521-5583-8(6))* Chronicle Bks. LLC.

Cahill, Byron. Space Pox. 2005. (J). pap. *(978-1-4108-4220-6(7))* Benchmark Education Co.

Calabrese, Diane Marie. My Dad's off to War. Swope, Brenda, illus. 2011. 28p. pap. 24.95 *(978-1-4560-0942-7(7))* America Star Bks.

Calabrese, Linda Lee. It Is What It Is: In a Kid's Mind. 2012. 28p. pap. 24.95 *(978-1-4626-5643-1(9))* America Star Bks.

Caletti, Deb. The Nature of Jade. 2008. (ENG.). 320p. (YA). (gr. 7-12). pap. 10.99 *(978-1-4169-1006-0(9)*, Simon Pulse) Simon Pulse.

—The Secret Life of Prince Charming. 2009. (ENG.). 336p. (YA). (gr. 7-18). 16.99 *(978-1-4169-5940-3(8)*, Simon Pulse) Simon Pulse.

Calhoun, Dia. After the River the Sun. Slater, Kate, illus. 2013. (ENG.). 368p. (J). (gr. 4-7). 16.99 *(978-1-4424-3985-6(8))* Simon & Schuster Children's Publishing.

Call of the Selkie: Individual Title Six-Packs. (Action Packs Ser.). 104p. (gr. 3-5). 44.00 *(978-0-7635-2991-8(5))* Rigby Education.

Callen, Sharon. Life at the Top, 1 vol. rev. ed. 2013. (Fiction Readers Ser.). (ENG., Illus.). 20p. (J). (gr. 1-1). pap. 15.96 *(978-1-4807-1143-3(8))*; pap. 4.99 *(978-1-4333-5487-8(X))* Shell Educational Publishing.

Calucag, Angela. Little Freddy S Journey. 2012. 32p. pap. 17.99 *(978-1-62419-840-3(6))* Salem Author Services.

Cameron, Sharon. The Dark Unwinding. 2013. (ENG.). 336p. (J). (gr. 7). pap. 9.99 *(978-0-545-32787-9(3)*, Scholastic Paperbacks) Scholastic, Inc.

Camp, V. Ray. The Little Mouse on the Prairie. Baker, David, illus. 2011. 28p. pap. 24.95 *(978-1-4560-1028-7(X))* America Star Bks.

Canady, Mary Monica. Why Is My Name Sam? Papeo, Maria Eugenia & Saumell, Marina, illus. 2008. 24p. pap. 24.95 *(978-1-60474-028-8(0))* America Star Bks.

Cannon, Anita. My Aunt Bonnie: A Child's Story of Love & Loss. 2011. 48p. pap. 20.45 *(978-1-4497-1617-2(2)*, WestBow Pr.) Author Solutions, Inc.

Cannon, Sherrill S. Peter & the Whimper-Whineys. 2010. 30p. pap. 13.00 *(978-1-60911-517-3(1)*, Strategic Bk. Publishing) Strategic Book Publishing & Rights Agency (SBPRA).

Capdevila, Roser & Vendrell, Maria Martinez. Los Conflictos de Ana. 2003.Tr. of Ana's Problems. (SPA.). 24p. (J). 7.95 *(978-84-233-1627-4(0))* Ediciones Destino ESP. Dist: Planeta Publishing Corp.

Caraballo, Samuel. Estas Manos: Manitas de Mi Familia. Costello, Shawn, illus. 2014.Tr. of These Hands: My Family's Hands. (ENG & SPA.). (J). 17.95 *(978-1-55885-795-7(8)*, Piñata Books) Arte Publico Pr.

Cardona, Nancy. Beethoven. Swope, Brenda, illus. 2011. 28p. pap. 24.95 *(978-1-4560-0961-8(3))* America Star Bks.

Carlson, Melody. A Not-So-Simple Life. 2008. (Diary of a Teenage Girl Ser.: Bk. 14). (ENG.). 256p. (YA). (gr. 7). pap. 14.99 *(978-1-60142-117-3(6)*, Multnomah) Doubleday Religious Publishing Group, The.

Carlson, Nancy. My Family Is Forever. Carlson, Nancy, illus. 2006. (ENG., Illus.). 32p. (J). (gr. -1-k). pap. 5.99 *(978-0-14-240561-1(2)*, Puffin Books) Penguin Young Readers Group.

Carmean, John. Moving Day: Adventures in Hogtown. l.t. ed. 2011. (ENG., Illus.). 33p. (J). pap. 16.99 *(978-0-9839799-1-3(X))* Carmean Productions LLC.

Carr, Karen. The Christmas Wishing Quilt. 2008. 24p. pap. 12.99 *(978-1-4389-1353-7(2))* AuthorHouse.

Carr, Lawrence. Under the Peach Tree. 2006. pap. 8.00 *(978-0-8059-7019-7(3))* Dorrance Publishing Co., Inc.

Carrillo, P. S. Desert Passage. 2008. (ENG.). 192p. (YA). (gr. 6-18). pap. 10.95 *(978-1-55885-517-5(3)*, Piñata Books) Arte Publico Pr.

Cart, Michael. Necessary Noise: Stories about Our Families as They Really Are. Noruzi, Charlotte, illus. 2006. (ENG.). 256p. (YA). (gr. 8-12). reprint ed. pap. 8.99 *(978-0-06-051437-2(X)*, HarperTeen) HarperCollins Pubs.

Carter, Alden R. Up Country. 2004. (ENG.). 256p. (YA). (gr. 7-5). 7.99 *(978-0-14-240243-6(5)*, Speak) Penguin Young Readers Group.

Carter, Kristin. What Matters Most: A Children's Book of Families. 2005. 47p. pap. 24.95 *(978-1-4137-3631-1(9))* PublishAmerica, Inc.

Carthage, Lynn. Haunted. 2015. (Arnaud Legacy Ser.: 1). (ENG.). 288p. (YA). (gr. 9). pap. 9.95 *(978-1-61773-626-1(0))* Kensington Publishing Corp.

Carttar, Debra. Picturing Lucy. 2010. pap. 14.95 *(978-0-7414-6195-7(1))* Infinity Publishing.

Carver, David. Lester Returns Home with His New Friend La'doo, 1 vol. Carver, Erin, illus. 2010. 28p. 24.95 *(978-1-4489-6340-9(0))* PublishAmerica, Inc.

Casanova, Mary. Frozen. 2013. (Fesler-Lampert Minnesota Heritage Ser.). (ENG.). 256p. pap. 11.95 *(978-0-8166-8057-3(4))* Univ. of Minnesota Pr.

Casselman, Grace. A Walk in the Park. 2005. (ENG., Illus.). 160p. (J). (gr. -1-7). pap. 8.95 *(978-1-894917-19-3(7)*, Napoleon & Co.) Dundurn CAN. Dist: Ingram Publisher Services.

Cassity, Brittney. Fiddlebug. 2008. 52p. pap. 22.49 *(978-1-4389-2537-0(8))* AuthorHouse.

Castillo, Ina. Red the Super Wiener. 2008. 24p. pap. 24.95 *(978-1-60474-897-0(4))* America Star Bks.

Castleberry, Stephen B., Sr. & Castleberry, Susie. Where There's Smoke. 2004. (Farm Mystery Ser.). (J). per. 8.50 *(978-1-891907-14-2(X))* Castleberry Farms Pr.

Castlemon, Harry. The Sportsman's Club among the Trappers. 2005. pap. 28.95 *(978-1-4179-5498-8(1))* Kessinger Publishing, LLC.

—Sportsmans Club in the Saddle. 2006. pap. 30.95 *(978-1-4286-5231-6(0))* Kessinger Publishing, LLC.

Castro, Adam-Troy. Gustav Gloom & the Four Terrors #3. Margiotta, Kristen, illus. 2014. (Gustav Gloom Ser.: 3). (ENG.). 248p. (J). (gr. 3-7). 7.99 *(978-0-448-48330-6(0)*, Grosset & Dunlap) Penguin Young Readers Group.

—Gustav Gloom & the People Taker #1. Margiotta, Kristen, illus. 2014. (Gustav Gloom Ser.: 1). (ENG.). 248p. (J). (gr. 3-7). 7.99 *(978-0-448-48328-3(9)*, Grosset & Dunlap) Penguin Young Readers Group.

Cataneo, D. M. Eggplant Alley. 2013. (ENG.). 352p. (YA). (gr. 7-9). 17.95 *(978-1-59373-146-5(9))* Bunker Hill Publishing, Inc.

Catran, Wendy. Katie Raven's Fire. 2003. 205p. (Orig.). pap. *(978-0-7344-0497-8(2)*, Lothian Children's Bks.) Hachette Australia.

Caudill, Rebecca. Happy Little Family. Merwin, Decie, illus. 2004. 107p. (J). pap. 10.95 *(978-1-883937-72-0(8))* Bethlehem Bks.

—Up & down the River. Merwin, Decie, illus. 2005. 143p. (J). (gr. -1-17). pap. 11.95 *(978-1-883937-81-2(7))* Bethlehem Bks.

Caught in the Storm: Individual Title Six-Packs. (gr. k-1). 23.00 *(978-0-7635-9046-8(0))* Rigby Education.

Celcer, Irene. The Gift. Gatto, Horacio, illus. 2009. (J). pap. *(978-0-9755810-6-3(6))* Graphite Pr.

Cesena, Denise. Caring - Companion Book. Perez, Maureen T., illus. l.t. ed. 2003. 12p. (J). 2.00 *(978-0-9740418-7-2(4))* Night Light Pubns., LLC.

Cesena, Denise & Perez, Maureen T. Caring. Perez, Maureen T., illus. l.t. ed. 2003. (Illus.). 28p. (J). 10.00 *(978-0-9740418-6-5(6))* Night Light Pubns., LLC.

Cesmat, Sheryl. Adopted Kitty from the City. 2013. 36p. pap. 18.41 *(978-1-4669-8285-7(3))* Trafford Publishing.

Chamberlin, Kate. Charles & David. Wroth, Dean, illus. 2010. 32p. (J). pap. 9.95 *(978-0-944727-37-9(9))*; lib. bdg. 15.95 *(978-0-944727-36-2(0))* Jason & Nordic Pubs. (Turtle Bks.).

Chapman, Brenda. Running Scared. 2004. (Jennifer Bannon Mystery Ser.: 1). (ENG.). 128p. (J). pap. 8.95 *(978-1-894917-14-8(6)*, Napoleon & Co.) Dundurn CAN. Dist: Ingram Publisher Services.

—Trail of Secrets. 2009. (Jennifer Bannon Mystery Ser.: 4). (ENG.). 144p. (YA). (gr. 7-18). pap. 9.95 *(978-1-894917-76-6(6)*, Napoleon & Co.) Dundurn CAN. Dist: Ingram Publisher Services.

Chatterton, Martin. Brain Full of Holes. 2008. 208p. *(978-1-921272-28-8(7))* Little Hare Bks. AUS. Dist: HarperCollins Pubs. Australia.

Cheng, Jack. See You in the Cosmos. 2017. (ENG.). 320p. (J). (gr. 5-9). 16.99 *(978-0-399-18637-0(9)*, Dial Bks) Penguin Young Readers Group.

Child, Lauren. Don't Look Now. Child, Lauren, illus. 2008. (Clarice Bean Ser.). (ENG., Illus.). 256p. (J). (gr. 3-7). pap. 5.99 *(978-0-7636-3935-8(4))* Candlewick Pr.

—I Am Not Sleepy & I Will Not Go to Bed. Child, Lauren, illus. 2008. (Charlie & Lola Ser.). (ENG., Illus.). 16p. (J). (gr. -1-2). 19.99 *(978-0-7636-4098-9(0))* Candlewick Pr.

Child, Lauren, et al. Carys Blodyn, Dyma Fi. 2005. (WEL., Illus.). 32p. pap. *(978-1-85596-670-3(0))* Dref Wen.

—Fi'n Hollol, Carys Blodyn. 2005. (WEL., Illus.). 192p. pap. *(978-1-85596-675-8(1))* Dref Wen.

Children's Press, contrib. by. Family Photo & Other Family Stories. 2008. (Rookie Reader Treasury Ser.). (ENG., Illus.). 128p. (J). 11.95 *(978-0-531-21725-2(6)*, Children's Pr.) Scholastic Library Publishing.

Choldenko, Gennifer. Notes from a Liar & Her Dog. 2003. (ENG.). 240p. (J). (gr. 3-7). pap. 7.99 *(978-0-14-250068-2(2)*, Puffin Books) Penguin Young Readers Group.

—Notes from a Liar & Her Dog. 2004. 224p. (J). (gr. 4-7). pap. 38.00 incl. audio *(978-0-8072-2097-9(3)*, Listening Library) Random Hse. Audio Publishing Group.

Choyce, Lesley. Crash, 1 vol. 2013. (Orca Soundings Ser.). (ENG.). 136p. (YA). (gr. 8-12). pap. 9.95 *(978-1-4598-0522-4(4))*; lib. bdg. 16.95 *(978-1-4598-0525-5(9))* Orca Bk. Pubs. USA.

Christelow, Eileen. Five Little Monkeys Jumping on the Bed Lap Board Book. 2008. (Five Little Monkeys Story Ser.). (ENG., Illus.). 30p. (J). (gr. -1 — 1). bds. 12.99 *(978-0-547-13176-4(3))* Houghton Mifflin Harcourt Publishing Co.

Christensen, Bob. Gaylord Goose. Marsh, Bobbi, illus. 2011. 28p. pap. 12.95 *(978-1-61493-014-3(7))* Peppertree Pr., The.

Christian Mauricio Constante. What a Catch! 2009. 24p. pap. 11.49 *(978-1-4389-6423-2(4))* AuthorHouse.

Christmas. 2004. (J). mass mkt. 8.99 *(978-0-9741215-4-3(1))* Stories of My Life, The.

Christopher, Danielle. Harley. 2009. 20p. pap. 9.29 *(978-1-4251-9004-0(9))* Trafford Publishing.

Christopher, Matt. Baseball World Series. (Little League Ser.: 5). (ENG., 208p. (J). (gr. 3-7). 2015. Illus.). pap. 7.00 *(978-0-316-21295-3(4))* 2014. 16.00 *(978-0-316-22046-0(9))* Little, Brown Bks. for Young Readers.

—Lacrosse Face-Off. 2010. (Matt Christopher Sports Library). 128p. (J). (gr. 4-6). lib. bdg. 26.60 *(978-1-59953-355-1(3))* Norwood Hse. Pr.

—Play Ball! 2013. (Little League Ser.: 1). (ENG.). 240p. (J). (gr. 3-7). pap. 7.99 *(978-0-316-19975-9(3))* Little, Brown Bks. for Young Readers.

—Zero's Slider. Delaney, Molly, illus. 2009. (New Peach Street Mudders Sports Library). 64p. (J). (gr. 2-4). lib. bdg. 23.93 *(978-1-59953-323-0(5))* Norwood Hse. Pr.

Church, Peggy Pond. The Pancake Stories: Cuentos Del Panqueque. Chilton, Noel, tr. Church, Elizabeth Comfort, illus. 2013. (ENG & SPA.). 96p. (J). 12.95 *(978-0-8263-5387-0(8))* Univ. of New Mexico Pr.

Ciencin, Scott, et al. Point-Blank Paintball, 1 vol. Aburto, Jesus, illus. 2010. (Sports Illustrated Kids Graphic Novels Ser.). (ENG.). 56p. (gr. 2-3). pap. 7.19 *(978-1-4342-2293-0(4))*; 26.65 *(978-1-4342-1914-5(3))* Stone Arch Bks.

Citak, Michael J. The Adventures of Leo- & the Curse of the Dreaded Doors. 2008. 51p. pap. 22.95 *(978-1-4357-5271-9(6))* Lulu Pr., Inc.

Citra, Becky. Never to Be Told, 1 vol. 2006. (ENG.). 224p. (J). (gr. 5-9). per. 8.95 *(978-1-55143-567-1(5))* Orca Bk. Pubs. USA.

—Whiteout, 1 vol. 2009. (Orca Young Readers Ser.). (ENG.). 112p. (J). (gr. 3-6). pap. 7.95 *(978-1-55469-083-1(8))* Orca Bk. Pubs. USA.

C.J. Elgert. The Elder Brothers & the Padstow Crystals. 2009. 284p. 27.95 *(978-1-4401-7678-4(7))*; pap. 17.95 *(978-1-4401-7676-0(0))* iUniverse, Inc.

Clark, Abbie. Way down Yonder in the Paw Paw Patch. Taylor, Jennifer, illus. 2006. 32p. (J). (gr. -1-3). per. 16.95 *(978-1-59858-129-4(5))* Dog Ear Publishing, LLC.

Clark, Anthony & Whybrow, Ian. Little Wolf's Book of Badness. 2008. (ENG.). 96p. (J). pap. 18.95 *(978-1-84002-823-2(8))* Oberon Bks., Ltd. GBR. Dist: Consortium Bk. Sales & Distribution.

Clark, Eleanor. Katie Sue: Heading West. 2007. (Eleanor Ser.: Bk. 3). 220p. 14.99 *(978-0-9788726-0-1(6))* HonorNet.

Clark, Kent & Snider, Brandon T. Peter Powers & the League of Lying Lizards! Bardin, Dave, illus. 2017. (Peter Powers Ser.: 4). (ENG.). 128p. (J). (gr. 1-5). 15.99 **(978-0-316-54640-9(2))** Little, Brown Bks. for Young Readers.

Clarke, Lorin. Our Last Trip to the Market. Vane, Mitch, illus. 2017. (ENG.). 32p. (J). (-k). 17.99 **(978-1-925266-96-2(6))** Allen & Unwin AUS. Dist: Independent Pubs. Group.

Clarke, Margaret Bruce. Hunter's Marjory. 2007. 148p. per. *(978-1-4068-4613-3(9))* Echo Library.

Clausman, Rachel. Miriam, Come Sit. 2011. 24p. pap. 11.32 *(978-1-4634-4812-7(0))* AuthorHouse.

Clay, Ian. Coyote Lake. 2007. 104p. per. 9.95 *(978-0-595-44590-5(X))* iUniverse, Inc.

Clay Iii, J. Percy. Sampson's Pumpkin Playhouse. 2012. 30p. 24.95 *(978-1-4626-7226-4(4))* America Star Bks.

Cleary, Beverly. Beezus & Ramona. Darling, Louis & Rogers, Jacqueline, illus. 2013. (Ramona Ser.: 1). (ENG.). 208p. (J). (gr. 3-7). pap. 6.99 *(978-0-380-70918-2(X))* HarperCollins Pubs.

—Beezus & Ramona. Darling, Louis et al, illus. 2013. (Ramona Ser.: 1). (ENG.). 208p. (J). (gr. 3-7). 16.99 *(978-0-688-21076-2(7))* HarperCollins Pubs.

—Beezus & Ramona. Dockray, Tracy & Rogers, Jacqueline, illus. movie tie-in ed. 2010. (Ramona Ser.: 1). (ENG.). 208p. (J). (gr. 3-7). pap. 5.99 *(978-0-06-191461-4(4)*, HarperFestival) HarperCollins Pubs.

—Beezus & Ramona. 2011. 9.01 *(978-0-7848-3570-8(5)*, Everbind) Marco Bk. Co.

—Beezus & Ramona. (Ramona Quimby Ser.). 142p. (J). (gr. 3-5). pap. 4.99 *(978-0-8072-1441-1(8)*, Listening Library) Random Hse. Audio Publishing Group.

—Beezus & Ramona. Darling, Louis, illus. (gr. 3-5). pap. *(978-0-545-24980-5(5))* Scholastic, Inc.

—Beezus & Ramona. (Ramona Quimby Ser.: 1). (J). 2013. lib. bdg. 17.20 *(978-0-88103-289-5(1))* 2010. lib. bdg. 16.00 *(978-0-606-15072-9(2))* Turtleback Bks. (Turtleback).

—Ramona Quimby, Age 8. Rogers, Jacqueline, illus. 2016. (Ramona Ser.: 6). 208p. (J). (gr. 3-7). 12.99 *(978-0-06-246454-5(X))* HarperCollins Pubs.
—Ramona Quimby, Age 8 Read-Aloud Edition. Rogers, Jacqueline, illus. 2016. (Ramona Ser.: 6). 208p. (J). (gr. 3-7). 17.99 *(978-0-06-245327-3(0))* HarperCollins Pubs.
Cleaver, Vera & Cleaver, Bill. Donde Florecen los Lirios. (SPA.). 168p. (YA). (gr. 5-8). *(978-84-204-3648-7(8),* AF0285) Ediciones Alfaguara ESP. Dist: Lectorum Pubns., Inc.
Clements, Andrew. Lost & Found. Elliott, Mark, illus. (ENG.). (J). (gr. 3-7). 2010. 192p. pap. 7.99 *(978-1-4169-0986-6(9))* 2008. 176p. 16.99 *(978-1-4169-0985-9(0))* Simon & Schuster Children's Publishing. (Atheneum Bks. for Young Readers).
—Lunch Money. Selznick, Brian, illus. 2005. (ENG.). 224p. (J). (gr. 3-7). 18.99 *(978-0-689-86683-8(6),* Atheneum Bks. for Young Readers) Simon & Schuster Children's Publishing.
Clifford, Ross. The Shiddakovich Adventure. 2009. 122p. pap. 12.88 *(978-1-4092-3520-0(3))* Lulu Pr., Inc.
Coates, Charmian. Secret Staircase. 2011. (Illus.). 88p. pap. 27.76 *(978-1-4567-8715-8(2))* AuthorHouse.
Coatsworth, Elizabeth. Away Goes Sally. Sewell, Helen, illus. 2004. 118p. (J). pap. 10.95 *(978-1-883937-83-6(3))* Bethlehem Bks.
Coe, Kimberly. My Dad Is A Marine. Coe, Kimberly, illus. 2007. (Illus.). 46p. (J). per. 12.00 *(978-0-9787113-1-3(9),* Ithaca Pr.) Authors & Artists Publishers of New York, Inc.
Cohagan, Carolyn. The Lost Children. 2010. (ENG.). 320p. (J). (gr. 3-7). 16.99 *(978-1-4169-8616-4(2),* Simon & Schuster/Paula Wiseman Bks.) Simon & Schuster/Paula Wiseman Bks.
Cohen, Marina. The Doll's Eye. 2017. (ENG.). 208p. (J). 16.99 *(978-1-62672-204-0(8),* 9781626722040) Roaring Brook Pr.
Cohn, Rachel. You Know Where to Find Me. 2009. (ENG.). 224p. (YA). (gr. 7). pap. 8.99 *(978-0-689-87860-2(5),* Simon & Schuster Bks. For Young Readers) Simon & Schuster Bks. For Young Readers.
Cohn, Rachel & Levithan, David. The Twelve Days of Dash & Lily. 2016. (ENG.). 224p. (YA). (gr. 7). 17.99 *(978-0-399-55380-6(0),* Knopf Bks. for Young Readers) Random Hse. Children's Bks.
Colbert, Catherine McNulty. Downsize Your Parents! Tips for Moving from a 2400 Sq Ft Home into an 800 Sq Ft Home. 2009. 34p. pap. 9.00 *(978-1-935125-48-8(6))* Robertson Publishing.
Cole, Babette. Los Problemas con Mi Tio.Tr. of Trouble with Uncle. (SPA.). 28p. (J). 12.95 *(978-84-233-2126-1(6))* Ediciones Destino ESP. Dist: Planeta Publishing Corp.
Cole, Penelope Ann. Magical Matthew. Collier, Kevin Scott, illus. 2012. 24p. pap. 10.95 *(978-1-61633-326-3(X))* Guardian Angel Publishing, Inc.
Cole, Penelope Anne. Magical Matthew. Collier, Kevin Scott, illus. 2012. 24p. 19.95 *(978-1-61633-325-6(1))* Guardian Angel Publishing, Inc.
Coleman, Emily. Christmas with Mary, Mom, Dad, & Dee. 2009. 20p. pap. 10.49 *(978-1-4490-4501-2(4))* AuthorHouse.
Coll, Ivar Da. Carlos. Coll, Ivar Da, illus. 2003. (SPA., Illus.). 52p. (J). (gr. k-3). pap. 9.95 *(978-958-8061-64-1(4))* Santillana USA Publishing Co., Inc.
Collins, Beth. Every Family Is Special. 2009. 24p. pap. 12.00 *(978-1-4389-5076-1(4))* AuthorHouse.
Collins, Rachel. Sidney Swallow's Baby Sister. 2010. 36p. pap. 16.95 *(978-0-557-44953-8(7))* Lulu Pr., Inc.
—Sidney Swallow's Christmas. 2010. 32p. pap. 16.95 *(978-0-557-62625-0(0))* Lulu Pr., Inc.
Collins, Yvonne & Rideout, Sandy. The Black Sheep. 2007. 348p. (J). *(978-1-4287-4665-7(X))* Hyperion Pr.
Colvin, S. R. R. The Krybosian Stairpath: Magnetic Reversal. 2009. 200p. pap. 14.95 *(978-1-4401-5927-5(0))* iUniverse, Inc.
Coman, Carolyn. Sneaking Suspicions. Shepperson, Rob, illus. 2007. (ENG.). 204p. (J). (gr. 4-6). 16.95 *(978-1-59078-491-4(X),* Front Street) Boyds Mills Pr.
Condi-Babich, Kris. 4Cam. us. 2004. 71p. pap. 19.95 *(978-1-4137-2241-3(5))* America Star Bks.
Conlin, Laura E. Winston's Wild Journeys: Live Outside Your Shell. 2011. 43p. (J). 18.95 *(978-1-4327-6885-0(9))* Outskirts Pr., Inc.
Conner, Sharon Landsberg. The Magnetizing Princess: A children's story that uses some of the most powerful tools available, to get more of what you Want. 2007. 56p. per. 8.95 *(978-0-595-44229-4(3))* iUniverse, Inc.
Conness, Steven A. George Huck, the Founding of Huckville: The Huck Family Chronicles, 1 vol. 2010. 78p. pap. 19.95 *(978-1-4489-4471-2(6))* PublishAmerica, Inc.
Cook, Jacqueline. The Little Bear Who Worried Too Much: Suzie Bear Goes to London. 2011. 34p. (gr. 1-4). pap. 13.50 *(978-1-60976-875-1(2),* Eloquent Bks.) Strategic Book Publishing & Rights Agency (SBPRA).
Cook, Julia. I Want to Be the Only Dog! DuFalla, Anita, illus. 2015. (ENG.). 32p. (J). pap. 10.95 *(978-1-934490-86-0(5))* Boys Town Pr.
Cook, William. Worth the Wait. Kim, Jeehyun, illus. 2007. 32p. (J). per. 15.00 *(978-0-9791387-0-6(1));* per. 15.00 *(978-0-9791387-1-3(X))* Yadda Yadda Pr.
Cooke, Trish. Look Back! Birch, Caroline, illus. 2014. (ENG.). 32p. (J). 17.95 *(978-1-56656-980-4(X),* Crocodile Bks.) Interlink Publishing Group, Inc.
—So Much! Oxenbury, Helen, illus. 2008. (ENG.). 48p. (J). (gr. -1-2). pap. 6.99 *(978-0-7636-4091-0(3))* Candlewick Pr.
Coolidge, Susan. Clover. Mcdermot, Jessie, illus. 2007. (ENG.). 168p. per. *(978-1-4065-1524-4(8))* Dodo Pr.
Cooney, Barbara. Miss Rumphius. Cooney, Barbara, illus. 2004. (Illus.). 28p. (J). (gr. k-2). reprint ed. pap. 6.00 *(978-0-7567-7107-2(2))* DIANE Publishing Co.
Cooney, Caroline B. Diamonds in the Shadow. 2009. (ENG.). 240p. (YA). 9.99 *(978-1-4000-7424-2(X),* WaterBrook Pr.) Crown Publishing Group.
—Diamonds in the Shadow. 2009. (ENG.). 240p. (YA). (gr. 7). pap. 9.99 *(978-0-385-73262-8(7),* Delacorte Bks. for Young Readers) Random Hse. Children's Bks.
—A Friend at Midnight. 2008. (ENG.). 192p. (YA). (gr. 7). pap. 8.99 *(978-1-4000-7209-5(3),* WaterBrook Pr.) Crown Publishing Group.
—A Friend at Midnight. 2008. (ENG.). 192p. (YA). (gr. 7). pap. 8.99 *(978-0-385-73327-4(5),* Delacorte Bks. for Young Readers) Random Hse. Children's Bks.
Coons, Mary. The Piglys & the Hundred-Year Mystery. 2013. 216p. (gr. 4-6). 33.99 *(978-1-4808-0141-7(0));* pap. 15.99 *(978-1-4808-0139-4(9))* Archway Publishing.
Cooper, Constance. Guile. 2017. (ENG.). 384p. (YA). (gr. 7). pap. 9.99 *(978-0-544-93691-1(4),* HMH Books For Young Readers) Houghton Mifflin Harcourt Publishing Co.
—Guile. 2016. (ENG.). 384p. (YA). (gr. 7). 17.99 *(978-0-544-45171-1(6),* Clarion Bks.) Houghton Mifflin Harcourt Trade & Reference Pubs.
—Guile. 2017. (ENG.). (YA). (gr. 7). lib. bdg. 20.85 ***(978-0-606-39821-3(X))*** Turtleback Bks.
Cooper, Judith. Many Moons. 2008. 28p. per. 24.95 *(978-1-4241-9284-7(6))* America Star Bks.
Corazon. (Coleccion Estrella). (SPA., Illus.). 64p. (J). 14.95 *(978-950-11-0005-1(7),* SGM005) Sigmar ARG. Dist: Continental Bk. Co., Inc.
Corbett Sampson, Natalie. Game Plan. 2013. 362p. pap. *(978-1-927746-09-7(4))* Fierce Ink Pr. Co-Op, Ltd.
Cordell, Matthew. Wish. Cordell, Matthew, illus. 2015. (ENG., Illus.). 48p. (J). (gr. -1-k). 16.99 *(978-1-4847-0875-0(X))* Hyperion Bks. for Children.
Córdova, Zoraida. Labyrinth Lost. (Brooklyn Brujas Ser.: 1). (ENG.). (YA). (gr. 8-12). 2017. 352p. pap. 10.99 *(978-1-4926-2316-8(4))* 2016. 336p. 17.99 *(978-1-4926-2094-5(7),* 9781492620945) Sourcebooks, Inc.
Corlyn, Ron. The House That Grew. 2013. 24p. pap. 24.95 *(978-1-63000-118-6(X))* America Star Bks.
Cory, Kim Delmar. Home to Mackinac: The Tale of Young Jack Murphy's Discovery of Loyalty, Family, & Forgiveness. Evans, Laura, illus. 2007. (ENG.). 175p. (J). (gr. 3-7). per. 9.95 *(978-0-911872-87-3(6))* Mackinac State Historic Parks.
Cosimano, Elle. The Suffering Tree. 2017. (ENG.). 368p. (YA). (gr. 9-17). 17.99 ***(978-1-4847-2659-4(6))*** Hyperion Bks. for Children.
Cosson, M. J. The Pirate, Big Fist, & Me, 1 vol. Garvey, Brann, illus. 2006. (Vortex Bks.). (ENG.). 112p. (gr. 2-3). 26.65 *(978-1-59889-068-6(9),* Vortex Bks.) Stone Arch Bks.
Cote, Nancy. Leonard's Beard. 2016. (ENG., Illus.). 32p. (J). (gr. -1-k). 16.99 *(978-1-5107-0796-2(4),* Sky Pony Pr.) Skyhorse Publishing Co., Inc.
Cotler, Steve. Cheesie Mack Is Not Exactly Famous. Holgate, Douglas, illus. 2014. (Cheesie Mack Ser.). (ENG.). 256p. (J). (gr. 3-7). 15.99 *(978-0-385-36984-8(0),* Random Hse. Bks. for Young Readers) Random Hse. Children's Bks.
Cottrell-Bentley, Lisa M. Wright on Time: Collection 1. Bauerle, Tanja, illus. 2012. 376p. pap. 19.99 *(978-1-937848-00-2(0))* Do Life Right, Inc.
Courcy, Jon. Scourges: Seeds of Dissent. 2005. (YA). per. 19.95 *(978-0-9741864-4-3(9))* NT Publishing, L.L.C.
Courgeon, Rémi. Toothpick. 2017. (ENG., Illus.). 36p. (J). (gr. k-4). 17.95 *(978-1-59270-210-7(4))* Enchanted Lion Bks., LLC.
CourseCrafters Staff, des. Interactive Storybooks - the Family Home. 2003. (J). spiral bd. 14.95 *(978-1-58605-965-1(3))* LeapFrog Enterprises, Inc.
Cousins Camp. 2010. 32p. pap. 12.99 *(978-1-4490-8387-8(0))* AuthorHouse.
Covey, Sean. When I Grow Up: Habit 2. Curtis, Stacy, illus. 2009. (7 Habits of Happy Kids Ser.: 2). (ENG.). 32p. (J). (gr. -1-1). 7.99 *(978-1-4169-9424-4(6),* Simon & Schuster Bks. For Young Readers) Simon & Schuster Bks. For Young Readers.
Coville, Bruce. Cursed. 2016. (Enchanted Files Ser.: 1). lib. bdg. 17.20 *(978-0-606-38460-5(X))* Turtleback Bks.
Cowan, Charlotte. Moose with Loose Poops. Neal, Penelope, illus. 2008. (Dr. Hippo Ser.). (ENG.). 32p. (J). (gr. -1-2). 17.95 *(978-0-9753516-5-9(6))* Hippocratic Pr., The.
Craddock, Sonia. Runaway Gran, 1 vol. 2006. (Lorimer Streetlights Ser.). (ENG.). 168p. (J). (gr. 2-5). 7.95 *(978-1-55028-953-4(5),* 9781550289534) Lorimer, James & Co., Ltd., Pubs. CAN. Dist: Casemate Pubs. & Bk. Distributors, LLC.
Craft, Jerry. Mama's Boyz: Because Learning Shouldn't Stop at 3 o'Clock!: Home Schoolin', 2 vols. 2007. (Illus.). 112p. (YA). per. 9.95 *(978-0-9796132-0-3(5))* Mama's Boyz, Inc.
Crane, Carol. The Brown Mountain Lights: A North Carolina Legend. Wyrick, Monica, illus. 2012. 36p. (J). pap. 11.99 *(978-1-935711-19-3(9))* Peak City Publishing, LLC.
Crawford-Haynes, Debra. Bedtime with Julian. 2010. 32p. 16.99 *(978-1-4520-6943-2(3))* AuthorHouse.
Crawford, Marie. Nutmeg, Ginger & Little Joan. 2012. 24p. pap. 17.99 *(978-1-62230-186-7(2))* Salem Author Services.
Creech, Sharon. Pleasing the Ghost. Schuett, Stacey, illus. 2013. (Trophy Bk.). 112p. (J). (gr. 3-7). reprint ed. pap. 5.99 *(978-0-06-440686-4(5))* HarperCollins Pubs.
Creech, Sharon. Walk Two Moons: a Harper Classic. 2017. (Harper Classic Ser.). 288p. (J). (gr. 3-7). 16.99 ***(978-0-06-265877-7(8))*** HarperCollins Pubs.
Crisis Maximus! Individual Title Six-Packs. (Bookweb Ser.). 32p. (gr. 6-18). 34.00 *(978-0-7578-0902-6(2))* Rigby Education.
Cronin, Doreen. Cyclone. 2017. (ENG., Illus.). 352p. (J). (gr. 4-8). 16.99 ***(978-1-4814-3525-3(6),*** Atheneum/Caitlyn Dlouhy Books) Simon & Schuster Children's Publishing.
Cronin, Doreen. Dark Shadows: Yes, Another Misadventure. Gilpin, Stephen, illus. 2017. (Chicken Squad Ser.: 4). (ENG.). 128p. (J). (gr. 2-5). 12.99 *(978-1-4814-5049-2(2),* Atheneum/Caitlyn Dlouhy Books) Simon & Schuster Children's Publishing.
Crosson, Denise D. Mommy's Gone to Treatment. Motz, Mike, illus. 2008. (ENG.). 44p. (J). (gr. k-3). pap. 14.95 *(978-0-9799869-1-8(5))* Central Recovery Pr.
Crowder, Melanie. A Nearer Moon. 2015. (ENG., Illus.). 160p. (J). (gr. 3-7). 16.99 *(978-1-4814-4148-3(5))* Simon & Schuster Children's Publishing.
—A Nearer Moon. 2016. (ENG.). 176p. (J). (gr. 3-7). 18.40 *(978-0-606-39238-9(6))* Turtleback Bks.
Crowley, Kieran Mark. Colm & the Lazarus Key. 2009. (ENG., Illus.). 224p. (J). pap. 14.95 *(978-1-85635-646-6(9))* Mercier Pr., Ltd., The IRL. Dist: Dufour Editions, Inc.
Crum, Karen Boyden. Family Angels. 2012. 32p. pap. 19.99 *(978-1-4772-7502-3(9))* AuthorHouse.
Crum, Shutta. Dozens of Cousins. Catrow, David, illus. 2013. (ENG.). 32p. (J). (gr. -1-3). 16.99 *(978-0-618-15874-4(X))* Houghton Mifflin Harcourt Publishing Co.
Crutcher, Chris. Chinese Handcuffs. 2004. (ENG.). 304p. (YA). (gr. 9). pap. 9.99 *(978-0-06-059839-6(5),* Greenwillow Bks.) HarperCollins Pubs.
Culwell, Lori. The Dirt. 2011. (ENG.). 208p. (YA). pap. 11.95 *(978-1-935961-36-9(5),* Booktrope Editions) Booktrope.
Cummings, Mag. Fishplates & Frogs. 2007. 272p. per. *(978-1-905529-99-5(6))* Grosvenor Hse. Publishing Ltd.
Cummings, Phil. Newspaper Hats. Swan, Owen, illus. 2016. (ENG.). 32p. (J). (gr. -1-2). lib. bdg. 16.95 *(978-1-58089-783-9(5))* Charlesbridge Publishing, Inc.
Cummings, Quasheba Giri. The World's First Submarine. 2008. 20p. pap. 15.49 *(978-1-4389-1273-8(0))* AuthorHouse.
Cumpiano, Ina. Quinito's Neighborhood (El Vecindario de Quinito) Ramirez, José, illus. 2013. (ENG & SPA.). 32p. (J). (gr. -1-3). pap. 9.95 *(978-0-89239-229-2(0))* Lee & Low Bks., Inc.
Cumyn, Alan. Dear Sylvia, 1 vol. 2009. (ENG.). 184p. (J). pap. 8.95 *(978-0-88899-848-4(1))* Groundwood Bks. CAN. Dist: Publishers Group West (PGW).
Cuno, Sabine. Abre, Cierra y Aprende! Caballero, D., tr. Senner, Katja, illus. 2007. 14p. (J). (gr. -1). *(978-970-718-489-3(2),* Silver Dolphin en Español) Advanced Marketing, S. de R. L. de C. V.
Curato, Mike. Little Elliot, Big Family. Curato, Mike, illus. 2015. (Little Elliot Ser.). (ENG., Illus.). 40p. (J). (gr. -1-3). 17.99 *(978-0-8050-9826-6(7),* 9780805098266, Holt, Henry & Co. Bks. For Young Readers) Holt, Henry & Co.
Currim, Nazli. Grandma Lives with Us. Tung, Kadhima Ren, illus. 2010. 46p. (J). 16.95 *(978-0-9814629-5-0(2))* Acacia Publishing, Inc.
Currinder, Michael. Running Full Tilt. 2017. (ENG.). 336p. (YA). (gr. 7). lib. bdg. 17.99 ***(978-1-58089-802-7(5),*** Charlesbridge Teen) Charlesbridge Publishing, Inc.
Curry, Jane Louise. The Egyptian Box. 2008. (ENG.). 196p. (J). (gr. 4-6). pap. 10.95 *(978-1-4169-7140-5(8),* Simon & Schuster/Paula Wiseman Bks.) Simon & Schuster/Paula Wiseman Bks.
Curtis, D. D. Catching Rodeo Fever. 2011. 32p. pap. 16.95 *(978-1-4560-7328-2(1))* America Star Bks.
Curtis, Jamie Lee. Jamie Lee Curtis's Books to Grow by Treasury. Cornell, Laura, illus. 2009. 208p. (J). (gr. -1-3). 24.99 *(978-0-06-180364-2(2))* HarperCollins Pubs.
Cutler, Jane. Family Dinner. 2011. 116p. pap. 9.95 *(978-1-4502-5374-1(1))* iUniverse, Inc.
Cuzzone, Beth. Two Lily Pads & One Froggie Family. 2009. 36p. pap. 16.95 *(978-1-4490-2179-5(4))* AuthorHouse.
Daddy Saved the Day: Six-Pack. (Greetings Ser.: Vol. 3). 24p. (gr. 2-3). 31.00 *(978-0-7635-9417-6(2))* Rigby Education.
Dahl, Michael. The Book That Ate My Brother, 1 vol. Kendall, Bradford, illus. 2010. (Return to the Library of Doom Ser.). (ENG.). 72p. (gr. 1-3). lib. bdg. 23.99 *(978-1-4342-2144-5(X),* Zone Bks.) Stone Arch Bks.
—Claws in the Snow, 1 vol. Evans, Mark & Vue, Tou, illus. 2009. (Dragonblood Ser.). (ENG.). 40p. (gr. 1-3). 23.99 *(978-1-4342-1262-7(9),* Zone Bks.) Stone Arch Bks.
Daines, Ellie. Lolly Luck. 2012. (ENG.). 186p. (J). (gr. 4-7). pap. 8.99 *(978-1-84939-396-6(6))* Andersen Pr. GBR. Dist: Independent Pubs. Group.
Dalhaimer Bartkowski, Anna. Maggie Visits Grandpa: A Coloring Adventure. Dalhaimer Bartkowski, Anna, illus. 2007. (Illus.). 32p. pap. 8.99 *(978-0-9790720-1-7(8))* Infinite Adventure.
Dalmatian Press Staff. My Family Tree. 2008. (ENG.). 11p. bds. 4.95 *(978-1-58117-718-3(6),* Intervisual/Piggy Toes) Bendon, Inc.
Damrell, John. The Flooring Family. 2008. 40p. pap. 24.95 *(978-1-60563-067-6(1))* America Star Bks.
Dana Kittendorf. Trail of Dreams. 2009. 136p. 21.95 *(978-1-4401-7787-3(2));* pap. 11.95 *(978-1-4401-7785-9(6))* iUniverse, Inc.
Daniels, Cheri & Nicewander, Carol. Shadow Tail Meets the Gang. 2008. 24p. pap. 11.49 *(978-1-4389-3259-0(6))* AuthorHouse.
Danneberg, Julie. Family Reminders. Shelley, John, illus. 2013. (ENG.). 112p. (J). (gr. 3-7). pap. 6.95 *(978-1-58089-321-3(X))* Charlesbridge Publishing, Inc.
Danziger, Paula. You Can't Eat Your Chicken Pox, Amber Brown. Ross, Tony, illus. 2006. (Amber Brown Ser.: No. 2). 100p. (gr. 2-5). 15.00 *(978-0-7569-6756-7(2))* Perfection Learning Corp.
D'Arcy, Megan. Be Happy. Gawthrop, Shaughn, illus. 2011. 32p. (J). 14.95 *(978-1-879094-95-6(9))* Momentum Bks., LLC.
Darcy N. Carmichael. Ember's Rising. 2009. 104p. pap. 9.95 *(978-1-4401-6368-5(5))* iUniverse, Inc.
Darke, J. A. Fade to Black. Evans, Neil, illus. 2016. (Spine Shivers Ser.). (ENG.). 128p. (gr. 3-4). lib. bdg. 26.65 *(978-1-4965-3070-7(5))* Stone Arch Bks.
—Tech Fury. Evergreen, Nelson, illus. 2015. (Spine Shivers Ser.). (ENG.). 128p. (gr. 3-4). lib. bdg. 26.65 *(978-1-4965-0218-6(3))* Stone Arch Bks.
Dasilva, D. Mom Has Left & Gone to Vegas. Craig, Dan, illus. 2008. 32p. pap. 19.95 *(978-1-59858-603-9(3))* Dog Ear Publishing, LLC.
David, Jamie. Johann Sebastian Humpbach. David, Jamie, illus. 2009. (Illus.). 167p. pap. 14.95 *(978-0-615-31840-0(1))* Chai Yo Maui Pr.
David, Lawrence. The Invasion of the Shag Carpet Creature. Gott, Barry, illus. 2004. (Horace Splattly Ser.). 151p. (J). (gr. 4-7). 12.65 *(978-0-7569-2818-6(4))* Perfection Learning Corp.
Davis, Catherine. Abby & Alex Feel Their Hearts' Little. 2006. 57p. pap. 16.95 *(978-1-4241-4586-7(4))* PublishAmerica, Inc.
Davis, Helen J. Good Times with Gregory: Airplanes: A Visit to A 747. Davis, Robyn L., illus. 2008. (Good Times with Gregory Ser.). 37p. (J). (gr. -1-4). 12.95 *(978-1-935122-11-1(8))* K&B Products.
Davis, Kesa Royette. The Adventures of Keitly Dee & Geode. 2012. 36p. pap. 20.99 *(978-1-4772-3754-0(2))* AuthorHouse.
Davis, L. J. A Simple Brown Leaf. Victoria, Lisa, illus. 2006. 32p. (J). (gr. -1-3). 17.95 *(978-0-9762007-8-9(3))* Abovo Publishing.
Davis, Lee. Beware the Last Cousins. 2003. (J). per. *(978-0-9741294-1-9(0),* MSP) Main St Publishing, Inc.
Davis, Pat. Estelle & the Escape from Mars: A Children's Novel By. 2009. 136p. pap. 10.99 *(978-1-4389-5432-5(8))* AuthorHouse.
de Brunhoff, Laurent. Babar in Famiglia. pap. 12.95 *(978-88-04-46271-2(X))* Mondadori ITA. Dist: Distribooks, Inc.
de Gramont, Nina. Meet Me at the River. 2013. (ENG., Illus.). 384p. (YA). (gr. 9). 17.99 *(978-1-4169-8014-8(8))* Simon & Schuster Children's Publishing.
De La Llata, Lorenza. Awaking the Mighty. 2008. 49p. pap. 16.95 *(978-1-60563-689-4(4))* America Star Bks.
De La Mora, Maribel, Sr. Andrés Chupadedos. Editorial Cultural, ed. 2012. (Illus.). 48p. pap. 10.45 *(978-1-56758-059-4(9))* Editorial Cultural, Inc.
De la Peña, Matt. Mexican WhiteBoy. 2010. (ENG.). 256p. (YA). (gr. 9). pap. 9.99 *(978-0-440-23938-3(9),* Ember) Random Hse. Children's Bks.
—Mexican WhiteBoy. 2010. lib. bdg. 20.85 *(978-0-606-12316-7(4),* Turtleback) Turtleback Bks.
De Saint-Exupéry, Antoine. The Little Prince Family Storybook: Unabridged Original Text. 2015. (Little Prince Ser.). (ENG., Illus.). 64p. (YA). (gr. 7). 17.99 *(978-0-544-79256-2(4),* HMH Books For Young Readers) Houghton Mifflin Harcourt Publishing Co.
Deans, Sis Boulos. Racing the Past. 2005. 151p. (J). (gr. 5-9). 13.65 *(978-0-7569-5068-2(6))* Perfection Learning Corp.
Deborah Sue. All Things Remembered. 2004. 56p. (YA). pap. 8.95 *(978-0-595-31286-3(1))* iUniverse, Inc.
Deen, Natasha. Sleight of Hand, 1 vol. 2015. (Orca Soundings Ser.). (ENG.). 144p. (YA). (gr. 8-12). pap. 9.95 *(978-1-4598-1120-1(8))* Orca Bk. Pubs. USA.
DeFatta Barattini, Kathryn. I Live in Shreveport-Bossier! by Louise E. Ana, Ladybug. 2006. 36p. (J). pap. 15.00 *(978-1-4116-5197-5(9))* Lulu Pr., Inc.
Defosse, Rosana Curiel. Santiago en el Mundo de me de la Gana. Barradas, Leticia, illus. (SPA.). 38p. (J). (gr. 3-5). pap. 7.95 *(978-970-29-0136-5(7))* Santillana USA Publishing Co., Inc.
Del Moral, Susana, tr. Sr. Cuadrado. 2005. (Mis figuras Geometricas Ser.). (SPA., Illus.). 6p. (J). (gr. -1-7). *(978-970-718-294-3(6),* Silver Dolphin en Español) Advanced Marketing, S. de R. L. de C. V.
del Rio, Tania. Warren the 13th & the All-Seeing Eye. Staehle, Will, illus. 2015. (Warren The 13th Ser.: 1). (ENG.). 224p. (J). (gr. 5). 16.95 *(978-1-59474-803-5(9))* Quirk Bks.
Delmonte, Ellis. Miracle Girl. 2007. (ENG.). 208p. (YA). per. *(978-0-9555096-4-3(5))* Hawkwood Bks.
Delton, Judy. Angel Bites the Bullet. Weber, Jill, illus. 2003. (ENG.). 144p. (J). (gr. 2-5). pap. 10.95 *(978-0-618-36920-1(1))* Houghton Mifflin Harcourt Publishing Co.
Demetris, Jean. Grandma's Box of Memories: Helping Grandma to Remember. Demetris, Alex, illus. 2014. (ENG.). 32p. 17.95 *(978-1-84905-993-0(4),* 2767) Kingsley, Jessica Pubs. GBR. Dist: Macmillan Distribution Ltd.
DeMico, Judy. The Bus Trip, 1 vol. Johnson, Catherine LeAnn, illus. 2010. 26p. pap. 24.95 *(978-1-4489-2767-8(6))* PublishAmerica, Inc.
DeMonte, Joe. Lucy & the Magic Factory. 2008. 79p. pap. 19.95 *(978-1-60813-119-8(X))* America Star Bks.
Denise, Carolyn. I Am Tan! Chatterji, Somnath, illus. 2012. (ENG.). 18p. (J). (gr. -1-3). pap. 19.95 *(978-0-9835651-3-0(9))* Levi Bass Publishing.
Denmark, Evangeline. Curio, 1 vol. 2016. (ENG.). 432p. (YA). 17.99 *(978-0-310-72966-2(1))* Blink.
Desimini, Lisa, illus. The Fleatastics. 2017. (ENG.). 32p. (J). (gr. -1-3). 16.95 *(978-1-62979-303-0(5))* Boyds Mills Pr.
Dessen, Sarah. Lock & Key. 2009. (ENG.). 448p. (YA). (gr. 7-18). 10.99 *(978-0-14-241472-9(7),* Speak) Penguin Young Readers Group.
—Lock & Key. 2009. lib. bdg. 22.10 *(978-0-606-14396-7(3),* Turtleback) Turtleback Bks.
deVet, L. J. Teddy's Christmas Wish. Zabarylo-Duma, Ewa, illus. 2013. (ENG.). 48p. (J). *(978-0-9873686-0-7(5));* pap. *(978-0-9873686-1-4(3))* Print-Rite Publishers.
DeVillers, Julia & Roy, Jennifer Rozines. Trading Faces. Smith, Alison, illus. 2009. (Mix Ser.). (ENG.). 320p. (J). (gr. 4-8). pap. 7.99 *(978-1-4169-6168-0(2),* Aladdin) Simon & Schuster Children's Publishing.
Dickinson, Peter. The Ropemaker. 2003. (ENG.). 384p. (YA). (gr. 7). pap. 8.99 *(978-0-385-73063-1(2),* Delacorte Bks. for Young Readers) Random Hse. Children's Bks.
Dillsworth-Swift, Tammy. The Bermuda Triangle & the Lost Island. 2009. 182p. pap. 16.53 *(978-0-557-14503-4(1))* Lulu Pr., Inc.
DiMaulo, Michael A. Maggie's Window, 1 vol. 2010. 48p. pap. 16.95 *(978-1-4489-5288-5(3))* America Star Bks.
Dion, Elayne. The Brass Button. 2008. 72p. pap. 9.95 *(978-0-557-01210-7(4))* Lulu Pr., Inc.
Dipucchio, Kelly. One Little, Two Little, Three Little Children. Lundquist, Mary, illus. 2016. 32p. (J). (gr. -1-3). 17.99 *(978-0-06-234866-1(3))* HarperCollins Pubs.
Disney Book Group Staff & Higginson, Sheila Sweeny. Henry Hugglemonster Daddo in Charge. Disney Storybook Art Team, illus. 2015. (ENG.). 12p. (J). (gr. -1-k). bds. 7.99 *(978-1-4847-0642-8(0))* Disney Pr.
Dittrich, Melissa Joy. Family Flower. 2008. 14p. pap. 24.95 *(978-1-60610-275-6(3))* America Star Bks.
Dodge, Mary Mapes. Po No Kah an Indian Tale of Long Ago. 2004. reprint ed. pap. 15.95 *(978-1-4191-4185-0(6))* Kessinger Publishing, LLC.
Doll, Nancy L. Buddee the Bugger & Me: Told by Mac, 1 vol. 2009. 48p. pap. 24.95 *(978-1-60749-979-4(7))* America Star Bks.
Dominado, Guia. The Fear of Max. 2013. 40p. pap. 15.95 *(978-1-4908-0971-7(6),* WestBow Pr.) Author Solutions, Inc.
Donaldson, Babette. Emma Lea's First Tea Party. Van Dijk, Jerianne, illus. 2007. (ENG.). 32p. (J). 16.95 *(978-0-9792612-0-6(1))* Blue Gate Bks.
—Emma Lea's Magic Teapot. Van Dijk, Jerianne, illus. 2007. 32p. (J). lib. bdg. 16.95 *(978-0-9792612-1-3(X))* Blue Gate Bks.

Donoghue, Emma. The Lotterys Plus One. Hadilaksono, Caroline, illus. 2017. (ENG.). 320p. (J). (gr. 3-7). 17.99 (978-0-545-92581-5(9)) Scholastic, Inc.

Donohoe, Helen. Birdy Flynn. 2017. (ENG.). 384p. pap. 11.99 (978-1-78074-939-6(2)) Oneworld Pubns. GBR. Dist: Publishers Group West (PGW).

Dorie & Me. 2003. (YA). per. (978-1-59431-071-3(8), Ebks. On The Net) Write Words, Inc.

Dorr, Shay. Khloe Dutch! 2011. 48p. pap. 8.95 (978-1-4502-8332-8(2)) iUniverse, Inc.

Doty, Linda. Hydrangea Hill: A New Home for Amy Manchester. 2008. 182p. pap. 24.95 (978-1-60610-840-6(9)) America Star Bks.

Double or Nothing. 2014. (It Takes Two Ser.: 3). (ENG., Illus.). 160p. (J). (gr. 3-7). pap. 6.99 (978-1-4814-1652-8(9), Simon Spotlight) Simon Spotlight.

Douglas, Erin. Get That Pest! Yee, Wong Herbert, illus. 2003. (Green Light Readers Level 2 Ser.). (ENG.). 24p. (J). (gr. -1-3). pap. 3.95 (978-0-15-204833-4(2)) Houghton Mifflin Harcourt Publishing Co.

Dowd, Siobhan. The London Eye Mystery. 2009. (ENG.). 336p. (J). (gr. 3-7). 7.99 (978-0-385-75184-1(2), Yearling) Random Hse. Children's Bks.

—The London Eye Mystery. 2009. lib. bdg. 18.40 (978-0-606-14413-1(7), Turtleback) Turtleback Bks.

Dowding, Philippa. The Gargoyle in My Yard. 2009. (Lost Gargoyle Ser.: 1). (ENG.). 128p. (J). (gr. 4-7). pap. 9.99 (978-1-894917-82-7(0), Napoleon & Co.) Dundurn CAN. Dist: Ingram Publisher Services.

Dowell, Frances O'Roark. Sam the Man & the Chicken Plan. Bates, Amy June, illus. 2017. (Sam the Man Ser.: 1). (ENG.). 144p. (J). (gr. 1-4). pap. 6.99 (978-1-4814-4067-7(5)) Simon & Schuster Children's Publishing.

—Sam the Man & the Chicken Plan. 2016. (Sam the Man Ser.: 1). (ENG., Illus.). 128p. (J). (gr. 1-4). 15.99 (978-1-4814-4066-0(7)) Simon & Schuster Children's Publishing.

Dowell, Vivian "Vee". I'm Da Muva, Said Miss Bossy. Huntley, Doris, illus. 2008. 32p. pap. 24.95 (978-1-60610-045-5(9)) America Star Bks.

Dower, Laura. For Emme, Baked with Love. Lazuli, Lilly, illus. 2016. (Dessert Diaries). (ENG.). 160p. (gr. 4-5). pap. 5.95 (978-1-4965-4142-0(1)); lib. bdg. 26.65 (978-1-4965-3122-3(1)) Stone Arch Bks.

—Kiki Takes the Cake. Lazuli, Lilly, illus. 2016. (Dessert Diaries). (ENG.). 160p. (gr. 4-5). lib. bdg. 26.65 (978-1-4965-3120-9(5)) Stone Arch Bks.

Downham, Jenny. Unbecoming. (ENG.). 384p. (J). (gr. 9-9). 2017. pap. 9.99 **(978-1-338-16072-7(9))** 2016. 17.99 (978-0-545-90717-0(9)) Scholastic, Inc.

—Unbecoming. 2017. lib. bdg. 20.85 **(978-0-606-40147-0(4))** Turtleback Bks.

Doyle, Brian. Uncle Ronald. 1 vol. 2nd ed. 2004. (ENG.). 138p. (J). (gr. 4). pap. 9.95 (978-0-88899-621-3(7)) Groundwood Bks. CAN. Dist: Publishers Group West (PGW).

Doyle, Catherine. Vendetta. 2015. (ENG.). 352p. (J). (gr. 9). 18.99 (978-0-545-69982-2(7)) Scholastic, Inc.

Doyle, Eugenie. Sleep Tight Farms: A Farm Prepares for Winter. Stadtlander, Becca, illus. 2016. (ENG.). 36p. (J). (gr. -1-k). 16.99 (978-1-4521-2901-3(0)) Chronicle Bks. LLC.

Dragonblood, A. The Whispering V: Children of the Others Collection. 2010. 84p. pap. 10.49 (978-1-4520-3250-4(5)) AuthorHouse.

Draper, Sharon M. The Battle of Jericho. (Jericho Trilogy Ser.: 1). (ENG., Illus.). (YA). (gr. 7). 2017. 320p. pap. 9.99 **(978-1-4814-9029-0(X)**, Atheneum/Caitlyn Dlouhy Books) 2003. 304p. 19.99 (978-0-689-84232-0(5), Atheneum Bks. for Young Readers) Simon & Schuster Children's Publishing.

—The Battle of Jericho. 2005. (Jericho Trilogy Ser.). (ENG., Illus.). 352p. (YA). (gr. 7). mass mkt. 7.99 (978-0-689-84233-7(3), Simon Pulse) Simon Pulse.

Draus, Naudia Burtwell. My Grandma Wears A Number: How One Girl Survived World War Ii. 2011. 40p. (gr. 4-6). pap. 19.57 (978-1-4269-3351-6(7)) Trafford Publishing.

Drawhorn, Barbara. Maddie Waaa! 2011. 32p. pap. 13.59 (978-1-4389-7509-2(0)) AuthorHouse.

Dream Boat: Individual Title Six-Packs. (Action Packs Ser.). 120p. (gr. 3-5). 44.00 (978-0-7635-8429-0(0)) Rigby Education.

Dreher, Ruth. Ralph the Red Engine. 2010. 36p. pap. 15.49 (978-1-4520-2169-0(4)) AuthorHouse.

Drogo, Susette. Five Blessings. Lukas, Mary, illus. 2008. 24p. (J). pap. 15.00 (978-0-9800611-8-5(0)) Orr Bks.

Drouhard, Brianne. Billie the Unicorn. 2011. (ENG., Illus.). 36p. (J). (gr. -1-3). 15.95 (978-1-59702-024-4(9)) Immedium.

Drown, Merle. Lighting the World. 2015. (ENG.). 278p. pap. 18.00 (978-0-9898971-4-3(1)) Whitepoint Pr.

Drummond, Karona. Along Came You. 1 vol. 2014. (ENG.). 24p. (J). bds. 7.99 (978-0-310-72859-7(2)) Zonderkidz.

Dube, Jasmine. Gratelle au Bois Mordant. 2004. (FRE., Illus.). (J). (gr. -1-3). spiral bd. (978-0-616-01848-4(7)) Canadian National Institute for the Blind/Institut National Canadien pour les Aveugles.

Dubisch, Mike, illus. The Haunted Cabin Mystery. 2009. (Boxcar Children Graphic Novels Ser.: 9). (ENG.). 32p. (J). (gr. 1-5). pap. 6.99 (978-0-8075-3180-8(4)) Whitman, Albert & Co.

—Tree House Mystery. 2009. (Boxcar Children Graphic Novels Ser.: 8). (ENG.). 32p. (J). (gr. 1-5). pap. 6.99 (978-0-8075-8088-2(0)) Whitman, Albert & Co.

Duble, Kathleen Benner. Bravo Zulu, Samantha!. 1 vol. 2007. (ENG.). 144p. (J). (gr. 3-7). 14.95 (978-1-56145-401-3(X)) Peachtree Pubs.

Duder, Tessa. Carpet of Dreams. Wilson, Mark, illus. 2008. 32p. pap. (978-0-207-19991-2(4)) HarperCollins Pubs. Australia.

Dudgeon and Oxenham, Dudgeon and Oxenham. Cyclones & Shadows. 2017. (ENG.). 168p. (J). (gr. 1-5). 9.95 **(978-1-925164-76-3(4))** Fremantle Pr. AUS. Dist: Independent Pubs. Group.

Dudney, Emma Mae. The Runaway. 2008. 144p. pap. 9.95 (978-0-9800654-0-2(3)) Authors' Discovery Cooperation, Inc.

Duffy, Jacqueline Ann. Dillon the Dog Finds His Family. 2008. 24p. pap. 24.95 (978-1-60563-331-2(3)) America Star Bks.

Dumont, Virginie, et al. Enredos de Familia. Boucher, Michel, illus. 2004. (Arbol de la Vida Ser.). (SPA.). 64p. (J). 13.99 (978-84-8488-098-1(2)) Serres, Ediciones, S. L. ESP. Dist: Lectorum Pubns., Inc.

Dunkle, Clare B. The Sky Inside. 2017. (ENG.). 240p. (YA). (gr. 7). pap. 11.99 **(978-1-5344-1875-2(X)**, Atheneum Bks. for Young Readers) Simon & Schuster Children's Publishing.

Dunlap, Susanne. The Musician's Daughter. 2010. (ENG.). 352p. (YA). (gr. 7). pap. 8.99 (978-1-59990-452-8(7), 9781599904528, Bloomsbury USA Childrens) Bloomsbury Publishing USA.

Dunn-Dern, Lisa. Dr. Duncan Dog on Duty! Yomtob, Andrea, illus. 2007. (J). (gr. -1-3). per. 16.99 (978-1-933156-20-0(1), Visikid Bks.) GSVQ Publishing.

Duras, Marguerite. La Pluie d'Ete. (FRE.). pap. 14.95 (978-2-07-038705-2(4)) Gallimard, Editions FRA. Dist: Distribooks, Inc.

Duren, Sheila Gregory. Pepper's Great Move! 2011. 28p. pap. 15.99 (978-1-4568-6766-9(0)) Xlibris Corp.

Durst, Sarah Beth. The Girl Who Could Not Dream. 2017. (ENG.). 384p. (J). (gr. 5-7). pap. 6.99 (978-0-544-93526-6(8), HMH Books For Young Readers) Houghton Mifflin Harcourt Publishing Co.

—The Girl Who Could Not Dream. 2015. (ENG.). 384p. (J). (gr. 5-7). 16.99 (978-0-544-46497-1(4), Clarion Bks.) Houghton Mifflin Harcourt Trade & Reference Pubs.

—The Girl Who Could Not Dream. 2017. (ENG.). (J). (gr. 5-7). lib. bdg. 17.20 **(978-0-606-39810-7(4))** Turtleback Bks.

Dyan, Penelope. Grandma's Suitcase — -Where a Kid Can Always Find a Surprise! Dyan, Penelope, illus. 2008. (Illus.). 44p. pap. 11.95 (978-1-935118-36-7(6)) Bellissima Publishing, LLC.

—The Musical Family — Sometimes a Song Says It All. Dyan, Penelope, illus. 2009. (Illus.). 42p. pap. 11.95 (978-1-935118-81-7(1)) Bellissima Publishing, LLC.

Dyer, Hadley. Johnny Kellock Died Today. 2007. (ENG.). 192p. (J). mass mkt. 6.92 **(978-0-00-639534-8(1)**, Harper Trophy) HarperCollins Pubs.

Dyer, K. C. A Walk Through a Window. 2009. (ENG.). 240p. (J). (gr. 5-7). pap. 12.50 (978-0-385-66637-4(3), Doubleday Canada) Penguin Random House Canada Young Readers CAN. Dist: Penguin Random Hse. LLC.

Dyson, Tony. The Crystal Wand. 2005. 242p. pap. 14.01 (978-1-4116-5596-6(6)) Lulu Pr., Inc.

Eagland, Jane. Wildthorn. 2012. (ENG.). 352p. (YA). (gr. 9). pap. 8.99 (978-0-547-57736-4(2)) Houghton Mifflin Harcourt Publishing Co.

Eagle, Rita. Farina & the Baby. 2011. 44p. pap. 17.99 (978-1-4568-5917-6(X)) Xlibris Corp.

Easton, Kelly. To Be Mona. 2009. (ENG.). 224p. (YA). (gr. 7). pap. 7.99 (978-1-4169-0055-9(1), McElderry, Margaret K. Bks.) McElderry, Margaret K. Bks.

Eastridge, Jim. Gregory & the Moon. 2008. 12p. pap. 24.95 (978-1-4241-9008-9(8)) America Star Bks.

Ebbeler, Jeffrey, illus. Jingle Bells. 2009. (ENG.). 20p. (J). (gr. -1-k). bds. 6.99 (978-0-8249-1827-9(4), Ideal Pubns.) Worthy Publishing.

Ebiringa, Chudy. The, Adventures of Ella at Bulukutu Stream. 2011. (ENG.). 50p. pap. 11.95 (978-1-4327-6655-9(4)) Outskirts Pr., Inc.

Echols, Jennifer. Going Too Far. 2009. (ENG.). 256p. pap. 16.99 (978-1-4165-7173-5(6), MTV Bks.) MTV Books.

Ecton, Emily. Boots & Pieces. 2008. (ENG.). 240p. (J). (gr. 3-7). pap. 11.99 (978-1-4169-6167-3(4), Aladdin) Simon & Schuster Children's Publishing.

Edman Lamote, Lisa. Booklet Goes to the Doctor. Wilson, Alisha, illus. 2006. (Bookmann Family Presents Ser.). 32p. (J). (gr. k-3). 15.99 (978-1-933673-02-8(8), BookMann Pr.) Mann Publishing Group.

—A Day Out for Opus. Wilson, Alisha, illus. 2006. (Bookmann Family Presents Ser.). 32p. (J). (gr. k-3). 15.99 (978-1-933673-03-5(6), BookMann Pr.) Mann Publishing Group.

—Don't Judge a Book by Its Cover. Wilson, Alisha, illus. 2006. (Bookmann Family Presents Ser.). 32p. (J). (gr. k-3). 15.99 (978-1-933673-01-1(X), BookMann Pr.) Mann Publishing Group.

Educational Adventures, creator. Blazin' Hot: Picture Book (Spanish) 9x9. 2006. (SPA., Illus.). (J). 5.99 (978-0-9770455-4-9(4)) Mighty Kids Media.

Edwards, Hazel. Fake ID. 2004. (Illus.). 144p. pap. (978-0-7344-0442-8(5), Lothian Children's Bks.) Hachette Australia.

Edwards, Melvin Neal. Sticks & Stones. 2013. 114p. (gr. 2-4). 19.88 (978-1-4669-8482-0(1)); pap. 9.88 (978-1-4669-8480-6(5)) Trafford Publishing.

Ehrlich, Amy. The Girl Who Wanted to Dance. Walsh, Rebecca, illus. 2009. (ENG.). 40p. (J). (gr. 1-4). 17.99 (978-0-7636-1345-7(2)) Candlewick Pr.

Elkeles, Simone. Chain Reaction. 2015. (Perfect Chemistry Novel Ser.). (ENG.). 336p. (YA). (gr. 9). pap. 9.99 (978-1-61963-703-0(0), 9781619637030, Bloomsbury USA Childrens) Bloomsbury Publishing USA.

Eller, Sylvia Klope. The Squirrel Who Hitchhiked to Atlanta. 2007. (Illus.). 32p. (J). pap. 8.00 (978-0-8059-7596-3(9)) Dorrance Publishing Co., Inc.

Eller, Tracy & Mason, Joan. Cousins & Kinship. 2008. 48p. pap. 28.45 (978-0-615-17808-0(1)) Aardvark Pubs.

Elliott, Rebecca. Zoo Girl. Elliott, Rebecca, illus. 2012. (ENG., Illus.). 32p. (J). (gr. k-2). 14.99 (978-0-7459-6323-5(4)) Lion Hudson PLC GBR. Dist: Independent Pubs. Group.

Elliott, Ruth & Elliott, David. The Richest Kid in the Poor House. Elliott, Ruth, illus. 2008. (Illus.). (J). pap. (978-0-9795017-4-6(1)) Edu Designs.

Ellis, Deborah. No Ordinary Day. 1 vol. (ENG.). (J). (gr. 3-7). 2014. 160p. pap. 9.95 (978-1-55498-108-3(5)) 2011. 144p. 16.95 (978-1-55498-134-2(4)) Groundwood Bks. CAN. Dist: Publishers Group West (PGW).

—Parvana's Journey. 1 vol. 2015. (Breadwinner Ser.). (ENG., Illus.). 200p. (J). (gr. 4-9). pap. 9.95 (978-1-55498-770-2(9)) Groundwood Bks. CAN. Dist: Publishers Group West (PGW).

Ellis, Sarah. Odd Man Out. 1 vol. 2008. (ENG.). 168p. (J). (gr. 3-7). pap. 8.95 (978-0-88899-703-6(5)) Groundwood Bks. CAN. Dist: Publishers Group West (PGW).

Else, Barbara. The Queen & the Nobody Boy. Broad, Sam, illus. 2013. (Tales of Fontania Ser.). (ENG.). 328p. (J). (gr. 4-7). (978-1-877579-49-3(1)) Gecko Pr.

Elston, Ashley. The Rules for Disappearing. 2014. (Rules Ser.). (ENG.). 336p. (YA). (gr. 7-12). pap. 8.99 (978-1-4231-6926-0(3)) Hyperion Bks. for Children.

Emory, Kb. Tyler Tales: What Is My Color/ Different Families. 2012. 36p. pap. 21.99 (978-1-4797-2504-5(8)) Xlibris Corp.

Encyclopaedia Britannica, Inc. Staff, compiled by. If Your Parents Drink. 2008. 49.95 (978-1-59339-649-7(X)) Encyclopaedia Britannica, Inc.

Enderlin, Lisa. Dad, There's a Bear in the Pool!!! 2012. 24p. pap. 24.95 (978-1-4626-8263-8(4)) America Star Bks.

Engel, Christiane. ABC Love: An Endearing Twist on Learning Your ABCs! 2017. (ABC for Me Ser.). (ENG., Illus.). 36p. (J). (gr. -1-1). 16.95 (978-1-63322-240-3(3), Walter Foster Jr) Quarto Publishing Group USA.

Engelman, Stephanie. A Single Bead. 2016. 199p. (YA). pap. (978-0-8198-9054-2(5)) Pauline Bks. & Media.

Engle, Margarita. Mountain Dog. Ivanov, Aleksey & Ivanov, Olga, illus. 2013. (ENG.). 224p. (J). (gr. 3-7). 17.99 (978-0-8050-9516-6(0), 9780805095166, Holt, Henry & Co. Bks. For Young Readers) Holt, Henry & Co.

English, Karen. Birthday Blues. Freeman, Laura, illus. 2010. (ENG.). 96p. (J). (gr. 1-4). pap. 5.99 (978-0-547-24893-6(8)) Houghton Mifflin Harcourt Publishing Co.

—Don't Feed the Geckos! The Carver Chronicles, Book Three. Freeman, Laura, illus. 2016. (Carver Chronicles Ser.). (ENG.). 144p. (J). (gr. 1-4). pap. 5.99 (978-0-544-81083-9(X), HMH Books For Young Readers) Houghton Mifflin Harcourt Publishing Co.

Ensor, Andrew. Luke Carter & the Sword of Kings. 2004. 427p. per. 27.95 (978-0-9758943-0-9(7), 1237945) WinDruid Publishing.

Erb, Sharlyne. A hug from Daddy. 2005. 83p. pap. 22.71 (978-1-4116-5970-4(8)) Lulu Pr., Inc.

Eriksen, Valanee. Christmas Bells & Hero's Tails. 2015. (Illus.). vi, 90p. (J). pap. 7.99 (978-1-4621-1737-6(6)) Cedar Fort, Inc./CFI Distribution.

Erlbruch, Wolf. The Miracle of Bears. Reynolds, Michael, tr. from GER. 2006. (ENG., Illus.). 32p. 14.95 (978-1-933372-21-1(4)) Europa Editions, Inc.

Erskine, Kathryn. Quaking. 2010. (ENG.). 256p. (YA). (gr. 7-18). 7.99 (978-0-14-241476-7(X), Speak) Penguin Young Readers Group.

Escalante, Travis. The Story of Rocks & Balloons. 2013. 28p. 16.99 (978-0-9897168-5-7(6)) Mindstir Media.

Evangelista, Gloria. In Search of the Perfect Pumpkin. Shea, Shawn, illus. 2008. (ENG.). 32p. (J). (gr. k). pap. 7.95 (978-1-55591-697-8(X)) Fulcrum Publishing.

Evans, Jane. How Are You Feeling Today Baby Bear? Exploring Big Feelings after Living in a Stormy Home. Jackson, Laurence, illus. 2014. (ENG.). 32p. (J). 15.95 (978-1-84905-424-9(X), 3151) Kingsley, Jessica Pubs. GBR. Dist: Macmillan Distribution Ltd.

Evans, Sandra. This Is Not a Werewolf Story. 2016. (ENG., Illus.). 352p. (J). (gr. 4-7). 16.99 (978-1-4814-4480-4(8), Atheneum Bks. for Young Readers) Simon & Schuster Children's Publishing.

Everest, D. D. Archie Greene & the Magician's Secret. 2015. (Archie Greene Ser.: 1). (ENG.). 320p. (J). (gr. 3-7). 16.99 (978-0-06-231211-2(1)) HarperCollins Pubs.

Everett Hale, Edward. Last of the Peterkins with Others of the. 2006. pap. (978-1-4068-1087-5(8)) Echo Library.

Everett, Reese. Jayla's Jitters. 2015. (ENG.). 48p. (gr. k-3). 27.07 (978-1-63430-374-3(1)) Rourke Educational Media.

Eversole, Barbara. My Name Is Zorro. 2005. 25p. 11.07 (978-1-4116-4438-0(7)) Lulu Pr., Inc.

Everstine, Andrew D. Seth: A Visitor's Pass. 2003. 286p. (YA). pap. 16.95 (978-0-595-26368-4(2), Writers Club Pr.) iUniverse, Inc.

Ewart, Francesca, et al. There's a Hamster in My Pocket! Bate, Helen, illus. 2012. (ENG.). 96p. (J). (gr. 3-6). pap. 7.95 (978-1-84780-118-0(8), Frances Lincoln) Quarto Publishing Group UK GBR. Dist: Hachette Bk. Group.

Face to Face: Individual Title Six-Packs. (Bookweb Ser.). 32p. (gr. 4-18). 34.00 (978-0-7635-3731-9(4)) Rigby Education.

Facia Kromah. Leah Toppings: The New Experience. 2010. 28p. pap. 15.99 (978-1-4535-2547-0(5)) Xlibris Corp.

Faerber, Jay. Noble Causes, Vol. 2. 2004. (ENG., Illus.). 120p. pap. 12.95 (978-1-58240-348-9(1), 9781582403489) Image Comics.

Fagan, Cary. Oy, Feh, So?. 1 vol. Clement, Gary, illus. 2013. (ENG.). 40p. (J). (gr. -1-3). 17.95 (978-1-55498-148-9(4)) Groundwood Bks. CAN. Dist: Publishers Group West (PGW).

—Ten Lessons for Kaspar Snit. 2008. (ENG.). 192p. (J). (gr. 3-7). pap. 9.95 (978-0-88776-835-4(0), Tundra Bks.) Tundra Bks. CAN. Dist: Penguin Random Hse. LLC.

Fajardo, Renee & Ruby, Carl. Ole Posole & Other Tummy Tales. Fajardo, Renee, ed. 2005. (Illus.). 110p. (YA). (gr. 4-8). pap. 14.00 (978-0-9724472-3-2(7)) Just Enjoyable Memorable Story Bks.

Falconer, Ian. Olivia Forms a Band. Falconer, Ian, illus. 2009. (ENG., Illus.). 50p. (J). (gr. -1-3). 12.99 (978-1-4169-8037-7(7), Atheneum Bks. for Young Readers) Simon & Schuster Children's Publishing.

Falletta, Bernadette & Gasparro, Marie. Reflections of the Dog That Learned English. 2005. 16p. (J). 14.95 (978-1-4116-6524-8(4)) Lulu Pr., Inc.

Falter, Laury. Residue. 2013. 306p. pap. 12.99 (978-0-9855110-0-5(1)) Falter, Laury.

Family Stories: Individual Packs Pack A. (SPA.). (gr. k-2). 15.40 (978-0-7362-0492-7(X)) CENGAGE Learning.

Family Stories: Individual Packs Pack B. (SPA.). (gr. k-2). 15.40 (978-0-7362-0494-1(6)) CENGAGE Learning.

Family Stories: Jumbo Packs. (SPA.). (gr. k-2). 157.08 (978-0-7362-0052-3(5)) CENGAGE Learning.

Fantasia, Kathryn. Pass It On. Flanagan, Jeff, illus. 2009. 28p. pap. 18.65 (978-1-4415-5446-8(7)) Xlibris Corp.

Fantich, Susanna. A Cat's Tale. 2012. 210p. 33.99 (978-1-4582-0527-8(4)); pap. 15.99 (978-1-4582-0525-4(8)) Author Solutions, Inc. (Abbott Pr.).

Farish, Terry. Luis Paints the World. Dominguez, Oliver, illus. 2016. (ENG.). 32p. (gr. k-4). 35.99 (978-1-5124-0667-2(8), Carolrhoda Bks.) Lerner Publishing Group.

Farmer, Merry. Balloons for Bella. 2010. 16p. 8.49 (978-1-4490-6497-6(3)) AuthorHouse.

Farnsworth-Simpson, Patricia Ann. Flick the Karate Pig. 2008. 163p. pap. 16.50 (978-1-4357-2843-1(2)) Lulu Pr., Inc.

Farre, Lluis. The Grey Boy. Willis, Judith, tr. from CAT. Gusti, illus. 2007. (ENG.). 44p. (J). (gr. k-2). 12.95 (978-1-905341-08-5(3)) WingedChariot Pr. GBR. Dist: Independent Pubs. Group.

Farrell, John. Dear Child. Manning, Maurie J., illus. 2008. (ENG.). 32p. (J). (gr. -1-k). 16.95 (978-1-59078-495-2(2)) Boyds Mills Pr.

Favorite, Deborah. The Tush People. Arinsberg, Norman, illus. (J). 11.95 (978-0-9722514-0-2(5)) Tush People, The.

Fearing, Mark. The Great Thanksgiving Escape. Fearing, Mark, illus. 2017. (ENG., Illus.). 32p. (J). (gr. k-3). 6.99 **(978-0-7636-9511-8(4))** Candlewick Pr.

Fehlbaum, Beth. Big Fat Disaster. 2015. (ENG.). 286p. (YA). pap. 9.99 (978-1-4405-9267-6(5), Simon Pulse) Simon Pulse.

Feil, Denise J. Praze B. a Growing, Loving Day: Forgiveness & Responsibility. Feil, Denise J., illus. 2004. (Illus.). (J). per. 5.50 (978-0-9741588-0-8(1)) Feil.

Feldhahn, Cathy J. Nosam. 2009. 37p. pap. 8.50 (978-1-4092-8290-7(2)) Lulu Pr., Inc.

Fennell, Haywood. Coota & the Magic Quilt. 2004. (J). (978-0-9720404-0-2(4)) Tri-Ad veterans League, Inc.

Fernandez, Nacho. La nueva era del sueno vol. 2: Los desiertos del Norte: The New Age of Dreams vol. 2: the Deserts of the North. 2007. (SPA.). 48p. 22.95 (978-1-59497-398-7(9)) Public Square Bks.

Fernandez, Rafael. Diego's Family Christmas. McGee, Warner, illus. 2008. (Go, Diego, Go! Ser.). (ENG.). 16p. (J). (gr. -1-k). bds. 5.99 (978-1-4169-5836-9(3), Simon Spotlight/Nickelodeon) Simon Spotlight/Nickelodeon.

Ferreira, Ann Devine & Bailey. Hi I'm Bailey & I'm Getting A New Special Family. 2011. 32p. 17.95 (978-1-4269-5303-3(8)) Trafford Publishing.

Ferris, Jean. Love among the Walnuts. 2008. (ENG., Illus.). 228p. (J). (gr. 5-7). pap. 7.99 (978-0-15-206227-9(0)) Houghton Mifflin Harcourt Publishing Co.

—Of Sound Mind. 2004. (ENG.). 224p. (YA). (gr. 7). reprint ed. pap. 10.99 (978-0-374-45584-2(8), 9780374455842, Farrar, Straus & Giroux (BYR)) Farrar, Straus & Giroux.

Field, Matthew S. Father Like a Tree. Hedderich, Tom, illus. 2005. (ENG.). (J). 19.95 (978-0-9761528-0-4(0)) Matting Leah Publishing Co.

Fields, Melissa. Auntie Silly & the Crazy Cousins Day Parade. 1 vol. Class, Virginia Tyree, illus. 2010. 20p. pap. 24.95 (978-1-4489-8140-3(9)) PublishAmerica, Inc.

Fienberg, Anna. Power to Burn. 167p. (J). pap. (978-0-340-70930-6(8)) Hodder & Stoughton.

Filkins, Allison J. The Amazings. 2007. 484p. per. 25.95 (978-0-595-47500-1(0)) iUniverse, Inc.

Fine, Anne. Blood Family. 2017. (ENG., Illus.). 304p. (YA). (gr. 9). 17.99 (978-1-4814-7773-4(0), Simon & Schuster Bks. For Young Readers) Simon & Schuster Bks. For Young Readers.

—Countdown. 2006. (Yellow Bananas Ser.). (ENG., Illus.). 48p. (J). (gr. -1-3). (978-0-7787-1004-2(1)) Crabtree Publishing Co.

Finley, Martha. Elsie's Girlhood. 2006. pap. 14.95 (978-1-4218-3093-3(0)) 1st World Publishing, Inc.

—Elsie's Girlhood. l.t. ed. 2007. (ENG.). 254p. pap. 23.99 (978-1-4264-3884-4(2)) Creative Media Partners, LLC.

—Elsie's Kith & Kin. 2006. 28.95 (978-1-4218-2994-4(0)); pap. 13.95 (978-1-4218-3094-0(9)) 1st World Publishing, Inc.

—Elsie's Motherhood. 2006. 29.95 (978-1-4218-2995-1(9)); pap. 14.95 (978-1-4218-3095-7(7)) 1st World Publishing, Inc.

—Elsie's New Relations. 2006. 28.95 (978-1-4218-2996-8(7)); pap. 13.95 (978-1-4218-3096-4(5)) 1st World Publishing, Inc.

Fiona Fox Staff, ed. The Swiss Family Robinson. 2012. (ENG., Illus.). 224p. (J). 15.00 (978-1-84135-839-0(8)) Award Pubns. Ltd. GBR. Dist: Parkwest Pubns., Inc.

Fiorella, Christina. My Brother Adam. 2012. 16p. pap. 15.99 (978-1-4772-1226-4(4)) AuthorHouse.

Fisk, Katie. Flying with the Angels. 2008. 62p. pap. 19.95 (978-1-60563-608-5(8)) America Star Bks.

FitzGerald, Helen. Deviant. 2014. (ENG.). (YA). (gr. 9). pap. 9.99 (978-1-61695-419-2(1), Soho Teen) Soho Pr., Inc.

Fitzgerald, John D. Me & My Little Brain. Mayer, Mercer, illus. 2004. (Great Brain Ser.). 137p. (gr. 3-7). 16.00 (978-0-7569-2541-3(X)) Perfection Learning Corp.

Fitzhugh, Louise. Nobody's Family Is Going to Change. 2016. (ENG.). 232p. (J). (-9). pap. 12.95 (978-1-939601-49-0(5)) Ig Publishing, Inc.

Fitzmaurice, Kathryn. Destiny, Rewritten. 2013. (ENG.). 352p. (J). (gr. 3-7). 16.99 (978-0-06-162501-5(9), Tegen, Katherine Bks) HarperCollins Pubs.

Fitzpatrick, Marie-Louise. Owl Bat Bat Owl. Fitzpatrick, Marie-Louise, illus. 2017. (ENG., Illus.). 32p. (J). (gr. -1-2). 15.99 (978-0-7636-9161-5(5)) Candlewick Pr.

Fleming, Ian. Chitty Chitty Bang Bang. Berger, Joe, illus. 2013. (Chitty Chitty Bang Bang Ser.). (ENG.). 160p. (J). (gr. 4-7). pap. 6.99 (978-0-7636-6666-8(1)) Candlewick Pr.

Flood, Nancy Bo. Soldier Sister, Fly Home. Begay, Shonto, illus. 2016. (ENG.). 176p. (YA). (gr. 5). lib. bdg. 16.95 (978-1-58089-702-0(9)) Charlesbridge Publishing, Inc.

Flood, Pansie Hart. Secret Holes. Marshall, Felicia, illus. 2004. 128p. (J). (gr. 3-6). 15.95 (978-0-87614-923-2(9), Carolrhoda Bks.) Lerner Publishing Group.

Florence, Leigh Anne. Mr. Dogwood Goes to Washington. Asher, James, illus. 2008. (Woody the Kentucky Wiener Ser.). 56p. (J). (gr. 2-8). pap. 12.95 (978-0-9741417-5-6(5)) HotDiggetyDog Pr.

Floyd, Brandi. Alex's Choice. 2012. 38p. 24.95 (978-1-4626-6028-5(2)) America Star Bks.

Fodi, Lee Edward. Kendra Kandlestar & the Crack in Kazah. Fodi, Lee Edward, illus. 2011. (ENG., Illus.). 282p. (J). (gr. 4-7). 16.95 (978-1-61254-018-4(X)) Brown Books Publishing Group.

Fontinalis. The Far Shore. 2011. 76p. pap. 6.99 (978-1-61667-309-3(5)) Raider Publishing International.

Forrester, Izola L. Kit of Greenacre Farm. 2007. (ENG.). 158p. pap. 19.99 (978-1-4264-8431-5(3)); 174p. pap. 21.99 (978-1-4264-8489-6(5)) Creative Media Partners, LLC.

Foster, Martha S. Ginger Box. Geer, Charles, illus. 2011. 126p. 40.95 (978-1-258-06588-1(6)) Literary Licensing, LLC.

Fowler, Orval Ray. Wally Gumper & Family Travel & Adventures: In Search of the Stones. 2010. 209p. pap. 71.95 *(978-1-4327-4719-0(3))* Outskirts Pr., Inc.

Fowley-Doyle, Moira. The Accident Season. 2015. (ENG.). 304p. (YA). (gr. 9). 17.99 *(978-0-525-42948-7(4),* Kathy Dawson Books) Penguin Young Readers Group.

—The Accident Season. 2016. (ENG.). 320p. (YA). (gr. 9). 22.10 *(978-0-606-39325-6(0))* Turtleback Bks.

Fox, Ben. The Great & the Grand. Robbins, Elizabeth, illus. 2015. (ENG.). 32p. (J). 16.95 *(978-1-942672-97-5(7))* Familius LLC.

Fox, Paula. La Habitacion de Mauricio. 2003.Tr. of Maurice's Room. (SPA., Illus.). 96p. (J). (gr. 3-5). *(978-84-279-3457-3(2),* NG4695) Noguer y Caralt Editores, S. A. ESP. Dist: Lectorum Pubns., Inc.

Francois, Rose Darlie. The Sixteen Eggs & the Frying Pan Clock. 2009. 41p. pap. 18.00 *(978-0-557-07155-5(0))* Lulu Pr., Inc.

Frank, E. R. Dime. 2015. (ENG., Illus.). 336p. (YA). (gr. 9). 18.99 *(978-1-4814-3160-6(9))* Simon & Schuster Children's Publishing.

Frederick, Heather Vogel. Yours Truly. 2017. (Pumpkin Falls Mystery Ser.). (ENG., Illus.). 336p. (J). (gr. 5-9). 16.99 *(978-1-4424-7186-3(7),* Simon & Schuster Bks. For Young Readers) Simon & Schuster Bks. For Young Readers.

Freeman, J. Miller. Creak in the Night - Mystery of the Crypts. Lavender, Todd, illus. 2012. 74p. pap. 9.99 *(978-0-9850410-1-4(3))* Akmaeon Publishing, LLC.

Freeman, Martha. The Case of the Missing Dinosaur Egg. 2013. (First Kids Mystery Ser.: 5). (ENG.). 144p. (J). (gr. 3-7). 16.95 *(978-0-8234-2523-5(1))* Holiday Hse., Inc.

—The Case of the Ruby Slippers. 2012. (First Kids Mystery Ser.: 3). (ENG.). 128p. (J). 16.95 *(978-0-8234-2409-2(X))* Holiday Hse., Inc.

—Effie Starr Zook Has One More Question. 2017. (ENG., Illus.). 224p. (J). (gr. 3-7). 16.99 *(978-1-4814-7264-7(X),* Simon & Schuster/Paula Wiseman Bks.) Simon & Schuster/Paula Wiseman Bks.

Freeman, Martha. P. S. Send More Cookies. 2017. (Secret Cookie Club Ser.). (ENG., Illus.). 336p. (J). (gr. 3-7). 16.99 ***(978-1-4814-4824-6(2),*** Simon & Schuster/Paula Wiseman Bks.) Simon & Schuster/Paula Wiseman Bks.

French, Jackie. One Big Wacky Family. 2008. (Illus.). 464p. pap. *(978-0-7322-8745-0(6))* HarperCollins Pubs. Australia.

French, Jennifer. Fidgets. 2007. 132p. pap. 9.95 *(978-1-59663-531-9(2),* Castle Keep Pr.) Rock, James A. & Co. Pubs.

Friedman, C. S. Dreamseeker. 2015. (Dreamwalker Ser.: 2). (ENG.). 336p. (gr. 12). 19.95 *(978-0-7564-0895-4(4),* DAW) DAW.

Friedman, Laurie. On the Road with Mallory. Kalis, Jennifer, illus. 2016. (Mallory Ser.: 25). (ENG.). 160p. (gr. 2-5). 31.99 *(978-1-4677-9567-8(4),* Darby Creek) Lerner Publishing Group.

Friedman, Stanley. I, Dinosaur. 2010. 166p. pap. 11.95 *(978-1-935118-91-6(9))* Bellissima Publishing, LLC.

Friesen, Gayle. For Now. 2007. (ENG.). 248p. (J). (gr. 5-9). 7.95 *(978-1-55453-133-2(0))* Kids Can Pr., Ltd. CAN. Dist: Hachette Bk. Group.

Froissart, Benedicte. Uncle Henry's Dinner Guests. 2004. (Illus.). (J). (gr. k-3). spiral bd. *(978-0-616-01644-2(1))* Canadian National Institute for the Blind/Institut National Canadien pour les Aveugles.

Fry, Erin. Losing It, 0 vols. 2014. (ENG.). 274p. (J). (gr. 5-7). pap. 9.99 *(978-1-4778-1668-4(2),* 9781477816684, Amazon Children's Publishing) Amazon Publishing.

Funke, Cornelia. Thief Lord. Birmingham, Christian, illus. 2010. (ENG.). 376p. (J). (gr. 3-7). 7.99 *(978-0-545-22770-4(4),* Chicken Hse., The) Scholastic, Inc.

Furcron, Bertha Phillips. No Half, No Step, Just a Whole. Hendrick, Betty Acey, illus. 2003. Orig. Title: Yes. 32p. (J). (gr. 1-3). lib. bdg. 15.95 *(978-1-884242-55-7(3));* pap. 7.95 *(978-1-884242-57-1(X))* Multicultural Pubns.

Furraway, Bec. Matthew's Family Moves / Robert's Family Moves. 2011. 30p. pap. 14.50 *(978-1-60860-995-6(2),* Strategic Bk. Publishing) Strategic Book Publishing & Rights Agency (SBPRA).

Fusco, Kimberly Newton. Tending to Grace. 2005. (ENG.). 184p. (YA). (gr. 7-12). per. 6.99 *(978-0-553-49423-5(6),* Laurel Leaf) Random Hse. Children's Bks.

Fussell, Bonnie. More Than a Stove. Sadler, Dale, illus. l.t. ed. 2004. 32p. (J). pap. 7.99 *(978-0-615-12702-6(9))* Blackberry Pubs.

Gainey, Gary. The Bonds. Gillen, Rosemarie, illus. 2012. 150p. pap. 9.99 *(978-1-937260-12-5(7))* Sleepytown Pr.

Galante, Cecilia. Hershey Herself. 2008. (Mix Ser.). (ENG.). 336p. (J). (gr. 4-8). pap. 15.99 *(978-1-4169-5463-7(5),* Simon & Schuster/Paula Wiseman Bks.) Simon & Schuster/Paula Wiseman Bks.

Galindo, Renata. My New Mom & Me. 2016. (ENG., Illus.). 32p. (J). (gr. -1-2). 19.99 *(978-0-553-52135-1(7),* Schwartz & Wade Bks.) Random Hse. Children's Bks.

Gallagher, Diana G. Beach Blues: The Complicated Life of Claudia Cristina Cortez, 1 vol. Garvey, Brann, illus. 2008. (Claudia Cristina Cortez Ser.). (ENG.). 88p. (gr. 2-3). pap. 6.10 *(978-1-4342-0869-9(9),* Claudia Cristina Cortez) Stone Arch Bks.

Gallagher, Mary. Mulhern Twins. 2007. (ENG., Illus.). 126p. (J). pap. 11.95 *(978-1-905172-17-7(6))* Collins Pr., The IRL. Dist: Dufour Editions, Inc.

Galusha, Carol. Same Birthday. 2008. 128p. pap. 10.95 *(978-1-60594-130-1(1),* Llumina Pr.) Aeon Publishing Inc.

Galvin, Laura Gates. Baby Duck Gets Lost. 2007. (Baby Animals Ser.). (ENG., Illus.). 16p. (gr. -1-k). 6.95 *(978-1-59249-747-8(0))* Soundprints.

—I Love My Family. 2011. (ENG.). 16p. (J). *(978-1-60727-621-0(6))* Soundprints.

Gamache, Line. Hello, Me Pretty. Cochrane, KerryAnn, tr. from FRE. 2007. (ENG., Illus.). 64p. per. *(978-1-894994-23-1(X))* Conundrum Pr.

Gambini, Josephine. Poetino Piccolino Saves the Day. Stafford, Jordan, illus. 2011. (ENG.). (J). pap. 19.95 *(978-0-9829496-3-4(4))* Giusti-Gambini, J.M. Publishing, LLC.

Gamble, Adam & Jasper, Mark. Good Night Alberta. Chan, Suwin, illus. 2017. (Good Night Our World Ser.). (ENG.). 20p. (J). (— 1). bds. 9.95 *(978-1-60219-442-7(4))* Good Night Bks.

Gamble, Adam, et al. Good Night New Baby. 2014. (Good Night Our World Ser.). (ENG., Illus.). 20p. (J). (— 1). bds. 9.95 *(978-1-60219-188-4(3))* Good Night Bks.

Gansworth, Eric L. If I Ever Get Out of Here. (ENG.). 368p. (J). (gr. 7). 2015. pap. 10.99 *(978-0-545-41731-0(7))* 2013. 17.99 *(978-0-545-41730-3(9))* Scholastic, Inc. (Levine, Arthur A. Bks.).

Gant, Gene. The Thunder in His Head [Library Edition]. 2012. 200p. (-18). pap. 14.99 *(978-1-62380-903-4(7),* Harmony Ink Pr.) Dreamspinner Pr.

Gantos, Jack. The Trouble in Me. 2017. (YA). lib. bdg. 20.85 ***(978-0-606-39592-2(X))*** Turtleback Bks.

Gantos, Jack. What Would Joey Do? 2004. (Joey Pigza Ser.: Bk. 3). 240p. (J). (gr. 5-9). pap. 36.00 incl. audio *(978-1-4000-9020-4(2),* Listening Library) Random Hse. Audio Publishing Group.

Ganzer, Diane & Swanson, Christopher. Called to Serve. 2008. 116p. pap. 9.99 *(978-1-935105-10-7(8))* Avid Readers Publishing Group.

García, Cristina. The Dog Who Loved the Moon. Serra, Sebastia, illus. 2011. (ENG.). 32p. (J). (gr. -1-3). 16.99 *(978-1-4424-3089-1(3),* Atheneum Bks. for Young Readers) Simon & Schuster Children's Publishing.

—I Wanna Be Your Shoebox. 2009. (ENG.). 208p. (J). (gr. 3-7). pap. 6.99 *(978-1-4169-7904-3(2),* Simon & Schuster Bks. For Young Readers) Simon & Schuster Bks. For Young Readers.

Garcia, Molly. G. G. The Diary fo a Space Case. 2007. 77p. pap. 9.95 *(978-0-7414-3838-6(0))* Infinity Publishing.

Garcia, Richard. Los Espiritus de Mi Tia Otilia. 2004. (ENG & SPA., Illus.). (J). (gr. k-3). spiral bd. *(978-0-616-14606-4(X))* Canadian National Institute for the Blind/Institut National Canadien pour les Aveugles.

Garis, Howard R. Curlytops at Uncle Frank's Ranch. 2011. 118p. 22.95 *(978-1-4638-9714-7(6))* 2009. 120p. pap. 10.95 *(978-1-60664-408-9(4))* Rodgers, Alan Bks.

Garis, Howard Roger. Uncle Wiggily's Happy Days. Date not set. 226p. (J). 21.95 *(978-0-8488-2650-5(7))* Amereon Ltd.

Garland, Michael. Super Snow Day Seek & Find. 2010. (ENG.). 32p. (J). (gr. -1-2). 16.99 *(978-0-525-42245-7(5),* Dutton Books for Young Readers) Penguin Young Readers Group.

Garland, Sally Anne. Share. Garland, Sally Anne, illus. 2014. (ENG., Illus.). 32p. (J). (gr. -1-3). 17.95 *(978-1-77147-005-6(4),* Owlkids) Owlkids Bks. Inc. CAN. Dist: Publishers Group West (PGW).

Garratt, Irene Joyce. Andrew's Activities: Two in One Stories. 2009. (Illus.). 20p. pap. 10.49 *(978-1-4389-4235-3(4))* AuthorHouse.

Gartlan, Daniel. Poor Hannah. 2012. 24p. pap. 24.95 *(978-1-4626-6030-8(4))* America Star Bks.

Garza, Xavier. Lucha Libre: The Man in the Silver Mask - A Bilingual Cuento. Garza, Xavier, illus. 2007. (SPA & ENG., Illus.). 40p. (J). (gr. 4-6). pap. 8.95 *(978-1-933693-10-1(X))* Cinco Puntos Pr.

Garza, Xavier, illus. Maximilian & the Mystery of the Guardian Angel. 2011. (Max's Lucha Libre Adventures Ser.). (SPA & ENG.). 160p. (J). (gr. 5-8). pap. 12.95 *(978-1-933693-98-9(3))* Cinco Puntos Pr.

Gauthier, Gilles. La Petite Lili Est un Genie. Derome, Pierre-André, illus. 2004. (Premier Roman Ser.). (FRE.). 64p. (J). (gr. 1-4). pap. *(978-2-89021-686-0(1))* Diffusion du livre Mirabel (DLM).

Gay, Homel D. On the Road Again! More Travels with My Family. Gay, Marie-Louise, illus. 2008. (ENG.). 120p. (J). (gr. 1-5). 15.95 *(978-0-88899-846-0(5))* Groundwood Bks. CAN. Dist: Publishers Group West (PGW).

Gaydos, Nora. I'M a New Big Brother: Little Steps for Big Kids. 2010. (ENG., Illus.). 30p. (J). (gr. -1-17). 8.99 *(978-1-60169-010-4(X))* Innovative Kids.

Gayken, D. Rae. Grandma's Baseball Card: A Braynard Family Story. 2007. 60p. per. 8.95 *(978-0-595-45439-6(9))* iUniverse, Inc.

Gehrke, William & Gehrke, Dolores. Sonia's Choice. 2011. 28p. pap. 15.99 *(978-1-4634-0825-1(0))* AuthorHouse.

Geller, Beverly. Ellies Shabbat Surprise. 2008. 32p. 13.95 *(978-965-229-390-9(3))* Gefen Publishing Hse., Ltd ISR. Dist: Gefen Bks.

George, Jessica Day. Silver in the Blood. 2016. (ENG.). 368p. (YA). pap. 9.99 *(978-1-68119-024-2(9),* 9781681190242, Bloomsbury USA Childrens) Bloomsbury Publishing USA.

Geras, Adèle. Watching the Roses: The Egerton Hall Novels, Volume Two, Vol. 2. 2005. (ENG.). 192p. (YA). (gr. 7-12). pap. 11.95 *(978-0-15-205531-8(2))* Houghton Mifflin Harcourt Publishing Co.

Gerber, Alyson. Braced. 2017. (ENG.). 304p. (J). (gr. 3-7). 16.99 *(978-0-545-90214-4(2))* Scholastic, Inc.

Gerlach-Babb nee Maines, Mary & Gerlach, Susan. Best Christmas Gift. 2007. (ENG.). 52p. per. 16.95 *(978-1-4241-6389-2(7))* America Star Bks.

Gervay, Susanne. Always Jack. Wilcox, Cathy, illus. 2013. 148p. (J). *(978-1-61067-226-9(7))* Kane Miller.

—Being Jack. Wilcox, Cathy, illus. 2015. 167p. (J). *(978-1-61067-455-3(3))* Kane Miller.

—I Am Jack. Cathy, Wilcox, illus. 2013. (ENG.). 144p. (J). pap. 5.99 *(978-1-61067-128-6(7))* Kane Miller.

Gervay, Susanne & Wilcox, Cathy. Always Jack. 2014. (ENG.). 160p. (J). pap. 5.99 *(978-1-61067-130-9(9))* Kane Miller.

Gewirtz, Adina Rishe. Zebra Forest. 2014. (ENG., Illus.). 208p. (J). (gr. 4-7). pap. 7.99 *(978-0-7636-7166-2(5))* Candlewick Pr.

Ghigna, Charles. Bobby Bear. East, Jacqueline, illus. 2015. (Tiny Tales Ser.). (ENG.). 64p. (gr. -1-2). lib. bdg. 23.99 *(978-1-4795-6531-3(8))* Tiny Tales.

Giff, Patricia Reilly. Pictures of Hollis Woods. 2014. (ENG.). 176p. (J). (gr. 3-7). 11.24 *(978-1-63245-318-1(5))* Lectorum Pubns., Inc.

—Pictures of Hollis Woods. 2004. (ENG.). 176p. (J). (gr. 3-7). 7.99 *(978-0-440-41578-7(0),* Yearling) Random Hse. Children's Bks.

—Storyteller. 2011. (ENG.). 176p. (J). (gr. 3-7). pap. 6.99 *(978-0-440-42175-7(6),* Yearling) Random Hse. Children's Bks.

—Water Street. 2008. (ENG.). 176p. (J). (gr. 3-7). 6.99 *(978-0-440-41921-1(2),* Yearling) Random Hse. Children's Bks.

Gikow, Louise. A Day with Daddy. Mazali, Gustavo, illus. 2004. (My First Reader Ser.). (ENG.). 32p. (J). (gr. k-1). pap. 3.95 *(978-0-516-25501-9(0),* Children's Pr.) Scholastic Library Publishing.

Giles, Gail. Right Behind You. 2008. (ENG.). 320p. (J). (gr. 10-17). pap. 10.99 *(978-0-316-16637-9(5))* Little, Brown Bks. for Young Readers.

Gillingham, Sara & Siminovich, Lorena. In My Tree. 2009. (ENG., Illus.). 12p. (J). (gr. -1 — 1). bds. 8.99 *(978-0-8118-7052-8(9))* Chronicle Bks. LLC.

Gingras, Marie Claude. Let's Spend Summer with Fred. 2012. 198p. 24.95 *(978-1-4626-4413-1(9))* America Star Bks.

Giuliani, Al. New Nanny. 2013. (Jessie Junior Novel Ser.). (ENG.). 128p. (J). (gr. 3-7). pap. 5.99 *(978-1-4231-8369-3(X))* Disney Pr.

Glick, Shifra. Shikufitsky, Vol. 2. Glick, Shifra, illus. (Illus.). 100p. (J). 19.99 *(978-1-58330-640-6(4))* Feldheim Pubs.

Glines, Abbi. Under the Lights. 2016. (Field Party Ser.: 2). (ENG., Illus.). 336p. (YA). (gr. 9). 17.99 *(978-1-4814-3889-6(1),* Simon Pulse) Simon Pulse.

Glover, Sandra. Dangerously Close. 2008. (ENG.). 176p. (YA). (gr. 7). pap. 9.99 *(978-1-84270-679-4(9))* Andersen Pr. GBR. Dist: Independent Pubs. Group.

Glynn, Eoin. Mischief at Se. 2009. 232p. pap. 14.49 *(978-1-4389-4919-2(7))* AuthorHouse.

Godbersen, Anna. Rumors. 2008. (Luxe Ser.: No. 2). (YA). (gr. 9-12). (ENG.). 304p. 17.99 *(978-0-06-134569-2(5));* 423p. lib. bdg. 18.89 *(978-0-06-134570-8(9))* HarperCollins Pubs. (HarperTeen).

Godby, Ron. The King of Imperial Hill. 2006. 76p. pap. 16.95 *(978-1-4241-1061-2(0))* PublishAmerica, Inc.

Goebel, Jenny. Fortune Falls. 2016. (ENG.). 208p. (J). (gr. 3-7). 16.99 *(978-0-545-81190-3(2),* Scholastic Pr.) Scholastic, Inc.

Going, K. L. King of the Screwups. 2010. (ENG., Illus.). 320p. (YA). (gr. 7). pap. 9.99 *(978-0-547-33166-9(5))* Houghton Mifflin Harcourt Publishing Co.

Golden Books Staff. Little Golden Book Favorites. Scarry, Richard & Golden Books Staff, illus. 2008. (Little Golden Book Favorites Ser.). (ENG.). 80p. (J). (gr. -1-2). 7.99 *(978-0-375-84580-2(1),* Golden Bks.) Random Hse. Children's Bks.

Goldin, Barbara Diamond. The Best Hanukkah Ever, 0 vols. 2013. (ENG.). 34p. (J). (gr. k-3). pap. 9.99 *(978-1-4778-1055-2(2),* 9781477810552, Amazon Children's Publishing) Amazon Publishing.

Goldstein, Bobby. The Story of the Pink Gorilla Monster. 2012. 40p. pap. 17.99 *(978-1-4490-6377-1(2))* AuthorHouse.

Gomes, Linda Nunes. Special Words: A Story about Multicultural Families & Their Pets. Levine, Lenora D., illus. 2007. (YA). per. 12.99 *(978-1-934400-02-9(5))* Rock Village Publishing.

Gonzalez, Gabriela & Triana, Gaby. Backstage Pass. 2004. (Illus.). 224p. (J). (gr. 7-18). lib. bdg. 16.89 *(978-0-06-056018-8(5))* HarperCollins Pubs.

Gonzalez, Maya Christina & Perez, Amada Irma. My Very Own Room: Mi Propio Cuartito. 2013. (ENG & SPA., Illus.). 32p. (J). (gr. k-4). pap. 9.95 *(978-0-89239-223-0(1))* Lee & Low Bks., Inc.

Gonzßlez Valdts, Alberto Domingo. Sueños de Obama/Obama's Dreams. 2008. (SPA.). 164p. pap. 15.00 *(978-1-4389-3773-1(3))* AuthorHouse.

Good Dog... Not So Good Dog. 2007. (J). *(978-0-9793568-1-0(4))* Merlin, Debbi.

Goodier, Eleanor, et al. The Vermin Family Adventures (Book 1) 2010. 68p. pap. 9.50 *(978-1-4457-5617-2(X))* Lulu Pr., Inc.

Goodman, Allegra. The Other Side of the Island. 2009. (ENG.). 288p. (YA). (gr. 7-18). pap. 8.99 *(978-1-59514-196-5(0),* Razorbill) Penguin Young Readers Group.

Goodman-Schneps, Oriana. The Seventh Chime. 2009. 52p. pap. 15.99 *(978-1-4415-2748-6(6))* Xlibris Corp.

Goodwin, Brian. Pineapple Soap. 2007. 130p. pap. 9.50 *(978-0-615-16104-4(9))* Goodwin, Brian.

Gopinath, Karin Ursula. Friends in the Garden. Sutanto, Tommy, illus. 2008. 34p. (J). per. 19.95 *(978-0-9800637-0-7(1))* Lotus Art Works Inc.

Goss, Jamie. The Snake Without a Hiss, 1 vol. 2010. 36p. pap. 24.95 *(978-1-4489-4446-0(5))* PublishAmerica, Inc.

Gould, M&R. The Bleeks: The Bleek Family's First Christmas, 1 vol. Hurst, Debbie, illus. 2010. 30p. pap. 24.95 *(978-1-4489-2770-8(6))* PublishAmerica, Inc.

Gownley, Jimmy. Her Permanent Record. Gownley, Jimmy, illus. 2012. (Amelia Rules! Ser.). (ENG., Illus.). 160p. (J). (gr. 2-7). 19.99 *(978-1-4169-8615-7(4));* pap. 11.99 *(978-1-4169-8614-0(6))* Simon & Schuster Children's Publishing. (Atheneum Bks. for Young Readers).

—What Makes You Happy. Gownley, Jimmy, illus. 2011. (Amelia Rules! Ser.). (ENG., Illus.). 176p. (J). (gr. 2-7). 19.99 *(978-1-4424-4539-0(4),* Atheneum Bks. for Young Readers) Simon & Schuster Children's Publishing.

—When the Past Is a Present. Gownley, Jimmy, illus. 2011. (Amelia Rules! Ser.). (ENG., Illus.). 176p. (J). (gr. 2-7). 19.99 *(978-1-4424-4541-3(6),* Atheneum Bks. for Young Readers) Simon & Schuster Children's Publishing.

Grady, Joi. I Like You & I Love You. 2012. 36p. pap. 20.99 *(978-1-4670-3953-6(5))* AuthorHouse.

Graff, Lisa. The Life & Crimes of Bernetta Wallflower: The Pros & Cons. 2015. (ENG.). 288p. (J). (gr. 3-7). 7.99 *(978-0-14-751675-6(7),* Puffin Books) Penguin Young Readers Group.

—The Thing about Georgie. 2008. (ENG.). 224p. (J). (gr. 3-7). pap. 6.99 *(978-0-06-087591-6(7))* HarperCollins Pubs.

Graham, Michael, illus. The Great Inhibinator. 2006. 44p. (J). *(978-0-9772977-0-2(5))* Bio Rx.

Grannie Annie, Vol. 1. 2006. (Illus.). 81p. (J). pap. 14.95 *(978-0-9677685-9-5(4))* Grannie Annie Family Story Celebration, The.

Grannie Annie: Selections from the Grannie Annie Family Story Celebration, Vol. 2. 2007. (Illus.). 86p. (J). pap. 14.95 *(978-0-9793296-1-6(2))* Grannie Annie Family Story Celebration, The.

Grant, Tess. Flying in the Dark. 2013. 186p. pap. 10.99 *(978-1-62237-167-9(4))* Turquoise Morning Pr.

Grant, Vicki. B Negative, 1 vol. 2011. (Orca Soundings Ser.). (ENG.). 136p. (YA). (gr. 8-12). pap. 9.95 *(978-1-55469-841-7(3));* lib. bdg. 16.95 *(978-1-55469-842-4(1))* Orca Bk. Pubs. USA.

Grantner, Anne M. & Haggart, Gary. Without a Home. Hannon, Kenneth, photos by. 2003. (Illus.). 35p. (YA). (gr. 5-18). pap. 12.95 *(978-0-9740929-0-4(8))* Shelter of Flint, Inc.

Gratz, Alan. Code of Honor. 2015. (ENG.). 288p. (J). (gr. 7). 17.99 *(978-0-545-69519-0(8),* Scholastic Pr.) Scholastic, Inc.

Graves, Anna Louise. How Can You Lose Something as Big as a Farm? 2007. 102p. pap. 10.95 *(978-0-7414-4029-7(6))* Infinity Publishing.

Gravley, Debbie Bybee. Golden Lace & the Magical Mossy Woods. 2005. 25.00 *(978-0-9771793-0-5(3))* Gravley, Debbie Bybee.

Gray, Kes. Daisy & the Trouble with Giants. Sharratt, Nick & Parsons, Garry, illus. 2010. (Daisy Ser.: 10). (ENG.). 256p. (J). (gr. 2-4). pap. 11.99 *(978-1-86230-495-6(5),* Red Fox) Random House Children's Books GBR. Dist: Independent Pubs. Group.

Gray, Laurie. Summer Sanctuary. 2010. (ENG.). 193p. (YA). (gr. 7). pap. 11.95 *(978-1-935462-34-7(2))* Luminis Bks., Inc.

Green, D. L. Zeke Meeks vs the Annoying Princess Sing-Along, 1 vol. Alves, Josh, illus. 2014. (Zeke Meeks Ser.). (ENG.). 128p. (gr. 2-2). 22.65 *(978-1-4795-4828-6(6),* Zeke Meeks) Picture Window Bks.

Green, Judith. A Family Secret. Hammah, Aisha, illus. 2013. 32p. pap. *(978-0-9810759-7-6(5))* WTL International.

Green, Tim. Home Run. 2016. (Baseball Great Ser.: 4). 352p. (J). (gr. 3-7). 16.99 *(978-0-06-231711-7(3))* HarperCollins Pubs.

Green with Envy. 2014. (Unicorn Magic Ser.: 3). (ENG., Illus.). 144p. (J). (gr. 1-4). pap. 5.99 *(978-1-4424-9826-6(9),* Aladdin) Simon & Schuster Children's Publishing.

Greenburg, J. C. In the Deep. Gerardi, Jan, illus. 2004. (Andrew Lost Ser.: 8). (ENG.). 96p. (J). (gr. 1-4). 3.99 *(978-0-375-82526-2(6),* Random Hse. Bks. for Young Readers) Random Hse. Children's Bks.

—In the Desert. Gerardi, Jan, illus. 2008. (Andrew Lost Ser.: 17). (ENG.). 96p. (J). (gr. 1-4). per. 3.99 *(978-0-375-84667-0(0),* Random Hse. Bks. for Young Readers) Random Hse. Children's Bks.

—In Uncle Al, No. 16. Gerardi, Jan, illus. 2007. (Andrew Lost Ser.: 16). (ENG.). 96p. (J). (gr. 1-4). 3.99 *(978-0-375-83565-0(2),* Random Hse. Bks. for Young Readers) Random Hse. Children's Bks.

—Under Water. Reed, Mike, illus. 2003. (Andrew Lost Ser.: 5). (ENG.). 96p. (J). (gr. 1-4). mass mkt. 3.99 *(978-0-375-82523-1(1),* Random Hse. Bks. for Young Readers) Random Hse. Children's Bks.

—With the Frogs. Gerardi, Jan, illus. 2008. (Andrew Lost Ser.: 18). (ENG.). 96p. (J). (gr. 1-4). 3.99 *(978-0-375-84668-7(9),* Random Hse. Bks. for Young Readers) Random Hse. Children's Bks.

Greene, Brenda. Dog Gone: Boomer's Story. Cheryl H. Hahn, illus. 2005. 127p. (YA). per. 8.99 *(978-0-9770279-0-3(2))* Three Willows Pr.

Greene, Kimberly. My Sister's a Pop Star. 2011. (My Sister's a Pop Star Ser.). 277p. (J). pap. 5.99 *(978-0-7945-2899-7(6),* Usborne) EDC Publishing.

Greenhalgh, Miranda. Rapid Duck. 2007. (Illus.). 38p. (J). per. 14.99 *(978-1-59879-348-2(9),* Lifevest) Lifevest Publishing, Inc.

Greenwald, Tommy. It's a Doggy Dog World. Stower, Adam, illus. 2016. (Crimebiters Ser.: 2). (ENG.). 240p. (J). (gr. 3-7). 12.99 *(978-0-545-78397-2(6),* Scholastic Pr.) Scholastic, Inc.

Gregory, Jeannette. Honor Your Father & Mother. 2004. (J). 6.99 *(978-0-9754779-5-3(1))* Chosen Word Publishing.

Gremila, Elaine Demetri. Seasons of the Heart. l.t. ed. 2003. (Illus.). 140p. per. 11.95 *(978-1-932338-16-4(0))* Lifevest Publishing, Inc.

Griffin, Adele. Sons of Liberty. 2003. (LRS Large Print Cornerstone Ser.). (J). lib. bdg. 29.95 *(978-1-58118-096-1(9),* 25333) LRS.

Griffis, Molly Levite. Simon Says. 2004. vi, 263p. (J). 22.95 *(978-1-57168-836-1(6));* pap. *(978-1-57168-847-7(1))* Eakin Pr. (Eakin Pr.).

Grimm, Jacob & Grimm, Wilhelm K. The Fisherman & His Wife: A Tale about Being Happy & Satisfied. Ebert, Len, illus. 2006. (J). *(978-1-59939-097-0(3),* Reader's Digest Young Families, Inc.) Studio Fun International.

Griser, Carol. Breona's New Life. 2009. 24p. pap. 14.00 *(978-1-4389-4975-8(8))* AuthorHouse.

Groening, Matt. Simpsons Comics Colossal Compendium Volume 2. 2014. (ENG., Illus.). 176p. pap. 17.99 *(978-0-06-233609-5(6),* Collins Design) HarperCollins Pubs.

Grogan, Shannon. From Where I Watch You. 2016. (ENG.). 304p. (YA). (gr. 9). pap. 10.99 *(978-1-61695-689-9(5),* Soho Teen) Soho Pr., Inc.

Gross, Kimberley & Gross, Kaiya. The Multiplication Monster. Gross, Sanai, illus. 2013. 84p. pap. 10.95 *(978-0-9886402-3-8(6))* G.E. Bks.

Grove, Ella. A Surprise for Tommy. 2005. (Illus.). 24p. (gr. -1-5). 2.70 *(978-0-7399-2341-2(2),* 2780) Rod & Staff Pubs., Inc.

Grover, Lorie Ann. Hold Me Tight. 2007. (ENG.). 352p. (J). (gr. 5-9). pap. 16.95 *(978-1-4169-6753-8(2),* McElderry, Margaret K. Bks.) McElderry, Margaret K. Bks.

Grubman, Bonnie. Oy Vey! Life in a Shoe. Mottram, Dave, illus. 2016. (J). *(978-1-68115-515-9(X))* Behrman Hse., Inc.

Guest, Jacqueline. Outcasts of River Falls, 1 vol. Peetoom, Laura, ed. 2012. (ENG.). 248p. (J). (gr. 4-7). pap. 9.95 *(978-1-55050-480-4(0))* Coteau Bks. CAN. Dist: Orca Bk. Pubs. USA.

—Wild Ride, 1 vol. 2005. (Lorimer SideStreets Ser.). (ENG.). 168p. (YA). (gr. 9-12). 16.95 *(978-1-55028-881-0(4),* 9781550288810) Lorimer, James & Co., Ltd., Pubs. CAN. Dist: Casemate Pubs. & Bk. Distributors, LLC.

Gurevich, Margaret. Gina's Balance. 2016. (What's Your Dream? Ser.). (ENG., Illus.). 96p. (gr. 3-4). lib. bdg. 25.32 *(978-1-4965-3443-9(3))* Capstone Press of Coughlan Cos.

Gurnick, Isabella Grace & Beals, Stephen Naayvek. Girls Have Eyelashes. 2004. 39p. pap. 11.63 *(978-1-4116-1696-7(0))* Lulu Pr., Inc.

Gutierrez, Debbi Miller. Cactus Factory. 2007. (J). pap. 5.99 *(978-0-9740173-4-1(5))* Prints By Mail.

Gutierrez-Green, Sandra. The Colors in My Garden. 2005. 36p. per. 19.25 *(978-1-4208-4266-1(8))* AuthorHouse.

E
F
G

Gwaltney, Doris. Homefront. 2009. (ENG.). 320p. (J). (gr. 5-9). pap. 6.99 (978-1-4169-9572-2(2), Simon & Schuster Bks. For Young Readers) Simon & Schuster Bks. For Young Readers.

Haddix, Margaret Peterson. Caught. 2012. (Missing Ser.: 5). (ENG.). 352p. (J). (gr. 3-7). 16.99 (978-1-4169-8982-0(X), Simon & Schuster Bks. For Young Readers) Simon & Schuster Bks. For Young Readers.

—Double Identity. 2007. (ENG.). 192p. (J). (gr. 5-9). pap. 7.99 (978-0-689-87379-9(4), Simon & Schuster Bks. For Young Readers) Simon & Schuster Bks. For Young Readers.

—Double Identity. rev. l.t. ed. 2007. (Literacy Bridge Young Adult Ser.). 299p. (J). (gr. 5-9). 22.95 (978-0-7862-9702-3(6)) Thorndike Pr.

—Into the Gauntlet. 2010. (39 Clues Ser.: 10). (ENG.). 336p. (J). (gr. 3-7). 12.99 (978-0-545-06050-9(8)) Scholastic, Inc.

—The Shadow Children: Among the Hidden; Among the Impostors; Among the Betrayed; Among the Barons; Among the Brave; Among the Enemy; Among the Free. 2012. (Shadow Children Ser.). (ENG., Illus.). 1424p. (J). (gr. 3-7). pap. 55.99 (978-1-4424-6864-1(5), Simon & Schuster Bks. For Young Readers) Simon & Schuster Bks. For Young Readers.

—Takeoffs & Landings. 2003. (ENG., Illus.). 208p. (J). (gr. 4-8). pap. 6.99 (978-0-689-85543-6(5), Simon & Schuster Bks. For Young Readers) Simon & Schuster Bks. For Young Readers.

Haesche, Richard, Sr. Ghost Wolf. 2007. (ENG.). 207p. (YA). 10.99 (978-0-9798536-5-4(6)) Kreative X-Pressions Pubns.

—The Mystery of Monster Manor. 2007. (ENG.). 306p. (YA). 11.99 (978-0-9798536-6-1(4)) Kreative X-Pressions Pubns.

Hahn, Blair. My Purple Kisses. Nation, Tate, illus. 2011. (My Purple Toes Ser.). 26p. (J). bds. 10.99 (978-0-9844556-7-6(1)) My Purple Toes, LLC.

Halahmy, Miriam. Behind Closed Doors. 2017. **(978-0-8234-3792-4(2))** Holiday Hse., Inc.

Halcomb, Suzanne. The Mcfee Family Harvest. 2012. 40p. pap. 19.75 (978-1-4269-9647-4(0)) Trafford Publishing.

Halcoop, Ursula Lily. Journey. 2012. 160p. pap. 12.50 (978-1-61204-959-5(1), Strategic Bk. Publishing) Strategic Book Publishing & Rights Agency (SBPRA).

Hale, Lucretia Peabody. The Last of the Peterkins: With Others of Their Kin. 2007. (ENG.). 142p. pap. 18.99 (978-1-4346-2126-9(X)); 154p. pap. 21.99 (978-1-4346-2145-0(6)) Creative Media Partners, LLC.

Hall, Barbara. That Is Choice! 2009. 192p. pap. (978-1-84748-314-0(3)) Athena Pr.

Hall, Hannah. God Bless Our Baby, 1 vol. Whitlow, Steve, illus. 2017. (God Bless Book Ser.). (ENG.). 20p. (J). bds. 9.99 (978-0-7180-8666-4(X)) Nelson, Thomas Inc.

Hall, Maggie. The Conspiracy of Us. 2015. (Conspiracy of Us Ser.). (ENG.). (YA). 336p. (gr. 7). 17.99 (978-0-399-16650-1(5));Pack. 161.91 (978-0-399-17404-9(4)) Penguin Young Readers Group. (G.P. Putnam's Sons Books for Young Readers).

Hall, Martha Gamble. A Note from Sant. 2008. 16p. pap. 10.99 (978-1-4389-2308-6(2)) AuthorHouse.

Hall, Susan, illus. Dora's Cousin Diego. 2011. (Dora & Diego Ser.). (ENG.). 24p. (J). pap. 3.99 (978-1-4424-1399-3(9), Simon Spotlight/Nickelodeon) Simon Spotlight/Nickelodeon.

Hall, Terri L. & Babeaux, Denise L. The Story of Chester the Chow Chow. 2011. 48p. pap. 24.95 (978-1-4560-3748-2(X)) America Star Bks.

Hallagin, Janet. The Way of Courage. 2006. 30.99 (978-1-4257-1249-5(5)); pap. 20.99 (978-1-4257-1248-8(7)) Xlibris Corp.

Hamilton, Virginia. Primos. 2003.Tr. of Cousins. (SPA., Illus.). 126p. (J). (gr. 5-8). pap. 9.95 (978-84-204-4747-6(1), LEC7471) Santillana USA Publishing Co., Inc.

Hamley, Dennis. Without Warning: Ellen's Story, 1914-1918. 2007. (ENG., Illus.). 336p. (YA). (gr. 7). 17.99 (978-0-7636-3338-7(0)) Candlewick Pr.

Hammond, Barbara, illus. The Duffy Chronicles. Hammond, Barbara, . 2007. 60p. pap. 11.99 (978-0-9800675-4-5(5)) Mirror Publishing.

Hampton, Randall. A Christmas Kiss. l.t. ed. 2005. (Illus.). 48p. (J). per. 16.95 (978-1-59879-048-1(X)) Lifevest Publishing, Inc.

Hankins, Larry. Stickboy at the Fair. 2011. 32p. pap. 24.95 (978-1-4512-2206-7(8)) America Star Bks.

Hanlon, Abby. Dory & the Real True Friend. 2016. (Dory Ser.: 2). lib. bdg. 18.40 (978-0-606-38846-7(X)) Turtleback Bks.

—Dory Fantasmagory. 2015. (Dory Fantasmagory Ser.: 1). (ENG., Illus.). 176p. (J). (gr. 1-3). 7.99 (978-0-14-751067-9(8), Puffin Books) Penguin Young Readers Group.

Hannam, John-Pierre M., Sr. Uncle Jake's Hat. 2009. 43p. pap. 20.00 (978-0-557-02568-8(0)) Lulu Pr., Inc.

Hannigan, Kate. Summer Showers. Hughes, Brooke Boynton, illus. 2016. (Cupcake Cousins Ser.: Bk. 2). (ENG.). 256p. (J). (gr. 3-7). pap. 6.99 (978-1-4847-2362-3(7)) Hyperion Bks. for Children.

Hansen, Francis & Hansen, Caroline. Finally a Friend. 2003. (Illus.). 117p. (J). per. (978-0-9722501-1-5(5)) Backwoods Publishing Co.

Hansen, Roland. The Story of a Butterfly Called Bee. 2010. 32p. pap. 9.96 (978-0-9843426-2-4(1)) G Publishing LLC.

Harding, Susan. Here I Am! 2008. 20p. pap. 24.95 (978-1-60474-093-6(0)) America Star Bks.

Hargis, Alvin. Kingdom of Mystique Series: Book 1. 2007. 25p. pap. 24.95 (978-1-4241-8635-8(8)) PublishAmerica, Inc.

Harlow, Joan Hiatt. Blown Away! 2008. (ENG.). 272p. (J). (gr. 4-7). pap. 7.99 (978-1-4169-0782-4(3), McElderry, Margaret K. Bks.) McElderry, Margaret K. Bks.

Harmon, Michael. Skate. 2008. (ENG.). 256p. (YA). (gr. 9). per. 6.99 (978-0-553-49510-2(0), Laurel Leaf) Random Hse. Children's Bks.

HarperCollins Publishers Ltd. Staff, et al. Paddington: Paddington's World. 2014. (Paddington Ser.). (ENG., Illus.). 24p. (J). (gr. -1-3). pap. 3.99 (978-0-06-234997-2(X)) HarperCollins Pubs.

Harrington, Claudia. My Grandparents, 1 vol. Persico, Zoe, illus. 2016. (ENG.). 32p. (J). (978-1-62402-105-3(0)) Magic Wagon.

—My Military Mom, 1 vol. Persico, Zoe, illus. 2016. (ENG.). 32p. (J). (978-1-62402-106-0(9)) Magic Wagon.

—My Mom & Dad, 1 vol. Persico, Zoe, illus. 2016. (ENG.). 32p. (J). (978-1-62402-107-7(7)) Magic Wagon.

—My Two Dads, 1 vol. Persico, Zoe, illus. 2016. (ENG.). 32p. (J). (978-1-62402-108-4(5)) Magic Wagon.

—My Two Homes, 1 vol. Persico, Zoe, illus. 2016. (ENG.). 32p. (J). (978-1-62402-109-1(3)) Magic Wagon.

—My Two Moms, 1 vol. Persico, Zoe, illus. 2016. (ENG.). 32p. (J). (978-1-62402-110-7(7)) Magic Wagon.

Harrington, Karen. Mayday. 2016. (ENG.). 352p. (J). (gr. 3-7). 16.99 (978-0-316-29801-8(8)) Little, Brown Bks. for Young Readers.

—Sure Signs of Crazy. 2014. (ENG.). 304p. (J). (gr. 5-17). pap. 7.99 (978-0-316-21049-2(8)) Little, Brown Bks. for Young Readers.

Harris, Missy. I'm Allergic. 2008. 16p. pap. 12.99 (978-1-4343-9421-7(2)) AuthorHouse.

Harris, Robie H. Who's in My Family? All about Our Families. Westcott, Nadine Bernard, illus. 2012. (Let's Talk about You & Me Ser.). (ENG.). 40p. (J). (gr. -1-2). 15.99 (978-0-7636-3631-9(2)) Candlewick Pr.

Harrod-Eagles, Cynthia. A Church Anniversary. 2011. 44p. pap. 18.46 (978-1-4567-6493-7(4)) AuthorHouse.

Hart, Christine. Best Laid Plans, 1 vol. 2009. (Lorimer SideStreets Ser.). (ENG.). 152p. (YA). (gr. 9-12). 9.95 (978-1-55277-446-5(5), 9781552774465) Lorimer, James & Co., Ltd., Pubs. CAN. Dist: Casemate Pubs. & Bk. Distributors, LLC.

Hart, Joy F. A New Family for Semoj. 2004. (Illus.). 242p. 9.65 (978-0-7399-2320-7(X), 2403) Rod & Staff Pubs., Inc.

Hart, Kate. After the Fall. 2017. (ENG.). 336p. (YA). 17.99 (978-0-374-30269-6(3), 9780374302696, Farrar, Straus & Giroux (BYR)) Farrar, Straus & Giroux.

Harvey-Fitzhenry, Alyxandra. Broken, 1 vol. 2010. (ENG., Illus.). 176p. (YA). (gr. 7-12). pap. 12.95 (978-1-896580-41-8(6)) Tradewind Bks. CAN. Dist: Orca Bk. Pubs. USA.

Harvey, Jacqueline. Clementine Rose & the Movie Magic. 2015. (Clementine Rose Ser.: 9). (ENG., Illus.). 128p. (J). (gr. 1-3). pap. 8.99 (978-0-85798-518-7(3)) Random Hse. Australia AUS. Dist: Independent Pubs. Group.

Harvey, Sarah N. Shattered, 1 vol. 2011. (Orca Soundings Ser.). (ENG.). 128p. (YA). (gr. 8-12). pap. 9.95 (978-1-55469-845-5(6)); lib. bdg. 16.95 (978-1-55469-846-2(4)) Orca Bk. Pubs. USA.

—Three Little Words, 1 vol. 2012. (ENG.). 224p. (YA). (gr. 8-12). pap. 14.95 (978-1-4598-0065-6(6)) Orca Bk. Pubs. USA.

Hatton, Jenny. Finding Aunt Joan. Rankin, Joan, illus. 2012. (Lucy Bks.). (ENG.). 32p. (J). (gr. k-2). pap. 6.95 (978-1-77009-803-9(8)) Jacana Media ZAF. Dist: Independent Pubs. Group.

Hautman, Pete. Mr. Was. 2012. (ENG.). 240p. (YA). (gr. 7). pap. 8.99 (978-1-4424-3337-3(X), Simon & Schuster Bks. For Young Readers) Simon & Schuster Bks. For Young Readers.

Hawthorne, Nathaniel. The House of the Seven Gables, 1 vol. Fisher, Scott, illus. 2011. (Calico Illustrated Classics Ser.). (ENG.). 112p. (J). (gr. 3-6). 27.07 (978-1-60270-746-7(4)) Magic Wagon.

Haxhia, Miranda. Andy's Cherry Tree. Deisadze, Zaur, illus. 2007. (POL & ENG.). 32p. (J). pap. 12.95 (978-1-60195-094-9(2)) International Step by Step Assn.

Hayes, Christine. Mothman's Curse. 2016. (J). lib. bdg. 18.40 (978-0-606-39560-1(1)) Turtleback Bks.

Hayes, Geoffrey. Benny & Penny in the Toy Breaker. Mouly, Francoise, ed. Hayes, Geoffrey, illus. 2010. (Benny & Penny Ser.). (ENG., Illus.). 32p. (J). (gr. -1-3). 12.95 (978-1-935179-07-8(1)) TOON Books / RAW Junior, LLC.

Haynes, Marilee. Pictures of Me. 2016. 149p. (J). pap. (978-0-8198-6019-4(0)) Pauline Bks. & Media.

Hayward, Laura. Why? 2004. 76p. (gr. 4-7). per. 11.50 (978-1-931195-25-6(0)) KiwE Publishing, Ltd.

Hayward, Linda. Monster Bug. Palmisciano, Diane, illus. 2004. 32p. (J). lib. bdg. 20.00 (978-1-4242-1097-8(6)) Fitzgerald Bks.

Headrick, Julianna. Our New Addition. Baker, David, illus. 2011. 28p. pap. 24.95 (978-1-4560-0933-5(8)) America Star Bks.

Heart, Sandra. Pernanna & Yerbo, the Toe-Tamals Family & Friends. 2011. 44p. pap. 21.99 (978-1-4568-3296-4(4)) Xlibris Corp.

Heather Heath Pruett. The Happy House. 2012. 24p. 24.95 (978-1-4626-6081-0(9)) America Star Bks.

Hecker, Vera, illus. A Home for Rainbow. 2007. 32p. (J). (978-0-9799729-0-4(6)) Banta, Sandra.

Hedderwick, Mairi. Katie Morag & the Big Boy Cousins. Hedderwick, Mairi, illus. 2010. (Katie Morag Ser.: 5). (ENG., Illus.). 32p. (J). (gr. k-2). pap. 12.99 (978-1-84941-089-2(5), Red Fox) Random House Children's Books GBR. Dist: Independent Pubs. Group.

Hegarty, Carol, ed. Teacher's Resource Guide. 2005. (Barclay Family Adventures 2 Ser.). (Illus.). 48p. (J). per. 9.95 (978-1-56254-813-1(1), SP8131) Saddleback Educational Publishing, Inc.

Hegarty, Patricia. We Are Family. Wheatcroft, Ryan, illus. 2017. (ENG.). 32p. (J). (gr. -1-2). 16.99 **(978-1-68010-054-9(8))** Tiger Tales.

Hegedus, Bethany. Between Us Baxters. 2009. 306p. (YA). (gr. 7-9). 17.95 (978-1-934813-02-7(8)) 2011. 9.14 (978-1-934813-18-8(4)) Westside Bks.

Heimerdinger, Chris. Escape from Zarahemla. 2011. 263p. (YA). pap. (978-1-60861-539-1(1)) Covenant Communications.

Helbig-Miller, Theresa. Nana & the Jabbywalker, 1 vol. Evans, Sherri, illus. 2008. (ENG.). 30p. 24.95 (978-1-60703-567-1(7)) America Star Bks.

Helget, Nicole. The End of the Wild. 2017. (ENG., Illus.). 272p. (J). (gr. 3-7). 16.99 (978-0-316-24511-1(9)) Little, Brown Bks. for Young Readers.

Hellings, Collete & Jacobs, Nadine. Un Bebe Caido del Cielo. Jacobs, Nadine, illus. 2003. (SPA., Illus.). 32p. (J). (gr. k-1). 16.95 (978-84-95150-10-3(7), COR4033) Corimbo, Editorial S.L. ESP. Dist: Distribooks, Inc.

Hemphill, Helen. The Adventurous Deeds of Deadwood Jones. 2008. (ENG.). 232p. (J). (gr. 5-18). 16.95 (978-1-59078-637-6(8), Front Street) Boyds Mills Pr.

Hennessey, M. G. The Other Boy. Monster, Sfe R., illus. 2016. 240p. (J). (gr. 3-7). 16.99 (978-0-06-242766-3(0)) HarperCollins Pubs.

Henry, Juliann. The Little Shepherd Girl: A Christmas Story. Madsen, Jim, illus. 2007. 32p. (J). (gr. -1-3). 14.99 (978-0-7814-4513-9(2)) Cook, David C.

Henry, Sherrie. Last of the Summer Tomatoes. 2016. (ENG., Illus.). (YA). (gr. 8-12). 24.99 **(978-1-63533-039-7(4))** 2013. 246p. pap. 14.99 (978-1-62380-959-1(2)) Dreamspinner Pr. (Harmony Ink Pr.).

Hensler, K. Why Worry? The Adventures of Bay/Bob/A/Loo/Bop Everything in Moderation. 2008. 48p. pap. 24.95 (978-1-60610-813-0(1)) America Star Bks.

Hensley, Judith Victoria. Terrible Tin. 2008. 136p. pap. 14.95 (978-0-9795103-3-5(3)) Ascended Ideas.

Hepler, Linda McGhee. How to Survive Seventh Grade (If You're Lucky) 2008. 146p. pap. 24.95 (978-1-60563-610-8(X)) America Star Bks.

Hepworth, Emily. Stray Dog. 2009. 39p. pap. 9.81 (978-0-557-21434-1(3)) Lulu Pr., Inc.

Hering, Marianne. Trouble on the Orphan Train. 2016. (AIO Imagination Station Bks.: 18). (ENG.). 144p. (J). pap. 4.99 (978-1-58997-805-8(6)) Focus on the Family Publishing.

Herlong, M. H. Buddy. 2013. (ENG.). 320p. (J). (gr. 5). pap. 7.99 (978-0-14-242544-2(3), Puffin Books) Penguin Young Readers Group.

—The Great Wide Sea. 2010. (ENG.). 288p. (YA). (gr. 7-18). 8.99 (978-0-14-241670-9(3), Puffin Books) Penguin Young Readers Group.

Hermes, Patricia. Emma Dilemma, the Nanny, & the Wedding, 0 vols. 2012. (Emma Dilemma Ser.: 7). (ENG.). 144p. (J). (gr. 3-6). 16.99 (978-0-7614-6210-1(4), 9780761462101, Amazon Children's Publishing) Amazon Publishing.

Herndon, Lee G. The Land of Always & Forever: The Trilogy, 1 vol. 2009. 77p. pap. 19.95 (978-1-60836-898-3(X)) America Star Bks.

Herrick, Steven. Love, Ghosts, & Facial Hair. 2004. (ENG., Illus.). 128p. (YA). (gr. 9). pap. 7.99 (978-0-689-86710-1(7), Simon Pulse) Simon Pulse.

Hest, Amy. Guess Who, Baby Duck! Barton, Jill, illus. 2004. (ENG.). 32p. (J). (gr. k-k). 15.99 (978-0-7636-1981-7(7)) Candlewick Pr.

Hickey, David. A Very Small Something. Griggs-Burr, Alexander & Griggs-Burr, Alexander, illus. 2012. (ENG.). 32p. (J). (gr. -1). 15.95 (978-1-926845-37-1(4)) Biblioasis CAN. Dist: Consortium Bk. Sales & Distribution.

Hicks, Deron R. Tower of the Five Orders. Geyer, Mark Edward, illus. 2013. (Shakespeare Mysteries Ser.: 2). (ENG.). 320p. (J). (gr. 5-7). 16.99 (978-0-547-83953-0(7)) Houghton Mifflin Harcourt Publishing Co.

Hicks, Jamara. Calvin Gets a Family. 2009. 24p. pap. 12.00 (978-1-4490-4754-2(8)) AuthorHouse.

Higgins, M. G. Family Fix-It Plan. Taylor, Jo, illus. 2016. (Sibling Split Ser.). (ENG.). 112p. (gr. 2-3). lib. bdg. 25.32 (978-1-4965-2590-1(6)) Stone Arch Bks.

—Fish Boy, 1 vol. 2015. (Red Rhino Ser.). (ENG.). 68p. (J). (gr. 4-6). pap. 7.95 (978-1-62250-953-9(6)) Saddleback Educational Publishing, Inc.

—The Impossible Wish. Taylor, Jo, illus. 2016. (Sibling Split Ser.). (ENG.). 112p. (gr. 2-3). lib. bdg. 25.32 (978-1-4965-2593-2(0)) Stone Arch Bks.

—Party of Nine. Taylor, Jo, illus. 2016. (Sibling Split Ser.). (ENG.). 112p. (gr. 2-3). lib. bdg. 25.32 (978-1-4965-2592-5(2)) Stone Arch Bks.

Hill, Grace Livingston. Cloudy Jewel. (J). reprint ed. lib. bdg. 24.95 (978-0-89190-037-5(3), Rivercity Pr.) Amereon Ltd.

Hinds, Ruth McNaughton. Puppy & I. 2006. (J). per. 7.95 (978-0-9764232-2-5(7)) River City Pr.

Hinton, S. E. The Outsiders. 50th anniv. ed. 2016. (ENG.). 224p. (YA). (gr. 7). 20.00 (978-0-425-28829-0(3), Penguin Books) Penguin Young Readers Group.

Hirota, Denise. The Circus Poster. 2011. 58p. pap. 9.99 (978-1-60911-292-9(X), Eloquent Bks.) Strategic Book Publishing & Rights Agency (SBPRA).

Hitchcock, Fleur. Sunk! A Shrunk! Adventure. 2016. (Shrunk! Adventure Ser.: 4). (ENG., Illus.). 240p. (J). (gr. 3-7). pap. 9.99 (978-1-84812-448-6(1)) Bonnier Publishing GBR. Dist: Independent Pubs. Group.

Hoban, Russell. The Little Brute Family. Hoban, Lillian, illus. 2011. (My Readers Ser.). (ENG.). 40p. (J). (gr. k-2). pap. 3.99 (978-0-312-56373-8(6), 9780312563738) Square Fish.

—Soonchild. Deacon, Alexis, illus. 2012. (ENG.). 144p. (YA). (gr. 9). 15.99 (978-0-7636-5920-2(7)) Candlewick Pr.

—The Sorely Trying Day. Hoban, Lillian, illus. 2010. (ENG.). 48p. (J). (gr. -1-3). 14.95 (978-1-59017-343-5(0), NYR Children's Collection) New York Review of Bks., Inc., The.

Hobbs, Olivia. The Summer of Violet. 2011. 56p. pap. 15.99 (978-1-4653-3539-5(0)) Xlibris Corp.

Hobbs, Will. Jackie's Wild Seattle. (ENG.). 208p. (J). (gr. 5-18). 2004. pap. 6.99 (978-0-380-73311-8(0)) 2003. 19.99 (978-0-688-17474-3(4)) HarperCollins Pubs.

—Take Me to the River. 2011. (ENG.). 192p. (J). (gr. 5-18). 15.99 (978-0-06-074144-0(9)) HarperCollins Pubs.

Hocutt, Rose (Webber). The Spoon Family. 2012. 44p. 24.95 (978-1-4560-0548-1(0)) America Star Bks.

Hodge, Deborah. Emma's Story. Zhang, Song Nan, illus. 2003. (ENG.). 24p. (J). (gr. k-3). 17.95 (978-0-88776-632-9(3), Tundra Bks.) Tundra Bks. CAN. Dist: Penguin Random Hse. LLC.

Hodge, Rosamund. Bright Smoke, Cold Fire. 2018. (Bright Smoke, Cold Fire Ser.: 1). (ENG.). 464p. (YA). (gr. 8). 9.99 **(978-0-06-236942-0(3)**, Balzer & Bray) HarperCollins Pubs.

Hodgkinson, Leigh. Troll Swap. Hodgkinson, Leigh, illus. 2014. (ENG., Illus.). 32p. (J). (gr. -1-2). 15.99 (978-0-7636-7101-3(0), Nosy Crow) Candlewick Pr.

Hoffman, Alice. Nightbird. 2015. (ENG., Illus.). 208p. (J). (gr. 5). 16.99 (978-0-385-38958-7(2), Lamb, Wendy Bks.) Random Hse. Children's Bks.

—Nightbird. 2016. lib. bdg. 18.40 (978-0-606-38451-3(0)) Turtleback Bks.

Hoffman, Nina Kiriki. A Stir of Bones. 2005. (ENG.). 224p. (YA). (gr. 7-7). 7.99 (978-0-14-240361-7(X), Firebird) Penguin Young Readers Group.

Hoffmann, E. T. A. The Nutcracker. Hess, Christina, illus. 2016. (Classic Edition Ser.: 10). (ENG.). 64p. (J). 19.95 (978-1-60433-630-6(7), Applesauce Pr.) Cider Mill Pr. Bk. Pubs., LLC.

Hofmeister, Nick. Adventures of Eli Deuce - SPECIAL EDITION - Fourth & Final Part Added. 2009. 360p. pap. 23.50 (978-0-557-12192-2(2)) Lulu Pr., Inc.

Hohenthal, K. D. Herman Goes Home: A Duffy Family Adventure. 2003. (Illus.). 46p. (J). per. 15.95 (978-0-9716907-3-8(1), Ridgewood Publishing) Ridgewood Group, The.

Holaves, Chris. Even the Dead Get up for Milk. Goomas, John, illus. 2008.Tr. of Hasta los muertos se levantan por Leche. (ENG & SPA.). 64p. (J). lib. bdg. 15.95 (978-0-9792991-0-0(1)) Astakos Publishing.

Holder, Nancy & Viguie, Debbie. Wicked: Witch & Curse. 2009. (978-1-4351-2000-6(0)) Barnes & Noble, Inc.

Holder, Nancy & Viguié, Debbie. Wicked: Witch & Curse. 2008. (Wicked Ser.). (ENG.). 672p. (YA). (gr. 9). pap. 9.99 (978-1-4169-7119-1(X), Simon Pulse) Simon Pulse.

Hole, Stian. Garmann's Summer. Bartlett, Don, tr. from NOR. Hole, Stian, illus. 2008. (ENG., Illus.). 42p. (J). (gr. k-3). 17.50 (978-0-8028-5339-4(0), Eerdmans Bks For Young Readers) Eerdmans, William B. Publishing Co.

Holland, L. Tam. The Counterfeit Family Tree of Vee Crawford-Wong. (ENG.). 368p. (YA). (gr. 9). 2014. pap. 9.99 (978-1-4424-1265-1(8)) 2013. 17.99 (978-1-4424-1264-4(X)) Simon & Schuster Children's Publishing.

Holliday, Patricia. You & me makes Two. 2008. 32p. pap. 17.35 (978-1-4357-5321-1(6)) Lulu Pr., Inc.

Holm, H. R. Forever Santa. 2009. 14p. (J). pap. 2.99 (978-1-59955-345-0(7)) Cedar Fort, Inc./CFI Distribution.

Holm, Jennifer L. The Fourteenth Goldfish. 2015. (CHI.). 264p. (J). pap. (978-986-320-783-2(7)) Commonwealth Publishing Co., Ltd.

—The Fourteenth Goldfish. (ENG.). (J). (gr. 3-7). 2016. 240p. 7.99 (978-0-375-87114-6(4), Yearling) 2014. 208p. 16.99 (978-0-375-87064-4(4), Random Hse. Bks. for Young Readers) 2014. 208p. lib. bdg. 19.99 (978-0-375-97064-1(9), Random Hse. Bks. for Young Readers) Random Hse. Children's Bks.

—The Fourteenth Goldfish. 2016. lib. bdg. 18.40 (978-0-606-38465-0(0)) Turtleback Bks.

Holm, M. S. The Arborist. Sayles, Susana, illus. 2007. (ENG.). 104p. (J). 16.95 (978-0-9796199-1-5(2)); pap. 11.95 (978-0-9796199-3-9(9)) Great West Publishing. (Sentry Bks.).

Holm, Matthew & Follett, Jonathan. Marvin & the Moths. 2016. (ENG.). 352p. (J). (gr. 3-7). 16.99 (978-0-545-87674-2(5), Scholastic Pr.) Scholastic, Inc.

Holmes, Sara Lewis. Operation Yes. 2009. (ENG.). 256p. (J). (gr. 4-7). 16.99 (978-0-545-10795-2(4), Levine, Arthur A. Bks.) Scholastic, Inc.

Holsather, Kent /Wilson. Sara's Moon. 2007. (Illus.). 176p. (YA). per. 12.95 (978-0-9729101-3-2(1)) Lonejack Mountain Pr.

Holt, K. A. House Arrest. 2016. (ENG.). 312p. (J). (gr. 5-9). pap. 7.99 (978-1-4521-5648-4(4)) Chronicle Bks. LLC.

Holyoke, Polly. The Neptune Project. 2014. (ENG.). 352p. (J). (gr. 3-7). pap. 7.99 (978-1-4231-5979-7(9)) Hyperion Bks. for Children.

Holzhauser-Peters, Leslie & Grizinski, Yolande. Thinking Through Problems at School: Social Problem Solving Scenarios to Enhance Communication, Thinking, & Decision Making Skills. 2008. 96p. pap. 13.95 (978-1-4327-2573-0(4)) Outskirts Pr., Inc.

Homan, Michael. Grendel Gander the Sinister Goose. Duggins, Peat, illus. 2012. 48p. pap. 14.95 (978-1-60808-049-6(8), WriteLife Publishing) Boutique of Quality Books Publishing Co., Inc.

Homel, David & Gay, Marie-Louise. Travels with My Family, 1 vol. 2007. (ENG., Illus.). 120p. (J). (gr. 1-5). pap. 8.95 (978-0-88899-833-0(3)) Groundwood Bks. CAN. Dist: Publishers Group West (PGW).

Honeycutt, Natalie. The Best-Laid Plans of Jonah Twist. 2014. (ENG.). 128p. (J). (gr. 2-5). pap. 13.99 (978-1-4814-3107-1(2), Simon & Schuster Bks. For Young Readers) Simon & Schuster Bks. For Young Readers.

Honeyman, Kay. Interference. 2016. (ENG.). 352p. (YA). (gr. 7). 17.99 (978-0-545-81232-0(1), Levine, Arthur A. Bks.) Scholastic, Inc.

Hope, Laura Lee. Six Little Bunkers at Cousin Tom's. rev. ed. 2006. 192p. 26.95 (978-1-4218-1795-8(0)); pap. 11.95 (978-1-4218-1895-5(7)) 1st World Publishing, Inc. (1st World Library - Literary Society).

—Six Little Bunkers at Cowboy Jack's. 2007. 180p. 25.96 (978-1-4218-3888-5(5), 1st World Library - Literary Society) 1st World Publishing, Inc.

—Six Little Bunkers at Grandpa Ford's. 2007. 188p. 25.96 (978-1-4218-3889-2(3), 1st World Library - Literary Society) 1st World Publishing, Inc.

Hopkins, Charles. Santa's Frost Covered Sleigh Lay Broken in the Snow. 2007. pap. 17.00 (978-0-8059-8935-9(8)) Dorrance Publishing Co., Inc.

Hopkins, Ellen. Tricks. (ENG.). (YA). (gr. 9). 2017. 656p. pap. 11.99 (978-1-4814-9824-1(X)) 2009. 640p. 22.99 (978-1-4169-5007-3(9)) McElderry, Margaret K. Bks. (McElderry, Margaret K. Bks.).

—Tricks. 2011. lib. bdg. 24.50 (978-0-606-23290-6(7), Turtleback) Turtleback Bks.

Hopkinson, Deborah. Cabin in the Snow. Faricy, Patrick, illus. 2005. 74p. (J). lib. bdg. 15.00 (978-1-59054-896-7(5)) Fitzgerald Bks.

—Our Kansas Home. Faricy, Patrick, illus. 2003. (Prairie Skies Ser.). 69p. (J). 11.65 (978-0-7569-3448-4(6)) Perfection Learning Corp.

Hoppey, Tim. The Good Fire Helmet. McElrath-Eslick, Lori, illus. 2010. (ENG.). 32p. (J). 16.95 (978-1-934617-06-9(7), Alma Little) Elva Resa Publishing, LLC.

Hord, Colleen. Everyone Visits Family. 2015. (ENG.). 24p. (gr. k-3). 28.50 (978-1-63430-364-4(4)) Rourke Educational Media.

Horvath, Polly. The Trolls. 2008. (ENG.). 160p. (J). (gr. 4-7). pap. 7.99 (978-0-312-38419-7(X), 9780312384197) Square Fish.

—The Vacation, 1 vol. (ENG.). 208p. pap. 12.95 (978-0-88899-693-0(4)) Groundwood Bks. CAN. Dist: Publishers Group West (PGW).

Hosch, Amanda. Mabel Opal Pear & the Rules for Spying. Sluyterman van Langeweyde, Ira, illus. 2017. (Middle-Grade

Novels Ser.). (ENG.). 272p. (gr. 4-7). lib. bdg. 26.65 (978-1-4965-4051-5(4)) Stone Arch Bks.

Hostetter, Joyce Moyer. Aim. 2016. (Bakers Mountain Stories Ser.). (ENG.). 288p. (J). (gr. 3-7). 17.99 (978-1-62979-673-4(5), Calkins Creek) Boyds Mills Pr.

Houran, Lori Haskins. A Dozen Cousins. Usher, Sam, illus. 2015. (ENG.). 32p. (J). (gr. k-1). 14.95 (978-1-4549-1062-6(3)) Sterling Publishing Co., Inc.

Howard, A. G. A Splintered Companion. 2015. (ENG.). 240p. (J). (gr. 9-17). pap. 7.95 (978-1-4197-1926-4(2)) Abrams, Inc.

Howard, Elizabeth Fitzgerald. Aunt Flossie's Hats (and Crab Cakes Later) Ransome, James, illus. 2015. 32p. pap. 8.00 (978-1-61003-491-3(0)) Center for the Collaborative Classroom.

Howell, Gail L. Sarah's World: Sarah Meets her Cousins by the Sea. 2009. 24p. pap. 11.49 (978-1-4389-4864-5(6)) AuthorHouse.

Howell, Julie Ann. The Pepper Tree, How the Seeds Were Planted! LaGrange, Tiffany, illus. 2008. 28p. pap. 12.95 (978-0-9820479-0-3(8)) Peppertree Pr., The.

Howland, Leila. The Brightest Stars of Summer. 2017. (Silver Sisters Ser.: 2). 384p. (J). (gr. 3-7). pap. 6.99 (978-0-06-231873-2(X)) HarperCollins Pubs.

Hucklesby, Jill. Samphire Song. 2013. (ENG.). 296p. (J). (gr. 3-7). 16.99 (978-0-8075-7224-5(1)) Whitman, Albert & Co.

Hudson, Judith. Bayo a Good African Boy. 2009. 28p. (J). pap. 12.95 (978-1-4327-4067-2(9)) Outskirts Pr., Inc.

Hughes, Diane. Wilbur Meets Aunt Lucy. 2009. 12p. pap. 8.49 (978-1-4490-1241-0(8)) AuthorHouse.

Hughes, Shirley. Hero on a Bicycle. 2013. (ENG., Illus.). 224p. (J). (gr. 5-9). 16.99 (978-0-7636-6037-6(X)) Candlewick Pr.

Hull, Norman. Robin's Big Brother. 2011. 56p. (gr. 4-6). pap. 9.99 (978-1-4634-3691-9(2)) AuthorHouse.

Humes, Kristin Joy. My Dad Wears Polka-Dotted Socks! Barr, Loel, illus. 2005. 32p. (J). (gr. -1-7). 15.95 (978-0-9744307-2-0(2)) Merry Lane Pr.

Hunter, C. C. Awake at Dawn. 2013. (Shadow Falls Novel Ser.: 2). (ENG.). 400p. (YA). (gr. 7-12). mass mkt. 9.99 (978-1-250-04679-6(3), 9781250046796, St. Martin's Paperbacks) St. Martin's Pr.

Hurwitz, Johanna. Amazing Monty. McGrory, Anik, illus. 2013. (Monty Ser.). (ENG.). 112p. (J). (gr. k-4). pap. 5.99 (978-0-7636-6561-6(4)) Candlewick Pr.

Husby, Greg. The Zoebirds. 2008. 40p. pap. 21.99 (978-1-4363-4941-3(9)) Xlibris Corp.

Hussey, Charmian. The Valley of Secrets. Crump, Christopher, illus. 2006. (ENG.). 400p. (J). (gr. 7-12). per. 17.99 (978-1-4169-0015-3(2), Simon Pulse) Simon Pulse.

Hylton, Maxine. True Friend: A Story for All about Healing. 2014. (ENG.). 104p. (J). pap. 7.95 (978-0-9845161-2-4(3)) Protective Hands Communications.

I Like Me. 2004. (J). per. (978-1-57657-395-2(8)) Paradise Pr., Inc.

I Like Me. 2004. 8p. (gr. k-2). 20.95 (978-0-322-00630-0(9)) Wright Group/McGraw-Hill.

Ilogienboh, Caroline. Nowhere to Hide. 2004. 220p. (YA). pap. 14.95 (978-0-9712781-4-1(8), 0-9712781) Sun Rose Pubs.

In My Father's House. 2004. (Literature Connections Ser.). (gr. 6-12). (978-0-395-88933-6(2), 2-70865) Holt McDougal.

Inchy Goes the Extra Mile, 3 bks. 2004. (Illus.). (J). 9.95 (978-0-9725286-1-0(X)) Sheppard Publishing.

Ingalls, Laura. En las Orillas del Lago de Plata. 2004. (SPA., Illus.). 192p. (gr. 5-8). pap. 12.99 (978-84-279-3227-2(8), NG5869) Noguer y Caralt Editores, S. A. ESP. Dist: Lectorum Pubns., Inc.

Ingham, Janis. Flip & Flop Celebrate Family. 2009. 32p. pap. 16.49 (978-1-4389-2152-5(7)) AuthorHouse.

Ingle, Rosalie Vandewater. The Stage Is Coming! Hallie's Stage Stop Journey. 2012. (Illus.). 36p. (J). pap. 12.95 (978-0-578-09876-0(8)) Ingle, Rosalie.

Ippolito, Heidi. Bobo's New Home. 2009. 24p. pap. 11.50 (978-1-60860-220-9(6), Strategic Bk. Publishing) Strategic Book Publishing & Rights Agency (SBPRA).

Ironside, Meredith. Spoon Creek Mystery. 2009. 244p. pap. 16.95 (978-0-595-53490-6(2)) iUniverse, Inc.

Irwin, Ms. Judy. What Did You Say? 2012. 78p. pap. (978-0-9877088-5-4(6)) Irwin, Judy.

Isaacs, John. A Doggone Good Story. 2009. 30p. pap. 16.50 (978-1-60693-471-5(6), Eloquent Bks.) Strategic Book Publishing & Rights Agency (SBPRA).

Isadora, Rachel. What a Family! A Fresh Look at Family Trees. 2006. (Illus.). (J). (978-1-4156-5634-1(7), Putnam Juvenile) Penguin Publishing Group.

Ivanoff, George. Long-Lost Relatives. Rankin, Bruce H., illus. 2004. iv, 36p. (J). pap. (978-0-7608-6740-2(2)) Sundance/Newbridge Educational Publishing.

J., Henry. The Big Gray House: The Adventures of Franklin Meyers. 2010. 96p. (gr. -1-2). pap. 12.00 (978-1-4269-4255-6(9)) Trafford Publishing.

Jack R. Wilder. Devil with a Halo. 2009. 256p. pap. 24.95 (978-1-4251-1283-7(8)) Trafford Publishing.

Jackson, Amani D. I'm a Big Boy Now. 2009. 16p. pap. 9.99 (978-1-4389-2195-2(0)) AuthorHouse.

Jacobs, Evan. Screaming Quietly, 1 vol. 2013. (Gravel Road Ser.). (ENG.). 212p. (YA). (gr. 9-12). pap. 9.95 (978-1-62250-003-1(2)) Saddleback Educational Publishing, Inc.

Jador, Monisha Annabel. Before You Were Born. 2013. 20p. pap. 15.29 (978-1-4669-9119-4(4)) Trafford Publishing.

Jakubowski, Michele. The Grass Is Always Greener. 2017. (Ashley Small & Ashlee Tall Ser.). (ENG., Illus.). 64p. (gr. 1-3). pap. 4.95 (978-1-5158-0016-3(4)) Picture Window Bks.

James, Henry. Washington Square. 2004. (gr. 7-12). reprint ed. pap. (978-0-87720-743-6(7), N387ALS) AMSCO Schl. Pubns., Inc.

James, Wilson. SONS & BROTHERS in SEATTLE. 2009. 158p. pap. 14.95 (978-0-557-07436-5(3)) Lulu Pr., Inc.

Jarrell, Pamela R. Caillou's Family & Friends. Meier, Kerry L., illus. I.t. ed. 2005. (HRL Board Book Ser.). (J). (gr. k-18). pap. 10.95 (978-1-57332-327-7(6), HighReach Learning, Incorporated) Carson-Dellosa Publishing, LLC.

Jasper, Rick & Reece, Richard. Thaw. 2010. (Night Fall Ser.). (ENG.). 112p. (YA). (gr. 6-12). pap. 7.95 (978-0-7613-6161-9(8)) Lerner Publishing Group.

Jaysree. Drama. 2004. 134p. (YA). pap. 11.95 (978-0-595-29662-0(9)) iUniverse, Inc.

Jeanne-Marie in Gay Paris. 2003. (Illus.). 32p. (J). mass mkt. 9.99 (978-0-9740599-1-4(9), 2) Omnibus Publishing.

Jeeva Raghunath & Nayar, Deeya. Malli. Nancy Raj, illus. 2005. (HIN & ENG.). 16p. (J). (978-81-8146-089-9(8)) Tulika Pubs.

Jeffries, Joyce. Meet Amy's Family, 1. 2012. (InfoMax Readers Ser.). (ENG., Illus.). 16p. (J). (gr. k-1). pap. 8.25 (978-1-4488-8902-0(2), Rosen Classroom) Rosen Publishing Group, Inc., The.

Jenisch, Betty. Rennie. 2007. 9.00 (978-0-8059-8947-2(1)) Dorrance Publishing Co., Inc.

Jenkins, Amanda. Wally Smithers Tames the River. Fagan, Martin, illus. 2017. (Text Connections Guided Close Reading Ser.). (J). (gr. 2). (978-1-4900-1842-3(5)) Benchmark Education Co.

Jenkins, Martin. Grandma Elephant's in Charge. Bates, Ivan, illus. 2014. (Read & Wonder Ser.). (ENG.). 32p. (J). (gr. k-3). 6.99 (978-0-7636-7381-9(1)) Candlewick Pr.

Jennings, Patrick. Hissy Fitz. Allen, Michael, illus. 2015. (ENG.). 128p. (J). (gr. 2-4). 14.99 (978-1-5124-0137-0(4), Carolrhoda Bks.) Lerner Publishing Group.

—Hissy Fitz. Austin, Michael Allen, illus. 2015. (ENG.). 128p. (gr. 2-4). 14.99 (978-1-60684-596-7(9), Carolrhoda Bks.) Lerner Publishing Group.

Jensen, Marion. Almost Super. (Almost Super Ser.: 1). (ENG.). (J). (gr. 3-7). 2015. 272p. pap. 6.99 (978-0-06-220962-7(0)) 2014. 256p. 14.99 (978-0-06-220961-0(2)) HarperCollins Pubs.

—Searching for Super. 2015. (Almost Super Ser.: 2). (ENG.). 256p. (J). (gr. 3-7). 14.99 (978-0-06-220958-0(2)) HarperCollins Pubs.

Jensen, Valerie K. Romeo & Juliet: The Coloring Book. 2011. 80p. pap. 11.99 (978-1-4567-5051-0(8)) AuthorHouse.

Jiménez, Francisco. Taking Hold: From Migrant Childhood to Columbia University. 2017. (ENG.). 208p. (YA). (gr. 9). pap. 8.99 (978-1-328-74209-4(1), HMH Books For Young Readers) Houghton Mifflin Harcourt Publishing Co.

Jimmy Gimmy & the Raid on Burkey Run. 2005. (Illus.). 192p. (J). pap. 12.95 (978-0-9767646-0-1(1)) Team EEK!

Johansson, J. R. Cut Me Free. 2015. (ENG.). 304p. (YA). (gr. 9-16). 17.99 (978-0-374-30023-4(2), 9780374300234, Farrar, Straus & Giroux (BYR)) Farrar, Straus & Giroux.

Johnson, Dawn M. I Have a Chuck. Klein, Ellen Marie, illus. 2013. 28p. pap. 24.95 (978-1-62709-628-7(0)) America Star Bks.

Johnson, Denise Donna. The Veridical Circle. 2011. 78p. pap. 19.95 (978-1-4626-0472-2(2)) America Star Bks.

Johnson, Donna. The Story of the Little Red Leaf. Johnson, Emily, illus. I.t. ed. 2006. (ENG.). 22p. (J). 25.00 (978-0-9778774-0-9(X)) Choice Point Editions.

Johnson, Janet. The Last Great Adventure of the PB & J Society. 2016. (ENG.). 256p. (gr. 4-8). 12.95 (978-1-62370-636-4(X)) Capstone Young Readers of Coughlan Cos.

Johnson, Kristin F. Wall of Water. 2017. (Day of Disaster Ser.). (ENG.). 112p. (gr. 6-12). (J). 26.65 (978-1-5124-2778-3(0)); (YA). 12.99 (978-1-5124-3516-0(3), Darby Creek); (YA). 39.99 (978-1-5124-2786-8(1), Darby Creek); (YA). 39.99 (978-1-5124-3515-3(5), Darby Creek) Lerner Publishing Group.

Johnson, Lindsay Lee. Worlds Apart. 2005. (ENG.). 168p. (J). (gr. 6-9). 16.95 (978-1-932425-28-4(4), Lemniscaat) Boyds Mills Pr.

Johnson, Maureen. Suite Scarlett. 2009. (ENG.). 368p. (J). (gr. 3-7). 8.99 (978-0-545-09632-4(4)) Scholastic, Inc.

—13 Little Blue Envelopes. (13 Little Blue Envelopes Ser.: 1). (ENG., Illus.). (YA). (gr. 8-18). 2005. 336p. 17.99 (978-0-06-054141-5(5)) 2010. 368p. reprint ed. pap. 9.99 (978-0-06-054143-9(1)) HarperCollins Pubs. (HarperTeen).

—13 Little Blue Envelopes. 2007. 317p. 20.00 (978-0-7569-7830-3(0)) Perfection Learning Corp.

Johnson-Simon. Anaya Visits the James E Lewis Museum of Art at Morgan State University. 2009. 40p. pap. 16.99 (978-1-4490-1884-9(X)) AuthorHouse.

Johnston, Annie Fell. Two Little Knights of Kentucky (Illustra. 2006. pap. (978-1-4065-1133-8(1)) Dodo Pr.

Johnston, Gayle. The Adventures of Jazzi G: Search for the Missing Peace. 2016. (Adventures of Jazzi G Ser.: 1). (ENG., Illus.). 202p. (J). 32.95 (978-1-63047-841-4(5)) Morgan James Publishing.

Johnston, Teresa. Thanksgiving for Emily Ann. Newton, Vanessa Brantley, illus. 2014. (ENG.). 32p. (J). (gr. -1-k). 6.99 (978-0-545-43413-3(0), Cartwheel Bks.) Scholastic, Inc.

Joiner, Sara K. After the Ashes. 2015. (ENG., Illus.). 352p. (J). (gr. 5-10). 17.95 (978-0-8234-3441-1(9)) Holiday Hse., Inc.

Jolin, Paula. In the Name of God. 2008. (ENG.). 224p. (YA). (gr. 9-12). pap. 18.99 (978-0-312-38455-5(6), 9780312384555) Square Fish.

Jonas. Three's a Crowd. 6th ed. 2010. 128p. pap. 4.99 (978-1-4231-2282-1(8)) Disney Pr.

Jones, Abigail. Still a Family. 2011. 24p. pap. 15.99 (978-1-4568-7941-9(3)) Xlibris Corp.

Jones, Christianne C. Dani el Dinosaurio, 1 vol. Lozano, Clara, tr. from ENG. Epstein, Len, illus. 2006. (Read-It! Readers en Español: Story Collection). (SPA.). 24p. (gr. -1-3). lib. bdg. 21.32 (978-1-4048-2706-6(4), Easy Readers) Picture Window Bks.

Jones, Diana Wynne. House of Many Ways. 2008. 404p. (J). 9.99 (978-0-06-147798-0(2), Greenwillow Bks.) HarperCollins Pubs.

—House of Many Ways, 7 vols. 2009. (J). 100.75 (978-1-4361-6132-9(0)); 245.75 (978-1-4361-6127-5(4)); 1.25 (978-1-4361-6123-7(1)); 79.75 (978-1-4361-6128-2(2)); 102.75 (978-1-4361-6130-5(4)) Recorded Bks., Inc.

Jones, Molly. Something in the Air. Welch, Sheila Kelly, illus. 2005. (J). (978-1-893516-03-8(2)) Our Child Pr.

Jones, Patrick. Always Faithful. 2015. (ENG.). 112p. (YA). (gr. 6-12). lib. bdg. 27.99 (978-1-4677-8052-0(9)); 7.99 (978-1-4677-9014-7(1)) Lerner Publishing Group. (Darby Creek).

—Body Shot. 2013. (Dojo Ser.). (ENG.). 112p. (YA). (gr. 6-12). pap. 7.95 (978-1-4677-1490-7(9)); lib. bdg. 27.93 (978-1-4677-0633-9(7)) Lerner Publishing Group. (Darby Creek).

—Fight or Flee. 2016. (Unbarred Ser.). (ENG.). 120p. (YA). (gr. 6-12). lib. bdg. 27.99 (978-1-5124-0004-5(1), Darby Creek) Lerner Publishing Group.

—Fight or Flee. 2016. (Unbarred Ser.). (ENG.). 120p. (YA). (gr. 6-12). pap. 7.99 (978-1-5124-0093-9(9), Darby Creek) Lerner Publishing Group.

—Fight or Flee. 2016. (Unbarred Ser.). (ENG.). 120p. (YA). (gr. 6-12). 42.65 (978-1-5124-0094-6(7), Darby Creek) Lerner Publishing Group.

—Head Kick. 2013. (Dojo Ser.). (ENG.). 120p. (YA). (gr. 6-12). pap. 7.95 (978-1-4677-1489-1(5)); lib. bdg. 27.93 (978-1-4677-0632-2(9)) Lerner Publishing Group. (Darby Creek).

Jones, Ralph E. The Adventures of Kele: Boy of the Rock Shelter. 2012. 156p. pap. 41.99 (978-1-4772-9405-5(8)); 56p. pap. 24.99 (978-1-4685-7696-2(8)) AuthorHouse.

Jopling, Heather. The Not-So-Only Child. 2006. (Illus.). (J). (978-0-9780739-4-7(0)) Nickname Pr.

Joseph, A. Valentine. The Forest Is Our Home. 2012. 88p. pap. 9.95 (978-1-4759-4400-6(4)) iUniverse, Inc.

Joyal, Lisa. Swahili for Beginners, 1 vol. 2008. (ENG., Illus.). 176p. (YA). (gr. 5-9). pap. (978-1-894549-69-1(4), Sumach Pr.) Canadian Scholars.

Joyce, Sandie May. Aunt Sandie Goes to School - the Comics. 2008. 55p. pap. 22.50 (978-0-557-02295-3(9)) Lulu Pr., Inc.

Joyner, Andrew. Boris on the Move. 2013. (Boris Ser.: 1). lib. bdg. 14.75 (978-0-606-31974-4(3), Turtleback) Turtleback Bks.

Jude, Sarah. The May Queen Murders. 2016. (ENG.). 304p. (YA). (gr. 9). 17.99 (978-0-544-64041-2(1), HMH Books For Young Readers) Houghton Mifflin Harcourt Publishing Co.

Jules, Jacqueline. My Fantástica Family. Smith, Kim, illus. 2017. (Sofia Martinez Ser.). (ENG.). 96p. (gr. k-2). pap. 4.95 (978-1-5158-0746-9(0), Sofia Martinez) Picture Window Bks.

Jung, Mike. Unidentified Suburban Object. (ENG.). 272p. (J). (gr. 3-7). 2017. pap. 6.99 (978-0-545-78227-2(9)) 2016. 16.99 (978-0-545-78226-5(0), Levine, Arthur A. Bks.) Scholastic, Inc.

Justesen, Kim Williams. The Deepest Blue. 2015. (ENG.). 292p. (J). (gr. 6). pap. 9.99 (978-1-939100-05-4(4)) Tanglewood Pr.

Kahler, Janet C. 1918 Covered Wagon Adventure. 2006. (Illus.). 94p. per. 10.95 (978-1-57258-444-0(0), 945-6305) TEACH Services, Inc.

Kain, P. G. & Frost, Michael. Picture Perfect. 2012. (Commercial Breaks Ser.: 2). (ENG.). 288p. (J). (gr. 4-9). pap. 6.99 (978-1-4169-9787-0(3), Aladdin) Simon & Schuster Children's Publishing.

Kann, Victoria. Pinkalicious - Eggstraordinary Easter. Kann, Victoria, illus. 2014. (Pinkalicious Ser.). (ENG., Illus.). 24p. (J). (gr. -1-3). pap. 4.99 (978-0-06-218772-7(4), HarperFestival) HarperCollins Pubs.

Kapai, Tommy. Cuzzies Meet the Motuhoa Shark. Henry, Mike, illus. 2006. (Cuzzies Adventures Ser.). (MAO & ENG.). 32p. (J). (gr. -1-3). pap. 9.00 (978-1-86969-100-4(8)) Huia Pubs. NZL. Dist: Univ. of Hawaii Pr.

Karlsson, Val. The Protectors. 2010. (Night Fall Ser.). (ENG.). 112p. (YA). (gr. 6-12). pap. 7.95 (978-0-7613-6159-6(6)) Lerner Publishing Group.

Kass, Pnina Moed. Real Time. 2006. (ENG.). 192p. (YA). (gr. 7-12). reprint ed. pap. 7.99 (978-0-618-69174-6(X)) Houghton Mifflin Harcourt Publishing Co.

Kastner, Erich. Lisa & Lottie. 2015. (ENG.). 168p. (gr. 3). pap. 12.95 (978-1-939601-33-9(9)) Ig Publishing, Inc.

Katz, Bebe Weinberg. A Best Friend for Claudia. 2008. 77p. pap. 19.95 (978-1-60563-485-2(9)) America Star Bks.

Katz, Jennifer A. The Era of Courting. 2006. 119p. pap. 19.95 (978-1-4241-3321-5(1)) PublishAmerica, Inc.

Katz, Karen. Baby's Box of Family Fun!: Set. Katz, Karen, illus. gif. ed. 2006. (ENG., Illus.). 56p. (J). (gr. -1 — 1). bds. 27.99 (978-1-4169-2795-2(6), Little Simon) Little Simon.

—Grandpa & Me. Katz, Karen, illus. 2004. (ENG., Illus.). 14p. (J). (gr. -1-k). bds. 6.99 (978-0-689-86644-9(5), Little Simon) Little Simon.

—What Does Baby Say? Katz, Karen, illus. 2004. (ENG., Illus.). 16p. (J). (gr. -1-k). bds. 6.99 (978-0-689-86645-6(3), Little Simon) Little Simon.

—Where Is Baby's Birthday Cake? Katz, Karen, illus. 2008. (ENG., Illus.). 14p. (J). (gr. -1 — 1). bds. 6.99 (978-1-4169-5817-8(7), Little Simon) Little Simon.

Kazerooni, Abbas. The Boy with Two Lives. 2016. (ENG.). 256p. (YA). (gr. 7). 12.99 (978-1-74331-483-8(3)) Allen & Unwin AUS. Dist: Independent Pubs. Group.

Kehoe, Lindy, illus. Home on a Giggle. 2004. (J). (978-0-9752801-0-2(4)) Beres, Nancy.

Kellogg, Elijah. The Young Shipbuilders of Elm Island by Rev Elijah Kellogg. 2006. 316p. per. 23.99 (978-1-4255-3063-1(X)) Michigan Publishing.

Kelly, David A. The All-Star Joker. Meyers, Mark, illus. 2012. (Ballpark Mysteries Ser.: 5). (ENG.). 112p. (J). (gr. 1-4). 4.99 (978-0-375-86884-9(4), Random Hse. Bks. for Young Readers) Random Hse. Children's Bks.

—The Astro Outlaw. Meyers, Mark, illus. 2012. (Ballpark Mysteries Ser.: Bk. 4). (ENG.). 112p. (J). (gr. 1-4). pap. 4.99 (978-0-375-86883-2(6), Random Hse. Bks. for Young Readers) Random Hse. Children's Bks.

—The Fenway Foul-Up. Meyers, Mark, illus. 2011. (Ballpark Mysteries Ser.: Bk. 1). (ENG.). 112p. (J). (gr. 1-4). pap. 4.99 (978-0-375-86703-3(1), Random Hse. Bks. for Young Readers) Random Hse. Children's Bks.

—The Pinstripe Ghost. Meyers, Mark, illus. 2011. (Ballpark Mysteries Ser.: 2). (ENG.). 112p. (J). (gr. 1-4). 4.99 (978-0-375-86704-0(X), Random Hse. Bks. for Young Readers) Random Hse. Children's Bks.

—The Rangers Rustlers. Meyers, Mark, illus. 2016. (Ballpark Mysteries Ser.: Bk. 12). (ENG.). 112p. (J). (gr. 1-4). pap. 4.99 (978-0-385-37881-9(5), Random Hse. Bks. for Young Readers) Random Hse. Children's Bks.

Kelly, Katy. Working Myself to Pieces & Bits. Ferguson, Peter, illus. 2008. (Lucy Rose Ser.). (ENG.). 208p. (J). (gr. 3-7). 6.99 (978-0-440-42186-3(1), Yearling) Random Hse. Children's Bks.

Kelly, Theresa. Aloha Cove Set, 7 vols. (Aloha Cove Ser.). (YA). 39.99 (978-0-7586-0005-9(4)) Concordia Publishing Hse.

Kelso, Mary Jean. One Family's Christmas. Snider, K. C., illus. 2008. 24p. pap. 10.95 (978-1-935137-05-4(0)) Guardian Angel Publishing, Inc.

Kemble, Mai S., illus. I'm So Not Wearing a Dress! 2010. (ENG.). 32p. (J). 11.99 (978-1-935703-05-1(6)) Downtown Bookworks.

Kendall, Jack. The Magic Apple Tree. Bostrom, Sally, illus. I.t. ed. 2006. (ENG.). 48p. (J). per. 9.95 (978-0-9787740-4-2(3)) Peppertree Pr., The.

Kendall, Jodi. The Unlikely Story of a Pig in the City. Campion, Pascal, illus. 2017. 336p. (J). (gr. 3-7). 16.99 (978-0-06-248453-6(2)) HarperCollins Pubs.

Kennedy, James. The Order of Odd-Fish. 2010. (ENG.). 416p. (YA). (gr. 7-18). mass mkt. 8.99 (978-0-440-24065-5(4), Laurel Leaf) Random Hse. Children's Bks.

Kent, Elizabeth. The Enchanted Adventures of the Caroline Kemps. 2007. 148p. pap. 24.95 (978-1-4241-9915-0(8)) America Star Bks.

Kephart, Beth. One Thing Stolen. 2016. (ENG.). 296p. (YA). pap. 9.99 (978-1-4521-5213-4(6)) Chronicle Bks. LLC.

Kerbel, Deborah. Feathered. 2016. (ENG., Illus.). 146p. (J). (gr. 4-8). 15.95 (978-1-77138-341-7(0)) Kids Can Pr., Ltd. CAN. Dist: Hachette Bk. Group.

Kerick, Mia. Not Broken, Just Bent [Library Edition]. 2014. 180p. pap. 14.99 (978-1-62798-529-1(8), Harmony Ink Pr.) Dreamspinner Pr.

Kerkow, Larry. Angel Goes to Sea. 2010. 24p. 12.56 (978-1-4269-3490-2(4)) Trafford Publishing.

Kerline, Joni M. Sebastian Breaks for Freedom, 1. 2006. (Illus.). 30p. (J). 19.95 (978-0-9776772-0-7(6)) KidBookInk Publishing, LLC.

Kerr, M. E., pseud. Slap Your Sides. 2003. 198p. (YA). 13.65 (978-0-7569-4240-3(3)) Perfection Learning Corp.

Kerrin, Jessica Scott. The Sky's the Limit! Kelly, Joseph, illus. 2008. (Martin Bridge Ser.). (ENG.). 112p. (J). (gr. 2-5). pap. 6.95 (978-1-55453-159-2(4)) Kids Can Pr., Ltd. CAN. Dist: Hachette Bk. Group.

Kertell, Lynn Maslen. Buddy to the Rescue. Hendra, Sue, illus. 2012. (Scholastic Reader Level 1 Ser.). (ENG.). 32p. (J). (gr. -1-2). pap. 3.99 (978-0-545-38273-1(4)) Scholastic, Inc.

—I Can Ride! Hendra, Sue, illus. 2012. (Scholastic Reader Level 1 Ser.). (ENG.). 32p. (J). (gr. -1-3). pap. 3.99 (978-0-545-38272-4(6)) Scholastic, Inc.

Ketchen, Susan. Born That Way. 2009. (ENG.). 176p. (YA). (gr. 7-10). pap. 12.95 (978-0-88982-254-2(9)) Oolichan Bks. CAN. Dist: Univ. of Toronto Pr.

Keyes, Pamela. Legend of Zamiel Zimbalist: Book Two of the Connedim Series. 2005. 280p. (YA). pap. 14.99 (978-1-59092-062-6(7)) Blue Forge Pr.

Kidd, Ronald. The Year of the Bomb. 2009. (ENG.). 208p. (YA). (gr. 7-18). 16.99 (978-1-4169-5892-5(4), Simon & Schuster Bks. For Young Readers) Simon & Schuster Bks. For Young Readers.

Killer Connections. 2010. (Hardy Boys (All New) Undercover Brothers Ser.: 33). (ENG.). 176p. (J). (gr. 3-7). pap. 6.99 (978-1-4169-8696-6(0), Aladdin) Simon & Schuster Children's Publishing.

Kimball, Michael D. Alligator Bay: A Beary Tale. 2009. 132p. pap. 11.95 (978-1-4401-1804-3(3)) iUniverse, Inc.

Kimmelman, Leslie. The Very Crowded Sukkah, 0 vols. 2013. (ENG.). 32p. (J). (gr. -1-k). 17.99 (978-1-4778-1716-2(6), 9781477817162, Amazon Children's Publishing) Amazon Publishing.

Kimura, Yasuko. You Look Yummy! 2015. (Tyrannosaurus Ser.). (ENG.). 40p. (J). (gr. k-2). 16.99 (978-1-940842-06-6(9)) Museyon.

King, Amy Sarig. Me & Marvin Gardens. 2017. (ENG.). 256p. (J). (gr. 3-7). 16.99 (978-0-545-87074-0(7), Levine, Arthur A. Bks.) Scholastic, Inc.

King, Dedie. I See the Sun in Afghanistan. Vahidi, Mohd, tr. Inglese, Judith, illus. 2011. (I See the Sun In ... Ser.: 0). (PER & ENG.). 40p. (J). (gr. k). pap. 12.95 (978-0-9818720-8-7(5)) Satya Hse. Pubns.

—I See the Sun in Mexico, 1 vol. Inglese, Judith, illus. 2012. (I See the Sun Ser.: 5). (ENG.). 40p. (J). (gr. 1-2). pap. 12.95 (978-1-935874-14-0(4)) Satya Hse. Pubns.

—I See the Sun in Russia. Ossipova, Irina, tr. Inglese, Judith, illus. 2012. (I See the Sun Ser.: 0). (RUS & ENG.). 40p. (J). (gr. 1-2). 12.95 (978-1-935874-08-9(X)) Satya Hse. Pubns.

King, Deja. Ride Wit' Me: A Novel. 2009. 151p. (YA). pap. (978-0-9755811-9-3(8)) King Production, A.

King James Bible Staff. Love Is ... Halperin, Wendy Anderson, illus. 2004. (ENG.). 32p. (J). 11.99 (978-0-689-86675-3(5), Simon & Schuster/Paula Wiseman Bks.) Simon & Schuster/Paula Wiseman Bks.

King, Lisa. The Gingerbread Baby in Search of a Family. 2013. 28p. pap. 24.95 (978-1-63004-147-2(5)) America Star Bks.

Kinney, Jeff. Double Down. 2016. (Diary of a Wimpy Kid Ser.: Bk. 11). (ENG., Illus.). 224p. (J). (gr. 3-7). 13.95 (978-1-4197-2344-5(8)); E-Book 12.56 (978-1-61312-992-0(0)) Abrams, Inc. (Amulet Bks.).

—Double Down. 2016. (Diary of a Wimpy Kid Ser.: 11). (J). lib. bdg. 25.70 (978-0-606-38998-3(9)) Turtleback Bks.

—Rodrick Rules. 2008. (Diary of a Wimpy Kid Ser.). (Illus.). (J). (ENG.). 224p. (gr. 3-7). 13.95 (978-0-8109-9473-7(9), Amulet Bks.); 216p. pap. 4.99 (978-0-8109-9552-9(2)) Abrams, Inc.

—Rodrick Rules. 2008. (Diary of a Wimpy Kid Ser.: Bk. 2). (JPN., Illus.). 220p. (J). (978-4-591-10464-4(8)) Poplar Publishing.

—Rodrick Rules, 2 vols. (Diary of a Wimpy Kid Ser.: 2). (J). 2010. 173.75 (978-1-4361-3864-2(7)) 2010. 75.75 (978-1-4407-0420-8(1)) 2009. 1.25 (978-1-4361-3860-4(4)) 2009. 46.75 (978-1-4361-3863-5(9)) 2009. 44.75 (978-1-4361-3869-7(8)) 2009. 44.75 (978-1-4361-3865-9(5)) 2009. (gr. 4-8). 46.75 (978-1-4361-3867-3(1)) Recorded Bks., Inc.

—Rodrick Rules. 2008. (Diary of a Wimpy Kid Ser.: 2). (J). lib. bdg. 25.70 (978-0-606-23663-8(5), Turtleback) Turtleback Bks.

Kinney, Jessica. The Pig Scramble, 1 vol. Brannen, Sarah S., illus. 2011. (ENG.). 36p. (J). 17.95 (978-1-934031-61-2(5), bd7fa2f2-9ea3-439a-9713-9f7979711a16) Islandport Pr., Inc.

Kirby, Jessi. The Secret History of Us. 2017. 288p. (YA). (gr. 9). 17.99 (978-0-06-229946-8(8), HarperTeen) HarperCollins Pubs.

Kirkman, Robert, et al. Eight Is Enough. 2004. (ENG., Illus.). 128p. (YA). pap. 12.99 (978-1-58240-347-2(3), 9781582403472) Image Comics.

EFG

Kirkpatrick, Teresa. Roscoe's Forest Adventures. 2008. 177p. pap. 24.95 *(978-1-60672-328-9(6))* America Star Bks.

Kirov, Erica. Magickeepers: The Eternal Hourglass. Fortune, Eric, illus. 2010. (ENG.). 256p. (J). (gr. 4-7). pap. 10.99 *(978-1-4022-3855-0(X),* Sourcebooks Jabberwocky) Sourcebooks, Inc.

Kitze, Carrie A. I Don't Have Your Eyes. Williams, Rob, illus. 2007. 32p. (J). (gr. -1-3). 16.95 *(978-0-9726244-2-8(2))* EMK Pr.

Klages, Ellen. White Sands, Red Menace. 2010. (ENG.). 352p. (J). (gr. 5-18). 8.99 *(978-0-14-241518-4(9),* Puffin Books) Penguin Young Readers Group.

Klein, Abby. The One Hundredth Day of School! McKinley, John, illus. 2008. (Ready, Freddy! Ser.: Bk. 13). 94p. (J). (gr. -1-3). 11.65 *(978-0-7569-8836-4(5))* Perfection Learning Corp.

Kleyla, Mary Pat. Identity Unknown. 2003. 154p. (YA). 22.95 *(978-0-595-65812-1(1));* pap. 12.95 *(978-0-595-28473-3(6))* iUniverse, Inc.

Klimo, Kate. The Dragon in the Sock Drawer. Shroades, John, illus. 2009. (Dragon Keepers Ser.). (ENG.). 192p. (J). (gr. 3-7). 6.99 *(978-0-375-85588-7(2),* Yearling) Random Hse. Children's Bks.

Klise, Kate. Homesick. 2014. (ENG.). 208p. (J). (gr. 5-9). pap. 7.99 *(978-1-250-06511-7(9),* 9781250065117) Square Fish.

Knapman, Timothy. Superhero Dad. Berger, Joe, illus. 2016. (ENG.). (J). (gr. -1-2). 15.99 *(978-0-7636-8657-4(3),* Nosy Crow) Candlewick Pr.

Knight, Barbara. The Lost Boy. 2008. (Illus.). 32p. (J). 14.95 *(978-0-9766270-3-6(5))* Mustang BKS.

Knight, Chris. The Statue. 2013. 52p. pap. *(978-1-78299-440-4(8))* FeedARead.com.

Knoch, Frank. The Big Rescue: The Greenwood Forest Series, 1 vol. Meierhofer, Brian, illus. 2010. 32p. pap. 24.95 *(978-1-4489-6158-0(0))* PublishAmerica, Inc.

Knott, Joan. Merry Christmas, Marushka! Frohliche Weihnachten, Marie! Knott, Marie, ed. 2006. (J). 7.95 *(978-0-9779895-1-5(8))* Knott, Joan.

Knowles, Jo. See You at Harry's. 2013. (ENG.). 320p. (J). (gr. 5). pap. 7.99 *(978-0-7636-6455-8(3))* Candlewick Pr.

Knox, Elizabeth. Dreamhunter. 2009. (Dreamhunter Duet Ser.: 1). (ENG.). 384p. (YA). (gr. 7-12). pap. 10.99 *(978-0-312-53571-1(6),* 9780312535711) Square Fish.

Knudsen, Michelle. Mother's Day Ribbons. Wallace, John, illus. 2005. (ENG.). 12p. (J). bds. 6.99 *(978-0-689-86381-3(0),* Little Simon) Little Simon.

Kohlhepp, Michael. Within the Hearthstone: Book 1: the Trea. 2006. 127p. pap. 19.95 *(978-1-4241-3744-2(6))* PublishAmerica, Inc.

Konigsberg, Bill. The Porcupine of Truth. 2015. (ENG.). 336p. (J). (gr. 9). 17.99 *(978-0-545-64893-6(9))* Scholastic, Inc.

Konigsburg, E. L. The Outcasts of 19 Schuyler Place. 2005. 296p. (J). (gr. 5). 13.65 *(978-0-7569-6307-1(9))* Perfection Learning Corp.

—The Outcasts of 19 Schuyler Place. 2006. (ENG.). 304p. (J). (gr. 5-9). reprint ed. pap. 7.99 *(978-0-689-86637-1(2),* Atheneum Bks. for Young Readers) Simon & Schuster Children's Publishing.

—T-Backs, T-Shirts, Coat, & Suit. 2008. (ENG.). 192p. (J). (gr. 4-8). pap. 6.99 *(978-1-4169-5877-2(0),* Atheneum Bks. for Young Readers) Simon & Schuster Children's Publishing.

Koniver, Laura. Together We Sleep. 2012. 54p. pap. 16.99 *(978-1-937848-01-9(9))* Do Life Right, Inc.

Koss, Amy Goldman. The Not-So-Great Depression. 2010. (ENG.). 272p. (YA). (gr. 7-18). pap. 19.99 *(978-1-59643-613-8(1))* Roaring Brook Pr.

Kozlowsky, M. P. Juniper Berry. Madrid, Erwin, illus. 2012. (ENG.). 240p. (J). (gr. 3-7). pap. 5.99 *(978-0-06-199870-6(2),* Waldon Pond Pr.) HarperCollins Pubs.

Kraegel, Kenneth. Green Pants. Kraegel, Kenneth, illus. 2017. (ENG., Illus.). 40p. (J). (gr. -1-2). 15.99 *(978-0-7636-8840-0(1))* Candlewick Pr.

Krakower, Harold. Sugarland. 2008. 28p. pap. 12.50 *(978-1-934925-12-6(8),* Eloquent Bks.) Strategic Book Publishing & Rights Agency (SBPRA).

Kranowitz, Carol Stock. The Goodenoughs Get in Sync: A Story for Kids about the Tough Day When Filibuster Grabbed Darwin's Rabbit's Foot... Wylie, T. J., illus. 2004. 86p. (J). 14.95 *(978-1-931615-17-4(9),* 978-1-931615-17-4) Sensory Resources.

Krensky, Stephen. The Magic Pomegranate: A Jewish Folktale. 2009. pap. 40.95 *(978-0-7613-4818-4(2))* Lerner Publishing Group.

Krossing, Karen. The Yo-Yo Prophet, 1 vol. 2011. (ENG.). 248p. (YA). (gr. 7-12). pap. 12.95 *(978-1-55469-827-1(8))* Orca Bk. Pubs. USA.

Krueger, Kathryn L. Road to Grandma's House. 2005. 128p. pap. 13.95 *(978-1-59800-366-6(6))* Outskirts Pr., Inc.

Kruk, Halya. The Littlest One. Morchiladze, Manana, illus. 2007. 32p. (J). (ARA & ENG.). pap. 14.95 *(978-1-60195-090-1(X));* (POL & ENG.). pap. 14.95 *(978-1-60195-102-1(7))* International Step by Step Assn.

Krulik, Nancy E. A Royal Pain in the Burp. 2015. (George Brown, Class Clown Ser.: 15). lib. bdg. 14.75 *(978-0-606-36764-6(0))* Turtleback Bks.

Kruse, Robyn A. Sammy the Sea Turtle, 1 vol. Litteral, Christopher, illus. 2010. 18p. 24.95 *(978-1-4489-4020-2(6))* PublishAmerica, Inc.

Kuehnel, Judy Lyons. Archie & Abigail. 2008. 64p. per. 17.95 *(978-1-4327-0565-7(2))* Outskirts Pr., Inc.

—The Autumn of Aunt Charlotte. 2006. (ENG.). 132p. per. 9.95 *(978-1-59800-688-9(6))* Outskirts Pr., Inc.

Kuhn, Douglas Wolcik. Uncle Kyle's Magic Kite. Kuhn, Douglas Wolcik, illus. 2012. (Illus.). 28p. pap. 24.95 *(978-1-4626-9699-4(6))* America Star Bks.

Kulman, Andrea M. Adventures of Charlie & Doo-Doo: Not a Baby Anymore, 1 vol. 2009. 53p. pap. 16.95 *(978-1-60703-861-0(7))* America Star Bks.

Kurtz, Jane. Anna Was Here. 2013. (ENG.). 288p. (J). (gr. 3-7). 16.99 *(978-0-06-056493-3(8),* Greenwillow Bks.) HarperCollins Pubs.

—Lemon Sand. 2011. (J). lib. bdg. 17.89 *(978-0-06-056494-0(6),* Greenwillow Bks.) HarperCollins Pubs.

—Planet Jupiter. 2017. 288p. (J). (gr. 3-7). 16.99 *(978-0-06-056486-5(5),* Greenwillow Bks.) HarperCollins Pubs.

—River Friendly, River Wild. Brennan, Neil, illus. 2007. (ENG.). 40p. (J). (gr. -1-3). 7.99 *(978-1-4169-3487-5(1),* Simon & Schuster/Paula Wiseman Bks.) Simon & Schuster/Paula Wiseman Bks.

La Flamme Beighey, Carole. The Waddodles of Hollow Lake: The Mighty Oak. 2009. 344p. 28.49 *(978-1-4389-4037-3(8))* 2008. 340p. pap. 17.99 *(978-1-4343-8201-6(X))* AuthorHouse.

La Rue, Mabel Guinnip. A Letter to Popsey. Lenski, Lois, illus. 2011. 28p. pap. 35.95 *(978-1-258-06342-9(5))* Literary Licensing, LLC.

Lacey, Josh. The Sultan's Tigers. 2014. (ENG.). 304p. (J). (gr. 5-7). pap. 6.99 *(978-0-544-33629-2(1),* HMH Books For Young Readers) Houghton Mifflin Harcourt Publishing Co.

LaCour, Nina. Everything Leads to You. 2014. (ENG.). 272p. (YA). (gr. 9). 17.99 *(978-0-525-42588-5(8),* Dutton Books for Young Readers) Penguin Young Readers Group.

Lacy, Sandy Allbee. Pepe & Lupita & the Great Yawn Jar. Schrom, Garren, illus. 2013. 36p. pap. 10.95 *(978-1-60494-923-0(6))* Wheatmark, Inc.

Lael, Anita. The Little Brick House. Gresham, Delia, illus. 2012. 30p. 24.95 *(978-1-4626-5972-2(1))* America Star Bks.

LaFevers, R. L. The Basilisk's Lair. Murphy, Kelly, illus. 2011. (Nathaniel Fludd, Beastologist Ser.: 2). (ENG.). 160p. (J). (gr. 1-4). pap. 6.99 *(978-0-547-54957-6(1))* Houghton Mifflin Harcourt Publishing Co.

—Flight of the Phoenix Bk. 1. Murphy, Kelly, illus. 2010. (Nathaniel Fludd, Beastologist Ser.: 1). (ENG.). 144p. (J). (gr. 1-4). pap. 5.99 *(978-0-547-40845-3(5))* Houghton Mifflin Harcourt Publishing Co.

Lai, Thanhhà. Listen, Slowly. 2016. 288p. (J). (gr. 3-7). pap. 6.99 *(978-0-06-222919-9(2))* HarperCollins Pubs.

Lai, Thanhha. Listen, Slowly. 2016. (J). lib. bdg. 17.20 *(978-0-606-38747-7(1))* Turtleback Bks.

Laird, Elizabeth. Lost Riders, 1. unabr. ed. 2010. (ENG., Illus.). 304p. (J). (gr. 4-7). pap. 8.99 *(978-0-330-45209-0(6))* Macmillan Pubs., Ltd. GBR. Dist: Independent Pubs. Group.

Lakin, Sunny. A Family for Anca. 2013. 48p. pap. 10.50 *(978-0-9891103-0-3(3))* Lakin, Laqwacia.

LaMarche, Una & Loftin, Nikki. Don't Fail Me Now. 2015. (ENG.). 288p. (YA). (gr. 7). 17.99 *(978-1-59514-817-9(5),* Razorbill) Penguin Young Readers Group.

Lambert, Janet. Just Jenifer. 2011. 184p. 42.95 *(978-1-258-09133-0(X))* Literary Licensing, LLC.

Lambert, Mary E. Family Game Night & Other Catastrophes. 2017. (ENG.). 256p. (J). (gr. 3-7). 16.99 *(978-0-545-93198-4(3),* Scholastic Pr.) Scholastic, Inc.

Landis, Mary M. Winter Days with the Treelo Triplets. 2012. (Illus.). 218p. (J). *(978-0-7399-2447-1(8))* Rod & Staff Pubs., Inc.

Lane, Queen, illus. & creator. It's Christmas Time (Babytown Storybook) Lane, Queen, creator. 2005. (BABYTOWN Ser.: Bk. 4). 36p. (J). spiral bd. 15.00 *(978-0-9772738-1-2(4))* Quebla.

Langan, Paul. Promises to Keep, 19. 2013. (Bluford Ser.: 19). pap. 5.95 *(978-1-59194-303-7(5))* Townsend Pr.

—Survivor, 20. 2013. (Bluford Ser.: 20). pap. 5.95 *(978-1-59194-304-4(3))* Townsend Pr.

Langer, Dana. Siren Sisters. 2017. (ENG., Illus.). 256p. (J). (gr. 4-8). 16.99 *(978-1-4814-6686-8(0),* Simon & Schuster/Paula Wiseman Bks.) Simon & Schuster/Paula Wiseman Bks.

Langill, Jill. Sweet Tea for Frankenstein. 2010. 212p. pap. 14.95 *(978-1-4490-6480-8(9))* AuthorHouse.

Langrish, Katherine. Troll Fell. 2004. (Illus.). 272p. (J). (gr. 5-18). (ENG.). 16.99 *(978-0-06-058304-0(5));* lib. bdg. 16.89 *(978-0-06-058305-7(3))* HarperCollins Pubs.

Langston, Laura. In Plain Sight. 2017. (Orca Soundings Ser.). lib. bdg. 20.80 ***(978-0-606-40455-6(4))*** Turtleback Bks.

Lariviere, Sarah. The Bad Kid. 2016. (ENG., Illus.). 304p. (J). (gr. 3-7). 16.99 *(978-1-4814-3581-9(7),* Simon & Schuster Bks. For Young Readers) Simon & Schuster Bks. For Young Readers.

Larsen, Elizabeth. Buster Hardings: Buster Makes New Friends. 2008. 104p. pap. 19.95 *(978-1-60563-951-2(6))* America Star Bks.

Larsen, Kirsten. Whoa! Ufo! 2009. pap. 34.95 *(978-0-8225-4797-6(X))* Lerner Publishing Group.

—Whoa! UFO! Gott, Barry, illus. 2009. (Science Solves It! Ser.). 32p. (J). (gr. k-2). pap. 5.95 *(978-1-57565-280-1(3))* Kane Press, Inc.

Larson, Kirby. Liberty. 2016. (Dogs of World War II Ser.). (ENG.). 240p. (J). (gr. 3-7). 16.99 *(978-0-545-84071-2(6),* Scholastic Pr.) Scholastic, Inc.

Latae, Lamura. Rooney Crooney's Second Chance. 2012. (Illus.). 48p. pap. 18.00 *(978-1-935914-20-4(0))* River Sanctuary Publishing.

Laura Lee Hope. Six Little Bunkers at Grandpa Ford's. 2007. 188p. per. 11.95 *(978-1-4218-3989-9(X),* 1st World Library - Literary Society) 1st World Publishing, Inc.

Law, Felicia. Family. Knight, Paula, illus. 2015. (Patchwork Ser.). (ENG.). 24p. (J). (gr. k-3). lib. bdg. 22.60 *(978-1-59953-711-5(7))* Norwood Hse. Pr.

Law, Ingrid. Switch. 2015. (ENG.). 368p. (J). (gr. 3-7). 16.99 *(978-0-8037-3862-1(5),* Dial Bks) Penguin Young Readers Group.

Lawrence, Lisa. Rodent, 1 vol. 2016. (ENG.). 288p. (YA). (gr. 8-12). pap. 14.95 *(978-1-4598-0976-5(9))* Orca Bk. Pubs. USA.

Le Feuvre, Amy. Harebell's Friend. 2004. (Golden Inheritance Ser.: Vol. 8). (Illus.). 140p. (J). pap. *(978-0-921100-84-3(1))* Inheritance Pubns.

Le Gras, Gilbert. Joaquin & Olivier en Haute Mer! On the High Seas. 2009. 24p. pap. 8.20 *(978-1-4251-1960-5(8))* Trafford Publishing.

Lease, Janice. Manny the Marmot. 2008. 48p. pap. 19.95 *(978-0-9800762-2-6(6))* Cinnamon Ridge Publishing.

—Marigold Little Squirrel in a Cactus Patch. 2008. 48p. pap. 19.95 *(978-0-9800762-0-2(X))* Cinnamon Ridge Publishing.

Leavey, Peggy Dymond. Trouble at Turtle Narrows. 2008. (ENG.). 144p. (J). (gr. 4-18). pap. 9.95 *(978-1-894917-71-1(5),* Napoleon & Co.) Dundurn CAN. Dist: Ingram Publisher Services.

Leavitt, Lindsey. Sean Griswold's Head. 2012. (ENG.). 304p. (YA). (gr. 7-12). pap. 9.99 *(978-1-59990-911-0(1),* 9781599909110, Bloomsbury USA Childrens) Bloomsbury Publishing USA.

Lectura en Familia: Jumbo Pack. (SPA.). (gr. -1-2). 392.63 *(978-0-7362-1489-6(5))* CENGAGE Learning.

Lee, Howard. Jamshid & the Lost Mountain of Light. 2008. (ENG.). 248p. pap. 14.99 *(978-1-4196-8958-1(4))* CreateSpace Independent Publishing Platform.

Lee, Mary Ellen. Danny & Life on Bluff Point: Lost in the Dark. 2009. 160p. (gr. 4-7). 22.95 *(978-1-4401-4607-7(1));* pap. 12.95 *(978-1-4401-4608-4(X))* iUniverse, Inc.

Leeuwen, Joke Van & Leeuwen, Joke van. Eep! Leeuwen, Joke van, illus. 2012. (Gecko Press Titles Ser.). (ENG., Illus.). 152p. (J). (gr. 2-5). pap. 7.95 *(978-1-877579-07-3(6))* Gecko Pr. NZL. Dist: Lerner Publishing Group.

Lehman-Wilzig, Tami. Zvuvi's Israel. Topaz, Ksenia, illus. 2009. (Israel Ser.). (ENG.). 32p. (J). (gr. -1-2). 16.95 *(978-0-8225-8759-0(9));* pap. 7.95 *(978-0-8225-8760-6(2))* Lerner Publishing Group. (Kar-Ben Publishing).

Lehmkuhl, Pat, illus. Starlight, Star Bright: (the Starlight Books, 3), 6 vols. 2003. (Starlight Bks.: Bk. 3). 192p. (J). (gr. 3-7). per. 12.00 *(978-0-9714161-2-3(5))* Raven Publishing Inc. of Montana.

Leinberger, Judy. The Man Who Talks with Eagles. 2010. 60p. pap. 14.00 *(978-1-4269-3396-7(7))* Trafford Publishing.

Lemna, Don. When the Sergeant Came Marching Home. 2009. (ENG.). 208p. (J). (gr. 3-7). pap. 7.95 *(978-0-8234-2211-1(9))* Holiday Hse., Inc.

L'Engle, Madeleine. The Other Dog. Davenier, Christine, illus. 2003. 37p. (J). (gr. 2-5). reprint ed. 16.00 *(978-0-7567-6970-3(1))* DIANE Publishing Co.

—A Ring of Endless Light Bk. 4. 2008. (Austin Family Ser.: 4). (ENG.). 352p. (J). (gr. 6-12). pap. 8.99 *(978-0-312-37935-3(8),* 9780312379353) Square Fish.

Leno, Katrina. The Lost & Found. 2016. 352p. (J). (gr. 8). 17.99 *(978-0-06-223120-8(0),* HarperTeen) HarperCollins Pubs.

Leon, Georgina Lazaro. El Mejor Es Mi Papa. Alvarez, David, illus. 2003. (Yellow Ser.). (SPA.). 31p. (gr. k-3). pap. 9.95 *(978-1-57581-442-1(0))* Santillana USA Publishing Co., Inc.

LernerClassroom Editors. Mallory Teaching Guide. 2009. pap. 7.95 *(978-0-8225-7448-4(9))* Lerner Publishing Group.

Les, Papa. Gio the Friendly T-Rex & Friends: Hide-and-Seek. 2009. 24p. pap. 24.95 *(978-1-60749-731-8(X))* America Star Bks.

Let's Go Downtown: Individual Title Six-Packs. (gr. -1-2). 27.00 *(978-0-7635-9458-9(X))* Rigby Education.

Leung, Helen. Toni. 2006. 251p. pap. 27.95 *(978-1-4137-8990-4(0))* PublishAmerica, Inc.

Levin, Mark & Flackett, Jennifer. The Family Hitchcock. 2011. (ENG.). 288p. (J). (gr. 4). 16.99 *(978-0-06-189394-0(3),* Tegen, Katherine Bks) HarperCollins Pubs.

Levine, Anna. Jodie's Passover Adventure. Topaz, Ksenia, illus. 2012. (Passover Ser.). (ENG.). 32p. (J). (gr. k-3). lib. bdg. 17.95 *(978-0-7613-5641-7(X),* Kar-Ben Publishing) Lerner Publishing Group.

Levine, Kristin. The Lions of Little Rock. 2013. (ENG.). 320p. (J). (gr. 5-9). pap. 7.99 *(978-0-14-242435-3(8),* Puffin Books) Penguin Young Readers Group.

—The Paper Cowboy. 2016. (ENG.). 368p. (J). (gr. 5). 8.99 *(978-0-14-242715-6(2),* Puffin Books) Penguin Young Readers Group.

Levine, Phyllis. At the Skylight with Matilda. 2007. (ENG.). 160p. per. 12.95 *(978-1-60047-089-9(0))* Wasteland Pr.

Levinson, Robin K. Miriam's Journey: Discovering a New World. 2006. (Illus.). 64p. (J). per. 12.00 *(978-0-9773673-0-6(4))* Gali Girls, Inc.

Levy, Joanne. Crushing It. 2017. (Mix Ser.). (ENG., Illus.). 240p. (J). (gr. 4-8). pap. 7.99 *(978-1-4814-6473-4(6),* Aladdin) Simon & Schuster Children's Publishing.

Lewis, Orane. Miss Henn & Family. Vest, Dianne, illus. l.t. ed. 2006. 27p. (J). per. 10.99 *(978-1-59879-141-9(9))* Lifevest Publishing, Inc.

Li-Qiong, Yu. A New Year's Reunion: A Chinese Story. Cheng-Liang, Zhu, illus. 2013. (ENG.). 40p. (J). (gr. -1-2). 6.99 *(978-0-7636-6748-1(X))* Candlewick Pr.

Lilly, Suzanne. Untellable. 2013. 158p. pap. 9.99 *(978-1-62237-218-8(2))* Turquoise Morning Pr.

Lilly, T. S. The Upgrade. 2008. 60p. pap. 16.95 *(978-1-60441-536-0(3))* America Star Bks.

Lindenbaum, Pija. Mini Mia & Her Darling Uncle. Dyssegaard, Elisabeth Kallick, tr. from SWE. 2007. (Illus.). 40p. (J). (gr. -1-3). 16.00 *(978-91-29-66734-9(8))* R & S Bks. SWE. Dist: Macmillan.

Lindgren, Astrid. Happy Times in Noisy Village. Wikland, Ilon, illus. 2003. Orig. Title: Bullerby Boken. 119p. (J). pap. 10.95 *(978-1-883937-66-9(3))* Bethlehem Bks.

Lindo, Elvira. Manolito Four-Eyes: the 2nd Volume of the Great Encyclopedia of My Life: The 2nd Volume of the Great Encyclopedia of My Life, 0 vols. Urberuaga, Emilio, illus. unabr. ed. 2013. (Manolito Four-Eyes Ser.: 2). (ENG.). 162p. (J). (gr. 3-7). pap. 9.99 *(978-1-4778-1700-1(X),* 9781477817001, Amazon Children's Publishing) Amazon Publishing.

Liphardt, Linda. Secret in the Old Barn. 2008. 116p. pap. 19.95 *(978-1-60703-615-9(0))* America Star Bks.

Lipsyte, Robert. Yellow Flag. 2009. (ENG.). 256p. (YA). (gr. 8). pap. 9.99 *(978-0-06-055709-6(5),* Tegen, Katherine Bks) HarperCollins Pubs.

Lisle, Janet Taylor. Afternoon of the Elves. 2017. (ENG., Illus.). 128p. (J). (gr. 3-7). 16.99 ***(978-1-4814-9908-8(4),*** Atheneum Bks. for Young Readers) Simon & Schuster Children's Publishing.

Littman, Sarah Darer. In Case You Missed It. (ENG.). 320p. (gr. 7). 2017. (J). pap. 9.99 ***(978-1-338-16065-9(6),*** Scholastic Paperbacks) 2016. (YA). 17.99 *(978-0-545-90437-7(4),* Scholastic Pr.) Scholastic, Inc.

Lively, Judy. Hanny Bonz. 2008. 24p. pap. 10.95 *(978-1-4327-2122-0(4))* Outskirts Pr., Inc.

Lloyd-Jones, Emily. The Hearts We Sold. 2017. (ENG.). 400p. (YA). (gr. 10-17). 17.99 ***(978-0-316-31459-6(5))*** Little Brown & Co.

Lloyd, Natalie. The Key to Extraordinary. 2016. (ENG.). 240p. (J). (gr. 3-7). 16.99 *(978-0-545-55274-5(5),* Scholastic Pr.) Scholastic, Inc.

Lo, Catherine. How It Ends. 2016. (ENG.). 304p. (YA). (gr. 9). 17.99 *(978-0-544-54006-4(9),* HMH Books For Young Readers) Houghton Mifflin Harcourt Publishing Co.

Lo, Malinda. Ash. 2010. (ENG.). 272p. (gr. 10-17). pap. 10.99 *(978-0-316-04010-5(X))* Little, Brown Bks. for Young Readers.

Lobel, Anita. Potatoes, Potatoes. 2004. 40p. (J). 15.99 *(978-0-06-023927-5(1));* lib. bdg. 16.89 *(978-0-06-023928-2(X))* HarperCollins Pubs.

Loccisano, Rina. Baby Dario Is Born. Baker, David, illus. 2012. 36p. pap. 24.95 *(978-1-4560-6099-2(6))* America Star Bks.

Lockhart, E. We Were Liars. 2014. (Illus.). 227p. (YA). *(978-0-385-39009-5(2),* Delacorte Pr) Random House Publishing Group.

—We Were Liars. (ENG., (YA). (gr. 7). 2014. Illus.). 240p. 17.99 *(978-0-385-74126-2(X))* 2017. 272p. 18.99 ***(978-1-5247-6458-6(2))*** Random Hse. Children's Bks. (Delacorte Pr.).

Loewen, Nancy. Baby Wants Mama, 0 vols. Melmon, Deborah, illus. 2013. (ENG.). 24p. (J). (gr. -1-k). 14.99 *(978-1-4778-1651-6(8),* 9781477816516, Amazon Children's Publishing) Amazon Publishing.

Logan, Dottie Colegrove. Picnic on the Beach: Nana & Me Series, Book Three. 2010. 16p. 12.99 *(978-1-4490-3689-8(9))* AuthorHouse.

Logsted, Greg. Alibi Junior High. (ENG.). 256p. (J). (gr. 5-9). 2011. pap. 6.99 *(978-1-4169-4814-8(7))* 2009. (Illus.). 16.99 *(978-1-4169-7959-3(X))* Simon & Schuster/Paula Wiseman Bks. (Simon & Schuster/Paula Wiseman Bks.).

Lois, Lowry. Anastasia on Her Own. de Groat, Diane, illus. 2016. (Anastasia Krupnik Story Ser.). (ENG.). 176p. (J). (gr. 5-7). pap. 7.99 *(978-0-544-54027-9(1),* HMH Books For Young Readers) Houghton Mifflin Harcourt Publishing Co.

London, Jonathan & Remkiewicz, Frank. Froggy Plays T-Ball. Remkiewicz, Frank, illus. 2009. (Froggy Ser.). (ENG., Illus.). 32p. (J). (gr. -1-k). pap. 6.99 *(978-0-14-241304-3(6),* Puffin Books) Penguin Young Readers Group.

Long, Ethan. Big Cat. Long, Ethan, illus. 2016. (I Like to Read(r) Ser.). (ENG., Illus.). 24p. (J). (gr. -1-3). 6.99 *(978-0-8234-3539-5(3))* Holiday Hse., Inc.

Long, Samantha Gail. Don't Let the Bedbugs Bite, 1 vol. Byers, Bradley, illus. 2010. 24p. 24.95 *(978-1-4512-8681-6(3))* PublishAmerica, Inc.

Longstreth, Galen Goodwin. Yes, Let's. Wicks, Maris, illus. 2013. (ENG.). 32p. (J). (gr. -1-3). 15.95 *(978-1-933718-87-3(0))* Tanglewood Pr.

Look, Lenore. Uncle Peter's Amazing Chinese Wedding. Heo, Yumi, illus. 2006. (ENG.). 40p. (J). (gr. -1-3). 17.99 *(978-0-689-84458-4(1),* Atheneum Bks. for Young Readers) Simon & Schuster Children's Publishing.

Looper, Grace W. Molasses Making Time. l.t. ed. 2004. 152p. (YA). pap. 8.95 *(978-0-9747685-5-7(3))* Bella Rosa Bks.

Lord, Emery. When We Collided. 2016. (ENG.). 352p. (YA). 17.99 *(978-1-61963-845-7(2),* 9781619638457, Bloomsbury USA Childrens) Bloomsbury Publishing USA.

Lorenzi, Natalie Dias. Flying the Dragon. (ENG.). 240p. (J). (gr. 4-7). 2014. pap. 8.95 *(978-1-58089-435-7(6))* 2012. 16.95 *(978-1-58089-434-0(8))* Charlesbridge Publishing, Inc.

—A Long Pitch Home. 2016. (ENG.). 256p. (J). (gr. 4-7). lib. bdg. 16.95 *(978-1-58089-713-6(4))* Charlesbridge Publishing, Inc.

The Lost Boy. 2008. (Illus.). 32p. (Orig.). (J). per. 14.95 *(978-0-9766720-3-6(0))* Mustang BKS.

Lottridge, Celia. Ticket to Curlew, 1 vol. 2nd ed. 2007. (ENG.). 144p. (J). (gr. 2-7). pap. 8.95 *(978-0-88899-843-9(0))* Groundwood Bks. CAN. Dist: Publishers Group West (PGW).

Lottridge, Celia Barker. Wings to Fly, 1 vol. 3rd ed. 2007. (ENG.). 144p. (J). (gr. 2-7). pap. 8.95 *(978-0-88899-844-6(9))* Groundwood Bks. CAN. Dist: Publishers Group West (PGW).

Love, D. Anne. Picture Perfect. 2010. (ENG.). 304p. (YA). (gr. 7). pap. 8.99 *(978-0-689-87391-1(3),* McElderry, Margaret K. Bks.) McElderry, Margaret K. Bks.

Lovett, Louise Sheppa, illus. A Happy Day. Lovett, Louise Sheppa, . 2008. 32p. (J). 18.50 *(978-0-9793419-0-8(6))* Tish & Co. LLC.

Lovins, Jennifer O. Ophi Baby. 2008. 32p. pap. 14.95 *(978-1-57306-285-5(5))* Bess Pr., Inc.

Lowes, Sarah. The Snow Queen. Clara, Miss, illus. 2013. (ENG.). 64p. (J). 17.99 *(978-1-84686-964-8(1))* Barefoot Bks., Inc.

Lowrey, Becky. Chirps. 2004. 45p. pap. 24.95 *(978-1-4137-2984-9(3))* PublishAmerica, Inc.

Lubar, David. Sophomores & Other Oxymorons. 2015. (ENG.). 432p. (YA). (gr. 7). 17.99 *(978-0-525-42970-8(0),* Dutton Books for Young Readers) Penguin Young Readers Group.

Luchesi, Dennis. Benji Rabbit. 2013. 24p. pap. 24.95 *(978-1-62709-894-6(1))* America Star Bks.

Ludwig, Sabine, tr. WINN-DIXIE. (GER.). pap. 17.95 *(978-3-423-70771-8(2))* Deutscher Taschenbuch Verlag GmbH & Co KG DEU. Dist: Distribooks, Inc.

Lunetta, Demitria. Bad Blood. 2017. (ENG.). 272p. (YA). (gr. 7). 17.99 *(978-1-101-93805-8(6),* Delacorte Pr.) Random Hse. Children's Bks.

Lupica, Mike. Heat. 2007. 18.40 *(978-1-4177-7264-3(6),* Turtleback) Turtleback Bks.

—Hot Hand. 2009. (Comeback Kids Ser.). (ENG.). 192p. (J). (gr. 3-7). pap. 6.99 *(978-0-14-241441-5(7),* Puffin Books) Penguin Young Readers Group.

—Million-Dollar Throw. 2010. (ENG.). 272p. (J). (gr. 5-18). 7.99 *(978-0-14-241558-0(8),* Puffin Books) Penguin Young Readers Group.

—Million-Dollar Throw. 2010. (Million Dollar Sports Ser.). lib. bdg. 18.40 *(978-0-606-25316-1(5),* Turtleback) Turtleback Bks.

—Safe at Home. 2009. (Comeback Kids Ser.). (ENG.). 192p. (J). (gr. 3-7). 6.99 *(978-0-14-241460-6(3),* Puffin Books) Penguin Young Readers Group.

Lynch, Janet Nichols. Messed Up. 2009. (ENG.). 320p. (YA). (gr. 7-18). 17.95 *(978-0-8234-2185-5(6))* Holiday Hse., Inc.

Lynch, Stephen D. The Travels of Kui, the African Spurred Tortoise. Richard, Keisha Luana, illus. 2007. 36p. per. 24.95 *(978-1-4137-1802-7(7))* America Star Bks.

Lyon, Annabel. All-Season Edie, 1 vol. 2008. (ENG., Illus.). 192p. (J). (gr. 5-10). pap. 13.00 *(978-1-55143-713-2(9))* Orca Bk. Pubs. USA.

Lysaght, Richard. The Black Bag Mystery. Wolfhound Publishing Editors, ed. (ENG., Illus.). 240p. pap. 6.95

(978-0-86327-886-0(8)) Wolfhound Pr. IRL. Dist: Interlink Publishing Group, Inc.

Mac, Carrie. Retribution. 2008. (ENG.). 320p. (J). (gr. 7-18). 11.00 *(978-0-14-305114-5(8),* Puffin Canada) Penguin Random House Canada Young Readers CAN. Dist: Penguin Random Hse. LLC.

Maccarone, Grace. The Gingerbread Family: A Scratch-and-Sniff Book. Gardner, Louise, illus. 2010. (ENG.). 14p. (J). (gr. -1-k). bds. 7.99 *(978-1-4424-0678-0(X),* Little Simon) Little Simon.

MacColl, Michaela & Nichols, Rosemary. Freedom's Price. 2015. (Hidden Histories Ser.). (ENG., Illus.). 288p. (J). (gr. 3-7). 17.95 *(978-1-62091-624-7(X),* Calkins Creek) Boyds Mills Pr.

MacCracken, Joan. Trisba & Sula: A Miskitu Folktale from Nicaragua (Una Leyenda de los Miskitos de Nicaragua) Macdonald, Isabel et al, trs. Silva, Augusto Alves da, illus. 2005. (ENG & SPA.). 16.95 *(978-0-9646018-2-6(6))* Tiffin Pr. of Maine.

The MacGregors & MacDougalls: Individual Title Six-Packs. (Bookweb Ser.). 32p. (gr. 5-18). 34.00 *(978-0-7635-3783-8(7))* Rigby Education.

MacHado, Ana Maria. Todo al Mismo Tiempo Ahora. 2003. (SPA.). (YA). 8.95 *(978-958-04-6030-5(2),* NR30567) Norma S.A. COL. Dist: Distribuidora Norma, Inc., Lectorum Pubns., Inc.

Mackall, Dandi Daley. Larger-Than-Life Lara. 2016. (ENG.). 176p. 14.99 *(978-1-4964-1429-8(2))* Tyndale Hse. Pubs.

Mackler, Carolyn. Infinite in Between. 2015. (ENG.). 480p. (YA). (gr. 8). 17.99 *(978-0-06-173107-5(2),* HarperTeen) HarperCollins Pubs.

MacLachlan, Patricia. Edward's Eyes. 2009. (ENG.). 128p. (J). (gr. 3-7). pap. 7.99 *(978-1-4169-2744-0(1),* Atheneum Bks. for Young Readers) Simon & Schuster Children's Publishing.

—Edward's Eyes. l.t. ed. 2008. (Literacy Bridge Middle Reader Ser.). 139p. (J). (gr. 3-7). 23.95 *(978-1-4104-0436-7(6))* Thorndike Pr.

—Just Dance. 2017. (ENG., Illus.). 128p. (J). (gr. 2). 15.99 ***(978-1-4814-7252-4(6),*** McElderry, Margaret K. Bks.) McElderry, Margaret K. Bks.

MacLachlan, Patricia. Your Moon, My Moon: A Grandmother's Words to a Faraway Child. Collier, Bryan, illus. 2011. (ENG.). 32p. (J). (gr. -1-3). 16.99 *(978-1-4169-7950-0(6),* Simon & Schuster Bks. For Young Readers) Simon & Schuster Bks. For Young Readers.

MacLean, Christine. Even Firefighters Hug Their Moms. Reed, Mike, illus. 2004. (ENG.). 32p. (J). (gr. k-3). pap. 5.99 *(978-0-14-240191-0(9),* Puffin Books) Penguin Young Readers Group.

Macor, Jim. Frazier Fir, A Christmas Fable. Macor, Jim, illus. 2007. (Illus.). 32p. (J). 17.95 *(978-0-9785551-3-9(9))* Zuber Publishing.

Maddox, Jake. On Guard, 1 vol. Tiffany, Sean, illus. 2010. (Team Jake Maddox Sports Stories Ser.). (ENG.). 72p. (gr. 2-3). pap. 5.95 *(978-1-4342-2279-4(9));* lib. bdg. 25.32 *(978-1-4342-1920-6(8))* Stone Arch Bks.

Madrzak, Carole. In the Shadows of Bington Manor. 2006. (ENG.). 132p. per. 24.95 *(978-1-4241-5168-4(6))* America Star Bks.

—Secrets Inside Bington Manor. 2005. 108p. pap. 19.95 *(978-1-4241-0720-9(2))* America Star Bks.

Magoon, Kekla. The Rock & the River. 2010. (ENG.). 304p. (J). (gr. 5-9). pap. 7.99 *(978-1-4169-7803-9(8),* Aladdin) Simon & Schuster Children's Publishing.

Magsamen, Sandra. Welcome Little One. 2015. (ENG., Illus.). 32p. (J). (gr. 3-8). 16.99 *(978-1-4926-1930-7(2),* Sourcebooks Jabberwocky) Sourcebooks, Inc.

Maguire, Gregory. What-the-Dickens: The Story of a Rogue Tooth Fairy. 2007. (ENG.). 304p. (J). (gr. 4-8). 24.80 *(978-1-4287-6555-9(7),* Follettbound) Follett School Solutions.

Mahoney, Jan. Moose Tales. 2010. 12p. 9.99 *(978-1-4520-6950-0(6))* AuthorHouse.

Malone, Jen. Changes in Latitudes. 2017. 384p. (YA). (gr. 8). pap. 9.99 *(978-0-06-238017-3(6),* HarperTeen) HarperCollins Pubs.

Mancil, Arlene. The Angel Explains Christmas Blessings. McKinnon, Joy, illus. 2008. 16p. pap. 24.95 *(978-1-60813-297-3(8))* America Star Bks.

Mandeville, Terry M. Just Waiting for My Family. l.t. ed. 2005. (Illus.). 52p. (J). 14.95 *(978-0-9762475-0-0(X))* Mandeville, Terry M.

Mann, Scott. Daddy Keeps Us Free. Pannell, Nick, illus. 2011. 36p. pap. 24.95 *(978-1-4560-6075-6(9))* America Star Bks.

Mann, T. L. The Adventures of Magellan. 2009. 23p. (J). pap. 13.95 *(978-1-4327-3490-9(3))* Outskirts Pr., Inc.

Manning, Maurie J. The Aunts Go Marching. 2003. (ENG., Illus.). 32p. (J). (gr. -1-18). 15.95 *(978-1-59078-026-8(4))* Boyds Mills Pr.

Manny's Aventura de Motorcyle. 2009. (ENG.). 24p. pap. 4.99 *(978-1-4231-2266-1(6))* Disney Pr.

Mansur, Motesem. The Terry Tornado Story: The Wake-up Call. 2004. 25p. pap. 24.95 *(978-1-4137-2133-1(8))* PublishAmerica, Inc.

Manushkin, Fran. Big Brothers Are the Best, 1 vol. Richards, Kirsten, illus. 2012. (Fiction Picture Bks.). (ENG.). 24p. (gr. -1 — 1). 6.95 *(978-1-4048-7224-0(8));* lib. bdg. 22.65 *(978-1-4048-7137-3(3))* Picture Window Bks. (Fiction Picture Bks.).

—Big Sisters Are the Best, 1 vol. Richards, Kirsten, illus. 2012. (Fiction Picture Bks.). (ENG.). 24p. (gr. -1 — 1). lib. bdg. 22.65 *(978-1-4048-7138-0(1),* Fiction Picture Bks.) Picture Window Bks.

—Katie Woo, Set. Lyon, Tammie, illus. Incl. Big Lie. 21.32 *(978-1-4048-5497-0(5));* Boss of the World. 21.32 *(978-1-4048-5493-2(2));* Goodbye to Goldie. 21.32 *(978-1-4048-5495-6(9));* Happy Day. 21.32 *(978-1-4048-5496-3(7));* No More Teasing. 21.32 *(978-1-4048-5492-5(4));* Too Much Rain. 21.32 *(978-1-4048-5494-9(0));* (gr. k-2). (Katie Woo Ser.). (ENG., Illus.). 32p. 2009. 127.92 *(978-1-4048-5679-0(X))* Picture Window Bks.

Manzano, Sonia. The Revolution of Evelyn Serrano. 2014. (ENG.). 224p. (J). (gr. 9). pap. 9.99 *(978-0-545-32506-6(4))* Scholastic, Inc.

Maracle, Lee. Will's Garden. 2nd rev. ed. 2008. (ENG.). 194p. pap. 16.95 *(978-1-894778-59-6(6))* Theytus Bks., Ltd. CAN. Dist: Univ. of Toronto Pr.

Marguerita, Ann. Fannie Annie & Her Little White Shoes. 2008. (Illus.). 68p. per. *(978-1-84748-259-4(7))* Athena Pr.

Marie, Brandi. Lily White & the Necklace of Doom, 1 vol. 2009. 147p. pap. 24.95 *(978-1-4489-7934-9(X))* America Star Bks.

Marie, Leann. The Ghost of Oberlin. 2008. pap. 16.95 *(978-1-4241-9597-8(7))* America Star Bks.

Marinaro, Stacy. Annabelle & the Meteor. 2008. 32p. pap. 8.95 *(978-1-4357-2841-7(6))* Lulu Pr., Inc.

Marino, Lia. Amelia & Gabby: More Than Just Sisters. Rankin, Shelly, illus. 2005. 31p. (J). 18.95 *(978-1-886057-30-2(3))* Warren Publishing, Inc.

Marley, Ziggy. I Love You Too. Jatkowska, Ag, illus. 2014. (ENG.). 48p. (J). (-2). 15.95 *(978-1-61775-310-7(6))* Akashic Bks.

Marlow, Susan K. River of Peril, 1 vol. 2014. (Goldtown Adventures Ser.: 4). 144p. (J). pap. 7.99 *(978-0-8254-4297-1(4))* Kregel Pubns.

Marrone, Amanda. Slayed. 2010. (ENG., Illus.). 272p. (YA). (gr. 9-18). pap. 9.99 *(978-1-4169-9487-9(4),* Simon Pulse) Simon Pulse.

Marsden, Carolyn & Niem, Thay. The Buddha's Diamonds. 2010. (ENG., Illus.). 112p. (J). (gr. 3-7). pap. 5.99 *(978-0-7636-4828-2(0))* Candlewick Pr.

Marsh, Carole. The Behemoth Blizzard Mystery. (Masters of Disasters Ser.). (Illus.). 118p. (J). (gr. 3-5). 2008. per. 5.99 *(978-0-635-06464-6(2))* 2007. 14.95 *(978-0-635-06467-7(7))* Gallopade International.

—The Horrendous Hurricane Mystery. 2007. (Masters of Disasters Ser.). (Illus.). 118p. (J). (gr. 2-9). 14.95 *(978-0-635-06396-0(4))* Gallopade International.

—The Mystery at Area 51. Friedlander, Randolyn, illus. 2011. (Carole Marsh Mysteries Ser.). 32p. pap. 7.99 *(978-0-635-07961-9(5),* Marsh, Carole Mysteries) Gallopade International.

—The Mystery at Cape Cod. 2010. (Real Kids, Real Places Ser.). (Illus.). 158p. (J). pap. 18.99 *(978-0-635-07594-9(6),* Marsh, Carole Mysteries) Gallopade International.

—The Mystery at Cape Cod. Friedlander, Randolyn, illus. 2010. (Real Kids, Real Places Teacher Guides). 32p. (J). pap. 7.99 *(978-0-635-07600-7(4))* Gallopade International.

—The Mystery at Death Valley. 2010. (Real Kids, Real Places Ser.). (Illus.). 158p. (J). 24.99 *(978-0-635-07608-3(X));* pap. 7.99 *(978-0-635-07596-3(2))* Gallopade International. (Marsh, Carole Mysteries).

—The Mystery at Hollywood. 2011. (Carole Marsh Mysteries Ser.). (J). pap. 7.99 *(978-0-635-07959-6(3),* Marsh, Carole Mysteries) Gallopade International.

—The Mystery at Motown. Friedlander, Randolyn, illus. 2011. (Carole Marsh Mysteries Ser.). 32p. pap. 7.99 *(978-0-635-07962-6(3),* Marsh, Carole Mysteries) Gallopade International.

—The Mystery in the Twin Cities. Baker, Janice, ed. 2011. (Carole Marsh Mysteries Ser.). (Illus.). (J). pap. 7.99 *(978-0-635-07960-2(7),* Marsh, Carole Mysteries) Gallopade International.

—The Treacherous Tornado Mystery. 2007. (Masters of Disasters Ser.). (Illus.). 118p. (J). (gr. 2-9). 14.95 *(978-0-635-06394-6(8))* Gallopade International.

Marsh, Sarah Glenn. Fear the Drowning Deep. 2016. (ENG.). 312p. (YA). (gr. 6). 16.99 *(978-1-5107-0348-3(9),* Sky Pony Pr.) Skyhorse Publishing Co., Inc.

Marshall, Denise. The Adventures of Hip Hop: Hip Hop & the Blueberry Pancakes. Champagne, Heather, illus. 2012. 36p. pap. 14.75 *(978-1-62212-331-5(X),* Strategic Bk. Publishing) Strategic Book Publishing & Rights Agency (SBPRA).

—The Adventures of Hip Hop: Hip Hop & the Yellow Hat. Schley, Cheri & Champagne, Heather, illus. 2011. 36p. pap. 14.75 *(978-1-60976-342-8(4),* Eloquent Bks.) Strategic Book Publishing & Rights Agency (SBPRA).

Marshall, Kate. Mokes, Mines & Mayhem. 2008. 120p. pap. 10.95 *(978-1-60693-357-2(4),* Eloquent Bks.) Strategic Book Publishing & Rights Agency (SBPRA).

Martha, Morales. Ariana Leaves San Francisco. Chiu, Bessie, illus. 2011. 28p. pap. 8.50 *(978-1-61170-017-6(5))* Robertson Publishing.

Martín Anguita, Carmen & Carmen, Martín Anguita. Marta y Mamá Juegan a Recordar. Cortazar, Alicia Canas, illus. 2008. (SPA.). 32p. (J). 10.99 *(978-84-241-5390-8(1))* Everest Editora ESP. Dist: Lectorum Pubns., Inc.

Martin, Ann M. Better to Wish. 2013. (Family Tree Ser.). (ENG.). 240p. (J). (gr. 3-7). 16.99 *(978-0-545-35942-9(2),* Scholastic Pr.) Scholastic, Inc.

—The Long Way Home. 2013. (Family Tree Ser.: 2). (ENG.). 224p. (J). (gr. 3-7). 16.99 *(978-0-545-35943-6(0),* Scholastic Pr.) Scholastic, Inc.

—Ten Good & Bad Things about My Life (So Far) 2012. (ENG.). 272p. (J). (gr. 4-7). 16.99 *(978-0-312-64299-0(7),* 9780312642990) Feiwel & Friends.

—Ten Good & Bad Things about My Life (So Far) 2013. (ENG.). 288p. (J). (gr. 4-7). pap. 7.99 *(978-1-250-03413-7(2),* 9781250034137) Square Fish.

—Tis the Season. 2007. (Main Street Ser.). (Illus.). 195p. (J). (gr. 4-7). 14.65 *(978-0-7569-8327-7(4))* Perfection Learning Corp.

Martin, Brian. The Lost Ring. McDonald, Kim, illus. 2007. 42p. (J). *(978-0-9798059-1-2(0))* Lunchbox Stories Inc.

Martin, Gary & Zondervan Bibles Staff. The Sword of Revenge, 1 vol. Rogers, Bud, ed. Cariello, Sergio, illus. 2009. (Z Graphic Novels / Son of Samson Ser.). (ENG.). 160p. (J). pap. 6.99 *(978-0-310-71285-5(8))* Zondervan.

Martin, Mildred A. Growing with the Millers. Burkholder, Edith, illus. 2012. 144p. (J). *(978-1-884377-23-5(8))* Green Pastures Pr.

Martin, Rebecca. Eyes for My Heart. 2003. (Illus.). 269p. 10.20 *(978-0-7399-2308-5(0),* 2231) Rod & Staff Pubs., Inc.

Martin, Tamra. My Wish, Our Little Oat. Tinker, Jason, illus. 2007. 36p. (J). 21.99 *(978-1-59879-522-6(8),* Lifevest) Lifevest Publishing, Inc.

Martinez, Claudia Guadalupe. Smell of Old Lady Perfume. 2011. (ENG., Illus.). 256p. (J). (gr. 4-10). pap. 7.95 *(978-1-933693-88-0(6))* Cinco Puntos Pr.

Martinez, Migdalia Fonseca & Martinez-Radio, Jorge Baez. Maina. 2004. (Yellow Ser.). (SPA., Illus.). 32p. (J). (gr. k-3). pap. 5.95 *(978-1-57581-441-4(2))* Santillana USA Publishing Co., Inc.

Mary E. Gale. Mountain Boy in the City. 2009. 136p. 21.95 *(978-1-4401-6771-3(0));* pap. 11.95 *(978-1-4401-6773-7(7))* iUniverse, Inc.

Maschari, Jennifer. Things That Surprise You. 2017. 288p. (J). (gr. 3-7). 16.99 ***(978-0-06-243892-8(1))*** HarperCollins Pubs.

Maslen, Bobby Lynn. Word Families, Set. Maslen, John R., illus. 2006. (Bob Bks.). (ENG.). 16p. (J). (gr. -1-3). pap. 16.99 *(978-0-439-84509-0(2),* Scholastic Paperbacks) Scholastic, Inc.

Matthews, Caroline. Uncle Orange. 2012. 30p. 24.95 *(978-1-4626-6623-2(X))* America Star Bks.

Matthews, Owen. The Fixes. 2016. 528p. (YA). (gr. 9). 17.99 *(978-0-06-233689-7(4),* HarperTeen) HarperCollins Pubs.

Matthies, Janna. Two Is Enough. Liddiard, Merrilee & Mourning, Tuesday, illus. 2015. (ENG.). 40p. (J). (gr. -1-17). 15.95 *(978-0-7624-5561-4(6),* Running Pr. Kids) Running Pr. Bk. Pubs.

Mauzy, Barbara. Don't Be a Schwoe: Embracing Differences, 1 vol. 2011. (ENG., Illus.). 80p. (J). 16.99 *(978-0-7643-3566-2(9),* 9780764335662) Schiffer Publishing, Ltd.

May, Maggie. Times Three. L, Joe, illus. 2011. 36p. pap. 24.95 *(978-1-4626-2504-8(5))* America Star Bks.

Mayer, Marvin S. Sammy Squirrel & the Sunflower Seeds. Johns, Dick, illus. 2008. 73p. pap. 19.95 *(978-1-60672-193-3(3))* America Star Bks.

Mayer, Mercer & Mayer, Gina. My Family: A Big Little Critter Book. 2013. (Big Little Critter Ser.: 2). (ENG., Illus.). 98p. (J). 12.95 *(978-1-60746-810-3(7),* Premiere) FastPrncil, Inc.

Mayeux, Gertie. Jesse the Oil Patch Kid. 2012. 36p. pap. 20.99 *(978-1-4772-3691-8(0))* AuthorHouse.

Mayher, Lauren. The Legend of Darien: A Hero Rises: Book 1. 2008. 423p. (J). per. 12.95 *(978-0-9794545-0-9(6))* Blue Eyed Mayhem Publishing.

Mayhew, Julie. Red Ink. 2016. (ENG.). 320p. (YA). (gr. 9). 16.99 *(978-0-7636-7731-2(0))* Candlewick Pr.

Mazer, Norma Fox. The Missing Girl. 2010. (ENG.). 304p. (YA). (gr. 8). pap. 8.99 *(978-0-06-447365-1(1),* HarperTeen) HarperCollins Pubs.

—Ten Ways to Make My Sister Disappear. l.t. ed. 2008. (Thorndike Literacy Bridge Ser.). 207p. (J). (gr. 4-7). 22.95 *(978-1-4104-0510-4(9))* Thorndike Pr.

McBratney, Sam. There, There. Bates, Ivan, illus. 2015. (ENG.). 32p. (J). (-k). bds. 7.99 *(978-0-7636-7565-3(2),* Templar) Candlewick Pr.

McBride, Linda Ray. Mema Has Cancer, 1 vol. DeNault, Shirl, illus. 2008. (ENG.). 29p. 24.95 *(978-1-60610-833-8(6))* America Star Bks.

McCabe, James Dabney, Jr. Planting the Wilderness or, the Pioneer Boys: a Story of Frontier Life. 2007. pap. 27.95 *(978-1-4304-8187-4(0))* Kessinger Publishing, LLC.

McCahan, Erin. The Lake Effect. 2017. (ENG.). 400p. (YA). (gr. 7). 17.99 ***(978-0-8037-4052-5(2),*** Dial Bks) Penguin Young Readers Group.

McCandless Iii, Bruce. Beatrice & the Basilisk. 2012. 66p. pap. 5.99 *(978-0-615-60901-0(5))* Ninth Planet Pr.

McCann, Thomas P. "Tom". The Tree Nobody Wanted: A Christmas Story. 2007. 14.95 *(978-0-9797407-0-1(3))* Exeter Pr.

McCarthy, Andrew. Just Fly Away. 2017. (ENG.). 272p. (YA). (gr. 9-12). 17.95 *(978-1-61620-629-1(2))* Algonquin Bks. of Chapel Hill.

McCarty, Peter. First Snow. McCarty, Peter, illus. 2015. (ENG., Illus.). 40p. (J). (gr. -1-3). 16.99 *(978-0-06-218996-7(4))* HarperCollins Pubs.

McCaughrean, Geraldine. The Kite Rider. 2003. (Illus.). 320p. (YA). (gr. 8-18). pap. 8.99 *(978-0-06-441091-5(9),* HarperTeen) HarperCollins Pubs.

McCaw, Neil. My Dad the Crab. 2008. 160p. pap. 10.95 *(978-1-4092-0156-4(2))* Lulu Pr., Inc.

McClintock, Barbara. Adèle & Simon in America. McClintock, Barbara, illus. 2008. (Adele & Simon Ser.). (ENG., Illus.). 40p. (J). (gr. -1-3). 18.99 *(978-0-374-39924-5(7),* 9780374399245, Farrar, Straus & Giroux (BYR)) Farrar, Straus & Giroux.

McClintock, Norah. Snitch, 1 vol. 2005. (Orca Soundings Ser.). (ENG.). 128p. (YA). (gr. 8-12). per. 9.95 *(978-1-55143-484-1(9))* Orca Bk. Pubs. USA.

McCormick, Patricia. Cut. 2011. (ENG.). 176p. (J). (gr. 7-7). pap. 8.99 *(978-0-545-29079-1(1),* PUSH) Scholastic, Inc.

—Sold. 2008. (ENG.). 272p. (J). (gr. 7-17). pap. 8.99 *(978-0-7868-5172-0(4))* Hyperion Pr.

—Sold. 2011. 10.36 *(978-0-7848-3420-6(2),* Everbind) Marco Bk. Co.

—Sold. 2008. 263p. (J). (gr. 7-12). 19.65 *(978-1-4178-1810-5(7),* Turtleback) Turtleback Bks.

McDaniel, Lurlene. The Year of Chasing Dreams. 2014. (ENG.). 336p. (YA). (gr. 7). 16.99 *(978-0-385-74173-6(1),* Delacorte Pr.) Random Hse. Children's Bks.

—The Year of Luminous Love. 2014. (ENG.). 384p. (YA). (gr. 7). pap. 9.99 *(978-0-385-74172-9(3),* Ember) Random Hse. Children's Bks.

McDonald, Diane O. The Adventures of Tweed. 2011. 52p. 24.99 *(978-1-4535-1701-7(4));* pap. 15.99 *(978-1-4535-1700-0(6))* Xlibris Corp.

McDonald, Megan. Judy Moody & the Not Bummer Summer. Reynolds, Peter H., illus. movie tie-in ed. (Judy Moody Ser.: Bk. 10). (ENG.). (J). (gr. 1-4). 2011. 128p. pap. 5.99 *(978-0-7636-5351-4(9))*Bk. 10. 2012. 208p. 15.99 *(978-0-7636-5711-6(5))*Bk. 10. 2012. 208p. pap. 5.99 *(978-0-7636-5710-9(7))* Candlewick Pr.

McDonough, Yona Zeldis. The Bicycle Spy. 2016. (ENG.). 208p. (J). (gr. 3-7). 16.99 *(978-0-545-85095-7(9),* Scholastic Pr.) Scholastic, Inc.

—The Cats in the Doll Shop. Maione, Heather, illus. 2012. (ENG.). 160p. (J). (gr. 3-7). pap. 5.99 *(978-0-14-242198-7(7),* Puffin Books) Penguin Young Readers Group.

McDougal-Littell Publishing Staff. Literature Connections English: Trouble River. 2004. (McDougal Littell Literature Connections Ser.). (ENG.). 144p. (gr. 6-6). stu. ed. 16.90 *(978-0-395-77526-4(4),* 2-80095) Great Source Education Group, Inc.

McElligott, Walter Lee. A Blessed Bethlehem Birth: As told by Abraham & Anna Mousenstern. Collier, Kevin Scott, illus. 2006. 28p. (J). E-Book 5.00 incl. cd-rom *(978-1-933090-21-4(9))* Guardian Angel Publishing, Inc.

McGee, Katharine. The Dazzling Heights. 2017. (Thousandth Floor Ser.: 2). 432p. (YA). (gr. 8). 18.99 ***(978-0-06-241862-3(9))*** HarperCollins Pubs.

—The Thousandth Floor. (Thousandth Floor Ser.: 1). (YA). (gr. 8). 2017. 496p. pap. 9.99 ***(978-0-06-241860-9(2))*** 2016. (ENG.). 448p. 18.99 *(978-0-06-241859-3(9))* HarperCollins Pubs.

Mcghee, Alison. Someday. Reynolds, Peter H., illus. 2015. (ENG.). 42p. (J). bds. 9.99 *(978-1-4814-6012-5(9),* Little Simon) Little Simon.

—Someday. 2014. pap. 29.95 *(978-0-545-79756-6(X))* Scholastic, Inc.

—Someday. Reynolds, Peter H., illus. 2007. (ENG.). 40p. (J). (gr. -1-3). 16.99 *(978-1-4169-2811-9(1),* Atheneum Bks. for Young Readers) Simon & Schuster Children's Publishing.

—Someday. Reynolds, Peter H., illus. 2008. (J). (gr. -1-2). 29.95 incl. audio compact disk *(978-0-8045-4200-5(7));* 27.95 incl. audio *(978-0-8045-6975-0(4))* Spoken Arts, Inc.

McGhee, Allison. Julia Gillian 3. 2010. *(978-0-545-10467-8(X))* Scholastic, Inc.

McGinnis, Mindy. This Darkness Mine. 2017. 384p. (YA). (gr. 9). 17.99 ***(978-0-06-256159-6(6),*** Tegen, Katherine Bks) HarperCollins Pubs.

McGovern, Cammie. Just My Luck. 2016. 240p. (J). (gr. 3-7). 16.99 *(978-0-06-233065-9(9))* HarperCollins Pubs.

McGowan, Angel. Stomp Out the Bullying! 2011. (ENG.). 28p. (J). pap. 14.95 *(978-1-4327-7994-8(X))* Outskirts Pr., Inc.

McGrath, Liz & Quick, Barbara. Even More/Todavía Más. de la Vega, Eida, tr. from ENG. McGrath, Liz, illus. 2004.Tr. of Todavía Más. (SPA & ENG., Illus.). 32p. (J). (gr. -1-3). 16.95 *(978-0-9720192-8-6(6),* 626999, Raven Tree Pr.,Csi) Continental Sales, Inc.

Mcintosh, Sharon. Grandma S Donut Hat. 2013. 22p. pap. 9.99 *(978-1-62697-407-4(1))* Salem Author Services.

McJarrow, Shandy. The Adventures of Papilio the Butterfly. 2009. 112p. 20.95 *(978-1-4401-3850-8(8));* pap. 10.95 *(978-1-4401-3840-9(0))* iUniverse, Inc.

McKay, Hilary. The Terrible Time Without Tilly. Scott, Kimberley, illus. 2014. (Red Bananas Ser.). (ENG.). 48p. (J). (gr. k-2). pap. 5.99 *(978-1-4052-6080-0(7))* Egmont Bks., Ltd. GBR. Dist: Independent Pubs. Group.

McKee, David. Not Now, Bernard. 2015. (ENG., Illus.). 32p. (J). (gr. -1-k). pap. 10.99 *(978-1-78344-290-4(5));* 35th ed. 24.99 *(978-1-78344-298-0(0))* Andersen Pr. GBR. Dist: Independent Pubs. Group.

McKelvie, Melissa, told to. Serena & the Turtle Eggs. 2007. (ENG.). 28p. pap. 15.99 *(978-1-4196-7780-9(2))* CreateSpace Independent Publishing Platform.

Mckenzie, Riford. The Witches of Dredmoore Hollow, 0 vols. unabr. ed. 2013. (ENG.). 274p. (J). (gr. 5-7). pap. 9.99 *(978-1-4778-1702-5(6),* 9781477817025, Amazon Children's Publishing) Amazon Publishing.

McKissack, Jenny & McKissack, Jennifer. Sanctuary. 2015. (ENG.). 320p. (J). (gr. 7). 17.99 *(978-0-545-58758-7(1),* Scholastic Pr.) Scholastic, Inc.

McKissack, Patricia C. Loved Best. Marshall, Felicia, illus. 2005. (ENG.). 64p. (J). (gr. 2-5). pap. 4.99 *(978-0-689-86151-2(6),* Simon & Schuster/Paula Wiseman Bks.) Simon & Schuster/Paula Wiseman Bks.

McLean, P. J. The Bears & the Baby. Jenkins, C. S., illus. 2012. 44p. pap. 17.44 *(978-1-4669-1335-6(5))* Trafford Publishing.

McMahon, Susan. Wee Mary from Derry. 2008. 12p. pap. 24.95 *(978-1-60610-876-5(X))* America Star Bks.

McMann, Lisa. Crash. 2013. (Visions Ser.: 1). (ENG.). 256p. (YA). (gr. 9). 16.99 *(978-1-4424-0391-8(8),* Simon Pulse) Simon Pulse.

McMillan, Ernest. Psalms of Passion. 2006. 48p. pap. 8.95 *(978-1-59800-224-9(4))* Outskirts Pr., Inc.

McMurchy-Barber, Gina. Reading the Bones. 2008. (Peggy Henderson Adventure Ser.: 1). (ENG.). 152p. (J). (gr. 6). pap. 11.99 *(978-1-55002-732-7(8),* Sandcastle Bks.) Dundurn CAN. Dist: Ingram Publisher Services.

McMurtrey, Martin. Loose to the Wilds. 2nd ed. 162p. (YA). reprint ed. pap. 6.00 *(978-0-9623961-0-6(9))* McMurtrey, Martin A.

McNamara, Margaret. Class Mom. Gordon, Mike, illus. 2009. (Robin Hill School Ser.). (ENG.). 32p. (J). (gr. -1-1). pap. 3.99 *(978-1-4169-5537-5(2),* Simon Spotlight) Simon Spotlight.

McNatt, Martha. Grandmother's Face in the Mirror. 2003. (YA). per. 14.00 *(978-0-9741294-0-2(2))* Main St Publishing, Inc.

McPhail, David. Pig Pig Returns. McPhail, David, illus. 2011. (ENG., Illus.). 32p. (J). (gr. -1-3). 15.95 *(978-1-58089-356-5(2))* Charlesbridge Publishing, Inc.

McPhail, J. A. Dawn of Day. Battis, Gwen, illus. 2012. 200p. 17.99 *(978-0-9851196-2-1(4))* Rowe Publishing and Design.

McQuestion, Karen. Favorite, 0 vols. unabr. ed. 2011. (ENG.). 172p. (gr. 7-9). pap. 9.95 *(978-1-935597-25-4(6),* 9781935597254, Skyscape) Amazon Publishing.

Meadows, Amy. Emma's American Chinese New Year. 2012. (ENG.). 31p. (J). pap. 12.95 *(978-1-4327-8694-6(6))* Outskirts Pr., Inc.

Meddaugh, Susan. Martha Speaks: Thanksgiving Reunion (Chapter Book) 2013. (Martha Speaks Ser.). (ENG., Illus.). 96p. (J). (gr. 1-4). 14.99 *(978-0-547-86580-5(5))* Houghton Mifflin Harcourt Publishing Co.

—Thanksgiving Reunion. 2013. (Martha Speaks Ser.). (ENG., Illus.). 96p. (J). (gr. 1-4). pap. 5.99 *(978-0-547-86581-2(3))* Houghton Mifflin Harcourt Publishing Co.

Medina, Meg. Tia Isa Quiere un Carro. Munoz, Claudio, illus. 2012.Tr. of Tia Isa Wants a Car. (SPA.). 32p. (J). (gr. -1-2). pap. 6.99 *(978-0-7636-5751-2(4))* Candlewick Pr.

—Tia Isa Wants a Car. Munoz, Claudio, illus. 2016. (ENG.). 32p. (J). (gr. -1-2). 6.99 *(978-0-7636-5752-9(2))* Candlewick Pr.

—Tia Isa Wants a Car. Muñoz, Claudio, illus. 2011. (ENG.). 32p. (J). (gr. -1-2). 15.99 *(978-0-7636-4156-6(1))* Candlewick Pr.

Meeks, Jane. Finding Home. 2011. 24p. pap. 15.99 *(978-1-4653-6606-1(7))* Xlibris Corp.

Meigs, Cornelia. The Windy Hill. 2017. (ENG.). 144p. (J). pap. 5.99 ***(978-0-486-81741-5(5))*** Dover Pubns., Inc.

Melcher, Rich. A Work in Progress. 2011. 148p. 29.99 *(978-1-4568-5192-7(6));* pap. 15.99 *(978-1-4568-5191-0(8))* Xlibris Corp.

_Meli, Ayani & D., Jessie. God Says I've Changed Your Dna: Walk As Children of the Light. Mallette, Dania, illus. 2013. 24p. pap. 12.00 (978-0-9846315-7-5(7)) JWD Publishing.

Meminger, Neesha. Shine, Coconut Moon. 2010. (ENG.). 256p. (YA). (gr. 9). pap. 10.99 (978-1-4424-0305-5(5), McElderry, Margaret K. Bks.) McElderry, Margaret K. Bks.

Meredith, Amberley. Bessie Bump Gets a New Family. Lee, Nikita, illus. 2010. 26p. pap. 13.95 (978-1-60911-901-0(0), Eloquent Bks.) Strategic Book Publishing & Rights Agency (SBPRA).

Meres, Jonathan. May Contain Nuts. 2012. (ENG., Illus.). 304p. (J). (gr. 4-6). pap. 10.99 (978-1-4083-1303-9(0)) Hodder & Stoughton GBR. Dist: Hachette Bk. Group.

Merkel, Ruth Vitrano. Hannah's Girls: Erin (Born 1988) 2009. (J). 9.99 (978-0-8280-1956-9(8)) Review & Herald Publishing Assn.

Messinger, Robert M. & Messinger, Laura M. Why Me? Why Did I Have to Get Diabetes? l.t. ed. 2004. (Illus.). 64p. 12.95 (978-1-893237-02-5(8)) Little Mai Pr.

Messner, Kate. All the Answers. 2016. (ENG.). 272p. (J). pap. 7.99 (978-1-68119-020-4(6), 9781681190204, Bloomsbury USA Childrens) Bloomsbury Publishing USA.

Metzger, Lois. A Trick of the Light. 2013. (ENG.). 208p. (YA). (gr. 9). 17.99 (978-0-06-213308-3(X)) HarperCollins Pubs.

Mewburn, Kyle. Kiss! Kiss! Yuck! Yuck!, 1 vol. Teo, Ali & O'Reilly, John, illus. (ENG.). 32p. (J). (gr. -1-3). 2017. pap. 7.95 **(978-1-56145-759-5(0))** 2008. 16.95 (978-1-56145-457-0(5)) Peachtree Pubs.

Michael, Alexander. Until Wishes Are Fulfilled. 2007. (ENG.). 154p. per. 13.50 (978-1-84426-408-7(4)) Upfront Publishing Ltd. GBR. Dist: Printondemand-worldwide.com.

Middleton, Dana. The Infinity Year of Avalon James. 2016. (ENG.). 224p. (J). 16.99 (978-1-250-08569-6(1), 9781250085696) Feiwel & Friends.

Miles, Robin, reader. Mufaro's Beautiful Daughters: An African Tale. 2003. (Illus.). (J). (gr. -1-2). pap. 35.95 incl. audio compact disk (978-1-59112-541-9(3)) Live Oak Media.

Miller-Burke, Jude. Snowball, Come Home! 2005. (Illus.). 32p. (J). bds. 16.95 (978-1-59298-093-2(7)) Beaver's Pond Pr., Inc.

Miller, Michael & Strickland, AdriAnne. Shadow Run. 2017. (ENG.). 400p. (YA). (gr. 7). 17.99 (978-0-399-55253-3(7), Delacorte Pr.) Random Hse. Children's Bks.

Millman, M. C. Always Something Else: The whimsical adventures of Elisheva Raskin. 2005. (Illus.). 160p. (J). 14.95 (978-1-932443-23-3(1), ASEH) Judaica Pr., Inc., The.

—Always Something Else 2. 2006. (Illus.). 160p. (J). 14.95 (978-1-932443-43-1(6), ASE2H) Judaica Pr., Inc., The.

Millman, Selena. Anyone Can Make A Difference. 2006. 109p. (YA). per. (978-0-9793058-6-3(1)) Millman, Selena.

Millner, Denene. Early Sunday Morning. Brantley-Newton, Vanessa, illus. 2017. (Denene Millner Bks.). (ENG.). 40p. (J). 17.95 (978-1-57284-211-3(3)) Agate Publishing, Inc.

Mills, Claudia. 7 X 9 = Trouble! Karas, G. Brian, illus. 2004. 103p. (J). (gr. 2-5). 13.60 (978-0-7569-3397-5(8)) Perfection Learning Corp.

Mills, David. Lima's Red Hot Chilli. Brazell, Derek, illus. 2004. (ENG & SPA.). 32p. (J). pap. (978-1-85269-942-0(6)) Mantra Lingua.

Mills, Emma. First & Then. 2015. (ENG.). 272p. (YA). (gr. 9-12). 17.99 (978-1-62779-235-6(X), 9781627792356, Holt, Henry & Co. Bks. For Young Readers) Holt, Henry & Co.

Mills, Linda Sue. Meet Toado & Friends. Mills, Lori, illus. l.t. ed. 2008. (ENG.). 30p. (J). 20.99 (978-1-59879-246-1(6), Lifevest) Lifevest Publishing, Inc.

Mills, Nathan & Beckett, David. My Family. 2012. (Rosen Readers Ser.). (ENG., Illus.). 16p. (J). (gr. k-1). pap. 7.00 (978-1-4488-8683-8(X), Rosen Classroom) Rosen Publishing Group, Inc., The.

Millsaps, Grace & Murphy, Ryan. You Wouldn't Like Me Without My Coffee. Marin, Danny, illus. 2014. (ENG.). 40p. (J). (gr. k-2). 17.95 (978-0-9904093-0-4(9)) Millfree Mursaps Media.

Milner, Claudette. Children of Plaines Estates. 2003. 165p. pap. 24.95 (978-1-4137-0424-2(7)) America Star Bks.

Minchin, Adele. The Beat Goes On. 2007. (ENG.). 224p. (YA). (gr. 7). pap. 11.95 (978-1-4169-6755-2(9), Simon Pulse) Simon Pulse.

Minter, J. The Insiders. 2004. (Insiders Ser.). (ENG.). 288p. (YA). (gr. 9-18). pap. 8.95 (978-1-58234-895-7(2), 9781582348957, Bloomsbury USA Childrens) Bloomsbury Publishing USA.

Minton, Ross. Baseball, from the Street to the Diamond, 1 vol. 2010. 94p. pap. 19.95 (978-1-4489-4918-2(1)) America Star Bks.

Mitchell, Carolann. The Song of the Snow. 2011. 68p. (gr. 4-6). pap. 8.95 (978-0-595-46609-2(5)) iUniverse, Inc.

Mitchell, Charlie. The Great M & M Caper. 2009. 82p. pap. 15.99 (978-1-4415-2242-9(5)) Xlibris Corp.

Mitchell, Christine. Family Day: Celebrating Ethan's Adoption Anniversary. 2009. 32p. pap. 13.95 (978-1-4389-5542-1(1)) AuthorHouse.

Mitchell, Melanie, illus. Who Do You Love? 2008. (ENG.). 6p. (J). bds. 5.95 (978-1-58117-707-7(0), Intervisual/Piggy Toes) Bendon, Inc.

Mittlefehldt, Rafi. It Looks Like This. 2016. (ENG.). 336p. (YA). (gr. 9). 16.99 (978-0-7636-8719-9(7)) Candlewick Pr.

Molesworth & Molesworth, Mary Louisa S. Peterkin. 2009. 128p. 23.95 (978-1-60664-659-5(1)) Rodgers, Alan Bks.

—Rosy. 2008. 120p. pap. 9.95 (978-1-60664-226-9(X)) Rodgers, Alan Bks.

Molesworth, Mary Louisa S. & Molesworth. Peterkin. 2009. 128p. pap. 10.95 (978-1-60664-287-0(1)) Rodgers, Alan Bks.

—Rosy. 2008. 120p. 22.95 (978-1-60664-727-1(X)) Rodgers, Alan Bks.

Molinet, Michael & Molinet, Kelly. Before You Were Born. Molinet, Michael, illus. 2003. (Illus.). 22p. (J). 12.99 (978-0-9705996-7-4(6)) Practical Christianity Foundation.

Monette, Roz. Alex & the Enderson Brothers: Book One, bks. 3. 2nd ed. 2013. (ENG., Illus.). 162p. (gr. 7-7). pap. 12.95 (978-0-9835077-1-0(6)) Cedar Grove Bks.

Monir, Alexandra. Timekeeper. (ENG.). (YA). (gr. 7). 2014. 304p. pap. 8.99 (978-0-385-73841-5(2), Ember) 2013. 288p. 16.99 (978-0-385-73840-8(4), Delacorte Bks. for Young Readers) Random Hse. Children's Bks.

—Timeless. 2012. (ENG.). 300p. (YA). (gr. 7). pap. 8.99 (978-0-385-73839-2(0), Ember) Random Hse. Children's Bks.

Monk, Isabell. Family. Porter, Janice Lee, illus. (Carolrhoda Picture Bks.). 32p. (J). 2005. (ENG.). (gr. k-4). per. 10.95 (978-1-57505-917-4(7)) 2003. (gr. -1-3). 15.95 (978-1-57505-485-8(X), Carolrhoda Bks.) Lerner Publishing Group.

Monnar, Alexander. Annoying Alex. Pileggi, Steven, illus. 2008. (J). per. 14.99 (978-0-9768035-9-1(3)) Readers Are Leaders U.S.A., Inc.

Montgomery Gibson, Jane. Daddy's Valentine. Montgomery Gibson, Jane, illus. 2005. (Illus.). (J). bds. 8.99 (978-1-4183-0046-3(2)) Christ Inspired, Inc.

Montgomery, L. M. A Tangled Web. 2014. (ENG.). 320p. (YA). (gr. 5-12). pap. 12.99 (978-1-4022-8933-0(2)) Sourcebooks, Inc.

—A Tangled Web. 2009. (Voyageur Classics Ser.). (ENG.). 296p. pap. 24.99 (978-1-55488-403-2(9)) Dundurn CAN. Dist: Ingram Publisher Services.

Moon, Keri & Fischer, Rita. Balduin. 2010. 364p. pap. 19.99 (978-1-4184-4716-8(1)) AuthorHouse.

Moore, Alice. Touched by Darkness. 2011. 208p. 24.95 (978-1-4502-9095-1(7)); pap. 14.95 (978-1-4502-9096-8(5)) iUniverse, Inc.

Moore, Deborah K. & Mulbah-Bondo, Gbolu. A Girl Like Me. 2013. 36p. pap. 15.99 (978-1-4497-9414-9(9), WestBow Pr.) Author Solutions, Inc.

Moore, Karen. Daddy Loves Me. Stanley, Mandy, illus. gif. ed. 2005. 10p. (J). (gr. -1-1). per., bds. 6.99 (978-1-57791-183-8(0)) Brighter Minds Children's Publishing.

Moore, Leslie. Guess What Ryan Saw at the Farm. 2008. 32p. pap. 19.50 (978-1-4357-5024-1(1)) Lulu Pr., Inc.

Moore, P. B. The Day the Buffalo Ran. 2008. 48p. pap. 16.95 (978-1-60563-461-6(1)) America Star Bks.

Moore, Shahari. It's Good Sunday. Waddington, Nicole, illus. 2003. (J). (978-0-9743394-0-5(7)) More Pr.

Moore, Ted. Eagle Eye & the Fall of Creek Canyon. 2007. 112p. per. 10.95 (978-0-595-43133-5(X)) iUniverse, Inc.

Mora, Pat. Here, Kitty, Kitty! (Ven, Gatita, Ven!) Suarez, Maribel, illus. 2008. (My Family: Mi Familia Ser.). (SPA & ENG.). 24p. (J). (gr. 4-7). lib. bdg. 15.89 (978-0-06-085045-6(0), Rayo) HarperCollins Pubs.

—Here Kitty Kitty!/Ven Gatita Ven! Suarez, Maribel, illus. 2008. (My Family: Mi Familia Ser.). (SPA & ENG.). 24p. (J). (gr. -1-1). 14.99 (978-0-06-085044-9(2), Rayo) HarperCollins Pubs.

—Sweet Dreams/Dulces Suenos. Suarez, Maribel, illus. 2008. (My Family: Mi Familia Ser.). (SPA & ENG.). 24p. (J). (gr. -1-1). 12.99 (978-0-06-085041-8(8), Rayo) HarperCollins Pubs.

More Than This. 2014. (ENG.). 480p. (YA). (gr. 9). pap. 10.99 (978-0-7636-7620-9(9)) Candlewick Pr.

Moreau, Laurent. My Wild Family. 2015. (ENG., Illus.). 32p. (J). (gr. -1-k). 17.99 (978-1-4521-4423-8(0)) Chronicle Bks. LLC.

Morganti, Jerre. The World of Priscilla Gingold. 2008. 135p. pap. 24.95 (978-1-60474-122-3(8)) America Star Bks.

Morpurgo, Michael. A Medal for Leroy. 2014. (ENG.). 144p. (YA). (gr. 5-9). 16.99 (978-1-250-03980-4(0), 9781250039804) Feiwel & Friends.

—Snakes & Ladders. Wilson, Anne, illus. 2006. (Yellow Bananas Ser.). (ENG.). 48p. (J). (gr. -1-3). (978-0-7787-0998-5(1)) Crabtree Publishing Co.

Morris, Deborah K. Here I Am Look at Me! Morris, Douglas, illus. 2010. 36p. pap. 13.95 (978-1-60911-739-9(5), Eloquent Bks.) Strategic Book Publishing & Rights Agency (SBPRA).

Morris, Jackie. Song of the Golden Hare. 2013. (ENG., Illus.). 40p. (J). (gr. k-3). 18.99 (978-1-84780-450-1(0), Frances Lincoln) Quarto Publishing Group UK GBR. Dist: Hachette Bk. Group.

Mortmain, Beatrice. I Help at Grandpa's House. Aguilera, Aurora, illus. 2017. (Ways I Help Ser.). 24p. (J). (gr. 4-6). pap. 8.25 **(978-1-5081-5677-2(8)**, PowerKids Pr.) Rosen Publishing Group, Inc., The.

Moses, Shelia P. Joseph's Grace. 2011. (ENG.). 160p. (YA). (gr. 7-18). 16.99 (978-1-4169-3942-9(3), McElderry, Margaret K. Bks.) McElderry, Margaret K. Bks.

—The Return of Buddy Bush. 2005. (ENG., Illus.). 160p. (J). (gr. 7-12). 15.95 (978-0-689-87431-4(6), McElderry, Margaret K. Bks.) McElderry, Margaret K. Bks.

Moskowitz, Hannah. Break. 2009. (ENG.). 272p. (YA). (gr. 9-18). pap. 10.99 (978-1-4169-8275-3(2), Simon Pulse) Simon Pulse.

Moss, Marissa. Amelia's Longest, Biggest, Most-Fights-Ever Family Reunion. Moss, Marissa, illus. 2006. (Amelia Ser.). (ENG., Illus.). 80p. (J). (gr. 4-7). 12.99 (978-0-689-87447-5(2), Simon & Schuster/Paula Wiseman Bks.) Simon & Schuster/Paula Wiseman Bks.

—Amelia's Summer Survival Guide: Amelia's Longest, Biggest, Most-Fights-Ever Family Reunion; Amelia's Itchy-Twitchy, Lovey-Dovey Summer at Camp Mosquito. Moss, Marissa, illus. 2011. (Amelia Ser.). (ENG., Illus.). 160p. (J). (gr. 5-8). 12.99 (978-1-4424-2331-2(5), Simon & Schuster/Paula Wiseman Bks.) Simon & Schuster/Paula Wiseman Bks.

Mostacchi, Massimo. El Rey Perezoso. Brignole, Giancarla, tr. Miceli, Monica, illus. rev. ed. 2006. (Fabulas De Familia Ser.). (SPA & ENG.). 32p. (J). (gr. k-4). pap. 6.95 (978-970-20-0274-1(5)) Castillo, Ediciones, S. A. de C. V. MEX. Dist: Macmillan.

Moynihan, Lindsay. The Waiting Tree, 0 vols. 2013. (ENG.). 218p. (YA). (gr. 9-12). 17.99 (978-1-4778-1634-9(8), 9781477816349, Amazon Children's Publishing) Amazon Publishing.

Mubiru, Bertha, ed. Kabaka,Kulabako & Kakookolo. 2004. (Illus.). 30p. pap. (978-9970-02-437-7(X)) Fountain Pubs. Ltd. UGA. Dist: Michigan State Univ. Pr.

Mubiru, Betha. Muzinge the Bird. 2004. (Illus.). 16p. pap. (978-9970-02-447-6(7)) Fountain Pubs. Ltd. UGA. Dist: Michigan State Univ. Pr.

Mueller, Paul G. Abigail & Blueboy. 2010. 152p. 22.95 (978-1-60860-881-2(6), Eloquent Bks.) Strategic Book Publishing & Rights Agency (SBPRA).

Mulder, Michelle. Out of the Box. 2011. 150p. (J). (978-1-55469-329-0(2)) Orca Bk. Pubs.

—Out of the Box, 1 vol. 2011. (ENG.). 160p. (J). (gr. 4-7). pap. 9.95 (978-1-55469-328-3(4)) Orca Bk. Pubs. USA.

Muller, Daniella L. Rumble, Rumble, Boom! 2009. 28p. pap. 12.99 (978-1-4389-7710-2(7)) AuthorHouse.

Muluka, B. Kandu & the Lake. 2004. (Illus.). 44p. pap. (978-9966-25-165-7(0)) Heinemann Kenya, Limited (East African Educational Publishers Ltd E.A.E.P.) KEN. Dist: Michigan State Univ. Pr.

Mumford, Carole. The Magnificent: Their Yellowstone Adventure, 1 vol. 2009. 73p. pap. 19.95 (978-1-60813-595-0(0)) America Star Bks.

Mundy, Dawn. The Gift: A Woodsong Story. Tigue, Terry & Turner, Diane, illus. 2003. (J). lib. bdg. (978-1-932139-16-7(8)) DEMDACO.

Munsch, Robert. Moose! Martchenko, Michael, illus. 2015. 28p. (J). pap. **(978-0-545-82631-0(4))** Scholastic, Inc.

Murciano, Carlos. El Mar Sigue Esperando. 2003. (SPA.). 112p. (978-84-279-3139-8(5), NG3602) Noguer y Caralt Editores, S. A. ESP. Dist: Lectorum Pubns., Inc.

Murphy, Barbara Beasley. Ace Flies Like an Eagle. 2003. (Can't Stop Ace Ser.: No. 3). 180p. (J). pap. 16.95 (978-0-86534-409-9(4)) Sunstone Pr.

Murphy, T. M. Saving Santa's Seals. Taylor, Adam, illus. 2009. (LeapKids Ser.). (ENG.). 170p. (J). (gr. 1-5). pap. 10.95 (978-0-9815148-8-8(X)) Leapfrog Pr.

Murray, Scott. Granny's Christmas Blunder. 2012. 28p. pap. 18.00 (978-1-4772-0990-5(5)) AuthorHouse.

Murrell, Belinda. The River Charm. l.t. ed. 2013. 504p. pap. (978-1-4596-6626-9(7)) ReadHowYouWant.com, Ltd.

Muse, Ludi. My Day at the Park. 2007. 32p. per. 13.95 (978-1-4259-6563-1(6)) AuthorHouse.

My Time on Nantucket Coloring Book. 2005. (J). 3.95 (978-0-9755078-1-0(8)) Sweet Punkin Pr.

Myers, Anna. Tumbleweed Baby. Vess, Charles, illus. 2014. (ENG.). 32p. (J). (gr. k-2). 16.95 (978-1-4197-1232-6(2), Abrams Bks. for Young Readers) Abrams, Inc.

Myers, Kate Kae. Inherit Midnight. (ENG.). (YA). 2016. 416p. pap. 9.99 (978-1-61963-936-2(X), 9781619639362) 2015. 400p. (gr. 7). 17.99 (978-1-61963-219-6(5), 9781619632196) Bloomsbury Publishing USA. (Bloomsbury USA Childrens).

Myers, Walter Dean. Game. 2009. (ENG.). 240p. (YA). (gr. 8). pap. 9.99 (978-0-06-058296-8(0), HarperTeen) HarperCollins Pubs.

—The Glory Field. 2008. (ENG.). 400p. (J). (gr. 7). pap. 9.99 (978-0-545-05575-8(X), Scholastic Paperbacks) Scholastic, Inc.

—Shooter. 2005. (ENG.). 256p. (YA). (gr. 9-17). reprint ed. pap. 9.99 (978-0-06-447290-6(6), Amistad) HarperCollins Pubs.

—What They Found: Love on 145th Street. 2009. (ENG.). 256p. (YA). (gr. 9). pap. 8.99 (978-0-375-84545-1(3), Lamb, Wendy Bks.) Random Hse. Children's Bks.

Myracle, Lauren. Thirteen. 2009. (Winnie Years Ser.). (ENG.). 272p. (J). (gr. 3-7). 7.99 (978-0-14-241370-8(4), Puffin Books) Penguin Young Readers Group.

Nadel, Carolina. Daddy's Home. Nadel, Carolina, illus. 2012. (Illus.). 32p. 19.95 (978-0-9792761-4-9(4)) Mookind Pr.

Nails, Jen. One Hundred Spaghetti Strings. 2017. 320p. (J). (gr. 3-7). 16.99 (978-0-06-242760-1(1)) HarperCollins Pubs.

Namukasa, Glaydah. Voice of a Dream. 2006. (Illus.). 97p. (978-1-4050-9592-1(X)) Macmillan/McGraw-Hill Schl. Div.

Nancy Elizabeth Bateman. Jason the Brat. 2009. 12p. pap. 8.96 (978-1-4389-6914-5(7)) AuthorHouse.

Napoli, Donna Jo. Alligator Bayou. 2010. (ENG.). 288p. (YA). (gr. 7). pap. 8.99 (978-0-553-49417-4(1), Lamb, Wendy Bks.) Random Hse. Children's Bks.

Nash, J. Q. The Fishin' Hole. 2008. 48p. pap. 24.95 (978-1-60563-621-4(5)) America Star Bks.

Nash, Susan Smith. The Good Deeds Society: Family Plot. 2008. (Illus.). 220p. (YA). pap. 18.00 (978-0-9797573-2-7(0)) Texture Pr.

Naylor, Phyllis Reynolds. The Boys Return. 2003. (Boys Against Girls Ser.: No. 7). 132p. (gr. 4-7). 16.00 (978-0-7569-1381-6(0)) Perfection Learning Corp.

—Lovingly Alice. 2004. (Alice Bks.). 166p. (J). (gr. 4-6). 13.65 (978-0-7569-6604-1(3)) Perfection Learning Corp.

Nealeigh, Thomas. See You in the Backlot. 2008. (Cutting Edge Ser.). (ENG.). 200p. pap. (978-1-84167-718-7(3)) Ransom Publishing Ltd.

Neely, Judith. And Even More. 2009. 24p. pap. 11.49 (978-1-4389-5649-7(5)) AuthorHouse.

Neer, P. J. A Home for Ruby: Helping Children Adjust to New Families. Blankenship, Robert, illus. 2015. (Let's Talk Ser.). (ENG.). 48p. (J). (gr. k-5). 9.95 (978-0-88282-488-8(0)) New Horizon Pr. Pubs., Inc.

Nees, Diane L. As Constant As the Stars. Elsen, Janis A., illus. 2012. 36p. 24.95 (978-1-4626-6886-1(0)); pap. 12.99 (978-1-4626-7919-5(6)) America Star Bks.

Neff, Fred. The Memory Tree. Montmeat, Jack, illus. 2008. 36p. pap. 14.99 (978-1-59858-854-5(0)) Dog Ear Publishing, LLC.

Nelid, Piper. A Special Dinner with My Moms, 01 vols., 1. 2016. (Rosen REAL Readers: Social Studies Nonfiction / Fiction: Family, Community, & the World Ser.). (ENG.). 8p. (J). pap. 5.46 (978-1-5081-1510-6(9), Rosen Classroom) Rosen Publishing Group, Inc., The.

Nelson, Jan. Signs of Love. Bohart, Lisa, illus. 2009. 24p. pap. 12.95 (978-1-936051-54-0(0)) Peppertree Pr., The.

Nesbit, E. New Treasure Seekers. 2009. 172p. (gr. 4-7). 25.95 (978-1-60664-665-6(6)); pap. 13.95 (978-1-60664-293-1(6)) Rodgers, Alan Bks.

Ness, Berthetta. Originals: Short Stories for Children. 2007. (YA). pap. (978-1-57579-351-1(2)) Pine Hill Pr.

Newbold, Keva N. The Family's Sorrow. 2009. 44p. pap. 16.99 (978-1-4389-4811-9(5)) AuthorHouse.

Newman, Lesléa. Donovan's Big Day. Dutton, Mike, illus. 2011. (ENG.). 32p. (J). (gr. -1-2). 15.99 (978-1-58246-332-2(8), Tricycle Pr.) Random Hse. Children's Bks.

—Heather Has Two Mommies. Cornell, Laura, illus. 2015. (ENG.). 32p. (J). (gr. -1-2). 16.99 (978-0-7636-6631-6(9)) Candlewick Pr.

Nicholls, Claire. In it to win It. 2011. 160p. (gr. 4-6). pap. 14.09 (978-1-4567-7994-8(X)) AuthorHouse.

Nickerson, Sara. The Secrets of Blueberries, Brothers, Moose & Me. (ENG.). 336p. (J). (gr. 5). 2016. 8.99 (978-0-14-751179-9(8), Puffin Books) 2015. 16.99 (978-0-525-42654-7(X), Dutton Books for Young Readers) Penguin Young Readers Group.

Nielsen, Amy. Victor & the Sun Orb. 2008. 144p. 21.95 (978-0-595-50307-0(1)); pap. 11.95 (978-0-595-51212-6(7)) iUniverse, Inc.

Nielsen, Jennifer A. A Night Divided. 2015. (ENG., Illus.). 336p. (J). (gr. 3-7). 16.99 (978-0-545-68242-8(8), Scholastic Pr.) Scholastic, Inc.

Nixon-Roulet, Mary F. Kalitan Our Little Alaskan Cousin. 2004. reprint ed. pap. 15.95 (978-1-4191-2838-7(8)); pap. 1.99 (978-1-4192-2838-4(2)) Kessinger Publishing, LLC.

No Extras: Individual Title, 6 packs. (Literatura 2000 Ser.). (gr. 1-2). 28.00 (978-0-7635-0103-7(4)) Rigby Education.

No Way Home: Individual Title Six-Packs. (Bookweb Ser.). 32p. (gr. 6-18). 34.00 (978-0-7578-0896-8(4)) Rigby Education.

Noensie, Pamela & Lamore, Garretta. Tari: the Little Balinese Dancer. 2013. (ENG., Illus.). 32p. (J). (gr. k-3). 14.95 (978-0-8048-4387-4(2)) Tuttle Publishing.

Noland, Monica. My Nana Looks Like a Telephone, 1 vol. 2007. (ENG.). 22p. 24.95 (978-1-4241-8532-0(7)) America Star Bks.

Norac, Carl. La Isla de los Mimos. 2003.Tr. of I Love to Cuddle. (SPA., Illus.). 32p. (J). (978-84-95150-66-0(2), COR3070) Corimbo, Editorial S.L.

—Las Palabras Dulces. 2003. (SPA., Illus.). 32p. (J). (978-84-95150-05-9(0), COR1690) Corimbo, Editorial S.L. ESP. Dist: Lectorum Pubns., Inc.

Norris II, Charles H. Fat Little Ugly Friend. 2008. 12p. per. 24.95 (978-1-4241-9222-9(6)) America Star Bks.

Northrop, Michael. Surrounded by Sharks. 2014. (ENG.). 224p. (J). (gr. 4-7). 17.99 (978-0-545-61545-7(3), Scholastic Pr.) Scholastic, Inc.

Norton, Mary. The Borrowers Aloft: Plus the Short Tale Poor Stainless. Krush, Beth & Krush, Joe, illus. 50th anniv. ed. 2003. (Borrowers Ser.: 4). (ENG.). 224p. (J). (gr. 2-5). pap. 7.99 (978-0-15-204734-4(4)) Houghton Mifflin Harcourt Publishing Co.

Novak, Ali. My Life with the Walter Boys. 2014. (ENG.). 368p. (YA). (gr. 7-12). pap. 10.99 (978-1-4022-9786-1(6), 9781402297861) Sourcebooks, Inc.

Novak, Matt. A Wish for You. Novak, Matt, illus. 2010. (Illus.). 32p. (J). 16.99 (978-0-06-155202-1(X), Greenwillow Bks.) HarperCollins Pubs.

Now I'll Tell You Everything. 2014. (Alice Ser.: 25). (ENG., Illus.). 544p. (YA). (gr. 9). pap. 12.99 (978-1-4424-4591-8(2), Atheneum Bks. for Young Readers) Simon & Schuster Children's Publishing.

Nugent, Cynthia. Francesca & the Magic Bike. 2005. 4p. (J). pap., tchr. ed. (978-1-55192-825-8(6)) Raincoast Bk. Distribution CAN. Dist: Publishers Group West (PGW).

Numeroff, Laura Joffe. What Brothers Do Best. Munsinger, Lynn, illus. 2012. (ENG.). 20p. (J). (gr. -1 — 1). bds. 7.99 (978-1-4521-1073-8(5)) Chronicle Bks. LLC.

—What Sisters Do Best. Munsinger, Lynn, illus. 2012. (ENG.). 20p. (J). (gr. -1 — 1). bds. 6.99 (978-1-4521-1074-5(3)) Chronicle Bks. LLC.

Nyikos, Stacy. Dragon Wishes. 2008. (ENG.). 256p. (J). (gr. 2-7). 16.95 (978-1-933831-11-4(1)) Blooming Tree Pr.

Oaks, J. Adams. Why I Fight. (ENG.). 240p. (YA). (gr. 7). 2010. pap. 9.99 (978-1-4424-0254-6(7), Atheneum Bks. for Young Readers) 2009. 17.99 (978-1-4169-1177-7(4), Atheneum/Richard Jackson Bks.) Simon & Schuster Children's Publishing.

Oates, Joyce Carol. Freaky Green Eyes. 2005. (ENG.). 368p. (YA). (gr. 8). reprint ed. pap. 9.99 (978-0-06-447348-4(1), HarperTeen) HarperCollins Pubs.

—Freaky Green Eyes. 2005. 341p. (YA). 15.65 (978-0-7569-6308-8(7)) Perfection Learning Corp.

—Where Is Little Reynard? Graham, Mark, illus. 2003. 32p. (J). 16.89 (978-0-06-029583-7(X)) HarperCollins Pubs.

O'Brien, Annemarie. Lara's Gift. 2014. (ENG.). 208p. (J). (gr. 5). 7.99 (978-0-307-93175-7(7), Yearling) Random Hse. Children's Bks.

O'Brien, Thomas E. The Magic of Finbar. 2011. 68p. pap. 19.95 (978-1-4560-4235-6(1)) America Star Bks.

Oceanak, Karla. Dumbstruck. Spanjer, Kendra, illus. 2011. (Aldo Zelnick Comic Novel Ser.: 4). (ENG.). 160p. (J). (gr. 3-7). 12.95 (978-1-934649-16-9(3)) Bailiwick Pr.

Ockler, Sarah. Twenty Boy Summer. 2010. (ENG.). 320p. (YA). (gr. 7-17). pap. 10.99 (978-0-316-05158-3(6)) Little, Brown Bks. for Young Readers.

O'Connor, Barbara. Wish. 2016. (ENG.). 240p. (J). 16.99 (978-0-374-30273-3(1), 9780374302733, Farrar, Straus & Giroux (BYR)) Farrar, Straus & Giroux.

O'Connor, Jane. Fancy Nancy & the Posh Puppy. Glasser, Robin Preiss, illus. 2012. (Fancy Nancy Ser.). (ENG.). 32p. (J). (gr. -1-2). 9.99 (978-0-06-221052-4(1)) HarperCollins Pubs.

—The Snow Globe Family. Schindler, S. D., illus. 2008. (ENG.). 40p. (J). (gr. 1-3). pap. 6.99 (978-0-14-241242-8(2), Puffin Books) Penguin Young Readers Group.

O'Dea, Michael, Rory and Cavanaugh & Benchmark Education Co. Staff. The Wall. 2014. (Text Connections Ser.). (J). (gr. 5). (978-1-4900-1387-9(3)) Benchmark Education Co.

Odu, Nkemakolam. My Horrible Trip to New York. 2012. (Illus.). 74p. (gr. 4-6). pap. 13.66 (978-1-4685-8217-8(8)) AuthorHouse.

Oelschlager, Vanita. Made in China: A Story of Adoption. Blackwood, Kristin, illus. 2008. (ENG.). 32p. (J). (gr. -1-3). 17.95 (978-0-9800162-3-9(1)) VanitaBooks.

OHora, Zachariah. My Cousin Momo. 2015. (ENG., Illus.). 32p. (J). (gr. -1-k). 17.99 (978-0-8037-4011-2(5), Dial Bks) Penguin Young Readers Group.

O'Leary, Sara. A Family Is a Family Is a Family, 1 vol. Leng, Qin, illus. 2016. (ENG.). 32p. (J). (gr. -1-2). 17.95 (978-1-55498-794-8(6)) Groundwood Bks. CAN. Dist: Publishers Group West (PGW).

Oliver, Lauren. Delirium Stories: Hana, Annabel, Raven & Alex. (Delirium Story Ser.). 224p. (YA). (gr. 9). 2016. pap. 9.99 (978-0-06-248432-1(X)) 2013. (ENG.). pap. 9.99 (978-0-06-226778-8(7)) HarperCollins Pubs.

—Delirium Stories: Hana, Annabel, Raven & Alex. (Delirium Ser.). (YA). 2016. lib. bdg. 20.85 (978-0-606-38920-4(2)) 2013. lib. bdg. 20.85 (978-0-606-31834-1(8), Turtleback) Turtleback Bks.

Oliver, Lin. Revenge of the Itty-Bitty Brothers. Gilpin, Stephen, illus. 2010. (Who Shrunk Daniel Funk? Ser.: 3). (ENG.). 176p. (J). (gr. 3-7). pap. 6.99 *(978-1-4169-0962-0(1),* Simon & Schuster Bks. For Young Readers) Simon & Schuster Bks. For Young Readers.

Oliver, Lin & Baker, Theo. The Shadow Mask, No. 2. 2013. (Sound Bender Ser.: 2). (ENG.). 368p. (J). (gr. 5-9). 16.99 *(978-0-545-19694-9(9),* Scholastic Pr.) Scholastic, Inc.

—Sound Bender. 2011. (ENG.). 272p. (J). (gr. 5-9). 16.99 *(978-0-545-19692-5(2),* Scholastic Pr.) Scholastic, Inc.

Ollweiler, Angela Messina. The Strange Wish. Ollweiler, D. R., illus. 2010. 112p. pap. 10.95 *(978-1-60844-274-4(8))* Dog Ear Publishing, LLC.

O'Loughlin, Erin. The Bluebird Dance. 2013. 44p. pap. 20.45 *(978-1-4908-0670-9(9),* WestBow Pr.) Author Solutions, Inc.

Olson, Mary W. Nice Try, Tooth Fairy. Tillotson, Katherine, illus. 2003. Orig. Title: Dear Tooth Fairy. (ENG.). 32p. (J). (gr. -1-2). 13.99 *(978-0-689-86141-3(9),* Aladdin) Simon & Schuster Children's Publishing.

Olson, Tod. How to Get Rich on the Oregon Trail. Proch, Gregory & Allred, Scott, illus. 2009. (How to Get Rich Ser.). (ENG.). 48p. (J). (gr. 5-9). lib. bdg. 27.90 *(978-1-4263-0413-2(7),* National Geographic Children's Bks.) National Geographic Society.

O'Malley Cerra, Kerry. Just a Drop of Water. 2016. (ENG.). 320p. (J). (gr. 2-7). pap. 7.99 *(978-1-5107-1234-8(8),* Sky Pony Pr.) Skyhorse Publishing Co., Inc.

O'Meara, Sandra F. Charli's First Christmas. 2010. 28p. pap. 28.03 *(978-1-4500-7325-7(5))* Xlibris Corp.

Oppel, Kenneth. Every Hidden Thing. 2016. (ENG., Illus.). 368p. (YA). (gr. 9). 17.99 *(978-1-4814-6416-1(7),* Simon & Schuster Bks. For Young Readers) Simon & Schuster Bks. For Young Readers.

O'Reilly, Jane. The Notations of Cooper Cameron. 2017. (ENG.). 320p. (J). (gr. 3-5). 17.99 ***(978-1-5124-0415-9(2),*** Carolrhoda Bks.) Lerner Publishing Group.

Orme, Helen. New Man. 2008. (Siti's Sisters Ser.). (ENG., Illus.). 36p. pap. *(978-1-84167-686-9(1))* Ransom Publishing Ltd.

Osborn, Valerie Huffman. A Week of Bunnies. Osborn, Kimberly, ed. 2007. (ENG., Illus.). 32p. (J). 19.95 *(978-1-932278-25-5(7))* Mayhaven Publishing, Inc.

Osborne Hale, Jennifer. Danny Blue! What Did You Do? 2009. 16p. pap. 9.95 *(978-1-4490-1171-0(3))* AuthorHouse.

Ostendorf, Jenifer Wirth & Bisbee, Richard J. Worthwhile Family Tales. 2010. 160p. pap. 11.99 *(978-1-4490-7605-4(X))* AuthorHouse.

Osterhold, Jared, illus. Cooks up a Surprise. 2011. (Olivia TV Tie-In Ser.). (ENG.). 24p. (J). (gr. -1-2). pap. 3.99 *(978-1-4424-1384-9(0),* Simon Spotlight) Simon Spotlight.

Ostow, Micol. Emily Goldberg Learns to Salsa. 2007. (ENG.). 208p. (YA). (gr. 7-18). 8.99 *(978-1-59514-144-6(8),* Razorbill) Penguin Young Readers Group.

Ot, Elli & Ot, Eli. Docto y los Jazmines. Brignole, Giancarla, tr. rev. ed. 2007. (Fabulas De Familia Ser.). (SPA & ENG.). 32p. (J). pap. 6.95 *(978-970-20-0267-3(2))* Castillo, Ediciones, S. A. de C. V. MEX. Dist: Macmillan.

Otitoloju/Blazing Ideas Ltd, Ololade/Adewunmi, retold by. Kunkuru Da Kare: The Tortoise & the Dog. 2008. (YOR & ENG., Illus.). 36p. 16.00 *(978-0-9801243-6-1(0))* Blazing Ideas Ltd.

Ovadia, Ron. Hank. 2013. 30p. 16.95 *(978-1-60844-834-0(7))* Dog Ear Publishing, LLC.

Owen, Bob. Billy. 2012. 24p. pap. 15.99 *(978-1-4653-9835-2(X))* Xlibris Corp.

Ozgur, Lynne Emily. Darryl & the Mountain. Abay, Ismail, illus. 2009. (ENG.). 32p. (J). (gr. 2-4). 9.95 *(978-1-59784-138-2(2))* Tughra Bks.

Pacheco, Miguel Angel. La Familia de Mic. Escriva, Ana Lopez, illus. 2003. (SPA.). (J). *(978-970-690-761-5(0))* Planeta Mexicana Editorial S. A. de C. V.

Packard, Robbi Anne. Two Daddies & Me. 2009. 32p. pap. 12.99 *(978-1-4389-5558-2(8))* AuthorHouse.

Padilla, Gerane & Sky. Penelope Potts & the Christmas Pup. 2009. 32p. pap. 16.49 *(978-1-4490-4781-8(5))* AuthorHouse.

Paiva, Teresa & Pinto, Helena Rebelo. Mein Freund, der Schlaf. 2011. (FRE.). 60p. (gr. 1-2). pap. 14.95 *(978-1-4567-8991-6(0))* AuthorHouse.

Palleschi, Sarah. Did I Really Dream Last Night? 2009. 48p. pap. 16.25 *(978-1-60693-814-0(2),* Eloquent Bks.) Strategic Book Publishing & Rights Agency (SBPRA).

Palmer, Nigel. The Heart Family Adventures. 2010. (Illus.). 28p. pap. 13.99 *(978-1-4520-0969-8(4))* AuthorHouse.

Palmer, Robin. Cindy Ella. 2008. (ENG.). 336p. (YA). (gr. 7-18). 9.99 *(978-0-14-240392-1(X),* Speak) Penguin Young Readers Group.

Palu, P. J. Who Loves You the Most of All? 2015. (ENG., Illus.). 38p. (J). pap. 9.99 *(978-1-63047-422-5(3))* Morgan James Publishing.

Panitch, Amanda. Never Missing, Never Found. 2016. (ENG.). 320p. (YA). (gr. 9). 17.99 *(978-0-553-50764-5(8),* Random Hse. Bks. for Young Readers) Random Hse. Children's Bks.

Papa's Gold. 2013. 196p. pap. 11.97 *(978-0-9851274-4-2(9))* Pen-L Publishing.

Paratore, Coleen Murtagh. The Wedding Planner's Daughter. 2005. (Wedding Planner's Daughter Ser.). (ENG.). 208p. (J). (gr. 3-7). 15.95 *(978-0-689-87340-9(9),* Simon & Schuster Bks. For Young Readers) Simon & Schuster Bks. For Young Readers.

Parish, Herman. Go West, Amelia Bedelia! Sweat, Lynn, illus. 2011. (Amelia Bedelia Ser.). 64p. (J). (gr. k-4). (ENG.). 17.99 *(978-0-06-084361-8(6));* lib. bdg. 18.89 *(978-0-06-084362-5(4))* HarperCollins Pubs. (Greenwillow Bks.).

Parish, Peggy. Amelia Bedelia's Family Album. Sweat, Lynn, illus. 2003. (I Can Read Level 2 Ser.). (ENG.). 48p. (J). (gr. k-3). pap. 3.99 *(978-0-06-051116-6(8),* Greenwillow Bks.) HarperCollins Pubs.

—Amelia Bedelia's Family Album. 2003. (Amelia Bedelia: I Can Read! Ser.: 12). (J). (gr. k-3). lib. bdg. 13.55 *(978-0-613-62129-8(8),* Turtleback) Turtleback Bks.

Park, Linda Sue. Keeping Score. 2010. (ENG.). 224p. (J). (gr. 2-5). pap. 7.99 *(978-0-547-24897-4(0))* Houghton Mifflin Harcourt Publishing Co.

—The Kite Fighters. 2010. (ENG., Illus.). 144p. (J). (gr. 2-5). pap. 7.99 *(978-0-547-32863-8(X))* Houghton Mifflin Harcourt Publishing Co.

Parker, Amy. Tiny Blessings: for My Family (large Trim) Walsh, Sarah, illus. 2017. (ENG.). 10p. (J). (gr. -1 — 1). bds. 9.95 ***(978-0-7624-6208-7(6),*** Running Pr.) Running Pr. Bk. Pubs.

Parkhurst, Johanna. Here's to You, Zeb Pike [Library Edition]. 2014. 180p. pap. 14.99 *(978-1-62798-526-0(3),* Harmony Ink Pr.) Dreamspinner Pr.

Parkinson, Curtis. Emily's Eighteen Aunts. 2004. (Illus.). (J). (gr. k-3). spiral bd. *(978-0-616-11134-5(7));* spiral bd. *(978-0-616-11135-2(5))* Canadian National Institute for the Blind/Institut National Canadien pour les Aveugles.

—Emily's Eighteen Aunts, 1 vol. von Königslöw, Andrea Wayne, illus. 2003. (ENG.). 30p. (J). *(978-0-7737-3336-7(1))* Fitzhenry & Whiteside, Ltd.

Parnell, Declan. Quack's Family Fun, 01 vols., 1. 2016. (Rosen REAL Readers: STEM & STEAM Collection). (ENG.). 8p. (J). pap. 5.46 *(978-1-5081-1395-9(5),* Rosen Classroom) Rosen Publishing Group, Inc., The.

Parr, Todd. The Family Book. 2010. (ENG., Illus.). 32p. (J). (gr. -1-1). pap. 8.00 *(978-0-316-07040-9(8))* Little, Brown Bks. for Young Readers.

Parsons, Julie. Julianne & the Jinn, the Evil Genie. 2008. 56p. pap. 16.95 *(978-1-60703-984-6(2))* America Star Bks.

Patricelli, Leslie. The Patterson Puppies & the Rainy Day. Patricelli, Leslie, illus. 2009. (ENG., Illus.). 40p. (J). (gr. -1-k). 14.99 *(978-0-7636-3242-7(2))* Candlewick Pr.

Patrick, Denise Lewis. Finding Someplace. 2016. (J). lib. bdg. 17.20 *(978-0-606-38560-2(6))* Turtleback Bks.

Patrick, Patsy S. Willie Wonders Why. Heiser, Aline L., illus. l.t. ed. 2003. 32p. (J). (gr. -1-6). 14.95 *(978-0-9726832-0-3(8))* Lu, Melissa Productions.

Patterson, James & Paetro, Maxine. Confessions: The Private School Murders. 2013. 422p. (YA). *(978-0-316-24263-9(2))* Little Brown & Co.

—Confessions: the Murder of an Angel. 2016. (Confessions Ser.: 4). (ENG.). 304p. (YA). (gr. 7-17). pap. 9.99 *(978-0-316-39218-1(9),* Jimmy Patterson) Little Brown & Co.

—The Private School Murders. 2015. (Confessions Ser.: 2). (ENG.). 400p. mass mkt. 8.00 *(978-1-4555-5946-6(6),* Jimmy Patterson) Grand Central Publishing.

—The Private School Murders. (Confessions Ser.: 2). (ENG.). (YA). (gr. 7-17). 2014. 448p. pap. 10.00 *(978-0-316-20764-5(0))* 2013. 448p. 18.00 *(978-0-316-20765-2(9))* 2013. 480p. 22.00 *(978-0-316-23992-9(5))* Little Brown & Co. (Jimmy Patterson).

—The Private School Murders. 2014. (Confessions Ser.: 2). (YA). lib. bdg. 20.85 *(978-0-606-35945-0(1))* Turtleback Bks.

Paul, Curtis Christopher. The Watsons Go to Birmingham 1963. 2014. (ENG.). 224p. (J). (gr. 12-12). 11.24 *(978-1-63245-108-8(5))* Lectorum Pubns., Inc.

Paul, Dominique. The Possibility of Fireflies. 2007. (ENG.). 224p. (YA). (gr. 8-12). pap. 8.99 *(978-1-4169-1311-5(4),* Simon & Schuster Bks. For Young Readers) Simon & Schuster Bks. For Young Readers.

Payton, Belle. Are You Thinking What I'm Thinking? 2015. (It Takes Two Ser.: 8). (ENG., Illus.). 160p. (J). (gr. 3-7). pap. 6.99 *(978-1-4814-3137-8(4),* Simon Spotlight) Simon Spotlight.

—A Whole New Ball Game. 2014. (It Takes Two Ser.: 1). (ENG., Illus.). 160p. (J). (gr. 3-7). pap. 6.99 *(978-1-4814-0641-3(8),* Simon Spotlight) Simon Spotlight.

Pearce, Jackson. The Doublecross: (And Other Skills I Learned As a Superspy) 2016. (ENG.). 304p. (J). pap. 7.99 *(978-1-61963-939-3(4),* 9781619639393, Bloomsbury USA Childrens) Bloomsbury Publishing USA.

Pearsall, Shelley. All of the Above. Steptoe, Javaka, illus. 2008. (ENG.). 256p. (J). (gr. 3-7). per. 8.00 *(978-0-316-11526-1(6))* Little, Brown Bks. for Young Readers.

Pedersen, Elsa. Alaska Harvest. Werth, Kurt, illus. 2012. 194p. 42.95 *(978-1-258-23211-5(1));* pap. 27.95 *(978-1-258-23973-2(6))* Literary Licensing, LLC.

Peirce, Lincoln. I Can't Take It! 2013. (Big Nate Graphic Novels Ser.). lib. bdg. 20.85 *(978-0-606-32313-0(9),* Turtleback) Turtleback Bks.

Pelow, Lawrence. Little Larry of Lewiston Meets Bobby the Backyard Bully. 2006. 2p. 6.71 *(978-1-4116-9172-8(5))* Lulu Pr., Inc.

Pennypacker, Sara. Completely Clementine. Frazee, Marla, illus. 2016. (Clementine Book Ser.). (ENG.). 208p. (J). (gr. 1-3). pap. 5.99 *(978-1-4231-2438-2(3))* Hyperion Bks. for Children.

Penrose, Margaret. Dorothy Dale. rev. ed. 2006. 196p. 26.95 *(978-1-4218-1801-6(9));* pap. 11.95 *(978-1-4218-1901-3(5))* 1st World Publishing, Inc. (1st World Library - Literary Society).

Perelman, Helen. The Peppermint Princess: Super Special. Waters, Erica-Jane, illus. 2016. (Candy Fairies Ser.). (ENG.). 176p. (J). (gr. 2-5). pap. 5.99 *(978-1-4814-4686-0(X),* Aladdin) Simon & Schuster Children's Publishing.

Perera, Anna. Guantanamo Boy. 2012. (ENG.). 352p. (YA). (gr. 8-12). 9.99 *(978-0-8075-3078-8(6))* Whitman, Albert & Co.

Perez, Angela J. Zack Attack! Hazard, Andrea, illus. 2007. 36p. (J). 17.95 *(978-0-9778328-9-7(9))* His Work Christian Publishing.

Perez, Jonathan. Sasp. 2005. (ENG., Illus.). 239p. (YA). per. 13.95 *(978-0-9708922-6-3(8),* 0970892268) Stansbury Publishing.

Perkins, Mitali. Rickshaw Girl. Hogan, Jamie, illus. 2008. (ENG.). 96p. (J). (gr. 2-5). pap. 6.95 *(978-1-58089-309-1(0))* Charlesbridge Publishing, Inc.

—Tiger Boy. 2017. (ENG.). 144p. (J). (gr. 2-5). pap. 6.99 *(978-1-58089-661-0(8))* Charlesbridge Publishing, Inc.

—Tiger Boy. Hogan, Jamie, illus. 2015. (ENG.). 144p. (J). (gr. 2-5). lib. bdg. 14.95 *(978-1-58089-660-3(X))* Charlesbridge Publishing, Inc.

Perl, Erica S. Aces Wild. 2015. (ENG.). 224p. (J). (gr. 3-7). 7.99 *(978-0-307-93173-3(0),* Yearling) Random Hse. Children's Bks.

Perreault, Diane Juttner. Breath of the Dragon. 2005. (ENG.). 208p. pap. 16.95 *(978-1-894283-54-0(6))* Great Plains Pubns. CAN. Dist: Publishers Group Canada.

Perrow, Angeli. Many Hands: A Penobscot Indian Story. Austin, Heather, illus. 2011. (ENG.). 32p. (J). (gr. -1-3). pap. 10.95 *(978-1-60893-014-2(9))* Down East Bks.

Perry, Laurie. Hello World, This Is Me!, 1 vol. 2009. 55p. pap. 16.95 *(978-1-4489-2013-6(2))* PublishAmerica, Inc.

Perryman, Kawanis. Gabrielle's Prayer: Gabrielle's Wish. 2011. 28p. pap. 13.59 *(978-1-4567-2731-4(1))* AuthorHouse.

Persaud, Sandhya S. One Day. Ahmad, Maryam & Ramotar, Alexandra, illus. 2009. 12p. pap. 12.99 *(978-1-4389-4437-1(3))* AuthorHouse.

Peschke, M. Vacation Queen. Mourning, Tuesday, illus. 2016. (Kylie Jean Ser.). (ENG.). 112p. (gr. 2-3). 8.95 *(978-1-5158-0059-0(8))* Picture Window Bks.

Peschke, Marci. Cooking Queen. Mourning, Tuesday, illus. 2017. (Kylie Jean Ser.). (ENG.). 112p. (gr. 2-3). lib. bdg. 22.65 ***(978-1-4795-9899-1(2),*** Kylie Jean) Picture Window Bks.

—Fashion Queen. Mourning, Tuesday, illus. 2015. (Kylie Jean Ser.). (ENG.). 112p. (gr. 2-3). 8.95 *(978-1-4795-5881-0(8),* Kylie Jean) Picture Window Bks.

—Fishing Queen. Mourning, Tuesday, illus. 2017. (Kylie Jean Ser.). (ENG.). 112p. (gr. 2-3). lib. bdg. 22.65 ***(978-1-4795-9900-4(X),*** Kylie Jean) Picture Window Bks.

—Gymnastics Queen. Mourning, Tuesday, illus. 2016. (Kylie Jean Ser.). (ENG.). 112p. (gr. 2-3). lib. bdg. 22.65 *(978-1-5158-0052-1(0))* Picture Window Bks.

—Soccer Queen. Mourning, Tuesday, illus. 2015. (Kylie Jean Ser.). (ENG.). 112p. (gr. 2-3). 22.65 *(978-1-4795-5882-7(6),* Kylie Jean) Picture Window Bks.

—Spelling Queen, 1 vol. Mourning, Tuesday, illus. 2012. (Kylie Jean Ser.). (ENG.). 112p. (gr. 2-3). pap. 5.95 *(978-1-4048-7212-7(4),* Kylie Jean) Picture Window Bks.

—Vacation Queen. Mourning, Tuesday, illus. 2016. (Kylie Jean Ser.). (ENG.). 112p. (gr. 2-3). lib. bdg. 22.65 *(978-1-5158-0058-3(X))* Picture Window Bks.

Peters, Julie Anne. Define Normal. 2003. (ENG., Illus.). 196p. (J). (gr. 7-17). pap. 9.99 *(978-0-316-73489-9(6))* Little, Brown Bks. for Young Readers.

—Luna. 2006. (ENG.). 256p. (YA). (gr. 10-17). reprint ed. pap. 10.99 *(978-0-316-01127-3(4),* Tingley, Megan Bks.) Little, Brown Bks. for Young Readers.

Peters, Kara L. The Adventures of the Peters Family: A Dolphin of a Time. 2013. 12p. pap. 15.99 *(978-1-4685-4404-6(7))* AuthorHouse.

Peterson, Lois. Meeting Miss 405, 1 vol. 2008. (Orca Young Readers Ser.). (ENG.). 112p. (J). (gr. 3-6). pap. 7.95 *(978-1-55469-015-2(3))* Orca Bk. Pubs. USA.

Philbrick, Rodman. The Big Dark. (ENG.). 192p. (J). (gr. 3-7). 2017. pap. 6.99 ***(978-0-545-78976-9(1))*** 2016. 17.99 *(978-0-545-78975-2(3))* Scholastic, Inc. (Blue Sky Pr., The).

Philips, Fleur. Crumble. 2013. 168p. (YA). pap. 8.99 *(978-0-9889299-0-6(2))* Philips, Fleur.

Phillips, Dixie. Baby Jesus Is Missing. Snider, K. C., illus. 2009. 16p. pap. 9.95 *(978-1-61633-000-2(7))* Guardian Angel Publishing, Inc.

Piccirillo, Renee. Big Mister Little Mister Baby Sister. Gumm, Susan Kathleen, illus. 2006. (J). per. 12.50 *(978-0-9771482-0-2(3),* Ithaca Pr.) Authors & Artists Publishers of New York, Inc.

Pichon, Liz. The Brilliant World of Tom Gates: Read It & Go Ha! Ha! Ha! Pichon, Liz, illus. 2014. (Tom Gates Ser.: 1). (ENG., Illus.). 256p. (J). (gr. 3-7). 12.99 *(978-0-7636-7472-4(9))* Candlewick Pr.

Pickering, Lynne. James & the Naughty Seagull. Pickering, Lynne, illus. 2013. (Illus.). 32p. pap. 13.50 *(978-1-62857-333-6(3),* Strategic Bk. Publishing) Strategic Book Publishing & Rights Agency (SBPRA).

Pierce, Tamora. Trickster's Choice. 2005. (Daughter of the Lioness Ser.: Bk. 1). (Illus.). 422p. (gr. 7). 20.00 *(978-0-7569-5746-9(X))* Perfection Learning Corp.

Pierro, Rita. Dear God, Will You Give Me A Dog?, 1 vol. French, David, illus. 2009. 35p. pap. 19.95 *(978-1-61582-589-9(4))* PublishAmerica, Inc.

Pighin, Marcel. Tickles the Bear Goes on a Cruise, 1 bk. Mitchell, Hazel, illus. 2006. 48p. (J). per. 10.49 *(978-0-9776679-7-0(9))* MP2ME Enterprise.

Pignat, Caroline & Loftin, Nikki. Unspeakable. 2016. (ENG., Illus.). 336p. (J). (gr. 7). 9.99 *(978-0-14-318756-1(2),* Razorbill Canada) Penguin Random House Canada Young Readers CAN. Dist: Penguin Random Hse. LLC.

Pilkey, Dav. Ricky Ricotta's Mighty Robot vs. the Unpleasant Penguins from Pluto. Santat, Dan, illus. 2016. (Ricky Ricotta's Mighty Robot Ser.: 9). (ENG.). 128p. (J). (gr. -1-3). 15.99 *(978-0-545-63016-0(9))* Scholastic, Inc.

Pincus, Gregory K. The Homework Strike. 2017. (ENG.). 272p. (J). (gr. 3-7). 16.99 *(978-0-439-91301-0(2))* Scholastic, Inc.

Pinfold, Levi. Black Dog. Pinfold, Levi, illus. 2012. (ENG., Illus.). 32p. (J). (gr. -1-3). 15.99 *(978-0-7636-6097-0(3),* Templar) Candlewick Pr.

Pirnot, Karen Hutchins. Rainbows Are the Best. Allen, Sandra Hutchins, illus. 2009. 24p. pap. 12.95 *(978-1-936051-01-4(X))* Peppertree Pr., The.

Pitchford, Dean. Captain Nobody. 2010. (ENG.). 208p. (J). (gr. 3-7). 6.99 *(978-0-14-241667-9(3),* Puffin Books) Penguin Young Readers Group.

Pittar, Gill. Milly, Molly & Different Dads. 2004. 28p. *(978-1-86972-019-3(9))* Milly Molly Bks.

—Milly, Molly & Different Dads (book W/dolls) 2006. 28p. pap. *(978-1-86972-099-5(7))* Milly Molly Bks.

Piumini, Roberto. Matias y el Abuelo. 2nd ed. 2003. (SPA., Illus.). 133p. pap. *(978-84-236-3261-9(X),* ED6273) La Galera, S.A. Editorial ESP. Dist: Lectorum Pubns., Inc.

Poblocki, Dan. The Book of Bad Things. 2014. (ENG.). 256p. (J). (gr. 5-9). 16.99 *(978-0-545-64553-9(0),* Scholastic Pr.) Scholastic, Inc.

Pointon, Janet. A Matter of Choice. 2008. 82p. pap. 11.51 *(978-1-4092-3108-0(9))* Lulu Pr., Inc.

Polacco, Patricia. The Graves Family. Polacco, Patricia, illus. 2006. (ENG., Illus.). 48p. (J). (gr. k-3). reprint ed. pap. 6.99 *(978-0-14-240635-9(X),* Puffin Books) Penguin Young Readers Group.

Polikoff, Barbara Garland. Her Mother's Secret. 2012. (ENG.). 184p. (YA). pap. 14.99 *(978-0-9831938-7-6(8))* Allium Pr. of Chicago.

Portal, Alex. The Applegates, 1 vol. 2009. 32p. pap. 24.95 *(978-1-60749-727-1(1))* America Star Bks.

Porter, Eleanor H. Pollyanna. Akib, Jamel, illus. 2007. (Classic Starts(tm) Ser.). (ENG.). 160p. (J). (gr. 2-4). 6.95 *(978-1-4027-3692-6(4))* Sterling Publishing Co., Inc.

Porter, Marylyn Kight. Speedy the Snail & His New Family. 2006. 10.00 *(978-0-8059-9134-5(4))* Dorrance Publishing Co., Inc.

Porter, Pamela. I'll Be Watching. 2013. 336p. pap. *(978-1-4596-6449-4(3))* ReadHowYouWant.com, Ltd.

Portis, Antoinette. Now. 2017. (ENG., Illus.). 32p. (J). 17.99 *(978-1-62672-137-1(8),* 9781626721371) Roaring Brook Pr.

Portis, Nathanial. Things in Between. 2008. (ENG.). 208p. (YA). per. 9.99 *(978-0-9760372-0-0(3))* Quick Quest Pubns. LLC.

Posner-Sanchez, Andrea. Fang-Tastic! (Disney Junior: Henry Hugglemonster) Laguna, Fabio & Gallego, James, illus. 2015. (Little Golden Book Ser.). (ENG.). 24p. (J). (-k). 4.99 *(978-0-7364-3348-8(1),* Golden/Disney) Random Hse. Children's Bks.

Potoma, Alison. The Smith Family Secret: Book 1. Reul, Sarah Lynne, illus. 2013. 122p. pap. 6.25 *(978-1-940602-00-4(9))* Potoma, Alison Elise.

Potter, Ellen. Olivia Kidney Stops for No One. Reynolds, Peter H., illus. 2007. (ENG.). 272p. (J). (gr. 3-7). 8.99 *(978-0-14-240772-1(0),* Puffin Books) Penguin Young Readers Group.

Potter, G. L. Keeping Secerts. 2003. 141p. (YA). per. *(978-1-931524-04-9(1))* Moondance Publishing.

Powell, Jimmie. The Squirrel the Worm & the Nut Trees. 2007. 48p. per. 15.95 *(978-1-4327-1326-3(4))* Outskirts Pr., Inc.

Power, Timothy. The Boy Who Howled. 2012. (ENG.). 272p. (YA). (gr. 3-12). pap. 7.99 *(978-1-59990-852-6(2),* 9781599908526, Bloomsbury USA Childrens) Bloomsbury Publishing USA.

Precourt, Barbara. Waiting for Mr. Right. 2004. 207p. (YA). per. 14.95 *(978-1-932338-42-3(X))* Lifevest Publishing, Inc.

Preller, James. Before You Go. 2013. (ENG.). 224p. (YA). (gr. 7-12). pap. 16.99 *(978-1-250-03421-2(3),* 9781250034212) Square Fish.

Preston, Natasha. Awake. 2015. (ENG.). 336p. (YA). (gr. 9-12). pap. 9.99 *(978-1-4926-1852-2(7),* 9781492618522) Sourcebooks, Inc.

Price, David. Sly the Fox & Advice from la Princessa Roja. 2008. (Illus.). 34p. (J). 14.95 *(978-0-9779701-2-4(4))* Wishingstone Publishing.

Price, Tom, illus. Champion Sleeper. 2008. 32p. (J). pap. 9.95 *(978-0-9748226-1-7(2))* Murphy's Bone Publishing.

Priddy, Roger. Best Friends: We Are a Family. 2015. (Best Friends Ser.). (ENG., Illus.). 20p. (J). (gr. -1-1). bds. 9.99 *(978-0-312-51923-0(0),* 9780312519230, Priddy Bks.) St. Martin's Pr.

—I Love You. 2015. (Mini Tab Ser.). (ENG.). 16p. (J). (gr. -1 — 1). bds. 5.99 *(978-0-312-51919-3(2),* 9780312519193, Priddy Bks.) St. Martin's Pr.

Prignano, Barbara. Angelo: The Underappreciated Ant. 2012. 28p. pap. 12.95 *(978-1-61897-177-7(8),* Strategic Bk. Publishing) Strategic Book Publishing & Rights Agency (SBPRA).

Primavera, Elise. Auntie Claus: Home for the Holidays. Primavera, Elise, illus. 2009. (ENG., Illus.). 40p. (J). (gr. -1-3). 17.99 *(978-1-4169-5485-9(6),* Simon & Schuster/Paula Wiseman Bks.) Simon & Schuster/Paula Wiseman Bks.

—Auntie Claus & the Key to Christmas. 2011. (ENG., Illus.). 40p. (J). (gr. -1-3). pap. 7.99 *(978-0-547-57679-4(X))* Houghton Mifflin Harcourt Publishing Co.

Probst, Jeff & Tebbetts, Christopher. Forbidden Passage. 2014. (Stranded Ser.: 4). (ENG.). 176p. (J). (gr. 3-7). 6.99 *(978-0-14-751388-5(X),* Puffin Books) Penguin Young Readers Group.

Prochovnic, Dawn Babb. Hip Hip Hooray! It's Family Day! Sign Language for Family, 1 vol. Bauer, Stephanie, illus. 2012. (ENG.). 32p. 28.50 *(978-1-61641-837-3(0),* Looking Glass Library) Magic Wagon.

Proimos, James. Todd's TV. Proimos, James, illus. 2010. (ENG., Illus.). 40p. (J). (gr. -1-3). 15.99 *(978-0-06-170985-2(9),* Tegen, Katherine Bks) HarperCollins Pubs.

Pruitt, Patti B. Meeting Paddy O'Rourke: Book One. 2007. 68p. (J). pap. 9.00 *(978-0-8059-7656-4(6))* Dorrance Publishing Co., Inc.

Pullman, Philip. Les Royaumes du Nord. (FRE.). pap. 19.95 *(978-2-07-054188-1(6))* Gallimard, Editions FRA. Dist: Distribooks, Inc.

—La Tour des Anges. (FRE.). pap. 19.95 *(978-2-07-054189-8(4))* Gallimard, Editions FRA. Dist: Distribooks, Inc.

Pung, Alice. Marly's Business. 2016. (Our Australian Girl Ser.: 2). (ENG.). 144p. (J). (gr. 3-7). 7.99 *(978-0-14-330850-8(5))* Penguin Books Australia AUS. Dist: Independent Pubs. Group.

Pung, Alice & Masciullo, Lucia. Marly Walks on the Moon. 2016. (Our Australian Girl Ser.: 4). (ENG.). 144p. (J). (gr. 3-7). 12.99 *(978-0-14-330852-2(1))* Penguin Books Australia AUS. Dist: Independent Pubs. Group.

Quin-Harkin, Janet. Four's a Crowd. 2014. (Tgif Ser.: 3). (ENG., Illus.). 128p. (J). (gr. 3-7). pap. 13.99 *(978-1-4814-2881-1(0),* Simon & Schuster/Paula Wiseman Bks.) Simon & Schuster/Paula Wiseman Bks.

Quinn, Spencer, pseud. ARF - A Bowser & Birdie Novel. 2016. (ENG.). 304p. (J). (gr. 3-7). 16.99 *(978-0-545-64334-4(1),* Scholastic Pr.) Scholastic, Inc.

Rabley, Stephen. The Twins & the Time Machine/Les Jumeaux et la Machine du Temps. Bougard, Marie-Therese, tr. Eudes-Pascal, Elisabeth, illus. 2008. (Let's Read! Bks.). (ENG & FRE.). 32p. (J). (gr. 3-7). pap. 5.99 *(978-0-7641-4048-8(5))* Barron's Educational Series, Inc.

Rader, Laura. The Twelve Days of Christmas in California. Rader, Laura, illus. 2009. (Twelve Days of Christmas in America Ser.). (ENG., Illus.). 40p. (J). (gr. k-3). 12.95 *(978-1-4027-6247-5(X))* Sterling Publishing Co., Inc.

Raether, Erin F. When Auntie Angie Left for Iraq & Remi Came to Stay. 2008. 15p. pap. 24.95 *(978-1-4241-8735-5(4))* America Star Bks.

Ragawa, Marimo. Baby & Me, Vol. 2. Ragawa, Marimo, illus. 2006. (Baby & Me Ser.). (ENG., Illus.). 208p. pap. 8.99 *(978-1-4215-0573-2(8))* Viz Media.

Ramos, Dania. Who's Ju? 2015. (ENG.). 174p. (J). pap. 9.95 *(978-1-937997-61-8(8))* Northampton Hse.

Ramos, Jorge. I'm Just Like My Mom. Gutierrez, Akemi, illus. 2008.Tr. of Me Parezco Tanto a mi Papá. (ENG & SPA.). 40p. (J). (gr. -1-1). 16.99 (978-0-06-123968-7(2), Rayo) HarperCollins Pubs.

Ramoutar, Christine L. Tales from the Pine Forest. 2012. 108p. pap. 10.95 (978-1-4620-7030-5(2)) iUniverse, Inc.

Ramsey, Jo. Opening Up. 2013. 266p. pap. 14.99 (978-1-60820-887-6(7)) MLR Pr., LLC.

Ramsey, Patricia. Mr. Quadrilateral & His Four Sided Family. 2011. 32p. pap. 14.51 (978-1-4269-6019-2(0)) Trafford Publishing.

Random House Disney Staff. Inside Out (Disney/Pixar Inside Out) Batson, Alan, illus. 2016. (Little Golden Book Ser.). (ENG.). 24p. (J). (-k). 4.99 (978-0-7364-3629-8(4), Golden/Disney) Random Hse. Children's Bks.

Ransburg, Ashley B. Evie Finds Her Family Tree. 2006. (Illus.). 34p. (J). (gr. -1-3). 14.95 (978-0-87195-187-8(8)) Indiana Historical Society.

Ransom, Candice. Iva Honeysuckle Meets Her Match. Ross, Heather, illus. 2014. (Iva Honeysuckle Book Ser.). (ENG.). 192p. (J). (gr. 1-3). pap. 4.99 (978-1-4231-3516-6(4)) Hyperion Bks. for Children.

—Iva Honeysuckle Meets Her Match. Ross, Heather, illus. 2013. (Iva Honeysuckle Book Ser.). (ENG.). 192p. (J). (gr. 2-5). 14.99 (978-1-4231-3514-2(8)) Hyperion Pr.

—The Twelve Days of Christmas in Washington, D. C. Hollander, Sarah, illus. 2010. (Twelve Days of Christmas in America Ser.). (ENG.). 40p. (J). (gr. k). 12.95 (978-1-4027-6394-6(8)) Sterling Publishing Co., Inc.

Rath, Tom & Reckmeyer, Mary. How Full Is Your Bucket? For Kids. Manning, Maurie J., illus. 2009. (ENG.). 32p. (J). (gr. -1-4). 17.95 (978-1-59562-027-9(3)) Gallup Pr.

Ratto, Linda Lee. Where Dreams Come True. 2004. (J). pap. (978-0-9748508-0-1(2)) Power Pr.

Rawlings, John S. Sometimes Boxes Make the Best Forts. Espina, Vito, illus. 2006. (J). pap. 15.00 (978-0-8059-7181-1(5)) Dorrance Publishing Co., Inc.

Ray, Christie Jones & Ray, Christie Jones. Eliza Has a Cousin. 2012. (Illus.). 32p. pap. 15.00 (978-0-9853223-5-9(7)) Rose Water Cottage Pr.

—Pick-A-Pick-a-Pumpkin. 2012. (Illus.). 36p. pap. 12.00 (978-0-9853223-4-2(9)) Rose Water Cottage Pr.

Ray, Delia. Finding Fortune. 2015. (ENG.). 288p. (J). (gr. 5-7). 16.99 (978-0-374-30065-4(8), 9780374300654, Farrar, Straus & Giroux (BYR)) Farrar, Straus & Giroux.

—Here Lies Linc. (ENG.). 320p. (J). (gr. 3-7). 2012. 7.99 (978-0-375-86538-1(1), Yearling) 2011. 16.99 (978-0-375-86757-6(0), Knopf Bks. for Young Readers) Random Hse. Children's Bks.

Ray, Keri. Dancing in the Rain: At the Zoo. 2009. 32p. pap. 12.99 (978-1-4490-0673-0(6)) AuthorHouse.

—The Saving Journey. 2009. 48p. pap. 10.49 (978-1-4389-5008-2(X)) AuthorHouse.

Rayment, Carolynn. Buster Batey & Mops. 2009. (Illus.). 16p. pap. 8.49 (978-1-4490-4163-2(9)) AuthorHouse.

Red & Green Choices by Green Irene: Niki's Next Grade. 2003. (J). per. 14.50 (978-0-9742280-1-3(X)) Green Irene.

Rees, Douglas. Uncle Pirate. Auth, Tony, illus. 2008. (ENG.). 112p. (J). (gr. 2-5). 15.99 (978-1-4169-4762-2(0), McElderry, Margaret K. Bks.) McElderry, Margaret K. Bks.

Reger, Rob & Gruner, Jessica. Dark Times. Reger, Rob & Parker, Buzz, illus. 2011. (Emily the Strange Ser.: 3). (ENG.). 248p. (YA). (gr. 8). pap. 8.99 (978-0-06-145237-6(8)) HarperCollins Pubs.

Reichardt, Marisa. Underwater. 2016. (ENG.). 288p. (YA). 17.99 (978-0-374-36886-9(4), 9780374368869, Farrar, Straus & Giroux (BYR)) Farrar, Straus & Giroux.

Reid, F. J. The Midwinter Child. 2009. 224p. pap. (978-1-84923-496-2(5)) YouWriteOn.

Reid, Lainey. Takari. 2008. 156p. pap. 24.95 (978-1-60672-717-1(6)) America Star Bks.

Reinhardt, Dana. The Things a Brother Knows. 2011. (ENG.). 256p. (YA). (gr. 9). pap. 8.99 (978-0-375-84456-0(2), Ember) Random Hse. Children's Bks.

Remkiewicz, Frank, illus. The Twelve Days of Christmas in Florida. (Twelve Days of Christmas in America Ser.). (ENG.). (J). (—1). 2017. 22p. bds. 7.95 **(978-1-4549-2283-4(4))** 2008. 40p. 12.95 (978-1-4027-3817-3(X)) Sterling Publishing Co., Inc.

Renero, Joaquin. The Enchanted Scrapbook: Welcome to the Wilburton Society. 2011. 320p. 29.95 (978-1-4502-6140-1(X)); pap. 19.95 (978-1-4502-6138-8(8)) iUniverse, Inc.

Renfroe, Vicki. Franklin. 2008. 63p. pap. 19.95 (978-1-60563-391-6(7)) America Star Bks.

Rennie-Pattison, Caroline. The Law of Three. 2007. (ENG.). 232p. (YA). (gr. 6). pap. 10.99 (978-1-55002-733-4(6), Boardwalk Bks.) Dundurn CAN. Dist: Ingram Publisher Services.

Resau, Laura. Red Glass. 2009. (ENG.). 304p. (YA). (gr. 7). pap. 8.99 (978-0-440-24025-9(5), Delacorte Bks. for Young Readers) Random Hse. Children's Bks.

Restivo, Andrea E. Arabella & the Perilous Pantheon. 2010. 28p. pap. 12.99 (978-1-60693-790-7(1), Strategic Bk. Publishing) Strategic Book Publishing & Rights Agency (SBPRA).

Reyes, Yolanda. Una Cama para Tres. Coll, Ivar Da, illus. 2004. (SPA.). 36p. (J). (gr. k-3). 14.95 (978-958-704-055-5(4)) Santillana USA Publishing Co., Inc.

Reynolds, Peter H. The Smallest Gift of Christmas. Reynolds, Peter H., illus. 2015. (ENG., Illus.). 40p. (J). (gr. -1-2). 10.00 (978-0-7636-7981-1(X)) Candlewick Pr.

Rhema, Dan. One Tiny Twig, 1. Leonard, Michael, illus. 2003. 32p. (J). per. 19.95 (978-0-9729835-0-1(3)) Mesquite Tress Pr., LLC.

Rhine, Linda H. The Ivory Buttons. 2008. 32p. per. 24.95 (978-1-4241-8949-6(7)) America Star Bks.

Rhodes, Morgan. Gathering Darkness. 2014. (Falling Kingdoms Ser.: 3). (ENG.). 430p. (YA). (gr. 7). 18.99 (978-1-59514-705-9(5), Razorbill) Penguin Young Readers Group.

Ribar, Lindsay. Rocks Fall Everyone Dies. 2016. (ENG.). 336p. (YA). (gr. 7). 17.99 (978-0-525-42868-8(2), Kathy Dawson Books) Penguin Young Readers Group.

Rice, David & Rice, David Talbot. Crazy Loco. Clayton, Christian, illus. 2003. (ENG.). 144p. (YA). (gr. 7-11). 6.99 (978-0-14-250056-9(9), Speak) Penguin Young Readers Group.

Richard Richtmyer. A Bit of Magic: A Novel. 2009. 116p. pap. 10.95 (978-1-4401-5565-9(8)) iUniverse, Inc.

Richards, Anthony Lee. The Golden Bird, 1 vol. 2009. 56p. pap. 16.95 (978-1-60703-712-5(2)) America Star Bks.

Richards, Lisa. Family Short Stories Book. 2011. 44p. pap. 24.95 (978-1-4560-6711-3(7)) America Star Bks.

Richardson, Sharde. Watched. 2011. (ENG.). 290p. (YA). pap. 12.99 (978-0-9831498-0-4(1)) Jolt.

Richardson, Timariay A. Billy Bean & the Chocolate Dragon. 2013. 44p. pap. 11.95 (978-0-9840456-7-9(8)) Universal Publishing LLC.

Richardson, Tom. Dominic Is Strong. 2005. (Illus.). 26p. (J). lib. bdg. 16.95 (978-1-932338-99-7(3)) Lifevest Publishing, Inc.

Richmond, Marianne. Dear Grandson. 2008. (ENG., Illus.). 40p. (gr. -1-3). 5.95 (978-1-934082-43-0(0), Marianne Richmond Studios, Inc.) Sourcebooks, Inc.

—You're a Big Brother. 2017. (ENG., Illus.). 32p. (J). (-3). 8.99 (978-1-4926-5049-2(8), 9781492650492, Sourcebooks Jabberwocky) Sourcebooks, Inc.

—You're a Big Sister. 2017. (ENG., Illus.). 32p. (J). (-3). 8.99 (978-1-4926-5051-5(X), 9781492650515, Sourcebooks Jabberwocky) Sourcebooks, Inc.

Richmond, Marianne R. I Wished for You: An Adoption Story. 2008. (ENG., Illus.). 40p. (J). (gr. -1-3). 15.95 (978-1-934082-06-5(6), Marianne Richmond Studios, Inc.) Sourcebooks, Inc.

Richter, Conrad. The Light in the Forest. (YA). (gr. 7-18). 21.95 (978-0-89190-333-8(X)) Amereon Ltd.

Rigby Education Staff. The Very Noisy Family. (Illus.). 16p. (J). bds. 30.00 (978-0-7635-6430-8(3), 764303C99) Rigby Education.

Riley, Elliot. Miguel's Family. Bassani, Srimalie, illus. 2017. (All Kinds of Families Ser.). (ENG.). (J). (gr. k-1). 28.51 **(978-1-68342-147-4(7))** Rourke Educational Media.

—Owen's Family. Bassani, Srimalie, illus. 2017. (All Kinds of Families Ser.). (ENG.). (J). (gr. k-1). 28.51 **(978-1-68342-148-1(5))** Rourke Educational Media.

Rinaldi, Ann. Come Juneteenth. 2009. (ENG., Illus.). 256p. (YA). (gr. 7). pap. 7.99 (978-0-15-206392-4(7)) Houghton Mifflin Harcourt Publishing Co.

—The Ever-After Bird. 2010. (ENG.). 240p. (J). (gr. 5-7). pap. 8.99 (978-0-547-25854-6(2)) Houghton Mifflin Harcourt Publishing Co.

Ringler, Matt. One Little, Two Little, Three Little Apples. Kennedy, Anne, illus. 2005. (J). pap. (978-0-439-77500-7(0)) Scholastic, Inc.

Ringwald, Whitaker. The Secret Box. (Secret Box Ser.: 1). (ENG.). (J). (gr. 3-7). 2015. 320p. pap. 6.99 (978-0-06-221615-1(5)) 2014. 304p. 16.99 (978-0-06-221614-4(7)) HarperCollins Pubs. (Tegen, Katherine Bks).

Rinker, Sherri Duskey. Silly Wonderful You. McDonnell, Patrick, illus. 2016. 40p. (J). (gr. -1-3). 17.99 (978-0-06-227105-1(9)) HarperCollins Pubs.

Riordan, Rick. The Maze of Bones. 2008. (39 Clues Ser.: 1). (ENG.). 224p. (J). (gr. 3-7). 12.99 (978-0-545-06039-4(7), Scholastic Pr.); (Illus.). 12.99 (978-0-545-09054-4(7)) Scholastic, Inc.

Rippin, Sally. The Crazy Cousins. Spartels, Stephanie, illus. 2013. (ENG.). 48p. (J). pap. 4.99 (978-1-61067-121-7(X)) Kane Miller.

Riseman, Daniel & D'Onofrio, J. J. The Greatest Ride of All. 2012. 48p. pap. 21.99 (978-1-4691-8388-6(9)) Xlibris Corp.

Ritchey, Melissa. The Kabeezles. 2006. (Illus.). 16p. (J). lib. bdg. 18.95 (978-0-9761128-5-3(X)) KB Bks. & More.

Rits, Susan Katherine. The Pirates of Bair Island. 2013. 234p. pap. 12.99 (978-0-9894891-1-9(6)) Imprint.li.

Rivadeneira, Alexa. Confessions from the Heart of a Teenage Girl. 2007. 248p. per. 16.95 (978-0-595-42432-0(5)) iUniverse, Inc.

Rivera-Ashford, Roni Capin & Johnson, Richard. Hip Hip Hooray, It's Monsoon Day! 2007. (ENG & SPA.). (YA). pap. 15.95 (978-1-886679-36-8(3)) Arizona Sonora Desert Museum Pr.

Rivera, Jeff. Forever My Lady: Young Adult. 2005. (YA). per. 12.95 (978-0-9762838-1-2(6)) Gumbo Multimedia Entertainment.

Robbins, Eliza & National Geographic Learning Staff. Nana's New Room. 2010. (Rise & Shine Ser.). (ENG.). 12p. (C). (gr. -1-3). pap. 9.95 (978-1-4042-6734-3(4)) National Geographic School Publishing, Inc.

Robe, Kim. Robbie's Trail Through Divorce. Gavet, Nathalie, illus. 2012. 40p. (-18). pap. 23.99 (978-1-935831-11-2(9)) Robe Communications, Inc.

—Robbie's Trail Through Divorce - Activity Book. Gavet, Nathalie, illus. 2012. 28p. (-18). pap. 16.99 (978-1-935831-12-9(7)) Robe Communications, Inc.

—Robbie's Trail Through Divorce - Adult Guide. Gavet, Nathalie, illus. 2012. 28p. (-18). pap. 16.99 (978-1-935831-13-6(5)) Robe Communications, Inc.

Roberts, Deborah. Mr Otagiri's Promise. Ju-Young Im, Joy & Da-Young Im, Linda, illus. 2012. 40p. pap. (978-1-77067-719-7(4)) FriesenPress.

Roberts, Dw. Pep Squad Mysteries Book: Mystery in the Lions' Maze. 2012. 102p. pap. 9.95 (978-1-257-92360-1(9)) Lulu Pr., Inc.

Roberts, In Pursuit of the Curious Bangle J. In Pursuit of the Curious Bangle. 2010. 170p. pap. 14.50 (978-1-4457-7210-3(8)) Lulu Pr., Inc.

Roberts, Nick H. Tyler the Tumbleweed & His Family Adventure. 2013. 28p. pap. 13.55 (978-1-4669-7782-2(5)) Trafford Publishing.

Roberts, Willo Davis. The Old House. 2016. (ENG., Illus.). 272p. (J). (gr. 3-7). pap. 6.99 (978-1-4814-5785-9(3), Aladdin) Simon & Schuster Children's Publishing.

—The Old House. 2016. (ENG., Illus.). 272p. (J). (gr. 3-7). 17.99 (978-1-4814-5786-6(1), Simon & Schuster/Paula Wiseman Bks.) Simon & Schuster/Paula Wiseman Bks.

Robinson, Elda L. Nathanial's Family. 2004. 32p. pap. 18.00 (978-1-4140-4943-4(9)) AuthorHouse.

Robinson, Gwen. The Renshaw Diversion. 2007. (Illus.). 204p. per. (978-0-7552-0275-1(9)) Authors OnLine, Ltd.

Robinson, Gwen G. The Jensen Case. 2010. (Illus.). 228p. pap. (978-0-7552-0496-0(4)) Authors OnLine, Ltd.

Robinson, Linda M. Dear Grandchild, When You Come for a Visit. Larkins, Mona, illus. 2005. 37p. (J). (gr. -1-4). 15.99 (978-0-9740841-4-5(X)) K&B Products.

Robinson, Sharon. Under the Same Sun. Ford, A. G., illus. 2014. (ENG.). 40p. (J). (gr. -1-3). 17.99 (978-0-545-16672-0(1), Scholastic Pr.) Scholastic, Inc.

Robinson, W. Heath. The Adventures of Uncle Lubin. 2013. (Dover Children's Classics Ser.). (ENG., Illus.). 128p. (J). (gr. 6-8). pap. 9.95 (978-0-486-49821-8(2)) Dover Pubns., Inc.

Robshaw, Brandon. Big Wish. 2016. (ENG.). 240p. (J). (gr. 3-7). 16.99 (978-0-545-90410-0(2), Chicken Hse., The) Scholastic, Inc.

Rocco, John & Primiano, Jay. Swim That Rock. Rocco, John, illus. 2014. (ENG., Illus.). 304p. (YA). (gr. 7). 16.99 (978-0-7636-6905-8(9)) Candlewick Pr.

Rodkey, Geoff. The Tapper Twins Go to War (with Each Other) 2016. (Tapper Twins Ser.: 1). (ENG., Illus.). 240p. (J). (gr. 3-7). pap. 5.99 (978-0-316-31597-5(4)) Little, Brown Bks. for Young Readers.

Rodriguez, Renae. Why You Are So Special. 2010. 16p. 9.99 (978-1-4520-3540-6(7)) AuthorHouse.

Romano, Juliana. First There Was Forever. 2016. (ENG.). 416p. (YA). (gr. 9). pap. 10.99 (978-0-14-751391-5(X), Speak) Penguin Young Readers Group.

Romero, Sensi. La Familia de Nieve. Serra, Armando, illus. 2004. (Cuentos con miga Ser.). 47p. (J). (gr. 1-5). pap. 11.00 (978-84-95895-22-6(6)) Editorial Brief ESP. Dist: Independent Pubs. Group.

Romo, Brandyn. Rustlings of an Old Tree. 2012. 28p. pap. 24.95 (978-1-4626-5581-6(5)) America Star Bks.

Rooney, Jodie C. Feather in Your Cap, 1 vol. 2008. (ENG.). 19p. 24.95 (978-1-60474-390-6(5)) America Star Bks.

Rose, Judith Robbins. Look Both Ways in the Barrio Blanco. 2015. (ENG.). 352p. (J). (gr. 5). 16.99 (978-0-7636-7235-5(1)) Candlewick Pr.

Rosen, Lucy. My Dad the Super Villain. 2010. (Despicable Me Ser.). (ENG., Illus.). 32p. (gr. -1-1). pap. 3.99 (978-0-316-08382-9(8), L,B Kids) Hachette Bk. Group.

Rosenberg, Madelyn & Shang, Wendy Wan-Long. This Is Just a Test: A Novel. 2017. (ENG.). 256p. (J). (gr. 3-7). 17.99 **(978-1-338-03772-2(2)**, Scholastic Pr.) Scholastic, Inc.

Rosenthal, Betsy R. Looking for Me: In This Great Big Family. 2013. (ENG., Illus.). 176p. (J). (gr. 5-7). pap. 6.99 (978-0-544-02271-3(8)) Houghton Mifflin Harcourt Publishing Co.

Ross, Jill. The Blake Family Vacation. Pruitt, Gwendolyn, illus. 2010. (ENG.). 130p. (J). (gr. 3-7). pap. 9.95 (978-1-59825-950-6(4)) Shenanigans Series.

—The Real Nitty-Gritty. Pruitt, Gwendolyn, illus. 2010. (ENG.). 60p. (J). (gr. 3-7). pap. 9.95 (978-1-59825-949-0(0)) Shenanigans Series.

Roth, Adam J. Checking up on Daddy! 2010. 36p. pap. 10.95 (978-1-60844-547-9(X)) Dog Ear Publishing, LLC.

Roth-Fisch, Marla. The Last Bedtime Story: That We Read Each Night. 2013. (ENG.). 32p. (J). pap. 9.95 (978-1-935567-43-1(8), 9781935567431) Sensory Resources.

Roth, Rhonda. The Most Important Thing. Grajczyk, Shane, illus. 2007. (ENG.). 32p. (J). (gr. -1-3). 16.95 (978-0-9770141-0-1(X), Crossing Guard Bks.) Crossing Guard Bks., LLC.

Roth, Veronica. Allegiant. (Divergent Ser.: 3). (YA). (gr. 9). 2016. 592p. pap. 12.99 (978-0-06-242009-1(7)) 2016. 592p. pap. 12.99 (978-0-06-202407-7(8)) 2013. (ENG.). 544p. 19.99 (978-0-06-202406-0(X)) 2016. 592p. 19.99 (978-0-06-242008-4(9)) HarperCollins Pubs. (Tegen, Katherine Bks).

—Allegiant. l.t. ed. 2016. (Divergent Ser.: 3). (ENG.). 580p. pap. 12.99 (978-1-59413-960-4(1), Large Print Pr.) Thorndike Pr.

—Allegiant. 2016. (Divergent Ser.: 3). lib. bdg. 24.50 (978-0-606-38141-3(4)); lib. bdg. 24.50 (978-0-606-38182-6(1)) Turtleback Bks.

—Divergent. 2013. (KOR.). **(978-89-5660-710-8(9))** Eunhaeng Namu Publishing Co.

—Divergent. Delort, Nicolas, photos by. 2014. (Divergent Ser.: 1). (ENG., Illus.). 576p. (YA). (gr. 9). pap. 12.99 (978-0-06-238724-0(3), Tegen, Katherine Bks) HarperCollins Pubs.

—Divergent. 2012. (ENG.). 512p. pap. (978-0-06-219406-0(2)) HarperCollins Pubs.

—Divergent, 3 vols. Delort, Nicolas, photos by. (Divergent Ser.: 1). (ENG., Illus.). (YA). (gr. 9-18). 2011. 496p. 17.99 (978-0-06-202402-2(7)) 2014. 576p. 19.99 (978-0-06-235217-0(2)) HarperCollins Pubs. (Tegen, Katherine Bks).

—Divergent. movie tie-in ed. 2014. (Divergent Ser.: Bk. 1). (ENG.). 496p. (YA). (gr. 9). 17.99 (978-0-06-228984-1(5), Tegen, Katherine Bks) HarperCollins Pubs.

—Divergent, 1. 2012. (ENG.). 496p. (978-0-00-742042-1(0)) HarperCollins Pubs. Ltd.

—Divergent. 2009. (Divergent Ser.: Bk. 1). 11.04 (978-0-7848-3786-3(4), Everbind) Marco Bk. Co.

—Divergent. 2014. (Divergent Trilogy Ser.). (ENG.). (YA). (gr. 9). lib. bdg. 23.60 **(978-1-62765-593-4(X))** Perfection Learning Corp.

—Divergent. l.t. ed. 2014. (Divergent Ser.: Bk. 1). (ENG.). 530p. pap. 12.99 (978-1-59413-745-7(5), Large Print Pr.) Thorndike Pr.

—Divergent. 2014. (Divergent Ser.: 1). (YA). lib. bdg. 24.50 (978-0-606-36515-4(X)) Turtleback Bks.

—Divergent; Insurgent; Allegiant, 3 vols., Set. 2013. (Divergent Ser.: Bks. 1-3). (ENG.). (YA). (gr. 9). 55.97 (978-0-06-227878-4(9), Tegen, Katherine Bks) HarperCollins Pubs.

—Divergente. 2013. (Divergent Ser.: Bk. 1).Tr. of Divergent. (SPA.). 464p. (YA). pap. 21.99 (978-84-272-0118-7(4)) Molino, Editorial ESP. Dist: Lectorum Pubns., Inc.

—Insurgent. 2014. (KOR.). **(978-89-5660-758-0(3))** Eunhaeng Namu Publishing Co.

—Insurgent. 2015. pap. (978-0-06-238845-2(2)) 2015. (Divergent Ser.: 2). (ENG.). 592p. (J). (gr. 9). pap. 12.99 (978-0-06-202405-3(1)) 2012. (Divergent Ser.: 2). (ENG.). 544p. (YA). (gr. 9). 17.99 (978-0-06-202404-6(3)) 2012. (Divergent Ser.: 2). 544p. (YA). (gr. 9). pap. 12.00 (978-0-06-212784-6(5)) 2012. (Divergent Ser.: 2). (ENG.). 592p. (YA). (gr. 9). 19.99 (978-0-06-223493-3(5)) 2015. (Divergent Ser.: 2). (ENG.). 544p. (YA). (gr. 9). 17.99 (978-0-06-237284-0(X)) 2015. (Divergent Ser.: Bk. 2). (ENG.). 592p. (YA). (gr. 9). pap. 12.99 (978-0-06-237285-7(8)) HarperCollins Pubs. (Tegen, Katherine Bks).

—Insurgent. 2015. (Divergent Trilogy Ser.). (ENG.). (YA). (gr. 9). lib. bdg. 23.60 **(978-1-62765-988-8(9))** Perfection Learning Corp.

—Insurgent. 2015. (Divergent Ser.: 2). (YA). lib. bdg. 24.50 (978-0-606-36475-1(7)) Turtleback Bks.

Rotstein, Adira. Little Jane & the Nameless Isle: A Little Jane Silver Adventure (Large Print 16pt) 2013. 324p. pap. (978-1-4596-6322-0(5)) ReadHowYouWant.com, Ltd.

Rottman, S. L. Shadow of a Doubt, 1 vol. (ENG.). 224p. (YA). (gr. 7-18). 2005. pap. 7.95 (978-1-56145-354-2(4)) 2003. 14.95 (978-1-56145-291-0(2)) Peachtree Pubs.

Roudon Jr., James. The Adventures of Ratsy & Kitten: Which Way Is Home? 2007. 56p. per. 16.95 (978-1-4241-8549-8(1)) America Star Bks.

Rounds, Harriet. The Magic Stairway, 1 vol. 2009. 48p. pap. 16.95 (978-1-60749-707-3(7)) America Star Bks.

Rouss, Sylvia A. Tali's Jerusalem Scrapbook. Oppenheimer, Nancy, illus. 2003. 32p. (J). (gr. 1-4). 14.95 (978-1-930143-68-5(0)); pap. 9.95 (978-1-930143-69-2(9)) Simcha Media Group. (Pitspopany Pr.).

Roy, Arundhati. Le Dieu des Petits Riens. pap. 19.95 (978-2-07-041172-6(9)) Gallimard, Editions FRA. Dist: Distribooks, Inc.

Roy, Ron. April Adventure. Gurney, John Steven, illus. 2010. (Calendar Mysteries Ser.: 4). (ENG.). 80p. (J). (gr. 1-4). 4.99 (978-0-375-86116-1(5), Random Hse. Bks. for Young Readers) Random Hse. Children's Bks.

—August Acrobat. Gurney, John Steven, illus. 2012. (Calendar Mysteries Ser.: 8). (ENG.). 80p. (J). (gr. 1-4). 4.99 (978-0-375-86886-3(0)); lib. bdg. 12.99 (978-0-375-96886-0(5)) Random Hse. Children's Bks. (Random Hse. Bks. for Young Readers).

—March Mischief. 2010. (Calendar Mysteries Ser.: 3). lib. bdg. 14.75 (978-0-606-12460-7(8), Turtleback) Turtleback Bks.

—October Ogre. 2013. (Calendar Mysteries Ser.: 10). lib. bdg. 14.75 (978-0-606-32232-4(9), Turtleback) Turtleback Bks.

Rubcic, Michael. Native Soul. 2004. 216p. (Orig.). (J). pap. 14.95 (978-0-9746848-0-2(5)) Native Sun Pr.

Rudnick, Paul. It's All Your Fault. (ENG.). 304p. (J). (gr. 9). 2017. pap. 10.99 (978-0-545-46429-1(3)) 2016. 19.99 (978-0-545-46428-4(5), Scholastic Pr.) Scholastic, Inc.

Ruellan, Susan. The Lost Treasure of Finistere. 2008. (ENG & FRE., Illus.). 83p. (J). (gr. 4-7). pap. 9.95 (978-1-933916-24-8(9)) Nelson Publishing & Marketing.

Rushton, Rosie. How Could You Do This to Me, Mum? 2005. 224p. (J). pap. 5.99 (978-0-7868-5187-4(2)) Hyperion Bks. for Children.

—Last Seen Wearing Trainers. 2003. 224p. (J). pap. 9.95 (978-1-84270-216-1(5)) Andersen Pr. GBR. Dist: Trafalgar Square Publishing.

Ruttledge, Nancy. If I Were My Mommy & Daddy. 2003. (J). per. 11.95 (978-1-932205-51-0(9)) Word Association Pubs.

Ruurs, Margriet. Families Around the World. Gordon, Jessica Rae, illus. 2014. (Around the World Ser.). (ENG.). 40p. (J). (gr. -1-2). 18.95 (978-1-894786-57-7(2)) Kids Can Pr., Ltd. CAN. Dist: Hachette Bk. Group.

Ryan, Darlene. Rules for Life, 1 vol. 2004. (ENG.). 176p. (YA). (gr. 8-12). pap. 9.95 (978-1-55143-350-9(8), 1234553) Orca Bk. Pubs. USA.

Ryan, Darlene & Manchester, Peter. Kisses, Kisses, Kisses. 2004. (Illus.). 24p. (J). (978-1-55131-092-3(9)) Univ. of New Brunswick, Dept. of Graphic Services.

Ryan, Pam Muñoz. Esperanza Rising. 2016. (gr. 5-8). lib. bdg. 17.20 (978-0-613-53807-7(2), Turtleback) Turtleback Bks.

—Mice & Beans. Cepeda, Joe, illus. 2005. (Bookshelf Ser.). (ENG.). 32p. (J). (gr. -1-3). pap. 6.99 (978-0-439-70136-5(8), Scholastic Paperbacks) Scholastic, Inc.

Ryan, Patrick. In Mike We Trust. 2009. 321p. (J). lib. bdg. 17.89 (978-0-06-085814-8(1), HarperTeen) HarperCollins Pubs.

Ryherd, Tim. My Hurricane Book. 2006. (Illus.). (J). 12.95 (978-0-9749974-1-4(2)) Ryherd, Tim Publishing.

Rylance, Maureen. The Spur on the Plate. 2005. 102p. (YA). pap. 12.15 (978-1-4120-5459-1(1)) Trafford Publishing.

Rylant, Cynthia. Annie & Snowball & the Teacup Club. Stevenson, Suçie, illus. (Annie & Snowball Ser.: 3). (ENG.). 40p. (J). (gr. k-2). 2009. pap. 3.99 (978-1-4169-1461-7(7)) 2008. 16.99 (978-1-4169-0940-8(0)) Simon Spotlight. (Simon Spotlight).

—Annie & Snowball & the Wintry Freeze. Stevenson, Suçie, illus. 2010. (Annie & Snowball Ser.: 8). (ENG.). 40p. (J). (gr. k-2). 16.99 (978-1-4169-7205-1(6), Simon Spotlight) Simon Spotlight.

—Henry & Mudge & the Funny Lunch. Bracken, Carolyn, illus. 2005. (Henry & Mudge Ser.: 24). (ENG.). 40p. (J). (gr. k-2). pap. 3.99 (978-0-689-83444-8(6), Simon Spotlight) Simon Spotlight.

—Henry & Mudge & the Tall Tree House. Bracken, Carolyn, illus. 2003. (Henry & Mudge Ser.). (ENG.). 40p. (J). (gr. k-2). pap. 3.99 (978-0-689-83445-5(4), Simon Spotlight) Simon Spotlight.

—Henry & Mudge & the Tall Tree House. 2003. (Henry & Mudge Ready-To-Read Ser.: 21). (gr. k-3). lib. bdg. 13.55 (978-0-613-90605-0(5), Turtleback) Turtleback Bks.

Sachar, Louis. The Cardturner. 2011. (ENG.). 352p. (YA). (gr. 7). pap. 9.99 (978-0-385-73663-3(0), Ember) Random Hse. Children's Bks.

—The Cardturner. 2011. lib. bdg. 20.85 (978-0-606-23428-3(4), Turtleback) Turtleback Bks.

—Marvin Redpost #1: Kidnapped at Birth? Record, Adam, illus. 2015. (Marvin Redpost Ser.: 1). (ENG.). 96p. (J). (gr. 1-4). lib. bdg. 12.99 (978-0-553-53540-2(4), Random Hse. Bks. for Young Readers) Random Hse. Children's Bks.

Sackanay, Kathleen. Adventures in the Forest. Wood, Morgan, illus. 2007. 24p. (J). pap. 8.45 (978-0-9791276-2-5(9)) Athanatos Publishing Group.

Sackett, Frances. The Misadventures of the Magician's Dog. 2013. (ENG.). 192p. (J). (gr. 2-7). 16.95 (978-0-8234-2869-4(9)) Holiday Hse., Inc.

Saddleback Educational Publishing Staff, ed. Blizzard, 1 vol. unabr. ed. 2011. (Heights Ser.). (ENG.). 49p. (gr. 5-8). 7.95

Smith, Tina. The Secret Love of Lone Wolf & Sarah. 2008. 55p. pap. 13.95 (978-1-4357-4550-6(7)) Lulu Pr., Inc.

Smothers, Ethel Footman. Auntee Edna. Clay, Wil, illus. 2004. 32p. (J). pap. 8.00 (978-0-8028-5246-5(7)); 16.00 (978-0-8028-5154-3(1)) Eerdmans, William B. Publishing Co.

Smythe, R. R. Into the Woods. 2007. 122p. (YA). per. 7.49 net. (978-0-9787139-4-2(X), Pandora) Highland Pr. Publishing.

Snadowsky, Daria. Anatomy of a Single Girl. 2014. (ENG.). 240p. (YA). (gr. 9). pap. 8.99 (978-0-385-73799-9(8), Ember) Random Hse. Children's Bks.

Snead, Kathi. My Mom Has a Job. Christine, Grove, illus. 2004. (J). (978-0-9747385-1-2(4)) City of Manassas Department of Social Services.

Snedeker, Caroline Dale. Lysis Goes to the Play. Clark, Elizabeth Palmer, illus. 2003. 62p. (J). per. 8.95 (978-0-9667067-4-1(9)) American Home-School Publishing, LLC.

Snelling, Lauraine. Golden Filly, No. 1. 2009. (ENG.). 624p. (J). pap. 16.00 (978-0-7642-0737-2(7)) Bethany Hse. Pubs.

—Golden Filly Collection 2. 2009. (ENG.). 624p. (J). pap. 16.00 (978-0-7642-0738-9(5)) Bethany Hse. Pubs.

Snicket, Lemony, pseud. The End. Helquist, Brett & Kupperman, Michael, illus. 2006. (Series of Unfortunate Events Ser.: 13). (ENG.). 368p. (J). (gr. 5-18). 13.99 (978-0-06-441016-8(1)) HarperCollins Pubs.

—The End. Helquist, Brett, illus. 2006. (Series of Unfortunate Events Ser.: Bk. 13). 368p. (J). lib. bdg. 15.89 (978-0-06-029644-5(5)) HarperCollins Pubs.

—The Grim Grotto. Helquist, Brett & Kupperman, Michael, illus. 2004. (Series of Unfortunate Events Ser.: 11). (ENG.). 352p. (J). (gr. 5-6). 13.99 (978-0-06-441014-4(5)) HarperCollins Pubs.

Snow, Carol. Bubble World. 2014. (ENG.). 352p. (YA). (gr. 7). pap. 9.99 (978-1-250-04441-9(3), 9781250044419) Square Fish.

Snow, Susie. The Old Cookie Jar. Motz, Mike, illus. 2012. 34p. pap. 19.99 (978-1-61996-595-9(X)) Salem Author Services.

Snowden, Gary. The Lost Treasure of Hawkins Cave. Pierce Clark, Donna, illus. 2013. 112p. pap. 7.99 (978-1-938768-10-1(8)) Gypsy Pubns.

Snyder, Zilpha Keatley. The Bronze Pen. 2008. (ENG.). 208p. (J). (gr. 3-7). 16.99 (978-1-4169-4201-6(7), Atheneum Bks. for Young Readers) Simon & Schuster Children's Publishing.

—William S. & the Great Escape. 2009. (ENG.). 224p. (J). (gr. 3-7). 16.99 (978-1-4169-6763-7(X), Atheneum Bks. for Young Readers) Simon & Schuster Children's Publishing.

Sobel, Sheila. Color Blind. 2016. (ENG.). 253p. (YA). 17.99 (978-1-4405-9746-6(4), Simon Pulse) Simon Pulse.

Sofranac, Rodo. Polly & the Peanut Pull. 2013. (Illus.). 62p. pap. (978-1-939625-24-3(6)) Inkwell Books LLC.

Solis, Javier Rene. The Adventures of Tony the Turtle: La Familia the Family. 2008. 24p. pap. 14.99 (978-1-4389-1421-3(0)) AuthorHouse.

Solomon, Sharon. A Walk With Grandpa/Un Paseo con el Abuelo. Del Risco, Eida, tr. Barcita, Pamela, illus. 2009. (ENG & SPA.). 32p. (J). (gr. -1-3). 16.95 (978-1-932748-91-8(1), Raven Tree Pr.,Csi) Continental Sales, Inc.

Solomon, Sharon K. A Walk with Grandpa. Barcita, Pamela, illus. 2009. (ENG.). 32p. (J). (gr. -1-3). 16.95 (978-1-934960-11-0(X), Raven Tree Pr.,Csi) Continental Sales, Inc.

Sommer, Carl. No Longer a Dilly Dally Read-Along 2003. (Another Sommer-Time Story Ser.). (Illus.). 48p. (J). lib. bdg. 23.95 incl. audio (978-1-57537-751-3(9)) Advance Publishing, Inc.

—No Longer a Dilly Dally Read-Along James, Kennon, illus. 2003. (Another Sommer-Time Story Ser.). (ENG.). 48p. (J). lib. bdg. 23.95 incl. audio compact disk (978-1-57537-701-8(2)) Advance Publishing, Inc.

—The Richest Poor Kid. Martínez, Jorge, illus. 2007. (Another Sommer-Time Story Ser.). (ENG.). 48p. (J). 23.95 incl. audio compact disk (978-1-57537-724-7(1)) Advance Publishing, Inc.

—You Move You Lose 2003. (Another Sommer-Time Story Ser.). (Illus.). 48p. (J). lib. bdg. 23.95 incl. audio (978-1-57537-755-1(1)) Advance Publishing, Inc.

—You Move You Lose James, Kennon, illus. 2003. (Another Sommer-Time Story Ser.). (ENG.). 48p. (J). lib. bdg. 23.95 incl. audio compact disk (978-1-57537-705-6(5)) Advance Publishing, Inc.

Son, John. Finding My Hat. 2005. (First Person Fiction Ser.). (ENG.). 192p. (J). (gr. 7). reprint ed. pap. 6.99 (978-0-439-43539-0(0), Scholastic Paperbacks) Scholastic, Inc.

Sones, Sonya. Saving Red. 2016. 448p. (YA). (gr. 8). 17.99 (978-0-06-237028-0(6), HarperTeen) HarperCollins Pubs.

Sonnenblick, Jordan. Curveball: The Year I Lost My Grip. 2012. 304p. pap. 17.99 (978-0-545-39311-9(6)) Scholastic, Inc.

Sonnichsen, A. L. Red Butterfly. Bates, Amy June, illus. 2015. (ENG.). 400p. (J). (gr. 3-7). 17.99 (978-1-4814-1109-7(8)) Simon & Schuster, Inc.

Soo, Kean, illus. The Race at Harewood. 2015. (March Grand Prix Ser.). (ENG.). 48p. (gr. 1-3). lib. bdg. 33.32 (978-1-4342-9639-9(3)) Capstone Young Readers of Coughlan Cos.

Sorrells, Walter. First Shot. 2009. (ENG.). 288p. (YA). (gr. 7-18). 8.99 (978-0-14-241421-7(2), Puffin Books) Penguin Young Readers Group.

Soto, Gary. Jesse. 2006. 166p. (gr. 7-12). 16.95 (978-0-7569-6688-1(4)) Perfection Learning Corp.

Soundprints Staff. Smithsonian's Backyard Collection Micro 4 Book Set. 2007. (ENG.). 32p. 14.95 (978-1-59249-751-5(9)); 14.95 (978-1-59249-750-8(0)) Soundprints.

Sourcebooks & Silverman, Laura. Girl Out of Water. 2017. (ENG.). 368p. (YA). (gr. 8-12). pap. 10.99 (978-1-4926-4686-0(5), 9781492646860) Sourcebooks, Inc.

Sovago-Royal, Sandra. Magimus. 2009. 33p. (J). pap. 19.95 (978-1-4327-4375-8(9)) Outskirts Pr., Inc.

Sovern, Megan Jean. The Meaning of Maggie. 2015. (ENG.). 232p. (J). (gr. 3-7). pap. 6.99 (978-1-4521-2876-4(6)) Chronicle Bks. LLC.

Sowards, Ben. Asleep on the Hay: A Dust Bowl Christmas. Sowards, Ben, illus. 2015. (Illus.). (J). 17.99 (978-1-62972-067-8(4), Ensign Peak) Deseret Bk. Co.

Spalding, Amy. Ink Is Thicker Than Water. 2013. (Entangled Teen Ser.). (ENG.). 320p. (YA). (gr. 7-12). pap. 9.99 (978-1-62266-040-7(4), 9781622660407) Entangled Publishing, LLC.

Spalding, Brenda M. Hayden's Garden. 2012. pap. 13.95 (978-0-7414-7961-7(3)) Infinity Publishing.

Spalding, Esta. Look Out for the Fitzgerald-Trouts. Smith, Sydney, illus. 2016. (ENG.). 256p. (J). (gr. 3-7). 16.99 (978-0-316-29858-2(1)) Little, Brown Bks. for Young Readers.

Spangler, Jon. The Sky Princess Moves to the Land of Peaches. 2009. 24p. pap. 11.95 (978-1-4490-0015-8(0)) AuthorHouse.

Sparling, Eric. Tantramar. 2012. (ENG.). 144p. pap. (978-1-55081-257-2(2)) Breakwater Bks., Ltd.

Spicer, Candace. Hopper & the Happy Houses. 2012. 18.95 (978-0-7414-6863-5(8)); pap. 11.95 (978-0-7414-6862-8(X)) Infinity Publishing.

Spinelli, Jerry. The Warden's Daughter. 2017. (ENG.). 352p. (J). (gr. 4-7). 16.99 (978-0-375-83199-7(1)); lib. bdg. 19.99 (978-0-375-93199-4(6)) Random Hse. Children's Bks. (Knopf Bks. for Young Readers).

Spoon, Cynthia. The Ice Angel. Harr, Lynn, illus. 2006. 24p. (J). (gr. -1-3). per. 8.50 (978-1-60002-280-7(4), 4233) Mountain Valley Publishing, LLC.

Sporn, Jessica. Old Enough to do Good in the World. 2010. 21p. 12.95 (978-0-557-34196-2(5)) Lulu Pr., Inc.

Spreng, Robert. Goin' Great in the Lone Star State. 2010. 39p. pap. 7.95 (978-0-557-58803-9(0)) Lulu Pr., Inc.

Springfield, Pepper. Meet the Bobs & Tweets. Caldwell, Kristy, illus. 2016. (Bobs & Tweets Ser.: No. 1). (ENG.). 80p. (J). (gr. -1-3). 9.99 (978-0-545-87072-6(0)) Scholastic, Inc.

Springfield, Pepper. Perfecto Pet Show. Caldwell, Kristy, illus. 2017. (Bobs & Tweets Ser.: 2). (ENG.). 80p. (J). (gr. -1-3). 9.99 **(978-0-545-87073-3(9))** Scholastic, Inc.

Springstubb, Tricia. Every Single Second. Sudyka, Diana, illus. 2016. 368p. (J). (gr. 3-7). 16.99 (978-0-06-236628-3(9)) HarperCollins Pubs.

Spruill, Ed. Jordan Wants a Brother. l.t. ed. 2005. (Illus.). 26p. (J). lib. bdg. 15.95 (978-0-9772578-0-5(0)) Tree Branch Publishing.

Spyropolous, Angelo. RV. 2005. pap. 12.99 (978-1-894869-98-0(2), PO 00128) Zumaya Pubns. LLC.

Squires, R. L. Peaches & Cream, 1 vol. Collier, Kevin Scott, illus. 2009. 31p. pap. 24.95 (978-1-60749-164-4(8)) America Star Bks.

St. Antoine, Sarah. Three Bird Summer. 2014. (ENG.). 256p. (J). (gr. 5). 16.99 (978-0-7636-6564-7(9)) Candlewick Pr.

St. John, Lauren. Kentucky Thriller. Dean, David, illus. 2014. (Jóvenes Lectores. Los Misterios de Laura Ser.). (SPA.). 248p. (J). (gr. 4-7). pap. 8.95 (978-84-8343-271-6(4), Bambu, Editorial) Combel Editorial, S.A. ESP. Dist: Independent Pubs. Group.

St. John, Patricia. Nothing Else Matters. 2003. 176p. 6.49 (978-0-85421-972-8(2)) Scripture Union GBR. Dist: Gabriel Resources.

Stadler, Alexander. Invasion of the Relatives. 2009. (Julian Rodriguez Ser.: 2). (ENG.). 144p. (J). (gr. 2-5). pap. 5.99 (978-0-439-91971-5(1), Scholastic Pr.) Scholastic, Inc.

Stalcup. La Loncheria. Arroyo, illus. 2008. (SPA & ENG.). 28p. (J). pap. 8.95 (978-1-60448-006-1(8)) Lectura Bks.

—La Loncheria. Arroyo, illus. 2008. (SPA & ENG.). 28p. (J). 15.95 (978-1-60448-005-4(X)) Lectura Bks.

Stan, Jaskiel, illus. Families are Forever Learning & Activity Guide. 2007. 20p. (J). 9.95 (978-0-9728666-2-0(0)) As Simple As That Publishing.

Stanek, Robert, pseud. The Bugville Critters Go on Vacation. 2008. (ENG., Illus.). (J). 32p. per. 9.95 (978-1-57545-148-0(4)); 52p. per. 19.95 (978-1-57545-125-1(5)) RP Media.

—The Bugville Critters Play Their First Big Game. 2008. (ENG., Illus.). (J). 32p. per. 9.95 (978-1-57545-149-7(2)); 52p. per. 16.95 (978-1-57545-127-5(1)) RP Media.

—The Bugville Critters Rush to the Hospital. 2008. (ENG., Illus.). (J). 32p. per. 9.95 (978-1-57545-150-3(6)); 52p. per. 19.95 (978-1-57545-126-8(3)) RP Media.

—The Bugville Critters Vacation Surprise: Buster Bee's School Days #3. 2008. (ENG., Illus.). 68p. (J). per. 18.95 (978-1-57545-172-5(7)) RP Media.

—The Bugville Critters Visit Dad & Mom at Work. 2007. (ENG.). (J). 28p. per. 9.99 (978-1-57545-144-2(1)); (Illus.). 52p. per. 19.95 (978-1-57545-121-3(2), Reagent Pr. Bks. for Young Readers) RP Media.

—Save Their Allowance. 2010. 32p. pap. 8.99 (978-1-57545-175-6(1), Reagent Pr. Bks. for Young Readers) RP Media.

—Start Summer Vacation. 2010. (Illus.). 32p. pap. 8.99 (978-1-57545-174-9(3), Reagent Pr. Bks. for Young Readers) RP Media.

Staniszewski, Anna. My Sort of Fairy Tale Ending. 2013. (My Very Unfairy Tale Life Ser.: 3). (ENG.). 224p. (J). (gr. 4-7). pap. 6.99 (978-1-4022-7933-1(7), Sourcebooks Jabberwocky) Sourcebooks, Inc.

Stanley, Diane. Joplin, Wishing. 2017. 272p. (J). (gr. 3-7). 16.99 (978-0-06-242370-2(3)) HarperCollins Pubs.

Stanton, Angie. Rock & a Hard Place. 2013. (Jamieson Brothers Ser.: 1). (ENG.). 304p. (YA). (gr. 9). pap. 9.99 (978-0-06-227254-6(3), HarperTeen) HarperCollins Pubs.

Starboortz Fish. 2007. (Illus.). 32p. (J). 18.95 (978-0-9792946-0-0(6)) Starlit Publishing LLC.

Steers, Billy. Tractor Mac Family Reunion. 2015. (Tractor Mac Ser.). (ENG., Illus.). 32p. (J). (gr. -1-k). 8.99 (978-0-374-30109-5(3), 9780374301095, Farrar, Straus & Giroux (BYR)) Farrar, Straus & Giroux.

Stern, D. G. Disappearing Diamonds: An Upton Charles Adventure. Bartlett, Rebecca, illus. 2008. (ENG.). 126p. (J). pap. 9.99 (978-0-9754676-9-5(7)) Yeoman Hse.

Sternberg, Julie. Friendship Over. Wright, Johanna, illus. 2014. (Top-Secret Diary of Celie Valentine Ser.). (ENG.). 160p. (J). (gr. 3-6). 15.95 (978-1-59078-993-3(8)) Boyds Mills Pr.

Stevens, A. P. The Volcano: The Adventures of Antboy & Mr Cricket. Finn, N. K., ed. Deskcube, illus. 2008. (ENG.). 29p. pap. 9.95 (978-0-9798886-0-1(3)) Mugsy and Sugar Pressed.

Stevenson, Robin. A Thousand Shades of Blue, 1 vol. 2008. (ENG.). 240p. (YA). (gr. 7-12). pap. 12.95 (978-1-55143-921-1(2)) Orca Bk. Pubs. USA.

Stewart, E. J. The Lyre Birds. 2008. 214p. pap. 16.95 (978-0-615-18762-4(5)) Leaf & Vine Bks.

Stewart, Elizabeth. Blue Gold: A Novel. 2014. (ENG., Illus.). 304p. (YA). (gr. 7-12). 21.95 (978-1-55451-635-3(8), 9781554516353) Annick Pr., Ltd. CAN. Dist: Publishers Group West (PGW).

Stewart, Jennifer J. The Twelve Days of Christmas in Arizona. Avril, Lynne, illus. 2010. (Twelve Days of Christmas in America Ser.). (ENG.). 40p. (J). (gr. k). 12.95 (978-1-4027-7036-4(7)) Sterling Publishing Co., Inc.

Stewart, Sarah. The Quiet Place, 1 vol. Small, David, illus. 2012. (ENG.). 44p. (J). (gr. k-4). 17.99 (978-0-374-32565-7(0), 9780374325657, Farrar, Straus & Giroux (BYR)) Farrar, Straus & Giroux.

Stiefvater, Maggie. Blue Lily, Lily Blue. 2015. (Raven Cycle Ser.: 3). lib. bdg. 20.85 (978-0-606-38004-1(3)) Turtleback Bks.

Stiegemeyer, Julie. Cheep! Cheep! Baicker-McKee, Carol, illus. 2006. (ENG.). 24p. (J). (gr. k-k). 9.95 (978-1-58234-682-3(8), 9781582346823, Bloomsbury USA Childrens) Bloomsbury Publishing USA.

Stilton, Geronimo. Geronimo Stilton Bk. 59: Welcome to Moldy Manor. 2014. (ENG., Illus.). 128p. (J). (gr. 2-5). pap. 7.99 (978-0-545-74613-7(2), Scholastic Paperbacks) Scholastic, Inc.

—Merry Christmas, Geronimo! Wolf, Matt, illus. 2004. (Geronimo Stilton Ser.: No. 12). 113p. (J). lib. bdg. 10.00 (978-1-4242-0281-2(7)) Fitzgerald Bks.

Stine, R. L. Planet of the Lawn Gnomes. 2012. (Goosebumps Most Wanted Ser.: 1). (ENG.). 160p. (J). (gr. 3-7). pap. 6.99 (978-0-545-41798-3(8), Scholastic Paperbacks) Scholastic, Inc.

—Terror Trips. Thompson, Jill et al, illus. 2007. (Goosebumps Graphix Ser.: 2). (ENG.). 144p. (J). (gr. 3-7). pap. 9.99 (978-0-439-85780-2(5), Graphix) Scholastic, Inc.

—Who's Your Mummy? 2009. (Goosebumps HorrorLand Ser.: 6). lib. bdg. 17.20 (978-0-606-05328-0(X), Turtleback) Turtleback Bks.

Stinson, Kathy. A Pocket Can Have a Treasure in It. Betteridge, Deirdre, illus. 2008. (ENG.). 32p. (J). (gr. -1-k). 18.95 (978-1-55451-126-6(7), 9781554511266); pap. 6.95 (978-1-55451-125-9(9), 9781554511259) Annick Pr., Ltd. CAN. Dist: Publishers Group West (PGW).

—Red Is Best. Lewis, Robin Baird, illus. 2006. (ENG.). 32p. (J). (gr. -1-1). 7th ed. 19.95 (978-1-55451-052-8(X), 9781554510528) 9th anniv. ed. pap. 6.95 (978-1-55451-051-1(1), 9781554510511) Annick Pr., Ltd. CAN. Dist: Publishers Group West (PGW).

Stolberg, Tina. Little Shrew Caboose. O'Neill, Philomena, illus. 2009. (ENG.). 32p. (J). (gr. k-2). 16.95 (978-0-9792035-7-2(0)) Pleasant St. Pr.

Stone Arch Books Staff. Cinderella: The Graphic Novel, 1 vol. Timmins, Jeffrey Stewart, illus. 2008. (Graphic Spin Ser.). (ENG.). 40p. (gr. 1-3). pap. 5.95 (978-1-4342-0860-6(5), Graphic Revolve) Stone Arch Bks.

Stone, Judith. Billie the Buffalo Goes to Great Sand Dunes National Park. 2009. 24p. pap. 15.95 (978-1-4490-1495-7(X)) AuthorHouse.

Stone, Phoebe. Paris for Two. 2016. (ENG.). 272p. (J). (gr. 3-7). 16.99 (978-0-545-44362-3(8), Levine, Arthur A. Bks.) Scholastic, Inc.

—The Romeo & Juliet Code. 2012. (ENG.). 320p. (J). (gr. 3-7). pap. 7.99 (978-0-545-21827-6(6), Levine, Arthur A. Bks.) Scholastic, Inc.

—Romeo Blue. 2015. (ENG.). 352p. (J). (gr. 3-7). pap. 7.99 (978-0-545-44361-6(X), Levine, Arthur A. Bks.) Scholastic, Inc.

Stork, Francisco X. The Memory of Light. 2016. (Arthur a Levine Novel Bks.). (ENG.). 336p. (YA). (gr. 7). 17.99 (978-0-545-47432-0(9)) Scholastic, Inc.

Stout, Shawn K. Ballerina Weather Girl. Martini, Angela, illus. 2013. (Not-So-Ordinary Girl Ser.: 1). (ENG.). 192p. (J). (gr. 1-5). pap. 5.99 (978-1-4424-7401-7(7), Aladdin) Simon & Schuster Children's Publishing.

—Ballerina Weather Girl. Martini, Angela, illus. 2013. (Not-So-Ordinary Girl Ser.: 1). (ENG.). 192p. (J). (gr. 1-5). 15.99 (978-1-4424-7402-4(5), Simon & Schuster/Paula Wiseman Bks.) Simon & Schuster/Paula Wiseman Bks.

—Penelope Crumb. 2013. (Penelope Crumb Ser.: 1). (ENG.). 240p. (J). (gr. 2-5). pap. 5.99 (978-0-14-242478-0(1), Puffin Books) Penguin Young Readers Group.

Stover, Jo Ann. If Everybody Did. 2014. 19.00 (978-1-63419-708-3(9)) Perfection Learning Corp.

The Strange & Beautiful Sorrows of Ava Lavender. 2014. 320p. (J). (gr. 9). E-Book 8.99 (978-0-7636-7034-4(0)) Candlewick Pr.

Strasnick, Lauren. Her & Me & You. 2010. (ENG.). 208p. (YA). (gr. 9-18). 16.99 (978-1-4169-8266-1(3), Simon Pulse) Simon Pulse.

Strasser, Todd. Fallout. (ENG.). 272p. (J). (gr. 5). 2015. pap. 6.99 (978-0-7636-7676-6(4)) 2013. 16.99 (978-0-7636-5534-1(1)) Candlewick Pr.

—For Money & Love. 2007. (Mob Princess Ser.: 1). (ENG.). 208p. (YA). (gr. 9-18). pap. 10.99 (978-1-4169-3533-9(9), Simon Pulse) Simon Pulse.

—Stolen Kisses, Secrets, & Lies. 2007. (Mob Princess Ser.: 2). (ENG., Illus.). 224p. (YA). (gr. 9-12). pap. 10.99 (978-1-4169-3541-4(X), Simon Pulse) Simon Pulse.

Stravinskas, Janice. Pam the Dog: A Hawaiian Adventure. 2009. 32p. pap. 13.00 (978-1-60860-692-4(9), Eloquent Bks.) Strategic Book Publishing & Rights Agency (SBPRA).

Stringam, Jean. How Not to Cry in Public. 2013. 390p. pap. 16.99 (978-0-9855540-1-9(0)) Dollison Road Bks.

Stuart, Wrigley. Who'd Have Thunk It? 2014. (Amazing World of Gumball Ser.). (ENG., Illus.). 208p. (J). (gr. 3-7). pap. 9.99 (978-0-8431-8106-7(0), Price Stern Sloan) Penguin Young Readers Group.

Stuber, Barbara. Crossing the Tracks. (ENG.). 272p. (YA). (gr. 7). 2011. pap. 8.99 (978-1-4169-9704-7(0)) 2010. 16.99 (978-1-4169-9703-0(2)) McElderry, Margaret K. Bks. (McElderry, Margaret K. Bks.).

Students of Galileo Academy of Science and Technology Staff. Home Wasn't Built in a Day: Constructing the Stories of Our Families. 2006. (ENG.). 279p. (J). (gr. 9-18). per. 16.00 (978-0-9770844-7-0(7)) 826 Valencia.

Sturgis, Brenda Reeves. Still a Family. Lee, Jo-Shin, illus. 2017. (ENG.). 32p. (J). (gr. -1-3). 16.99 (978-0-8075-7707-3(3)) Whitman, Albert & Co.

Sturman, Jennifer. And Then Everything Unraveled. 2010. (ENG.). 256p. (J). (gr. 7). 8.99 (978-0-545-08723-0(6)) Scholastic, Inc.

Style Guide, Style, illus. Lovely, Love My Family. 2011. (Yo Gabba Gabba! Ser.). (ENG.). 14p. (J). (gr. -1-1). bds. 5.99 (978-1-4424-2134-9(7), Simon Spotlight) Simon Spotlight.

Sue. The Whinermans. 2010. 72p. (gr. 1-2). pap. 8.95 (978-1-4502-4998-0(1)) iUniverse, Inc.

Sullivan, Maureen. Cabbages & Queens. Ferrando, Carol, illus. 2010. 57p. (J). pap. (978-0-9820381-3-0(5)) MoJo InkWorks.

Sullivan-Ringe, Laurie. Noise in the Night. Matiuzzo, Nick, illus. 2008. 37p. pap. 24.95 (978-1-60672-476-7(2)) America Star Bks.

Sullivan, Sarah. All That's Missing. 2013. (ENG.). 368p. (J). (gr. 3-7). 16.99 (978-0-7636-6102-1(3)) Candlewick Pr.

—Dear Baby: Letters from Your Big Brother. Meisel, Paul, illus. 2005. (ENG.). 40p. (J). (gr. k-3). 14.99 (978-0-7636-2126-1(9)) Candlewick Pr.

Sullivan, Tara. The Bitter Side of Sweet. 2017. lib. bdg. 22.10 **(978-0-606-39795-7(7))** Turtleback Bks.

Summer of Dreaming. 2010. (Illus.). 157p. (YA). pap. (978-1-936021-22-2(6), Banana Oil Bks.) Cyberwizard Productions.

Sumner Johnson, Janet. The Last Great Adventure of the PB & J Society. 2016. (Middle-Grade Novels Ser.). (ENG.). 256p. (gr. 4-7). lib. bdg. 26.65 (978-1-4965-2695-3(3)) Stone Arch Bks.

Sundance/Newbridge LLC Staff. The Lost Jewels of Nafouti. 2005. (Choose Your Own Adventure Ser.). (gr. 4-8). pap. 5.50 (978-0-7608-9691-4(7)) Sundance/Newbridge Educational Publishing.

Sundberg, Angela M., et al. The Pottamus Family & the Unhappy Pottamus. Sundberg, Angela M. et al, illus. 2007. (J). pap. 16.00 (978-0-8059-7478-2(4)) Dorrance Publishing Co., Inc.

Supplee, Kathryn. Choose Happy. 2013. 34p. pap. 11.99 (978-1-939268-05-1(2)) Pilot Communications Group, Inc.

Susanne, Gervay & Gervay, Susanne. Being Jack. Wilcox, Cathy, illus. 2016. (ENG.), 192p. (J). pap. 5.99 (978-1-61067-379-2(4)) Kane Miller.

Sutherland, Suzanne. Something Wiki. 2015. (ENG.). 160p. (J). pap. 12.99 (978-1-4597-2821-9(1)) Dundurn CAN. Dist: Ingram Publisher Services.

Sutter, Daniel R. Is a Tattoo Right for You? 2012. (ENG.). pap. (978-1-4675-1738-6(0)) Independent Pub.

Swigut, Bernadetta. First Star: Vigilja- First Star. 2006. (J). 16.99 (978-0-9790026-0-1(5)) Steinschneider, Bernadetta.

Sydor, Colleen. Timmerman Was Here. Debon, Nicolas, illus. 2009. (ENG.). 32p. (J). (gr. -1-1). 19.95 (978-0-88776-890-3(3), Tundra Bks.) Tundra Bks. CAN. Dist: Penguin Random Hse. LLC.

Sykes, Shelley & Szymanski, Lois. The Soldier in the Cellar. 2011. (Gettysburg Ghost Gang Ser.: Vol. 5). 96p. (J). pap. 7.95 (978-1-57249-299-8(6), White Mane Kids) White Mane Publishing Co., Inc.

Symington, Martha M. Emily: Dream Believe Achieve. Nolan, Amanda M., illus. 2008. 36p. pap. (978-1-897435-21-2(5)) Agio Publishing Hse.

Synoracki, Amy R. Don't They Know I'm a Kid? 2009. 20p. pap. 13.00 (978-1-4389-9462-8(1)) AuthorHouse.

Tackett, Wendy. The Jefferson Wish. 2011. 124p. (gr. 4-6). 20.95 (978-1-4620-3771-1(2)); pap. 10.95 (978-1-4620-3768-1(2)) iUniverse, Inc.

Tague, James E. The Krankel Family. 2008. 32p. pap. 21.99 (978-1-4363-7170-4(8)) Xlibris Corp.

Tanabe, Yellow. Kekkaishi, Vol. 6. Tanabe, Yellow, illus. 2006. (ENG., Illus.). 208p. pap. 9.99 (978-1-4215-0487-2(1)) Viz Media.

Tani, Branca. Sam the Cat. 2015. (Rosen REAL Readers: STEM & STEAM Collection). (ENG.). 12p. (gr. 1-2). pap. 6.33 (978-1-4994-9623-9(0), Rosen Classroom) Rosen Publishing Group, Inc., The.

Tarasova, Julia. Daniel's Travels. 2008. 48p. 21.50 (978-1-4357-1249-2(8)) Lulu Pr., Inc.

Tate, Eleanora E. A Blessing in Disguise. 2004. 192p. (J). pap. 6.95 (978-0-940975-66-8(1), Sankofa Bks.) Just Us Bks., Inc.

Taylor, Chet. Last, but Not Least. 2007. (Illus.). 20p. (J). per. 11.99 (978-0-9797574-8-8(7)) Dragonfly Publishing, Inc.

Taylor, Janet B. Into the Dim. 2016. (ENG.). 432p. (YA). (gr. 9). 17.99 (978-0-544-60200-7(5), HMH Books For Young Readers) Houghton Mifflin Harcourt Publishing Co.

—Sparks of Light. 2017. (ENG.). 448p. (YA). (gr. 9). 16.99 (978-0-544-60957-0(3), HMH Books For Young Readers) Houghton Mifflin Harcourt Publishing Co.

Taylor, Jeannie St. John & St. John Taylor, Jeannie. Out at Home: A Novel. 2004. 144p. (J). pap. 7.99 (978-0-8254-3724-3(5)) Kregel Pubns.

Taylor, Joanne. Making Room. Rankin, Peter, illus. 2004. (ENG.). 24p. (J). (gr. 1-4). 15.95 (978-0-88776-651-0(X), Tundra Bks.) Tundra Bks. CAN. Dist: Penguin Random Hse. LLC.

—There You Are. 2004. (ENG.). 208p. (J). (gr. 3-7). pap. 8.95 (978-0-88776-658-9(7), Tundra Bks.) Tundra Bks. CAN. Dist: Penguin Random Hse. LLC.

Taylor, Sydney. All-Of-a-Kind Family Uptown. 2014. (ENG.). 200p. (J). (gr. 3). pap. 12.95 (978-1-939601-17-9(7)) Ig Publishing, Inc.

Teaster, Gerald Fred. Spirit up the People: Four Days to the Cowpens. 2006. (Illus.). 236p. per. 12.95 (978-0-9744556-2-4(8)) Junior History Pr.

Teckentrup, Britta, illus. Busy Bunny Days: In the Town, on the Farm & at the Port. 2014. (ENG.). 56p. (J). (gr. -1-3). 17.99 (978-1-4521-1700-3(4)) Chronicle Bks. LLC.

Telgemeier, Raina. Ghosts. Telgemeier, Raina, illus. 2016. (ENG., Illus.). 256p. (J). (gr. 3-7). 24.99 (978-0-545-54061-2(5), Graphix) Scholastic, Inc.

TenNapel, Doug. Bad Island. 2011. (ENG.). 224p. (J). (gr. 4-7). pap. 10.99 (978-0-545-31480-0(1), Graphix) Scholastic, Inc.

Tercio, Ricardo, illus. Jack & the Beanstalk: The Graphic Novel. 2008. (Graphic Spin Ser.). (ENG.). 40p. (gr. 1-3). 25.32 (978-1-4342-0766-1(8), Graphic Revolve) Stone Arch Bks.

Terrell, Brandon. Grit & Gold. Max, Iman & Garcia, Eduardo, illus. 2016. (Time Machine Magazine Ser.). (ENG.). 128p. (gr. 3-4). lib. bdg. 22.65 (978-1-4965-2597-0(3)) Capstone Press of Coughlan Cos.

The Terrible Twos: 6 Small Books. (gr. k-3). 24.00 (978-0-7635-6244-1(0)) Rigby Education.

Terrill, Cristin. Here Lies Daniel Tate. 2017. (ENG., Illus.). 400p. (YA). (gr. 9). 17.99 **(978-1-4814-8076-5(6)**, Simon & Schuster Bks. For Young Readers) Simon & Schuster Bks. For Young Readers.

Terry, Chris L. Zero Fade. Knabb, Jacob & Vance, Leonard, eds. 2013. (ENG., Illus.). 294p. (gr. 6). pap. 12.00 (978-0-9884804-3-8(3), 1362831) Curbside Splendor Publishing.

Terry, Teri. The Book of Lies. 2017. (ENG.). 384p. (YA). (gr. 7). 17.99 **(978-0-544-90048-6(0)**, Clarion Bks.) Houghton Mifflin Harcourt Trade & Reference Pubs.

Terry, Teri. Slated. 2013. (Slated Ser.: 1). (ENG.). 368p. (YA). (gr. 7). pap. 9.99 (978-0-14-242503-9(6), Speak) Penguin Young Readers Group.

Testa, Maggie. The Power of Po. 2015. (Kung Fu Panda 8x8 Ser.). lib. bdg. 13.55 (978-0-606-38258-8(5)) Turtleback Bks.

The Man From A.N.K.L.E. Myles a Hedd. 2008. 76p. (gr. -1). pap. 8.95 (978-0-595-51515-8(0)) iUniverse, Inc.

Thiel, Annie. Chloe's New Baby Brother. Marjoribanks, Karen & Edwards, William M., illus. 2006. (Playdate Kids Ser.). 32p. (J). (gr. -1-3). 14.95 (978-1-933721-01-9(4)) Playdate Kids Publishing.

—Cosmos' Mom & Dad Are Moving Apart. Edwards, William M. & Marjoribanks, Karen, illus. 2006. (Playdate Kids Ser.). 32p. (J). (gr. -1-3). 14.95 (978-1-933721-04-0(9)) Playdate Kids Publishing.

—Dakota's Mom Goes to the Hospital. Edwards, William M. & Marjoribanks, Karen, illus. 2006. (Playdate Kids Ser.). 32p. (J). (gr. -1-3). 14.95 (978-1-933721-03-3(0)) Playdate Kids Publishing.

Thomas, Jacquelin. It's a Curl Thing. 2009. (Divine & Friends Ser.). (ENG., Illus.). 288p. pap. 18.99 (978-1-4165-9878-7(2)) Pocket Books.

Thomas, Linda. The Cats of Dogwood Lane: Daisy Finds a Home. 2009. 28p. pap. 15.00 (978-1-4389-3831-8(4)) AuthorHouse.

Thomas, Lori. The Daisy Family. 2008. 16p. pap. 24.95 (978-1-60610-274-9(5)) America Star Bks.

Thomas, Shelley Moore. Secrets of Selkie Bay. 2015. (ENG.). 208p. (J). (gr. 3-7). 15.99 (978-0-374-36749-7(3), 9780374367497, Farrar, Straus & Giroux (BYR)) Farrar, Straus & Giroux.

Thomas, Susan. Beyond the Mist: Sequel to Mist on the Window. 2012. 352p. pap. 24.34 (978-1-4772-4627-6(4)) AuthorHouse.

Thompson, Anne. Arrow Sparrow. 2009. (Illus.). 32p. pap. (978-1-84549-369-1(9), Swirl) arima publishing.

Thompson, Bill. The Legend of Gunners Cove. 2012. (ENG.). 132p. pap. 14.95 (978-1-4327-9817-8(0)) Outskirts Pr., Inc.

Thompson, Emma. Nanny Mcphee Returns, Vol. 2. 2010. (ENG., Illus.). 304p. (J). (gr. 3-6). pap. 7.99 (978-1-59990-472-6(1), 9781599904726, Bloomsbury USA Childrens) Bloomsbury Publishing USA.

Thompson Ii, Roger E. A Sister's Love: A Novel. 2007. 80p. per. 8.95 (978-0-595-44549-3(7)) iUniverse, Inc.

Thompson, J. E. The Girl from Felony Bay. 2014. (Felony Bay Mysteries Ser.: 1). (ENG.). 400p. (J). (gr. 3-7). pap. 6.99 (978-0-06-210447-2(0), Waldon Pond Pr.) HarperCollins Pubs.

Thompson, Lauren. Little Quack's Opposites. Anderson, Derek, illus. 2010. (Super Chubbies Ser.). (ENG.). 26p. (J). (gr. -1 — 1). bds. 5.99 (978-1-4169-6092-8(9), Little Simon) Little Simon.

Thompson, Lisa. Digging for Buried Treasure. Cantell, Brenda, illus. 2006. (Treasure Trackers Ser.). 80p. (J). (gr. 3-4). lib. bdg. 19.00 (978-0-7910-8872-2(3), Chelsea Hse.) Facts On File, Inc.

Thoms, Susan Collins. The Twelve Days of Christmas in Michigan. Pilutti, Deb, illus. (Twelve Days of Christmas in America Ser.). (ENG.). (J). (— 1). 2017. 22p. bds. 7.95 **(978-1-4549-2284-1(2))** 2010. 40p. 12.95 (978-1-4027-6351-9(4)) Sterling Publishing Co., Inc.

Thorp, Gloria J. & Ruotsala, Charity Aili. Anna's Hats: Anna has a hat for every Adventure. 2009. 40p. pap. 19.49 (978-1-4389-8967-9(9)) AuthorHouse.

Thorup, Bryce. Doctor Matthews' Family Christmas. Muller, Ruth, illus. 2005. (J). 18.95 (978-0-9765964-1-7(5)) Round Tower Pr.

Thrasher, Grady. Tim & Sally's Beach Adventure. Rabon, Elaine Hearn, illus. 2008. 48p. (J). (gr. -1-3). 18.95 (978-1-58818-161-9(8)) Hill Street Pr., LLC.

Tiernan, Cate. Darkest Fear. 2014. (Birthright Ser.: 1). (ENG., Illus.). 368p. (YA). (gr. 9). pap. 9.99 (978-1-4424-8245-6(1), Simon Pulse) Simon Pulse.

—Eternally Yours. 2013. (Immortal Beloved Ser.: 3). (ENG.). 464p. (YA). (gr. 7-17). pap. 10.00 (978-0-316-03595-8(5), Poppy) Little, Brown Bks. for Young Readers.

Tillit, L. B. Unchained. 2012. (Gravel Road Ser.). (YA). lib. bdg. 20.80 (978-0-606-25250-8(9), Turtleback) Turtleback Bks.

Timmins, Jeffrey Stewart, illus. Cinderella: The Graphic Novel, 1 vol. 2008. (Graphic Spin Ser.). (ENG.). 40p. (gr. 1-3). 25.32 (978-1-4342-0764-7(1), Graphic Revolve) Stone Arch Bks.

Todd, Ilima. Remake. 2014. (Remake Ser.: 1). (ENG.). 304p. (YA). (gr. 7). 17.99 (978-1-60907-924-6(8), Shadow Mountain) Shadow Mountain Publishing.

Tomblin, Marian Strong. The Mystery at Hotel Ormond 2004. (Illus.). 142p. (J). per. 9.95 (978-0-9766620-0-6(0)) Avery Goode-Reid Pubs.

—Where's Capone's Cash? 2005. (Illus.). 232p. (J). per. 9.95 (978-0-9766620-1-3(9)) Avery Goode-Reid Pubs.

Toombs, Tom. The Mysterious Money Tree: Little Tommy Learns a Lesson in Giving. Smith, Abby, illus. 2012. 28p. (J). pap. 12.95 (978-1-61314-033-8(9), Innovo Pr.) Innovo Publishing, LLC.

Townsend, Daniel. Trumpet. 2008. 24p. pap. 24.95 (978-1-4241-9387-5(7)) America Star Bks.

Townsend, Marjorie. Wee's Moving Day. 2008. 24p. pap. 14.95 (978-1-4327-2828-1(8)) Outskirts Pr., Inc.

Toybox Innovations, creator. Meet the Robinson's. 2007. (Disney's Read Along Ser.). (ENG.). 24p. (J). (gr. -1-3). pap. (978-0-7634-2187-8(1)) Walt Disney Records.

Toz, Karen Pokras. Nate Rocks the World. 2nd ed. 2011. (ENG.). (J). pap. 7.99 (978-0-9848608-0-7(0)) Grand Daisy Pr.

Tracy, Roseann. Whose Toes Are Those? 2008. 24p. pap. 12.99 (978-1-4343-9291-6(0)) AuthorHouse.

Trail, George. Moby & Family. 2009. 103p. pap. 20.95 (978-0-9559927-0-4(2)) Trail, George GBR. Dist: Lulu Pr., Inc.

Travers, Georgia. The Wily Woodchucks. Gag, Flavia, illus. 2009. (Fesler-Lampert Minnesota Heritage Ser.). (ENG.). 32p. 14.95 (978-0-8166-6548-8(6)) Univ. of Minnesota Pr.

Treadway, Clifton. Benny & Bugsy. 2013. 36p. pap. 15.95 (978-1-4624-0492-6(8), Inspiring Voices) Author Solutions, Inc.

Trees, Annie Mae. The Old Apartment Building: A Tale from the Trees. 2012. 24p. 24.95 (978-1-4626-6093-3(2)) America Star Bks.

Tregay, Sarah. Love & Leftovers. 2014. (ENG.). 464p. (YA). (gr. 8). pap. 9.99 (978-0-06-202360-5(8), Tegen, Katherine Bks) HarperCollins Pubs.

Treis, Connie. Bartrob. 2003. 44p. per. 12.95 (978-1-932344-52-3(7)) Thornton Publishing, Inc.

Tremblay, Amanda. The Tornado Trial. 2010. 65p. pap. 12.00 (978-0-557-14051-0(X)) Lulu Pr., Inc.

Trice, Linda. Kenya's Song. Johnson, Pamela, illus. 2013. (ENG.). 32p. (J). (gr. -1-3). pap. 7.95 (978-1-57091-847-6(3)); lib. bdg. 17.95 (978-1-57091-846-9(5)) Charlesbridge Publishing, Inc.

Tricking Tracy: 6 Small Books. (gr. k-3). 24.00 (978-0-7635-6245-8(9)) Rigby Education.

Trigg, Roberta. Haworth Idyll: A Fantasy. Dashiell, Margaret, illus. 2012. 88p. 38.95 (978-1-258-23556-7(0)); pap. 23.95 (978-1-258-24510-8(8)) Literary Licensing, LLC.

Trilling, Richard J. Still More Stories of Stephanie & Friends: Volume 3 in the Stephanie Series. 2011. 72p. pap. 21.00 (978-1-61204-546-7(4), Strategic Bk. Publishing) Strategic Book Publishing & Rights Agency (SBPRA).

Trotter, Deborah W. A Summer's Trade/Shiigo Na'iini' Toddy, Irving, illus. 2007. (ENG & NAV.). 32p. (J). (gr. -1-3). 17.95 (978-1-893354-71-5(7)) Salina Bookshelf Inc.

Troughton, Ruth. The Invisible Ones. 2003. 88p. pap. 9.95 (978-0-595-29592-0(4)) iUniverse, Inc.

Trout, Holly Christian. The Firefly Who Lost Her Way. 2013. 24p. pap. 24.95 (978-1-62709-594-5(2)) America Star Bks.

Tsahiridis, Van. Peree' & the Magic Fish: Fairy Tale from Pontos. 2010. 64p. pap. 10.16 (978-1-4269-2335-7(X)) Trafford Publishing.

Tubb, Kristin O'Donnell. Selling Hope. 2010. (ENG.). 224p. (YA). (gr. 5-9). 29.99 (978-0-312-61122-4(6), 9780312611224) Feiwel & Friends.

Tulloch, S. A. The Night Prayers. 2008. 40p. 18.95 (978-1-4357-0962-1(4)) Lulu Pr., Inc.

Tunis, John Roberts. Keystone Kids. 2006. (Odyssey/Harcourt Young Classic Ser.). 239p. (J). (gr. 3). 13.65 (978-0-7569-7102-1(0)) Perfection Learning Corp.

Turner, Brenda. Cimarron Sunrise. 2011. 162p. pap. 12.99 (978-0-88144-265-6(8)) Yorkshire Publishing Group.

—Cimarron Sunrise: Teacher's Guide. 2011. 44p. pap. 8.99 (978-1-936750-49-8(X)) Yorkshire Publishing Group.

Turner, Daniel. Cinnamon the Adventurous Guinea Pig Goes to Devil's Island. Skinner, Gayle, illus. 2013. (ENG.). 48p. (J). pap. 10.95 (978-1-4787-1753-9(X)) Outskirts Pr., Inc.

Turnquist, Myrtle Moose. How Do Dandelions Grow. 2011. 48p. pap. 20.50 (978-1-4634-3776-3(5)) AuthorHouse.

Ungerer, Tomi. Christmas Eve at the Mellops' 2011. (ENG., Illus.). 32p. (gr. -1-2). 12.95 (978-0-7148-6250-7(9)) Phaidon Pr., Inc.

—The Mellops Strike Oil. 2011. (ENG., Illus.). 32p. (gr. -1-2). 12.95 (978-0-7148-6249-1(5)) Phaidon Pr., Inc.

Unknown & Grosset and Dunlap Staff, (AU). Fun with Our Family. 2004. (Dick & Jane Ser.). (ENG., Illus.). 144p. (J). (gr. -1-1). 8.99 (978-0-448-43568-8(3), Grosset & Dunlap) Penguin Young Readers Group.

Unrau, Adela. A Big Change, 1 vol. Friesen, Anni, illus. 2010. 16p. pap. 24.95 (978-1-4489-7672-0(3)) PublishAmerica, Inc.

Upham, Linda. Divided Loyalties. Littlejohn, Anna, illus. 2007. 188p. per. (978-0-7552-0302-4(X)) Authors OnLine, Ltd.

Urban, Linda. The Center of Everything. (ENG.). 208p. (J). (gr. 5-7). 2015. pap. 7.99 (978-0-544-34069-5(8), HMH Books For Young Readers) 2013. 15.99 (978-0-547-76348-4(4)) Houghton Mifflin Harcourt Publishing Co.

—Little Red Henry. Valentine, Madeline, illus. 2015. (ENG.). 40p. (J). (gr. -1-3). 16.99 (978-0-7636-6176-2(7)) Candlewick Pr.

Urbanovic, Jackie. Ducks in a Row. Urbanovic, Jackie & Mathieu, Joe, illus. 2011. (I Can Read Level 1 Ser.). (ENG.). 32p. (J). (gr. k-3). 16.99 (978-0-06-186438-4(2)); pap. 3.99 (978-0-06-186437-7(4)) HarperCollins Pubs.

Ure, Jean. Family Fan Club. Donnelly, Karen, illus. 2011. (ENG.). 160p. (J). (gr. 4-7). pap. 7.99 (978-0-00-717237-5(0), HarperCollins Children's Bks.) HarperCollins Pubs. Ltd. GBR. Dist: HarperCollins Pubs.

Vail, Rachel. Kiss Me Again. 2013. (If We Kiss Ser.: 2). (ENG.). 272p. (YA). (gr. 8). pap. 9.99 (978-0-06-194719-3(9), HarperTeen) HarperCollins Pubs.

Vail, Rochelle Kelly. Critters: A Dog's Tale. 2007. 140p. per. 11.95 (978-1-4327-0826-9(0)) Outskirts Pr., Inc.

Valentine, Jenny. Broken Soup. 2009. 216p. (YA). 17.89 (978-0-06-085072-2(8), HarperTeen) HarperCollins Pubs.

Vallejo-Nagera, Alejandra. Los Bigotes de Chocolate. 2003.Tr. of Chocolate Mustache. (SPA., Illus.). 27p. (J). (gr. k-1). 8.95 (978-968-19-1020-4(6)) Santillana USA Publishing Co., Inc.

—Cuanto me Quieren! Guerrero, Andres, illus. 2003. (SPA.). 23p. (J). (gr. k-1). 8.95 (978-84-204-4951-7(2)) Santillana USA Publishing Co., Inc.

Van Dyne, Edith. Aunt Jane's Nieces. l.t. ed. 2007. (ENG.). 170p. pap. 19.99 (978-1-4264-3951-3(2)); 462p. pap. 30.99 (978-1-4264-4009-0(X)) Creative Media Partners, LLC.

—Aunt Jane's Nieces Abroad. l.t. ed. 2007. (ENG.). 204p. pap. 22.99 (978-1-4346-0259-6(1)) Creative Media Partners, LLC.

—Aunt Jane's Nieces at Millville. l.t. ed. 2006. 158p. pap. 19.99 (978-1-4264-4058-8(8)); 172p. pap. 22.99 (978-1-4264-4117-2(7)) Creative Media Partners, LLC.

—Aunt Jane's Nieces at Work. 2005. 27.95 (978-1-4218-1423-0(4)); 204p. pap. 12.95 (978-1-4218-1523-7(0)) 1st World Publishing, Inc. (1st World Library - Literary Society).

—Aunt Jane's Nieces in Society. 2007. (ENG.). 144p. pap. 18.99 (978-1-4264-4161-5(4)); 156p. pap. 21.99 (978-1-4264-4202-5(5)) Creative Media Partners, LLC.

—Aunt Jane's Nieces Out West. 2007. (ENG.). 180p. pap. 21.99 (978-1-4264-4188-2(6)); 164p. pap. 19.99 (978-1-4264-4145-5(2)) Creative Media Partners, LLC.

van Genechten, Guido. Con los Abuelos. 2003. (SPA.). 32p. (J). (gr. k-1). 19.99 (978-84-261-3268-0(5)) Juventud, Editorial ESP. Dist: Lectorum Pubns., Inc.

Van Leeuwen, Jean. Amanda Pig & the Awful, Scary Monster. Schweninger, Ann, illus. 2004. (Oliver & Amanda Ser.). (ENG.). 48p. (J). (gr. 1-3). mass mkt. 3.99 (978-0-14-240203-0(6), Penguin Young Readers) Penguin Young Readers Group.

Van, Muon. In a Village by the Sea. Chu, April, illus. 2015. (ENG.). 32p. (J). (gr. -1-5). 16.95 (978-1-939547-15-6(6)) Creston Bks.

Van Vleet, Carmella. Eliza Bing Is (Not) a Big, Fat Quitter. Donnelly, Karen, illus. 2014. (ENG.). 176p. (J). (gr. 2-6). 16.95 (978-0-8234-2944-8(X)) Holiday Hse., Inc.

Vande Velde, Vivian. 23 Minutes. 2016. (ENG.). 176p. (J). (gr. 6-10). 16.95 (978-1-62979-441-9(4)) Boyds Mills Pr.

Vander Zee, Ruth & Sneider, Marian. Eli Remembers. Farnsworth, Bill, illus. 2007. (ENG.). 32p. (J). (gr. -1-3). 18.00 (978-0-8028-5309-7(9), Eerdmans Bks For Young Readers) Eerdmans, William B. Publishing Co.

Vasiliu, Mircea. A Day at the Beach. 2007. (Illus.). 36p. (J). 7.95 (978-1-59091-068-9(0)) Eastern National.

Vasquez, Paula. When I Grow Up, 1 vol. 2017. (ENG., Illus.). 40p. (J). 14.99 (978-1-4236-4689-1(4)) Gibbs Smith, Publisher.

Vasylenko, Veronica. Jingle Bells. Tiger Tales Staff, ed. 2011. (ENG., Illus.). 20p. bds. 8.95 (978-1-58925-869-3(X)) Tiger Tales.

Vaught, Susan. Things Too Huge to Fix by Saying Sorry. 2016. (ENG., Illus.). 352p. (J). (gr. 5-9). 16.99 (978-1-4814-2279-6(0), Simon & Schuster Bks. For Young Readers) Simon & Schuster Bks. For Young Readers.

—Things Too Huge to Fix by Saying Sorry. 2017. (ENG.). 368p. (J). (gr. 5-9). pap. 7.99 **(978-1-4814-2280-2(4)**, Simon & Schuster/Paula Wiseman Bks.) Simon & Schuster/Paula Wiseman Bks.

Veneziano, Chuckie. My Time on Nantucket. 2005. (Illus.). 56p. (J). lib. bdg. 17.95 (978-0-9755078-0-3(X)) Sweet Punkin Pr.

Venkatraman, Padma. Climbing the Stairs. 2010. (ENG., Illus.). 272p. (YA). (gr. 7-18). 9.99 (978-0-14-241490-3(5), Speak) Penguin Young Readers Group.

Vernon, Ursula. Revenge of the Horned Bunnies, No. 6. 6th ed. 2012. (Dragonbreath Ser.: 6). (ENG.). 208p. (J). (gr. 3-7). 12.99 (978-0-8037-3677-1(0), Dial Bks) Penguin Young Readers Group.

The Very Noisy Family: Lap Book. (Pebble Soup Explorations Ser.). 16p. (gr. -1-18). 21.00 (978-0-7578-2109-7(X)) Rigby Education.

The Very Noisy Family: Small Book. (Pebble Soup Explorations Ser.). 16p. (gr. -1-18). 5.00 (978-0-7578-2110-3(3)) Rigby Education.

Vescio & LohnRiver, Jenna. Rainbow Journey Screen Play (with Pictures) 2005. 65p. pap. 20.00 (978-1-4116-3288-2(5)) Lulu Pr., Inc.

Viau, Nancy. Storm Song. Gynux, illus. 2013. 24p. pap. 12.99 (978-1-4778-6646-7(9)) Amazon Publishing.

Viau, Nancy & Bolinao, Mela. Storm Song, 0 vols. Gynux, illus. 2013. (ENG.). 24p. (J). (gr. k-3). 12.99 (978-1-4778-1646-2(1), 9781477816462, Amazon Children's Publishing) Amazon Publishing.

Vickers, Elaine. Paper Chains. Not, Sara, illus. 2017. 304p. (J). (gr. 3-7). 16.99 **(978-0-06-241434-2(8))** HarperCollins Pubs.

Victoria & the Baby Tree. 2005. pap. 14.95 (978-1-59526-525-8(2)) Aeon Publishing Inc.

Viky Toma Unas Vacaciones Divetidas. 2003. (SPA.). 62p. (J). (gr. -1-1). (978-968-5308-80-9(2), Silver Dolphin en Español) Advanced Marketing, S. de R. L. de C. V.

Villines, Carol. Clean Your Room. Villines, Leo, illus. 2008. 20p. pap. 24.95 (978-1-60441-166-9(X)) America Star Bks.

Vinsh, Aara J. Ben, the Miracle Horse, 1 vol. 2010. 193p. pap. 24.95 (978-1-4489-7591-4(3)) America Star Bks.

Violo, Linda. Don't Talka Me! 2011. 24p. (gr. -1). pap. 13.95 (978-1-4567-6641-2(4)) AuthorHouse.

Vision, David & Vision, Mutiya Sahar. Missing You. Alcantara, Ignacio, illus. 2009. 32p. 17.00 (978-0-9659538-6-3(6)) Von Curtis Publishing.

Viswanath, Shobha. An Elephant in My Backyard. Jawa, Sadhvi, illus. 2013. (ENG.). 28p. (J). (gr. -1). 11.95 (978-81-8190-240-5(8)) Karadi Tales Co. Pvt, Ltd. IND. Dist: Consortium Bk. Sales & Distribution.

Vitello, Suzy. The Moment Before. 2014. (ENG.). 216p. pap. 12.99 (978-1-62681-167-6(9)) Diversion Publishing Corp.

Vivat, Booki. Frazzled: Everyday Disasters & Impending Doom. Vivat, Booki, illus. 2016. (Illus.). 240p. (J). (gr. 3-7). 12.99 (978-0-06-239879-6(2)) HarperCollins Pubs.

Vogel, Mark A. This Fun Family Has Fun with Numbers. 2012. 28p. pap. 24.95 (978-1-4626-7085-7(7)) America Star Bks.

Voigt, Cynthia. Dicey's Song. 2012. (Tillerman Cycle Ser.: 2). (ENG., Illus.). 256p. (YA). (gr. 7). 19.99 (978-1-4424-5060-8(6)); pap. 9.99 (978-1-4424-2879-9(1)) Simon & Schuster Children's Publishing. (Atheneum Bks. for Young Readers).

—Dicey's Song. 2012. (Tillerman Ser.: 2). lib. bdg. 20.85 (978-0-606-25260-7(6), Turtleback) Turtleback Bks.

Voiles, Alison. My Family Forest. Mikle, Toby, illus. 2010. 28p. pap. 13.99 (978-1-4389-1682-8(5)) AuthorHouse.

Volp, Denise. Gregory the Greedy Duck. 2013. 32p. pap. 23.35 (978-1-4669-3216-6(3)) Trafford Publishing.

Volponi, Paul. Rooftop. 2007. 199p. 17.00 (978-0-7569-7958-4(7)) Perfection Learning Corp.

Voyager, Beatrice Nambouy. Mama Minko: A Survival Quest. 2010. (Illus.). 28p. pap. 15.49 (978-1-4490-5797-8(7)) AuthorHouse.

Vrabel, Beth. Pack of Dorks. 2014. (ENG.). 240p. (J). (gr. 2-7). 15.95 (978-1-62914-623-2(4), Sky Pony Pr.) Skyhorse Publishing Co., Inc.

Vrettos, Adrienne Maria. Skin. 2006. (ENG., Illus.). 240p. (YA). (gr. 7-12). 16.95 (978-1-4169-0655-1(X), McElderry, Margaret K. Bks.) McElderry, Margaret K. Bks.

Waddell, Martin. Owl Babies: Candlewick Storybook Animations. Benson, Patrick, illus. 2008. (Candlewick Storybook Animations Ser.). (ENG.). 32p. (J). (gr. k-k). 14.99 (978-0-7636-3538-1(3)) Candlewick Pr.

Waggener, Anna. Grim. 2012. (ENG.). 320p. (J). (gr. 7-7). 17.99 (978-0-545-38480-3(X), Scholastic Pr.) Scholastic, Inc.

Waggoner, Sandra. Son of an Honest Man. 2013. 136p. (J). pap. 10.95 (978-0-9890667-2-3(X)) Sable Creek Pr. LLC.

Wagler, Elizabeth. Sojourn in Africa. 2003. (Travels with Aunt Laura Ser.: Vol. 1). (Illus.). v, 256p. (J). (978-0-87813-607-0(X)) Christian Light Pubns., Inc.

Wagner, Laura Rose. Hold Tight, Don't Let Go. 2015. (ENG.). 272p. (YA). (gr. 9-17). 17.95 (978-1-4197-1204-3(7), Amulet Bks.) Abrams, Inc.

Wagner, Lloyd S. Ghosts at Gettysburg: An Oliver Family Adventure. 2007. 144p. 21.95 (978-0-595-70995-3(8)); per. 11.95 (978-0-595-46877-5(2)) iUniverse, Inc.

Wait for Me. 2007. 169p. (gr. 4-7). 18.00 (978-0-7569-7959-1(5)) Perfection Learning Corp.

Wakefield, Nelida. Little Flathead & the Black Pearl. Smith, Nathan, illus. 2009. 36p. pap. 12.99 (978-1-59858-828-6(1)) Dog Ear Publishing, LLC.

Walker, Landry. Secrets & Lies. Takara, Marcio, illus. 2010. (Incredibles Ser.). 112p. (J). (gr. 3-8). pap. 9.99 (978-1-60886-583-3(5)) Boom! Studios.

Walker, Melzina. Little Melvin's Blue Coat. 2007. (Illus.). 32p. (J). pap. 8.00 (978-0-8059-7389-1(3)) Dorrance Publishing Co., Inc.

Walker-Renner, Christa. Santa's Magic. 2009. 20p. pap. 11.00 (978-1-4389-8206-9(2)) AuthorHouse.

Walker, Susan Eileen. I Know the Quigglebush Heroes. 2008. 53p. pap. 16.95 (978-1-60672-587-0(4)) America Star Bks.

—Secret of the Dance. 2006. (ENG.). 232p. (J). (gr. -1-12). per. 15.00 (978-0-9766805-4-3(8)) Keene Publishing.

Wallace, Karen. Wendy. 2005. 307p. (gr. 7-12). 17.00 (978-0-7569-5658-5(7)) Perfection Learning Corp.

—Wendy. 2005. (ENG.). 320p. (YA). (gr. 6). reprint ed. pap. 14.99 (978-1-4169-0314-7(3), Simon & Schuster Bks. For Young Readers) Simon & Schuster Bks. For Young Readers.

Wallace, Michael. You, Mommy & Me. 2006. 22p. spiral bd. 8.50 (978-1-4116-9761-4(8)) Lulu Pr., Inc.

Wallace, Rich. Takedown, No. 8. 2007. (Winning Season Ser.: Bk. 8). (ENG.). 128p. (J). (gr. 3-7). 5.99 (978-0-14-240919-0(7), Puffin Books) Penguin Young Readers Group.

Wallace, Sally. A Big Secret: A Nativity Story. 2009. 40p. pap. 16.99 (978-1-4490-1660-9(X)) AuthorHouse.

Walsh, Alice. Uncle Farley's False Teeth. 2004. (Illus.). (J). (gr. k-3). spiral bd. (978-0-616-01807-1(X)) Canadian National Institute for the Blind/Institut National Canadien pour les Aveugles.

Walsh, Ann. The Ghost of Soda Creek. 2009. (ENG.). 176p. (J). pap. 11.99 (978-1-55002-830-0(8), Sandcastle Bks.) Dundurn CAN. Dist: Ingram Publisher Services.

Walsh, Laurence & Walsh, Suella. In the Middle of the Night. 2006. (J). pap. (978-0-88092-473-3(X)) Royal Fireworks Publishing Co.

Walsh, Sheila. Gigi, God's Little Princess, 1 vol. Johnson, Meredith, illus. 2005. (Gigi, God's Little Princess Ser.: 1). (ENG.). 32p. 14.99 (978-1-4003-0529-2(2)) Nelson, Thomas Inc.

Walton, Leslye. The Strange & Beautiful Sorrows of Ava Lavender. (ENG.). 320p. (YA). (gr. 9). 2015. pap. 8.99 (978-0-7636-8027-5(3)) 2014. 17.99 (978-0-7636-6566-1(5)) Candlewick Pr.

—The Strange & Beautiful Sorrows of Ava Lavender. 2015. lib. bdg. 19.65 (978-0-606-36879-7(5)) Turtleback Bks.

Wang, Adria. My World: My Family. Nicholls, Paul, illus. 2005. (My World Bks.). 10p. (J). 4.95 (978-1-58117-252-2(4), Intervisual/Piggy Toes) Bendon, Inc.

Ward, Matthew. The Fantastic Family Whipple. 2014. (Fantastic Family Whipple Ser.: 1). (ENG.). 400p. (J). (gr. 3-7). pap. 8.99 (978-1-59514-690-8(3), Razorbill) Penguin Young Readers Group.

—War of the World Records. 2nd ed. 2015. (Fantastic Family Whipple Ser.: 2). (ENG.). 384p. (J). (gr. 3-7). pap. 8.99 (978-1-59514-692-2(X), Razorbill) Penguin Young Readers Group.

Ward, Rachel. The Drowning. 2014. (ENG.). 272p. (J). (gr. 9). 17.99 (978-0-545-62771-9(0), Chicken Hse., The) Scholastic, Inc.

Wargin, Kathy-jo. Mitt & Minn at the Wisconsin Cheese Jamboree. Holman, Karen Busch, illus. 2007. (Mitt Midwest Ser.: 3). (ENG.). 144p. (J). (gr. k-7). 14.95 (978-1-58726-305-7(X), Mitten Pr.) Ann Arbor Editions LLC.

Warner, Gertrude Chandler. Snowbound Mystery. Dubisch, Mike, illus. 2009. (Boxcar Children Graphic Novels Ser.: 7). (ENG.). 32p. (J). (gr. 1-5). pap. 6.99 (978-0-8075-7515-4(1)) Whitman, Albert & Co.

—The Yellow House Mystery, No. 3. Dubisch, Mike, illus. 2009. (Boxcar Children Graphic Novels Ser.). (ENG.). 32p. (J). (gr. 2-5). 6.99 (978-0-8075-2869-3(2)) Whitman, Albert & Co.

Warner, Jodi. Shia's Tail. 2012. 24p. pap. 10.99 (978-1-4624-0182-6(1), Inspiring Voices) Author Solutions, Inc.

Warner, Sally. EllRay Jakes Is a Rock Star, 2 vols. Harper, Jamie, illus. 2012. (EllRay Jakes Ser.: 2). (ENG.). 128p. (J). (gr. 1-3). 5.99 (978-0-14-241989-2(3), Puffin Books) Penguin Young Readers Group.

—EllRay Jakes Is Not a Chicken, 1 vol. Harper, Jamie, illus. 2012. (EllRay Jakes Ser.: 1). (ENG.). 128p. (J). (gr. 1-3). 5.99 (978-0-14-241988-5(5), Puffin Books) Penguin Young Readers Group.

—Ellray Jakes Rocks the Holidays! 2014. (EllRay Jakes Ser.: 7). lib. bdg. 16.00 (978-0-606-36188-0(X)) Turtleback Bks.

—Ellray Jakes Stands Tall. 2016. (EllRay Jakes Ser.: 9). lib. bdg. 16.00 (978-0-606-38420-9(0)) Turtleback Bks.

—Ellray Jakes the Dragon Slayer, No. 4. Biggs, Brian, illus. 2013. (EllRay Jakes Ser.: 4). (ENG.). 144p. (J). (gr. 1-3). pap. 5.99 (978-0-14-242358-5(0), Puffin Books) Penguin Young Readers Group.

Warner, Susan & Wetherell, Elizabeth. Daisy in the Field. 2011. 272p. 29.95 (978-1-4638-9964-6(5)); pap. 16.95 (978-1-4638-0163-2(7)) Rodgers, Alan Bks.

Wasserman, Sand. The Sun's Special Blessing: Happens Only Once in 28 Years - French Flap. Koffsky, Ann, illus. 2009. 36p. 12.95 (978-1-934440-76-6(0), Pitspopany Pr.) Simcha Media Group.

—The Sun's Special Blessing: Happens Only Once in 28 Years - HC. Koffsky, Ann, illus. 2009. 36p. 17.95 (978-1-934440-92-6(2), Pitspopany Pr.) Simcha Media Group.

Waters, Graham. The Raindrops & the Wrong Cloud. 2009. (Illus.). 28p. pap. 15.49 (978-1-4490-0685-3(X)) AuthorHouse.

Watson, Jean & Bunyan, John. The Family Pilgrim's Progress: Adapted from John Bunyan's Classic. 2013. (ENG., Illus.). 128p. (J). 17.99 (978-1-84550-232-4(9), a27dc5b1-6b3c-43a6-ac3a-3756f774adec) Christian Focus Pubns. GBR. Dist: Bookmasters Distribution.

Watson, Jude. The 39 Clues # 6: En Las Profundidades. 2012. (SPA.). 208p. (J). (gr. 5-8). pap. 14.99 (978-84-08-10768-2(2)) Noguer y Caralt Editores, S. A. ESP. Dist: Lectorum Pubns., Inc.

Watts, Jeri. A Piece of Home. Yum, Hyewon, illus. 2016. (ENG.). 32p. (J). (gr. k-3). 16.99 (978-0-7636-6971-3(7)) Candlewick Pr.

Weatherly, L. A. Them. 2013. (ENG.). 80p. (YA). (gr. 6-12). pap. 6.95 (978-1-78112-185-6(0)); lib. bdg. 22.60 (978-1-78112-184-9(2)) Lerner Publishing Group.

Webb, Melissa & Webb, Lexy. Zoe the Earless Kitten: Zoe Meets the Family. 2011. 40p. pap. 21.99 (978-1-4628-8462-9(8)) Xlibris Corp.

Webb Quest, Sara. Aydil Vice & Her Disgustin' Hair Knots. 2008. 72p. pap. 7.00 (978-1-4357-5150-7(7)) Lulu Pr., Inc.

Webb, Sarah. Boy Trouble. 2011. (Ask Amy Green Ser.: 1). (ENG., Illus.). 288p. (YA). (gr. 7). 6.99 (978-0-7636-5063-6(3)) Candlewick Pr.

—Bridesmaid Blitz. 2012. (Ask Amy Green Ser.: 3). (ENG., Illus.). 320p. (YA). (gr. 7). pap. 6.99 (978-0-7636-5157-2(5)) Candlewick Pr.

—Summer Secrets. 2011. (Ask Amy Green Ser.: 2). (ENG., Illus.). 288p. (YA). (gr. 7-18). 16.99 (978-0-7636-5071-1(4)) Candlewick Pr.

Webber, Barbara. Feeling Loved: A Ted E. Bear Story. 2013. 40p. pap. 15.95 (978-1-4525-7162-1(7), Balboa Pr.) Author Solutions, Inc.

Webster, Christy. Mom, Dad & Me. Random House Disney Staff, illus. 2016. (Step into Reading Ser.). (ENG.). 24p. (J). (gr. -1-1). lib. bdg. 12.99 (978-0-7364-8238-7(5), RH/Disney) Random Hse. Children's Bks.

—Mom, Dad, & Me. Random House Disney Staff, illus. 2016. (Step into Reading Ser.). (ENG.). 24p. (J). (gr. -1-1). 4.99 (978-0-7364-3536-9(0), RH/Disney) Random Hse. Children's Bks.

Webster, Raelyn & Rasmussen, Kenneth L. My Grandma Mary. Johnson, Kimberli Anne, illus. 2013. 38p. 22.95 (978-1-940379-00-5(8)) Telling Family Tales.

Weeks, Sarah. Jumping the Scratch. 2007. (J). 1.25 (978-1-4193-8222-2(5)) Recorded Bks., Inc.

Weeks, Sophie. The Soured Earth. 2013. 156p. pap. 12.95 (978-1-62015-184-6(7), Booktrope Editions) Booktrope.

Weimer, Heidi. I Love You More Than... . 2006. (Ideals Interactive Ser.). (ENG., Illus.). 16p. (J). (gr. -1-k). bds. 12.99 (978-0-8249-6679-9(1), Ideal Pubns.) Worthy Publishing.

Weis, Michael David. Diamond & the Fosters. Avant, Matthew, illus. 2013. 64p. 21.95 (978-1-59663-635-4(1), Castle Keep Pr.) Rock, James A. & Co. Pubs.

Welch, Sheila Kelly. The Shadowed Unicorn. 2011. 192p. (gr. -1). pap. 12.95 (978-1-4502-6991-9(5)) iUniverse, Inc.

Welles, Lee. Way of Water. Coogan, Carol, illus. 2007. (Gaia Girls Ser.: 2). (ENG.). 336p. (YA). (gr. 4-7). pap. 19.95 (978-1-933609-03-4(6)) Chelsea Green Publishing.

Wells, Carolyn. Marjorie's Maytime. 2007. (ENG.). 152p. pap. 19.99 (978-1-4264-8435-3(6)) Creative Media Partners, LLC.

—Patty at Home. 2007. (ENG.). 204p. per. 12.95 (978-1-4218-3321-7(2)) 1st World Publishing, Inc.

Wells, Rosemary. Stella's Starliner. Wells, Rosemary, illus. 2014. (ENG., Illus.). 32p. (J). (gr. -1-3). 15.99 (978-0-7636-1495-9(5)) Candlewick Pr.

Wells-Sanders, Glenora. Trinny Bear & Dallas. Wells, Quierra LaQuelle, illus. 2012. 24p. pap. 11.50 (978-1-61897-763-2(6), Strategic Bk. Publishing) Strategic Book Publishing & Rights Agency (SBPRA).

Wells, Tom. Strange Seasons: Summer. 2008. 212p. 24.95 (978-0-595-50888-4(X)); pap. 14.95 (978-0-595-52016-9(2)) iUniverse, Inc.

Welshman, Kate. Anais Butt & the Hairy-Handed Gent. 2013. 164p. pap. 16.50 (978-1-61213-187-0(5)) Writer's Coffee Shop, The.

Wentz, Lorraine. Who Has Barney. 2013. 38p. pap. 10.99 (978-1-62697-124-0(2)) Salem Author Services.

Wesley, Valerie Wilson. How to Fish for Trouble. Roos, Maryn, illus. 2004. 89p. (J). lib. bdg. 15.00 (978-1-4242-0643-8(X)) Fitzgerald Bks.

Westcott, Jim. The Gift. 2014. (Red Rhino Ser.). (J). lib. bdg. 18.40 (978-0-606-36201-6(0)) Turtleback Bks.

Westerman, Robert. Alohalani Kalikimaka Auntie: Sheet Music & Lyrics. Westerman, Robert, . 2006. (Illus.). 12p. (J). 6.95 (978-0-9761992-1-2(1)) Gold Boy Music & Pubn.

Weyland, Jack. Brianna, My Brother, & the Blog. 2009. (YA). (978-1-60641-140-7(3)) Deseret Bk. Co.

Weyn, Suzanne. The Diamond Secret. 2009. (Once upon a Time Ser.). (ENG.). 240p. (YA). (gr. 7-18). mass mkt. 7.99 (978-1-4169-7530-4(6), Simon Pulse) Simon Pulse.

Whale Watch, 6 Packs. (Bookweb Ser.). 32p. (gr. 6-18). 34.00 (978-0-7578-0895-1(6)) Rigby Education.

Wharton, Laura Spanton, et al. Mystery at the Phoenix Festival. 2012. 140p. pap. 9.99 (978-0-9837148-8-0(6)) Broad Creek Pr.

What Kind of a Name Is That? 2006. (J). per. 6.49 net. (978-0-9759665-3-2(7)) Pilate, Victoria.

Wheeler, Jordan & Jackson, Dennis. Christmas at Wapos Bay, 1 vol. 2005. (From Many Peoples Ser.). (ENG.). 152p. (J). (gr. 4-7). per. 7.95 (978-1-55050-324-1(3)) Coteau Bks. CAN. Dist: Orca Bk. Pubs. USA.

Whint, Ana Lee. Espalemit. 2003. (ENG.). 112p. pap. 9.95 (978-0-595-26259-5(7), Writers Club Pr.) iUniverse, Inc.

White, Aaron D. Creek Babies. 2013. 44p. pap. 16.95 (978-1-63000-671-6(8)) America Star Bks.

White, Kiersten. The Chaos of Stars. 2013. (ENG.). 288p. (YA). pap. (978-0-06-229412-8(1), HarperTeen) HarperCollins Pubs.

White, Ruth. Belle Prater's Boy. unabr. ed. 2004. 196p. (J). (gr. 5-9). pap. 38.00 incl. audio (978-0-8072-8682-1(6), YA234SP, Listening Library) Random Hse. Audio Publishing Group.

—A Month of Sundays. 2013. (ENG.). 192p. (YA). (gr. 5-9). pap. 6.99 (978-1-250-02730-6(6), 9781250027306) Square Fish.

—The Search for Belle Prater. 2007. 169p. (J). (gr. 4-7). 14.15 (978-0-7569-7274-5(4)) Perfection Learning Corp.

Whitehouse, Elizabeth. The Bag Babies & the Secret of Civilization: A Jensen Family Story. 2004. (Illus.). 96p. (J). pap. 5.95 (978-1-933031-54-5(9)) Whitehouse Publishing.

Whiting, Sue. Portraits of Celina. 2015. (ENG.). 352p. 16.95 (978-1-63079-024-0(9)) Switch Pr.

Whitney, A. D. T. Sights & Insights: Patience Strong's Story of over the Way. Vol. 1. 2006. 356p. per. 26.99 (978-1-4255-3625-1(5)) Michigan Publishing.

—Sights & Insights: Patience Strong's Story of over the Way. Vol. 2. 2006. 344p. per. 23.99 (978-1-4255-3480-6(5)) Michigan Publishing.

Who Will Look Out for Danny? Individual Title Six-Packs. (Action Packs Ser.). 120p. (gr. 3-5). 44.00 (978-0-7635-8420-7(7)) Rigby Education.

Whos's in My Family? (Peek A Boo Pockets Ser.). 12p. (J). bds. (978-2-7643-0107-4(3)) Phidal Publishing, Inc./Editions Phidal, Inc.

Whyman, Matt. The Savages. 2014. (ENG.). 288p. (gr. 8-14). 16.99 (978-1-4683-0856-3(4), 460856) Overlook Pr., The.

Wiechman, Kathy Canon. Empty Places. 2016. (ENG., Illus.). 240p. (J). (gr. 3-7). 17.95 (978-1-62979-451-8(1), Calkins Creek) Boyds Mills Pr.

Wiesner, David, adapted by. Gonna Roll the Bones. 2004. (ENG., Illus.). 32p. (J). (gr. -1-12). 16.95 (978-1-59687-176-2(8)) IBks., Inc.

Wiggin, Kate Douglas. New Chronicles of Rebecc. 2008. 152p. (gr. 4-7). pap. 12.95 (978-1-60664-257-3(X)) Rodgers, Alan Bks.

—New Chronicles of Rebecca. 2006. 128p. pap. (978-1-84637-648-1(3)) Echo Library.

—Rebecca of Sunnybrook Farm. (J). 23.95 (978-0-8488-0854-9(1)) Amereon Ltd.

—Rebecca of Sunnybrook Farm. 2003. (Dover Children's Evergreen Classics Ser.). (ENG.). 240p. (J). (gr. 3-8). pap. 4.50 (978-0-486-42845-1(1)) Dover Pubns., Inc.

—Rebecca of Sunnybrook Farm. 2003. (Aladdin Classics Ser.). (ENG.). 368p. (J). pap. 7.99 (978-0-689-86001-0(3), Aladdin) Simon & Schuster Children's Publishing.

—Rebecca of Sunnybrook Farm. Akib, Jamel, illus. 2007. (Classic Starts(tm) Ser.). (ENG.). 160p. (J). (gr. 2-4). 6.95 (978-1-4027-3693-3(2)) Sterling Publishing Co., Inc.

—Rebecca of Sunnybrook Farm. 2004. reprint ed. pap. 19.95 (978-1-4179-9996-5(9)); pap. 1.99 (978-1-4179-9946-0(2)) Kessinger Publishing, LLC.

—A Summer in a Canyon. 2007. 140p. 24.95 (978-1-60312-626-7(0)) Aegypan.

—Susanna & Sue. 2011. 102p. 22.95 (978-1-4638-9980-6(7)); pap. 9.95 (978-1-60664-691-5(5)) Rodgers, Alan Bks.

Wiles, Deborah. Countdown. 2013. (ENG.). 400p. (J). (gr. 3-7). pap. 8.99 (978-0-545-10606-1(0), Scholastic Paperbacks) Scholastic, Inc.

Wiley, Gordon. Journey Finds Family. 2009. 68p. pap. 10.49 (978-1-4389-5265-9(1)) AuthorHouse.

Wilkins, LaTanya. The Adventures of Dedan & Dylan Jackson: The Second Day of School. 2010. 48p. pap. 13.99 (978-1-4520-5963-1(2)) AuthorHouse.

Williams, C. G., illus. The Incredibly Helpful Helper. 2008. (ENG.). 40p. (J). (gr. -1-k). 14.95 (978-0-7892-1001-2(0), Abbeville Kids) Abbeville Pr., Inc.

Williams-Garcia, Rita. Gone Crazy in Alabama. (J). (gr. 3-7). 2016. 320p. pap. 6.99 (978-0-06-221589-5(2), Amistad) 2015. (ENG., Illus.). 304p. 16.99 (978-0-06-221587-1(6)) HarperCollins Pubs.

Williams, Kethette. The Ghosts on the Hill. 2007. (ENG.). 56p. per. 16.95 (978-1-4241-6767-8(1)) America Star Bks.

Williams, Raymond. The House of Useful Things. 2012. (Illus.). 44p. pap. 13.50 (978-1-78035-396-8(0), Fastprint Publishing) Upfront Publishing Ltd. GBR. Dist: Printondemand-worldwide.com.

Williams, Suzanne Morgan. Bull Rider. 2010. (ENG.). 256p. (YA). (gr. 7). pap. 8.99 (978-1-4424-1252-1(6), McElderry, Margaret K. Bks.) McElderry, Margaret K. Bks.

Williams, Tad & Beale, Deborah. The Dragons of Ordinary Farm. Swearingen, Greg, illus. 2009. (ENG.). 416p. (J). (gr. 4-7). 16.99 (978-0-06-154345-6(4)) HarperCollins Pubs.

Williamson, Jan. A Special Day in May. 2006. (Neighborhood Readers Ser.). (ENG.). 16p. (gr. 1-3). pap. 6.50 (978-1-4042-7276-7(3), Rosen Classroom) Rosen Publishing Group, Inc., The.

Williamson, Linda. Groundhog Breakfast, Soft Petals, & a Roof That Don't Leak Too Much, 1 vol. Mollett, Irene, illus. 2009. 23p. pap. 24.95 (978-1-60749-618-2(6)) America Star Bks.

Willink, Jocko. Way of the Warrior Kid: From Wimpy to Warrior the Navy SEAL Way. Bozak, Jon, illus. 2017. (Way of the Warrior Kid Ser.: 1). (ENG.). 192p. (J). 13.99 (**978-1-250-15107-0(4)**, 9781250151070) Feiwel & Friends.

Willis, S. J. The Wishwasher. 2011. 128p. (gr. 4-6). pap. 13.32 (978-1-4567-8751-6(9)) AuthorHouse.

Wilson, Angela. My Aunt & Me. Basta, Stormie, illus. 2012. 26p. 24.95 (978-1-4626-6630-0(2)) America Star Bks.

Wilson, Anna. The Family Fiasco. 2017. (Mortifying Life of Skye Green Ser.: 2). (ENG.). 240p. (J). (gr. 4-7). 9.99 (**978-1-5098-0129-9(4)**) Pan Macmillan GBR. Dist: Independent Pubs. Group.

Wilson, Jacqueline. Best Friends. Sharratt, Nick, illus. 2009. (ENG.). 256p. (J). (gr. 4-7). pap. 8.99 (978-0-312-58144-2(0), 9780312581442) Square Fish.

Wilson, N. D. The Chestnut King. 2011. (100 Cupboards Ser.: 3). (ENG., Illus.). 512p. (J). (gr. 3-7). 8.99 (978-0-375-83886-6(4), Yearling) Random Hse. Children's Bks.

—Dandelion Fire. 2009. (100 Cupboards Ser.: 2). (ENG.). 480p. (J). (gr. 3-7). 8.99 (978-0-375-83884-2(8), Yearling) Random Hse. Children's Bks.

Winbolt-Lewis, Martin. Owliviah. Cressey, Roger, illus. 2013. 56p. (J). pap. (978-1-78222-075-6(5)) Paragon Publishing, Rothersthorpe.

Wingart, Ramona A. Where Is Brother Beaver?, 1 vol. 2010. 30p. 24.95 (978-1-4489-4773-7(1)) PublishAmerica, Inc.

Winget, Dianna Dorisi. A Smidgen of Sky. 2012. (ENG.). 208p. (J). (gr. 5-7). 16.99 (978-0-547-80798-0(8)) Houghton Mifflin Harcourt Publishing Co.

Winkler, Henry & Oliver, Lin. Dump Trucks & Dogsleds - I'm on My Way, Mom! Watson, Jesse Joshua, illus. 2009. (Hank Zipzer Ser.: 16). (ENG.). 160p. (J). (gr. 3-7). pap. 5.99 (978-0-448-44380-5(5), Grosset & Dunlap) Penguin Young Readers Group.

Winn, Christine M. & Walsh, David. Clover's Secret. Winn, Christine M., illus. 2004. (Illus.). 28p. (J). (gr. k-4). reprint ed. 15.00 (978-0-7567-7653-4(8)) DIANE Publishing Co.

Winsor, Michael & Daidoji, Yoko. Going Somewhere. 2007. (Illus.). (J). 18.00 (978-0-9799470-0-1(6)) yomitobi.

Wiseman, Eva. No One Must Know. 2004. (ENG.). 200p. (J). (gr. 5). pap. 9.95 (978-0-88776-680-0(3), Tundra Bks.) Tundra Bks. CAN. Dist: Penguin Random Hse. LLC.

Wixom, Jason Kay & Wixom, Tedi Tuttle. Cock-a-Doodle-Doo, I Love You. Lancaster, Derek, illus. 2nd ed. 2003. (Ralph Rooster Ser.: Vol. 1). 16p. (J). (gr. -1-2). 6.95 (978-1-885227-05-8(1)) TNT Bks.

Wizards of Waverly Place Insider's Guide. 2009. 128p. pap. 8.99 (978-1-4231-2473-3(1)) Disney Pr.

Wold, Justin And Janet. This Thing I Made Can Make Anything but Can't Make Friends & Family. 2013. 24p. pap. 14.93 (978-1-4669-9572-7(6)) Trafford Publishing.

Wolek, Guy, illus. Dinner with OLIVIA. 2009. (Olivia TV Tie-In Ser.). (ENG.). 24p. (J). (gr. -1-2). pap. 3.99 (978-1-4169-7187-0(4), Simon Spotlight) Simon Spotlight.

Wolf, Mária. Black Dog. 2013. 12p. pap. 15.99 (978-1-4817-0405-2(2)) AuthorHouse.

Wolff, Jan, et al. Chiquita's Children: Teaching Children about Foster Families. Dey, Lorraine, illus. 2016. (ENG.). 48p. (gr. -1-4). 9.95 (978-0-88282-516-8(X)) New Horizon Pr. Pubs., Inc.

Wood Jr, Richard L. The Stick Family. 2011. 28p. pap. 15.00 (978-1-4634-2564-7(3)) AuthorHouse.

Wood, June Rae. The Man Who Loved Clowns. 2005. 224p. (gr. 3-7). 16.00 (978-0-7569-5516-8(5)) Perfection Learning Corp.

Woods, Brenda. Blossoming Universe of Violet Diamond. 2014. (ENG.). 240p. (J). (gr. 3-7). 16.99 (978-0-399-25714-8(4), Nancy Paulsen Books) Penguin Young Readers Group.

Woods, Brenda. Zoe in Wonderland. 2017. (ENG.). 224p. (J). (gr. 3-7). 8.99 (**978-0-425-28891-7(9)**, Puffin Books) Penguin Young Readers Group.

Woods, Brenda & Airgood, Ellen. Zoe in Wonderland. 2016. (ENG.). 208p. (J). (gr. 3-7). 16.99 (978-0-399-17097-3(9), Nancy Paulsen Books) Penguin Young Readers Group.

Woodson, Jacqueline. Feathers. 2010. (ENG.). 160p. (J). (gr. 5-18). 8.99 (978-0-14-241550-4(2), Speak) Penguin Young Readers Group.

Woodson, Jacqueline. This Is the Rope: A Story from the Great Migration. Ransome, James, illus. (ENG.). 32p. (J). (gr. k-3). 2017. pap. 8.99 (**978-0-425-28894-8(3)**, Puffin Books) 2013. 16.99 (978-0-399-23986-1(3), Nancy Paulsen Books) Penguin Young Readers Group.

Woollatt, Margaret. The Twelve Days of Christmas in New Jersey. Rossi, Richard, illus. 2008. (Twelve Days of Christmas in America Ser.). (ENG.). 40p. (J). (gr. k). 12.95 (978-1-4027-3816-6(1)) Sterling Publishing Co., Inc.

Woolson, Constance Fenimore (A. K. A. Anne March). The Old Stone House. 2006. 140p. pap. (978-1-84637-478-4(2)) Echo Library.

Worley, Carla. Freedom Choice: A Book that Allows You to Consider Your Options. 2010. 76p. pap. 23.50 (978-1-60860-624-5(4), Strategic Bk. Publishing) Strategic Book Publishing & Rights Agency (SBPRA).

Wortham, Caledra. Way up High in the Sky. 2011. 40p. pap. 21.99 (978-1-4568-3931-4(4)) Xlibris Corp.

Wright, Betty Ren. Crandalls' Castle. 2005. (ENG.). 184p. (YA). (gr. 4-6). tchr. ed. 17.95 (978-0-8234-1726-1(3)) Holiday Hse., Inc.

Wright, Bud. My Momma Raised Ugly Children Not Stupid Ones: The Ruminations & Reminiscences of a Gentle Southern Man. 2008. 332p. pap. 22.95 (978-1-4327-2880-9(6)) Outskirts Pr., Inc.

Wright, Kiyah. Vacation Fun. 2011. 24p. pap. 14.95 (978-1-4634-4055-8(3)) AuthorHouse.

Wright, Pauline. Why Did My Dad Go to War? 2008. 48p. pap. 19.49 (978-1-4343-4677-3(3)) AuthorHouse.

Wyss, Johann David. The Swiss Family Robinson. 2006. (Charming Classics). 208p. (J). pap. 6.99 (978-0-06-087587-9(9), HarperFestival) HarperCollins Pubs.

—The Swiss Family Robinson. Tayal, Amit, illus. 2011. (Campfire Graphic Novels Ser.). (ENG.). 88p. (YA). (gr. 3-7). pap. 11.99 (978-93-80028-47-7(4), Campfire) Steerforth Pr.

—The Swiss Family Robinson. Akib, Jamel, illus. 2007. (Classic Starts(tm) Ser.). (ENG.). 160p. (J). (gr. 2-4). 6.95 (978-1-4027-3694-0(0)) Sterling Publishing Co., Inc.

—The Swiss Family Robinson: Or Adventures in a Desert Island. l.t. ed. 2007. (ENG.). 354p. pap. 26.99 (978-1-4264-5633-6(6)) Creative Media Partners, LLC.

Yaccarino, Dan. Zorgoochi Intergalactic Pizza: Delivery of Doom. Yaccarino, Dan, illus. 2014. (ENG., Illus.). 336p. (J). (gr. 3-7). 16.99 (978-1-250-00844-2(1), 9781250008442) Feiwel & Friends.

Yacoubou, Jeanne. I Am a Rainbow Child Coloring-Story Book. Stebakova, Elena, illus. 2005. 16p. (J). (978-0-9788737-4-5(2)) Alaafia Kids Co.

Yamasaki, Katie, illus. When the Cousins Came. 2016. (J). (978-0-8234-3457-2(5)) Holiday Hse., Inc.

Yang, Gene Luen & Pham, Thien. Level Up. 2016. (YA). lib. bdg. 20.85 (978-0-606-38563-3(0)) Turtleback Bks.

Yarrow, Peter. Day Is Done. Sweet, Melissa, illus. 2009. (ENG.). 24p. (J). (gr. k-2). 16.95 (978-1-4027-4806-6(X)) Sterling Publishing Co., Inc.

Yee, Lisa. The Kidney Hypothetical: or How to Ruin Your Life in Seven Days:Or How to Ruin Your Life in Seven Days. 2015. (ENG.). 272p. (J). (gr. 7). 17.99 (978-0-545-23094-0(2)) Scholastic, Inc.

—The Kidney Hypothetical, or, How to Ruin Your Life in Seven Days. 2016. (ENG.). 272p. (J). (gr. 7). pap. 9.99 (978-0-545-23095-7(0)) Scholastic, Inc.

Yep, Laurence. Mia, Bk. 1. England, Tamara, ed. Papp, Robert, illus. 2008. (ENG.). 136p. (gr. 3-18). pap. 6.95 (978-1-59369-409-8(1)) American Girl Publishing, Inc.

—Skunk Scout. 2009. (Journeys Ser.). (ENG.). 192p. (gr. 5-5). pap. 7.45 (978-0-547-07397-2(6)) Houghton Mifflin Harcourt Publishing Co.

Ylvisaker, Anne. The Curse of the Buttons. 2014. (ENG.). 240p. (J). (gr. 3-7). 15.99 (978-0-7636-6138-0(4)) Candlewick Pr.

—Little Klein. 2009. (ENG.). 192p. (J). (gr. 3-7). pap. 6.99 (978-0-7636-4338-6(6)) Candlewick Pr.

Yonge, Charlotte M. Little Lucy's Wonderful Globe. 2008. 152p. 36.95 (978-0-548-97272-4(9)) Kessinger Publishing, LLC.

—The Stokesley Secret. 2005. 28.95 (978-1-4218-0319-7(4), 1st World Library - Literary Society) 1st World Publishing, Inc.

—The Trial. 2005. 39.95 (978-1-55742-448-8(9)); pap. 22.95 (978-1-55742-428-0(4)) Wildside Pr., LLC.

Yoon, Salina. Stormy Night. 2016. (ENG., Illus.). 32p. (J). bds. 7.99 (978-1-68119-165-2(2), 9781681191652, Bloomsbury USA Childrens) Bloomsbury Publishing USA.

Young, Andrea. Finny & the Boy from Horse Mountain. 2013. (ENG.). 320p. (J). (gr. 6-8). 16.95 (978-1-62087-682-4(5), 620682, Sky Pony Pr.) Skyhorse Publishing Co., Inc.

Young, Jessica. Art-Rageous. Secheret, Jessica, illus. 2015. (Finley Flowers Ser.). (ENG.). 128p. (gr. 2-3). 8.95 (978-1-4795-5960-2(1), Finley Flowers) Picture Window Bks.

Young, Judy. The Lucky Star. Ellison, Chris, illus. 2008. (Tales of Young Americans Ser.). (ENG.). 32p. (J). (gr. 3-7). 17.95 (978-1-58536-348-3(0)) Sleeping Bear Pr.

Young, Karen Romano. Hundred Percent. 2016. (ENG., Illus.). 256p. (J). (gr. 3-7). 16.99 (978-1-4521-3890-9(7)) Chronicle Bks. LLC.

Young, Ruth. Aunty Marmalade. 2009. 218p. pap. 13.78 (978-1-60693-893-5(2), Eloquent Bks.) Strategic Book Publishing & Rights Agency (SBPRA).

Young, T. M. Playing Church. Washington, Victoria, ed. Cromwell, Danielle, illus. 2012. 32p. pap. 24.95 (978-1-4626-7883-9(1)) America Star Bks.

Yrjana, Colleen. Carry Me to Kinshasa Our Adoption Journey. Ulrich, Kelly, illus. 2012. 24p. pap. (978-1-77097-655-9(8)) FriesenPress.

Yu, Li Qiong. A New Year's Reunion: A Chinese Story. Liang, Zhu Chen, illus. 2011. (ENG.). 40p. (J). (gr. -1-2). 15.99 (978-0-7636-5881-6(2)) Candlewick Pr.

Yuki, Kaori. Godchild. 2007. (GodChild Ser.: 4). (ENG., Illus.). 200p. pap. 8.99 (978-1-4215-0478-0(2)) Viz Media.

Yukkie the Yorkie, A. K. A. Marilyn J. Sanders. The Adventures of Yukkie the Yorkie: The Beginning. 2008. (Illus.). 32p. (J). 16.00 (978-0-8059-7606-9(X)) Dorrance Publishing Co., Inc.

Zaikine, Zak. A Mother's Love. Zaikine, Zak & O'Keefe, Karin, eds. deluxe ed. 2005. (Illus.). 42p. (J). 24.95 (978-0-934290-01-2(6)) Moon Valley Productions.

Zia, Farhana. The Garden of My Imaan, 1 vol. 2016. (ENG.). 232p. (J). (gr. 3-6). pap. 7.95 (978-1-56145-921-6(6)) Peachtree Pubs.

Ziegler, Jennifer. Revenge of the Angels. 2015. (ENG.). 256p. (J). (gr. 3-7). 16.99 (978-0-545-83899-3(1), Scholastic Pr.) Scholastic, Inc.

Zimmerman, Dorothy. Why Am I Different? 2008. 128p. pap. 9.95 (978-1-4327-2555-6(6)) Outskirts Pr., Inc.

Zubizarreta, Patxi. Paloma, Llegaste Por el Aire. Balzola, Asun, illus. 2003. (SPA.). 24p. (978-84-246-5913-4(9), GL3212) La Galera, S.A. Editorial ESP. Dist: Lectorum Pubns., Inc.

Zucker, Jonny. Lighting a Lamp: A Diwali Story. Cohen, Jan Barger, illus. 2004. (Festival Time Ser.). (ENG.). 24p. (J). pap. 8.99 (978-0-7641-2670-3(9)) Barron's Educational Series, Inc.

50 Cent Staff. Playground. Akana, Lizzi, illus. 2012. (ENG.). 320p. (YA). (gr. 7). pap. 9.99 (978-1-59514-478-2(1), Razorbill) Penguin Young Readers Group.

FAMILY BUDGET

see Home Economics—Accounting

FAMILY LIFE

Armstrong, Aldona. Every Family Is Special. 2013. (Illus.). 20p. pap. 11.59 (978-1-4669-8913-9(0)) Trafford Publishing.

Berry, Joy. Teach Me about Special Times Nutshell Pack. 2009. (ENG.). 180p. (J). (gr. k — 1). 39.95 (978-1-60577-035-2(3)) Berry, Joy Enterprises.

Bishop, Jennie. Jesus Must Be Really Special. Wummer, Amy, illus. 2006. (Heritage Builders Ser.). 32p. (J). 14.99 (978-0-7847-1379-2(0), 04029) Standard Publishing.

Boom, Rosie. Where Lions Roar at Night. 2nd ed. 2013. (Illus.). 240p. (978-1-921161-18-6(3)) Boom Tree Publishing.

Building a Culture of Life Leader's Manual. 2nd ed. 2004. (YA). per. 19.95 (978-0-9764572-0-6(2)) Together, Inc.

Building a Culture of Life Study Guide. 2004. (YA). per. 17.95 (978-0-9764572-1-3(0)) Together, Inc.

Burton, Margie, et al. Families. 2011. (Early Connections Ser.). (J). (978-1-61672-487-0(0)) Benchmark Education Co.

Clement, Christine. My Family Reunion: Learning to Recognize Fractions as Part of a Group. 2009. (Math for the REAL World Ser.). 16p. (gr. 2-3). pap. 7.05 (978-0-8239-8923-2(2), Rosen Classroom) Rosen Publishing Group, Inc., The.

Concepcion, Jorge L., creator. A Tale of Innovation & Persistence. 2004. (Illus.). 125p. (YA). per. 12.95 (978-0-9761779-0-6(0)) Concepcion, Jorge.

Demars, Sue. Jesus Loves You More. 2009. 20p. pap. 10.95 (978-1-60860-695-5(3), Eloquent Bks.) Strategic Book Publishing & Rights Agency (SBPRA).

Dorling Kindersley Publishing Staff, ed. Buenos Dias, Bebe! 2004. (Soft-To-Touch Bks.).Tr. of Good Morning, Baby! (SPA & ENG., Illus.). 18p. (J). (gr. -1 — 1). bds. 5.99 (978-0-7566-0437-0(0), DK Children) Dorling Kindersley Publishing, Inc.

Dyan, Penelope. The Big Mikey & Me Workbook. 2011. 48p. pap. 11.95 (978-1-935630-70-8(9)) Bellissima Publishing, LLC.

Faye, Joanne & Whaley, Stacey Lynn. Conversations with Kids Ages 3 to 6. l.t. ed. 2004. (Illus.). 24p. (J). 9.95 *(978-0-9747375-0-8(X))* Joanne Faye Pr.

Flor Ada, Alma. Where the Flame Trees Bloom. 2007. (ENG.). 80p. (J). (gr. 4-6). pap. 9.95 *(978-1-4169-6840-5(7)*, Simon & Schuster/Paula Wiseman Bks.) Simon & Schuster/Paula Wiseman Bks.

Focus on Family Matters. (Focus on Family Matters Ser.). (gr. 5-8). 2005. 225.00 *(978-0-7910-9163-0(5))*Set. (Illus.). 64p. (YA). 118.50 *(978-0-7910-6689-8(4))* Facts On File, Inc. (Chelsea Hse.).

Gallagher, Debbie. Families, 6 bks., Set. Incl. Family Celebrations. lib. bdg. 18.56 *(978-0-7614-3133-6(0))*; Family Homes. lib. bdg. 18.56 *(978-0-7614-3136-7(5))*; Family Meals. lib. bdg. 18.56 *(978-0-7614-3138-1(1))*; Family Members. lib. bdg. 18.56 *(978-0-7614-3139-8(X))*; Family Responsibilities. lib. bdg. 18.56 *(978-0-7614-3141-1(1))*; Family Stories. lib. bdg. 18.56 *(978-0-7614-3142-8(X))*; 32p. (gr. 1-2). (Families Ser.). 2008. Set lib. bdg. 111.36 *(978-0-7614-3132-9(2)*, Benchmark Bks.) Marshall Cavendish Corp.

Gamble, Adam & Jasper, Mark. Good Night Little Brother. Kelly, Cooper, illus. 2016. (Good Night Our World Ser.). (ENG.). 20p. (J). (— 1). bds. 9.95 *(978-1-60219-505-9(6))* Good Night Bks.

Gesme, Carole & Pearson, Douglas. Time Together Learning about Family Values. (Time-Together Ser.). (J). (gr. k-6). wbk. ed. 9.95 *(978-1-888384-02-4(6))* Time-Together Pr.

Giacobello, John. You & Violence in Your Family. 2005. (Family Matters Ser.). (Illus.). 48p. (J). (gr. 5-8). lib. bdg. 29.25 *(978-0-8239-3353-2(9))* Rosen Publishing Group, Inc., The.

Gilbreth, Frank B., Jr. & Carey, Ernestine Gilbreth. Cheaper by the Dozen. 188p. (YA). (gr. 7-18). reprint ed. lib. bdg. 24.95 *(978-0-88411-289-1(6))* Amereon Ltd.

—Cheaper by the Dozen. 180p. (YA). (gr. 7-18). pap. 5.50 *(978-0-8072-8308-0(8))*; 2004. (J). (gr. 4-7). pap. 38.00 incl. audio *(978-0-8072-8307-3(X)*, YA157SP) Random Hse. Audio Publishing Group. (Listening Library).

Grippo, Daniel. When Mom or Dad Dies: A Book of Comfort for Kids. Alley, R. W., illus. 2008. (J). pap. 7.95 *(978-0-87029-415-0(6))* Abbey Pr.

Hartley, Susan. A Family Celebration: Set Of 6. 2011. (Early Connections Ser.). (J). 37.00 net. *(978-1-4108-1078-6(X))* Benchmark Education Co.

Hoffman, Mary. The Great Big Book of Families. Asquith, Ros, illus. 2011. (ENG.). 40p. (J). (gr. k-3). 17.99 *(978-0-8037-3516-3(2)*, Dial Bks) Penguin Young Readers Group.

Hood, Karen Jean Matsko. Karen Jean Matsko Hood, Inc. Parenting Book & Gift Catalog. Whispering Pine Press International, ed. Artistic Design Service Staff, illus. 2014. 50p. pap. 4.99 *(978-1-59210-715-5(X))* Whispering Pine Pr. International, Inc.

Hord, Janice. The Walking Stick Adventure. 2007. 52p. per. 19.95 *(978-1-934335-05-5(3))* WordWright.biz, Inc.

Jackson, J. S. Keeping Family First: A Kid's Guide. Alley, R. W., illus. 2004. (J). per. 7.95 *(978-0-87029-390-0(7))* Abbey Pr.

Jones, Marla F. Ponder Learns to Be Thankful. 2010. 28p. pap. 13.99 *(978-1-4490-8570-4(9))* AuthorHouse.

Lawrence, D. H. The Rocking-Horse Winner. 2010. (Illus.). 40p. (J). 19.95 *(978-1-58341-924-3(1)*, Creative Education) Creative Co., The.

Lindemann, Lindy. Kicklighter Shadow & the Beeples. White, David, illus. 2009. 24p. pap. 12.95 *(978-0-9822540-9-7(1))* Peppertree Pr., The.

Lobo, Julia. Guess How Much I Miss You. 2011. (Record A Story Ser.). 14p. (J). ring bd. 29.99 *(978-1-60130-256-4(8)*, Usborne) EDC Publishing.

Look Who's Popping Up: At Home. 2003. (J). (gr. -1-k). 4.98 *(978-0-7525-8901-5(6))* Parragon, Inc.

Marcovitz, Hal. Teens & Family Issues. Developed in Association with the Gallup Organization Staff, ed. 2013. (Gallup Youth Survey: Major Issues & Trends Ser.: 14). 112p. (J). (gr. 7-18). 24.95 *(978-1-4222-2952-1(1))* Mason Crest.

Markowitz, Siri. HELP with RAISING YOUR NURSERY or PRESCHOOL CHILDREN - 26 great ideas for parents & preschool Teachers. 2009. 44p. pap. 19.99 *(978-0-557-09610-7(3))* Lulu Pr., Inc.

Masters, Barbara. King Jack the Fourth. 2011. 24p. 13.00 *(978-1-4567-1344-7(2))* AuthorHouse.

McCurry, Janice. Grandma's Wish: A Keepsake Book for All Grandchildren. 2008. 24p. pap. 19.95 *(978-1-59858-821-7(4))* Dog Ear Publishing, LLC.

Michels, Dia L. Look What I See! Where Can I Be? 5 Book Set, 5 vols. Bowles, Michael J. N., photos by. 2005. (Look What I See! Where Can I Be? Ser.: 1-5). (ENG., Illus.). 32p. (J). (gr. -1-12). 69.95 *(978-1-930775-22-0(9))* Platypus Media, L.L.C.

Mitchell, Sherry. Growing up on the Lake: Sherry Mitchell. 2012. 24p. pap. 17.99 *(978-1-4772-0302-6(8))* AuthorHouse.

Moore-Mallinos, Jennifer. Do You Have a Secret? Fabrega, Marta, illus. 2005. (Let's Talk about It! Ser.). (ENG.). 32p. (J). (gr. -1-3). pap. 7.99 *(978-0-7641-3170-7(2))* Barron's Educational Series, Inc.

Moskal, G. Family Fun: Learning the F Sound. 2009. (PowerPhonics Ser.). 24p. (gr. 1-1). 39.90 *(978-1-60851-441-0(2)*, PowerKids Pr.) Rosen Publishing Group, Inc., The.

Mundy, Michaelene. One Caring Kid: A Book about You-and What Your Kindness Can Do! 2008. (Elf-Help Books for Kids Ser.). (Illus.). (J). per. 7.95 *(978-0-87029-414-3(8))* Abbey Pr.

Nelson, Robin. Where Is My Home? 2005. (First Step Nonfiction Ser.). (Illus.). 24p. (gr. k-2). lib. bdg. 17.27 *(978-0-8225-0189-3(9))* Lerner Publishing Group.

Nelson, Robin & National Geographic Learning Staff. Where Is My Home? 2012. (ENG.). 24p. (C). (gr. k-2). pap. 10.95 *(978-0-8225-1978-2(X))* National Geographic School Publishing, Inc.

Perry, Lucinda. The Ninth Child: Third Edition. 2008. 256p. pap. 19.95 *(978-0-595-52455-6(9))* iUniverse, Inc.

Power Twins Handbook Volume One. 2006. (J). spiral bd. *(978-0-9742355-1-6(2))* Brda, Tracy.

Quattlebaum, Mary. Family Reunion. Shine, Andrea, illus. 2004. 32p. (J). 16.00 *(978-0-8028-5237-3(8))* Eerdmans, William B. Publishing Co.

Rice, David L. Because Brian Hugged His Mother. 2004. (Sharing Nature with Children Book Ser.). (Illus.). 32p. (YA). (gr. -1-3). 16.95 *(978-1-883220-90-7(4))* Dawn Pubns.

—Because Brian Hugged His Mother, 1 vol. Thompson, K. Dyble, illus. 2004. (Sharing Nature with Children Book Ser.). (ENG.). 32p. (YA). (gr. -1-3). pap. 7.95 *(978-1-883220-89-1(0))* Dawn Pubns.

Robinson, Hilda & Kunkel, Jeff. Didn't We Have Fun! Robinson, Hilda, illus. 2012. (Illus.). 48p. (J). 19.95 *(978-1-933987-17-0(0)*, Crickhollow Bks.) Great Lakes Literary, LLC.

Rosa-Mendoza, Gladys. My Family & I/Mi Familia y Yo. Snider, Jackie, illus. 2007. (English Spanish Foundations Ser.). 20p. (gr. -1-k). pap. 19.95 *(978-1-931398-80-0(1))* Me+Mi Publishing.

Russell Johnson, Charlotte. A Journey to Hell & Back: The Flip Side. 2004. (Illus.). 255p. per. 15.95 *(978-0-9741893-2-1(4))* Reaching Beyond, Inc.

Shumway, Lindsey. I Chose You. 2005. (Illus.). 31p. (J). 15.99 *(978-1-55517-861-1(8))* Cedar Fort, Inc./CFI Distribution.

Thomas, Brenda. The Feelings from Autumn. 2012. 12p. pap. 15.99 *(978-1-4685-8878-1(8))* AuthorHouse.

Thomas, Pat. I Miss My Pet: A First Look at When a Pet Dies. Harker, Lesley, illus. 2012. (First Look At... Ser.). (ENG.). 32p. (J). (gr. -1-3). pap. 7.99 *(978-1-4380-0188-3(6))* Barron's Educational Series, Inc.

—This Is My Family: A First Look at Same-Sex Parents. Harker, Lesley, illus. 2012. (First Look At... Ser.). (ENG.). 32p. (J). (gr. -1-3). pap. 7.99 *(978-1-4380-0187-6(8))* Barron's Educational Series, Inc.

Townes-Richards, Carolyn. Nothing Like Christine: Living Through Literature with Aunt Curly's Collection. 2009. 90p. pap. 13.50 *(978-1-4251-1129-8(7))* Trafford Publishing.

Wall, Joanne. Anna of Allegheny. Wall, Joanne, ed. 2009. (Illus.). 110p. (YA). pap. 20.00 *(978-0-9644283-9-3(3))* Wall, Mary Joanne.

Weimer, Heidi. You're My Little Love Bug. Sharp, Chris, illus. 2008. (ENG.). 16p. (J). bds. 12.99 *(978-0-8249-6589-1(2)*, Ideal Pubns.) Worthy Publishing.

Weitzman, Elizabeth. Living in a Blended Family. 2004. (Let's Talk Library). (Illus.). 24p. (J). lib. bdg. 22.60 *(978-0-8239-6929-6(0)*, PowerKids Pr.) Rosen Publishing Group, Inc., The.

Willard, Nancy. Cracked Corn & Snow Ice Cream: A Family Almanac. Dyer, Jane, illus. 2005. 56p. (YA). (gr. 4-8). 18.00 *(978-0-7567-8835-3(8))* DIANE Publishing Co.

Williams, Dave. Windgalore Farm. 2005. (Illus.). 182p. pap. 21.95 *(978-0-937921-56-2(4))* Acorn Publishing.

FAMILY LIFE—FICTION

Aboff, Marcie. Giant Jelly Bean Jar. Billin-Frye, Paige & Frye, Paige Billin, illus. 2004. (Penguin Young Readers, Level 3 Ser.). (ENG.). 32p. (J). (gr. 1-3). mass mkt. 3.99 *(978-0-14-240049-4(1)*, Penguin Young Readers) Penguin Young Readers Group.

Abraham, Michelle Shapiro. Good Morning, Boker Tov. Alko, Selina, illus. 2004. pap. 6.95 *(978-0-8074-0783-7(6)*, 101974) URJ Pr.

—Good Night, Lilah Tov. Alko, Selina, illus. 2004. pap. 6.95 *(978-0-8074-0784-4(4)*, 101975) URJ Pr.

Abraham, Susan Gonzales & Abraham, Denise Gonzales. Cecilia's Year. (Latino Fiction for Young Adults Ser.). (ENG., Illus.). (J). 2007. 210p. (gr. 4-6). pap. 11.95 *(978-1-933693-02-6(9))* 2004. 160p. (gr. 7-9). 16.95 *(978-0-938317-87-6(3))* Cinco Puntos Pr.

—Surprising Cecilia. 2005. (Latino Fiction for Young Adults Ser.). (ENG., Illus.). 216p. (J). (gr. -1-7). 16.95 *(978-0-938317-96-8(2))* Cinco Puntos Pr.

Acampora, Paul. Rachel Spinelli Punched Me in the Face. 2013. (ENG.). 192p. (J). (gr. 3-7). pap. 8.99 *(978-1-250-01669-0(X)*, 9781250016690) Square Fish.

Acheson, Alison. Grandpa's Music: A Story about Alzheimer's. Farnsworth, Bill, illus. 2009. (ENG.). 32p. (J). (gr. 3-3). 16.99 *(978-0-8075-3052-8(2))* Whitman, Albert & Co.

Ackerman, Peter & Dalton, Max. The Lonely Typewriter. 2014. (Illus.). 32p. (J). 16.95 *(978-1-56792-518-0(9))* Godine, David R. Pub.

Acton, Vanessa. Skeleton Tower. 2016. (Atlas of Cursed Places Ser.). (ENG.). 104p. (YA). (gr. 6-12). lib. bdg. 26.65 *(978-1-5124-1322-9(4)*, Darby Creek) Lerner Publishing Group.

Adams, Chanelle. Myra. 2006. 22p. 12.16 *(978-1-4116-9426-2(0))* Lulu Pr., Inc.

Adams, Diane. Two Hands to Love You. Davis, Jon & Keiser, Paige, illus. 2014. (ENG.). 40p. (J). (gr. -1 — 1). 15.99 *(978-0-8118-7797-8(3))* Chronicle Bks. LLC.

Adams, Julie. Kem's Adventures: The Fishing Trip. 2009. 40p. pap. 16.99 *(978-1-4389-8458-2(8))* AuthorHouse.

Adams, L. Happy Memories: A Continuing Family Saga for Young Adults. 2003. 516p. pap. 26.95 *(978-0-595-29210-3(0))* iUniverse, Inc.

Adams, Lenora. Baby Girl. 2007. (ENG.). 240p. (YA). (gr. 9). pap. 6.99 *(978-1-4169-2512-5(0)*, Simon Pulse) Simon Pulse.

Adams, Mark. A Boy Named Bucky, Vol. 1. Dolan, Amy, illus. 2006. 17p. (J). pap. 5.00 *(978-0-9670245-5-4(2))* Enthusi Adams, Inc.

Adderson, Caroline. Jasper John Dooley: Not in Love. Clanton, Ben, illus. 2015. (Jasper John Dooley Ser.). (ENG.). 132p. (J). (gr. 2-5). pap. 7.95 *(978-1-77138-343-1(7))* Kids Can Pr., Ltd. CAN. Dist: Hachette Bk. Group.

—Jasper John Dooley: Star of the Week. Clanton, Ben, illus. 2014. (Jasper John Dooley Ser.). (ENG.). 128p. (J). (gr. 2-5). pap. 7.95 *(978-1-77138-119-2(1))* Kids Can Pr., Ltd. CAN. Dist: Hachette Bk. Group.

Adler, David A. Andy & Tamika. Hillenbrand, Will, illus. 2005. (Andy Russell Ser.: 2). (ENG.). 144p. (J). (gr. 1-4). pap. 5.99 *(978-0-15-205446-5(4))* Houghton Mifflin Harcourt Publishing Co.

—Andy & Tamika. Hillenbrand, Will, illus. 2005. (Andy Russell Ser.: Bk. 2). 129p. 16.00 *(978-0-7569-4898-6(3))* Perfection Learning Corp.

—Don't Talk to Me about the War. 2009. (ENG.). 224p. (J). (gr. 3-7). 7.99 *(978-0-14-241372-2(0)*, Puffin Books) Penguin Young Readers Group.

—It's a Baby, Andy Russell. Franson, Leanne, illus. 2006. (Andy Russell Ser.: Bk. 6). (ENG.). 128p. (J). (gr. 1-4). pap. 9.95 *(978-0-15-205610-0(6))* Houghton Mifflin Harcourt Publishing Co.

—The Many Troubles of Andy Russell. Hillenbrand, Will, illus. 2005. (Andy Russell Ser.: 1). (ENG.). 144p. (J). (gr. 1-4). pap. 6.99 *(978-0-15-205440-3(5))* Houghton Mifflin Harcourt Publishing Co.

—The Many Troubles of Andy Russell. 2008. (J). (gr. 2-4). pap. 24.95 incl. audio *(978-1-4301-0479-7(1))* Live Oak Media.

Adoff, Arnold. Black Is Brown Is Tan. McCully, Emily Arnold, illus. 2004. (ENG.). 40p. (J). (gr. -1-3). reprint ed. pap. 6.99 *(978-0-06-443644-1(6)*, Amistad) HarperCollins Pubs.

Adrian, Emily. Like It Never Happened. 2015. (ENG.). 368p. (J). (gr. 9). 17.99 *(978-0-525-42823-7(2)*, Dial Bks) Penguin Young Readers Group.

Adrian, Susan. Tunnel Vision: A Novel. 2015. (ENG.). 320p. (YA). (gr. 8-12). 18.99 *(978-1-250-04792-2(7)*, 9781250047922, St. Martin's Griffin) St. Martin's Pr.

The Adventures of Bug & Roofus: Clean Your Room Roofus. 2008. (Illus.). 32p. (J). 9.95 *(978-0-615-17074-9(9))* Big Bk. Pubns.

Aiken, Joan. The Serial Garden. 2012. (ENG.). 320p. (J). (gr. 4). pap. 16.00 *(978-1-931520-82-9(8)*, Big Mouth Hse.) Small Beer Pr.

Ain, Beth. Starring Jules (Third Grade Debut) 2014. (Starring Jules Ser.: 4). (ENG.). 176p. (J). (gr. 2-5). 14.99 *(978-0-545-44358-6(X)*, Scholastic Pr.) Scholastic, Inc.

Airgood, Ellen. The Education of Ivy Blake. 2015. (ENG.). 240p. (J). (gr. 5). 16.99 *(978-0-399-16278-7(X)*, Nancy Paulsen Books) Penguin Young Readers Group.

—Prairie Evers. 2012. (ENG.). 224p. (J). (gr. 3-7). 15.99 *(978-0-399-25691-2(1)*, Nancy Paulsen Books) Penguin Young Readers Group.

Akin, Sara Laux. Three Scoops & a Fig, 1 vol. Hartung, Susan Kathleen, illus. 2010. (ENG.). 32p. (J). (gr. -1-3). 15.95 *(978-1-56145-522-5(9))* Peachtree Pubs.

Albee, Sarah. Off to Bed. Ebert, Len, illus. 2006. (Step-By-Step Readers Ser.). (J). pap. *(978-1-59939-060-4(4)*, Reader's Digest Young Families, Inc.) Studio Fun International.

Alberto, Daisy. No Rules for Rex! Smath, Jerry, illus. 2005. (Social Studies Connects). 32p. (J). pap. 5.95 *(978-1-57565-146-0(7))* Kane Press, Inc.

Alcott, Louisa May. Eight Cousins. 2005. 29.95 *(978-1-4218-0976-2(1))*; 300p. pap. 14.95 *(978-1-59540-676-7(X))* 1st World Publishing, Inc. (1st World Library - Literary Society).

—Eight Cousins. 2005. 120p. per. 4.95 *(978-1-4209-2569-2(5))* Digireads.com Publishing.

—Eight Cousins. 2007. (Dover Children's Evergreen Classics Ser.). (ENG.). 224p. (J). (gr. 4-7). per. 5.99 *(978-0-486-45559-4(9))* Dover Pubns., Inc.

—Eight Cousins. 2004. reprint ed. pap. 1.99 *(978-1-4192-1740-1(2))* Kessinger Publishing, LLC.

—Eight Cousins. 2013. (Works of Louisa May Alcott). 291p. reprint ed. lthr. 79.00 *(978-0-7812-1633-3(8))* Reprint Services Corp.

—Eight Cousins, or, the Aunt-Hill. 2010. 250p. pap. 16.95 *(978-1-60444-100-0(3))* IndoEuropeanPublishing.com.

—Jack & Jill. 2005. 29.95 *(978-1-4218-1069-0(7))*; 320p. pap. 14.95 *(978-1-4218-1169-7(3))* 1st World Publishing, Inc. (1st World Library - Literary Society).

—Jack & Jill. Date not set. 352p. (YA). 25.95 *(978-0-8488-2671-0(X))* Amereon Ltd.

—Jack & Jill. 2012. (ENG., Illus.). 368p. (J). (gr. 3-9). pap. 17.95 *(978-1-4290-9310-1(2))* Applewood Bks.

—Jack & Jill. 2007. (ENG.). 252p. pap. 21.99 *(978-1-4346-2587-8(7))*; 276p. pap. 23.99 *(978-1-4346-2665-3(2))* Creative Media Partners, LLC.

—Jack & Jill. 2005. pap. *(978-1-4065-0100-1(X))* Dodo Pr.

—Jack & Jill. 2013. (Works of Louisa May Alcott). 425p. reprint ed. lthr. 79.00 *(978-0-7812-1638-8(9))* Reprint Services Corp.

—Jo's Boys. l.t. ed. 2007. (ENG.). 288p. pap. 23.99 *(978-1-4346-0451-4(9))* Creative Media Partners, LLC.

—Jo's Boys. 2005. pap. *(978-1-4065-0107-0(7))* Dodo Pr.

—Jo's Boys. abr. ed. 2011. (Dover Children's Thrift Classics Ser.). (ENG., Illus.). 112p. (J). (gr. 3-8). pap. 4.00 *(978-0-486-40789-0(6))* Dover Pubns., Inc.

—Jo's Boys. l.t. ed. 2005. 424p. pap. *(978-1-84637-067-0(1))* Echo Library.

—Jo's Boys. 2013. (Works of Louisa May Alcott). 366p. reprint ed. lthr. 79.00 *(978-0-7812-1642-5(7))* Reprint Services Corp.

—Kitty's Class Day & Other Stories. 2005. 28.95 *(978-1-4218-1485-8(4))*; 268p. pap. 13.95 *(978-1-4218-1585-5(0))* 1st World Publishing, Inc. (1st World Library - Literary Society).

—Little Men. Andreasen, Dan, illus. 2009. (Classic Starts(tm) Ser.). (ENG.). 160p. (J). (gr. 2-4). 6.95 *(978-1-4027-5423-4(X))* Sterling Publishing Co., Inc.

—Little Men. rev. ed. 2006. 352p. 31.95 *(978-1-4218-1800-9(0))*; pap. 15.95 *(978-1-4218-1900-6(7))* 1st World Publishing, Inc. (1st World Library - Literary Society).

—Little Men. l.t. ed. 2005. 564p. pap. *(978-1-84637-068-7(X))* Echo Library.

—Little Men: Life at Plumfield with Jo's Boys. 2013. (Works of Louisa May Alcott). 292p. reprint ed. lthr. 79.00 *(978-0-7812-1629-6(X))* Reprint Services Corp.

—Little Women. Corvino, Lucy, illus. 2005. (Classic Starts(tm) Ser.). (ENG.). 160p. (J). (gr. 2-4). 6.95 *(978-1-4027-1236-4(7))* Sterling Publishing Co., Inc.

—Little Women. Dunn, Robert, illus. 2013. 46p. (J). *(978-1-4351-4813-0(4))* Barnes & Noble, Inc.

—Little Women. 2007. 264p. (YA). 11.95 *(978-1-933486-01-7(5))* Core Knowledge Foundation.

—Little Women. 2013. (ENG., Illus.). 426p. (J). (gr. 4-7). pap. 10.99 *(978-0-09-957296-1(6))* Random Hse. GBR. Dist: Independent Pubs. Group.

—Little Women. 2013. (Works of Louisa May Alcott). 451p. reprint ed. lthr. 79.00 *(978-0-7812-1627-2(3))* Reprint Services Corp.

—Little Women: Bring the Classics to Life. 2008. (Bring the Classics to Life Ser.). (Illus.). 72p. (gr. 1-12). pap., act. bk. ed. 10.95 *(978-1-55576-047-2(3)*, EDCTR-103B) EDCON Publishing Group.

—Little Women: With a Discussion of Family. Lauter, Richard, illus. 2003. (Values in Action Illustrated Classics Ser.). 191p. (J). *(978-1-59203-032-3(7))* Learning Challenge, Inc.

—A Modern Cinderella. l.t. ed. 2005. 224p. pap. *(978-1-84637-050-2(7))* Echo Library.

—Modern Cinderella or the Little Old Shoe. 2006. pap. 44.99 *(978-1-4219-8892-4(5))* IndyPublish.com.

—A Modern Mephistopheles. Date not set. (J). lib. bdg. 16.95 *(978-0-8488-0412-1(0))* Amereon Ltd.

—Mujercitas.Tr. of Little Women. (SPA., Illus.). 192p. (YA). 11.95 *(978-84-7281-101-0(8)*, AF1101) Auriga, Ediciones S.A. ESP. Dist: Continental Bk. Co., Inc.

—Mujercitas. 2004.Tr. of Little Women. (SPA.). lib. bdg. *(978-1-4135-2067-5(7))* El Cid Editor Incorporated.

—Mujercitas. (Coleccion Estrella).Tr. of Little Women. (SPA., Illus.). 64p. (J). 14.95 *(978-950-11-0010-5(3)*, SGM010) Sigmar ARG. Dist: Continental Bk. Co., Inc.

—An Old-Fashioned Thanksgiving. Wheeler, Jody, illus. 2010. 40p. (J). (gr. -1-3). 14.99 *(978-0-8249-5620-2(6)*, Ideal Pubns.) Worthy Publishing.

—The Works of Louisa May Alcott. (J). (gr. 5-6). 40.95 *(978-0-88411-173-3(3))* Amereon Ltd.

Alcott, Louisa May & Barbarese, J. T. Little Men. 2012. (ENG.). 368p. (gr. 12). mass mkt. 5.95 *(978-0-451-53223-7(6)*, Signet) Penguin Publishing Group.

Alcott, Louisa May & Lacey, Mike. Little Women, 1 vol. 2012. (Calico Illustrated Classics Ser.: No. 4). (ENG., Illus.). 112p. (J). (gr. 3-6). 27.07 *(978-1-61641-617-1(3))* Magic Wagon.

Alcott, Louisa May & Naxos of America Staff. Little Women. Mims, Ashley, illus. 3rd ed. 2008. (Hear It Read It Classics Ser.: 0). (ENG.). 128p. (J). (gr. 2-4). 9.99 *(978-1-4022-1169-0(4)*, Sourcebooks Jabberwocky) Sourcebooks, Inc.

Alda, Arlene. Iris Has a Virus. Desimini, Lisa, illus. 2008. (ENG.). 24p. (J). (gr. -1-1). 18.95 *(978-0-88776-844-6(X)*, Tundra Bks.) Tundra Bks. CAN. Dist: Penguin Random Hse. LLC.

Alden-Tirrill, Anna. The Promise Box. 2013. 284p. pap. 14.95 *(978-1-885831-05-7(6))* Proclaim Publishing.

Alender, Katie. The Dead Girls of Hysteria Hall. 2015. (ENG.). 336p. (J). (gr. 7). 18.99 *(978-0-545-63999-6(9))* Scholastic, Inc.

Alexander, Carol. When My Name Was Keoko. Friedland, Joyce & Kessler, Rikki, eds. 2008. (Novel-Ties Ser.). 29p. pap. 16.95 *(978-0-7675-1520-7(X))* Learning Links Inc.

Alexander, Sarah. The Art of Not Breathing. 2016. (ENG.). 288p. (YA). (gr. 9). 17.99 *(978-0-544-63388-9(1)*, HMH Books For Young Readers) Houghton Mifflin Harcourt Publishing Co.

Alger, Horatio. Five Hundred Dollars: Or: Jacob Marlowe's Secret. 2007. (ENG.). 192p. per. 19.99 *(978-1-4346-5063-4(4))*; 206p. per. 22.99 *(978-1-4346-5064-1(2))* Creative Media Partners, LLC.

Alice B. Emerson. Ruth Fielding of the Red Mill: Or Jasper Parloe's Secret. 2007. (ENG.). 134p. per. 18.99 *(978-1-4346-3930-1(4))*; 146p. per. 19.99 *(978-1-4346-3931-8(2))* Creative Media Partners, LLC.

Alko, Selina. Daddy Christmas & Hanukkah Mama. 2012. (ENG., Illus.). 32p. (J). (gr. k-3). 16.99 *(978-0-375-86093-5(2)*, Knopf Bks. for Young Readers) Random Hse. Children's Bks.

All My Noble Dreams & Then What Happens. 2013. (ENG.). 272p. (J). (gr. 4-7). 15.99 *(978-1-4424-4976-3(4))*, Simon & Schuster/Paula Wiseman Bks.) Simon & Schuster/Paula Wiseman Bks.

Allen, Nancy. Amazing Grace: A Kentucky Girl with Gumption During World War II. 2014. Orig. Title: Amazing Grace: a Kentucky Girl with Gumption During World War II. (ENG., Illus.). 160p. (gr. 4-7). pap. 14.99 *(978-1-62619-405-2(X)*, History Pr., The) Arcadia Publishing.

Allison, Jennifer. Gilda Joyce, Psychic Investigator. 2006. (Gilda Joyce Ser.). (ENG.). 336p. (J). (gr. 5-18). reprint ed. 8.99 *(978-0-14-240698-4(8)*, Puffin Books) Penguin Young Readers Group.

Allstun, Gina. Related. 2007. 63p. pap. 8.50 *(978-1-4303-1229-1(7))* Lulu Pr., Inc.

Almond, David. En el Lugar de las Alas. (Barco de Vapor). (SPA.). 218p. (YA). (gr. 5-8). *(978-84-348-6421-4(5))* SM Ediciones.

—My Name Is Mina. (ENG.). 304p. (J). 2012. (gr. 5). 6.99 *(978-0-375-87327-0(9)*, Yearling) 2011. (gr. 3-7). 15.99 *(978-0-385-74073-9(5)*, Delacorte Bks. for Young Readers) Random Hse. Children's Bks.

—Skellig. 2009. 9.14 *(978-0-7848-2973-8(X)*, Everbind) Marco Bk. Co.

Alongi, Anthony & Davidson, MaryJanice. Jennifer Scales & the Ancient Furnace. 2007. (Jennifer Scales Ser.: 1). (ENG.). 224p. (gr. 12-18). 7.99 *(978-0-441-01474-3(7)*, Ace Bks.) Penguin Publishing Group.

—Jennifer Scales & the Messenger of Light. 2007. (Jennifer Scales Ser.: 2). (ENG.). 288p. (gr. 12-18). 7.99 *(978-0-441-01510-8(7)*, Ace Bks.) Penguin Publishing Group.

Alpine, Rachele. A Void the Size of the World. 2017. (ENG., Illus.). 368p. (YA). (gr. 9). 17.99 ***(978-1-4814-8571-5(7)***, Simon Pulse) Simon Pulse.

Altebrando, Tara. My Life in Dioramas. 2015. (ENG., Illus.). 256p. (J). (gr. 2-7). 14.95 *(978-0-7624-5681-9(7)*, Running Pr. Kids) Running Pr. Bk. Pubs.

Alvarez, Julia. Antes de Ser Libres. 2004.Tr. of Before We Were Free. (SPA.). (gr. 7-12). lib. bdg. 17.20 *(978-0-613-71931-5(X)*, Turtleback) Turtleback Bks.

—De Como la Tia Lola Aprendio a Ensenar. 2011. (Tia Lola Stories Ser.). (SPA & ENG.). 160p. (J). (gr. 3-7). 7.99 *(978-0-375-85793-5(1)*, Yearling) Random Hse. Children's Bks.

—De Como Tia Lola Salvo el Verano. 2012. (Tia Lola Stories Ser.). (ENG & SPA.). 192p. (J). (gr. 3-7). 6.99 *(978-0-307-93023-1(8)*, Yearling) Random Hse. Children's Bks.

—De Como Tia Lola Termino Empezando Otra Vez. 2012. (Tia Lola Stories Ser.). (ENG & SPA.). 192p. (J). (gr. 3-7). 7.99 *(978-0-307-93034-7(3)*, Yearling) Random Hse. Children's Bks.

—Devolver Al Remitente. 2010.Tr. of Return to Sender. (SPA & ENG.). 368p. (J). (gr. 3-7). 7.99 *(978-0-375-85124-7(0)*, Yearling) Random Hse. Children's Bks.

E F G

—How the Garcia Girls Lost Their Accent. 2011. 13.46 (978-0-7848-3532-6(2), Everbind) Marco Bk. Co.

—How Tia Lola Came to Visit Stay. 2004. 147p. (gr. 3-7). 17.00 (978-0-7569-3641-9(1)) Perfection Learning Corp.

—How Tia Lola Ended up Starting Over. 2012. (Tia Lola Stories Ser.). (ENG.). 160p. (J). (gr. 3-7). pap. 6.99 (978-0-375-87320-1(1), Yearling) Random Hse. Children's Bks.

—How Tia Lola Learned to Teach. 2011. (Tia Lola Stories Ser.). (ENG., Illus.). 144p. (J). (gr. 3-7). pap. 7.99 (978-0-375-85792-8(3), Yearling) Random Hse. Children's Bks.

—How Tia Lola Saved the Summer. (Tia Lola Stories Ser.). (ENG.). (J). (gr. 3-7). 2012. 176p. 6.99 (978-0-375-86687-6(6), Yearling) 2011. 160p. 15.99 (978-0-375-86727-9(9), Knopf Bks. for Young Readers) Random Hse. Children's Bks.

Amado, Elisa. Primas, 1 vol. Iribarren, Elena & Iribarren, Leopoldo, trs. from ENG. Garay, Luis, illus. 2004. (SPA & ENG.). 32p. (J). 16.95 (978-0-88899-548-3(2)) Groundwood Bks. CAN. Dist: Publishers Group West (PGW).

Amoss, Berthe. Secret Lives. 2014. (ENG., Illus.). 200p. (gr. 4). pap. 12.95 (978-1-939601-05-6(3)) Ig Publishing, Inc.

Andersen, C. B. The Forgotten Treasure. 2004. 215p. (J). pap. (978-1-59038-314-8(1)) Deseret Bk. Co.

—The Secret Mission. 2008. (J). (978-1-59038-906-5(9)) Deseret Bk. Co.

Anderson, Claire. Talking to the Stars. 2009. 24p. pap. 12.99 (978-1-4389-7268-8(7)) AuthorHouse.

Anderson, Janet. The Last Treasure. 2004. (ENG.). 272p. (J). (gr. 3-7). 8.99 (978-0-14-240217-7(6), Puffin Books) Penguin Young Readers Group.

Anderson, Jodi Lynn. Love & Peaches. 2008. 256p. (YA). (gr. 7-18). lib. bdg. 17.89 (978-0-06-073312-4(8), HarperTeen) HarperCollins Pubs.

—My Diary from the Edge of the World. 2015. (ENG., Illus.). 432p. (J). (gr. 3-7). 16.99 (978-1-4424-8387-3(3), Aladdin) Simon & Schuster Children's Publishing.

—My Diary from the Edge of the World. 2017. (ENG., Illus.). 448p. (J). (gr. 3-7). pap. 7.99 (978-1-4424-8388-0(1), Simon & Schuster/Paula Wiseman Bks.) Simon & Schuster/Paula Wiseman Bks.

—Peaches. (ENG.). (YA). 2005. 320p. (gr. 7-12). 15.99 (978-0-06-073305-6(5)) 2012. (Peaches Ser.: 1). 368p. (gr. 9-12). reprint ed. pap. 8.99 (978-0-06-073307-0(1), HarperTeen) HarperCollins Pubs.

Anderson, Laurie Halse. Fever 1793. unabr. ed. 2004. 256p. (J). (gr. 5-9). pap. 38.00 incl. audio (978-0-8072-8719-4(9), LYA 246 SP, Listening Library) Random Hse. Audio Publishing Group.

—The Impossible Knife of Memory. 2015. (ENG.). 416p. (YA). (gr. 7). pap. 9.99 (978-0-14-751072-3(4), Speak) Penguin Publishing Group.

—The Impossible Knife of Memory. 2014. (ENG.). 384p. (YA). (gr. 7). 18.99 (978-0-670-01209-1(2), Viking Books for Young Readers) Penguin Young Readers Group.

—The Impossible Knife of Memory. 2015. (ENG.). (YA). (gr. 7). lib. bdg. 20.60 **(978-1-68065-510-0(8))** Perfection Learning Corp.

—The Impossible Knife of Memory. 2015. lib. bdg. 20.85 (978-0-606-36798-1(5)) Turtleback Bks.

—Prom. 2006. (ENG.). 240p. (YA). (gr. 7-18). reprint ed. 8.99 (978-0-14-240570-3(1), Speak) Penguin Young Readers Group.

—Prom. 2006. (YA). 1.25 (978-1-4193-5096-2(X)) Recorded Bks., Inc.

—Twisted. 2008. (ENG.). 288p. (YA). (gr. 7-18). 9.99 (978-0-14-241184-1(1), Speak) Penguin Young Readers Group.

—Twisted. l.t. ed. 2007. (Literacy Bridge Young Adult Ser.). 299p. (YA). (gr. 7-12). 23.95 (978-0-7862-9885-3(5)) Thorndike Pr.

Anderson, Libby. The Richest Boy on Earth. 2008. 20p. pap. 24.95 (978-1-60563-109-7(4)) America Star Bks.

Anderson, Lynda & Bennett, Melanie. The Micro Meanies. 2008. 180p. pap. (978-0-9783204-7-8(6)) Aaspirations.

Andreae, Giles. Heaven Is Having You. Cabban, Vanessa, illus. 2007. (Padded Board Bks.). 18p. (J). (gr. -1-1). bds. 7.95 (978-1-58925-820-4(7)) Tiger Tales.

Andrews, Jesse. Me & Earl & the Dying Girl. (ENG.). 304p. (YA). (gr. 9-17). 2012. 17.95 (978-1-4197-0176-4(2), Amulet Bks.) 2015. 17.95 (978-1-4197-2027-7(9)) 2015. 17.95 (978-1-4197-2013-0(9), Amulet Bks.) 2015. pap. 9.95 (978-1-4197-1960-8(2), Amulet Bks.) Abrams, Inc.

—Me & Earl & the Dying Girl. 2015. (CHI.). 320p. (YA). (gr. 9-17). pap. (978-986-344-282-0(8)) Rye Field Publishing, Co.

—Me & Earl & the Dying Girl. 2015. lib. bdg. 20.80 (978-0-606-37113-1(3)) Turtleback Bks.

Andros, Camille. Charlotte the Scientist Is Squished. Farley, Brianne, illus. 2017. (ENG.). 40p. (J). (gr. -1-3). 16.99 (978-0-544-78583-0(5)) Houghton Mifflin Harcourt Publishing Co.

Angelini, Josephine. Trail of Tears. 2015. (Worldwalker Trilogy Ser.: 2). (SPA & ENG.). 352p. (YA). (gr. 7). 17.99 (978-1-250-05090-8(1), 9781250050908) Feiwel & Friends.

Anhalt, Ariela. Freefall. 2011. (ENG.). 252p. (YA). (gr. 9). pap. 14.99 (978-0-547-55216-3(5)) Houghton Mifflin Harcourt Publishing Co.

Anholt, Laurence. Rude Ruby. Ross, Tony, illus. 2015. (My Freaky Family Ser.: 1). (ENG.). 48p. (J). (gr. k-2). pap. 8.99 (978-1-4083-3639-7(1)) Hodder & Stoughton GBR. Dist: Hachette Bk. Group.

Ann, Cameron. The Stories Julian Tells. 2014. (Stepping Stone Book Ser.). (ENG.). 80p. (J). 9.24 (978-1-63245-217-7(0)) Lectorum Pubns., Inc.

Antieau, Kim. Mercy, Unbound. 2006. (ENG., Illus.). 176p. (YA). (gr. 9). pap. 9.99 (978-1-4169-0893-7(5), Simon Pulse) Simon Pulse.

Anton, Maggie. Secret Scholar. 2008. (ENG.). 160p. (gr. 4-7). pap. 14.00 (978-0-8276-0869-6(1)) Jewish Pubn. Society.

Appelt, Kathi. Oh My Baby, Little One. Dyer, Jane, illus. 2005. (ENG.). 32p. (J). (gr. -1 — 1). reprint ed. pap. 6.99 (978-0-15-205242-3(9)) Houghton Mifflin Harcourt Publishing Co.

Archer, Jennifer. The Shadow Girl. 2013. (ENG.). 336p. (YA). (gr. 8). pap. 9.99 (978-0-06-183460-8(2), HarperTeen) HarperCollins Pubs.

—Through Her Eyes. 2012. (ENG.). 400p. (YA). (gr. 8). pap. 9.99 (978-0-06-183459-2(9), HarperTeen) HarperCollins Pubs.

Archer, Nick & McDonald, Megan. Rule of Three. Consolazio, Pamela A., illus. 2009. (Sisters Club Ser.: 2). (ENG.). 240p. (J). (gr. 3-7). 15.99 (978-0-7636-4153-5(7)) Candlewick Pr.

Arcos, Carrie. There Will Come a Time. 2014. (ENG., Illus.). 320p. (YA). (gr. 9). 17.99 (978-1-4424-9585-2(5), Simon Pulse) Simon Pulse.

Ardizzone, Edward. Sarah & Simon & No Red Paint. Ardizzone, Edward, illus. 2011. (Illus.). 48p. (J). 17.95 (978-1-56792-410-7(7)) Godine, David R. Pub.

Armentrout, Jennifer L. Don't Look Back. 2014. (Novel Ser.: 1). (ENG.). 384p. (YA). (gr. 9-17). 16.99 (978-1-4231-7512-4(3)) Hyperion Bks. for Children.

Armstrong, Kelley. The Gathering. (Darkness Rising Ser.: 1). (YA). (gr. 8). 2012. 384p. pap. 9.99 (978-0-06-179703-3(0)) 2011. 368p. 17.99 (978-0-06-179702-6(2)) HarperCollins Pubs.

—The Gathering. (Darkness Rising Ser.: Bk. 1). (YA). 1.25 (978-1-4498-6189-6(X)); 100.75 (978-1-4498-6186-5(5)); 2013. 102.75 (978-1-4498-6184-1(9)) Recorded Bks., Inc.

Armstrong, William H. Sounder. l.t. ed. 2005. 111p. (YA). pap. 10.95 (978-0-7862-7915-9(X)) Thorndike Pr.

Arnold, Elana K. Far from Fair. 2016. (ENG.). 240p. (J). (gr. 5-7). 16.99 (978-0-544-60227-4(7), HMH Books For Young Readers) Houghton Mifflin Harcourt Publishing Co.

Arnold, Elana K. What Girls Are Made Of. 2017. (ENG.). 208p. (YA). (gr. 8-12). 18.99 (978-1-5124-1024-2(1)); 9.99 **(978-1-5124-3437-8(X)**, Carolrhoda Lab™); 38.65 **(978-1-5124-3438-5(8)**, Carolrhoda Lab™); 38.65 **(978-1-5124-2694-6(6)**, Carolrhoda Lab™) Lerner Publishing Group.

Arnold, Tedd. Big Family. Arnold, Tedd, illus. 2017. (Fly Guy Ser.: 17). (ENG., Illus.). 32p. (J). (gr. -1-3). 6.99 **(978-0-545-86316-8(4))** Scholastic, Inc.

Arnold, Tedd, et al. Noodlehead Nightmares. Arnold, Tedd, illus. 2016. (ENG., Illus.). 48p. (J). (gr. 1-5). 15.95 (978-0-8234-3566-1(0)) Holiday Hse., Inc.

Arnosky, Jim. The Pirates of Crocodile Swamp. 2009. (ENG.). 240p. (J). (gr. 4-7). 15.99 (978-0-399-25068-2(9), G.P. Putnam's Sons Books for Young Readers) Penguin Young Readers Group.

Aronson, Rosy. A Tale of Serendipity: the Adventure Begins! 2010. 370p. pap. 24.84 (978-0-557-12641-5(X)) Lulu Pr., Inc.

Arrington, Gladys. Dallas: On Book One: Jo/Jo KIDS. Arrington, Chiquila, illus. 2006. 49p. pap. 16.95 (978-1-4241-1162-6(5)) PublishAmerica, Inc.

Asch, Frank. Just Like Daddy. 2015. lib. bdg. 17.20 (978-0-606-36293-1(2)) Turtleback Bks.

Ashburn, Boni. The Fort That Jack Built. Helquist, Brett, illus. 2013. (ENG.). 32p. (J). (gr. k-2). 18.95 (978-1-4197-0795-7(7), Abrams Bks. for Young Readers) Abrams, Inc.

Asher, Penny & Booker, Ricki. Mommy & Daddy Are Going on a Trip. Kassab, Selena, illus. 2006. 32p. (J). 12.95 (978-0-9755902-1-8(9)) Change Is Strange, Inc.

—We're Having a Baby. Kassab, Selena, illus. 2006. 32p. 12.95 (978-0-9755902-0-1(0)) Change Is Strange, Inc.

Ashford Frame, Jeron & Christie, R. Gregory. Yesterday I Had the Blues. 2nd rev. ed. 2008. (ENG., Illus.). 32p. (J). (gr. -1-2). pap. 7.99 (978-1-58246-260-8(7), Tricycle Pr.) Random Hse. Children's Bks.

Ashman, Linda. Henry Wants More! Hughes, Brooke Boynton, illus. 2016. (ENG.). 32p. (J). (gr. -1-2). 20.99 (978-0-375-97348-2(6), Random Hse. Bks. for Young Readers) Random Hse. Children's Bks.

Ashton, Anna. Molly & Ben. 2007. (Illus.). 76p. per. (978-1-84401-178-0(X)) Athena Pr.

Atkinson, Elizabeth. From Alice to Zen & Everyone in Between. (gr. 4-7). 2013. (ENG.). 248p. (J). pap. 9.95 (978-1-4677-0861-6(5), Carolrhoda Bks.) 2008. 247p. (YA). 16.95 (978-0-8225-7271-8(0)) Lerner Publishing Group.

—I, Emma Freke. (Exceptional Reading & Language Arts Titles for Intermediate Grades Ser.). (ENG.). 240p. (J). (gr. 4-7). 2012. 9.95 (978-0-7613-8500-4(2)) 2010. 16.95 (978-0-7613-5604-2(5)) Lerner Publishing Group. (Carolrhoda Bks.).

—The Island of Beyond. 2016. (ENG.). 288p. (gr. 4-7). 35.99 (978-1-4677-9557-9(7), Carolrhoda Bks.) Lerner Publishing Group.

Auch, M. J. Guitar Boy. 2012. (ENG.). 288p. (J). (gr. 5-9). pap. 14.99 (978-0-312-64124-5(9), 9780312641245) Square Fish.

—One-Handed Catch. 2009. (ENG.). 272p. (J). (gr. 5-9). pap. 6.99 (978-0-312-53575-9(9), 9780312535759) Square Fish.

Auch, Mary Jane. One-Handed Catch. 2009. 272p. (J). (gr. 5-9). pap. 6.99 (978-0-312-58002-5(9)) Square Fish.

Aunt Lucy's Rolls. 2005. (J). per. (978-0-9772209-0-8(7)) Spann Productions.

Auseon, Andrew. Freak Magnet. 2010. (ENG.). 304p. (YA). (gr. 9-18). 16.99 (978-0-06-113926-0(2), HarperTeen) HarperCollins Pubs.

Austen, Catherine. Walking Backward, 1 vol. 2009. (ENG., Illus.). 176p. (J). (gr. 4-7). pap. 9.95 (978-1-55469-147-0(8)) Orca Bk. Pubs. USA.

Austen, Jane. Pride & Prejudice. Miralles, Joseph, illus. 2005. (Great Illustrated Classics Ser.). 236p. (gr. 3-8). 21.35 (978-1-59679-249-4(3)) Spotlight.

Austen, Jane & Fisher, Eric Scott. Pride & Prejudice, 1 vol. 2012. (Calico Illustrated Classics Ser.: No. 4). (ENG., Illus.). 112p. (J). (gr. 3-6). 27.07 (978-1-61641-619-5(X)) Magic Wagon.

Auth, Jeannine. Emmy's Question. 2010. 155p. pap. 11.99 (978-0-9790395-3-9(3)) Morningtide Pr.

Authement, Louise. Diaries of the Fifth Grade Miseries. 2013. 68p. pap. 10.95 (978-1-4327-9996-0(7)) Outskirts Pr., Inc.

Autumn Moon, 6 Pcks. (Bookweb Ser.). 32p. (gr. 6-18). 34.00 (978-0-7578-0894-4(8)) Rigby Education.

Avasthi, Swati. Chasing Shadows. Phillips, Craig, illus. 2015. (ENG.). 336p. (YA). (gr. 9). pap. 10.99 (978-0-375-86343-1(5), Ember) Random Hse. Children's Bks.

Averbeck, Jim. One Word from Sophia. Ismail, Yasmeen, illus. 2015. (ENG.). 40p. (J). (gr. -1-3). 17.99 (978-1-4814-0514-0(4)) Simon & Schuster Children's Publishing.

Avi. City of Orphans. Ruth, Greg, illus. (ENG.). 368p. (J). (gr. 5-9). 2012. pap. 8.99 (978-1-4169-7108-5(4), Atheneum Bks. for Young Readers) 2011. 17.99 (978-1-4169-7102-3(5), Atheneum/Richard Jackson Bks.) Simon & Schuster Children's Publishing.

—The Traitors' Gate. Raude, Karina, illus. 2007. (ENG.). 368p. (J). (gr. 5-8). 17.99 (978-0-689-85335-7(1), Atheneum/Richard Jackson Bks.) Simon & Schuster Children's Publishing.

Axelrod, Amy. Your Friend in Fashion, Abby Shapiro. 2011. (ENG.). 288p. (J). (gr. 3-7). 17.95 (978-0-8234-2340-8(9)) Holiday Hse., Inc.

Ayarbe, Heidi. Compromised. (ENG.). (YA). (gr. 8). 2011. 480p. pap. 8.99 (978-0-06-172851-8(9)) 2010. 464p. 16.99 (978-0-06-172849-5(7)) HarperCollins Pubs. (HarperTeen).

Ayres, Katherine. Macaroni Boy. 2004. (ENG.). 192p. (J). (gr. 3-7). per. 6.99 (978-0-440-41884-9(4), Yearling) Random Hse. Children's Bks.

Baca, Ana. Tía's Tamales. Chilton, Noel, illus. 2012. (ENG & SPA.). 32p. (J). pap. 16.95 (978-0-8263-5027-5(5)) Univ. of New Mexico Pr.

Badoe, Adwoa. Nana's Cold Days, 1 vol. Junaid, Bushra, illus. 2009. (ENG.). 24p. (J). (gr. k-k). pap. 6.95 (978-0-88899-937-5(2)) Groundwood Bks. CAN. Dist: Publishers Group West (PGW).

Baer, Marianna. The Inconceivable Life of Quinn. 2017. (ENG.). 384p. (YA). 18.95 (978-1-4197-2302-5(2), Amulet Bks.) Abrams, Inc.

Bains-Fort. It's Keen to Be Green. 2009. 40p. pap. 23.49 (978-1-4389-9145-0(2)) AuthorHouse.

Bair, Sheila. Rock, Brock, & the Savings Shock. Gott, Barry, illus. 2017. (ENG.). 32p. (J). (gr. -1-3). pap. 7.99 **(978-0-8075-7095-1(8))** Whitman, Albert & Co.

Bajaj, Varsha. How Many Kisses Do You Want Tonight? Bates, Ivan, illus. 2007. (ENG.). 26p. (J). (gr. -1 — 1). bds. 6.99 (978-0-316-06735-5(0)) Little, Brown Bks. for Young Readers.

Baker, Barbara. One Saturday Evening. Duke, Kate, illus. 2007. (J). (978-0-525-47850-8(7), Dutton Juvenile) Penguin Publishing Group.

Baker, Jennifer. Just Like Sisters. 2014. (ENG., Illus.). 192p. (YA). (gr. 7). pap. 13.99 (978-1-4814-2876-7(4), Simon Pulse) Simon Pulse.

Balaban, Bob. Boy or Beast. Rash, Andy, illus. (Creature from the 7th Grade Ser.: 1). (ENG.). (J). (gr. 5). 2013. 272p. pap. 7.99 (978-0-14-242542-8(7), Puffin Books) 2012. 256p. 15.99 (978-0-670-01271-8(8), Viking Books for Young Readers) Penguin Young Readers Group.

Ballengee, Fran. Sara Elizabeth, an Adoption Story. 2008. 22p. pap. 24.95 (978-1-60610-557-3(4)) PublishAmerica, Inc.

Balliett, Blue. The Danger Box. 2012. (ENG.). 320p. (J). (gr. 3-7). pap. 7.99 (978-0-439-85210-4(2), Scholastic Paperbacks) Scholastic, Inc.

—Hold Fast. 2015. (ENG.). 288p. (J). (gr. 3-7). pap. 6.99 (978-0-545-29989-3(6), Scholastic Paperbacks) Scholastic, Inc.

Balzola, Asun. Munia y Sra. Piltronera (Munia & Mrs. Piltronera) (SPA.). 36p. (J). 16.95 (978-84-233-1290-0(9)) Ediciones Destino ESP. Dist: AIMS International Bks., Inc.

Balzola, Asun & Asun, Balzola. Babi es Barbara. (SPA.). 72p. 8.95 (978-84-392-8113-9(7)) Baker & Taylor Bks.

Bancks, Tristan. On the Run. 2015. (ENG.). 240p. (J). (gr. 5-7). 16.99 (978-0-374-30153-8(0), 9780374301538, Farrar, Straus & Giroux (BYR)) Farrar, Straus & Giroux.

Banks, Kate. Max's Words. 2011. (J). (gr. k-2). 29.95 (978-0-545-04373-1(5)) Weston Woods Studios, Inc.

Banks, Lynne Reid. The Key to the Indian. 2004. (Indian in the Cupboard Ser.: 5). (J). (gr. 3-6). lib. bdg. 17.20 (978-0-613-23006-3(X), Turtleback) Turtleback Bks.

—The Mystery of the Cupboard. Newsom, Tom, illus. 2004. (Indian in the Cupboard Ser.: No. 4). (ENG.). 256p. (J). (gr. 4-18). pap. 6.99 (978-0-380-72013-2(2)) HarperCollins Pubs.

Banks, Sara Harrell. The Everlasting Now, 1 vol. 2010. (ENG.). 168p. (J). (gr. 3-7). 15.95 (978-1-56145-525-6(3), Peachtree Junior) Peachtree Pubs.

Banting, Celia. I only said I was telling the Truth. 2006. 240p. (YA). per. 14.99 (978-0-9786648-4-8(1)) Wighita Pr.

—I Only Said Yes So That They'd Like Me. 2006. (Illus.). 224p. (YA). per. 14.99 (978-0-9786648-1-7(7)) Wighita Pr.

Barash, Chris. Is It Hanukkah Yet? Psacharopulo, Alessandra, illus. 2015. (ENG.). 32p. (J). (gr. -1-3). 16.99 (978-0-8075-3384-0(X)) Whitman, Albert & Co.

—Is It Passover Yet? Psacharopulo, Alessandra, illus. 2015. (ENG.). 32p. (J). (gr. -1-3). 16.99 (978-0-8075-6330-4(7)) Whitman, Albert & Co.

Baratz-Logsted, Lauren. I Love You, Michael Collins. 2017. (ENG.). 240p. (J). 16.99 (978-0-374-30385-3(1), 9780374303853, Farrar, Straus & Giroux (BYR)) Farrar, Straus & Giroux.

—Red Girl, Blue Boy: An If Only Novel. 2015. (If Only... Ser.). (ENG.). 304p. (YA). (gr. 7). pap. 9.99 (978-1-61963-685-9(9), 9781619636859, Bloomsbury USA Childrens) Bloomsbury Publishing USA.

Barber, Tiki & Barber, Ronde. Goal Line. 2013. (Barber Game Time Bks.). (ENG., Illus.). 176p. (J). (gr. 3-7). pap. 6.99 (978-1-4169-9096-3(8), Simon & Schuster/Paula Wiseman Bks.) Simon & Schuster/Paula Wiseman Bks.

—Jump Shot. 2013. (Barber Game Time Bks.). (ENG., Illus.). 160p. (J). (gr. 3-7). 16.99 (978-1-4424-5729-4(5), Simon & Schuster/Paula Wiseman Bks.) Simon & Schuster/Paula Wiseman Bks.

Barden, Stephanie. Cinderella Smith. Goode, Diane, illus. (Cinderella Smith Ser.: 1). (ENG.). (J). 2011. 160p. (gr. 3-7). 16.99 (978-0-06-196423-7(9)) Vol. 3. 2013. 144p. (gr. 1-5). 16.99 (978-0-06-200443-7(3)) HarperCollins Pubs.

—The More the Merrier. Goode, Diane, illus. (Cinderella Smith Ser.: 2). (ENG.). (J). (gr. 3-7). 2013. 160p. pap. 5.99 (978-0-06-200442-0(5)) 2012. 144p. 15.99 (978-0-06-200440-6(9)) HarperCollins Pubs.

Barnaby, Hannah Rodgers. Bad Guy. Yamada, Mike, illus. 2017. (ENG.). 32p. (J). (gr. -1-3). 17.99 (978-1-4814-6010-1(2), Simon & Schuster Bks. For Young Readers) Simon & Schuster Bks. For Young Readers.

Barnes, Derrick D. We Could Be Brothers. 2010. (J). (978-0-545-13574-0(5), Scholastic Pr.) Scholastic, Inc.

Barnett, Mac. Billy Twitters & His Blue Whale Problem. Rex, Adam, illus. 2009. (ENG.). 48p. (J). (gr. -1-2). 16.99 (978-0-7868-4958-1(4)) Hyperion Pr.

Barnett, Wm. Billy's Wish. Kiste, Tori Lynn, illus. 2008. 28p. pap. 24.95 (978-1-60563-330-5(5)) America Star Bks.

Barnhill, Kelly. The Mostly True Story of Jack. 2012. (ENG.). 352p. (J). (gr. 3-7). pap. 8.99 (978-0-316-05672-4(3)) Little, Brown Bks. for Young Readers.

—The Witch's Boy. 2014. (ENG.). 384p. (J). (gr. 4). 17.95 (978-1-61620-351-1(X), 73351) Algonquin Bks. of Chapel Hill.

Barnholdt, Lauren. Hailey Twitch & the Great Teacher Switch. Beaky, Suzanne, illus. 2010. (Hailey Twitch Ser.: 2). (ENG.). 176p. (J). (gr. 2-4). pap. 6.99 (978-1-4022-2445-4(1), Sourcebooks Jabberwocky) Sourcebooks, Inc.

—Hailey Twitch Is Not a Snitch. Beaky, Suzanne, illus. 2010. (Hailey Twitch Ser.: 1). (ENG.). 160p. (J). (gr. 2-4). pap. 6.99 (978-1-4022-2444-7(3), Sourcebooks Jabberwocky) Sourcebooks, Inc.

—Right of Way. 2014. (ENG., Illus.). 336p. (YA). (gr. 9). pap. 9.99 (978-1-4424-5128-5(9), Simon Pulse) Simon Pulse.

Barraclough, Lindsey. Long Lankin. 2014. (ENG.). 464p. (YA). (gr. 7). pap. 9.99 (978-0-7636-6937-9(7)) Candlewick Pr.

Barrow, Randi. Saving Zasha. 2013. (ENG.). 256p. (J). (gr. 3-7). pap. 6.99 (978-0-545-20633-4(2), Scholastic Paperbacks) Scholastic, Inc.

Barrows, Annie. Bound to Be Bad. 2009. (Ivy & Bean Ser.: 5). (J). lib. bdg. 16.00 (978-0-606-14473-5(0), Turtleback) Turtleback Bks.

—Ivy + Bean Bound to Be Bad. Blackall, Sophie, illus. (Ivy & Bean Ser.: IVYB). (ENG.). (J). (gr. 1-5). 2009. 128p. pap. 5.99 (978-0-8118-6857-0(5)) 2008. 124p. 14.99 (978-0-8118-6265-3(8)) Chronicle Bks. LLC.

Barrows, Annie & Blackall, Sophie. Ivy + Bean Bound to Be Bad, 1 vol. 2011. (Ivy & Bean Ser.). (ENG., Illus.). 128p. (J). (gr. 1-4). 24.21 (978-1-59961-932-3(6)) Spotlight.

Barry, Cotter. By the Numbers. 2010. 16p. 12.99 (978-1-4520-1476-0(0)) AuthorHouse.

Barshaw, Ruth McNally. Ellie McDoodle: Have Pen, Will Travel. Barshaw, Ruth McNally, illus. 2nd ed. 2011. (Ellie Mcdoodle Ser.). (ENG., Illus.). 192p. (YA). (gr. 3-6). pap. 7.99 (978-1-59990-715-4(1), 9781599907154, Bloomsbury USA Childrens) Bloomsbury Publishing USA.

—The Ellie McDoodle Diaries: Ellie for President. Barshaw, Ruth McNally, illus. 2014. (Ellie Mcdoodle Ser.). (ENG., Illus.). 176p. (J). (gr. 3-6). 12.99 (978-1-61963-061-1(3), 9781619630611, Bloomsbury USA Childrens) Bloomsbury Publishing USA.

—Have Pen, Will Travel. Barshaw, Ruth McNally, illus. 2013. (Ellie Mcdoodle Diaries). (ENG., Illus.). 192p. (YA). (gr. 3-6). 12.99 (978-1-61963-173-1(3), 9781619631731, Bloomsbury USA Childrens) Bloomsbury Publishing USA.

—New Kid in School. Barshaw, Ruth McNally, illus. 2013. (Ellie Mcdoodle Diaries). (ENG., Illus.). 192p. (YA). (gr. 3-6). 12.99 (978-1-61963-174-8(1), 9781619631748, Bloomsbury USA Childrens) Bloomsbury Publishing USA.

—The Show Must Go On. Barshaw, Ruth McNally, illus. 2013. (Ellie Mcdoodle Diaries). (ENG., Illus.). 176p. (YA). (gr. 3-6). 12.99 (978-1-61963-059-8(1), 9781619630598, Bloomsbury USA Childrens) Bloomsbury Publishing USA.

Baskin, Nora Raleigh. Anything but Typical. (ENG.). 208p. (J). (gr. 5-9). 2010. pap. 8.99 (978-1-4169-9500-5(5)) 2009. (Illus.). 17.99 (978-1-4169-6378-3(2)) Simon & Schuster Bks. For Young Readers. (Simon & Schuster Bks. For Young Readers).

—Basketball (or Something Like It) 176p. (J). 2007. (ENG.). (gr. 4-7). pap. 6.99 (978-0-06-059612-5(0)) 2005. (ENG.). 15.99 (978-0-06-059610-1(4)) 2005. lib. bdg. 16.89 (978-0-06-059611-8(2)) HarperCollins Pubs.

Bass, Alexis. What's Broken Between Us. 2015. (ENG.). 304p. (YA). (gr. 9). 17.99 (978-0-06-227535-6(6), HarperTeen) HarperCollins Pubs.

Bateson, Catherine. Being Bee. (ENG.). 136p. (J). 2008. (gr. 3-7). pap. 7.95 (978-0-8234-2208-1(9)) 2007. (Illus.). (gr. 4-7). 16.95 (978-0-8234-2104-6(X)) Holiday Hse., Inc.

Bauer, Joan. Backwater. rev. ed. 2005. (ENG.). 192p. (YA). (gr. 7-12). pap. 7.99 (978-0-14-240434-8(9), Speak) Penguin Young Readers Group.

—Backwater. 2005. 185p. 18.00 (978-0-7569-5779-7(6)) Perfection Learning Corp.

—Best Foot Forward. 2006. (ENG.). 192p. (YA). (gr. 7-18). reprint ed. 7.99 (978-0-14-240690-8(2), Speak) Penguin Young Readers Group.

—Best Foot Forward. 2006. 183p. (gr. 7-12). 18.00 (978-0-7569-6767-3(8)) Perfection Learning Corp.

Bauer, Marion Dane. Killing Miss Kitty & Other Sins. 2008. (ENG.). 176p. (YA). (gr. 7). pap. 12.95 (978-0-547-07614-0(2)) Houghton Mifflin Harcourt Publishing Co.

Bauman, Beth Ann. Rosie & Skate. 2011. (ENG.). 224p. (YA). (gr. 9). pap. 8.99 (978-0-385-73736-4(X), Ember) Random Hse. Children's Bks.

Beale, Fleur. The Boy in the Olive Grove. 2013. 368p. pap. (978-1-4596-5723-6(3)) ReadHowYouWant.com, Ltd.

Beam, Jon. Jardien's Dream, 1 vol. 2009. 185p. pap. 24.95 (978-1-4489-2613-8(0)) America Star Bks.

Bean, Jonathan. This Is My Home, This Is My School. 2015. (ENG., Illus.). 48p. (J). (gr. -1-1). 18.99 (978-0-374-38020-5(1), 9780374380205, Farrar, Straus & Giroux (BYR)) Farrar, Straus & Giroux.

Beaty, Andrea. Dorko the Magnificent. (ENG.). (J). (gr. 3-7). 2014. 240p. pap. 7.95 (978-1-4197-1019-3(2)) 2013. (Illus.). 224p. 17.95 (978-1-4197-0638-7(1)) Abrams, Inc. (Amulet Bks.).

Beaumont, Karen. Crybaby. Yelchin, Eugene, illus. 2015. (ENG.). 40p. (J). (gr. -1-1). 17.99 (978-0-8050-8974-5(8), 9780805089745, Holt, Henry & Co. Bks. For Young Readers) Holt, Henry & Co.

Beauty of the Broken. 2014. (ENG., Illus.). 368p. (YA). (gr. 9). 17.99 (978-1-4814-0709-0(0), Simon Pulse) Simon Pulse.

Beauvais, Clémentine. Sleuth on Skates. Horne, Sarah, illus. 2014. (Sesame Seade Mystery Ser.: 1). (ENG.). 224p. (J). (gr. 2-5). 16.95 (978-0-8234-3197-7(5)) Holiday Hse., Inc.

Beck, Glenn, et al. The Snow Angel. Dorman, Brandon, illus. 2011. (ENG.). 40p. (J). (gr. -1-2). 7.99 *(978-1-4424-4448-5(7),* Simon & Schuster/Paula Wiseman Bks.) Simon & Schuster/Paula Wiseman Bks.

Becker, Suzy. Kate the Great Except When She's Not. Becker, Suzy, illus. 2014. (Kate the Great Ser.: 1). (ENG., Illus.). 272p. (J). (gr. 3-7). 12.99 *(978-0-385-38742-2(3),* Crown Books For Young Readers) Random Hse. Children's Bks.

—Kate the Great, Except When She's Not. Becker, Suzy, illus. 2014. (Kate the Great Ser.). (ENG., Illus.). 272p. (J). (gr. 3-7). lib. bdg. 15.99 *(978-0-385-38743-9(1),* Crown Books For Young Readers) Random Hse. Children's Bks.

Beckley, N. K. The Writer's Corner: Book 3. 2012. 90p. 24.99 *(978-1-4797-1241-0(8));* pap. 15.99 *(978-1-4797-1240-3(X))* Xlibris Corp.

Beer, Henry, photos by. Girl Defective. 2015. (ENG., Illus.). 320p. (YA). (gr. 9). pap. 10.99 *(978-1-4424-9761-0(0))* Simon & Schuster Children's Publishing.

Behar, Ruth. Lucky Broken Girl. 2017. (ENG.). 256p. (J). (gr. 5). 16.99 *(978-0-399-54644-0(8),* Nancy Paulsen Books) Penguin Young Readers Group.

Believarexic, 1 vol. 2015. (ENG.). 464p. (YA). (gr. 8-11). 18.95 *(978-1-56145-771-7(X))* Peachtree Pubs.

Bell, Cathleen Davitt. Little Blog on the Prairie. 2011. (ENG.). 288p. (YA). (gr. 7). pap. 9.99 *(978-1-59990-677-5(5),* 9781599906775, Bloomsbury USA Childrens) Bloomsbury Publishing USA.

Bell, Eric. Alan Cole Is Not a Coward. 2017. 272p. (J). (gr. 3-7). 16.99 ***(978-0-06-256702-4(0),*** Tegen, Katherine Bks) HarperCollins Pubs.

Bell, Hilari. Trickster's Girl: The Raven Duet Book #1. 2011. (Raven Duet Ser.). (ENG.). 288p. (YA). (gr. 7). pap. 15.99 *(978-0-547-57724-1(9))* Houghton Mifflin Harcourt Publishing Co.

Bell, Jennifer. The Crooked Sixpence. Helquist, Brett, illus. 2017. (Uncommoners Ser.: 1). (ENG.). 320p. (J). (gr. 3-7). 16.99 *(978-0-553-49843-1(6),* Crown Books For Young Readers) Random Hse. Children's Bks.

Bell, Julia. Massive. 2006. (ENG., Illus.). 272p. (YA). (gr. 7-18). pap. 8.99 *(978-1-4169-0207-2(4),* Simon Pulse) Simon Pulse.

Bell, Juliet. Kepler's Dream. 2013. (ENG.). 256p. (J). (gr. 5). pap. 6.99 *(978-0-14-242648-7(2),* Puffin Books) Penguin Young Readers Group.

Bell, Liz. Amarie & Her Family. 2011. 24p. pap. 24.95 *(978-1-4560-5430-4(9))* America Star Bks.

Bell, Shelia. The Life of Payne: Book II Fairley High Series. 2014. (ENG.). (YA). (gr. 7-18). pap. 9.95 *(978-0-9838935-7-8(8),* Seraphina) Bonita and Hodge Publishing Group.

Bencastro, Mario. A Promise to Keep. Giersbach-Rascon, Susan, tr. from SPA. 2005. 134p. (J). (gr. 3-7). pap. 9.95 *(978-1-55885-457-4(6),* Piñata Books) Arte Publico Pr.

Benchmark Education Co., LLC. OH BRODIE! Big Book. 2014. (Shared Reading Foundations Ser.). (J). (gr. -1). *(978-1-4509-9430-9(X))* Benchmark Education Co.

Bender, Carrie. Hemlock Hill Hideaway: Whispering Brook Series #4. 2007. (Illus.). 168p. pap. 8.99 *(978-1-60126-022-2(9))* Masthof Pr.

—Summerville Days: Whispering Brook Series #2. 2007. (Illus.). 224p. pap. 8.99 *(978-1-60126-023-9(7))* Masthof Pr.

—Timber Lane Cove. 2003. (ENG.). 144p. (YA). pap. 8.99 *(978-0-8361-9202-5(8))* Herald Pr.

Bender, Esther. Elisabeth & the Windmill. 2003. (ENG.). 112p. (J). (gr. 3-7). pap. 6.99 *(978-0-8361-9204-9(4))* Herald Pr.

Benedis-Grab, Daphne. Clementine for Christmas. 2015. (ENG.). 256p. (J). (gr. 3-7). 16.99 *(978-0-545-83951-8(3),* Scholastic Pr.) Scholastic, Inc.

Benjamin, Ruth. The Lost Treasure of Chelton. 2004. viii, 170p. (J). 13.95 *(978-1-932443-02-8(9))* Judaica Pr., Inc., The.

—The Mysterious Lighthouse of Chelton. 2006. (ENG.). 160p. (J). 14.95 *(978-1-932443-57-8(6))* Judaica Pr., Inc., The.

Bennett, Jenn. The Anatomical Shape of a Heart. 2015. (ENG.). 304p. (YA). (gr. 7). 17.99 *(978-1-250-06645-9(X),* 9781250066459) Feiwel & Friends.

Bennett, Jill. Grandad's Tree: Poems about Families. Cairns, Julia, illus. 2003. 32p. (J). 16.99 *(978-1-84148-541-6(1))* Barefoot Bks., Inc.

Bennett, Sophia. The Look. 2013. (J). (ENG.). 336p. (gr. 7). 17.99 *(978-0-545-46438-3(2)); (978-0-545-46439-0(0))* Scholastic, Inc. (Chicken Hse., The).

Benson, Jeffrey. The Adventures of Avortit & Rooney. 2005. pap. *(978-1-84401-490-3(8))* Athena Pr.

Benson, Linda. Finding Chance. Lane, Nancy, illus. 2006. 112p. (J). *(978-1-59336-696-4(5))* Mondo Publishing.

Benson, Linda Sue. It's Okay, Leon, 1 vol. 2009. 74p. pap. 19.95 *(978-1-4489-2173-7(2))* America Star Bks.

Benson, Sherry. Introducing Jelly Bean. 2008. 27p. pap. 24.95 *(978-1-60672-427-9(4))* America Star Bks.

Benyo, Richard. The South Street Gang vs. the Coalcracker Cyclops. 2010. (ENG.). 151p. pap. 8.00 *(978-1-58966-208-7(3))* Univ. of Scranton Pr.

Berenstain, Jan & Berenstain, Mike. Bear Country Blessings, 1 vol. 2013. (Berenstain Bears/Living Lights Ser.). (ENG.). 96p. (J). 7.99 *(978-0-310-73503-8(3))* Zonderkidz.

—The Berenstain Bears at the Aquarium. 2012. (Berenstain Bears: I Can Read! Ser.). (J). lib. bdg. 13.55 *(978-0-606-23594-5(9),* Turtleback) Turtleback Bks.

—God Bless Our Home, 1 vol. 2012. (Berenstain Bears/Living Lights Ser.). (ENG., Illus.). 32p. (J). pap. 3.99 *(978-0-310-72089-8(3))* Zonderkidz.

Berenstain, Mike. The Berenstain Bears Play Football! Berenstain, Mike, illus. 2017. (I Can Read Level 1 Ser.). (Illus.). 32p. (J). (gr. -1-3). pap. 3.99 ***(978-0-06-235033-6(1))*** HarperCollins Pubs.

Berenstain, Mike, illus. The Berenstain Bears Love One Another. 2016. (J). *(978-0-8249-1983-2(1),* Ideal Pubns.) Worthy Publishing.

—The Berenstain Bears' Please & Thank You Book. 2015. (J). *(978-0-8249-1945-0(9),* Ideal Pubns.) Worthy Publishing.

—The Berenstain Bears' Sleepy Time Book. 2015. (J). *(978-0-8249-1946-7(7),* Ideal Pubns.) Worthy Publishing.

Berenstain, Stan & Berenstain, Jan. The Berenstain Bears & the Trouble with Chores. Berenstain, Jan, illus. 2005. (Berenstain Bears Ser.). (ENG., Illus.). 32p. (J). (gr. -1-3). pap. 3.99 *(978-0-06-057382-9(1),* HarperFestival) HarperCollins Pubs.

—The Berenstain Bears & Too Much Car Trip. Berenstain, Stan & Berenstain, Jan, illus. 2006. (Berenstain Bears Ser.). (Illus.). 32p. (J). (gr. -1-2). 10.99 *(978-0-06-057400-0(3));* (ENG., pap. 3.99 *(978-0-06-057384-3(8))* HarperCollins Pubs. (HarperFestival).

—The Berenstain Bears' Report Card Trouble. 2004. (Berenstain Bears First Time Bks.). (J). (gr. k-3). spiral bd. *(978-0-616-11096-6(0));* spiral bd. *(978-0-616-11095-9(2))* Canadian National Institute for the Blind/Institut National Canadien pour les Aveugles.

—The Berenstain Bears' Storytime Treasury. 2012. (ENG., Illus.). 104p. (J). (gr. k-3). pap. 12.99 *(978-0-486-49836-2(0))* Dover Pubns., Inc.

Berenstain, Stan, et al. The Berenstain Bears. 2012. (Dover Paper Dolls Ser.). (ENG.). 32p. (J). (gr. 1-5). pap. 9.99 *(978-0-486-49835-5(2))* Dover Pubns., Inc.

—The Berenstain Bears & the Big Spelling Bee, No. 6. Berenstain, Stan et al, illus. 2007. (Berenstain Bears Ser.). (ENG.). 32p. (J). (gr. -1-2). pap. 3.99 *(978-0-06-057386-7(4),* HarperFestival) HarperCollins Pubs.

—The Berenstain Bears Hug & Make Up. Berenstain, Stan & Berenstain, Jan, illus. 2006. (Berenstain Bears Ser.). (ENG.). 32p. (J). (gr. -1-2). pap. 3.99 *(978-0-06-057385-0(6),* HarperFestival) HarperCollins Pubs.

Beres, E. Jean. The Sugaring Season. 2008. 92p. pap. 19.95 *(978-1-60610-633-4(3))* America Star Bks.

Berman, Seryl. Around the Shabbos Table. Binus, Ari, illus. 2008. 40p. (J). (gr. -1-k). pap. 10.95 *(978-1-929628-44-5(7))* Hachai Publishing.

Bernard, Margaret Mitchell. Kate & the Family Tree. Duncan, Shirley, ed. Ciesinska, Izabela, illus. 2009. 24p. pap. 14.99 *(978-1-4251-7408-8(6))* Trafford Publishing.

Berni, K. S. Angels of Children: Sarafina Teaches the Importance of Prayer. 2012. 40p. pap. 20.99 *(978-1-4772-7708-9(0))* AuthorHouse.

Bernstein, Jonathan. Bridget Wilder: Spy-In-Training. 2016. (Bridget Wilder Ser.: 1). (J). lib. bdg. 17.20 *(978-0-606-38746-0(3))* Turtleback Bks.

—Bridget Wilder: Spy-In-Training. 2015. (Bridget Wilder Ser.: 1). (ENG.). 320p. (J). (gr. 3-7). 16.99 *(978-0-06-238266-5(7),* Tegen, Katherine Bks) HarperCollins Pubs.

Bertrand, Diane Gonzales. El Dilema de Trino. Castilla, Julia Mercedes, tr. from ENG. 2005. (SPA.). 136p. (J). (gr. 3-7). per. 9.95 *(978-1-55885-458-1(4),* Piñata Books) Arte Publico Pr.

—The F Factor. 2010. 256p. (YA). (gr. 6-18). pap. 12.95 *(978-1-55885-598-4(X),* Piñata Books) Arte Publico Pr.

—El Momento de Trino. Sanmiguel, Rosario, tr. from ENG. 2006. (SPA.). 181p. (J). (gr. 3-7). per. 9.95 *(978-1-55885-473-4(8),* Piñata Books) Arte Publico Pr.

—Sip, Slurp, Soup, Soup/Caldo, Caldo, Caldo. Castilla, Julia Mercedes, tr. Delange, Alex Pardo, illus. 2008. (SPA & ENG.). 32p. (J). (gr. -1-2). pap. 7.95 *(978-1-55885-241-9(7),* Piñata Books) Arte Publico Pr.

—Sip, Slurp, Soup Soup/Caldo Caldo Caldo: CD & Book Set. DeLange, Alex Pardo, illus. 2008. 32p. (J). pap. 19.95 *(978-0-9815686-1-4(0))* Lorito Bks., Inc.

Beserra, Donna. Twirly Shirley & the Brother Like No Other. 2004. (J). pap. 12.00 *(978-0-9729484-2-5(2))* Seventh Street Pr.

Bess, Clayton, et al. Story for a Black Night. 2004. (ENG.). 112p. (YA). (gr. 7). pap. 8.95 *(978-0-618-49483-5(9))* Houghton Mifflin Harcourt Publishing Co.

Best, Cari. When We Go Walking, 0 vols. Brooker, Kyrsten, illus. 2013. (ENG.). 32p. (J). (gr. -1-3). 17.99 *(978-1-4778-1648-6(8),* 9781477816486, Amazon Children's Publishing) Amazon Publishing.

Bick, Ilsa J. Drowning Instinct. 2013. (ENG.). 352p. (YA). (gr. 9-12). pap. 9.95 *(978-1-4677-0912-5(3),* Carolrhoda Lab™) Lerner Publishing Group.

The Big Mix-up: Individual Title Six-Packs. (gr. -1-2). 27.00 *(978-0-7635-9438-1(5))* Rigby Education.

Bildner, Phil. Tournament of Champions. Probert, Tim, illus. 2017. (Rip & Red Ser.: 3). (ENG.). 256p. (J). 16.99 *(978-0-374-30507-9(2),* 9780374305079, Farrar, Straus & Giroux (BYR)) Farrar, Straus & Giroux.

—Turkey Bowl. Payne, C. F., illus. 2008. (ENG.). 32p. (J). (gr. k-3). 15.99 *(978-0-689-87896-1(6),* Simon & Schuster Bks. For Young Readers) Simon & Schuster Bks. For Young Readers.

Birdsall, Jeanne. The Penderwicks at Point Mouette. 2011. (Playaway Children Ser.). (J). (gr. k). 44.99 *(978-1-61707-434-9(9))* Findaway World, LLC.

—The Penderwicks at Point Mouette. (Penderwicks Ser.). (ENG.). (J). (gr. 3-7). 2012. 320p. 7.99 *(978-0-375-85135-3(6),* Yearling) 2011. 304p. 16.99 *(978-0-375-85851-2(2),* Knopf Bks. for Young Readers) Random Hse. Children's Bks.

—The Penderwicks in Spring. 2015. (Penderwicks Ser.). (ENG.). 352p. (J). (gr. 3-7). 16.99 *(978-0-375-87077-4(6),* Knopf Bks. for Young Readers) Random Hse. Children's Bks.

—The Penderwicks on Gardam Street. 2011. (Playaway Children Ser.). (J). (gr. 3-6). 44.99 *(978-1-61707-435-6(7))* Findaway World, LLC.

—The Penderwicks on Gardam Street. (Penderwicks Ser.). (ENG.). (J). (gr. 3-7). 2010. 336p. 7.99 *(978-0-440-42203-7(5),* Yearling) 2008. 320p. 16.99 *(978-0-375-84090-6(7),* Knopf Bks. for Young Readers) Random Hse. Children's Bks.

—The Penderwicks on Gardam Street. 2010. (Penderwicks Ser.: 2). lib. bdg. 18.40 *(978-0-606-14418-6(8),* Turtleback) Turtleback Bks.

Birney, Betty G. The Princess & the Peabodys. 2007. (ENG.). 256p. (J). (gr. 5-9). 15.99 *(978-0-06-084720-3(4))* HarperCollins Pubs.

—The Seven Wonders of Sassafras Springs. Phelan, Matt, illus. 2007. 210p. 17.00 *(978-0-7569-8075-7(5))* Perfection Learning Corp.

—The Seven Wonders of Sassafras Springs. Phelan, Matt, illus. (ENG.). 224p. (J). (gr. 3-7). 2007. pap. 7.99 *(978-1-4169-3489-9(8))* 2005. 16.95 *(978-0-689-87136-8(8))* Simon & Schuster Children's Publishing. (Atheneum Bks. for Young Readers).

Birtha, Becky. Lucky Beans. Tadgell, Nicole, illus. 2012. (J). 34.28 *(978-1-61913-129-3(3))* Weigl Pubs., Inc.

—Lucky Beans. Tadgell, Nicole, illus. 2010. (ENG.). 32p. (J). (gr. 2-3). 16.99 *(978-0-8075-4782-3(4))* Whitman, Albert & Co.

Bishop, Jenn. 14 Hollow Road. 2017. (ENG.). 288p. (J). (gr. 3-7). 16.99 ***(978-1-101-93875-1(7));*** lib. bdg. 19.99 ***(978-1-101-93876-8(5))*** Random Hse. Children's Bks. (Knopf Bks. for Young Readers).

Bjornsen, Holly. Red Book Pets Vets & Snakes. Phillips, Linda T., illus. 2011. 51p. (YA). pap. 16.95 *(978-0-9828950-1-6(1))* Digi-Tall Media.

Black, Chuck. Rise of the Fallen: Wars of the Realm, Book 2. 2015. (Wars of the Realm Ser.). (ENG.). 320p. (YA). (gr. 7). pap. 11.99 *(978-1-60142-504-1(X),* Multnomah Bks.) Crown Publishing Group.

Black, Holly. Doll Bones. Wheeler, Eliza, illus. 2013. (ENG.). 256p. (J). (gr. 5-9). 18.99 *(978-1-4169-6398-1(7),* McElderry, Margaret K. Bks.) McElderry, Margaret K. Bks.

—Doll Bones. 2015. lib. bdg. 18.40 *(978-0-606-36308-2(4))* Turtleback Bks.

Black, Holly & DiTerlizzi, Tony. Lucinda's Secret. DiTerlizzi, Tony, illus. 2013. (Spiderwick Chronicles Ser.: 3). (ENG., Illus.). (J). (gr. 1-5). 128p. 15.99 *(978-1-4424-8700-0(3));* 144p. pap. 7.99 *(978-1-4424-8697-3(X))* Simon & Schuster Bks. For Young Readers. (Simon & Schuster Bks. For Young Readers).

Black, Joe. Afikomen Mambo. Prater, Linda, illus. 2011. (ENG.). 24p. (J). (gr. -1 — 1). pap. 8.95 *(978-0-7613-5639-4(8),* Kar-Ben Publishing) Lerner Publishing Group.

—Afikomen Mambo. Brown, Richard E. & Prater, Linda, illus. 2011. (Passover Ser.). (ENG.). 24p. (J). (gr. -1 — 1). lib. bdg. 17.95 *(978-0-7613-5638-7(X),* Kar-Ben Publishing) Lerner Publishing Group.

Blackaby, Susan. Moving Day, 1 vol. Haugen, Ryan, illus. 2005. (Read-It! Readers Ser.). (ENG.). 24p. (gr. -1-3). 21.32 *(978-1-4048-1006-8(4),* Easy Readers) Picture Window Bks.

Blacker, Terence. The Angel Factory. 2012. (ENG., Illus.). 224p. (J). (gr. 5-9). pap. 10.99 *(978-0-689-86413-1(2),* Simon & Schuster/Paula Wiseman Bks.) Simon & Schuster/Paula Wiseman Bks.

Blackstone, Stella. La Familia Ocupada de Oso. 2012. (ENG & SPA.). (J). 6.99 *(978-1-84686-771-2(1))* Barefoot Bks., Inc.

—La Famille Active de l'Ours. 2012.Tr. of Bear's Busy Family. (FRE & ENG.). (J). pap. 6.99 *(978-1-84686-772-9(X))* Barefoot Bks., Inc.

Blackwell, Paul E. Undercurrent. 2013. 320p. (YA). (gr. 9). 17.99 *(978-0-06-212350-3(5),* HarperTeen) HarperCollins Pubs.

Blair, Eric. El Pescador y Su Mujer: Versión del Cuento de los Hermanos Grimm. Abello, Patricia, tr. Ouren, Todd, illus. 2006. (Read-It! Readers en Español: Cuentos de Hadas Ser.). (SPA.). 32p. (gr. k-3). 21.32 *(978-1-4048-1630-5(5),* Easy Readers) Picture Window Bks.

Blake, Ashley Herring. Suffer Love. 2016. (ENG.). 352p. (YA). (gr. 9). 17.99 *(978-0-544-59632-0(3),* HMH Books For Young Readers) Houghton Mifflin Harcourt Publishing Co.

—Suffer Love. 2017. (ENG.). (YA). (gr. 9). lib. bdg. 20.85 ***(978-0-606-39817-6(1))*** Turtleback Bks.

Blake, Stephanie J. The Marble Queen, 0 vols. 2012. (ENG.). 192p. (YA). (gr. 5-9). 16.99 *(978-0-7614-6227-9(9),* 9780761462279, Amazon Children's Publishing) Amazon Publishing.

Blakemore, Megan Frazer. Very in Pieces. 2015. (ENG.). 384p. (YA). (gr. 8). 17.99 *(978-0-06-234839-5(6),* HarperTeen) HarperCollins Pubs.

Bland, Nick. The Runaway Hug. Blackwood, Freya, illus. 2013. (ENG.). 32p. (J). (gr. -1-2). 16.99 *(978-0-449-81825-1(X),* Random Hse. Bks. for Young Readers) Random Hse. Children's Bks.

Blasi, Kathleen McAlpin. A Name of Honor. Bowman, Leslie W., illus. 2006. (J). *(978-1-59336-692-6(2))* Mondo Publishing.

Blejwas, Emily. Once You Know This. 2017. (ENG.). 240p. (J). (gr. 4-7). 16.99 ***(978-1-5247-0097-3(5));*** lib. bdg. 19.99 ***(978-1-5247-0098-0(3))*** Random Hse. Children's Bks. (Delacorte Bks. for Young Readers).

Block, F. L. My Miserable Life. Hemingway, Edward, illus. 2016. (ENG.). 192p. (J). 13.99 *(978-0-8050-9628-6(0),* 9780805096286, Holt, Henry & Co. Bks. For Young Readers) Holt, Henry & Co.

Blomgren, Jennifer. The Tale of Alice's Quilt. 2008. (That Patchwork Place Ser.). (ENG., Illus.). 95p. (YA). (gr. 8-12). per. 14.95 *(978-1-56477-833-8(9),* That Patchwork Place) Martingale & Co.

Blue, Martha. Little Prankster Girl: At'Eed Adilahi Yazhi. Ruffenach, Jessie, ed. Thomas, Peter, tr. from NAV. Smith, Keith, illus. 2008. (NAV & ENG.). 32p. (J). (gr. -1-3). 17.95 *(978-1-893354-36-4(9))* Salina Bookshelf Inc.

Bluemle, Elizabeth. Dogs on the Bed. Wilsdorf, Anne, illus. 2013. (ENG.). 32p. (J). (gr. -1-2). pap. 6.99 *(978-0-7636-6736-8(6))* Candlewick Pr.

Blume, Judy. BFF: Just as Long as We're Together/Here's to You, Rachel Robinson. 2007. (ENG., Illus.). 512p. (J). (gr. 3-7). 18.99 *(978-0-385-73407-3(7),* Delacorte Bks. for Young Readers) Random Hse. Children's Bks.

—Cool Zone with the Pain & the Great One. Stevenson, James, illus. 2009. (ENG.). 128p. (J). (gr. 3-7). 5.99 *(978-0-440-42093-4(8),* Yearling) Random Hse. Children's Bks.

—Double Fudge. 2004. (ENG.). 192p. (J). (gr. 3-7). 5.99 *(978-0-425-19647-2(X),* Berkley) Penguin Publishing Group.

—Double Fudge. 2007. (ENG.). 240p. (J). (gr. 3-7). 7.99 *(978-0-14-240878-0(6),* Puffin Books) Penguin Young Readers Group.

—Double Fudge. 2004. (Fudge Ser.). 160p. (J). (gr. 3-7). pap. 36.00 incl. audio *(978-0-8072-2036-8(1),* Listening Library) Random Hse. Audio Publishing Group.

—Double Fudge. 2007. (Fudge Bks.: 5). lib. bdg. 18.40 *(978-1-4177-8371-7(0),* Turtleback) Turtleback Bks.

—Friend or Fiend? With the Pain & the Great One. Stevenson, James, illus. 2010. (ENG.). 128p. (J). (gr. 3-7). 5.99 *(978-0-440-42095-8(4),* Yearling) Random Hse. Children's Bks.

—Fudge-a-Mania. 2004. (ENG.). 176p. (J). (gr. 3-7). 6.99 *(978-0-425-19382-2(9),* Berkley) Penguin Publishing Group.

—Fudge-a-Mania. 2007. (ENG.). 176p. (J). (gr. 3-7). 7.99 *(978-0-14-240877-3(8),* Puffin Books) Penguin Young Readers Group.

—Going, Going, Gone! with the Pain & the Great One. Stevenson, James, illus. 2010. (ENG.). 128p. (J). (gr. 3-7). 5.99 *(978-0-440-42094-1(6),* Yearling) Random Hse. Children's Bks.

—Here's to You, Rachel Robinson. 2010. (ENG.). 208p. (J). (gr. 5). pap. 8.99 *(978-0-385-73987-0(7),* Delacorte Bks. for Young Readers) Random Hse. Children's Bks.

—It's Not the End of the World. 174p. (YA). (gr. 5-18). pap. 4.50 *(978-0-8072-1365-0(9),* Listening Library) Random Hse. Audio Publishing Group.

—Just As Long As We're Together. 2010. (ENG.). 288p. (YA). (gr. 7). pap. 8.99 *(978-0-385-73988-7(5),* Delacorte Bks. for Young Readers) Random Hse. Children's Bks.

—The One in the Middle Is the Green Kangaroo. Ohi, Debbie Ridpath, illus. 2014. (ENG.). 48p. (J). (gr. 1-5). pap. 5.99 *(978-1-4814-1131-8(4),* Atheneum Bks. for Young Readers) Simon & Schuster Children's Publishing.

—Starring Sally J. Freedman As Herself. 2014. (ENG., Illus.). (J). (gr. 3-7). 384p. 17.99 *(978-1-4814-1437-1(2));* 400p. pap. 7.99 *(978-1-4814-1355-8(4))* Simon & Schuster Children's Publishing. (Atheneum Bks. for Young Readers).

—Superfudge. 2004.Tr. of Superfudge. (ENG.). 192p. (J). (gr. 3-7). 6.99 *(978-0-425-19381-5(0),* Berkley) Penguin Publishing Group.

—Superfudge. (Fudge Ser.).Tr. of Superfudge. 166p. (J). (gr. 2-4). pap. 4.99 *(978-0-8072-1457-2(4),* Listening Library) Random Hse. Audio Publishing Group.

—Superfudge. 2007. (Fudge Bks.: 3).Tr. of Superfudge. lib. bdg. 18.40 *(978-1-4177-8843-9(7),* Turtleback) Turtleback Bks.

—Tales of a Fourth Grade Nothing. 2009. 8.32 *(978-0-7848-3046-8(0));* 8.32 *(978-0-7848-0332-5(3))* Marco Bk. Co. (Everbind).

—Tales of a Fourth Grade Nothing. 2007. 17.00 *(978-0-7569-7937-9(4))* 2004. (ENG.). 144p. (J). (gr. 3-7). 7.99 *(978-0-425-19379-2(9),* Berkley) Penguin Publishing Group.

—Tales of a Fourth Grade Nothing. 2007. (ENG.). 160p. (J). (gr. 3-7). 7.99 *(978-0-14-240881-0(6),* Puffin Books) Penguin Young Readers Group.

—Tales of a Fourth Grade Nothing. (Fudge Ser.). 120p. (J). (gr. 3-5). pap. 4.99 *(978-0-8072-1496-1(5),* Listening Library) Random Hse. Audio Publishing Group.

—Tales of a Fourth Grade Nothing. 2003. pap. *(978-0-439-57779-3(9),* Scholastic) Scholastic, Inc.

Blythe, Daniel. Shadow Breakers. 2013. (J). *(978-0-545-47980-6(0));* (ENG.). 256p. (gr. 5-9). 16.99 *(978-0-545-47979-0(7))* Scholastic, Inc. (Chicken Hse., The).

Blyton, Enid. Adventures of the Six Cousins. Pape, Jane, illus. 2013. (ENG.). 330p. (J). 16.50 *(978-1-84135-589-4(5))* Award Pubns. Ltd. GBR. Dist: Parkwest Pubns., Inc.

—Family at Red-Roofs. 2013. (ENG.). 256p. (J). pap. 9.99 *(978-1-84135-648-8(4))* Award Pubns. Ltd. GBR. Dist: Parkwest Pubns., Inc.

—Family Christmas. (Illus.). 160p. (J). pap. 6.95 *(978-0-09-987830-8(5))* Random Hse. GBR. Dist: Trafalgar Square Publishing.

—Four Cousins. (Illus.). 96p. (J). pap. 5.95 *(978-0-09-926640-2(7))* Random Hse. GBR. Dist: Trafalgar Square Publishing.

Bobulski, Chelsea. The Wood. 2017. (ENG.). 320p. (YA). 17.99 *(978-1-250-09426-1(7),* 9781250094261) Feiwel & Friends.

Bodeen, S. A. Shipwreck Island. 2014. (Shipwreck Island Ser.: 1). (ENG.). 192p. (J). (gr. 5-8). 16.99 *(978-1-250-02777-1(2),* 9781250027771) Feiwel & Friends.

Bodger, Holly. 5 to 1. 2015. (ENG.). 256p. (YA). (gr. 7). 17.99 *(978-0-385-39153-5(6),* Knopf Bks. for Young Readers) Random Hse. Children's Bks.

Bolger, Kevin. Zombiekins 2. Blecha, Aaron, illus. 2011. (J). 10.99 *(978-1-59514-432-4(3),* Razorbill) Penguin Publishing Group.

Boling, Katharine. January 1905. 2006. (ENG., Illus.). 192p. (J). (gr. 5-7). pap. 6.99 *(978-0-15-205121-1(X))* Houghton Mifflin Harcourt Publishing Co.

Bollendorf, Robert F. & Makely, William. Flight of the Loon: One Family's Battle with Recovery. Donlon, Eleanor, ed. 2007. 8.95 *(978-1-932514-15-5(5))* College of DuPage Pr.

Bongiovanni, Debbie. Kindness Pays Off, 1 vol. 2010. 58p. pap. 16.95 *(978-1-4489-6320-1(6))* America Star Bks.

Bonwill, Ann. The Frazzle Family Finds a Way. Gammell, Stephen, illus. 2013. (ENG.). 32p. (J). (gr. -1-3). 16.95 *(978-0-8234-2405-4(7))* Holiday Hse., Inc.

Booth, Coe. Kinda Like Brothers. 2015. lib. bdg. 17.20 *(978-0-606-37783-6(2))* Turtleback Bks.

Borntrager, Mary Christner. Andy. 2015. (Ellie's People Ser.: Vol. 6). (ENG.). 200p. (YA). (gr. 7-18). pap. 9.99 *(978-0-8361-3633-3(0))* Herald Pr.

—Ellie. 2014. (Ellie's People, Book One Ser.: Vol. 1). (ENG.). 193p. (J). (gr. 3-7). pap. 9.99 *(978-0-8361-3468-1(0))* Herald Pr.

—Rebecca. 2014. (Ellie's People, Book Two Ser.: Vol. 2). (ENG.). 234p. (J). (gr. 4-7). pap. 9.99 *(978-0-8361-3500-8(8))* Herald Pr.

Bose, Janet Von. The Noun Family. 2011. 24p. pap. 15.99 *(978-1-4628-5987-0(9))* Xlibris Corp.

Bourgeois, Paulette & Paulette, Bourgeois. El Principe y el Mendigo. Jorisch, Stéphane, illus. 2003.Tr. of Oma's Quilt. (SPA.). 32p. (J). (gr. k-2). 14.99 *(978-84-241-8644-9(3))* Everest Editora ESP. Dist: Lectorum Pubns., Inc.

Bowe, Julie. Birthday Glamour! 2015. (Victoria Torres, Unfortunately Average Ser.). (ENG.). 160p. (gr. 4-4). lib. bdg. 26.65 *(978-1-4965-0533-0(6))* Stone Arch Bks.

Bowen, Anne. Christmas Is Coming. Bogacki, Tomek, illus. 2007. (Carolrhoda Picture Bks.). 28p. (J). (gr. -1-3). 16.95 *(978-1-57505-934-1(7),* Carolrhoda Bks.) Lerner Publishing Group.

Bowler, Tim. Buried Thunder. 2011. (ENG.). 224p. (J). 16.95 *(978-0-8234-2397-2(2))* Holiday Hse., Inc.

—Storm Catchers. 2003. (ENG., Illus.). 208p. (YA). (gr. 7). 18.99 *(978-0-689-84573-4(1),* McElderry, Margaret K. Bks.) McElderry, Margaret K. Bks.

EFG

Bowman, Erin. Taken. 2013. (Taken Ser.: 1). (ENG.). 368p. (YA). (gr. 8). 17.99 *(978-0-06-211726-7(2)*, HarperTeen) HarperCollins Pubs.
Boyce, Frank Cottrell. Chitty Chitty Bang Bang & the Race Against Time. Berger, Joe, illus. 2014. (Chitty Chitty Bang Bang Ser.). (ENG.). 240p. (J). (gr. 4-7). pap. 6.99 *(978-0-7636-6931-7(8))* Candlewick Pr.
—Framed. (J). (gr. 3). 2008. (Illus.). 320p. per. 8.99 *(978-0-06-073404-6(3))* 2006. 306p. lib. bdg. 17.89 *(978-0-06-073403-9(5))* HarperCollins Pubs.
Bozarth, Jan. Kerka's Book. Burden, Andrea, illus. 2010. (Fairy Godmother Academy Ser.: No. 2). (ENG.). 224p. (J). (gr. 3-7). pap. 6.99 *(978-0-375-85183-4(6)*, Yearling) Random Hse. Children's Bks.
Bracken, Beth. Terrible, Awful, Horrible Manners!, 1 vol. Watson, Richard, illus. 2011. (Little Boost Ser.). (ENG.). 32p. (gr. k-3). lib. bdg. 23.99 *(978-1-4048-6653-9(1)*, Little Boost) Picture Window Bks.
—Terrible, Awful, Horrible Manners, 1 vol. Watson, Richard, illus. 2012. (Little Boost Ser.). (ENG.). 32p. (gr. k-3). 7.95 *(978-1-4048-7419-0(4)*, Little Boost) Picture Window Bks.
Bradbury, Jennifer. A Moment Comes. 2013. (ENG., Illus.). 288p. (YA). (gr. 7). 17.99 *(978-1-4169-7876-3(3))* Simon & Schuster Children's Publishing.
Bradby, Marie. Some Friend. 2007. (ENG.). 240p. (J). (gr. 3-7). pap. 7.99 *(978-1-4169-3452-3(9)*, Atheneum Bks. for Young Readers) Simon & Schuster Children's Publishing.
Bradfield, Carl. Hawaii Calls Wendell & Myrtle: The Wendells Family Make It to the Big Island. (Illus.). 196p. (Orig.). (YA). (gr. 8-12). pap. *(978-0-9632319-5-6(2))* ASDA Publishing, Inc.
Bradman, Tony. The Mummy Family Find Fame. 2006. (Red Bananas Ser.). (ENG., Illus.). 48p. (J). (gr. -1-3). lib. bdg. *(978-0-7787-1076-9(9))* Crabtree Publishing Co.
Bragg, Jane. Teddy Bears Christmas Miracle. 2009. 49p. pap. 18.70 *(978-0-557-22087-8(4))* Lulu Pr., Inc.
Brahmachari, Sita. Jasmine Skies. 2014. (ENG.). 336p. (J). (gr. 3-7). 16.99 *(978-0-8075-3782-4(9))* Whitman, Albert & Co.
—Mira in the Present Tense. (ENG.). 288p. (J). (gr. 3-7). 2015. pap. 9.99 *(978-0-8075-5151-6(1))* 2013. 16.99 *(978-0-8075-5149-3(X))* Whitman, Albert & Co.
Braids for Naya, 6, Pack. (gr. -1-2). 27.00 *(978-0-7635-9439-8(3))* Rigby Education.
Brandeis, Batsheva. Faiga Finds the Way. Levitas, Alexander, illus. 2005. (Fun to Read Book Ser.). 120p. (J). pap. 9.95 *(978-1-929628-28-5(5))* Hachai Publishing.
Brandeis, Gayle. My Life with the Lincolns. 2010. (ENG.). 256p. (J). (gr. 5-9). 34.99 *(978-0-8050-9013-0(4)*, 9780805090130, Holt, Henry & Co. Bks. For Young Readers) Holt, Henry & Co.
Branford, Anna. Violet Mackerel's Natural Habitat. Allen, Elanna, illus. 2013. (Violet Mackerel Ser.). (ENG.). 112p. (J). (gr. 1-5). 15.99 *(978-1-4424-3594-0(1))*; pap. 5.99 *(978-1-4424-3595-7(X))* Simon & Schuster Children's Publishing.
—Violet Mackerel's Personal Space. Allen, Elanna, illus. 2013. (Violet Mackerel Ser.). (ENG.). 128p. (J). (gr. 1-5). 15.99 *(978-1-4424-3591-9(7))*; pap. 5.99 *(978-1-4424-3592-6(5))* Simon & Schuster Children's Publishing. (Atheneum Bks. for Young Readers).
—Violet Mackerel's Possible Friend. Allen, Elanna, illus. 2014. (Violet Mackerel Ser.). (ENG.). 128p. (J). (gr. 1-5). 15.99 *(978-1-4424-9455-8(7)*, Atheneum Bks. for Young Readers) Simon & Schuster Children's Publishing.
Brauning, Kate. How We Fall. 2014. (ENG.). 304p. (YA). 17.99 *(978-1-4405-8179-3(7)*, Simon Pulse) Simon Pulse.
Bredsdorff, Bodil. The Crow-Girl: The Children of Crow Cove. Ingwersen, Faith, tr. from DAN. 2007. (Illus.). 155p. (gr. 3-7). 18.00 *(978-0-7569-8186-0(7))* Perfection Learning Corp.
—The Crow-Girl: The Children of Crow Cove. Ingwersen, Faith, tr. 2006. (Children of Crow Cove Ser.: 1). (ENG., Illus.). 160p. (J). (gr. 3-7). reprint ed. pap. 8.99 *(978-0-374-40003-3(2)*, 9780374400033, Farrar, Straus & Giroux (BYR)) Farrar, Straus & Giroux.
Brendler, Carol. Radio Girl. 2014. (ENG.). 224p. (J). (gr. 5-9). pap. 6.99 *(978-0-8234-3192-2(4))* Holiday Hse., Inc.
Brennan, Herbie. Faerie Lord. 2009. 1.00 *(978-1-4074-4311-9(9))* Recorded Bks., Inc.
—Faerie Wars. 2007. (ENG.). 384p. (gr. 7-12). per. 6.99 *(978-0-7653-5674-1(0)*, 9780765356741, Tor Bks.) Doherty, Tom Assocs., LLC.
—Faerie Wars. 1.00 *(978-1-4074-5906-6(6))* Recorded Bks., Inc.
Brennan-Nelson, Denise. Someday Is Not a Day of the Week. O'Malley, Kevin, illus. 2005. (ENG.). 32p. (J). (gr. 1-4). 15.95 *(978-1-58536-243-1(3)*, 202066) Sleeping Bear Pr.
Brennan, Sarah Rees. Unmade. 2014. (Lynburn Legacy Ser.: Bk. 3). (ENG., Illus.). 384p. (YA). (gr. 7). 17.99 *(978-0-375-87043-9(1)*, Random Hse. Bks. for Young Readers) Random Hse. Children's Bks.
—Untold. Fochesato, Giorgio, illus. 2013. (Lynburn Legacy Ser.: Bk. 2). (ENG.). 384p. (YA). (gr. 7). 18.99 *(978-0-375-87042-2(3)*, Random Hse. Bks. for Young Readers) Random Hse. Children's Bks.
Brett, Jan. Home for Christmas. Brett, Jan, illus. 2011. (ENG., Illus.). 32p. (J). (gr. -1-k). 17.99 *(978-0-399-25653-0(9)*, G.P. Putnam's Sons Books for Young Readers) Penguin Young Readers Group.
Brezenoff, Steve. The Absolute Value of -1. 2010. (Carolrhoda YA Ser.). (ENG.). 296p. (YA). (gr. 9-12). lib. bdg. 16.95 *(978-0-7613-5417-8(4)*, Carolrhoda Bks.) Lerner Publishing Group.
Brisson, Pat. Sometimes We Were Brave. Brassard, France, illus. 2010. (ENG.). 32p. (J). (gr. k-2). 16.95 *(978-1-59078-586-7(X))* Boyds Mills Pr.
Bristow, Catherine. My Strange & Terrible Malady. 2008. (YA). pap. 15.95 *(978-1-934575-19-2(4))* Autism Asperger Publishing Co.
Broach, Elise. Revenge of Superstition Mountain. Ivanov, Olga & Ivanov, Aleksey, illus. 2015. (Superstition Mountain Mysteries Ser.: 3). (ENG.). 320p. (J). (gr. 3-7). pap. 8.99 *(978-1-250-05686-3(1)*, 9781250056863) Square Fish.
Brochu, Lisa. Dad Still Smiles. Butterfield, Ned, illus. 2003. (Books for Young Learners). (ENG.). 12p. (J). pap. 5.75 net. *(978-1-57274-601-5(7)*, 2731, Bks. for Young Learners) Owen, Richard C. Pubs., Inc.
Brodien-Jones, Chris. The Glass Puzzle. 2013. (Illus.). 319p. (J). *(978-0-385-74298-6(3)*, Delacorte Pr) Random House Publishing Group.
Brodien-Jones, Christine. The Glass Puzzle. 2013. (ENG., Illus.). 336p. (J). (gr. 4-7). 16.99 *(978-0-385-74297-9(5)*, Delacorte Bks. for Young Readers) Random Hse. Children's Bks.
Brooks, Kevin. Dawn. 2010. (ENG.). 272p. (J). (gr. 9). pap. 8.99 *(978-0-545-06092-9(3)*, PUSH) Scholastic, Inc.
—Martyn Pig. 2003. 230p. (J). (gr. 5-9). 15.65 *(978-0-7569-7217-2(5))* Perfection Learning Corp.
Brooks, Martha. Queen of Hearts. 2011. (ENG.). 224p. (YA). (gr. 7-12). 17.99 *(978-0-374-34229-6(6)*, 9780374342296, Farrar, Straus & Giroux (BYR)) Farrar, Straus & Giroux.
Brouwer, Sigmund. Hitmen Triumph, 1 vol. 2007. (Orca Sports Ser.). (ENG.). 168p. (YA). (gr. 6-10). per. 9.95 *(978-1-55143-873-3(9))* Orca Bk. Pubs. USA.
—Timberwolf Prey, 1 vol. Ross, Graham, illus. 2010. (Orca Echoes Ser.). (ENG.). 64p. (J). (gr. 2-3). pap. 6.95 *(978-1-55469-109-8(5))* Orca Bk. Pubs. USA.
Brown, Elizabeth Ferguson & Boyds Mills Press Staff. Coal Country Christmas. Stevenson, Harvey, illus. 2003. (ENG.). 32p. (J). (gr. 1-7). 15.95 *(978-1-59078-020-6(5))* Boyds Mills Pr.
Brown, Gavin. Josh Baxter Levels Up. 2016. (ENG., Illus.). 192p. (J). (gr. 3-7). 12.99 *(978-0-545-77294-5(X)*, Scholastic Pr.) Scholastic, Inc.
Brown, Jeff. Flat Stanley. Nash, Scott, illus. 2006. (Flat Stanley Ser.). (ENG.). 40p. (J). (gr. -1-3). 17.99 *(978-0-06-112904-9(6))* HarperCollins Pubs.
Brown, Jennifer. Life on Mars. 2014. (ENG.). 240p. (YA). (gr. 3-6). 16.99 *(978-1-61963-252-3(7)*, 9781619632523, Bloomsbury USA Childrens) Bloomsbury Publishing USA.
Brown Lcsw, Jennifer. Star's Unexpected News. 2011. 32p. pap. 13.49 *(978-1-4389-3567-6(6))* AuthorHouse.
Brown, Margaret Wise. My World: A Companion to Goodnight Moon. Hurd, Clement, illus. (ENG.). (J). (gr. -1 — 1). 2004. 32p. pap. 6.99 *(978-0-694-01660-0(8))* 2003. 36p. bds. 8.99 *(978-0-694-00862-9(1)*, HarperFestival) HarperCollins Pubs.
—Where Have You Been? Dillon, Leo & Dillon, Diane, illus. 2004. (ENG.). 32p. (J). (gr. -1-1). 16.99 *(978-0-06-028378-0(5))* HarperCollins Pubs.
—Where Have You Been? rev. ed. Date not set. (ENG.). 32p. (J). (gr. -1-1). pap. 6.99 *(978-0-06-443569-7(5))* HarperCollins Pubs.
Brown, Mary. An Ear for Graci. 2011. 16p. 8.99 *(978-1-4520-9702-2(X))* AuthorHouse.
Brown, Monica. Drama Queen. 2016. (Lola Levine Ser.: 2). (J). lib. bdg. 16.00 *(978-0-606-38329-5(8))* Turtleback Bks.
—Lola Levine, Drama Queen. 2016. (Lola Levine Ser.: 2). (ENG., Illus.). (J). (gr. 1-5). 112p. pap. 5.99 *(978-0-316-25842-5(3))*; 96p. 15.99 *(978-0-316-25843-2(1))* Little, Brown Bks. for Young Readers.
Brown, Monica & Ventura, Gabriela Baeza. Clara & the Curandera / Clara y la Curandera. Muraida, Thelma, illus. 2011. (J). 16.95 *(978-1-55885-700-1(1)*, Piñata Books) Arte Publico Pr.
Brown, Ruth. The Big Sneeze. Date not set. (ENG., Illus.). 32p. (J). pap. *(978-0-05-004391-2(9))* Addison-Wesley Longman, Inc.
Brown-Wood, Janay & Burris, Priscilla. Grandma's Tiny House. 2017. (ENG., Illus.). 32p. (J). (-k). lib. bdg. 16.99 *(978-1-58089-712-9(6))* Charlesbridge Publishing, Inc.
Bryan, Jennifer. El Dragón Diferente. Hosler, Danamarie, illus. 2nd ed. 2015.Tr. of Different Dragon. (SPA.). 36p. (Orig.). (J). pap. 12.95 *(978-0-9674468-9-9(9))* Two Lives Publishing.
Bryant, Ann. She's No Angel. 2005. (Step-Chain Ser.). 190p. (J). pap. 4.95 *(978-1-894222-75-4(X))* Lobster Pr. CAN. Dist: Univ. of Toronto Pr.
—Too Good to Be True. 2005. (Step-Chain Ser.). 190p. (J). pap. 4.95 *(978-1-894222-76-1(8))* Lobster Pr. CAN. Dist: Univ. of Toronto Pr.
Bryant, Annie. Katani's Jamaican Holiday. 2008. (Beacon Street Girls Ser.: No. 4). (ENG., Illus.). 192p. (J). (gr. 4-8). pap. 6.99 *(978-1-4169-6443-8(6)*, Aladdin) Simon & Schuster Children's Publishing.
—Letters from the Heart. 2008. (Beacon Street Girls Ser.: 3). (ENG., Illus.). 256p. (J). (gr. 4-8). pap. 6.99 *(978-1-4169-6426-1(6)*, Aladdin) Simon & Schuster Children's Publishing.
Bryant, Jen. Kaleidoscope Eyes. 2010. (ENG.). 272p. (J). (gr. 3-7). 7.99 *(978-0-440-42190-0(X)*, Yearling) Random Hse. Children's Bks.
Bryce, Celia. Anthem for Jackson Dawes. 2013. (ENG.). 240p. (YA). (gr. 7-12). 16.99 *(978-1-59990-975-2(8)*, 9781599909752, Bloomsbury USA Childrens) Bloomsbury Publishing USA.
Bryson, Clyde, the Elf That Santa Fired. 2004. 364p. 31.00 *(978-1-4184-3736-7(0))*; pap. 22.95 *(978-1-4184-3737-4(9))* AuthorHouse.
Buchwald, Claire. Are You Ready for Me? Hansen, Amelia, illus. 2007. (Sit! Stay! Read! Ser.). (ENG.). 24p. (J). (gr. k-1). 15.95 *(978-0-940719-04-0(5))* Gryphon Pr., The.
Buckle, J. A. Half My Facebook Friends Are Ferrets, 1 vol. 2014. (ENG.). 224p. (gr. 9-12). 16.95 *(978-1-63079-000-4(1))* Switch Pr.
Budhos, Marina. Ask Me No Questions. 2007. 159p. (gr. 7-12). 20.00 *(978-0-7569-8114-3(X))* Perfection Learning Corp.
—Ask Me No Questions. 2007. (ENG.). 192p. (YA). (gr. 7-12). pap. 10.99 *(978-1-4169-4920-6(8)*, Atheneum Bks. for Young Readers) Simon & Schuster Children's Publishing.
Bulion, Leslie. The Trouble with Rules, 1 vol. (ENG.). 160p. (J). 2011. pap. 6.95 *(978-1-56145-576-8(8))* 2008. (gr. 2-6). 14.95 *(978-1-56145-440-2(0))* Peachtree Pubs.
Bundy, Tamara. Walking with Miss Millie. 2017. (ENG.). 240p. (J). (gr. 5). 16.99 ***(978-0-399-54456-9(9)***, Nancy Paulsen Books) Penguin Young Readers Group.
Bunker, Lisa. Felix Yz. 2017. (ENG.). 288p. (J). (gr. 5-9). 16.99 *(978-0-425-28850-4(1)*, Viking Books for Young Readers) Penguin Young Readers Group.
Bunting, Eve. The Banshee. McCully, Emily Arnold, illus. 2009. (ENG.). 32p. (J). (gr. -1-3). 16.00 *(978-0-618-82162-4(7))* Houghton Mifflin Harcourt Publishing Co.
—Jamaica Tag-Along. Hewitt, Kathryn, illus. 2015. 32p. pap. 7.00 *(978-1-61003-504-0(6))* Center for the Collaborative Classroom.
—Will It Be a Baby Brother? Spiegel, Beth, illus. 2010. (ENG.). 32p. (J). (gr. -1-1). 16.95 *(978-1-59078-439-6(1))* Boyds Mills Pr.
—You Were Loved Before You Were Born. Barbour, Karen, illus. 2008. (J). pap. *(978-0-439-04062-4(0)*, Blue Sky Pr., The) Scholastic, Inc.
Burch, Christian. Hit the Road, Manny: A Manny Files Novel. 2008. (ENG.). 240p. (J). (gr. 3-7). 16.99 *(978-1-4169-2812-6(X)*, Atheneum Bks. for Young Readers) Simon & Schuster Children's Publishing.
—The Manny Files. 2008. (Mix Ser.). (ENG.). 304p. (J). (gr. 4-8). pap. 14.99 *(978-1-4169-5534-4(8)*, Aladdin) Simon & Schuster Children's Publishing.
Burchill, Julie. Sweet, 1. unabr. ed. 2008. (ENG.). 240p. (gr. 8-12). pap. 15.95 *(978-0-330-45371-4(8)*, Picador) Pan Macmillan GBR. Dist: Trans-Atlantic Pubns., Inc.
Burg, Ann E. Serafina's Promise. 2013. (ENG.). 304p. (J). (gr. 3-7). 16.99 *(978-0-545-53564-9(6)*, Scholastic Pr.) Scholastic, Inc.
—Unbound. 2016. (ENG.). 352p. (J). (gr. 4-6). 16.99 *(978-0-545-93427-5(3)*, Scholastic Pr.) Scholastic, Inc.
Burgess, Melvin. The Hit. 2014. (ENG.). 304p. (J). (gr. 9). 17.99 *(978-0-545-55699-6(6)*, Chicken Hse., The) Scholastic, Inc.
Burgis, Stephanie. Kat, Incorrigible. 2012. (Kat, Incorrigible Ser.: 1). (ENG., Illus.). 320p. (J). (gr. 5-9). pap. 7.99 *(978-1-4169-9448-0(3)*, Atheneum Bks. for Young Readers) Simon & Schuster Children's Publishing.
—Renegade Magic. 2012. (Kat, Incorrigible Ser.: 2). (ENG., Illus.). 336p. (J). (gr. 5-9). 16.99 *(978-1-4169-9449-7(1)*, Atheneum Bks. for Young Readers) Simon & Schuster Children's Publishing.
Burgis, Stephanie & Ward, Barnaby. Kat, Incorrigible. 2011. (Kat, Incorrigible Ser.: 1). (ENG., Illus.). 304p. (J). (gr. 5-9). 16.99 *(978-1-4169-9447-3(5)*, Atheneum Bks. for Young Readers) Simon & Schuster Children's Publishing.
Burkinshaw, Kathleen. The Last Cherry Blossom. 2016. (J). ***(978-1-63450-618-2(9))*** Skyhorse Publishing Co., Inc.
Burnett, Frances Hodgson. The Head of the House of Coombe. 2008. 252p. 29.95 *(978-1-60664-769-1(5))*; pap. 15.95 *(978-1-60664-142-2(5))* Aegypan.
Burney. Exorsistah: X Returns. 2016. (ENG., Illus.). 336p. pap. 20.99 *(978-1-5011-0261-5(3))* Simon & Schuster, Inc.
Burnham, Molly B. Teddy Mars: Almost a World Record Breaker. Spencer, Trevor, illus. (Teddy Mars Ser.: 2). (J). (gr. 3-7). 2016. 288p. 16.99 *(978-0-06-227813-5(4)*, Tegen, Katherine Bks) 2015. (ENG.). 224p. 16.99 *(978-0-06-227810-4(X))* HarperCollins Pubs.
Burnham, Niki. Royally Crushed: Royally Jacked; Spin Control; Do-Over. 2011. (ENG.). 624p. (YA). (gr. 7). pap. 11.99 *(978-1-4424-0648-3(8)*, Simon Pulse) Simon Pulse.
Burns, Catherine Lloyd. The Good, the Bad & the Beagle. 2014. (ENG.). 336p. (J). (gr. 5-7). 16.99 *(978-0-374-30039-5(9)*, 9780374300395, Farrar, Straus & Giroux (BYR)) Farrar, Straus & Giroux.
—The Half-True Lies of Cricket Cohen. 2017. (ENG.). 256p. (J). 16.99 *(978-0-374-30041-8(0)*, 9780374300418, Farrar, Straus & Giroux (BYR)) Farrar, Straus & Giroux.
Butcher, Kristin. Zee's Way, 1 vol. 2004. (Orca Soundings Ser.). (ENG.). 128p. (YA). (gr. 8-12). pap. 9.95 *(978-1-55143-279-3(X))* Orca Bk. Pubs. USA.
Buyea, Rob. Because of Mr. Terupt. (ENG.). (J). (gr. 3-7). 2011. 304p. 7.99 *(978-0-375-85824-6(5)*, Yearling) 2010. 288p. 16.99 *(978-0-385-73882-8(X)*, Delacorte Bks. for Young Readers) Random Hse. Children's Bks.
Buzbee, Lewis. Steinbeck's Ghost. 2010. (ENG.). 368p. (J). (gr. 5-9). pap. 18.99 *(978-0-312-60211-6(1)*, 9780312602116) Square Fish.
Byars, Betsy. A Blossom Promise. Haley, Amanda, illus. 4th ed. 2008. (Blossom Family Book Ser.: Bk. 4). (ENG.). 192p. (J). (gr. 4-7). pap. 6.95 *(978-0-8234-2147-3(3))* Holiday Hse., Inc.
—The Blossoms & the Green Phantom. Haley, Amanda, illus. 2008. (Blossom Family Book Ser.: 3). (ENG.). 176p. (J). (gr. 4-7). pap. 6.95 *(978-0-8234-2146-6(5))* Holiday Hse., Inc.
—The Blossoms Meet the Vulture Lady. 2008. (Blossom Family Book Ser.: 2). (ENG., Illus.). 134p. (J). (gr. 4-7). 6.95 *(978-0-8234-2144-2(9))* Holiday Hse., Inc.
—Keeper of the Doves. 2004. (ENG., Illus.). 128p. (J). (gr. 3-7). reprint ed. 7.99 *(978-0-14-240063-0(7)*, Puffin Books) Penguin Young Readers Group.
—The Summer of the Swans. 2004. (Puffin Modern Classics Ser.). (ENG.). 144p. (J). (gr. 3-7). pap. 6.99 *(978-0-14-240114-9(5)*, Puffin Books) Penguin Young Readers Group.
—Wanted... Mud Blossom. Haley, Amanda, illus. 5th ed. 2008. (Blossom Family Book Ser.: Bk. 5). (ENG.). 192p. (J). (gr. 4-7). pap. 8.95 *(978-0-8234-2148-0(1))* Holiday Hse., Inc.
Byers, Shaunette. The Story: The Legend of Fearless Fred. Lollino, Jessica, ed. 2008. (Mimi's Kids Ser.: vol. 3). (ENG., Illus.). 32p. (J). pap. 12.95 *(978-0-9712383-7-4(5))* Culturatti Ink.
Byrd, Cari Grigsby. Where Did Pop Pop Go? 2013. 24p. pap. 24.95 *(978-1-62709-967-7(0))* America Star Bks.
Cabot, Meg. Abandon. 2011. (ENG.). 320p. (J). (gr. 9-18). 17.99 *(978-0-545-28410-3(4))* Scholastic, Inc.
—Awaken. 2013. (ENG.). 336p. (J). (gr. 9). 17.99 *(978-0-545-28412-7(0))* Scholastic, Inc.
—Jinx. 2009. (ENG.). 288p. (YA). (gr. 8). pap. 8.99 *(978-0-06-083766-2(7)*, HarperTeen) HarperCollins Pubs.
—Moving Day. 2009. (Allie Finkle's Rules for Girls Ser.: 1). lib. bdg. 17.20 *(978-0-606-06818-5(X)*, Turtleback) Turtleback Bks.
—The New Girl. 2008. (Allie Finkle's Rules for Girls Ser.: 2). (ENG.). 240p. (J). (gr. 3-7). 15.99 *(978-0-545-04049-5(3)*, Scholastic Pr.) Scholastic, Inc.
—Ready or Not. (All-American Girl Ser.: 2). (ENG.). 2008. 336p. (YA). (gr. 8). pap. 8.99 *(978-0-06-147996-0(9)*, HarperTeen) 2005. 256p. (J). (gr. 7-18). 16.99 *(978-0-06-072450-4(1))* HarperCollins Pubs.
—Stage Fright. 2010. (Allie Finkle's Rules for Girls Ser.: 4). (ENG.). 240p. (J). (gr. 3-7). 6.99 *(978-0-545-04046-4(9))* Scholastic, Inc.
—Underworld. 2012. (Abandon Ser.). (ENG.). 336p. (J). (gr. 9). 17.99 *(978-0-545-28411-0(2))* Scholastic, Inc.
Cagan, Kayla. Piper Perish. 2017. (ENG., Illus.). 416p. (YA). 17.99 *(978-1-4521-5583-8(6))* Chronicle Bks. LLC.
Calabrese, Dianne. The Inspirational Guide, 1 vol. 2010. 24p. 24.95 *(978-1-4489-4844-4(4))* PublishAmerica, Inc.
Caletti, Deb. The Fortunes of Indigo Skye. (ENG.). (YA). (gr. 7). 2009. 320p. pap. 9.99 *(978-1-4169-1008-4(5))* 2008. 304p. 15.99 *(978-1-4169-1007-7(7))* Simon Pulse. (Simon Pulse).
—The Secret Life of Prince Charming. 2010. (ENG.). 352p. (YA). (gr. 7). pap. 11.99 *(978-1-4169-5941-0(6)*, Simon Pulse) Simon Pulse.
—The Six Rules of Maybe. 2010. (ENG.). 336p. (YA). (gr. 7-18). 16.99 *(978-1-4169-7969-2(7)*, Simon Pulse) Simon Pulse.
Calhoun, Dia. Eva of the Farm. Slater, Kate, illus. 2013. (ENG.). 272p. (J). (gr. 4-7). pap. 6.99 *(978-1-4424-1701-4(3)*, Atheneum Bks. for Young Readers) Simon & Schuster Children's Publishing.
Calkhoven, Laurie. Daniel at the Siege of Boston 1776. (Boys of Wartime Ser.: 1). (ENG.). (J). (gr. 4-7). 2011. 224p. 6.99 *(978-0-14-241750-8(5)*, Puffin Books) 2010. 208p. 16.99 *(978-0-525-42144-3(0)*, Dutton Books for Young Readers) Penguin Young Readers Group.
Callahan, Thera S. All Wrapped Up. 2004. (Rookie Reader Español Ser.). (ENG., Illus.). 32p. (J). (gr. k-2). pap. 4.95 *(978-0-516-21949-3(9)*, Children's Pr.) Scholastic Library Publishing.
Calonita, Jen. Belles. 2012. (Belles Ser.: 1). (ENG.). 384p. (YA). (gr. 7-17). pap. 8.99 *(978-0-316-09112-1(X)*, Poppy) Little, Brown Bks. for Young Readers.
—The Grass Is Always Greener. 2014. (Belles Ser.: 3). (ENG.). 320p. (YA). (gr. 7-17). pap. 10.00 *(978-0-316-09109-1(X)*, Poppy) Little, Brown Bks. for Young Readers.
Cameron, Ann. The Secret Life of Amanda K. Woods. 2014. (ENG.). 208p. (J). (gr. 5-9). pap. 6.99 *(978-1-250-04419-8(7)*, 9781250044198) Square Fish.
Cameron, Sharon. A Spark Unseen. 2013. (ENG.). 352p. (J). (gr. 7). 17.99 *(978-0-545-32813-5(6)*, Scholastic Pr.) Scholastic, Inc.
Campbell, Isaiah. The Struggles of Johnny Cannon. 2015. 322p. (J). pap. *(978-1-4814-2632-9(X)*, Simon & Schuster Bks. For Young Readers) Simon & Schuster Bks. For Young Readers.
Canales, Viola. The Tequila Worm. 2007. (ENG., Illus.). 208p. (YA). (gr. 7-11). pap. 7.99 *(978-0-375-84089-0(3)*, Lamb, Wendy Bks.) Random Hse. Children's Bks.
Candlewick Press, Candlewick. Peppa Pig & the Day at Snowy Mountain. 2014. (Peppa Pig Ser.). (ENG.). 32p. (J). (-k). 12.99 *(978-0-7636-7455-7(9)*, Candlewick Entertainment) Candlewick Pr.
Cantor, Jillian. The Life of Glass. 2010. (ENG.). 352p. (YA). (gr. 8-18). 16.99 *(978-0-06-168651-1(4)*, HarperTeen) HarperCollins Pubs.
—The September Sisters. 2009. (ENG.). 368p. (YA). (gr. 8-18). 16.99 *(978-0-06-168648-1(4)*, HarperTeen) HarperCollins Pubs.
Capstone Press Staff. Flood, 1 vol. Vila, Alvaro F., illus. 2013. (Fiction Picture Bks.). (ENG.). 32p. (gr. 1-3). 22.60 *(978-1-4048-8006-1(2)*, Fiction Picture Bks.) Picture Window Bks.
Capucilli, Alyssa Satin. Biscuit's First Trip. 2010. (Biscuit 8x8 Ser.). (J). lib. bdg. 13.55 *(978-0-606-10115-8(2)*, Turtleback) Turtleback Bks.
Cardi, Annie. The Chance You Won't Return. 2014. (ENG.). 352p. (YA). (gr. 7). 16.99 *(978-0-7636-6292-9(5))* Candlewick Pr.
Cardillo, Linda. The Smallest Christmas Tree. Cardillo, Linda & Albert, Dar, illus. 2013. 42p. pap. 9.49 *(978-0-9910861-0-8(4))* Bellastoria Pr.
Carestio, Michael A. Black Jack Jetty: A Boy's Journey Through Grief. 2010. (Illus.). 64p. (J). (gr. 3-8). 14.95 *(978-1-4338-0784-8(X))*; pap. 9.95 *(978-1-4338-0786-2(6))* American Psychological Assn. (Magination Pr.).
Carey, Edward. Heap House. 2014. (Iremonger Trilogy Ser.: 1). (ENG.). 416p. (gr. 4-13). 16.99 *(978-1-4683-0953-9(6)*, 460953) Overlook Pr., The.
Carey, Janet Lee. The Double Life of Zoe Flynn. 2007. (ENG.). 240p. (J). (gr. 3-7). pap. 12.95 *(978-1-4169-6754-5(0)*, Simon & Schuster/Paula Wiseman Bks.) Simon & Schuster/Paula Wiseman Bks.
Carlson, Nancy. Louanne Pig in the Perfect Family. 2nd rev. ed. 2004. (Nancy Carlson's Neighborhood Ser.). (ENG., Illus.). 32p. (J). (gr. k-2). 15.95 *(978-1-57505-611-1(9))*; pap. 6.95 *(978-1-57505-616-6(X))* Lerner Publishing Group.
—Take Time to Relax! Carlson, Nancy, illus. 2012. (Nancy Carlson Picture Bks). (Illus.). 32p. (J). (gr. k-2). 56.72 *(978-0-7613-9304-7(8)*, Carolrhoda Bks.) Lerner Publishing Group.
Carlson, Ron. The Speed of Light. 2003. (ENG., Illus.). 288p. (J). 15.99 *(978-0-380-97837-3(7)*, HarperTeen) HarperCollins Pubs.
Carmichael, Clay. Wild Things. (ENG.). (J). 2012. 184p. (gr. 5-8). pap. 9.95 *(978-1-59078-914-8(8))* 2009. 248p. (gr. 4-6). 18.95 *(978-1-59078-627-7(0)*, Front Street) Boyds Mills Pr.
—Wild Things, 6 vols. 2010. (J). 77.75 *(978-1-4498-0632-3(5))* Recorded Bks., Inc.
Carmichael, Katrina. Back Together Again. 2008. 20p. pap. 7.95 *(978-0-9814650-5-0(6))* G Publishing LLC.
Carroll, Michael Shane. Bye-Bye Brewster. Carroll, Katie, illus. 2012. 20p. pap. 5.00 *(978-1-937260-14-9(3))* Sleepytown Pr.
Carson, Diana Pastora. All the Muchos in the World: A Special Story about Love. Pruitt, Ginny, illus. 2006. 32p. (J). pap. 8.95 *(978-0-8198-0779-3(6))* Pauline Bks. & Media.
Cartaya, Pablo. The Epic Fail of Arturo Zamora. 2017. (ENG.). 256p. (J). (gr. 5). 16.99 *(978-1-101-99723-9(0)*, Viking Books for Young Readers) Penguin Young Readers Group.
Carter, Caela. Forever, or a Long, Long Time. 2017. 320p. (J). (gr. 3-7). 16.99 *(978-0-06-238568-0(2))* HarperCollins Pubs.
Carthage, Lynn. Haunted. 2015. (Arnaud Legacy Ser.: 1). (ENG.). 288p. (YA). (gr. 9). pap. 9.95 *(978-1-61773-626-1(0))* Kensington Publishing Corp.
Carvalho, Marcela. Three Sisters, Three Weddings, & One Dress. 2011. 38p. pap. 24.94 *(978-0-557-52962-9(X))* Lulu Pr., Inc.
Casanova, Mary. Ice-Out. 2016. (ENG., Illus.). 264p. (YA). 16.95 *(978-0-8166-9417-4(6))* Univ. of Minnesota Pr.
—The Klipfish Code. 2012. (ENG.). 240p. (J). (gr. 5-7). pap. 6.99 *(978-0-547-74447-6(1))* Houghton Mifflin Harcourt Publishing Co.

Casella, Jody. Thin Space. 2013. (ENG.). 256p. (YA). (gr. 7). 16.99 *(978-1-58270-435-7(X))*; pap. 10.99 *(978-1-58270-392-3(2))* Simon Pulse. (Simon Pulse).

Casey, Sean. My Dad Cancelled Christmas! Casey, Quinn, illus. 2008. 25p. (J). 15.95 *(978-0-9797297-0-6(X))* Cool Kids Create.

Cassidy, Cathy. Indigo Blue. 2006. (ENG.). 240p. (J). (gr. 5-18). 7.99 *(978-0-14-240703-5(8))*, Puffin Books) Penguin Young Readers Group.

Cassidy, Sara. Skylark, 1 vol. 2014. (Orca Soundings Ser.). (ENG.). 136p. (YA). (gr. 8-12). pap. 9.95 *(978-1-4598-0590-3(9))* Orca Bk. Pubs. USA.

Castilla, Julia Mercedes. Strange Parents. 2009. 144p. (J). (gr. 6-18). pap. 9.95 *(978-1-55885-590-8(4))*, Piñata Books) Arte Publico Pr.

Cataneo, D. M. Eggplant Alley. 2013. (ENG.). 352p. (YA). (gr. 7-9). 17.95 *(978-1-59373-146-5(9))* Bunker Hill Publishing, Inc.

Catchpole, Barbara. Dead Ed in My Head. 2013. 118p. pap. *(978-0-7552-1604-8(0))*, Bright Pen) Authors OnLine, Ltd.

Chabon, Michael. The Astonishing Secret of Awesome Man. Parker, Jake, illus. 2011. (ENG.). 40p. (J). (gr. -1-3). 17.99 *(978-0-06-191462-1(2))* HarperCollins Pubs.

Chaconas, Dori. Hurry down to Derry Fair. Tyler, Gillian, illus. 2011. (ENG.). 36p. (J). (gr. -1-2). 16.99 *(978-0-7636-3208-3(2))* Candlewick Pr.

Chalifour, Francis. After. 2005. (ENG.). 144p. (J). (gr. 7). pap. 7.95 *(978-0-88776-705-0(2))*, Tundra Bks.) Tundra Bks. CAN. Dist: Penguin Random Hse. LLC.

Chaltas, Thalia. Because I Am Furniture. 2010. (ENG.). 368p. (YA). (gr. 7-18). 8.99 *(978-0-14-241510-8(3))*, Speak) Penguin Young Readers Group.

Chambers, Aidan. Breaktime. 2008. (ENG.). 192p. (YA). (gr. 9-17). pap. 9.95 *(978-0-8109-7262-9(X))*, Amulet Bks.) Abrams, Inc.

Chambers, Melissa. The Summer Before Forever. 2016. (ENG., Illus.). (YA). (gr. 8-12). pap. 15.99 ***(978-1-68281-282-2(0))*** Entangled Publishing, LLC.

Chambers, Veronica. The Go-Between. 2017. (ENG.). 208p. (YA). (gr. 7). 16.99 ***(978-1-101-93095-3(0)***, Delacorte Pr.) Random Hse. Children's Bks.

Chandler, Elizabeth. No Time to Die - The Deep End of Fear No. 2. 2010. (Dark Secrets Ser.: 2). (ENG.). 624p. (YA). (gr. 7). pap. 9.99 *(978-1-4169-9462-6(9))*, Simon Pulse) Simon Pulse.

Chang, Margaret. Celia's Robot. 2009. (ENG.). 208p. (J). (gr. 3-7). 16.95 *(978-0-8234-2181-7(3))* Holiday Hse., Inc.

Chari, Sheela. Finding Mighty. 2017. (ENG., Illus.). 320p. (J). (gr. 5-9). 16.95 *(978-1-4197-2296-7(4))*, Amulet Bks.) Abrams, Inc.

Charlie Bumpers vs. the Squeaking Skull, 1 vol. 2014. (Charlie Bumpers Ser.). (ENG., Illus.). (J). (gr. 2-4). 10p. 16.95 *(978-1-56145-809-7(0))*; 160p. 13.95 *(978-1-56145-808-0(2))* Peachtree Pubs.

Cheaney, J. B. I Don't Know How the Story Ends. 2015. (ENG.). 288p. (J). (gr. 4-7). 16.99 *(978-1-4926-0944-5(7))*, 9781492609445, Sourcebooks Jabberwocky) Sourcebooks, Inc.

—My Friend the Enemy. 2007. 266p. (gr. 4-7). 16.50 *(978-0-7569-7946-1(3))* Perfection Learning Corp.

Chen, Justina. Return to Me. 2013. (ENG.). 352p. (YA). (gr. 7-17). 17.99 *(978-0-316-10255-1(5))* Little Brown & Co.

Chen, Shan-Shan & Goodman, Heidi. Mei-Mei's Lucky Birthday Noodles: A Loving Story of Adoption, Chinese Culture & a Special Birthday Treat. 2014. (ENG., Illus.). 32p. (J). (gr. -1-3). 13.95 *(978-0-8048-4461-1(5))* Tuttle Publishing.

Cheng, Andrea. The Bear Makers. 2008. (ENG., Illus.). 176p. (J). (gr. 6-9). 16.95 *(978-1-59078-518-8(5))*, Front Street) Boyds Mills Pr.

—Shanghai Messenger, 1 vol. Young, Ed, illus. 2005. (ENG.). 40p. (J). (gr. 3-7). 17.95 *(978-1-58430-238-4(0))* Lee & Low Bks., Inc.

Cheng, Andrea & Young, Ed. Shanghai Messenger. 2015. (ENG.). 40p. (J). pap. 10.95 *(978-1-62014-230-1(9))* Lee & Low Bks., Inc.

Chew, Ruth. No Such Thing as a Witch. 2013. (Matter-Of-Fact Magic Book Ser.). (ENG., Illus.). 128p. (J). (gr. 2-5). 5.99 *(978-0-449-81562-5(5))*; 15.99 *(978-0-449-81559-5(5))* Random Hse. Children's Bks. (Random Hse. Bks. for Young Readers).

Chichester Clark, Emma, illus. No More Kissing! 2015. (J). ***(978-1-4351-5751-4(6))*** Barnes & Noble, Inc.

Child, Lauren. Clarice Bean Spells Trouble. Child, Lauren, illus. 2006. (Clarice Bean Ser.). (Illus.). 189p. (J). (gr. 3-6). 13.65 *(978-0-7569-7919-5(6))* Perfection Learning Corp.

—Clarice Bean, That's Me. Child, Lauren, illus. 2010. (Clarice Bean Ser.). (ENG., Illus.). 32p. (J). (gr. 1-4). pap. 8.99 *(978-0-7636-4795-7(0))* Candlewick Pr.

—Guess Who's Babysitting? Child, Lauren, illus. 2010. (Clarice Bean Ser.). (ENG., Illus.). 32p. (J). (gr. 1-4). pap. 8.99 *(978-0-7636-4797-1(7))* Candlewick Pr.

—Spells Trouble. Child, Lauren, illus. 2006. (Clarice Bean Ser.). (ENG., Illus.). 192p. (J). (gr. 3-7). pap. 6.99 *(978-0-7636-2903-8(0))* Candlewick Pr.

—Utterly Me, Clarice Bean. Child, Lauren, illus. 2005. (Clarice Bean Ser.). (ENG., Illus.). 208p. (J). (gr. 3-7). reprint ed. pap. 5.99 *(978-0-7636-2788-1(7))* Candlewick Pr.

—Utterly Me, Clarice Bean. Child, Lauren, illus. 2006. (Clarice Bean Ser.). (Illus.). 16.00 *(978-0-7569-6567-9(5))* Perfection Learning Corp.

Choldenko, Gennifer. Al Capone Does My Shirts. 2006. (Tales from Alcatraz Ser.). (ENG., Illus.). 288p. (J). (gr. 5-18). reprint ed. pap. 7.99 *(978-0-14-240370-9(9))*, Puffin Books) Penguin Young Readers Group.

—If a Tree Falls at Lunch Period. 2009. (ENG., Illus.). 224p. (J). (gr. 5-7). pap. 7.99 *(978-0-15-206644-4(6))* Houghton Mifflin Harcourt Publishing Co.

Christopher, Lucy. Flyaway. 2011. (ENG.). 336p. (J). (gr. 5-9). 16.99 *(978-0-545-31771-9(1))*, Chicken Hse., The) Scholastic, Inc.

Christopher, Matt. Soccer Halfback. l.t. ed. 2007. (New Matt Christopher Sports Library). 160p. (J). (gr. 4-6). lib. bdg. 26.60 *(978-1-59953-110-6(0))* Norwood Hse. Pr.

—Stealing Home. 2004. (ENG.). 144p. (J). (gr. 3-7). pap. 5.99 *(978-0-316-60742-1(8))* Little, Brown Bks. for Young Readers.

Chung, Arree. Ninja! Chung, Arree, illus. 2016. (Ninja! Ser.). (ENG., Illus.). 40p. (J). 16.99 *(978-0-8050-9916-4(6))*, 9780805099164, Holt, Henry & Co. Bks. For Young Readers) Holt, Henry & Co.

Ciocca, Gina. Last Year's Mistake. 2015. (ENG., Illus.). 320p. (YA). (gr. 9). 17.99 *(978-1-4814-3223-8(0))*, Simon Pulse) Simon Pulse.

Citra, Becky. Missing, 1 vol. 2011. (ENG.). 184p. (J). (gr. 4-7). pap. 9.95 *(978-1-55469-345-0(4))* Orca Bk. Pubs. USA.

Clara Mulholland. Naughty Miss Bunny. 2007. 128p. per. 10.95 *(978-1-4218-3938-7(5))*, 1st World Library - Literary Society) 1st World Publishing, Inc.

Clark, Catherine. Frozen Rodeo. 2003. (ENG.). 304p. (J). (gr. 8-18). 15.99 *(978-0-06-009070-8(7))* HarperCollins Pubs.

Clark, Jay. The Edumacation of Jay Baker. 2012. (ENG.). 288p. (YA). (gr. 9-12). pap. 9.99 *(978-1-250-01675-1(4))* Square Fish.

Clark, Kent & Snider, Brandon. Peter Powers. Bardin, Dave, illus. 2016. (Peter Powers Ser.: 1). (ENG.). 128p. (J). (gr. 1-5). 15.99 *(978-0-316-35932-0(7))* Little, Brown Bks. for Young Readers.

Clark, Kent & Snider, Brandon T. Peter Powers & the Rowdy Robot Raiders! Bardin, Dave, illus. 2016. (Peter Powers Ser.: 2). (ENG.). 128p. (J). (gr. 1-5). 15.99 *(978-0-316-35941-2(6))* Little, Brown Bks. for Young Readers.

Clarke, Cat. The Pants Project. 2017. (ENG.). 272p. (J). (gr. 4-9). 16.99 *(978-1-4926-3809-4(9))*, 9781492638094, Sourcebooks Jabberwocky) Sourcebooks, Inc.

Clarke, Henry. Miss Merivale's Mistake. 2007. 68p. per. *(978-1-4068-4614-0(7))* Echo Library.

Clarke, Judith. One Whole & Perfect Day. 2007. (ENG.). 250p. (J). (gr. 8-13). 16.95 *(978-1-932425-95-6(0))*, Front Street) Boyds Mills Pr.

Cleary, Beverly. Beezus & Ramona. Darling, Louis & Rogers, Jacqueline, illus. 2013. (Ramona Ser.: 1). (ENG.). 208p. (J). (gr. 3-7). pap. 6.99 *(978-0-380-70918-2(X))* HarperCollins Pubs.

—Beezus & Ramona. Darling, Louis et al, illus. 2013. (Ramona Ser.: 1). (ENG.). 208p. (J). (gr. 3-7). 16.99 *(978-0-688-21076-2(7))* HarperCollins Pubs.

—Beezus & Ramona. Dockray, Tracy & Rogers, Jacqueline, illus. movie tie-in ed. 2010. (Ramona Ser.: 1). (ENG.). 208p. (J). (gr. 3-7). pap. 5.99 *(978-0-06-191461-4(4))*, HarperFestival) HarperCollins Pubs.

—Beezus & Ramona. 2011. 9.01 *(978-0-7848-3570-8(5))*, Everbind) Marco Bk. Co.

—Beezus & Ramona. (Ramona Quimby Ser.). 142p. (J). (gr. 3-5). pap. 4.99 *(978-0-8072-1441-1(8))*, Listening Library) Random Hse. Audio Publishing Group.

—Beezus & Ramona. Darling, Louis, illus. (gr. 3-5). pap. *(978-0-545-24980-5(5))* Scholastic, Inc.

—Beezus & Ramona. (Ramona Quimby Ser.: 1). (J). 2013. lib. bdg. 17.20 *(978-0-88103-289-5(1))* 2010. lib. bdg. 16.00 *(978-0-606-15072-9(2))* Turtleback Bks. (Turtleback).

—Ramona & Her Family. (J). Random House Publishing Group.

—Ramona & Her Father. Tiegreen, Alan & Rogers, Jacqueline, illus. 2013. (Ramona Ser.: 4). (ENG.). 192p. (J). (gr. 3-7). pap. 6.99 *(978-0-380-70916-8(3))* HarperCollins Pubs.

—Ramona & Her Father. Tiegreen, Alan et al, illus. 2013. (Ramona Ser.: 4). (ENG.). 192p. (J). (gr. 3-7). 16.99 *(978-0-688-22114-0(9))* HarperCollins Pubs.

—Ramona & Her Father. 2009. 8.32 *(978-0-88483-705-3(X))*, Everbind) Marco Bk. Co.

—Ramona & Her Father. (Ramona Quimby Ser.). 186p. (J). (gr. 3-5). pap. 4.99 *(978-0-8072-1439-8(6))*, Listening Library) Random Hse. Audio Publishing Group.

—Ramona & Her Mother. Tiegreen, Alan et al, illus. 2013. (Ramona Ser.: 5). (ENG.). 224p. (J). (gr. 3-7). 16.99 *(978-0-688-22195-9(5))* HarperCollins Pubs.

—Ramona & Her Mother. Tiegreen, Alan & Rogers, Jacqueline, illus. 2013. (Ramona Ser.: 5). (ENG.). 224p. (J). (gr. 3-7). reprint ed. pap. 7.99 *(978-0-380-70952-6(X))* HarperCollins Pubs.

—Ramona & Her Mother. (Ramona Quimby Ser.). 208p. (J). (gr. 3-5). pap. 4.99 *(978-0-8072-1435-0(3))*, Listening Library) Random Hse. Audio Publishing Group.

—Ramona Empieza el Curso, 1 vol. Bustelo, Gabriela, tr. Giegreen, Alan et al, illus. 2006. (Ramona Ser.: 6).Tr. of Ramona Quimby, Age 8. (SPA.). 224p. (J). (gr. 3-7). pap. *(978-0-688-15487-5(5))*, MR7554) HarperCollins Pubs.

—Ramona Forever. Tiegreen, Alan et al, illus. 2013. (Ramona Ser.: 7). (ENG.). 208p. (J). (gr. 3-7). 16.99 *(978-0-688-03785-7(2))* HarperCollins Pubs.

—Ramona Forever. Tiegreen, Alan & Rogers, Jacqueline, illus. 2013. (Ramona Ser.: 7). (ENG.). 208p. (J). (gr. 3-7). reprint ed. pap. 7.99 *(978-0-380-70960-1(0))* HarperCollins Pubs.

—Ramona Forever. (Ramona Quimby Ser.). 182p. (J). (gr. 3-5). pap. 4.99 *(978-0-8072-1437-4(X))*, Listening Library) Random Hse. Audio Publishing Group.

—Ramona Forever. 2013. (Ramona Quimby Ser.: 7). (J). (gr. 3-6). lib. bdg. 17.20 *(978-0-8085-5273-4(2))*, Turtleback) Turtleback Bks.

—Ramona la Chinche, 1 vol. Darling, Louis et al, illus. 2006. (Ramona Ser.: 2).Tr. of Ramona the Pest. (SPA.). 192p. (J). (gr. 3-7). pap. 5.99 *(978-0-688-14888-1(3))*, MR2295) HarperCollins Pubs.

—Ramona la Chinche. Palacios, Argentina, tr. Darling, Louis, illus. 2006. (Ramona Quimby Spanish Ser.: 2).Tr. of Ramona the Pest. (SPA.). 181p. (J). (gr. 4-7). lib. bdg. 16.00 *(978-0-613-00464-0(7))*, Turtleback) Turtleback Bks.

—Ramona Quimby, Age 8. Rogers, Jacqueline, illus. 2016. (Ramona Ser.: 6). 208p. (J). (gr. 3-7). 12.99 *(978-0-06-246454-5(X))* HarperCollins Pubs.

—Ramona Quimby, Age 8. Tiegreen, Alan & Rogers, Jacqueline, illus. 2016. (Ramona Ser.: 6). (ENG.). 208p. (J). (gr. 3-7). pap. 6.99 *(978-0-380-70956-4(2))* HarperCollins Pubs.

—Ramona Quimby, Age 8. Tiegreen, Alan et al, illus. 2014. (Ramona Ser.: 6). (ENG.). 208p. (J). (gr. 3-7). 16.99 *(978-0-688-00477-4(6))* HarperCollins Pubs.

—Ramona Quimby, Age 8. (Ramona Quimby Ser.). (J). (gr. 3-5). Random House Publishing Group.

—Ramona Quimby, Age 8. (Ramona Quimby Ser.). 190p. (J). (gr. 3-5). pap. 4.99 *(978-0-8072-1436-7(1))*, Listening Library) Random Hse. Audio Publishing Group.

—Ramona Quimby, Age 8 Read-Aloud Edition. Rogers, Jacqueline, illus. 2016. (Ramona Ser.: 6). 208p. (J). (gr. 3-7). 17.99 *(978-0-06-245327-3(0))* HarperCollins Pubs.

—Ramona the Brave. Tiegreen, Alan et al, illus. 2013. (Ramona Ser.: 3). (ENG.). 208p. (J). (gr. 3-7). 16.99 *(978-0-688-22015-0(0))*; pap. 6.99 *(978-0-380-70959-5(7))* HarperCollins Pubs.

—Ramona the Brave. (Ramona Quimby Ser.). 190p. (J). (gr. 3-5). pap. 4.99 *(978-0-8072-1440-4(X))*, Listening Library) Random Hse. Audio Publishing Group.

—Ramona the Pest. Darling, Louis & Rogers, Jacqueline, illus. 2013. (Ramona Ser.: 2). (SPA & ENG.). 240p. (J). (gr. 3-7). pap. 6.99 *(978-0-380-70954-0(6))* HarperCollins Pubs.

—Ramona the Pest. Darling, Louis et al, illus. 2013. (Ramona Ser.: 2). (ENG.). 240p. (J). (gr. 3-7). 16.99 *(978-0-688-21721-1(4))* HarperCollins Pubs.

—Ramona the Pest. (Ramona Quimby Ser.). (J). (gr. 3-5). Random House Publishing Group.

—Ramona the Pest. (Ramona Quimby Ser.). 192p. (J). (gr. 3-5). pap. 4.99 *(978-0-8072-1438-1(8))*, Listening Library) Random Hse. Audio Publishing Group.

—Ramona's World. Tiegreen, Alan et al, illus. 2014. (Ramona Ser.: 8). (ENG.). 240p. (J). (gr. 3-7). 16.99 *(978-0-688-16816-2(7))* HarperCollins Pubs.

—Ramona's World. Tiegreen, Alan & Rogers, Jacqueline, illus. 2013. (Ramona Ser.: 8). (ENG.). 240p. (J). (gr. 3-7). pap. 7.99 *(978-0-380-73272-2(6))* HarperCollins Pubs.

—Ramona's World. unabr. ed. 2004. (Ramona Quimby Ser.). 194p. (J). (gr. 3-7). pap. 29.00 incl. audio *(978-0-8072-8169-7(7))*, Listening Library) Random Hse. Audio Publishing Group.

—Ramona's World. 2013. (Ramona Quimby Ser.: 8). (J). (gr. 3-6). lib. bdg. 17.20 *(978-0-613-35794-4(9))*, Turtleback) Turtleback Bks.

Cleary, Jon. The Sundowners. (J). 25.95 *(978-0-88411-467-3(8))* Amereon Ltd.

Clements, Andrew. Extra Credit. Elliott, Mark, illus. (ENG.). (J). (gr. 3-7). 2011. 224p. pap. 7.99 *(978-1-4169-4931-2(3))* 2009. 192p. 16.99 *(978-1-4169-4929-9(1))* Simon & Schuster Children's Publishing. (Atheneum Bks. for Young Readers).

—In Harm's Way. Stower, Adam, illus. (Benjamin Pratt & the Keepers of the School Ser.: 4). (ENG.). (J). (gr. 2-5). 2014. 240p. pap. 7.99 *(978-1-4169-3910-8(5))* 2013. 224p. 14.99 *(978-1-4169-3889-7(3))* Simon & Schuster Children's Publishing. (Atheneum Bks. for Young Readers).

Clifton, Lutricia. Freaky Fast Frankie Joe. (ENG.). 272p. (J). 2013. pap. 7.99 *(978-0-8234-2867-0(2))* 2012. 16.95 *(978-0-8234-2367-5(0))* Holiday Hse., Inc.

Clinton, Cathryn. A Stone in My Hand. 2010. (ENG., Illus.). 208p. (J). (gr. 5). pap. 6.99 *(978-0-7636-4772-8(1))* Candlewick Pr.

Clymer, Susan. There's a Rabbit in My Backpack. 2007. 100p. pap. 8.50 *(978-1-4303-2959-6(9))* Lulu Pr., Inc.

Cocca-Leffler, Maryann. A Homemade Together Christmas. Cocca-Leffler, Maryann, illus. 2015. (ENG., Illus.). 32p. (J). (gr. -1-3). 16.99 *(978-0-8075-3366-6(1))* Whitman, Albert & Co.

Cochard, Nadège. A Daycare for Connor. Fanny, illus. 2009. (My First Stories Ser.). 24p. (J). (gr. -1-3). 22.60 *(978-1-60754-353-4(2))*; pap. 8.15 *(978-1-60754-354-1(0))* Windmill Bks.

Cocks, Nancy & Marton, Jirina. Fergie Counts His Blessings. 2003. (Illus.). 16p. pap. *(978-2-89507-302-4(3))* Novalis Publishing.

Cody, Matthew. Powerless. 2011. (Supers of Noble's Green Ser.). (ENG.). 288p. (J). (gr. 3-7). 7.99 *(978-0-375-84489-8(9))*, Yearling) Random Hse. Children's Bks.

Coffelt, Nancy. Catch That Baby! Nash, Scott, illus. 2011. (ENG.). 40p. (J). (gr. -1-3). 16.99 *(978-1-4169-9148-9(4))*, Aladdin) Simon & Schuster Children's Publishing.

—Uh-Oh, Baby! Nash, Scott, illus. 2013. (ENG.). 40p. (J). (gr. -1-3). 16.99 *(978-1-4169-9149-6(2))*, Simon & Schuster/Paula Wiseman Bks.) Simon & Schuster/Paula Wiseman Bks.

Coh, Smiljana. I Have a Brother. 2012. (ENG.). 24p. (J). *(978-1-58925-124-3(5))* Tiger Tales.

Cohagan, Carolyn. The Lost Children. 2011. (ENG.). 320p. (J). (gr. 3-7). pap. 7.99 *(978-1-4169-8617-1(0))*, Aladdin) Simon & Schuster Children's Publishing.

Cohen, Miriam. My Big Brother, 1 vol. Himler, Ronald, illus. 2005. (ENG.). 32p. (J). 15.95 *(978-1-59572-007-8(3))*; pap. 6.95 *(978-1-59572-158-7(4))* Star Bright Bks., Inc.

—My Big Brother (Spanish/English), 1 vol. Himler, Ronald, illus. 2008. (ABK, SPA & ENG.). 32p. (J). (gr. -1-3). pap. 5.95 *(978-1-59572-037-5(5))* Star Bright Bks., Inc.

Cohn, Rachel. Beta. 2013. (Beta Novel Ser.). (ENG., Illus.). 336p. (YA). (gr. 9-17). pap. 9.99 *(978-1-4231-5734-2(6))* Hyperion Pr.

—Emergent. 2014. (Beta Novel Ser.). (ENG.). 288p. (YA). (gr. 9-17). 17.99 *(978-1-4231-5720-5(6))* Hyperion Bks. for Children.

—The Steps. 2004. (ENG.). 144p. (J). (gr. 3-7). reprint ed. pap. 6.99 *(978-0-689-87414-7(6))*, Simon & Schuster Bks. For Young Readers) Simon & Schuster Bks. For Young Readers.

—Two Steps Forward. 2006. (ENG., Illus.). 240p. (YA). 15.95 *(978-0-689-86614-2(3))*, Simon & Schuster Bks. For Young Readers) Simon & Schuster Bks. For Young Readers.

—You Know Where to Find Me. 2008. (ENG.). 208p. (YA). (gr. 7-12). 16.99 *(978-0-689-87859-6(1))*, Simon & Schuster Bks. For Young Readers) Simon & Schuster Bks. For Young Readers.

Cohn, Scott M. Daddy Sat on a Duck. 2015. (Daddy Ser.: 1). (ENG., Illus.). 32p. (J). (gr. -1-3). 15.00 *(978-0-316-40749-6(6))* Little Brown & Co.

Colasanti, Susane. Waiting for You. 2010. (ENG.). 336p. (YA). (gr. 7-18). 9.99 *(978-0-14-241575-7(8))*, Speak) Penguin Young Readers Group.

Colbert, Brandy. Little & Lion. 2017. (ENG.). 336p. (YA). (gr. 9-17). 17.99 ***(978-0-316-34900-0(3))*** Little, Brown Bks. for Young Readers.

Colbert, Brandy. Pointe. (ENG.). 352p. (YA). (gr. 9). 2015. pap. 9.99 *(978-0-14-751441-7(X))*, Speak) 2014. 17.99 *(978-0-399-16034-9(5))*, G.P. Putnam's Sons Books for Young Readers) Penguin Young Readers Group.

Cole, Tom Clohosy. Wall. Cole, Tom Clohosy, illus. 2014. (ENG., Illus.). 32p. (J). (gr. -1-3). 16.99 *(978-0-7636-7560-8(1))*, Templar) Candlewick Pr.

Coleman, Evelyn. Freedom Train. 2012. (ENG.). 160p. (J). (gr. 3-7). pap. 7.99 *(978-1-4424-3652-7(2))*, McElderry, Margaret K. Bks.) McElderry, Margaret K. Bks.

—Freedom Train. Riley, David, illus. 2008. (ENG.). 160p. (J). (gr. 3-7). 17.99 *(978-0-689-84716-5(5))*, McElderry, Margaret K. Bks.) McElderry, Margaret K. Bks.

Coley, Liz. Pretty Girl-13. 2013. (ENG.). 352p. (YA). (gr. 9). 17.99 *(978-0-06-212737-2(3))*, Tegen, Katherine Bks) HarperCollins Pubs.

Colfer, Eoin. Benny & Omar. 2003. 240p. (YA). (gr. 5-18). pap. 7.95 *(978-0-86278-567-3(7))* O'Brien Pr., Ltd., The IRL. Dist: Independent Pubs. Group.

Colin, Beatrice & Pinto, Sara. My Invisible Sister. Pinto, Sara, illus. 2011. (ENG., Illus.). 128p. (YA). (gr. 3-6). pap. 6.99 *(978-1-59990-678-2(3))*, 9781599906782, Bloomsbury USA Childrens) Bloomsbury Publishing USA.

Collicott, Sharleen. Mildred & Sam & Their Babies. Collicott, Sharleen, illus. 2005. (I Can Read Bks.). (Illus.). 48p. (J). (gr. -1-2). 15.99 *(978-0-06-058111-4(5))*, Geringer, Laura Book) HarperCollins Pubs.

Columbro, Judy. The Gift That Grows. Scottorosano, Deborah, illus. 2011. 28p. pap. 24.95 *(978-1-4626-1800-2(6))* America Star Bks.

Coman, Carolyn. Many Stones. 2009. (ENG.). 160p. (YA). pap. 12.95 *(978-1-59078-782-3(X))*, Front Street) Boyds Mills Pr.

—Many Stones. 2011. 14.12 *(978-0-7848-3598-2(5))*, Everbind) Marco Bk. Co.

—What Jamie Saw. unabr. ed. 2004. 128p. (J). (gr. 7-18). pap. 29.00 incl. audio *(978-0-8072-8788-0(1))*, YA268SP, Listening Library) Random Hse. Audio Publishing Group.

Compestine, Ying Chang. Revolution Is Not a Dinner Party. 2009. (ENG.). 272p. (J). (gr. 5-9). pap. 9.99 *(978-0-312-58149-7(1))*, 9780312581497) Square Fish.

Condie, Ally. Being Sixteen. 2010. (YA). *(978-1-60641-233-6(7))* Deseret Bk. Co.

—Freshman for President. 2008. (ENG.). 304p. (YA). (gr. 8-12). pap. 15.99 *(978-1-59038-913-3(1))*, Shadow Mountain) Shadow Mountain Publishing.

Condra, Estelle. See the Ocean. 7.95 *(978-1-57102-178-6(7))*, Ideal Pubns.) Worthy Publishing.

Conford, Ellen. And This Is Laura. 2014. (ENG.). 228p. (J). (gr. 3). pap. 12.95 *(978-1-939601-18-6(5))* Ig Publishing, Inc.

Conklin, Melanie. Counting Thyme. 2016. (ENG.). 320p. (J). (gr. 5). 16.99 *(978-0-399-17330-1(7))*, G.P. Putnam's Sons Books for Young Readers) Penguin Young Readers Group.

Conlon-McKenna, Marita. The Fields of Home. 2009. (ENG.). 176p. (J). (gr. 4-6). pap. 7.99 *(978-1-4022-1908-5(3))*, Sourcebooks Jabberwocky) Sourcebooks, Inc.

Connelly, Neil. The Miracle Stealer. 2010. (ENG.). 240p. (J). (gr. 9-18). 17.99 *(978-0-545-13195-7(2))*, Levine, Arthur A. Bks.) Scholastic, Inc.

Connelly, Neil O. The Miracle Stealer. 2012. (ENG.). 240p. (J). (gr. 9-9). pap. 9.99 *(978-0-545-13312-8(2))*, Levine, Arthur A. Bks.) Scholastic, Inc.

Connor, Leslie. Crunch. 2012. (ENG.). 336p. (J). (gr. 5). pap. 6.99 *(978-0-06-169234-5(4))*, Tegen, Katherine Bks) HarperCollins Pubs.

—Waiting for Normal. (ENG.). (J). (gr. 5). 2010. 320p. pap. 6.99 *(978-0-06-089090-2(8))* 2008. 304p. 16.99 *(978-0-06-089088-9(6))* HarperCollins Pubs. (Tegen, Katherine Bks).

Conti, Alexis. One Blue Shoe. Beth, Shannon, illus. 2013. (ENG.). (J). (gr. -1-3). 14.95 *(978-1-937406-11-0(3))* Mascot Bks., Inc.

Converse, P. J. Subway Girl. 2011. (ENG.). 224p. (YA). (gr. 9-18). 16.99 *(978-0-06-157514-3(3))*, HarperTeen) HarperCollins Pubs.

Conway, Celeste. When You Open Your Eyes. 2012. (ENG.). 320p. (YA). (gr. 9). pap. 9.99 *(978-1-4424-3031-0(1))*, Simon Pulse) Simon Pulse.

Cook, Kristi. Magnolia. 2014. (ENG., Illus.). 336p. (YA). (gr. 9). 17.99 *(978-1-4424-8535-8(3))*; pap. 10.99 *(978-1-4424-8534-1(5))* Simon Pulse. (Simon Pulse).

Cooke, Trish. So Much! Oxenbury, Helen, illus. 2008. (ENG.). 48p. (J). (gr. -1-2). pap. 6.99 *(978-0-7636-4091-0(3))* Candlewick Pr.

—So Much! Oxenbury, Helen, illus. 2008. (J). (gr. -1-1). lib. bdg. 17.20 *(978-0-613-08774-2(7))*, Turtleback) Turtleback Bks.

Coolidge, Susan. Clover. 2005. (Illus.). 133p. pap. *(978-1-59569-026-5(3))* Mondial.

—What Katy Did. 2012. 246p. pap. *(978-1-78139-262-1(5))* Benediction Classics.

—What Katy Did. 2012. 302p. pap. 29.75 *(978-1-286-07372-8(3))* 2012. 300p. pap. 29.75 *(978-1-286-00091-5(2))* 2011. 290p. (gr. 3-7). pap. 28.75 *(978-1-179-65265-8(7))* 2010. (ENG.). 300p. pap. 29.75 *(978-1-178-00783-1(9))* 2010. (ENG.). 282p. (gr. 3-7). pap. 28.75 *(978-1-177-27477-7(9))* 2010. 302p. pap. 29.75 *(978-1-145-74830-9(9))* 2008. 164p. (gr. 4-7). 25.99 *(978-0-554-28634-1(3))* 2008. 164p. (gr. 4-7). 22.99 *(978-0-554-37937-1(6))* 2007. (ENG.). 144p. pap. 18.99 *(978-1-4346-5943-9(7))* 2007. (ENG.). 160p. pap. 21.99 *(978-1-4346-5944-6(5))* Creative Media Partners, LLC.

—What Katy Did. 2007. (ENG.). 148p. per. *(978-1-4065-1527-5(2))* Dodo Pr.

—What Katy Did. 2006. (Dover Children's Classics Ser.). (ENG., Illus.). 160p. (J). (gr. 3-8). per. 6.95 *(978-0-486-44760-5(X))* Dover Pubns., Inc.

—What Katy Did. 2007. (ENG.). 104p. per. *(978-1-4068-4855-7(7))* Echo Library.

—What Katy Did. 2010. (Illus.). 92p. (gr. 3-7). pap. 19.99 *(978-1-153-74507-9(0))* 2009. 104p. pap. 6.40 *(978-0-217-53637-0(9))* General Bks. LLC.

—What Katy Did. 2010. 132p. pap. *(978-1-4076-5115-6(3))* HardPr.

—What Katy Did. Ledyard, Addie, illus. 284p. 2010. 35.16 *(978-1-163-85079-4(9))* 2010. pap. 23.16 *(978-1-163-77965-1(2))* 2007. 43.95 *(978-0-548-53870-8(0))* 2007. per. 28.95 *(978-0-548-48700-6(6))* Kessinger Publishing, LLC.

E
F
G

—What Katy Did. 2010. (Puffin Classics Ser.). (ENG., Illus.). 240p. (J). (gr. 5-7). pap. 5.99 *(978-0-14-132671-9(9),* Puffin Books) Penguin Young Readers Group.
—What Katy Did. 2013. (ENG., Illus.). 256p. (J). (gr. 4-7). pap. 12.99 *(978-0-09-957312-8(1))* Random Hse. GBR. Dist: Independent Pubs. Group.
—What Katy Did. 2007. (ENG.). 192p. pap. 12.45 *(978-1-60424-403-8(8),* Book Jungle) Standard Pubns., Inc.
—What Katy Did. 2011. 162p. (gr. 3-7). pap. *(978-3-8424-6664-7(1))* Tredition GmbH.
—What Katy Did. 2010. 144p. pap. 4.99 *(978-1-61720-100-4(6))* Wilder Pubns., Corp.
Coolidge, Susan & Ledyard, Addie. What Katy Did. 2010. (ENG.). 292p. pap. 28.75 *(978-1-172-34659-2(3))* Creative Media Partners, LLC.
Cooney, Caroline B. A Friend at Midnight. 2008. (ENG.). 192p. (YA). (gr. 7). pap. 8.99 *(978-1-4000-7209-5(3),* WaterBrook Pr.) Crown Publishing Group.
—If the Witness Lied. 2010. (ENG.). 224p. (YA). (gr. 7). pap. 8.99 *(978-0-385-73449-3(2),* Ember) Random Hse. Children's Bks.
—Janie Face to Face. 2013. (ENG.). 352p. (YA). (gr. 7). 17.99 *(978-0-385-74206-1(1),* Delacorte Bks. for Young Readers) Random Hse. Children's Bks.
Cooper, Alison. Adrian's Journey. 2017. (ENG.). 462p. pap. 16.95 ***(978-1-78629-571-2(7),*** 2bcdc6a2-796f-48f1-8b02-af290ff5dffa) Austin, Stan AUS. Dist: Bookmasters Distribution.
Cooper, Ilene. Lucy's Holiday Surprise. Fitzgerald, Royce, illus. 2015. (Lucy Ser.: 7). (ENG.). 112p. (J). (gr. 1-4). 12.99 *(978-0-385-39131-3(5),* Random Hse. Bks. for Young Readers) Random Hse. Children's Bks.
Cooper, Michelle. A Brief History of Montmaray. 2011. (Montmaray Journals). (ENG.). 324p. (YA). (gr. 7). pap. 8.99 *(978-0-375-85154-4(2),* Knopf Bks. for Young Readers) Random Hse. Children's Bks.
—The FitzOsbornes at War. 2013. (Montmaray Journals). (ENG.). 560p. (YA). (gr. 7). pap. 10.99 *(978-0-307-93058-3(0),* Ember) Random Hse. Children's Bks.
—The FitzOsbornes in Exile. 2012. (Montmaray Journals). (ENG.). 464p. (YA). (gr. 7). pap. 10.99 *(978-0-375-85155-1(0),* Ember) Random Hse. Children's Bks.
Cordell, Matthew. Another Brother. Cordell, Matthew, illus. 2012. (ENG., Illus.). 36p. (J). (gr. -1-1). 16.99 *(978-0-312-64324-9(1),* 9780312643249) Feiwel & Friends.
—Hello! Hello! Cordell, Matthew, illus. 2012. (ENG., Illus.). 56p. (J). (gr. -1-4). 16.99 *(978-1-4231-5906-3(3))* Hyperion Pr.
Corn, Tori. What Will It Be, Penelope? Ceccolini, Danielle, illus. 2013. (ENG.). 32p. (J). (gr. -1-k). 16.95 *(978-1-62087-542-1(X),* 620542, Sky Pony Pr.) Skyhorse Publishing Co., Inc.
Cornman, Sabrina. Lepi's Golden America. Pierce, Kim, illus. 2003. 108p. 20.00 *(978-0-9719167-6-0(4));* per. 12.00 *(978-0-9719167-5-3(6))* Open Bk. Publishing.
Corriveau, Art. 13 Hangmen. 2012. (ENG.). 352p. (J). (gr. 3-7). 17.95 *(978-1-4197-0159-7(2),* Amulet Bks.) Abrams, Inc.
Corso, Erika. The Day You Came. Corso, Erika & Corso, Bertina, illus. 2006. (ENG.). 20p. (J). per. 12.95 *(978-1-59800-242-3(2))* Outskirts Pr., Inc.
Corthron, Kara Lee. The Truth of Right Now. 2017. (ENG., Illus.). 288p. (YA). (gr. 9). 17.99 *(978-1-4814-5947-1(3),* Simon Pulse) Simon Pulse.
Corwin, Jeff. The Great Alaska Adventure!, 2 vols., Bk. 2. 2010. (Jeff Corwin Ser.: 2). (ENG.). 112p. (J). (gr. 1-3). 4.99 *(978-0-14-241409-5(3),* Puffin Books) Penguin Young Readers Group.
—Your Backyard Is Wild. 2009. (Jeff Corwin Ser.: 1). (ENG.). 96p. (J). (gr. 1-3). 4.99 *(978-0-14-241404-0(2),* Puffin Books) Penguin Young Readers Group.
Cory, Kim Delmar. Tending Ben's Garden. 2009. (J). pap. *(978-0-88092-778-9(X))* Royal Fireworks Publishing Co.
Cosgrove, Stephen. The Bigg Family: Getting along with Others. Arroyo, Fian, illus. 2004. (J). *(978-1-58804-354-2(1))* P C I Education.
—Flynn "Flea" Flicker: Sticking to the Truth. Arroyo, Fian, illus. 2004. (J). *(978-1-58804-353-5(3))* P C I Education.
—Katy Didd Bigg: Standing up for Yourself. Arroyo, Fian, illus. 2004. (J). *(978-1-58804-378-8(9))* P C I Education.
Costales, Amy. Sundays on Fourth Street/Los Domingos en la Calle Cuatro. Jerome, Elaine, illus. 2009. (SPA & ENG.). 32p. (J). (gr. -1-3). 16.95 *(978-1-55885-520-5(3))* Arte Publico Pr.
Coster, Simon. My Dinosaur Is More Awesome! 2015. (ENG., Illus.). 48p. (J). (gr. -1-k). 16.99 *(978-1-63220-416-5(9),* Sky Pony Pr.) Skyhorse Publishing Co., Inc.
Cotler, Steve. Cheesie Mack Is Not a Genius or Anything. McCauley, Adam, illus. (Cheesie Mack Ser.). (ENG.). 240p. (J). (gr. 3-7). 2012. 6.99 *(978-0-375-86394-3(X),* Yearling) 2011. 15.99 *(978-0-375-86437-7(7),* Random Hse. Bks. for Young Readers) Random Hse. Children's Bks.
—Cheesie Mack Is Sort of Freaked Out. Holgate, Douglas, illus. 2014. (Cheesie Mack Ser.). (ENG.). 256p. (J). (gr. 3-7). 15.99 *(978-0-385-36988-6(3),* Random Hse. Bks. for Young Readers) Random Hse. Children's Bks.
Courgeon, Rémi. Toothpick. 2017. (ENG., Illus.). 36p. (J). (gr. k-4). 17.95 *(978-1-59270-210-7(4))* Enchanted Lion Bks., LLC.
Cousins, Dave. Waiting for Gonzo. 2015. (ENG.). 288p. (YA). pap. 9.99 *(978-0-7387-4199-4(X),* Flux) North Star Editions.
Coven, Wanda. Heidi Heckelbeck Gets Glasses. Burris, Priscilla, illus. 2012. (Heidi Heckelbeck Ser.: 5). (ENG.). 128p. (J). (gr. k-2). pap. 5.99 *(978-1-4424-4171-2(2));* 15.99 *(978-1-4424-4172-9(0))* Little Simon. (Little Simon).
—Heidi Heckelbeck Gets Glasses. 2012. (Heidi Heckelbeck Ser.: 5). lib. bdg. 16.00 *(978-0-606-26888-2(X),* Turtleback) Turtleback Bks.
—Heidi Heckelbeck Has a Secret. Burris, Priscilla, illus. 2012. (Heidi Heckelbeck Ser.: 1). (ENG.). 128p. (J). (gr. k-4). 16.99 *(978-1-4424-4087-6(2));* pap. 5.99 *(978-1-4424-3565-0(8))* Little Simon. (Little Simon).
—Heidi Heckelbeck Has a Secret. 2012. (Heidi Heckelbeck Ser.: 1). lib. bdg. 16.00 *(978-0-606-26326-9(8),* Turtleback) Turtleback Bks.
Coville, Bruce. Diary of a Mad Brownie. 2015. (Enchanted Files Ser.). (ENG., Illus.). 256p. (J). (gr. 3-7). lib. bdg. 19.99 *(978-0-385-39248-8(6),* Random Hse. Bks. for Young Readers) Random Hse. Children's Bks.
—The Skull of Truth: A Magic Shop Book. Lippincott, Gary A., illus. 2007. (Magic Shop Book Ser.: 4). (ENG.). 208p. (J). (gr. 5-7). pap. 7.99 *(978-0-15-206084-8(7))* Houghton Mifflin Harcourt Publishing Co.
Coward, Fiona. Swing High, Swing Low. Manna, Giovanni, illus. 2005. (ENG.). 32p. (J). 16.99 *(978-1-84148-170-8(X))* Barefoot Bks., Inc.
Cowley, Joy. Freddy Bear & the Beach. Webb, Philip, illus. 2016. (Freddy Bear Ser.). (ENG.). 20p. (J). (gr. -1-k). bds. 12.99 *(978-1-927262-56-6(9))* Upstart Pr. NZL. Dist: Independent Pubs. Group.
—Stories of the Wild West Gang. Pye, Trevor, illus. 2012. (Gecko Press Titles Ser.). (ENG.). 368p. (gr. -1-1). 16.95 *(978-1-877579-21-9(1))* Gecko Pr. NZL. Dist: Lerner Publishing Group.
Cox, Judy. The Secret Chicken Society. Haley, Amanda, illus. (ENG.). 96p. (J). 2013. pap. 5.99 *(978-0-8234-2765-9(X))* 2012. 15.95 *(978-0-8234-2372-9(7))* Holiday Hse., Inc.
Coy, John. Eyes on the Goal, Bk. 2. 2012. (4 For 4 Ser.: 2). (ENG.). 192p. (J). (gr. 3-7). pap. 7.99 *(978-0-312-65922-6(9),* 9780312659226) Square Fish.
—Love of the Game. 2011. (4 For 4 Ser.: 3). (ENG.). 192p. (J). (gr. 3-7). 16.99 *(978-0-312-37331-3(7),* 9780312373313) Feiwel & Friends.
—Love of the Game. 2011. (4 For 4 Ser.: 3). (ENG.). 192p. (J). (gr. 3-7). pap. 8.99 *(978-1-250-00637-0(6),* 9781250006370) Square Fish.
—Take Your Best Shot. 2012. (4 For 4 Ser.: 4). (ENG.). 192p. (J). (gr. 3-7). 16.99 *(978-0-312-37332-0(5),* 9780312373320) Feiwel & Friends.
—Top of the Order. 2010. (4 For 4 Ser.: 1). (ENG.). 208p. (J). (gr. 3-7). pap. 8.99 *(978-0-312-61111-8(0),* 9780312611118) Square Fish.
Coyle, Carmela Lavigna. Do Princesses Make Happy Campers? Gordon, Mike, illus. 2015. (ENG.). 32p. (J). (gr. -1-2). 15.95 *(978-1-63076-054-0(4))* Taylor Trade Publishing.
Cozzo, Karole. How to Keep Rolling after a Fall. 2016. (ENG.). 272p. (YA). pap. 9.99 *(978-1-250-07928-2(4),* 9781250079282) Feiwel & Friends.
—How to Say I Love You Out Loud. 2015. (ENG.). 240p. (YA). (gr. 7). pap. 9.99 *(978-1-250-06359-5(0))* Feiwel & Friends.
Craig, Ellen. Making a Book a Best Seller: Marketing Techniques above & Beyond the Rest. 2009. (ENG., Illus.). 130p. per. 24.97 *(978-0-9779960-7-0(7),* Books To Believe In) Thornton Publishing, Inc.
Creech, Sharon. Absolutely Normal Chaos. 2012. (Walk Two Moons Ser.: 2). (ENG.). 256p. (J). (gr. 4-18). pap. 7.99 *(978-0-06-440632-1(6))* HarperCollins Pubs.
—Bloomability. unabr. ed. 2004. 273p. (J). (gr. 4-7). pap. 38.00 incl. audio *(978-0-8072-8754-5(7),* YA257SP, Listening Library) Random Hse. Audio Publishing Group.
—Bloomability. 2012. (J). (gr. 3-6). 17.20 *(978-0-613-22826-8(X),* Turtleback) Turtleback Bks.
—Fishing in the Air. Raschka, Chris, illus. 2003. (J). 25.95 incl. audio *(978-1-59112-225-8(2));* pap. 37.95 incl. audio *(978-1-59112-226-5(0));* pap. 39.95 incl. audio compact disk *(978-1-59112-521-1(9))* Live Oak Media.
—Replay. (J). (gr. 3-7). 2013. (ENG.). 224p. pap. 6.99 *(978-0-06-054021-0(4))* 2005. 240p. lib. bdg. 16.89 *(978-0-06-054020-3(6),* Cotler, Joanna Books) HarperCollins Pubs.
—Walk Two Moons. 2003. (Walk Two Moons Ser.: 1). 304p. (J). (gr. 3-7). pap. 7.99 *(978-0-06-056013-3(4),* HarperTeen) HarperCollins Pubs.
—Walk Two Moons. 280p. (J). (gr. 4-6). pap. 4.95 *(978-0-8072-1509-8(0),* Listening Library) Random Hse. Audio Publishing Group.
—Walk Two Moons. (J). 2011. (gr. 5-8). lib. bdg. 18.40 *(978-0-613-00204-2(0))* 2003. (gr. 7-12). 18.40 *(978-0-613-81971-8(3))* Turtleback Bks. (Turtleback).
—The Wanderer. Diaz, David, illus. 2011. (ENG.). 304p. (J). (gr. 3-7). pap. 6.99 *(978-0-06-441032-8(3))* HarperCollins Pubs.
Crews, Deborah Sue. Broken Slippers. 2013. 92p. pap. 12.00 *(978-1-936688-82-1(4),* Compass Flower Pr.) AKA:yoLa.
Crockett-Blassingame, Linda, illus. See the Ocean. 2006. 32p. (J). 14.95 *(978-0-9778143-0-5(0))* Inclusive Books LLC.
Cronkhite, Lisa. Disconnected. 2014. (ENG.). 196p. (YA). pap. 10.95 *(978-1-929345-02-1(X))* Poisoned Pen Pr.
Cronn-Mills, Kirstin. Original Fake. Johnson, E. Eero, illus. 2016. (ENG.). 352p. (YA). (gr. 7). 17.99 *(978-0-399-17326-4(9),* G.P. Putnam's Sons Books for Young Readers) Penguin Young Readers Group.
Crossan, Sarah. Apple & Rain. 2015. (ENG.). 352p. (YA). (gr. 7). 17.99 *(978-1-61963-690-3(5),* 9781619636903, Bloomsbury USA Childrens) Bloomsbury Publishing USA.
—One. 2015. (ENG.). 400p. (YA). (gr. 8). 17.99 *(978-0-06-211875-2(7),* Greenwillow Bks.) HarperCollins Pubs.
Crow, Kristyn. Bedtime at the Swamp. Pamintuan, Macky, illus. 2008. (ENG.). 32p. (J). (gr. -1-1). 16.99 *(978-0-06-083951-2(1))* HarperCollins Pubs.
Crow, Marilee. So Silly. Snider, K. C., illus. 2013. 28p. pap. 10.95 *(978-1-61633-443-7(6))* Guardian Angel Publishing, Inc.
Crow, Melinda Melton. Little Lizard's Family Fun, 1 vol. Rowland, Andrew, illus. 2010. (Little Lizards Ser.). (ENG.). 32p. (gr. -1-1). lib. bdg. 22.65 *(978-1-4342-2006-6(0))* Stone Arch Bks.
—Little Lizard's Family Fun. Rowland, Andrew & Rowlands, Andy, illus. 2010. (Little Lizards Ser.). (ENG.). 32p. (gr. -1-1). pap. 6.25 *(978-1-4342-2790-4(1))* Stone Arch Bks.
Crowder, Melanie. A Nearer Moon. (ENG., Illus.). (J). (gr. 3-7). 2016. 176p. pap. 7.99 *(978-1-4814-4149-0(3),* Atheneum Bks. for Young Readers) 2015. 160p. 16.99 *(978-1-4814-4148-3(5))* Simon & Schuster Children's Publishing.
—An Uninterrupted View of the Sky. 2017. (ENG.). 304p. (YA). (gr. 7). 17.99 *(978-0-399-16900-7(8),* Philomel Bks.) Penguin Young Readers Group.
Crowley, Suzanne. The Very Ordered Existence of Merilee Marvelous. 2007. 380p. (J). (gr. 5-9). 16.99 *(978-0-06-123197-1(5),* Greenwillow Bks.) HarperCollins Pubs.
Cruz, Maria Colleen. Border Crossing. 2003. 128p. (J). pap. 9.95 *(978-1-55885-405-5(3),* Piñata Books) Arte Publico Pr.
—Border Crossing. 2006. 122p. (gr. 8-12). 19.95 *(978-0-7569-6587-7(X))* Perfection Learning Corp.
Cuevas, Michelle. Beyond the Laughing Sky. Morstad, Julie, illus. 2014. (ENG.). 160p. (J). (gr. 3-7). 16.99 *(978-0-8037-3867-6(6),* Dial Bks) Penguin Young Readers Group.
Cummings, John Michael. Ugly to Start With. 2011. (ENG.). pap. 16.99 *(978-1-935978-08-4(X),* Vandalia Pr.) West Virginia Univ. Pr.
Cumpiano, Ina & Ramirez, Jose. Quinito, Day & Night. 2008.Tr. of Quinito, Dia y Noche. (SPA & ENG., Illus.). 24p. (J). (gr. -1-3). 16.95 *(978-0-89239-226-1(6))* Lee & Low Bks., Inc.
Cumyn, Alan. The Secret Life of Owen Skye. 2nd ed. 2008. (ENG.). 176p. (J). (gr. 3-7). pap. 9.95 *(978-0-88899-867-5(8))* Groundwood Bks. CAN. Dist: Publishers Group West (PGW).
—Tilt. 2013. 260p. pap. *(978-1-4596-6448-7(5))* ReadHowYouWant.com, Ltd.
Cupala, Holly. Don't Breathe a Word. 2012. (ENG.). 320p. (YA). (gr. 9). pap. 8.99 *(978-0-06-176669-5(0),* HarperTeen) HarperCollins Pubs.
—Tell Me a Secret. 2010. (ENG.). 304p. (YA). (gr. 9-18). 16.99 *(978-0-06-176666-4(6),* HarperTeen) HarperCollins Pubs.
Currey, Anna. Truffle Goes to Town. Currey, Anna, illus. 2003. (Illus.). 32p. (YA). *(978-1-85602-429-7(6),* Pavilion Children's Books) Pavilion Bks.
Curtis, Christopher Paul. The Mighty Miss Malone. (ENG.). 320p. (J). (gr. 4-7). 2013. pap. 7.99 *(978-0-440-42214-3(0),* Yearling) 2012. 15.99 *(978-0-385-73491-2(3),* Lamb, Wendy Bks.) Random Hse. Children's Bks.
—The Mighty Miss Malone. 2013. lib. bdg. 18.40 *(978-0-606-27007-6(8),* Turtleback) Turtleback Bks.
—The Watsons Go to Birmingham — 1963. 2013. (ENG.). 224p. (J). (gr. 3-7). 7.99 *(978-0-385-38294-6(4),* Yearling) Random Hse. Children's Bks.
—The Watsons Go to Birmingham 1963. 210p. (YA). (gr. 5-18). pap. 5.50 *(978-0-8072-8336-3(3));* 2004. (J). (gr. 4-18). pap. 38.00 incl. audio *(978-0-8072-8335-6(5),* YA166SP) Random Hse. Audio Publishing Group. (Listening Library).
Curtis, Christopher Paul & Vega, Eida de la. Los Watson Van a Birmingham - 1963. 2016. (SPA.). 200p. (J). (gr. 5-12). pap. 12.99 ***(978-1-63245-640-3(0))*** Lectorum Pubns., Inc.
Curtis, Marci Lyn. The One Thing. 2015. (ENG., Illus.). 336p. (YA). (gr. 7-12). 17.99 *(978-1-4847-0902-3(0))* Hyperion Bks. for Children.
Curtis, Morgan. Second-hand Alligata: A Cajun Tale. 2010. 20p. 13.99 *(978-1-4520-1673-3(9))* AuthorHouse.
Curtis, Vanessa. The Baking Life of Amelie Day. Eccles, Jane, illus. 2015. (Middle-Grade Novels Ser.). (ENG.). 176p. (gr. 4-7). lib. bdg. 25.27 *(978-1-4965-2216-0(8))* Stone Arch Bks.
Cusick, John M. Girl Parts. 2010. (ENG., Illus.). 240p. (YA). (gr. 9-18). 16.99 *(978-0-7636-4930-2(9))* Candlewick Pr.
Cusick, Richie Tankersley. The Unseen 1 It Begins. 2005. (Unseen Ser.: 1). (ENG.). 304p. (YA). (gr. 7-7). 8.99 *(978-0-14-240463-8(2),* Speak) Penguin Young Readers Group.
Cutler, Jane. Susan Marcus Bends the Rules. 2014. (ENG.). 112p. (J). (gr. 3-7). pap. 16.95 *(978-0-8234-3047-5(2))* Holiday Hse., Inc.
D C Thomson Staff, ed. The Broons 2004. 2003. (Illus.). 96p. (J). 9.95 *(978-0-85116-835-7(3))* Thomson, D.C. & Co., Ltd. GBR. Dist: APG Sales & Distribution Services.
—The Broons & Oor Wullie 2004: More Classics from the Fifties. 2003. (Illus.). 144p. (J). 12.95 *(978-0-85116-836-4(1))* Thomson, D.C. & Co., Ltd. GBR. Dist: APG Sales & Distribution Services.
Da Costa, Deborah. Hanukkah Moon. Mosz, Gosia, illus. 2007. (Hanukkah Ser.). (ENG.). 32p. (J). (gr. 1-4). 10.95 *(978-1-58013-245-9(6),* Kar-Ben Publishing) Lerner Publishing Group.
Dairman, Tara. All Four Stars. 2014. (All Four Stars Ser.: Bk. 1). (ENG.). 288p. (J). (gr. 3-7). 16.99 *(978-0-399-16252-7(6),* G.P. Putnam's Sons Books for Young Readers) Penguin Young Readers Group.
Dalton, Michelle. Fifteenth Summer. 2013. (ENG.). 272p. (YA). (gr. 7). 17.99 *(978-1-4424-7267-9(7));* (Illus.). pap. 10.99 *(978-1-4424-7266-2(9))* Simon Pulse. (Simon Pulse).
—Pulled Under. 2014. (Sixteenth Summer Ser.). (ENG., Illus.). 288p. (YA). (gr. 7). pap. 9.99 *(978-1-4814-0700-7(7),* Simon Pulse) Simon Pulse.
Daly, Niki & Quarto Generic Staff. No More Kisses for Bernard! 2012. (ENG., Illus.). 32p. (J). (gr. -1-1). 17.99 *(978-1-84780-105-0(6),* Frances Lincoln) Quarto Publishing Group UK GBR. Dist: Hachette Bk. Group.
Dana, Katherine. Family Picture Day. 2013. 40p. pap. 14.99 *(978-1-4575-2349-6(3))* Dog Ear Publishing, LLC.
Danczyk, Kenneth. Grandpas Farm. 2008. 35p. pap. 16.00 *(978-1-4357-4021-1(1))* Lulu Pr., Inc.
Daniels, Darla. Carrie Goes Camping. 2011. 24p. pap. 16.95 *(978-1-4626-0642-9(3))* America Star Bks.
Danneberg, Julie. Family Reminders. Shelley, John, illus. 2009. (ENG.). 112p. (J). (gr. 3-7). 14.95 *(978-1-58089-320-6(1))* Charlesbridge Publishing, Inc.
Danowski, Edwin K. The Green Turkey & Other Holiday Classics: (for Kids of All Ages & All Seasons Plus Reflections from the Heart -for Those a Little Older) 2007. 284p. per. 27.95 *(978-1-4241-8271-8(9))* America Star Bks.
Danticat, Edwidge. Untwine: A Novel. 2015. (ENG.). 320p. (J). (gr. 7). 16.99 *(978-0-545-42303-8(1),* Scholastic Pr.) Scholastic, Inc.
Danziger, Paula. Amber Brown Is Green with Envy. 2014. (Amber Brown Ser.: 9). (ENG., Illus.). 176p. (J). (gr. 2-5). pap. 5.99 *(978-0-14-242699-9(7),* Puffin Books) Penguin Young Readers Group.
—Amber Brown Is Green with Envy. Ross, Tony, illus. 2004. (Amber Brown Ser.: No. 9). 151p. (J). (gr. 2-5). 12.65 *(978-0-7569-2978-7(4))* Perfection Learning Corp.
—Can You Sue Your Parents for Malpractice? (gr. 5-6). 144p. (J). pap. 3.99 *(978-0-8072-1375-9(6));* 152p. (YA). pap. 3.99 *(978-0-8072-1540-1(6))* Random Hse. Audio Publishing Group. (Listening Library).
—Forever Amber Brown. 2008. (Amber Brown Ser.: 5). (ENG.). 128p. (J). (gr. 2-5). 5.99 *(978-0-14-241201-5(5),* Puffin Books) Penguin Young Readers Group.
—Orange You Glad It's Halloween, Amber Brown? Ross, Tony, illus. 2007. (Amber Brown Ser.). 48p. (J). (gr. k-3). 11.65 *(978-0-7569-8154-9(9))* Perfection Learning Corp.
—The Pistachio Prescription. 2006. (ENG.). 208p. (J). (gr. 5-18). 8.99 *(978-0-14-240682-3(1),* Puffin Books) Penguin Young Readers Group.
Danziger, Paula & Martin, Ann M. Snail Mail No More. unabr. ed. 2004. (Tara Starr & Elizabeth Ser.). 307p. (J). (gr. 3-7). pap. 36.00 incl. audio *(978-0-8072-8413-1(0),* Listening Library) Random Hse. Audio Publishing Group.
Danziger, Paula & Mazer, Anne. Is Green with Envy. Ross, Tony, illus. 2004. (Amber Brown Ser.: 9). (ENG.). 160p. (J). (gr. 2-5). pap. 4.99 *(978-0-439-07171-0(2),* Scholastic Paperbacks) Scholastic, Inc.
Danziger, Paula, et al. Amber Brown Horses Around. Lewis, Anthony, illus. 2014. (Amber Brown Ser.: 12). (ENG.). 208p. (J). (gr. 2-5). 14.99 *(978-0-399-16170-4(8),* G.P. Putnam's Sons Books for Young Readers) Penguin Young Readers Group.
—Amber Brown Is on the Move. Lewis, Anthony, illus. 2014. (Amber Brown Ser.: 11). (ENG.). 192p. (J). (gr. 2-5). pap. 6.99 *(978-0-14-751223-9(9),* Puffin Books) Penguin Young Readers Group.
Dashner, James. The Journal of Curious Letters. Beus, Bryan, illus. 2008. (13th Reality Ser.: Bk. 1). 434p. (J). (gr. 4-7). 17.95 *(978-1-59038-831-0(3),* Shadow Mountain) Shadow Mountain Publishing.
—The Journal of Curious Letters. Beus, Bryan, illus. 2009. (13th Reality Ser.: 1). (ENG.). 528p. (J). (gr. 3-7). pap. 8.99 *(978-1-4169-9152-6(2),* Aladdin) Simon & Schuster Children's Publishing.
Daswani, Kavita. Lovetorn. 2012. (ENG.). 256p. (YA). (gr. 8). 17.99 *(978-0-06-167311-5(0),* HarperTeen) HarperCollins Pubs.
Daval, Josie. The Wright Twist. 2006. (Illus.). 151p. (J). (gr. 3-7). 14.95 *(978-1-933197-19-7(6))* Orange Frazer Pr.
Davidson, Lg. Supernova's Unique Family. 2012. 36p. pap. 20.99 *(978-1-4772-6322-8(5))* AuthorHouse.
Davies, Katie. The Great Cat Conspiracy. Shaw, Hannah, illus. 2012. (Great Critter Capers Ser.). (ENG.). 224p. (J). (gr. 3-7). 12.99 *(978-1-4424-4513-0(0),* Beach Lane Bks.) Beach Lane Bks.
—The Great Dog Disaster. Shaw, Hannah, illus. 2013. (Great Critter Capers Ser.). (ENG.). 208p. (J). (gr. 3-7). 12.99 *(978-1-4424-4517-8(3),* Beach Lane Bks.) Beach Lane Bks.
—The Great Hamster Massacre. Shaw, Hannah, illus. 2011. (Great Critter Capers Ser.). (ENG.). 208p. (J). (gr. 3-7). 12.99 *(978-1-4424-2062-5(6),* Beach Lane Bks.) Beach Lane Bks.
Davies, Stephen. Don't Spill the Milk! Corr, Christopher, illus. 2013. 32p. 16.95 *(978-1-4677-2028-1(3))* Anderson Pr.
Davis, Diane. Something Is Wrong at My House: A Book about Parents' Fighting. Neely, Keith R., illus. 2010.Tr. of Algo anda mal en mi Casa. (SPA & ENG.). 32p. (J). (gr. -1-3). pap. 9.95 *(978-1-884734-65-6(0))* Parenting Pr., Inc.
Davis, Katie. The Curse of Addy Mcmahon. 2008. (ENG., Illus.). 288p. (J). (gr. 5-9). 16.99 *(978-0-06-128711-4(3),* Greenwillow Bks.) HarperCollins Pubs.
—The Curse of Addy McMahon. 2008. (Illus.). 288p. (J). (gr. 5-9). lib. bdg. 17.89 *(978-0-06-128712-1(1),* Greenwillow Bks.) HarperCollins Pubs.
Day, Alexandra. Carl's Sleepy Afternoon. Day, Alexandra, illus. 2005. (Carl Ser.). (ENG., Illus.). 40p. (J). (gr. -1-1). 15.99 *(978-0-374-31088-2(2),* 9780374310882, Farrar, Straus & Giroux (BYR)) Farrar, Straus & Giroux.
Day, Karen. A Million Miles from Boston. 2012. (ENG.). 224p. (J). (gr. 3-7). pap. 6.99 *(978-0-375-85974-8(8),* Yearling) Random Hse. Children's Bks.
Day, Susie. Serafina67 - "Urgently Requires Life" 2010. (ENG.). 256p. (J). (gr. 7-12). 8.99 *(978-0-545-07352-3(9),* Scholastic Paperbacks) Scholastic, Inc.
De Goldi, Kate. The 10 PM Question. (ENG., Illus.). 256p. (YA). (gr. 7). 2012. pap. 6.99 *(978-0-7636-5848-9(0))* 2010. 15.99 *(978-0-7636-4939-5(2))* Candlewick Pr.
de Gramont, Nina. Meet Me at the River. (ENG., Illus.). 384p. (YA). (gr. 9). 2014. pap. 11.99 *(978-1-4169-8016-2(4),* Atheneum Bks. for Young Readers) 2013. 17.99 *(978-1-4169-8014-8(8))* Simon & Schuster Children's Publishing.
De Kockere, Geert & Dom, An. Dragon Fire. Van Hemeldonck, Tineke, illus. 2015. (ENG.). 32p. (J). (gr. -1-k). 16.99 *(978-1-63220-599-5(8),* Sky Pony Pr.) Skyhorse Publishing Co., Inc.
De Laurentiis, Giada. Hong Kong! #3. Gambatesa, Francesca, illus. 2014. (Recipe for Adventure Ser.: 3). (ENG.). 144p. (J). (gr. 2-5). 6.99 *(978-0-448-46258-5(3));* 16.99 *(978-0-448-48040-4(9))* Penguin Young Readers Group. (Grosset & Dunlap).
de Vigan, Delphine. No & Me. Miller, George, tr. from FRE. 2010. (ENG.). 256p. (YA). (gr. 7-12). 16.99 *(978-1-59990-479-5(9),* 9781599904795, Bloomsbury USA Childrens) Bloomsbury Publishing USA.
Deák, Erzsi. Pumpkin Time! Cushman, Doug, illus. 2014. (ENG.). 32p. (J). (-3). 14.99 *(978-1-4022-9526-3(X),* 9781402295263, Sourcebooks Jabberwocky) Sourcebooks, Inc.
Dean, Carolee. Comfort. 2004. (ENG.). 256p. (YA). (gr. 7-18). pap. 14.95 *(978-0-618-43912-6(9))* Houghton Mifflin Harcourt Publishing Co.
—Take Me There. 2010. (ENG.). 336p. (YA). (gr. 9-18). pap. 8.99 *(978-1-4169-8950-9(1),* Simon Pulse) Simon Pulse.
DeAnda, Diane. The Monster in the Mattress & Other Stories: El Monstruo en el Colchón y Otros Cuentos. 2011. (SPA & ENG., Illus.). 90p. (J). (gr. 3-7). pap. 9.95 *(978-1-55885-693-6(5),* Piñata Books) Arte Publico Pr.
DeCamp, Alison. My Near-Death Adventures: I Almost Died. Again. 2016. (ENG., Illus.). 288p. (J). (gr. 3-7). 16.99 *(978-0-385-39048-4(3),* Crown Books For Young Readers) Random Hse. Children's Bks.
Dee, Barbara. Just Another Day in My Insanely Real Life. 2007. (Mix Ser.). (ENG.). 256p. (J). (gr. 4-8). pap. 7.99 *(978-1-4169-4739-4(6),* Aladdin) Simon & Schuster Children's Publishing.

—Solving Zoe. 2010. (Mix Ser.). (ENG.). 256p. (J). (gr. 4-8). pap. 7.99 *(978-1-4169-9159-5(X)*, Aladdin) Simon & Schuster Children's Publishing.

—Star-Crossed. 2017. (ENG., Illus.). 288p. (J). (gr. 4-8). 16.99 *(978-1-4814-7848-9(6)*, Simon & Schuster/Paula Wiseman Bks.) Simon & Schuster/Paula Wiseman Bks.

DeFelice, Cynthia. Fort. 2015. (ENG.). 208p. (J). (gr. 3-7). 16.99 *(978-0-374-32427-8(1)*, 9780374324278, Farrar, Straus & Giroux (BYR)) Farrar, Straus & Giroux.

—Fort. 2016. (ENG.). 224p. (J). pap. 6.99 *(978-1-250-07973-2(X)*, 9781250079732) Square Fish.

—The Ghost of Cutler Creek. 2011. (Ghost Mysteries Ser.: 3). (ENG.). 208p. (J). (gr. 3-7). pap. 9.99 *(978-0-312-62967-0(2)*, 9780312629670) Square Fish.

—Wild Life. 2011. (ENG.). 192p. (J). (gr. 3-7). 17.99 *(978-0-374-38001-4(5)*, 9780374380014, Farrar, Straus & Giroux (BYR)) Farrar, Straus & Giroux.

—Wild Life. 2013. (ENG.). 208p. (J). (gr. 3-7). pap. 7.99 *(978-1-250-03407-6(8)*, 9781250034076) Square Fish.

DeFelice, Cynthia C. The Ghost of Cutler Creek. 2006. (Ghost Mysteries Ser.). 181p. (J). (gr. 3-7). 13.60 *(978-0-7569-8185-3(9))* Perfection Learning Corp.

—The Missing Manatee. 2008. (ENG.). 192p. (J). (gr. 3-7). pap. 8.99 *(978-0-374-40020-0(2)*, 9780374400200) Square Fish.

Degnan, Robert W. Fife's Lessons: The Tao of Cool. 2013. 38p. 24.99 *(978-1-4575-2081-5(8))* Dog Ear Publishing, LLC.

Delacre, Lulu. Alicia Afterimage. 2008. (ENG.). 144p. (YA). (gr. 7-18). 19.95 *(978-1-60060-242-9(8))* Lee & Low Bks., Inc.

Dellasega, Cheryl. Nugrl90, 0 vols. LaPierre, Karina, illus. 2007. (Bloggrls Ser.: 1). (ENG.). 192p. (YA). (gr. 7-11). pap. 9.99 *(978-0-7614-5396-3(2)*, 9780761453963, Amazon Children's Publishing) Amazon Publishing.

DelleCava, Karen. A Closer Look. 2011. 304p. (YA). (gr. 9-18). 16.95 *(978-1-934813-49-2(4))* Westside Bks.

Dellicurti, Dana. Christopher's Little Blue Backpack. 2007. 32p. per. 12.95 *(978-1-59800-806-7(4))* Outskirts Pr., Inc.

delMazo, Deborah. No Cookies for Christmas: The Story of Grandma's Missing Package. Horsfall, Jacqueline, ed. Balvanz, Gwynessa, illus. 2010. 32p. (J). pap. 9.95 *(978-0-615-32691-7(9))* Zoombird Bks.

Demas, Corinne. Everything I Was. (Carolrhoda YA Ser.). (ENG.). 216p. (YA). (gr. 6-10). 2012. pap. 9.95 *(978-0-7613-9011-4(1))* 2011. 17.95 *(978-0-7613-7303-2(9))* Lerner Publishing Group. (Carolrhoda Lab™).

Demetrios, Heather. Something Real. 2014. (ENG.). 416p. (YA). (gr. 7). 17.99 *(978-0-8050-9794-8(5)*, Holt, Henry & Co. Bks. For Young Readers) Holt, Henry & Co.

Dennett, Kathleen. The 4 Corners Mystery. 2008. 32p. pap. 24.95 *(978-1-4137-2603-9(8))* America Star Bks.

Dent, Grace & Dent, Grace. Diva Without a Cause. 2009. (ENG.). 240p. (YA). (gr. 10-17). pap. 18.99 *(978-0-316-03482-1(7)*, Poppy) Little, Brown Bks. for Young Readers.

Denton, Shannon Eric & Warner, Gertrude Chandler. The Boxcar Children, 1 vol. Dubisch, Michael, illus. 2009. (Boxcar Children Graphic Novels Ser.). (ENG.). 32p. (J). (gr. 2-5). lib. bdg. 28.50 *(978-1-60270-586-9(0))* ABDO Publishing Co.

dePaola, Tomie. Now One Foot, Now the Other. dePaola, Tomie, illus. 2006. (ENG., Illus.). 48p. (J). (gr. k-3). pap. 7.99 *(978-0-14-240104-0(8)*, Puffin Books) Penguin Young Readers Group.

—Things Will Never Be the Same. 2004. (26 Fairmount Avenue Book Ser.: 5). (ENG., Illus.). 80p. (J). (gr. 2-5). reprint ed. 6.99 *(978-0-14-240155-2(2)*, Puffin Books) Penguin Young Readers Group.

Derby, Sally. Kyle's Island. (ENG.). 192p. (J). (gr. 5). 2014. pap. 7.95 *(978-1-58089-317-6(1))* 2010. 16.95 *(978-1-58089-316-9(3))* Charlesbridge Publishing, Inc.

—No Mush Today, 1 vol. Tadgell, Nicole, illus. 2008. (ENG.). 32p. (J). (gr. -1-3). 17.95 *(978-1-60060-238-2(X))* Lee & Low Bks., Inc.

Deriso, Christine Hurley. The Right-Under Club: Second Stage. 2010. (J). *(978-0-385-73621-3(5))*; lib. bdg. *(978-0-385-90593-0(9))* Random House Publishing Group. (Delacorte Pr).

—Thirty Sunsets. 2014. (ENG.). 240p. (YA). pap. 9.99 *(978-0-7387-3991-5(X)*, Flux) North Star Editions.

Derkez, Linda. Chip's Sharing Day. Doehring, Phoebe, illus. 2012. 16p. pap. 9.95 *(978-1-61633-245-7(X))* Guardian Angel Publishing, Inc.

DeRosa Bodie, Leona. One Is Fun. Davis, Catherine Baptista, illus. 2007. 30p. (J). (gr. -1). bds. 12.95 *(978-1-4243-2961-8(2))* Independent Publisher Services.

Desnick, Chaim. The Little Room. Zwebner, Janet, illus. 2005. 32p. (J). (gr. -1-1). 14.95 *(978-1-930143-81-4(8))*; pap. 9.95 *(978-1-930143-86-9(9))* Simcha Media Group. (Devora Publishing).

Despain, Bree. The Dark Divine. 2010. (ENG.). 384p. (gr. 7). pap. 9.99 *(978-1-60684-154-9(8)*, Carolrhoda Lab™) Lerner Publishing Group.

Desrosiers, Sylvie & Franson, Leanne. Je Suis Thomas. 2003. (Premier Roman Ser.). (FRE., Illus.). 64p. (J). (gr. 1-4). pap. *(978-2-89021-617-4(9))* Diffusion du livre Mirabel (DLM).

Dessen, Sarah. Just Listen. 2008. (ENG.). 400p. (YA). (gr. 7-18). 10.99 *(978-0-14-241097-4(7)*, Speak) Penguin Young Readers Group.

—Just Listen. 2007. 20.00 *(978-0-7569-8270-6(7))* Perfection Learning Corp.

—Just Listen. 2008. 22.10 *(978-1-4178-2016-0(0)*, Turtleback) Turtleback Bks.

—Saint Anything. (ENG.). (YA). (gr. 7). 2016. 448p. pap. 10.99 *(978-0-14-751603-9(X)*, Speak) 2015. 432p. 19.99 *(978-0-451-47470-4(8)*, Viking Books for Young Readers) Penguin Young Readers Group.

—Saint Anything. 2016. lib. bdg. 22.10 *(978-0-606-38833-7(8))* Turtleback Bks.

DeStefano, Lauren. A Curious Tale of the In-Between. 2015. (ENG.). 240p. (YA). (gr. 3-6). 16.99 *(978-1-61963-600-2(X)*, 9781619636002, Bloomsbury USA Childrens) Bloomsbury Publishing USA.

Destiny, A. & Helms, Rhonda. Sparks in Scotland. 2015. (Flirt Ser.). (ENG.). 224p. (YA). (gr. 7). pap. 9.99 *(978-1-4814-2121-8(2)*, Simon Pulse) Simon Pulse.

Detweiler, Katelyn & Wells, Rosemary. Immaculate. 2015. (ENG.). 464p. (YA). (gr. 9). bds. 17.99 *(978-0-451-46962-5(3)*, Viking Books for Young Readers) Penguin Young Readers Group.

Deuker, Carl. Gym Candy. 2008. (ENG.). 320p. (YA). (gr. 7). pap. 9.99 *(978-0-547-07631-7(2))* Houghton Mifflin Harcourt Publishing Co.

—Gym Candy. 2008. 313p. 19.00 *(978-1-60686-376-3(2))* Perfection Learning Corp.

DeVillers, Julia. Liberty Porter, First Daughter. Pooler, Paige, illus. (Liberty Porter, First Daughter Ser.: 1). (ENG.). (J). (gr. 3-7). 2010. 192p. pap. 6.99 *(978-1-4169-9127-4(1))* 2009. 176p. 15.99 *(978-1-4169-9126-7(3))* Simon & Schuster/Paula Wiseman Bks. (Simon & Schuster/Paula Wiseman Bks.).

DeWoskin, Rachel. Blind. 2014. (ENG.). 416p. (YA). (gr. 7). 17.99 *(978-0-670-78522-3(9)*, Viking Books for Young Readers) Penguin Young Readers Group.

Dewoskin, Rachel. Blind. 2016. (ENG.). 416p. (YA). (gr. 7). pap. 10.99 *(978-0-14-242455-1(2)*, Speak) Penguin Young Readers Group.

DiCamillo, Kate. Raymie Nightingale. 2016. (ENG.). 272p. (J). (gr. 5-7). 16.99 *(978-0-7636-8117-3(2))* Candlewick Pr.

—Raymie Nightingale. 2016. (J). lib. bdg. 29.40 *(978-0-606-37935-9(5))* Turtleback Bks.

Dickens, Monica. Summer at World's End. 2012. (ENG.). 168p. (YA). pap. 13.99 *(978-1-4482-0313-0(9)*, 9781448203130, Bloomsbury Reader) Bloomsbury Publishing Plc GBR. Dist: Macmillan.

Dickinson, Mary & Charlotte. Alex's Bed. Date not set. 32p. (J). pap. *(978-0-05-004389-9(7))* Addison-Wesley Longman, Inc.

Diersch, Sandra. No Contact, 1 vol. 2008. (Lorimer Sports Stories Ser.). (ENG.). 136p. (J). (gr. 4-8). 16.95 *(978-1-55277-025-2(7)*, 9781552770252); 8.95 *(978-1-55277-024-5(9)*, 9781552770245) Lorimer, James & Co., Ltd., Pubs. CAN. Dist: Casemate Pubs. & Bk. Distributors, LLC.

A Different Kind of Family. 2006. (J). *(978-0-9793568-0-3(6))* Merlin, Debbi.

Dill, Margo L. Finding My Place: One Girl's Strength at Vicksburg. 2012. (ENG.). 202p. (J). pap. 8.95 *(978-1-57249-408-4(5)*, White Mane Kids) White Mane Publishing Co., Inc.

Dion. Fishing with Balloons. 2004. (Illus.). 57p. (J). pap. 4.95 *(978-1-881929-34-5(5))* Oxton Hse., Pubs.

Dionne, Erin. Notes from an Accidental Band Geek. 2012. (ENG.). 304p. (J). (gr. 5). pap. 6.99 *(978-0-14-242247-2(9)*, Puffin Books) Penguin Young Readers Group.

Dipucchio, Kelly. Littles: And How They Grow. Ford, A. G., illus. 2017. (ENG.). 32p. (J). (gr. -1 — 1). 17.99 ***(978-0-399-55526-8(9))***; lib. bdg. 20.99 ***(978-0-399-55527-5(7))*** Random Hse. Children's Bks. (Doubleday Bks. for Young Readers).

Disney Book Group Staff & Hapka, Catherine. Me & Our Mom. Disney Storybook Art Team, illus. 2015. (ENG.). 24p. (J). (gr. -1-k). pap. 4.99 *(978-1-4847-0668-6(9))* Disney Pr.

Ditmars, Maribeth R. The Bald-Headed Princess: Cancer, Chemo, & Courage. 2010. 80p. (J). (gr. 3-8). 14.95 *(978-1-4338-0737-4(8))*; pap. 9.95 *(978-1-4338-0738-1(6))* American Psychological Assn. (Magination Pr.).

Dockter, Debra. Deadly Design. 2015. (ENG.). 368p. (YA). (gr. 7). 17.99 *(978-0-399-17105-5(3)*, G.P. Putnam's Sons Books for Young Readers) Penguin Young Readers Group.

Dokey, Cameron. Belle: A Retelling of Beauty & the Beast. 2008. (Once upon a Time Ser.). (ENG.). 224p. (YA). (gr. 7-18). mass mkt. 6.99 *(978-1-4169-6131-4(3)*, Simon Pulse) Simon Pulse.

Doktorski, Jennifer Salvato. The Summer after You & Me. 2015. (ENG.). 304p. (YA). (gr. 8-12). pap. 10.99 *(978-1-4926-1903-1(5))* Sourcebooks, Inc.

Doller, Trish. Something Like Normal. 2012. (ENG.). 224p. (YA). (gr. 9-12). 16.99 *(978-1-59990-844-1(1)*, 9781599908441, Bloomsbury USA Childrens) Bloomsbury Publishing USA.

—Where the Stars Still Shine. 2013. (ENG.). 352p. (YA). (gr. 9). 17.99 *(978-1-61963-144-1(X)*, 9781619631441, Bloomsbury USA Childrens); 256p. 17.99 *(978-1-61963-145-8(8))* Bloomsbury Publishing USA.

Donald, Margaret. Tipsy: The Hurricane Hero. 2007. (ENG.). 26p. (J). (gr. k-2). *(978-81-8386-050-5(8))* India Research Pr. IND. Dist: Independent Pubs. Group.

Donaldson, Joan. On Viney's Mountain. 2009. (ENG.). 192p. (YA). (gr. 5-18). 16.95 *(978-0-8234-2129-9(5))* Holiday Hse., Inc.

Donnelly, Jennifer. Revolution. 2011. (ENG.). 512p. (YA). (gr. 9). pap. 9.99 *(978-0-385-73764-7(5)*, Ember) Random Hse. Children's Bks.

Donnelly, Rebecca. How to Stage a Catastrophe. 2017. (ENG.). 256p. (gr. 4-7). 12.95 *(978-1-62370-807-8(9))* Capstone Young Readers of Coughlan Cos.

Donoghue, Emma. The Lotterys Plus One. Hadilaksono, Caroline, illus. 2017. (ENG.). 320p. (J). (gr. 3-7). 17.99 *(978-0-545-92581-5(9))* Scholastic, Inc.

Donwerth-Chikamatsu, Annie. Somewhere Among. Chaghatzbanian, Sonia, illus. 2016. (ENG.). 448p. (J). (gr. 4-7). 16.99 *(978-1-4814-3786-8(0)*, Atheneum/Caitlyn Dlouhy Books) Simon & Schuster Children's Publishing.

Dopirak, Kate. You're My Boo. Withrow, Lesley Breen, illus. 2016. (ENG.). 40p. (J). (gr. -1-3). 17.99 *(978-1-4424-4160-6(7)*, Beach Lane Bks.) Beach Lane Bks.

Dopson, Jennifer. Life Goes On. 2008. 202p. pap. 12.96 *(978-0-557-01741-6(6))* Lulu Pr., Inc.

Dorfman, Joaquin. The Long Wait for Tomorrow. 2009. (YA). *(978-0-375-84696-0(4))* Random Hse., Inc.

Dorman, Brandon. Hoolie & the Hooligans, Book 1: The Alien That Ate My Socks. Dorman, Brandon, illus. 2016. (Hoolie & the Hooligans Ser.: 1). (ENG., Illus.). 224p. (J). (gr. 2-7). 13.99 *(978-1-62972-222-1(7)*, Shadow Mountain) Shadow Mountain Publishing.

Dostis, Isaac & Haddad Ikonomopoulos, Marcia. Ten Gold Medals: Glory or Freedom. 2005. (Illus.). ii, 72p. (J). *(978-0-8197-0770-3(8))* Bloch Publishing Co.

Dotlich, Rebecca Kai. Mama Loves. Brown, Kathryn, illus. 2004. 32p. (J). (gr. -1-2). lib. bdg. 15.89 *(978-0-06-029408-3(6))* HarperCollins Pubs.

Doucet, Sharon Arms. Fiddle Fever. 2007. (ENG.). 176p. (J). (gr. 5-7). pap. 12.95 *(978-0-618-77682-5(6))* Houghton Mifflin Harcourt Publishing Co.

Dougherty, Meghan. Rise of the Undead Redhead. Birnbach, Alecia, illus. 2014. (Dorothy's Derby Chronicles Ser.: 1). (ENG.). 256p. (J). (gr. 3-6). pap. 6.99 *(978-1-4022-9535-5(9)*, Sourcebooks Jabberwocky) Sourcebooks, Inc.

Dowd, Siobhan. Bog Child. 2010. (ENG.). 336p. (YA). (gr. 7). pap. 9.99 *(978-0-375-84135-4(0))* Fickling, David Bks. GBR. Dist: Penguin Random Hse. LLC.

—A Swift Pure Cry. 2008. (ENG.). 320p. (YA). (gr. 7). pap. 8.99 *(978-0-440-42218-1(3))* Fickling, David Bks. GBR. Dist: Penguin Random Hse. LLC.

—A Swift Pure Cry. 2011. 10.54 *(978-0-7848-3500-5(4)*, Everbind) Marco Bk. Co.

Dowell, Frances O'Roark. Chicken Boy. Krause, George, photos by. 2007. (ENG., Illus.). 224p. (J). (gr. 5-9). pap. 6.99 *(978-1-4169-3482-0(0)*, Atheneum Bks. for Young Readers) Simon & Schuster Children's Publishing.

—Chicken Boy. 2005. (ENG., Illus.). 208p. (J). (gr. 5-9). 17.99 *(978-0-689-85816-1(7)*, Atheneum Bks. for Young Readers) Simon & Schuster Children's Publishing.

—Sam the Man & the Chicken Plan. Bates, Amy June, illus. 2017. (Sam the Man Ser.: 1). (ENG.). 144p. (J). (gr. 1-4). pap. 6.99 *(978-1-4814-4067-7(5))* Simon & Schuster Children's Publishing.

—Sam the Man & the Chicken Plan. 2016. (Sam the Man Ser.: 1). (ENG., Illus.). 128p. (J). (gr. 1-4). 15.99 *(978-1-4814-4066-0(7))* Simon & Schuster Children's Publishing.

—Trouble the Water. (ENG.). (J). (gr. 4-8). 2017. 304p. pap. 7.99 *(978-1-4814-2464-6(5))* 2016. (Illus.). 288p. 16.99 *(978-1-4814-2463-9(7))* Simon & Schuster Children's Publishing.

—Trouble the Water. 2017. lib. bdg. 18.40 ***(978-0-606-40126-5(1))*** Turtleback Bks.

Dower, Laura. For Emme, Baked with Love. Lazuli, Lilly, illus. 2016. (Dessert Diaries). (ENG.). 160p. (gr. 4-5). lib. bdg. 26.65 *(978-1-4965-3122-3(1))* Stone Arch Bks.

Downham, Jenny. Unbecoming. (ENG.). 384p. (J). (gr. 9-9). 2017. pap. 9.99 ***(978-1-338-16072-7(9))*** 2016. 17.99 *(978-0-545-90717-0(9))* Scholastic, Inc.

Downing, Erin. Kiss It. 2010. (ENG.). 288p. (YA). (gr. 9-18). pap. 9.99 *(978-1-4169-9700-9(8)*, Simon Pulse) Simon Pulse.

Doyle, Bill. The Prizewinners of Piedmont Place. Jack, Colin, illus. 2016. (Prizewinners of Piedmont Place Ser.: 1). (ENG.). 192p. (J). (gr. 3-7). 15.99 *(978-0-553-52177-1(2)*, Random Hse. Bks. for Young Readers) Random Hse. Children's Bks.

Doyle, Bill H. Extreme Home Takeover/C by Bill Doyle; Illustrated by Colin Jack. Jack, Colin, illus. 2017. (Prizewinners of Piedmont Place Ser.). (ENG.). 208p. (J). (gr. 3-7). 15.99 *(978-0-553-52181-8(0)*, Random Hse. Bks. for Young Readers) Random Hse. Children's Bks.

Doyle, Brian. Boy O'Boy, 1 vol. 2005. (ENG.). (YA). 176p. pap. *(978-0-88899-590-2(3)*, Libros Tigrillo); 162p. pap. 6.95 *(978-0-88899-654-1(3))* Groundwood Bks. CAN. Dist: Publishers Group West (PGW).

Doyle, Eugenie. Sleep Tight Farms: A Farm Prepares for Winter. Stadtlander, Becca, illus. 2016. (ENG.). 36p. (J). (gr. -1-k). 16.99 *(978-1-4521-2901-3(0))* Chronicle Bks. LLC.

Dragon, Laura. Hurricane Boy, 1 vol. 2014. (ENG., Illus.). 160p. (J). (gr. 3-7). pap. 8.95 *(978-1-4556-1916-0(7))* Pelican Publishing Co., Inc.

Draper, Penny. Ice Storm!, 1 vol. 2011. (Disaster Strikes! Ser.: 6). (ENG.). 192p. (J). (gr. 4-8). pap. 8.95 *(978-1-55050-451-4(7))* Coteau Bks. CAN. Dist: Orca Bk. Pubs. USA.

Draper, Sharon M. Fire from the Rock. 2014. (ENG.). 240p. (YA). (gr. 7-12). 12.24 *(978-1-63245-286-3(3))* Lectorum Pubns., Inc.

—Fire from the Rock. 2008. (ENG.). 240p. (YA). (gr. 7-18). 7.99 *(978-0-14-241199-5(X)*, Speak) Penguin Young Readers Group.

—The Silver Secret. 2010. (J). *(978-0-545-07157-4(7)*, Scholastic Pr.) Scholastic, Inc.

Dreyer, Ellen. The Glow Stone, 1 vol. 2006. (ENG.). 224p. (YA). (gr. 7-18). 15.95 *(978-1-56145-370-2(6))* Peachtree Pubs.

Dudley, David L. Caleb's Wars. 2011. (ENG.). 272p. (YA). (gr. 9). 17.99 *(978-0-547-23997-2(1))* Houghton Mifflin Harcourt Publishing Co.

Duff, Justin. Big Boy. 2012. 36p. pap. 21.99 *(978-1-4771-3592-1(8))* Xlibris Corp.

Dugger, Elizabeth L. & Kanell, Beth. The Darkness under the Water. 2008. (ENG., Illus.). 320p. (YA). (gr. 7). 16.99 *(978-0-7636-3719-4(X))* Candlewick Pr.

Dunbar, Polly. Arthur's Dream Boat. Dunbar, Polly, illus. 2012. (ENG., Illus.). 40p. (J). (gr. -1-k). 15.99 *(978-0-7636-5867-0(7))* Candlewick Pr.

Dungy, Tony. You Can Do It! Bates, Amy June, illus. 2008. (ENG.). 32p. (J). (gr. -1-2). 17.99 *(978-1-4169-5461-3(9)*, Little Simon Inspirations) Little Simon Inspirations.

Dungy, Tony & Dungy, Lauren. Here Comes the Parade! Newton, Vanessa Brantley, illus. 2014. (Tony & Lauren Dungy Ready-To-Reads Ser.). (ENG.). 32p. (J). (gr. k-2). pap. 3.99 *(978-1-4424-5469-9(5)*, Simon Spotlight) Simon Spotlight.

—The Missing Cupcake Mystery. Newton, Vanessa Brantley, illus. 2013. (Tony & Lauren Dungy Ready-To-Reads Ser.). (ENG.). 32p. (J). (gr. k-2). 16.99 *(978-1-4424-5464-4(4))*; pap. 3.99 *(978-1-4424-5463-7(6))* Simon Spotlight. (Simon Spotlight).

—The Missing Cupcake Mystery. 2013. (Simon & Schuster Ready-To-Read Level 2 Ser.). lib. bdg. 13.55 *(978-0-606-27055-7(8)*, Turtleback) Turtleback Bks.

—Ruby's New Home. Newton, Vanessa Brantley, illus. 2011. (Tony & Lauren Dungy Ready-To-Reads Ser.). (ENG.). 32p. (J). (gr. k-2). pap. 3.99 *(978-1-4169-9784-9(9))*; lib. bdg. 15.99 *(978-1-4424-2948-2(8))* Simon Spotlight. (Simon Spotlight).

Dunham, Wendy. Hope Girl. 2016. (ENG.). 144p. (J). (gr. 2-7). pap. 7.99 *(978-0-7369-6495-1(9))* Harvest Hse. Pubs.

Dunivan, Dennis W. Escape from Communist Heaven. 2013. (ENG., Illus.). 392p. 17.99 *(978-1-59181-229-6(1))* Sentient Pubns.

Dunkle, Clare B. The Walls Have Eyes. 2009. (ENG.). 240p. (YA). (gr. 7). 16.99 *(978-1-4169-5379-1(5)*, Atheneum Bks. for Young Readers) Simon & Schuster Children's Publishing.

Dunlap, Susanne. The Musician's Daughter. (ENG.). (YA). (gr. 7). 2010. 352p. pap. 8.99 *(978-1-59990-452-8(7)*, 9781599904528) 2009. 336p. 16.99 *(978-1-59990-332-3(6)*, 9781599903323) Bloomsbury Publishing USA. (Bloomsbury USA Childrens).

Dupuy, W. The Story of Poppy's Frankentoe, 1 vol. 2010. 24p. 24.95 *(978-1-4489-7585-3(9))* PublishAmerica, Inc.

Durand, Hallie. Dessert First. Davenier, Christine, illus. (ENG.). (J). (gr. 2-5). 2010. 176p. pap. 5.99 *(978-1-4169-6386-8(3))* 2009. 160p. 14.99 *(978-1-4169-6385-1(5))* Simon & Schuster Children's Publishing. (Atheneum Bks. for Young Readers).

—Just Desserts. Davenier, Christine, illus. (ENG.). (J). (gr. 2-5). 2011. 224p. pap. 5.99 *(978-1-4169-6388-2(X))* 2010. 208p. 15.99 *(978-1-4169-6387-5(1))* Simon & Schuster Children's Publishing. (Atheneum Bks. for Young Readers).

—No Room for Dessert. Davenier, Christine, illus. (ENG.). 192p. (J). (gr. 2-5). 2012. pap. 6.99 *(978-1-4424-0361-1(6))* 2011. 15.99 *(978-1-4424-0360-4(8))* Simon & Schuster Children's Publishing. (Atheneum Bks. for Young Readers).

Duvoisin, Roger. The House of Four Seasons. 2017. (ENG., Illus.). 40p. (J). (gr. -1-1). 16.95 *(978-1-68137-098-9(0)*, NYR Children's Collection) New York Review of Bks., Inc., The.

Dyan, Penelope. The Carousel. Dyan, Penelope, illus. 2010. (Illus.). 34p. pap. 11.95 *(978-1-935630-26-5(1))* Bellissima Publishing, LLC.

—I Did It, & I Hid It! a Book about Taking Responsibility. Dyan, Penelope, illus. 2009. (Illus.). 44p. pap. 11.95 *(978-1-935118-68-8(4))* Bellissima Publishing, LLC.

—My Mother Always Says. Dyan, Penelope, illus. 2010. (Illus.). 42p. pap. 11.95 *(978-1-935118-98-5(6))* Bellissima Publishing, LLC.

—My Two Cents Worth! 2011. 34p. pap. 11.95 *(978-1-935630-69-2(5))* Bellissima Publishing, LLC.

—Someone's Getting Married! 2011. 34p. pap. 11.95 *(978-1-935630-64-7(4))* Bellissima Publishing, LLC.

Dycus, Warren. Monyum Bay - Time Travel. 2010. 24p. 13.99 *(978-0-557-45202-6(3))* Lulu Pr., Inc.

Eagland, Jane. The World Within: A Novel of Emily Bronte. 2015. (ENG.). 336p. (J). (gr. 7). 18.99 *(978-0-545-49295-9(5))* Scholastic, Inc.

Earle, Phil. The Bubble Wrap Boy. (ENG.). 288p. (J). (gr. 5). 2016. 7.99 *(978-0-553-51318-9(4)*, Yearling) 2015. (Illus.). 19.99 *(978-0-553-51316-5(8)*, Delacorte Bks. for Young Readers) 2015. (Illus.). 16.99 *(978-0-553-51315-8(X)*, Delacorte Bks. for Young Readers) Random Hse. Children's Bks.

—The Bubble Wrap Boy. 2016. (ENG.). 288p. (J). (gr. 5). 18.40 *(978-0-606-39343-0(9))* Turtleback Bks.

Easer, Katherine. Vicious Little Darlings. 2012. (ENG.). 320p. (YA). (gr. 9-12). pap. 9.99 *(978-1-59990-854-0(9)*, 9781599908540, Bloomsbury USA Childrens) Bloomsbury Publishing USA.

Easton, Kelly. The Outlandish Adventures of Liberty Aimes. Swearingen, Greg, illus. 2011. (ENG.). 224p. (J). (gr. 3-7). pap. 6.99 *(978-0-375-83772-2(8)*, Yearling) Random Hse. Children's Bks.

—Walking on Air. 2010. (ENG.). 240p. (YA). (gr. 7). pap. 11.99 *(978-1-4424-1437-2(5)*, McElderry, Margaret K. Bks.) McElderry, Margaret K. Bks.

Easton, T. S. Boys Don't Knit. 2015. (ENG.). 272p. (YA). (gr. 8). 16.99 *(978-1-250-05331-2(5)*, 9781250053312) Feiwel & Friends.

—Boys Don't Knit. 2016. (ENG.). 272p. (YA). pap. 9.99 *(978-1-250-07354-9(5)*, 9781250073549) Square Fish.

Eberhard, Phyllis Lunde Brees. Little Miss Neat-As-A-Pin. Jacoby, Nickolina Dye, illus. 2007. (J). *(978-0-9722741-7-3(0))* Publishing Factory, The.

Eboch, Chris. The Ghost on the Stairs. 2009. (Haunted Ser.). (ENG.). 176p. (J). (gr. 3-7). pap. 5.99 *(978-1-4169-7548-9(9)*, Aladdin) Simon & Schuster Children's Publishing.

—The Riverboat Phantom. 2009. (Haunted Ser.). (ENG.). 192p. (J). (gr. 3-7). pap. 5.99 *(978-1-4169-7549-6(7)*, Aladdin) Simon & Schuster Children's Publishing.

Echols, Jennifer. Perfect Couple. 2015. (Superlatives Ser.). (ENG., Illus.). 336p. (YA). (gr. 9). pap. 10.99 *(978-1-4424-7448-2(3)*, Simon Pulse) Simon Pulse.

Ecton, Anne Massey. Passing Through Camelot. 2006. (J). *(978-0-88092-620-1(1))* Royal Fireworks Publishing Co.

Eddy, Olivia. The Hatchling. 2008. 112p. pap. 9.99 *(978-1-60693-546-0(1)*, Strategic Bk. Publishing) Strategic Book Publishing & Rights Agency (SBPRA).

Edwards, Jeannell. A New House for Jennie. 2011. 20p. pap. 16.95 *(978-1-4512-2485-6(0))* America Star Bks.

Edwards, Nancy. Mom for Mayor. Chesworth, Michael D., illus. 2006. (ENG.). 96p. (J). (gr. 1-5). 16.95 *(978-0-8126-2743-5(1))* Cricket Bks.

Edwards, Nicholas & White, Ellen Emerson. The Rescue. 2009. (Dog Whisperer Ser.: 1). (ENG.). 224p. (J). (gr. 3-7). pap. 9.99 *(978-0-312-36768-8(6)*, 9780312367688) Square Fish.

Edwards, Sal A. A Forever Family: Living in the Big House. 2012. 42p. (-18). pap. 17.45 *(978-1-4624-0329-5(8)*, Inspiring Voices) Author Solutions, Inc.

Efaw, Amy. After. 2010. (ENG.). 368p. (YA). (gr. 7-18). 8.99 *(978-0-14-241590-0(1)*, Speak) Penguin Young Readers Group.

Ehrlich, Amy. The Wild Swans. Jeffers, Susan, illus. 2008. (ENG.). 32p. (J). (gr. -1-3). 17.99 *(978-0-525-47914-7(7)*, Dutton Books for Young Readers) Penguin Young Readers Group.

Ehrlich, Esther. Nest. (ENG.). 336p. (J). (gr. 5). 2016. pap. 7.99 *(978-0-385-38610-4(9)*, Yearling) 2014. 16.99 *(978-0-385-38607-4(9)*, Lamb, Wendy Bks.) Random Hse. Children's Bks.

Eland, Lindsay. A Summer of Sundays. (ENG.). 336p. (J). (gr. 3-7). 2014. pap. 8.99 *(978-1-60684-541-7(1))* 2013. 16.99 *(978-1-60684-030-6(4))* Lerner Publishing Group. (Carolrhoda Bks.).

Eleanor Gates. The Poor Little Rich Girl. l.t. ed. 2007. 506p. pap. 21.99 *(978-1-4264-8948-8(X))* Creative Media Partners, LLC.

Elias, Megan J. Stir It Up: Home Economics in American Culture. 2010. (ENG., Illus.). 240p. (C). pap. 22.50 *(978-0-8122-2121-3(4))* Univ. of Pennsylvania Pr.

EFG

Elkeles, Simone. Better Than Perfect. 2014. (Wild Cards Ser.). (ENG.). 352p. (YA). (gr. 9). pap. 9.99 *(978-0-8027-3725-0(0),* 9780802737250, Bloomsbury USA Childrens) Bloomsbury Publishing USA.

—Leaving Paradise. 2007. 20.80 *(978-1-4177-8393-9(1),* Turtleback) Turtleback Bks.

Elliott, David. Nobody's Perfect. Zuppardi, Sam, illus. 2015. (ENG.). 32p. (J). (gr. -1-3). 16.99 *(978-0-7636-6699-6(8))* Candlewick Pr.

Elliott, L. M. Suspect Red. 2017. (ENG.). 304p. (J). (gr. 5-9). 16.99 ***(978-1-4231-5754-0(0))*** Hyperion Bks. for Children.

Elliott, Zetta & Strickland, Shadra. Bird, 1 vol. 2008. (ENG., Illus.). 48p. (J). (gr. 3-7). 19.95 *(978-1-60060-241-2(X))* Lee & Low Bks., Inc.

Elliott, Zetta & Terasaki, Stanley Todd. Bird. Shinjo, Shelly, illus. 2016. (ENG.). 32p. (J). (gr. 2-5). pap. 9.95 ***(978-1-62014-350-6(X))*** Lee & Low Bks., Inc.

Ellison, Elizabeth Stow. Flight. 2008. (ENG.). 192p. (YA). (gr. 3-7). 16.95 *(978-0-8234-2128-2(7))* Holiday Hse., Inc.

Ellison, Laura. Hard Rock, Hard Times: Coming of Age in Butte Montana, 1911-1917. 2005. 195p. (YA). per. *(978-0-9722217-7-1(8))* Horse Creek Pubns.

Elliston, Beth. A Baby Book as told by ME! the Big Sister. 2009. 32p. pap. 14.95 *(978-0-557-07646-8(3))* Lulu Pr., Inc.

Elston, Ashley. The Rules for Breaking. 2014. (Rules Ser.). (ENG.). 320p. (YA). (gr. 7-12). 16.99 *(978-1-4231-6898-0(4))* Hyperion Bks. for Children.

Elvgren, Jennifer. Josias, Hold the Book. Tadgell, Nicole, illus. 2011. (ENG.). 32p. (J). (gr. 2-4). pap. 10.95 *(978-1-59078-856-1(7))* Boyds Mills Pr.

Emerson, Kevin. Breakout. 2015. (ENG.). 304p. (YA). (gr. 7). 17.99 *(978-0-385-39112-2(9),* Crown Books For Young Readers) Random Hse. Children's Bks.

—The Fellowship for Alien Detection. 2013. (ENG.). 432p. (J). (gr. 3-7). 16.99 *(978-0-06-207185-9(8),* Waldon Pond Pr.) HarperCollins Pubs.

Emond, Stephen. Winter Town. 2012. (ENG., Illus.). 352p. (YA). (gr. 7-17). pap. 10.99 *(978-0-316-13331-9(0))* Little, Brown Bks. for Young Readers.

Enderle, Dotti. Hidden, 1 vol. Gentry, T. Kyle, illus. 2007. (ENG.). 104p. (J). (gr. 3-7). per. 8.95 *(978-1-58980-481-4(3))* Pelican Publishing Co., Inc.

—Tell No One!, 1 vol. McWilliam, Howard, illus. 2010. (Ghost Detectors Ser.: No. 1). (ENG.). 80p. (J). (gr. 2-5). 27.07 *(978-1-60270-692-7(1))* Magic Wagon.

Enderlin, Darlene C. Pathways of Hermie. 2008. 48p. pap. 16.95 *(978-1-60672-086-8(4))* America Star Bks.

Engelbreit, Mary. Baby Booky: Honey Bunny. Engelbreit, Mary, illus. 2004. (ENG., Illus.). 14p. (J). (gr. -1-18). 6.99 *(978-0-06-008135-5(X),* HarperFestival) HarperCollins Pubs.

Engelman, Stephanie. A Single Bead. 2016. 199p. (YA). pap. *(978-0-8198-9054-2(5))* Pauline Bks. & Media.

Engle, Margarita. All the Way to Havana. Curato, Mike, illus. 2017. (ENG.). 40p. (J). 17.99 *(978-1-62779-642-2(8),* 9781627796422, Holt, Henry & Co. Bks. For Young Readers) Holt, Henry & Co.

Engle, Margarita. Forest World. 2017. (ENG., Illus.). 208p. (J). (gr. 5). 16.99 ***(978-1-4814-9057-3(5),*** Atheneum Bks. for Young Readers) Simon & Schuster Children's Publishing.

English, Karen. It All Comes down to This. 2017. (ENG.). 368p. (J). (gr. 5-7). 16.99 *(978-0-544-83957-1(9),* Clarion Bks.) Houghton Mifflin Harcourt Trade & Reference Pubs.

English, Travis. Knights of Paris. 2004. (J). per. 11.95 *(978-0-9759903-1-5(4))* Blue Tiger Publishing.

Enright, Elizabeth. The Saturdays. Enright, Elizabeth, illus. 3rd ed. 2008. (Melendy Quartet Ser.: 1). (ENG., Illus.). 192p. (J). (gr. 3-7). per. 7.99 *(978-0-312-37598-0(0),* 9780312375980) Square Fish.

—Spiderweb for Two: A Melendy Maze. Enright, Elizabeth, illus. 3rd ed. 2008. (Melendy Quartet Ser.: 4). (ENG., Illus.). 224p. (J). (gr. 3-7). per. 8.99 *(978-0-312-37601-7(4),* 9780312376017) Square Fish.

Epstein, Estelle Pottern. I Heard My Father's Voice. 2007. 124p. pap. 11.95 *(978-0-7414-4053-2(9))* Infinity Publishing.

Erdman, Loula Grace. The Good Land. 2008. (Living History Library). 185p. (YA). (gr. 6). pap. 12.95 *(978-1-932350-13-5(6))* Bethlehem Bks.

Erdrich, Louise. Chickadee. Erdrich, Louise, illus. (Birchbark House Ser.: 4). (Illus.). (J). (gr. 3-7). 2013. (ENG.). 224p. pap. 6.99 *(978-0-06-057792-6(4))* 2012. (ENG., 208p. 16.99 *(978-0-06-057790-2(8))* 2012. 208p. lib. bdg. 17.89 *(978-0-06-057791-9(6))* HarperCollins Pubs.

—The Porcupine Year. Erdrich, Louise, illus. 2010. (Birchbark House Ser.: 3). (Illus.). 224p. (J). (gr. 3-7). pap. 6.99 *(978-0-06-441030-4(7))* HarperCollins Pubs.

Eriksson, Eva E. A Crash Course for Molly. Dyssegaard, Elisabeth Kallick, tr. from SWE. 2005. (Illus.). 32p. (J). 16.00 *(978-91-29-66156-9(0))* R & S Bks. SWE. Dist: Macmillan.

Erskine, Kathryn. Mockingbird. (ENG.). (J). (gr. 5-18). 2011. 256p. 7.99 *(978-0-14-241775-1(0),* Puffin Books) 2010. 240p. 16.99 *(978-0-399-25264-8(9),* Philomel Bks.) Penguin Young Readers Group.

—Mockingbird. (J). 2012. 1.25 *(978-1-4407-4671-0(0))* 2010. 72.75 *(978-1-4407-4667-3(2))* 2010. 74.75 *(978-1-4407-4665-9(6))* 2010. 210.75 *(978-1-4407-4662-8(1))* 2010. 64.75 *(978-1-4407-4661-1(3))* 2010. (SPA.). 62.75 *(978-1-4407-4663-5(X))* Recorded Bks., Inc.

—Mockingbird. 2011. lib. bdg. 18.40 *(978-0-606-15356-0(X),* Turtleback) Turtleback Bks.

—Quaking. 2010. (ENG.). 256p. (YA). (gr. 7-18). 7.99 *(978-0-14-241476-7(X),* Speak) Penguin Young Readers Group.

—Seeing Red. 2013. (YA). *(978-0-545-57645-1(8));* (ENG.). 352p. (J). (gr. 5-9). 16.99 *(978-0-545-46440-6(4))* Scholastic, Inc. (Scholastic Pr.).

Estevis, Anne. Down Garrapata Road. 2003. 128p. (J). pap. 12.95 *(978-1-55885-397-3(9))* Arte Publico Pr.

Evatt, Harriet. The Secret of the Old Coach Inn. Stone, David, illus. 2011. 190p. 42.95 *(978-1-258-08239-0(X))* Literary Licensing, LLC.

Eversole, Barbara. Adventures of Zorro. 2005. 42p. 14.49 *(978-1-4116-5523-2(0))* Lulu Pr., Inc.

Ewing, Juliana Horatia. Six To. 2007. 196p. per. *(978-1-4065-2535-9(9))* Dodo Pr.

—Six to Sixteen. 2007. (ENG.). 190p. pap. 19.99 *(978-1-4264-9664-6(8));* 206p. pap. 22.99 *(978-1-4264-9206-8(5))* Creative Media Partners, LLC.

Fajardo, Renee & Ruby, Carl. Chili Today, Hot Tamale & Other Tummy Tales. Fajardo, Renee & Ruby, Carl, eds. 2004. (Illus.). 110p. (YA). (gr. 4-8). pap. 14.00 *(978-0-9724472-2-5(9))* Just Enjoyable Memorable Story Bks.

Falconer, Ian. Olivia Forma una Banda. Mlawer, Teresa, tr. from ENG. Falconer, Ian, illus. 2007. (SPA., Illus.). 39p. (J). (gr. -1-3). 17.99 *(978-1-933032-23-8(5))* Lectorum Pubns., Inc.

Falwell, Cathryn. Feast for 10, 1 vol. Falwell, Cathryn, illus. (Read along Book & CD Ser.). (ENG., Illus.). (J). (gr. -1-3). 2008. 32p. audio compact disk 10.99 *(978-0-547-06431-4(4))* 2003. 28p. bds. 4.95 *(978-0-618-38226-2(7))* Houghton Mifflin Harcourt Publishing Co.

—The Nesting Quilt, 1 vol. 2015. (ENG., Illus.). 32p. (gr. -1-3). 16.95 *(978-0-88448-418-9(1),* 884418) Tilbury Hse. Pubs.

Fames, Catherine. Snowblind. 2004. 108p. (J). *(978-1-59166-329-4(6))* BJU Pr.

Farrant, Natasha. After Iris. 2013. (ENG.). 272p. (J). (gr. 5). 16.99 *(978-0-8037-3982-6(6),* Dial Bks) Penguin Young Readers Group.

Federle, Tim. Tommy Can't Stop! Fearing, Mark, illus. 2015. (ENG.). 32p. (J). (gr. -1-k). 16.99 *(978-1-4231-6917-8(4))* Disney Pr.

Feehan, Mary Edward. Mary's Rainbow. 2007. 116p. per. *(978-1-4065-1697-5(X))* Dodo Pr.

Fehlbaum, Beth. Big Fat Disaster. (ENG.). (YA). 2015. 286p. pap. 9.99 *(978-1-4405-9267-6(5))* 2014. 288p. 17.99 *(978-1-4405-7048-3(5))* Simon Pulse. (Simon Pulse).

—Hope in Patience. 2010. 312p. (YA). (gr. 8-18). 16.95 *(978-1-934813-41-6(9))* Westside Bks.

Fehler, Gene. Never Blame the Umpire, 1 vol. 2010. (ENG.). 192p. (J). (gr. 4-7). 12.99 *(978-0-310-71941-0(0))* Zonderkidz.

Feiffer, Jules. The House Across the Street. Feiffer, Jules, illus. 2003. (Illus.). 28p. (J). (gr. 1-4). reprint ed. 16.00 *(978-0-7567-6845-4(4))* DIANE Publishing Co.

—A Room with a Zoo. Feiffer, Jules, illus. 2007. (ENG., Illus.). 192p. (gr. 2-7). per. 7.99 *(978-0-7868-3703-8(9),* di Capua, Michael Bks.) Hyperion Bks. for Children.

Feiffer, Kate. But I Wanted a Baby Brother! Goode, Diane, illus. 2010. (ENG.). 32p. (J). (gr. -1-3). 16.99 *(978-1-4169-3941-2(5),* Simon & Schuster/Paula Wiseman Bks.) Simon & Schuster/Paula Wiseman Bks.

—The Problem with the Puddles. Tusa, Tricia, illus. 2011. (ENG.). 208p. (J). (gr. 3-7). pap. 7.99 *(978-1-4424-2101-1(0),* Simon & Schuster/Paula Wiseman Bks.) Simon & Schuster/Paula Wiseman Bks.

—The Wild, Wild Inside: A View from Mommy's Tummy! Huliska-Beith, Laura, illus. 2010. (ENG.). 32p. (J). (gr. -1-3). 15.99 *(978-1-4169-4099-9(5),* Simon & Schuster/Paula Wiseman Bks.) Simon & Schuster/Paula Wiseman Bks.

Felin, M. Sindy. Touching Snow. 2007. (ENG., Illus.). 240p. (YA). (gr. 7-12). 16.99 *(978-1-4169-1795-3(0),* Atheneum Bks. for Young Readers) Simon & Schuster Children's Publishing.

Fenner, Carol. Yolonda's Genius. unabr. ed. 2004. 211p. (J). (gr. 4-6). pap. 38.00 incl. audio *(978-0-8072-0462-7(5),* Listening Library) Random Hse. Audio Publishing Group.

Ferguson, Ann M. A Fine New Home for Young James Madison. 2012. 24p. pap. 15.99 *(978-1-4691-6978-1(9))* Xlibris Corp.

Ferrari, Michael. Born to Fly. 2011. (ENG.). 224p. (J). (gr. 3-7). 6.99 *(978-0-375-84607-6(7),* Yearling) Random Hse. Children's Bks.

Ferris, Jean. Of Sound Mind. 2004. 215p. (YA). (gr. 7). 14.60 *(978-0-7569-2970-1(9))* Perfection Learning Corp.

—Once upon a Marigold. 2004. 275p. (gr. 5). 17.00 *(978-0-7569-3613-6(6))* Perfection Learning Corp.

Feuerbach, Jennifer. Chef Philip Has Autism. Wroth, Dean, illus. 2014. 32p. (J). pap. 10.49 *(978-0-944727-61-4(1),* Turtle Bks.) Jason & Nordic Pubs.

Few, Cyndi. My Family Loves Me: For My Grandson, Talon. 2005. 27p. pap. 24.95 *(978-1-4137-3189-7(9))* PublishAmerica, Inc.

Fidler, Mark. Pond Puckster. 2nd ed. 2003. 148p. (J). (gr. 4-8). reprint ed. pap. 11.95 *(978-0-9721839-0-1(6))* BLR Bks.

Figley, Marthy Rhodes & Figley, Marty Rhodes. The Night the Chimneys Fell. Marschall, Felicia, illus. 2011. 48p. (J). pap. 6.95 *(978-0-7613-3939-7(6),* First Avenue Editions) Lerner Publishing Group.

Figley, Marty Rhodes. The Night the Chimneys Fell. Marschall, Felicia, illus. 2011. (On My Own History Ser.). 48p. (J). pap. 39.62 *(978-0-7613-7622-4(4),* First Avenue Editions) Lerner Publishing Group.

—The Night the Chimneys Fell. Marshall, Felicia, illus. 2009. (On My Own History Ser.). (ENG.). 48p. (gr. 2-4). 25.26 *(978-0-8225-7894-9(8))* Lerner Publishing Group.

Findlay, Chris. Ae Sma Voice. 2008. 152p. pap. *(978-1-84923-144-2(3))* YouWriteOn.

Fine, Anne. Friday Surprise. Flook, Helen, illus. 2nd ed. 2016. (Reading Ladder Ser.). (ENG.). 48p. (J). (gr. k-2). pap. 7.99 *(978-1-4052-8246-8(0))* Egmont Bks., Ltd. GBR. Dist: Independent Pubs. Group.

Finley, Martha. Elsie's Girlhood. 2006. 29.95 *(978-1-4218-2993-7(2))* 1st World Publishing, Inc.

—Elsie's New Relations. 2007. (ENG.). 200p. pap. 19.99 *(978-1-4346-2507-6(9));* 224p. pap. 22.99 *(978-1-4346-2549-6(4))* Creative Media Partners, LLC.

Finn, Felicity. Jeremy & the Aunties, 1 vol. 2005. (Jeremy Ser.). (ENG., Illus.). 199p. (J). (gr. 4-8). pap. 5.95 *(978-0-929005-40-9(6))* Second Story Pr. CAN. Dist: Orca Bk. Pubs. USA.

Finnegan, Evelyn M. My Little Friend Goes to a Baseball Game. Houghton, Diane R., illus. 2006. 32p. (J). (gr. -1-3). reprint ed. pap. 7.00 *(978-1-4223-5403-2(2))* DIANE Publishing Co.

Finney, Patricia. I, Jack. Bailey, Peter, illus. 2004. 192p. (J). 15.99 *(978-0-06-052207-0(0));* lib. bdg. 16.89 *(978-0-06-052208-7(9))* HarperCollins Pubs.

Finneyfrock, Karen. The Sweet Revenge of Celia Door. 2014. (ENG.). 288p. (YA). (gr. 7). pap. 9.99 *(978-0-14-750995-6(5),* Speak) Penguin Young Readers Group.

Finotti, M. C. The Treasure of Amelia Island. 2008. (Florida Historical Fiction for Youth Ser.). (ENG., Illus.). 97p. (J). (gr. 3-7). 14.95 *(978-1-56164-416-2(1))* Pineapple Pr., Inc.

Finotti, M. C. & National Geographic Learning Staff. The Treasure of Amelia Island. 2012. (ENG.). 108p. (C). pap. 14.95 *(978-1-56164-536-7(2))* National Geographic School Publishing, Inc.

Fiona Fox Staff, ed. The Railway Children. 2012. (ENG., Illus.). 64p. (J). 15.00 *(978-1-84135-840-6(1))* Award Pubns. Ltd. GBR. Dist: Parkwest Pubns., Inc.

Firestone, Carrie. The Loose Ends List. 2016. (ENG.). 352p. (YA). (gr. 9-17). 17.99 *(978-0-316-38282-3(5))* Little, Brown Bks. for Young Readers.

Fisher, Stacey & Paner, Amy, Illustrator. No Nuts for Nutty. 2008. 26p. 14.95 *(978-0-615-19778-4(7))* Fisher-Paner Publishing.

Fitch, Michele. When Lizzi & Kathryn Get Together. 2007. 18p. 10.00 *(978-0-615-14996-7(0))* Fitch, Michele Marko.

FitzGerald, Dawn. Soccer Chick Rules. 2007. (ENG.). 160p. (J). (gr. 5-9). per. 9.99 *(978-0-312-37662-8(6),* 9780312376628) Square Fish.

Fitzhugh, Louise. Nobody's Family Is Going to Change. 2016. (ENG.). 232p. (J). (-9). pap. 12.95 *(978-1-939601-49-0(5))* Ig Publishing, Inc.

Fitzpatrick, Huntley. My Life Next Door. 2012. (ENG.). 400p. (YA). (gr. 7-18). 18.99 *(978-0-8037-3699-3(1),* Dial Bks) Penguin Young Readers Group.

—What I Thought Was True. 2014. (ENG.). 416p. (YA). (gr. 9). 17.99 *(978-0-8037-3909-3(5),* Dial Bks) Penguin Young Readers Group.

Flaherty, Kathleen Marion. An Octopus Named Mom. Donehey, Jennifer Caulfield, illus. 2012. (ENG.). 32p. (J). 16.95 *(978-0-9767276-8-2(4))* Three Bean Pr.

Flake, Sharon G. Bang! 2007. (ENG., Illus.). 304p. (J). (gr. 5-9). pap. 9.99 *(978-0-7868-4955-0(X),* Jump at the Sun) Hyperion Bks. for Children.

—Bang! 2007. (J). 20.85 *(978-1-4177-7952-9(7),* Turtleback) Turtleback Bks.

—Money Hungry. Disney Press Staff, illus. rev. ed. 2007. (ENG.). 192p. (J). (gr. 5-9). pap. 8.99 *(978-1-4231-0386-8(6),* Jump at the Sun) Hyperion Bks. for Children.

Flam, Chanie. Good Night. (Goldie Gold Board Book Ser.: Vol. 6). (Illus.). (J). (gr. -1-1). bds. 4.95 *(978-1-58330-030-5(9))* Feldheim Pubs.

Fleischman, Paul. Glass Slipper, Gold Sandal: A Worldwide Cinderella. Paschkis, Julie, illus. 2007. (ENG.). 32p. (J). (gr. k-5). 17.99 *(978-0-8050-7953-1(X),* 9780805079531, Holt, Henry & Co. Bks. For Young Readers) Holt, Henry & Co.

Fleming, Candace. Papa's Mechanical Fish. Kulikov, Boris, illus. 2013. (ENG.). 40p. (J). (gr. k-3). 17.99 *(978-0-374-39908-5(5),* 9780374399085, Farrar, Straus & Giroux (BYR)) Farrar, Straus & Giroux.

Fleming, David. Saturday Boy. 2013. (ENG.). 272p. (J). (gr. 5). 16.99 *(978-0-670-78551-3(2),* Viking Books for Young Readers) Penguin Young Readers Group.

Fliess, Sue. The Hug Book. Kennedy, Anne, illus. 2014. (Little Golden Book Ser.). (ENG.). 24p. (J). (-k). 4.99 *(978-0-385-37907-6(2),* Golden Bks.) Random Hse. Children's Bks.

Flinn, Alex. A Kiss in Time. 2009. (ENG.). 384p. (YA). (gr. 8-18). 17.99 *(978-0-06-087419-3(8),* HarperTeen) HarperCollins Pubs.

Flood, Nancy Bo. The Hogan That Great-Grandfather Built. Yazzie, Peterson, illus. 2012. (ENG & NAV.). 32p. (J). (gr. -1-3). 17.95 *(978-1-893354-97-5(0))* Salina Bookshelf Inc.

Flood, Pansie Hart. Secret Holes. Marshall, Felicia, illus. 2004. 128p. (J). (gr. 3-6). 15.95 *(978-0-87614-923-2(9),* Carolrhoda Bks.) Lerner Publishing Group.

—Sometimey Friend. Marshall, Felicia, illus. 2005. 124p. (J). (gr. 3-7). 15.95 *(978-1-57505-866-5(9))* Lerner Publishing Group.

—Sylvia & Miz Lula Maye. Marshall, Felicia, illus. 2003. (Middle Grade Fiction Ser.). 120p. (J). (gr. 3-6). 15.95 *(978-0-87614-204-2(8),* Carolrhoda Bks.) Lerner Publishing Group.

Flor Ada, Alma & Zubizarreta, Gabriel M. Con Cariño, Amalia. (SPA., Illus.). (J). (gr. 3-7). 2013. 160p. pap. 6.99 *(978-1-4424-2406-7(0))* 2012. 144p. 15.99 *(978-1-4424-2405-0(2),* Atheneum Bks. for Young Readers) Simon & Schuster Children's Publishing.

—Dancing Home. (ENG., (J). (gr. 3-7). 2013. Illus.). 176p. pap. 7.99 *(978-1-4424-8175-6(7))* 2011. 160p. 15.99 *(978-1-4169-0088-7(8))* Simon & Schuster Children's Publishing. (Atheneum Bks. for Young Readers).

—Love, Amalia. (ENG., Illus.). (J). (gr. 3-7). 2013. 160p. pap. 6.99 *(978-1-4424-2403-6(6))* 2012. 144p. 15.99 *(978-1-4424-2402-9(8))* Simon & Schuster Children's Publishing. (Atheneum Bks. for Young Readers).

—Nacer Bailando (Dancing Home) 2011. (SPA.). 160p. (J). (gr. 3-7). lib. bdg. 16.99 *(978-1-4424-2061-8(8),* Atheneum Bks. for Young Readers) Simon & Schuster Children's Publishing.

Florence, Debbi Michiko. Jasmine Toguchi, Mochi Queen. 2017. (J). pap. ***(978-0-374-30411-9(4))*** Farrar, Straus & Giroux.

—Jasmine Toguchi, Super Sleuth. Vukovic, Elizabet, illus. 2017. (J). pap. ***(978-0-374-30414-0(9))*** Farrar, Straus & Giroux.

Flores-Scott, Patrick. Jumped In. 2013. (ENG.). 304p. (YA). (gr. 7). 16.99 *(978-0-8050-9514-2(4),* 9780805095142, Holt, Henry & Co. Bks. For Young Readers) Holt, Henry & Co.

—Jumped In. 2014. (ENG., Illus.). 304p. (YA). (gr. 7). pap. 10.99 *(978-1-250-05398-5(6),* 9781250053985) Square Fish.

Floyd, Lucy. A Place for Nicholas. McPhail, David, illus. 2005. (Green Light Readers Level 2 Ser.). (ENG.). 24p. (J). (gr. -1-3). pap. 3.95 *(978-0-15-205149-5(X))* Houghton Mifflin Harcourt Publishing Co.

—A Place for Nicholas. McPhail, David, illus. 2005. (Green Light Readers Level 2 Ser.). 18p. (gr. k-2). 13.95 *(978-0-7569-5243-3(3))* Perfection Learning Corp.

Fogelin, Adrian. My Brother's Hero, 1 vol. 2005. (ENG.). 224p. (J). (gr. 3-7). reprint ed. pap. 7.95 *(978-1-56145-352-8(8))* Peachtree Pubs.

—Sister Spider Knows All, 1 vol. 2007. (ENG.). 224p. (J). (gr. 3-7). pap. 6.95 *(978-1-56145-386-3(2))* Peachtree Pubs.

Forbes, Dillon. Careful Enough? 2008. (YA). 8.99 *(978-1-59166-835-0(2))* BJU Pr.

Forde, Catherine. Slippy. 2012. (Stoke Books Titles Ser.). 72p. (J). (gr. 5-8). pap. 45.32 *(978-0-7613-9223-1(8));* pap. 7.95 *(978-1-78112-032-3(3));* lib. bdg. 22.60 *(978-1-78112-031-6(5))* Stoke Bks.

Forman, Gayle. If I Stay. 2011. (If I Stay Ser.: BK.1). (YA). 10.36 *(978-0-7848-3573-9(X),* Everbind) Marco Bk. Co.

—If I Stay. movie tie-in ed. 2014. (If I Stay Ser.: BK.1). (ENG.). 304p. (YA). (gr. 9). pap. 10.99 *(978-0-14-751453-0(3))* Penguin Publishing Group.

—If I Stay. (If I Stay Ser.: BK.1). (ENG.). (YA). (gr. 9-18). 2010. 320p. 10.99 *(978-0-14-241543-6(X),* Speak) 2009. 208p. 17.99 *(978-0-525-42103-0(3),* Dutton Books for Young Readers) 2014. 304p. 17.99 *(978-0-451-47464-3(3),* Viking Books for Young Readers) Penguin Young Readers Group.

—If I Stay. 2010. (If I Stay Ser.: BK.1). (ENG.). 262p. (YA). (gr. 9-12). 18.45 *(978-1-60686-742-6(3))* Perfection Learning Corp.

—If I Stay. l.t. ed. 2014. (If I Stay Ser.: BK.1). (ENG.). (YA). 482p. 23.99 *(978-1-4104-7543-5(3));* 480p. pap. 12.99 *(978-1-59413-814-0(1),* Large Print Pr.) Thorndike Pr.

—If I Stay. 2010. (If I Stay Ser.: BK.1). (YA). lib. bdg. 22.10 *(978-0-606-14395-0(5),* Turtleback) Turtleback Bks.

Formento, Alison Ashley. Twigs. 2013. (ENG.). 272p. (YA). 17.99 *(978-1-4405-6565-6(1),* Simon Pulse) Simon Pulse.

Fox, Mem. Noam Mechapes Zichronot. Dash Greenspan, Shari, tr. from ENG. Vivas, Julie, illus. 2005. Orig. Title: Wilfrid Gordon McDonald Partridge. (HEB.). 32p. 14.00 *(978-965-7108-43-7(8))* Urim Pubns. ISR. Dist: Coronet Bks.

Fox, Paula. Maurice's Room. Fetz, Ingrid, illus. 2010. (ENG.). 64p. (J). (gr. 2-5). pap. 6.99 *(978-1-4424-1678-9(5),* Simon & Schuster/Paula Wiseman Bks.) Simon & Schuster/Paula Wiseman Bks.

Foxlee, Karen. The Anatomy of Wings. 2010. (ENG.). 384p. (Orig.). (YA). (gr. 9). pap. 9.99 *(978-0-375-84761-5(8),* Knopf Bks. for Young Readers) Random Hse. Children's Bks.

Frank, E. R. Life Is Funny. 2016. (ENG., Illus.). 288p. (YA). (gr. 9). 17.99 *(978-1-4814-3164-4(1),* Atheneum Bks. for Young Readers) Simon & Schuster Children's Publishing.

—Wrecked. 2007. (ENG.). 256p. (YA). (gr. 7-12). pap. 9.99 *(978-0-689-87384-3(0),* Atheneum Bks. for Young Readers) Simon & Schuster Children's Publishing.

Frank, Hillary. I Can't Tell You. 2004. (ENG.). 208p. (YA). (gr. 7). pap. 7.99 *(978-0-618-49491-0(X))* Houghton Mifflin Harcourt Publishing Co.

—I Can't Tell You. 2004. 208p. (YA). (gr. 7). 16.00 *(978-0-618-41202-0(6))* Houghton Mifflin Harcourt Trade & Reference Pubs.

Franklin, Kristine L. Dove Song. 2006. (ENG.). 192p. (J). (gr. 5-9). per. 5.99 *(978-0-7636-3219-9(8))* Candlewick Pr.

Fraustino, Lisa Rowe. The Hole in the Wall. (ENG.). (J). (gr. 2-8). 2011. 232p. pap. 8.00 *(978-1-57131-698-1(1))* 2010. 280p. 16.95 *(978-1-57131-696-7(5))* Milkweed Editions.

Frazier, Angie. The Mastermind Plot. 2012. (ENG.). 240p. (J). (gr. 3-7). 16.99 *(978-0-545-20864-2(5),* Scholastic Pr.) Scholastic, Inc.

—The Midnight Tunnel: A Suzanna Snow Mystery. 2011. (ENG.). 288p. (J). (gr. 3-7). 17.99 *(978-0-545-20862-8(9),* Scholastic Pr.) Scholastic, Inc.

Frazier, Sundee T. Brendan Buckley's Universe & Everything in It. 2008. (ENG.). 208p. (J). (gr. 3-7). 6.99 *(978-0-440-42206-8(X),* Yearling) Random Hse. Children's Bks.

Frederick, Heather Vogel. A Little Women Christmas. Ibatoulline, Bagram, illus. 2014. (ENG.). 32p. (J). (gr. -1-3). 17.99 *(978-1-4424-1359-7(X),* Simon & Schuster Bks. For Young Readers) Simon & Schuster Bks. For Young Readers.

Fredericks, Mariah. Life. Watkins, Liselotte, illus. 2009. (In the Cards Ser.: No. 3). (ENG.). 272p. (J). pap. 5.99 *(978-0-689-87659-2(9),* Simon & Schuster/Paula Wiseman Bks.) Simon & Schuster/Paula Wiseman Bks.

Freeman, Martha. The Secret Cookie Club. 2015. (Secret Cookie Club Ser.). (ENG., Illus.). 304p. (J). (gr. 3-7). 16.99 *(978-1-4814-1046-5(6),* Simon & Schuster Bks. For Young Readers) Simon & Schuster Bks. For Young Readers.

—Strudel's Forever Home. 2016. (ENG.). 192p. (J). 16.95 *(978-0-8234-3534-0(2))* Holiday Hse., Inc.

—The Trouble with Twins. Smith, Cat Bowman, illus. 2007. (ENG.). 112p. (J). (gr. 2-6). 16.95 *(978-0-8234-2025-4(6))* Holiday Hse., Inc.

—Who Stole Uncle Sam? 2008. (Chickadee Court Mystery Ser.). (ENG., Illus.). 128p. (J). (gr. 3-7). 16.95 *(978-0-8234-2091-9(4))* Holiday Hse., Inc.

Freeman, Ruth. One Good Thing about America. Honesta, Kathrin, illus. 2017. (ENG.). 160p. (J). (gr. 3-6). 16.95 *(978-0-8234-3695-8(0))* Holiday Hse., Inc.

Freitas, Donna. Gold Medal Summer. (ENG.). 240p. (J). 2014. (gr. 5-9). pap. 6.99 *(978-0-545-32789-3(X))* 2012. (gr. 4-7). 16.99 *(978-0-545-32788-6(1))* Scholastic, Inc. (Levine, Arthur A. Bks.).

French, Jackie. My Dog the Dinosaur. King, Stephen Michael, illus. 2006. (Wacky Families Ser.). (ENG.). 112p. *(978-0-207-19941-7(8))* HarperCollins Pubs. Australia.

Friedland, Joyce, ed. Cool Zone with Pain & the Great One: Novel-Ties Study Guide. 2011. 29p. pap. 16.95 *(978-0-7675-4471-9(4))* Learning Links Inc.

Friedman, Becky. Tiger Family Trip. 2017. (Daniel Tiger's Neighborhood 8X8 Ser.). lib. bdg. 13.55 ***(978-0-606-39755-1(8))*** Turtleback Bks.

Friedman, Laurie. Back to School, Mallory. Schmitz, Tamara, illus. (Mallory Ser.: 2). (ENG.). 176p. (J). (gr. 2-5). 2005. per. 5.95 *(978-1-57505-865-8(0))* 2004. 15.95 *(978-1-57505-658-6(5))* Lerner Publishing Group.

—Can You Say Catastrophe? 2014. (Mostly Miserable Life of April Sinclair Ser.: 1). (ENG.). 160p. (J). (gr. 5-9). pap. 5.95 *(978-1-4677-0941-5(7),* Darby Creek) 2013. 151p. pap. 17.95 *(978-1-4677-1620-8(0))* 2013. (Mostly Miserable Life of April Sinclair Ser.: 1). (ENG.). 160p. (J). (gr. 5-9). 17.95 *(978-1-4677-0925-5(5),* Darby Creek) Lerner Publishing Group.

—A Clases Otra Vez, Mallory. Anaya, Josefina, tr. from ENG. Schmitz, Tamara, illus. 2008. (Mallory en español (Mallory in Spanish) Ser.).Tr. of Back to School, Mallory. (SPA & ENG.). 176p. (J). (gr. 2-5). pap. 5.95 *(978-0-7613-3904-5(3))* Lerner Publishing Group.

—Happy New Year, Mallory! Kalis, Jennifer, illus. (Mallory Ser.: 12). (ENG.). 176p. (J). (gr. 2-5). 2010. pap. 5.95 (978-0-7613-3947-2(7)) 2009. 15.95 (978-0-8225-8883-2(8)) Lerner Publishing Group. (Carolrhoda Bks.).

—Life, Loss, & Lemonade. Shaloshvili, Natasha, illus. 2017. (Mostly Miserable Life of April Sinclair Ser.: 8). (ENG.). 168p. (gr. 5-9). (J). 17.95 (978-1-4677-8591-4(1)); 35.99 **(978-1-5124-2699-1(7))** Lerner Publishing Group. (Darby Creek).

—Mallory Makes a Difference. Kalis, Jennifer, illus. 2017. (Mallory Ser.: 28). (ENG.). 152p. (gr. 2-5). 15.95 **(978-1-4677-5032-5(8))** Lerner Publishing Group.

—Mallory McDonald, Super Snoop. Kalis, Jennifer, illus. (Mallory Ser.: 18). (ENG.). 152p. (J). (gr. 2-5). 2013. pap. 5.95 (978-1-4677-0929-3(8), Darby Creek) 2012. 15.95 (978-0-7613-6073-5(5)) Lerner Publishing Group.

—Mallory on Board. 2008. pap. 34.95 (978-0-8225-9440-6(4)) Lerner Publishing Group.

—Mallory on Board. Pollak, Barbara, illus. (Mallory Ser.: 7). (ENG.). 176p. (J). (gr. 2-5). 2008. per. 5.95 (978-0-8225-9023-1(9), First Avenue Editions) 2007. 15.95 (978-0-8225-6194-1(8), Carolrhoda Bks.) Lerner Publishing Group.

—Mallory Se Muda. Schmitz, Tamara, illus. 2007. (Mallory en español (Mallory in Spanish) Ser.). (SPA.). 160p. (J). (gr. 4-7). per. 5.95 (978-0-8225-7493-4(4), Ediciones Lerner) Lerner Publishing Group.

—Mallory vs. Max. Schmitz, Tamara, illus. (Mallory Ser.: 3). (ENG.). 160p. (J). (gr. 2-5). 2006. per. 5.95 (978-1-57505-863-4(4), First Avenue Editions) 2005. 15.95 (978-1-57505-795-8(6)) Lerner Publishing Group.

—Mallory's Guide to Boys, Brothers, Dads, & Dogs. Kalis, Jennifer, illus. (Mallory Ser.). 160p. (J). (gr. 2-5). 2012. pap. 33.92 (978-0-7613-9206-4(8), Darby Creek) 2012. (ENG.). pap. 5.95 (978-0-7613-5250-1(3), Darby Creek) 2011. (ENG.). 15.95 (978-0-8225-8886-3(2), Carolrhoda Bks.) Lerner Publishing Group.

—Not What I Expected. Shaloshvili, Natasha, illus. 2015. (Mostly Miserable Life of April Sinclair Ser.: 5). (ENG.). 176p. (J). (gr. 5-9). 17.99 (978-1-4677-8829-8(5), Darby Creek) Lerner Publishing Group.

—On the Road with Mallory. Kalis, Jennifer, illus. 2016. (Mallory Ser.: 25). (ENG.). 160p. (J). (gr. 2-5). 15.95 (978-1-4677-5029-5(8), Darby Creek) Lerner Publishing Group.

—Thanksgiving Rules. Murfin, Teresa, illus. 2009. (Carolrhoda Picture Bks.). (ENG.). 32p. (J). (gr. k-3). 16.95 (978-0-8225-7983-0(9)) Lerner Publishing Group.

—A Twist of Fate. Shaloshvili, Natasha, illus. (Mostly Miserable Life of April Sinclair Ser.: Vol. 7). (ENG.). 168p. (gr. 5-9). 2017. (J). pap. 5.95 **(978-1-5124-5866-4(X))** 2016. 17.95 (978-1-4677-8590-7(3)) 2016. 35.99 (978-1-5124-0899-7(9)) Lerner Publishing Group. (Darby Creek).

Friedman, Laurie B. Love or Something Like It. 2015. (J). 5.99 (978-1-4677-7790-2(0)); (Mostly Miserable Life of April Sinclair Ser.: 4). (ENG.). 184p. (gr. 5-9). 17.95 (978-1-4677-0928-6(X)) Lerner Publishing Group.

—Not What I Expected. Shaloshvili, Natasha, illus. 2015. (ENG.). 176p. (J). (gr. 5-9). 17.95 (978-1-4677-8588-4(1)) Lerner Publishing Group.

Friend, Alison. Freddy & Frito & the Clubhouse Rules. Friend, Alison, illus. 2015. (ENG., Illus.). 40p. (J). (gr. -1-3). 17.99 (978-0-06-228580-5(7)) HarperCollins Pubs.

Friend, Natasha. For Keeps. 2011. (ENG.). 272p. (YA). (gr. 7-18). 7.99 (978-0-14-241846-8(3), Speak) Penguin Young Readers Group.

Friesen, Jonathan. Jerk, California. 2008. (ENG.). 352p. (YA). (gr. 7-18). 9.99 (978-0-14-241203-9(1), Speak) Penguin Young Readers Group.

—Rush. 2010. (ENG.). 320p. (YA). (gr. 7-18). 9.99 (978-0-14-241258-9(9), Speak) Penguin Young Readers Group.

Frost, Helen. Applesauce Weather. Bates, Amy June, illus. 2016. (ENG.). 112p. (J). (gr. 3-7). 14.99 (978-0-7636-7576-9(8)) Candlewick Pr.

—Crossing Stones. 2009. (ENG., Illus.). 192p. (YA). (gr. 7-18). 18.99 (978-0-374-31653-2(8), 9780374316532, Farrar, Straus & Giroux (BYR)) Farrar, Straus & Giroux.

—Diamond Willow. 2011. (ENG.). 144p. (J). (gr. 5-9). pap. 7.99 (978-0-312-60383-0(5), 9780312603830) Square Fish.

—Keesha's House. 2011. 9.46 (978-0-7848-3534-0(9), Everbind) Marco Bk. Co.

Frueh, Pamela. Me & My Best Cousin Joy. 2007. 80p. pap. 8.95 (978-1-4303-2193-4(8)) Lulu Pr., Inc.

Funke, Cornelia. Igraine the Brave. Bell, Anthea, tr. Funke, Cornelia, illus. l.t. ed. 2008. (Thorndike Literacy Bridge Middle Reader Ser.). (Illus.). 259p. (J). (gr. 4-7). 23.95 (978-1-4104-0341-4(6)) Thorndike Pr.

Gail, Cornelia. Juvey. 2015. 153p. (YA). per. 14.95 (978-0-9674454-4-1(2)) Girls In Da Game Publishing.

Galang, M. Evelina. Angel de la Luna & the 5th Glorious Mystery. 2013. (ENG.). 304p. (J). (gr. 6). pap. 12.00 (978-1-56689-333-6(X)) Coffee Hse. Pr.

Galante, Cecilia. The Sweetness of Salt. 2012. (ENG.). 320p. (YA). (gr. 7). pap. 9.99 (978-1-59990-853-3(0), 9781599908533, Bloomsbury USA Childrens) Bloomsbury Publishing USA.

Gale, Emily. The Other Side of Summer. 2017. 336p. (J). (gr. 3-7). 16.99 (978-0-06-265674-2(0)) HarperCollins Pubs.

Gallagher, Diana G. Advice about Family: Claudia Cristina Cortez Uncomplicates Your Life. Garvey, Brann, illus. 2010. (Claudia Cristina Cortez Ser.). (ENG.). 80p. (gr. 2-3). pap. 6.10 (978-1-4342-2250-3(0), Claudia Cristina Cortez) Stone Arch Bks.

Gallenkamp, Kirk Charles. Pages in Tyme: The River's Journey. 2009. 336p. pap. 18.99 (978-1-61579-605-2(3)) Salem Author Services.

Galusha, Carol. Same Birthday. 2008. 128p. pap. 10.95 (978-1-60594-130-1(1), Llumina Pr.) Aeon Publishing Inc.

Gamble, Adam & Jasper, Mark. Good Night Families. Kelly, Cooper, illus. 2017. (Good Night Our World Ser.). (ENG.). 20p. (J). (— 1). bds. 9.95 **(978-1-60219-465-6(3))** Good Night Bks.

Ganeshram, Ramin. Stir It Up! 2011. (J). (978-0-545-16583-9(0)); (ENG.). 176p. (gr. 5-9). 16.99 (978-0-545-16582-2(2), Scholastic Pr.) Scholastic, Inc.

Gannon, Nicholas. The Doldrums. 368p. (J). (gr. 3-7). 2017. pap. 7.99 **(978-0-06-232095-7(5))** 2015. (ENG., Illus.). 17.99 (978-0-06-232094-0(7)) HarperCollins Pubs. (Greenwillow Bks.).

Gantos, Jack. What Would Joey Do? 2004. (Joey Pigza Ser.). 229p. (J). (gr. 5-9). 13.65 (978-0-7569-2597-0(5)) Perfection Learning Corp.

—What Would Joey Do? 2004. (Joey Pigza Ser.: Bk. 3). 240p. (J). (gr. 5-9). pap. 36.00 incl. audio (978-1-4000-9020-4(2), Listening Library) Random Hse. Audio Publishing Group.

Garcia, Nasario & Aragon, Dolores, illus. Grandpa Lolo's Matanza: A New Mexican Tradition = la Matanza de Abuelito Lolo: Una Tradición Nuevo Mexicana. 2015. (SPA & ENG.). 70p. (J). (978-1-936744-47-3(3), Rio Grande Bks.) LPD Pr.

Garcia, Norma Lee. A Day with Smiles. 2012. 28p. pap. 24.95 (978-1-4626-8823-4(3)) America Star Bks.

Gardner, Graham. Inventing Elliot. 2005. 181p. (YA). 13.65 (978-0-7569-5704-9(4)) Perfection Learning Corp.

Garis, Howard R. The Curlytops at Silver Lake. 2007. 260p. 29.95 (978-1-4344-9207-4(9)); per. 19.95 (978-1-4344-9113-8(7)) Wildside Pr., LLC.

Garis, Howard Roger. Lulu, Alice & Jammie Wibble Wobble. 2005. 152p. pap. 11.95 (978-1-4218-1564-0(8), 1st World Library - Literary Society) 1st World Publishing, Inc.

—Lulu, Alice & Jimmie Wibblewobble. 2005. 26.95 (978-1-4218-1464-3(1), 1st World Library - Literary Society) 1st World Publishing, Inc.

—Sammie & Susie Littletail. 2005. 26.95 (978-1-4218-1465-0(X)); 182p. pap. 11.95 (978-1-4218-1565-7(6)) 1st World Publishing, Inc. (1st World Library - Literary Society).

—Uncle Wiggily's Fortune. Date not set. 192p. (J). 20.95 (978-0-8488-2280-4(3)) Amereon Ltd.

Garris, Rebekah. Whither Thou Goest, I Will Go. 2005. pap. 24.95 (978-1-4137-8823-5(8)) PublishAmerica, Inc.

Garrott, Dawn E. How Riley Tamed the Invisible Monster. 2008. (J). pap. (978-0-87743-709-3(2)) Baha'i Publishing Trust, U.S.

Garza, Jenny. Beautiful. 2007. 56p. per. 8.95 (978-0-595-46756-3(3)) iUniverse, Inc.

Garza, Xavier, illus. Maximilian & the Mystery of the Guardian Angel. 2011. (Max's Lucha Libre Adventures Ser.). (SPA & ENG.). 160p. (J). (gr. 5-8). pap. 12.95 (978-1-933693-98-9(3)) Cinco Puntos Pr.

Gaskins, Terry & Treigle, Jimmy. The Very Big Storm: Created by Terry Gaskins Inspired by Jimmy Treigle. 2009. 28p. pap. 13.99 (978-1-4389-4220-9(6)) AuthorHouse.

Gavalda, Anna. 95 Libras de Esperanza. 2004.Tr. of 95 Pounds of Hope. (SPA.). (YA). 13.99 (978-1-930332-64-5(5)) Lectorum Pubns., Inc.

Gavin, Sherrie. Baptism & Boomerangs. 2015. (Illus.). (J). 14.99 (978-1-4621-1681-2(7)) Cedar Fort, Inc./CFI Distribution.

Gay, Marie-Louise. Summer in the City. 2013. 148p. pap. (978-1-4596-6493-7(0)) ReadHowYouWant.com, Ltd.

Gennifer, Choldenko. Al Capone Does My Shirts. 2014. (ENG.). 240p. (J). (gr. 6-12). 12.24 (978-1-63245-251-1(0)) Lectorum Pubns., Inc.

George, Jessica Day. Silver in the Blood. (ENG.). 368p. (YA). 2016. pap. 9.99 (978-1-68119-024-2(9), 9781681190242) 2015. (gr. 7). 17.99 (978-1-61963-431-2(7), 9781619634312) Bloomsbury Publishing USA. (Bloomsbury USA Childrens).

Gerber, Alyson. Braced. 2017. (ENG.). 304p. (J). (gr. 3-7). 16.99 (978-0-545-90214-4(2)) Scholastic, Inc.

Gerber, Carole. The Twelve Days of Christmas in Ohio. Ebbeler, Jeffrey, illus. 2014. (Twelve Days of Christmas in America Ser.). (ENG.). 40p. (J). (gr. k). 12.95 (978-1-4549-0890-6(4)) Sterling Publishing Co., Inc.

Gerber, Linda. Now & Zen. 2006. (S. A. S. S. Ser.). (ENG., Illus.). 224p. (YA). (gr. 7-18). 7.99 (978-0-14-240657-1(0), Speak) Penguin Young Readers Group.

Gerber, Mary Lichty. Mary's Family Stories. Whitehead, Victoria E. & Shirk, Linda, illus. 2015. 124p. (J). **(978-0-7399-2512-6(1))** Rod & Staff Pubs., Inc.

Gerdner, Linda & Langford, Sarah. Grandfather's Story Cloth. Loughridge, Stuart, illus. 2008. (Grandfather's Story Cloth Ser.). 32p. (J). (gr. 2-4). 16.95 (978-1-885008-34-3(1), Shen's Bks.) Lee & Low Bks., Inc.

Gerrard, K. A. My Family Is a Zoo. Dodd, Emma, illus. 2016. (ENG.). 32p. (J). 16.99 (978-1-61963-851-8(7), 9781619638518, Bloomsbury USA Childrens) Bloomsbury Publishing USA.

Gervay, Susanne. Super Jack. Wilcox, Cathy, illus. 2003. 192p. (978-0-207-19918-9(3)) HarperCollins Pubs. Australia.

—SuperJack. Wilcox, Cathy, illus. 2013. (ENG.). 192p. (J). pap. 5.99 (978-1-61067-129-3(5)) Kane Miller.

Gewirtz, Adina Rishe. Zebra Forest. 2013. (ENG.). 208p. (J). (gr. 4-7). 15.99 (978-0-7636-6041-3(8)) Candlewick Pr.

Gibbs, Stuart. Poached. 2014. (FunJungle Ser.). (ENG., Illus.). 352p. (J). (gr. 3-7). 17.99 (978-1-4424-6777-4(0), Simon & Schuster Bks. For Young Readers) Simon & Schuster Bks. For Young Readers.

Gibney, Shannon. See No Color. 2015. (ENG.). 192p. (YA). (gr. 7-12). 18.99 (978-1-4677-8814-4(7), Carolrhoda Lab™); 18.99 (978-1-4677-7682-0(3)) Lerner Publishing Group.

Gibson, Narie. Judah the Barracuda. 2013. 42p. pap. 16.95 (978-1-4908-1495-7(7), WestBow Pr.) Author Solutions, Inc.

Gier, Kerstin. Emerald Green. Bell, Anthea, tr. 2013. (Ruby Red Trilogy Ser.: Vol. 3). (ENG.). 464p. (YA). (gr. 7). 17.99 (978-0-8050-9267-7(6), 9780805092677, Holt, Henry & Co. Bks. For Young Readers) Holt, Henry & Co.

—Ruby Red. Bell, Anthea, tr. from GER. 2011. (Ruby Red Trilogy Ser.: 1). (ENG.). 336p. (YA). (gr. 7-12). 18.99 (978-0-8050-9252-3(8), 9780805092523, Holt, Henry & Co. Bks. For Young Readers) Holt, Henry & Co.

—Ruby Red. Bell, Anthea, tr. 2012. (Ruby Red Trilogy Ser.: 1). (ENG.). 352p. (YA). (gr. 7-12). pap. 10.99 (978-0-312-55151-3(7), 9780312551513) Square Fish.

—Sapphire Blue. Bell, Anthea, tr. from GER. 2012. (Ruby Red Trilogy Ser.: 2). (ENG.). 368p. (YA). (gr. 7). 18.99 (978-0-8050-9266-0(8), 9780805092660, Holt, Henry & Co. Bks. For Young Readers) Holt, Henry & Co.

—Sapphire Blue. Bell, Anthea, tr. 2013. (Ruby Red Trilogy Ser.: 2). (ENG.). 384p. (YA). (gr. 7). pap. 10.99 (978-1-250-03416-8(7), 9781250034168) Square Fish.

Giff, Patricia Reilly. Gingersnap. 2014. (ENG.). 160p. (J). (gr. 3-7). 6.99 (978-0-440-42178-8(0), Yearling) Random Hse. Children's Bks.

—Hunter Moran Hangs Out. (ENG.). 144p. (J). (gr. 3-7). 2014. pap. 6.99 (978-0-8234-3189-2(4)) 2013. (Illus.). 16.95 (978-0-8234-2859-5(1)) Holiday Hse., Inc.

—Hunter Moran Saves the Universe. (ENG.). 128p. (J). (gr. 2-7). 2013. pap. 6.99 (978-0-8234-2917-2(2)) 2012. 16.95 (978-0-8234-1949-4(5)) Holiday Hse., Inc.

—Wild Girl. 2011. (ENG.). 160p. (J). (gr. 3-7). pap. 6.99 (978-0-440-42177-1(2), Yearling) Random Hse. Children's Bks.

—Winter Sky. 2014. (ENG.). 160p. (J). (gr. 3-7). 15.99 (978-0-375-83892-7(9), Lamb, Wendy Bks.) Random Hse. Children's Bks.

Gifford, Griselda. Second Sight. 2003. (ENG., Illus.). 96p. (YA). pap. 9.99 (978-1-84270-217-8(3)) Andersen Pr. GBR. Dist: Independent Pubs. Group.

Gifford, Peggy. Moxy Maxwell Does Not Love Stuart Little. Fisher, Valorie, photos by. 2008. (Moxy Maxwell Ser.). (ENG., Illus.). 112p. (J). (gr. 2-5). 5.99 (978-0-440-42230-3(2), Yearling) Random Hse. Children's Bks.

—Moxy Maxwell Does Not Love Writing Thank-You Notes. Fisher, Valorie, illus. 2009. (Moxy Maxwell Ser.). (ENG.). 192p. (J). (gr. 2-5). 6.99 (978-0-375-84343-3(4), Yearling) Random Hse. Children's Bks.

Gilbert, Paul T. Bertram & His Funny Animals. Rousseff, Minnie H., illus. 2016. (ENG.). 140p. (J). 24.95 (978-0-7649-7372-7(X), POMEGRANATE KIDS) Pomegranate Communications, Inc.

Giles, Gail. What Happened to Cass McBride? 2007. (ENG.). 240p. (J). (gr. 10-17). per. 9.99 (978-0-316-16639-3(1)) Little, Brown Bks. for Young Readers.

—What Happened to Cass McBride? 2007. 211p. 18.00 (978-0-7569-8178-5(6)) Perfection Learning Corp.

—What Happened to Cass McBride? A Novel. 2006. (ENG.). 224p. pap. (978-0-00-639197-5(4), Harper Trophy) HarperCollins Pubs.

Gill, J. Duddy. The Secret of Ferrell Savage. Chaghatzbanian, Sonia, illus. (ENG.). 176p. (J). (gr. 3-7). 2015. pap. 7.99 (978-1-4424-6018-8(0)) 2014. 15.99 (978-1-4424-6017-1(2)) Simon & Schuster Children's Publishing. (Atheneum Bks. for Young Readers).

Gilleland, Rebecca. The Swiss Family Robinson Study Guide. 2003. stu. ed., ring bd. 14.99 (978-1-58609-194-1(8)) Progeny Pr.

Gillmor, Don. The Fabulous Song. Gay, Marie-Louise, illus. 2003. 32p. (J). pap. 7.95 (978-1-929132-48-5(4)) Kane Miller.

Gillmor, Don, et al. The Fabulous Song. Gay, Marie-Louise, illus. 2006. (ENG.). 44p. (J). (gr. -1-2). 16.95 (978-2-923163-17-8(6)) La Montagne Secrete CAN. Dist: Independent Pubs. Group.

Gilmore, Grace. The Big City. Brown, Petra, illus. 2015. (Tales from Maple Ridge Ser.: 3). (ENG.). 128p. (J). (gr. k-4). pap. 5.99 (978-1-4814-3006-7(6), Little Simon) Little Simon.

—Logan Pryce Makes a Mess. Brown, Petra, illus. 2015. (Tales from Maple Ridge Ser.: 1). (ENG.). 128p. (J). (gr. k-4). pap. 5.99 (978-1-4814-2624-4(9), Little Simon) Little Simon.

—The Lucky Wheel. Brown, Petra, illus. 2015. (Tales from Maple Ridge Ser.: 2). (ENG.). 128p. (J). (gr. k-4). pap. 5.99 (978-1-4814-2627-5(3), Little Simon) Little Simon.

Glaser, Karina. The Vanderbeekers of 141st Street. 2017. (Vanderbeekers Ser.: 1). (ENG., Illus.). 304p. (J). (gr. 2-5). 16.99 **(978-0-544-87639-2(3)**, HMH Books For Young Readers) Houghton Mifflin Harcourt Publishing Co.

Glassman, Miriam. Call Me Oklahoma! 2013. (ENG.). 128p. (J). (gr. 2-7). 16.95 (978-0-8234-2742-0(0)) Holiday Hse., Inc.

Glavin, Kevin. All the Things You'll Do! Grepo, Sarah, illus. 2012. 80p. 17.95 (978-0-9825466-3-5(7)) Glavin, Kevin.

Glines, Abbi. Because of Low. 2013. (Sea Breeze Ser.). (ENG., Illus.). 320p. (YA). (gr. 11). 17.99 (978-1-4424-8864-9(6)); pap. 10.99 (978-1-4424-8863-2(8)) Simon Pulse. (Simon Pulse).

Gloster, Dean. Dessert First. 2016. (ENG.). 304p. (YA). 17.99 (978-1-4405-9454-0(6), Simon Pulse) Simon Pulse.

Godolphin, Mary. The Swiss Family Robinson Told in Words. 2004. reprint ed. pap. 15.95 (978-1-4191-8466-6(0)) Kessinger Publishing, LLC.

—The Swiss Family Robinson Told in Words of One Syllable. 2004. reprint ed. pap. 1.99 (978-1-4192-8466-3(5)) Kessinger Publishing, LLC.

Gohman, Amy. I Have Just the Gift for You. 2005. (Illus.). 47p. per. 9.99 (978-1-932338-87-4(X)) Lifevest Publishing, Inc.

Going, K. L. The Garden of Eve. 2009. (ENG., Illus.). 240p. (J). (gr. 2-5). pap. 14.95 (978-0-15-206614-7(4)) Houghton Mifflin Harcourt Publishing Co.

Goldberg, Whoopi. Terrible Terrel. Roos, Maryn, illus. 2010. (ENG.). 160p. (J). (gr. 1-17). pap. 4.99 (978-0-7868-5263-5(1), Jump at the Sun) Hyperion Bks. for Children.

Golden Books Staff. Eloise Wilkin Stories. Wilkin, Eloise, illus. 2005. (Little Golden Book Treasury Ser.). (ENG.). 224p. (J). (gr. -1-2). 10.95 (978-0-375-82928-4(8), Golden Bks.) Random Hse. Children's Bks.

Goldin, Barbara Diamond. Mountain of Blintzes, 0 vols. McGrory, Anik, illus. 2010. (ENG.). 32p. (J). (gr. -1-2). pap. 6.99 (978-0-7614-5790-9(9), 9780761457909, Amazon Children's Publishing) Amazon Publishing.

Golding Moore, Michelle. Normal Is Me. 2009. 24p. pap. 15.95 (978-1-4327-4303-1(1)) Outskirts Pr., Inc.

Goniwicha, William. Spike a Relli: A Week at the Lake. 2009. 28p. pap. 13.99 (978-1-4389-2902-6(1)) AuthorHouse.

Gonzales Bertrand, Diane. Sofia & the Purple Dress / Sofia y el Vestido Morado. Baeza Ventura, Gabriela, tr. Fields, Lisa, illus. 2012. (SPA & ENG.). (J). 17.95 (978-1-55885-701-8(X), Piñata Books) Arte Publico Pr.

Gonzales, Rebecca. Beauty & the Basketcase. 2007. 103p. pap. 14.94 (978-1-4303-2379-2(5)) Lulu Pr., Inc.

Gonzalez, Christina Diaz. The Red Umbrella. 2011. (ENG.). 304p. (J). (gr. 3-7). 7.99 (978-0-375-85489-7(4), Yearling) Random Hse. Children's Bks.

Gonzalez, Gabriela & Triana, Gaby. Backstage Pass. 2004. (Illus.). 224p. (J). (gr. 7-18). 15.99 (978-0-06-056017-1(7)) HarperCollins Pubs.

Gonzalez, Genaro. A So-Called Vacation. 2009. 192p. (YA). (gr. 9-18). pap. 10.95 (978-1-55885-545-8(9), Piñata Books) Arte Publico Pr.

Gonzalez, Maya Christina & Perez, Amada Irma. My Very Own Room: Mi Propio Cuartito. 2013. (ENG & SPA., Illus.). 32p. (J). (gr. k-4). pap. 9.95 (978-0-89239-223-0(1)) Lee & Low Bks., Inc.

Goobie, Beth. The Lottery, 1 vol. 2004. (ENG.). 272p. (YA). (gr. 8-12). pap. 14.95 (978-1-55143-280-9(3)) Orca Bk. Pubs. USA.

Goodhart, Pippa. House that Jack Built. Parker, Andy, illus. 2004. (ENG.). 24p. (J). lib. bdg. 23.65 (978-1-59646-700-2(2)) Dingles & Co.

Goodman, Shawn. Kindness for Weakness. 2015. (ENG.). 272p. (YA). (gr. 9). pap. 9.99 (978-0-385-74325-9(4), Ember) Random Hse. Children's Bks.

Gordon, Amy. The Shadow Collector's Apprentice. 2012. (ENG.). 208p. (J). 16.95 (978-0-8234-2359-0(X)) Holiday Hse., Inc.

Goring, Ruth. Adriana's Angels. Meza, Erika, illus. 2017. (J). 16.99 **(978-1-5064-1832-2(5)**, Sparkhouse Family) Augsburg Fortress, Pubs.

Goring, Ruth & Meza, Erika. Los Angeles de Adriana (Spanish Edition) Meza, Erika, illus. 2017. (SPA., Illus.). (J). 16.99 **(978-1-5064-2507-8(0)**, Sparkhouse Family) Augsburg Fortress, Pubs.

Goscinny, René & Bell, Anthea. Nicholas. Sempé, Jean-Jacques, illus. 2011. (ENG.). 136p. (gr. 7-17). pap. 9.95 (978-0-7148-6115-9(4)) Phaidon Pr., Inc.

Gourley, Robbin. Bring Me Some Apples & I'll Make You a Pie: A Story about Edna Lewis. 2016. (ENG., Illus.). 48p. (J). (gr. -1-3). pap. 6.99 (978-0-544-80901-7(7), HMH Books For Young Readers) Houghton Mifflin Harcourt Publishing Co.

Gownley, Jim. Amelia in Loosely in Disguise & Frightened: #3, 1 vol. Gownley, Jim, illus. 2011. (Amelia Rules! Ser.). (ENG., Illus.). 36p. 24.21 (978-1-59961-789-3(7)) Spotlight.

Gownley, Jimmy. Amelia & Her Three Kisses, 1 vol. 2013. (Amelia Rules! Set 2 Ser.). (ENG.). 36p. (J). (gr. 3-6). 24.21 (978-1-61479-068-6(X)) Spotlight.

—Her Permanent Record. 2012. (Amelia Rules! Ser.: 8). lib. bdg. 23.30 (978-0-606-26885-1(5), Turtleback) Turtleback Bks.

—True Things: Adults Don't Want Kids to Know. Gownley, Jimmy, illus. 2010. (Amelia Rules! Ser.). (ENG., Illus.). 176p. (J). (gr. 2-7). 19.99 (978-1-4169-8611-9(1)); pap. 11.99 (978-1-4169-8609-6(X)) Simon & Schuster Children's Publishing. (Atheneum Bks. for Young Readers).

Grab, Daphne. Alive & Well in Prague, New York. 2008. (Laura Geringer Bks.). 247p. (YA). (gr. 7-18). lib. bdg. 17.89 (978-0-06-125671-4(4), Geringer, Laura Book) HarperCollins Pubs.

—Halftime. 2010. (J). (978-0-385-90693-7(5)); (978-0-385-73783-8(1)) Random House Publishing Group. (Delacorte Pr).

Grabenstein, Chris. The Crossroads. 2009. (Haunted Mystery Ser.: 1). (ENG.). 352p. (J). (gr. 3-7). 7.99 (978-0-375-84698-4(0), Yearling) Random Hse. Children's Bks.

Graff, Lisa. Absolutely Almost. 2014. (ENG.). 304p. (J). (gr. 3-7). 16.99 (978-0-399-16405-7(7), Philomel Bks.) Penguin Young Readers Group.

—A Tangle of Knots. 2013. (ENG.). 240p. (J). (gr. 3-7). 16.99 (978-0-399-25517-5(6), Philomel Bks.) Penguin Young Readers Group.

Graham, Rita Z. Big Brother Little Brother. Vadalia, Hemali, illus. 2013. 42p. pap. 9.95 (978-0-578-13165-8(X)) Graham, Rita.

Graham, Rosemary. Thou Shalt Not Dump the Skater Dude: And Other Commandments I Have Broken. 2008. (ENG.). 288p. (YA). (gr. 7-18). 8.99 (978-0-14-240851-3(4), Speak) Penguin Young Readers Group.

Grahame, Abby. Wentworth Hall. (ENG.). 288p. (YA). (gr. 7). 2013. pap. 9.99 (978-1-4424-5197-1(1)) 2012. 16.99 (978-1-4424-5196-4(3)) Simon & Schuster Bks. For Young Readers. (Simon & Schuster Bks. For Young Readers).

Grandma Moves In: Six-Pack. (Greetings Ser.: Vol. 2). (gr. 2-3). 31.00 (978-0-7635-9429-9(6)) Rigby Education.

Grandma's Pictures: Individual Title Six-Packs. (gr. k-1). 23.00 (978-0-7635-8842-7(3)) Rigby Education.

Grant, Alice. Dear Mr President, Please Send My Daddy Home. 2008. 23p. pap. 24.95 (978-1-60441-293-2(3)) America Star Bks.

Grant, Holly. The League of Beastly Dreadfuls. 2015. (League of Beastly Dreadfuls Ser.: Bk. 1). (ENG., Illus.). 320p. (J). (gr. 3-7). 16.99 (978-0-385-37007-3(5), Random Hse. Bks. for Young Readers) Random Hse. Children's Bks.

Grant, Katy. Hide & Seek, 1 vol. (ENG.). 240p. (J). 2012. pap. 7.95 (978-1-56145-669-7(1)) 2010. (gr. 3-7). 15.95 (978-1-56145-542-3(3)) Peachtree Pubs.

Grant, Vicki. No te Vayas, 1 vol. 2011. (Spanish Soundings Ser.). (SPA.). 160p. (J). (gr. 8-12). pap. 9.95 (978-1-55469-970-4(3)) Orca Bk. Pubs. USA.

Gratton, Tessa. Blood Magic. 2011. (YA). pap. (978-0-375-86486-5(5)) Random Hse. Children's Bks.

Gratz, Alan. Something Rotten. 2009. (ENG.). 224p. (YA). (gr. 7-18). 7.99 (978-0-14-241297-8(X), Puffin Books) Penguin Young Readers Group.

Graves, Annie. Frankenkids. McElhinney, Glenn, illus. 2015. (Nightmare Club Ser.: 5). (ENG.). 64p. (J). (gr. 2-5). lib. bdg. 25.32 (978-1-4677-4352-5(6)) Lerner Publishing Group.

—Help! My Brother's a Zombie. McElhinney, Glenn, illus. 2015. (J). (Nightmare Club Ser.: 2). (ENG.). 64p. (gr. 2-5). lib. bdg. 25.32 (978-1-4677-4348-8(8)); 6.99 (978-1-4677-7871-8(0)) Lerner Publishing Group.

Gravett, Emily. The Rabbit Problem. Gravett, Emily, illus. 2010. (ENG., Illus.). 32p. (J). (gr. -1-3). 17.99 (978-1-4424-1255-2(0), Simon & Schuster Bks. For Young Readers) Simon & Schuster Bks. For Young Readers.

Gray, Claudia. Spellcaster. 2013. (Spellcaster Ser.: 1). (ENG.). 400p. (YA). (gr. 8). 17.99 (978-0-06-196120-5(5), HarperTeen) HarperCollins Pubs.

—Steadfast. (Spellcaster Ser.: 2). (ENG.). (YA). (gr. 8). 2015. 368p. pap. 9.99 (978-0-06-196123-6(X)) 2014. 352p. 17.99 (978-0-06-196122-9(1)) HarperCollins Pubs. (HarperTeen).

Gray, Michael Loyd. King Biscuit. 2013. (J). pap. (978-1-938237-04-1(8)) Tempest Bk. Shop.

EFG

Greathouse, Cindy. Wilbur Learns to Forgive, 1 vol. 2010. 18p. 24.95 *(978-1-4489-7374-3(0))* PublishAmerica, Inc.

Green, Connie Jordan. Emmy. 2nd ed. 2007. (J). pap. 15.00 *(978-1-60454-000-0(1))* Iris Publishing Group, Inc., The.

Green, D. L. Kaitlyn & the Competition. 2016. (Babysitter Chronicles Ser.). (ENG.). 160p. (gr. 4-7). pap. 6.95 *(978-1-4914-8861-4(1))* Stone Arch Bks.

Green, Jessica. Diary of a Would-Be Princess: The Journal of Jillian Jones, 5b. 2007. (Illus.). 236p. (J). (gr. 4-7). 15.95 *(978-1-58089-166-0(7))* Charlesbridge Publishing, Inc.

Green, Jose. Castro's Diary. 2004. 174p. pap. 24.95 *(978-1-4137-4556-6(3))* America Star Bks.

Green, Julia. Hunter's Heart. 2007. 264p. (YA). (gr. 7-12). 16.95 *(978-0-7613-9493-8(1)*, Carolrhoda Bks.) Lerner Publishing Group.

Green, S. E. Killer Instinct. 2014. (ENG., Illus.). 272p. (YA). (gr. 9). 17.99 *(978-1-4814-0285-9(4)*, Simon Pulse) Simon Pulse.

—Killer Within. 2015. (ENG.). 304p. (YA). (gr. 9). 17.99 *(978-1-4814-0288-0(9)*, Simon Pulse) Simon Pulse.

Green, Sally. Half Bad. (ENG.). (YA). 2015. (Half Bad Trilogy Ser.: 1). 432p. (gr. 7). pap. 9.99 *(978-0-14-751146-1(1)*, Speak) 2014. (Half Bad Trilogy Ser.: 1). 416p. (gr. 7). 18.99 *(978-0-670-01678-5(0)*, Viking Books for Young Readers)Pack. 2015. pap. 89.91 *(978-0-14-751591-9(2)*, Speak) Penguin Young Readers Group.

Green, Terry. Moonstone. 2010. 188p. pap. 14.49 *(978-1-4520-4634-1(4))* AuthorHouse.

Green, Tim. Football Hero. (Football Genius Ser.: 2). (ENG.). (J). (gr. 3-7). 2009. 320p. pap. 6.99 *(978-0-06-112276-7(9))* 2008. (Illus.). 304p. 16.99 *(978-0-06-112274-3(2))* HarperCollins Pubs.

—Football Hero. l.t. ed. 2008. (YA). 23.95 *(978-1-4104-1116-7(8))* Thorndike Pr.

—Home Run. 2016. (Baseball Great Ser.: 4). 352p. (J). (gr. 3-7). 16.99 *(978-0-06-231711-7(3))* HarperCollins Pubs.

—Pinch Hit. (ENG.). (J). (gr. 3-7). 2013. 336p. pap. 6.99 *(978-0-06-201247-0(9))* 2012. 320p. 16.99 *(978-0-06-201246-3(0))* HarperCollins Pubs.

Greene, Constance C. Beat the Turtle Drum. 128p. (J). (gr. 4-6). pap. 3.99 *(978-0-8072-1411-4(6)*, Listening Library) Random Hse. Audio Publishing Group.

Greene, Stephanie. Christmas at Stony Creek. Sheban, Chris, illus. 2007. 96p. (gr. -1-3). lib. bdg. 15.89 *(978-0-06-121487-5(6))* HarperCollins Pubs.

—Falling into Place. 2006. (ENG.). 128p. (J). (gr. 5-7). pap. 8.95 *(978-0-618-68928-6(1))* Houghton Mifflin Harcourt Publishing Co.

—Happy Birthday, Sophie Hartley. 2011. (ENG.). 128p. (J). (gr. 2-5). pap. 6.99 *(978-0-547-55025-1(1))* Houghton Mifflin Harcourt Publishing Co.

—Owen Foote, Money Man. Weston, Martha, illus. 2003. 88p. (gr. 2-4). 14.95 *(978-0-7569-1559-9(7))* Perfection Learning Corp.

—Princess Posey & the Crazy, Lazy Vacation. Sisson, Stéphanie Roth, illus. 2016. (Princess Posey, First Grader Ser.: 10). (ENG.). 96p. (J). (gr. k-3). 5.99 *(978-0-14-751293-2(X)*, Puffin Books) Penguin Young Readers Group.

—Queen Sophie Hartley. 2011. (ENG.). 144p. (J). (gr. 2-5). pap. 5.99 *(978-0-547-55021-3(9))* Houghton Mifflin Harcourt Publishing Co.

—Sophie Hartley & the Facts of Life. 2015. (ENG.). 144p. (J). (gr. 5-7). pap. 5.99 *(978-0-544-43938-2(4)*, HMH Books For Young Readers) Houghton Mifflin Harcourt Publishing Co.

—Sophie Hartley, on Strike. 2011. (ENG.). 156p. (J). (gr. 2-5). pap. 11.95 *(978-0-547-55018-3(9))* Houghton Mifflin Harcourt Publishing Co.

Greenwald, Lisa. My Life in Pink & Green. (Pink & Green Ser.). (ENG.). (gr. 3-7). 2010. 288p. (J). pap. 7.95 *(978-0-8109-8984-9(0))* 2009. 272p. (YA). 17.95 *(978-0-8109-8352-6(4))* Abrams, Inc. (Amulet Bks.).

—My Summer of Pink & Green. 2013. (Pink & Green Ser.). (ENG.). 272p. (YA). (gr. 3-7). 17.95 *(978-1-4197-0413-0(3)*, Amulet Bks.); (J). (gr. 5-9). 5.00 *(978-1-4197-0932-6(1))* Abrams, Inc.

—My Summer of Pink & Green: Pink & Green Book Two. 2014. (Pink & Green Ser.). (ENG.). 288p. (YA). (gr. 3-7). pap. 7.95 *(978-1-4197-0931-9(3)*, Amulet Bks.) Abrams, Inc.

—Reel Life Starring Us. (ENG.). (YA). (gr. 3-7). 2013. 320p. pap. 7.95 *(978-1-4197-0426-0(5))* 2011. 304p. 16.95 *(978-1-4197-0026-2(X))* Abrams, Inc. (Amulet Bks.).

Greenwald, Tommy. Jack Strong Takes a Stand. Mendes, Melissa, illus. 2013. (ENG.). 240p. (J). (gr. 4-7). 15.99 *(978-1-59643-836-1(3)*, 9781596438361) Roaring Brook Pr.

—Jack Strong Takes a Stand. 2015. (Charlie Joe Jackson's Guide Ser.). (J). lib. bdg. 17.20 *(978-0-606-36717-2(9))* Turtleback Bks.

Gregerson, Judy. Bad Girls Club. 2007. (ENG.). 288p. (YA). (gr. 9-13). 16.95 *(978-1-933831-01-5(4))* Blooming Tree Pr.

Gregory, Dee. The Accidental Daughter: A Children's Story about Hope. 2008. 96p. pap. 10.49 *(978-1-4389-3338-2(X))* AuthorHouse.

Gregory, Kristiana. My Darlin' Clementine. 2009. (ENG.). 192p. (J). (gr. 5-18). 16.95 *(978-0-8234-2198-5(8))* Holiday Hse., Inc.

Greves, Julie, et al. Upside down & Backwards: A Sibling's Journey Through Childhood Cancer. 2014. (Illus.). 112p. (J). *(978-1-4338-1637-6(7)*, Magination Pr.) American Psychological Assn.

Griffin, Adele. The Knaveheart's Curse. 2009. (Vampire Island Ser.). (ENG.). 160p. (J). (gr. 3-7). 6.99 *(978-0-14-241407-1(7)*, Puffin Books) Penguin Young Readers Group.

Griffin, Donna. The Twelve Days of Christmas in Indiana. Cummings, Troy, illus. 2014. (Twelve Days of Christmas in America Ser.). (ENG.). 40p. (J). (gr. k). 12.95 *(978-1-4549-0888-3(2))* Sterling Publishing Co., Inc.

Griffin, N. The Whole Stupid Way We Are. 2013. (ENG., Illus.). 368p. (YA). (gr. 9). 16.99 *(978-1-4424-3155-3(5)*, Atheneum Bks. for Young Readers) Simon & Schuster Children's Publishing.

Griffiths, Corinne Escobar. Corky Eckelsbriar. 2004. (J). pap. 6.95 *(978-0-9760271-0-2(0))* Cappella Publishing, A.

Grimes, Nikki. Planet Middle School. 2011. (ENG.). 160p. (YA). 15.99 *(978-1-59990-284-5(2)*, 9781599902845, Bloomsbury USA Childrens) Bloomsbury Publishing USA.

Grindley, Sally. Hurricane Wills. 2012. (ENG.). 256p. (J). (gr. -1-k). pap. 6.95 *(978-1-61608-732-6(3)*, 608732, Sky Pony Pr.) Skyhorse Publishing Co., Inc.

Grisham, John. La Casa Dipinta. pap. 21.95 *(978-88-04-50528-0(1))* Mondadori ITA. Dist: Distribooks, Inc.

Grogan, Shannon. From Where I Watch You. 2015. (ENG.). 304p. (YA). (gr. 9). 18.99 *(978-1-61695-554-0(6)*, Soho Teen) Soho Pr., Inc.

Grossnickle, Mary. A Place in My Heart. Relyea, Alison, illus. 2014. (ENG.). 36p. 15.95 *(978-1-84905-771-4(0)*, 3958) Kingsley, Jessica Pubs. GBR. Dist: Macmillan Distribution Ltd.

Grosso, Alissa. Ferocity Summer. 2012. (ENG., Illus.). 288p. (YA). pap. 9.95 *(978-0-7387-3070-7(X)*, Flux) North Star Editions.

Grosso, Mike. I Am Drums. 2016. (ENG.). 256p. (J). (gr. 5-7). 16.99 *(978-0-544-70710-8(9))* Houghton Mifflin Harcourt Publishing Co.

Groves. Best Duster Bk. 5. Date not set. (Illus.). 16p. (J). pap. 129.15 *(978-0-582-18766-5(4))* Addison-Wesley Longman, Ltd. GBR. Dist: Trans-Atlantic Pubns., Inc.

—Sticky Trousers. Date not set. (Illus.). 32p. (J). pap. 129.15 *(978-0-582-18304-9(9))* Addison-Wesley Longman, Ltd. GBR. Dist: Trans-Atlantic Pubns., Inc.

Grund, Carol A. Anna Mei, Blessing in Disguise. 2011. 181p. (J). pap. *(978-0-8198-0796-0(6))* Pauline Bks. & Media.

—Anna Mei, Escape Artist. 2011. 168p. (J). (gr. 4-7). pap. 8.95 *(978-0-8198-0794-6(X))* Pauline Bks. & Media.

Guerra, Stephanie. Torn, 0 vols. 2012. (ENG.). 272p. (YA). (gr. 10-12). 17.99 *(978-0-7614-6272-9(4)*, 9780761462729, Amazon Children's Publishing) Amazon Publishing.

Guest, Elissa Haden. Bella's Rules. Halpin, Abigail, illus. 2013. (ENG.). 32p. (J). (gr. -1-k). 16.99 *(978-0-8037-3393-0(3)*, Dial Bks) Penguin Young Readers Group.

—Harriet's Had Enough! Meisel, Paul, illus. 2009. (ENG.). 32p. (J). (gr. -1-2). 15.99 *(978-0-7636-3454-4(9))* Candlewick Pr.

Guinn, Dolores Hollyfield. Frederick Frog & His Family: Being a Bully. 2008. 16p. per. 24.95 *(978-1-4241-9223-6(4))* America Star Bks.

Gunderson, Jessica. Emma's New Beginning. Foti, Anthony J., illus. 2015. (U. S. Immigration in The 1900s Ser.). (ENG.). 96p. (gr. 3-4). pap. 7.95 *(978-1-4965-0501-9(8))* Stone Arch Bks.

Gunning, Monica. Under the Breadfruit Tree: Island Poems. Broeck, Fabricio Vanden, illus. 2004. (ENG.). 48p. (J). (gr. 2-5). pap. 9.95 *(978-1-59078-258-3(5))* Boyds Mills Pr.

Gurtler, Janet. The Truth about Us. 2015. (ENG.). 320p. (YA). (gr. 8-12). pap. 9.99 *(978-1-4022-7800-6(4)*, 9781402278006) Sourcebooks, Inc.

Gutch, Michael. Sticky, Sticky, Stuck! Björkman, Steve, illus. 2013. (ENG.). 32p. (J). (gr. -1-3). 17.99 *(978-0-06-199818-8(4))* HarperCollins Pubs.

Gutman, Dan. From Texas with Love. 2014. (ENG.). (J): (gr. 3-7). (Genius Files Ser.: 4). 304p. pap. 6.99 *(978-0-06-182775-4(4))*; (Genius Files Ser.: Bk. 4). (Illus.). 288p. 16.99 *(978-0-06-182773-0(8))* HarperCollins Pubs.

—From Texas with Love. 2014. (Genius Files Ser.: 4). (J). lib. bdg. 17.20 *(978-0-606-36462-1(5))* Turtleback Bks.

—The Genius Files #4: from Texas with Love. 2014. (Genius Files Ser.: 4). 288p. (J). (gr. 3-7). lib. bdg. 17.89 *(978-0-06-182774-7(6))* HarperCollins Pubs.

—License to Thrill. 2015. (Genius Files Ser.: 5). (ENG.). 272p. (J). (gr. 3-7). 16.99 *(978-0-06-223632-6(6))* HarperCollins Pubs.

—Mission Unstoppable. 2011. (Genius Files Ser.: 1). (ENG.). 304p. (J). (gr. 3-7). pap. 6.99 *(978-0-06-182766-2(5))*; (Illus.). 16.99 *(978-0-06-182764-8(9))* HarperCollins Pubs.

—Mission Unstoppable. 2011. (Genius Files Ser.: 1). (J). lib. bdg. 17.20 *(978-0-606-23559-4(0)*, Turtleback) Turtleback Bks.

—Never Say Genius. 2012. (Genius Files Ser.: 2). (J). (gr. 3-7). (ENG.). 304p. pap. 6.99 *(978-0-06-182769-3(X))*; (ENG.). 288p. 16.99 *(978-0-06-182767-9(3))*; 288p. lib. bdg. 17.89 *(978-0-06-182768-6(1))* HarperCollins Pubs.

—Never Say Genius. 2012. (Genius Files Ser.: 2). (J). lib. bdg. 17.20 *(978-0-606-27128-8(7)*, Turtleback) Turtleback Bks.

—You Only Die Twice. 2013. (Genius Files Ser.: 3). (J). (gr. 3-7). (ENG.). 320p. pap. 6.99 *(978-0-06-182772-3(X))*; (ENG., Illus.). 304p. 16.99 *(978-0-06-182770-9(3))*; (Illus.). 304p. lib. bdg. 17.89 *(978-0-06-182771-6(1))* HarperCollins Pubs.

—You Only Die Twice. 2013. (Genius Files Ser.: 3). (J). lib. bdg. 17.20 *(978-0-606-35043-3(8)*, Turtleback) Turtleback Bks.

Guy, Joseph. One Childs Cry for Hope. 2010. 32p. 18.60 *(978-0-557-28780-2(4))* Lulu Pr., Inc.

Haas, Jessie. Saige. Davis, Sarah, illus. 2012. (American Girl Today Ser.: Bk. 1). lib. bdg. 17.15 *(978-0-606-31568-5(3)*, Turtleback) Turtleback Bks.

—Saige Paints the Sky. Davis, Sarah, illus. 2012. (American Girl Today Ser.: Bk. 2). lib. bdg. 17.15 *(978-0-606-31569-2(1)*, Turtleback) Turtleback Bks.

Haddix, Margaret Peterson. Redeemed. 2015. (Missing Ser.: 8). (ENG.). 416p. (J). (gr. 3-7). 17.99 *(978-1-4424-9756-6(4)*, Simon & Schuster Bks. For Young Readers) Simon & Schuster Bks. For Young Readers.

Hahn, Mary Downing. The Dead Man in Indian Creek. 2009. (ENG.). 144p. (J). (gr. 2-5). pap. 7.99 *(978-0-547-24880-6(6))* Houghton Mifflin Harcourt Publishing Co.

Haight, Jessica & Robinson, Stephanie. The Secret Files of Fairday Morrow. Muradov, Roman, illus. 2015. (ENG.). 272p. (J). (gr. 4-7). 18.99 *(978-0-375-99182-0(4)*, Delacorte Bks. for Young Readers) Random Hse. Children's Bks.

Haines, Lise. Girl in the Arena. (ENG.). 336p. (YA). (gr. 9-13). 2010. pap. 9.99 *(978-1-59990-521-1(3)*, 9781599905211) 2009. 16.99 *(978-1-59990-372-9(5)*, 9781599903729) Bloomsbury Publishing USA. (Bloomsbury USA Childrens).

Halahmy, Miriam. Behind Closed Doors. 2017. (ENG.). 208p. (J). (gr. 9). 16.95 *(978-0-8234-3641-5(1))* Holiday Hse., Inc.

—Hidden. 2016. (ENG.). 224p. (J). 16.95 *(978-0-8234-3694-1(2))* Holiday Hse., Inc.

Hale, Lucretia. The Peterkin Papers. Brett, Harold M., illus. 2005. reprint ed. pap. 24.95 *(978-1-4179-3265-8(1))* Kessinger Publishing, LLC.

Hale, Lucretia P. The Peterkin Papers. 2009. (Dover Children's Classics Ser.). (ENG., Illus.). 224p. (J). (gr. k-6). pap. 7.99 *(978-0-486-47170-9(5))* Dover Pubns., Inc.

—The Peterkin Papers. 2004. reprint ed. pap. 20.95 *(978-1-4191-7709-5(5))*; pap. 1.99 *(978-1-4192-7709-2(X))* Kessinger Publishing, LLC.

—The Peterkin Papers. 2006. (New York Review Children's Collection). (ENG., Illus.). 324p. (J). (gr. 4-7). 18.95 *(978-1-59017-212-4(4)*, NYR Children's Collection) New York Review of Bks., Inc., The.

Hale, Marian. Dark Water Rising. 2010. (ENG.). 256p. (J). (gr. 5-9). pap. 7.99 *(978-0-312-62908-3(7)*, 9780312629083) Square Fish.

—The Goodbye Season. 2009. (ENG.). 288p. (YA). (gr. 7-12). 16.99 *(978-0-8050-8855-7(5)*, 9780805088557, Holt, Henry & Co. Bks. For Young Readers) Holt, Henry & Co.

—The Truth about Sparrows. 2007. (ENG.). 288p. (YA). (gr. 7-12). per. 9.99 *(978-0-312-37133-3(0)*, 9780312371333) Square Fish.

Hale, Sheila. I Am Me. 2012. 32p. pap. 21.99 *(978-1-4691-9312-0(4))* Xlibris Corp.

Hall, Barbara. Dixie Storms. 2006. (ENG., Illus.). 224p. (YA). (gr. 7-12). pap. 12.95 *(978-0-15-205756-5(0))* Houghton Mifflin Harcourt Publishing Co.

Hall, Kate W. Richmond Rocks! 2009. (Illus.). (J). 14.95 *(978-1-61623-975-6(1)*, Richmondmom.com Publishing) Palari Publishing LLP.

Hallinan, P. K. Thanksgiving at Our House. 2006. (ENG., Illus.). 32p. (J). (gr. -1-3). 9.85 *(978-0-8249-5534-2(X)*, 1262730, Ideal Pubns.) Worthy Publishing.

Hamburg, Jennifer. Hazy Bloom & the Tomorrow Power. Mourning, Tuesday & Hamie, Jenn, illus. 2017. (Hazy Bloom Ser.). (ENG.). 176p. (J). 15.99 *(978-0-374-30494-2(7)*, 9780374304942, Farrar, Straus & Giroux (BYR)) Farrar, Straus & Giroux.

Hamilton, Virginia. M. C. Higgins, the Great. 2006. 271p. (gr. 8-12). 18.00 *(978-0-7569-6809-0(7))* Perfection Learning Corp.

—M. C. Higgins, the Great. 3rd ed. (J). pap. 3.95 *(978-0-13-800137-7(5))*; pap. 23.70 *(978-0-13-620220-2(9))* Prentice Hall (Schl. Div.).

—M. C. Higgins, the Great. 2006. (ENG., Illus.). 288p. (J). (gr. 3-7). pap. 7.99 *(978-1-4169-1407-5(2)*, Aladdin) Simon & Schuster Children's Publishing.

Hamley, Dennis. Divided Loyalties. 2010. (J). *(978-0-7636-3418-6(2))* Candlewick Pr.

Hampstead, Tom. The Kingdom of the Two Great Houses. 2011. 86p. pap. 10.95 *(978-1-60911-895-2(2)*, Strategic Bk. Publishing) Strategic Book Publishing & Rights Agency (SBPRA).

Han, Jenny. Clara Lee & the Apple Pie Dream. 2014. (ENG.). 160p. (J). (gr. 3-7). pap. 5.99 *(978-0-316-07037-9(8))* Little, Brown Bks. for Young Readers.

Hand, Cynthia. Boundless. 2013. (Unearthly Ser.: 3). (ENG.). 448p. (YA). (gr. 8). pap. 9.99 *(978-0-06-199621-4(1))*; 17.99 *(978-0-06-199620-7(3))* HarperCollins Pubs. (HarperTeen).

—The Last Time We Say Goodbye. 400p. (YA). (gr. 8). 2016. pap. 9.99 *(978-0-06-231848-0(9))* 2015. (ENG.). 17.99 *(978-0-06-231847-3(0))* HarperCollins Pubs. (HarperTeen).

—The Last Time We Say Goodbye. 2016. (YA). lib. bdg. 20.85 *(978-0-606-38130-7(9))* Turtleback Bks.

Hanks, Larry R. Stickboy, 1 vol. 2010. 28p. 24.95 *(978-1-4489-5141-3(0))* PublishAmerica, Inc.

Hanlon, Abby. Dory Fantasmagory. (Dory Fantasmagory Ser.: 1). (ENG.). (J). (gr. 1-3). 2015. Illus.). 176p. 7.99 *(978-0-14-751067-9(8)*, Puffin Books) 2014. 160p. 14.99 *(978-0-8037-4088-4(3)*, Dial Bks) Penguin Young Readers Group.

—The Real True Friend. 2015. (Dory Fantasmagory Ser.: 2). (ENG., Illus.). 160p. (J). (gr. 1-3). 14.99 *(978-0-525-42866-4(6)*, Dial Bks) Penguin Young Readers Group.

Hannan, Peter. Freddy! Deep-Space Food Fighter. Hannan, Peter, illus. 2011. (Freddy! Ser.: 2). (ENG., Illus.). 144p. (J). (gr. 2-6). pap. 5.99 *(978-0-06-128468-7(8))* HarperCollins Pubs.

—Freddy! Locked in Space. Hannan, Peter, illus. 2011. (Freddy! Ser.: 3). (ENG., Illus.). 160p. (J). (gr. 2-6). pap. 5.99 *(978-0-06-128470-0(X))* HarperCollins Pubs.

Hannigan, Kate. Summer Showers. Hughes, Brooke Boynton, illus. (Cupcake Cousins Ser.: Bk. 2). (ENG.). (J). (gr. 3-7). 2016. 256p. pap. 6.99 *(978-1-4847-2362-3(7))*Bk. 2. 2015. 240p. 16.99 *(978-1-4847-1662-5(0))* Hyperion Bks. for Children.

—Winter Wonders. Hughes, Brooke Boynton, illus. 2016. (Cupcake Cousins Ser.: Bk. 3). (ENG.). 240p. (J). (gr. 3-7). 16.99 *(978-1-4847-1663-2(9))* Hyperion Bks. for Children.

Hannigan, Katherine. Ida B: ... And Her Plans to Maximize Fun, Avoid Disaster, & (Possibly) Save the World. 2004. 256p. (gr. 4-18). lib. bdg. 16.89 *(978-0-06-073025-3(0))*; (ENG.). (J). 17.99 *(978-0-06-073024-6(2)*, Greenwillow Bks.) HarperCollins Pubs.

—Ida B: And Her Plans to Maximize Fun Avoid Disaster, & (Possibly) Save the World. 2011. (ENG.). 272p. (J). (gr. 5-9). reprint ed. pap. 6.99 *(978-0-06-073026-0(9)*, Greenwillow Bks.) HarperCollins Pubs.

Harbor, Missy. Susan of Bluebonnet Hill, 1 vol. 2009. 28p. pap. 24.95 *(978-1-61546-207-0(4))* America Star Bks.

Hardesty, Ann A. Lucy's Trials in the Black Hills. 2009. 104p. pap. 10.99 *(978-1-4490-5368-0(8))* AuthorHouse.

Hardinge, Frances. Cuckoo Song. (ENG.). (YA). (gr. 7-12). 2016. 432p. pap. 9.95 *(978-1-4197-1939-4(4))* 2015. 416p. 17.95 *(978-1-4197-1480-1(5))* Abrams, Inc. (Amulet Bks.).

Harkey, Faith. Genuine Sweet. (ENG.). 288p. (J). (gr. 5-7). 2016. pap. 6.99 *(978-0-544-66853-9(7)*, HMH Books For Young Readers) 2015. 16.99 *(978-0-544-28366-4(X))* Houghton Mifflin Harcourt Publishing Co.

Harley, Bill. Charlie Bumpers vs. the Perfect Little Turkey, 1 vol. Gustavson, Adam, illus. (Charlie Bumpers Ser.: 4). (ENG.). (J). (gr. 2-4). 2016. 176p. pap. 6.95 *(978-1-56145-963-6(1))* 2015. 164p. 13.95 *(978-1-56145-835-6(X))* Peachtree Pubs.

—Charlie Bumpers vs. the Puny Pirates, 1 vol. Gustavson, Adam, illus. (Charlie Bumpers Ser.). (ENG.). (J). (gr. 2-4). 2017. 186p. pap. 6.95 ***(978-1-68263-001-3(3))*** 2016. 160p. 14.95 *(978-1-56145-939-1(9))* Peachtree Pubs.

—Charlie Bumpers vs. the Really Nice Gnome, 1 vol. Gustavson, Adam, illus. 2014. (Charlie Bumpers Ser.). (ENG.). 160p. (J). (gr. 2-4). 13.95 *(978-1-56145-740-3(X))* Peachtree Pubs.

—Charlie Bumpers vs. the Squeaking Skull, 1 vol. Gustavson, Adam, illus. 2015. (Charlie Bumpers Ser.). (ENG.). 176p. (J). (gr. 2-4). pap. 6.95 *(978-1-56145-888-2(0))* Peachtree Pubs.

—Charlie Bumpers vs. the Teacher of the Year, 1 vol. Gustavson, Adam, illus. (Charlie Bumpers Ser.). (ENG.). 160p. (J). 2014. pap. 6.95 *(978-1-56145-824-0(4))* 2013. (gr. 2-4). 14.95 *(978-1-56145-732-8(9))* Peachtree Pubs.

Harlow, Joan Hiatt. Blown Away! (ENG.). 272p. (J). (gr. 4-7). 2008. pap. 7.99 *(978-1-4169-0782-4(3))* 2007. 16.99 *(978-1-4169-0781-7(5))* McElderry, Margaret K. Bks. (McElderry, Margaret K. Bks.).

—Firestorm! (ENG.). 336p. (J). (gr. 3-7). 2011. pap. 7.99 *(978-1-4169-8486-3(0))* 2010. (Illus.). 16.99 *(978-1-4169-8485-6(2))* McElderry, Margaret K. Bks. (McElderry, Margaret K. Bks.).

—Secret of the Night Ponies. 2010. (ENG.). 352p. (J). (gr. 3-7). pap. 7.99 *(978-1-4169-0784-8(X)*, McElderry, Margaret K. Bks.) McElderry, Margaret K. Bks.

—Thunder from the Sea. 2004. (ENG., Illus.). 208p. (J). (gr. 3-7). 17.99 *(978-0-689-86403-2(5)*, McElderry, Margaret K. Bks.) McElderry, Margaret K. Bks.

Harper, Benjamin & Scieszka, Jon. All Around Trucktown. Shannon, David et al, illus. 2008. (Jon Scieszka's Trucktown Ser.). (ENG.). 32p. (J). (gr. -1-1). 3.99 *(978-1-4169-4194-1(0)*, Simon Scribbles) Simon Scribbles.

Harper, Charise Mericle. Alien Encounter. Harper, Charise Mericle, illus. 2014. (Sasquatch & Aliens Ser.: 1). (ENG., Illus.). 208p. (J). (gr. 2-5). 12.99 *(978-0-8050-9621-7(3)*, 9780805096217, Holt, Henry & Co. Bks. For Young Readers) Holt, Henry & Co.

—Just Grace & the Snack Attack. 2010. (Just Grace Ser.: 5). (ENG., Illus.). 176p. (J). (gr. 1-4). pap. 5.99 *(978-0-547-40629-9(0))* Houghton Mifflin Harcourt Publishing Co.

Harper, Demetria R. God, Help Me, I Keep Falling! The Cries of a Young Teenager's Heart. 2011. 64p. (gr. 3-3). pap. 9.99 *(978-1-4567-5263-7(4))* AuthorHouse.

Harper, Suzanne. A Gaggle of Goblins. 2012. (Unseen World of Poppy Malone Ser.: 1). (ENG.). 320p. (J). (gr. 3-7). pap. 6.99 *(978-0-06-199609-2(2)*, Greenwillow Bks.) HarperCollins Pubs.

—A Gust of Ghosts. (ENG.). 320p. (J). (gr. 3-7). 2075. 6.99 *(978-0-06-199612-2(2))* 2012. (Unseen World of Poppy Malone Ser.: 2). 16.99 *(978-0-06-199610-8(6))* HarperCollins Pubs. (Greenwillow Bks.).

—A Mischief of Mermaids. 2013. (Unseen World of Poppy Malone Ser.: 3). (ENG.). 288p. (J). (gr. 3-7). 16.99 *(978-0-06-199613-9(0)*, Greenwillow Bks.) HarperCollins Pubs.

—The Secret Life of Sparrow Delaney. (YA). 2008. (ENG.). 368p. (gr. 8-12). pap. 8.99 *(978-0-06-113160-8(1)*, Greenwillow Bks.) 2007. 224p. (gr. 7-12). 16.99 *(978-0-06-113158-5(X))* 2007. 362p. (gr. 7-12). lib. bdg. 17.89 *(978-0-06-113159-2(8))* HarperCollins Pubs.

—The Unseen World of Poppy Malone No. 1: A Gaggle of Goblins. 2011. (Unseen World of Poppy Malone Ser.: 1). (ENG., Illus.). 304p. (J). (gr. 3-7). 16.99 *(978-0-06-199607-8(6)*, Greenwillow Bks.) HarperCollins Pubs.

Harrington, Claudia. My Two Dads, 1 vol. Persico, Zoe, illus. 2016. (ENG.). 32p. (J). *(978-1-62402-108-4(5))* Magic Wagon.

—My Two Moms, 1 vol. Persico, Zoe, illus. 2016. (ENG.). 32p. (J). *(978-1-62402-110-7(7))* Magic Wagon.

Harrington, K. A. Forget Me. 2014. (ENG.). 288p. (YA). (gr. 7). 17.99 *(978-0-399-16529-0(0)*, G.P. Putnam's Sons Books for Young Readers) Penguin Young Readers Group.

Harrington, Karen. Sure Signs of Crazy. 2013. (ENG.). 288p. (J). (gr. 4-17). 17.00 *(978-0-316-21058-4(7))* Little, Brown Bks. for Young Readers.

Harris, Joel Chandler. Mingo. 2007. 108p. 22.95 *(978-1-60312-654-0(6))*; per. 9.95 *(978-1-60312-396-9(2))* Aegypan.

Harrison, Emma. Finding What's Real. 2017. (ENG., Illus.). 304p. (YA). (gr. 9). 17.99 *(978-1-4814-4215-2(5)*, Simon Pulse) Simon Pulse.

Harrison, Jean & Cristnogol, Cymorth. Shompa o India. 2005. *(978-0-904379-43-3(4))* Christian Aid.

Harrod-Eagles, Cynthia. It's Holiday Time! Baccala, Gladys, illus. 2012. (ENG.). 18p. (J). bds. *(978-1-58925-640-8(9))* Tiger Tales.

Harshman, Marc. One Big Family. Palacios, Sara, illus. 2016. (ENG.). 40p. (J). 17.00 *(978-0-8028-5388-2(9)*, Eerdmans Bks For Young Readers) Eerdmans, William B. Publishing Co.

Hart, Christine. Best Laid Plans, 1 vol. 2009. (Lorimer SideStreets Ser.). (ENG.). 152p. (YA). (gr. 9-12). 16.95 *(978-1-55277-447-2(3)*, 9781552774472) Lorimer, James & Co., Ltd., Pubs. CAN. Dist: Casemate Pubs. & Bk. Distributors, LLC.

Hartinger, Brent. Split Screen: Attack of the Soul-Sucking Brain Zombies; Bride of the Soul-Sucking Brain Zombies. 2007. 304p. (YA). (gr. 9-12). lib. bdg. 17.89 *(978-0-06-082409-9(3)*, HarperTeen) HarperCollins Pubs.

Hartman, Brett. Cadillac Chronicles. 2012. (ENG.). 304p. (J). (gr. 10). 16.95 *(978-1-935955-41-2(1))* Cinco Puntos Pr.

Hartnett, Sonya. Butterfly. (ENG.). 240p. (YA). (gr. 9). 2013. pap. 7.99 *(978-0-7636-6334-6(4))* 2010. (Illus.). 16.99 *(978-0-7636-4760-5(8))* Candlewick Pr.

—Stripes of the Sidestep Wolf. 2005. (ENG.). 208p. (YA). (gr. 7-18). 16.99 *(978-0-7636-2644-0(9))* Candlewick Pr.

Harvey, Gwen. Esperanza Means Hope. Porfirio, Guy, illus. 2010. (J). *(978-0-910037-51-8(5))*; pap. *(978-0-910037-52-5(3))* Arizona Historical Society.

Harvey, Jacqueline. Alice-Miranda on Vacation. 2013. (ENG.). 288p. (J). (gr. 2-5). 7.99 *(978-0-385-73996-2(6)*, Yearling) Random Hse. Children's Bks.

Harvey, Sarah N. Bull's Eye, 1 vol. 2007. (Orca Soundings Ser.). (ENG.). 112p. (YA). (gr. 8-12). 9.95 *(978-1-55143-679-1(5))* Orca Bk. Pubs. USA.

Haskins, James. The March on Washington. 2004. (Illus.). 192p. (J). (gr. 5-18). pap. 10.95 *(978-0-940975-93-4(9)*, Sankofa Bks.) Just Us Bks., Inc.

Hathom, Libby. Eu Amo Você, Livro. Dalla, Juliana, tr. from ENG. McKenzie, Heath, illus. 2012.Tr. of I love Your Book.

(POR.). 36p. pap. (978-1-921869-82-2(8), IP Kidz) Interactive Pubns. Pty, Ltd.

Hattrup, Karen. Frannie & Tru. 2016. 320p. (YA). (gr. 9). 17.99 (978-0-06-241020-7(2), HarperTeen) HarperCollins Pubs.

Hautman, Pete. The Big Crunch. 2011. (ENG.). 288p. (J). (gr. 7-8). 17.99 (978-0-545-24075-8(1), Scholastic Pr.) Scholastic, Inc.

—The Flinkwater Factor: A Novel in Five Thrilling Episodes. 2015. (Flinkwater Chronicles Ser.: 1). (ENG.). 256p. (J). (gr. 4-8). 16.99 (978-1-4814-3251-1(6), Simon & Schuster Bks. For Young Readers) Simon & Schuster Bks. For Young Readers.

—How to Steal a Car. (ENG.). 176p. (J). 2011. (gr. 2-5). pap. 9.99 (978-0-545-11287-1(7), Scholastic Paperbacks) 2009. (gr. 7-18). 16.99 (978-0-545-11318-2(0), Scholastic Pr.) Scholastic, Inc.

Hautzig, Deborah. Little Witch Learns to Read. Wickstrom, Sylvie K., illus. 2003. (Step into Reading Ser.). (ENG.). 48p. (J). (gr. k-3). pap. 3.99 (978-0-375-82179-0(1), Random Hse. Bks. for Young Readers) Random Hse. Children's Bks.

Haworth-Attard, Barbara. My Life from Air-Bras to Zits. 2009. (ENG.). 288p. (YA). (gr. 7-10). pap. 9.95 (978-0-7387-1483-7(6), Flux) North Star Editions.

Haydu, Corey Ann. Rules for Stealing Stars. (J). (gr. 3-7). 2017. 352p. pap. 6.99 (978-0-06-235273-6(3)) 2015. (ENG.). 336p. 16.99 (978-0-06-235271-2(7)) HarperCollins Pubs. (Tegen, Katherine Bks).

Hayes, Angela. Just an Existence, 1 vol. 2010. 50p. pap. 16.95 (978-1-60749-035-7(8)) PublishAmerica, Inc.

Hayes, Christine. The Mothman's Curse. Hindle, James K., illus. 2015. (ENG.). 320p. (J). (gr. 3-7). 15.99 (978-1-62672-027-5(4), 9781626720275) Roaring Brook Pr.

Hayes, Joe. A Spoon for Every Bite. Leer, Rebecca, illus. 2005. (SPA & ENG.). 32p. (J). (gr. 1-4). reprint ed. pap. 8.95 (978-0-938317-93-7(8)) Cinco Puntos Pr.

Hayes, Michael. James Little Elk: Meeting His Family. 2011. 32p. pap. 18.50 (978-1-4567-1491-8(0)) AuthorHouse.

Haynes, Marilee. Pictures of Me. 2016. 149p. (J). pap. (978-0-8198-6019-4(0)) Pauline Bks. & Media.

Haywood, Carolyn. Here's a Penny. 2005. (ENG., Illus.). 160p. (J). (gr. 1-4). pap. 6.99 (978-0-15-205225-6(9)) Houghton Mifflin Harcourt Publishing Co.

Hazell, Mark. Gift of the Wind Dancers. 2004. 140p. pap. (978-1-84401-029-5(5)) Athena Pr.

—Miners of the Rainbow Stone (the Forest Children Series) 2006. 308p. pap. (978-1-84401-625-9(0)) Athena Pr.

Hearn, Julie. Hazel. 2009. (ENG.). 400p. (YA). (gr. 7-18). 17.99 (978-1-4169-2504-0(X), Atheneum Bks. for Young Readers) Simon & Schuster Children's Publishing.

Heasley, Gwendolyn. Where I Belong. 2011. (Where I Belong Ser.: 1). (ENG.). 304p. (YA). (gr. 8-18). pap. 9.99 (978-0-06-197884-5(1), HarperTeen) HarperCollins Pubs.

Hedlund, Daniel Levine. The Trouble with Tomatoes. 2003. 108p. 19.95 (978-0-595-74776-4(0)); pap. 9.95 (978-0-595-28313-2(6)) iUniverse, Inc.

Heibel, Dorothy. Message for a Spy. 2004. (Illus.). 94p. (J). pap. (978-1-932663-07-5(X)) History Compass, LLC.

Helakoski, Leslie. Doggone Feet! Helakoski, Leslie, illus. 2013. (ENG., Illus.). 40p. (J). (gr. -1-2). 16.95 (978-1-59078-933-9(4)) Boyds Mills Pr.

Heldring, Thatcher. The Football Girl. 2017. (YA). **(978-0-375-99026-7(7)**, Delacorte Pr) Random House Publishing Group.

Helget, Nicole. Wonder at the Edge of the World. 2015. (ENG., Illus.). 384p. (J). (gr. 3-7). 17.00 (978-0-316-24510-4(0)) Little, Brown Bks. for Young Readers.

Hellisen, Cat. Beastkeeper. 2015. (ENG.). 208p. (YA). (gr. 7-9). 16.99 (978-0-8050-9980-5(8), Holt, Henry & Co. Bks. For Young Readers) Holt, Henry & Co.

Helmso, Candy Grant. Freedom Quilt. Friar, Joanne, illus. 2003. (Books for Young Learners). (ENG.). 16p. (J). 5.75 net. (978-1-57274-529-2(0), 2744, Bks. for Young Learners) Owen, Richard C. Pubs., Inc.

Hemphill, Helen. Runaround. (ENG.). 117p. (J). (gr. 6-9). 2009. pap. 10.95 (978-1-59078-777-9(3)) 2007. (Illus.). 16.95 (978-1-932425-83-3(7)) Boyds Mills Pr. (Front Street).

Hendershot, Eric. At Season's End. 2012. pap. 13.99 (978-1-59955-995-7(1)) Cedar Fort, Inc./CFI Distribution.

Henderson, Aileen Kilgore. Hard Times for Jake Smith: A Story of the Depression Era. 2004. (Historical Fiction for Young Readers Ser.). (ENG.). 232p. (J). pap. 8.00 (978-1-57131-649-3(3)) Milkweed Editions.

Henkes, Kevin. Bird Lake Moon. (ENG.). 192p. (J). (gr. 3-7). 2010. pap. 5.99 (978-0-06-147079-0(1)) 2008. 17.99 (978-0-06-147076-9(7)) HarperCollins Pubs. (Greenwillow Bks.).

—The Birthday Room. unabr. ed. 2004. 160p. (J). (gr. 3-7). pap. 29.00 incl. audio (978-0-8072-0444-3(7), Listening Library) Random Hse. Audio Publishing Group.

—Olive's Ocean. 2005. (HarperClassics Ser.). (ENG.). 224p. (J). (gr. 3-7). reprint ed. pap. 6.99 (978-0-06-053545-2(8), Greenwillow Bks.) HarperCollins Pubs.

—Penny & Her Doll. Henkes, Kevin, illus. 2012. (Illus.). 32p. (J). (gr. -1-3). (ENG.). 12.99 (978-0-06-208199-5(3)); lib. bdg. 14.89 (978-0-06-208200-8(0)) HarperCollins Pubs. (Greenwillow Bks.).

—Penny & Her Doll. 2013. (I Can Read! Level 1 Ser.). (J). lib. bdg. 13.55 (978-0-606-27147-9(3), Turtleback) Turtleback Bks.

—Penny & Her Song. Henkes, Kevin, illus. 2012. (I Can Read Level 1 Ser.). (Illus.). 32p. (J). (gr. -1-3). (ENG.). pap. 3.99 (978-0-06-208197-1(7)); (ENG., 12.99 (978-0-06-208195-7(0)); lib. bdg. 14.89 (978-0-06-208196-4(9)) HarperCollins Pubs. (Greenwillow Bks.).

—Penny & Her Song. 2012. (J). lib. bdg. 13.55 (978-0-606-26847-9(2), Turtleback) Turtleback Bks.

—The Year of Billy Miller. Henkes, Kevin, illus. 2013. (Illus.). 240p. (J). (gr. 3-7). (ENG.). 16.99 (978-0-06-226812-9(0)); lib. bdg. 17.89 (978-0-06-226813-6(9)) HarperCollins Pubs. (Greenwillow Bks.).

—The Year of Billy Miller. Henkes, Kevin, illus. 2015. (ENG., Illus.). (J). (gr. 3-7). lib. bdg. 17.60 **(978-1-62765-762-4(2))** Perfection Learning Corp.

—The Year of Billy Miller. 2015. (J). lib. bdg. 17.20 (978-0-606-36977-0(5)) Turtleback Bks.

Hennessy, Claire. Afterwards. 2005. 188p. (YA). pap. (978-1-84223-207-1(X)) Poolbeg Pr.

Hensley, Nathaniel. The Strange Tale of Hector & Hannah Crowe. 2015. (ENG.). 222p. (J). (gr. 8-18). 13.95 (978-1-937240-49-3(5)) Casa de Snapdragon LLC.

Henson, Heather. Here's How I See It — Here's How It Is. 2010. (ENG., Illus.). 304p. (J). (gr. 5-9). pap. 6.99 (978-1-4169-9773-3(3), Atheneum Bks. for Young Readers) Simon & Schuster Children's Publishing.

Heo, Yumi. Ten Days & Nine Nights: An Adoption Story. Heo, Yumi, illus. 2009. (Rise & Shine Ser.). (ENG., Illus.). 40p. (J). (gr. -1-3). 17.99 (978-0-375-84718-9(9), Schwartz & Wade Bks.) Random Hse. Children's Bks.

Hepler, Heather. The Cupcake Queen. 2010. (ENG.). 256p. (YA). (gr. 7-18). 7.99 (978-0-14-241668-6(1), Speak) Penguin Young Readers Group.

Herbach, Geoff. Fat Boy vs. the Cheerleaders. 2014. (ENG.). 320p. (YA). (gr. 7-12). 16.99 (978-1-4022-9141-8(8), 9781402291418) Sourcebooks, Inc.

—Gabe Johnson Takes Over. 2015. (ENG.). 352p. (YA). (gr. 6-12). pap. 9.99 (978-1-4926-0865-3(3)) Sourcebooks, Inc.

Herlong, M. H. Buddy. 2013. (ENG.). 320p. (J). (gr. 5). pap. 7.99 (978-0-14-242544-2(3), Puffin Books) Penguin Young Readers Group.

Herman, Charlotte. My Chocolate Year: A Novel with 12 Recipes. Pham, LeUyen, illus. 2008. (ENG.). 176p. (J). (gr. 3-7). 15.99 (978-1-4169-3341-0(7), Simon & Schuster Bks. For Young Readers) Simon & Schuster Bks. For Young Readers.

Hermes, Patricia. Emma Dilemma & the Camping Nanny, 0 vols. Carter, Abby, illus. 2009. (Emma Dilemma Ser.: 4). (ENG.). 144p. (J). (gr. 3-6). 15.99 (978-0-7614-5534-9(5), 9780761455349, Amazon Children's Publishing) Amazon Publishing.

—Emma Dilemma & the New Nanny, 0 vols. Carter, Abby, illus. 2010. (Emma Dilemma Ser.: 1). (ENG.). 114p. (J). (gr. 3-6). pap. 6.99 (978-0-7614-5619-3(8), 9780761456193, Amazon Children's Publishing) Amazon Publishing.

—Emma Dilemma & the Two Nannies, 0 vols. Carter, Abby, illus. 2011. (Emma Dilemma Ser.: 2). (ENG.). 126p. (J). (gr. 3-6). pap. 7.99 (978-0-7614-5835-7(2), 9780761458357, Amazon Children's Publishing) Amazon Publishing.

—Emma Dilemma, the Nanny, & the Best Horse Ever, 0 vols. Carter, Abby, illus. 2013. (Emma Dilemma Ser.: 6). (ENG.). 144p. (J). (gr. 3-6). pap. 9.99 (978-1-4778-1633-2(X), 9781477816332, Amazon Children's Publishing) Amazon Publishing.

—Emma Dilemma, the Nanny, & the Secret Ferret, 0 vols. Carter, Abby, illus. 2010. (Emma Dilemma Ser.: 5). (ENG.). 112p. (J). (gr. 3-6). 15.99 (978-0-7614-5650-6(3), 9780761456506, Amazon Children's Publishing) Amazon Publishing.

—Fly Away Home. 2005. (Illus.). 160p. pap. 7.95 (978-1-55704-308-5(6)) Newmarket Pr.

Hernandez, David. Suckerpunch. 2007. (ENG.). 224p. (YA). (gr. 9-18). 17.99 (978-0-06-117330-1(4), HarperTeen) HarperCollins Pubs.

Herrick, Steven. The Wolf. 2007. (ENG.). 216p. (J). (gr. 7-18). 17.95 (978-1-932425-75-8(6), Front Street) Boyds Mills Pr.

Hesse, Karen. Brooklyn Bridge. Sheban, Chris, illus. 2011. (ENG.). 256p. (J). (gr. 5-9). pap. 9.99 (978-0-312-67428-1(7), 9780312674281) Square Fish.

Hetherington, Sally. Where's Pa? Hetherington, Jan, illus. 2013. 28p. pap. 15.97 (978-1-62516-299-1(5), Strategic Bk. Publishing) Strategic Book Publishing & Rights Agency (SBPRA).

Hewlett, Stefanie & Foulk, Allison. Heart Stockings. McCann, Caroline, illus. 2015. (J). pap. 7.99 (978-1-62972-159-0(X)) Deseret Bk. Co.

Heyne, Kara. The Locket's Secret. 2013. (ENG.). 162p. (J). pap. 8.95 (978-0-8198-7484-9(1)) Pauline Bks. & Media.

Hicks, Deron R. Secrets of Shakespeare's Grave, Bk. 1. Geyer, Mark Edward, illus. 2013. (Shakespeare Mysteries Ser.: 1). (ENG.). 320p. (J). (gr. 2-5). pap. 7.99 (978-0-544-10504-1(4)) Houghton Mifflin Harcourt Publishing Co.

Higgins, M. G. The Impossible Wish. Taylor, Jo, illus. 2016. (Sibling Split Ser.). (ENG.). 112p. (gr. 2-3). lib. bdg. 25.32 (978-1-4965-2593-2(0)) Stone Arch Bks.

—Party of Nine. Taylor, Jo, illus. 2016. (Sibling Split Ser.). (ENG.). 112p. (gr. 2-3). lib. bdg. 25.32 (978-1-4965-2592-5(2)) Stone Arch Bks.

—Trouble in the City. Taylor, Jo, illus. 2016. (Sibling Split Ser.). (ENG.). 112p. (gr. 2-3). lib. bdg. 25.32 (978-1-4965-2591-8(4)) Stone Arch Bks.

Highway, Tomson. Dragonfly Kites: Kiweeginapiseek. 2004. (Illus.). (J). (gr. k-3). spiral bd. (978-0-616-14619-4(1)) Canadian National Institute for the Blind/Institut National Canadien pour les Aveugles.

Hill, David. My Brother's War. 2015. (ENG.). 252p. (gr. 3-7). pap. 20.95 (978-1-906582-63-0(7)) Aurora Metro Pubns. Ltd. GBR. Dist: Consortium Bk. Sales & Distribution.

Hill, Eric. Spot Loves His Mommy. Hill, Eric, illus. 2006. (Spot Ser.). (ENG., Illus.). 14p. (J). (gr. -1 — 1). bds. 5.99 (978-0-399-24511-4(1), Warne) Penguin Young Readers Group.

Hill, Janet Muirhead. Miranda & Starlight: (the Starlight Books, 1) Revised Edition, 6 vols. Lehmkuhl, Pat, illus. 2nd rev. ed. 2003. (Starlight Bks.: 1). 168p. (J). (gr. 3-7). per. 9.00 (978-0-9714161-4-7(1)) Raven Publishing Inc. of Montana.

Hill, Kirkpatrick. Bo at Iditarod Creek. Pham, LeUyen, illus. 2014. (ENG.). 288p. (J). (gr. 3-7). 15.99 (978-0-8050-9352-0(4), 9780805093520, Holt, Henry & Co. Bks. For Young Readers) Holt, Henry & Co.

—Do Not Pass Go. (ENG.). 240p. (J). (gr. 4-9). 2011. pap. 6.99 (978-1-4424-2122-6(3)) 2007. 16.99 (978-1-4169-1400-6(5)) McElderry, Margaret K. Bks. (McElderry, Margaret K. Bks.).

Hill, Tara Theresa. What Can You Do with Two Mommies? 2012. 40p. pap. 18.00 (978-1-105-50649-9(5)) Lulu Pr., Inc.

Hillert, Margaret. Who Feels Mad, Dear Dragon? Pullan, Jack, illus. 2017. (BeginningtoRead Ser.). (ENG.). 32p. (J). (-2). 22.60 **(978-1-59953-822-8(9))**; pap. 11.94 **(978-1-68404-000-1(0))** Norwood Hse. Pr.

—Who Feels Sad, Dear Dragon? Pullan, Jack, illus. 2017. (BeginningtoRead Ser.). (ENG.). 32p. (J). (-2). 22.60 **(978-1-59953-823-5(7))**; pap. 11.94 **(978-1-68404-001-8(9))** Norwood Hse. Pr.

Hills, Curt. Hannah's Legalized Kidnapping: A Rush to React Took Her Away for 207 Days. 2007. 68p. per. 12.95 (978-1-4327-0668-5(3)) Outskirts Pr., Inc.

Hilton, Marilyn. Found Things. (ENG.). 240p. (J). (gr. 4-7). 2015. pap. 7.99 (978-1-4424-6088-1(1)) 2014. 16.99 (978-1-4424-6087-4(3)) Simon & Schuster Children's Publishing.

Hinton, Cheryl. Kayla's Magic Eyes. Ellis, Althia Melody, ed. Coates, Sean, illus. 2013. 26p. 13.00 (978-0-578-11929-8(3)) Mosaic Paradigm Group, LLC.

Hinton, S. E. The Outsiders. 2006. (ENG.). 224p. (YA). (gr. 7-7). 10.00 (978-0-14-240733-2(X), Speak) Penguin Young Readers Group.

—The Outsiders. 156p. (YA). (gr. 7-18). pap. 5.99 (978-0-8072-1430-5(2), Listening Library) Random Hse. Audio Publishing Group.

—The Outsiders. 2006. (ENG.). 160p. (gr. 12-18). 15.00 (978-0-14-303985-3(7), Penguin Classics) Penguin Publishing Group.

—The Outsiders. l.t. ed. 2005. (ENG.). 253p. pap. 10.95 (978-0-7862-7362-1(3), Large Print Pr.) Thorndike Pr.

Hiskey, Iris. Hannah & the Hippo's No Mud Day. 2014. (ENG., Illus.). 32p. (J). (gr. -1-3). 16.99 (978-1-4814-2537-7(4), Simon & Schuster Bks. For Young Readers) Simon & Schuster Bks. For Young Readers.

Hoban, Russell. A Baby Sister for Frances. Hoban, Lillian, illus. 2011. (I Can Read Level 2 Ser.). (ENG.). 48p. (J). (gr. k-3). 16.99 (978-0-06-083804-1(3)); pap. 3.99 (978-0-06-083806-5(X)) HarperCollins Pubs.

—The Little Brute Family. Peck, Lillian Hoban, illus. 2004. (Sunburst Bks.). 17.00 (978-0-7569-3301-2(3)) Perfection Learning Corp.

Hobbs, Will. The Big Wander. 2004. (Illus.). 181p. (J). (gr. 5-9). 13.65 (978-0-7569-4970-9(X)) Perfection Learning Corp.

—Changes in Latitudes. 2004. (ENG.). 176p. (YA). (gr. 7). pap. 9.95 (978-0-689-87069-9(8), Simon Pulse) Simon Pulse.

Hobbs, William. Leaving Protection. 2004. 192p. (J). (gr. 5-18). lib. bdg. 16.89 (978-0-06-051632-1(1)) HarperCollins Pubs.

Hodge, Merle. For the Life of Laetitia. 2003. 21.25 (978-0-8446-7246-5(7)) Smith, Peter Pub., Inc.

Hodkin, Michelle. The Unbecoming of Mara Dyer. (Mara Dyer Trilogy Ser.: 1). (ENG., Illus.). (YA). (gr. 9). 2012. 480p. pap. 12.99 (978-1-4424-2177-6(0)) 2011. 464p. 21.99 (978-1-4424-2176-9(2)) Simon & Schuster Bks. For Young Readers. (Simon & Schuster Bks. For Young Readers).

Hof, Marjolijn. Against the Odds, 1 vol. Prins, Johanna, tr. 2011.Tr. of Een Kleine Kans. (ENG.). 128p. (J). (gr. 3-7). pap. 8.95 (978-0-88899-950-4(X)) Groundwood Bks. CAN. Dist: Publishers Group West (PGW).

Hofer, Ernst & Hofer, Nelly, illus. The Wild Swans. 2003. (ENG.). 40p. (J). (gr. 2-5). 17.95 (978-0-88776-615-2(3), Tundra Bks.) Tundra Bks. CAN. Dist: Penguin Random Hse. LLC.

Hoffman, Alice. Nightbird. 2016. (ENG., Illus.). 208p. (J). (gr. 5). pap. 7.99 (978-0-385-38961-7(2), Yearling) Random Hse. Children's Bks.

Hoffman, Eric. A Dark, Dark Cave. Tabor, Corey R., illus. 2016. (ENG.). 40p. (J). (gr. -1-1). 17.99 (978-0-670-01636-5(5), Viking Books for Young Readers) Penguin Young Readers Group.

Hoffmeister, Peter Brown. This Is the Part Where You Laugh. 2016. (ENG.). 336p. (YA). (gr. 9). 17.99 (978-0-553-53810-6(1), Knopf Bks. for Young Readers) Random Hse. Children's Bks.

Hogan, Mary. The Serious Kiss. 2005. (ENG.). 256p. (YA). (gr. 8). pap. 7.99 (978-0-06-072208-1(8), HarperTeen); (gr. 7-18). 16.99 (978-0-06-072206-7(1)) HarperCollins Pubs.

Holbrook, James. Emily I Think I Saw Heaven. Brittingham, Jennifer, illus. 2007. 40p. per. 14.95 (978-1-934246-56-6(5)) Peppertree Pr., The.

Holden, Pam. Pin the Tail on the Donkey, 6 pack. Hawley, Kelvin, illus. 2009. (Red Rocket Readers Ser.). (ENG.). 16p. pap. (978-1-877363-78-8(2)) Flying Start Bks.

Holder, Nancy. The Rose Bride: A Retelling of "The White Bride & the Black Bride" 2007. (Once upon a Time Ser.). (ENG.). 256p. (YA). (gr. 7-12). mass mkt. 6.99 (978-1-4169-3535-3(5), Simon Pulse) Simon Pulse.

Hole, Stian. Garmann's Summer. Bartlett, Don, tr. from NOR. Hole, Stian, illus. 2008. (ENG., Illus.). 42p. (J). (gr. k-3). 17.50 (978-0-8028-5339-4(0), Eerdmans Bks For Young Readers) Eerdmans, William B. Publishing Co.

Holland, Trish. I Can Do It! Newton, Vanessa Brantley, illus. 2014. (Little Golden Book Ser.). (ENG.). 24p. (J). (-k). 4.99 (978-0-449-81310-2(X), Golden Bks.) Random Hse. Children's Bks.

Hollyer, Belinda. Secrets, Lies & My Sister Kate. 2009. (ENG.). 144p. (J). (gr. 3-7). 16.95 (978-0-8234-2179-4(1)) Holiday Hse., Inc.

Holm, H. R. Forever Santa. 2009. 14p. (J). pap. 2.99 (978-1-59955-345-0(7)) Cedar Fort, Inc./CFI Distribution.

Holm, Jennifer L. Eighth Grade Is Making Me Sick: Ginny Davis's Year in Stuff. Castaldi, Elicia, illus. 2012. (Ginny Davis's Year in Stuff Ser.). (ENG.). 128p. (J). (gr. 3-7). 15.99 (978-0-375-86851-1(8), Random Hse. Bks. for Young Readers) Random Hse. Children's Bks.

—Middle School Is Worse Than Meatloaf: A Year Told Through Stuff. Castaldi, Elicia, illus. 2011. (ENG.). 128p. (J). (gr. 3-7). pap. 8.99 (978-1-4424-3663-3(8), Atheneum Bks. for Young Readers) Simon & Schuster Children's Publishing.

—Penny from Heaven. 2007. 265p. (gr. 3-7). 17.00 (978-0-7569-8206-5(5)) Perfection Learning Corp.

—Penny from Heaven. 2007. (ENG., Illus.). 304p. (J). (gr. 3-7). 7.99 (978-0-375-83689-3(6), Yearling) Random Hse. Children's Bks.

—Penny from Heaven. l.t. ed. 2007. (Literacy Bridge Middle Reader Ser.). (Illus.). 285p. (J). (gr. 5-7). 23.95 (978-0-7862-9698-9(4)) Thorndike Pr.

—Swing It, Sunny. Holm, Matthew, illus. 2017. (Sunny Ser.: 2). (ENG.). 224p. (J). (gr. 3-7). 24.99 **(978-0-545-74170-5(X))**; pap. 12.99 **(978-0-545-74172-9(6))** Scholastic, Inc. (Graphix).

Holm, Jennifer L. Turtle in Paradise. 2012. (CHI.). 187p. (J). (gr. 3-7). pap. (978-7-221-10316-1(X)) Guizhou People's Publishing Hse.

—Turtle in Paradise. 2009. 9.14 (978-0-7848-3781-8(3), Everbind) Marco Bk. Co.

—Turtle in Paradise. 2011. (ENG.). 224p. (J). (gr. 3-7). pap. 7.99 (978-0-375-83690-9(X), Yearling) Random Hse. Children's Bks.

—Turtle in Paradise. 2011. lib. bdg. 18.40 (978-0-606-23877-9(8), Turtleback) Turtleback Bks.

Holm, Jennifer L., et al. Sunny Side Up. 2015. (Illus.). 216p. (J). **(978-0-545-89934-5(6)**, Graphix) Scholastic, Inc.

Holm, Matthew & Follett, Jonathan. Marvin & the Moths. 2016. (ENG.). 352p. (J). (gr. 3-7). 16.99 (978-0-545-87674-2(5), Scholastic Pr.) Scholastic, Inc.

Holman, T. A. Stop It, Tyrone! (Illus.). 42p. (J). (gr. k-4). pap. 7.50 (978-0-9660617-1-0(3)) PLEO.

Holmes, Sara. Operation Yes. 2009. 234p. (J). pap. (978-0-545-20418-7(6)) Scholastic, Inc.

Holt, K. A. Mike Stellar: Nerves of Steel. 2010. (ENG.). 272p. (J). (gr. 3-7). 7.99 (978-0-375-84557-4(7), Yearling) Random Hse. Children's Bks.

—Rhyme Schemer. 2014. (ENG., Illus.). 176p. (J). (gr. 5-9). 15.99 (978-1-4521-2700-2(X)) Chronicle Bks. LLC.

Holt, Kimberly Willis. Dancing in Cadillac Light. 2003. (ENG.). 176p. (J). (gr. 5-9). 5.99 (978-0-698-11970-3(3), Puffin Books) Penguin Young Readers Group.

—Dancing in Cadillac Light. 2004. 176p. (J). (gr. 4-7). pap. 36.00 incl. audio (978-0-8072-2095-5(7), Listening Library) Random Hse. Audio Publishing Group.

—Dear Hank Williams. 2015. (ENG.). 224p. (J). (gr. 4-7). 16.99 (978-0-8050-8022-3(8), 9780805080223, Holt, Henry & Co. Bks. For Young Readers) Holt, Henry & Co.

—Dear Hank Williams. 2016. (J). lib. bdg. 18.40 (978-0-606-38551-0(7)) Turtleback Bks.

—Keeper of the Night. 2011. (ENG.). 336p. (YA). (gr. 7-12). pap. 14.99 (978-0-312-66103-8(7), 9780312661038) Square Fish.

—Navy Brat. Davenier, Christine, illus. 2011. (Piper Reed Ser.: 1). (ENG.). 176p. (J). (gr. 3-6). pap. 6.99 (978-0-312-62548-1(0), 9780312625481) Square Fish.

—Part of Me: Stories of a Louisiana Family. 2009. (ENG.). 240p. (J). (gr. 5-10). pap. 9.99 (978-0-312-58145-9(9), 9780312581459) Square Fish.

—Part of Me: Stories of a Louisiana Family. rev. l.t. ed. 2007. (Thorndike Literacy Bridge Ser.). 223p. (J). (gr. 3-7). 23.95 (978-0-7862-9184-7(2)) Thorndike Pr.

—Piper Reed, Campfire Girl. Davenier, Christine, illus. 2010. (Piper Reed Ser.: 4). (ENG.). 160p. (J). (gr. 3-6). 15.99 (978-0-8050-9006-2(1), 9780805090062, Holt, Henry & Co. Bks. For Young Readers) Holt, Henry & Co.

—Piper Reed, Campfire Girl. Davenier, Christine, illus. 2011. (Piper Reed Ser.: 4). (ENG.). 176p. (J). (gr. 3-6). pap. 6.99 (978-0-312-67482-3(1), 9780312674823) Square Fish.

—Piper Reed, Clubhouse Queen. Davenier, Christine, illus. 2011. (Piper Reed Ser.: 2). (ENG.). 160p. (J). (gr. 3-6). 15.99 (978-0-8050-9431-2(8), 9780805094312, Holt, Henry & Co. Bks. For Young Readers) Holt, Henry & Co.

—Piper Reed, Clubhouse Queen. Davenier, Christine, illus. 2011. (Piper Reed Ser.: 2). (ENG.). 176p. (J). (gr. 3-6). pap. 6.99 (978-0-312-61676-2(7), 9780312616762) Square Fish.

—Piper Reed, Forever Friend. Davenier, Christine, illus. 2012. (Piper Reed Ser.: 6). (ENG.). 160p. (J). (gr. 3-6). 15.99 (978-0-8050-9008-6(8), 9780805090086, Holt, Henry & Co. Bks. For Young Readers) Holt, Henry & Co.

—Piper Reed, Forever Friend. Davenier, Christine, illus. 2013. (Piper Reed Ser.: 6). (ENG.). 176p. (J). (gr. 3-6). pap. 6.99 (978-1-250-02725-2(X), 9781250027252) Square Fish.

—Piper Reed Gets a Job. Davenier, Christine, illus. 2009. (Piper Reed Ser.: 3). (ENG.). 160p. (J). (gr. 3-6). 14.99 (978-0-8050-8199-2(2), 9780805081992, Holt, Henry & Co. Bks. For Young Readers) Holt, Henry & Co.

—Piper Reed, Party Planner. Davenier, Christine, illus. 2011. (Piper Reed Ser.: 3). (ENG.). 176p. (J). (gr. 3-6). pap. 7.99 (978-0-312-61677-9(5), 9780312616779) Square Fish.

—Piper Reed, Rodeo Star. Davenier, Christine, illus. 2011. (Piper Reed Ser.: 5). (ENG.). 160p. (J). (gr. 3-6). 15.99 (978-0-8050-9007-9(X), 9780805090079, Holt, Henry & Co. Bks. For Young Readers) Holt, Henry & Co.

—Piper Reed, Rodeo Star. Davenier, Christine, illus. 2012. (Piper Reed Ser.: 5). (ENG.). 176p. (J). (gr. 3-6). pap. 6.99 (978-1-250-00409-3(8), 9781250004093) Square Fish.

Holub, Joan. Itty Bitty Kitty. Burks, James, illus. 2015. (ENG.). 32p. (J). (gr. -1-3). 17.99 (978-0-06-232219-7(2)) HarperCollins Pubs.

Honey, Elizabeth. Hop up! Wriggle Over! 2017. (ENG., Illus.). 40p. (J). (gr. -1-3). 16.99 (978-0-544-79084-1(7), Clarion Bks.) Houghton Mifflin Harcourt Trade & Reference Pubs.

Hood-Caddy, Karen. Howl. 2011. (Wild Place Adventure Ser.: 1). (ENG.). 256p. (J). (gr. 6-8). pap. 9.99 (978-1-926607-25-2(2)) Dundurn CAN. Dist: Ingram Publisher Services.

Hooper, Jaci. Gary: #Exodus 20. 2013. 32p. pap. 16.95 (978-1-4908-1120-8(6), WestBow Pr.) Author Solutions, Inc.

Hooray for Midsommar! 6 Small Books. (Greetings Ser.: Vol. 1). 24p. (gr. 2-3). 31.00 (978-0-7635-9410-7(5)) Rigby Education.

Hooray for Midsommar! Big Book. (Greetings Ser.: Vol. 1). 24p. (gr. 2-3). 31.00 (978-0-7635-5694-5(7)) Rigby Education.

Hope, Laura. The Bobbsey Twins at the County Fair. 2005. pap. 14.95 (978-1-55742-397-9(0)) Wildside Pr., LLC.

Hopkins, Ellen. Burned. 2006. (ENG., Illus.). 544p. (YA). (gr. 9-12). 21.99 (978-1-4169-0354-3(2), McElderry, Margaret K. Bks.) McElderry, Margaret K. Bks.

—Crank. 2010. (ENG.). 544p. (YA). (gr. 9). 21.99 (978-1-4169-9513-5(7), McElderry, Margaret K. Bks.) McElderry, Margaret K. Bks.

—The Crank Trilogy: Crank; Glass; Fallout. 2013. (ENG., Illus.). 1952p. (YA). (gr. 9). pap. 38.99 (978-1-4424-9959-1(1), McElderry, Margaret K. Bks.) McElderry, Margaret K. Bks.

—Fallout. 2010. (ENG.). 672p. (YA). (gr. 9-18). 18.99 (978-1-4169-5009-7(5), McElderry, Margaret K. Bks.) McElderry, Margaret K. Bks.

—Glass. (ENG., (YA). (gr. 9). 2013. Illus.). 720p. pap. 12.99 (978-1-4424-7182-5(4)) 2007. 688p. 21.99 (978-1-4169-4090-6(1)) McElderry, Margaret K. Bks. (McElderry, Margaret K. Bks.).

—Identical. (ENG.). (YA). (gr. 9-18). 2010. 592p. pap. 12.99 (978-1-4169-5006-6(0)) 2008. 576p. 17.99 (978-1-4169-5005-9(2)) McElderry, Margaret K. Bks. (McElderry, Margaret K. Bks.).

—Perfect. (ENG., (YA). (gr. 9). 2013. Illus.). 656p. pap. 12.99 *(978-1-4169-8325-5(2))* 2011. 640p. 18.99 *(978-1-4169-8324-8(4))* McElderry, Margaret K. Bks. (McElderry, Margaret K. Bks.).

—Tilt. (ENG., (YA). (gr. 9). 2014. Illus.). 624p. pap. 12.99 *(978-1-4169-8331-6(7))* 2012. 608p. 18.99 *(978-1-4169-8330-9(9))* McElderry, Margaret K. Bks. (McElderry, Margaret K. Bks.).

Hopkinson, Deborah. Our Kansas Home. Faricy, Patrick, illus. 2003. (Prairie Skies Ser.). 69p. (J). 11.65 *(978-0-7569-3448-4(6))* Perfection Learning Corp.

Hopkinson, Nalo. The Chaos. (ENG., 256p. (YA). (gr. 9). 2013. Illus.). pap. 9.99 *(978-1-4424-5926-7(3))* 2012. 16.99 *(978-1-4169-5488-0(0))* McElderry, Margaret K. Bks. (McElderry, Margaret K. Bks.).

Horning, Katherine. World of Shadows. 2005. 128p. pap. 19.95 *(978-1-4137-6500-7(9))* America Star Bks.

Horvath, Polly. The Canning Season. 2012. (ENG., Illus.). 224p. (YA). (gr. 7-12). pap. 11.99 *(978-0-312-53564-3(3),* 9780312535643) Square Fish.

—Everything on a Waffle. 2008. (ENG., Illus.). 176p. (J). (gr. 5-9). pap. 7.99 *(978-0-312-38004-5(6),* 9780312380045) Square Fish.

—Northward to the Moon. 2012. (ENG.). 256p. (J). (gr. 5-8). 7.99 *(978-0-307-92980-8(9),* Yearling) Random Hse. Children's Bks.

—The Trolls. 2008. (ENG.). 160p. (J). (gr. 4-7). pap. 7.99 *(978-0-312-38419-7(X),* 9780312384197) Square Fish.

House, Peggy. Prairie Anna. 2012. (J). *(978-1-60682-395-8(7))* BJU Pr.

Howard, Elizabeth Fitzgerald. Flower Girl Butterflies. Kromer, Christiane, illus. 2004. 32p. (J). 16.89 *(978-0-688-17810-9(3))* HarperCollins Pubs.

Howard, Ellen. The Log Cabin Wedding. Himler, Ronald, illus. 2006. (ENG.). 64p. (J). (gr. -1-3). 15.95 *(978-0-8234-1989-0(4))* Holiday Hse., Inc.

Howe, James. Also Known As Elvis. (Misfits Ser.). (ENG., Illus.). (J). (gr. 5-9). 2015. 304p. pap. 7.99 *(978-1-4424-4511-6(4))* 2014. 288p. 16.99 *(978-1-4424-4510-9(6),* Atheneum Bks. for Young Readers) Simon & Schuster Children's Publishing.

—Totally Joe. (Misfits Ser.). (ENG.). (J). 2007. 224p. (gr. 4-8). pap. 7.99 *(978-0-689-83958-0(8))* 2005. (Illus.). 208p. (gr. 5-9). 17.99 *(978-0-689-83957-3(X))* Simon & Schuster Children's Publishing. (Atheneum Bks. for Young Readers).

Howell, Julie. The Pepper Tree, How the Seeds Were Planted! LaGrange, Tiffany, illus. 2007. 28p. per. 12.95 *(978-1-934246-51-1(4))* Peppertree Pr., The.

Hubbard, Kirsten. Watch the Sky. 2015. (ENG.). 272p. (J). (gr. 3-7). 16.99 *(978-1-4847-0833-0(4))* Hyperion Bks. for Children.

Hudson, Tara. Arise. (Hereafter Trilogy Ser.: 2). (ENG.). (YA). (gr. 8). 2013. 432p. pap. 9.99 *(978-0-06-202680-4(1))* 2012. 416p. 17.99 *(978-0-06-202679-8(8))* HarperCollins Pubs. (HarperTeen).

—Elegy. 2013. (Hereafter Trilogy Ser.: 3). (ENG.). 400p. (YA). (gr. 8). 17.99 *(978-0-06-202681-1(X),* HarperTeen) HarperCollins Pubs.

—Hereafter. 2012. (Hereafter Trilogy Ser.: 1). (ENG.). 432p. (YA). (gr. 8). pap. 8.99 *(978-0-06-202678-1(X),* HarperTeen) HarperCollins Pubs.

Hugelmeyer, Michele. Alex King, Famous Fourth Grader. 2007. 78p. pap. 8.99 *(978-1-4303-0821-8(4))* Lulu Pr., Inc.

Hughes, Dean. As Wide As the River. 2005. 156p. (J). pap. *(978-1-59038-450-3(4))* Deseret Bk. Co.

—Facing the Enemy. 2005. (Illus.). 153p. (J). pap. *(978-1-59038-449-7(0))* Deseret Bk. Co.

—Missing in Action. 2010. (ENG.). 240p. (J). (gr. 5-9). 16.99 *(978-1-4169-1502-7(8),* Atheneum Bks. for Young Readers) Simon & Schuster Children's Publishing.

—Under the Same Stars. 2005. viii, 152p. (J). pap. *(978-1-59038-448-0(2))* Deseret Bk. Co.

Hughes, Mark Peter. A Crack in the Sky. 2011. (Greenhouse Chronicles Ser.). (ENG.). 416p. (J). (gr. 3-7). 9.99 *(978-0-385-73709-8(2),* Yearling) Random Hse. Children's Bks.

—I Am the Wallpaper. 2007. (Readers Circle Ser.). (ENG.). 256p. (YA). (gr. 7-11). pap. 8.99 *(978-0-440-42046-0(6),* Delacorte Bks. for Young Readers) Random Hse. Children's Bks.

Hughes, Shirley. An Evening at Alfie's. Hughes, Shirley, illus. 2009. (Alfie Ser.). (ENG., Illus.). 32p. (J). (gr. k-k). pap. 11.99 *(978-1-86230-786-5(5),* Red Fox) Random House Children's Books GBR. Dist: Independent Pubs. Group.

Hulme-Cross, Benjamin. The Gladiator's Victory. Rinaldi, Angelo, illus. 2015. (ENG.). 160p. (J). *(978-0-7787-1764-5(X))* Crabtree Publishing Co.

—The Knight's Enemies. Rinaldi, Angelo, illus. 2015. (ENG.). 160p. (J). *(978-0-7787-1765-2(8))* Crabtree Publishing Co.

—The Samurai's Assassin. Rinaldi, Angelo, illus. 2015. (ENG.). 160p. (J). *(978-0-7787-1766-9(6))* Crabtree Publishing Co.

—The Viking's Revenge. Rinaldi, Angelo, illus. 2015. (ENG.). 160p. (J). *(978-0-7787-1767-6(4))* Crabtree Publishing Co.

Hulslander, Dyan. God's Precious Gift. 2009. 24p. pap. 14.99 *(978-1-4389-6903-9(1))* AuthorHouse.

Hulst, W. G. van de & Hulst, Willem G. van de, illus. The Black Kitten. 2014. (J). *(978-1-928136-07-1(9))* Inheritance Pubns.

—The Secret in the Box. 2014. (J). *(978-1-928136-17-0(6))* Inheritance Pubns.

Huneck, Stephen. Sally at the Farm. 2014. (Sally Board Bks.). (ENG., Illus.). 20p. (J). (gr. -1 — 1). bds. 7.95 *(978-1-4197-1030-8(3),* Abrams Appleseed) Abrams, Inc.

Hunt, Irene. Up a Road Slowly. 2003. (gr. 3-6). lib. bdg. 16.00 *(978-0-613-58744-0(8),* Turtleback) Turtleback Bks.

Hunt, Lynda Mullaly. One for the Murphys. (ENG.). (J). (gr. 5). 2013. 256p. pap. 7.99 *(978-0-14-242652-4(0),* Puffin Books) 2012. 288p. 16.99 *(978-0-399-25615-8(6),* Nancy Paulsen Books) Penguin Young Readers Group.

Hunt, Tiffani "Paradise". Glamorous 5: In the City of Garden Valley. 2012. 24p. pap. 17.99 *(978-1-4772-7922-9(9))* AuthorHouse.

Hurst, Elva. Autumn Days: Based on a True Story. 2015. (Farm Life Ser.). (ENG., Illus.). 80p. (J). pap. 6.99 *(978-0-7369-6094-6(5))* Harvest Hse. Pubs.

—Summer on the Farm. 2014. (Farm Life Ser.). 80p. pap. 6.99 *(978-0-7369-6091-5(0))* Harvest Hse. Pubs.

—Summer on the Farm: A True Story. 2014. (Farm Life Ser.). (ENG., Illus.). 80p. (J). pap. 6.99 *(978-0-7369-6090-8(2))* Harvest Hse. Pubs.

Hurwitz, Johanna. E Is for Elisa. Tilley, Debbie, illus. 2003. (Riverside Kids Ser.). (ENG.). 96p. (J). (gr. 1-4). pap. 4.25 *(978-0-06-054374-7(4))* HarperCollins Pubs.

Hurwitz, Michele Weber. Calli Be Gold. 2012. (ENG.). 208p. (J). (gr. 3-7). 6.99 *(978-0-375-86528-2(4),* Yearling) Random Hse. Children's Bks.

—The Summer I Saved the World ... in 65 Days. 2015. (ENG.). 272p. (J). (gr. 5). pap. 9.99 *(978-0-385-37109-4(8),* Ember) Random Hse. Children's Bks.

Ibbotson, Eva. One Dog & His Boy. 2012. (ENG.). 288p. (J). (gr. 3-7). 16.99 *(978-0-545-35196-6(0),* Scholastic Pr.) Scholastic, Inc.

I'll Run Away: Individual Title Six-Packs. (gr. -1-2). 23.00 *(978-0-7635-8793-2(1))* Rigby Education.

Immel, Mary Blair. Giant Steps: Suffragettes & Soldiers. 2016. (J). pap. ***(978-0-87195-406-0(0))*** Indiana Historical Society.

Ing, Dean. It's up to Charlie Hardin. 2015. (Baen Ser.: 1). (ENG.). 256p. (YA). (gr. 5). 16.99 *(978-1-4767-8030-6(7))* Baen Bks.

Ingle, Sheila. Courageous Kate: A Daughter of the American Revolution. 2006. (ENG.). 130p. pap. 11.95 *(978-1-891885-52-5(9))* Hub City Pr.

Ingold, Jeanette. Mountain Solo. 2005. (ENG.). 320p. (YA). (gr. 7-12). pap. 15.95 *(978-0-15-205358-1(1))* Houghton Mifflin Harcourt Publishing Co.

—The Window. 2003. (ENG.). 208p. (YA). (gr. 7-12). pap. 13.95 *(978-0-15-204926-3(6))* Houghton Mifflin Harcourt Publishing Co.

Ioannides, Mara W. Cohen. A Shout in the Sunshine. 2007. (ENG.). 120p. (gr. 5). per. 14.95 *(978-0-8276-0838-2(1))* Jewish Pubn. Society.

Irwin, Gayle. Sage Learns to Share, 1 vol. Araujo, Katie, illus. 2009. 45p. pap. 24.95 *(978-1-60836-409-1(7))* America Star Bks.

Ishida, S. E. M. Nick Newton Is Not a Genius. 2016. (Illus.). 151p. (J). *(978-1-62856-235-4(8))* BJU Pr.

Jablonski, Carla. Thicker Than Water. 2007. (ENG.). 272p. (YA). (gr. 9-12). 8.99 *(978-1-59514-123-1(5),* Razorbill) Penguin Young Readers Group.

Jacobson, Darlene Beck. Wheels of Change. 2014. (ENG., Illus.). 180p. (J). (gr. 2-8). 12.95 *(978-1-939547-13-2(X))* Creston Bks.

Jacques, Karen. Monsters Have My Brother. Cahanes, Erin, illus. 2015. (ENG.). 16.95 *(978-1-59298-863-1(6))* Beaver's Pond Pr., Inc.

Jakubowski, Michele. The Grass Is Always Greener. (Ashley Small & Ashlee Tall Ser.). (ENG., Illus.). 64p. (gr. 1-3). 2017. pap. 4.95 *(978-1-5158-0016-3(4))* 2016. lib. bdg. 20.65 *(978-1-5158-0012-5(1))* Picture Window Bks.

James, Tina. Sarabeth Palmer: 1963-1964. 2010. 91p. (J). *(978-0-615-37484-0(0))* Afrolez Productions, LLC.

Jamieson, Victoria. All's Faire in Middle School, 9 vols. 2017. (ENG.). (J). pap. 116.91 ***(978-0-525-48668-8(2))***; (Illus.). 248p. (gr. 4-7). 20.99 ***(978-0-525-42998-2(0))***; (Illus.). 248p. (gr. 4-7). pap. 12.99 ***(978-0-525-42999-9(9))*** Penguin Young Readers Group. (Dial Bks).

—All's Faire in Middle School. 2017. lib. bdg. 24.50 ***(978-0-606-40484-6(8))*** Turtleback Bks.

Jarman, Benjamin. Tony's Last Touchdown. 2012. (Champion Sports Story Ser.). 104p. (J). (gr. 3-18). pap. 10.95 *(978-1-4644-0004-9(0))* Enslow Pubs., Inc.

Jeffers, Oliver. It Wasn't Me: A Hueys Book. Jeffers, Oliver, illus. 2014. (Hueys Ser.: 2). (ENG., Illus.). 32p. (J). (gr. -1-k). 17.99 *(978-0-399-25768-1(3),* Philomel Bks.) Penguin Young Readers Group.

Jenkins, Emily. Dangerous Pumpkins. Bliss, Harry, illus. 2012. (Invisible Inkling Ser.: 2). (ENG.). 160p. (J). (gr. 1-5). 14.99 *(978-0-06-180223-2(9))* HarperCollins Pubs.

—Five Creatures. Bogacki, Tomek, illus. 2005. (ENG.). 32p. (J). (gr. -1-1). reprint ed. per. 8.99 *(978-0-374-42328-5(8),* 9780374423285) Square Fish.

—The Whoopie Pie War. Bliss, Harry, illus. 2013. (Invisible Inkling Ser.: 3). (ENG.). 160p. (J). (gr. 1-5). 14.99 *(978-0-06-180226-3(3))* HarperCollins Pubs.

Jenkins, Jerry B. & Fabry, Chris. Double Fault. 2005. (Red Rock Mysteries Ser.: 7). (ENG.). 272p. (YA). pap. 6.99 *(978-1-4143-0146-4(4),* Tyndale Kids) Tyndale Hse. Pubs.

—Phantom Writer. 2005. (Red Rock Mysteries Ser.: 6). (ENG.). 256p. (YA). pap. 5.99 *(978-1-4143-0145-7(6),* Tyndale Kids) Tyndale Hse. Pubs.

—Stolen Secrets. 2005. (Red Rock Mysteries Ser.: 2). (ENG., Illus.). 224p. (YA). (gr. -1-7). pap. 6.99 *(978-1-4143-0141-9(3),* Tyndale Kids) Tyndale Hse. Pubs.

Jennings, Patrick. Guinea Dog. (Guinea Dog Ser.). (ENG.). 192p. (gr. 3-7). 2011. (J). 6.99 *(978-1-60684-153-2(X))* 2010. 15.99 *(978-1-60684-053-5(3))* Lerner Publishing Group. (Darby Creek).

—Guinea Dog 2. 2013. (Guinea Dog Ser.). (ENG.). 176p. (J). (gr. 3-7). 15.99 *(978-1-60684-452-6(0),* Darby Creek) Lerner Publishing Group.

—Hissy Fitz. Allen, Michael, illus. 2015. (ENG.). 128p. (J). (gr. 2-4). 14.99 *(978-1-5124-0137-0(4),* Carolrhoda Bks.) Lerner Publishing Group.

—My Homework Ate My Homework. 2013. (ENG.). 224p. (J). (gr. 4-7). 15.99 *(978-1-60684-286-7(2),* Carolrhoda Bks.) Lerner Publishing Group.

Jensen, Patricia. My House. 2004. (My First Reader Ser.). (ENG.). 32p. (J). (gr. k-1). pap. 3.95 *(978-0-516-24636-9(4),* Children's Pr.) Scholastic Library Publishing.

Jerry, Spinelli. Blue Ribbon Blues. 2014. (Stepping Stone Book Ser. Vol. 2 Ser.). (ENG.). 80p. (J). (gr. 7-12). 8.24 *(978-1-63245-269-6(3))* Lectorum Pubns., Inc.

—Loser. 2014. (ENG.). 224p. (J). (gr. 7-7). 11.24 *(978-1-63245-207-8(3))* Lectorum Pubns., Inc.

Jocelyn, Marthe. Would You. 2008. (ENG.). 176p. (YA). (gr. 4-7). 19.99 *(978-0-88776-816-3(4),* Tundra Bks.) Tundra Bks. CAN. Dist: Penguin Random Hse. LLC.

Johann David Wyss Staff. The Swiss Family Robinson. 2005. pap. *(978-1-905432-50-9(X))* Dodo Pr.

Johansson, J. R. Mania. 2015. (Night Walkers Ser.: 3). (ENG.). 408p. (YA). pap. 9.99 *(978-0-7387-4431-5(X),* Flux) North Star Editions.

Johnson, Angela. Daddy Calls Me Man. Mitchell, Rhonda, illus. 2014. 32p. pap. 7.00 *(978-1-61003-309-1(4))* Center for the Collaborative Classroom.

Johnson, J. J. Believarexic, 1 vol. 2017. (ENG.). 464p. (YA). (gr. 8-11). pap. 9.95 ***(978-1-68263-007-5(2))*** Peachtree Pubs.

Johnson, Kristel. Even When We Are Apart. 2008. 20p. pap. 24.95 *(978-1-60610-435-4(7))* America Star Bks.

Johnson, Maureen. The Last Little Blue Envelope. 2012. (13 Little Blue Envelopes Ser.: 2). (ENG.). 288p. (YA). (gr. 8). pap. 9.99 *(978-0-06-197681-0(4),* HarperTeen) HarperCollins Pubs.

—Scarlett Fever. (ENG.). 352p. (J). (gr. 7-7). 2011. pap. 9.99 *(978-0-545-09633-1(2))* 2010. 16.99 *(978-0-439-89928-4(1))* Scholastic, Inc.

Johnson, Mo. Noah's Garden: When Someone You Love Is in the Hospital. Josse, Annabelle, illus. 2010. (ENG.). 32p. (J). (gr. -1-2). 15.99 *(978-0-7636-4782-7(9))* Candlewick Pr.

Johnson, Peter. The Amazing Adventures of John Smith, Jr. Aka Houdini. 2012. (ENG.). 176p. (J). (gr. 3-7). 16.99 *(978-0-06-198890-5(1))* HarperCollins Pubs.

—The Amazing Adventures of John Smith, Jr. AKA Houdini. 2014. (ENG.). 192p. (J). (gr. 3-7). pap. 6.99 *(978-0-06-198891-2(X))* HarperCollins Pubs.

—The Life & Times of Benny Alvarez. 2014. (ENG.). 224p. (J). (gr. 3-7). 16.99 *(978-0-06-221596-3(5))* HarperCollins Pubs.

Johnston, Annie Fell. The Story of Dago. 2006. (Illus.). pap. *(978-1-4065-1127-7(7))* Dodo Pr.

Johnston, Annie Fellows. The Little Colonel's Hero. 2007. (ENG.). 164p. pap. 19.99 *(978-1-4264-8448-3(8))*; 182p. pap. 21.99 *(978-1-4264-8506-0(9))* Creative Media Partners, LLC.

Johnston, E. K. Prairie Fire. 2015. (J). 18.99 *(978-1-4677-6181-9(8))*; (ENG.). 304p. (gr. 6-12). 18.99 *(978-1-4677-3909-2(X))* Lerner Publishing Group.

—The Story of Owen: Dragon Slayer of Trondheim. 2014. 312p. (J). (gr. 6-12). 17.95 *(978-1-4677-1066-4(0),* Carolrhoda Lab™) Lerner Publishing Group.

Johnston, Teresa. Thanksgiving for Emily Ann. Newton, Vanessa Brantley, illus. 2014. (ENG.). 32p. (J). (gr. -1-k). 6.99 *(978-0-545-43413-3(0),* Cartwheel Bks.) Scholastic, Inc.

Johnston, Tony. Any Small Goodness: A Novel of the Barrio. Colón, Raúl, illus. 2005. (Reader's Workshop Ser.). (ENG.). 120p. (C). pap. 19.95 *(978-0-7362-2797-1(0))* CENGAGE Learning.

—Laugh-Out-Loud Baby. Gammell, Stephen, illus. 2012. (ENG.). 32p. (J). (gr. -1-3). 16.99 *(978-1-4424-1380-1(8),* Simon & Schuster Bks. For Young Readers) Simon & Schuster/Paula Wiseman Bks.

Jolin, Paula. In the Name of God. 2008. (ENG.). 224p. (YA). (gr. 9-12). pap. 18.99 *(978-0-312-38455-5(6),* 9780312384555) Square Fish.

Jones, Diana Wynne & Jones, Ursula. The Islands of Chaldea. 2015. 368p. (J). (gr. 3-7). pap. 9.99 *(978-0-06-229508-8(X),* Greenwillow Bks.) HarperCollins Pubs.

Jones, Jenny B. So Not Happening, 1 vol. 2009. (Charmed Life Ser.: 1). (ENG.). 336p. (YA). (gr. 7-18). pap. 12.99 *(978-1-59554-541-1(7))* Nelson, Thomas Inc.

Jones, Kimberly K. Sand Dollar Summer. 2008. (ENG., Illus.). 224p. (J). (gr. 4-8). pap. 5.99 *(978-1-4169-5834-5(7),* McElderry, Margaret K. Bks.) McElderry, Margaret K. Bks.

Jones, Molly. The Choosing Tree. 2006. 126p. pap. 19.95 *(978-1-4241-5076-2(0))* PublishAmerica, Inc.

Jones, Patrick. Always Faithful. 2015. (ENG.). 112p. (YA). (gr. 6-12). lib. bdg. 27.99 *(978-1-4677-8052-0(9))*; 7.99 *(978-1-4677-9014-7(1))* Lerner Publishing Group. (Darby Creek).

—Barrier. 2014. (Alternative Ser.). (ENG.). 104p. (YA). (gr. 6-12). lib. bdg. 27.93 *(978-1-4677-3899-6(9))* Lerner Publishing Group.

—Controlled. 2014. (Alternative Ser.). (ENG.). 112p. (YA). (gr. 6-12). pap. 7.95 *(978-1-4677-4483-6(2),* Darby Creek); lib. bdg. 27.93 *(978-1-4677-3902-3(2))* Lerner Publishing Group.

—Guarding Secrets. 2015. (Locked Out Ser.). (ENG.). 96p. (J). (gr. 6-12). lib. bdg. 27.99 *(978-1-4677-5801-7(9))* Lerner Publishing Group.

—Out of the Tunnel. 2014. (Red Zone Ser.: 1). (ENG.). 104p. (YA). (gr. 6-12). pap. 7.95 *(978-1-4677-4471-3(9),* Darby Creek); lib. bdg. 27.93 *(978-1-4677-2126-4(3))* Lerner Publishing Group.

—Target. 2014. (Alternative Ser.). (ENG.). 128p. (YA). (gr. 6-12). pap. 7.95 *(978-1-4677-4485-0(9),* Darby Creek); lib. bdg. 27.93 *(978-1-4677-3900-9(6))* Lerner Publishing Group.

Jones, Traci L. Silhouetted by the Blue. 2011. (ENG.). 208p. (J). (gr. 5-9). 16.99 *(978-0-374-36914-9(3),* 9780374369149, Farrar, Straus & Giroux (BYR)) Farrar, Straus & Giroux.

Jonsberg, Barry. The Categorical Universe of Candice Phee. 2014. (ENG.). 242p. (J). (gr. 5-8). 16.99 *(978-1-4521-3351-5(4))* Chronicle Bks. LLC.

Jordan, Rosa. The Goatnappers. 2007. (ENG.). 224p. (J). (gr. 3-7). 14.95 *(978-1-56145-400-6(1))* Peachtree Pubs.

—Lost Goat Lane, 1 vol. 2004. (ENG.). 192p. (J). (gr. 3-7). 14.95 *(978-1-56145-325-2(0))* Peachtree Pubs.

Joseph, Lynn. El Color de Mis Palabras. 2004. (SPA., Illus.). (YA). pap. 5.99 *(978-1-930332-75-1(0))* Lectorum Pubns., Inc.

Jougla, Frederic. Tricked on Halloween: Rina & Jax's Stories. Jougla, Karina, illus. l.t. ed. 2004. 36p. (J). bds. 14.99 *(978-0-9754287-0-2(5))* Imagery Pr.

Juby, Susan. Another Kind of Cowboy. 2007. 344p. (YA). lib. bdg. 6.99 *(978-0-06-076521-7(6),* HarperTeen) HarperCollins Pubs.

—Miss Smithers. 2004. (Illus.). 336p. (J). 15.99 *(978-0-06-051546-1(5),* HarperTeen) HarperCollins Pubs.

Juby, Susan & Wells, Rosemary. The Truth Commission. 2015. (ENG., Illus.). 320p. (YA). (gr. 9). bds. 18.99 *(978-0-451-46877-2(5),* Viking Books for Young Readers) Penguin Young Readers Group.

Jules, Jacqueline. Abuela's Special Letters. Smith, Kim, illus. 2017. (Sofia Martinez Ser.). (ENG.). 32p. (gr. k-2). lib. bdg. 21.32 *(978-1-5158-0728-5(2),* Sofia Martinez) Picture Window Bks.

—The Beach Trip. Smith, Kim, illus. 2016. (Sofia Martinez Ser.). (ENG.). 32p. (gr. k-2). lib. bdg. 21.32 *(978-1-4795-8719-3(2),* Sofia Martinez) Picture Window Bks.

—Lights Out. Smith, Kim, illus. 2016. (Sofia Martinez Ser.). (ENG.). 32p. (gr. k-2). lib. bdg. 21.32 *(978-1-4795-8718-6(4))* Picture Window Bks.

—The Marigold Mess. Smith, Kim, illus. 2015. (Sofia Martinez Ser.). (ENG.). 32p. (gr. k-2). lib. bdg. 21.32 *(978-1-4795-5776-9(5),* Sofia Martinez) Picture Window Bks.

—My Family Adventure. Smith, Kim, illus. 2015. (Sofia Martinez Ser.). (ENG.). 96p. (gr. k-2). pap. 4.95 *(978-1-4795-5790-5(0),* Sofia Martinez) Picture Window Bks.

—My Vida Loca. Smith, Kim, illus. 2016. (Sofia Martinez Ser.). (ENG.). 96p. (gr. k-2). pap. 4.95 *(978-1-4795-8720-9(6),* Sofia Martinez) Picture Window Bks.

—Shopping Trip Trouble Smith, Kim, illus. 2017. (Sofia Martinez Ser.). (ENG.). 32p. (gr. k-2). lib. bdg. 21.32 *(978-1-5158-0729-2(0),* Sofia Martinez) Picture Window Bks.

—Singing Superstar. Smith, Kim, illus. 2016. (Sofia Martinez Ser.). (ENG.). 32p. (gr. k-2). lib. bdg. 21.32 *(978-1-4795-8716-2(8),* Sofia Martinez) Picture Window Bks.

Julia, Alvarez. Before We Were Free. 2014. (ENG.). 192p. (YA). 11.24 *(978-1-63245-139-2(5))* Lectorum Pubns., Inc.

—How Tia Lola Came to Visit Stay. 2014. (Tia Lola Stories Ser.). (ENG.). 160p. (J). (gr. 3-7). 11.24 *(978-1-63245-289-4(8))* Lectorum Pubns., Inc.

Jung, Mike. Unidentified Suburban Object. 2016. (ENG.). 272p. (J). (gr. 3-7). 16.99 *(978-0-545-78226-5(0),* Levine, Arthur A. Bks.) Scholastic, Inc.

Justus, Barbara & Starbird, Caroline. The Day Papa Came Home Newman, Timothy, ed. Bennett, Brent, illus. 2004. 20p. (YA). *(978-0-9755996-0-0(7))* Heifer Project International.

Kade, Stacey. The Ghost & the Goth. 2011. (ENG.). 304p. (J). (gr. 7-17). pap. 8.99 *(978-1-4231-2487-0(1))* Hyperion Pr.

Kafka, Rebecca. Alef Is for Abba. Basaluzzo, Constanza, illus. 2014. (ENG.). 24p. (J). (gr. -1-1). 17.95 *(978-1-4677-2156-1(5),* Kar-Ben Publishing) Lerner Publishing Group.

Kalar, Bonnie. Clair at Home. Spreen, Kathe, illus. Date not set. 12p. (J). (gr. -1-2). pap. *(978-1-891619-44-1(6))* Corona Pr.

—A Good Day. Spreen, Kathe, illus. Date not set. 12p. (J). (gr. -1-2). pap. *(978-1-891619-41-0(1))* Corona Pr.

Kallander, Susan & Boomgaarden, Larry. Up in Smoke. 2010. (Illus.). 24p. pap. 11.50 *(978-1-60860-934-5(0),* Eloquent Bks.) Strategic Book Publishing & Rights Agency (SBPRA).

Kane, Sharon. Little Mommy. Kane, Sharon, illus. 2008. (Little Golden Book Ser.). (ENG., Illus.). 24p. (J). (gr. -1-2). 4.99 *(978-0-375-84820-9(7),* Golden Bks.) Random Hse. Children's Bks.

Kantor, Melissa. Better Than Perfect. 2015. (ENG.). 336p. (YA). (gr. 8). 17.99 *(978-0-06-227923-1(8),* HarperTeen) HarperCollins Pubs.

—Maybe One Day. 2014. (ENG.). 400p. (YA). (gr. 8). 17.99 *(978-0-06-227920-0(3),* HarperTeen) HarperCollins Pubs.

Kapai, Tommy. Cuzzies Find the Rainbow's End. Henry, Mike, illus. 2004. (Cuzzies Adventures Ser.). (MAO & ENG.). 32p. (J). (gr. -1-3). pap. 9.00 *(978-0-9582517-0-9(3),* Kina) Huia Pubs. NZL. Dist: Univ. of Hawaii Pr.

Kaplan, Michael B. Betty Bunny Didn't Do It. Jorisch, Stéphane, illus. 2013. (Betty Bunny Ser.). (ENG.). 32p. (J). (gr. -1-k). 16.99 *(978-0-8037-3858-4(7),* Dial Bks) Penguin Young Readers Group.

—Betty Bunny Loves Chocolate Cake. Jorisch, Stéphane, illus. 2011. (Betty Bunny Ser.). (ENG.). 36p. (J). (gr. -1-k). 17.99 *(978-0-8037-3407-4(7),* Dial Bks) Penguin Young Readers Group.

—Betty Bunny Wants a Goal. Jorisch, Stéphane, illus. 2014. (Betty Bunny Ser.). (ENG.). 32p. (J). (gr. -1-k). 16.99 *(978-0-8037-3859-1(5),* Dial Bks) Penguin Young Readers Group.

—Betty Bunny Wants Everything. Jorisch, Stéphane, illus. 2012. (Betty Bunny Ser.). (ENG.). 32p. (J). (gr. -1-k). 17.99 *(978-0-8037-3408-1(5),* Dial Bks) Penguin Young Readers Group.

Karwoski, Gail Langer. When Hurricane Katrina Hit Home. Marshall, Julia, illus. 2013. Orig. Title: When Hurricane Katrina Hit Home. (ENG.). 192p. (gr. 4-7). 15.99 *(978-1-62619-083-2(6),* History Pr., The) Arcadia Publishing.

Kats, Jewel. Miss Popular Steals the Show: Girls in Wheelchairs Rule! Stenton, Murray, illus. 2014. 37p. (J). pap. 14.95 *(978-1-61599-236-2(7))* Loving Healing Pr., Inc.

Katz, Karen. Best-Ever Big Brother. 2006. (ENG., Illus.). 14p. (J). (gr. -1-k). 6.99 *(978-0-448-43914-3(X),* Grosset & Dunlap) Penguin Young Readers Group.

—Best-Ever Big Sister. 2006. (ENG., Illus.). 14p. (J). (gr. -1-k). 6.99 *(978-0-448-43915-0(8),* Grosset & Dunlap) Penguin Young Readers Group.

Kay, Alan N. Crossroads at Gettysburg. 2005. (Young Heroes of History Ser.: 6). (Illus.). 166p. (J). (gr. 3-7). per. 7.95 *(978-1-57249-359-9(3),* White Mane Kids) White Mane Publishing Co., Inc.

Kaye, Deborah. Stubby the Frog: Three Journeys Beyond the Pond, 1 vol. 2010. 74p. pap. 19.95 *(978-1-4489-4087-5(7))* America Star Bks.

Kaye, Marilyn. Penelope. movie tie-in ed. 2007. (ENG.). 240p. (YA). (gr. 8-13). pap. 18.99 *(978-0-312-37559-1(X),* 9780312375591, St. Martin's Griffin) St. Martin's Pr.

Keating, Jess. How to Outrun a Crocodile When Your Shoes Are Untied. 2014. (My Life Is a Zoo Ser.: 1). (ENG.). 288p. (J). (gr. 4-7). pap. 7.99 *(978-1-4022-9755-7(6),* 9781402297557, Sourcebooks Jabberwocky) Sourcebooks, Inc.

—How to Outswim a Shark Without a Snorkel. 2015. (My Life Is a Zoo Ser.: 2). (ENG.). 304p. (J). (gr. 4-7). pap. 7.99 *(978-1-4022-9758-8(0),* 9781402297588, Sourcebooks Jabberwocky) Sourcebooks, Inc.

Keeble, Helen. Fang Girl. 2012. (ENG.). 352p. (YA). (gr. 8). pap. 9.99 *(978-0-06-208225-1(6),* HarperTeen) HarperCollins Pubs.

Keenan-Bolger, Andrew, et al. Jack & Louisa - Act 1. Webster, Kyle T., illus. 2015. (Jack & Louisa Ser.: 1). (ENG.). 240p. (J). (gr. 3-7). bds. 16.99 *(978-0-448-47839-5(0),* Grosset & Dunlap) Penguin Young Readers Group.

Kelley, Jane. The Girl Behind the Glass. 2012. (ENG.). 192p. (J). (gr. 4-7). pap. 6.99 *(978-0-375-86219-9(6),* Yearling) Random Hse. Children's Bks.

Kelly, David A. The Rookie Blue Jay. Meyers, Mark, illus. 2015. (Ballpark Mysteries Ser.: 10). (ENG.). 112p. (J). (gr. 1-4).

4.99 *(978-0-385-37875-8(0)*, Random Hse. Bks. for Young Readers) Random Hse. Children's Bks.
—The Tiger Troubles. Meyers, Mark, illus. 2015. (Ballpark Mysteries Ser.: 11). (ENG.). 112p. (J). (gr. 1-4). pap. 4.99 *(978-0-385-37878-9(5)*, Random Hse. Bks. for Young Readers) Random Hse. Children's Bks.
—The Wrigley Riddle. Meyers, Mark, illus. 2013. (Ballpark Mysteries Ser.: Bk. 6). (ENG.). 112p. (J). (gr. 1-4). pap. 4.99 *(978-0-307-97776-2(5)*, Random Hse. Bks. for Young Readers) Random Hse. Children's Bks.
Kelly, Erin Entrada. The Land of Forgotten Girls. 2017. 320p. (J). (gr. 3-7). pap. 6.99 *(978-0-06-223865-8(5)*, Greenwillow Bks.) HarperCollins Pubs.
Kelly, J. M. Speed of Life. 2016. (ENG.). 352p. (YA). (gr. 9). 17.99 *(978-0-544-74782-1(8)*, HMH Books For Young Readers) Houghton Mifflin Harcourt Publishing Co.
Kelly, Jacqueline. Counting Sheep: Calpurnia Tate, Girl Vet. White, Teagan & Meyer, Jennifer L., illus. 2017. (Calpurnia Tate, Girl Vet Ser.). (ENG.). 112p. (J). 15.99 *(978-1-62779-870-9(6)*, 9781627798709, Holt, Henry & Co. Bks. For Young Readers) Holt, Henry & Co.
—The Curious World of Calpurnia Tate. 2015. (Calpurnia Tate Ser.: 2). (ENG.). 320p. (J). (gr. 4-7). 16.99 *(978-0-8050-9744-3(9)*, 9780805097443, Holt, Henry & Co. Bks. For Young Readers) Holt, Henry & Co.
—The Curious World of Calpurnia Tate. 2017. (Calpurnia Tate Ser.: 2). (J). lib. bdg. 18.40 ***(978-0-606-39939-5(9))*** Turtleback Bks.
—La Evolución de Calpurnia Tate. 2010.Tr. of Evolution of Calpurnia Tate. (SPA.). 272p. (YA). pap. 20.95 *(978-84-9918-103-5(1))* Roca Editorial ESP. Dist: Spanish Pubs., LLC.
—La Evolucion de Calpurnia Tate, Vol. 2. 2011.Tr. of Evolution of Calpurnia Tate. (SPA.). 272p. pap. 12.95 *(978-84-92833-15-3(7))* Roca Editorial ESP. Dist: Spanish Pubs., LLC.
—The Evolution of Calpurnia Tate. 2009. (Calpurnia Tate Ser.: 1). (ENG.). 352p. (J). (gr. 4-7). 17.99 *(978-0-8050-8841-0(5)*, 9780805088410, Holt, Henry & Co. Bks. For Young Readers) Holt, Henry & Co.
—The Evolution of Calpurnia Tate. 2010. 340p. 18.00 *(978-1-60686-849-2(7))* Perfection Learning Corp.
—The Evolution of Calpurnia Tate. 2011. (Calpurnia Tate Ser.: 1). (ENG.). 368p. (J). (gr. 4-7). pap. 7.99 *(978-0-312-65930-1(X)*, 9780312659301) Square Fish.
—The Evolution of Calpurnia Tate. 2011. (Calpurnia Tate Ser.: 1). (J). lib. bdg. 18.40 *(978-0-606-20974-8(3)*, Turtleback) Turtleback Bks.
—Skunked! White, Teagan & Meyer, Jennifer L., illus. 2016. (Calpurnia Tate, Girl Vet Ser.). (ENG.). 112p. (J). 15.99 *(978-1-62779-868-6(4)*, 9781627798686, Holt, Henry & Co. Bks. For Young Readers) Holt, Henry & Co.
Kelly, Jacqueline. Who Gives a Hoot?: Calpurnia Tate, Girl Vet. Meyer, Jennifer L., illus. 2017. (Calpurnia Tate, Girl Vet Ser.). (ENG.). 112p. (J). 15.99 ***(978-1-62779-873-0(0)***, 9781627798730, Holt, Henry & Co. Bks. For Young Readers) Holt, Henry & Co.
Kelly, Katy. Here's the Thing about Me. Rex, Adam, illus. 2006. (Lucy Rose Ser.). (ENG.). 160p. (J). (gr. 3-7). reprint ed. per. 6.99 *(978-0-440-42026-2(1)*, Yearling) Random Hse. Children's Bks.
—Melonhead & the Undercover Operation. Johnson, Gillian, illus. 2012. (Melonhead Ser.). (ENG.). 256p. (J). (gr. 3-7). 7.99 *(978-0-375-84528-4(3)*, Yearling) Random Hse. Children's Bks.
Kemnitz, Dianna. Meet Jack & His New Friend. 2011. 36p. pap. 24.95 *(978-1-4560-8776-0(2))* America Star Bks.
Kendall, Grace, ed. I See Reality: Twelve Short Stories about Real Life. 2016. (ENG.). 304p. (YA). 17.99 *(978-0-374-30258-0(8)*, 9780374302580, Farrar, Straus & Giroux (BYR)) Farrar, Straus & Giroux.
Kennedy, Kim. Misty Gordon & the Mystery of the Ghost Pirates. 2010. (ENG., Illus.). 240p. (YA). (gr. 3-7). 15.95 *(978-0-8109-9357-0(0)*, Amulet Bks.) Abrams, Inc.
Kennedy, Marlane. The Dog Days of Charlotte Hayes. 2009. (ENG., Illus.). 240p. (J). (gr. 3-7). 15.99 *(978-0-06-145241-3(6)*, Greenwillow Bks.) HarperCollins Pubs.
Kennedy, Pamela. Moving Day for Sam: A Story about Change. Petrov, Anton, illus. 2007. 32p. (J). (gr. -1-3). 8.99 *(978-0-8249-5558-8(7)*, Ideal Pubns.) Worthy Publishing.
Kennemore, Tim. Alice's Shooting Star. 2009. 100p. (J). (gr. 2-6). 12.00 *(978-0-8028-5337-0(4)*, Eerdmans Bks For Young Readers) Eerdmans, William B. Publishing Co.
Kenney, Rebecca. The Silent. 2009. (YA). 8.99 *(978-1-60682-054-4(0)*, JourneyForth) BJU Pr.
Kent, Renee Holmes. Girl Talk, Vol. 7. 2004. (Adventures in Misty Falls Ser.: Vol. 7). (Illus.). 100p. (J). (gr. 4-7). pap. 4.99 *(978-1-56309-455-2(X)*, N017103) New Hope Pubs.
Kent, Rose. Kimchi & Calamari. 2010. (ENG.). 240p. (J). (gr. 3-7). pap. 6.99 *(978-0-06-083771-6(3))* HarperCollins Pubs.
Kephart, Beth. One Thing Stolen. 2015. (ENG.). 272p. (YA). (gr. 7-12). 17.99 *(978-1-4521-2831-3(6))* Chronicle Bks. LLC.
Keplinger, Kody. The DUFF: Designated Ugly Fat Friend. (ENG.). (YA). (gr. 10-17). 2011. 304p. pap., pap. 10.99 *(978-0-316-08424-6(7))* 2015. 320p. pap. 10.00 *(978-0-316-38180-2(2))* Little, Brown Bks. for Young Readers. (Poppy).
—The Swift Boys & Me. 2014. (ENG.). 272p. (J). (gr. 3-7). 16.99 *(978-0-545-56200-3(7)*, Scholastic Pr.) Scholastic, Inc.
Kerbel, Deborah. Girl on the Other Side. 2009. (ENG., Illus.). 152p. (YA). (gr. 6-18). pap. 10.99 *(978-1-55488-443-8(8)*, Dundurn Pr.) Dundurn CAN. Dist: Ingram Publisher Services.
Kerr, Judith. When Hitler Stole Pink Rabbit. (SPA.). 172p. (J). 11.95 *(978-84-204-3201-4(6))* Santillana USA Publishing Co., Inc.
—When Hitler Stole Pink Rabbit. 2009. (gr. 3-6). lib. bdg. 17.20 *(978-0-8085-9123-8(1)*, Turtleback) Turtleback Bks.
Kerr, M. E., pseud. Your Eyes in Stars. 2006. (YA). (gr. 7-12). (ENG.). 240p. 16.99 *(978-0-06-075682-6(9))*; 229p. lib. bdg. 17.89 *(978-0-06-075683-3(7))* HarperCollins Pubs.
Kerr, P. B., pseud. One Small Step. 2009. (ENG.). 320p. (J). (gr. 3-9). pap. 8.99 *(978-1-4169-4214-6(9)*, McElderry, Margaret K. Bks.) McElderry, Margaret K. Bks.
Kerz, Anna. The Gnome's Eye, 1 vol. 2010. (ENG.). 224p. (J). (gr. 4-7). pap. 9.95 *(978-1-55469-195-1(8))* Orca Bk. Pubs. USA.
Kessler, Liz. A Year Without Autumn. (ENG.). 304p. (J). (gr. 4-7). 2012. pap. 7.99 *(978-0-7636-6060-4(4))* 2011. (Illus.). 15.99 *(978-0-7636-5595-2(3))* Candlewick Pr.
Key, Janet Rhyme. Rosa in Bloom. 2013. 86p. (J). pap. 13.95 *(978-1-4817-1956-8(4))* AuthorHouse.
Kidd, Ronald. Year of the Bomb. 2009. 208p. 5.99 *(978-1-4169-9504-3(8))* Studio Fun International.
Kim, YeShil. We Are Proud of You. The Pope Twins, illus. rev. ed. 2014. (MySELF Bookshelf Ser.). (ENG.). 32p. (J). (gr. k-2). pap. 11.94 *(978-1-60357-651-2(7))*; lib. bdg. 25.27 *(978-1-59953-642-2(0))* Norwood Hse. Pr.
Kimmel, Elizabeth Cody. Lily B. on the Brink of Cool. 2005. 245p. (J). (gr. 5-9). 14.65 *(978-0-7569-5653-0(6))* Perfection Learning Corp.
Kimmel, Smith Robert. The War with Grandpa. 2014. (Yearling Ser.). (ENG.). 160p. (J). (gr. 3-7). 11.24 *(978-1-63245-333-4(9))* Lectorum Pubns., Inc.
Kimmelman, Leslie. Round the Turkey: A Grateful Thanksgiving. Cote, Nancy, illus. 2012. (J). 34.28 *(978-1-61913-130-9(7))* Weigl Pubs., Inc.
Kinde, Christa. The Hidden Deep, 1 vol. 2013. (Threshold Ser.). (ENG.). 272p. (J). 14.99 *(978-0-310-72489-6(9))* Zonderkidz.
King, A. S. Everybody Sees the Ants. 2011. (ENG.). 288p. (YA). (gr. 10-17). 18.00 *(978-0-316-12928-2(3))* Little Brown & Co.
—Everybody Sees the Ants. 2012. (ENG.). 320p. (YA). (gr. 10-17). pap. 10.00 *(978-0-316-12927-5(5))* Little, Brown Bks. for Young Readers.
—Still Life with Tornado. 2016. (ENG.). 304p. (YA). (gr. 9). 17.99 *(978-1-101-99488-7(6)*, Dutton Books for Young Readers) Penguin Young Readers Group.
King, Amy Sarig. Me & Marvin Gardens. 2017. (ENG.). 256p. (J). (gr. 3-7). 16.99 *(978-0-545-87074-0(7)*, Levine, Arthur A. Bks.) Scholastic, Inc.
Kinkade, Thomas. Katherine's Story. 2004. (Girls of Lighthouse Lane Ser.). 176p. (J). (gr. 5-18). 13.89 *(978-0-06-054342-6(6))* HarperCollins Pubs.
Kinkade, Thomas & Tamar, Erika. Rose's Story. 2004. (Girls of Lighthouse Lane Ser.: No. 2). (Illus.). 192p. (J). (gr. 5-18). 12.99 *(978-0-06-054344-0(2))* HarperCollins Pubs.
Kinney, Jeff. Cabin Fever. 2011. (Diary of a Wimpy Kid Ser.). (ENG., Illus.). 224p. (J). (gr. 3-7). 13.95 *(978-1-4197-0223-5(8)*, Amulet Bks.) Abrams, Inc.
—Cabin Fever. 2011. (Diary of a Wimpy Kid Ser.: 6). (J). 1.25 *(978-1-4640-4524-0(0))*; *(978-1-4640-2149-7(X))*; 44.75 *(978-1-4640-2151-0(1))*; 44.75 *(978-1-4640-2152-7(X))*; 46.75 *(978-1-4640-2148-0(1))* Recorded Bks., Inc.
—Cabin Fever. 2011. (Diary of a Wimpy Kid Ser.: 6). (J). lib. bdg. 25.70 *(978-0-606-23667-6(8)*, Turtleback) Turtleback Bks.
—The Last Straw. 2009. (Diary of a Wimpy Kid Ser.). (Illus.). (J). (gr. 3-7). (ENG.). 224p. 13.95 *(978-0-8109-7068-7(6)*, Amulet Bks.); 218p. pap. *(978-0-8109-7108-0(0))* Abrams, Inc.
—The Last Straw. 2009. (Diary of a Wimpy Kid Ser.: 3). (ENG.). 224p. (J). (gr. 4-6). pap. 17.95 *(978-1-4395-8262-6(9)*, 0008062297, Paw Prints) Baker & Taylor, CATS.
—The Last Straw. 2009. (Diary of a Wimpy Kid Ser.: Bk. 3). (JPN., Illus.). 221p. (J). *(978-4-591-10910-6(0))* Poplar Publishing.
—The Last Straw. 2010. (Diary of a Wimpy Kid Ser.: 3). (J). 1.25 *(978-1-4407-2984-3(0))* 2010. (Diary of a Wimpy Kid Ser.: 3). (J). 46.75 *(978-1-4407-2976-8(X))* 2009. (Diary of a Wimpy Kid Ser.: 3). (J). 75.75 *(978-1-4407-2986-7(7))* 2009. (Diary of a Wimpy Kid Ser.: 3). (J). 44.75 *(978-1-4407-2982-9(4))* 2009. (Diary of a Wimpy Kid Ser.: 3). (J). 45.75 *(978-1-4407-2980-5(8))* 2009. (Diary of a Wimpy Kid Ser.: 3). (J). 173.75 *(978-1-4407-2977-5(8))* 2009. (Diary of a Wimpy Kid Ser.: 3). (J). 44.75 *(978-1-4407-2978-2(6))* 2009. (Diary of a Wimpy Kid Ser.: Bk. 3). 1.00 *(978-1-4416-1788-0(4))* Recorded Bks., Inc.
—The Last Straw. 2009. (Diary of a Wimpy Kid Ser.: 3). (Illus.). 217p. (J). lib. bdg. 25.70 *(978-0-606-23664-5(3)*, Turtleback) Turtleback Bks.
—The Long Haul. Kinney, Jeff, illus. 2014. (Diary of a Wimpy Kid Ser.: Bk. 9). (ENG., Illus.). 224p. (J). (gr. 3-7). 13.95 *(978-1-4197-1189-3(X)*, Amulet Bks.) Abrams, Inc.
—The Long Haul. (CHI.). (J). 2015. 368p. (gr. 4-8). pap. *(978-986-6104-59-6(1))* 2014. *(978-986-6104-52-7(4))* DaskoviK, Izdatel'sko-torgovaja korporacija.
—The Long Haul. 2014. (JPN.). 221p. (J). *(978-4-591-14196-0(9))* Poplar Publishing.
—The Long Haul. 2013. (Diary of a Wimpy Kid Ser.: 9). (J). 43.75 *(978-1-4906-4058-7(4))*; 40.75 *(978-1-4906-4383-0(4))* Recorded Bks., Inc.
—The Long Haul. 2014. (Diary of a Wimpy Kid Ser.: 9). (J). lib. bdg. 25.70 *(978-0-606-36074-6(3))* Turtleback Bks.
—Old School. 2015. (Diary of a Wimpy Kid Ser.: Bk. 10). (ENG., Illus.). 224p. (J). (gr. 3-7). 13.95 *(978-1-4197-1701-7(4)*, Amulet Bks.) Abrams, Inc.
—Old School. 2015. (Diary of a Wimpy Kid Ser.: 10). (J). lib. bdg. 25.70 *(978-0-606-37422-4(1))* Turtleback Bks.
—The Third Wheel. 2012. (ENG.). (J). (gr. 3-7). pap. 8.49 *(978-1-4197-0729-2(9))* Abrams, Inc.
—The Ugly Truth. 2010. (Diary of a Wimpy Kid Ser.). (ENG.). 224p. (J). (gr. 3-7). 13.95 *(978-0-8109-8491-2(1)*, Amulet Bks.) Abrams, Inc.
—The Ugly Truth. 2010. (Diary of a Wimpy Kid Ser.: Bk. 5). (JPN., Illus.). 221p. (J). (gr. 4-7). *(978-4-591-12117-7(8))* Poplar Publishing.
—The Ugly Truth, 2 vols. 2010. (Diary of a Wimpy Kid Ser.: 5). (J). 44.75 *(978-1-4498-4534-6(7))*; 46.75 *(978-1-4498-4532-2(0))*; 173.75 *(978-1-4498-4530-8(4))*; 44.75 *(978-1-4498-4531-5(2))*; 1.25 *(978-1-4498-4535-3(5))* Recorded Bks., Inc.
—The Ugly Truth. 2010. (Diary of a Wimpy Kid Ser.: 5). (J). lib. bdg. 25.70 *(978-0-606-23666-9(X)*, Turtleback) Turtleback Bks.
Kirby, Jessi. Golden. (ENG.). 288p. (YA). (gr. 7). 2014. pap. 9.99 *(978-1-4424-5218-3(8))* 2013. 16.99 *(978-1-4424-5216-9(1))* Simon & Schuster Bks. For Young Readers. (Simon & Schuster Bks. For Young Readers).
Kirby, Susan E. A No-Fuss Christmas. 2010. (J). *(978-1-60682-059-9(1))* BJU Pr.
Kircher, Jean. Bertie Can't Fly. 2007. 24p. pap. 24.95 *(978-1-4241-8477-4(0))* America Star Bks.
Kirkle, Diane Luise. Rachel Serves a Stew. Batson, Susann, illus. 2009. 28p. pap. 10.95 *(978-1-935137-59-7(X))* Guardian Angel Publishing, Inc.
Kisseloff, Jeff & Wells, Rosemary. Ruby's Tea for Two. 2003. (Max & Ruby Ser.). (ENG.). 12p. (J). (gr. -1 — 1). bds. 6.99 *(978-0-670-03652-3(8)*, Viking Books for Young Readers) Penguin Young Readers Group.
Klassen, Kirsten L. Katelyn's Affection. 2004. (ENG.). 280p. pap. 11.99 *(978-0-8361-9281-0(8))* Herald Pr.
Klein, Abby. The One Hundredth Day of School! McKinley, John, illus. 2008. (Ready, Freddy! Ser.: Bk. 13). 94p. (J). (gr. -1-3). 11.65 *(978-0-7569-8836-4(5))* Perfection Learning Corp.
—Thanksgiving Turkey Trouble. McKinley, John, illus. 2008. (Ready, Freddy! Ser.: Bk. 15). 95p. (gr. -1-3). 16.00 *(978-0-7569-8838-8(1))* Perfection Learning Corp.
Kleinman, Estelle. Al Capone Does My Shirts. Friedland, Joyce & Kessler, Rikki, eds. 2007. (Al Capone on Alcatraz Ser.: Bk. 1). (Illus.). 38p. pap. 16.95 *(978-0-7675-3758-2(0))* Learning Links Inc.
Kletter, Kerry. The First Time She Drowned. 2016. (ENG.). 352p. (YA). (gr. 9). 17.99 *(978-0-399-17103-1(7)*, Philomel Bks.) Penguin Young Readers Group.
Klimo, Kate. Dragon Keepers #3: the Dragon in the Library. Shroades, John, illus. 2011. (Dragon Keepers Ser.). (ENG.). 240p. (J). (gr. 3-7). 6.99 *(978-0-375-85592-4(0)*, Yearling) Random Hse. Children's Bks.
—Dragon Keepers #4: the Dragon in the Volcano. Shroades, John, illus. 2012. (Dragon Keepers Ser.). (ENG.). 256p. (J). (gr. 3-7). 6.99 *(978-0-375-86688-3(4)*, Yearling) Random Hse. Children's Bks.
Klise, Kate. Homesick. 2014. (ENG.). 208p. (J). (gr. 5-9). pap. 7.99 *(978-1-250-06511-7(9)*, 9781250065117) Square Fish.
Knowles, Jo. Living with Jackie Chan. 2013. (ENG.). 384p. (YA). (gr. 9). 16.99 *(978-0-7636-6280-6(1))* Candlewick Pr.
—See You at Harry's. 2012. (ENG., Illus.). 310p. (J). (gr. 5). 16.99 *(978-0-7636-5407-8(8))* Candlewick Pr.
Knox, E. C. Don't Call Me Honey! Call Me Cherry Pie. Knox, E. C., illus. 2011. (Illus.). 38p. pap. 14.50 *(978-1-60976-192-9(8)*, Eloquent Bks.) Strategic Book Publishing & Rights Agency (SBPRA).
Knox, Elizabeth. Dreamquake. 2007. (Dreamhunter Duet Ser.: No. 2). 528p. *(978-0-7322-8194-6(6)*, Fourth Estate) HarperCollins Pubs. Australia.
—Dreamquake. 2009. (Dreamhunter Duet Ser.: 2). (ENG., Illus.). 464p. (YA). (gr. 7-12). pap. 12.99 *(978-0-312-58147-3(5)*, 9780312581473) Square Fish.
Knutson, Barbara. Love & Roast Chicken: A Trickster Tale from the Andes Mountains. 2005. (Libros Ilustrados (Picture Bks.)). (SPA., Illus.). 40p. (J). (gr. k-3). 16.95 *(978-0-8225-3190-6(9)*, Ediciones Lerner) Lerner Publishing Group.
Knutsson, Catherine. Shadows Cast by Stars. (ENG., Illus.). 464p. (YA). (gr. 7). 2013. pap. 11.99 *(978-1-4424-0192-1(3))* 2012. 17.99 *(978-1-4424-0191-4(5))* Simon & Schuster Children's Publishing. (Atheneum Bks. for Young Readers).
Koenig, Faydra. Two Homes for Daniel. 2013. 30p. pap. 10.95 *(978-0-9891471-1-8(8))* Alpine River Pr.
Kogler, Jennifer Anne. Ruby Tuesday. 2005. (ENG.). 320p. (J). (gr. 7-18). 15.99 *(978-0-06-073956-0(8))* HarperCollins Pubs.
Koller, Jackie French. Someday. 2010. 228p. pap. 14.95 *(978-1-4401-8675-2(8))* iUniverse, Inc.
Komaiko, Leah. Annie Bananie. Cornell, Laura, illus. 2003. (ENG.). 32p. (J). (gr. -1-3). pap. 6.99 *(978-0-06-051912-4(6))* HarperCollins Pubs.
Kongyin. Gooby & the Dreamwalker. 2011. 296p. pap. *(978-0-9869858-4-3(8))* Kima Global Pubs.
Konigsburg, E. L. About the B'nai Bagels. Konigsburg, E. L., illus. 2008. (ENG., Illus.). 208p. (J). (gr. 3-7). pap. 7.99 *(978-1-4169-5798-0(7)*, Atheneum Bks. for Young Readers) Simon & Schuster Children's Publishing.
—George. Konigsburg, E. L., illus. 2007. (ENG., Illus.). 192p. (J). (gr. 3-7). pap. 7.99 *(978-1-4169-4957-2(7)*, Atheneum Bks. for Young Readers) Simon & Schuster Children's Publishing.
—Journey to an 800 Number. 2008. (ENG.). 160p. (J). (gr. 4-8). pap. 6.99 *(978-1-4169-5875-8(4)*, Atheneum Bks. for Young Readers) Simon & Schuster Children's Publishing.
Konopka, Annie. The Tale of A Parkie Princess. 2008. 20p. 12.50 *(978-0-615-18598-9(3))* Konopka, Ann Marie.
Koss, Amy Goldman. Side Effects. 2006. 143p. (J). *(978-1-4287-0203-5(2))* Roaring Brook Pr.
—Side Effects. 2010. (ENG.). 160p. (YA). (gr. 4-7). pap. 8.99 *(978-0-312-60276-5(6)*, 9780312602765) Square Fish.
Kozlowsky, M. P. The Dyerville Tales. Thompson, Brian, illus. 2014. (ENG.). 336p. (J). (gr. 3-7). 16.99 *(978-0-06-199871-3(0)*, Walden Pond Pr.) HarperCollins Pubs.
Kramer, Paul M. Divorce Stinks. 2012. (ENG & ABK.). 32p. 15.95 *(978-0-9819745-4-5(6))* Aloha Wellness Pubs.
Kramer, Stacy & Thomas, Valerie. Karma Bites. 2010. (ENG.). 348p. (J). (gr. 5-7). pap. 18.99 *(978-0-547-36301-1(X))* Houghton Mifflin Harcourt Publishing Co.
Krasnesky, Thad. I Always, Always Get My Way. Parkins, David, illus. 2009. (ENG.). 32p. (J). (gr. k-2). 16.95 *(978-0-9799746-4-9(X))* Flashlight Pr.
Kraus, Daniel. Scowler. 2014. (ENG.). 304p. (YA). (gr. 9). pap. 9.99 *(978-0-385-74310-5(6)*, Ember) Random Hse. Children's Bks.
Krauss, Ruth. The Backward Day. Simont, Marc, illus. 2007. (ENG.). 40p. (J). (gr. -1-2). 14.95 *(978-1-59017-237-7(X)*, NYR Children's Collection) New York Review of Bks., Inc., The.
Krishnaswami, Uma. Chachaji's Cup. Sitaraman, Soumya, illus. 2013. (ENG.). 32p. (J). (gr. 1-18). 16.95 *(978-0-89239-178-3(2))* Lee & Low Bks., Inc.
Krosoczka, Jarrett J. Ollie the Purple Elephant. 2011. (ENG.). 40p. (J). (gr. -1-2). 16.99 *(978-0-375-86654-8(X)*, Knopf Bks. for Young Readers) Random Hse. Children's Bks.
Krossing, Karen. Take the Stairs, 1 vol. 2003. (ENG.). 184p. (YA). (gr. 8-12). pap. 9.95 *(978-1-896764-76-4(2))* Second Story Pr. CAN. Dist: Orca Bk. Pubs. USA.
Krupic, Janice. Felicia's Family Divorces. 2004. 72p. *(978-0-9745219-0-9(6))* Children Concept Publishing.
Kuhlman, Evan. Brother from a Box. Bruno, Iacopo, illus. (ENG.). 288p. (J). (gr. 4-7). 2013. pap. 6.99 *(978-1-4424-2659-7(4))* 2012. 16.99 *(978-1-4424-2658-0(6))* Simon & Schuster Children's Publishing. (Atheneum Bks. for Young Readers).
—The Last Invisible Boy. Coovert, J. P., illus. (ENG.). 240p. (J). (gr. 5-9). 2010. pap. 6.99 *(978-1-4169-6089-8(9))* 2008. 16.99 *(978-1-4169-5797-3(9))* Simon & Schuster Children's Publishing. (Atheneum Bks. for Young Readers).
Kuijer, Guus & Nieuwenhuizen, John. The Book of Everything. 2006. ix, 101p. (J). 16.99 *(978-0-439-74919-0(0)*, Levine, Arthur A. Bks.) Scholastic, Inc.
Kulka, Joe. The Rope, 1 vol. 2008. (ENG., Illus.). 32p. (J). (gr. k-3). 16.99 *(978-1-58980-487-6(2))* Pelican Publishing Co., Inc.
Kurkosky, Tina. Bunny Brothers. 2011. 24p. pap. 24.95 *(978-1-4626-3608-2(X))* America Star Bks.
Kurtz, Carmen. Veva. (SPA.). 128p. (J). (gr. 3-5). *(978-84-279-3120-6(4))* Noguer y Caralt Editores, S. A. ESP. Dist: Lectorum Pubns., Inc.
Kurtz, Jane. Lanie's Real Adventures. Papp, Robert, illus. 2010. (American Girl Today Ser.). (ENG.). 112p. (YA). (gr. 3-18). 12.95 *(978-1-59369-685-6(X))* American Girl Publishing, Inc.
Kyi, Tanya Lloyd. Truth. 2003. (YA). (gr. 7-18). pap. 7.95 *(978-1-55143-235-9(8))* Orca Bk. Pubs. USA.
Kyle, Sherry. Love, Lexi: Letters to God. 2016. (ENG.). 224p. (YA). pap. 12.99 *(978-1-4964-0963-8(9))* Tyndale Hse. Pubs.
Lachtman, Ofelia Dumas. The Trouble with Tessa. 2005. 122p. (J). (gr. 3-7). per. 9.95 *(978-1-55885-448-2(7)*, Piñata Books) Arte Publico Pr.
Lacont'e. Overcoming Obstacles. 2012. 28p. 19.95 *(978-1-4626-7076-5(8))* America Star Bks.
LaFevers, R. L. The Wyverns' Treasure. 2012. (Nathaniel Fludd, Beastologist Ser.: 3). lib. bdg. 16.00 *(978-0-606-24516-6(2)*, Turtleback) Turtleback Bks.
LaFleur, Suzanne. Eight Keys. 2012. (ENG.). 224p. (J). (gr. 4-7). 6.99 *(978-0-375-87213-6(2)*, Yearling) Random Hse. Children's Bks.
—Listening for Lucca. 2015. (ENG.). 240p. (J). (gr. 4-7). pap. 7.99 *(978-0-307-98030-4(8)*, Yearling) Random Hse. Children's Bks.
Lai, Thanhhà. Listen, Slowly. (J). (gr. 3-7). 2016. 288p. pap. 6.99 *(978-0-06-222919-9(2))* 2015. (ENG.). 272p. 16.99 *(978-0-06-222918-2(4))* 2015. (ENG.). 288p. E-Book *(978-0-06-222920-5(6))* HarperCollins Pubs.
Lainez, René Colato. From North to South/Del Norte Al Sur. Cepeda, Joe, illus. 2010.Tr. of Del norte al Sur. (ENG & SPA.). 32p. (J). (gr. k-3). 17.95 *(978-0-89239-231-5(2))* Lee & Low Bks., Inc.
Lamana, Julie T. Upside down in the Middle of Nowhere. (ENG.). (J). 2015. 328p. (gr. 4-7). pap. 7.99 *(978-1-4521-2880-1(4))* 2014. 320p. (gr. 3-7). 16.99 *(978-1-4521-2456-8(6))* Chronicle Bks. LLC.
Lamb, Steven. Eliot. 2007. 56p. per. 16.95 *(978-1-4241-9042-3(8))* America Star Bks.
Laminack, Lester L. Saturdays & Teacakes, 1 vol. Soentpiet, Chris K., illus. 2004. (ENG.). 32p. (J). (gr. k-3). 16.95 *(978-1-56145-303-0(X))* Peachtree Pubs.
Lancaster, Mike A. The Future We Left Behind. 2012. (ENG.). 384p. (J). (gr. 7). 16.99 *(978-1-60684-410-6(5)*, Carolrhoda Lab™) Lerner Publishing Group.
—Human. 4. 2012. (ENG.). 240p. (J). (gr. 7). pap. 8.99 *(978-1-60684-309-3(5)*, Carolrhoda Lab™) Lerner Publishing Group.
Lancett, Peter. Seeing Red, 1 vol. unabr. ed. 2012. (Cutting Edge Ser.). (ENG.). 221p. (YA). (gr. 9-12). pap. 9.95 *(978-1-61651-759-5(X))* Saddleback Educational Publishing, Inc.
Landau, Orna. Leopardpox! Sadie Is Having the Funniest Sick Day Ever! Hoffmann, Omer, illus. 2015. (ENG.). 40p. (J). (gr. -1-3). 16.99 *(978-0-544-29001-3(1))* Houghton Mifflin Harcourt Publishing Co.
Landry, Leo. Space Boy. Landry, Leo, illus. 2007. (ENG., Illus.). 32p. (J). (gr. -1-3). 16.99 *(978-0-618-60568-2(1))* Houghton Mifflin Harcourt Publishing Co.
Lane, Alison Hoffman. Uncle Arnel & the Awful, Angry Alligator. 2009. (Uncle Arnel Ser.). (Illus.). 32p. (J). 15.95 *(978-1-58980-645-0(X))* Pelican Publishing Co., Inc.
Lane, Bryan. Stepbrothers. 2010. 16p. 9.00 *(978-1-4520-1305-3(5))* AuthorHouse.
Lane, Dakota. Gothic Lolita: A Mystical Thriller. Lane, Dakota, illus. 2008. (ENG., Illus.). 208p. (YA). (gr. 7-18). 17.99 *(978-1-4169-1396-2(3)*, Atheneum Bks. for Young Readers) Simon & Schuster Children's Publishing.
—Orpheus Obsession. 2005. (Illus.). 288p. (J). lib. bdg. 17.89 *(978-0-06-074174-7(0)*, HarperTeen) HarperCollins Pubs.
—The Orpheus Obsession. 2008. (ENG., Illus.). 288p. (YA). (gr. 9). pap. 8.99 *(978-0-06-074175-4(9)*, HarperTeen) HarperCollins Pubs.
Langhorne Folan, Karyn & Langan, Paul. Breaking Point. 2011. (Bluford Ser.: 16). (J). (gr. k-12). pap. 4.95 *(978-1-59194-232-0(2))* Townsend Pr.
Lantigua, Lizette M. Mision Libertad. 2012. (ENG.). 192p. (YA). pap. 9.95 *(978-0-8198-4900-7(6))* Pauline Bks. & Media.
Lanton, Sandy. The Littlest Levine. Keay, Claire, illus. 2014. (Passover Ser.). (ENG.). 24p. (J). (gr. -1-2). 7.95 *(978-0-7613-9046-6(4))*; 17.95 *(978-0-7613-9045-9(6))* Lerner Publishing Group. (Kar-Ben Publishing).
Larson, Hope. Mercury. Larson, Hope, illus. 2010. (ENG., Illus.). 240p. (YA). (gr. 7-18). 19.99 *(978-1-4169-3585-8(1))*; pap. 15.99 *(978-1-4169-3588-9(6))* Simon & Schuster Children's Publishing. (Atheneum Bks. for Young Readers).
Larson, Kirby. Liberty. 2016. (Dogs of World War II Ser.). (ENG.). 240p. (J). (gr. 3-7). 16.99 *(978-0-545-84071-2(6)*, Scholastic Pr.) Scholastic, Inc.
Lascarso, Laura. Counting Backwards. (ENG., Illus.). 288p. (YA). (gr. 9). 2013. pap. 9.99 *(978-1-4424-0691-9(7))* 2012. 16.99 *(978-1-4424-0690-2(9)*, Atheneum Bks. for Young Readers) Simon & Schuster Children's Publishing.
Laskas, Gretchen Moran. The Miner's Daughter. 2007. (ENG.). 256p. (YA). (gr. 7-12). 17.99 *(978-1-4169-1262-0(2)*, Simon & Schuster Bks. For Young Readers) Simon & Schuster Bks. For Young Readers.

E
F
G

Laski, Deirdre. Hidden in the Next Step. 2008. 224p. 25.95 *(978-0-595-50565-4(1))*; pap. 15.95 *(978-0-595-50807-5(3))* iUniverse, Inc.

Lasky, Kathryn. Ashes. 2010. (ENG.). 320p. (J). (gr. 5-18). 16.99 *(978-0-670-01157-5(6)*, Viking Books for Young Readers) Penguin Young Readers Group.

—Christmas after All. 2012. (Dear America Ser.). (ENG.). 192p. (J). (gr. 3-7). 12.99 *(978-0-545-38177-2(0))* Scholastic, Inc.

—Spiders on the Case. Gilpin, Stephen, illus. (Deadlies Ser.). (ENG.). 176p. (J). (gr. 2-5). 2012. pap. 5.99 *(978-0-545-11731-9(3))*Bk. 2. 2011. 15.99 *(978-0-545-11682-4(1))* Scholastic, Inc. (Scholastic Pr.).

The Last Wild Run. 2006. (J). per. 14.95 *(978-1-933791-05-0(5))* Finial Publishing.

Lat. Kampung Boy. Lat, illus. rev. ed. 2006. Orig. Title: The Kampung Boy. (ENG., Illus.). 144p. (YA). (gr. 7-8). pap. 19.99 *(978-1-59643-121-8(0)*, 9781596431218, First Second Bks.) Roaring Brook Pr.

Latham, Irene. Don't Feed the Boy. Graegin, Stephanie, illus. 2012. (ENG.). 288p. (J). (gr. 3-7). 17.99 *(978-1-59643-755-5(3)*, 9781596437555) Roaring Brook Pr.

—Don't Feed the Boy. Graegin, Stephanie, illus. 2014. (ENG.). 304p. (J). (gr. 3-7). pap. 9.99 *(978-1-250-04428-0(6)*, 9781250044280) Square Fish.

Latimer, Miriam. Shrinking Sam. Latimer, Miriam, illus. 2007. (ENG., Illus.). 32p. (J). (gr. -1-3). 16.99 *(978-1-84686-038-6(5))* Barefoot Bks., Inc.

Laughlin, Florence. The Little Leftover Witch. 2013. (ENG.). 96p. (J). (gr. 3-7). 15.99 *(978-1-4424-8677-5(5))*; pap. 5.99 *(978-1-4424-8672-0(4))* Simon & Schuster Bks. For Young Readers. (Simon & Schuster Bks. For Young Readers).

Laure, Estelle. These Mighty Forces. 2017. (ENG.). 320p. (YA). (gr. 9). 17.99 *(978-0-544-53126-0(4)*, HMH Books For Young Readers) Houghton Mifflin Harcourt Publishing Co.

Lauter, Richard, illus. Little Women. (Young Collector's Illustrated Classics Ser.). 192p. (J). 9.95 *(978-1-56156-371-5(4))* Kidsbooks, LLC.

Lawson-Goins, Helen. Surprise in the Garden. 2012. 40p. pap. 21.99 *(978-1-4771-1258-8(8))* Xlibris Corp.

Lawson, Jessica. The Actual & Truthful Adventures of Becky Thatcher. Bruno, Iacopo, illus. 2014. (ENG.). 224p. (J). (gr. 3-7). 16.99 *(978-1-4814-0150-0(5)*, Simon & Schuster Bks. For Young Readers) Simon & Schuster Bks. For Young Readers.

Leavitt, Lindsey. The Chapel Wars. 2014. (ENG.). 304p. (YA). (gr. 7). 17.99 *(978-1-59990-788-8(7)*, 9781599907888, Bloomsbury USA Childrens) Bloomsbury Publishing USA.

—Going Vintage. 2013. (ENG.). 320p. (YA). (gr. 7-12). 16.99 *(978-1-59990-787-1(9)*, 9781599907871, Bloomsbury USA Childrens) Bloomsbury Publishing USA.

—Sean Griswold's Head. (ENG.). (YA). (gr. 7-12). 2012. 304p. pap. 9.99 *(978-1-59990-911-0(1)*, 9781599909110) 2011. 288p. 16.99 *(978-1-59990-498-6(5)*, 9781599904986) Bloomsbury Publishing USA. (Bloomsbury USA Childrens).

Lee, Ingrid. Cat Found. 2013. (ENG.). 176p. (J). (gr. 3-7). pap. 6.99 *(978-0-545-35108-9(1)*, Chicken Hse., The) Scholastic, Inc.

Lee, Jenny. Elvis & the Underdogs. Light, Kelly, illus. 2013. (Elvis & the Underdogs Ser.: 1). (ENG.). 304p. (J). (gr. 3-7). 16.99 *(978-0-06-223554-1(0))* HarperCollins Pubs.

Lee, Margaret A. Grandpa, What Are Lasers? 2012. 32p. pap. 19.99 *(978-1-4685-6343-6(2))* AuthorHouse.

Lee, Mary Ellen. Danny & Life on Bluff Point: Blizzard of '95 revised Edition. 2009. 160p. (gr. 4-7). pap. 12.95 *(978-0-595-53308-4(6))* iUniverse, Inc.

Lee Wardlaw. Seventh-Grade Weirdo. 2010. 160p. pap. 11.95 *(978-1-4401-8263-1(9))* iUniverse, Inc.

Leeuwen, Joke Van & Leeuwen, Joke van. Eep! Leeuwen, Joke van, illus. 2012. (Gecko Press Titles Ser.). (ENG., Illus.). 152p. (J). (gr. 2-5). pap. 7.95 *(978-1-877579-07-3(6))* Gecko Pr. NZL. Dist: Lerner Publishing Group.

LeFlore, Lyah B. The World Is Mine. Warfield, D. L., illus. 2009. (Come Up Ser.). (ENG.). 304p. (YA). (gr. 9-18). pap. 8.99 *(978-1-4169-7963-0(8)*, Simon Pulse) Simon Pulse.

Legrand, Claire. The Year of Shadows. Kwasny, Karl, illus. 2013. (ENG.). 416p. (J). (gr. 3-7). 16.99 *(978-1-4424-4294-8(8)*, Simon & Schuster Bks. For Young Readers) Simon & Schuster Bks. For Young Readers.

Lemna, Don. Out in Left Field. Collins, Matt, illus. 2013. (ENG.). 217p. (J). pap. 7.99 *(978-0-8234-2766-6(8))* Holiday Hse., Inc.

—When the Sergeant Came Marching Home. 2008. (ENG., Illus.). 208p. (J). (gr. 3-7). 17.95 *(978-0-8234-2083-4(3))* Holiday Hse., Inc.

Lendler, Ian & Bloch, Serge. Saturday. 2016. (ENG., Illus.). 40p. (J). 16.99 *(978-1-59643-965-8(3)*, 9781596439658) Roaring Brook Pr.

L'Engle, Madeleine. Camilla. 2009. (ENG.). 272p. (YA). (gr. 7-12). pap. 18.99 *(978-0-312-56132-1(6)*, 9780312561321) Square Fish.

—Meet the Austins. 2008. (Austin Family Ser.: 1). (ENG., Illus.). 240p. (J). (gr. 6-12). pap. 8.99 *(978-0-312-37931-5(5)*, 9780312379315) Square Fish.

—The Moon by Night, Bk. 2. 2008. (Austin Family Ser.: 2). (ENG.). 288p. (J). (gr. 6-12). pap. 9.99 *(978-0-312-37932-2(3)*, 9780312379322) Square Fish.

—The Young Unicorns. 2008. (Austin Family Ser.: 3). (ENG.). 304p. (J). (gr. 7-12). pap. 11.99 *(978-0-312-37933-9(1)*, 9780312379339) Square Fish.

Lennon, Maria T. Confessions of a So-Called Middle Child. (ENG.). (J). (gr. 3-7). 2014. 304p. pap. 6.99 *(978-0-06-212691-7(1))* 2013. 288p. 16.99 *(978-0-06-212690-0(3))* HarperCollins Pubs.

Leonard, Julia Platt. Cold Case. 2012. (ENG.). 288p. (J). (gr. 3-7). pap. 5.99 *(978-1-4424-2010-6(3)*, Simon & Schuster/Paula Wiseman Bks.) Simon & Schuster/Paula Wiseman Bks.

—Cold Case. Mauro, Tony, illus. 2011. (ENG.). 288p. (J). (gr. 3-7). 15.99 *(978-1-4424-2009-0(X)*, Simon & Schuster/Paula Wiseman Bks.) Simon & Schuster/Paula Wiseman Bks.

Leopold-Strauss, Linda. A Different Kind of Passover. Tugeau, Jeremy, illus. 2017. (ENG.). 32p. (gr. -1-3). 17.99 *(978-1-5124-0097-7(1)*, Kar-Ben Publishing) Lerner Publishing Group.

Leppard, Lois Gladys. The Mandie Collection. (ENG.). (J). (gr. 3-8). 2011. 368p. pap. 12.99 *(978-0-7642-0932-1(9))* 2011. 384p. pap. 13.00 *(978-0-7642-0878-2(0))* 2011. 368p. pap. 12.99 *(978-0-7642-0877-5(2))* 2011. 368p. pap. 10.99 *(978-0-7642-0689-4(3))* Vol. 1. 2007. 544p. pap. 15.99 *(978-0-7642-0446-3(7))* Vol. 2. 2008. (Illus.). 576p. pap. 15.99 *(978-0-7642-0538-5(2))* Bethany Hse. Pubs.

—Mandie Collection, Vol. 3. 2008. (ENG.). 608p. (J). pap. 15.99 *(978-0-7642-0593-4(5))* Bethany Hse. Pubs.

Leslie, Emma. For Merrie England: A Tale of the Weavers of Norfolk. Taylor, R., illus. 2010. 168p. 20.95 *(978-1-934671-38-2(X))*; pap. 10.95 *(978-1-934671-39-9(8))* Salem Ridge Press LLC.

Leveen, Tom. Party. 2011. (ENG.). 240p. (YA). (gr. 9). pap. 8.99 *(978-0-375-86392-9(3)*, Ember) Random Hse. Children's Bks.

—Random. 2014. (ENG., Illus.). 224p. (YA). (gr. 9). 17.99 *(978-1-4424-9956-0(7)*, Simon Pulse) Simon Pulse.

Levine, Caroline. David's Secret Soccer Goals. 2004. (ENG.). 40p. (J). pap. 13.95 *(978-1-84310-772-9(4)*, 3659) Kingsley, Jessica Pubs. GBR. Dist: Macmillan Distribution Ltd.

Levine, Ellen. In Trouble. 2011. (Carolrhoda YA Ser.). (ENG.). 208p. (YA). (gr. 9-12). 17.95 *(978-0-7613-6558-7(3)*, Carolrhoda Lab™) Lerner Publishing Group.

Levine, Karen R. Daddy's Picture. Stasuyk, Max, illus. 2013. 24p. pap. 14.95 *(978-1-57258-794-6(6)*, Aspect Bk.) TEACH Services, Inc.

Levine, Kristin. The Best Bad Luck I Ever Had. 2010. (ENG.). 272p. (J). (gr. 5-18). 7.99 *(978-0-14-241648-8(7)*, Puffin Books) Penguin Young Readers Group.

—The Lions of Little Rock. 2012. (ENG.). 304p. (J). (gr. 5-18). 16.99 *(978-0-399-25644-8(X)*, G.P. Putnam's Sons Books for Young Readers) Penguin Young Readers Group.

Levine, Phyllis. Matilda's Way. 2007. (ENG.). 188p. per. 12.95 *(978-1-60047-073-8(4))* Wasteland Pr.

Levine, Rhoda. He Was There from the Day We Moved In. Gorey, Edward, illus. 2012. (ENG.). 32p. (J). (gr. -1-2). 14.95 *(978-1-59017-515-6(8)*, NYR Children's Collection) New York Review of Bks., Inc., The.

Levinson, Lara. Zachary's Dinnertime, 1 vol. Van Wright, Cornelius, illus. 2012. (ENG.). 32p. (J). 16.95 *(978-1-59572-329-1(3))*; pap. 6.95 *(978-1-59572-330-7(7))* Star Bright Bks., Inc.

Levitin, Sonia. Junk Man's Daughter. Porfirio, Guy, illus. rev. ed. 2007. (Tales of Young Americans Ser.). (ENG.). 32p. (J). (gr. 3-7). 17.95 *(978-1-58536-315-5(4))* Sleeping Bear Pr.

Levy, Barry. How the Rules Were Made. 2005. 31p. (J). 7.99 *(978-1-4116-3482-4(9))* Lulu Pr., Inc.

Levy, Dana Alison. The Family Fletcher Takes Rock Island. (ENG.). 272p. (J). (gr. 4-7). 2017. 6.99 ***(978-0-553-52133-7(0)**, Yearling)* 2016. 16.99 *(978-0-553-52130-6(6)*, Delacorte Bks. for Young Readers) Random Hse. Children's Bks.

—This Would Make a Good Story Someday. 2017. (ENG.). 320p. (J). (gr. 4-7). 16.99 ***(978-1-101-93817-1(X))***; lib. bdg. 19.99 ***(978-1-101-93818-8(8))*** Random Hse. Children's Bks. (Delacorte Bks. for Young Readers).

Levy, Marilyn. Checkpoints. 2009. (ENG.). 256p. (gr. 7). pap. 14.95 *(978-0-8276-0870-2(5))* Jewish Pubn. Society.

Lewin, Terry. God Remembered Us. Gumm, Susan Kathleen, illus. 2006. 36p. (J). per. 19.00 *(978-0-9771482-1-9(1)*, Ithaca Pr.) Authors & Artists Publishers of New York, Inc.

Lewis-Brown, Alscess. Mosquito Get in Trouble Too. Hatfield, Cynthia, illus. 2009. (J). *(978-1-934370-09-4(6))* Editorial Campana.

Lidh, Jessica. The Number 7. 2014. 272p. pap. 17.99 *(978-1-4405-8307-0(2))* Adams Media Corp.

Lieb, Josh. I Am a Genius of Unspeakable Evil & I Want to Be Your Class President. 2010. (ENG.). 304p. (J). (gr. 5-7). 8.99 *(978-1-59514-354-9(8)*, Razorbill) Penguin Young Readers Group.

Lin, Grace. Dim Sum for Everyone! Lin, Grace, illus. 2003. (ENG., Illus.). 32p. (J). (gr. -1-2). 7.99 *(978-0-440-41770-5(8)*, Dragonfly Bks.) Random Hse. Children's Bks.

—Dumpling Days. 2012. (Pacy Lin Novel Ser.). (ENG.). 272p. (J). (gr. 3-7). 15.99 *(978-0-316-12590-1(3))* Little Brown & Co.

—Dumpling Days. 2013. (Pacy Lin Novel Ser.). (ENG.). 272p. (J). (gr. 3-7). pap. 7.99 *(978-0-316-12589-5(X))* Little, Brown Bks. for Young Readers.

—The Year of the Dog. 2007. (Pacy Lin Novel Ser.). (ENG., Illus.). 160p. (J). (gr. 3-7). per. 6.99 *(978-0-316-06002-8(X))* Little, Brown Bks. for Young Readers.

—The Year of the Dog. 2007. (Illus.). 134p. (gr. 3-7). 16.00 *(978-0-7569-8143-3(3))* Perfection Learning Corp.

Lindelauf, Benny. Nine Open Arms. 2014. (ENG., Illus.). 264p. (J). (gr. 3). 16.95 *(978-1-59270-146-9(9))* Enchanted Lion Bks., LLC.

Lindgren, Astrid. Seacrow Island. Ramsden, Evelyn, tr. from SWE. 2015. (ENG.). 256p. (J). (gr. 3-7). 17.95 *(978-1-59017-868-3(8)*, NYR Children's Collection) New York Review of Bks., Inc., The.

Lindo, Elvira. Manolito Four-Eyes, 0 vols. Emilio, Urberuaga & Urberuaga, Emilio, illus. 2010. (Manolito Four-Eyes Ser.: 1). (ENG.). 155p. (J). (gr. 3-7). pap. 9.99 *(978-0-7614-5729-9(1)*, 9780761457299, Amazon Children's Publishing) Amazon Publishing.

—Manolito Gafotas, 0 vols. Urberuaga, Emilio, illus. 2010. (SPA & ENG.). 192p. (J). (gr. 3-7). pap. 9.99 *(978-0-7614-5730-5(5)*, 9780761457305, Amazon Children's Publishing) Amazon Publishing.

Lindon, David A. The Lost Children of the Namuh & the Chamber of Souls - the First of a Trilogy. 2008. 376p. pap. *(978-1-906210-88-5(8))* Grosvenor Hse. Publishing Ltd.

Lindsey, Kathleen D. Sweet Potato Pie. Riley-Webb, Charlotte, illus. 2003. (J). 16.95 *(978-1-58430-061-8(2))* Lee & Low Bks., Inc.

Linker, Julie. Disenchanted Princess. 2007. (ENG.). 240p. (YA). (gr. 9-18). pap. 11.99 *(978-1-4169-3472-1(3)*, Simon Pulse) Simon Pulse.

Liparulo, Robert. House of Dark Shadows, 1 vol. 2009. (Dreamhouse Kings Ser.: 1). (ENG.). 304p. pap. 9.99 *(978-1-59554-727-9(4))* Nelson, Thomas Inc.

—Watcher in the Woods, 1 vol. 2009. (Dreamhouse Kings Ser.: 2). (ENG.). 304p. pap. 9.99 *(978-1-59554-728-6(2))* Nelson, Thomas Inc.

Lipsyte, Robert. Center Field. 2010. (ENG.). 288p. (YA). (gr. 8-18). 17.99 *(978-0-06-055704-1(4)*, HarperTeen) HarperCollins Pubs.

—Yellow Flag. 2009. (ENG.). 256p. (YA). (gr. 8). pap. 9.99 *(978-0-06-055709-6(5)*, Tegen, Katherine Bks) HarperCollins Pubs.

Littke, Lael. Searching for Selene. 2003. 203p. (J). pap. 13.95 *(978-1-59038-179-3(3))* Deseret Bk. Co.

Little, Kimberley Griffiths. The Healing Spell. 2010. (ENG.). 368p. (J). (gr. 3-7). 17.99 *(978-0-545-16559-4(8)*, Scholastic Pr.) Scholastic, Inc.

Littman, Sarah Darer. Backlash. 2015. (ENG.). 336p. (J). (gr. 7). 17.99 *(978-0-545-65126-4(3)*, Scholastic Pr.) Scholastic, Inc.

—Confessions of a Closet Catholic. 2006. (ENG.). 208p. (J). (gr. 5-18). reprint ed. 7.99 *(978-0-14-240597-0(3)*, Puffin Books) Penguin Young Readers Group.

—In Case You Missed It. 2016. (ENG.). 320p. (YA). (gr. 7). 17.99 *(978-0-545-90437-7(4)*, Scholastic Pr.) Scholastic, Inc.

—Want to Go Private? (ENG.). 336p. (J). 2013. (gr. 7). pap. 10.99 *(978-0-545-15147-4(3))* 2011. (gr. 9-9). 17.99 *(978-0-545-15146-7(5)*, Scholastic Pr.) Scholastic, Inc.

Litwin, Eric. The Nuts: Bedtime at the Nut House. Magoon, Scott, illus. 2014. (ENG.). 32p. (J). (gr. -1-3). 18.00 *(978-0-316-32244-7(X))* Little, Brown Bks. for Young Readers.

—The Nuts: Sing & Dance in Your Polka Dot Pants. Magoon, Scott, illus. 2015. (ENG.). 32p. (J). (gr. -1-3). 18.00 *(978-0-316-32250-8(4))* Little Brown & Co.

Livshits, Larisa. Seven Little Brothers. Wilson, Phil, illus. 2012. 40p. pap. *(978-1-77097-322-0(2))* FriesenPress.

Llama, Gram. The Bunny Fuzz Mystery. 2007. 32p. per. 24.95 *(978-1-4241-8371-5(5))* America Star Bks.

Lloyd-Jones, Sally. The Ultimate Guide to Grandmas & Grandpas! Emberley, Michael, illus. 2008. (ENG.). 32p. (J). (gr. -1-3). 14.99 *(978-0-06-075687-1(X))* HarperCollins Pubs.

Lloyd-Jones, Sally & Dyer, Jane. The House That's Your Home. 2015. (ENG., Illus.). 40p. (J). (gr. -1-2). 17.99 *(978-0-375-85884-0(9)*, Schwartz & Wade Bks.) Random Hse. Children's Bks.

Lloyd, Natalie. A Snicker of Magic. (ENG.). 320p. (J). (gr. 3-7). 2015. pap. 6.99 *(978-0-545-55273-8(7))* 2014. 16.99 *(978-0-545-55270-7(2))* Scholastic, Inc. (Scholastic Pr.).

—A Snicker of Magic. 2015. lib. bdg. 17.20 *(978-0-606-37089-9(7))* Turtleback Bks.

Lloyd, Natalie, et al. A Snicker of Magic. 2014. (ENG.). mass mkt. *(978-0-545-68447-7(1))* Scholastic, Inc.

Lloyd, Saci. The Carbon Diaries 2015. 2008. (ENG., Illus.). 384p. (YA). pap. *(978-0-340-97015-7(4)*, Hodder Children's Books) Hachette Children's Group.

—The Carbon Diaries 2015. 2009. (ENG.). 384p. (YA). (gr. 9-18). 17.95 *(978-0-8234-2190-9(2))* Holiday Hse., Inc.

Lo, Ginnie & Lo, Beth. Auntie Yang's Great Soybean Picnic. 2012. (ENG., Illus.). 32p. (J). 18.95 *(978-1-60060-442-3(0))* Lee & Low Bks., Inc.

Loftin, Nikki. Nightingale's Nest. 2015. (ENG.). 272p. (J). (gr. 3-7). pap. 8.99 *(978-1-59514-623-6(7)*, Razorbill) Penguin Young Readers Group.

—Wish Girl. 2015. (ENG.). 256p. (J). (gr. 3-7). 16.99 *(978-1-59514-686-1(5)*, Razorbill) Penguin Young Readers Group.

Loiodice, Lisa M. Through His Eyes. 2009. 32p. pap. 16.99 *(978-1-4389-5132-4(9))* AuthorHouse.

Lois, Lowry. Anastasia Esta al Mando. 2003. (Anastasia Krupnik Ser.).Tr. of Anastasia on Her Own. (SPA.). 168p. (J). *(978-84-239-7095-7(7))* Espasa Calpe, S.A.

—Anastasia on Her Own. de Groat, Diane, illus. 2016. (Anastasia Krupnik Story Ser.). (ENG.). 176p. (J). (gr. 5-7). pap. 7.99 *(978-0-544-54027-9(1)*, HMH Books For Young Readers) Houghton Mifflin Harcourt Publishing Co.

—The Willoughbys. Lois, Lowry, illus. 2008. (ENG., Illus.). 176p. (J). (gr. 1-4). 17.99 *(978-0-618-97974-5(3))* Houghton Mifflin Harcourt Publishing Co.

—The Willoughbys. 2010. (ENG.). 176p. (J). (gr. 3-7). 6.99 *(978-0-385-73776-0(9)*, Yearling) Random Hse. Children's Bks.

Lollino, Jessica. Little Lily Mays & the Daddy Dilemma. Kendrick-TaZiyah, Brandi, illus. 2006. (Little Lily Mays Ser.: vol. 1). 32p. (J). per. 20.00 *(978-0-9712383-1-2(6))* Culturatti Ink.

Lombard, Jenny. Drita, My Homegirl. 2008. (ENG.). 144p. (J). (gr. 3-7). 5.99 *(978-0-14-240905-3(7)*, Puffin Books) Penguin Young Readers Group.

—Drita, My Homegirl. 2008. 135p. (J). (gr. 4-6). 13.65 *(978-0-7569-8919-4(1))* Perfection Learning Corp.

Long, Ethan. Big Cat. Long, Ethan, illus. 2016. (I Like to Read(r) Ser.). (ENG., Illus.). 24p. (J). (gr. -1-3). 14.95 *(978-0-8234-3538-8(5))* Holiday Hse., Inc.

Long, Heather & Long, Ethan. Max & Milo the Mixed-Up Message. Long, Ethan, illus. 2013. (ENG., Illus.). 32p. (J). (gr. -1-3). 14.99 *(978-1-4424-5140-7(8)*, Simon & Schuster/Paula Wiseman Bks.) Simon & Schuster/Paula Wiseman Bks.

Long, Loren. Otis. Long, Loren, illus. 2013. (Otis Ser.). (SPA & ENG., Illus.). 40p. (J). (gr. -1-k). 7.99 *(978-0-14-751124-9(0)*, Puffin Books) Penguin Young Readers Group.

The Long Walk Home: Individual Title Six-Packs. (Action Packs Ser.). 120p. (gr. 3-5). 44.00 *(978-0-7635-8430-6(4))* Rigby Education.

Longo, Jennifer. Six Feet over It. 2014. (ENG.). 352p. (YA). (gr. 7). 17.99 *(978-0-449-81871-8(3)*, Random Hse. Bks. for Young Readers) Random Hse. Children's Bks.

Look, Lenore. Ruby Lu, Brave & True. 2004. (Illus.). 104p. (J). lib. bdg. 15.00 *(978-1-4242-0914-9(5))* Fitzgerald Bks.

—Ruby Lu, Brave & True. Wilsdorf, Anne, illus. 2006. (ENG.). 112p. (J). (gr. 1-5). pap. 6.99 *(978-1-4169-1389-4(0)*, Atheneum Bks. for Young Readers) Simon & Schuster Children's Publishing.

—Ruby Lu, Star of the Show. Choi, Stef, illus. (ENG.). 144p. (J). (gr. 1-5). 2012. pap. 6.99 *(978-1-4169-1776-2(4))* 2011. 15.99 *(978-1-4169-1775-5(6))* Simon & Schuster Children's Publishing. (Atheneum Bks. for Young Readers).

López, Diana. Ask My Mood Ring How I Feel. 2013. (ENG.). 336p. (J). (gr. 3-7). 17.00 *(978-0-316-20996-0(1))* Little Brown & Co.

—Confetti Girl. 2010. (ENG.). 208p. (J). (gr. 3-7). pap. 8.00 *(978-0-316-02956-8(4))* Little, Brown Bks. for Young Readers.

Lord, Emery. The Start of Me & You. 2015. (ENG.). 384p. (YA). (gr. 7). 17.99 *(978-1-61963-359-9(0)*, 9781619633599, Bloomsbury USA Childrens) Bloomsbury Publishing USA.

Love, D. Anne. Picture Perfect. 2010. (ENG.). 304p. (YA). (gr. 7). pap. 8.99 *(978-0-689-87391-1(3)*, McElderry, Margaret K. Bks.) McElderry, Margaret K. Bks.

—Semiprecious. (ENG.). 304p. (J). (gr. 5-9). 2009. pap. 6.99 *(978-0-689-87389-8(1))* 2006. (Illus.). 17.99 *(978-0-689-85638-9(5))* McElderry, Margaret K. Bks. (McElderry, Margaret K. Bks.).

Lowe, Natasha. The Power of Poppy Pendle. (Poppy Pendle Ser.). (ENG., 272p. (J). (gr. 3-7). 2013. Illus.). pap. 7.99 *(978-1-4424-4926-8(8))* 2012. 16.99 *(978-1-4424-4679-3(X))* Simon & Schuster/Paula Wiseman Bks. (Simon & Schuster/Paula Wiseman Bks.).

Lowery, Linda. Truth & Salsa, 1 vol. (ENG.). 176p. (J). 2009. pap. 7.95 *(978-1-56145-498-3(2))* 2006. (gr. 3-7). 15.95 *(978-1-56145-366-5(8))* Peachtree Pubs.

Lowery, Marie Hayes. Beau & Friends. 2012. 20p. pap. 17.99 *(978-1-4817-0106-8(1))* AuthorHouse.

Lowitz, Leza & Oketani, Shogo. Jet Black & the Ninja Wind. 2013. (ENG., Illus.). 320p. (J). (gr. 7-12). 17.99 *(978-4-8053-1284-1(X))* Tuttle Publishing.

Lowry, Brigid. Things You Either Hate or Love. 2006. (ENG.). 179p. (YA). (gr. 7-12). 16.95 *(978-0-8234-2004-9(3))* Holiday Hse., Inc.

—Things You Either Hate or Love. 2007. (ENG.). 192p. (YA). (gr. 8-12). pap. 18.99 *(978-0-312-36308-6(7)*, 9780312363086, St. Martin's Griffin) St. Martin's Pr.

Lozano, José. Little Chanclas. 2015. (ENG & SPA., Illus.). 32p. (J). (gr. k-3). 16.95 *(978-1-935955-85-6(3))* Cinco Puntos Pr.

Lubar, David. Sophomores & Other Oxymorons. 2015. (ENG.). 432p. (YA). (gr. 7). 17.99 *(978-0-525-42970-8(0)*, Dutton Books for Young Readers) Penguin Young Readers Group.

Lubner, Susan. The Upside of Ordinary. 2012. (ENG.). 128p. (J). 16.95 *(978-0-8234-2417-7(0))* Holiday Hse., Inc.

Luddy, Karon. Spelldown: The Big-Time Dreams of a Small-Town Word Whiz. 2008. (Mix Ser.). (ENG.). 224p. (J). (gr. 4-8). pap. 10.99 *(978-1-4169-5452-1(X)*, Simon & Schuster/Paula Wiseman Bks.) Simon & Schuster/Paula Wiseman Bks.

Luedtke, Courtney. Baby Boo: The Happy Beginning. 2009. (Illus.). 72p. pap. 27.49 *(978-1-4389-2696-4(0))* AuthorHouse.

Lupica, Mike. Hero. (ENG.). 304p. (J). (gr. 5-18). 2011. 7.99 *(978-0-14-241960-1(5)*, Puffin Books) 2010. 17.99 *(978-0-399-25283-9(5)*, Philomel Bks.) Penguin Young Readers Group.

—Hero. 2011. lib. bdg. 18.40 *(978-0-606-23142-8(0)*, Turtleback) Turtleback Bks.

—Last Man Out. (ENG.). (J). (gr. 5). 2017. 272p. 8.99 ***(978-0-14-751491-2(6)***, Puffin Books) 2016. 256p. 17.99 *(978-0-399-17279-3(3)*, Philomel Bks.) Penguin Young Readers Group.

Lupica, Mike. Qb 1. 2013. (ENG.). 272p. (J). (gr. 5). 17.99 *(978-0-399-25228-0(2)*, Philomel Bks.) Penguin Publishing Group.

—Qb 1. 2014. (ENG.). 288p. (J). (gr. 5). pap. 7.99 *(978-0-14-751152-2(6)*, Puffin Books) Penguin Young Readers Group.

Lupton, Hugh. The Gingerbread Man. Mayo, Diana, illus. 2003. 24p. (J). (gr. k-3). 14.99 *(978-1-84148-056-5(8))* Barefoot Bks., Inc.

Lyga, Barry. Bang. 2017. (ENG.). 304p. (J). (gr. 7-17). 17.99 *(978-0-316-31550-0(8))* Little, Brown Bks. for Young Readers.

—The Secret Sea. 2016. (ENG.). 448p. (J). 16.99 *(978-1-250-07283-2(2)*, 9781250072832) Feiwel & Friends.

Lynch, Chris. The Gravedigger's Cottage. 2004. (ENG.). 208p. (J). (gr. 7-18). 15.99 *(978-0-06-623940-8(0))* HarperCollins Pubs.

—Inexcusable. 2005. (ENG., Illus.). 176p. (YA). (gr. 7-18). 19.99 *(978-0-689-84789-9(0)*, Atheneum Bks. for Young Readers) Simon & Schuster Children's Publishing.

—Inexcusable: 10th Anniversary Edition. 10th ed. 2015. (ENG., Illus.). 192p. (YA). (gr. 8). pap. 9.99 *(978-1-4814-3202-3(8)*, Simon & Schuster Bks. For Young Readers) Simon & Schuster Bks. For Young Readers.

—Irreversible. 2016. (ENG., Illus.). 352p. (YA). (gr. 7). 17.99 *(978-1-4814-2985-6(X)*, Simon & Schuster Bks. For Young Readers) Simon & Schuster Bks. For Young Readers.

—Me, Dead Dad, & Alcatraz. 3rd ed. 2005. (ENG.). 240p. (J). 15.99 *(978-0-06-059709-2(7))* HarperCollins Pubs.

—Shadow Boxer. 2013. (ENG.). 176p. (YA). (gr. 7). 16.99 *(978-1-4424-5811-6(9)*, Simon & Schuster Bks. For Young Readers) Simon & Schuster Bks. For Young Readers.

Lynch, Diane M., ed. Family Ties: Thirteen Short Stories. 2010. 112p. (J). (gr. 4-7). pap. 7.95 *(978-0-8198-2688-6(X))* Pauline Bks. & Media.

Lyne, Jennifer H. Catch Rider. (ENG.). 288p. (YA). (gr. 7). 2014. pap. 8.99 *(978-0-544-30182-5(X)*, HMH Books For Young Readers) 2013. (Illus.). 16.99 *(978-0-547-86871-4(5))* Houghton Mifflin Harcourt Publishing Co.

Lynn, Erin. Speed Demon. 2008. (ENG.). 192p. (YA). (gr. 9-18). 9.99 *(978-0-425-22366-6(3)*, Berkley) Penguin Publishing Group.

Lynn, Joseph. Color of My Words. 2014. (ENG.). 144p. (J). (gr. 5-12). 10.24 *(978-1-63245-277-1(4))* Lectorum Pubns., Inc.

Lyon, George Ella. Sonny's House of Spies. 2007. (ENG.). 304p. (J). (gr. 6-9). pap. 14.95 *(978-1-4169-6815-3(6)*, Simon & Schuster/Paula Wiseman Bks.) Simon & Schuster/Paula Wiseman Bks.

Lyons, C. J. Broken. 2014. (ENG.). 320p. (YA). (gr. 7-12). pap. 9.99 *(978-1-4022-9230-9(9))* Sourcebooks, Inc.

Lyons, Stefanie. Dating Down. 2015. (ENG., Illus.). 312p. (YA). pap. 9.99 *(978-0-7387-4337-0(2)*, Flux) North Star Editions.

Maberry, Jonathan. Flesh & Bone. 2013. (Rot & Ruin Ser.: 3). (ENG., Illus.). 496p. (YA). (gr. 7). pap. 11.99 *(978-1-4424-3990-0(4)*, Simon & Schuster Bks. For Young Readers) Simon & Schuster Bks. For Young Readers.

MacCready, Robin Merrow. Snapshot. 2017. (ENG.). 208p. (YA). 16.99 *(978-0-8050-9109-0(2)*, 9780805091090, Holt, Henry & Co. Bks. For Young Readers) Holt, Henry & Co.

MacDonald, George. History of GuttaPercha Willie. 2006. 116p. 22.95 (978-1-59818-157-9(2)) Aegypan.
MacDonald, Maryann. No Room for Francie. Richards, Virginia Helen, illus. 2010. 64p. (J). (gr. 1-3). pap. 6.95 (978-0-8198-5168-0(X)) Pauline Bks. & Media.
—Starring Francie O'Leary. Richards, Virginia Helen, illus. 2010. 64p. (J). (gr. 1-3). pap. 6.95 (978-0-8198-7132-9(X)) Pauline Bks. & Media.
MacDonald, Steven. Just Clowning Around: Two Stories. McPhail, David, illus. 2003. (Green Light Readers Level 1 Ser.). (ENG.). 24p. (J). (gr. -1-3). pap. 3.95 (978-0-15-204856-3(1)) Houghton Mifflin Harcourt Publishing Co.
Mack, Jeff. Clueless McGee & the Inflatable Pants, Bk. 2. Mack, Jeff, illus. 2013. (Clueless Mcgee Ser.: 2). (ENG., Illus.). 256p. (J). (gr. 3-7). 12.99 (978-0-399-25750-6(0), Philomel Bks.) Penguin Young Readers Group.
Mackall, Dandi Daley. Natalie Wants a Puppy, 1 vol. Blakeslee, Lys, illus. 2009. (That's Nat! Ser.). (ENG.). 96p. (J). (gr. 1-4). pap. 4.99 (978-0-310-71571-9(7)) Zonderkidz.
—The Secrets of Tree Taylor. 2014. (ENG.). 288p. (J). (gr. 5). 16.99 (978-0-375-86897-9(6), Knopf Bks. for Young Readers) Random Hse. Children's Bks.
Mackey, Weezie Kerr. Throwing Like a Girl, 0 vols. 2010. (ENG.). 272p. (YA). (gr. 7-9). pap. 9.99 (978-0-7614-5606-3(6), 9780761456063, Amazon Children's Publishing) Amazon Publishing.
Mackler, Carolyn. Infinite in Between. 2015. (ENG.). 480p. (YA). (gr. 8). 17.99 (978-0-06-173107-5(2), HarperTeen) HarperCollins Pubs.
—Tangled. 2009. (ENG.). 320p. (YA). (gr. 9-18). 16.99 (978-0-06-173104-4(8), HarperTeen) HarperCollins Pubs.
MacLachlan, Patricia. The Boxcar Children Beginning. Jessell, Tim, illus. 2012. (Boxcar Children Mysteries Ser.). (ENG.). 144p. (J). (gr. 1-5). 16.99 (978-0-8075-6616-9(0)) Whitman, Albert & Co.
—Edward's Eyes. 2009. (ENG.). 128p. (J). (gr. 3-7). pap. 7.99 (978-1-4169-2744-0(1), Atheneum Bks. for Young Readers) Simon & Schuster Children's Publishing.
—Fly Away. 2014. (ENG., Illus.). 128p. (J). (gr. 2). 15.99 (978-1-4424-6008-9(3), McElderry, Margaret K. Bks.) McElderry, Margaret K. Bks.
—Grandfather's Dance. (Sarah, Plain & Tall Ser.: 5). (J). 2007. (ENG.). 96p. (gr. 1-5). pap. 5.99 (978-0-06-134003-1(0)) 2006. 84p. (gr. 3-5). lib. bdg. 15.89 (978-0-06-027561-7(8), Cotler, Joanna Books) HarperCollins Pubs.
—Kindred Souls. (J). (gr. 1-5). 2013. (ENG.). 144p. pap. 5.99 (978-0-06-052299-5(2)) 2012. (ENG.). 128p. 16.99 (978-0-06-052297-1(6)) 2012. 128p. lib. bdg. 17.89 (978-0-06-052298-8(4)) HarperCollins Pubs. (Tegen, Katherine Bks).
—Lala Salama: A Tanzanian Lullaby. Zunon, Elizabeth, illus. 2011. (ENG.). 32p. (J). (gr. -1-2). 16.99 (978-0-7636-4747-6(0)) Candlewick Pr.
—More Perfect Than the Moon. 2005. (Sarah, Plain & Tall Ser.: 4). (ENG.). 96p. (J). (gr. 1-5). pap. 5.99 (978-0-06-075179-1(7)) HarperCollins Pubs.
—Waiting for the Magic. Bates, Amy June, illus. (ENG.). (J). (gr. 3-7). 2012. 176p. pap. 6.99 (978-1-4169-2746-4(8)) 2011. 160p. 16.99 (978-1-4169-2745-7(X)) Simon & Schuster Children's Publishing. (Atheneum Bks. for Young Readers).
Madden, Kerry. Gentle's Holler. 2007. (Maggie Valley Ser.). 237p. (gr. 4-7). 17.00 (978-0-7569-8090-0(9)) Perfection Learning Corp.
Maddox, Jake. Skateboard Struggle, 1 vol. Tiffany, Sean, illus. 2011. (Jake Maddox Sports Stories Ser.). (ENG.). 72p. (gr. 2-3). lib. bdg. 25.32 (978-1-4342-2987-8(4)) Stone Arch Bks.
—Touchdown Triumph. Aburto, Jesus, illus. 2015. (Jake Maddox Sports Stories Ser.). (ENG.). 72p. (gr. 2-3). lib. bdg. 25.32 (978-1-4965-0492-0(5)) Stone Arch Bks.
Madormo, John V. The Homemade Stuffing Caper, Bk. 1. 2013. (Charlie Collier, Snoop for Hire Ser.: 1). (ENG.). 272p. (J). (gr. 5). pap. 7.99 (978-0-14-242380-6(7), Puffin Books) Penguin Young Readers Group.
Magnin, Joyce. Carrying Mason, 1 vol. 2013. (ENG.). 176p. (J). pap. 6.99 (978-0-310-72682-1(4)) Zonderkidz.
Magusin, Matthew. Diary of a Nerd. the Start of Middle School. 2012. 72p. pap. 8.25 (978-1-61170-103-6(1)) Robertson Publishing.
Mahmoodian, Maryam. Muslim Teens In: Pitfalls & Pranks. 2008. (YA). per. 10.95 (978-0-9793577-3-2(X)) Muslim Writers Publishing.
Maizel, Rebecca. Between Us & the Moon. 2015. (ENG.). 384p. (YA). (gr. 9). 17.99 (978-0-06-232761-1(5)) HarperCollins Pubs.
Malaspina, Ann. Touch the Sky: Alice Coachman, Olympic High Jumper. Velasquez, Eric, illus. 2012. (ENG.). 32p. (J). (gr. 1-3). 16.99 (978-0-8075-8035-6(X)) Whitman, Albert & Co.
—Yasmin's Hammer. Chayka, Doug, illus. 2010. (ENG.). 40p. (J). (gr. k-6). 18.95 (978-1-60060-359-4(9)) Lee & Low Bks., Inc.
Malizia, Laura. Nonna's Kitchen. 2010. 70p. pap. 7.99 (978-0-88144-236-6(4)) Yorkshire Publishing Group.
Malokas, Ann. The Tag-a-long Trio: Zak, Lizze & Ben Too! Nicholas, Corasue, illus. 2007. (J). 15.95 (978-0-9708415-8-2(2)) Guilty Mom Pr.
Mammay, Judith. Knowing Joseph. (ENG., Illus.). 256p. (J). (gr. 2-7). 2009. pap. 8.95 (978-1-933831-06-0(5)) 2008. 13.95 (978-1-933831-05-3(7)) Blooming Tree Pr.
—Ryan's Victory. Fargo, Todd, illus. 2009. 32p. (J). pap. 9.95 (978-0-944727-53-9(0)); lib. bdg. 15.95 (978-0-944727-54-6(9)) Jason & Nordic Pubs. (Turtle Bks.).
Mancini, Aly. Layne at Home. 2012. 24p. pap. 21.99 (978-1-4797-5397-0(1)) Xlibris Corp.
Manivong, Laura. Escaping the Tiger. 2010. (ENG.). 224p. (J). (gr. 5-18). 15.99 (978-0-06-166177-8(5)) HarperCollins Pubs.
Manley, Candace. Skeeter's Dream. 2010. (ENG.). 192p. (J). (gr. 7-18). pap. 14.95 (978-0-9785634-8-6(4)) La Frontera Publishing.
Mann, Elizabeth. Little Man: A Novel. 2014. (ENG., Illus.). 208p. (J). (gr. 5-7). 18.95 (978-1-931414-49-4(1), 9781931414494) Mikaya Pr.
Manning, Maurie J. Kitchen Dance. Manning, Maurie J., illus. 2008. (ENG., Illus.). 32p. (J). (gr. -1-3). 17.99 (978-0-618-99110-5(7)) Houghton Mifflin Harcourt Publishing Co.
Manushkin, Fran. Big Brothers Are the Best, 1 vol. Richards, Kirsten, illus. 2012. (Fiction Picture Bks.). (ENG.). 24p. (gr. -1 — 1). 6.95 (978-1-4048-7224-0(8)); lib. bdg. 22.65 (978-1-4048-7137-3(3)) Picture Window Bks. (Fiction Picture Bks.).
—Big Sisters Are the Best, 1 vol. Richards, Kirsten, illus. 2012. (Fiction Picture Bks.). (ENG.). 24p. (gr. -1 — 1). 6.95 (978-1-4048-7225-7(6)); lib. bdg. 22.65 (978-1-4048-7138-0(1)) Picture Window Bks. (Fiction Picture Bks.).
—Katie Woo, Don't Be Blue, 1 vol. Lyon, Tammie, illus. 2013. (Katie Woo Ser.). (ENG.). 96p. (gr. k-2). pap. 4.95 (978-1-4048-8101-3(8)) Picture Window Bks.
—Katie Woo, Every Day's an Adventure, 1 vol. Lyon, Tammie, illus. 2014. (Katie Woo Ser.). (ENG.). 96p. (gr. k-2). pap. 4.95 (978-1-4795-5211-5(9)) Picture Window Bks.
—Moving Day, 1 vol. Lyon, Tammie, illus. 2010. (Katie Woo Ser.). (ENG.). 32p. (gr. k-2). pap. 5.95 (978-1-4048-6059-9(2)); lib. bdg. 21.32 (978-1-4048-5733-9(8)) Picture Window Bks.
Manzano, Sonia. The Revolution of Evelyn Serrano. 2012. (ENG.). 224p. (J). (gr. 7-9). 17.99 (978-0-545-32505-9(6), Scholastic Pr.) Scholastic, Inc.
Manzer, Jenny. Save Me, Kurt Cobain. 2016. (ENG.). 272p. (YA). (gr. 7). 17.99 (978-0-553-52126-9(8), Delacorte Pr.) Random Hse. Children's Bks.
Marchetta, Melina. The Piper's Son. (ENG.). 336p. (YA). (gr. 9). 2012. pap. 7.99 (978-0-7636-6062-8(0)) 2011. (Illus.). 17.99 (978-0-7636-4758-2(6)) Candlewick Pr.
—Saving Francesca. 2006. (ENG.). 258p. (YA). (gr. 7-12). reprint ed. per. 8.99 (978-0-375-82983-3(0), Knopf Bks. for Young Readers) Random Hse. Children's Bks.
Marciano, John Bemelmans. Respect Your Ghosts. Blackall, Sophie, illus. 2017. (Witches of Benevento Ser.: 4). (ENG.). 128p. (J). (gr. 2-5). 13.99 (978-0-451-47183-3(0), Viking Books for Young Readers) Penguin Young Readers Group.
Marciniak, Christine. Lights, Camera, Ali! 2013. 232p. pap. 13.99 (978-1-61271-214-7(2)) Zumaya Pubns. LLC.
Margolis, Leslie. Everybody Bugs Out. (Annabelle Unleashed Ser.). (ENG.). (YA). (gr. 3-12). 2012. 224p. pap. 6.99 (978-1-59990-828-1(X), 9781599908281) 2011. 208p. 15.99 (978-1-59990-526-6(4), 9781599905266) Bloomsbury Publishing USA. (Bloomsbury USA Childrens).
—Girls Acting Catty. (Annabelle Unleashed Ser.). (ENG.). (YA). (gr. 3-6). 2010. 208p. pap. 6.99 (978-1-59990-520-4(5), 9781599905204) 2009. 192p. 15.99 (978-1-59990-237-1(0), 9781599902371) Bloomsbury Publishing USA. (Bloomsbury USA Childrens).
—Girl's Best Friend. (Maggie Brooklyn Mystery Ser.). (ENG.). (YA). (gr. 3-12). 2011. 288p. pap. 7.99 (978-1-59990-690-4(2), 9781599906904) 2010. 272p. 14.99 (978-1-59990-525-9(6), 9781599905259) Bloomsbury Publishing USA. (Bloomsbury USA Childrens).
—One Tough Chick. 2013. (Annabelle Unleashed Ser.). (ENG.). 176p. (YA). (gr. 3-6). 15.99 (978-1-59990-961-5(8), 9781599909615, Bloomsbury USA Childrens) Bloomsbury Publishing USA.
Marie, Jill Jana. Anna Lee Enis Bee. 2010. 24p. pap. 11.00 (978-1-60860-907-9(3), Eloquent Bks.) Strategic Book Publishing & Rights Agency (SBPRA).
Marie, Tina. Raccoon Round-Up at the Diamond R Ranch. 2012. 30p. 24.95 (978-1-62709-237-1(4)) America Star Bks.
Marino, Peter. Dough Boy. 2007. (ENG.). 176p. (YA). (gr. 7-12). pap. 6.95 (978-0-8234-2096-4(5)) Holiday Hse., Inc.
Marinsky, Jane. Just Perfect. 2012. (Illus.). 32p. (J). (gr. k). 16.95 (978-1-56792-428-2(X)) Godine, David R. Pub.
Marsh, Laura F. Steps to Liberty. Wright, John R., illus. 2007. 32p. (J). 17.95 (978-0-615-16563-9(X)) Junior League of Central Westchester.
Marston, Carrie. Catch Me If You Can. 2012. 82p. (gr. 10-12). pap. 9.95 (978-1-4497-6706-8(0), WestBow Pr.) Author Solutions, Inc.
Martin, Ann M. Belle Teal. 2004. (Illus.). 214p. (gr. 4-7). 17.00 (978-0-7569-2929-9(6)) Perfection Learning Corp.
—Better to Wish. 2013. (Family Tree Ser.). (ENG.). 240p. (J). (gr. 3-7). 16.99 (978-0-545-35942-9(2), Scholastic Pr.) Scholastic, Inc.
—Coming Apart. 2010. (Main Street Ser.: 9). (ENG.). 208p. (J). (gr. 3-7). pap. 6.99 (978-0-545-06896-3(7), Scholastic Paperbacks) Scholastic, Inc.
—A Corner of the Universe. 2004. (ENG.). 208p. (J). (gr. 3-7). pap. 7.99 (978-0-439-38881-8(3), Scholastic Paperbacks) Scholastic, Inc.
—Dawn on the Coast. (Baby-Sitters Club Ser.: No. 23). 10p. (J). (gr. 3-7). pap. 3.95 (978-0-590-42007-5(0)) Scholastic, Inc.
—Family Tree Book One: Better to Wish. 2014. (Family Tree Ser.: 1). (ENG.). 240p. (J). (gr. 3-7). pap. 6.99 (978-0-545-67518-5(9)) Scholastic, Inc.
—Family Tree Book Three: Best Kept Secret. 2014. (ENG.). 224p. (J). (gr. 3-7). 16.99 (978-0-545-35944-3(9), Scholastic Pr.) Scholastic, Inc.
—Here Today. 2005. 308p. (gr. 5-9). 18.00 (978-0-7569-5104-7(6)) Perfection Learning Corp.
—Here Today. 2005. (ENG.). 336p. (J). (gr. 3-7). pap. 7.99 (978-0-439-57945-2(7), Scholastic Paperbacks) Scholastic, Inc.
—Home Is the Place. 2014. (Family Tree Ser.: 4). (ENG.). 224p. (J). (gr. 3-7). 16.99 (978-0-545-35945-0(7), Scholastic Pr.) Scholastic, Inc.
—The Long Way Home. 2013. (Family Tree Ser.: 2). (ENG.). 224p. (J). (gr. 3-7). 16.99 (978-0-545-35943-6(0), Scholastic Pr.) Scholastic, Inc.
—Needle & Thread. 2007. (Main Street Ser.). (Illus.). 205p. (J). (gr. 4-7). 14.65 (978-0-7569-8328-4(2)) Perfection Learning Corp.
—Needle & Thread. Andreasen, Dan, illus. 2007. 205p. (J). pap. (978-0-545-03660-3(7)) Scholastic, Inc.
—The Summer Before. 2010. (Baby-Sitters Club Ser.). (ENG.). 224p. (J). (gr. 3-7). 16.99 (978-0-545-16093-3(6)) Scholastic, Inc.
—Ten Good & Bad Things about My Life (So Far) 2013. (ENG.). 288p. (J). (gr. 4-7). pap. 7.99 (978-1-250-03413-7(2), 9781250034137) Square Fish.
—Ten Rules for Living with My Sister. 2011. (ENG.). 240p. (J). (gr. 4-7). 16.99 (978-0-312-36766-4(X), 9780312367664) Feiwel & Friends.
—Ten Rules for Living with My Sister. 2012. (ENG.). 256p. (J). (gr. 4-7). pap. 7.99 (978-1-250-01021-6(7), 9781250010216) Square Fish.
Martin, Emily Winfield. The Littlest Family's Big Day. 2016. (ENG., Illus.). 36p. (J). (gr. -1-2). 17.99 (978-0-553-51101-7(7)); lib. bdg. 20.99 (978-0-375-97431-1(8)) Random Hse. Children's Bks. (Random Hse. Bks. for Young Readers).
Martin, Matthew. Cleatus Goes Camping. 2011. 44p. pap. 19.95 (978-1-4634-3646-9(7)) AuthorHouse.
Martin, Rebecca. Blossoms on the Roof. 2015. (Amish Frontier Ser.). (ENG.). 160p. (J). (gr. 2-7). pap. 8.99 (978-0-7369-6367-1(7)) Harvest Hse. Pubs.
Martinez, Claudia Guadalupe. Pig Park. 2014. (ENG.). 248p. (J). 15.95 (978-1-935955-76-4(4)) Cinco Puntos Pr.
—The Smell of Old Lady Perfume. 2008. (ENG., Illus.). 248p. (J). (gr. 4-9). 15.95 (978-1-933693-18-7(5)) Cinco Puntos Pr.
Martínez, Claudia Guadalupe. Smell of Old Lady Perfume. 2011. (ENG., Illus.). 256p. (J). (gr. 4-10). pap. 7.95 (978-1-933693-88-0(6)) Cinco Puntos Pr.
Martinez, Raul. Rooly & Flora's Reunion: A Story of Cuba. Prieto, Antonio, illus. 2006. (ENG.). 32p. (J). pap. 6.95 (978-1-59249-658-7(X)) Soundprints.
Martinez, Victor. Parrot in the Oven. Scott, Steve, illus. rev. ed. 2004. (ENG.). 240p. (YA). (gr. 8-18). pap. 8.99 (978-0-06-447186-2(1), Rayo) HarperCollins Pubs.
Martins, E. V. Cookie Nana's Story Book: Featuring " Grumpy Granddad " 2009. (Illus.). 40p. pap. 16.99 (978-1-4389-2325-3(2)) AuthorHouse.
Martinusen-Coloma, Cindy. Ruby Unscripted, 1 vol. 2009. (ENG.). 272p. (YA). (gr. 7-18). pap. 12.99 (978-1-59554-356-1(2)) Nelson, Thomas Inc.
Marusak, Elaine. Truly Tales & Girl Fish Stories. 2006. 93p. pap. 16.95 (978-1-4241-3244-7(4)) PublishAmerica, Inc.
Masilela, Johnny. We Shall Not Weep. 2010. (ENG.). 132p. pap. (978-0-7957-0147-4(0)) NB Pubs. Ltd.
Mass, Wendy. Finally. 2011. (ENG.). 304p. (J). (gr. 3-7). pap. 6.99 (978-0-545-05243-6(2), Scholastic Paperbacks) Scholastic, Inc.
—A Mango-Shaped Space. 2005. (ENG.). 240p. (YA). (gr. 3-7). per. 8.99 (978-0-316-05825-4(4)) Little, Brown Bks. for Young Readers.
Mateos, Pilar. El Cuento Interrumpido. (SPA.). 128p. (YA). (gr. 5-8). (978-84-279-3149-7(2), NG0388) Noguer y Caralt Editores, S. A. ESP. Dist: Lectorum Pubns., Inc.
Mathieu, Jennifer. Devoted. 2015. (ENG.). 336p. (YA). (gr. 7). 16.99 (978-1-59643-911-5(4), 9781596439115) Roaring Brook Pr.
Mathis, Sharon Bell. The Hundred Penny Box. Dillon, Diane & Dillon, Leo, illus. 2006. (ENG.). 48p. (J). (gr. 1-4). pap. 7.99 (978-0-14-240702-8(X), Puffin Books) Penguin Young Readers Group.
—The Hundred Penny Box. Dillon, Leo & Dillon, Diane, illus. 2006. 47p. (gr. 1-4). 18.00 (978-0-7569-6786-4(4)) Perfection Learning Corp.
Matson, Morgan. Second Chance Summer. (ENG.). (YA). (gr. 7). 2013. 496p. pap. 10.99 (978-1-4169-9068-0(2)) 2012. 480p. 19.99 (978-1-4169-9067-3(4)) Simon & Schuster Bks. For Young Readers. (Simon & Schuster Bks. For Young Readers).
Matthews, Gail. Our Forever Family, 1 vol. 2010. 32p. 24.95 (978-1-4512-1055-2(8)) America Star Bks.
Matthews, Leeana. The Dimetriuses. 2007. 128p. per. 19.95 (978-1-4241-7528-4(3)) America Star Bks.
Matthies, Jana. The Goodbye Cancer Garden, 1 vol. Valiant, Kristi, illus. 2011. (ENG.). 32p. (J). (gr. 1-3). 16.99 (978-0-8075-2994-2(X)) Whitman, Albert & Co.
Mattingley, Christobel. Asmir No Quiere Pistolas. Balseiro, Maria Luisa, tr. Honey, Elizabeth, illus.Tr. of No Gun for Asmir. (SPA.). 129p. (J). (gr. 5-8). pap. 9.95 (978-84-204-4891-6(5)) Santillana USA Publishing Co., Inc.
Matute, Ana María. El Polizón del Ulises. (SPA.). 96p. (J). (978-84-264-3401-2(0), LM4015) Editorial Lumen ESP. Dist: Lectorum Pubns., Inc.
Maunder, Roger. Mundy Pond. 2006. (ENG.). 195p. per. (978-1-897174-09-8(8), Tuckamore Bks) Creative Bk. Publishing.
Maurer, Shari. Change of Heart. 2010. 290p. (YA). 16.95 (978-1-934813-36-2(2)) Westside Bks.
May, Kyla. Mika: My New Life. 2013. (Lotus Lane Ser.: 4). (ENG.). 96p. (J). (gr. 1-3). pap. 4.99 (978-0-545-44519-1(1)) Scholastic, Inc.
—Mika: My New Life. 2013. (Lotus Lane Ser.: 4). lib. bdg. 14.75 (978-0-606-32365-9(1), Turtleback) Turtleback Bks.
Mayer, Mercer. The Best Teacher Ever No. 6. Mayer, Mercer, illus. 2008. (Little Critter Ser.). (ENG., Illus.). 24p. (J). (gr. -1-2). pap. 3.99 (978-0-06-053960-3(7), HarperFestival) HarperCollins Pubs.
—Bye-Bye, Mom & Dad. Mayer, Mercer, illus. 2004. (Little Critter Ser.). (ENG., Illus.). 24p. (J). (gr. -1-2). pap. 3.99 (978-0-06-053945-0(3), HarperFestival) HarperCollins Pubs.
Mayhall, Robin. He Loves Me, He Loves Me Not. Cella, Kristen & Tiede, Dirk, illus. 2013. (My Boyfriend Is a Monster Ser.: 7). (ENG.). 128p. (YA). (gr. 7-12). lib. bdg. 29.27 (978-0-7613-6005-6(0), Graphic Universe™) Lerner Publishing Group.
—He Loves Me, He Loves Me Not. Cella, Kristen et al, illus. 2013. (My Boyfriend Is a Monster Ser.: 7). (ENG.). 128p. (YA). (gr. 7-12). pap. 9.95 (978-0-7613-8548-6(7), Graphic Universe™) Lerner Publishing Group.
Mazer, Norma Fox. Babyface. 2007. (ENG., Illus.). 176p. (YA). (gr. 7). pap. 11.95 (978-0-15-206277-4(7)) Houghton Mifflin Harcourt Publishing Co.
—The Missing Girl. 2010. (ENG.). 304p. (YA). (gr. 8). pap. 8.99 (978-0-06-447365-1(1), HarperTeen) HarperCollins Pubs.
—Ten Ways to Make My Sister Disappear. 2007. (ENG.). 128p. (J). (gr. 4-7). 16.99 (978-0-439-83983-9(1), Levine, Arthur A. Bks.) Scholastic, Inc.
—Ten Ways to Make My Sister Disappear. l.t. ed. 2008. (Thorndike Literacy Bridge Ser.). 207p. (J). (gr. 4-7). 22.95 (978-1-4104-0510-4(9)) Thorndike Pr.
—What I Believe. 2007. (ENG., Illus.). 176p. (J). (gr. 5-9). pap. 12.95 (978-0-15-206283-5(1)) Houghton Mifflin Harcourt Publishing Co.
McAlpine, Gordon. Once upon a Midnight Eerie: Book #2. Zuppardi, Sam, illus. 2014. (Misadventures of Edgar & Allan Poe Ser.: 2). (ENG.). 192p. (J). (gr. 3-7). 16.99 (978-0-670-78493-6(1), Viking Books for Young Readers) Penguin Young Readers Group.
McAnulty, Stacy. Excellent Ed. Sarcone-Roach, Julia, illus. 2016. (ENG.). 32p. (J). (gr. -1-3). 16.99 (978-0-553-51023-2(1), Knopf Bks. for Young Readers) Random Hse. Children's Bks.
—It's Not a Dinosaur! Boldt, Mike, illus. 2016. (Dino Files Ser.: 3). (ENG.). 128p. (J). (gr. 2-5). 9.99 (978-0-553-52197-9(7), Random Hse. Bks. for Young Readers) Random Hse. Children's Bks.
McBratney, Sam. There, There. Bates, Ivan, illus. 2013. (ENG.). 40p. (J). (gr. -1-2). 15.99 (978-0-7636-6702-3(1), Templar) Candlewick Pr.
McBride, Kristina. One Moment. 2017. (ENG.). 272p. (YA). (gr. 8). pap. 9.99 (978-1-5107-1455-7(3), Sky Pony Pr.) Skyhorse Publishing Co., Inc.
McCafferty, Megan. The (Totally Not) Guaranteed Guide to Popularity, Prettiness & Perfection. 2014. (Jessica Darling's It List Ser.: 1). (ENG.). 240p. (J). (gr. 3-7). pap. 8.99 (978-0-316-24498-5(8), Poppy) Little, Brown Bks. for Young Readers.
McCahan, Erin. I Now Pronounce You Someone Else. 2010. (ENG.). 272p. (J). (gr. 7-18). 16.99 (978-0-545-08818-3(6), Levine, Arthur A. Bks.) Scholastic, Inc.
McCall, Guadalupe Garcia. Summer of the Mariposas. 2012. (ENG.). 352p. (YA). 19.95 (978-1-60060-900-8(7), Tu Bks.) Lee & Low Bks., Inc.
—Under the Mesquite. 2013. (ENG., Illus.). 224p. (J). (gr. 7-18). 17.95 (978-1-60060-429-4(3)) Lee & Low Bks., Inc.
McCarthy, Jenna. Lola Knows a Lot. Palacios, Sara, illus. 2016. 32p. (J). (gr. -1-3). 17.99 (978-0-06-225017-9(5)) HarperCollins Pubs.
McCarty, Peter. Chloe. McCarty, Peter, illus. 2012. (Illus.). 40p. (J). (gr. -1-1). (ENG.). 16.99 (978-0-06-114291-8(3)); lib. bdg. 17.89 (978-0-06-114292-5(1)) HarperCollins Pubs.
McClements, George. Night of the Veggie Monster. McClements, George, illus. 2008. (ENG., Illus.). 32p. (J). (gr. -1-1). 16.99 (978-1-59990-061-2(0), 9781599900612, Bloomsbury USA Childrens) Bloomsbury Publishing USA.
McClure, Nikki. Waiting for High Tide. 2016. (ENG., Illus.). 48p. (J). (gr. k-2). 19.95 (978-1-4197-1656-0(5), Abrams Bks. for Young Readers) Abrams, Inc.
McCombie, Karen. My Big (Strange) Happy Family. Monks, Lydia, illus. 2009. (J). pap. (978-0-385-73597-1(9), Yearling) Random Hse. Children's Bks.
McCormack, Caren McNelly. The Fiesta Dress: A Quinceanera Tale, 0 vols. Aviles, Martha, illus. 2012. (ENG.). 42p. (J). (gr. k-4). pap. 7.99 (978-0-7614-6236-1(8), 9780761462361, Amazon Children's Publishing) Amazon Publishing.
McCormick, Patricia. Cut. unabr. ed. 2004. 168p. (J). (gr. 7-18). pap. 36.00 incl. audio (978-0-8072-0868-7(X), LYA 320 SP, Listening Library) Random Hse. Audio Publishing Group.
—Cut. 2011. (gr. 7-12). lib. bdg. 19.65 (978-0-613-49394-9(X), Turtleback) Turtleback Bks.
McCourt, Lisa. Te Quiero, Carita Sucia. 2006. (SPA., Illus.). 30p. (J). (gr. 1-2). 10.40 (978-84-95620-66-8(9), BRO33536) Brosquil Edicions, S.L. ESP. Dist: Lectorum Pubns., Inc.
McCreely, Havelock. My Zombie Hamster. 2014. (ENG.). 200p. (J). (gr. 3-7). 15.99 (978-1-60684-491-5(1), Carolrhoda Bks.) Lerner Publishing Group.
McCusker, Paul. Danger Lies Ahead! 2006. (Adventures in Odyssey Bks.: No. 2). (ENG.). 336p. (J). (gr. 8-12). per. 15.99 (978-1-58997-329-9(1)) Tyndale Hse. Pubs.
McDaniel, Lurlene. Garden of Angels. 2005. 272p. (gr. 7). 16.50 (978-0-7569-5756-8(7)) Perfection Learning Corp.
—Letting Go of Lisa. 2007. (ENG.). 192p. (YA). (gr. 7-12). mass mkt. 6.99 (978-0-440-23868-3(4), Laurel Leaf) Random Hse. Children's Bks.
—The Year of Luminous Love. 2013. (ENG.). 384p. (YA). (gr. 7). 16.99 (978-0-385-74171-2(5), Delacorte Bks. for Young Readers) Random Hse. Children's Bks.
McDonald, Joyce. Swallowing Stones. 2012. (ENG.). 256p. (YA). (gr. 7). pap. 9.99 (978-0-307-97609-3(2), Ember) Random Hse. Children's Bks.
McDonald, Kirsten. The Big Rain, 1 vol. Meza, Erika, illus. 2016. (Carlos & Carmen Ser.). (ENG.). 32p. (J). (gr. k-3). 27.07 (978-1-62402-137-4(9)) Magic Wagon.
—The Green Surprise, 1 vol. Meza, Erika, illus. 2016. (Carlos & Carmen Ser.). (ENG.). 32p. (J). (gr. k-3). 27.07 (978-1-62402-138-1(7)) Magic Wagon.
—The One-Tire House, 1 vol. Meza, Erika, illus. 2016. (Carlos & Carmen Ser.). (ENG.). 32p. (J). (gr. k-3). 27.07 (978-1-62402-140-4(9)) Magic Wagon.
—Tío Time, 1 vol. Meza, Erika, illus. 2016. (ENG.). 32p. (J). (978-1-62402-143-5(3)) Magic Wagon.
—The Wobbly Wheels, 1 vol. Meza, Erika, illus. 2016. (ENG.). 32p. (J). (978-1-62402-144-2(1)) Magic Wagon.
—The Yummy Mistake. Meza, Erika, illus. 2016. (ENG.). 32p. (J). (978-1-62402-145-9(X)) Magic Wagon.
McDonald, Marion. The Missing Mom. McDonald, Marion & Brown, Marion, illus. 2012. 30p. pap. 9.00 (978-1-4349-8628-3(4), RoseDog Bks.) Dorrance Publishing Co., Inc.
McDonald, Megan. Cloudy with a Chance of Boys. (Sisters Club Ser.: 3). (ENG., Illus.). 272p. (J). (gr. 3-7). 2012. pap. 5.99 (978-0-7636-5577-8(5)) 2011. 15.99 (978-0-7636-4615-8(6)) Candlewick Pr.
—Judy Moody & the Bad Luck Charm. 2013. (Judy Moody Ser.: 11). lib. bdg. 16.00 (978-0-606-32099-3(7), Turtleback) Turtleback Bks.
—The Sisters Club. 2008. (Sisters Club Ser.: 1). (ENG., Illus.). 208p. (J). (gr. 3-7). pap. 5.99 (978-0-7636-3251-9(1)) Candlewick Pr.
—The Sisters Club. 2008. (Sisters Club Ser.: 1). lib. bdg. 16.00 (978-1-4178-1785-6(2), Turtleback) Turtleback Bks.
—Stink & the Ultimate Thumb-Wrestling Smackdown. Reynolds, Peter H., illus. 2013. (Stink Ser.: 6). (ENG.). 144p. (J). (gr. 1-4). pap. 4.99 (978-0-7636-6423-7(5));Bk. 6. 12.99 (978-0-7636-6393-3(X)) Candlewick Pr.
—Stink & the Ultimate Thumb-Wrestling Smackdown, 1 vol. Reynolds, Peter H., illus. 2012. (Stink Ser.: No. 2). (ENG.). 144p. (J). (gr. 2-5). 24.21 (978-1-59961-194-5(5)) Spotlight.
McDonald, Megan & Michalak, Jamie. The Poop Picnic. Reynolds, Peter H. & Candlewick Press Staff, illus. 2011.

(Judy Moody Ser.). (ENG.). 48p. (J). (gr. k-3). pap. 3.99 (978-0-7636-5553-2(8)) Candlewick Pr.

McDonough, Yona Zeldis. The Doll Shop Downstairs. Maione, Heather, illus. 2011. (ENG.). 128p. (J). (gr. 2-5). 5.99 (978-0-14-241691-4(6), Puffin Books) Penguin Young Readers Group.

McEwan, Ian. The Daydreamer, 2 vols. 2004. (J). 33.75 (978-1-4025-9960-6(9)); 36.75 (978-1-4025-8430-5(X)) Recorded Bks., Inc.

Mcghee, Alison. Julia Gillian - And the Art of Knowing. Kozjan, Drazen, illus. 2009. (Julia Gillian Ser.). (ENG.). 304p. (J). (gr. 3-7). 6.99 (978-0-545-03349-7(7), Scholastic Paperbacks) Scholastic, Inc.

McGill, Justin. Friends Forever, Signed Jeremy E. 2007. 48p. per. 16.95 (978-1-4241-8794-2(X)) America Star Bks.

McGlotham, L. R. E. Special Place. 2013. 24p. pap. 17.00 (978-1-4817-0013-9(8)) AuthorHouse.

McGovern, Kate. Rules for 50/50 Chances: If You could Find Out How it All Ends, Would You? 2015. (ENG.). 352p. (YA). (gr. 7). 17.99 (978-0-374-30158-3(1), 9780374301583, Farrar, Straus & Giroux (BYR)) Farrar, Straus & Giroux.

McGuigan, Mary Ann. Crossing into Brooklyn. 2015. (ENG.). 224p. (YA). 17.99 (978-1-4405-8463-3(X), Simon Pulse) Simon Pulse.

—Morning in a Different Place. 2009. (ENG.). 195p. (YA). (gr. 7-18). 17.95 (978-1-59078-551-5(7), Front Street) Boyds Mills Pr.

McGuirk, Leslie. The Moogees Move House. McGuirk, Leslie, illus. 2012. (ENG., Illus.). 32p. (J). (gr. -1-2). 14.99 (978-0-7636-5558-7(9)) Candlewick Pr.

McIsaac, Meaghan. The Boys of Fire & Ash. 2015. (ENG.). 336p. (J). (gr. 5). 19.99 (978-0-375-99167-7(0), Delacorte Bks. for Young Readers) Random Hse. Children's Bks.

McKay, Hilary. Binny for Short. Player, Micah, illus. (ENG.). (J). (gr. 3-7). 2014. 320p. pap. 7.99 (978-1-4424-8276-0(1)) 2013. 304p. 16.99 (978-1-4424-8275-3(3)) McElderry, Margaret K. Bks. (McElderry, Margaret K. Bks.).

—Caddy Ever After. (ENG.). 224p. (J). 2007. (gr. 4-8). per. 6.99 (978-1-4169-0931-6(1)) 2006. (gr. 5-9). 16.99 (978-1-4169-0930-9(3)) McElderry, Margaret K. Bks. (McElderry, Margaret K. Bks.).

—Caddy's World. (ENG.). (J). (gr. 5-9). 2013. 288p. pap. 6.99 (978-1-4424-4106-4(2)) 2012. 272p. 16.99 (978-1-4424-4105-7(4)) McElderry, Margaret K. Bks. (McElderry, Margaret K. Bks.).

—The Exiles at Home. 2007. (ENG.). 208p. (J). (gr. 3-7). pap. 12.95 (978-1-4169-6729-3(X), McElderry, Margaret K. Bks.) McElderry, Margaret K. Bks.

—Forever Rose. (ENG.). 304p. (J). 2009. (gr. 4-9). pap. 6.99 (978-1-4169-5487-3(2)) 2008. (Illus.). (gr. 5-9). 17.99 (978-1-4169-5486-6(4)) McElderry, Margaret K. Bks. (McElderry, Margaret K. Bks.).

—Indigo's Star. 2006. (ENG.). 272p. (J). (gr. 3-7). reprint ed. per. 7.99 (978-1-4169-1403-7(X), McElderry, Margaret K. Bks.) McElderry, Margaret K. Bks.

—Permanent Rose. 2006. (ENG.). 256p. (J). (gr. 3-7). reprint ed. per. 7.99 (978-1-4169-2804-1(9), McElderry, Margaret K. Bks.) McElderry, Margaret K. Bks.

—Saffy's Angel. 2003. (ENG., Illus.). 160p. (J). (gr. 3-7). pap. 7.99 (978-0-689-84934-3(6), McElderry, Margaret K. Bks.) McElderry, Margaret K. Bks.

—Saffy's Angel. 2004. (Casson Family Ser.: Bk. 1). 160p. (J). (gr. 4-7). pap. 36.00 incl. audio (978-0-8072-2098-6(1), Listening Library) Random Hse. Audio Publishing Group.

McKay, Hilary & McKay, Hilary. El Perro Viernes. (Barco de Vapor). (SPA.). (YA). (gr. 5-8). pap. (978-84-348-6214-2(X)) SM Ediciones.

McKay, Lise Y. The Mysterious Well. 2012. 130p. pap. 14.95 (978-1-59663-865-5(6), Mount Helicon Pr.) Rock, James A. & Co. Pubs.

McKennon, Tony. You're Moving Where?! 2008. 40p. pap. 18.55 (978-1-4389-1397-1(4)) AuthorHouse.

McKinnon, Hannah Roberts. The Properties of Water. 2010. (ENG.). 176p. (YA). (gr. 5-9). 27.99 (978-0-374-36145-7(2), 9780374361457, Farrar, Straus & Giroux (BYR)) Farrar, Straus & Giroux.

McKinty, Adrian. Deviant. 2011. (ENG.). 368p. (YA). (gr. 9-17). 16.95 (978-0-8109-8420-2(2), Amulet Bks.) Abrams, Inc.

McKnight, Penny. Nix. 2006. (Illus.). 84p. (J). (gr. 3-7). per. 8.99 (978-1-59166-610-3(4)) BJU Pr.

McKy, Katie. Wolf Camp. Leick, Bonnie, illus. 2009. (ENG.). 32p. (J). (gr. -1-3). pap. 8.95 (978-1-933718-25-5(0)) Tanglewood Pr.

McLaren, Clemence. Dance for the Aina. 2003. 160p. 9.95 (978-1-57306-151-3(4)) Bess Pr., Inc.

McLaughlin, Lauren. The Free. 2017. (ENG.). 288p. (YA). (gr. 9). 18.99 (978-1-61695-731-5(X), Soho Teen) Soho Pr., Inc.

McMahon, Kathleen A. Mister Pudge Meets Baby Beth. 2011. 44p. 22.00 (978-1-4269-5800-7(5)) Trafford Publishing.

McMann, Lisa. Bang. 2014. (Visions Ser.: 2). (ENG., Illus.). 272p. (YA). (gr. 9). pap. 9.99 (978-1-4424-6628-9(6), Simon Pulse) Simon Pulse.

—Dead to You. 2012. (ENG.). (YA). (gr. 9). 272p. pap. 10.99 (978-1-4424-0389-5(6)); 256p. 16.99 (978-1-4424-0388-8(8)) Simon Pulse. (Simon Pulse).

—Island of Fire. 2013. (Unwanteds Ser.: Bk. 3). (ENG., Illus.). 464p. (J). (gr. 3-7). 19.99 (978-1-4424-5845-1(3), Aladdin) Simon & Schuster Children's Publishing.

—Island of Silence. 2013. (Unwanteds Ser.: 2). (ENG., Illus.). 432p. (J). (gr. 3-7). pap. 8.99 (978-1-4424-0772-5(7), Aladdin) Simon & Schuster Children's Publishing.

McMorrow, T. E. & Hoffmann, E. T. A. Nutcracker in Harlem. Ransome, James, illus. 2017. 32p. (J). (gr. -1-3). 17.99 (978-0-06-117598-5(6)) HarperCollins Pubs.

McMullan, Kate. School! Adventures at the Harvey N. Trouble Elementary School. Booth, George, illus. 2012. (ENG.). 176p. (J). (gr. 1-4). pap. 8.99 (978-0-312-55595-5(4), 9780312555955) Square Fish.

—Sir Lancelot, Where Are You?, 1 vol. Basso, Bill, illus. 2007. (Dragon Slayers' Academy Ser.: No. 6). (ENG.). 109p. (gr. 2-5). 24.21 (978-1-59961-379-6(4)) Spotlight.

McMullan, Margaret. How I Found the Strong: A Civil War Story. 2006. (ENG.). 144p. (YA). (gr. 7-12). reprint ed. mass mkt. 5.99 (978-0-553-49492-1(9), Laurel Leaf) Random Hse. Children's Bks.

McNeal, Laura. Dark Water. 2011. (ENG.). 324p. (YA). (gr. 7). pap. 9.99 (978-0-375-84330-3(2), Ember) Random Hse. Children's Bks.

McNish, Cliff. Angel. 2008. (Exceptional Reading & Language Arts Titles for Intermediate Grades Ser.). 311p. (YA). (gr. 8-12). 16.95 (978-0-8225-8900-6(1)) Lerner Publishing Group.

McQuestion, Karen. Favorite, 0 vols. unabr. ed. 2011. (ENG.). 172p. (gr. 7-9). pap. 9.95 (978-1-935597-25-4(6), 9781935597254, Skyscape) Amazon Publishing.

McQuinn, Anna. Lola Plants a Garden. Beardshaw, Rosalind, illus. 2014. (ENG.). 28p. (J). (-k). 15.95 (978-1-58089-694-8(4)) Charlesbridge Publishing, Inc.

McQuinn, Anna & Calvo, Carlos E. Lola Planta un Jardin. Beardshaw, Rosalind, illus. 2017. (SPA.). 28p. (J). (-k). pap. 7.99 (978-1-58089-786-0(X)) Charlesbridge Publishing, Inc.

McStay, Moriah. Everything That Makes You. 2015. (ENG.). 352p. (YA). (gr. 8). 17.99 (978-0-06-229548-4(9), Tegen, Katherine Bks) HarperCollins Pubs.

McVoy, Terra Elan. Criminal. 2014. (ENG., Illus.). 304p. (YA). (gr. 9). pap. 9.99 (978-1-4424-2163-9(0), Simon Pulse) Simon Pulse.

Meddaugh, Susan. Martha Speaks: Meet Martha (Picture Reader) 2010. (Martha Speaks Ser.). (ENG., Illus.). 24p. (J). (gr. -1-3). 12.99 (978-0-547-36904-4(2)) Houghton Mifflin Harcourt Publishing Co.

—Meet Martha. 2010. (Martha Speaks Ser.). (ENG., Illus.). 24p. (J). (gr. -1-3). pap. 3.99 (978-0-547-21079-7(5)) Houghton Mifflin Harcourt Publishing Co.

Medina, Meg. The Girl Who Could Silence the Wind. (ENG.). 256p. (YA). (gr. 9). 2013. pap. 8.99 (978-0-7636-6419-0(7)) 2012. (Illus.). 17.99 (978-0-7636-4602-8(4)) Candlewick Pr.

—Tía Isa Quiere un Carro. 2012.Tr. of Tia Isa Wants a Car. (SPA.). lib. bdg. 17.20 (978-0-606-23801-4(8), Turtleback) Turtleback Bks.

Meierhenry, Mark & Volk, David. The Mystery of the Pheasants. Turnbull, Susan, illus. 2012. 44p. (J). 14.95 (978-0-9845041-9-0(2)) South Dakota State Historical Society Pr.

Melling, David. Dont Worry Douglas. Melling, David, illus. 2011. (ENG., Illus.). 32p. 12.95 (978-1-58925-106-9(7)) Tiger Tales.

Meltzer, Amy. The Shabbat Princess. Avilés, Martha, illus. 2011. (Shabbat Ser.). (ENG.). 32p. (J). (gr. -1-2). pap. 7.95 (978-0-7613-5106-1(X)); lib. bdg. 17.95 (978-0-7613-5142-9(6)) Lerner Publishing Group. (Kar-Ben Publishing).

Menard, Michele R. The Cherub in the Lily Field. 2013. 50p. pap. 13.50 (978-0-9887969-3-5(7)) Four Menards, The.

Mendle, Jane. My Ultimate Sister Disaster: A Novel. 2010. (ENG.). 208p. (YA). (gr. 7-18). pap. 18.99 (978-0-312-36904-0(2), 9780312369040, St. Martin's Griffin) St. Martin's Pr.

Menon, Sandhya. When Dimple Met Rishi. 2017. (ENG., Illus.). 384p. (YA). (gr. 7). 17.99 **(978-1-4814-7868-7(0)**, Simon Pulse) Simon Pulse.

Mentyka, Sharon. Chasing at the Surface. 2016. (ENG., Illus.). 228p. (J). pap. 12.99 (978-1-943328-60-4(9), West Winds Pr.) Graphic Arts Ctr. Publishing Co.

Meredith, Christina. Kiss Crush Collide. (ENG.). 320p. (YA). (gr. 9). 2012. pap. 9.99 (978-0-06-206225-3(5)) 2011. 16.99 (978-0-06-206224-6(7)) HarperCollins Pubs. (Greenwillow Bks.).

Merkel, Ruth Vitrano. Ann: 1833-1897. 2006. (Hannah's Girls Ser.). (Illus.). 112p. (J). (gr. 4-7). per. 9.99 (978-0-8280-1951-4(7)) Review & Herald Publishing Assn.

—Grace: 1890-1973, 6. 2006. (Hannah's Girls Ser.). (Illus.). 128p. (J). (gr. 4-7). per. 9.99 (978-0-8280-1953-8(3)) Review & Herald Publishing Assn.

—Hannah's Girls: Elaine. 2008. (Hannah's Girls Ser.: 5). (Illus.). 176p. (J). pap. 9.99 (978-0-8280-1955-2(X)) Review & Herald Publishing Assn.

—Marilla 1851-1916, 6 bks. 2006. (Hannah's Girls Ser.). (Illus.). 144p. (J). (gr. 4-7). per. 9.99 (978-0-8280-1952-1(5)) Review & Herald Publishing Assn.

—Ruthie: Born 1931. 2007. (Hannah's Girls Ser.). (Illus.). 144p. (J). (gr. 4-7). per. 9.99 (978-0-8280-1954-5(1)) Review & Herald Publishing Assn.

Merritt, Ginny. The Window in the Wall. 2013. 78p. (J). (978-1-60682-781-9(2)) BJU Pr.

Messner, Kate. All the Answers. (ENG.). 2016. 272p. (J). pap. 7.99 (978-1-68119-020-4(6), 9781681190204) 2015. 256p. (YA). (gr. 3-6). 16.99 (978-1-61963-374-2(4), 9781619633742) Bloomsbury Publishing USA. (Bloomsbury USA Childrens).

—The Brilliant Fall of Gianna Z. (ENG.). 224p. 2017. (J). pap. 8.99 **(978-1-68119-547-6(X)**, 9781681195476) 2010. (YA). (gr. 3-6). pap. 8.99 (978-0-8027-2173-0(7), 9780802721730) Bloomsbury Publishing USA. (Bloomsbury USA Childrens).

—The Brilliant Fall of Gianna Z. 2017. (J). lib. bdg. 19.65 **(978-0-606-40595-9(X))** Turtleback Bks.

Messner, Kate. The Seventh Wish. 2016. (ENG.). 240p. (J). 16.99 (978-1-61963-376-6(0), 9781619633766, Bloomsbury USA Childrens) Bloomsbury Publishing USA.

Metzler, Chris & Kim, Sunyoung. Me & 10 Babies. (Illus.). 36p. (978-0-9688338-4-1(5)) Cadence Publishing.

Meyer, Franklyn. More Me & Caleb Again. 2008. (Illus.). 191p. (J). 16.95 (978-0-9789388-2-6(8)) Hester Publishing.

Meyer, Jane G. The Suitcase: A Story to Learn How to Give. Pasqualotto, Chiara, illus. 2017. (ENG.). (J). (gr. -1). pap. 16.99 (978-1-61261-776-3(X)) Paraclete Pr., Inc.

Meyer, Susan Lynn. Skating with the Statue of Liberty. 2016. (ENG.). 320p. (J). (gr. 3-7). 19.99 (978-0-375-99010-6(0), Delacorte Bks. for Young Readers) Random Hse. Children's Bks.

Meyerhoff, Jenny. The Barftastic Life of Louie Burger. Week, Jason, illus. 2013. (Barftastic Life of Louie Burger Ser.: 1). (ENG.). 240p. (J). (gr. 3-6). 13.99 (978-0-374-30518-5(8), 9780374305185, Farrar, Straus & Giroux (BYR)) Farrar, Straus & Giroux.

—Class B. U. R. P. Week, Jason, illus. 2014. (Barftastic Life of Louie Burger Ser.: 2). (ENG.). 288p. (J). (gr. 3-6). 13.99 (978-0-374-30521-5(8), 9780374305215, Farrar, Straus & Giroux (BYR)) Farrar, Straus & Giroux.

—Green Thumbs-Up! Chatelain, Éva, illus. 2015. (Friendship Garden Ser.: 1). (ENG.). 176p. (J). (gr. 2-5). pap. 5.99 (978-1-4814-3904-6(9), Aladdin) Simon & Schuster Children's Publishing.

Michalak, Jamie. The Coziest Place. Davis, Jon, illus. 2013. (ENG.). 32p. (J). (gr. -1-k). 14.99 (978-1-58925-121-2(0)) Tiger Tales.

Michels, Dia. Look What I See! Where Can I Be? With My Animal Friends. Bowles, Michael J. N. & Bowles, Michael J. N., photos by. 2007. (ENG., Illus.). 32p. (J). 9.95 (978-1-930775-08-4(3)) Platypus Media, L.L.C.

Michels, Dia L. Look What I See! Where Can I Be? At Home. Bowles, Michael J. N., photos by. 2005. (ENG., Illus.). 32p. (J). (gr. -1-12). 9.95 (978-1-930775-06-0(7)) Platypus Media, L.L.C.

—Look What I See! Where Can I Be? With My Animal Friends. Bowles, Michael J. N., photos by. l.t. ed. 2005. (Look What I See! Where Can I Be? Ser.: Vol. 3). (ENG., Illus.). 32p. (J). (gr. -1-12). 9.95 (978-1-930775-07-7(5)) Platypus Media, L.L.C.

—Zack in the Middle. Bell, Fred, illus. 2005. (Newly Independent Reader Ser.). (ENG.). 48p. (J). (gr. -1-3). 9.95 (978-1-930775-01-5(6)) Platypus Media, L.L.C.

Michiko Florence, Debbi. Jasmine Toguchi, Mochi Queen. Vukovic, Elizabet, illus. 2017. (Jasmine Toguchi Ser.). (ENG.). 128p. (J). 15.99 (978-0-374-30410-2(6), 9780374304102, Farrar, Straus & Giroux (BYR)) Farrar, Straus & Giroux.

Middleton, William. The Chipmunk Jamboree. 2013. 24p. pap. 12.45 (978-1-4624-0669-2(6), Inspiring Voices) Author Solutions, Inc.

Miller, Daniel, et al. A Miller Cousin Mystery. 2010. 120p. pap. 49.00 (978-0-557-57235-9(5)); pap. 17.80 (978-0-557-57118-5(9)) Lulu Pr., Inc.

Miller, Jennifer. Christmas Tails. Knight, Vanessa, illus. 2009. 56p. pap. 17.26 (978-1-4251-8987-7(3)) Trafford Publishing.

Miller, Mary Beth. Aimee. 2005. 276p. (gr. 9-12). 17.00 (978-0-7569-6303-3(6)) Perfection Learning Corp.

Miller, Pat Zietlow. Sharing the Bread: An Old-Fashioned Thanksgiving Story. McElmurry, Jill, illus. 2015. (ENG.). 32p. (J). (gr. -1-3). 17.99 (978-0-307-98182-0(7), Schwartz & Wade Bks.) Random Hse. Children's Bks.

Miller, Paula. One-Eyed Jack. Forrest, Chris, illus. (J). 2007. (ENG.). 133p. (gr. 2-7). pap. 8.95 (978-0-9769417-0-5(8)) 2006. 144p. 13.95 (978-0-9718348-8-0(1)) Blooming Tree Pr.

Mills, Charles. Wings over Oshkosh. 2005. (Honors Club Story Ser.: Vol. 5). 127p. (J). 7.99 (978-0-8163-2089-9(6)) Pacific Pr. Publishing Assn.

Milner, Claudette. Silent Tears: Children of Plains Estates. 2011. 132p. pap. 24.95 (978-1-4626-3943-4(7)) PublishAmerica, Inc.

Mindel, Nissan. Eight Chanukah Tales. Toron, Eli & Graybar, Shmuel, illus. 2007. 78p. (J). 10.95 (978-0-8266-0039-4(5)) Kehot Pubn. Society.

Miranda, Conchita. Yago's Heartbeat. 2011. (Light (Cuento de Luz) Ser.). (ENG., Illus.). 42p. (J). (gr. 1-4). (978-84-938240-3-7(8)) D P & G Military Pubs.

Miraucourt, Christophe. The Pirate's Daughter. 2015. (Race Further with Reading Ser.). (ENG., Illus.). 48p. (J). (978-0-7787-2088-1(8)) Crabtree Publishing Co.

Mobley, Jeannie. Katerina's Wish. (ENG., Illus.). (J). (gr. 3-7). 2014. 272p. pap. 8.99 (978-1-4424-3344-1(2)) 2012. 256p. 15.99 (978-1-4424-3343-4(4)) McElderry, Margaret K. Bks. (McElderry, Margaret K. Bks.).

Moceanu, Dominique & Thompson, Alicia. Reaching High. 2012. (Go-For-Gold Gymnasts Ser.). (ENG.). 224p. (J). (gr. 5-9). pap. 5.99 (978-1-4231-3657-6(8)) Hyperion Pr.

Molina, Silvia & Silvia, Molina. Le Comieron la Lengua los Ratones. Rodriguez, Mari, illus. 2005. (Montana Encantada Ser.). (SPA.). 96p. (YA). (gr. 3-5). pap. 9.50 (978-84-241-8557-2(9)) Everest Editora ESP. Dist: Lectorum Pubns., Inc.

Molinari, Laurice E. Pillars of Fire, 1 vol. 2016. (Ether Novel Ser.). (ENG.). 368p. (J). pap. 8.99 (978-0-310-73562-5(9)) Zonderkidz.

Molinari, Laurice Elehwany. Pillars of Fire, 1 vol. 2015. (Ether Novel Ser.). (ENG.). 368p. (J). 16.99 (978-0-310-73556-4(4)) Zonderkidz.

Montalbano, Andrea. Breakaway. 2011. (ENG.). 208p. (J). (gr. 3-7). 6.99 (978-0-14-241903-8(6), Puffin Books) Penguin Young Readers Group.

—Out of Bounds. 2017. (Soccer Sisters Ser.: 1). (ENG.). 176p. (J). (gr. 3-7). pap. 7.99 (978-1-4926-4481-1(1), 9781492644811, Sourcebooks Jabberwocky) Sourcebooks, Inc.

Montanari, Susan McElroy. My Dog's a Chicken. Wilsdorf, Anne, illus. 2016. (ENG.). 40p. (J). (gr. -1-3). 16.99 (978-0-385-38490-2(4), Schwartz & Wade Bks.) Random Hse. Children's Bks.

Montes, Marisa. A Crazy Mixed-Up Spanglish Day. Cepeda, Joe, illus. 2004. (Get Ready for Gabi Ser.). 120p. (gr. 2-5). 14.00 (978-0-7569-3403-3(6)) Perfection Learning Corp.

—A Crazy Mixed-Up Spanglish Day. Cepeda, Joe, illus. 2003. (Get Ready for Gabi Ser.). 128p. (J). 12.95 (978-0-439-51710-2(9), Scholastic Paperbacks) Scholastic, Inc.

Montgomery, Corey. Ask Grandma Pearl. 2011. 28p. pap. 15.99 (978-1-4628-9498-7(4)) Xlibris Corp.

Montgomery, L. M. Akin to Anne: Tales of Other Orphans. (YA). 22.95 (978-0-8488-2656-7(6)) Amereon Ltd.

—Jane of Lantern Hill. 2014. (ENG.). 272p. (YA). (gr. 5-12). pap. 11.99 (978-1-4022-8930-9(8)) Sourcebooks, Inc.

—Magic for Marigold. 2014. (ENG.). 336p. (YA). (gr. 5-12). pap. 8.99 (978-1-4022-8921-7(9)) Sourcebooks, Inc.

—Rainbow Valley. 2007. (ENG.). 234p. pap. 20.99 (978-1-4346-5245-4(9)); 258p. pap. 23.99 (978-1-4346-5246-1(7)) Creative Media Partners, LLC.

—Rainbow Valley. 2004. 184p. (YA). pap. 8.95 (978-1-57646-890-6(9)) Quiet Vision Publishing.

—The Story Girl. Date not set. 22.95 (978-0-8488-2372-6(9)) Amereon Ltd.

Moore, Kelly, et al. Amber House. 2013. (Amber House Ser.: 1). (ENG.). 384p. (J). (gr. 7). pap. 9.99 (978-0-545-43417-1(3), Levine, Arthur A. Bks.) Scholastic, Inc.

—Neverwas. 2014. (YA). pap. (978-0-545-43419-5(X)); (Amber House Ser.: 2). (ENG.). 320p. (J). (gr. 9). 17.99 (978-0-545-43418-8(1), Levine, Arthur A. Bks.) Scholastic, Inc.

Moore, Stephanie. Make Something of It. 2014. (Sharp Sisters Ser.: 1). (ENG.). 152p. (YA). (gr. 6-12). pap. 7.95 (978-1-4677-4488-1(3), Darby Creek) Lerner Publishing Group.

Moore, Stephanie Perry. Enjoying True Peace, 1 vol. 2010. (Yasmin Peace Ser.: 5). (ENG.). 176p. pap. 6.99 (978-0-8024-8606-6(1), Lift Every Voice) Moody Pubs.

—Experiencing the Joy, 1 vol. 2009. (Yasmin Peace Ser.: 3). (ENG.). 160p. (gr. 7-10). pap. 7.99 (978-0-8024-8604-2(5), Lift Every Voice) Moody Pubs.

—Golden Spirit. 2006. (Carmen Browne Ser.: 3). (ENG.). 144p. (YA). (gr. 3-7). per. 6.99 (978-0-8024-8169-6(8), Lift Every Voice) Moody Pubs.

—Make Something of It. 2014. (Sharp Sisters Ser.: 1). (ENG.). 152p. (YA). (gr. 6-12). lib. bdg. 27.93 (978-1-4677-3722-7(4)) Lerner Publishing Group.

—Turn up for Real. 2014. (Sharp Sisters Ser.: 3). (ENG.). 168p. (YA). (gr. 6-12). pap. 7.95 (978-1-4677-4490-4(5), Darby Creek); lib. bdg. 27.93 (978-1-4677-3726-5(7)) Lerner Publishing Group.

Moore, Stephanie Perry & Moody Publishing Staff. Believing in Hope. 2009. (Yasmin Peace Ser.: 2). (ENG.). 176p. (gr. 7-10). pap. 7.99 (978-0-8024-8603-5(7), Lift Every Voice) Moody Pubs.

—Finding Your Faith 2009. (Yasmin Peace Ser.: 1). (ENG.). 176p. (gr. 7-10). pap. 7.99 (978-0-8024-8602-8(9), Lift Every Voice) Moody Pubs.

Mora, Pat. Let's Eat! - ¡A Comer! Suarez, Maribel, illus. 2008. (My Family: Mi Familia Ser.). (SPA & ENG.). 24p. (J). (gr. -1-3). 12.99 (978-0-06-085038-8(8), Rayo) HarperCollins Pubs.

—Wiggling Pockets (Los Bolsillos Saltarines) Suarez, Maribel, illus. 2009. (My Family: Mi Familia Ser.). (SPA & ENG.). 24p. (J). (gr. -1-1). 12.99 (978-0-06-085047-0(7), Rayo) HarperCollins Pubs.

Morait, Tracey. Goalden Girl. 2007. 160p. pap. 13.95 (978-1-84799-758-6(9)) Lulu Pr., Inc.

Morey, Walt. Year of the Black Pony. 2006. (Living History Library). 171p. (J). (gr. 4-7). pap. 11.95 (978-1-932350-08-1(X)) Bethlehem Bks.

Morgan, Alex. Sabotage Season. 2013. (Kicks Ser.). (ENG., Illus.). 176p. (J). (gr. 3-7). 15.99 (978-1-4424-8574-7(4), Simon & Schuster Bks. For Young Readers) Simon & Schuster Bks. For Young Readers.

—Win or Lose. 2014. (Kicks Ser.). (ENG., Illus.). 160p. (J). (gr. 3-7). 15.99 (978-1-4424-8580-8(9), Simon & Schuster Bks. For Young Readers) Simon & Schuster Bks. For Young Readers.

Morgan, Melissa J. Politically Incorrect. 2010. (Camp Confidential Ser.: 23). (ENG.). 176p. (J). (gr. 3-7). pap. 4.99 (978-0-448-45267-8(7), Grosset & Dunlap) Penguin Young Readers Group.

Morgan, Phillip. Abused, Alone & Forsaken: Mommy, Don't Leave Me. 2009. 212p. pap. 24.95 (978-1-4489-2733-3(1)) America Star Bks.

Moriarty, Jaclyn. The Spell Book of Listen Taylor. 2007. (YA). (978-0-439-84679-0(X), Levine, Arthur A. Bks.) Scholastic, Inc.

Morrill, Lauren. Being Sloane Jacobs. 2015. (ENG.). 352p. (YA). (gr. 7). pap. 9.99 (978-0-385-74180-4(4), Ember) Random Hse. Children's Bks.

Morris, Taylor. Class Favorite. 2007. (Mix Ser.). (ENG., Illus.). 304p. (J). (gr. 4-8). pap. 5.99 (978-1-4169-3598-8(3), Simon & Schuster/Paula Wiseman Bks.) Simon & Schuster/Paula Wiseman Bks.

Morrison, Toni. Little Brother. 2011. 14.75 (978-0-7848-3494-7(6), Everbind) Marco Bk. Co.

Morrow, Dj. Two Bears Short. 2013. 28p. pap. 24.95 (978-1-62709-822-9(4)) America Star Bks.

Moser, Elise. Lily & Taylor. 2013. (ENG.). 224p. E-Book (978-1-55498-336-0(3)) Groundwood Bks.

Moses, Albert. The Hawk & the Turtles. Roberts, Pam, illus. 2011. 16p. pap. 24.95 (978-1-4626-4261-8(6)) America Star Bks.

Moses, Antoinette. Vinnie's Vacation Level 1 Beginner/Elementary American English Edition. 2012. (ENG.). 48p. pap. 9.50 (978-1-107-62130-5(5)) Cambridge Univ. Pr.

Moses, Shelia P. The Baptism. (ENG., 144p. 2008. Illus.). (J). (gr. 5-9). pap. 5.99 (978-1-4169-5833-8(9)) 2007. (YA). (gr. 7-12). 15.99 (978-1-4169-0671-1(1)) McElderry, Margaret K. Bks. (McElderry, Margaret K. Bks.).

—Joseph. 2008. (ENG., Illus.). 176p. (YA). (gr. 7-18). 16.99 (978-1-4169-1752-6(7), McElderry, Margaret K. Bks.) McElderry, Margaret K. Bks.

—The Legend of Buddy Bush. 2004. (ENG., Illus.). 224p. (YA). (gr. 7). 19.99 (978-0-689-85839-0(6), McElderry, Margaret K. Bks.) McElderry, Margaret K. Bks.

—The Legend of Buddy Bush. 2005. (Illus.). 211p. (gr. 7-12). 17.00 (978-0-7569-5459-8(2)) Perfection Learning Corp.

—The Legend of Buddy Bush, 3 vols. unabr. ed. 2005. (YA). (gr. 3-7). 54.75 (978-1-4193-3575-4(8), 42043) Recorded Bks., Inc.

Moskowitz, Hannah. Invincible Summer. 2011. (ENG.). 288p. (YA). (gr. 9-18). pap. 9.99 (978-1-4424-0751-0(4), Simon Pulse) Simon Pulse.

Moss, Marissa. Amelia Writes Again. Moss, Marissa, illus. (Amelia Ser.). (ENG., Illus.). (J). (gr. 2-5). 2012. 32p. pap. 6.99 (978-1-4169-1285-9(1)) 2006. 40p. 12.99 (978-1-4169-0904-0(4)) Simon & Schuster/Paula Wiseman Bks. (Simon & Schuster/Paula Wiseman Bks.).

—Amelia's 5th-Grade Notebook. Moss, Marissa, illus. 2006. (Amelia Ser.). (ENG., Illus.). (J). 5.99 (978-1-4169-1292-7(4), Simon & Schuster/Paula Wiseman Bks.) Simon & Schuster/Paula Wiseman Bks.

—Amelia's Guide to Babysitting. Moss, Marissa, illus. 2008. (Amelia Ser.). (ENG., Illus.). 80p. (J). (gr. 5-8). 9.99 (978-1-4169-5051-6(6), Simon & Schuster/Paula Wiseman Bks.) Simon & Schuster/Paula Wiseman Bks.

—The Fake Friend! Moss, Marissa, illus. 2012. (Daphne's Diary of Daily Disasters Ser.). (ENG., Illus.). 96p. (J). (gr. 2-5). 9.99 (978-1-4424-4014-2(7)); pap. 5.99 (978-1-4424-4015-9(5)) Simon & Schuster/Paula Wiseman Bks. (Simon & Schuster/Paula Wiseman Bks.).

—The Name Game! Moss, Marissa, illus. 2011. (Daphne's Diary of Daily Disasters Ser.). (ENG., Illus.). 80p. (J). (gr. 2-5). pap. 5.99 (978-1-4424-1738-0(2)); lib. bdg. 9.99 (978-1-4424-2676-4(4)) Simon & Schuster/Paula Wiseman Bks. (Simon & Schuster/Paula Wiseman Bks.).

—Rose's Journal: The Story of a Girl in the Great Depression. 2003. (Young American Voices Ser.). (ENG., Illus.). 56p. (J). (gr. 2-5). pap. 7.99 (978-0-15-204605-7(4)) Houghton Mifflin Harcourt Publishing Co.

—Rose's Journal: The Story of a Girl in the Great Depression. 2004. (Young American Voice Bks.). (Illus.). (gr. 3-7). 17.00 (978-0-7569-4230-4(6)) Perfection Learning Corp.

—The Vampire Dare! Moss, Marissa, illus. 2011. (Daphne's Diary of Daily Disasters Ser.). (ENG., Illus.). 80p. (J). (gr. 2-5). pap. 5.99 (978-1-4424-1737-3(4)); lib. bdg. 9.99 (978-1-4424-2677-1(2)) Simon & Schuster/Paula Wiseman Bks. (Simon & Schuster/Paula Wiseman Bks.).

Moulder, Holly. Crystal City Lights. 2013. (ENG.). 190p. (J). pap. 8.99 (978-0-9885295-0-2(5)) Blue Marlin Pubns.

Moulton, Erin E. Chasing the Milky Way. 2014. (ENG.). 288p. (J). (gr. 3-7). 16.99 (978-0-399-16449-1(9), Philomel Bks.) Penguin Young Readers Group.

—Flutter: The Story of Four Sisters & an Incredible Journey. 2012. (ENG.). 224p. (J). (gr. 3-7). pap. 6.99 (978-0-14-242133-8(2), Puffin Books) Penguin Young Readers Group.

Mueller, Dagmar H. David's World: A Picture Book about Living with Autism. Ballhaus, Verena, illus. 2012. (ENG.). 28p. (J). (gr. -1-k). 16.95 (978-1-61608-962-7(8), 608962, Sky Pony Pr.) Skyhorse Publishing Co., Inc.

Mueller, Miranda, illus. Mishka: An Adoption Tale. 2007. 32p. (J). 16.95 (978-1-933084-01-5(4)) DRT Pr.

Mulder, Michelle. Out of the Box. 2011. 150p. (J). (978-1-55469-329-0(2)) Orca Bk. Pubs.

—Out of the Box, 1 vol. 2011. (ENG.). 160p. (J). (gr. 4-7). pap. 9.95 (978-1-55469-328-3(4)) Orca Bk. Pubs. USA.

Muldrow, Diane. Everything I Need to Know about Family I Learned from a Little Golden Book. 2017. (ENG., Illus.). 96p. (gr. 7-12). 9.99 (978-0-553-53851-9(9), Golden Bks.) Random Hse. Children's Bks.

Mulholland, Clara. Naughty Miss Bunny. 2007. 128p. 25.95 (978-1-4218-3838-0(9), 1st World Library - Literary Society) 1st World Publishing, Inc.

Mullen, Paul Michael. The Day I Hit a Home Run at Great American Ball Park. 2007. 146p. (J). (978-1-933197-30-2(7)) Orange Frazer Pr.

Mullinax, Jerry. Enoree. 2009. (YA). pap. (978-0-88092-646-1(5)) Royal Fireworks Publishing Co.

Muncaster, Harriet. The Biggest Smallest Christmas Present. Muncaster, Harriet, illus. 2016. (ENG., Illus.). 32p. (J). (-k). 16.99 (978-0-399-16432-3(4), G.P. Putnam's Sons Books for Young Readers) Penguin Young Readers Group.

Munsch, Robert. On Partage Tout! 2004. (FRE., Illus.). (J). (gr. k-3). spiral bd. (978-0-616-01838-5(X)) Canadian National Institute for the Blind/Institut National Canadien pour les Aveugles.

—Up, up, Down. 2004. (Illus.). (J). (gr. k-3). spiral bd. (978-0-616-11126-0(6)); spiral bd. (978-0-616-11127-7(4)) Canadian National Institute for the Blind/Institut National Canadien pour les Aveugles.

Murdoch, Emily. If You Find Me. (ENG.). (YA). (gr. 7). 2014. 288p. pap. 10.99 (978-1-250-03327-7(6), 9781250033277) 2013. 256p. 17.99 (978-1-250-02152-6(9), 9781250021526) St. Martin's Pr. (St. Martin's Griffin).

Mure, Nancy & Keene, Kateline. Irregular Joe. 2014. (ENG., Illus.). 30p. (J). pap. 9.98 (978-0-7443-2141-8(7)) SynergEbks.

Murphy, Barbara & Murphy, Barbara Beasley. Life! How I Love You! Baca, Elena, illus. 2004. (ENG.). 136p. (J). 9.95 (978-0-89013-468-9(5)) Museum of New Mexico Pr.

Murphy, Jill. Five Minutes' Peace. Murphy, Jill, illus. 2012. (ENG., Illus.). 24p. (J). (gr. -1 — 1). bds. 7.99 (978-0-399-25707-0(1), G.P. Putnam's Sons Books for Young Readers) Penguin Young Readers Group.

—Mr. Large in Charge. Murphy, Jill, illus. 2007. (ENG., Illus.). 40p. (J). (gr. -1-3). 16.99 (978-0-7636-3504-6(9)) Candlewick Pr.

Murphy, Julie. Ramona Blue. (YA). (gr. 8). 2018. (ENG.). 448p. pap. 9.99 (978-0-06-241836-4(X)) 2017. 432p. 17.99 (978-0-06-241835-7(1)) HarperCollins Pubs.

Murphy, Pat. The Wild Girls. unabr. ed. 2007. (YA). (gr. 6-9). audio compact disk 45.00 (978-0-7393-5988-4(6)) Random Hse. Audio Publishing Group.

Murphy, Sally. Pearl Verses the World. Potter, Heather, illus. 2011. (ENG.). 80p. (J). (gr. 3-7). 14.99 (978-0-7636-4821-3(3)) Candlewick Pr.

Murray, Martine. Henrietta: There's No One Better. 2010. (Henrietta Ser.). (ENG., Illus.). 96p. (J). (gr. k-2). pap. 10.99 (978-1-74114-718-6(2)) Allen & Unwin AUS. Dist: Independent Pubs. Group.

—Henrietta: There's No One Better. 2006. (Illus.). 88p. (J). 9.99 (978-0-439-80749-4(2), Levine, Arthur A. Bks.) Scholastic, Inc.

Muschla, Gary Robert. The Sword & the Cross. 2009. (YA). pap. (978-0-88092-472-6(1)) Royal Fireworks Publishing Co.

My Great Grandma Clara. 2006. (J). pap. 12.95 (978-0-9677047-8-4(2)) Marble Hse. Editions.

My little Brother, 6 vols., Pack. (gr. 1-2). 22.00 (978-0-7635-9164-9(5)) Rigby Education.

Myers, Anna. Tumbleweed Baby. Vess, Charles, illus. 2014. (ENG.). 32p. (J). (gr. k-2). 16.95 (978-1-4197-1232-6(2), Abrams Bks. for Young Readers) Abrams, Inc.

Myers, Walter Dean. The Dream Bearer. 2003. (ENG.). 192p. (J). (gr. 5-18). 15.99 (978-0-06-029521-9(X), Amistad) HarperCollins Pubs.

—The Dream Bearer. 2004. 16.00 (978-0-7569-3242-8(4)) Perfection Learning Corp.

—Game. 2008. (ENG.). 224p. (YA). (gr. 8-18). 17.99 (978-0-06-058294-4(4), HarperTeen) HarperCollins Pubs.

—It Ain't All for Nothin' 2003. (Amistad Ser.). (ENG.). 240p. (YA). (gr. 8-18). pap. 6.99 (978-0-06-447311-8(2), Amistad) HarperCollins Pubs.

—Looking Like Me. Myers, Christopher, illus. 2009. (ENG.). 32p. (J). (gr. k-4). 18.99 (978-1-60684-001-6(0), Carolrhoda Bks.) Lerner Publishing Group.

—Shooter. 2004. (ENG.). 224p. (J). 15.99 (978-0-06-029519-6(8), HarperTeen) HarperCollins Pubs.

—What They Found: Love on 145th Street. 2011. 10.54 (978-0-7848-3499-2(7)); 10.54 (978-0-7848-3386-5(9)) Marco Bk. Co. (Everbind).

Myers, Walter Dean & Workman, Ross. Kick. 2011. (ENG.). 208p. (YA). (gr. 9-18). 16.99 (978-0-06-200489-5(1), HarperTeen) HarperCollins Pubs.

Myracle, Lauren. Eleven. 2005. (Winnie Years Ser.). (ENG.). 224p. (J). (gr. 3-7). reprint ed. pap. 7.99 (978-0-14-240346-4(6), Puffin Books) Penguin Young Readers Group.

—The Fashion Disaster That Changed My Life. 2008. (ENG.). 160p. (J). (gr. 5-18). 6.99 (978-0-14-240717-2(8), Puffin Books) Penguin Young Readers Group.

—The Infinite Moment of Us. (ENG.). 336p. (YA). (gr. 9-17). 2014. pap. 8.95 (978-1-4197-1358-3(2)) 2013. 18.95 (978-1-4197-0793-3(0)) Abrams, Inc. (Amulet Bks.).

—Ten. 2011. (Winnie Years Ser.). (ENG.). 272p. (J). (gr. 3-7). 16.99 (978-0-525-42356-0(7), Dutton Books for Young Readers) Penguin Young Readers Group.

—Thirteen. 2009. (Winnie Years Ser.). (ENG.). 272p. (J). (gr. 3-7). 7.99 (978-0-14-241370-8(4), Puffin Books) Penguin Young Readers Group.

—Twelve. 2008. (Winnie Years Ser.). (ENG.). 224p. (J). (gr. 5-18). 7.99 (978-0-14-241091-2(8), Puffin Books) Penguin Young Readers Group.

Nall, Gail. Breaking the Ice. 2015. (ENG., Illus.). 320p. (J). (gr. 3-7). 16.99 (978-1-4814-1911-6(0), Aladdin) Simon & Schuster Children's Publishing.

Namioka, Lensey. Half & Half. 2005. 136p. (gr. 3-7). 16.00 (978-0-7569-5680-6(3)) Perfection Learning Corp.

—Half & Half. 2004. (ENG.). 144p. (J). (gr. 3-7). 5.99 (978-0-440-41890-0(9), Yearling) Random Hse. Children's Bks.

Nanji, Shenaaz. Child of Dandelions. 2008. (ENG., Illus.). 208p. (J). (gr. 6-9). 17.95 (978-1-932425-93-2(4), Front Street) Boyds Mills Pr.

Napoli, Donna Jo. Daughter of Venice. 2003. (ENG.). 288p. (YA). (gr. 7). mass mkt. 7.99 (978-0-440-22928-5(6), Laurel Leaf) Random Hse. Children's Bks.

Naylor, Phyllis Reynolds. Alice in April. 2011. (Alice Ser.: 5). (ENG.). 192p. (J). (gr. 5-9). pap. 6.99 (978-1-4424-2757-0(4), Atheneum Bks. for Young Readers) Simon & Schuster Children's Publishing.

—Alice In-Between. 2011. (Alice Ser.: 6). (ENG.). 192p. (J). (gr. 5-9). pap. 6.99 (978-1-4424-2758-7(2), Atheneum Bks. for Young Readers) Simon & Schuster Children's Publishing.

—Alice In-Between. 2008. (Alice McKinley Ser.: No. 6). (ENG.). 176p. (J). pap. 5.99 (978-1-4169-6770-5(2), Simon & Schuster/Paula Wiseman Bks.) Simon & Schuster/Paula Wiseman Bks.

—Alice in Charge. (Alice Ser.: 22). (ENG., (YA). (gr. 9). 2011. Illus.). 304p. pap. 8.99 (978-1-4169-7555-7(1)) 2010. 336p. 16.99 (978-1-4169-7552-6(7)) Simon & Schuster Children's Publishing. (Atheneum Bks. for Young Readers).

—Alice in Lace. 2009. (Alice McKinley Ser.: No. 8). (ENG.). 160p. (J). pap. 7.99 (978-1-4169-7543-4(8), Simon & Schuster/Paula Wiseman Bks.) Simon & Schuster/Paula Wiseman Bks.

—Alice on Her Way. 2006. (Alice McKinley Ser.: No. 17). 322p. (gr. 9-12). 17.00 (978-0-7569-6909-7(3)) Perfection Learning Corp.

—Alice on Her Way. 2006. (Alice Ser.: No. 17). (ENG.). 352p. (YA). (gr. 9-12). mass mkt. 6.99 (978-0-689-87091-0(4), Simon Pulse) Simon Pulse.

—Alice the Brave. (Alice Ser.: 7). (ENG., (J). 2011. Illus.). 176p. (gr. 5-9). pap. 7.99 (978-1-4424-2851-5(1), Atheneum Bks. for Young Readers) 2009. 160p. (gr. 4-8). pap. 7.99 (978-1-4169-7542-7(X), Aladdin) Simon & Schuster Children's Publishing.

—Dangerously Alice. 2007. (Alice Ser.: 19). (ENG.). 304p. (YA). (gr. 9-12). 15.99 (978-0-689-87094-1(9), Atheneum Bks. for Young Readers) Simon & Schuster Children's Publishing.

—Dangerously Alice. 2008. (Alice Ser.: No. 19). (ENG.). 320p. (YA). mass mkt. 6.99 (978-0-689-87095-8(7), Simon Pulse) Simon Pulse.

—I Like Him, He Likes Her: Alice Alone; Simply Alice; Patiently Alice. 2010. (Alice Ser.). (ENG.). 640p. (YA). (gr. 7). pap. 12.99 (978-1-4424-0978-1(9), Atheneum Bks. for Young Readers) Simon & Schuster Children's Publishing.

—Incredibly Alice. (Alice Ser.: 23). (ENG., (YA). (gr. 9). 2012. Illus.). 304p. pap. 8.99 (978-1-4169-7556-4(X)) 2011. 288p. 16.99 (978-1-4169-7553-3(5)) Simon & Schuster Children's Publishing. (Atheneum Bks. for Young Readers).

—Lovingly Alice. 2006. (Alice Ser.). (ENG., Illus.). 176p. (J). (gr. 4-7). pap. 5.99 (978-0-689-84400-3(X), Atheneum Bks. for Young Readers) Simon & Schuster Children's Publishing.

—Now I'll Tell You Everything. 2013. (Alice Ser.: 25). (ENG., Illus.). 528p. (YA). (gr. 9). 17.99 (978-1-4424-4590-1(4)) Simon & Schuster Children's Publishing.

—Outrageously Alice. 2011. (Alice Ser.: 9). (ENG., Illus.). 176p. (J). (gr. 5-9). pap. 6.99 (978-1-4424-2853-9(8), Atheneum Bks. for Young Readers) Simon & Schuster Children's Publishing.

—Please Don't Be True: Dangerously Alice; Almost Alice; Intensely Alice. 2011. (Alice Ser.). (ENG., Illus.). 768p. (YA). (gr. 9). pap. 12.99 (978-1-4424-1721-2(8), Atheneum Bks. for Young Readers) Simon & Schuster Children's Publishing.

—Reluctantly Alice. 2011. (Alice Ser.: 3). (ENG.). 240p. (J). (gr. 5-9). pap. 6.99 (978-1-4424-2361-9(7), Atheneum Bks. for Young Readers) Simon & Schuster Children's Publishing.

—Reluctantly Alice. 2008. (Alice McKinley Ser.: No. 3). (ENG.). 208p. (J). pap. 5.99 (978-1-4169-5876-5(2), Simon & Schuster/Paula Wiseman Bks.) Simon & Schuster/Paula Wiseman Bks.

—Shiloh. 144p. (J). (Shiloh Ser.: No. 1). (gr. 4-7). pap. 4.99 (978-0-8072-8330-1(4));No. 1. 2004. (gr. 3-7). pap. 29.00 incl. audio (978-0-8072-8329-5(0), YA164SP) Random Hse. Audio Publishing Group. (Listening Library).

—A Shiloh Christmas. 2015. (Shiloh Quartet Ser.). (ENG., Illus.). 256p. (J). (gr. 3-7). 17.99 (978-1-4814-4151-3(5)) Simon & Schuster Children's Publishing.

—Shiloh Season. unabr. ed. 2004. (Shiloh Ser.: No. 2). 120p. (J). (gr. 3-7). pap. 29.00 incl. audio (978-0-8072-8707-1(5), YA242SP, Listening Library) Random Hse. Audio Publishing Group.

—Starting with Alice. 2004. (Alice Bks.). 181p. (J). (gr. 4-7). 12.65 (978-0-7569-2940-4(7)) Perfection Learning Corp.

—Starting with Alice. 2012. (Alice Ser.). (ENG., Illus.). 224p. (J). (gr. 2-7). pap. 6.99 (978-1-4424-4642-7(0), Atheneum Bks. for Young Readers) Simon & Schuster Children's Publishing.

—Walker's Crossing. unabr. ed. 2004. 232p. (J). (gr. 5-9). pap. 36.00 incl. audio (978-0-8072-8410-0(6), Listening Library) Random Hse. Audio Publishing Group.

—You & Me & the Space in Between: Alice in Charge; Incredibly Alice; Alice on Board. 2013. (Alice Ser.). (ENG., Illus.). 880p. (YA). (gr. 9). pap. 10.99 (978-1-4424-8664-5(3), Atheneum Bks. for Young Readers) Simon & Schuster Children's Publishing.

Neale, Cynthia. Hope in New York City: The Continuing Story of the Irish Dresser. 2008. (ENG.). 176p. (J). pap. 7.95 (978-1-57249-387-2(9), White Mane Kids) White Mane Publishing Co., Inc.

Neilsen, David. Beyond the Doors. 2017. (ENG.). 368p. (J). (gr. 3-7). 16.99 **(978-1-101-93582-8(0)**, Crown Books For Young Readers) Random Hse. Children's Bks.

Nelson, Annabelle. Ricardo's Pain: A Story for Young People & Their Parents about Staying Strong, Finding Courage & Overcoming Adversity. Palomares, Franz, illus. 2003. (SPA.). (978-0-9656732-8-0(6)) WHEEL Council, Inc., The.

Nelson, Blake. Destroy All Cars. 2011. (ENG.). 224p. (J). (gr. 9-10). pap. 9.99 (978-0-545-10475-3(0), Scholastic Paperbacks) Scholastic, Inc.

Nelson, Jandy. I'll Give You the Sun. 2015. (CHI.). 384p. (YA). (gr. 9). pap. (978-986-359-180-1(7)) Ecus Publishing Hse.

—I'll Give You the Sun. 2014. (ENG.). 384p. (YA). (gr. 9). 17.99 (978-0-8037-3496-8(4), Dial Bks) Penguin Publishing Group.

—I'll Give You the Sun. 2015. (ENG.). 400p. (YA). (gr. 9-12). pap. 10.99 (978-0-14-242576-3(1), Speak) Penguin Young Readers Group.

—I'll Give You the Sun. 2015. (ENG.). 400p. (YA). (gr. 9). 21.30 (978-1-68065-512-4(4)) Perfection Learning Corp.

—I'll Give You the Sun. 2015. lib. bdg. 22.10 (978-0-606-37572-6(4)) Turtleback Bks.

Nelson, Marilyn. American Ace. 2016. (ENG.). 128p. (YA). (gr. 7). 17.99 (978-0-8037-3305-3(4), Dial Bks) Penguin Young Readers Group.

Nelson, R. A. Breathe My Name. 2008. (ENG.). 320p. (YA). (gr. 7-18). 9.99 (978-1-59514-186-6(3), Razorbill) Penguin Young Readers Group.

Nervelle, Rosemarie. The Witch of Beaver Creek Mine. 2007. (ENG.). 160p. (J). (gr. 3-7). 14.95 (978-0-89272-741-4(1)) Down East Bks.

Nesbet, Anne. The Cabinet of Earths. 2013. (ENG.). 288p. (J). (gr. 3-7). pap. 6.99 (978-0-06-196319-3(4)) HarperCollins Pubs.

Nesbit, E. Harding's Luck. 2006. 164p. (gr. 4-7). per. 13.95 (978-1-59818-878-3(X)); 25.95 (978-1-59818-170-8(X)) Aegypan.

—The Railway Children. 2007. 236p. per. 12.95 (978-1-4218-3945-5(8)); (ENG.). (gr. 4-7). 27.95 (978-1-4218-3845-8(1)) 1st World Publishing, Inc. (1st World Library - Literary Society).

—The Railway Children. 2006. (ENG.). 228p. (gr. 4-7). per. 14.95 (978-1-59818-933-9(6)); 26.95 (978-1-59818-179-1(3)) Aegypan.

—The Railway Children. 2013. 140p. pap. (978-1-908388-94-0(3)) Aziloth Bks.

—The Railway Children. 2008. (J). 8.99 (978-1-59166-924-1(3)) BJU Pr.

—The Railway Children. Brock, C. E., illus. (YA). 14.95 (978-0-8118-4933-3(3)) Chronicle Bks. LLC.

—The Railway Children. 2012. (ENG.). 234p. pap. 14.99 (978-1-4812-4818-1(9)) CreateSpace Independent Publishing Platform.

—The Railway Children. 2008. 204p. (gr. 4-7). 27.99 (978-0-554-26706-7(3)); 24.99 (978-0-554-36009-6(8)) Creative Media Partners, LLC.

—The Railway Children. 2008. (gr. 4-7). pap. 5.99 (978-1-4209-3105-1(9)) Digireads.com Publishing.

—The Railway Children. Brock, C. E., illus. 2008. (ENG.). 248p. per. (978-1-4065-9815-5(1)) Dodo Pr.

—The Railway Children. 2007. (ENG.). 204p. per. (978-1-4065-3083-4(2)) Dodo Pr.

—The Railway Children. 2006. pap. (978-1-4068-3505-2(6)) 2005. 348p. pap. (978-1-84637-205-6(4)) Echo Library.

—The Railway Children. Brock, Charles Edmund, illus. 2012. 232p. pap. (978-1-78201-004-3(1)) Evertype.

—The Railway Children. 2010. (Illus.). 118p. pap. 19.99 (978-1-153-71841-7(3)) General Bks. LLC.

—The Railway Children. Dryhurst, Dinah, tr. Dryhurst, Dinah, illus. 2004. 184p. 18.95 (978-1-56792-261-5(9)) Godine, David R. Pub.

—The Railway Children. 2010. 184p. pap. (978-1-4076-1891-3(1)) HardPr.

—The Railway Children. (J). (978-0-340-71497-3(2)) Hodder & Stoughton.

—The Railway Children. 2010. 194p. 30.36 (978-1-169-28328-2(4)) 2010. 194p. pap. 18.36 (978-1-162-70632-0(5)) 2010. 194p. 37.95 (978-1-161-47496-1(X)) 2004. reprint ed. pap. 22.95 (978-1-4191-7972-3(1)) 2004. reprint ed. pap. 1.99 (978-1-4192-7972-0(6)) Kessinger Publishing, LLC.

—The Railway Children. 2006. (Twelve-Point Ser.). lib. bdg. 25.00 (978-1-58287-399-2(2)); lib. bdg. 26.00 (978-1-58287-890-4(0)) North Bks.

—The Railway Children. 2012. (Oxford Children's Classics Ser.). (ENG.). 240p. 9.95 (978-0-19-275819-4(5)) Oxford Univ. Pr., Inc.

—The Railway Children. unabr. ed. 2004. (Chrysalis Childrens Classics Ser.). (Illus.). 128p. (YA). pap. (978-1-84365-050-8(9), Pavilion Children's Books) Pavilion Bks.

—The Railway Children. 2nd ed. 2008. (ENG., Illus.). 48p. pap. 11.99 (978-1-4058-6964-5(X)) Pearson Education.

—The Railway Children. 2nd ed. 2011. (Puffin Classics Ser.). (ENG., Illus.). 304p. (J). (gr. 5-7). pap. 5.99 (978-0-14-132160-8(1), Puffin Books) Penguin Young Readers Group.

—The Railway Children. (ENG.). (J). (gr. 4-7). 2013. 320p. pap. 10.99 (978-0-09-957299-2(0)) 2012. 290p. 10.99 (978-0-09-957715-7(1)) Random Hse. GBR. Dist: Independent Pubs. Group.

—The Railway Children. 2010. 146p. (gr. 4-7). pap. 8.95 (978-1-61104-337-2(9)) ReadaClassic.com.

—The Railway Children. 2004. (ENG.). 580p. (978-0-9548401-2-9(7)) Shoes & Ships & Sealing Wax Ltd.

—The Railway Children. 2011. 200p. (gr. 4-7). pap. (978-3-8424-4120-0(7)) Tredition GmbH.

—The Railway Children. 2009. 156p. (gr. 4-7). pap. 6.99 (978-1-60459-698-4(8)) Wilder Pubns., Corp.

—Story of the Treasure Seekers. 2006. pap. (978-1-4068-3507-6(2)) Echo Library.

—The Story of the Treasure Seekers: Being the Adventures of the Bastable Children in Search of a Fortune. 2007. (ENG.). 150p. pap. 18.99 (978-1-4346-5163-1(0)); 170p. pap. 21.99 (978-1-4346-5164-8(9)) Creative Media Partners, LLC.

—The Story of the Treasure Seekers: Being the Adventures of the Bastable Children in Search of A Fortune. l.t. ed. 2005. 288p. pap. (978-1-84637-207-0(0)) Echo Library.

Newman, Catherine. One Mixed-Up Night. 2017. (ENG.). 208p. (J). (gr. 3-7). 16.99 **(978-0-399-55388-2(6))**; lib. bdg. 19.99 **(978-0-399-55389-9(4))** Random Hse. Children's Bks. (Random Hse. Bks. for Young Readers).

Newman, John. Mimi. 2011. (ENG., Illus.). 192p. (J). (gr. 3-7). 15.99 (978-0-7636-5415-3(9)) Candlewick Pr.

Newman, Tracy. Shabbat Hiccups. Exelby, Ilana, illus. 2016. (ENG.). 32p. (J). (gr. -1-3). 16.99 (978-0-8075-7312-9(4)) Whitman, Albert & Co.

Newswanger, Rebecca. God Gave Us Fathers & Mothers. Steiner, Maria, illus. 2009. (Little Jewel Book Ser.). 24p. (J). (gr. 2). pap. 2.70 (978-0-7399-2408-2(7)) Rod & Staff Pubs., Inc.

Newton, Samantha. Being Nine Isn't So Bad. 2006. 52p. pap. 16.95 (978-1-4241-1902-8(2)) PublishAmerica, Inc.

Nicholls, Sally. Season of Secrets. 2011. 225p. (J). pap. (978-0-545-21826-9(8), Levine, Arthur A. Bks.) Scholastic, Inc.

Nichols, Travis. Matthew Meets the Man. 2012. (ENG., Illus.). 176p. (YA). (gr. 6-9). 24.99 (978-1-59643-545-2(3), 9781596435452) Roaring Brook Pr.

Nickerson, Sara. How to Disappear Completely & Never Be Found. Comport, Sally Wern, illus. 2003. (ENG.). 288p. (J). (gr. 5-18). pap. 5.99 (978-0-06-441027-4(7)) HarperCollins Pubs.

Nielsen, Jennifer A. A Night Divided. 2015. (ENG., Illus.). 336p. (J). (gr. 3-7). 16.99 (978-0-545-68242-8(8), Scholastic Pr.) Scholastic, Inc.

Nielsen, Susin. Dear George Clooney: Please Marry My Mom. 2012. (ENG., Illus.). 232p. (J). (gr. 5-9). 10.95 (978-1-77049-295-0(X), Tundra Bks.) Tundra Bks. CAN. Dist: Penguin Random Hse. LLC.

Nielson, Ane O. The Lone Star G Brand on My Behind. 2004. (Illus.). 96p. (J). per. 9.95 (978-1-930580-56-5(8), Luminary Media Group) Pine Orchard, Inc.

Nitz, Kristin Wolden. Suspect, 1 vol. 2010. (ENG.). 224p. (YA). (gr. 7-11). 16.95 (978-1-56145-543-0(1)) Peachtree Pubs.

Nixon, Joan Lowery. John's Story, 1775. 2004. (J). (978-0-87935-228-8(0)) Colonial Williamsburg Foundation.

Noble, Trinka Hakes. The Orange Shoes. Ettlinger, Doris, illus. rev. ed. 2007. (ENG.). 40p. (J). (gr. k-6). 16.95 (978-1-58536-277-6(8)) Sleeping Bear Pr.

Noe, Katherine Schlick. Something to Hold. 2011. (ENG., Illus.). 256p. (J). (gr. 5-7). 17.99 (978-0-547-55813-4(9)) Houghton Mifflin Harcourt Publishing Co.

Noël, Alyson. Forever Summer. 2011. (ENG.). 464p. (YA). (gr. 8-12). pap. 9.99 (978-0-312-60439-4(4), 9780312604394, St. Martin's Griffin) St. Martin's Pr.

Nolan, Han. Crazy. 2010. (ENG.). 352p. (YA). (gr. 7-18). 17.00 (978-0-15-205109-9(0)) Houghton Mifflin Harcourt Publishing Co.

—Dancing on the Edge. 2007. (ENG., Illus.). 272p. (YA). (gr. 7-12). pap. 7.99 (978-0-15-205884-5(2)) Houghton Mifflin Harcourt Publishing Co.

—A Face in Every Window. 2008. (ENG., Illus.). 276p. (YA). (gr. 7). pap. 15.95 (978-0-15-206418-1(4)) Houghton Mifflin Harcourt Publishing Co.

—Pregnant Pause. 2012. (ENG.). 352p. (YA). (gr. 9). pap. 8.99 (978-0-547-85414-4(5)) Houghton Mifflin Harcourt Publishing Co.

—A Summer of Kings. 2006. 334p. (J). (978-1-4156-7340-9(3)) Harcourt Trade Pubs.

Nolen, Gale. Johnny, My Favorite Mouse. Cain, Doreyl Ammons, illus. 2007. 32p. (J). per. 18.95 (978-0-9753023-7-8(X)) Ammons Communications, Ltd.

Nolen, Jerdine. Calico Girl. 2017. (ENG., Illus.). 192p. (J). (gr. 3-7). 16.99 (978-1-4814-5981-5(3), Simon & Schuster/Paula Wiseman Bks.) Simon & Schuster/Paula Wiseman Bks.

—Pitching in for Eubie. Lewis, E. B., illus. 2007. (ENG.). 32p. (J). (gr. k-3). 16.99 (978-0-688-14917-8(0), Amistad) HarperCollins Pubs.

Nolen, Jerdine, et al. Bradford Street Buddies: Backyard Camp-Out. Henninger, Michelle, illus. 2015. (Green Light Readers Level 3 Ser.). (ENG.). 48p. (J). (gr. 1-4). pap. 3.99 (978-0-544-36844-6(4), HMH Books For Young Readers) Houghton Mifflin Harcourt Publishing Co.

—Bradford Street Buddies: Backyard Camp-Out. Henninger, Michelle, illus. 2015. (Green Light Readers Level 3 Ser.). (ENG.). 48p. (J). (gr. 1-4). 12.99 (978-0-544-36843-9(6), HMH Books For Young Readers) Houghton Mifflin Harcourt Publishing Co.

Norris, Elizabeth. Unraveling. (Unraveling Ser.: 1). (ENG.). (YA). (gr. 8). 2013. 480p. pap. 9.99 (978-0-06-210374-1(1)) 2012. 464p. 17.99 (978-0-06-210373-4(3)) HarperCollins Pubs.

Norton, Tamra. Make Me a Home. 2008. 159p. (J). (gr. 3-7). pap. 12.99 (978-1-59955-113-5(6)) Cedar Fort, Inc./CFI Distribution.

Novara, Joe. Road Wrangler: Cowboys on Wheels. Lawson, Robert & Spatrisano, Kimberly, illus. 2007. 112p. (J). pap. 8.95 (978-1-58980-507-1(0)) Pelican Publishing Co., Inc.

Ntihemuka, Patty Froese. Hyacinth Doesn't Go to Jail: And, Hyacinth Doesn't Miss Christmas. 2009. (J). pap. 10.99 (978-0-8163-2372-2(0)) Pacific Pr. Publishing Assn.

—Hyacinth Doesn't Grow Up: And Hyacinth Doesn't Drown. 2010. (J). pap. 10.99 (978-0-8163-2386-9(0)) Pacific Pr. Publishing Assn.

Oborowsky, S. L. S. Ivy: The Stem of a Rose. 2011. (ENG.). 112p. (YA). pap. 10.95 (978-1-59299-654-4(X)) Inkwater Pr.

O'Brien, Annemarie. Lara's Gift. 2014. (ENG.). 208p. (J). (gr. 5). 7.99 (978-0-307-93175-7(7), Yearling) Random Hse. Children's Bks.

Ochsner, Gina. The Hidden Letters of Velta B. 2017. (ENG.). 320p. pap. 14.99 (978-0-544-70304-9(9)) Houghton Mifflin Harcourt Publishing Co.

Ockler, Sarah. The Book of Broken Hearts. (ENG., Illus.). (YA). (gr. 9). 2014. 384p. pap. 9.99 (978-1-4424-3039-6(7)) 2013. 368p. 17.99 (978-1-4424-3038-9(9)) Simon Pulse. (Simon Pulse).

O'Connell, Jenny. Rich Boys: An Island Summer Novel. 2008. (ENG.). 288p. pap. 18.99 (978-1-4165-6336-5(9), MTV Bks.) MTV Books.

O'Connor, Barbara. The Fantastic Secret of Owen Jester. 2010. (ENG.). 176p. (J). (gr. 3-7). 15.99 (978-0-374-36850-0(3), 9780374368500, Farrar, Straus & Giroux (BYR)) Farrar, Straus & Giroux.

—The Fantastic Secret of Owen Jester. 2011. (ENG.). 192p. (J). (gr. 3-7). pap. 7.99 (978-0-312-67430-4(9), 9780312674304) Square Fish.

O'Connor, Jane. Apples Galore! 2013. (Fancy Nancy - I Can Read! Ser.). (J). lib. bdg. 13.55 (978-0-606-32150-1(0), Turtleback) Turtleback Bks.

—Every Day Is Earth Day. Ivanov, Aleksey et al, illus. 2010. (I Can Read Level 1 Ser.). (ENG.). 32p. (J). (gr. -1-3). 16.99 (978-0-06-187327-0(6)) HarperCollins Pubs.

—Every Day Is Earth Day. Ivanov, Aleksey et al, illus. 2010. (I Can Read Level 1 Ser.). (ENG.). 32p. (J). (gr. -1-3). pap. 3.99 (978-0-06-187326-3(8)) HarperCollins Pubs.

—Fancy Nancy. Glasser, Robin Preiss, illus. 2005. (Fancy Nancy Ser.). 32p. (J). (gr. -1-3). 17.89 (978-0-06-054210-8(1)); (ENG.). 17.99 (978-0-06-054209-2(8)) HarperCollins Pubs.

—Fancy Nancy: Too Many Tutus. Glasser, Robin Preiss, illus. 2012. (I Can Read Level 1 Ser.). (ENG.). 32p. (J). (gr. -1-3). 16.99 (978-0-06-208308-1(2)) HarperCollins Pubs.

—Fancy Nancy & the Posh Puppy. Glasser, Robin Preiss, illus. 2012. (Fancy Nancy Ser.). (ENG.). 32p. (J). (gr. -1-2). 9.99 (978-0-06-221052-4(1)) HarperCollins Pubs.

—Fancy Nancy & the Posh Puppy (Nancy la Elegante y la Perrita Popoff), 1 vol. Glasser, Robin Preiss, illus. 2011. (Fancy Nancy Ser.). (SPA & ENG.). 32p. (J). (gr. -1-3). 16.99 (978-0-06-179961-7(0)) HarperCollins Pubs.

—Fancy Nancy's Marvelous Mother's Day Brunch. Glasser, Robin Preiss, illus. 2011. (Fancy Nancy Ser.). (ENG.). 16p. (J). (gr. -1-3). pap. 6.99 (978-0-06-170380-5(X), HarperFestival) HarperCollins Pubs.

—Nancy la Elegante, 1 vol. Valenzuela, Liliana, tr. from ENG. Glasser, Robin Preiss, illus. 2008. (Fancy Nancy Ser.). (SPA.). 32p. (J). (gr. -1-2). 17.99 (978-0-06-143528-7(7)) HarperCollins Pubs.

—Splendiferous Christmas. Glasser, Robin Preiss, illus. (Fancy Nancy Ser.). 32p. (J). (gr. -1-2). 2011. (ENG.). 17.99 (978-0-06-123590-0(3)) 2009. lib. bdg. 18.89 (978-0-06-123591-7(1)) HarperCollins Pubs.

—Too Many Tutus. Glasser, Robin Preiss, illus. 2012. (I Can Read Level 1 Ser.). (ENG.). 32p. (J). (gr. -1-3). pap. 3.99 (978-0-06-208307-4(4)) HarperCollins Pubs.

Oelschlager, Vanita. A Tale of Two Mommies. Blanc, Mike, illus. 2011. (ENG.). 40p. (J). (gr. -1-3). 15.95 (978-0-9826366-6-4(0)); pap. 8.95 (978-0-9826366-7-1(9)) VanitaBooks.

Ogilvie, Elizabeth. The Pigeon Pair. (J). reprint ed. lib. bdg. 19.95 (978-0-88411-336-2(1)) Amereon Ltd.

Oh, Jina, reader. A Step from Heaven. 2004. 160p. (J). (gr. 6-18). pap. 36.00 incl. audio (978-0-8072-2287-4(9), Listening Library) Random Hse. Audio Publishing Group.

O'Keefe, Susan Heyboer. My Life & Death by Alexandra Canarsie, 1 vol. 2006. (ENG.). 217p. (YA). (gr. 7-18). pap. 7.95 (978-1-56145-387-0(0)) Peachtree Pubs.

Olin, Sean. Reckless Hearts. 2015. (Wicked Games Ser.: 2). (ENG.). 336p. (YA). (gr. 9). 17.99 (978-0-06-219241-7(8), Tegen, Katherine Bks) HarperCollins Pubs.

Oliver, Lauren. Delirium. (Delirium Trilogy Ser.: 1). (ENG.). 480p. (YA). (gr. 9-18). 2016. pap. 9.99 (978-0-06-172683-5(4)) 2011. 17.99 (978-0-06-211243-9(0)) HarperCollins Pubs.

—Delirium. 2016. (Delirium Ser.: 1). (YA). lib. bdg. 20.85 (978-0-606-23575-4(2), Turtleback) Turtleback Bks.

Oliver, Lin. Almost Identical. 2012. (Almost Identical Ser.: 1). (ENG.). 224p. (J). (gr. 3-7). pap. 7.99 (978-0-448-45191-6(3), Grosset & Dunlap) Penguin Young Readers Group.

—Attack of the Growling Eyeballs. Gilpin, Stephen, illus. 2009. (Who Shrunk Daniel Funk? Ser.: 1). (ENG.). 160p. (J). (gr. 3-7). pap. 6.99 (978-1-4169-0958-3(3), Simon & Schuster Bks. For Young Readers) Simon & Schuster Bks. For Young Readers.

—Revenge of the Itty-Bitty Brothers. Gilpin, Stephen, illus. 2009. (Who Shrunk Daniel Funk? Ser.: 3). (ENG.). 176p. (J). (gr. 3-7). 14.99 (978-1-4169-0961-3(3), Simon & Schuster Bks. For Young Readers) Simon & Schuster Bks. For Young Readers.

—Secret of the Super-Small Superstar. Gilpin, Stephen, illus. 2010. (Who Shrunk Daniel Funk? Ser.: 4). (ENG.). 160p. (J). (gr. 3-7). 14.99 (978-1-4169-0963-7(X), Simon & Schuster Bks. For Young Readers) Simon & Schuster Bks. For Young Readers.

—Two-Faced, No. 2. 2012. (Almost Identical Ser.: 2). (ENG.). 224p. (J). (gr. 3-7). pap. 7.99 (978-0-448-45192-3(1), Grosset & Dunlap) Penguin Young Readers Group.

Once upon a Time. Date not set. (978-0-517-80128-4(0)) Random Hse. Value Publishing.

O'Neal, Shaquille. Little Shaq. Taylor, Theodore, III, illus. 2015. (ENG.). 80p. (J). (gr. k-2). 9.99 (978-1-61963-721-4(9), 9781619637214, Bloomsbury USA Childrens) Bloomsbury Publishing USA.

O'Neil, Paula. Valley of the Moon. 2011. pap. 10.95 (978-0-7414-6333-3(4)) Infinity Publishing.

Onley, Sandra. Halley the Sheepdog. 2011. (Illus.). 28p. pap. 12.50 (978-1-61204-237-4(6), Strategic Bk. Publishing) Strategic Book Publishing & Rights Agency (SBPRA).

Onyefulu, Ifeoma & Quarto Generic Staff. Omer's Favorite Place. 2011. (First Experiences Ser.). (ENG., Illus.). 32p. (J). (gr. -1-1). 17.95 (978-1-84780-241-5(9), Frances Lincoln) Quarto Publishing Group UK GBR. Dist: Hachette Bk. Group.

Optic, Oliver, pseud. Watch & Wait; or, the Young Fugitives a Story for Young People by Oliver Optic [Pseud]. 2006. 284p. per. 23.99 (978-1-4255-2683-2(7)) Michigan Publishing.

Orlando, Kristen, et al. You Don't Know My Name. 2017. (Black Angel Chronicles Ser.). (ENG.). 304p. (YA). 16.99 (978-1-250-08411-8(3), 9781250084118) Feiwel & Friends.

Orlando, Linda M. Island Boy. 2004. (ENG.). (YA). pap. 14.95 (978-1-59088-776-9(X)) Wings ePress, Inc.

Orlev, Uri. Lidia, Reina de Palestina. (SPA.). 158p. (YA). (gr. 5-8). (978-84-279-3237-1(5), NG8035) Noguer y Caralt Editores, S. A. ESP. Dist: Lectorum Pubns., Inc.

Orloff, Karen Kaufman. I Wanna Go Home. Catrow, David, illus. 2014. (ENG.). 32p. (J). (gr. k-3). 16.99 (978-0-399-25407-9(2), G.P. Putnam's Sons Books for Young Readers) Penguin Young Readers Group.

—I Wanna New Room. Catrow, David, III, illus. 2010. (ENG.). 32p. (J). (gr. k-3). 16.99 (978-0-399-25405-5(6), G.P. Putnam's Sons Books for Young Readers) Penguin Young Readers Group.

Osborn, Valerie Huffman. A Week of Bunnies. Osborn, Kimberly, ed. 2007. (ENG., Illus.). 32p. (J). 19.95 (978-1-932278-25-5(7)) Mayhaven Publishing, Inc.

Osborne, Rick. Legend of the Christmas Stocking: An Inspirational Story of a Wish Come True, 1 vol. Griffin, Jim, illus. 2004. (ENG.). 32p. (J). 17.99 (978-0-310-70898-8(2)) Zonderkidz.

Osmond, Jimmy. The Awesome Possum Family Band. 2014. (ENG., Illus.). 40p. (J). (gr. -1-3). 16.99 (978-1-62157-211-4(0), Regnery Kids) Regnery Publishing, Inc., An Eagle Publishing Co.

Ostow, Micol. Amity. 2014. (ENG.). 362p. (J). (gr. 9). 18.99 (978-1-60684-156-3(4), Carolrhoda Lab™) Lerner Publishing Group.

—What Would My Cell Phone Do? 2011. (ENG.). 272p. (YA). (gr. 7-18). 7.99 (978-0-14-241469-9(7), Speak) Penguin Young Readers Group.

Padian, Maria. Brett McCarthy: Work in Progress. 2009. (ENG.). 288p. (YA). (gr. 7). pap. 8.99 (978-0-440-24055-6(7), Knopf Bks. for Young Readers) Random Hse. Children's Bks.

Pagratis, Maggie. My Sister the Bee. 2004. 29p. (J). per. 16.68 (978-1-4116-1098-9(9)) Lulu Pr., Inc.

Pakkala, Christine. Last-But-Not-Least Lola Going Green. Hoppe, Paul, illus. 2014. (Last-But-Not-Least Lola Ser.). (ENG.). 192p. (J). (gr. 2-5). pap. 7.95 (978-1-62979-113-5(X)) Boyds Mills Pr.

Palatini, Margie. Isabella for Real. Pham, LeUyen, illus. 2016. (ENG.). 208p. (J). (gr. 5-7). 16.99 (978-0-544-14846-8(0), HMH Books For Young Readers) Houghton Mifflin Harcourt Publishing Co.

Palmer, Angela Elsberry. Promise Wishes. 2005. (J). 19.95 (978-1-58597-311-8(4)) Leathers Publishing.

Paradine, Mike. King of Toys. 2006. 83p. pap. 19.95 (978-1-4241-2694-1(0)) America Star Bks.

Paratore, Coleen Murtagh. Dreamsleeves. 2012. (ENG.). 288p. (J). (gr. 5-9). 16.99 (978-0-545-31020-8(2), Scholastic Pr.) Scholastic, Inc.

—The Funeral Director's Son. 2008. (Funeral Director's Son Ser.). (ENG.). 144p. (J). (gr. 3-7). 15.99 (978-1-4169-3594-0(0), Simon & Schuster Bks. For Young Readers) Simon & Schuster Bks. For Young Readers.

—Kip Campbell's Gift. 2009. (ENG.). 160p. (J). (gr. 3-7). 15.99 (978-1-4169-3596-4(7), Simon & Schuster Bks. For Young Readers) Simon & Schuster Bks. For Young Readers.

Paris, Harper. The Mystery at the Coral Reef. Calo, Marcos, illus. 2015. (Greetings from Somewhere Ser.: 8). (ENG.). 128p. (J). (gr. k-4). pap. 5.99 (978-1-4814-2370-0(3), Little Simon) Little Simon.

Parish, Herman. Amelia Bedelia Chapter Book #3: Amelia Bedelia Road Trip! (Special Edition) 2013. (ENG., Illus.). 160p. (J). (978-0-06-227057-3(5), Collins Design) HarperCollins Pubs.

—Amelia Bedelia Makes a Splash. Avril, Lynne, illus. 2017. (Amelia Bedelia Ser.). 160p. (J). (gr. 1-5). pap. 4.99 (978-0-06-265839-5(5), Greenwillow Bks.) HarperCollins Pubs.

—Amelia Bedelia Road Trip! 2013. (Amelia Bedelia Chapter Book Ser.: 3). (J). lib. bdg. 14.75 (978-0-606-32453-3(4), Turtleback) Turtleback Bks.

—Amelia Bedelia Sets Sail. Avril, Lynne, illus. 2015. (Amelia Bedelia Ser.). (ENG.). 160p. (J). (gr. 1-5). pap. 4.99 (978-0-06-233404-6(2), Greenwillow Bks.) HarperCollins Pubs.

—Amelia Bedelia Ties the Knot. 2016. (Amelia Bedelia Chapter Book Ser.: 10). (J). lib. bdg. 14.75 (978-0-606-38762-0(5)) Turtleback Bks.

—Amelia Bedelia's First Valentine. Avril, Lynne, illus. (Amelia Bedelia Ser.). (ENG.). 32p. (J). (gr. -1-3). 2014. pap. 6.99 (978-0-06-154460-6(4)) 2011. 9.99 (978-0-06-203275-1(5)) 2009. 16.99 (978-0-06-154458-3(2)) HarperCollins Pubs. (Greenwillow Bks.).

—Amelia Bedelia's First Valentine. 2014. (Amelia Bedelia Picture Bks.). (J). lib. bdg. 17.20 (978-0-606-35971-9(0)) Turtleback Bks.

—Go West, Amelia Bedelia! Sweat, Lynn, illus. 2012. (I Can Read Level 2 Ser.). (ENG.). 64p. (J). (gr. k-4). pap. 3.99 (978-0-06-084363-2(2), Greenwillow Bks.) HarperCollins Pubs.

—Sets Sail. Avril, Lynne, illus. 2015. (Amelia Bedelia Ser.). (ENG.). 160p. (J). (gr. 1-5). 15.99 (978-0-06-233405-3(0), Greenwillow Bks.) HarperCollins Pubs.

Park, Jennifer. The Shadows We Know by Heart. 2017. (ENG., Illus.). 304p. (YA). (gr. 7). 17.99 (978-1-4814-6351-5(9), Simon Pulse) Simon Pulse.

Park, Linda Sue. Project Mulberry. 2017. (ENG.). 272p. (J). (gr. 5-7). pap. 6.99 (978-0-544-93521-1(7), HMH Books For Young Readers) Houghton Mifflin Harcourt Publishing Co.

—Project Mulberry. 2007. 225p. (gr. 4-7). 17.00 (978-0-7569-7921-8(8)) Perfection Learning Corp.

—Project Mulberry. 2007. (ENG.). 240p. (J). (gr. 3-7). 6.99 (978-0-440-42163-4(2), Yearling) Random Hse. Children's Bks.

—When My Name Was Keoko. 2004. 199p. (J). (gr. 5). 14.65 (978-0-7569-2928-2(8)) Perfection Learning Corp.

—When My Name Was Keoko. 2012. lib. bdg. 18.40 (978-0-606-24716-0(5), Turtleback) Turtleback Bks.

Parker, Amy. Tiny Blessings: for My Family. Walsh, Sarah, illus. 2017. (ENG.). 10p. (J). (gr. -1 — 1). bds. 7.99 (978-0-7624-6178-3(0), Running Pr.) Running Pr. Bk. Pubs.

Parker, John. Chaos Mountain. 2007. 96p. (YA). pap. (978-1-4207-0734-2(5)) Sundance/Newbridge Educational Publishing.

Parker, Ms. Alichia R. My Aunt & Me. Brown, Chris L., illus. 2013. 24p. pap. 9.99 (978-0-578-12712-5(1)) A PAR Educational, LLC.

Parry, Rosanne. Heart of a Shepherd. 2010. (ENG.). 176p. (J). (gr. 3-7). pap. 7.99 (978-0-375-84803-2(7), Yearling) Random Hse. Children's Bks.

Partridge, Elizabeth. Dogtag Summer. (ENG.). 240p. (YA). (gr. 3-12). 2012. pap. 7.99 (978-1-59990-829-8(8), 9781599908298) 2011. 16.99 (978-1-59990-183-1(8), 9781599901831) Bloomsbury Publishing USA. (Bloomsbury USA Childrens).

Pascal, Francine. Atrapada. Orig. Title: Married Woman. (SPA.). 208p. (J). 10.50 (978-84-272-3165-8(2)) Molino, Editorial ESP. Dist: AIMS International Bks., Inc.

Patel, Sonia. Rani Patel in Full Effect. 2016. (ENG.). 224p. (J). (gr. 6). 16.95 (978-1-941026-49-6(4)) Cinco Puntos Pr.

Paterson, Katherine. Preacher's Boy. 2013. (ENG.). 176p. (J). (gr. 5-7). pap. 7.99 (978-0-544-10490-7(0)) Houghton Mifflin Harcourt Publishing Co.

—The Same Stuff as Stars. 2004. 270p. (gr. 3-7). 17.00 (978-0-7569-2801-8(X)) Perfection Learning Corp.

Patrick, Cat. Forgotten. 2012. (ENG.). 320p. (J). (gr. 7-17). pap. 8.99 (978-0-316-09460-3(9)) Little, Brown Bks. for Young Readers.

Patrick, Denise Lewis. Finding Someplace. 2015. (ENG.). 224p. (J). (gr. 3-7). 16.99 (978-0-8050-4716-5(6), 9780805047165, Holt, Henry & Co. Bks. For Young Readers) Holt, Henry & Co.

—Finding Someplace. 2016. (ENG.). 224p. (J). pap. 7.99 (978-1-250-07982-4(9), 9781250079824) Square Fish.

—Finding Someplace. 2016. (J). lib. bdg. 17.20 (978-0-606-38560-2(6)) Turtleback Bks.

—MaDear's Old Green House. Sadler, Sonia Lynn, illus. 2004. 32p. (J). (gr. k-3). 16.95 (978-0-940975-55-2(6), Sankofa Bks.) Just Us Bks., Inc.

Patterson, James. House of Robots: Robot Revolution. Neufeld, Juliana, illus. 2017. (House of Robots Ser.: 3). (ENG.). 336p. (J). (gr. 3-7). 13.99 (978-0-316-34958-1(5), Jimmy Patterson) Little Brown & Co.

—The Worst Years of My Life. 2014. lthr. 79.00 (978-1-62715-524-3(4)) Leatherbound Bestsellers.

—The Worst Years of My Life. 2012. 18.00 (978-1-61383-331-5(8)) Perfection Learning Corp.

Patterson, James & Grabenstein, Chris. House of Robots. Neufeld, Juliana, illus. (House of Robots Ser.: 1). (ENG.). (J). (gr. 3-7). 2015. 336p. pap. 7.99 (978-0-316-34679-5(9)) 2014. 352p. 13.99 (978-0-316-40591-1(4)) Little Brown & Co. (Jimmy Patterson).

—House of Robots. 2015. (J). lib. bdg. 18.40 (978-0-606-37527-6(9)) Turtleback Bks.

—Jacky Ha-Ha. Kerascoët, illus. 2016. (ENG.). 384p. (J). (gr. 3-7). 13.99 (978-0-316-26249-1(8), Jimmy Patterson) Little Brown & Co.

—Jacky Ha-Ha. 2017. (Jacky Ha-Ha Ser.). (J). lib. bdg. 18.40 **(978-0-606-40732-8(4))** Turtleback Bks.

Patterson, James & Grabenstein, Chris. Robots Go Wild. Neufeld, Juliana, illus. 2015. (House of Robots Ser.: 2). (ENG.). 336p. (J). (gr. 3-7). 13.99 (978-0-316-28479-0(3), Jimmy Patterson) Little Brown & Co.

Patterson, James & Paetro, Maxine. Confessions: The Paris Mysteries. 2014. (Confessions Ser.). (ENG.). 320p. (YA). (gr. 7-17). 18.00 (978-0-316-37084-4(3), Jimmy Patterson) Little Brown & Co.

—Confessions of a Murder Suspect. 2014. (Confessions Ser.: 1). (ENG.). 352p. (gr. 7-17). mass mkt. 8.00 (978-1-4555-4774-6(3), Jimmy Patterson) 2013. (ENG.). 400p. (J). (gr. 7-17). pap. 10.00 (978-0-316-20700-3(4), Jimmy Patterson) 2012. (Confessions Ser.: 1). (ENG.). 384p. (YA). (gr. 7-17). 19.99 (978-0-316-20698-3(9), Jimmy Patterson) 2012. 372p. (J). 11.99 (978-0-316-22641-7(6)) 2012. (Confessions Ser.: 1). (ENG.). 400p. (YA). (gr. 7-17). 31.99 (978-0-316-22418-5(9), Jimmy Patterson) Little Brown & Co.

—Confessions of a Murder Suspect. 2013. (Confessions Ser.: 1). lib. bdg. 20.85 (978-0-606-32278-2(7), Turtleback) Turtleback Bks.

—Confessions: the Murder of an Angel. 2015. (Confessions Ser.: 4). (ENG.). 304p. (YA). (gr. 7-12). 18.00 (978-0-316-30102-2(7), Jimmy Patterson) Little Brown & Co.

—The Paris Mysteries. l.t. ed. 2014. (Confessions Ser.: 3). (ENG.). 352p. (YA). (gr. 7-17). 30.99 (978-0-316-40963-6(4), Jimmy Patterson) Little Brown & Co.

—The Paris Mysteries. 2015. (Confessions Ser.: 3). (YA). lib. bdg. 20.85 (978-0-606-37526-9(0)) Turtleback Bks.

Patterson, James & Tebbetts, Chris. The Worst Years of My Life. Park, Laura, illus. (Middle School Ser.: Bk. 1). (ENG.). (J). (gr. 3-7). 2014. 320p. 13.99 (978-0-316-32202-7(4), Jimmy Patterson) 2013. pap. 0.01 (978-0-316-25251-5(4)) 2012. 336p. pap. 8.00 (978-0-316-10169-1(9), Jimmy Patterson) Little Brown & Co.

—The Worst Years of My Life. Park, Laura, illus. 2012. (Middle School Ser.: 1). (J). lib. bdg. 18.45 (978-0-606-26164-7(8), Turtleback) Turtleback Bks.

Patti, Caroline. The World Spins Madly On. 2008. 144p. 21.95 (978-0-595-71087-4(5)); pap. 11.95 (978-0-595-47439-4(X)) iUniverse, Inc.

Paul, Curtis Christopher. The Watsons Go to Birmingham 1963. 2014. (ENG.). 224p. (J). (gr. 12-12). 11.24 (978-1-63245-108-8(5)) Lectorum Pubns., Inc.

Pauley, Kimberly. Cat Girl's Day Off, 1 vol. 2012. (ENG.). 336p. (YA). 17.95 (978-1-60060-883-4(3), Tu Bks.) Lee & Low Bks., Inc.

Paulsen, Gary. Family Ties. 2014. (ENG.). 144p. (J). (gr. 4-7). 12.99 (978-0-385-37380-7(5), Lamb, Wendy Bks.) Random Hse. Children's Bks.

—Flat Broke: The Theory, Practice & Destructive Properties of Greed. (ENG.). 128p. (J). (gr. 3-7). 2012. pap. 6.99 (978-0-375-86612-8(4), Yearling) 2011. 12.99 (978-0-385-74002-9(6), Lamb, Wendy Bks.) Random Hse. Children's Bks.

Pavlicin, Karen. Perch, Mrs. Sackets, & Crow's Nest. 2007. (J). (ENG.). 160p. 16.95 (978-1-934617-00-7(8)); pap. (978-1-934617-01-4(6)) Elva Resa Publishing, LLC. (Alma Little).

—Summer of Courage. 2014. (ENG.). 160p. (J). pap. 12.95 (978-1-934617-24-3(5), Alma Little) Elva Resa Publishing, LLC.

Payne, C. C. Lula Bell on Geekdom, Freakdom, & the Challenges of Bad Hair, 0 vols. 2012. (ENG.). 276p. (J). (gr. 3-7). 16.99 (978-0-7614-6225-5(2), 9780761462255, Amazon Children's Publishing) Amazon Publishing.

—Something to Sing About. 2008. (ENG.). 167p. (J). (gr. 4-7). pap. 8.50 (978-0-8028-5344-8(7)) Eerdmans, William B. Publishing Co.

—The Thing about Leftovers. 2016. (ENG.). 288p. (J). (gr. 5). 16.99 (978-0-399-17204-5(1), Nancy Paulsen Books) Penguin Young Readers Group.

Peacock, Hilda V. Eye-Jack & Hey-Oh. 2008. 20p. pap. 10.49 (978-1-4389-3239-2(1)) AuthorHouse.

Pearce, Emily Smith. Slowpoke. Ritchie, Scot, illus. 2010. (ENG.). 40p. (J). (gr. 2-4). 16.95 (978-1-59078-705-2(6)) Boyds Mills Pr.

Pearce, Jackson. The Doublecross: (And Other Skills I Learned As a Superspy) 2015. (ENG.). 304p. (YA). (gr. 3-6). 16.99 (978-1-61963-414-5(7), 9781619634145, Bloomsbury USA Childrens) Bloomsbury Publishing USA.

Pearce, Jonathan. John-Browne's Body & Sole: A Semester of Life. 2nd ed. 2004. (Illus.). 150p. (J). pap. 15.95 (978-1-59411-053-5(0)) Writers' Collective, The.

Pearce, Margaret. A Beautiful Day. van Garderen, Ilse, illus. 2012. 24p. pap. 10.95 (978-1-61633-251-8(4)) Guardian Angel Publishing, Inc.

Pearsall, Shelley. Crooked River. 2007. 249p. (gr. 5-9). 17.00 (978-0-7569-7771-9(1)) Perfection Learning Corp.

—Crooked River. 2007. (ENG.). 272p. (J). (gr. 3-7). 7.99 (978-0-440-42101-6(2), Yearling) Random Hse. Children's Bks.

Pearson, Joanna. The Rites & Wrongs of Janice Wills. 2011. (YA). pap. (978-0-545-19774-8(0)); (ENG.). 224p. (J). (gr. 9-7). 16.99 (978-0-545-19773-1(2)) Scholastic, Inc. (Levine, Arthur A. Bks.).

Pearson, Mary E. A Room on Lorelei Street. 2008. (ENG.). 288p. (YA). (gr. 9-13). pap. 19.99 (978-0-312-38019-9(4), 9780312380199) Square Fish.

Peaslee Levine, Martha. The Twelve Days of Christmas in Pennsylvania. Dougherty, Rachel, illus. 2014. (Twelve Days of Christmas in America Ser.). (ENG.). 40p. (J). (gr. k). 12.95 (978-1-4549-0889-0(0)) Sterling Publishing Co., Inc.

Peck, Richard. The Best Man, 5 vols. (ENG.). (J). 2017. 44.95 **(978-0-525-48687-9(9)**, Puffin Books) 2017. 256p. (gr. 4-7). 8.99 **(978-0-14-751579-7(3)**, Puffin Books) 2016. 240p. (gr. 4-7). 16.99 (978-0-8037-3839-3(0), Dial Bks) Penguin Young Readers Group.

—Fair Weather. 2003. (ENG., Illus.). 160p. (J). (gr. 3-7). pap. 7.99 (978-0-14-250034-7(8), Puffin Books) Penguin Young Readers Group.

—Fair Weather. 2003. (Illus.). 146p. (gr. 4-7). 17.00 (978-0-7569-1376-2(4)) Perfection Learning Corp.

—Fair Weather. 2004. 146p. (J). (gr. 5-9). pap. 36.00 incl. audio (978-0-8072-2038-2(8), Listening Library) Random Hse. Audio Publishing Group.

—The River Between Us. 2005. (ENG.). 176p. (J). (gr. 3-7). reprint ed. pap. 7.99 (978-0-14-240310-5(5), Puffin Books) Penguin Young Readers Group.

Pedersen, Laura & Weber, Penny. Unplugged: Ella Gets Her Family Back, 1 vol. 2012. (ENG., Illus.). 32p. (gr. 2-6). 16.95 (978-0-88448-337-3(1), 884337) Tilbury Hse. Pubs.

Peifer, Jane Hoober. The Family Song. Hess, Ingrid, illus. 2008. 64p. (J). (gr. -1-3). pap. 18.99 incl. audio compact disk (978-0-8361-9414-2(4)) Herald Pr.

Pellicioli, Anna. Where You End. 2015. (ENG.). 312p. (YA). pap. 9.99 (978-0-7387-4403-2(4), Flux) North Star Editions.

Penn, Audrey. The Miracle Jar: A Hanukkah Story. Lyon, Lea, illus. 2009. (ENG.). 32p. (J). (gr. -1-3). pap. 8.95 (978-1-933718-26-2(9)) Tanglewood Pr.

—A Pocket Full of Kisses. Gibson, Barbara Leonard, illus. 2004. (New Child & Family Press Titles Ser.). 32p. (gr. -1-1). 16.95 (978-0-87868-894-4(3), 8943, Child & Family Pr.) Child Welfare League of America, Inc.

—A Pocket Full of Kisses. Gibson, Barbara Leonard, illus. 2006. (Kissing Hand Ser.). (ENG.). 32p. (J). (gr. -1-3). 16.95 (978-1-933718-02-6(1)) Tanglewood Pr.

Pennypacker, Sara. Clementine. Frazee, Marla, illus. (ENG.). (J). 2008. 160p. (gr. 2-5). pap. 5.99 (978-0-7868-3883-7(3)) 2006. 144p. (gr. 1-3). 14.99 (978-0-7868-3882-0(5)) Hyperion Pr.

—Clementine & the Family Meeting. Frazee, Marla, illus. (ENG.). 176p. (J). (gr. 2-5). 2012. pap. 5.99 (978-1-4231-2436-8(7)) 2011. 14.99 (978-1-4231-2356-9(5)) Hyperion Pr.

—Clementine & the Family Meeting. 2012. (Clementine Ser.: 5). (J). lib. bdg. 16.00 (978-0-606-26093-0(5), Turtleback) Turtleback Bks.

—Clementine & the Spring Trip. Frazee, Marla, illus. 2013. (ENG.). 160p. (J). (gr. 2-5). 14.99 (978-1-4231-2357-6(3)) Hyperion Pr.

—Clementine & the Spring Trip. 2014. (Clementine Ser.: 6). (J). lib. bdg. 16.00 (978-0-606-32287-4(6), Turtleback) Turtleback Bks.

—Clementine, Friend of the Week. Frazee, Marla, illus. (Clementine Book Ser.). (ENG.). 176p. (J). 2011. (gr. 1-3). pap. 5.99 (978-1-4231-1560-1(0)) 2010. (gr. 2-5). 14.99 (978-1-4231-1355-3(1)) Hyperion Pr.

—Completely Clementine. Frazee, Marla, illus. 2015. (Clementine Book Ser.). (ENG.). 192p. (J). (gr. 1-3). 14.99 (978-1-4231-2358-3(1)) Disney Pr.

—Completely Clementine. Frazee, Marla, illus. 2016. (Clementine Book Ser.). (ENG.). 208p. (J). (gr. 1-3). pap. 5.99 (978-1-4231-2438-2(3)) Hyperion Bks. for Children.

—Meet the Dullards. Salmieri, Daniel, illus. 2015. (ENG.). 32p. (J). (gr. -1-3). 17.99 (978-0-06-219856-3(4)) HarperCollins Pubs.

Penson, Mary E. Martha Mary Overstreet, M. D. 2007. (Chaparral Bks.). (ENG.). 142p. (J). per. 11.95 (978-0-87565-345-7(6)) Texas Christian Univ. Pr.

Perego, Jeanne. Joseph & Chico: The Life of Pope Benedict XVI as Told by a Cat. Matt, Andrew, tr. from ITA. Casagrande, Donata Dal Molin, illus. 2008. 36p. (J). (gr. k-7). 17.95 *(978-1-58617-252-7(2))* Ignatius Pr.

Pérez, Amada Irma. Mi Diario de Aquí Hasta Allá. Gonzalez, Maya Christina, illus. 2013.Tr. of My Diary from Here to There. (ENG & SPA.). 32p. (J). (gr. k). pap. 9.95 *(978-0-89239-230-8(4))* Lee & Low Bks., Inc.

Perez, Amada Irma. Mi Propio Cuartito. 2004. (SPA & ENG., Illus.). (J). (gr. k-3). spiral bd. *(978-0-616-14609-5(4))* Canadian National Institute for the Blind/Institut National Canadien pour les Aveugles.

Pérez, Ashley Hope. What Can't Wait. 2011. (Carolrhoda YA Ser.). (ENG.). 240p. (YA). (gr. 9-12). 17.95 *(978-0-7613-6155-8(3),* Carolrhoda Bks.) Lerner Publishing Group.

Perez, Marlene. Dead Is a State of Mind. 2009. (Dead Is Ser.: 2). (ENG., Illus.). 192p. (YA). (gr. 7-18). pap. 7.99 *(978-0-15-206210-1(6))* Houghton Mifflin Harcourt Publishing Co.

Perkins, Larry B. Jake the Cow Hand. 2004. 27p. pap. 9.97 *(978-1-4116-1344-7(9))* Lulu Pr., Inc.

Perkins, Lynne Rae. Pictures from Our Vacation. Perkins, Lynne Rae, illus. 2007. (Illus.). 32p. (J). (gr. k-3). 17.89 *(978-0-06-085098-2(1),* Greenwillow Bks.) HarperCollins Pubs.

Perkins, Lynne Rae & Perkins, Lynne R. All Alone in the Universe. 2007. (ENG., Illus.). 224p. (J). (gr. 5-18). reprint ed. pap. 6.99 *(978-0-380-73302-6(1),* Greenwillow Bks.) HarperCollins Pubs.

—Pictures from Our Vacation. Perkins, Lynne Rae, illus. 2007. (ENG., Illus.). 32p. (J). (gr. k-3). 17.99 *(978-0-06-085097-5(3),* Greenwillow Bks.) HarperCollins Pubs.

Perkins, Mitali. Rickshaw Girl. Hogan, Jamie, illus. 2007. (ENG.). 96p. (J). (gr. 2-5). 14.95 *(978-1-58089-308-4(2))* Charlesbridge Publishing, Inc.

—Secret Keeper. 2010. (ENG.). 240p. (YA). (gr. 7). pap. 8.99 *(978-0-440-23955-0(9),* Ember) Random Hse. Children's Bks.

Perkins, Mitali. You Bring the Distant Near. 2017. (ENG.). 320p. (YA). 17.99 ***(978-0-374-30490-4(4),*** 9780374304904, Farrar, Straus & Giroux (BYR)) Farrar, Straus & Giroux.

Perl, Erica S. Aces Wild. 2013. (ENG.). 224p. (J). (gr. 3-7). 15.99 *(978-0-307-93172-6(2),* Knopf Bks. for Young Readers) Random Hse. Children's Bks.

—When Life Gives You O. J. (ENG.). 224p. (J). (gr. 3-7). 2013. 6.99 *(978-0-375-85902-1(0),* Yearling) 2011. 15.99 *(978-0-375-85924-3(1),* Knopf Bks. for Young Readers) Random Hse. Children's Bks.

Perret, Delphine. Pablo & His Chair. 2016. (ENG., Illus.). 32p. (J). (gr. -1-3). 17.95 *(978-1-61689-490-0(3))* Princeton Architectural Pr.

Perrin, Randy, et al. Time Like a River. 2004. 144p. (gr. 5-18). 14.95 *(978-1-57143-061-8(X))* RDR Bks.

Perry, Alma. Gently Smiling Jaws. 2011. 120p. 39.95 *(978-1-258-06411-2(1))* Literary Licensing, LLC.

Perry, Jolene. Stronger Than You Know. 2014. (ENG.). 256p. (YA). (gr. 8-12). 16.99 *(978-0-8075-3155-6(3))* Whitman, Albert & Co.

Perry, Michael. The Scavengers. 2014. (ENG.). 336p. (J). (gr. 3-7). 16.99 *(978-0-06-202616-3(X))* HarperCollins Pubs.

Perry, Naresha S. Zora's Valentine. 2005. (J). per. 13.00 *(978-0-9767189-0-1(1))* Better Day Publishing LLC.

Peschke, Marci. Cooking Queen. Mourning, Tuesday, illus. 2017. (Kylie Jean Ser.). (ENG.). 112p. (gr. 2-3). lib. bdg. 22.65 ***(978-1-4795-9899-1(2),*** Kylie Jean) Picture Window Bks.

—Fashion Queen. Mourning, Tuesday, illus. 2015. (Kylie Jean Ser.). (ENG.). 112p. (gr. 2-3). 8.95 *(978-1-4795-5881-0(8),* Kylie Jean) Picture Window Bks.

—Gymnastics Queen. Mourning, Tuesday, illus. 2016. (Kylie Jean Ser.). (ENG.). 112p. (gr. 2-3). lib. bdg. 22.65 *(978-1-5158-0052-1(0))* Picture Window Bks.

—Soccer Queen. Mourning, Tuesday, illus. 2015. (Kylie Jean Ser.). (ENG.). 112p. (gr. 2-3). 22.65 *(978-1-4795-5882-7(6),* Kylie Jean) Picture Window Bks.

—Spelling Queen, 1 vol. Mourning, Tuesday, illus. 2012. (Kylie Jean Ser.). (ENG.). 112p. (gr. 2-3). lib. bdg. 22.65 *(978-1-4048-6801-4(1),* Kylie Jean) Picture Window Bks.

—Valentine Queen, 1 vol. Mourning, Tuesday, illus. 2014. (Kylie Jean Ser.). (ENG.). 112p. (gr. 2-3). 22.65 *(978-1-4795-2352-8(6),* Kylie Jean) Picture Window Bks.

Peterfreund, Diana. For Darkness Shows the Stars. 2012. (Stars Ser.: 1). (ENG.). 416p. (YA). (gr. 8). 17.99 *(978-0-06-200614-1(2))* HarperCollins Pubs.

Peters, Judy. The Little Blue Curtain. 2008. pap. 9.00 *(978-0-8059-8790-4(8))* Dorrance Publishing Co., Inc.

Peters, Julie Anne. Rage: A Love Story. 2010. (ENG.). 306p. (YA). (gr. 9). pap. 9.99 *(978-0-375-84411-9(2),* Knopf Bks. for Young Readers) Random Hse. Children's Bks.

Petersen, Alicia. Out of Darkness. 2007. (Illus.). 177p. (J). (gr. 3-7). per. 8.99 *(978-1-59166-822-0(0))* BJU Pr.

Peterson, David. 10 Days Until Forever. 2011. 32p. 14.99 *(978-1-59955-266-8(3),* Bonneville Bks.) Cedar Fort, Inc./CFI Distribution.

Peterson, Donna. The Misadventures of Phillip Isaac Penn. 2011. 96p. pap. 7.99 *(978-1-59955-893-6(9))* Cedar Fort, Inc./CFI Distribution.

Peterson, Jeanne Whitehouse. Don't Forget Winona. Root, Kimberly Bulcken, illus. 2004. 32p. (J). (gr. -1-3). lib. bdg. 15.89 *(978-0-06-027198-5(1))* HarperCollins Pubs.

Peterson, Sheryl. The Best Part of a Sauna, 1 vol. Dupre, Kelly, illus. 2013. 32p. (J). (gr. 1-2). 17.95 *(978-0-9883508-0-9(7));* (ENG.). pap. 9.95 *(978-0-9883508-1-6(5))* Raven Productions, Inc.

Petty, Kate. Ha Ha, Baby! Birkett, Georgie, illus. 2008. (ENG.). 32p. (J). (gr. -1-k). 14.95 *(978-1-905417-12-4(8))* Boxer Bks., Ltd. GBR. Dist: Sterling Publishing Co., Inc.

Pfeffer, Susan Beth. Life As We Knew It. 2008. (Life As We Knew It Ser.: 1). (ENG., Illus.). 352p. (YA). (gr. 7-18). pap. 9.99 *(978-0-15-206154-8(1))* Houghton Mifflin Harcourt Publishing Co.

—Life As We Knew It. Howard, Arthur, illus. 2006. (Life As We Knew It Ser.: 1). (ENG.). 352p. (YA). (gr. 7-12). 17.99 *(978-0-15-205826-5(5))* Houghton Mifflin Harcourt Publishing Co.

—Life As We Knew It. 2008. (Last Survivors Ser.: 1). 347p. (gr. 7-12). lib. bdg. 19.65 *(978-1-4178-1541-8(8),* Turtleback) Turtleback Bks.

—The Life As We Knew It Collection. 2015. (Life As We Knew It Ser.). (ENG.). 1252p. (YA). (gr. 7). 29.99 *(978-0-544-54263-1(0),* HMH Books For Young Readers) Houghton Mifflin Harcourt Publishing Co.

—The Shade of the Moon. (Life As We Knew It Ser.: 4). (ENG.). 304p. (YA). (gr. 7). 2014. pap. 8.99 *(978-0-544-33615-5(1),* HMH Books For Young Readers) 2013. 17.99 *(978-0-547-81337-0(6))* Houghton Mifflin Harcourt Publishing Co.

—This World We Live In, Bk. 3. 2011. (Life As We Knew It Ser.: 3). (ENG.). 256p. (YA). (gr. 7). pap. 8.99 *(978-0-547-55028-2(6))* Houghton Mifflin Harcourt Publishing Co.

Philbrick, Rodman. The Big Dark. (ENG.). 192p. (J). (gr. 3-7). 2017. pap. 6.99 ***(978-0-545-78976-9(1))*** 2016. 17.99 *(978-0-545-78975-2(3))* Scholastic, Inc. (Blue Sky Pr., The).

Philbrick, Rodman. The Young Man & the Sea. 2005. (ENG.). 192p. (J). (gr. 3-7). reprint ed. pap. 6.99 *(978-0-439-36830-8(8),* Scholastic Paperbacks) Scholastic, Inc.

Phillipps, J. C. The Simples Love a Picnic. 2014. (ENG., Illus.). 32p. (J). (gr. -1-3). 16.99 *(978-0-544-16667-7(1),* HMH Books For Young Readers) Houghton Mifflin Harcourt Publishing Co.

Phillips, Clifton. Ten Spunky Monkeys. Jung, Shirley, illus. 2007. 32p. (J). 8.99 *(978-0-9797106-4-3(2))* Avid Readers Publishing Group.

Phillips, Jan. Just for Today. Shapiro, Alison Bonds, illus. 2005. (ENG.). 32p. (J). (gr. -1-5). 15.95 *(978-1-932073-07-2(8))* Kramer, H.J. Inc.

Phillips, Rebecca. Faking Perfect. 2015. (ENG.). 272p. (J). (gr. 9). pap. 9.95 *(978-1-61773-880-7(8))* Kensington Publishing Corp.

Pickett, Anola. Callahan Crossroads. 2015. (ENG.). 192p. (J). pap. 12.99 *(978-1-4621-1715-4(5),* Sweetwater Bks.) Cedar Fort, Inc./CFI Distribution.

—Whisper Island. 2013. (ENG.). 235p. (J). (gr. 3-7). pap. 14.99 *(978-1-4621-1167-1(X),* Sweetwater Bks.) Cedar Fort, Inc./CFI Distribution.

Pierce, Seth J. The Day the School Blew Up. 2009. (J). pap. 12.99 *(978-0-8163-2329-6(1))* Pacific Pr. Publishing Assn.

Pierotti, Jr. Toward the Setting Sun. 2007. 268p. per. 17.95 *(978-0-595-45469-3(0))* iUniverse, Inc.

Pierre, Eileen. Why Is Life So Confusing? 2009. 40p. pap. 12.00 *(978-1-60693-025-0(7),* Eloquent Bks.) Strategic Book Publishing & Rights Agency (SBPRA).

Pike, Aprilynne. Life after Theft. 2013. (Life after Theft Ser.). (ENG.). 352p. (YA). (gr. 8). 17.99 *(978-0-06-199900-0(8),* HarperTeen) HarperCollins Pubs.

Pike, Kenneth & Stewart, Isaac. Jacob's Journal of Doom: Confessions of an Almost-Deacon. 2012. (J). 14.99 *(978-1-60907-016-8(X))* Deseret Bk. Co.

Pincus, Gregory K. The Homework Strike. 2017. (ENG.). 272p. (J). (gr. 3-7). 16.99 *(978-0-439-91301-0(2))* Scholastic, Inc.

Pinkney, Andrea Davis. Raven in a Dove House. 2014. (ENG.). 224p. (J). (gr. 5-7). pap. 8.99 *(978-0-544-23016-3(7),* HMH Books For Young Readers) Houghton Mifflin Harcourt Publishing Co.

—The Red Pencil. 2015. (J). lib. bdg. 19.65 *(978-0-606-37523-8(6))* Turtleback Bks.

Pintozzi, Nick. Bentley & the Great Fire. Pintozzi, Nick et al, illus. l.t. ed. 2004. 120p. per. 17.95 *(978-0-9749465-1-1(6))* BentDaiSha, LLC.

Pirola, Isabella. Steadfast. Tucker, Hilary, illus. 2016. (ENG.). 28p. (J). 19.99 *(978-1-63413-894-9(5))* Salem Author Services.

Pitcher, Annabel. Ketchup Clouds. 2013. (ENG.). 272p. (YA). (gr. 7-17). 18.00 *(978-0-316-24676-7(X))* Little Brown & Co.

—My Sister Lives on the Mantelpiece. (ENG.). (YA). (gr. 7-17). 2013. 240p. pap. 10.00 *(978-0-316-17689-7(3))* 2012. 224p. 18.00 *(978-0-316-17690-3(7))* Little, Brown Bks. for Young Readers.

—Yours Truly. 2014. (ENG., Illus.). 288p. (YA). (gr. 7-17). pap. 9.99 *(978-0-316-24678-1(6))* Little, Brown Bks. for Young Readers.

Pitcock, Tiffany. Just Friends. 2017. (ENG.). 320p. (YA). pap. 10.99 *(978-1-250-08405-7(9),* 9781250084057) Feiwel & Friends.

Piven, Hanoch. My Dog Is As Smelly As Dirty Socks. 2012. lib. bdg. 18.40 *(978-0-606-26384-9(5),* Turtleback) Turtleback Bks.

—My Dog Is As Smelly As Dirty Socks: And Other Funny Family Portraits. Piven, Hanoch, illus. 2012. (ENG., Illus.). 40p. (J). (gr. -1-3). pap. 7.99 *(978-0-307-93089-7(0),* Dragonfly Bks.) Random Hse. Children's Bks.

Pizzoli, Greg. Templeton Gets His Wish. Pizzoli, Greg, illus. 2015. (ENG., Illus.). 48p. (J). (gr. -1-k). 16.99 *(978-1-4847-1274-0(9))* Disney Pr.

Platt, Randall Beth. Liberty's Christmas. 2012. (ENG.). 224p. (YA). (gr. 7-12). 19.95 *(978-0-89672-766-3(1))* Texas Tech Univ. Pr.

Platt, Richard. The Visitor. 2014. 168p. pap. *(978-1-78222-179-1(4))* Paragon Publishing, Rothersthorpe.

Poblocki, Dan. The Book of Bad Things. 2014. (ENG.). 256p. (J). (gr. 5-9). 16.99 *(978-0-545-64553-9(0),* Scholastic Pr.) Scholastic, Inc.

Polacco, Ernest L. When Lightning Comes in a Jar. Polacco, Patricia, illus. 2007. (ENG.). 40p. (J). (gr. k-3). 6.99 *(978-0-14-240350-1(4),* Puffin Books) Penguin Young Readers Group.

Polacco, Patricia. The Blessing Cup. Polacco, Patricia, illus. 2013. (ENG., Illus.). 48p. (J). (gr. -1-3). 17.99 *(978-1-4424-5047-9(9),* Simon & Schuster Bks. For Young Readers) Simon & Schuster Bks. For Young Readers.

—In Our Mothers' House. Polacco, Patricia, illus. 2009. (ENG., Illus.). 48p. (J). (gr. 1-3). 17.99 *(978-0-399-25076-7(X),* Philomel Bks.) Penguin Young Readers Group.

—January's Sparrow. Polacco, Patricia, illus. 2009. (ENG., Illus.). 96p. (J). (gr. 3-7). 23.99 *(978-0-399-25077-4(8),* Philomel Bks.) Penguin Young Readers Group.

—When Lightning Comes in a Jar. 2007. (Illus.). (gr. -1-3). 17.00 *(978-0-7569-8196-9(4))* Perfection Learning Corp.

Polak, Monique. Home Invasion, 1 vol. 2005. (Orca Soundings Ser.). (ENG.). 128p. (YA). (gr. 8-12). per. 9.95 *(978-1-55143-482-7(2))* Orca Bk. Pubs. USA.

—Pyro, 1 vol. 2012. (Orca Currents Ser.). (ENG.). 128p. (J). (gr. 5-9). pap. 9.95 *(978-1-4598-0228-5(4));* lib. bdg. 16.95 *(978-1-4598-0229-2(2))* Orca Bk. Pubs. USA.

Polonsky, Ami. Gracefully Grayson. 2016. (ENG., Illus.). 250p. (J). (gr. 5-9). pap. 8.99 *(978-1-4847-2365-4(1))* Hyperion Bks. for Children.

—Gracefully Grayson. 2014. (ENG.). 256p. (J). (gr. 5-9). 16.99 *(978-1-4231-8527-7(7))* Hyperion Pr.

Pons, Lele & De la Cruz, Melissa. Surviving High School: Do It for the Vine: A Novel. 2017. (ENG.). 272p. (gr. 8). pap. 11.99 *(978-1-5011-2054-1(9),* Gallery Bks.) Gallery Bks.

Pooker, J. D. The Ifs. 2013. (ENG.). 148p. (J). pap. 7.95 *(978-0-9858280-3-5(X))* Little Devil Bks.

Poon, Janice. Claire & the Bakery Thief. Poon, Janice, illus. 2008. (ENG., Illus.). 104p. (J). (gr. 2-5). 15.95 *(978-1-55453-286-5(8));* pap. 7.95 *(978-1-55453-245-2(0))* Kids Can Pr., Ltd. CAN. Dist: Hachette Bk. Group.

Pope, Cheryl Lynn. The Adventures of Princess Zari. Nyamor, Eric, illus. 2009. 34p. pap. 12.99 *(978-0-9840660-1-8(2))* Second Time Media & Communications.

Poploff, Michelle. Where Triplets Go, Trouble Follows. Jamieson, Victoria, illus. 2015. (ENG.). 96p. (J). (gr. 2-6). 16.95 *(978-0-8234-3289-9(0))* Holiday Hse., Inc.

Porter, Eleanor H. Pollyanna. (J). 21.95 *(978-0-8488-1445-8(2))* Amereon Ltd.

—Pollyanna. Date not set. (J). 14.99 *(978-0-06-028226-4(6));* 32p. pap. 4.99 *(978-0-06-443536-9(9))* HarperCollins Pubs.

—Pollyanna. McKowen, Scott, illus. 2013. (Sterling Unabridged Classics Ser.). (ENG.). 208p. (J). (gr. 5). 9.95 *(978-1-4027-9718-7(4))* Sterling Publishing Co., Inc.

—Pollyanna & Pollyanna Grows Up. 2004. pap. 11.95 *(978-1-4145-0603-6(1))* Pavilion Pr., Inc.

—Pollyanna Grows Up. Date not set. 216p. (J). 21.95 *(978-0-8488-1447-2(9))* Amereon Ltd.

Porter, Pamela. I'll Be Watching. 2013. 336p. pap. *(978-1-4596-6449-4(3))* ReadHowYouWant.com, Ltd.

Porter, Tracey. Lark. 2011. (ENG.). 192p. (YA). (gr. 8-18). 15.99 *(978-0-06-112287-3(4),* HarperTeen) HarperCollins Pubs.

Portman, Frank. Andromeda Klein. 2010. (ENG.). 432p. (YA). (gr. 9). pap. 9.99 *(978-0-385-73526-1(X),* Delacorte Bks. for Young Readers) Random Hse. Children's Bks.

Portnoy, Mindy Avra. A Tale of Two Seders. Cis, Valeria, illus. 2010. (ENG.). 32p. (J). (gr. k-4). lib. bdg. 17.95 *(978-0-8225-9907-4(4));* pap. 7.95 *(978-0-8225-9931-9(7))* Lerner Publishing Group. (Kar-Ben Publishing).

Poskitt, Kjartan. Agatha Parrot & the Heart of Mud. Hargis, Wes, illus. 2016. (Agatha Parrot Ser.). (ENG.). 160p. (J). (gr. 2-5). 16.99 *(978-0-544-50876-7(9))* Houghton Mifflin Harcourt Publishing Co.

Postgate, Daniel. Love Stinks. 2012. (J). *(978-1-61913-132-3(3))* Weigl Pubs., Inc.

Potter, Ellen. Piper Green & the Fairy Tree. Leng, Qin, illus. 2015. (Piper Green & the Fairy Tree Ser.). (ENG.). 112p. (J). (gr. 2-4). pap. 5.99 *(978-0-553-49926-1(2),* Yearling) Random Hse. Children's Bks.

Powell, Jillian. Henry & the Hand-Me-Downs. Worsley, Belinda, illus. 2005. 32p. (J). lib. bdg. 9.00 *(978-1-4242-0886-9(6))* Fitzgerald Bks.

Powell, Maud Macrory. City of Grit & Gold. 2017. (ENG.). 164p. (J). (gr. 4-6). pap. 16.99 ***(978-0-9967558-5-6(3))*** Allium Pr. of Chicago.

Preble, Joy. Haunted. 2011. (ENG.). 304p. (YA). (gr. 7-12). pap. 9.99 *(978-1-4022-4468-1(1))* Sourcebooks, Inc.

Precious. Dymond in the Rough. 2004. (Platinum Teen Ser.). 111p. per. 6.99 *(978-0-9729325-2-3(6))* Precioustymes Entertainment, LLC.

Preller, James. Before You Go. 2013. (ENG.). 224p. (YA). (gr. 7-12). pap. 16.99 *(978-1-250-03421-2(3),* 9781250034212) Square Fish.

—Bystander. 2011. (ENG.). 256p. (YA). (gr. 5-9). pap. 8.99 *(978-0-312-54796-7(X),* 9780312547967) Square Fish.

Prestwood, Donna. Center World. 2006. 120p. per. 10.95 *(978-1-59824-206-5(7))* E-BookTime LLC.

Price, Bc. Mabel & Her Litter Of. 2008. 132p. pap. 12.00 *(978-0-615-20692-9(1))* BCP Pubns.

Prince, Ricky. What Made That Noise? 2008. 35p. pap. 24.95 *(978-1-60474-601-3(7))* America Star Bks.

Prosek, James. The Day My Mother Left. Prosek, James, illus. 2009. (ENG., Illus.). 304p. (J). (gr. 4-7). pap. 7.99 *(978-1-4169-0771-8(8),* Simon & Schuster Bks. For Young Readers) Simon & Schuster Bks. For Young Readers.

Prozeller, Ellen Lucey. 32 Days: A Story of Faith & Courage. 2016. (J). pap. *(978-0-8198-0657-4(9))* Pauline Bks. & Media.

Pryor, Bonnie. Simon's Escape: A Story of the Holocaust. 2010. (Historical Fiction Adventures (HFA) Ser.). (Illus.). 160p. (J). pap. 10.95 *(978-1-59845-216-7(9));* (gr. 3-6). 29.27 *(978-0-7660-3388-7(0))* Enslow Pubs., Inc.

Puccinelli, Joanne. Naughty Nello & the Sleds. Elam, Brock, illus. 2012. 34p. (J). pap. 12.95 *(978-1-938707-00-1(1))* Stoneydale Pr. Publishing Co.

Puccini, Giacomo. Madame Butterfly. Fucíková, Renata, illus. 2005. (ENG.). 40p. (Orig.). (J). 15.95 *(978-1-933327-04-4(9))* Purple Bear Bks., Inc.

Puentes, Christina. On the Way to Granny's House. 2005. 28p. per. 17.32 *(978-1-4134-3612-9(9))* Xlibris Corp.

Purmell, Ann. Maple Syrup Season. Weber, Jill, illus. 2008. (ENG.). 32p. (J). (gr. -1-k). 16.95 *(978-0-8234-1891-6(X))* Holiday Hse., Inc.

Pyke, Helen Godfrey. Julia. 2012. (J). pap. *(978-0-8163-3400-1(5))* Pacific Pr. Publishing Assn.

Qamar, Amjed. Beneath My Mother's Feet. (ENG.). 208p. (YA). (gr. 7). 2011. pap. 10.99 *(978-1-4424-1451-8(0))* 2008. 16.99 *(978-1-4169-4728-8(0))* Simon & Schuster Children's Publishing. (Atheneum Bks. for Young Readers).

Quan, Adalucia. The Song of the Coconut. 2008. (SPA & ENG., Illus.). (J). *(978-0-9742956-2-6(0))* Cholita Prints & Pub. Co.

Quinn, Kate Karyus. Another Little Piece. 2013. (ENG.). 432p. (YA). (gr. 9). 17.99 *(978-0-06-213595-7(3),* HarperTeen) HarperCollins Pubs.

Quinn, Spencer, pseud. ARF - A Bowser & Birdie Novel. 2016. (ENG.). 304p. (J). (gr. 3-7). 16.99 *(978-0-545-64334-4(1),* Scholastic Pr.) Scholastic, Inc.

Quintero, Isabel. Gabi, a Girl in Pieces. 2014. (ENG.). 208p. (J). pap. 11.95 *(978-1-935955-95-5(0));* (YA). 17.95 *(978-1-935955-94-8(2))* Cinco Puntos Pr.

Quinton, Sasha. Florabelle. Barrager, Brigette & Tcherevkoff, Michel, illus. 2015. (ENG.). 40p. (J). (gr. -1-3). 15.99 *(978-0-06-229182-0(3))* HarperCollins Pubs.

R. Friend -Panic in the PigPen. 2007. (J). per. *(978-0-9743627-7-9(8))* Sunflower Seeds Pr.

Raabe, Emily. Lost Children of the Far Islands. 2014. (ENG.). 288p. (J). (gr. 3-7). 16.99 *(978-0-375-87091-0(1),* Knopf Bks. for Young Readers) Random Hse. Children's Bks.

Rainforth, Hannah. Barnaby Bennett, 1 vol. Teo, Ali, illus. 2008. (ENG.). 32p. (J). (gr. -1-3). pap. 5.95 *(978-1-59572-156-3(8))* Star Bright Bks., Inc.

Ramona Quimby, Age 8. 2005. (J). *(978-1-59564-976-8(X))* Steps To Literacy, LLC.

Rankin, Laura. Ruthie & the (Not So) Very Busy Day. Rankin, Laura, illus. 2014. (ENG., Illus.). 32p. (J). (gr. -1-1). 17.99 *(978-1-59990-052-0(1),* 9781599900520, Bloomsbury USA Childrens) Bloomsbury Publishing USA.

Ransom, Candice. Iva Honeysuckle Meets Her Match. Ross, Heather, illus. 2014. (Iva Honeysuckle Book Ser.). (ENG.). 192p. (J). (gr. 1-3). pap. 4.99 *(978-1-4231-3516-6(4))* Hyperion Bks. for Children.

—Iva Honeysuckle Meets Her Match. Ross, Heather, illus. 2013. (Iva Honeysuckle Book Ser.). (ENG.). 192p. (J). (gr. 2-5). 14.99 *(978-1-4231-3514-2(8))* Hyperion Pr.

Rapp, Adam. Punkzilla. 2009. (ENG., Illus.). 256p. (YA). (gr. 9). 16.99 *(978-0-7636-3031-7(4))* Candlewick Pr.

Raskin, Ellen. Figgs & Phantoms. Raskin, Ellen, illus. 2011. (ENG., Illus.). 176p. (J). (gr. 5-18). 6.99 *(978-0-14-241169-8(8),* Puffin Books) Penguin Young Readers Group.

Raskin, Joyce. My Misadventures As a Teenage Rock Star. Chu, Carol, illus. 2011. (ENG.). 112p. (YA). (gr. 7-18). pap. 8.99 *(978-0-547-39311-7(3))* Houghton Mifflin Harcourt Publishing Co.

Rathore, Jazz Kopecek & Niederhofer, Renate. Adler the Eagle Boy. 2012. 44p. pap. *(978-1-908341-83-9(1))* Paragon Publishing, Rothersthorpe.

Raudenbush, Amy. Lucy More Needs Less. 2006. 48p. (J). pap. 13.99 *(978-1-4116-6120-2(6))* Lulu Pr., Inc.

Rawlings, Marjorie Kinnan. The Yearling. Wyeth, N. C., illus. 2013. (Scribner Classics Ser.). (ENG.). 416p. (J). (gr. 5-9). 29.99 *(978-1-4424-8209-8(5),* Atheneum Bks. for Young Readers) Simon & Schuster Children's Publishing.

Rayburn, Tricia. The Melting of Maggie Bean. 2007. (ENG.). 256p. (J). (gr. 4-8). pap. 6.99 *(978-1-4169-3348-9(4),* Aladdin) Simon & Schuster Children's Publishing.

Reader's Digest Staff. Busy Day Bunnies: A Carry along Treasury. McCue, Lisa, illus. 2011. (Carry along Bks.). (ENG.). 20p. (J). (gr. -1-k). 14.99 *(978-0-7944-2168-7(7))* Reader's Digest Assn., Inc., The.

Reed, Amy. Beautiful. 2010. (ENG.). 256p. (YA). (gr. 9). pap. 10.99 *(978-1-4169-7831-2(3),* Simon Pulse) Simon Pulse.

—Clean. 2011. (ENG.). 288p. (YA). (gr. 9-18). 16.99 *(978-1-4424-1344-3(1),* Simon Pulse) Simon Pulse.

—Over You. 2014. (ENG., Illus.). 336p. (YA). (gr. 9). pap. 9.99 *(978-1-4424-5697-6(3),* Simon Pulse) Simon Pulse.

Reed, Amy Lynn. Beautiful. 2009. (ENG.). 240p. (YA). (gr. 9-18). 16.99 *(978-1-4169-7830-5(5),* Simon Pulse) Simon Pulse.

Reed, Amy Lynn. The Nowhere Girls. 2017. (YA). pap. ***(978-1-4814-8174-8(6),*** Simon Pulse) Simon Pulse.

Reed, Stephanie. The Light Across the River, 1 vol. 2008. (Illus.). 216p. (J). (gr. 4-7). pap. 10.99 *(978-0-8254-3574-4(9))* Kregel Pubns.

Reedy, Trent. Words in the Dust. (ENG.). 272p. (J). 2013. (gr. 5-9). pap. 6.99 *(978-0-545-26126-5(0))* 2011. (gr. 4-7). 17.99 *(978-0-545-26125-8(2))* Scholastic, Inc. (Levine, Arthur A. Bks.).

Reely, Mary Katharine. The Blue Mittens. Wiese, Kurt, illus. 2011. 164p. 41.95 *(978-1-258-10114-5(9))* Literary Licensing, LLC.

Reinhardt, Dana. A Brief Chapter in My Impossible Life. 2007. (ENG.). 256p. (YA). (gr. 9-12). pap. 8.99 *(978-0-375-84691-5(3),* Ember) Random Hse. Children's Bks.

—The Things a Brother Knows. 2011. (ENG.). 256p. (YA). (gr. 9). pap. 8.99 *(978-0-375-84456-0(2),* Ember) Random Hse. Children's Bks.

Reiss, Kathryn. Riddle of the Prairie Bride. 2009. (Mysteries Through Time Ser.). 144 - 176p. (YA). (gr. 4-8). 31.95 *(978-1-60754-421-0(0));* pap. 15.25 *(978-1-60754-420-3(2))* Windmill Bks.

Rempel, Leah. Hey, Hmong Girl, Whassup? The Journal of Choua Vang. 2004. (Illus.). v, 138p. (YA). pap. *(978-0-9723721-5-2(6))* Hamline Univ. Pr.

Remza, Freddie. The Journey to Mei. 2007. 164p. (YA). per. 10.95 *(978-1-4327-0459-9(1))* Outskirts Pr., Inc.

Rennison, Louise. Dancing in My Nuddy-Pants. 2006. (Confessions of Georgia Nicolson Ser.: 4). (ENG.). 240p. (YA). (gr. 8). reprint ed. pap. 8.99 *(978-0-06-009748-6(5),* HarperTeen) HarperCollins Pubs.

—On the Bright Side, I'm Now the Girlfriend of a Sex God: Further Confessions of Georgia Nicolson. (Confessions of Georgia Nicolson Ser.: 2). (ENG.). 2006. 272p. (YA). (gr. 8). pap. 8.99 *(978-0-06-447226-5(4),* HarperTeen) 2003. 256p. (J). pap. 6.99 *(978-0-06-052185-1(6))* HarperCollins Pubs.

Rettig, Liz. My Desperate Love Diary. 2007. (ENG.). 314p. (YA). (gr. 9-12). 16.95 *(978-0-8234-2033-9(7))* Holiday Hse., Inc.

Revell, Mike. Stormwalker. 2016. (ENG.). 304p. (J). (gr. 5-9). 16.99 *(978-1-68144-493-2(3))* Quercus NA.

Reynolds, Cynthia Furlong. Across the Reach. 2007. 269p. (J). (gr. 3-7). 16.95 *(978-1-58726-518-1(4),* Mitten Pr.) Ann Arbor Editions LLC.

Reynolds, Jason. The Boy in the Black Suit. 2015. (ENG., Illus.). 272p. (YA). (gr. 7). 17.99 *(978-1-4424-5950-2(6))* Simon & Schuster Children's Publishing.

—The Boy in the Black Suit. 2016. (ENG.). (J). lib. bdg. 22.10 *(978-0-606-38272-4(0))* Turtleback Bks.

—Patina. 2017. (J). pap. ***(978-1-4814-5019-5(0));*** (Track Ser.: 2). (ENG., Illus.). 240p. (gr. 5). 16.99 ***(978-1-4814-5018-8(2),*** Atheneum/Caitlyn Dlouhy Books) Simon & Schuster Children's Publishing.

Reynolds, Jason. When I Was the Greatest. Frost, Michael, photos by. 2014. (ENG., Illus.). 240p. (YA). (gr. 7). 17.99 *(978-1-4424-5947-2(6),* Atheneum Bks. for Young Readers) Simon & Schuster Children's Publishing.

Reynolds, Peter H. My Very Big Little World. Reynolds, Peter H., illus. 2006. (ENG., Illus.). 40p. (J). (gr. -1-3). 17.99 *(978-0-689-87621-9(1),* Atheneum Bks. for Young Readers) Simon & Schuster Children's Publishing.

Rhodes, Jewell Parker. Towers Falling. 2016. (ENG., Illus.). 240p. (J). (gr. 3-7). 16.99 *(978-0-316-26222-4(6))* Little, Brown Bks. for Young Readers.

Rhuday-Perkovich, Olugbemisola & Vernick, Audrey. Two Naomis. 2016. 208p. (J). (gr. 3-7). 16.99 *(978-0-06-241425-0(9))* HarperCollins Pubs.

Rhyason, Sharon. Utopia, Where Are You? 2003. 164p. (YA). pap. 11.95 *(978-0-595-26401-8(8),* Writers Club Pr.) iUniverse, Inc.

Rice, David L. Because Brian Hugged His Mother. 2004. (Sharing Nature with Children Book Ser.). (Illus.). 32p. (YA). (gr. -1-3). 16.95 *(978-1-883220-90-7(4))* Dawn Pubns.

—Because Brian Hugged His Mother, 1 vol. Thompson, K. Dyble, illus. 2004. (Sharing Nature with Children Book Ser.). (ENG.). 32p. (YA). (gr. -1-3). pap. 7.95 *(978-1-883220-89-1(0))* Dawn Pubns.

Richards, Lisa. Family Stories: A Collection of Short Stories by Lisa Richards, 1 vol. 2010. 52p. pap. 16.95 *(978-1-4512-8988-6(X))* America Star Bks.

Richter, Conrad. The Light in the Forest. 2005. (ENG., Illus.). 176p. *(978-1-85715-515-0(7))* Knopf, Alfred A. Inc.

Riley, Elliot. Sonya's Family. Bassani, Srimalie, illus. 2017. (All Kinds of Families Ser.). (ENG.). (J). (gr. k-1). 28.51 ***(978-1-68342-146-7(9))*** Rourke Educational Media.

Rinaldi, Ann. Come Juneteenth. 2009. (ENG., Illus.). 256p. (YA). (gr. 7). pap. 7.99 *(978-0-15-206392-4(7))* Houghton Mifflin Harcourt Publishing Co.

—Leigh Ann's Civil War. 2011. (ENG.). 320p. (YA). (gr. 7). pap. 17.99 *(978-0-547-54999-6(7))* Houghton Mifflin Harcourt Publishing Co.

—My Vicksburg. 2011. (ENG.). 160p. (YA). (gr. 7). pap. 11.95 *(978-0-547-55000-8(6))* Houghton Mifflin Harcourt Publishing Co.

—Or Give Me Death. 2004. (Great Episodes Ser.). 226p. (gr. 5-9). 17.00 *(978-0-7569-3462-0(1))* Perfection Learning Corp.

—Or Give Me Death: A Novel of Patrick Henry's Family. 2004. (Great Episodes Ser.). (ENG.). 240p. (YA). (gr. 7-8). pap. 6.99 *(978-0-15-205076-4(0))* Houghton Mifflin Harcourt Publishing Co.

Ripken, Cal, Jr. Hothead. aut. ed. 2011. 16.99 *(978-1-4231-5168-5(2))* Disney Pr.

—Hothead. 2011. (Playaway Children Ser.). (J). (gr. 4-6). 44.99 *(978-1-61707-430-1(6))* Random Hse., Inc.

Ripken, Cal, Jr. & Cowherd, Kevin. Hothead. 2012. (ENG.). 160p. (J). (gr. 3-7). pap. 6.99 *(978-1-4231-4003-0(6))* Hyperion Pr.

Rippin, Sally. The Best Project. Fukuoka, Aki, illus. 2015. (ENG.). 48p. (J). pap. 4.99 *(978-1-61067-258-0(5))* Kane Miller.

—The Crazy Cousins. Spartels, Stephanie, illus. 2012. 42p. (J). *(978-1-61067-135-4(X))* Kane Miller.

Rissi, Anica Mrose. Anna, Banana, & the Friendship Split. Park, Meg, illus. 2015. (Anna, Banana Ser.: 1). (ENG.). 128p. (J). (gr. 1-5). 16.99 *(978-1-4814-1605-4(7),* Simon & Schuster Bks. For Young Readers) Simon & Schuster Bks. For Young Readers.

—Anna, Banana, & the Monkey in the Middle. Park, Meg, illus. 2015. (Anna, Banana Ser.: 2). (ENG.). 128p. (J). (gr. 1-5). 15.99 *(978-1-4814-1608-5(1),* Simon & Schuster Bks. For Young Readers) Simon & Schuster Bks. For Young Readers.

Rivera, Lilliam. The Education of Margot Sanchez. 2017. (ENG., Illus.). 304p. (YA). (gr. 9). 17.99 *(978-1-4814-7211-1(9),* Simon & Schuster Bks. For Young Readers) Simon & Schuster Bks. For Young Readers.

Roberts, Willo Davis. Blood on His Hands. 2014. (ENG., Illus.). 192p. (YA). (gr. 7). pap. 13.99 *(978-1-4814-4461-3(1),* Simon Pulse) Simon Pulse.

Robinson, A. M. Vampire Crush. 2010. (ENG.). 416p. (YA). (gr. 8-18). pap. 8.99 *(978-0-06-198971-1(1),* HarperTeen) HarperCollins Pubs.

Robinson, Gary. Paranormal: A Billy Buckhorn Supernatural Adventure. 2014. (PathFinders Ser.). (ENG.). 147p. (J). pap. *(978-1-939053-08-4(0))* Book Publishing Co.

Robshaw, Brandon. Big Wish. 2016. (ENG.). 240p. (J). (gr. 3-7). 16.99 *(978-0-545-90410-0(2),* Chicken Hse., The) Scholastic, Inc.

Rocco, John. Blackout. Rocco, John, illus. 2011. (ENG., Illus.). 40p. (J). (gr. -1-k). 17.99 *(978-1-4231-2190-9(2))* Hyperion Pr.

Rocco, John & Primiano, Jay. Swim That Rock. Rocco, John, illus. 2017. (ENG., Illus.). 304p. (J). (gr. 7). pap. 7.99 *(978-0-7636-9447-0(9))* Candlewick Pr.

Rochea, Vanessa. Kamlyn's Journal, 1 vol. 2009. 48p. pap. 16.95 *(978-1-4489-1937-6(1))* America Star Bks.

Rocklin, Joanne. Fleabrain Loves Franny. (ENG.). 288p. (J). (gr. 3-7). 2015. pap. 8.95 *(978-1-4197-1676-8(X))* 2014. 16.95 *(978-1-4197-1068-1(0))* Abrams, Inc. (Amulet Bks.).

—One Day & One Amazing Morning on Orange Street. 2012. (ENG., Illus.). 240p. (J). (gr. 3-7). pap. 8.95 *(978-1-4197-0181-8(9),* Amulet Bks.) Abrams, Inc.

Roddy, Lee. Eye of the Hurricane. 2007. (Ladd Family Adventure Ser.: Vol. 9). (Illus.). 161p. (J). (gr. 3-7). per. 7.99 *(978-0-88062-258-5(X))* Mott Media.

—Stranded on Terror Island. 2007. (Ladd Family Adventure Ser.: Vol. 14). 137p. (J). (gr. 3-7). pap. 6.99 *(978-0-88062-263-9(6))* Mott Media.

Rodkey, Geoff. The Tapper Twins Go to War (with Each Other) 2015. (Tapper Twins Ser.: 1). (ENG., Illus.). 240p. (J). (gr. 3-7). 13.99 *(978-0-316-29779-0(8))* Little Brown & Co.

—The Tapper Twins Go Viral. 2017. (Tapper Twins Ser.: 4). (ENG., Illus.). 256p. (J). (gr. 3-7). 13.99 *(978-0-316-29784-4(4))* Little Brown & Co.

Rolle Williams, Joyce. Chris's Story: A Family Voting Secret Revealed. 2008. 24p. pap. 12.99 *(978-1-4389-4258-2(3))* AuthorHouse.

Roman Saint-Pierre, Erika. Hoppa's Big Move. Newman, J. Heidi, ed. 2009. (Mimi's Kids Ser.: vol. 1). (ENG., Illus.). 32p. (J). pap. 12.95 *(978-0-9712383-5-0(9))* Culturatti Ink.

Romano, Jennifer. Saturday Morning. 2010. 44p. pap. 16.99 *(978-1-4520-0165-4(0))* AuthorHouse.

Romano, Ray. Raymie, Dickie, & the Bean: Why I Love & Hate My Brothers. Locke, Gary, illus. 2007. 30p. (J). 18.00 *(978-1-4223-6806-0(8))* DIANE Publishing Co.

Room for One More, 6 Packs. (gr. -1-2). 27.00 *(978-0-7635-9472-5(5))* Rigby Education.

Roop, Peter & Roop, Connie. An Eye for an Eye. 2004. 168p. (J). lib. bdg. 16.92 *(978-1-4242-0772-5(X))* Fitzgerald Bks.

Rosa-Casanova, Sylvia. Mama Provi & the Pot of Rice. 2004. (Illus.). (J). (gr. k-3). spiral bd. *(978-0-616-07257-8(0))* Canadian National Institute for the Blind/Institut National Canadien pour les Aveugles.

Rose, Phyllis & de Brunhoff, Laurent. Babar & the New Baby. 2013. (ENG., Illus.). 22p. (J). (gr. -1 — 1). bds. 7.95 *(978-1-4197-0620-2(9),* Abrams Appleseed) Abrams, Inc.

Rosen, Chaya & Braverman, Rivkie. Our New Special Baby. 2013. *(978-1-59826-960-4(7))* Feldheim Pubs.

Rosen, Michael J. A Drive in the Country. Burckhardt, Marc, illus. 2007. (ENG.). 32p. (J). (gr. k-4). 16.99 *(978-0-7636-2140-7(4))* Candlewick Pr.

Rosenberg, Natascha & Kempter, Christa. When Mama Can't Sleep. 2011. (ENG., Illus.). 24p. (J). (gr. -1 — 1). 6.95 *(978-0-7358-4015-7(6))* North-South Bks., Inc.

Roskos, Evan. Dr. Bird's Advice for Sad Poets. 2013. (ENG.). 320p. (YA). (gr. 9). 17.99 *(978-0-547-92853-1(X))* Houghton Mifflin Harcourt Publishing Co.

Rosoff, Meg. How I Live Now. (ENG.). (YA). (gr. 7). 2013. 208p. pap. 8.99 *(978-0-449-81960-9(4),* Ember) 2006. 224p. reprint ed. pap. 8.99 *(978-0-553-37605-0(5),* Lamb, Wendy Bks.) Random Hse. Children's Bks.

Ross, Chudney. Lone Bean. 2012. (ENG.). 208p. (J). (gr. 3-7). 16.99 *(978-0-06-166011-5(6),* Amistad) HarperCollins Pubs.

Ross, Jeff. Coming Clean, 1 vol. 2012. (Orca Soundings Ser.). (ENG.). 128p. (YA). (gr. 8-12). lib. bdg. 16.95 *(978-1-4598-0332-9(9))* Orca Bk. Pubs. USA.

Rosseau, Paul. Lucifer, Mon Grand-Père, Tome 1. Guénette, Geneviève, illus. 2004. (Mon Roman Ser.). (FRE.). 160p. (J). (gr. 2). pap. *(978-2-89021-650-1(0))* Diffusion du livre Mirabel (DLM).

Roth, Veronica. Divergent. 2014. (Divergent Ser.). (ENG.). 496p. (J). 14.24 *(978-1-63245-208-5(1))* Lectorum Pubns., Inc.

Rothstein, Nancy H. & Gilpin, Stephen. My Daddy Snores. 2006. (Illus.). (J). pap. *(978-0-439-87142-6(5))* Scholastic, Inc.

Rowley, Deborah. The Miracle of the Wooden Shoes. 2008. 32p. (J). 18.95 *(978-1-59038-990-4(5))* Deseret Bk. Co.

Roy, Jennifer. Cordially Uninvited. 2012. (ENG., Illus.). 256p. (J). (gr. 3-7). 15.99 *(978-1-4424-3920-7(3),* Simon & Schuster Bks. For Young Readers) Simon & Schuster Bks. For Young Readers.

—Yellow Star, 0 vols. 2014. (ENG.). 256p. (gr. 5-7). pap. 9.99 *(978-0-7614-6310-8(0),* 9780761463108, Amazon Children's Publishing) Amazon Publishing.

Roy, Ron. July Jitters. 2012. (Calendar Mysteries Ser.: 7). lib. bdg. 14.75 *(978-0-606-26402-0(7),* Turtleback) Turtleback Bks.

—September Sneakers. 2013. (Calendar Mysteries Ser.: 9). lib. bdg. 14.75 *(978-0-606-32231-7(0),* Turtleback) Turtleback Bks.

Rubens, Michael. Sons of The 613. 2012. (ENG.). 320p. (YA). (gr. 7). 16.99 *(978-0-547-61216-4(8))* Houghton Mifflin Harcourt Publishing Co.

Ruby, Jeff. Penelope March Is Melting. 2017. (J). ***(978-1-5247-1829-9(7),*** Delacorte Pr) Random House Publishing Group.

Ruby, Laura. Bad Apple. 2009. (ENG.). 256p. (YA). (gr. 8-18). 16.99 *(978-0-06-124330-1(2),* HarperTeen) HarperCollins Pubs.

Ruby, Lois. Shanghai Shadows. 2006. (ENG.). 256p. (YA). 16.95 *(978-0-8234-1960-9(6))* Holiday Hse., Inc.

Rue, Nancy N. Motorcycles, Sushi & One Strange Book, 1 vol. 2010. (Real Life Ser.). (ENG.). 224p. (YA). (gr. 8-11). pap. 9.99 *(978-0-310-71484-2(2))* Zondervan.

Ruelle, Karen Gray. Spookier Than a Ghost. (Holiday House Readers Ser.). (ENG., Illus.). 32p. (J). (gr. k-3). pap. 4.95 *(978-0-8234-1801-5(4))* Holiday Hse., Inc.

Ruiz Zafón, Carlos. The Prince of Mist. 2011. (ENG.). 256p. (YA). (gr. 7-17). pap., pap. 10.99 *(978-0-316-04480-6(6))* Little, Brown Bks. for Young Readers.

Rumbaugh, Melinda. Somebunny Loves You! Biscoe, Cee, illus. 2015. (ENG.). 16p. (J). 12.99 *(978-0-8249-1950-4(5),* Ideal Pubns.) Worthy Publishing.

Rumble. 2014. (ENG., Illus.). 560p. (YA). (gr. 9). 19.99 *(978-1-4424-8284-5(2),* McElderry, Margaret K. Bks.) McElderry, Margaret K. Bks.

Rupp, Rebecca. After Eli. 2012. (ENG., Illus.). 256p. (J). (gr. 4-7). 15.99 *(978-0-7636-5810-6(3))* Candlewick Pr.

—Octavia Boone's Big Questions about Life, the Universe & Everything. 2010. (ENG., Illus.). 192p. (J). (gr. 4-7). 15.99 *(978-0-7636-4491-8(9))* Candlewick Pr.

—Sarah Simpson's Rules for Living. 2008. (ENG., Illus.). 96p. (J). (gr. 3-7). 14.99 *(978-0-7636-3220-5(1))* Candlewick Pr.

Rushford, Patricia H. Secrets of Ghost Island. 2007. (J). *(978-88-02-46255-4(0))* Moody Pubs.

Ryan, Amy Kathleen. Vibes. 2010. (ENG.). 264p. (YA). (gr. 9). pap. 14.95 *(978-0-547-24889-9(X))* Houghton Mifflin Harcourt Publishing Co.

—Zen & Xander Undone. 2011. (ENG.). 228p. (YA). (gr. 9). pap. 13.99 *(978-0-547-55030-5(8))* Houghton Mifflin Harcourt Publishing Co.

Ryan, Carrie. The Dead-Tossed Waves. 2011. (Forest of Hands & Teeth Ser.: Bk. 2). (ENG.). 432p. (YA). (gr. 9). pap. 9.99 *(978-0-385-73685-5(1),* Delacorte Bks. for Young Readers) Random Hse. Children's Bks.

Ryan, Pam Muñoz. Echo. 2015. (ENG., Illus.). 512p. (J). (gr. 5-9). 19.99 *(978-0-439-87402-1(5),* Scholastic Pr.) Scholastic, Inc.

Ryan, Pam Muñoz & McInerney, Kathleen. Paint the Wind. 2009. (ENG.). 352p. (J). (gr. 3-7). pap. 7.99 *(978-0-545-10176-9(X),* Scholastic Paperbacks) Scholastic, Inc.

Ryan, Patrick. Gemini Bites. 2011. (ENG.). 240p. (J). (gr. 7-8). 17.99 *(978-0-545-22128-3(5),* Scholastic Pr.) Scholastic, Inc.

Ryan, Shawn. Right Now I'm Small, & I Have a Long Time to Grow. 2010. 32p. pap. 17.95 *(978-1-4269-3769-9(5))* Trafford Publishing.

Rylant, Cynthia. Annie & Snowball & the Wintry Freeze. Stevenson, Suçie, illus. 2011. (Annie & Snowball Ser.: 8). (ENG.). 40p. (J). (gr. k-2). pap. 3.99 *(978-1-4169-7206-8(4),* Simon Spotlight) Simon Spotlight.

—Old Town in the Green Groves. 2007. (Little House Ser.). (ENG.). 192p. (J). (gr. 3-7). pap. 6.99 *(978-0-06-088546-5(7))* HarperCollins Pubs.

—We Love You, Rosie! Davick, Linda, illus. 2017. (ENG.). 48p. (J). (gr. -1-2). 17.99 *(978-1-4424-6511-4(5),* Beach Lane Bks.) Beach Lane Bks.

—Wedding Flowers. Halperin, Wendy Anderson, illus. 2003. (Cobble Street Cousins Ser.). 72p. (gr. 2-5). 15.00 *(978-0-7569-1476-9(0))* Perfection Learning Corp.

Sackier, Shelley. Dear OPL. 2015. (ENG.). 240p. (J). (gr. 5-8). pap. 7.99 *(978-1-4926-0859-2(9),* 9781492608592) Sourcebooks, Inc.

Sacre, Antonio. A Mango in the Hand: A Story Told Through Proverbs. Serra, Sebastia, illus. 2011. (ENG.). 32p. (J). (gr. k-2). 16.95 *(978-0-8109-9734-9(7),* Abrams Bks. for Young Readers) Abrams, Inc.

—La Noche Buena: A Christmas Story. Dominguez, Angela, illus. 2010. (ENG.). 32p. (J). (gr. k-2). 17.95 *(978-0-8109-8967-2(0),* Abrams Bks. for Young Readers) Abrams, Inc.

Saddleback Educational Publishing Staff, ed. Camp, 1 vol. unabr. ed. 2011. (Heights Ser.). (ENG.). 50p. (gr. 5-8). pap. 7.95 *(978-1-61651-284-2(9))* Saddleback Educational Publishing, Inc.

—Crash, 1 vol. unabr. ed. 2011. (Heights Ser.). (ENG.). 49p. (gr. 5-8). pap. 7.95 *(978-1-61651-283-5(0))* Saddleback Educational Publishing, Inc.

—Dive, 1 vol. unabr. ed. 2011. (Heights Ser.). (ENG.). 50p. (gr. 5-8). pap. 7.95 *(978-1-61651-282-8(2))* Saddleback Educational Publishing, Inc.

—Neptune, 1 vol. unabr. ed. 2011. (Heights Ser.). (ENG.). 50p. (gr. 5-8). pap. 7.95 *(978-1-61651-285-9(7))* Saddleback Educational Publishing, Inc.

—River, 1 vol. unabr. ed. 2011. (Heights Ser.). (ENG.). 49p. (gr. 5-8). pap. 7.95 *(978-1-61651-281-1(4))* Saddleback Educational Publishing, Inc.

Sáenz, Benjamin Alire. He Forgot to Say Goodbye. 2008. (ENG.). 336p. (YA). (gr. 7-12). 18.99 *(978-1-4169-4963-3(1),* Simon & Schuster Bks. For Young Readers) Simon & Schuster Bks. For Young Readers.

—La Perrita Que le Encantaban las Tortillas. Garcia, Geronimo, illus. 2009. (Little Diego Book Ser.).Tr. of Dog Who Loved Tortillas. (SPA & ENG.). 40p. (J). (gr. 1-4). 17.95 *(978-1-933693-54-5(1))* Cinco Puntos Pr.

Saldana, Rene, Jr. The Jumping Tree. 2008. 181p. (gr. 5-7). 16.50 *(978-0-7569-8950-7(7))* Perfection Learning Corp.

Saldana, Theresa. The Almost Murder & Other Stories. 2008. (ENG.). 144p. (YA). (gr. 6-18). pap. 10.95 *(978-1-55885-507-6(6),* Piñata Books) Arte Publico Pr.

Salisbury, Graham. Calvin Coconut: Dog Heaven. Rogers, Jacqueline, illus. 2011. (Calvin Coconut Ser.). (ENG.). 160p. (J). (gr. 3-7). 6.99 *(978-0-375-84602-1(6),* Yearling) Random Hse. Children's Bks.

—Calvin Coconut: Man Trip. Rogers, Jacqueline, illus. 2013. (Calvin Coconut Ser.). (ENG.). 144p. (J). (gr. 2-5). pap. 6.99 *(978-0-375-86507-7(1),* Yearling) Random Hse. Children's Bks.

—Calvin Coconut: Zoo Breath. Rogers, Jacqueline, illus. 2011. (Calvin Coconut Ser.). (ENG.). 160p. (J). (gr. 3-7). 6.99 *(978-0-375-84603-8(4),* Yearling) Random Hse. Children's Bks.

—Extra Famous. Rogers, Jacqueline, illus. 2014. (Calvin Coconut Ser.). (ENG.). 176p. (J). (gr. 2-5). pap. 6.99 *(978-0-307-93075-0(0),* Yearling) Random Hse. Children's Bks.

—Kung Fooey. Rogers, Jacqueline, illus. 2012. (Calvin Coconut Ser.). (ENG.). 144p. (J). (gr. 2-5). 6.99 *(978-0-375-86506-0(3),* Yearling) Random Hse. Children's Bks.

—Trouble Magnet. Rogers, Jacqueline, illus. 2010. (Calvin Coconut Ser.). (ENG.). 160p. (J). (gr. 3-7). pap. 6.99 *(978-0-375-84600-7(X),* Yearling) Random Hse. Children's Bks.

—Under the Blood-Red Sun. 2014. (ENG.). 272p. (YA). (gr. 7-7). pap. 9.99 *(978-0-385-38655-5(9),* Ember) Random Hse. Children's Bks.

—The Zippy Fix. Rogers, Jacqueline, illus. 2010. (Calvin Coconut Ser.). (ENG.). 176p. (J). (gr. 3-7). pap. 6.99 *(978-0-375-84601-4(8),* Yearling) Random Hse. Children's Bks.

Salm, Arthur. Anyway: A Story about Me with 138 Footnotes, 27 Exaggerations, & 1 Plate of Spaghetti. 2012. (ENG., Illus.). 192p. (J). (gr. 3-7). 15.99 *(978-1-4424-2930-7(5),* Simon & Schuster Bks. For Young Readers) Simon & Schuster Bks. For Young Readers.

Samphire, Patrick. Secrets of the Dragon Tomb. Holmes, Jeremy, illus. 2016. (ENG.). 336p. (J). (gr. 5-8). 16.99 *(978-0-8050-9906-5(9),* 9780805099065, Holt, Henry & Co. Bks. For Young Readers) Holt, Henry & Co.

Sanchez, Alex. Bait. 2010. (ENG.). 256p. (YA). (gr. 7). pap. 12.99 *(978-1-4169-3774-6(9),* Simon & Schuster Bks. For Young Readers) Simon & Schuster Bks. For Young Readers.

Sanchez, Jenny Torres. Because of the Sun. 2017. (ENG.). 272p. (YA). (gr. 7). 17.99 *(978-0-399-55145-1(X),* Delacorte Pr.) Random Hse. Children's Bks.

Sanders-Wells, Linda. Maggie's Monkeys. Carter, Abby, illus. 2009. (ENG.). 32p. (J). (gr. -1-2). 16.99 *(978-0-7636-3326-4(7))* Candlewick Pr.

Sandoval, Victor. Roll over, Big Toben. 2003. 128p. (J). pap. 9.95 *(978-1-55885-401-7(0),* Piñata Books) Arte Publico Pr.

Sanroman, Susana. Senora Reganona: A Mexican Bedtime Story. 2004. (SPA., Illus.). (J). (gr. k-3). spiral bd. *(978-0-616-07280-6(5))* Canadian National Institute for the Blind/Institut National Canadien pour les Aveugles.

Santillo, LuAnn. Family Fun, 6 vols. Santillo, LuAnn, ed. 2003. (Half-Pint Kids Readers Ser.). (Illus.). 42p. (J). (gr. -1-1). pap. 6.95 *(978-1-59256-098-1(9))* Half-Pint Kids, Inc.

Sargent-Barker, Erika. Casey Moore, the Littlest Leprechaun, 1 vol. 2010. 16p. pap. 24.95 *(978-1-4489-5419-3(3))* PublishAmerica, Inc.

Sargent, Dave & Sargent, Pat. Amy Armadillo: Mind Your Mama, 15 vols. Huff, Jeane, illus. 2003. (Animal Pride Ser.: 15). 42p. (J). pap. 6.95 *(978-1-56763-788-5(4));* lib. bdg. 20.95 *(978-1-56763-787-8(6))* Ozark Publishing.

—Bandit: I Help Others, 38 vols., Vol. 14. Huff, Jeane, illus. 2nd rev. ed. 2003. (Animal Pride Ser.: No. 14). 42p. (J). pap. 10.95 *(978-1-56763-786-1(8))* Ozark Publishing.

Sargent, Pat L. The Cheetah, 6 vols., Vol. 6. Lenoir, Jane, illus. l.t. ed. 2004. (Barney the Bear Killer Ser.: No. 6). 146p. (YA). pap. 10.95 *(978-1-56763-974-2(7))* Ozark Publishing.

Sartorius, Evohn. Bobbie, His Family & Dog Bingo, 1 vol. 2009. 42p. pap. 24.95 *(978-1-61546-409-8(3))* America Star Bks.

Sauer, Tammi. Your Alien. Fujita, Goro, illus. 2015. (ENG.). 32p. (J). (gr. -1). 14.95 *(978-1-4549-1129-6(8))* Sterling Publishing Co., Inc.

Sawyer, Kim Vogel. Katy's New World, 1 vol. 2010. (Katy Lambright Ser.: No. 1). (ENG.). 208p. (YA). (gr. 8-11). pap. 9.99 *(978-0-310-71924-3(0))* Zondervan.

Sazaklis, John. The Dangers of Dog Walking. Robinson, Lee, illus. 2016. (Billy Burger, Model Citizen Ser.). (ENG.). 96p. (gr. 2-3). lib. bdg. 22.65 *(978-1-4965-2587-1(6))* Stone Arch Bks.

—Jumping for Junk Food. Robinson, Lee, illus. 2016. (Billy Burger, Model Citizen Ser.). (ENG.). 96p. (gr. 2-3). lib. bdg. 22.65 *(978-1-4965-2586-4(8))* Stone Arch Bks.

Scaletta, Kurtis. Mudville. 2010. (ENG.). 272p. (J). (gr. 3-7). 8.99 *(978-0-375-84472-0(4),* Yearling) Random Hse. Children's Bks.

—The Tanglewood Terror. (ENG.). 272p. (J). 2012. (gr. 4-7). 7.99 *(978-0-375-86542-8(X),* Yearling) 2011. (gr. 3-7). 16.99 *(978-0-375-86758-3(9),* Knopf Bks. for Young Readers) Random Hse. Children's Bks.

Scelsa, Kate. Fans of the Impossible Life. 2015. (ENG.). 368p. (YA). (gr. 9). 17.99 *(978-0-06-233175-5(2))* HarperCollins Pubs.

Schaefer, Laura. Littler Women: A Modern Retelling. 2017. (ENG., Illus.). 224p. (J). (gr. 3-7). 16.99 ***(978-1-4814-8761-0(2),*** Simon & Schuster/Paula Wiseman Bks.) Simon & Schuster/Paula Wiseman Bks.

Schaefer, Lola M. Frankie Stein, 0 vols. Atteberry, Kevan, illus. 2009. (ENG.). 34p. (J). (gr. k-3). pap. 6.99 *(978-0-7614-5608-7(2),* 9780761456087, Amazon Children's Publishing) Amazon Publishing.

Schanback, Mindy. Princess from Another Planet. 2005. (ENG.). 254p. (J). (gr. 5-9). 16.95 *(978-0-8234-1847-3(2))* Holiday Hse., Inc.

Schantz, Sarah Elizabeth. Fig. 2016. (ENG.). 352p. (YA). (gr. 9). pap. 10.99 *(978-1-4814-2359-5(2),* McElderry, Margaret K. Bks.) McElderry, Margaret K. Bks.

Schindler, Holly. A Blue So Dark. 2010. (ENG.). 288p. (YA). (gr. 9-18). pap. 11.99 *(978-0-7387-1926-9(9),* Flux) North Star Editions.

Schippers, Mary Kay. A Year on the Family Farm: And the Life Lessons Learned. 2013. 168p. pap. *(978-1-4602-2597-4(X))* FriesenPress.

Schmidt, Gary D. The Wednesday Wars. (ENG.). 272p. (J). (gr. 5-7). 2009. pap. 7.99 *(978-0-547-23760-2(X))* 2007. 16.99 *(978-0-618-72483-3(4))* Houghton Mifflin Harcourt Publishing Co.

—The Wednesday Wars. 2008. *(978-0-545-10562-0(5))* Scholastic, Inc.

—The Wednesday Wars. 2009. lib. bdg. 18.40 *(978-0-606-10573-6(5),* Turtleback) Turtleback Bks.

Schmidt, Tiffany. Break Me Like a Promise: Once upon a Crime Family. 2016. (ENG.). 416p. (YA). 17.99 *(978-0-8027-3783-0(8),* 9780802737830, Bloomsbury USA Childrens) Bloomsbury Publishing USA.

—Hold Me Like a Breath. 2015. (Once upon a Crime Family Ser.: Bk. 1). (ENG.). 400p. (YA). 17.99 *(978-0-8027-3782-3(X),* 9780802737823, Bloomsbury USA Childrens) Bloomsbury Publishing USA.

Schneider, Robyn. The Beginning of Everything. (ENG.). 352p. (YA). (gr. 8). 2014. pap. 9.99 *(978-0-06-221714-1(3),* Tegen, Katherine Bks) 2013. 17.99 *(978-0-06-221713-4(5))* HarperCollins Pubs.

Schoenberg, Jane. Stuey Lewis Against All Odds: Stories from the Third Grade, 1 vol. Evans, Cambria, illus. 2012. (Stuey Lewis Ser.: 2). (ENG.). 144p. (J). (gr. 1-4). 15.99 *(978-0-374-39901-6(8),* 9780374399016, Farrar, Straus & Giroux (BYR)) Farrar, Straus & Giroux.

—Stuey Lewis Against All Odds: Stories from the Third Grade. Evans, Cambria, illus. 2013. (Stuey Lewis Ser.: 2). (ENG.). 160p. (J). (gr. 1-4). pap. 8.99 *(978-1-250-03404-5(3),* 9781250034045) Square Fish.

Scholastic, Inc. Staff & Black, Sonia. Mommy's Bed. Kindert, Jennifer, illus. 2004. (Just for You Ser.). (ENG.). 32p. pap. 3.99 *(978-0-439-56857-9(9),* Teaching Resources) Scholastic, Inc.

Schotter, Roni. When the Wizzy Foot Goes Walking. Wohnoutka, Mike, illus. 2007. (J). *(978-5-525-47791-9(2),* Dutton Juvenile) Penguin Publishing Group.

Schraff, Anne. A Boy Called Twister, 1 vol. unabr. ed. 2010. (Urban Underground Ser.). (ENG.). 180p. (YA). (gr. 9-12). pap. 9.95 *(978-1-61651-002-2(1))* Saddleback Educational Publishing, Inc.

—Dark Secrets, 1 vol. unabr. ed. 2011. (Urban Underground Ser.). (ENG.). 201p. (YA). (gr. 9-12). pap. 9.95 *(978-1-61651-267-5(9))* Saddleback Educational Publishing, Inc.

—Like a Broken Doll, 1 vol. unabr. ed. 2011. (Urban Underground Ser.). (ENG.). 182p. (YA). (gr. 9-12). pap. 9.95 *(978-1-61651-005-3(6))* Saddleback Educational Publishing, Inc.

—Lost & Found. 2007. (Bluford High — Scholastic Ser.: 1). lib. bdg. 16.00 *(978-1-4177-7141-7(0),* Turtleback) Turtleback Bks.

—Memories Are Forever. 2008. (Passages Ser.). 135p. lib. bdg. 13.95 *(978-0-7569-8405-2(X))* Perfection Learning Corp.

—The One for Me, 1 vol. 2013. (Urban Underground Ser.). (ENG.). 199p. (YA). (gr. 9-12). pap. 9.95 *(978-1-62250-042-0(3))* Saddleback Educational Publishing, Inc.

—Second Chances, 1 vol. 2013. (Urban Underground Ser.). (ENG.). 192p. (YA). (gr. 9-12). pap. 9.95 *(978-1-62250-044-4(X))* Saddleback Educational Publishing, Inc.
—A Song to Sing. 2008. (Passages Ser.). 130p. (YA). (gr. 7-9). lib. bdg. 13.95 *(978-0-7569-8384-0(3))* Perfection Learning Corp.
—Sounds of Terror, 1 vol. unabr. ed. 2010. (Q Reads Ser.). (ENG.). 32p. (YA). (gr. 9-12). pap. 6.95 *(978-1-61651-206-4(7))* Saddleback Educational Publishing, Inc.
—Stolen Treasure. 2014. (Red Rhino Ser.). (J). lib. bdg. 18.40 *(978-0-606-36203-0(7))* Turtleback Bks.
—Time of Courage, 1 vol. unabr. ed. 2011. (Urban Underground Ser.). (ENG.). 197p. (YA). (gr. 9-12). pap. 9.95 *(978-1-61651-270-5(9))* Saddleback Educational Publishing, Inc.
—To Catch a Dream, 1 vol. unabr. ed. 2011. (Urban Underground Ser.). (ENG.). 198p. (YA). (gr. 9-12). pap. 9.95 *(978-1-61651-269-9(5))* Saddleback Educational Publishing, Inc.
—Wildflower. 2011. (Urban Underground — Harriet Tubman High School Ser.). (YA). lib. bdg. 20.80 *(978-0-606-14816-0(7),* Turtleback) Turtleback Bks.
Schreiber, Ellen. Royal Blood No. 6. 2009. (Vampire Kisses Ser.: 6). (ENG.). 208p. (YA). (gr. 8-18). 17.99 *(978-0-06-128887-6(X),* Tegen, Katherine Bks) HarperCollins Pubs.
Schröder, Monika. The Dog in the Wood. 2009. (ENG.). 168p. (J). (gr. 5-9). 17.95 *(978-1-59078-701-4(3),* Front Street) Boyds Mills Pr.
Schroeder, Lisa. Caitlin's Lucky Charm. 2014. (Charmed Life Ser.: 1). lib. bdg. 16.00 *(978-0-606-35849-1(8))* Turtleback Bks.
—The Day Before. (ENG.). (YA). (gr. 9). 2012. 336p. pap. 9.99 *(978-1-4424-1744-1(7))* 2011. 320p. 16.99 *(978-1-4424-1743-4(9))* Simon Pulse. (Simon Pulse).
—It's Raining Cupcakes. (ENG., Illus.). 208p. (J). (gr. 3-7). 2011. pap. 6.99 *(978-1-4169-9085-7(2))* 2010. 17.99 *(978-1-4169-9084-0(4))* Simon & Schuster Children's Publishing. (Aladdin).
—My Secret Guide to Paris. 2015. (ENG.). 224p. (J). (gr. 3-7). 16.99 *(978-0-545-70808-1(7),* Scholastic Pr.) Scholastic, Inc.
—Sealed with a Secret. 2016. (ENG.). 224p. (J). (gr. 3-7). 16.99 *(978-0-545-90734-7(9),* Scholastic Pr.) Scholastic, Inc.
Schubert, Leda. Reading to Peanut. Haley, Amanda, illus. 2011. (ENG.). 32p. (J). 16.95 *(978-0-8234-2339-2(5))* Holiday Hse., Inc.
Schulte, Mary. Who Do I Look Like? Roos, Maryn, illus. 2006. (Rookie Reader Skill Set Ser.). (ENG.). 32p. (J). (gr. k-2). pap. 4.95 *(978-0-516-24758-8(1),* Children's Pr.) Scholastic Library Publishing.
Schumacher, Julie. Black Box. 2010. (ENG.). 176p. (YA). (gr. 7-18). pap. 7.99 *(978-0-440-24064-8(6),* Delacorte Bks. for Young Readers) Random Hse. Children's Bks.
Schwartz, Amy. I Can't Wait! Schwartz, Amy, illus. 2015. (ENG., Illus.). 40p. (J). (gr. k-3). 17.99 *(978-1-4424-8231-9(1),* Beach Lane Bks.) Beach Lane Bks.
—Willie & Uncle Bill. 2012. (ENG.). 40p. (J). (gr. -1-3). 16.95 *(978-0-8234-2203-6(8))* Holiday Hse., Inc.
Schwemm, Diane. The Year I Turned Sixteen: Rose, Daisy, Laurel, Lily. 2010. (ENG.). 720p. (YA). (gr. 7). pap. 12.99 *(978-1-4169-8597-6(2),* Simon Pulse) Simon Pulse.
Scieszka, Jon. Spaceheadz. Prigmore, Shane, illus. (Spaceheadz Ser.: 3). (ENG.). (J). (gr. 2-5). 2012. 224p. pap. 7.99 *(978-1-4169-7956-2(5))* 2011. 224p. 15.99 *(978-1-4169-7955-5(7))* 2010. 176p. 14.99 *(978-1-4169-7951-7(4))* Simon & Schuster Bks. For Young Readers. (Simon & Schuster Bks. For Young Readers).
—SPHDZ 4 Life! Prigmore, Shane, illus. 2013. (Spaceheadz Ser.: 4). (ENG.). 192p. (J). (gr. 2-5). pap. 5.99 *(978-1-4169-7958-6(1));*Bk. 4. 16.99 *(978-1-4169-7957-9(3))* Simon & Schuster Bks. For Young Readers. (Simon & Schuster Bks. For Young Readers).
—SPHDZ Book #2! Prigmore, Shane, illus. (Spaceheadz Ser.: 2). (ENG.). (J). (gr. 2-5). 2011. 256p. pap. 7.99 *(978-1-4169-7954-8(9))* 2010. 240p. 14.99 *(978-1-4169-7953-1(0))* Simon & Schuster Bks. For Young Readers. (Simon & Schuster Bks. For Young Readers).
Scillian, Devin. Johnny Kaw: A Tall Tale. Sneed, Brad, illus. 2013. (ENG.). 32p. (J). (gr. 1-4). 15.95 *(978-1-58536-791-7(5),* 202353) Sleeping Bear Pr.
—Pappy's Handkerchief. Ellison, Chris, illus. rev. ed. 2007. (Tales of Young Americans Ser.). (ENG.). 32p. (J). (gr. 3-7). 17.95 *(978-1-58536-316-2(2))* Sleeping Bear Pr.
Scott, Elizabeth. Miracle. (ENG., Illus.). (YA). (gr. 9). 2013. 240p. pap. 9.99 *(978-1-4424-1707-6(2))* 2012. 220p. 16.99 *(978-1-4424-1706-9(4))* Simon Pulse. (Simon Pulse).
Scott, Kate. Spies in Disguise: Boy in Tights. 2016. (ENG., Illus.). 192p. (J). (gr. 1-5). pap. 7.99 *(978-1-63450-689-2(8),* Sky Pony Pr.) Skyhorse Publishing Co., Inc.
Scott, Kieran. He's So Not Worth It. (He's So/She's So Trilogy Ser.). (ENG.). (YA). (gr. 7). 2012. 384p. pap. 9.99 *(978-1-4169-9954-6(X))* 2011. 368p. 17.99 *(978-1-4169-9953-9(1))* Simon & Schuster Bks. For Young Readers. (Simon & Schuster Bks. For Young Readers).
—She's So Dead to Us. (He's So/She's So Trilogy Ser.). (ENG.). (YA). (gr. 7). 2011. 304p. pap. 9.99 *(978-1-4169-9952-2(3))* 2010. 288p. 16.99 *(978-1-4169-9951-5(5))* Simon & Schuster Bks. For Young Readers. (Simon & Schuster Bks. For Young Readers).
—This Is So Not Happening. (He's So/She's So Trilogy Ser.). (ENG., 320p. (YA). (gr. 7). 2013. Illus.). pap. 9.99 *(978-1-4169-9956-0(6))* 2012. 16.99 *(978-1-4169-9955-3(8))* Simon & Schuster Bks. For Young Readers. (Simon & Schuster Bks. For Young Readers).
Scott, Lisa Ann. School of Charm. 2014. (ENG.). 304p. (J). (gr. 3-7). 16.99 *(978-0-06-220758-6(X),* Tegen, Katherine Bks) HarperCollins Pubs.
Scott, Mindi. Live Through This. 2012. (ENG.). 304p. (YA). (gr. 9). 17.99 *(978-1-4424-4059-3(7));* pap. 9.99 *(978-1-4424-4060-9(0))* Simon Pulse. (Simon Pulse).
Seabrooke, Brenda. Cemetery Street. 2008. 144p. (J). (gr. 3-7). 16.95 *(978-0-8234-2115-2(5))* Holiday Hse., Inc.
Self, Jeffery. Drag Teen. 2016. (ENG.). 272p. (YA). (gr. 9). 17.99 *(978-0-545-82993-9(3),* PUSH) Scholastic, Inc.
Sellen, Sandi. The Splendiddly Fazztabulous Grandmas. Maltman Dinwoodie, Heather, illus. 2013. 32p. pap. *(978-1-77069-893-2(0))* Word Alive Pr.
Selznick, Brian. The Marvels. Selznick, Brian, illus. 2015. (ENG., Illus.). 672p. (J). (gr. 5-7). 32.99 *(978-0-545-44868-0(9),* Scholastic Pr.) Scholastic, Inc.
Senzai, N. H. Saving Kabul Corner. 2014. (Kabul Chronicles Ser.). (ENG., Illus.). 288p. (J). (gr. 3-7). 16.99 *(978-1-4424-8494-8(2),* Simon & Schuster/Paula Wiseman Bks.) Simon & Schuster/Paula Wiseman Bks.
Sepahban, Lois. Paper Wishes. 2016. (ENG.). 192p. (J). 16.99 *(978-0-374-30216-0(2),* 9780374302160, Farrar, Straus & Giroux (BYR)) Farrar, Straus & Giroux.
Seredy, Kate. The Chestry Oak. 2015. (Illus.). 253p. (J). pap. 12.95 *(978-1-930900-81-3(3))* Purple Hse. Pr.
Seuling, Barbara. Robert & the Lemming Problem. Brewer, Paul, illus. 2003. (Robert Bks.). (ENG.). 120p. (J). 15.95 *(978-0-8126-2686-5(9))* Cricket Bks.
—Robert Finds a Way. Brewer, Paul, illus. 2005. (Robert Bks.). (ENG.). 150p. (J). 15.95 *(978-0-8126-2734-3(2))* Cricket Bks.
Sévigny, Eric, illus. Caillou: Family Fun Story Box, 4 vols. 2014. (Boxset Ser.). (ENG.). 40p. (J). (gr. -1-k). bds. 12.99 *(978-2-89718-123-9(0))* Caillouet, Gerry.
Shang, Wendy Wan-Long. The Great Wall of Lucy Wu. 2013. (ENG.). 320p. (J). (gr. 3-7). pap. 7.99 *(978-0-545-16216-6(5),* Scholastic Paperbacks) Scholastic, Inc.
—The Way Home Looks Now. 2015. (ENG.). 272p. (J). (gr. 3-7). 16.99 *(978-0-545-60956-2(9),* Scholastic Pr.) Scholastic, Inc.
Sharenow, Robert. The Berlin Boxing Club. (ENG.). (YA). (gr. 8). 2012. 432p. pap. 9.99 *(978-0-06-157970-7(X))* 2011. 416p. 17.99 *(978-0-06-157968-4(8))* HarperCollins Pubs. (HarperTeen).
—The Berlin Boxing Club. 2012. (YA). lib. bdg. 20.85 *(978-0-606-26871-4(5),* Turtleback) Turtleback Bks.
Sharmat, Mitchell. Gregory, the Terrible Eater. Dewey, Ariane & Aruego, Jose, illus. 2009. (ENG.). 32p. (J). (gr. -1-3). pap. 6.99 *(978-0-545-12931-2(1))* Scholastic, Inc.
Shaw, Nancy. Elena's Story. 2012. (Tales of the World Ser.). (ENG., Illus.). 32p. (J). (gr. 1-5). 16.95 *(978-1-58536-528-9(9))* Sleeping Bear Pr.
Shawver, Margaret. What's Wrong with Grandma? A Family's Experience with Alzheimer's. Bagby, Jeffrey K., illus. 2003. (ENG.). 62p. (J). (gr. -1-3). pap. 16.99 *(978-1-59102-174-2(X))* Prometheus Bks., Pubs.
Sheinmel, Courtney. All the Things You Are. (ENG.). 256p. (J). (gr. 4-8). 2012. pap. 6.99 *(978-1-4169-9718-4(0))* 2011. 15.99 *(978-1-4169-9717-7(2))* Simon & Schuster Bks. For Young Readers. (Simon & Schuster Bks. For Young Readers).
—Broken Birthday. Bell, Jennifer A., illus. 2017. (Stella Batts Ser.). (ENG.). 160p. (J). (gr. 2-3). 9.99 *(978-1-58536-921-8(7),* 204228) Sleeping Bear Pr.
—My So-Called Family. 2008. (ENG.). 208p. (J). (gr. 4-7). 15.99 *(978-1-4169-5785-0(5),* Simon & Schuster Bks. For Young Readers) Simon & Schuster Bks. For Young Readers.
—Sincerely: Sincerely, Sophie; Sincerely, Katie. 2010. (ENG.). 400p. (J). (gr. 3-7). 15.99 *(978-1-4169-4010-4(3),* Simon & Schuster Bks. For Young Readers) Simon & Schuster Bks. For Young Readers.
—Stella Batts: None of Your Beeswax. Bell, Jennifer A., illus. 2014. (Stella Batts Ser.). (ENG.). 160p. (J). (gr. 1-3). 9.99 *(978-1-58536-853-2(9),* 203677) Sleeping Bear Pr.
—Stella Batts: Pardon Me. Bell, Jennifer A., illus. 2012. (Stella Batts Ser.: 3). (ENG.). 160p. (J). (gr. 1-3). 9.99 *(978-1-58536-193-9(3),* 202270); pap. 5.99 *(978-1-58536-194-6(1),* 202271) Sleeping Bear Pr.
—Stella Batts Something Blue. Bell, Jennifer A., illus. 2014. (Stella Batts Ser.). (ENG.). 162p. (J). (gr. 1-3). 9.99 *(978-1-58536-851-8(2),* 203016) Sleeping Bear Pr.
—Superstar. Bell, Jennifer A., illus. 2015. (Stella Batts Ser.). (ENG.). 184p. (J). (gr. 1-3). pap. 5.99 *(978-1-58536-856-3(3),* 203956) Sleeping Bear Pr.
Sheinmel, Courtney & Bell, Jennifer A. Stella Batts: Hair Today, Gone Tomorrow. 2012. (Stella Batts Ser.). (ENG., Illus.). (J). (gr. 1-3). 152p. pap. 5.99 *(978-1-58536-191-5(7),* 202269); 160p. lib. bdg. 9.99 *(978-1-58536-189-2(5),* 202268) Sleeping Bear Pr.
—Stella Batts: Needs a New Name. 2012. (Stella Batts Ser.). (ENG., Illus.). 160p. (J). (gr. 1-3). pap. 5.99 *(978-1-58536-183-0(6),* 202266); lib. bdg. 9.99 *(978-1-58536-185-4(2),* 202267) Sleeping Bear Pr.
Sheldon, Dyan. Confessions of a Teenage Drama Queen. movie tie-in ed. 2004. (J). 107.82 *(978-0-7636-2538-2(8))* Candlewick Pr.
Shemin, Craig. Families Are Forever. McCoy, John, illus. 2006. 34p. (J). (gr. -1-2). 16.95 *(978-0-9728666-6-8(3))* As Simple As That Publishing.
—Families Are Forever McCoy, John, illus. l.t. ed. 2003. 34p. 9.95 *(978-0-9728666-0-6(4),* 1) As Simple As That Publishing.
Shepard, Sara. Hide & Seek. 2012. (YA). (Lying Game Ser.: 4). (ENG.). 304p. (gr. 9). 17.99 *(978-0-06-186976-1(7));* (Lying Game Ser.: Bk. 4). 289p. 9.99 *(978-0-06-219369-8(4))* HarperCollins Pubs. (HarperTeen).
Shephard, H. Ferebee. Jonathan & Roscoe. 2011. 24p. pap. 14.39 *(978-1-4634-4881-3(3))* AuthorHouse.
Shepherd, David & Plummer, William K. We Were There at the Driving of the Golden Spike. 2013. (ENG., Illus.). 192p. (J). (gr. 3-8). pap. 6.99 *(978-0-486-49259-9(1))* Dover Pubns., Inc.
Sheppard, Caroline H. Shadow Moves: A Story for Families & Children Experiencing a Difficult or Traumatic Move. Manikoff, John, illus. 2003. (J). pap. 10.00 *(978-1-931310-26-0(2))* National Institute for Trauma & Loss in Children (TLC), The.
Sher, Abby. All the Ways the World Can End. 2017. (ENG.). 320p. (YA). 17.99 *(978-0-374-30425-6(4),* 9780374304256, Farrar, Straus & Giroux (BYR)) Farrar, Straus & Giroux.
Sheth, Kashmira. Koyal Dark, Mango Sweet. (ENG.). 224p. (gr. 7-17). 2006. 15.99 *(978-0-7868-3857-8(4))* 2007. pap. 7.99 *(978-0-7868-3858-5(2))* Hyperion Pr.
—Sona & the Wedding Game, 1 vol. Jaeggi, Yoshiko, illus. 2015. (ENG.). 32p. (J). (gr. 1-3). 16.95 *(978-1-56145-735-9(3))* Peachtree Pubs.
Shields, Gillian. When the World Is Ready for Bed. Currey, Anna, illus. 2010. (ENG.). 26p. (J). (gr. -1 — 1). bds. 7.99 *(978-1-59990-533-4(7),* 9781599905334, Bloomsbury USA Childrens) Bloomsbury Publishing USA.
Shinoda, Anna. Learning Not to Drown. 2014. (ENG., Illus.). 352p. (YA). (gr. 9). 17.99 *(978-1-4169-9393-3(2),* Atheneum Bks. for Young Readers) Simon & Schuster Children's Publishing.
Shipton, Jonathan. Baby Baby Blah Blah Blah! Chessa, Francesca, illus. 2009. (ENG.). 32p. (J). (gr. -1-1). 16.95 *(978-0-8234-2213-5(5))* Holiday Hse., Inc.
Shirvington, Jessica. One Past Midnight. 2014. (ENG.). 352p. (YA). (gr. 9). 17.99 *(978-0-8027-3702-1(1),* 9780802737021, Bloomsbury USA Childrens) Bloomsbury Publishing USA.
Shorrock, Anne. The Secret Adventures of Amelia & Rainbow. 2008. 36p. pap. 15.95 *(978-1-60693-011-3(7),* Eloquent Bks.) Strategic Book Publishing & Rights Agency (SBPRA).
Shoulders, Michael. Goodnight Baby Bear. Weidner, Teri, illus. 2010. (ENG.). 32p. (J). (gr. -1-k). 15.95 *(978-1-58536-471-8(1))* Sleeping Bear Pr.
—Say Daddy! Weidner, Teri, illus. 2013. (ENG.). 26p. (J). (gr. -1-k). 8.99 *(978-1-58536-863-1(6),* 202383) Sleeping Bear Pr.
Shreve, Susan. The Search for Baby Ruby. 2015. 213p. (J). pap. *(978-0-545-41784-6(8))* Scholastic, Inc.
Shum, Benson. Holly's Day at the Pool: A Walt Disney Animation Studios Artist Showcase. Shum, Benson, illus. 2017. (Walt Disney Animation Studios Artist Showcase Ser.). (ENG., Illus.). 40p. (J). (gr. -1-k). 16.99 *(978-1-4847-0938-2(1))* Disney Pr.
Shusterman, Neal. Bruiser. 2010. (ENG.). 336p. (YA). (gr. 9-18). 17.99 *(978-0-06-113408-1(2),* HarperTeen) HarperCollins Pubs.
—Dread Locks. 2006. (Dark Fusion Ser.: 1). (ENG.). 176p. (YA). (gr. 7-18). 7.99 *(978-0-14-240599-4(X),* Speak) Penguin Young Readers Group.
Sidney, Margaret. Five Little Peppers Abroad. 2008. 212p. (gr. 4-7). 26.95 *(978-1-60664-996-1(5));* per. 14.95 *(978-1-60312-546-8(9))* Aegypan.
—Five Little Peppers & How They Grew. 2006. (Dover Children's Classics Ser.). (ENG., Illus.). 224p. (J). (gr. 3-5). per. 6.95 *(978-0-486-45267-8(0))* Dover Pubns., Inc.
—Five Little Peppers & How They Grew. Andreasen, Dan, illus. 2009. (Classic Starts(tm) Ser.). (ENG.). 160p. (J). (gr. 2-4). 6.95 *(978-1-4027-5420-3(5))* Sterling Publishing Co., Inc.
—Five Little Peppers Grown Up. 2008. 196p. (gr. -1-3). 26.95 *(978-1-60664-805-6(5));* pap. 14.95 *(978-1-60664-177-4(8))* Aegypan.
—Five Little Peppers Grown Up. 2007. (ENG.). 236p. pap. 20.99 *(978-1-4264-2517-2(1))* Creative Media Partners, LLC.
—Five Little Peppers Grown up. l.t. ed. 2006. 250p. pap. 22.99 *(978-1-4264-2540-0(6))* Creative Media Partners, LLC.
—Polly Pepper's Book. 2011. 316p. 50.95 *(978-1-258-10539-6(X))* Literary Licensing, LLC.
Siegrist, Bonnie. Little Farm down the Lane -Book IV. 2007. pap. 10.99 *(978-1-60034-912-6(9))* Salem Author Services.
Silberberg, Alan. The Awesome, Almost 100% True Adventures of Matt & Craz. Silberberg, Alan, illus. (ENG., Illus.). 336p. (J). (gr. 4-8). 2014. pap. 7.99 *(978-1-4169-9433-6(5))* 2013. 16.99 *(978-1-4169-9432-9(7))* Simon & Schuster Children's Publishing. (Aladdin).
Silver Dolphin en Español Staff, creator. Mis Figuras Geometricas. 2005. (Mis figuras Geometricas Ser.). (SPA., Illus.). 6p. (J). (gr. -1-k). *(978-970-718-296-7(2),* Silver Dolphin en Español) Advanced Marketing, S. de R. L. de C. V.
Silvey, Craig. Jasper Jones. 2012. 20.00 *(978-1-61383-806-8(9))* Perfection Learning Corp.
—Jasper Jones. 2012. (ENG.). 320p. (YA). (gr. 7). pap. 9.99 *(978-0-375-86627-2(2),* Ember) Random Hse. Children's Bks.
Simmons, H. J. The Little House on the Corner. 2004. 63p. pap. 19.95 *(978-1-4137-2934-4(7))* America Star Bks.
Simmons, Michael. Pool Boy. 2005. 164p. (gr. 7). 17.95 *(978-0-7569-5064-4(3))* Perfection Learning Corp.
—Pool Boy. 2005. (ENG.). 192p. (YA). (gr. 7). reprint ed. pap. 7.99 *(978-0-385-73196-6(5),* Delacorte Bks. for Young Readers) Random Hse. Children's Bks.
Simon, Chaman. Pumpkin Fever. Bryan-Hunt, Jan, illus. 2011. (Rookie Ready to Learn Ser.). 40p. (J). (ENG.). pap. 5.95 *(978-0-531-26803-2(9));* (gr. -1-k). lib. bdg. 23.00 *(978-0-531-25643-5(X))* Scholastic Library Publishing. (Children's Pr.).
—Tressa the Musical Princess. Allen, Joy, illus. 2005. 25p. (J). *(978-1-58987-112-0(X))* Kindermusik International.
Simon, Leslie & Kelley, Trevor. Wish You Were Here: An Essential Guide to Your Favorite Music Scenes - From Punk to Indie & Everything in Between. Dobi, Rob, illus. 2009. (ENG.). 256p. pap. 14.99 *(978-0-06-157371-2(X))* HarperCollins Pubs.
Simon, Norma. All Families Are Special. Flavin, Teresa, illus. 2013. (AV2 Fiction Readalong Ser.: Vol. 59). (ENG.). 32p. (J). (gr. k-3). 34.28 *(978-1-62127-867-2(0),* AV2 by Weigl) Weigl Pubs., Inc.
Simonds, William. Marcus; or, the Boy-Tamer by Walter Aimwell [Pseud.]. 2006. 336p. per. 23.99 *(978-1-4255-3348-9(5))* Michigan Publishing.
Sims, Stacy. Rainbow Butterflies. 2007. 39p. 25.95 *(978-0-615-15922-5(2))* Blue Peach Publishing.
Singleton, Linda Joy. Dead Girl Walking. 2008. (Dead Girl Ser.: 1). (ENG.). 312p. (YA). (gr. 8-18). pap. 9.95 *(978-0-7387-1405-9(4),* Flux) North Star Editions.
Sise, Katie. The Pretty App. 2015. (ENG.). 352p. (YA). (gr. 8). 17.99 *(978-0-06-219529-6(8))* HarperCollins Pubs.
Sitomer, Alan Lawrence. The Secret Story of Sonia Rodriguez. 2010. (ENG.). 320p. (J). (gr. 6-8). pap. 9.99 *(978-1-4231-3027-7(8),* Jump at the Sun) Hyperion Bks. for Children.
Skelton, Matthew. Endymion Spring. 2008. (ENG.). 416p. (YA). (gr. 7). pap. 9.99 *(978-0-385-73456-1(5),* Delacorte Bks. for Young Readers) Random Hse. Children's Bks.
Skolmoski, Stephanie. A Paper Hug. Bennion, Anneliese, illus. 2006. 36p. (J). 6.95 *(978-0-9786425-0-1(3))* DesignAbility.
Skye, obert. Pinocula. Skye, obert, illus. 2013. (Creature from My Closet Ser.: 3). (ENG., Illus.). 256p. (J). (gr. 4-7). 12.99 *(978-0-8050-9689-7(2),* 9780805096897, Holt, Henry & Co. Bks. For Young Readers) Holt, Henry & Co.
—Potterwookiee. Skye, obert, illus. 2012. (Creature from My Closet Ser.: 2). (ENG., Illus.). 256p. (J). (gr. 4-7). 13.99 *(978-0-8050-9451-0(2),* 9780805094510, Holt, Henry & Co. Bks. For Young Readers) Holt, Henry & Co.
—Wonkenstein. Skye, obert, illus. 2011. (Creature from My Closet Ser.: 1). (ENG., Illus.). 240p. (J). (gr. 4-7). 12.99 *(978-0-8050-9268-4(4),* 9780805092684, Holt, Henry & Co. Bks. For Young Readers) Holt, Henry & Co.
—Wonkenstein. Skye, obert, illus. 2015. (Creature from My Closet Ser.: 1). (ENG., Illus.). 256p. (J). (gr. 4-7). pap. 6.99 *(978-1-250-01022-3(5),* 9781250010223) Square Fish.
Slater, David Michael. Westley the Wicked & the Rascally Ring Bear. Brooks, S. G., illus. 2012. 36p. pap. 10.95 *(978-1-61413-028-4(0))* Puddletown Publishing Group, Inc.
Slayton, Fran. When the Whistle Blows. 2010. (ENG.). 176p. (J). (gr. 5-18). 6.99 *(978-0-14-241732-4(7),* Puffin Books) Penguin Young Readers Group.
Sleiman, Dina L. Chivalrous. 2015. (Valiant Hearts Ser.: 2). (ENG.). 368p. (YA). pap. 16.00 *(978-0-7642-1313-7(X))* Bethany Hse. Pubs.
Sliwerski, Jessica Reid. Cancer Hates Kisses. Song, Mika, illus. 2017. (ENG.). 40p. (J). (-k). 17.99 ***(978-0-7352-2781-1(0),*** Dial Bks) Penguin Young Readers Group.
Sloan, Holly Goldberg. I'll Be There. (ENG.). (YA). (gr. 7-17). 2012. 416p. pap. 11.99 *(978-0-316-12276-4(9))* 2011. (Illus.). 400p. 18.00 *(978-0-316-12279-5(3))* Little, Brown Bks. for Young Readers.
Smiley, Jane. Gee Whiz. Clayton, Elaine, illus. 2013. (Horses of Oak Valley Ranch Ser.: Bk. 5). (ENG.). 272p. (J). (gr. 5). 16.99 *(978-0-375-86969-3(7),* Knopf Bks. for Young Readers) Random Hse. Children's Bks.
—The Georges & the Jewels. 2010. (Horses of Oak Valley Ranch Ser.: Bk. 1). (ENG.). 240p. (J). (gr. 5). 6.99 *(978-0-375-86228-1(5),* Yearling) Random Hse. Children's Bks.
—A Good Horse. 2011. (Horses of Oak Valley Ranch Ser.: Bk. 2). (ENG.). 256p. (J). (gr. 5). 6.99 *(978-0-375-86230-4(7),* Yearling) Random Hse. Children's Bks.
—Pie in the Sky. 2013. (Horses of Oak Valley Ranch Ser.). (ENG.). 272p. (J). (gr. 5). 6.99 *(978-0-375-87131-3(4),* Yearling) Random Hse. Children's Bks.
—True Blue. 2012. (Horses of Oak Valley Ranch Ser.: Bk. 3). (ENG.). 304p. (J). (gr. 5). 6.99 *(978-0-375-86232-8(3),* Yearling) Random Hse. Children's Bks.
Smith, Andrew. Grasshopper Jungle. 2015. (ENG.). 416p. (YA). (gr. 9). pap. 10.99 *(978-0-14-242500-8(1),* Speak) Penguin Young Readers Group.
—In the Path of Falling Objects. 2010. (ENG.). 352p. (YA). (gr. 8-12). pap. 12.99 *(978-0-312-65929-5(6),* 9780312659295) Square Fish.
Smith, D. James. The Boys of San Joaquin. 2006. (ENG.). 240p. (J). (gr. 3-7). pap. 11.99 *(978-1-4169-1619-2(9),* Atheneum Bks. for Young Readers) Simon & Schuster Children's Publishing.
—It Was September When We Ran Away the First Time. 2012. (ENG.). 240p. (J). (gr. 3-7). pap. 11.99 *(978-1-4169-3810-1(9),* Atheneum Bks. for Young Readers) Simon & Schuster Children's Publishing.
—Probably the World's Best Story about a Dog & the Girl Who Loved Me. 2011. (ENG.). 256p. (J). pap. 5.99 *(978-1-4169-9652-1(4),* Atheneum Bks. for Young Readers) Simon & Schuster Children's Publishing.
—Probably the World's Best Story about a Dog & The Girl Who Loved Me. 2010. (ENG.). 240p. (J). (gr. 4-7). pap. 11.99 *(978-1-4424-2194-3(0),* Atheneum Bks. for Young Readers) Simon & Schuster Children's Publishing.
Smith, Debra West. Hattie Marshall & the Prowling Panther, 1 vol. 2005. (Hattie Marshall Ser.). (ENG.). 144p. (J). (gr. 4-6). pap. 7.95 *(978-1-56554-940-1(6))* Pelican Publishing Co., Inc.
Smith, Heather. Baygirl, 1 vol. 2013. (ENG.). 288p. (YA). (gr. 8-12). pap. 12.95 *(978-1-4598-0274-2(8))* Orca Bk. Pubs. USA.
Smith, Hope Anita. Keeping the Night Watch. Lewis, E. B., illus. 2014. (ENG.). 80p. (J). (gr. 5-8). pap. 9.99 *(978-0-312-65936-3(9),* 9780312659363) Square Fish.
Smith, Icy. Mystery of the Giant Mask of Sanxingdui. Roski, Gayle Garner, illus. 2015. (J). *(978-0-9913454-8-9(7))* East West Discovery Pr.
Smith, Jennifer E. The Comeback Season. 2008. (ENG.). 256p. (YA). (gr. 8). 15.99 *(978-1-4169-3847-7(8),* Simon & Schuster Bks. For Young Readers) Simon & Schuster Bks. For Young Readers.
—The Storm Makers. Helquist, Brett, illus. 2013. (ENG.). 384p. (J). (gr. 3-7). pap. 8.00 *(978-0-316-17959-1(0))* Little, Brown Bks. for Young Readers.
Smith, Lane. Return to Augie Hobble. 2015. (ENG., Illus.). 288p. (J). (gr. 3-7). 16.99 *(978-1-62672-054-1(1),* 9781626720541) Roaring Brook Pr.
Smith-Mansell, Dana. The Smith Family's New Puppy: Helping Children Cope with a New Family Member. Voerg, Kathy, illus. 2008. (Let's Talk Ser.). (ENG.). 48p. (J). (gr. -1-4). pap. 8.95 *(978-0-88282-327-0(2))* New Horizon Pr. Pubs., Inc.
Smith-Ready, Jeri. This Side of Salvation. 2014. (ENG., Illus.). 384p. (YA). (gr. 9). 17.99 *(978-1-4424-3948-1(3),* Simon Pulse) Simon Pulse.
Smith, Robert F. Bitten: A Romantic Comedy. 2008. (YA). pap. *(978-1-59038-904-1(2))* Deseret Bk. Co.
Smith, Ronald L. Hoodoo. 2015. (ENG.). 224p. (J). (gr. 5-7). 16.99 *(978-0-544-44525-3(2),* Clarion Bks.) Houghton Mifflin Harcourt Trade & Reference Pubs.
—Hoodoo. 2017. (ENG.). (J). (gr. 5-7). lib. bdg. 18.40 ***(978-0-606-39820-6(1))*** Turtleback Bks.
Smith, Yeardley. I, Lorelei. 2009. 352p. (J). (gr. 3-7). lib. bdg. 17.89 *(978-0-06-149345-4(7),* Geringer, Laura Book) HarperCollins Pubs.
Smothers, Ethel Footman. Down in the Piney Woods. 2004. 128p. (J). pap. 7.00 *(978-0-8028-5248-9(3))* Eerdmans, William B. Publishing Co.

E
F
G

Smucker, Barbara. Nubes Negras. (SPA.). (YA). (gr. 5-8). pap. *(978-84-279-3148-0(4),* NG3493) Noguer y Caralt Editores, S. A. ESP. Dist: Lectorum Pubns., Inc.

Snadowsky, Daria. Anatomy of a Boyfriend. 2008. (ENG.). 272p. (YA). (gr. 9). pap. 8.99 *(978-0-440-23944-4(3),* Ember) Random Hse. Children's Bks.

Snedeker, Caroline. Downright Dencey. Barney, Maginel Wright, illus. 2003. (Young Adult Library). 268p. (YA). pap. 12.95 *(978-1-883937-79-9(5))* Bethlehem Bks.

Snelling, Lauraine. What about Cimmaron? 2008. (J). 8.99 *(978-1-59166-872-5(7))* BJU Pr.

Snyder, Laurel. Charlie & Mouse. Hughes, Emily, illus. 2017. (Charlie & Mouse Ser.: 1). (ENG.). 48p. (J). 14.99 *(978-1-4521-3153-5(8))* Chronicle Bks. LLC.

—Penny Dreadful. Halpin, Abigail, illus. 2011. (ENG.). 320p. (J). (gr. 3-7). 8.99 *(978-0-375-86169-7(6),* Yearling) Random Hse. Children's Bks.

Snyder, Zilpha Keatley. The Bronze Pen. 2009. (ENG.). 208p. (J). (gr. 3-7). pap. 5.99 *(978-1-4169-4208-5(4),* Atheneum Bks. for Young Readers) Simon & Schuster Children's Publishing.

—The Headless Cupid. Raible, Alton, illus. 2009. (Stanley Family Ser.). (ENG.). 224p. (J). (gr. 3-7). 16.99 *(978-1-4169-9532-6(3),* Atheneum Bks. for Young Readers) Simon & Schuster Children's Publishing.

—The Treasures of Weatherby. 2008. (ENG.). 240p. (J). (gr. 3-7). pap. 7.99 *(978-1-4169-1399-3(8),* Atheneum Bks. for Young Readers) Simon & Schuster Children's Publishing.

—The Unseen. 2005. 199p. 16.00 *(978-0-7569-5670-7(6))* Perfection Learning Corp.

—William S. & the Great Escape. 2010. (ENG.). 240p. (J). (gr. 3-7). pap. 7.99 *(978-1-4169-6764-4(8),* Atheneum Bks. for Young Readers) Simon & Schuster Children's Publishing.

Soderberg, Erin. The Quirks & the Freaky Field Trip. Jack, Colin, illus. 2015. (Quirks Ser.). (ENG.). 208p. (YA). (gr. 3-6). 13.99 *(978-1-61963-668-2(9),* 9781619636682, Bloomsbury USA Childrens) Bloomsbury Publishing USA.

—The Quirks & the Quirkalicious Birthday. Light, Kelly, illus. 2015. (Quirks Ser.). (ENG.). 208p. (YA). (gr. 3-6). 13.99 *(978-1-61963-370-4(1),* 9781619633704, Bloomsbury USA Childrens) Bloomsbury Publishing USA.

—The Quirks in Circus Quirkus. 2014. (Quirks Ser.). (ENG., Illus.). (YA). (gr. 3-6). 256p. pap. 7.99 *(978-1-61963-663-7(8),* 9781619636637); 240p. 13.99 *(978-1-59990-790-1(9),* 9781599907901) Bloomsbury Publishing USA. (Bloomsbury USA Childrens).

Soderberg, Erin & Munford, Rebecca. Welcome to Normal. 2013. (Quirks Ser.). (ENG., Illus.). 240p. (YA). (gr. 3-6). 13.99 *(978-1-59990-789-5(5),* 9781599907895, Bloomsbury USA Childrens) Bloomsbury Publishing USA.

Solages, Mahalia. What Morning Is This? 2009. 26p. 12.50 *(978-0-557-07760-1(5))* Lulu Pr., Inc.

Solomon, Jef. Right in My Own Neighborhood. 2009. 53p. pap. 15.50 *(978-0-557-05790-0(6))* Lulu Pr., Inc.

Solomon, Martha. Christmas in Da Hood. 2012. 28p. pap. 12.50 *(978-0-9883126-3-0(8))* iScribe Pubns. LLC.

Sommer, Carl. No Longer a Dilly Dally, 1 bk. 2003. (Another Sommer-Time Story Ser.). (Illus.). 48p. (J). 16.95 incl. audio *(978-1-57537-550-2(8))* Advance Publishing, Inc.

—No Longer a Dilly Dally, 11 vols. James, Kennon, illus. 2003. (Another Sommer-Time Story Ser.). (ENG.). 48p. (J). (gr. 1-4). 16.95 incl. audio compact disk *(978-1-57537-501-4(X))* Advance Publishing, Inc.

—The Richest Poor Kid. Martinez, Jorge, illus. 2014. (J). pap. *(978-1-57537-965-4(1))* Advance Publishing, Inc.

—The Richest Poor Kid. Martinez, Jorge, illus. 2007. (Another Sommer-Time Story Ser.). (ENG.). 48p. (J). (gr. -1-3). 16.95 incl. audio compact disk *(978-1-57537-524-3(9));* (gr. -1-3). 9.95 *(978-1-57537-025-5(5));* (gr. k-4). 16.95 *(978-1-57537-074-3(3))* Advance Publishing, Inc.

—Your Job Is Easy. James, Kennon, illus. 2014. (J). pap. *(978-1-57537-973-9(2))* Advance Publishing, Inc.

—Your Job Is Easy(Tu Trabajo Es Facil) James, Kennon, illus. 2009. (Another Sommer-Time Story Bilingual Ser.). (SPA & ENG.). 48p. (J). lib. bdg. 16.95 *(978-1-57537-173-3(1))* Advance Publishing, Inc.

Sommers, Jackie Lea. Truest. 2015. (ENG.). 384p. (YA). (gr. 8). 17.99 *(978-0-06-234825-8(6),* Tegen, Katherine Bks) HarperCollins Pubs.

Sonnenblick, Jordan. After Ever After. (ENG.). 272p. (J). 2014. pap. 9.99 *(978-0-545-72287-2(X))* 2010. (gr. 7-12). 17.99 *(978-0-439-83706-4(5),* Scholastic Pr.) Scholastic, Inc.

—Curveball: The Year I Lost My Grip. 2014. (ENG.). 304p. (J). (gr. 7). pap. 9.99 *(978-0-545-32070-2(4),* Scholastic Paperbacks) Scholastic, Inc.

—Falling over Sideways. (ENG.). 272p. (J). (gr. 7). 2017. pap. 9.99 ***(978-0-545-86325-4(2))*** 2016. 17.99 *(978-0-545-86324-7(4),* Scholastic Pr.) Scholastic, Inc.

Sonnenblick, Jordan. Notes from the Midnight Driver. 2009. 265p. 18.00 *(978-1-60686-516-3(1))* Perfection Learning Corp.

—Notes from the Midnight Driver. 2007. (ENG.). 288p. (J). (gr. 7-12). pap. 9.99 *(978-0-439-75781-2(9),* Scholastic Paperbacks) Scholastic, Inc.

Sorensen, Virginia. Miracles on Maple Hill. Krush, Joe & Krush, Beth, illus. 2003. (ENG.). 256p. (J). (gr. 2-5). pap. 7.99 *(978-0-15-204718-4(2))* Houghton Mifflin Harcourt Publishing Co.

Souliere, Lisa. Guess What? I Have Diabetes. 2008. 36p. pap. 14.95 *(978-1-60693-287-2(X),* Eloquent Bks.) Strategic Book Publishing & Rights Agency (SBPRA).

Soup, Cuthbert. Another Whole Nother Story. Timmins, Jeffrey Stewart, illus. (Whole Nother Story Ser.). (ENG.). (YA). (gr. 3-6). 2012. 320p. pap. 7.99 *(978-1-59990-737-6(2),* 9781599907376) 2010. 304p. 16.99 *(978-1-59990-436-8(5),* 9781599904368) Bloomsbury Publishing USA. (Bloomsbury USA Childrens).

—No Other Story. (Whole Nother Story Ser.). (ENG., Illus.). 256p. (YA). (gr. 3-6). 2013. pap. 7.99 *(978-1-61963-120-5(2),* 9781619631205) 2012. 16.99 *(978-1-59990-824-3(7),* 9781599908243) Bloomsbury Publishing USA. (Bloomsbury USA Childrens).

—A Whole Nother Story. Timmins, Jeffrey Stewart, illus. 2010. (Whole Nother Story Ser.). (ENG.). 288p. (YA). (gr. 3-6). pap. 7.99 *(978-1-59990-518-1(3),* 9781599905181, Bloomsbury USA Childrens) Bloomsbury Publishing USA.

Sovern, Megan Jean. The Meaning of Maggie. 2015. (ENG.). 232p. (J). (gr. 3-7). pap. 6.99 *(978-1-4521-2876-4(6))* Chronicle Bks. LLC.

Spalding, Andrea. Heart of the Hill, 1 vol. 2005. (Summer of Magic Quartet Ser.: 3). (ENG., Illus.). 192p. (J). (gr. 3-7). per. 7.95 *(978-1-55143-486-5(5))* Orca Bk. Pubs. USA.

Spalding, Esta. Knock about with the Fitzgerald-Trouts. Smith, Sydney, illus. 2017. (ENG.). 320p. (J). (gr. 3-7). 16.99 *(978-0-316-29860-5(3))* Little, Brown Bks. for Young Readers.

Sparkes, Ali. Anaconda Adventure. Collins, Ross, illus. 2014. (S. W. I. T. C. H. Ser.: 13). (ENG.). 104p. (J). (gr. 2-5). lib. bdg. 27.93 *(978-1-4677-2116-5(6),* Darby Creek) Lerner Publishing Group.

—Ant Attack. Collins, Ross, illus. 2013. (S. W. I. T. C. H. Ser.: 4). (ENG.). 104p. (J). (gr. 2-5). pap. 7.95 *(978-1-4677-0713-8(9),* Darby Creek) Lerner Publishing Group.

—Beetle Blast. Collins, Ross, illus. 2013. (S. W. I. T. C. H. Ser.: 6). (ENG.). 104p. (J). (gr. 2-5). pap. 7.95 *(978-1-4677-0715-2(5),* Darby Creek) Lerner Publishing Group.

—Frog Freakout. Collins, Ross, illus. 2014. (S. W. I. T. C. H. Ser.: 7). (ENG.). 88p. (J). (gr. 2-5). lib. bdg. 27.93 *(978-1-4677-2111-0(5),* Darby Creek) Lerner Publishing Group.

—Gecko Gladiator. Collins, Ross, illus. 2014. (S. W. I. T. C. H. Ser.: 12). (ENG.). 104p. (J). (gr. 2-5). lib. bdg. 27.93 *(978-1-4677-2115-8(8),* Darby Creek) Lerner Publishing Group.

—Lizard Loopy. Collins, Ross, illus. 2014. (S. W. I. T. C. H. Ser.: 9). (ENG.). 104p. (J). (gr. 2-5). lib. bdg. 27.93 *(978-1-4677-2112-7(3),* Darby Creek) Lerner Publishing Group.

—Newt Nemesis. Collins, Ross, illus. 2014. (S. W. I. T. C. H. Ser.: 8). (ENG.). 88p. (J). (gr. 2-5). lib. bdg. 27.93 *(978-1-4677-3233-8(8),* Darby Creek) Lerner Publishing Group.

Spinelli, Eileen. Another Day As Emily. Lew-Vriethoff, Joanne, illus. 2015. (ENG.). 240p. (J). (gr. 3-7). 6.99 *(978-0-449-80989-1(7),* Yearling) Random Hse. Children's Bks.

—The Dancing Pancake. Lew-Vriethoff, Joanne, illus. 2011. (ENG.). 256p. (J). (gr. 3-7). 6.99 *(978-0-375-85348-7(0),* Yearling) Random Hse. Children's Bks.

—God's Amazing World! Florian, Mlanie, illus. 2014. 32p. (J). 15.99 *(978-0-8249-5661-5(3),* Ideal Pubns.) Worthy Publishing.

—The Perfect Thanksgiving. Adinolfi, JoAnn, illus. 2007. (ENG.). 32p. (J). (gr. -1-2). 7.99 *(978-0-312-37505-8(0),* 9780312375058) Square Fish.

—Someday. Winstead, Rosie, illus. 2007. (ENG.). 32p. (J). (gr. -1-3). 17.99 *(978-0-8037-2941-4(3),* Dial Bks) Penguin Young Readers Group.

—Summerhouse Time. Lew-Vriethoff, Joanne, illus. 2009. (ENG.). 224p. (J). (gr. 3-7). 6.99 *(978-0-440-42224-2(8),* Yearling) Random Hse. Children's Bks.

—Thanksgiving at the Tappletons' Lloyd, Megan, illus. 2005. (gr. -1-3). 17.00 *(978-0-7569-5762-9(1))* Perfection Learning Corp.

—When You Are Happy. Valério, Geraldo, illus. 2006. (ENG.). 40p. (J). (gr. -1-3). 19.99 *(978-0-689-86251-9(2),* Simon & Schuster Bks. For Young Readers) Simon & Schuster Bks. For Young Readers.

Spinelli, Jerry. Loser. 2003. (ENG.). 224p. (J). (gr. 3-7). pap. 6.99 *(978-0-06-054074-6(5))* HarperCollins Pubs.

—Loser. 2003. (J). (gr. 3-6). lib. bdg. 17.20 *(978-0-613-66899-6(5),* Turtleback) Turtleback Bks.

—Mama Seeton's Whistle. 2015. (ENG., Illus.). 40p. (J). (gr. -1-3). 17.00 *(978-0-316-12217-7(3))* Little, Brown Bks. for Young Readers.

—Smiles to Go. 2009. (ENG.). 272p. (J). (gr. 5). pap. 6.99 *(978-0-06-447197-8(7))* HarperCollins Pubs.

Spizman, Robyn Freedman & Johnston, Mark. Secret Agent. 2006. (ENG.). 240p. (J). (gr. 4-7). pap. 11.99 *(978-1-4169-1862-2(0),* Atheneum Bks. for Young Readers) Simon & Schuster Children's Publishing.

Spotswood, Jessica. Born Wicked. 2013. (Cahill Witch Chronicles Ser.: 1). (ENG.). 352p. (YA). (gr. 7). pap. 10.99 *(978-0-14-242187-1(1),* Speak) Penguin Young Readers Group.

—Born Wicked. 2013. lib. bdg. 22.10 *(978-0-606-26729-8(8),* Turtleback) Turtleback Bks.

Springstubb, Tricia. Mo Wren, Lost & Found. Ross, Heather, illus. 2011. (Fox Street Ser.: 2). (ENG.). 256p. (J). (gr. 3-7). 15.99 *(978-0-06-199039-7(6))* HarperCollins Pubs.

—What Happened on Fox Street. Ross, Heather, illus. 2011. (Fox Street Ser.: 1). (ENG.). 240p. (J). (gr. 3-7). pap. 6.99 *(978-0-06-198636-9(4))* HarperCollins Pubs.

Sproul, R. C. The Barber Who Wanted to Pray. Fluharty, T. Lively, illus. 2011. 40p. (J). 17.99 *(978-1-4335-2703-6(0))* Crossway.

Spykman, E. C. Terrible, Horrible Edie. 2010. (ENG.). 232p. (J). (gr. 4-7). 16.95 *(978-1-59017-353-4(8),* NYR Children's Collection) New York Review of Bks., Inc., The.

Spyri, Johanna. Gritli's Children. 2006. 144p. (gr. 4-7). per. 11.95 *(978-1-59818-921-6(2));* 24.95 *(978-1-59818-413-6(X))* Aegypan.

—Gritli's Children. 2006. pap. *(978-1-4068-0693-9(5))* Echo Library.

—Heidi. 2013. 425p. reprint ed. lthr. 69.00 *(978-0-7426-1047-7(0))* Classic Bks.

—Heidi. l.t. ed. 2004. (Large Print Ser.). 433p. 26.00 *(978-1-58287-666-5(5))* North Bks.

—Heidi. 2013. (ENG., Illus.). 336p. (J). (gr. 2-7). 14.95 *(978-1-62087-686-2(8),* 620686, Sky Pony Pr.) Skyhorse Publishing Co., Inc.

St. Anthony, Jane. Grace above All. 2015. (Fesler-Lampert Minnesota Heritage Ser.). (ENG.). 176p. pap. 9.95 *(978-0-8166-9814-1(7))* Univ. of Minnesota Pr.

—The Summer Sherman Loved Me. 2015. (Fesler-Lampert Minnesota Heritage Ser.). (ENG.). 144p. pap. 9.95 *(978-0-8166-9815-8(5))* Univ. of Minnesota Pr.

St. George, Judith. The Ghost, the White House & Me. 2007. (ENG.). 128p. (J). (gr. 4-7). 16.95 *(978-0-8234-2045-2(0))* Holiday Hse., Inc.

St. John, Patricia. I Needed a Neighbour. 2003. 128p. 6.49 *(978-0-86201-454-4(9))* Scripture Union GBR. Dist: Gabriel Resources.

Stahler, David, Jr. Doppelganger. 2006. (Illus.). (YA). (gr. 7-12). 272p. 16.99 *(978-0-06-087232-8(2));* 258p. lib. bdg. 17.89 *(978-0-06-087233-5(0))* HarperCollins Pubs.

Stamper, Judith Bauer. The Quinceañera. Varma, Ishan, illus. 2010. (J). *(978-1-60617-121-9(6))* Teaching Strategies, LLC.

Standiford, Natalie. Confessions of the Sullivan Sisters. (ENG.). 320p. (J). 2012. (gr. 9). pap. 9.99 *(978-0-545-10711-2(3),* Scholastic Paperbacks) 2010. (gr. 8-18). 17.99 *(978-0-545-10710-5(5),* Scholastic Pr.) Scholastic, Inc.

—How to Say Goodbye in Robot. 2009. (ENG.). 288p. (J). (gr. 7-18). 17.99 *(978-0-545-10708-2(3),* Scholastic Pr.) Scholastic, Inc.

Stanley, Diane. Saving Sky. (ENG.). 208p. (J). (gr. 3-7). 2012. pap. 6.99 *(978-0-06-123907-6(0))* 2010. 15.99 *(978-0-06-123905-2(4))* HarperCollins Pubs.

Staples, Suzanne Fisher. The House of Djinn. 2012. (ENG.). 222p. (YA). (gr. 7). pap. 8.99 *(978-0-307-97642-0(4),* Ember) Random Hse. Children's Bks.

Starcher, Michele. The Ornery Angel. 2005. 68p. per. 13.95 *(978-1-59858-039-6(6))* Dog Ear Publishing, LLC.

Starmer, Aaron. The Storyteller. 2016. (Riverman Trilogy Ser.: 3). (ENG.). 336p. (J). 16.99 *(978-0-374-36313-0(7),* 9780374363130, Farrar, Straus & Giroux (BYR)) Farrar, Straus & Giroux.

Stauffacher, Sue. Animal Rescue Team: Gator on the Loose! Lamont, Priscilla, illus. 2011. (Animal Rescue Team Ser.). (ENG.). 160p. (J). (gr. 3-7). 5.99 *(978-0-375-85131-5(3),* Yearling) Random Hse. Children's Bks.

—Animal Rescue Team: Hide & Seek. Lamont, Priscilla, illus. 2011. (Animal Rescue Team Ser.). (ENG.). 160p. (J). (gr. 3-7). 5.99 *(978-0-375-85133-9(X),* Yearling) Random Hse. Children's Bks.

—Animal Rescue Team: Special Delivery! Lamont, Priscilla, illus. 2011. (Animal Rescue Team Ser.). (ENG.). 176p. (J). (gr. 3-7). 6.99 *(978-0-375-85132-2(1),* Yearling) Random Hse. Children's Bks.

—Show Time. Lamont, Priscilla, illus. 2011. (Animal Rescue Team Ser.). (ENG.). 160p. (J). (gr. 3-7). 5.99 *(978-0-375-85134-6(8),* Yearling) Random Hse. Children's Bks.

—Special Delivery! Lamont, Priscilla, illus. 2010. (Animal Rescue Team Ser.: No. 2). (ENG.). 176p. (J). (gr. 3-7). 12.99 *(978-0-375-85848-2(2),* Knopf Bks. for Young Readers) Random Hse. Children's Bks.

St.Clair, Jennifer. A Beth-Hill Novel: Full Moon. Cummins, Sandy, ed. 2004. (ENG.). pap. *(978-1-920741-10-5(0))* Writers Exchange E-Publishing.

Stead, Rebecca. Goodbye Stranger. (ENG.). (J). (gr. 5). 2017. 320p. 7.99 *(978-0-307-98086-1(3),* Yearling) 2015. 304p. 16.99 *(978-0-385-74317-4(3),* Lamb, Wendy Bks.) 2015. 304p. lib. bdg. 19.99 *(978-0-375-99098-4(4),* Lamb, Wendy Bks.) Random Hse. Children's Bks.

—Liar & Spy. (ENG.). (J). (gr. 3-7). 2013. 208p. 7.99 *(978-0-375-85087-5(2),* Yearling) 2012. 192p. 15.99 *(978-0-385-73743-2(2),* Lamb, Wendy Bks.) Random Hse. Children's Bks.

Steig, William. Spinky Sulks. Steig, William, illus. 2011. (ENG., Illus.). 32p. (J). (gr. -1-3). pap. 7.99 *(978-0-312-67246-1(2),* 9780312672461) Square Fish.

Steinkellner, Elisabeth. My New Granny. Roher, Michael, illus. 2012. (ENG.). 32p. (J). (gr. -1-3). 16.95 *(978-1-62087-223-9(4),* 620223, Sky Pony Pr.) Skyhorse Publishing Co., Inc.

Steinkellner, Teddy. Trash Can Days: A Middle School Saga. 2013. (Trash Can Days Ser.). (ENG.). 352p. (J). (gr. 5-9). 16.99 *(978-1-4231-6632-0(9))* Disney Pr.

Stern, A. J. Doggy Day Care, 2 vols. Marts, Doreen Mulryan, illus. 2010. (Frankly, Frannie Ser.: 2). (ENG.). 128p. (J). (gr. 1-3). pap. 4.99 *(978-0-448-45350-7(9),* Grosset & Dunlap) Penguin Young Readers Group.

Stevens, Eric. Finn Reeder, Flu Fighter: How I Survived a Worldwide Pandemic, the School Bully, & the Craziest Game of Dodge Ball Ever. Fraser, Kay, illus. 2009. (Finn Reeder Ser.). (ENG.). 80p. (gr. 2-3). lib. bdg. 26.65 *(978-1-4342-2450-7(3))* Capstone Digital.

—Flu Fighter: How I Survived a Worldwide Pandemic, the School Bully, & the Craziest Game of Dodge Ball Ever. Fraser, Kay, illus. 2010. (Finn Reeder Ser.). (ENG.). 80p. (gr. 3-4). 9.99 *(978-1-4342-2562-7(3))* Capstone Digital.

Stevenson, Robin. Impossible Things, 1 vol. 2008. (ENG.). 192p. (J). (gr. 4-8). pap. 8.95 *(978-1-55143-736-1(8))* Orca Bk. Pubs. USA.

Stevenson, Sarah Jamila. The Latte Rebellion. 2011. (ENG., Illus.). 336p. (YA). (gr. 9-18). pap. 9.95 *(978-0-7387-2278-8(2),* Flux) North Star Editions.

Stewart, Justus. Kyle Oaks: A Traitor on Nighta. 2007. 144p. per. 11.95 *(978-0-595-47708-1(9))* iUniverse, Inc.

Stewart, Kiera. The Summer of Bad Ideas. 2017. 304p. (J). (gr. 3-7). 16.99 *(978-0-06-236021-2(3))* HarperCollins Pubs.

Stewart, Sarah. The Gardener. Small, David, illus. 2007. (ENG.). 40p. (J). (gr. -1-2). per. 8.99 *(978-0-312-36749-7(X),* 9780312367497) Square Fish.

Stiefvater, Maggie. The Dream Thieves. (Raven Cycle Ser.: 2). (ENG.). 448p. (J). (gr. 9). 2014. pap. 9.99 *(978-0-545-42495-0(X),* Scholastic Paperbacks) 2013. 18.99 *(978-0-545-42494-3(1),* Scholastic Pr.) Scholastic, Inc.

—The Dream Thieves. 2014. (Raven Cycle Ser.: 2). lib. bdg. 20.85 *(978-0-606-36029-6(8))* Turtleback Bks.

Still, Teresa B. Tessa Has Two Homes. 2009. 28p. pap. 14.99 *(978-1-4389-8202-1(X))* AuthorHouse.

Stille, Ljuba & Mundt, Anja. Mia's Thumb. Stille, Ljuba, illus. 2014. (ENG., Illus.). 32p. (J). (gr. -1-k). 16.95 *(978-0-8234-3067-3(7))* Holiday Hse., Inc.

Stites, Clara. Rosalba of Santa Juanita: A California Story. 2015. (ENG., Illus.). 100p. (J). pap. 8.95 *(978-1-56474-394-7(2),* Fithian Pr) Daniel & Daniel, Pubs., Inc.

Stone, Phoebe. Deep down Popular. 2010. (ENG.). 288p. (J). (gr. 4-7). 6.99 *(978-0-439-80244-4(X),* Levine, Arthur A. Bks.) Scholastic, Inc.

Stone, Tamara Ireland. Time after Time. 2014. (ENG.). 368p. (YA). (gr. 7-12). pap. 9.99 *(978-1-4231-5981-0(0))* Hyperion Bks. for Children.

Stout, Shawn K. Fiona Finkelstein, Big-Time Ballerina!! Martini, Angela, illus. 2010. (ENG.). 192p. (J). pap. 4.99 *(978-1-4169-7109-2(2),* Simon & Schuster/Paula Wiseman Bks.) Simon & Schuster/Paula Wiseman Bks.

—Miss Matched. Martini, Angela, illus. 2013. (Not-So-Ordinary Girl Ser.: 2). (ENG.). 176p. (J). (gr. 1-5). pap. 5.99 *(978-1-4424-7404-8(1),* Aladdin) Simon & Schuster Children's Publishing.

—Miss Matched. Martini, Angela, illus. 2013. (Not-So-Ordinary Girl Ser.: 2). (ENG.). 160p. (J). (gr. 1-5). 15.99 *(978-1-4424-7405-5(X),* Simon & Schuster/Paula Wiseman Bks.) Simon & Schuster/Paula Wiseman Bks.

—Penelope Crumb Never Forgets. Docampo, Valeria, illus. 2013. (Penelope Crumb Ser.: 2). (ENG.). 208p. (J). (gr. 2-5). pap. 5.99 *(978-0-14-751009-9(0),* Puffin Books) Penguin Young Readers Group.

Strasnick, Lauren. Her & Me & You. 2011. (ENG.). 208p. (YA). (gr. 9). pap. 9.99 *(978-1-4169-8267-8(1),* Simon Pulse) Simon Pulse.

—Then You Were Gone. (ENG., 272p. (YA). (gr. 9). 2014. Illus.). pap. 9.99 *(978-1-4424-2716-7(7))* 2013. 16.99 *(978-1-4424-2715-0(9))* Simon Pulse. (Simon Pulse).

Strasser, Todd. Boot Camp. 2012. (ENG.). 272p. (YA). (gr. 7). pap. 11.99 *(978-1-4424-3358-8(2),* Simon & Schuster Bks. For Young Readers) Simon & Schuster Bks. For Young Readers.

—Boot Camp. 2007. (ENG.). 256p. (YA). (gr. 7-12). 16.99 *(978-1-4169-0848-7(X))* Simon & Schuster Children's Publishing.

—Boot Camp. 2008. (ENG., Illus.). 256p. (YA). (gr. 7). mass mkt. 7.99 *(978-1-4169-5942-7(4),* Simon Pulse) Simon Pulse.

—Count Your Blessings. 2007. (Mob Princess Ser.: 3). (ENG.). 240p. (YA). (gr. 9-12). pap. 11.99 *(978-1-4169-3542-1(8),* Simon Pulse) Simon Pulse.

Stringham, Jean. Balance. 2011. 208p. (J). pap. 14.99 *(978-1-59955-518-8(2),* Bonneville Bks.) Cedar Fort, Inc./CFI Distribution.

Stromberg, Ronica. A Shadow in the Dark. 2009. (J). pap. *(978-0-88092-751-2(8));* lib. bdg. *(978-0-88092-750-5(X))* Royal Fireworks Publishing Co.

Stuart, Pamela Haught. Just like my Papa. 2008. 40p. per. 16.99 *(978-1-4343-5369-6(9))* AuthorHouse.

Stuchner, Joan Betty. A Time to Be Brave. Nugent, Cynthia, illus. 2014. (Stepping Stone Book(TM) Ser.). (ENG.). 112p. (J). (gr. 2-5). 4.99 *(978-0-385-39205-1(2),* Random Hse. Bks. for Young Readers) Random Hse. Children's Bks.

Stuve-Bodeen, Stephanie. La Escuela de Elizabeti. Sarfatti, Esther, tr. from ENG. Hale, Christy, illus. 2007. (SPA.). 32p. (J). (gr. -1-2). pap. 9.95 *(978-1-60060-235-1(5))* Lee & Low Bks., Inc.

Sugiura, Misa. It's Not Like It's a Secret. 2017. 400p. (YA). (gr. 8). 17.99 *(978-0-06-247341-7(7),* HarperTeen) HarperCollins Pubs.

Sullivan, Jacqueline Levering. Annie's War. 2007. (Illus.). 183p. (J). (gr. 3-7). 15.00 *(978-0-8028-5325-7(0),* Eerdmans Bks For Young Readers) Eerdmans, William B. Publishing Co.

Sullivan, Kevin & Morgan, Elizabeth. Anne's New Home. 2010. (Anne of Green Gables Picture Bks.). (ENG.). 32p. (J). (gr. k-2). pap. 4.95 *(978-0-9736803-7-9(7))* Davenport Pr. CAN. Dist: Independent Pubs. Group.

Sullivan, Laura L. Love by the Morning Star. 2014. (ENG.). 320p. (YA). (gr. 7-12). 17.99 *(978-0-547-68951-7(9),* HMH Books For Young Readers) Houghton Mifflin Harcourt Publishing Co.

Sullivan, Therese M. & Bitner, Pamela. A Gift from Valentine. 2007. 24p. (J). per. 12.95 *(978-1-58939-981-5(1))* Virtualbookworm.com Publishing, Inc.

Summers, Courtney. This Is Not a Test. 2012. (ENG.). 336p. (YA). (gr. 8). pap. 10.99 *(978-0-312-65674-4(2),* 9780312656744, St. Martin's Griffin) St. Martin's Pr.

Sumner Johnson, Janet. The Last Great Adventure of the PB & J Society. 2016. (Middle-Grade Novels Ser.). (ENG.). 256p. (gr. 4-7). lib. bdg. 26.65 *(978-1-4965-2695-3(3))* Stone Arch Bks.

Surprise Cake: Individual Title Six-Packs. (Literatura 2000 Ser.). (gr. k-1). 28.00 *(978-0-7635-0065-8(8))* Rigby Education.

Surviving the Applewhites. (J). tchr. ed. *(978-0-06-058369-9(X))* HarperCollins Pubs.

Sutton, Kelsey. The Lonely Ones. 2016. (ENG.). 240p. (J). (gr. 5). 16.99 *(978-0-399-17289-2(0),* Philomel Bks.) Penguin Young Readers Group.

—Some Quiet Place. 2013. (ENG.). 336p. (YA). pap. 9.99 *(978-0-7387-3643-3(0),* Flux) North Star Editions.

Swaby, Barbara. When Will Daddy Be Home? 2012. 32p. pap. 19.99 *(978-1-4772-6439-3(6))* AuthorHouse.

Swank, Denise Grover. One Paris Summer, 1 vol. 2016. (ENG.). 352p. (YA). pap. 14.99 *(978-0-310-75516-6(6))* Blink.

Sweeney, Linda Booth. When the Wind Blows. Christy, Jana, illus. 2015. (ENG.). 32p. (J). (gr. -1-k). 16.99 *(978-0-399-16015-8(9),* G.P. Putnam's Sons Books for Young Readers) Penguin Young Readers Group.

Swerling, Lisa & Lazar, Ralph. We Without You. 2013. (ENG., Illus.). 96p. 9.95 *(978-1-4521-2232-8(6))* Chronicle Bks. LLC.

Swinger-Elibogen, Sue. Campfire Kids, 1 vol. 2010. 54p. pap. 16.95 *(978-1-4489-5493-3(2))* America Star Bks.

Tabby, Abigail. The KnitWits Make a Move! Wildish, Lee, illus. Frost, Michael, photos by. 2013. (ENG.). 32p. (J). (gr. -1-1). 14.99 *(978-1-4424-5342-5(7),* Little Simon) Little Simon.

Tafuri, Nancy. Mama's Little Bears. 2004. (J). bds. 7.99 *(978-0-439-57357-3(2))* Scholastic, Inc.

Tagged. 2015. (ENG.). 288p. (YA). (gr. 7). lib. bdg. 16.95 *(978-1-58089-583-5(2))* Charlesbridge Publishing, Inc.

Tait, Chris & Wyss, Johann David. The Swiss Family Robinson. Akib, Jamel, illus. 2007. 151p. (J). *(978-1-4287-4213-0(1))* Sterling Publishing Co., Inc.

Tak, Bibi Dumon. Mikis & the Donkey. Hopman, Philip, illus. 2014. (ENG.). 89p. (J). 13.00 *(978-0-8028-5430-8(3),* Eerdmans Bks For Young Readers) Eerdmans, William B. Publishing Co.

Takabayashi, Mari. I Live in Brooklyn. 2004. (ENG., Illus.). 32p. (J). (gr. -1-3). tchr. ed. 17.99 *(978-0-618-30899-6(7))* Houghton Mifflin Harcourt Publishing Co.

Talley, Rebecca Cornish. Heaven Scent. 2008. 229p. (gr. 8-12). pap. 15.99 *(978-1-59955-100-5(4))* Cedar Fort, Inc./CFI Distribution.

Tamaki, Mariko. Saving Montgomery Sole. 2016. (ENG.). 240p. (YA). 17.99 *(978-1-62672-271-2(4),* 9781626722712) Roaring Brook Pr.

—Saving Montgomery Sole. 2017. (ENG.). 240p. (YA). pap. 9.99 *(978-1-250-10440-3(8),* 9781250104403) Square Fish.

Tamanini, Kara T. I Promised Not to Tell. 2009. 44p. pap. 18.50 *(978-1-60860-470-8(5),* Eloquent Bks.) Strategic Book Publishing & Rights Agency (SBPRA).

Tan, Susan. Cilla Lee-Jenkins: Future Author Extraordinaire. Wulfekotte, Dana, illus. 2017. (Cilla Lee-Jenkins Ser.). (ENG.). 256p. (J). 16.99 *(978-1-62672-551-5(9),* 9781626725515) Roaring Brook Pr.

Tashjian, Janet. For What It's Worth. 2012. (ENG.). 288p. (YA). (gr. 7-12). 16.99 *(978-0-8050-9365-0(6),* 9780805093650, Holt, Henry & Co. Bks. For Young Readers) Holt, Henry & Co.

—My Life As a Book. Tashjian, Jake, illus. 2010. (My Life Ser.: 1). (ENG.). 224p. (J). (gr. 4-7). 17.99 *(978-0-8050-8903-5(9),* 9780805089035, Holt, Henry & Co. Bks. For Young Readers) Holt, Henry & Co.

—My Life As a Book. Tashjian, Jake, illus. 2011. (My Life Ser.: 1). (ENG.). 240p. (J). (gr. 4-7). pap. 7.99 *(978-0-312-67289-8(6),* 9780312672898) Square Fish.

—My Life As a Gamer. Tashjian, Jake, illus. 2015. (My Life Ser.: 5). (ENG.). 272p. (J). (gr. 4-7). 13.99 *(978-0-8050-9851-8(8),* 9780805098518, Holt, Henry & Co. Bks. For Young Readers) Holt, Henry & Co.

—My Life As a Joke. Tashjian, Jake, illus. 2014. (My Life Ser.: 4). (ENG.). 272p. (J). (gr. 4-7). 13.99 *(978-0-8050-9850-1(X),* 9780805098501, Holt, Henry & Co. Bks. For Young Readers) Holt, Henry & Co.

—My Life as a Stuntboy. Tashjian, Jake, illus. 2011. (My Life Ser.: 2). (ENG.). 272p. (J). (gr. 4-7). 15.99 *(978-0-8050-8904-2(7),* 9780805089042, Holt, Henry & Co. Bks. For Young Readers) Holt, Henry & Co.

—My Life as a Stuntboy. Tashjian, Jake, illus. 2015. (My Life Ser.: 2). (ENG.). 288p. (J). (gr. 4-7). pap. 7.99 *(978-1-250-01038-4(1),* 9781250010384) Square Fish.

Tayleur, Karen. Famous (Scholastic) The Awesome Life of David Mortimore Baxter. Garvey, Brann, illus. 2009. (David Mortimore Baxter Ser.). 88p. pap. 0.80 *(978-1-4342-2503-0(8),* David Mortimore Baxter) Stone Arch Bks.

Taylor, Billy. Thieving Weasels. 2016. (ENG.). 256p. (YA). (gr. 7). 17.99 *(978-0-525-42924-1(7),* Dial Bks) Penguin Young Readers Group.

Taylor, Cora. Champlain & Cartier, 1 vol. 2004. (Ghost Voyages Ser.: No. 4). (ENG., Illus.). 128p. (J). (gr. 3-6). pap. 7.95 *(978-1-55050-374-6(X))* Coteau Bks. CAN. Dist: Orca Bk. Pubs. USA.

Taylor, Kim. Cissy Funk. Date not set. 224p. (YA). (gr. 5-18). mass mkt. 4.99 *(978-0-06-440880-6(9))* HarperCollins Pubs.

Taylor, Sydney. Ella of All-Of-a-Kind Family. 2014. (ENG.). 200p. (J). (gr. 3-8). pap. 12.95 *(978-1-939601-26-1(6))* Ig Publishing, Inc.

Taylor, Theodore. The Maldonado Miracle. 2003. (ENG.). 176p. (J). (gr. 2-5). pap. 6.95 *(978-0-15-205036-8(1))* Houghton Mifflin Harcourt Publishing Co.

A Teeny Tiny Taste: Individual Title Six-Packs. (gr. -1-2). 27.00 *(978-0-7635-9478-7(4))* Rigby Education.

Telgemeier, Raina. Ghosts. Telgemeier, Raina, illus. 2016. (ENG., Illus.). 256p. (J). (gr. 3-7). 24.99 *(978-0-545-54061-2(5),* Graphix) Scholastic, Inc.

Ten Turtles on Tuesday: A Story for Children about Obsessive-Compulsive Disorder. 2014. (Illus.). 80p. (J). *(978-1-4338-1643-7(1),* Magination Pr.) American Psychological Assn.

Tenney, Richard L. Conflict & Calling. 2012. 184p. *(978-1-77097-461-6(X));* pap. *(978-1-77097-462-3(8))* FriesenPress.

Terzis, Kara. Frayed. 2016. (ENG.). 304p. (YA). (gr. 8-12). pap. 10.99 *(978-1-4926-3173-6(6),* 9781492631736) Sourcebooks, Inc.

Tetzlaff, Wendy Jo. A Girl Named Frannie. 2008. 28p. pap. 24.95 *(978-1-60703-055-3(1))* America Star Bks.

Tharp, Tim. The Spectacular Now. (ENG.). 304p. (YA). (gr. 9). 2010. pap. 8.99 *(978-0-375-86502-2(0),* Knopf Bks. for Young Readers) 2013. pap. 9.99 *(978-0-385-75430-9(2),* Ember) Random Hse. Children's Bks.

Thermes, Jennifer. Sam Bennett's New Shoes. 2006. (Illus.). (J). 15.95 *(978-1-57505-822-1(7),* Carolrhoda Bks.) Lerner Publishing Group.

Thiel, Annie. Cosmos' Blended Family. Edwards, William M., illus. 2007. (Playdate Kids: Let's Be Friends! Ser.). 27p. (J). (gr. -1-3). per. 6.95 *(978-1-933721-23-1(5))* Playdate Kids Publishing.

Thiel Annie. Playdate Kids Cosmos' Blended Family. 2007. 32p. 12.95 *(978-1-933721-10-1(3))* Playdate Kids Publishing.

Thomas, Shelley Moore. Secrets of Selkie Bay. 2015. (ENG.). 208p. (J). (gr. 3-7). 15.99 *(978-0-374-36749-7(3),* 9780374367497, Farrar, Straus & Giroux (BYR)) Farrar, Straus & Giroux.

Thompson, Gwendolyn. Tiniest Angel with the Strongest Weapons. 2009. 24p. pap. 11.49 *(978-1-4490-1728-6(2))* AuthorHouse.

Thompson, Jan & Sharpe, Jaime. Amara's Magical Playhouse: The Adventure Begins. 2010. 108p. pap. 37.99 *(978-1-4520-8284-4(7))* AuthorHouse.

Thompson, Kate. The Last of the High Kings. (YA). 2010. (New Policeman Trilogy Ser.: 2). (ENG.). 336p. (gr. 8). pap. 8.99 *(978-0-06-117597-8(8),* Greenwillow Bks.) 2008. 323p. (gr. 7-18). lib. bdg. 17.89 *(978-0-06-117596-1(X),* HarperTeen) HarperCollins Pubs.

—Most Wanted. 2010. (ENG.). 144p. (J). (gr. 3-18). 15.99 *(978-0-06-173037-5(8),* Greenwillow Bks.) HarperCollins Pubs.

Thompson, Lisa. The Goldfish Boy. 2017. (ENG.). 320p. (J). (gr. 3-7). 16.99 *(978-1-338-05392-0(2),* Scholastic Pr.) Scholastic, Inc.

Thompson, Tyler. Sneaker Freak, 1 vol. 2010. 164p. pap. 24.95 *(978-1-4489-6191-7(2))* America Star Bks.

A Thousand Pieces of You. 2014. (Firebird Ser.: 1). (ENG.). 368p. (YA). (gr. 9). 17.99 *(978-0-06-227896-8(7))* HarperCollins Pubs.

Tillman, Nancy. On the Night You Were Born, 1. l.t. ed. 2005. (Illus.). 32p. (J). 17.95 *(978-0-9765761-0-5(4))* Darling Pr. LLC.

Todd, Pamela. The Blind Faith Hotel. (ENG.). 320p. (YA). (gr. 7). 2010. pap. 8.99 *(978-1-4169-9509-8(9))* 2008. 16.99 *(978-1-4169-5494-1(5))* McElderry, Margaret K. Bks. (McElderry, Margaret K. Bks.).

Toft, Di. Wolven, Bk. 1. 2011. (Wolven Ser.: 1). (ENG.). 352p. (J). (gr. 3-7). pap. 7.99 *(978-0-545-17110-6(5),* Chicken Hse., The) Scholastic, Inc.

Tolan, Stephanie S. Applewhites at Wit's End. (Applewhites Ser.: 2). (J). (gr. 5). 2013. (ENG.). 288p. pap. 6.99 *(978-0-06-057940-1(4))* 2012. (ENG.). 272p. 16.99 *(978-0-06-057938-8(2))* 2012. 272p. lib. bdg. 17.89 *(978-0-06-057939-5(0))* HarperCollins Pubs.

Tolan, Stephanie S. & Tolan, R. J. Applewhites Coast to Coast. 2017. 320p. (J). (gr. 3-7). 16.99 ***(978-0-06-213320-5(9))*** HarperCollins Pubs.

Torres, Jennifer. Stef Soto, Taco Queen. 2017. (ENG.). 176p. (J). (gr. 3-7). 16.99 *(978-0-316-30686-7(X))* Little Brown & Co.

Torrey, Richard. Moe Is Best. 2014. (I Like to Read(r) Ser.). (ENG., Illus.). 24p. (J). (gr. -1-3). 14.95 *(978-0-8234-2837-3(0))* Holiday Hse., Inc.

Toten, Teresa. Better Than Blonde. 2007. (ENG.). 224p. (J). (gr. 3-7). pap. 11.99 *(978-0-14-305314-9(0),* Puffin Canada) Penguin Random House Canada Young Readers CAN. Dist: Penguin Random Hse. LLC.

—Me & the Blondes. 2006. (ENG.). 232p. (J). (gr. 3-7). 11.99 *(978-0-14-305307-1(8),* Puffin Canada) Penguin Random House Canada Young Readers CAN. Dist: Penguin Random Hse. LLC.

Tougas, Shelley. Finders Keepers. 2015. (ENG.). 288p. (J). (gr. 3-7). 16.99 *(978-1-59643-990-0(4),* 9781596439900) Roaring Brook Pr.

—A Patron Saint for Junior Bridesmaids. 2016. (ENG.). 272p. (J). 16.99 *(978-1-62672-403-7(2),* 9781626724037) Roaring Brook Pr.

Townley, Roderick. A Bitter Magic. 2015. (ENG.). 304p. (J). (gr. 4-7). 16.99 *(978-0-449-81649-3(4),* Knopf Bks. for Young Readers) Random Hse. Children's Bks.

—The Red Thread: A Novel in Three Incarnations. 2012. (ENG.). 304p. (YA). (gr. 7). pap. 14.99 *(978-1-4169-0895-1(1),* Atheneum Bks. for Young Readers) Simon & Schuster Children's Publishing.

Tracy, Kristen. Camille McPhee Fell under the Bus. 2010. (ENG.). 304p. (J). (gr. 3-7). 7.99 *(978-0-375-84546-8(1),* Yearling) Random Hse. Children's Bks.

—Too Cool for This School. 2015. (ENG.). 288p. (J). (gr. 5). 6.99 *(978-0-375-87296-9(5),* Yearling) Random Hse. Children's Bks.

The Trail of the Wooden Horse. 2007. 32p. pap. 4.50 *(978-0-8341-2284-0(7),* 083-412-2847) Beacon Hill Pr. of Kansas City.

Travers, P. L. Mary Poppins. (Mary Poppins Ser.: No. 1). 202p. (J). (gr. 3-5). pap. 6.00 *(978-0-8072-1536-4(8),* Listening Library) Random Hse. Audio Publishing Group.

—Mary Poppins from A to Z. Shepard, Mary, illus. 2006. (Mary Poppins Ser.). (ENG.). 64p. (J). (gr. 5-7). 16.99 *(978-0-15-205834-0(6))* Houghton Mifflin Harcourt Publishing Co.

Tregay, Sarah. Love & Leftovers. 2011. (ENG.). 448p. (YA). (gr. 8). 17.99 *(978-0-06-202358-2(6),* Tegen, Katherine Bks) HarperCollins Pubs.

Tremblay, Alain Ulysse. L' Héritage de Julien. Malépart, Céline, illus. 2004. (Roman Jeunesse Ser.). (FRE.). 96p. (J). (gr. 4-7). pap. *(978-2-89021-682-2(9))* Diffusion du livre Mirabel (DLM).

Treyes, Jill. Brooke & Brandon Welcome Brandon. 2010. 28p. pap. 12.99 *(978-1-4389-1939-3(5))* AuthorHouse.

Trice, Linda. Kenya's Art. Mitchell, Hazel, illus. 2016. (ENG.). 32p. (J). (gr. -1-3). 16.95 *(978-1-57091-848-3(1))* Charlesbridge Publishing, Inc.

Trigiani, Adriana. Viola in the Spotlight. 2012. (Viola Ser.: 2). (ENG.). 288p. (YA). (gr. 8). pap. 8.99 *(978-0-06-145107-2(X),* HarperTeen) HarperCollins Pubs.

Tristan, Sarah. Cheat Codes. 2003. 234p. (YA). pap. 15.95 *(978-0-595-29670-5(X))* iUniverse, Inc.

Trivas, Tracy. The Wish Stealers. 2011. (ENG.). 288p. (J). (gr. 3-7). pap. 7.99 *(978-1-4169-8726-0(6),* Aladdin) Simon & Schuster Children's Publishing.

Trueman, Terry. Cruise Control. 2005. (Stuck in Neutral Ser.: 2). (ENG.). 160p. (YA). (gr. 9). pap. 8.99 *(978-0-06-447377-4(5),* HarperTeen) HarperCollins Pubs.

—Life Happens Next. 2012. (Stuck in Neutral Ser.: 3). (ENG.). 144p. (YA). (gr. 9). 17.99 *(978-0-06-202803-7(0),* HarperTeen) HarperCollins Pubs.

Trumbore, Cindy. The Genie in the Book. Alley, R. W., illus. 2004. (ENG.). 120p. (J). (gr. -1-7). 15.95 *(978-1-59354-042-5(6),* Handprint Bks.) Chronicle Bks. LLC.

Truss, Jan. Red. (J). pap. 6.95 *(978-0-88899-135-5(5))* Groundwood Bks. CAN. Dist: Publishers Group West (PGW).

Tuck, Pamela M. As Fast As Words Could Fly, 1 vol. Velasquez, Eric, illus. 2013. (ENG.). 40p. (J). 18.95 *(978-1-60060-348-8(3))* Lee & Low Bks., Inc.

Tuell, Todd. Ninja, Ninja, Never Stop! Carpenter, Tad, illus. 2014. (ENG.). 32p. (J). (gr. -1-k). 14.95 *(978-1-4197-1027-8(3),* Abrams Appleseed) Abrams, Inc.

Tuey, Doug E Do. Martin, Susan, illus. 2006. 76p. pap. 16.95 *(978-1-4241-0295-2(2))* PublishAmerica, Inc.

Turetsky, Bianca. The Time-Traveling Fashionista at the Palace of Marie Antoinette. 2013. (Time-Traveling Fashionista Ser.: 2). (ENG., Illus.). 272p. (J). (gr. 3-7). pap. 9.00 *(978-0-316-10535-4(X),* Poppy) Little, Brown Bks. for Young Readers.

Turnbull, Betty. A Sergeant in the House. Senning, Susan, illus. 2013. 44p. (J). 19.95 *(978-1-61153-059-9(8))* Light Messages Publishing.

Turnbull, Betty J. A Sergeant in the House. Senning, Susan, illus. 2013. 44p. pap. 14.95 *(978-1-61153-060-5(1))* Light Messages Publishing.

Turner, Henry. Ask the Dark. 2015. (ENG.). 256p. (YA). (gr. 9-12). 17.99 *(978-0-544-30827-5(1),* Clarion Bks.) Houghton Mifflin Harcourt Publishing Co.

Tym, Kate. Be Nice. 2008. (Manners Ser.). (Illus.). 24p. (J). (gr. -1-1). lib. bdg. 16.95 *(978-1-59566-590-4(0))* QEB Publishing Inc.

Tyner, Christopher. I'll Do It Tommarra Laura. 2004. 37p. (J). pap. 24.95 *(978-1-4137-2753-1(0))* PublishAmerica, Inc.

Tyre, Lisa Lewis & Airgood, Ellen. Last in a Long Line of Rebels. 2015. (ENG.). 288p. (J). (gr. 5). 16.99 *(978-0-399-16838-3(9),* Nancy Paulsen Books) Penguin Young Readers Group.

Udvari, Joseph G. Courage. 2012. 132p. pap. *(978-1-84961-169-5(6))* RealTime Publishing.

Ulch, Virginia. I Love You Anyway. 2007. 32p. per. 18.95 *(978-1-59858-433-2(2))* Dog Ear Publishing, LLC.

Uncle Tease: Individual Title Six-Packs. (Action Packs Ser.). 120p. (gr. 3-5). 44.00 *(978-0-7635-8388-0(X))* Rigby Education.

Underwood, Deborah. Part-Time Princess. Evans, Cambria, illus. 2013. (ENG.). 40p. (J). (gr. -1-k). 16.99 *(978-1-4231-2485-6(5))* Hyperion Pr.

Underwood, Kim. The Wonderful World of Sparkle Girl & Doobins. Goldman, Garnet, illus. 2009. 48p. (J). pap. 16.95 *(978-0-89587-373-6(7))* Blair, John F. Pub.

Unstead, Sue. Say Hello. 2004. (Illus.). 24p. (J). (gr. k-18). 14.95 *(978-1-58728-438-0(3),* Creative Publishing International) Quarto Publishing Group USA.

Upperman, Katy. Kissing Max Holden. Brzozowski, Kat, ed. 2017. (ENG.). 304p. (YA). 17.99 *(978-1-250-11116-6(1),* 9781250111166) Feiwel & Friends.

Urban, Linda. A Crooked Kind of Perfect. (ENG., Illus.). 224p. (J). (gr. 5-7). 2009. pap. 7.99 *(978-0-15-206608-6(X))* 2007. 16.00 *(978-0-15-206007-7(3))* Houghton Mifflin Harcourt Publishing Co.

Vail, Rachel. Gorgeous. (Avery Sisters Trilogy Ser.: 2). (ENG.). (YA). (gr. 8). 2010. 304p. pap. 9.99 *(978-0-06-089048-3(7))* 2009. 288p. 16.99 *(978-0-06-089046-9(0))* HarperCollins Pubs.

—If You Only Knew. 2014. (Friendship Ring Ser.: 1). (ENG.). 176p. (J). (gr. 5). pap. 7.99 *(978-0-14-751118-6(8),* Puffin Books) Penguin Young Readers Group.

—Well, That Was Awkward. 2017. (ENG.). 320p. (J). (gr. 5). 16.99 *(978-0-670-01308-1(0),* Viking Books for Young Readers) Penguin Young Readers Group.

Valentin, Karen. Allie's World: Abuela & Abuelo Move: Abuela & Abuelo Move. 2009. 32p. 6.95 *(978-1-60349-021-4(3),* Marimba Bks.) Hudson Publishing Group, The.

Valentine, Jenny. Broken Soup. 2009. 224p. (YA). (gr. 9-18). 16.99 *(978-0-06-085071-5(X),* HarperTeen) HarperCollins Pubs.

Valentine, Stephen J. The Lazarus Game. 2015. 311p. (YA). pap. 19.99 *(978-1-4621-1554-9(3))* Cedar Fort, Inc./CFI Distribution.

Valentino, Carla. When Can We Run, Play & Dance Again? An Enchanting Story about Family, Learning & Imagination. 2011. 32p. (gr. 2-4). pap. 17.95 *(978-1-4567-5495-2(5))* AuthorHouse.

Vallejo-Nagera, Alejandra. Mira Como He Crecido. Guerrero, Andres, illus. (SPA.). 31p. (J). (gr. k-1). 8.95 *(978-1-58986-547-1(2))* Santillana USA Publishing Co., Inc.

Van Ark, Katie. The Boy Next Door. 2015. (ENG.). 368p. (YA). (gr. 7). pap. 9.99 *(978-1-250-06146-1(6))* Feiwel & Friends.

van de Ruit, John. Spud. 2005. 300p. pap. *(978-0-14-302484-2(1))* Penguin Publishing Group.

—Spud. 2008. (ENG.). 336p. (YA). (gr. 7-18). 9.99 *(978-1-59514-187-3(1),* Razorbill) Penguin Young Readers Group.

Van De Ruit, John. Spud - The Madness Continues. 2009. (ENG.). 352p. (YA). (gr. 7-18). 9.99 *(978-1-59514-245-0(2),* Razorbill) Penguin Young Readers Group.

van Diepen, Allison. Light of Day. 2015. (ENG.). 320p. (YA). (gr. 9). 17.99 *(978-0-06-230347-9(3))* HarperCollins Pubs.

Van Dolzer, Krista. The Sound of Life & Everything. 2015. (ENG.). 272p. (J). (gr. 5). 16.99 *(978-0-399-16775-1(7),* G.P. Putnam's Sons Books for Young Readers) Penguin Young Readers Group.

Van Draanen, Wendelin. Confessions of a Serial Kisser. 2009. (ENG.). 304p. (YA). (gr. 7-18). pap. 9.99 *(978-0-375-84249-8(7),* Ember) Random Hse. Children's Bks.

—Flipped. 2003. (ENG.). 256p. (YA). (gr. 7-9). pap. 9.99 *(978-0-375-82544-6(4),* Ember) Random Hse. Children's Bks.

Van Dyne, Edith. Aunt Jane's Nieces. 2005. 27.95 *(978-1-4218-1025-6(5));* 228p. pap. 12.95 *(978-1-4218-1125-3(1))* 1st World Publishing, Inc. (1st World Library - Literary Society).

—Aunt Jane's Nieces & Uncle John. 2005. 26.95 *(978-1-4218-1024-9(7));* 176p. pap. 11.95 *(978-1-4218-1124-6(3))* 1st World Publishing, Inc. (1st World Library - Literary Society).

—Aunt Jane's Nieces at Millville. 2005. 27.95 *(978-1-4218-1026-3(3),* 1st World Library - Literary Society) 1st World Publishing, Inc.

—Aunt Jane's Nieces on Vacation. 2005. 27.95 *(978-1-4218-1027-0(1));* 200p. pap. 12.95 *(978-1-4218-1127-7(8))* 1st World Publishing, Inc. (1st World Library - Literary Society).

Van Leeuwen, Jean. Amanda Pig & the Really Hot Day. Schweninger, Ann, illus. 2007. (Oliver & Amanda Ser.). (ENG.). 48p. (J). (gr. 1-3). pap. 3.99 *(978-0-14-240775-2(5),* Penguin Young Readers) Penguin Young Readers Group.

—Amanda Pig & the Really Hot Day. Schweninger, Ann, illus. 2007. (Oliver & Amanda Ser.). 47p. (J). (gr. -1-3). 11.65 *(978-0-7569-8152-5(2))* Perfection Learning Corp.

Van Vleet, Carmella. Eliza Bing Is (Not) a Big, Fat Quitter. Donnelly, Karen, illus. 2014. (ENG.). 176p. (J). (gr. 2-6). 16.95 *(978-0-8234-2944-8(X))* Holiday Hse., Inc.

Vaughn, J. D. Paula & the Parrot. Brisiane, Niche, illus. 2009. 16p. pap. 8.49 *(978-1-4389-8634-0(3))* AuthorHouse.

Vaught, Susan. Footer Davis Probably Is Crazy. Reinhardt, Jennifer Black, illus. 2015. (ENG.). 240p. (J). (gr. 5-9). 16.99 *(978-1-4814-2276-5(6),* Simon & Schuster Bks. For Young Readers) Simon & Schuster Bks. For Young Readers.

Vawter, Vince. Paperboy. 2013. (ENG.). 240p. (J). (gr. 5). 16.99 *(978-0-385-74244-3(4));* lib. bdg. 19.99 *(978-0-375-99058-8(5))* Random Hse. Children's Bks. (Delacorte Bks. for Young Readers).

Velásquez, Gloria. Rudy's Memory Walk. 2009. (Roosevelt High School Ser.). 140p. (YA). (gr. 6-18). pap. 9.95 *(978-1-55885-593-9(9))* Arte Publico Pr.

Velasquez, Gloria. Tyrone's Betrayal. 2006. (Roosevelt High School Series Bks.). 135p. (J). (gr. 3-7). per. 9.95 *(978-1-55885-465-9(7),* Piñata Books) Arte Publico Pr.

Verhoeff, Carolyn. All about Johnnie Jones. 2007. 80p. per. *(978-1-4068-1628-0(0))* Echo Library.

Verne, Jules. Los Hijos del Capitan Grant (Captain Grant's Children) (SPA., Illus.). 192p. (YA). 11.95 *(978-84-7281-077-8(1),* AF1077) Auriga, Ediciones S.A. ESP. Dist: Continental Bk. Co., Inc.

Vernon, Ursula. Knight-Napped! 2015. (Dragonbreath Ser.: 10). (ENG.). 208p. (J). (gr. 3-7). 12.99 *(978-0-8037-3849-2(8),* Dial Bks) Penguin Young Readers Group.

Viau, Nancy. Storm Song. Gynux, illus. 2013. 24p. pap. 12.99 *(978-1-4778-6646-7(9))* Amazon Publishing.

Viorst, Judith. Alexander, Who's Trying His Best to Be the Best Boy Ever. 2014. (ENG., Illus.). 40p. (J). (gr. -1-3). 17.99 *(978-1-4814-2353-3(3),* Atheneum Bks. for Young Readers) Simon & Schuster Children's Publishing.

Vipont, Elfrida. The Lark in the Morn. Freeman, T. R., illus. 2007. 196p. (YA). pap. 12.95 *(978-1-932350-22-7(5))* Bethlehem Bks.

Vision, David & Vision, Mutiya Sahar. Daddy Loves His Baby Girl. Vision, Mutiya Sahar, illus. 2009. (Illus.). 32p. 16.00 *(978-0-9659538-7-0(4))* Visor Bks.

Vivian, Siobhan. Same Difference. 2014. (ENG.). 304p. (J). pap. 9.99 *(978-0-545-75802-4(5))* Scholastic, Inc.

Vlahos, Len. The Scar Boys. 2014. (ENG.). 256p. (J). (gr. 9). 17.99 *(978-1-60684-439-7(3))* Lerner Publishing Group.

Voigt, Cynthia. LOS TILLERMAN ENCUENTRAN HOGAR. (SPA.). 190p. (YA). (gr. 5-8). *(978-84-279-3219-7(7),* NG1573) Noguer y Caralt Editores, S. A. ESP. Dist: Lectorum Pubns., Inc.

—The Runner. 2005. (Tillerman Cycle Ser.: Bk. 4). (ENG., Illus.). 320p. (YA). (gr. 7). mass mkt. 7.99 *(978-1-4169-0341-3(0),* Simon Pulse) Simon Pulse.

Volponi, Paul. Crossing Lines. 2011. (ENG.). 256p. (YA). (gr. 7). E-Book *(978-1-101-52904-1(0));* 16.99 *(978-0-670-01214-5(9))* Penguin Young Readers Group. (Viking Books for Young Readers).

—Rooftop. 2007. (ENG.). 224p. (YA). (gr. 7-18). 6.99 *(978-0-14-240844-5(1),* Puffin Books) Penguin Young Readers Group.

—Rooftop. 2007. 199p. 17.00 *(978-0-7569-7958-4(7))* Perfection Learning Corp.

Vrettos, Adrienne Maria. Skin. 2007. (ENG.). 272p. (YA). (gr. 7-12). pap. 9.99 *(978-1-4169-0656-8(8),* McElderry, Margaret K. Bks.) McElderry, Margaret K. Bks.

Waber, Bernard. Lyle, Lyle, Crocodile Storybook Treasury. 2012. (Lyle the Crocodile Ser.). (ENG., Illus.). 192p. (J). (gr. -1-3). 11.99 *(978-0-547-51618-9(5))* Houghton Mifflin Harcourt Publishing Co.

Wade, Rebecca. The Whispering House. 2012. (ENG.). 272p. (J). (gr. 3-7). 16.99 *(978-0-06-077497-4(5),* Tegen, Katherine Bks) HarperCollins Pubs.

Wagman, Diana. Extraordinary October. 2016. (ENG.). 264p. (YA). (gr. 6). 18.95 *(978-1-63246-036-3(X))* Ig Publishing, Inc.

Wagner, Sandra Glahn. The Ants Have Dyed. Wagner, Sandra Glahn, illus. 2013. (Illus.). 20p. pap. 12.95 *(978-1-61493-171-3(2))* Peppertree Pr., The.

Wait, Lea. Wintering Well. 2006. (ENG., Illus.). 192p. (J). (gr. 3-7). pap. 6.99 *(978-0-689-85647-1(4),* McElderry, Margaret K. Bks.) McElderry, Margaret K. Bks.

Walker, Dan. Summer of Trespass. 2016. (ENG.). 182p. (YA). pap. 12.99 *(978-1-943328-42-0(0),* Alaska Northwest Bks.) Graphic Arts Ctr. Publishing Co.

Walker, Melissa. Unbreak My Heart. (ENG., (YA). (gr. 7). 2013. Illus.). 256p. pap. 9.99 *(978-1-61963-007-9(9),* 9781619630079) 2012. 240p. 16.99 *(978-1-59990-528-0(0),* 9781599905280) Bloomsbury Publishing USA. (Bloomsbury USA Childrens).

Walker, Patricia. Tommy's New Barn Mates. 2009. 44p. pap. 18.95 *(978-1-4389-6024-1(7))* AuthorHouse.

Wallace, Bill. The Dog Who Thought He Was Santa. 2007. (ENG., Illus.). 224p. (J). (gr. 4-7). 17.95 *(978-0-8234-2114-5(7))* Holiday Hse., Inc.

—The Dog Who Thought He Was Santa. 2008. (ENG.). 192p. (J). (gr. 3-7). pap. 5.99 *(978-1-4169-4816-2(3),* Aladdin) Simon & Schuster Children's Publishing.

—No Dogs Allowed! 2004. (ENG.). 214p. (J). (gr. 4-6). tchr. ed. 16.95 *(978-0-8234-1818-3(9))* Holiday Hse., Inc.

Wallace, Brandon. The Journey Home. 2016. (Wilder Boys Ser.). (ENG., Illus.). 208p. (J). (gr. 3-7). 16.99 *(978-1-4814-3267-2(2),* Aladdin) Simon & Schuster Children's Publishing.

Wallace-Brodeur, Ruth. Stories from the Big Chair. 2010. (ENG.). 48p. (J). (gr. -1-3). 6.99 *(978-1-4424-1439-6(1),* McElderry, Margaret K. Bks.) McElderry, Margaret K. Bks.

Wallace, Carol. The Santa Secret. Björkman, Steve, illus. 2007. (Holiday House Readers: Level 2 Ser.). (ENG.). 40p. (J). (gr. -1-3). 15.95 *(978-0-8234-2022-3(1));* pap. 4.95 *(978-0-8234-2126-8(0))* Holiday Hse., Inc.

Wallace, Nancy Elizabeth. Ready, Set, 100th Day!, 0 vols. 2011. (ENG.). 40p. (J). (gr. -1-3). 17.99 *(978-0-7614-5956-9(1),* 9780761459569, Amazon Children's Publishing) Amazon Publishing.

Wallace, Rich. Fake Out. Holder, Jimmy, illus. 2011. (Kickers Ser.: Bk. 2). (ENG.). 128p. (J). (gr. 1-4). 6.99 *(978-0-375-85093-6(7),* Yearling) Random Hse. Children's Bks.

—Game-Day Jitters. Holder, Jimmy, illus. 2012. (Kickers Ser.). (ENG.). 128p. (J). (gr. 2-5). 5.99 *(978-0-375-85095-0(3),* Yearling) Random Hse. Children's Bks.

—Second-String Center. 2008. (Winning Season Ser.: 10). (ENG.). 128p. (J). (gr. 3-7). 5.99 *(978-0-14-241216-9(3),* Puffin Books) Penguin Young Readers Group.

—War & Watermelon. 2012. (ENG.). 192p. (J). (gr. 5-18). pap. 6.99 *(978-0-14-242138-3(3),* Puffin Books) Penguin Young Readers Group.

E F G

Walmsley, Tom. Kid Stuff: A Novel. 2004. (ENG.). 288p. 17.95 *(978-1-55152-153-4(9)*, 187) Arsenal Pulp Pr. CAN. Dist: Consortium Bk. Sales & Distribution.

Walsh, Meg. Mama, Won't You Play with Me? 2009. 28p. pap. 13.99 *(978-1-4490-1424-7(0))* AuthorHouse.

Walter, Mildred Pitts. Justin & the Best Biscuits in the World. Stock, Catherine, illus. 2010. (ENG.). 144p. (J). (gr. 3-7). pap. 5.99 *(978-0-06-195891-5(3)*, Amistad) HarperCollins Pubs.

—Justin & the Best Biscuits in the World. 2011. 8.32 *(978-0-7848-3586-9(1)*, Everbind) Marco Bk. Co.

Walton, K. M. Ultimatum. 2017. (ENG.). 320p. (YA). (gr. 7-12). 17.99 *(978-1-4926-3507-9(3)*, 9781492635079) Sourcebooks, Inc.

Walton, Rick. Bunny Christmas: A Family Celebration. Miglio, Paige, illus. 2004. 32p. (J). (ENG.). 15.99 *(978-0-06-008415-8(4))*; lib. bdg. 16.89 *(978-0-06-008416-5(2))* HarperCollins Pubs.

—I Need My Own Country! Hargis, Wes, illus. 2012. (ENG.). 40p. (J). (gr. -1-3). 17.89 *(978-1-59990-560-0(4)*, 9781599905600, Bloomsbury USA Childrens) Bloomsbury Publishing USA.

Walton, Rick & Kraus, Franz. I Need My Own Country! Hargis, Wes, illus. 2012. (ENG.). 40p. (J). (gr. -1-8). 16.99 *(978-1-59990-559-4(0)*, 9781599905594, Bloomsbury USA Childrens) Bloomsbury Publishing USA.

Wardlaw, Lee. 101 Ways to Bug Your Friends & Enemies. 2011. (ENG.). 288p. (J). (gr. 5-18). 6.99 *(978-0-14-241949-6(4)*, Puffin Books) Penguin Young Readers Group.

Wargin, Kathy-jo. The Voyageur's Paddle. Geister, David & Van Frankenhuyzen, Gijsbert, illus. rev. ed. 2007. (Myths, Legends, Fairy & Folktales Ser.). (ENG.). 40p. (J). (gr. 1-4). 19.99 *(978-1-58536-007-9(4)*, 201942) Sleeping Bear Pr.

Warner, Gertrude Chandler. Blue Bay Mystery, 1 vol. Dubisch, Michael, illus. 2009. (Boxcar Children Graphic Novels Ser.). (ENG.). 32p. (J). (gr. 2-5). 28.50 *(978-1-60270-591-3(7))* ABDO Publishing Co.

—The Boxcar Children. Date not set. (Boxcar Children Ser.: No. 1). (J). (gr. 2-5). lib. bdg. 18.95 *(978-0-8488-1712-1(5))* Amereon Ltd.

—Mike's Mystery, 1 vol. Dubisch, Michael, illus. 2009. (Boxcar Children Graphic Novels Ser.). (ENG.). 32p. (J). (gr. 2-5). 28.50 *(978-1-60270-590-6(9))* ABDO Publishing Co.

—Mystery Ranch, 1 vol. Dubisch, Michael, illus. 2009. (Boxcar Children Graphic Novels Ser.). (ENG.). 32p. (J). (gr. 2-5). 28.50 *(978-1-60270-589-0(5))* ABDO Publishing Co.

—The Yellow House Mystery, 1 vol. Dubisch, Michael, illus. 2009. (Boxcar Children Graphic Novels Ser.). (ENG.). 32p. (J). (gr. 2-5). 28.50 *(978-1-60270-588-3(7))* ABDO Publishing Co.

Warner, Sally. The Dragon Slayer! Biggs, Brian, illus. 2013. (EllRay Jakes Ser.: 4). (ENG.). 144p. (J). (gr. 1-3). 14.99 *(978-0-670-78497-4(4)*, Viking Books for Young Readers) Penguin Young Readers Group.

—Ellray Jakes Is a Rock Star! 2012. (EllRay Jakes Ser.: 2). lib. bdg. 16.00 *(978-0-606-23633-1(3)*, Turtleback) Turtleback Bks.

—EllRay Jakes Is Magic. Biggs, Brian, illus. 2014. (EllRay Jakes Ser.: 6). (ENG.). (J). (gr. 1-3). 160p. 14.99 *(978-0-670-78500-1(8)*, Viking Books for Young Readers); 176p. pap. 5.99 *(978-0-14-242360-8(2)*, Puffin Books) Penguin Young Readers Group.

—Ellray Jakes Is Magic. 2014. (EllRay Jakes Ser.: 6). lib. bdg. 16.00 *(978-0-606-34215-5(X)*, Turtleback) Turtleback Bks.

—EllRay Jakes Is Not a Chicken! 2012. (EllRay Jakes Ser.: 1). lib. bdg. 16.00 *(978-0-606-23632-4(5)*, Turtleback) Turtleback Bks.

—Ellray Jakes Rocks the Holidays! 2014. (EllRay Jakes Ser.: 7). lib. bdg. 16.00 *(978-0-606-36188-0(X))* Turtleback Bks.

—EllRay Jakes the Dragon Slayer. 2013. (EllRay Jakes Ser.: 4). lib. bdg. 16.00 *(978-0-606-32136-5(5)*, Turtleback) Turtleback Bks.

—EllRay Jakes the Recess King! Biggs, Brian, illus. 2015. (EllRay Jakes Ser.: 8). (ENG.). 176p. (J). (gr. 1-3). 5.99 *(978-0-14-751252-9(2)*, Puffin Books); 14.99 *(978-0-451-46911-3(9)*, Viking Books for Young Readers) Penguin Young Readers Group.

—Rocks the Holidays! Biggs, Brian, illus. 2014. (EllRay Jakes Ser.: 7). (ENG.). 160p. (J). (gr. 1-3). 14.99 *(978-0-451-46909-0(7)*, Viking Books for Young Readers) Penguin Young Readers Group.

Watkins, Steve. Down Sand Mountain. (ENG., Illus.). 336p. (YA). (gr. 7). 2011. pap. 7.99 *(978-0-7636-4835-0(3))* 2008. 16.99 *(978-0-7636-3839-9(0))* Candlewick Pr.

—Great Falls. 2016. (ENG.). 256p. (YA). (gr. 9). 17.99 *(978-0-7636-7155-6(X))* Candlewick Pr.

Watson, K. R. Little Gabby Meets Her New Family. 2008. 44p. pap. 17.99 *(978-1-4389-1767-2(8))* AuthorHouse.

Watson, Myrtle. Kite Flying in the Village: A Guyanese Girl's Story. 2011. 20p. 10.03 *(978-1-4520-8632-3(X))* AuthorHouse.

Watson, Renée. What Momma Left Me. 2012. (ENG.). 240p. (YA). pap. 7.99 *(978-1-59990-704-8(6)*, 9781599907048, Bloomsbury USA Childrens) Bloomsbury Publishing USA.

Wayland, April Halprin. More Than Enough. Kath, Katie, illus. 2016. (ENG.). 40p. (J). (-k). 16.99 *(978-0-8037-4126-3(X)*, Dial Bks) Penguin Young Readers Group.

Weatherford, Carole Boston. Celebremos Juneteenth! de La Vega, Eida, tr. from ENG. Buchanan, Yvonne, illus. 2007. (SPA.). 32p. (J). (gr. -1-3). pap. 7.95 *(978-1-60060-247-4(9))* Lee & Low Bks., Inc.

Weatherly, Lee. Child X. 2004. 211p. 16.00 *(978-0-7569-3211-4(4))* Perfection Learning Corp.

Weaver, Will. Clay. 2004. 232p. (YA). (gr. 8-12). 14.65 *(978-0-7569-4594-7(1))* Perfection Learning Corp.

—Memory Boy. 2012. Orig. Title: The Boy on Platform One. (ENG.). 240p. (YA). (gr. 8). pap. 8.99 *(978-0-06-201814-4(0)*, HarperTeen) HarperCollins Pubs.

—The Survivors. 2012. (ENG.). 320p. (YA). (gr. 8). 17.99 *(978-0-06-009476-8(1)*, HarperTeen) HarperCollins Pubs.

Webb, Sarah. Ask Amy Green: Love & Other Drama-Ramas! 2012. (Ask Amy Green Ser.: 4). (ENG., Illus.). 224p. (YA). (gr. 7). 15.99 *(978-0-7636-5582-2(1))* Candlewick Pr.

Webb, Susan. A Tale of Two Brothers. 2012. 24p. pap. 12.95 *(978-1-4497-6053-3(8)*, WestBow Pr.) Author Solutions, Inc.

Weber, John. Orphan. 2010. 266p. (YA). (gr. 7-18). 16.95 *(978-1-934813-38-6(9))* Westside Bks.

Weber, Lori. Split, 1 vol. 2005. (Lorimer SideStreets Ser.). (ENG.). 152p. (YA). (gr. 9-12). 16.95 *(978-1-55028-879-7(2)*, 9781550288797); 8.95 *(978-1-55028-878-0(4)*, 9781550288780) Lorimer, James & Co., Ltd., Pubs. CAN. Dist: Casemate Pubs. & Bk. Distributors, LLC.

Weeks, Sarah. As Simple as It Seems. (ENG.). 192p. (J). (gr. 3-7). 2011. pap. 5.99 *(978-0-06-084665-7(8))* 2010. 15.99 *(978-0-06-084663-3(1))* HarperCollins Pubs.

—Pie. 2013. (ENG.). 192p. (J). (gr. 3-7). pap. 6.99 *(978-0-545-27012-0(X)*, Scholastic Paperbacks) Scholastic, Inc.

Weigel, Jeff. Atomic Ace & the Robot Rampage. Weigel, Jeff, illus. 2006. (ENG., Illus.). 32p. (J). (gr. 1-5). 6.95 *(978-0-8075-0485-7(8))*; 15.95 *(978-0-8075-0484-0(X))* Whitman, Albert & Co.

Weihrich, Carroll. In the Meantime. 2007. 208p. per. 15.00 *(978-1-932621-36-5(9))* Open Bk. Publishing.

Weinbrenner, Darlene. Hannah, Mable, & the Moving Van. 2007. 76p. per. 19.95 *(978-1-4241-6563-6(6))* America Star Bks.

Weiner, Kimberly. Not My Reality. 2004. pap. 12.50 *(978-0-9753262-0-6(1))* YNR Media L.L.C.

Welch, Leah. Pretty on the Inside. 2007. (J). per. 10.00 *(978-1-59872-779-1(6))* Instant Pub.

Wells, Rosemary. Julieta, Estate Quieta! (SPA.). 43p. (J). 5.50 *(978-84-372-1523-5(4))* Santillana USA Publishing Co., Inc.

—Max & Ruby's Show-and-Tell. 2006. (Max & Ruby Ser.). (ENG., Illus.). 32p. (J). (gr. -1-k). mass mkt. 3.99 *(978-0-448-43952-5(2)*, Grosset & Dunlap) Penguin Young Readers Group.

—Max's ABC. 2006. (Max & Ruby Ser.). (ENG., Illus.). 32p. (J). (gr. -1-k). 16.99 *(978-0-670-06074-0(7)*, Viking Books for Young Readers) Penguin Young Readers Group.

—Noisy Nora. Wells, Rosemary, illus. 2007. (Illus.). 28p. (gr. -1-2). 17.00 *(978-0-7569-7870-9(X))* Perfection Learning Corp.

—Say Hello, Sophie! 2017. (ENG., Illus.). 32p. (J). (— 1). 17.99 *(978-1-101-99925-7(X)*, Viking Books for Young Readers) Penguin Young Readers Group.

—Sophie's Terrible Twos. Wells, Rosemary, illus. 2014. (ENG., Illus.). 32p. (J). (gr. -1-k). 16.99 *(978-0-670-78512-4(1)*, Viking Books for Young Readers) Penguin Young Readers Group.

—Ten Kisses for Sophie! Wells, Rosemary, illus. 2016. (ENG., Illus.). 32p. (J). (— 1). 16.99 *(978-0-670-01665-5(9)*, Viking Books for Young Readers) Penguin Young Readers Group.

—Time-Out for Sophie. Wells, Rosemary, illus. (ENG., Illus.). (J). (gr. -1). 2015. 26p. bds. 6.99 *(978-0-451-47766-8(9))* 2013. 32p. 15.99 *(978-0-670-78511-7(3))* Penguin Young Readers Group. (Viking Books for Young Readers).

Wells, Rosemary, et al. My Havana: Memories of a Cuban Boyhood. Ferguson, Peter, illus. 2010. (ENG.). 72p. (J). (gr. 2-5). 17.99 *(978-0-7636-4305-8(X))* Candlewick Pr.

Wenberg, Michael. Stringz. 2010. 216p. (YA). (gr. 6-10). 16.95 *(978-1-934813-33-1(8))* Westside Bks.

Werlin, Nancy. Are You Alone on Purpose? 2007. (ENG.). 208p. (YA). (gr. 7-18). 7.99 *(978-0-14-240777-6(1)*, Speak) Penguin Young Readers Group.

—The Killer's Cousin. 2009. (ENG.). 240p. (YA). (gr. 7-18). 7.99 *(978-0-14-241373-9(9)*, Speak) Penguin Young Readers Group.

Wertheim, L. Jon & Moskowitz, Tobias J. The Rookie Bookie. (ENG., Illus.). 272p. (J). (gr. 3-7). 2015. pap. 7.00 *(978-0-316-24979-9(3))* 2014. 17.00 *(978-0-316-24981-2(5))* Little, Brown Bks. for Young Readers.

Wesley, Mary. Haphazard House. Date not set. (Sky Bks.). 200p. pap. 54.75 *(978-0-582-08108-6(4))* Addison-Wesley Longman, Ltd. GBR. Dist: Trans-Atlantic Pubns., Inc.

West, Kasie. On the Fence. 2014. (ENG.). 304p. (YA). (gr. 8). pap. 9.99 *(978-0-06-223567-1(2)*, HarperTeen) HarperCollins Pubs.

—Split Second. 2015. (Pivot Point Ser.: Bk. 2). (ENG.). 384p. (YA). (gr. 8). pap. 9.99 *(978-0-06-211739-7(4)*, HarperTeen) HarperCollins Pubs.

West, Lily June Wolford. A Trip to the Cellar. West, June & Wright, Shannon, illus. 2007. (J). (gr. -1-3). 16.99 *(978-1-59879-347-5(0))* Lifevest Publishing, Inc.

Westaway, Kylie. A Whale in the Bathtub. Jellett, Tom, illus. 2016. (ENG.). 40p. (J). (gr. -1-3). 16.99 *(978-0-544-53535-0(9))* Houghton Mifflin Harcourt Publishing Co.

Westcott, Jim. The Gift. 2014. (Red Rhino Ser.). (J). lib. bdg. 18.40 *(978-0-606-36201-6(0))* Turtleback Bks.

Weston, Carol. Ava & Pip. (Ava & Pip Ser.: 1). (ENG.). 224p. (J). (gr. 5-7). 2015. pap. 6.99 *(978-1-4926-0183-8(7))* 2014. 15.99 *(978-1-4022-8870-8(0)*, 9781402288708) Sourcebooks, Inc. (Sourcebooks Jabberwocky).

Weston Woods Staff, creator. Elizabeti's Doll. 2011. 38.75 *(978-0-439-84574-8(2))*; 18.95 *(978-0-439-73629-9(3))* Weston Woods Studios, Inc.

—Five Creatures. 2011. 18.95 *(978-0-439-80441-7(8))*; 38.75 *(978-0-439-80444-8(2))* Weston Woods Studios, Inc.

—Too Many Tamales. 2004. (J). (gr. -1-3). 29.95 *(978-1-55592-137-8(X))* Weston Woods Studios, Inc.

Whaley, John Corey. Noggin. (ENG., Illus.). (YA). (gr. 9). 2015. 368p. pap. 12.99 *(978-1-4424-5873-4(9))* 2014. 352p. 18.99 *(978-1-4424-5872-7(0))* Simon & Schuster Children's Publishing. (Atheneum Bks. for Young Readers).

—Where Things Come Back. (ENG., Illus.). (YA). (gr. 9). 2012. 256p. pap. 11.99 *(978-1-4424-1334-4(4))* 2011. 240p. 16.99 *(978-1-4424-1333-7(6))* Simon & Schuster Children's Publishing. (Atheneum Bks. for Young Readers).

Wheeler, Lisa. Uncles & Antlers. Floca, Brian, illus. 2014. (ENG.). 40p. (J). (gr. -1-3). 17.99 *(978-1-4814-3018-0(1)*, Atheneum Bks. for Young Readers) Simon & Schuster Children's Publishing.

Wheeler, Ron. Stinky Stevens: Escape from Aunt Smoochie-Kiss (Book 4) 2012. 114p. pap. 6.95 *(978-0-9829377-7-8(6))* Written World Communications.

Whelan, Gloria. The Boy Who Wanted to Cook. Adams, Steve, illus. 2011. (Tales of the World Ser.). (ENG.). 40p. (gr. k-5). lib. bdg. 16.95 *(978-1-58536-534-0(3))* Sleeping Bear Pr.

—Chu Ju's House. 2005. (ENG.). 240p. (J). (gr. 5). reprint ed. pap. 7.99 *(978-0-06-050726-8(8))* HarperCollins Pubs.

—Farewell to the Island. 2004. 200p. (J). (gr. 4-7). per. 7.95 *(978-1-882376-92-6(7))* Thunder Bay Pr.

—Megan's Year: An Irish Traveler's Story. Peck, Beth, illus. 2011. (Tales of the World Ser.). (ENG.). 32p. (gr. k-5). lib. bdg. 16.95 *(978-1-58536-449-7(5))* Sleeping Bear Pr.

—Summer of the War. 2006. 163p. (J). (gr. 5-9). lib. bdg. 16.89 *(978-0-06-008073-0(6))*; *(978-1-4287-0030-7(7))* HarperCollins Pubs.

When I Go. 2003. (Illus.). (J). bds. 7.98 *(978-0-7525-8657-1(2))* Parragon, Inc.

Whitaker, Kenneth. Hood-Hearted Child, Life as a Nobody: Based on a True Story, 1 vol. 2009. 48p. pap. 16.95 *(978-1-61546-369-5(0))* America Star Bks.

Whitaker, Nathan. Snap Decision, 1 vol. 2015. (Game Face Ser.). (ENG.). 272p. (J). pap. 8.99 *(978-0-310-73703-2(6))* Zonderkidz.

Whitby, Adele. Beth's Story 1914. 2014. (Secrets of the Manor Ser.: 1). (ENG., Illus.). 160p. (J). (gr. 3-7). 16.99 *(978-1-4814-0632-1(9)*, Simon Spotlight) Simon Spotlight.

—Kate's Story 1914. 2014. (Secrets of the Manor Ser.: 2). (ENG., Illus.). 160p. (J). (gr. 3-7). 16.99 *(978-1-4814-0635-2(3)*, Simon Spotlight) Simon Spotlight.

White, Ruth. The Search for Belle Prater. 2007. 169p. (J). (gr. 4-7). 14.15 *(978-0-7569-7274-5(4))* Perfection Learning Corp.

—You'll Like It Here (Everybody Does) 2012. (ENG.). 272p. (J). (gr. 4-7). 7.99 *(978-0-375-86596-1(9)*, Yearling) Random Hse. Children's Bks.

Whitehouse, Elizabeth. Ogham in Orkney: A Jensen Family Story. 2004. (J). pap. 5.95 *(978-1-933031-36-1(0))* Whitehouse Publishing.

Whitmore, Arvella. The Bread Winner. 2004. (ENG.). 144p. (J). (gr. 5-7). pap. 6.99 *(978-0-618-49479-8(0))* Houghton Mifflin Harcourt Publishing Co.

Whitney, Kim Ablon. See You down the Road. 14.85 *(978-0-7569-5710-0(9))* Perfection Learning Corp.

Whittemore, Jo. Colonial Madness. 2015. (ENG., Illus.). 240p. (J). (gr. 4-8). 17.99 *(978-1-4814-0508-9(X)*, Aladdin) Simon & Schuster Children's Publishing.

Whyman, Matt. The Savages. 2015. (ENG.). 288p. (gr. 8-14). pap. 9.99 *(978-1-4683-1071-9(2)*, 461071) Overlook Pr., The.

Wiesner, Karen Sue. Cody Knows. Hardy, Candace J., illus. 2012. 16p. pap. 9.95 *(978-1-61633-260-0(3))* Guardian Angel Publishing, Inc.

Wiess, Laura. Leftovers. 2008. (ENG.). 256p. (gr. 8-18). pap. 12.99 *(978-1-4165-4662-7(6)*, MTV Bks.) MTV Books.

Wiggin, Kate Douglas. New Chronicles of Rebecca. 2004. reprint ed. pap. 28.95 *(978-1-4179-2096-9(3))*; pap. 15.95 *(978-1-4179-9994-1(2))*; pap. 1.99 *(978-1-4179-9944-6(6))* Kessinger Publishing, LLC.

Wiggins, Leah Holder. My Neighbor Is Gone. Wiggins, Margaret W., illus. 2006. 28p. (J). per. 17.99 *(978-0-9768579-5-2(2))* eVision, LLC.

Wight, Eric. Frankie Pickle & the Closet of Doom. Wight, Eric, illus. (Frankie Pickle Ser.). (ENG., Illus.). 96p. (J). (gr. 2-5). 2010. pap. 5.99 *(978-1-4424-1304-7(2))* 2009. 9.99 *(978-1-4169-6484-1(3))* Simon & Schuster Bks. For Young Readers. (Simon & Schuster Bks. For Young Readers).

—Frankie Pickle & the Pine Run 3000. Wight, Eric, illus. 2010. (Frankie Pickle Ser.). (ENG., Illus.). 96p. (J). (gr. 2-5). 9.99 *(978-1-4169-6485-8(1)*, Simon & Schuster Bks. For Young Readers) Simon & Schuster Bks. For Young Readers.

Wigington, Patti. Summer's Ashes. 2007. (ENG.). 208p. (gr. 8-12). per. 15.00 *(978-0-9766805-9-8(9))* Keene Publishing.

Wilder, Laura Ingalls. Farmer Boy. Williams, Garth, illus. (Little House Ser.: 2). (ENG.). 384p. (J). (gr. 3-7). 2008. pap. 7.99 *(978-0-06-440003-9(4))* 2004. pap. 8.99 *(978-0-06-058182-4(4))* HarperCollins Pubs.

—A Little House Christmas Treasury: Festive Holiday Stories. Williams, Garth, illus. 2005. (Little House Ser.). (ENG.). 144p. (J). (gr. 3-7). 14.99 *(978-0-06-076918-5(1))* HarperCollins Pubs.

—The Little House Collection, Set. Williams, Garth, illus. 2004. (Little House Ser.). (J). (gr. 3-7). pap. 44.99 *(978-0-06-075428-0(1))* HarperCollins Pubs.

—Little House in the Big Woods. Williams, Garth, illus. 2008. (Little House Ser.: 1). (ENG.). 256p. (J). (gr. 3-7). pap. 7.99 *(978-0-06-440001-5(8))* HarperCollins Pubs.

—Little House in the Big Woods. 2007. (Little House Ser.). 224p. (J). (gr. 3-7). pap. 6.99 *(978-0-06-088537-3(8)*, Harper Trophy) HarperCollins Pubs.

—Little House in the Big Woods. Williams, Garth, illus. 2004. (Little House Ser.: 1). (ENG.). 256p. (J). (gr. 3-7). pap. 8.99 *(978-0-06-058180-0(8))* HarperCollins Pubs.

—Little House on the Prairie. 2007. (Little House Ser.). 336p. (J). (gr. 3-7). pap. 6.99 *(978-0-06-088539-7(4)*, Harper Trophy) HarperCollins Pubs.

—Little House on the Prairie. Williams, Garth, illus. 75th anniv. ed. 2010. (Little House Ser.: 3). (ENG.). 368p. (J). (gr. 3-7). 16.99 *(978-0-06-195827-4(1))* HarperCollins Pubs.

—Little House on the Prairie. 2008. (Little House Bks.: 2). (J). 17.20 *(978-1-4177-7357-2(X)*, Turtleback) Turtleback Bks.

—Little Town on the Prairie. 2007. (Little House Ser.). 320p. (J). (gr. 3-7). pap. 6.99 *(978-0-06-088543-4(2)*, Harper Trophy) HarperCollins Pubs.

—The Long Winter. Williams, Garth, illus. (Little House Ser.: 6). (ENG.). 352p. (J). (gr. 3-7). 2008. pap. 8.99 *(978-0-06-440006-0(9))* 2004. pap. 8.99 *(978-0-06-058185-5(9))* HarperCollins Pubs.

—On the Banks of Plum Creek. 2007. (Little House Ser.). 384p. (J). (gr. 3-7). pap., pap., pap. 6.99 *(978-0-06-088540-3(8)*, Harper Trophy) HarperCollins Pubs.

—These Happy Golden Years. 2007. (Little House Ser.). (ENG.). 304p. (J). (gr. 3-7). pap., pap. 6.99 *(978-0-06-088544-1(0)*, Harper Trophy) HarperCollins Pubs.

Wiles, Deborah. Each Little Bird That Sings. 2006. (ENG., Illus.). 288p. (J). (gr. 2-5). reprint ed. pap. 7.99 *(978-0-15-205657-5(2))* Houghton Mifflin Harcourt Publishing Co.

Wiley, Melissa. Beyond the Heather Hills. Graef, Renee, illus. 2003. (Little House Ser.). 189p. (J). (gr. 3-7). 14.65 *(978-0-7569-3467-5(2))* Perfection Learning Corp.

—Little House by Boston Bay. 2007. (Little House Prequel Ser.). (ENG.). 160p. (J). (gr. 3-7). pap. 5.99 *(978-0-06-114828-6(8))* HarperCollins Pubs.

—Little House in the Highlands. 2007. (Little House Prequel Ser.). (ENG.). 160p. (J). (gr. 3-7). pap. 6.99 *(978-0-06-114817-0(2))* HarperCollins Pubs.

Wilkes, Maria D. Little House in Brookfield. abr. ed. 2007. (Little House Ser.). (ENG.). 144p. (J). (gr. 3-7). pap. 6.99 *(978-0-06-114821-7(0))* HarperCollins Pubs.

Wilkinson, Lili. Pink. (ENG.). 320p. (YA). (gr. 8). 2012. pap. 9.99 *(978-0-06-192654-9(X))* 2011. 16.99 *(978-0-06-192653-2(1))* HarperCollins Pubs. (HarperTeen).

Willems, Mo, illus. Nanette's Baguette. 2016. (ENG.). 40p. (J). (gr. -1-k). 17.99 *(978-1-4847-2286-2(8))* Disney Pr.

Williams, Carol Lynch. The Chosen One. 2010. (ENG.). 240p. (YA). (gr. 7). pap. 10.99 *(978-0-312-62775-1(0)*, 9780312627751, St. Martin's Griffin) St. Martin's Pr.

—Waiting. (ENG.). 352p. (YA). (gr. 9). 2013. pap. 9.99 *(978-1-4424-4354-9(5))* 2012. 16.99 *(978-1-4424-4353-2(7))* Simon & Schuster/Paula Wiseman Bks. (Simon & Schuster/Paula Wiseman Bks.).

Williams-Garcia, Rita. Clayton Byrd Goes Underground. Morrison, Frank, illus. 2017. 176p. (J). (gr. 3-7). 16.99 *(978-0-06-221591-8(4))*; (ENG.). E-Book *(978-0-06-221594-9(9))* HarperCollins Pubs. (Amistad).

Williams, Heather. Farmer Boy Goes West. 2012. (Little House Sequel Ser.). (ENG.). 320p. (J). (gr. 3-7). 16.99 *(978-0-06-124251-9(9))* HarperCollins Pubs.

Williams, Julie. Drama Queens in the House. 2014. (ENG.). 432p. (YA). (gr. 7). 17.99 *(978-1-59643-735-7(9)*, 9781596437357) Roaring Brook Pr.

Williams, Lori Aurelia. Shayla's Double Brown Baby Blues. 2003. (ENG., Illus.). 304p. (YA). (gr. 7). pap. 12.99 *(978-0-689-85670-9(9)*, Simon & Schuster Bks. For Young Readers) Simon & Schuster Bks. For Young Readers.

—When Kambia Elaine Flew in from Neptune. unabr. ed. 2004. 246p. (J). (gr. 7-18). pap. 50.00 incl. audio *(978-0-8072-8851-1(9)*, Listening Library) Random Hse. Audio Publishing Group.

Williams, Sarah DeFord. Palace Beautiful. 2011. (ENG.). 240p. (J). (gr. 5-18). 6.99 *(978-0-14-241745-4(9)*, Puffin Books) Penguin Young Readers Group.

Williams, Venus & Williams, Serena. SisterTales 2. 2010. (gr. 5-9). *(978-0-618-44915-6(9))* Houghton Mifflin Harcourt Trade & Reference Pubs.

Williams, Vera B. A Chair for Always. Williams, Vera B., illus. 2009. (SPA & ENG., Illus.). 40p. (J). (gr. -1-3). 16.99 *(978-0-06-172279-0(0)*, Greenwillow Bks.) HarperCollins Pubs.

—A Chair for My Mother. Williams, Vera B., illus. 25th anniv. ed. 2007. (Reading Rainbow Bks.). (ENG., Illus.). 32p. (J). (gr. -1-3). pap. 7.99 *(978-0-688-04074-1(8)*, Greenwillow Bks.) HarperCollins Pubs.

—A Chair for My Mother. 2014. (Reading Rainbow Bks). (ENG.). 32p. (J). (gr. k-3). 11.24 *(978-1-63245-340-2(1))* Lectorum Pubns., Inc.

—A Chair for My Mother. 2007. (Reading Rainbow Bks.). (Illus.). 32p. (J). (gr. -1-3). 18.40 *(978-0-8085-3385-6(1)*, Turtleback) Turtleback Bks.

—Un Sillón para Siempre, 1 vol. Williams, Vera B., illus. 2009.Tr. of Chair for Always. (SPA & ENG., Illus.). 40p. (J). (gr. -1-3). 17.99 *(978-0-06-172283-7(9)*, Greenwillow Bks.) HarperCollins Pubs.

Willis, Meredith Sue. Billie of Fish House Lane. 2006. (J). pap. 12.95 *(978-1-932727-02-9(7))* Montemayor Pr.

Wilson, Budge. A Fiddle for Angus. Tooke, Susan, illus. 2006. (ENG.). 32p. (J). (gr. 1-4). pap. 13.95 *(978-0-88776-785-2(0)*, Tundra Bks.) Tundra Bks. CAN. Dist: Penguin Random Hse. LLC.

Wilson, Diane Lee. Firehorse. (ENG.). 336p. (YA). (gr. 7). 2010. pap. 8.99 *(978-1-4424-0331-4(4))* 2006. (Illus.). 17.99 *(978-1-4169-1551-5(6))* McElderry, Margaret K. Bks. (McElderry, Margaret K. Bks.).

Wilson, Geraline. Billy & Willy Learn to Share. 2012. 24p. pap. 24.95 *(978-1-4626-8135-8(2))* America Star Bks.

Wilson, Jacqueline. Cookie. Sharratt, Nick, illus. 2010. (ENG.). 352p. (J). (gr. 4-7). pap. 11.99 *(978-0-312-64290-7(3)*, 9780312642907) Square Fish.

Wilson, John. Adrift in Time. 2005. (ENG., Illus.). 136p. (J). pap. 9.95 *(978-1-55380-007-1(9))* Ronsdale Pr. CAN. Dist: Literary Pr. Group of Canada.

Wilson, Karma. What's in the Egg, Little Pip? Chapman, Jane, illus. 2010. (ENG.). 40p. (J). (gr. -1-3). 17.99 *(978-1-4169-4204-7(1)*, McElderry, Margaret K. Bks.) McElderry, Margaret K. Bks.

Wilson, Martin. What They Always Tell Us. 2010. (ENG.). 304p. (YA). (gr. 9). pap. 8.99 *(978-0-385-73508-7(1)*, Delacorte Bks. for Young Readers) Random Hse. Children's Bks.

Wilson, N. D. The Chestnut King. 2011. (100 Cupboards Ser.: 3). (ENG., Illus.). 512p. (J). (gr. 3-7). 8.99 *(978-0-375-83886-6(4)*, Yearling) Random Hse. Children's Bks.

—Dandelion Fire. 2009. (100 Cupboards Ser.: 2). (ENG.). 480p. (J). (gr. 3-7). 8.99 *(978-0-375-83884-2(8)*, Yearling) Random Hse. Children's Bks.

—100 Cupboards. 2008. (100 Cupboards Ser.: 1). (ENG.). 320p. (J). (gr. 3-7). 7.99 *(978-0-375-83882-8(1)*, Yearling) Random Hse. Children's Bks.

Wilson, Rosalee. A Mushy Mouse Tale. 2009. 69p. pap. 24.58 *(978-0-557-10084-2(4))* Lulu Pr., Inc.

Wilson, Wayne L. Kate, the Ghost Dog: Coping with the Death of a Pet. Soud, illus. 2009. 48p. (J). (gr. 3-8). 14.95 *(978-1-4338-0554-7(5))*; pap. 9.95 *(978-1-4338-0555-4(3))* American Psychological Assn. (Magination Pr.).

Winfrey, Kerry. Love & Other Alien Experiences. 2017. (ENG.). 272p. (YA). pap. 10.99 *(978-1-250-11952-0(9)*, 9781250119520) Feiwel & Friends.

Wing, Natasha. The Night Before Hanukkah. Wummer, Amy, illus. 2014. (Night Before Ser.). (ENG.). 32p. (J). (gr. -1-k). 4.99 *(978-0-448-48140-1(5)*, Grosset & Dunlap) Penguin Young Readers Group.

—The Night Before Hanukkah. 2014. (Night Before Ser.). lib. bdg. 13.55 *(978-0-606-36160-6(X))* Turtleback Bks.

Wing, Natasha & dePaola, Tomie. The Night Before the Fourth of July. Wummer, Amy, illus. 2015. (Night Before Ser.). (ENG.). 32p. (J). (gr. -1-k). bds. 4.99 *(978-0-448-48712-0(8)*, Grosset & Dunlap) Penguin Young Readers Group.

Winkler, Henry & Oliver, Lin. Barfing in the Backseat: How I Survived My Family Road Trip. Watson, Jesse Joshua, illus.

2007. (Hank Zipzer Ser.: No. 12). 152p. (gr. 4-7). 15.00 *(978-0-7569-8162-4(X))* Perfection Learning Corp.
—Fake Snakes & Weird Wizards. Garrett, Scott, illus. 2015. (Here's Hank Ser.: No. 4). (ENG.). 128p. (J). (gr. 1-3). 5.99 *(978-0-448-48252-1(5)*, Grosset & Dunlap) Penguin Young Readers Group.
—Who Ordered This Baby? Definitely Not Me! Watson, Jesse Joshua & Heitz, Tim, illus. 2007. (Hank Zipzer Ser.: 13). (ENG.). 160p. (J). (gr. 3-7). pap. 5.99 *(978-0-448-44374-4(0)*, Grosset & Dunlap) Penguin Young Readers Group.
Wittlinger, Ellen. Blind Faith. 2007. (ENG.). 304p. (YA). (gr. 7-12). pap. 9.99 *(978-1-4169-4906-0(2)*, Simon & Schuster Bks. For Young Readers) Simon & Schuster Bks. For Young Readers.
—Heart on My Sleeve. 2006. (ENG., Illus.). 240p. (YA). (gr. 7). reprint ed. pap. 10.99 *(978-0-689-84999-2(0)*, Simon & Schuster Bks. For Young Readers) Simon & Schuster Bks. For Young Readers.
—Parrotfish. 2007. (ENG., Illus.). 304p. (YA). (gr. 7-12). 19.99 *(978-1-4169-1622-2(9)*, Simon & Schuster Bks. For Young Readers) Simon & Schuster Bks. For Young Readers.
Wojciechowski, Susan. Beany & the Dreaded Wedding. Natti, Susanna, illus. 2005. (Beany Adventures Ser.). 121p. (J). 13.65 *(978-0-7569-6498-6(9))* Perfection Learning Corp.
Wolf, Elisabeth. Lulu in la la Land. 2013. (Lulu in la la Land Ser.: 1). (ENG.). 272p. (J). (gr. 3-6). pap. 6.99 *(978-1-4022-8504-2(3)*, 9781402285042, Sourcebooks Jabberwocky) Sourcebooks, Inc.
Wolfe, Jaymie Stuart. Family Matters: Thirteen Short Stories. 2011. 126p. (J). pap. *(978-0-8198-2694-7(4))* Pauline Bks. & Media.
Wolk, Lauren. Wolf Hollow. 2016. (ENG.). 304p. (J). (gr. 5-7). 16.99 *(978-1-101-99482-5(7)*, Dutton Books for Young Readers) Penguin Young Readers Group.
Wollman, Jessica. The Chipster's Sister. MacNeil, Chris, illus. 2005. (Penelope Fritter: Super-Sitter Ser.: 1). (ENG.). 128p. (J). (gr. 3-7). pap. 7.99 *(978-1-4169-0089-4(6)*, Simon & Schuster/Paula Wiseman Bks.) Simon & Schuster/Paula Wiseman Bks.
Wolper, Joanna. The Man Who Could Be Santa. 2008. (Illus.). 78p. (J). pap. *(978-0-88092-765-9(8))*; lib. bdg. *(978-0-88092-764-2(X))* Royal Fireworks Publishing Co.
Wong, Janet S. Minn & Jake's Almost Terrible Summer. Côté, Geneviève, illus. 2008. (ENG.). 112p. (J). (gr. 2-5). 15.99 *(978-0-374-34977-6(0)*, 9780374349776, Farrar, Straus & Giroux (BYR)) Farrar, Straus & Giroux.
Wong, Joyce Lee. Seeing Emily. 2005. (ENG., Illus.). 288p. (J). (gr. 7-11). 16.95 *(978-0-8109-5757-2(4)*, Abrams Bks. for Young Readers) Abrams, Inc.
Wood, Amanda. Rainbow. 2009. 208p. pap. 13.50 *(978-1-60860-343-5(1)*, Strategic Bk. Publishing) Strategic Book Publishing & Rights Agency (SBPRA).
Wood, Douglas. Aunt Mary's Rose. Shed, Greg & Pham, LeUyen, illus. 2010. (ENG.). 32p. (J). (gr. -1-3). 16.99 *(978-0-7636-1090-6(9))* Candlewick Pr.
—What Dads Can't Do. 2004. (Illus.). (J). (gr. k-3). spiral bd. *(978-0-616-07247-9(3))* Canadian National Institute for the Blind/Institut National Canadien pour les Aveugles.
Wood, Gail. Lizzie & the Big Lake Mystery. 2015. (Illus.). ix, 93p. (J). pap. *(978-1-57249-416-9(6)*, White Mane Kids) White Mane Publishing Co., Inc.
—Lizzie, Light Feather & the Quarry Bluff Storm. 2015. (Illus.). viii, 88p. (J). pap. *(978-1-57249-415-2(8)*, White Mane Kids) White Mane Publishing Co., Inc.
Wood, Lena. Elijah Creek & the Armor of Gift Set. 2006. 576p. (J). Bks. 1-3. 17.99 *(978-0-7847-1966-4(7))*Bks. 4-6. 17.99 *(978-0-7847-1967-1(5))* Standard Publishing.
Wood, Maryrose. How I Found the Perfect Dress. 2008. (ENG.). 240p. (YA). (gr. 9-18). 11.00 *(978-0-425-21939-3(9)*, Berkley) Penguin Publishing Group.
Woodson, Jacqueline. Feathers. 2007. (ENG.). 128p. (J). (gr. 5-7). 16.99 *(978-0-399-23989-2(8)*, G.P. Putnam's Sons Books for Young Readers) Penguin Young Readers Group.
—If You Come Softly & Behind You. 2010. (ENG.). 352p. (YA). (gr. 7-18). 8.99 *(978-0-14-241918-2(4)*, Puffin Books) Penguin Young Readers Group.
—Miracle's Boys. 2010. (ENG.). 176p. (YA). (gr. 7-18). 8.99 *(978-0-14-241553-5(7)*, Speak) Penguin Young Readers Group.
—Miracle's Boys. unabr. ed. 2004. 192p. (J). (gr. 7-18). pap. 20.00 incl. audio *(978-0-8072-0789-5(6)*, LYA 322 SP, Listening Library) Random Hse. Audio Publishing Group.
—Peace, Locomotion. 2010. (ENG.). 176p. (J). (gr. 5-18). 8.99 *(978-0-14-241512-2(X)*, Puffin Books) Penguin Young Readers Group.
Woolston, Blythe. MARTians. 2015. (ENG.). 224p. (YA). (gr. 7). 16.99 *(978-0-7636-7756-5(6))* Candlewick Pr.
Worley, Rob M. & Warner, Gertrude Chandler. Surprise Island, 1 vol. Dubisch, Michael, illus. 2009. (Boxcar Children Graphic Novels Ser.). (ENG.). 32p. (J). (gr. 2-5). 28.50 *(978-1-60270-587-6(9))* ABDO Publishing Co.
Wright, Barbara. Crow. 2013. (ENG.). 320p. (J). (gr. 5-7). pap. 7.99 *(978-0-375-87367-6(8)*, Yearling) Random Hse. Children's Bks.
Wright, Betty Ren. Crandalls' Castle. 2005. (ENG.). 184p. (YA). (gr. 4-6). tchr. ed. 17.95 *(978-0-8234-1726-1(3))* Holiday Hse., Inc.
Wright, Bil. Putting Makeup on the Fat Boy. (ENG., 240p. (YA). (gr. 7). 2012. Illus.). pap. 9.99 *(978-1-4169-4004-3(9))* 2011. 16.99 *(978-1-4169-3996-2(2))* Simon & Schuster Bks. For Young Readers. (Simon & Schuster Bks. For Young Readers).
Wright, Kiyah. Joshua's Surprise. 2010. 28p. pap. 16.95 *(978-1-4490-8234-5(3))* AuthorHouse.
Wyatt, Leslie J. Poor Is Just a Starting Place. 2005. (ENG.). 192p. (J). (gr. 6-17). 16.95 *(978-0-8234-1884-8(7))* Holiday Hse., Inc.
Wylie, Sarah. All These Lives. 1 vol. 2012. (ENG.). 256p. (YA). (gr. 7-12). 24.99 *(978-0-374-30208-5(1)*, 9780374302085, Farrar, Straus & Giroux (BYR)) Farrar, Straus & Giroux.
Wynne-Jones, Tim. Rex Zero & the End of the World. 2013. (ENG.). 208p. (J). (gr. 3-7). pap. 8.99 *(978-0-312-64460-4(4)*, 9780312644604) Square Fish.
—Rex Zero, King of Nothing. 2013. (ENG.). 240p. (J). (gr. 3-7). pap. 6.99 *(978-0-312-67478-6(3)*, 9780312674786) Square Fish.
—Stephen Fair. (J). pap. 6.95 *(978-0-88899-360-1(9))* Groundwood Bks. CAN. Dist: Publishers Group West (PGW).
Wyss, J. D. The Swiss Family Robinson. Goodwin, William, tr. from GER. 200th rev. anniv. ed. 2004. (ENG., Illus.). 352p. (gr. 12-18). 4.95 *(978-0-451-52961-9(8)*, Signet) Penguin Publishing Group.
Wyss, Johann. The Swiss Family Robinson. 2006. (Illus.). 61p. (J). lib. bdg. 30.77 *(978-1-4242-1334-4(7))* Fitzgerald Bks.
—The Swiss Family Robinson. 2005. pap. 16.95 *(978-1-59818-422-8(9))* Rodgers, Alan Bks.
—Swiss Family Robinson Study Guide. 2003. (Saddleback Classics Ser.). (Illus.). 48p. (J). (gr. 4-7). per. 17.95 *(978-1-56254-532-1(9)*, SP5329) Saddleback Educational Publishing, Inc.
Wyss, Johann David. Swiss Family Robinson. 2008. (Bring the Classics to Life Ser.). (ENG., Illus.). 72p. (gr. 1-12). pap., act. bk. ed. 10.95 *(978-1-55576-049-6(X)*, EDCTR-104B) EDCON Publishing Group.
—The Swiss Family Robinson. McKowen, Scott, illus. 2006. (Sterling Unabridged Classics Ser.). (ENG.). 352p. (J). (gr. 5-7). 14.95 *(978-1-4027-2602-6(3))* Sterling Publishing Co., Inc.
—Swiss Family Robinson. Hunt, Robert, illus. 2006. (Stepping Stone Book(TM) Ser.). (ENG.). 112p. (J). (gr. 1-4). per. 3.99 *(978-0-375-87525-0(5)*, Random Hse. Bks. for Young Readers) Random Hse. Children's Bks.
—Swiss Family Robinson: A Classic Story about Initiative. 2003. (Illus.). 32p. per. 3.95 *(978-0-9747133-3-5(3)*, Values to Live By Classic Stories) Thomas, Frederic Inc.
—Swiss Family Robinson: With a Discussion of Teamwork. Butterfield, Ned, illus. 2003. (Values in Action Illustrated Classics Ser.). 191p. (J). *(978-1-59203-036-1(X))* Learning Challenge, Inc.
Wyss, Johann David, illus. The Swiss Family Robinson. 2004. reprint ed. pap. 1.99 *(978-1-4192-5012-5(4))*; pap. 30.95 *(978-1-4191-5012-8(X))* Kessinger Publishing, LLC.
Wyss, Johann David & Kingston, William Henry Giles. The Swiss Family Robinson: A Translation from the Original German. 2016. (J). pap. *(978-1-5124-2612-0(1))* Lerner Publishing Group.
Yaccarino, Dan. Where the Four Winds Blow. Yaccarino, Dan, illus. 2003. (Illus.). 104p. (J). 17.89 *(978-0-06-623627-8(4)*, Cotler, Joanna Books) HarperCollins Pubs.
Yager, Fred. Sound from a Star: A Novel. 2011. 150p. (YA). 31.95 *(978-1-889262-90-1(0))* Hannacroix Creek Bks., Inc.
Yang, Gene Luen. Level Up. Pham, Thien, illus. 2011. (ENG.). 160p. (YA). (gr. 7). 19.99 *(978-1-59643-714-2(6)*, 9781596437142, First Second Bks.) Roaring Brook Pr.
Yates, Alma J. Sammy's Song: A Novel. 2005. 272p. (J). *(978-1-59156-945-9(1))* Covenant Communications.
Yee, Lisa. The Kidney Hypothetical: or How to Ruin Your Life in Seven Days:Or How to Ruin Your Life in Seven Days. 2015. (ENG.). 272p. (J). (gr. 7). 17.99 *(978-0-545-23094-0(2))* Scholastic, Inc.
—Stanford Wong Flunks Big-Time. 2007. (Apple Signature Edition Ser.). (ENG., Illus.). 320p. (J). (gr. 3-7). per. 6.99 *(978-0-439-62248-6(4)*, Levine, Arthur A. Bks.) Scholastic, Inc.
—Warp Speed. (ENG.). 320p. (J). 2013. (gr. 3-7). pap. 6.99 *(978-0-545-15400-0(6))* 2011. (gr. 4-7). 16.99 *(978-0-545-12276-4(7))* Scholastic, Inc. (Levine, Arthur A. Bks.).
Yee, Paul. The Jade Necklace. Lin, Grace, illus. 2006. 29p. (J). (gr. 4-8). reprint ed. 16.00 *(978-1-4223-5135-2(1))* DIANE Publishing Co.
Yeh, Kat. The Way to Bea. 2017. (ENG.). 352p. (J). (gr. 3-7). 16.99 ***(978-0-316-23667-6(5))*** Little, Brown Bks. for Young Readers.
Yep, Laurence. Bravo, Mia! England, Tamara, ed. Papp, Robert, illus. 2008. (ENG.). 136p. (J). (gr. 3). pap. 6.95 *(978-1-59369-410-4(5))* American Girl Publishing, Inc.
Ylvisaker, Anne. Button Down. (ENG.). 192p. (J). (gr. 3-7). 2013. pap. 6.99 *(978-0-7636-6463-3(4))* 2012. (Illus.). 15.99 *(978-0-7636-5396-5(9))* Candlewick Pr.
—The Luck of the Buttons. 2012. (ENG., Illus.). 240p. (J). (gr. 3-7). pap. 6.99 *(978-0-7636-6061-1(2))* Candlewick Pr.
Yolen, Jane. Curse of the Thirteenth Fey: The True Tale of Sleeping Beauty. 2013. (ENG.). 320p. (J). (gr. 5). pap. 7.99 *(978-0-14-242761-3(6)*, Puffin Books) Penguin Young Readers Group.
Yoon, Salina. Stormy Night. (ENG., Illus.). (J). 2016. 32p. bds. 7.99 *(978-1-68119-165-2(2)*, 9781681191652) 2015. 40p. (gr. -1-1). 14.99 *(978-0-8027-3780-9(3)*, 9780802737809) Bloomsbury Publishing USA. (Bloomsbury USA Childrens).
Young, Amy. Don't Eat the Baby! 2013. (ENG.). 32p. (J). (gr. -1-k). 16.99 *(978-0-670-78513-1(X)*, Viking Books for Young Readers) Penguin Young Readers Group.
Young, Janet Ruth. The Babysitter Murders. 2011. (ENG., Illus.). 336p. (YA). (gr. 9-18). 16.99 *(978-1-4169-5944-1(0)*, Atheneum Bks. for Young Readers) Simon & Schuster Children's Publishing.
—My Beautiful Failure. (ENG., Illus.). 320p. (YA). (gr. 7). 2013. pap. 9.99 *(978-1-4424-8269-2(9))* 2012. 16.99 *(978-1-4169-5489-7(9))* Simon & Schuster Children's Publishing. (Atheneum Bks. for Young Readers).
Young, Jessica. Art-Rageous. Secheret, Jessica, illus. 2015. (Finley Flowers Ser.). (ENG.). 128p. (gr. 2-3). 8.95 *(978-1-4795-5960-2(1)*, Finley Flowers) Picture Window Bks.
Young, Karen Romano. Hundred Percent. 2016. (ENG., Illus.). 256p. (J). (gr. 3-7). 16.99 *(978-1-4521-3890-9(7))* Chronicle Bks. LLC.
Young, Kathy Chase. The Gift. 2005. (Illus.). 32p. (J). pap. 16.99 *(978-0-9768861-0-5(3)*, 1001) Tishomingo Tree Pr., The.
Young, Suzanne. All in Pieces. 2016. (ENG., Illus.). 272p. (YA). (gr. 9). 17.99 *(978-1-4814-1883-6(1)*, Simon Pulse) Simon Pulse.
Yovanoff, Brenna. The Replacement. 2011. (ENG.). 368p. (YA). (gr. 7-18). 8.99 *(978-1-59514-381-5(5)*, Razorbill) Penguin Young Readers Group.
Yue, Gui & Farrow, Clare. Little Leap Forward: A Boy in Beijing. Cann, Helen, illus. 2011. (ENG.). 120p. (J). (gr. 3-6). pap. 12.99 *(978-1-84686-539-8(5))* Barefoot Bks., Inc.
Yue, Guo & Farrow, Clare. Little Leap Forward: A Boy in Beijing. Cann, Helen, illus. 2008. (ENG.). 128p. (YA). (gr. 4-7). 16.99 *(978-1-84686-114-7(4))* Barefoot Bks., Inc.
Yum, Hyewon. This Is Our House. Yum, Hyewon, illus. 2013. (ENG., Illus.). 36p. (J). (gr. -1-2). 16.99 *(978-0-374-37487-7(2)*, 9780374374877, Farrar, Straus & Giroux (BYR)) Farrar, Straus & Giroux.
Zafón, Carlos Ruiz. The Watcher in the Shadows. (ENG.). (YA). (gr. 7-17). 2014. 288p. pap. 10.99 *(978-0-316-04475-2(X))* 2013. 272p. 18.00 *(978-0-316-04476-9(8))* Little, Brown Bks. for Young Readers.
Zamorano, Ana, et al. Let's Eat! Vivas, Julie, illus. 2003. (Avenues Ser.). (ENG.). 32p. (C). (gr. -1 — 1). pap. 8.95 *(978-0-439-06758-4(8)*, SO1095) National Geographic School Publishing, Inc.
Zarr, Sara. How to Save a Life. 2012. (ENG.). 368p. (YA). (gr. 7-17). pap. 10.99 *(978-0-316-03605-4(6))* Little, Brown Bks. for Young Readers.
—The Lucy Variations. 2014. (ENG.). 336p. (YA). (gr. 7-17). pap. 10.00 *(978-0-316-20500-9(1))* Little, Brown Bks. for Young Readers.
—Story of a Girl. 2008. (ENG.). 224p. (YA). (gr. 7-17). per. 10.99 *(978-0-316-01454-0(0))* Little, Brown Bks. for Young Readers.
Zarr, Sara & Altebrando, Tara. Roomies. 2013. (ENG.). 288p. (YA). (gr. 7-17). 18.00 *(978-0-316-21749-1(2))* Little, Brown Bks. for Young Readers.
Zaugg, Sandra L. Secret of the Desert Lights: A Story about Following God's Laws. 2009. (J). pap. 9.99 *(978-0-8163-2294-7(5))* Pacific Pr. Publishing Assn.
Zeitlin, Meredith. Freshman Year & Other Unnatural Disasters. 2013. (ENG.). 288p. (YA). (gr. 7). pap. 8.99 *(978-0-14-242421-6(8)*, Speak) Penguin Young Readers Group.
Zevin, Gabrielle. Because It Is My Blood, 1 vol. 2012. (Birthright Ser.: 2). (ENG.). 368p. (YA). (gr. 7). 17.99 *(978-0-374-38074-8(0)*, 9780374380748, Farrar, Straus & Giroux (BYR)) Farrar, Straus & Giroux.
—Because It Is My Blood. 2013. (Birthright Ser.: 2). (ENG.). 384p. (YA). (gr. 7). pap. 9.99 *(978-1-250-03422-9(1)*, 9781250034229) Square Fish.
—In the Age of Love & Chocolate. 2014. (Birthright Ser.: 3). (ENG.). 320p. (YA). (gr. 7). pap. 10.99 *(978-1-250-05071-7(5)*, 9781250050717) Square Fish.
Zhang, Kat. The Emperor's Riddle. 2017. (ENG., Illus.). 256p. (J). (gr. 3-7). 16.99 ***(978-1-4814-7862-5(1)***, Aladdin) Simon & Schuster Children's Publishing.
Zia, Farhana. Child of Spring, 1 vol. 2016. (ENG., Illus.). 192p. (J). (gr. 3-6). 16.95 *(978-1-56145-904-9(6))* Peachtree Pubs.
—The Garden of My Imaan, 1 vol. 2013. (ENG.). 192p. (J). (gr. 3-5). 15.95 *(978-1-56145-698-7(5))* Peachtree Pubs.
Ziegler, Jennifer. How Not to Be Popular. 2010. (ENG.). 348p. (YA). (gr. 7). mass mkt. 8.99 *(978-0-440-24024-2(7)*, Delacorte Bks. for Young Readers) Random Hse. Children's Bks.
—Revenge of the Angels. 2015. (ENG.). 256p. (J). (gr. 3-7). 16.99 *(978-0-545-83899-3(1)*, Scholastic Pr.) Scholastic, Inc.
Zima, Marjorie H. Meghan's Military Family. 2008. 23p. pap. 24.95 *(978-1-60563-437-1(9))* America Star Bks.
Zink, Michelle. Lies I Told. 2015. (Lies I Told Ser.: 1). (ENG.). 352p. (YA). (gr. 8). 17.99 *(978-0-06-232712-3(7))* HarperCollins Pubs.
Zink, Rui. The Boy Who Did Not Like Television. Dreher, Patrick, tr. from POR. Ramos, Manuel Joao, illus. 2004. (ENG.). 24p. (J). *(978-1-931561-96-9(6))* MacAdam/Cage Publishing, Inc.
Zuppardi, Sam. The Nowhere Box. Zuppardi, Sam, illus. 2013. (ENG., Illus.). 40p. (J). (gr. -1-3). 15.99 *(978-0-7636-6367-4(0))* Candlewick Pr.
Zweibel, Alan. Our Tree Named Steve. Catrow, David & David, Catrow, illus. 2007. (ENG.). 32p. (J). (gr. -1-k). pap. 5.99 *(978-0-14-240743-1(7)*, Puffin Books) Penguin Young Readers Group.
—Our Tree Named Steve. 2007. 16.00 *(978-1-4177-6974-2(2)*, Turtleback) Turtleback Bks.

FAMILY LIFE EDUCATION

Johnson, Leona. Strengthening Family & Self. 2005. 750p. (J). 61.28 *(978-1-59070-495-0(9))* Goodheart-Willcox Pub.
—Strengthening Family & Self: Teaching Package Teacher's Annotated Edition. annot. ed. 845p. (gr. 9-12). tchr. ed. 69.00 *(978-1-59070-123-2(2))* Goodheart-Willcox Pub.
—Strengthening Family & Self: Teaching Package Teacher's Resource Guide. 424p. (gr. 9-12). tchr. ed. 64.00 *(978-1-59070-125-6(9))* Goodheart-Willcox Pub.
—Strengthening Family & Self: Teaching Package Teacher's Resource Portfolio. 460p. (gr. 9-12). tchr. ed. 136.00 *(978-1-59070-126-3(7))* Goodheart-Willcox Pub.

FAMILY PLANNING

see Birth Control

FAMILY RELATIONS

see Domestic Relations

FAMINE

Allan, Tony. The Irish Famine: The Birth of Irish America. 2003. (Point of Impact Ser.). (Illus.). 32p. (J). (gr. 5-7). per. 7.50 *(978-1-4034-4113-3(8))* Heinemann-Raintree.
Brezina, Corona. Disappearing Forests: Deforestation, Desertification, & Drought. 2009. (Extreme Environmental Threats Ser.). (ENG., Illus.). 64p. (J). (gr. 7-12). pap. 12.95 *(978-1-4358-5374-4(1)*, 1291449); (YA). (gr. 5-9). lib. bdg. 31.95 *(978-1-4358-5018-7(1))* Rosen Publishing Group, Inc., The.
Connolly, Sean. Famines & Droughts. 2003. (J). lib. bdg. 27.10 *(978-1-58340-389-1(2))* Black Rabbit Bks.
—Oxfam. 2009. (Global Organizations Ser.). (Illus.). 46p. (J). (gr. 4-7). pap. *(978-1-897563-36-6(1))* Saunders Bk. Co.
Henningfeld, Diane Andrews. Famine. 2009. (Global Viewpoints Ser.). (ENG., Illus.). 224p. (YA). (gr. 10-12). 27.95 *(978-0-7377-4331-9(X)*, LML02109-245286); pap. 40.45 *(978-0-7377-4332-6(8)*, LML02109-245288) Cengage Gale. (Greenhaven Pr., Inc.).
Sherman, Jill. The Irish Potato Famine: A Cause-And-Effect Investigation. 2016. (Cause-And-Effect Disasters Ser.). (ENG., Illus.). 40p. (J). (gr. 4-6). lib. bdg. 30.65 *(978-1-5124-1119-5(1))* Lerner Publishing Group.
Thornton, Jeremy. The Irish Potato Famine: Irish Immigrants Come to America, 1845-1850. 2004. (Primary Sources of Immigration & Migration in America Ser.). (ENG., Illus.). 24p. (gr. 4-8). pap. 9.40 *(978-0-8239-8957-7(7)*, PowerKids Pr.) Rosen Publishing Group, Inc., The.

FANTASTIC FICTION

see Fantasy Fiction

FANTASY

see Fantasy Fiction

FANTASY FICTION

see also Ghost Stories; Science Fiction

A., Vartika. The Secrets of Destiny. 2012. 448p. pap. 23.95 *(978-1-4697-5536-6(X))* iUniverse, Inc.
Aaron, Chester. Home to the Sea 2004. (Illus.). 125p. (YA). (gr. 8-12). per. 10.95 *(978-0-9746481-2-5(4))* Brown Barn Bks.
Abbott, Charles R. Patches & Leif. 2003. pap. 9.00 *(978-0-8059-6077-8(5))* Dorrance Publishing Co., Inc.
Abbott, Ellen Jensen. Watersmeet, 0 vols. 2012. (Watersmeet Ser.: 1). (ENG.). 352p. (YA). (gr. 7-11). pap. 8.99 *(978-0-7614-5992-7(8)*, 9780761459927, Amazon Children's Publishing) Amazon Publishing.
Abbott, Tony. City in the Clouds. Jessell, Tim, illus. 2004. (Secrets of Droon Ser.: No. 4). 88p. 15.00 *(978-0-7569-3930-4(5))* Perfection Learning Corp.
—Flight of the Genie. Jessell, Tim, illus. 2004. (Secrets of Droon Ser.: No. 21). 122p. (J). lib. bdg. 15.38 *(978-1-4242-0314-7(7))* Fitzgerald Bks.
—The Fortress of the Treasure Queen. Merrell, David, illus. 2004. (Secrets of Droon Ser.: No. 23). 115p. (J). lib. bdg. 15.38 *(978-1-4242-0312-3(0))* Fitzgerald Bks.
—The Hidden Stairs & the Magic Carpet. Jessell, Tim, illus. 2004. (Secrets of Droon Ser.: No. 1). 80p. (gr. 2-5). 15.00 *(978-0-7569-3939-7(9))* Perfection Learning Corp.
—The Ice Dragon. Caparó, Antonio Javier, illus. 2012. (Underworlds Ser.: 4). (ENG.). 128p. (J). (gr. 2-5). pap. 4.99 *(978-0-545-30834-2(8)*, Scholastic Paperbacks) Scholastic, Inc.
—In the Ice Caves of Krog. Adams, Gil & Jessell, Tim, illus. 2003. (Secrets of Droon Ser.: No. 20). 114p. (J). (gr. 2-5). 12.65 *(978-0-7569-3940-3(2))* Perfection Learning Corp.
—The Magic Escapes. Jessell, Tim, illus. 2004. (Secrets of Droon Ser.: No. 1). 161p. (gr. 2-5). 16.00 *(978-0-7569-3944-1(5))* Perfection Learning Corp.
—The Moon Scroll. Jessell, Tim, illus. 2004. (Secrets of Droon Ser.: No. 15). 129p. (gr. 2-5). 15.00 *(978-0-7569-3946-5(1))* Perfection Learning Corp.
—The Riddle of Zorfendorf Castle. Merrell, David, illus. 2005. (Secrets of Droon Ser.: No. 25). 124p. (J). lib. bdg. 15.38 *(978-1-4242-0310-9(4))* Fitzgerald Bks.
—The Secrets of Droon Vol. 2: City in the Clouds; The Great Ice Battle; The Sleeping Giant of Goll. 2005. (Secrets of Droon Ser.: Nos. 4-6). 389p. (J). *(978-0-7607-9540-8(1))* Scholastic, Inc.
Abdo Publishing. The Mystical Pencil, 1 vol. 2013. (Mystical Pencil Ser.: 4). (ENG.). 32p. (J). (gr. 3-6). lib. bdg. 114.00 *(978-1-61641-925-7(3)*, Graphic Planet) Magic Wagon.
—Nascar Heroes, 1 vol. 2013. (NASCAR Heroes Ser.: 8). (ENG.). 32p. (J). (gr. 3-9). lib. bdg. 216.56 *(978-1-61783-659-6(1)*, SportsZone) ABDO Publishing Co.
—Skylanders: The Kaos Trap. 2015. (Skylanders: the Kaos Trap Ser.: Vol. 4). (ENG.). 24p. (J). (gr. 2-5). lib. bdg. 96.84 *(978-1-61479-384-7(0))* ABDO Publishing Co.
ABDO Publishing Company Staff. Fairy Realm - 10 Titles. 2007. (Fairy Realm Ser.). (ENG., Illus.). 110p. 256.50 *(978-1-59961-322-2(0))* Spotlight.
Abedi, C. J. Fae. 2013. (Fae Ser.: 1). (ENG.). 348p. pap. 16.99 *(978-1-62681-161-4(X))* Diversion Publishing Corp.
Abner, Jessil. Kingsview Kids Adventures: Internet Friend & Adventure in Africa. 2012. 228p. pap. 16.95 *(978-1-4678-7915-6(0))* AuthorHouse.
Abnett, Dan. Dragon Frontier. 2015. (Dragon Frontier Ser.). (ENG., Illus.). 330p. (J). (gr. 4). pap. 9.99 *(978-0-14-134296-2(X))* Penguin Bks., Ltd. GBR. Dist: Independent Pubs. Group.
Abnett, Dan & Lanning, Andy. Dragon Frontier: Burning Moon. 2nd ed. 2015. (Dragon Frontier Ser.: 2). (ENG.). 352p. (J). (gr. 4). pap. 9.99 *(978-0-14-134298-6(6))* Penguin Bks., Ltd. GBR. Dist: Independent Pubs. Group.
Accardo, Jus. Tremble. 2013. (Denazen Ser.). (ENG.). 352p. (YA). (gr. 9). pap. 9.99 *(978-1-62061-018-3(3)*, 9781620610183) Entangled Publishing, LLC.
Acevedo, Jenny. Ginger's Grand Adventure. 2012. 36p. pap. 24.95 *(978-1-4626-2472-0(3))* America Star Bks.
Achi, Taro. Mamoru the Shadow Protector Volume 1. 2008. (ENG., Illus.). 176p. (YA). pap. 9.95 *(978-1-59796-183-7(3))* DrMaster Pubns. Inc.
Achikeobi-Lewis, Omileye. E. Rainbow Goddess. 2013. 26p. pap. *(978-0-9542066-9-7(X))* Naked Truth Pr.
Adam D. Levine. Knights: Reign of Hellfire. 2010. (ENG.). 184p. 23.95 *(978-1-4401-7614-2(0))*; pap. 13.95 *(978-1-4401-7618-0(3))* iUniverse, Inc.
Adamchuk, Rachelle G. Disappearance: The First Part of Trickery & Honest Deception. 2006. 169p. pap. 16.99 *(978-1-4120-8991-3(3))* Trafford Publishing.
Adams, Ea "Beth". A Tiny Wish Granted: A tiny fairy meets a tiny Troll. 2010. 28p. pap. 13.59 *(978-1-4490-7565-1(7))* AuthorHouse.
Adams, Leon. Dragon Pearls. 2008. 176p. pap. 13.95 *(978-1-4357-0395-7(2))* Lulu Pr., Inc.
—Jewel of Light. 2008. 182p. pap. 14.00 *(978-1-4357-1538-7(1))* Lulu Pr., Inc.
Adams, Leonard. Two Girls & Two Monsters. 2008. 48p. pap. 7.95 *(978-0-557-01456-9(5))* Lulu Pr., Inc.
Adams, "Little John". Legend of the Mono Gnome: A Story from Gnome Hollow. 2013. 32p. pap. 16.95 *(978-1-4497-9816-1(0)*, WestBow Pr.) Author Solutions, Inc.
Adams, Richard. Watership Down. 2005. (ENG., Illus.). 496p. pap. 18.99 *(978-0-7432-7770-9(8)*, Scribner) Scribner.
Adams, Robert. Growing up in Charis. 2007. 48p. per. 16.95 *(978-1-4241-9518-3(7))* PublishAmerica, Inc.
Adams, Sandi. Watch What You Wish: Kajsa Conquers Her World. 2009. 36p. pap. 15.49 *(978-1-4490-3513-6(2))* AuthorHouse.
Adams, W. Royce. The Computer's Nerd. 2004. 136p. (J). pap. 9.95 *(978-0-9712206-4-5(6))* Rairarubia Bks.
—Raid on Rairarubi. 2008. 148p. (gr. 4-7). pap. 10.95 *(978-0-9712206-8-3(9))* Rairarubia Bks.
—Return to Rairarubi. 2008. 148p. (gr. 3-7). pap. 10.95 *(978-0-9712206-7-6(0))* Rairarubia Bks.

E
F
G

—The Ring from Rairarubia. 2003. (Rairarubia Tales Ser.: Bk. 5). (Illus.). 126p. (J). (gr. 5-18). pap. 10.95 *(978-0-9712206-3-8(8))* Rairarubia Bks.

Adlington, L. J. Glittering Eye. 2009. (ENG.). 320p. (J). (gr. 4-6). pap. 8.99 *(978-0-340-95681-6(X))* Hodder & Stoughton GBR. Dist: Hachette Bk. Group.

Adornetto, Alexandra. Hades. 2011. (Halo Trilogy Ser.: 2). (ENG.). 432p. (J). (gr. 7-12). 17.99 *(978-0-312-65627-0(0))* Feiwel & Friends.

—Hades. 2012. (Halo Trilogy Ser.: 2). (ENG.). 448p. (YA). (gr. 7-12). pap. 10.99 *(978-1-250-01030-8(6))* Square Fish.

—HADES. 2011. (SPA.). 360p. (YA). pap. 21.95 *(978-84-9918-290-2(9))* Roca Editorial ESP. Dist: Spanish Pubs., LLC.

—Heaven. 2013. (Halo Trilogy Ser.: 3). (ENG.). 448p. (YA). (gr. 7-12). pap. 10.99 *(978-1-250-02941-6(4)*, 9781250029416) Square Fish.

Adrien, Gilles & Broders, Alain. The Planet of the Giant. Élyum Studio, illus. 2013. (Little Prince Ser.: 9). (ENG.). 56p. (J). (gr. 4-8). lib. bdg. 26.60 *(978-0-7613-8759-6(5)*, Graphic Universe™) Lerner Publishing Group.

Aesop. The Aesop for Children. Winter, Milo, illus. 2013. 236p. pap. 9.97 *(978-1-60386-613-2(2))* Rough Draft Printing.

Affleck, D. S. The Wish. 2014. 312p. pap. *(978-1-910162-31-6(0))* Legend Pr.

Aguirre-Sacasa, Roberto. Wolf at the Door. 2004. (Fantastic Four Ser.: Vol. 1). (Illus.). 168p. (YA). pap. 16.99 *(978-0-7851-1471-0(8))* Marvel Worldwide, Inc.

Ahdieh, Renée. Flame in the Mist. 2017. (ENG.). 416p. (YA). (gr. 7). 17.99 *(978-0-399-17163-5(0)*, G.P. Putnam's Sons Books for Young Readers) Penguin Young Readers Group.

—The Rose & the Dagger. (Wrath & the Dawn Ser.). (ENG., Illus.). (YA). (gr. 7). 2017. 448p. pap. 10.99 *(978-0-14-751386-1(3)*, Speak) 2016. 432p. 17.99 *(978-0-399-17162-8(2)*, G.P. Putnam's Sons Books for Young Readers) Penguin Young Readers Group.

—The Rose & the Dagger. 2017. (Wrath & the Dawn Ser.: 2). lib. bdg. 22.10 ***(978-0-606-40106-7(7))*** Turtleback Bks.

Ahiers, Sarah. Assassin's Heart. 2016. 432p. (YA). (gr. 9). 17.99 *(978-0-06-236378-7(6)*, HarperTeen) HarperCollins Pubs.

Ahmad, M. I. Aldebaram. 2009. 95p. pap. 13.00 *(978-0-557-08323-7(0))* Lulu Pr., Inc.

Aikins, Dave, illus. Big Sister Dora! 2005. (Dora the Explorer Ser.). (ENG.). 24p. (J). pap. 3.99 *(978-0-689-87846-6(X)*, Simon Spotlight/Nickelodeon) Simon Spotlight/Nickelodeon.

Ailes, Mark Cusco. The Tree of No Boundaries: Book One. 2009. 196p. pap. 14.95 *(978-0-595-52834-9(1))* iUniverse, Inc.

Aira, Luis. Somewhere. 2011. 130p. pap. 14.00 *(978-0-557-18746-1(X))* Lulu Pr., Inc.

Akainy, Boma. Angel Legn. 2011. 28p. pap. 15.99 *(978-1-4628-8214-4(5))* Xlibris Corp.

Akatsuki, Natsume. God's Blessing on This Wonderful World! You are Being Summoned Darkness. Mishima, Kurone, illus. 2017. (Konosuba (light Novel) Ser.: 3). (ENG.). 192p. (YA). (gr. 8-17). pap. 14.00 ***(978-0-316-46873-2(8)***, Yen Pr.) Orbit.

Akatsuki, Natsume & Steinbach, Kevin. Konosuba, God's Blessing on This Wonderful World! Mishima, Kurone, illus. 2017. (YA). ***(978-0-316-46880-0(0))***; ***(978-0-316-46885-5(1))***; ***(978-0-316-46882-4(7))*** Yen Pr. LLC.

Akihiro. Light of Love, Forever. 2009. 76p. pap. 8.99 *(978-0-557-03693-6(3))* Lulu Pr., Inc.

Akira, Shouko. Times Two. Akira, Shouko, illus. 2005. (Times Two Ser.). (ENG., Illus.). 200p. (YA). pap. 9.99 *(978-1-59116-736-5(1))* Viz Media.

Akita, Yoshinobu. Orphen, Vol. 4. 2006. (Orphen Ser.). (Illus.). 168p. (YA). pap. 9.99 *(978-1-4139-0269-3(3))* ADV Manga.

Akley, Jason. The Candlestick. 2007. 40p. per. 17.95 *(978-1-4327-0312-7(9))* Outskirts Pr., Inc.

Alberti, Robert. Mitlanyal: The Gods of Stability, Vol. 1. 10th ed. 2004. (Illus.). 152p. (YA). pap. 19.95 *(978-0-9725880-2-7(7)*, mit1) Zottola Publishing, Inc.

—Mitlanyal: The Gods of Change, Vol. 2. 10th ed. 2004. (Illus.). 184p. (YA). pap. 19.95 *(978-0-9725880-3-4(5)*, mit2) Zottola Publishing, Inc.

Albright, David Edward. The Journals of Aiden Hunter: The Marakata Shard. Haight, Joelle, illus. 2012. 262p. 24.99 *(978-0-9858325-0-6(9))* Storm Leaf.

Aldrich, Sandra D. Danny Dolphin. 2012. 30p. 19.95 *(978-1-4626-6594-5(2))* America Star Bks.

Alerson, Sue Ann, et al. Time for Flowers Time for Snow, 1 vol. 2013. (ENG., Illus.). 54p. (J). (gr. k-5). 18.95 *(978-1-896580-26-5(2))* Tradewind Bks. CAN. Dist: Orca Bk. Pubs. USA.

Alexander, Alma. Gift of the Unmage. 2007. (Worldweavers Ser.: Bk. 1). (ENG.). 400p. (YA). (gr. 7-12). 16.99 *(978-0-06-083955-0(4))* HarperCollins Pubs.

—Spellspam. 2008. (Worldweavers Ser.: Bk. 2). (YA). (gr. 7-18). (ENG.). 448p. 17.99 *(978-0-06-083958-1(9))*; 437p. lib. bdg. 18.89 *(978-0-06-083959-8(7))* HarperCollins Pubs. (Eos).

Alexander, Jason, illus. Alice's Adventures in Wonderland. 2009. (ENG.). 12p. (J). 8.95 *(978-1-58117-855-5(7)*, Intervisual/Piggy Toes) Bendon, Inc.

Alexander, Lloyd. The Arkadians. 272p. (YA). (gr. 5-18). pap. 4.99 *(978-0-8072-1527-2(9)*, Listening Library) Random Hse. Audio Publishing Group.

—The Black Cauldron. 2006. (Chronicles of Prydain: Bk. 2). (Illus.). 182p. (gr. 3-7). 17.00 *(978-0-7569-6813-7(5))* Perfection Learning Corp.

—The Black Cauldron. 2004. (Chronicles of Prydain: Bk. 2). 240p. (J). (gr. 4-7). pap. 38.00 incl. audio *(978-1-4000-8636-8(1)*, Listening Library) Random Hse. Audio Publishing Group.

—The Black Cauldron. Wyatt, David, illus. 2nd rev. ed. 2006. (Chronicles of Prydain Ser.: 2). (ENG.). 208p. (J). (gr. 3-7). pap. 7.99 *(978-0-8050-8049-0(X)*, 9780805080490) Square Fish.

—The Book of Three. Wyatt, David, illus. 2006. (Chronicles of Prydain Ser.: 1). (ENG.). 224p. (J). (gr. 3-7). pap. 7.99 *(978-0-8050-8048-3(1)*, 9780805080483) Square Fish.

—The Castle of Llyr. 2004. (Chronicles of Prydain: Bk. 3). 208p. (J). (gr. 4-7). pap. 36.00 incl. audio *(978-1-4000-9019-8(9)*, Listening Library) Random Hse. Audio Publishing Group.

—The Castle of Llyr. Wyatt, David, illus. 3rd rev. ed. 2006. (Chronicles of Prydain Ser.: 3). (ENG.). 208p. (J). (gr. 3-7). pap. 6.99 *(978-0-8050-8050-6(3)*, 9780805080506) Square Fish.

—The Foundling: And Other Tales of Prydain. Wyatt, David, illus. 6th rev. ed. 2006. (Chronicles of Prydain Ser.: 6). (ENG.). 112p. (J). (gr. 3-7). pap. 6.99 *(978-0-8050-8053-7(8)*, 9780805080537) Square Fish.

—The High King. 2006. (Chronicles of Prydain: Bk. 5). (Illus.). 253p. (gr. 3-7). 17.00 *(978-0-7569-6816-8(X))* Perfection Learning Corp.

—The High King. Wyatt, David, illus. 5th rev. ed. 2006. (Chronicles of Prydain Ser.: 5). (ENG.). 272p. (J). (gr. 3-7). pap. 7.99 *(978-0-8050-8052-0(X)*, 9780805080520) Square Fish.

—The Remarkable Journey of Prince Jen. 2004. (ENG., Illus.). 288p. (J). (gr. 3-7). 6.99 *(978-0-14-240225-2(7)*, Puffin Books) Penguin Young Readers Group.

—Taran Wanderer. 2006. (Chronicles of Prydain: Bk. 4). 222p. (gr. 3-7). 17.00 *(978-0-7569-6815-1(1))* Perfection Learning Corp.

—Taran Wanderer. Wyatt, David, illus. 4th rev. ed. 2006. (Chronicles of Prydain Ser.: 4). (ENG.). 256p. (J). (gr. 3-7). pap. 6.99 *(978-0-8050-8051-3(1)*, 9780805080513) Square Fish.

Alexander, Lloyd, et al. Firebirds: An Anthology of Original Fantasy & Science Fiction. Sharyn, November, ed. Vess, Charles, illus. 2005. (ENG.). 432p. (YA). (gr. 7-11). 9.99 *(978-0-14-240320-4(2)*, Firebird) Penguin Young Readers Group.

Alexander, Lyndi. Windmills. 2013. 248p. (J). pap. 14.99 *(978-1-61271-226-0(6))* Zumaya Pubns. LLC.

Alexander, William. Ghoulish Song. (ENG., Illus.). (J). (gr. 3-7). 2014. 192p. pap. 6.99 *(978-1-4424-2730-3(2))* 2013. 176p. 16.99 *(978-1-4424-2729-7(9))* McElderry, Margaret K. Bks. (McElderry, Margaret K. Bks.).

—Goblin Secrets. (ENG., Illus.). (J). (gr. 3-7). 2013. 256p. pap. 7.99 *(978-1-4424-2727-3(2))* 2012. 240p. 16.99 *(978-1-4424-2726-6(4))* McElderry, Margaret K. Bks. (McElderry, Margaret K. Bks.).

Alice in Wonderland. 2003. (Illus.). 288p. (J). 9.98 *(978-1-4054-1674-0(2))* Parragon, Inc.

Allem, Jolyia. The Maiden & the Prince: A Tale of Devotion. 2009. 16p. pap. 8.75 *(978-1-4490-2350-8(9))* AuthorHouse.

Allen, Becky. Bound by Blood & Sand. 2016. (ENG.). 320p. (YA). (gr. 9). 17.99 *(978-1-101-93214-8(7)*, Delacorte Pr.) Random Hse. Children's Bks.

Allen, Dan. Fall of the Dragon Prince. 2017. (Forgotten Heirs Trilogy Ser.). (ENG.). 378p. (YA). (gr. 8). pap. 17.99 *(978-1-63163-086-6(5)*, Jolly Fish Pr.) North Star Editions.

Allen, Skye. The Songbird Thief. 2016. (Oaktown Fey Ser.). (ENG., Illus.). (YA). pap. 14.99 ***(978-1-63477-003-3(X)***, Harmony Ink Pr.) Dreamspinner Pr.

Allen, Traudi. The Knife & the Fork Go Dancing. 2012. 36p. pap. 16.95 *(978-1-4525-0447-6(4))* Balboa Pr.

Allen, Will. Swords for Hire: Two of the Most Unlikely Heroes You'll Ever Meet. Beck, David Michael, illus. 2003. 168p. (gr. 3-18). pap. 6.95 *(978-0-9724882-0-4(0))* Centerpunch Pr.

Allende, Isabel. Kingdom of the Golden Dragon. Peden, Margaret Sayers, tr. from SPA. 2005. (City of the Beasts Ser.: Bk. 2).Tr. of Reino del Dragón de Oro. (ENG.). 464p. (J). (gr. 5-12). pap. 10.99 *(978-0-06-058944-8(2)*, Rayo) HarperCollins Pubs.

Allison, Joseph. Petal Peel & the Ghost Dragon. 2013. 154p. pap. 12.50 *(978-1-62857-198-1(5)*, Strategic Bk. Publishing) Strategic Book Publishing & Rights Agency (SBPRA).

Alloway, Kit. Dream Forever: A Novel. 2017. (Dream Walker Trilogy Ser.). (ENG.). 320p. (YA). pap. 19.99 *(978-1-250-00125-2(0)*, 9781250001252, St. Martin's Griffin) St. Martin's Pr.

—Dreamfire. 2015. (Dream Walker Trilogy Ser.: 1). (ENG.). 368p. (YA). (gr. 8-12). 18.99 *(978-1-250-06366-3(3)*, 9781250063663, St. Martin's Griffin) St. Martin's Pr.

—Dreamworld: Two Books in One: Dreamfire & Dreamfever. 2017. (Dream Walker Trilogy Ser.: 3). (ENG.). 704p. (YA). pap. 14.99 *(978-1-250-12251-3(1)*, 9781250122513, St. Martin's Griffin) St. Martin's Pr.

Almand, M. Nicholas. Orphan Blade. 2014. (ENG., Illus.). 160p. (YA). pap. 19.99 *(978-1-62010-120-9(3)*, 9781620101209) Oni Pr., Inc.

Almeida, Jose-Gabriel. Lodiville: Adventure Land. 2008. 52p. pap. 16.95 *(978-1-60563-989-5(3))* America Star Bks.

Almhjell, Tone. Thornghost. 2016. (ENG., Illus.). 368p. (J). (gr. 5). 16.99 *(978-0-8037-3897-3(8)*, Dial Bks) Penguin Young Readers Group.

—The Twistrose Key. Schoenherr, Ian, illus. 2014. (ENG.). 384p. (J). (gr. 5). pap. 8.99 *(978-0-14-242345-5(9)*, Puffin Books) Penguin Young Readers Group.

Alonso, Fernando & Fernando, Alonso. La Historia de un Hombrecillo de Papel. (Leer Es Vivir Serie Teatro). (SPA.). 96p. (J). (gr. 3-5). 6.36 *(978-84-241-7711-9(8))* Everest Editora ESP. Dist: Lectorum Pubns., Inc.

Alonso, Manuel L. Extrano, Muy Extrano. Schubert, Karin, illus. 2003. (SPA.). 124p. (J). (gr. 3-5). pap. 10.95 *(978-84-204-4906-7(7))* Santillana USA Publishing Co., Inc.

Alpha Blox. (J). pap. 9.95 *(978-1-886647-07-7(0))* ALPI International, Ltd.

Alston, E. B. The Last Voyage of the Dan-D. Garrett, Toni, illus. l.t. ed. 2003. 47p. (J). per. 8.00 *(978-0-9747735-0-6(6))* Righter Publishing Co., Inc.

Aluris: The Book of Annua, 1, 4. 2006. (Illus.). 320p. (YA). per. 20.00 *(978-0-9786177-0-7(3))* Michalek, Curtis.

Alva, Kristian. The Balborite Curse: Book Four of the Dragon Stones Saga. 2013. 240p. pap. 9.98 *(978-1-937361-11-2(X)*, Defiant Pr.) Passkey Pubns.

Alvarado, I. J. The Adventures of Saleiah & Emm: Book 1. Zacker, Sandi, illus. 2009. 16p. pap. 11.99 *(978-1-4490-0515-3(2))* AuthorHouse.

Alvarez, Jennifer Lynn. The Guardian Herd: Windborn. McClellan, David, illus. 2017. (Guardian Herd Ser.: 4). 432p. (J). (gr. 3-7). pap. 6.99 ***(978-0-06-228616-1(1))*** HarperCollins Pubs.

—Landfall. 2016. (Guardian Herd Ser.: 3). (Illus.). 352p. (J). (gr. 3-7). 16.99 *(978-0-06-228612-3(9))* HarperCollins Pubs.

—Landfall. 2016. (Guardian Herd Ser.: 3). (J). lib. bdg. 17.20 ***(978-0-606-40049-7(4))*** Turtleback Bks.

—The Pet Washer. 2nd ed. 2012. (ENG.). 171p. (J). (gr. 3-7). pap. 8.99 *(978-0-9848484-5-4(2))* Dreamcatcher Bks.

—Starfire. (Guardian Herd Ser.: 1). (ENG., Illus.). (J). (gr. 3-7). 2015. 320p. pap. 6.99 *(978-0-06-228607-9(2))* 2014. 272p. 16.99 *(978-0-06-228606-2(4))* HarperCollins Pubs.

—Starfire. 2015. (Guardian Herd Ser.: 1). (J). lib. bdg. 17.20 *(978-0-606-36951-0(1))* Turtleback Bks.

—Stormbound. McClellan, David, illus. (Guardian Herd Ser.: 2). (J). (gr. 3-7). 2016. 368p. pap. 6.99 *(978-0-06-228610-9(2))* 2015. (ENG.). 320p. 16.99 *(978-0-06-228609-3(9))* HarperCollins Pubs.

Amanda Rose. Sara James & the Mermaid Tale. 2009. 160p. pap. 11.99 *(978-1-4389-7247-3(4))* AuthorHouse.

Ambrus, Victor G., illus. The Iliad. 2004. (Kingfisher Epics Ser.). (ENG.). 165p. (YA). (gr. 3-7). pap. 8.99 *(978-0-7534-5722-1(9)*, 9780753457221, Kingfisher) Roaring Brook Pr.

Amin, Ahmed. The Mountains of Kohqaf. 2013. 88p. (gr. 4-6). pap. 11.25 *(978-1-4907-0959-8(2))* Trafford Publishing.

Amirkhan, Michele. Princess Elian's Quest. 2008. 112p. 20.95 *(978-0-595-50870-9(7))*; pap. 10.95 *(978-0-595-51400-7(6))* iUniverse, Inc.

Amma, Jill. The Indaba Tree Odyssey: An African Tale. 2006. 360p. pap. 18.95 *(978-0-7414-3172-1(6))* Infinity Publishing.

Amundson, Sandi. Zach & Dougie Dragonfly's Adventure. 2011. 55p. pap. 23.95 *(978-1-4327-3536-4(5))* Outskirts Pr., Inc.

Ana, Moh. Kookaburra Tales: Shy Not, My Friend. 2013. 16p. pap. 17.03 *(978-1-4669-3193-0(0))* Trafford Publishing.

Anders, Lou. Nightborn. 2015. (Thrones & Bones Ser.). (ENG.). 368p. (J). (gr. 3-7). 16.99 *(978-0-385-39036-1(X)*, Crown Books For Young Readers) Random Hse. Children's Bks.

Anders, Lou. Skyborn. (Thrones & Bones Ser.: 3). (ENG., Illus.). (J). (gr. 3-7). 2017. 400p. 7.99 ***(978-0-385-39043-9(2)***, Yearling) 2016. 384p. 16.99 *(978-0-385-39040-8(8)*, Crown Books For Young Readers) Random Hse. Children's Bks.

Andersen, Alan Lance. Wizard Academies - Rumpots, Crackpots, & Pooka-Mazed Halfwits. 2008. 174p. pap. 19.96 *(978-0-615-18594-1(0))* Wizard Academies, LLC.

Andersen, Hans Christian. Fairy Tales of Hans Christian Andersen. 2011. 892p. pap. 19.99 *(978-1-61382-020-9(8))* Simon & Brown.

—The Wild Swans & Other Tales. 2012. (Fairy Tales of Hans Christian Andersen Ser.). (ENG.). 152p. pap. 19.99 *(978-1-909438-12-5(X)*, Sovereign) Bollinger, Max GBR. Dist: Lightning Source UK, Ltd.

Andersen, Hans Christian & Capstone Press Staff. Caperucita Roja. Rivas, Victor, illus. 2010. (Graphic Spin en Español Ser.). (SPA.). 40p. (gr. 1-3). lib. bdg. 25.32 *(978-1-4342-1903-9(8)*, Graphic Spin en Español) Stone Arch Bks.

—Cenicienta. Feely, Maria Luisa, tr. Timmins, Jeffrey Stewart, illus. 2010. (Graphic Spin en Español Ser.). (SPA.). 40p. (gr. 1-3). lib. bdg. 25.32 *(978-1-4342-1900-8(3)*, Graphic Spin en Español) Stone Arch Bks.

Andersen, Hans Christian & Fowler, Gloria. The Red Shoes. Yung Yoo, Sun, illus. 2008. (ENG.). 32p. (J). (gr. -1-3). 16.95 *(978-1-934429-06-8(6))* AMMO Bks., LLC.

Andersen, Hans Christian & Stone Arch Books Staff. Caperucita Roja. Rivas, Victor, illus. 2010. (Graphic Spin en Español Ser.). (SPA & ENG.). 40p. (gr. 1-3). pap. 5.95 *(978-1-4342-2315-9(9)*, Graphic Spin en Español) Stone Arch Bks.

—Cenicienta: La Novela Grafica. Timmins, Jeffrey Stewart, illus. 2010. (Graphic Spin en Español Ser.). (SPA & ENG.). 40p. (gr. 1-3). pap. 5.95 *(978-1-4342-2270-1(5)*, Graphic Spin en Español) Stone Arch Bks.

Andersen, Hans Christian & Tatar, Maria. Hans Christian Andersen. Allen, Julie K., tr. from DAN. 2007. (ENG., Illus.). 496p. 39.95 *(978-0-393-06081-2(0)*, 6081) Norton, W. W. & Co., Inc.

Anderson, Clay. Mary Margaret Hammersmith & the Lady of the Roundtable, 1 vol. 2009. 134p. pap. 24.95 *(978-1-4489-1892-8(8))* America Star Bks.

Anderson, Holli. Five: Out of the Dark. 2013. 250p. (YA). pap. 15.99 *(978-1-62007-299-8(8))* Curiosity Quills Pr.

Anderson, Jodi Lynn. Among the Stars. 2014. (May Bird Ser.: 2). (ENG., Illus.). 304p. (J). (gr. 3-7). 17.99 *(978-1-4424-9579-1(0)*, Simon & Schuster/Paula Wiseman Bks.) Simon & Schuster/Paula Wiseman Bks.

—The Ever After. 2014. (May Bird Ser.: 1). (ENG., Illus.). 368p. (J). (gr. 3-7). pap. 7.99 *(978-1-4424-9576-0(6)*, Aladdin) Simon & Schuster Children's Publishing.

—The May Bird Trilogy: The Ever after; among the Stars; Warrior Princess. 2014. (May Bird Ser.). (ENG., Illus.). 960p. (J). (gr. 3-7). pap. 22.99 *(978-1-4814-1673-3(1)*, Aladdin) Simon & Schuster Children's Publishing.

—Warrior Princess. 2014. (May Bird Ser.: 3). (ENG., Illus.). 288p. (J). (gr. 3-7). pap. 6.99 *(978-1-4424-9580-7(4)*, Aladdin) Simon & Schuster Children's Publishing.

Anderson, John David. The Dungeoneers. 2015. (ENG.). 448p. (J). (gr. 3-7). 16.99 *(978-0-06-233814-3(5)*, Waldon Pond Pr.) HarperCollins Pubs.

Anderson, Leone Castell. Sean's Quest. Welch, Sheila Kelly, illus. 2003. 162p. (J). 16.95 *(978-0-9638819-6-0(5))*; pap. 10.95 *(978-0-9638819-7-7(3))* ShadowPlay Pr.

Anderson, Matt & Hutchins, Eric. White Picket Fences: Red Scare TP: Red Scare TP. 2011. (Illus.). 104p. (J). pap. 12.99 *(978-1-934944-30-1(0))* Ape Entertainment.

Anderson, Matt & Lambert, Chad. Kung Fu Panda Vol. 2: It's Elemental & Other Stories. 2012. (ENG., Illus.). 24p. pap., pap. 6.95 *(978-1-936340-56-9(9)*, 9781936340569) Ape Entertainment.

Anderson, Paris. The Sisters Kennington. 2004. 140p. (J). per. 16.00 *(978-1-58982-195-8(5)*, Millennial Mind Publishing) American Bk. Publishing Group.

Anderson, R. J. A Pocket Full of Murder. 2015. (ENG., Illus.). 352p. (J). (gr. 4-7). 18.99 *(978-1-4814-3771-4(2))* Simon & Schuster Children's Publishing.

—Wayfarer. 2010. (ENG.). 304p. (J). (gr. 8-18). 16.99 *(978-0-06-155477-3(4)*, HarperTeen) HarperCollins Pubs.

Anderson, Robert L. Dreamland. 2015. (ENG.). 336p. (YA). (gr. 9). 17.99 *(978-0-06-233867-9(6)*, HarperTeen) HarperCollins Pubs.

Anderson, Scoular. Bubble Trouble. Anderson, Scoular, illus. 2010. (Wizzbang Wizard Ser.: 2). (ENG., Illus.). 96p. (J). (gr. 2-4). pap. 5.99 *(978-0-00-719006-5(9))* HarperCollins Pubs. Ltd. GBR. Dist: HarperCollins Pubs.

—Super Slosh. Anderson, Scoular, illus. 2011. (Wizzbang Wizard Ser.: 1). (ENG., Illus.). 96p. (J). (gr. 2-4). pap. 5.99 *(978-0-00-719005-8(0))* HarperCollins Pubs. Ltd. GBR. Dist: HarperCollins Pubs.

Anderson, Trey. Jesse & Midnight. 2007. 56p. per. 16.95 *(978-1-60474-062-2(0))* America Star Bks.

Andre Norton. 2010. (Who Wrote That? Ser.). (Illus.). 128p. (gr. 6-12). 35.00 *(978-1-60413-682-1(0)*, Chelsea Hse.) Facts On File, Inc.

Andrews, D. M. The Serpent in the Glass. 2012. 234p. pap. *(978-1-78176-773-3(4))* FeedARead.com.

Andrews, Julie & Edwards, Julie Andrews. The Last of the Really Great Whangdoodles. 2003. (J). (gr. 3-6). 17.20 *(978-0-8335-6918-9(X)*, Turtleback) Turtleback Bks.

Andrisano, Micheal. Harold the High Knight & Princess Megan: Harold & Megan. 2013. (ENG.). 221p. (YA). pap. 16.95 *(978-1-4327-9451-4(5))* Outskirts Pr., Inc.

Anfuso, Dennis & Lindsay, Alan. Oz House. 2012. (ENG.). 321p. pap. 19.95 *(978-1-57433-041-0(1))* Interset Pr.

Angelini, Josephine. Dreamless. 2012. (Starcrossed Trilogy Ser.: 2). (ENG.). 496p. (YA). (gr. 8). 17.99 *(978-0-06-201201-2(0)*, HarperTeen) HarperCollins Pubs.

Angelique, Aj. Lady Cy. 2011. 108p. pap. 7.95 *(978-1-4583-5494-5(6))* Lulu Pr., Inc.

Angelo, Linda. The Three Secrets of Happiness. 2012. (ENG.). 31p. (J). pap. 14.95 *(978-1-4327-9349-4(7))* Outskirts Pr., Inc.

Anna. The Magic Money Tree. 2009. (Illus.). 20p. pap. 15.49 *(978-1-4389-0472-6(X))* AuthorHouse.

Anna, Jennifer. Year of the Dragon. 2nd ed. 2007. (Illus.). 56p. (J). pap. 24.99 *(978-1-59092-155-5(0))* Blue Forge Pr.

Anthony, David & David, Charles. Knightscares #1 No. 1: (Knightscares): Cauldron Cooker's Night. 2003. (Knightscares Ser.: Vol. 1). (Illus.). 200p. (J). per. 5.99 *(978-0-9728461-0-3(7))* Sigil Publishing.

—Knightscares #4: (Knightscares) 2004. (Illus.). 208p. (J). per. 5.99 *(978-0-9728461-3-4(1))* Sigil Publishing.

Anthony, Piers. Key to Chroma. 2003. (ChroMagic Ser.: Bk. 2). 550p. (J). 34.99 *(978-1-59426-017-9(6))*; 554p. per. 22.50 *(978-1-59426-018-6(4))* Mundania Pr.

—Key to Havoc. 2003. (ChroMagic Ser.: Bk. 1). (ENG.). 496p. 29.00 *(978-0-9723670-7-3(1)*, khhb01, Mundania Pr.) Mundania Pr.

—Pandora Park. 2013. (ENG.). 120p. pap. 9.99 *(978-1-62467-203-3(5)*, 9781624672033) Open Road Integrated Media, Inc.

Anton, Robert & Marie, Madeline. Flames of Fortune: Dragonia, Tales of the Golden Talon, 1 bk. 2004. (Illus.). 308p. (YA). per. 19.95 *(978-0-9742460-2-4(6))* Timtu Ink.

—The Hope for Zargahn: Dragonia, Tales of the Golden Talon. 2004. (Illus.). 308p. (YA). per. 19.95 *(978-0-9742460-3-1(4))* Timtu Ink.

Anton, Robert Wayne & Anton, Madeline Marie. A Portal in the Storm: Dragonia, Tales of the Golden Talon. 2004. (Illus.). 350p. (YA). per. 19.95 *(978-0-9742460-1-7(8))* Timtu Ink.

Anzai, Nobuyuki & Caselman, Lance. Flame of Recca. Anzai, Nobuyuki, illus. (Flame of Recca Ser.: 19). (ENG., Illus.). 2006. 208p. pap. 9.99 *(978-1-4215-0455-1(3))* 2006. 208p. pap. 9.99 *(978-1-4215-0454-4(5))* 2006. 208p. pap. 9.99 *(978-1-4215-0250-2(X))* 2005. 200p. pap. 9.99 *(978-1-4215-0131-4(7))* Vol. 14. 2005. 184p. pap. 9.99 *(978-1-4215-0014-0(0))* Vol. 17. 2006. 208p. pap. 9.99 *(978-1-4215-0381-3(6))* Viz Media.

Appel, Julie & Guglielmo, Amy. Find King Henry's Treasure. 2010. (Touch the Art Ser.). (ENG., Illus.). 24p. (J). (gr. -1-1). bds. 12.95 *(978-1-4027-6324-3(7))* Sterling Publishing Co., Inc.

Applegate, K. A., pseud. Animorphs #7: the Stranger. 2012. (Animorphs Ser.: 7). (ENG.). 176p. (J). (gr. 3-7). pap. 6.99 *(978-0-545-42414-1(3)*, Scholastic Paperbacks) Scholastic, Inc.

—The Message. 2011. (Animorphs Ser.: 4). (ENG.). 192p. (J). (gr. 3-7). pap. 6.99 *(978-0-545-29156-9(9)*, Scholastic Paperbacks) Scholastic, Inc.

—The Predator. 2011. (Animorphs Ser.: 5). (ENG.). 160p. (J). (gr. 3-7). pap. 6.99 *(978-0-545-29157-6(7)*, Scholastic Paperbacks) Scholastic, Inc.

Applegate, Katherine. Crenshaw. 2015. (ENG.). 256p. (J). (gr. 5-9). 16.99 *(978-1-250-04323-8(9)*, 9781250043238) Feiwel & Friends.

—Crenshaw. 2017. (ENG.). 272p. (J). pap. 7.99 ***(978-1-250-09166-6(7)***, 9781250091666) Square Fish.

—Crenshaw. 2017. (J). lib. bdg. 18.40 ***(978-0-606-40539-3(9))*** Turtleback Bks.

—Crenshaw. 2016. (SPA.). 192p. (J). (gr. 5-8). pap. 13.99 *(978-987-747-067-3(5))* V&R Editoras.

—The Stranger. 2012. (Animorphs Ser.: 7). lib. bdg. 17.20 *(978-0-606-26195-1(8)*, Turtleback) Turtleback Bks.

Applequist, Frances. Fangs, Claws, & Camouflage: Zombie Problems. 2016. (ENG., Illus.). (YA). 18.95 ***(978-1-5069-0242-5(1))***; pap. 14.95 ***(978-1-5069-0241-8(3))*** First Edition Design eBook Publishing.

Appleton, Nancy. The Rescue: Cecelia's Story. 2012. 24p. 24.95 *(978-1-4626-6713-0(9))* America Star Bks.

Appleton-Smith, Laura. Oh My, It Must Be the Sky! Neel, Preston, illus. 2004. (Book to Remember Ser.). (ENG.). 52p. pap. 8.95 *(978-1-929262-21-2(3)*, Books To Remember) Flyleaf Publishing.

Appleton, Victor. Tom Swift & His Electric Rifle. 2004. (J). 21.95 *(978-0-8488-2725-0(2))* Amereon Ltd.

Arakawa, Hiromu. Fullmetal Alchemist (3-in-1 Edition), Vol. 7, 3 in 1. 7th ed. 2014. (ENG., Illus.). 568p. pap. 14.99 *(978-1-4215-5494-5(1))* Viz Media.

—Fullmetal Alchemist, Vol. 26. Arakawa, Hiromu, illus. 2011. (ENG., Illus.). 193p. pap. 9.99 *(978-1-4215-3962-1(4))* Viz Media.

Aranha, Marc. The Queen of Spiders. 2003. 210p. pap. 14.95 *(978-0-595-29275-2(5))* iUniverse, Inc.

Arbuthnott, Gill. The Chaos Clock, 1 vol. 2003. (Kelpies Ser.). (ENG.). 160p. 10.00 *(978-0-86315-422-5(0))* Floris Bks. GBR. Dist: SteinerBooks, Inc.

—The Keepers' Tattoo. 2010. (ENG.). 432p. (J). (gr. 3-7). 17.99 *(978-0-545-17166-3(0)*, Chicken Hse., The) Scholastic, Inc.

Archer, Chris. Aftershock. 2010. (Mindwarp Ser.: 6). (ENG.). 144p. (YA). (gr. 11). pap. 8.99 *(978-1-4424-1415-0(4)*, Simon Pulse) Simon Pulse.
Archer, E. Geek Fantasy Novel. 2011. (ENG.). 320p. (J). (gr. 7-7). 17.99 *(978-0-545-16040-7(5)*, Scholastic Pr.) Scholastic, Inc.
Arevalo, Luis Paquime. Juan & the Magic Shoes. 2005. (J). per. 3.99 *(978-0-9748598-1-1(8))* L. A. Eng Bks.
Argiento, Cindy. Doris in Dreamland. 2007. pap. 8.00 *(978-0-8059-7461-4(X))* Dorrance Publishing Co., Inc.
Armstrong, K. L. & Marr, M. A. Thor's Serpents. 2016. (Blackwell Pages Ser.: 3). (ENG.). 368p. (J). (gr. 3-7). pap. 8.99 *(978-0-316-20493-4(5))* Little, Brown Bks. for Young Readers.
Armstrong, Kelley. Empire of Night. 2015. (Age of Legends Trilogy Ser.: 2). 432p. (YA). (gr. 8). 17.99 *(978-0-06-207127-9(0))* HarperCollins Pubs.
—Forest of Ruin. 2016. (Age of Legends Trilogy Ser.: 3). 448p. (YA). (gr. 8). 17.99 *(978-0-06-207130-9(0))* HarperCollins Pubs.
—The Reckoning. 2010. (Darkest Powers Ser.: 3). 400p. (YA). (gr. 8-18). 17.99 *(978-0-06-166283-6(6))* HarperCollins Pubs.
—Sea of Shadows. (gr. 8). 2015. (Age of Legends Trilogy Ser.: 1). 432p. (YA). pap. 9.99 *(978-0-06-207125-5(4))* 2014. (Age of Legends Trilogy: Bk. 1). 416p. (J). 17.99 *(978-0-06-207124-8(6))* HarperCollins Pubs.
—Sea of Shadows. 2015. (Age of Legends Ser.: 1). (YA). lib. bdg. 20.85 *(978-0-606-36511-6(7))* Turtleback Bks.
Armstrong, Rachel. Fair Folk in Knob's End. 2013. 274p. pap. 14.99 *(978-1-60820-851-7(6))* MLR Pr., LLC.
Armstrong, Tony. The Water Troll. 2008. (ENG.). 16p. 8.49 *(978-1-4389-1925-6(5))* AuthorHouse.
Arnauld, D. S. Zertelo & the Road of Fire: Book Two. Scott, Sara, ed. 2007. 210p. (J). per. 9.95 *(978-0-9801408-1-1(1))* Heroes & Leaders.
Aronson, Sarah. The Worst Fairy Godmother Ever! 2017. (Wish List Ser.: 1). (ENG.). 176p. (J). (gr. 3-7). 14.99 ***(978-0-545-94151-8(2)***, Scholastic Pr.) Scholastic, Inc.
Arrigan, Mary. Milo & One Dead Angry Druid. Arrigan, Mary, illus. 2014. (Milo Adventures Ser.: 1). (ENG., Illus.). 112p. (J). pap. 12.95 *(978-1-84717-351-5(9))* O'Brien Pr., Ltd., The IRL. Dist: Dufour Editions, Inc.
Arthur, Anne. The Pigeon with the Sticky Stuck Neck. Liebman, Simean, illus. 2004. (J). per. 7.99 *(978-0-9753320-0-9(7))* Riverbank Publishing.
Arthur, Sherry. Magical Hallows Eve. 2009. 44p. pap. 24.00 *(978-0-557-07264-4(6))* Lulu Pr., Inc.
Artz, D. M. Maggie & the Magic Sparkle Seed. 2007. 30p. 16.95 *(978-1-4357-0152-6(6))* Lulu Pr., Inc.
Arvidson, Douglas N. The Eye of the Stallion Bk. 1: The Face in Amber. 2006. 237p. (YA). pap. 14.95 *(978-1-890109-81-3(9)*, Cross Time) Crossquarter Publishing Group.
Asare, Meshack. L' Appel de Sosu (Sosu's Call) Keita, Fatou, tr. 2003. (FRE., Illus.). 37p. pap. *(978-9988-550-48-6(0))* Sub-Saharan Pubs. & Traders GHA. Dist: Michigan State Univ. Pr.
Aschermann, Kurt. Bj & the Amazing Doctor Directions. 2008. 172p. pap. 11.99 *(978-1-4343-7708-1(3))* AuthorHouse.
Ashby, Norman. Magic Fireplace. 2003. (Illus.). 50p. pap. *(978-1-84401-066-0(X))* Athena Pr.
Ashe, Gregory. The Imagineer (Fire Eye Edition) A Book of Miracles. Whittaker, Kay, illus. 3rd ed. 2005. 198p. pap. *(978-1-905532-01-8(6))* Humdrumming, Ltd.
—The Imagineer (Snow Scene Edition) A Book of Miracles. Whittaker, Kay, illus. 2nd ed. 2005. 198p. (YA). pap. *(978-1-905532-00-1(8))* Humdrumming, Ltd.
Ashford, Kathy. Little Grace. 2011. 36p. pap. 24.95 *(978-1-4489-3936-7(4))* America Star Bks.
Ashland, Monk & Ashland, Nigel. The Sky Village, Bk. 1. 2008. (Kaimira Ser.: 1). (ENG., Illus.). 416p. (J). (gr. 5). 17.99 *(978-0-7636-3524-4(3))* Candlewick Pr.
Ashley, John A. The Gathering of the Fairy Horses Series. 2009. 59p. pap. 16.84 *(978-1-4092-0638-5(6))* 2008. 64p. 44.58 *(978-1-4092-2152-4(0))* Lulu Pr., Inc.
Ashworth, Caspian. Copper Smith & the Battle of the Bands. 2012. (Illus.). 228p. pap. 18.24 *(978-1-4772-5071-6(9))* AuthorHouse.
Askew, Gee. The Starstiller. 2008. 216p. pap. *(978-1-84923-034-6(X))* YouWriteOn.
Askounis, Christina. The Dream of the Stone. 2007. (ENG.). 304p. (YA). (gr. 7). pap. 13.99 *(978-1-4169-1187-6(1)*, Simon Pulse) Simon Pulse.
Atkin, Jean. The Crow House. 2013. 270p. pap. *(978-1-78299-650-7(8))* FeedARead.com.
Atnip, Linda. Miranda's Magic Garden. 2004. cd-rom 15.98 *(978-1-885394-25-5(X))* Amber Lotus Publishing.
—Miranda's Magic Garden. Rothan, Ann, illus. 2004. 32p. (gr. -1-7). 19.95 *(978-1-885394-21-7(7))* Amber Lotus Publishing.
Atwater-Rhodes, Amelia. Bloodwitch. 2015. lib. bdg. 20.85 *(978-0-606-37648-8(8))* Turtleback Bks.
—Falcondance. 2007. (Kiesha'ra Ser.: Bk. 3). (ENG.). 208p. (YA). (gr. 7-12). per. 7.99 *(978-0-440-23885-0(4)*, Delacorte Pr.) Random Hse. Children's Bks.
—The Shapeshifters: The Kiesha'ra of the Den of Shadows. 2010. (ENG.). 976p. (YA). (gr. 7). pap. 14.99 *(978-0-385-73950-4(8)*, Delacorte Pr.) Random Hse. Children's Bks.
—Snakecharm. (Kiesha'ra Ser.: Bk. 2). (ENG.). 176p. (YA). (gr. 7-12). 2007. per. 7.99 *(978-0-385-73493-6(X)*, Delacorte Pr.) 2006. per. 6.99 *(978-0-440-23804-1(8)*, Laurel Leaf) Random Hse. Children's Bks.
—Wolfcry. 2008. (Kiesha'ra Ser.: Bk. 4). (ENG.). 208p. (YA). (gr. 9-12). pap. 7.99 *(978-0-440-23886-7(2)*, Delacorte Pr.) Random Hse. Children's Bks.
—Wyvernhail, Vol. 5. 2008. (Kiesha'ra Ser.: Bk. 5). (ENG.). 192p. (YA). (gr. 7). pap. 7.99 *(978-0-440-24003-7(4)*, Delacorte Pr.) Random Hse. Children's Bks.
Atwell, A. Erika Laura. 2008. 157p. pap. 24.95 *(978-1-60703-006-5(3))* PublishAmerica, Inc.
Audouin-Mamikonian, H. R. H. Princess Sophie. Tara Duncan & the Forbidden Book. Rodarmor, William, tr. 2016. (Tara Duncan Ser.). (ENG.). 476p. (J). (gr. 2-7). pap. 9.99 *(978-1-5107-0388-9(8)*, Sky Pony Pr.) Skyhorse Publishing Co., Inc.
—Tara Duncan & the Spellbinders. Rodarmor, William, tr. 2016. (Tara Duncan Ser.). (ENG.). 480p. (J). (gr. 2-7). pap. 9.99 *(978-1-5107-0387-2(X)*, Sky Pony Pr.) Skyhorse Publishing Co., Inc.
Audouin-Mamikonian, Princess Sophie. Tara Duncan & the Forbidden Book. Rodarmor, William, tr. from FRE. 2013. (ENG.). 480p. (J). (gr. 2-7). 16.95 *(978-1-61608-969-6(5)*, 608969, Sky Pony Pr.) Skyhorse Publishing Co., Inc.
—Tara Duncan & the Spellbinders. Rodarmor, Williams, tr. 2012. (ENG.). 480p. (J). (gr. 2-7). 16.95 *(978-1-61608-733-3(1)*, 608733, Sky Pony Pr.) Skyhorse Publishing Co., Inc.
Auerbach, Annie. Attack of the Boggans. 2013. (Epic Ser.). (ENG., Illus.). 24p. (J). (gr. -1-3). pap. 3.99 *(978-0-06-220989-4(2)*, HarperFestival) HarperCollins Pubs.
—Epic. 2013. (Epic Ser.). (ENG., Illus.). 144p. (J). (gr. 3-7). pap. 5.99 *(978-0-06-220995-5(7)*, HarperFestival) HarperCollins Pubs.
—Welcome to Moonhaven. 2013. (Epic Ser.). (ENG., Illus.). 24p. (J). (gr. -1-3). pap. 3.99 *(978-0-06-220987-0(6)*, HarperFestival) HarperCollins Pubs.
Auerbach, Annie & PopCap Games Staff. Brains & the Beanstalk. Grosvenor, Charles & Roberts, Jeremy, illus. 2013. (Plants vs. Zombies Ser.). (ENG.). 24p. (J). (gr. -1-3). pap. 4.99 *(978-0-06-222836-9(6)*, HarperFestival) HarperCollins Pubs.
Augenstein, Marianne R. The Quest for Kair, 1 vol. 2009. 152p. pap. 24.95 *(978-1-60813-899-9(2))* America Star Bks.
Auger, Dale. Mwâkwa Talks to the Loon: A Cree Story for Children, 1 vol. Auger, Dale, illus. 2007. (ENG., Illus.). 32p. (J). (gr. k-3). pap. 12.95 *(978-1-894974-32-5(8))* Heritage Hse. CAN. Dist: Orca Bk. Pubs. USA.
August, Elaine. Fira Gani: An Earthly Fable. 2012. 40p. pap. 24.95 *(978-1-4626-7589-0(1))* America Star Bks.
Augustin, Lucus. Traeh: The Portal. 2007. 208p. per. 14.95 *(978-0-595-45890-5(4))* iUniverse, Inc.
Auntie Annie. Knute: In the Magical Meadow. 2013. 32p. pap. 17.25 *(978-1-4669-9778-3(8))* Trafford Publishing.
—Knute: Meets Mike in the Magical Meadow. 2013. 28p. pap. 16.09 *(978-1-4669-9780-6(X))* Trafford Publishing.
Auxier, Jonathan. Sophie Quire & the Last Storyguard. 2017. (ENG.). 464p. (J). (gr. 3-7). pap. 8.95 *(978-1-4197-2202-8(6)*, Amulet Bks.) Abrams, Inc.
Avanti, Michele. GreeHee the Journey of Five: Tales of Tamoor Book One. 2008. (Illus.). 304p. (J). per. 14.99 *(978-0-9779590-4-4(X))* GreeHee Publishing.
Avery, Ben G. Turtle Trouble, 1 vol. Gaudiamo, Adi Darda, illus. 2007. (Z Graphic Novels / TimeFlyz Ser.). (ENG.). 160p. (J). (gr. 3-7). pap. 6.99 *(978-0-310-71362-3(5))* Zondervan.
Aveyard, Victoria. Cruel Crown. 2016. (Red Queen Novella Ser.). 208p. (YA). (gr. 8-12). pap. 9.99 *(978-0-06-243534-7(5)*, HarperTeen) HarperCollins Pubs.
—Glass Sword. l.t. ed. 2016. (Red Queen Ser.: 2). (ENG.). 656p. 24.99 *(978-1-4104-8668-4(0))* Cengage Gale.
—Glass Sword. (Red Queen Ser.: 2). 464p. (YA). (gr. 8). 2018. pap. 12.99 ***(978-0-06-231067-5(4))*** 2016. (ENG.). 19.99 *(978-0-06-231066-8(6))* HarperCollins Pubs. (HarperTeen).
—King's Cage. 2017. (Red Queen Ser.: 3). (Illus.). 528p. (YA). (gr. 8). 19.99 *(978-0-06-231069-9(0)*, HarperTeen) HarperCollins Pubs.
—Red Queen. l.t. ed. 2016. (Red Queen Ser.: 1). (ENG.). 562p. (YA). 24.99 *(978-1-4104-8669-1(9))* Cengage Gale.
—Red Queen. (YA). (gr. 8). 2016. (Red Queen Ser.). 864p. 37.98 *(978-0-06-256866-3(3))* 2016. (Red Queen Ser.: 1). (ENG.). 416p. pap. 12.99 *(978-0-06-231064-4(X))* 2015. (ENG.). 400p. 17.99 *(978-0-06-231063-7(1))* 2015. (Red Queen Ser.: 1). 400p. pap. 12.00 *(978-0-06-236271-1(2))* HarperCollins Pubs. (HarperTeen).
—Red Queen. 2016. (Red Queen Ser.: 1). 416p. lib. bdg. 22.10 *(978-0-606-38918-1(0))* Turtleback Bks.
Aveyard, Victoria. Red Queen Collector's Edition. 2017. (Red Queen Ser.: 1). 416p. (YA). (gr. 8). 22.99 ***(978-0-06-284000-4(2))*** HarperCollins Pubs.
Avi. City of Light, City of Dark. Floca, Brian, illus. 2013. (ENG.). 192p. (J). (gr. 3-7). 19.99 *(978-0-545-54256-2(1))*; pap. 12.99 *(978-0-545-39880-0(0))* Scholastic, Inc. (Graphix).
—Poppy's Return. Floca, Brian, illus. (Poppy Stories Ser.). (J). 2006. (ENG.). 256p. (gr. 3-7). pap. 6.99 *(978-0-06-000014-1(7))* 2005. 240p. lib. bdg. 16.89 *(978-0-06-000013-4(9))* HarperCollins Pubs.
Avila, Kat. Hanako Loves Monsters. 2008. 32p. 14.98 *(978-1-4357-0188-5(7))* Lulu Pr., Inc.
AWRP Meet Superkids. (J). pap., stu. ed. *(978-0-201-21600-4(0))* Addison-Wesley Longman, Inc.
Ayaz, Huda. Freeze-Land: A New Beginning. 2013. 110p. pap. 11.99 *(978-1-4808-0267-4(0))* Archway Publishing.
Ayers, Linda. The Time Bridge Travelers, 3 bks., Bk. 1. Ayers, Ryan, illus. 56p. (J). 2006. 13.95 *(978-0-9760505-8-2(7))* 2004. per. 7.95 *(978-0-9760505-0-6(1))* Blue Thistle Pr.
—The Time Bridge Travelers & the Mysterious Map, 3 bks., Bk. 2. Ayers, Ryan, illus. l.t. ed. (Time Bridge Travelers Ser.: 2). 80p. (J). 2006. 13.95 *(978-0-9760505-6-8(0))* 2005. per. 7.95 *(978-0-9760505-3-7(6))* Blue Thistle Pr.
AZ Books, creator. My Favorite Pet. 2013. (Velvet Fantasy Ser.). (ENG., Illus.). 16p. (J). (gr. k-3). pap. 4.95 *(978-1-61889-293-5(2))* AZ Bks. LLC.
Azerier, Gary. Constellation Station. 2011. (ENG.). 54p. pap. 15.99 *(978-0-615-55249-1(8))* IFWG Publishing Inc.
Aziz, Khalif. The Magikh Series: The Black Phoenix Book 1. 2012. 140p. 30.99 *(978-1-4771-2780-3(1))* Xlibris Corp.
Azuma, Kiyohiko. Azumanga Daioh, Vol. 3. 2004. (Illus.). 172p. (YA). pap. 9.99 *(978-1-4139-0030-9(5))* ADV Manga.
Babbitt, Ellen C. More Jataka Tales. Young, Ellsworth, illus. 2008. 92p. pap. 7.95 *(978-1-59915-310-0(6))* Yesterday's Classics.
Babbitt, Natalie. The Search for Delicious. 167p. (J). pap. 3.95 *(978-0-8072-1481-7(7)*, Listening Library) Random Hse. Audio Publishing Group.
—The Search for Delicious. Babbitt, Natalie, illus. 2007. (ENG., Illus.). 192p. (J). (gr. 3-7). per. 7.99 *(978-0-312-36982-8(4)*, 9780312369828) Square Fish.
—Tuck Everlasting. 139p. (J). (gr. 4-6). pap. 4.95 *(978-0-8072-1385-8(3)*, Listening Library) Random Hse. Audio Publishing Group.
Babinsky, Joseph. The Magical Dream Forest. 2008. 164p. pap. 15.95 *(978-1-4116-3517-3(5))* Lulu Pr., Inc.
Baccalario, Pierdomenico. Enchanted Emporium. Pernigotti, Chiara, tr. Bruno, Iacopo, illus. (Enchanted Emporium Ser.). (ENG.). 240p. (gr. 4-8). 2015. 79.95 *(978-1-4965-0047-2(4))* 2014. 53.30 *(978-1-4342-9603-0(2))* Stone Arch Bks.
Baccellia, Kim. No More Goddesses. 2013. (ENG.). 252p. (YA). (gr. 3-7). pap. 14.99 *(978-1-61271-012-9(3)*, Zumaya Thresholds) Zumaya Pubns. LLC.
Bachmann, Stefan. The Peculiar. (Peculiar Ser.: 1). (ENG.). (J). (gr. 4). 2013. 400p. pap. 8.99 *(978-0-06-219519-7(0))* 2012. 384p. 16.99 *(978-0-06-219518-0(2))* HarperCollins Pubs. (Greenwillow Bks.).
—The Whatnot. (J). 2014. (Peculiar Ser.: 2). (ENG.). 432p. (gr. 3-7). pap. 8.99 *(978-0-06-219522-7(0)*, Greenwillow Bks.) 2013. (Peculiar Ser.: 2). (ENG.). 432p. (gr. 3-7). 16.99 *(978-0-06-219521-0(2)*, Greenwillow Bks.) 2013. 421p. *(978-0-06-228630-7(7)*, Collins Design) HarperCollins Pubs.
Bacon, Lee. The Battle for Urth. 2016. (Legendtopia Ser.). (ENG., Illus.). 288p. (J). (gr. 4-7). 16.99 *(978-0-553-53402-3(5)*, Delacorte Bks. for Young Readers) Random Hse. Children's Bks.
Bacon, Lee. Legendtopia Book #2: the Shadow Queen. 2017. (Legendtopia Ser.: 2). (ENG.). 272p. (J). (gr. 4-7). 16.99 ***(978-0-553-53406-1(8)***, Delacorte Bks. for Young Readers) Random Hse. Children's Bks.
Badalian, Lucy. George the Dragonslayer & His Friends: On Earth. Badalian, Lucy, illus. 2003. (Illus.). 312p. (YA). per. 18.95 *(978-0-9725344-0-6(7)*, 9725344) Millennium Workshop Production.
Bagdanov, Patricia. The Adventures of Charlie & a Dragon Named Trevor. 2013. 26p. pap. 16.95 *(978-1-63004-985-0(9))* PublishAmerica, Inc.
Bailey, J. L. Children's Gate. 2005. 292p. 21.95 *(978-1-58939-814-6(9))* Virtualbookworm.com Publishing, Inc.
Bailey, Kristin. The Silver Gate. 2017. 320p. (J). (gr. 3-7). 16.99 *(978-0-06-239857-4(1)*, Tegen, Katherine Bks) HarperCollins Pubs.
Bailey-Peiffer, Stefanie & Bailey-Yarbrough, Caroline. Modie & the Power of the BellKeys. 2004. pap. 8.95 *(978-0-9762502-0-3(9))* Hudson Bks.
Bailey, Wendy R. Mary the Doll. 2012. 66p. pap. 24.99 *(978-1-300-18820-9(0))* Lulu Pr., Inc.
Baird, Jeri. Curses & Warfare. 2017. (Tokens & Omens Ser.). (ENG.). 312p. (YA). pap. 16.99 *(978-1-63163-126-9(8)*, Jolly Fish Pr.) North Star Editions.
—Tokens & Omens. 2016. (Tokens & Omens Ser.). (ENG.). 284p. (YA). (gr. 8). pap. 16.99 *(978-1-63163-082-8(2)*, Jolly Fish Pr.) North Star Editions.
Baker, E. D. Fairy Wings: A Fairy Tale. 2012. (ENG.). 336p. (YA). (gr. 5-14). pap. 8.99 *(978-1-59990-756-7(9)*, 9781599907567, Bloomsbury USA Childrens) Bloomsbury Publishing USA.
Baker, Kage. The Hotel under the Sand. Law, Stephanie Pui-Mun, illus. 2009. (ENG.). 179p. (J). (gr. 2-7). pap. *(978-1-892391-89-6(9))* Temmen, Edition, Horst Temmen.
Baker-King, Lisa. The Zealous Zebecs from the Midnight Ocean's Zenith. 2015. (ENG., Illus.). 58p. (J). pap. 10.95 *(978-1-63047-437-9(1))* Morgan James Publishing.
Balch, Betty Neff & Poythress, Jean Hill. Tales of the Cinnamon Dragon Book I: Adventures in Farr Elvenhome. Balch, Betty Neff, illus. 2004. (Illus.). 152p. (J). lib. bdg. 16.95 *(978-1-930580-46-6(0)*, Luminary Media Group) Pine Orchard, Inc.
Baldacci, David. The Finisher. (ENG.). 512p. (J). (gr. 5-9). 2015. (Vega Jane Ser.: Bk. 1). mass mkt. 7.99 *(978-0-545-88854-7(9))* 2015. (Vega Jane Ser.: 1). pap. 9.99 *(978-0-545-65226-1(X))* 2014. 17.99 *(978-0-545-65220-9(0))* Scholastic, Inc. (Scholastic Pr.).
—The Finisher. 2015. (Vega Jane Ser.: 1). lib. bdg. 20.85 *(978-0-606-36740-0(3))* Turtleback Bks.
—The Keeper. 2015. (Vega Jane Ser.: 2). (ENG.). 448p. (J). (gr. 5-9). 17.99 *(978-0-545-83194-9(6))*; 428p. (YA). *(978-0-545-88230-9(3))* Scholastic, Inc. (Scholastic Pr.).
—The Keeper. 2016. (Vega Jane Ser.: 2). (ENG.). 428p. (J). (gr. 5-9). 20.85 *(978-0-606-39127-6(4))* Turtleback Bks.
—The Keeper (Vega Jane, Book 2) 2017. (Vega Jane Ser.: 2). (ENG.). 464p. (J). (gr. 4-7). pap. 7.99 *(978-1-338-05360-9(4))* Scholastic, Inc.
—The Width of the World. 2017. (Vega Jane Ser.: 3). (ENG.). 448p. (J). (gr. 5-9). 17.99 *(978-0-545-83196-3(2)*, Scholastic Pr.) Scholastic, Inc.
Baldry, Cherith. The Emerald Throne. Wyatt, David, illus. 2003. (Eaglesmount Ser.). (J). 144p. 15.95 *(978-1-59034-584-9(3))*; 141p. pap. *(978-1-59034-585-6(1))* Mondo Publishing.
—The Lake of Darkness. Wyatt, David, illus. 2004. (Eaglesmount Ser.). 144p. (J). 15.95 *(978-1-59034-586-3(X))*; pap. *(978-1-59034-587-0(8))* Mondo Publishing.
Baldwin, James. Fifty Famous Stories Retold. 2008. 100p. pap. 9.50 *(978-1-60459-518-5(3))* Wilder Pubns., Corp.
—The Story of Roland. 2013. pap. 31.93 *(978-1-4400-6789-1(9))* Forgotten Bks.
—The Story of Siegfried. 2005. 256p. pap. 13.95 *(978-1-4218-1152-9(9)*, 1st World Library - Literary Society) 1st World Publishing, Inc.
—The Story of Siegfried. 2006. (Dover Children's Classics Ser.). (ENG.). 224p. (J). (gr. 3-5). per. 9.95 *(978-0-486-44574-8(7))* Dover Pubns., Inc.
—The Story of Siegfried. 2004. reprint ed. pap. 22.95 *(978-1-4191-8401-7(6))*; pap. 1.99 *(978-1-4192-8401-4(0))* Kessinger Publishing, LLC.
Baldwin, Kathleen. Exile for Dreamers: A Stranje House Novel. 2016. (Stranje House Ser.: 2). (ENG.). 384p. (J). 17.99 *(978-0-7653-7602-2(4)*, 9780765376022, Tor Teen) Doherty, Tom Assocs., LLC.
Baldwin, Stephen. Spirit, No. 1. Simko, Joe, illus. 2006. (ENG.). 208p. (gr. 8-12). per. 9.99 *(978-0-8054-4357-8(6))* B&H Publishing Group.
—Spirit Warriors: Number Three. 2007. (Spirit Warriors Ser.). (Illus.). 208p. (YA). per. 9.99 *(978-0-8054-4356-1(8))* B&H Publishing Group.
Ballesta, Juan. Tommy y el Elefante. (SPA., Illus.). 28p. (J). (gr. k-3). *(978-84-264-3578-1(5)*, LM1605) Editorial Lumen ESP. Dist: Lectorum Pubns., Inc.
Balletta, Janet. The Legend of the Colombian Mermaid. Mejía, Estella, illus. 2013. 36p. (J). pap. 14.95 *(978-0-9856762-9-2(9))* WRB Pub.
Banerjee, Anjali. The Silver Spell. Fiegenshuh, Emily, illus. 2005. (Knights of the Silver Dragon Ser.: Bk. 8). 174p. (J). *(978-1-4156-1645-1(0)*, Mirrorstone) Wizards of the Coast.
Bangs, John Kendrick, et al. Rollo in Emblemland: A Tale Inspired by Lewis Carroll's Wonderland. 2010. (Illus.). 132p. pap. *(978-1-904808-58-9(1))* Evertype.
Bangs, Jude Hatcher. The Elf King, 2 vols. 2005. *(978-0-9724979-7-8(8))*; *(978-0-9724979-8-5(6))* A Cappela Publishing. (Advocate Hse.).
Banks, Anna. Nemesis. 2016. (Nemesis Ser.). (ENG.). 368p. (YA). 17.99 *(978-1-250-07017-3(1)*, 9781250070173) Feiwel & Friends.
—Of Neptune. 2014. (Syrena Legacy Ser.: 3). (ENG.). 336p. (YA). (gr. 8-12). 17.99 *(978-1-250-03960-6(6)*, 9781250039606) Feiwel & Friends.
—Of Poseidon. 2013. (Syrena Legacy Ser.: 1). (ENG.). 384p. (YA). (gr. 8-12). pap. 10.99 *(978-1-250-02736-8(5)*, 9781250027368) Square Fish.
—Of Triton. 2013. (Syrena Legacy Ser.: 2). (ENG.). 256p. (YA). (gr. 8-12). 17.99 *(978-1-250-00333-1(4)*, 9781250003331) Feiwel & Friends.
—Of Triton. 2014. (Syrena Legacy Ser.: 2). (ENG., Illus.). 304p. (YA). (gr. 8-12). pap. 9.99 *(978-1-250-04431-0(6)*, 9781250044310) Square Fish.
Banks, Kate. The Magician's Apprentice. Sís, Peter, illus. 2012. (ENG.). 224p. (J). (gr. 5-9). 16.99 *(978-0-374-34716-1(6)*, 9780374347161, Farrar, Straus & Giroux (BYR)) Farrar, Straus & Giroux.
Banks, Lynne Reid. The Fairy Rebel. 2004. (ENG., Illus.). 128p. (J). (gr. 3-7). 5.99 *(978-0-440-41925-9(5)*, Yearling) Random Hse. Children's Bks.
—I, Houdini: The Amazing Story of an Escape-Artist Hamster. 127p. (J). (gr. 4-5). pap. 4.99 *(978-0-8072-1493-0(0)*, Listening Library) Random Hse. Audio Publishing Group.
—The Indian in the Cupboard. 181p. (J). (Indian in the Cupboard Ser.: No. 1). (gr. 4-7). pap. 4.99 *(978-0-8072-1433-6(7))*; 2004. (Indian in the Cupboard Ser.). (gr. 3-7). pap. 36.00 incl. audio *(978-0-8072-7308-1(2)*, YA809SP) Random Hse. Audio Publishing Group. (Listening Library).
—The Key to the Indian. Watling, James, illus. 2004. (Indian in the Cupboard Ser.: No. 5). (ENG.). 288p. (J). (gr. 4-18). pap. 6.99 *(978-0-380-80373-6(9))* HarperCollins Pubs.
—The Key to the Indian. (Indian in the Cupboard Ser.: No. 5). 240p. (J). (gr. 4-7). pap. 4.99 *(978-0-8072-1551-7(1)*, Listening Library) Random Hse. Audio Publishing Group.
—The Mystery of the Cupboard. Newsom, Tom, illus. 2004. (Indian in the Cupboard Ser.: No. 4). (ENG.). 256p. (J). (gr. 4-18). pap. 6.99 *(978-0-380-72013-2(2))* HarperCollins Pubs.
—The Return of the Indian. (Indian in the Cupboard Ser.: No. 2). 189p. (J). (gr. 4-7). pap. 4.99 *(978-0-8072-1434-3(5)*, Listening Library) Random Hse. Audio Publishing Group.
—Return of the Indian. 2003. (ENG., Illus.). 192p. pap. *(978-0-00-714899-8(2))* HarperCollins Pubs. Ltd.
Banks, Rosie. Bubble Volcano. 2013. (ENG., Illus.). 128p. (J). (gr. k-2). pap. 4.99 *(978-1-4083-2376-2(1)*, Orchard Bks.) Hachette Children's Group GBR. Dist: Hachette Bk. Group.
—Candy Cove Pirates. 2016. (Secret Kingdom Ser.). (ENG., Illus.). 208p. (J). (gr. 1-17). pap. 5.99 *(978-1-4083-3307-5(4)*, Orchard Bks.) Hachette Children's Group GBR. Dist: Hachette Bk. Group.
—Christmas Castle. 2013. (ENG., Illus.). 208p. (J). (gr. k-2). pap. 5.99 *(978-1-4083-2038-9(X)*, Orchard Bks.) Hachette Children's Group GBR. Dist: Hachette Bk. Group.
—Fairy Charm. 2016. (Secret Kingdom Ser.). (ENG., Illus.). 128p. (J). (gr. 1-17). pap. 4.99 *(978-1-4083-3998-5(6)*, Orchard Bks.) Hachette Children's Group GBR. Dist: Hachette Bk. Group.
—Fairytale Forest. 2013. (ENG., Illus.). 128p. (J). (gr. k-2). pap. 4.99 *(978-1-4083-2380-9(X)*, Orchard Bks.) Hachette Children's Group GBR. Dist: Hachette Bk. Group.
—Fancy Dress Party. 2013. (ENG., Illus.). 128p. (J). (gr. k-2). pap. 4.99 *(978-1-4083-2342-7(7)*, Orchard Bks.) Hachette Children's Group GBR. Dist: Hachette Bk. Group.
—Genie Wish. 2016. (Secret Kingdom Ser.). (ENG., Illus.). 128p. (J). (gr. 1-17). pap. 4.99 *(978-1-4083-4008-0(9)*, Orchard Bks.) Hachette Children's Group GBR. Dist: Hachette Bk. Group.
—Jewel Cavern. 2013. (ENG., Illus.). 128p. (J). (gr. k-2). pap. 4.99 *(978-1-4083-2343-4(5)*, Orchard Bks.) Hachette Children's Group GBR. Dist: Hachette Bk. Group.
—Magic Mountain. 2014. (Secret Kingdom Ser.: 5). lib. bdg. 14.75 *(978-0-606-36062-3(X))* Turtleback Bks.
—Melody Medal. 2016. (Secret Kingdom Ser.). (ENG., Illus.). 128p. (J). (gr. 1-17). pap. 4.99 *(978-1-4083-3288-7(4)*, Orchard Bks.) Hachette Children's Group GBR. Dist: Hachette Bk. Group.
—Mermaid Magic. 2016. (Secret Kingdom Ser.). (ENG., Illus.). 128p. (J). (gr. 1-17). pap. 4.99 *(978-1-4083-4012-7(7)*, Orchard Bks.) Hachette Children's Group GBR. Dist: Hachette Bk. Group.
—Mermaid Reef. 2014. (Secret Kingdom Ser.: 4). lib. bdg. 14.75 *(978-0-606-35842-2(0))* Turtleback Bks.
—Midnight Maze. 2013. (ENG., Illus.). 128p. (J). (gr. k-2). pap. 4.99 *(978-1-4083-2381-6(8)*, Orchard Bks.) Hachette Children's Group GBR. Dist: Hachette Bk. Group.
—My Dreams & Wishes Notebook. 2017. (Secret Kingdom Ser.). (ENG.). 208p. (J). (gr. k-2). 9.99 ***(978-1-4083-3586-4(7)***, Orchard Bks.) Hachette Children's Group GBR. Dist: Hachette Bk. Group.
—My Magical Story Collection. 2017. (Secret Kingdom Ser.). (ENG., Illus.). 352p. (J). (gr. k-2). 17.99 ***(978-1-4083-3016-6(4)***, Orchard Bks.) Hachette Children's Group GBR. Dist: Hachette Bk. Group.
—Pet Show Prize, Bk. 29. 2016. (Secret Kingdom Ser.). (ENG., Illus.). 128p. (J). (gr. 1-17). pap. 4.99 *(978-1-4083-3289-4(2)*, Orchard Bks.) Hachette Children's Group GBR. Dist: Hachette Bk. Group.
—Petal Parade. 2016. (Secret Kingdom Ser.). (ENG., Illus.). 208p. (J). (gr. 1-17). pap. 5.99 *(978-1-4083-3308-2(2)*, Orchard Bks.) Hachette Children's Group GBR. Dist: Hachette Bk. Group.

EFG

—Phoenix Festival. 2013. (ENG., Illus.). 128p. (J). (gr. k-2). pap. 4.99 *(978-1-4083-2341-0(9),* Orchard Bks.) Hachette Children's Group GBR. Dist: Hachette Bk. Group.

—Pixie Spell. 2016. (Secret Kingdom Ser.). (ENG., Illus.). 128p. (J). (gr. 1-17). pap. 4.99 *(978-1-4083-4010-3(0),* Orchard Bks.) Hachette Children's Group GBR. Dist: Hachette Bk. Group.

—Royal Bridesmaids. 2016. (Secret Kingdom Ser.). (ENG., Illus.). 208p. (J). (gr. 1-17). pap. 5.99 *(978-1-4083-4038-7(0),* Orchard Bks.) Hachette Children's Group GBR. Dist: Hachette Bk. Group.

—Secret Kingdom #4: Mermaid Reef. 2014. (Secret Kingdom Ser.: 4). (ENG.). 128p. (J). (gr. 2-5). pap. 4.99 *(978-0-545-53556-4(5),* Scholastic Paperbacks) Scholastic, Inc.

—Snow Bear Sanctuary. 2013. (ENG., Illus.). 128p. (J). (gr. k-2). pap. 4.99 *(978-1-4083-2340-3(0),* Orchard Bks.) Hachette Children's Group GBR. Dist: Hachette Bk. Group.

—Starlight Adventure. 2017. (Secret Kingdom Ser.). (ENG., Illus.). 208p. (J). (gr. k-2). pap. 5.99 ***(978-1-4083-2918-4(2),*** Orchard Bks.) Hachette Children's Group GBR. Dist: Hachette Bk. Group.

—Swan Palace. 2013. (ENG., Illus.). 128p. (J). (gr. k-2). pap. 4.99 *(978-1-4083-2339-7(7),* Orchard Bks.) Hachette Children's Group GBR. Dist: Hachette Bk. Group.

—Twinkle Trophy. 2016. (Secret Kingdom Ser.). (ENG., Illus.). 128p. (J). (gr. 1-17). pap. 4.99 *(978-1-4083-3305-1(8),* Orchard Bks.) Hachette Children's Group GBR. Dist: Hachette Bk. Group.

—Wildflower Wood. 2013. (ENG., Illus.). 128p. (J). (gr. k-2). pap. 4.99 *(978-1-4083-2338-0(9),* Orchard Bks.) Hachette Children's Group GBR. Dist: Hachette Bk. Group.

Bankston, John. Ray Bradbury. 2011. (Who Wrote That? Ser.). (Illus.). 140p. (gr. 6-12). 35.00 *(978-1-60413-778-1(9),* Chelsea Hse.) Facts On File, Inc.

Barbie of Swan Lake. 10p. 9.98 *(978-0-7853-9372-6(2))* Publications International, Ltd.

Barbieri, Sandra Birriel. Cristal & the Secret of the Enchanted Forest: Cristal y el Secreto Del Bosque Encantado. 2013. 64p. pap. 23.99 *(978-1-4525-6512-5(0))* Balboa Pr.

Barbot, Daniel. El Auto del Sr. Pulga. Mas, Maribel, illus. 2004. (SPA.). 28p. (J). pap. 6.99 *(978-980-257-260-1(8))* Ekare, Ediciones VEN. Dist: Lectorum Pubns., Inc.

Bardsley-Sirois, Lois. Katherine's Winter Garden. 2012. 24p. pap. 12.99 *(978-1-4525-6269-8(5))* Balboa Pr.

Bardugo, Leigh. Crooked Kingdom. 2016. (Six of Crows Ser.: 2). (ENG.). 560p. (YA). (gr. 7-12). 18.99 *(978-1-62779-213-4(9),* 9781627792134, Holt, Henry & Co. Bks. For Young Readers) Holt, Henry & Co.

—The Language of Thorns: Midnight Tales & Dangerous Magic. Kipin, Sara, illus. 2017. (ENG.). 288p. (YA). 18.99 ***(978-1-250-12252-0(X),*** 9781250122520) Imprint IND. Dist: Macmillan.

—Ruin & Rising. 2014. (Grisha Trilogy: Vol. 3). (ENG., Illus.). 432p. (YA). (gr. 7-12). 19.99 *(978-0-8050-9461-9(X),* 9780805094619, Holt, Henry & Co. Bks. For Young Readers) Holt, Henry & Co.

—Ruin & Rising. 2015. (Grisha Trilogy Ser.: 3). (YA). lib. bdg. 22.10 *(978-0-606-37283-1(0))* Turtleback Bks.

—Shadow & Bone. 2012. (Shadow & Bone Trilogy Ser.: 1). (ENG.). 368p. (YA). (gr. 7-12). 19.99 *(978-0-8050-9459-6(8),* 9780805094596, Holt, Henry & Co. Bks. For Young Readers) Holt, Henry & Co.

—Shadow & Bone. 2013. (Shadow & Bone Trilogy Ser.: 1). (ENG.). 416p. (YA). (gr. 7-12). pap. 10.99 *(978-1-250-02743-6(8),* 9781250027436) Square Fish.

—Shadow & Bone. 2013. (Grisha Trilogy Ser.: 1). (YA). lib. bdg. 22.10 *(978-0-606-31903-4(4),* Turtleback) Turtleback Bks.

—Siege & Storm. 2013. (Shadow & Bone Trilogy Ser.: 2). (ENG., Illus.). 448p. (YA). (gr. 7). 19.99 *(978-0-8050-9460-2(1),* 9780805094602, Holt, Henry & Co. Bks. For Young Readers) Holt, Henry & Co.

—Siege & Storm. 2014. (Shadow & Bone Trilogy Ser.: 2). (ENG.). 496p. (YA). (gr. 7). pap. 10.99 *(978-1-250-04443-3(X),* 9781250044433) Square Fish.

—Six of Crows. 2015. (Illus.). (YA). pap. *(978-1-62779-509-8(X))* Holt, Henry & Co.

—Six of Crows. Stein, Erin, ed. 2015. (Six of Crows Ser.: 1). (ENG., Illus.). 480p. (YA). (gr. 7-17). 18.99 *(978-1-62779-212-7(0),* 9781627792127, Holt, Henry & Co. Bks. For Young Readers) Holt, Henry & Co.

—Six of Crows. 2018. (Six of Crows Ser.: 1). (YA). lib. bdg. 22.10 ***(978-0-606-39944-9(5))*** Turtleback Bks.

Barker, Cicely Mary. How to Find Flower Fairies. 2007. (Flower Fairies Ser.). (ENG., Illus.). 24p. (J). (gr. k-4). 22.99 *(978-0-7232-5890-2(2),* Warne) Penguin Young Readers Group.

—Magical Doors: Discover the Doors to Fairyopolis. 2009. (Flower Fairies Ser.). (ENG.). 16p. (J). (gr. k-4). 22.99 *(978-0-7232-6351-7(5),* Warne) Penguin Young Readers Group.

Barker, Clive. Abarat. 119.90 *(978-0-06-056894-8(1))* HarperCollins Pubs.

—Abarat. Barker, Clive, illus. (Abarat Ser.: 1). (ENG., Illus.). (YA). (gr. 8). 2011. 528p. pap. 9.99 *(978-0-06-209410-0(6))* 2004. 496p. reprint ed. pap. 8.99 *(978-0-06-059637-8(6))* HarperCollins Pubs.

—Abarat: Days of Magic, Nights of War, 4 vols., Vol. 2. Barker, Clive, illus. ltd. num. aut. ed. 2004. (Illus.). 493p. 175.00 *(978-1-890885-17-5(7))* Trice, B.E. Publishing.

—Absolute Midnight. Barker, Clive, illus. 2013. (Abarat Ser.: 3). (ENG., Illus.). 640p. (YA). (gr. 8). pap. 9.99 *(978-0-06-440933-9(3))* HarperCollins Pubs.

—Days of Magic, Nights of War. Barker, Clive, illus. (Abarat Ser.: 2). (ENG., Illus.). (YA). (gr. 8). 2011. 624p. pap. 9.99 *(978-0-06-209411-7(4))* 2006. 576p. reprint ed. pap. 7.99 *(978-0-06-059638-5(4))* HarperCollins Pubs.

—The Thief of Always. 2008. (ENG.). 288p. pap. 15.99 *(978-0-06-168426-5(0),* Harper Perennial) HarperCollins Pubs.

Barker, Laraine Anne. Lord of Obsidian: Quest for Earthlight Trilogy. 2004. (Quest for Earthlight Trilogy: 2). 184p. (YA). pap. 10.95 *(978-0-7599-0502-3(9))* Hard Shell Word Factory.

Barkow, Henriette. Buri & the Marrow. Finlay, Lizzie, illus. 2004. (ENG & SPA.). 24p. (J). pap. *(978-1-85269-589-7(7));* pap. *(978-1-85269-584-2(6));* pap. *(978-1-85269-592-7(7));* pap. *(978-1-85269-585-9(4));* pap. *(978-1-85269-582-8(X));* pap. *(978-1-85269-581-1(1));* pap. *(978-1-85269-579-8(X));* pap. *(978-1-85269-588-0(9))* Mantra Lingua.

—Pandora's Box. Mayo, Diana, illus. 2004. (ENG & SOM.). 32p. (J). pap. *(978-1-85269-874-4(8));* pap. *(978-1-85269-819-5(5));* pap. *(978-1-85269-824-9(1));* pap. *(978-1-85269-829-4(2));* pap. *(978-1-85269-834-8(9));* pap. *(978-1-85269-839-3(X));* pap. *(978-1-85269-844-7(6));* pap. *(978-1-85269-849-2(7));* pap. *(978-1-85269-854-6(3));* pap. *(978-1-85269-859-1(4));* pap. *(978-1-85269-864-5(0));* pap. *(978-1-85269-869-0(1));* pap. *(978-1-85269-898-0(5));* pap. *(978-1-85269-894-2(2));* pap. *(978-1-85269-893-5(4));* pap. *(978-1-85269-889-8(6));* pap. *(978-1-85269-884-3(5));* pap. *(978-1-85269-879-9(9))* Mantra Lingua.

Barkow, Henriette & Reed, Nathan, illus. The Buskers of Bremen: Les Chanteurs de Rues de Bremen. 2004. (FRE & ENG.). 24p. (J). pap. *(978-1-85269-769-3(5))* Mantra Lingua.

Barlow, Steve & Skidmore, Steve. Stone Me! Ross, Tony, illus. 2005. (Mad Myths Ser.). 122p. (J). pap. 5.95 *(978-1-903015-43-8(X))* Barn Owl Bks, London GBR. Dist: Independent Pubs. Group.

Barna, Beverly. The Daughter of Dreams, a Fable of Destiny. White, David, illus. 2009. 28p. pap. 14.95 *(978-1-936051-09-0(5))* Peppertree Pr., The.

Barnacott, Anthony Royce. Permanoids of Chilon. 2009. 260p. 27.99 *(978-1-4389-3824-0(1))* AuthorHouse.

Barnard, Sarah. The Map & the Stone. 2nd ed. 2010. (Illus.). 142p. pap. 16.95 *(978-0-9556887-2-0(8))* Ethics Trading GBR. Dist: Lulu Pr., Inc.

Barnett, Brandi. Glamour. 2008. 231p. 19.95 *(978-1-930709-68-3(4))* HAWK Publishing Group.

Barnhill, Kelly. The Witch's Boy. 2014. (ENG.). 384p. (J). (gr. 4). 17.95 *(978-1-61620-351-1(X),* 73351) Algonquin Bks. of Chapel Hill.

Barrera, F. M. Tales of the Blue Wizard: The Children of Jamomere. 2005. (Illus.). 180p. (YA). (gr. 4-9). per. 10.99 *(978-0-9670848-1-7(4))* Talisman Pr.

Barrera, J. Mario. Nine Moons. 2005. (ENG & SPA., Illus.). (YA). cd-rom 21.99 *(978-0-9752725-2-7(7))* Orion-Cosmos.

BARRIE / LEFFLER. Peter Pan. 2016. (ENG., Illus.). 176p. 25.00 *(978-0-7358-4259-5(0))* North-South Bks., Inc.

Barrie, J. M. The Complete Adventures of Peter Pan Includes: The Little White Bird, Peter Pan in Kensington Gardens(Illustrated) & Peter. Rackham, Arthur & Bedford, F. D., illus. 2013. 326p. *(978-1-78139-361-1(3))* Benediction Classics.

—J. M. Barrie's Peter Pan. White, Stephen, illus. 2016. (ENG.). 96p. (J). (gr. 2-4). pap. *(978-1-78027-290-0(1))* Birlinn, Ltd.

—Peter Pan. 2008. 124p. (gr. 5-18). 23.95 *(978-1-60664-889-6(6));* pap. 10.95 *(978-1-60664-007-4(0))* Aegypan.

—Peter Pan. (SPA.). 191p. 15.95 *(978-84-206-3689-4(4))* Alianza Editorial, S. A. ESP. Dist: Distribooks, Inc.

—Peter Pan. 2005. 112p. per. 6.95 *(978-1-933652-07-8(1))* Bed Bks.

—Peter Pan. Date not set. (C). pap. *(978-0-7593-9877-1(1),* Cengage Learning) CENGAGE Learning.

—Peter Pan. Cowley, Joy, ed. Jang, Yeong-seon, illus. 2015. (World Classics Ser.). (ENG.). 32p. (J). (gr. k-4). 26.65 *(978-1-925246-45-2(0));* 7.99 *(978-1-925246-71-1(X));* 26.65 *(978-1-925246-19-3(1))* ChoiceMaker Pty. Ltd., The AUS. (Big and SMALL). Dist: Lerner Publishing Group.

—Peter Pan. 2005. 96p. per. 4.95 *(978-1-4209-2538-8(5))* Digireads.com Publishing.

—Peter Pan. 2006. pap. *(978-1-4065-0949-6(3))* Dodo Pr.

—Peter Pan. 2009. 276p. (gr. 3-7). pap. *(978-1-4068-9291-8(2))* Echo Library.

—Peter Pan. Bustelo, Gabriela, tr. Vicente, Fernando, illus. 2006. (Alfaguara Infantil y Juvenil Ser.). 229p. (J). (gr. 4-7). pap. *(978-970-770-677-4(5))* Ediciones Alfaguara.

—Peter Pan. pap. 16.95 *(978-2-07-051627-8(X))* Gallimard, Editions FRA. Dist: Distribooks, Inc.

—Peter Pan. Minalima Staff, illus. 2015. (ENG.). 256p. 27.99 *(978-0-06-236222-3(4),* Collins Design) HarperCollins Pubs.

—Peter Pan. (J). pap. *(978-0-340-71498-0(0))* Hodder & Stoughton.

—Peter Pan. Cowley, Joy, ed. Jang, Yeong-seon, illus. 2015. (World Classics Ser.). (ENG.). 32p. (J). (gr. k-4). 26.65 *(978-1-925186-71-0(7));* pap. 7.99 *(978-1-925186-65-9(2))* Lerner Publishing Group.

—Peter Pan, 1 vol. Mullarkey, Lisa, illus. 2010. (Calico Illustrated Classics Ser.: No. 1). (ENG.). 112p. (J). (gr. 3-6). 27.07 *(978-1-60270-710-8(3))* Magic Wagon.

—Peter Pan. Barrie, J. M., ed. Bedford, F. D. & Rackham, Arthur, illus. 2009. (ENG.). 287p. *(978-1-905716-40-1(0),* Collector's Library, The) Pan Macmillan.

—Peter Pan. 160p. pap. *(978-1-85471-231-8(4))* Penguin Bks., Ltd.

—Peter Pan. 2009. (Puffin Classics Ser.). (ENG., Illus.). 240p. (J). (gr. 5-7). 5.99 *(978-0-14-132257-5(8),* Puffin Books) Penguin Young Readers Group.

—Peter Pan. 2003. (Aladdin Classics Ser.). (ENG.). 256p. (J). (gr. 3-7). pap. 7.99 *(978-0-689-86691-3(7),* Aladdin) Simon & Schuster Children's Publishing.

—Peter Pan. McKowen, Scott, illus. 2008. (Sterling Unabridged Classics Ser.). (ENG.). 160p. (J). 9.95 *(978-1-4027-5426-5(4))* Sterling Publishing Co., Inc.

—Peter Pan. Bedford, F. D., illus. 2004. (Modern Library Classics Ser.). (ENG.). 192p. (J). (gr. 3-7). pap. 10.00 *(978-0-8129-7297-9(X),* Modern Library) Random House Publishing Group.

—Peter Pan. Andreasen, Dan, illus. 2009. (Classic Starts(tm) Ser.). (ENG.). 160p. (J). (gr. 2-4). 6.95 *(978-1-4027-5421-0(3))* Sterling Publishing Co., Inc.

—Peter Pan. Bedford, F. D., illus. 2005. (Barnes & Noble Classics Ser.). (ENG.). 208p. per. 7.95 *(978-1-59308-213-0(4))* Barnes & Noble, Inc.

—Peter Pan: A Bed Book First Edition Classic. 2005. 112p. 12.95 *(978-1-933652-30-6(6))* Bed Bks.

—Peter Pan: An Illustrated Classic for Kids & Young Readers (Excellent for Bedtime & Young Readers) eMusic, Tom, ed. Friday, Arthur, illus. 2013. 38p. pap. 6.99 *(978-1-62321-067-0(4))* Tommye-music Corp. DBA Tom eMusic.

—Peter Pan: Complete & Unabridged. Barrie, J. M., illus. 2005. (Illus.). 176p. reprint ed. pap. 17.00 *(978-0-7567-9445-3(5))* DIANE Publishing Co.

—Peter Pan: Peter & Wendy & Peter Pan in Kensington Gardens. 2004. (ENG., Illus.). 352p. (gr. 12-18). 11.00 *(978-0-14-243793-3(X),* Penguin Classics) Penguin Publishing Group.

—Peter Pan: The Original Tale of Neverland. Jaramillo, Raquel, illus. Jaramillo, Raquel, photos by. unabr. ed. 2003. 135p. (YA). (gr. 5-8). reprint ed. 25.00 *(978-0-7567-6883-6(7))* DIANE Publishing Co.

—Peter Pan: The Story of Peter & Wendy [Photoplay Edition]. 2007. 244p. (gr. 4-7). 29.95 *(978-1-4344-8379-9(7));* per. 17.95 *(978-1-4344-8378-2(9))* Wildside Pr., LLC.

—Peter Pan - the Original Classic Edition. 2011. pap. *(978-1-74244-781-0(3),* Tebbo) Emereo Pty Ltd.

—Peter Pan & Wendy. 2013. (ENG.). 172p. (YA). 14.95 *(978-1-940849-05-8(5))* Ancient Wisdom Pubns.

—Peter Pan & Wendy. 2010. 224p. pap. 19.95 *(978-0-557-36915-7(0))* Lulu Pr., Inc.

—Peter Pan & Wendy. Foreman, Michael, illus. 2003. (Chrysalis Childrens Classics Ser.). 176p. (YA). pap. *(978-1-84365-039-3(8),* Pavilion Children's Books) Pavilion Bks.

—Peter Pan & Wendy: Centenary Edition. Ingpen, Robert R., illus. 2004. (ENG.). 216p. (J). *(978-1-897035-12-2(8),* Blue Heron Bks.) Raincoast Bk. Distribution.

—Peter Pan, by J. M. Barrie - the Original Classic Edition. 2011. mass mkt. *(978-1-74244-961-6(1),* Tebbo) Emereo Pty Ltd.

—Peter Pan in Kensington Gardens. (J). 18.95 *(978-0-8488-0427-5(9))* Amereon Ltd.

—Peter Pan in Kensington Gardens. 2013. 123p. reprint ed. lthr. 69.00 *(978-0-7426-2518-1(4))* Classic Bks.

—Peter Pan in Kensington Gardens. 2006. pap. *(978-1-4065-0950-2(7))* Dodo Pr.

—Peter Pan in Kensington Gardens. unabr. ed. 2012. (Illus.). 147p. 39.99 *(978-1-4622-8152-7(4))* Repressed Publishing LLC.

—Peter Pan in Kensington Gardens. 2009. 108p. (gr. -1-18). pap. 9.95 *(978-1-60664-381-5(9))* Rodgers, Alan Bks.

—Peter Pan in Kensington Gardens & Peter & Wendy. 2009. 120p. pap. 7.99 *(978-1-4209-3191-4(1))* Digireads.com Publishing.

—The Story of Peter Pan. Woodward, Alice B., illus. unabr. ed. 2011. (Dover Children's Thrift Classics Ser.). (ENG.). 96p. (J). (gr. 3-8). reprint ed. pap. 3.50 *(978-0-486-27294-8(X))* Dover Pubns., Inc.

Barrie, J. M. & Bedford, F. D. Peter Pan. 2012. (Illus.). 200p. *(978-1-4351-4201-5(2))* Barnes & Noble, Inc.

Barrie, J. M. & Edens, Cooper. Peter Pan. (SPA.). 174p. 26.95 *(978-84-666-0760-5(9))* Ediciones B ESP. Dist: Spanish Pubs., LLC.

Barrie, J. M. & Lindner, Brooke. Peter Pan. Bedford, Francis Donkin & Rackham, Arthur, illus. 2015. (Word Cloud Classics Ser.). (ENG.). 272p. pap. 14.99 *(978-1-62686-392-7(X),* Thunder Bay Pr.) Readerlink Distribution Services, LLC.

Barrie, J. M. & Naxos of America Staff. Peter Pan. 3rd ed. 2008. (Hear It Read It Classics Ser.: 0). (ENG.). 144p. (J). (gr. 2-4). 9.99 *(978-1-4022-1170-6(8),* Sourcebooks Jabberwocky) Sourcebooks, Inc.

Barrie, J. M. & Sterne, Laurence. The Life & Opinions of Tristram Shandy, Gentleman. 2015. (Vintage Classics Ser.). (ENG.). 762p. pap. 13.95 *(978-0-09-951915-7(1))* Random Hse. GBR. Dist: Independent Pubs. Group.

Barron, Liz. Salcombe Seaside Fairies: Louise the Lobster Pot Fairy. 2009. (Illus.). 24p. pap. 11.49 *(978-1-4389-8525-1(8))* AuthorHouse.

Barron, T. A. The Ancient One. 2003. (Illus.). 304p. 14.65 *(978-0-7569-6642-3(6))* Perfection Learning Corp.

—Atlantis in Peril. 2015. (Atlantis Saga Ser.: 2). (ENG., Illus.). 272p. (J). (gr. 5). 17.99 *(978-0-399-16804-8(4),* Philomel Bks.) Penguin Young Readers Group.

—Atlantis Lost. 2016. (Atlantis Saga Ser.: 3). (ENG.). 224p. (J). (gr. 5). 17.99 *(978-0-399-16805-5(2),* Philomel Bks.) Penguin Young Readers Group.

—Atlantis Rising. 2014. (Atlantis Saga Ser.: 1). (ENG.). 400p. (J). (gr. 5). pap. 8.99 *(978-0-14-751221-5(2),* Puffin Books) Penguin Young Readers Group.

—The Book of Magic, 12 vols., Bk. 12. Hall, August, illus. 2011. (Merlin Saga Ser.: 12). (ENG.). 160p. (J). (gr. 5-18). 17.99 *(978-0-399-24741-5(6),* Philomel Bks.) Penguin Young Readers Group.

—Child of the Dark Prophecy. 2004. (Merlin Saga Ser.: 9). (ENG.). 432p. (J). (gr. 5-18). 21.99 *(978-0-399-23763-8(1),* Philomel Bks.) Penguin Young Readers Group.

—Doomraga's Revenge. (Merlin Saga Ser.: 7). (ENG.). (J). (gr. 5-18). 2009. 256p. 19.99 *(978-0-399-25212-9(6),* Philomel Bks.)Bk. 7. 2011. 272p. 8.99 *(978-0-14-241925-0(7),* Puffin Books) Penguin Young Readers Group.

—The Eternal Flame: Book 11, 11 vols. 2011. (Merlin Saga Ser.: 11). (ENG.). 416p. (J). (gr. 5-18). 8.99 *(978-0-14-241929-8(X),* Puffin Books) Penguin Young Readers Group.

—The Great Tree of Avalon: Book 9, 9 vols. 2011. (Merlin Saga Ser.: 9). (ENG.). 464p. (J). (gr. 5-18). 8.99 *(978-0-14-241927-4(3),* Puffin Books) Penguin Young Readers Group.

—The Lost Years, Bk. 1. 2011. (Merlin Saga Ser.: 1). (ENG.). 352p. (J). (gr. 5-18). 8.99 *(978-0-14-241889-5(7),* Puffin Books) Penguin Young Readers Group.

—Merlin's Dragon. 2008. (Merlin Saga Ser.: 6). (ENG.). 336p. (J). (gr. 5-18). 19.99 *(978-0-399-24750-7(5),* Philomel Bks.) Penguin Young Readers Group.

—The Mirror of Fate, Bk. 4. 2011. (Merlin Saga Ser.: 4). (ENG.). 272p. (J). (gr. 5-18). 8.99 *(978-0-14-241922-9(2),* Puffin Books) Penguin Young Readers Group.

—The Raging Fires, Bk. 3. 2011. (Merlin Saga Ser.: 2). (ENG.). 288p. (J). (gr. 5-18). 8.99 *(978-0-14-241921-2(4),* Puffin Books) Penguin Young Readers Group.

—The Seven Songs, Bk. 2. 2011. (Merlin Saga Ser.: 2). (ENG.). 336p. (J). (gr. 5-18). 8.99 *(978-0-14-241920-5(6),* Puffin Books) Penguin Young Readers Group.

—Shadows on the Stars: Book 10, 10 vols. 2011. (Merlin Saga Ser.: 10). (ENG.). 464p. (J). (gr. 5-18). 8.99 *(978-0-14-241928-1(1),* Puffin Books) Penguin Young Readers Group.

—Tree Girl. 2013. (ENG.). 144p. (J). (gr. 3-7). pap. 7.99 *(978-0-14-242708-8(X),* Puffin Books) Penguin Young Readers Group.

—Ultimate Magic, 8 vols., Bk. 8. 2011. (Merlin Saga Ser.: 8). (ENG.). 256p. (J). (gr. 5-18). 8.99 *(978-0-14-241926-7(5),* Puffin Books) Penguin Young Readers Group.

—The Wizard's Wings, Bk. 5. 2011. (Merlin Saga Ser.: 5). (ENG.). 384p. (J). (gr. 5-18). 8.99 *(978-0-14-241923-6(0),* Puffin Books) Penguin Young Readers Group.

Barron, Tom. The Ancient One. 2016. (ENG.). 320p. (J). (gr. 5). 8.99 *(978-1-101-99702-4(8),* Puffin Books) Penguin Young Readers Group.

Barrowman, John & Barrowman, Carole E. The Bone Quill. 2013. (Hollow Earth Ser.). (ENG.). 304p. (J). (gr. 3-7). 16.99 *(978-1-4424-8928-8(6),* Aladdin) Simon & Schuster Children's Publishing.

—Conjuror. 2016. (Orion Chronicles Ser.). (ENG.). 320p. (YA). (gr. 7). 16.99 *(978-1-78185-637-6(0))* Head of Zeus GBR. Dist: Independent Pubs. Group.

—Hollow Earth. (Hollow Earth Ser.). (ENG., (J). (gr. 3-7). 2013. Illus.). 416p. pap. 7.99 *(978-1-4424-5853-6(4))* 2012. 400p. 16.99 *(978-1-4424-5852-9(6))* Simon & Schuster Children's Publishing. (Aladdin).

Barrowman, John & Barrowman, Carole E. Nephilim. 2017. (Orion Chronicles Ser.: 2). (ENG.). 320p. (YA). (gr. 7). 16.99 ***(978-1-78185-641-3(9))*** Head of Zeus GBR. Dist: Independent Pubs. Group.

Barrows, Robert. Milestones - the Sixth World. 2009. 312p. pap. 16.98 *(978-0-557-02589-3(3))* Lulu Pr., Inc.

Barry, Dave & Pearson, Ridley. Peter & the Shadow Thieves. Call, Greg, illus. 2007. (Starcatchers Ser.: Bk. 2). 556p. (gr. 5-9). 19.00 *(978-0-7569-8060-3(7))* Perfection Learning Corp.

—Peter & the Sword of Mercy. Call, Greg, illus. 2011. (Peter & the Starcatchers Ser.: Bk. 4). (ENG.). 528p. (J). (gr. 5-9). pap. 9.99 *(978-1-4231-3070-3(7))* Hyperion Pr.

Barry, William J. Forever Awakening. 2014. 242p. pap. 18.50 *(978-1-61213-113-9(1))* Writer's Coffee Shop, The.

Barthelme, Donald. The Slightly Irregular Fire Engine. 2006. (ENG., Illus.). 32p. (gr. 4-13). 19.95 *(978-1-58567-828-0(7),* 856828) Overlook Pr., The.

Bartholomeusz, James. The Grey Star. 2013. (Seven Stars Trilogy Ser.: 3). (ENG.). 384p. (YA). (gr. 6). pap. 9.99 *(978-1-60542-700-3(4))* Nodin Pr.

Bartlett, Roberta. How I Met an Alien. 2011. 74p. pap. 19.95 *(978-1-4560-7818-8(6))* America Star Bks.

Batchler, Darla. If I Were a Monkey. Parris, Kitty, illus. 2005. 24p. (J). bds. 12.95 *(978-0-9746959-2-1(0))* Falcon Publishing LTD.

Bate, Tharah. White Arrow. 2012. 20p. pap. 13.77 *(978-1-4669-0991-5(9))* Trafford Publishing.

Bates, Emily. Demon's Heart. 2014. 263p. (YA). pap. 16.99 *(978-1-4621-1515-0(2))* Cedar Fort, Inc./CFI Distribution.

Bates, Robert L. Lopaka's Legends of Hawaii. 2008. 28p. pap. 19.95 *(978-1-4327-3655-2(8))* Outskirts Pr., Inc.

Bateson-Hill, Margaret. Chanda & the Mirror of Moonlight. Littlewood, Karin, illus. 2003. (Folk Tales Ser.). 32p. (J). (gr. 3-4). *(978-1-84089-217-8(X))* Zero to Ten, Ltd.

Bateson Hill, Margaret. Masha & the Firebird. Wilson, Anne, illus. 2005. (Folk Tales Ser.: 1). (RUS & ENG.). 32p. (J). pap. *(978-1-84089-201-7(3))* Zero to Ten, Ltd.

Bath, K. P. The Secret of Castle Cant. 2005. 1.00 *(978-1-4237-3189-4(1))* Recorded Bks., Inc.

Batham, Matthew. Lightsleep. 2006. 167p. pap. *(978-1-904623-39-7(5))* WritersPrintShop.

Batson, Wayne. The War for the Waking World, 1 vol. 2015. (Dreamtreaders Ser.). (ENG.). 288p. (J). pap. 9.99 *(978-1-4003-2368-5(1))* Nelson, Thomas Inc.

Batson, Wayne Thomas. Dreamtreaders, 1 vol. 2014. (Dreamtreaders Ser.). (ENG.). 304p. (J). pap. 9.99 *(978-1-4003-2366-1(5))* Nelson, Thomas Inc.

—Search for the Shadow Key, 1 vol. 2014. (Dreamtreaders Ser.). (ENG.). 336p. (J). pap. 9.99 *(978-1-4003-2367-8(3))* Nelson, Thomas Inc.

Batson, Wayne Thomas & Hopper, Christopher. Curse of the Spider King: The Berinfell Prophecies Series - Book One. 2014. (ENG.). 384p. (J). pap. 14.99 *(978-0-7180-2987-6(9))* Nelson, Thomas Inc.

Batt, Tanya Robyn. The Faerie's Gift. Ceccoli, Nicoletta, illus. 2008. (ENG.). 32p. (J). (gr. -1-3). 17.99 *(978-1-84686-230-4(2))* Barefoot Bks., Inc.

Battah, Suzan. Basatai: Outside In. 2012. 330p. pap. *(978-0-9872632-1-6(8))* Battah, Suzan.

Batterson, Mark, et al. Jack Staples & the Ring of Time. 2014. (ENG.). 240p. (J). pap. 9.99 *(978-0-7814-1107-3(6))* Cook, David C.

Baum, L. Frank. Adventures in Oz: Dorothy & the Wizard in Oz, the Road to Oz, the Emerald City of Oz. 2007. 296p. 24.95 *(978-1-60459-017-3(3));* per. 12.95 *(978-1-60459-016-6(5))* Wilder Pubns., Corp.

—Adventures in Oz: The Patchwork Girl of Oz, Little Wizard Stories of Oz, Tik-Tok of Oz. 2007. 268p. 24.95 *(978-1-60459-019-7(X));* per. 12.99 *(978-1-60459-018-0(1))* Wilder Pubns., Corp.

—Adventures in Oz: The Scarecrow of Oz, Rinkitink in Oz, the Lost Princess of Oz. 2007. 324p. 24.95 *(978-1-60459-021-0(1));* per. 12.99 *(978-1-60459-020-3(3))* Wilder Pubns., Corp.

—Adventures in Oz: The Tin Woodman of Oz, the Magic of Oz, Glinda of Oz. 2007. 284p. 24.95 *(978-1-60459-023-4(8));* per. 12.99 *(978-1-60459-022-7(X))* Wilder Pubns., Corp.

—Adventures in Oz: The Wonderful Wizard of Oz, the Marvelous Land of Oz, Ozma of Oz. 2007. 264p. per. 12.99 *(978-1-60459-014-2(9));* per. 24.95 *(978-1-60459-015-9(7))* Wilder Pubns., Corp.

—Dorothy & the Wizard in Oz; the Road to Oz; the Emerald City of Oz, Vol. 2. 2013. (Oz, the Complete Collection: 2). (ENG.). 656p. (J). (gr. 3-7). pap. 12.99 *(978-1-4424-8548-8(5),* Aladdin) Simon & Schuster Children's Publishing.

—Dorothy & the Wizard of Oz. 2005. pap. *(978-1-4065-0075-2(5))* Dodo Pr.

—Dorothy & the Wizard of Oz. 2004. (Twelve-Point Ser.). lib. bdg. 24.00 *(978-1-58287-273-5(2))* North Bks.

—Dot & Tot of Merryland. 2008. 124p. (gr. 4-10). 23.95 *(978-1-60664-767-7(9))*; pap. 11.95 *(978-1-60664-139-2(5))* Aegypan.
—The Emerald City if Oz. 2005. 256p. pap. 13.95 *(978-1-4218-0464-4(6)*, 1st World Library - Literary Society) 1st World Publishing, Inc.
—The Emerald City of Oz. 2007. 144p. per. 11.95 *(978-1-60312-256-6(7))* Aegypan.
—The Emerald City of Oz. (Oz Ser.). (YA). (gr. 5-8). 21.95 *(978-0-8488-0733-7(2))* Amereon Ltd.
—The Emerald City of Oz. 2003. (Twelve-Point Ser.). lib. bdg. 24.00 *(978-1-58287-254-4(6))* North Bks.
—The Enchanted Island of Yew. 2005. 26.95 *(978-1-4218-1480-3(3))*; 184p. pap. 11.95 *(978-1-4218-1580-0(X))* 1st World Publishing, Inc. (1st World Library - Literary Society).
—The Enchanted Island of Yew. 2007. 116p. (gr. -1-7). per. 9.95 *(978-1-60312-332-7(6))*; 22.95 *(978-1-60312-672-4(4))* Aegypan.
—The Enchanted Island of Yew. 2008. 140p. 21.99 *(978-0-554-31893-6(8))* 2008. 140p. 24.99 *(978-0-554-22590-6(5))* 2007. (ENG.). 128p. pap. 18.99 *(978-1-4264-2666-7(6))* Creative Media Partners, LLC.
—The Enchanted Island of Yew. 2007. 128p. per. *(978-1-4065-3666-9(0))* Dodo Pr.
—The Enchanted Island of Yew. 2003. (Twelve-Point Ser.). (J). lib. bdg. 24.00 *(978-1-58287-253-7(8))* North Bks.
—Enchanted Island of Yew. 2006. 268p. pap. 11.45 *(978-1-59462-396-7(1)*, Book Jungle) Standard Pubns., Inc.
—The Enchanted Island of Yew. 2008. 128p. pap. 10.45 *(978-1-4385-0427-8(6)*, Book Jungle) Standard Pubns., Inc.
—The Enchanted Island of Yew. l.t. ed. 2007. (ENG.). 136p. pap. 19.99 *(978-1-4264-2723-7(9))* Creative Media Partners, LLC.
—The Enchanted Island of Yew. l.t. ed. 2005. 228p. pap. *(978-1-84637-102-8(3))* Echo Library.
—The Enchanted Island of Yew. 2004. reprint ed. pap. 19.95 *(978-1-4191-6093-6(1))*; pap. 1.99 *(978-1-4192-6093-3(6))* Kessinger Publishing, LLC.
—The Enchanted Island of Yew. l.t. ed. 2004. (Large Print Ser.). 207p. 25.00 *(978-1-58287-737-2(8))* North Bks.
—Glinda of Oz. rev. ed. 2006. 184p. 26.95 *(978-1-4218-1786-6(1))*; pap. 11.95 *(978-1-4218-1886-3(8))* 1st World Publishing, Inc. (1st World Library - Literary Society).
—Glinda of Oz. 2007. 108p. 22.95 *(978-1-60312-591-8(4))* Aegypan.
—Glinda of Oz. (Oz Ser.). (YA). (gr. 5-8). 21.95 *(978-0-8488-0784-9(7))* Amereon Ltd.
—Glinda of Oz. (Twelve-Point Ser.). 2003. lib. bdg. 24.00 *(978-1-58287-256-8(2))* 2004. 210p. 25.00 *(978-1-58287-740-2(8))* North Bks.
—L Frank Baum's Book of Santa Claus. 2007. 84p. per. 7.99 *(978-1-60459-118-7(8))* Wilder Pubns., Corp.
—Little Wizard Stories of Oz. Neill, John R., illus. 2011. (Dover Children's Classics Ser.). (ENG.). 160p. (J). (gr. 3-5). pap. 14.99 *(978-0-486-47644-5(8))* Dover Pubns., Inc.
—Little Wizard Stories of Oz. 2011. 80p. (gr. 3-18). 18.95 *(978-1-4638-9617-1(4))* Rodgers, Alan Bks.
—The Lost Princess of Oz. 208p. 2005. 27.95 *(978-1-4218-0647-1(9)*, 1st World Library - Literary Society) 2004. per. 12.95 *(978-1-59540-047-5(8))* 1st World Publishing, Inc.
—The Lost Princess of Oz. (Oz Ser.). (YA). (gr. 5-8). 22.95 *(978-0-8488-0786-3(3))* Amereon Ltd.
—The Lost Princess of Oz. 2004. reprint ed. pap. 20.95 *(978-1-4191-7079-9(1))*; pap. 1.99 *(978-1-4192-7079-6(6))* Kessinger Publishing, LLC.
—The Lost Princess of Oz. (Twelve-Point Ser.). 2003. lib. bdg. 24.00 *(978-1-58287-255-1(4))* 2004. 241p. 25.00 *(978-1-58287-739-6(4))* North Bks.
—The Magic of Oz. 184p. 2005. 26.95 *(978-1-4218-0651-8(7))* 2004. pap. 11.95 *(978-1-59540-101-4(6))* 1st World Publishing, Inc. (1st World Library - Literary Society).
—The Magic of Oz. 2007. 108p. (gr. 4-7). per. 9.95 *(978-1-60312-334-1(2))*; 22.95 *(978-1-60312-671-7(6))* Aegypan.
—The Magic of Oz. 2004. reprint ed. pap. 1.99 *(978-1-4192-7118-2(0))*; pap. 19.95 *(978-1-4191-7118-5(6))* Kessinger Publishing, LLC.
—The Magic of Oz. 2004. (Twelve-Point Ser.). lib. bdg. 24.00 *(978-1-58287-279-7(1))*; lib. bdg. 25.00 *(978-1-58287-775-4(0))* North Bks.
—El Maravilloso Mago de Oz. (Oz Ser.).Tr. of Wonderful Wizard of Oz. (SPA., Illus.). 160p. (YA). (gr. 5-8). 14.95 *(978-84-7281-184-3(0)*, AF1184) Auriga, Ediciones S.A. ESP. Dist: Continental Bk. Co., Inc.
—The Marvelous Land of Oz. 2004. 208p. per. 12.95 *(978-1-59540-100-7(8))* 1st World Publishing, Inc.
—The Marvelous Land of Oz. 2007. 120p. per. 10.95 *(978-1-60312-149-1(8))* Aegypan.
—The Marvelous Land of Oz. 2004. reprint ed. pap. 1.99 *(978-1-4192-7194-6(6))*; pap. 21.95 *(978-1-4191-7194-9(1))* Kessinger Publishing, LLC.
—The Marvelous Land of Oz. 2004. (Twelve-Point Ser.). lib. bdg. 24.00 *(978-1-58287-272-8(4))*; lib. bdg. 25.00 *(978-1-58287-768-6(8))* North Bks.
—The Master Key. 2004. reprint ed. pap. 15.95 *(978-1-4191-7199-4(2))*; pap. 1.99 *(978-1-4192-7199-1(7))* Kessinger Publishing, LLC.
—The Master Key: An Electrical Fairy Tale. 2007. 120p. per. *(978-1-4065-3669-0(5))* Dodo Pr.
—Michael Foreman's the Wonderful Wizard of Oz. Foreman, Michael, illus. 2010. (ENG.). 160p. (J). (gr. 2-7). 19.99 *(978-1-84365-157-4(2)*, Pavilion Children's Books) Pavilion Bks. GBR. Dist: Independent Pubs. Group.
—La Mirinda Sorchisto de Oz. Broadribb, Donald, tr. Denslow, W. W., illus. 2012. 278p. pap. 24.00 *(978-1-59569-245-0(2))* Mondial.
—Oz, the Complete Collection, Volume 1: The Wonderful Wizard of Oz; the Marvelous Land of Oz; Ozma of Oz. 2013. (Oz, the Complete Collection: 1). (ENG., Illus.). 592p. (J). (gr. 3-7). 19.99 *(978-1-4424-8889-2(1)*, Aladdin) Simon & Schuster Children's Publishing.
—Oz, the Complete Collection, Volume 2: Dorothy & the Wizard in Oz; the Road to Oz; the Emerald City of Oz. 2013. (Oz, the Complete Collection: 2). (ENG.). 656p. (J). (gr. 3-7). 19.99 *(978-1-4424-8890-8(5)*, Simon & Schuster/Paula Wiseman Bks.) Simon & Schuster/Paula Wiseman Bks.
—Oz, the Complete Collection, Volume 3: The Patchwork Girl of Oz; Tik-Tok of Oz; the Scarecrow of Oz. 2013. (Oz, the Complete Collection: 3). (ENG.). 720p. (J). (gr. 3-7). 19.99 *(978-1-4424-8892-2(1)*, Aladdin) Simon & Schuster Children's Publishing.
—Oz, the Complete Collection, Volume 4: Rinkitink in Oz; the Lost Princess of Oz; the Tin Woodman of Oz. 2013. (Oz, the Complete Collection: 4). (ENG.). 656p. (J). (gr. 3-7). 19.99 *(978-1-4424-8893-9(X)*, Aladdin) Simon & Schuster Children's Publishing.
—Oz, the Complete Hardcover Collection. 2013. (Oz, the Complete Collection). (ENG.). 3200p. (J). (gr. 3-7). 99.99 *(978-1-4424-8903-5(0)*, Aladdin) Simon & Schuster Children's Publishing.
—Ozma of Oz. 2007. 108p. (gr. 4-7). per. 9.95 *(978-1-60312-150-7(1))* Aegypan.
—Ozma of Oz. (Twelve-Point Ser.). 2003. lib. bdg. 24.00 *(978-1-58287-252-0(X))* 2004. 210p. 25.00 *(978-1-58287-736-5(X))* North Bks.
—The Patchwork Girl of Oz. 2007. 152p. (gr. -1-7). 24.95 *(978-1-60312-632-8(5))*; per. 12.95 *(978-1-60312-374-7(1))* Aegypan.
—The Patchwork Girl of Oz. (Oz Ser.). (YA). (gr. 5-8). 25.95 *(978-0-8488-0705-4(7))* Amereon Ltd.
—The Patchwork Girl of OZ. l.t. ed. 2004. (Large Print Ser.). lib. bdg. 25.00 *(978-1-58287-771-6(8))* North Bks.
—Rinkitink in Oz. rev. ed. 2006. 216p. 27.95 *(978-1-4218-1791-0(8))*; pap. 12.95 *(978-1-4218-1891-7(4))* 1st World Publishing, Inc. (1st World Library - Literary Society).
—Rinkitink in Oz. (Oz Ser.). (YA). (gr. 5-8). 22.95 *(978-0-8488-0735-1(9))* Amereon Ltd.
—Rinkitink in Oz. 2004. reprint ed. pap. 20.95 *(978-1-4191-6718-8(9))*; pap. 1.99 *(978-1-4192-6718-5(3))* Kessinger Publishing, LLC.
—Rinkitink in Oz. 2004. (Twelve-Point Ser.). lib. bdg. 24.00 *(978-1-58287-278-0(3))*; lib. bdg. 25.00 *(978-1-58287-774-7(2))* North Bks.
—Rinkitink in Oz; the Lost Princess of Oz; the Tin Woodman of Oz, Vol. 4. 2013. (Oz, the Complete Collection: 4). (ENG.). 656p. (J). (gr. 3-7). pap. 11.99 *(978-1-4424-8550-1(7)*, Aladdin) Simon & Schuster Children's Publishing.
—The Road to Oz. 2005. 192p. pap. 11.95 *(978-1-4218-0165-0(5))*; 26.95 *(978-1-4218-0065-3(9))* 1st World Publishing, Inc. (1st World Library - Literary Society).
—The Road to Oz. (Oz Ser.). (YA). (gr. 5-8). 20.95 *(978-0-8488-0788-7(X))* Amereon Ltd.
—The Road to Oz. 2004. reprint ed. pap. 20.95 *(978-1-4191-8077-4(0))*; pap. 1.99 *(978-1-4192-8077-1(5))* Kessinger Publishing, LLC.
—The Road to Oz. 2004. (Twelve-Point Ser.). lib. bdg. 24.00 *(978-1-58287-274-2(0))*; lib. bdg. 25.00 *(978-1-58287-770-9(X))* North Bks.
—The Road to Oz. 2009. (Little Golden Book Ser.). (ENG., Illus.). 24p. (J). (gr. -1-2). 3.99 *(978-0-375-84757-8(X)*, Golden Bks.) Random Hse. Children's Bks.
—The Scarecrow of Oz. rev. ed. 2006. 208p. 27.95 *(978-1-4218-1790-3(X))*; pap. 12.95 *(978-1-4218-1890-0(6))* 1st World Publishing, Inc. (1st World Library - Literary Society).
—The Scarecrow of Oz. (Oz Ser.). (YA). (gr. 5-8). 20.95 *(978-0-8488-0707-8(3))* Amereon Ltd.
—The Scarecrow of Oz. 2004. reprint ed. pap. 20.95 *(978-1-4191-8147-4(5))*; pap. 1.99 *(978-1-4192-8147-1(X))* Kessinger Publishing, LLC.
—The Scarecrow of Oz. 2004. (Twelve-Point Ser.). lib. bdg. 24.00 *(978-1-58287-277-3(5))*; lib. bdg. 25.00 *(978-1-58287-773-0(4))* North Bks.
—The Sea Fairies. rev. ed. 2006. 192p. 26.95 *(978-1-4218-1788-0(8))*; pap. 11.95 *(978-1-4218-1888-7(4))* 1st World Publishing, Inc. (1st World Library - Literary Society).
—The Sea Fairies. 2007. 112p. per. 9.95 *(978-1-60312-375-4(X))* Aegypan.
—The Sea Fairies. 2004. reprint ed. pap. 20.95 *(978-1-4191-8165-8(3))*; pap. 1.99 *(978-1-4192-8165-5(8))* Kessinger Publishing, LLC.
—The Sea Fairies. l.t. ed. 2004. (Large Print Ser.). lib. bdg. 25.00 *(978-1-58287-793-8(9))* North Bks.
—Sky Island. 2007. 144p. (gr. 4-7). per. 11.95 *(978-1-60312-253-5(2))* Aegypan.
—Sky Island. 2004. (Twelve-Point Ser.). lib. bdg. 24.00 *(978-1-58287-280-3(5))*; lib. bdg. 25.00 *(978-1-58287-792-1(0))* North Bks.
—The Patchwork Girl of Oz; Tik-Tok of Oz; the Scarecrow of Oz, Vol. 3. 2013. (Oz, the Complete Collection: 3). (ENG.). 720p. (J). (gr. 3-7). pap. 12.99 *(978-1-4424-8549-5(3)*, Aladdin) Simon & Schuster Children's Publishing.
—The Wonderful Wizard of Oz; the Marvelous Land of Oz; Ozma of Oz. 2013. (Oz, the Complete Collection: 1). (ENG., Illus.). 592p. (J). (gr. 3-7). pap. 12.99 *(978-1-4424-8547-1(7)*, Aladdin) Simon & Schuster Children's Publishing.
—Tik-Tok of Oz. rev. ed. 2006. 232p. 27.95 *(978-1-4218-1792-7(6))*; pap. 12.95 *(978-1-4218-1892-4(2))* 1st World Publishing, Inc. (1st World Library - Literary Society).
—Tik-Tok of Oz. 2007. 128p. (gr. -1-7). per. 10.95 *(978-1-60312-333-4(4))*; 23.95 *(978-1-60312-670-0(8))* Aegypan.
—Tik-Tok of Oz. 2004. (Twelve-Point Ser.). lib. bdg. 24.00 *(978-1-58287-276-6(7))*; lib. bdg. 25.00 *(978-1-58287-772-3(6))* North Bks.
—The Tin Woodman of Oz. rev. ed. 2006. 204p. 27.95 *(978-1-4218-1789-7(6))*; pap. 12.95 *(978-1-4218-1889-4(2))* 1st World Publishing, Inc. (1st World Library - Literary Society).
—The Tin Woodman of Oz. 2008. 116p. (gr. 4-7). 22.95 *(978-1-60664-947-3(7))*; per. 9.95 *(978-1-60312-497-3(7))* Aegypan.
—The Tin Woodman of Oz. 2009. 174p. (gr. 4-7). 25.99 *(978-1-60512-317-2(X))*; pap. 12.99 *(978-1-60512-417-9(6))* Akasha Publishing, LLC. (Akasha Classics).
—The Tin Woodman of Oz. (J). 20.95 *(978-0-8488-0709-2(X))* Amereon Ltd.
—The Tin Woodman of Oz. 2008. 160p. 25.99 *(978-0-554-28352-4(2))* 2008. 160p. 22.99 *(978-0-554-37655-4(5))* 2007. (ENG.). 142p. pap. 18.99 *(978-1-4346-5199-0(1))* 2007. (ENG.). 156p. pap. 21.99 *(978-1-4346-5200-3(9))* Creative Media Partners, LLC.
—The Tin Woodman of Oz. 2005. pap. *(978-1-4065-0079-0(8))* Dodo Pr.
—The Tin Woodman of Oz. l.t. ed. 2005. 256p. pap. *(978-1-84637-112-7(0))* Echo Library.
—The Tin Woodman of Oz. (Twelve-Point Ser.). 2003. lib. bdg. 24.00 *(978-1-58287-257-5(0))* 2004. 230p. 25.00 *(978-1-58287-741-9(6))* North Bks.
—The Tin Woodman of Oz. 2009. 136p. pap. 10.95 *(978-1-4385-2196-1(0)*, Book Jungle) Standard Pubns., Inc.
—The Tin Woodman of Oz. 2008. 308p. (gr. 4-7). 32.95 *(978-1-4344-7192-5(6))*; pap. 19.95 *(978-1-4344-7191-8(8))* Wildside Pr., LLC.
—The Treasury of Oz. 2007. 784p. 49.99 *(978-1-60459-028-9(9))* Wilder Pubns., Corp.
—The Tresury of Oz: The Wonderful Wizard of Oz, the Marvelous Land of Oz, Ozma of Oz, Dorothy & the Wizard in Oz, the Road to Oz, the Emerald City Of. 2007. 548p. per. 19.49 *(978-1-60459-029-6(7))* Wilder Pubns., Corp.
—Twinkle & Chubbins. 2011. 106p. pap. 9.95 *(978-1-60664-470-6(X))* Rodgers, Alan Bks.
—The Wizard of Oz. Evangelista, Mauro, illus. (Usborne Young Reading: Series Two Ser.). 64p. (J). 2010. 6.99 *(978-0-7945-2826-3(0))* 2007. (gr. 3-7). 8.99 *(978-0-7945-1457-0(X)*, Usborne) EDC Publishing.
—The Wizard of Oz. 2013. (ENG., Illus.). 176p. *(978-1-907360-90-9(5)*, Collector's Library, The) Pan Macmillan.
—The Wizard of Oz. Denslow, W. W., illus. 2012. (Stepping Stone Book Ser.). (ENG.). 112p. (J). (gr. 1-4). 4.99 *(978-0-375-86994-5(8)*, Random Hse. Bks. for Young Readers) Random Hse. Children's Bks.
—The Wizard of Oz. (SPA.). 256p. (J). 9.95 *(978-84-204-3509-1(0))* Santillana USA Publishing Co., Inc.
—The Wizard of Oz. 2012. (ENG., Illus.). (J). (gr. 4-7). 14.99 ***(978-1-61382-935-6(3))*** Simon & Brown.
—The Wizard of Oz. Zwerger, Lisbeth, illus. 2004. 103p. (J). (gr. 4-8). reprint ed. 20.00 *(978-0-7567-7708-1(9))* DIANE Publishing Co.
—The Wizard of Oz. 2004. reprint ed. pap. 19.95 *(978-1-4191-8832-9(1))* Kessinger Publishing, LLC.
—The Wizard of Oz: And Other Wonderful Books of Oz - The Emerald City of Oz & Glinda of Oz. Sumpter, Rachell, illus. deluxe ed. 2012. (Penguin Classics Deluxe Edition Ser.). (ENG.). 432p. (gr. 5). pap. 17.00 *(978-0-14-310663-0(5)*, Penguin Classics) Penguin Publishing Group.
—The Wizard of Oz Book & Charm. deluxe ed. 2005. (Charming Classics). 208p. (J). 9.99 *(978-0-06-075772-4(8)*, HarperFestival) HarperCollins Pubs.
—The Woggle-Bug Book. 2008. 52p. pap. 7.95 *(978-1-60664-008-1(9))* Aegypan.
—The Woggle-Bug Book. 2011. 52p. 14.95 *(978-1-4638-9578-5(X))* Rodgers, Alan Bks.
—A Wonderful Welcome to Oz: The Marvelous Land of Oz, Ozma of Oz, & the Emerald City of Oz. Maguire, Gregory, ed. Neill, John R., illus. 2006. (Modern Library Classics Ser.). (ENG.). 624p. per. 17.00 *(978-0-8129-7494-2(8)*, Modern Library) Random House Publishing Group.
—The Wonderful Wizard of Oz. 180p. 2005. 26.95 *(978-1-4218-0652-5(5))* 2004. pap. 11.95 *(978-1-59540-102-1(4))* 1st World Publishing, Inc. (1st World Library - Literary Society).
—The Wonderful Wizard of Oz. (Oz Ser.). (YA). (gr. 5-8). 20.95 *(978-0-88411-772-8(3))* Amereon Ltd.
—The Wonderful Wizard of Oz. 2014. (ENG., Illus.). 167p. 17.50 *(978-1-78270-042-5(0))* Award Pubns. Ltd. GBR. Dist: Parkwest Pubns., Inc.
—The Wonderful Wizard of Oz. 2007. (ENG.). 134p. pap. 19.99 *(978-1-4264-4884-3(8))*; 374p. pap. 18.99 *(978-1-4264-4841-6(4))* Creative Media Partners, LLC.
—The Wonderful Wizard of Oz. Denslow, W. W., illus. 2015. (Dover Children's Classics Ser.). (ENG.). 308p. (J). (gr. 3-6). reprint ed. pap. 14.99 *(978-0-486-20691-2(2))* Dover Pubns., Inc.
—The Wonderful Wizard of Oz. 2003. (Modern Library Classics Ser.). (ENG., Illus.). 224p. pap. 15.00 *(978-0-8129-7011-1(X)*, Modern Library) Random House Publishing Group.
—The Wonderful Wizard of Oz. (ENG., Illus.). (J). (gr. 1-7). 2012. 14.99 ***(978-1-61382-939-4(6))*** 2011. 14.99 ***(978-1-61382-942-4(6))*** Simon & Brown.
—The Wonderful Wizard of Oz: A Classic Story about Cooperation. 2003. (Illus.). 32p. per. 3.95 *(978-0-9747133-5-9(X)*, Values to Live By Classic Stories) Thomas, Frederic Inc.
—The Wonderful Wizard of Oz: The Marvelous Land of Oz - Ozma of Oz. 2013. (Oz, the Complete Collection). (ENG.). 3200p. (J). (gr. 3-7). pap. 54.99 *(978-1-4424-8902-8(2)*, Aladdin) Simon & Schuster Children's Publishing.
—7 Books In: L. Frank Baum's Original Oz Series, Volume 1 of 2. the Wonderful Wizard of Oz, the Marvelous Land of Oz, Ozma of Oz, Dorothy & the W. 2008. 820p. *(978-1-905921-02-7(0))* Shoes & Ships & Sealing Wax Ltd.
—7 Books In: L. Frank Baum's Oz Series, volume 1 of 2. the Wonderful Wizard of Oz, the Marvelous Land of Oz, Ozma of Oz, Dorothy & the Wizard In. 2008. 824p. pap. *(978-1-905921-01-0(2))* Shoes & Ships & Sealing Wax Ltd.
—8 Books In: L. Frank Baum's Original Oz Series, volume 2 of 2. Little Wizard Stories of Oz, Tik-Tok of Oz, the Scarecrow of Oz, Rinkitink in Oz, T. 2008. 764p. *(978-1-905921-03-4(9))* Shoes & Ships & Sealing Wax Ltd.
—8 Books In: L. Frank Baum's Oz Series, volume 2 of 2. Little Wizard Stories of Oz, Tik-Tok of Oz, the Scarecrow of Oz, Rinkitink in Oz, the Lost P. 2008. 812p. pap. *(978-1-905921-09-6(8))* Shoes & Ships & Sealing Wax Ltd.
Baum, L. Frank, told to. The Emerald City of Oz. l.t. ed. 2004. (Large Print Ser.). 285p. 25.00 *(978-1-58287-738-9(6))* North Bks.
Baum, L. Frank & Bancroft, Laura. Policeman Bluejay. 2009. 116p. pap. 9.95 *(978-1-60664-382-2(7))* Rodgers, Alan Bks.
—Twinkle & Chubbins. 2011. 106p. 22.95 *(978-1-4638-9604-1(2))* Rodgers, Alan Bks.
Baum, L. Frank & Denslow, W. W. The Wonderful Wizard of Oz. 2012. (Illus.). 232p. *(978-1-4351-3973-2(9))* Barnes & Noble, Inc.
Baum, L. Frank & Thompson, Ruth Plumly. Oz - The Complete Collection Vol. 5: The Magic of Oz; Glinda of Oz; The Royal Book of Oz. 2013. (Oz, the Complete Collection: 5). (ENG.). 576p. (J). (gr. 3-7). 19.99 *(978-1-4424-8894-6(8)*, Aladdin) Simon & Schuster Children's Publishing.
—The Royal Book of Oz. 2011. 160p. (gr. -1-7). pap. 13.95 *(978-1-60664-507-9(2))* Rodgers, Alan Bks.
—The Royal Book of Oz. 2009. 112p. pap. 8.99 *(978-1-60459-763-9(1))* Wilder Pubns., Corp.
—The Magic of Oz; Glinda of Oz; the Royal Book of Oz. 2013. (Oz, the Complete Collection: 5). (ENG.). 576p. (J). (gr. 3-7). pap. 12.99 *(978-1-4424-8551-8(5)*, Aladdin) Simon & Schuster Children's Publishing.
Baum, L. Frank & van Dyne, Edith. Aunt Jane's Nieces. 2009. 136p. 24.95 *(978-1-60664-647-2(8))*; pap. 11.95 *(978-1-60664-272-6(3))* Rodgers, Alan Bks.
Baum, L. Frank & Wolek, Guy. The Wonderful Wizard of Oz, 1 vol. 2012. (Calico Illustrated Classics Ser.: No. 4). (ENG., Illus.). 112p. (J). (gr. 3-6). 27.07 *(978-1-61641-621-8(1))* Magic Wagon.
Baum, L. Frank & Zwerger, Lisbeth. The Wizard of Oz. 2011. (ENG., Illus.). 160p. (J). (gr. 4-3). 22.95 *(978-0-7358-4042-3(3))* North-South Bks., Inc.
Baum, L. Frank, et al. A Children's Treasury. 2007. 792p. per. 24.95 *(978-1-60459-011-1(4))* Wilder Pubns., Corp.
Baum, Roger S. The Lion of Oz & the Badge of Courage. Coons, Dean, illus. 2nd ed. 2003. 247p. (J). 24.95 *(978-1-57072-255-4(2))* Overmountain Pr.
—The Oz Odyssey. Seitzinger, Victoria, illus. 2006. 176p. (J). 19.95 *(978-1-57072-299-8(4))* Overmountain Pr.
Baumgartner, Edward Louis. Wabash Boy. 2011. 236p. (gr. 4-6). pap. 16.26 *(978-1-4269-7615-5(1))* Trafford Publishing.
Baynes, Pauline & Lewis, C. S. Prince Caspian, Bk. 7. Baynes, Pauline, illus. 2008. (Chronicles of Narnia Ser.). (Illus.). 768p. (J). (gr. 3). pap. 99.99 *(978-0-06-076552-1(6))* HarperCollins Pubs.
Beahm, George. Passport to Narnia: The Unofficial Giude. Kirk, Tim, illus. 2005. (J). lib. bdg. 15.95 *(978-1-57174-481-4(9))* Hampton Roads Publishing Co., Inc.
Beale, Edith. Angela's Odyssey. 2010. 50p. pap. 9.99 *(978-0-557-32690-7(7))* Lulu Pr., Inc.
Bealer-Wynton, Cheryl. Blinky's Island. 2008. 60p. pap. 6.50 *(978-1-4303-1146-1(0))* Lulu Pr., Inc.
Beamer, Winona Desha, et al. Naupaka: By Nona Beamer: Illustrations by Caren Loebel-Fried: Hawaiian Translation by Kaliko Beamer-Trapp: Music by Keola Beamer. Loebel-Fried, Caren, illus. 2008. (J). 14.95 *(978-1-58178-089-5(3))* Bishop Museum Pr.
Bear, F. T. Connor Finn: The Secret of Snow. 2013. 258p. pap. *(978-0-646-91485-5(5))* F. T. Bear.
Beastly Boys Staff, et al. Battle of the Zombies. 2012. (Awfully Beastly Business Ser.: 5). (ENG., Illus.). 208p. (J). (gr. 4-7). pap. 8.99 *(978-0-85707-522-2(5))* Simon & Schuster, Ltd. GBR. Dist: Simon & Schuster, Inc.
Beauty & the Boy: An old man's story for a dying Boy. 2006. (Illus.). 270p. (YA). per. 19.95 *(978-0-9759902-0-9(9))* Before Christmas Pr.
Beck, A. E. Master-E: Travel into Mystical Dragon Dimensions: Collision of Fantasy, Science Fiction & Physics. 2010. 212p. pap. 49.49 *(978-1-4490-3612-6(0))* AuthorHouse.
Becker, Aaron. Journey. Becker, Aaron, illus. 2013. (ENG., Illus.). 40p. (J). (gr. -1-3). 15.99 *(978-0-7636-6053-6(1))* Candlewick Pr.
—Quest. 2014. (ENG., Illus.). 40p. (J). (gr. -1-3). 15.99 *(978-0-7636-6595-1(9))* Candlewick Pr.
—Quest. 2015. (CHI.). 40p. (J). *(978-7-5133-1677-4(5))* New Star Publishing Hse.
—Return. Becker, Aaron, illus. 2016. (ENG., Illus.). 40p. (J). (gr. -1-3). 15.99 *(978-0-7636-7730-5(2))* Candlewick Pr.
Becker-Doyle, Eve & Doyle, Evan Brain. Evan Brain's Christmas List & Other Shenanigans: Boy Warrior Fights Evil. Doyle, Evan Brain, illus. 2008. (ENG., Illus.). 64p. pap. 15.95 *(978-0-9794716-3-6(X))* BDA Publishing.
Becker, Lindsey. The Star Thief. 2017. (ENG., Illus.). 416p. (J). (gr. 3-7). 16.99 *(978-0-316-34856-0(2))* Little, Brown Bks. for Young Readers.
Beckerman, Menucha. The Crying Clown. 2003. (My Little World Ser.: Vol. 2). (Illus.). 34p. (J). (gr. k-5). 5.95 *(978-1-931681-07-0(4))* Israel Bookshop Pubns.
—Gitty's Dream Comes True. 2003. (My Little World Ser.: Vol. 1). (Illus.). (J). (gr. k-5). 5.95 *(978-1-931681-06-3(6))* Israel Bookshop Pubns.
—My Middos World: Dina-dee Is a Goody, 4. Gaash, Elisheva, illus. 2003. (My Middos World Ser.: Vol. 4). 24p. (J). (gr. k-5). 11.95 *(978-1-931681-03-2(1))* Israel Bookshop Pubns.
—My Middos World: Dina-dee Loves Shabbos, 5. Gaash, Elisheva, illus. 2003. (My Middos World Ser.: Vol. 5). 24p. (J). (gr. k-5). 11.95 *(978-1-931681-04-9(X))* Israel Bookshop Pubns.
—My Middos World: Hurray! Michael Is Big. 2003. (My Middos World Ser.: Vol. 3). (Illus.). 24p. (J). (gr. k-5). 11.95 *(978-1-931681-02-5(3))* Israel Bookshop Pubns.
—My Middos World: Michael & the Raindrops, 7. 2003. (My Middos World Ser.: Vol. 7). (Illus.). 24p. (J). (gr. k-5). 11.95 *(978-1-931681-17-9(1))* Israel Bookshop Pubns.
—My Middos World: Michael & the Secret of Making Friends, 9. 2003. (My Middos World Ser.: Vol. 9). (Illus.). 24p. (J). (gr. k-5). 11.95 *(978-1-931681-15-5(5))* Israel Bookshop Pubns.
—My Middos World: Michael Wants Patience, 2. 2003. (My Middos World Ser.: Vol. 2). (Illus.). 24p. (J). (gr. k-5). 11.95 *(978-1-931681-01-8(5))* Israel Bookshop Pubns.
Becket. Key the Steampunk Vampire Girl - Book One: And the Dungeon of Despair. 2013. 242p. (J). pap. 9.99 *(978-0-9898785-2-4(X))* Becket.
Beckham, David. Charlie Barker & the Secret of the Deep Dark Woods. 2006. 570p. pap. 33.20 *(978-1-4120-9264-7(7))* Trafford Publishing.
Bedard, Michael. The Green Man. 2012. (ENG., Illus.). 308p. (YA). (gr. 5-9). 19.95 *(978-1-77049-285-1(2)*, Tundra Bks.) Tundra Bks. CAN. Dist: Penguin Random Hse. LLC.
—Painted Devil. 2007. (ENG.). 240p. (YA). (gr. 7-12). pap. 13.95 *(978-1-4169-6139-0(9)*, Atheneum Bks. for Young Readers) Simon & Schuster Children's Publishing.

EFG

Bedard, Tony. Mystic: The Mathemagician, Vol. 6. Lopresti, Aaron et al, illus. 2004. (Mystic Ser.). 160p. (YA). pap. 15.95 (978-1-59314-039-7(8)) CrossGeneration Comics, Inc.

Beddor, Frank. Arch Enemy. 2010. (Looking Glass Wars Ser.: 3). lib. bdg. 20.85 (978-0-606-14997-6(X), Turtleback) Turtleback Bks.

—ArchEnemy: The Looking Glass Wars, Book Three, 3 vols. 2010. (Looking Glass Wars Ser.: 3). (ENG.). 384p. (YA). (gr. 7-18). 9.99 (978-0-14-241689-1(4), Speak) Penguin Young Readers Group.

—The Looking Glass Wars, 1 vol. 2007. (Looking Glass Wars Ser.: 1). (ENG., Illus.). 400p. (YA). (gr. 7-18). 9.99 (978-0-14-240941-1(3), Speak) Penguin Young Readers Group.

—Seeing Redd. (Looking Glass Wars Ser.: 2). (ENG.). (YA). (gr. 7-18). 2008. 400p. 9.99 (978-0-14-241209-1(0), Speak) 2007. (Illus.). 384p. 17.99 (978-0-8037-3155-4(8), Dial Bks) Penguin Young Readers Group.

Beddor, Frank & Cavalier, Liz. Hatter M: The Looking Glass Wars - Love of Wonder. Wrobel, C. J., ed. 2010. (ENG., Illus.). 176p. (gr. 7). pap. 14.99 (978-0-9892221-4-3(4)) Automatic Pictures Publishing.

—The Nature of Wonder, Vol. 3. Wrobel, C. J., ed. 2010. (ENG., Illus.). 192p. (gr. 7). 24.99 (978-0-9818737-4-9(X)) Automatic Pictures Publishing.

—The Nature of Wonder, Vol. 3. Wrobel, C. J., ed. 2010. (ENG., Illus.). 192p. (gr. 7). pap. 14.95 (978-0-9818737-5-6(8)) Automatic Pictures Publishing.

—Zen of Wonder, Vol. 4. 2013. (ENG., Illus.). 140p. (gr. 7). pap. 14.95 (978-0-9818737-8-7(2)) Automatic Pictures Publishing.

—Zen of Wonder, Vol. 4. 2013. (ENG., Illus.). 142p. (gr. 7). 24.99 (978-0-9818737-7-0(4)) Automatic Pictures Publishing.

Bee, Ersila. The Everywhere Armchair. 2010. 26p. pap. 9.99 (978-1-60911-110-6(9), Eloquent Bks.) Strategic Book Publishing & Rights Agency (SBPRA).

Beekman, Kelley Lee. Sir Eli & the Halloween Dragon: The Legend of the Toasted Marshmallow. 2006. 55p. pap. 16.95 (978-1-4241-4047-3(1)) PublishAmerica, Inc.

Beiko, S. M. The Lake & the Library. l.t. ed. 2013. 542p. pap. (978-1-4596-6871-3(5)) ReadHowYouWant.com, Ltd.

Bell, Amber Dawn. Cave of Terror. 2008. 280p. pap. 12.95 (978-0-9818550-3-5(2)) Highland Pr. Publishing.

Bell, Anita & Bell, Belinda. 'Twas Ever. 2011. 208p. 28.99 (978-0-557-41894-7(1)); 210p. pap. 11.99 (978-1-257-00131-6(0)) Lulu Pr., Inc.

Bell, Braden. The Kindling. 2012. (YA). (978-1-4621-1027-8(4)) Cedar Fort, Inc./CFI Distribution.

—Luminescence. 2014. pap. 14.99 (978-1-4621-1405-4(9), Horizon Pubs.) Cedar Fort, Inc./CFI Distribution.

Bell, Clare. Clan Ground. 2010. (Named Ser.: Bk. 2). (ENG.). 307p. (YA). pap. 14.95 (978-0-9745603-7-3(5)) Imaginator Pr.

—Ratha's Challenge. 2011. (Named Ser.: Bk. 4). (ENG.). 252p. (YA). pap. 14.95 (978-0-9745603-9-7(1)) Imaginator Pr.

—Ratha's Creature. 2011. (Named Ser.: Bk. 1). (ENG.). 296p. (YA). pap. 14.95 (978-1-936917-01-3(7)) Imaginator Pr.

Bell, David. Dawn Grays Cosmic Adventure 1. 2007. (Dawn Gray Ser.). (ENG., Illus.). 260p. pap. (978-1-84167-558-9(X)) Ransom Publishing Ltd.

—Pink Alert! 2007. (Dawn Gray Ser.). (ENG.). 260p. pap. (978-1-84167-581-7(4)) Ransom Publishing Ltd.

—Pyjamas in Space. 2007. (Dawn Gray Ser.). (ENG.). 260p. pap. (978-1-84167-580-0(6)) Ransom Publishing Ltd.

Bell, Frank. Panda Patrol to the Rescue. Seaman, Paul, illus. 2004. 24p. pap. 7.00 (978-1-84161-068-9(2)) Ravette Publishing, Ltd. GBR. Dist: Parkwest Pubns., Inc.

Bell, Hilari. Crown of Earth. Willis, Drew, illus. 2010. (Shield, Sword, & Crown Ser.: 3). (ENG.). 272p. (J). (gr. 3-7). pap. 5.99 (978-1-4169-0599-8(5), Aladdin) Simon & Schuster Children's Publishing.

—Crown of Earth. Willis, Drew, illus. 2009. (Shield, Sword, & Crown Ser.: 3). (ENG.). 272p. (J). (gr. 3-7). 16.99 (978-1-4169-0598-1(7), Simon & Schuster/Paula Wiseman Bks.) Simon & Schuster/Paula Wiseman Bks.

—Fall of a Kingdom. 2005. (Farsala Trilogy Ser.: 1). (ENG.). 448p. (YA). (gr. 7). pap. 6.99 (978-0-689-85414-9(5), Simon Pulse) Simon Pulse.

—The Goblin Gate. (ENG.). (YA). (gr. 8). 2011. 400p. pap. 8.99 (978-0-06-165104-5(4)) 2010. 384p. 16.99 (978-0-06-165102-1(8)) HarperCollins Pubs. (HarperTeen).

—The Goblin War. 2011. (ENG.). 304p. (J). (gr. 8). 17.99 (978-0-06-165105-2(2), HarperTeen) HarperCollins Pubs.

—The Last Knight. 2007. (Knight & Rogue Ser.: 1). (ENG.). 368p. (YA). (gr. 8-12). 16.99 (978-0-06-082503-4(0), HarperTeen) HarperCollins Pubs.

—Player's Ruse. 2010. (Knight & Rogue Ser.: 3). (ENG.). 384p. (YA). (gr. 8-10). 17.99 (978-0-06-082509-6(X), HarperTeen) HarperCollins Pubs.

—Rogue's Home. 2008. (Knight & Rogue Ser.: 2). (ENG.). 432p. (YA). (gr. 8-18). 17.99 (978-0-06-082506-5(5), HarperTeen) HarperCollins Pubs.

—Shield of Stars, No. 1. 2008. (Shield, Sword, & Crown Ser.: 1). (ENG.). 288p. (J). (gr. 3-7). pap. 13.99 (978-1-4169-0595-0(2), Simon & Schuster/Paula Wiseman Bks.) Simon & Schuster/Paula Wiseman Bks.

—Sword of Waters. Willis, Drew, illus. 2009. (Shield, Sword, & Crown Ser.: 2). (ENG.). 384p. (J). (gr. 3-7). pap. 6.99 (978-1-4169-0597-4(9), Aladdin) Simon & Schuster Children's Publishing.

—Sword of Waters, No. 2. Willis, Drew, illus. 2008. (Shield, Sword, & Crown Ser.: 2). (ENG.). 368p. (J). (gr. 3-7). 16.99 (978-1-4169-0596-7(0), Simon & Schuster/Paula Wiseman Bks.) Simon & Schuster/Paula Wiseman Bks.

Bell, Jaime R. Terra. 2011. 68p. pap. 27.68 (978-1-4269-6115-1(4)) Trafford Publishing.

Bell, James Stuart, et al. Inside the Lion, the Witch & the Wardrobe: Myths, Mysteries, & Magic from the Chronicles of Narnia. 2005. (ENG., Illus.). 240p. (YA). (gr. 8-13). pap. 18.99 (978-0-312-34744-4(8), 9780312347444, St. Martin's Griffin) St. Martin's Pr.

Bell, Jennifer. The Crooked Sixpence. Helquist, Brett, illus. 2017. (Uncommoners Ser.: 1). (ENG.). 320p. (J). (gr. 3-7). 16.99 (978-0-553-49843-1(6), Crown Books For Young Readers) Random Hse. Children's Bks.

Bell, Nancy Marie. A Step Sideways. 2013. 134p. (J). pap. (978-1-77127-162-2(0)) MuseItUp Publishing.

Bell, Parker. Tale of the Hundred. 2012. (ENG.). pap. (978-1-4675-2062-1(4)) Independent Pub.

Bell, Ted. The Time Pirate. 2011. (Nick McIver Adventures Through Time Ser.: 2). (ENG., Illus.). 480p. (J). (gr. 5-9). pap. 10.99 (978-0-312-66549-4(0), 9780312665494) Square Fish.

Bellairs, John. The Mansion in the Mist. Gorey, Edward, illus. 2004. (Anthony Monday Ser.: No. 4). (ENG.). 176p. (J). (gr. 3-7). 6.99 (978-0-14-240262-7(1), Puffin Books) Penguin Young Readers Group.

Belle, Magnolia. Teen Titans Go! (TM): Silkie Time. 2017. (Passport to Reading Level 2 Ser.). (ENG., Illus.). 32p. (J). (gr. -1-3). pap. 3.99 (978-0-316-31580-7(X)) Little, Brown Bks. for Young Readers.

Bellisario, Gina. Ellie Ultra. von Innerebner, Jessika, illus. 2017. (Ellie Ultra Ser.). (ENG.). 128p. (gr. 2-3). pap. 27.80 **(978-1-4965-5345-4(4))** Stone Arch Bks.

Bellisario, Gina. Team Earth Takeover. von Innerebner, Jessika, illus. 2017. (Ellie Ultra Ser.). (ENG.). 128p. (gr. 2-3). pap. 6.95 (978-1-4965-3147-6(7)) Stone Arch Bks.

Bemis, John Claude. The Nine Pound Hammer. 2010. (Clockwork Dark Ser.: Bk. 1). (ENG.). 384p. (J). (gr. 3-7). pap. 7.99 (978-0-375-85565-8(3), Yearling) Random Hse. Children's Bks.

—Out of Abaton, Book 1 the Wooden Prince. 2017. (Out of Abaton Ser.). (ENG.). 336p. (J). (gr. 3-7). pap. 7.99 (978-1-4847-0742-5(7)) Hyperion Bks. for Children.

—The Wooden Prince. 2016. (Out of Abaton Ser.: Bk. 1). (ENG., Illus.). 318p. (J). (gr. 3-7). 16.99 (978-1-4847-0727-2(3)) Disney Pr.

Bender, Carol. The Doctor's Little Stowaway. 2009. 28p. pap. 13.99 (978-1-4490-3711-6(9)) AuthorHouse.

—Picky Eater, That Peter. 2011. 25p. (J). 24.95 (978-1-4327-7055-6(1)) Outskirts Pr., Inc.

Bendis, Brian Michael, et al. What If... ? Why Not?, Vol. 1. 2005. (Marvel Heroes Ser.). (Illus.). 152p. pap. 16.99 (978-0-7851-1593-9(5)) Marvel Worldwide, Inc.

Benedetti, Martha J. Fantasy Fairytale: 7 short Stories. 2009. 108p. pap. 44.99 (978-1-4389-1096-3(7)) AuthorHouse.

Benesch, Walter. Adam Cox Meets the CrackleCrunch for Lunch. Jamieson, Sandy, illus. 2004. 32p. (J). 24.95 (978-1-932053-09-8(3)) Nonetheless Pr.

Benjamin, A. H. Shamwood. 2006. 140p. pap. 24.95 (978-1-4137-9193-8(X)) PublishAmerica, Inc.

Bennett, Holly. The Bonemender's Oath, 1 vol. 2006. (Bonemender Ser.: 2). (ENG.). 176p. (YA). (gr. 8-12). per. 9.95 (978-1-55143-443-8(1)) Orca Bk. Pubs. USA.

Bennett, Steven. The Adventures of Super Dad: Colossal Encounters (Book #1) 2005. 98p. pap. 10.49 (978-1-4116-5947-6(3)) Lulu Pr., Inc.

Bentley, Cheryl. Petronella & the Janjilons. 2015. (Petronella Ser.: 2). (ENG.). 144p. (J). 14.95 (978-1-907230-60-8(2)) Sparkling Bks. GBR. Dist: Silvermine International Bks., LLC.

Bentley, Sue. A Circus Wish. 2009. (Magic Kitten Ser.: 6). lib. bdg. 14.75 (978-0-606-06970-0(4), Turtleback) Turtleback Bks.

Beobi & the Magic Coloring Book A Visit to the Doctor. 2005. (J). 3.99 (978-0-9743847-3-3(9)) Cohn, Tricia.

Berarie, Denis. The Little Soul & His Friend. 2012. (Illus.). 32p. pap. 21.35 (978-1-4772-2634-6(6)) AuthorHouse.

Berenato, Dave. Medlocks: The Peractio Blackout. 2011. 284p. (gr. 10-12). 27.95 (978-1-4620-5219-6(3)); pap. 17.95 (978-1-4620-5217-2(7)) iUniverse, Inc.

Berger, Susan J. Growing up Dreams. Bell, Samantha, illus. 2010. 24p. pap. 10.95 (978-1-61633-029-3(5)) Guardian Angel Publishing, Inc.

Berger, Thomas. Stan Bolivan & the Dragon. (Illus.). 30p. (J). 17.95 (978-0-86315-152-1(3), 1585) Floris Bks. GBR. Dist: SteinerBooks, Inc.

Bergsma, Jody. Wizard. 2nd ed. 2008. (Illus.). 32p. (J). 15.95 (978-0-9740190-9-3(7)) Illumination Arts Publishing Co., Inc.

Bergvinson, M. E. St. George's Mysterious Cross. 2013. 208p. pap. 23.16 (978-1-300-13979-9(X)) Lulu Pr., Inc.

Berk, Ari. Death Watch. (Undertaken Trilogy Ser.: 1). (ENG.). (YA). (gr. 7). 2012. 560p. pap. 9.99 (978-1-4169-9116-8(6)) 2011. 544p. 17.99 (978-1-4169-9115-1(8)) Simon & Schuster Bks. For Young Readers. (Simon & Schuster Bks. For Young Readers).

—Lych Way. 2014. (Undertaken Trilogy Ser.: 3). (ENG., Illus.). 336p. (YA). (gr. 7). 17.99 (978-1-4169-9119-9(0), Simon & Schuster Bks. For Young Readers) Simon & Schuster Bks. For Young Readers.

—Mistle Child. (Undertaken Trilogy Ser.: 2). (ENG., (YA). (gr. 7). 2014. Illus.). 368p. pap. 9.99 (978-1-4169-9118-2(2)) 2013. 352p. 17.99 (978-1-4169-9117-5(4)) Simon & Schuster Bks. For Young Readers. (Simon & Schuster Bks. For Young Readers).

Berkley, Shea. The Fallen Prince. 2013. (ENG.). 330p. (YA). (gr. 9). pap. 9.99 (978-1-62061-226-2(7), 9781620612262) Entangled Publishing, LLC.

Bernstein, David D. The Enchanted Rope. 2010. 25p. (J). pap. 13.95 (978-1-4327-5175-3(1)) Outskirts Pr., Inc.

Berrow, G. M. Applejack & the Honest-To-Goodness Switcheroo. 2014. (My Little Pony Chapter Bks.). (J). lib. bdg. 16.00 (978-0-606-35301-4(1)) Turtleback Bks.

—My Little Pony: Equestria Girls: Through the Mirror. 2013. (Equestria Girls Ser.: 1). (ENG.). 240p. (J). (gr. 3-7). 9.99 (978-0-316-24762-7(6)) Little, Brown Bks. for Young Readers.

—The Trouble with Trixie. 2017. (My Little Pony Chapter Bks.). (J). lib. bdg. 16.00 (978-0-606-39477-2(X)) Turtleback Bks.

Berry, Eileen M., retold by. Sticky Flies, Whirling Squirrels, & Plucky Ducks. 2009. (J). (978-1-60682-009-4(5)) BJU Pr.

Berry, Julie. The Amaranth Enchantment. (ENG.). (YA). (gr. 5-8). 2010. 336p. pap. 7.99 (978-1-59990-449-8(7), 9781599904498) 2009. 320p. 16.99 (978-1-59990-334-7(2), 9781599903347) Bloomsbury Publishing USA. (Bloomsbury USA Childrens).

—Secondhand Charm. 2010. (ENG.). 352p. (YA). (gr. 5-8). 16.99 (978-1-59990-511-2(6), 9781599905112, Bloomsbury USA Childrens) Bloomsbury Publishing USA.

Berry, Nina. Othermoon. 2013. (ENG.). 320p. (YA). (gr. 9). pap. 9.95 (978-0-7582-7693-3(1), K-Teen) Kensington Publishing Corp.

Berry, R. A. Buddy's Blue Day. 2010. 16p. 10.99 (978-1-4520-2413-4(8)) AuthorHouse.

Berry, Ron. My Guardian Angel. Sharp, Chris, illus. 2008. 12p. (J). (gr. -1-k). bds. 12.99 (978-0-8249-1819-4(3), Ideal Pubns.) Worthy Publishing.

Berryhill, Shane. Dragon Island. 2013. 216p. pap. 9.99 (978-1-937530-23-5(X)) Crossroad Pr.

Bess, Alex Marie. The Scrapper. 2011. 188p. (J). pap. 13.95 (978-1-936184-85-9(0)) Kidpub Pr.

Bessen, Luc. Arthur & the Minimoys. Sowchek, Ellen, tr. from FRE. 2005. (ENG.). 240p. (J). 15.99 (978-0-06-059623-1(6)) HarperCollins Pubs.

Besson, Luc. Arthur & the Minimoys. 2005. (Illus.). 240p. (J). lib. bdg. 16.89 (978-0-06-059624-8(4)) HarperCollins Pubs.

BeSwitched. 2004. (YA). mass mkt. 7.99 (978-0-9759784-0-5(3)) Breezy Reads.

Bette, Grandma. The Excellent Adventures of Max & Madison: Bedtime stories for Youngsters. 2012. 116p. pap. 42.95 (978-1-4525-0432-2(6)) Balboa Pr.

Bevis, Kaitlin. Persephone. 2015. (ENG., Illus.). 194p. (J). pap. 14.95 (978-1-61194-622-2(0)) BelleBks., Inc.

Bewitched in Oz. 2016. (Bewitched in Oz Ser.). (ENG.). 256p. (gr. 4-8). 61.30 (978-1-4965-2605-2(8)) Stone Arch Bks.

Bhadresa, G. N. Tymrose a Fantasy. 2012. 120p. (978-1-4602-0561-7(8)); pap. (978-1-4602-0560-0(X)) FriesenPress.

Bice, Charles. What Lies Beneath. 2009. 208p. pap. 16.50 (978-0-578-03340-2(2)) Wimabi Pr.

Bidaud, Agnès. The Planet of Libris. Élyum Studio, illus. 2013. (Little Prince Ser.: 11). (ENG.). 48p. (J). (gr. 4-8). lib. bdg. 26.60 (978-0-7613-8761-9(7), Graphic Universe™) Lerner Publishing Group.

Biederman, Ashley. The Witches Keys. 2012. 250p. 28.99 (978-1-105-52163-8(X)) Lulu Pr., Inc.

Biel, Valerie. Circle of Nine: Beltany. 2014. (ENG., Illus.). 307p. (YA). pap. 13.99 (978-0-9906450-0-9(2)) Lost Lake Pr.

Biggs, Stephen. The Time Barrel. 2009. 152p. pap. (978-1-84923-434-4(5)) YouWriteOn.

Bigonette, John, Jr. The Island. 2005. 334p. (YA). 29.95 (978-0-595-78170-6(5)) iUniverse, Inc.

Bilgrey, Marc. And Don't Forget to Rescue the Other Princess. 2009. 252p. 25.95 (978-1-59414-744-9(2), Five Star) Cengage Gale.

Bill Henry Edge. Blip & the Seat of Arthur. 2009. 500p. pap. 24.99 (978-1-4389-5971-9(0)) AuthorHouse.

Billingsley, Franny. The Folk Keeper. unabr. ed. 2004. 176p. (J). (gr. 5-9). pap. 36.00 incl. audio (978-0-8072-0662-1(8), Listening Library) Random Hse. Audio Publishing Group.

Binfet, Eric. The Ninja with Bunny Rabbit Slippers. 2012. 34p. pap. 19.99 (978-1-105-44896-6(7)) Lulu.com GBR. Dist: Lulu Pr., Inc.

Bingham, Laura. Älvor. 2009. pap. 17.99 (978-1-59955-272-9(8)) Cedar Fort, Inc./CFI Distribution.

—Wings of Light. 2011. 240p. pap. 15.99 (978-1-59955-492-1(5), Sweetwater Bks.) Cedar Fort, Inc./CFI Distribution.

Binns, Paul J. Paul & the Porch Gnome. 2011. 24p. pap. 12.99 (978-1-4634-3226-3(7)) AuthorHouse.

Birchfield, Elaine. Wilbur Two the Woodland Road. 2012. pap. 12.95 (978-1-4675-2830-6(7)) Independent Pub.

Bishop, Anne. Anne Bishop's Christmas Dram: The Gift of Three. 2013. 28p. pap. 24.95 (978-1-4626-8276-8(6)) America Star Bks.

Bishop, Debbie. The Fairies of Bladderwhack Pond. Park, Andy, illus. 2003. (Fairies of Bladderwhack Pond Ser.: Vol. 1). (ENG.). 152p. (J). (gr. 4-9). 19.99 (978-1-932431-01-8(2)) Left Field,Angel Gate.

—MYST of the Lost Shadow Boys. 2008. (ENG.). 228p. (J). (gr. 4-9). pap. 6.99 (978-1-932431-79-7(9)) Left Field,Angel Gate.

Bishop, Rose. Arielle's Pursuit. 2007. 100p. pap. 10.95 (978-0-7414-3804-1(6)) Infinity Publishing.

Bixley, Donovan. Dogfight. 2016. (Flying Furballs Ser.: 1). (ENG., Illus.). 112p. (J). (gr. 2-4). pap. 8.99 (978-1-927262-53-5(4)) Upstart Pr. NZL. Dist: Independent Pubs. Group.

Bixley, Donovan. Hot Air. Bixley, Donovan, illus. 2017. (Flying Furballs Ser.: 2). (ENG., Illus.). 112p. (J). (gr. 2-4). pap. 8.99 **(978-1-927262-54-2(2))** Upstart Pr. NZL. Dist: Independent Pubs. Group.

Black, Chuck. Sir Kendrick & the Castle of Bel Lione. 2008. (Knights of Arrethtrae Ser.). (ENG., Illus.). 208p. (YA). (gr. 7-7). pap. 9.99 (978-1-60142-124-1(9), Multnomah Bks.) Crown Publishing Group.

Black, Holly. Kind. Naifeh, Ted, illus. (Good Neighbors Ser.: 3). (ENG.). 128p. (J). 2011. (gr. 7-7). pap. 12.99 (978-0-439-85567-9(5)) 2010. (gr. 3-7). 16.99 (978-0-439-85564-8(0)) Scholastic, Inc. (Graphix).

—The Poison Eaters: And Other Stories. Black, Theo, illus. 2011. (ENG.). 224p. (YA). (gr. 9). pap. 9.99 (978-1-4424-1232-3(1), McElderry, Margaret K. Bks.) McElderry, Margaret K. Bks.

Black, Holly & Clare, Cassandra. The Copper Gauntlet. 2016. (Magisterium Ser.). (ENG.). (J). (gr. 4-7). lib. bdg. 18.40 **(978-0-606-38811-5(7))** Turtleback Bks.

Black, Holly & DiTerlizzi, Tony. Arthur Spiderwick's Field Guide to the Fantastical World Around You. Black, Holly & DiTerlizzi, Tony, illus. 2005. (Spiderwick Chronicles Ser.). (ENG., Illus.). 142p. (J). (gr. 3). 24.99 (978-0-689-85941-0(4), Simon & Schuster Bks. For Young Readers) Simon & Schuster Bks. For Young Readers.

—Arthur Spiderwick's Field Guide to the Fantastical World Around You. DiTerlizzi, Tony, illus. movie tie-in ed. 2008. (Spiderwick Chronicles Ser.). (ENG., Illus.). 142p. (J). (gr. 3-7). 24.99 (978-1-4169-6095-9(3), Simon & Schuster Bks. For Young Readers) Simon & Schuster Bks. For Young Readers.

—The Spiderwick. DiTerlizzi, Tony, illus. 2009. (Spiderwick Chronicles Ser.). (ENG., Illus.). 608p. (J). (gr. 3-7). 29.99 (978-1-4169-8685-0(5), Simon & Schuster Bks. For Young Readers) Simon & Schuster Bks. For Young Readers.

—The Spiderwick Chronicles Set: The Field Guide - The Seeing Stone - Lucinda's Secret - The Ironwood Tree - The Wrath of Mulgrath. DiTerlizzi, Tony, illus. 2013. (Spiderwick Chronicles Ser.). (ENG., Illus.). (J). (gr. 1-5). 752p. pap. 39.99 (978-1-4424-8798-7(4)); 672p. 79.99

(978-1-4424-8797-0(6)) Simon & Schuster Bks. For Young Readers. (Simon & Schuster Bks. For Young Readers).

—The Wyrm King. DiTerlizzi, Tony, illus. 2009. (Beyond the Spiderwick Chronicles Ser.: 3). (ENG., Illus.). 224p. (J). (gr. 2-7). 11.99 (978-0-689-87133-7(3), Simon & Schuster Bks. For Young Readers) Simon & Schuster Bks. For Young Readers.

Blackburn, Jessica. The Echoing. 2016. (ENG.). (YA). pap. 14.99 (978-1-4621-1894-6(1), Bonneville Bks.) Cedar Fort, Inc./CFI Distribution.

Blackburne, Livia. Daughter of Dusk. (ENG., Illus.). (YA). (gr. 7-12). 2016. 384p. pap. 9.99 (978-1-4847-2366-1(X)) 2015. 380p. 17.99 (978-1-4847-2208-4(6)) Hyperion Bks. for Children.

—Midnight Thief. (Midnight Thief Ser.). (ENG., Illus.). (YA). (gr. 7-12). 2014. 380p. 16.99 (978-1-4231-7638-1(3))Bk. 1. 2015. 394p. pap. 9.99 (978-1-4231-9461-3(6)) Hyperion Bks. for Children.

Blackford, Holly. The Plight of Persephone in Girls' Fantasy Literature. 2011. (Children's Literature & Culture Ser.). (ENG.). 260p. (C). 141.00 (978-0-415-89541-5(3), Y119731) Routledge.

Blackthorn, J. D. & Rinehart, J. D. Crown of Three. 2015. (Crown of Three Ser.: 1). (ENG.). 416p. (J). (gr. 4-8). 17.99 (978-1-4814-2443-1(2), Aladdin) Simon & Schuster Children's Publishing.

Blackwood, Sage. Jinx. (Jinx Ser.: 3). (J). (gr. 3-7). 2016. 400p. pap. 7.99 (978-0-06-212997-0(X), Tegen, Katherine Bks) 2015. (ENG.). 400p. 16.99 (978-0-06-212996-3(1), Tegen, Katherine Bks) 2014. (ENG.). 400p. 16.99 (978-0-06-212993-2(7), Tegen, Katherine Bks) 2013. (ENG.). 368p. 16.99 (978-0-06-212990-1(2)) HarperCollins Pubs.

—Miss Ellicott's School for the Magically Minded. 2017. 368p. (J). (gr. 3-7). 16.99 (978-0-06-240263-9(3), Tegen, Katherine Bks) HarperCollins Pubs.

Blade, Adam. Amictus: The Bug Queen. 2015. (Beast Quest Ser.). (ENG., Illus.). 144p. (J). (gr. 2-4). pap. 5.99 (978-1-4083-0442-6(2)) Hodder & Stoughton GBR. Dist: Hachette Bk. Group.

—Anoret: The First Beast. 2014. (Beast Quest Ser.: 12). (ENG., Illus.). 192p. (J). (gr. 2-4). pap. 5.99 (978-1-4083-2410-3(5)) Hodder & Stoughton GBR. Dist: Hachette Bk. Group.

—Arax: The Soul Stealer. 2014. (Beast Quest Ser.). (ENG., Illus.). 192p. (J). (gr. 2-4). pap. 5.99 (978-1-4083-0382-5(5)) Hodder & Stoughton GBR. Dist: Hachette Bk. Group.

—Battle of the Beasts: Ferno vs Epos. 2014. (Beast Quest Ser.: 1). (ENG., Illus.). 192p. (J). (gr. 2-4). pap. 5.99 (978-1-4083-1867-6(9)) Hodder & Stoughton GBR. Dist: Hachette Bk. Group.

—Brutus: The Hound of Horror. 2014. (Beast Quest Ser.: 63). (ENG., Illus.). 144p. (J). (gr. 2-4). pap. 5.99 (978-1-4083-1843-0(1)) Hodder & Stoughton GBR. Dist: Hachette Bk. Group.

—Carnivora: The Winged Scavenger. 2015. (Beast Quest Ser.). (ENG., Illus.). 144p. (J). (gr. 2-4). pap. 5.99 (978-1-4083-0734-2(0)) Hodder & Stoughton GBR. Dist: Hachette Bk. Group.

—Chasing Evil. (Chronicles of Avantia Ser.). (ENG.). 176p. (J). (gr. 3-7). 2013. pap. 5.99 (978-0-545-36157-6(5), Scholastic Paperbacks) 2012. 15.99 (978-0-545-36158-3(3), Scholastic Pr.) Scholastic, Inc.

—The Chronicles of Avantia #3: Call to War. 2012. (Chronicles of Avantia Ser.: 3). (ENG.). 176p. (J). (gr. 3-7). 15.99 (978-0-545-36156-9(7), Scholastic Pr.) Scholastic, Inc.

—Convol: The Cold-Blooded Brute. 2015. (Beast Quest Ser.). (ENG., Illus.). 144p. (J). (gr. 2-4). pap. 5.99 (978-1-4083-0729-8(4)) Hodder & Stoughton GBR. Dist: Hachette Bk. Group.

—Creta: The Winged Terror. 2016. (Beast Quest Ser.). (ENG., Illus.). 80p. (J). (gr. k-17). pap. 5.99 (978-1-4083-3924-4(2), Orchard Bks.) Hachette Children's Group GBR. Dist: Hachette Bk. Group.

—Creta the Winged Terror. 2014. (Beast Quest Ser.: 5). (ENG., Illus.). 192p. (J). (gr. 2-4). pap. 5.99 (978-1-4083-0735-9(9)) Hodder & Stoughton GBR. Dist: Hachette Bk. Group.

—The Dagger of Doom. 2014. (Beast Quest Ser.). (ENG., Illus.). 128p. (J). (gr. 2-4). 5.99 (978-1-4083-1406-7(1)) Hodder & Stoughton GBR. Dist: Hachette Bk. Group.

—The Dark Cauldron. 2014. (Beast Quest Ser.). (ENG., Illus.). 112p. (J). (gr. 2-4). pap. 5.99 (978-1-4083-0943-8(2)) Hodder & Stoughton GBR. Dist: Hachette Bk. Group.

—Doomskull Bk. 60: The King of Fear. 2014. (Beast Quest Ser.: 60). (ENG., Illus.). 128p. (J). (gr. 2-4). pap. 5.99 (978-1-4083-1523-1(8)) Hodder & Stoughton GBR. Dist: Hachette Bk. Group.

—Drogan: The Jungle Menace. 2016. (Beast Quest Ser.). (ENG., Illus.). 144p. (J). (gr. 2-4). pap. 5.99 (978-1-4083-4295-4(2), Orchard Bks.) Hachette Children's Group GBR. Dist: Hachette Bk. Group.

—Elko: Lord of the Sea. 2014. (Beast Quest Ser.: 61). (ENG., Illus.). 128p. (J). (gr. 2-4). 5.99 (978-1-4083-1841-6(5)) Hodder & Stoughton GBR. Dist: Hachette Bk. Group.

—Ellik: The Lightning Horror. 2015. (Beast Quest Ser.). (ENG., Illus.). 144p. (J). (gr. 2-4). pap. 5.99 (978-1-4083-0733-5(2)) Hodder & Stoughton GBR. Dist: Hachette Bk. Group.

—Falkor: The Coiled Terror. 2017. (Beast Quest Ser.). (ENG., Illus.). 192p. (J). (gr. 2-4). pap. 5.99 (978-1-4083-4297-8(9), Orchard Bks.) Hachette Children's Group GBR. Dist: Hachette Bk. Group.

—Falra Bk. 82: The Snow Phoenix. 2016. (Beast Quest Ser.). (ENG., Illus.). 144p. (J). (gr. 2-4). pap. 5.99 (978-1-4083-2923-8(9), Orchard Bks.) Hachette Children's Group GBR. Dist: Hachette Bk. Group.

—Fang: The Bat Fiend. 2015. (Beast Quest Ser.). (ENG., Illus.). 144p. (J). (gr. 2-4). pap. 5.99 (978-1-4083-0725-0(1)) Hodder & Stoughton GBR. Dist: Hachette Bk. Group.

—Fire & Fury. 2013. (Chronicles of Avantia Ser.: 4). (ENG.). 192p. (J). (gr. 3-7). 15.99 (978-0-545-36154-5(0), Scholastic Pr.) Scholastic, Inc.

—First Hero. 2012. (Chronicles of Avantia Ser.). (ENG.). 176p. (J). (gr. 3-7). 15.99 (978-0-545-36160-6(5), Scholastic Pr.) Scholastic, Inc.

—Flaymar: The Scorched Blaze. 2014. (Beast Quest Ser.: 64). (ENG., Illus.). 144p. (J). (gr. 2-4). pap. 5.99

(978-1-4083-1844-7(X)) Hodder & Stoughton GBR. Dist: Hachette Bk. Group.
—The Ghost Warrior. 2016. (Beast Quest Ser.). (ENG., Illus.). 192p. (J). (gr. 2-4). pap. 5.99 (978-1-4083-3497-3(6), Orchard Bks.) Hachette Children's Group GBR. Dist: Hachette Bk. Group.
—Grashkor: The Beast Guard. 2015. (Beast Quest Ser.: 9). (ENG., Illus.). 192p. (J). (gr. 2-4). pap. 5.99 (978-1-4083-1517-0(3)) Hodder & Stoughton GBR. Dist: Hachette Bk. Group.
—Gryph: The Feathered Fiend. 2016. (Beast Quest Ser.). (ENG., Illus.). 144p. (J). (gr. 2-17). pap. 5.99 (978-1-4083-4076-9(3), Orchard Bks.) Hachette Children's Group GBR. Dist: Hachette Bk. Group.
—Hawkite: Arrow of the Air. 2015. (Beast Quest Ser.). (ENG., Illus.). 144p. (J). (gr. 2-4). pap. 5.99 (978-1-4083-0438-9(4)) Hodder & Stoughton GBR. Dist: Hachette Bk. Group.
—Hellion: The Fiery Foe. 2015. (Beast Quest Ser.). (ENG., Illus.). 144p. (J). (gr. 2-4). pap. 5.99 (978-1-4083-0730-4(8)) Hodder & Stoughton GBR. Dist: Hachette Bk. Group.
—Kanis: The Shadow Hound. 2016. (Beast Quest Ser.). (ENG., Illus.). 144p. (J). (gr. 2-17). pap. 5.99 (978-1-4083-3994-7(3), Orchard Bks.) Hachette Children's Group GBR. Dist: Hachette Bk. Group.
—Karixa: The Diamond Warrior. 2016. (Beast Quest Ser.). (ENG., Illus.). 144p. (J). (gr. 2-4). pap. 5.99 (978-1-4083-4309-8(6), Orchard Bks.) Hachette Children's Group GBR. Dist: Hachette Bk. Group.
—Koba: Ghoul of the Shadows. 2015. (Beast Quest Ser.: 78). (ENG., Illus.). 128p. (J). (gr. 2-4). pap. 5.99 (978-1-4083-2407-3(5)) Hodder & Stoughton GBR. Dist: Hachette Bk. Group.
—Koldo: The Arctic Warrior. 2015. (Beast Quest Ser.). (ENG., Illus.). 144p. (J). (gr. 2-4). pap. 5.99 (978-1-4083-0440-2(6)) Hodder & Stoughton GBR. Dist: Hachette Bk. Group.
—Komodo Bk. 31: The Lizard King. 2015. (Beast Quest Ser.). (ENG., Illus.). 144p. (J). (gr. 2-4). pap. 5.99 (978-1-4083-0723-6(5)) Hodder & Stoughton GBR. Dist: Hachette Bk. Group.
—Koraka: The Winged Assassin. 2014. (Beast Quest Ser.: 51). (ENG., Illus.). 128p. (J). (gr. 2-4). pap. 5.99 (978-1-4083-1318-3(9)) Hodder & Stoughton GBR. Dist: Hachette Bk. Group.
—Korvax: The Sea Dragon. 2017. (Beast Quest Ser.). (ENG., Illus.). 144p. (J). (gr. 2-4). 5.99 **(978-1-4083-4313-5(4)**, Orchard Bks.) Hachette Children's Group GBR. Dist: Hachette Bk. Group.
—Krabb Bk. 25: Master of the Sea. 2015. (Beast Quest Ser.). (ENG., Illus.). 144p. (J). (gr. 2-4). pap. 5.99 (978-1-4083-0437-2(6)) Hodder & Stoughton GBR. Dist: Hachette Bk. Group.
—Kragos & Kildor: The Two-Headed Demon. 2016. (Beast Quest Ser.). (ENG., Illus.). 80p. (J). (gr. 2-4). pap. 5.99 (978-1-4083-3514-7(X), Orchard Bks.) Hachette Children's Group GBR. Dist: Hachette Bk. Group.
—Kragos & Kildor: The Two-Headed Demon. 2014. (Beast Quest Ser.: 4). (ENG., Illus.). 192p. (J). (gr. 2-4). pap. 5.99 (978-1-4083-0436-5(8)) Hodder & Stoughton GBR. Dist: Hachette Bk. Group.
—Krestor: The Crushing Terror. 2015. (Beast Quest Ser.). (ENG., Illus.). 144p. (J). (gr. 2-4). pap. 5.99 (978-1-4083-0731-1(6)) Hodder & Stoughton GBR. Dist: Hachette Bk. Group.
—Krytor: The Blood Bat. 2016. (Beast Quest Ser.). (ENG., Illus.). 144p. (J). (gr. 2-4). pap. 5.99 (978-1-4083-4086-8(0), Orchard Bks.) Hachette Children's Group GBR. Dist: Hachette Bk. Group.
—Kyrax: The Metal Warrior. 2017. (Beast Quest Ser.). (ENG., Illus.). 192p. (J). (gr. 2-17). 5.99 (978-1-4083-4299-2(5), Orchard Bks.) Hachette Children's Group GBR. Dist: Hachette Bk. Group.
—Linka Bk. 76: The Sky Conqueror. 2015. (Beast Quest Ser.: 76). (ENG., Illus.). 128p. (J). (gr. 2-4). pap. 5.99 (978-1-4083-2405-9(9)) Hodder & Stoughton GBR. Dist: Hachette Bk. Group.
—Lustor: The Acid Dart. 2014. (Beast Quest Ser.: 57). (ENG., Illus.). 128p. (J). (gr. 2-4). pap. 5.99 (978-1-4083-1520-0(3)) Hodder & Stoughton GBR. Dist: Hachette Bk. Group.
—Minos: The Demon Bull. 2014. (Beast Quest Ser.: 50). (ENG., Illus.). 128p. (J). (gr. 2-4). pap. 5.99 (978-1-4083-1317-6(0)) Hodder & Stoughton GBR. Dist: Hachette Bk. Group.
—Mortaxe: The Skeleton Warrior. 2016. (Beast Quest Ser.). (ENG., Illus.). 80p. (J). (gr. k-17). pap. 5.99 (978-1-4083-4182-7(4), Orchard Bks.) Hachette Children's Group GBR. Dist: Hachette Bk. Group.
—Murk: The Swamp Man. 2015. (Beast Quest Ser.). (ENG., Illus.). 144p. (J). (gr. 2-4). pap. 5.99 (978-1-4083-0726-7(X)) Hodder & Stoughton GBR. Dist: Hachette Bk. Group.
—Muro: The Rat Monster. 2015. (Beast Quest Ser.). (ENG., Illus.). 144p. (J). (gr. 2-4). pap. 5.99 (978-1-4083-0724-3(3)) Hodder & Stoughton GBR. Dist: Hachette Bk. Group.
—Noctila: The Death Owl. 2014. (Beast Quest Ser.: 55). (ENG., Illus.). 128p. (J). (gr. 2-4). pap. 5.99 (978-1-4083-1518-7(1)) Hodder & Stoughton GBR. Dist: Hachette Bk. Group.
—The Pirate's Curse. 2016. (Beast Quest Ser.). (ENG., Illus.). 144p. (J). (gr. 2-4). pap. 5.99 (978-1-4083-1840-9(7)) Hodder & Stoughton GBR. Dist: Hachette Bk. Group.
—Plexor: The Raging Reptile. 2016. (Beast Quest Ser.). (ENG., Illus.). 144p. (J). (gr. 2-4). pap. 5.99 (978-1-4083-3491-1(7), Orchard Bks.) Hachette Children's Group GBR. Dist: Hachette Bk. Group.
—Quagos the Armoured Beetle. 2016. (Beast Quest Ser.). (ENG., Illus.). 144p. (J). (gr. 2-4). pap. 5.99 (978-1-4083-3493-5(3), Orchard Bks.) Hachette Children's Group GBR. Dist: Hachette Bk. Group.
—Quarg: The Stone Dragon. 2017. (Beast Quest Ser.). (ENG., Illus.). 144p. (J). (gr. 2-4). 5.99 **(978-1-4083-4311-1(8)**, Orchard Bks.) Hachette Children's Group GBR. Dist: Hachette Bk. Group.
—Raffkor Bk. 79: The Stampeding Brute. 2016. (Beast Quest Ser.). (ENG., Illus.). 144p. (J). (gr. 2-4). pap. 5.99 (978-1-4083-2920-7(4), Orchard Bks.) Hachette Children's Group GBR. Dist: Hachette Bk. Group.
—Ravira: Ruler of the Underworld. 2016. (Beast Quest Ser.). (ENG., Illus.). 80p. (J). (gr. k-2). pap. 5.99 (978-1-4083-4184-1(0), Orchard Bks.) Hachette Children's Group GBR. Dist: Hachette Bk. Group.
—Ronak: The Toxic Terror. 2016. (Beast Quest Ser.). (ENG., Illus.). 144p. (J). (gr. 2-17). pap. 5.99 (978-1-4083-3996-1(X), Orchard Bks.) Hachette Children's Group GBR. Dist: Hachette Bk. Group.
—Saurex the Silent Creeper. 2016. (Beast Quest Ser.). (ENG., Illus.). 144p. (J). (gr. 2-17). pap. 5.99 (978-1-4083-4084-4(4), Orchard Bks.) Hachette Children's Group GBR. Dist: Hachette Bk. Group.
—Serpio: The Slithering Shadow. 2014. (Beast Quest Ser.: 65). (ENG., Illus.). 144p. (J). (gr. 2-4). pap. 5.99 (978-1-4083-1845-4(8)) Hodder & Stoughton GBR. Dist: Hachette Bk. Group.
—Shamani: The Raging Flame. 2014. (Beast Quest Ser.: 56). (ENG., Illus.). 128p. (J). (gr. 2-4). pap. 5.99 (978-1-4083-1519-4(X)) Hodder & Stoughton GBR. Dist: Hachette Bk. Group.
—Silver: The Wild Terror. 2014. (Beast Quest Ser.: 52). (ENG., Illus.). 128p. (J). (gr. 2-4). pap. 5.99 (978-1-4083-1319-0(7)) Hodder & Stoughton GBR. Dist: Hachette Bk. Group.
—Skolo: The Bladed Monster. 2016. (Beast Quest Ser.). (ENG., Illus.). 192p. (J). (gr. 2-4). pap. 5.99 (978-1-4083-2930-6(1), Orchard Bks.) Hachette Children's Group GBR. Dist: Hachette Bk. Group.
—Skurik Bk. 73: The Forest Demon. 2015. (Beast Quest Ser.: 73). (ENG., Illus.). 128p. (J). (gr. 2-4). pap. 5.99 (978-1-4083-2402-8(4)) Hodder & Stoughton GBR. Dist: Hachette Bk. Group.
—Slivka: The Cold-Hearted Curse. 2015. (Beast Quest Ser.: 75). (ENG., Illus.). 128p. (J). (gr. 2-4). pap. 5.99 (978-1-4083-2404-2(0)) Hodder & Stoughton GBR. Dist: Hachette Bk. Group.
—Soara: The Stinging Spectre. 2016. (Beast Quest Ser.). (ENG., Illus.). 144p. (J). (gr. 2-4). pap. 5.99 (978-1-4083-4088-2(7), Orchard Bks.) Hachette Children's Group GBR. Dist: Hachette Bk. Group.
—Solix Bk. 89: The Deadly Swarm. 2016. (Beast Quest Ser.). (ENG., Illus.). 144p. (J). (gr. 2-17). pap. 5.99 (978-1-4083-3988-6(9), Orchard Bks.) Hachette Children's Group GBR. Dist: Hachette Bk. Group.
—Spikefin: The Water King. 2014. (Beast Quest Ser.: 53). (ENG., Illus.). 128p. (J). (gr. 2-4). pap. 5.99 (978-1-4083-1320-6(0)) Hodder & Stoughton GBR. Dist: Hachette Bk. Group.
—Strytor the Skeleton Dragon. 2017. (Beast Quest Ser.). (ENG., Illus.). 144p. (J). (gr. 2-4). 5.99 **(978-1-4083-4317-3(7)**, Orchard Bks.) Hachette Children's Group GBR. Dist: Hachette Bk. Group.
—Styro: The Snapping Brute. 2016. (Beast Quest Ser.). (ENG., Illus.). 144p. (J). (gr. 2-17). pap. 5.99 (978-1-4083-3986-2(2), Orchard Bks.) Hachette Children's Group GBR. Dist: Hachette Bk. Group.
—Targro: The Arctic Menace. 2015. (Beast Quest Ser.: 74). (ENG., Illus.). 128p. (J). (gr. 2-4). pap. 5.99 (978-1-4083-2403-5(2)) Hodder & Stoughton GBR. Dist: Hachette Bk. Group.
—Tarrok the Blood Spike. 2014. (Beast Quest Ser.: 62). (ENG., Illus.). 144p. (J). (gr. 2-4). pap. 5.99 (978-1-4083-1842-3(3)) Hodder & Stoughton GBR. Dist: Hachette Bk. Group.
—Tauron: The Pounding Fury. 2014. (Beast Quest Ser.: 66). (ENG., Illus.). 144p. (J). (gr. 2-4). pap. 5.99 (978-1-4083-1846-1(6)) Hodder & Stoughton GBR. Dist: Hachette Bk. Group.
—Tecton: The Armoured Giant. 2014. (Beast Quest Ser.: 59). (ENG., Illus.). 128p. (J). (gr. 2-4). pap. 5.99 (978-1-4083-1522-4(X)) Hodder & Stoughton GBR. Dist: Hachette Bk. Group.
—Tempra: Thee Time Stealer. 2016. (Beast Quest Ser.). (ENG., Illus.). 192p. (J). (gr. 2-4). pap. 5.99 (978-1-4083-4078-3(X), Orchard Bks.) Hachette Children's Group GBR. Dist: Hachette Bk. Group.
—Terra: Curse of the Forest. 2015. (Beast Quest Ser.). (ENG., Illus.). 144p. (J). (gr. 2-4). pap. 5.99 (978-1-4083-0727-4(8)) Hodder & Stoughton GBR. Dist: Hachette Bk. Group.
—The Ultimate Story Collection. 2016. (Beast Quest Ser.). (ENG., Illus.). 384p. (J). (gr. 2-4). 16.99 (978-1-4083-4547-4(1), Orchard Bks.) Hachette Children's Group GBR. Dist: Hachette Bk. Group.
—Thoron: The Living Storm. 2016. (Beast Quest Ser.). (ENG., Illus.). 144p. (J). (gr. 2-17). pap. 5.99 (978-1-4083-4080-6(1), Orchard Bks.) Hachette Children's Group GBR. Dist: Hachette Bk. Group.
—Tikron Bk. 81: The Jungle Master. 2016. (Beast Quest Ser.). (ENG., Illus.). 144p. (J). (gr. 2-4). pap. 5.99 (978-1-4083-2922-1(0), Orchard Bks.) Hachette Children's Group GBR. Dist: Hachette Bk. Group.
—Torpix: The Twisting Serpent. 2014. (Beast Quest Ser.: 54). (ENG., Illus.). 128p. (J). (gr. 2-4). pap. 5.99 (978-1-4083-1321-3(9)) Hodder & Stoughton GBR. Dist: Hachette Bk. Group.
—Trema: The Earth Lord. 2015. (Beast Quest Ser.). (ENG., Illus.). 144p. (J). (gr. 2-4). pap. 5.99 (978-1-4083-0441-9(4)) Hodder & Stoughton GBR. Dist: Hachette Bk. Group.
—Ursus Bk. 49: The Clawed Roar. 2014. (Beast Quest Ser.: 49). (ENG., Illus.). 128p. (J). (gr. 2-4). pap. 5.99 (978-1-4083-1316-9(2)) Hodder & Stoughton GBR. Dist: Hachette Bk. Group.
—Vedra & Krimon: Twin Beasts of Avantia. 2015. (Beast Quest Ser.). (ENG., Illus.). 80p. (J). (gr. 2-4). pap. 5.99 (978-1-4083-3500-0(X)) Hodder & Stoughton GBR. Dist: Hachette Bk. Group.
—Vedra & Krimon the Twin Dragons. 2012. (Beast Quest Special Edition Ser.: 2). lib. bdg. 16.00 (978-0-606-26187-6(7), Turtleback) Turtleback Bks.
—Vermok: The Spiteful Scavenger. 2015. (Beast Quest Ser.: 77). (ENG., Illus.). 128p. (J). (gr. 2-4). pap. 5.99 (978-1-4083-2406-6(7)) Hodder & Stoughton GBR. Dist: Hachette Bk. Group.
—Vespick Bk. 36: The Wasp Queen. 2015. (Beast Quest Ser.). (ENG., Illus.). 144p. (J). (gr. 2-4). pap. 5.99 (978-1-4083-0728-1(6)) Hodder & Stoughton GBR. Dist: Hachette Bk. Group.
—Vetrix the Poison Dragon. 2017. (Beast Quest Ser.). (ENG., Illus.). 144p. (J). (gr. 2-4). 5.99 **(978-1-4083-4315-9(0)**, Orchard Bks.) Hachette Children's Group GBR. Dist: Hachette Bk. Group.
—Viktor: The Deadly Archer. 2015. (Beast Quest Ser.: 11). (ENG., Illus.). 192p. (J). (gr. 2-4). pap. 5.99 (978-1-4083-2408-0(3)) Hodder & Stoughton GBR. Dist: Hachette Bk. Group.
—Vislak Bk. 80: The Slithering Serpent. 2016. (Beast Quest Ser.). (ENG., Illus.). 144p. (J). (gr. 2-4). pap. 5.99 (978-1-4083-2921-4(2), Orchard Bks.) Hachette Children's Group GBR. Dist: Hachette Bk. Group.
—Voltrex: The Two-Headed Octopus. 2014. (Beast Quest Ser.: 58). (ENG., Illus.). 144p. (J). (gr. 2-4). pap. 5.99 (978-1-4083-1521-7(1)) Hodder & Stoughton GBR. Dist: Hachette Bk. Group.
—Wardok the Sky Terror. 2016. (Beast Quest Ser.). (ENG., Illus.). 144p. (J). (gr. 2-4). pap. 5.99 (978-1-4083-3487-4(9), Orchard Bks.) Hachette Children's Group GBR. Dist: Hachette Bk. Group.
—Xerik: The Bone Cruncher. 2016. (Beast Quest Ser.). (ENG., Illus.). 144p. (J). (gr. 2-4). pap. 5.99 (978-1-4083-3489-8(5), Orchard Bks.) Hachette Children's Group GBR. Dist: Hachette Bk. Group.
—Yakorix: The Ice Bear. 2016. (Beast Quest Ser.). (ENG., Illus.). 192p. (J). (gr. 2-4). pap. 5.99 (978-1-4083-3495-9(X), Orchard Bks.) Hachette Children's Group GBR. Dist: Hachette Bk. Group.
Blaha-Black, Caroline. Anika & the Magic Top. 2008. 60p. pap. 11.95 (978-1-4357-1194-5(7)) Lulu Pr., Inc.
Blaine, Jack. The Nightworld. 2012. (ENG.). 240p. (YA). (gr. 9). pap. 8.99 (978-0-06-213380-9(2)) HarperCollins Pubs.
Blair, Eric. The Boy Who Cried Wolf, 1 vol. Silverman, Dianne, illus. 2011. (My First Classic Story Ser.). (ENG.). 24p. (gr. k-3). pap. 7.10 (978-1-4048-7364-3(3), My First Classic Story) Picture Window Bks.
—Rumpelstiltskin. Abello, Patricia, tr. from ENG. Shaw, David, illus. 2006. (Read-It! Readers en Español: Cuentos de Hadas Ser.). (SPA.). 32p. (gr. k-3). 21.32 (978-1-4048-1637-4(2), Easy Readers) Picture Window Bks.
Blair, Eric & Aesop Enterprise Inc. Staff. Belling the Cat: A Retelling of Aesop's Fable, 1 vol. Silverman, Dianne, illus. 2011. (My First Classic Story Ser.). (ENG.). 24p. (gr. k-3). lib. bdg. 22.65 (978-1-4048-6504-4(7), My First Classic Story) Picture Window Bks.
—The Boy Who Cried Wolf: A Retelling of Aesop's Fable, 1 vol. Silverman, Dianne, illus. 2011. (My First Classic Story Ser.). (ENG.). 24p. (gr. k-3). lib. bdg. 22.65 (978-1-4048-6507-5(1), My First Classic Story) Picture Window Bks.
—The Country Mouse & the City Mouse: A Retelling of Aesop's Fable, 1 vol. Silverman, Dianne, illus. 2011. (My First Classic Story Ser.). (ENG.). 24p. (gr. k-3). lib. bdg. 22.65 (978-1-4048-6510-5(1), My First Classic Story) Picture Window Bks.
—The Donkey in the Lion's Skin: A Retelling of Aesop's Fable, 1 vol. Silverman, Dianne, illus. 2011. (My First Classic Story Ser.). (ENG.). 24p. (gr. k-3). lib. bdg. 22.65 (978-1-4048-6506-8(3), My First Classic Story) Picture Window Bks.
Blair, Eric & Peterson, Ben. The Pied Piper, 1 vol. 2010. (My First Classic Story Ser.). (ENG.). 32p. (gr. k-3). lib. bdg. 22.65 (978-1-4048-6084-1(3), My First Classic Story) Picture Window Bks.
Blair, Eric, et al. The Brave Little Tailor: A Retelling of the Grimm's Fairy Tale, 1 vol. Shaw, David, illus. 2010. (My First Classic Story Ser.). (ENG.). 32p. (gr. k-3). lib. bdg. 22.65 (978-1-4048-6074-2(6), My First Classic Story) Picture Window Bks.
—Sleeping Beauty: A Retelling of the Grimm's Fairy Tale, 1 vol. Ouren, Todd, illus. 2010. (My First Classic Story Ser.). (ENG.). 32p. (gr. k-3). lib. bdg. 22.65 (978-1-4048-6080-3(0), My First Classic Story) Picture Window Bks.
—Tom Thumb: A Retelling of the Grimm's Fairy Tale, 1 vol. Ouren, Todd, illus. 2010. (My First Classic Story Ser.). (ENG.). 32p. (gr. k-3). lib. bdg. 22.65 (978-1-4048-6071-1(1), My First Classic Story) Picture Window Bks.
Blair, Thomas L. The Sabatini Prophecy. 2006. 469p. 22.95 (978-0-9760237-1-5(7)) Axiom Hse.
Blake, Drew. Engineer's Spell. 2007. 380p. per. 21.95 (978-0-595-45249-1(3)) iUniverse, Inc.
Blake, Elly. Fireblood. 2017. (Frostblood Saga Ser.: 2). (ENG.). 416p. (YA). (gr. 7-17). 17.99 **(978-0-316-27332-9(5))** Little, Brown Bks. for Young Readers.
Blake, Elly. Frostblood. 2017. (Frostblood Saga Ser.: 1). (ENG.). (YA). (gr. 7-17). 400p. pap. 9.99 **(978-0-316-27318-3(X))**; 384p. 17.99 (978-0-316-27325-1(2)) Little, Brown Bks. for Young Readers.
Blake-Garrett, Andrea. The Adventures of Izzy & Juju: Twin Detective Investigators (T. D. I.) 2012. 28p. pap. 19.99 (978-1-4685-0683-9(8)) AuthorHouse.
—Las Aventuras de Izzy y Juju: Gemelos Detectives Investigadores (G. D. I.) 2012. 28p. pap. 19.99 (978-1-4772-2523-3(4)) AuthorHouse.
Blake, Kendare. One Dark Throne. 2017. (Three Dark Crowns Ser.: 2). 464p. (YA). (gr. 9). 18.99 **(978-0-06-238546-8(1)**, HarperTeen) HarperCollins Pubs.
Blake, Kendare. Ungodly. 2015. (Goddess War Ser.: 3). (ENG.). 368p. (YA). (gr. 8). 17.99 (978-0-7653-3445-9(3), 9780765334459, Tor Teen) Doherty, Tom Assocs., LLC.
Blankenship, Paula. We Both Read-Lulu's Lost Shoes Big Book: Lulu's Lost Shoes Big Book. Reinhart, Larry, illus. 2005. 44p. (J). (gr. k-1). 29.95 (978-1-891327-90-2(9)) Treasure Bay, Inc.
Blashfield, Jean F. Realm of the Enchanter. 2007. (Paths of Doom Ser.). (Illus.). 127p. (J). per. 4.99 (978-1-931567-73-2(5)) Margaret Weis Productions, Ltd.
Blaylock, Josh. Misplaced. O'Reilly, Sean Patrick, ed. 2011. (Illus.). 126p. (YA). pap. 14.95 (978-1-926914-17-6(1)) Arcana Studio, Inc.
Bledsoe, C. L. The Necro-Files. 2013. 174p. pap. 10.99 (978-1-939194-93-0(8)) Etopia Pr.
Bliss, Bob, illus. The Hardest Lessons: The Lost Babies Series #3. 2007. 118p. (J). per. 5.99 (978-0-9792499-2-1(9)) Eagle Tree Pr.
—The Ruby Hind: The Lost Babies Series #1. 2007. 116p. (J). per. 5.99 (978-0-9792499-0-7(2)) Eagle Tree Pr.
—Too Many Parents: The Lost Babies Series #2. 2007. 109p. (J). per. 5.99 (978-0-9792499-1-4(0)) Eagle Tree Pr.
Bliss, Emily. Flash's Dash. Hanson, Sydney, illus. 2017. (Unicorn Princesses Ser.). (ENG.). 128p. (J). 15.99 (978-1-68119-329-8(9), 9781681193298, Bloomsbury USA Childrens) Bloomsbury Publishing USA.
Block, Betty Mitchell. The Magic Pork Chop Bone. 2013. (ENG.). 76p. (YA). pap. 8.95 (978-1-4787-1482-8(4)) Outskirts Pr., Inc.
Block, Francesca Lia. Ecstasia. 2004. (ENG., Illus.). 208p. (Orig.). (YA). (gr. 7-7). pap. 7.99 (978-0-14-240037-1(8), Firebird) Penguin Young Readers Group.
Bloom, Harold, ed. The Chronicles of Narnia. 2006. (Bloom's Modern Critical Interpretations Ser.). 248p. (C). (gr. 9). lib. bdg. 45.00 (978-0-7910-9310-8(7), Chelsea Hse.) Facts On File, Inc.
Bloom, Janice Stitziel. A Grateful Heart under My Bed. Woodcock, Marcy, illus. 2007. 36p. (J). per. 15.99 (978-1-934643-06-8(8)) Villager Bk. Publishing.
—Wonderfully Made under My Bed. Woodcock, Marcy, illus. 2007. 36p. (J). per. 15.99 (978-1-934643-00-6(9)) Villager Bk. Publishing.
Bloumis, Joy. An Adventure in Fairyland. 2013. 84p. pap. 10.50 (978-1-62212-835-8(4), Strategic Bk. Publishing) Strategic Book Publishing & Rights Agency (SBPRA).
Blue, Parker. Try Me. 2010. 218p. pap. 14.95 (978-0-9843256-6-5(2), Bell Bridge Bks.) BelleBks., Inc.
Blue, Sebastien. Liquid Diamond. 2013. 176p. (978-1-4602-3345-0(X)) FriesenPress.
Blum, Vicki. The Dragon Prince. Sourwine, David, illus. 2005. (ENG.). 160p. pap. (978-0-439-95668-0(4)) Scholastic Canada, Ltd.
Blume, Rebecca. When the World Was Green! Blume, Rebecca, illus. 2007. (Illus.). 32p. (J). per. 14.00 (978-0-9785427-1-9(1)) Liberty Artists Management.
Blundell, Gerald Lee. Bunkalunken Goes to Washington & Other Stories, 1 vol. 2010. 138p. pap. 24.95 (978-1-4489-5234-2(4)) America Star Bks.
Blunden, Alan. Tommy & the Garden Shed. 2008. 104p. pap. (978-1-84923-111-4(7)) YouWriteOn.
Boatwright-Cook, Jane. The Skeleton Leaf Stories: Behind the Shutters. 2012. 124p. 23.99 (978-1-4772-1346-9(5)); pap. 14.95 (978-1-4772-1347-6(3)) AuthorHouse.
Bobet, Leah. Above. 2012. (ENG.). 368p. (J). (gr. 9). 17.99 (978-0-545-29670-0(6), Levine, Arthur A. Bks.) Scholastic, Inc.
—An Inheritance of Ashes. (ENG.). 400p. (YA). (gr. 7). 2016. pap. 9.99 (978-0-544-81322-9(7), HMH Books For Young Readers) 2015. 17.99 (978-0-544-28111-0(X)) Houghton Mifflin Harcourt Publishing Co.
Bobowicz, Pamela. Alice in Wonderland (Disney Alice in Wonderland) Disney Storybook Artists Staff, illus. 2013. (Step into Reading Ser.). (ENG.). 32p. (J). (gr. -1-1). pap. 3.99 (978-0-7364-3027-2(X), RH/Disney) Random Hse. Children's Bks.
—Disney Alice in Wonderland. 2013. (Step into Reading Level 2 Ser.). lib. bdg. 13.55 (978-0-606-26972-8(X), Turtleback) Turtleback Bks.
Bodecker, N. M. The Mushroom Center Disaster. Blegvad, Erik & Starr, Branka, illus. 2004. (ENG.). 48p. (J). reprint ed. (978-1-931561-98-3(2)) MacAdam/Cage Publishing, Inc.
—Quimble Wood. Starr, Branka, illus. 2004. (ENG.). 32p. (J). reprint ed. (978-1-931561-97-6(4)) MacAdam/Cage Publishing, Inc.
Boecker, Virginia. The King Slayer. 2016. (Witch Hunter Ser.: 2). (ENG.). 368p. (YA). (gr. 10-17). 17.99 (978-0-316-32723-7(9)) Little, Brown Bks. for Young Readers.
Boen, Sherry. The Fish Who Made a Magical Wish, 1 vol. 2009. 21p. pap. 24.95 (978-1-61582-726-8(9)) America Star Bks.
Bogardus, Ray & Bogardus, Karin. Hannah the Magic Shelter Dog. Seltzer, Jerry, illus. 2005. 143p. (J). pap. 14.99 (978-1-932864-30-4(X)) Masthof Pr.
Bogel, Rachel Anne. A Ride on the Monster's Back. Greenfelder, Jill, illus. 2008. 28p. pap. 15.99 (978-1-59858-752-4(8)) Dog Ear Publishing, LLC.
Boggs, Danielle. The Snow Globe. 2008. 55p. pap. 16.95 (978-1-60703-588-6(X)) America Star Bks.
Bogumill, Mark P. KingMaker: The Swamp Crusade, 4 vols. 2003. 310p. (YA). bds. 25.00 (978-0-9744870-0-7(7)) KingMaker Bks. LLC.
Bohn, Kendall. Fantasy Adventure. 2008. (Kaleidoscopia Coloring Book Ser.). (Illus.). 56p. (J). (gr. -1-7). 8.95 (978-0-929636-83-2(X)) Syren Bk. Co.
Boles Levy, Anne. The Temple of Doubt. 2015. (Temple of Doubt Ser.). (ENG., Illus.). 316p. (J). (gr. 6). 16.99 (978-1-63220-427-1(4), Sky Pony Pr.) Skyhorse Publishing Co., Inc.
—The Well of Prayers. 2016. (Temple of Doubt Ser.). (ENG., Illus.). 364p. (J). (gr. 6). 17.99 (978-1-63450-193-4(4), Sky Pony Pr.) Skyhorse Publishing Co., Inc.
Bolton, Chris A. Smash: Trial by Fire. Bolton, Kyle, illus. 2013. (ENG.). 160p. (J). (gr. 4-7). 18.99 (978-0-7636-5596-9(1)) Candlewick Pr.
Bolton, Nicola Joanne. The WeatherGens. 2010. (ENG.). 89p. pap. 10.50 (978-1-4452-7936-7(3)) Lulu Pr., Inc.
Bomgaars, Sharon. The Best Clubhouse Ever. 2009. 232p. pap. 14.49 (978-1-4259-9306-1(0)) AuthorHouse.
Bonner, Sally. Millie's Daydream. 2010. 32p. 12.99 (978-1-4520-8101-4(8)) AuthorHouse.
Bonniol, Magali. El Ogro De Mariuchi. 2003. (SPA.). 40p. (978-84-8470-112-5(3)) Corimbo, Editorial S.L.
Bontempelli, Massimo. The Chess Set in the Mirror. Gilson, Estelle, tr. from ITA. sto, illus. 2007. (Nautilus Ser.). (ENG.). 114p. (J). (gr. 7-9). per. 9.95 (978-1-58988-031-3(5)) Dry, Paul Bks., Inc.
Boor, Annarie. Bapsie in the Bushveld. 2007. 148p. 26.50 (978-1-4251-2717-6(7)) Trafford Publishing.
Boorman, Kate A. Darkthaw: A Winterkill Novel. 2015. (Winterkill Ser.). (ENG.). 336p. (YA). (gr. 7-17). 17.95 (978-1-4197-1663-6(8), Amulet Bks.) Abrams, Inc.
—Heartfire: A Winterkill Novel. 2016. (Winterkill Ser.: 3). (ENG.). 336p. (YA). (gr. 7-17). 17.95 (978-1-4197-2124-3(0), Amulet Bks.) Abrams, Inc.

E
F
G

—Winterkill. 2014. (Winterkill Ser.). (ENG.). 336p. (YA). (gr. 7-17). 17.95 *(978-1-4197-1235-7(7),* Amulet Bks.) Abrams, Inc.

Boos, Ben. Fantasy: An Artist's Realm. Boos, Ben, illus. 2010. (ENG., Illus.). 96p. (J). (gr. 5-9). 19.99 *(978-0-7636-4056-9(5))* Candlewick Pr.

Booth, Richard A. The Valley of Gillhista. 2003. (Valley Ser.: Bk. 4). 145p. (YA). pap. 9.95 *(978-1-885813-11-4(2))* B&B Publishing.

Booth, Sara. Poppy. Horne, Nathan, illus. 2012. 28p. pap. 12.50 *(978-1-61897-666-6(4),* Strategic Bk. Publishing) Strategic Book Publishing & Rights Agency (SBPRA).

Boroughs, Allan. Ironheart. 1. unabr. ed. 2015. (Legend of Ironheart Ser.: 1). (ENG., Illus.). 320p. (YA). (gr. 7). pap. 9.99 *(978-1-4472-3599-6(1))* Pan Macmillan GBR. Dist: Independent Pubs. Group.

Bosch, Pseudonymous. Bad News. 2017. (Bad Bks.: 3). (ENG.). 352p. (J). (gr. 3-7). 16.99 *(978-0-316-32048-1(X))* Little, Brown Bks. for Young Readers.

—The Name of This Book Is Secret. (Secret Ser.: 1). (ENG.). 400p. (J). (gr. 3-7). 2008. pap. 8.99 *(978-0-316-11369-4(7))* 2015. 12.99 *(978-0-316-26502-7(0))* Little, Brown Bks. for Young Readers.

—The Name of This Book Is Secret. Ford, Gilbert, illus. rev. ed. 2007. (Secret Ser.: 1). (ENG.). 384p. (J). (gr. 3-7). 17.99 *(978-0-316-11366-3(2))* Little, Brown Bks. for Young Readers.

—The Name of This Book Is Secret. 2009. 18.00 *(978-1-60686-518-7(8))* Perfection Learning Corp.

—The Name of This Book Is Secret. 2008. (Secret Ser.: 1). (J). lib. bdg. 19.65 *(978-1-4178-2975-0(3),* Turtleback) Turtleback Bks.

—This Book Is Not Good for You. 2009. (Secret Ser.: 3). (ENG.). 400p. (J). (gr. 3-7). 17.99 *(978-0-316-04086-0(X))* Little, Brown Bks. for Young Readers.

Boston, Ruth. Super Hero for A Day. 2007. 152p. per. 13.95 *(978-1-4327-1427-7(9))* Outskirts Pr., Inc.

Botha, Ingrid. Chikin & Scrub. 2011. 108p. pap. 10.50 *(978-1-60976-295-7(9),* Strategic Bk. Publishing) Strategic Book Publishing & Rights Agency (SBPRA).

Botha, Si. Goosala Goop. 2009. 48p. pap. 16.50 *(978-1-60860-124-0(2),* Strategic Bk. Publishing) Strategic Book Publishing & Rights Agency (SBPRA).

Bouwman, H. M. A Crack in the Sea. 2017. (ENG., Illus.). 368p. (J). (gr. 5). 16.99 *(978-0-399-54519-1(0),* G.P. Putnam's Sons Books for Young Readers) Penguin Young Readers Group.

Bow, Erin. Plain Kate. (ENG.). 320p. (J). (gr. 7-7). 2012. pap. 9.99 *(978-0-545-16665-2(9))* 2010. 17.99 *(978-0-545-16664-5(0))* Scholastic, Inc. (Levine, Arthur A. Bks.).

Bow, James. Fathom Five: The Unwritten Books. 2007. (Unwritten Bks.: 2). (ENG.). 232p. (YA). (gr. 7). pap. 12.99 *(978-1-55002-692-4(5))* Dundurn CAN. Dist: Ingram Publisher Services.

Bow, Patricia. The Prism Blade. 2008. (Passage to Mythrin Ser.: 2). (ENG.). 272p. (YA). (gr. 7-12). pap. 12.99 *(978-1-55002-809-6(X),* Boardwalk Bks.) Dundurn CAN. Dist: Ingram Publisher Services.

Bowen, J. L. Ryker's Revenge. 2013. 282p. pap. 14.99 *(978-1-60820-855-5(9))* MLR Pr., LLC.

Bowers, Chuck. Leprechaun Legacy. 2009. 156p. pap. 12.95 *(978-1-4401-2248-4(2))* iUniverse, Inc.

Bowes, Kyle J. The Crossroads of the Other World. 2013. 240p. pap. *(978-1-4602-1892-1(2))* FriesenPress.

Bowler, Michael J. Children of the Knight. 2016. (ENG., Illus.). (J). 29.99 ***(978-1-63477-952-4(5))*** 2013. 344p. pap. 17.99 *(978-1-62380-655-2(0))* Dreamspinner Pr. (Harmony Ink Pr.).

Bowling, Athena. Malice: The Magicka Barney Chronicles, 1 vol. 2010. 388p. pap. 29.95 *(978-1-4489-4066-0(4))* PublishAmerica, Inc.

Bowman, Erin. Frozen. (Taken Ser.). (ENG.). (YA). (gr. 8). 2015. 384p. pap. 9.99 *(978-0-06-211730-4(0))* 2014. 368p. 17.99 *(978-0-06-211729-8(7))* HarperCollins Pubs. (HarperTeen).

—Taken. 2013. (Taken Ser.: 1). (ENG.). 368p. (YA). (gr. 8). 17.99 *(978-0-06-211726-7(2),* HarperTeen) HarperCollins Pubs.

Bowyer, Clifford B. The Apprentice of Zoldex: The Imperium Saga: the Adventures of Kyria, 12 vols., Vol. 8. Brigman, June, illus. 2008. (Imperium Saga: 8). (ENG.). 208p. (J). 5.99 *(978-0-9787782-2-4(7),* BK0023) Silver Leaf Bks., LLC.

—The Awakening: The Imperium Saga: the Adventures of Kyria, 12 vols., Vol. 2. Brigman, June, illus. 2004. (Imperium Saga: 2). (ENG.). 182p. (J). 5.99 *(978-0-9744354-1-1(4),* BK0004) Silver Leaf Bks., LLC.

—The Child of Prophecy: The Imperium Saga: the Adventures of Kyria, 12 vols., Vol. 1. Brigman, June, illus. 2004. (Imperium Saga: 1). (ENG.). 182p. (J). 5.99 *(978-0-9744354-0-4(6),* BK0002) Silver Leaf Bks., LLC.

—The Darkness Within: The Imperium Saga: the Adventures of Kyria, 12 vols., Vol. 9. Brigman, June, illus. 2009. (Imperium Saga: 9). (ENG.). (J). 5.99 *(978-0-9787782-4-8(3))* Silver Leaf Bks., LLC.

—The Mage's Council: The Imperium Saga: the Adventures of Kyria, 12 vols., Vol. 3. Brigman, June, illus. 2005. (Imperium Saga: 3). (ENG.). 182p. (J). 5.99 *(978-0-9744354-2-8(2),* BK0006) Silver Leaf Bks., LLC.

—Quest for the Shard: The Imperium Saga: the Adventures of Kyria, 12 vols., Vol. 6. Brigman, June, illus. 2007. (Imperium Saga: 6). (ENG.). 166p. (J). 5.99 *(978-0-9744354-8-0(1),* BK0020) Silver Leaf Bks., LLC.

—The Spread of Darkness: The Imperium Saga: the Adventures of Kyria, 12 vols., Vol. 7. Brigman, June, illus. 2007. (Imperium Saga: 7). (ENG.). 158p. (J). 5.99 *(978-0-9787782-1-7(9),* BK0022) Silver Leaf Bks., LLC.

—Trapped in Time: The Imperium Saga: the Adventures of Kyria, 12 vols., Vol. 5. Brigman, June, illus. 2006. (Imperium Saga: 5). (ENG.). 150p. (J). 5.99 *(978-0-9744354-7-3(3),* BK0008) Silver Leaf Bks., LLC.

Boyce, Frank Cottrell. Chitty Chitty Bang Bang Flies Again. Berger, Joe, illus. 2012. (Chitty Chitty Bang Bang Ser.). (ENG.). 192p. (J). (gr. 4-7). 15.99 *(978-0-7636-5957-8(6))* Candlewick Pr.

Boyd, Charles O'Halloran. Mountains of the North. 2009. 172p. pap. 13.95 *(978-1-4401-4228-4(9))* iUniverse, Inc.

Boyd, David. Khan of Khans: An Adventure with Genghis Khan. 2003. (Milo the Wonderdog Adventures Ser.). 64p. pap. *(978-0-921156-90-1(1))* Rubicon Publishing, Inc.

Boyd, G. A. Alchemy Jones & the Source of Magic. 2011. 324p. (gr. -1). 29.95 *(978-1-4620-2234-2(0));* pap. 19.95 *(978-1-4620-2232-8(4))* iUniverse, Inc.

Boyd, Johnny. First Tracks. 2004. 32p. 17.95 *(978-0-9760187-0-4(5))* PTO Pr.

Boylan, Jennifer Finney. Falcon Quinn & the Black Mirror. Dorman, Brandon, illus. (Falcon Quinn Ser.: 1). (ENG.). (J). (gr. 5-9). 2011. 512p. pap. 7.99 *(978-0-06-172834-1(9))* 2010. 496p. 16.99 *(978-0-06-172832-7(2))* HarperCollins Pubs. (Tegen, Katherine Bks).

—Falcon Quinn & the Crimson Vapor. 2011. (Falcon Quinn Ser.: 2). (ENG.). 384p. (J). (gr. 5-9). 16.99 *(978-0-06-172835-8(7),* Tegen, Katherine Bks) HarperCollins Pubs.

Bracken, Alexandra. The Dreadful Tale of Prosper Redding. 2017. (Prosper Redding Ser.). (ENG.). 368p. (J). (gr. 3-7). 16.99 ***(978-1-4847-7817-3(0))*** Hyperion Bks. for Children.

Bracken, Beth. The Wizard of Oz, 1 vol. 2013. (Wizard of Oz Ser.). (ENG., Illus.). 32p. (gr. k-3). 14.95 *(978-1-62370-026-3(4))* Capstone Young Readers of Coughlan Cos.

Bracken, Beth & Fraser, Kay. Faerieground, 1 vol. Sawyer, Odessa, illus. 2014. (Faerieground Ser.). (ENG.). 96p. (gr. 1-3). 95.96 *(978-1-4342-9465-4(X),* Faerieground) Stone Arch Bks.

—Hope, 1 vol. Sawyer, Odessa, illus. 2013. (Faerieground Ser.). (ENG.). 288p. (gr. 4-8). 12.95 *(978-1-62370-010-2(8))* Capstone Young Readers of Coughlan Cos.

Bradfield, Jolly Roger. Benjamin Dilley's Thirsty Camel. Bradfield, Jolly Roger, illus. 2012. (ENG., Illus.). 64p. (J). (gr. 4-7). 18.95 *(978-1-930900-60-8(0))* Purple Hse. Pr.

Brafman, Joshua. Death Bunny! 2008. 248p. 26.95 *(978-0-595-51446-5(4));* pap. 16.95 *(978-0-595-52098-5(7))* iUniverse, Inc.

Brandeis, Madeline. The Little Dutch Tulip Girl. 2011. 194p. 42.95 *(978-1-258-09813-1(X))* Literary Licensing, LLC.

Brannin, Kaitlyn & Brannin, Sandy. Return to Arteo. 2010. (Illus.). 64p. (J). *(978-0-929915-51-7(8))* Headline Bks., Inc.

Brannon, Dj. The Angelic Soldiers: The Way Back. 2012. 138p. (gr. 4-6). 28.95 *(978-1-4497-5971-1(8));* pap. 11.95 *(978-1-4497-5972-8(6))* Author Solutions, Inc. (WestBow Pr.).

Branson, Eve. Sarky Puddleboat. Lowe, Wes, illus. 2011. 44p. (J). 14.99 *(978-1-4520-9754-1(2))* AuthorHouse.

Branson, Terri. Tyler on the Moon. Taylor, Chet, illus. I.t. ed. 2004. 24p. (J). 18.99 *(978-0-9755888-2-6(6))* Dragonfly Publishing, Inc.

Braswell, Liz. As Old As Time: A Twisted Tale. 2016. (Twisted Tale Ser.). (ENG.). 496p. (YA). (gr. 7-17). 17.99 *(978-1-4847-0728-9(1))* Disney Pr.

—Once upon a Dream: A Twisted Tale. 2017. (Twisted Tale Ser.). (ENG.). 464p. (YA). (gr. 7-17). pap. 9.99 *(978-1-4847-0730-2(3))* Disney Pr.

—A Whole New World: A Twisted Tale. (Twisted Tale Ser.). (ENG.). (YA). (gr. 7-12). 2016. 400p. pap. 9.99 *(978-1-4847-0732-6(X))* 2015. 384p. 17.99 *(978-1-4847-0729-6(X))* Disney Pr.

Breckenridge, Trula & Breckenridge, Scott. Squiggly the Roach. Breckenridge, Trula & Breckenridge, Scott, illus. 2004. (Illus.). (J). per. *(978-0-9749480-6-5(3),* MSPpress) Mama Specific Productions.

Breckenridge, Trula & Palmore, Iyende. FiFi the Leaf. Breckenridge, Trula & Palmore, Iyende, illus. 2004. (Illus.). (J). per. *(978-0-9749480-7-2(1),* MSPpress) Mama Specific Productions.

Bredeson, Michelle. Legends. 2012. 220p. pap. *(978-1-61706-158-5(1))* Roxby Media Ltd.

Brege, K. B. All Isn't Well in Roswell! 2005. (Mick Morris Myth Solver Ser.: No. 1). (Illus.). 188p. (J). pap. 6.99 *(978-0-9774119-0-0(7))* Team B Creative LLC.

BreMaud, R. E. Simon, Friends, & the Dream Stealer: Book One. 2010. 152p. 24.50 *(978-1-4269-4552-6(3));* pap. 14.50 *(978-1-4269-4551-9(5))* Trafford Publishing.

Brennan, Herbie. Faerie Wars, Vol. 1. 2004. (Faerie Wars Chronicles Ser.). (ENG.). 384p. (YA). reprint ed. pap. 8.99 *(978-1-58234-943-5(6),* 9781582349435, Bloomsbury USA Childrens) Bloomsbury Publishing USA.

Brennan, Sarah Rees. In Other Lands. Nowak, Carolyn, illus. 2017. (ENG.). 432p. 19.95 *(978-1-61873-120-3(3),* Big Mouth Hse.) Small Beer Pr.

—Tell the Wind & Fire. (ENG.). 368p. (YA). (gr. 7). 2017. pap. 9.99 *(978-0-544-93887-8(9),* HMH Books For Young Readers) 2016. 17.99 *(978-0-544-31817-5(X))* Houghton Mifflin Harcourt Publishing Co.

—Untold. Fochesato, Giorgio, illus. 2014. (Lynburn Legacy Ser.: Bk. 2). (ENG.). 400p. (YA). (gr. 7). pap. 9.99 *(978-0-375-87104-7(7),* Ember) Random Hse. Children's Bks.

Brett, James. Infaeter. Englund, Jonathon, illus. 2nd ed. 2013. 238p. pap. *(978-1-908462-03-9(5))* New Dawn Pubs.

Brewer, Nancy B. Princess Bertha & the Goose. 2011. 32p. pap. 24.95 *(978-1-4560-7868-3(2))* America Star Bks.

Brezenoff, Steve. Guy in Real Life. 2015. (ENG.). 400p. (YA). (gr. 9). pap. 9.99 *(978-0-06-226684-2(5))* HarperCollins Pubs.

Brian, Kate, pseud. Perfect Mistake. 2009. (Privilege Ser.: No. 3). (ENG.). 240p. (YA). (gr. 9-18). pap. 9.99 *(978-1-4169-6761-3(3),* Simon & Schuster Bks. For Young Readers) Simon & Schuster Bks. For Young Readers.

Bridges, Robin. The Katerina Trilogy, Vol. II: the Unfailing Light. 2013. (ENG.). 320p. (YA). (gr. 7). pap. 9.99 *(978-0-385-74025-8(5),* Ember) Random Hse. Children's Bks.

Bridgman, Rae. Kingdom of Trolls: A Middlegate Book. 2010. (Illus.). 287p. (J). pap. 15.00 *(978-0-9864974-1-4(X))* Sybertooth, Inc. CAN. Dist: Lightning Source, Inc.

Brier, Bill. The Crystal Heart. 2005. 52p. pap. 3.95 *(978-1-4184-6327-4(2))* AuthorHouse.

Bright, J. E. & West, Alexandra. Super Hero Adventures: Save the Day! Laufman, Derek, illus. 2017. (ENG.). 14p. (J). (gr. -1-k). bds. 10.99 ***(978-1-4847-8859-2(1),*** Marvel Pr.) Disney Publishing Worldwide.

Bright, Phoebe. Lucky Stars #1: Wish upon a Friend. 2012. (Lucky Stars Ser.). (ENG.). 96p. (J). (gr. 2-5). pap. 5.99 *(978-0-545-41998-7(0),* Scholastic Paperbacks) Scholastic, Inc.

—Lucky Stars #2: Wish upon a Pet. 2012. (Lucky Stars Ser.). (ENG.). 96p. (J). (gr. 2-5). 5.99 *(978-0-545-41999-4(9),* Scholastic Paperbacks) Scholastic, Inc.

—Lucky Stars #3: Wish upon a Song. 2012. (Lucky Stars Ser.: 3). (ENG.). 96p. (J). (gr. 2-5). pap. 5.99 *(978-0-545-42000-6(8),* Scholastic Paperbacks) Scholastic, Inc.

—Lucky Stars #5: Wish upon a Superstar. 2012. (Lucky Stars Ser.). (ENG.). 96p. (J). (gr. 2-5). pap. 5.99 *(978-0-545-42002-0(4),* Scholastic Paperbacks) Scholastic, Inc.

Brighton, Wendy. Bosley Beats the Burglars. 2005. (Illus.). pap. 11.45 *(978-1-4208-6436-6(X))* AuthorHouse.

Brightwood, Laura, illus. The House That Talked to Itself. 2006. (J). *(978-0-9779290-3-0(5))* 3-C Institute for Social Development.

Brignole, Giancarla, tr. El Gigante y el Mar. Gazzaneo, Lucia, illus. (Fabulas De Familia Ser.). (SPA.). 32p. *(978-970-20-0268-0(0))* Castillo, Ediciones, S. A. de C. V.

Brignull, Irena. The Hawkweed Prophecy. 2017. (Hawkweed Ser.: 1). (ENG.). 384p. (gr. 7-17). pap. 10.99 ***(978-1-60286-313-2(X),*** Weinstein Bks.) Perseus Bks. Group.

Briley, Randy. Mr Underneath. 2013. 134p. pap. 12.99 *(978-0-9896269-0-3(3))* Raven Mad Studios.

Brinkerhoff, Phillip. To the Magical Pond. 2004. 116p. (YA). pap. 11.95 *(978-0-7414-1982-8(3))* Infinity Publishing.

Brisebois, Ro. Sherlock & Elf: The Mystery of the Thicket Behind the Shed. 2008. 100p. pap. 12.99 *(978-1-4343-9987-8(7))* AuthorHouse.

Broadribb, Donald. Marcia. 2009. 423p. 39.47 *(978-1-4092-6754-6(7))* Lulu Pr., Inc.

Broderick, Paula. The Quest: The First Toby & Sox Adventure. 2011. (ENG., Illus.). 160p. pap. *(978-1-84876-626-6(2))* Troubador Publishing Ltd.

Brodhead, Kimberly. Gaden's Tower: Book One. 2007. 164p. per. 24.95 *(978-1-60441-038-9(8))* America Star Bks.

Brodien-Jones, Christine. The Owl Keeper. Kneen, Maggie, illus. 2011. (ENG.). 320p. (J). (gr. 3-7). 8.99 *(978-0-385-73815-6(3),* Yearling) Random Hse. Children's Bks.

—The Scorpions of Zahir. Murphy, Kelly, illus. 2012. (ENG.). 384p. (J). (gr. 5). 17.99 *(978-0-385-73933-7(8),* Delacorte Bks. for Young Readers) Random Hse. Children's Bks.

Brondos, Pam. The Last Remnant, 0 vols. 2016. (Fourline Trilogy Ser.: 3). (ENG.). 320p. (J). pap. 9.99 *(978-1-61218-470-8(7),* 9781612184708, Skyscape) Amazon Publishing.

—On the Meldon Plain, 0 vols. 2016. (Fourline Trilogy Ser.: 2). (ENG.). 356p. (YA). (gr. 9-13). pap. 9.99 *(978-1-5039-5320-8(3),* 9781503953208, Skyscape) Amazon Publishing.

Brooks, Charlie. Greystone Valley. Grundy, Jessica, illus. 2013. 166p. 17.99 *(978-1-938821-33-2(5));* 198p. pap. 9.99 *(978-1-938821-41-7(6))* Grey Gecko Pr.

Brooks, Donna. The Golden Spindle. 2010. 112p. pap. 30.00 *(978-1-60860-852-2(2),* Eloquent Bks.) Strategic Book Publishing & Rights Agency (SBPRA).

Brooks, Elizabeth. Montefiore's Goddaughter. 2012. (ENG.). 304p. (YA). (gr. 4-6). 15.95 *(978-1-84982-099-8(6))* MP Publishing Ltd. GBR. Dist: Midpoint Trade Bks., Inc.

Brooks-Scrivanich, Olivia. Fiscal Pear & Shimmer in the Call of River Whale. 2008. (ENG.). 92p. pap. 14.99 *(978-1-4196-9589-6(4))* CreateSpace Independent Publishing Platform.

Broom, Jenny. The Lion & the Mouse: Turn-And-Tell Tales. Noj, Nahta, illus. 2014. (ENG.). 32p. (J). (gr. -1-2). 14.99 *(978-0-7636-6619-4(X),* Templar) Candlewick Pr.

Brothers Grimm. Rapunzel & Other Tales: Includes the Ugly Duckling & the Boy Pirate. 2008. (J). 34.99 *(978-1-60514-832-8(6))* Findaway World, LLC.

Brothers, Marilee. Shadow Moon. 2011. 230p. (YA). pap. *(978-1-61194-058-9(3))* BelleBks., Inc.

Brown, Alan James. Michael & the Monkey King. 2008. 180p. pap. 16.95 *(978-1-4092-0241-7(0))* Lulu Pr., Inc.

Brown, Anne Greenwood. Promise Bound. 2014. (ENG.). 368p. (YA). (gr. 7). 17.99 *(978-0-385-74383-9(1),* Delacorte Pr.) Random Hse. Children's Bks.

Brown, Cara D. Isabelle's Wish. 2013. 48p. (gr. 2-2). pap. 8.95 *(978-1-4759-7421-8(3))* iUniverse, Inc.

Brown, E.A. Gossamer. 2012. 24p. pap. 24.95 *(978-1-4626-5043-9(0))* America Star Bks.

Brown, Frank. Among the Pandemoniumous Mismaides: A Fantasy. 2008. 148p. 22.95 *(978-0-595-71458-2(7))* iUniverse, Inc.

Brown, Hazel. Prince Henry St. Clair Earl of Orkney. Bramadat, Dawn, ed. Brown, Hazel, illus. 2013. (Illus.). 106p. pap. 25.95 *(978-1-935786-57-3(1))* St. Clair Pubns.

Brown, Jeff Allan. Floom Shroom the Battling Mushroom. 2009. 100p. pap. 28.99 *(978-1-60693-485-2(6),* Strategic Bk. Publishing) Strategic Book Publishing & Rights Agency (SBPRA).

Brown, Jeffrey. Sulk. 2009. (Sulk Ser.: 3). (ENG., Illus.). 64p. pap. 6.00 *(978-1-60309-055-1(X),* 9781603090551) Top Shelf Productions.

Brown, Kevin. In a Field of Sunflowers. 2006. pap. 9.00 *(978-0-8059-6921-4(7))* Dorrance Publishing Co., Inc.

Brown, Margaret Wise. The Quiet Noisy Book Board Book. Weisgard, Leonard, illus. 2017. 34p. (J). (gr. -1 — 1). bds. 7.99 ***(978-0-06-248466-6(4),*** HarperFestival) HarperCollins Pubs.

Brown, Palmer. Beyond the Pawpaw Trees. Brown, Palmer, illus. 2011. (ENG., Illus.). 136p. (J). (gr. k-4). 14.95 *(978-1-59017-461-6(5),* NYR Children's Collection) New York Review of Bks., Inc., The.

—The Silver Nutmeg. Brown, Palmer, illus. 2012. (ENG., Illus.). 152p. (J). (gr. k-4). 15.95 *(978-1-59017-500-2(X),* NYR Children's Collection) New York Review of Bks., Inc., The.

Brown, Rachael. Faerie Wings. 2008. 58p. pap. 10.50 *(978-1-4092-0908-9(3))* Lulu Pr., Inc.

Brown, Tara. Imaginations. 2013. 382p. pap. *(978-0-9918411-8-9(2))* Brown, Tara Publishing.

Browning, Frances G. Dillow. Neon Ned. 2009. 20p. pap. 10.95 *(978-1-60860-152-3(8),* Strategic Bk. Publishing) Strategic Book Publishing & Rights Agency (SBPRA).

Brubaker, William. The Dark King. 2012. (ENG.). (J). pap. *(978-1-4675-2086-7(1))* Independent Pub.

Bruce, Karl. Annie Apple & the Teleportation Phantoms from Outer Space. 2006. (YA). pap. 16.00 *(978-0-8059-7156-9(4))* Dorrance Publishing Co., Inc.

Brueggeman, Karen & Paddock, Briana. Fruzzle's Mystery Talent: A Bed Time Fantasy Story for Children Ages 3-10. Brueggeman, Bryan, illus. 2013. 48p. pap. 10.99 *(978-0-9892565-0-6(2))* Dolphins Publishing.

Brundage, Frances, illus. Cinderella: A Fairy Story. 2004. reprint ed. pap. 15.95 *(978-1-4179-8713-9(8))* Kessinger Publishing, LLC.

Brundin, Anders & Dranger, Joanna Rubin. Dudley the Daydreamer. Perry, Frank, tr. from SWE. 2008. (ENG., Illus.). 32p. (J). (gr. k-2). pap. 12.95 *(978-1-905341-10-8(5))* WingedChariot Pr. GBR. Dist: Independent Pubs. Group.

Bruneau, Clotilde, et al. The Planet of Bamalias. 2015. (ENG., Illus.). 48p. (J). (gr. 4-8). pap. 7.95 *(978-1-4677-6026-3(9),* Graphic Universe™) Lerner Publishing Group.

Brunson, Marya. The Light of Rigel. 2013. 178p. pap. 9.95 *(978-0-9801414-2-9(7))* Lotus Blossom Bks.

Bruton, Georgia. Escape. 2012. 210p. pap. 11.95 *(978-1-936083-10-5(5))* Silver Knight Publishing, LLC.

Bryant, Clorinda. Imaginary World: The Stone of Amajara. 2012. 252p. 30.50 *(978-0-557-54922-1(1))* Lulu Pr., Inc.

Bryant, Samantha. Innocent Child. 2012. pap. 15.95 *(978-0-7414-7874-0(9))* Infinity Publishing.

Buchan, John. The Magic Walking Stick & Stories from the Arabian Nights. Soper, Vernon, illus. 2007. 336p. per. 19.95 *(978-0-9791702-8-7(1))* Capricorn Hse. Publishing.

Buchanan, Andrea J. Gift. 2012. (ENG.). 326p. (YA). (gr. 7-12). pap. 9.99 *(978-1-4532-2023-8(2),* Open Road Media E-riginal) Open Road Integrated Media, Inc.

Buck, Alicia. Out of the Ashes. 2015. 281p. (YA). pap. 17.99 *(978-1-4621-1727-7(9))* Cedar Fort, Inc./CFI Distribution.

Buckeridge, Anthony. Jennings Again! 2008. (Jennings Ser.: 23). (ENG.). 132p. (J). (gr. -1-12). pap. 10.95 *(978-0-7551-0155-9(3))* House of Stratus, Inc. GBR. Dist: Gardners Bks. Ltd.

Buckley, Michael. M Is for Mama's Boy, Bk. 2. 2011. (Nerds Ser.). (ENG., Illus.). 304p. (J). (gr. 3-7). pap. 7.95 *(978-1-4197-0023-1(5),* Amulet Bks.) Abrams, Inc.

—Undertow. (Undertow Trilogy Ser.). (ENG.). (gr. 7). 2016. 400p. (YA). pap. 10.99 *(978-0-544-81319-9(7))* 2015. 384p. (J). 18.99 *(978-0-544-34825-7(7))* Houghton Mifflin Harcourt Publishing Co. (HMH Books For Young Readers).

Buckmaster, Heath L. Box of Hair: A Fairy Tale, 3 bks., Bk. 1. (Illus.). (YA). 2007. 102p. pap. 12.99 *(978-0-9771802-5-7(5))* 2008. 108p. lib. bdg. 25.00 *(978-0-9771802-4-0(7))* Transaltar Publishing.

—Box of Hair: A Fairy Tale. 2008. 104p. pap. 12.50 *(978-1-4357-2690-1(1))* Lulu Pr., Inc.

—The Venus Diary. 2008. 136p. pap. 13.50 *(978-0-615-20678-3(6));* Bk. 2. 132p. (YA). lib. bdg. 19.95 *(978-0-9771802-6-4(3))* Transaltar Publishing.

Bueno, Carlos. Lauren Ipsum: A Story about Computer Science & Other Improbable Things. 2014. (ENG., Illus.). 192p. (J). (gr. 5). pap. 16.95 *(978-1-59327-574-7(9))* No Starch Pr., Inc.

Bujor, Flavia. The Prophecy of the Stones. Coverdale, Linda, tr. 2005. 386p. (J). (gr. 5-9). 15.65 *(978-0-7569-5668-4(4))* Perfection Learning Corp.

Bulbring, Edyth. Cornelia Button & the Globe of Gamagion. 2009. (ENG.). 208p. (J). (gr. 4-7). pap. 18.00 *(978-1-77009-501-4(2))* Jacana Media ZAF. Dist: Independent Pubs. Group.

Bulger, Melissa. We Can Dream. 2009. 36p. pap. 15.65 *(978-1-4490-1170-3(5))* AuthorHouse.

Bulkowski, James. O'Briah: A Bedtime Story. 2011. 64p. pap. 8.95 *(978-1-4620-1333-3(3))* iUniverse, Inc.

Bulla, Lynda. Katydid. 2003. (Illus.). 20p. (J). lib. bdg. 17.99 *(978-0-9724272-1-0(X))* Katydid Publishing LLC.

Bullock, Rob. Noah Ramsbottom & the Cave Elves. 2009. 48p. pap. 12.25 *(978-1-60860-335-0(0),* Strategic Bk. Publishing) Strategic Book Publishing & Rights Agency (SBPRA).

Bunce, Elizabeth C. Liar's Moon. 2011. (YA). pap. *(978-0-545-13607-5(5));* (ENG.). 368p. (J). (gr. 7-7). 17.99 *(978-0-545-13608-2(3))* Scholastic, Inc. (Levine, Arthur A. Bks.).

—StarCrossed. 2011. (ENG.). 368p. (YA). pap. 9.99 *(978-0-545-13606-8(7),* Levine, Arthur A. Bks.) Scholastic, Inc.

Bundy, E. A. Phillip Marrow, Jr. 2013. (ENG.). 206p. (YA). pap. 10.99 *(978-1-61955-008-7(3))* Singing Winds Pr.

Bunton, M. Catherine. The Fairy Tale Keeper. 2012. 134p. pap. 8.95 *(978-1-60594-783-9(0))* Aeon Publishing Inc.

Burchell, Graham. The Ice Spells of Krollinad. 2005. 213p. pap. 11.99 *(978-1-4116-5258-3(4))* Lulu Pr., Inc.

Burden, Meg. The King Commands. 2010. (Tales of the Borderlands Ser.: Bk. 2). 312p. (YA). (gr. 7-18). pap. 8.95 *(978-0-9798824-1-8(9))* Brown Barn Bks.

Burgess, Barbara. The Magic Manuscript: The Nine Companions. 2013. 234p. pap. 12.99 *(978-0-9918574-3-2(7))* Sulby Hall Publishing.

—The Magic Manuscript: Voyage to Eve Ilion. 2013. 202p. pap. 9.99 *(978-0-9918574-4-9(5))* Sulby Hall Publishing.

Burgess, Jennifer. Dj Daring & the Dangerous Dragon. 2013. 20p. pap. 11.97 *(978-1-61204-287-9(2),* Strategic Bk. Publishing) Strategic Book Publishing & Rights Agency (SBPRA).

Burgess, Sushila. Jasmine's Unicorn. 2010. 115p. pap. 18.95 *(978-1-4452-5662-7(2))* Lulu Pr., Inc.

Burgess, Thornton W. Bowser the Hound. 2007. 128p. (gr. 4-7). per. 10.95 *(978-1-60312-295-5(8));* 23.95 *(978-1-60312-713-4(5))* Aegypan.

—Tommy & the Wishing Stone. (J). 19.95 *(978-0-8488-0932-4(7))* Amereon Ltd.

—Tommy's Change of Heart. (J). 19.95 *(978-0-8488-1418-2(5))* Amereon Ltd.

—Tommy's Wishes Come True. (J). 19.95 *(978-0-8488-1419-9(3))* Amereon Ltd.

—While the Story-Log Burns. (J). 18.95 *(978-0-8488-0401-5(5))* Amereon Ltd.

Burgess, V. L. The Mapmaker's Sons. 2012. (ENG.). 176p. (J). (gr. 4-7). 16.99 *(978-0-9854810-0-1(5))* Move Bks., LLC.

Burghall, Johan. The Vale of the Faeries. 2012. 274p. (-18). pap. *(978-0-9571863-3-0(9))* Burghall, Johan.

Burgos-Diaz, Mercedes. Meenah, the Mystical Princess of Zantel. 2011. 56p. pap. 8.95 *(978-1-4620-5928-7(7))* iUniverse, Inc.

Burick, Rebecca. Little Daisy Tutu. Burick, Rebecca & Burick Jr., Michael, illus. 2012. 28p. pap. 24.95 *(978-1-4560-6883-7(0))* America Star Bks.

Burke, Merrilee. Dreamcatcher Garden: A Sacred Journey. 2012. 108p. (gr. 4-6). 28.99 *(978-1-4525-5786-1(1))*; pap. 8.99 *(978-1-4525-5784-7(5))* Balboa Pr.

Burkhart, Jessica. Bella's Birthday Unicorn. Ying, Victoria, illus. 2014. (Unicorn Magic Ser.: 1). (ENG.). 144p. (J). (gr. 1-4). 15.99 *(978-1-4814-1105-9(5),* Aladdin) Simon & Schuster Children's Publishing.

Burnell, Pamela H. The Light Keeper: An Epps Kids Mystery. 2008. 76p. pap. 19.95 *(978-1-60474-847-5(8))* America Star Bks.

Burnett, Frances Hodgson. The Land of Blue Flower. 2007. 76p. pap. 14.45 *(978-1-59462-742-2(8),* Book Jungle) Standard Pubns., Inc.

—The Land of the Blue Flower. 2007. 76p. per. 9.45 *(978-1-59462-779-8(7),* Book Jungle) Standard Pubns., Inc.

Burningham, John. La Cama Mágica. 2004. (SPA., Illus.). (J). 19.99 *(978-84-88342-46-1(2))* S.A. Kokinos ESP. Dist: Lectorum Pubns., Inc.

—Cloudland. Burningham, John, illus. 2007. (ENG., Illus.). 48p. (J). (gr. -1-2). 16.95 *(978-0-09-971161-2(3),* Red Fox) Random House Children's Books GBR. Dist: Independent Pubs. Group.

—It's a Secret! Burningham, John, illus. 2009. (ENG., Illus.). 56p. (J). (gr. -1-2). 16.99 *(978-0-7636-4275-4(4))* Candlewick Pr.

—The Way to the Zoo. Burningham, John, illus. 2014. (ENG., Illus.). 40p. (J). (gr. -1-2). 15.99 *(978-0-7636-7317-8(X))* Candlewick Pr.

Burns, A. M. Hunters. 2016. (ENG., Illus.). (J). 24.99 ***(978-1-63533-031-1(9),*** Harmony Ink Pr.) Dreamspinner Pr.

Burns, Helen Marie. Ryleigh's Little Bug Book, 1 vol. 2010. 22p. 24.95 *(978-1-4512-1464-2(2))* America Star Bks.

Burns, Jason M. Sesame Street: I Is for Imagination: I Is for Imagination. 2016. 32p. (J). 7.99 *(978-1-937676-91-9(9))* Ape Entertainment.

Burns, Jennifer N. Magic in Time: Fairy Tale Stories. 2012. 198p. 24.95 *(978-1-4759-3965-1(5))*; pap. 14.95 *(978-1-4759-3964-4(7))* iUniverse, Inc.

Burns, Laura J. Bewitched in Oz, 1 vol. Peters, Liam, illus. 2014. (Bewitched in Oz Ser.). (ENG.). 256p. (gr. 4-8). 12.95 *(978-1-62370-129-1(5))*; lib. bdg. 30.65 *(978-1-4342-9207-0(X))* Stone Arch Bks.

Burt, Isabel. Toxics. 2013. (Illus.). 258p. pap. *(978-1-78132-186-7(8))* SilverWood Bks.

Burt, Marissa. A Legend of Starfire. (J). (gr. 3-7). 2017. 416p. pap. 6.99 ***(978-0-06-229159-2(9))*** 2016. 400p. 16.99 *(978-0-06-229158-5(0))* HarperCollins Pubs.

—A Sliver of Stardust. (J). (gr. 3-7). 2016. 400p. pap. 7.99 *(978-0-06-229156-1(4))* 2015. (ENG.). 384p. 16.99 *(978-0-06-229155-4(6))* HarperCollins Pubs.

—Story's End. 2013. (Storybound Ser.: 2). (ENG.). 368p. (J). (gr. 3-7). 16.99 *(978-0-06-202054-3(4))* HarperCollins Pubs.

Burtenshaw, Jenna. Blackwatch. 2013. (Secrets of Wintercraft Ser.: 2). (ENG.). 336p. (YA). (gr. 8). pap. 9.99 *(978-0-06-202645-3(3),* Greenwillow Bks.) HarperCollins Pubs.

—Shadowcry. (Secrets of Wintercraft Ser.: 1). (ENG.). (YA). (gr. 8). 2012. 336p. pap. 8.99 *(978-0-06-202643-9(7))* 2011. 320p. 16.99 *(978-0-06-202642-2(9))* HarperCollins Pubs. (Greenwillow Bks.).

—Winterveil. 2013. (Secrets of Wintercraft Ser.: 3). (ENG.). 304p. (YA). (gr. 8). 17.99 *(978-0-06-202646-0(1),* Greenwillow Bks.) HarperCollins Pubs.

Burton, Elizabeth K. The Everdark Gate: The Everdark Wars Book 3. 2008. (ENG.). 280p. pap. 15.50 *(978-1-934135-79-2(8),* Zumaya Otherworlds) Zumaya Pubns. LLC.

Burton, Hallie. Tapestry. 2016. (ENG., Illus.). (J). 27.99 ***(978-1-63533-078-6(5))*** 2013. 276p. pap. 16.99 *(978-1-62380-355-1(1))* Dreamspinner Pr. (Harmony Ink Pr.).

Burton, Hallie. Tapestry [Library Edition]. 2013. 276p. pap. 16.99 *(978-1-62380-926-3(6),* Harmony Ink Pr.) Dreamspinner Pr.

Burton, Martin Nelson. Fooling the Tooth Fairy. Hansen, Clint, illus. Tanner, Dean, photos by. 2005. (ENG.). 32p. (J). 17.00 *(978-0-9666490-2-4(8))* London Town Pr.

Busch, Darcy J. Lily & the Hidden Secrets, 1 vol. 2009. 164p. pap. 24.95 *(978-1-60836-498-5(4))* America Star Bks.

Bush, Randall B. Gabriel's Magic Ornament. Schunemann, Ryan, illus. 2003. 120p. (gr. 5-8). pap. 11.95 *(978-0-9716633-0-5(0))* Pristine Pubs., Inc.

Bush, Ty. Marcus Jones & the Mastery of the Scripture Balls. 2011. 270p. pap. 27.95 *(978-1-4626-0461-6(7))* America Star Bks.

Busiek, Kurt. Wizard's Tale. 2013. (ENG., Illus.). 144p. pap. 19.99 *(978-1-61377-593-6(8),* 9781613775936) Idea & Design Works, LLC.

But I Knew Better: Individual Title, 6 pack. (gr. k-1). 23.00 *(978-0-7635-9033-8(9))* Rigby Education.

Butcher, Kristin & Butcher, Kristen. The Tomorrow Tunnel. 2006. (ENG.). 188p. pap. 14.95 *(978-1-895449-90-7(1))* Thistledown Pr., Ltd. CAN. Dist: Univ. of Toronto Pr.

Butler, Berwyn. Dinky the Doorknob: The Adventures of Sir Dinkum Wilhelm, the Third Earl of Surridge. 2005. (J). per. 11.95 *(978-1-933732-02-2(4))* Big Ransom Studio.

Butler, Berwyn & McClean, Shorty. Dinky the Doorknob. 2006. (J). lib. bdg. 21.95 *(978-1-933732-04-6(0))* Big Ransom Studio.

Butler, Charles. The Fetch of Mardy Watt: Can You Believe Your Eyes? 2011. (ENG.). 224p. (Orig.). (J). pap. 9.99 *(978-0-00-712857-0(6),* Voyager) HarperCollins Pubs. Ltd. GBR. Dist: HarperCollins Pubs.

Butler, Dave. The Giant's Seat (the Extraordinary Journeys of Clockwork Charlie) 2017. (Extraordinary Journeys of Clockwork Charlie Ser.: 2). (ENG.). 352p. (J). (gr. 3-7). 16.99 ***(978-0-553-51299-1(4),*** Knopf Bks. for Young Readers) Random Hse. Children's Bks.

—The Kidnap Plot (the Extraordinary Journeys of Clockwork Charlie) 2017. (Extraordinary Journeys of Clockwork Charlie Ser.). (ENG.). 336p. (J). (gr. 3-7). 7.99 ***(978-0-553-51298-4(6),*** Yearling) Random Hse. Children's Bks.

Buxton, W. J. Winkiedough Twinkletoe: Upon the Window Ledge. 2012. 36p. pap. 20.99 *(978-1-4685-3050-6(X))* AuthorHouse.

Byars, Betsy. Burbujas, el Pez de una Tonelada. 2003.Tr. of Two-Thousand-Pound Goldfish. (SPA., Illus.). 160p. (YA). (gr. 5-8). pap. 11.99 *(978-84-279-3191-6(3),* NG3953) Noguer y Caralt Editores, S. A. ESP. Dist: Lectorum Pubns., Inc.

Byrne, Jean Livingstone. Legends of Newgrange. 2014. 54p. pap. 12.99 *(978-1-84386-818-7(0))* Vanguard Pr.

Cabot, Meg. Haunted. 2004. (Mediator Ser.: 5). (ENG.). 288p. (YA). (gr. 8-18). pap. 8.99 *(978-0-06-075164-7(9),* HarperTeen) HarperCollins Pubs.

—Missing You. 2006. (1-800-Where-R-You Ser.: 5). (ENG.). 288p. (YA). (gr. 8-12). pap. 6.99 *(978-0-06-087430-8(9),* HarperTeen) HarperCollins Pubs.

Caddy, Meg. Waer. 2017. (ENG., Illus.). 320p. (J). (gr. 8). 11.95 *(978-1-922182-21-0(4))* Text Publishing Co. AUS. Dist: Consortium Bk. Sales & Distribution.

Caicco, Joseph. Adventures of the Rainbow Guardians: When the Color Came Down. 2013. 40p. pap. *(978-1-4602-1451-0(X))* FriesenPress.

Cain, Tommy. Tan & the Bowl of Time. 2011. (ENG.). 150p. (gr. 3-9). pap. 11.95 *(978-988-18094-3-8(6))* Haven Bks.

Caine, Rachel, pseud. Fall of Night. 2013. (Morganville Vampires Ser.: 14). (ENG.). 368p. (YA). (gr. 9). pap. 9.99 *(978-0-451-41426-7(8),* Berkley) Penguin Publishing Group.

—Kiss of Death, 8 vols. 2010. (Morganville Vampires Ser.: 8). (ENG.). 256p. (YA). (gr. 9-18). 6.99 *(978-0-451-22973-1(8),* Berkley) Penguin Publishing Group.

—The Morganville Vampires. (Morganville Vampires Ser.: Bks. 1-2). (ENG.). (YA). (gr. 9-18). 2009. 480p. 9.99 *(978-0-451-23054-6(X))* Vol. 2. 2010. 464p. 9.99 *(978-0-451-23289-2(5))* Vol. 3. 2011. 464p. 9.99 *(978-0-451-23355-4(7))* Vol. 4. 2011. 464p. 9.99 *(978-0-451-23426-1(X))* Penguin Publishing Group. (Berkley).

Caine, Rachel, pseud, et al. Immortal: Love Stories with Bite. Cast, P. C., ed. 2009. (ENG., Illus.). 280p. (J). (gr. 9-12). pap. 8.95 *(978-1-933771-92-2(5))* BenBella Bks.

Calhoun, Dia. Avielle of Rhia, 1 vol. 2006. (ENG.). 400p. (J). (gr. 6). 16.99 *(978-0-7614-5320-8(2))* Marshall Cavendish Corp.

—Firegold. 2003. (Sunburst Bks.). 284p. (YA). 16.60 *(978-0-7569-2809-4(5))* Perfection Learning Corp.

—Firegold. l.t. ed. 2005. (Thorndike Literacy Bridge Ser.). 415p. (YA). (gr. 7-12). per. 21.95 *(978-0-7862-7696-7(7),* Large Print Pr.) Thorndike Pr.

Calhoun, Megan. Oscar the Pig: Mommy Goes to Work. 2008. 32p. 18.50 *(978-0-615-25193-6(5))* Silly String Media.

Calhoun, Terry. The Muggwapps. 2007. (J). pap. 8.00 *(978-0-8059-7223-8(4))* Dorrance Publishing Co., Inc.

Callaghan, Cindy. Just Add Magic. 2010. (Just Add Magic Ser.: 1). (ENG., Illus.). 240p. (J). (gr. 4-8). pap. 7.99 *(978-1-4424-0268-3(7),* Aladdin) Simon & Schuster Children's Publishing.

Camargo, F. T. Shanti & the Magic Mandala. 2014. (ENG.). 336p. pap. 12.95 *(978-1-78279-500-1(6),* Lodestone Bks.) Hunt, John Publishing Ltd. GBR. Dist: National Bk. Network.

Cameron, Anne. Dreamspeaker. unabr. ed. 2005. (ENG.). 128p. pap. 9.95 *(978-1-55017-364-2(2))* Harbour Publishing Co., Ltd. CAN. Dist: Midpoint Trade Bks., Inc.

—The Fire Dragon Storm. 2016. (Lightning Catcher Ser.: 4). 464p. (J). (gr. 3-7). 16.99 *(978-0-06-211286-6(4),* Greenwillow Bks.) HarperCollins Pubs.

—The Lightning Catcher. Jamieson, Victoria, illus. 2013. (Lightning Catcher Ser.: 1). (ENG.). 432p. (J). (gr. 3-7). 16.99 *(978-0-06-211276-7(7),* Greenwillow Bks.) HarperCollins Pubs.

Cameron, Sharon. The Forgetting. 2017. lib. bdg. 20.85 ***(978-0-606-40148-7(2))*** Turtleback Bks.

Cammuso, Frank. Big Birthday Bash. 2014. (Misadventures of Salem Hyde Ser.). (ENG., Illus.). 96p. (J). (gr. 1-4). 14.95 *(978-1-4197-1025-4(7),* Amulet Bks.) Abrams, Inc.

—The Misadventures of Salem Hyde: Cookie Catastrophe. 2014. (Misadventures of Salem Hyde Ser.). (ENG., Illus.). 96p. (J). (gr. 1-4). 14.95 *(978-1-4197-1198-5(9),* Amulet Bks.) Abrams, Inc.

Campana, Augustine. The Last Fairy. 2008. 204p. (gr. -1 — 1). 24.95 *(978-0-595-50892-1(8))*; pap. 14.95 *(978-0-595-52086-2(3))* iUniverse, Inc.

Campbell, Charles K. La Magic Coin. 2004. (YA). (gr. 3-18). per. 15.00 *(978-0-9742064-3-1(1))* Unmistakably C K C.

Campbell, D. Andrew. Catharsis. 2013. 340p. pap. 12.50 *(978-0-9897522-0-6(8))* Broviak Publishing.

Campos, Paula. The Turtle's Shell. Ortega, Macarena, illus. 2008.Tr. of tortuga Golosa. (J). pap. 14.95 *(978-0-9801147-5-1(6))* Jorge Pinto Bks.

Candlewick Press Staff. Magical Film Projections: Creatures. 2017. (J. K. Rowling's Wizarding World Ser.). (ENG.). 16p. (J). (gr. 2-5). 16.99 *(978-0-7636-9585-9(8))* Candlewick Pr.

Cannizzaro, Debbie. We Live in Mandeville: 0. l.t. ed. 2005. (Illus.). 32p. (J). lib. bdg. 9.99 *(978-0-9762262-0-8(0))* DeCa Communications, LLC.

Capehart, Staci. Furry Tails: The Adventures of Mr. Mackie. 2009. 40p. pap. 16.99 *(978-1-4343-6974-1(9))* AuthorHouse.

Capone, Deb. Tooth Fairy Tales. 2005. (J). 14.95 *(978-0-9728666-7-5(1))* As Simple As That Publishing.

Cardwell, Helen. Amber Janusson & the Battle for the Magic Lands. 2004. 124p. (YA). pap. 10.95 *(978-0-595-33006-5(1))* iUniverse, Inc.

Carey, Anna. Deadfall. 2016. (Blackbird Ser.: 2). 272p. (YA). (gr. 9). pap. 9.99 *(978-0-06-229977-2(8),* HarperTeen) HarperCollins Pubs.

Carey, Edward. Foulsham: The Iremonger Trilogy: Book 2. 2015. (Iremonger Trilogy Ser.: 0). (ENG., Illus.). 336p. (gr. 5-17). 16.99 *(978-1-4683-0954-6(4),* 460954) Overlook Pr., The.

—Foulsham: The Iremonger Trilogy: Book Two. 2015. (Iremonger Trilogy Ser.: 0). (ENG.). 336p. (gr. 5-9). pap. 10.99 *(978-1-4683-1178-5(6),* 461178) Overlook Pr., The.

—Heap House: The Iremonger Trilogy: Book One. 2015. (Iremonger Trilogy Ser.: 1). (ENG., Illus.). 416p. pap. 10.99 *(978-1-4683-1118-1(2),* 461118) Overlook Pr., The.

—Lungdon: The Iremonger Trilogy: Book Three. 2015. (Iremonger Trilogy Ser.: 0). (ENG., Illus.). 512p. (gr. 5-12). 17.99 *(978-1-4683-0955-3(2),* 460955) Overlook Pr., The.

Carey, Janet Lee. The Beast of Noor. (ENG., Illus.). 512p. (J). (gr. 5-9). 2011. pap. 7.99 *(978-1-4424-4338-9(3))* 2006. 19.99 *(978-0-689-87644-8(0))* Simon & Schuster Children's Publishing. (Atheneum Bks. for Young Readers).

—Dragonswood. 2013. (ENG.). 416p. (YA). (gr. 7). pap. 9.99 *(978-0-14-242432-2(3),* Firebird) Penguin Young Readers Group.

—In the Time of Dragon Moon. (ENG.). 480p. (YA). (gr. 7). 2016. pap. 10.99 *(978-0-14-242574-9(5),* Speak) 2015. 17.99 *(978-0-8037-3810-2(2),* Kathy Dawson Books) Penguin Young Readers Group.

Carlson, Caroline. Magic Marks the Spot. Phillips, Dave, illus. 2014. (Very Nearly Honorable League of Pirates Ser.: 1). (ENG.). 384p. (J). (gr. 3-7). pap. 6.99 *(978-0-06-219435-0(6))* HarperCollins Pubs.

—The Very Nearly Honorable League of Pirates - The Terror of the Southlands. Phillips, Dave, illus. 2014. (Very Nearly Honorable League of Pirates Ser.: 2). (ENG.). 336p. (J). (gr. 3-7). 16.99 *(978-0-06-219436-7(4))* HarperCollins Pubs.

Carlson, Lavelle. Rocks in My Socks & Rainbows Too, 10 vols. Adams, Lucas, illus. 2003. 32p. (J). per. 16.95 *(978-0-9725803-2-8(8))* Children's Publishing.

Carmack, Cora. Roar. 2017. (Stormheart Ser.). (ENG.). (YA). 384p. 17.99 *(978-0-7653-8631-1(3),* 9780765386311); (gr. 8-12). pap. 11.99 ***(978-0-7653-9705-8(6))*** Doherty, Tom Assocs., LLC. (Tor Teen).

Carman, Patrick. The Dark Hills Divide. 2003. (Land of Elyon Ser.: Bk. 1). 200p. (J). pap. 11.95 *(978-0-9742287-0-9(2))* Amped Media.

—The Dark Planet. 2010. (Atherton Ser.: 3). (ENG., Illus.). 368p. (J). (gr. 3-7). pap. 9.99 *(978-0-316-16675-1(8))* Little, Brown Bks. for Young Readers.

—Rivers of Fire. 2009. (Atherton Ser.: 2). (ENG., Illus.). 336p. (J). (gr. 3-7). pap. 9.99 *(978-0-316-16673-7(1))* Little Brown & Co.

Carmody, Isobelle. A Fox Called Sorrow. 2008. (Little Fur Ser.: Bk. 2). (ENG., Illus.). 272p. (J). (gr. 3-7). 5.99 *(978-0-375-83857-6(0),* Yearling) Random Hse. Children's Bks.

—A Mystery of Wolves. 2009. (Little Fur Ser.: Bk. 3). (ENG., Illus.). 256p. (J). (gr. 3-7). 6.99 *(978-0-375-83859-0(7),* Yearling) Random Hse. Children's Bks.

—The Red Queen. 7th ed. 2016. (Obernewtyn Chronicles Ser.: 7). (ENG.). 1120p. (YA). (gr. 7). 29.99 *(978-0-670-07640-6(6))* Penguin Books Australia AUS. Dist: Independent Pubs. Group.

—The Red Queen. 2011. (Obernewtyn Chronicles: Bk. 7). 544p. (YA). (gr. 7-18). mass mkt. 7.99 *(978-0-375-85774-4(5),* Random Hse. Bks. for Young Readers) Random Hse. Children's Bks.

—A Riddle of Green. 2009. (Little Fur Ser.: Bk. 4). (J). *(978-0-375-83860-6(0))* Random House Children's Books.

Carney, Larry, adapted by. Jack & the Beanstalk. 2009. (ENG., Illus.). 24p. (J). 6.95 *(978-1-60072-115-1(X))* PC Treasures, Inc.

—Rapunzel. 2009. (ENG., Illus.). 24p. (J). 6.95 *(978-1-60072-113-7(3))* PC Treasures, Inc.

—Sleeping Beauty. 2009. (ENG., Illus.). 24p. (J). 6.95 *(978-1-60072-116-8(8))* PC Treasures, Inc.

—Snow White. 2009. (ENG., Illus.). 24p. (J). 6.95 *(978-1-60072-117-5(6))* PC Treasures, Inc.

Carney, Riley. The Final Alliance: Book Five of the Reign of the Elements. 2012. (Reign of the Elements Ser.: Bk. 5). (Illus.). 312p. (J). 20.95 *(978-0-9841307-9-5(9))* BookLight Pr.

Carriger, Gail. Manners & Mutiny. 2016. (Finishing School Ser.: 4). (ENG., Illus.). 352p. (YA). (gr. 7-17). pap. 10.99 *(978-0-316-19029-9(2))* Little, Brown Bks. for Young Readers.

Carroll, Emma. In Darkling Wood. 2017. (ENG.). 240p. (J). (gr. 5). 16.99 *(978-0-399-55601-2(X),* Delacorte Bks. for Young Readers) Random Hse. Children's Bks.

Carroll, Harlisha. Miracle Mouse & Jesus - Book: (Short Stories 1) 2012. 36p. pap. 24.95 *(978-1-4626-6615-7(9))* America Star Bks.

Carroll, Jenny, pseud & Cabot, Meg. Reunion. 2004. (Mediator Ser.: 3). (ENG.). 304p. (YA). (gr. 8-18). pap. 7.99 *(978-0-06-072513-6(3),* HarperTeen) HarperCollins Pubs.

Carroll, Katie L. Elixir Bound. 2013. 158p. pap. *(978-1-77127-465-4(4))* MuseItUp Publishing.

Carroll, Lewis, pseud. AILICE'S ANTERS IN FERLIELANN. 2012. (GER., Illus.). 144p. pap. *(978-1-78201-016-6(5))* Evertype.

—AILIS'S ANTERINS I THE LAUN O FERLIES. 2013. (GER., Illus.). 138p. pap. *(978-1-78201-026-5(2))* Evertype.

—Alice in Wonderland. Steadman, Ralph, illus. 2010. (ENG.). 128p. pap. 19.95 *(978-1-55407-203-3(4),* 9781554072033) Firefly Bks., Ltd.

—Alice in Wonderland. 2009. (Stepping Stone Book Ser.). (ENG.). 112p. (J). (gr. 1-4). 4.99 *(978-0-375-86641-8(8),* Random Hse. Bks. for Young Readers) Random Hse. Children's Bks.

—Alice in Wonderland & Through the Looking-Glass. Andreasen, Dan, illus. 2009. (Classic Starts(tm) Ser.). (ENG.). 160p. (J). (gr. 2-4). 6.95 *(978-1-4027-5422-7(1))* Sterling Publishing Co., Inc.

—Alice's Abenteuer im Wunderland. Zimmermann, Antonie, tr. Tenniel, John, illus. 2012. (Dover Dual Language German Ser.).Tr. of Alice's Adventures in Wonderland. (GER & ENG.). 192p. (J). reprint ed. pap. 8.95 *(978-0-486-20668-4(8))* Dover Pubns., Inc.

—ALICE'S ADVENTIRS IN WONDERLAAND. 2012. (GER., Illus.). 140p. pap. *(978-1-78201-008-1(4))* Evertype.

—Alice's Adventures in Wonderland. Date not set. (J). lib. bdg. 16.95 *(978-0-8488-1262-1(X))* Amereon Ltd.

—Alice's Adventures in Wonderland. Robinson, Gordon, illus. 2009. 118p. (gr. 3-18). pap. 4.50 *(978-1-60450-761-4(6),* Serenity Pubs.) Arc Manor.

—Alice's Adventures in Wonderland. Tenniel, John, illus. Date not set. 248p. (YA). 14.95 *(978-1-884807-19-0(4))* Blushing Rose Publishing.

—Alice's Adventures in Wonderland. Tenniel, John, illus. 2013. (Cambridge Library Collection - Fiction & Poetry Ser.). (ENG.). 210p. 57.00 *(978-1-108-06037-0(4))*; pap. 29.99 *(978-1-108-05958-9(9))* Cambridge Univ. Pr.

—Alice's Adventures in Wonderland. Oxenbury, Helen, illus. 2003. (ENG.). 208p. (J). (gr. 3-7). pap. 16.99 *(978-0-7636-2049-3(1))* Candlewick Pr.

—Alice's Adventures in Wonderland. Tenniel, John, illus. 2007. 204p. (J). 24.95 *(978-1-58218-791-4(6))*; (ENG.). (YA). per. 14.95 *(978-1-58218-790-7(8))* Digital Scanning, Inc.

—Alice's Adventures in Wonderland. Rountree, Harry, illus. 2011. (Calla Editions Ser.). (ENG.). 248p. (gr. 3). 40.00 *(978-1-60660-014-6(1))* Dover Pubns., Inc.

—Alice's Adventures in Wonderland. Evangelista, Mauro, illus. 2006. 63p. (J). (gr. 2). 8.99 *(978-0-7945-1239-2(9),* Usborne) EDC Publishing.

—Alice's Adventures in Wonderland. Lornie, June, illus. 2013. 104p. pap. *(978-1-78201-037-1(8))* Evertype.

—Alice's Adventures in Wonderland. Tenniel, John, illus. 2009. 68p. pap. 14.14 *(978-1-151-46988-5(2))* General Bks. LLC.

—Alice's Adventures in Wonderland. 2009. 80p. pap. 14.14 *(978-1-4590-2482-3(6))*; 78p. (gr. 4-18). pap. 14.14 *(978-1-4590-2479-3(6))* General Bks. LLC.

—Alice's Adventures in Wonderland. 2008. (Green Apple Starter Ser.). 64p. (J). (gr. 4). pap. 24.95 incl. cd-rom *(978-88-530-0768-1(0),* Black Cat) Grove/Atlantic, Inc.

—Alice's Adventures in Wonderland. Date not set. 192p. (YA). (gr. 3-18). mass mkt. 8.99 *(978-0-06-440929-2(5))*; (ENG., Illus.). 176p. (J). 14.95 *(978-0-06-095770-4(0))* HarperCollins Pubs.

—Alice's Adventures in Wonderland. Garcia, Camille Rose, illus. 2010. (ENG.). 160p. 16.99 *(978-0-06-188657-7(2),* Collins Design) HarperCollins Pubs.

—Alice's Adventures in Wonderland. Sabuda, Robert, illus. 2003. (ENG.). 12p. (J). (gr. -1-3). 34.99 *(978-0-689-84743-1(2),* Little Simon) Little Simon.

—Alice's Adventures in Wonderland. 2010. 208p. pap. 24.95 *(978-0-557-01173-5(6))* 2009. 67p. pap. 12.36 *(978-0-557-15604-7(1))* Lulu Pr., Inc.

—Alice's Adventures in Wonderland. 2009. pap. 2.95 *(978-1-61600-010-3(4))* Mizzou Publishing - The Mizzou Store.

—Alice's Adventures in Wonderland. 2015. (Macmillan Classics Ser.). (ENG., Illus.). 192p. (J). (gr. 2-4). 16.99 *(978-1-4472-7308-0(7),* Macmillan Children's Bks.) Pan Macmillan GBR. Dist: Independent Pubs. Group.

—Alice's Adventures in Wonderland. (Charm Book Classics Ser.). 26p. *(978-1-4054-9107-5(8))* Parragon, Inc.

—Alice's Adventures in Wonderland. 2013. (ENG., Illus.). 368p. (J). (gr. 4-7). pap. 10.99 *(978-0-09-957292-3(3))* Random Hse. GBR. Dist: Independent Pubs. Group.

—Alice's Adventures in Wonderland. (J). 2006. 34.75 *(978-1-4193-1123-9(9))* 2004. 36.75 *(978-1-4025-8106-9(8))* Recorded Bks., Inc.

—Alice's Adventures in Wonderland. Ingpen, Robert R., illus. 2009. (Sterling Illustrated Classics Ser.). (ENG.). 192p. (J). (gr. 5-18). 19.95 *(978-1-4027-6835-4(4))* Sterling Publishing Co., Inc.

—Alice's Adventures in Wonderland. Lipchenko, Oleg, illus. 2009. (ENG.). 104p. (J). (gr. k-12). 22.95 *(978-0-88776-932-0(2),* Tundra Bks.) Tundra Bks. CAN. Dist: Penguin Random Hse. LLC.

—Alice's Adventures in Wonderland. Wiley, Nancy, illus. 2009. 88p. 35.00 *(978-0-615-29492-6(8))* OBrien, Wiley Workspace.

—Alice's Adventures in Wonderland. Ghiuselev, Iassen, illus. rev. ed. 2012. (ENG.). 120p. (J). (gr. 3). 29.95 *(978-1-897476-42-0(6))* Simply Read Bks. CAN. Dist: Ingram Publisher Services.

—Alice's Adventures in Wonderland. 2008. (Puffin Classics Ser.). (gr. 5-8). lib. bdg. 16.00 *(978-0-613-63916-3(2),* Turtleback) Turtleback Bks.

—Alice's Adventures in Wonderland. D'Aquino, Andrea, illus. unabr. ed. 2015. (Classics Reimagined Ser.). (ENG.). 248p. 25.00 *(978-1-63159-075-7(8),* Rockport Publishers) Quarto Publishing Group USA.

—Alice's Adventures in Wonderland, 1. Tenniel, John, illus. 2011. (Macmillan Alice Ser.). (ENG.). 208p. (J). (gr. 2). 26.99 *(978-0-230-75538-3(0))* Pan Macmillan GBR. Dist: Independent Pubs. Group.

—Alice's Adventures in Wonderland. Bond, Anna, illus. 150th anniv. ed. 2015. (ENG.). 192p. (J). (gr. 5). 30.00 *(978-0-14-751587-2(4),* Puffin Books) Penguin Young Readers Group.

—Alice's Adventures in Wonderland: And Other Stories. Tenniel, John, illus. 2013. (Leather-Bound Classics Ser.). (ENG.). 544p. lthr. 24.99 *(978-1-60710-933-4(6),* Thunder Bay Pr.) Readerlink Distribution Services, LLC.

—Alice's Adventures in Wonderland: With a Discussion of Imagination. Schneider, Rex, tr. Schneider, Rex, illus. 2003. (J). *(978-1-59203-046-0(7))* Learning Challenge, Inc.

—Alice's Adventures in Wonderland & Through the Looking Glass. Tenniel, John & Bickford-smith, Coralie, illus. 2010. (Penguin Classics Hardcover Ser.). (ENG.). 448p. (gr. 12). 24.00 *(978-0-14-119246-8(1),* Penguin Classics) Penguin Publishing Group.

—Alice's Adventures in Wonderland & Through the Looking Glass. 2010. (Enriched Classics Ser.). (ENG.). 336p. mass mkt. 5.99 *(978-1-4391-6947-6(0))* Simon & Schuster.

—Alice's Adventures in Wonderland & Through the Looking-Glass. Haughton, Hugh, ed. Tenniel, John, illus. rev. ed. 2003. (ENG.). 400p. (gr. 12-18). pap. 11.00 *(978-0-14-143976-1(9),* Penguin Classics) Penguin Publishing Group.

—Alice's Adventures under Ground: Being the Book Afterwards Developed into Alice's Adventures in Wonderland. 2009. (Illus.). 72p. pap. *(978-1-904808-39-8(5))* Evertype.

—Alicia en el Pais de las Maravillas. Aranguren, Dolores, tr. 2010.Tr. of Alice's Adventures in Wonderland. (SPA.). 264p. (YA). (gr. 5-8). pap. *(978-607-07-0359-1(6))* Editorial Planeta Mexicana.

—Alicia en el País de las Maravillas. (SPA.). 152p. 24.95 *(978-84-261-2700-6(2))* Juventud, Editorial ESP. Dist: Distribooks, Inc.

—Alicia en el País de las Maravillas. 2011. (Vintage Espanol Ser.). (SPA.). 384p. pap. 15.00 *(978-0-307-74514-9(7),* Vintage Espanol) Knopf Doubleday Publishing Group.

—Las Aventuras de Alicia. (Coleccion Clasicos de la Juventud).Tr. of Alice's Adventures in Wonderland. (SPA., Illus.). 240p. (J). 12.95 *(978-84-7189-060-3(7),* ORT308)

EFG

Ortells, Alfredo Editorial S.L. ESP. Dist: Continental Bk. Co., Inc.
—Eachdraidh Ealasaid Ann an Tir Nan Iongantas. Watson, Moray, tr. from ENG. Tenniel, John, illus. 2012. 156p. pap. *(978-1-78201-015-9(7))* Evertype.
—Michael Foreman's Alice's Adventures in Wonderland. Foreman, Michael, illus. 2010. (ENG.). 176p. (J). (gr. 2-7). 19.99 *(978-1-84365-142-0(4),* Pavilion) Pavilion Bks. GBR. Dist: Independent Pubs. Group.
—The Nursery Alice. 2013. 425p. reprint ed. lthr. 69.00 *(978-0-7426-2289-0(4))* Classic Bks.
—The Nursery Alice. Tenniel, Sir John & Thomson, E. Gertrude, illus. 2014. 64p. *(978-1-907960-09-3(0))* English Rose Publishing.
—The Nursery Alice. Tenniel, John & Thomson, E. Gertrude, illus. 2010. 64p. pap. *(978-1-907960-00-0(7))* English Rose Publishing.
—The Nursery Alice. Tenniel, John, illus. 2010. 86p. pap. *(978-1-904808-42-8(5))* Evertype.
—The Nursery Alice. Tenniel, John, illus. 2013. 74p. (J). pap. 18.58 *(978-1-939652-68-3(5))* Lire Bks.
—The Nursery Alice. Tenniel, John, illus. 2009. 56p. *(978-973-88826-8-3(0))* Mediamorphosis.
—The Nursery Alice. Tenniel, John, illus. 2015. (Macmillan Alice Ser.). (ENG.). 72p. (J). (-k). 19.99 *(978-1-4472-8711-7(8))* Pan Macmillan GBR. Dist: Independent Pubs. Group.
—'O Tafaoga a 'Alise I Le Nu'o O Mea Ofoofogia. Simanu-Klutz, Luafata, tr. from ENG. Tenniel, John, illus. 2013. 152p. pap. *(978-1-78201-023-4(8))* Evertype.
—The Story of Sylvie & Bruno. 2005. pap. 31.95 *(978-0-7661-9697-1(6))* Kessinger Publishing, LLC.
—Sylvie & Bruno. 304p. 2005. 29.95 *(978-1-4218-0843-7(9))* 2004. pap. 14.95 *(978-1-59540-443-5(0))* 1st World Publishing, Inc. (1st World Library - Literary Society).
—Sylvie & Bruno. 2013. 425p. reprint ed. lthr. 69.00 *(978-0-7426-2290-6(8))* Classic Bks.
—Sylvie & Bruno. 2008. 224p. 24.99 *(978-0-554-32690-0(6))* 2008. 224p. 27.99 *(978-0-554-23387-1(8))* 2007. 328p. pap. 20.99 *(978-1-4264-4275-9(0))* Creative Media Partners, LLC.
—Sylvie & Bruno. 2007. (ENG.). 216p. per. *(978-1-4065-9750-9(3))* Dodo Pr.
—Sylvie & Bruno. 2008. 148p. pap. *(978-1-4068-9052-5(9))* 2006. 380p. pap. *(978-1-84637-327-5(1))* Echo Library.
—Sylvie & Bruno. 2010. (Illus.). 130p. pap. 19.99 *(978-1-153-73795-1(7))* 2009. 158p. pap. 21.89 *(978-1-151-23618-0(7))* 2009. 162p. pap. 19.99 *(978-1-150-59969-9(3))* General Bks. LLC.
—Sylvie & Bruno. 2004. reprint ed. pap. 1.99 *(978-1-4192-5019-4(1))* Kessinger Publishing, LLC.
—Sylvie & Bruno. 2010. (CAM.). 200p. pap. 13.95 *(978-1-4385-3644-6(5),* Book Jungle) Standard Pubns., Inc.
—Sylvie & Bruno Concluded. 2013. 425p. reprint ed. lthr. 69.00 *(978-0-7426-2294-4(0))* Classic Bks.
—Sylvie & Bruno Concluded. 2009. 176p. pap. 21.89 *(978-1-150-29096-1(X))* General Bks. LLC.
—Sylvie & Bruno Concluded. Furniss, Harry, illus. 462p. 2010. 42.36 *(978-1-167-13605-4(5))* 2010. pap. 30.36 *(978-1-167-01946-3(6))* 2009. 52.95 *(978-1-120-84142-1(9))* 2009. pap. 37.95 *(978-1-120-71925-6(9))* Kessinger Publishing, LLC.
—Sylvie & Bruno Concluded. 2004. reprint ed. pap. 1.99 *(978-1-4192-5020-0(5))* Kessinger Publishing, LLC.
—Through the Looking Glass. 2010. 84p. pap. 9.95 *(978-1-59594-837-3(6),* Wingspan Pr.) WingSpan Publishing.
—Through the Looking-Glass. Date not set. 176p. (J). 19.95 *(978-0-8488-2629-1(9))* Amereon Ltd.
—Through the Looking-Glass. l.t. ed. 2006. 176p. pap. *(978-1-84637-329-9(8))* Echo Library.
—Through the Looking-Glass, & What Alice Found There, Original Version: Alice Through the Looking Glass. Tenniel, John, illus. 2010. (ENG.). 210p. pap. 25.95 *(978-4-87187-304-8(8))* Ishi Pr. International.
Carroll, Lewis, pseud & Baker, Kyle. Through the Looking-Glass. (Classics Illustrated Ser.). (Illus.). 52p. (YA). pap. 4.95 *(978-1-57209-002-6(2))* Classics International Entertainment, Inc.
Carroll, Lewis, pseud & Burstein, Mark. Sonja in a Kingdom of Wonder. 2013. (RUS., Illus.). 206p. pap. *(978-1-78201-040-1(8))* Evertype.
Carroll, Lewis, pseud & Everson, Michael. Alice's Adventures in Wonderland: Retold in Words of One Syllable. 2010. (Illus.). 108p. pap. *(978-1-904808-44-2(1))* Evertype.
Carroll, Lewis, pseud & Faraday, L. Winifred. Sylvie & Bruno. 2007. (ENG.). 222p. pap. 22.99 *(978-1-4264-4339-8(0))* Creative Media Partners, LLC.
Carroll, Lewis, pseud & Furniss, Harry. Sylvie & Bruno. 2010. 438p. pap. 35.75 *(978-1-177-81979-4(1));* (ENG.). 428p. pap. 35.75 *(978-1-177-54729-1(5));* 432p. pap. 35.75 *(978-1-144-73477-8(0))* Creative Media Partners, LLC.
—Sylvie & Bruno Concluded. 2011. 470p. pap. 37.75 *(978-1-172-76819-6(6))* 2010. (ENG.). 470p. pap. 37.75 *(978-1-177-60596-0(1))* 2010. (ENG.). 468p. pap. 37.75 *(978-1-177-97833-0(4))* 2010. 472p. pap. 37.75 *(978-1-142-48842-0(X))* Creative Media Partners, LLC.
Carroll, Lewis, pseud & Ladybird Books Staff. Alice in Wonderland. García-Cortés, Ester, illus. 2015. (Ladybird Classics Ser.). (ENG.). 72p. (J). (gr. k-3). 8.99 *(978-1-4093-1123-2(6))* Penguin Bks., Ltd. GBR. Dist: Independent Pubs. Group.
Carroll, Lewis, pseud & Roberts, Selyf. Anturiaethau Alys Yng Ngwlad Hud. 2010.Tr. of Alice in Wonderland. (WEL., Illus.). 126p. pap. *(978-1-904808-46-6(8))* Evertype.
Carroll, Lewis, pseud & Stowell, Brian. Contoyryssyn Ealish Ayns Cheer Ny Yindyssyn. 2010. (Illus.). 144p. pap. *(978-1-904808-48-0(4))* Evertype.
Carroll, Lewis, pseud, et al. Sylvie & Bruno. 2011. 434p. pap. 35.75 *(978-1-172-76473-0(5))* 2010. 438p. pap. 35.75 *(978-1-177-93122-9(2))* Creative Media Partners, LLC.
Carroll, Lewis, pseud & Þórarinn Eldjárn. Ævintýri Lísu Undralandi. 2nd ed. 2013. (ICE., Illus.). 142p. pap. *(978-1-78201-025-8(4))* Evertype.
Carroll, Michael. The Ascension. 2011. (Super Human Ser.: 2). (ENG.). 384p. (YA). (gr. 7-18). 16.99 *(978-0-399-25624-0(5),* Philomel Bks.) Penguin Young Readers Group.
—Super Human. 2011. (Super Human Ser.: 1). (ENG.). 400p. (YA). (gr. 7-18). 9.99 *(978-0-14-241905-2(2),* Speak) Penguin Young Readers Group.
Carryl, Charles E. The Admiral's Caravan: A Tale Inspired by Lewis Carroll's Wonderland. 2011. 110p. pap. *(978-1-904808-66-4(2))* Evertype.
—Davy & the Goblin: Or, What Followed Reading 'Alice's Adventures in Wonderland' 2011. (Illus.). 128p. pap. *(978-1-904808-65-7(4))* Evertype.
Carson, Andrew. Cocoa Blasting Home. 2015. (ENG.). 123p. (J). (gr. 1-2). mass mkt. 13.95 *(978-1-78455-947-2(4),* af1cd2a7-ad9a-450a-984d-23569d822d96) Austin, Stan AUS. Dist: Bookmasters Distribution.
Carson, Rae. The Bitter Kingdom. 2013. (Girl of Fire & Thorns Ser.: 3). (ENG.). 448p. (YA). (gr. 8). 17.99 *(978-0-06-202654-5(2),* Greenwillow Bks.) HarperCollins Pubs.
—The Crown of Embers. 2012. (Girl of Fire & Thorns Ser.: 2). (ENG.). 416p. (YA). (gr. 8). 17.99 *(978-0-06-202651-4(8),* Greenwillow Bks.) HarperCollins Pubs.
Carter, Aimée. The Goddess Test. 2011. (Goddess Test Ser.: 1). lib. bdg. 20.85 *(978-0-606-26943-8(6),* Turtleback) Turtleback Bks.
Carter, David. The Nutters of Pendle Forest - Part 1 the Enchanted Valley. 2012. (Illus.). 222p. pap. *(978-1-908098-54-2(6))* 2QT, Ltd. (Publishing).
Carter, Liane. The Chronicles of Joy. 2008. 244p. pap. *(978-1-84923-001-8(3))* YouWriteOn.
Carter, R. J. Alices Journey Beyond Moon, 1 vol. Wright, Lucy, illus. 2004. (ENG.). 98p. *(978-1-903889-76-3(6))* Telos Publishing, Ltd. GBR. Dist: Fitzhenry & Whiteside, Ltd.
Casado, Dami. Como Comes Tu? (SPA.). 8p. 9.95 *(978-84-272-8325-1(3))* Molino, Editorial ESP. Dist: Distribooks, Inc.
—Como Te Lavas? (SPA.). 8p. 9.95 *(978-84-272-8326-8(1))* Molino, Editorial ESP. Dist: Distribooks, Inc.
—Como Te Vistes? (SPA.). 8p. 9.95 *(978-84-272-8328-2(8))* Molino, Editorial ESP. Dist: Distribooks, Inc.
Casey, C. A. Dragon Drool. 2nd ed. 2010. (ENG.). 128p. (J). (gr. 4-7). pap. 7.95 *(978-1-934452-47-9(5),* Dragonfeather Bks.) Bedazzled Ink Publishing Co.
Casey, Jane. How to Fall. 2014. (Jess Tennant Mysteries Ser.: 1). (ENG.). 352p. (YA). (gr. 8-11). 18.99 *(978-1-250-04065-7(5),* 9781250040657, St. Martin's Griffin) St. Martin's Pr.
Casey, Joe. Rock Bottom. 2012. (ENG., Illus.). 120p. (YA). 19.99 *(978-1-60706-619-4(X),* 9781607066194) Image Comics.
Cashore, Kristin. Bitterblue. Schoenherr, Ian, illus. 2013. (ENG.). 608p. (YA). (gr. 9). pap. 10.99 *(978-0-14-242601-2(6),* Firebird) Penguin Young Readers Group.
—Bitterblue. 2012. (SPA.). 384p. (YA). pap. 24.95 *(978-84-9918-435-7(9))* Roca Editorial ESP. Dist: Spanish Pubs., LLC.
—Bitterblue. 2013. (Graceling Realm Ser.: 3). lib. bdg. 22.10 *(978-0-606-32142-6(X),* Turtleback) Turtleback Bks.
—Fire. November, S., ed. 2011. (ENG.). 528p. (YA). (gr. 7-18). pap. 10.99 *(978-0-14-241591-7(X),* Firebird) Penguin Young Readers Group.
—Fire. 2011. (Graceling Realm Ser.: 2). lib. bdg. 22.10 *(978-0-606-23085-8(8),* Turtleback) Turtleback Bks.
Cashore, Kristin. Graceling. (ENG.). (YA). 2009. 512p. (gr. 9). pap. 9.99 *(978-0-547-25830-0(5))* 2008. (Illus.). 480p. (gr. 7-18). 17.99 *(978-0-15-206396-2(X))* Houghton Mifflin Harcourt Publishing Co.
—Graceling. 2011. (Fantasy Ser.). (FRE.). pap. ***(978-2-253-15763-2(5)**,* Le Livre de poche) Librairie Generale Francaise, LGF.
—Graceling. 2009. (Graceling Ser.). (ENG., Illus.). 471p. (gr. 8-12). 20.00 *(978-1-60686-533-0(1))* Perfection Learning Corp.
—Graceling. 2009. (SPA.). 402p. (YA). 23.95 *(978-84-92429-81-3(X))* Roca Editorial ESP. Dist: Spanish Pubs., LLC.
—Graceling. 2009. (Graceling Realm Ser.: 1). lib. bdg. 20.85 *(978-0-606-07993-8(9),* Turtleback) Turtleback Bks.
Caso, George R. The Mission. Caso, George R., illus. 2003. (Illus.). 16p. (J). (gr. -1-6). pap. 4.95 *(978-0-9719290-1-2(7))* Caso, George R.
Cass, Kiera. The Selection 4-Book Box Set. 2016. (Selection Ser.). 1456p. (YA). (gr. 8). pap. 39.96 *(978-0-06-242440-2(8),* HarperTeen) HarperCollins Pubs.
—The Siren. (YA). 2017. 352p. (gr. 8). pap. 9.99 *(978-0-06-239200-8(X),* HarperTeen) 2016. 327p. pap. *(978-0-06-244954-2(0))* 2016. 336p. (gr. 8-12). 18.99 *(978-0-06-239199-5(2),* HarperTeen) HarperCollins Pubs.
—The Siren. 2017. lib. bdg. 20.85 ***(978-0-606-40073-2(7))*** Turtleback Bks.
—The Siren. 2009. 276p. pap. 16.95 *(978-1-4401-5423-2(6))* iUniverse, Inc.
Cassaday, John, illus. Astonishing X-Men - Gifted, Vol. 1. gif. ed. 2006. (ENG.). 152p. (YA). (gr. 8-17). pap. 14.99 *(978-0-7851-1531-1(5))* Marvel Worldwide, Inc.
Cast, P. C. Moon Chosen. 2016. (Tales of a New World Ser.: 1). (ENG., Illus.). 608p. (YA). (gr. 7-12). 18.99 *(978-1-250-10072-6(0),* 9781250100726, St. Martin's Griffin) St. Martin's Pr.
Cast, P. C. & Cast, Kristin. Awakened. (House of Night Novels Ser.: 8). (ENG.). 304p. (YA). (gr. 7-12). 2013. mass mkt. 9.99 *(978-1-250-04692-5(0),* 9781250046925, St. Martin's Paperbacks) 2012. pap. 10.99 *(978-0-312-38797-6(0),* 9780312387976, St. Martin's Griffin) 2011. 17.99 *(978-0-312-65024-7(8),* 9780312650247, St. Martin's Griffin) St. Martin's Pr.
—Awakened. l.t. ed. 2011. (House of Night Ser.). (ENG.). 436p. 23.99 *(978-1-4104-3776-1(0))* Thorndike Pr.
—Betrayed. (House of Night Novels Ser.: 2). (ENG.). 320p. (YA). (gr. 7-12). 2013. mass mkt. 9.99 *(978-1-250-04693-2(9),* 9781250046932, St. Martin's Paperbacks) 2009. 19.99 *(978-0-312-59629-3(4),* 9780312596293) 2007. pap. 10.99 *(978-0-312-36028-3(2),* 9780312360283, St. Martin's Griffin) St. Martin's Pr.
—Betrayed. l.t. ed. 2008. (House of Night Ser.: No. 2). (ENG.). 472p. (YA). 23.95 *(978-1-4104-1025-2(0))* Thorndike Pr.
—Burned. l.t. ed. 2011. (House of Night Ser.). (ENG.). 552p. 23.99 *(978-1-4104-3440-1(0))* Thorndike Pr.
—Chosen. 2010. (House of Night Novels (Quality) Ser.). (CHI.). 367p. pap. *(978-957-0316-42-1(X))* Locus Publishing Co.
—Chosen. 2008. (House of Night Novels Ser.: 3). (ENG.). 320p. (YA). (gr. 8-12). pap. 10.99 *(978-0-312-36030-6(4),* 9780312360306, St. Martin's Griffin) St. Martin's Pr.
—Chosen. l.t. ed. 2009. (House of Night Ser.: Bk. 3). (ENG.). 406p. (YA). 23.95 *(978-1-4104-1608-7(9))* Thorndike Pr.
—Destined. 2013. (House of Night Novels Ser.: 9). (ENG.). 336p. (YA). (gr. 7-12). pap. 10.99 *(978-0-312-38798-3(9),* 9780312387983, St. Martin's Griffin) St. Martin's Pr.
—House of Night: the Beginning: Marked & Betrayed. 2013. (House of Night Novels Ser.). (ENG.). 640p. (YA). (gr. 7-12). pap. 11.99 *(978-1-250-03723-7(9),* 9781250037237, St. Martin's Griffin) St. Martin's Pr.
—Hunted. (House of Night Novels Ser.: 5). (ENG.). 336p. (YA). (gr. 7-12). 2013. mass mkt. 9.99 *(978-1-250-04696-3(3),* 9781250046963, St. Martin's Paperbacks) 2010. pap. 10.99 *(978-0-312-57799-5(0),* 9780312577995, St. Martin's Griffin) St. Martin's Pr.
—Hunted. l.t. ed. 2010. (House of Night Ser.: Bk. 5). (ENG.). 548p. 23.95 *(978-1-4104-1951-4(7))* Thorndike Pr.
—Marked. (House of Night Novels Ser.: 1). (ENG.). 320p. (YA). (gr. 8-12). 2009. 19.99 *(978-0-312-36025-2(8),* 9780312360252) 2007. pap. 10.99 *(978-0-312-36026-9(6),* 9780312360269, St. Martin's Griffin) St. Martin's Pr.
—Marked. l.t. ed. 2008. (House of Night Ser.: No. 1). (ENG.). 442p. (YA). 23.95 *(978-1-4104-1021-4(8))* Thorndike Pr.
—Marked. 2007. (House of Night Ser.: 1). 306p. (YA). lib. bdg. 22.10 *(978-1-4178-0853-3(5),* Turtleback) Turtleback Bks.
—Tempted. (House of Night Novels Ser.: 6). (ENG.). (YA). (gr. 7-12). 2013. 352p. mass mkt. 9.99 *(978-1-250-04698-7(X),* 9781250046987, St. Martin's Paperbacks) 2011. 336p. pap. 10.99 *(978-0-312-60938-2(8),* 9780312609382, St. Martin's Griffin) 2009. 336p. 17.99 *(978-0-312-56748-4(0),* 9780312567484, St. Martin's Griffin) St. Martin's Pr.
—Tempted. l.t. ed. 2010. (House of Night Novel Ser.). (ENG.). 552p. 23.99 *(978-1-4104-3141-7(X))* Thorndike Pr.
—Untamed. 2008. (House of Night Novels Ser.: 4). (ENG.). 352p. (YA). (gr. 8-12). pap. 10.99 *(978-0-312-37983-4(8),* 9780312379834, St. Martin's Griffin) St. Martin's Pr.
—Untamed. l.t. ed. 2009. (House of Night Ser.: Bk. 4). (ENG.). 510p. (YA). 23.95 *(978-1-4104-1965-1(7))* Thorndike Pr.
Castaneda, Huguette. Mariella y Los Obsequios Del Mar. 2012. 56p. pap. 20.99 *(978-1-4525-6215-5(6))* Balboa Pr.
—Mariella's Gifts from the Se. 2012. 56p. pap. 20.95 *(978-1-4525-5865-3(5))* Balboa Pr.
Castenetto, Christiana. Dante's Journey. Ceva, Aline Cantono di, illus. 2009. (ENG.). 28p. (J). (gr. 4-7). 15.00 *(978-88-7461-113-3(7))* Mandragora ITA. Dist: National Bk. Network.
Castle, Amber. Evie the Swan Sister. Hall, Mary, illus. 2012. (ENG.). 160p. (J). (gr. 2-4). pap. 7.99 *(978-0-85707-252-8(8),* Simon & Schuster Children's) Simon & Schuster, Ltd. GBR. Dist: Simon & Schuster, Inc.
—Grace the Sea Sister. Hall, Mary, illus. 2012. (ENG.). 160p. (J). (gr. 2-4). pap. 5.99 *(978-0-85707-251-1(X),* Simon & Schuster Children's) Simon & Schuster, Ltd. GBR. Dist: Simon & Schuster, Inc.
—Isabella: The Butterfly Sister. Hall, Mary, illus. 2012. (ENG.). 160p. (J). (gr. 2-4). pap. 7.99 *(978-0-85707-249-8(8),* Simon & Schuster Children's) Simon & Schuster, Ltd. GBR. Dist: Simon & Schuster, Inc.
—Olivia the Otter Sister. Hall, Mary, illus. 2013. (ENG.). 160p. (J). (gr. 2-4). pap. 7.99 *(978-0-85707-253-5(6),* Simon & Schuster Children's) Simon & Schuster, Ltd. GBR. Dist: Simon & Schuster, Inc.
—The Silver Sister. Hall, Mary, illus. 2012. (ENG.). 160p. (J). (gr. 2-4). pap. 7.99 *(978-0-85707-250-4(1),* Simon & Schuster Children's) Simon & Schuster, Ltd. GBR. Dist: Simon & Schuster, Inc.
—Sophia: The Flame Sister. Hall, Mary, illus. 2012. (ENG.). 160p. (J). (gr. 2-4). pap. 7.99 *(978-0-85707-247-4(1),* Simon & Schuster Children's) Simon & Schuster, Ltd. GBR. Dist: Simon & Schuster, Inc.
Castle, J. R. The Flame Dragon. 2016. (Dragon Knights Ser.: 1). (ENG., Illus.). 224p. (J). (gr. 4-7). pap. 7.99 *(978-1-84812-459-2(7))* Bonnier Publishing GBR. Dist: Independent Pubs. Group.
—The Shadow Dragon. 2016. (Dragon Knights Ser.: 2). (ENG., Illus.). 192p. (J). (gr. 4-7). pap. 7.99 *(978-1-84812-460-8(0))* Bonnier Publishing GBR. Dist: Independent Pubs. Group.
—The Storm Dragon. 2017. (Dragon Knights Ser.: 3). (ENG., Illus.). 192p. (J). (gr. 4-7). pap. 7.99 *(978-1-84812-515-5(1))* Bonnier Publishing GBR. Dist: Independent Pubs. Group.
Castles & Kingdoms. 2014. (Dream Doodle Draw! Ser.). (ENG., Illus.). 96p. (J). (gr. -1-2). pap. 7.99 *(978-1-4814-1712-9(6),* Little Simon) Little Simon.
Castro, Adam-Troy. Gustav Gloom & the Cryptic Carousel #4. Margiotta, Kristen, illus. 2014. (Gustav Gloom Ser.: 4). (ENG.). 248p. (J). (gr. 3-7). 12.99 *(978-0-448-45836-6(5),* Grosset & Dunlap) Penguin Young Readers Group.
—Gustav Gloom & the Four Terrors #3. Margiotta, Kristen, illus. 2014. (Gustav Gloom Ser.: 3). (ENG.). 248p. (J). (gr. 3-7). 7.99 *(978-0-448-48330-6(0),* Grosset & Dunlap) Penguin Young Readers Group.
Catalano, Nikki. Mitsu: The Dark Witch & the Dream Wilderness. 2010. 88p. pap. 25.13 *(978-1-4251-7411-8(6))* Trafford Publishing.
Catanese, P. W. Dragon Games. Ho, David, illus. (Books of Umber Ser.: 2). (ENG.). (J). (gr. 3-7). 2011. 400p. pap. 7.99 *(978-1-4169-5383-8(3))* 2010. 384p. 17.99 *(978-1-4169-7521-2(7))* Simon & Schuster Children's Publishing. (Aladdin).
—The End of Time. Ho, David, illus. 2012. (Books of Umber Ser.: 3). (ENG.). 432p. (J). (gr. 3-7). pap. 6.99 *(978-1-4169-5384-5(1),* Aladdin) Simon & Schuster Children's Publishing.
—The End of Time. Ho, David, illus. 2011. (Books of Umber Ser.: 3). (ENG.). 432p. (J). (gr. 3-7). 16.99 *(978-1-4169-7520-5(9),* Simon & Schuster/Paula Wiseman Bks.) Simon & Schuster/Paula Wiseman Bks.
—Happenstance Found, No. 1. 2009. (Books of Umber Ser.: 1). (ENG.). 368p. (J). (gr. 3-7). pap. 6.99 *(978-1-4169-5382-1(5),* Aladdin) Simon & Schuster Children's Publishing.
—Happenstance Found. 2009. (Books of Umber Ser.: 1). (ENG.). 352p. (J). (gr. 3-7). 16.99 *(978-1-4169-7519-9(5),* Simon & Schuster/Paula Wiseman Bks.) Simon & Schuster/Paula Wiseman Bks.
—The Riddle of the Gnome: A Further Tale Adventure. 2007. (ENG.). 256p. (J). (gr. 5-9). pap. 5.99 *(978-1-4169-1252-1(5),* Aladdin) Simon & Schuster Children's Publishing.
Catmull, Katherine. Summer & Bird. 2014. (ENG.). 352p. (J). (gr. 5). pap. 8.99 *(978-0-14-242505-3(2),* Puffin Books) Penguin Young Readers Group.
Catran, Ken. Voyage with Jason. 2005. 208p. pap. *(978-0-7344-0151-9(5),* Lothian Children's Bks.) Hachette Australia.
Caviezel, Giovanni. Ballerina. Mesturini, C., illus. 2011. (Mini People Shape Bks.). (ENG.). 10p. (J). bds. 5.99 *(978-0-7641-6436-1(8))* Barron's Educational Series, Inc.
—Builder. Mesturini, C., illus. 2011. (Mini People Shape Bks.). (ENG.). 10p. (J). bds. 5.99 *(978-0-7641-6437-8(6))* Barron's Educational Series, Inc.
—Cowboy. Mesturini, C., illus. 2011. (Mini People Shape Bks.). (ENG.). 10p. (J). bds. 5.99 *(978-0-7641-6438-5(4))* Barron's Educational Series, Inc.
—Farmer. Mesturini, C., illus. 2011. (Mini People Shape Bks.). (ENG.). 10p. (J). bds. 5.99 *(978-0-7641-6439-2(2))* Barron's Educational Series, Inc.
Cefalo, Andrea. The Fairytale Keeper: Avenging the Queen. 2012. (ENG., Illus.). 274p. pap. 11.99 *(978-0-9851678-1-3(5))* Scarlet Primrose Pr.
Celano, June. Dripsy the Cloud. 2008. 28p. per. 24.95 *(978-1-4241-9958-7(1))* America Star Bks.
Chabon, Michael. Summerland. l.t. ed. 2003. 615p. (J). 25.95 *(978-0-7862-5143-8(3))* Thorndike Pr.
Chabot, Jacob & Mcginty, Ian. Delicious! 2014. (Hello Kitty Graphic Novel Ser.). lib. bdg. 18.40 *(978-0-606-35470-7(0))* Turtleback Bks.
Chadwick, J. R. Thomas & the Dragon's Pearl. 2008. (Illus.). v, 181p. pap. *(978-0-7552-0430-4(1))* Authors OnLine, Ltd.
Chaffey, Tim & Westbrook, Joe. The Truth Chronicles: The Ark. 2013. 146p. pap. *(978-1-936835-15-7(0))* Roxby Media Ltd.
Chainani, Soman. The Ever Never. Blank, Michael, illus. 2016. (School for Good & Evil Ser.). 304p. (J). (gr. 3-7). 17.99 *(978-0-06-242305-4(3))* HarperCollins Pubs.
—The Last Ever After. Bruno, Iacopo, illus. 2015. 655p. (J). *(978-0-06-241756-5(8))* Harper & Row Ltd.
—The Last Ever After. 2015. (School for Good & Evil Ser.: 3). (ENG., Illus.). 672p. (J). (gr. 3-7). 17.99 *(978-0-06-210495-3(0))* HarperCollins Pubs.
—Never Handbook. 2016. (ENG., Illus.). 304p. (J). ***(978-0-00-818179-6(9))*** Harper & Row Ltd.
—The School for Good & Evil. (School for Good & Evil Ser.). (J). (gr. 3). 2016. 1760p. pap. 23.97 *(978-0-06-245624-3(5))* 2015. (ENG.). 1334p. 53.97 *(978-0-06-243497-5(7))* HarperCollins Pubs.
—The School for Good & Evil. Bruno, Iacopo, illus. (ENG.). (J). (gr. 3-7). 2014. (School for Good & Evil Ser.: 1). 544p. pap. 7.99 *(978-0-06-210490-8(X))* 2013. (School for Good & Evil Trilogy: No. 1). 400p. 17.99 *(978-0-06-210489-2(6))* HarperCollins Pubs.
—The School for Good & Evil. Bruno, Iacopo, illus. 2014. (School for Good & Evil Ser.: 1). 496p. (J). lib. bdg. 17.20 *(978-0-606-36513-0(3))* Turtleback Bks.
—The School for Good & Evil #4: Quests for Glory. 2017. (School for Good & Evil Ser.: 4). 576p. (J). (gr. 3-7). 17.99 ***(978-0-06-265847-0(6))*** HarperCollins Pubs.
Chainani, Soman. A World Without Princes. 2014. (School for Good & Evil Trilogy: No. 2). 448p. (J). pap. *(978-0-06-233135-9(3))* Harper & Row Ltd.
—A World Without Princes. Bruno, Iacopo, illus. 2014. (School for Good & Evil Trilogy: No. 2). (ENG.). 400p. (J). *(978-0-06-234072-6(7))* Harper & Row Ltd.
—A World Without Princes. Bruno, Iacopo, illus. 2015. (School for Good & Evil Ser.: 2). (ENG.). 512p. (J). (gr. 3-7). pap. 7.99 *(978-0-06-210493-9(4))* HarperCollins Pubs.
—A World Without Princes. 2014. (School for Good & Evil Trilogy: No. 2). (ENG., Illus.). 448p. (J). (gr. 3-7). 17.99 *(978-0-06-210492-2(6))* HarperCollins Pubs.
—A World Without Princes. 2015. (School for Good & Evil Ser.: 2). (J). lib. bdg. 17.20 *(978-0-606-36514-7(1))* Turtleback Bks.
Chan, San Wei, illus. Spear & Shield. *(978-0-9744905-0-2(4))* Santoon Bks.
Chananie, Gloria. Fearful Frannie's African Safari. 2006. 95p. pap. 16.95 *(978-1-4241-2617-0(7))* PublishAmerica, Inc.
Chance, Megan. The Veil, 0 vols. 2015. (Fianna Trilogy Ser.: 3). (ENG.). 366p. (YA). (gr. 7-12). 16.99 *(978-1-5039-4571-5(5),* 9781503945715, Skyscape) Amazon Publishing.
Chankhamma, Shari. The Sisters' Luck. 2010. (ENG., Illus.). 144p. (YA). pap. 12.95 *(978-1-59362-190-2(6),* 9781593621902) Slave Labor Bks.
Chantler, Scott. Tower of Treasure. Chantler, Scott, illus. 2010. (Three Thieves Ser.). (ENG., Illus.). 112p. (J). (gr. 4-7). pap. 7.95 *(978-1-55453-415-9(1))* Kids Can Pr., Ltd. CAN. Dist: Hachette Bk. Group.
Chapman, Allan W. Mr. Wugidgem & the Phoenix Journey. 2012. 74p. pap. 7.99 *(978-0-9796780-4-2(8))* AC Writings.
Chapman, Catherine. The Magical Scarecrows' Garden. 2009. 160p. pap. 35.95 *(978-1-60860-481-4(0),* Strategic Bk. Publishing) Strategic Book Publishing & Rights Agency (SBPRA).
Chapman, Lara. Accidentally Evil. 2015. (Mix Ser.). (ENG., Illus.). 240p. (J). (gr. 4-8). pap. 7.99 *(978-1-4814-0110-4(6),* Aladdin) Simon & Schuster Children's Publishing.
—The XYZs of Being Wicked. 2014. (ENG., Illus.). 272p. (J). (gr. 4-8). pap. 6.99 *(978-1-4814-0107-4(6),* Aladdin) Simon & Schuster Children's Publishing.
Charbonneau, Joelle. Dividing Eden. 2017. 336p. (YA). (gr. 8). 17.99 *(978-0-06-245384-6(X),* HarperTeen) HarperCollins Pubs.
Charlton, Dan & Weiss, Stacy. Silver Surfer, Vol. 2. 2005. (Silver Surfer Ser.: Vol. 2). (Illus.). 192p. (YA). pap. 19.99 *(978-0-7851-1575-5(7))* Marvel Worldwide, Inc.
Charles L. Wilson. The Search Is On: The Wild Adventures of Lester & Dora. 2009. 200p. 24.99 *(978-1-4269-1813-1(5));* pap. 14.99 *(978-1-4269-1812-4(7))* Trafford Publishing.

Charles, Novalyn. Wagabuibui, the Four Eyed Eagle. Manasau, Amos, illus. 2012. 38p. pap. (978-9980-945-66-2(4)) University of Papua New Guinea Press.
Charlie & Champ. 2nd ed. 2004. (J). 4.95 (978-0-943864-57-0(7)) Davenport, May Pubs.
Charnee, David. P T Mudd in the Land of Lies: A Novel for Children of All Ages. 2007. 196p. 23.95 (978-0-595-70152-0(3)); per. 13.95 (978-0-595-46307-7(X)) iUniverse, Inc.
Chase, Dakota. Mad about the Hatter. (ENG., Illus.). (YA). 2016. 24.99 **(978-1-63533-045-8(9))** 2015. 190p. pap. 14.99 (978-1-63476-148-2(0)) Dreamspinner Pr. (Harmony Ink Pr.).
Chastain, Sandra. Kaseybelle: The Tiniest Fairy in the Kingdom, 1 bk. Chadwick, Cindy, illus. 2004. 32p. (J). 14.95 (978-0-9673035-6-7(7), 24) BelleBks., Inc.
Cheasebro, Margaret. The Healing Tree. 2015. (ENG.). 304p. (YA). 15.95 (978-1-937240-60-8(6)) Casa de Snapdragon LLC.
Chee, Traci. The Reader. (Sea of Ink & Gold Ser.: 1). (ENG.). 464p. (YA). (gr. 7). 2017. pap. 10.99 **(978-0-14-751805-7(9)**, Speak)Bk. 1. 2016. 19.99 (978-0-399-17677-7(2), G.P. Putnam's Sons Books for Young Readers) Penguin Young Readers Group.
—The Reader. 2017. (Sea of Ink & Gold Ser.: 1). lib. bdg. 22.10 **(978-0-606-40001-5(X))** Turtleback Bks.
Chen, Wei Dong. The Expulsion of Sun Wu Kong. Peng, Chao, illus. 2013. (Monkey King Ser.: 7). 176p. (YA). (gr. 6-12). lib. bdg. 29.27 (978-89-94208-75-6(5)) Lerner Publishing Group.
—The Lost Children. Peng, Chao, illus. 2013. (Monkey King Ser.: 12). 176p. (YA). (gr. 6-12). lib. bdg. 29.27 (978-89-94208-80-0(1)) Lerner Publishing Group.
—Monkey King: Journey to the West. Peng, Chao, illus. 2012. (Monkey King Ser.: 3). (ENG.). 176p. (gr. 5-8). lib. bdg. 29.27 (978-89-94208-71-8(2)) JR Comics KOR. Dist: Lerner Publishing Group.
—Monkey King: The Bane of Heaven. Peng, Chao, illus. 2012. (Monkey King Ser.: 2). (ENG.). 176p. (gr. 5-8). lib. bdg. 29.27 (978-89-94208-70-1(4)) JR Comics KOR. Dist: Lerner Publishing Group.
—Monkey King: Three Trials. Peng, Chao, illus. 2012. (Monkey King Ser.: 5). (ENG.). 176p. (gr. 5-8). lib. bdg. 29.27 (978-89-94208-73-2(9)) JR Comics KOR. Dist: Lerner Publishing Group.
—The Realm of the Infant King. Peng, Chao, illus. 2013. (Monkey King Ser.: 10). 176p. (YA). (gr. 6-12). lib. bdg. 29.27 (978-89-94208-78-7(X)) Lerner Publishing Group.
—The Stolen Kingdom. Peng, Chao, illus. 2013. (Monkey King Ser.: 9). 176p. (YA). (gr. 6-12). lib. bdg. 29.27 (978-89-94208-77-0(1)) Lerner Publishing Group.
—Treasures of the Mountain Kings. Peng, Chao, illus. 2013. (Monkey King Ser.: 8). 176p. (YA). (gr. 6-12). lib. bdg. 29.27 (978-89-94208-76-3(3)) Lerner Publishing Group.
Cheng'en, Wu. Journey to the West. Chiang, Shirley, illus. 2013. (Chinese Classics Ser.). (ENG.). 64p. pap. 6.95 (978-1-906230-34-0(X)) Real Reads Ltd. GBR. Dist: Casemate Pubs. & Bk. Distributors, LLC.
Cheshire, Simon. The Frankenstein Inheritance. 2012. 204p. pap. (978-0-9565049-7-5(3)) Cheshire, Simon.
Chester, Laura. Marvel the Marvelous. Lippincott, Gary A., illus. 2008. (ENG.). 176p. (J). 18.95 (978-1-59543-841-6(6)) Willow Creek Pr., Inc.
Chester, Malcolm. Elysia: The World in Children's Dreams. 2012. 320p. 29.11 (978-1-4669-4812-9(4)); pap. 19.11 (978-1-4669-4810-5(8)) Trafford Publishing.
Chetwin, Grace. The Foundling of Snawbyr Crygg: Part 2 of the Lords of Aelyth-kintalyn. 2003. (Ulm Ser.: 3). (Illus.). 140p. (YA). pap. 15.00 net. (978-1-930094-13-0(2), Rivet Bks.) Feral Pr., Inc.
—Jason's Wonderful Week of Fabulous Night Rides. 2003. Orig. Title: Jason's Seven Magical Night Rides. (Illus.). 116p. (J). pap. 25.00 net. (978-1-930094-12-3(4), Rivet Bks.) Feral Pr., Inc.
Chew, Ruth. Magic in the Park. 2014. (Matter-Of-Fact Magic Book Ser.). (ENG., Illus.). 144p. (J). (gr. 2-5). 5.99 (978-0-449-81376-8(2), Random Hse. Bks. for Young Readers) Random Hse. Children's Bks.
Chic, Suzy & Touvay, Monique. Watching. 2007. (ENG.). 48p. (J). (gr. k-2). 12.00 (978-1-905341-07-8(5)) WingedChariot Pr. GBR. Dist: Independent Pubs. Group.
Chick, Bryan. The Secret Zoo. 2010. (Secret Zoo Ser.: 1). (ENG.). 304p. (J). (gr. 3-7). 16.99 (978-0-06-198750-2(6), Greenwillow Bks.) HarperCollins Pubs.
Chikuhwa, Jacob. From the Cradle to the Bonfire. 2012. 78p. pap. 16.95 (978-1-4626-9859-2(X)) America Star Bks.
Child, Lauren. I Can Do Anything That's Everything All on My Own. 2008. (Charlie & Lola Ser.). (ENG., Illus.). 24p. (J). (gr. -1-k). mass mkt. 3.99 (978-0-448-44792-6(4), Grosset & Dunlap) Penguin Young Readers Group.
Childress, Jamie. Galactic Treasure Hunt 5: Lost Fortress of Light. Braun, Chris, illus. 2010. (Galactic Treasure Hunt Ser.). (ENG.). 230p. pap. 6.99 (978-1-935487-06-7(X)) Adventures Unlimited Pr.
—Lost Universe. Braun, Chris, illus. 2015. (ENG.). 100p. (J). (gr. 4-7). per. 4.99 (978-1-931882-74-3(6)) Adventures Unlimited Pr.
Childress, Jenna Lynn. Dragon Soul: Book One of the Triune Jewels. 2003. 262p. (YA). per. 8.00 (978-0-9704006-2-8(4)) Bound & Determined Pubs.
Childs, Karin Alfelt. The Balm of Gilead. 2007. 356p. (YA). 15.95 (978-0-9748423-7-0(0)) Fountain Publishing.
Childs, Tera Lynn & Deebs, Tracy. Relentless. 2016. (Hero Agenda Ser.: 2). (ENG.). 288p. (YA). (gr. 7-12). 17.99 (978-1-4926-1661-0(3), 9781492616610) Sourcebooks, Inc.
Chilton, Andrew. The Goblin's Puzzle: Being the Adventures of a Boy with No Name & Two Girls Called Alice. 2016. (ENG.). 288p. (J). (gr. 3-7). 16.99 (978-0-553-52070-5(9), Knopf Bks. for Young Readers) Random Hse. Children's Bks.
Chilton, Claire. Shattered. 2012. 268p. pap. (978-1-908822-10-9(4)) Ragz Bks.
Chima, Cinda Williams. The Crimson Crown. (Seven Realms Novel Ser.). (ENG.). (J). (gr. 5-9). 2013. 624p. pap. 9.99 (978-1-4231-5214-9(X)) 2012. 608p. 18.99 (978-1-4231-4433-5(3)) Hyperion Pr.
—The Demon King. 2010. (ENG.). 528p. (J). (gr. 5-6). pap. 9.99 (978-1-4231-2136-7(8)) Hyperion Pr.
—The Dragon Heir. 2009. (Heir Chronicles Ser.). (ENG., Illus.). 528p. (J). (gr. 5-9). pap. 9.99 (978-1-4231-1071-2(4)) Hyperion Pr.
—The Enchanter Heir. 2013. 464p. 18.99 (978-1-4231-8789-9(X)) Disney Pr.
—The Enchanter Heir. 2013. (Heir Chronicles Ser.). (ENG.). 464p. (YA). (gr. 7-17). 18.99 (978-1-4231-4434-2(1)) Hyperion Pr.
—The Exiled Queen. 2011. (Seven Realms Novel Ser.). (ENG.). 608p. (J). (gr. 5-17). pap. 9.99 (978-1-4231-2137-4(6)) Hyperion Pr.
—Flamecaster. (Shattered Realms Ser.: 1). (gr. 8). 2017. 560p. (YA). pap. 9.99 (978-0-06-238095-1(8)) 2016. 544p. (J). pap. 12.00 (978-0-06-245490-4(0)) 2016. (ENG.). 544p. (YA). 18.99 (978-0-06-238094-4(X)) HarperCollins Pubs. (HarperTeen).
—The Gray Wolf Throne. 2012. (ENG.). 544p. (YA). (gr. 7-17). pap. 9.99 (978-1-4231-2138-1(4)) Hyperion Pr.
—The Seven Realms Box Set. 2013. (Seven Realms Novel Ser.). (ENG.). 2272p. (YA). (gr. 7-12). pap. 37.99 (978-1-4231-9961-8(8)) Hyperion Bks. for Children.
—Shadowcaster. (Shattered Realms Ser.: 2). (YA). (gr. 8). 2018. (ENG.). 576p. pap. 9.99 **(978-0-06-238098-2(2))** 2017. 560p. 18.99 (978-0-06-238097-5(4)) HarperCollins Pubs. (HarperTeen).
—The Sorcerer Heir. 2016. (Heir Chronicles Ser.). (ENG.). 560p. (J). (gr. 5-9). pap. 9.99 (978-1-4231-9475-0(6)) Hyperion Bks. for Children.
—The Warrior Heir. 2007. (Heir Chronicles Ser.). (ENG.). 448p. (J). (gr. 5-9). pap. 9.99 (978-0-7868-3917-9(1)) Hyperion Pr.
—The Warrior Heir. 2006. (Heir Chronicles: No. 1). 1.00 (978-1-4294-0323-8(3)) Recorded Bks., Inc.
—The Wizard Heir. 2008. (Heir Chronicles Ser.). (ENG.). 480p. (J). (gr. 5-9). pap. 9.99 (978-1-4231-0488-9(9)) Hyperion Pr.
Chime, P. K. Moonrise. 2013. 452p. pap. (978-1-78299-644-6(3)) FeedARead.com.
Chinery, Michael & Michael, Chinery. Enciclopedia de los Animales Salvajes, 8 vols.Tr. of Wild World of Animals. (SPA.). 346p. (J). (gr. 3-5). 100.00 (978-84-241-2059-7(0)) Everest Editora ESP. Dist: Lectorum Pubns., Inc.
Chipley, John. The Secret Place: A Boy's Journey into the Woods. 2011. 92p. (gr. 1-1). pap. 13.95 (978-1-4567-4593-6(X)) AuthorHouse.
Chiu, Harry. Enve Lopt Unfolded. 2007. 268p. per. 17.95 (978-0-595-44707-7(4)) iUniverse, Inc.
Chizuru, Mio. The Pirate & the Princess Volume 1: the Timelight Stone: The Timelight Stone. 2007. 110p. (J). pap. 5.99 (978-1-933164-43-4(3)) Seven Seas Entertainment, LLC.
—The Pirate & the Princess Volume 2: the Red Crystal: The Red Crystal. 2007. 110p. (J). pap. 5.99 (978-1-933164-44-1(1)) Seven Seas Entertainment, LLC.
Chokshi, Roshani. A Crown of Wishes. 2017. (Star-Touched Ser.). (ENG.). 384p. (YA). 18.99 (978-1-250-08549-8(7), 9781250085498, St. Martin's Griffin) St. Martin's Pr.
—The Star-Touched Queen. Rothschild, Eileen, ed. 2017. (Star-Touched Ser.). (ENG.). 368p. (YA). pap. 10.99 (978-1-250-10020-7(8), 9781250100207, St. Martin's Griffin) St. Martin's Pr.
—The Star-Touched Queen. 2016. (ENG.). 352p. (YA). (gr. 9). 18.99 (978-1-250-08547-4(0), 9781250085474, St. Martin's Griffin) St. Martin's Pr.
Choldenko, Gennifer. No Passengers Beyond This Point. 2012. (ENG.). 272p. (J). (gr. 5-18). 7.99 (978-0-14-242052-2(2), Puffin Books) Penguin Young Readers Group.
—No Passengers Beyond This Point. 2012. lib. bdg. 17.20 (978-0-606-23637-9(6), Turtleback) Turtleback Bks.
Choldenko, Gennifer, et al. No Passengers Beyond This Point. 2011. (Playaway Children Ser.). (J). 49.99 (978-1-61707-000-6(9)) Findaway World, LLC.
Choyce, Lesley. Thin Places. 2017. (ENG., Illus.). 176p. (YA). pap. 12.99 **(978-1-4597-3957-4(4))** Dundurn CAN. Dist: Ingram Publisher Services.
Christen, Dennis H. Lundon Bridge wa seagae wa Yolsae. Lee, Kathryn, tr. 2008.Tr. of Lundon Bridge wa seagae wa Yolsae. (KOR., Illus.). 280p. (J). pap. 12.95 (978-0-9718151-4-8(3)) C-It Entertainment Group, LLC.
—Lundon's Bridge & the Three Keys. 2008. 221p. (J). pap. 12.95 (978-0-9718151-5-5(1)) C-It Entertainment Group, LLC.
Christensen, Margaret Kate. The Hollyhock Fairies. 2004. 48p. per. (978-1-932077-85-8(5)) Athena Pr.
Christian, Norma. A Christmas Mouse. 2012. 32p. pap. 13.99 (978-1-4624-0328-8(X), Inspiring Voices) Author Solutions, Inc.
Christianson, Leslie Rose. Malinda Matters: And Priscilla the Praying Mantis. 2010. 36p. pap. 15.49 (978-1-4490-6914-8(2)) AuthorHouse.
—Malinda Matters: Malinda's Birthday Surprise. 2010. 44p. pap. 16.99 (978-1-4490-6915-5(0)) AuthorHouse.
Christopher, John. Dragon Dance. 2015. (Fireball Trilogy Ser.: 3). (ENG., Illus.). 224p. (J). (gr. 4-8). pap. 7.99 (978-1-4814-2015-0(1), Aladdin) Simon & Schuster Children's Publishing.
Christopher Paolini. 2010. (Who Wrote That? Ser.). (Illus.). 136p. (J). (gr. 6-12). 35.00 (978-1-60413-727-9(4), Chelsea Hse.) Facts On File, Inc.
Christy, Jana, illus. The Never Girls Collecton #3 (Disney: the Never Girls), 4 vols. 2016. (ENG.). 512p. (J). (gr. 1-4). 23.96 (978-0-7364-3521-5(2), RH/Disney) Random Hse. Children's Bks.
Chupeco, Rin. The Bone Witch. 2017. (Bone Witch Ser.: 1). (ENG.). 432p. (YA). (gr. 7-12). 17.99 (978-1-4926-3582-6(0), 9781492635826) Sourcebooks, Inc.
Church, Alfred J. The Aeneid for Boys & Girls. 2008. 100p. pap. 9.05 (978-1-60459-519-2(1)) Wilder Pubns., Corp.
Ciccarelli, Kristen. The Last Namsara. 2017. (Iskari Ser.: 1). 432p. (YA). (gr. 8). 17.99 **(978-0-06-256798-7(5)**, HarperTeen) HarperCollins Pubs.
Ciccone, Tiziana. Taylor, Please Stop Talking! Cannavicci, Luigi A., illus. 2013. 32p. pap. 12.95 (978-1-62516-817-7(9), Strategic Bk. Publishing) Strategic Book Publishing & Rights Agency (SBPRA).
Cicierega, Emmy. Gravity Falls Don't Color This Book! A Cursed Coloring Book. Ramirez, Stephanie, illus. 2017. (ENG.). 64p. pap. 12.99 **(978-1-368-00899-0(2))** Disney Pr.
Ciencin, Scott & Burge, Constance M. Luck Be a Lady. 2004. (Charmed Ser.). (ENG., Illus.). 224p. (YA). pap. 16.95 (978-0-689-85793-5(4), Gallery Bks.) Gallery Bks.
Cinderella. 2005. 124p. 26.95 (978-1-4218-0600-6(2), 1st World Library - Literary Society) 1st World Publishing, Inc.
Circle of Friends: The Camelot Rabbitry Series - Volume Three. 2006. (Camelot Rabbitry Ser.: 3). (Illus.). 98p. (J). per. 9.95 (978-0-9672375-3-4(X)) Camelot Tales.
City of a Thousand Dolls. 2014. (ENG.). 384p. (YA). (gr. 8). pap. 9.99 (978-0-06-212132-5(4)) HarperCollins Pubs.
CLAMP. X, Vol. 6. 6th ed. 2013. (ENG., Illus.). 192p. pap. 19.99 (978-1-4215-4046-7(0)) Viz Media.
Clamp Staff. Blood-C Volume 3. Simon, Philip, ed. Kotone, Ranmaru, illus. 2014. (ENG.). 192p. pap. 12.99 (978-1-61655-314-2(6)) Dark Horse Comics.
—Cardcaptor Sakura, 4 vols., Bk. 4. Horn, Carl Gustav, ed. 2012. (ENG., Illus.). 592p. pap. 19.99 (978-1-59582-889-7(3)) Dark Horse Comics.
—Cardcaptor Sakura, 4 vols., Vol. 1. 2010. (ENG., Illus.). 600p. pap. 19.99 (978-1-59582-522-3(3)) Dark Horse Comics.
—Cardcaptor Sakura, 4 vols., Vol. 3. Clamp Staff, illus. 2012. (ENG., Illus.). 600p. pap. 19.99 (978-1-59582-808-8(7)) Dark Horse Comics.
—Cardcaptor Sakura, Vol. 4. Clamp Staff, illus. rev. ed. 2005. (Illus.). 200p. (J). pap. 9.99 (978-1-59182-881-5(3), Tokyopop Kids) TOKYOPOP, Inc.
Clancy, Kaycee. Sky Painters. 2007. 41p. per. 11.95 (978-0-9776777-8-8(8)) Legacy Publishing Services, Inc.
Clare, Cassandra. Clockwork Angel. (Infernal Devices Ser.: Bk. 1). (ENG., Illus.). (YA). (gr. 9). 2015. 544p. pap. 13.99 (978-1-4814-5602-9(4)) 2010. 496p. 24.99 (978-1-4169-7586-1(1)) McElderry, Margaret K. Bks. (McElderry, Margaret K. Bks.).
—Clockwork Angel. 2012. (Infernal Devices Ser.: 1). (ENG.). 240p. (gr. 8-17). pap. 13.00 (978-0-316-20098-1(0), Yen Pr.) Orbit.
—Clockwork Angel. 2015. (Infernal Devices Ser.: Bk. 1). 544p. (YA). lib. bdg. 25.75 (978-0-606-37737-9(9)) 2012. (Infernal Devices Graphic Novel Ser.: 1). lib. bdg. 24.55 (978-0-606-32257-7(4), Turtleback) Turtleback Bks.
—The Infernal Devices: Clockwork Angel; Clockwork Prince; Clockwork Princess. 2013. (Infernal Devices Ser.: Bks. 1-3). (ENG.). 1520p. (YA). (gr. 9). 74.99 (978-1-4424-8372-9(5), McElderry, Margaret K. Bks.) McElderry, Margaret K. Bks.
—Lord of Shadows. 2017. (Dark Artifices Ser.: 2). (ENG., Illus.). 720p. (YA). (gr. 9). 24.99 (978-1-4424-6840-5(8), McElderry, Margaret K. Bks.) McElderry, Margaret K. Bks.
Clarizio, Laura. If I Had a Magic Carpet. 2005. 48p. pap. 16.95 (978-1-4137-8557-9(3)) America Star Bks.
—If I Had a Magic Carpet III: Haunted Holidays. 2008. 73p. pap. 19.95 (978-1-60563-240-7(6)) America Star Bks.
—Traveling Through Time: If I Had a Magic Carpet IV. 2012. 100p. 21.95 (978-1-4489-3229-0(7)) 2010. 98p. pap. 16.95 (978-1-4489-5428-5(2)) America Star Bks.
Clark, Hannah L. Uncovering Cobbogoth. 2014. pap. 17.99 (978-1-4621-1426-9(1)) Cedar Fort, Inc./CFI Distribution.
Clark, Jr. Metrognomes. 2007. 292p. per. 17.95 (978-0-595-42973-8(4)) iUniverse, Inc.
Clark, Kent & Snider, Brandon T. Peter Powers & His Not-So-Super Powers. Bardin, Dave, illus. 2017. (Peter Powers Ser.: 1). (ENG.). 128p. (J). (gr. 1-5). pap. 5.99 (978-0-316-35934-4(3)) Little, Brown Bks. for Young Readers.
—Peter Powers & the Itchy Insect Invasion! Bardin, Dave, illus. 2017. (Peter Powers Ser.: 3). (ENG.). 128p. (J). (gr. 1-5). 15.99 (978-0-316-35947-4(5)) Little, Brown Bks. for Young Readers.
Clark, Malcolm. Bounty's Cave. 2007. (ENG.). 156p. per. 19.95 (978-1-932762-82-2(5)) Elderberry Press, Inc.
Clark, Platte F. Bad Unicorn. 2013. (Bad Unicorn Trilogy Ser.: 1). (ENG., Illus.). 432p. (J). (gr. 3-7). 15.99 (978-1-4424-5012-7(6), Aladdin) Simon & Schuster Children's Publishing.
—Fluff Dragon. 2014. (Bad Unicorn Trilogy Ser.: 2). (ENG., Illus.). 384p. (J). (gr. 3-7). 16.99 (978-1-4424-5015-8(0), Aladdin) Simon & Schuster Children's Publishing.
—Good Ogre. 2015. (Bad Unicorn Trilogy Ser.: 3). (ENG., Illus.). 384p. (J). (gr. 3-7). 17.99 (978-1-4424-5018-9(5), Aladdin) Simon & Schuster Children's Publishing.
Clark, Steven & Clark, Justin. The Golden Knight #1: The Boy Is Summoned. Gibson, Taylor, illus. 2011. (ENG.). 80p. (J). pap. 5.99 (978-0-9647933-9-2(3)) New Horizons Pr.
Clarke, Lizzy. The Spirit of the Jaguar. 2013. 92p. pap. 11.38 (978-1-4907-0600-9(3)); (gr. -1). 21.38 (978-1-4907-0602-3(X)) Trafford Publishing.
Clausen, Andrew. Prince Caspian. 2003. stu. ed., ring bd. 14.99 (978-1-58609-195-8(6)) Progeny Pr.
Clement-Davies, David. Fell. 2009. (ENG.). 544p. (YA). (gr. 7-11). pap. 10.95 (978-0-8109-7266-7(2), Amulet Bks.) Abrams, Inc.
Clement, Maryceleste. Mr. Tooties & the Polka-Dot Lollypops. Schexnayder, Paul, illus. 2005. (Tootle Tales Ser.: Vol. 2). 32p. (J). 14.95 (978-0-9721706-1-1(8)) Tootle Time Publishing Co.
Cleofas-Moore, Ramona. Tiffany. 2008. 60p. pap. 16.95 (978-1-60474-238-1(0)) America Star Bks.
Clifford, Leah. A Touch Morbid. 2012. (Touch Mortal Trilogy Ser.: 2). (ENG.). 304p. (YA). (gr. 9). 16.99 (978-0-06-200502-1(2), Greenwillow Bks.) HarperCollins Pubs.
Cline, Barbara Jean. Seth's' Journey. 2012. 44p. pap. 21.99 (978-1-4685-6313-9(0)) AuthorHouse.
Cluess, Jessica. A Poison Dark & Drowning (Kingdom on Fire, Book Two) 2017. (Kingdom on Fire Ser.: 2). (ENG.). 432p. (YA). (gr. 7). 17.99 **(978-0-553-53594-5(3)**, Random Hse. Bks. for Young Readers) Random Hse. Children's Bks.
Cluess, Jessica. A Shadow Bright & Burning. 2016. (Kingdom on Fire Ser.: 1). (ENG.). 416p. (YA). (gr. 7). 17.99 (978-0-553-53590-7(0)); lib. bdg. 20.99 (978-0-553-53591-4(9)) Random Hse. Children's Bks. (Random Hse. Bks. for Young Readers).
Coakley, Lena. Witchlanders. (ENG., Illus.). 416p. (YA). (gr. 7). 2012. pap. 9.99 (978-1-4424-2005-2(7)) 2011. 16.99 (978-1-4424-2004-5(9)) Simon & Schuster Children's Publishing. (Atheneum Bks. for Young Readers).
—Worlds of Ink & Shadow. 2016. (ENG.). 352p. (YA). (gr. 8-17). 17.95 (978-1-4197-1034-6(6), Amulet Bks.) Abrams, Inc.
Coates, Theresa. Imaginary Time of Life. 2007. 102p. pap. 10.95 (978-0-7414-4067-9(9)) Infinity Publishing.
Coats, Lucy. Zeus's Eagle. 2016. (Beasts of Olympus Ser.: 6). lib. bdg. 17.20 (978-0-606-38837-5(0)) Turtleback Bks.
Coburn, Ann. Alex & the Winter Star. 2009. pap. 18.95 (978-1-84002-894-2(7)) Theatre Communications Group, Inc.
Cody, Matthew. The Peddler's Road. 2015. (Secrets of the Pied Piper Ser.: 1). (ENG., Illus.). 368p. (J). (gr. 3-7). 17.99 (978-0-385-75522-1(8), Knopf Bks. for Young Readers) Random Hse. Children's Bks.
—The Secrets of the Pied Piper 1: the Peddler's Road. 2016. (Secrets of the Pied Piper Ser.: 1). (ENG.). 384p. (J). (gr. 3-7). 7.99 (978-0-385-75525-2(2), Yearling) Random Hse. Children's Bks.
—The Secrets of the Pied Piper 2: the Magician's Key. 2016. (Secrets of the Pied Piper Ser.: 2). (ENG., Illus.). 336p. (J). (gr. 3-7). 17.99 (978-0-385-75526-9(0), Knopf Bks. for Young Readers) Random Hse. Children's Bks.
Coe, Mary. The Prince of Betherland. 2007. 100p. pap. 9.95 (978-1-4303-2521-5(6)) Lulu Pr., Inc.
Coe, Mary E. The Prince of Betherland. 2008. 117p. 24.95 (978-0-557-03112-2(5)) Lulu Pr., Inc.
—The Prince of Betherland A Wonderful World of Fantasy. 2009. 66p. pap. 9.95 (978-0-557-08499-9(7)) Lulu Pr., Inc.
—The Prince of Betherland a Wonderful World of Fantasy. 2009. 112p. pap. 9.95 (978-0-557-09297-0(3)) Lulu Pr., Inc.
Coelho, Rogério. Boat of Dreams, 1 vol. 2017. (ENG., Illus.). 80p. (gr. 2-17). 22.95 (978-0-88448-528-5(5), 884528) Tilbury Hse. Pubs.
Cofer, Amadeus. Aloha Adventure: The Magic of Imagination on a Rainy Day. l.t. ed. 2004. (Illus.). 36p. (J). 14.00 (978-1-932957-01-3(4)) Legacy Pubs.
Cohen, Lawrence J. The Dragon's Familiar. 2008. 236p. 25.95 (978-0-595-63430-9(3)) iUniverse, Inc.
Coia, Kristina. Lymeria. 2007. 120p. (YA). 20.95 (978-0-595-69347-4(4)); per. 10.95 (978-0-595-45268-2(X)) iUniverse, Inc.
Coiner, Tea Railene. Hear the Song of the Fairies. 2009. 74p. pap. 19.95 (978-1-61582-833-3(8)) America Star Bks.
Cokal, Susann. The Kingdom of Little Wounds. 2013. (ENG., Illus.). 576p. (YA). (gr. 11). 22.99 (978-0-7636-6694-1(7)) Candlewick Pr.
Cola, Arthur. Papa & the Gingerbread Man. 2006. 14.95 (978-0-9789423-0-4(2)) Cola, Arthur.
Cold Moon. 2nd ed. 2014. 180p. pap. 14.99 (978-1-62798-459-1(3), Harmony Ink Pr.) Dreamspinner Pr.
Cole, Henry. Brambleheart. Cole, Henry, illus. 2016. (Brambleheart Ser.: 1). (Illus.). 272p. (J). (gr. 3-7). 16.99 (978-0-06-224546-5(5)) HarperCollins Pubs.
—Brambleheart: A Story about Finding Treasure & the Unexpected Magic of Friendship. Cole, Henry, illus. 2017. (Brambleheart Ser.: 1). (Illus.). 288p. (J). (gr. 3-7). pap. 6.99 (978-0-06-224544-1(9), Tegen, Katherine Bks) HarperCollins Pubs.
Cole, Myke. The Wildsidhe Chronicles Bk. 6: Car Trouble. 2003. (J). pap. 7.99 (978-1-890096-18-2(0)) Padwolf Publishing, Inc.
Cole, Nikki. Princess Hope. 2012. 40p. pap. 14.95 (978-1-886528-39-0(X)) ASA Publishing Corp.
Colebourn, Craig. The Knights of Videnland: Passing the Torch. 2007. 428p. per. 23.95 (978-0-595-46989-5(2)) iUniverse, Inc.
Coleman, Wim & Perrin, Pat. The Death of the Good Wizard. 2011. (Red Monocle Ser.: 2). (ENG.). 196p. (YA). pap. 7.95 (978-1-935178-04-0(0), ChironBooks) Coleman/Perrin.
Colfer, Chris. An Author's Odyssey. 2016. (Land of Stories Ser.: 5). (ENG.). (J). (gr. 3-7). 496p. pap. 11.99 (978-0-316-27214-8(0)); (Illus.). 464p. 19.99 (978-0-316-38329-5(5)) Little, Brown Bks. for Young Readers.
—Queen Red Riding Hood's Guide to Royalty. Dorman, Brandon, illus. 2015. 118p. (J). (978-0-316-38339-4(2)) Little Brown & Co.
Colfer, Eoin. The Time Paradox. 2009. (Artemis Fowl Ser.). (ENG.). 448p. (J). (gr. 5-9). pap. 8.99 (978-1-4231-0837-5(X)) Hyperion Pr.
—The Time Paradox. 2009. (Artemis Fowl Ser.: 6). (J). lib. bdg. 19.65 (978-0-606-10579-8(4), Turtleback) Turtleback Bks.
Collins, Christine. The Knight Meets Ole Dragon. 2009. 100p. pap. 28.95 (978-1-4327-4128-0(4)) Outskirts Pr., Inc.
Collins, Diana Sue. Elfin, the Elf. 2011. 44p. pap. 24.95 (978-1-4560-8493-6(3)) America Star Bks.
Collins, Lynette. The Round Door: The Willow Tree. 2017. (Round Door Ser.: Bk. 2). (ENG., Illus.). (J). pap. 28.22 **(978-1-5245-6171-0(1))** Xlibris Corp.
Collins, Michael. Anu & the Blue. 2009. 166p. pap. 16.68 (978-0-557-20316-1(3)) Lulu Pr., Inc.
Collins, Paul. Dragonlinks: Book One in the Jelindel Chronicles (Large Print 16pt) l.t. ed. 2013. 486p. pap. (978-1-4596-6927-7(4)) ReadHowYouWant.com, Ltd.
—Slaves of Quentaris. (Illus.). 160p. pap. (978-0-7344-0557-9(X), Lothian Children's Bks.) Hachette Australia.
—The Spell of Undoing. 2009. (ENG., Illus.). 178p. pap. 10.95 (978-1-876462-53-6(1), Ford Street Publishing) Hybrid Pubs. AUS. Dist: International Publishers Marketing.
—Swords of Quentaris. 2005. 160p. pap. (978-0-7344-0470-1(0), Lothian Children's Bks.) Hachette Australia.
Collins, Suzanne. Gregor, Set, Nos. 1-5. 2009. (Underland Chronicles Ser.). (ENG.). (J). (gr. 3-7). pap., pap., pap. 39.95 (978-0-545-16681-2(0)) Scholastic, Inc.
—Gregor & the Code of Claw. 2008. (Underland Chronicles Ser.: 5). (ENG., Illus.). 416p. (J). (gr. 3-7). pap. 7.99 (978-0-439-79144-1(8), Scholastic Paperbacks) Scholastic, Inc.
—Gregor & the Code of Claw. l.t. ed. 2007. (Underland Chronicles: Bk. 5). 413p. (YA). (gr. 8-12). 22.95 (978-0-7862-9696-5(8)) Thorndike Pr.
—Gregor & the Curse of the Warmbloods. 2006. (Underland Chronicles: Bk. 3). 358p. (gr. 4-7). 17.00 (978-0-7569-6766-6(X)) Perfection Learning Corp.

—Gregor & the Curse of the Warmbloods, Bk. 3. 2006. (Underland Chronicles Ser.: 3). (ENG.). 368p. (J). (gr. 3-7). pap. 7.99 *(978-0-439-65624-5(9),* Scholastic Paperbacks) Scholastic, Inc.

—Gregor & the Marks of Secret. 2007. (Underland Chronicles Ser.: 4). (ENG., Illus.). 352p. (J). (gr. 3-7). 7.99 *(978-0-439-79146-5(4),* Scholastic Paperbacks) Scholastic, Inc.

—Gregor & the Marks of Secret. 2007. (Underland Chronicles Ser.: 4). 343p. (gr. 4-7). lib. bdg. 18.40 *(978-1-4177-8358-8(3),* Turtleback) Turtleback Bks.

—Gregor & the Prophecy of Bane. 2005. (Underland Chronicles Ser.: 2). (ENG.). 320p. (J). (gr. 3-7). pap. 7.99 *(978-0-439-65076-2(3))* Scholastic, Inc.

Collins, Tim. Fang-Tastic Collection! Notes from a Totally Lame Vampire; Prince of Dorkness; Notes from a Hairy-Not-Scary Werewolf; Fangs a Lot. Pindar, Andrew, illus. 2016. (ENG.). 1280p. (J). (gr. 3-7). 52.99 *(978-1-4814-6980-7(0),* Aladdin) Simon & Schuster Children's Publishing.

Collodi, C. The Adventures of Pinocchio. 2007. 108p. (gr. 4-7). per. 7.99 *(978-1-60459-012-8(2))* Wilder Pubns., Corp.

Collodi, Carlo, et al. Pinocchio & Peter Pan: Selections from Two Classic Children's Novels. Palmer, James, illus. 2014. (Text Connections Ser.). (J). (gr. 3). *(978-1-4509-9648-8(5))* Benchmark Education Co.

Colossal, Eric. Rutabaga: the Adventure Chef. 2015. (Rutabaga the Adventure Chef Ser.). (ENG., Illus.). 128p. (J). (gr. 3-7). 16.95 *(978-1-4197-1380-4(9),* Amulet Bks.) Abrams, Inc.

Colum, Padraic. The Adventures of Odysseus & Tales of Troy. 2005. pap. *(978-1-4065-0125-4(5))* Dodo Pr.

Columbus, Chris & Vizzini, Ned. House of Secrets. 2015. (House of Secrets Ser.: Vol. 1). (KOR.). 580p. (J). *(978-89-491-7127-2(9))* Biryongso Publishing Co.

—House of Secrets. Call, Greg, illus. (House of Secrets Ser.: 1). (J). 2014. (ENG.). 512p. (gr. 3-7). pap. 7.99 *(978-0-06-219247-9(7))* 2013. (ENG.). 496p. (gr. 3-7). 17.99 *(978-0-06-219246-2(9))* 2013. 490p. *(978-0-06-225964-6(4))* HarperCollins Pubs.

—House of Secrets. 2014. (House of Secrets Ser.: 1). (J). lib. bdg. 18.40 *(978-0-606-35070-9(5),* Turtleback) Turtleback Bks.

Columbus, Chris, et al. Clash of the Worlds. 2016. (House of Secrets Ser.: 3). 528p. (J). (gr. 3-7). 17.99 *(978-0-06-219251-6(5))* HarperCollins Pubs.

—House of Secrets: Clash of the Worlds. 2017. (House of Secrets Ser.: 3). 528p. (J). (gr. 3-7). pap. 7.99 *(978-0-06-219254-7(X))* HarperCollins Pubs.

Common, Gabriel. The Demon of Basile High: The Return of Cassius. 2007. 132p. per. 11.95 *(978-1-4327-0664-7(0))* Outskirts Pr., Inc.

Condie, Ally. Atlantia. (ENG.). 320p. (gr. 7). 2015. (YA). pap. 10.99 *(978-0-14-751065-5(1),* Speak) 2014. (J). 18.99 *(978-0-525-42644-8(2),* Dutton Books for Young Readers) Penguin Young Readers Group.

—Atlantia. 2015. lib. bdg. 22.10 *(978-0-606-37576-4(7))* Turtleback Bks.

—Crossed. 2013. (Matched Ser.: 2). (ENG.). 400p. (YA). (gr. 7). pap. 9.99 *(978-0-14-242171-0(5),* Speak) Penguin Publishing Group.

—Crossed, 2 vols. 2011. (Matched Ser.: 2). (ENG.). 384p. (YA). (gr. 7-18). 17.99 *(978-0-525-42365-2(6),* Dutton Books for Young Readers) Penguin Young Readers Group.

—Crossed. l.t. ed. 2011. (Matched Trilogy: Bk. 2). (ENG.). 448p. (J). 23.99 *(978-1-4104-4325-0(6))* Thorndike Pr.

—Crossed. 2013. (Matched Trilogy Ser.: 2). lib. bdg. 20.85 *(978-0-606-26634-5(8),* Turtleback) Turtleback Bks.

—Juntos. 2011. (Vintage Espanol Ser.).Tr. of Matched. (SPA.). 352p. (YA). (gr. 7). pap. 10.95 *(978-0-307-94778-9(5),* Vintage Espanol) Knopf Doubleday Publishing Group.

—Matched. 2009. (Matched Trilogy: Bk. 1). 11.04 *(978-0-7848-3716-0(3),* Everbind) Marco Bk. Co.

—Matched. (Matched Ser.: 1). (ENG.). (YA). (gr. 7-18). 2011. 416p. 9.99 *(978-0-14-241977-9(X),* Speak) 2010. 384p. 17.99 *(978-0-525-42364-5(8),* Dutton Books for Young Readers) Penguin Young Readers Group.

—Matched. 2011. pap. *(978-0-545-39990-6(4))* Scholastic, Inc.

—Matched. l.t. ed. 2011. (Matched Trilogy: Bk. 1). (ENG.). 450p. 23.99 *(978-1-4104-3954-3(2))* Thorndike Pr.

—Matched. 2011. (Matched Trilogy Ser.: 1). lib. bdg. 20.85 *(978-0-606-23140-4(4),* Turtleback) Turtleback Bks.

—Reached. (Matched Ser.: 3). (ENG.). (YA). (gr. 7). 2013. 544p. pap. 9.99 *(978-0-14-242599-2(0),* Speak) 2012. 528p. 17.99 *(978-0-525-42366-9(4),* Dutton Books for Young Readers) Penguin Young Readers Group.

—Reached. l.t. ed. 2012. (Matched Trilogy: Bk. 3). (ENG.). 614p. 23.99 *(978-1-4104-5366-2(9))* Thorndike Pr.

—Reached. 2013. (Matched Trilogy Ser.: 3). lib. bdg. 20.85 *(978-0-606-34456-2(X),* Turtleback) Turtleback Bks.

Cone, Carl. There's a Season for All. Cone, Carl, illus. 2008. (ENG., Illus.). pap. 14.95 *(978-0-9801555-6-3(8))* Argus Enterprises International, Inc.

Conner, Guy. Elizabeth & Parr. 2013. 90p. 24.00 *(978-0-578-12011-9(9))* GRC Bks.

Connolly, John. The Book of Lost Things. 2011. (ENG.). 368p. (J). (gr. 5-9). pap. 7.99 *(978-1-4424-2934-5(8),* Simon & Schuster Bks. For Young Readers) Simon & Schuster Bks. For Young Readers.

—The Gates. 2009. (ENG.). 304p. 24.00 *(978-1-4391-7263-6(3),* Beyond Words/Atria Bks.) Atria Bks.

—The Gates. 2011. (Samuel Lord Ser.: 1). (ENG.). 320p. (J). (gr. 5-9). pap. 8.99 *(978-1-4424-2933-8(X),* Simon & Schuster Bks. For Young Readers) Simon & Schuster Bks. For Young Readers.

Connolly, Tina. Seriously Wicked. 2015. (ENG.). 208p. (YA). (gr. 8-12). 17.99 *(978-0-7653-7516-2(8),* 9780765375162, Tor Teen) Doherty, Tom Assocs., LLC.

Connor, D. E. L. Spirit Warriors: The Concealing. 2013. 186p. pap. 13.95 *(978-1-62015-180-8(4),* Booktrope Editions) Booktrope.

Conrad, Cody And Arnetta. The Gerbil & the Arabian Nights: Jamal's Night Trip for Water. 2012. 16p. pap. 15.99 *(978-1-4772-2430-4(0))* AuthorHouse.

Constantine, Clélia. The Planet of Ludokaa. Élyum Studio, illus. 2013. (Little Prince Ser.: 12). (ENG.). 48p. (J). (gr. 4-8). lib. bdg. 26.60 *(978-0-7613-8762-6(5),* Graphic Universe™) Lerner Publishing Group.

Conway, Gerry. Crawling with Zombies. 2010. (Hardy Boys the New Case Files Ser.). (ENG., Illus.). 64p. (J). (gr. 3-7). pap. 6.99 *(978-1-59707-219-9(2),* 9781597072199) Papercutz.

Cook, Jeremy. Illusion Meets Reality. 2008. 116p. pap. 19.95 *(978-1-60813-059-7(2))* America Star Bks.

—The Illusion Stick. 2008. 115p. pap. 19.95 *(978-1-60474-705-8(6))* America Star Bks.

Cook, Katie. Little Big Benny: The Boy Who Didn't Know He Was the Universe. 2012. 144p. pap. 9.99 *(978-0-9883554-0-8(X))* Katie Cook.

Cook, Philip. Erden: Flame of the Creator. 2014. xiii, 259p. (YA). *(978-1-4908-2033-0(7),* WestBow Pr.) Author Solutions, Inc.

Cooke, C. W. Wrath of the Titans: Cyclops. 2012. (ENG.). 40p. pap. 7.99 *(978-1-4507-8964-6(1))* Bluewater Productions, Inc.

Coonan, Candace N. The Darkest Hour: Tales from Fadreama: Book 1. 2012. 328p. (gr. 4-6). pap. 19.11 *(978-1-4669-3565-5(0))* Trafford Publishing.

—Where Shadows Linger: Tales from Fadreama: Book 2. 2012. 304p. (gr. 2-4). pap. 18.30 *(978-1-4669-3541-9(3))* Trafford Publishing.

Coons, Susan Anderson. Lighthouse Mouse Meets Simon the Cat. Sanne, Don, illus. 2012. 52p. pap. 10.03 *(978-1-4669-1223-6(5))* Trafford Publishing.

Cooper, Clare. Time Ball. 2003. (ENG.). 72p. pap. 11.95 *(978-1-84323-255-1(3))* Beekman Bks., Inc.

Cooper, Constance. Guile. 2017. (ENG.). 384p. (YA). (gr. 7). pap. 9.99 *(978-0-544-93691-1(4),* HMH Books For Young Readers) Houghton Mifflin Harcourt Publishing Co.

—Guile. 2016. (ENG.). 384p. (YA). (gr. 7). 17.99 *(978-0-544-45171-1(6),* Clarion Bks.) Houghton Mifflin Harcourt Trade & Reference Pubs.

—Guile. 2017. (ENG.). (YA). (gr. 7). lib. bdg. 20.85 ***(978-0-606-39821-3(X))*** Turtleback Bks.

Cooper, Polly. The Adventures of Sir George & His Friends. 2008. (Illus.). 48p. pap. 17.49 *(978-1-4343-4057-3(0))* AuthorHouse.

Cooper, Susan. The Boggart. Rayyan, Omar & Dillon, Julie, illus. 2004. (Boggart Ser.). (ENG.). 224p. (J). (gr. 3-7). pap. 7.99 *(978-0-689-86930-3(4),* McElderry, Margaret K. Bks.) McElderry, Margaret K. Bks.

—The Boggart & the Monster. Rayyan, Omar & Dillon, Julie, illus. 2004. (Boggart Ser.). (ENG.). 224p. (J). (gr. 3-7). pap. 7.99 *(978-0-689-86931-0(2),* McElderry, Margaret K. Bks.) McElderry, Margaret K. Bks.

—The Dark Is Rising. 2009. 7.64 *(978-0-7848-2212-8(3));* 10.36 *(978-0-7848-3502-9(0))* Marco Bk. Co. (Everbind).

—The Dark Is Rising. 15.85 *(978-0-7569-8464-9(5))* Perfection Learning Corp.

—The Dark Is Rising. (Dark Is Rising Sequence Ser.). 244p. (YA). (gr. 5-18). pap. 4.99 *(978-0-8072-1533-3(3),* Listening Library) Random Hse. Audio Publishing Group.

—The Dark Is Rising. 2007. (YA). 1.25 *(978-1-4193-7923-9(2))* Recorded Bks., Inc.

—The Dark Is Rising Sequence: Over Sea, under Stone - The Dark Is Rising - Greenwitch - The Grey King - Silver on the Tree. 2013. (Dark Is Rising Sequence Ser.). (ENG.). 1088p. (J). (gr. 3-7). pap. 39.99 *(978-1-4424-8967-7(7),* McElderry, Margaret K. Bks.) McElderry, Margaret K. Bks.

—The Dark Is Rising Sequence Set: Over Sea, under Stone; The Dark Is Rising; Greenwitch; The Grey King; Silver on the Tree. 2013. (Dark Is Rising Sequence Ser.). (ENG.). 1088p. (J). (gr. 3-7). 89.99 *(978-1-4424-8968-4(5),* McElderry, Margaret K. Bks.) McElderry, Margaret K. Bks.

—Green Boy. 2003. (ENG., Illus.). 208p. (J). (gr. 4-7). pap. 7.99 *(978-0-689-84760-8(2),* McElderry, Margaret K. Bks.) McElderry, Margaret K. Bks.

—King of Shadows. unabr. ed. 2004. 192p. (J). (gr. 5-9). pap. 36.00 incl. audio *(978-0-8072-8388-2(6),* Listening Library) Random Hse. Audio Publishing Group.

—Over Sea, under Stone. 2013. (Dark Is Rising Sequence Ser.: 1). (ENG., Illus.). 288p. (J). (gr. 3-7). 17.99 *(978-1-4424-9592-0(8),* McElderry, Margaret K. Bks.) McElderry, Margaret K. Bks.

—Seaward. 2013. (ENG., Illus.). 240p. (J). (gr. 3-7). 17.99 *(978-1-4424-7327-0(4));* pap. 6.99 *(978-1-4424-7326-3(6))* McElderry, Margaret K. Bks. (McElderry, Margaret K. Bks.).

Corder, Zizou. Lion Boy - The Chase. 2005. (ENG., Illus.). 288p. (J). (gr. 3-7). 8.99 *(978-0-14-240454-6(3),* Puffin Books) Penguin Young Readers Group.

Cordero, Silvia Jaeger & Cordero, Silvia Jaegar. El Huevo Azul. Sunset Producciones & Producciones, Sunset, illus. rev. ed. 2005. (Castillo de la Lectura Verde Ser.). (SPA & ENG.). 136p. (J). (gr. -1-7). pap. 7.95 *(978-970-20-0127-0(7))* Castillo, Ediciones, S. A. de C. V. MEX. Dist: Macmillan.

Corderoy, Tracey. The Great Granny Cake Contest! Hubble Bubble. Berger, Joe, illus. 2017. (ENG.). 128p. (J). (gr. 1-4). pap. 6.99 *(978-0-7636-8849-3(5),* Nosy Crow) Candlewick Pr.

Cordery-Maring, Jeanee. Climbing over Rainbows. 2008. 76p. pap. 19.95 *(978-1-4241-6243-7(2))* America Star Bks.

Córdova, Zoraida. The Savage Blue. 2013. (Vicious Deep Ser.: 2). (ENG., Illus.). 416p. (YA). (gr. 7-12). 16.99 *(978-1-4022-8206-5(0),* 9781402282065) Sourcebooks, Inc.

—The Vicious Deep. 2012. (Vicious Deep Ser.: 1). (ENG.). 384p. (YA). (gr. 7-12). pap. 9.99 *(978-1-4022-7441-1(6))* Sourcebooks, Inc.

Corlett, William. The Bridge in the Clouds. 2003. 20.25 *(978-0-8446-7239-7(4))* Smith, Peter Pub., Inc.

—The Tunnel Behind the Waterfall. 2010. (Magician's House Quartet Ser.: 3). (ENG.). 320p. (YA). (gr. 5-8). pap. 14.99 *(978-1-4424-1413-6(8),* Simon Pulse) Simon Pulse.

Corman, Dick. Fountain of Age. 2006. 185p. (YA). pap. 12.95 *(978-0-9655749-2-1(X))* Corman Productions.

Cormier, Shawn P. Necromancer. 2008. 276p. (YA). per. 12.95 *(978-0-9740151-4-9(8))* Pine View Pr.

—Nomadin. 2003. 296p. (YA). per. 12.95 *(978-0-9740151-0-1(5))* Pine View Pr.

Cornerstonia Books. Cornerstonia: The Rose River Journey, vol. 1. 2010. (ENG., Illus.). 195p. pap. 10.99 *(978-0-9828588-0-6(9))* Cornerstonia.

Cornish, D. M. Foundling. Cornish, D. M., illus. 2007. (Monster Blood Tattoo Ser.). (Illus.). 434p. (gr. 7-12). 20.00 *(978-0-7569-7957-7(9))* Perfection Learning Corp.

Coro, Edys. Edys' Collection of Short Tales. 2008. 64p. pap. 19.95 *(978-1-60672-856-7(3))* America Star Bks.

Corp, Carey & Langdon, Lorie. Shades of Doon, 1 vol. 2015. (Doon Novel Ser.). (ENG.). 352p. (YA). 17.99 *(978-0-310-74235-7(8))* Blink.

Corr, Katharine & Corr, Elizabeth. The Witch's Kiss. 2017. (Witch's Kiss Ser.: 1). (ENG.). 320p. (YA). 9.99 ***(978-0-00-825120-8(7),*** HarperCollins Children's Bks.) HarperCollins Pubs. Ltd. GBR. Dist: HarperCollins Pubs.

Corre, Lorraine. Book #1, Just for Fun. 2009. 116p. pap. 14.95 *(978-1-4401-2812-7(X))* iUniverse, Inc.

Corwin, Susan Simon. The Cryptic Cat. Corwin, Stuart, illus. 2006. 99p. (YA). *(978-0-9790632-0-6(5))* Lucky Duck Designs.

Cosby, Andrew. Mary Scary. Nixey, Troy, illus. 2007. (ENG.). 56p. (gr. 7). pap. 9.95 *(978-1-59307-730-3(0))* Dark Horse Comics.

Cosby, Sam & Metzger, Clancy. Ceruladons: Blue dreams rain to Tears. 2008. 304p. 28.95 *(978-0-595-51125-9(2));* pap. 18.95 *(978-0-595-52400-6(1))* iUniverse, Inc.

Cosentino, Ralph. Superman: The Story of the Man of Steel. 2010. (ENG., Illus.). 40p. (J). (gr. -1-2). 16.99 *(978-0-670-06285-0(5),* Viking Books for Young Readers) Penguin Young Readers Group.

Cosgrove, Stephen. Buttermilk. James, Robin, illus. 2013. (Serendipity Ser.: 2). (ENG.). 32p. (J). (gr. k-4). pap. 7.95 *(978-1-939011-52-7(3))* Heritage Builders, LLC.

—Button Breaker. 2016. (Treasure Trolls Ser.). (ENG., Illus.). 32p. (J). (gr. k-4). pap. 7.95 *(978-1-941437-79-7(6))* Heritage Builders, LLC.

—Creole. James, Robin, illus. 2013. (Serendipity Ser.: 3). (ENG.). 32p. (J). (gr. k-4). pap. 7.95 *(978-1-939011-53-4(1))* Heritage Builders, LLC.

—Fanny. James, Robin, illus. 2013. (Serendipity Ser.: 4). (ENG.). 32p. (J). (gr. k-4). pap. 7.95 *(978-1-939011-54-1(X))* Heritage Builders, LLC.

—Flutterby. James, Robin, illus. 2013. (Serendipity Ser.: 5). (ENG.). 32p. (J). (gr. k-4). pap. 7.95 *(978-1-939011-55-8(8))* Heritage Builders, LLC.

—Leo the Lop. James, Robin, illus. 2013. (Serendipity Ser.: 6). (ENG.). 32p. (J). (gr. k-4). pap. 7.95 *(978-1-939011-56-5(6))* Heritage Builders, LLC.

—Morgan & Me. James, Robin, illus. 2013. (Serendipity Ser.: 7). (ENG.). 32p. (J). (gr. k-4). pap. 7.95 *(978-1-939011-57-2(4))* Heritage Builders, LLC.

—The Muffin Dragon. James, Robin, illus. 2013. (Serendipity Ser.: 8). (ENG.). 32p. (J). (gr. k-4). pap. 7.95 *(978-1-939011-59-6(0))* Heritage Builders, LLC.

—Nitter Pitter. James, Robin, illus. 2015. (Serendipity Ser.: 20). (ENG.). 32p. (J). (gr. k-4). pap. 7.95 *(978-1-941437-38-4(9))* Heritage Builders, LLC.

—Sniffles. James, Robin, illus. 2013. (Serendipity Ser.: 1). (ENG.). 32p. (J). (gr. k-4). pap. 7.95 *(978-1-939011-58-9(2))* Heritage Builders, LLC.

Cosper, Andy. The Adventures of Drew Kreeger: Book 1. 2008. 56p. pap. 14.95 *(978-1-4327-3320-9(6))* Outskirts Pr., Inc.

Cote, Denis. Les Chemins de Mirlande. 2003. (Roman + Ser.). 160p. (YA). (gr. 8-18). pap. *(978-2-89021-310-4(2))* Diffusion du livre Mirabel (DLM).

Côté, Denis. La Forêt aux Mille et un Périls, Tome 2. Poulin, Stephane, illus. 2004. (Roman Jeunesse Ser.). (FRE.). 96p. (J). (gr. 4-7). pap. *(978-2-89021-696-9(9))* Diffusion du livre Mirabel (DLM).

—La Machination du Scorpion Noir. 2004. (Mon Roman Ser.). (FRE.). 160p. (J). (gr. 2). pap. *(978-2-89021-667-9(5))* Diffusion du livre Mirabel (DLM).

Cote, Jenny. The Ark, the Reed & the Fire Cloud: The Amazing Tales of Max & Liz Book One, 2 bks, Bk 1. 2008. (Amazing Tales of Max & Liz Ser.: 1). (ENG., Illus.). 432p. (J). (gr. 5-11). pap. 16.99 *(978-0-89957-198-0(0),* Living Ink Bks.) AMG Pubs.

Cottrell, Kim. Izaboo, Izaboo, What Are We to Do. 2009. 36p. pap. 15.49 *(978-1-4389-5210-9(4))* AuthorHouse.

Coulthurst, Audrey. Of Fire & Stars. Saia, Jordan, illus. 2016. 400p. (YA). (gr. 8). 17.99 *(978-0-06-243325-1(3))* HarperCollins Pubs.

Courtauld, Sarah & Burniac, Lauren. The Perilous Princess Plot. 2015. (Buckle & Squash Ser.). (ENG., Illus.). 192p. (J). (gr. 2-5). 14.99 *(978-1-250-05277-3(7),* 9781250052773) Feiwel & Friends.

Coven, Wanda. Heidi Heckelbeck & the Never-Ending Day. Burris, Priscilla, illus. 2017. (Heidi Heckelbeck Ser.: 21). (ENG.). 128p. (J). (gr. k-4). 16.99 ***(978-1-4814-9525-7(9));*** pap. 5.99 ***(978-1-4814-9524-0(0))*** Little Simon. (Little Simon).

Coville, Bruce. Into the Land of the Unicorns. 2008. (Unicorn Chronicles Ser.). (Illus.). 159p. (J). (gr. 4-7). 14.65 *(978-0-7569-9061-9(0))* Perfection Learning Corp.

—Into the Land of the Unicorns. (Unicorn Chronicles: Bk. 1). 159p. (J). (gr. 4-7). pap. 4.50 *(978-0-8072-1518-0(X),* Listening Library) Random Hse. Audio Publishing Group.

Coville, Katherine. Ivy. 2017. (ENG.). 144p. (J). (gr. 2-5). 16.99 *(978-0-553-53975-2(2),* Knopf Bks. for Young Readers) Random Hse. Children's Bks.

Cowan, Catherine. My Life with the Wave. Buehner, Mark, illus. 2004. (J). (gr. k-3). spiral bd. *(978-0-616-11863-4(5))* Canadian National Institute for the Blind/Institut National Canadien pour les Aveugles.

Cowden, Matt. Emma Mcdougal & the Quest for Father Time. Black, Ilene, illus. 2008. 190p. (J). 24.95 *(978-0-9799189-0-2(1))* His Work Christian Publishing.

Cowell, Cressida. How to Cheat a Dragon's Curse. 2010. (ENG., Illus.). 256p. (J). *(978-0-340-99910-3(1),* Hodder Children's Books) Hachette Children's Group GBR. Dist: Hachette Bk. Group.

—How to Cheat a Dragon's Curse. Cowell, Cressida, illus. 2007. (How to Train Your Dragon Ser.: 4). (ENG., Illus.). 256p. (J). (gr. 3-7). 14.99 *(978-0-316-11425-7(1))* Little, Brown Bks. for Young Readers.

—How to Twist a Dragon's Tale. 2010. (ENG., Illus.). 272p. (J). *(978-0-340-99911-0(X),* Hodder Children's Books) Hachette Children's Group GBR. Dist: Hachette Bk. Group.

—How to Twist a Dragon's Tale. 2008. (How to Train Your Dragon Ser.: 5). (ENG., Illus.). 256p. (J). (gr. 3-7). 10.99 *(978-0-316-11774-6(9))* Little, Brown Bks. for Young Readers.

Cowey, James. William Snottengrout - Gangor's Reign. 2006. 104p. per. *(978-1-84667-006-0(3))* Derwent Pr., The.

—William Snottengrout - Quapta's Revenge. 2006. 104p. per. *(978-1-84667-023-7(3))* Derwent Pr., The.

Cowley, Joseph. Alice's Adventures in Wonderland by Lewis Carroll: (Adapted by Joseph Cowley) 2012. 102p. pap. 9.95 *(978-1-4759-3276-8(6))* iUniverse, Inc.

Cowley, Joy. Starbright & the Dream Eater. Date not set. 208p. (J). (gr. 4-18). pap. 4.99 *(978-0-06-440791-5(8))* HarperCollins Pubs.

Cox, Greg. Riese: Kingdom Falling. 2012. (ENG.). 288p. (YA). (gr. 7). 16.99 *(978-1-4424-2969-7(0),* Simon & Schuster Bks. For Young Readers) Simon & Schuster Bks. For Young Readers.

Cox, M. M. The Condemned. 2016. (ENG., Illus.). 274p. (J). pap. *(978-0-908325-23-8(1))* Bluewood Publishing, Ltd.

Crane, Phyllis F. Anything but the Most Boring Place on Earth. 2011. 174p. pap. 24.95 *(978-1-4560-6802-8(4))* America Star Bks.

Craw, Gloria. Atlantis Rising. 2015. (Atlantis Rising Ser.: 1). (ENG.). 352p. (YA). 16.99 *(978-1-62266-519-8(8),* 9781622665198) Entangled Publishing, LLC.

Crawley, Oksanna. So, You Be Keon & I'll Be Mahovlich. 2009. 28p. pap. 13.99 *(978-1-4490-0243-5(9))* AuthorHouse.

Crippa, Luca, et al. The Discovery of America. Cooper-McGuinness, Nanette, tr. de Pretto, Lorenzo, illus. 2009. (Geronimo Stilton Graphic Novels Ser.). (ENG.). 56p. (J). (gr. 2-6). 9.99 *(978-1-59707-158-1(7),* 9781597071581) Papercutz.

Crofoot, Betty & Arledge, Roo. The Great Celebration Ceremony - My Genie & Me Series Book 2. 2012. 84p. pap. 8.95 *(978-1-60862-430-0(7))* E-BookTime LLC.

Croggon, Alison. The Bone Queen. 2017. (Pellinor Ser.). (ENG.). 416p. (YA). (gr. 7). 17.99 *(978-0-7636-8974-2(2))* Candlewick Pr.

—The Crow: Book Three of Pellinor. 2017. (Pellinor Ser.). (ENG.). 528p. (J). (gr. 7). pap. 9.99 *(978-0-7636-9445-6(2))* Candlewick Pr.

—The Naming: Book One of Pellinor. 2017. (ENG.). 512p. (J). (gr. 7). pap. 9.99 *(978-0-7636-9443-2(6))* Candlewick Pr.

—The Riddle: Book Two of Pellinor. 2017. (Pellinor Ser.). (ENG.). 512p. (J). (gr. 7). pap. 9.99 *(978-0-7636-9444-9(4))* Candlewick Pr.

Cronshaw, Joseph. Podge & Dodge. 2009. 32p. pap. 13.50 *(978-1-60693-868-3(1),* Strategic Bk. Publishing) Strategic Book Publishing & Rights Agency (SBPRA).

Cross, Frances. Boy the Witch & the Blobber 1. 2007. (Blobber Ser.). (Illus.). 98p. pap. *(978-1-84167-560-2(1))* Ransom Publishing Ltd.

Cross, P. W. The Idea Miners: The Lost Lake Dig. 2009. 288p. (J). pap. 7.99 *(978-0-9662800-8-1(3))* Appalachian Hse.

Croteau, Marie-Danielle & St. Aubin, Bruno. Des Fantomes Sous la Mer. 2003. (Roman Jeunesse Ser.). (FRE., Illus.). 96p. (J). (gr. 4-7). pap. *(978-2-89021-610-5(1))* Diffusion du livre Mirabel (DLM).

Crothers, Julia. Solari. 2016. (ENG.). 127p. pap. 10.95 *(978-1-78455-809-3(5),* c5e99ca9-fd9c-4a05-9ebb-bb7d20b14ce1) Austin, Stan AUS. Dist: Bookmasters Distribution.

Crow, Gary & Crow, Brock. JimJim Meets PosterGuy. 2006. 100p. (J). pap. 14.95 *(978-0-9759621-5-2(9))* Koenisha Pubns.

Crowe, A. B. The Protectors of Dromgoon: The Crossing. 2017. (ENG.). 160p. pap. 13.95 ***(978-1-78629-805-8(8),*** 2473b89d-f919-4774-8e34-a6b22314fce2) Austin, Stan AUS. Dist: Bookmasters Distribution.

Crowley, James. Monsterland. 2017. (ENG.). 384p. (J). (gr. 5). 16.99 *(978-0-399-17589-3(X),* G.P. Putnam's Sons Books for Young Readers) Penguin Young Readers Group.

Crum, Shutta. Thomas & the Dragon Queen. Wildish, Lee, illus. 2011. (ENG.). 272p. (J). (gr. 3-7). 6.99 *(978-0-375-84634-2(4),* Yearling) Random Hse. Children's Bks.

Cuartas, Jennifer M. So Many Things. 2012. 28p. 24.95 *(978-1-4626-6328-6(1))* America Star Bks.

Cue, Ian J. The Renewal: First Encounter. 2003. 192p. (YA). per. 9.95 *(978-0-9741989-0-3(0))* Mill Creek Metro Publishing.

Culici, Tonia. Kiku Gecko & Rainbow Girl. 2012. 44p. pap. 20.45 *(978-1-4525-0584-8(5))* Balboa Pr.

Cullen, Sean. Hamish X Goes to Providence, Rhode Island. 2008. (ENG.). 336p. (J). ***(978-0-670-06854-8(3))*** Penguin Bks., Ltd.

Culpepper, R. B. W. Ellena & the Magic Lamp. 2011. 182p. pap. 24.95 *(978-1-4626-2830-8(3))* America Star Bks.

Cumming, Hannah. The Red Boat. Cumming, Hannah, illus. 2012. (Child's Play Library). (ENG., Illus.). 32p. (J). *(978-1-84643-493-8(9))* Child's Play International Ltd.

Cummings, Lindsay. The Fires of Calderon. (Balance Keepers Ser.: 1). (ENG., (J). (gr. 3-7). 2015. Illus.). 368p. pap. 6.99 *(978-0-06-227519-6(4))* 2014. 352p. 16.99 *(978-0-06-227518-9(6))* HarperCollins Pubs. (Tegen, Katherine Bks).

—The Pillars of Ponderay. 2016. (Balance Keepers Ser.: 2). 400p. (J). (gr. 3-7). pap. 6.99 *(978-0-06-227522-6(4),* Tegen, Katherine Bks) HarperCollins Pubs.

—The Traitor of Belltroll. 2016. (Balance Keepers Ser.: 3). (Illus.). 384p. (J). (gr. 3-7). 16.99 *(978-0-06-227524-0(0),* Tegen, Katherine Bks) HarperCollins Pubs.

Cunningham, Mary. Curse of the Bayou. 2007. (Cynthia's Attic Ser.). 157p. (J). per. 9.99 *(978-1-59080-575-6(5))* Echelon Press Publishing.

—Cynthias Attic Magicians Castle. 2009. 158p. pap. 10.99 *(978-1-59080-656-2(5))* Echelon Press Publishing.

—The Missing Locket. 2005. (Cynthia's Attic Ser.). 152p. (J). (gr. 5). per. 9.99 *(978-1-59080-441-4(4))* Echelon Press Publishing.

Curran, Steven Earl. Whales used to Fly in the Sky. 2005. 9.00 *(978-0-8059-8086-8(5))* Dorrance Publishing Co., Inc.

Curry, Cicero. The Tickle Man. Ledbetter, John'el, illus. 2013. 44p. 24.95 *(978-1-63004-279-0(X))* America Star Bks.

Curry, Jane Louise. The Egyptian Box. 2008. (ENG.). 196p. (J). (gr. 4-6). pap. 10.95 *(978-1-4169-7140-5(8),* Simon & Schuster/Paula Wiseman Bks.) Simon & Schuster/Paula Wiseman Bks.

Curry, Kenneth. The Legend of the Dancing Trees: An African American Folk Tale. 2007. 111p. (J). per. 14.95 (978-0-9798364-0-4(9)) Curry Brothers Publishing Group.

Curry, Kenneth, et al. The Legend of the Dancing Tees Teachers Resource: The Legend of the Dancing Trees. 2007.Tr. of Teachers Resource. per. 19.95 (978-0-9798364-1-1(7)) Curry Brothers Publishing Group.

Curtis, Philip. El Senor Browser y los Afilacerebros. Ross, Tony, illus. (SPA.). 112p. (YA). (gr. 5-8). (978-84-239-2754-8(7), EC2750) Espasa Calpe, S.A. ESP. Dist: Lectorum Pubns., Inc.

Cutler, Ivor. El Desayuno de Tomas. (SPA., Illus.). 30p. (J). (gr. k-3). pap. 8.95 (978-1-56014-162-4(X)) Aguilar Editorial MEX. Dist: Santillana USA Publishing Co., Inc.

—El Desayuno de Tomas. Oxenbury, Helen, illus. (SPA.). 30p. (J). (gr. k-3). pap. 6.95 (978-1-56014-629-2(X)) Santillana USA Publishing Co., Inc.

Cyber. The Transdimensional War Series. 2006. 67p. pap. 16.95 (978-1-4241-2778-8(5)) PublishAmerica, Inc.

Cynthia, A. Sears. A World Divided: The Fairy Princess Chronicles - Book 1. 2012. 656p. (978-1-4602-0516-7(2)); pap. (978-1-4602-0514-3(6)) FriesenPress.

Cypess, Leah. Death Marked. 400p. (YA). (gr. 8). 2016. pap. 9.99 (978-0-06-222125-4(6)) 2015. (ENG.). 17.99 (978-0-06-222124-7(8)) HarperCollins Pubs. (Greenwillow Bks.).

—Death Sworn. 2014. (ENG.). 352p. (YA). (gr. 8). 17.99 (978-0-06-222121-6(3), Greenwillow Bks.) HarperCollins Pubs.

—Mistwood. (ENG., 320p. (YA). (gr. 8). 2011. Illus.). pap. 8.99 (978-0-06-195701-7(1)) 2010. 16.99 (978-0-06-195699-7(6)) HarperCollins Pubs. (Greenwillow Bks.).

—Nightspell. 2012. (ENG.). 368p. (YA). (gr. 8). pap. 8.99 (978-0-06-195704-8(6), Greenwillow Bks.) HarperCollins Pubs.

Dade, Barbara A. Story Time with Grandm. 2008. 88p. pap. 41.99 (978-1-4363-5325-0(4)) Xlibris Corp.

Dadey, Debbie & Jones, Marcia Thornton. Inside the Magic. 2009. (Keyholders Ser.: 3). (ENG.). 128p. (J). (gr. 2-5). 4.99 (978-0-7653-5984-1(7), 9780765359841, Starscape) Doherty, Tom Assocs., LLC.

—The Wrong Side of Magic. 2009. (Keyholders Ser.: 4). (ENG.). 128p. (J). (gr. 2-5). pap. 4.99 (978-0-7653-5985-8(5), 9780765359858, Starscape) Doherty, Tom Assocs., LLC.

Daffern, Brian. Prince Albert Bk. 2: The Beast School. 2005. 160p. (YA). per. 10.95 (978-0-9709104-6-2(0)) Hickory Tales Publishing.

—Prince Albert in a Can, Bk. 1. 2004. 256p. (YA). per. 13.95 (978-0-9709104-5-5(2)) Hickory Tales Publishing.

Dahl, M. B. Through the Balustrade. 2013. 376p. pap. 17.95 (978-0-9891064-0-5(3), Taberah Pr.) Sonfire Media, LLC.

Dahl, Michael. The Creeping Bookends, 1 vol. Kendall, Bradford, illus. 2008. (Library of Doom Ser.). (ENG.). 40p. (gr. 1-3). pap. 6.25 (978-1-4342-0546-9(0)); lib. bdg. 23.99 (978-1-4342-0486-8(3)) Stone Arch Bks. (Zone Bks.).

—Escape from the Pop-Up Prison. Kendall, Bradford, illus. 2008. (Library of Doom Ser.). (ENG.). 40p. (gr. 1-3). pap. 6.25 (978-1-4342-0550-6(9), Zone Bks.) Stone Arch Bks.

—The Golden Book of Death. Souleiman, Serg, illus. 2008. (Library of Doom Ser.). (ENG.). 40p. (gr. 1-3). lib. bdg. 23.99 (978-1-4342-0487-5(1), Zone Bks.) Stone Arch Bks.

—The Last City of Krypton. Levins, Tim & Vecchio, Luciano, illus. 2017. (Superman Tales of the Fortress of Solitude Ser.). (ENG.). 40p. (gr. 1-3). lib. bdg. 24.65 (978-1-4965-4394-3(7), DC Super Heroes) Stone Arch Bks.

—Rays of Doom. Levins, Tim & Vecchio, Luciano, illus. 2017. (Superman Tales of the Fortress of Solitude Ser.). (ENG.). 40p. (gr. 1-3). lib. bdg. 24.65 (978-1-4965-4396-7(3), DC Super Heroes) Stone Arch Bks.

—The Robot That Barked. Levins, Tim & Vecchio, Luciano, illus. 2017. (Superman Tales of the Fortress of Solitude Ser.). (ENG.). 40p. (gr. 1-3). lib. bdg. 24.65 (978-1-4965-4397-4(1), DC Super Heroes) Stone Arch Bks.

—Skyfall, 1 vol. Kovar, Ben, illus. 2012. (Troll Hunters Ser.). (ENG.). 112p. (gr. 2-3). lib. bdg. 25.32 (978-1-4342-3307-3(3), Troll Hunters) Stone Arch Bks.

—Superman Tales of the Fortress of Solitude. 2017. (Superman Tales of the Fortress of Solitude Ser.). (ENG.). 40p. (gr. 1-3). 98.60 (978-1-4965-4414-8(5), DC Super Heroes) Stone Arch Bks.

—Twilight of the Gods: A Viking Graphic Novel. Garcia, Eduardo, illus. 2016. (Norse Myths: a Viking Graphic Novel Ser.). (ENG.). 56p. (gr. 3-4). lib. bdg. 27.99 (978-1-4965-3489-7(1)) Stone Arch Bks.

—The Twister Trap, 1 vol. Kendall, Bradford, illus. 2008. (Library of Doom Ser.). (ENG.). 40p. (gr. 1-3). pap. 6.25 (978-1-4342-0548-3(7)); lib. bdg. 23.99 (978-1-4342-0488-2(X)) Stone Arch Bks. (Zone Bks.).

—The Word Eater, 1 vol. Kendall, Bradford, illus. 2008. (Library of Doom Ser.). (ENG.). 40p. (gr. 1-3). lib. bdg. 23.99 (978-1-4342-0491-2(X)); per. 6.25 (978-1-4342-0551-3(7)) Stone Arch Bks. (Zone Bks.).

Dahl, Roald. Charlie y la Fabrica de Chocolate.Tr. of Charlie & the Chocolate Factory. (SPA.). (J). pap. (978-84-204-5999-8(2), KZ992) Ediciones Alfaguara.

—Charlie y la Fabrica de Chocolate. Jacques, Faith, illus. 2003.Tr. of Charlie & the Chocolate Factory. (FRE & SPA.). 176p. (J). (gr. 4-7). (978-84-204-4771-1(4), AF0153) Ediciones Alfaguara.

—CHARLIE Y LA FABRICA DE CHOCOLATE. 51st ed. (SPA., Illus.). 172p. (J). (gr. 5-8). pap. 9.95 (978-84-204-6450-3(3)) Santillana USA Publishing Co., Inc.

—Fantastic Mr. Fox. 2007. 18.40 (978-1-4177-8615-2(9), Turtleback) Turtleback Bks.

—James & the Giant Peach. 2014. (ENG.). 144p. (J). (gr. 12-12). 12.24 (978-1-63245-219-1(7)) Lectorum Pubns., Inc.

—James & the Giant Peach. 2011. 9.00 (978-0-7848-3560-9(8)) 2009. 9.00 (978-0-7848-0470-4(2)) Marco Bk. Co. (Everbind).

—James & the Giant Peach. Crane, Jordan & Burkert, Nancy E., illus. 2011. (Penguin Classics Deluxe Edition Ser.). (ENG.). 160p. (gr. 3-7). 16.00 (978-0-14-310634-0(1), Penguin Classics) Penguin Publishing Group.

—James & the Giant Peach. 2005. 18.00 (978-0-7569-5911-1(X)) Penguin Publishing Group.

—James & the Giant Peach. Blake, Quentin, illus. (ENG.). (J). (gr. 3-7). 2016. 176p. 16.99 (978-0-425-28765-1(3)) 2011. 128p. pap. 15.99 (978-0-14-241823-9(4)) 2007. 176p. 7.99 (978-0-14-241036-3(5)) Penguin Young Readers Group. (Puffin Books).

—James & the Giant Peach. Blake, Quentin, illus. 2007. 146p. (gr. 4-7). 18.40 (978-1-4177-8608-4(6), Turtleback) Turtleback Bks.

—James et la Grosse Peche.Tr. of James & the Giant Peach. (FRE.). (J). pap. 17.95 (978-2-07-051374-1(2)) Gallimard, Editions FRA. Dist: Distribooks, Inc.

—James und der Riesenpfirsich: (Das Buch zum Film)Tr. of James & the Giant Peach. pap. 17.95 (978-3-499-21183-6(1)) Rowohlt Taschenbuch Verlag GmbH DEU. Dist: Distribooks, Inc.

—James y el Melocoton Gigante. Blake, Quentin, illus. 2003.Tr. of James & the Giant Peach. (SPA.). 184p. pap. 9.95 (978-968-19-0625-2(X)) Aguilar, Altea, Taurus, Alfaguara, S.A. de C.V MEX. Dist: Santillana USA Publishing Co., Inc.

—Matilda. 2007.Tr. of Matilda. 18.40 (978-1-4177-8613-8(2), Turtleback) Turtleback Bks.

—The Minpins. 2009. (ENG.). 32p. (J). (gr. 1-3). pap. 7.99 (978-0-14-241474-3(3), Puffin Books) Penguin Young Readers Group.

—La Potion Magique de Georges Bouillon.Tr. of George's Marvellous Medicine. (FRE.). (J). pap. 17.95 (978-2-07-051340-6(8)) Gallimard, Editions FRA. Dist: Distribooks, Inc.

—The Witches. Blake, Quentin, illus. 2007. 206p. (gr. 4-7). 17.00 (978-0-7569-8229-4(4)) Perfection Learning Corp.

Dahl, Roald & Wood, David. James & the Giant Peach. 2010. 51p. pap. (978-0-573-05138-8(0)) French, Samuel Ltd.

Daily, Lorrie Ann. The Castlewood Twins, the Magic Begins. 2008. 196p. pap. 12.95 (978-0-9820479-8-9(3)) Peppertree Pr., The.

Daines, Julie. Unraveled: A Tale of True Love. 2014. 192p. (J). pap. 14.99 (978-1-62108-627-7(5)) Covenant Communications, Inc.

Dal Santo, Sandy. I See a Zoo up in the Sky. 2009. 28p. pap. 12.89 (978-1-4389-4871-3(9)) AuthorHouse.

—My Fantasy Forest. 2009. 36p. pap. 15.65 (978-1-4389-6035-7(2)) AuthorHouse.

Dallion 7th, David W. Tales of Tura. 2007. 188p. per. 24.95 (978-1-4241-7131-6(8)) America Star Bks.

Dalton, Andrew & Boatfield, Jonny. The Lost People of Malplaquet. 2007. (ENG., Illus.). 144p. (C). (gr. 4-7). 34.00 (978-0-7188-3049-6(0)); per. 17.00 (978-0-7188-3050-2(4)) Lutherworth Pr., The GBR. Dist: Casemate Academic.

—The New Empire of Malplaquet. 2009. (ENG., Illus.). 192p. (gr. 4-7). 35.00 (978-0-7188-3096-0(2)); pap. 17.50 (978-0-7188-3093-9(8)) Lutherworth Pr., The GBR. Dist: Casemate Academic.

—Temples of Malplaquet. 2005. (Malplaquet Trilogy Ser.). (ENG., Illus.). 192p. (978-0-7188-3046-5(6)) Lutherworth Pr., The.

Dalton, Annie. Budding Star: Mission - Rescue a Pop Princess. 2008. (Mel Beeby Agent Angel Ser.). (ENG.). 208p. (J). (gr. 4-7). pap. 6.95 (978-0-00-720478-6(7)) HarperCollins Pubs. Ltd. GBR. Dist: Independent Pubs. Group.

—The Divine Collection: Three Amazing Missions in One Book! 2008. (Mel Beeby Agent Angel Ser.). (ENG., Illus.). 608p. (J). (gr. 4-7). pap. 19.95 (978-0-00-719074-4(3)) HarperCollins Pubs. Ltd. GBR. Dist: Independent Pubs. Group.

—Feeling the Vibes: Babysit a Buddha! 2008. (Mel Beeby Agent Angel Ser.). (ENG.). 208p. (J). (gr. 4-7). pap. 6.95 (978-0-00-716140-9(9)) HarperCollins Pubs. Ltd. GBR. Dist: Independent Pubs. Group.

—Fighting Fit: Mission - Get into the Gladiator Groove! 2009. (Mel Beeby, Agent Angel Ser.: 6). (ENG.). 192p. (J). (gr. 4-7). pap. 7.99 (978-0-00-720476-2(0)) HarperCollins Pubs. Ltd. GBR. Dist: HarperCollins Pubs.

—Flying High: Mission - Prepare to Party! 2010. (Mel Beeby, Agent Angel Ser.: 3). (ENG.). 144p. (J). (gr. 4-7). pap. 7.99 (978-0-00-720473-1(6)) HarperCollins Pubs. Ltd. GBR. Dist: HarperCollins Pubs.

—Fogging Over: Mission - Take a Trip down Under. 2010. (Mel Beeby, Agent Angel Ser.: 5). (ENG.). 160p. (J). (gr. 4-7). pap. 7.99 (978-0-00-720475-5(2)) HarperCollins Pubs. Ltd. GBR. Dist: HarperCollins Pubs.

—The Heavenly Collection: Three Amazing Missions in One Book! 2010. (Angels Unlimited Ser.). (ENG.). 400p. (J). pap., pap., pap. 14.99 (978-0-00-714406-8(7), HarperCollins Children's Bks.) HarperCollins Pubs. Ltd. GBR. Dist: HarperCollins Pubs.

—Losing the Plot: Mission: Rescue a Teenage Trio! 2008. (Mel Beeby Agent Angel Ser.). (ENG.). 160p. (J). (gr. 4-7). pap. 6.95 (978-0-00-720472-4(8)) HarperCollins Pubs. Ltd. GBR. Dist: Independent Pubs. Group.

—Making Waves: Mission - Foil the Pirates. 2010. (Mel Beeby, Agent Angel Ser.: 7). (ENG.). 208p. (J). (gr. 4-7). pap. 9.99 (978-0-00-720477-9(9)) HarperCollins Pubs. Ltd. GBR. Dist: HarperCollins Pubs.

—Winging It: Mission: Enrol at Angel School! 2008. (Mel Beeby Agent Angel Ser.). (ENG.). 144p. (J). (gr. 4-7). pap. 6.95 (978-0-00-720471-7(X)) HarperCollins Pubs. Ltd. GBR. Dist: Independent Pubs. Group.

Dalton, R. M. The Sisters' Story: The Legend of Queen Brighton & Sister Jasmine. 2012. 146p. 46.72 (978-1-4771-4886-0(8)); pap. 28.03 (978-1-4771-4885-3(X)) Xlibris Corp.

Daly, Stuart. The Final Battle. 2016. (Brotherhood of Thieves Ser.: 3). (ENG.). 336p. (J). (gr. 4-7). pap. 9.99 (978-0-85798-538-5(8)) Random Hse. Australia AUS. Dist: Independent Pubs. Group.

Damian, Gabriela Georgeta. The Chocolate Tree. 2010. 50p. pap. 19.88 (978-0-557-14739-7(5)) Lulu Pr., Inc.

Damiani, AU, Kathleen. Molly O'Brien & the Mark of the Dragon Slayer. 2011. (ENG.). 272p. pap. 15.95 (978-1-936012-55-8(3)) Larson Pubns.

Dandridge, Gwen. The Stone Lions. 2013. 230p. pap. 10.99 (978-0-9893157-8-4(9)) Hickory Tree Publishing.

Dane, Dichira A. Pathway of Pebbles. 2008. 20p. pap. 24.95 (978-1-60703-801-6(3)) America Star Bks.

Daniel, Tony. The Amber Arrow. 2017. (Wulf's Saga Ser.: 2). (ENG.). 416p. (J). (gr. 8-8). 18.99 **(978-1-4814-8253-0(X))** Baen Bks.

Daniel, Tony. The Dragon Hammer. 2016. (Wulf's Saga Ser.: 1). (ENG., Illus.). 512p. (YA). (gr. 8). pap. 11.99 (978-1-4767-8155-6(9)) Baen Bks.

Daniels, April. Dreadnought. 2017. (Nemesis Ser.: 1). (ENG.). 280p. pap. 14.99 (978-1-68230-068-8(4)) Diversion Publishing Corp.

Daniels, Darla. The Magic Ring: Summer Vacation in London. 2012. 30p. 16.95 (978-1-4626-6252-4(8)) America Star Bks.

Daniels, Linda. The Magic Gazebo. 2012. 36p. pap. 18.41 (978-1-4669-6165-4(1)) Trafford Publishing.

Daniels, W. J. The Empress Academy: The Secret of Glittershine. 2009. 144p. pap. 16.95 (978-1-4327-2335-4(9)) Outskirts Pr., Inc.

Darden, Amy. Yesterday Once Again: Guenevere's Quest. 2003. (J). pap. 11.00 (978-0-8059-9238-0(3), RoseDog Bks.) Dorrance Publishing Co., Inc.

D'Argenzio, Gertilyn Elinor. What Color Is Your Happiness? 2012. 24p. pap. 15.99 (978-1-4669-1443-8(2)) Trafford Publishing.

Darkbeast Rebellion. 2014. (ENG., Illus.). 352p. (J). (gr. 5-9). pap. 7.99 (978-1-4424-4209-2(3), McElderry, Margaret K. Bks.) McElderry, Margaret K. Bks.

Darling, Fiona. The Horse's Curse. 2003. 144p. (J). pap. 7.95 (978-0-86327-904-1(X)) Wolfhound Pr. IRL. Dist: Interlink Publishing Group, Inc.

Darling, Tellulah. My Date from Hell. 2013. (Blooming Goddess Trilogy: 2). (ENG.). 388p. (YA). pap. (978-0-9880540-6-6(X)) Te Da Media.

—My Life from Hell. 2014. (Blooming Goddess Trilogy: 3). (ENG.). 414p. (YA). pap. (978-0-9880540-9-7(4)) Te Da Media.

Dashner, James. 13th Reality Complete Set: The Journal of Curious Letters; the Hunt for Dark Infinity; the Blade of Shattered Hope; the Void of Mist & Thunder. 2013. (13th Reality Ser.: Bks. 1-4). (ENG., Illus.). 2096p. (J). (gr. 3-7). pap. 35.99 (978-1-4424-8452-8(7), Aladdin) Simon & Schuster Children's Publishing.

D'Ath, Justin. Pool. 2009. (ENG.). 288p. (Orig.). (YA). 13.95 (978-1-876462-51-2(5), Ford Street Publishing) Hybrid Pubs. AUS. Dist: International Publishers Marketing.

Datsiouk, Andrew. Kristo. 2011. 140p. (gr. 4-6). pap. 12.87 (978-1-4269-5083-4(7)) Trafford Publishing.

Dauphin, Vaya. The Greenstone Garden: The Elementals of Aotearoa, Vol. 2. 2013. viii, 297p. pap. (978-1-74284-346-9(8)) ReadOnTime.

David, Beth. Zorena: And the Medallion of Corandu. 2003. (Illus.). 238p. (YA). per. 13.99 (978-0-9740170-0-6(0), 0-9740170-0-0) David, Elizabeth A.

David, Erica. All Hail the Queen. RH Disney Staff & Robinson, Bill, illus. 2015. (Stepping Stone Book(TM) Ser.: 1). (ENG.). 128p. (J). (gr. 1-4). lib. bdg. 12.99 (978-0-7364-8216-5(4), RH/Disney) Random Hse. Children's Bks.

—Anna & Elsa: Books 1-4 (Disney Frozen), 4 vols. Random House Disney Staff, illus. 2015. (ENG.). 512p. (J). (gr. 1-4). 39.96 (978-0-7364-3459-1(3), RH/Disney) Random Hse. Children's Bks.

David, Karen. The Kingdom of Puli. 2017. (ENG.). 137p. (J). pap. 19.95 **(978-1-78629-744-0(2)**, 67fb35cd-ac8b-44d4-b35b-a168e5be81e7) Austin, Stan AUS. Dist: Bookmasters Distribution.

Davidge, James. Driftwood Ellesmere. Palmer, Judd, illus. 2010. (Driftwood Saga Ser.). (ENG.). 216p. (J). (gr. 8-12). 7.95 (978-1-896209-81-4(5)) Bayeux Arts, Inc. CAN. Dist: Chicago Distribution Ctr.

Davids, Paul. The Fountain of Youth. Davids, Paul, photos by. (Illus.). 56p. (Orig.). (YA). (gr. 5-9). pap. 9.95 (978-0-939031-01-6(9)) Pictorial Legends.

Davidsen, Keith & Hayes, Drew. Hyena, 2 vols., Vol. 1. 2006. (Poison Elves Ser.). (Illus.). 128p. pap. 14.95 (978-1-57989-084-1(9)) Sirius Entertainment, Inc.

Davidson, Danica. Attack on the Overworld: The Overworld Adventures, Book 2. 2015. (Unofficial Overworld Adventure Ser.). (ENG.). 112p. (J). (gr. 1-7). pap. 7.99 (978-1-5107-0276-9(8), Sky Pony Pr.) Skyhorse Publishing Co., Inc.

—Battle with the Wither: An Unofficial Overworld Adventure, Book Six. 2016. (Unofficial Overworld Adventure Ser.). (ENG.). 112p. (J). (gr. 1-7). pap. 7.99 (978-1-5107-1621-6(1), Sky Pony Pr.) Skyhorse Publishing Co., Inc.

Davidson L. Haworth. The Dragon of Prali. 2010. 168p. 22.95 (978-1-4502-0147-6(4)); pap. 12.95 (978-1-4502-0145-2(8)) iUniverse, Inc.

Davidson, Susanna. Stories of Mermaids. 2009. (Young Reading 1 Ser.). 48p. (J). (gr. 2). 6.99 (978-0-7945-2589-7(X), Usborne) EDC Publishing.

—Usborne Stories of Dolls & Fairies. Wanert, Amandine, illus. 2007. (Usborne Ser.). 96p. (J). 9.99 (978-0-7945-1779-3(X), Usborne) EDC Publishing.

Davie, Jan. Arthur's Amulet. 2004. 86p. pap. (978-1-84401-228-2(X)) Athena Pr.

—The Nexus Facilitator. 2006. 96p. pap. (978-1-84401-798-0(2)) Athena Pr.

Davies, Jocelyn. A Radiant Sky. (ENG.). (YA). (gr. 8). 2014. 384p. pap. 9.99 (978-0-06-199070-0(1)) 2013. 368p. 17.99 (978-0-06-199069-4(8)) HarperCollins Pubs. (HarperTeen).

Davis, Adam. Hulk to the Rescue. Lim, Ronald et al, illus. 2015. 32p. (J). **(978-1-4844-5268-4(2))** Little Brown & Co.

Davis, Aubrey. La Grosse Patate. 2004.Tr. of Enormous Potato. (FRE., Illus.). (J). (gr. k-3). spiral bd. (978-0-616-14598-2(5)) Canadian National Institute for the Blind/Institut National Canadien pour les Aveugles.

Davis, Bryan. Beyond the Gateway (Reapers Trilogy V2) 2015. (ENG.). 384p. (YA). pap. 12.99 (978-0-9898122-4-5(3)) Scrub Jay Journeys.

—From the Mouth of Elijah. 2012. (Children of the Bard Ser.: 2). (ENG.). 512p. (YA). (gr. 7). pap. 14.99 (978-0-89957-881-1(0)) AMG Pubs.

Davis, Christine. The Shelter Dog. Davis, Christine, illus. 2008. (Illus.). 32p. (J). (gr. -1-3). 11.95 (978-0-9659225-4-8(5)) Lighthearted Pr., Inc.

Davis, Darren & Davis, Darren G. ABC's for Superheroes. l.t. ed. 2006. (Atlas Ser.). (ENG., Illus.). 12p. (J). (gr. -1-12). 5.99 (978-1-59559-110-4(9)) Bluewater Productions, Inc.

Davis, Darren G. & Misuraca, Thomas J. Maze of the Minotaur. 2003. (10th Muse Ser.: Vol. 1). (ENG., Illus.). 198p. (J). (gr. 4-7). pap. 7.95 (978-0-9664737-4-2(4)) Left Field,Angel Gate.

Davis, Graeme. Re-Read Harry Potter & the Chamber of Secrets Today! an Unauthorized Guide. 2008. 112p. pap. 15.49 (978-1-934840-72-6(6)) Nimble Bks. LLC.

Davis, Izzy. The Croaks at Roaring River, 1 vol. 2009. 40p. pap. 24.95 (978-1-60813-245-4(5)) America Star Bks.

Davis, Kent. A Riddle in Ruby. (Riddle in Ruby Ser.: 1). (J). (gr. 3-7). 2016. 448p. pap. 7.99 (978-0-06-236835-5(4)) 2015. (ENG.). 432p. 17.99 (978-0-06-236834-8(6)) HarperCollins Pubs. (Greenwillow Bks.).

Davis, Kent. A Riddle in Ruby #2: the Changer's Key. 2017. (Riddle in Ruby Ser.: 2). 464p. (J). (gr. 3-7). pap. 7.99 **(978-0-06-236838-6(9)**, Greenwillow Bks.) HarperCollins Pubs.

Davis, Linda. A Chanukah Story. Taub, Udi, illus. 2003. 24p. 12.99 (978-1-58330-652-9(8)) Feldheim Pubs.

Davis, Milton J. Amber & the Hidden City. 2013. 220p. pap. 16.95 (978-0-9800842-7-6(X)) MVmedia.

Davis, Toby K. The Ever Part of Always: Keely Tucker's First Adventure. 2012. 208p. (gr. 4-6). 24.95 (978-1-4697-4592-3(5)); pap. 14.95 (978-1-4697-4591-6(7)) iUniverse, Inc.

Davison, Gail. Prince Alexander. PellerinUndo, Joel Ray, illus. 2016. (ENG.). 28p. (J). pap. 28.22 **(978-1-5245-1787-8(9))** Xlibris Corp.

Dawley, Linda. The Tooth Fairy's Mistake. 2nd ed. 2014. (ENG.). 114p. (J). pap. (978-0-9941011-6-7(3), The Little Red Hen Community Pr.) CCB Publishing.

Dawson, Paola. A Dancing Dream. 2013. 38p. pap. 16.95 (978-1-4497-8297-9(3), WestBow Pr.) Author Solutions, Inc.

Day, K. The Silver Bullet: Tour of the Universe. 2010. 120p. pap. 12.49 (978-1-4490-6534-8(1)) AuthorHouse.

Day, Tracy. The Silver Lining: Book the First of the Kadnohkka Grey Series. 2007. 96p. per. 11.95 (978-1-59858-440-0(5)) Dog Ear Publishing, LLC.

DC Comics Staff. DC Super Friends: Girl Power! 2017. (ENG., Illus.). 16p. (J). bds. 10.99 (978-0-374-30397-6(5), 9780374303976, Farrar, Straus & Giroux (BYR)) Farrar, Straus & Giroux.

DC Super Friends, 1 vol. 2014. (DC Super Friends Ser.). (ENG.). 32p. (gr. 1-2). 271.20 (978-1-4342-9525-5(7)) Stone Arch Bks.

De Bie, Erik Scott. Ghostwalker. 2005. (Fighters Ser.). 318p. (978-1-4156-3838-5(1)) Wizards of the Coast.

De Bonneval, Gwen. William & the Lost Spirit. Smith, Anne, tr. Bonhomme, Matthieu, illus. 2013. (ENG.). 160p. (YA). (gr. 8-12). pap. 9.95 (978-1-4677-0807-4(0), Graphic Universe™) Lerner Publishing Group.

De la Cruz, Melissa. Return to the Isle of the Lost: A Descendants Novel. 2016. (Descendants Ser.). (ENG.). 320p. (J). (gr. 4-7). 17.99 (978-1-4847-8521-8(5)); 17.99 (978-1-4847-8522-5(3)); 17.99 (978-1-4847-8520-1(7)); (Illus.). 17.99 (978-1-4847-5071-1(3)) Hyperion Bks. for Children.

De la Peña, Matt. Eternity. 2014. (Infinity Ring Ser.: 8). (ENG.). 192p. (J). (gr. 3-7). lib. bdg. 16.99 (978-0-545-66770-8(4)); (Illus.). lib. bdg. 12.99 (978-0-545-66535-3(3)) Scholastic, Inc.

de Lint, Charles. The Cats of Tanglewood Forest. Vess, Charles, illus. 2013. (ENG.). 304p. (J). (gr. 3-7). 18.00 (978-0-316-05357-0(0)) Little, Brown Bks. for Young Readers.

—Dingo. 2008. (ENG.). 224p. (YA). (gr. 7-18). 11.99 (978-0-14-240816-2(6), Firebird) Penguin Young Readers Group.

—Seven Wild Sisters: A Modern Fairy Tale. Vess, Charles, illus. 2014. (ENG.). 272p. (J). (gr. 3-7). 18.00 (978-0-316-05356-3(2)) Little, Brown Bks. for Young Readers.

De Long, Robert & De Long, Janice. Redwall Study Guide. 2003. ring bd. 14.99 (978-1-58609-196-5(4)) Progeny Pr.

De Regniers, Beatrice Schenk. Little Sister & the Month Brothers, 0 vols. Tomes, Margot, illus. 2009. (ENG.). 48p. (J). (gr. -1-3). 17.99 (978-0-7614-5546-2(9), 9780761455462, Amazon Children's Publishing) Amazon Publishing.

De Saint-Exupéry, Antoine. The Little Prince. 2015.Tr. of Petit Prince. (HEB.). (J). **(978-965-13-1323-3(4))** Am Oved Pubs., Ltd.

—The Little Prince.Tr. of Petit Prince. 17.95 (978-0-89190-331-4(3)) Amereon Ltd.

—The Little Prince. deluxe ed. 2015. (Little Prince Ser.).Tr. of Petit Prince. (ENG., Illus.). 72p. (J). (gr. 5-7). 35.00 (978-0-544-65649-9(0), HMH Books For Young Readers) Houghton Mifflin Harcourt Publishing Co.

—The Little Prince. Kahler, Evan & Woods, Katherine, trs. 2016.Tr. of Petit Prince. (ENG., Illus.). (J). (gr. 3-7). **(978-1-77323-014-6(X))** Rehak, David.

—The Little Prince. Hill, Rowland, tr. Gormand, Caroline, illus. 2016.Tr. of Petit Prince. (ENG.). (J). (gr. 3-6). pap. **(978-2-89687-592-4(1))** chouetteditions.com.

—The Little Prince Coloring Book: Beautiful Images for You to Color & Enjoy... 2015. (Little Prince Ser.). (ENG., Illus.). 96p. (gr. 6). 12.99 (978-0-544-79258-6(0), HMH Books For Young Readers) Houghton Mifflin Harcourt Publishing Co.

—Le Petit Prince. 2016. (FRE., Illus.). (J). pap. **(978-5-521-00151-4(4))** Books on Demand.

—Le Petit Prince. 2010. (CHI., Illus.). 128p. (J). (gr. 3-7). (978-986-7897-01-5(3)) Ecus Publishing Hse.

—Le Petit Prince. 2010. (CHI.). 132p. (J). (gr. 5-8). pap. (978-986-189-225-2(7)) Grimm Cultural Ent., Co., Ltd.

—Le Petit Prince. Gormand, Caroline, illus. 2016. (FRE.). (J). (gr. 3-6). pap. **(978-2-89687-593-1(X))** chouetteditions.com.

—Il Piccolo Principe.Tr. of Little Prince. (ITA.). 2014. 106p. pap. 6.50 (978-1-4992-7698-5(2)) 2013. 96p. pap. 12.00 (978-1-4948-5566-6(6)) 2013. 106p. pap. 6.50 (978-1-4948-4773-9(6)) CreateSpace Independent Publishing Platform.

—Il Piccolo Principe.Tr. of Little Prince. (ITA.). pap. 17.95 (978-88-452-4741-5(4)) Fabbri Editori - RCS Libri ITA. Dist: Distribooks, Inc.

—EL PRINCIPITO. 2016. (SPA.). 96p. (YA). (gr. 6-9). 16.95 (978-84-7888-629-6(X)) Publicaciones y Ediciones Salamandra, S.A. ESP. Dist: Spanish Pubs., LLC.

De Saint-Exupéry, Antoine & Hemerman, Ilana. The Little Prince. 2013.Tr. of Petit Prince. (HEB.). (J). **(978-965-13-0883-3(4))**; 90p. *(978-965-13-2376-8(0))* Am Oved Pubs., Ltd.

Deak, Mike. The Magical Land of Kallamazoo. 2011. 52p. pap. 22.28 *(978-1-4520-4915-1(7))* AuthorHouse.

Dean, Pamela. The Secret Country. 2003. (ENG.). 384p. (YA). (gr. 7-18). pap. 8.99 *(978-0-14-250153-5(0)*, Firebird) Penguin Young Readers Group.

—The Whim of the Dragon. 2003. (ENG.). 400p. (YA). (gr. 7). 8.99 *(978-0-14-250161-0(1)*, Firebird) Penguin Young Readers Group.

Deary, Terry. The Fire Thief. 2005. (Fire Thief Trilogy: Bk. 1). 253p. (J). *(978-1-4156-3464-6(5)*, Kingfisher) Roaring Brook Pr.

Deas, Stephen. The Thief-Taker's Apprentice: With a Sword, Comes Blood... 2011. (ENG.). 320p. (gr. 13-17). 14.99 *(978-0-575-09449-9(4)*, Gollancz) Orion Publishing Group, Ltd. GBR. Dist: Hachette Bk. Group.

Debaer-Levoy, Carole. The Story of Candyland. 2007. 40p. per. 13.95 *(978-1-59858-328-1(X))* Dog Ear Publishing, LLC.

DeBonis, Todd DeBonis. The SwordMaster of Ashland -Book One- 2007. 300p. (YA). per. 20.00 net. *(978-0-9678094-1-0(X))* DVTVFilm.

Decker, Wendy. The Bedazzling Bowl. 2006. pap. 13.99 *(978-1-60034-468-8(2))* Salem Author Services.

DEE and AMA, The Toybox Grannies. Katie & Savannah - Special Edition. 2009. 216p. pap. 21.89 *(978-0-557-04568-6(1))* Lulu Pr., Inc.

Dee, Katya. Orna Puella, 1 vol. 2009. 194p. pap. 24.95 *(978-1-61582-195-2(3))* PublishAmerica, Inc.

Defabio, Richard Bryan. The Magic Spoon. 2011. 42p. pap. 21.99 *(978-1-4568-1773-2(6))* Xlibris Corp.

Defalco, Tom, et al. Thor Epic Collection: War of the Pantheons. Frenz, Ron et al, illus. 2013. (ENG.). 472p. (J). (gr. 4-17). pap. 34.99 *(978-0-7851-8788-2(X))* Marvel Worldwide, Inc.

Defilippis, Nunzio & Weir, Christina. The Avalon Chronicles, Vol. 2. 2013. (ENG., Illus.). 152p. (YA). 19.99 *(978-1-934964-90-3(5)*, 9781934964903) Oni Pr., Inc.

—Avalon Chronicles Volume 1: Once in a Blue Moon. 2012. (ENG., Illus.). 152p. 19.99 *(978-1-934964-75-0(1)*, 9781934964750) Oni Pr., Inc.

DeGreeff, Davy. Tommy Bomani: Land of Legend, 1 vol. Brookins, Sam, illus. 2010. (Tommy Bomani: Teen Warrior Ser.: Bk. 2). (ENG.). 112p. (gr. 3-8). 27.07 *(978-1-60270-698-9(0)*, Calico Chapter Bks) Magic Wagon.

—Tommy Bomani: Prophecy Fulfilled, 1 vol. Brookins, Sam, illus. 2010. (Tommy Bomani: Teen Warrior Ser.: Bk. 4). (ENG.). 112p. (gr. 3-8). 27.07 *(978-1-60270-700-9(6)*, Calico Chapter Bks) Magic Wagon.

Deisher, Kathleen E. Beyond the Gloesmur: In the Gloesmur Scrolls. Deisher, Kathleen E., illus. 2003. (Gloesmur Scrolls Ser.: Bk. 1). (Illus.). 270p. (J). pap. 13.95 *(978-1-892135-00-1(0))* Lamp Post Publishing, Inc.

Deiss, A. G. & Emi. The Sad Tale of Emmaline Austin, Monkey-Girl. 2005. 23p. 10.67 *(978-1-4116-5439-6(0))* Lulu Pr., Inc.

del Rio, Tania. Sabrina the Teenage Witch: the Magic Within 1. 2013. (Sabrina Manga Ser.). (ENG., Illus.). 256p. (J). (gr. 4-7). 10.99 *(978-1-936975-39-6(4)*, Archie Comics) Archie Comic Pubns., Inc.

—Sabrina the Teenage Witch: the Magic Within 3. 2013. (Sabrina Manga Ser.: 3). (ENG., Illus.). 256p. (J). (gr. 4-7). pap. 10.99 *(978-1-936975-60-0(2)*, Archie Comics) Archie Comic Pubns., Inc.

—Sabrina the Teenage Witch: the Magic Within 4. 2014. (Sabrina Manga Ser.: 4). (ENG., Illus.). 272p. (J). (gr. 4-7). pap. 10.99 *(978-1-936975-76-1(9)*, Archie Comics) Archie Comic Pubns., Inc.

del Toro, Guillermo & Kraus, Daniel. Trollhunters. Murray, Sean, illus. (Trollhunters Ser.). (ENG.). 320p. (YA). (gr. 7-12). 2016. pap. 9.99 **(978-1-368-01218-8(3)**, 1380291) 2015. 18.99 *(978-1-4231-2598-3(3)*, 1380291) Hyperion Bks. for Children.

Del Vecchio, Gene. The Pearl of Anton, 1 vol. 2004. (ENG., Illus.). 256p. (YA). (gr. 6-10). 16.95 *(978-1-58980-172-1(5))* Pelican Publishing Co., Inc.

del Vecchio, Gene & Del Vecchio, Gene. The Sword of Anton, 1 vol. 2006. (ENG., Illus.). 248p. (YA). (gr. 6-10). 16.95 *(978-1-58980-304-6(3))* Pelican Publishing Co., Inc.

Delaney, Joseph. The Dark Army. 2017. 416p. (YA). (gr. 8). pap. 9.99 **(978-0-06-233457-2(3)**, Greenwillow Bks.) HarperCollins Pubs.

—Grimalkin the Witch Assassin, Bk. 9. Arrasmith, Patrick, illus. 2013. (Last Apprentice Ser.: 9). (ENG.). 416p. (YA). (gr. 8). pap. 9.99 *(978-0-06-208208-4(6)*, Greenwillow Bks.) HarperCollins Pubs.

—I Am Alice, Bk. 12. Arrasmith, Patrick, illus. 2014. (Last Apprentice Ser.: 12). (ENG.). 464p. (YA). (gr. 8). pap. 9.99 *(978-0-06-171515-0(8)*, Greenwillow Bks.) HarperCollins Pubs.

—The Last Apprentice - I Am Alice, Bk. 12. Arrasmith, Patrick, illus. 2013. (Last Apprentice Ser.: 12). (ENG.). 448p. (YA). (gr. 8). 17.99 *(978-0-06-171513-6(1)*, Greenwillow Bks.) HarperCollins Pubs.

—The Last Apprentice: the Spook's Bestiary: The Guide to Creatures of the Dark. Heller, Julek, illus. 2014. (Last Apprentice Short Fiction Ser.: 3). (ENG.). 240p. (YA). (gr. 8). pap. 8.99 *(978-0-06-208115-5(2)*, Greenwillow Bks.) HarperCollins Pubs.

—Lure of the Dead. Arrasmith, Patrick, illus. (Last Apprentice Ser.: 10). (ENG.). (YA). (gr. 8). 2013. 448p. pap. 9.99 *(978-0-06-202762-7(X))*Bk. 10. 2012. 432p. 17.99 *(978-0-06-202760-3(3))* HarperCollins Pubs. (Greenwillow Bks.).

—The Seventh Son, Bks. 1 & 2. 2014. (Last Apprentice Ser.). (ENG.). 704p. (J). (gr. 8). pap. 10.99 *(978-0-06-220970-2(1)*, Greenwillow Bks.) HarperCollins Pubs.

Deluca, Alison. Christmas O'Clock: A Collection. Daly, Lisa, illus. 2013. 198p. pap. 9.99 *(978-1-939296-98-6(6))* Myrddin Publishing Group.

DeLuise, Dom & Brown, Tim. No Place Like Home. 2007. 240p. pap. 9.95 *(978-0-9769369-1-6(7))* Bacchus Bks.

DeMasque, Catherine. The Quest of the White Stag. 2011. (ENG.). 346p. per. 16.95 *(978-0-9725230-3-5(0))* Wandering Sage Pubns., LLC.

DeMatteis, J. M. Stardust Kid. Ploog, Mike, illus. 2008. (ENG.). 128p. pap. 14.99 *(978-1-934506-04-2(4))* Boom! Studios.

Demetrios, Heather. Blood Passage. 2017. (Dark Caravan Cycle Ser.: 2). 512p. (YA). (gr. 8). pap. 9.99 *(978-0-06-231860-2(8))* HarperCollins Pubs.

—Freedom's Slave. 2017. (Dark Caravan Cycle Ser.: 3). 608p. (YA). (gr. 8). 17.99 *(978-0-06-231862-6(4))* HarperCollins Pubs.

DeMeulemeester, Linda. The Forgotten Secret. 2016. (ENG.). 208p. (J). pap. **(978-1-77203-100-3(3)**, Wandering Fox) Heritage Hse.

DeMonte, Joe. Lucy & the Magic Factory. 2008. 79p. pap. 19.95 *(978-1-60813-119-8(X))* America Star Bks.

Denkhaus, Henry. Anna & the Magical Horse - Henry the Hobo - the Pond. 2013. 50p. pap. 8.99 *(978-1-4624-0734-7(X)*, Inspiring Voices) Author Solutions, Inc.

Dennard, Susan. A Darkness Strange & Lovely. (Something Strange & Deadly Trilogy Ser.: 2). 432p. (YA). (gr. 9). 2017. pap. 9.99 *(978-0-06-265816-6(6))* 2014. (ENG.). pap. 9.99 *(978-0-06-208330-2(9))* HarperCollins Pubs. (HarperTeen).

—Windwitch. 2017. (ENG., Illus.). (Witchlands Ser.). 380p. (J). (gr. 8-12). pap. 12.99 **(978-0-7653-9579-5(7))**; (Witchlands Ser.: 2). 384p. (YA). 18.99 *(978-0-7653-7930-6(9)*, 9780765379306) Doherty, Tom Assocs., LLC. (Tor Teen).

Denning, Richard. The Catacombs of Vanaheim. 2013. (Illus.). 240p. (J). pap. *(978-0-9568103-4-2(9))* Mercia Bks.

Dennis, Kingsley L. Mundus Grundy: Trouble in Grundusland. 2015. (ENG.). 160p. (J). (gr. -1-12). pap. 11.95 *(978-1-78535-047-4(1)*, Our Street Bks.) Hunt, John Publishing Ltd. GBR. Dist: National Bk. Network.

Dennis, Peter, illus. The Adventures of King Arthur. 2003. (Usborne Young Reading: Series Two Ser.). 64p. (J). (gr. k-7). 8.99 *(978-0-7945-1871-4(0)*, Usborne) EDC Publishing.

Dent, Sue. Never Ceese: Can Two Who Were Wronged Make It Right? 2006. 336p. (YA). lib. bdg. 17.99 *(978-1-59958-017-3(9))* Journey Stone Creations, LLC.

dePaola, Tomie. Strega Nona Does It Again. dePaola, Tomie, illus. 2013. (ENG., Illus.). 40p. (J). (gr. -1-3). 17.99 *(978-0-399-25781-0(0)*, Nancy Paulsen Books) Penguin Young Readers Group.

Derdowski, Chad. All Robots Must Die: Nacho-Geddon. 2013. 187p. (J). pap. 7.99 *(978-1-933925-50-9(7)*, Agent of Danger) Komikwerks, LLC.

Derting, Kimberly. The Essence. 2013. (Pledge Trilogy Ser.). (ENG., Illus.). (YA). (gr. 9). 368p. pap. 9.99 *(978-1-4424-4560-4(2))*; 352p. 16.99 *(978-1-4424-4559-8(9))* McElderry, Margaret K. Bks. (McElderry, Margaret K. Bks.).

—The Offering: A Pledge Novel. 2015. (Pledge Trilogy Ser.). (ENG., Illus.). 304p. (YA). (gr. 9). pap. 11.99 *(978-1-4424-4563-5(7)*, McElderry, Margaret K. Bks.) McElderry, Margaret K. Bks.

—The Pledge. (Pledge Trilogy Ser.). (ENG., Illus.). (YA). (gr. 9). 2012. 352p. pap. 10.99 *(978-1-4424-2202-5(5))* 2011. 336p. 16.99 *(978-1-4424-2201-8(7))* McElderry, Margaret K. Bks. (McElderry, Margaret K. Bks.).

Desautels, Jodi. There Were Always Noises. 2012. 20p. pap. 24.95 *(978-1-4626-8628-5(1))* PublishAmerica, Inc.

Despain, Bree. The Savage Grace. 2013. (ENG.). 496p. (J). (gr. 7). pap. 9.99 *(978-1-60684-416-8(4)*, Carolrhoda Lab™) Lerner Publishing Group.

Desrosiers, Sylvie. Aimez-Vous la Musique? Sylvestre, Daniel, illus. 2004. (Roman Jeunesse Ser.). (FRE.). 96p. (J). (gr. 4-7). pap. *(978-2-89021-709-6(4))* Diffusion du livre Mirabel (DLM).

Dessen, Sarah. Dreamland. 2004. (ENG.). 272p. (YA). (gr. 7-11). pap. 10.99 *(978-0-14-240175-0(7)*, Speak) Penguin Young Readers Group.

DeStefano, Lauren. A Curious Tale of the In-Between. 2016. (ENG.). 256p. (J). pap. 7.99 *(978-1-61963-602-6(6)*, 9781619636026, Bloomsbury USA Childrens) Bloomsbury Publishing USA.

DeStefano, Lauren. The Glass Spare. 2017. (Glass Spare Ser.: 1). 416p. (YA). (gr. 8). 17.99 **(978-0-06-249128-2(8))** HarperCollins Pubs.

Deutsch, Barry & Hansen Literary Agency Staff. Hereville: How Mirka Got Her Sword. 2010. (Hereville Ser.). (ENG., Illus.). 144p. (J). (gr. 3-7). 17.99 *(978-0-8109-8422-6(9)*, Amulet Bks.) Abrams, Inc.

Devers, Joe. Dungeons of Torgar. (Illus.). (J). (gr. k-6). 5.95 *(978-0-09-951250-9(5))* Random Hse. GBR. Dist: Trafalgar Square Publishing.

DeVita, James. The Silenced. 2007. 512p. (J). (gr. 8-12). lib. bdg. 18.89 *(978-0-06-078464-5(4)*, HarperTeen) HarperCollins Pubs.

—The Silenced: A Novel. 2015. (ENG.). 448p. (gr. 6). pap. 12.00 *(978-1-57131-937-1(9))* Milkweed Editions.

DeVita, James & Devita, James. The Silenced. 2007. (ENG.). 368p. (J). (gr. 8-12). 17.99 *(978-0-06-078462-1(8)*, HarperTeen) HarperCollins Pubs.

Dhariwal, Radhika R. The Tale of a No-Name Squirrel. Benjaminsen, Audrey, illus. 2016. (ENG.). 384p. (J). (gr. 3-7). 16.99 *(978-1-4814-4475-0(1)*, Simon & Schuster Bks. For Young Readers) Simon & Schuster Bks. For Young Readers.

Dharma Publishing Staff. Great Gift & the Wish-Fulfilling Gem: A Story about the Wish to Help Others. 2010. (ENG.). 36p. (gr. -1-7). pap. 8.95 *(978-0-89800-600-1(7))* Dharma Publishing.

—The King Who Understood Animals: A Story about Using Knowledge Wisely. 2nd ed. 2013. (ENG.). 36p. (gr. -1-7). pap. 8.95 *(978-0-89800-520-2(5))* Dharma Publishing.

—The Power of a Promise: A Story about the Power of Keeping Promises. 2010. (ENG.). 36p. (gr. -1-7). pap. 8.95 *(978-0-89800-603-2(1))* Dharma Publishing.

Di Fabbio, Nancy. Midnight Magic: Be Careful What You Wish For! 2011. 240p. (gr. 4-6). 25.95 *(978-1-4502-9147-7(3))*; pap. 15.95 *(978-1-4502-9145-3(7))* iUniverse, Inc.

Di Santo, Melina. Mel & her Magic Journey. 2010. (Illus.). 32p. 14.49 *(978-1-4490-6889-9(8))* AuthorHouse.

Diablo - Race Against Time. 2006. (J). *(978-1-933343-29-7(X)*, PONY) Stabenfeldt Inc.

Diamond, Laura. Shifting Pride. 2013. 270p. pap. 13.99 *(978-1-940223-02-5(4))* Etopia Pr.

Diaz, Luis. The Dream. 2010. 166p. pap. 12.98 *(978-0-557-09653-4(7))* Lulu Pr., Inc.

DiCamillo, Kate. Flora & Ulysses: The Illuminated Adventures. Campbell, K. G., illus. (ENG.). (J). (gr. 3-7). 2016. pap. 6.99 *(978-0-7636-8764-9(2))* 2013. 240p. 17.99 *(978-0-7636-6040-6(X))* Candlewick Pr.

—Flora & Ulysses: The Illuminated Adventures. Campbell, K. G., illus. 2016. (ENG.). 256p. (J). (gr. 3-7). 17.20 *(978-0-606-39100-9(2))* Turtleback Bks.

—Flora & Ulysses: The Illuminated Adventures. 2015. lib. bdg. 19.65 *(978-0-606-36861-2(2))* Turtleback Bks.

—The Magician's Elephant. Tanaka, Yoko, illus. (ENG.). (J). (gr. 3-7). 2015. 224p. pap. 7.99 *(978-0-7636-8088-6(5))* 2009. 208p. 16.99 *(978-0-7636-4410-9(2))* Candlewick Pr.

—The Magician's Elephant. Lt. ed. 2010. (ENG.). 242p. 23.95 *(978-1-4104-2493-8(6))* Thorndike Pr.

—The Magician's Elephant. 2015. lib. bdg. 17.20 *(978-0-606-37891-8(X))* 2011. lib. bdg. 17.20 *(978-0-606-15375-1(6)*, Turtleback) Turtleback Bks.

Dickens, Charles. A Christmas Carol. Lynch, P. J., illus. 2006. (ENG.). 160p. (Orig.). (J). (gr. 5-6). 19.99 *(978-0-7636-3120-8(5))* Candlewick Pr.

Dickinson, Peter. Earth & Air: Tales of Elemental Creatures. 2012. (ENG.). 256p. (J). (gr. 4). pap. 14.95 *(978-1-61873-038-1(X)*, Big Mouth Hse.) Small Beer Pr.

—The Lion Tamer's Daughter & Other Stories. 2015. (ENG.). 230p. (J). (gr. 7-10). pap. 12.99 *(978-1-5040-1499-1(5))* Open Road Integrated Media, Inc.

—The Ropemaker. Andrew, Ian, illus. 2004. 375p. (gr. 7). 17.95 *(978-0-7569-1935-1(5))* Perfection Learning Corp.

—The Ropemaker. 2003. (ENG.). 384p. (YA). (gr. 7). pap. 8.99 *(978-0-385-73063-1(2)*, Delacorte Bks. for Young Readers) Random Hse. Children's Bks.

Dickson, Diane. Daisy & the Dust Angel. 2010. 35p. pap. 20.50 *(978-1-4452-1375-0(3))* Lulu Pr., Inc.

Digby, Anne. First Term at Trebizon. 2016. (Trebizon Ser.). (ENG., Illus.). 192p. (J). (gr. 3-5). pap. 10.99 *(978-1-4052-8063-1(8))* Egmont Bks., Ltd. GBR. Dist: Independent Pubs. Group.

DiGenti, Victor. Windrusher. 2nd ed. 2004. 280p. per. 15.95 *(978-1-59411-098-6(0))* Writers' Collective, The.

DiGerolamo, Tony. The Wildsidhe Chronicles Bk. 5: The Undercover Dragon. 2003. (J). pap. 7.99 *(978-1-890096-17-5(2))* Padwolf Publishing, Inc.

Dillon, Doug. Stepping off a Cliff [the St. Augustine Trilogy: The St. Augustine Trilogy: Book II. 2013. (ENG., Illus.). 394p. (YA). pap. 13.99 *(978-0-9833684-3-4(0))* Old St. Augustine Pubns.

Dillon, Sally Pierson. Exile of the Chosen: God's Heroes from Solomon to Malachi. 2003. (Pathfinder Junior Book Club Ser.). 223p. (J). pap. 10.99 *(978-0-8280-1703-9(4)*, 58-710) Review & Herald Publishing Assn.

Dilloway, Margaret. Momotaro Xander & the Lost Island of Monsters. Yung, Choong, illus. 2016. (Momotaro Ser.). (ENG.). 310p. (J). (gr. 3-7). 16.99 *(978-1-4847-2487-3(9))* Disney Publishing Worldwide.

Dimarco, Tony. The Three Keys. Mallette, Dania, illus. 2010. 146p. pap. 9.95 *(978-0-9818391-2-7(6))* Panoply Pubns.

DiMartino, Michael Dante. Rebel Genius. 2016. (Rebel Geniuses Ser.). (ENG., Illus.). 384p. (J). 16.99 *(978-1-62672-336-8(2)*, 9781626723368) Roaring Brook Pr.

DiMartino, Michael Dante & Konietzko, Bryan, creators. Avatar, Vol. 5. 2007. (Avatar Ser.). (Illus.). 104p. pap. 7.99 *(978-1-59816-929-4(7)*, Tokyopop Kids) TOKYOPOP, Inc.

Dimpel, Matt. The War of the Serpent Swords. 2011. 230p. pap. 24.95 *(978-1-4626-3169-8(X))* PublishAmerica, Inc.

Ding, Sean. Zediogram. 2013. 118p. pap. *(978-981-07-5534-8(1))* Lukano Publishing Pte, Ltd.

Ding, Yuhui Andrew. Warrior Soul. 2009. 28p. pap. 15.99 *(978-1-4415-6734-5(8))* Xlibris Corp.

Dinn, Philip & Jones, Andy. Peg Bearskin. Cohen, Elly, illus. 2003. (ENG.). 32p. (J). pap. *(978-0-9688712-7-0(5))* Running the Goat.

Dinsdale, Christopher. Broken Circle. 2004. (ENG.). 104p. (J). pap. 7.95 *(978-1-894917-15-5(4)*, Napoleon & Co.) Dundurn CAN. Dist: Ingram Publisher Services.

Disney, ed. Big Learning Superstar: Read & Sing. 2009. (ENG.). 20p. 16.99 *(978-1-59069-835-8(5))* Studio Mouse LLC.

Disney Book Group. Descendants: Mal's Diary. Disney Storybook Art Team, illus. 2015. (ENG.). 192p. (J). (gr. 3-7). 9.99 *(978-1-4847-2685-3(5))* Disney Pr.

—Descendants: Mal's Spell Book. Disney Storybook Art Team, illus. 2015. (ENG.). 192p. (J). (gr. 3-7). 11.99 *(978-1-4847-2638-9(3))* Disney Pr.

—Goldie & Bear Training of the Broom. 2017. (ENG.). 24p. (J). (gr. -1-k). pap. 4.99 **(978-1-368-00856-3(9))** Disney Pr.

—Mal's Spell, Bk. 2. Disney Storybook Art Team, illus. 2017. (ENG.). 192p. (J). (gr. 3-7). 12.99 **(978-1-368-00041-3(X))** Disney Pr.

—World of Reading: Elena of Avalor the Secret Spell Book: Level 2. Disney Storybook Art Team, illus. 2017. (World of Reading Ser.). (ENG.). 32p. (J). (gr. 1-3). pap. 4.99 *(978-1-4847-4793-3(3))* Disney Pr.

—World of Reading Star Wars Rebels Kanan's Jedi Training: Level 2. 2015. (World of Reading Ser.). (ENG.). 32p. (J). (gr. 1-3). pap. 3.99 *(978-1-4847-0563-6(7)*, Disney Lucasfilm Press) Disney Publishing Worldwide.

—5-Minute Spider-Man Stories. Disney Book Group, illus. 2013. (5-Minute Stories Ser.). (ENG., Illus.). 192p. (J). (gr. 1-3). 12.99 *(978-1-4231-7786-9(X))* Marvel Worldwide, Inc.

Disney Book Group & Rucka, Greg. Guardians of the Whills. 2017. (ENG.). 240p. (J). (gr. 5-9). 12.99 *(978-1-4847-8081-7(7)*, Disney Lucasfilm Press) Disney Publishing Worldwide.

Disney Book Group & Rudnick, Elizabeth. A Frozen Heart. Disney Storybook Art Team, illus. 2015. (ENG.). 304p. (J). (gr. 5-9). 14.99 *(978-1-4847-3051-5(8))* Disney Pr.

Disney Book Group, et al. Stealing Starlight. Disney Storybook Art Team, illus. 2017. (Star Darlings Ser.: 1). (ENG.). 224p. (J). (gr. 3-7). 12.99 *(978-1-4847-5639-3(8))* Disney Pr.

Disney Book Group Staff. Brave. 2012. (Read-Along Storybook & CD Ser.). (ENG.). 32p. (J). (gr. -1-k). pap. 6.99 *(978-1-4231-3770-2(1))* Disney Pr.

—Cinderella. Disney Storybook Artists Staff, illus. 2nd ed. 2012. (Read-Along Storybook & CD Ser.). (ENG.). 32p. (J). (gr. -1 — 1). pap. 6.99 *(978-1-4231-6321-3(4))* Disney Pr.

—Disney Bedtime Favorites. Disney Storybook Artists Staff & Disney Book Group Staff, illus. 2012. (Storybook Collection). (ENG.). 304p. (J). (gr. -1 — 1). 15.99 *(978-1-4231-6034-2(7))* Disney Pr.

—Disney Princess, Set. 2012. (ENG.). 272p. pap. 12.99 *(978-1-4231-5533-1(5))* Disney Pr.

—Finding Nemo. 2012. (Read-Along Storybook & CD Ser.). (ENG.). 912p. (J). (gr. -1 — 1). pap. 6.99 *(978-1-4231-6028-1(2))* Disney Pr.

—Iron Man vs. Titanium Man. Disney Storybook Artists Staff, illus. 2013. (Marvel Super Hero vs. Book Ser.). (ENG.). 24p. (J). (gr. -1-k). pap. 3.99 *(978-1-4231-5469-3(X))* Marvel Worldwide, Inc.

—The Little Mermaid Read-Along Storybook & CD. Disney Storybook Artists Staff, illus. 2013. (Read-Along Storybook & CD Ser.). (ENG.). 32p. (J). (gr. -1-k). pap. 6.99 *(978-1-4231-6889-8(5))* Disney Pr.

—Peter Pan Read-Along Storybook & CD. Disney Storybook Art Team, illus. 2013. (Read-Along Storybook & CD Ser.). (ENG.). 32p. (J). (gr. -1-k). pap. 6.99 *(978-1-4231-8034-0(8))* Disney Pr.

—Teen Beach Movie. 2013. (ENG.). 128p. (J). (gr. 5-9). pap. 5.99 *(978-1-4231-7790-6(8))* Disney Pr.

Disney Book Group Staff & Green, Rico. Descendants: Junior Novel. Disney Storybook Art Team, illus. 2015. (ENG.). 176p. (J). (gr. 5-9). 10.99 *(978-1-4847-2614-3(6))* Disney Pr.

Disney Book Group Staff & Hapka, Catherine. Sofia the First. Lee, Grace, illus. 2012. (ENG.). 40p. (J). (gr. -1-k). 15.99 *(978-1-4231-6986-4(7))* Disney Pr.

Disney Book Group Staff & Richards, Kitty. The Lost Tiara. Disney Storybook Art Team & Studio Iboix Staff, illus. 2012. (Jewel Story Ser.). (ENG.). 96p. (J). (gr. 1-3). pap. 4.99 *(978-1-4231-5197-5(6))* Disney Pr.

Disney Book Group Staff, et al. The Avengers. 2015. (Beginnings Ser.). (ENG.). 48p. (J). (gr. 1-3). 12.99 *(978-1-4847-1382-2(6)*, Marvel Pr.) Disney Publishing Worldwide.

Disney Editors. Opposites Attract. 2017. (Tales of Rapunzel Ser.: 2). lib. bdg. 16.00 **(978-0-606-40248-4(9))** Turtleback Bks.

Disney Press Staff. School's Out. 2010. 128p. pap. 4.99 *(978-1-4231-2677-5(7))* Disney Pr.

Disney Princess Staff, adapted by. Princess Enchanted Palace: Storybook & Play Castle. 2010. (Playbox Ser.). (ENG., Illus.). 32p. (J). (gr. -1-2). bds. 19.99 *(978-0-7944-2035-2(4))* Reader's Digest Assn., Inc., The.

Disney Sofia the First, Disney Sofia. Disney Sofia the First Movie Theater Storybook & Movie Projector. 2014. (Movie Theater Ser.: 15). (ENG.). 32p. (J). (gr. -1-1). 19.99 *(978-0-7944-3138-9(0)*, Reader's Digest Children's Bks.) Studio Fun International.

Disney Storybook Art Team, illus. Disney Deluxe Storybook Treasury. 2016. (Storybook Treasury Ser.). (ENG.). 256p. (J). (gr. 1-3). 30.00 *(978-1-4847-8960-5(1))* Disney Pr.

—Legend of the Neverbeast. 2015. (Read-Along Storybook & CD Ser.). (ENG.). 32p. (J). (gr. 1-3). pap. 6.99 *(978-1-4847-1075-3(4))* Disney Pr.

Disney Storybook Artists Staff. Rapunzel's Dream: Storybook with Musical Hairbrush. 2010. (ENG., Illus.). 32p. (J). (gr. -1-3). 19.99 *(978-0-7944-2024-6(9))* Reader's Digest Assn., Inc., The.

Disneys Cinderella Palace. 2005. (Illus.). 10p. (J). bds. 10.50 *(978-1-4127-3349-6(9)*, 7249700) Publications International, Ltd.

Distler, Christine A. Pegasus: The Introduction. 2005. 84p. pap. 11.95 *(978-1-59113-763-4(2))* Booklocker.com, Inc.

DiTerlizzi, Tony & Black, Holly. Lucinda's Secret, BK. 3. DiTerlizzi, Tony, illus. 3rd ed. 2003. (Spiderwick Chronicles Ser.: 3). (ENG., Illus.). 128p. (J). (gr. 2-7). 12.99 *(978-0-689-85938-0(4)*, Simon & Schuster Bks. For Young Readers) Simon & Schuster Bks. For Young Readers.

—The Spiderwick Chronicles Vols. 1-5, Set: The Field Guide - The Seeing Stone - Lucinda's Secret - The Ironwood Tree - The Wrath of Mulgrath. DiTerlizzi, Tony & Black, Holly, illus. 2004. (Spiderwick Chronicles Ser.). (ENG., Illus.). 672p. (J). (gr. 2-6). 59.99 *(978-0-689-04034-4(2)*, Simon & Schuster Bks. For Young Readers) Simon & Schuster Bks. For Young Readers.

DiTerlizzi, Tony, et al. El Anteojo Asombroso. 2007. (Spiderwick Cronicas). (SPA., Illus.). 116p. (J). (gr. 4-7). 13.95 *(978-84-666-1280-7(7))* Ediciones B ESP. Dist: Spanish Pubs., LLC.

—El Libro Fantástico. Abreu, Carlos, tr. 2007. (Crónicas Spiderwick). (SPA., Illus.). 116p. (J). (gr. 4-7). 13.95 *(978-84-666-1279-1(3))* Ediciones B ESP. Dist: Spanish Pubs., LLC.

DiTocco, Robyn & DiTocco, Tony. Atlas' Revenge: Another Mad Myth Mystery. 2005. 234p. 19.95 *(978-0-9723429-2-6(3))*; pap. 11.95 *(978-0-9723429-3-3(1))* Brainstorm Pubns., Inc.

—The Hero Perseus: A Mad Myth Mystery. 2004. 220p. (gr. 3-12). 19.95 *(978-0-9723429-0-2(7))*; pap. 11.95 *(978-0-9723429-1-9(5))* Brainstorm Pubns., Inc.

Divakaruni, Chitra Banerjee. The Conch Bearer. 2005. (ENG.). 272p. (J). (gr. 3-7). reprint ed. pap. 8.99 *(978-0-689-87242-6(9)*, Aladdin) Simon & Schuster Children's Publishing.

Divine, Miss Jill. The alien who came to Tea. 2009. (Illus.). 88p. pap. 10.50 *(978-1-4092-8010-1(1))* Lulu Pr., Inc.

Dixon, Andy. Dragon Quest. Brooks, Felicity, ed. Harris, Nick, illus. rev. ed. 2005. (Usborne Fantasy Puzzle Bks.). 32p. (J). (gr. 3-7). per. 7.99 *(978-0-7945-1098-5(1)*, Usborne) EDC Publishing.

—Star Quest. Brooks, Felicity, ed. Harris, Nick, illus. 2006. (Usborne Fantasy Puzzle Bks.). 32p. (YA). (gr. 7). lib. bdg. 15.99 *(978-1-58086-906-5(8)*, Usborne) EDC Publishing.

—Sword Quest. Brooks, Felicity, ed. Boni, Simone, illus. rev. ed. 2005. (Usborne Fantasy Puzzle Bks.). 31p. (J). (gr. 3-7). pap., pap. 7.95 *(978-0-7945-1096-1(5)*, Usborne) EDC Publishing.

Dixon, Danielle. Project: Purest. 2012. 370p. pap. 19.99 *(978-1-4691-8247-6(5))* Xlibris Corp.

Dixon, Heather. Entwined. (ENG.). 480p. (YA). (gr. 8). 2012. pap. 9.99 *(978-0-06-200104-7(3))* 2011. 17.99 *(978-0-06-200103-0(5))* HarperCollins Pubs. (Greenwillow Bks.).

d'Lacey, Chris. A Crown of Dragons. 2016. (UFiles Ser.: 3). (ENG.). 320p. (J). (gr. 3-7). 16.99 *(978-0-545-60883-1(X)*, Scholastic Pr.) Scholastic, Inc.

—The Fire Ascending. (ENG.). 576p. (J). (gr. 3-7). 2013. pap. 9.99 *(978-0-545-40293-4(X)*, Scholastic Paperbacks) 2012. (Last Dragon Chronicles Ser.: 7). 18.99 *(978-0-545-40216-3(6)*, Orchard Bks.) Scholastic, Inc.
—The Fire Ascending. 2013. (Last Dragon Chronicles Ser.: 7). lib. bdg. 20.85 *(978-0-606-31958-4(1)*, Turtleback) Turtleback Bks.
—The Fire Eternal. 2010. (Last Dragon Chronicles Ser.: 4). (ENG.). 512p. (J). (gr. 3-7). 8.99 *(978-0-545-05164-4(9)*, Orchard Bks.) Scholastic, Inc.
—Fire World. 2012. (Last Dragon Chronicles Ser.: 6). lib. bdg. 19.65 *(978-0-606-23967-7(7)*, Turtleback) Turtleback Bks.
—Icefire. d'Lacey, Chris, illus. 2007. (Last Dragon Chronicles Ser.: 2). (Illus.). lib. bdg. 19.65 *(978-1-4177-9138-5(1)*, Turtleback) Turtleback Bks.
—The Wearle. 2016. (Erth Dragons Ser.: 1). (ENG.). 320p. (J). (gr. 3-7). 16.99 *(978-0-545-90018-8(2)*, Scholastic Pr.) Scholastic, Inc.
d'Lacey, Jay & d'Lacey, Chris. Rain & Fire. 2012. (Last Dragon Chronicles Ser.). (ENG.). 304p. (J). (gr. 3-7). 16.99 *(978-0-545-41453-1(9)*, Orchard Bks.) Scholastic, Inc.
Doherty, Berlie. Jack the Giant Killer. (Illus.). 139p. pap. 8.99 *(978-0-340-76452-7(X))* Hodder & Stoughton GBR. Dist: Trafalgar Square Publishing.
Doherty, Gillian. Stories of Wizards. Edwards, Linda, illus. 2008. (Stories for Young Children Ser.). 95p. (J). (gr. 1). 16.99 *(978-0-7945-1915-5(6)*, Usborne) EDC Publishing.
Doige, Vania & Doige, Jay. The Lost Souls: The Story of Hakiki. 2013. 186p. pap. *(978-1-909220-57-7(4))* Mirador Publishing.
Dokey, Cameron. Beauty Sleep: A Retelling of Sleeping Beauty. 2006. (Once upon a Time Ser.). (ENG.). 208p. (YA). (gr. 9-12). mass mkt. 6.99 *(978-1-4169-4014-2(6)*, Simon Pulse) Simon Pulse.
—Once: Before Midnight; Golden; Wild Orchid. 2012. (ENG.). 640p. (YA). (gr. 7). pap. 11.99 *(978-1-4424-2283-4(1)*, Simon Pulse) Simon Pulse.
—Sunlight & Shadow: Her Love Is Trapped Between Night & Day.... 2004. (ENG., Illus.). 192p. (YA). (gr. 9). pap. 6.99 *(978-0-689-86999-0(1)*, Simon Pulse) Simon Pulse.
Dolamore, Jaclyn. Glittering Shadows. 2016. (Dark Metropolis Ser.). (ENG., Illus.). 442p. (YA). (gr. 7-12). pap. 9.99 *(978-1-4231-6477-7(6))* Hyperion Bks. for Children.
—Magic under Glass. (Magic under Glass Ser.). (ENG.). (YA). (gr. 7). 2011. 256p. pap. 8.99 *(978-1-59990-587-7(6)*, 9781599905877) 2010. 240p. 16.99 *(978-1-59990-430-6(6)*, 9781599904306) Bloomsbury Publishing USA. (Bloomsbury USA Childrens).
—Magic under Stone. 2012. (Magic under Glass Ser.). (ENG.). 304p. (YA). 16.99 *(978-1-59990-643-0(0)*, 9781599906430, Bloomsbury USA Childrens) Bloomsbury Publishing USA.
Dolan, Francis. Meg & Jen: Daffyd & the Sacred Oath. 2016. (ENG.). 191p. (J). pap. 10.95 *(978-1-78612-491-3(2)*, 158c72bc-f505-4282-9754-d6f3db5451db) Austin, Stan AUS. Dist: Bookmasters Distribution.
Dolbeck, Andrew. Fever Jenny, Bk. 1. 2006. 120p. pap. 10.99 *(978-1-59092-324-5(3))* Blue Forge Pr.
Dolenz, Ami. Harold & Agatha: The Mysterious Jewel. 2013. 176p. *(978-1-4602-0520-4(0))*; pap. *(978-1-4602-0420-7(4))* FriesenPress.
Dollak, Nicholas. Jenna of Erdovon: The Philosopher's Egg. 2007. (Illus.). 220p. (J). (gr. 4-7). per. 19.95 *(978-1-929084-14-2(5))* Malibu Bks. for Children.
Dolye, Brittlyn. Waking Beauty. 2017. (ENG.). 320p. pap. 15.99 ***(978-1-4621-2053-6(9)**, Sweetwater Bks.) Cedar Fort, Inc./CFI Distribution.
Dompieri, Patricia Lynn. Lemon Bee & Other Peculiar Tales. 2013. 136p. pap. 11.95 *(978-1-4787-2240-3(1))* Outskirts Pr., Inc.
Don, Freeman. Corduroy. 2014. (Corduroy Ser.). (ENG.). 32p. (J). (gr. k-12). 11.24 *(978-1-63245-291-7(X))* Lectorum Pubns., Inc.
Donald, David R. Tikoloshe & the Three Fox Cubs. 2012. (Illus.). 56p. pap. 13.66 *(978-1-4772-3496-9(9))* AuthorHouse.
Donaldson, Julia. The Giants & the Joneses. Swearingen, Greg, illus. 2008. (ENG.). 224p. (J). (gr. 3-5). pap. 14.99 *(978-0-312-37961-2(7)*, 9780312379612) Square Fish.
Dong Chen, Wei. Lost Children. Peng, Chao, illus. 2013. (Monkey King Ser.: 12). (ENG.). 176p. (YA). (gr. 6-12). pap. 9.99 *(978-89-94208-57-2(7))* Lerner Publishing Group.
—Realm of Infant King. Peng, Chao, illus. 2013. (Monkey King Ser.: 10). (ENG.). 176p. (YA). (gr. 6-12). pap. 9.99 *(978-89-94208-54-1(2))* Lerner Publishing Group.
—Stolen Kingdom. Peng, Chao, illus. 2013. (Monkey King Ser.: 9). (ENG.). 176p. (YA). (gr. 6-12). pap. 9.99 *(978-89-94208-53-4(4))* Lerner Publishing Group.
—Treasures of the Mountain Kings. Peng, Chao, illus. 2013. (Monkey King Ser.: 8). (ENG.). 176p. (YA). (gr. 6-12). pap. 9.99 *(978-89-94208-52-7(6))* Lerner Publishing Group.
Dong Chen, Wei & Peng, Chao. Bane of Heaven. 2012. (Monkey King Ser.: 2). (ENG., Illus.). 176p. (gr. 5-8). pap. 9.99 *(978-89-94208-46-6(1))* JR Comics KOR. Dist: Lerner Publishing Group.
—Birth of Stone Monkey. 2012. (Monkey King Ser.: 1). (ENG., Illus.). 176p. (gr. 5-8). pap. 9.99 *(978-89-94208-45-9(3))* JR Comics KOR. Dist: Lerner Publishing Group.
—Enemies & New Friend. 2012. (Monkey King Ser.: 4). (ENG., Illus.). 176p. (gr. 5-8). pap. 9.99 *(978-89-94208-48-0(8))* JR Comics KOR. Dist: Lerner Publishing Group.
—Journey to the West. 2012. (Monkey King Ser.: 3). (ENG., Illus.). 176p. (gr. 5-8). pap. 9.99 *(978-89-94208-47-3(X))* JR Comics KOR. Dist: Lerner Publishing Group.
—Sacred Tree. 2012. (Monkey King Ser.: 6). (ENG., Illus.). 176p. (gr. 5-8). pap. 9.99 *(978-89-94208-50-3(X))* JR Comics KOR. Dist: Lerner Publishing Group.
—Three Trials. 2012. (Monkey King Ser.: 5). (ENG., Illus.). 176p. (gr. 5-8). pap. 9.99 *(978-89-94208-49-7(6))* JR Comics KOR. Dist: Lerner Publishing Group.
Donovan, Kim. St Viper's School for Super Villains. the Big Bank Burglary. Bean, Izzy, illus. 2013. 160p. pap. *(978-0-9571300-2-9(3))* Squawk Bks.
Dora's Magical Adventures, Set. 2008. (Dora the Explorer Ser.). (ENG.). 144p. (J). pap. 10.99 *(978-1-4169-7583-0(7)*, Simon Spotlight/Nickelodeon) Simon Spotlight/Nickelodeon.
Dorison, Xavier & Nury, Fabian. Century Club. Ross, C., illus. 2012. (Spooks Ser.: 2). (ENG.). 56p. (J). (gr. 10-12). pap. 13.95 *(978-1-84918-129-7(2))* CineBook GBR. Dist: National Bk. Network.
Dorling Kindersley Publishing Staff. LEGO DC Comics Super Heroes Character Encyclopedia. 2016. (ENG., Illus.). 208p. (J). (gr. 1-3). 18.99 *(978-1-4654-4454-7(8)*, DK Children) Dorling Kindersley Publishing, Inc.
—Tangled. 2010. (Ultimate Sticker Bks.). (ENG.). 16p. (J). (gr. k-3). pap. 6.99 *(978-0-7566-6687-3(2)*, DK Children) Dorling Kindersley Publishing, Inc.
Dorling Kindersley Publishing Staff, et al. Alice Through the Looking Glass: The Complete Visual Guide. 2016. (ENG., Illus.). 96p. (J). (gr. 3-7). 16.99 *(978-1-4654-5255-9(9)*, DK Children) Dorling Kindersley Publishing, Inc.
Dorsey, Angela. Autumn in Snake Canyon. 2012. 122p. pap. *(978-1-927100-23-3(2))* Enchanted Pony Bks.
Dorsey, Angela & Miller, Marina. Sun Chaser. 2012. 112p. pap. *(978-1-927100-21-9(6))* Enchanted Pony Bks.
Dotson, Kyt. The Specter in the Spectacles. 2003. 126p. pap. 10.95 *(978-0-595-28251-7(2))* iUniverse, Inc.
Dove, Debra. The Fur Flew. 2010. 42p. pap. 19.99 *(978-1-60957-425-3(7))* Salem Author Services.
Dowding, Philippa. The Strange Gift of Gwendolyn Golden. 2014. (Night Flyer's Handbook Ser.: 1). (ENG., Illus.). 200p. (J). pap. 9.99 *(978-1-4597-0735-1(4)*, 9781459707351) Dundurn CAN. Dist: Ingram Publisher Services.
Dowell, Frances O'Roark. Falling In. (ENG., 256p. (J). (gr. 3-7). 2012. Illus.). pap. 8.99 *(978-1-4424-2205-6(X))* 2010. 16.99 *(978-1-4169-5032-5(X))* Simon & Schuster Children's Publishing. (Atheneum Bks. for Young Readers).
Downer, Ann. The Books of the Keepers. 2012. (ENG.). 256p. (YA). (gr. 8). pap. 12.99 *(978-1-4424-7232-7(4)*, Atheneum Bks. for Young Readers) Simon & Schuster Children's Publishing.
—The Glass Salamander. 2012. (ENG.). 224p. (YA). (gr. 8). pap. 10.99 *(978-1-4424-7231-0(6)*, Atheneum Bks. for Young Readers) Simon & Schuster Children's Publishing.
—The Spellkey. 2012. (ENG.). 224p. (YA). (gr. 8). pap. 10.99 *(978-1-4424-7230-3(8)*, Atheneum Bks. for Young Readers) Simon & Schuster Children's Publishing.
Downes, Alice & Hargreaves, Roger. Little Miss Splendid & the Beast. 2014. (Mr. Men & Little Miss Ser.). (ENG.). 32p. (J). (gr. -1-2). 3.99 *(978-0-8431-8242-2(3)*, Price Stern Sloan) Penguin Young Readers Group.
Dowson, Jonas. Meteor Man. 2012. 48p. pap. 37.37 *(978-1-4771-3435-1(2))* Xlibris Corp.
Doyle, Helen. The Rainbow Pals. 2011. 96p. pap. 39.39 *(978-1-4567-0169-7(X))* AuthorHouse.
Doyle, Malachy. Hair Scare. Allen, Jonathan, illus. 2005. (ENG.). 24p. (J). lib. bdg. 23.65 *(978-1-59646-724-8(X))* Dingles & Co.
Dragon: Enter the Realm. 2007. (YA). per. *(978-1-934345-43-6(1))* SouthWest Pubns.
Dragon: The Fantasy Continues. 2007. (YA). per. *(978-1-934345-44-3(X))* SouthWest Pubns.
Dragonfang. l.t. ed. 2013. 466p. (Orig.). pap. *(978-1-4596-7055-6(8))* ReadHowYouWant.com, Ltd.
Dragons, Phantoms, & Secrets: The Best New Fantasy from Arrow Writers. 2005. 63p. (J). *(978-0-439-74432-4(6))* Scholastic, Inc.
Drake, Brenda. Thief of Lies. 2016. (Library Jumpers Ser.: 1). (ENG.). 400p. (YA). 16.99 *(978-1-63375-221-4(6)*, 9781633752214) Entangled Publishing, LLC.
Drake, Emily. The Curse of Arkady. (Magickers Ser.: 2). (ENG.). (gr. 12-18). Bk. 2. 2003. 384p. 6.99 *(978-0-7564-0103-0(8))* Vol. 1. 2010. (Illus.). 624p. 9.99 *(978-0-7564-0636-3(6))* DAW. (DAW).
Drake, Raelyn. Realm of Mystics. 2017. (Level Up Ser.). (ENG.). (YA). (gr. 6-12). 120p. pap. 7.99 ***(978-1-5124-5359-1(5))**; lib. bdg. 26.65 ***(978-1-5124-3989-2(4))** Lerner Publishing Group. (Darby Creek).
DreamWorks Animation Staff. Shrek 2. 2004. (Illus.). pap. 14.99 *(978-1-59182-912-6(7)*, Tokyopop Kids) TOKYOPOP, Inc.
Driscoll, Roger K. Echo Mccool, Outlaw Through Time. 2011. 190p. pap. *(978-1-908105-26-4(7))* Grosvenor Hse. Publishing Ltd.
Drouin, Véronique. L' Île D'Aurélie. 2004. (Mon Roman Ser.). (FRE.). 304p. (J). (gr. 2). pap. *(978-2-89021-690-7(X))* Diffusion du livre Mirabel (DLM).
Du Lac, Leo J. Moon Fruit & the Dragons: Santa Claus & the Flying Carpet 3. Washington, Victoria, ed. Baker, David, illus. 2012. 26p. 24.95 *(978-1-4560-1037-9(9))* America Star Bks.
Duane, Diane. High Wizardry. 7 vols. (Young Wizards Ser.: 3). (J). 2006. 90.75 *(978-1-4025-9917-0(X))* 2004. 93.75 *(978-1-4025-8355-1(9))* Recorded Bks., Inc.
—A Wizard Alone. 2003. (Young Wizards Ser.: 6). (ENG.). 352p. (J). (gr. 5-7). pap. 8.99 *(978-0-15-204911-9(8))* Houghton Mifflin Harcourt Publishing Co.
—A Wizard of Mars Bk. 9. 2011. (Young Wizards Ser.: 9). (ENG.). 560p. (YA). (gr. 7-9). pap. 8.99 *(978-0-15-205449-6(9))* Houghton Mifflin Harcourt Publishing Co.
—Wizards at War Bk. 8. 2007. (Young Wizards Ser.: 8). (ENG., Illus.). 560p. (YA). (gr. 7-9). pap. 8.99 *(978-0-15-205223-2(2))* Houghton Mifflin Harcourt Publishing Co.
Duarte, Gustavo. Monsters! & Other Stories. Hahn, Sierra, ed. Duarte, Gustavo, illus. 2014. (ENG., Illus.). 152p. pap. 12.99 *(978-1-61655-309-8(X))* Dark Horse Comics.
Dubrovin, Barbara. Fantasy Fair: Bright Stories of Imagination. Dubrovin, Barbara, illus. 2007. (Illus.). 128p. (J). pap. 17.50 *(978-0-9638339-6-9(0))* Storycraft Publishing.
Duce, Gillian. Magic & Mayhem. 2006. (ENG.). 212p. per. *(978-1-894936-64-4(7))* Saga Bks.
Duchêne, Mique. The Mystery of Foo & the Great Chasm. 2012. 32p. (-18). pap. 17.99 *(978-1-4772-7211-4(9))* AuthorHouse.
Dudek, V. A. Soldiers of Fate. 2009. 94p. pap. 15.99 *(978-1-4415-2702-8(8))* Xlibris Corp.
Due, Kirsten L. Bearen Bear & the Bunbury Tales. Berends, Jenny, illus. 2013. 194p. pap. *(978-0-9884916-3-2(X))* Roxby Media Ltd.
Duerr, Doug. The Adventures of Jazz & Elliott: Danielle goes to the Magical Land of Roop-E-Doo. 2010. 29p. (J). pap. 17.95 *(978-1-4327-5405-1(X))* Outskirts Pr., Inc.
Duey, Kathleen. Sacred Scars, No. 2. Rayyan, Sheila, illus. 2009. (Resurrection of Magic Ser.: 2). (ENG.). 560p. (YA). (gr. 7-18). 18.99 *(978-0-689-84095-1(0)*, Atheneum Bks. for Young Readers) Simon & Schuster Children's Publishing.
—Skin Hunger. 2008. (Resurrection of Magic Ser.: 1). (ENG.). 368p. (YA). (gr. 7-7). pap. 12.99 *(978-0-689-84094-4(2)*, Atheneum Bks. for Young Readers) Simon & Schuster Children's Publishing.
—True Heart. Rayyan, Omar, illus. 2005. 76p. (J). lib. bdg. 15.00 *(978-1-59054-920-9(1))* Fitzgerald Bks.
DuFalla, Anita, illus. Sumac & the Magic Lake. 2004. (Reader's Theater Ser.). (J). pap. *(978-1-4108-2291-8(5)*, A22915) Benchmark Education Co.
Dufaux, Jean. Blackmore Vol. 2: Lament of the Lost Moors, Volume 2. Rosinski, Grzegorz, illus. 2014. (Lament of the Lost Moors Ser.: 2). (ENG.). 64p. pap. 15.95 *(978-1-84918-187-7(X))* CineBook GBR. Dist: National Bk. Network.
—Siobhan. Rosinski, Grzegorz, illus. 2014. (Lament of the Lost Moors Ser.: 1). (ENG.). 64p. pap. 15.95 *(978-1-84918-169-3(1))* CineBook GBR. Dist: National Bk. Network.
Dugan, David J. The Missing Prince of Distria. 2008. 36p. pap. 24.95 *(978-1-60563-587-3(1))* America Star Bks.
Dukes, Martin. Worm Winds of Zanzibar. 2013. 420p. pap. *(978-0-9575679-0-0(1))* Dukes, Martin.
Duncalf, Joanne. The Zookeeper's Menagerie. 2007. pap. 15.95 *(978-0-9797232-1-6(3))* Twelve Star Pr.
Duncan, Lois. Stranger with My Face. 235p. (YA). (gr. 7-18). pap. 4.99 *(978-0-8072-1371-1(3)*, Listening Library) Random Hse. Audio Publishing Group.
Duncan, S. L. The Revelation of Gabriel Adam. 2014. (Revelation Saga Ser.). (ENG.). 384p. (gr. 6). pap. 9.99 *(978-1-60542-737-9(3))* Nodin Pr.
Dunkle, Clare B. The Sky Inside. 2017. (ENG.). 240p. (YA). (gr. 7). pap. 11.99 ***(978-1-5344-1875-2(X)**, Atheneum Bks. for Young Readers) Simon & Schuster Children's Publishing.
Dunmore, Helen. The Crossing of Ingo. 2009. (ENG.). 368p. (J). 15.99 *(978-1-55468-247-8(9))* HarperCollins Pubs.
—The Deep. 2009. (Ingo Ser.: 3). 336p. (YA). (gr. 5-18). 16.99 *(978-0-06-081858-6(1))* HarperCollins Pubs.
—Ingo. 2006. 328p. (J). (gr. 5-9). lib. bdg. 17.89 *(978-0-06-081853-1(0))* HarperCollins Pubs.
Dunn, Edward Grieves. Crinkles Academy for Wizards. 2008. 424p. pap. *(978-1-906210-98-4(5))* Grosvenor Hse. Publishing Ltd.
Dunn, Layne. The Light of the Moon. Dunn Jr., Howard Alfred, illus. 2012. 16p. pap. 24.95 *(978-1-4626-5501-4(7))* America Star Bks.
Dunn, Matthew. Day One. 2007. 192p. (YA). per. 15.00 *(978-0-9794908-0-4(4))* Onondaga Hill Publishing.
Dunseith, Peter. Bird of Heaven: The Story of a Swazi Sangoma. 2010. 257p. pap. *(978-0-624-04557-1(9))* NB Pubs. Ltd.
DuPrau, Jeanne. The City of Ember. 2008. (Book of Ember Ser.). (J). 44.99 *(978-0-7393-7097-1(9))* Findaway World, LLC.
—The City of Ember. (City of Ember Ser.: 1). (ENG.). 288p. (J). (gr. 3-7). 2004. 7.99 *(978-0-375-82274-2(7)*, Yearling) 2003. 16.99 *(978-0-375-82273-5(9)*, Random Hse. Bks. for Young Readers) Random Hse. Children's Bks.
—The City of Ember Complete Boxed Set, 4 vols. 2016. (ENG.). 352p. (J). (gr. 3-7). 31.96 *(978-0-399-55164-2(6)*, Yearling) Random Hse. Children's Bks.
—The Diamond of Darkhold. 2010. (City of Ember Ser.: 3). (ENG., Illus.). 304p. (J). (gr. 3-7). pap. 7.99 *(978-0-375-85572-6(6)*, Yearling) Random Hse. Children's Bks.
—The People of Sparks. 2005. (City of Ember Ser.: 2). (ENG.). 352p. (J). (gr. 3-7). reprint ed. 7.99 *(978-0-375-82825-6(7)*, Yearling) Random Hse. Children's Bks.
—The Prophet of Yonwood. 2007. (City of Ember Ser.: 4). (ENG.). 304p. (J). (gr. 3-7). 7.99 *(978-0-440-42124-5(1)*, Yearling) Random Hse. Children's Bks.
—The Prophet of Yonwood. 2007. (City of Ember Ser.: 3). 289p. (gr. 4-8). lib. bdg. 18.40 *(978-1-4178-1984-3(7)*, Turtleback) Turtleback Bks.
Durham, Paul. Fork-Tongue Charmers. Antonsson, Petur, illus. 2015. (Luck Uglies Ser.: 2). (ENG.). 416p. (J). (gr. 3-7). 16.99 *(978-0-06-227153-2(9))* HarperCollins Pubs.
—The Luck Uglies. Antonsson, Petur, illus. 2014. (Luck Uglies Ser.: 1). (ENG.). 400p. (J). (gr. 3-7). 16.99 *(978-0-06-227150-1(4))* HarperCollins Pubs.
—The Luck Uglies #2: Fork-Tongue Charmers. Antonsson, Petur, illus. 2016. (Luck Uglies Ser.: 2). 432p. (J). (gr. 3-7). pap. 7.99 *(978-0-06-227154-9(7))* HarperCollins Pubs.
—The Luck Uglies #3: Rise of the Ragged Clover. Antonsson, Petur, illus. 2016. (Luck Uglies Ser.: 3). 400p. (J). (gr. 3-7). 16.99 *(978-0-06-227156-3(3))* HarperCollins Pubs.
Durst, Sarah Beth. Journey Across the Hidden Islands. 2017. (ENG., Illus.). 352p. (J). (gr. 5-7). 16.99 *(978-0-544-70679-8(X)*, Clarion Bks.) Houghton Mifflin Harcourt Trade & Reference Pubs.
—Vessel. (ENG., Illus.). 432p. (YA). (gr. 7). 2013. pap. 9.99 *(978-1-4424-2377-0(3))* 2012. 16.99 *(978-1-4424-2376-3(5))* McElderry, Margaret K. Bks. (McElderry, Margaret K. Bks.).
Dutton, John. Tiger's Island. Dutton, John, illus. unabr. ed. Date not set. (Dreamguard Ser.: Vol. 2). (Illus.). viii, 245p. (J). pap. 12.95 *(978-0-9577556-1-1(9))* Samara Pr.
Duval, Alex. Bloodlust - Initiation. 2010. (Vampire Beach Ser.: 1). (ENG.). 416p. (YA). (gr. 9). pap. 9.99 *(978-1-4424-0693-3(3)*, Simon Pulse) Simon Pulse.
Dyan, Penelope. Introducing Fabulous Marie, a Girl with a Good Head on Her Shoulders. Dyan, Penelope, illus. 2009. (Illus.). 44p. pap. 11.95 *(978-1-935118-55-8(2))* Bellissima Publishing, LLC.
—The Warrior Mouse of Forest Hollow. Quinn, Courtney, illus. 2008. 108p. 17.95 *(978-1-935118-00-8(5))* Bellissima Publishing, LLC.
—The Warrior Mouse of Forest Hollow. 2005. (J). per. 5.95 *(978-0-9771916-5-9(6))* Bellissima Publishing, LLC.
Dyer, K. C. A Walk Through a Window. 2009. (ENG.). 240p. (J). (gr. 5-7). pap. 12.50 *(978-0-385-66637-4(3)*, Doubleday Canada) Penguin Random House Canada Young Readers CAN. Dist: Penguin Random Hse. LLC.
Dynyel. Windy the Winged Unicorn. 2004. 140p. 24.95 *(978-1-4184-8615-0(9))* AuthorHouse.
Earl, Cheri Pray & Williams, Carol Lynch. The Rescue Begins in Delaware. Oliphant, Manelle, illus. 2013. (Just in Time Ser.: 1). (ENG.). 144p. (J). (gr. 3-7). pap. 9.95 *(978-1-938301-74-2(9))* Familius LLC.
Early, Alan. Arthur Quinn & Hell's Keeper. 2014. (Father of Lies Chronicles Ser.: 03). (ENG.). 384p. (J). pap. 14.95 *(978-1-78117-158-5(0))* Mercier Pr., Ltd., The IRL. Dist: Dufour Editions, Inc.
—Arthur Quinn & the Fenris Wolf. 2013. (Father of Lies Chronicles Ser.: 02). (ENG.). 384p. (J). pap. 14.95 *(978-1-85635-998-6(0))* Mercier Pr., Ltd., The IRL. Dist: Dufour Editions, Inc.
—Arthur Quinn & the World Serpent. 2012. (Father of Lies Chronicles Ser.: 01). (ENG., Illus.). 320p. (J). pap. 14.95 *(978-1-85635-827-9(5))* Mercier Pr., Ltd., The IRL. Dist: Dufour Editions, Inc.
East, Bob. Tommy Cat & the Giant Chickens. East, Matt, illus. 2008. 24p. per. 24.95 *(978-1-4241-9242-7(0))* America Star Bks.
Eastburn, Mark. Earning My Spots. 2016. (ENG.). 288p. (J). (gr. 2-7). 15.99 *(978-1-5107-0778-6(8)*, Sky Pony Pr.) Skyhorse Publishing Co., Inc.
Eaton, Anthony. Nightpeople. 2005. (Darklands Ser.: Bk. 1). 392p. (Orig.). (YA). pap. *(978-0-7022-3494-1(X))* Univ. of Queensland Pr.
Eberly, Chelsea. Magic Friends. 2014. (Step into Reading Ser.). (ENG., Illus.). 32p. (J). (gr. -1-1). 3.99 *(978-0-385-38296-0(0)*, Random Hse. Bks. for Young Readers) Random Hse. Children's Bks.
—Magic Friends. 2014. (Barbie Step into Reading Level 2 Ser.). lib. bdg. 13.55 *(978-0-606-35991-7(5))* Turtleback Bks.
Ebner, Abra. Ladybird, Ladybird. 2011. 172p. (J). 16.99 *(978-0-9829505-4-8(3))* Crimson Oak Publishing LLC.
Ecton, Emily. Project Jackalope. 2015. (ENG.). 256p. (J). (gr. 3-7). pap. 6.99 *(978-1-4521-5346-9(9))* Chronicle Bks. LLC.
Edge, A. M. Frankie Feinstein & the Fenworld Thief-Takers. 2013. 156p. (J). pap. *(978-1-78299-419-0(X))* FeedARead.com.
Edmondson, Frank. Mr. Frank's Magic School Bus: Rainbow's End Adventure. Edmondson, Brad, illus. 2007. 20p. per. 24.95 *(978-1-4241-8617-4(X))* America Star Bks.
Edward Eggleston. Queer Stories for Boys & Girls. 2007. 168p. per. 11.95 *(978-1-4218-3949-3(0)*, 1st World Library - Literary Society) 1st World Publishing, Inc.
Edwards, Christine. The Charmed Enchanted Book. 2010. 24p. pap. 16.49 *(978-1-4490-7091-5(4))* AuthorHouse.
Edwards, Mark. The Gang Book 1 the Saint's Bones. 2004. (YA). per. 10.95 *(978-0-9755704-0-1(4))* New Classics Pr.
Edwards, Marnie. Pets & Parties. Hodgkinson, Leigh, illus. 2013. (Magical Mix-Ups Ser.). (ENG.). 96p. (J). (gr. 2-5). pap. 6.99 *(978-0-7636-6371-1(9)*, Nosy Crow) Candlewick Pr.
Edwards, Stuart. Dragon Jack. 2006. 42p. 15.99 *(978-1-4116-7499-8(5))* Lulu Pr., Inc.
Edwards, Wayne. Ali & the Magic Ball. Golden, Rayna, illus. 2009. 24p. pap. 12.50 *(978-1-60860-367-1(9)*, Eloquent Bks.) Strategic Book Publishing & Rights Agency (SBPRA).
Ee, Susan. Angelfall, 0 vols. 2012. (Penryn & the End of Days Ser.: 1). (ENG.). 288p. (YA). (gr. 9-12). pap. 7.99 *(978-0-7614-6327-6(5)*, 9780761463276, Amazon Children's Publishing) Amazon Publishing.
—Angelfall. 2012. 256p. pap. 12.99 *(978-0-9835970-1-8(4))* Dream, Feral LLC.
Egan, Catherine. Bone, Fog, Ash & Star, 1 vol. 2014. (Last Days of Tian Di Ser.: 3). (ENG.). 320p. (J). (gr. 6-10). pap. 12.95 *(978-1-55050-593-1(9))* Coteau Bks. CAN. Dist: Orca Bk. Pubs. USA.
—Julia Defiant. 2017. (Witch's Child Ser.: 2). (ENG.). 464p. (YA). (gr. 9). 17.99 ***(978-0-553-53335-4(5)**, Knopf Bks. for Young Readers) Random Hse. Children's Bks.
—Shade & Sorceress Bk. 1: The Last Days of Tian Di, 1 vol. 2012. (Last Days of Tian Di Ser.: 1). (ENG., Illus.). 352p. (J). (gr. 4-8). pap. 12.95 *(978-1-55050-514-6(9))* Coteau Bks. CAN. Dist: Orca Bk. Pubs. USA.
—The Unmaking, 1 vol. 2013. (Last Days of Tian Di Ser.: 2). (ENG.). 248p. (J). (gr. 4-6). pap. 12.95 *(978-1-55050-559-7(9))* Coteau Bks. CAN. Dist: Orca Bk. Pubs. USA.
Egan, Kate. Evil Comes in Pairs. Merkel, Joe F., illus. 2009. (Spider-Man Ser.). 64p. (J). (gr. 2-5). pap. 4.99 *(978-0-06-162625-8(2)*, HarperFestival) HarperCollins Pubs.
Eggleton, Jill. Turtle's Trouble. Cammell, Sandra, illus. 2003. (Rigby Sails Early Ser.). (ENG.). 16p. (gr. 1-2). pap. 6.95 *(978-0-7578-8672-0(8))* Houghton Mifflin Harcourt Publishing Co.
Ehrlich, Amy. The Wild Swans. Jeffers, Susan, illus. 2008. (ENG.). 32p. (J). (gr. -1-3). 17.99 *(978-0-525-47914-7(7)*, Dutton Books for Young Readers) Penguin Young Readers Group.
Eisele, Barbara. Curious Cozy. 2011. 48p. pap. 9.99 *(978-1-4567-1746-9(4))* AuthorHouse.
Eisner, Fern. Saba's Room. 2009. 28p. pap. 15.99 *(978-1-4415-1843-9(6))* Xlibris Corp.
Ejsing, Jesper. Jarvis: the Sorcerer's Apprentice: The Sorcerer's Apprentice. 2010. (Illus.). 608p. (YA). 19.95 *(978-1-58994-321-6(X))* Fantasy Flight Games.
Elaine Vanier. Crystal Lights: Awaken the Power. 2009. 116p. pap. 10.95 *(978-1-4401-8357-7(0))* iUniverse, Inc.
Eleanor Gates. The Poor Little Rich Girl. l.t. ed. 2007. 506p. pap. 21.99 *(978-1-4264-8948-8(X))* Creative Media Partners, LLC.
Elfakir, Mahamad Ali. Blueberry Bubble Gum. 2013. 44p. 16.95 *(978-0-578-10978-7(6))*; (J). pap. 11.95 *(978-0-578-10974-9(3))* Elfa Bks.
Elfgren, Sara B. & Strandberg, Mats. The Circle. 2014. (Engelsfors Trilogy Ser.: 1). (ENG.). 608p. (gr. 9-13). pap. 13.99 *(978-1-4683-0819-8(X)*, 460819) Overlook Pr., The.
—Fire. 2015. (Engelsfors Trilogy Ser.: 0). (ENG.). 608p. (gr. 9-13). pap. 14.99 *(978-1-4683-1007-8(0)*, 461007) Overlook Pr., The.
—The Key. 2016. (Engelsfors Trilogy Ser.: 0). (ENG.). 864p. (YA). (gr. 5-16). pap. 14.99 *(978-1-4683-1280-5(4)*, 461280) Overlook Pr., The.
—The Key: The Engelsfors Trilogy — Book 3. 2015. (Engelsfors Trilogy Ser.: 3). (ENG.). 864p. (gr. 9-17). 19.99 *(978-1-4683-0673-6(1)*, 460673) Overlook Pr., The.

E
F
G

Elgert, C. J. The Elder Brothers & the Dragon's Portal. 2011. 236p. (gr. 4-6). 25.95 (978-1-4620-1467-5(4)); pap. 15.95 (978-1-4620-1466-8(6)) iUniverse, Inc.

—The Elder Brothers & the Therian Teacher. 2013. 200p. (978-1-4602-3567-6(3)) FriesenPress.

Eliotte, Lisa J. The Adventures of Derby Doodle. 2009. 640p. pap. 25.99 (978-1-4389-3058-9(5)) AuthorHouse.

Elise, Christy. Beez Take Flight. 2012. 56p. pap. 24.99 (978-1-4685-6265-1(7)) AuthorHouse.

Elizabeth, Mary. The Graveyard Book: A Teaching Guide. 2015. (Discovering Literature Series: Challengi Ser.). (ENG.). 112p. (gr. 7). pap. 13.95 (978-0-931993-09-1(1)) Garlic Pr.

Ella, Sara. Unblemished, 1 vol. 2016. (Unblemished Trilogy Ser.). (ENG., Illus.). 384p. (YA). 15.99 (978-0-7180-8101-0(3)) Nelson, Thomas Inc.

Ella, Sara. Unraveling, 1 vol. 2017. (Unblemished Trilogy Ser.). (ENG.). 368p. (YA). 15.99 **(978-0-7180-8103-4(X))** Nelson, Thomas Inc.

Elliott, Kate, pseud. Buried Heart. 2017. (Court of Fives Ser.: 3). (ENG., Illus.). 480p. (YA). (gr. 7-17). 17.99 **(978-0-316-34441-8(9))** Little, Brown Bks. for Young Readers.

—Court of Fives. 2015. (Court of Fives Ser.: Bk. 1). (ENG., Illus.). 448p. (YA). (gr. 7-17). 18.00 (978-0-316-36419-5(3)) Little Brown & Co.

—Court of Fives. 2016. (Court of Fives Ser.: 1). (ENG., Illus.). 464p. (YA). (gr. 7-17). pap. 10.99 (978-0-316-36430-0(4)) Little, Brown Bks. for Young Readers.

—Court of Fives. 2016. (YA). lib. bdg. 22.10 **(978-0-606-39996-8(8))** Turtleback Bks.

Elliott, Kate, pseud. Poisoned Blade. (Court of Fives Ser.: 2). (ENG., Illus.). (YA). (gr. 7-17). 2017. 496p. pap. 10.99 **(978-0-316-34438-8(9))** 2016. 480p. 17.99 (978-0-316-34437-1(0)) Little, Brown Bks. for Young Readers.

—Poisoned Blade. 2017. (YA). lib. bdg. 22.10 **(978-0-606-40219-4(5))** Turtleback Bks.

Elliott, M. G. The Magic Wheel: And the Adventures of Ding-How, Ah-So, & Mi-Tu. 2011. 220p. (gr. 4-6). 33.95 (978-1-4497-3050-5(7)); pap. 17.95 (978-1-4497-3049-9(3)) Author Solutions, Inc. (WestBow Pr.).

Elliott, Sherry. The Great Veiled Pearl. 2009. 48p. pap. 10.49 (978-1-4389-1263-9(3)) AuthorHouse.

ELLIS, B. J. Mrs. Morgan's Adventures with Aliens. 2008. 249p. 29.50 (978-0-557-00095-1(5)) Lulu Pr., Inc.

Ellis, M. Henderson. Petra K & the Blackhearts: A Novel. 2014. (Young Europe Bks.). (ENG., Illus.). 202p. (J). (gr. 9). pap. 11.99 (978-0-9850623-8-5(X)) New Europe Bks.

Ellison, Harlan. Troublemakers. 2009. 272p. pap. 13.95 (978-0-7592-9198-0(5)) Open Road Integrated Media, Inc.

Ellsworth, Theo. Eyes of War. 2006. 385p. (YA). pap. 14.99 (978-0-9776114-0-9(X)) Hidden Talent Pr.

Ellwand, Ruth & Ellwand, David. The Mystery of the Fool & the Vanisher. Ellwand, David, illus. 2008. (ENG., Illus.). 104p. (J). (gr. 5). 18.99 (978-0-7636-2096-7(3)) Candlewick Pr.

Ellynby, Christy. 24th Room: The Vale Legend. 2013. (ENG., Illus.). 104p. pap. (978-1-78306-132-7(4)) Troubador Publishing Ltd.

Elmer, Robert. Trion Rising, 1 vol. 2008. (Shadowside Trilogy Ser.). (ENG.). 352p. (YA). (gr. 8-11). pap. 9.99 (978-0-310-71421-7(4)) Zondervan.

Else, Barbara. The Queen & the Nobody Boy. Broad, Sam, illus. 2013. (Tales of Fontania Ser.). (ENG.). 328p. (J). (gr. 4-7). (978-1-877579-49-3(1)) Gecko Pr.

—The Traveling Restaurant: Jasper's Voyage in Three Parts. 2012. (Gecko Press Titles Ser.). (ENG.). 304p. (J). (gr. 5-8). 17.95 (978-1-877579-03-5(3)) Gecko Pr. NZL. Dist: Lerner Publishing Group.

Eltoukhy, G. N. Fattopia a C: The Tablet Legacy. 2012. 28p. pap. 16.09 (978-1-4669-3706-2(8)) Trafford Publishing.

Elves & the Shoemaker. 2005. (J). bds. 3.99 (978-1-933200-07-1(3)) Family Bks. at Home.

Elwell, Sharon. Jeremy & the Wappo. Gentry, Debra, illus. 126p. (Orig.). (J). (gr. 3-4). pap. 10.50 (978-0-9626210-0-0(5)) Rattle OK Pubns.

Elwell, Susan. Madigan's Discoveries: Book One - the Magic of Transformation. 2009. 106p. pap. 12.95 (978-1-933063-22-5(X)) Global Partnership, LLC.

Elys Dayton, Arwen. Seeker. 2015. lib. bdg. 20.85 (978-0-606-38458-2(8)) Turtleback Bks.

Ember, Julia. Unicorn Tracks. 2016. (ENG., Illus.). (YA). (gr. 8-12). 24.99 **(978-1-63477-987-6(8))**; 180p. (J). pap. 14.99 (978-1-63476-878-8(7)) Dreamspinner Pr. (Harmony Ink Pr.).

Emberley, Ed & Emberley, Rebecca. Chicken Little. Emberley, Ed, illus. 2009. (ENG., Illus.). 34p. (J). (gr. -1-2). 18.99 (978-1-59643-464-6(3), 9781596434646) Roaring Brook Pr.

Emerson, Kevin. The Dark Shore. 2014. (Atlanteans Ser.: 2). (ENG.). 496p. (YA). (gr. 8). pap. 9.99 (978-0-06-206283-3(2), Tegen, Katherine Bks) HarperCollins Pubs.

Empire of Shadows. 2014. (ENG.). 496p. (YA). (gr. 8). 17.99 (978-0-06-212133-2(2)) HarperCollins Pubs.

Emshwiller, Carol. The Mount. 2005. (ENG.). 240p. (YA). (gr. 7-7). 7.99 (978-0-14-240302-0(4), Firebird) Penguin Young Readers Group.

Encyclopaedia Britannica, Inc. Staff, compiled by. Cinderella. 2008. 49.95 (978-1-59339-683-1(X)) Encyclopaedia Britannica, Inc.

—Familiar Tales Around the World. 2008. 49.95 (978-1-59339-676-3(7)) Encyclopaedia Britannica, Inc.

—Hansel & Gretel. 2008. 49.95 (978-1-59339-687-9(2)) Encyclopaedia Britannica, Inc.

—Rapunzel. 2008. 49.95 (978-1-59339-688-6(0)) Encyclopaedia Britannica, Inc.

—Rumpelstiltskin. 2008. 49.95 (978-1-59339-686-2(4)) Encyclopaedia Britannica, Inc.

Ende, Michael. La Historia Interminable.Tr. of Unendliche Geschichte. (SPA.). 432p. (YA). (gr. 5-8). 13.95 (978-84-204-2522-1(2), LEC5222) Ediciones Alfaguara ESP. Dist: Lectorum Pubns., Inc.

—La Historia Interminable. Quadflieg, Roswitha & Sáenz, Miguel, trs. Quadflieg, Roswitha, illus.Tr. of Unendliche Geschichte. (SPA.). 424p. (J). 9.95 (978-84-204-3226-7(1)) Ediciones Alfaguara ESP. Dist: Santillana USA Publishing Co., Inc.

—La Historia Interminable. Quadflieg, Roswitha, tr. 57th ed. 2014.Tr. of Unendliche Geschichte. (SPA., Illus.). 419p. 17.95 (978-84-204-6439-8(2)) Ediciones Alfaguara ESP. Dist: Santillana USA Publishing Co., Inc.

—La Historia Interminable. 2003.Tr. of Unendliche Geschichte. (SPA., Illus.). 420p. (J). (gr. 5-8). pap. 12.95 (978-968-19-0254-4(8)) Santillana USA Publishing Co., Inc.

Engelbreit, Mary. Mary Engelbreit's Nutcracker. Engelbreit, Mary, illus. 2014. (ENG., Illus.). 40p. (J). (gr. -1-3). 9.99 (978-0-06-222417-0(4)) HarperCollins Pubs.

—Twelve Timeless Treasures. Engelbreit, Mary, illus. 2010. (ENG., Illus.). 128p. (J). 19.99 (978-0-06-088583-0(1)) HarperCollins Pubs.

England, Nora. The Witches of Dorkdom. 2013. 180p. pap. 9.95 (978-0-9676344-4-9(X)) Penury Pr.

Ennis, Brenda. The Secret of Sleeveen. 2013. (Illus.). 142p. pap. (978-1-78201-041-8(6)) Evertype.

Enos, K. D. The Chronicles of Artici: Children of the Dead. 2012. 324p. 29.95 (978-1-59330-781-3(0)); pap. 18.95 (978-1-59330-780-6(2)) Aventine Pr.

Ensor, Rod. Getting It. 2007. 216p. per. 14.95 (978-0-595-44800-5(3)) iUniverse, Inc.

Epstein, Adam Jay & Jacobson, Andrew. Circle of Heroes. (Familiars Ser.: 3). (ENG.). 336p. (J). (gr. 3-7). 2013. pap. 6.99 (978-0-06-196116-8(7)) 2012. (Illus.). 16.99 (978-0-06-196114-4(0)) HarperCollins Pubs.

—The Familiars. 2011. (Familiars Ser.: 1). (ENG.). 384p. (J). (gr. 3-7). pap. 6.99 (978-0-06-196110-6(8)) HarperCollins Pubs.

—The Familiars. Chiu, Bobby, illus. 2010. (Familiars Ser.: 1). (ENG.). 368p. (J). (gr. 3-7). 16.99 (978-0-06-196108-3(6)) HarperCollins Pubs.

—Palace of Dreams. Phillips, Dave, illus. (Familiars Ser.: 4). (ENG.). 336p. (J). (gr. 3-7). 2015. pap. 6.99 (978-0-06-212031-1(X))No. 4. 2013. 16.99 (978-0-06-212029-8(8)) HarperCollins Pubs.

—Secrets of the Crown. (Familiars Ser.: 2). (ENG.). (J). (gr. 3-7). 2012. 400p. pap. 6.99 (978-0-06-196113-7(2)) 2011. 384p. 16.99 (978-0-06-196111-3(6)) HarperCollins Pubs.

Epstein, Alex. The Circle Cast, 1 vol. 2011. (ENG., Illus.). 304p. (YA). (gr. 2-4). pap. 12.95 (978-1-896580-63-0(7)) Tradewind Bks. CAN. Dist: Orca Bk. Pubs. USA.

Erich, James. Dreams of Fire & Gods: Dreams. 2016. (ENG., Illus.). (J). 27.99 **(978-1-63533-005-2(X)**, Harmony Ink Pr.) Dreamspinner Pr.

—Dreams of Fire & Gods: Fire. 2016. (ENG., Illus.). (J). 24.99 **(978-1-63533-006-9(8)**, Harmony Ink Pr.) Dreamspinner Pr.

—Dreams of Fire & Gods: Gods. 2016. (ENG., Illus.). (J). 24.99 **(978-1-63533-007-6(6)**, Harmony Ink Pr.) Dreamspinner Pr.

Erich, James. Dreams of Fire & Gods: Gods [Library Edition]. 2014. 200p. pap. 14.99 (978-1-62798-380-8(5), Harmony Ink Pr.) Dreamspinner Pr.

Errico, Jessica / C. Grandpa's Magical Accordion. Star, Brenda, illus. 2007. 28p. (J). pap. 17.95 incl. cd-rom (978-0-9800577-0-6(1)) Three Part Harmony LLC.

Eschler, Linda. The Strawberry Fairies Save Sandcastle Island. 2007. 52p. per. 16.95 (978-1-4241-9175-8(0)) America Star Bks.

Escott, John & Falkner, John Meade. Moonfleet. Date not set. (Nelson Readers Ser.). (Illus.). 47p. (J). pap. (978-0-17-557052-2(3)) Addison-Wesley Longman, Inc.

Eshbaugh, Julie. Ivory & Bone. 2016. 272p. (YA). (gr. 9). 17.99 (978-0-06-239925-0(X), HarperTeen) HarperCollins Pubs.

Esparza- Vela, Mary. You Can't Take the Dinosaur Home. Motz, Mike, illus. 2013. 16p. pap. 9.95 (978-1-61633-364-5(2)) Guardian Angel Publishing, Inc.

Espinosa, Rod. The Courageous Princess Pocket Manga. 2012. (Illus.). 232p. pap. 14.99 (978-0-9841107-9-7(8)) Antarctic Pr., Inc.

Essig, Helene & Perez, Victoria. Angela's Angel. 2007. 112p. per. 11.95 (978-1-4327-1348-5(5)) Outskirts Pr., Inc.

Estep, Jennifer. Midnight Frost. 2013. (Mythos Academy Ser.). (ENG.). 400p. pap. 9.95 (978-0-7582-8149-4(8), K-Teen) Kensington Publishing Corp.

Ethel Cook Eliot. The Little House in Fairy Wood. 2005. pap. (978-1-905432-33-2(X)) Dodo Pr.

Etheridge, Judy. Olivia's Wish. 2009. 32p. pap. 21.99 (978-1-4415-3915-1(8)) Xlibris Corp.

Etherly, L. D. When I Fall Asleep. Velarde, Chase, illus. 2013. 36p. pap. 11.95 (978-0-9833877-6-3(1)) Inkspil Publishing.

Etting, Jessica Koosed & Schwartz, Alyssa Embree. The Lost Causes. 2017. (ENG.). 344p. (YA). (gr. 9-17). 17.99 **(978-1-77138-844-3(7))** Kids Can Pr., Ltd. CAN. Dist: Hachette Bk. Group.

Evans, D. R. Palindor. 2008. 268p. pap. 18.95 (978-0-615-20663-9(8)) Engine Hse. Bks.

Evans, Florence Adéle. Alice's Adventures in Pictureland: A Tale Inspired by Lewis Carroll's Wonderland. 2011. (Illus.). 152p. pap. (978-1-904808-63-3(8)) Evertype.

Evans, Margaret. The Tale of Rainbow's End. 2007. pap. 11.00 (978-0-8059-8716-4(9)) Dorrance Publishing Co., Inc.

Everblaze. 2014. (Keeper of the Lost Cities Ser.: 3). (ENG., Illus.). 624p. (J). (gr. 3-7). 18.99 (978-1-4424-4599-4(8), Aladdin) Simon & Schuster Children's Publishing.

Everburg, R. S. Audrika's Magic. 2011. 264p. 29.99 (978-1-4628-5596-4(2)); pap. 19.99 (978-1-4628-5595-7(4)) Xlibris Corp.

Everest, D. D. Archie Greene & the Magician's Secret. 2016. (Archie Greene Ser.: 1). 336p. (J). (gr. 3-7). pap. 6.99 (978-0-06-231212-9(X)) HarperCollins Pubs.

Evert, Robert. Quests of the Kings: The Quests of the Kings Trilogy - Book One. 2017. (Quest of Kings Trilogy Ser.: 1). (ENG.). 322p. pap. 14.99 (978-1-68230-699-4(2)) Diversion Publishing Corp.

Eves, Rosalyn. Blood Rose Rebellion. 2017. (Blood Rose Rebellion Ser.). (ENG.). 416p. (YA). (gr. 7). 17.99 (978-1-101-93599-6(5), Knopf Bks. for Young Readers) Random Hse. Children's Bks.

Ewan, Ann. Brondings' Honour. 2006. (ENG., Illus.). 144p. (gr. 8-12). per. 15.95 (978-1-897235-01-0(1)) Thistledown Pr., Ltd. CAN. Dist: Univ. of Toronto Pr.

—Firedrake. 2006. (ENG.). 264p. pap. 12.95 (978-1-894345-45-3(2)) Thistledown Pr., Ltd. CAN. Dist: Univ. of Toronto Pr.

Ewing, Amy. The Black Key. 2017. (Lone City Trilogy Ser.: 3). 304p. (YA). (gr. 9). pap. 9.99 **(978-0-06-223585-5(0)**, HarperTeen) 2016. 295p. (J). **(978-0-06-256581-5(8))** HarperCollins Pubs.

—The Jewel. (Lone City Trilogy Ser.: 1). (ENG.). (YA). (gr. 9). 2015. 400p. pap. 9.99 (978-0-06-223578-7(8)) 2014. 368p. 17.99 (978-0-06-223579-4(6)) HarperCollins Pubs. (HarperTeen).

—The White Rose. 2016. (Lone City Trilogy Ser.: 2). 336p. (YA). (gr. 9). pap. 9.99 (978-0-06-223582-4(6), HarperTeen) 2015. (Lone City Trilogy Ser.: 2). (ENG.). 320p. (YA). (gr. 9). 17.99 (978-0-06-223581-7(8), HarperTeen) 2015. 320p. pap. 17.99 (978-0-06-241475-5(5)) HarperCollins Pubs.

Exony's Excursion. (Tales of Planet Artembo Ser.: Bk. 6). (Illus.). 56p. (J). (gr. 5-7). pap. 20.00 (978-0-9600792-7-8(0)) Rymer Bks.

Eyre, David. White Rainbow Black Curse. 2007. 31p. 14.95 (978-0-87336-117-0(2)) Kamehameha Publishing.

Fagan, Cary. Ten Lessons for Kaspar Snit. 2008. (ENG.). 192p. (J). (gr. 3-7). pap. 9.95 (978-0-88776-835-4(0), Tundra Bks.) Tundra Bks. CAN. Dist: Penguin Random Hse. LLC.

Fahnestock, Todd. The Wishing World. 2016. (ENG.). 224p. (J). 17.99 (978-0-7653-8588-8(0), 9780765385888, Starscape) Doherty, Tom Assocs., LLC.

Fairbanks, Letitia. Princess April Morning-Glory: What Kind of a World Would You Create, If You Had to Do Three Dood Deeds to Make Ii Home Again? Fairbanks, Letitia, illus. 2013. (ENG., Illus.). 66p. pap. 24.00 (978-0-9887848-0-2(7)) Sandramantos Publishing.

Fairy Tales. (J). 2.29 (978-1-59445-060-0(9)) Dogs in Hats Children's Publishing Co.

Fairy Tales. 2003. (J). per. (978-1-57657-913-8(1)); per. (978-1-57657-912-1(3)) Paradise Pr., Inc.

Fajardo, Alexis E. The Song of Roland. 2017. (Kid Beowulf Ser.: 2). (ENG., Illus.). 280p. (J). pap. 12.99 (978-1-4494-7590-1(6)) Andrews McMeel Publishing.

Fake, Vol. 8. 2004. (YA). pap. 9.99 (978-1-59182-454-1(0)) TOKYOPOP, Inc.

Falls, Kat. Inhuman. 2013. (ENG.). 384p. (J). (gr. 7). 17.99 (978-0-545-37099-8(X), Scholastic Pr.) Scholastic, Inc.

Falter, Laury. Savior. 2013. 304p. pap. 12.99 (978-0-9855110-2-9(8)) Falter, Laury.

Fan, Nancy Yi. Sword Mountain. 2012. (Swordbird Ser.: 3). (ENG., Illus.). 336p. (J). (gr. 3-7). 16.99 (978-0-06-165108-3(7)) HarperCollins Pubs.

—Swordbird. 2008. (J). 54.99 (978-1-60514-800-7(8)) Findaway World, LLC.

—Swordbird. Zug, Mark, illus. 2007. (Swordbird Ser.). (J). (gr. 3-7). 219p. 15.99 (978-0-06-113099-1(0), HarperCollins); 217p. lib. bdg. 16.89 (978-0-06-113100-4(8)) HarperCollins Pubs.

Fancher, Joseph. Sydney's Travels Through Dreamland Part. 2006. 48p. pap. 16.95 (978-1-4241-3690-2(3)) PublishAmerica, Inc.

Fantich, Susanna. A Cat's Tale. 2012. 210p. 33.99 (978-1-4582-0527-8(4)); pap. 15.99 (978-1-4582-0525-4(8)) Author Solutions, Inc. (Abbott Pr.).

Farah, Barbara. Parabola O Jednom Mostu. Conway, Tricia, illus. 2006. 44p. (gr. 4-7). per. 14.99 (978-1-59919-011-2(7)) Elim Publishing.

Farley, Steven. The Black Stallion & the Shape-Shifter. 2010. (Black Stallion Ser.). (ENG.). 272p. (J). (gr. 3-7). 8.99 (978-0-375-84532-1(1), Yearling) Random Hse. Children's Bks.

Farley, Terri. Phantom Stallion - Wild Horse Island Bk. 2: The Shining Stallion. 2007. (Phantom Stallion: Wild Horse Island Ser.: 2). (ENG., Illus.). 224p. (J). (gr. 5-9). pap. 4.99 (978-0-06-081543-1(4)) HarperCollins Pubs.

Farmer, Nancy. The Land of the Silver Apples. 2009. (ENG., Illus.). 528p. (YA). (gr. 7). pap. 11.99 (978-1-4169-0736-7(X), Atheneum Bks. for Young Readers) Simon & Schuster Children's Publishing.

—The Land of the Silver Apples. Sardinha, Rick, illus. 2007. (ENG.). 512p. (J). (gr. 5-9). 18.99 (978-1-4169-0735-0(1), Atheneum/Richard Jackson Bks.) Simon & Schuster Children's Publishing.

Farnsworth-Simpson,, Patricia Ann. The Twinkles Fairy Story. 2008. 115p. pap. 12.50 (978-1-4092-4951-1(4)) Lulu Pr., Inc.

Farooqi, Imran A. The Spell of the Witch-Queen. 2006. (Illus.). 60p. pap. (978-1-84401-816-1(4)) Athena Pr.

Farrey, Brian. The Secret of Dreadwillow Carse. 2017. (ENG.). (J). (gr. 4-8). lib. bdg. 17.15 **(978-0-606-39831-2(7))** Turtleback Bks.

—The Shadowhand Covenant. Helquist, Brett, illus. (Vengekeep Prophecies Ser.: 2). (ENG.). (J). (gr. 3-7). 2014. 400p. pap. 7.99 (978-0-06-204932-2(1)) 2013. 384p. 16.99 (978-0-06-204931-5(3)) HarperCollins Pubs.

—The Vengekeep Prophecies. Helquist, Brett, illus. (Vengekeep Prophecies Ser.: 1). (ENG.). (J). (gr. 3-7). 2013. 416p. pap. 7.99 (978-0-06-204929-2(1)) 2012. 400p. 16.99 (978-0-06-204928-5(3)) HarperCollins Pubs.

Farrow, G. e. & Farrow, G. E. The Wallypug in London. 2011. 106p. 23.95 (978-1-4638-9696-6(4)) Rodgers, Alan Bks.

Farrow, George Edward. The Mysterious Shin Shira. Easton, W. G., illus. 2007. 120p. per. (978-1-4065-1690-6(2)) Dodo Pr.

Fast, David R. Doctor Dave's Dragon Tales. Ciesinska, Izabela, illus. 2007. 160p. (J). per. 13.95 (978-0-9793944-8-5(1)) Digi-Tall Media.

Father of Dragons. 2007. (Binding of the Blade Ser.). (Illus.). 486p. per. 16.99 (978-0-87552-723-9(X)) P & R Publishing.

Faulconer, Charlotte. The Green Button Wish. 2010. 28p. pap. 12.49 (978-1-4490-8003-7(0)) AuthorHouse.

Faust, Jon. Helicopter Harry & the Copter Kids. 2016. (ENG., Illus.). (J). pap. 9.95 **(978-0-692-78184-5(6))** Mother Lode Pr. LLC.

Faust, Lauren. The Magic Begins, Vol. 1. 2013. (My Little Pony Ser.). (ENG., Illus.). 112p. (J). (gr. 2-5). pap. 7.99 (978-1-61377-754-1(X), 9781613777541) Idea & Design Works, LLC.

Favretto, Robert. Cat-Astrophe. 2012. 40p. pap. (978-0-9859147-9-0(3)) Morris Publishing Australia.

Fawcett, Heather. Even the Darkest Stars. 2017. (Even the Darkest Stars Ser.: 1). 432p. (YA). (gr. 8). 17.99 **(978-0-06-246338-8(1))** HarperCollins Pubs.

Faye Morningstar. Little Dream Athe: The Sand Prince. 2012. 20p. pap. 17.99 (978-1-4772-9540-3(2)) AuthorHouse.

Fearnley, Jan. Mr Wolf's Pancakes. 2008. (ENG., Illus.). 32p. (J). (gr. -1-2). 12.95 (978-1-4052-3872-4(0)) Egmont Bks., Ltd. GBR. Dist: Independent Pubs. Group.

Feasey, Steve. Wereling. 2010. (Wereling Ser.: 1). (ENG.). 288p. (YA). (gr. 7-18). pap. 9.99 (978-0-312-59612-5(X), 9780312596125) Feiwel & Friends.

FeatherHill, Annaha. Little Britches. 2007. 76p. per. 19.95 (978-1-4241-5303-9(4)) America Star Bks.

Feder, Joel A. The Legend of Sidney Snowflake. 2009. 24p. pap. 14.99 (978-1-4490-0828-4(3)) AuthorHouse.

Fei, Kanara. Kalani's Wish. 2009. 44p. pap. 16.99 (978-1-4389-8118-5(X)) AuthorHouse.

Feiffer, Jules. Bark, George. 2004. 29.95 (978-1-55592-700-4(9)) Weston Woods Studios, Inc.

Fell, K. The Dragon Stones. 2009. 352p. 30.95 (978-0-595-51644-5(0)); pap. 20.95 (978-0-595-52712-0(4)) iUniverse, Inc.

Fénelon, Marie Jirlande. The Two Best Friends & the Old Lady. 2004. (Illus.). 28p. (J). bds. 19.00 (978-1-58432-128-6(8)) Educa Vision Inc.

Ferguson, Adrian. Hamburger Man: Resurrection. 2008. 155p. pap. 17.95 (978-1-4092-4500-1(4)) Lulu Pr., Inc.

Ferrier, Paul Eugene. Kavaldo & His Diamond Pills. Gettys, Katherine, illus. 2013. (ENG.). 72p. pap. 12.99 (978-1-940395-07-4(0)) Yawn's Bks. & More, Inc.

Fforde, Jasper. The Eye of Zoltar. 2014. (Chronicles of Kazam Ser.). (ENG.). 416p. (J). (gr. 5-7). 16.99 (978-0-547-73849-9(8), HMH Books For Young Readers) Houghton Mifflin Harcourt Publishing Co.

—The Last Dragonslayer. 2011. 352p. pap. (978-1-4447-0720-5(5), Hodder Faith) Hodder & Stoughton.

—The Last Dragonslayer. (Chronicles of Kazam Ser.). (ENG.). (gr. 5-9). 2013. 306p. (YA). pap. 7.99 (978-0-544-10471-6(4))Bk. 1. 2012. 296p. (J). 16.99 (978-0-547-73847-5(1)) Houghton Mifflin Harcourt Publishing Co.

—The Song of the Quarkbeast. 2013. (Chronicles of Kazam Ser.: 2). (ENG.). 304p. (J). (gr. 5-7). 16.99 (978-0-547-73848-2(X)) Houghton Mifflin Harcourt Publishing Co.

—The Song of the Quarkbeast: The Chronicles of Kazam, Book 2. 2014. (Chronicles of Kazam Ser.). (ENG.). 304p. (J). (gr. 5-7). pap. 7.99 (978-0-544-33662-9(3), HMH Books For Young Readers) Houghton Mifflin Harcourt Publishing Co.

Fiedler, Lisa. A Fiery Friendship. Giacobino, Sebastian, illus. 2017. (Ages of Oz Ser.). (ENG.). 432p. (J). (gr. 3-7). 17.99 **(978-1-4814-6971-5(1)**, McElderry, Margaret K. Bks.) McElderry, Margaret K. Bks.

Fiedler, Lisa. Mouseheart. To, Vivienne, illus. 2014. (Mouseheart Ser.: 1). (ENG.). 320p. (J). (gr. 3-7). 16.99 (978-1-4424-8781-9(X), McElderry, Margaret K. Bks.) McElderry, Margaret K. Bks.

Fienberg, Anna. Power to Burn. 167p. (J). pap. (978-0-340-70930-6(8)) Hodder & Stoughton.

Fienberg, Anna & Fienberg, Barbara. Tashi & the Royal Tomb. Gamble, Kim, illus. 10th ed. 2007. (Tashi Ser.: 10). (ENG.). 64p. (Orig.). (J). (gr. k-2). pap. 8.99 (978-1-74114-973-9(8)) Allen & Unwin AUS. Dist: Independent Pubs. Group.

Figurska, A. B. The Island of Harklitt, 1 vol. 2010. 108p. pap. 19.95 (978-1-4489-4176-6(8)) PublishAmerica, Inc.

Filaretos, William. The Potion of Time: A Story of Demetrios. 2006. per. 12.95 (978-0-9724520-0-7(1)) Filaretos, William.

Fillisetti, Celeste. Just a Dream. 2013. 28p. pap. 13.95 (978-1-4787-1254-1(6)) Outskirts Pr., Inc.

Finch, David, illus. Disassembled. 2006. (ENG.). 176p. (YA). (gr. 8-17). pap. 15.99 (978-0-7851-1482-6(3)) Marvel Worldwide, Inc.

Findlay, Jamieson. The Blue Roan Child. 2004. (ENG., Illus.). 416p. (J). (gr. 5). mass mkt. 6.99 (978-0-7704-2876-1(2), Seal Bks.) Penguin Random House Canada Young Readers CAN. Dist: Penguin Random Hse. LLC.

Findlay, Lisa & Swift, Jonathan. Gulliver in Lilliput. Caparó, Antonio Javier, illus. 2010. (Step into Reading Ser.). (ENG.). 48p. (J). (gr. k-3). pap. 3.99 (978-0-375-86585-5(3), Random Hse. Bks. for Young Readers) Random Hse. Children's Bks.

Fine, Sarah. The Cursed Queen. 2017. (Impostor Queen Ser.: 2). (ENG., Illus.). 432p. (YA). (gr. 7). 17.99 (978-1-4814-4193-3(0), McElderry, Margaret K. Bks.) McElderry, Margaret K. Bks.

—The Impostor Queen. (ENG., Illus.). (YA). (gr. 7). 2017. (Impostor Queen Ser.: 1). 448p. pap. 11.99 (978-1-4814-4191-9(4)) 2016. 432p. 18.99 (978-1-4814-4190-2(6)) McElderry, Margaret K. Bks. (McElderry, Margaret K. Bks.).

—Sanctum, 0 vols. 2014. (Guards of the Shadowlands Ser.: 1). (ENG., Illus.). 448p. (YA). (gr. 9-11). pap. 9.99 (978-1-4778-1033-0(1), 9781477810330, Skyscape) Amazon Publishing.

Finlay, Lizzie, illus. Buri & the Marrow. 2004. 24p. (J). pap. (978-1-85269-590-3(0)); pap. (978-1-85269-587-3(0)); (ENG & TUR.). pap. (978-1-85269-591-0(9)) Mantra Lingua.

Finley, Leah. Ms T. 2007. 108p. (J). per. 8.95 (978-0-9794815-1-2(1)) Bellissima Publishing, LLC.

Finn, Perdita. Ever after High. 2016. (ENG.). 144p. (J). (gr. 3-7). 9.99 (978-0-316-39394-2(0)) Little, Brown Bks. for Young Readers.

—Rainbow Rocks. 2014. (Equestria Girls Ser.: 2). (ENG.). 192p. (J). (gr. 3-7). 9.99 (978-0-316-28486-8(6)) Little, Brown Bks. for Young Readers.

Finneron, Karyn A. Susu of the Frufru. Provencher, Annematie, illus. 2012. 32p. (-18). pap. 9.99 (978-0-9857362-0-0(8)) Nana's Stories.

Finnish, V. K. The Society's Traitor. Oshida, Tim, illus. 2012. (The Discoveries of Arthur Grey ser.: 1). (ENG.). 298p. (J). (gr. 4-8). 27.99 (978-0-9852202-0-4(1)) Panama Hat Publishing, Ltd.

Fisch, Sholly, et al. Through the Looking Glass! 2015. (All-New Batman: the Brave & the Bold Ser.). (ENG., Illus.). 32p. (gr. 2-3). lib. bdg. 22.60 (978-1-4342-9660-3(1)) Stone Arch Bks.

Fischel, Ana. The Twelve Quests - Book 2, a Dragon's Tooth. 2009. 158p. pap. (978-1-84923-874-8(X)) YouWriteOn.

—The Twelve Quests - Book 3, the Pied Piper's Flute. 2009. 158p. pap. (978-1-84923-875-5(8)) YouWriteOn.

—The Twelve Quests - Book 4, Rapunzel's Hair. 2009. 158p. pap. (978-1-84923-876-2(6)) YouWriteOn.

—The Twelve Quests - Book 5, a Firebird's Feather. 2009. 158p. pap. (978-1-84923-877-9(4)) YouWriteOn.

—The Twelve Quests - Book 6, the Enchanted Harp. 2009. 158p. pap. (978-1-84923-878-6(2)) YouWriteOn.

—The Twelve Quests - Book 7, a Bottled Genie. 2010. 158p. pap. *(978-1-84923-463-4(9))* YouWriteOn.
Fischer, JoAnn. Our Teacher Is A Fish! 2008. (ENG.). 34p. pap. 10.00 *(978-1-4196-7477-8(3))* CreateSpace Independent Publishing Platform.
Fishburne, Melody. Three Little Faeries in the Baby Lady Bug Adventure, 1 vol. 2009. 48p. pap. 16.95 *(978-1-4489-8897-6(7))* America Star Bks.
Fisher, Catherine. Darkhenge. 2006. 340p. (YA). (gr. 7-12). 15.99 *(978-0-06-078582-6(9))* HarperCollins Pubs.
—Incarceron. 2010. (Playaway Children Ser.). (J). 64.99 *(978-1-61637-331-3(8))* Findaway World, LLC.
—Incarceron. 2010. (Incarceron Ser.). (FRE.). 498p. (YA). (gr. 7-12). pap. *(978-2-266-17793-1(1))* Le Robert.
—Incarceron. November, S., ed. Yuen, Sammy, illus. 2011. (ENG.). 464p. (YA). (gr. 7-18). pap. 10.99 *(978-0-14-241852-9(8),* Firebird) Penguin Young Readers Group.
—Incarceron. 2011. (Incarceron Ser.). (ENG.). 442p. (gr. 7-12). 20.00 *(978-1-61383-117-5(X))* Perfection Learning Corp.
—INCARCERON. 2010. (SPA.). 512p. (J). (gr. 8-12). pap. 19.99 *(978-84-272-0047-0(1))* RBA Libros, S.A. ESP. Dist: Lectorum Pubns., Inc.
—Incarceron. l.t. ed. 2010. (Incarceron Ser.). (ENG.). 526p. 23.99 *(978-1-4104-2991-9(1))* Thorndike Pr.
—Incarceron. 2011. lib. bdg. 22.10 *(978-0-606-22590-8(0),* Turtleback) Turtleback Bks.
—The Oracle Betrayed. (Oracle Prophecies Ser.: Bk. 1). 352p. (J). 2004. (gr. 7-18). lib. bdg. 17.89 *(978-0-06-057158-0(6))* 2005. (gr. 8-18). reprint ed. pap. 7.99 *(978-0-06-057159-7(4),* Greenwillow Bks.) HarperCollins Pubs.
—The Oracle Betrayed. 2005. (Oracle Prophecies Ser.). (Illus.). 332p. (YA). (gr. 7-12). 14.65 *(978-0-7569-5269-3(7))* Perfection Learning Corp.
—Relic Master Part 1. 2013. (Relic Master Ser.). (ENG.). 752p. (YA). (gr. 7). pap. 9.99 *(978-0-14-242687-6(3),* Firebird) Penguin Young Readers Group.
—Relic Master Part 2. 2013. (Relic Master Ser.). (ENG.). 880p. (YA). (gr. 7). pap. 9.99 *(978-0-14-242686-9(5),* Firebird) Penguin Young Readers Group.
—Sapphique. (ENG.). (YA). (gr. 7-18). 2011. 480p. 10.99 *(978-0-14-241979-3(6),* Firebird) 2010. 464p. 17.99 *(978-0-8037-3397-8(6),* Dial Bks) Penguin Young Readers Group.
—The Scarab. 2006. (Oracle Prophecies Ser.: Bk. 3). 400p. (J). (gr. 5). lib. bdg. 18.89 *(978-0-06-057164-1(0))* HarperCollins Pubs.
—The Sphere of Secrets. 2006. (Oracle Prophecies Ser.: Bk. 2). 344p. (J). (gr. 5-9). per. 6.99 *(978-0-06-057160-3(8))* HarperCollins Pubs.
—The Speed of Darkness. 2016. (Obsidian Mirror Ser.). (ENG.). 400p. (YA). pap. 10.99 *(978-1-4449-2632-3(2))* Hachette Children's Group GBR. Dist: Hachette Bk. Group.
Fisher, Edward J. The Little Girl with the Magic Shoes: And Other Delights. 2008. 40p. 31.99 *(978-1-4363-4210-0(4))* Xlibris Corp.
Fisher, Jude. El Senor de los Anillos: Las Dos Torres. Torres, Estela Gutierrez, tr. 2003. (Lord of the Rings Ser.). (SPA., Illus.). 67p. (J). 14.95 *(978-84-450-7413-8(X))* Minotauro Ediciones ESP. Dist: Planeta Publishing Corp.
Fisher, Maire & Beautement, Tiah, eds. Follow the Road. 2015. (ENG., Illus.). 154p. (J). pap. *(978-1-920590-98-7(6))* Modajaji Bks.
Fisher, Rusty. Littlest Zombie's Story, 1 vol. 2014. (Story Time for Little Monsters Ser.). (ENG.). 24p. (J). (gr. -1-4). lib. bdg. 27.07 *(978-1-62402-023-0(2),* Looking Glass Library) Magic Wagon.
Fishman, Linda Charles. The Little Girl Who Loves Make Believe: Book 2 of Grandma's Girls. 2012. 24p. pap. 17.99 *(978-1-4685-4467-1(5))* AuthorHouse.
Fisk, Nicholas. Flip Side. 140p. pap. 8.99 *(978-0-340-71019-7(5))* Hodder & Stoughton GBR. Dist: Trafalgar Square Publishing.
Fisk, Pauline. Midnight Blue. 2005. 217p. (gr. -1). 16.95 *(978-0-7569-5683-7(8))* Perfection Learning Corp.
Fitzgerald, D. M. The True Story of the Big Red Onion. Cudd, Savannah, illus. 2013. 36p. 18.99 *(978-0-9890288-7-5(9));* pap. 10.99 *(978-0-9890288-5-1(2))* Mindstir Media.
Fitzgerald, Gyleen Xavier. The Dream: A Magical Journey in Colourful Stitches. 2005. (ENG., Illus.). 90p. (J). (gr. 4-7). 29.95 *(978-0-9768215-1-9(6))* FPI Publishing.
Fitzpatrick, Becca. The Complete Hush, Hush Saga: Hush, Hush; Crescendo; Silence; Finale. 2013. (Hush, Hush Saga Ser.). (ENG., Illus.). 1824p. (YA). (gr. 9). pap. 47.99 *(978-1-4814-0084-8(3),* Simon & Schuster Bks. For Young Readers) Simon & Schuster Bks. For Young Readers.
—Finale. 2012. (Hush, Hush Saga Ser.: Bk. 4). (ENG.). 464p. (YA). (gr. 9). 19.99 *(978-1-4424-2667-2(5),* Simon & Schuster Bks. For Young Readers) Simon & Schuster Bks. For Young Readers.
Five Children & It. 2013. 58p. pap. 5.60 *(978-1-236-72792-3(4))* General Bks. LLC.
Five Children & It. 2010. (CAM.). 142p. pap. 10.95 *(978-1-4385-3539-5(2),* Book Jungle) Standard Pubns., Inc.
Flambaum, Victor & Flambaum, Andrew. How to Make a Big Bang: A Cosmic Journey. 2012. (ENG.). 226p. (J). (gr. 7-10). pap. 14.95 *(978-1-936782-72-7(3))* Salem Author Services.
Flammer, JoAnn. The Last Wish. 2007. 80p. pap. 10.00 *(978-0-615-16197-6(9))* Flammer, Josephine.
Flanagan, John. The Battle for Skandia. (Ranger's Apprentice Ser.: 4). (ENG.). (J). (gr. 5-18). 2008. 304p. 18.99 *(978-0-399-24457-5(3),* Philomel Bks.)Bk. 4. 2009. 336p. 8.99 *(978-0-14-241340-1(2),* Puffin Books) Penguin Young Readers Group.
—The Battle for Skandia. 2009. (Ranger's Apprentice Ser.: 4). lib. bdg. 19.65 *(978-0-606-02208-8(2),* Turtleback) Turtleback Bks.
—The Battle of Hackham Heath. 2016. (Ranger's Apprentice: the Early Years Ser.: 2). (ENG., Illus.). 352p. (J). (gr. 5). 18.99 *(978-0-399-16362-3(X),* Philomel Bks.) Penguin Young Readers Group.
—The Burning Bridge, Bk. 2. 2007. (Ranger's Apprentice Ser.: 2). (ENG.). 304p. (J). (gr. 5-18). 8.99 *(978-0-14-240842-1(5),* Puffin Books) Penguin Young Readers Group.
—The Burning Bridge. 2007. (Ranger's Apprentice Ser.: 2). 262p. lib. bdg. 19.65 *(978-1-4177-9330-3(9),* Turtleback) Turtleback Bks.
—The Emperor of Nihon-Ja, 10 vols., Bk. 10. (Ranger's Apprentice Ser.: 10). (ENG.). (J). (gr. 5-18). 2012. 464p. 8.99 *(978-0-14-241859-8(5),* Puffin Books) 2011. 448p. 18.99 *(978-0-399-25500-7(1),* Philomel Bks.) Penguin Young Readers Group.
—The Emperor of Nihon-Ja. 2012. (Ranger's Apprentice Ser.: 10). lib. bdg. 19.65 *(978-0-606-23641-6(4),* Turtleback) Turtleback Bks.
—Erak's Ransom, Bk. 7. (Ranger's Apprentice Ser.: 7). (ENG.). (J). (gr. 5-18). 2011. 416p. 8.99 *(978-0-14-241525-2(1),* Puffin Books) 2010. 384p. 18.99 *(978-0-399-25205-1(3),* Philomel Bks.) Penguin Young Readers Group.
—The Ghostfaces. 2016. (Brotherband Chronicles Ser.: 6). (ENG.). 400p. (J). (gr. 5). 18.99 *(978-0-399-16357-9(3),* Philomel Bks.) Penguin Young Readers Group.
—Halt's Peril, Bk. 9. (Ranger's Apprentice Ser.: 9). (ENG.). (J). (gr. 5-18). 2012. 416p. 8.99 *(978-0-14-241858-1(7),* Puffin Books) 2010. 400p. 18.99 *(978-0-399-25207-5(X),* Philomel Bks.) Penguin Young Readers Group.
—Halt's Peril. 2012. (Ranger's Apprentice Ser.: 9). lib. bdg. 19.65 *(978-0-606-23640-9(6),* Turtleback) Turtleback Bks.
—The Hunters. (Brotherband Chronicles Ser.: 3). (ENG.). (J). (gr. 5). 2014. 448p. pap. 8.99 *(978-0-14-242664-7(4),* Puffin Books) 2012. 416p. 18.99 *(978-0-399-25621-9(0),* Philomel Bks.) Penguin Young Readers Group.
—The Hunters. 2014. (Brotherband Chronicles Ser.: 3). lib. bdg. 19.65 *(978-0-606-35708-1(4))* Turtleback Bks.
—The Icebound Land. 2007. (Ranger's Apprentice Ser.: Bk. 3). 260p. (J). 25.66 *(978-1-4287-4632-9(3),* Follettbound) Follett School Solutions.
—The Icebound Land, Bk. 3. (Ranger's Apprentice Ser.: 3). (ENG.). (J). (gr. 5-18). 2008. 304p. 8.99 *(978-0-14-241075-2(6),* Puffin Books) 2007. 272p. 18.99 *(978-0-399-24456-8(5),* Philomel Bks.) Penguin Young Readers Group.
—The Invaders. (Brotherband Chronicles Ser.: 2). (ENG.). (J). (gr. 5). 2013. 448p. pap. 8.99 *(978-0-14-242663-0(6),* Puffin Books) 2012. 432p. 18.99 *(978-0-399-25620-2(2),* Philomel Bks.) Penguin Young Readers Group.
—The Invaders. 2013. (Brotherband Chronicles Ser.: 2). lib. bdg. 19.65 *(978-0-606-26637-6(2),* Turtleback) Turtleback Bks.
—The Kings of Clonmel, Bk. 8. (Ranger's Apprentice Ser.: 8). (ENG.). (J). (gr. 5-18). 2011. 400p. 8.99 *(978-0-14-241857-4(9),* Puffin Books) 2010. 368p. 18.99 *(978-0-399-25206-8(1),* Philomel Bks.) Penguin Young Readers Group.
—The Lost Stories. (Ranger's Apprentice Ser.: 11). (ENG.). (J). (gr. 5). 2013. 464p. pap. 8.99 *(978-0-14-242195-6(2),* Puffin Books) 2011. (Illus.). 432p. 18.99 *(978-0-399-25618-9(0),* Philomel Bks.) Penguin Young Readers Group.
—The Outcasts. 2011. (Brotherband Chronicles: Bk. 1). (ENG.). (J). (gr. 3-7). 54.99 *(978-1-61657-043-9(1))* Findaway World, LLC.
—The Outcasts. (Brotherband Chronicles Ser.: 1). (ENG.). (J). (gr. 5). 2012. 464p. pap. 8.99 *(978-0-14-242194-9(4),* Puffin Books) 2011. 448p. 18.99 *(978-0-399-25619-6(9),* Philomel Bks.) Penguin Young Readers Group.
—The Outcasts. 2012. (Brotherband Chronicles Ser.: 1). lib. bdg. 19.65 *(978-0-606-26636-9(4),* Turtleback) Turtleback Bks.
—The Royal Ranger. 2013. (Ranger's Apprentice Ser.: 12). (ENG.). 464p. (J). (gr. 5). 18.99 *(978-0-399-16360-9(3),* Philomel Bks.) Penguin Publishing Group.
—The Royal Ranger. 2014. (Ranger's Apprentice Ser.: 12). (ENG.). 480p. (J). (gr. 5). pap. 8.99 *(978-0-14-242731-6(4),* Puffin Books) Penguin Young Readers Group.
—The Royal Ranger. 2014. (Ranger's Apprentice Ser.: 12). lib. bdg. 19.65 *(978-0-606-36604-5(0))* Turtleback Bks.
—The Ruins of Gorlan, Bk. 1. 2006. (Ranger's Apprentice Ser.: 1). (ENG.). 288p. (J). (gr. 5-18). 8.99 *(978-0-14-240663-2(5),* Puffin Books) Penguin Young Readers Group.
—Scorpion Mountain. 2014. (Brotherband Chronicles Ser.: 5). (ENG., Illus.). 464p. (J). (gr. 5). 18.99 *(978-0-399-16356-2(5),* Philomel Bks.) Penguin Publishing Group.
—Scorpion Mountain. 2015. (Brotherband Chronicles Ser.: 5). (ENG.). 480p. (J). (gr. 5). 8.99 *(978-0-14-242727-9(6),* Puffin Books) Penguin Young Readers Group.
—Scorpion Mountain. 2015. (Brotherband Chronicles Ser.: 5). lib. bdg. 19.65 *(978-0-606-37563-4(5))* Turtleback Bks.
—The Siege of Macindaw, Bk. 6. (Ranger's Apprentice Ser.: 6). (ENG.). (J). (gr. 5-18). 2010. 336p. 8.99 *(978-0-14-241524-5(3),* Puffin Books) 2009. 304p. 18.99 *(978-0-399-25033-0(6),* Philomel Bks.) Penguin Young Readers Group.
—Slaves of Socorro. 2014. (Brotherband Chronicles Ser.: Bk. 4). (ENG., Illus.). 480p. (J). 18.99 *(978-0-399-16355-5(7),* Philomel Bks.) Penguin Publishing Group.
—Slaves of Socorro. 2015. (Brotherband Chronicles Ser.: 4). (ENG.). 496p. (J). (gr. 5). pap. 8.99 *(978-0-14-242726-2(8),* Puffin Books) Penguin Young Readers Group.
—Slaves of Socorro. 2015. (Brotherband Chronicles Ser.: 4). lib. bdg. 19.65 *(978-0-606-36771-4(3))* Turtleback Bks.
—The Sorcerer of the North, 5 vols., Bk. 5. (Ranger's Apprentice Ser.: 5). (ENG.). (J). (gr. 5-18). 2009. 336p. pap. 8.99 *(978-0-14-241429-3(8),* Puffin Books) 2008. 304p. 18.99 *(978-0-399-25032-3(8),* Philomel Bks.) Penguin Young Readers Group.
—The Sorcerer of the North. 2009. (Ranger's Apprentice Ser.: 5). lib. bdg. 19.65 *(978-0-606-02237-8(6),* Turtleback) Turtleback Bks.
—The Tournament at Gorlan. 2015. (Ranger's Apprentice: the Early Years Ser.: 1). (ENG., Illus.). 384p. (J). (gr. 5). 18.99 *(978-0-399-16361-6(1),* Philomel Bks.) Penguin Young Readers Group.
Flanagan, John A. The Tournament at Gorlan. 2016. (Ranger's Apprentice the Early Years Ser.: 1). lib. bdg. 19.65 *(978-0-606-39332-4(3))* Turtleback Bks.
Fletcher, Pamela. Who Is Freddy Farlittle? 2011. 40p. pap. 16.99 *(978-1-4634-1086-5(7))* AuthorHouse.
Fletcher, Susan. Ancient, Strange, & Lovely. (Dragon Chronicles Ser.). (ENG.). 336p. (J). (gr. 3-7). 2011. pap. 10.99 *(978-1-4169-5787-4(1))* 2010. 16.99 *(978-1-4169-5786-7(3))* Simon & Schuster Children's Publishing. (Atheneum Bks. for Young Readers).
—Dadblamed Union Army Cow. Root, Kimberly Bulcken, illus. 2007. (ENG.). 32p. (J). (gr. k-3). 16.99 *(978-0-7636-2263-3(X))* Candlewick Pr.
—Flight of the Dragon Kyn. 2010. (Dragon Chronicles Ser.). (ENG.). 240p. (J). (gr. 3-7). pap. 10.99 *(978-1-4169-9713-9(X),* Atheneum Bks. for Young Readers) Simon & Schuster Children's Publishing.
—Sign of the Dove. 2010. (Dragon Chronicles Ser.). (ENG.). 240p. (J). (gr. 3-7). pap. 10.99 *(978-1-4169-9714-6(8),* Atheneum Bks. for Young Readers) Simon & Schuster Children's Publishing.
Flinn, Alex. Beastly. (Kendra Chronicles Ser.: 1). (ENG.). (YA). (gr. 9). 2009. 336p. pap. 9.99 *(978-0-06-199866-9(4))* 2007. 320p. 17.99 *(978-0-06-087416-2(3))* 2012. 512p. pap. 9.99 *(978-0-06-211391-7(7))* 2011. 336p. pap. 9.99 *(978-0-06-196328-5(3))* HarperCollins Pubs. (HarperTeen).
—Beheld. 2017. 368p. (YA). (gr. 8). 17.99 *(978-0-06-213455-4(8),* HarperTeen) HarperCollins Pubs.
—Bewitching: The Kendra Chronicles. 2013. (Kendra Chronicles Ser.: 2). (ENG.). 368p. (YA). (gr. 8). pap. 9.99 *(978-0-06-202416-9(7),* HarperTeen) HarperCollins Pubs.
—Cloaked. 2012. (ENG.). 368p. (YA). (gr. 8). pap. 9.99 *(978-0-06-087424-7(4),* HarperTeen) HarperCollins Pubs.
Flood, Tony. Jody Richards & the Secret Potion. 2nd ed. 2012. 146p. pap. *(978-0-9569682-9-6(5))* My Voice Publishing.
Flor Ada, Alma. Extra! Extra! Fairy-Tale News from Hidden Forest. Tryon, Leslie, illus. 2007. (ENG.). 32p. (J). (gr. k-3). 17.99 *(978-0-689-82582-8(X),* Atheneum Bks. for Young Readers) Simon & Schuster Children's Publishing.
Flor Ada, Alma & Campoy, F. Isabel. Ratoncito Prez, Cartero. Escriva, Sandra Lopez, illus. 2015. (Santillana USA Ser.).Tr. of New Job for Pérez, the Mouse. (SPA.). 32p. (J). (gr. 6-6). pap. 15.95 *(978-1-63113-547-7(3),* Santillana) Santillana USA Publishing Co., Inc.
Flores, Eileen. To All a Good Knight. 2008. 92p. pap. 12.50 *(978-1-4389-2267-6(1))* AuthorHouse.
Floyd, Donyell. The Curious Child. 2008. 16p. per. 11.95 *(978-1-59800-046-7(2))* Outskirts Pr., Inc.
Floyd, Lucy. Conejo y Tortuga van a la Escuela. Flor Ada, Alma & Campoy, F. Isabel, trs. from ENG. Denise, Christopher, illus. 2010. (Green Light Readers Level 1 Ser.).Tr. of Rabbit & Turtle Go to School. (SPA & ENG.). 28p. (J). (gr. -1-3). pap. 3.99 *(978-0-547-33898-9(8))* Houghton Mifflin Harcourt Publishing Co.
The Flying Hockey Stick. 2007. (Illus.). 64p. (J). (gr. -1-3). 18.95 *(978-1-930900-31-8(7))* Purple Hse. Pr.
Flynn, Dave. Nick & the Old Man of the Mountain. 2010. 40p. pap. 18.49 *(978-1-4389-9356-0(0))* AuthorHouse.
Fodi, Lee Edward. Kendra Kandlestar & the Box of Whispers. Fodi, Lee Edward, illus. 2005. (Illus.). 227p. (J). (gr. 2). 16.95 *(978-1-933285-10-8(9));* per. 8.95 *(978-1-933285-11-5(7))* Brown Books Publishing Group.
—Kendra Kandlestar & the Crack in Kazah. 2011. (Illus.). 294p. (J). pap. 8.95 *(978-1-61254-019-1(8))* Brown Books Publishing Group.
—Kendra Kandlestar & the Crack in Kazah. 2014. (Kendra Kandlestar Ser.: 4). (ENG., Illus.). 274p. (J). (gr. 3-6). pap. 8.95 *(978-1-927018-28-6(5),* 9781927018286) Simply Read Bks. CAN. Dist: Ingram Publisher Services.
—Kendra Kandlestar & the Search for Arazeen. 2015. (Kendra Kandlestar Ser.: 5). (ENG., Illus.). 240p. (J). (gr. 3-6). pap. 9.95 *(978-1-927018-29-3(3))* Simply Read Bks. CAN. Dist: Ingram Publisher Services.
—Kendra Kandlestar & the Shard from Greeve. 2014. (Kendra Kandlestar Ser.: 3). (ENG., Illus.). 284p. (J). (gr. 3-6). pap. 8.95 *(978-1-927018-27-9(7),* 9781927018279) Simply Read Bks. CAN. Dist: Ingram Publisher Services.
Födi, Lee Edward, illus. Kendra Kandlestar & the Box of Whispers. 2013. (Kendra Kandlestar Ser.: 1). (ENG.). 228p. (J). (gr. 3-6). pap. 8.95 *(978-1-927018-25-5(0))* Simply Read Bks. CAN. Dist: Ingram Publisher Services.
—Kendra Kandlestar & the Door to Unger. 2013. (Kendra Kandlestar Ser.: 2). (ENG.). 260p. (J). (gr. 2-5). pap. 8.95 *(978-1-927018-26-2(9))* Simply Read Bks. CAN. Dist: Ingram Publisher Services.
Fonseca, Mireya (Adaptación), adapted by. NEREO -el anciano del Mar. 2005. (SPA.). 32p. *(978-958-30-1909-8(7))* Panamericana Editorial.
Fontes, Justine. Barbie in the Pink Shoes. 2013. (Book & Jewelry Ser.: 1). (ENG.). 24p. (J). (gr. -1-3). 10.99 *(978-0-7944-2785-6(5))* Reader's Digest Assn., Inc., The.
Fontes, Justine & Fontes, Ron. Casebook: Vampires. 2009. (Top Secret Graphica Mysteries Ser.). (Illus.). 48p. (YA). (gr. 2-6). 29.25 *(978-1-60754-606-1(X));* pap. 11.75 *(978-1-60754-607-8(8))* Windmill Bks.
—Casebook: Werewolves. 2009. (Top Secret Graphica Mysteries Ser.). (Illus.). 48p. (YA). (gr. 2-6). 29.25 *(978-1-60754-609-2(4));* pap. 11.75 *(978-1-60754-611-5(6))* Windmill Bks.
Foody, Amanda. Daughter of the Burning City. 2017. (ENG.). 384p. 19.99 ***(978-0-373-21243-9(7),*** Harlequin Teen) Harlequin Enterprises, Ltd. CAN. Dist: HarperCollins Pubs.
Forbes, Anne. Dragonfire, 1 vol. 2006. (ENG.). 256p. (J). per. 11.95 *(978-0-86315-552-9(9))* Floris Bks. GBR. Dist: SteinerBooks, Inc.
—The Underground City. 2008. (Contemporary Kelpies Ser.). (ENG.). 272p. (J). pap. *(978-0-86315-637-3(1))* Floris Bks.
Ford, Jayme. The Adventures of Glop-A-Lopikins. 2012. 32p. pap. 24.95 *(978-1-62709-207-4(2))* America Star Bks.
Ford, RoShawn T. Marty & the Magical Christmas Tree. 2012. 24p. pap. 17.99 *(978-1-4772-3719-9(4))* AuthorHouse.
Ford, Sharon Lea. The Pages of Lost Time. 2010. 212p. 24.95 *(978-1-60911-127-4(3),* Eloquent Bks.) Strategic Book Publishing & Rights Agency (SBPRA).
Foreman, Colin. A Moment Comes. Colin Foreman. 2007. (Keepers & Seekers Ser.). (ENG., Illus.). 320p. pap. *(978-0-9548949-2-4(8))* Myroy Bks. Ltd.
The Forest of the Frendibles. 2006. (J). mass mkt. *(978-0-9791982-0-5(8))* Pine Cone Pr.
Forgey, Winchester. Chronicle of the Bent Nail. 2004. (J). per. *(978-0-9666572-7-2(6))* Acacia Publishing, Inc.
Forman, M. L. Adventurers Wanted, Book 1: Slathbog's Gold. 2011. 400p. mass mkt. 7.99 *(978-1-60641-681-5(2))* Deseret Bk. Co.
—Adventurers Wanted, Book 2: The Horn of Moran. 2012. (J). pap. 7.99 *(978-1-60908-911-5(1))* 2011. 400p. 39.99 *(978-1-60641-255-8(8))* Deseret Bk. Co.
—Adventurers Wanted, Book 3: Albrek's Tomb. 2013. (Adventurers Wanted Ser.: 3). (ENG.). 504p. (J). (gr. 5). pap. 9.99 *(978-1-60907-339-8(8),* Shadow Mountain) Shadow Mountain Publishing.
—Adventurers Wanted, Book 4: Sands of Nezza. 2013. (Adventurers Wanted Ser.: 4). (ENG.). 400p. (J). (gr. 5). 19.99 *(978-1-60907-329-9(0),* Shadow Mountain) Shadow Mountain Publishing.
—Adventures Wanted, Book 3: Albrek's Tomb. 2012. (YA). 19.99 *(978-1-60908-892-7(1))* Deseret Bk. Co.
Forman, Mark. Slathbog's Gold. 2009. (Adventurers Wanted Ser.: Bk. 1). 432p. (J). 17.95 *(978-1-60641-029-5(6),* Shadow Mountain) Shadow Mountain Publishing.
Formento, Alison Ashley. Twigs. 2013. (ENG.). 272p. (YA). 17.99 *(978-1-4405-6565-6(1),* Simon Pulse) Simon Pulse.
Forney, Lane. The Super Power Teens 2: A Blast from the Past. 2010. 137p. pap. 14.99 *(978-0-557-09707-4(X))* Lulu Pr., Inc.
Forsberg, Victoria. Little Irma Shirley & the Wand of Better: City Adventures. 2013. (ENG.). 23p. (J). pap. 10.95 *(978-1-4327-9671-6(2))* Outskirts Pr., Inc.
Forster, Miriam. City of a Thousand Dolls. 2013. (ENG.). 368p. (YA). (gr. 8). 17.99 *(978-0-06-212130-1(8),* HarperTeen) HarperCollins Pubs.
Forward, Toby. Dragonborn. (Dragonborn Ser.: 1). (ENG.). (YA). (gr. 3-6). 2013. 368p. pap. 8.99 *(978-1-59990-983-7(9),* 9781599909837) 2012. 352p. 16.99 *(978-1-59990-724-6(0),* 9781599907246) Bloomsbury Publishing USA. (Bloomsbury USA Childrens).
—Starborn: A Dragonborn Novel. 2016. (Dragonborn Ser.: 4). (ENG.). 448p. (J). 16.99 *(978-1-61963-842-6(8),* 9781619638426, Bloomsbury USA Childrens) Bloomsbury Publishing USA.
Fosse, Mika. Garage People. 2008. 84p. pap. 9.95 *(978-1-60693-500-2(3),* Eloquent Bks.) Strategic Book Publishing & Rights Agency (SBPRA).
Foster, D. S. The Stone Heart. Lewis, Jesse, illus. 2012. (J). pap. 12.99 *(978-1-937331-14-6(8))* ShadeTree Publishing, LLC.
Foster, Patricia. Where Did You Come from, Tiny Drop? 2008. 24p. pap. 24.95 *(978-1-60610-224-4(9))* America Star Bks.
Fournier, Elizabeth. Sailboat Dreams: Monkey Island. 2012. 16p. pap. 15.99 *(978-1-4772-7670-9(X))* AuthorHouse.
Fox, Jennifer. Meet the Boxtrolls. 2014. (Passport to Reading Level 2 Ser.). (J). lib. bdg. 13.55 *(978-0-606-36529-1(X))* Turtleback Bks.
—My Little Pony: Hearts & Hooves. 2013. (Passport to Reading Level 1 Ser.). (ENG., Illus.). 32p. (J). (gr. -1-3). 4.99 *(978-0-316-24797-9(9))* Little, Brown Bks. for Young Readers.
Fox, Lee White. Toby Erdrich & the Golden Eclipse. Selyov, Trebor E., ed. 2005. 170p. (YA). (gr. 7-12). pap. 11.95 *(978-0-9665055-7-3(3),* 5) Hallmark Emporium.
Fox, Lucy. Keeper of the Enchanted Pool. 2009. 184p. pap. *(978-1-84923-437-5(X))* YouWriteOn.
Fox Mazer, Norma. Saturday, the Twelfth of October. 2015. (ENG.). 274p. (J). (gr. 3). pap. 13.95 *(978-1-939601-31-5(2))* Ig Publishing, Inc.
Fox, R. J. Stuart & His Incredibly Obnoxious Magical Book: Soccer, 1 vol. 2009. 86p. pap. 19.95 *(978-1-4489-9833-3(6))* America Star Bks.
Foxlee, Karen. Ophelia & the Marvelous Boy. 2014. (ENG.). 240p. (J). (gr. 3-7). 16.99 *(978-0-385-75354-8(3),* Knopf Bks. for Young Readers) Random Hse. Children's Bks.
Fragoza, Samuel. Josh & the Sock Army. 2012. 24p. pap. 17.99 *(978-1-4772-9532-8(1))* AuthorHouse.
Franco. Itty Bitty Comics: Grimmiss Island. Baltazar, Art, illus. 2015. (Itty Bitty Comics Ser.). (ENG.). 104p. (J). (gr. 3-7). pap. 12.99 *(978-1-61655-768-3(0))* Dark Horse Comics.
Frantz, Jennifer, adapted by. Narnia: Welcome to Narnia. 2005. (Illus.). 32p. (J). lib. bdg. 13.85 *(978-1-4242-0617-9(0))* Fitzgerald Bks.
Frazin, Julian. A Little Dab of Paint. Schirmer, Susan, illus. 2012. 32p. (J). 22.95 *(978-0-9838846-5-1(X))* Berwick Court Publishing.
Frederick Edward Pitts. Tale of the Hummingopotomus: The Flight for Life. 2009. 40p. pap. 18.49 *(978-1-4389-6453-9(6))* AuthorHouse.
Freeman, Greg. The Legend of Booga Bearia: Land of the. 2005. 128p. pap. 19.95 *(978-1-4137-8411-4(9))* PublishAmerica, Inc.
Freeman, Melita. The Knight of Lord Greengate's Castle. Freeman, Melita, illus. 2012. (Illus.). 28p. pap. 10.00 *(978-1-936750-90-0(2))* Yorkshire Publishing Group.
Freeman, R. Gregory. A Carpenter's Tale: The Mystery of Kidron Valley. 2006. (Illus.). 34p. per. 10.95 *(978-1-60002-118-3(2),* 3901) Mountain Valley Publishing, LLC.
Freeman, Richard. The Legend of Booga Bearia. 2004. 117p. pap. 19.95 *(978-1-4137-2016-7(1))* America Star Bks.
Freer, Dave. Changeling's Island. 2016. (ENG.). 256p. (YA). (gr. 6). pap. 10.99 *(978-1-4767-8120-4(6))* Baen Bks.
French, Vivian. The Flight of Dragons: The Fourth Tale from the Five Kingdoms. Collins, Ross, illus. 2011. (Tales from the Five Kingdoms Ser.: 4). (ENG.). 208p. (J). (gr. 3-7). 15.99 *(978-0-7636-5083-4(8))* Candlewick Pr.
—The Flight of Dragons: The Fourth Tale from the Five Kingdoms. Collins, Ross, illus. 2012. (Tales from the Five Kingdoms Ser.: 4). (ENG.). 256p. (J). (gr. 3-7). pap. 5.99 *(978-0-7636-5133-6(8))* Candlewick Pr.
—The Heart of Glass: The Third Tale from the Five Kingdoms. Collins, Ross, illus. 2010. (Tales from the Five Kingdoms Ser.: 3). (ENG.). 256p. (J). (gr. 3-7). 14.99 *(978-0-7636-4814-5(0))* Candlewick Pr.
—The Music of Zombies. Collins, Ross, illus. 2013. (Tales from the Five Kingdoms Ser.). (ENG.). 304p. (J). (gr. 3-7). 15.99 *(978-0-7636-5930-1(4))* Candlewick Pr.
—Princess Georgia & the Shimmering Pearl. Gibb, Sarah, illus. 2008. (Tiara Club Ser.: No. 3). (ENG.). 80p. (J). (gr. 1-4). pap. 3.99 *(978-0-06-143486-0(8),* Harper Trophy) HarperCollins Pubs.
Frewin Jones, Allan. The Mole & Beverley Miller. l.t. ed. 2007. 232p. per. *(978-1-905665-34-1(2))* Pollinger In Print.
Frie, Robert R. & Zahradnik, Kristen M. Windy Wildwood: The Secret in the Attic. 2004. 103p. (J). per. 9.95 *(978-0-9753641-0-9(3))* Zahrob Publishing Co.

Friel, Maeve. Watch-in-Train Vol. 2: Spelling Trouble. Reed, Nathan, illus. 2011. (Witch-In-Training Ser.: 2). (ENG.). 96p. (J). pap. 5.99 *(978-0-00-713342-0(1))* HarperCollins Pubs. Ltd. GBR. Dist: HarperCollins Pubs.

Friend, Catherine. When Night & Day Meet. 2005. 32p. (J). *(978-0-7868-0112-1(3))* Hyperion Pr.

Friend, Gaythel & Miller, Dalton. The Mystery of the Green Box. 2006. 88p. per. 8.95 *(978-1-59824-147-1(8))* E-BookTime LLC.

Friend, Gaythel Boggs & Miller, Dalton. Foundation of a Clown, 1 vol. 2010. 58p. pap. 19.95 *(978-1-4489-8253-0(7))* America Star Bks.

Friesner, Esther & Friesner, Esther M. Nobody's Princess. 2008. (Princesses of Myth Ser.). (ENG., Illus.). 336p. (YA). (gr. 7-11). pap. 8.99 *(978-0-375-87529-8(8)*, Ember) Random Hse. Children's Bks.

Frisch, Aaron. Pirates at the Plate. Summers, Mark, illus. 2012. (ENG.). 32p. (J). (gr. 1-3). 17.99 *(978-1-56846-210-3(7)*, Creative Editions) Creative Co., The.

Froeb, Lori C. Butterphants & Eleflies. Rinaldo, Luana, illus. 2010. (Sliding Surprise Ser.). (ENG.). 10p. (J). bds. 7.99 *(978-0-7944-1932-5(1))* Reader's Digest Assn., Inc., The.

Frontiera, Deborah K. Eric & the Enchanted Leaf / Eric y la Hoja Encantada: A Visit with Canis Lupis / una Visita con Canis Lupis. Santillan-Cruz, Silvia R., tr. Scott, Korey, illus. 2nd l.t. ed. 2005. (SPA & ENG.). 32p. (J). lib. bdg. 16.95 *(978-0-9663629-8-5(5))* By Grace Enterprises.

Frost, C. Amethyst. Mourning under the Bridge. 2012. 280p. pap. 9.99 *(978-0-9847236-2-1(5))* Frost, C. A.

Frost, Robert Temple. Long Trip Home: Stand up Paddleboard Fantasy. 2013. 82p. pap. 10.95 *(978-1-62212-924-9(5)*, Strategic Bk. Publishing) Strategic Book Publishing & Rights Agency (SBPRA).

Froud, Brian, illus. Chelsea Morning. 2004. (ENG.). 32p. (J). (gr. -1-3). 17.95 *(978-1-59687-178-6(4))* IBks., Inc.

Fry, Erin. Secrets of the Book, 0 vols. 2014. (ENG.). 304p. (YA). (gr. 7-9). 14.99 *(978-1-4778-4716-9(2)*, 9781477847169, Two Lions) Amazon Publishing.

Fryer, Samantha. A Sorcerer's Tale. 2008. 116p. pap. 14.95 *(978-1-84799-366-3(4))* Lulu Pr., Inc.

Fujimoto, Yoshie. The Ninjas & Goblins. 2008. pap. 13.00 *(978-0-8059-8638-9(3))* Dorrance Publishing Co., Inc.

Fujishima, Kosuke. Oh My Goddess!, Vol. 25. Fujishima, Kosuke, illus. 2007. (Oh My Goddess! Ser.). (ENG., Illus.). 176p. pap. 10.95 *(978-1-59307-644-3(4))* Dark Horse Comics.

—Oh My Goddess! Volume 43. Horn, Carl Gustav, ed. Fujishima, Kosuke, illus. 2013. (ENG., Illus.). 176p. pap. 12.99 *(978-1-61655-082-0(1))* Dark Horse Comics.

Fukuda, Andrew. The Trap. 2013. (Hunt Trilogy Ser.: 3). (ENG.). 320p. (YA). (gr. 7). 18.99 *(978-1-250-00512-0(4)*, 9781250005120, St. Martin's Griffin) St. Martin's Pr.

Fukui, Isamu. Truancy. 2010. (Truancy Ser.: 1). (ENG.). 432p. (YA). (gr. 8-12). pap. 24.99 *(978-0-7653-2258-6(7)*, 9780765322586, Tor Teen) Doherty, Tom Assocs., LLC.

—Truancy Origins. 2011. (Truancy Ser.: 2). (ENG.). 384p. (YA). (gr. 8-12). pap. 19.99 *(978-0-7653-2264-7(1)*, 9780765322647, Tor Teen) Doherty, Tom Assocs., LLC.

Fuller, Dawn. Looper: Bullying. 2012. 32p. pap. 14.51 *(978-1-4669-1989-1(2))* Trafford Publishing.

Fuller, Niki. The Cat from M-31. 2009. 24p. pap. 15.99 *(978-1-4415-3826-0(7))* Xlibris Corp.

Funderburg, April. Soul Snatcher. 2009. 84p. pap. 19.95 *(978-1-60749-765-3(4))* America Star Bks.

Funk, Rachel. Christabelle in the Museum of Time. 2007. 217p. pap. 14.95 *(978-1-4303-2572-7(0))* Lulu Pr., Inc.

Funke, Cornelia. Dragon Rider. 2011.Tr. of Drachenreiter. (ENG.). 560p. (J). (gr. 2-5). pap. 9.99 *(978-0-545-31648-4(0)*, Chicken Hse., The) Scholastic, Inc.

—Igraine the Brave. Bell, Anthea, tr. Funke, Cornelia, illus. l.t. ed. 2008. (Thorndike Literacy Bridge Middle Reader Ser.). (Illus.). 259p. (J). (gr. 4-7). 23.95 *(978-1-4104-0341-4(6))* Thorndike Pr.

Funny Faces. 120p. 19.99 *(978-1-58279-127-2(9)*, 92) Standard International Media.

Fuqua, J. Scott. Secrets of the Greaser Hotel. 2014. (ENG., Illus.). 280p. 25.00 *(978-1-61088-130-2(3))* Bancroft Pr.

Furman, Ben. Sam's Quest. 2008. 240p. pap. 8.95 *(978-0-9778731-4-2(5))* Black Hawk Pr., Inc., The.

—Sam's Quest for the Crimson Crystal. 2007. 189p. (J). per. 8.95 *(978-0-9778731-8-0(8))* Black Hawk Pr., Inc., The.

Furman, Simon. Dragons: Defenders of Berk Volume 1. Nazif, Iwan & Lawrence, Jack, illus. 2016. (ENG.). 112p. (J). (gr. 1-4). pap. 12.99 *(978-1-78585-678-5(2))* Titan Bks. Ltd. GBR. Dist: Penguin Random Hse. LLC.

Furman, Simon & Nazif, Iwan. Dragons - Riders of Berk. 2015. (ENG., Illus.). 112p. (J). 22.99 *(978-1-78276-766-4(5))* Titan Bks. Ltd. GBR. Dist: Penguin Random Hse. LLC.

Gabolinscy, Jack & Oppatt, Karen. Danny's Dream. 2008. (Rigby Focus Forward: Level O Ser.). (Illus.). 24p. pap. *(978-1-4190-3843-3(5)*, Rigby) Pearson Education Australia.

Gabriel, Thora. Chessie Bligh & the Scroll of Andelthor. 2006. 284p. (J). 27.95 *(978-0-595-83579-9(1))* iUniverse, Inc.

Gage, Christos. What You Want, Not What You Need. Allie, Scott & Hahn, Sierra, eds. 2014. (ENG., Illus.). 136p. pap. 17.99 *(978-1-61655-253-4(0))* Dark Horse Comics.

Gaiman, NEil. Gaiman Mid Grade Novel. 2005. 176p. (J). 15.99 *(978-0-06-088123-8(2))*; pap. 5.99 *(978-0-06-088125-2(9)*, Harper Trophy); lib. bdg. 16.89 *(978-0-06-088124-5(0))* HarperCollins Pubs.

—The Graveyard Book: a Harper Classic. McKean, Dave, illus. 2017. (Harper Classic Ser.). 368p. (J). (gr. 3-7). 16.99 ***(978-0-06-266703-8(3))*** HarperCollins Pubs.

—The Graveyard Book Graphic Novel Single Volume. Russell, P. Craig, illus. 368p. (J). (gr. 3-7). 2017. pap. 20.00 ***(978-0-06-242189-0(1))*** 2016. 35.00 *(978-0-06-242188-3(3))* HarperCollins Pubs.

—The Graveyard Book Graphic Novel Single Volume Special Limited Edition. Russell, P. Craig, illus. 2016. 384p. (J). (gr. 3-7). 175.00 *(978-0-06-239449-1(5))* HarperCollins Pubs.

—Instructions. Vess, Charles, illus. 2010. 40p. (J). (gr. -1-3). (ENG.). 14.99 *(978-0-06-196030-7(6))*; lib. bdg. 15.89 *(978-0-06-196031-4(4))* HarperCollins Pubs.

—Instructions. Vess, Charles, illus. 2015. (ENG.). 40p. (J). (gr. -1-3). 8.99 *(978-0-06-196032-1(2))* HarperCollins Pubs.

—M Is for Magic. Kristiansen, Teddy, illus. 272p. (J). (gr. 5-9). 2008. (ENG.). pap. 7.99 *(978-0-06-118647-9(3))* 2007. 16.99 *(978-0-06-118642-4(2))* HarperCollins Pubs.

—M Is for Magic. 2007. (Illus.). 151p. (J). (gr. 5-9). 60.00 *(978-1-59606-123-1(5))* Subterranean Pr.

—Odd & the Frost Giants. Riddell, Chris, illus. 2016. 128p. (J). (gr. 3-7). 19.99 *(978-0-06-256795-6(0))* HarperCollins Pubs.

—Odd & the Frost Giants. Helquist, Brett, illus. 128p. (J). 2009. (ENG.). (gr. 3-18). 14.99 *(978-0-06-167173-9(8))* 2008. lib. bdg. 15.89 *(978-0-06-167175-3(4))* HarperCollins Pubs.

—The Sleeper & the Spindle. Riddell, Chris, illus. 2015. (ENG.). 64p. (YA). (gr. 8). 19.99 *(978-0-06-239824-6(5))* HarperCollins Pubs.

—Unnatural Creatures: Stories Selected by Neil Gaiman. 2013. (ENG., Illus.). 480p. (YA). (gr. 8). 17.99 *(978-0-06-223629-6(0))*; pap. 9.99 *(978-0-06-223630-2(X))* HarperCollins Pubs.

—Unnatural Creatures: Stories Selected by Neil Gaiman. 2013. (YA). lib. bdg. 20.85 *(978-0-606-31804-4(6)*, Turtleback) Turtleback Bks.

Gaiman, NEil & Reaves, Michael. Interworld. 2007. (InterWorld Trilogy Ser.: 1). (ENG.). 256p. (YA). (gr. 8-9). 17.99 *(978-0-06-123896-3(1))* HarperCollins Pubs.

—Interworld. 2008. (Illus.). 181p. (J). (gr. 5-9). 60.00 *(978-1-59606-173-6(1))* Subterranean Pr.

Galasso, Marina. I Wish. 2009. (Illus.). 24p. pap. 12.95 *(978-1-4269-1087-6(8))* Trafford Publishing.

Gale, Gabriel. A Fiery Friendship. Giacobino, Sebastian, illus. 2017. (J). pap. ***(978-1-4814-6972-2(X)***, McElderry, Margaret K. Bks.) McElderry, Margaret K. Bks.

Gall, Allan R. Of Mouse & Magic. 2011. (ENG., Illus.). 269p. (J). (gr. 3-7). pap. 12.95 *(978-1-936401-78-9(9))* Salem Author Services.

Gallagher, Diana G. & Burge, Constance M. Trickery Treat. 2008. (Charmed Ser.). (ENG.). 208p. (YA). (gr. 8-12). mass mkt. 6.99 *(978-1-4169-3670-1(X))* Pocket Books.

Gallagher, Michael. X-Men, Scourge of the Savage Land. Severin, Marie, illus. 24p. (YA). (gr. k-18). 12.95 *(978-0-9627001-7-0(7))* Futech Educational Products, Inc.

Gallardo, Adam. 100 Girls Vol. 1: Vol 1: the First Girl, Vol. 1. Demong, Todd, illus. 2008. (YA). 9.95 *(978-0-9763095-3-6(X))* Arcana Studio, Inc.

Gallardo, Adam J. Zomburbia. 2014. (Zombie Apocalypse Ser.). (ENG.). 368p. (YA). (gr. 13). pap. 9.95 *(978-1-61773-098-6(X)*, K-Teen) Kensington Publishing Corp.

Gallop to the Sea. 2005. (J). *(978-1-933343-12-9(5))* Stabenfeldt Inc.

Gannett, Ruth Stiles. The Dragons of Blueland. Gannett, Ruth Chrisman, illus. (Tales of My Father's Dragon Ser.: Bk. 3). 88p. (J). (gr. 3-6). pap. 4.99 incl. audio *(978-0-8072-1287-5(3)*, Listening Library) Random Hse. Audio Publishing Group.

—Elmer & the Dragon. Gannett, Ruth Chrisman, illus. (Tales of My Father's Dragon Ser.: Bk. 2). 87p. (J). (gr. 3-6). pap. 4.99 incl. audio *(978-0-8072-1288-2(1)*, Listening Library) Random Hse. Audio Publishing Group.

—My Father's Dragon. Gannett, Ruth Chrisman, illus. 2014. (ENG.). 96p. (J). (gr. 1-4). pap. 5.99 *(978-0-486-49283-4(4))* Dover Pubns., Inc.

Garber, Stephanie. Caraval. 2017. (SPA.). 432p. pap. 16.95 ***(978-607-07-4044-2(0))*** Editorial Planeta, S. A. ESP. Dist: Two Rivers Distribution.

—Caraval. 2017. (Caraval Ser.). (ENG.). (YA). 416p. 18.99 *(978-1-250-09525-1(5)*, 9781250095251); (gr. 8-12). pap. 11.99 ***(978-1-250-14149-1(4))*** Flatiron Bks.

Garcia, Kami & Stohl, Margaret. The Beautiful Creatures Complete Paperback Collection: Beautiful Creatures; Beautiful Darkness; Beautiful Chaos; Beautiful Redemption. 2013. (Beautiful Creatures Ser.: Bks. 1-4). (ENG.). 2272p. (YA). (gr. 7-17). pap. 50.00 *(978-0-316-25090-0(2))* Little, Brown Bks. for Young Readers.

García Márquez, Gabriel. Un Senor muy Viejo con unas Alas Enormes.Tr. of Very Old Man with Large Wings. (SPA.). 28p. 10.50 *(978-958-04-5570-7(8))* Norma S.A. COL. Dist: Distribuidora Norma, Inc.

Gardner, Dianne Lynn. Rubies & Robbers. 2013. (ENG.). 176p. (J). pap. 14.99 *(978-0-615-81113-0(2))* Hydra Pubns.

Gardner, Lyn. Out of the Woods. 2011. (ENG., Illus.). 368p. (J). (gr. 3-7). 7.99 *(978-0-385-75226-8(1)*, Yearling) Random Hse. Children's Bks.

Gardner, Sally. I, Coriander. 2007. (Illus.). 280p. (J). (gr. 5-9). 14.65 *(978-0-7569-8130-3(1))* Perfection Learning Corp.

—Maggot Moon. Crouch, Julian, illus. 2013. (ENG.). 288p. (YA). (gr. 7). 16.99 *(978-0-7636-6553-1(3))* Candlewick Pr.

—Tinder. Roberts, David, illus. (Moments in History Ser.). (ENG.). 352p. 2015. (J). (gr. 7-17). 8.99 *(978-1-78062-148-7(5))* 2014. (YA). 18.99 *(978-1-78062-149-4(3))* Hachette Children's Group GBR. (Orion Children's Bks.). Dist: Hachette Bk. Group.

Garis, Howard R. Umboo, the Elephant. 2008. 108p. 22.95 *(978-1-60664-782-0(2))*; pap. 9.95 *(978-1-60664-156-9(5))* Aegypan.

Garis, Howard Roger. Lulu, Alice & Jammie Wibble Wobble. 2005. 152p. pap. 11.95 *(978-1-4218-1564-0(8)*, 1st World Library - Literary Society) 1st World Publishing, Inc.

—Lulu, Alice & Jimmie Wibblewobble. 2005. 26.95 *(978-1-4218-1464-3(1)*, 1st World Library - Literary Society) 1st World Publishing, Inc.

Garner, Alan. Elidor. 192p. (YA). (gr. 5-18). pap. 6.00 *(978-0-8072-1545-6(7)*, Listening Library) Random Hse. Audio Publishing Group.

—The Moon of Gomrath: A Tale of Alderley. 2006. (ENG., Illus.). 216p. (J). (gr. 4-8). pap. 13.95 *(978-0-15-205630-8(0))* Houghton Mifflin Harcourt Publishing Co.

—The Weirdstone of Brisingamen: A Tale of Alderley. 2006. (ENG., Illus.). 288p. (J). (gr. 4-8). pap. 16.95 *(978-0-15-205636-0(X))* Houghton Mifflin Harcourt Publishing Co.

Garrett, Christine. Dream Bunny's Tales - Saving the Land of Dreams. 2009. (Illus.). 48p. pap. 13.95 *(978-1-60860-451-7(9)*, Eloquent Bks.) Strategic Book Publishing & Rights Agency (SBPRA).

Garrido, Pedro Gelabert. El Libro del Abuelo: Un Mundo de Aventuras Entre la Realidad y la Fantasma. Velert, Miriam, illus. 2003. (Ficcion Interactiva Ser.). (SPA.). 160p. pap. 14.95 *(978-84-89984-11-0(5))* Recursos, Ediciones ESP. Dist: Independent Pubs. Group.

Garton, Carol. The Land of Carin. 2007. 108p. 19.95 *(978-1-4327-1027-9(3))*; 104p. per. 10.95 *(978-1-4327-1634-9(4))* Outskirts Pr., Inc.

Gates, Josephine Scribner. The April fool Doll. Keep, Virginia, illus. 2007. 152p. (J). lib. bdg. 59.00 *(978-1-60304-009-9(9))* Dollworks.

—Captain Billie: Leads the way to the land of I don't want To. Sichel, Harold, illus. 2007. 96p. (J). lib. bdg. 59.00 *(978-1-60304-019-8(6))* Dollworks.

—The dolls in Fairyland. Keep, Virginia, illus. 2007. 136p. (J). lib. bdg. 59.00 *(978-1-60304-013-6(7))* Dollworks.

—Little girl Blue: Lives in the woods til she learns to say Please. Keep, Virginia, illus. 2007. 54p. (J). lib. bdg. 59.00 *(978-1-60304-012-9(9))* Dollworks.

—Little Girl Blue plays I Spy. 2007. (Illus.). 64p. (J). lib. bdg. 59.00 *(978-1-60304-017-4(X))* Dollworks.

—Little red white & Blue. Keep, Virginia, illus. 2007. 118p. (J). lib. bdg. 59.00 *(978-1-60304-006-8(4))* Dollworks.

—The live dolls' busy Days. Keep, Virginia, illus. 2007. 106p. (J). lib. bdg. 59.00 *(978-1-60304-007-5(2))* Dollworks.

—The live dolls' house Party. Keep, Virginia, illus. 2007. 104p. (J). lib. bdg. 59.00 *(978-1-60304-005-1(6))* Dollworks.

—The live dolls in Wonderland. Keep, Virginia, illus. 2007. 150p. (J). lib. bdg. 59.00 *(978-1-60304-015-0(3))* Dollworks.

—The live dolls' play Days. Keep, Virginia, illus. 2007. 110p. (J). lib. bdg. 59.00 *(978-1-60304-008-2(0))* Dollworks.

—More about live Dolls. Keep, Virginia, illus. 2007. 106p. (J). lib. bdg. 59.00 *(978-1-60304-002-0(1))* Dollworks.

—Nannette & the baby Monkey. 2007. (Illus.). 50p. (J). lib. bdg. 59.00 *(978-1-60304-020-4(X))* Dollworks.

—Nannette goes to visit her Grandmother. 2007. (J). lib. bdg. 59.00 *(978-1-60304-021-1(8))* Dollworks.

—One day in Betty,s Life. Stuart, B. S., illus. 2007. 58p. (J). lib. bdg. 59.00 *(978-1-60304-018-1(8))* Dollworks.

—The secret of the live Dolls. Archibald, A. L., illus. 2007. (J). lib. bdg. 59.00 *(978-1-60304-024-2(2))* Dollworks.

—The Story of Live Dolls: Being an account by Josephine Scribner Gates of how, on a certian June morning, all of the dolls in the Cloverdale came Alive. Keep, Virginia, illus. 2007. 102p. (J). lib. bdg. 59.00 *(978-1-60304-001-3(3))* Dollworks.

—The story of the lost Doll. Keep, Virginia, illus. 2007. 108p. (J). lib. bdg. 59.00 *(978-1-60304-003-7(X))* Dollworks.

—The Story of the three Dolls. Keep, Virginia, illus. 2007. 148p. (J). lib. bdg. 59.00 *(978-1-60304-004-4(8))* Dollworks.

—Sunshine Annie. Cory, Fanny Y., illus. 2007. 148p. (J). lib. bdg. 59.00 *(978-1-60304-011-2(0))* Dollworks.

—Tommy Sweet-Tooth & Little girl Blue. Churbuck, Esther V., illus. 2007. 64p. (J). lib. bdg. 59.00 *(978-1-60304-014-3(5))* Dollworks.

—The Turkey Doll. Flass, E. C., illus. 2007. 62p. (J). lib. bdg. 59.00 *(978-1-60304-016-7(1))* Dollworks.

Gathering Place Publishers. Stones' Quest in Search of Its Master: In Search of Its Master 2005. (Stones' Quest Ser.: 1). (ENG., Illus.). 489p. (J). pap. 19.95 *(978-0-9754622-0-1(2))* Gathering Place Pubs., Inc.

Gavioli, Gino & Gavoili, G. Candido, el Limpiador de Chimeneas. Brignole, Giancarla, tr. Gavioli, Gino, illus. rev. ed. 2006. (Fabulas De Familia Ser.). (SPA & ENG., Illus.). 32p. (J). (gr. k-4). pap. 6.95 *(978-970-20-0264-2(8))* Castillo, Ediciones, S. A. de C. V. MEX. Dist: Macmillan.

Gay, Marie-Louise. Stella, Princess of the Sky, 1 vol. 2004. (Stella & Sam Ser.). (ENG., Illus.). 32p. (J). 15.95 *(978-0-88899-601-5(2))* Groundwood Bks. CAN. Dist: Publishers Group West (PGW).

Gayatri Stein, Mari. Puddle Moon. 2010. (ENG., Illus.). 32p. 17.95 *(978-0-9793840-0-4(1)*, Riverwood Bks.) White Cloud Pr.

Gayle, Emi. Night & Day. 2014. 132p. (YA). *(978-1-937744-55-7(8))* J. Taylor Publishing.

Gayton, Sam. Lilliput, 1 vol. Ratterree, Alice, illus. 256p. (J). (gr. 3-6). 2017. (ENG.). pap. 8.95 ***(978-1-68263-006-8(4))*** 2016. (SPA & ENG.). 16.95 *(978-1-56145-806-6(6))* Peachtree Pubs.

Gazdag, Adam. The Non Born Heir. 2010. 313p. pap. 19.27 *(978-0-557-17709-7(X))* Lulu Pr., Inc.

Gee, Maurice. Gool, 1 vol. 2012. (Salt Trilogy Ser.: 2). (ENG.). 240p. (YA). (gr. 7-12). pap. 12.95 *(978-1-4598-0196-7(2))* Orca Bk. Pubs. USA.

—The Limping Man, 1 vol. 2011. (Salt Trilogy Ser.: 3). (ENG.). 208p. (YA). (gr. 7-12). lib. bdg. 18.00 *(978-1-55469-216-3(4))* Orca Bk. Pubs. USA.

—Salt, 1 vol. (Salt Trilogy Ser.: 1). (ENG., Illus.). 272p. (gr. 7-12). 2011. (J). pap. 12.95 *(978-1-55469-369-6(1))* 2009. (YA). 18.00 *(978-1-55469-209-5(1))* Orca Bk. Pubs. USA.

Gelsey, James, adapted by. Opposing Force. 2004. (Illus.). 92p. (J). *(978-1-4156-3935-1(3)*, Volo) Hyperion Bks. for Children.

Geneviève Douyon Flambert. Grace: The Mystical Caribbean Mission. 2009. 152p. 22.95 *(978-0-595-50709-2(3))*; pap. 12.95 *(978-0-595-51639-1(4))* iUniverse, Inc.

Gentry, Jennifer Mills. Maria the Cat, 1 vol. 2010. 24p. pap. 24.95 *(978-1-4489-7748-2(7))* PublishAmerica, Inc.

George, Jessica Day. Dragon Flight. 2009. (Dragon Slippers Ser.). (ENG.). 288p. (YA). (gr. 5-8). pap. 8.99 *(978-1-59990-359-0(8)*, 9781599903590, Bloomsbury USA Childrens) Bloomsbury Publishing USA.

—Dragon Slippers. 2008. (Dragon Slippers Ser.). (ENG., Illus.). 352p. (YA). (gr. 5). pap. 8.99 *(978-1-59990-275-3(3)*, 9781599902753, Bloomsbury USA Childrens) Bloomsbury Publishing USA.

—Dragon Slippers. l.t. ed. 2008. (Thorndike Literacy Bridge Middle Reader Ser.). 391p. (J). (gr. 4-7). 22.95 *(978-1-4104-0337-7(8))* Thorndike Pr.

—Dragon Spear. (Dragon Slippers Ser.). (ENG.). (YA). (gr. 5-8). 2010. 272p. pap. 8.99 *(978-1-59990-516-7(7)*, 9781599905167) 2009. 256p. 16.99 *(978-1-59990-369-9(5)*, 9781599903699) Bloomsbury Publishing USA. (Bloomsbury USA Childrens).

—Wednesdays in the Tower. 2017. (Tuesdays at the Castle Ser.). (ENG.). 256p. (J). pap. 7.99 *(978-1-68119-219-2(5)*, 9781681192192, Bloomsbury USA Childrens) 2014. (Tuesdays at the Castle Ser.: 2). (ENG.). 256p. (YA). (gr. 3-6). pap. 7.99 *(978-1-61963-265-3(9)*, 9781619632653, Bloomsbury USA Childrens) 2013. 240p. E-Book 16.99 *(978-1-61963-051-2(6))* 2013. (Tuesdays at the Castle Ser.: 2). (ENG.). 240p. (YA). (gr. 3-6). 16.99 *(978-1-59990-645-4(7)*, 9781599906454, Bloomsbury USA Childrens) Bloomsbury Publishing USA.

George, Kallie. The Missing Magic. 2017. (Magical Animal Adoption Agency Ser.: 3). (J). lib. bdg. 16.00 ***(978-0-606-39973-9(9))*** Turtleback Bks.

Gerald, A. I. Hathlin Behind the Gates of Hell. 2005. 104p. pap. 14.95 *(978-1-4208-5567-8(0))* AuthorHouse.

Gerard, Justin, illus. Beowulf Bk. 1: Grendel the Ghastly. 2007. 32p. (J). (gr. 4-6). 17.95 *(978-0-9797183-0-4(9))* Portland Studios, Inc.

Gerard, Kevin. Diego's Dragon, Book Three: Battle at Tenochtitlan. Dreadfuls, Penny, ed. Gallegos, Benito, illus. 2013. 298p. pap. 14.99 *(978-0-9859802-3-8(0))* Crying Cougar Pr.

Geron, Eric. Descendants 2 Junior Novel. 2017. (Descendants Junior Novel Ser.). (ENG.). 208p. (J). (gr. 3-7). 10.99 ***(978-1-4847-9970-3(4))*** Disney Pr.

Gerry's 4. The World of Round. 2012. 24p. pap. 12.56 *(978-1-4669-6882-0(6))* Trafford Publishing.

Gershon, Neil. The Other Side of the Frame. 2007. 184p. (J). per. 13.95 *(978-0-595-40618-0(1))* iUniverse, Inc.

Gibbs, Jon. Barnum's Revenge. 2013. 246p. pap. 12.99 *(978-1-59080-722-4(7))* Echelon Press Publishing.

Gibson, Jo. Afraid. 2014. (ENG.). 336p. (YA). (gr. 13). pap. 9.95 *(978-1-61773-242-3(7)*, K-Teen) Kensington Publishing Corp.

Gibson, Julia Mary. Copper Magic. 2014. (ENG., Illus.). 336p. (J). (gr. 5-9). 16.99 *(978-0-7653-3211-0(6)*, 9780765332110, Starscape) Doherty, Tom Assocs., LLC.

Gibson, Sherri L. In the Mind of a Child: Children's Stories. 2013. 36p. pap. 24.95 *(978-1-62709-750-5(3))* America Star Bks.

Gidwitz, Adam. The Grimm Conclusion. D'Andrade, Hugh, illus. 2013. (ENG.). 368p. (J). (gr. 5). 16.99 *(978-0-525-42615-8(9)*, Dutton Books for Young Readers) Penguin Young Readers Group.

Gier, Kerstin. Dream a Little Dream. Bell, Anthea, tr. from GER. 2015. (Silver Trilogy Ser.: 1). (ENG.). 336p. (YA). (gr. 7). 17.99 *(978-1-62779-027-7(6)*, 9781627790277, Holt, Henry & Co. Bks. For Young Readers) Holt, Henry & Co.

Gilbert, Julie. Dark Waters. 2017. (Dark Waters Ser.). (ENG.). 160p. (gr. 2-4). lib. bdg. 106.60 *(978-1-4965-4192-5(8))* Stone Arch Bks.

Giles, Katharine. The Princess of Skye, an Archer Adventure. 2013. (ENG.). 280p. (YA). pap. 12.99 *(978-1-939927-79-8(X))* Telemachus Pr., LLC.

Gili, Phillida. Cinderella: A Pop-up Book. Gili, Phillida, illus. 2007. (Illus.). 12p. (J). 25.00 *(978-1-4223-9031-3(4))* DIANE Publishing Co.

Gill, Margaret. The Brain Changers. 2004. 160p. (YA). pap. 12.95 *(978-0-595-31161-3(X))* iUniverse, Inc.

Gill, Paul. The Centaurs: An Adventure Fantasy. 2003. 54p. pap. 8.95 *(978-0-595-30260-4(2))* iUniverse, Inc.

Gilliam, Jessie. Geno, 1 vol. 2010. 48p. pap. 16.95 *(978-1-4489-5473-5(8))* America Star Bks.

Gilligan, Shannon. Cup of Death. Nugent, Suzanne, illus. 2006. (Choose Your Own Adventure Ser.). 144p. (J). (gr. 4-8). per. 6.99 *(978-1-933390-70-3(0))* Chooseco LLC.

Gillott, C. M. Nelson 'n' Deck & Friends: How the Adventures Began. 2010. (Illus.). 48p. pap. 17.49 *(978-1-4490-9593-2(3))* AuthorHouse.

Gilman, Charles. The Slither Sisters. 2013. (Tales from Lovecraft Middle School Ser.: 2). (ENG., Illus.). 160p. (J). (gr. 4-7). 13.99 *(978-1-59474-593-5(5))* Quirk Bks.

Gilmartin, Mary. Adventures with Easton: The Magical Journey. 2012. (ENG.). (J). pap. 16.95 *(978-1-4675-2418-6(2))* Independent Pub.

Gingeleski, Randolph J. The War of Lord Capani. 2008. 58p. pap. 16.95 *(978-1-60563-758-7(0))* America Star Bks.

Ginoschio De Osceola, Ibrahim. Enter the Corn Bunny, Vol. 1. 2007. 56p. per. 8.95 *(978-0-595-45273-6(6))* iUniverse, Inc.

Giordano, Anne. Spencer, the Magic Rabbit. 2009. 40p. pap. 16.99 *(978-1-4490-3296-8(6))* AuthorHouse.

Givner, Joan. The Hills Are Shadows. 2014. (ENG.). 264p. pap. 12.95 *(978-1-927068-91-5(6)*, 0fe8d3e0-6759-43f3-8) Thistledown Pr., Ltd. CAN. Dist: Univ. of Toronto Pr.

Gladman, Marjorie-Ann. Bozzled. 2015. (ENG., Illus.). 44p. (J). (gr. 3-4). 24.95 *(978-1-78455-563-4(0)*, dfeed516-ee4b-4fdb-ae7b-ba3b422a6887); pap. 14.95 *(978-1-78455-562-7(2)*, b63aa545-6ff4-4fb9-9c91-421775d1a7ff) Austin, Stan AUS. Dist: Bookmasters Distribution.

Glanville, K. L. The Realm: The Awakening Begins, bk. 1. 2008. (ENG.). 314p. (YA). pap. 12.99 *(978-0-9821199-1-4(7))* Luminations Media Group, Inc.

Glaser, P. H. Chrystallia & the Source of Light. 2011. (Illus.). 196p. (J). 18.99 *(978-1-60832-232-9(7))* Greenleaf Book Group.

Glass, Bryan J. L. Mice Templar, Vol. 3. 2012. (ENG., Illus.). 250p. (YA). 29.99 *(978-1-60706-457-2(X)*, 9781607064572) Image Comics.

Glewwe, Eleanor. Sparkers. 2014. (ENG.). 336p. (J). (gr. 5-8). 16.99 *(978-0-451-46876-5(7)*, Viking Books for Young Readers) Penguin Young Readers Group.

—Widings. 2016. (ENG.). 336p. (J). (gr. 5). 16.99 *(978-0-451-46885-7(6)*, Viking Books for Young Readers) Penguin Young Readers Group.

Glori, Debi. Witch Baby & Me. 2010. (ENG., Illus.). 256p. (J). (gr. 2-4). pap. 12.99 *(978-0-552-55676-7(9))* Transworld Publishers Ltd. GBR. Dist: Independent Pubs. Group.

Gloria North. Dragon Dreams: Tales of Fun & Fantasy. 2005. 77p. pap. 10.00 *(978-1-59926-471-4(4))* Xlibris Corp.

Glover, Ruth E. The Lost Labyrinth. 2008. 239p. pap. 15.95 *(978-1-4092-1076-4(6))* Lulu Pr., Inc.

Glur, D. L' Empire Contre Attaque.Tr. of Empire Strikes Back. (FRE.). (J). pap. 11.95 *(978-2-265-06729-5(6))* Fleuve Noir FRA. Dist: Distribooks, Inc.

Godbout, Neil. Disintegrate, Vol. 1. 2013. (ENG.). 240p. (YA). pap. 14.95 *(978-0-9782052-8-7(6)*, 9780978205287) Bundoran Pr. CAN. Dist: Diamond Comic Distributors, Inc.

Godden, Rumer. The Dolls' House. 126p. (J). (gr. 3-5). pap. 4.99 *(978-0-8072-1408-4(6)*, Listening Library) Random Hse. Audio Publishing Group.

Goebel, Kelly. Adventures in the Weeping Willow Tree. Murfield, Anna, illus. 2013. 26p. pap. 9.99 *(978-1-937165-49-9(3))* Orange Hat Publishing.

Gogonya, Carol. The Magical Crystal Island of Morzzagal Where the King & His Three Sons Lived. 2012. 28p. pap. 32.70 *(978-1-4771-3159-6(0))* Xlibris Corp.

Golden Books. The Big Golden Book of Starships, Speeders, & Space Stations (Star Wars) Golden Books, illus. 2017. (Big Golden Book Ser.). (ENG., Illus.). 48p. (J). (gr. -1-2). 10.99 ***(978-0-7364-3693-9(6)***, Golden Bks.) Random Hse. Children's Bks.

—Shimmer & Shine Awesome Sticker Collection (Shimmer & Shine) Golden Books, illus. 2017. (4 Color Plus 1,000 Stickers Ser.). (ENG., Illus.). 64p. (J). (gr. -1-2). pap. 12.99 ***(978-1-5247-1680-6(4)***, Golden Bks.) Random Hse. Children's Bks.

—Shimmer & Shine Little Golden Book Favorites (Shimmer & Shine) Golden Books, illus. 2017. (Little Golden Book Favorites Ser.). (ENG., Illus.). 80p. (J). (gr. -1-2). 7.99 ***(978-1-5247-1720-9(7)***, Random Hse. Bks. for Young Readers) Random Hse. Children's Bks.

Golden Books Staff. Rainbow Adventure. Miller, Victoria, illus. 2010. (Super Color with Stickers Ser.). (ENG.). 96p. (J). (gr. -1-2). pap. 3.99 *(978-0-375-86350-9(8)*, Golden Bks.) Random Hse. Children's Bks.

Golden, Christopher. When Rose Wakes. 2010. (ENG.). 320p. pap. 19.99 *(978-1-4391-4823-5(6)*, MTV Bks.) MTV Books.

Golding, Julia. The Glass Swallow, 0 vols. 2011. (ENG.). 320p. (gr. 7-12). 17.99 *(978-0-7614-5979-8(0)*, 9780761459798, Amazon Children's Publishing) Amazon Publishing.

Goldstein, Lori A. Becoming Jinn. 2015. (Becoming Jinn Ser.: 1). (ENG.). 384p. (YA). (gr. 7). 17.99 *(978-1-250-05539-2(3)*, 9781250055392) Feiwel & Friends.

Gollahon, Carleen Anderson. Sophie & the Mysterious Ring. 2012. 62p. (gr. 4-18). pap. 8.99 *(978-1-4624-0379-0(4)*, Inspiring Voices) Author Solutions, Inc.

Gologan, Trena. Alexandru's Gift. 2008. 35p. pap. 17.00 *(978-1-4357-3486-9(6))* Lulu Pr., Inc.

Goly, Rozz. The WOB: Where Does Bubblegum Come From?, 2 sizes, 7x10. 2010. (ENG., Illus.). 46p. (J). per. 16.89 *(978-1-933300-10-8(8))* Wandering Sage Pubns., LLC.

Goode, John. Eye of the Storm. 2016. (ENG., Illus.). (J). 24.99 ***(978-1-63533-011-3(4)***, Harmony Ink Pr.) Dreamspinner Pr.

Goode, John & Morgan, J.G. The Unseen Tempest. (ENG., Illus.). (YA). 2016. (Lords of Arcadia Ser.: Vol. 3). (gr. 8-12). 24.99 ***(978-1-63477-980-7(0))*** 2014. 248p. pap. 14.99 *(978-1-63216-189-5(3))* Dreamspinner Pr. (Harmony Ink Pr.).

Goode, Suzi. The Lost Wizard Series Bk 1. 2007. pap. 11.95 *(978-1-59374-817-3(5))* Whiskey Creek Pr., LLC.

Gooden, Sean Lawrence. The Mother of the Green Bear, 1 vol. 2009. (ENG.). 191p. pap. 24.95 *(978-1-60749-815-5(4))* America Star Bks.

Goodin, Carolyn M. Candy Land. Goodin, Carolyn M., illus. 2007. (Illus.). 38p. (J). per. 14.99 *(978-0-9797879-1-1(2))* Family Legacy Ministries.

Goodman, Alison. Eon: Dragoneye Reborn. 2010. (ENG.). 576p. (YA). (gr. 7-18). 10.99 *(978-0-14-241711-9(4)*, Firebird) Penguin Young Readers Group.

—Eon: Dragoneye Reborn. 2010. (Eon Ser.: 1). lib. bdg. 22.10 *(978-0-606-23647-8(3)*, Turtleback) Turtleback Bks.

—The Last Dragoneye. 2012. (ENG.). 672p. (YA). (gr. 7-18). 11.99 *(978-0-14-242093-5(X)*, Firebird) Penguin Young Readers Group.

—The Last Dragoneye. 2012. (Eon Ser.: 2). lib. bdg. 23.30 *(978-0-606-23648-5(1)*, Turtleback) Turtleback Bks.

Goodman, John. Percy's Magical Adventures. 2005. (Illus.). 170p. pap. *(978-1-84401-556-6(4))* Athena Pr.

Gordon, Mike & Gordon, Carl, illus. The Magic Porridge Pot. 2008. (Usborne First Reading: Level 3 Ser.). 48p. (J). (gr. -1-3). 8.99 *(978-0-7945-1883-7(4)*, Usborne) EDC Publishing.

Goscinny, René. Iznogoud & the Magic Carpet. Tabary, illus. 2010. (Iznogoud Ser.: 6). (ENG.). 46p. (J). (gr. 3-17). pap. 11.95 *(978-1-84918-044-3(X))* CineBook GBR. Dist: National Bk. Network.

Goudge, Elizabeth. The Little White Horse. movie tie-in ed. 2008. (ENG., Illus.). 248p. (J). (gr. 4-7). pap. *(978-0-7459-6118-7(5))* Lion Hudson PLC GBR. Dist: Independent Pubs. Group.

Gouveia, Keith. Children of the Dragon. 2005. (ENG.). 174p. pap. *(978-1-897217-03-0(X))* Coscom Entertainment.

Gow, Kailin. Reborn #1: Queen B Superheroine Series. 2005. 168p. (YA). per. 7.99 *(978-1-59748-855-6(0))* Sparklesoup LLC.

Goyer, Deb. Billy's Fantasies. 2008. 36p. pap. 24.95 *(978-1-60474-176-6(7))* America Star Bks.

Grace, Ann Marie. The Secret Gift. 2013. 18p. pap. 12.99 *(978-1-4808-0411-1(8))* Archway Publishing.

Grace, N. B. Rev It Up! 9th ed. 2010. (Wizards of Waverly Place Ser.: No. 9). 128p. (J). (gr. 3-7). pap. 4.99 *(978-1-4231-2676-8(9))* Disney Pr.

Graff, Lisa. A Clatter of Jars. 2016. (ENG.). 224p. (J). (gr. 3-7). 16.99 *(978-0-399-17499-5(0)*, Philomel Bks.) Penguin Young Readers Group.

Graham, Judith A. The Didley-Doo's Go on an Adventure, 1 vol. 2009. 33p. pap. 24.95 *(978-1-60749-897-1(9))* America Star Bks.

Graham, L. B. All My Holy Mountain. 2008. (YA). pap. *(978-0-87552-724-6(8))* P & R Publishing.

—Beyond the Summerland. 2004. (Binding of the Blade Ser.: 1). (Illus.). 608p. (J). per. 16.99 *(978-0-87552-720-8(5)*, 5000) P & R Publishing.

Graham, Richard. Jack y el Monstruo. Varley, Susan, illus. (Cotton Cloud Ser.). (SPA.). 32p. (J). (gr. 1-3). *(978-84-7722-680-2(6))* Timun Mas, Editorial S.A. ESP. Dist: Lectorum Pubns., Inc.

Grahame, Howard. The Wishing Book. 2009. 110p. (J). pap. *(978-1-905809-64-6(6))* Pneuma Springs Publishing.

—The Wishing Book 2 - Return to Mars. 2009. 102p. (J). pap. *(978-1-905809-80-6(8))* Pneuma Springs Publishing.

Gran, Meredith. Marceline & the Scream Queens. Gran, Meredith, illus. 2013. (Adventure Time Ser.). (ENG., Illus.). 128p. (J). (gr. 4). pap. 19.99 *(978-1-60886-313-6(1))* Boom! Studios.

Granata, Nancy. The Perfect Porch for Witch Watching. 2008. 52p. pap. 22.49 *(978-1-4389-0107-7(0))* AuthorHouse.

Grandpa Peeps. The Squire & the White Dragon. 2011. 24p. 11.95 *(978-1-4567-1872-5(X))* AuthorHouse.

Grannis, Greg. Lottie Bright & the Starmaker's Universe. Vargas, Robert, illus. 2006. (ENG.). 280p. (J). per. *(978-0-9778205-9-7(9))* Helm Publishing.

Granson, Steven. Zando. 2009. 124p. pap. 10.95 *(978-1-4401-5658-8(1))* iUniverse, Inc.

Grant, Crystal. Warrior Boy. 2007. (ENG.). 92p. per. 16.95 *(978-1-4241-3978-1(3))* PublishAmerica, Inc.

Grant, Holly. The Dastardly Deed. 2017. (League of Beastly Dreadfuls Ser.: Bk. 2). (ENG., Illus.). 368p. (J). (gr. 3-7). 7.99 *(978-0-385-37028-8(8)*, Yearling) Random Hse. Children's Bks.

Grant, Mark J. Lila: The Sign of the Elven Queen. 2013. (ENG.). 230p. (J). (gr. 3-7). 14.95 *(978-1-62086-357-2(X))* Mascot Bks., Inc.

Grant, Michael. The Call. (Magnificent 12 Ser.: 1). (ENG.). (J). (gr. 3-7). 2011. 272p. pap. 6.99 *(978-0-06-183367-0(3))* 2010. (Illus.). 256p. 16.99 *(978-0-06-183366-3(5))* HarperCollins Pubs. (Tegen, Katherine Bks).

—Fear. 2014. (Gone Ser.: 5). (ENG.). 544p. (YA). (gr. 9). pap. 9.99 *(978-0-06-144917-8(2)*, Tegen, Katherine Bks) HarperCollins Pubs.

—The Key. (Magnificent 12 Ser.: 3). (ENG.). (J). (gr. 3-7). 2013. 304p. pap. 5.99 *(978-0-06-183371-7(1))* 2012. (Illus.). 288p. 16.99 *(978-0-06-183370-0(3))* HarperCollins Pubs. (Tegen, Katherine Bks).

—The Power. 2013. (Magnificent 12 Ser.: 4). (ENG.). 288p. (J). (gr. 3-7). 16.99 *(978-0-06-183372-4(X)*, Tegen, Katherine Bks) HarperCollins Pubs.

—The Trap. (Magnificent 12 Ser.: 2). (ENG.). (J). (gr. 3-7). 2012. 320p. pap. 5.99 *(978-0-06-183369-4(X))* 2011. 304p. 16.99 *(978-0-06-183368-7(1))* HarperCollins Pubs. (Tegen, Katherine Bks).

Gratton, Tessa. Blood Magic. 2012. (Blood Journals). (ENG.). 432p. (YA). (gr. 9). pap. 9.99 *(978-0-375-86485-8(7)*, Bluefire) Random Hse. Children's Bks.

Gratz, Alan. The Dragon Lantern: A League of Seven Novel. 2016. (League of Seven Ser.: 2). (ENG., Illus.). 336p. (J). pap. 9.99 *(978-0-7653-3826-6(2)*, 9780765338266, Starscape) Doherty, Tom Assocs., LLC.

—The Monster War: A League of Seven Novel. 2016. (League of Seven Ser.: 3). (ENG., Illus.). 336p. (J). 17.99 *(978-0-7653-3824-2(6)*, 9780765338242, Starscape) Doherty, Tom Assocs., LLC.

Graudin, Ryan. Blood for Blood. (Wolf by Wolf Ser.: 1). (ENG.). (YA). (gr. 10-17). 2017. 592p. pap. 10.99 ***(978-0-316-40516-4(7))*** 2016. 496p. 17.99 *(978-0-316-40515-7(9))* Little, Brown Bks. for Young Readers.

Graves, Judith. Second Skin. 2011. 280p. (J). pap. 16.99 *(978-1-61603-006-3(2))* Leap Bks.

—Under My Skin. Cox, Val, illus. 2010. 328p. (YA). (gr. 8-18). pap. 16.99 *(978-1-61603-000-1(3))* Leap Bks.

Gray, Anne. Healer's Touch, 1 vol. 2009. (ENG.). 288p. (YA). (gr. 7-11). pap. *(978-1-894549-77-6(5)*, Sumach Pr.) Canadian Scholars.

—Rites of the Healer, 1 vol. 2007. (ENG.). 288p. (YA). (gr. 7-12). per. *(978-1-894549-59-2(7)*, Sumach Pr.) Canadian Scholars.

Gray, Betty. The Legend of CaseyRock. 2007. (Illus.). 40p. (J). per. 12.00 *(978-0-9779601-2-5(9))* BareBones Publishing.

Gray, Claudia. Spellcaster. 2014. (Spellcaster Ser.: 1). (ENG., Illus.). 416p. (YA). (gr. 8). pap. 9.99 *(978-0-06-196121-2(3)*, HarperTeen) HarperCollins Pubs.

Gray, Jennifer. Atticus Claw Settles a Score. Ecob, Mark, illus. 2016. (Atticus Claw Ser.). (ENG.). 240p. (gr. 1-4). 7.95 *(978-0-571-28681-2(X))* Faber & Faber, Inc.

Gray, P. J. Book 1: the Dream, 1 vol. 2016. (Message Ser.). (ENG.). (YA). (gr. 9-12). pap. 8.95 *(978-1-68021-149-8(8))* Saddleback Educational Publishing, Inc.

—Book 2: Dark Waters, 1 vol. 2016. (Message Ser.). (ENG.). (YA). (gr. 9-12). pap. 8.95 *(978-1-68021-150-4(1))* Saddleback Educational Publishing, Inc.

—Book 3: the Hunted, 1 vol. 2016. (Message Ser.). (ENG.). (YA). (gr. 9-12). pap. 8.95 *(978-1-68021-151-1(X))* Saddleback Educational Publishing, Inc.

Gray, Stephen J. For the Love of a Cloud Maker. 2013. 28p. pap. 13.55 *(978-1-4669-8004-4(4))* Trafford Publishing.

Greban, Tanguy. Sarah So Small. Greban, Quentin, illus. 2004. (ENG.). 32p. (J). (gr. 4-7). 16.95 *(978-1-59687-179-3(2))* IBks., Inc.

Green, Amy. Escape from Riddler's Pass, Vol. 2. 2011. (ENG., Illus.). 176p. (J). pap. 7.99 *(978-1-59317-433-0(0))* Warner Pr., Inc.

Green, Dawn A. Marianne Wellman's School for Girls. 2011. 236p. pap. 24.95 *(978-1-4626-0715-0(2))* America Star Bks.

Green, Sally. Half Lost. 2017. (Half Bad Trilogy Ser.: 3). lib. bdg. 22.10 ***(978-0-606-39798-8(1))*** Turtleback Bks.

Green, Scooter. Ituke's First Hunt. 2012. 32p. 24.95 *(978-1-4626-6903-5(4))* America Star Bks.

Greenberg, Doris & Shandley, Pandré. The Legend of L'Esprit: Dance Legacy Series. 2011. 272p. pap. 15.95 *(978-1-4634-1800-7(0))* AuthorHouse.

Greenburg, Dan. Secrets of Dripping Fang, Book One: The Onts. Fischer, Scott M., illus. 2005. (Secrets of Dripping Fang Ser.: Bk. 1). (ENG.). 144p. (J). (gr. 2-5). 12.99 *(978-0-15-205457-1(X))* Houghton Mifflin Harcourt Publishing Co.

Greenhill, Ms Jane. Jolly Olde Teenage Alien. 2013. 258p. pap. *(978-0-9918766-2-4(8))* Greenhill, Jane.

Greer, Hannah. The Castle Ivengless: The Velvet Bag Memoirs, Bk. 3. 2009. 145p. pap. 24.95 *(978-1-60749-105-7(2))* America Star Bks.

—The Pharos Legacy Book: The Whiz Kids Adventures. 2010. 122p. 21.95 *(978-1-60860-902-4(2)*, Strategic Bk. Publishing) Strategic Book Publishing & Rights Agency (SBPRA).

Gregory, David. Visions of Reality. 2007. 236p. per. 15.95 *(978-0-595-44969-9(7))* iUniverse, Inc.

Gregory, Manju. The Dragon's Tears. Le, Guo, illus. 2004. (ENG & BEN.). 24p. (J). pap. *(978-1-85269-687-0(7))*; pap. *(978-1-85269-810-2(1))*; pap. *(978-1-85269-805-8(5))*; pap. *(978-1-85269-787-7(3))*; pap. *(978-1-85269-699-3(0))*; pap. *(978-1-85269-698-6(2))*; pap. *(978-1-85269-697-9(4))*; pap. *(978-1-85269-696-2(6))*; pap. *(978-1-85269-695-5(8))*; pap. *(978-1-85269-694-8(X))*; pap. *(978-1-85269-692-4(3))*; pap. *(978-1-85269-691-7(5))*; pap. *(978-1-85269-688-7(5))*; pap. *(978-1-85269-686-3(9))* Mantra Lingua.

—The Dragon's Tears: Les Larmes du Dragon. Le, Guo, illus. 2004. (ENG & FRE.). 24p. (J). pap. *(978-1-85269-689-4(3))* Mantra Lingua.

Gregory, Nicky. Georgie Jones ... & You Thought Your Family Was Weird! 2013. 204p. pap. 9.95 *(978-0-9560537-3-2(4))* FBS Publishing Co.

Gresh, Lois H. The Ultimate Unauthorized Eragon Guide: The Hidden Facts Behind the World of Alagaesia. 2006. (ENG., Illus.). 176p. (J). (gr. 4-7). pap. 17.99 *(978-0-312-35792-4(3)*, 9780312357924, St. Martin's Griffin) St. Martin's Pr.

Gresham, P. A. Anything Could Be Any Thing. 2005. 128p. pap. 12.95 *(978-1-4116-4353-6(4))* Lulu Pr., Inc.

Grethe, James. Weird & Wondrous Tales of Woodland Wyre. 2009. 60p. pap. 11.00 *(978-1-4269-1527-7(6))* Trafford Publishing.

Grey, Allan. Alienology. Steer, Dugald A., ed. Carrell, Douglas, illus. 2010. (Ologies Ser.: 10). (ENG.). 32p. (J). (gr. 3-7). 21.99 *(978-0-7636-4565-6(6))* Candlewick Pr.

Grey, C. R. Animas, Book One Legacy of the Claw. Madsen, Jim, illus. 2015. (Animas Ser.). (ENG.). 320p. (J). (gr. 3-7). pap. 7.99 *(978-1-4231-8466-9(1))* Hyperion Bks. for Children.

—Animas, Book Two Flight of the King. 2015. (Animas Ser.). (ENG., Illus.). 304p. (J). (gr. 3-7). 16.99 *(978-1-4231-8343-3(6))* Hyperion Bks. for Children.

—Legacy of the Claw. Madsen, Jim, illus. 2014. (Animas Ser.). (ENG.). 304p. (J). (gr. 3-7). 16.99 *(978-1-4231-8038-8(0))* Disney Pr.

Grey, Melissa. The Savage Dawn. 2017. (Girl at Midnight Ser.: 3). (ENG.). 496p. (YA). (gr. 9). 17.99 ***(978-0-385-74469-0(2))***; lib. bdg. 20.99 ***(978-0-375-99181-3(6))*** Random Hse. Children's Bks. (Delacorte Pr.).

—The Shadow Hour. (Girl at Midnight Ser.: 2). (ENG.). (YA). (gr. 9). 2017. 448p. pap. 9.99 ***(978-0-385-74468-3(4)***, Ember) 2016. 432p. lib. bdg. 20.99 *(978-0-375-99180-6(8)*, Delacorte Pr.) Random Hse. Children's Bks.

Grey, Mini & Gardner, Lyn. Into the Woods. Grey, Mini, illus. 2009. (ENG.). 448p. (J). (gr. 3-7). 8.99 *(978-0-440-42223-5(X)*, Yearling) Random Hse. Children's Bks.

Griffin, Bethany. The Dance of the Red Death. 2013. (Masque of the Red Death Ser.: 2). (ENG.). 336p. (YA). (gr. 9). 17.99 *(978-0-06-210782-4(8)*, Greenwillow Bks.) HarperCollins Pubs.

Griffith, Diane. Granny's Magic Garden. 2010. 66p. pap. 19.95 *(978-1-60693-925-3(4)*, Eloquent Bks.) Strategic Book Publishing & Rights Agency (SBPRA).

Grimes, Linda. Jiggery-Jee's Eden Valley Stories. 2004. 84p. pap. 19.95 *(978-1-4137-0677-2(0))* America Star Bks.

Grimm, Jacob. Cinderella/Cenicienta. 2004. (Illus.). (J). *(978-1-933530-13-0(8))* Bingo Bks., Inc.

—Cinderella/Cenicienta Take Home Version. 2004. (Illus.). (J). cd-rom *(978-1-933530-39-0(1))* Bingo Bks., Inc.

Grimm, Jacob & Grimm, Wilhelm K. Grimm's Fairy Tales. Hunt, Margaret, tr. from GER. 2007. (Dover Thrift Editions Ser.). (ENG., Illus.). 208p. per. 5.00 *(978-0-486-45656-0(0))* Dover Pubns., Inc.

—Rumpelstiltskin. 2004. (Illus.). (J). *(978-1-933530-17-8(0))* Bingo Bks., Inc.

Griswold-Ford, Valerie. Last Rites. 2013. 322p. pap. *(978-1-897492-66-6(9))* Dragon Moon Pr.

Groethe, Kd. The Boy Who Would Walk on Air. 2012. 118p. (gr. -1). 23.99 *(978-1-4772-9164-1(4))*; pap. 14.95 *(978-1-4772-9165-8(2))* AuthorHouse.

Grotholt, Yannick. The Power of Fire Chi. 2015. (LEGO Legends of Chima Graphic Novels Ser.: 4). (J). lib. bdg. 18.40 *(978-0-606-36452-2(8))* Turtleback Bks.

Grove, Malachai. Malachai Grove Plunt Solinatry: The Song of Malachai. 2010. 24p. 14.99 *(978-1-4520-6441-3(5))* AuthorHouse.

—The Return of Malachai. 2011. 24p. pap. 14.99 *(978-1-4567-6257-5(5))* AuthorHouse.

Grove, S. E. The Crimson Skew. (Mapmakers Trilogy Ser.: 3). (ENG.). (J). (gr. 5). 2017. 464p. 8.99 ***(978-0-14-242368-4(8)***, Puffin Books) 2016. (Illus.). 448p. 17.99 *(978-0-670-78504-9(0)*, Viking Books for Young Readers) Penguin Young Readers Group.

—The Glass Sentence. (Mapmakers Trilogy Ser.: 1). (ENG., Illus.). (J). (gr. 5). 2015. 528p. 8.99 *(978-0-14-242366-0(1)*, Puffin Books) 2014. 512p. 17.99 *(978-0-670-78502-5(4)*, Viking Books for Young Readers) Penguin Young Readers Group.

—The Golden Specific. 2015. (Mapmakers Trilogy Ser.: 2). (ENG., Illus.). 528p. (J). (gr. 5). 17.99 *(978-0-670-78503-2(2)*, Viking Books for Young Readers) Penguin Young Readers Group.

—The Golden Specific. 2016. (Mapmakers Ser.: 2). lib. bdg. 19.65 *(978-0-606-38836-8(2))* Turtleback Bks.

Gruber, Daveda. Red Barn & other Short Stories. 2010. 45p. pap. 19.50 *(978-0-557-41998-2(0))* Lulu Pr., Inc.

Gruelle, Johnny. Raggedy Ann in Cookie Land: (Classic) Gruelle, Johnny, illus. 2010. (Raggedy Ann Ser.). (ENG., Illus.). 96p. (J). 21.99 *(978-1-4424-2199-8(1)*, Simon & Schuster Bks. For Young Readers) Simon & Schuster Bks. For Young Readers.

Guarnaccia, Steven. The Three Little Pigs: An Architectural Tale. 2010. (ENG., Illus.). 32p. (J). (gr. -1-2). 19.95 *(978-0-8109-8941-2(7)*, Abrams Bks. for Young Readers) Abrams, Inc.

Guarneri, Cristina. The Invincible, 1 vol. 2010. 48p. pap. 16.95 *(978-1-4489-4086-8(9))* America Star Bks.

Gubernatis, Loretto. Dimitrius & the Gladiolas. 2011. 356p. pap. 19.99 *(978-1-4568-2907-0(6))* Xlibris Corp.

—Dragons N Things. 2009. 316p. pap. 19.99 *(978-1-4363-9969-2(6))* Xlibris Corp.

Guffrey, Lindsey. A Psalm for the Solar System. 2013. 24p. pap. 9.00 *(978-0-9896518-0-6(0))* Yorkshire Publishing Group.

Guignard, Lars. The Yogi's Curse. 2013. 342p. pap. *(978-0-9877753-9-9(1))* Guignard, Lars.

Guillain, Adam. Bella Balistica & the Izta Warriors. 2012. (Bella Balistica Ser.). (ENG., Illus.). 170p. (J). (gr. 4-7). pap. 9.95 *(978-1-84059-771-4(2))* Milet Publishing.

—Bella Balistica & the Temple of Tikal. 2004. (Bella Balistica Ser.). (ENG., Illus.). 350p. (J). (gr. 4-7). pap. 9.95 *(978-1-84059-394-5(6))* Milet Publishing.

Gunson, Jonathan. The Divine Calling. 2006. 289p. 24.30 *(978-1-4116-7790-6(0))* Lulu Pr., Inc.

Guptara, Suresh & Guptara, Jyoti. Conspiracy of Calaspia. 2007. (ENG.). 226p. (gr. 7). pap. *(978-81-8386-026-0(5))* India Research Pr. IND. Dist: Independent Pubs. Group.

Gurney, James. Dinotopia: Journey to Chandara. 2016. (ENG., Illus.). 160p. pap. 19.99 *(978-1-4494-7984-8(7))* Andrews McMeel Publishing.

—Dinotopia: The World Beneath. 20th anniv. ed. 2012. (Calla Editions Ser.). (ENG., Illus.). 192p. (gr. 3). 30.00 *(978-1-60660-033-7(8))* Dover Pubns., Inc.

—Dinotopia - First Flight. 20th anniv. ed. 2014. (ENG., Illus.). 112p. (gr. 5). 25.00 *(978-1-60660-057-3(5))* Dover Pubns., Inc.

Gurney, James & Gurney, James. A Land Apart from Time. Gurney, James & Gurney, James, illus. 2003. (Dinotopia Ser.). (ENG., Illus.). 160p. (J). (gr. 3-7). pap. 21.99 *(978-0-06-053064-8(2))* HarperCollins Pubs.

Guzzardi, Mary. The Magical Ice Skates. 2011. 50p. pap. 24.95 *(978-1-4560-3246-3(1))* PublishAmerica, Inc.

Habel, Lia. Dearly, Departed. 2012. (ENG.). 496p. (YA). (gr. 8-12). pap. 10.99 *(978-0-345-52332-7(6)*, Del Rey) Random House Publishing Group.

Haberlin, Brian. Manhunter Project Vol. 1, Vol. 1. 2003. (ENG., Illus.). 240p. (gr. 11-18). pap. 19.95 *(978-1-58240-303-8(1)*, 9781582403038) Image Comics.

Haddix, Margaret Peterson. Palace of Lies. 2015. (Palace Chronicles Ser.: 3). (ENG., Illus.). 368p. (YA). (gr. 7). 17.99 *(978-1-4424-4281-8(6))* Simon & Schuster Children's Publishing.

—Palace of Mirrors. 2010. (Palace Chronicles Ser.: 2). (ENG.). 320p. (J). (gr. 5-9). pap. 7.99 *(978-1-4424-0667-4(4)*, Simon & Schuster Bks. For Young Readers) Simon & Schuster Bks. For Young Readers.

Haddon, Dawn. Paddy Stories. 2013. 66p. pap. *(978-1-78407-272-6(9))* FeedARead.com.

Hadnot, Victor. The Wheels of God. 2003. 140p. (YA). pap. 11.95 *(978-0-595-27507-6(9)*, Writers Club Pr.) iUniverse, Inc.

Haesche, Richard, Sr. A Dog Named Wishbone. 2007. 155p. (J). 6.75 *(978-0-9798536-2-3(1))* Kreative X-Pressions Pubns.

—The Legend of the Unicorn. 2007. (ENG.). 61p. (J). 8.99 *(978-0-9798536-9-2(9))* Kreative X-Pressions Pubns.

Haesche, Richard Paul, Sr. The Magic of the Leprechaun. 2007. (ENG.). 182p. (YA). *(978-0-9798536-3-0(X))* Kreative X-Pressions Pubns.

—My Pet Dinosaur. 2007. (ENG.). 60p. (J). 6.99 *(978-0-9800552-0-7(2))* Kreative X-Pressions Pubns.

Hafiz, Caroline Owen. The Return of the Fossil. 2007. 76p. per. *(978-1-897312-26-1(1))* Adlibbed Ltd.

Hagen, George. Gabriel Finley & the Raven's Riddle. 2016. (ENG.). 384p. (J). (gr. 4-7). 7.99 *(978-0-399-55222-9(7)*, Yearling) Random Hse. Children's Bks.

Haggard, H. Rider. Allan Quatermain #3: Allan+s Wife. 2007. 116p. per. 7.99 *(978-1-934451-87-8(8))* Wilder Pubns., Corp.

Hahn, Mary Downing. The Doll in the Garden: A Ghost Story. 2007. (ENG.). 144p. (J). (gr. 1-4). pap. 7.99 *(978-0-618-87315-9(5))* Houghton Mifflin Harcourt Publishing Co.

Hahn, Rebecca. A Creature of Moonlight. 2014. (ENG.). 224p. (YA). (gr. 7-12). 17.99 *(978-0-544-10935-3(X)*, HMH Books For Young Readers) Houghton Mifflin Harcourt Publishing Co.

Haig, Matt. Samuel Blink & the Forbidden Forest. 2008. (ENG.). 352p. (J). (gr. 3-7). 7.99 *(978-0-14-241191-9(4)*, Puffin Books) Penguin Young Readers Group.

Haining, Peter. Magicians' Circle. 2012. 348p. (-18). pap. *(978-1-4596-4365-9(8))* ReadHowYouWant.com, Ltd.

Haining, Peter, ed. Magician's Circle: More Spellbinding Stories of Wizards & Wizardry. 2004. (ENG., Illus.). 256p. (J). (gr. 5). 19.95 *(978-0-285-63681-1(2))* Souvenir Pr. Ltd. GBR. Dist: Independent Pubs. Group.

Hainsworth, Emily. Through to You. 2012. (ENG.). 272p. (YA). (gr. 8). 17.99 *(978-0-06-209419-3(X))* HarperCollins Pubs.

Haldane, Rachael. Nymphas' World. 2009. 392p. pap. 13.99 *(978-1-61667-003-0(7))* Raider Publishing International.

Hale, Aaron. Addy Gets Made. 2008. 27p. pap. 24.95 *(978-1-60610-339-5(3))* America Star Bks.

Hale, Shannon. The Book of a Thousand Days. Smith, James Noel, illus. 2007. (ENG.). 320p. (YA). (gr. 7-12). 17.95 *(978-1-59990-051-3(3)*, 9781599900513, Bloomsbury USA Childrens) Bloomsbury Publishing USA.

—Enna Burning. 2017. (Books of Bayern Ser.). (ENG.). 368p. (YA). pap. 9.99 *(978-1-68119-317-5(5)*, 9781681193175, Bloomsbury USA Childrens) Bloomsbury Publishing USA.

—Ever after High: Once upon a Time: A Story Collection. 2014. (ENG.). 272p. (J). (gr. 3-7). 12.99 *(978-0-316-25821-0(0))* Little, Brown Bks. for Young Readers.

—Ever after High: the Storybox of Legends Boxed Set. 2014. (ENG.). 900p. (J). (gr. 3-7). 45.00 *(978-0-316-28720-3(2))* Little, Brown Bks. for Young Readers.

—Fire & Ice. 2014. (Spirit Animals Ser.: 4). (ENG., Illus.). 192p. (J). (gr. 3-7). 16.99 *(978-0-545-59974-0(1))*; 12.99 *(978-0-545-52246-5(3))* Scholastic, Inc.

—Palace of Stone. (Princess Academy Ser.: 2). (ENG.). (YA). (gr. 5-8). 2015. 352p. pap. 7.99 *(978-1-61963-257-8(8)*, 9781619632578) 2012. 336p. 17.99 *(978-1-59990-873-1(5)*, 9781599908731) Bloomsbury Publishing USA. (Bloomsbury USA Childrens).

—Palace of Stone. 2015. (Princess Academy Ser.: 2). (YA). lib. bdg. 18.40 *(978-0-606-36439-3(0))* Turtleback Bks.

—The Storybook of Legends. 2013. (Ever after High Ser.). (ENG., Illus.). 320p. (J). (gr. 3-7). 14.99 *(978-0-316-40122-7(6))* Little, Brown Bks. for Young Readers.

—The Storybook of Legends. 2017. (Ever after High Ser.: 1). (J). lib. bdg. 18.40 ***(978-0-606-40630-7(1))*** Turtleback Bks.

—The Unfairest of Them All. 2014. (Ever after High Ser.). (ENG.). 336p. (J). (gr. 3-7). 14.99 *(978-0-316-28201-7(4))* Little, Brown Bks. for Young Readers.

—A Wonderlandiful World. 2014. (Ever after High Ser.: 3). (ENG.). 336p. (J). (gr. 3-7). 14.99 *(978-0-316-28209-3(X))* Little, Brown Bks. for Young Readers.

EFG

Hale, Shannon & Hale, Dean. The Princess in Black Takes a Vacation. 2017. (Princess in Black Ser.: 4). (ENG.). (J). (gr. k-3). lib. bdg. 17.20 **(978-0-606-39839-8(2))** Turtleback Bks.

Hale, Shannon & Hale, Dean. Rapunzel's Revenge. Hale, Nathan, illus. 2008. (ENG.). 144p. (YA). (gr. 5-8). pap. 16.99 *(978-1-59990-288-3(5)*, 9781599902883, Bloomsbury USA Childrens) Bloomsbury Publishing USA.

Hale, Susan Elizabeth. Emma Oliver & the Song of Creation. 2016. (ENG.). 178p. (J). (gr. -1-12). pap. 11.95 *(978-1-78535-386-4(1)*, Our Street Bks.) Hunt, John Publishing Ltd. GBR. Dist: National Bk. Network.

Halevy, Hanita H. Dragonlions & the Spacemen. Heler, Shraga, illus. 2012. (ENG.). 140p. (J). pap. 13.00 *(978-965-550-085-1(3))* Contento De Semrik ISR. Dist: Bookmasters Distribution.

Hall, C. Aubrey. The Call of Eirian, 0 vols. 2012. (Faelin Chronicles Ser.: 2). (ENG.). 352p. (YA). (gr. 7-11). 17.99 *(978-0-7614-6262-0(7)*, 9780761462620, Amazon Children's Publishing) Amazon Publishing.

Hall, Francois, illus. The Emperor's New Clothes. 2007. (First Fairy Tales Ser.). 32p. (J). (gr. -1-3). lib. bdg. 28.50 *(978-1-59771-071-8(7)*, 1262700) Sea-To-Sea Pubns.

Hall, Frank. The Prince Who Did Not Want to be King. 2011. 132p. 28.95 *(978-1-4497-1440-6(4))*; (J). pap. 11.95 *(978-1-4497-1438-3(2))* Author Solutions, Inc. (WestBow Pr.).

Hall, Jennie. The Viking Tales. 2008. 88p. pap. 8.15 *(978-1-60459-529-1(9))* Wilder Pubns., Corp.

Hall, John & Gilpin, Stephen. If the Earth Had a Zipper. 2006. (Illus.). 48p. 15.99 *(978-1-59379-069-1(4))* White Stone Bks.

Hall, Shirley. A Fairy Tale. 2012. 20p. pap. 15.99 *(978-1-4685-5242-3(2))* AuthorHouse.

Hall, Traci. Wiccan Cool. 2010. (Rhiannon Godfrey Ser.). (ENG.). 264p. pap. 15.00 *(978-1-60504-611-2(6))* Samhain Publishing, LTD.

Hallam, Gwion. Creadyn. 2005. (WEL.). 176p. pap. 5.99 *(978-1-84323-247-6(2))* Gomer Pr. GBR. Dist: Gomer Pr.

Halloran, Craig. The Chronicles of Dragon: Dragon Bones & Tombstones (Book 2) 2013. 226p. pap. 9.99 *(978-0-9896216-0-1(X))* Two-Ten Bk. Pr.

—The Chronicles of Dragon: Terror at the Temple (Book 3) 2013. 276p. pap. 9.99 *(978-0-9896216-2-5(6))* Two-Ten Bk. Pr.

—The Chronicles of Dragon: The Hero, the Sword & the Dragons (Book 1) 2013. 136p. pap. 9.99 *(978-0-9884642-6-1(8))* Two-Ten Bk. Pr.

Halpern, Jake & Kujawinski, Peter. Dormia. 2010. (ENG.). 528p. (J). (gr. 5-7). pap. 7.99 *(978-0-547-32887-4(7))* Houghton Mifflin Harcourt Publishing Co.

—Edgeland. 2017. (ENG., Illus.). 272p. (J). (gr. 5). 17.99 *(978-0-399-17581-7(4)*, G.P. Putnam's Sons Books for Young Readers) Penguin Young Readers Group.

—Nightfall. 2015. (ENG., Illus.). 368p. (YA). (gr. 7). 17.99 *(978-0-399-17580-0(6)*, G.P. Putnam's Sons Books for Young Readers) Penguin Young Readers Group.

Hamazaki, Tatsuya. .hack //Legend of the Twilight, Volume 1: Kaplan SAT/ACT Vocabulary-Building Manga. Izumi, Rei, illus. 2007. (Kaplan SAT/ACT Score-Raising Manga Ser.). 192p. pap. 9.99 *(978-1-4277-5497-4(7))* Kaplan Publishing.

Hamilton, Alwyn. Rebel of the Sands. (Rebel of the Sands Ser.). (ENG.). (YA). (gr. 7). 2017. 336p. pap. 10.99 *(978-0-14-751797-5(4)*, Speak) 2016. 320p. 18.99 *(978-0-451-47753-8(7)*, Viking Books for Young Readers) Penguin Young Readers Group.

Hamilton, C. After Ever Happily. 2006. 80p. pap. 16.95 *(978-1-4241-3190-7(1))* PublishAmerica, Inc.

Hamilton, Kersten. The Mesmer Menace. Hamilton, James, illus. 2015. (Gadgets & Gears Ser.: 1). (ENG.). 160p. (J). (gr. 2-5). pap. 6.99 *(978-0-544-43934-4(1)*, HMH Books For Young Readers) Houghton Mifflin Harcourt Publishing Co.

—The Tick-Tock Man: Gadgets & Gears, Book 3. Hamilton, James, illus. 2017. (Gadgets & Gears Ser.: 3). (ENG.). 144p. (J). (gr. 2-5). pap. 6.99 *(978-0-544-93715-4(5)*, HMH Books For Young Readers) Houghton Mifflin Harcourt Publishing Co.

Hamilton, Peter F. The Hunting of the Princes. 2016. (Queen of Dreams Ser.: 2). (ENG., Illus.). 320p. (J). (gr. 4-7). pap. 11.99 *(978-1-4472-9114-5(X))* Pan Macmillan GBR. Dist: Independent Pubs. Group.

Hamilton, Seymour. The Laughing Princess. 2012. (ENG.). 146p. (J). pap. 7.99 *(978-1-937291-45-7(6))* Acedrex Publishing.

Hamilton-Sturdy, K. The Tree of Dreams. 2013. 138p. pap. *(978-1-78299-683-5(4))* FeedARead.com.

Hamley, Dennis. Pageants of Despair. 2006. (ENG.). 175p. (J). (gr. 7-12). per. 9.95 *(978-1-58988-028-3(5))* Consortium Bk. Sales & Distribution.

Hamme, Van. Giants. Rosinski, illus. 2013. (Thorgal Ser.: 14). (ENG.). 48p. pap. 11.95 *(978-1-84918-156-3(X))* CineBook GBR. Dist: National Bk. Network.

Hammock, Mary B. Msn Cpnp. Princess Reagan & the Paci Fairy. 2012. 24p. pap. 15.99 *(978-1-4797-1074-4(1))* Xlibris Corp.

Hammond, John, as told by. Lucky in Life. 2003. 150p. (YA). per. 13.95 *(978-1-885631-76-3(6))* Hutchison, G.F. Pr.

Hampton, Brooke. Enchanted Cedar: The Journey Home. 2013. 38p. pap. 16.99 *(978-1-4525-6896-6(0))* Balboa Pr.

Han, Xuemei. Brave Little Mongolian Sisters. Han, Xuemei, illus. 2007. (Illus.). (J). pap. 12.99 *(978-0-9763168-7-9(0))* DigitalKu.

—The Radish & the Girl with Long Hair. Han, Xuemei, illus. 2008. (Illus.). (J). per. *(978-0-9763168-6-2(2))* DigitalKu.

Hancock, R. C. An Uncommon Blue. 2014. (Illus.). xi, 275p. (YA). pap. 16.99 *(978-1-4621-1488-7(1))* Cedar Fort, Inc./CFI Distribution.

Hand, Cynthia. The Afterlife of Holly Chase. 2017. 400p. (YA). (gr. 8). 17.99 **(978-0-06-231850-3(0)**, HarperTeen) HarperCollins Pubs.

Hand, Cynthia, et al. My Lady Jane. 512p. (YA). (gr. 8). 2017. pap. 9.99 *(978-0-06-239176-6(3))* 2016. 17.99 *(978-0-06-239174-2(7))* HarperCollins Pubs. (HarperTeen).

Hanley, Victoria. Seize the Story: A Handbook for Teens Who Like to Write. 2008. (ENG.). 208p. (J). (gr. 6). pap. 15.95 *(978-1-877673-81-8(1))* Cottonwood Pr., Inc.

Hanna, John Fairbanks. Vincent J Muggs: What If? 2009. 48p. pap. 17.50 *(978-1-60693-874-4(6)*, Eloquent Bks.) Strategic Book Publishing & Rights Agency (SBPRA).

Hanna, Kevin & Fagan, Dave. Creature Academy GN. 2011. (Illus.). 80p. (YA). pap. 14.95 *(978-1-897548-53-0(2))* Arcana Studio, Inc.

Hannibal, James R. The Lost Property Office. 2016. (Section 13 Ser.: 1). (ENG., Illus.). 400p. (J). (gr. 3-7). 16.99 *(978-1-4814-6709-4(3)*, Simon & Schuster Bks. For Young Readers) Simon & Schuster Bks. For Young Readers.

Hano, Patricia. Tyler Meets the Moon. 2010. 28p. pap. 11.99 *(978-1-60911-189-2(3)*, Eloquent Bks.) Strategic Book Publishing & Rights Agency (SBPRA).

Hanson, Ann. Flicker's Round Trip. 2003. (Illus.). per. 12.95 *(978-1-888345-51-3(9))* Paper Jam Publishing.

Hanson, Robert Karl. Bluey & the Great Spirit Moon. 2012. 48p. pap. 17.45 *(978-1-4525-0730-9(9))* Balboa Pr.

Hapka, Catherine, pseud. Don't Meddle with Miss Nettle. 2014. (Sofia the First Ser.). (J). lib. bdg. 24.50 *(978-0-606-34101-1(3)*, Turtleback) Turtleback Bks.

Hapka, Catherine, pseud & Disney Book Group Staff. The Amulet & the Anthem. Disney Storybook Art Team, illus. 2013. (ENG.). 24p. (J). (gr. -1-k). pap. 4.99 *(978-1-4231-8023-4(2))* Disney Pr.

Hapka, Cathy, pseud & Disney Book Group Staff. Sofia Makes a Friend. Disney Storybook Artists Staff, illus. 2013. (World of Reading Ser.). (ENG.). 32p. (J). (gr. -1-k). pap. 3.99 *(978-1-4231-6408-1(3))* Disney Pr.

Hapka, Cathy, pseud, et al. The Royal Slumber Party. Disney Storybook Art Team, illus. 2013. (ENG.). 24p. (J). (gr. -1-k). pap. 3.99 *(978-1-4231-6410-4(5))* Disney Pr.

Haptie, Charlotte. Otto & the Bird Charmers: The Second Book of the Karmidee. 2005. (Illus.). 417p. (J). 17.95 *(978-0-8234-1883-1(9))* Holiday Hse., Inc.

Harbridge, Paul. Helena's Voyage: A Mystic Adventure. 2008. (HEB, ARA & ENG., Illus.). 48p. (J). (gr. -1-2). pap. 9.95 *(978-1-84694-114-6(8)*, Our Street Bks.) Hunt, John Publishing Ltd. GBR. Dist: National Bk. Network.

Hardegree, Maureen. If It Haint Broke. 2015. (ENG., Illus.). 196p. (J). pap. 12.95 *(978-1-61194-597-3(6))* BelleBks., Inc.

Hardin, J. R. Kalvin the Kudzu Monster. 2010. 76p. (J). pap. 8.95 *(978-1-4502-5764-0(X))* iUniverse, Inc.

Hardinge, Frances. A Face Like Glass. 2017. (ENG.). 496p. (YA). (gr. 7-17). 19.95 *(978-1-4197-2484-8(3)*, Amulet Bks.) Abrams, Inc.

—Fly by Night. (J). (gr. 5-9). 2008. 512p. per. 7.99 *(978-0-06-087630-2(1))* 2006. 487p. 16.99 *(978-0-06-087627-2(1))* 2006. 496p. lib. bdg. 17.89 *(978-0-06-087629-6(8))* HarperCollins Pubs.

—Fly Trap. 592p. (J). (gr. 5). 2012. pap. 7.99 *(978-0-06-088046-0(5))* 2011. 16.99 *(978-0-06-088044-6(9))* HarperCollins Pubs.

—The Lost Conspiracy. 2009. 576p. (J). (gr. 5). lib. bdg. 17.89 *(978-0-06-088042-2(2))*; 16.99 *(978-0-06-088041-5(4))* HarperCollins Pubs.

Hardy, Emma-Rose. Vampuric Slayer Blood. 2010. 155p. pap. 7.94 *(978-1-4461-5652-0(4))* Lulu Pr., Inc.

Hardy, Janice. A Blue Fire, Bk. 2. 2010. (Healing Wars Ser.: II). (ENG.). 384p. (J). (gr. 5-18). 16.99 *(978-0-06-174741-0(6))* HarperCollins Pubs.

—The Healing Wars: Book II: Blue Fire. 2011. (Healing Wars Ser.: II). (ENG.). 400p. (J). (gr. 5). pap. 7.99 *(978-0-06-174744-1(0))* HarperCollins Pubs.

—The Shifter. (J). (gr. 5). 2010. (Healing Wars Ser.: I). (ENG.). 400p. pap. 7.99 *(978-0-06-174708-3(4))* 2009. (Healing Wars Ser.). 384p. lib. bdg. 17.89 *(978-0-06-176177-5(X))* HarperCollins Pubs.

Harel, Moshe. Elf Prince. 2012. (ENG.). 258p. pap. *(978-965-550-089-9(6))* Contento De Semrik.

Harland, Richard. Liberator. (ENG.). 496p. (YA). (gr. 7). 2013. Illus.). pap. 9.99 *(978-1-4424-2334-3(X))* 2012. 17.99 *(978-1-4424-2333-6(1))* Simon & Schuster Bks. For Young Readers. (Simon & Schuster Bks. For Young Readers).

—Worldshaker. (ENG.). (YA). (gr. 7). 2011. 416p. pap. 9.99 *(978-1-4169-9553-1(6))* 2010. 400p. 16.99 *(978-1-4169-9552-4(8))* Simon & Schuster Bks. For Young Readers. (Simon & Schuster Bks. For Young Readers).

Harman, Ian. The Adventures of Terry Tool Bench: Book 1 Terry Is Born. 2009. 36p. pap. 16.99 *(978-1-4490-0048-6(7))* AuthorHouse.

Harmening, Gail. How Did Clancey Get His Color?, 1 vol. 2009. 45p. pap. 24.95 *(978-1-60836-440-4(2))* America Star Bks.

Harper, John. Time Lapse: Collapse. 2011. 184p. 24.99 *(978-1-4490-7045-8(0))*; pap. 17.99 *(978-1-4490-7044-1(2))* AuthorHouse.

Harrington, James. The Last Laugh. 2009. (Illus.). 24p. pap. 11.50 *(978-1-60860-187-5(0)*, Strategic Bk. Publishing) Strategic Book Publishing & Rights Agency (SBPRA).

Harris, Charles Edward. Ice Angels. 2007. 60p. pap. 30.50 *(978-1-84799-750-0(3))* Lulu Pr., Inc.

Harris, J. Henry & Everson, Michael. Phyllis in Piskie-Land: A Tale of Cornwall, Inspired by Lewis Carroll's Wonderland. 2012. (Illus.). 102p. pap. *(978-1-904808-84-8(0))* Evertype.

Harris, Joe. Wars in Toyland. 2013. (ENG., Illus.). 104p. 19.99 *(978-1-934964-93-4(X)*, 9781934964934) Oni Pr., Inc.

Harris, Robert & Yolen, Jane. Girl in a Cage. 2004. (ENG.). 240p. (YA). (gr. 7-7). 6.99 *(978-0-14-240132-3(3)*, Speak) Penguin Young Readers Group.

Harris, Todd V. Heroes & Haters. 2008. 75p. pap. 19.95 *(978-1-60563-157-8(4))* America Star Bks.

Harris, Tony, illus. The Invincible Iron Man(r): Disassembled. 2007. (ENG.). 144p. (YA). (gr. 8-17). pap. 14.99 *(978-0-7851-1653-0(2))* Marvel Worldwide, Inc.

Harrison, Cora. Wolf in the Midnight Forest. (ENG., Illus.). 240p. pap. 5.95 *(978-0-86327-882-2(5))* Wolfhound Pr. IRL. Dist: Interlink Publishing Group, Inc.

Harrison, Kim, pseud. Early to Death, Early to Rise. 2011. (Madison Avery Ser.: 2). (ENG., Illus.). 256p. (YA). (gr. 9). pap. 8.99 *(978-0-06-144169-1(4))* HarperCollins Pubs.

—Once Dead, Twice Shy. (Madison Avery Ser.: 1). 2010. (ENG.). 256p. (YA). (gr. 8). pap. 8.99 *(978-0-06-144168-4(6))* 2009. 240p. (J). lib. bdg. 17.89 *(978-0-06-171820-5(3)*, HarperTeen) 2009. 240p. (J). (gr. 9-18). 16.99 *(978-0-06-171816-8(5)*, HarperTeen) HarperCollins Pubs.

—Something Deadly This Way Comes. 2011. (Madison Avery Ser.: 3). (ENG.). 256p. (YA). (gr. 9-18). 16.99 *(978-0-06-171819-9(X))* HarperCollins Pubs.

Harrison, Paula. The Baby Firebird. Williams, Sophy, illus. 2017. (Secret Rescuers Ser.: 3). (ENG.). 128p. (J). (gr. 2-5). pap. 5.99 **(978-1-4814-7613-3(0)**, Aladdin) Simon & Schuster Children's Publishing.

Harrison, Troon. The Dream Collector. 2004. (Illus.). (J). (gr. k-3). spiral bd. *(978-0-616-01671-8(9))* Canadian National Institute for the Blind/Institut National Canadien pour les Aveugles.

—The Twilight Box. 2007. (Tales of Terre Ser.: No. 2). (Illus.). 362p. (gr. 7-18). per. 10.95 *(978-0-9768126-7-8(3))* Brown Barn Bks.

Harry Potter y el Misterio del Principe. 2006. (Harry Potter Ser.: Year 6). (SPA.). 602p. (J). (gr. 4-7). per. 15.99 *(978-84-7888-996-9(5))* Publicaciones y Ediciones Salamandra, S.A. ESP. Dist: Lectorum Pubns., Inc.

Harry Potter y el Misterio del Principe. 2006. (Harry Potter Ser.: Year 6). (SPA.). 602p. (J). (gr. 4-7). 19.99 *(978-84-7888-993-8(0))* Publicaciones y Ediciones Salamandra, S.A. ESP. Dist: Lectorum Pubns., Inc.

Hart, Carla. A Kid Named Cancer: A Story about a Bully & How He Got Treated. 2009. 50p. pap. 16.50 *(978-1-60693-659-7(X)*, Eloquent Bks.) Strategic Book Publishing & Rights Agency (SBPRA).

Hartley, A. J. Firebrand: A Steeplejack Novel. 2017. (Steeplejack Ser.: 2). (ENG.). 336p. (YA). 17.99 *(978-0-7653-8813-1(8)*, 9780765388131, Tor Teen) Doherty, Tom Assocs., LLC.

—Steeplejack. 2016. (Steeplejack Ser.: 1). (ENG.). 336p. (YA). 17.99 *(978-0-7653-8342-6(X)*, 9780765383426, Tor Teen) Doherty, Tom Assocs., LLC.

Hartman, Rachel. Seraphina. (ENG.). (YA). (gr. 7). 2014. 528p. pap. 10.99 *(978-0-375-86622-7(1)*, Ember) 2012. 512p. lib. bdg. 20.99 *(978-0-375-96656-9(0)*, Random Hse. Bks. for Young Readers) Random Hse. Children's Bks.

—Shadow Scale. 2015. (ENG., Illus.). 608p. (J). (gr. 7). 18.99 *(978-0-375-86657-9(4)*, Random Hse. Bks. for Young Readers) Random Hse. Children's Bks.

Hastings, Brian. Merryn's Journey. 2016. (ENG., Illus.). 40p. (J). (gr. -1). 14.95 *(978-1-4549-2161-5(7))* Sterling Publishing Co., Inc.

Hasty, Vicki Sterling. Eliza & the Analogies of Burnshire. 2009. 150p. pap. 24.95 *(978-1-60813-216-4(1))* America Star Bks.

Hatton, L. J. Sing down the Stars, 0 vols. 2015. (Sing down the Stars Ser.: 1). (ENG.). 380p. (YA). (gr. 8-13). pap. 9.99 *(978-1-5039-4656-9(8)*, 9781503946569, Skyscape) Amazon Publishing.

Haugen, Timothy A. The Castle of Gloom, 1 vol. 2009. (ENG.). 175p. pap. 24.95 *(978-1-61546-106-6(X))* America Star Bks.

A Haunting Melody. 80p. (YA). (gr. 6-12). pap. 10.95 *(978-0-8224-3943-1(3))* Globe Fearon Educational Publishing.

Hauser, Michele. The Crystal Palace: Rescue of the Baby Fairy Prince. 2009. (Illus.). 84p. pap. 9.95 *(978-1-4327-1157-3(1))* Outskirts Pr., Inc.

—The Crystal Palace II: Rebellion in Fairyland. 2009. (Illus.). 130p. pap. 9.95 *(978-1-4327-1153-5(9))* Outskirts Pr., Inc.

Hausman, Gerald. Timeswimmer. 2009. (Island Fiction Ser.). 187p. (J). (gr. 5-16). pap. *(978-1-4050-9898-4(8))* Macmillan Caribbean.

Hautzig, Deborah. Lewis Carroll's Alice in Wonderland. Rathke, Kathryn, illus. 2010. (Penguin Young Readers, Level 4 Ser.). (ENG.). 48p. (J). (gr. 3-4). mass mkt. 3.99 *(978-0-448-45269-2(3)*, Penguin Young Readers) Penguin Young Readers Group.

Havard, Amanda. The Survivors. 2011. (ENG.). (YA). 294p. 21.99 *(978-0-9833190-0-9(6))*; 300p. pap. 11.99 *(978-0-9833190-2-3(2))* Chafie Pr., LLC.

Haviland, C. S. Faith & Fairies. rev. ed. 2005. (ENG.). 253p. (YA). reprint ed. pap. 14.95 *(978-0-9759355-1-4(8))* LegendMaker Scriptoria.

Hawk, Delores. The Edge of Finali. 2012. 350p. pap. 14.25 *(978-0-9859522-0-4(2))* Asimow, Dyanne.

Hawkins, A. D. The Time Princess. 2013. 208p. pap. *(978-1-78299-661-3(3))* FeedARead.com.

Hawkins, Linda J. Alexander & the Great Vegetable Feud. Bowles, Jennifer, illus. 2004. 40p. (J). (gr. k-5). 19.99 *(978-0-9742806-1-5(5))* Heart to Heart Publishing, Inc.

Hawkins, Rachel. Hex Hall, Bk. 1. 2010. (ENG.). 336p. (J). (gr. 7-17). 16.99 *(978-1-4231-2130-5(9))* Hyperion Pr.

—Rebel Belle. 2014. (Rebel Belle Ser.: 1). (ENG.). 352p. (YA). (gr. 7). 17.99 *(978-0-399-25693-6(8)*, G.P. Putnam's Sons Books for Young Readers) Penguin Young Readers Group.

Hawks, K. J. Lu-Don & the Kingdoms of Trent. 2012. 72p. pap. 27.49 *(978-1-4520-6359-1(1))* AuthorHouse.

Hawley, Bobby. Matt & the Wonder of Wishes, 1 vol. 2009. 165p. pap. 24.95 *(978-1-60836-743-6(6))* America Star Bks.

Haws, Jacob. Telarthia: The Taln Crystal. 2013. 336p. pap. 29.95 *(978-1-63000-906-9(7))* PublishAmerica, Inc.

Hawthorn, P. Little Book of Fairy Stories. 2004. (Mini Storybooks Ser.). (ENG., Illus.). 128p. (J). 7.95 *(978-0-7945-0297-3(0)*, Usborne) EDC Publishing.

Hawthorne, Rachel. Dark of the Moon. 2009. (Dark Guardian Ser.: 3). (ENG.). 272p. (YA). (gr. 9-18). pap. 9.99 *(978-0-06-170957-9(3)*, HarperTeen) HarperCollins Pubs.

Haydon, Elizabeth. The Tree of Water. Dorman, Brandon, illus. 2014. (Lost Journals of Ven Polypheme Ser.: 4). (ENG.). 400p. (J). (gr. 5-9). 17.99 *(978-0-7653-2059-9(2)*, 9780765320599, Starscape) Doherty, Tom Assocs., LLC.

Hayes, Joe. El Dia que Nevaron Tortillas. Hayes, Joe, tr. Lopez, Antonio Castro & Castro L., Antonio, illus. 2003.Tr. of Day It Snowed Tortillas. (SPA & ENG.). 160p. (J). (gr. 4-6). pap. 12.95 *(978-0-938317-76-0(8))* Cinco Puntos Pr.

—Pajaro Verde. Castro L., Antonio, illus. 2005. (ENG & SPA.). 40p. (J). (gr. 4-6). pap. 8.95 *(978-0-938317-90-6(3))* Cinco Puntos Pr.

Hayes, Malcolm. The Dreamcatchers. 2006. 282p. pap. 20.14 *(978-1-4120-8320-1(6))* Trafford Publishing.

Hayhurst, James L. The Adventures of Mercury Lane: Bad Commandments, Book No. 1. 2008. (Illus.). 212p. (YA). pap. 13.95 *(978-0-9729380-1-3(X)*, Parascension Pr.) Parascension, Inc.

Hayhurst/Parascension Press, James/Lyle. The Adventures of Mercury Lane: Bad Commandments, Book No.1. 2008. (Illus.). 212p. (YA). lib. bdg. 21.95 *(978-0-615-18212-4(7)*, Parascension Pr.) Parascension, Inc.

Haynes, Betsy. The Creepazoid's Nostrils. 2013. 118p. pap. 9.99 *(978-1-60820-858-6(3))* MLR Pr., LLC.

Haynes, Cate. Groovy Granny. Tholen, Shane, illus. 2003. 32p. (J). pap. 13.50 *(978-1-86368-332-6(1))* Fremantle Pr. AUS. Dist: Independent Pubs. Group.

Hays, K. D. & Weidman, Meg. Toto's Tale. Martinez, April, illus. 2010. 248p. (J). pap. 14.99 *(978-1-936144-61-7(1)*, Zumaya Thresholds) Zumaya Pubns. LLC.

Hays, Steve. Beauty & the Boy: An Old Man's Story for a Dying Boy. 2006. (YA). 24.95 *(978-0-9759902-1-6(7))* Before Christmas Pr.

Haze, Armand. Beautiful Blossom. 2012. 322p. 29.95 *(978-1-4626-7056-7(3))* America Star Bks.

Hazel, Jan. Marshall Meets the Little Dragons. 2013. 38p. pap. 9.99 *(978-1-62509-396-7(9))* Salem Author Services.

Hazell, Carolyn. Pav the Plumber Saves the Day. 2011. 84p. (gr. 4-6). pap. 11.76 *(978-1-4567-8148-4(0))* AuthorHouse.

Hazell, Mark. Flight of the Cloud Sailor. 2004. 172p. pap. *(978-1-84401-137-7(2))* Athena Pr.

—Gift of the Wind Dancers. 2004. 140p. pap. *(978-1-84401-029-5(5))* Athena Pr.

Heacock, David & Giles, Inga. Child of Oz. 2010. (J). pap. *(978-0-88092-479-5(9))* Royal Fireworks Publishing Co.

Headley, Maria Dahvana. Magonia. (Magonia Ser.: 1). (YA). (gr. 8). 2016. 336p. pap. 9.99 *(978-0-06-232053-7(X))* 2015. (ENG.). 320p. 17.99 *(978-0-06-232052-0(1)*, HarperTeen) HarperCollins Pubs.

Heap, Sue. A Fabulous Fairy Feast. Heap, Sue, illus. 2009. (ENG., Illus.). 32p. (J). (gr. -1-k). pap. 8.99 *(978-1-4052-3644-7(2))* Egmont Bks., Ltd. GBR. Dist: Independent Pubs. Group.

Hearn, Jeff. Cutting Yards on Mars: Writer's Block. 2007. 172p. per. 15.95 *(978-1-4327-1688-2(3))* Outskirts Pr., Inc.

Hearn, Julie & Yankus, Marc. Sign of the Raven. 2005. (ENG., Illus.). 336p. (YA). 16.95 *(978-0-689-85734-8(9)*, Atheneum Bks. for Young Readers) Simon & Schuster Children's Publishing.

Hearn, Lian. Heaven's Net Is Wide. unabr. ed. 2008. (Illus.). 592p. pap. *(978-0-330-45428-5(5)*, Macmillan Children's Bks.) Pan Macmillan.

Heather Rose Brabant. The Moon Princess. 2009. 20p. pap. 11.95 *(978-1-4389-2980-4(3))* AuthorHouse.

Heddle, Rebecca. Puzzle Journey through Time. Spenceley, Annabel, illus. 2003. 32p. (J). pap. 6.95 *(978-0-7945-0440-3(X)*, Usborne) EDC Publishing.

Heer, Dusty Rhoades. The Forest That Rains Frogs. 2012. (ENG.). 58p. pap. 19.95 *(978-1-4327-9303-6(9))* Outskirts Pr., Inc.

Heffernan, Margaret McKay. The Crystal Grove. 2012. 126p. pap. *(978-1-926876-36-8(9))* Soul Asylum Poetry.

Hegarty, Shane. Chaos Descends. 2017. (Darkmouth Ser.: 3). 432p. (J). (gr. 3-7). 17.99 *(978-0-06-231135-1(2))* HarperCollins Pubs.

Heil, Christopher. Wish Rings: A Second Beginning. 2003. 196p. pap. 14.95 *(978-0-595-29582-1(7)*, Writers Club Pr.) iUniverse, Inc.

Heilig, Heidi. The Girl from Everywhere. 2016. 464p. (YA). (gr. 8). 17.99 *(978-0-06-238075-3(3)*, Greenwillow Bks.) HarperCollins Pubs.

The Heir of King Meldh: Book One of the Geometry of Power. 2004. (YA). per. 10.95 *(978-0-9747441-0-0(7))* Brainerd Enterprises.

Helgerson, Joseph. Horns & Wrinkles. Ceccoli, Nicoletta, illus. 2008. (ENG.). 240p. (J). (gr. 5-7). pap. 6.99 *(978-0-618-98178-6(0))* Houghton Mifflin Harcourt Publishing Co.

Hellisen, Cat. Beastkeeper. 2015. (ENG.). 208p. (YA). (gr. 7-9). 16.99 *(978-0-8050-9980-5(8)*, Holt, Henry & Co. Bks. For Young Readers) Holt, Henry & Co.

Helliwell, Sheila. Hoonraki Moon: The Murphy Stories. 2006. (J). pap. 9.00 *(978-0-8059-7027-2(4))* Dorrance Publishing Co., Inc.

Hemphill, Stephanie. Wicked Girls: A Novel of the Salem Witch Trials. 2010. (YA). 336p. (gr. 7-18). lib. bdg. 17.89 *(978-0-06-185329-6(1))*; (ENG.). 416p. (gr. 8-18). 17.99 *(978-0-06-185328-9(3))* HarperCollins Pubs.

Henderson, Hugh. VanDland. 2012. 112p. pap. 10.95 *(978-1-61204-859-8(5)*, Strategic Bk. Publishing) Strategic Book Publishing & Rights Agency (SBPRA).

Hendesi, Roya. The Ancient Queendom. 2011. 52p. pap. 29.05 *(978-1-4568-2783-0(9))* Xlibris Corp.

Heneghan, Lou. The Turnarounders & the Arbuckle Rescue. Maguire, Jake, illus. 2013. 496p. pap. *(978-0-9573523-1-5(X))* Natus Publishing.

Henham, R. D. Bronze Dragon Codex. 2008. (Dragon Codices Ser.). (ENG., Illus.). 256p. (J). (gr. 4-7). 9.95 *(978-0-7869-4930-4(9)*, Mirrorstone) Wizards of the Coast.

—Red Dragon Codex. 2008. (Dragon Codices Ser.). (ENG., Illus.). 256p. (J). (gr. 4-7). 9.95 *(978-0-7869-4925-0(2)*, Mirrorstone) Wizards of the Coast.

Henighan, Tom. Demon in My View. 2007. (ENG.). 176p. (J). (gr. 4). pap. 12.99 *(978-1-55002-656-6(9)*, Boardwalk Bks.) Dundurn CAN. Dist: Ingram Publisher Services.

Henkes, Kevin. Wemberly's Ice-Cream Star. Henkes, Kevin, illus. 2003. (ENG., Illus.). 24p. (J). (gr. -1-k). bds. 6.99 *(978-0-06-050405-2(6)*, Greenwillow Bks.) HarperCollins Pubs.

Hennessy, Barbara G. The Once upon a Time Map Book: Take a Tour of Six Enchanted Lands. Joyce, Peter, illus. 2013. (ENG.). 16p. (J). (gr. 1-4). 24.99 *(978-0-7636-6475-6(8))* Candlewick Pr.

Hennesy, Carolyn. Pandora Gets Jealous. 2009. (Mythic Misadventures Ser.). (ENG., Illus.). 288p. (YA). (gr. 3-6). pap. 7.99 *(978-1-59990-291-3(5)*, 9781599902913, Bloomsbury USA Childrens) Bloomsbury Publishing USA.

Herda, Frank A. The Cup of Death: Chronicles of the Dragons of the Magi. 2007. 180p. 16.95 *(978-1-4327-0922-8(4))*; 212p. per. 9.95 *(978-1-4327-1412-3(0))* Outskirts Pr., Inc.

Herman, Eleanor. Empire of Dust. 2016. (Blood of Gods & Royals Ser.: 2). (ENG., Illus.). 384p. 19.99 *(978-0-373-21192-0(9)*, Harlequin Teen) Harlequin Enterprises, Ltd. CAN. Dist: HarperCollins Pubs.

Hermes, Patricia. Emma Dilemma, the Nanny, & the Secret Ferret, 0 vols. Carter, Abby, illus. 2010. (Emma Dilemma Ser.: 5). (ENG.). 112p. (J). (gr. 3-6). 15.99 *(978-0-7614-5650-6(3)*, 9780761456506, Amazon Children's Publishing) Amazon Publishing.

Hernandez, Janice. Lisa & the Light Dancer. 2009. 48p. pap. 9.95 *(978-1-60860-243-8(5),* Eloquent Bks.) Strategic Book Publishing & Rights Agency (SBPRA).

Herrera, Joaquin. Horris, Little Eli & the Lens of Truth. 2007. (DreamFever Chronicles Ser.: Bk. 1). 208p. *(978-1-59258-245-7(1))* Hylas Publishing.

Herrick, Amy. The Time Fetch. 2014. (ENG.). 336p. (J). (gr. 4-7). pap. 6.95 *(978-1-61620-453-2(2),* 73453) Algonquin Bks. of Chapel Hill.

Herskowitz, Sol. The Horrible Happening. 2004. (J). per. *(978-1-932203-66-0(4))* Sundog, Ltd.

Hess, Brian F. Lynquest & the Search for Greatness. 2006. (ENG.). 116p. per. 19.95 *(978-1-4241-4503-4(1))* PublishAmerica, Inc.

Hesse, George. Malcolm & the Magic Shoe... a Peek into Heaven. 2012. 30p. pap. 17.99 *(978-1-62419-858-8(9))* Salem Author Services.

Hewitt, Megan. Eagle Rises. 2013. 118p. (J). pap. 12.99 *(978-1-300-55242-0(5))* Lulu Pr., Inc.

Higgins, F. E. The Lunatic's Curse. 2011. (ENG.). 352p. (J). (gr. 5-9). 29.99 *(978-0-312-56682-1(4),* 9780312566821) Feiwel & Friends.

Higgins, Lawrence. Demons & Dragons: Time, Space & Magic. 2010. (ENG., Illus.). 93p. pap. 20.99 *(978-1-906791-68-1(6))* Arena Bks. GBR. Dist: Lightning Source UK, Ltd.

Higgins, Wendy. The Great Pursuit. 2017. 512p. (YA). (gr. 8). 17.99 *(978-0-06-238136-1(9),* HarperTeen) HarperCollins Pubs.

Hikawa, Kyoko. From Far Away, Vol. 2. Hikawa, Kyoko, illus. 2005. (ENG., Illus.). 184p. pap. 9.99 *(978-1-59116-601-6(2))* Viz Media.

Hildreth, Joann R. Nicholas James & Missy. Aughe, Roger, illus. 2011. 28p. pap. 24.95 *(978-1-4626-0041-0(7))* America Star Bks.

Hili, Marvin. Playland. 2007. 96p. pap. 14.95 *(978-1-84799-888-0(7))* Lulu Pr., Inc.

Hill, Alan J. Tremain, Book One: The Seven Faiths. 2009. (Illus.). 274p. pap. *(978-1-84748-647-9(9))* Athena Pr.

—Tremain Book Two: Underworld & Overland. 2010. 274p. pap. *(978-1-84748-682-0(7))* Athena Pr.

Hill, C. J. Slayers. 2011. (Slayers Ser.: 1). (ENG.). 384p. (YA). (gr. 7). 16.99 *(978-0-312-61414-0(4))* Feiwel & Friends.

—Slayers: Friends & Traitors. 2013. (Slayers Ser.: 2). (ENG.). 400p. (YA). (gr. 7). 16.99 *(978-1-250-02461-9(7),* 9781250024619) Feiwel & Friends.

Hill, Douglas. The Dragon Charmer. Melnyczuk, Peter, illus. 2005. 151p. (J). (gr. -1-k). pap. 4.95 *(978-1-903015-36-0(7))* Barn Owl Bks, London GBR. Dist: Independent Pubs. Group.

—Warriors Wasteland: The Huntsmen. (ENG.). 144p. pap. *(978-0-330-35384-7(5))* Pan Macmillan.

Hill, Kevin Kelvin. The Red Baron, the Knight of Many Talents. 2009. 40p. pap. 20.99 *(978-1-4490-0642-6(6))* AuthorHouse.

Hill, Sarah. Posie Pixie & the Lost Matchbox. O'Gorman, Sarah, ed. Mauchline, Sarah, illus. 2013. 60p. pap. *(978-1-909302-31-0(7))* Abela Publishing.

Hill, Stuart. Blade of Fire. 2007. 574p. (J). pap. *(978-0-545-01969-9(9))*; (Illus.). *(978-1-4287-2169-2(X),* Chicken Hse., The) Scholastic, Inc.

—Last Battle of the Icemark. 2009. (Icemark Chronicl Ser.: 3). (ENG.). 480p. (J). (gr. 3-7). 18.99 *(978-0-545-09329-3(5),* Chicken Hse., The) Scholastic, Inc.

Hillenburg, Steven. SpongeBob SquarePants, Vol. 7. 2005. (SpongeBob SquarePants Ser.). (Illus.). 89p. pap. 14.99 *(978-1-59532-678-2(2),* Tokyopop Kids) TOKYOPOP, Inc.

Hillenburg, Steven, creator. Saves the Day, Vol. 8. 2005. (Nickelodeon Ser.). (Illus.). 88p. pap. 14.99 *(978-1-59532-679-9(0),* Tokyopop Kids) TOKYOPOP, Inc.

Hillner, Brenda. The Invisible Girl. 2012. 86p. 19.10 *(978-1-4669-5398-7(5))*; pap. 9.10 *(978-1-4669-5396-3(9))* Trafford Publishing.

Hillyer, Rhonda. Butterfly Magic. Wood, Steve, illus. 2013. 84p. pap. 12.00 *(978-1-62212-306-3(9),* Strategic Bk. Publishing) Strategic Book Publishing & Rights Agency (SBPRA).

Himler, Ronald. The Girl on the Yellow Giraffe, 1 vol. Himler, Ronald, illus. 2004. (ENG., Illus.). 32p. (J). 15.95 *(978-1-932065-93-0(8))* Star Bright Bks., Inc.

hines, j. Finding Raven. 2007. 101p. pap. 8.95 *(978-0-615-17723-6(9))* Hines, Jerry.

Hinkler Books Staff. CD Storybook: Beauty & the Beast; The Little Mermaid; Cinderella; Snow White. rev. ed. 2004. (Illus.). 128p. (J). (gr. 4-12). 14.95 incl. cd-rom *(978-1-86515-754-2(6))* Hinkler Bks. Pty, Ltd. AUS. Dist: Penton Overseas, Inc.

Hinks, Roy H. Cybo Soccer & Heavens Above. 2011. 116p. pap. 13.32 *(978-1-4567-7327-4(5))* AuthorHouse.

Hiwatari, Saki. Please Save My Earth, Vol. 18. Hiwatari, Saki, illus. 2006. (Please Save My Earth Ser.: 18). (ENG., Illus.). 208p. pap. 9.99 *(978-1-4215-0551-0(7))* Viz Media.

—Please Save My Earth, Vol. 17. Hiwatari, Saki, illus. 2006. (ENG., Illus.). 208p. pap. 9.99 *(978-1-4215-0550-3(9))* Viz Media.

Hliva, Diana. My Pet Lunecat. 2010. 36p. pap. 18.41 *(978-1-4269-3208-3(1))* Trafford Publishing.

Hocking, Amanda. Ascend. l.t. ed. 2012. (Trylle Trilogy: Bk. 3). (ENG.). 412p. (J). (gr. 8-12). 23.99 *(978-1-4104-5014-2(7))* Thorndike Pr.

—Crystal Kingdom. 2015. (Kanin Chronicles Ser.: 3). (ENG., Illus.). 432p. (YA). (gr. 7). pap. 9.99 *(978-1-250-04988-9(1),* 9781250049889, St. Martin's Griffin) St. Martin's Pr.

—Elegy. (Watersong Novel Ser.: 4). (ENG.). 560p. (YA). (gr. 7). 2014. pap. 10.99 *(978-1-250-00809-1(3),* 9781250008091) 2013. 17.99 *(978-1-250-00567-0(1),* 9781250005670) St. Martin's Pr. (St. Martin's Griffin).

—Frostfire. 2015. (Kanin Chronicles Ser.: 1). (ENG.). 336p. (YA). (gr. 7). pap. 9.99 *(978-1-250-04982-7(2),* 9781250049827, St. Martin's Griffin) St. Martin's Pr.

—Ice Kissed. 2015. (Kanin Chronicles Ser.: 2). (ENG., Illus.). 320p. (YA). (gr. 7-12). 22.99 *(978-1-250-07534-5(3),* 9781250075345); pap. 10.99 *(978-1-250-04987-2(3),* 9781250049872) St. Martin's Pr. (St. Martin's Griffin).

—Lullaby. 2013. (Watersong Novel Ser.: 2). (ENG.). 368p. (YA). (gr. 7). mass mkt. 9.99 *(978-1-250-04675-8(0),* 9781250046758, St. Martin's Paperbacks); pap. 10.99 *(978-1-250-00810-7(7),* 9781250008107, St. Martin's Griffin) St. Martin's Pr.

Hodge, Rosamund. Crimson Bound. (YA). (gr. 8). 2016. 464p. pap. 9.99 *(978-0-06-222477-4(8))* 2015. (ENG.). 448p. 17.99 *(978-0-06-222476-7(X))* HarperCollins Pubs.

—Cruel Beauty. (ENG.). (YA). (gr. 8). 2015. 368p. pap. 9.99 *(978-0-06-222474-3(3))* 2014. 352p. 17.99 *(978-0-06-222473-6(5))* HarperCollins Pubs.

Hodgson, Julie. Earth Child. 2008. 81p. pap. 6.95 *(978-1-4092-2764-9(2))* Lulu Pr., Inc.

—The Mothaich. 2008. 185p. 41.95 *(978-1-4092-3819-5(9))* Lulu Pr., Inc.

Hoehn, Ron. The Windy Night: It happened one Night. 2011. 23p. (J). pap. 16.95 *(978-1-4327-6408-1(X))* Outskirts Pr., Inc.

Hoes, Holly. When Aliens Took over the World. 2012. 44p. pap. 21.99 *(978-1-4797-4870-9(6))* Xlibris Corp.

Hoffmann, E. T. A. The Nutcracker. (Illus.). 12p. (J). 4.95 *(978-1-58989-100-5(7))* Thurman Hse., LLC.

Hoffmann, E. T. A. & Ventura, Paola Fratalocchi. The Nutcracker. 2010. (ENG., Illus.). 32p. (J). 14.99 *(978-0-7944-2044-4(3))* Reader's Digest Assn., Inc., The.

Hoffmann, Lou. Wraith Queen's Veil. 2016. (Sun Child Chronicles Ser.: Vol. 2). (ENG., Illus.). (YA). pap. 17.99 ***(978-1-63477-414-7(0),*** Harmony Ink Pr.) Dreamspinner Pr.

Holder, Nancy. On Fire. 2012. (ENG.). 256p. pap. 11.00 *(978-1-4516-7447-7(3),* MTV Bks.) MTV Books.

—Spirited. 2004. (Once upon a Time Ser.). (ENG.). 272p. (YA). (gr. 9). pap. 13.95 *(978-0-689-87063-7(9),* Simon Pulse) Simon Pulse.

Holl, Kristi D. Invisible Alex. 126p. (J). (gr. 3-7). pap. 9.99 *(978-0-88092-340-8(7))* Royal Fireworks Publishing Co.

Hollaway, David. Quigley Mccormick: And the Curse of the Polka Dotted Pig, 3 vols. l.t. ed. 2005. (Illus.). 156p. (J). (gr. -1-3). per. 15.95 *(978-1-933211-54-1(7))* Quackenworth Publishing.

Holliday, Susan. Dream Cave. l.t. ed. 2007. 216p. per. *(978-1-905665-23-5(7))* Pollinger In Print.

Holloway, Christina. Irish Selkie. 2008. 12p. pap. 24.95 *(978-1-60610-693-8(7))* America Star Bks.

Holloway, Christopher. Gloumain Chronicles Book 1. the Aznadac Heir. 2013. 262p. (J). pap. *(978-1-78299-219-6(7))* FeedARead.com.

Holm, Jennifer L. & Holm, Matthew. Game On! 2013. (Squish Ser.: 5). lib. bdg. 17.20 *(978-0-606-31946-1(8),* Turtleback) Turtleback Bks.

Holman, Felice. The Cricket Winter. Thomas, Robyn, illus. 2006. 91p. (J). (gr. 3-7). 15.00 *(978-0-8028-5289-2(0),* Eerdmans Bks For Young Readers) Eerdmans, William B. Publishing Co.

Holsey, Alvin I. Dinosaur Haunt. 2008. 188p. pap. 13.95 *(978-1-60693-282-7(9),* Eloquent Bks.) Strategic Book Publishing & Rights Agency (SBPRA).

Holston-Holloway, Angela M. The Apple Pie Kids. 2006. (J). pap. 8.00 *(978-0-8059-6899-6(7))* Dorrance Publishing Co., Inc.

Holt, K. A. Gnome-A-geddon. Jack, Colin, illus. 2017. (ENG.). 304p. (J). (gr. 3-7). 16.99 ***(978-1-4814-7845-8(1),*** McElderry, Margaret K. Bks.) McElderry, Margaret K. Bks.

Holub, Joan & Williams, Suzanne. Apollo & the Battle of the Birds. Phillips, Craig, illus. 2014. (Heroes in Training Ser.: 6). (ENG.). 128p. (J). (gr. 1-4). pap. 5.99 *(978-1-4424-8845-8(X),* Aladdin) Simon & Schuster Children's Publishing.

—Apollo & the Battle of the Birds. 2014. (Heroes in Training Ser.: 6). lib. bdg. 16.00 *(978-0-606-35442-4(5))* Turtleback Bks.

—Artemis the Loyal. 2011. (Goddess Girls Ser.: 7). (ENG.). 288p. (J). (gr. 3-7). pap. 7.99 *(978-1-4424-3377-9(9),* Aladdin) Simon & Schuster Children's Publishing.

—Athena the Proud. 2014. (Goddess Girls Ser.: 13). lib. bdg. 18.40 *(978-0-606-35441-7(7))* Turtleback Bks.

—Crius & the Night of Fright. 2015. (Heroes in Training Ser.: 9). lib. bdg. 16.00 *(978-0-606-36302-0(5))* Turtleback Bks.

—Echo the Copycat. 2016. (Goddess Girls Ser.: 19). (ENG., Illus.). 272p. (J). (gr. 3-7). pap. 7.99 *(978-1-4814-5001-0(8),* Aladdin) Simon & Schuster Children's Publishing.

—Goddess Girls Set, Bks. 1-4: Athena the Brave - Persephone the Phony; Aphrodite the Beauty; Artemis the Brave. 2012. (Goddess Girls Ser.). (ENG., Illus.). 752p. (J). (gr. 3-7). pap. 31.99 *(978-1-4424-8210-4(9),* Aladdin) Simon & Schuster Children's Publishing.

—Gretel Pushes Back. 2016. (Grimmtastic Girls Ser.: 8). (ENG.). 192p. (J). (gr. 3-7). 16.00 *(978-0-606-39144-3(4))* Turtleback Bks.

—Heroes in Training 4-Books-In-1! Volume Two: Typhon & the Winds of Destruction; Apollo & the Battle of the Birds; Ares & the Spear of Fear; Cronus & the Threads of Dread. Phillips, Craig, illus. 2016. (Heroes in Training Ser.). (ENG.). 464p. (J). (gr. 1-4). 14.99 *(978-1-4814-7595-2(9),* Aladdin) Simon & Schuster Children's Publishing.

—Hestia the Invisible. 2015. (Goddess Girls Ser.: 18). lib. bdg. 18.40 *(978-0-606-37854-3(5))* Turtleback Bks.

—Persephone the Daring. 2013. (Goddess Girls Ser.: 11). (ENG., Illus.). 256p. (J). (gr. 3-7). 17.99 *(978-1-4424-8158-9(7))*; pap. 7.99 *(978-1-4424-4939-8(X))* Simon & Schuster Children's Publishing. (Aladdin).

—Perseus & the Monstrous Medusa. Phillips, Craig, illus. 2016. (Heroes in Training Ser.: 12). (ENG.). 128p. (J). (gr. 1-4). 16.99 *(978-1-4814-3516-1(7))*; pap. 5.99 *(978-1-4814-3515-4(9))* Simon & Schuster Children's Publishing. (Aladdin).

—Perseus & the Monstrous Medusa. 2016. (Heroes in Training Ser.: 12). lib. bdg. 16.00 *(978-0-606-38248-9(8))* Turtleback Bks.

—Pheme the Gossip. 2013. (Goddess Girls Ser.: 10). (ENG.). 272p. (J). (gr. 3-7). pap. 7.99 *(978-1-4424-4937-4(3),* Aladdin) Simon & Schuster Children's Publishing.

—Pheme the Gossip. 2013. (Goddess Girls Ser.: 10). (ENG.). 272p. (J). (gr. 3-7). 16.99 *(978-1-4424-6138-3(1),* Simon & Schuster/Paula Wiseman Bks.) Simon & Schuster/Paula Wiseman Bks.

—Rapunzel Cuts Loose. 2014. (Grimmtastic Girls Ser.: 4). (ENG.). 192p. (J). (gr. 3-7). pap. 5.99 *(978-0-545-51986-1(1),* Scholastic Paperbacks) Scholastic, Inc.

—Red Riding Hood Gets Lost. 2014. (Grimmtastic Girls Ser.: 2). (ENG.). 192p. (J). (gr. 3-7). pap. 5.99 *(978-0-545-51984-7(5))* Scholastic, Inc.

—Red Riding Hood Gets Lost. 2014. (Grimmtastic Girls Ser.: 2). lib. bdg. 16.00 *(978-0-606-35396-0(8))* Turtleback Bks.

—Zeus & the Thunderbolt of Doom. Phillips, Craig, illus. 2012. (Heroes in Training Ser.: 1). (ENG.). 112p. (J). (gr. 1-4). 16.99 *(978-1-4424-5787-4(2))*; pap. 5.99 *(978-1-4424-5263-3(3))* Simon & Schuster Children's Publishing. (Aladdin).

Holyoak, Kathleen & Summers, Sherry. Flowers in Heaven. 2009. 32p. pap. 14.49 *(978-1-4389-4607-8(4))* AuthorHouse.

Homer, Elizabeth. Peter Wolfe & the Scepter of Myleah. 2008. 212p. pap. 13.95 *(978-1-60693-197-4(0),* Eloquent Bks.) Strategic Book Publishing & Rights Agency (SBPRA).

Hondo. Dream World Tales. 2005. pap. 9.99 *(978-0-9773016-0-7(5))* Capital Publishing.

The Honey Tree, 6 Packs. (Literatura 2000 Ser.). (gr. 2-3). 33.00 *(978-0-7635-0262-1(6))* Rigby Education.

Hood, Karen Jean Matsko. Dewberry Farm. Whispering Pine Press International, ed. Artistic Design Service Staff, illus. 2017. (Magic Farmhouse Ser.). 160p. (J). 25.95 *(978-1-59649-415-2(8))*; per. 14.95 *(978-1-59649-562-3(6))* Whispering Pine Pr. International, Inc.

Hooper, R. M. J. The Secret of Crescent Grey. 2009. 340p. pap. 19.99 *(978-1-4363-3206-4(0))* Xlibris Corp.

Hoopmann, Kathy & Kiss, J. S. Elemental Island. 2015. (ENG.). 224p. (J). 19.95 *(978-1-84905-658-8(7),* 7980) Kingsley, Jessica Pubs. GBR. Dist: Macmillan Distribution Ltd.

Hooton, David James. Carrots in Candy Land. 2008. 25p. pap. 24.95 *(978-1-60672-828-4(8))* America Star Bks.

Hoover, Krystal Dawn. Tabby Town. 2011. 40p. pap. *(978-1-4269-7276-8(8))* Trafford Publishing (UK) Ltd.

Hoover, Laney Laube. The Tale of the Tailless Cat. 2007. (ENG.). 90p. pap. 7.99 *(978-1-4196-7441-9(2))* CreateSpace Independent Publishing Platform.

Hoover, P. J. The Emerald Tablet. 2012. (ENG.). 296p. (J). (gr. 6-9). pap. 8.95 *(978-1-933767-19-2(7))* CBAY Bks.

—The Navel of the World. 2013. (ENG.). 304p. (J). (gr. 6-9). pap. 8.95 *(978-1-933767-20-8(0))* CBAY Bks.

—Tut: My Epic Battle to Save the World. 2017. (Tut: My Immortal Life Ser.: 2). (ENG.). 336p. (J). 16.99 *(978-0-7653-9082-0(5),* 9780765390820, Starscape) Doherty, Tom Assocs., LLC.

Hope, Harry S. The Elements of Lore - Volume 1 of the Books of Lore. 2008. 272p. pap. *(978-1-906210-83-0(7))* Grosvenor Hse. Publishing Ltd.

Hopkins, Ellen, ed. A New Dawn: Your Favorite Authors on Stephenie Meyer's Twilight Series. 2009. (ENG., Illus.). 200p. (J). (gr. 9-12). pap. 12.95 *(978-1-933771-93-9(3))* BenBella Bks.

Hopton, Stan. To Dance Beneath a Diamond Sky. 2005. 118p. pap. 19.95 *(978-1-4241-0032-3(1))* PublishAmerica, Inc.

Horan, Pamela. Newman the Gnome. 2012. 66p. pap. 17.95 *(978-1-4626-9461-7(6))* America Star Bks.

Horne, Glenda Burton & Burton, Beth Windsor. My Daydreams, 1 vol. 2009. 21p. pap. 24.95 *(978-1-60749-284-9(9))* America Star Bks.

Horning, Mandy Cha'rae. The Defenders: Rise of the Perfected. 2012. 118p. (gr. 10-12). 23.99 *(978-1-4772-5327-4(0))*; pap. 14.95 *(978-1-4772-5328-1(9))* AuthorHouse.

Hornsby, Ashley Brooke. Pretty Little Lilly & the Land of Sweet Dreams (Hard Bound) Hranilovich, Barbara, illus. 2007. (J). 15.95 *(978-0-9777241-2-3(3))* Cepia LLC.

—Pretty Little Lilly & the Land of Sweet Dreams (Paperback) Hranilovich, Barbara, illus. 2007. (J). *(978-0-9777241-3-0(1))* Cepia LLC.

Horowitz, Alena Netia. The Tlytiettlym Tree. Horowitz, Alena Netia & De La Fuente, Mary, illus. l.t. ed. 2003. 64p. (J). per. 12.95 *(978-0-923550-42-4(9))* Tetrahedron Publishing LLC.

Horowitz, Anthony. Oblivion. 2014. (Gatekeepers Ser.: 5). lib. bdg. 20.85 *(978-0-606-36035-7(2))* Turtleback Bks.

Horton, Steve. Amala's Blade - Spirits of Naamaron, Vol. 1. Warner, Chris, ed. 2014. (ENG., Illus.). 144p. pap. 18.99 *(978-1-61655-332-6(4))* Dark Horse Comics.

Houle, Kelly. Gracie's Gallery: A Magic Mirror Book. 2008. (ENG., Illus.). 28p. (J). (gr. -1). 14.95 *(978-1-58117-784-8(4),* Intervisual/Piggy Toes) Bendon, Inc.

Hourlier, Sylvaine. Blacky & the Enchanted Mountain, 1 vol. 2010. 48p. pap. 16.95 *(978-1-4512-1140-5(6))* America Star Bks.

House, David James. The Key to Space. 2006. (ENM.). 364p. (YA). 24.95 *(978-0-9777086-0-4(8))* House, David.

Houston, Meradeth. Colors Like Memories. 2013. 178p. pap. *(978-1-77127-371-8(2))* MuseItUp Publishing.

Howard, A. G. RoseBlood. 2017. (ENG.). (gr. 8-17). 400p. (J). pap. 8.95 ***(978-1-4197-2342-1(1))***; 432p. (YA). 18.95 *(978-1-4197-1909-7(2),* Amulet Bks.) Abrams, Inc.

—RoseBlood. 2018. lib. bdg. 20.85 ***(978-0-606-40729-8(4))*** Turtleback Bks.

—A Splintered Companion. 2015. (ENG.). 240p. (J). (gr. 9-17). pap. 7.95 *(978-1-4197-1926-4(2))* Abrams, Inc.

—Untamed. 2016. (Splintered Ser.). (J). lib. bdg. 20.80 *(978-0-606-39020-0(0))* Turtleback Bks.

—Untamed: A Splintered Companion. 2015. (Splintered Ser.). (ENG.). 288p. (YA). (gr. 9-17). 16.95 *(978-1-4197-1869-4(X),* Amulet Bks.) Abrams, Inc.

—Untamed (Splintered Series Companion) A Splintered Companion. 2016. (Splintered Ser.). (ENG., Illus.). 304p. (J). (gr. 9-17). pap. 9.95 *(978-1-4197-2203-5(4),* Amulet Bks.) Abrams, Inc.

Howard, Amalie. The Fallen Prince. 2016. (Riven Chronicles Ser.). (ENG.). 384p. (YA). (gr. 6). 17.99 *(978-1-5107-0170-0(2),* Sky Pony Pr.) Skyhorse Publishing Co., Inc.

Howard, Ann. The Mystery of Dragon Bridge: A Peach Blossom Village Story. 2014. (ENG & CHI., Illus.). 40p. (J). (gr. 2-5). pap. 16.95 *(978-1-58394-813-2(9))* North Atlantic Bks.

Howard, Cheryl L. Mikhael the Mighty: Be True to Who You Are & You Can Never Go Wrong. 2009. 52p. pap. 18.50 *(978-1-60860-760-0(7),* Strategic Bk. Publishing) Strategic Book Publishing & Rights Agency (SBPRA).

Howard, Grahame. The Wishing Book 3 - Extermination. 2010. 170p. (J). pap. *(978-1-905809-90-5(5))* Pneuma Springs Publishing.

Howard, Jennifer. Lucy & the Land of Lost Socks. 2009. 56p. pap. 10.49 *(978-1-4389-5362-5(3))* AuthorHouse.

Howard, Jonathan L. Katya's World. 2012. (Strange Chemistry Ser.). (ENG.). 320p. (J). (gr. 9-12). pap. 9.99 *(978-1-908844-13-2(2),* Strange Chemistry) Watkins Media Limited GBR. Dist: Penguin Random Hse. LLC.

Howard, Kate. The Search for Zane. 2015. (Lego Ninjago Ser.: 7). (ENG.). 80p. (J). (gr. 2-5). pap. 4.99 *(978-0-545-75054-7(7))* Scholastic, Inc.

Howard, Kate, adapted by. Fright Knight! 2016. 71p. (J). ***(978-1-4844-8023-6(6))*** Scholastic, Inc.

Howard, Martin. The Wild Winter. Stimpson, Colin, illus. 2012. (Witches at War! Ser.: 3). (ENG.). 214p. (J). (gr. 3-7). 12.99 *(978-1-84365-180-2(7),* Pavilion Children's Books) Pavilion Bks. GBR. Dist: Independent Pubs. Group.

Howard, Peggy Ann. Zorees: Land of Dreams. 2007. (YA). per. 16.95 *(978-0-9795519-0-1(0))* Dream Scape Publishing, LLC.

Howard, Velma Swanston, tr. Wonderful Adventures of Nils. 2013. 354p. pap. *(978-1-78139-369-7(9))* Benediction Classics.

Howe, James. Screaming Mummies of the Pharaoh's Tomb II. Helquist, Brett, illus. 2004. (Tales from the House of Bunnicula Ser.: 4). (ENG.). 112p. (J). (gr. 2-5). pap. 6.99 *(978-0-689-83954-2(5),* Atheneum Bks. for Young Readers) Simon & Schuster Children's Publishing.

Howe, Peter. Warriors of the Black Shroud. 2012. (ENG.). 272p. (J). (gr. 3-7). 16.99 *(978-0-06-172987-4(6))* HarperCollins Pubs.

Howe, Tina Field. Alysa of the Fields: Book One in the Tellings of Xunar-kun. 2006. (Illus.). 320p. (YA). pap. 16.95 *(978-0-9768585-1-5(7),* 002) Howe, Tina Field.

Howe, Tom. Stonebringer: A Novel of Individuation. 2004. (Illus.). (YA). pap. 16.69 *(978-0-9717280-5-9(4))* Roundsquare Pr.

Howell, David. Swan Songs-in Search of the Staffstone. 2005. per. 13.99 *(978-1-59781-002-9(9))* Salem Author Services.

Howell, Heather. Emily's Ballet Recital. 2010. 32p. pap. 12.99 *(978-1-4490-8457-8(5))* AuthorHouse.

Howell, Robert. Third Times the Charm. 2007. (ENG.). 224p. (gr. 4-7). per. 12.95 *(978-1-897235-20-1(8))* Thistledown Pr., Ltd. CAN. Dist: Univ. of Toronto Pr.

Howell, Trisha Adelena. Talia & the Great Sapphire of Knowledge. Hohn, David, illus. 2005. 128p. (J). pap. 11.95 *(978-1-931210-11-9(X))* Howell Canyon Pr.

Howells, Andrea. Finding Peace & the True Soul. 2006. 60p. (J). per. *(978-0-9765072-4-6(2))* Tribute Bks.

Howland, Michele. The Flying Boy, 1 vol. 2009. 21p. pap. 19.95 *(978-1-61582-678-0(5))* PublishAmerica, Inc.

Hoyle, K. B. The Scroll. 2016. (ENG., Illus.). (J). 29.99 ***(978-1-61213-400-0(9))*** 2013. 266p. pap. 18.99 *(978-1-61213-169-6(7))* Writer's Coffee Shop, The.

—The Six. 2016. (ENG., Illus.). (J). 29.99 ***(978-1-61213-396-6(7))*** 2012. 230p. pap. 22.50 *(978-1-61213-052-1(6))* Writer's Coffee Shop, The.

Hoylie, Gerry. Byron Unleashed. 2005. 60p. pap. 14.95 *(978-1-59113-670-5(9))* Booklocker.com, Inc.

Hoyt, Holly. The Purple Widow. 2009. 314p. 28.25 *(978-1-60860-688-7(0),* Eloquent Bks.) Strategic Book Publishing & Rights Agency (SBPRA).

Hoyt, Sarah, et al, eds. Something Magic This Way Comes. 2008. (ENG.). 320p. (gr. 12-18). 7.99 *(978-0-7564-0472-7(X),* DAW) DAW.

Hsia, Pei Chen. The Little Dumpling. 2012. 82p. pap. 19.95 *(978-1-4626-8041-2(0))* America Star Bks.

Hsiao, Christie. Journey to Rainbow Island. 2013. (ENG., Illus.). 400p. (J). (gr. 2-7). 17.95 *(978-1-939529-24-4(7))* BenBella Bks.

Hu, Vicky. The Muses: Greek Mythology (Mitologia Griega) 2009. 44p. pap. 21.99 *(978-1-4415-3415-6(6))* Xlibris Corp.

Hubbard, L. Ron, contrib. by. The Crossroads: Literature Guide for Teachers & Librarians, Based on Common Core ELA Standards for Classrooms 6-9. 2013. (Stories from the Golden Age Ser.). (ENG.). 35p. (gr. 6-9). pap., tchr. ed. 14.95 *(978-1-59212-810-5(6))* Galaxy Pr., LLC.

Hubbell, Mary A. The Miracle of Annie's Ring. 2010. 138p. pap. 11.50 *(978-1-60911-530-2(9),* Eloquent Bks.) Strategic Book Publishing & Rights Agency (SBPRA).

Hudson, Margaret Parker. The Blue Umbrella. 2005. (Illus.). (J). 15.95 *(978-0-9771301-0-8(X))* FayRe Pr.

Hudspith, Will. Stairgate - Gordon's Adventures on Everest. 2013. 64p. pap. *(978-1-4602-1219-6(3))* FriesenPress.

Hughes, Devon. Unnaturals: the Battle Begins. Richardson, Owen, illus. 2017. (Unnaturals Ser.: 1). 368p. (J). (gr. 3-7). pap. 6.99 *(978-0-06-225755-0(2),* Tegen, Katherine Bks) HarperCollins Pubs.

Hughes, Monica. The Keeper of the Isis Light. 2008. Orig. Title: Summerspell. (ENG.). 240p. (J). (gr. 3-7). pap. 11.99 *(978-1-4169-8963-9(3),* Atheneum Bks. for Young Readers) Simon & Schuster Children's Publishing.

Hulin, Rachel, photos by. Flying Henry. 2013. (ENG., Illus.). 40p. (J). (-k). 12.95 *(978-1-57687-626-8(8),* powerHouse Bks.) powerHouse Cultural Entertainment, Inc.

Hume, Maureen. The Pizza Gang: Facing the Witch. 2009. 80p. pap. 9.95 *(978-1-60860-337-4(7),* Eloquent Bks.) Strategic Book Publishing & Rights Agency (SBPRA).

Hummel, Jim. Imagination: On Planet Hic-Cup. 2013. 36p. pap. 15.49 *(978-1-4669-8903-0(3))* Trafford Publishing.

Hunt, B. B. Samantha Stone & the Mermaid's Quest. 2007. (J). 14.95 *(978-0-9789041-1-1(7))* Press Americana.

Hunter, Alex. Game Over. Rew, Jen, illus. 2012. 126p. pap. *(978-1-78176-771-9(8))* FeedARead.com.

Hunter, Erin. The Apprentice's Quest. 2017. (Warriors — a Vision of Shadows Ser.: 1). (J). lib. bdg. 18.40 ***(978-0-606-39643-1(8))*** Turtleback Bks.

—Battles of the Clans. 2010. (Warriors Field Guide Ser.). 208p. (J). (gr. 3-7). (ENG.). 16.99 *(978-0-06-170230-3(7))*; lib. bdg. 17.89 *(978-0-06-170231-0(5))* HarperCollins Pubs.

—Bluestar's Prophecy. McLoughlin, Wayne, illus. (Warriors Super Edition Ser.: 2). (ENG.). (J). (gr. 3-7). 2010. 560p. pap. 7.99 *(978-0-06-158250-9(6))* 2009. 544p. 17.99 *(978-0-06-158247-9(6))* HarperCollins Pubs.

—The Broken Path. 2014. (Survivors Ser.: 4). 320p. (J). (gr. 3-7). lib. bdg. 17.89 *(978-0-06-210269-0(9))* HarperCollins Pubs.

—Broken Pride. Richardson, Owen, illus. 2017. (Bravelands Ser.: 1). (ENG.). 336p. (J). (gr. 3-7). 16.99 *(978-0-06-264202-8(2))* HarperCollins Pubs.

—The Burning Horizon. 2015. (Seekers: Return to the Wild Ser.: 5). (ENG., Illus.). 304p. (J). (gr. 3-7). 16.99 *(978-0-06-199646-7(7))* HarperCollins Pubs.

—The Burning Horizon. 2016. (Seekers: Return to the Wild Ser.: 5). (J). lib. bdg. 18.40 *(978-0-606-38147-5(3))* Turtleback Bks.

—Cats of the Clans. McLoughlin, Wayne, illus. 2008. (Warriors Field Guide Ser.: No. 2). (ENG.). 112p. (J). (gr. 3-7). 16.99 *(978-0-06-145856-9(2))* HarperCollins Pubs.

—Code of the Clans. McLoughlin, Wayne, illus. 2009. (Warriors Field Guide Ser.: No. 3). 176p. (J). (gr. 3-7). (ENG.). 16.99 *(978-0-06-166009-2(4))*; lib. bdg. 17.89 *(978-0-06-166010-8(8))* HarperCollins Pubs.

—Crookedstar's Promise. (Warriors Super Edition Ser.: 4). 528p. (J). (gr. 3-7). 2012. (ENG.). pap. 7.99 *(978-0-06-198099-2(4))* 2011. (ENG.). 17.99 *(978-0-06-198097-8(8))* 2011. lib. bdg. 18.89 *(978-0-06-198098-5(6))* HarperCollins Pubs.

—Crookedstar's Promise. 2012. (Warriors Ser.: No. 4). (J). lib. bdg. 18.40 *(978-0-606-26263-7(6),* Turtleback) Turtleback Bks.

—A Dangerous Path. Richardson, Owen & Stevenson, Dave, illus. 2015. (Warriors: the Prophecies Begin Ser.: 5). (ENG.). 368p. (J). (gr. 3-7). pap. 7.99 *(978-0-06-236700-6(5))* HarperCollins Pubs.

—A Dangerous Path. Stevenson, Dave, illus. 2004. (Warriors: the Prophecies Begin Ser.: 5). (ENG.). 336p. (J). (gr. 3-7). 16.99 *(978-0-06-000006-6(6))* HarperCollins Pubs.

—A Dangerous Path. 2015. (Warriors Ser.: 5). (J). lib. bdg. 18.40 *(978-0-606-36498-0(6))* Turtleback Bks.

—Dark River. (Warriors: Power of Three Ser.: 2). (ENG.). (J). (gr. 3-7). 2015. 368p. pap. 7.99 *(978-0-06-236709-9(9))* 2008. 368p. pap. 6.99 *(978-0-06-089207-4(2))* 2007. (Illus.). 352p. 16.99 *(978-0-06-089205-0(6))* HarperCollins Pubs.

—The Darkest Hour. Richardson, Owen & Stevenson, Dave, illus. 2015. (Warriors: the Prophecies Begin Ser.: 6). (ENG.). 368p. (J). (gr. 3-7). pap. 7.99 *(978-0-06-236701-3(3))* HarperCollins Pubs.

—The Darkest Hour. Stevenson, Dave, illus. (Warriors: the Prophecies Begin Ser.: 6). (ENG.). 336p. (J). (gr. 3-7). 2005. pap. 6.99 *(978-0-06-052585-9(1))* 2004. 17.99 *(978-0-06-000007-3(4))* HarperCollins Pubs.

—The Darkest Hour. 2015. (Warriors Ser.: 6). (J). lib. bdg. 18.40 *(978-0-606-36499-7(4))* Turtleback Bks.

—Darkness Falls. 2014. (Survivors Ser.: 3). (ENG.). 320p. (J). (gr. 3-7). pap. 7.99 *(978-0-06-210266-9(4))* HarperCollins Pubs.

—Darkness Falls. 2014. (Survivors Ser.: 3). (J). lib. bdg. 18.40 *(978-0-606-35496-7(4))* Turtleback Bks.

—Dawn. Stevenson, Dave, illus. (Warriors: the New Prophecy Ser.: 3). (ENG.). 352p. (J). (gr. 3-7). 2006. pap. 6.99 *(978-0-06-074457-1(X))* 2005. 16.99 *(978-0-06-074455-7(3))* HarperCollins Pubs.

—Eclipse. (Warriors: Power of Three Ser.: 4). (ENG.). (J). (gr. 3-7). 2015. 368p. pap. 7.99 *(978-0-06-236711-2(0))* 2009. 336p. pap. 7.99 *(978-0-06-089213-5(7))* 2008. (Illus.). 336p. 16.99 *(978-0-06-089211-1(0))* HarperCollins Pubs.

—The Empty City. (Survivors Ser.: 1). (J). (gr. 3-7). 2013. (ENG.). 304p. pap. 7.99 *(978-0-06-210258-4(3))* 2012. (ENG.). 288p. 16.99 *(978-0-06-210256-0(7))* 2012. 288p. lib. bdg. 17.89 *(978-0-06-210257-7(5))* HarperCollins Pubs.

—The Empty City. 2013. (Survivors Ser.: 1). (J). lib. bdg. 18.40 *(978-0-606-31803-7(8),* Turtleback) Turtleback Bks.

—The Empty City & a Hidden Enemy. 2014. (Survivors Ser.). (ENG.). 592p. (J). (gr. 3-7). pap. 7.99 *(978-0-06-232146-6(3))* HarperCollins Pubs.

—The Endless Lake. 2014. (Survivors Ser.: 5). 320p. (J). (gr. 3-7). (ENG.). 16.99 *(978-0-06-210272-0(9))*; lib. bdg. 17.89 *(978-0-06-210273-7(7))* HarperCollins Pubs.

—Enter the Clans. 2012. (Warriors Field Guide Ser.: Nos. 1-2). (ENG.). 400p. (J). (gr. 3-7). pap. 7.99 *(978-0-06-210239-3(7))* HarperCollins Pubs.

—Enter the Clans. 2012. (Warriors Ser.). (J). lib. bdg. 18.40 *(978-0-606-26296-5(2,* Turtleback) Turtleback Bks.

—Fading Echoes. Richardson, Owen & Douglas, Allen, illus. (Warriors: Omen of the Stars Ser.: 2). (ENG.). (J). (gr. 3-7). 2011. 368p. pap. 6.99 *(978-0-06-155514-5(2))* 2010. 352p. 16.99 *(978-0-06-155512-1(6))* HarperCollins Pubs.

—Fire & Ice. Richardson, Owen & Stevenson, Dave, illus. 2015. (Warriors: the Prophecies Begin Ser.: 2). (ENG.). 368p. (J). (gr. 3-7). pap. 7.99 *(978-0-06-236697-9(1))* HarperCollins Pubs.

—Fire & Ice. Stevenson, Dave, illus. (Warriors: the Prophecies Begin Ser.: 2). (ENG.). 336p. (J). (gr. 3-7). 2004. pap. 6.99 *(978-0-06-052559-0(2))* 2003. 16.99 *(978-0-06-000003-5(1))* HarperCollins Pubs.

—Fire in the Sky. (Seekers Ser.: 5). (ENG.). (J). (gr. 3-7). 2011. 288p. pap. 6.99 *(978-0-06-087136-9(9))* 2010. 272p. 16.99 *(978-0-06-087134-5(2))* HarperCollins Pubs.

—Firestar's Quest. Chalk, Gary, illus. 2008. (Warriors Super Edition Ser.: 1). (ENG.). 544p. (J). (gr. 3-7). pap. 7.99 *(978-0-06-113167-9(9))* HarperCollins Pubs.

—Firestar's Quest. 2007. (Warriors Super Edition Ser.: 1). (ENG., Illus.). 528p. (J). (gr. 3-7). 17.99 *(978-0-06-113164-6(4))* HarperCollins Pubs.

—The First Battle. McLoughlin, Wayne & Douglas, Allen, illus. 2015. (Warriors: Dawn of the Clans Ser.: 3). (ENG.). 352p. (J). (gr. 3-7). pap. 6.99 *(978-0-06-206356-4(1))* HarperCollins Pubs.

—The First Battle. 2016. (Warriors — Dawn of the Clans Ser.: 3). (J). lib. bdg. 18.40 *(978-0-606-38163-5(5))* Turtleback Bks.

—A Forest Divided. McLoughlin, Wayne & Douglas, Allen, illus. 2015. (Warriors Ser.: Bk. 5). (ENG.). 384p. (J). (gr. 3-7). 16.99 *(978-0-06-206362-5(6))* HarperCollins Pubs.

—Forest of Secrets. Richardson, Owen & Stevenson, Dave, illus. 2015. (Warriors: the Prophecies Begin Ser.: 3). (ENG.). 368p. (J). (gr. 3-7). pap. 7.99 *(978-0-06-236698-6(X))* HarperCollins Pubs.

—Forest of Secrets. Stevenson, Dave, illus. 2003. (Warriors Ser.: 3). 336p. (J). (gr. 3-7). lib. bdg. 17.89 *(978-0-06-052560-6(6))* HarperCollins Pubs.

—Forest of Secrets. 2015. (Warriors Ser.: 3). (J). lib. bdg. 18.40 *(978-0-606-36496-6(X))* Turtleback Bks.

—Forest of Wolves. 2014. (Seekers: Return to the Wild Ser.: 4). (ENG.). 288p. (J). (gr. 3-7). 16.99 *(978-0-06-199643-6(2))* HarperCollins Pubs.

—Forest of Wolves. 2015. (Seekers: Return to the Wild Ser.: 4). (J). lib. bdg. 17.20 *(978-0-606-36472-0(2))* Turtleback Bks.

—The Forgotten Warrior. Richardson, Owen & Douglas, Allen, illus. 2012. (Warriors: Omen of the Stars Ser.: 5). (ENG.). 384p. (J). (gr. 3-7). pap. 6.99 *(978-0-06-155526-8(6))* HarperCollins Pubs.

—The Forgotten Warrior. 2015. (Warriors — Omen of the Stars Ser.: 5). (J). lib. bdg. 18.40 *(978-0-606-37726-3(3))* Turtleback Bks.

—The Fourth Apprentice. Richardson, Owen & Douglas, Allen, illus. (Warriors: Omen of the Stars Ser.: 1). (ENG.). (J). (gr. 3-7). 2010. 368p. pap. 7.99 *(978-0-06-155511-4(8))* 2009. 352p. 16.99 *(978-0-06-155509-1(6))* HarperCollins Pubs.

—The Fourth Apprentice. 2015. (Warriors — Omen of the Stars Ser.: 1). (J). lib. bdg. 18.40 *(978-0-606-37728-7(X))* Turtleback Bks.

—Great Bear Lake. (Seekers Ser.: 2). (ENG.). 320p. (J). (gr. 3-7). 2010. pap. 6.99 *(978-0-06-087127-7(X))* 2009. 16.99 *(978-0-06-087125-3(3))* HarperCollins Pubs.

—Hawkwing's Journey. Barry, James L., illus. 2016. (Warriors Super Edition Ser.: 9). 480p. (J). (gr. 3-7). 18.99 *(978-0-06-246768-3(9))* HarperCollins Pubs.

—The Heart of a Warrior. Barry, James L., illus. 2010. (Warriors Manga Ser.: 3). (ENG.). 112p. (J). (gr. 3-7). pap. 6.99 *(978-0-06-168867-6(3))* HarperCollins Pubs.

—A Hidden Enemy. (Survivors Ser.: 2). (J). (gr. 3-7). 2014. (ENG.). 304p. pap. 7.99 *(978-0-06-210262-1(1))* 2013. 288p. lib. bdg. 17.89 *(978-0-06-210261-4(3))* 2013. (ENG.). 288p. 16.99 *(978-0-06-210260-7(5))* HarperCollins Pubs.

—A Hidden Enemy. 2014. (Survivors Ser.: 2). (J). lib. bdg. 18.40 *(978-0-606-35056-3(X),* Turtleback) Turtleback Bks.

—Into the Wild. Stevenson, Dave, illus. 2003. (Warriors: the Prophecies Begin Ser.: 1). (ENG.). 288p. (J). (gr. 3-7). 16.99 *(978-0-06-000002-8(3))* HarperCollins Pubs.

—Island of Shadows. (Seekers: Return to the Wild Ser.: 1). 320p. (J). (gr. 3-7). 2013. (ENG.). pap. 6.99 *(978-0-06-199636-8(X))* 2012. (ENG.). 16.99 *(978-0-06-199634-4(3))* 2012. lib. bdg. 17.89 *(978-0-06-199635-1(1))* HarperCollins Pubs.

—Island of Shadows. 2013. (Seekers: Return to the Wild Ser.: 1). (J). lib. bdg. 17.20 *(978-0-606-27127-1(9),* Turtleback) Turtleback Bks.

—The Last Hope. Richardson, Owen & Douglas, Allen, illus. (Warriors: Omen of the Stars Ser.: 6). (ENG.). (J). (gr. 3-7). 2013. 400p. pap. 7.99 *(978-0-06-155529-9(0))* 2012. 384p. 16.99 *(978-0-06-155527-5(4))* HarperCollins Pubs.

—The Last Hope. 2015. (Warriors — Omen of the Stars Ser.: 6). (J). lib. bdg. 18.40 *(978-0-606-37727-0(1))* Turtleback Bks.

—The Last Wilderness. (Seekers Ser.: 4). (J). 2011. (ENG.). 288p. (gr. 3-7). pap. 6.99 *(978-0-06-087133-8(4))* 2010. (ENG.). 288p. (gr. 3-7). 16.99 *(978-0-06-087131-4(8))* 2010. (Illus.). 265p. 9.99 *(978-0-06-198681-9(X))* HarperCollins Pubs.

—Long Shadows. (Warriors: Power of Three Ser.: 5). (ENG.). (J). (gr. 3-7). 2015. 368p. pap. 7.99 *(978-0-06-236712-9(9))* 2009. 352p. pap. 7.99 *(978-0-06-089216-6(1))* HarperCollins Pubs.

—The Melting Sea. (Seekers: Return to the Wild Ser.: 2). (J). (gr. 3-7). 2013. (ENG.). 304p. pap. 6.99 *(978-0-06-199639-9(4))* 2012. (ENG., Illus.). 288p. 16.99 *(978-0-06-199637-5(8))* 2012. (Illus.). 288p. lib. bdg. 17.89 *(978-0-06-199638-2(6))* HarperCollins Pubs.

—The Melting Sea. 2013. (Seekers: Return to the Wild Ser.: 2). (J). lib. bdg. 17.20 *(978-0-606-31816-7(X,* Turtleback) Turtleback Bks.

—Middle Grade Series Launch. Richardson, Owen, illus. 2017. (Bravelands Ser.: 1). 336p. (J). (gr. 3-7). lib. bdg. 17.89 *(978-0-06-264203-5(0))* HarperCollins Pubs.

—Midnight. 2005. (Warriors Ser.: Bk. 1). (Illus.). 320p. (J). (gr. 5-18). lib. bdg. 17.89 *(978-0-06-074450-2(2))* HarperCollins Pubs.

—Midnight. Stevenson, Dave, illus. 2005. (Warriors: the New Prophecy Ser.: 1). (ENG.). 320p. (J). (gr. 3-7). 16.99 *(978-0-06-074449-6(9))* HarperCollins Pubs.

—Moonrise. Richardson, Owen & Stevenson, Dave, illus. 2015. (Warriors: the New Prophecy Ser.: 2). (ENG.). 336p. (J). (gr. 3-7). pap. 7.99 *(978-0-06-236703-7(X))* HarperCollins Pubs.

—Moonrise. Stevenson, Dave, illus. (Warriors: the New Prophecy Ser.: 2). (ENG.). (J). (gr. 3-7). 2006. 320p. pap. 6.99 *(978-0-06-074454-0(5))* 2005. 304p. 16.99 *(978-0-06-074452-6(9))* HarperCollins Pubs.

—The New Prophecy, Vols. 1-6. 2008. (Warriors: the New Prophecy Ser.: Bks. 1-6). (J). (gr. 3-7). pap. 36.99 *(978-0-06-144898-0(2))* HarperCollins Pubs.

—Night Whispers. Richardson, Owen & Douglas, Allen, illus. (Warriors: Omen of the Stars Ser.: 3). (ENG.). (J). (gr. 3-7). 2011. 368p. pap. 6.99 *(978-0-06-155517-6(7))* 2010. 352p. 16.99 *(978-0-06-155515-2(0))* HarperCollins Pubs.

—Night Whispers. 2015. (Warriors — Omen of the Stars Ser.: 3). (J). lib. bdg. 17.20 *(978-0-606-37724-9(7))* Turtleback Bks.

—Outcast. (Warriors: Power of Three Ser.: 3). (ENG.). (J). (gr. 3-7). 2015. 368p. pap. 7.99 *(978-0-06-236710-5(2))* 2008. (Illus.). 352p. 16.99 *(978-0-06-089208-1(0))* HarperCollins Pubs.

—A Pack Divided. 2016. (Survivors Gathering Darkness Ser.: 1). (J). lib. bdg. 18.40 *(978-0-606-38767-5(6))* Turtleback Bks.

—The Quest Begins. Chalk, Gary, illus. 2008. (Seekers Ser.: 1). (ENG.). 320p. (J). (gr. 3-7). 16.99 *(978-0-06-087122-2(9))* HarperCollins Pubs.

—The Quest Begins. Lt. ed. 2008. (Seekers Ser.: No. 1). 372p. (J). pap. 16.99 *(978-0-06-170951-7(4))* HarperCollins Pubs.

—Return to the Clans. Hudson, Don, illus. 2009. (Warriors Manga Ser.: 3). (ENG.). 112p. (J). (gr. 3-7). pap. 6.99 *(978-0-06-154794-2(8))* HarperCollins Pubs.

—Rising Storm. Richardson, Owen & Stevenson, Dave, illus. 2015. (Warriors: the Prophecies Begin Ser.: 4). (ENG.). 368p. (J). (gr. 3-7). pap. 7.99 *(978-0-06-236699-3(8))* HarperCollins Pubs.

—Rising Storm. Stevenson, Dave, illus. (Warriors: the Prophecies Begin Ser.: 4). (ENG.). 336p. (J). (gr. 3-7). 2005. pap. 6.99 *(978-0-06-052563-7(0))* 2004. 16.99 *(978-0-06-000005-9(8))* HarperCollins Pubs.

—River of Lost Bearsrs No. 3. 2013. (Seekers: Return to the Wild Ser.: 3). (ENG., Illus.). 320p. (J). (gr. 3-7). 16.99 *(978-0-06-199640-5(8))* HarperCollins Pubs.

—Seekers: Return to the Wild #6: the Longest Day. 2016. (Seekers: Return to the Wild Ser.: 6). (Illus.). 336p. (J). (gr. 3-7). 16.99 *(978-0-06-199649-8(1))* HarperCollins Pubs.

—Shadows of the Clans. 2016. (Warriors Ser.). (J). lib. bdg. 18.40 *(978-0-606-38146-8(5))* Turtleback Bks.

—Shattered Peace. Barry, James L., illus. 2009. (Warriors Manga Ser.: 1). (ENG.). 112p. (J). (gr. 3-7). pap. 6.99 *(978-0-06-168865-2(7))* HarperCollins Pubs.

—Sign of the Moon. Richardson, Owen & Douglas, Allen, illus. (Warriors: Omen of the Stars Ser.: 4). (J). (gr. 3-7). 2011. (ENG.). 352p. 16.99 *(978-0-06-155518-3(5))* 2011. 352p. lib. bdg. 17.89 *(978-0-06-155520-6(7))*No. 4. 2012. (ENG.). 368p. pap. 6.99 *(978-0-06-155521-3(5))* HarperCollins Pubs.

—Sign of the Moon. 2015. (Warriors — Omen of the Stars Ser.: 4). (J). lib. bdg. 17.20 *(978-0-606-37725-6(5))* Turtleback Bks.

—Skyclan's Destiny. McLoughlin, Wayne, illus. (Warriors Super Edition Ser.: 3). (ENG.). 528p. (J). (gr. 3-7). 2011. pap. 7.99 *(978-0-06-169996-2(9))* 2010. 17.99 *(978-0-06-169994-8(2))* HarperCollins Pubs.

—Smoke Mountain. (Seekers Ser.: 3). (ENG.). 288p. (J). (gr. 3-7). 2010. pap. 6.99 *(978-0-06-087130-7(X))* 2009. 16.99 *(978-0-06-087128-4(8))* HarperCollins Pubs.

—Spirits in the Stars. (Seekers Ser.: 6). (ENG.). 304p. (J). (gr. 3-7). 2012. pap. 6.99 *(978-0-06-087142-0(3))* 2011. 16.99 *(978-0-06-087140-6(7))* HarperCollins Pubs.

—Starlight. Richardson, Owen & Stevenson, Dave, illus. 2015. (Warriors: the New Prophecy Ser.: 4). (ENG.). 368p. (J). (gr. 3-7). pap. 7.99 *(978-0-06-236705-1(6))* HarperCollins Pubs.

—Starlight. Stevenson, Dave, illus. 2006. (Warriors: the New Prophecy Ser.: 4). (ENG.). 336p. (J). (gr. 3-7). 16.99 *(978-0-06-082758-8(0))* HarperCollins Pubs.

—Starlight. 2015. (Warriors — the New Prophecy Ser.: 4). (J). lib. bdg. 18.40 *(978-0-606-36503-1(6))* Turtleback Bks.

—Storm of Dogs. 2015. (Survivors Ser.: 6). 288p. (J). (gr. 3-7). (ENG.). 16.99 *(978-0-06-210276-8(1))*; lib. bdg. 17.89 *(978-0-06-210277-5(X))* HarperCollins Pubs.

—The Sun Trail. McLoughlin, Wayne & Douglas, Allen, illus. (Warriors: Dawn of the Clans Ser.: 1). (ENG.). (J). (gr. 3-7). 2014. 368p. pap. 7.99 *(978-0-06-206348-9(0))* 2013. 352p. 16.99 *(978-0-06-206346-5(4))* HarperCollins Pubs.

—The Sun Trail. 2016. (Warriors — Dawn of the Clans Ser.: 1). (J). lib. bdg. 18.40 *(978-0-606-38161-1(9))* Turtleback Bks.

—Sunrise. (Warriors: Power of Three Ser.: 6). (ENG.). (J). (gr. 3-7). 2010. 368p. pap. 7.99 *(978-0-06-089219-7(6))* 6th ed. 2009. 352p. 16.99 *(978-0-06-089217-3(X))* HarperCollins Pubs.

—Sunset. Richardson, Owen & Stevenson, Dave, illus. 2015. (Warriors: the New Prophecy Ser.: 6). (ENG.). 352p. (J). (gr. 3-7). pap. 7.99 *(978-0-06-236707-5(2))* HarperCollins Pubs.

—Survivors: the Gathering Darkness #1: a Pack Divided. Kubinyi, Laszlo & Green, Julia, illus. 2015. (Survivors: the Gathering Darkness Ser.: 1). (ENG.). 304p. (J). (gr. 3-7). 16.99 *(978-0-06-234333-8(5))* HarperCollins Pubs.

—Survivors: the Gathering Darkness #2: Dead of Night. Kubinyi, Laszlo & Green, Julia, illus. 2016. (Survivors: the Gathering Darkness Ser.: 2). 304p. (J). (gr. 3-7). 16.99 *(978-0-06-234337-6(8))* HarperCollins Pubs.

—Survivors: the Gathering Darkness #3: into the Shadows. Kubinyi, Laszlo & Green, Julia, illus. 2017. (Survivors: the Gathering Darkness Ser.: 3). (J). (gr. 3-7). 336p. pap. 7.99 ***(978-0-06-234343-7(2))***; 320p. 16.99 *(978-0-06-234341-3(6))* HarperCollins Pubs.

—Survivors: the Gathering Darkness #4: Red Moon Rising. Kubinyi, Laszlo & Green, Julia, illus. 2017. (Survivors: the Gathering Darkness Ser.: 4). 304p. (J). (gr. 3-7). 16.99 ***(978-0-06-234345-1(9))*** HarperCollins Pubs.

—Tallstar's Revenge. Barry, James L., illus. 2014. (Warriors Super Edition Ser.: 6). (ENG.). 560p. (J). (gr. 3-7). pap. 7.99 *(978-0-06-221806-3(9))* HarperCollins Pubs.

—Tallstar's Revenge. 2014. (Warriors Super Edition Ser.). (J). lib. bdg. 18.40 *(978-0-606-35954-2(0))* Turtleback Bks.

—The Fourth Apprentice. Richardson, Owen & Douglas, Allen, illus. 2015. (Warriors: Omen of the Stars Ser.: 1). (ENG.). 384p. (J). (gr. 3-7). pap. 7.99 *(978-0-06-238257-3(8))* HarperCollins Pubs.

—Thunder & Shadow. 2016. (Illus.). 376p. (J). ***(978-0-06-257415-2(9))*** Harper & Row Ltd.

—Thunder Rising. McLoughlin, Wayne & Douglas, Allen, illus. (Warriors: Dawn of the Clans Ser.: 2). (J). (gr. 3-7). 2014. (ENG.). 368p. pap. 7.99 *(978-0-06-206352-6(9))* 2013. (ENG.). 352p. 16.99 *(978-0-06-206350-2(2))* 2013. 352p. lib. bdg. 17.89 *(978-0-06-206351-9(0))* HarperCollins Pubs.

—Twilight. Richardson, Owen & Stevenson, Dave, illus. 2015. (Warriors: the New Prophecy Ser.: 5). (ENG.). 368p. (J). (gr. 3-7). pap. 7.99 *(978-0-06-236706-8(4))* HarperCollins Pubs.

—Twilight. Stevenson, Dave, illus. 2006. (Warriors: the New Prophecy Ser.: 5). (ENG.). 336p. (J). (gr. 3-7). 16.99 *(978-0-06-082764-9(5))* HarperCollins Pubs.

—Twilight. 2015. (Warriors — the New Prophecy Ser.: 5). (J). lib. bdg. 18.40 *(978-0-606-36506-2(0))* Turtleback Bks.

—Warriors. 2015. (Warriors: the Prophecies Begin Ser.). (ENG.). (J). (gr. 3-7). Vols. 1-6. 2112p. pap. 42.99 *(978-0-06-236714-3(5))*Vols. 1 to 6. 2256p. pap. 44.99 *(978-0-06-236716-7(1))* HarperCollins Pubs.

—Warriors: The First Battle. 2014. (Warriors: Dawn of the Clans Ser.: 3). (ENG., Illus.). 352p. (J). (gr. 3-7). 16.99 *(978-0-06-206353-3(7))* HarperCollins Pubs.

—Warriors: The Ultimate Guide. McLoughlin, Wayne, illus. 2013. (Warriors Ser.). (ENG.). 304p. (J). (gr. 3-7). 19.99 *(978-0-06-224533-5(3))* HarperCollins Pubs.

—Warriors - Sunrise. 2015. (Warriors: Power of Three Ser.: 6). (ENG.). 368p. (J). (gr. 3-7). pap. 7.99 *(978-0-06-236713-6(7))* HarperCollins Pubs.

—Warriors - The New Prophecy, Vol. 1-6. Richardson, Owen, illus. 2015. (Warriors: the New Prophecy Ser.). (ENG.). 2176p. (J). (gr. 3-7). pap. 44.99 *(978-0-06-236715-0(3))* HarperCollins Pubs.

—Warriors: a Vision of Shadows #1: the Apprentice's Quest. (Warriors: a Vision of Shadows Ser.: 1). (J). (gr. 3-7). 2017. 352p. pap. 7.99 *(978-0-06-238639-7(5))* 2016. (ENG., Illus.). 336p. 16.99 *(978-0-06-238637-3(9))* 2016. (Illus.). 336p. lib. bdg. 17.89 *(978-0-06-238638-0(7))* HarperCollins Pubs.

—Warriors: a Vision of Shadows #2: Thunder & Shadow. (Warriors: a Vision of Shadows Ser.: 2). (J). (gr. 3-7). 2017. 416p. pap. 7.99 ***(978-0-06-238643-4(3))*** 2016. (Illus.). 400p. 16.99 *(978-0-06-238641-0(7))* 2016. (Illus.). 400p. lib. bdg. 17.89 *(978-0-06-238642-7(5))* HarperCollins Pubs.

—Warriors: a Vision of Shadows #3: Shattered Sky. 2017. (Warriors: a Vision of Shadows Ser.: 3). 320p. (J). (gr. 3-7). 16.99 *(978-0-06-238645-8(X))*; lib. bdg. 17.89 *(978-0-06-238646-5(8))* HarperCollins Pubs.

—Warriors: a Vision of Shadows #4: Darkest Night. 2017. (Warriors: a Vision of Shadows Ser.: 4). 336p. (J). (gr. 3-7). 16.99 ***(978-0-06-238649-6(2))***; (ENG.). lib. bdg. 17.89 ***(978-0-06-238650-2(6))*** HarperCollins Pubs.

—Warriors Boxed Set: Rising Storm; A Dangerous Path; The Darkest Hour. 2007. (Warriors Ser.: Nos. 4-6). (J). pap. 19.99 *(978-0-06-128452-6(1),* Harper Trophy) HarperCollins Pubs.

—Warriors: Dawn of the Clans #1: the Sun Trail. McLoughlin, Wayne & Douglas, Allen, illus. 2016. (Warriors: Dawn of the Clans Ser.: 1). 368p. (J). (gr. 3-7). pap. 7.99 *(978-0-06-241000-9(8))* HarperCollins Pubs.

—Warriors: Dawn of the Clans #2: Thunder Rising. McLoughlin, Wayne & Douglas, Allen, illus. 2016. (Warriors: Dawn of the Clans Ser.: 2). 368p. (J). (gr. 3-7). pap. 7.99 *(978-0-06-241001-6(6))* HarperCollins Pubs.

—Warriors: Dawn of the Clans #3: the First Battle. McLoughlin, Wayne & Douglas, Allen, illus. 2016. (Warriors: Dawn of the Clans Ser.: 3). 352p. (J). (gr. 3-7). pap. 7.99 *(978-0-06-241002-3(4))* HarperCollins Pubs.

—Warriors: Dawn of the Clans #4: the Blazing Star. McLoughlin, Wayne & Douglas, Allen, illus. 2016. (Warriors: Dawn of the Clans Ser.: 4). 336p. (J). (gr. 3-7). pap. 7.99 *(978-0-06-241003-0(2))* HarperCollins Pubs.

—Warriors: Dawn of the Clans #6: Path of Stars. McLoughlin, Wayne & Douglas, Allen, illus. 2015. (Warriors: Dawn of the Clans Ser.: 6). (ENG.). 352p. (J). (gr. 3-7). 16.99 *(978-0-06-206366-3(9))* HarperCollins Pubs.

—Warriors: Dawn of the Clans Box Set: Volumes 1 To 3. McLoughlin, Wayne, illus. 2016. (Warriors: Dawn of the Clans Ser.). 1088p. (J). (gr. 3-7). pap. 20.97 *(978-0-06-234325-3(4))* HarperCollins Pubs.

—Warriors: Legends of the Clans. 2017. (Warriors Novella Ser.). 336p. (J). (gr. 3-7). pap. 7.99 *(978-0-06-256087-2(5))* HarperCollins Pubs.

—Warriors: Omen of the Stars #2: Fading Echoes. Richardson, Owen & Douglas, Allen, illus. 2015. (Warriors: Omen of the Stars Ser.: 2). (ENG.). 384p. (J). (gr. 3-7). pap. 7.99 *(978-0-06-238259-7(4))* HarperCollins Pubs.

—Warriors: Omen of the Stars #3: Night Whispers. Richardson, Owen & Douglas, Allen, illus. 2015. (Warriors: Omen of the Stars Ser.: 3). (ENG.). 368p. (J). (gr. 3-7). pap. 7.99 *(978-0-06-238260-3(8))* HarperCollins Pubs.

—Warriors: Omen of the Stars #4: Sign of the Moon. Richardson, Owen & Douglas, Allen, illus. 2015. (Warriors: Omen of the Stars Ser.: 4). (ENG.). 368p. (J). (gr. 3-7). pap. 7.99 *(978-0-06-238261-0(6))* HarperCollins Pubs.

—Warriors: Omen of the Stars #5: the Forgotten Warrior. Richardson, Owen & Douglas, Allen, illus. 2015. (Warriors: Omen of the Stars Ser.: 5). (ENG.). 384p. (J). (gr. 3-7). pap. 7.99 *(978-0-06-238262-7(4))* HarperCollins Pubs.

—Warriors: Omen of the Stars #6: the Last Hope. Richardson, Owen & Douglas, Allen, illus. 2015. (Warriors: Omen of the Stars Ser.: 6). (ENG.). 400p. (J). (gr. 3-7). pap. 7.99 *(978-0-06-238263-4(2))* HarperCollins Pubs.

—Warriors: Shadows of the Clans. 2016. (Warriors Novella Ser.). 336p. (J). (gr. 3-7). pap. 7.99 *(978-0-06-234332-1(7))* HarperCollins Pubs.

—Warriors Super Edition: Bramblestar's Storm. 2014. (Warriors Ser.). (ENG., Illus.). 512p. (J). (gr. 3-7). 18.99 *(978-0-06-229143-1(2))* HarperCollins Pubs.

—Yellowfang's Secret. Barry, James L., illus. (Warriors Super Edition Ser.: 5). (J). (gr. 3-7). 2014. (ENG.). 544p. pap. 7.99 *(978-0-06-208216-9(7))* 2012. (ENG.). 528p. 18.99 *(978-0-06-208214-5(0))* 2012. 528p. lib. bdg. 19.89 *(978-0-06-208215-2(9))* HarperCollins Pubs.

—Yellowfang's Secret. 2014. (Warriors Super Edition Ser.). (J). lib. bdg. 18.40 *(978-0-606-35074-7(8),* Turtleback) Turtleback Bks.

Hunter, Erin & Jolley, Dan. Bramblestar's Storm. 2016. (Warriors Super Edition Ser.). (J). lib. bdg. 18.40 *(978-0-606-38180-2(5))* Turtleback Bks.

—Escape from the Forest. Hudson, Don, illus. 2008. (Warriors Manga Ser.: 2). (ENG.). 112p. (J). (gr. 3-7). pap. 7.99 *(978-0-06-154793-5(X))* HarperCollins Pubs.

Hunter, Erin, et al. Moth Flight's Vision. Barry, James L. & Richardson, Owen, illus. 2015. (Warriors Super Edition Ser.: 8). (ENG.). 528p. (J). (gr. 3-7). 18.99 *(978-0-06-229147-9(5))* HarperCollins Pubs.

Hunter, K. N. Hollow: N2 the Hollow World. 2008. 62p. pap. 16.95 *(978-1-4241-0220-4(0))* PublishAmerica, Inc.

Hunter, R. C. Moon Kids. 2010. 64p. pap. 11.99 *(978-1-4490-7846-1(X))* AuthorHouse.

Huntington, Geoffrey. Blood Moon. 2013. (Ravenscliff Ser.: 3). (ENG.). 260p. pap. 17.99 *(978-1-62681-169-0(5))* Diversion Publishing Corp.

Hunton, Robert L. Secrets of the Medicine Pouch. 2012. 260p. pap. *(978-0-9852737-4-3(7))* Roxby Media Ltd.

Hutchins, M. K. Drift, 1 vol. 2014. (ENG.). 352p. (YA). 19.95 *(978-1-62014-145-8(0))* Lee & Low Bks., Inc.

Hutchison, Barry. Mr Mumbles, 1. 2010. (Invisible Fiends Ser.: 1). (ENG.). 288p. (J). 8.99 *(978-0-00-731515-4(5),* HarperCollins Children's Bks.) HarperCollins Pubs. Ltd. GBR. Dist: HarperCollins Pubs.

Hutton, Fiona. The Adventures of Henrietta - the Camden Girl. 2012. 24p. pap. *(978-1-78222-056-5(9))* Paragon Publishing, Rothersthorpe.

Hyperion Staff. Enchanted Music. rev. ed. 2006. (W. I. T. C. H. Adventures Ser.: Bk. 5). 112p. (J). pap. 4.99 *(978-0-7868-0978-3(7),* Volo) Hyperion Bks. for Children.

Ibbott, Penny. Scarcode. 2013. 358p. pap. *(978-1-78299-864-8(0))* FeedARead.com.

Idowu, Cathy. Light for the Sacra Vellum: The Graceville Chronicles Book One. 2008. (Illus.). (J). *(978-0-9801484-0-4(5))* Rite Quest.

Ikin, Susan. Alex & the Night-tide Dragon. 2010. (Illus.). 68p. pap. 18.95 *(978-1-4461-4894-5(7))* Lulu Pr., Inc.

Illich, Maria. The Morcant Twins & the Curse of the Griseum. 2013. 248p. pap. *(978-1-927384-11-4(7))* Zeta Comics.

Impey, Rose. Peter Pan. Beck, Ian, illus. 2015. (ENG.). 96p. (J). (gr. k-2). pap. 11.99 *(978-1-4083-3822-3(X))* Hodder & Stoughton GBR. Dist: Hachette Bk. Group.

Impey, Rose & Huws, Emily. Dymuniad Mewn Eiliad. 2005. (WEL., Illus.). 64p. pap. *(978-0-86381-912-4(5))* Gwasg Carreg Gwalch.

Inches, Alison. Big Sister Dora! Aikins, Dave, illus. 2005. (Dora the Explorer Ser.: 13). 32p. (J). lib. bdg. 15.00 *(978-1-59054-790-8(X))* Fitzgerald Bks.

Ingram, Richard. Land of the Giddiwonks. 2004. (J). pap. 12.50 net. *(978-0-9745741-1-0(2))* Quality Publishing Inc.

The Invisible Boat. 1 vol. 2013. (ENG.). 336p. pap. 18.00 *(978-1-936367-44-3(0))* Waldorf Publications.

Inzana, Ryan. Ichiro. (ENG., Illus.). 288p. (YA). (gr. 7). 2014. pap. 12.99 *(978-0-547-61789-3(5),* HMH Books For Young Readers) 2012. 24.99 *(978-0-547-25269-8(2))* Houghton Mifflin Harcourt Publishing Co.

Irvine, Alex. Phase Three: Marvel's Captain America: Civil War. 2017. (ENG.). 208p. (J). (gr. 3-7). 12.99 *(978-0-316-27150-9(0))* Little, Brown Bks. for Young Readers.

Isadora, Rachel. Hansel & Gretel. Isadora, Rachel, illus. 2009. (ENG., Illus.). 32p. (J). (gr. 1-3). 16.99 *(978-0-399-25028-6(X),* G.P. Putnam's Sons Books for Young Readers) Penguin Young Readers Group.

Isbell, Tom. The Release. 2017. (Prey Trilogy Ser.: 3). 368p. (J). (gr. 8). 17.99 *(978-0-06-221608-3(2),* HarperTeen) HarperCollins Pubs.

Isenhoff, Michelle. The Quill Pen. 2011. (ENG.). 168p. pap. 9.98 *(978-1-4664-9691-0(6))* CreateSpace Independent Publishing Platform.

Ivanoff, George. Gamers' Quest. 2009. (Gamers Ser.: Bk. 1). (ENG.). 208p. (YA). pap. *(978-1-876462-86-4(8),* Ford Street Publishing) Hybrid Pubs.

Jablonski, Carla. Shadow of the Sphinx. 2007. (Charmed Ser.). (ENG.). 192p. (YA). pap. 14.95 *(978-1-4169-6756-9(7),* Gallery Bks.) Gallery Bks.

Jackson, Corrine. Ignited. 2014. (Sense Thieves Ser.). (ENG.). 368p. (YA). (gr. 13). pap. 9.95 *(978-0-7582-7335-2(5),* K-Teen) Kensington Publishing Corp.

Jackson, Ladain. Rare Vision. 2013. 100p. pap. 8.99 *(978-1-937165-35-2(3))* Orange Hat Publishing.

Jackson, Stephen. Mundoespejo. 2005. (SPA., Illus.). 28p. (J). (gr. 2-4). 15.95 *(978-84-666-1495-5(8))* Ediciones B ESP. Dist: Independent Pubs. Group.

Jackson, Steve. The Citadel of Chaos. 2003. 208p. pap. *(978-0-7434-7510-5(0))* ibooks, Inc.

Jackson, Steve & Livingstone, Ian. The Worlock of Firetop Mountain. 2003. 192p. pap. 6.99 *(978-0-7434-7511-2(9))* ibooks, Inc.

Jackson, Sue Ann. A Vessel for the King. 2013. (Illus.). 40p. pap. 7.99 *(978-1-936688-55-5(7))* AKA:yoLa.

Jacob, Violet. The Golden Heart, & Other Fairy Stories. Sandheim, May, illus. 2011. 168p. pap. *(978-1-84921-098-0(5))* Kennedy & Boyd.

Jacques, Brian. Castaways of the Flying Dutchman. Schoenherr, Ian, illus. 2003. (ENG.). 336p. (J). (gr. 3-7). pap. 9.99 *(978-0-14-250118-4(2),* Firebird) Penguin Young Readers Group.

—Doomwyte. 2010. (Redwall Ser.: 20). (ENG.). 368p. (J). (gr. 5). pap. 8.99 *(978-0-441-01778-2(9),* Ace Bks.) Penguin Publishing Group.

—Doomwyte. Elliot, David, illus. 2011. (Redwall Ser.). (ENG.). 384p. (J). (gr. 5-18). 8.99 *(978-0-14-241853-6(6),* Firebird) Penguin Young Readers Group.

—High Rhulain. 18 vols. Elliott, David, illus. 2007. (Redwall Ser.: 18). (ENG.). 336p. (J). (gr. 5-18). 7.99 *(978-0-441-01436-1(4),* Ace Bks.) Penguin Publishing Group.

—High Rhulain. Elliot, David, illus. 2008. (Redwall Ser.). (ENG.). 352p. (J). (gr. 5-18). 8.99 *(978-0-14-240938-1(3),* Firebird) Penguin Young Readers Group.

—High Rhulain. Elliot, David, illus. 2007. (Redwall Ser.). 320p. (gr. 3-7). 18.00 *(978-0-7569-7763-4(0))* Perfection Learning Corp.

—High Rhulain. 2007. (Redwall Ser.: 18). 18.40 *(978-1-4177-7458-6(4),* Turtleback) Turtleback Bks.

—The Legend of Luke. 2005. (Redwall Ser.). (ENG., Illus.). 384p. (J). (gr. 5-7). pap. 8.99 *(978-0-14-250109-2(3),* Firebird) Penguin Young Readers Group.

—Loamhedge. Elliot, David, illus. 2005. (Redwall Ser.). (ENG.). 432p. (J). (gr. 5-5). 8.99 *(978-0-14-240377-8(6),* Firebird) Penguin Young Readers Group.

—Lord Brocktree. Fangorn, illus. 2005. (Redwall Ser.). (ENG.). 384p. (J). (gr. 5-7). pap. 8.99 *(978-0-14-250110-8(7),* Firebird) Penguin Young Readers Group.

—Mariel of Redwall. Chalk, Gary, illus. 2003. (Redwall Ser.). (ENG.). 400p. (J). (gr. 5-5). pap. 9.99 *(978-0-14-230239-2(2),* Firebird) Penguin Young Readers Group.

—Mariel of Redwall. 2004. (Redwall Ser.). 1.00 *(978-1-4175-6449-1(0))* Recorded Bks., Inc.

—Martfox: A Tale from Redwall. 2005. (Redwall Ser.). (ENG.). 400p. (J). (gr. 5-5). reprint ed. 8.99 *(978-0-14-250108-5(5),* Firebird) Penguin Young Readers Group.

—Martin the Warrior. Chalk, Gary, illus. 2004. (Redwall Ser.). (ENG.). 384p. (J). (gr. 5-18). pap. 9.99 *(978-0-14-240055-5(6),* Firebird) Penguin Young Readers Group.

—Mattimeo. Chalk, Gary, illus. 2003. (Redwall Ser.). (ENG.). 448p. (J). (gr. 5-7). pap. 9.99 *(978-0-14-230240-8(6),* Firebird) Penguin Young Readers Group.

—Mattimeo. 2003. (Redwall Ser.). 1.00 *(978-1-4175-5316-7(2))* Recorded Bks., Inc.

—Outcast of Redwall. 2006. (Redwall Ser.). 1.00 *(978-1-4237-8693-1(9))* Recorded Bks., Inc.

—Pearls of Lutra. 2004. (Redwall Ser.). (ENG., Illus.). 416p. (J). (gr. 5-5). 8.99 *(978-0-14-240144-6(7),* Firebird) Penguin Young Readers Group.

—Rakkety Tam. 17 vols. 2005. (Redwall Ser.: 17). (ENG.). 384p. (J). (gr. 5-18). mass mkt. 8.99 *(978-0-441-01318-0(X),* Ace Bks.) Penguin Publishing Group.

—Rakkety Tam. Elliot, David, illus. 2006. (Redwall Ser.). (ENG.). 384p. (J). (gr. 5-18). 8.99 *(978-0-14-240683-0(X),* Firebird) Penguin Young Readers Group.

—Rakkety Tam. 2004. (Redwall Ser.). 1.00 *(978-1-4175-5517-8(3))* Recorded Bks., Inc.

—Redwall. Blevins, Bret, illus. 2007. (Redwall Ser.). (ENG.). 148p. (J). (gr. 5-18). 12.99 *(978-0-399-24481-0(6),* Philomel Bks.) Penguin Young Readers Group.

—Redwall. Chalk, Gary, illus. 20th anniv. ed. 2007. (Redwall Ser.). (ENG.). 352p. (J). (gr. 5-18). 23.99 *(978-0-399-24794-1(7),* Philomel Bks.) Penguin Young Readers Group.

—The Rogue Crew. 2012. (Redwall Ser.: 22). (ENG.). 368p. (J). (gr. 5). 8.99 *(978-1-937007-48-5(0),* Ace Bks.) Penguin Publishing Group.

—The Rogue Crew. Rubin, Sean, illus. 2011. (Redwall Ser.). (ENG.). 400p. (J). (gr. 5-18). 23.99 *(978-0-399-25416-1(1),* Philomel Bks.) Penguin Young Readers Group.

—The Rogue Crew. 2013. (Redwall Ser.: 22). lib. bdg. 20.85 *(978-0-606-31702-3(3),* Turtleback) Turtleback Bks.

—The Sable Quean. 21 vols. 2011. (Redwall Ser.: 21). (ENG.). 368p. (J). (gr. 5). 8.99 *(978-0-441-01998-4(6),* Ace Bks.) Penguin Publishing Group.

—The Sable Quean. 21 vols. Elliot, David, illus. 2010. (Redwall Ser.: 21). (ENG.). 448p. (J). (gr. 5-18). 23.99 *(978-0-399-25164-1(2),* Philomel Bks.) Penguin Young Readers Group.

—The Sable Quean. Elliot, David, illus. 2012. (Redwall Ser.: 21). lib. bdg. 19.65 *(978-0-606-23646-1(5),* Turtleback) Turtleback Bks.

—Salamandastron. Chalk, Gary, illus. 2003. (Redwall Ser.). (ENG.). 400p. (J). (gr. 5-3). pap. 9.99 *(978-0-14-250152-8(2),* Firebird) Penguin Young Readers Group.

—Taggerung. Standley, Peter & Chalk, Gary, illus. 2003. (Redwall Ser.). (ENG.). 448p. (J). (gr. 5-18). pap. 8.99 *(978-0-14-250154-2(9),* Firebird) Penguin Young Readers Group.

—Taggerung. 2003. (Redwall Ser.). 1.00 *(978-1-4175-5326-6(X))* Recorded Bks., Inc.

—Triss. Elliot, David & Curless, Allan, illus. 2004. (Redwall Ser.). (ENG.). 400p. (J). (gr. 5-7). pap. 8.99 *(978-0-14-240248-1(6),* Firebird) Penguin Young Readers Group.

—Triss. l.t. ed. 2004. (Redwall Ser.). 596p. (J). 23.95 *(978-0-7862-6207-6(9))* Thorndike Pr.

Jae, Ava. Beyond the Red. 2016. (ENG., Illus.). 360p. (J). (gr. 8). 17.99 *(978-1-63450-644-1(8),* Sky Pony Pr.) Skyhorse Publishing Co., Inc.

Jae-Jones, S. Wintersong. 2017. (ENG.). 448p. (YA). 18.99 *(978-1-250-07921-3(7),* 9781250079213) St. Martin's Pr.

Jakubsen, Ryan. Portals III, Band of Rogues. 2011. 128p. pap. 10.00 *(978-0-9846320-0-8(X))* Alabaster Bk. Pub.

Jamal L. Q'Ettelle. Jayden & the Return of the Jalon Warriors. 2010. 120p. pap. 10.95 *(978-1-4502-0288-6(8))* iUniverse, Inc.

James, Arthur. Jason & the Kodikats. 2013. 118p. pap. *(978-0-9918166-2-0(5))* Flower Pr.

James, Betsy. Listening at the Gate. James, Betsy, illus. 2007. (Seeker Chronicles Ser.). (ENG., Illus.). 512p. (YA). (gr. 7-12). pap. 22.99 *(978-0-689-85069-1(7),* Atheneum Bks. for Young Readers) Simon & Schuster Children's Publishing.

James, Carol Ann. Baby's Sleepy Time Adventure. 2008. 19p. pap. 24.95 *(978-1-60563-500-2(6))* America Star Bks.

James, M. R. The Five Jars. 2008. 96p. pap. *(978-1-84830-112-2(X),* Wildhern Pr.) Echo Library.

Janicke, Gregory. The Conquerors. 1 vol. Janicke, Gregory, illus. 2008. (Outcasts Ser.: Bk. 4). (ENG., Illus.). 328p. (YA). (gr. 5-18). pap. 7.99 *(978-0-7614-5442-7(X))* Marshall Cavendish Corp.

—The Dark Mystery of the Shadow Beasts. 2004. (Illus.). 168p. *(978-983-58-0993-4(3))* Times Edition.

—Lost & Found. 1 vol. 2008. (Outcasts Ser.: Bk. 3). (ENG., Illus.). 276p. (YA). (gr. 8-12). pap. 7.99 *(978-0-7614-5426-7(8))* Marshall Cavendish Corp.

—The Shadow Beasts. 1 vol. Janicke, Gregory, illus. 2007. (Outcasts Ser.: Bk. 1). (ENG., Illus.). 276p. (YA). (gr. 8-12). pap. 6.99 *(978-0-7614-5364-2(4))* Marshall Cavendish Corp.

Janik, Dan. Sourdough Scott's Bedtime Fairy Tales from Alaska. 2005. (Illus.). (J). 12.95 *(978-1-59433-031-5(X))* Publication Consultants.

Janney, Connie. The Most Extraordinary Farm. 2012. 30p. (-18). pap. 13.99 *(978-1-4525-6213-1(X))* Balboa Pr.

Janowski, Alice. The Adventures of Inka the Feline. Smith, Jerry, illus. 2010. 36p. pap. 14.00 *(978-1-60844-576-9(3))* Dog Ear Publishing, LLC.

Janry, illus. Spirou & Fantasio - Valley of the Exiles. 2013. (Spirou & Fantasio Ser.: 4). Orig. Title: Vol. 4. (ENG.). 48p. pap. 11.95 *(978-1-84918-157-0(8))* CineBook GBR. Dist: National Bk. Network.

Jansen, Patty. The Far Horizon. 2012. 176p. pap. *(978-0-9872009-4-5(1))* Capricornica Pubns.

Jansen Van Rensburg, Bianca. When Tomorrow Doesn't Come. 2012. 320p. pap. 16.99 *(978-1-105-92516-0(1))* Lulu Pr., Inc.

Jansson, Tove. The Book about Moomin, Mymble & Little My. Hannah, Sophie, tr. from SWE. 2009. (Moomin Ser.). Orig. Title: Boken om Mymlan, Mumintrollet och Lilla My. (ENG., Illus.). 20p. (J). (gr. k-5). 16.95 *(978-1-897299-95-1(8),* 9781897299951) Drawn & Quarterly Pubns. CAN. Dist: Macmillan.

—Comet in Moominland. Portch, Elizabeth, tr. Jansson, Tove, illus. 2010. (Moomins Ser.: 1). (ENG., Illus.). 192p. (J). (gr. 4-7). pap. 7.99 *(978-0-312-60888-0(8),* 9780312608880) Square Fish.

—Finn Family Moomintroll. Portch, Elizabeth, tr. from SWE. Jansson, Tove, illus. 2010. (Moomins Ser.: 2). (ENG., Illus.). 176p. (J). (gr. 4-7). pap. 7.99 *(978-0-312-60889-7(6),* 9780312608897) Square Fish.

—Lift-the-Flap Hide & Seek. 2011. (Moomins Ser.). (ENG., Illus.). 24p. (J). (gr. -1 — 1). 8.99 *(978-0-374-35051-2(5),* 9780374350512, Farrar, Straus & Giroux (BYR)) Farrar, Straus & Giroux.

—Moomin & the Martians. 2015. (Moomin Ser.). (ENG., Illus.). 56p. (J). (gr. -1-5). pap. 9.95 *(978-1-77046-203-8(1),* 9781770462038) Drawn & Quarterly Pubns. CAN. Dist: Macmillan.

—Moominland Midwinter. Warburton, Thomas, tr. Jansson, Tove, illus. 2010. (Moomins Ser.: 5). (ENG., Illus.). 160p. (J). (gr. 4-7). pap. 7.99 *(978-0-312-62541-2(3),* 9780312625412) Square Fish.

—Moominpappa at Sea. Hart, Kingsley, tr. Jansson, Tove, illus. 2010. (Moomins Ser.: 7). (ENG., Illus.). 240p. (J). (gr. 4-7). pap. 7.99 *(978-0-312-60892-7(6),* 9780312608927) Square Fish.

—Moominpappa's Memoirs. Warburton, Thomas, tr. Jansson, Tove, illus. 2010. (Moomins Ser.: 4). (ENG., Illus.). 192p. (J). (gr. 4-7). pap. 7.99 *(978-0-312-62543-6(X),* 9780312625436) Square Fish.

—Moominsummer Madness. Warburton, Thomas, tr. Jansson, Tove, illus. 2010. (Moomins Ser.: 4). (ENG., Illus.). 176p. (J). (gr. 4-7). pap. 7.99 *(978-0-312-60891-0(8),* 9780312608910) Square Fish.

—Moominvalley in November. Hart, Kingsley, tr. Jansson, Tove, illus. 2010. (Moomins Ser.: 8). (ENG., Illus.). 208p. (J). (gr. 4-7). pap. 7.99 *(978-0-312-62544-3(8),* 9780312625443) Square Fish.

—Tales from Moominvalley. Warburton, Thomas, tr. Jansson, Tove, illus. 2010. (Moomins Ser.: 6).Tr. of Osynliga Barnet. (ENG., Illus.). 192p. (J). (gr. 4-7). pap. 7.99 *(978-0-312-62542-9(1),* 9780312625429) Square Fish.

Januarius. James & the Pixie. Wigmore, Kitty, illus. 2015. (ENG.). 50p. (J). (gr. 3-4). 24.95 *(978-1-78455-540-5(1),* 5bd61eeb-94b8-41ac-94aa-57a16cb4eeda); pap. 13.95 *(978-1-78455-538-2(X),* 0a59afd6-d79f-4a96-b3d0-d19a1af0e939) Austin, Stan AUS. Dist: Bookmasters Distribution.

Jarman, Julia. Time-Travelling Cat & the Great Victorian Stink. 2011. (Time-Travelling Cat Ser.: 6). (ENG.). 160p. (J). (gr. 4-7). pap. 12.99 *(978-1-84939-019-4(3))* Andersen Pr. GBR. Dist: Independent Pubs. Group.

—The Time-Travelling Cat & the Roman Eagle. 2008. (Time-Travelling Cat Ser.: 3). (ENG., Illus.). 156p. (J). (gr. 4-7). pap. 13.99 *(978-1-84270-617-6(9))* Andersen Pr. GBR. Dist: Independent Pubs. Group.

—The Time-Travelling Cat & the Viking Terror. 2008. (Time-Travelling Cat Ser.: 4). (ENG., Illus.). 176p. (J). (gr. 4-7). pap. 11.99 *(978-1-84270-686-2(1))* Andersen Pr. GBR. Dist: Independent Pubs. Group.

Jarvis, Robin. Fighting Pax. 2014. (Dancing Jax Ser.: 3). (ENG., Illus.). 576p. (J). 8.99 *(978-0-00-745130-2(X),* HarperCollins Children's Bks.) HarperCollins Pubs. Ltd. GBR. Dist: HarperCollins Pubs.

—Thorn Ogres of Hagwood. 2013. (Hagwood Trilogy Ser.: 1). (ENG.). 210p. (J). (gr. 4-6). pap. 11.99 *(978-1-4532-9921-0(1))* Open Road Integrated Media, Inc.

—War in Hagwood. 2016. (Hagwood Trilogy Ser.: 3). (ENG.). 310p. (J). (gr. 4-6). pap. 14.99 *(978-1-4532-9922-7(X),* Open Road Media E-riginal) Open Road Integrated Media, Inc.

Jarvis, Robin. The Whitby Witches. 2017. (Modern Classics Ser.). (ENG., Illus.). 336p. (YA). (gr. 6). pap. 9.99 ***(978-1-4052-8540-7(0))*** Egmont Bks., Ltd. GBR. Dist: Independent Pubs. Group.

Jay, Alison. Alice's Adventures in Wonderland Board Book. 2015. (ENG.). 22p. (J). (— 1). bds. 6.99 *(978-0-525-42979-1(4),* Dial Bks) Penguin Young Readers Group.

Jay, Annabelle. The Sun Dragon. 2016. (ENG., Illus.). (YA). 24.99 ***(978-1-63477-977-7(0))***; 180p. (J). pap. 14.99 *(978-1-63476-339-4(4))* Dreamspinner Pr. (Harmony Ink Pr.).

Jay, Stacey. Of Beast & Beauty. 2014. (ENG.). 400p. (YA). (gr. 9). pap. 9.99 *(978-0-385-74321-1(1),* Ember) Random Hse. Children's Bks.

—Princess of Thorns. 2016. (ENG.). 400p. (YA). (gr. 9). pap. 9.99 *(978-0-385-74323-5(8),* Ember) Random Hse. Children's Bks.

Jazwierska, Jennifer & Popiel, Candice Bataille. Discovery of Glow. 2008. (Glowmundo Ser.). (J). (gr. 2-6). pap. 12.95 *(978-0-9814930-0-8(9))* Elora Media, LLC.

Jeanmarie, Michele. Curiosity, Curiosity: Lost in an Array. 2008. 74p. pap. 19.95 *(978-1-60610-169-8(2))* America Star Bks.

Jeanne, DuPrau. The City of Ember. 2014. (Books of Ember Ser. Bk. 1 Ser.). (ENG.). 288p. (J). (gr. 12-12). 11.24 *(978-1-63245-182-8(4))* Lectorum Pubns., Inc.

Jeanne Taylor Thomas Illustrator: Pr. Austin & Harlow's First Adventure. Hardy, Pris, illus. 2011. 28p. pap. 24.95 *(978-1-4560-8383-0(X))* America Star Bks.

Jeb. Destinations in Time. 2008. 101p. pap. 19.95 *(978-1-60672-653-2(6))* America Star Bks.

Jeffers, Dawn. Beautiful Moon. Leick, Bonnie, illus. 2009. (ENG.). 32p. (J). (gr. -1-3). 16.95 *(978-1-934960-05-9(5),* Raven Tree Pr.,Csi) Continental Sales, Inc.

Jefferson, E. Louis. The Little Tadpole-A Story of Friendship: Companion Coloring Book. 2012. 48p. pap. 7.00 *(978-1-105-51123-0(X))* Lulu.com GBR. Dist: Lulu Pr., Inc.

Jeffrey, Leonard J. Journeys of the Mind-Book. 2012. 140p. pap. 39.88 *(978-1-4669-3873-1(0))* Trafford Publishing.

Jenkins, Emily. Toys Come Home: Being the Early Experiences of an Intelligent Stingray, a Brave Buffalo, & a Brand-New Someone Called Plastic. Zelinsky, Paul O., illus. 2016. (Toys Go Out Ser.). (ENG.). 144p. (J). (gr. 1-4). 6.99 *(978-0-449-81592-2(7),* Yearling) Random Hse. Children's Bks.

Jenkins, Gloria. Storm: The Peace Maker. 2006. (J). pap. 8.00 *(978-0-8059-7116-3(5))* Dorrance Publishing Co., Inc.

Jenkins, Jerry B. & Fabry, Chris. The Author's Blood. 2008. (Wormling Ser.: 5). (ENG.). 368p. (J). (gr. 5-9). per. 7.99 *(978-1-4143-0159-4(6),* Tyndale Kids) Tyndale Hse. Pubs.

—The Minions of Time. 2008. (Wormling Ser.: 4). (ENG.). 336p. (J). (gr. 5-9). per. 7.99 *(978-1-4143-0158-7(8))* Tyndale Hse. Pubs.

—Sword of the Wormling. 2007. (Wormling Ser.: 2). (ENG.). 336p. (J). (gr. 5-9). per. 7.99 *(978-1-4143-0156-3(1))* Tyndale Hse. Pubs.

Jennette, Mairead. Ten Green Bottles. 2013. 98p. pap. *(978-3-7103-0181-0(5))* united p.c. Verlag.

Jennewein, James & Parker, Tom S. RuneWarriors. 2008. (RuneWarriors Ser.). 320p. (J). (gr. 3-7). lib. bdg. 17.89 *(978-0-06-144937-6(7),* Geringer, Laura Book) HarperCollins Pubs.

Jennings, L. N. Seven Splinters. 2012. 426p. pap. 22.50 *(978-1-105-54636-5(5))* Lulu Pr., Inc.

Jensen, Danielle L. Stolen Songbird. 2014. (Malediction Trilogy Ser.: 1). (ENG.). 480p. (YA). (gr. 9). pap. 9.99 *(978-1-908844-96-5(5),* Angry Robot, Limited) Watkins Media Limited GBR. Dist: Penguin Random Hse. LLC.

Jesperson, Per. Wonder & Magic: The David Tales. 2003. 50p. pap. *(978-1-84401-017-2(1))* Athena Pr.

Jesus, Opal De. The Golden Apple Kingdom. 1 vol. 2009. 48p. pap. 16.95 *(978-1-60749-414-0(0))* America Star Bks.

Jewell, M. B. Tales of Amanda O' 2008. 80p. pap. 15.99 *(978-1-4363-2215-7(4))* Xlibris Corp.

Jewish. 2004. (YA). spiral bd. *(978-0-9754913-2-4(6),* Gap Tooth Publishing) Charles River Pr.

Jiya, Tapiwa. The Epic of Goz. 2008. 144p. pap. 11.99 *(978-1-4343-5730-4(9))* AuthorHouse.

Jobin, Matthew. The Nethergrim. (Nethergrim Ser.: 1). (ENG.). 368p. (J). (gr. 5). 2015. 8.99 *(978-0-14-242268-7(1),* Puffin Books) 2014. 17.99 *(978-0-399-15998-5(3),* Philomel Bks.) Penguin Young Readers Group.

—The Skeleth. 2016. (Nethergrim Ser.: 2). (ENG.). 400p. (J). (gr. 5). 17.99 *(978-0-399-15999-2(1),* Philomel Bks.) Penguin Young Readers Group.

Jobling, Curtis. Nest of Serpents. 2015. (Wereworld Ser.: 4). (ENG.). 512p. (J). (gr. 5). 8.99 *(978-0-14-242193-2(6),* Puffin Books) Penguin Young Readers Group.

—Rage of Lions. 2013. (Wereworld Ser.: 2). (ENG.). 432p. (J). (gr. 5). pap. 8.99 *(978-0-14-242202-1(9),* Puffin Books) Penguin Young Readers Group.

—Rise of the Wolf. 2012. (Wereworld Ser.: 1). (ENG.). 432p. (J). (gr. 5-18). pap. 8.99 *(978-0-14-242108-6(1),* Puffin Books) Penguin Young Readers Group.

—Rise of the Wolf. 2012. (Wereworld Ser.: 1). lib. bdg. 19.65 *(978-0-606-26084-8(6),* Turtleback) Turtleback Bks.

—Shadow of the Hawk. 2013. (Wereworld Ser.: 3). (ENG.). 496p. (J). (gr. 5). pap. 8.99 *(978-0-14-242192-5(8),* Puffin Books) Penguin Young Readers Group.

—Shadow of the Hawk. 2013. (Wereworld Ser.: 3). lib. bdg. 19.65 *(978-0-606-30044-5(9),* Turtleback) Turtleback Bks.

—Storm of Sharks. (Wereworld Ser.: 5). (ENG.). 480p. (J). (gr. 5). 2015. 8.99 *(978-0-14-242577-0(X),* Puffin Books) 2013. 16.99 *(978-0-670-78558-2(X),* Viking Books for Young Readers) Penguin Young Readers Group.

—War of the Werelords. 2013. (Wereworld Ser.: 6). (ENG.). 528p. (J). (gr. 5). 16.99 *(978-0-670-78559-9(8),* Viking Books for Young Readers) Penguin Young Readers Group.

Jocelyn, Marthe. Earthly Astonishments. 2003. (ENG.). 192p. (J). (gr. 3-7). pap. 7.95 *(978-0-88776-628-2(5))* Tundra Bks. CAN. Dist: Random Hse., Inc.

Johansen, K. V. Nightwalker. 1 vol. 2007. (ENG.). 208p. (YA). (gr. 8-12). per. 9.95 *(978-1-55143-481-0(4))* Orca Bk. Pubs. USA.

—Treason in Eswy. 1 vol. 2008. (ENG., Illus.). 192p. (YA). (gr. 7-12). pap. 9.95 *(978-1-55143-888-7(7))* Orca Bk. Pubs. USA.

John, Antony. Elemental. (ENG., (YA). (gr. 7). 2013. Illus.). 352p. pap. 8.99 *(978-0-14-242516-9(8),* Speak) 2012. 336p. 17.99 *(978-0-8037-3682-5(7),* Dial Bks) Penguin Young Readers Group.

—Renegade. 2014. (ENG.). 304p. (YA). (gr. 7). 17.99 *(978-0-8037-3685-6(1),* Dial Bks) Penguin Young Readers Group.

Johns, Eric. The Giraffe Tree & Other Tall Stories. 2012. 180p. (-18). pap. 12.95 *(978-1-291-03279-6(7))* Lulu Pr., Inc.

—Mindreaders. 2007. 184p. pap. 16.95 *(978-1-4357-0121-2(6))* Lulu Pr., Inc.

Johnson, Amy. The Princess & the Frog. 2010. 24p. 14.93 *(978-1-4269-3712-5(1))* Trafford Publishing.

Johnson, Bob. The Lost Mine of the Mechanical Spider. Johnson, Bob, illus. 2006. (Squatland Chronicles Ser.). (Illus.). 53p. (J). (gr. -1-3). per. 11.00 *(978-1-60002-185-5(9),* 3977) Mountain Valley Publishing, LLC.

Johnson, Cheryl. Marlow. Ciesinki, Izabela, illus. 2007. 27p. (J). 14.95 *(978-0-9785728-4-6(X))* Digi-Tall Media.

Johnson, Christine. The Gathering Dark. (ENG., (YA). (gr. 9). 2014. Illus.). 528p. pap. 9.99 *(978-1-4424-3904-7(1))* 2013. 512p. 16.99 *(978-1-4424-3903-0(3))* Simon Pulse. (Simon Pulse).

Johnson, Crockett. Harold & the Purple Crayon. Johnson, Crockett, illus. 50th anniv. ed. 2015. (ENG., Illus.). 64p. (J). (gr. -1-3). pap. 6.99 *(978-0-06-443022-7(7))*; 16.99 *(978-0-06-022935-1(7))* HarperCollins Pubs.

—Harold at the North Pole. Johnson, Crockett, illus. 2015. (ENG., Illus.). 48p. (J). (gr. -1-3). 16.99 *(978-0-06-242861-5(6))* HarperCollins Pubs.

—Magic Beach. 2005. (ENG., Illus.). 64p. (J). (gr. -1-3). 18.95 *(978-1-932425-27-6(6),* Lemniscaat) Boyds Mills Pr.

Johnson, D. C. & Rowan, Ron. The Secret of MeadowBrook Orphanage. 2012. 528p. (gr. -1). pap. 18.30 *(978-1-4669-1866-5(7))* Trafford Publishing.

Johnson, Elizabeth. And Then Nicholas Sang: The Story of the Trisagion Hymn. Lobastov, Masha, illus. 2010. 32p. (J). 18.95 *(978-1-936270-05-7(6))* Ancient Faith Publishing.

Johnson, H. E. Sequoia Secret Place: Redeeming the Stolen Kingdom. 2011. 74p. (gr. -1). pap. 10.77 *(978-1-4567-5923-0(X))* AuthorHouse.

Johnson, Jahleigh. The Mark of the Dragonfly. (ENG.). 400p. (J). (gr. 5). 2015. 7.99 *(978-0-385-37647-1(2),* Yearling) 2014. 16.99 *(978-0-385-37615-0(4),* Delacorte Bks. for Young Readers) Random Hse. Children's Bks.

—The Mark of the Dragonfly. 2015. lib. bdg. 18.40 *(978-0-606-37701-0(8))* Turtleback Bks.

Johnson, Jaleigh. The Quest to the Uncharted Lands. 2017. (ENG.). 352p. (J). (gr. 5). 16.99 ***(978-1-101-93312-1(7),*** Delacorte Bks. for Young Readers) Random Hse. Children's Bks.

Johnson, Jaleigh. The Secrets of Solace. (ENG.). (J). (gr. 5). 2017. 400p. 7.99 ***(978-0-385-37651-8(0),*** Yearling) 2016. 384p. 16.99 *(978-0-385-37648-8(0),* Delacorte Bks. for Young Readers) Random Hse. Children's Bks.

Johnson, Jane. Legends of the Shadow World: The Secret Country; the Shadow World; Dragon's Fire. Stower, Adam, illus. 2010. (ENG.). 1120p. (J). (gr. 3-7). pap. 14.99 *(978-1-4169-9082-6(8),* Simon & Schuster Bks. For Young Readers) Simon & Schuster Bks. For Young Readers.

—The Secret Country. Stower, Adam, illus. 2007. (Eidolon Chronicles Ser.: 1). (ENG.). 336p. (J). (gr. 3-7). per. 15.99

EFG

(978-1-4169-3815-6(X), Simon & Schuster Bks. For Young Readers) Simon & Schuster Bks. For Young Readers.

Johnson, Kathleen Jeffrie. A Fast & Brutal Wing. unabr. ed. 2005. (YA). 46.70 incl. audio (978-1-4193-3247-0(3), 42029) Recorded Bks., Inc.

Johnson, R. Kikuo. The Shark King. Loeffler, Trade & Johnson, R. Kikuo, illus. 2012. (ENG.). 40p. (J). (gr. -1-3). 12.95 (978-1-935179-16-0(0)) TOON Books / RAW Junior, LLC.

Johnson, Sarah Blake. Crossings. 2017. (YA). pap. 17.99 **(978-1-4621-1957-8(3))** Cedar Fort, Inc./CFI Distribution.

Johnson-Shelton, Nils. The Dragon King. 2013. (Otherworld Chronicles Ser.: 3). (ENG.). 352p. (J). (gr. 3-7). 16.99 (978-0-06-207097-5(5)) HarperCollins Pubs.

—The Invisible Tower. 2012. (Otherworld Chronicles Ser.: 1). (ENG.). 368p. (J). (gr. 5). pap. 6.99 (978-0-06-207088-3(6)) HarperCollins Pubs.

—Otherworld Chronicles #2: the Seven Swords. 2013. (Otherworld Chronicles Ser.: 2). (ENG.). 384p. (J). (gr. 3-7). pap. 6.99 (978-0-06-207095-1(9)) HarperCollins Pubs.

Johnson, Varian. The Return. 2016. (Spirit Animals: Fall of the Beasts Ser.: 3). (ENG.). 192p. (J). (gr. 3-7). 12.99 (978-0-545-84207-5(7)) Scholastic, Inc.

Johnston, Annie Fellows. The Giant Scissors. Barry, Etheldred B., illus. 2005. reprint ed. pap. 22.95 (978-1-4179-0341-2(4)) Kessinger Publishing, LLC.

Johnston, Jack. The Ice Cream Hotel. 2012. 32p. (J). 17.95 (978-0-9852869-0-3(3)) Norwen Pubns.

Johnston, Tamra L. Libby the Little Leprechaun. 2012. 42p. pap. 20.99 (978-1-4772-0750-5(3)) AuthorHouse.

Johnstone, Ian. The Bell Between Worlds. 2016. (Mirror Chronicles Ser.: 1). (J). lib. bdg. 20.85 (978-0-606-38185-7(6)) Turtleback Bks.

—The Bell Between Worlds (the Mirror Chronicles) 2016. (Mirror Chronicles Ser.). (ENG.). 512p. (J). pap. 9.99 (978-0-00-815428-8(7), HarperCollins Children's Bks.) HarperCollins Pubs. Ltd. GBR. Dist: HarperCollins Pubs.

—Circles of Stone. 2015. (Mirror Chronicles Ser.: 2). (ENG.). 512p. (J). 8.99 (978-0-00-749117-9(4), HarperCollins Children's Bks.) HarperCollins Pubs. Ltd. GBR. Dist: HarperCollins Pubs.

—The Bell Between Worlds. 2015. (Mirror Chronicles Ser.). (ENG.). 512p. (J). 8.99 (978-0-00-749121-6(2), HarperCollins Children's Bks.) HarperCollins Pubs. Ltd. GBR. Dist: HarperCollins Pubs.

Jolley, Dan. The Emerald Tablet. 2016. (Five Elements Ser.: 1). 304p. (J). (gr. 3-7). 16.99 (978-0-06-241165-5(9)) HarperCollins Pubs.

—The Emerald Tablet. 2017. (Five Elements Ser.: 1). (ENG.). (J). (gr. 3-7). lib. bdg. 17.20 **(978-0-606-40054-1(0))** Turtleback Bks.

—Five Elements #1: the Emerald Tablet. 2017. (Five Elements Ser.: 1). (Illus.). 320p. (J). (gr. 3-7). pap. 6.99 **(978-0-06-241166-2(7))** HarperCollins Pubs.

—Five Elements #2: the Shadow City. (Five Elements Ser.: 2). (J). (gr. 3-7). 2018. 288p. pap. 6.99 **(978-0-06-241168-6(3))** 2017. 272p. 16.99 **(978-0-06-241167-9(5))** HarperCollins Pubs.

Jonell, Lynne. The Sign of the Cat. 2015. (ENG., Illus.). 368p. (J). (gr. 3-7). 16.99 (978-0-8050-9683-5(3), 9780805096835, Holt, Henry & Co. Bks. For Young Readers) Holt, Henry & Co.

Jones, Allan. The Six Crowns: Full Circle. Chalk, Gary, illus. 2013. (Six Crowns Ser.: 6). 176p. (J). (gr. 3-7). 16.99 (978-0-06-200639-4(8), Greenwillow Bks.) HarperCollins Pubs.

—The Six Crowns: Sargasso Skies. Chalk, Gary, illus. 2013. (Six Crowns Ser.: 5). 176p. (J). (gr. 3-7). 16.99 (978-0-06-200636-3(3), Greenwillow Bks.) HarperCollins Pubs.

Jones, Anne Marie. Mother Hen's Family Time Rhymes for Thought Book II. 2004. (YA). per. (978-1-4134-5837-4(8)) Borders Personal Publishing.

Jones, Carrie. Quest for the Golden Arrow. 2017. (Time Stoppers Ser.). (ENG.). 464p. (J). 16.99 (978-1-61963-863-1(0), 9781619638631, Bloomsbury USA Childrens) Bloomsbury Publishing USA.

—Time Stoppers. (Time Stoppers Ser.). (ENG.). (J). 2017. 400p. pap. 7.99 (978-1-68119-437-0(6), 9781681194370) 2016. 384p. 16.99 (978-1-61963-861-7(4), 9781619638617) Bloomsbury Publishing USA. (Bloomsbury USA Childrens).

Jones, Chris. Cameron Jack & the Key to the Universe. 2010. (Illus.). 136p. pap. 10.99 (978-1-4490-6547-8(3)) AuthorHouse.

Jones, Christianne C. Chicken Little, 1 vol. Hermanson, Kyle, illus. 2010. (My First Classic Story Ser.). (ENG.). 32p. (gr. k-3). lib. bdg. 22.65 (978-1-4048-6072-8(X), My First Classic Story) Picture Window Bks.

—John Henry, 1 vol. Robledo, Sol, tr. Peterson, Ben, illus. 2008. (Read-It! Readers en Español: Cuentos Exagerados Ser.).Tr. of John Henry. (SPA.). 32p. (gr. k-3). per. 3.95 (978-1-4048-2174-3(0), Easy Readers) Picture Window Bks.

—The Little Red Hen, 1 vol. Magnuson, Natalie, illus. 2010. (My First Classic Story Ser.). (ENG.). 32p. (gr. k-3). lib. bdg. 22.65 (978-1-4048-6073-5(8), My First Classic Story) Picture Window Bks.

Jones, Darynda. Death, Doom, & Detention. 2013. (Darklight Ser.: 2). (ENG.). 320p. (YA). (gr. 8-11). pap. 17.99 (978-0-312-62521-4(9), 9780312625214, St. Martin's Griffin) St. Martin's Pr.

Jones, Diana Wynne. Castle in the Air. 2008. (World of Howl Ser.: 2). 400p. (J). (gr. 3-7). pap. 7.99 (978-0-06-147877-2(6), Greenwillow Bks.) HarperCollins Pubs.

—Castle in the Air, 7 vols. 2009. (J). 94.75 (978-1-4361-6119-0(3)); 91.75 (978-1-4361-6121-3(5)); 73.75 (978-1-4361-6115-2(0)); 70.75 (978-1-4361-6117-6(7)); 156.75 (978-1-4361-6116-9(9)); 1.25 (978-1-4361-6112-1(6)) Recorded Bks., Inc.

—The Chronicles of Chrestomanci. (Chronicles of Chrestomanci Ser.: Nos. 1-2). (YA). (gr. 8-12). Vol. 1. 2007. 608p. pap. 8.99 (978-0-06-447268-5(X)) Vol. 2. 2007. 560p. pap. 8.99 (978-0-06-447269-2(8)) Vol. 3. 2008. 688p. pap. 8.99 (978-0-06-114832-3(6)) HarperCollins Pubs. (Greenwillow Bks.).

—The Chronicles of Chrestomanci Vol. 1: Charmed Life; The Lives of Christopher Chant, Vol. 1. 2007. (Chrestomanci Ser.). (YA). (gr. 5-8). lib. bdg. 19.65 (978-0-613-31070-3(5), Turtleback) Turtleback Bks.

—Conrad's Fate. 2006. (ENG., Illus.). 352p. (978-0-00-719087-4(5)) HarperCollins Children's Bks.

—Conrad's Fate. (J). 2006. (Chronicles of Chrestomanci Ser.: 3). 400p. (gr. 3-7). per. 6.99 (978-0-06-074745-9(5), Greenwillow Bks.) 2005. (Chrestomanci Ser.: No. 5). 384p. (gr. k-17). lib. bdg. 17.89 (978-0-06-074744-2(7)) 2005. (Chrestomanci Ser.: No. 5). 384p. (gr. 5-18). 16.99 (978-0-06-074743-5(9)) HarperCollins Pubs.

—Conrad's Fate: Read-Along/Homework Pack, 6 vols. 2005. (Chrestomanci Ser.: No. 5). (J). (gr. 5-8). 86.75 (978-1-4193-3551-8(0), 42039) Recorded Bks., Inc.

—Dogsbody. 2012. (ENG.). 288p. (YA). (gr. 7-18). 9.99 (978-0-14-242013-3(1), Firebird) Penguin Young Readers Group.

—Enchanted Glass. 2011. 304p. (J). (gr. 3-7). pap. 6.99 (978-0-06-186685-2(7), Greenwillow Bks.) HarperCollins Pubs.

—Fire & Hemlock. 2012. (ENG.). 496p. (YA). (gr. 7-18). 9.99 (978-0-14-242014-0(X), Firebird) Penguin Young Readers Group.

—House of Many Ways. 2008. 404p. (J). 9.99 (978-0-06-147798-0(2), Greenwillow Bks.) HarperCollins Pubs.

—House of Many Ways. 2009. (J). 1.25 (978-1-4361-6123-7(1)); 102.75 (978-1-4361-6130-5(4)); 245.75 (978-1-4361-6127-5(4)); 100.75 (978-1-4361-6132-9(0)); 79.75 (978-1-4361-6128-2(2)) Recorded Bks., Inc.

—Howl's Moving Castle. 2008. (World of Howl Ser.: 1). (ENG.). 448p. (J). (gr. 3-7). pap. 7.99 (978-0-06-147878-9(4), Greenwillow Bks.) HarperCollins Pubs.

—Howl's Moving Castle. 2009. 9.00 (978-0-7848-2484-9(3), Everbind) Marco Bk. Co.

—Howl's Moving Castle, 8 vols. 2008. (YA). 101.75 (978-1-4361-5953-1(9)); 1.25 (978-1-4361-5944-9(X)); 78.75 (978-1-4361-5947-0(4)); 75.75 (978-1-4361-5949-4(0)); 104.75 (978-1-4361-5951-7(2)); 179.75 (978-1-4361-5948-7(2)) Recorded Bks., Inc.

—The Merlin Conspiracy. 480p. (J). 2004. (Magids Ser.: 2). (gr. 3-7). pap. 9.99 (978-0-06-052320-6(4), Greenwillow Bks.) 2003. (gr. 5-18). 17.89 (978-0-06-052319-0(0)) HarperCollins Pubs.

—The Pinhoe Egg. (J). 2007. (Chronicles of Chrestomanci Ser.: 6). 480p. (gr. 3-7). per. 7.99 (978-0-06-113126-4(1), Greenwillow Bks.) 2006. (Chrestomanci Ser.: No. 6). 528p. lib. bdg. 18.89 (978-0-06-113125-7(3)) HarperCollins Pubs.

—Unexpected Magic: Collected Stories. 2006. 608p. (J). (gr. 3-7). per. 7.99 (978-0-06-055535-1(1), Greenwillow Bks.) HarperCollins Pubs.

Jones, Diana Wynne & Jones, Ursula. The Islands of Chaldea. 368p. (J). (gr. 3-7). 2015. pap. 9.99 (978-0-06-229508-8(X)) 2014. 17.99 (978-0-06-229507-1(1)) HarperCollins Pubs. (Greenwillow Bks.).

Jones, Frewin. The Charmed Return. 2011. (Faerie Path Ser.: 6). (ENG.). 368p. (YA). (gr. 8-18). 17.99 (978-0-06-087161-1(X), HarperTeen) HarperCollins Pubs.

—The Enchanted Quest. (Faerie Path Ser.: 5). (ENG.). 368p. (YA). (gr. 8). 2011. pap. 9.99 (978-0-06-087160-4(1)) 2010. 16.99 (978-0-06-087158-1(X)) HarperCollins Pubs. (HarperTeen).

—The Faerie Path. (Faerie Path Ser.: 1). (YA). 2008. (ENG., Illus.). 336p. (gr. 8-12). pap. 8.99 (978-0-06-087104-8(0), HarperTeen) 2007. (ENG.). 320p. (gr. 7-12). 16.99 (978-0-06-087102-4(4)) 2007. 312p. (gr. 7-12). lib. bdg. 17.89 (978-0-06-087103-1(2)) HarperCollins Pubs.

—The Faerie Path Bk. 4: The Immortal Realm. 2010. (Faerie Path Ser.: 4). (ENG.). 368p. (YA). (gr. 8). pap. 9.99 (978-0-06-087157-4(1), HarperTeen) HarperCollins Pubs.

—The Lost Queen. (Faerie Path Ser.: 2). (YA). 2008. (ENG.). 352p. (gr. 8). pap. 8.99 (978-0-06-087107-9(5), HarperTeen) 2007. 335p. (gr. 7). lib. bdg. 17.89 (978-0-06-087106-2(7), Eos) 2007. (ENG.). 352p. (gr. 7-12). 16.99 (978-0-06-087105-5(9), Eos) HarperCollins Pubs.

—The Seventh Daughter. 2009. (Faerie Path Ser.: 3). (ENG.). 352p. (YA). (gr. 8). pap. 9.99 (978-0-06-087110-9(5), HarperTeen) HarperCollins Pubs.

Jones, Gareth P. The Clan of the Scorpion. Finlayson, Luke, illus. 2013. (Ninja Meerkats Ser.: 1). (ENG.). 128p. (J). (gr. 2-4). pap. 5.99 (978-1-250-01664-5(9), 9781250016645) Square Fish.

—The Eye of the Monkey. Finlayson, Luke, illus. 2013. (Ninja Meerkats Ser.: 2). (ENG.). 128p. (J). (gr. 2-4). pap. 5.99 (978-1-250-01665-2(7), 9781250016652) Square Fish.

Jones, Heulwen. O'Grady's Well. 2005. (Illus.). 96p. pap. (978-1-84401-578-8(5)) Athena Pr.

Jones, Marcia Thornton & Dadey, Debbie. This Side of Magic. Stower, Adam, illus. 2009. (Keyholders Ser.: 1). (ENG.). 144p. (J). (gr. 2-5). 3.99 (978-0-7653-5982-7(0), 9780765359827, Starscape) Doherty, Tom Assocs., LLC.

Jones, Michael. Finding Imagine Nation. 2007. (YA). per. 10.95 (978-0-9789386-4-2(X)) Lucy Rose Publishing LLC.

Jones, Nathan Smith. Dragonkyn. 2017. (YA). pap. 14.99 **(978-1-4621-1978-3(6))** Cedar Fort, Inc./CFI Distribution.

Jones, P. T. & Tremblay, Paul. Floating Boy & the Girl Who Couldn't Fly. 2014. (ENG.). 280p. (J). (gr. 6). pap. 12.99 (978-1-77148-173-1(0)) ChiZine Pubns. CAN. Dist: Consortium Bk. Sales & Distribution.

Jones, T. W. Derth. 2006. 165p. pap. 24.95 (978-1-4241-0806-0(3)) PublishAmerica, Inc.

Jones, Ursula. The Lost King Trilogy: Part 1. 2012. (ENG.). 56p. (gr. 5-12). pap. (978-1-908458-12-4(7)) Inside Pocket Publishing, Ltd.

Jordan, Annie Laurie. Bogwaddle Pond. La Grange, Myrtle, illus. 2004. 25p. pap. 24.95 (978-1-4137-2013-6(7)) PublishAmerica, Inc.

Jordan, Robert. The Hunt Begins. Keegan, Charles, illus. 2005. (Great Hunt Ser.: Bk. 1). 397p. (gr. 5-9). 16.00 (978-0-7569-5065-1(1)) Perfection Learning Corp.

Jordan, Sophie. Hidden. 2012. (Firelight Ser.: 3). (ENG.). 272p. (YA). (gr. 8). 17.99 (978-0-06-193512-1(3)) HarperCollins Pubs.

—Reign of Shadows. 2016. (Reign of Shadows Ser.: 1). 304p. (YA). (gr. 8). 17.99 (978-0-06-237764-7(7), HarperTeen) HarperCollins Pubs.

—Rise of Fire. 2017. (Reign of Shadows Ser.: 2). 304p. (YA). (gr. 8). 17.99 (978-0-06-237767-8(1), HarperTeen) HarperCollins Pubs.

Joseph, A. Valentine. The Forest Is Our Home. 2012. 88p. pap. 9.95 (978-1-4759-4400-6(4)) iUniverse, Inc.

Joseph, Lila. The Boy Who Could Talk to Animals. 2008. 36p. pap. 18.95 (978-1-4327-2873-1(3)) Outskirts Pr., Inc.

Joslin, Nikolai. Life Beyond the Temple. 2016. (ENG., Illus.). (J). 27.99 **(978-1-63533-041-0(6)**, Harmony Ink Pr.) Dreamspinner Pr.

Joyce, William. The Fantastic Flying Books of Mr. Morris Lessmore. 2006. (978-0-06-050838-8(8)) HarperCollins Canada, Ltd.

—The Fantastic Flying Books of Mr. Morris Lessmore. Joyce, William & Bluhm, Joe, illus. 2012. (ENG.). 56p. (J). (gr. -1-3). 18.99 (978-1-4424-5702-7(3), Atheneum Bks. for Young Readers) Simon & Schuster Children's Publishing.

—Jack Frost. Joyce, William, illus. 2015. (Guardians of Childhood Ser.). (ENG., Illus.). 48p. (J). (gr. -1-3). 17.99 (978-1-4424-3043-3(5), Atheneum Bks. for Young Readers) Simon & Schuster Children's Publishing.

—The Sandman & the War of Dreams. Joyce, William, illus. 2013. (Guardians Ser.: 4). (ENG., Illus.). 240p. (J). (gr. 2-6). 15.99 (978-1-4424-3054-9(0), Atheneum Bks. for Young Readers) Simon & Schuster Children's Publishing.

Jubert, Hervé. Dance of the Assassins. Bell, Anthea, tr. from FRE. 2005. (Devil's Dances Ser.: Bk. 1). 400p. (J). (gr. 9-18). lib. bdg. 17.89 (978-0-06-077718-0(4)) HarperCollins Pubs.

Jubert, Herve. Devil's Tango. Bell, Anthea, tr. from FRE. 2006. (Devil's Dances Ser.). 376p. (YA). (gr. 7-12). lib. bdg. 17.89 (978-0-06-077721-0(4)) HarperCollins Pubs.

Juckes, Deborah Sioux. Meesha, Guardian of Grand Mountain: Book One of the Guardian Series. McCleary, Twila, illus. 2005. (YA). 18.95 (978-0-9767748-1-5(X)) Red Earth Publishing.

Jules. Bubble's World: Book Four Enchanted England. 2010. 40p. 16.99 (978-1-4520-5407-0(X)) AuthorHouse.

—Bubble's World: Isabella's Magic Dream. 2012. 58p. pap. 24.99 (978-1-4772-6956-5(8)) AuthorHouse.

Jules, Laurie. Tales from a Magical Kingdom. 2013. (ENG., Illus.). 176p. pap. (978-1-78088-328-1(5)) Troubador Publishing Ltd.

Julius, Nicholas. The Mythfitz: Unee the Unicorn. 2012. (ENG., Illus.). 62p. 28.95 (978-1-4327-9868-0(5)); pap. 23.95 (978-1-4327-9365-4(9)) Outskirts Pr., Inc.

Juncar, Nicola. The Legend of Thornton Wood. 2012. 238p. pap. (978-1-78176-184-7(1)) FeedARead.com.

Juster, Norton. The Annotated Phantom Tollbooth. Feiffer, Jules, illus. 2011. (ENG.). 320p. (J). (gr. 3-7). 29.99 (978-0-375-85715-7(X), Knopf Bks. for Young Readers) Random Hse. Children's Bks.

—The Odious Ogre. Feiffer, Jules, illus. 2010. (ENG.). 32p. (J). (gr. -1-2). 17.95 (978-0-545-16202-9(5), Di Capua, Michael) Scholastic, Inc.

—The Phantom Tollbooth. 2009. 9.14 (978-0-7848-0345-5(5), Everbind) Marco Bk. Co.

—The Phantom Tollbooth. Feiffer, Jules, illus. 2003. (J). mass mkt. 5.99 (978-0-440-23808-9(0), Laurel) Random House Publishing Group.

—The Phantom Tollbooth. Feiffer, Jules, illus. 256p. (J). pap. 4.99 (978-0-8072-1400-8(0), Listening Library) Random Hse. Audio Publishing Group.

Kaaberbøl, Lene. Life Stealer. Barslund, Charlotte, tr. from DAN. Eason, Rohan Daniel, illus. 2017. (Wildwitch Ser.). (ENG.). 160p. (J). (gr. 4-7). pap. 9.99 (978-1-78269-085-6(9), Pushkin Children's Bks.) Steerforth Pr.

—Oblivion. Barslund, Charlotte, tr. from DAN. Eason, Rohan, illus. 2016. (Wildwitch Ser.). (ENG.). 160p. (J). (gr. 4-7). pap. 9.99 (978-1-78269-084-9(0), Pushkin Press) Steerforth Pr.

—The Serpent Gift. 3rd ed. 2007. (Shamer Chronicles Ser.: 3). Orig. Title: Slangens Gave. (ENG.). 384p. (J). (gr. 5-9). pap. 22.99 (978-0-8050-8655-3(2), 9780805086553, Holt, Henry & Co. Bks. For Young Readers) Holt, Henry & Co.

—The Shamer's Daughter. 2006. (Shamer Chronicles Ser.: 1).Tr. of Skammerens Datter. (ENG.). 240p. (J). (gr. 5-9). pap. 14.99 (978-0-8050-8111-4(9), 9780805081114, Holt, Henry & Co. Bks. For Young Readers) Holt, Henry & Co.

—Wildfire. Barslund, Charlotte, tr. from DAN. Eason, Rohan, illus. 2016. (ENG.). 160p. (J). (gr. 4-7). pap. 9.99 (978-1-78269-083-2(2), Pushkin Children's Bks.) Steerforth Pr.

Kagawa, Julie. The Iron Daughter. 2010. (Iron Fey Ser.: 2). lib. bdg. 20.85 (978-0-606-14917-4(1), Turtleback) Turtleback Bks.

—The Iron Knight. 2011. (Iron Fey Ser.: 4). lib. bdg. 20.85 (978-0-606-23259-3(1), Turtleback) Turtleback Bks.

—The Iron Queen. 2011. (Iron Fey Ser.: 3). lib. bdg. 20.85 (978-0-606-23258-6(3), Turtleback) Turtleback Bks.

—The Iron Traitor. 2013. (Iron Fey Ser.: 6). lib. bdg. 20.85 (978-0-606-35037-2(3), Turtleback) Turtleback Bks.

—The Lost Prince. 2012. (Iron Fey Ser.: 5). lib. bdg. 20.85 (978-0-606-26946-9(0), Turtleback) Turtleback Bks.

Kahanek, Kristine Elizabeth. Katie & the Magic Umbrella: A Stormy Adventure. 2008. (Katie & the Magic Umbrella Ser.). (Illus.). 44p. (J). (gr. -1-4). 14.95 (978-0-9801423-0-3(X)) K.Co.Kids, LLC.

Kahn, J. Le Retour du Jedi, Vol. II.Tr. of Return of the Jedi. (FRE.). (J). pap. 11.95 (978-2-265-06728-8(8)) Fleuve Noir FRA. Dist: Distribooks, Inc.

Kaishaku. Eternal Alice Rondo, Vol. 4. 2007. (ENG., Illus.). 192p. pap. 9.95 (978-1-59796-123-3(X)) DrMaster Pubns. Inc.

Kamachi, Kazuma. A Certain Magical Index, Vol. 4. Haimura, Kiyotaka, illus. 2015. (Certain Magical Index Ser.: 4). (ENG.). 240p. (YA). (gr. 8-17). pap. 14.00 (978-0-316-34056-4(1), Yen Pr.) Orbit.

Kaminsky, Stuart M. Fever Pitch. 2003. (ENG., Illus.). 48p. (gr. 11-18). pap. 6.95 (978-0-9710129-9-8(7), 9780971012998) Moonstone.

Kananen, Barbara L. Fairies in My Garden. 2007. 106p. (YA). (gr. 2-2). per. 10.95 (978-0-595-45082-4(2)) iUniverse, Inc.

—Fairies in My Garden. 2007. 106p. (YA). (gr. 2-2). 20.95 (978-0-595-91014-4(9)) iUniverse, Inc.

Kane, Doug. Ariel's Journey. 2008. 256p. pap. 8.95 (978-0-9817234-0-2(3)) Blue Ink Pr.

Kane, Gil, et al, illus. Thor Epic Collection: A Kingdom Lost. 2014. (ENG.). 480p. (J). (gr. 4-17). pap. 34.99 (978-0-7851-8862-9(2)) Marvel Worldwide, Inc.

Kane, P. B. & Kane, Paul. The Rainbow Man. 2013. 162p. pap. 9.99 (978-0-9823322-3-8(8)) Rocket Ride Bks.

Kanemaki, Tomoco, et al. Kingdom Hearts II. 2017. (Kingdom Hearts II: the Novel Ser.: 1). (ENG.). 272p. pap. 16.00 **(978-0-316-47193-0(3)**, Yen Pr.) Orbit.

Kanietzko, Bryan & DiMartino, Michael Dante. Avatar. 2007. (Illus.). 96p. pap. 7.99 (978-1-59816-928-7(9), Tokyopop Kids) TOKYOPOP, Inc.

Kanzaka, Hajime & Yoshinaka, Shoko. Super-Explosive Demon Story: Return, 7 vols., Vol. 4. 2004. (Slayers Ser.). (Illus.). 192p. 9.99 (978-1-58664-914-2(0), CMX 64604G, CPM Manga) Central Park Media Corp.

Karandeev, Oleg. Dmitri: The Kind Storyteller Book One of Five. Ciesinska, Izabela, illus. 2006. 76p. (YA). per. 15.95 (978-0-9785728-9-1(0)) Digi-Tall Media.

Karchut, Darby. Gideon's Spear. 2014. (Finn Finnegan Ser.: 2). (ENG.). 240p. (J). (gr. 4-6). pap. 9.95 (978-1-937053-94-9(6), Spencer Hill Middle Grade) Spencer Hill Pr.

—The Hound at the Gate. 2015. (Adventures of Finn MacCullen Ser.: 3). (ENG.). 272p. (J). (gr. 4-8). pap. 9.95 (978-1-939392-48-0(9), Spencer Hill Middle Grade) Spencer Hill Pr.

Karcz, Lauren. The Gallery of Unfinished Girls. 2017. 352p. (YA). (gr. 8). 17.99 (978-0-06-246777-5(8), HarperTeen) HarperCollins Pubs.

Karesh, Tracy Ann. Brave Little Soldier. 2005. (J). pap. 15.00 (978-0-8059-6742-5(7)) Dorrance Publishing Co., Inc.

Kastigar, Jessica. The King of Hearts. 2006. 49p. pap. 16.95 (978-1-4241-3875-3(2)) PublishAmerica, Inc.

Kate, Lauren. Atlántida. 2015. (SPA.). 368p. pap. 10.95 (978-1-101-91062-7(3), Vintage Espanol) Knopf Doubleday Publishing Group.

Katheryn, Shelly. Legends of the New Worlds: In the Beginning. 2012. 116p. (J). (gr. -1). 22.19 (978-1-4669-2112-2(9)); pap. 12.19 (978-1-4669-2114-6(5)) Trafford Publishing.

Kaufman, Seufert. Wee Wilhelmina & Her Magic Marbles. 2012. (ENG.). pap. (978-1-4675-4364-4(0)) Independent Pub.

Kawahara, Reki. Red Storm Princess, Vol. 2. 2014. (Accel World Ser.: 2). (ENG.). 256p. (YA). (gr. 8-17). pap. 13.00 (978-0-316-29636-6(8), Yen Pr.) Orbit.

Kawahara, Yumiko. Dolls, 1. Kawahara, Yumiko, illus. 2004. (Dolls Ser.: 1). (ENG., Illus.). 200p. pap. 9.99 (978-1-59116-508-8(3)) Viz Media.

Kay, Elizabeth. Fury. 2012. (Stoke Books Titles Ser.). (ENG.). 80p. (YA). (gr. 8-12). pap. 6.95 (978-1-78112-097-2(8)); lib. bdg. 22.60 (978-1-78112-098-9(6)) Lerner Publishing Group.

Kazenbroot, Nelly. Down the Chimney with Googol & Googolplex, 1 vol. 2004. (Orca Echoes Ser.). (ENG., Illus.). 64p. (J). (gr. 2-3). pap. 6.95 (978-1-55143-290-8(0), 1234537) Orca Bk. Pubs. USA.

Kazimierski, Diana. The Star. 2009. 24p. pap. 11.99 (978-1-4389-3799-1(7)) AuthorHouse.

Keegan, Shannon. Legend of the Sea Fairies. 2006. (Illus.). (J). per. 14.99 (978-0-9773433-0-0(8)) Bixie Gate Publishing.

Keene, Carolyn. Green-Eyed Monster: Book One in the Eco Mystery Trilogy. 2009. (Nancy Drew (All New) Girl Detective Ser.: 39). (ENG.). 176p. (J). (gr. 3-7). pap. 5.99 (978-1-4169-7844-2(5), Aladdin) Simon & Schuster Children's Publishing.

Kehret, Peg. Flood Disaster. 2008. (ENG.). 160p. (J). (gr. 3-7). pap. 8.99 (978-1-4169-9109-0(3), Simon & Schuster/Paula Wiseman Bks.) Simon & Schuster/Paula Wiseman Bks.

Kelahan, Renee. Agua, the Mysterious Portuguese Water Dog. 2009. 108p. 20.95 (978-1-4401-5443-0(0)); pap. 10.95 (978-1-4401-5442-3(2)) iUniverse, Inc.

Kelborne, Wenna. The Stinkozimus. 2012. 356p. pap. 24.34 (978-1-4772-2282-9(0)) AuthorHouse.

Kelly, Joe, et al. Justice League Elite, Vol. 1. rev. ed. 2005. (ENG., Illus.). 208p. (YA). pap. 19.99 (978-1-4012-0481-5(3)) DC Comics.

Kelly, Lisa. The Many Adventures of Elysse: Her Journey Begins. 2012. 36p. pap. 16.99 (978-1-4525-5760-1(8)) Balboa Pr.

Kelly, Mij. A Bed of Your Own. McQuillan, Mary, illus. 2011. 32p. (J). (gr. -1-1). pap. 8.99 (978-0-7641-4768-5(4)) Barron's Educational Series, Inc.

Kelly, Nikki. Jonah. 2017. (Styclar Saga Ser.: 3). (ENG.). 352p. (YA). 17.99 (978-1-250-05154-7(1), 9781250051547) Feiwel & Friends.

—Lailah. 2014. (Styclar Saga Ser.: 1). (ENG.). 416p. (YA). (gr. 7). 17.99 (978-1-250-05151-6(7), 9781250051516) Feiwel & Friends.

Kelso, Mary Jean. Andy & Spirit Meet the Rodeo Queen. Snider, K. C., illus. 2010. 24p. pap. 10.95 (978-1-61633-031-6(7)) Guardian Angel Publishing, Inc.

Kemmerer, Brigid. Spirit. 2013. (ENG.). 432p. (YA). (gr. 9). pap. 9.95 (978-0-7582-7283-6(9), K-Teen) Kensington Publishing Corp.

Kemp, Dane. Imaginary Tales. 2011. 186p. pap. 24.95 (978-1-4560-4686-6(1)) America Star Bks.

Kennedy, Hugh J. The Flowers & the Fairies. 2009. 32p. pap. 18.97 (978-1-4490-0265-7(X)) AuthorHouse.

Kennedy, J. Aday. Cobbledom's Curse. Foster, Jack, illus. 2012. 20p. pap. 9.95 (978-1-61633-265-5(4)) Guardian Angel Publishing, Inc.

Kennedy, James. The Order of Odd-Fish. 2010. (ENG.). 416p. (YA). (gr. 7-18). mass mkt. 8.99 (978-0-440-24065-5(4), Laurel Leaf) Random Hse. Children's Bks.

Kennedy Tosten, S. Troy's Amazing Universe: A for Aliens. 2005. 124p. pap. 13.95 (978-1-59113-672-9(5)) Booklocker.com, Inc.

Kenner, Crystal R. The King of All Tickle Bugs & Other Stories. 2011. (Illus.). 124p. (gr. -1). pap. 10.95 (978-1-4502-9466-9(9)) iUniverse, Inc.

Kennerson, Vern. Love Stories for Children. Falk, Cathy Kennerson, illus. 2013. (ENG.). 67p. (YA). pap. 17.95 (978-1-4787-1665-5(7)) Outskirts Pr., Inc.

Kent, Elizabeth. The Enchanted Adventures of the Caroline Kemps. 2007. 148p. pap. 24.95 (978-1-4241-9915-0(8)) America Star Bks.

Kent, Neville. The Secrets of the Forest - the Time Zone. 2013. 88p. pap. (978-1-78299-795-5(4)) FeedARead.com.

Kenyon, Sherrilyn. Illusion. 2014. (Chronicles of Nick Ser.: Bk. 5). (ENG.). 464p. (YA). (gr. 7-12). 18.99 (978-1-250-00284-6(2), 9781250002846, St. Martin's Griffin) St. Martin's Pr.

—Inferno. 2013. (Chronicles of Nick Ser.: 4). (ENG.). 464p. (YA). (gr. 7). 18.99 (978-1-250-00283-9(4), 9781250002839, St. Martin's Griffin) St. Martin's Pr.

—Invision. 2016. (Chronicles of Nick Ser.: 7). (ENG.). 400p. (YA). (gr. 7-12). 19.99 (978-1-250-06388-5(4), 9781250063885, St. Martin's Griffin) St. Martin's Pr.

Kerbel, Deborah. Lure. 2010. (ENG.). 200p. (YA). (gr. 9). pap. 12.99 (978-1-55488-754-5(2)) Dundurn CAN. Dist: Ingram Publisher Services.

Kernaghan, Eileen. The Alchemist's Daughter. 2006. (ENG., Illus.). 144p. pap. 15.95 (978-1-894345-79-8(7)) Thistledown Pr., Ltd. CAN. Dist: Univ. of Toronto Pr.

—The Snow Queen. 2006. (ENG.). 160p. mass mkt. 14.95 (978-1-894345-14-9(2)) Thistledown Pr., Ltd. CAN. Dist: Univ. of Toronto Pr.

Kerwin, Betsy. The Adventures of Floret the Woodland Fairy: The Adventures Begin. 2008. 44p. pap. 18.49 (978-1-4343-9426-2(3)) AuthorHouse.

Kessler, Liz. The Castle in the Mist. Ledwidge, Natacha & Gibb, Sarah, illus. 2007. (Emily Windsnap Ser.: 3). (ENG.). 208p. (J). (gr. 3-7). 15.99 (978-0-7636-3330-1(5)) Candlewick Pr.

—The Castle in the Mist. 2012. (Emily Windsnap Ser.: 3). lib. bdg. 16.00 (978-0-606-25596-7(6), Turtleback) Turtleback Bks.

—Emily Windsnap & the Castle in the Mist. Ledwidge, Natacha, illus. 2012. (Emily Windsnap Ser.: 3). (ENG.). 208p. (J). (gr. 3-7). pap. 5.99 (978-0-7636-6017-8(5)) Candlewick Pr.

—Emily Windsnap & the Land of the Midnight Sun. Gibb, Sarah & Ledwidge, Natacha, illus. 2013. (Emily Windsnap Ser.: 5). (ENG.). 288p. (J). (gr. 3-7). 15.99 (978-0-7636-5824-3(3)) Candlewick Pr.

—Emily Windsnap & the Land of the Midnight Sun. 2014. (Emily Windsnap Ser.: 5). lib. bdg. 16.00 (978-0-606-35165-2(5)) Turtleback Bks.

—Emily Windsnap & the Monster from the Deep. Gibb, Sarah, illus. 2012. (Emily Windsnap Ser.: 2). (ENG.). 240p. (J). (gr. 3-7). pap. 5.99 (978-0-7636-6018-5(3)) Candlewick Pr.

—Emily Windsnap & the Monster from the Deep. 2012. (Emily Windsnap Ser.: 2). lib. bdg. 16.00 (978-0-606-25573-8(7), Turtleback) Turtleback Bks.

—Emily Windsnap & the Ship of Lost Souls. Gibb, Sarah, illus. 2015. (Emily Windsnap Ser.). (ENG.). 288p. (J). (gr. 3-7). 15.99 (978-0-7636-7688-9(8)) Candlewick Pr.

—Emily Windsnap & the Siren's Secret. (Emily Windsnap Ser.: 4). (ENG., Illus.). 304p. (J). (gr. 3-7). 2012. pap. 5.99 (978-0-7636-6019-2(1)) 2010. 15.99 (978-0-7636-4374-4(2)) Candlewick Pr.

—Emily Windsnap & the Siren's Secret. 2012. (Emily Windsnap Ser.: 4). lib. bdg. 16.00 (978-0-606-25601-8(6), Turtleback) Turtleback Bks.

—Haunt Me. 2017. (ENG.). (YA). (gr. 7). 17.99 **(978-0-7636-9162-2(3))** Candlewick Pr.

—Philippa Fisher & the Dream-Maker's Daughter. 2009. (Philippa Fisher Ser.: 2). (ENG., Illus.). 288p. (J). (gr. 3-7). 15.99 (978-0-7636-4202-0(9)) Candlewick Pr.

—Philippa Fisher's Fairy Godsister. 2008. (Philippa Fisher Ser.: 1). (ENG., Illus.). 256p. (J). (gr. 3-7). 15.99 (978-0-7636-4070-5(0)) Candlewick Pr.

Keyes, Morgan. Darkbeast. (ENG., (J). (gr. 5-9). 2013. Illus.). 304p. pap. 7.99 (978-1-4424-4206-1(9)) 2012. 288p. 16.99 (978-1-4424-4205-4(0)) McElderry, Margaret K. Bks. (McElderry, Margaret K. Bks.).

—Darkbeast Rebellion. 2013. (ENG., Illus.). 352p. (J). (gr. 5-9). 16.99 (978-1-4424-4208-5(5), McElderry, Margaret K. Bks.) McElderry, Margaret K. Bks.

Keyes, Pamela. Legend of Zamiel Zimbalist: Book Two of the Connedim Series. 2005. 280p. (YA). pap. 14.99 (978-1-59092-062-6(7)) Blue Forge Pr.

—Rune of Zachary Zimbalist: Book One of the Connedim Series. 2005. 280p. (YA). pap. 14.99 (978-1-59092-131-9(3)) Blue Forge Pr.

Khan, Joshua. Dream Magic. 2017. (ENG.). 352p. (J). (gr. 3-7). 16.99 (978-1-4847-3762-0(8)) Hyperion Bks. for Children.

—Shadow Magic. Hibon, Ben, illus. 2016. (ENG.). 336p. (J). (gr. 3-7). 16.99 (978-1-4847-3272-4(3)) Hyperion Bks. for Children.

Khoury, Jessica. The Forbidden Wish. 2017. lib. bdg. 20.85 **(978-0-606-40000-8(1))** Turtleback Bks.

Kibuishi, Kazu. Amulet, Bks. 1-7, Set. Kibuishi, Kazu, illus. 2016. (Amulet Ser.). (ENG., Illus.). 1344p. (J). (gr. 3-7). pap., pap., pap. 90.93 (978-1-338-04564-2(4)) Scholastic, Inc.

—The Cloud Searchers. (Amulet Ser.: 3). (ENG.). 208p. (J). (gr. 3-7). 2015. 24.99 (978-0-545-20884-0(X)) 2010. pap. 12.99 (978-0-545-20885-7(8)) Scholastic, Inc. (Graphix).

—Escape from Lucien. 2014. (Amulet Ser.: Bk. 6). (ENG., Illus.). 224p. (J). (gr. 3-7). pap. 12.99 (978-0-545-43315-0(0), Graphix) Scholastic, Inc.

—Escape from Lucien. 2014. (Amulet Ser.: 6). lib. bdg. 24.50 (978-0-606-36039-5(5)) Turtleback Bks.

—Firelight. 2016. (Amulet Ser.: 7). (ENG., Illus.). 208p. (J). (gr. 3-7). 24.99 (978-0-545-83966-2(1)); pap. 12.99 (978-0-545-43316-7(9)) Scholastic, Inc. (Graphix).

—Firelight. 2016. (Amulet Ser.: 7). (ENG., Illus.). 224p. (J). (gr. 3-7). lib. bdg. 24.50 (978-0-606-38070-6(1)) Turtleback Bks.

—The Last Council. (Amulet Ser.: 4). (ENG.). 224p. (J). (gr. 3-7). 2015. 24.99 (978-0-545-20886-4(6)) 2011. pap. 12.99 (978-0-545-20887-1(4)) Scholastic, Inc. (Graphix).

—The Lost Islands. 2013. (Explorer Ser.). (ENG., Illus.). 128p. (J). (gr. 3-7). 19.95 (978-1-4197-0881-7(3)); pap. 10.95 (978-1-4197-0883-1(X)) Abrams, Inc. (Amulet Bks.).

—Prince of the Elves. 2012. (Amulet Ser.: 5). (ENG., Illus.). 208p. (J). (gr. 3-7). pap. 12.99 (978-0-545-20889-5(0), Graphix) Scholastic, Inc.

—Prince of the Elves. 2012. (Amulet Ser.: 5). lib. bdg. 24.50 (978-0-606-26499-0(X), Turtleback) Turtleback Bks.

—The Stonekeeper's Curse. 2009. (Amulet Ser.: 2). (ENG., Illus.). 224p. (J). (gr. 3-7). pap. 12.99 (978-0-439-84683-7(8)); (gr. 4-7). 24.99 (978-0-439-84682-0(X)) Scholastic, Inc. (Graphix).

Kidd, Paul T. Father Christmas Adventures: Unexpected Tales of Christmas Magic. 2012. (ENG.). 92p. pap. (978-1-901864-12-0(X)) Cheshire Henbury.

Kidd, Ronald. Dreambender. (ENG.). 256p. (J). (gr. 3-7). 2017. pap. 9.99 **(978-0-8075-1726-0(7))** 2016. (Illus.). 16.99 (978-0-8075-1725-3(9)) Whitman, Albert & Co.

Kidwell, Justina. The Enchanted Garden & the Curse of the Evil Witch: The Kent Boys' Adventures. 2009. 68p. pap. 19.95 (978-1-60749-163-7(X)) America Star Bks.

Kiem, Elizabeth. Hider, Seeker, Secret Keeper. 2017. (Bolshoi Saga Ser.: 2). (ENG., Illus.). 272p. (YA). (gr. 9). pap. 10.99 (978-1-61695-569-4(4), Soho Teen) Soho Pr., Inc.

Kilgore, Lee. Widga's Quest, 1 vol. 2009. 48p. pap. 16.95 (978-1-4489-2517-9(7)) America Star Bks.

Kilworth, Garry. Attica. 2007. (ENG.). 352p. (gr. 7). pap. 11.95 (978-1-904233-56-5(2)) Little, Brown Book Group Ltd. GBR. Dist: Hachette Bk. Group.

Kim, Raeshin. The Legend of Goo-Shu: Journal 1. 2003. (Illus.). 179p. (YA). per. 17.95 net. (978-0-9743775-0-6(3)) RK Enterprises, Inc.

Kim, Susan & Klavan, Laurence. Wanderers. 2014. (Wasteland Ser.: 2). (ENG.). 368p. (YA). (gr. 9). 17.99 (978-0-06-211854-7(4), HarperTeen) HarperCollins Pubs.

Kimberly, Anne. Dark Well of Decision. 2007. 136p. per. 7.99 (978-0-9800356-5-0(1)) HIghland Pr. Publishing.

Kimberly Vogel. Everyone's Price: Book 4 of Rae's Story. 2006. 91p. 20.00 (978-1-4257-1610-3(5)); pap. 10.00 (978-1-4257-1611-0(3)) Xlibris Corp.

Kimmel, Elizabeth Cody. The Boxtrolls: A Novel. 2014. (Illus.). 246p. (J). (978-0-316-33263-7(1)) Little Brown & Co.

—Legend of the Ghost Dog. 2012. (ENG.). 208p. (J). (gr. 3-7). 16.99 (978-0-545-39127-6(X), Scholastic Pr.) Scholastic, Inc.

—Suddenly Supernatural: School Spirit. 2010. (Suddenly Supernatural Ser.: 1). (ENG.). 336p. (J). (gr. 3-7). pap. 7.99 (978-0-316-07821-4(2)) Little, Brown Bks. for Young Readers.

Kimmel, Eric A. Even Higher! A Rosh Hashanah Story by I. L. Peretz. Weber, Jill, illus. 2010. (ENG.). 32p. (J). (gr. -1-3). pap. 6.95 (978-0-8234-2298-2(4)) Holiday Hse., Inc.

—Joha Makes a Wish: A Middle Eastern Tale, 0 vols. Rayyan, Omar, illus. 2013. (ENG.). 40p. (J). (gr. k-3). pap. 7.99 (978-1-4778-1687-5(9), 9781477816875, Amazon Children's Publishing) Amazon Publishing.

—Joseph & the Sabbath Fish. Peluso, Martina, illus. 2011. (Shabbat Ser.). (ENG.). 32p. (J). (gr. k-3). lib. bdg. 17.95 (978-0-7613-5908-1(7), Kar-Ben Publishing) Lerner Publishing Group.

—The Three Princes. Fisher, Leonard Everett, illus. 2005. (Ala Notable Book Ser.). (ENG.). 32p. (J). (gr. k-3). pap. 6.95 (978-0-8234-1553-3(8)) Holiday Hse., Inc.

Kimmel, Jordan L. The Magic Gown. 2007. (Illus.). 144p. (J). (gr. 3-6). pap. (978-0-9785007-0-2(9)) Spring Tree Pr.

Kimmelman, Leslie. The Little Red Hen & the Passover Matzah. Meisel, Paul, illus. 2010. (ENG.). 32p. (J). (gr. -1-3). 16.95 (978-0-8234-1952-4(5)) Holiday Hse., Inc.

Kindler, Jennifer. Rita's Fairytale. 2011. 68p. pap. 10.95 (978-1-4575-0277-4(1)) Dog Ear Publishing, LLC.

King, Caro. Seven Sorcerers. 2011. (ENG.). 352p. (J). (gr. 3-7). 15.99 (978-1-4424-2042-7(1), Aladdin) Simon & Schuster Children's Publishing.

—Shadow Spell. 2012. (ENG.). 320p. (J). (gr. 3-7). pap. 6.99 (978-1-4423-3908-8(X), Aladdin) Simon & Schuster Children's Publishing.

—Shadow Spell. 2012. (ENG.). 320p. (J). (gr. 3-7). 15.99 (978-1-4424-2045-8(6), Simon & Schuster/Paula Wiseman Bks.) Simon & Schuster/Paula Wiseman Bks.

King, Clive. The Town That Went South. 2014. (ENG., Illus.). 128p. (J). (gr. 3-7). pap. 13.99 (978-1-4814-4487-3(5), Atheneum Bks. for Young Readers) Simon & Schuster Children's Publishing.

King, Emily R. The Fire Queen. 2017. (Hundredth Queen Ser.: 2). (ENG.). 286p. (YA). pap. 9.99 **(978-1-61109-749-8(5)**, 9781611097498, Skyscape) Amazon Publishing.

—The Hundredth Queen. 2017. (Hundredth Queen Ser.: 1). (YA). (ENG.). 300p. pap. 9.99 **(978-1-5039-4365-0(8)**, 9781503943650, Amazon Children's Publishing); **(978-1-5039-9865-0(7))** Amazon Publishing.

King, J. R. Arianna Kelt & the Renegades of Time: Signature Edition, Wizards of Skyhall Book 2. 2008. (ENG.). 256p. (J). 18.95 (978-1-57545-165-7(4), Reagent Pr. Echo) RP Media.

—Arianna Kelt & the Wizards of Skyhall. (J). 2008. (ENG.). 200p. 18.95 (978-1-57545-164-0(6), Reagent Pr. Echo) 2006. (Illus.). 200p. pap. 11.95 (978-1-57545-115-2(8)) 2006. (Illus.). 148p. per. 18.95 (978-1-57545-106-0(9), Reagent Pr. Echo) RP Media.

King, Jeremy Jordan. In Stone: A Grotesque Faerie Tale. 2012. (ENG.). 264p. (gr. 7). pap. 11.95 (978-1-60282-761-5(3)) Bold Strokes Bks.

King, Jo. A Flight of Fancy. 2011. 58p. 24.99 (978-1-4691-3665-3(1)); pap. 15.99 (978-1-4653-9298-5(X)) Xlibris Corp.

King, Ken. The Sunflower. Kearney, Jennifer, illus. 2008. 24p. (J). pap. 14.99 (978-1-4343-8463-8(2)) AuthorHouse.

KING, R. O. N. S. A trilogy of magical Tales. 2010. 500p. pap. 26.95 (978-1-4461-4016-1(4)) Lulu Pr., Inc.

King, Sharon. Oops Was Bullied? Hey, Why Did You Hurt Me That Way? LaRoe, Misty Bailey, illus. 2013. (ENG.). 32p. (J). pap. 16.95 (978-1-4787-1364-7(X)) Outskirts Pr., Inc.

King-smith, Dick. The Merman. unabr. ed. 2004. 102p. (J). (gr. 3-7). pap. 29.00 incl. audio (978-0-8072-8132-1(8), Listening Library) Random Hse. Audio Publishing Group.

King, Steve. The Stone Dragon. 2005. 80p. pap. 16.95 (978-1-4137-9628-5(1)) PublishAmerica, Inc.

King, Susan. A Place for Me Beneath the Se. 2009. 36p. pap. 15.49 (978-1-4343-8674-8(0)) AuthorHouse.

King, Wesley. Dragons vs. Drones. 2016. (Dragons vs. Drones Ser.: 1). (ENG.). 288p. (J). (gr. 3-7). 16.99 (978-1-59514-797-4(7), Razorbill) Penguin Young Readers Group.

—Enemy of the Realm. 2017. (Dragons vs. Drones Ser.: 2). (ENG.). 256p. (J). (gr. 3-7). 8.99 (978-1-59514-799-8(3), Razorbill) Penguin Young Readers Group.

Kingsley, Kaza. The Dragon's Eye. 2007. (Erec Rex Ser.). (Illus.). 384p. (J). (gr. 3-7). per. 9.99 (978-0-9786555-3-2(2)) Firelight Press, Inc.

—The Dragon's Eye. Grant, Melvyn, illus. 2009. (Erec Rex Ser.: 1). (ENG.). 368p. (J). (gr. 5-9). pap. 12.99 (978-1-4169-7933-3(6), Simon & Schuster Bks. For Young Readers) Simon & Schuster Bks. For Young Readers.

—Erec Rex: The Dragon's Eye. Payne, John, ed. Grant, Melvyn, illus. 2006. 360p. (J). 17.99 (978-0-9786555-6-3(7)) Firelight Press, Inc.

—Erec Rex: the Monsters of Otherness. 2007. (Erec Rex Ser.). (Illus.). 344p. (J). (gr. 3-7). 18.99 (978-0-9786555-7-0(5)) Firelight Press, Inc.

—The Monsters of Otherness. Grant, Melvyn, illus. 2009. (Erec Rex Ser.: 2). (ENG.). 352p. (J). (gr. 5-9). pap. 9.99 (978-1-4169-7934-0(4), Simon & Schuster Bks. For Young Readers) Simon & Schuster Bks. For Young Readers.

—The Search for Truth. Jacobus, Tim, illus. (Erec Rex Ser.: 3). (ENG.). (J). (gr. 5-9). 2010. 464p. pap. 9.99 (978-1-4169-7989-0(1)) 2009. 448p. 17.99 (978-1-4169-7988-3(3)) Simon & Schuster Bks. For Young Readers. (Simon & Schuster Bks. For Young Readers).

—The Secret of Ashona. Ng, James, illus. (Erec Rex Ser.: 5). (ENG.). 528p. (J). (gr. 5-9). 2013. pap. 8.99 (978-1-4169-7993-7(X)) 2012. 16.99 (978-1-4169-7992-0(1)) Simon & Schuster Bks. For Young Readers. (Simon & Schuster Bks. For Young Readers).

—The Three Furies. Ng, James & Mohrbacher, Peter, illus. 2011. (Erec Rex Ser.: 4). (ENG.). 576p. (J). (gr. 5-9). pap. 8.99 (978-1-4169-7991-3(3), Simon & Schuster Bks. For Young Readers) Simon & Schuster Bks. For Young Readers.

—The Three Furies. Mohrbacher, Peter, illus. 2010. (Erec Rex Ser.: 4). (ENG.). 576p. (J). (gr. 5-9). 16.99 (978-1-4169-7990-6(5), Simon & Schuster Bks. For Young Readers) Simon & Schuster Bks. For Young Readers.

Kipling, Rudyard. How the Elephant Got His Trunk: The Graphic Novel, 1 vol. Rodriguez, Pedro, illus. 2012. (Graphic Spin Ser.). (ENG.). 40p. (gr. 1-3). pap. 5.95 (978-1-4342-3880-1(6)); lib. bdg. 23.99 (978-1-4342-3222-9(0)) Stone Arch Bks. (Graphic Revolve).

—How the Rhinoceros Got His Skin: The Graphic Novel, 1 vol. Rodriguez, Pedro, illus. 2012. (Graphic Spin Ser.). (ENG.). 40p. (gr. 1-3). pap. 5.95 (978-1-4342-3882-5(2), Graphic Revolve) Stone Arch Bks.

—How the Rhinoceros Got His Skin: The Graphic Novel, 1 vol. Rodríguez, Pedro, illus. 2012. (Graphic Spin Ser.). (ENG.). 40p. (gr. 1-3). lib. bdg. 23.99 (978-1-4342-3025-6(2), Graphic Revolve) Stone Arch Bks.

Kirby, Matthew. Spider Stories. 2007. (ENG.). 242p. pap. 14.99 (978-1-4196-6359-8(3)) CreateSpace Independent Publishing Platform.

Kirby, Matthew J. Cave of Wonders. 2013. (Infinity Ring Ser.: 5). (ENG.). 192p. (J). (gr. 3-7). 16.99 (978-0-545-48460-2(X)) Scholastic, Inc.

—Icefall. (ENG.). 336p. (J). (gr. 3-7). 2013. pap. 6.99 (978-0-545-27425-8(7), Scholastic Paperbacks) 2011. 17.99 (978-0-545-27424-1(9), Scholastic Pr.) Scholastic, Inc.

—Island of the Sun. 2016. (Dark Gravity Sequence Ser.: 2). 384p. (J). (gr. 3-7). 16.99 (978-0-06-222490-3(5)) HarperCollins Pubs.

Kirk, Daniel. Elf Realm: The High Road. 2009. (Elf Realm Ser.). (ENG., Illus.). 576p. (YA). (gr. 7-11). 19.95 (978-0-8109-4075-8(2), Amulet Bks.) Abrams, Inc.

Kirkman, Robert. Marvel Knights 2099. 2005. (Marvel Heroes Ser.). (Illus.). 120p. (YA). pap. 13.99 (978-0-7851-1613-4(3)) Marvel Worldwide, Inc.

Kirkpatrick, Teresa. The Adventures of Four Friends on Vacation, 1 vol. 2009. 119p. pap. 19.95 (978-1-60836-927-0(7)) America Star Bks.

Kirkup, Mary. More Tales of Granny Grunt. 2012. (Illus.). 32p. (-18). pap. 19.76 (978-1-4490-9161-3(X)) AuthorHouse.

Kirsch, R. A. The Big One: (A Bicycle Tale), 1 vol. 2009. 191p. pap. 24.95 (978-1-60703-341-7(0)) PublishAmerica, Inc.

Kishimoto, Masashi. Naruto, Vol. 52. Kishimoto, Masashi, illus. 2011. (ENG., Illus.). 192p. pap. 9.99 (978-1-4215-3957-7(8)) Viz Media.

—Zatch Bell. 2004. 192p. pap. 9.95 (978-1-59116-679-5(9)) Viz Media.

Kittredge, Caitlin. The Iron Thorn. 2012. (Iron Codex Ser.). (ENG.). 512p. (YA). (gr. 7). pap. 10.99 (978-0-385-73830-9(7), Ember) Random Hse. Children's Bks.

—The Mirrored Shard: the Iron Codex Book Three. 2013. (Iron Codex Ser.). (ENG.). 304p. (YA). (gr. 7). 17.99 (978-0-385-73833-0(1), Delacorte Bks. for Young Readers) Random Hse. Children's Bks.

—The Nightmare Garden: the Iron Codex Book Two. 2013. (Iron Codex Ser.). (ENG.). 432p. (YA). (gr. 7). pap. 10.99 (978-0-385-73832-3(3), Ember) Random Hse. Children's Bks.

Kladstrup, Kristin. Garden Princess. 2015. (ENG.). 272p. (J). (gr. 5). pap. 7.99 (978-0-7636-7668-1(3)) Candlewick Pr.

Klein Bernstein, Sandy. The Door in the Sky. 2012. 268p. pap. 12.95 (978-1-4575-1111-0(8)) Dog Ear Publishing, LLC.

Klett, David E. Rachel & the Wizard of Lake Lure: The Lake Lure Chronicles - Book 2. 2006. (Illus.). (J). lib. bdg. 17.95 (978-0-9779325-1-1(6)) Five Oaks Pr.

Klimo, Kate. A Gathering of Wings. 2014. (Centauriad Ser.). (ENG.). 368p. (YA). (gr. 7). pap. 9.99 (978-0-375-87139-9(X), Ember) Random Hse. Children's Bks.

Kline, Suzy. Horrible Harry & the Mud Gremlins. Remkiewicz, Frank, illus. 2004. (Horrible Harry Ser.). (ENG.). 64p. (J). (gr. 2-4). 4.99 (978-0-14-240123-1(4), Puffin Books) Penguin Young Readers Group.

Klingele, Lindsey. The Broken World. 2017. 432p. (YA). (gr. 8). 17.99 **(978-0-06-238036-4(2)**, HarperTeen) HarperCollins Pubs.

Kloepfer, John. The Zombie Chasers. Wolfhard, Steve, illus. 2010. (Zombie Chasers Ser.: 1). (ENG.). 224p. (J). (gr. 3-7). 16.99 (978-0-06-185304-3(6)) HarperCollins Pubs.

Klutz Editors & Rose, Amber. Monsters. 2009. (Hammond Undercover Ser.). 72p. (J). (gr. 3-7). pap. 13.99 (978-0-8416-1497-0(0)) Hammond World Atlas Corp.

K.M. Mohr, John Kelley and. Waking Dalifi. 2005. 72p. pap. 9.95 (978-1-4116-6364-0(0)) Lulu Pr., Inc.

Kneff, Steff F. Emlyn & the Gremlin: Emlyn & the Gremlin Series. Spooner, Luke, illus. l.t. ed. 2014. 1. (ENG.). 52p. (gr. k-3). 26.95 (978-1-62253-399-2(2)); pap. 10.95 (978-1-62253-398-5(4)) Evolved Publishing.

Knickerbocker, S. J. King of the Ball. 2008. 24p. pap. 13.50 (978-1-60693-215-5(2), Eloquent Bks.) Strategic Book Publishing & Rights Agency (SBPRA).

Knight, Aya. The Chronicles of Kale: Dawn of Retribution. 2012. 456p. 28.95 (978-1-938083-13-6(X)); pap. 15.95 (978-1-938083-12-9(1)) Silver Knight Publishing, LLC.

Knight, Paul. Abbabuwas Mountain. 2006. 252p. per. (978-1-905529-65-0(1)) Grosvenor Hse. Publishing Ltd.

Knowles, Daniel S. Rodent. 2010. 718p. 34.99 (978-1-4535-2562-3(9)); pap. 23.99 (978-1-4535-2561-6(0)) Xlibris Corp.

Knox, Elizabeth. Dreamhunter. 2009. (Dreamhunter Duet Ser.: 1). (ENG.). 384p. (YA). (gr. 7-12). pap. 10.99 (978-0-312-53571-1(6), 9780312535711) Square Fish.

—Dreamquake. 2007. (Dreamhunter Duet Ser.: No. 2). 528p. (978-0-7322-8194-6(6), Fourth Estate) HarperCollins Pubs. Australia.

—Dreamquake. 2009. (Dreamhunter Duet Ser.: 2). (ENG., Illus.). 464p. (YA). (gr. 7-12). pap. 12.99 (978-0-312-58147-3(5), 9780312581473) Square Fish.

—Mortal Fire. 2014. (ENG.). 464p. (YA). (gr. 7). pap. 10.99 (978-1-250-05069-4(3), 9781250050694) Square Fish.

Knox nee Ramsamugh, Lorna. Fire the Wolf & His Magical Kingdom, 1 vol. 2010. 24p. pap. 24.95 (978-1-4489-6677-6(9)) PublishAmerica, Inc.

Knudsen, Michelle. The Dragon of Trelian. (Trelian Ser.). (ENG., Illus.). 416p. (J). (gr. 5-7). 2011. pap. 8.99 (978-0-7636-4993-7(7)) 2009. 16.99 (978-0-7636-3455-1(7)) Candlewick Pr.

—Mage of Trelian. 2016. (Trelian Ser.). (ENG.). 432p. (J). (gr. 5). 17.99 (978-0-7636-7436-6(2)) Candlewick Pr.

—The Princess of Trelian. (Trelian Ser.: 2). (ENG.). 448p. (J). (gr. 5). 2017. pap. 9.99 (978-0-7636-9455-5(X)) 2014. pap. 8.99 (978-0-7636-6935-5(0)) 2012. (Illus.). 16.99 (978-0-7636-5062-9(5)) Candlewick Pr.

Kobernick, J. W. Mary Margaret & the Magical Mall. 2010. (ENG., Illus.). 380p. (YA). 13.99 (978-0-615-38779-6(9)) Eryn Lace.

Kochalka, James. Dragon Puncher Book 1. 2010. (Dragon Puncher Ser.: 1). (ENG., Illus.). 40p. (J). (gr. 2-5). 9.95 (978-1-60309-057-5(6), 9781603090575) Top Shelf Productions.

—Dragon Puncher Book 2: Dragon Puncher Island: Dragon Puncher Island. 2011. (Dragon Puncher Ser.: 2). (ENG., Illus.). 40p. (J). (gr. 2-5). 9.95 (978-1-60309-085-8(1), 9781603090858) Top Shelf Productions.

Koehler, Hanne Lore & Laraya-Coutts, Corie. A Tale of a Malipayon Warrior. 2010. 128p. 21.95 (978-1-4502-1344-8(8)); pap. 11.95 (978-1-4502-1346-2(4)) iUniverse, Inc.

Koller, Jackie French. The Wizard's Scepter. 2012. (ENG., Illus.). 176p. (J). (gr. 3-7). pap. 9.99 (978-0-689-85593-1(1), Aladdin) Simon & Schuster Children's Publishing.

Komarnitsky, Kara. The Grimalkin's Secret. 2013. 242p. pap. 16.99 (978-0-9825528-1-0(5)) Stone Arrow Bks.

Komorn, Julie, adapted by. Out of the Dark. 2004. (W. I. T. C. H. Ser.: Bk. 8). (Illus.). 128p. (J). lib. bdg. 16.92 (978-1-4242-0789-3(4)) Fitzgerald Bks.

Komorn, Julie & Lenhard, Elizabeth, adapted by. The Light of Meridian. 2004. (W. I. T. C. H. Ser.: Bk. 7). (Illus.). 144p. (J). lib. bdg. 16.92 (978-1-4242-0794-7(0)) Fitzgerald Bks.

Kongyin. Gooby & the Dreamwalker. 2011. 296p. pap. (978-0-9869858-4-3(8)) Kima Global Pubs.

Koralek, Jenny. War Games. 216p. (J). pap. 8.99 (978-1-4052-0074-5(X)) Egmont Bks., Ltd. GBR. Dist: Trafalgar Square Publishing.

Kornher-Stace, Nicole. Archivist Wasp: A Novel. 2015. (ENG.). 256p. (YA). (gr. 6). pap. 14.00 (978-1-61873-097-8(5), Big Mouth Hse.) Small Beer Pr.

Kortvely, Zolton. Stories of a Lost Sock. 2012. 32p. pap. 14.50 (978-1-4669-6714-4(5)) Trafford Publishing.

Kova, Elise. The Crown's Dog. 2016. (Golden Guard Trilogy Ser.: Vol. 1). (ENG., Illus.). (YA). (gr. 7-12). 22.99 **(978-1-61984-590-9(3))**; pap. 11.99 **(978-1-61984-591-6(1))** Price World Publishing.

Kovac, Tommy. Wonderland #1. 2006. (Illus.). 24p. (YA). pap. 3.50 (978-1-59362-039-4(X), Slave Labor Graphics) Slave Labor Bks.

Kovalkova-McKenna, Svetlana & McKenna, Konstantin. Oberon. 2009. 44p. pap. 7.26 (978-0-557-06114-3(8)) Lulu Pr., Inc.

Krafft, Melody A. Finding Me. 2010. 40p. pap. 21.99 (978-1-4500-3932-1(4)) Xlibris Corp.

Krakower, Harold. Sugarland. 2008. 28p. pap. 12.50 (978-1-934925-12-6(8), Eloquent Bks.) Strategic Book Publishing & Rights Agency (SBPRA).

Kramer, Alan. The Three Little Pigs Wise up & the Princess Prince & the Vegetables. 2011. (Navigators Ser.). (J). pap. (978-1-61672-962-2(7)) Benchmark Education Co.

Kraszewski. Surf Angel. 2009. 40p. (978-0-9821989-0-2(6)) Kraszewski, Terry.

Kratzert, Barbara & Probst, Sharon Patrice. Bobby Bubblebug in the Bubblegum Tree Forest. 2009. 24p. pap. 11.49 (978-1-4389-4480-7(2)) AuthorHouse.

Kretzer, Joyce B. Shane & the Jackadoo: A Butcher Hollow Fantasy. 2008. 24p. pap. 11.49 (978-1-4389-1894-5(1)) AuthorHouse.

Kreuger, Jim & Averdonz, N. R. My Double-Edged Life, 1 vol. Padilla, Ariel, illus. 2007. (Z Graphic Novels / Tomo Ser.). (ENG.). 160p. (J). (gr. 3-7). pap. 6.99 (978-0-310-71301-2(3)) Zondervan.

Krise, Gale. It's a Colorful Candy Birthday. 2012. 24p. pap. 24.95 (978-1-4626-7604-0(9)) America Star Bks.

Krisp, Caleb. Somebody Stop Ivy Pocket. 2016. (Ivy Pocket Ser.: 2). (Illus.). 416p. (J). (gr. 3-7). 17.99 (978-0-06-236437-1(5), Greenwillow Bks.) HarperCollins Pubs.

Krohn, Genendel. I Wish I Were a King. Pelleg, Tirtsa, illus. 50p. 13.95 (978-1-58330-590-4(4)) Feldheim Pubs.

Krpata, Mitch. The Secret Society. Merritt, Kory, illus. 2017. (Poptropica Ser.). (ENG.). 112p. (J). (gr. 1-4). 9.95 (978-1-4197-2311-7(1), Amulet Bks.) Abrams, Inc.

Krueger, Jim & Rogers, Bud. The Argon Deception, 1 vol. Padilla, Ariel, illus. 2008. (Z Graphic Novels / Tomo Ser.). (ENG.). 160p. (J). (gr. 4-7). pap. 6.99 (978-0-310-71303-6(X)) Zondervan.

—Child of Destiny, 1 vol. Padilla, Ariel, illus. 2008. (Z Graphic Novels / Tomo Ser.). (ENG.). 160p. (J). (gr. 4-7). pap. 6.99 (978-0-310-71302-9(1)) Zondervan.

Krueger, Jim & Zondervan Staff. Betrayal of Trust, 1 vol. Rogers, Bud, ed. Padilla, Ariel, illus. 2009. (Z Graphic Novels / Tomo Ser.). (ENG.). 160p. (J). pap. 6.99 (978-0-310-71306-7(4)) Zondervan.

Krueger, K. S. Traegonia: The Ember Rune. 2011. 295p. 24.95 (978-1-4327-7718-0(1)); 304p. pap. 17.95 (978-1-4327-7604-6(5)) Outskirts Pr., Inc.

Krulik, Nancy. A Collection of Katie: Books 1-4. John and Wendy, illus. 2012. (Katie Kazoo, Switcheroo Ser.). (ENG.). 320p. (J). (gr. 2-4). pap. 7.99 (978-0-448-46304-9(0), Grosset & Dunlap) Penguin Young Readers Group.

—Let the Burping Begin. Blecha, Aaron, illus. 2012. (George Brown, Class Clown Ser.). (ENG.). 384p. (J). (gr. 2-4). pap. 8.99 (978-0-448-46284-4(2), Grosset & Dunlap) Penguin Young Readers Group.

—My Pops Is Tops! John and Wendy Staff, illus. 2007. (Katie Kazoo, Switcheroo Ser.: 25). (ENG.). 80p. (J). (gr. 2-4). pap. 3.99 (978-0-448-44441-3(0), Grosset & Dunlap) Penguin Young Readers Group.

—On Thin Ice. John and Wendy Staff, illus. 2007. (Katie Kazoo, Switcheroo Ser.: No. 6). (ENG.). 160p. (J). (gr. 2-4). pap. 5.99 (978-0-448-44447-5(X), Grosset & Dunlap) Penguin Young Readers Group.

—Three Burps & You're Out! 2013. (George Brown, Class Clown Ser.: 10). lib. bdg. 14.75 (978-0-606-31682-8(5), Turtleback) Turtleback Bks.

Krum, Atticus. The Taming. Donaera, Patrizia, illus. 2014. (ENG.). 227p. (J). pap. 12.99 (978-0-9885349-1-9(6)) Huntly Hse.

Krumwiede, Lana. Archon. 2015. (Psi Chronicles Ser.). (ENG.). 320p. (J). (gr. 5). pap. 7.99 (978-0-7636-7659-9(4)) Candlewick Pr.

—Freakling. 2014. (Psi Chronicles Ser.). (ENG.). 320p. (J). (gr. 5). pap. 7.99 (978-0-7636-6938-6(5)) Candlewick Pr.

Kubert, Andy. Cry Wolf, Vol. 10. 2007. (ENG., Illus.). 96p. (YA). (gr. 8-17). pap. 8.99 (978-0-7851-1405-5(X)) Marvel Worldwide, Inc.

Kueng, Christian Roulland. Three Genie Brothers. 2012. 270p. 27.95 (978-1-4759-6184-3(7)); pap. 17.95 (978-1-4759-6185-0(5)) iUniverse, Inc.

Kuhl, Debra. Sammy's Magic Carpet Ride, 1 vol. 2009. 73p. pap. 14.95 (978-1-4489-9204-1(4)) PublishAmerica, Inc.

Kuhn, Douglas Wolcik. Uncle Kyle's Magic Kite. Kuhn, Douglas Wolcik, illus. 2012. (Illus.). 28p. pap. 24.95 (978-1-4626-9699-4(6)) America Star Bks.

Kuipers, Jennifer L. Lynn's Magic Trunk: An Adventure in King Arthur's Court. 2007. 76p. per. 19.95 (978-1-4241-9860-3(7)) America Star Bks.

Kumar, Nishanth. The Book of the Heavens. 2013. 162p. (J). pap. 12.95 (978-1-62516-128-4(X), Strategic Bk. Publishing) Strategic Book Publishing & Rights Agency (SBPRA).

Kuplenk, Martina. The Angelettes. 2012. 28p. pap. 18.95 (978-1-4525-5256-9(8)) Balboa Pr.

Kupperberg, Paul & Loughridge, Lee. The Shadow Masters. Burchett, Rick, illus. 2014. (Superman Ser.). (ENG.). 56p. (gr. 2-3). pap. 4.95 (978-1-4342-2768-3(5), DC Super Heroes) Stone Arch Bks.

Kurchinski, Alessandra. Disney Story. 2010. 36p. pap. 17.30 (978-0-557-25447-7(7)) Lulu Pr., Inc.

Kurlander, Keith. Tommy the Fishboy. Belomlinsky, Alex, illus. 2012. 34p. 24.95 (978-1-4626-4527-5(5)) America Star Bks.

Kuroda, Yosuke & Hayashiya, Shizuru. Onegai Teacher, No. 2. 2003. 120p. pap. 9.95 (978-1-58899-179-9(2)) ComicsOne Corp./Dr. Masters.

Kurty, G. Thomas the Treemaker: a Short Story about a Tall Tale. 2007. (ENG.). 76p. per. 19.95 (978-1-4241-6219-2(X)) America Star Bks.

Kurumada, Masami. Knights of the Zodiac (Saint Seiya), Vol. 6. Kurumada, Masami, illus. 2004. (ENG., Illus.). 200p. pap. 7.95 (978-1-59116-525-5(3)) Viz Media.

—Knights of the Zodiac, Vol. 5. Kurumada, Masami, illus. 2004. (ENG., Illus.). 200p. pap. 7.95 (978-1-59116-470-8(2)) Viz Media.

Kusaka, Hidenori. Pokémon Black & White, Vol. 17. Yamamoto, Satoshi, illus. 2014. (ENG.). 88p. (J). pap. 4.99 (978-1-4215-6769-3(5)) Viz Media.

Kuykendoll, Kim. The Adventures of the Coral Way Gang. 2008. 160p. pap. 13.99 (978-1-60477-840-3(7)) Salem Author Services.

Kuyper, Sjoerd. The Swan's Child. Jutte, Jan, illus. 2005. (ENG.). 128p. (J). (gr. 5-9). 16.95 (978-0-8234-1861-9(8)) Holiday Hse., Inc.

Kwaymullina, Ambelin. The Foretelling of Georgie Spider: The Tribe Book 3. 2017. (Tribe Ser.). (ENG.). 448p. (J). (gr. 7). 17.99 (978-0-7636-9210-0(7)) Candlewick Pr.

Kyber, Manifred. Fables & Fairytales to Delight All Ages Book Two: Gossamer Kingdoms, 3 vols. 2007. (ENG., Illus.). 140p. per. (978-1-84401-985-4(3)) Athena Pr.

LaBaff, Stephanie. Draw Princesses in 4 Easy Steps: Then Write a Story. LaBaff, Tom, illus. 2012. (Drawing in 4 Easy Steps Ser.). 48p. (J). (gr. 3-18). 25.27 (978-0-7660-3838-7(6)) Enslow Pubs., Inc.

Labaff, Stephanie. Draw Princesses in 4 Easy Steps: Then Write a Story. LaBaff, Tom, illus. 2012. (Drawing in 4 Easy Steps Ser.). 48p. (J). (gr. 3-18). pap. 8.95 (978-1-4644-0011-7(3), Enslow Elementary) Enslow Pubs., Inc.

Labenne, Jonathan A. Annual Bear Dance. 2013. (Illus.). 64p. pap. 23.95 (978-1-4525-6633-7(X)) Balboa Pr.

Lacek, Carolyn. Destiny Awakened. 2009. 52p. pap. 18.25 (978-1-60860-736-5(4), Eloquent Bks.) Strategic Book Publishing & Rights Agency (SBPRA).

Lachtman, Ofelia Dumas. The Truth about las Mariposas. 2007. 144p. (J). (gr. 6-18). pap. 9.95 (978-1-55885-494-9(0), Piñata Books) Arte Publico Pr.

Lackey, Mercedes. Apex. 2017. (Hunter Ser.: 3). (ENG.). 304p. (YA). (gr. 7-17). 18.99 **(978-1-4847-0786-9(9))** Hyperion Bks. for Children.

—Elite: A Hunter Novel. (Hunter Ser.). (ENG.). (YA). (gr. 7-17). 2017. 384p. pap. 9.99 **(978-1-4847-4784-1(4))** 2016. (Illus.). 368p. 17.99 (978-1-4847-0785-2(0)) Hyperion Bks. for Children.

—Elite: A Hunter Novel. 2017. (Hunter Ser.: 2). (YA). lib. bdg. 20.85 **(978-0-606-40645-1(X))** Turtleback Bks.

Lackey, Mercedes. Hunter. 2016. (Hunter Ser.). (ENG., Illus.). 400p. (YA). (gr. 7-12). pap. 9.99 (978-1-4847-2543-6(3)) Hyperion Bks. for Children.

—Hunter. 2016. (Hunter Ser.: 1). (YA). lib. bdg. 20.85 (978-0-606-38309-7(3)) Turtleback Bks.

Lackey, Mercedes, ed. Hunter. 2015. (Hunter Ser.). (ENG., Illus.). 380p. (YA). (gr. 7-12). 17.99 (978-1-4847-0784-5(2)) Hyperion Bks. for Children.

Lackey, Mercedes & Edghill, Rosemary. Legacies, No. 1. 2010. (Shadow Grail Ser.: 1). (ENG.). 320p. (YA). (gr. 8-12). pap. 11.99 (978-0-7653-1761-2(3), Tor Teen) Doherty, Tom Assocs., LLC.

Lacy, Kendra. The Stone Garden. 2004. 72p. (YA). pap. 8.95 (978-0-595-30719-7(1)) iUniverse, Inc.

LaFevers, R. L. The Forging of the Blade. 2006. (ENG.). 144p. (J). (gr. 3-7). 5.99 (978-0-14-240557-4(4), Puffin Books) Penguin Young Readers Group.

Lagerlof, Selma. The Wonderful Adventures of Nils. 2004. reprint ed. pap. 1.99 (978-1-4192-8845-6(8)); pap. 34.95 (978-1-4191-8845-9(3)) Kessinger Publishing, LLC.

—The Wonderful Adventures of Nils. Latyk, Olivier, illus. 2016. (ENG.). 64p. (J). (gr. 3-6). 19.95 **(978-1-910277-19-5(3)**, Words & Pictures) Quarto Publishing Group UK GBR. Dist: Hachette Bk. Group.

—The Wonderful Adventures of Nils. Howard, Velma Swanston, tr. 2003. 284p. pap. 14.95 (978-1-59224-322-8(3)) Wildside Pr., LLC.

—The Wonderful Adventures of Nils. 2003. 32.95 (978-1-59224-745-5(8)) Wildside Pr., LLC.

Lagonegro, Melissa. Barbie in Princess Power - Saving the Day! 2015. (Step into Reading Ser.). (ENG., Illus.). 24p. (J). (gr. -1-1). 4.99 (978-0-553-50890-1(3), Random Hse. Bks. for Young Readers) Random Hse. Children's Bks.

LAIKA & Rosen, Lucy. Kubo & the Two Strings: His Adventure Begins. 2016. (ENG.). 24p. (J). (gr. -1-3). pap. 5.99 (978-0-316-36140-8(2)) Little, Brown Bks. for Young Readers.

Lake, A. J. The Coming of Dragons: The Darkest Age. 2007. (Darkest Age Ser.). (ENG., Illus.). 256p. (YA). (gr. 4-7). per. 7.99 (978-1-58234-902-2(9), 9781582349022, Bloomsbury USA Childrens) Bloomsbury Publishing USA.

Lalwani, Shalaka. Mrs. Mulberry's Winter, 1 vol. 2010. 32p. 24.95 (978-1-4512-2436-8(2)) PublishAmerica, Inc.

Lam, Laura. Pantomime. 2017. (Micah Grey Trilogy Ser.: 1). (ENG.). 400p. (YA). (gr. 7). 12.99 (978-1-5098-0777-2(2)) Pan Macmillan GBR. Dist: Independent Pubs. Group.

LaMar, Brad A. The Megalith Union. Adasikov, Igor, illus. 2013. (Celtic Mythos Ser.). (ENG.). 342p. pap. 16.99 (978-1-61153-070-4(9)) Light Messages Publishing.

Lamb, Enelle. Christopher Collin & the True Okemus - the Adventure Begins. 2009. 123p. pap. 13.00 (978-0-557-05783-2(3)) Lulu Pr., Inc.

Lambert, George J. 8 Boys & 8 Beasts, 1 vol. Lambert, Celeste, illus. 2010. 24p. 24.95 (978-1-4489-5901-3(2)) PublishAmerica, Inc.

Lamere, Jill. The King's Crown. 2007. (Illus.). 5p. (J). (gr. -1). vinyl bd. 14.95 (978-0-9772320-2-4(6)) Minikin Pr.

Lamond, Peter. The Rainforest Family & Those Terrible Toads. Purnell, Teresa, illus. 2011. 92p. pap. 27.25 (978-1-60976-297-1(5), Eloquent Bks.) Strategic Book Publishing & Rights Agency (SBPRA).

Lamont, Jess. Peter's Garden. 2003. 230p. (YA). pap. 14.95 (978-0-9740319-0-3(9)) Added Upon, Inc.

Lamont, Kelton. Super K: The Attack of the Popcorn Chicken. 2010. 48p. (gr. -1). pap. 10.95 (978-1-4490-9939-8(4)) AuthorHouse.

Lampman, Annette. Nicole's Wish. 2006. 23.00 (978-0-8059-9146-8(8)) Dorrance Publishing Co., Inc.

Lanagan, Margo. Tender Morsels. 2010. (ENG.). 464p. (YA). (gr. 9-18). pap. 11.99 (978-0-375-84305-1(1), Ember) Random Hse. Children's Bks.

Lancaster, Janie. Julie & the Lost Fairy Tale. 2006. (Illus.). 116p. (J). per. 10.95 (978-1-932993-60-8(6)) Star Publish LLC.

Lancett, Peter. Escape from the Dark (Blue Series), 1 vol. 2015. (Dark Man Ser.). (ENG.). 36p. (YA). (gr. 9-12). pap. 7.95 (978-1-68021-126-9(9)) Saddleback Educational Publishing, Inc.

—The Shadow in the Dark, 1 vol. unabr. ed. 2010. (Dark Man Ser.). (ENG.). 34p. (YA). (gr. 9-12). pap. 7.95 (978-1-61651-021-3(8)) Saddleback Educational Publishing, Inc.

Land, Linda C. The Mysterious Traveling Trunk. 2011. 156p. 23.50 (978-1-4269-6160-1(X)); pap. 13.50 (978-1-4269-6161-8(8)) Trafford Publishing.

Land of Dawny Dusk: Fruit. 2003. (978-0-9720334-0-4(8)) Nicewood Imagined.

The Land of the Blue Flower. 2006. 76p. pap. 7.45 (978-1-59462-377-6(5), 413, Book Jungle) Standard Pubns., Inc.

Land of the Dawny Dusk: Seashell. 2003. (978-0-9720334-1-1(6)) Nicewood Imagined.

Landers, Ace. Anakin to the Rescue! White, David A., illus. 2012. (Lego Star Wars Ser.). (ENG.). 24p. (J). (gr. -1-3). pap. 3.99 (978-0-545-47066-7(8)) Scholastic, Inc.

Landy, Derek. And He's the Good Guy. Percival, Tom, illus. 2007. (Skulduggery Pleasant Ser.: 1). (ENG.). 400p. (J). (gr. 5-7). 17.99 (978-0-06-123115-5(0)) HarperCollins Pubs.

—Dark Days, 4. (ENG.). 416p. pap. (978-0-00-732597-9(5)) HarperCollins Children's Bks.

—The Faceless Ones. (Skulduggery Pleasant Ser.: 3). (ENG.). 432p. (J). (gr. 5). 2010. pap. 7.99 (978-0-06-124093-5(1)) 2009. 16.99 (978-0-06-124091-1(5)) HarperCollins Pubs.

—The Faceless Ones: A California Gothic. 2007. (Skulduggery Pleasant Ser.: Bk. 3). (SPA.). 335p. (978-84-675-1984-6(3)) SM Ediciones.

—Playing with Fire. (Skulduggery Pleasant Ser.: 2). (ENG.). (J). (gr. 5). 2009. 416p. pap. 7.99 (978-0-06-124090-4(7)) 2008. 400p. 16.99 (978-0-06-124088-1(5)) HarperCollins Pubs.

—Scepter of the Ancients. Percival, Tom, illus. 2008. (Skulduggery Pleasant Ser.: 1). (ENG.). 416p. (J). (gr. 5). pap. 7.99 (978-0-06-123117-9(7)) HarperCollins Pubs.

Lane, Amy. Triane's Son Fighting. 2nd ed. 2016. (ENG., Illus.). (J). 32.99 **(978-1-63477-982-1(7))** 2014. (Bitter Moon Ser.: Bk. 3). 350p. pap. 17.99 (978-1-62798-340-2(6)) Dreamspinner Pr. (Harmony Ink Pr.).

—Triane's Son Learning. 2nd ed. 2016. (ENG., Illus.). (J). 29.99 **(978-1-63477-983-8(5))** 2014. (Bitter Moon Ser.: Bk. 2). 324p. pap. 17.99 (978-1-62798-339-6(2)) Dreamspinner Pr. (Harmony Ink Pr.).

Lane, Amy. Triane's Son Reigning. 2nd ed. 2016. (ENG., Illus.). (J). 29.99 **(978-1-63477-984-5(3))** 2014. (Bitter Moon Ser.: Bk. 4). 320p. pap. 17.99 (978-1-62798-343-3(0)) Dreamspinner Pr. (Harmony Ink Pr.).

Lane, Andy. Glendale: Nashville's Magical Park. Sloan, Michael, illus. 2009. 88p. (J). 22.95 (978-1-57736-408-5(2)) Providence Hse Pubs.

Lane, Leonie. The Retford Witch Catchers. 2005. 144p. per. (978-1-84667-002-2(0)) Derwent Pr., The.

Lang, Andrew. The Crimson Fairy Book. 2007. 384p. 29.95 (978-1-4344-9149-7(8)); per. 19.95 (978-1-4344-9055-1(6)) Wildside Pr., LLC.

—The Green Fairy Book. 2007. 384p. 31.95 (978-1-4218-3823-6(0)); per. 15.95 (978-1-4218-3923-3(7)) 1st World Publishing, Inc. (1st World Library - Literary Society).

—The Grey Fairy Book. 2007. 332p. per. 14.95 (978-1-4218-3924-0(5), 1st World Library - Literary Society) 1st World Publishing, Inc.

—The Lilac Fairy Book. l.t. ed. 2005. 508p. pap. (978-1-84637-149-3(X)) Echo Library.

—The Orange Fairy Book. 2007. 332p. per. 14.95 (978-1-4218-3925-7(3), 1st World Library - Literary Society) 1st World Publishing, Inc.

—The Red Fairy Book. 2007. 444p. per. 18.95 (978-1-4218-3926-4(1), 1st World Library - Literary Society) 1st World Publishing, Inc.

—The Yellow Fairy Book. 2007. 396p. per. 15.95 (978-1-4218-4502-9(4)); 31.95 (978-1-4218-4418-3(4)) 1st World Publishing, Inc. (1st World Library - Literary Society).

Lang, Andrew, ed. The Green Fairy Book. 2007. 316p. per. (978-1-4065-2615-8(0)) Dodo Pr.

Lang, Heidi & Bartkowski, Kati. A Dash of Dragon. 2017. (ENG., Illus.). 320p. (J). (gr. 3-7). 17.99 **(978-1-4814-7793-2(5)**, Aladdin) Simon & Schuster Children's Publishing.

Langlois, Annie. Victorine et la Pièce D'or. Beshwaty, Steve, tr. 2003. (Picture Bks.). (FRE., Illus.). 32p. (J). (gr. -1). pap. (978-2-89021-658-7(6)) Diffusion du livre Mirabel (DLM).

Langner, Mark Eugene. The One Window. 2012. 264p. pap. 13.95 (978-0-9840120-2-2(8)) Aliso Street Productions.

Langrish, Katherine. The Shadow Hunt. 2010. 322p. lib. bdg. (978-0-06-111678-0(5)) HarperCollins Pubs.

—Troll Blood. 2011. (ENG., Illus.). 416p. (J). pap. 14.99 (978-0-00-721488-4(X), HarperCollins Children's Bks.) HarperCollins Pubs. Ltd. GBR. Dist: HarperCollins Pubs.

Lanza, Barbara. Time to Fly: A Fairy Lane Book. Lanza, Barbara, illus. 2005. (ENG., Illus.). 32p. (J). (gr. 4-7). 19.95 (978-0-9724853-7-1(6)) Keene Publishing.

Laplante, Carole. The Magic Is in You. Byrne-Walker, Mary Ann, illus. 2012. 36p. pap. 9.95 (978-1-62006-055-1(8)) Sunbury Press, Inc.

Larbalestier, Justine. How to Ditch Your Fairy. 2009. (ENG.). 336p. (YA). (gr. 7). pap. 8.99 (978-1-59990-379-8(2), 9781599903798, Bloomsbury USA Childrens) Bloomsbury Publishing USA.

LaRose, Melinda & Disney Book Group Staff. The Croc Takes the Cake. Disney Storybook Artists Staff, illus. 2012. (World of Reading Ser.). (ENG.). 32p. (J). (gr. -1-k). pap. 3.99 (978-1-4231-5543-0(2)) Disney Pr.

—Jake Hatches a Plan, Pre-Level 1. Disney Storybook Art Team, illus. 2012. (World of Reading Ser.). (ENG.). 32p. (J). (gr. -1-k). pap. 3.99 (978-1-4231-5542-3(4)) Disney Pr.

Larsen, Angela Sage. Broken Record, Bk. 4. 2013. (Fifties Chix Ser.: 4). (ENG., Illus.). 200p. (YA). pap. 9.95 (978-1-60746-446-4(2), Premiere) FastPrncil, Inc.

—Third Time's a Charm, Bk. 3. 2013. (Fifties Chix Ser.: 3). (ENG.). 200p. (YA). pap. 9.95 (978-1-60746-155-5(2), Premiere) FastPrncil, Inc.

Larsen, C. S. The Chronicles of Marvin Archibald Trekker: Boy Magician Book 1 - Penguins of Choice. l.t. ed. 2006. (Illus.). 163p. (YA). per. 5.99 (978-0-9779844-1-1(9)) KnowledgeGain Inc.

Larsen, Erik. Savage Dragon on Trial TP. 2013. (ENG., Illus.). 128p. (YA). pap. 16.99 (978-1-60706-755-9(2), 9781607067559) Image Comics.

Larsen, Patti. Sassafras. 2013. 290p. pap. (978-1-927464-36-6(6)) Larsen, Patti.

Larson, M. A. Pennyroyal Academy. 2014. (Pennyroyal Academy Ser.: 1). (ENG.). 320p. (J). (gr. 5). 16.99 (978-0-399-16324-1(7), G.P. Putnam's Sons Books for Young Readers) Penguin Young Readers Group.

Larson, Sara B. Ignite. 2015. (Defy Trilogy: Bk. 2). (ENG.). 304p. (J). (gr. 7). pap. 9.99 (978-0-545-83563-3(1), Scholastic Paperbacks) Scholastic, Inc.

Larwood, Kieran. Podkin One-Ear. Wyatt, David, illus. 2017. (Longburrow Ser.). (ENG.). 256p. (J). (gr. 5-7). 16.99 **(978-1-328-69582-6(4))** Houghton Mifflin Harcourt Publishing Co.

Lascurain, Anna. Apollo in the Moon House. 2006. Orig. Title: The Moonboy. (J). per. 7.99 (978-0-9769612-3-9(7)) Darker Intentions Pr.

Lasky, Kathryn. The Coming of Hoole. 2006. (Guardians of Ga'hoole Ser.: 10). (ENG., Illus.). 240p. (J). (gr. 3-7). 6.99 (978-0-439-79569-2(9), Scholastic Paperbacks) Scholastic, Inc.

—Exile. 2008. (Guardians of Ga'hoole Ser.: 14). (ENG., Illus.). 224p. (J). (gr. 3-7). 6.99 (978-0-439-88808-0(5), Scholastic Paperbacks) Scholastic, Inc.

—Frost Wolf. 2012. (Wolves of the Beyond Ser.: 4). (ENG.). 256p. (J). (gr. 3-7). pap. 6.99 (978-0-545-09317-0(1), Scholastic Pr.) Scholastic, Inc.

—Frost Wolf. 2012. (Wolves of the Beyond Ser.: 4). lib. bdg. 17.20 (978-0-606-26739-7(5), Turtleback) Turtleback Bks.

—The Golden Tree. 2007. (Guardians of Ga'Hoole Ser.: 12). (Illus.). 192p. lib. bdg. 17.20 (978-1-4177-8260-4(9), Turtleback) Turtleback Bks.

—The Journey. 2003. (Guardians of Ga'hoole Ser.: 2). (ENG.). 256p. (J). (gr. 3-7). mass mkt. 6.99 (978-0-439-40558-4(0), Scholastic Paperbacks) Scholastic, Inc.

—The Journey. l.t. ed. 2007. (Guardians of Ga'Hoole Ser.: Bk. 2). (Illus.). 271p. (J). (gr. 3-7). 22.95 (978-1-4104-0293-6(2)) Thorndike Pr.

—The Journey. 2003. (Guardians of Ga'Hoole Ser.: 2). (gr. 3-6). lib. bdg. 17.20 (978-0-613-72135-6(7), Turtleback) Turtleback Bks.

—Lone Wolf. 2011. (Wolves of the Beyond Ser.: 1). (ENG.). 240p. (J). (gr. 3-7). pap. 6.99 (978-0-545-09311-8(2)) Scholastic, Inc.

—Lost Tales of Ga'Hoole. Huang, Kathryn, illus. 2010. (Guardians of Ga'hoole Ser.). (ENG.). 192p. (J). (gr. 3-7). 6.99 (978-0-545-10244-5(8), Scholastic Paperbacks) Scholastic, Inc.

—The Rise of a Legend. 2015. (Guardians of Ga'Hoole Ser.: 0). lib. bdg. 17.20 (978-0-606-37024-0(2)) Turtleback Bks.

—The River of Wind. 2007. (Guardians of Ga'Hoole Ser.: 13). lib. bdg. 17.20 (978-1-4177-8261-1(7), Turtleback) Turtleback Bks.

—Shadow Wolf. (Wolves of the Beyond Ser.: 2). (ENG.). (J). (gr. 3-7). 2011. 288p. pap. 6.99 (978-0-545-09313-2(9)) 2010. 272p. 17.99 (978-0-545-09312-5(0)) Scholastic, Inc. (Scholastic Pr.).

—Spirit Wolf. Cowdrey, Richard, illus. 2013. (Wolves of the Beyond Ser.: 5). (ENG.). 240p. (J). (gr. 3-7). pap. 6.99 (978-0-545-27971-0(2), Scholastic Pr.) Scholastic, Inc.

—Spirit Wolf. 2012. (Wolves of the Beyond Ser.: 5). (ENG.). 240p. (J). (gr. 3-7). 16.99 (978-0-545-27961-1(5), Scholastic Pr.) Scholastic, Inc.

—Star Wolf. 2013. (Wolves of the Beyond Ser.: 6). (ENG., Illus.). 256p. (J). (gr. 3-7). 16.99 (978-0-545-27962-8(3), Scholastic Pr.) Scholastic, Inc.

—Watch Wolf. 2011. (Wolves of the Beyond Ser.: 3). (ENG.). 240p. (J). (gr. 3-7). 17.99 (978-0-545-09314-9(7), Scholastic Pr.) Scholastic, Inc.

Laudati, Joe. Faela: A Fairy's Tale. 2008. 190p. pap. 14.50 (978-0-615-20324-9(8)) Laudati, Joe.

Launchbury, Jane. Witch & Wizard Stories. 2012. (ENG., Illus.). 64p. (J). 9.95 (978-1-84135-103-2(2)) Award Pubns. Ltd. GBR. Dist: Parkwest Pubns., Inc.

Launier, Veronique. Deliverance. 2014. (Hearts of Stone Ser.: 2). (ENG.). 288p. (YA). pap. 9.99 (978-0-7387-3075-2(0), Flux) Llewellyn Pubns.

Launier, Véronique & Launier, Veronique. Redemption. 2012. (Hearts of Stone Ser.: 1). (ENG.). 360p. (YA). pap. 9.99 (978-0-7387-3074-5(2), Flux) North Star Editions.

Laura & the Leprechauns. 2007. (J). 19.95 (978-0-9795933-0-7(1)) Chrysalis Pr.

Laura Beth. Two Girls 2 Cats: A Magical Mystery, 1 vol. 2010. 130p. pap. 24.95 (978-1-4489-4235-0(7)) PublishAmerica, Inc.

Laura Grey Wahl. The Magic Town of Stuart Easterly. 2009. 16p. pap. 15.00 (978-1-4389-4703-7(8)) AuthorHouse.

Laureano, C. E. Beneath the Forsaken City. 2015. (Song of Seare Ser.: 2). (ENG., Illus.). 416p. (YA). pap. 14.99 (978-1-61291-631-6(7)) Tyndale Hse. Pubs.

Laurence, Margaret. The Olden Days Coat. Wood, Muriel, illus. 2004. (ENG.). 32p. (J). (gr. 2-5). pap. 8.99 (978-0-88776-704-3(4), Tundra Bks.) Tundra Bks. CAN. Dist: Penguin Random Hse. LLC.

Law, Jerel. Truth Runner, 1 vol. 2013. (Son of Angels, Jonah Stone Ser.). (ENG.). 272p. (J). pap. 9.99 (978-1-4003-2287-9(1)) Nelson, Thomas Inc.

Lawes, Alexander. Peter & the Enchanted Cavern. 2012. 140p. pap. (978-1-909395-25-1(0)) Legend Pr.

Lawhead, Stephen R. The Dragon King Trilogy: n the Hall of the Dragon King; The Warlords of Nin; The Sword & the Flame. 2008. (Dragon King Trilogy: Bks. 1-3). 1168p. 19.99 (978-1-59554-518-3(2)) Nelson, Thomas Inc.

Lawhorn, Mary Joyce. When Annie Dreams. 2012. 74p. pap. 8.95 (978-1-4697-8819-7(5)) iUniverse, Inc.

Lawrence, David, et al. El Niño Escarabajo. 2004. (SPA.). 32p. (978-84-7720-794-8(1)) Ediciones Obelisco.

Lawrence, Iain. The Giant-Slayer. 2012. (ENG.). 304p. (J). (gr. 3-7). 6.99 (978-0-440-23971-0(0), Yearling) Random Hse. Children's Bks.

Layne, Steven L. This Side of Paradise, 1 vol. 2005. (ENG.). 224p. (YA). (gr. 6-10). pap. 8.95 (978-1-58980-254-4(3)) Pelican Publishing Co., Inc.

Layton, Dan. Adventures in the Kingdom, the Dreamer. 2004. 64p. pap. 5.99 (978-0-9707919-4-8(1)) Mercy Place, Inc.

Lazear, Suzanne. Fragile Destiny. 2014. (Aether Chronicles Ser.: 3). (ENG.). 432p. (YA). pap. 9.99 (978-0-7387-3986-1(3), Flux) North Star Editions.

—Innocent Darkness. 2012. (Aether Chronicles Ser.: 1). (ENG.). 408p. (YA). pap. 9.95 (978-0-7387-3248-0(6), Flux) North Star Editions.

Le Guin, Ursula K. Catwings. 2003. (Catwings Ser.: 1). (gr. 3-6). lib. bdg. 16.00 (978-0-613-70842-5(3), Turtleback) Turtleback Bks.

—Catwings Return. 2003. (Catwings Ser.: 2). (gr. 3-6). lib. bdg. 16.00 (978-0-613-65072-4(7), Turtleback) Turtleback Bks.

—The Daughter of Odren. 2014. (ENG.). 42p. (YA). (gr. 7). E-Book 1.99 (978-0-544-35838-6(4), HMH Books For Young Readers) Houghton Mifflin Harcourt Publishing Co.

—The Farthest Shore. 2012. (Earthsea Cycle Ser.: 3). (ENG., Illus.). (YA). (gr. 7). 272p. 17.99 (978-1-4424-5992-2(1)); 288p. pap. 9.99 (978-1-4424-5993-9(X)) Simon & Schuster Children's Publishing. (Atheneum Bks. for Young Readers).

—Gifts. 2006. (Annals of the Western Shore Ser.: 1). (ENG., Illus.). 304p. (YA). (gr. 7-12). reprint ed. pap. 7.95 (978-0-15-205124-2(4)) Houghton Mifflin Harcourt Publishing Co.

—Powers. 2009. (Annals of the Western Shore Ser.: 3). (ENG., Illus.). 512p. (J). (gr. 7-12). pap. 7.99 (978-0-15-206674-1(8)) Houghton Mifflin Harcourt Publishing Co.

—Tehanu. 2012. (Earthsea Cycle Ser.: 4). (ENG., Illus.). (YA). (gr. 7). 288p. 16.99 (978-1-4424-5995-3(6)); 320p. pap. 9.99 (978-1-4424-5996-0(4)) Simon & Schuster Children's Publishing. (Atheneum Bks. for Young Readers).

—The Tombs of Atuan. 2012. (Earthsea Cycle Ser.: 2). (ENG., Illus.). (YA). (gr. 7). 208p. 17.99 (978-1-4424-5990-8(5)); 224p. pap. 10.99 (978-1-4424-5991-5(3)) Simon & Schuster Children's Publishing. (Atheneum Bks. for Young Readers).

—Voices. 2008. (Annals of the Western Shore Ser.: 2). (ENG., Illus.). 368p. (YA). (gr. 7-12). pap. 8.99 (978-0-15-206242-2(4)) Houghton Mifflin Harcourt Publishing Co.

Le Guin, Ursula K. A Wizard of Earthsea. 2012. (Earthsea Cycle Ser.: 1). (ENG.). (YA). (gr. 7). 240p. 17.99

(978-0-547-85139-6(1)); 264p. pap. 8.99 *(978-0-547-72202-3(8))*; 320p. mass mkt. 8.99 *(978-0-547-77374-2(9))* Houghton Mifflin Harcourt Publishing Co.
—A Wizard of Earthsea. 2012. (Earthsea Cycle Ser.: Vol. 1). (ENG.). (YA). (gr. 7). lib. bdg. 19.60 ***(978-1-68065-210-9(9))*** Perfection Learning Corp.
—A Wizard of Earthsea. 2012. (Earthsea Ser.: 1). lib. bdg. 19.65 *(978-0-606-26624-6(0)*, Turtleback) Turtleback Bks.
Le, Guo, illus. The Dragon's Tears. 2004. (ENG & POR.). 24p. (J). pap. *(978-1-85269-693-1(1))*; pap. *(978-1-85269-700-6(8))* Mantra Lingua.
Leavell, Tracy. Lily. 2012. 118p. pap. 19.95 *(978-1-4626-9353-5(9))* America Star Bks.
Leaves: Look & Find. 2004. (J). pap. 12.95 *(978-1-932762-03-7(5))* Elderberry Press, Inc.
Lebbon, Tim. Contagion. 2013. (Toxic City Ser.). (ENG.). 219p. (J). (gr. 7). 17.99 *(978-1-61614-821-8(7))* Prometheus Bks., Pubs.
Leblanc, Louise. Le Bon, la Brute et le Vampire. 2003. (Premier Roman Ser.). (FRE., Illus.). 64p. (J). (gr. 2-5). pap. *(978-2-89021-365-4(X))* Diffusion du livre Mirabel (DLM).
Lee, H. Chuku. Beauty & the Beast. Cummings, Pat, illus. 2014. (ENG.). 32p. (J). (gr. -1-3). 17.99 *(978-0-688-14819-5(0)*, Amistad) HarperCollins Pubs.
Lee, Imani K., illus. Clever! Clever! & the Book of Forever. 2005. 17p. (YA). per. 9.99 *(978-0-9768429-2-7(0))* Genius In A Bottle Technology Corp.
Lee, Silver Ann. Amazing Bedtime Stories. 2010. 32p. pap. 19.99 *(978-1-4490-6094-7(3))* AuthorHouse.
Lee, Stan & Moore, Stuart. The Balance of Power. Tong, Andie, illus. 2017. (Zodiac Ser.: 3). (ENG.). 448p. (J). (gr. 3-7). 16.99 *(978-1-4847-1351-8(6))* Disney Pr.
Lee, Suzy. Shadow. 2010. (ENG., Illus.). 44p. (J). (gr. -1-3). 15.99 *(978-0-8118-7280-5(7))* Chronicle Bks. LLC.
Lee, Tanith. Black Unicorn. 2005. (ENG., Illus.). 144p. (J). (gr. -1-12). per. 12.00 *(978-1-59687-162-5(8))* IBks., Inc.
Lee, Zaina. Sun Takes a Holiday. 2009. 28p. pap. 13.99 *(978-1-4389-9992-0(5))* AuthorHouse.
Leeuwen, Joke Van & Leeuwen, Joke van. Eep! Leeuwen, Joke van, illus. 2012. (Gecko Press Titles Ser.). (ENG., Illus.). 152p. (J). (gr. 2-5). pap. 7.95 *(978-1-877579-07-3(6))* Gecko Pr. NZL. Dist: Lerner Publishing Group.
LeGette, M. L. The Unicorn Girl. 2008. (ENG.). 416p. pap. 10.00 *(978-1-4196-8696-2(8))* CreateSpace Independent Publishing Platform.
Lego, et al. Fire Truck to the Rescue!, No. 1. 2009. (Lego City Ser.). (ENG.). 32p. (J). (gr. -1-k). pap. 3.99 *(978-0-545-11543-8(4))* Scholastic, Inc.
Legrand, Claire. Foxheart. Zollars, Jaime, illus. 2016. 480p. (J). (gr. 3-7). 16.99 *(978-0-06-242773-1(3)*, Greenwillow Bks.) HarperCollins Pubs.
—Some Kind of Happiness. 2016. (ENG., Illus.). 384p. (J). (gr. 3-7). 17.99 *(978-1-4424-6601-2(4)*, Simon & Schuster Bks. For Young Readers) Simon & Schuster Bks. For Young Readers.
Lehane, Pearse. The Train That Never Came. 2008. 328p. pap. *(978-1-84923-249-4(0))* YouWriteOn.
Lehman, Barbara. The Red Book. Lehman, Barbara, illus. 2004. (ENG., Illus.). 32p. (J). (gr. -1-3). 16.99 *(978-0-618-42858-8(5))* Houghton Mifflin Harcourt Publishing Co.
Lehman, Seth. The Color Pets. 2006. (Illus.). 52p. (J). 7.00 net. *(978-0-9787986-0-4(0))* 4All Ages LLC.
Lehmann, Christian. Ultimate Game. Rodarmor, William, tr. 2003. (ENG.). 192p. pap. 10.95 *(978-1-56792-215-8(5))* Godine, David R. Pub.
Lei, Xu. Grave Robbers' Chronicles Vol 1-6 Box Set. Mok, Kathy, tr. 2014. (Grave Robbers' Chronicles Ser.). (ENG.). pap. 29.95 *(978-1-934159-37-8(9))* ThingsAsian Pr.
Leiderman, Lucy. Lives of Magic. 2014. (Seven Wanderers Trilogy Ser.: 1). (ENG., Illus.). 384p. (YA). pap. 12.99 *(978-1-4597-0846-4(6)*, 9781459708464) Dundurn CAN. Dist: Ingram Publisher Services.
Leigh, Anita L. Willow's Gift, 1 vol. 2009. 48p. pap. 16.95 *(978-1-4489-9202-7(8))* America Star Bks.
Lemke, Donald. Bizarro's Last Laugh. 2017. (Justice League Classic: I Can Read! Ser.). (J). lib. bdg. 13.55 ***(978-0-606-39632-5(2))*** Turtleback Bks.
—Rat Trap. 2016. (Batman 8X8 Storybooks Ser.). (J). lib. bdg. 13.55 *(978-0-606-38768-2(4))* Turtleback Bks.
—Superman Classic: Pranking News. Spaziante, Patrick, illus. 2016. (I Can Read Level 2 Ser.). 32p. (J). (gr. -1-3). pap. 3.99 *(978-0-06-236085-4(X))* HarperCollins Pubs.
Lenahan, John. The Sons of Macha. 2013. (Shadowmagic Ser.: 3). (ENG., Illus.). 288p. (J). 6.99 *(978-0-00-745674-1(3)*, Friday Project) HarperCollins Pubs. Ltd. GBR. Dist: HarperCollins Pubs.
L'Engle, Madeleine. Many Waters. 2007. (Wrinkle in Time Quintet Ser.: 3). (ENG.). 368p. (J). (gr. 5-9). per. 6.99 *(978-0-312-36857-9(7)*, 9780312368579) Square Fish.
—A Swiftly Tilting Planet. 228p. (YA). (gr. 5-18). pap. 5.50 *(978-0-8072-1495-4(7)*, Listening Library) Random Hse. Audio Publishing Group.
—A Swiftly Tilting Planet. 2007. (Wrinkle in Time Quintet Ser.: 4). (ENG.). 320p. (J). (gr. 5-9). per. 7.99 *(978-0-312-36856-2(9)*, 9780312368562) Square Fish.
—A Wind in the Door. 211p. (YA). (gr. 5-18). pap. 5.50 *(978-0-8072-1466-4(3)*, Listening Library) Random Hse. Audio Publishing Group.
—A Wind in the Door. 2007. (Wrinkle in Time Quintet Ser.: 2). (ENG.). 256p. (J). (gr. 5-9). per. 6.99 *(978-0-312-36854-8(2)*, 9780312368548) Square Fish.
—A Wrinkle in Time, 2 vols., Set. 20.00 *(978-0-89064-014-2(9))* National Assn. for Visually Handicapped.
—A Wrinkle in Time. 211p. (YA). (gr. 5-18). pap. 5.99 *(978-0-8072-1460-2(4)*, Listening Library) Random Hse. Audio Publishing Group.
—A Wrinkle in Time. l.t. ed. 2005. 273p. pap. 10.95 *(978-0-7862-7335-5(6)*, Large Print Pr.) Thorndike Pr.
Lenhard, Elizabeth. A Bridge Between Worlds. 2004. (W. I. T. C. H. Ser.: Bk. 10). 158p. (J). lib. bdg. 16.92 *(978-1-4242-0796-1(7))* Fitzgerald Bks.
—The Disappearance. 2004. (W. I. T. C. H. Ser.: Bk. 2). 158p. (J). lib. bdg. 16.92 *(978-1-4242-0799-2(1))* Fitzgerald Bks.
—Finding Meridian. 2004. (W. I. T. C. H. Ser.: Bk. 3). 158p. (J). lib. bdg. 16.92 *(978-1-4242-0801-2(7))* Fitzgerald Bks.
Lenhard, Elizabeth, adapted by. The Disappearance. 2004. (W. I. T. C. H. Ser.). (Illus.). 144p. (J). 12.65 *(978-0-7569-4620-3(4))* Perfection Learning Corp.
Lennard, Daric. My Name Is Berta. 2008. 48p. pap. 16.95 *(978-1-60672-036-3(8))* America Star Bks.
Leno, Katrina. Everything All at Once. 2017. 368p. (YA). (gr. 8). 17.99 *(978-0-06-249309-5(4)*, HarperTeen) HarperCollins Pubs.
Leo, Domenic. The Messengers: The Secret of the Orbs. 2007. 324p. per. 19.95 *(978-0-595-42668-3(9))* iUniverse, Inc.
Leone, Jason, illus. the Enchantress of Caratunk. Manna, Elizabeth, photos by. 2003. 30p. (J). (gr. 1-5). pap. 9.95 *(978-0-9729807-0-8(9))* Murray, David M.
Leonhard, Herb. Sir Norman & the Dreaming Dragon. Leonhard, Herb, illus. 2008. (ENG., Illus.). 32p. (J). 17.95 *(978-0-9763555-1-9(5))* Prancing Pony, The.
Lerangis, Peter. The Colossus Rises, Bk. 1. Norstrand, Torstein & Reagan, Mike, illus. 2013. (Seven Wonders Ser.: 1). (ENG.). 384p. (J). (gr. 3-7). pap. 6.99 *(978-0-06-207041-8(X))* HarperCollins Pubs.
—The Colossus Rises, Bk. 1. Reagan, Mike & Norstrand, Torstein, illus. 2013. (Seven Wonders Ser.: 1). (ENG.). 368p. (J). (gr. 3-7). 17.99 *(978-0-06-207040-1(1))* HarperCollins Pubs.
—The Colossus Rises, No. 1. Lerangis, Peter, illus. 2012. (Seven Wonders Ser.). (ENG., Illus.). 112p. (J). (gr. 3-7). 2.99 *(978-0-06-223889-4(2))* HarperCollins Pubs.
—The Colossus Rises. 2013. (Seven Wonders Ser.: 1). (J). lib. bdg. 17.20 *(978-0-606-32166-2(7)*, Turtleback) Turtleback Bks.
—The Legend of the Rift. 2016. (Seven Wonders Ser.: 5). (J). lib. bdg. 17.20 *(978-0-606-38738-5(2))* Turtleback Bks.
—Lost in Babylon. Norstrand, Torstein, illus. 2014. (Seven Wonders Ser.: 2). (ENG.). 400p. (J). (gr. 3-7). pap. 6.99 *(978-0-06-207044-9(4))* HarperCollins Pubs.
—Lost in Babylon. 2013. (Seven Wonders Ser.). (ENG., Illus.). 384p. (J). (gr. 3-7). 17.99 *(978-0-06-207043-2(6))* HarperCollins Pubs.
—Lost in Babylon. 2014. (Seven Wonders Ser.: 2). (J). lib. bdg. 17.20 *(978-0-606-35483-7(2))* Turtleback Bks.
—The Select & the Orphan. 2014. (Seven Wonders Journals). (ENG.). 144p. (J). (gr. 3-7). pap. 2.99 *(978-0-06-223891-7(4))* HarperCollins Pubs.
—The Select & the Orphans. 2014. (Seven Wonders Journals). (J). lib. bdg. 12.35 *(978-0-606-35484-4(0))* Turtleback Bks.
—Seven Wonders Book 5: the Legend of the Rift. Norstrand, Torstein, illus. 2016. (Seven Wonders Ser.: 5). 448p. (J). (gr. 3-7). 17.99 *(978-0-06-207052-4(5))* HarperCollins Pubs.
—The Sword Thief. 2009. (39 Clues Ser.: 3). (ENG.). 160p. (J). (gr. 3-7). 12.99 *(978-0-545-06043-1(5)*, Scholastic Pr.); (Illus.). 12.99 *(978-0-545-09059-9(8))* Scholastic, Inc.
—The Tomb of Shadows. Norstrand, Torstein, illus. (Seven Wonders Ser.: 3). (ENG.). (J). (gr. 3-7). 2015. 368p. pap. 6.99 *(978-0-06-207047-0(9))* 2014. 304p. 17.99 *(978-0-06-207046-3(0))* HarperCollins Pubs.
—The Tomb of Shadows. 2015. (Seven Wonders Ser.: 3). (J). lib. bdg. 17.20 *(978-0-606-36484-3(6))* Turtleback Bks.
Leslie, Dawn Marie. Orthify. 2007. 33p. pap. 24.95 *(978-1-4241-8468-2(1))* America Star Bks.
Lestelle, Wende. Science Mouse. 2004. pap. *(978-1-930493-65-0(7))* Athena Pr.
Leth, Kate. Adventure Time Vol. 4. 2014. lib. bdg. 24.50 *(978-0-606-36119-4(7))* Turtleback Bks.
Lethcoe, Jason. Song, 3 vols. Altmann, Scott, illus. 2009. (Mysterious Mr. Spines Ser.: 3). (ENG.). 208p. (J). (gr. 5-18). pap. 7.99 *(978-0-448-44655-4(3)*, Grosset & Dunlap) Penguin Young Readers Group.
Let's Go! A Snap-Back Book. (Illus.). (J). 4.00 net. *(978-1-56021-383-3(3))* W.J. Fantasy, Inc.
Levin, Betty. Thorn. 2005. (ENG.). 176p. (J). (gr. 9-12). 16.95 *(978-1-932425-46-8(2)*, Lemniscaat) Boyds Mills Pr.
Levine, Gail Carson. Ella Enchanted. 2008. (J). 39.99 *(978-0-7393-7107-7(X))* Findaway World, LLC.
—Ella Enchanted. 2017. (ENG.). 288p. (J). (gr. 3-7). pap. 7.99 *(978-0-06-440705-2(5))* HarperCollins Pubs.
—Ella Enchanted. unabr. ed. 2004. 232p. (J). (gr. 4-7). pap. 38.00 incl. audio *(978-0-8072-8694-4(X)*, YA238SP, Listening Library) Random Hse. Audio Publishing Group.
—The Enchanted Collection Box Set: Ella Enchanted, the Two Princesses of Bamarre, Fairest. 2008. (J). (gr. 3-7). pap. 19.99 *(978-0-06-143100-5(1))* HarperCollins Pubs.
—Fairy Haven & the Quest for the Wand. Christiana, David, illus. 2007. 191p. (J). *(978-1-4287-6391-3(0))* Disney Pr.
—The Lost Kingdom of Bamarre. 2017. 400p. (J). (gr. 3-7). 16.99 *(978-0-06-207466-9(0))* HarperCollins Pubs.
—A Tale of Two Castles. Call, Greg, illus. (ENG.). (J). (gr. 3-7). 2012. 352p. pap. 6.99 *(978-0-06-122967-1(9))* 2011. 336p. 16.99 *(978-0-06-122965-7(2))* HarperCollins Pubs.
Levithan, David. Every Day. 2015. (KOR.). 424p. (J). pap. *(978-89-374-3204-0(8))* Min-enumsa Publishing Co., Ltd.
—Every Day. (ENG.). (YA). (gr. 7). 2013. 400p. pap. 9.99 *(978-0-307-93189-4(7)*, Ember) 2012. 336p. 17.99 *(978-0-307-93188-7(9)*, Knopf Bks. for Young Readers) Random Hse. Children's Bks.
—Every Day. 2013. lib. bdg. 20.85 *(978-0-606-32238-6(8)*, Turtleback) Turtleback Bks.
Lewis, Anne. Dragonchild. 2003. (Bwgan-Wood Ser.: 3). (ENG., Illus.). 208p. (J). (gr. 3-6). pap. 7.95 *(978-1-870206-55-6(X))* Honno Welsh Women's Pr. GBR. Dist: Independent Pubs. Group.
Lewis, Anne Margaret. Fly Blanky Fly. Chavarri, Elisa, illus. 2012. (ENG.). 40p. (J). (gr. -1-2). 16.99 *(978-0-06-199996-3(2))* HarperCollins Pubs.
Lewis, C. Robbie. Rapunzel. 2004. 228p. 23.95 *(978-1-4184-8779-9(1))* AuthorHouse.
Lewis, C. S. L' Armoire Magique. Orig. Title: The Lion, the Witch & the Wardrobe. (FRE.). pap. 12.95 *(978-2-08-161994-4(6))* Flammarion et Cie FRA. Dist: Distribooks, Inc.
—The Chronicles of Narnia. Baynes, Pauline, illus. (Chronicles of Narnia Ser.). (J). 2004. (ENG.). 784p. (gr. 5). 32.99 *(978-0-06-059824-2(7))*Set. 2007. (gr. 3-18). 120.00 *(978-0-06-024488-0(7))* HarperCollins Pubs.
—Las Cronicas de Narnia, 1 vol. Baynes, Pauline, illus. 2006. (Cronicas de Narnia Ser.). (SPA.). 816p. (gr. 4-7). pap. 19.99 *(978-0-06-119900-4(1))* HarperCollins Pubs.
—The Horse & His Boy. Baynes, Pauline, illus. (Chronicles of Narnia Ser.: 3). (ENG.). 240p. (J). (gr. 3-18). 2008. pap. 8.99 *(978-0-06-440501-0(X))* 2007. 17.99 *(978-0-06-023488-1(1))* HarperCollins Pubs.
—The Last Battle. Baynes, Pauline, illus. (Chronicles of Narnia Ser.: 7). (ENG.). 224p. (J). (gr. 3-18). 2008. pap. 7.99 *(978-0-06-440503-4(6))* 2007. 17.99 *(978-0-06-023493-5(8))* HarperCollins Pubs.
—El Leon, la Bruja y el Ropero, 1 vol. 2005. (Cronicas de Narnia Ser.). (ESP, SPA & ENG.). 208p. pap. 9.99 *(978-0-06-084253-6(9))* HarperCollins Pubs.
—The Lion, the Witch & the Wardrobe. Baynes, Pauline, illus. movie tie-in ed. 2005. (Chronicles of Narnia Ser.: 2). (ENG.). 224p. (J). (gr. 3-7). pap. 6.99 *(978-0-06-076548-4(8)*, HarperFestival) HarperCollins Pubs.
—The Magician's Nephew. Baynes, Pauline, illus. 2008. (Chronicles of Narnia Ser.: 1). (ENG.). 208p. (J). (gr. 3-18). pap. 7.99 *(978-0-06-440505-8(2))* HarperCollins Pubs.
—The Magician's Nephew. Baynes, Pauline & Van Allsburg, Chris, illus. 2007. (Chronicles of Narnia Ser.: 1). (ENG.). 208p. (J). (gr. 3-18). 17.99 *(978-0-06-023497-3(0))* HarperCollins Pubs.
—Prince Caspian. Baynes, Pauline, illus. 2007. (Chronicles of Narnia Ser.: 4). (ENG.). 240p. (J). (gr. 3-18). 17.99 *(978-0-06-023483-6(0))* HarperCollins Pubs.
—Prince Caspian: The Return to Narnia. Baynes, Pauline, illus. 2008. (Chronicles of Narnia Ser.: 4). (ENG.). 240p. (J). (gr. 3-18). pap. 8.99 *(978-0-06-440500-3(1))* HarperCollins Pubs.
—La Silla de Plata, 1 vol. Gallart, Gemma, tr. Baynes, Pauline, illus. 2005. (Cronicas de Narnia Ser.). (ESP, SPA & ENG.). 304p. (gr. 4-7). per. 9.99 *(978-0-06-088430-7(4))* HarperCollins Pubs.
—The Silver Chair. Baynes, Pauline, illus. (Chronicles of Narnia Ser.: 6). (ENG.). 256p. (J). (gr. 3-18). 2008. pap. 8.99 *(978-0-06-440504-1(4))* 2007. 17.99 *(978-0-06-023495-9(4))* HarperCollins Pubs.
—The Voyage of the Dawn Treader. Baynes, Pauline, illus. (Chronicles of Narnia Ser.: 5). (ENG.). 256p. (J). (gr. 3-18). 2008. pap. 8.99 *(978-0-06-440502-7(8))* 2007. 17.99 *(978-0-06-023486-7(5))* HarperCollins Pubs.
Lewis-Domenech, Shanty. Toot, 1 vol. 2010. 16p. pap. 24.95 *(978-1-4489-5311-0(1))* PublishAmerica, Inc.
Lewis, Karlanna. Gladyus & the Voodoo Priestess. 2012. 24p. pap. 15.99 *(978-1-300-00528-5(9))* Lulu Pr., Inc.
Lewis, Regina N. The Smallest Forest. Moore, P. M., illus. 2013. 60p. pap. 12.95 *(978-1-935083-12-2(0))* CyPress Pubns.
Lewis, Steven & Parker, Shelley. Return to Allapatria. 2006. 395p. (J). pap. *(978-0-9547092-9-7(2))* Accent Pr. Ltd.
Lewis, Sylvia. Beautiful Decay. 2013. (ENG.). 304p. (YA). (gr. 2-17). pap. 9.95 *(978-0-7624-4611-7(0)*, Running Pr. Kids) Running Pr. Bk. Pubs.
Lewman, David. Truck or Treat! (Blaze & the Monster Machines) Fruchter, Jason, illus. 2017. (Big Golden Book Ser.). (ENG.). 48p. (J). (gr. -1-2). 9.99 ***(978-1-5247-1669-1(3)***, Golden Bks.) Random Hse. Children's Bks.
Liang, Kuan & Yung, Kao. Magic Lover's Tower, Vol. 1. 2008. (ENG., Illus.). 176p. (YA). pap. 9.95 *(978-1-59796-153-0(1))* DrMaster Pubns. Inc.
Liano, Dante, et al. The Honey Jar, 1 vol. Unger, David, tr. from SPA. Domi, illus. 2006. (ENG.). 56p. (J). (gr. 3). 18.95 *(978-0-88899-670-1(5))* Groundwood Bks. CAN. Dist: Publishers Group West (PGW).
Lijewski, Christy. Next Exit, Vol. 1. 2006. (ENG., Illus.). 168p. (YA). pap. 12.95 *(978-1-59362-037-0(3)*, 9781593620370) Slave Labor Bks.
Limb, Lisa. The Wishing Wheelchair. 2009. 40p. pap. 16.99 *(978-1-4389-4205-6(2))* AuthorHouse.
Lin, Grace. The Red Thread: An Adoption Fairy Tale. Lin, Grace, illus. 2007. (ENG., Illus.). 32p. (J). (gr. -1-3). 16.99 *(978-0-8075-6922-1(4))* Whitman, Albert & Co.
Lincoln, Jerri Kay. Dancing with Unicorns. 2013. 254p. pap. 14.99 *(978-1-938322-21-1(5))* Ralston Store Publishing.
Lindsay, Elizabeth. Annie to the Rescue. Kavanagh, Peter, illus. 2003. 94p. (J). *(978-0-439-56006-1(3))* Scholastic, Inc.
Lindsay, Norman. The Magic Pudding. 2012. (Dover Children's Classics Ser.). (ENG., Illus.). 144p. (J). (gr. 3-8). per. 8.95 *(978-0-486-45281-4(6))* Dover Pubns., Inc.
—The Magic Pudding. deluxe ed. (Illus.). 180p. 20.00 *(978-0-207-18355-3(4))* HarperCollins Pubs.
—The Magic Pudding. 2004. reprint ed. pap. 15.95 *(978-1-4191-7119-2(4))*; pap. 1.99 *(978-1-4192-7119-9(9))* Kessinger Publishing, LLC.
—The Magic Pudding: The Adventures of Bunyip Bluegum. 2008. 208p. *(978-0-7322-8432-9(5))* HarperCollins Pubs. Australia.
Lindsey, Julie Anne. Deceived. 2013. (ENG.). 320p. (YA). 17.99 *(978-1-4405-6389-8(6)*, Simon Pulse) Simon Pulse.
Lininger, Dianne. The Kingdom of Cydinah. 2006. (J). *(978-0-9790337-0-4(5))* Crosam Pr.
Link, Kelly. Pretty Monsters. 2010. (ENG., Illus.). 416p. (YA). (gr. 7-18). 9.99 *(978-0-14-241672-3(X)*, Speak) Penguin Young Readers Group.
Link, Kelly & Grant, Gavin J., eds. Monstrous Affections: An Anthology of Beastly Tales. 2014. (ENG., Illus.). 480p. (YA). (gr. 9). 22.99 *(978-0-7636-6473-2(1))* Candlewick Pr.
Linka, Catherine. A Girl Undone: A Novel. 2015. (Girl Called Fearless Ser.: 2). (ENG.). 304p. (YA). (gr. 7-12). 19.99 *(978-1-250-06867-5(3)*, 9781250068675, St. Martin's Griffin) St. Martin's Pr.
Linn, Susie. Fairies. Ellis, Lauren, illus. 2017. (Search & Find Ser.). (ENG.). 48p. (J). (gr. k-2). pap. 6.99 ***(978-1-78700-036-0(2))*** Top That! Publishing PLC GBR. Dist: Independent Pubs. Group.
Linton, Chandra S. Colors, Colors, Colors, A World Filled with Colors, Who Made Them? 2011. 20p. (gr. 2-4). pap. 15.49 *(978-1-4567-6355-8(5))* AuthorHouse.
Lisle, Holly. Ruby Key, Bk. 1. 2008. (ENG.). 384p. (J). *(978-0-545-00013-0(0)*, Orchard Bks.) Scholastic, Inc.
Litke, Erin. Crystal Shards. 2007. 528p. per. 16.95 *(978-1-4327-1548-9(8))* Outskirts Pr., Inc.
Litrel, Suzanne. Jackie Tempo & the House of Wisdom. 2012. 150p. (gr. 10-12). 21.95 *(978-1-4620-5887-7(6))*; pap. 11.95 *(978-1-4620-5886-0(8))* iUniverse, Inc.
Littman, Sarah Darer. Fairest of Them All. 2017. (ENG., Illus.). 224p. (J). (gr. 3-7). pap. 7.99 ***(978-1-4814-5129-1(4)***, Aladdin) Simon & Schuster Children's Publishing.
The live dolls' party Days. 2007. (Illus.). 160p. (J). lib. bdg. 59.00 *(978-1-60304-010-5(2))* Dollworks.
Livingston, Eric. Brandon Marlowe & the Spirit Snatcher. 2011. 216p. 25.95 *(978-1-4502-9221-4(6))*; pap. 15.95 *(978-1-4502-9220-7(8))* iUniverse, Inc.
Livingston, Lesley. Starling. 2075. (ENG.). 368p. (J). (gr. 8). 9.99 *(978-0-06-206308-3(1)*, HarperTeen) HarperCollins Pubs.
—Tempestuous. 2012. (Wondrous Strange Trilogy Ser.: 3). (ENG.). 384p. (YA). (gr. 8). pap. 8.99 *(978-0-06-174002-2(0)*, HarperTeen) HarperCollins Pubs.
—Transcendent. 2014. (Starling Trilogy Ser.: 3). (ENG.). 352p. (YA). (gr. 8). 17.99 *(978-0-06-206313-7(8)*, HarperTeen) HarperCollins Pubs.
—Wondrous Strange. 2009. (Wondrous Strange Trilogy Ser.: 1). (ENG.). 352p. (YA). (gr. 8). pap. 9.99 *(978-0-06-157539-6(9)*, HarperTeen) HarperCollins Pubs.
Livingstone, Ian. Deathtrap Dungeon. 2003. 224p. pap. 6.99 *(978-0-7434-7967-7(X))* ibooks, Inc.
Liz Smith And Kate Spohrer. Jangelle the Adhd Angel - Training the Dunelm Way. 2010. 56p. pap. 8.95 *(978-1-4502-0879-6(7))* iUniverse, Inc.
Llewellyn, Sam. The Well Between the Worlds. 2010. (Lyonesse Ser.: 1). (ENG.). 368p. (J). (gr. 3-7). 7.99 *(978-0-439-93470-1(2)*, Scholastic Paperbacks) Scholastic, Inc.
Llongueras, Joan & Masnou, Merce. Kadingir: El Cetro de Zink. 2007. (SPA.). 365p. (J). 18.95 *(978-84-96544-64-2(8))* Roca Editorial ESP. Dist: Spanish Pubs., LLC.
Lockard, Lynn. Gone Batty!!! 2009. 40p. pap. 16.99 *(978-1-4389-8516-9(9))* AuthorHouse.
Locke, Pamela K. Centaur's Door. 2007. (Young Writers Ser.). 143p. (YA). (gr. 8-14). per. 5.99 *(978-1-58158-111-9(4))* McDougal Publishing Co.
Lofting, Hugh. The Story of Doctor Dolittle. 2005. 128p. pap. 10.95 *(978-1-4218-0147-6(7))*; 26.95 *(978-1-4218-0047-9(0))* 1st World Publishing, Inc. (1st World Library - Literary Society).
—The Story of Doctor Dolittle. 2005. 96p. per. 4.95 *(978-1-4209-2544-9(X))* Digireads.com Publishing.
—The Story of Doctor Dolittle. 2016. (J). pap. *(978-1-5124-2606-9(7)*, First Avenue Editions) Lerner Publishing Group.
—The Story of Doctor Dolittle. unabr. ed. 2011. (Dover Children's Thrift Classics Ser.). (ENG., Illus.). 96p. (J). (gr. 3-8). reprint ed. pap. 4.00 *(978-0-486-29350-9(5))* Dover Pubns., Inc.
—The Story of Doctor Dolittle. 2004. reprint ed. pap. 15.95 *(978-1-4191-8383-6(4))*; pap. 1.99 *(978-1-4192-8383-3(9))* Kessinger Publishing, LLC.
—The Story of Doctor Dolittle, Original Version. Lofting, Hugh, illus. 2010. (ENG., Illus.). 204p. (J). pap. 25.95 *(978-4-87187-305-5(6))* Ishi Pr. International.
—The Voyages of Doctor Dolittle. 2005. 340p. pap. 14.95 *(978-1-4218-0148-3(5)*, 1st World Library - Literary Society) 1st World Publishing, Inc.
—The Voyages of Doctor Dolittle. 2003. (Signet Classics Ser.). (Illus.). 254p. 14.95 *(978-0-7569-1855-2(3))* Perfection Learning Corp.
—The Voyages of Doctor Dolittle. McKowen, Scott, illus. 2012. (Sterling Unabridged Classics Ser.). (ENG.). 256p. (J). (gr. 5). 9.95 *(978-1-4027-9721-7(4))* Sterling Publishing Co., Inc.
—The Voyages of Doctor Dolittle. Corvino, Lucy, illus. 2008. (Classic Starts(tm) Ser.). (ENG.). 160p. (J). (gr. 2-4). 6.95 *(978-1-4027-4574-4(5))* Sterling Publishing Co., Inc.
Lombardo, G. Where the Trees Grow Gumballs. 2006. 57p. pap. 16.95 *(978-1-4241-2978-2(8))* PublishAmerica, Inc.
London, C. Alexander. Moonlight Brigade. 2016. (Wild Ones Ser.: 2). (ENG.). 240p. (J). (gr. 3-7). 17.99 *(978-0-399-17100-0(2)*, Philomel Bks.) Penguin Young Readers Group.
London, C. Alexander & Mack, Jeff. The Wild Ones. 2015. (Wild Ones Ser.: 1). (ENG., Illus.). 256p. (J). (gr. 3-7). bds. 17.99 *(978-0-399-17099-7(5)*, Philomel Bks.) Penguin Young Readers Group.
Long, Chad M. The Lycan Journal. 2007. (Illus.). 141p. (YA). per. 12.95 *(978-0-615-15295-0(3))* Long Stories LLC.
Long, Ruth Frances. The Treachery of Beautiful Things. 2013. (ENG.). 384p. (YA). (gr. 7). pap. 9.99 *(978-0-14-242606-7(7)*, Speak) Penguin Young Readers Group.
Longoria, Eugene R., Jr. Junior y la Llorona en la Montana de Nieve. 2006. (SPA., Illus.). 40p. (J). 12.00 *(978-0-9796818-0-6(4))* Longoria, Eugene R.
Longus. The ADVENTURES of SILVANA & the MAGIC UNICORN. 2008. 48p. 18.95 *(978-1-4357-1877-7(1))* Lulu Pr., Inc.
Lopez Dekker, Anna. Everwhere. 2008. 137p. 31.95 *(978-1-4092-0318-6(2))* Lulu Pr., Inc.
Lopresti, Kirsten. Bright Coin Moon: A Novel. 2014. (ENG.). 272p. (J). (gr. 6). 16.95 *(978-1-62914-751-2(6)*, Sky Pony Pr.) Skyhorse Publishing Co., Inc.
Lord, David R. The Figment Wars: Through the Portals. 2015. (ENG.). 184p. pap. 11.95 *(978-1-78455-183-4(X)*, e9670af4-858e-4d5b-b10f-395a3bb1d534) Austin, Stan AUS. Dist: Bookmasters Distribution.
Lore, Pittacus. I Am Number Four. 2012. (Lorien Legacies: the Lost Files Ser.). (ENG.). 416p. (YA). (gr. 9). pap. 9.99 *(978-0-06-221110-1(2))* HarperCollins Pubs.
Lorentzen, Bent. Krona: Dragons of Nistala. 2009. 266p. (J). pap. 18.95 *(978-1-60619-091-3(1))* Twilight Times Bks.
Lorenz Guest, Donna. The Enchanted Ride. 2009. 32p. pap. 14.99 *(978-1-4389-8116-1(3))* AuthorHouse.
Lorey, Dean. Monster Law. 2009. 304p. 10.99 *(978-0-06-134048-2(0))* HarperCollins Pubs.
Lou, Rachel. The Bridge. 2016. (ENG., Illus.). (YA). (gr. 8-12). 24.99 ***(978-1-63477-964-7(9)***, Harmony Ink Pr.) Dreamspinner Pr.
Love, Angela. 'Gwyngallion' Guardian of Little Children Lost in the Woods. 2009. (Illus.). 40p. pap. 16.99 *(978-1-4389-2017-7(2))* AuthorHouse.

Lovegrove, James. The Lord of Fire (Five Lords of Pain Book 5) 2013. (Five Lords of Pain Ser.: 5). (ENG.). 96p. (YA). (gr. 8-12). pap. 7.95 *(978-1-78112-262-4(8))* Lerner Publishing Group.

—The Lord of Tears (Five Lords of Pain Book 3) 2013. (Five Lords of Pain Ser.: 3). (ENG.). 96p. (YA). (gr. 8-12). pap. 7.95 *(978-1-78112-256-3(3))* Lerner Publishing Group.

—The Lord of the Mountain (Five Lords of Pain Book 1) 2013. (Five Lords of Pain Ser.: 1). (ENG.). 96p. (YA). (gr. 8-12). pap. 7.95 *(978-1-78112-250-1(4))* Lerner Publishing Group.

—The Lord of the Typhoon (Five Lords of Pain Book 4) 2013. (Five Lords of Pain Ser.: 4). (ENG.). 96p. (YA). (gr. 8-12). pap. 7.95 *(978-1-78112-259-4(8))* Lerner Publishing Group.

—The Lord of the Void (Five Lords of Pain Book 2) 2013. (Five Lords of Pain Ser.: 2). (ENG.). 96p. (YA). (gr. 8-12). pap. 7.95 *(978-1-78112-253-2(9))* Lerner Publishing Group.

Lovett, Vienna. Mission from God. 2013. 256p. *(978-1-77069-833-8(7))* Word Alive Pr.

Lovhaug, Lewis J. Angel Armor: Just a Boy. 2003. 224p. (YA). pap. 15.95 *(978-0-595-28475-7(2))* iUniverse, Inc.

Lowe, E. Van. Never Slow Dance with a Zombie. 2009. (ENG.). 256p. (J). (gr. 8-12). pap. 18.99 *(978-0-7653-2040-7(1)*, 9780765320407, Tor Teen) Doherty, Tom Assocs., LLC.

Lowe, Wesley. The Griffin's Gauntlet. 2003. (Illus.). (YA). per. 14.95 *(978-0-9723011-2-1(7))* Helm Publishing.

Lowery, Linda & Keep, Richard. The Chocolate Tree: [A Mayan Folktale]. Porter, Janice, illus. 2009. (On My Own Folklore Ser.). (ENG.). 48p. (gr. 2-4). pap. 6.95 *(978-1-58013-851-2(9)*, First Avenue Editions) Lerner Publishing Group.

Lowry, Amy & Aesop. Fox Tails: Four Fables from Aesop. 2012. (ENG., Illus.). 32p. (J). 17.95 *(978-0-8234-2400-9(6))* Holiday Hse., Inc.

Lu, Marie. The Evertree. 2015. (Spirit Animals Ser.: 7). (ENG., Illus.). 192p. (J). (gr. 3-7). 12.99 *(978-0-545-53521-2(2))* Scholastic, Inc.

—The Rose Society. 2015. (Young Elites Ser.: 2). (ENG., Illus.). 416p. (YA). (gr. 7). 18.99 *(978-0-399-16784-3(6)*, G.P. Putnam's Sons Books for Young Readers) Penguin Publishing Group.

—The Rose Society. 2016. (Young Elites Novel Ser.). (ENG.). 432p. (YA). (gr. 7). pap. 10.99 *(978-0-14-751169-0(0)*, Speak) Penguin Young Readers Group.

—The Rose Society. Lt. ed. 2015. (Young Elites Ser.). (ENG.). 24.99 *(978-1-4104-8465-9(3))* Thorndike Pr.

—The Rose Society. 2016. (Young Elites Ser.: 2). (ENG.). 432p. (YA). (gr. 7). 22.10 *(978-0-606-39314-0(5))* Turtleback Bks.

Lu, Marie. The Young Elites. 2014. (ENG., Illus.). 368p. (YA). (gr. 7). 18.99 *(978-0-399-16783-6(8)*, G.P. Putnam's Sons Books for Young Readers) Penguin Publishing Group.

—The Young Elites. 2015. (Young Elites Novel Ser.). (ENG.). 384p. (YA). (gr. 7). pap. 10.99 *(978-0-14-751168-3(2)*, Speak) Penguin Young Readers Group.

—The Young Elites. 2015. (ENG.). (YA). (gr. 7). lib. bdg. 21.60 ***(978-1-68065-052-5(1))*** Perfection Learning Corp.

—The Young Elites. 2015. (Young Elites Ser.: 1). lib. bdg. 22.10 *(978-0-606-37575-7(9))* Turtleback Bks.

Lubar, David. The Big Stink. 2010. (Nathan Abercrombie, Accidental Zombie Ser.: 4). (ENG.). 176p. (J). (gr. 3-7). pap. 7.99 *(978-0-7653-2510-5(1)*, 9780765325105, Starscape) Doherty, Tom Assocs., LLC.

—Goop Soup. 2010. (Nathan Abercrombie, Accidental Zombie Ser.: 3). (ENG.). 176p. (J). (gr. 3-7). pap. 7.99 *(978-0-7653-2509-9(8)*, 9780765325099, Starscape) Doherty, Tom Assocs., LLC.

—Strikeout of the Bleacher Weenies: And Other Warped & Creepy Tales. 2016. (Weenies Stories Ser.: 8). (ENG.). 208p. (J). 15.99 *(978-0-7653-7726-5(8)*, 9780765377265, Starscape) Doherty, Tom Assocs., LLC.

Luberto, Bradley. Clide & Druce: A Repulsive Tale of Trolls & Tax Money. 2006. (ENG.). 48p. per. 16.95 *(978-1-4241-5012-0(4))* PublishAmerica, Inc.

Lucas, George. La Guerre des Etoiles, Tome 1.Tr. of Star Wars. (FRE.). (J). pap. 11.95 *(978-2-265-06730-1(X))* Fleuve Noir FRA. Dist: Distribooks, Inc.

Lucas, Matthew. A Roar in the Pinelands. 2010. 308p. 28.95 *(978-1-4502-3193-0(4))*; pap. 18.95 *(978-1-4502-3191-6(8))* iUniverse, Inc.

Luciano, Sonia. Mr. I Forgot. 2009. 48p. pap. 16.95 *(978-1-61582-765-7(X))* America Star Bks.

Lucken, Eve M. The Tree, the Crazy Leaf, & Me. 2012. 64p. pap. 20.99 *(978-1-4525-5016-9(6))* Balboa Pr.

Luiken, Nicole. Dreamfire. 2009. (Dreamfire Ser.: 1). (ENG.). 192p. pap. 14.95 *(978-1-894283-88-5(0)*, Great Plains Teen Fiction) Great Plains Pubns. CAN. Dist: Publishers Group Canada.

Luiz, Fernando, illus. How to Be a Princess: A Girly Girl Book. 2009. 12p. (J). bds. 6.95 *(978-1-58117-850-0(6)*, Intervisual/Piggy Toes) Bendon, Inc.

Lund, Fiauna. Indigo. 2013. 268p. pap. 13.99 *(978-1-936850-82-2(6))* Rhemalda Publishing.

Lund, J. L. The Temple of Kahmahrgx. 2013. (ENG.). 352p. (YA). pap. 14.99 *(978-0-9889537-0-3(6))* Prepare For Rain Pr.

Lundquist, Jenny. The Opal Crown. 2014. (ENG.). 368p. (YA). (gr. 2-17). pap. 9.95 *(978-0-7624-5422-8(9)*, Running Pr. Kids) Running Pr. Bk. Pubs.

—The Princess in the Opal Mask. 2013. (ENG.). 352p. (YA). (gr. 2-17). pap. 9.95 *(978-0-7624-5109-8(2)*, Running Pr. Kids) Running Pr. Bk. Pubs.

Lupin III 2nd Series, Vol. 2. 2004. (YA). pap. 9.99 *(978-1-59182-494-7(X))* TOKYOPOP, Inc.

Lupin III Series 2. 2004. (YA). pap. 9.99 *(978-1-59182-493-0(1))* TOKYOPOP, Inc.

Lupton, Hugh. The Gingerbread Man. Mayo, Diana, illus. 2003. 24p. (J). (gr. k-3). 14.99 *(978-1-84148-056-5(8))* Barefoot Bks., Inc.

—Tales of Wisdom & Wonder. Sharkey, Niamh, illus. (ENG.). 64p. (J). 2008. 19.99 *(978-1-84686-243-4(4))* 2006. 15.99 *(978-1-905236-84-8(0))* Barefoot Bks., Inc.

Lux, Josephine Kei & Doerflinger, Marion. Daydreaming Daisy Part of the Daydreamer's Club Series. 2009. 40p. pap. 17.50 *(978-1-60860-252-0(4)*, Eloquent Bks.) Strategic Book Publishing & Rights Agency (SBPRA).

Lydia Jane. Fifth Moon: The First Installment in the Gates Trilogy. 2007. 480p. 35.95 *(978-0-595-91408-1(X))*; per. 25.95 *(978-0-595-43671-2(4))* iUniverse, Inc.

Lying as Still as I Can: Six-Pack. (Greetings Ser.: Vol. 3). (gr. 2-3). 31.00 *(978-0-7635-9433-6(4))* Rigby Education.

Lyle, Cindy. The Creation Chronicles - the Dragon Within. 2013. 320p. *(978-1-4602-2618-6(6))* FriesenPress.

Lyons, Jayne. 100% Wolf. Rivas, Victor, illus. 2010. (ENG.). 256p. (J). (gr. 2-7). pap. 7.99 *(978-1-4424-0252-2(0)*, Atheneum Bks. for Young Readers) Simon & Schuster Children's Publishing.

Lyrrek, E. Dawne. A Page Turns 12 & Comes of Age. 2004. (J). 8.95 *(978-1-59590-009-8(8))* Books2Go.

Maar, Paul. El Viaje de Lisa. Kasparavicius, Kestutis, illus. 2008. (la Orilla del Viento Ser.). (SPA.). 28p. (J). (gr. -1-3). 12.99 *(978-968-16-7452-6(9))* Fondo de Cultura Economica USA.

Maas, Sarah J. The Assassin's Blade. 2014. (Throne of Glass Ser.). (ENG., Illus.). 464p. (YA). (gr. 9). 18.99 *(978-1-61963-361-2(2)*, 9781619633612, Bloomsbury USA Childrens) Bloomsbury Publishing USA.

—A Court of Mist & Fury. (Court of Thorns & Roses Ser.: 2). (ENG.). (YA). 2017. 656p. pap. 10.99 *(978-1-61963-519-7(4)*, 9781619635197) 2016. (Illus.). 640p. (gr. 9). 18.99 *(978-1-61963-446-6(5)*, 9781619634466) Bloomsbury Publishing USA. (Bloomsbury USA Childrens).

—A Court of Mist & Fury. 2017. (Court of Thorns & Roses Ser.: 2). (YA). lib. bdg. 22.10 ***(978-0-606-40562-1(3))*** Turtleback Bks.

—A Court of Thorns & Roses. (Court of Thorns & Roses Ser.). (ENG.). (YA). 2017. 56.97 ***(978-1-68119-774-6(X)***, 9781681197746) 2017. 96p. pap. 15.99 *(978-1-68119-576-6(3)*, 9781681195766) 2016. 448p. (gr. 9). pap. 10.99 *(978-1-61963-518-0(6)*, 9781619635180) 2015. 432p. (gr. 9). 18.99 *(978-1-61963-444-2(9)*, 9781619634442) Bloomsbury Publishing USA. (Bloomsbury USA Childrens).

—A Court of Thorns & Roses. 2016. lib. bdg. 22.10 *(978-0-606-38548-0(7))* Turtleback Bks.

—A Court of Wings & Ruin. 2017. (Court of Thorns & Roses Ser.: bk.3). (ENG.). 720p. (YA). 18.99 *(978-1-61963-448-0(1)*, 9781619634480, Bloomsbury USA Childrens) Bloomsbury Publishing USA.

—Crown of Midnight. (Throne of Glass Ser.: 2). (ENG.). (YA). (gr. 9). 2014. 448p. pap. 10.99 *(978-1-61963-064-2(8)*, 9781619630642) 2013. (Illus.). 432p. 18.99 *(978-1-61963-062-8(1)*, 9781619630628) Bloomsbury Publishing USA. (Bloomsbury USA Childrens).

—Crown of Midnight. 2014. (Throne of Glass Ser.: 2). (YA). lib. bdg. 22.10 *(978-0-606-36441-6(2))* Turtleback Bks.

—Empire of Storms. (Throne of Glass Ser.). (ENG.). (YA). 2017. 720p. pap. 10.99 ***(978-1-61963-609-5(3)***, 9781619636095) 2016. 704p. (gr. 9). 18.99 *(978-1-61963-607-1(7)*, 9781619636071) Bloomsbury Publishing USA. (Bloomsbury USA Childrens).

—Empire of Storms. 2017. (Throne of Glass Ser.: 5). (YA). lib. bdg. 22.10 ***(978-0-606-40598-0(4))*** Turtleback Bks.

—Heir of Fire. 2014. (Throne of Glass Ser.: Bk. 3). (ENG., Illus.). 576p. (YA). (gr. 9). 18.99 *(978-1-61963-065-9(6)*, 9781619630659, Bloomsbury USA Childrens) Bloomsbury Publishing USA.

—Queen of Shadows. (Throne of Glass Ser.). (ENG.). (YA). (gr. 9). 2016. 672p. pap. 10.99 *(978-1-61963-606-4(9)*, 9781619636064) 2015. (Illus.). 656p. 18.99 *(978-1-61963-604-0(2)*, 9781619636040) Bloomsbury Publishing USA. (Bloomsbury USA Childrens).

—Queen of Shadows. 2016. (Throne of Glass Ser.: 4). (ENG.). 384p. (YA). (gr. 9-12). 22.10 *(978-0-606-39288-4(2))* Turtleback Bks.

—Throne of Glass. (Throne of Glass Ser.: 1). (ENG., Illus.). (YA). (gr. 9). 2013. 432p. pap. 10.99 *(978-1-61963-034-5(6)*, 9781619630345) 2012. 416p. 18.99 *(978-1-59990-695-9(3)*, 9781599906959) Bloomsbury Publishing USA. (Bloomsbury USA Childrens).

—Throne of Glass. 2013. (Throne of Glass Ser.: 1). (YA). lib. bdg. 22.10 *(978-0-606-31888-4(7)*, Turtleback) Turtleback Bks.

—Tower of Dawn. 2017. (Throne of Glass Ser.). (ENG.). 672p. (YA). 18.99 *(978-1-68119-577-3(1)*, 9781681195773, Bloomsbury USA Childrens) Bloomsbury Publishing USA.

Mabbitt, Will. Mabel Jones & the Doomsday Book. 2016. (Mabel Jones Ser.). (ENG., Illus.). 336p. (J). (gr. 3-7). 16.99 *(978-1-101-99962-2(4)*, Viking Books for Young Readers) Penguin Young Readers Group.

Mabille, Christine. Potato-Kid & the Adventure: Treasures Within, 1 vol. 2009. 76p. pap. 19.95 *(978-1-61582-981-1(4))* America Star Bks.

Mabry, Samantha. A Fierce & Subtle Poison. 2017. (ENG.). 288p. (YA). (gr. 8-12). pap. 9.95 *(978-1-61620-698-7(5))* Algonquin Bks. of Chapel Hill.

Mac, Carrie. The Droughtlanders, Bk. 1. 2007. (ENG.). 360p. (J). (gr. k-12). 13.50 *(978-0-14-305666-9(2)*, Puffin Canada) Penguin Random House Canada Young Readers CAN. Dist: Penguin Random Hse. LLC.

—Storm. 2009. (ENG.). 304p. (J). (gr. k-12). 14.00 *(978-0-14-305115-2(6)*, Puffin Canada) Penguin Random House Canada Young Readers CAN. Dist: Penguin Random Hse. LLC.

Macauley, Michael. The Inheritance Almanac. Vaz, Mark Cotta, ed. 2010. (ENG.). 224p. (YA). (gr. 7). 18.99 *(978-0-375-86493-3(8))*; pap. 12.99 *(978-0-375-86672-2(8))* Random Hse. Children's Bks. (Knopf Bks. for Young Readers).

Macaw, Grant. Vigil's End. 2005. (ENG.). 310p. (YA). (gr. 7). per. *(978-1-933255-13-2(7))* DNA Pr.

MacDonald, George. The Carasoyn. 2008. 108p. 22.95 *(978-1-60664-921-3(3))*; pap. 9.95 *(978-1-60664-041-8(0))* Aegypan.

—George MacDonald's Fantasy Novels for Children Including: The Princess & the Goblin, the Princess & Curdie & at the Ba. 2013. 444p. *(978-1-78139-368-0(0))* Benediction Classics.

—The Golden Key: Classic fairy Tales. McCabe, Steve, illus. 2008. 104p. (J). pap. *(978-0-88835-045-9(7))* Meany, P. D. Pubs.

—The Light Princess. 110p. (J). (gr. 4-5). pap. 5.95 *(978-0-8072-1396-4(9)*, Listening Library) Random Hse. Audio Publishing Group.

—Phantastes, a Faerie Romance. 2007. 164p. per. 12.95 *(978-1-60312-241-2(9))*; 24.95 *(978-1-60312-819-3(0))* Aegypan.

—The Princess & Curdie. Lt. ed. 2005. 320p. pap. *(978-1-84637-020-5(5))* Echo Library.

—Princess & the Goblin. Hughes, Arthur, illus. 2nd ed. 2011. (Puffin Classics Ser.). (ENG.). 256p. (J). (gr. 5-7). 5.99 *(978-0-14-133248-2(4)*, Puffin Books) Penguin Young Readers Group.

—The Princess Treasury. 2008. 372p. pap. 12.99 *(978-1-60459-458-4(6))* Wilder Pubns., Corp.

—The Wise Woman. 2009. 128p. 23.95 *(978-1-60664-614-4(1))*; pap. 10.95 *(978-1-60664-352-5(5))* Rodgers, Alan Bks.

MacHale, D. J. Black Water. 2007. (Pendragon Ser.: 5). (ENG., Illus.). 448p. (J). (gr. 5-9). 18.99 *(978-1-4169-5779-9(0)*, Aladdin) Simon & Schuster Children's Publishing.

—The Lost City of Faar. 2003. (Pendragon Ser.: 2). (ENG.). 400p. (J). (gr. 5-9). pap. 9.99 *(978-0-7434-3732-5(2)*, Aladdin) Simon & Schuster Children's Publishing.

—The Merchant of Death; The Lost City of Faar. 2005. (Pendragon Ser.: Bks. 1-2). 758p. (YA). 9.99 *(978-0-681-05434-9(4))* Borders Pr.

—Pendragon: The Merchant of Death; The Lost City of Faar; The Never War; The Reality Bug; Black Water. 2013. (Pendragon Ser.). (ENG., Illus.). 1968p. (J). (gr. 5-9). pap. 49.99 *(978-1-4424-9926-3(5)*, Simon & Schuster/Paula Wiseman Bks.) Simon & Schuster/Paula Wiseman Bks.

—The Pilgrims of Rayne. (Pendragon Ser.: 8). (ENG.). (J). (gr. 5-9). 2008. 576p. pap. 9.99 *(978-1-4169-1417-4(X))* 2007. 560p. 19.99 *(978-1-4169-1416-7(1))* Simon & Schuster Children's Publishing. (Aladdin).

—The Quillan Games. 2007. (Pendragon Ser.: 7). (ENG.). 512p. (J). (gr. 5-9). pap. 9.99 *(978-0-689-86913-6(4)*, Aladdin) Simon & Schuster Children's Publishing.

—Raven Rise. 2008. (Pendragon Ser.: 9). (ENG.). 560p. (J). (gr. 5-9). 18.99 *(978-1-4169-1418-1(8)*, Aladdin) Simon & Schuster Children's Publishing.

—The Rivers of Zadaa. (Pendragon Ser.: 6). (ENG.). 416p. (J). (gr. 5-9). 2006. pap. 9.99 *(978-0-689-86912-9(6))* 2005. 19.99 *(978-1-4169-0710-7(6))* Simon & Schuster Children's Publishing. (Aladdin).

—The Soldiers of Halla. (Pendragon Ser.: 10). (ENG.). 608p. (J). (gr. 5-9). 2010. pap. 9.99 *(978-1-4169-1421-1(8))* 2009. 17.99 *(978-1-4169-1420-4(X))* Simon & Schuster Children's Publishing. (Aladdin).

MacInnis, Katherine. Kelsar. 2006. pap. 12.95 *(978-1-58939-876-4(9))* Virtualbookworm.com Publishing, Inc.

MacInnis, Katherine Grace. Kelsar. 2006. 140p. 19.95 *(978-1-58939-877-1(7))* Virtualbookworm.com Publishing, Inc.

Mack, Crystal. The Pentrals. 2013. (The Pentrals Ser.). (ENG.). 246p. (YA). pap. 12.95 *(978-0-9819825-1-9(4))* Apologue Entertainment, LLC.

Mackall, Dandi Daley. Little Shepherd. 2004. 32p. (J). 6.99 *(978-0-7586-0324-1(X))* Concordia Publishing Hse.

Mackan, Paul. Dream Girl, Dream! A Story for Children to Share with Groan-Ups, 1 vol. 2010. 55p. pap. 16.95 *(978-1-4489-7842-7(4))* America Star Bks.

MacKenzie, Ross. Zac & the Dream Stealers. (J). 2013. 297p. *(978-0-545-40107-4(0))* 2012. (ENG.). 304p. (gr. 3-7). 16.99 *(978-0-545-40106-7(2))* Scholastic, Inc. (Chicken Hse., The).

MacMillan, Kathy. Sword & Verse. 2016. 384p. (YA). (gr. 9). 17.99 *(978-0-06-232461-0(6)*, HarperTeen) HarperCollins Pubs.

Maconie, Robin. Alice & Her Fabulous Teeth! Fruisen, Catherine Myler, illus. 2004. 32p. (J). per. *(978-1-893974-21-0(9)*, Design Pr. Bks.) Savannah College of Art & Design Exhibitions.

Macri, Thomas. The Story of the X-Men Level 2 Reader. Olliffe, Pat, illus. 2013. (World of Reading Ser.). (ENG.). 32p. (J). (gr. 1-3). pap. 3.99 *(978-1-4231-7224-6(8))* Marvel Worldwide, Inc.

Madiwale, Frances. Special Creatures. 2005. (Illus.). 20p. (J). per. 9.99 *(978-1-59879-011-5(0))* Lifevest Publishing, Inc.

The Madrona Heroes Register: Echoes of the Past. 2013. (Illus.). 344p. pap. 12.43 *(978-0-9899905-4-7(0))* Atelier Mythologie.

Madsen, Shane. The Stevenson Chronicles: Deltorn. 2013. 170p. (gr. 10-12). 23.96 *(978-1-4669-7614-6(4))*; pap. 13.96 *(978-1-4669-7612-2(8))* Trafford Publishing.

Madsen, W. J. Arkeepers: Episode One. 2012. 142p. pap. 7.95 *(978-0-9830487-0-1(3))* little m Bks.

—Arkeepers: Episode Two. 2012. 206p. pap. 9.30 *(978-0-9830487-1-8(1))* little m Bks.

Mafi, Tahereh. Furthermore. 2016. (ENG.). 416p. (J). (gr. 4-7). 17.99 *(978-1-101-99476-4(2)*, Dutton Books for Young Readers) Penguin Young Readers Group.

—Furthermore. 2017. lib. bdg. 19.65 ***(978-0-606-40493-8(7))*** Turtleback Bks.

Magness, Lee. Silver Dasher. 2003. 164p. pap. 12.95 *(978-0-595-29043-7(4))* iUniverse, Inc.

Magone, Teresa. Little Bunny Has Belly Surgery. 2012. 38p. pap. 9.50 *(978-0-615-58595-6(7))* Little Bunny Bks.

Maguire, Gregory. Egg & Spoon. 2014. (ENG., Illus.). 496p. (YA). (gr. 7). 17.99 *(978-0-7636-7220-1(3))* Candlewick Pr.

Maguire, Suzanne & Maguire, Eve. Spellbound Chronicles - Blood Line. 2014. (ENG.). 184p. pap. *(978-1-78306-469-4(2))* Troubador Publishing Ltd.

Mahalik, Cathy. The Longest Hair Ever. 2011. 40p. 18.41 *(978-1-4269-4396-6(2))* Trafford Publishing.

Mahon, Matthew. The Defenders of All Thats Fall. 2008. 56p. pap. 24.95 *(978-1-4327-3169-4(6))* Outskirts Pr., Inc.

Mahoney, Karen. The Stone Demon. 2013. (Iron Witch Ser.: 3). (ENG.). 336p. (YA). pap. 9.99 *(978-0-7387-3340-1(7)*, Flux) North Star Editions.

—The Wood Queen: An Iron Witch Novel. 2012. (Iron Witch Ser.: 2). (ENG.). 336p. (YA). pap. 9.95 *(978-0-7387-2662-5(1)*, Flux) North Star Editions.

Mahy, Margaret. Maddigan's Fantasia. 2005. 320p. *(978-1-86950-561-5(1))* HarperCollins Pubs. Australia.

—Maddigan's Fantasia. 2012. (ENG.). 512p. (J). (gr. 5-9). pap. 22.99 *(978-1-4424-6053-9(9)*, McElderry, Margaret K. Bks.) McElderry, Margaret K. Bks.

—The Magician of Hoad. (ENG.). 432p. (YA). (gr. 9). 2010. pap. 9.99 *(978-1-4169-7808-4(9))* 2009. 18.99 *(978-1-4169-7807-7(0))* McElderry, Margaret K. Bks. (McElderry, Margaret K. Bks.).

—Shock Forest: And Other Stories. 2004. *(978-0-7136-7652-5(3)*, A&C Black) Bloomsbury Publishing Plc.

Maier, Gary B. Key Masters: The Tyrannosaur Rebellion. 2013. 124p. pap. 11.50 *(978-1-62516-403-2(3)*, Strategic Bk. Publishing) Strategic Book Publishing & Rights Agency (SBPRA).

Maizel, Rebecca. Infinite Days. 2010. (Vampire Queen Ser.: 1). (ENG.). 336p. (YA). (gr. 7-18). pap. 9.99 *(978-0-312-64991-3(6)*, 9780312649913, St. Martin's Griffin) St. Martin's Pr.

Major, Roberta Olsen. The Bad Heir Day. 2009. (Royal Pains Ser.: 8). (ENG.). (YA). pap. 11.95 *(978-1-59705-624-3(3))* Wings ePress, Inc.

—The Bottle of Djinn. 2006. (Royal Pains Ser.: 4). (ENG.). 116p. (YA). pap. 11.95 *(978-1-59705-824-7(6))* Wings ePress, Inc.

—The Good Knight Kiss. 2003. (Royal Pains Ser.: 3). pap. 12.95 *(978-1-59088-698-4(4))* Wings ePress, Inc.

Mäkinen, Kirsti. The Kalevala: Tales of Magic & Adventure. Brooks, Kaarina, tr. from FIN. Surojegin, Pirkko-Liisa, illus. 2009. (ENG.). 214p. (YA). (gr. 4-18). 24.95 *(978-1-897476-00-0(0))* Simply Read Bks. CAN. Dist: Ingram Publisher Services.

Malchow, Hal & Malchow, Alex. The Sword of Darrow. 2011. (ENG.). (gr. 3-7). 372p. pap. 12.99 *(978-1-935618-47-8(4))*; 532p. 17.99 *(978-1-935618-46-1(6))* BenBella Bks.

Malloy, Chris. Wizard Academies - A Special Kind of Talent. 2008. 142p. pap. 19.95 *(978-0-615-18505-7(3))* Wizard Academies, LLC.

Maloof, Torrey. Young Adult Literature: Magical Worlds (Grade 6) 2016. (TIME for KIDS(r) Nonfiction Readers Ser.). (Illus.). 48p. (J). (gr. 6-6). pap. 9.99 *(978-1-4938-3597-3(1))* Teacher Created Materials, Inc.

Malouf, Ranya. Blue Fish's Secret Wish. 2011. 32p. pap. *(978-9963-610-72-3(2))* Rimal Pubns.

Mammina, David. The Circle Stone Group: Book 1: the Beginning. 2009. 112p. pap. 13.35 *(978-1-4269-1478-2(4))* Trafford Publishing.

Man-Kong, Mary. Fairy Dreams. Random House Staff, illus. 2013. (Step into Reading Ser.). (ENG.). 32p. (J). (gr. -1-1). 3.99 *(978-0-449-81628-8(1)*, Random Hse. Bks. for Young Readers) Random Hse. Children's Bks.

—A Fairy-Tail Adventure. 2012. (Barbie 8X8 Ser.). lib. bdg. 13.55 *(978-0-606-23850-2(6)*, Turtleback) Turtleback Bks.

Manatee Moon. 2006. (J). per. 9.95 *(978-0-9766620-3-7(5))* Avery Goode-Reid Pubs.

Mancil, Arlene. The Garden Fairy. 2008. 32p. pap. 24.95 *(978-1-60441-735-7(8))* PublishAmerica, Inc.

Mangels, Andy, et al. Dragon's Lair, Vol. 1. O'Reilly, Sean Patrick, ed. Bluth, Don, illus. 2008. 164p. (YA). 19.95 *(978-0-9763095-5-0(6))* Arcana Studio, Inc.

Mangual, Cynthia Ines. 3 Super Hero Tales (DC Super Friends) Random House & Doescher, Erik, illus. 2017. (Padded Board Book Ser.). (ENG.). 30p. (J). (— 1). bds. 11.99 ***(978-1-5247-1714-8(2)***, Random Hse. Bks. for Young Readers) Random Hse. Children's Bks.

Mann, Emma. Amelia's Star. 2006. 110p. pap. 19.95 *(978-1-4241-2363-6(1))* PublishAmerica, Inc.

Mann, Greyson. Lost in the Jungle: Secrets of a Minecraft Survivor. Sandford, Grace, illus. 2017. (Secrets of an Overworld Survivor Ser.). (ENG.). 112p. (J). (gr. 1-4). 13.99 *(978-1-5107-1325-3(5)*, Sky Pony Pr.) Skyhorse Publishing Co., Inc.

Mannering, G. R. Roses. 2013. (ENG., Illus.). 320p. (YA). (gr. 6-12). 16.95 *(978-1-62087-988-7(3)*, 620988, Sky Pony Pr.) Skyhorse Publishing Co., Inc.

Mannering, Rose. Feathers: The Tales Trilogy, Book 2. 2016. (Tales Trilogy Ser.). (ENG.). 288p. (YA). (gr. 6). 17.99 *(978-1-63450-165-1(9)*, Sky Pony Pr.) Skyhorse Publishing Co., Inc.

—Roses: The Tales Trilogy, Book 1. 2016. (Tales Trilogy Ser.). (ENG.). 328p. (J). (gr. 6). pap. 9.99 *(978-1-63450-188-0(8)*, Sky Pony Pr.) Skyhorse Publishing Co., Inc.

Manning, Matthew. Batgirl: New Hero of the Night (Backstories) 2017. (Backstories Ser.). lib. bdg. 16.00 ***(978-0-606-39731-5(0))*** Turtleback Bks.

Manning, Matthew K. DC Super Hero Stories. Beavers, Ethen, illus. 2017. (DC Super Hero Stories Ser.). (ENG.). 56p. (gr. 1-3). 101.28 *(978-1-4965-4636-4(9)*, DC Super Heroes) Stone Arch Bks.

—The Flash Races the Rogues. Beavers, Ethen, illus. 2017. (DC Super Hero Stories Ser.). (ENG.). 56p. (gr. 1-3). lib. bdg. 25.32 *(978-1-4965-4633-3(4)*, DC Super Heroes) Stone Arch Bks.

Manoa, J. One. 2016. (One Ser.: 6). (ENG.). 200p. (YA). (gr. 6-12). lib. bdg. 162.78 *(978-1-68076-049-1(1)*, Epic Pr.) ABDO Publishing Co.

Manson, Beverlie, illus. The Mermaid's Secret Diaries. 2013. (ENG.). 96p. (J). (gr. -1-2). 9.95 *(978-1-907967-59-7(1))* Boxer Bks., Ltd. GBR. Dist: Sterling Publishing Co., Inc.

Mara, Cate. The Great Kieranski & the Bardbuy. 2012. 114p. pap. *(978-0-9873204-2-1(4))* Breedles Publishing.

Maraja, illus. Alice in Wonderland Picture Book. 2013. (Shape Bks.). (ENG.). 16p. (J). pap. 9.95 *(978-1-59583-701-1(9))* Laughing Elephant.

Marathon, creator. When You're Having Fun, Vol. 2. 2005. (Illus.). 92p. pap. 14.99 *(978-1-59532-682-9(0)*, Tokyopop Kids) TOKYOPOP, Inc.

Marchetta, Melina. Finnikin of the Rock. 2011. (Lumatere Chronicles Ser.: 1). (ENG., Illus.). 416p. (YA). (gr. 9). pap. 10.99 *(978-0-7636-5292-0(X))* Candlewick Pr.

—Quintana of Charyn: The Lumatere Chronicles. (Lumatere Chronicles Ser.). (ENG.). 528p. (YA). (gr. 9). 2014. pap. 10.99 *(978-0-7636-6930-0(X))* 2013. 18.99 *(978-0-7636-5835-9(9))* Candlewick Pr.

Marchi, Mary V. The Web in the Halo: A Tale of a Spider Who Learns about Christmas. 2012. 32p. pap. 19.99 *(978-1-4685-6624-6(5))* AuthorHouse.

Marchi, Sergio. The Emerald Table. 2008. 192p. pap. 19.95 (978-1-84799-226-0(9)) Lulu Pr., Inc.

Marciano, John Bemelmans. The All Powerful Ring. Blackall, Sophie, illus. 2016. (Witches of Benevento Ser.: 2). (ENG.). 144p. (J). (gr. 2-5). 13.99 (978-0-451-47180-2(6), Viking Books for Young Readers) Penguin Young Readers Group.

—Mischief Season. Blackall, Sophie, illus. 2016. (Witches of Benevento Ser.: 1). (ENG.). 128p. (J). (gr. 2-5). 13.99 (978-0-451-47181-9(4), Viking Books for Young Readers) Penguin Young Readers Group.

—Respect Your Ghosts. Blackall, Sophie, illus. 2017. (Witches of Benevento Ser.: 4). (ENG.). 128p. (J). (gr. 2-5). 13.99 (978-0-451-47183-3(0), Viking Books for Young Readers) Penguin Young Readers Group.

Marcotte, Jennifer. The Nightly Knight. 2009. 28p. pap. 14.99 (978-1-4490-1943-3(9)) AuthorHouse.

Marcoux, Tom. Crystal Pegasus. 2012. 92p. pap. 18.24 (978-0-9800511-9-3(3)) Marcoux, Tom Media, LLC.

Marcus, Richard. What Will Happen in Eragon IV: Who Lives, Who Dies, Who Becomes the Third Dragon Rider & How Will the Inheritance Cycle Finally End? 2009. (ENG.). 180p. (J). (gr. 3). pap. 12.95 (978-1-56975-728-4(3)) Ulysses Pr.

Mariconda, Barbara. The Voyage of Lucy P. Simmons. 2012. (Voyage of Lucy P. Simmons Ser.: 1). (ENG.). 256p. (J). (gr. 3-7). 16.99 (978-0-06-211979-7(6), Tegen, Katherine Bks) HarperCollins Pubs.

Marie, Dani. The Tale of Prince George. 2012. 28p. pap. 24.95 (978-1-4626-8264-5(2)) America Star Bks.

Marillier, Juliet. Cybele's Secret. 2011. (ENG.). 444p. (YA). (gr. 7). pap. 9.99 (978-0-553-49486-0(4), Knopf Bks. for Young Readers) Random Hse. Children's Bks.

—Raven Flight. (ENG.). 416p. (YA). (gr. 7). 2014. pap. 9.99 (978-0-375-87197-9(7), Ember) 2013. 16.99 (978-0-375-86955-6(7), Knopf Bks. for Young Readers) Random Hse. Children's Bks.

—Shadowfell. 2013. (ENG.). 416p. (YA). (gr. 7). pap. 10.99 (978-0-375-87196-2(9), Ember) Random Hse. Children's Bks.

Marini, Enrico & Dufaux, Jean. Rapaces, Vol. 4. 2005. (SPA., Illus.). 56p. pap. 17.95 (978-1-59497-107-5(2)) Public Square Bks.

Marino, Michael. Magi Adventure. 2012. 80p. 24.99 (978-1-4691-3712-4(7)); pap. 15.99 (978-1-4691-3711-7(9)) Xlibris Corp.

Mark, Yudel. The Jewish Pope: A Yiddish Tale. Goodman, Ruth Fisher, tr. from YID. Krupin, Connie G., illus. 2015. (ENG.). 100p. per. 14.95 (978-1-56474-459-3(0), Fithian Pr) Daniel & Daniel, Pubs., Inc.

Marlowe, Paul. Sporeville. 2007. (Wellborn Conspiracy Ser.: Bk. 1). 250p. (YA). (gr. 8-12). pap. 10.95 (978-0-9739505-4-0(4)) Sybertooth, Inc. CAN. Dist: Lightning Source, Inc.

Marmell, Ari. Covenant's End: A Widdershins Adventure. 2015. (ENG.). 271p. (YA). (gr. 7). 17.99 (978-1-61614-986-4(8), Pyr Bks.) Prometheus Bks., Pubs.

—Lost Covenant: A Widdershins Adventure. 2013. (ENG.). 279p. (YA). (gr. 7). 17.99 (978-1-61614-811-9(X), Pyr Bks.) Prometheus Bks., Pubs.

Marr, Andrew. Creatures We Dream of Knowing: Stories of Our Life Together. 2011. 208p. 24.95 (978-1-4502-8071-6(4)); pap. 14.95 (978-1-4502-8070-9(6)) iUniverse, Inc.

Marr, Melissa. Carnival of Souls. 2012. (ENG.). 320p. (J). pap. 143.92 (978-0-06-221668-7(6)) HarperCollins Pubs.

—Challenge. Xian Nu Studio Staff, illus. 2010. (Wicked Lovely: Desert Tales Ser.: 2). (ENG.). 176p. (YA). (gr. 8-18). pap. 9.99 (978-0-06-149349-2(X)) HarperCollins Pubs.

—Darkest Mercy. 2012. (Wicked Lovely Ser.: 5). (ENG.). 336p. (YA). (gr. 8). pap. 9.99 (978-0-06-165927-0(4)) HarperCollins Pubs.

—Darkest Mercy, 7 vols. (Wicked Lovely Ser.: 5). (YA). 78.75 (978-1-4498-6206-0(3)); 1.25 (978-1-4498-6214-5(4)); 235.75 (978-1-4498-6205-3(5)); 2011. 101.75 (978-1-4498-6208-4(X)); 2011. 99.75 (978-1-4498-6210-7(1)) Recorded Bks., Inc.

—Desert Tales. 2013. (Wicked Lovely Ser.). (ENG.). 272p. (YA). (gr. 8). pap. 9.99 (978-0-06-228756-4(7)) HarperCollins Pubs.

—Faery Tales & Nightmares. 2013. (ENG.). 432p. (YA). (gr. 8). pap. 9.99 (978-0-06-185273-2(2)) HarperCollins Pubs.

—Fragile Eternity. 2010. (Wicked Lovely Ser.: 3). (ENG.). 448p. (YA). (gr. 8). pap. 8.99 (978-0-06-121473-8(6)) HarperCollins Pubs.

—Fragile Eternity, 9 vols. 2009. (Wicked Lovely Ser.: 3). (YA). 130.75 (978-1-4407-3042-9(3)); 265.75 (978-1-4407-3037-5(7)); 1.25 (978-1-4407-3044-3(X)); 112.75 (978-1-4407-3036-8(9)); 110.75 (978-1-4407-3038-2(5)); 132.75 (978-1-4407-3040-5(7)) Recorded Bks., Inc.

—Ink Exchange. (Wicked Lovely Ser.: 2). (ENG.). (YA). (gr. 8). 2009. 352p. pap. 9.99 (978-0-06-121470-7(1)) 2008. 336p. 17.99 (978-0-06-121468-4(X)) HarperCollins Pubs.

—One Blood Ruby. 2017. 368p. (YA). (gr. 9). 17.99 (978-0-06-208416-3(X)) HarperCollins Pubs.

—Radiant Shadows. 2011. (Wicked Lovely Ser.: 4). (ENG.). 368p. (YA). (gr. 8). pap. 9.99 (978-0-06-165924-9(X)) HarperCollins Pubs.

—Untamed City - Carnival of Secrets. 2015. (Untamed City Ser.). (ENG.). 368p. (YA). (gr. 8). pap. 9.99 (978-0-06-235494-5(9)) HarperCollins Pubs.

—Wicked Lovely. 2008. (Wicked Lovely Ser.: 1). (ENG.). 352p. (YA). (gr. 8-12). pap. 9.99 (978-0-06-121467-7(1)) HarperCollins Pubs.

Marr Osb, Andrew. From Beyond to Here: Merendael's Gift & Other Stories. 2012. 320p. (gr. 4-6). 29.95 (978-1-4759-3460-1(2)); pap. 19.95 (978-1-4759-3458-8(0)) iUniverse, Inc.

Marriott, Zoë. Swan Kingdom. 2009. (ENG., Illus.). 272p. (YA). (gr. 7). pap. 8.99 (978-0-7636-4293-8(2)) Candlewick Pr.

Marrone, Amanda. Devoured. 2009. (ENG.). 304p. (YA). (gr. 9-18). pap. 9.99 (978-1-4169-7890-9(9), Simon Pulse) Simon Pulse.

—Master of Mirrors. 2011. (Magic Repair Shop Ser.: 3). (ENG.). 192p. (J). (gr. 3-7). pap. 5.99 (978-1-4169-9035-2(6), Aladdin) Simon & Schuster Children's Publishing.

—Revealers. 2008. (ENG.). 288p. (YA). (gr. 9-18). pap. 8.99 (978-1-4169-5874-1(6), Simon Pulse) Simon Pulse.

Marsh, Carole. Adventure to the Eight Wonders of the World. 2007. (Field Trips (Gallopade International) Ser.). (Illus.). 118p. (J). (gr. 2-9). per. 5.99 (978-0-635-06335-9(2)) Gallopade International.

—Adventure to the Pioneer Prairie! 2007. (Field Trips (Gallopade International) Ser.). (Illus.). 114p. (J). (gr. 2-9). pap. 14.95 (978-0-635-06393-9(X)) Gallopade International.

—Adventure to the Planet Mars! 2007. (Field Trips (Gallopade International) Ser.). (Illus.). 114p. (J). (gr. 4-9). per. 5.99 (978-0-635-06336-6(0)) Gallopade International.

Marsh, Mike. The Skyrats Capture the Grumblies! Jain, Priti, illus. 2012. 28p. pap. (978-1-927506-01-1(8)) Yellow Toadstool Pr.

Marsh, Richard Phillip. Mattress People Go to Bear Park. 2009. 44p. pap. 10.95 (978-1-935125-39-6(7)) Robertson Publishing.

Marshall, Gwendolyn. Saving Crystallia, 1 vol. 2010. 32p. pap. 24.95 (978-1-4489-5637-1(4)) PublishAmerica, Inc.

Marshland, Brad. The Imagicators & the Wind Between the Worlds. 2008. 184p. pap. 13.95 (978-0-595-53370-1(1)) iUniverse, Inc.

Marsoli, Lisa Ann. Harold Takes a Trip: Harold & the Purple Crayon. Chiang, Andy, illus. 2005. 10p. (J). 7.95 (978-1-58117-262-1(1), Intervisual/Piggy Toes) Bendon, Inc.

Marsoli, Lisa Ann & Disney Book Group Staff. The Halloween Ball. Disney Storybook Art Team, illus. 2013. (ENG.). 24p. (J). (gr. -1-k). pap. 5.99 (978-1-4231-7144-7(6)) Disney Pr.

Martin, Benjamin. Revenge of the Akuma Clan. 2013. (ENG.). 320p. (J). (gr. 7-12). 17.99 (978-4-8053-1274-2(2)) Tuttle Publishing.

Martin, Cynthia Bloom. Tryloc: The Quest. 2006. (J). per. 22.95 (978-0-9787015-0-5(X)) T.C. McSears Publishing.

Martin, Dick. The Ozmapolitan of Oz. 2006. (J). 24.95 (978-1-930764-11-8(1)) International Wizard of Oz Club, The.

Martin, Gary & Rogers, Bud. The Raiders of Joppa, 1 vol. Cariello, Sergio, illus. 2008. (Z Graphic Novels / Son of Samson Ser.). (ENG.). 160p. (J). (gr. 4-7). pap. 6.99 (978-0-310-71282-4(3)) Zonderkidz.

Martin, George R. R. The Ice Dragon. Royo, Luis, illus. 2014. (ENG.). 128p. (YA). (gr. 7-12). 14.99 (978-0-7653-7877-4(9), 9780765378774, Tor Teen) Doherty, Tom Assocs., LLC.

Martin, Gina. Mother Moon: Magic Pool in the Sky. 2008. 28p. pap. 12.49 (978-1-4389-0138-1(0)) AuthorHouse.

Martín, JoElle. A Bridge in the Forest, Vol. 1. 2008. (ENG.). 224p. (YA). pap. 14.99 (978-1-59092-372-6(3)) Blue Forge Pr.

—A Promise in the Forest, Vol. 2. 2008. (ENG.). 172p. (YA). pap. 14.99 (978-1-59092-541-6(6)) Blue Forge Pr.

Martin, Nicole. The Werewolf. 2006. 146p. pap. 14.99 (978-1-4120-8802-2(X)) Trafford Publishing.

Martin, W. Lyon. An Ordinary Girl, A Magical Child. Martin, W. Lyon, illus. 2008. (ENG., Illus.). 48p. (J). lib. bdg. 16.95 (978-0-9796834-3-5(2), Magical Child Bks.) Shades of White.

Martinez, G. O. Count Von Ice Dela Cream & the Golden Ice Cream. 2011. 56p. pap. 27.99 (978-1-4568-6522-1(6)) Xlibris Corp.

Marvel & Davis, Adam. Hulk to the Rescue. 2015. (Passport to Reading Level 2 Ser.). (ENG., Illus.). 32p. (J). (gr. -1-3). pap. 3.99 (978-0-316-25640-7(4)) Little, Brown Bks. for Young Readers.

Marvel & Palacios, Tomas. Friends & Foes. 2015. (Passport to Reading Level 2 Ser.). (ENG., Illus.). 32p. (J). (gr. -1-3). pap. 3.99 (978-0-316-25641-4(2)) Little, Brown Bks. for Young Readers.

Marvel & Wyatt, Chris. Marvel's Ant-Man: the Junior Novel. 2015. (ENG.). 144p. (J). (gr. 3-7). pap. 6.99 (978-0-316-25674-2(9)) Little, Brown Bks. for Young Readers.

—Marvel's Avengers: Age of Ultron: the Deluxe Junior Novel. 2015. (ENG., Illus.). 144p. (J). (gr. 3-7). 9.99 (978-0-316-30105-3(1)) Little, Brown Bks. for Young Readers.

Marvel Book Group. The Avengers Storybook Collection. 2015. (Storybook Collection). (ENG.). 304p. (J). (gr. 1-3). 16.99 (978-1-4847-0242-0(5), Marvel Pr.) Disney Publishing Worldwide.

—World of Reading: Avengers the New Team: Level 1. 2015. (World of Reading Ser.). (ENG.). 32p. (J). (gr. -1-1). pap. 3.99 (978-1-4847-1454-6(7), Marvel Pr.) Disney Publishing Worldwide.

Marvel Book Group & West, Alexandra. World of Reading Super Hero Adventures: Thwip! You Are It! Level Pre-1. 2017. (World of Reading Ser.). (ENG.). 32p. (J). (gr. -1-k). pap. 3.99 (978-1-4847-8643-7(2), Marvel Pr.) Disney Publishing Worldwide.

—World of Reading Super Hero Adventures: Tricky Trouble! Level Pre-1. 2017. (World of Reading Ser.). (ENG.). 32p. (J). (gr. -1-k). pap. 3.99 (978-1-4847-8644-4(0), Marvel Pr.) Disney Publishing Worldwide.

Marvel Book Group & Wong, Clarissa S. World of Reading Falcon: This Is Falcon: Level 1. Lim, Ron & Rosenberg, Rachelle, illus. 2015. (World of Reading Ser.). (ENG.). 32p. (J). (gr. 1-3). pap. 3.99 (978-1-4847-2259-6(0), Marvel Pr.) Disney Publishing Worldwide.

Marvel Book Group & Wyatt, Chris. World of Reading: Hulk This Is Hulk. 2015. (World of Reading Ser.). (ENG.). 32p. (J). (gr. 1-3). pap. 3.99 (978-1-4847-1658-8(2), Marvel Pr.) Disney Publishing Worldwide.

Marvel Book Group Staff, et al. Doctor Strange Attack of the Doubt Demons. Lim, Ron, illus. 2016. (ENG.). 24p. (J). (gr. 1-3). pap. 4.99 (978-1-4847-8137-1(6), Marvel Pr.) Disney Publishing Worldwide.

Marvel Books Group & Macri, Thomas. This Is Wolverine. 2013. (Marvel World of Reading Level 1 Ser.). (J). lib. bdg. 13.55 (978-0-606-31751-1(1), Turtleback) Turtleback Bks.

Marvel Books Staff & Strathearn, Chris. Marvel's Ant-Man. 2015. (ENG., Illus.). 24p. (J). (gr. -1-3). pap. 3.99 (978-0-316-25668-1(4)) Little, Brown Bks. for Young Readers.

Marvel Press Group & Disney Book Group Staff. Marvel Super Heroes. Disney Book Group Staff, illus. 2013. (Storybook Collection). (ENG., Illus.). 304p. (J). (gr. -1-k). 15.99 (978-1-4231-7223-9(X)) Marvel Worldwide, Inc.

Marvel Press Staff & Palacios, Tomas. Suits of Armor. Disney Book Group Staff, illus. 2013. (ENG.). 24p. (J). (gr. -1-k). pap. 3.99 (978-1-4231-7246-8(9)) Marvel Worldwide, Inc.

Marvel Press Staff, et al. Thor: the Dark World Junior Novel. Disney Book Group Staff, illus. 2013. (ENG.). 128p. (J). (gr. 3-7). pap. 5.99 (978-1-4231-7245-1(0)) Marvel Worldwide, Inc.

Marvel Staff & Palacios, Tomas. Marvel's Ant-Man: Reader. 2015. (Passport to Reading Level 2 Ser.). (ENG., Illus.). 32p. (J). (gr. -1-3). pap. 3.99 (978-0-316-25671-1(4)) Little, Brown Bks. for Young Readers.

Marz, Ron. Artifacts, Vol. 5. 2013. (ENG., Illus.). 160p. (YA). pap. 16.99 (978-1-60706-664-4(5), 9781607066644) Image Comics.

—Mystic Traveler: The Demon Queen, Vol. 2. Peterson, Brandon et al, illus. 2004. (Mystic Traveler Ser.). 160p. (YA). pap. 9.95 (978-1-59314-037-3(1)) CrossGeneration Comics, Inc.

—Scion Vol. 6: The Royal Wedding. Cheung, Jim et al, illus. 2004. (Scion Ser.). 160p. (YA). pap. 15.95 (978-1-59314-034-2(7)) CrossGeneration Comics, Inc.

Masefield, John. The Box of Delights. Masefield, Judith, illus. 2007. (ENG.). 312p. (J). (gr. 4-7). 17.95 (978-1-59017-251-3(5), NYR Children's Collection) New York Review of Bks., Inc., The.

—The Midnight Folk. Hilder, Rowland, illus. 2008. (ENG.). 256p. (J). (gr. 4-7). 17.95 (978-1-59017-290-2(6), NYR Children's Collection) New York Review of Bks., Inc., The.

Masi, Sue. A Journey Through Fantasy Forest. 2012. 44p. pap. 21.99 (978-1-4691-4837-3(4)) Xlibris Corp.

Mason, Christine. The Mystery of Nan Madol a Pacific Island Adventure. 2011. 166p. pap. 11.95 (978-1-61170-025-1(6)) Robertson Publishing.

Mason, Mike. The Blue Umbrella. 2009. (ENG.). 448p. (YA). pap. 10.99 (978-1-4347-6526-0(1)) Cook, David C.

Mass, Wendy. Every Soul a Star. 2009. (ENG.). 336p. (J). (gr. 3-7). pap. 8.99 (978-0-316-00257-8(7)) Little, Brown Bks. for Young Readers.

—The Last Present. 2015. (ENG.). 256p. (J). (gr. 3-7). pap. 6.99 (978-0-545-31017-8(2)) Scholastic, Inc.

—The Last Present. 2015. (Willow Falls Ser.: 4). lib. bdg. 17.20 (978-0-606-37015-8(3)) Turtleback Bks.

Massey, Eithne. Blood Brother, Swan Sister: 1014 Clontarf - a Battle Begins. 2014. (ENG.). 208p. (J). pap. 14.00 (978-1-84717-567-0(8)) O'Brien Pr., Ltd., The IRL. Dist: Dufour Editions, Inc.

Massie, Elizabeth. Ameri-Scares: Virginia. 2013. 150p. pap. 12.99 (978-1-937530-52-5(3)) Crossroad Pr.

Mastro, M. L. Return to Baladah. 2011. 88p. (gr. 10-12). pap. 9.99 (978-1-4520-7377-4(5)) AuthorHouse.

Matas, Carol & Nodelman, Perry. Of Two Minds. 2013. 156p. pap. (978-0-9919012-1-0(5)) Starburst.

Matharu, Taran. The Battlemage. 2017. (Summoner Trilogy Ser.: bk.3). (ENG., Illus.). 384p. (YA). 18.99 (978-1-250-07632-8(3), 9781250076328) Feiwel & Friends.

—The Inquisition. 2016. (Summoner Trilogy: Bk. 2). (ENG.). 368p. (YA). (gr. 7). 17.99 (978-1-250-07631-1(5), 9781250076311) Feiwel & Friends.

—The Inquisition. 2017. (Summoner Trilogy Ser.: Bk. 2). (ENG.). 384p. (YA). pap. 10.99 (978-1-250-11521-8(3), 9781250115218) Square Fish.

—The Inquisition. 2017. (Summoner Ser.: 2). (YA). lib. bdg. 22.10 (978-0-606-39945-6(3)) Turtleback Bks.

Matharu, Taran. The Novice. 2015. (Summoner Trilogy: Bk. 1). (ENG.). 384p. (YA). (gr. 7). 18.99 (978-1-250-06712-8(X), 9781250067128) Feiwel & Friends.

—The Novice. Barcellona, Christine, ed. 2016. (Summoner Trilogy Ser.: Bk. 1). (ENG.). 384p. (YA). pap. 10.99 (978-1-250-08005-9(3), 9781250080059) Square Fish.

—The Novice. 2016. (Summoner Trilogy: Bk. 1). (ENG.). (YA). (gr. 7-12). lib. bdg. 22.10 (978-0-606-39884-8(8)) Turtleback Bks.

Mathews, Temple. The Sword of Armageddon. 2012. (ENG.). 274p. (J). (gr. 6-11). pap. 9.99 (978-1-937856-19-9(4)) BenBella Bks.

Mathis, Kate. Moon over Monsters. 2013. 318p. pap. 12.95 (978-0-9819789-9-4(1)) PowWow Publishing.

Matott, J. P. & Baker, Margaret. When I Was a Girl ... I Dreamed. Ludy, Mark, illus. 2005. (ENG.). 32p. (J). (gr. -1-4). (978-0-9664276-3-9(7)) Green Pastures Publishing, Inc.

Matott, Justin. When I Was a Boy... I Dreamed. Ludy, Mark, illus. 2004. (ENG.). 32p. (J). (gr. -1-4). (978-0-9664276-2-2(9)) Green Pastures Publishing, Inc.

Matsakis, Cynthia. Sister Sun, Brother Storm. Silver, Jane, illus. 2012. 32p. 24.95 (978-1-4575-0768-7(4)) Dog Ear Publishing, LLC.

Matsi, Maria. A Week in the Life of the Chromasomas. 2009. (Illus.). 156p. pap. (978-1-84748-619-6(3)) Athena Pr.

Matthew-Barnes, David. Wonderland. 2013. (ENG.). 264p. (gr. 7). pap. 11.95 (978-1-60282-788-2(5)) Bold Strokes Bks.

Matthews, Caitlín, et al. Tales from Celtic Lands. Whelan, Olwyn, illus. 2008. (ENG.). 80p. (J). (gr. -1-3). 21.99 (978-1-84686-213-7(2)) Barefoot Bks., Inc.

Matthews, Helen. In a Pocket of Time. 2012. 84p. pap. (978-1-78176-789-4(0)) FeedARead.com.

Matthews, John. The Barefoot Book of Giants, Ghosts, & Goblins. Manna, Giovanni, illus. 2008. (ENG.). 80p. (J). 21.99 (978-1-84686-235-9(3)) Barefoot Bks., Inc.

—The Chronicles of Arthur: Sword of Fire & Ice. Collins, Mike, illus. 2009. (ENG.). 128p. (J). (gr. 3-7). pap. 14.99 (978-1-4169-5908-3(4), Aladdin) Simon & Schuster Children's Publishing.

—Henry Hunter & the Beast of Snagov: Henry Hunter Series #1. 2016. (Henry Hunter Ser.). (ENG., Illus.). 240p. (J). (gr. 2-7). 15.99 (978-1-5107-1038-2(8), Sky Pony Pr.) Skyhorse Publishing Co., Inc.

Matuszak, Pat. Simone's Secret, 2, Bk 2. 2009. (Angel Light Ser.: 2). (ENG.). 192p. (gr. 11). pap. 12.99 (978-0-89957-876-7(4)) AMG Pubs.

Mawhinney, Art, illus. Look & Find Disney Princess Worlds of Wonder. 2006. (Look & Find Books). (J). pap. 24.98 (978-1-4127-6490-2(4)) Publications International, Ltd.

Maxey. Keeko & the Beastie Three. 2010. (Illus.). 40p. (J). 14.99 (978-0-615-38690-4(3)) MonsterHaven.

Maxwell, Lisa. The Last Magician. 2017. (ENG., Illus.). 512p. (YA). (gr. 9). 18.99 (978-1-4814-3207-8(9), Simon Pulse) Simon Pulse.

—Unhooked. 2016. (ENG., Illus.). 352p. (YA). (gr. 9). 17.99 (978-1-4814-3204-7(4), Simon Pulse) Simon Pulse.

May, Elizabeth. The Vanishing Throne. 2016. (Falconer Ser.: 2). (ENG., Illus.). 458p. (YA). (gr. 7-12). 17.99 (978-1-4521-2882-5(0)) Chronicle Bks. LLC.

—The Vanishing Throne: Book Two of the Falconer Trilogy. 2017. (Falconer Ser.: 2). (ENG.). 480p. (YA). pap. 10.99 (978-1-4521-6140-2(2)) Chronicle Bks. LLC.

Mayer, Jeffrey J. Si Javais Gorille. (FRE.). (J). pap. (978-2-07-050613-2(4)) Gallimard, Editions FRA. Dist: Distribooks, Inc.

Mayher, Lauren. The Legend of Darien: A Hero Rises: Book 1. 2008. 423p. (J). per. 12.95 (978-0-9794545-0-9(6)) Blue Eyed Mayhem Publishing.

Mayhew, James. Ella Bella Ballerina & Cinderella. 2009. (Ella Bella Ballerina Ser.). (ENG.). 32p. (J). (gr. -1-3). 14.99 (978-0-7641-6268-8(3)) Barron's Educational Series, Inc.

Mazzola, Lori. Tales of the Tree People to Tree... or. 2006. 48p. pap. 16.95 (978-1-4241-5065-6(5)) PublishAmerica, Inc.

Mc Collin, Alethea. The Cloud Catcher. 2005. (J). per. 3.99 (978-0-9764163-0-2(1)) Bookmark Bks., LLC.

Mc Shane, Mary. Karena the Fairy. 2011. 112p. pap. 10.95 (978-1-4502-9297-9(6)) iUniverse, Inc.

McBride, Earvin, Jr. Earvin MacBride's Amazing Sci-Fi & Adventure Heroes, 7 vols. McBride, Earvin, Jr., illus. 2nd unabr. ed. 2003. (Illus.). (J). (gr. 7-12). pap. 25.95 (978-1-892511-05-8(3)) MacBride, E. J. Pubn., Inc.

McBride, Lish. Firebug. 2014. (ENG.). 336p. (YA). (gr. 9-12). 17.99 (978-0-8050-9862-4(3), 9780805098624, Holt, Henry & Co. Bks. For Young Readers) Holt, Henry & Co.

McBroom, Danielle Loiselle. A Painted Dream. 2008. 20p. pap. 24.95 (978-1-60441-694-7(7)) America Star Bks.

McCaffrey, Anne. If Wishes Were Horses. 2014. (ENG.). 144p. (YA). pap. 10.00 (978-1-4344-4242-0(X), 9781434442420) Wildside Pr., LLC.

Mccall, Philip, 2nd. Adaxxis Nightshade. 2012. 300p. pap. 14.99 (978-0-9822656-9-7(7), Mythix Studios) McCall, Philip Lee II.

McCandless Iii, Bruce. Beatrice & the Basilisk. 2012. 66p. pap. 5.99 (978-0-615-60901-0(5)) Ninth Planet Pr.

McCarthy, Jon-Paul. Eddie the Egg. 2010. (Illus.). 32p. pap. 12.99 (978-1-4490-4125-0(6)) AuthorHouse.

McCarthy, Kai. Unpredictable Prophecies. 2012. 324p. 29.95 (978-1-4626-7644-6(8)) America Star Bks.

McCarty, Bryan. Devyn's Gold. 2008. pap. 17.00 (978-0-8059-8640-2(5)) Dorrance Publishing Co., Inc.

McCarty, Marty. Hard Girl Goes to a Scary Movie. 2004. (J). 7.99 (978-0-9748712-0-2(6)) hard girl bk. club.

McCaughrean, Geraldine. Peter Pan de Rojo Escarlata. Gonzalez-Gallarza, Isabel, tr. Wyatt, David, illus. 2006. 296p. (J). (gr. 5-8). 17.95 (978-958-704-467-6(3)) Ediciones Alfaguara ESP. Dist: Santillana USA Publishing Co., Inc.

—The Stones Are Hatching. unabr. ed. 2004. 240p. (J). (gr. 5-9). pap. 38.00 incl. audio (978-0-8072-0866-3(3), LYA 318 SP, Listening Library) Random Hse. Audio Publishing Group.

McClinton, Theresa. The Stone Guardian. 2013. 300p. pap. 11.99 (978-1-939194-78-7(4)) Etopia Pr.

McClymer, Kelly. Must Love Black. 2008. (ENG.). 192p. (YA). (gr. 7-18). pap. 8.99 (978-1-4169-4903-9(8), Simon Pulse) Simon Pulse.

Mcconaghy, Taylor. Too Good to Be True: Book One of the Beholder Trilogy. 2012. 226p. 25.95 (978-1-4759-3323-9(1)); pap. 15.95 (978-1-4759-3322-2(3)) iUniverse, Inc.

McCooke, Valerie J. Grandfather's Chest. 2012. 40p. pap. 32.70 (978-1-4771-0543-6(3)) Xlibris Corp.

McCormick, Lisa Wade. Christopher Paolini. 2012. (All about the Author Ser.). (ENG., Illus.). 112p. (J). (gr. 7-12). lib. bdg. 34.60 (978-1-4488-6939-8(0)) Rosen Publishing Group, Inc., The.

McCoy, Angie. Starchild's Adventures on Earth. McCoy, Derrick, illus. 2011. 24p. pap. 24.95 (978-1-4560-5053-5(2)) America Star Bks.

McCray, Ed. Jill Chill & the Baron of Glacier Mountain: Wonder Tales from the Book of Ed. Brewer, Tammy & Harms, Cathy, eds. McCray, Ed, illus. 2003. (Illus.). 150p. (J). mass mkt. 14.95 (978-1-929515-26-4(X), Solovisions) Comic Library International.

McCulloch, Amy. The Oathbreaker's Shadow. 2015. (ENG.). 384p. (YA). pap. 11.99 (978-0-7387-4405-6(0), Flux) North Star Editions.

—The Shadow's Curse. 2016. (ENG., Illus.). 456p. (YA). pap. 11.99 (978-0-7387-4512-1(X), Flux) North Star Editions.

McCullough, Jerletha. Fairies of the Lilies. 2009. 20p. pap. 16.49 (978-1-4389-2286-7(8)) AuthorHouse.

Mccullough, Kelly. School for Sidekicks. 2016. (J). lib. bdg. 18.40 (978-0-606-38559-6(2)) Turtleback Bks.

McCune, Joshua. Invisible Monsters. 2015. (Talker 25 Ser.: 2). (ENG.). 448p. (YA). (gr. 8). 17.99 (978-0-06-212194-3(4), Greenwillow Bks.) HarperCollins Pubs.

—Talker 25. 2015. (Talker 25 Ser.: 1). (ENG.). 448p. (YA). (gr. 9). pap. 9.99 (978-0-06-212193-6(6), Greenwillow Bks.) HarperCollins Pubs.

McDonald, Megan. Judy Moody, Mood Martian. 2015. (Judy Moody Ser.: 12). lib. bdg. 16.00 (978-0-606-36876-6(0)) Turtleback Bks.

McDougal-Littell Publishing Staff. Literature Connections English: Tuck Everlasting. 2004. (McDougal Littell Literature Connections Ser.). (ENG.). 152p. (gr. 6-6). 16.90 (978-0-395-77522-6(1), 2-80091) Great Source Education Group, Inc.

McDowell, Andrew. Beyond the Forest. 2007. 286p. pap. 16.95 (978-0-7414-4238-3(8)) Infinity Publishing.

McDowell, Nigel. The Black North. 2016. (ENG., Illus.). 432p. (YA). (gr. 8). 11.99 (978-1-4714-0067-4(0)) Bonnier Publishing GBR. Dist: Independent Pubs. Group.

McDunn, Rosemary. When Kids Dream & Trucks Fly. 2007. (ENG.). 52p. per. 12.99 (978-0-9792258-6-4(8)) Bezalel Bks.

McEntee, Jackie. Reality & Dreams. 2010. 120p. (gr. -1). pap. 12.49 (978-1-4389-9551-9(2)) AuthorHouse.

Mcfaul, Jason & Macdonald, Eric. What A Trip. 2007. pap. 77.53 (978-0-7575-4014-1(7)) Kendall Hunt Publishing Co.

McGalliard, Julie. Waking up Naked in Strange Places. 2015. (YA). 24.99 (978-1-941662-09-0(9)) Per Aspera Pr.

—Waking Up Naked in Strange Places. 2015. (YA). pap. 14.99 (978-1-941662-10-6(2)) Per Aspera Pr.

McGann, Oisín. Under Fragile Stone, Vol. 2. 2005. (ENG., Illus.). 384p. (J). pap. 12.95 *(978-0-86278-835-3(8))* O'Brien Pr., Ltd., The IRL. Dist: Dufour Editions, Inc.
McGinnis, Mindy. Given to the Sea. 2017. (Given Duet Ser.). (ENG.). 352p. (YA). (gr. 9). 17.99 *(978-0-399-54461-3(5),* G.P. Putnam's Sons Books for Young Readers) Penguin Young Readers Group.
Mcginty, Ian. Surprise! 2014. (Hello Kitty Graphic Novel Ser.). lib. bdg. 18.40 *(978-0-606-35471-4(9))* Turtleback Bks.
McGinty, Ian. Welcome to Showside. 2016. (ENG., Illus.). 176p. (J). pap. 19.99 *(978-1-940878-07-2(1),* 9781940878072) Z2 Comics.
McGlame, Jack. Majik: The Beginning. 2012. 132p. 21.95 *(978-1-4759-3289-8(8))* iUniverse, Inc.
McGonagle, Riona. The Crystal Tower of Light. 2007. (Illus.). 192p. (J). (gr. 3-7). pap. *(978-1-903631-34-8(3))* Arlen Hse.
McGowan, Maureen. Sleeping Beauty: Vampire Slayer. 2010. 320p. pap. 8.95 *(978-1-60747-779-2(3),* Pickwick Pr.) Phoenix Bks., Inc.
McGrath, Alister. Chosen Ones, 1 vol. 2010. (Aedyn Chronicles Ser.). (ENG.). 208p. (J). (gr. 4-7). 14.99 *(978-0-310-71812-3(0))* Zondervan.
McGrath, Barbara Barbieri. The Little Red Elf. Bonnet, Rosalinde, illus. 2009. (ENG.). 32p. (J). (gr. -1-2). 14.95 *(978-1-58089-236-0(1))* Charlesbridge Publishing, Inc.
McGraw, Eloise. The Moorchild. 2006. 241p. (gr. 4-7). 17.00 *(978-0-7569-6823-6(2))* Perfection Learning Corp.
McGraw, Eloise Jarvis & McGraw, Lauren Lynn. The Forbidden Fountain of Oz. 2006. (J). 24.95 *(978-1-930764-12-5(X))* International Wizard of Oz Club, The.
McGregor, Suzy. Moon Leopard. 2013. 40p. pap. 11.95 *(978-0-9824926-5-9(0))* Lollipop Media Productions, LP.
McGuire, Jeremy. O'shaughnessey: Boy & His Leprechaun. 2007. 140p. per. 14.95 *(978-1-4327-0892-4(9))* Outskirts Pr., Inc.
McIsaac, Meaghan. The Boys of Fire & Ash. 2015. (ENG.). 336p. (J). (gr. 5). 19.99 *(978-0-375-99167-7(0),* Delacorte Bks. for Young Readers) Random Hse. Children's Bks.
McKay, Laurie. Realm Breaker. 2017. (Last Dragon Charmer Ser.: 3). 368p. (J). (gr. 3-7). 16.99 *(978-0-06-230849-8(1))* HarperCollins Pubs.
—The Villain Keeper. 2016. (Last Dragon Charmer Ser.: 1). 368p. (J). (gr. 3-7). pap. 6.99 *(978-0-06-230844-3(0))* HarperCollins Pubs.
McKendall, Kerry. My Imagination Book. 2009. 48p. pap. 17.49 *(978-1-4389-1299-8(4))* AuthorHouse.
McKenna, James. The Mind Traveller. 2013. 212p. pap. *(978-0-9569723-8-5(1))* Lone Cloud Publishing.
McKenzie, Hugh Galt & Bradshaw-White, Karl. The Four Dreamers Return to Loch Brochan. 2015. (ENG., Illus.). 275p. (J). (gr. 1-2). pap. 14.95 *(978-1-78455-600-6(9),* 81f774d5-6673-435e-b5de-3720511a5997) Austin, Stan AUS. Dist: Bookmasters Distribution.
McKenzie, J. Lee. Vampires Don't Believe in Mermaids. 2011. 54p. pap. 16.95 *(978-1-4560-1157-4(X))* America Star Bks.
McKenzie, Tiffany M. The Adventures of Alan & the Man-Eating Rabbits. 2013. 24p. pap. 24.95 *(978-1-63000-143-8(0))* America Star Bks.
McKillip, Patricia A. The Changeling Sea. 2003. (ENG., Illus.). 144p. (YA). (gr. 7-7). 5.99 *(978-0-14-131262-0(9),* Firebird) Penguin Young Readers Group.
—The Forgotten Beasts of Eld. 2006. (ENG., Illus.). 352p. (YA). (gr. 7-12). pap. 16.95 *(978-0-15-205536-3(3))* Houghton Mifflin Harcourt Publishing Co.
McKinley, Robin. Beauty: A Retelling of the Story of Beauty & the Beast. 2005. (ENG.). 336p. (YA). (gr. 3-7). pap. 8.99 *(978-0-06-075310-8(2),* HarperTeen) HarperCollins Pubs.
—Beauty: A Retelling of the Story of Beauty & the Beast. 325p. (YA). (gr. 3-18). 23.25 *(978-0-8446-7317-2(X))* Smith, Peter Pub., Inc.
—Chalice. 2010. (ENG.). 288p. (YA). (gr. 7-18). 8.99 *(978-0-14-241720-1(3),* Firebird) Penguin Young Readers Group.
—Dragonhaven. 2009. (ENG.). 368p. (YA). (gr. 7-18). 9.99 *(978-0-14-241494-1(8),* Firebird) Penguin Young Readers Group.
—Pegasus. 2010. (ENG.). 416p. (YA). (gr. 7-18). 18.99 *(978-0-399-24677-7(0),* G.P. Putnam's Sons Books for Young Readers) Penguin Young Readers Group.
—Shadows. 2013. 356p. (YA). *(978-0-399-25625-7(3))* Penguin Publishing Group.
—Shadows. 2014. (ENG.). 384p. (YA). (gr. 7). pap. 9.99 *(978-0-14-751220-8(4),* Speak) Penguin Young Readers Group.
McKinley, Ryan. The Lost Crew. 2012. (ENG.). 144p. pap. 14.95 *(978-1-4327-9659-4(3));* pap. 9.95 *(978-1-4327-9658-7(5))* Outskirts Pr., Inc.
McKinty, Adrian. The Lighthouse Land. 2006. (ENG., Illus.). 200p. (YA). (gr. 6-10). 16.95 *(978-0-8109-5480-9(X))* Abrams, Inc.
McLaren, Heather. Mythos. 2013. (ENG.). 260p. pap. 17.95 *(978-1-60619-093-7(8))* Twilight Times Bks.
McLean, Wendy & Book Company Staff. Follow an Elf. Worthington, Leonie, illus. 2003. (Sparkle Bks.). 10p. (J). bds. 8.95 *(978-1-74047-314-9(0))* Book Co. Publishing Pty, Ltd., The AUS. Dist: Penton Overseas, Inc.
McLeod, Kris Aro. Hush-a-Bye Counting: A Bedtime Book. Allyn, Virginia, illus. 2008. (ENG.). 20p. (J). (gr. -1). 14.95 *(978-1-58117-785-5(2),* Intervisual/Piggy Toes) Bendon, Inc.
McLoughlin, Wayne, illus. Warriors - Tales from the Clans. 2014. (Warriors Novella Ser.). (ENG.). 320p. (J). (gr. 3-7). pap. 6.99 *(978-0-06-229085-4(1))* HarperCollins Pubs.
McMahen, Chris. Box of Shocks, 1 vol. 2011. (ENG.). 168p. (J). (gr. 4-7). pap. 9.95 *(978-1-55469-917-9(7))* Orca Bk. Pubs. USA.
McMakin, Jordan. Prince Ezrick & the Morpheas Curse, 4 vols. 2005. (Illus.). 304p. (J). per. 11.95 *(978-0-9764184-0-5(1))* Canterwine Pr.
McMann, Laney. Tied. 2013. (ENG.). 286p. (YA). pap. 13.99 *(978-1-937744-30-4(2))* J. Taylor Publishing.
McMann, Lisa. Dragon Captives. 2017. (Unwanteds Quests Ser.: 1). (ENG., Illus.). 432p. (J). (gr. 3-7). 17.99 *(978-1-4814-5681-4(4),* Simon & Schuster/Paula Wiseman Bks.) Simon & Schuster/Paula Wiseman Bks.
—Dragon Captives. 2018. (Unwanteds Quests Ser.: 1). lib. bdg. 18.40 ***(978-0-606-40846-2(0))*** Turtleback Bks.
—Island of Dragons. 2016. (Unwanteds Ser.: 7). (ENG., Illus.). 544p. (J). (gr. 3-7). 17.99 *(978-1-4424-9337-7(2),* Aladdin) Simon & Schuster Children's Publishing.
—Island of Fire. (Unwanteds Ser.: 3). (ENG., Illus.). (J). (gr. 3-7). 2014. 480p. pap. 8.99 *(978-1-4424-5846-8(1))* 2013. 464p. 19.99 *(978-1-4424-5845-1(3))* Simon & Schuster Children's Publishing. (Aladdin).
—Island of Fire. 2014. (Unwanteds Ser.: 3). lib. bdg. 19.65 *(978-0-606-35796-8(3))* Turtleback Bks.
—Island of Graves. (Unwanteds Ser.: 6). (ENG., Illus.). (J). (gr. 3-7). 2016. 560p. pap. 8.99 *(978-1-4424-9335-3(6))* 2015. 528p. 18.99 *(978-1-4424-9334-6(8))* Simon & Schuster Children's Publishing. (Aladdin).
—Island of Graves. 2016. (Unwanteds Ser.: 6). lib. bdg. 19.65 *(978-0-606-38497-1(9))* Turtleback Bks.
—Island of Legends. 2015. (Unwanteds Ser.: 4). lib. bdg. 19.65 *(978-0-606-37134-6(6))* Turtleback Bks.
—Island of Shipwrecks. 2015. (Unwanteds Ser.: 5). (ENG., Illus.). 480p. (J). (gr. 3-7). pap. 8.99 *(978-1-4424-9332-2(1),* Aladdin) Simon & Schuster Children's Publishing.
—The Unwanteds, 6 vols. 2011. (Unwanteds Ser.: Bk. 1). (J). 90.75 *(978-1-4618-4113-5(5));* 88.75 *(978-1-4618-4117-3(8));* 245.75 *(978-1-4618-4114-2(3));* 1.25 *(978-1-4640-2489-4(8));* 88.75 *(978-1-4618-4116-6(X))* Recorded Bks., Inc.
—The Unwanteds. (Unwanteds Ser.: 1). (ENG., Illus.). (J). (gr. 3-7). 2012. 416p. pap. 7.99 *(978-1-4424-0769-5(7))* 2011. 400p. 18.99 *(978-1-4424-0768-8(9))* Simon & Schuster Children's Publishing. (Aladdin).
—The Unwanteds. 2012. (Unwanteds Ser.: 1). lib. bdg. 18.40 *(978-0-606-26953-7(3),* Turtleback) Turtleback Bks.
—The Unwanteds Set: The Unwanteds; Island of Silence; Island of Fire. 2013. (Unwanteds Ser.). (ENG.). 1280p. (J). (gr. 3-7). 51.99 *(978-1-4424-9450-3(6),* Aladdin) Simon & Schuster Children's Publishing.
—The Wake Trilogy: Wake; Fade; Gone. 2011. (Wake Ser.: Bks. 1-3). (ENG.). 768p. (YA). (gr. 9). pap. 29.99 *(978-1-4424-2826-3(0),* Simon Pulse) Simon Pulse.
McMillion, Gloria. Whirlwinds Whirl Around. 2007. 136p. per. 11.95 *(978-0-595-42248-7(9))* iUniverse, Inc.
McMullan, Kate. Dragon Slayers' Academy Set 2. Basso, Bill, illus. 2007. (Dragon Slayers' Academy Ser.). (ENG.). 112p. 145.26 *(978-1-59961-375-8(1))* Spotlight.
—The Ghost of Sir Herbert Dungeonstone. Basso, Bill, illus. 2004. (Dragon Slayers' Academy Ser.: 12). (ENG.). 112p. (J). (gr. 2-5). pap. 4.99 *(978-0-448-43530-5(6),* Grosset & Dunlap) Penguin Young Readers Group.
—Stop That Bull, Theseus! LaFleur, David, illus. 2003. (Myth-o-Mania Ser.: Bk. 5). (ENG.). 160p. (J). (gr. 3-7). 9.99 *(978-0-7868-0861-8(6))* Hyperion Bks. for Children.
—A Wedding for Wiglaf? Basso, Bill, illus. 2003. (Dragon Slayers' Academy Ser.: 4). (ENG.). 112p. (J). (gr. 2-5). pap. 5.99 *(978-0-448-43111-6(4),* Grosset & Dunlap) Penguin Young Readers Group.
—Wheel of Misfortune, 1 vol. Basso, Bill, illus. 2007. (Dragon Slayers' Academy Ser.: No. 7). (ENG.). 109p. (gr. 2-5). 24.21 *(978-1-59961-381-9(6))* Spotlight.
McMullen, Judy Benson, ed. Ghost in the Gazebo. 2012. (ENG.). (YA). pap. *(978-1-4675-3218-1(5))* Independent Pub.
McMullin, Perry. The Boy Who Could Fly. 2009. 44p. pap. 18.95 *(978-1-4490-0904-5(2))* AuthorHouse.
McNabb, Linda. Dragons' Bane. 2008. 208p. *(978-1-86950-655-1(3))* HarperCollins Pubs. Australia.
McNaney, Jeanne. Miracle in Sumatra: The Story of Gutsy Gus. Cochard, David, illus. 2009. (ENG.). 32p. (J). (gr. -1-3). 16.95 *(978-0-9814534-6-0(5))* Ovation Bks.
McNeil, Natalie. Wylli Nilly's Amazing Adventures. 2011. (Illus.). 56p. pap. 20.38 *(978-1-4567-7672-5(X))* AuthorHouse.
McNish, Cliff. The Silver Child. 192p. (J). 2015. (ENG.). (gr. 4-7). 9.99 *(978-1-4677-9452-7(X),* Carolrhoda Bks.) 2006. (gr. 3-7). per. 6.95 *(978-0-8225-6503-1(X),* First Avenue Editions) 2005. (ENG.). (gr. 4-7). 15.95 *(978-1-57505-825-2(1))* Lerner Publishing Group.
—Silver City. 2007. (Exceptional Reading & Language Arts Titles for Intermediate Grades Ser.). (ENG.). 256p. (J). (gr. 4-7). per. 6.95 *(978-0-8225-6780-6(6),* First Avenue Editions) Lerner Publishing Group.
—Silver World. (ENG.). 248p. (J). (gr. 4-7). 2008. pap. 6.95 *(978-1-58013-879-6(9),* First Avenue Editions) 2007. 15.95 *(978-1-57505-897-9(9),* Carolrhoda Bks.) Lerner Publishing Group.
McOmber, Rachel B., ed. McOmber Phonics Storybooks: Robin Hood's Cook. rev. ed. (Illus.). (J). *(978-0-944991-64-0(5))* Swift Learning Resources.
—McOmber Phonics Storybooks: Under the Rainbow. rev. ed. (Illus.). (J). *(978-0-944991-81-7(5))* Swift Learning Resources.
McPartland, Dorothy. Wishing Stars. McPartland, Dorothy, illus. 2004. (Illus.). 34p. (J). bds. 15.95 *(978-0-9755374-0-4(7))* Little Light Pr.
McPhail, J. A. Dawn of Day. Battis, Gwen, illus. 2012. 200p. pap. 10.99 *(978-0-9851196-1-4(6))* Rowe Publishing and Design.
McPhate, Paul J. The Puggle King. 2008. 52p. pap. 16.95 *(978-1-60703-709-5(2))* America Star Bks.
McShane, Pol. The Button That Should Never, Ever, Ever Be Pushed! 2008. 140p. pap. 11.95 *(978-0-595-53194-3(6),* iUniverse, Inc.) iUniverse, Inc.
McVeigh, Mark W. The Lizard's Legacy. Sazaklis, John, illus. 2009. (Spider-Man Ser.). 64p. (J). (gr. 2-5). pap. 4.99 *(978-0-06-162627-2(9),* HarperFestival) HarperCollins Pubs.
Mead, Richelle. Bloodlines. 2012. (Bloodlines Ser.: 1). (ENG.). 448p. (YA). (gr. 7-18). pap. 10.99 *(978-1-59514-473-7(0),* Razorbill) Penguin Young Readers Group.
—The Glittering Court. 2016. 416p. (YA). pap. *(978-0-448-49385-5(3),* Razorbill) Penguin Publishing Group.
—The Glittering Court. (Glittering Court Ser.: 1). (ENG.). (YA). (gr. 7). 2017. 432p. pap. 10.99 *(978-1-59514-842-1(6))* 2016. 416p. 19.99 *(978-1-59514-841-4(8))* Penguin Young Readers Group. (Razorbill).
—The Indigo Spell. 2013. (Bloodlines Ser.: Bk. 3). (ENG.). 416p. (YA). (gr. 7). 18.99 *(978-1-59514-319-8(X),* Razorbill) Penguin Publishing Group.
—The Indigo Spell. 2013. (Bloodlines Ser.: 3). (ENG.). 448p. (YA). (gr. 7). pap. 10.99 *(978-1-59514-613-7(X),* Razorbill) Penguin Young Readers Group.
—The Ruby Circle. 2015. (Bloodlines Ser.: 6). (ENG.). 384p. (YA). (gr. 7). pap. 10.99 *(978-1-59514-633-5(4),* Razorbill) Penguin Young Readers Group.
—Shadow Kiss. 2008. (Vampire Academy Ser.: 3). (ENG.). 448p. (YA). (gr. 7-18). pap. 10.99 *(978-1-59514-197-2(9),* Razorbill) Penguin Publishing Group.
—Soundless. l.t. ed. 2016. (ENG.). 352p. 25.99 *(978-1-4104-8817-6(9))* Cengage Gale.
—Soundless. 2015. (ENG.). 272p. (YA). (gr. 7-10). 19.99 *(978-1-59514-763-9(2),* Razorbill) Penguin Publishing Group.
Mead, Richelle & Loftin, Nikki. Soundless. 2016. (ENG.). 288p. (YA). (gr. 7). 10.99 *(978-1-59514-764-6(0),* Razorbill) Penguin Young Readers Group.
Meadows, Daisy. Addison the April Fool's Day Fairy. 2014. (Rainbow Magic — Special Edition Ser.). lib. bdg. 17.20 *(978-0-606-35378-6(X))* Turtleback Bks.
—Alexa the Fashion Editor Fairy. 2013. (Rainbow Magic — the Fashion Fairies Ser.: 4). lib. bdg. 14.75 *(978-0-606-31994-2(8),* Turtleback) Turtleback Bks.
—Angelica the Angel Fairy (Rainbow Magic: Special Edition) 2015. (Rainbow Magic Special Edition Ser.). (ENG., Illus.). 176p. (J). (gr. 2-5). pap. 6.99 *(978-0-545-70828-9(1),* Scholastic Paperbacks) Scholastic, Inc.
—Ashley the Dragon Fairy. 2012. (Illus.). (J). (Magical Animal Fairies Ser.: 1). (ENG.). 80p. (gr. 2-5). pap. 4.99 *(978-0-545-38417-9(6),* Scholastic Paperbacks); 65p. *(978-0-545-42595-7(6))* Scholastic, Inc.
—Autumn the Falling Leaves Fairy. 2013. (Rainbow Magic — Special Edition Ser.). lib. bdg. 17.20 *(978-0-606-32370-3(8),* Turtleback) Turtleback Bks.
—Ava the Sunset Fairy. 2011. (Illus.). 63p. (J). *(978-0-545-38040-9(5))* Scholastic, Inc.
—Cara the Camp Fairy. 2011. (Rainbow Magic Ser.). (ENG., Illus.). 176p. (J). (gr. 2-5). pap. 6.99 *(978-0-545-30877-9(1),* Scholastic Paperbacks) Scholastic, Inc.
—Cassidy the Costume Fairy. 2012. (Rainbow Magic — the Princess Fairies Ser.: 2). lib. bdg. 14.75 *(978-0-606-26170-8(2),* Turtleback) Turtleback Bks.
—Crystal the Snow Fairy. Ripper, Georgie, illus. 2006. (Weather Fairies Ser.: 1). (ENG.). 80p. (Orig.). (J). (gr. -1-3). mass mkt. 4.99 *(978-0-439-81387-7(5),* Scholastic Paperbacks) Scholastic, Inc.
—Elisa the Royal Adventure Fairy. 2012. (Rainbow Magic — the Princess Fairies Ser.: 4). lib. bdg. 14.75 *(978-0-606-26172-2(9),* Turtleback) Turtleback Bks.
—Emily, the Emerald Fairy. Ripper, Georgie, illus. 2005. 65p. (J). pap. *(978-0-545-01190-7(6))* Scholastic, Inc.
—Erin the Phoenix Fairy. 2012. (Illus.). 64p. (J). *(978-0-545-42597-1(2))* Scholastic, Inc.
—Eva the Enchanted Ball Fairy. 2012. (Rainbow Magic — the Princess Fairies Ser.: 7). lib. bdg. 14.75 *(978-0-606-26175-3(3),* Turtleback) Turtleback Bks.
—The Fairies' Birthday Surprise. 2010. (Scholastic Reader Level 2 Ser.). (ENG.). 32p. (J). (gr. 1-3). pap. 3.99 *(978-0-545-22292-1(3),* Cartwheel Bks.) Scholastic, Inc.
—Gabriella the Snow Kingdom Fairy. 2009. (Rainbow Magic Ser.). (ENG.). 176p. (J). (gr. 2-5). 6.99 *(978-0-545-10614-6(1),* Scholastic Paperbacks) Scholastic, Inc.
—Grace Woollyhop's Musical Mystery (Magic Animal Friends #12) 2016. (Magic Animal Friends Ser.: 12). (ENG., Illus.). 112p. (J). (gr. 2-5). pap. 4.99 *(978-0-545-94079-5(6),* Scholastic Paperbacks) Scholastic, Inc.
—Harriet the Hamster Fairy. Ripper, Georgie, illus. 2008. (Rainbow Magic — the Pet Fairies Ser.). 67p. (gr. -1-3). lib. bdg. 14.75 *(978-1-4178-3007-7(7),* Turtleback) Turtleback Bks.
—Hayley the Rain Fairy. 2007. (Rainbow Magic — the Weather Fairies Ser.: 7). (Orig.). lib. bdg. 14.75 *(978-1-4177-7082-3(1),* Turtleback) Turtleback Bks.
—Heather the Violet Fairy. 2005. (Rainbow Magic Ser.). 71p. (J). *(978-0-439-69192-5(3))* Scholastic, Inc.
—Helena the Horse-Riding Fairy. 2010. (Sports Fairies Ser.: 1). (ENG.). 80p. (J). (gr. 2-5). 4.99 *(978-0-545-20252-7(3),* Scholastic Paperbacks) Scholastic, Inc.
—Joy the Summer Vacation Fairy. Ripper, Georgie, illus. 2007. (Rainbow Magic — Special Edition Ser.). 177p. (gr. -1-3). lib. bdg. 17.20 *(978-1-4177-7081-6(3),* Turtleback) Turtleback Bks.
—Katie the Kitten Fairy. Ripper, Georgie, illus. 2008. (J). (Pet Fairies Ser.: 1). (ENG.). 80p. (gr. -1-3). pap. 4.99 *(978-0-545-02816-5(7),* Scholastic Paperbacks); 65p. pap. *(978-0-545-13320-3(3))* Scholastic, Inc.
—Katie the Kitten Fairy. Ripper, Georgie, illus. 2008. (Rainbow Magic — the Pet Fairies Ser.). 65p. (gr. 1-4). lib. bdg. 14.75 *(978-1-4178-2999-6(0),* Turtleback) Turtleback Bks.
—Lara the Black Cat Fairy. 2012. (Illus.). 65p. (J). *(978-0-545-42596-4(4))* Scholastic, Inc.
—Lisa the Lollipop Fairy. 2014. (Sugar & Spice Fairies Ser.: 1). (ENG.). 80p. (J). (gr. 2-5). pap. 4.99 *(978-0-545-60531-1(8),* Scholastic Paperbacks) Scholastic, Inc.
—Lizzie the Sweet Treats Fairy. 2012. (Rainbow Magic — the Princess Fairies Ser.: 5). lib. bdg. 14.75 *(978-0-606-26173-9(7),* Turtleback) Turtleback Bks.
—Mia the Bridesmaid Fairy. 2010. (Rainbow Magic Ser.). (ENG.). 176p. (J). (gr. 2-5). 6.99 *(978-0-545-20251-0(5),* Scholastic Paperbacks) Scholastic, Inc.
—Molly the Goldfish Fairy. Ripper, Georgie, illus. 2008. (Pet Fairies Ser.: 6). (ENG.). 80p. (J). (gr. -1-3). pap. 4.99 *(978-0-545-04189-8(9),* Scholastic Paperbacks) Scholastic, Inc.
—Molly the Goldfish Fairy. Ripper, Georgie, illus. 2008. (Rainbow Magic — the Pet Fairies Ser.). 68p. (gr. -1-3). lib. bdg. 14.75 *(978-1-4178-3001-5(8),* Turtleback) Turtleback Bks.
—Rainbow Magic Special Edition: Autumn the Falling Leaves Fairy. 2013. (Rainbow Magic Special Edition Ser.). (ENG.). 176p. (J). (gr. 2-5). pap. 6.99 *(978-0-545-48495-4(2),* Scholastic Paperbacks) Scholastic, Inc.
—Rainbow Magic Special Edition: Lindsay the Luck Fairy. Dynamo Limited Staff, illus. 2013. (Rainbow Magic Special Edition Ser.). (ENG.). 192p. (J). (gr. 2-5). pap. 6.99 *(978-0-545-48492-3(8),* Scholastic Paperbacks) Scholastic, Inc.
—Rihanna the Seahorse Fairy. 2012. (Illus.). 65p. (J). *(978-0-545-42599-5(9))* Scholastic, Inc.
—Rita the Frog Princess Fairy. 2016. (Fairy Tale Fairies Ser.: 4). (ENG., Illus.). 80p. (J). (gr. 2-5). pap. 4.99 *(978-0-545-85197-8(1),* Scholastic Paperbacks) Scholastic, Inc.
—Rosalie the Rapunzel Fairy. 2017. (Storybook Fairies Ser.: 3). (ENG.). 80p. (J). (gr. 2-5). pap. 4.99 *(978-1-338-05502-3(X),* Scholastic Paperbacks) Scholastic, Inc.
—Ruby the Red Fairy. Ripper, Georgie, illus. 2005. (Rainbow Magic Ser.: 1). (ENG.). 80p. (Orig.). (J). (gr. -1-3). pap. 4.99 *(978-0-439-73861-3(X))* Scholastic, Inc.
—Scholastic Reader Level 2: Rainbow Magic: Pet Fairies to the Rescue! Artful Doodlers Ltd Staff, illus. 2013. (Scholastic Reader Level 2 Ser.). (ENG.). 32p. (J). (gr. -1-3). pap. 3.99 *(978-0-545-46295-2(9),* Scholastic Paperbacks) Scholastic, Inc.
—Sophia the Snow Swan Fairy. 2012. (Illus.). 65p. (J). *(978-0-545-42600-8(6))* Scholastic, Inc.
—Stacey the Soccer Fairy. 2010. (Sports Fairies Ser.: 2). (ENG.). 80p. (J). (gr. 2-5). 4.99 *(978-0-545-20253-4(1),* Scholastic Paperbacks) Scholastic, Inc.
—Vanessa the Choreography Fairy. 2013. (Rainbow Magic — the Superstar Fairies Ser.: 3). lib. bdg. 14.75 *(978-0-606-31515-9(2),* Turtleback) Turtleback Bks.
Meadows, Jodi. Asunder. 2013. (Incarnate Trilogy Ser.: 2). (ENG.). (YA). (gr. 8). 432p. pap. 9.99 *(978-0-06-206079-2(1));* 416p. 17.99 *(978-0-06-206078-5(3))* HarperCollins Pubs. (Tegen, Katherine Bks).
—Before She Ignites. 2017. (Fallen Isles Ser.: 1). 496p. (YA). (gr. 8). 17.99 ***(978-0-06-246940-3(1),*** Tegen, Katherine Bks) HarperCollins Pubs.
—Incarnate. 2013. (Incarnate Trilogy Ser.: 1). (ENG.). 400p. (YA). (gr. 8). pap. 9.99 *(978-0-06-206076-1(7),* Tegen, Katherine Bks) HarperCollins Pubs.
—Infinite. (Incarnate Trilogy Ser.: 3). (ENG.). (YA). (gr. 8). 2015. 448p. pap. 9.99 *(978-0-06-206082-2(1))* 2014. 432p. 17.99 *(978-0-06-206081-5(3))* HarperCollins Pubs. (Tegen, Katherine Bks).
—The Mirror King. 2016. (Orphan Queen Ser.: 2). (Illus.). 544p. (YA). (gr. 8). 17.99 *(978-0-06-231741-4(5),* Tegen, Katherine Bks) HarperCollins Pubs.
—The Orphan Queen. 2015. (Orphan Queen Ser.: 1). (ENG., Illus.). 400p. (YA). (gr. 8). 17.99 *(978-0-06-231738-4(5),* Tegen, Katherine Bks) HarperCollins Pubs.
Means, J. D. Millie & Honey: The Incredible, Instantaneous, Interplanetary Adventure - Volume Ii - Appleopolis. 2012. 112p. pap. 12.95 *(978-1-4575-1394-7(3))* Dog Ear Publishing, LLC.
Mebus, Scott. Gods of Manhattan, 1 vol. 2009. (ENG.). 368p. (J). (gr. 3-7). 8.99 *(978-0-14-241307-4(0),* Puffin Books) Penguin Young Readers Group.
—The Sorcerer's Secret, Bk. 3. 2011. (ENG.). 384p. (J). (gr. 5-18). 8.99 *(978-0-14-241878-9(1),* Puffin Books) Penguin Young Readers Group.
—Spirits in the Park. 2009. (Gods of Manhattan Ser.: No. 2). (J). *(978-0-525-47963-5(5),* Dutton Juvenile) Penguin Publishing Group.
—Spirits in the Park, Vol. 2. 2010. (ENG.). 400p. (J). (gr. 3-7). 8.99 *(978-0-14-241645-7(2),* Puffin Books) Penguin Young Readers Group.
Medders, James. The Tooth Fairy's Quest. Hardin, Teresa, illus. 2008. 32p. pap. 24.95 *(978-1-60672-549-8(1))* America Star Bks.
Medina, Kathleen. Born into Greyworld. 2008. 220p. 29.99 *(978-1-4363-2619-3(2));* pap. 19.99 *(978-1-4363-2618-6(4))* Xlibris Corp.
Meehan, Kelly. A Star Named Symphony. 2009. 24p. pap. 12.99 *(978-1-4389-6652-6(0))* AuthorHouse.
Meehan, William. Amulets of Acacia. 2003. 184p. 23.95 *(978-0-595-74755-9(8));* pap. 13.95 *(978-0-595-27163-4(4))* iUniverse, Inc.
Meer, Pippa Lee. Matilda's Marvellous Monday. 2008. 32p. pap. 14.49 *(978-1-4389-0421-4(5))* AuthorHouse.
Melling, David & Whybrow, Ian. The Flying Diggers. 2010. (ENG., Illus.). 32p. (J). (gr. -1-k). pap. 9.99 *(978-0-340-90313-1(9))* Hodder & Stoughton GBR. Dist: Hachette Bk. Group.
Melling, O. R. The Chronicles of Faerie: The Book of Dreams. 2010. (Chronicles of Faerie Ser.). (ENG.). 720p. (YA). (gr. 2-8). pap. 12.95 *(978-0-8109-8418-9(0),* Amulet Bks.) Abrams, Inc.
Mellon, Gray. The Weird Worlds of Willoughby Wren Wren & the Pigeons. 2010. 196p. pap. *(978-1-907652-06-6(X))* Grosvenor Hse. Publishing Ltd.
Meloy, Colin. Under Wildwood. Ellis, Carson, illus. (Wildwood Chronicles Ser.: 2). (ENG.). (J). (gr. 3). 2013. 592p. pap. 9.99 *(978-0-06-202473-2(6))* 2012. 576p. 17.99 *(978-0-06-202471-8(X))* HarperCollins Pubs.
—The Whiz Mob & the Grenadine Kid. Ellis, Carson, illus. 2017. 432p. (J). (gr. 3-7). 17.99 ***(978-0-06-234245-4(2))*** HarperCollins Pubs.
—Wildwood. Ellis, Carson, illus. (Wildwood Chronicles Ser.: 1). (ENG.). (J). (gr. 3). 2012. 576p. pap. 9.99 *(978-0-06-202470-1(1))* 2011. 560p. 17.99 *(978-0-06-202468-8(X))* HarperCollins Pubs.
—Wildwood. Ellis, Carson, illus. 2012. (Wildwood Chronicles Ser.: 1). (J). lib. bdg. 20.85 *(978-0-606-26864-6(2),* Turtleback) Turtleback Bks.
—Wildwood Imperium. Ellis, Carson, illus. 2014. (Wildwood Chronicles: Bk. 3). (ENG.). 592p. (J). (gr. 3). 17.99 *(978-0-06-202474-9(4))* HarperCollins Pubs.
—Wildwood Imperium: The Wildwood Chronicles, Book III. Ellis, Carson, illus. 2015. (Wildwood Chronicles Ser.: 3). (ENG.). 592p. (J). (gr. 3). pap. 9.99 *(978-0-06-202476-3(0))* HarperCollins Pubs.
Melrose, Laurie. Willow Wood. 2013. 238p. pap. 15.95 *(978-1-62646-375-2(1))* Booklocker.com, Inc.
Memoirs of Gulls: Growing Up. l.t. ed. 2005. (Illus.). 28p. (J). pap. 14.95 *(978-0-9768752-1-5(7))* Open Spaces Publishing (Rupen), LLC.
Menard, Michele. The Invisible Giant's Whisper. 2013. 48p. 24.95 *(978-0-9891734-9-0(6))* Four Menards, The.

Menchen, Antonio Martinez. Fosco. (SPA.). 104p. (YA). (gr. 5-8). *(978-84-204-4101-6(5),* AF1750) Ediciones Alfaguara ESP. Dist: Lectorum Pubns., Inc.

Menchú, Rigoberta & Liano, Dante. The Secret Legacy. Unger, David, tr. from SPA. Domi, Carlos, illus. 2008. (ENG.). 64p. (J). (gr. -1). 19.95 *(978-0-88899-896-5(1))* Groundwood Bks. CAN. Dist: Publishers Group West (PGW).

Merce Company Staff. Don Gil y el Paraguas Magico. (Barril Sin Fondo Ser.). (SPA.). (J). (gr. 3-5). pap. *(978-968-6465-02-0(2))* Casa de Estudios de Literatura y Talleres Artisticos Amaquemecan A.C. MEX. Dist: Lectorum Pubns., Inc.

Merlin. Wizardology: The Book of the Secrets of Merlin. Steer, Dugald A., ed. gif. ed. 2005. (Ologies Ser.). (ENG., Illus.). 32p. (J). (gr. 3-7). 24.99 *(978-0-7636-2895-6(6))* Candlewick Pr.

Merrick, M.R. Endure. 2013. 382p. pap. *(978-0-9917862-4-4(6))* Merrick, M.R.

Mertz, Alyssa. The Lucky Farm Boy, 1 vol. Crum, A. M., illus. 2009. 28p. pap. 24.95 *(978-1-60813-892-0(5))* PublishAmerica, Inc.

Mesibere, Ellen. The Curse of the Laulau Tree. Manasau, Amos, illus. 2012. 34p. pap. *(978-9980-945-67-9(2))* University of Papua New Guinea Press.

—The Magic Log. Naime, Sophie, ed. Joseph, Albert, illus. 2012. 24p. pap. *(978-9980-945-68-6(0))* University of Papua New Guinea Press.

Meskill, Elizia. The Heart Pendant: A Princess' Search for True Love Resplendent. 2012. (ENG.). 22p. (J). 21.95 *(978-1-4327-8003-6(4));* pap. 13.95 *(978-1-4327-7774-6(2))* Outskirts Pr., Inc.

Messenger, Shannon. Exile. (Keeper of the Lost Cities Ser.: 2). (ENG., Illus.). (J). (gr. 3-7). 2014. 592p. pap. 9.99 *(978-1-4424-4597-0(1))* 2013. 576p. 19.99 *(978-1-4424-4596-3(3))* Simon & Schuster Children's Publishing. (Aladdin).

—Keeper of the Lost Cities. (Keeper of the Lost Cities Ser.: 1). (ENG., Illus.). (J). (gr. 3-7). 2013. 512p. pap. 8.99 *(978-1-4424-4594-9(7))* 2012. 496p. 16.99 *(978-1-4424-4593-2(9))* 2015. 1744p. pap. 26.99 *(978-1-4814-5112-3(X))* Simon & Schuster Children's Publishing. (Aladdin).

—Let the Wind Rise. (Sky Fall Ser.: 3). (ENG., Illus.). (YA). (gr. 7). 2017. 432p. pap. 10.99 *(978-1-4814-4655-6(X))* 2016. 416p. 17.99 *(978-1-4814-4654-9(1))* Simon Pulse. (Simon Pulse).

—Lodestar. 2016. (Keeper of the Lost Cities Ser.: 5). (ENG., Illus.). 688p. (J). (gr. 3-7). 18.99 *(978-1-4814-7495-5(2),* Aladdin) Simon & Schuster Children's Publishing.

—Neverseen. (Keeper of the Lost Cities Ser.: 4). (ENG., Illus.). 688p. (J). (gr. 3-7). 2016. pap. 9.99 *(978-1-4814-3230-6(3))* 2015. 19.99 *(978-1-4814-3229-0(X))* Simon & Schuster Children's Publishing. (Aladdin).

Messner, Kate. The Seventh Wish. 2017. (ENG.). 256p. (J). pap. 7.99 *(978-1-68119-431-8(7),* 9781681194318, Bloomsbury USA Childrens) Bloomsbury Publishing USA.

Mestas, Nolan & the Magic Bridge. 2009. 28p. pap. 13.99 *(978-1-4490-0812-3(7))* AuthorHouse.

Metaxas, Eric. The Fool & the Flying Ship, 1 vol. Drescher, Henrick, illus. 2007. (Rabbit Ears: A Classic Tale Ser.). (ENG.). 36p. (gr. -1-3). 25.65 *(978-1-59961-308-6(5))* Spotlight.

Meteor & the Mighty Monster Trucks: Shifting Gears. 24p. (J). pap. 3.29 *(978-1-59445-043-3(9))* Dogs in Hats Children's Publishing Co.

Metz, Diana. Brinn & the Dragons of Pallan Cliffs. 2003. 352p. (J). pap. *(978-0-9718431-2-7(0))* M.O.T.H.E.R. Publishing Co., Inc., The.

Metzger, Steve. Ice Cream King. Downing, Julie, illus. 2011. (ENG.). 32p. (J). (gr. -1-2). 15.95 *(978-1-58925-096-3(6));* pap. 7.95 *(978-1-58925-427-5(9))* Tiger Tales.

Meyer, Kai. Arcadia Awakens. 2013. (Arcadia Ser.: 1). (ENG.). 480p. (YA). (gr. 9). pap. 9.99 *(978-0-06-200607-3(X))* HarperCollins Pubs.

—Dark Reflections: The Water Mirror - The Stone Light; the Glass Word. Crawford, Elizabeth D., tr. from GER. 2010. (Dark Reflections Trilogy Ser.). (ENG.). 896p. (YA). (gr. 7). pap. 9.99 *(978-1-4424-0938-5(X),* McElderry, Margaret K. Bks.) McElderry, Margaret K. Bks.

—The Glass Word. Crawford, Elizabeth D., tr. from GER. 2008. (ENG.). 288p. (YA). (gr. 7). (Dark Reflections Trilogy Ser.: 3). pap. 9.99 *(978-0-689-87792-6(7));* (Dark Reflections Trilogy: Bk. 3). 16.99 *(978-0-689-87791-9(9))* McElderry, Margaret K. Bks. (McElderry, Margaret K. Bks.).

—Pirate Wars. Crawford, Elizabeth D., tr. 2008. (Wave Walkers Ser.: 3). (ENG.). 384p. (J). (gr. 5-9). pap. 6.99 *(978-1-4169-2477-7(9),* McElderry, Margaret K. Bks.) McElderry, Margaret K. Bks.

—The Stone Light. Crawford, Elizabeth D., tr. 2007. (Dark Reflections Trilogy Ser.: 2). (ENG.). 384p. (YA). (gr. 7-12). pap. 8.99 *(978-0-689-87790-2(0),* McElderry, Margaret K. Bks.) McElderry, Margaret K. Bks.

Meyer, Maggie. Big Foot Adventures down Under: Book One in the Series 'Spirits Alive' 2013. 244p. (gr. 1-1). 46.72 *(978-1-4797-4547-0(2));* pap. 28.03 *(978-1-4797-4546-3(4))* Xlibris Corp.

Meyer, Marissa. Heartless. 2016. (ENG.). 464p. (YA). 19.99 *(978-1-250-04465-5(0),* 9781250044655) Feiwel & Friends.

—Heartless. 2016. (ENG.). (YA). (gr. 8-12). pap. 12.99 ***(978-1-250-11486-0(1))*** St. Martin's Pr.

—Heartless. 2017. 592p. (YA). pap. 17.99 ***(978-987-747-254-7(6))*** V&R Editoras.

—Stars Above. 2017. (Lunar Chronicles Ser.). (YA). lib. bdg. 22.10 ***(978-0-606-39949-4(6))*** Turtleback Bks.

Mi-Leing. Chrystal's Castle. 2007. 40p. 18.50 *(978-1-4303-2242-9(X))* Lulu Pr., Inc.

Miceli, Mary Anne. Boston North Shore's ... Salem's Golden Broomstick. 2013. 44p. pap. 20.00 *(978-0-9888654-0-2(8))* Miceli, Mary Anne.

—Boston North Shore's... Mouse Tales of Early Salem. 2013. 44p. pap. 20.00 *(978-0-9888654-1-9(6))* Miceli, Mary Anne.

Michael. Bedwin, 1 vol. David, Amanda, illus. 2009. (ENG.). 46p. 24.95 *(978-1-60813-258-4(7))* America Star Bks.

Michaelides, M. Rainbow Angel. 2012. 120p. (gr. 4-6). 20.95 *(978-1-4759-6249-5(9));* pap. 10.95 *(978-1-4759-6248-2(7))* iUniverse, Inc.

Michel, Pauline. Haunted Childhoods. Spencer, Nigel, tr. from FRE. 2006. (ENG.). 18p. pap. 19.95 *(978-1-894852-21-0(4))* Dundurn CAN. Dist: Ingram Publisher Services.

—Haunted Childhoods. 2006. (ENG & FRE.). 94p. (J). *(978-2-89261-460-2(0))* X Y Z Publishing.

Mickel, Sharon. Uniquely Me, Nicci B. 2009. 24p. pap. 12.99 *(978-1-4389-4972-7(3))* AuthorHouse.

Middleton, Julian. Joanna Beyond the Veil. 2012. 116p. pap. *(978-1-78176-977-5(X))* FeedARead.com.

—Rebecca's Book of Dreams. 2013. 110p. pap. *(978-1-78407-136-3(6))* FeedARead.com.

Midorikawa, Yuki. Natsume's Book of Friends. Midorikawa, Yuki, illus. 2010. (ENG., Illus.). Vol. 1. 208p. pap. 9.99 *(978-1-4215-3243-1(3))* Vol. 3. 200p. pap. 9.99 *(978-1-4215-3245-5(X))* Vol. 4. 200p. pap. 9.99 *(978-1-4215-3246-2(8))* Viz Media.

—Natsume's Book of Friends, Vol. 2. Midorikawa, Yuki, illus. 2010. (ENG., Illus.). 208p. pap. 9.99 *(978-1-4215-3244-8(1))* Viz Media.

Miéville, China. Railsea. 2013. (ENG., Illus.). 448p. pap. 12.00 *(978-0-345-52453-9(5),* Del Rey) Random House Publishing Group.

Milford, Kate. The Broken Lands. Offermann, Andrea, illus. 2015. (ENG.). 464p. (J). (gr. 5-7). pap. 8.99 *(978-0-544-43942-9(2),* HMH Books For Young Readers) Houghton Mifflin Harcourt Publishing Co.

Millard, Adam. Peter Crombie, Teenage Zombie. 2012. 238p. pap. *(978-0-9573999-7-6(9))* Crowded Quarantine Pubns.

Miller, Deanna. Sky Bounce. 2003. (Illus.). 210p. (YA). per. 7.99 *(978-0-9725424-1-8(8))* Miller, Deanna.

Miller-Johnston, Renee. Double Trouble for Courtney Logan Kennedy, 1 vol. 2009. 88p. pap. 19.95 *(978-1-60836-384-1(8))* America Star Bks.

Miller, Kristine Elizabeth. Albert's Lunch Box. 2008. 24p. pap. 24.95 *(978-1-60672-096-7(1))* America Star Bks.

Miller, Linsey. Mask of Shadows. 2017. (Mask of Shadows Ser.: 1). (ENG.). 352p. (YA). (gr. 8-12). 17.99 ***(978-1-4926-4749-2(7))*** Sourcebooks, Inc.

Miller, Victoria, illus. Dora & the Unicorn King. 2011. (Dora the Explorer Ser.). (ENG.). 24p. (J). pap. 3.99 *(978-1-4424-1312-2(3),* Simon Spotlight/Nickelodeon) Simon Spotlight/Nickelodeon.

Millet, Lydia. Bodies of the Ancients. 2017. (Dissenters Ser.). (ENG.). 256p. (J). (gr. 4). 16.95 *(978-1-61873-128-9(9),* Big Mouth Hse.) Small Beer Pr.

—The Fires Beneath the Sea. 2012. (Dissenters Ser.). (ENG.). 256p. (J). (gr. 3-7). pap. 12.00 *(978-1-931520-47-8(X),* Big Mouth Hse.) Small Beer Pr.

Millin, Christopher. The King of Arugula. 2007. (ENG.). 208p. (J). (gr. 1-7). per. 12.95 *(978-1-897235-21-8(6))* Thistledown Pr., Ltd. CAN. Dist: Univ. of Toronto Pr.

Milson, Matthew R. Young Arcan & the Garden of Loc. 2007. (Tales from Emberthel Ser.). 221p. (J). (gr. 3-7). per. 14.95 *(978-1-933770-03-1(1))* Avari Pr.

Mindler, Jason. Giralon. 2003. 122p. (YA). 20.95 *(978-0-595-74854-9(6));* pap. 10.95 *(978-0-595-28581-5(3))* iUniverse, Inc. (Writers Club Pr.).

Minix, Holly. What Does Mommy Do at Night? 2009. 68p. pap. 25.00 *(978-1-60693-705-1(7),* Strategic Bk. Publishing) Strategic Book Publishing & Rights Agency (SBPRA).

The Mission. 2nd ed. 2003. 200p. (YA). per. 10.95 *(978-0-9713292-2-5(2))* Aim Higher Bks.

Mitchell, Devon L. The Candy Dragon: Torchy's Adventures of Starting School. 2009. 40p. pap. 16.99 *(978-1-4389-4626-9(0))* AuthorHouse.

Mitchell, Lee Ann. Milo the Mighty Protector. 2010. 32p. pap. 12.99 *(978-1-4490-5447-2(1))* AuthorHouse.

Mitchell, Rae. Anna's Wish. 2009. 24p. pap. 13.50 *(978-1-60860-441-8(1),* Eloquent Bks.) Strategic Book Publishing & Rights Agency (SBPRA).

Mittal, Amitabh. The Heir Apparent. 2009. 32p. pap. 14.99 *(978-1-4389-7845-1(6))* AuthorHouse.

Miura, Taro. Crazy Days. 2009. (ENG., Illus.). 24p. (J). (gr. -1-3). 14.50 *(978-1-85437-850-7(3))* Tate Publishing, Ltd. GBR. Dist: Abrams, Inc.

Miyasaka, Kaho. Kare First Love, 10 vols. Miyasaka, Kaho, illus. 2004. (Kare First Love Ser.: 2). (ENG., Illus.). 200p. pap. 9.95 *(978-1-59116-395-4(1))* Viz Media.

—Kare First Love, 10 vols. Watanabe, Akira, tr. from JPN. Miyasaka, Kaho, illus. 2004. (Kare First Love Ser.: 1). (ENG., Illus.). 200p. pap. 9.95 *(978-1-59116-394-7(3))* Viz Media.

Miyazaki, Hayao. My Neighbor Totoro Picture Book (New Edition) 2013. (ENG., Illus.). 112p. (J). 19.99 *(978-1-4215-6122-6(0))* Viz Media.

—Nausicaä of the Valley of the Wind. Miyazaki, Hayao, illus. 2nd ed. 2004. (ENG., Illus.). Vol. 6. 168p. pap. 12.99 *(978-1-59116-354-1(4))* Vol. 7. 232p. pap. 12.99 *(978-1-59116-355-8(2))* Viz Media.

—Ponyo Film Comic, Vol. 1. Miyazaki, Hayao, illus. movie tie-in ed. 2009. (ENG., Illus.). 172p. (J). pap. 9.99 *(978-1-4215-3077-2(5))* Viz Media.

Mlynowski, Sarah. Abby in Wonderland. 2017. (Whatever After Ser.). (ENG.). 256p. (J). (gr. 3-7). 16.99 ***(978-0-545-74664-9(7),*** Scholastic Pr.) Scholastic, Inc.

Mlynowski, Sarah. Magic in Manhattan: Bras & Broomsticks Frogs; French Kisses. 2012. (Magic in Manhattan Ser.). (ENG.). 608p. (YA). (gr. 7). pap. 10.99 *(978-0-385-74232-0(0),* Ember) Random Hse. Children's Bks.

Mlynowski, Sarah, et al. Upside-Down Magic. 2015. (J). (Upside-down Magic Ser.: No. 1). (ENG.). 208p. (gr. 3-7). 14.99 *(978-0-545-80045-7(5));* 196p. pap. *(978-0-545-90822-1(1))* Scholastic, Inc. (Scholastic Pr.).

Modesto, Michelle. Revenge & the Wild. 2016. 384p. (YA). (gr. 9). 17.99 *(978-0-06-236615-3(7))* HarperCollins Pubs.

Moerbeck, Kees, illus. & des. Cinderella. Moerbeck, Kees, des. 2006. (Roly Poly Box Bks.). (ENG.). 24p. (J). *(978-1-84643-019-0(4))* Child's Play International Ltd.

Molesworth. The Cuckoo Clock. 2007. (ENG.). 122p. pap. 18.99 *(978-1-4346-4245-5(3))* Creative Media Partners, LLC.

—Cuckoo Clock. 2006. 216p. per. *(978-1-4067-1668-9(5),* Hesperides Pr.) Read Bks.

—The Cuckoo Clock. l.t. ed. 2007. 132p. pap. 19.99 *(978-1-4346-4246-2(1))* Creative Media Partners, LLC.

Molinari, Laurice Elehwany. The Dragon's Descent, 1 vol. 2016. (Ether Novel Ser.). (ENG.). 384p. (J). 16.99 *(978-0-310-73557-1(2))* Zonderkidz.

Moloney, James. The Book of Lies. 2004. (Illus.). 416p. *(978-0-207-19831-1(4))* HarperCollins Pubs. Australia.

Moloney, Maria. The Changeling Quest: Children of the Fae. 2013. (ENG.). 210p. (J). (gr. -1-12). pap. 9.95 *(978-1-78099-405-5(2),* Our Street Bks.) Hunt, John Publishing Ltd. GBR. Dist: National Bk. Network.

Molyneux, Caroline. Red for Stop. Green for Go. Yellow for Be Careful. 2010. 32p. 14.49 *(978-1-4490-5824-1(8))* AuthorHouse.

Mongredien, Sue. Oliver Moon & the Broomstick Battle. 2011. (Oliver Moon Ser.). 94p. (J). pap. 4.99 *(978-0-7945-3038-9(9),* Usborne) EDC Publishing.

Moniz, Michael. My Little Superhero. 2013. 42p. 15.95 *(978-1-938083-19-8(9))* Silver Knight Publishing, LLC.

—Tristan: The Changeling Prince (Book 2) 2013. 252p. (J). pap. 11.95 *(978-1-938083-25-9(3))* Silver Knight Publishing, LLC.

Monson, Marianne. The Enchanted Tunnel Vol. 3: Journey to Jerusalem. Burr, Dan, illus. 2011. (J). (gr. 3-6). pap. 7.99 *(978-1-60908-068-6(8))* Deseret Bk. Co.

—Escape from Egypt. 2010. (J). *(978-1-60641-670-9(7))* Deseret Bk. Co.

—Pioneer Puzzle. 2010. (J). *(978-1-60641-669-3(3))* Deseret Bk. Co.

Mont, Eve Marie. A Phantom Enchantment. 2014. (Unbound Ser.). (ENG.). 288p. (YA). (gr. 13). pap. 9.95 *(978-0-7582-6950-8(1),* K-Teen) Kensington Publishing Corp.

Montgomery, L. M. Ana la de Alamos Ventosos. Fantín de Bellocq, Constanza, tr. (Ana la de Tejas Verdes Ser.: 4).Tr. of Anne of Windy Poplars. (SPA.). 288p. (J). (gr. 5-8). *(978-84-7888-636-4(2),* SAL3944) Emece Editores ESP. Dist: Lectorum Pubns., Inc.

Montgomery, R. A. Sand Castle. Newton, Keith, illus. 2008. 80p. (J). (gr. k-3). pap. 7.99 *(978-1-933390-59-8(X))* Chooseco LLC.

—The Trail of Lost Time. 2011. (Illus.). 144p. (J). mass mkt. 6.99 *(978-1-937133-03-0(6))* Chooseco LLC.

Moon, Adam. The Fuzzle. 2007. (J). per. 7.95 *(978-1-934345-28-3(8))* SouthWest Pubns.

Moone, Colin. Wonderful Adventures of the Margicans: The One Bad Apple. 2003. 164p. pap. *(978-1-84426-189-5(1))* Upfront Publishing Ltd.

Mooney, Ms Olive. The Chronicles of Cadaver College: Book of Omis. 2013. 110p. pap. *(978-0-9575130-1-3(1))* Olive Mooney.

Moonshower, Candie. Vivian Vande Velde: Author of Fantasy Fiction. 2009. (Authors Teens Love Ser.). (Illus.). 128p. (J). (gr. 6). lib. bdg. 33.27 *(978-0-7660-2964-4(6))* Enslow Pubs., Inc.

Moore, Kevin. The Road Maker. 2008. 52p. pap. 31.99 *(978-1-4363-7007-3(8))* Xlibris Corp.

Moore, Lorraine. Lidoo Woodo's Goes to Daycare. 2012. 28p. pap. 21.99 *(978-1-4691-6576-9(7))* Xlibris Corp.

Moore, Rosey. Dreams. 2010. 228p. pap. 14.49 *(978-1-4520-7485-6(2))* AuthorHouse.

Moore Thomas, Shelley & Thomas, Shelley Moore. The Seven Tales of Trinket, 1 vol. 2012. (ENG., Illus.). 384p. (J). (gr. 3-7). 16.99 *(978-0-374-36745-9(0),* 9780374367459, Farrar, Straus & Giroux (BYR)) Farrar, Straus & Giroux.

Moore, Victor L. The Pentacle of Northumbria. 2013. 432p. pap. *(978-1-78222-073-2(9))* Paragon Publishing, Rothersthorpe.

Moore, Yvonne. The Listening Gift. 2012. 24p. pap. 17.99 *(978-1-4772-9313-3(2))* AuthorHouse.

Morano, John. Makoona. 2nd rev. ed. 2005. (Morano Eco-Adventure Ser.: 2). 236p. (YA). (gr. 8-12). per. 14.99 *(978-1-59092-111-1(9))* Blue Forge Pr.

Moredun, P. R. The World of Eldaterra Vol. 1: The Dragon Conspiracy. 2005. (World of Eldaterra Ser.). (Illus.). 304p. (J). (gr. 7-18). lib. bdg. 17.89 *(978-0-06-076664-1(6))* HarperCollins Pubs.

Moredun, P.R. The World of Eldaterra: The Dragon Conspiracy, Vol. 1. 2005. (World of Eldaterra Ser.). 304p. (J). (gr. 7-18). 16.99 *(978-0-06-076663-4(8))* HarperCollins Pubs.

Moreira, Carol. Membrane, 1 vol. 2013. (ENG.). 269p. pap. *(978-1-927746-05-9(1))* Fierce ink Pr. Co-Op, Ltd.

Morena - di Palma, Alicia. One Dampy Dawn. 2004. (J). 5.95 *(978-0-9729454-1-7(5),* MomGeek.com) Wood Designs, Inc.

Morgan, Allen. Matthew & the Midnight Wrecker. 2004. (Illus.). (J). (gr. k-3). spiral bd. *(978-0-616-11123-9(1))* Canadian National Institute for the Blind/Institut National Canadien pour les Aveugles.

Morgan, C. M. Silver Doorway #1: A Gnome Away from Home. 2003. 104p. (J). pap. 6.99 *(978-0-9702189-2-6(3))* Sabledrake Enterprises.

—Silver Doorway #3: An Elf's Adventure. 2004. 104p. (J). pap. 6.99 *(978-0-9702189-4-0(X))* Sabledrake Enterprises.

MOrgan, C. M. Silver Doorway #4: Dragon on the Loose. 2004. 104p. (J). pap. 6.99 *(978-0-9702189-7-1(4))* Sabledrake Enterprises.

Morgan, C. M. Silver Doorway #5: Orcs Ahoy! 2005. 104p. (J). pap. 6.99 *(978-0-9702189-8-8(2))* Sabledrake Enterprises.

Morgan, G. A. Chantarelle, 1 vol. 2015. (Five Stones Trilogy Ser.: 2). (ENG.). 316p. (J). pap. 18.95 *(978-1-939017-63-5(7),* a178678b-3da7-4c5c-96c5-09386c28787e) Islandport Pr., Inc.

—The Kinfolk, 1 vol. 2016. (Five Stones Trilogy Ser.: 3). (ENG.). 300p. (J). 18.95 *(978-1-934031-82-7(8),* 8d77caad-23f8-4ae6-8704-a88c1b35f25d) Islandport Pr., Inc.

Morgan, Nikki. Mithendrove: Escaping Callendae. 2003. 110p. (YA). pap. 9.95 *(978-0-595-27138-2(3),* Writer's Showcase Pr.) iUniverse, Inc.

Morgan, Retta & Morgan, Kris. Love Hates. 2011. 152p. pap. 11.99 *(978-1-4567-1448-2(1))* AuthorHouse.

Morgan, Winter. Lost in the End: Lost Minecraft Journals, Book Three. 2016. (Lost Minecraft Journals Ser.). (ENG.). 112p. (J). (gr. 1-7). pap. 7.99 *(978-1-5107-0352-0(7),* Sky Pony Pr.) Skyhorse Publishing Co., Inc.

Morganti, Jerre. The World of Priscilla Gingold. 2008. 135p. pap. 24.95 *(978-1-60474-122-3(8))* America Star Bks.

Mori, Kotaro. Stray Little Devil. (Stray Little Devil Ser.). (ENG., Illus.). (YA). Vol. 1. 2006. 200p. pap. 9.95 *(978-1-59796-043-4(8))* Vol. 2. 2006. 200p. pap. 9.95 *(978-1-59796-044-1(6))* Vol. 3. 2006. 200p. pap. 9.95 *(978-1-59796-045-8(4))* Vol. 4. 2007. 208p. pap. 9.95 *(978-1-59796-046-5(2))* DrMaster Pubns. Inc.

Moriarty, Chris. The Inquisitor's Apprentice. Geyer, Mark Edward, illus. 2013. (ENG.). 352p. (J). (gr. 5-7). pap. 7.99 *(978-0-547-85084-9(0))* Houghton Mifflin Harcourt Publishing Co.

Morimoto, Sango. Taro & the Terror of Eats Street. Morimoto, Sango, illus. 2011. (Adventures of Taro Ser.). (ENG., Illus.). 96p. (J). (gr. 1-4). pap. 7.99 *(978-1-4215-3525-8(4))* Viz Media.

Morin, James F. Rothshield Chasing Shadows. 2006. pap. 14.95 *(978-1-59330-422-5(6))* Aventine Pr.

Morison, M. C. Time Knot: A Timepathway Book. 2017. (ENG.). 416p. (YA). (gr. 8-17). pap. 15.95 ***(978-1-78535-490-8(6),*** Lodestone Bks.) Hunt, John Publishing Ltd. GBR. Dist: National Bk. Network.

Moriyama, Daisuke. Chrono Crusade. 2004. (Illus.). (YA). Vol. 2. 200p. pap. 9.99 *(978-1-4139-0104-7(2))* Vol. 3. 198p. pap. 9.99 *(978-1-4139-0045-3(3))* ADV Manga.

Morris, Chad. Cragbridge Hall, Book 1: The Inventor's Secret. 2013. (Cragbridge Hall Ser.: 1). (ENG., Illus.). 352p. (J). (gr. 3-9). 17.99 *(978-1-60907-326-8(6),* Shadow Mountain) Shadow Mountain Publishing.

—Cragbridge Hall, Book 2: The Avatar Battle. 2014. (Cragbridge Hall Ser.: 2). (ENG., Illus.). 360p. (J). (gr. 3-9). 17.99 *(978-1-60907-809-6(8),* Shadow Mountain) Shadow Mountain Publishing.

—Cragbridge Hall, Book 3: The Impossible Race. 2015. (Cragbridge Hall Ser.: 3). (ENG., Illus.). 432p. (J). (gr. 3-9). 18.99 *(978-1-60907-979-6(5),* Shadow Mountain) Shadow Mountain Publishing.

Morris, Dave. Kingdom of Dream. (Chronicles of Magi Ser.: No. 2). (Illus.). 198p. (J). (gr. k-6). pap. *(978-0-340-67299-0(4))* Hodder & Stoughton.

Morris, Elizabeth. The Quest for the Tellings. Troy, Michael, illus. 2012. 52p. (-18). pap. *(978-1-78222-055-8(0))* Paragon Publishing, Rothersthorpe.

Morris, Rooster. The Gate of No Return. Cummins, Scott, illus. 2004. (ENG.). (J). per. 7.95 *(978-0-9755895-1-9(2),* 0-9755895-1-2) Axle Publishing Co., Inc.

Morton, Ken, illus. Cinderella. 2012. (ENG.). 24p. (J). (gr. -1-12). 5.99 *(978-1-84322-803-5(3))* Anness Publishing GBR. Dist: National Bk. Network.

Mosel, Arlene. Tikki Tikki Tembo. Lent, Blair, illus. 2008. (gr. k-2). 16.95 *(978-0-7569-8457-1(2))* Perfection Learning Corp.

Moskowitz, Hannah. A History of Glitter & Blood. 2015. (ENG., Illus.). 280p. (YA). (gr. 9-17). 18.99 *(978-1-4521-2942-6(8))* Chronicle Bks. LLC.

Moss, Marissa. Alien Eraser Reveals the Secret of Evolution. Moss, Marissa, illus. 2009. (ENG., Illus.). 56p. (J). (gr. 3-7). pap. 6.99 *(978-0-7636-4419-2(6));* (Max Disaster Ser.: Bk. 3). 15.99 *(978-0-7636-3579-4(0))* Candlewick Pr.

Moss, Ronald. The Wizard Next Door. 2009. 198p. pap. 14.95 *(978-1-60911-077-2(3),* Eloquent Bks.) Strategic Book Publishing & Rights Agency (SBPRA).

Mounter, Paddy. Aladdin & His Magical Lamp. 2004. (Young Reading Ser.: Vol. 1). 48p. (J). (gr. 2-18). lib. bdg. 13.95 *(978-1-58086-559-3(3),* Usborne) EDC Publishing.

Mourlevat, Jean-Claude. Winter's End. Bell, Anthea, tr. from FRE. 2009. (ENG., Illus.). 432p. (YA). (gr. 9-18). 17.99 *(978-0-7636-4450-5(1))* Candlewick Pr.

Mudenda, Duly & Nagunga, Kansi. Syankombo. 2004. (Illus.). 20p. 16.95 *(978-1-77936-005-2(3))* Africa Community Publishing & Development Trust ZWE. Dist: Michigan State Univ. Pr.

Muir, Nicola. Baba Didi & the Godwits Fly, 1 vol. Hayward, Annie, illus. 2013. (ENG.). 32p. (J). (gr. k-4). 8.95 *(978-1-78026-130-0(6))* New Internationalist Pubns., Ltd. GBR. Dist: Consortium Bk. Sales & Distribution.

Mulholland, Marie. A Study Guide for the Necklace of Terrersylvanous. 2007. 38p. (J). ring bd. 11.95 *(978-0-9797715-0-7(1))* Sonic Sword Productions.

mulholland, robin. Bolivia & the sunshine King. 2008. 147p. pap. 14.98 *(978-0-557-01401-9(8))* Lulu Pr., Inc.

Mull, Brandon. The Caretaker's Guide to Fablehaven. Dorman, Brandon, illus. 2015. (ENG.). 128p. (J). (gr. 4). 24.99 *(978-1-62972-091-3(7),* Shadow Mountain) Shadow Mountain Publishing.

—Chasing the Prophecy. (Beyonders Ser.: 3). (ENG.). (J). (gr. 3-7). 2014. 528p. pap. 8.99 *(978-1-4169-9797-9(0))* 2013. 512p. 19.99 *(978-1-4169-9796-2(2))* Simon & Schuster Children's Publishing. (Aladdin).

—Chasing the Prophecy. 2014. (Beyonders Ser.: 3). lib. bdg. 19.65 *(978-0-606-35435-6(2))* Turtleback Bks.

—Crystal Keepers. (Five Kingdoms Ser.: 3). (ENG., Illus.). (J). (gr. 3-7). 2016. 512p. pap. 8.99 *(978-1-4424-9707-8(6),* Aladdin) 2015. 496p. 17.99 *(978-1-4424-9706-1(8),* Aladdin Library) Simon & Schuster Children's Publishing.

—Death Weavers. 2016. (Five Kingdoms Ser.: 4). (ENG., Illus.). 512p. (J). (gr. 3-7). 17.99 *(978-1-4424-9709-2(2),* Aladdin) Simon & Schuster Children's Publishing.

—Grip of the Shadow Plague. Dorman, Brandon, illus. 2009. (Fablehaven Ser.: 3). (ENG.). 512p. (J). (gr. 3-8). pap. 8.99 *(978-1-4169-8603-4(0),* Aladdin) Simon & Schuster Children's Publishing.

—Keys to the Demon Prison. 2010. (Fablehaven Ser.: 5). (ENG., Illus.). 600p. (J). (gr. 3). 21.99 *(978-1-60641-238-1(8),* Shadow Mountain) Shadow Mountain Publishing.

—Keys to the Demon Prison. Dorman, Brandon, illus. 2011. (Fablehaven Ser.: 5). (ENG.). 640p. (J). (gr. 3-8). pap. 8.99 *(978-1-4169-9029-1(1),* Aladdin) Simon & Schuster Children's Publishing.

—Rogue Knight. (Five Kingdoms Ser.: 2). (ENG., Illus.). (J). (gr. 3-7). 2015. 496p. pap. 8.99 *(978-1-4424-9704-7(1))* 2014. 480p. 17.99 *(978-1-4424-9703-0(3))* Simon & Schuster Children's Publishing. (Aladdin).

—Rogue Knight. 2015. (Five Kingdoms Ser.: 2). lib. bdg. 19.65 *(978-0-606-38254-0(2))* Turtleback Bks.

—Secrets of the Dragon Sanctuary. Dorman, Brandon, illus. 2010. (Fablehaven Ser.: 4). (ENG.). 560p. (J). (gr. 3-8). pap. 8.99 *(978-1-4169-9028-4(3),* Aladdin) Simon & Schuster Children's Publishing.

—Secrets of the Dragon Sanctuary. 2010. (Fablehaven Ser.: 4). lib. bdg. 19.65 (978-0-606-10685-6(5), Turtleback) Turtleback Bks.
—Seeds of Rebellion. (Beyonders Ser.: 2). (ENG., Illus.). (J). (gr. 3-7). 2013. 528p. pap. 8.99 (978-1-4169-9795-5(4)) 2012. 512p. 19.99 (978-1-4169-9794-8(6)) Simon & Schuster Children's Publishing. (Aladdin).
—Seeds of Rebellion. 2012. (Beyonders Ser.: Bk. 2). (ENG., Illus.). 512p. (J). pap. 10.99 (978-1-4424-4965-7(9), Simon & Schuster/Paula Wiseman Bks.) Simon & Schuster/Paula Wiseman Bks.
—Seeds of Rebellion. 2013. (Beyonders Ser.: 2). lib. bdg. 19.65 (978-0-606-27030-4(2), Turtleback) Turtleback Bks.
—Sky Raiders. (Five Kingdoms Ser.: 1). (ENG., Illus.). (J). (gr. 3-7). 2015. 448p. pap. 7.99 (978-1-4424-9701-6(7)) 2014. 432p. 17.99 (978-1-4424-9700-9(9)) Simon & Schuster Children's Publishing. (Aladdin).
—Sky Raiders. 2015. (Five Kingdoms Ser.: 1). lib. bdg. 18.40 (978-0-606-36303-7(3)) Turtleback Bks.
—Wild Born. 2013. (Spirit Animals Ser.: 1). (ENG., Illus.). 224p. (J). (gr. 3-7). 12.99 (978-0-545-52243-4(9)) Scholastic, Inc.
—A World Without Heroes. (J). 2011. (Beyonders Ser.: 1). 1.25 (978-1-4640-0920-4(1)) (Beyonders Ser.: 1). 92.75 (978-1-4618-0338-6(1)) 2011. (Beyonders Ser.: 1). 124.75 (978-1-4618-0353-9(5)) 2011. 122.75 (978-1-4618-0363-8(2)) Recorded Bks., Inc.
—A World Without Heroes. (Beyonders Ser.: 1). (ENG.). (J). (gr. 3-7). 2012. 496p. pap. 8.99 (978-1-4169-9793-1(8)) 2011. 464p. 19.99 (978-1-4169-9792-4(X)) Simon & Schuster Children's Publishing. (Aladdin).
—A World Without Heroes. 2011. (Beyonders Ser.: Bk. 1). (ENG.). 464p. (J). pap. 10.99 (978-1-4424-3530-8(5), Simon & Schuster/Paula Wiseman Bks.) Simon & Schuster/Paula Wiseman Bks.
—A World Without Heroes. 2012. (Beyonders Ser.: 1). lib. bdg. 19.65 (978-0-606-23675-1(9), Turtleback) Turtleback Bks.
—A World Without Heroes; Seeds of Rebellion; Chasing the Prophecy, Set. 2013. (Beyonders Ser.). (ENG., Illus.). 1456p. (J). (gr. 3-7). 59.99 (978-1-4424-8593-8(0), Aladdin) Simon & Schuster Children's Publishing.
Mull, Brandon, et al. Tales of the Fallen Beasts. 2016. (Spirit Animals Ser.). (ENG.). 192p. (J). (gr. 3-7). 12.99 (978-0-545-90129-1(4)) Scholastic, Inc.
Mullaney, Polly. Three Kids Gripped by Evil. 2013. 158p. pap. 10.62 (978-1-291-38027-9(2)) Lulu Pr., Inc.
Muller, Jean Powers. Rudolph's Sniffalator. 2011. 20p. pap. 13.77 (978-1-4269-7065-8(X)) Trafford Publishing.
—Santa's New Reindeer, RUBIN. 2011. 32p. pap. 14.50 (978-1-4269-6572-2(9)) Trafford Publishing.
Muncaster, Harriet. Isadora Moon Goes Camping. 2017. (Isadora Moon Ser.: 2). (ENG.). 128p. (J). (gr. 1-4). 5.99 **(978-0-399-55827-6(6))**; 14.99 **(978-0-399-55825-2(X))**; lib. bdg. 17.99 **(978-0-399-55826-9(8))** Random Hse. Children's Bks. (Random Hse. Bks. for Young Readers).
—Isadora Moon Goes to School. 2017. (Isadora Moon Ser.: 1). (ENG.). 128p. (J). (gr. 1-4). 5.99 **(978-0-399-55823-8(3))**; 14.99 **(978-0-399-55821-4(7))**; lib. bdg. 17.99 **(978-0-399-55822-1(5))** Random Hse. Children's Bks. (Random Hse. Bks. for Young Readers).
Munday, Dj. The Secret Dummy of Joshua Bean. 2008. 84p. pap. (978-1-84923-029-2(3)) YouWriteOn.
Mungin, Shanyece. Entwined, 1 vol. 2010. 117p. pap. 19.95 (978-1-4489-9685-8(6)) America Star Bks.
Murayama, Kei. A Centaur's Life, Vol. 2. 2014. (Centaur's Life Ser.). (ENG., Illus.). 175p. pap. 12.99 (978-1-62692-000-2(1), 9781626920002) Seven Seas Entertainment, LLC.
Murguia, Bethanie Deeney. I Feel Five! Murguia, Bethanie Deeney, illus. 2014. (ENG., Illus.). 32p. (J). (gr. -1-3). 14.99 (978-0-7636-6291-2(7)) Candlewick Pr.
Murphy, Timothy. Sugarbowl. 2013. 140p. pap. 11.95 (978-1-62857-019-9(9), Strategic Bk. Publishing) Strategic Book Publishing & Rights Agency (SBPRA).
Murray, E. R. The Book of Shadows. 2017. (Nine Lives Trilogy Ser.: 02). (ENG.). 384p. pap. 14.00 **(978-1-78117-452-4(0))** Mercier Pr., Ltd., The IRL. Dist: Dufour Editions, Inc.
Murray, Shannon & Groenendyk, Doretta. Bounce & Beans & Bum, 1 vol. 2008. (ENG., Illus.). 24p. (J). (gr. -1-3). 7.95 (978-1-894838-28-3(9)) Acorn Pr., The CAN. Dist: Orca Bk. Pubs. USA.
Muscia, Marilena Carrubba. Misses Cowy to the Rescue. 2011. 24p. (gr. -1). 12.99 (978-1-4567-3582-1(9)) AuthorHouse.
Mwangi, Nyaruai. Argwings & the Lamplighters. 2008. 96p. (YA). pap. 13.95 (978-0-9796476-8-0(1)) HM Bks.
My Time on Nantucket. 2005. (J). cd-rom 11.95 (978-0-9755078-2-7(6)) Sweet Punkin Pr.
Myklusch, Matt. The End of Infinity. 2013. (Jack Blank Adventure Ser.: 3). (ENG., Illus.). 416p. (J). (gr. 3-7). pap. 8.99 (978-1-4169-9568-5(4), Aladdin) Simon & Schuster Children's Publishing.
—The End of Infinity. 2012. (Jack Blank Adventure Ser.: 3). (ENG., Illus.). 416p. (J). (gr. 3-7). 16.99 (978-1-4169-9567-8(6), Simon & Schuster/Paula Wiseman Bks.) Simon & Schuster/Paula Wiseman Bks.
—The Secret War. 2012. (Jack Blank Adventure Ser.: 2). (ENG., Illus.). 560p. (J). (gr. 3-7). pap. 7.99 (978-1-4169-9565-4(X), Aladdin) Simon & Schuster Children's Publishing.
—The Secret War. 2011. (Jack Blank Adventure Ser.: 2). (ENG., Illus.). 544p. (J). (gr. 3-7). lib. bdg. 16.99 (978-1-4169-9564-7(1), Simon & Schuster/Paula Wiseman Bks.) Simon & Schuster/Paula Wiseman Bks.
Myracle, Lauren. Wishing Day. McLaughlin, Julie, illus. 2016. (Wishing Day Ser.: 1). 336p. (J). (gr. 3-7). 16.99 (978-0-06-234206-5(1), Tegen, Katherine Bks) HarperCollins Pubs.
!Myster?Ous M! & Courageous $Oul. The Lonely Flower. Courageous $oul, illus. 2011. 20p. pap. 24.95 (978-1-4560-6950-6(0)) America Star Bks.
Mystical World of Nebe: Sky of Dreams. 2006. (YA). 14.95 (978-0-9779369-0-8(2)) Adamson, Mac.
Nagatsuki, Tappei & Otsuka, Shinichirou. Starting Life in Another World. 2016. (Re:ZERO -Starting Life in Another World- Ser.: 1). (ENG., Illus.). 240p. (gr. 8-17). pap. 14.00 (978-0-316-31530-2(3), Yen Pr.) Orbit.
Namjoshi, Suniti & Jain, Shefalee. Aditi & the Marine Sage. 2004. (Simply a Story Ser.). (Illus.). 80p. (J). (978-81-8146-040-0(5)) Tulika Pubs.
Nanavati, Daniel. Midrak Earthshaker. Pryor, John-Thomas, illus. 2013. 132p. pap. (978-1-908867-06-3(X)) FootSteps Pr.
Narine, Vidya D. Kari. 2011. 66p. 24.99 (978-1-4568-5348-8(1)); pap. 15.99 (978-1-4568-5347-1(3)) Xlibris Corp.
Narsimhan, Mahtab. The Third Eye. 2007. (Tara Trilogy Ser.: 1). (ENG.). 240p. (YA). (gr. 5-7). pap. 12.99 (978-1-55002-750-1(6), Boardwalk Bks.) Dundurn CAN. Dist: Ingram Publisher Services.
Narvick, the Whark (or a Shwale) 2003. (J). 8.95 (978-0-9729703-1-0(2)) Kidderature Publishing.
Nash, Scott. The High-Skies Adventures of Blue Jay the Pirate. Nash, Scott, illus. 2012. (ENG., Illus.). 368p. (J). (gr. 4-7). 17.99 (978-0-7636-3264-9(3)) Candlewick Pr.
Na'Shae. The Magic Chronicles: Ice. 2008. 80p. pap. 9.99 (978-0-9814650-6-7(4)) G Publishing LLC.
Nasu, Yukie. Here Is Greenwood. Nasu, Yukie, illus. 2005. (Here Is Greenwood Ser.). (ENG., Illus.). (YA). Vol. 2. 216p. pap. 9.99 (978-1-59116-605-4(5)) Vol. 3. 200p. pap. 9.99 (978-1-59116-606-1(3)) Viz Media.
Nasu, Yukie & Smith, Joe. Here is Greenwood, 1. Nasu, Yukie, illus. 2004. (ENG., Illus.). 208p. (YA). pap. 9.99 (978-1-59116-604-7(7)) Viz Media.
Nation, Kaleb. The Specter Key. 2010. (ENG.). 352p. (J). (gr. 4-7). pap. 7.99 (978-1-4022-4059-1(7), Sourcebooks Jabberwocky) Sourcebooks, Inc.
Nayeri, Daniel & Nayeri, Dina. Another Pan. 2011. (ENG., Illus.). 400p. (YA). (gr. 9). pap. 8.99 (978-0-7636-5664-5(X)) Candlewick Pr.
Nayeri, Daniel and Dina. Another Pan. 2010. (ENG., Illus.). 400p. (YA). (gr. 9-18). 16.99 (978-0-7636-3712-5(2)) Candlewick Pr.
Nazemi, Mary. Kaveh, Jolly & the Super Giant. 2006. (J). pap. 15.00 (978-0-8059-7001-2(0)) Dorrance Publishing Co., Inc.
Neff, Henry H. Impyrium. (Impyrium Ser.: 1). 592p. (J). (gr. 3-7). 2017. pap. 7.99 **(978-0-06-239206-0(9))** 2016. (Illus.). 17.99 (978-0-06-239205-3(0)) HarperCollins Pubs.
Neill, Chloe. Firespell: A Novel of the Dark Elite. 2010. (Dark Elite Ser.: 1). (ENG.). 256p. (YA). (gr. 9-18). 6.99 (978-0-451-22886-4(3), Berkley) Penguin Publishing Group.
Neilson, G. E. F. Cosmic Aviators - Nathaniel's 1st Adventure. 2013. 332p. pap. (978-0-9576132-0-1(2)) Buzzword Pr.
Neimark, Gillian. The Golden Rectangle. (ENG., 160p. (J). (gr. 3-7). 2014. Illus.). pap. 6.99 (978-1-4169-8043-8(1)) 2013. 15.99 (978-1-4169-8042-1(3)) Simon & Schuster Children's Publishing. (Aladdin).
—The Secret Spiral. 2013. (ENG.). 224p. (J). (gr. 3-7). pap. 5.99 (978-1-4169-8041-4(5), Aladdin) Simon & Schuster Children's Publishing.
Nelson, D. J. The One-Eyed Spotogon. 2012. (Illus.). 24p. pap. 19.82 (978-1-4772-1965-2(X)) AuthorHouse.
Nelson, Michael Alan. Hexed: The Sisters of Witchdown. 2015. (ENG., Illus.). 281p. (YA). (gr. 7). pap. 14.99 (978-1-63388-056-6(7), Pyr Bks.) Prometheus Bks., Pubs.
Nelson, Sybil. Priscilla the Great: The Kiss of Life. 2013. 218p. 17.99 (978-1-939947-01-7(4)) Little Prince Publishing.
Nesbet, Anne. The Wrinkled Crown. 2015. (ENG.). 400p. (J). (gr. 3-7). 17.99 (978-0-06-210429-8(2)) HarperCollins Pubs.
Nesbit, E. The Enchanted Castle. 2007. 252p. per. 13.95 (978-1-4218-3942-4(3)); (gr. -1-7). 28.95 (978-1-4218-3842-7(7)) 1st World Publishing, Inc. (1st World Library - Literary Society).
—The Enchanted Castle. 2007. (ENG.). 190p. pap. 19.99 (978-1-4346-5225-6(4)); 212p. pap. 22.99 (978-1-4346-5226-3(2)) Creative Media Partners, LLC.
—Five Children & It. 2007. 192p. per. 12.95 (978-1-4218-3940-0(7)); (gr. 4-7). 27.95 (978-1-4218-3840-3(0)) 1st World Publishing, Inc. (1st World Library - Literary Society).
—Five Children & It. 207p. 20.95 (978-0-8488-2523-2(3)) Amereon Ltd.
—Five Children & It. 2013. 132p. pap. (978-1-908388-99-5(4)) Aziloth Bks.
—Five Children & It. (gr. 4-6). 2011. 428p. pap. 35.75 (978-1-179-45023-0(X)) 2008. 200p. 22.99 (978-0-554-38716-1(6)) 2008. 200p. 25.99 (978-0-554-29413-1(3)) Creative Media Partners, LLC.
—Five Children & It. Millar, H. R., illus. 2007. (ENG.). 178p. pap. 19.99 (978-1-4346-7586-6(6)); 198p. pap. 21.99 (978-1-4346-7587-3(4)) Creative Media Partners, LLC.
—Five Children & It. 2005. 96p. per. 4.95 (978-1-4209-2587-6(3)) Digireads.com Publishing.
—Five Children & It. Millar, H. R., illus. 2007. (ENG.). 204p. per. (978-1-4065-3077-3(8)) Dodo Pr.
—Five Children & It. 2017. (Dover Children's Evergreen Classics Ser.). (ENG., Illus.). 160p. (J). (gr. 3-8). pap. 4.00 (978-0-486-42366-1(2)) Dover Pubns., Inc.
—Five Children & It. 2006. pap. (978-1-4068-3501-4(3)) 2005. 296p. pap. (978-1-84637-200-1(3)) Echo Library.
—Five Children & It. 2010. 98p. pap. 19.99 (978-1-153-62213-4(0)) General Bks. LLC.
—Five Children & It. 2010. 144p. pap. (978-1-4076-4577-3(3)) HardPr.
—Five Children & It. 2010. 152p. pap. 17.56 (978-1-162-66290-9(5)) 2010. 152p. (gr. 3-7). 29.56 (978-1-169-26518-9(9)) 2010. 152p. 36.95 (978-1-161-43155-1(1)) 2004. reprint ed. pap. 1.99 (978-1-4192-1987-0(1)) 2004. reprint ed. pap. 21.95 (978-1-4191-1987-3(7)) Kessinger Publishing, LLC.
—Five Children & It. 2013. (Oxford Children's Classics Ser.). (ENG.). 208p. 9.95 (978-0-19-273343-6(5)) Oxford Univ. Pr., Inc.
—Five Children & It. Hische, Jessica, illus. 2013. (Penguin Drop Caps Ser.). (ENG.). 256p. (gr. 12). 25.00 (978-0-14-312466-5(8), Penguin Books) Penguin Publishing Group.
—Five Children & It. Nesbit, E. & Millar, H. R., illus. 2004. (ENG.). 240p. (gr. 12-18). 14.00 (978-0-14-303915-0(6), Penguin Classics) Penguin Publishing Group.
—Five Children & It. 2008. (Puffin Classics Ser.). (ENG., Illus.). 272p. (J). (gr. 5-7). 5.99 (978-0-14-132161-5(X), Puffin Books) Penguin Young Readers Group.
—Five Children & It. 2013. (ENG., Illus.). 272p. (J). (gr. 4-7). pap. 10.99 (978-0-09-957298-5(2)) Random Hse. GBR. Dist: Independent Pubs. Group.
—Five Children & It. 2005. (J). 1.25 (978-1-4025-4084-4(1)) Recorded Bks., Inc.
—Five Children & It. 2013. 160p. (978-3-8495-1928-5(7)) 2013. 160p. pap. (978-3-8495-0897-5(8)) 2011. 208p. pap. (978-3-8424-8390-3(2)) Tredition GmbH.
—Five Children & It. 2009. 128p. (gr. 4-7). pap. 4.95 (978-1-60459-692-2(9)) Wilder Pubns., Corp.
—Five Children & It. 2005. (ENG.). 29.95 (978-1-55742-510-2(8)); pap. 14.95 (978-1-55742-506-5(X)) Wildside Pr., LLC.
—Harding's Luck. 2006. 164p. (gr. 4-7). 25.95 (978-1-59818-170-8(X)) Aegypan.
—The Magic City. 2008. 144p. (gr. 4-7). 24.95 (978-1-60664-925-1(6)); pap. 11.95 (978-1-60664-045-6(3)) Aegypan.
—Magic World. 2006. 156p. (gr. -1-7). per. 12.95 (978-1-59818-966-7(2)) Aegypan.
—New Treasure Seekers. 2009. 172p. (gr. 4-7). 25.95 (978-1-60664-665-6(6)); pap. 13.95 (978-1-60664-293-1(6)) Rodgers, Alan Bks.
—The Phoenix & the Carpet. 2007. 236p. per. 12.95 (978-1-4218-3944-8(X), 1st World Library - Literary Society) 1st World Publishing, Inc.
—The Phoenix & the Carpet. 2007. (ENG.). 184p. pap. 19.99 (978-1-4346-5187-7(8)); 204p. pap. 22.99 (978-1-4346-5188-4(6)) Creative Media Partners, LLC.
—The Phoenix & the Carpet. Millar, H., illus. 2012. (Puffin Classics Ser.). (ENG.). 304p. (J). (gr. 5). pap. 5.99 (978-0-14-134086-9(X), Puffin Books) Penguin Young Readers Group.
—The Phoenix & the Carpet. 2009. 156p. pap. 4.95 (978-1-60459-693-9(7)) Wilder Pubns., Corp.
—The Red House. 2006. 140p. per. 11.95 (978-1-59818-965-0(4)) Aegypan.
—The Seven Dragons & Other Stories. 2006. 140p. 24.95 (978-1-59818-171-5(8)) Aegypan.
—The Story of the Amulet. 2009. 176p. (gr. -1-7). pap. 4.95 (978-1-60459-694-6(5)) Wilder Pubns., Corp.
—The Story of the Treasure Seekers. 2009. 128p. (gr. 4-7). pap. 5.50 (978-1-60459-695-3(3)) Wilder Pubns., Corp.
—Wet Magic. 2006. 188p. (gr. -1-7). per. 13.95 (978-1-59818-932-2(8)); 26.95 (978-1-59818-174-6(2)) Aegypan.
Nesbit, Edith. Phoenix & the Carpet. 2003. (Children's Classics). (ENG., Illus.). 224p. (J). (gr. 3-6). pap. 4.99 (978-1-85326-155-8(6)) Wordsworth Editions, Ltd. GBR. Dist: May, L. B. & Assocs.
Ness, Patrick. The Rest of Us Just Live Here. 2015. 342p. (YA). pap. (978-1-4063-6179-7(8)) HarperCollins Pubs.
Nettrour, Nelani. Banshees Bk. 2: Dragon Lands. Nettrour, Heather, illus. I.t. ed. 2003. 114p. (J). pap. 11.95 (978-1-932657-03-6(7)) Third Millennium Pubns.
—Nunkey's Adventures, Bk. 1. Nettrour, Autumn, illus. 2003. 70p. (J). pap. 11.95 (978-1-929381-17-3(4), Third Millennium Publishing) Sci Fi-Arizona, Inc.
Neubert, Oliver. Chantel's Quest for the Enchanted Medallion. 2009. (Cozy Classics Ser.). (ENG., Illus.). 224p. (J). (gr. 3-6). 16.95 (978-1-897476-15-4(9)) Simply Read Bks. CAN. Dist: Ingram Publisher Services.
—Chantel's Quest for the Golden Sword. 2014. (Cozy Classics Ser.). (ENG., Illus.). 224p. (J). (gr. 3-6). pap. 9.95 (978-1-897476-16-1(7)) Simply Read Bks. CAN. Dist: Ingram Publisher Services.
—Chantel's Quest for the Silver Leaf. 2012. (Chantel's Quest Ser.). (ENG., Illus.). 200p. (J). (gr. 4-7). pap. 9.95 (978-1-897476-43-7(4)) Simply Read Bks. CAN. Dist: Ingram Publisher Services.
Neumeier, Rachel. The Floating Islands. 2012. (ENG.). 400p. (YA). (gr. 7). pap. 9.99 (978-0-440-24060-0(3)) Random Hse. Children's Bks.
—The Keeper of the Mist. 2016. (ENG.). 400p. (YA). (gr. 7). lib. bdg. 20.99 (978-0-553-50929-8(2), Knopf Bks. for Young Readers) Random Hse. Children's Bks.
—The White Road of the Moon. 2017. (ENG.). 384p. (YA). (gr. 7). 17.99 (978-0-553-50932-8(2), Knopf Bks. for Young Readers) Random Hse. Children's Bks.
The New Olympians. 2014. (Pegasus Ser.: 3). (ENG., Illus.). 448p. (J). (gr. 3-7). pap. 8.99 (978-1-4424-4416-4(9), Simon & Schuster/Paula Wiseman Bks.) Simon & Schuster/Paula Wiseman Bks.
Newton Driscoll, Ell. The Dragons of Candlewood. 2006. pap. 15.95 (978-1-932196-92-4(7)) WordWright.biz, Inc.
Newton Driscoll, Ellen. The Legend of the Dragon Sword. 2009. 204p. pap. 14.95 (978-1-934335-36-9(3)) WordWright.biz, Inc.
Nguyen, Hoang & Gardner, Paul. Daughters of Stone, Vol. 2. 2013. (ENG., Illus.). 128p. (YA). pap. 14.99 (978-1-60706-789-4(7), 9781607067894) Image Comics.
Nichills, Dee. Visit the Rainforest. 2013. 42p. pap. 9.99 (978-1-60820-857-9(5)) MLR Pr., LLC.
Nicholson, William. Jango. 2007. 409p. (YA). (978-1-4287-4812-5(1)) Harcourt Trade Pubs.
—Jango: Book Two of the Noble Warriors. 2008. (Noble Warriors Ser.: 2). (ENG., Illus.). 432p. (YA). (gr. 7). pap. 25.95 (978-0-15-206160-9(6)) Houghton Mifflin Harcourt Publishing Co.
—Noman: Book Three of the Noble Warriors. 2009. (Noble Warriors Ser.: 3). (ENG., Illus.). 368p. (J). (gr. 7). pap. 15.95 (978-0-15-206656-7(X)) Houghton Mifflin Harcourt Publishing Co.
—Noman: La Orden de los Guerreros Misticos. 2009. (SPA.). 352p. (YA). 18.95 (978-84-666-4051-0(7)) Ediciones B ESP. Dist: Spanish Pubs., LLC.
—Seeker: Book One of the Noble Warriors. 2007. (Noble Warriors Ser.: 1). (ENG., Illus.). 448p. (YA). (gr. 7-12). pap. 23.99 (978-0-15-205866-1(4)) Houghton Mifflin Harcourt Publishing Co.
Nicklas, Rita. The B-Liminator & I Fight Cancer. 2009. 40p. pap. 18.50 (978-0-557-04764-2(1)) Lulu Pr., Inc.
Nicola Baxter Staff. Fairy Palace Pop up. 2009. (978-1-84322-574-4(3)) Bookmart Ltd.
Nicoll, David. Bean at the Fair. 2012. 24p. pap. 15.99 (978-1-4691-4706-2(8)) Xlibris Corp.
—Bean on the Farm. 2012. 24p. pap. 15.99 (978-1-4691-7837-0(0)) Xlibris Corp.
Nicolle, Malachai. Axe Cop, Vol. 1. 2011. (ENG., Illus.). 144p. (J). (gr. 5-12). pap. 14.99 (978-1-59582-681-7(5)) Dark Horse Comics.
—Axe Cop, Vol. 3. 2012. (ENG., Illus.). 120p. (J). (gr. 5-12). pap. 14.99 (978-1-59582-911-5(3)) Dark Horse Comics.
—Bad Guy Earth, Vol. 1. 2011. (ENG., Illus.). 120p. (J). (gr. 5-12). pap. 14.99 (978-1-59582-825-5(7)) Dark Horse Comics.
Nielsen, Jennifer A. Elliot & the Last Underworld War. Kendall, Gideon, illus. 2012. (ENG.). 208p. (J). (gr. 3-8). 12.99 (978-1-4022-4021-8(X), Sourcebooks Jabberwocky) Sourcebooks, Inc.
—Elliot & the Pixie Plot. Kendall, Gideon, illus. 2011. (Underworld Chronicles: Bk. 2). (ENG.). 208p. (J). (gr. 3-8). 12.99 (978-1-4022-4020-1(1), Sourcebooks Jabberwocky) Sourcebooks, Inc.
—Mark of the Thief. 2015. (Mark of the Thief Ser.: 1). lib. bdg. 18.40 (978-0-606-38064-5(7)) Turtleback Bks.
Nielson, Kelli S. Stone Mage Wars, Book 1: Journey to the Fringe. 2011. (YA). 17.99 (978-1-60908-833-0(6)) Deseret Bk. Co.
Niemann, Christoph. The Pet Dragon: A Story about Adventure, Friendship, & Chinese Characters. Niemann, Christoph, illus. 2008. (ENG., Illus.). 40p. (J). (gr. -1-3). 16.99 (978-0-06-157776-5(6), Greenwillow Bks.) HarperCollins Pubs.
Night, P. J. Read It & Weep! 2013. (Creepover Ser.: 13). lib. bdg. 16.00 (978-0-606-27039-7(6), Turtleback) Turtleback Bks.
Nightingale, Clare Theresa. The Adventures of Fishkins & Pepperjacket. 2011. (Illus.). 220p. pap. 56.49 (978-1-4520-8803-7(9)) AuthorHouse.
Niles, Steve & Santoro, Matt. Breath of Bones: a Tale of the Golem: A Tale of the Golem. Allie, Scott, ed. Wachter, Dave, illus. 2014. (ENG.). 80p. 14.99 (978-1-61655-344-9(8)) Dark Horse Comics.
Nimmo, Jenny. Chestnut Soldier. 2009. (Magician Trilogy Ser.). (ENG.). 208p. (J). (gr. 3-7). 5.99 (978-0-545-07127-7(5), Scholastic Paperbacks) Scholastic, Inc.
—Midnight for Charlie Bone. 2003. (Children of the Red King Ser.: Bk. 1). (J). (gr. 2-6). per. 4.99 (978-0-439-48839-6(7)) Scholastic, Inc.
Nishi, Yoshiyuki. Muhyo & Roji's Bureau of Supernatural Investigation, Vol. 18. Nishi, Yoshiyuki, illus. 2010. (ENG., Illus.). 192p. pap. 9.99 (978-1-4215-2840-3(1)) Viz Media.
Nix, Garth. Abhorsen. (Old Kingdom Ser.: 3). (ENG.). (YA). (gr. 8). 2014. 384p. pap. 9.99 (978-0-06-231557-1(9)) 2008. 368p. pap. 9.99 (978-0-06-147433-0(9), HarperTeen) 2004. 528p. pap. 8.99 (978-0-06-052873-7(7), HarperTeen) HarperCollins Pubs.
—Abhorsen. 2004. (Abhorsen Trilogy). (Illus.). 518p. 19.00 (978-0-7569-3180-3(0)) Perfection Learning Corp.
—Abhorsen. Filipetto, Celia, tr. 2006. (Old Kingdom Ser.: No. 3). (SPA.). 315p. (J). 25.99 (978-84-7871-508-4(8)) RBA Libros, S.A. ESP. Dist: Santillana USA Publishing Co., Inc.
—The Abhorsen Chronicles. 2008. (Old Kingdom Ser.: Nos. 1-3). (ENG.). 1232p. (YA). (gr. 8). pap. 19.99 (978-0-06-144182-0(1), HarperTeen) HarperCollins Pubs.
—The Abhorsen Trilogy Set: Sabriel - Lirael - Abhorsen. 2005. (Old Kingdom Ser.: Nos. 1-3). (YA). (gr. 8). pap. 26.99 (978-0-06-073419-0(1), HarperTeen) HarperCollins Pubs.
—Across the Wall: A Tale of the Abhorsen & Other Stories. 2006. (ENG.). 432p. (YA). (gr. 8-12). pap. 8.99 (978-0-06-074715-2(3), HarperTeen) HarperCollins Pubs.
—Aenir. 2004. (Seventh Tower Ser.). 233p. (gr. 3-7). 18.00 (978-0-7569-3525-2(3)) Perfection Learning Corp.
—Clariel: The Lost Abhorsen. 2014. (Old Kingdom Ser.: Bk. 4). (ENG., Illus.). 400p. (YA). (gr. 8). 18.99 (978-0-06-156155-9(X)) HarperCollins Pubs.
—Drowned Wednesday. 2006. (Keys to the Kingdom Ser.: No. 3). 389p. (gr. 4-7). 18.00 (978-0-7569-6939-4(5)) Perfection Learning Corp.
—The Fall. 2004. (Seventh Tower Ser.). 195p. (gr. 4-7). 18.00 (978-0-7569-3516-0(4)) Perfection Learning Corp.
—Goldenhand. 2016. (Old Kingdom Ser.: 5). (Illus.). 368p. (YA). (gr. 8). 19.99 (978-0-06-156158-0(4)) HarperCollins Pubs.
—Into Battle. 2004. (Seventh Tower Ser.). 201p. (gr. 3-7). 17.00 (978-0-7569-3515-3(6)) Perfection Learning Corp.
—Lirael. 2014. (Old Kingdom Ser.: 2). (ENG.). 512p. (YA). (gr. 8). pap. 9.99 (978-0-06-231556-4(0)) HarperCollins Pubs.
—Lirael, Daughter of the Clayr. 2009. 9.68 (978-0-7848-2612-6(9), Everbind) Marco Bk. Co.
—One Beastly Beast: Two Aliens, Three Inventors, Four Fantastic Tales. Biggs, Brian, illus. 2007. 176p. (J). (gr. 2-6). lib. bdg. 16.89 (978-0-06-084320-5(9), Eos) HarperCollins Pubs.
—The Ragwitch. 2004. 391p. (YA). (gr. 7-12). 14.65 (978-0-7569-5709-4(5)) Perfection Learning Corp.
—Sabriel. (Old Kingdom Ser.: 1). (ENG.). (YA). (gr. 8). 2014. 352p. pap. 9.99 (978-0-06-231555-7(2)) 2008. (Illus.). 336p. pap. 9.99 (978-0-06-147435-4(5), HarperTeen) HarperCollins Pubs.
—Sabriel. 2014. (Abhorsen Trilogy Ser.: 1). (YA). lib. bdg. 20.85 (978-0-606-35499-8(9)) Turtleback Bks.
—Sir Thursday. 2007. (Keys to the Kingdom Ser.: No. 4). 344p. (gr. 4-7). 18.00 (978-0-7569-8121-1(2)) Perfection Learning Corp.
—Sir Thursday. 2007. (Keys to the Kingdom Ser.: 4). (ENG.). 352p. (J). (gr. 3-7). pap. 7.99 (978-0-439-43657-1(5), Scholastic Paperbacks) Scholastic, Inc.
—Superior Saturday. 2010. (Keys to the Kingdom Ser.: 6). (ENG.). 288p. (J). (gr. 3-7). 7.99 (978-0-439-43659-5(1), Scholastic Paperbacks) Scholastic, Inc.
—To Hold the Bridge. 2015. (ENG.). 416p. (YA). (gr. 8). 17.99 (978-0-06-229252-0(8)) HarperCollins Pubs.
—The Violet Keystone. 2004. (Seventh Tower Ser.: Bk. 6). 233p. (gr. 4-7). 17.00 (978-0-7569-3506-1(7)) Perfection Learning Corp.
Nix, Garth & Williams, Sean. Blood Ties. 2014. (Spirit Animals Ser.: 3). (ENG., Illus.). 224p. (J). (gr. 3-7). 12.99 (978-0-545-52245-8(5)) Scholastic, Inc.
—The Magic, Bk. 1. 2012. (Troubletwisters Ser.: 1). (ENG.). 304p. (J). (gr. 3-7). pap. 7.99 (978-0-545-25903-3(7), Scholastic Paperbacks) Scholastic, Inc.

—The Monster. (Troubletwisters Ser.: 2). (ENG.). 304p. (J). (gr. 3-7). 2013. pap. 6.99 *(978-0-545-25904-0(5)*, Scholastic Paperbacks) 2012. 16.99 *(978-0-545-25898-2(7)*, Scholastic Pr.) Scholastic, Inc.
—Troubletwisters, Bk. 1. 2011. (Troubletwisters Ser.: 1). (ENG.). 304p. (J). (gr. 3-7). 16.99 *(978-0-545-25897-5(9)*, Scholastic Pr.) Scholastic, Inc.
N'Leh, Anne-Claire. The Planet of Trainiacs. Élyum Studio, illus. 2013. (Little Prince Ser.: 10). (ENG.). 56p. (J). (gr. 4-8). lib. bdg. 26.60 *(978-0-7613-8760-2(9)*, Graphic Universe™) Lerner Publishing Group.
Noël, Alyson. Blue Moon. 2009. (Immortals Ser.: 2). (ENG.). 304p. (YA). (gr. 7-12). pap. 11.99 *(978-0-312-53276-5(8)*, 9780312532765, St. Martin's Griffin) St. Martin's Pr.
—Blue Moon. 2009. (Immortals Ser.: 2). (YA). lib. bdg. 20.85 *(978-0-606-07221-2(7)*, Turtleback) Turtleback Bks.
—La Cazadora de Almas. 2013. (Vintage Espanol Ser.). (SPA.). 464p. (YA). (gr. 7). pap. 10.95 *(978-0-345-80541-6(0)*, Vintage Espanol) Knopf Doubleday Publishing Group.
—Dark Flame. (Immortals Ser.: 4). (ENG.). 336p. (YA). (gr. 7-12). 2012. pap. 10.99 *(978-0-312-58375-0(3)*, 9780312583750) 2010. 17.99 *(978-0-312-59097-0(0)*, 9780312590970) St. Martin's Pr. (St. Martin's Griffin).
—Echo. 2012. (Soul Seekers Ser.: 2). (ENG.). 352p. (YA). (gr. 7). pap. 10.99 *(978-0-312-57566-3(1)*, 9780312575663, St. Martin's Griffin) St. Martin's Pr.
—Fated. 2012. (Soul Seekers Ser.: 1). (ENG.). 368p. (YA). (gr. 7). 18.99 *(978-0-312-66485-5(0)*, 9780312664855, St. Martin's Griffin) St. Martin's Pr.
—Horizon. 2013. (Soul Seekers Ser.: 4). (ENG.). 336p. (YA). (gr. 7). 18.99 *(978-0-312-57717-9(6)*, 9780312577179, St. Martin's Griffin); pap. 9.99 *(978-0-312-66489-3(3)*, 9780312664893, St. Martin's Griffin); mass mkt. 9.99 *(978-1-250-05435-7(4)*, 9781250054357, St. Martin's Paperbacks) St. Martin's Pr.
—Night Star. 2010. (Immortals Ser.: 5). (ENG.). 320p. (YA). (gr. 7-12). 17.99 *(978-0-312-59098-7(9)*, 9780312590987, St. Martin's Griffin) St. Martin's Pr.
—Shadowland. (Immortals Ser.: 3). (ENG.). 368p. (YA). 2010. (gr. 7-12). pap. 9.99 *(978-0-312-65005-6(1)*, 9780312650056) 2009. (gr. 8-12). 17.99 *(978-0-312-59044-4(X)*, 9780312590444) St. Martin's Pr. (St. Martin's Griffin).
Nolan, Lea. Allure. 2013. (Hoodoo Apprentice Ser.: 2). (ENG.). 304p. (YA). (gr. 7-12). pap. 9.99 *(978-1-62266-022-3(6)*, 9781622660223) Entangled Publishing, LLC.
Nolan, Lucy. The Lizard Man of Crabtree County, 1 vol. Kastner, Jill, illus. 2003. (ENG.). 32p. (J). (gr. 1-4). pap. 5.95 *(978-0-7614-5144-0(7))* Marshall Cavendish Corp.
Noland, Charles. The Adventures of Drew & Ellie: The Daring Rescue. Moyer, Tom, illus. 2nd ed. 2006. 92p. (J). per. 7.95 *(978-0-9789297-2-5(1))* TMD Enterprises.
Nolen, T. K. The Magical Fantastical Big Red Balloon. 2009. 20p. pap. 11.49 *(978-1-4389-5183-6(3))* AuthorHouse.
Nomura, Mizuki. Book Girl & the Undine Who Bore a Moonflower. 2013. (Book Girl Ser.: 6). (ENG., Illus.). 240p. (YA). (gr. 8-17). pap. 11.99 *(978-0-316-07696-8(1)*, Yen Pr.) Orbit.
Nordling, Lee. The Bramble. Zick, Bruce, illus. 2013. (ENG.). 32p. (J). (gr. k-3). 16.95 *(978-0-7613-5856-5(0)*, Carolrhoda Bks.) Lerner Publishing Group.
Nordquist, Donna M. Petey the Pigasaurus. Fortune, Leslie, illus. 2011. 32p. pap. 24.95 *(978-1-4560-6051-0(1))* America Star Bks.
Norman, Claire. At the End of the Lane. 2012. (Illus.). 48p. (gr. 1-2). pap. 13.66 *(978-1-4685-8237-6(2))* AuthorHouse.
Norris, Christine. Talisman of Zandria. 1. Nagy, Robert, illus. 2005. 187p. (YA). pap. 14.95 *(978-1-885093-44-8(6)*, LBF/Hadrosaur) Hadrosaur Pr.
—The Talisman of Zandria. 2013. 240p. pap. 14.99 *(978-1-61271-220-8(7))* Zumaya Pubns. LLC.
Norris-Gooding, S. M. The Legend of Kerloup. 2011. 340p. (gr. -1). pap. 23.03 *(978-1-4343-5229-3(3))* AuthorHouse.
North, Lynne. Gerties Gets It Right. 2008. 204p. pap. *(978-1-84923-231-9(8))* YouWriteOn.
North, Pearl. Libyrinth. 2010. (Libyrinth Ser.: 1). (ENG.). 336p. (YA). (gr. 7). pap. 22.99 *(978-0-7653-2687-4(6)*, 9780765326874, Tor Teen) Doherty, Tom Assocs., LLC.
North, Poppy. The Ruby Stone. 2013. 52p. pap. 15.99 *(978-1-4797-6920-9(7))* Xlibris Corp.
Northrop, Michael. Valley of Kings. 2015. (TombQuest Ser.: 3). (ENG.). 192p. (J). (gr. 3-7). 16.99 *(978-0-545-87104-4(2))*; 12.99 *(978-0-545-72340-4(X)*, Scholastic Pr.) Scholastic, Inc.
Norton, Andre. The Monster's Legacy. Lee, Jody A., illus. 2017. (ENG.). 160p. (YA). (gr. 7). pap. 13.99 ***(978-1-5344-1247-7(6)**, Atheneum Bks. for Young Readers)* Simon & Schuster Children's Publishing.
Norton, Mary. The Borrowers. Krush, Beth & Krush, Joe, illus. 2003. (Borrowers Ser.: 1). (ENG.). 192p. (J). (gr. 2-5). pap. 7.99 *(978-0-15-204737-5(9))* Houghton Mifflin Harcourt Publishing Co.
—The Borrowers. Krush, Beth & Krush, Joe, illus. l.t. ed. 2005. 215p. (J). (gr. 3). per. 10.95 *(978-0-7862-7954-8(0))* Thorndike Pr.
—The Borrowers. Krush, Beth & Krush, Joe, illus. 2003. (Odyssey Classic Ser.). 180p. (gr. 4-7). 17.20 *(978-0-613-63581-3(7)*, Turtleback) Turtleback Bks.
—Borrowers. 50th anniv. ed. 2003. (Illus.). (YA). *(978-0-15-204768-9(9)*, Harcourt Children's Bks) Harcourt Children's Bks.
—The Borrowers Afield. Krush, Beth & Krush, Joe, illus. 50th anniv. ed. 2003. (Borrowers Ser.: 2). (ENG.). 224p. (J). (gr. 2-5). pap. 7.99 *(978-0-15-204732-0(8))* Houghton Mifflin Harcourt Publishing Co.
—The Borrowers Afloat. Krush, Beth & Krush, Joe, illus. 2003. (Borrowers Ser.: 3). (ENG.). 192p. (J). (gr. 2-5). pap. 7.99 *(978-0-15-204733-7(6))* Houghton Mifflin Harcourt Publishing Co.
—The Borrowers Avenged. Krush, Joe et al, illus. 50th anniv. ed. 2003. (Borrowers Ser.: 5). (ENG.). 304p. (J). (gr. 2-5). pap. 7.99 *(978-0-15-204731-3(X))* Houghton Mifflin Harcourt Publishing Co.
—Borrowers Collection. 2016. (Borrowers Ser.). (ENG., Illus.). 1104p. (J). (gr. 2-5). 24.99 *(978-0-544-84213-7(8)*, HMH Books For Young Readers) Houghton Mifflin Harcourt Publishing Co.
Norton, Tamra. Shayla Witherwood: A Half-Faerie Tale. 2012. pap. 16.99 *(978-1-59955-963-6(3))* Cedar Fort, Inc./CFI Distribution.
Nosov, Nikolai. The Adventures of Dunno & His Friends. Kay, Nicole, tr. from ENG. 2006. (RUS.). (J). *(978-0-9754433-2-3(1)*, Language Transformer Bks.) Velichko, Vera.
Nova, Jacy & Nova, Nick. City of the Lost Souls. 2008. (ENG., Illus.). 224p. (YA). (gr. 8-12). 9.99 *(978-0-7582-2528-3(8)*, K-Teen) Kensington Publishing Corp.
Noyce, Pendred. Lost in Lexicon: An Adventure in Words & Numbers. Charles, Joan, illus. 2011. (ENG.). 368p. (J). (gr. 3). pap. 12.95 *(978-0-9830219-2-6(9))* Mighty Media Pr.
Noyes, Deborah. Angel & Apostle. 2007. (ENG.). 304p. per. 14.95 *(978-1-932961-29-4(1))* Unbridled Bks.
Nunes, Lygia Bojunga. La Cuerda Floja. (SPA.). 136p. (YA). (gr. 5-8). *(978-84-204-3122-2(2)*, AF1749) Ediciones Alfaguara ESP. Dist: Lectorum Pubns., Inc.
Nunez, Kent Hamilton. Mish: The Desert. 2007. 152p. per. 11.95 *(978-0-595-47808-8(5))* iUniverse, Inc.
Nye, Barry. Hannah & the Magic Blanket - Land of the Robots. 2009. 40p. pap. 18.50 *(978-0-557-06602-5(6))* Lulu Pr., Inc.
Nygren, Kelsie. The Line Between. 2007. (Young Writers Ser.). 176p. (YA). (gr. 8-12). per. 5.99 *(978-1-58158-109-6(2))* McDougal Publishing Co.
Nytra, David. The Secret of the Stone Frog. Nytra, David, illus. 2012. (Leah & Alan Adventures Ser.). (ENG., Illus.). 80p. (J). (gr. 2-7). 14.95 *(978-1-935179-18-4(7))* TOON Books / RAW Junior, LLC.
O' Byrne, Lorraine. The Hippity Dippity Witch. Martin, Laura & Kennedy, Seamus, illus. 2012. 138p. pap. *(978-1-78176-391-9(7))* FeedARead.com.
O., Lila. Lulabelle's Jewels: The Christmas Wish of Mrs. Claus. 2008. 20p. pap. 12.49 *(978-1-4389-3189-0(1))* AuthorHouse.
Oakes, Colleen. Queen of Hearts. 2016. (Queen of Hearts Ser.: 1). 320p. (YA). (gr. 8). 17.99 *(978-0-06-240972-0(7)*, HarperTeen) HarperCollins Pubs.
Oakes, Stephanie. The Sacred Lies of Minnow Bly. 2016. (ENG.). 416p. (YA). (gr. 9). 22.10 *(978-0-606-39335-5(8))* Turtleback Bks.
Oberne, Sharon. Kelsey. 2006. 88p. (YA). pap. 13.95 *(978-1-58909-340-9(2))* Bookstand Publishing.
Oberon, Daphne. The Ghost Tree: Tonantzin's Blessing. 2009. 50p. pap. 23.95 *(978-1-4327-3153-3(X))* Outskirts Pr., Inc.
Oceanak, Karla. Goodnight Unicorn: A Magical Parody. Spanjer, Kendra, illus. 2016. (ENG.). 32p. (gr. -1-3). 16.95 *(978-1-934649-63-3(5))* Bailiwick Pr.
Ocelot, Michel. Kirikou et la Sorciere. pap. 14.95 *(978-2-01-321877-1(X))* Hachette Groupe Livre FRA. Dist: Distribooks, Inc.
O'Connor, Daniel & Barrie, J. M. The Peter Pan Picture Book. Woodward, Alice B., illus. 2015. (ENG.). 96p. (J). (gr. k-3). pap. 12.99 *(978-0-486-79430-3(X))* Dover Pubns., Inc.
O'Connor, George. Artemis: Goddess of the Hunt. 2017. (Olympians Ser.: 9). (ENG., Illus.). 80p. (J). 17.99 *(978-1-62672-521-8(7)*, 9781626725218, First Second Bks.) Roaring Brook Pr.
—Athena Bk. 2: Grey-Eyed Goddess. O'Connor, George, illus. 2010. (Olympians Ser.: 2). (ENG., Illus.). 80p. (J). (gr. 4-9). 17.99 *(978-1-59643-649-7(2)*, 9781596436497, First Second Bks.) Roaring Brook Pr.
O'Dell, Patrick Timothy Wayne. Elvin. 2009. 58p. pap. 16.95 *(978-1-61546-576-7(6))* America Star Bks.
O'Dell, Scott. The Seven Serpents Trilogy. 2009. (ENG.). 560p. (J). (gr. 4-6). pap. 19.99 *(978-1-4022-1836-1(2)*, Sourcebooks Jabberwocky) Sourcebooks, Inc.
Odems, Carlee. A Thin Line. 2008. 88p. pap. 9.95 *(978-0-595-50829-7(4))* iUniverse, Inc.
Odezi, Jesse. Little Sunny & the Giants: The World's Greatest. 2012. 76p. pap. 30.00 *(978-1-4669-0270-1(1))* Trafford Publishing.
Odjick, Jay & Tenascon, Patrick. Kagagi: the Raven: The Raven. O'Reilly, Sean Patrick, ed. 2011. (Illus.). 78p. (YA). pap. 14.95 *(978-1-926914-29-9(5))* Arcana Studio, Inc.
Oeming, Michael Avon & Glass, Bryan J. L. Mice Templar Volume 4. 1 HC. 2013. (ENG., Illus.). 248p. (YA). 29.99 *(978-1-60706-822-8(2)*, 9781607068228) Image Comics.
—Mice Templar Volume 4. 1: Legend Part 1 TP: Legend Part 1 TP. 2014. (ENG., Illus.). 304p. (YA). pap. 17.99 *(978-1-60706-857-0(5)*, 9781607068570) Image Comics.
Oh, Ellen. Prophecy. 2013. (Prophecy Ser.: 1). (ENG.). (YA). (gr. 8). 352p. pap. 9.99 *(978-0-06-209110-9(7))*; (Illus.). 320p. 17.99 *(978-0-06-209109-3(3))* HarperCollins Pubs. (HarperTeen).
—Warrior. (Prophecy Ser.: 2). (ENG.). (YA). (gr. 8). 2015. 352p. pap. 9.99 *(978-0-06-209113-0(1))* 2013. 336p. 17.99 *(978-0-06-209112-3(3))* HarperCollins Pubs. (HarperTeen).
O'Hearn, Kate. The Flame of Olympus. (Pegasus Ser.: 1). (ENG.). (J). (gr. 3-7). 2013. 416p. pap. 7.99 *(978-1-4424-4410-2(X))* 2012. 400p. 17.99 *(978-1-4424-4409-6(6))* Simon & Schuster/Paula Wiseman Bks. (Simon & Schuster/Paula Wiseman Bks.).
—The New Olympians. 2014. (Pegasus Ser.: 3). (ENG., Illus.). 432p. (J). (gr. 3-7). 17.99 *(978-1-4424-4415-7(0)*, Simon & Schuster/Paula Wiseman Bks.) Simon & Schuster/Paula Wiseman Bks.
—Olympus at War. 2013. (Pegasus Ser.: 2). (ENG., Illus.). 416p. (J). (gr. 3-7). pap. 8.99 *(978-1-4424-4413-3(4)*, Simon & Schuster/Paula Wiseman Bks.) Simon & Schuster/Paula Wiseman Bks.
—Origins of Olympus. 2015. (Pegasus Ser.: 4). lib. bdg. 19.65 *(978-0-606-38366-0(2))* Turtleback Bks.
—Rise of the Titans. 2015. (Pegasus Ser.: 5). (ENG., Illus.). 448p. (J). (gr. 3-7). 17.99 *(978-1-4814-4714-0(9)*, Simon & Schuster/Paula Wiseman Bks.) Simon & Schuster/Paula Wiseman Bks.
Okorafor-Mbachu, Nnedi. Zahrah the Windseeker. 2008. (ENG., Illus.). 320p. (J). (gr. 5-7). pap. 8.99 *(978-0-547-02028-0(7))* Houghton Mifflin Harcourt Publishing Co.
Olds, Laurie. Cars on Vacation. 2009. 24p. pap. 12.25 *(978-1-4490-1633-3(2))* AuthorHouse.
Olfet, Omid. In the Dark: Parts 3 And 4. 2009. 74p. pap. 8.95 *(978-1-4401-5811-7(8))* iUniverse, Inc.
Oliver, Jan. Heart of Fire. 2009. 176p. pap. 18.95 *(978-1-4092-6660-0(5))* Lulu Pr., Inc.
Oliver, Jana. Foretold. 2012. (Demon Trappers Ser.: 4). (ENG.). 368p. (YA). (gr. 7). pap. 9.99 *(978-1-250-02184-7(7)*, 9781250021847, St. Martin's Griffin) St. Martin's Pr.
Oliver, Lauren. The Spindlers. Bruno, Iacopo, illus. (ENG.). (J). (gr. 3-7). 2013. 272p. pap. 8.99 *(978-0-06-197809-8(4))* 2012. 256p. 16.99 *(978-0-06-197808-1(6))* HarperCollins Pubs.
Oliver, Lauren & Chester, H. C. The Screaming Statue. 2016. (Curiosity House Ser.: 2). 368p. (J). (gr. 3-7). 16.99 *(978-0-06-227084-9(2))* HarperCollins Pubs.
—The Shrunken Head. Lacombe, Benjamin, illus. 2016. (Curiosity House Ser.: 1). 384p. (J). (gr. 3-7). pap. 6.99 *(978-0-06-227082-5(6))* HarperCollins Pubs.
Oliveto, Michelle. My Dog the Faker. 2012. 24p. 24.95 *(978-1-4560-2194-8(X))* America Star Bks.
Olsen, Erik. Garden of the Lost Souls. 2012. (J). *(978-1-4621-1010-0(X))* Cedar Fort, Inc./CFI Distribution.
—Quest & Honor (Flin's Destiny 4) 2013. pap. 14.99 *(978-1-4621-1012-4(6)*, Horizon Pubs.) Cedar Fort, Inc./CFI Distribution.
Olsen, J. J. The Mystic Kingdom: A Jenny Dewberry Series. 2008. 400p. pap. 17.99 *(978-1-4389-2598-1(0))* AuthorHouse.
Olshan, Matthew. The Flown Sky, 1. 2007. (Illus.). 352p. 19.95 *(978-0-9789391-0-6(7))* Chacmool Pr.
Olson, Kevin Noel. Eerey Tocsin in the Cryptoid Zoo. Hammack, Debi, illus. 2006. (ENG.). 176p. (YA). per. 15.95 *(978-1-887560-17-7(3)*, Cornerstone Bk. Publishers) Poll, Michael Publishing.
Once upon a Time- Fantasy Flight. 2005. (J). bds. *(978-1-4194-0095-7(9))* Paradise Pr., Inc.
O'Neill, Josh, et al, eds. Little Nemo's Big Dreams: A Toon Graphic. 2015. (ENG., Illus.). 72p. (J). (gr. 6). 16.95 *(978-1-935179-87-0(X))* TOON Books / RAW Junior, LLC.
O'Neill, Teresa. Dear Jesus. 2008. 17p. pap. 24.95 *(978-1-60441-643-5(2))* America Star Bks.
O'Neill, Tom. Old Friends. 2010. (ENG.). 436p. (J). (gr. 3-7). pap. 12.99 *(978-1-84840-941-5(9))* Little Island IRL. Dist: Independent Pubs. Group.
Onus, Katie. Island of the Wolves. 2012. 180p. pap. 11.99 *(978-0-9823271-7-3(X))* Adventure Bks. of Seattle.
Oppel, Kenneth. Airborn. (Illus.). (YA). (gr. 8-18). 2004. 368p. 18.99 *(978-0-06-053180-5(0))* 2005. 544p. reprint ed. pap. 8.99 *(978-0-06-053182-9(7))* HarperCollins Pubs.
—Firewing. 2008. (Silverwing Trilogy Ser.). (ENG.). 336p. (J). (gr. 3-7). pap. 7.99 *(978-1-4169-4999-2(2)*, Simon & Schuster Bks. For Young Readers) Simon & Schuster Bks. For Young Readers.
—Skybreaker. (Illus.). 2007. 560p. (YA). (gr. 8). per. 9.99 *(978-0-06-053229-1(7))* 2005. (ENG., 384p. (J). (gr. 6-10). 16.99 *(978-0-06-053227-7(0))* HarperCollins Pubs.
—Skybreaker. 2007. (Illus.). 544p. (YA). (gr. 8-12). lib. bdg. 20.85 *(978-1-4177-8130-0(0)*, Turtleback) Turtleback Bks.
—Starclimber. 400p. (YA). (gr. 8). 2010. pap. 9.99 *(978-0-06-085059-3(0))* 2009. (Illus.). 17.99 *(978-0-06-085057-9(4))* HarperCollins Pubs.
Oram, Hiawyn. The Giant Surprise: A Narnia Story. Humphries, Tudor, illus. 2005. (Step into Narnia Ser.). 40p. (J). (gr. -1-2). lib. bdg. 16.89 *(978-0-06-001360-8(5))* HarperCollins Pubs.
Orchard, Eric. Maddy Kettle Book 1: the Adventure of the Thimblewitch: The Adventure of the Thimblewitch. 2014. (ENG., Illus.). 96p. (J). (gr. 2-5). pap. 14.95 *(978-1-60309-072-8(X)*, 9781603090728) Top Shelf Productions.
O'Reilly, Avril. A Fairy in the Family. 2009. 32p. pap. 22.50 *(978-1-4092-8061-3(6))* Lulu Pr., Inc.
O'Reilly, Sean. Ezra: Egyptian Exchange. 2005. (YA). 9.95 *(978-0-9763095-4-3(8))* Arcana Studio, Inc.
—Kade: Identity, 5 vols. 2005. (Illus.). (YA). 9.95 *(978-0-9763095-1-2(3))* Arcana Studio, Inc.
The Origins of Olympus. 2014. (Pegasus Ser.: 4). (ENG., Illus.). 432p. (J). (gr. 3-7). 18.99 *(978-1-4424-9715-3(7)*, Simon & Schuster/Paula Wiseman Bks.) Simon & Schuster/Paula Wiseman Bks.
Ormerod, Nicola. Roxy May, Help My Boyfriend Is a Fairy. 2012. 224p. pap. *(978-1-909402-03-4(6))* Vamptasy Publishing.
Ormondroyd, Edward. David & the Phoenix. Raysor, Joan, illus. 2012. (ENG.). 191p. (J). (gr. 3-6). pap. 2.99 *(978-1-930900-58-5(9))* Purple Hse. Pr.
—David & the Phoenix. 2009. 76p. (gr. 4-7). pap. 4.75 *(978-1-60459-691-5(0))* Wilder Pubns., Corp.
—Time at the Top & All in Good Time: Two Novels. Ericksen, Barb et al, illus. 2011. (ENG.). 379p. (J). (gr. 4-7). pap. 12.95 *(978-1-930900-55-4(4))* Purple Hse. Pr.
Ormsbee, K. E. The Water & the Wild. 2016. (ENG., Illus.). 456p. (J). (gr. 3-7). pap. 8.99 *(978-1-4521-2881-8(2))* Chronicle Bks. LLC.
Orr, Judith. A Fairy Walk. 2004. 47p. (J). (gr. k-9). pap. 18.95 *(978-1-930002-66-1(1))* I & L Publishing.
Ortiz, Andrea. Snowflakes in June. Ortega, James, illus. 2013. 36p. 14.00 *(978-0-9884237-9-4(0))* CLF Publishing.
Osa, Nancy. Battalion Banished: Defenders of the Overworld #2. 2015. (Defenders of the Overworld Ser.). (ENG.). 272p. (J). (gr. 6). pap. 9.99 *(978-1-63450-997-8(8)*, Sky Pony Pr.) Skyhorse Publishing Co., Inc.
—Deep Ocean Six: Defenders of the Overworld #4. 2016. (Defenders of the Overworld Ser.). (ENG.). 272p. (J). (gr. 6). pap. 9.99 *(978-1-5107-0323-0(3)*, Sky Pony Pr.) Skyhorse Publishing Co., Inc.
Osborne, Mary Pope. Abe Lincoln at Last! Murdocca, Sal, illus. 2011. (Magic Tree House Merlin Mission Ser.: No. 19). (ENG.). 128p. (J). (gr. 2-5). 12.99 *(978-0-375-86825-2(9)*, Random Hse. Bks. for Young Readers) Random Hse. Children's Bks.
—The Brave Little Seamstress. Potter, Giselle, illus. 2006. 32p. (gr. -1-3). 17.00 *(978-0-7569-6613-3(2))* Perfection Learning Corp.
—Buffalo Before Breakfast. 2004. (Magic Tree House Ser.: No. 18). 72p. (J). (gr. k-3). pap. 17.00 incl. audio *(978-0-8072-0927-1(9)*, Listening Library) Random Hse. Audio Publishing Group.
—Civil War on Sunday. unabr. ed. 2004. (Magic Tree House Ser.: No. 21). 76p. (J). (gr. k-3). pap. 17.00 incl. audio *(978-0-8072-0930-1(9)*, S FTR 253 SP, Listening Library) Random Hse. Audio Publishing Group.
—Day of the Dragon King. unabr. ed. 2004. (Magic Tree House Ser.: No. 14). 68p. (J). (gr. k-3). pap. 17.00 incl. audio *(978-0-8072-0783-3(7)*, S FTR 242 SP, Listening Library) Random Hse. Audio Publishing Group.
—Dinosaurios al Atardecer. 2003. (Magic Tree House Ser.: 1). (SPA.). (gr. 3-6). lib. bdg. 16.00 *(978-0-613-64486-0(7)*, Turtleback) Turtleback Bks.
—Dinosaurs Before Dark. unabr. ed. 2004. (Magic Tree House Ser.: No. 1). 68p. (J). (gr. k-5). pap. 17.00 incl. audio *(978-0-8072-0330-9(0)*, FTR208SP, Listening Library) Random Hse. Audio Publishing Group.
—A Good Night for Ghosts. Murdocca, Sal, illus. 2009. (Magic Tree House Merlin Mission Ser.: 42). (ENG.). 128p. (J). (gr. 2-5). 12.99 *(978-0-375-85648-8(X)*, Random Hse. Bks. for Young Readers) Random Hse. Children's Bks.
—Haunted Waters. 2006. (ENG.). 160p. (YA). (gr. 7-12). 14.99 *(978-0-7636-2995-3(2))* Candlewick Pr.
—The Knight at Dawn. unabr. ed. 2004. (Magic Tree House Ser.: No. 2). 66p. (J). (gr. k-3). pap. 17.00 incl. audio *(978-0-8072-0331-6(9)*, Listening Library) Random Hse. Audio Publishing Group.
—Medianoche en la Luna. 2004. (Casa del Arbol Ser.: 8).Tr. of Midnight on the Moon. (SPA.). (J). pap. 5.99 *(978-1-930332-69-0(6))* Lectorum Pubns., Inc.
—Soccer on Sunday. Murdocca, Sal, illus. 2014. (Magic Tree House Merlin Missions Ser.: No. 24). (ENG.). 128p. (J). (gr. 2-5). 12.99 *(978-0-307-98053-3(7)*, Random Hse. Bks. for Young Readers) Random Hse. Children's Bks.
—Winter of the Ice Wizard. Murdocca, Sal, illus. (Magic Tree House Merlin Mission Ser.: 4). (ENG.). (J). (gr. 2-5). 2011. 144p. 5.99 *(978-0-375-87395-9(3))* 2004. 128p. 11.95 *(978-0-375-82736-5(6))* Random Hse. Children's Bks. (Random Hse. Bks. for Young Readers).
O'Shea, M.J. Blood Moon [Library Edition]. 3rd ed. 2014. 160p. pap. 14.99 *(978-1-62798-454-6(2)*, Harmony Ink Pr.) Dreamspinner Pr.
—Cold Moon. 2nd ed. 2016. (ENG., Illus.). (J). 24.99 ***(978-1-63477-954-8(1)**, Harmony Ink Pr.)* Dreamspinner Pr.
—Hunter's Moon. 3rd ed. 2016. (ENG., Illus.). (J). 27.99 ***(978-1-63533-032-8(7)**, Harmony Ink Pr.)* Dreamspinner Pr.
Oshida, Tim, illus. The Society's Traitor. 2nd ed. 2015. (The Discoveries of Arthur Grey ser.: 1). (ENG.). 304p. (J). (gr. 4-8). 27.99 *(978-1-943317-00-4(3))* Panama Hat Publishing, Ltd.
Osorio, Rick. The Great Adventure of Sally Rock & the Secret of Man, 1 vol. 2009. 164p. pap. 24.95 *(978-1-60813-596-7(9))* America Star Bks.
Osteen, Victoria. Unexpected Treasures. Palmisciano, Diane, illus. 2009. (ENG.). 32p. (J). (gr. -1-3). 17.99 *(978-1-4169-5550-4(X)*, Little Simon Inspirations) Little Simon Inspirations.
Ostler, Heather. The Siren's Secret. 2013. 16.99 *(978-1-4621-1223-4(4)*, Horizon Pubs.) Cedar Fort, Inc./CFI Distribution.
O'Sullivan, Darren. The Sleep Taker. 2013. 158p. pap. *(978-1-78333-233-5(6)*, AUK Authors) Andrews UK Ltd.
Otoshi, Kathryn. What Emily Saw. Otoshi, Kathryn, illus. 2004. (ENG., Illus.). 36p. (J). (gr. -1-12). 16.95 *(978-0-9723946-0-4(5))* KO Kids Bks.
Ott, Alexandra. Rules for Thieves. 2017. (Rules for Thieves Ser.: 1). (ENG., Illus.). 320p. (J). (gr. 3-7). 17.99 ***(978-1-4814-7274-6(7)**, Aladdin)* Simon & Schuster Children's Publishing.
—Rules for Thieves. 2017. (J). pap. ***(978-1-4814-7275-3(5)**,* Simon & Schuster/Paula Wiseman Bks.) Simon & Schuster/Paula Wiseman Bks.
Otte, John W. Failstate, 1 vol. 2012. (Failstate Ser.: 1). (ENG.). 416p. (YA). pap. 15.99 *(978-1-935929-48-2(8)*, Enclave) Gilead Publishing, LLC.
—Failstate: Legends, 1 vol. 2013. (Failstate Ser.: 2). 464p. (YA). pap. 15.99 *(978-1-935929-94-9(1)*, Enclave) Gilead Publishing, LLC.
Owen, James A. Dawn of the Dragons: Here, There Be Dragons; the Search for the Red Dragon. 2015. (Age of Dragons Ser.: 1). (ENG., Illus.). 688p. pap. 21.99 *(978-1-4814-2996-2(5)*, SAGA Press) Simon & Schuster Bks. For Young Readers.
—The Dragon's Apprentice. Owen, James A., illus. (Chronicles of the Imaginarium Geographica Ser.: 5). (ENG., Illus.). (YA). (gr. 7). 2012. 400p. pap. 9.99 *(978-1-4169-5898-7(3))* 2010. 384p. 17.99 *(978-1-4169-5897-0(5))* Simon & Schuster Bks. For Young Readers. (Simon & Schuster Bks. For Young Readers).
—The Dragons of Winter. Owen, James A., illus. (Chronicles of the Imaginarium Geographica Ser.: 6). (ENG., Illus.). (YA). (gr. 7). 2013. 416p. pap. 9.99 *(978-1-4424-1224-8(0))* 2012. 400p. 17.99 *(978-1-4424-1223-1(2))* Simon & Schuster Bks. For Young Readers. (Simon & Schuster Bks. For Young Readers).
—Fall of the Dragons: The Dragon's Apprentice; the Dragons of Winter; the First Dragon. 2016. (Age of Dragons Ser.: 3). (ENG., Illus.). 1056p. pap. 21.99 *(978-1-4814-2998-6(1)*, SAGA Press) Simon & Schuster Bks. For Young Readers.
—The First Dragon. Owen, James A., illus. (Chronicles of the Imaginarium Geographica Ser.: 7). (ENG., Illus.). 304p. (YA). (gr. 7). 2014. pap. 12.99 *(978-1-4424-1227-9(5))* 2013. 17.99 *(978-1-4424-1226-2(7))* Simon & Schuster Bks. For Young Readers. (Simon & Schuster Bks. For Young Readers).
—Here, There Be Dragons. 2008. (Playaway Children Ser.). (YA). (gr. 7-12). 59.99 *(978-1-60640-959-6(X))* Findaway World, LLC.
—Here, There Be Dragons. Owen, James A., illus. (Chronicles of the Imaginarium Geographica Ser.: 1). (ENG., Illus.). (YA). (gr. 7-12). 2007. 352p. pap. 11.99 *(978-1-4169-1228-6(2))* 2006. 336p. 21.99 *(978-1-4169-1227-9(4))* Simon & Schuster Bks. For Young Readers. (Simon & Schuster Bks. For Young Readers).
—The Indigo King. Owen, James A., illus. (Chronicles of the Imaginarium Geographica Ser.: 3). (ENG., Illus.). (YA). (gr. 7). 2010. 400p. pap. 12.99 *(978-1-4169-5108-7(3))* 2008. 384p. 17.99 *(978-1-4169-5107-0(5))* Simon & Schuster Bks. For Young Readers. (Simon & Schuster Bks. For Young Readers).
—The Search for the Red Dragon. Owen, James A., illus. 2008. (Chronicles of the Imaginarium Geographica Ser.: 2). (ENG., Illus.). (YA). (gr. 7). 400p. pap. 9.99

(978-1-4169-4851-3(1)); 384p. 17.99 *(978-1-4169-4850-6(3))* Simon & Schuster Bks. For Young Readers. (Simon & Schuster Bks. For Young Readers).

—The Shadow Dragons. Owen, James A., illus. 2009. (Chronicles of the Imaginarium Geographica Ser.: 4). (ENG., Illus.). 432p. (YA). (gr. 7-18). 21.99 *(978-1-4169-5879-6(7))*, Simon & Schuster Bks. For Young Readers) Simon & Schuster Bks. For Young Readers.

Owings, Lisa. The Constellation Cassiopeia: The Story of the Queen. Morrow, J. T., illus. 2013. (Constellations Ser.). (ENG.). 32p. (J). (gr. 2-5). 29.93 *(978-1-62323-484-3(0)*, 206252) Child's World, Inc., The.

Oxridge, Panama. Justin Thyme. 2012. (Tartan of Thyme Ser.). (Illus.). 368p. (YA). (gr. 5-12). pap. 9.99 *(978-0-9567122-8-8(2))* Lerner Publishing Group.

—Justin Thyme. Poxmage, Adrian, illus. 2011. (Tartan of Thyme Ser.). 368p. (YA). 18.99 *(978-0-9562315-9-8(4))* Lerner Publishing Group.

—Thyme Running Out. 2012. (ENG., Illus.). 80p. (gr. 5-12). pap. *(978-1-908458-00-1(3))* Inside Pocket Publishing, Ltd.

—Thyme Running Out. 2012. (Tartan of Thyme Ser.). (Illus.). 368p. (YA). (gr. 5-12). 18.99 *(978-0-9567122-0-2(7))* Lerner Publishing Group.

Pabbaraju, S. Adventures of Andreux: Book One - Aranya. 2008. 176p. 23.95 *(978-1-4401-0075-8(6))*; pap. 13.95 *(978-0-595-40964-8(4))* iUniverse, Inc.

Pacat, C. S. Kings Rising. 2016. (Captive Prince Trilogy Ser.: 3). (ENG., Illus.). 368p. pap. 16.00 *(978-0-425-27399-9(7)*, Berkley) Penguin Publishing Group.

Pace, Jessica. The Truth Finally Comes Out. 2012. 54p. 19.95 *(978-1-4626-6345-3(1))* America Star Bks.

Pace, Renee. The Forsaken. 2013. 204p. pap. 10.99 *(978-1-939194-79-4(2))* Etopia Pr.

Pace, Terri L. The Christmas Dream, 1 vol. 2009. 116p. pap. 19.95 *(978-1-60813-532-5(2))* America Star Bks.

Packard, Albert. Cavern of Babel. Boyles, Shawn, illus. 2006. (J). per. 14.95 *(978-0-9790652-0-0(8))* Diamond Triple C Ranch.

Page, Chris. Veneficus - Stones of the Chosen. 2008. 252p. 26.50 *(978-1-60693-473-9(2)*, Eloquent Bks.) Strategic Book Publishing & Rights Agency (SBPRA).

Paige, Danielle. Dorothy Must Die. (Dorothy Must Die Ser.: 1). (ENG.). (gr. 9). 2015. 480p. (J). pap. 9.99 *(978-0-06-228068-8(6))* 2014. 464p. (YA). 17.99 *(978-0-06-228067-1(8)*, HarperTeen) HarperCollins Pubs.

—Dorothy Must Die. 2015. (Dorothy Must Die Ser.: 1). (YA). lib. bdg. 20.85 *(978-0-606-36510-9(9))* Turtleback Bks.

—Dorothy Must Die 2-Book Box Set: Dorothy Must Die, the Wicked Will Rise. 2016. (Dorothy Must Die). 800p. (YA). (gr. 9). pap. 19.98 *(978-0-06-256982-0(1))* HarperCollins Pubs.

—Dorothy Must Die Stories: No Place Like Oz - The Witch Must Burn; the Wizard Returns. 2015. (Dorothy Must Die Novella Ser.). (ENG., Illus.). 416p. (YA). (gr. 9). pap. 9.99 *(978-0-06-228079-4(1))* HarperCollins Pubs.

—Dorothy Must Die Stories: No Place Like Oz, the Witch Must Burn, the Wizard Returns. 2015. (Dorothy Must Die Ser.). (YA). lib. bdg. 20.85 *(978-0-606-37248-0(2))* Turtleback Bks.

—Dorothy Must Die Stories Volume 2. 2016. (Dorothy Must Die Novella Ser.). 336p. (YA). (gr. 9). pap. 9.99 *(978-0-06-240397-1(4))* HarperCollins Pubs.

—Dorothy Must Die Stories Volume 3. 2017. (Dorothy Must Die Novella Ser.). 288p. (YA). (gr. 9). pap. 9.99 *(978-0-06-242383-2(5))* HarperCollins Pubs.

—The End of Oz. 2017. (Dorothy Must Die Ser.: 4). 304p. (YA). (gr. 9). 18.99 *(978-0-06-242377-1(0))* HarperCollins Pubs.

—Stealing Snow. 2016. (Stealing Snow Ser.). (ENG.). 384p. (YA). (gr. 9-12). 18.99 *(978-1-68119-076-1(1)*, 9781681190761, Bloomsbury USA Childrens) Bloomsbury Publishing USA.

—Stealing Snow. 2017. (SPA.). 384p. (YA). 18.95 ***(978-84-16700-68-4(0))*** Roca Editorial ESP. Dist: Spanish Pubs., LLC.

—The Wicked Will Rise. (Dorothy Must Die Ser.: 2). (YA). (gr. 9). 2016. 320p. pap. 9.99 *(978-0-06-228071-8(6))* 2015. (ENG.). 304p. 17.99 *(978-0-06-228070-1(8))* HarperCollins Pubs.

—The Wicked Will Rise. 2016. (Dorothy Must Die Ser.: 2). (YA). lib. bdg. 20.85 *(978-0-606-38170-3(8))* Turtleback Bks.

—Yellow Brick War. 2017. (Dorothy Must Die Ser.: 3). 304p. (YA). (gr. 9). pap. 9.99 *(978-0-06-228074-9(0))* 2016. *(978-0-06-245860-5(4))* 2016. (Dorothy Must Die Ser.: 3). (ENG.). 288p. (YA). (gr. 9-12). 18.99 *(978-0-06-228073-2(2))* HarperCollins Pubs.

Palfrey, Bernard. No Match for Uncle Charlie. 2009. 141p. pap. 23.50 *(978-1-4092-3981-9(0))* Lulu Pr., Inc.

Palka, Yvonne. Dragon Fire Ocean Mist. 2009. pap. 12.95 *(978-0-9817668-0-5(3))* Heartrock Pr.

Palleschi, Sarah. Did I Really Dream Last Night? 2009. 48p. pap. 16.25 *(978-1-60693-814-0(2)*, Eloquent Bks.) Strategic Book Publishing & Rights Agency (SBPRA).

Palmer, Judd. Wolf King No. 3: Preposterous Fables for Unusual Children. 2003. (Prepost Fable Unusual Children Ser.: 3). (ENG., Illus.). 136p. (gr. 5-18). 10.95 *(978-1-896209-82-1(3))* Bayeux Arts, Inc. CAN. Dist: Chicago Distribution Ctr.

Palus, Benji Alexander. The Magic Pumpkin. 2013. 314p. (gr. 10-12). 28.95 *(978-1-4759-7046-3(3))*; pap. 18.95 *(978-1-4759-7048-7(X))* iUniverse, Inc.

Pandora, Ankh: Conquering the Seven Deadly Sins. 2013. 100p. pap. 10.95 *(978-1-62212-908-9(3)*, Strategic Bk. Publishing) Strategic Book Publishing & Rights Agency (SBPRA).

Panes, Kerry. Knowledge of Good & Evil. 2012. 406p. pap. 22.95 *(978-1-4759-4035-0(1))* iUniverse, Inc.

Pankiw, Dr Mary & Pankiw, Mary. Misilla Mouse. 2011. 32p. pap. *(978-1-4269-5476-4(X))* Trafford Publishing (UK) Ltd.

Pantages, Joanna. Fairytale Fitness: Holygrain. 2009. 24p. pap. 12.49 *(978-1-4389-4494-4(2))* AuthorHouse.

—Fairytale Fitness: The Goobyland Race. 2009. 20p. pap. 11.95 *(978-1-4389-5480-6(8))* AuthorHouse.

Paolini, Christopher. Brisingr. 2009. (Inheritance Cycle Ser.: Bk. 3). (CHI., Illus.). 560p. (YA). pap. *(978-7-5448-0634-3(0))* Jieli Publishing Hse.

—Brisingr. 2009. (Inheritance Cycle Ser.: Bk. 3). (CHI., Illus.). 822p. (YA). pap. *(978-957-08-3421-5(8))* Linking Publishing Co., Ltd.

—Brisingr, Bk. 3. 2011. (ENG., Illus.). 784p. pap. *(978-0-552-55212-7(7)*, Corgi Bks. Ltd.) Random House Children's Books.

—Brisingr. (ENG.). 2010. (Inheritance Cycle Ser.: 3). 800p. (YA). (gr. 7-18). pap. 14.99 *(978-0-375-82674-0(2))* 2008. (Inheritance Cycle Ser.: Bk. 3). 784p. (J). 27.50 *(978-0-375-85117-9(8))* 2008. (Inheritance Cycle Ser.: Bk. 3). 784p. (YA). (gr. 7). 27.50 *(978-0-375-82672-6(6))* 2009. (Inheritance Cycle Ser.: Bk. 3). 800p. (YA). (gr. 7-18). 29.99 *(978-0-375-85481-1(9))* Random Hse. Children's Bks. (Knopf Bks. for Young Readers).

—Brisingr, Vol. 1. Isern, Carol & Rizzo, Jorge, trs. 2008. (Inheritance Cycle Ser.: Bk. 3). (SPA.). 704p. (YA). (gr. 7-12). pap. 21.95 *(978-84-92429-39-4(9))* Roca Editorial ESP. Dist: Spanish Pubs., LLC.

—Brisingr. 2010. (Inheritance Ser.: 03). lib. bdg. 26.95 *(978-0-606-14109-3(X)*, Turtleback) Turtleback Bks.

—Eldest. abr. ed. 2009. (Inheritance Cycle Ser.: Bk. 2). (SPA.). (J). 59.99 *(978-1-60847-564-3(6))* Findaway World, LLC.

—Eldest. (Inheritance Cycle Ser.: Bk. 2). (ENG.). 704p. (YA). (gr. 7-18). 2007. pap. 12.99 *(978-0-375-84040-1(0))* 2005. (Illus.). 21.00 *(978-0-375-82670-2(X))* Random Hse. Children's Bks. (Knopf Bks. for Young Readers).

—Eldest. de Heriz, Enrique, tr. 2006. (Inheritance Cycle Ser.: Bk. 2). (SPA.). (YA). 832p. (gr. 7-12). 22.95 *(978-84-96284-96-8(4))*; 831p. (gr. 8-12). per. 22.95 *(978-84-96544-07-9(9))* Roca Editorial ESP. Dist: Spanish Pubs., LLC.

—Eldest. 2007. (Inheritance Ser.: 2). 24.50 *(978-1-4177-7363-3(4)*, Turtleback) Turtleback Bks.

—Eragon. 2006. (Inheritance Cycle Ser.: Bk. 1). (YA). cd-rom 39.99 *(978-1-59895-406-7(7))* Findaway World, LLC.

—Eragon. (Inheritance Cycle Ser.: Bk. 1). (ENG., 528p. (YA). (gr. 7-18). 2003. Illus.). 18.95 *(978-0-375-82668-9(8))* 2005. reprint ed. pap. 11.99 *(978-0-375-82669-6(6))* Random Hse. Children's Bks. (Knopf Bks. for Young Readers).

—Eragon. (Inheritance Cycle Ser.: Bk. 1). (SPA.). (YA). pap. *(978-84-96284-44-9(1))* Roca Editorial.

—Eragon; Eldest. (Inheritance Cycle Ser.: Bks. 1-2). (ENG.). (YA). (gr. 7). 2008. 1216p. pap. 19.99 *(978-0-375-85704-1(4))*Set. 2005. 1232p. 39.95 *(978-0-375-83658-9(6))* Random Hse. Children's Bks. (Knopf Bks. for Young Readers).

—Eragon, Eldest, Brisingr, 3 vols., Set. 2010. (Inheritance Cycle Ser.: Bk. 4). (ENG.). 800p. (YA). (gr. 7). pap., pap., pap. 38.97 *(978-0-375-87203-7(5)*, Knopf Bks. for Young Readers) Random Hse. Children's Bks.

—Inheritance. (Inheritance Cycle Ser.: Bk. 4). (ENG.). (YA). (gr. 7). 2012. 880p. pap. 15.99 *(978-0-375-84631-1(X))* 2011. 880p. 27.99 *(978-0-375-85611-2(0))* 2012. (Illus.). 896p. 29.99 *(978-0-449-81319-5(3))* Random Hse. Children's Bks. (Knopf Bks. for Young Readers).

—Inheritance Set: Eragon; Eldest; Brisingr, 3 vols. 2008. (Inheritance Cycle Ser.: Bks. 1-3). (ENG.). (YA). (gr. 7). 67.45 *(978-0-375-84615-1(8)*, Knopf Bks. for Young Readers) Random Hse. Children's Bks.

—The Inheritance Cycle, 3 vols. 2008. (Inheritance Cycle Ser.: Bks. 1-3). (ENG.). (J). (gr. 7). 67.45 *(978-0-375-85141-4(0)*, Knopf Bks. for Young Readers) Random Hse. Children's Bks.

Paourou, Maria. Bubblebea Wants to Be a Hero. 2009. (Illus.). 40p. pap. 16.99 *(978-1-4343-7330-4(4))* AuthorHouse.

Papp, Robert L., illus. The Vampire Mystery. 2009. (Boxcar Children Mysteries Ser.: 120). (ENG.). 128p. (J). (gr. 1-5). pap. 5.99 *(978-0-8075-8461-3(4))*; lib. bdg. 14.99 *(978-0-8075-8460-6(6))* Whitman, Albert & Co.

Paradise, Elizabeth. The Lost Dreamer. 2013. 192p. pap. 9.99 *(978-0-615-77563-0(2))* EJMP.

Paris, Tom. Tom & Pearl's Udder Stand. 2012. 44p. pap. 17.45 *(978-1-4669-4829-7(9))* Trafford Publishing.

Park, Linda Sue. Cavern of Secrets. Madsen, Jim, illus. 2017. (Wing & Claw Ser.: 2). 320p. (J). (gr. 3-7). 16.99 *(978-0-06-232741-3(0))* HarperCollins Pubs.

—Forest of Wonders. Madsen, Jim, illus. 2017. (Wing & Claw Ser.: 1). 352p. (J). (gr. 3-7). pap. 6.99 *(978-0-06-232739-0(9))* HarperCollins Pubs.

Parker, C. Brad. Chosen Generation. 2007. 118p. (YA). pap. 12.86 *(978-1-4116-3497-8(7))* Lulu Pr., Inc.

Parker, Daniel. August. 2014. (Countdown Ser.: 8). (ENG.). 144p. (YA). (gr. 7). pap. 13.99 *(978-1-4814-2593-3(5)*, Simon Pulse) Simon Pulse.

—February. 2014. (Countdown Ser.: 2). (ENG.). 144p. (J). (gr. 7). pap. 13.99 *(978-1-4814-2587-2(0)*, Simon Pulse) Simon Pulse.

—November. 2014. (Countdown Ser.: 11). (ENG.). 144p. (YA). (gr. 7). pap. 13.99 *(978-1-4814-2596-4(X)*, Simon Pulse) Simon Pulse.

—October. 2014. (Countdown Ser.: 10). (ENG.). 144p. (YA). (gr. 7). pap. 13.99 *(978-1-4814-2595-7(1)*, Simon Pulse) Simon Pulse.

Parker, John F. Rosezinda: Riding Rainbows. 2003. 148p. pap. 11.95 *(978-0-595-28042-1(0))* iUniverse, Inc.

Parker, Meeta. Cookie the Clown. 2007. 56p. per. 16.95 *(978-1-4241-7917-6(3))* America Star Bks.

Parker, Patti. Book of Ominook: The Journey Begins. 2012. 28p. pap. 9.95 *(978-1-936587-98-8(X))* Brighton Publishing LLC.

Parker, Ron. Teen Wars. 2010. 170p. pap. 9.42 *(978-1-4452-5000-7(4))* Lulu Pr., Inc.

Parkhouse, David. Lucy's Spoons. 2004. 52p. pap. *(978-1-84401-276-3(X))* Athena Pr.

Parks, James & Costa, Ben. The Road to Epoli. 2017. (Rickety Stitch & the Gelatinous Goo Ser.: Bk. 1). (ENG.). 208p. (YA). (gr. 7). 18.99 ***(978-0-399-55613-5(3))***; pap. 14.99 ***(978-0-399-55614-2(1))*** Random Hse. Children's Bks. (Knopf Bks. for Young Readers).

Parlato, Stephen. The World That Loved Books. rev. ed. 2008. (ENG., Illus.). 32p. (J). (gr. -1-3). 16.95 *(978-1-894965-98-9(1))* Simply Read Bks. CAN. Dist: Ingram Publisher Services.

Parnell, Paul. Talking Rocks. 2009. 52p. pap. 16.95 *(978-1-61546-651-1(7))* America Star Bks.

Parragon Staff. Dumbo: The Magical Story. 2010. (Disney Padded Magical Storybks.). (Illus.). 32p. (J). (gr. -1-1). *(978-1-4075-8452-2(9))* Parragon, Inc.

—Pinocchio: The Magical Story. 2010. (Disney Padded Magical Storybks.). (Illus.). 32p. (J). (gr. -1-1). *(978-1-4075-8451-5(0))* Parragon, Inc.

Parrish, Harry. Kate & Alice. 2009. 28p. pap. 13.40 *(978-1-4389-3120-3(4))* AuthorHouse.

Parry, Michael. The Nanobot. 2013. 198p. pap. *(978-1-78148-599-6(2))* Grosvenor Hse. Publishing Ltd.

Pasca, Pamela. If I Lived in a Balloon. 2009. 24p. pap. 12.99 *(978-1-4389-2242-3(6))* AuthorHouse.

Pascoe, Matt. Chaos Island: A Daisy Albright Adventure. 2010. 72p. pap. 9.99 *(978-1-60911-208-0(3)*, Eloquent Bks.) Strategic Book Publishing & Rights Agency (SBPRA).

Pashley, Hilton. Sammael's Wings. 2016. (ENG., Illus.). 262p. (J). (gr. 4-7). pap. 12.99 *(978-1-78344-325-3(1))* Andersen Pr. GBR. Dist: Independent Pubs. Group.

Pastor, N. Allie Mckay: And the Keepers of the Golden Cross. 2008. 280p. 25.99 *(978-1-60647-248-4(8))*; pap. 15.99 *(978-1-60647-247-7(X))* Salem Author Services.

Pastor, Norma. The Young Alchemists & the Vatican's Legion of Evil. 2013. 472p. pap. 30.95 *(978-1-4633-6179-2(3))* Palibrio.

Patey, Nicola. Aspireland & the story of George. 2010. 101p. pap. 16.95 *(978-1-4457-2458-4(8))* Lulu Pr., Inc.

Patrick, Ruthven. Prisoners under Glass. 2005. (YA). per. *(978-0-9735422-2-6(5))* Scroll Pr.

Patten, E. J. The Legend Thief. Rocco, John, illus. 2014. (Hunter Chronicles Ser.: 2). (ENG.). 384p. (J). (gr. 3-7). pap. 7.99 *(978-1-4424-2036-6(7)*, Simon & Schuster Bks. For Young Readers) Simon & Schuster Bks. For Young Readers.

Patterson, Christine. Conversation in the Crayon Box. 2004. 12p. (J). per. 9.33 *(978-1-4116-0672-2(8))* Lulu Pr., Inc.

Patterson, Christine D. Conversation in the Crayon Box. 2008. 24p. per. 12.95 *(978-1-4327-1469-7(4))* Outskirts Pr., Inc.

Patterson, Eric. Nature Boy. Wright, Christopher, illus. 2007. 112p. (J). pap. 6.95 *(978-0-9797106-0-5(X))* Avid Readers Publishing Group.

Patterson, James. The Fire. 2011. (Playaway Children Ser.). (ENG.). (YA). (gr. 8-12). 59.99 *(978-1-61113-385-1(8))* Hachette Audio.

—The Gift. 2010. (Witch & Wizard Ser.: No. 2). (J). 59.99 *(978-1-60941-012-4(2))* Findaway World, LLC.

—The Gift. 2014. lthr. 79.00 *(978-1-62715-523-6(6))* Leatherbound Bestsellers.

—Witch & Wizard. 2014. lthr. 79.00 *(978-1-62715-529-8(5))* Leatherbound Bestsellers.

—Witch & Wizard. 2010. (Witch & Wizard Ser.: 1). (ENG.). 336p. (YA). (gr. 5-17). pap. 10.00 *(978-0-316-03834-8(2)*, Jimmy Patterson) Little Brown & Co.

—Witch & Wizard. 2010. (Witch & Wizard Ser.: 1). (YA). lib. bdg. 20.85 *(978-0-606-15119-1(2)*, Turtleback) Turtleback Bks.

Patterson, James & Charbonnet, Gabrielle. Witch & Wizard. 2011. (Witch & Wizard Ser.: 1). (ENG.). 368p. mass mkt. 8.00 *(978-0-446-56243-0(2)*, Jimmy Patterson) Little Brown & Co.

—Witch & Wizard. 2011. (Witch & Wizard Ser.: 1). lib. bdg. 18.45 *(978-0-606-26452-5(3)*, Turtleback) Turtleback Bks.

Patterson, James & Dembowski, Jill. The Fire. 2011. (Witch & Wizard Ser.: 3). (ENG.). 352p. (YA). (gr. 5-17). 17.99 *(978-0-316-10190-5(7)*, Jimmy Patterson) Little Brown & Co.

—The Kiss. 2013. (Witch & Wizard Ser.: 4). (ENG.). 384p. (YA). (gr. 7-17). pap. 10.00 *(978-0-316-10176-9(1)*, Jimmy Patterson) Little Brown & Co.

Patterson, James & Rust, Ned. The Gift. (Witch & Wizard Ser.: 2). (ENG.). 2012. 352p. mass mkt. 7.99 *(978-0-446-56245-4(9))* 2011. 400p. (gr. 5-17). pap. 9.99 *(978-0-316-03835-5(0))* 2010. 352p. (gr. 5-17). 17.99 *(978-0-316-03625-2(0))* Little Brown & Co. (Jimmy Patterson).

—The Gift. 2012. (Witch & Wizard Ser.: 2). lib. bdg. 18.40 *(978-0-606-26451-8(5)*, Turtleback) Turtleback Bks.

Patterson, Jim. Lisa B's Cookie Tree. 2011. 36p. pap. 24.95 *(978-1-4560-3599-0(1))* America Star Bks.

Patterson, Shannon. The Princess & the Cheese. 2010. 43p. pap. 19.95 *(978-0-557-51615-5(3))* Lulu Pr., Inc.

Patton, Jack. The Chameleon Attack (Battle Bugs #4) 2015. (Battle Bugs Ser.: 4). (ENG., Illus.). 128p. (J). (gr. 2-5). pap. 4.99 *(978-0-545-70784-8(6)*, Scholastic Paperbacks) Scholastic, Inc.

—The Dragonfly Defense. 2016. (Battle Bugs Ser.: 7). (ENG.). 128p. (J). (gr. 2-5). pap. 4.99 *(978-0-545-94509-7(7)*, Scholastic Paperbacks) Scholastic, Inc.

—The Lizard War. 2015. (Battle Bugs Ser.: 1). (ENG.). 128p. (J). (gr. 2-5). pap. 4.99 *(978-0-545-70741-1(2)*, Scholastic Paperbacks) Scholastic, Inc.

—The Poison Frog Assault (Battle Bugs #3) 2015. (Battle Bugs Ser.: 3). (ENG.). 128p. (J). (gr. 2-5). pap. 4.99 *(978-0-545-70744-2(7)*, Scholastic Paperbacks) Scholastic, Inc.

Pau Pau. The Princess' Adventure. 2007. 52p. pap. 16.95 *(978-1-60441-069-3(8))* America Star Bks.

Paul, Donita K. Two Renegade Realms, 1 vol. 2014. (Realm Walkers Ser.). (ENG.). 416p. (YA). pap. 13.99 *(978-0-310-73581-6(5))* Zondervan.

Paul, John. Copters. Young, Bill, illus. 2012. 36p. 24.95 *(978-1-4626-9458-7(6))* America Star Bks.

Paulk, William. The Creatures of Vision City: Pokie's Party, Book One. 2009. 48p. pap. 10.99 *(978-1-4389-5659-6(2))* AuthorHouse.

Pausacker, Jenny. The Perfect Princess. 2006. (Illus.). 160p. pap. *(978-0-7344-0586-9(3)*, Lothian Children's Bks.) Hachette Australia.

Paver, Michelle. Ghost Hunter. Taylor, Geoff, illus. (Chronicles of Ancient Darkness Ser.: 6). 304p. (J). (gr. 5). 2011. pap. 7.99 *(978-0-06-072842-7(6))* 2010. 16.99 *(978-0-06-072840-3(X))* HarperCollins Pubs. (Tegen, Katherine Bks).

—Oath Breaker. Taylor, Geoff, illus. (Chronicles of Ancient Darkness Ser.: 5). (J). (gr. 5). 2010. 320p. pap. 6.99 *(978-0-06-072839-7(6))* 2009. 304p. 16.99 *(978-0-06-072837-3(X))* HarperCollins Pubs. (Tegen, Katherine Bks).

—Wolf Brother. Taylor, Geoff, illus. 2006. (Chronicles of Ancient Darkness Ser.: 1). 320p. (J). (gr. 5-9). reprint ed. pap. 6.99 *(978-0-06-072827-4(2)*, Tegen, Katherine Bks) HarperCollins Pubs.

—Wolf Brother, 6 vols. 2005. (Chronicles of Ancient Darkness Ser.: 1). (J). 89.75 *(978-1-4193-3811-3(0))*; 76.75 *(978-1-4193-2628-8(7))*; 91.75 *(978-1-4193-3809-0(9))*; 73.75 *(978-1-4193-2630-1(9))* Recorded Bks., Inc.

Pavlova, Elena. Adventures at Tall Oaks: New Friends. 2004. (Illus.). 80p. (J). 19.95 *(978-0-9755839-0-6(5))* Read 2 Children.

Pavón Córdoba, María del Mar. ¡SELENA, SELEEENA! 2005. (Caballo Alado Series-Al Galope Ser.). (SPA & ENG., Illus.). 24p. (J). (gr. k-2). pap. 5.95 *(978-84-7864-885-6(2))* Combel Editorial, S.A. ESP. Dist: Independent Pubs. Group.

Payne, Laurie. Mush & the Big Blue Flower. Campbell, Ruth, illus. 2007. (ENG.). 104p. (J). (gr. -1). pap. 12.95 *(978-0-88982-242-9(5))* Oolichan Bks. CAN. Dist: Univ. of Toronto Pr.

Peabody, Richard. Alice Redux: New Stories of Alice, Lewis, & Wonderland. 2006. (Illus.). xvi, 319p. pap. *(978-0-931181-22-1(4))* Paycock Pr.

Peacock, Ann & Lewis, C. S. The Chronicles of Narnia. Barbera, Tony et al, illus. Barbera, Tony et al, photos by. 2005. (Chronicles of Narnia Ser.). 64p. (J). *(978-1-4156-3678-7(8))* HarperCollins Pubs.

Peacock, Kathleen. Willowgrove. 2016. (Hemlock Trilogy Ser.: 3). 384p. (YA). (gr. 9). pap. 9.99 *(978-0-06-204872-1(4)*, Tegen, Katherine Bks) HarperCollins Pubs.

Peacock, L. A. Panic in Pompeii. Hale, Nathan, illus. 2011. 92p. (J). pap. *(978-0-545-34062-5(4))* Scholastic, Inc.

—Terror at Troy. Hale, Nathan, illus. 2012. 90p. (J). *(978-0-545-34063-2(2))* Scholastic, Inc.

Peak, Danielle. The Enchanted Conquest. 2003. 145p. pap. 13.95 *(978-0-7414-1355-0(8))* Infinity Publishing.

Pearce, Margaret. A Belinda Robinson Novel Book 1: Belinda & the Witch's Cat. 2013. 82p. pap. *(978-1-922066-58-9(3))* Writers Exchange E-Publishing.

—A Belinda Robinson Novel Book 2: Belinda & the Holidays It Rained. 2013. 78p. pap. *(978-1-922233-22-6(6))* Writers Exchange E-Publishing.

—A Belinda Robinson Novel Book 3: Belinda & the Missing Will. 2013. 80p. pap. *(978-1-922233-23-3(4))* Writers Exchange E-Publishing.

Pearl, B. B. Poerava's Heaven. 2011. (Illus.). 88p. pap. 12.85 *(978-1-4567-8985-5(6))* AuthorHouse.

Pearson, Kimberly Ann. Mystling Glen Book I: The Tale of A Prince. 2009. 207p. pap. 14.95 *(978-1-4327-4169-3(1))* Outskirts Pr., Inc.

Pearson, Mary E. The Beauty of Darkness. 2016. (Remnant Chronicles Ser.: 3). (ENG., Illus.). 688p. (YA). (gr. 9-12). 18.99 *(978-0-8050-9925-6(5)*, 9780805099256, Holt, Henry & Co. Bks. For Young Readers) Holt, Henry & Co.

—The Beauty of Darkness. 2017. (Remnant Chronicles Ser.: Bk. 3). (ENG.). 688p. (YA). pap. 10.99 *(978-1-250-11531-7(0)*, 9781250115317) Square Fish.

—The Heart of Betrayal. 2015. (Remnant Chronicles: Bk. 2). (ENG.). 480p. (YA). (gr. 9). 18.99 *(978-0-8050-9924-9(7)*, 9780805099249, Holt, Henry & Co. Bks. For Young Readers) Holt, Henry & Co.

—The Heart of Betrayal. 2016. (Remnant Chronicles Ser.: 2). (ENG.). 496p. (YA). pap. 10.99 *(978-1-250-08002-8(9)*, 9781250080028) Square Fish.

—The Kiss of Deception. 2014. (Remnant Chronicles Ser.: 1). (ENG.). 496p. (YA). (gr. 9-12). 18.99 *(978-0-8050-9923-2(9)*, 9780805099232); E-Book *(978-1-62779-218-9(X)*, 9781627792189) Holt, Henry & Co. (Holt, Henry & Co. Bks. For Young Readers).

—The Kiss of Deception. 2015. (Remnant Chronicles Ser.: 1). (ENG.). 512p. (YA). (gr. 9-12). pap. 10.99 *(978-1-250-06315-1(9)*, 9781250063151) Square Fish.

Pearson, Ridley. Dark Passage. 2014. (Kingdom Keepers Ser.). (ENG., Illus.). 256p. (J). (gr. 5-9). pap. 8.99 *(978-1-4231-6523-1(3))* Hyperion Bks. for Children.

—Disney after Dark. 2005. (Kingdom Keepers Ser.: Bk. 1). 324p. *(978-1-4156-2836-2(X))* Disney Pr.

—Disney after Dark. Elwell, Tristan, illus. 2009. (Kingdom Keepers Ser.: Bk. 1). (ENG.). 336p. (J). (gr. 5-9). pap. 8.99 *(978-1-4231-2311-8(5))* Hyperion Pr.

—Disney at Dawn. Elwell, Tristan, illus. 2009. (Kingdom Keepers Ser.: Bk. 2). (ENG.). 384p. (J). (gr. 5-9). pap. 8.99 *(978-1-4231-0708-8(X))* Hyperion Pr.

—Disney in Shadow. Elwell, Tristan, illus. 2011. (Kingdom Keepers Ser.: Bk. 3). (ENG.). 576p. (J). (gr. 5-17). pap. 8.99 *(978-1-4231-3856-3(2))* Hyperion Pr.

—Disney Lands. 2016. (Kingdom Keepers: the Return Ser.: Bk. 1). (ENG., Illus.). 362p. (J). (gr. 3-7). pap. 8.99 *(978-1-4847-3275-5(8))* Hyperion Bks. for Children.

—The Insider. (Kingdom Keepers Ser.). (ENG., Illus.). (J). (gr. 5-9). 2015. 626p. pap. 9.99 *(978-1-4231-6524-8(1))* 2014. 614p. 17.99 *(978-1-4231-6490-6(3))* Hyperion Bks. for Children.

—Kingdom Keepers Boxed Set. 2014. (Kingdom Keepers Ser.). (ENG., Illus.). 1296p. (J). (gr. 3-7). pap. 25.99 *(978-1-4847-0402-8(9))* Hyperion Bks. for Children.

—Kingdom Keepers the Return. 2017. (Kingdom Keepers Ser.). (ENG.). 480p. (J). (gr. 5-9). 17.99 *(978-1-4231-8433-1(5))* Hyperion Bks. for Children.

—Kingdom Keepers: the Return Book Two Legacy of Secrets. 2017. (Kingdom Keepers: the Return Ser.). (ENG.). 416p. (J). (gr. 3-7). pap. 8.99 *(978-1-4847-3414-8(9))* Hyperion Bks. for Children.

—Legacy of Secrets. 2017. (Kingdom Keepers - the Return Ser.: 2). (J). lib. bdg. 19.65 *(978-0-606-39497-0(4))* Turtleback Bks.

—Power Play. Elwell, Tristan, illus. 2011. (Kingdom Keepers Ser.: Bk. 4). (ENG.). 448p. (J). (gr. 5-9). 17.99 *(978-1-4231-3857-0(0))* Hyperion Pr.

Pearson, Ridley & Barry, Dave. Peter & the Secret of Rundoon. Call, Greg, illus. rev. ed. 2009. (Peter & the Starcatchers Ser.: Bk. 3). (ENG.). 496p. (J). (gr. 5-9). pap. 9.99 *(978-1-4231-2326-2(3))* Hyperion Pr.

Peck, Steven L. The Rifts of Rime (Quickened Chronicles) 2012. pap. 14.99 *(978-1-59955-967-4(6))* Cedar Fort, Inc./CFI Distribution.

Pedro y el Lobo. 2004. (SPA., Illus.). (J). *(978-1-84458-109-2(8)*, Pavilion Children's Books) Pavilion Bks.

Pelelo-Ray, Sam. Athenrei. 2006. 56p. pap. 16.95 *(978-1-4137-9946-0(9))* PublishAmerica, Inc.

Penberthy, Stephen. The Adventures of Bird Dog & Friends. 2009. 24p. pap. 10.99 *(978-1-4269-0977-1(2))* Trafford Publishing.

Penick Phillips-Cermak, Mosetta. The Wishing Flower. 2007. 24p. 16.50 *(978-0-615-15573-9(1))* PM Moon Pubs., Ltd.

Pennington, Norma C. & Schuller, Sheldon V. The Unopened Gift, 1 vol. 2010. 18p. 24.95 *(978-1-4489-7670-6(7))* PublishAmerica, Inc.

Pepper, Cally. Bird Without Wings: Faebles. 2013. (ENG.). 283p. (YA). (gr. 8-17). pap. 12.95 *(978-1-78099-902-9(X)*, Lodestone Bks.) Hunt, John Publishing Ltd. GBR. Dist: National Bk. Network.

Perelman, Helen. The Coconut Clue. Waters, Erica-Jane, illus. 2015. (Candy Fairies Ser.: 17). (ENG.). 128p. (J). (gr. 2-5). pap. 5.99 *(978-1-4814-0616-1(7)*, Aladdin) Simon & Schuster Children's Publishing.

—Cool Mint. Waters, Erica-Jane, illus. 2010. (Candy Fairies Ser.: 4). (ENG.). 128p. (J). (gr. 2-5). pap. 5.99 *(978-1-4169-9457-2(2)*, Aladdin) Simon & Schuster Children's Publishing.

—Jelly Bean Jumble. Waters, Erica-Jane, illus. 2013. (Candy Fairies Ser.: 10). (ENG.). 128p. (J). (gr. 2-5). pap. 5.99 *(978-1-4424-5297-8(8)*, Aladdin) Simon & Schuster Children's Publishing.

—Jelly Bean Jumble. Waters, Erica-Jane, illus. 2013. (Candy Fairies Ser.: 10). (ENG.). 128p. (J). (gr. 2-5). 15.99 *(978-1-4424-6000-3(8)*, Simon & Schuster/Paula Wiseman Bks.) Simon & Schuster/Paula Wiseman Bks.

Peretti, Frank E. Escape from the Island of Aquarius. 2004. (Cooper Kids Adventure Ser.: No. 2). 160p. (gr. 4-7). 5.99 *(978-0-89107-592-9(5))* Crossway.

Peretti, Frank E., et al. The Door in the Dragon's Throat. 2004. (Cooper Kids Adventure Ser.: No. 1). 125p. (YA). (gr. 4-7). 5.99 *(978-0-89107-591-2(7))* Crossway.

Pérez-Foncea, Juan Antonio & Caro, Stephen. Ivan of Aldenuri: The Forest of the Taurocs. 2007. (J). *(978-1-59835-058-6(7))* Cambridge BrickHouse, Inc.

Perez, Marlene. Dead Is Just a Rumor. 2010. (Dead Is Ser.: 4). lib. bdg. 18.40 *(978-0-606-14958-7(9)*, Turtleback) Turtleback Bks.

Perkins, Kevin. The Little Blue Gnome. 2013. 210p. pap. *(978-1-78148-649-8(2))* Grosvenor Hse. Publishing Ltd.

Perkins, Kevin John. The Circlet. 2010. 316p. pap. *(978-1-907211-33-1(0))* Grosvenor Hse. Publishing Ltd.

Perone, S. P. Star of the Future. 2010. 176p. 23.95 *(978-1-4502-6861-5(7))*; pap. 13.95 *(978-1-4502-6859-2(5))* iUniverse, Inc.

Perrault, Charles. OXFORD WORLD'S CLASSICS: THE COMPLETE FAIRY TALES. 2010. (Oxford World's Classics Ser.). (ENG., Illus.). 256p. pap. 13.95 *(978-0-19-958580-9(6))* Oxford Univ. Pr., Inc.

Perret, Gene. Clean Underwear. 2003. *(978-1-893860-88-9(4))* Arizona Highways.

Perro, Bryan. Amos Daragon #2: the Key of Braha. 2013. (Amos Daragon Ser.). (ENG.). 192p. (J). (gr. 3-7). 6.99 *(978-0-375-85977-9(2))* Random Hse. Children's Bks.

Perry, Dakota. Brim's Journey. 2008. 36p. pap. 24.95 *(978-1-60703-938-9(9))* America Star Bks.

Perry, Fred. Gold Digger - Platinum, Vol. 2. 2011. (ENG.). 132p. (YA). pap., pap. 14.99 *(978-0-9831823-4-4(5)*, 9780983182344) Antarctic Pr., Inc.

—Gold Digger Platinum, Vol. 4. 2012. (ENG., Illus.). 132p. (YA). pap. 14.95 *(978-0-9850925-0-4(5)*, 9780985092504) Antarctic Pr., Inc.

Perry, John. The Book That Eats People. Fearing, Mark, illus. 2009. (ENG.). 38p. (J). (gr. -1-2). 15.99 *(978-1-58246-268-4(2)*, Tricycle Pr.) Random Hse. Children's Bks.

Perry, Pete. The Saints in Paradise: Another Crazy Story for Crazy Kids. 2009. (Illus.). 76p. pap. 24.99 *(978-1-4490-1311-0(2))* AuthorHouse.

—The Secret of Bedside Manor. 2009. (Illus.). 140p. pap. 36.49 *(978-1-4389-6668-7(7))* AuthorHouse.

Peter L. Ward. Freya & the Fenris-Wolf. 2010. 184p. 24.50 *(978-1-4269-2511-5(5))*; pap. 14.50 *(978-1-4269-2510-8(7))* Trafford Publishing.

Peter Pantm. 2003. (J). 173.68 *(978-0-06-056911-2(5))* HarperCollins Pubs.

Peterfreund, Diana. The Forbidden Fortress. 2017. (Omega City Ser.: 2). 304p. (J). (gr. 3-7). 16.99 *(978-0-06-231088-0(7))* HarperCollins Pubs.

Peters, Anna. The Friendly Rubbish Monsters. 2011. 92p. pap. 10.00 *(978-1-60911-878-5(2)*, Eloquent Bks.) Strategic Book Publishing & Rights Agency (SBPRA).

Peterson, Alyson. The Cursed Dagger. 2016. (YA). pap. *(978-1-4621-1865-6(8))* Cedar Fort, Inc./CFI Distribution.

—The Exiled Prince. 2017. (ENG.). (YA). (gr. 8-12). pap. 17.99 ***(978-1-4621-2035-2(0)***, Sweetwater Bks.) Cedar Fort, Inc./CFI Distribution.

Peterson, Alyson. Ian Quicksilver: The Warrior's Return. 2015. vii, 309p. (YA). pap. 17.99 *(978-1-4621-1629-4(9))* Cedar Fort, Inc./CFI Distribution.

Peterson, Andrew. On the Edge of the Dark Sea of Darkness: Adventure. Peril. Lost Jewels. & the Fearsome Toothy Cows of Skree. 2008. (Wingfeather Saga Ser.). (ENG., Illus.). 304p. pap. 15.99 *(978-1-4000-7384-9(7)*, WaterBrook Pr.) Crown Publishing Group.

Peterson, Brandon & Brereton, Dan. Giant Killer. 2006. (ENG., Illus.). 128p. (YA). pap. 14.99 *(978-1-58240-539-1(5)*, 9781582405391) Image Comics.

Peterson, Brian. The Popcornmaker. 2007. 232p. 25.95 *(978-0-595-70458-3(1))*; per. 15.95 *(978-0-595-46727-3(X))* iUniverse, Inc.

Peterson, Joel & Rogers, Jacqueline, illus. The Littles & the Surprise Thanksgiving Guests. 2004. (Littles First Readers Ser.). 105p. (J). *(978-0-439-68704-1(7))* Scholastic, Inc.

Peterson, Mark. The Tater Tot King. 2011. 16p. 12.68 *(978-1-4269-5395-8(X))* Trafford Publishing.

Peterson, Scott. The Ultimate Returns. 4th ed. 2009. (Spectrobes Ser.: No. 3). (ENG.). 144p. (J). (gr. 3-7). pap. 4.99 *(978-1-4231-0811-5(6))* Disney Pr.

Petit, Cheryl. Fairy Princess Melina, 1 vol. 2010. 26p. pap. 24.95 *(978-1-4489-7915-8(3))* PublishAmerica, Inc.

Petri, Michelle. The Fvantom: Omegapocalypse. 2007. 212p. per. 14.95 *(978-0-595-45723-6(1))* iUniverse, Inc.

Petrucha, Stefan. Harry Potty & the Deathly Boring. 2010. (Papercutz Slices Ser.). (ENG., Illus.). 64p. (J). (gr. 5-12). pap. 7.99 *(978-1-59707-217-5(6)*, 9781597072175) Papercutz.

Petrucha, Stefan & Kinney-Petrucha, Margo. Percy Jackson & the Ovolactovegetarians, No. 3. 2011. (Papercutz Slices Ser.). (ENG., Illus.). 64p. (J). (gr. 5-12). pap. 6.99 *(978-1-59707-264-9(8)*, 9781597072649) Papercutz.

Pevear, Ted F. & Pevear, Linda W. The Date in the Junk Yard. 2012. 28p. (-18). pap. 24.95 *(978-1-4626-8994-1(9))* America Star Bks.

Peymani, Christine. Kitai's Journal. Katzenstein, Jason A., illus. 2013. (ENG.). 144p. (J). (gr. 3-7). pap. 5.99 *(978-0-06-226857-0(0))* HarperCollins Pubs.

Peyo. Meet Smurfette. Peyo, illus. 2011. (Smurfs Classic Ser.). (ENG., Illus.). 24p. (J). (gr. -1-2). pap. 3.99 *(978-1-4424-2290-2(4)*, Simon Spotlight) Simon Spotlight.

—Off to School! Peyo, illus. 2011. (Smurfs Classic Ser.). (ENG., Illus.). 32p. (J). (gr. k-2). pap. 3.99 *(978-1-4424-2138-7(X))*; lib. bdg. 15.99 *(978-1-4424-3062-4(1))* Simon Spotlight. (Simon Spotlight).

—The Smurfs #14: the Baby Smurf. 2013. (Smurfs Graphic Novels Ser.). (ENG., Illus.). 56p. (J). (gr. 1-5). 10.99 *(978-1-59707-382-0(2)*, 9781597073820) Papercutz.

—The Smurfs & the Magic Egg. Peyo, illus. 2014. (Smurfs Classic Ser.). (ENG., Illus.). 32p. (J). (gr. k-2). pap. 3.99 *(978-1-4424-9570-8(7)*, Simon Spotlight) Simon Spotlight.

Peyo & Delporte, Yvan. The Smurf Olympics. 2012. (Smurfs Graphic Novels Ser.). (ENG., Illus.). 56p. (J). (gr. 2-5). 10.99 *(978-1-59707-302-8(4)*, 9781597073028) Papercutz.

—The Smurfette. 2011. (Smurfs Graphic Novels Ser.). (ENG., Illus.). 64p. (J). (gr. 2-5). pap. 5.99 *(978-1-59707-236-6(2)*, 9781597072366);No. 4. 10.99 *(978-1-59707-237-3(0)*, 9781597072373) Papercutz.

—The Smurfs, 3 Vols., Set. 2011. (Smurfs Graphic Novels Ser.). (ENG., Illus.). 184p. (J). (gr. 2-5). 17.99 *(978-1-59707-273-1(7)*, 9781597072731) Papercutz.

—The Smurfs #9: Gargamel & the Smurfs. 2011. (Smurfs Graphic Novels Ser.). (ENG., Illus.). 56p. (J). (gr. 2-5). 10.99 *(978-1-59707-290-8(7)*, 9781597072908); pap. 5.99 *(978-1-59707-289-2(3)*, 9781597072892) Papercutz.

—The Smurfs & the Egg. 2011. (Smurfs Graphic Novels Ser.). (ENG., Illus.). 64p. (J). (gr. 2-5). 10.99 *(978-1-59707-247-2(8)*, 9781597072472); pap. 5.99 *(978-1-59707-246-5(X)*, 9781597072465) Papercutz.

Peyo, et al. The Smurfs #8: the Smurf Apprentice. 2011. (Smurfs Graphic Novels Ser.). (ENG., Illus.). 56p. (J). (gr. 2-5). 10.99 *(978-1-59707-280-9(X)*, 9781597072809); pap. 5.99 *(978-1-59707-279-3(6)*, 9781597072793) Papercutz.

Phanton, Rick. Boston & the Bean. 2012. 112p. pap. 19.95 *(978-1-4626-4809-2(6))* America Star Bks.

Phillips, Joanne M. Angelique & the Green Planet. 2013. 112p. 28.99 *(978-1-4525-7587-2(8))*; pap. 11.99 *(978-1-4525-7585-8(1))* Author Solutions, Inc. (Balboa Pr.).

Phillips, Kent. The Red Eyed Black Dragon. 2011. 28p. pap. 15.99 *(978-1-4568-3795-2(8))* Xlibris Corp.

Phillips, Michael. The Sword, the Garden, & the King. 2013. 248p. pap. 12.99 *(978-0-940652-70-5(6))* Sunrise Bks.

Phillpotts, Eden. The Flint Heart; a Fairy Story. 2010. 376p. pap. 33.75 *(978-1-171-85836-2(1))* Creative Media Partners, LLC.

—The Flint Heart; a Fairy Story. 2010. (Illus.). 98p. pap. 20.00 *(978-1-154-70758-8(X))* 2009. 134p. pap. 19.99 *(978-1-150-78588-7(8))* General Bks. LLC.

Philpot, Graham, illus. The Emperor & the Nightingale. 2007. (First Reading Level 4 Ser.). 48p. (J). (gr. -1-3). 8.99 *(978-0-7945-1614-7(9)*, Usborne) EDC Publishing.

Phoenix, Three. Daughter of the Sun. 2012. 36p. pap. 11.99 *(978-0-9830686-3-1(1))* Capital Apple Pr.

Pickering, Sean & Morrill, Scott. The Adventures of Danny & Spike: Underground. 2007. 92p. per. 9.95 *(978-0-595-44365-9(6))* iUniverse, Inc.

Pickett, Lanaya A. Walking with Angels. 2011. 192p. 23.95 *(978-1-4620-2306-6(1))*; pap. 13.95 *(978-1-4620-2307-3(X))* iUniverse, Inc.

Picoult, Jodi & van Leer, Samantha. Between the Lines. (ENG., Illus.). 368p. (YA). (gr. 7). 2013. pap. 12.99 *(978-1-4516-3581-2(8))* 2012. 19.99 *(978-1-4516-3575-1(3))* Atria/Emily Bestler Bks. (Atria/Emily Bestler Bks.).

—Off the Page. Gilbert, Yvonne, illus. 2015. (YA). lib. bdg. *(978-0-553-53557-0(9)*, Delacorte Pr) Random House Publishing Group.

—Off the Page. Gilbert, Yvonne, illus. (ENG.). (YA). (gr. 7). 2016. 368p. pap. 9.99 *(978-0-553-53559-4(5)*, Ember) 2015. 384p. 19.99 *(978-0-553-53556-3(0)*, Delacorte Pr.) Random Hse. Children's Bks.

Picouly, Daniel. Thumbelina of Toulaba. Bedrick, Claudia Z., tr. from FRE. Tallec, Olivier & Sorman, Joy, illus. 2007. (ENG.). 36p. (J). (gr. -1-3). 16.95 *(978-1-59270-069-1(1))* Enchanted Lion Bks., LLC.

Pierce, Meredith Ann. The Birth of the Firebringer, Vol. 1. 2003. (ENG.). 208p. (YA). (gr. 7-18). pap. 7.99 *(978-0-14-250053-8(4)*, Firebird) Penguin Young Readers Group.

—The Dark Moon. 2003. (ENG.). 256p. (YA). (gr. 7-11). 7.99 *(978-0-14-250057-6(7)*, Firebird) Penguin Young Readers Group.

—The Pearl of the Soul of the World. 2008. (Darkangel Trilogy Ser.: Bk. 3). (ENG.). 256p. (YA). (gr. 7-17). per. 7.99 *(978-0-316-06724-9(5))* Little, Brown Bks. for Young Readers.

—The Son of Summer Stars, Vol. 3. 2003. (ENG.). 256p. (YA). (gr. 7-7). 7.99 *(978-0-14-250074-3(7)*, Firebird) Penguin Young Readers Group.

Pierce, Ricky. Bouncing Billy. 2008. 24p. per. 10.95 *(978-1-4327-1696-7(4))* Outskirts Pr., Inc.

Pierce, Tamora. Alanna: The First Adventure. unabr. ed. 2004. (Song of the Lioness Ser.: Bk. 1). 216p. (J). (gr. 6-18). pap. 36.00 incl. audio *(978-0-8072-8772-9(5)*, YA263SP, Listening Library) Random Hse. Audio Publishing Group.

—Bloodhound. 2010. (Beka Cooper Ser.: Bk. 2). (ENG., Illus.). 576p. (YA). (gr. 7-11). pap. 10.99 *(978-0-375-83817-0(1)*, Random Hse. Bks. for Young Readers) Random Hse. Children's Bks.

—Cold Fire. 2003. (Circle Opens Ser.: 3). (ENG.). 384p. (J). (gr. 7). mass mkt. 7.99 *(978-0-590-39656-1(0)*, Scholastic Paperbacks) Scholastic, Inc.

—Emperor Mage. 2015. (Immortals Ser.: 3). (ENG., Illus.). 368p. (YA). (gr. 7). pap. 10.99 *(978-1-4814-4026-4(8))* Simon & Schuster Children's Publishing.

—Emperor Mage. 2005. (Immortals Ser.: 3). (ENG.). 384p. (YA). (gr. 7). pap. 7.99 *(978-1-4169-0337-6(2)*, Simon Pulse) Simon Pulse.

—First Test. 2004. (Protector of the Small Ser.: No. 1). (ENG.). 240p. (YA). (gr. 7). pap. 9.99 *(978-0-375-82905-5(9)*, Ember) Random Hse. Children's Bks.

—In the Hand of the Goddess. unabr. ed. 2004. (Song of the Lioness Ser.: Bk. 2). 206p. (J). (gr. 6-18). pap. 36.00 incl. audio *(978-0-8072-0665-2(2)*, S YA 338 SP, Listening Library) Random Hse. Audio Publishing Group.

—Lady Knight. 2004. (Protector of the Small Ser.: 4). (ENG.). 464p. (YA). (gr. 7-12). pap. 9.99 *(978-0-375-82908-6(3)*, Ember) Random Hse. Children's Bks.

—Lady Knight. l.t. ed. 2003. (Protector of the Small Ser.: No. 4). (J). (gr. 3-6). 23.95 *(978-0-7862-5217-6(0))* Thorndike Pr.

—Lioness Rampant. unabr. ed. 2004. (Song of the Lioness Ser.: Bk. 4). 308p. (J). (gr. 6-18). pap. 38.00 incl. audio *(978-0-8072-0985-1(6)*, S YA 388 SP, Listening Library) Random Hse. Audio Publishing Group.

—Lioness Rampant. 2011. (Song of the Lioness Ser.: 4). (ENG., Illus.). 384p. (YA). (gr. 7). pap. 10.99 *(978-1-4424-2766-2(3)*, Atheneum Bks. for Young Readers) Simon & Schuster Children's Publishing.

—Lioness Rampant. 2005. (Song of the Lioness Ser.: 4). (ENG.). 400p. (YA). (gr. 7). mass mkt. 7.99 *(978-0-689-87857-2(5)*, Simon Pulse) Simon Pulse.

—Mastiff. 2012. (Beka Cooper Ser.). (ENG.). 608p. (YA). (gr. 7-11). pap. 10.99 *(978-0-375-83818-7(X)*, Ember) Random Hse. Children's Bks.

—Page. 2004. (Protector of the Small Ser.: 2). (ENG.). 288p. (YA). (gr. 7). pap. 9.99 *(978-0-375-82907-9(5)*, Ember) Random Hse. Children's Bks.

—The Realms of the Gods. 2005. (Immortals Ser.: No. 4). 347p. (gr. 7-12). 18.00 *(978-0-7569-5775-9(3))* Perfection Learning Corp.

—The Realms of the Gods. 2015. (Immortals Ser.: 4). (ENG., Illus.). 352p. (YA). (gr. 7). pap. 10.99 *(978-1-4814-4028-8(4))* Simon & Schuster Children's Publishing.

—Shatterglass. 2004. (Circle Opens Ser.: 4). (ENG.). 368p. (J). (gr. 3-7). pap. 8.99 *(978-0-590-39696-7(X)*, Scholastic Paperbacks) Scholastic, Inc.

—Squire. 2004. (Protector of the Small Ser.: 3). (ENG.). 432p. (YA). (gr. 7). pap. 9.99 *(978-0-375-82906-2(7)*, Ember) Random Hse. Children's Bks.

—Terrier. 2007. (Beka Cooper Ser.: Bk. 1). (ENG.). 608p. (YA). (gr. 7-11). pap. 10.99 *(978-0-375-83816-3(3)*, Ember) Random Hse. Children's Bks.

—Tortall & Other Lands: A Collection of Tales. 2012. (Beka Cooper Ser.). (ENG.). 400p. (YA). (gr. 7). pap. 10.99 *(978-0-375-86633-3(7)*, Bluefire) Random Hse. Children's Bks.

—Trickster's Choice. 2005. (Daughter of the Lioness Ser.: Bk. 1). (Illus.). 422p. (gr. 7). 20.00 *(978-0-7569-5746-9(X))* Perfection Learning Corp.

—Trickster's Choice. 2004. (Trickster's Duet Ser.: 1). (ENG., Illus.). 448p. (YA). (gr. 7). reprint ed. pap. 9.99 *(978-0-375-82879-9(6)*, Ember) Random Hse. Children's Bks.

—Trickster's Queen. 2005. (Daughter of the Lioness Ser.: Bk. 2). (Illus.). 467p. (gr. 7-12). 20.00 *(978-0-7569-5482-6(7))* Perfection Learning Corp.

—Trickster's Queen. 2005. (Trickster's Duet Ser.: 2). (ENG., Illus.). 496p. (YA). (gr. 7-12). per. 9.99 *(978-0-375-82878-2(8)*, Ember) Random Hse. Children's Bks.

—Wild Magic. 2005. (Immortals Ser.: No. 1). (Illus.). 362p. (gr. 7-12). 18.00 *(978-0-7569-5508-3(4))* Perfection Learning Corp.

—Wild Magic. 2015. (Immortals Ser.: 1). (ENG., Illus.). 368p. (YA). (gr. 7). pap. 10.99 *(978-1-4814-4022-6(5))* Simon & Schuster Children's Publishing.

—Wolf-Speaker. 2005. (Immortals Ser.: No. 2). 344p. (gr. 7-12). 18.00 *(978-0-7569-5509-0(2))* Perfection Learning Corp.

—Wolf-Speaker. 2015. (Immortals Ser.: 2). (ENG., Illus.). 352p. (YA). (gr. 7). pap. 10.99 *(978-1-4814-4024-0(1))* Simon & Schuster Children's Publishing.

—The Woman Who Rides Like a Man. unabr. ed. 2004. (Song of the Lioness Ser.: Bk. 3). 228p. (J). (gr. 6-18). pap. 38.00 incl. audio *(978-0-8072-0797-0(7)*, LYA 357 SP, Listening Library) Random Hse. Audio Publishing Group.

—The Woman Who Rides Like a Man. 2014. (Song of the Lioness Ser.: 3). (ENG., Illus.). 288p. (YA). (gr. 7). 19.99 *(978-1-4814-3962-6(6)*, Atheneum Bks. for Young Readers) Simon & Schuster Children's Publishing.

—The Woman Who Rides Like a Man. 2005. (Song of the Lioness Ser.: Bk. 3). (ENG., Illus.). 304p. (YA). mass mkt. 6.99 *(978-0-689-87858-9(3)*, Simon Pulse) Simon Pulse.

Pierce, Walter. Dreams Unseen: The Dragon of Mists. 2007. 260p. (YA). per. 16.95 *(978-0-595-45171-5(3))* iUniverse, Inc.

Pierson, D. C. Crap Kingdom. 2014. (ENG.). 368p. (YA). (gr. 7). pap. 9.99 *(978-0-14-242231-1(2)*, Speak) Penguin Young Readers Group.

Pike, Aprilynne. Destined. (Wings Ser.: 4). (ENG.). (YA). (gr. 8). 2013. 336p. pap. 9.99 *(978-0-06-166814-2(1))* 2012. 320p. 17.99 *(978-0-06-166812-8(5))* HarperCollins Pubs. (HarperTeen).

—Wings. 2011. (Wings Ser.: 1). (ENG.). 320p. (YA). (gr. 8). pap. 8.99 *(978-0-06-166805-0(2)*, HarperTeen) HarperCollins Pubs.

Pike, Christopher, pseud. The Midnight Club. 2012. (ENG.). 224p. (YA). (gr. 11). pap. 10.99 *(978-1-4424-6054-6(7)*, Simon Pulse) Simon Pulse.

—The Secret of Ka. 2011. (ENG.). 416p. (YA). (gr. 7). pap. 8.99 *(978-0-547-57729-6(X))* Houghton Mifflin Harcourt Publishing Co.

—The Witch's Revenge. 2015. (Spooksville Ser.: 6). (ENG., Illus.). 128p. (J). (gr. 3-7). pap. 6.99 *(978-1-4814-1069-4(5)*, Aladdin) Simon & Schuster Children's Publishing.

Pike, Tabitha R. Dragon Tears: The Legacy. 2011. 232p. pap. 24.95 *(978-1-4560-6664-2(1))* America Star Bks.

Pikey, Mikey. The Diamond Tree. 2007. 378p. pap. 31.95 *(978-1-84728-234-7(2))* Lulu Pr., Inc.

Pilkey, Dav. El Capitán Calzoncillos y la Feroz Batalla Contra el Niño Mocobionico: La Noche de los Mocos Vivientes. Pilkey, Dav, illus. 2005. (Capitán Calzoncillos Ser.: 6). Orig. Title: Captain Underpants & the Big, Bad Battle of the Bionic Booger Boy: the Night of the Nasty Nostril Nuggets. (SPA & ENG., Illus.). 176p. (J). (gr. 2-5). mass mkt. 5.99 *(978-0-439-66204-8(4)*, Scholastic en Espanol) Scholastic, Inc.

Pillsworth, Anne M. Fathomless. 2015. (Redemption's Heir Ser.: 2). (ENG.). 320p. (YA). 18.99 *(978-0-7653-3590-6(5)*, 9780765335906, Tor Teen) Doherty, Tom Assocs., LLC.

Pilumeli, Tanya. The Dragonfly Keeper. 2008. 264p. (J). per. 12.95 *(978-0-9801396-0-0(0))* FAVA Pr.

Pipera, Lady. The Enchanted Meadow. 2009. 52p. pap. 17.50 *(978-1-60860-100-4(5)*, Eloquent Bks.) Strategic Book Publishing & Rights Agency (SBPRA).

Pitcher, Caroline. Cloud Cat. 2005. (Year of Changes Ser.: 1). (ENG.). 154p. (J). (gr. 4-7). pap. 9.99 *(978-1-4052-0849-9(X))* Egmont Bks., Ltd. GBR. Dist: Independent Pubs. Group.

Pitcher, Chelsea. The Last Changeling. 2014. (ENG.). 360p. (YA). pap. 11.99 *(978-0-7387-4084-3(5)*, Flux) North Star Editions.

Pittman, Eddie. Red's Planet. 2016. (Red's Planet Ser.). (ENG., Illus.). 192p. (J). (gr. 3-7). 19.95 *(978-1-4197-1907-3(6)*, Amulet Bks.) Abrams, Inc.

Pixie, B. R. Just a Little Human. 2011. 98p. pap. 19.95 *(978-1-4512-3551-7(8))* America Star Bks.

Plante, Raymond. Le Monde de Xéros. Delezenne, Christine, illus. 2004. (Roman Jeunesse Ser.). (FRE.). 96p. (J). (gr. 4-7). pap. *(978-2-89021-615-0(2))* Diffusion du livre Mirabel (DLM).

Pockat, Alison A. Adam's Bubble. 2010. 76p. pap. 10.49 *(978-1-4490-9287-0(X))* AuthorHouse.

Podwitch. 2014. (ENG.). 304p. pap. *(978-1-78306-380-2(7))* Troubador Publishing Ltd.

Poe, Edgar Allen. The Raven & Other Writings. 2003. (Aladdin Classics Ser.). (ENG.). 448p. (J). (gr. 4-7). pap. 7.99 *(978-0-689-86352-3(7)*, Aladdin) Simon & Schuster Children's Publishing.

Pohl-Weary, Emily. Not Your Ordinary Wolf Girl, 0 vols. 2013. (ENG.). 224p. (YA). (gr. 9-12). pap. 9.99 *(978-1-4778-1688-2(7)*, 9781477816882, Amazon Children's Publishing) Amazon Publishing.

Polette, Keith. Isabel & the Hungry Coyote. 2009. (ENG.). 32p. (J). (gr. 4-7). 16.95 *(978-1-934960-72-1(1)*, Raven Tree Pr.,Csi) Continental Sales, Inc.

—Moon over the Mountain. 2009. (ENG.). 32p. (J). (gr. -1-3). 16.95 *(978-1-934960-07-3(1)*, Raven Tree Pr.,Csi) Continental Sales, Inc.

—Moon over the Mountain/Luna Sobre la Montana. 2009. (ENG & SPA.). 32p. (J). (gr. -1-3). 16.95 *(978-1-932748-85-7(7))*; pap. 7.95 *(978-1-932748-84-0(9))* Continental Sales, Inc. (Raven Tree Pr.,Csi).

Poling, Atarah L. Forbidden Secret: Shadows Behind Locked Doors. 2011. 162p. pap. 24.95 *(978-1-4560-5477-9(5))* America Star Bks.

Pollock, Tom. The Glass Republic. 2016. (Skyscraper Throne Ser.: 2). (ENG.). 448p. (YA). (gr. 7-9). pap. 14.99 *(978-1-68144-348-5(1)*, Jo Fletcher Books) Quercus NA.

—Our Lady of the Streets. 2017. (Skyscraper Throne Ser.: 3). (ENG.). 464p. (YA). (gr. 7-9). pap. 14.99 *(978-1-68144-381-2(3)*, Jo Fletcher Books) Quercus NA.

Pomaska, Anna. Scruffy & Muffin in the Land of Enchantment: A Dot-to-Dot Storybook. 2004. (Dover Children's Activity Bks.). (ENG., Illus.). 32p. (J). (gr. -1-2). pap. 3.95 *(978-0-486-43566-4(0))* Dover Pubns., Inc.

Ponti, James. Blue Moon. 2013. (Dead City Ser.: 2). (ENG., Illus.). 336p. (J). (gr. 4-8). 17.99 *(978-1-4424-4131-6(3)*, Aladdin) Simon & Schuster Children's Publishing.

Pooker, J. D. The Ifs. 2013. (ENG.). 148p. (J). pap. 7.95 *(978-0-9858280-3-5(X))* Little Devil Bks.

Pool, Catherine. Catrina's Journey to Her Musical Friends, 1 vol. 2010. 18p. pap. 24.95 *(978-1-4489-7237-1(X))* PublishAmerica, Inc.

Poole, Josephine. BLANCANIEVES. 2007. (SPA., Illus.). 30p. (J). (gr. -1-5). 24.95 *(978-84-96629-17-2(1))* S.A. Kokinos ESP. Dist: Lectorum Pubns., Inc.

Poole, Richard. Jewel & Thorn. 2007. (Book of Lowmoor Ser.: 1). (ENG., Illus.). 400p. (J). (gr. 7-12). pap. 11.95 *(978-0-689-87290-7(9))* Simon & Schuster, Ltd. GBR. Dist: Simon & Schuster, Inc.

Pope, Paul. Battling Boy. Pope, Paul, illus. 2013. (Battling Boy Ser.: 1). (ENG., Illus.). 208p. (J). (gr. 5-12). 24.99 *(978-1-59643-805-7(3)*, 9781596438057); pap. 16.99 *(978-1-59643-145-4(8)*, 9781596431454) Roaring Brook Pr. (First Second Bks.).

Pope, Paul & Petty, J. T. The Fall of the House of West. Rubín, David, illus. 2015. (Battling Boy Ser.: 2). (ENG.). 160p. (J). (gr. 5). pap. 9.99 *(978-1-62672-010-7(X)*, 9781626720107, First Second Bks.) Roaring Brook Pr.

Portal, Alex. The Applegates, 1 vol. 2009. 32p. pap. 24.95 *(978-1-60749-727-1(1))* America Star Bks.

Porter, Sarah. Waking Storms. 2013. (Lost Voices Trilogy Ser.: 2). (ENG.). 416p. (YA). (gr. 7). pap. 8.99 *(978-0-547-48254-5(X))* Houghton Mifflin Harcourt Publishing Co.

Porter, Todd. Firefly Fred. Patenaude, Brian, illus. 2004. (ENG.). 36p. (J). (gr. -1-3). 19.95 *(978-1-932278-00-2(1))* Mayhaven Publishing, Inc.

Poryes, Michael, illus. The Trouble with Boys, 2 vols., Vol. 2. 2004. (That's So Raven Ser.). 96p. pap. 14.99 *(978-1-59182-807-5(4)*, Tokyopop Kids) TOKYOPOP, Inc.

Posadas, Carmen. Dorilda. 2nd ed. 2003. (SPA., Illus.). 127p. (J). (gr. 3-5). pap. 13.95 *(978-84-204-5800-7(7))* Santillana USA Publishing Co., Inc.

Posner-Sanchez, Andrea. Pixie Puzzles, Games, & More! Christy, Jana, illus. 2014. (Never Girls Ser.). (ENG.). 256p. (J). (gr. 1-4). 6.99 *(978-0-7364-3152-1(7)*, Golden/Disney) Random Hse. Children's Bks.

E
F
G

Post, Bobby. The Adventures of Jimmy. 2007. 48p. per. 16.95 *(978-1-4137-8704-7(5))* America Star Bks.

Potey Molina, José Luis. El pergamino de Zenit y el descubrimiento de los sellos Divinos. 2010. (SPA.). 224p. (YA). pap. 18.99 *(978-1-59835-099-9(4)*, CBH Bks.) Cambridge BrickHouse, Inc.

Potter, Beatrix. The Tale of Peter Rabbit. 2012. 26p. pap. 12.00 *(978-0-9880821-2-0(8))* Birch Tree Publishing.

Powell, Christine. Bootsie's Underground Adventure. 2012. 28p. pap. 24.95 *(978-1-4626-7449-7(6))* America Star Bks.

Powell, Gregg E. Goobadabers. Lea, Corinne, illus. 2011. 24p. pap. 24.95 *(978-1-4626-0734-1(9))* America Star Bks.

Powell, J. Frederick. Puffy & the Witch's Revenge. 2004. (Illus.). 96p. pap. *(978-1-84401-329-6(4))* Athena Pr.

Powell, Jim S. The Mystery of the Totem Trees: A Plumroy Pack Adventure. 2009. 124p. pap. 10.95 *(978-1-4401-3921-5(0))* iUniverse, Inc.

Powell, Martin. The Seven Voyages of Sinbad, 1 vol. Pérez, Daniel et al, illus. 2010. (Classic Fiction Ser.). (ENG.). 72p. (gr. 2-3). 27.99 *(978-1-4342-1987-9(9)*, Graphic Revolve) Stone Arch Bks.

—The Seven Voyages of Sinbad. Pérez, Daniel et al, illus. 2010. (Classic Fiction Ser.). (ENG.). 72p. (gr. 2-3). pap. 7.15 *(978-1-4342-2775-1(8)*, Graphic Revolve) Stone Arch Bks.

Power, Nicholas D. Paudie's Magical Adventures. 2009. 236p. 24.75 *(978-1-60693-534-7(8)*, Strategic Bk. Publishing) Strategic Book Publishing & Rights Agency (SBPRA).

Powers, Mark & Powers, Megan. Tara's Tiara: Paperback. Powers, Mark & Powers, Megan, illus. Powers, Marilia, illus. 2012. 130p. (J). pap. 14.95 *(978-0-9853817-0-7(1))* Pendentive Pubns.

Pranali. The Secret Storybook. 2013. 64p. pap. 23.95 *(978-1-4828-0147-7(7))* Partridge Pub.

Pratchett, Terry. The Carpet People. (ENG., Illus.). 304p. (J). (gr. 2-5). 2015. pap. 6.99 *(978-0-544-43954-2(6)*, HMH Books For Young Readers) 2013. 17.99 *(978-0-544-21247-3(9))* Houghton Mifflin Harcourt Publishing Co.

—Dodger. 368p. (YA). (gr. 8). 2013. pap. 9.99 *(978-0-06-200951-7(6))* 2012. 17.99 *(978-0-06-200949-4(4))* 2012. lib. bdg. 18.89 *(978-0-06-200950-0(8))* HarperCollins Pubs.

—Eric. 2013. (Discworld Ser.: 9). (gr. 5-8). 18.40 *(978-0-613-57205-7(X)*, Turtleback) Turtleback Bks.

—A Hat Full of Sky. (Tiffany Aching Ser.: 2). (YA). (gr. 8). 2015. (ENG.). 400p. pap. 9.99 *(978-0-06-243527-9(2))* 2004. 288p. 17.99 *(978-0-06-058660-7(5))* HarperCollins Pubs.

—A Hat Full of Sky. 2005. 407p. (gr. 7). 19.00 *(978-0-7569-5126-9(7))* Perfection Learning Corp.

—A Hat Full of Sky. 2005. (Discworld Ser.: 32). 407p. (YA). 19.65 *(978-1-4177-2658-5(X)*, Turtleback) Turtleback Bks.

—I Shall Wear Midnight. (Tiffany Aching Ser.: 4). (YA). (gr. 8). 2015. (ENG.). 464p. pap. 9.99 *(978-0-06-243529-3(9))* 2011. 368p. pap. 9.99 *(978-0-06-143306-1(3))* 2010. 368p. 16.99 *(978-0-06-143304-7(7))* HarperCollins Pubs.

—Sourcery. 2013. (Discworld Ser.: 5). (gr. 5-8). 20.85 *(978-0-613-57278-1(5)*, Turtleback) Turtleback Bks.

—The Truth. 2014. (Discworld Ser.: 25). (gr. 5-8). 20.85 *(978-0-613-57290-3(4)*, Turtleback) Turtleback Bks.

—The Wee Free Men. (Tiffany Aching Ser.: 1). (YA). (gr. 8). 2015. (ENG.). 352p. pap. 9.99 *(978-0-06-243526-2(4))* 2010. 576p. pap. 9.99 *(978-0-06-201217-3(7))* 2006. 400p. reprint ed. pap. 8.99 *(978-0-06-001238-0(2))* HarperCollins Pubs.

—The Wee Free Men. 2004. 19.00 *(978-0-7569-3252-7(1))* Perfection Learning Corp.

—The Wee Free Men. 2006. (Discworld Ser.: 28). (YA). 19.65 *(978-1-4176-2764-6(6)*, Turtleback) Turtleback Bks.

—Where's My Cow? 2005. (Discworld Ser.). (Illus.). 32p. 16.99 *(978-0-06-087267-0(5))* HarperCollins Pubs.

—Wintersmith. (YA). 2015. (Tiffany Aching Ser.: 3). (ENG.). 416p. (gr. 8). pap. 9.99 *(978-0-06-243528-6(0))* 2007. (Tiffany Aching Ser.: 3). 464p. (gr. 8-12). per. 8.99 *(978-0-06-089033-9(9))* 2006. (Discworld Novels Ser.). 323p. (gr. 7-12). 16.99 *(978-0-06-089031-5(2)*, HarperTeen) 2006. (Discworld Novels Ser.). 323p. (gr. 7-12). lib. bdg. 17.89 *(978-0-06-089032-2(0)*, HarperTeen) HarperCollins Pubs.

—Wintersmith. 2007. 450p. (gr. 7). 19.00 *(978-0-7569-8091-7(7))* Perfection Learning Corp.

—The Witch's Vacuum Cleaner. 2017. 256p. (YA). (gr. 8). 18.99 *(978-0-06-265311-6(3)*, Tegen, Katherine Bks) HarperCollins Pubs.

Press, Pikachu. Guide to Pokemon Legends. 2012. (ENG.). 32p. (J). 17.99 *(978-1-60438-175-7(2))* Pokemon, USA, Inc.

Price, Allison W. A. The Dragons & the Works of Knowledge. 2009. 112p. pap. 14.98 *(978-0-557-05766-5(3))* Lulu Pr., Inc.

Price, David J. Tom & Emily's Incredible Adventure to the World of the Gossamerians. 2013. 130p. pap. *(978-1-909740-41-9(1))* Legend Pr.

Price, Jennifer L. Half Moon: Phases of the Moon: Book 2, 1 vol. 2009. 252p. pap. 27.95 *(978-1-4489-2193-5(7))* PublishAmerica, Inc.

Price, Nick, illus. The Wonderful Wizard of Oz. 2009. (ENG.). 12p. (J). 8.95 *(978-1-58117-856-2(5)*, Intervisual/Piggy Toes) Bendon, Inc.

Prichard, Kathy. Tree Twitters: An Earth Dragons Tale, 1 vol. 2009. 23p. pap. 19.95 *(978-1-61582-620-9(3))* PublishAmerica, Inc.

Priebe, Trisha & Jenkins, Jerry B. The Glass Castle. 2016. (Thirteen Ser.). (ENG.). 256p. (J). 14.99 *(978-1-63409-389-7(5))* Barbour Publishing, Inc.

—The Ruby Moon. 2016. (Thirteen Ser.). (ENG.). 240p. 14.99 *(978-1-63409-903-5(6))* Barbour Publishing, Inc.

Priest, Christopher. Brothers & Keepers. 2005. (Captain America & the Falcon Ser.: Vol. 2). (Illus.). 168p. (YA). pap. 17.99 *(978-0-7851-1568-7(4))* Marvel Worldwide, Inc.

Priest, Robert. The Paper Sword. 2014. (Spell Crossed Ser.: 1). (ENG.). 224p. (YA). pap. 12.99 *(978-1-4597-0826-6(1)*, 9781459708266) Dundurn CAN. Dist: Ingram Publisher Services.

—Second Kiss: Spell Crossed. 2015. (Spell Crossed Ser.: 2). (ENG., Illus.). 328p. (YA). pap. 12.99 *(978-1-4597-3020-5(8))* Dundurn CAN. Dist: Ingram Publisher Services.

Priestley, Chris. Billy Wizard. Priestley, Chris, illus. 2005. (Young Corgi Ser.). (ENG., Illus.). 96p. (J). per. 6.99 *(978-0-552-54689-8(5))* Transworld Publishers Ltd. GBR. Dist: Independent Pubs. Group.

Primavera, Elise. Secret Order Gumm Street Girl, No. 2. 2006. *(978-0-06-056950-1(6))*; *(978-0-06-056949-5(2))* HarperCollins Canada, Ltd.

—The Secret Order of the Gumm Street Girls. Primavera, Elise, illus. 2008. (ENG., Illus.). 464p. (J). (gr. 3-7). pap. 9.99 *(978-0-06-056948-8(4))* HarperCollins Pubs.

Prince Caspian Chapter Book #1. 2008. (Chronicles of Narnia Ser.). 96p. (J). pap. 3.99 *(978-0-06-147260-2(3)*, Harper Trophy) HarperCollins Pubs.

Prince Caspian Chapter Book #2. 2008. (Chronicles of Narnia Ser.). 96p. (J). pap. 3.99 *(978-0-06-147261-9(1)*, Harper Trophy) HarperCollins Pubs.

Prince Caspian Chapter Book #3. 2008. (Chronicles of Narnia Ser.). 96p. (J). pap. 3.99 *(978-0-06-147262-6(X)*, Harper Trophy) HarperCollins Pubs.

Prince Caspian Chapter Book #4. 2008. (Chronicles of Narnia Ser.). 96p. (J). pap. 3.99 *(978-0-06-147263-3(8)*, Harper Trophy) HarperCollins Pubs.

Princess Madeline & the Dragon. 2013. (Illus.). 118p. (YA). pap. 5.99 *(978-1-62375-070-1(9)*, Caliburn Bks.) MQuills Publishing.

Princesses. 2009. (FACT ATLAS Ser.). 72p. (J). 15.99 *(978-0-8416-1101-6(7))* Hammond World Atlas Corp.

Prineas, Sarah. Found. Caparo, Antonio Javier, illus. 2011. (Magic Thief Ser.: 3). (ENG.). 384p. (J). (gr. 5). pap. 7.99 *(978-0-06-137595-8(0))* HarperCollins Pubs.

—Heart of the Land. 2017. (Spirit Animals: Fall of the Beasts Ser.: 5). (ENG.). 192p. (J). (gr. 3-7). 12.99 ***(978-1-338-11665-6(7))*** Scholastic, Inc.

—Lost. Caparo, Antonio Javier, illus. 2009. (Magic Thief Ser.: 2). (ENG.). 400p. (J). (gr. 5-18). 17.99 *(978-0-06-137589-7(6))* HarperCollins Pubs.

—Lost. 2009. (Magic Thief Ser.: 2). (J). 88.75 *(978-1-4407-3133-4(0))*; 130.75 *(978-1-4407-3129-7(2))*; 132.75 *(978-1-4407-3127-3(6))*; 110.75 *(978-1-4407-3125-9(X))*; (SPA.). 265.75 *(978-1-4407-3124-2(1))*; 112.75 *(978-1-4407-3123-5(3))*; 1.25 *(978-1-4407-3131-0(4))* Recorded Bks., Inc.

—The Magic Thief. Caparo, Antonio Javier, illus. 2009. (Magic Thief Ser.: 1). (ENG.). 448p. (J). (gr. 5). pap. 7.99 *(978-0-06-137590-3(X))* HarperCollins Pubs.

—The Magic Thief - Found. Caparo, Antonio Javier, illus. 2010. (Magic Thief Ser.: 3). (ENG.). 368p. (J). (gr. 5-18). 16.99 *(978-0-06-137593-4(4))* HarperCollins Pubs.

—The Magic Thief - Home. Caparo, Antonio Javier, illus. 2015. (Magic Thief Ser.: 4). (ENG.). 416p. (J). (gr. 3-7). pap. 7.99 *(978-0-06-220956-6(6))* HarperCollins Pubs.

—The Magic Thief - Lost. Caparo, Antonio Javier, illus. 2010. (Magic Thief Ser.: 2). (ENG.). 416p. (J). (gr. 5). pap. 7.99 *(978-0-06-137592-7(6))* HarperCollins Pubs.

—The Magic Thief: Home. Caparo, Antonio Javier, illus. 2014. (Magic Thief Ser.: 4). (ENG.). 416p. (J). (gr. 3-7). 17.99 *(978-0-06-220954-2(X))* HarperCollins Pubs.

—Moonkind. (Summerlands Ser.: 3). (ENG.). 272p. (J). (gr. 3-7). 2014. pap. 6.99 *(978-0-06-192111-7(4))* 2013. 16.99 *(978-0-06-192109-4(2))* HarperCollins Pubs.

—Summerkin. 2013. (Summerlands Ser.: 2). (ENG.). (J). (gr. 3-7). 288p. pap. 6.99 *(978-0-06-192108-7(4))*; 272p. 16.99 *(978-0-06-192106-3(8))* HarperCollins Pubs.

—Winterling. (J). (gr. 5-7). 2013. (Summerlands Ser.: 1). (ENG.). 272p. pap. 6.99 *(978-0-06-192105-6(X))* 2012. 256p. lib. bdg. 17.89 *(978-0-06-192104-9(1))* 2012. (Summerlands Ser.: 1). (ENG.). 256p. 16.99 *(978-0-06-192103-2(3))* HarperCollins Pubs.

—Winterling, 5 vols. 2012. (Winterling Ser.: 1). (J). 75.75 *(978-1-4640-1032-3(3))*; 230.75 *(978-1-4640-1034-7(X))*; 73.75 *(978-1-4640-1037-8(4))*; 73.75 *(978-1-4640-1036-1(6))* Recorded Bks., Inc.

The Princess Who Lost Her Smile. 2006. (J). 19.95 *(978-0-9790682-0-1(7))* Clear Braces L.L.C.

Prior, Natalie. Lily Quench & the Dragon of Ashby, No. 1. Dawson, Janine, illus. 2004. (ENG.). 160p. (J). (gr. 3-7). 6.99 *(978-0-14-240020-3(3)*, Puffin Books) Penguin Young Readers Group.

Prior, Natalie Jane. Lily Quench 6 Hand of Manuelo, Vol. 6. Dawson, Janine, illus. 2004. (ENG.). 176p. (J). (gr. 3-7). 6.99 *(978-0-14-240222-1(2)*, Puffin Books) Penguin Young Readers Group.

—The Search for King Dragon. Dawson, Janine, illus. 2005. (ENG.). 192p. (J). (gr. 3-7). 6.99 *(978-0-14-240267-2(2)*, Puffin Books) Penguin Young Readers Group.

Priscilla Asks, Why? The Rest of the Story. 2010. (YA). pap. 11.95 *(978-0-9742732-9-7(5))* My Grandma & Me Pubs.

Pritchard, Mark A. Billy Christmas. 2012. (ENG.). 350p. (YA). (gr. 7). pap. 16.95 *(978-0-9826251-8-7(9))* Santa Fe Writers Project.

Prm, Katherine & Dee, Stacy. The Veil. 2010. 233p. (YA). pap. 15.95 *(978-1-59705-540-6(9))* Wings ePress, Inc.

Prom Etiquette Scrapbook. 2011. 128p. 8.99 *(978-1-4231-4566-0(6))* Disney Pr.

Prom: He Said/She Said. 2011. 256p. (J). 12.99 *(978-1-4231-4565-3(8))* Disney Pr.

The Prophesied. 2013. 152p. *(978-1-4602-3111-1(2))* FriesenPress.

Pryce, Denise. Alexander & the Ring of Destiny. 2009. 72p. pap. 24.99 *(978-1-4251-8887-0(7))* Trafford Publishing.

Pryce, Trevor. Amphibians' End. Greene, Sanford, illus. 2016. (Kulipari Ser.). (ENG.). 304p. (J). (gr. 3-7). pap. 8.95 *(978-1-4197-2194-6(1)*, Amulet Bks.) Abrams, Inc.

—An Army of Frogs. Greene, Sanford, illus. 2013. (Kulipari Ser.). (ENG.). 288p. (J). (gr. 3-7). 15.95 *(978-1-4197-0172-6(X)*, Amulet Bks.) Abrams, Inc.

Pryce, Trevor & Naftali, Joel. Amphibians' End. 2015. (Kulipari Ser.). (ENG., Illus.). 304p. (J). (gr. 3-7). 15.95 *(978-1-4197-1648-5(4)*, Amulet Bks.) Abrams, Inc.

—An Army of Frogs. Greene, Sanford, illus. 2014. (Kulipari Ser.). (ENG.). 304p. (J). (gr. 3-7). pap. 8.95 *(978-1-4197-1381-1(7)*, Amulet Bks.) Abrams, Inc.

—The Rainbow Serpent. Greene, Sanford, illus. 2014. (Kulipari Ser.). (ENG.). 304p. (J). (gr. 3-7). 15.95 *(978-1-4197-1309-5(4)*, Amulet Bks.) Abrams, Inc.

Pryor, Michael. Beneath Quentaris. (Illus.). 160p. pap. *(978-0-7344-0556-2(1)*, Lothian Children's Bks.) Hachette Australia.

—The Missing Kin. 2009. (Chronicles of Krangor Ser.: 2). (ENG.). 208p. (J). (gr. 4-7). pap. 7.99 *(978-1-74166-175-0(7))* Random Hse. Australia AUS. Dist: Independent Pubs. Group.

—Quentaris in Flames. 2005. (Illus.). 160p. pap. *(978-0-7344-0469-5(7)*, Lothian Children's Bks.) Hachette Australia.

Publications International Ltd. Staff, creator. Once upon a Time: A Treasury of Fairy Tales. 2007. (Illus.). 318p. 15.98 *(978-1-4127-8732-1(7))* Publications International, Ltd.

Publications International Ltd. Staff, ed. Captain America Large Play a Sound. 2011. 24p. (J). 14.98 *(978-1-4508-1608-3(8))* Publications International, Ltd.

Puffy: The Cloud That Couldn't Rain. 2005. (J). 8.95 *(978-0-9755348-0-9(7))* Kids Life Pr.

Pullman, Philip. The Amber Spyglass. unabr. ed. 2004. (His Dark Materials Ser.: Bk. 3). 465p. (YA). (gr. 7-18). pap. 63.00 incl. audio *(978-0-8072-1593-7(7)*, S YA 169 SP, Listening Library) Random Hse. Audio Publishing Group.

—The Amber Spyglass. 2003. (His Dark Materials Ser.: 3). (ENG.). (J). (gr. 5-12). 480p. mass mkt. 8.99 *(978-0-440-23815-7(3)*, Laurel Leaf); (Illus.). 560p. pap. 8.99 *(978-0-440-41856-6(9)*, Yearling) Random Hse. Children's Bks.

—La Daga. Gallart, Dolors, tr. 7th ed. 2005. (Escritura desatada Ser.).Tr. of Subtle Knife. (SPA., Illus.). 283p. (YA). (gr. 7-11). 13.95 *(978-84-406-8409-7(6))* Ediciones B ESP. Dist: Independent Pubs. Group.

—La Daga.Tr. of Subtle Knife. (SPA.). 448p. 18.95 *(978-84-663-0742-0(7))* Suma de Letras, S.L. ESP. Dist: Distribooks, Inc.

—The Golden Compass. 2003. (His Dark Materials Ser.: 1). (ENG.). 368p. (J). (gr. 5-12). mass mkt. 8.99 *(978-0-440-23813-3(7)*, Laurel Leaf) Random Hse. Children's Bks.

—The Golden Compass Graphic Novel, Complete Edition. 2017. (His Dark Materials Ser.). (ENG.). 224p. (J). (gr. 5). 21.99 ***(978-0-553-53516-7(1))***; pap. 12.99 ***(978-0-553-53517-4(X))***; lib. bdg. 24.99 ***(978-0-553-53518-1(8))*** Random Hse. Children's Bks. (Knopf Bks. for Young Readers).

—The Golden Compass Graphic Novel, Volume 2. 2016. (His Dark Materials Ser.). (ENG.). 80p. (J). (gr. 5). 18.99 *(978-0-553-53512-9(9)*, Knopf Bks. for Young Readers) Random Hse. Children's Bks.

—His Dark Materials: The Golden Compass - The Subtle Knife - The Amber Spyglass, 3 vols. (His Dark Materials Ser.). (ENG.). (J). (gr. 5-12). 2007. 1312p. 60.00 *(978-0-375-84238-2(1)*, Knopf Bks. for Young Readers) 2003. mass mkt., mass mkt., mass mkt. 26.97 *(978-0-440-23860-7(9)*, Laurel Leaf) Random Hse. Children's Bks.

—His Dark Materials: The Golden Compass, the Subtle Knife, the Amber Spyglass. 2011. (Everyman's Library Contemporary Classics Ser.). (ENG.). 1144p. 35.00 *(978-0-307-95783-2(7)*, Everyman's Library) Knopf Doubleday Publishing Group.

—His Dark Materials Set: The Golden Compass - The Subtle Knife - The Amber Spyglass, 3 vols. 2003. (His Dark Materials Ser.: Bks. 1-3). (ENG.). 560p. (J). (gr. 5). 26.97 *(978-0-440-41951-8(4)*, Yearling) Random Hse. Children's Bks.

—Lyra's Oxford. Lawrence, John, illus. 2006. (His Dark Materials Ser.). 49p. (YA). reprint ed. 11.00 *(978-1-4223-5410-0(5))* DIANE Publishing Co.

—Lyra's Oxford. Lawrence, John, illus. (His Dark Materials Ser.). (ENG.). 64p. (J). (gr. 5-12). 2007. per. 6.99 *(978-0-375-84369-3(8))* 2003. 12.99 *(978-0-375-82819-5(2))* Random Hse. Children's Bks. (Knopf Bks. for Young Readers).

—Le Miroir d'Ambre. (FRE.). pap. 18.95 *(978-2-07-054376-2(5))* Gallimard, Editions FRA. Dist: Distribooks, Inc.

—Once upon a Time in the North. 2008. (His Dark Materials Ser.). (ENG., Illus.). 112p. *(978-0-385-61432-0(2))* Fickling, David Bks.

—Once upon a Time in the North. Lawrence, John, illus. 2008. (His Dark Materials Ser.). (ENG.). 112p. (J). (gr. 5-12). 12.99 *(978-0-375-84510-9(0)*, Knopf Bks. for Young Readers) Random Hse. Children's Bks.

—Les Royaumes du Nord. (FRE.). pap. 19.95 *(978-2-07-054188-1(6))* Gallimard, Editions FRA. Dist: Distribooks, Inc.

—The Subtle Knife, Vol. 2. unabr. ed. 2004. (His Dark Materials Ser.: Bk. 2). 326p. (J). (gr. 7-18). pap. 58.00 incl. audio *(978-0-8072-0567-9(2)*, S YA 136 SP, Listening Library) Random Hse. Audio Publishing Group.

—The Subtle Knife, Bk. 2. 2003. (His Dark Materials Ser.: 2). (ENG.). 304p. (J). (gr. 5-12). mass mkt. 8.99 *(978-0-440-23814-0(5)*, Laurel Leaf) Random Hse. Children's Bks.

—La Tour des Anges. (FRE.). pap. 19.95 *(978-2-07-054189-8(4))* Gallimard, Editions FRA. Dist: Distribooks, Inc.

Purday, Paul. The Two Lands. 2006. 310p. (J). pap. *(978-1-905809-11-0(5))* Pneuma Springs Publishing.

Purdie, Kathryn. Burning Glass. (Burning Glass Ser.: 1). (YA). (gr. 9). 2017. 528p. pap. 9.99 *(978-0-06-241237-9(X))* 2016. (Illus.). 512p. 17.99 *(978-0-06-241236-2(1))* HarperCollins Pubs. (Tegen, Katherine Bks).

—Crystal Blade. 2017. (Burning Glass Ser.: 2). 368p. (YA). (gr. 9). 17.99 *(978-0-06-241239-3(6)*, Tegen, Katherine Bks) HarperCollins Pubs.

Purdy, Rebekah L. Summer Marked. 2015. (ENG.). 304p. (YA). 16.99 *(978-1-63375-009-8(4)*, 9781633750098) Entangled Publishing, LLC.

Pyatt, A. K. Old Woman's Garbage. Hill, Lynn, illus. 2003. *(978-0-9718431-3-4(9))* M.O.T.H.E.R. Publishing Co., Inc., The.

Pyle, Howard. The Garden Behind the Moon: A Real Story of the Moon-Angel. 2005. (Dover Children's Classics Ser.). (ENG., Illus.). 128p. (gr. 3-8). pap. 7.95 *(978-0-486-44073-6(7))* Dover Pubns., Inc.

—Twilight Land. 2006. (ENG.). 192p. pap. 19.99 *(978-1-4264-0425-2(5))* Creative Media Partners, LLC.

—Twilight Land. 2004. reprint ed. pap. 1.99 *(978-1-4192-9142-5(4))* Kessinger Publishing, LLC.

Pyrtle Second Graders & Writers' Circle. Poetry & a Fifth Grade Cinderell: An Anthology from Nebraska. 2009. 60p. pap. 8.95 *(978-0-595-53233-9(0))* iUniverse, Inc.

Quinn, Jordan. The Bard & the Beast. McPhillips, Robert, illus. 2015. (Kingdom of Wrenly Ser.: 9). (ENG.). 128p. (J). (gr. k-4). pap. 5.99 *(978-1-4814-4396-8(8)*, Little Simon) Little Simon.

Quinn, Kate Karyus. (Don't You) Forget about Me. 2014. (ENG.). 352p. (YA). (gr. 8). 17.99 *(978-0-06-213596-4(1)*, HarperTeen) HarperCollins Pubs.

—Down with the Shine. 2016. 368p. (YA). (gr. 8). 17.99 *(978-0-06-235604-8(6)*, HarperTeen) HarperCollins Pubs.

Quinones, Juan Carlos. La Pandilla Bajo el Arbol. Ortiz Montanez, Nivea, illus. 2004. (Purple Ser.). (SPA.). 44p. (J). (gr. 3-5). pap. 5.95 *(978-1-57581-439-1(0))* Santillana USA Publishing Co., Inc.

R. Dixon, Jackie. Gilroy the Fairy Collector. 2015. (ENG.). 369p. (J). (gr. 4-6). mass mkt. 11.95 *(978-1-78455-407-1(3)*, ef247b99-9022-425a-8ff9-42e8f9da0689) Austin, Stan AUS. Dist: Bookmasters Distribution.

Raasch, Sara. Frost Like Night. (Snow Like Ashes Ser.: 3). (YA). (gr. 9). 2017. 512p. pap. 9.99 ***(978-0-06-228699-4(4))*** 2016. (Illus.). 496p. 17.99 *(978-0-06-228698-7(6))* HarperCollins Pubs.

—Ice Like Fire. (YA). 2016. (Snow Like Ashes Ser.: 2). 512p. (gr. 9). pap. 9.99 *(978-0-06-228696-3(X))* 2015. (Snow Like Ashes Ser.: Bk. 2). (ENG., Illus.). 496p. (gr. 9-12). 17.99 *(978-0-06-228695-6(1))* 2015. (Illus.). 496p. pap. ***(978-0-06-242793-9(8))*** HarperCollins Pubs.

—Snow Like Ashes. (Snow Like Ashes Ser.: 1). (ENG., Illus.). (YA). (gr. 9). 2015. 448p. pap. 9.99 *(978-0-06-228693-2(5))* 2014. 432p. 17.99 *(978-0-06-228692-5(7))* HarperCollins Pubs.

Radford, Ruby Lorraine. Rose Colored Glasses. White, Iris Weddell, illus. 2011. 46p. 35.95 *(978-1-258-03586-0(3))* Literary Licensing, LLC.

A Ragged Magic. 2014. (ENG.). (YA). 24.95 *(978-1-941662-03-8(X))* Per Aspera Pr.

Raheb, Donna. The Adventures of Henrietta Ham. 2007. 32p. per. 14.95 *(978-1-4327-0142-0(8))* Outskirts Pr., Inc.

Rahnama, Seyed Javad. Minty Ear. 2011. (Illus.). 20p. pap. 14.11 *(978-1-4567-8188-0(X))* AuthorHouse.

Rai, Sarbjit. Elfins in San Francisco. 2009. 24p. pap. 11.49 *(978-1-4389-8014-0(0))* AuthorHouse.

Raiku, Makoto. Animal Land 7. 2013. (Animal Land Ser.). (ENG., Illus.). 200p. (gr. 8-12). pap. 10.99 *(978-1-61262-249-1(6))* Kodansha America, Inc.

—Animal Land 8. 2013. (Animal Land Ser.). (ENG., Illus.). 208p. (gr. 8-12). pap. 10.99 *(978-1-61262-250-7(X))* Kodansha America, Inc.

—Animal Land 9. 2014. (Animal Land Ser.). (ENG., Illus.). 208p. pap. 10.99 *(978-1-61262-546-1(0))* Kodansha America, Inc.

Raine, Arne. A Ray of Light: Key Keepers Book #3. 2008. 180p. pap. 13.95 *(978-0-595-53464-7(3))* iUniverse, Inc.

Raine, Bonnie. Islands. MacMenamin, John, illus. 2003. 48p. (J). per. *(978-1-931456-74-6(7))* Athena Pr.

Ralles, H. J. Keeper of the Empire, Vol. 3. 2004. (Illus.). 235p. (J). pap. 9.95 *(978-1-929976-25-6(9))* Top Pubns., Ltd.

Ralison, Janette. The Wrong Side of Magic. 2016. (ENG.). 336p. (J). 16.99 *(978-1-250-07428-7(2)*, 9781250074287) Feiwel & Friends.

Ramakar, Ram. Little Crow Feather. 2006. (ENG.). 48p. per. 16.95 *(978-1-4241-5134-9(1))* America Star Bks.

Ramdayal, Mia. Learning How to Fly. 2012. 28p. pap. 15.99 *(978-1-4691-5897-6(3))* Xlibris Corp.

Ramirez, Ken. You, Me, Naideen & a Bee. 2009. 278p. (YA). pap. 19.95 *(978-1-60619-208-5(6))* Twilight Times Bks.

Ramirez, Martha. The Fabulous Adventures of Fred the Frog. 2008. 48p. pap. 24.95 *(978-1-60474-799-7(4))* America Star Bks.

Ramsey, Jo. Jet Black. 2012. 220p. pap. 12.99 *(978-1-60820-630-8(0))* MLR Pr., LLC.

—Time of Darkness. 2013. 234p. pap. 12.99 *(978-1-60820-870-8(2))* MLR Pr., LLC.

Rand, Johnathan. American Chillers #15 Nebraska Nightcrawlers, Vol. 15. 2004. (American Chillers Ser.: 15). 208p. (J). pap. 5.99 *(978-1-893699-67-0(6))* AudioCraft Publishing, Inc.

—Freddie Fernortner #1 the Fantastic Flying Bicycle. 2005. 89p. (J). pap. 4.99 *(978-1-893699-78-6(1))* AudioCraft Publishing, Inc.

Randall, David. Clovermead: In the Shadow of the Bear. 2010. (ENG.). 304p. (YA). (gr. 7). pap. 14.99 *(978-1-4424-2740-2(X)*, McElderry, Margaret K. Bks.) McElderry, Margaret K. Bks.

Randolph, Grace. Muppet Peter Pan. Mebberson, Amy, illus. 2010. (Muppet Show Ser.). (ENG.). 112p. (J). pap. 9.99 *(978-1-60886-507-9(X))* Boom! Studios.

Randolph, Grace & Barks, Carl. Muppet Peter Pan. Mebberson, Amy, illus. 2010. (Muppet Show Ser.). (ENG.). 112p. (J). 24.99 *(978-1-60886-531-4(2))* Boom! Studios.

Random House Disney Staff. Jasmine & the Star of Persia (Disney Princess) Random House Disney Staff, illus. 2015. (Pictureback Ser.). (ENG., Illus.). 16p. (J). (gr. -1-2). pap. 4.99 *(978-0-7364-3048-7(2)*, RH/Disney) Random Hse. Children's Bks.

Random House Disney Staff & Peymani, Christine. Tangled. Disney Storybook Artists Staff & Orpinas, Jean-Paul, illus. 2010. (Read-Aloud Storybook Ser.). (ENG.). 72p. (J). (gr. -1-2). 9.99 *(978-0-7364-2718-0(X)*, RH/Disney) Random Hse. Children's Bks.

Random House Disney Staff & Smiley, Ben. Tangled. Disney Storybook Artists Staff & Ying, Victoria, illus. 2010. (Little Golden Book Ser.). (ENG.). 24p. (J). (gr. -1-2). 4.99 *(978-0-7364-2684-8(1)*, Golden/Disney) Random Hse. Children's Bks.

Random House Disney Staff & Yuu, Kristen. Teeny Genies. Random House Disney Staff et al, illus. 2017. (Official Guide Ser.). (ENG.). 64p. (J). (gr. -1-1). pap. 8.99 *(978-1-5247-1919-7(6)*, Random Hse. Bks. for Young Readers) Random Hse. Children's Bks.

Random House Editors. Disney Peter Pan. 2013. (Step into Reading Level 1 Ser.). lib. bdg. 13.55 *(978-0-606-26973-5(8)*, Turtleback) Turtleback Bks.

—Wishes & Surprises! (Shimmer & Shine) Random House Editors & Cho, Mu Young, illus. 2017. (Nifty Lift-And-Look

Ser.). (ENG.). 12p. (J). (-k). bds. 9.99 *(978-1-101-93983-3(4)*, Random Hse. Bks. for Young Readers) Random Hse. Children's Bks.

Randy. Charlie the Fox & Mr Cricket. 2009. 28p. pap. 15.99 *(978-1-4415-4254-0(X))* Xlibris Corp.

Rankin, H. L. Chaya & the Spider Gem. White, Siobhán, illus. 2011. 152p. (YA). pap. 9.95 *(978-2-930583-10-5(X))* White & MacLean Publishing BEL. Dist: Gardners Bks. Ltd.

Ransom, Candice. Key to the Griffon's Lair. Fiegenshuh, Emily, illus. 2005. (Knights of the Silver Dragon Ser.: Bk. 9). 182p. (J). *(978-1-4156-3032-7(1)*, Mirrorstone) Wizards of the Coast.

Ransome, Arthur. Old Peter's Russian Tales. 2007. (ENG.). 200p. pap. 19.99 *(978-1-4346-0606-8(6))*; 222p. pap. 22.99 *(978-1-4346-0681-5(3))* Creative Media Partners, LLC.

Rasheed, Winona. Sugar & Spice Fairy Tales for Girls. 2008. 69p. pap. 20.51 *(978-1-4357-4619-0(8))* Lulu Pr., Inc.

Rauscher, C D. The Fairies of the Clouds. 2008. 68p. pap. 25.49 *(978-1-4343-5153-1(X))* AuthorHouse.

Ravishankar, Anushka. Today Is My Day. Grobler, Piet, illus. 2005. (ENG.). 40p. (J). *(978-81-86211-76-2(4))* Tara Publishing.

Rawson, Christopher. Gnomes & Goblins. Cartwright, Stephen, illus. 2004. (Young Reading Series One Ser.). 48p. (J). (gr. 2-18). pap. 5.95 *(978-0-7945-0407-6(8)*, Usborne) EDC Publishing.

Ray, Belinda. Unicorn. 2003. 131p. (J). *(978-0-439-56012-2(8))* Scholastic, Inc.

Ray, Christie Jones & Ray, Christie Jones. Eliza Celebrates a Royal Wedding. 2012. (Illus.). 48p. pap. 15.00 *(978-0-9853223-6-6(5))* Rose Water Cottage Pr.

—Eliza Has a Cousin. 2012. (Illus.). 32p. pap. 15.00 *(978-0-9853223-5-9(7))* Rose Water Cottage Pr.

—Fox Family of Franklin. 2012. (Illus.). 16p. pap. 10.00 *(978-0-9853223-3-5(0))* Rose Water Cottage Pr.

—Pick-A-Pick-a-Pumpkin. 2012. (Illus.). 36p. pap. 12.00 *(978-0-9853223-4-2(9))* Rose Water Cottage Pr.

Rayburn, Tricia. Ruby's Slippers. 2010. (ENG.). 352p. (J). (gr. 4-8). pap. 7.99 *(978-1-4169-8701-7(0)*, Aladdin) Simon & Schuster Children's Publishing.

Rayment, Carolynn. Buster Batey & Mops. 2009. (Illus.). 16p. pap. 8.49 *(978-1-4490-4163-2(9))* AuthorHouse.

Rea, Monique. Toulouse the Moose & the Mystery Guests. 2012. 34p. pap. 13.99 *(978-0-9788926-4-7(X))* Trails of Discovery.

Reader's Digest Staff & Disney Storybook Artists Staff. Rapunzel's Dream Walmart Edition Storybook with Musical Hairbrush. 2010. (Disney Tangled Ser.). (ENG., Illus.). 32p. (J). bds. 19.99 *(978-0-7944-2048-2(6))* Reader's Digest Assn., Inc., The.

Reardon, A. C. Galish: The adventure of Isabelle & Eva. 2011. 168p. pap. 14.69 *(978-1-4567-7818-7(8))* AuthorHouse.

The Rebel Princess. 2014. pap. 12.99 *(978-1-4621-1430-6(X))* Cedar Fort, Inc./CFI Distribution.

Reber, Kelseyleigh. If I Fall: The Circle & Cross: Book One. 2013. (ENG.). 238p. (J). pap. 14.99 *(978-0-9889351-3-6(9))* Aperture Pr., LLC.

Red Fox Picture Books Staff & Transworld Publishing Staff. Better Play Times. 2006. (ENG., Illus.). 24p. (J). (gr. k-k). pap. 7.95 *(978-1-86230-164-1(6)*, Red Fox) Random House Children's Books GBR. Dist: Independent Pubs. Group.

Redinger, Robert. The Sylvan Horn: Book One of the Sylvan Chord. 2009. 220p. 25.95 *(978-0-595-50536-4(8))*; pap. 15.95 *(978-0-595-48489-8(1))* iUniverse, Inc.

Redwine, C. J. Defiance. (Defiance Trilogy Ser.: 1). (ENG.). (YA). (gr. 8). 2013. 432p. pap. 9.99 *(978-0-06-211717-5(3))* 2012. 416p. 17.99 *(978-0-06-211718-2(1))* HarperCollins Pubs.

—Deliverance. 2014. (Defiance Trilogy Ser.: 3). (ENG.). 480p. (YA). (gr. 8). 17.99 *(978-0-06-211723-6(8))* HarperCollins Pubs.

—The Shadow Queen. 2016. (YA). (gr. 8). (Ravenspire Ser.: 1). 416p. pap. 9.99 *(978-0-06-236025-0(6))*; (ENG., Illus.). 400p. 17.99 *(978-0-06-236024-3(8))* HarperCollins Pubs.

—The Shadow Queen. 2016. (Ravenspire Ser.: 1). (YA). lib. bdg. 20.85 *(978-0-606-39615-8(2))* Turtleback Bks.

—The Wish Granter. 2017. (Ravenspire Ser.: 2). (Illus.). 432p. (YA). (gr. 8). 17.99 *(978-0-06-236027-4(2))* HarperCollins Pubs.

Reece, Eva. The Boinking Bubble MacHine. Davis, Shelley L. A., illus. 2013. 24p. pap. 12.99 *(978-0-9886360-2-6(6))* Kids At Heart Publishing, LLC.

Reed, Bliss & Reed, Sinclair. This Summer I Plan to Rule the World. rev. ed. 2009. (ENG., Illus.). 100p. (J). (gr. k-7). pap. *(978-0-9822200-2-3(2))* Temmen, Edition, Horst Temmen.

Reed, T. K. Quasar & the Eye of the Serpent. 2009. 136p. 21.95 *(978-1-4401-2753-3(0))*; pap. 11.95 *(978-1-4401-2751-9(4))* iUniverse, Inc.

Reed, Wilfred. Andy & Mark & the Time Machine: Custer's Last Stand. 2003. 240p. (YA). pap. 15.95 *(978-0-595-26496-4(4)*, Writers Club Pr.) iUniverse, Inc.

Reeder, Marty. How to Become a Pirate Hunter. 2017. (ENG.). (J). pap. 14.99 ***(978-1-4621-1980-6(8)***, Sweetwater Bks.) Cedar Fort, Inc./CFI Distribution.

Reef Rescue (Book 4) 2017. (Secret Mermaid Ser.). (ENG.). (J). pap. 4.99 ***(978-0-7945-3686-2(7)***, Usborne) EDC Publishing.

Reeve, Philip. No Such Thing As Dragons. 2010. (ENG.). 192p. (J). (gr. 3-7). 16.99 *(978-0-545-22224-2(9)*, Scholastic Pr.) Scholastic, Inc.

Regan, Dian. Cam's Quest: The Continuing Story of Princess Nevermore & the Wizard's Apprentice. 2007. (Junior Library Guild Selection Ser.). 334p. (J). (gr. 4-8). 17.95 *(978-1-58196-056-3(5)*, Darby Creek) Lerner Publishing Group.

—Princess Nevermore. rev. ed. 2007. (Junior Library Guild Selection Ser.). (ENG.). 256p. (J). (gr. 4-8). 17.95 *(978-1-58196-055-6(7)*, Darby Creek) Lerner Publishing Group.

Reger, Rob & Gruner, Jessica. Piece of Mind. Reger, Rob & Parker, Buzz, illus. 2013. (Emily the Strange Ser.: 4). (ENG.). 288p. (YA). (gr. 8). pap. 9.99 *(978-0-06-145240-6(8))* HarperCollins Pubs.

Regordosa, Adria. Dustrats. 2017. (ENG., Illus.). 32p. (J). (gr. -1-2). 16.99 *(978-1-57687-821-7(X)*, powerHouse Bks.) powerHouse Cultural Entertainment, Inc.

Reid, Alastair. Supposing. Gill, Bob, illus. 2010. (ENG.). 48p. (J). (gr. -1-3). 15.95 *(978-1-59017-369-5(4)*, NYR Children's Collection) New York Review of Bks., Inc., The.

Reid, F. J. The Midwinter Child. 2009. 224p. pap. *(978-1-84923-496-2(5))* YouWriteOn.

Reid, Isabelle. Serafina Moon. 2009. 48p. pap. *(978-1-84923-771-0(9))* YouWriteOn.

Reid, Julia. Could You Own a Dinosaur? 2008. 44p. pap. 24.95 *(978-1-60563-375-6(5))* America Star Bks.

Reiffel, J. A., et al. Once upon an Antigmule: (... or, the Day Roseanna's Dreams Came True) 2012. 44p. pap. 21.99 *(978-1-4772-9618-9(2))* AuthorHouse.

Reilly, Antoinette. Mr. Lobster & the Mermaid. 2011. 24p. pap. 14.93 *(978-1-4269-5683-6(5))* Trafford Publishing.

Reilly, Carmel & Young, Karen. Buzz Takes Over. 2008. (Rigby Focus Forward: Level I Ser.). (Illus.). 24p. (J). (gr. 4-7). pap. *(978-1-4190-3743-6(9)*, Rigby) Pearson Education Australia.

Reinhart, Matthew. Marvel's the Avengers - Age of Ultron: A Pop-Up Book. Reinhart, Matthew, illus. 2015. (ENG., Illus.). 10p. (J). (gr. 1-17). 14.99 *(978-0-316-34086-1(3))* Little, Brown Bks. for Young Readers.

Reintjes, Susan B. Through the Fairy Door. Sparling, Bren M., illus. 2012. 128p. (J). pap. 16.95 *(978-1-59715-085-9(1))* Chapel Hill Press, Inc.

Reisz, Kristopher. Unleashed. (ENG.). 352p. (YA). (gr. 9). 2010. pap. 9.99 *(978-1-4424-0637-7(2))* 2008. pap. 7.99 *(978-1-4169-4001-2(4))* Simon Pulse. (Simon Pulse).

Remey, Grace Anne. Lion's Pride: A Tail of Deployment. Remey, Grace Anne, illus. 2012. (ENG., Illus.). 38p. pap. 12.95 *(978-0-9855445-0-8(3))* Remey, Lisa.

Remole, Arnulf. The Island of Alphebia. 2007. 34p. 24.55 *(978-1-4303-2720-2(0))* Lulu Pr., Inc.

René, Richard. The Edge of Mysterion: Another Tale of Mysterion. 2011. (ENG.). 224p. (YA). pap. 14.95 *(978-1-936270-34-7(X))* Ancient Faith Publishing.

Renfroe, Vicki. Franklin. 2008. 63p. pap. 19.95 *(978-1-60563-391-6(7))* America Star Bks.

Renier, Aaron. The Unsinkable Walker Bean. Renier, Aaron, illus. 2010. (Unsinkable Walker Bean Ser.: 1). (ENG., Illus.). 208p. (J). (gr. 4-9). pap. 15.99 *(978-1-59643-453-0(8)*, 9781596434530, First Second Bks.) Roaring Brook Pr.

Renzetti, Rob & Hirsch, Alex. Gravity Falls Journal 3. Disney Storybook Art Team, illus. 2016. (ENG.). 288p. (J). (gr. 3-7). 19.99 *(978-1-4847-4669-1(4))* Disney Pr.

Rere The Storyteller. I Am a Wish. 2013. 36p. 25.99 *(978-1-4808-0090-8(2))* Archway Publishing.

Rewalt, Nancy E. Aerial Meets Farmer Fedamore. Cranford, Darren, illus. 2012. 64p. (J). 17.95 *(978-0-9821110-3-1(7))* Ronan Enterprises, Inc.

Reyes, Laurisa White. The Last Enchanter. 2013. (Celestine Chronicles Ser.: Bk. 2). (ENG.). 404p. (J). (gr. 2-7). 16.95 *(978-1-933718-93-4(5))* Tanglewood Pr.

—The Rock of Ivanore. (Celestine Chronicles Ser.). (ENG.). (J). (gr. 2-7). 2013. 349p. pap. 9.95 *(978-1-933718-92-7(7))* 2012. (Illus.). 356p. 16.95 *(978-1-933718-60-6(9))* Tanglewood Pr.

Reyes, Yazmin. Fairies vs. Wizards: The Last Battle, 1 vol. 2009. 48p. pap. 16.95 *(978-1-4489-9527-1(2))* America Star Bks.

Reynolds, A. J. The Chrysalid Conspiracy - the Sanddancer. 2013. 482p. pap. *(978-1-78148-136-3(9))* Grosvenor Hse. Publishing Ltd.

Reynolds, Jean. Gwen & the Talking Napkin. 2007. (Grandma Ser.: 4). (J). per. 7.99 *(978-1-59872-897-2(0))* Instant Pub.

Reynolds, Mariem. The World in Between. 2008. 87p. pap. 16.95 *(978-1-60672-144-5(5))* PublishAmerica, Inc.

RH Disney. Mulan Is Loyal/Merida Is Brave (Disney Princess) RH Disney, illus. 2017. (Step into Reading Ser.). (ENG., Illus.). 48p. (J). (gr. -1-1). lib. bdg. 12.99 ***(978-0-7364-9017-7(5)***, RH/Disney) Random Hse. Children's Bks.

RH Disney Staff. Amazing Ariel! (Disney Princess) RH Disney Staff, illus. 2013. (Pictureback(R) Ser.). (ENG., Illus.). 16p. (J). (gr. -1-2). 4.99 *(978-0-7364-2994-8(8)*, RH/Disney) Random Hse. Children's Bks.

—Never Girls - In a Blink, 2 bks. in 1. Christy, Jana, illus. 2015. (Never Girls Ser.). (ENG.). 256p. (J). (gr. 1-4). 9.99 *(978-0-7364-3432-4(1)*, RH/Disney) Random Hse. Children's Bks.

—Walt Disney's Alice in Wonderland. RH Disney Staff, illus. 2010. (Little Golden Book Ser.). (ENG., Illus.). 24p. (J). (gr. -1-2). 4.99 *(978-0-7364-2670-1(1)*, Golden/Disney) Random Hse. Children's Bks.

Rhodes, Morgan. The Darkest Magic. 2016. (Book of Spirits & Thieves Ser.: 2). (ENG.). 368p. (YA). (gr. 7). 18.99 *(978-1-59514-761-5(6)*, Razorbill) Penguin Young Readers Group.

—Falling Kingdoms. (Falling Kingdoms Ser.: 1). (ENG.). (YA). (gr. 7). 2014. 448p. pap. 10.99 *(978-1-59514-585-7(0))* 2012. (Illus.). 432p. 18.99 *(978-1-59514-584-0(2))* Penguin Young Readers Group. (Razorbill).

—Gathering Darkness. 2014. (Falling Kingdoms Ser.: 3). (ENG.). 430p. (YA). (gr. 7). 18.99 *(978-1-59514-705-9(5)*, Razorbill) Penguin Young Readers Group.

—Rebel Spring. (Falling Kingdoms Ser.: 2). (ENG.). (YA). (gr. 7). 2014. 432p. pap. 10.99 *(978-1-59514-592-5(3))* 2013. 416p. 18.99 *(978-1-59514-593-2(1))* Penguin Young Readers Group. (Razorbill).

Rhodes, Morgan & Loftin, Nikki. Frozen Tides. 2015. (Falling Kingdoms Ser.: 4). (ENG., Illus.). 432p. (YA). (gr. 7). 18.99 *(978-1-59514-707-3(1)*, Razorbill) Penguin Young Readers Group.

Rice, Morgan. Night of the Bold (Kings & Sorcerers — Book 6) 2016. (ENG., Illus.). 162p. (J). pap. 12.99 *(978-1-63291-497-2(2)*, Morgan Rice) Morgan Rice Bks.

—A Quest of Heroes. 2012. (Sorcerer's Ring Ser.: Bk. 1). (ENG.). 348p. (YA). 22.99 *(978-1-939416-21-6(3))*; pap. 10.99 *(978-1-939416-20-9(5))* Morgan Rice Bks.

—Queste der Helden (Band 1 Im Ring der Zauberei) 2015. (ENG & GEM., Illus.). 264p. (J). pap. 10.99 *(978-1-63291-306-7(2))* Morgan Rice Bks.

—A Rule of Queens (Book #13 in the Sorcerer's Ring) 2014. 238p. (YA). pap. 15.99 *(978-1-939416-92-6(2)*, Morgan Rice) Morgan Rice Bks.

—A Vow of Glory. 2013. (Sorcerer's Ring Ser.: Bk. 5). 274p. pap. 13.99 *(978-1-939416-28-5(0))* Morgan Rice Bks.

Rich, Jamie S. Spell Checkers Volume 3: Careless Whisper: Careless Whisper. 2013. (ENG., Illus.). 144p. (YA). pap. 11.99 *(978-1-62010-094-3(0)*, 9781620100943) Oni Pr., Inc.

Richards, Anna Matlack & Carroll, Lewis. A New Alice in the Old Wonderland. 2009. (Illus.). 178p. *(978-1-904808-35-0(2))* Evertype.

Richards, Claire. Mai's Garden: Mickamoo's Rescue. 2011. (Illus.). 56p. (gr. -1). pap. 12.51 *(978-1-4567-7559-9(6))* AuthorHouse.

Richards, Elizabeth. Black City. 2013. (Black City Novel Ser.: 1). (ENG., Illus.). 400p. (YA). (gr. 9). pap. 9.99 *(978-0-14-242722-4(5)*, Speak) Penguin Young Readers Group.

—Phoenix. 2nd ed. 2014. (Black City Novel Ser.: 2). (ENG.). 368p. (YA). (gr. 9). pap. 9.99 *(978-0-14-751137-9(2)*, Speak) Penguin Young Readers Group.

Richards, Jasmine. The Book of Wonders. 2012. (ENG.). 416p. (J). (gr. 3-7). 16.99 *(978-0-06-201007-0(7))* HarperCollins Pubs.

—Keeper of Myths. 2017. (Secrets of Valhalla Ser.: 2). 256p. (J). (gr. 3-7). 16.99 *(978-0-06-201011-7(5))* HarperCollins Pubs.

—Secrets of Valhalla. 2016. (Secrets of Valhalla Ser.: 1). 320p. (J). (gr. 3-7). 16.99 *(978-0-06-201009-4(3))* HarperCollins Pubs.

Richardson, J. J. It's about Time. 2008. (ENG.). 92p. pap. 12.99 *(978-1-4196-5707-8(0))* CreateSpace Independent Publishing Platform.

Richardson, Jeffery. Wormwood Adventures New Friends. 2010. 49p. pap. 8.50 *(978-1-4452-5758-7(0))* Lulu Pr., Inc.

Richardson, Sharde. Watched. 2011. (ENG.). 290p. (YA). pap. 12.99 *(978-0-9831498-0-4(1))* Jolt.

Richardville, Carol. Beau Bandit's Tale. Davis, Kaley, illus. 2004. (J). per. 16.99 *(978-1-932503-23-4(4))* Insight Publishing Group.

Richler, Mordecai. Jacob Two-Two & the Dinosaur. Eyolfson, Norman, illus. 2004. (Jacob Two-Two Ser.). (ENG.). 96p. (J). (gr. 3-7). pap. 6.95 *(978-0-88776-712-8(5))* Tundra Bks. CAN. Dist: Random Hse., Inc.

—Jacob Two-Two & the Dinosaur. Petricic, Dusan, illus. 2009. (Jacob Two-Two Ser.). (ENG.). 104p. (J). (gr. 4-7). 10.95 *(978-0-88776-926-9(8))* Tundra Bks. CAN. Dist: Random Hse., Inc.

—Jacob Two-Two Meets the Hooded Fang. Petricic, Dusan, illus. 2009. (Jacob Two-Two Ser.). (ENG.). 96p. (J). (gr. 4-7). 10.95 *(978-0-88776-925-2(X)*, Tundra Bks.) Tundra Bks. CAN. Dist: Penguin Random Hse. LLC.

Ricker, Jeffrey. The Unwanted. 2014. (ENG.). 264p. (J). (gr. 9-12). pap. 11.95 *(978-1-62639-048-5(7))* Bold Strokes Bks.

Riddell, Chris. The Emperor of Absurdia. 3rd ed. 2007. (ENG., Illus.). 32p. (J). (gr. -1-k). pap. 11.99 *(978-1-4050-9028-5(6))* Pan Macmillan GBR. Dist: Independent Pubs. Group.

—Goth Girl & the Fete Worse Than Death. unabr. ed. 2016. (Goth Girl Ser.: 2). (ENG., Illus.). 224p. (J). (gr. 2-6). 14.99 *(978-0-230-75982-4(3))* Pan Macmillan GBR. Dist: Independent Pubs. Group.

Riddell, Chris & Stewart, Paul. The Curse of the Gloamglozer. 2009. (Edge Chronicles Ser.). (ENG.). 384p. (J). (gr. 3-7). 8.99 *(978-0-440-42099-6(7)*, Yearling) Random Hse. Children's Bks.

—Edge Chronicles: Freeglader. 2010. (Edge Chronicles Ser.). (ENG.). 416p. (J). (gr. 3-7). 8.99 *(978-0-385-73611-4(8)*, Yearling) Random Hse. Children's Bks.

Rider, Jason. Dawn of Hope. 2008. 180p. pap. 11.95 *(978-1-935118-10-7(2))* Bellissima Publishing, LLC.

Ridley, R. W. Dèlon City: Book Two of the Oz Chronicles. 2006. (YA). per. 9.99 *(978-0-9792067-0-2(7))* Middlebury Hse. Publishing.

Riebe, C. V. Jonathan Jameson in the Crossroad Chronicles: Adventures in Heaven, Vol. 1. 2008. 64p. pap. 10.95 *(978-1-4327-3709-2(0))* Outskirts Pr., Inc.

Rifkin, L. Life Four. 2008. (Nine Lives of Romeo Crumb Ser.). (Illus.). 201p. (gr. 6-8). per. 8.95 *(978-0-9743221-9-3(9))* Sunrise Publishing Co.

—The Nine Lives of Romeo Crumb: Life Seven. 2011. 218p. (J). pap. 8.95 *(978-0-9835480-0-3(5))* Sunrise Publishing Co.

Rifkin, L. (Lauren). The Nine Lives of Romeo Crumb: Life Five. Hartman, Kurt, illus. 2009. 169p. (YA). pap. 8.95 *(978-0-9743221-7-9(2))* Sunrise Publishing Co.

Rifkin, Lauren I. The Nine Lives of Romeo Crumb: Life Eight. 2013. (ENG.). 224p. (YA). pap. 8.95 *(978-0-9886853-8-3(8))* Sunrise Publishing Co.

Rigby Education Staff. Rumpelstiltskin: Jumbled Tumble. (gr. k-2). 26.00 *(978-0-7635-2421-0(2))* Rigby Education.

Riggs, Mary L. Dragon Forge the Ballad of Beighn. 2009. 110p. pap. 9.95 *(978-1-60860-499-3(3)*, Strategic Bk. Publishing) Strategic Book Publishing & Rights Agency (SBPRA).

Riggs, Ransom. Hollow City. 2015. (Miss Peregrine's Peculiar Children Ser.: Bk. 2). (ENG., Illus.). 416p. (YA). pap. 10.99 *(978-1-59474-735-9(0))* Quirk Bks.

—Hollow City. Riggs, Ransom, illus. 2014. (ENG., Illus.). 352p. (YA). (gr. 9). 18.99 *(978-1-59474-612-3(5))* Quirk Bks.

—Hollow City. Riggs, Ransom, illus. 2015. (Miss Peregrine's Peculiar Children Ser.: 2). (Illus.). lib. bdg. 22.10 *(978-0-606-36394-5(7))* Turtleback Bks.

—Library of Souls. 2015. (Miss Peregrine's Peculiar Children Ser.: Bk. 3). (ENG., Illus.). 464p. (YA). (gr. 9). 18.99 *(978-1-59474-758-8(X))* Quirk Bks.

—Library of Souls. 2017. (Miss Peregrine's Peculiar Children Ser.: 3). (ENG.). (YA). (gr. 9). lib. bdg. 23.30 ***(978-0-606-39808-4(2))*** Turtleback Bks.

—Miss Peregrine, Set. 2015. (Miss Peregrine's Peculiar Children Ser.). (ENG., Illus.). 1152p. (YA). (gr. 9). 56.97 *(978-1-59474-838-7(1))* Quirk Bks.

—Miss Peregrine's Home for Peculiar Children. (ENG., Illus.). (YA). (gr. 9). 2013. 368p. pap. 10.99 *(978-1-59474-603-1(6))* 2011. (Miss Peregrine's Peculiar Children Ser.: 1). 352p. 18.99 *(978-1-59474-476-1(9))* 2016. (Miss Peregrine's Peculiar Children Ser.: 1). 392p. pap. 11.99 *(978-1-59474-902-5(7))* Quirk Bks.

—Miss Peregrine's Home for Peculiar Children. l.t. ed. 2012. (ENG.). 484p. (J). (gr. 8-12). 23.99 *(978-1-4104-5023-4(6))* Thorndike Pr.

—Miss Peregrine's Home for Peculiar Children. 2013. (Miss Peregrine's Peculiar Children Ser.: 1). lib. bdg. 22.10 *(978-0-606-32081-8(4)*, Turtleback) Turtleback Bks.

Right, Emma. Keeper of Reign. 2013. 340p. pap. 17.99 *(978-1-939337-69-6(0))* Telemachus Pr., LLC.

Riley, Analynn. Legend of the Mountains & the Valleys: The Nine Gifts of Theodosia, the Final Question, Kenelm's Quest, Yedda Sings. 2013. 152p. (J). (gr. 4-6). 30.95 *(978-1-4497-8372-3(4))*; pap. 13.95 *(978-1-4497-8371-6(6))* Author Solutions, Inc. (WestBow Pr.).

Riley, James. The Half upon a Time Trilogy: Half upon a Time; Twice upon a Time; Once upon the End. 2014. (Half upon a Time Ser.). (ENG., Illus.). 1168p. (J). (gr. 3-7). pap. 23.99 *(978-1-4424-9966-9(4)*, Aladdin) Simon & Schuster Children's Publishing.

—Once upon the End. 2013. (Half upon a Time Ser.: 3). (ENG.). 384p. (J). (gr. 3-7). 17.99 *(978-1-4424-7422-2(X)*, Simon & Schuster/Paula Wiseman Bks.) Simon & Schuster/Paula Wiseman Bks.

Rinaldo, Jessica. Key to the Gate Book 1. 2005. 324p. (YA). pap. 14.98 *(978-1-4116-5262-0(2))* Lulu Pr., Inc.

Rinehart, J. D. Crown of Three. 2016. (Crown of Three Ser.: 1). (ENG., Illus.). 432p. (J). (gr. 4-8). pap. 7.99 *(978-1-4814-2444-8(0)*, Aladdin) Simon & Schuster Children's Publishing.

—A Kingdom Rises. 2017. (Crown of Three Ser.: 3). (ENG., Illus.). 432p. (J). (gr. 4-8). 18.99 ***(978-1-4814-2449-3(1)***, Aladdin) Simon & Schuster Children's Publishing.

—The Lost Realm. (Crown of Three Ser.: 2). (ENG., Illus.). (J). (gr. 4-8). 2017. 512p. pap. 8.99 ***(978-1-4814-2447-9(5))*** 2016. 496p. 17.99 *(978-1-4814-2446-2(7))* Simon & Schuster Children's Publishing. (Aladdin).

Rininger, Alyce. Ka-Boom. Lucas, Diane, illus. 2012. 46p. pap. 13.95 *(978-1-61244-069-9(X))* Halo Publishing International.

Riordan, Betty J. The Imaginary Journeys of Bj & Dobbin. 2008. 108p. pap. 11.99 *(978-1-60647-432-7(4))* Salem Author Services.

Riordan, Rick. The Battle of the Labyrinth, Bk. 4. (Percy Jackson & the Olympians Ser.). (ENG.). (J). (gr. 5-9). 2009. 400p. pap. 7.99 *(978-1-4231-0149-9(9))* 2008. 384p. 17.99 *(978-1-4231-0146-8(4))* Hyperion Pr.

—The Battle of the Labyrinth. l.t. ed. 2008. (Percy Jackson & the Olympians Ser.: Bk. 4). (ENG.). 462p. (J). (gr. 4-7). 23.95 *(978-1-4104-1018-4(8))* Thorndike Pr.

—The Dark Prophecy. 2017. (Trials of Apollo Ser.: bk.2). (ENG.). 432p. (J). (gr. 5-9). 19.99 *(978-1-4847-4642-4(2))* Hyperion Bks. for Children.

—The Demigod Diaries. 2012. (ENG.). 256p. (YA). (gr. 5-9). 12.99 *(978-1-4231-6300-8(1))* Hyperion Pr.

—The Demigod Files. James, Steve, illus. 2009. (ENG.). 160p. (J). (gr. 5-6). 12.99 *(978-1-4231-2166-4(X))* Hyperion Pr.

—For Magnus Chase: Hotel Valhalla Guide to the Norse Worlds: Your Introduction to Deities, Mythical Beings, & Fantastic Creatures. 2016. (Magnus Chase & the Gods of Asgard Ser.). (ENG.). 176p. (J). (gr. 3-7). 9.99 *(978-1-4847-8554-6(1))* Hyperion Bks. for Children.

—From Percy Jackson: Camp Half-Blood Confidential: Your Real Guide to the Demigod Training Camp. 2017. (Trials of Apollo Ser.). (ENG.). 192p. (J). (gr. 3-7). 9.99 *(978-1-4847-8555-3(X))* Hyperion Bks. for Children.

—The Hammer of Thor. 2016. (Magnus Chase & the Gods of Asgard Ser.: Bk. 2). (ENG.). 480p. (J). (gr. 5-9). 19.99 *(978-1-4231-6092-2(4))* Hyperion Bks. for Children.

—The Heroes of Olympus, Book Five the Blood of Olympus. 2016. (Heroes of Olympus Ser.). (ENG.). 544p. (J). (gr. 5-9). pap. 9.99 *(978-1-4231-4678-0(6))* Hyperion Bks. for Children.

—The Hidden Oracle. l.t. ed. 2016. (Trials of Apollo Ser.: 1). (ENG.). 488p. (J). 25.99 *(978-1-4104-8945-6(0))* Cengage Gale.

—The Hidden Oracle. 2016. (Trials of Apollo Ser.: Bk. 1). (ENG.). 384p. (J). (gr. 5-9). 19.99 *(978-1-4847-3274-8(X))* Hyperion Bks. for Children.

—The Hidden Oracle. 2017. (Trials of Apollo Ser.: 1). (J). lib. bdg. 20.85 ***(978-0-606-40605-5(0))*** Turtleback Bks.

—The House of Hades. 2013. (Heroes of Olympus Ser.). (ENG.). 608p. (J). (gr. 5-17). 19.99 *(978-1-4231-4672-8(7))* Hyperion Pr.

—The House of Hades. 2015. (Heroes of Olympus Ser.: 4). (J). lib. bdg. 20.85 *(978-0-606-36895-7(7))* Turtleback Bks.

—The Last Olympian, Bk. 5. (Percy Jackson & the Olympians Ser.). (ENG.). (J). (gr. 5-9). 2011. 432p. pap. 7.99 *(978-1-4231-0150-5(2))* 5th ed. 2009. 400p. 17.99 *(978-1-4231-0147-5(2))* Hyperion Pr.

—The Lightning Thief. (Percy Jackson & the Olympians Ser.: Bk. 1). (ENG.). (J). (gr. 5-9). 2005. 384p. 17.99 *(978-0-7868-5629-9(7))*Bk. 1. 2006. 416p. reprint ed. per. 7.99 *(978-0-7868-3865-3(5))* Disney Publishing Worldwide.

—The Lightning Thief. 2008. (J). 54.99 *(978-0-7393-7113-8(4))* Findaway World, LLC.

—The Lightning Thief. 2006. (Percy Jackson & the Olympians Ser.: Bk. 1). 377p. (J). (gr. 5-12). 15.65 *(978-0-7569-6603-4(5))* Perfection Learning Corp.

—The Lightning Thief. rev. l.t. ed. 2006. (Percy Jackson & the Olympians Ser.: 1). (ENG.). 483p. (gr. 5-18). 22.95 *(978-0-7862-8225-8(8))* Thorndike Pr.

—The Lightning Thief. 2006. (Percy Jackson & the Olympians Ser.: 1). (J). lib. bdg. 18.40 *(978-1-4177-3247-0(4)*, Turtleback) Turtleback Bks.

—The Lost Hero. 2011. (Heroes of Olympus Ser.: Bk. 1). (ENG.). 576p. pap. 9.99 *(978-1-4231-5537-9(8))* Disney Pr.

—The Lost Hero. 2010. (Heroes of Olympus Ser.). (ENG.). 576p. (YA). (gr. 5-9). pap. 12.00 *(978-1-4231-4265-2(9))* Hyperion Bks. for Children.

—The Lost Hero. (Heroes of Olympus Ser.). (ENG.). (J). (gr. 5-9). 2012. 592p. pap. 9.99 *(978-1-4231-1346-1(2))* 2010. 576p. 19.99 *(978-1-4231-1339-3(X))* Hyperion Pr.

—The Lost Hero. l.t. ed. 2010. (Heroes of Olympus Ser.: Bk. 1). (ENG.). 708p. 23.99 *(978-1-4104-3359-6(5))* Thorndike Pr.

—The Lost Hero. 2012. (Heroes of Olympus Ser.: 1). (J). lib. bdg. 20.85 *(978-0-606-23615-7(5)*, Turtleback) Turtleback Bks.

—The Mark of Athena. 2012. (Heroes of Olympus Ser.). (ENG.). 608p. (J). (gr. 5-17). 19.99 *(978-1-4231-4060-3(5))* Hyperion Pr.

E
F
G

—The Mark of Athena. l.t. ed. 2012. (Heroes of Olympus Ser.: Bk. 3). (ENG.). 698p. 23.99 *(978-1-4104-5205-4(0))* Thorndike Pr.

—Percy Jackson & the Olympians, Set. 2010. (ENG.). 1744p. (J). (gr. 5-17). 89.99 *(978-1-4231-4189-1(X))* Hyperion Pr.

—Percy Jackson & the Olympians. l.t. ed. 2009. (Percy Jackson & the Olympians Ser.). (ENG.). 485p. (YA). 23.95 *(978-1-4104-1678-0(X))* Thorndike Pr.

—Percy Jackson & the Olympians. 2011. (Percy Jackson & the Olympians Ser.: 5). (J). lib. bdg. 18.40 *(978-0-606-10567-5(0)*, Turtleback) Turtleback Bks.

—Percy Jackson & the Olympians the Percy Jackson Coloring Book. Robinson, Keith, illus. 2017. (Percy Jackson & the Olympians Ser.). (ENG.). 96p. (J). (gr. 3-7). pap. 15.99 ***(978-1-4847-8779-3(X))*** Hyperion Bks. for Children.

—The Red Pyramid. 2011. (ENG.). 544p. (J). (gr. 5-17). pap. 9.99 *(978-1-4231-1345-4(4))* Disney Publishing Worldwide.

—The Red Pyramid. 2010. (Kane Chronicles Ser.). (ENG.). 528p. (J). (gr. 5-9). 17.99 *(978-1-4231-1338-6(1))* Hyperion Pr.

—The Red Pyramid, Bk. 1. Collar, Orpheus, illus. 2012. (Kane Chronicles Ser.). (ENG.). 192p. (J). (gr. 5-9). pap. 12.99 *(978-1-4231-5069-5(4))* Hyperion Pr.

—The Red Pyramid. 2009. (Kane Chronicles: Bk. 1). 11.04 *(978-0-7848-3733-7(3)*, Everbind) Marco Bk. Co.

—The Red Pyramid. 2012. 20.00 *(978-1-61383-660-6(0))* Perfection Learning Corp.

—The Red Pyramid. 2010. pap. *(978-0-545-40016-9(3))* Scholastic, Inc.

—The Red Pyramid. l.t. ed. 2010. (Kane Chronicles: Bk. 1). (ENG.). 671p. 23.95 *(978-1-4104-2536-2(3))* Thorndike Pr.

—The Red Pyramid. (Kane Chronicles Graphic Novels Ser.: 1). (J). 2012. lib. bdg. 24.50 *(978-0-606-37510-8(4))* 2011. lib. bdg. 20.85 *(978-0-606-39216-7(5))* Turtleback Bks.

—The Sea of Monsters, Bk. 2. 2nd rev. ed. 2006. (Percy Jackson & the Olympians Ser.: Bk. 2). (ENG.). 288p. (J). (gr. 5-9). 17.99 *(978-0-7868-5686-2(6))* Disney Publishing Worldwide.

—The Sea of Monsters. l.t. ed. 2006. (Percy Jackson & the Olympians Ser.: Bk. 2). 361p. (J). (gr. 5-9). 22.95 *(978-0-7862-9074-1(9))* Thorndike Pr.

—The Sea of Monsters. 2007. (Percy Jackson & the Olympians Ser.: 2). 279p. (J). (gr. 4-7). lib. bdg. 18.40 *(978-1-4177-7612-2(9)*, Turtleback) Turtleback Bks.

—The Serpent's Shadow, Bk. 3. 2012. (Kane Chronicles Ser.). (ENG.). 416p. (YA). (gr. 5-17). 19.99 *(978-1-4231-4057-3(5))* Hyperion Pr.

—The Serpent's Shadow. 2012. 416p. *(978-0-14-133568-1(8)*, Puffin) Penguin Bks., Ltd.

—The Serpent's Shadow. l.t. ed. 2012. (Kane Chronicles: Bk. 3). (ENG.). 521p. (gr. 5-12). 23.99 *(978-1-4104-4789-0(8))* Thorndike Pr.

—The Son of Neptune. (Heroes of Olympus Ser.: Bk. 2). (ENG.). (J). (gr. 5-9). 2013. 560p. pap. 9.99 *(978-1-4231-4199-0(7))* 2011. (Illus.). 544p. 19.99 *(978-1-4231-4059-7(1))* Hyperion Pr.

—The Son of Neptune. l.t. ed. 2011. (Heroes of Olympus Ser.: Bk. 2). (ENG.). 616p. 23.99 *(978-1-4104-4122-5(9))* Thorndike Pr.

—The Son of Neptune. 2013. (Heroes of Olympus Ser.: 2). (J). lib. bdg. 20.85 *(978-0-606-31759-7(7)*, Turtleback) Turtleback Bks.

—The Son of Neptune: The Graphic Novel. 2017. (Heroes of Olympus Ser.). (ENG.). 192p. (J). (gr. 5-9). 21.99 *(978-1-4847-1621-2(3))* Disney Pr.

—The Sword of Summer. l.t. ed. 2015. (Magnus Chase & the Gods of Asgard Ser.: Bk. 1). (ENG.). 698p. 24.99 *(978-1-4104-8316-4(9))* Cengage Gale.

—The Sword of Summer. (Magnus Chase & the Gods of Asgard Ser.: Bk. 1). (ENG.). (J). 2017. 544p. (gr. 3-7). pap. 9.99 *(978-1-4231-6337-4(0))* 2015. 512p. (gr. 5-9). 19.99 *(978-1-4231-6091-5(6))* Hyperion Bks. for Children.

—The Sword of Summer. Rocco, John, illus. ltd. ed. 2015. (Magnus Chase & the Gods of Asgard Ser.: Bk. 1). (ENG.). 512p. (J). (gr. 5-9). 100.00 *(978-1-4847-1871-1(2))* Hyperion Bks. for Children.

—The Sword of Summer. 2017. (Magnus Chase & the Gods of Asgard Ser.: 1). (J). lib. bdg. 20.85 ***(978-0-606-39972-2(0))*** Turtleback Bks.

—The Throne of Fire. 2011. (Kane Chronicles: Bk. 2). 452p. (J). pap. *(978-1-4231-5059-6(7))* Disney Pr.

—The Throne of Fire. 2nd ed. 2012. (ENG.). 464p. (YA). (gr. 5-9). pap. 9.99 *(978-1-4231-6703-7(1))* Hyperion Bks. for Children.

—The Throne of Fire, Bk. 2. (ENG.). 464p. (gr. 5-17). 2012. (YA). pap. 9.99 *(978-1-4231-4201-0(2))* 2011. (J). 18.99 *(978-1-4231-4056-6(7))* Hyperion Pr.

—The Throne of Fire. 2011. (Kane Chronicles: Bk. 2). (ENG., Illus.). 451p. 28.25 *(978-0-85757-231-8(8))*; 2nd ed. 554p. pap. *(978-0-14-133566-7(1))* Penguin Publishing Group. (Puffin).

—The Throne of Fire. l.t. ed. 2011. (Kane Chronicles: Bk. 2). (ENG.). 591p. 23.99 *(978-1-4104-3607-8(1))* Thorndike Pr.

—The Throne of Fire. (Kane Chronicles Graphic Novels Ser.: 2). 2015. lib. bdg. 24.50 *(978-0-606-37509-2(0))* 2012. (YA). lib. bdg. 20.85 *(978-0-606-39217-4(3))* Turtleback Bks.

—The Titan's Curse, Bk. 3. rev. ed. 2007. (Percy Jackson & the Olympians Ser.: Bk. 3). (ENG.). 320p. (J). (gr. 5-9). 17.99 *(978-1-4231-0145-1(6))* Disney Publishing Worldwide.

—The Titan's Curse. 2008. (Percy Jackson & the Olympians Ser.: No. 3). 312p. (J). lib. bdg. 20.00 *(978-1-4242-4710-3(1))* Fitzgerald Bks.

—The Titan's Curse, Bk. 3. 2008. (Percy Jackson & the Olympians Ser.). (ENG.). 352p. (J). (gr. 5-9). pap. 7.99 *(978-1-4231-0148-2(0))* Hyperion Pr.

—The Titan's Curse. 2011. 9.68 *(978-0-7848-3441-1(5)*, Everbind) Marco Bk. Co.

—The Titan's Curse. l.t. rev. ed. 2007. (Percy Jackson & the Olympians Ser.: 3). (ENG.). 402p. (gr. 5-9). 23.95 *(978-0-7862-9701-6(8))* Thorndike Pr.

Riordan, Rick & Venditti, Robert. Heroes of Olympus, Book One the Lost Hero: the Graphic Novel. Powell, Nathan, illus. 2014. (Heroes of Olympus Ser.). (ENG.). 192p. (J). (gr. 5-9). pap. 12.99 *(978-1-4231-6325-1(7))* Hyperion Bks. for Children.

—The Lightning Thief. Futaki, Attila & Villarrubia, Jose, illus. 2010. (Percy Jackson & the Olympians Ser.). (ENG.). 128p. (J). (gr. 5-9). 21.99 *(978-1-4231-1696-7(8))*; pap. 12.99 *(978-1-4231-1710-0(7))* Hyperion Pr.

Rios, Yuri M. The Kingdom of Ice. Rios, Margarita, tr. 2012. 26p. pap. 9.99 *(978-1-61897-223-1(5)*, Strategic Bk. Publishing) Strategic Book Publishing & Rights Agency (SBPRA).

Rioux, Jo. The Golden Twine. Rioux, Jo, illus. 2012. (Cat's Cradle Ser.: 1). (ENG., Illus.). 112p. (J). (gr. 4-7). 9.95 *(978-1-55453-637-5(5))* Kids Can Pr., Ltd. CAN. Dist: Hachette Bk. Group.

Riseman, Daniel. They Return. 2012. 48p. pap. 21.99 *(978-1-4771-3649-2(5))* Xlibris Corp.

Risso, Eduardo. Mysteries of the Red Moon, Vol. 3. 2006. (SPA.). 48p. pap. 16.95 *(978-1-59497-163-1(3))* Public Square Bks.

Risso, Eduardo & Trillo, Carlos. Los Misterios de la Luna Roja Vol. 2: El Ataque del Circo. 2006. (SPA., Illus.). 72p. (J). (gr. 1). per. 16.95 *(978-1-59497-162-4(5))* Public Square Bks.

Riva, Jim. Marvin Mallard & the Magic Medallion. Steinmark, Sharyl, illus. 2004. 64p. (YA). pap. 14.95 *(978-1-891262-03-6(3))* Soaring Sparrow Pr.

Rivers, Phoebe. A Perfect Storm. 2013. (Saranormal Ser.: 10). (ENG., Illus.). 160p. (J). (gr. 3-7). 15.99 *(978-1-4424-8959-2(6))*; pap. 5.99 *(978-1-4424-8958-5(8))* Simon Spotlight. (Simon Spotlight).

Rjk. Little Hero's Frown. Stubbing, Lori, illus. 2012. 36p. pap. 24.95 *(978-1-4626-7786-3(X))* America Star Bks.

Robert, Na'ima Bint, tr. The Swirling Hijaab: Percja Valezuese. Mistry, Nilesh, illus. 2004. (ALB & ENG.). 24p. (J). pap. *(978-1-85269-105-9(0))* Mantra Lingua.

Roberts, Constance. Sigil in Shadow. 2016. (ENG.). (J). pap. 15.99 *(978-1-4621-1873-1(9)*, Sweetwater Bks.) Cedar Fort, Inc./CFI Distribution.

Roberts, Rachel. All That Glitters. (gr. 3-6). 2008. (Avalon: Web of Magic Ser.: 2). (ENG., Illus.). 216p. (YA). pap. 6.95 *(978-1-933164-67-0(0)*, 9781933164670) 2007. (Avalon Ser.: Bk. 2). 175p. (J). 9.99 *(978-1-933164-65-6(4))* Seven Seas Entertainment, LLC.

—Omnibus Collection No. 1, Bk. 1-3. 2012. (Avalon: Web of Magic Ser.: 1). (ENG., Illus.). 640p. (YA). (gr. 3-6). pap. 14.95 *(978-1-935934-29-5(5)*, 9781935934295) Seven Seas Entertainment, LLC.

—The Warlock Diaries Omnibus. Shiei, illus. 2010. (Avalon: Web of Magic Ser.). (ENG.). 304p. (J). (gr. 3-6). pap. 11.99 *(978-1-934876-88-6(7)*, 9781934876886) Seven Seas Entertainment, LLC.

Roberts, Roxanne. Angel Wings, Faery Dust & Other Magical Things: A Story about Guardian Angels. 2012. 16p. pap. 10.00 *(978-1-61897-252-1(9)*, Eloquent Bks.) Strategic Book Publishing & Rights Agency (SBPRA).

Roberts, Tina. Dream Watchman: Quest for the Missing Talisman Book I. 2011. 244p. pap. 15.95 *(978-1-60976-636-8(9)*, Eloquent Bks.) Strategic Book Publishing & Rights Agency (SBPRA).

Roberts, William. Thomas & Caitlin Bk. 1: The Caves of Caerdraig. 2016. (ENG.). 188p. (J). pap. 11.95 *(978-1-78612-737-2(7)*, 4da30275-fed8-42d1-97ec-2212ae49829b) Austin, Stan AUS. Dist: Bookmasters Distribution.

Robertson, M. P. The Egg. 2004. (ENG., Illus.). 32p. (J). (gr. k-3). pap. 6.99 *(978-0-14-240038-8(6)*, Puffin Books) Penguin Young Readers Group.

Robichaud, Yves. Tomes of Tari: Kaylen's Rising. 2013. 240p. *(978-1-4602-0526-6(X))*; pap. *(978-1-4602-0524-2(3))* FriesenPress.

Robinson, Fay. Fish Wish. 2005. (Illus.). 32p. (J). *(978-1-84011-605-2(6))* Templar Publishing.

Robinson, Hilary & Catling, Andy. Aladdin & the Lamp. 2009. (Hopscotch Adventures Ser.). (Illus.). 31p. (J). (gr. 1). lib. bdg. 25.65 *(978-1-59771-181-4(0))* Sea-To-Sea Pubns.

Robinson, Kathleen Marie. The Magic Doorknob, 1 vol. 2009. 56p. pap. 16.95 *(978-1-60813-362-8(1))* America Star Bks.

Robinson, Keith. Chamber of Ghosts. 2013. 222p. pap. *(978-0-9843906-5-6(0))* Roxby Media Ltd.

Robinson, Kelley. Naming: Book One of the Magic of Io Series. Curtiss, Melody, illus. 2013. 138p. pap. 8.95 *(978-0-9745865-1-9(X)*, SarahRose Children's Bks.) SarahRose Publishing.

Robinson, Rob. The Princess & the Juggler. 2004. 154p. pap. 12.95 *(978-0-595-30831-6(7))* iUniverse, Inc.

Robinson, Robin, illus. L. Frank Baum's Wizard of Oz. 2013. (Penguin Young Readers, Level 4 Ser.). (ENG.). 48p. (J). (gr. 3-4). mass mkt. 3.99 *(978-0-448-45588-4(9)*, Penguin Young Readers) Penguin Young Readers Group.

Robinson, T. J. The Academy Defenders. 2nd ed. 2012. 326p. pap. 14.99 *(978-1-936850-76-1(1))* Rhemalda Publishing.

Robinson, Vickie J. Use Your Imagination. Long, Corey, illus. 2008. 24p. pap. 24.95 *(978-1-60703-825-2(0))* America Star Bks.

Robinson, W. Heath. The Adventures of Uncle Lubin. 2013. (Dover Children's Classics Ser.). (ENG., Illus.). 128p. (J). (gr. 6-8). pap. 9.95 *(978-0-486-49821-8(2))* Dover Pubns., Inc.

Rochelle, Warren. The Called. 2010. (ENG.). 367p. 24.95 *(978-1-930846-63-0(0))* Golden Gryphon Pr.

Rockhill, Dennis. Meadow Dance. 2007. (Wonderlands Ser.).Tr. of Danza de la Pradera. (ENG., Illus.). 32p. (J). (gr. -1-3). per. 7.95 *(978-1-932748-70-3(9)*, Raven Tree Pr.,Csi) Continental Sales, Inc.

—Polar Slumber/Sueño Polar. Raven Tree Press Staff, ed. de la Vega, Eida, tr. Rockhill, Dennis, illus. 2004.Tr. of Sueño Polar. (SPA & ENG., Illus.). 32p. (J). (gr. -1-3). 16.95 *(978-0-9724973-1-2(5)*, 1234791, Raven Tree Pr.,Csi) Continental Sales, Inc.

Rockwood, Roy. On a Torn-Away World. 2008. 136p. pap. 12.95 *(978-1-60664-174-3(3))* Aegypan.

—The Wizard of the Se. 2008. 124p. 23.95 *(978-1-60664-931-2(0))*; pap. 10.95 *(978-1-60664-051-7(8))* Aegypan.

Rodda, Emily. City of the Rats. 2012. (Deltora Quest Ser.). (ENG.). 160p. (J). (gr. 3-7). pap. 5.99 *(978-0-545-46022-4(0))* Scholastic, Inc.

—Deltora Quest 1. Niwano, Makoto, illus. 2011. (Deltora Quest Ser.). (ENG.). 202p. (gr. 8-12). pap. 10.99 *(978-1-935429-28-9(0))* Kodansha America, Inc.

—Deltora Quest 2. Niwano, Makoto, illus. 2011. (Deltora Quest Ser.). (ENG.). 206p. (gr. 8-12). pap. 10.99 *(978-1-935429-29-6(9))* Kodansha America, Inc.

—Deltora Quest 3. Niwano, Makoto, illus. 2011. (Deltora Quest Ser.). (ENG.). 208p. (gr. 8-12). pap. 10.99 *(978-1-935429-30-2(2))* Kodansha America, Inc.

—Deltora Quest 4. Niwano, Makoto, illus. 2012. (Deltora Quest Ser.). (ENG.). 208p. (gr. 8-12). pap. 10.99 *(978-1-935429-31-9(0))* Kodansha America, Inc.

—Deltora Quest 5. 2012. (Deltora Quest Ser.). (ENG., Illus.). 208p. (gr. 8-12). pap. 10.99 *(978-1-61262-011-4(6))* Kodansha America, Inc.

—Deltora Quest 6. 2012. (Deltora Quest Ser.). (ENG., Illus.). 200p. (gr. 8-12). pap. 10.99 *(978-1-61262-012-1(4))* Kodansha America, Inc.

—Deltora Quest #6: the Maze of the Beast. 2012. (Deltora Quest Ser.). (ENG.). 160p. (J). (gr. 3-7). pap. 5.99 *(978-0-545-46026-2(3))* Scholastic, Inc.

—Deltora Quest 7. 2012. (Deltora Quest Ser.). (ENG., Illus.). 200p. (gr. 8-12). pap. 10.99 *(978-1-61262-013-8(2))* Kodansha America, Inc.

—Deltora Quest #7: the Valley of the Lost. 2012. (Deltora Quest Ser.). (ENG.). 160p. (J). (gr. 3-7). pap. 5.99 *(978-0-545-46027-9(1))* Scholastic, Inc.

—Deltora Quest 8. 2012. (Deltora Quest Ser.). (ENG., Illus.). 200p. (gr. 8-12). pap. 10.99 *(978-1-61262-014-5(0))* Kodansha America, Inc.

—Deltora Quest 9. 2012. (Deltora Quest Ser.). (ENG., Illus.). 200p. (gr. 8-12). pap. 10.99 *(978-1-61262-015-2(9))* Kodansha America, Inc.

—Isle of the Dead. 2004. (Dragons of Deltora Ser.: No. 3). 195p. (J). lib. bdg. 16.92 *(978-1-4242-0273-7(6))* Fitzgerald Bks.

—Return to Del. 2012. (Deltora Quest Ser.). (ENG.). 160p. (J). (gr. 3-7). pap. 5.99 *(978-0-545-46028-6(X))* Scholastic, Inc.

—Rowan & the Ice Creepers. 2003. (Rowan of Rin Ser.). 272p. (J). (gr. 3-18). 15.99 *(978-0-06-029780-0(8))* HarperCollins Pubs.

—Rowan & the Travelers. 2004. (Rowan of Rin Ser.). (ENG.). 192p. (J). (gr. 3-18). pap. 6.99 *(978-0-06-056072-0(X)*, Greenwillow Bks.) HarperCollins Pubs.

—Rowan & the Zebak. 2003. (Rowan of Rin Ser.). (ENG., Illus.). 208p. (J). (gr. 2-18). pap. 5.99 *(978-0-06-441024-3(2)*, Harper Trophy) HarperCollins Pubs.

—Rowan of Rin. 2004. (Rowan of Rin Ser.). (ENG., Illus.). 176p. (J). (gr. 3-18). pap. 6.99 *(978-0-06-056071-3(1)*, Greenwillow Bks.) HarperCollins Pubs.

—Shadowgate. 2004. (Dragons of Deltora Ser.: No. 2). 195p. (J). lib. bdg. 16.92 *(978-1-4242-0274-4(4))* Fitzgerald Bks.

—The Sister of the South. 2004. (Dragons of Deltora Ser.: No. 4). 205p. (J). lib. bdg. 16.92 *(978-1-4242-0275-1(2))* Fitzgerald Bks.

—The Star Cloak. Vitale, Raoul, illus. 2007. (Fairy Realm Ser.). (ENG.). 112p. (gr. 3-7). 25.65 *(978-1-59961-329-1(8))* Spotlight.

—The Unicorn. Vitale, Raoul, illus. 2007. (Fairy Realm Ser.). 106p. (gr. 3-7). 25.65 *(978-1-59961-328-4(X))* Spotlight.

—The Water Sprites. Vitale, Raoul, illus. 2007. (Fairy Realm Ser.). 104p. (gr. 3-7). 25.65 *(978-1-59961-330-7(1))* Spotlight.

Rodgers, Mary. Freaky Friday. 2009. (Trophy Bk.). (ENG.). 192p. (J). (gr. 5-18). reprint ed. pap. 5.99 *(978-0-06-440046-6(8))* HarperCollins Pubs.

Rodi, Robert & Richards, Cliff. Rogue: Going Rogue. 2005. (X-Men Ser.). (Illus.). 144p. pap. 14.99 *(978-0-7851-1336-2(3))* Marvel Worldwide, Inc.

Rodriguez, David. Shadowgirls - Season One. Nelson, Angela, ed. 2013. (ENG., Illus.). 240p. (YA). 29.95 *(978-0-9832161-1-7(8)*, 9780983216117) Th3rd World Studios.

Rodriguez, Elaine M. Nerposito & Planet Earth. 2012. 36p. pap. 15.49 *(978-1-4669-5972-9(X))* Trafford Publishing.

Rodriguez, Lourdes. Mandy, Princess of la la Land: The Green Monster. 2013. 52p. pap. 24.99 *(978-1-4817-0077-1(4))* AuthorHouse.

Rodriguez, Odette B. Lezama. The Last Golden Egg. 2011. 32p. pap. 19.95 *(978-1-4327-5931-5(0))* Outskirts Pr., Inc.

Rodriguez, Sergio R. Little Santa & Snowboy: The Childhood Adventures of Santa Claus. 2007. (Illus.). 32p. (J). pap. 8.95 *(978-0-615-17411-2(6))* Little Santa Bks., Inc.

Rodriguez, Susan R. The Meadow of Mine. 2009. 52p. pap. 22.49 *(978-1-4389-9979-1(8))* AuthorHouse.

Rogers, Anne. The magic rainbow large Print. 2008. 332p. pap. 30.95 *(978-1-4092-3059-5(7))* Lulu Pr., Inc.

—The magic rainbow very large Print. 2008. 502p. pap. 39.50 *(978-1-4092-3065-6(1))* Lulu Pr., Inc.

Rogers, Bud & Martin, Gary. The Witch of Endor, 1 vol. Cariello, Sergio, illus. 2008. (Z Graphic Novels / Son of Samson Ser.). (ENG.). 160p. (J). pap. 6.99 *(978-0-310-71283-1(1))* Zonderkidz.

Rogers, Bud, et al. Truth Revealed, 1 vol. Padilla, Ariel, illus. 2009. (Z Graphic Novels / Tomo Ser.). (ENG.). 160p. (J). pap. 6.99 *(978-0-310-71305-0(6))* Zondervan.

Rogers, Don. The Adventures of Shawn & Jeremy. 2011. 20p. pap. 24.95 *(978-1-4626-3674-7(8))* America Star Bks.

Rogers, Jennifer H. Chasing Grace. 2013. 30p. pap. 13.95 *(978-1-4525-8739-4(6)*, Balboa Pr.) Author Solutions, Inc.

Rogers, John. Dungeons & Dragons Volume 3: Down: Down. Ponce, Andres & Arranz, Nacho, illus. 2012. (Dungeons & Dragons Ser.). (ENG.). 132p. 21.99 *(978-1-61377-178-5(9)*, 9781613771785) Idea & Design Works, LLC.

Rogers, John & Di Vito, Andrea. First Encounters, Vol. 2. Alcazar, Vicente et al, illus. 2012. (Dungeons & Dragons Ser.). (ENG.). 156p. pap. 19.99 *(978-1-61377-534-9(2)*, 9781613775349) Idea & Design Works, LLC.

Rogers, Kerima. Far from Far, Far Away: A Fractured Tale. 2012. 28p. pap. 21.99 *(978-1-4653-8523-9(1))* Xlibris Corp.

Rogers, Kirsteen. Haunted House Sticker Book. 2012. (Sticker Activity Book Ser.). 24p. (J). pap. 8.99 *(978-0-7945-3163-8(6)*, Usborne) EDC Publishing.

Rogers, Suzanne J. Cody Meets A Butterfly. 2008. 72p. pap. 19.95 *(978-1-4327-2069-8(4))* Outskirts Pr., Inc.

Rohan, Julia K. Weaverworld: Grimsnipe's Revenge. 2012. 382p. 31.95 *(978-1-4697-0031-1(X))*; pap. 21.95 *(978-1-4697-0032-8(8))* iUniverse, Inc.

Rollins, Danielle. Burning. 2017. (ENG.). 368p. (YA). pap. 9.99 *(978-1-68119-205-5(5)*, 9781681192055, Bloomsbury USA Childrens) Bloomsbury Publishing USA.

Rollins, James. Jake Ransom & the Howling Sphinx. 2011. (Jake Ransom Ser.: 2). (ENG.). 384p. (J). (gr. 5-18). 16.99 *(978-0-06-147382-1(0))* HarperCollins Pubs.

—Jake Ransom & the Skull King's Shadow. 2010. (Jake Ransom Ser.: 1). (ENG.). 432p. (J). (gr. 5). pap. 7.99 *(978-0-06-147381-4(2))* HarperCollins Pubs.

Rollins, L. G. Shadows of Angels. 2015. 315p. (YA). pap. 18.99 *(978-1-4621-1746-8(5))* Cedar Fort, Inc./CFI Distribution.

Roman, Dave. Teen Boat! The Race for Boatlantis. Green, John, illus. 2015. (ENG.). 160p. (YA). (gr. 7). 14.99 *(978-0-547-86563-8(5))* Houghton Mifflin Harcourt Publishing Co.

Romansky, Sally Rosenberg. Invincible. Ott, Margot Janet, illus. 2006. (J). pap. 8.95 *(978-0-9723729-4-7(6))* Imagination Stage, Inc.

Romey, Elizabeth A. Dragon Magic. (YA). pap. 9.99 *(978-0-88092-625-6(2))* Royal Fireworks Publishing Co.

Root, Laura L. Quail in My Garden: Book One of Adventures in My Garden. 2012. 64p. pap. 26.99 *(978-1-4490-6963-6(0))* AuthorHouse.

Rooyen, Suzanne Van. The Other Me. 2016. (ENG., Illus.). (J). 24.99 ***(978-1-63477-973-9(8)***, Harmony Ink Pr.) Dreamspinner Pr.

Rooyen, Suzanne Van. The Other Me [Library Edition]. 2014. 216p. pap. 14.99 *(978-1-62798-645-8(6)*, Harmony Ink Pr.) Dreamspinner Pr.

Rose, Alice. Maria Dracula: A Fantasy Novel for Children. 2007. (Illus.). 191p. pap. 13.50 *(978-0-615-15099-4(3))* DUENDE Bks.

Rose, Christine & Rose, Ethan. Rowan of the Wood. 2008. 240p. (YA). pap. 14.95 *(978-0-9817443-1-5(1))* Dalton Publishing GBR. Dist: Midpoint Trade Bks., Inc.

Rose, John. Wikker. 2007. 248p. pap. 17.95 *(978-1-4303-1523-0(7))* Lulu Pr., Inc.

Rose, Lynda J. Assignment Earth. 2008. (ENG.). 160p. (J). (gr. 4-7). pap. 8.95 *(978-0-7459-6063-0(4))* Lion Hudson PLC GBR. Dist: Independent Pubs. Group.

Rose, S. J. Plant Agriculture Education: 2012 Edition. collector's ed. 2011. (ENG., Illus.). 176p. per. 5.00 *(978-0-9729057-2-5(3))* Training Grounds.

Rose, Simon. The Emerald Curse, 1 vol. Nugent, Cynthia, illus. 384th ed. 2006. (ENG.). 96p. (J). (gr. 3-6). per. 7.95 *(978-1-896580-90-6(4))* Tradewind Bks. CAN. Dist: Orca Bk. Pubs. USA.

—The Heretic's Tomb, 1 vol. 2008. (ENG., Illus.). 176p. (J). (gr. 2-5). per. 9.95 *(978-1-896580-92-0(0))* Tradewind Bks. CAN. Dist: Orca Bk. Pubs. USA.

—The Sorcerer's Letterbox, 1 vol. 2004. (ENG., Illus.). 114p. (J). (gr. 4-6). per. 7.95 *(978-1-896580-52-4(1))* Tradewind Bks. CAN. Dist: Orca Bk. Pubs. USA.

Rose, Tammy Marie. Majik the Black Unicorn, 1 vol. 2009. 74p. pap. 19.95 *(978-1-60749-824-7(3))* America Star Bks.

—Munchkin. 2012. 24p. 24.95 *(978-1-4626-6095-7(9))* America Star Bks.

Rosen, Lucy. M. K. Saves the Day. 2013. (I Can Read Level 2 Ser.). (ENG., Illus.). 32p. (J). (gr. -1-3). pap. 3.99 *(978-0-06-220991-7(4))* HarperCollins Pubs.

—Meet the Leafmen. 2013. (I Can Read Level 2 Ser.). (ENG., Illus.). 32p. (J). (gr. -1-3). pap. 3.99 *(978-0-06-220993-1(0))* HarperCollins Pubs.

Rosen, Michael. Send for a Superhero! McEwen, Katharine, illus. 2014. (ENG.). 40p. (J). (gr. -1-2). 16.99 *(978-0-7636-6438-1(3))* Candlewick Pr.

Rosenow, Ty. The Historical Adventures of Thomas Balfour. 2012. 186p. pap. 17.95 *(978-1-105-94011-8(X))* Lulu Pr., Inc.

Ross, Dev. We Both Read-Fox's Best Trick Ever: Level 1. Reinhart, Larry, illus. 2006. (We Both Read Ser.). 44p. (J). (gr. -1-3). 7.99 *(978-1-891327-69-8(0))* Treasure Bay, Inc.

Rossi, Veronica. Seeker. 2017. (Riders Ser.: 2). (ENG.). 352p. (YA). 17.99 *(978-0-7653-8256-6(3)*, 9780765382566, Tor Teen) Doherty, Tom Assocs., LLC.

—Through the Ever Night. 2013. 341p. (YA). *(978-0-06-224710-0(7))* Harper & Row Ltd.

—Through the Ever Night. 2013. (Under the Never Sky Trilogy Ser.: 2). (ENG.). 368p. (YA). (gr. 9). pap. 9.99 *(978-0-06-207207-8(2))* HarperCollins Pubs.

Rossignol, Manon Éléonor & Lecor, Tex. Isory Poutch et le Sortilege de Cacouna. 2004. (FRE., Illus.). 398p. (J). *(978-2-9807852-1-4(0)*, Spotlight Poets) Éditions le Poutchoman.

Rothchild, Erik. The Garden Adventures: The Mishaps of Martha & Matilda. Hief, Gina, illus. 2013. 44p. *(978-0-9883568-5-6(6))* Inkwell Books LLC.

Rothman, Lorne. Southcrop Forest. 2008. 184p. pap. 13.95 *(978-0-595-49588-7(5))* iUniverse, Inc.

Rothwell, David. The Voyage of the Pilchard. 2009. 162p. pap. 13.95 *(978-1-4092-1071-9(5))* Lulu Pr., Inc.

Rotter, Laura. Terratorv. 2009. 32p. pap. 12.99 *(978-1-4490-3092-6(0))* AuthorHouse.

Rouncville, Bibi. Sea Bugs & Moose Eggs. 2009. 52p. pap. 9.50 *(978-1-4357-4004-4(1))* Lulu Pr., Inc.

Round, J. The Catcher. 2008. 168p. pap. 14.95 *(978-1-4092-0372-8(7))* Lulu Pr., Inc.

Rowe, W. W. Jerry's Mystery. 2016. (ENG., Illus.). 96p. (J). (gr. 6-9). pap. 8.95 *(978-1-936012-70-1(7))* Larson Pubns.

—The Wand Goes Wild. 2011. 120p. (gr. 3-7). pap. 12.95 *(978-0-9843754-4-8(9))* Sanctuary Publishing, Inc.

—The Wizard's Wayward Wand. 2010. (ENG.). 99p. (J). (gr. 3-7). pap. 12.95 *(978-0-9843754-0-0(6))* Sanctuary Publishing, Inc.

Rowley, M'lin. The Silver Coat. 2009. (Knights of Right Ser.: Bk. 2). 71p. (J). (gr. 1-5). pap. 6.99 *(978-1-60641-104-9(7)*, Shadow Mountain) Shadow Mountain Publishing.

Rowling, J. K. Fantastic Beasts & Where to Find Them. 2017. (Harry Potter Ser.). (ENG.). 128p. (J). (gr. 3). 12.99 *(978-1-338-13231-1(8))* Scholastic, Inc.

—Harrius Potter et Philosophi Lapis. Needham, Peter, tr. from ENG. 2003. (Harry Potter Ser.).Tr. of Harry Potter & the Philosopher's Stone. (LAT & ENG., Illus.). 256p. (YA). (gr. 7). 29.99 *(978-1-58234-825-4(1)*, 9781582348254, Bloomsbury USA Childrens) Bloomsbury Publishing USA.

—Harry Potter à l'École des Sorciers. Menard, Jean-François, tr. from ENG. 2007. (Harry Potter Ser.: Year 1).Tr. of Harry Potter & the Sorcerer's Stone. 311p. (J). per. 14.95 *(978-2-07-061236-9(8))* Gallimard, Editions FRA. Dist: Distribooks, Inc.

—Harry Potter & the Chamber of Secrets. 2009. 9.64 *(978-0-7848-1444-4(9),* Everbind) Marco Bk. Co.
—Harry Potter & the Chamber of Secrets. unabr. ed. 2004. (Harry Potter Ser.: Year 2). 352p. (J). (gr. 3-18). pap. 46.00 incl. audio *(978-0-8072-8207-6(3),* S YA 137 SP, Listening Library) Random Hse. Audio Publishing Group.
—Harry Potter & the Chamber of Secrets. (Harry Potter Ser.: 2). (J). 2006. 1.25 *(978-1-4193-8079-2(6))* 2003. 78.75 *(978-1-4025-6698-1(0))* Recorded Bks., Inc.
—Harry Potter & the Chamber of Secrets. (Harry Potter Ser.: Year 2). (RUS., Illus.). 28.95 *(978-5-8451-0947-7(7))* Rosmen-Izdat RUS. Dist: Distribooks, Inc.
—Harry Potter & the Chamber of Secrets. Kay, Jim, illus. 2016. (Harry Potter Ser.: 2). (ENG.). 272p. (J). (gr. 3). 39.99 *(978-0-545-79132-8(4));* 275.00 *(978-1-338-11986-2(9))* Scholastic, Inc. (Levine, Arthur A. Bks.).
—Harry Potter & the Chamber of Secrets. l.t. ed. 2003. (Harry Potter Ser.: Year 2). (ENG.). 466p. pap. 13.95 *(978-1-59413-001-4(9))* Thorndike Pr.
—Harry Potter & the Chamber of Secrets. 2013. (Harry Potter (Kazu Kibuishi Illustrations) Ser.: 2). lib. bdg. 24.50 *(978-0-606-32346-8(5),* Turtleback) Turtleback Bks.
—Harry Potter & the Deathly Hallows. (Illus.). 2008. 832p. pap. *(978-0-7475-9586-1(0))* 2007. (ENG., 608p. *(978-0-7475-9106-1(7))* Bloomsbury Publishing Plc.
—Harry Potter & the Deathly Hallows. braille ed. 2007. (Harry Potter Ser.: Year 7). (J). (gr. 4-7). 34.99 *(978-0-939173-57-0(3))* National Braille Pr.
—Harry Potter & the Deathly Hallows. 2010. 25.00 *(978-1-60686-882-9(9))* Perfection Learning Corp.
—Harry Potter & the Deathly Hallows, 17 vols. 2007. (Harry Potter Ser.: 7). (YA). 129.79 *(978-1-4281-6654-7(8));* 131.75 *(978-1-4281-6652-3(1))* Recorded Bks., Inc.
—Harry Potter & the Deathly Hallows. GrandPré, Mary, illus. (Harry Potter Ser.: 7). (ENG.). (J). 2009. 784p. (gr. 4-7). pap. 14.99 *(978-0-545-13970-0(8),* Levine, Arthur A. Bks.) 2007. 784p. (gr. 5-9). 34.99 *(978-0-545-01022-1(5))* 2007. 816p. (gr. 4-7). 65.00 *(978-0-545-02937-7(6),* Levine, Arthur A. Bks.) Scholastic, Inc.
—Harry Potter & the Deathly Hallows. l.t. ed. 2009. (ENG.). 970p. pap. 14.95 *(978-1-59413-355-8(7),* Large Print Pr.) 2007. (Harry Potter Ser.: Year 7). (Illus.). 969p. (J). (gr. 4-7). 34.95 *(978-0-7862-9665-1(8))* Thorndike Pr.
—Harry Potter & the Deathly Hallows. (Harry Potter (Kazu Kibuishi Illustrations) Ser.: 7). 2013. lib. bdg. 29.40 *(978-0-606-32351-2(1))* 2009. lib. bdg. 26.95 *(978-0-606-00420-6(3))* Turtleback Bks. (Turtleback).
—Harry Potter & the Deathly Hallows. Bar-hillel, Gili, tr. from ENG. 2007. (Harry Potter Ser.: Year 7). (HEB., Illus.). 568p. (J). (gr. 4-7). pap. *(978-965-482-635-8(6))* Yediot Aharonot Bks., Miscal.
—Harry Potter & the Goblet of Fire. 2009. 10.24 *(978-0-7848-1587-8(9),* Everbind) Marco Bk. Co.
—Harry Potter & the Goblet of Fire. (Harry Potter Ser.: 4). (J). 2006. 1.25 *(978-1-4193-8531-5(3))* 2003. 101.75 *(978-1-4025-6702-5(2))* Recorded Bks., Inc.
—Harry Potter & the Goblet of Fire. GrandPré, Mary, illus. l.t. ed. 2003. (Harry Potter Ser.: Vol. 4). (ENG.). 936p. pap. 11.66 *(978-1-59413-003-8(5))* Thorndike Pr.
—Harry Potter & the Goblet of Fire. 2013. (Harry Potter (Kazu Kibuishi Illustrations) Ser.: 4). lib. bdg. 26.95 *(978-0-606-32348-2(1),* Turtleback) Turtleback Bks.
—Harry Potter & the Half-Blood Prince. 2005. (ENG.). cd-rom *(978-0-7475-8258-8(0))* Bloomsbury Publishing Plc.
—Harry Potter & the Half-Blood Prince, 9 vols. braille ed. 2005. (Harry Potter Ser.: Year 6). (J). (gr. 4-8). 29.99 *(978-0-939173-39-6(5),* HALF) National Braille Pr.
—Harry Potter & the Half-Blood Prince. GrandPré, Mary, illus. 2006. (Harry Potter Ser.: Year 6). 652p. (gr. 4-8). 23.00 *(978-0-7569-6765-9(1))* Perfection Learning Corp.
—Harry Potter & the Half-Blood Prince. (Harry Potter Ser.: 6). (J). 2007. 1.25 *(978-1-4193-5430-4(2))* 2006. 110.75 *(978-1-4193-5436-6(1))* 2006. 193.75 *(978-1-4193-5432-8(9))* 2005. 113.75 *(978-1-4193-5434-2(5))* Recorded Bks., Inc.
—Harry Potter & the Half-Blood Prince. GrandPré, Mary, illus. (Harry Potter Ser.: 6). (ENG.). 672p. (J). (gr. 4-8). 2005. 29.99 *(978-0-439-78454-2(9))* 2006. reprint ed. per. 12.99 *(978-0-439-78596-9(0))* Scholastic, Inc. (Levine, Arthur A. Bks.).
—Harry Potter & the Half-Blood Prince. (Illus.). (J). (gr. 4-7). 2007. (ENG.). 832p. per. 14.95 *(978-1-59413-221-6(0))* 2005. (Harry Potter Ser.: Year 6). 831p. 29.95 *(978-0-7862-7745-2(9))* Thorndike Pr. (Large Print Pr.).
—Harry Potter & the Half-Blood Prince. 2013. (Harry Potter (Kazu Kibuishi Illustrations) Ser.: 6). lib. bdg. 26.95 *(978-0-606-32350-5(3),* Turtleback) Turtleback Bks.
—Harry Potter & the Half Blood Prince - Chinese Language. 2005. (Harry Potter Ser.: Year 6). (CHI.). 496p. (YA). (gr. 4-8). pap. 28.95 *(978-7-02-005323-0(8),* HAP06) People's Literature Publishing Hse. CHN. Dist: Chinasprout, Inc.
—Harry Potter & the Order of the Phoenix. (ENG.). 768p. (J). (gr. 6-10). pap. *(978-0-7475-6107-1(9))* Bloomsbury Publishing Plc.
—Harry Potter & the Order of the Phoenix. 2008. *(978-977-14-2697-4(4))* Nahdat Misr Bkshop for Printing and Pubs.
—Harry Potter & the Order of the Phoenix, 13 vols. braille ed. 2003. (Harry Potter Ser.: Year 5). (YA). 29.99 *(978-0-939173-38-9(7))* National Braille Pr.
—Harry Potter & the Order of the Phoenix. 2003. (Harry Potter Ser.: Year 5). (CHI.). 575p. (YA). pap. 26.95 *(978-7-02-004327-9(5),* HAP05) People's Literature Publishing Hse. CHN. Dist: Chinasprout, Inc.
—Harry Potter & the Order of the Phoenix. 2004. (Harry Potter Ser.). 870p. (gr. 4-6). 16.49 *(978-0-7569-4163-5(6))* Perfection Learning Corp.
—Harry Potter & the Order of the Phoenix. 2003. (ENG.). 768p. *(978-1-55192-570-7(2))* Raincoast Bk. Distribution.
—Harry Potter & the Order of the Phoenix. GrandPré, Mary, illus. (Harry Potter Ser.: 5). (ENG.). (J). (gr. 3-7). 2004. 896p. mass mkt. 12.99 *(978-0-439-35807-1(8),* Scholastic Paperbacks) 2003. 870p. 29.99 *(978-0-439-35806-4(X))* Scholastic, Inc.
—Harry Potter & the Order of the Phoenix. l.t. ed. 2003. (Harry Potter Ser.: Year 5). 1093p. 29.95 *(978-0-7862-5778-2(4),* Large Print Pr.) Thorndike Pr.
—Harry Potter & the Order of the Phoenix. GrandPré, Mary, illus. l.t. ed. 2003. (Thorndike Young Adult Ser.). (ENG.). 1232p. (J). (gr. 4-7). per. 14.95 *(978-1-59413-112-7(0),* Large Print Pr.) Thorndike Pr.
—Harry Potter & the Order of the Phoenix. (Harry Potter (Kazu Kibuishi Illustrations) Ser.: 5). 2013. lib. bdg. 26.95 *(978-0-606-32349-9(X))* 2004. lib. bdg. 24.50 *(978-0-613-99916-8(9))* Turtleback Bks. (Turtleback).
—Harry Potter & the Philosopher's Stone. 2014. (ENG., Illus.). 352p. *(978-1-4088-5589-8(5))* Bloomsbury Publishing Plc.
—Harry Potter & the Prisoner of Azkaban. 2009. 9.64 *(978-0-7848-1542-7(9),* Everbind) Marco Bk. Co.
—Harry Potter & the Prisoner of Azkaban. 2005. (Harry Potter Ser.: Year 3). (CHI.). 260p. (YA). pap. 16.95 *(978-7-02-003345-4(8),* HAP03) People's Literature Publishing Hse. CHN. Dist: Chinasprout, Inc.
—Harry Potter & the Prisoner of Azkaban, 10 vols. 2003. (Harry Potter Ser.: 3). (J). 84.75 *(978-1-4025-6700-1(6))* Recorded Bks., Inc.
—Harry Potter & the Prisoner of Azkaban. l.t. ed. 2003. (Harry Potter Ser.: Year 3). (ENG.). 592p. pap. 13.95 *(978-1-59413-002-1(7),* Large Print Pr.) Thorndike Pr.
—Harry Potter & the Prisoner of Azkaban. 2013. (Harry Potter (Kazu Kibuishi Illustrations) Ser.: 3). lib. bdg. 24.50 *(978-0-606-32347-5(3),* Turtleback) Turtleback Bks.
—Harry Potter & the Sorcerer's Stone. 2014. (ENG.). lthr. 79.00 *(978-1-62715-772-8(7))* Leatherbound Bestsellers.
—Harry Potter & the Sorcerer's Stone. 2009. 8.44 *(978-0-7848-2438-2(X));* 10.84 *(978-0-7848-1357-7(4))* Marco Bk. Co. (Everbind).
—Harry Potter & the Sorcerer's Stone. 2003. (Harry Potter Ser.: Year 1). (CHI.). 191p. (YA). pap. 14.95 *(978-7-02-003343-0(1),* HAP01) People's Literature Publishing Hse. CHN. Dist: Chinasprout, Inc.
—Harry Potter & the Sorcerer's Stone. (Harry Potter Ser.: 1). (J). 2004. 1.25 *(978-1-4025-6757-5(X))* 2003. 80.75 *(978-1-4025-6696-7(4))* Recorded Bks., Inc.
—Harry Potter & the Sorcerer's Stone. Kay, Jim, illus. 2015. (Harry Potter Ser.: 1). (ENG.). 256p. (J). (gr. 3). 39.99 *(978-0-545-79035-2(2),* Levine, Arthur A. Bks.) Scholastic, Inc.
—Harry Potter & the Sorcerer's Stone, Bk. 1. 2013. (Harry Potter Ser.: 1). (ENG., Illus.). 336p. (J). (gr. 4). pap. 12.99 *(978-0-545-58288-9(1))* Scholastic, Inc.
—Harry Potter & the Sorcerer's Stone. 2013. (Harry Potter (Kazu Kibuishi Illustrations) Ser.: 1). lib. bdg. 24.50 *(978-0-606-32345-1(7),* Turtleback) Turtleback Bks.
—Harry Potter e il Prigioniero di Azkaban. (Harry Potter Ser.: Year 3).Tr. of Harry Potter & the Prisoner of Azkaban. (ITA.). pap. 32.95 *(978-88-7782-852-1(8))* Salani ITA. Dist: Distribooks, Inc.
—Harry Potter e la camera dei segreti. (Harry Potter Ser.: Year 2). (ITA.). pap. 32.95 *(978-88-7782-703-6(3))* Salani ITA. Dist: Distribooks, Inc.
—Harry Potter e la Pietra Filosofale. (Harry Potter Ser.: Year 1).Tr. of Harry Potter & the Philosopher's Stone. (ITA., Illus.). 293p. pap. 32.95 *(978-88-7782-702-9(5))* Salani ITA. Dist: Distribooks, Inc.
—Harry Potter et l'Ordre du Phenix. 2003. (Harry Potter Ser.: Year 5).Tr. of Harry Potter & the Order of the Phoenix. 975p. pap. 75.00 *(978-0-320-04839-5(X))* French & European Pubns., Inc.
—Harry Potter y el Caliz de Fuego. 2004. (Harry Potter Ser.: Year 4).Tr. of Harry Potter & the Goblet of Fire. (SPA., Illus.). 240p. (YA). 19.95 *(978-84-7888-645-6(1),* SAL30169) Emece Editores ESP. Dist: Lectorum Pubns., Inc.
—Harry Potter y el Prisionero de Azkaban. 2004. (Harry Potter Ser.: Year 3).Tr. of Harry Potter & the Prisoner of Azkaban. (SPA., Illus.). 360p. (gr. 3-18). 17.95 *(978-84-7888-519-0(6),* SAL1889) Emece Editores ESP. Dist: Lectorum Pubns., Inc.
—Harry Potter y el Prisionero de Azkaban. 2015. (Harry Potter Spanish Ser.: 3).Tr. of Harry Potter & the Prisoner of Azkaban. (SPA.). (gr. 3-6). lib. bdg. 28.10 *(978-0-613-35958-0(5),* Turtleback) Turtleback Bks.
—Harry Potter y la Camara Secreta. 2004. (Harry Potter Ser.: Year 2).Tr. of Harry Potter & the Chamber of Secrets. (SPA., Illus.). 288p. (YA). (gr. 3-18). 15.95 *(978-84-7888-495-7(5),* SAL4595) Emece Editores ESP. Dist: Lectorum Pubns., Inc.
—Harry Potter Y la Orden del Fenix. 2004. (Harry Potter Ser.: Year 5).Tr. of Harry Potter & the Order of the Phoenix. (SPA.). 893p. (YA). 23.99 *(978-84-7888-901-3(9))* Emece Editores ESP. Dist: Lectorum Pubns., Inc.
—Harry Potter Y la Orden del Fenix. Ortega, Gemma Rovira, tr. from ENG. 2004. (Harry Potter Ser.: Year 5).Tr. of Harry Potter & the Order of the Phoenix. (SPA.). 893p. (YA). pap. 17.99 *(978-84-7888-884-9(5))* Emece Editores ESP. Dist: Lectorum Pubns., Inc.
—Harry Potter y la Piedra Filosofal. 2004. (Harry Potter Ser.: Year 1).Tr. of Harry Potter & the Sorcerer's Stone. (SPA., Illus.). 256p. (YA). (gr. 7-18). 15.95 *(978-84-7888-445-2(9),* SAL2819) Emece Editores ESP. Dist: Lectorum Pubns., Inc.
—The Tales of Beedle the Bard. GrandPré, Mary, illus. 2008. (ENG.). 128p. *(978-0-7475-9987-6(4))* Bloomsbury Publishing Plc.
—The Tales of Beedle the Bard. GrandPré, Mary, illus. collector's ed. 2008. 184p. *(978-0-9560109-0-2(3))* Children's High Level Group.
—The Tales of Beedle the Bard. 2017. (Harry Potter Ser.). (ENG.). 128p. (J). (gr. 3-3). 12.99 *(978-1-338-12568-9(0),* Levine, Arthur A. Bks.) Scholastic, Inc.
—The Tales of Beedle the Bard. 2017. (ENG.). (J). (gr. 3). lib. bdg. 24.50 ***(978-0-606-39695-0(0))*** Turtleback Bks.
Rowling, J. K. & Scholastic, Inc. Staff. Harry Potter. 2007. (Harry Potter Ser.: Years 1-7). (ENG.). (J). (gr. 3-7). 205.93 *(978-0-545-04425-7(1),* Levine, Arthur A. Bks.) Scholastic, Inc.
Rowntree, G. M. Wizards Spell Magic in the Legends of Mere Leander. 2010. 291p. pap. 32.50 *(978-1-4452-6812-5(4))* Lulu Pr., Inc.
—Wizards Spell Magic in the Legends of Mere Leander - US Trade Size. 2010. 291p. pap. 24.95 *(978-1-4452-9266-3(1))* Lulu Pr., Inc.
Roy, Keri Anne & Holt, K. A. Brains for Lunch: A Zombie Novel in Haiku?! Wilson, Gahan, illus. 2010. (ENG.). 96p. (J). (gr. 4-9). 22.99 *(978-1-59643-629-9(8),* 9781596436299) Roaring Brook Pr.
Roy, Lauren M. The Fire Children. 2015. (ENG.). 272p. (YA). (gr. 8-13). mass mkt. 9.99 *(978-1-78108-353-6(3),* Ravenstone) Rebellion GBR. Dist: Simon & Schuster, Inc.
Roy, Lillian Elizabeth. Alice in Beeland: A Tale of Cornwall, Inspired by Lewis Carroll's Wonderland. 2nd ed. 2012. (Illus.). 128p. pap. *(978-1-78201-018-0(1))* Evertype.
Ruble, Kam. Princess Annado Tandy's Versery Rhymes. McMullen, T. C., illus. l.t. ed. 2007. 88p. (J). per. *(978-0-9779680-4-6(9))* Global Authors Pubns.
Ruby, Anne. Children of the Sea. Meier, Ty, illus. 2007. (YA). per. *(978-0-9787881-0-0(9))* Seachild.
Ruditis, Paul. Ready to Glow. Choi Sung Hwan, Aragon Noel, illus. 2005. (Trollz Ser.). (ENG.). 80p. (J). pap. 5.99 *(978-0-439-80313-7(6))* Scholastic, Inc.
Ruebush, McKenna. Enter a Glossy Web. Zollars, Jaime, illus. 2016. (ENG.). 400p. (YA). 16.99 *(978-1-62779-370-4(4),* 9781627793704, Holt, Henry & Co. Bks. For Young Readers) Holt, Henry & Co.
Ruellan, Susan. The Lost Treasure of Finistere. 2008. (ENG & FRE., Illus.). 83p. (J). (gr. 4-7). pap. 9.95 *(978-1-933916-24-8(9))* Nelson Publishing & Marketing.
Ruggieri, J. G. Weather Changes, Mountains Move, & Islands Disappear. 2012. 168p. pap. 15.00 *(978-0-9860300-0-0(7))* Alabaster Bk. Pub.
Ruiz, Frances. Fairy Bond: Book Two of the Key to Embralia. 2010. 290p. (YA). pap. 14.95 *(978-0-9818880-2-6(X))* Hinterland Sky Pr.
Ruiz, Margarita, illus. Pinocho. (SPA & ENG.). (J). (gr. -1-5). pap. 5.95 incl. audio compact disk *(978-88-8148-253-5(3))* EMC/Paradigm Publishing.
Ruley, Garrett. Hollin. 2011. 226p. pap. 15.00 *(978-0-557-55873-5(5))* Lulu Pr., Inc.
Ruley, Rose. Quest for a Moose: An Alaska Tale of Searching for an Animal that Doesn't Exist — until it Is Found. 2004. (J). pap. 12.95 *(978-1-59433-019-3(0))* Publication Consultants.
Rumpelstiltskin: 6 Small Books. (gr. k-2). 23.00 *(978-0-7635-8515-0(7))* Rigby Education.
Running Press, Running. Walking Dead Blood Globe. 2016. (Miniature Editions Ser.). (ENG., Illus.). 32p. pap. 12.95 *(978-0-7624-6070-0(9),* Running Pr. Minature Editions) Running Pr. Bk. Pubs.
Running Press Staff, ed. Harry Potter Golden Snitch Sticker Kit, Kit. 2006. (Miniature Editions Ser.). (ENG.). 16p. pap. 9.95 *(978-0-7624-2821-2(X))* Running Pr. Bk. Pubs.
Runstedler, Nancy. Beautiful Goodbye. 2012. (ENG., Illus.). 152p. (YA). pap. 12.99 *(978-1-4597-0553-1(X))* Dundurn CAN. Dist: Ingram Publisher Services.
Rupp, Rebecca. The Dragon of Lonely Island. 2006. (Dragon of Lonely Island Ser.). (ENG.). 192p. (J). (gr. 4-7). 6.99 *(978-0-7636-2805-5(0))* Candlewick Pr.
—Journey to the Blue Moon: In Which Time Is Lost & Then Found Again. 2006. (ENG., Illus.). 272p. (J). (gr. 5-7). 15.99 *(978-0-7636-2544-3(2))* Candlewick Pr.
Rusch, Elizabeth. Muddy Max: The Mystery of Marsh Creek. Lawrence, Mike, illus. 2014. (ENG.). 224p. (J). pap. 9.99 *(978-1-4494-3561-5(0))* Andrews McMeel Publishing.
Rusch, Elizabeth & Lawrence, Mike. Muddy Max: The Mystery of Marsh Creek. 2016. (ENG., Illus.). (J). (gr. 2-6). 37.99 ***(978-1-4494-7388-4(1))*** Andrews McMeel Publishing.
Rushdie, Salman. Luka & the Fire of Life. 2009. 14.75 *(978-0-7848-3731-3(7),* Everbind) Marco Bk. Co.
—Luka & the Fire of Life. 2011. (ENG.). 240p. (J). (gr. 7). pap. 17.00 *(978-0-679-78347-3(4),* Random Hse. Trade Paperbacks) Random House Publishing Group.
Russell, Kitty, compiled by. Fairy Lovely: Stories of Yesteryear. 2012. (ENG.). 416p. 29.95 *(978-1-937922-04-7(9))* Kittyco Pr.
Russell, Mark James. Young-Hee & the Pullocho. 2015. (ENG.). 256p. (J). (gr. 7-12). pap. 8.99 *(978-0-8048-4497-0(6))* Tuttle Publishing.
Russell, Romina. Black Moon. 2016. (Zodiac Ser.: 3). (ENG.). 320p. (YA). (gr. 7). 18.99 *(978-1-59514-745-5(4),* Razorbill) Penguin Young Readers Group.
—Zodiac. 2014. (Zodiac Ser.: 1). (ENG.). 336p. (YA). (gr. 7). 17.99 *(978-1-59514-740-0(3),* Razorbill) Penguin Young Readers Group.
Russell, Romina & Loftin, Nikki. Wandering Star. 2015. (Zodiac Ser.: 2). (ENG., Illus.). 320p. (YA). (gr. 7). 18.99 *(978-1-59514-743-1(8),* Razorbill) Penguin Young Readers Group.
—Zodiac. 2015. (Zodiac Ser.: 1). (ENG.). 480p. (YA). (gr. 7). pap. 10.99 *(978-1-59514-741-7(1),* Razorbill) Penguin Young Readers Group.
Rust, Ned. Patrick Griffin's Last Breakfast on Earth. 2016. (Patrick Griffin & the Three Worlds Ser.: 1). (ENG.). 416p. (J). 16.99 *(978-1-62672-342-9(7),* 9781626723429) Roaring Brook Pr.
Ruth, Greg. The Lost Boy. 2013. (ENG.). 192p. (J). (gr. 3-7). pap. 12.99 *(978-0-439-82332-6(3),* Graphix) Scholastic, Inc.
Ruth, Nick. The Dark Dreamweaver. Concannon, Sue, illus. 2007. (Remin Chronicles: 1). (ENG.). 256p. (J). (gr. 4-7). per. 11.95 *(978-0-9745603-5-9(9))* Imaginator Pr.
Rutkoski, Marie. The Cabinet of Wonders. 2013. (Kronos Chronicles Ser.: 1). (ENG.). 288p. (J). (gr. 5-9). pap. 10.99 *(978-1-250-01804-5(8),* 9781250018045) Square Fish.
—The Celestial Globe. 2013. (Kronos Chronicles Ser.: 2). (ENG.). 320p. (J). (gr. 5-9). pap. 7.99 *(978-1-250-02732-0(2),* 9781250027320) Square Fish.
—The Jewel of the Kalderash. 3rd ed. 2011. (Kronos Chronicles Ser.: 3). (ENG.). 336p. (J). (gr. 5-9). 16.99 *(978-0-374-33678-3(4),* 9780374336783, Farrar, Straus & Giroux (BYR)) Farrar, Straus & Giroux.
—The Jewel of the Kalderash. 2013. (Kronos Chronicles Ser.: 3). (ENG.). 336p. (J). (gr. 5-9). pap. 7.99 *(978-1-250-01025-4(X),* 9781250010254) Square Fish.
—The Winner's Crime. 2015. (Winner's Trilogy: Vol. 2). (ENG., Illus.). 416p. (YA). (gr. 7-12). 18.99 *(978-0-374-38470-8(3),* 9780374384708, Farrar, Straus & Giroux (BYR)) Farrar, Straus & Giroux.
—The Winner's Curse. 2014. (Winner's Trilogy Ser.: 1). (ENG.). 368p. (YA). (gr. 7). 18.99 *(978-0-374-38467-8(3),* 9780374384678, Farrar, Straus & Giroux (BYR)) Farrar, Straus & Giroux.
—The Winner's Curse. 2015. (Winner's Trilogy Ser.: 1). (ENG.). 384p. (YA). (gr. 7). pap. 10.99 *(978-1-250-05697-9(7),* 9781250056979) Square Fish.
Ruzycki, Dan Dan. The Adventures of Pillow Head: The Fallen Star. Hunter, Robbie Chase, illus. 2012. 26p. (J). 13.95 *(978-0-9834315-5-8(8))* Dan Dan Fantasy.
Ryan, Carrie. The Dark & Hollow Places. (Forest of Hands & Teeth Ser.: Bk. 3). (ENG.). 384p. (YA). (gr. 9). 2012. pap. 8.99 *(978-0-385-73860-6(9),* Ember) 2011. 17.99 *(978-0-385-73859-0(5),* Delacorte Bks. for Young Readers) Random Hse. Children's Bks.
—The Dead-Tossed Waves. 2011. (Forest of Hands & Teeth Ser.: Bk. 2). (J). 59.99 *(978-1-61707-144-7(7))* Findaway World, LLC.
—The Dead-Tossed Waves. (Forest of Hands & Teeth Ser.: Bk. 2). (ENG.). (YA). (gr. 9). 2011. 432p. pap. 9.99 *(978-0-385-73685-5(1))* 2010. 416p. 17.99 *(978-0-385-73684-8(3))* Random Hse. Children's Bks. (Delacorte Bks. for Young Readers).
—The Forest of Hands & Teeth. 2011. (Forest of Hands & Teeth Ser.: Bk. 1). (YA). 59.99 *(978-1-61707-145-4(5))* Findaway World, LLC.
—The Forest of Hands & Teeth. 2010. (Forest of Hands & Teeth Ser.: Bk. 1). (ENG.). 310p. (gr. 9-12). 20.00 *(978-1-60686-909-3(4))* Perfection Learning Corp.
—The Forest of Hands & Teeth. 2010. (Forest of Hands & Teeth Ser.: Bk. 1). (ENG.). 336p. (YA). (gr. 9-18). pap. 9.99 *(978-0-385-73682-4(7),* Ember) Random Hse. Children's Bks.
—The Forest of Hands & Teeth. 2010. (Forest of Hands & Teeth Ser.: Bk. 1). lib. bdg. 20.85 *(978-0-606-23881-6(6),* Turtleback) Turtleback Bks.
Ryan, Carrie & Davis, John Parke. City of Thirst. (Map to Everywhere Ser.: 2). (ENG., Illus.). (J). (gr. 3-7). 2016. 416p. pap. 7.99 *(978-0-316-24082-6(6))* 2015. 400p. 17.00 *(978-0-316-24084-0(2))* Little, Brown Bks. for Young Readers.
—The Map to Everywhere. 2014. (Map to Everywhere Ser.: Bk. 1). (ENG., Illus.). 448p. (J). (gr. 3-7). 17.00 *(978-0-316-24077-2(X))* Little Brown & Co.
—The Map to Everywhere. 2015. (Map to Everywhere Ser.: 1). (J). lib. bdg. 18.45 *(978-0-606-37521-4(X))* Turtleback Bks.
—Shadows of the Lost Sun. 2017. (Map to Everywhere Ser.: 3). (ENG., Illus.). 368p. (J). (gr. 3-7). 17.99 *(978-0-316-24088-8(5))* Little, Brown Bks. for Young Readers.
Ryan, Frank P. The Snowmelt River. 2013. (Three Powers Ser.: 1). (ENG.). 720p. (J). (gr. 7-17). 15.95 *(978-1-62365-048-3(8),* Jo Fletcher Books) Quercus NA.
Ryan, Margaret. Littlest Dragon Gets the Giggles. Smith, Jamie, illus. 2011. (ENG.). 80p. (J). pap. 5.99 *(978-0-00-718029-5(2),* HarperCollins Children's Bks.) HarperCollins Pubs. Ltd. GBR. Dist: HarperCollins Pubs.
Rylance, Ulrike. Emma in Buttonland. Morby, Connie Stradling, tr. from GER. Leffler, Silke, illus. 2013. (ENG.). 120p. (J). (gr. 1-5). 12.95 *(978-1-62087-992-4(1),* 620992, Sky Pony Pr.) Skyhorse Publishing Co., Inc.
Rylant, Cynthia. The Wonderful Happens. Dowley, Coco, illus. 2003. (ENG.). 40p. (J). (gr. -1-3). pap. 8.99 *(978-0-689-86355-4(1),* Simon & Schuster Bks. For Young Readers) Simon & Schuster Bks. For Young Readers.
Sabel, Lauren. Lies I Live By. 2016. 432p. (YA). (gr. 8). 17.99 *(978-0-06-223198-7(7),* Tegen, Katherine Bks) HarperCollins Pubs.
Saccheri, Josephine. Magic on the Wall, 1 vol. Carrescia, Reid, illus. 2009. 11p. pap. 24.95 *(978-1-61546-374-9(7))* America Star Bks.
Saddlewick, A. B. Monstrous Maud: Freaky Sleepover. Home, Sarah, illus. 2013. (Monstrous Maud Ser.: 3). (ENG.). 128p. (J). (gr. k-2). pap. 6.99 *(978-1-78055-074-9(X))* O'Mara, Michael Bks., Ltd. GBR. Dist: Independent Pubs. Group.
—Monstrous Maud: School Scare. Home, Sarah, illus. 2013. (Monstrous Maud Ser.: 4). (ENG.). 128p. (J). (gr. k-2). pap. 6.99 *(978-1-78055-075-6(8))* O'Mara, Michael Bks., Ltd. GBR. Dist: Independent Pubs. Group.
Sagar, Marie. Cuddly Sam. 2009. 24p. pap. 12.99 *(978-1-4389-9334-8(X))* AuthorHouse.
—Jimmy's Adventures: I'm Bored & Mr. Gray Bat. 2007. 20p. (J). 7.00 *(978-0-8059-7494-2(6))* Dorrance Publishing Co., Inc.
—Pirate Hill. 2008. 17p. pap. 24.95 *(978-1-60610-705-8(4))* America Star Bks.
—Princess Samantha? 2009. 20p. pap. 12.49 *(978-1-4389-5297-0(X))* AuthorHouse.
Sage, Angie. Darke. Zug, Mark, illus. (Septimus Heap Ser.: 6). 656p. (J). (gr. 4). 2012. (ENG.). pap. 7.99 *(978-0-06-124244-1(6))* 2011. lib. bdg. 18.89 *(978-0-06-124243-4(8))*Bk. 6. 2011. (ENG.). 17.99 *(978-0-06-124242-7(X))* HarperCollins Pubs. (Tegen, Katherine Bks).
—Darke, 12 vols. (Septimus Heap Ser.: 6). (J). 297.75 *(978-1-4498-6217-6(9));* 1.25 *(978-1-4498-6226-8(8));* 131.75 *(978-1-4498-6218-3(7));* 2013. 92.75 *(978-1-4498-6225-1(X));* 2011. 133.75 *(978-1-4498-6220-6(9));* 2011. 131.75 *(978-1-4498-6222-0(5))* Recorded Bks., Inc.
—Darke. Zug, Mark, illus. 2012. (Septimus Heap Ser.: 6). (J). lib. bdg. 18.40 *(978-0-606-26264-4(4),* Turtleback) Turtleback Bks.
—Flyte. Zug, Mark, illus. (Septimus Heap Ser.: 2). (ENG.). 544p. (J). (gr. 4-7). 2007. pap. 7.99 *(978-0-06-057736-0(3))* 2006. 17.99 *(978-0-06-057734-6(7))* HarperCollins Pubs. (Tegen, Katherine Bks).
—Flyte. (Septimus Heap Ser.: 2). (J). 2009. 84.49 *(978-1-4361-5831-2(1))* 2008. 1.25 *(978-1-4193-9383-9(9))* 2006. 114.75 *(978-1-4193-9386-0(3))* 2006. 133.75 *(978-1-4193-9390-7(1))* 2006. 282.75 *(978-1-4193-9387-7(1))* 2006. 111.75 *(978-1-4193-9388-4(X))* 2006. 131.75 *(978-1-4193-9392-1(8))* Recorded Bks., Inc.
—Fyre. Zug, Mark, illus. 2013. (J). (Septimus Heap Ser.: 7). (ENG.). 720p. (gr. 3-7). 17.99 *(978-0-06-124245-8(4),* Tegen, Katherine Bks); 702p. *(978-0-06-224697-4(6))* HarperCollins Pubs.
—Fyre. 2014. (Septimus Heap Ser.: 7). (J). lib. bdg. 18.40 *(978-0-606-35067-9(5),* Turtleback) Turtleback Bks.
—Magyk. Zug, Mark, illus. (Septimus Heap Ser.: 1). (J). (gr. 4-18). 2005. (ENG.). 576p. 17.99 *(978-0-06-057731-5(2))* 2005. 576p. lib. bdg. 18.89 *(978-0-06-057732-2(0))* 2006.

(ENG.). 608p. reprint ed. pap. 7.99 (978-0-06-057733-9(9)) HarperCollins Pubs. (Tegen, Katherine Bks).

—Magyk. Zug, Mark, illus. 2007. (Septimus Heap Ser.: Bk. 1). 564p. (gr. 4-7). 18.00 (978-0-7569-7760-3(6)) Perfection Learning Corp.

—Magyk. (Septimus Heap Ser.: 1). (J). 2008. 79.75 (978-1-4361-0584-2(6)) 2007. 1.25 (978-1-4193-2619-6(8)) 2006. 123.75 (978-1-4193-3807-6(2)) 2005. 106.75 (978-1-4193-2622-6(8)) 2005. 126.75 (978-1-4193-3805-2(6)) 2005. 103.75 (978-1-4193-2624-0(4)) Recorded Bks., Inc.

—Magyk. 2006. (Septimus Heap Ser.: 1). (J). lib. bdg. 18.40 (978-1-4177-3321-7(7), Turtleback) Turtleback Bks.

—The Magykal Papers. Zug, Mark, illus. 2009. (Septimus Heap Ser.). (ENG.). 176p. (J). (gr. 3-7). 17.99 (978-0-06-170416-1(4), Tegen, Katherine Bks) HarperCollins Pubs.

—Pathfinder. 2015. (Septimus Heap: TodHunter Moon Ser.: 1). (J). lib. bdg. 18.40 (978-0-606-37612-9(7)) Turtleback Bks.

—Physik. Zug, Mark, illus. (Septimus Heap Ser.: 3). (ENG.). (J). (gr. 4-7). 2007. 560p. 17.99 (978-0-06-057737-7(1))Bk. 3. 2008. 576p. pap. 7.99 (978-0-06-057739-1(8)) HarperCollins Pubs. (Tegen, Katherine Bks).

—Physik, 11 vols. 2007. (Septimus Heap Ser.: 3). (J). 113.75 (978-1-4281-4576-4(1)); (SPA.). 131.75 (978-1-4281-4582-5(6)); 133.75 (978-1-4281-4580-1(X)); 111.75 (978-1-4281-4578-8(8)); 1.25 (978-1-4281-4573-3(7)); 277.75 (978-1-4281-4577-1(X)) Recorded Bks., Inc.

—Physik. 2008. (Septimus Heap Ser.: 3). (J). lib. bdg. 18.40 (978-1-4178-1565-4(5), Turtleback) Turtleback Bks.

—Queste. Zug, Mark, illus. (Septimus Heap Ser.: 4). (ENG.). (J). (gr. 4). 2009. 624p. pap. 7.99 (978-0-06-088209-9(3)) 2008. 608p. 17.99 (978-0-06-088207-5(7)) HarperCollins Pubs. (Tegen, Katherine Bks).

—Queste. Zug, Mark, illus. 2009. (Septimus Heap Ser.: 4). 596p. (J). lib. bdg. 18.40 (978-0-606-02607-9(X), Turtleback) Turtleback Bks.

—Sandrider. 2015. (World of Septimus Heap Ser.: 2). (ENG., Illus.). 480p. (J). (gr. 3-7). 17.99 (978-0-06-227248-5(9), Tegen, Katherine Bks) HarperCollins Pubs.

—Septimus Heap, Set. Zug, Mark, illus. 2007. (Septimus Heap Ser.: Bks. 1-2). (J). (gr. 4). pap. 15.99 (978-0-06-136195-1(X), Tegen, Katherine Bks) HarperCollins Pubs.

—Septimus Heap - Todhunter Moon. Zug, Mark, illus. 2014. (World of Septimus Heap Ser.: 1). (ENG.). 480p. (J). (gr. 3-7). 17.99 (978-0-06-227245-4(4), Tegen, Katherine Bks) HarperCollins Pubs.

—Syren. Zug, Mark, illus. (Septimus Heap Ser.: 5). (J). (gr. 4). 2011. (ENG.). 656p. pap. 7.99 (978-0-06-088212-9(3)) 2009. 640p. lib. bdg. 18.89 (978-0-06-088211-2(5)) 2009. (ENG.). 640p. 17.99 (978-0-06-088210-5(7)) HarperCollins Pubs. (Tegen, Katherine Bks).

—Todhunter Moon. Zug, Mark, illus. 2015. (World of Septimus Heap Ser.: 1). (ENG.). 496p. (J). (gr. 3-7). pap. 7.99 (978-0-06-227246-1(2), Tegen, Katherine Bks) HarperCollins Pubs.

—Todhunter Moon: Sandrider. Zug, Mark, illus. 2016. (Septimus Heap: TodHunter Moon Ser.: 2). (ENG.). 496p. (J). (gr. 3-7). 18.40 (978-0-606-39255-6(6)) Turtleback Bks.

—Todhunter Moon: Starchaser. Zug, Mark, illus. 2016. (World of Septimus Heap Ser.: 3). 496p. (J). (gr. 3-7). 17.99 (978-0-06-227251-5(9), Tegen, Katherine Bks) HarperCollins Pubs.

—TodHunter Moon, Book Three: StarChaser. Zug, Mark, illus. 2017. (World of Septimus Heap Ser.: 3). 496p. (J). (gr. 3-7). pap. 7.99 **(978-0-06-227252-2(7)**, Tegen, Katherine Bks) HarperCollins Pubs.

Sage, Angie. Vampire Brat. Pickering, Jimmy, illus. 2009. (Araminta Spookie Ser.: 4). (ENG.). 224p. (J). (gr. 2-5). pap. 6.99 (978-0-06-077492-9(4), Tegen, Katherine Bks) HarperCollins Pubs.

Saha, Tulika. 'Kosho & Sid on the Rainbow' 2014. 22p. pap. 13.99 (978-1-4828-1762-1(4)) Partridge Pub.

Saki. Gabriel-Ernest & Other Tales. Blake, Quentin, illus. 2015. (ENG.). 128p. (J). pap. 9.99 **(978-1-84749-592-1(3)**, 9781847495921, Alma Classics) Bloomsbury Publishing USA.

Salazar, L. J. Chin & the Magic Stones: Book One - Becoming Guardians. 2009. 108p. 20.95 (978-0-595-63627-3(6)); pap. 10.95 (978-0-595-53157-8(1)) iUniverse, Inc.

Salemi, Dianne K. The Inquisitor's Mark. 2015. (Eighth Day Ser.: 2). (ENG.). 352p. (J). (gr. 3-7). 16.99 (978-0-06-227218-8(7)) HarperCollins Pubs.

Salisbury, Melinda. The Sin Eater's Daughter. 2015. (ENG.). 320p. (J). (gr. 9). 17.99 (978-0-545-81062-3(0), Scholastic Pr.) Scholastic, Inc.

Salmon, Nina. Nola & the Sprickle. 2012. 232p. pap. (978-1-78148-137-0(7)) Grosvenor Hse. Publishing Ltd.

Salti, Kim. Riley's Imagination Super Highway - Adventures in Dreamworld. 2012. 56p. pap. 12.00 (978-1-105-81460-0(2)) Lulu Pr., Inc.

Salvatore, R. A. Road of the Patriarch. 2007. (Sellswords Ser.: Bk. 3). (ENG., Illus.). 384p. mass mkt. 7.99 (978-0-7869-4277-0(0), Wizards of the Coast) Wizards of the Coast.

Sammarco, Teresa "T". The What If Book. Curley, Carol, illus. 2013. (J). lib. bdg. 16.95 (978-1-59598-236-0(1)) HenschelHAUS Publishing.

Sammartino, Joseph & Ozimkowski, Edward. The Legend of Kringle. 2009. 48p. pap. 19.95 (978-1-4490-5241-6(X)) AuthorHouse.

Sampson, Fay. The Sorcerer's Daughter. 2007. (ENG.). 224p. (J). (gr. 4-7). per. 9.95 (978-0-7459-6072-2(3)) Lion Hudson PLC GBR. Dist: Independent Pubs. Group.

Samuels, Vallerie. The Village of Time. 2005. 9.00 (978-0-8059-9709-5(1)) Dorrance Publishing Co., Inc.

Sánchez, Juanvi. Cinco. (SPA.). 16p. (J). (978-84-348-7183-0(1)) SM Ediciones ESP. Dist: Lectorum Pubns., Inc.

—Cuatro. (SPA.). 16p. (J). (978-84-348-7182-3(3)) SM Ediciones ESP. Dist: Lectorum Pubns., Inc.

Sánchez, Juanvi & Sánchez, Juanvi. Un Dos Con Lunares. (SPA.). 16p. (J). (978-84-348-7180-9(7)) SM Ediciones ESP. Dist: Lectorum Pubns., Inc.

—El Tres de Lunares. (SPA.). 16p. (J). (978-84-348-7181-6(5)) SM Ediciones ESP. Dist: Lectorum Pubns., Inc.

—Uno. (SPA.). 16p. (J). (978-84-348-7179-3(3)) SM Ediciones ESP. Dist: Lectorum Pubns., Inc.

Sanders, Ted. The Keepers #2: the Harp & the Ravenvine. Bruno, Iacopo, illus. 2017. (Keepers Ser.: 2). 688p. (J). (gr. 3-7). pap. 7.99 (978-0-06-227586-8(0)) HarperCollins Pubs.

Sanders, Ted. The Keepers #3: the Portal & the Veil. 2017. (Keepers Ser.: 3). 592p. (J). (gr. 3-7). 16.99 **(978-0-06-227588-2(7))** HarperCollins Pubs.

Sanderson, Brandon. Alcatraz Versus the Evil Librarians. Lazo, Hayley, illus. 2016. (Alcatraz Versus the Evil Librarians Ser.: 1). (ENG.). 320p. (J). 16.99 (978-0-7653-7894-1(9), 9780765378941, Starscape) Doherty, Tom Assocs., LLC.

—Alcatraz Versus the Knights of Crystallia. 2016. (Alcatraz Versus the Evil Librarians Ser.: 3). (ENG.). 320p. (J). 16.99 (978-0-7653-7898-9(1), 9780765378989, Starscape) Doherty, Tom Assocs., LLC.

—Alcatraz Versus the Shattered Lens. 2016. (Alcatraz Versus the Evil Librarians Ser.: 4). (ENG.). 336p. (J). 16.99 (978-0-7653-7900-9(7), 9780765379009, Starscape) Doherty, Tom Assocs., LLC.

—Calamity. 2017. (Reckoners Ser.). (ENG.). 448p. (YA). (gr. 7). pap. 10.99 (978-0-385-74361-7(0), Ember) Random Hse. Children's Bks.

—The Hero of Ages, 3 vols. 2014. (Mistborn Ser.: 3). (ENG.). 768p. (YA). (gr. 8-12). pap. 12.99 (978-0-7653-7715-9(2), 9780765377159, Tor Teen) Doherty, Tom Assocs., LLC.

—The Rithmatist. McSweeney, Ben, illus. 2014. (ENG.). 384p. (YA). (gr. 7). pap. 10.99 (978-0-7653-3844-0(0), 9780765338440, Tor Teen) Doherty, Tom Assocs., LLC.

—The Rithmatist. 2013. (ENG., Illus.). 384p. (YA). (gr. 7). 17.99 (978-0-7653-2032-2(0), 9780765320322, Tor Teen) Doherty, Tom Assocs., LLC.

—The Rithmatist. 2014. (YA). lib. bdg. 22.10 (978-0-606-38512-1(6)) Turtleback Bks.

—The Scrivener's Bones. 2016. (Alcatraz Versus the Evil Librarians Ser.: 2). (ENG.). 368p. (J). 16.99 (978-0-7653-7896-5(5), 9780765378965, Starscape) Doherty, Tom Assocs., LLC.

Sandrey, Alexander & Sellers, Carolyn. Cold Weather Bro's Arctic Adventure. 2012. 36p. 17.95 (978-1-4575-1701-3(9)) Dog Ear Publishing, LLC.

Sands, Kathryn N. Billy's Big Adventure. 2012. 32p. pap. 24.95 (978-1-4626-2327-3(1)) America Star Bks.

Sanjo, Riku. Beet the Vandel Buster, Vol. 1. Inada, Koji, illus. 2004. (ENG.). 200p. pap. 7.99 (978-1-59116-690-0(X)) Viz Media.

Sanschagrin, Joceline. Le Visage Masqué. Brignaud, Pierre, illus. 2004. (Mon Roman Ser.). (FRE.). 160p. (J). (gr. 2). pap. (978-2-89021-651-8(9)) Diffusion du livre Mirabel (DLM).

Santan. Good & Evil: The Princess & Devil. 2011. (Illus.). 64p. pap. 25.80 (978-1-4567-9683-9(6)) AuthorHouse.

Santaniello, Shelly W. Tommy's Needham Rocket. 2011. 53p. pap. 10.95 (978-1-4327-7000-6(4)) Outskirts Pr., Inc.

Sargent, Daina. Arkansas: Dream Big. Lenoir, Jane, illus. l.t. ed. 2004. (Double Trouble Ser.). 48p. (J). pap. 10.95 (978-1-59381-123-5(3)); lib. bdg. (978-1-59381-122-8(5)) Ozark Publishing.

Sargent, Dave & Sargent, Pat. Bo Bo's Big Imagination/la Gran Imaginacion de Bo Bo, 10 vols., Vol. 13. Robinson, Laura, illus. 2004. (Learn to Read Ser.: 10). (ENG & SPA.). 18p. (J). pap. 10.95 (978-1-56763-986-5(0)) Ozark Publishing.

Sarrasin, Alex. The Guardians of Neoegypti: Book One. 2007. 300p. per. 18.95 (978-0-595-45710-6(X)) iUniverse, Inc.

Sassone, Richard. Galangous. Sassone, Richard, illus. 2009. (Illus.). 62p. pap. 14.95 (978-1-936051-14-4(1)) Peppertree Pr., The.

Sastrias, Marta. Cuentos de Todo y de Nada. Martinez y Luis San Vicente, Enrique, illus. 2003. (SPA.). 82p. (J). (gr. 3-5). (978-968-19-0551-4(2)) Aguilar, Altea, Taurus, Alfaguara, S.A. de C.V.

Sataram, Nikita. Zatheria: The Hidden Realm. 2013. 194p. (gr. -1). 24.77 (978-1-4907-0938-3(X)); pap. 14.77 (978-1-4907-0936-9(3)) Trafford Publishing.

Satou, Tsutomu. Nine School Competition Arc II. 2017. (Irregular at Magic High School Ser.: 4). (ENG., Illus.). 336p. (gr. 8-17). pap. 14.00 (978-0-316-39031-6(3), Yen Pr.) Orbit.

Saugstad, Edward. Oakee Doakee & the Hate Wave. 2008. 88p. pap. 18.95 (978-0-9551503-6-4(1)) Checkpoint Pr. IRL. Dist: Printondemand-worldwide.com.

Saunders, Catherine. The Legendary Yoda. 2013. (Star Wars DK Readers Level 3 Ser.). lib. bdg. 13.55 (978-0-606-31479-4(2), Turtleback) Turtleback Bks.

Saunders, George. The Very Persistent Gappers of Frip. 2008. (ENG.). 88p. pap. 8.50 (978-1-58342-557-2(8)) Dramatic Publishing Co.

—The Very Persistent Gappers of Frip. Smith, Lane, illus. 2015. (ENG.). 96p. 22.00 (978-0-8129-8963-2(5), Random House) Random House Publishing Group.

Saunders, George P. The Last Elf. 2007. 180p. per. 13.95 (978-0-595-40843-6(5)) iUniverse, Inc.

Saunders, Kate. The Little Secret. Carman, William, illus. 2012. (ENG.). 240p. (J). (gr. 3-6). pap. 10.99 (978-0-312-67427-4(9), 9780312674274) Square Fish.

Sautereau, Francois. La Extrana Navidad de Jonas.Tr. of Jonas's Extraordinary Christmas. (SPA.). 92p. (YA). (gr. 5-8). (978-84-279-3163-3(8), NG3472) Noguer y Caralt Editores, S. A. ESP. Dist: Lectorum Pubns., Inc.

Savage, J. Scott. Air Keep. 2013. (Farworld Ser.: Bk. 3). 19.99 (978-1-60907-325-1(8), Shadow Mountain) Shadow Mountain Publishing.

—Gears of Revolution. 2016. (Mysteries of Cove Ser.: 2). 342p. (J). 17.99 (978-1-62972-223-8(5), Shadow Mountain) Deseret Bk. Co.

—Land Keep. (Farworld Ser.: 2). (gr. 5). 2013. (ENG., Illus.). 384p. (J). pap. 9.99 (978-1-60907-331-2(2)) 2009. 432p. (YA). 18.95 (978-1-60641-164-3(0)) Shadow Mountain Publishing. (Shadow Mountain).

—Water Keep. 2013. (Farworld Ser.: 1). (ENG., Illus.). 432p. (J). (gr. 5). pap. 12.99 (978-1-60907-330-5(4), Shadow Mountain) Shadow Mountain Publishing.

Saveley, Barb. Curse of Moonstone Island. 2009. (Illus.). 36p. pap. 16.99 (978-1-4389-4938-3(3)) AuthorHouse.

—Dusky: The Lost Unicorn. 2008. 24p. pap. 24.95 (978-1-60441-909-2(1)) America Star Bks.

—Dusky II: Journey of Tears. 2010. 40p. 18.95 (978-1-4389-8243-4(7)) AuthorHouse.

Savoy, Simona. The Faerwald's Secret, 1 vol. 2010. 218p. pap. 24.95 (978-1-4512-9417-0(4)) PublishAmerica, Inc.

Saxon, Lucy. Take Back the Skies. 2014. (ENG.). 384p. (YA). (gr. 7). 17.99 (978-1-61963-367-4(1), 9781619633674, Bloomsbury USA Childrens) Bloomsbury Publishing USA.

Sazaklis, John. Deep-Sea Duel, 1 vol. Baltazar, Art, illus. 2012. (DC Super-Pets Ser.). (ENG.). 56p. (gr. 2-2). pap. 4.95 (978-1-4048-7662-0(6)); lib. bdg. 23.99 (978-1-4048-6489-4(X)) Picture Window Bks. (DC Super-Pets).

—Swamp Thing vs the Zombie Pets, 1 vol. Baltazar, Art, illus. 2012. (DC Super-Pets Ser.). (ENG.). 56p. (gr. 2-2). pap. 4.95 (978-1-4048-7667-5(7)); lib. bdg. 23.99 (978-1-4048-6491-7(1)) Picture Window Bks. (DC Super-Pets).

Sazaklis, John. Thunder Strike! (Marvel: Thor) Spaziante, Patrick, illus. 2017. (Little Golden Book Ser.). (ENG.). 24p. (J). (-k). 4.99 **(978-1-5247-1730-8(4)**, Golden Bks.) Random Hse. Children's Bks.

Sazaklis, John & Foxe, Steve. Justice League: Versus. 2015. (ENG.). 48p. (J). (gr. 3-7). pap. 8.99 (978-0-545-89062-5(4)) Scholastic, Inc.

Scarry, Janet. The Land of Whodunnit. 2013. 22p. pap. 11.99 (978-1-62839-326-2(2)) Salem Author Services.

Schachner, Judy. Up, up, & Away! 2009. (Skippyjon Jones Ser.). (ENG.). 16p. (J). (gr. -1-k). pap. 5.99 (978-0-448-45082-7(8), Grosset & Dunlap) Penguin Young Readers Group.

Schaefer, Elizabeth. The Force Awakens. White, Dave, illus. 2016. (Lego Star Wars Ser.). (ENG.). 24p. (J). (gr. -1-3). pap. 3.99 (978-0-545-94072-6(9)) Scholastic, Inc.

Schaffer, Jacqueline. Porsha & the Great Snowmen Adventure. 2009. 36p. pap. 15.99 (978-1-4490-5421-2(8)) AuthorHouse.

Scharf, J. L. Grace & the Ice Prince: The Diamond Heart Quest. 2006. (ENG.). 262p. (J). per. 16.95 (978-1-897235-09-6(7)) Thistledown Pr., Ltd. CAN. Dist: Univ. of Toronto Pr.

Schemery, Beau. The Unlikely Hero. 2016. (ENG., Illus.). (J). 24.99 **(978-1-63477-979-1(7))** 2013. 160p. pap. 14.99 (978-1-62380-451-0(5)) Dreamspinner Pr. (Harmony Ink Pr.).

Scherer, Donovan Harold. Fear & Sunshine. Scherer, Donovan Harold, illus. 2009. (Illus.). 248p. (J). pap. 14.95 (978-0-9841746-1-4(3)) Studio Moonfall.

Schmidt, Gary D. What Came from the Stars. 2014. (ENG.). 304p. (J). (gr. 5-7). pap. 6.99 (978-0-544-33636-0(4), HMH Books For Young Readers) Houghton Mifflin Harcourt Publishing Co.

Schmidt, Karen, retold by. The Gingerbread Man. 2007. (J). (gr. -1-2). pap. 9.95 incl. audio compact disk (978-0-545-01773-2(4)) Scholastic, Inc.

Scholastic & Howard, Kate. Fright Knight!, Bk. 2. 2016. (LEGO NEXO Knights Ser.). (ENG.). 80p. (J). (gr. 2-5). pap. 4.99 (978-0-545-92555-6(X)) Scholastic, Inc.

Scholastic, et al. Forbidden Power. 2017. (LEGO NEXO Knights Ser.: 1). (ENG.). 192p. (J). (gr. 2-5). 12.99 (978-1-338-04183-5(5)) Scholastic, Inc.

Scholastic, Inc. Staff, contrib. by. Stats & Facts on over 150 Brand-New Pokémon! 2011. (Pokemon Ser.). (ENG.). 112p. (J). (gr. 2-5). pap., instr.'s hndbk. ed. 7.99 (978-0-545-31652-1(9), Scholastic Paperbacks) Scholastic, Inc.

Scholastic, Inc. Staff & Ameet Studio Staff. NEXO Powers Rule! 2016. (LEGO NEXO Knights Ser.). (ENG.). 32p. (J). (gr. 2-5). pap., act. bk. ed. 8.99 (978-0-545-90584-8(2)) Scholastic, Inc.

Scholastic, Inc. Staff & Schmidt, Rebecca L. The Power of the Fortrex. 2016. (Scholastic Reader, Level 2 Ser.: 1). (ENG.). 32p. (J). (gr. 1-3). pap. 3.99 (978-0-545-93338-4(2)) Scholastic, Inc.

Scholastic, Inc. Staff & West, Tracey. Graduation Day, Bk. 1. 2016. (LEGO NEXO Knights Ser.). (ENG.). 80p. (J). (gr. 2-5). pap. 4.99 (978-0-545-92554-9(1)) Scholastic, Inc.

Scholistic Editors & Rusu, Meredith. Official Guide. 2016. (Yo-Kai Watch Ser.). (ENG.). 128p. (J). (gr. 2-5). pap. 7.99 (978-1-338-05442-2(2)) Scholastic, Inc.

Schow, Betsy. Wanted. 2017. (Storymakers Ser.: 2). (ENG.). 320p. (YA). (gr. 6-12). pap. 10.99 (978-1-4926-3599-4(5), 9781492635994) Sourcebooks, Inc.

Schram, Kristina. The Chronicles of Anaedor. 2010. 416p. pap. 9.95 (978-1-935142-10-2(0)) Variance Publishing, LLC.

—The Chronicles of Anaedor: The Lost Ones. 2013. 442p. pap. 15.99 (978-0-9884774-5-2(9)) Hive Collective.

—The Chronicles of Anaedor: The Uprising. 2013. 462p. pap. 15.99 (978-0-9884774-6-9(7)) Hive Collective.

Schrefer, Eliot. Rise & Fall. 2014. (Spirit Animals Ser.: 6). (ENG., Illus.). 192p. (J). (gr. 3-7). 12.99 (978-0-545-52248-9(X)) Scholastic, Inc.

Schuler, Betty Jo. Brainman & Double Trouble Ditto Box. Cummins, Sandy, ed. 2007. (J). pap. (978-1-876962-67-8(4)) Writers Exchange E-Publishing.

Schulz, Charles. Necesito Todos los Amigos Que Pueda Tener. (SPA.). (J). 7.00 (978-84-7655-665-8(9), PI3928) Plaza Joven, S.A. ESP. Dist: Lectorum Pubns., Inc.

Schwab, Victoria. The Archived. 2014. (Archived Ser.). (ENG., Illus.). 352p. (YA). (gr. 7-12). pap. 9.99 (978-1-4231-7108-9(X)) Hyperion Bks. for Children.

—Our Dark Duet. 2018. (Monsters of Verity Ser.: 2). 368p. (YA). (gr. 9). pap. 9.99 **(978-0-06-238089-0(3))** 2017. 528p. pap. **(978-0-06-267203-2(7))** 2017. (Monsters of Verity Ser.: bk.2). (ENG.). 528p. (YA). (gr. 9). 17.99 (978-0-06-238088-3(5)) HarperCollins Pubs. (Greenwillow Bks.).

Schwab, Victoria. This Savage Song. (Monsters of Verity Ser.: 1). (YA). (gr. 9). 2017. 480p. pap. 9.99 (978-0-06-238086-9(9)) 2016. (ENG.). 464p. 17.99 (978-0-06-238085-2(0)) HarperCollins Pubs. (Greenwillow Bks.).

—This Savage Song. 2017. (Monsters of Verity Ser.: 1). lib. bdg. 20.85 **(978-0-606-40071-8(0))** Turtleback Bks.

Schwartz, Alvin. Scary Stories to Tell in the Dark. Helquist, Brett, illus. 2010. (Scary Stories Ser.). (ENG.). 128p. (J). (gr. 4-18). 16.99 (978-0-06-083519-4(2)); pap. 5.99 (978-0-06-083520-0(6)) HarperCollins Pubs.

Schwartz, Alvin. Scary Stories to Tell in the Dark. Gammell, Stephen, illus. 2017. (Scary Stories Ser.: 1). 128p. (J). (gr. 3-7). pap. 6.99 **(978-0-06-268282-6(2))** HarperCollins Pubs.

Schwartz, Bennett L. Khadim & the Wanderers. 2010. 227p. 39.08 (978-0-557-22262-9(1)) Lulu Pr., Inc.

Scieszka, Jon. Baloney (Henry P.) Smith, Lane, illus. 2005. (ENG.). 40p. (J). (gr. k-k). pap. 6.99 (978-0-14-240430-0(6), Puffin Books) Penguin Young Readers Group.

Scieszka, Jon, et al. Guys Read: Heroes & Villains. 2017. (Guys Read Ser.: 7). 288p. (J). (gr. 3-7). pap. 6.99 (978-0-06-238560-4(7), Waldon Pond Pr.) HarperCollins Pubs.

Scott, Eric. The Day the Rainbow Ended. 2013. 90p. pap. 7.99 (978-1-78333-419-3(3)) Acorn Bks.

—The Great Fairytale Robbery. 2013. 102p. pap. 7.99 (978-1-78333-400-1(2)) Acorn Bks.

—The Island of Lost Dolls. 2013. 86p. pap. 7.99 (978-1-78333-403-2(7)) Acorn Bks.

Scott, Gwen. In Between the Cracks: The Search for Zar. 2013. 20p. pap. 16.95 (978-1-63000-080-6(9)) America Star Bks.

Scott, Jeff. The Discovery of Monkey Island. 2008. 64p. pap. 19.95 (978-1-60610-921-2(9)) America Star Bks.

Scott, Luke. Through a Crystal Doorknob. 2012. 88p. 24.95 (978-1-4626-9420-4(9)) America Star Bks.

Scott, Michael. The Sorceress. 2009. (Secrets of the Immortal Nicholas Flamel Ser.: Bk. 3). (ENG.). 512p. (YA). (gr. 7-18). 17.99 (978-0-385-73529-2(4), Delacorte Bks. for Young Readers) Random Hse. Children's Bks.

Scott, Molly. Broken Bones Are No Fun, but Broken Bones Won't Stop My Play! Baker, David, illus. 2012. 32p. pap. 24.95 (978-1-4626-7424-4(0)) America Star Bks.

Scott, Stephen K. Grunions with Onions: A Children's Food Fantasy. 2011. 36p. pap. 16.99 (978-1-4634-4550-8(4)) AuthorHouse.

Seagull, Robert. The Adventure to Septumus Sevusere & the Magic Glowing Rings. 2013. 60p. pap. 7.00 (978-1-927558-43-0(3)) Birch Tree Publishing.

Sealey, Philip. The Sorcerer's Tome. 2013. 254p. pap. (978-1-78407-199-8(4)) FeedARead.com.

Sealls, Arthur. The Three Little Heroes: Book One of Kirk, Chelsea, & Samantha's Adventures. 2007. 84p. per. 8.95 (978-0-595-44083-2(5)) iUniverse, Inc.

Seaman, John E. The Captain's Secret: A Lost Boy's Odyssey in Old New York. 2008. 220p. pap. 15.95 (978-0-595-51753-4(6)) iUniverse, Inc.

Seamus. The Company of the Flaming Sword: Buried Treasure. 2016. (ENG.). 152p. (J). (gr. -1-12). pap. 11.95 (978-1-78535-275-1(X), Our Street Bks.) Hunt, John Publishing Ltd. GBR. Dist: National Bk. Network.

Sears, Cynthia A. The Dragon Lord: The Fairy Princess Chronicles - Book 2. 2013. 376p. (978-1-4602-3081-7(7)) FriesenPress.

Seda, Gus. Prohex the Cat. 2012. 44p. pap. 24.95 (978-1-4626-7704-7(5)) America Star Bks.

Seeger, K R. Asa-Birdie Corn. 2007. 244p. 26.95 (978-0-595-69522-5(1)); per. 16.95 (978-0-595-45553-9(0)) iUniverse, Inc.

Seeley, Tim, et al. Rebirth, Vol. 4. 2013. (ENG., Illus.). 160p. (YA). pap. 16.99 (978-1-60706-800-6(1), 9781607068006) Image Comics.

Seever, Berni. A Supernatural Tale. 2007. 62p. pap. 20.00 (978-1-4196-7788-5(8)) CreateSpace Independent Publishing Platform.

Seiss, Ellie & Random House Staff. Dora & the Unicorn King. 2013. (Dora the Explorer Step into Reading Ser.). lib. bdg. 13.55 (978-0-606-32415-1(1), Turtleback) Turtleback Bks.

Selfors, Suzanne. The Fairy Swarm. Santat, Dan, illus. 2016. (Imaginary Veterinary Ser.: 6). (ENG.). 240p. (J). (gr. 2-7). pap. 7.99 (978-0-316-28692-3(3)) Little, Brown Bks. for Young Readers.

—To Catch a Mermaid. 2009. (ENG.). 272p. (J). (gr. 3-7). pap. 8.00 (978-0-316-01817-3(1)) Little, Brown Bks. for Young Readers.

Sellaro, Brendan. Space Santa Holiday Hero. 2012. (ENG., Illus.). 32p. (J). 16.95 (978-0-938467-60-1(3)) Headline Bks., Inc.

Sempebwa, Christina. Tales of Zindan. 2012. 154p. pap. (978-1-908895-48-6(9)) FeedARead.com.

Sendak, Maurice. In the Night Kitchen. 2009. (Illus.). 19.00 (978-0-7569-9298-9(2)) Perfection Learning Corp.

—Where the Wild Things Are. Sendak, Maurice, illus. 25th anniv. ed. 2012. (ENG., Illus.). 48p. (J). (gr. -1-3). 18.95 (978-0-06-025492-6(0)); pap. 8.95 (978-0-06-443178-1(9)) HarperCollins Pubs.

—Where the Wild Things Are. 2010. (HEB., Illus.). 38p. (J). (978-965-07-1793-3(5)) Keter Publishing Hse.

—Where the Wild Things Are. (J). pap. 12.95 incl. audio Weston Woods Studios, Inc.

Senior, Patricia. Mischief on Mumpit Mountain. 2009. 36p. pap. 14.75 (978-1-60693-661-0(1), Eloquent Bks.) Strategic Book Publishing & Rights Agency (SBPRA).

Sensel, Joni. The Farwalker's Quest. (ENG.). 384p. (YA). (gr. 3-6). 2010. pap. 7.99 (978-1-59990-450-4(0), 9781599904504) 2009. 16.99 (978-1-59990-272-2(9), 9781599902722) Bloomsbury Publishing USA. (Bloomsbury USA Childrens).

Sesso, Karen A. Off They Swam, 1 vol. 2009. 37p. pap. 19.95 (978-1-61546-453-1(0)) PublishAmerica, Inc.

Seuss, Dr. The Big Orange Book of Beginner Books. 2015. (Beginner Books(R) Ser.). (ENG., Illus.). 240p. (J). (gr. -1-2). 16.99 (978-0-553-52425-3(9), Random Hse. Bks. for Young Readers) Random Hse. Children's Bks.

—The Cat in the Hat. 2012. (Beginner Books(R) Ser.). (ENG.). 72p. (J). (gr. k-3). 17.99 (978-0-449-81086-6(0), Random Hse. Bks. for Young Readers) Random Hse. Children's Bks.

—The Cat in the Hat Book & Hat. 2012. (Beginner Books Ser.). (ENG.). 72p. (J). (gr. k-3). 24.99 (978-0-307-93044-6(0), Random Hse. Bks. for Young Readers) Random Hse. Children's Bks.

—Fox in Socks: Dr. Seuss's Book of Tongue Tanglers. 2011. (Bright & Early Board Books Ser.). (ENG., Illus.). 24p. (J). (gr. k-1). bds. 4.99 (978-0-307-93180-1(3), Random Hse. Bks. for Young Readers) Random Hse. Children's Bks.

—Horton Hears a Who Pop-Up! 2008. (ENG., Illus.). 22p. (J). (gr. k-12). 25.99 (978-0-375-84194-1(6), Robin Corey Bks.) Random Hse. Children's Bks.

—Oh, the Thinks You Can Think! (Big Bright & Early Board Book Ser.). (ENG., Illus.). 24p. (J). (-k). 2014. bds. 6.99 (978-0-385-38713-2(X)) 2009. bds. 4.99 (978-0-375-85794-2(X)) Random Hse. Children's Bks. (Random Hse. Bks. for Young Readers).

Seven, John. The Time-Tripping Faradays, 1 vol. Phillips, Craig, illus. 2014. (Time-Tripping Faradays Ser.). (ENG.). 160p. (gr. 4-5). 53.30 (978-1-4342-9473-9(0)) Stone Arch Bks.

Sewell, Byron W. Alix's Adventures in Wonderland: Lewis Carroll's Nightmare. 2011. (Illus.). 130p. pap. (978-1-904808-72-5(7)) Evertype.

—Snarkmaster: A Destiny in Eight Fits. a Tale Inspired by Lewis Carroll's the Hunting of the Snark. Sewell, Byron W., illus. 2012. (Illus.). 138p. pap. (978-1-78201-002-9(5)) Evertype.

Sewell, Byron W. & Carroll, Lewis. Álbok's Adventures in Goatland. 2011. (Illus.). 140p. pap. (978-1-904808-76-3(X)) Evertype.

Sewell, Byron W. & Everson, Michael. Alice's Bad Hair Day in Wonderland: A Tangled Tale. 2013. (Illus.). 112p. pap. (978-1-78201-009-8(2)) Evertype.

Sexton, Shirley. Fairy with an Attitude. 2009. 142p. 22.50 (978-1-60860-616-0(3), Strategic Bk. Publishing) Strategic Book Publishing & Rights Agency (SBPRA).

SFX Fantasy. Tween Tales - Robots, Dragons & the Interworld Machine. 2007. 131p. pap. 12.99 (978-1-4303-2546-8(1)) Lulu Pr., Inc.

Shaffer, Jan. A Summoning Stone Book Two: Vision Caster. 2009. 96p. pap. 9.00 (978-0-557-06040-5(0)) Lulu Pr., Inc.

Shah, Idries. Neem el Media Nino. Wirkala, Rita, tr. Mori, Midori & Revels, Robert, illus. 2007. 32p. (J). 18.00 (978-1-883536-96-1(0)); pap. 7.99 (978-1-883536-97-8(9)) I S H K. (Hoopoe Bks.).

—Neem the Half-Boy. Mori, Midori & Revels, Robert, illus. 2007. 32p. (J). (gr. -1). pap. 7.99 (978-1-883536-95-4(2), Hoopoe Bks.) I S H K.

Shah, Yasmin. Abby & the Feather Quest. 2010. (Illus.). 48p. pap. 10.49 (978-1-4343-9839-0(0)) AuthorHouse.

Shahan, Sherry. Fountain of Weird. 2003. (ENG., Illus.). 128p. (J). mass mkt. 6.99 (978-0-330-37072-1(3), Pan) Pan Macmillan GBR. Dist: Trafalgar Square Publishing.

Shakespeare, William. A Midsummer Night's Dream. Bryant, Clive, ed. Nicholson, Kat & Cardy, Jason, illus. 2012. (ENG.). 144p. (gr. 6). lib. bdg. 24.95 (978-1-907127-44-1(5)) Classical Comics GBR. Dist: Publishers Group West (PGW).

Shalant, Phyllis. When Pirates Came to Brooklyn. 2010. 224p. pap. 14.95 (978-1-4401-8338-6(4)) iUniverse, Inc.

Shan, Darren, pseud. Bec. 2008. (ENG.). 256p. (YA). (gr. 10-17). pap. 10.00 (978-0-316-01390-1(0)) Little, Brown Bks. for Young Readers.

—The Thin Executioner. 2011. (ENG.). 512p. (YA). (gr. 10-17). pap. 10.99 (978-0-316-07864-1(6)) Little, Brown Bks. for Young Readers.

—Vampire Mountain. Vol. 4. 2010. (Cirque du Freak, the Manga Ser.: 4). lib. bdg. 24.55 (978-0-606-14433-9(1), Turtleback) Turtleback Bks.

—Wolf Island. 2010. (ENG.). 216p. (YA). (gr. 10-17). pap. 10.00 (978-0-316-04881-1(X)) Little, Brown Bks. for Young Readers.

Shanghai Animation Studio Staff & Tang, Sanmu. Monkey Makes Havoc in Heaven. Xiaozhen, Wu, tr. from CHI. 2010. (Favorite Children's Ser.). (ENG., Illus.). 32p. (J). (gr. -1-3). pap. 5.95 (978-1-60220-974-9(X)) BetterLink Pr., Inc.

—Nezha Conquers the Dragon King. Yawtsong, Lee, tr. from CHI. 2010. (Favorite Children's Ser.). (ENG., Illus.). 32p. (J). (gr. -1-3). pap. 5.95 (978-1-60220-975-6(8)) BetterLink Pr., Inc.

Shankman, Ed. The Bourbon Street Band Is Back. O'Neill, Dave, illus. 2011. (Shankman & O'Neill Ser.). (ENG.). 32p. (gr. -1-3). 14.95 (978-1-933212-79-1(9), Commonwealth Editions) Applewood Bks.

Shannon, David. Alice the Fairy. Shannon, David, illus. 2009. (ENG., Illus.). (J). (gr. -1-k). pap. 9.95 incl. audio compact disk (978-0-545-11758-6(5)) Scholastic, Inc.

Shannon, R. J. Rita Rain & the Shadow Apprentice: Book 1. 2012. 472p. 29.95 (978-1-4626-7390-2(2)) America Star Bks.

Shannon, Ronnie Jay. Samurai Force: the Final Hope: The Junior Novel. 2007. (ENG.). 76p. per. 19.95 (978-1-4241-6528-5(8)) America Star Bks.

Shanower, Eric. Adventures in Oz Volume 1. 2014. (Adventures in Oz Ser.). (ENG., Illus.). 160p. (J). (gr. 2-5). 34.99 (978-1-63140-150-3(5), 9781631401503) Idea & Design Works, LLC.

—The Giant Garden of Oz. 2015. (ENG., Illus.). 192p. (gr. 4). pap. 9.95 (978-0-486-79835-6(6)) Dover Pubns., Inc.

—Wonderful Wizard of Oz: Vol. 3, 1 vol. 2014. (ENG.). 24p. 24.21 (978-1-61479-228-4(3)) ABDO Publishing Co.

Shanower, Eric & Baum, L. Frank. The Marvelous Land of Oz: Adapted from the Novel by L. Frank Baum, 1 vol. Young, Skottie, illus. 2014. (ENG.). 24p. (J). (978-1-61479-238-3(0)) Spotlight.

—The Wonderful Wizard of Oz, 1 vol. Young, Skottie, illus. 2014. (ENG.). 24p. (J). (978-1-61479-229-1(1)) Spotlight.

Sharma, Shivan. The Castle, Dragons & a Cricket Ball. 2009. 76p. pap. (978-1-84549-415-5(6), Swirl) arima publishing.

Sharp, J. L. Persephia. 2009. 73p. pap. 19.95 (978-1-60813-836-4(4)) America Star Bks.

Sharp, Margery. The Rescuers. Williams, Garth, illus. 2016. (ENG.). 160p. (J). (gr. 4-7). pap. 9.99 (978-1-68137-007-1(7), NYRB Kids) New York Review of Bks., Inc., The.

Sharp, Sharon. The Planet Chaos, 1 vol. 2010. 48p. pap. 16.95 (978-1-61546-034-2(9)) America Star Bks.

Sharpe, Gerald. Parade of Lights. Moya, Patricia, illus. 2007. (What Lies Beneath the Bed Ser.). 487p. (J). per. 11.00 (978-1-933894-01-0(6)) IJN Publishing, Inc.

—Tommy's Tales. Moya, Patricia, illus. 2006. (Tommy's Tales Ser.). 300p. (J). per. 7.00 (978-1-933894-00-3(8)) IJN Publishing, Inc.

—What Lies Beneath the Bed: Tommy's Tales (Revised) 2nd rev. ed. 2008. 320p. pap. 7.95 (978-1-933894-04-1(0)) IJN Publishing, Inc.

Sharplin, Emory. Scrap. 2013. 352p. (J). pap. 10.95 (978-1-938416-35-4(X)) River Grove Bks.

Shaughnessy, Adam. The Entirely True Story of the Unbelievable FIB. 2015. (Unbelievable FIB Ser.: 1). (ENG.). 272p. (J). (gr. 3-7). 16.95 (978-1-61620-498-3(2)) Algonquin Bks. of Chapel Hill.

—Over the Underworld. 2016. (Unbelievable FIB Ser.: 2). (ENG.). 304p. (J). (gr. 3-7). 16.95 (978-1-61620-499-0(0)) Algonquin Bks. of Chapel Hill.

—The Trickster's Tale, Bk. 1. 2016. (Unbelievable FIB Ser.: 1). (ENG.). 288p. (J). (gr. 3-7). pap. 6.95 (978-1-61620-637-6(3)) Algonquin Bks. of Chapel Hill.

Shaw, Ellie. Together Again. 2012. 24p. pap. 24.95 (978-1-4626-6427-6(X)) America Star Bks.

Shaw, Esther. The Winter Mare. 2005. (ENG., Illus.). 198p. pap. (978-1-84401-447-7(9)) Athena Pr.

Shaw, Heather. Smallfish Clover. 2007. 368p. (J). pap. 20.00 (978-1-4243-4242-6(2)) Independent Publisher Services.

Shaw, Natalie & Barton, Elizabeth Dennis. The Smurfin' Guide to the Smurfs. 2011. (Smurfs Classic Ser.). (ENG., Illus.). 96p. (J). (gr. 1-5). pap. 5.99 (978-1-4424-2291-9(2), Simon Spotlight) Simon Spotlight.

Shaw, Scott. Shrek - Living Green, Vol. 2. 2012. (ENG.). 52p. pap. 6.95 (978-1-936340-19-4(4), 9781936340194) Ape Entertainment.

Shealy, Dennis & Random House Staff. Heroes United! - Attack of the Robot! Doescher, Erik et al, illus. 2008. (Pictureback(R) Ser.). (ENG.). 32p. (J). (gr. -1-2). pap. 4.99 (978-0-375-84409-6(0), Random Hse. Bks. for Young Readers) Random Hse. Children's Bks.

Sheard, Jean. A Chinese Fantasy - Cave in a Casket. 2007. 128p. 34.95 (978-1-84753-349-4(3)); (Illus.). pap. 10.50 (978-1-84753-249-7(7)) Lulu Pr., Inc.

Shearer, Tony. The Praying Flute: Song of the Earth Mother. rev. ed. 2006. (Illus.). 96p. pap. 16.95 (978-0-87961-268-9(1)) Naturegraph Pubs., Inc.

Sheen, C. D. McKnight. Morphani: And the Valley of the Coloured Doorway's. 2012. 76p. 37.37 (978-1-4691-7680-2(7)); pap. 18.68 (978-1-4691-7679-6(3)) Xlibris Corp.

Shelton, Angela. Tilda Pinkerton's Magical Hats. 2013. 196p. 19.95 (978-0-9859443-8-4(2)) Quiet Owl Bks.

Shepard, Aaron. The Magic Flyswatter: A Superhero Tale of Africa, Retold from the Mwindo Epic. 2008. (Ancient Fantasy Ser.: 3). 44p. (J). pap. 6.00 (978-0-938497-39-4(1)); lib. bdg. 15.00 (978-0-938497-38-7(3)) Shepard Pubns. (Skyhook Pr.).

—The Monkey King: A Superhero Tale of China, Retold from the Journey to the West. 2008. (Ancient Fantasy Ser.: 4). (J). 50p. lib. bdg. 15.00 (978-0-938497-40-0(5)); 44p. lib. bdg. 6.00 (978-0-938497-41-7(3)) Shepard Pubns. (Skyhook Pr.).

—The Mountain of Marvels: A Celtic Tale of Magic, Retold from the Mabinogion. 2007. (Ancient Fantasy Ser.: 1). 46p. (J). pap. 6.00 (978-0-938497-36-3(7)); lib. bdg. 15.00 (978-0-938497-34-9(0)) Shepard Pubns. (Skyhook Pr.).

—The Songs of Power: A Finnish Tale of Magic, Retold from the Kalevala. 2007. (Ancient Fantasy Ser.: 2). 54p. (J). lib. bdg. 15.00 (978-0-938497-35-6(9)); lib. bdg. 6.00 (978-0-938497-37-0(5)) Shepard Pubns. (Skyhook Pr.).

Shepherd, JaiLeen. Anan: Lea's Special Friend — Part II of the Lea Trilogy. 2006. (J). per. 15.95 (978-1-889743-55-4(0)) Robbie Dean Pr.

Shepherd, Megan. The Hunt. 2016. (Cage Ser.: 2). 368p. (YA). (gr. 8). 17.99 (978-0-06-224308-9(X)) HarperCollins Pubs.

Shepherd, Wilf. Behind the Whiskers: Tales for the Young at Heart. 2012. 282p. pap. 28.03 (978-1-4797-0473-6(3)) Xlibris Corp.

Sheppard, Keith. In the Kingdom of the Fair-Eyes. 2013. (Illus.). 212p. pap. (978-1-78201-039-5(4)) Evertype.

—Wonderland Revisited & the Games Alice Played There. 2009. (Illus.). 128p. (gr. 3-7). pap. (978-1-904808-34-3(4)) Evertype.

Sheridan, Luke. Luke & His Amazing Space Bed. McCartney, Jen, illus. 2010. (ENG.). 32p. (J). (gr. -1-3). 17.95 (978-0-9814536-6-8(X), Cambridge House Pr.) Sterling & Ross Pubs.

Sherman, Delia. The Evil Wizard Smallbone. 2016. (ENG.). 416p. (J). (gr. 3-7). 17.99 (978-0-7636-8805-9(3)) Candlewick Pr.

Sherman, Susan & Poryes, Michael. That's So Raven, 2 vols., Vol. 1. 2004. (Illus.). 192p. pap. 14.99 (978-1-59182-806-8(6), Tokyopop Kids) TOKYOPOP, Inc.

Shetterly, Will. Elsewhere. 2004. (ENG.). 264p. (YA). (gr. 9-12). pap. 14.99 (978-0-15-205209-6(7)) Houghton Mifflin Harcourt Publishing Co.

—Nevernever. 2004. (ENG.). 240p. (YA). (gr. 9-12). pap. 14.95 (978-0-15-205210-2(0)) Houghton Mifflin Harcourt Publishing Co.

Shi, Charleston. The Quest of the Phoenix: Book Two, Storm of the Kraken. 2010. 180p. pap. 14.95 (978-1-60844-352-9(3)) Dog Ear Publishing, LLC.

Shickman, Allan Richard. Zan-Gah: A Prehistoric Adventure. 2007. 160p. (J). (gr. 4-7). per. 9.95 (978-0-9790357-0-8(8)) Earthshaker Bks.

Shields, Breeana. Poison's Kiss. 2017. (Serpent's Promise Ser.). (ENG.). 304p. (YA). (gr. 7). 17.99 (978-1-101-93782-2(3), Random Hse. Bks. for Young Readers) Random Hse. Children's Bks.

Shinn, Sharon. The Dream-Maker's Magic. 2008. (ENG.). 288p. (YA). (gr. 7-18). pap. 8.99 (978-0-14-241096-7(9), Speak) Penguin Young Readers Group.

Shipton, Paul. The Games Player of Zob. McCafferty, Jan, illus. 2007. (Collins Big Cat Ser.). (ENG.). 1p. (J). (gr. 3-4). pap. 8.99 (978-0-00-723094-5(X)) HarperCollins Pubs. Ltd. GBR. Dist: Independent Pubs. Group.

Shiro, S. P. Postcards from the Beyond. 2012. 194p. pap. (978-1-78176-408-4(5)) FeedARead.com.

Shook, Karl. The Family Thing. 2004. 166p. (YA). pap. 12.95 (978-0-595-31121-7(0)) iUniverse, Inc.

Shoopman, Jim. Zachary Hamm in the Land of Eggs. 2012. 82p. pap. 14.95 (978-0-9846558-1-6(6)) Taylor and Seale Publishing, LLC.

Shouoto, Aya. He's My Only Vampire, Vol. 9. 2016. (He's My Only Vampire Ser.: 9). (ENG., Illus.). 160p. (gr. 11-17). pap. 13.00 (978-0-316-34584-2(9), Yen Pr.) Orbit.

Showalter, Gena. Firstlife. 2016. (Harlequin Teen Ser.). (ENG.). 480p. (YA). (gr. 9-9). 18.99 (978-0-373-21227-9(5)) Blackstone Audio, Inc.

—Firstlife. (Everlife Novel Ser.). (ENG.). 2017. 448p. (gr. 8-12). pap. 9.99 (978-0-373-21221-7(6)) 2016. 480p. (YA). (gr. 9-12). 18.99 (978-0-373-21157-9(0)) Harlequin Enterprises, Ltd. CAN. (Harlequin Teen). Dist: HarperCollins Pubs.

—Lifeblood. 2017. (Everlife Novel Ser.). (ENG.). 448p. 18.99 (978-0-373-21219-4(4), Harlequin Teen) Harlequin Enterprises, Ltd. CAN. Dist: HarperCollins Pubs.

Showers, Barbara. Angel Jubilee. 2008. 28p. pap. 12.95 (978-1-4327-2084-1(8)) Outskirts Pr., Inc.

Shrum, Brianna. Never Never. 2015. (ENG.). 368p. (YA). (gr. 10-12). pap. 9.95 (978-1-63392-039-2(9)) Spencer Hill Pr.

Shusterman, Neal. The Dark Side of Nowhere. unabr. ed. 2004. 192p. (J). (gr. 4-7). pap. 36.00 incl. audio (978-0-8072-8757-6(1), YA258SP, Listening Library) Random Hse. Audio Publishing Group.

Shvarts, Andrew. Royal Bastards. 2017. (Royal Bastards Ser.). (ENG.). 352p. (YA). (gr. 9-17). 18.99 **(978-1-4847-6765-8(9))** Hyperion Bks. for Children.

Sibille, Lucinda. Dragon Swirl: Book II. 2009. 28p. pap. 14.95 (978-1-4490-1057-7(1)) AuthorHouse.

—Dragon Swirl: Book III. 2009. 32p. pap. 14.95 (978-1-4490-1072-0(5)) AuthorHouse.

—Dragon Swirl: Book IV. 2009. 32p. pap. 14.95 (978-1-4490-1075-1(X)) AuthorHouse.

—Dragon Swirl: In the Beginning. 2009. 32p. pap. 14.95 (978-1-4490-0965-6(4)) AuthorHouse.

Sidwell, Beth. Zack the Zombie. 2012. 24p. pap. 15.99 (978-1-4797-0962-5(X)) Xlibris Corp.

Siegel, Jan. The Devil's Apprentice. 2013. (ENG.). 384p. (YA). (gr. 6). pap. 9.99 (978-1-78108-147-1(6), Ravenstone) Rebellion GBR. Dist: Simon & Schuster, Inc.

Sierra, JulieAnn. Legacy & the Dark Prince, 1 vol. 2009. 209p. pap. 24.95 (978-1-61582-693-3(9)) America Star Bks.

Signorino, John. Billy & the Aliens of Alpha-C, 1 vol. 2008. (ENG.). 36p. pap. 24.95 (978-1-60474-882-6(6)) America Star Bks.

Silver Dolphin en Español Staff, creator. Caritas Felices. 2007. (Disney Princesa (Silver Dolphin) Ser.). (Illus.). 10p. (J). (gr. -1). bds. (978-970-718-390-2(X), Silver Dolphin en Español) Advanced Marketing, S. de R. L. de C. V.

Silver, Ruth. Aberrant. 2013. 250p. pap. 14.99 (978-0-9917897-8-8(4)) Patchwork Pr.

—Isaura. 2013. 242p. pap. 14.99 (978-1-927940-02-0(8)) Patchwork Pr.

Silverberry, A. R. Wyndano's Cloak. 2010. 424p. 21.95 (978-0-9841037-6-8(7)) Tree Tunnel Pr.

Sim, Tara. Timekeeper. 2016. (ENG.). 424p. (YA). (gr. 8). 17.99 (978-1-5107-0618-7(6), Sky Pony Pr.) Skyhorse Publishing Co., Inc.

Simko, Joe. The Sweet Rot Book 3: The Purple Meltdown, 1 vol. Simko, Joe, illus. 2012. (ENG., Illus.). 32p. (J). 19.99 (978-0-7643-3977-6(X), 9780764339776) Schiffer Publishing, Ltd.

Simms, Mattie. Q. 2006. (J). pap. 2.99 (978-0-9772077-1-8(4)) Kanleam, Inc.

Simon, Elizabeth. Tyler Adams & the Adventures of Bravura: the First Quest. 2009. 49p. pap. 19.95 (978-0-557-06290-4(X)) Lulu Pr., Inc.

Simon, Jay. Deep Freeze. 2004. 255p. (YA). per. 7.99 (978-0-931764-17-2(3)) Roberts Publishing Co.

Simon, Morris. Wizards Keep. 2007. 124p. pap. 4.99 (978-1-931567-67-1(0)) Margaret Weis Productions, Ltd.

Simon, Nadine. Flickers of True Destiny. 2010. 58p. pap. 11.95 (978-1-60860-948-2(0), Eloquent Bks.) Strategic Book Publishing & Rights Agency (SBPRA).

—The Treasured Dream. 2009. 52p. pap. 9.95 (978-1-60693-274-2(8), Eloquent Bks.) Strategic Book Publishing & Rights Agency (SBPRA).

Simonson, Bill. Itt 'N' Ott's Pizza Journey. 2013. 32p. 16.99 (978-0-9892711-6-5(1)) Mindstir Media.

Simpson, C. E. & Smith, C. E. Eighth Grade Witch. Utomo, Gabhor, illus. 2014. (ENG.). 144p. (J). mass mkt. 6.99 (978-1-937133-45-0(1)) Chooseco LLC.

Sims, C. Bailey. Candlewax. 2012. (ENG., Illus.). 384p. (YA). 18.99 (978-0-9839877-1-0(8)); pap. 13.99 (978-0-9839877-0-3(X)) Terabyte Pr. LLC.

Sinclair, Alison. Lightborn. 2011. (Darkborn Trilogy Ser.: 2). (ENG., Illus.). 312p. (gr. 12). 7.99 (978-0-451-46358-6(7), Ace Bks.) Penguin Publishing Group.

Sinclair, Lynn. Key to Aten 2005. (Chronicles of Aten Ser.). 179p. (YA). (gr. 7). per. 8.95 (978-0-9746481-7-0(5)) Brown Barn Bks.

Sinden, David, et al. Bang Goes a Troll, Bk. 3. Duddle, Jonny, illus. 2009. (Awfully Beastly Business Ser.: 3). (ENG.). 208p. (J). (gr. 3-7). 9.99 (978-1-4169-8651-5(0), Aladdin) Simon & Schuster Children's Publishing.

—Werewolf Versus Dragon. Duddle, Jonny, illus. 2009. (Awfully Beastly Business Ser.: 1). (ENG.). 192p. (J). (gr. 3-7). 9.99 (978-1-4169-8649-2(9), Aladdin) Simon & Schuster Children's Publishing.

Singh, Navneet. The Key to Light & Darkness: Everything Can Feel Like a Dream... 2013. 344p. pap. 19.92 (978-1-4907-0948-2(7)) Trafford Publishing.

Singleton, Linda Joy. Dead Girl Dancing. 2009. (Dead Girl Ser.: 2). (ENG.). 264p. (YA). pap. 9.95 (978-0-7387-1406-6(2), Flux) Llewellyn Pubns.

—Dead Girl in Love. 2009. (Dead Girl Ser.: 3). (ENG.). 288p. (YA). pap. 9.95 (978-0-7387-1407-3(0), B06XZ9TSKM, Flux) North Star Editions.

—Magician's Muse. 2010. (Seer Ser.: 6). (ENG.). 312p. (YA). (gr. 6-18). pap. 9.95 (978-0-7387-1957-3(9), Flux) Llewellyn Pubns.

—Sword Play. 2006. (Seer Ser.: 4). (ENG.). 288p. (YA). (gr. 7). per. 9.99 (978-0-7387-0880-5(1), Flux) Llewellyn Pubns.

Sinke, Janet Mary. Priscilla Mcdoodlenut Doodle Mcmae Asks, Why? Pennington, Craig, illus. 2007. 40p. (J). 17.95 (978-0-9742732-8-0(7)) My Grandma & Me Pubs.

Sioux Rose. Cassandra's Tale: Invitation to the Circle. 2010. 200p. pap. 16.95 (978-1-4401-9510-5(2)) iUniverse, Inc.

Skinner, Teresa. Casaq the Eagle. 2012. 29.95 (978-0-7414-7075-1(6)); pap. 19.95 (978-0-7414-7313-4(5)) Infinity Publishing.

Sklyar, Igor. King & the Star. 2005. (Illus.). 50p. pap. (978-1-84401-048-6(1)) Athena Pr.

Skogen, Jennifer. Tyger, Tyger #6. 2015. (Haunting of Grey Hills Ser.). (ENG.). 200-216p. (YA). (gr. 9-12). lib. bdg. 27.13 (978-1-68076-034-7(3), Epic Pr.) ABDO Publishing Co.

Skovron, Jon. Man Made Boy. 2015. (ENG.). 384p. (YA). (gr. 7). pap. 10.99 (978-0-14-242743-9(8), Speak) Penguin Young Readers Group.

Skrutskie, Emily. The Abyss Surrounds Us. 2016. (ENG., Illus.). 288p. (YA). pap. 11.99 (978-0-7387-4691-3(6), Flux) North Star Editions.

—The Abyss Surrounds Us. 2016. lib. bdg. 23.30 (978-0-606-38499-5(5)) Turtleback Bks.

Skurzynski, Gloria. Virtual War: The Virtual War Chronologs — Book 1. 2008. (ENG.). 188p. (YA). (gr. 7). pap. 10.99 (978-1-4169-7577-9(2), Simon Pulse) Simon Pulse.

Skye. Beyond Foo, Book 1: Geth & the Return of the Lithens. 2011. (978-1-60641-339-5(2), Shadow Mountain) Shadow Mountain Publishing.

Skye, Evelyn. The Crown's Fate. (Crown's Game Ser.: 2). (ENG.). 432p. (YA). (gr. 8). 2018. pap. 9.99 **(978-0-06-242262-0(6)**, Balzer & Bray) 2017. 17.99 (978-0-06-242261-3(8)) HarperCollins Pubs.

Skye, Evelyn. The Crown's Game. (Crown's Game Ser.: 1). (ENG.). (YA). (gr. 8). 2017. 432p. pap. 9.99 (978-0-06-242259-0(6)) 2016. 416p. 17.99 (978-0-06-242258-3(8)) HarperCollins Pubs.

—The Crown's Game. 2017. (Crown's Game Ser.: bk.1). (ENG.). (J). lib. bdg. 20.85 **(978-0-606-39645-5(4))** Turtleback Bks.

Skye, obert. Beyond Foo: Geth & the Return of the Lithens. 2011. 224p. (YA). (gr. 3-18). 14.99 (978-1-60908-050-1(5)) Deseret Bk. Co.

—Choke. 2010. (Pillage Ser.: 2). (ENG., Illus.). 336p. (YA). (gr. 7). 17.99 (978-1-60641-653-2(7), Shadow Mountain) Shadow Mountain Publishing.

—The Eyes of the Want. Sowards, Ben, illus. 2008. (Leven Thumps Ser.: 3). (ENG.). 464p. (J). (gr. 3-7). pap. 9.99 (978-1-4169-4719-6(1), Aladdin) Simon & Schuster Children's Publishing.

—The Gateway. Sowards, Ben, illus. 2006. (Leven Thumps Ser.: 1). (ENG.). 400p. (J). (gr. 3-7). pap. 9.99 (978-1-4169-2806-5(5), Aladdin) Simon & Schuster Children's Publishing.

—Leven Thumps 5 Volume Set. 2009. (ENG.). (J). (978-1-60641-220-6(5), Shadow Mountain) Shadow Mountain Publishing.

—Leven Thumps & the Eyes of the Want. 2007. (Leven Thumps Ser.: Bk. 3). (Illus.). 406p. (J). (gr. 4-7). 18.95 (978-1-59038-800-6(3), Shadow Mountain) Shadow Mountain Publishing.

—Leven Thumps & the Gateway to Foo. (Leven Thumps Ser.: 1). (J). 2008. 74.75 (978-1-4361-1570-4(1)) 2007. 85.75 (978-1-4281-4616-7(4)) 2007. 112.75 (978-1-4281-4622-8(9)) 2007. 115.75 (978-1-4281-4620-4(2)) 2007. 1.25 (978-1-4281-4613-6(X)) 2007. 178.75 (978-1-4281-4617-4(2)) 2007. 82.75 (978-1-4281-4618-1(0)) Recorded Bks., Inc.

—Leven Thumps & the Gateway to Foo. 2005. (Leven Thumps Ser.: Bk. 1). (Illus.). 384p. (J). 17.95 (978-1-59038-369-8(9), Shadow Mountain) Shadow Mountain Publishing.

—Leven Thumps & the Ruins of Alder. 2009. (Leven Thumps Ser.: Bk. 5). 384p. (YA). (gr. 5-18). 19.95 (978-1-60641-146-9(2), Shadow Mountain) Shadow Mountain Publishing.

—Leven Thumps & the Wrath of Ezra. 2008. (Leven Thumps Ser.: Bk. 4). (Illus.). 388p. (J). 19.95 (978-1-59038-963-8(8), Shadow Mountain) Shadow Mountain Publishing.

—Pillagy: The Complete Trilogy. 2013. (ENG., Illus.). 712p. (YA). (gr. 6). pap. 17.99 (978-1-60907-706-8(7), Shadow Mountain) Shadow Mountain Publishing.

—The Ruins of Alder. Sowards, Ben, illus. 2010. (Leven Thumps Ser.: 5). (ENG.). 416p. (J). (gr. 4-9). pap. 9.99 (978-1-4169-9093-2(3), Aladdin) Simon & Schuster Children's Publishing.

—The Whispered Secret. Sowards, Ben, illus. 2007. (Leven Thumps Ser.: 2). (ENG.). 464p. (J). (gr. 3-7). pap. 9.99 (978-1-4169-4718-9(3), Aladdin) Simon & Schuster Children's Publishing.

—The Wrath of Ezra. Sowards, Ben, illus. 2009. (Leven Thumps Ser.: 4). (ENG.). 464p. (J). (gr. 4-9). pap. 9.99 (978-1-4169-9092-5(5), Aladdin) Simon & Schuster Children's Publishing.

Slade, Nicholas. Joon the Zsun & His Magical Spoon. 2009. (Illus.). 32p. pap. 12.99 (978-1-4389-3496-9(3)) AuthorHouse.

Slate, Jenny & Fleischer-Camp, Dean. Marcel the Shell with Shoes On: Things about Me, 1 vol. 2011. (Marcel the Shell Ser.: 1). (ENG.). 42p. (J). (gr. k-3). 18.99 (978-1-59514-455-3(2), Razorbill) Penguin Young Readers Group.

Slater, Teddy. Beauty & the Beast. Dias, Ron et al, illus. 2004. (Little Golden Book Ser.). (ENG.). 24p. (J). (gr. -1-2). 4.99 (978-0-7364-2197-3(1), Golden/Disney) Random Hse. Children's Bks.

Sleigh, Barbara. Carbonel & Calidor: Being the Further Adventures of a Royal Cat. Front, Charles, illus. 2009. (ENG.). 224p. (J). (gr. 4-7). 17.95 (978-1-59017-333-6(3), NYR Children's Collection) New York Review of Bks., Inc., The.

Sloat, Teri & Huffman, Betty. Berry Magic. 2004. (ENG., Illus.). 32p. (J). pap. 11.99 (978-0-88240-576-6(4)) Graphic Arts Ctr. Publishing Co.

Slote, Alfred. My Trip to Alpha I. 96p. (J). (gr. 3-5). pap. 96.00 (978-0-8072-1402-2(7), Listening Library) Random Hse. Audio Publishing Group.

Small, Wylie J. The Great Prune Caper. 2009. 94p. pap. 9.98 (978-1-84728-350-4(0)) Lulu Pr., Inc.

Smedman, Lisa. Sacrifice of the Widow. 2007. (Lady Penitent Ser.: Bk. 1). 311p. (978-1-4287-1497-7(9)) Wizards of the Coast.

Smibert, Angie. The Meme Plague, 0 vols. (ENG.). 240p. (YA). (gr. 7-12). 2016. pap. 9.99 (978-1-4778-1689-9(5), 9781477816899, Skyscape) 2013. 16.99 (978-1-4778-1660-8(7), 9781477816608, Amazon Children's Publishing) Amazon Publishing.

Smiles from the Deep. 2004. (Illus.). 50p. (J). per. 12.00 (978-0-9745249-0-0(5)) Sounds Devine.

Smith, A. Valentine. A Circle of Three: Book of Newport. Smith, Frederick J. & Davis, Cynthia, eds. 2003. 464p. (YA). pap.

16.98 *(978-0-9727309-4-5(X)*, 097273094X) Alien Time Treasure.
Smith, Andrew. Passenger. 2012. (ENG.). 480p. (YA). (gr. 9-13). 17.99 *(978-1-250-00487-1(X))* Feiwel & Friends.
Smith, Ann Pierce. Esmerelda Hedgepath's First Date. 2010. 16p. 12.50 *(978-1-4520-3493-5(1))* AuthorHouse.
Smith, Blanche Z. A Gift from God. 2012. 20p. pap. 17.99 *(978-1-4685-8376-2(X))* AuthorHouse.
Smith, C. E. Giants of Anglesey. 2011. 176p. (gr. 4-6). 23.95 *(978-1-4620-3361-4(X))* iUniverse, Inc.
Smith, Cleveland W. Billabongo. 2008. 172p. pap. *(978-1-84923-100-8(1))* YouWriteOn.
Smith, Cliff. New Magical Holiday Stories. 2005. pap. 31.99 *(978-1-4134-7971-3(5))* Xlibris Corp.
Smith, J. L. The Abominators & the Forces of Evil. Hearn, Sam, illus. 2013. (ENG.). 240p. (J). (gr. 2-4). pap. 7.99 *(978-1-907411-64-9(X))* Little, Brown Book Group Ltd. GBR. Dist: Hachette Bk. Group.
—The Abominators in the Wild. Hearn, Sam, illus. 2013. (ENG.). 144p. (J). (gr. 2-4). 7.99 *(978-1-907411-63-2(1))* Little, Brown Book Group Ltd. GBR. Dist: Hachette Bk. Group.
Smith, Jeff. Bone Vol. 2: La Gran Carrera de Vacas. 2007. (SPA., Illus.). 144p. reprint ed. 24.95 *(978-1-59497-347-5(4))* Public Square Bks.
—Bone Vol. 3: Los Ojos de la Tormenta. 2007. (SPA., Illus.). 144p. reprint ed. 24.95 *(978-1-59497-348-2(2))* Public Square Bks.
—Crown of Horns. Smith, Jeff, illus. 2009. (Bone Ser.: 9). (ENG., Illus.). 224p. (J). (gr. 4-7). 26.99 *(978-0-439-70631-5(9)*, Graphix) Scholastic, Inc.
—Ghost Circles. Smith, Jeff & Hamaker, Steve, illus. 2008. (Bone Ser.: 7). (ENG.). 160p. (J). (gr. 4-7). 26.99 *(978-0-439-70629-2(7)*, Graphix) Scholastic, Inc.
—The Great Cow Race. Smith, Jeff & Hamaker, Steve, illus. 2005. (Bone Ser.: 2). (ENG.). 144p. (J). (gr. 4-7). pap. 12.99 *(978-0-439-70639-1(4)*, Graphix) Scholastic, Inc.
—Out from Boneville. Smith, Jeff, illus. 2005. (Bone Ser.: 1). (ENG., Illus.). 144p. (J). pap. 26.99 *(978-0-439-70623-0(8)*, Graphix) Scholastic, Inc.
—Out from Boneville. Smith, Jeff & Hamaker, Steve, illus. 2005. (Bone Ser.: 1). (ENG.). 144p. (J). pap. 12.99 *(978-0-439-70640-7(8)*, Graphix) Scholastic, Inc.
Smith, L. J. Dark Visions: The Strange Power - The Possessed - The Passion. 2009. (Dark Visions Ser.: Bks 1-3). (ENG.). 752p. (YA). (gr. 7). pap. 9.99 *(978-1-4169-8956-1(0)*, Simon Pulse) Simon Pulse.
—Heart of Valor. 2008. (ENG.). 244p. (YA). pap. 11.99 *(978-1-4169-8966-0(8)*, Simon & Schuster Bks. For Young Readers) Simon & Schuster Bks. For Young Readers.
—Heart of Valor. 2010. (ENG.). 352p. (J). (gr. 3-7). pap. 7.99 *(978-1-4169-9841-9(1)*, Aladdin) Simon & Schuster Children's Publishing.
—The Night of the Solstice. 2010. (ENG.). 352p. (J). (gr. 3-7). pap. 7.99 *(978-1-4169-9840-2(3)*, Aladdin) Simon & Schuster Children's Publishing.
—The Struggle. 2010. (Vampire Diaries: 2). (ENG.). 304p. (YA). (gr. 8). mass mkt. 7.99 *(978-0-06-199076-2(0))* HarperCollins Pubs.
Smith, L. J. & Clark, Aubrey. Unspoken, 0 vols. 2013. (Vampire Diaries: the Salvation Ser.: 2). (ENG.). 308p. (YA). (gr. 7-12). pap. 9.99 *(978-1-61218-462-3(6)*, 9781612184623, 47North) Amazon Publishing.
Smith, L. J. & Smith, Tom. The Night of the Solstice. 2008. (ENG.). 244p. (YA). pap. 11.99 *(978-1-4169-8965-3(X)*, Simon & Schuster Bks. For Young Readers) Simon & Schuster Bks. For Young Readers.
Smith, Linda. The Broken Thread, 1 vol. 2008. (ENG.). 248p. (YA). (gr. 8-12). pap. 12.95 *(978-1-55050-398-2(7))* Coteau Bks. CAN. Dist: Orca Bk. Pubs. USA.
—The Piper of Shadonia, 1 vol. 2012. (ENG.). 352p. (YA). (gr. 7-12). pap. 14.95 *(978-1-55050-516-0(5))* Coteau Bks. CAN. Dist: Orca Bk. Pubs. USA.
Smith, Lindsay. Dreamstrider. 2015. (ENG., Illus.). 400p. (YA). (gr. 7). 17.99 *(978-1-62672-042-8(8)*, 9781626720428) Roaring Brook Pr.
Smith, Matt. Barbarian Lord. Smith, Matt, illus. 2014. (ENG., Illus.). 176p. (YA). (gr. 7-12). 17.99 *(978-0-547-85906-4(6))* Houghton Mifflin Harcourt Publishing Co.
Smith, Melinda. Soldiers for Battle. 2008. 192p. 24.50 *(978-1-60693-398-5(1)*, Eloquent Bks.) Strategic Book Publishing & Rights Agency (SBPRA).
Smith, Molly K. Cassie's Guardian Angel. 2009. 24p. pap. 17.50 *(978-1-4490-4065-9(9))* AuthorHouse.
Smith, R. L. The Journals of Underwich: Book One. 2007. 253p. pap. 27.95 *(978-1-60441-490-5(1))* America Star Bks.
Smith, Roland. Shatterproof. 2012. (39 Clues: Cahills vs. Vespers Ser.: 4). (ENG.). 192p. (J). (gr. 3-7). 12.99 *(978-0-545-29842-1(3))*; Bk. 4. (Illus.). lib. bdg. 12.99 *(978-0-545-32413-7(0))* Scholastic, Inc.
Smith, Ronald L. Hoodoo. 2017. (ENG.). 224p. (J). (gr. 5-7). pap. 7.99 *(978-0-544-93561-7(6)*, HMH Books For Young Readers) Houghton Mifflin Harcourt Publishing Co.
Smith, Rosemary. Three Wishes for Maddy. 2012. 48p. pap. 10.00 *(978-1-61204-798-0(X)*, Strategic Bk. Publishing) Strategic Book Publishing & Rights Agency (SBPRA).
Smith, Sharon. Speedy the Squirrel. 2012. 32p. pap. 17.25 *(978-1-4669-6438-9(3))* Trafford Publishing.
Smith, Sherwood. The Emerald Wand of Oz. Stout, William, illus. 2007. 262p. (J). 17.00 *(978-1-4223-6710-0(X))* DIANE Publishing Co.
—The Emerald Wand of Oz. Stout, William, illus. 2005. (ENG.). 272p. (J). (gr. -1-17). 16.99 *(978-0-06-029607-0(0))* HarperCollins Pubs.
—Over the Sea: CJ's First Notebook. 2007. (Illus.). 260p. (YA). pap. 12.95 *(978-1-934648-36-0(1)*, YA Angst) Norilana Bks.
Smith, W. J. Gorte 2: The Awakening. 2010. 174p. pap. *(978-1-84748-452-9(2))* Athena Pr.
Smythe, R. R. Into the Woods. 2007. 122p. (YA). per. 7.49 net. *(978-0-9787139-4-2(X)*, Pandora) Highland Pr. Publishing.
Snelson, Brian & Sellars, Rodney. Shaturanga: The Story of Onus. 2003. 244p. (YA). 26.95 *(978-0-595-66019-3(3))* iUniverse, Inc.
Sniegoski, Thomas E. The Brimstone Network. 2008. (Brimstone Network Ser.: 1). (ENG.). 304p. (J). (gr. 4-8). pap. 14.99 *(978-1-4169-5104-9(0)*, Simon & Schuster/Paula Wiseman Bks.) Simon & Schuster/Paula Wiseman Bks.
—The Shroud of A'Ranka. Howard, Zachariah, illus. 2008. (Brimstone Network Ser.: 2). (ENG.). 288p. (J). (gr. 4-8). pap. 5.99 *(978-1-4169-5105-6(9)*, Simon & Schuster/Paula Wiseman Bks.) Simon & Schuster/Paula Wiseman Bks.
—Specter Rising. 2009. (Brimstone Network Ser.: 3). (ENG.). 288p. (J). pap. 5.99 *(978-1-4169-5106-3(7)*, Simon & Schuster/Paula Wiseman Bks.) Simon & Schuster/Paula Wiseman Bks.
Sniegoski, Thomas E. & Golden, Christopher. Battle for Arcanum. 2013. (Magic Zero Ser.: 4). (ENG., Illus.). 240p. (J). (gr. 3-7). pap. 6.99 *(978-1-4424-7315-7(0)*, Aladdin) Simon & Schuster Children's Publishing.
—Battle for Arcanum. 2013. (Magic Zero Ser.: 4). (ENG., Illus.). 240p. (J). (gr. 3-7). 17.99 *(978-1-4424-7316-4(9)*, Simon & Schuster/Paula Wiseman Bks.) Simon & Schuster/Paula Wiseman Bks.
—Ghostfire. 2013. (Magic Zero Ser.: 3). (ENG., Illus.). 304p. (J). (gr. 5-9). pap. 6.99 *(978-1-4424-7313-3(4)*, Aladdin) Simon & Schuster Children's Publishing.
—Ghostfire. 2013. (Magic Zero Ser.: 3). (ENG.). 304p. (J). (gr. 3-7). 17.99 *(978-1-4424-7314-0(2)*, Simon & Schuster/Paula Wiseman Bks.) Simon & Schuster/Paula Wiseman Bks.
—Magic Zero. 2013. (Magic Zero Ser.: 1). (ENG., Illus.). 304p. (J). (gr. 3-7). 17.99 *(978-1-4424-7312-6(6))*; pap. 6.99 *(978-1-4424-7311-9(8))* Simon & Schuster Children's Publishing. (Aladdin).
Sniegoski, Tom. Quest for the Spark. Smith, Jeff, illus. (Bone Ser.). (ENG.). (J). (gr. 3-7). 2012. 240p. pap. 10.99 *(978-0-545-14104-8(4))*Bk. 2. 2012. 240p. 26.99 *(978-0-545-14103-1(6))*Bk. 3. 2013. 288p. pap. 10.99 *(978-0-545-14106-2(0))*No. 3. 2013. 288p. 22.99 *(978-0-545-14105-5(2))* Scholastic, Inc. (Graphix).
—Quest for the Spark. 2012. (Bone: Quest for the Spark Ser.: 2). lib. bdg. 22.10 *(978-0-606-23947-9(2)*, Turtleback) Turtleback Bks.
Sniegoski, Tom & Smith, Jeff. Quest for the Spark, Bk. 1. Smith, Jeff, illus. 2011. (BONE: Quest for the Spark Ser.: 1). (ENG., Illus.). 224p. (J). (gr. 3-7). 26.99 *(978-0-545-14101-7(X)*, Graphix) Scholastic, Inc.
Snow, Alan. Here Be Monsters! Snow, Alan, illus. (Ratbridge Chronicles Ser.: 1). (ENG., Illus.). 544p. (J). (gr. 3-9). 2007. per. 9.99 *(978-0-689-87048-4(5))* 2006. 17.95 *(978-0-689-87047-7(7))* Simon & Schuster Children's Publishing. (Atheneum Bks. for Young Readers).
Snow, Carol. Snap. 2009. (ENG.). 224p. (YA). (gr. 8-18). 16.99 *(978-0-06-145211-6(4)*, HarperTeen) HarperCollins Pubs.
Snow White & the Seven Dwarfs. 2008. (Read & Learn Sticker Books Ser.). 48p. pap. *(978-1-4075-3197-7(2))* Parragon, Inc.
Snyder, Laurel. Bigger Than a Bread Box. 2012. (ENG.). 240p. (J). (gr. 3-7). 7.99 *(978-0-375-87325-6(2)*, Yearling) Random Hse. Children's Bks.
Snyder, Maria V. Dawn Study. 2017. (Study Ser.: 6). (ENG.). 480p. pap. 16.99 *(978-0-7783-1985-6(7)*, Mira Bks.) Harlequin Enterprises, Ltd. CAN. Dist: HarperCollins Pubs.
Snyder, Zilpha Keatley. Black & Blue Magic. 2016. (ENG.). 200p. (J). (gr. 4-6). pap. 11.99 *(978-1-5040-3560-6(7))* Open Road Integrated Media, Inc.
Sobat, Gail Sidonie. A Glass Darkly. 2006. (Ingamald Ser.: 3). (ENG., Illus.). 192p. (YA). (gr. 8-12). per. 14.95 *(978-1-894283-69-4(4))* Great Plains Pubns. CAN. Dist: Publishers Group Canada.
Sobel, Gerrie. Jacob & His Magical Flying Bears. Torres, Dottie, illus. 2009. 32p. pap. 12.95 *(978-1-936051-16-8(8))* Peppertree Pr., The.
Soffe, Caroline Dawn. Billy Barnet & the House of Fern: An Environmental Story. 2011. 222p. pap. 24.95 *(978-1-4560-5201-0(2))* America Star Bks.
Sommer, Carl. Three Little Pigs(Los Tres Cerditos) Budwine, Greg & Vignolo, Enrique, illus. 2009. (Another Sommer-Time Story Bilingual Ser.). (SPA & ENG.). 48p. (J). lib. bdg. 16.95 *(978-1-57537-168-9(5))* Advance Publishing, Inc.
Sommer, Carl & Aesop. Divide to Conquer. Mercado, Jorge, illus. 2009. (Quest for Success Ser.). (ENG.). 40p. (YA). pap. 4.95 *(978-1-57537-275-4(4))*; lib. bdg. 12.95 *(978-1-57537-250-1(9))* Advance Publishing, Inc.
—Divide to Conquer(Divide y Venceras) Mercado, Jorge, illus. 2009. (Quest for Success Bilingual Ser.). (ENG & SPA.). 72p. (YA). lib. bdg. 14.95 *(978-1-57537-225-9(8))* Advance Publishing, Inc.
—The Silent Scream. Bogdan, Enache, illus. 2009. (Quest for Success Ser.). (ENG.). 40p. (YA). pap. 4.95 *(978-1-57537-285-3(1))*; lib. bdg. 12.95 *(978-1-57537-260-0(6))* Advance Publishing, Inc.
—The Tiny Giant. Mercado, Jorge, illus. 2009. (Quest for Success Ser.). (ENG.). 40p. (YA). pap. 4.95 *(978-1-57537-286-0(X))*; lib. bdg. 12.95 *(978-1-57537-261-7(4))* Advance Publishing, Inc.
—Tiny Giant(La Gigante Pequeña) Mercado, Jorge, illus. 2009. (Quest for Success Bilingual Ser.). (ENG & SPA.). 72p. (YA). lib. bdg. 14.95 *(978-1-57537-236-5(3))* Advance Publishing, Inc.
Somper, Justin. Allies & Assassins. 2014. (Allies & Assassins Ser.). (ENG.). 496p. (YA). (gr. 7-17). 18.00 *(978-0-316-25393-2(6))* Little, Brown Bks. for Young Readers.
—A Conspiracy of Princes. 2015. (Allies & Assassins Ser.: 2). (ENG., Illus.). 496p. (J). (gr. 7-17). 18.00 *(978-0-316-25397-0(9))* Little, Brown Bks. for Young Readers.
The Song of the Lioness Quartet. 2014. (Song of the Lioness Ser.). (ENG., Illus.). 1168p. (YA). (gr. 7). pap. 42.99 *(978-1-4814-1649-8(9)*, Atheneum Bks. for Young Readers) Simon & Schuster Children's Publishing.
Sonneborn, Scott. Supergirl vs. Brainiac, 1 vol. Vecchio, Luciano, illus. 2013. (DC Super Heroes Ser.). (ENG.). 56p. (gr. 2-3). lib. bdg. 26.65 *(978-1-4342-6015-4(1))* Stone Arch Bks.
Sonoda, Hideki. Pokémon: Zoroark: Master of Illusions. 2011. (ENG.). 192p. (J). pap. 7.99 *(978-1-4215-4221-8(8))* Viz Media.
Soontornvat, Christina. The Changelings. (Changelings Ser.: 1). (ENG.). (J). (gr. 5-8). 2017. 304p. pap. 7.99 ***(978-1-4926-4795-9(0))*** 2016. 288p. 16.99 *(978-1-4926-3260-3(0)*, 9781492632603) Sourcebooks, Inc. (Sourcebooks Jabberwocky).
Sorenson, Jack R. Eibhlin & Her Dragon, 1 vol. 2009. 131p. pap. 24.95 *(978-1-60749-634-2(8))* America Star Bks.
Sorrells, Walter. Book Three of the Travelers. 2009. (Pendragon: 3). (ENG.). 224p. (J). (gr. 5-9). pap. 6.99 *(978-1-4169-6524-4(6)*, Aladdin) Simon & Schuster Children's Publishing.
Soto, Manuel. Mi & Two. Duggan, Micheal, illus. 2008. 27p. pap. 24.95 *(978-1-60610-877-2(8))* America Star Bks.
Soundprints Staff. Fairy Tales. 2005. (Studio Mouse Ser.). (Illus.). 256p. (J). (gr. -1-2). 14.95 *(978-1-59069-229-5(2))* Studio Mouse LLC.
—Pat-a-Cake: And Othe Favorites. 2005. (Meet Mother Goose Ser.). (ENG., Illus.). 36p. (J). 14.95 *(978-1-931465-48-9(7)*, MPD1104) Soundprints.
—Pat-a-Cake: And Other Favorites. 2005. (Meet Mother Goose Ser.). (ENG., Illus.). 36p. (J). 10.95 *(978-1-931465-28-1(2)*, MD1104) Soundprints.
Sowles, Joann I. Martin. Darkness (the Brookehaven Vampires Series #2) The Brookehaven Vampires. 2011. (YA). *(978-0-9844867-3-1(9))* Brookehaven Publishing.
Spalding, Andrea. Behind the Sorcerer's Cloak, 1 vol. 2006. (Summer of Magic Quartet Ser.: 4). (ENG., Illus.). 240p. (J). (gr. 4-7). per. 8.95 *(978-1-55143-627-2(2))* Orca Bk. Pubs. USA.
Spaziano, Layna. Shane & Molly's Magical Journey, 1 vol. 2010. 28p. pap. 24.95 *(978-1-4489-6261-7(7))* PublishAmerica, Inc.
Speaker-Yuan, Margaret & Yuan, Margaret Speaker. Phillip Pullman. 2005. (Who Wrote That? Ser.). (Illus.). 120p. (gr. 6-12). lib. bdg. 35.00 *(978-0-7910-8658-2(5)*, Chelsea Hse.) Facts On File, Inc.
Speakman, Peter & Galvin, Michael. Rebels of the Lamp, Book 1 Rebels of the Lamp. 2017. (Rebels of the Lamp Ser.). (ENG.). 304p. (J). (gr. 5-9). pap. 7.99 *(978-1-4847-0847-7(4))* Hyperion Bks. for Children.
Speer, Cindy Lynn. Unbalanced. 2010. pap. *(978-1-934841-90-7(0))* Zumaya Pubns. LLC.
Speer, Scott. Battle Angel. 2014. (Immortal City Ser.: 3). (ENG.). 320p. (YA). (gr. 7). pap. 9.99 *(978-1-59514-598-7(2)*, Razorbill) Penguin Young Readers Group.
Spees, Melanie. Run for Hawk's Bay. 2010. (ENG.). 176p. (J). pap. 11.95 *(978-0-9841658-9-6(4)*, Excite Kids Pr.) Publishing Services @ Thomson-Shore.
Speicher, Diane Carty. Brighton One Star's Journey to Shine. Robinson, Lenord, illus. 2005. 84p. (J). 19.95 *(978-0-9749806-0-7(9))* Shine On Pubns.
Spence, Craig. Josh & the Magic Vial. 2006. (ENG.). 396p. (J). per. 17.95 *(978-1-897235-10-2(0))* Thistledown Pr., Ltd. CAN. Dist: Univ. of Toronto Pr.
Spendlove, Joanna. The Adventures of Gooky & Spinnet: The Universe, Our Wonderland. 2011. 24p. 14.99 *(978-1-4567-1066-8(4))* AuthorHouse.
Spendlove, Owen. Stanley Brambles & the Pirate's Treasure. 2007. 320p. per. 18.95 *(978-0-595-43792-4(3))* iUniverse, Inc.
Sperry, Brendan. Captain Dino & the Revenge of Roberto. 2012. 20p. pap. 24.95 *(978-1-4626-8260-7(X))* America Star Bks.
Spika, Jana. Locket & the Mask. 2004. 12.99 *(978-0-9727103-0-5(2))* Tree of Life Pr.
Spinner, Stephanie. The Magic of Merlin. Sokolova, Valerie, illus. 2004. (Stepping Stones: A Chapter Book: Fantasy Ser.). 42p. (J). 11.65 *(978-0-7569-0905-5(8))* Perfection Learning Corp.
Spirin, Gennady. Goldilocks & the Three Bears, 0 vols. Spirin, Gennady, illus. 2009. (ENG., Illus.). 32p. (J). (gr. -1-2). 17.99 *(978-0-7614-5596-7(5)*, 9780761455967, Amazon Children's Publishing) Amazon Publishing.
Spitzer, Linda & Myers, Sarah. Tales of the Paper Bag Fairies/Color Version. 2005. 54p. (J). pap. 14.95 *(978-1-4116-4095-5(0))* Lulu Pr., Inc.
Spizman, Robyn F. Lollipop Grapes & Clothespin Critters: Quick on the Spot Remedies for Restless Children. (J). pap. 89.50 *(978-0-201-57753-2(4))* Addison-Wesley Longman, Inc.
Spooner, Meagan. Lark Ascending. 2014. (ENG.). 328p. (YA). 17.95 *(978-0-7613-8867-8(2))* Lerner Publishing Group.
—Shadowlark. 2013. 327p. pap. 17.95 *(978-1-4677-1664-2(2))*; (ENG.). 336p. (YA). (gr. 7-12). 17.95 *(978-0-7613-8866-1(4)*, Carolrhoda Lab™) Lerner Publishing Group.
—Skylark. 2012. (Skylark Trilogy Ser.). (ENG.). 344p. (YA). (gr. 7-12). 17.95 *(978-0-7613-8865-4(6))* Lerner Publishing Group.
Spring, Manda. Emerald & the Withered Willow. 2007. 148p. pap. 18.00 *(978-1-4303-1353-3(6))* Lulu Pr., Inc.
Springer, Nancy. Lionclaw: A Tale of Rowan Hood. 2004. (ENG.). 128p. (J). (gr. 3-7). 7.99 *(978-0-14-240053-1(X)*, Puffin Books) Penguin Young Readers Group.
Springham, James. Earth-n-Bones: Blue Things. 2006. 54p. pap. 16.95 *(978-1-4137-9738-1(5))* America Star Bks.
Squatrito, J. Michael, Jr. The Talisman of Unification: The Overlords. 2007. (ENG., Illus.). 424p. (YA). per. 22.95 *(978-0-595-47343-4(1))* iUniverse, Inc.
St. Aubyn, Douglas. Caribbean Fables. 2007. 72p. pap. *(978-976-8054-72-2(7))* Paria Publishing Co., Ltd.
St. Crow, Lili. Jealousy. 2010. (Strange Angels Ser.: 3). (ENG.). 320p. (YA). (gr. 7-18). 9.99 *(978-1-59514-290-0(8)*, Razorbill) Penguin Young Readers Group.
—Jealousy, 10 vols. 2010. (Strange Angels Ser.: 3). (J). 86.75 *(978-1-4498-2774-8(8))*; 209.75 *(978-1-4498-2772-4(1))*; 68.75 *(978-1-4498-2773-1(X))*; 83.75 *(978-1-4498-2776-2(4))*; 1.25 *(978-1-4498-2777-9(2))* Recorded Bks., Inc.
—Jealousy. 2010. (Strange Angels Ser.: 3). lib. bdg. 20.85 *(978-0-606-14566-4(4)*, Turtleback) Turtleback Bks.
—Strange Angels. 2009. (Strange Angels Ser.: 1). (ENG., Illus.). 304p. (YA). (gr. 7-18). pap. 9.99 *(978-1-59514-251-1(7)*, Razorbill) Penguin Young Readers Group.
—Strange Angels, 9 vols. 2009. (Strange Angels Ser.: 1). (J). 114.75 *(978-1-4407-6199-7(X))*; 84.75 *(978-1-4407-6195-9(7))*; 181.75 *(978-1-4407-6194-2(9))*; 117.75 *(978-1-4407-6197-3(3))*; 87.75 *(978-1-4407-6193-5(0))* Recorded Bks., Inc.
—Strange Angels. 2009. (Strange Angels Ser.: 1). lib. bdg. 20.85 *(978-0-606-08957-9(8)*, Turtleback) Turtleback Bks.
—Wayfarer. 2014. (Tales of Beauty & Madness Ser.). (ENG.). 352p. (YA). (gr. 7). pap. 9.99 *(978-1-59514-620-5(2)*, Razorbill) Penguin Young Readers Group.
St. Jean, Alan. Aidan of Oren: The Journey Begins. Friedman, Judith, illus. 2004. (ENG.). 208p. (J). (gr. 4-7). 19.95 *(978-0-9724853-5-7(X))* Keene Publishing.
St. John, Laurence. Metatron: The Angel Has Risen. 2012. 102p. pap. *(978-1-926997-64-3(6))* Imajin Bks.
St-Onge, Donna Na-Tasa Katherine. The Eye of Isis, 1 vol. 2009. 155p. pap. 24.95 *(978-1-60836-986-7(2))* America Star Bks.
Stadther, Michael. Secrets of the Alchemist Dar. Stadther, Michael, illus. 2006. (Treasure's Trove Ser.). (ENG., Illus.). 144p. (J). 21.99 *(978-1-4169-2653-5(4))*; 39.99 *(978-1-4169-2661-0(5))* Treasure Trove, Inc.
Stairs-Oberlick, Anita Ruth. Helen the Transartist. 2004. (Illus.). 256p. (J). per. 15.95 *(978-0-9759738-0-6(0))* Carleton Bks.
Stamey, Marsha. The Man in the Clouds, 1 vol. Jones, Seth, illus. 2009. 21p. pap. 24.95 *(978-1-60836-730-6(4))* PublishAmerica, Inc.
Stan, Adrianna. The Letters. 2012. 24p. pap. *(978-1-4602-0045-2(4))* FriesenPress.
Stanek, Robert, pseud. The Art of Ruin Mist: Heroes & Villains. 2007. (ENG.). 60p. (YA). per. 16.00 *(978-1-57545-163-3(8))* RP Media.
—The Elf Queen & the King III. 2007. 232p. (YA). pap. 15.00 *(978-1-57545-086-5(0))* RP Media.
—The Elf Queen & the King IV. 2008. 238p. (YA). pap. 15.00 *(978-1-57545-087-2(9))* RP Media.
—Illustrated Encyclopedia of Ruin Mist. 2008. pap. 15.00 *(978-1-57545-157-2(3)*, Ruin Mist Pubns.) RP Media.
—In the Service of Dragons: Keeper Martin's Tales, Book 5. 2005. 252p. (YA). (gr. 4-9). pap. 14.00 *(978-1-57545-089-6(5))* RP Media.
—In the Service of Dragons II: Keeper Martin's Tales, Book 6. 2005. (Illus.). 256p. (YA). (gr. 4-9). pap. 14.00 *(978-1-57545-090-2(9))* RP Media.
—In the Service of Dragons III: Keeper Martin's Tales, Book 7. 2005. (Keeper Martin's Tales Ser.). (Illus.). 240p. (J). (gr. 4-7). per. 14.00 *(978-1-57545-093-3(3))* RP Media.
—In the Service of Dragons IV: Keeper Martin's Tales, Book 8. 2005. (Keeper Martin's Tales Ser.). (ENG., Illus.). 240p. (YA). (gr. 8-12). per. 14.00 *(978-1-57545-094-0(1))* RP Media.
—Into the Stone Land. 2011. (Best Fantasy Ser.: Bk. 2). 242p. (J). pap. 11.00 *(978-1-57545-092-6(5))* RP Media.
—Journey Beyond the Beyond. 2008. (Magic Lands (Playaway) Ser.). 54.99 *(978-1-60514-596-9(3))* Findaway World, LLC.
—Journey Beyond the Beyond. (J). 2007. (ENG.). 156p. per. 14.00 *(978-1-57545-132-9(8))* 2007. (ENG., Illus.). 156p. 18.95 *(978-1-57545-133-6(6))* 2006. (Illus.). 112p. pap. 14.95 *(978-1-57545-108-4(5))* RP Media.
—The Kingdoms & the Elves of the Reaches. Stanek, Robert, illus. alt. gif. ed. 2004. (Illus.). 176p. (YA). pap. 10.99 *(978-1-57545-501-3(3)*, Reagent Pr. Echo) RP Media.
—The Kingdoms & the Elves of the Reaches: Keeper Martin's Tales, Book 1. (Keeper Martin's Tales Ser.: Bk. 1). (Illus.). 2006. 256p. (YA). pap. 18.95 *(978-1-57545-505-1(6)*, Reagent Pr. Signature Editions) 2005. 240p. (J). pap. 14.00 *(978-1-57545-059-9(3))* RP Media.
—The Kingdoms & the Elves of the Reaches: Signature, Keeper Martin's Tales, Bk. 1. 2007. (Illus.). 240p. (YA). 35.00 *(978-1-57545-128-2(X))* RP Media.
—The Kingdoms & the Elves of the Reaches II. Stanek, Robert, illus. alt. gif. ed. 2004. (ENG., Illus.). 180p. (YA). pap. 10.99 *(978-1-57545-502-0(1)*, Reagent Pr. Echo) RP Media.
—The Kingdoms & the Elves of the Reaches II: Keeper Martin's Tales, Book 2. 2008. (Keeper Martin's Tales (Playaway) Ser.). (J). 54.99 *(978-1-60514-649-2(8))* Findaway World, LLC.
—The Kingdoms & the Elves of the Reaches II: Keeper Martin's Tales, Book 2. (Keeper Martin's Tales Ser.: Bk. 2). (Illus.). 2007. 260p. (YA). pap. 18.95 *(978-1-57545-506-8(4)*, Reagent Pr. Signature Editions) 2005. 240p. (J). pap. 14.00 *(978-1-57545-060-5(7))* RP Media.
—The Kingdoms & the Elves of the Reaches II: Signature, Keeper Martin's Tales, Bk. 2. 2007. (Illus.). 244p. (J). (gr. 4-7). 35.00 *(978-1-57545-129-9(8))* RP Media.
—The Kingdoms & the Elves of the Reaches III. Stanek, Robert, illus. alt. gif. ed. 2004. (ENG., Illus.). 172p. (YA). pap. 10.99 *(978-1-57545-503-7(X)*, Reagent Pr. Echo) RP Media.
—The Kingdoms & the Elves of the Reaches III: Keeper Martin's Tales, Bk. 3. 2008. (Keeper Martin's Tales Ser.: Bk. 3). (Illus.). 188p. (YA). per. 18.95 *(978-1-57545-507-5(2)*, Reagent Pr. Signature Editions) RP Media.
—The Kingdoms & the Elves of the Reaches III: Keeper Martin's Tales, Book 3. deluxe ed. 2005. (Keeper Martin's Tales Ser.: Vol. 3). (Illus.). 240p. (J). pap. 14.00 *(978-1-57545-063-6(1))* RP Media.
—The Kingdoms & the Elves of the Reaches III: Signature, Keeper Martin's Tales, Bk. 3. 2008. (Illus.). 244p. (J). (gr. 4-7). 35.00 *(978-1-57545-130-5(1))* RP Media.
—The Kingdoms & the Elves of the Reaches IV. 2009. (Keeper Martin's Tales Ser.: Bk. 4). (Illus.). 188p. (YA). per. 18.95 *(978-1-57545-508-2(0)*, Reagent Pr. Signature Editions) RP Media.
—The Kingdoms & the Elves of the Reaches IV. Stanek, Robert, illus. alt. gif. ed. 2005. (Illus.). 172p. (YA). pap. 10.99 *(978-1-57545-504-4(8)*, Reagent Pr. Echo) RP Media.
—The Kingdoms & the Elves of the Reaches IV: Keeper Martin's Tales, Book 4. deluxe ed. 2005. (Keeper Martin's Tales Ser.: Vol. 4). (Illus.). 240p. (YA). pap. 14.00 *(978-1-57545-065-0(8))* RP Media.
Stanek, Robert, pseud & Ruin Mist Publications Staff. The Magic of Ruin Mist: A Candid Look at Robert Stanek's Life, Work & Books. 2003. 150p. pap. 9.99 *(978-1-57545-031-5(3)*, Ruin Mist Pubns.) RP Media.
Stanford, K. B. Sixteen Wishes (paperback) 2008. 188p. pap. 15.47 *(978-1-4357-1773-2(2))* Lulu Pr., Inc.
Stanley, Diane. The Cup & the Crown. (Silver Bowl Ser.: 2). (ENG.). (J). (gr. 3-7). 2013. 368p. pap. 6.99 *(978-0-06-196323-0(2))* 2012. 352p. 16.99 *(978-0-06-196321-6(6))* HarperCollins Pubs.
—The Princess of Cortova. (J). 2015. (Silver Bowl Ser.: 3). (ENG.). 336p. (gr. 3-7). pap. 6.99 *(978-0-06-204732-8(9))* 2013. (Silver Bowl Ser.: 3). (ENG.). 320p. (gr. 3-7). 16.99

(978-0-06-204730-4(2)) 2013. 311p. lib. bdg. *(978-0-06-204731-1(0))* HarperCollins Pubs.
—The Silver Bowl. (Silver Bowl Ser.: 1). (ENG.). (J). (gr. 5). 2012. 336p. pap. 6.99 *(978-0-06-157546-4(1))* 2011. 320p. 16.99 *(978-0-06-157543-3(7))* HarperCollins Pubs.
—Stanley Mid Grade Novel #11. 2018. 368p. (J). (gr. 3-7). 17.99 *(978-0-06-265803-6(4))* HarperCollins Pubs.
—The Trouble with Wishes. Stanley, Diane, illus. 2007. (Illus.). 32p. (J). (gr. k-3). lib. bdg. 17.89 *(978-0-06-055452-1(5))* HarperCollins Pubs.
Stanley, Pauline. The Children & the Witches Magic. 2010. (Illus.). 48p. pap. 10.49 *(978-1-4490-9544-4(5))* AuthorHouse.
Stansberry, Don. Inky & the Missing Gold. 2007. (Illus.). 128p. (YA). per. 15.95 *(978-0-929915-10-4(0)*, Publisher Page) Headline Bks., Inc.
Stapylton, K. E. The Terror of Prism Fading. 2008. 260p. pap. 15.90 *(978-1-4357-5457-7(3))* Lulu Pr., Inc.
Star Wars Staff & Valois, Rob. Sticker Storyteller. 2008. (Star Wars). (ENG.). 48p. (J). (gr. 1-3). pap. 12.99 *(978-0-448-45058-2(5))* Penguin Publishing Group.
Star Wars Staff, et al. Renegade. 2009. (Star Wars: Rebel For Ser.: 3). (ENG.). 176p. (J). (gr. 3-7). pap. 6.99 *(978-0-545-11211-6(7))* Scholastic, Inc.
Starmer, Aaron. The Riverman. 2014. (Riverman Trilogy Ser.: 1). (ENG.). 320p. (YA). (gr. 5-9). 15.99 *(978-0-374-36309-3(9)*, 9780374363093, Farrar, Straus & Giroux (BYR)) Farrar, Straus & Giroux.
—The Storyteller. 2016. (Riverman Trilogy Ser.: 3). (ENG.). 336p. (J). 16.99 *(978-0-374-36313-0(7)*, 9780374363130, Farrar, Straus & Giroux (BYR)) Farrar, Straus & Giroux.
—The Whisper. 2015. (Riverman Trilogy Ser.: 2). (ENG.). 368p. (YA). (gr. 5-9). 16.99 *(978-0-374-36311-6(0)*, 9780374363116, Farrar, Straus & Giroux (BYR)) Farrar, Straus & Giroux.
Starrenburg, Hasko. The Queen's Orb. 2012. (Illus.). 144p. pap. 8.00 *(978-1-4349-8782-2(5)*, RoseDog Bks.) Dorrance Publishing Co., Inc.
Steadman, Ralph. The Little Red Computer. 2004. (Illus.). 46p. 100.00 *(978-0-9673004-9-8(5))* Sylph Pubns.
Steampunk City: An Alphabetical Journey. 2014. (ENG., Illus.). 56p. (J). (gr. 2-5). 16.95 *(978-1-57687-703-6(5)*, powerHouse Bks.) powerHouse Cultural Entertainment, Inc.
Steel, Flora Annie. English Fairy Tales. 2007. (ENG.). 262p. pap. 21.99 *(978-1-4346-0692-1(9))*; 296p. pap. 23.99 *(978-1-4346-0752-2(6))* Creative Media Partners, LLC.
Stef. Be Careful What You Wish For. 2008. 380p. 29.99 *(978-1-4363-5233-8(9))*; pap. 19.99 *(978-1-4363-5232-1(0))* Xlibris Corp.
Stein, Clem. Scotty's Feeder & the Secret Tower. Prouix, Denis, illus. 2011. 40p. 16.99 *(978-1-4567-3191-5(2))* AuthorHouse.
Stephanie K. McMahan. Sylvan Tales: The Secret of Elfenore. 2009. 152p. 22.95 *(978-1-4401-5507-9(0))*; pap. 12.95 *(978-1-4401-5505-5(4))* iUniverse, Inc.
Stephens, Ann Marie. Stella Eats Out. Bolan, Michael, illus. 2004. 32p. (J). per. 12.95 *(978-0-9729285-2-6(9)*, 2-9) Kinkachoo Pr., The.
Stephens, Sarah Hines. Poison Ivy's Rainforest Revenge. Levins, Tim, illus. 2017. (Batman & Robin Adventures Ser.). (ENG.). 88p. (gr. 2-3). lib. bdg. 26.65 ***(978-1-4965-5352-2(7)***, DC Super Heroes) Stone Arch Bks.
Stephenson, Kenniqueca. The Magical Land of Norms. 2010. 24p. pap. 12.99 *(978-1-4490-5146-4(4))* AuthorHouse.
Steps To Literacy Staff, compiled by. Beast Quest Collection Grades 2-5: Class Pack (6 Titles, 6 Each) 2010. (ENG.). (J). pap. 170.75 *(978-1-60923-616-8(5))* Steps To Literacy, LLC.
—Beast Quest Collection Grades 2-5: Variety Pack (6 Titles, 1 Each) 2010. (ENG.). (J). pap. 29.90 *(978-1-60923-615-1(7))* Steps To Literacy, LLC.
—Eragon/Eldest Box Set: Variety Pack (2 Titles, 1 Each) 2010. (ENG.). (J). pap. 23.85 *(978-1-61267-194-9(2))* Steps To Literacy, LLC.
—Percy Jackson & the Olympians Series: Variety Pack (5 Titles, 1 Each) 2010. (J). pap. 39.95 *(978-1-60923-745-5(5))* Steps To Literacy, LLC.
Steven, Ruth Lauren & Lauren, Ruth. Prisoner of Ice & Snow. 2017. (ENG.). 288p. (J). 16.99 *(978-1-68119-131-7(8)*, 9781681191317, Bloomsbury USA Childrens) Bloomsbury Publishing USA.
Stevens, Cara J. The Battle for the Dragon's Temple: An Unofficial Graphic Novel for Minecrafters, #4. 2017. (Unofficial Graphic Novel for Minecrafters Ser.). (ENG., Illus.). 192p. (J). (gr. 2-7). pap. 11.99 *(978-1-5107-1798-5(6)*, Sky Pony Pr.) Skyhorse Publishing Co., Inc.
Stevens, Dan. The Magic of the Brass Ring. 2009. 84p. pap. 19.95 *(978-1-4489-7759-8(2))* America Star Bks.
Stevens, Terry. Tommy, the Wizard & the Magic Umbrella. 2006. (Illus.). 60p. pap. *(978-1-84401-752-2(4))* Athena Pr.
Stevenson, Noelle. Nimona. Stevenson, Noelle, illus. 2015. (ENG., Illus.). 272p. (YA). (gr. 8). 17.99 *(978-0-06-227823-4(1))*; pap. 14.99 *(978-0-06-227822-7(3))* HarperCollins Pubs. (HarperTeen).
Stevenson, Robert Louis. Classics Illustrated #7: Dr. Jekyll & Mr. Hyde. 2009. (Classics Illustrated Graphic Novels Ser.). (ENG., Illus.). 56p. (J). (gr. 3-9). 9.95 *(978-1-59707-171-0(4)*, 9781597071710) Papercutz.
Stevenson, S. Roy. The Magic Act: A Mystery by S. Roy Stevenson. 2008. 108p. 20.95 *(978-0-595-51841-8(9))*; pap. 10.95 *(978-0-595-53062-5(1))* iUniverse, Inc.
Stewart, E. J. The Lyre Birds. 2008. 214p. pap. 16.95 *(978-0-615-18762-4(5))* Leaf & Vine Bks.
Stewart-Goodair, Madonna. Key to the Golden Gates: The Mystic Soldier, Book 1, 1 vol. 2009. 48p. pap. 16.95 *(978-1-61582-625-4(4))* PublishAmerica, Inc.
Stewart, Martin. Riverkeep. (ENG.). 416p. (YA). (gr. 7). 2017. pap. 10.99 ***(978-1-101-99831-1(8)***, Speak) 2016. (Illus.). 17.99 *(978-1-101-99829-8(6)*, Viking Books for Young Readers) Penguin Young Readers Group.
—Riverkeep. 2017. lib. bdg. 22.10 ***(978-0-606-40100-5(8))*** Turtleback Bks.
Stewart, Paul. The Curse of Magoria. 2008. (Thrillers Ser.). 125p. (YA). (gr. 5-18). per. 4.99 *(978-0-7945-1816-5(8)*, Usborne) EDC Publishing.
—Edge - The Nameless One, Bk. 1. Riddell, Chris, illus. 2014. (Edge Chronicles Ser.). (ENG.). 368p. (J). (gr. 4-6). 24.99 *(978-0-85753-234-3(0))* Transworld Publishers Ltd. GBR. Dist: Independent Pubs. Group.
—Far-Flung Adventures: Hugo Pepper. 2012. (Far-Flung Adventures Ser.). (ENG.). 272p. (J). (gr. 3-7). 7.99 *(978-0-385-75223-7(7)*, Yearling) Random Hse. Children's Bks.
Stewart, Paul & Riddell, Chris. Beyond the Deepwoods. 2008. (Edge Chronicles Ser.: Bk. 1). (ENG.). 288p. (J). (gr. 3-7). 8.99 *(978-0-440-42087-3(3)*, Bluefire) Random Hse. Children's Bks.
—Edge Chronicles: Clash of the Sky Galleons. 2010. (Edge Chronicles Ser.). (ENG.). 432p. (J). (gr. 3-7). 8.99 *(978-0-385-73613-8(4)*, Yearling) Random Hse. Children's Bks.
—Edge Chronicles: the Winter Knights. 2010. (Edge Chronicles Ser.). (ENG.). 400p. (J). (gr. 3-7). 8.99 *(978-0-385-73612-1(6)*, Yearling) Random Hse. Children's Bks.
—Last of the Sky Pirates. 2009. (Edge Chronicles Ser.). (ENG.). 384p. (J). (gr. 3-7). 8.99 *(978-0-440-42100-9(4)*, Yearling) Random Hse. Children's Bks.
—Midnight over Sanctaphrax. 2008. (Edge Chronicles Ser.: No. 3). (ENG.). 368p. (J). (gr. 3-7). 7.99 *(978-0-440-42098-9(9)*, Yearling) Random Hse. Children's Bks.
—Stormchaser. 2008. (Edge Chronicles Ser.: Bk. 2). (ENG., Illus.). 400p. (J). (gr. 3-7). 8.99 *(978-0-440-42088-0(1)*, Yearling) Random Hse. Children's Bks.
Stewart, Sharon. Raven Quest. 2005. (ENG.). 320p. (J). (gr. 4-6). 15.95 *(978-1-57505-894-8(4)*, Carolrhoda Bks.) Lerner Publishing Group.
Stiefvater, Maggie. Ballad: A Gathering of Faerie. 2009. (Lament Novel Ser.: 2). (ENG.). 360p. (YA). (gr. 7-18). pap. 9.95 *(978-0-7387-1484-4(4)*, Flux) North Star Editions.
—Hunted, Bk. 2. 2014. (Spirit Animals Ser.: 2). (ENG., Illus.). 192p. (J). (gr. 3-7). 12.99 *(978-0-545-52244-1(7))* Scholastic, Inc.
—The Raven King. 2016. 439p. (J). ***(978-0-605-90184-1(8)***, Scholastic Pr.) Scholastic, Inc.
Stiefvater, Maggie. The Scorpio Races. 2011. (ENG.). 416p. (J). (gr. 9). 17.99 *(978-0-545-22490-1(X)*, Scholastic Pr.) Scholastic, Inc.
Stilton, Geronimo. Kingdom of Fantasy. 2009. (Kingdom of Fantasy Ser.: No. 1). 320p. 14.99 *(978-0-439-69148-2(6)*, Scholastic Paperbacks) Scholastic, Inc.
—The Kingdom of Fantasy. 2009. (Geronimo Stilton & the Kingdom of Fantasy Ser.: 1). (ENG., Illus.). 288p. (J). (gr. 2-5). 14.99 *(978-0-545-98025-8(9))* Scholastic, Inc.
—The Quest for Paradise. 2010. (Geronimo Stilton & the Kingdom of Fantasy Ser.: 2). (ENG.). 320p. (J). (gr. 2-5). 14.99 *(978-0-545-25307-9(1))* Scholastic, Inc.
—The Treasure of Easter Island. 2015. (Geronimo Stilton Ser.: 60). lib. bdg. 17.20 *(978-0-606-37057-8(9))* Turtleback Bks.
Stilton, Geronimo & Dami, Elisabetta. The Enchanted Charms: The Seventh Adventure in the Kingdom of Fantasy. Barozzi, Danilo, illus. 2015. (ENG.). 320p. (J). (gr. 2-5). 14.99 *(978-0-545-74615-1(9))* Scholastic, Inc.
Stims, Robert. The Chain of Wisdom, Bk. I. 2003. 166p. (YA). pap. 12.95 *(978-0-595-29235-6(6))* iUniverse, Inc.
Stine, Faye. The Magic Forest: The Magic of Childhood. 2009. 117p. (J). pap. 10.95 *(978-1-4327-3617-0(5))* Outskirts Pr., Inc.
Stine, R. L. Can You Keep a Secret? 2016. (Fear Street Ser.). (ENG.). 272p. (YA). 18.99 *(978-1-250-05894-2(5)*, 9781250058942, St. Martin's Griffin) St. Martin's Pr.
—Deep Trouble. 2008. (Classic Goosebumps Ser.: 2). (ENG.). 144p. (J). (gr. 3-7). 6.99 *(978-0-545-03519-4(8)*, Scholastic Paperbacks) Scholastic, Inc.
—Ghost Beach. 2010. (Classic Goosebumps Ser.: 15). (ENG.). 160p. (J). (gr. 3-7). 6.99 *(978-0-545-17803-7(7)*, Scholastic Paperbacks) Scholastic, Inc.
—The Haunted Mask. 2013. lib. bdg. 17.20 *(978-0-606-32005-4(9)*, Turtleback) Turtleback Bks.
—Heads, You Lose. 2010. (Goosebumps Horrorland Ser.: 15). (ENG.). 160p. (J). (gr. 3-7). 6.99 *(978-0-545-16196-1(7)*, Scholastic Paperbacks) Scholastic, Inc.
—Little Shop of Hamsters. 2010. (Goosebumps Horrorland Ser.: 14). (ENG.). 160p. (J). (gr. 3-7). 6.99 *(978-0-545-16195-4(9)*, Scholastic Paperbacks) Scholastic, Inc.
—A Midsummer Night's Scream. 2013. (ENG.). 256p. (YA). (gr. 7). 17.99 *(978-1-250-02434-3(X)*, 9781250024343) Feiwel & Friends.
—A Midsummer Night's Scream. 2014. (ENG.). 256p. (YA). (gr. 7-12). pap. 10.99 *(978-1-250-04434-1(0)*, 9781250044341) Square Fish.
—Phantom of the Auditorium. 2011. (Classic Goosebumps Ser.: 20). (ENG.). 160p. (J). (gr. 3-7). pap. 6.99 *(978-0-545-29836-0(9)*, Scholastic Paperbacks) Scholastic, Inc.
—Planet of the Lawn Gnomes. 2012. (Goosebumps Most Wanted Ser.: 1). (ENG.). 160p. (J). (gr. 3-7). pap. 6.99 *(978-0-545-41798-3(8)*, Scholastic Paperbacks) Scholastic, Inc.
—Return of the Mummy. 2010. (Classic Goosebumps Ser.: 18). (ENG.). 160p. (J). (gr. 3-7). pap. 6.99 *(978-0-545-17794-8(4)*, Scholastic Paperbacks) Scholastic, Inc.
—Who's Your Mummy? 2009. (Goosebumps Horrorland Ser.: 6). (ENG.). 160p. (J). (gr. 3-7). 6.99 *(978-0-439-91874-9(X)*, Scholastic Paperbacks) Scholastic, Inc.
—Wizard of Ooze. 2010. (Goosebumps Horrorland Ser.: 17). (ENG.). 160p. (J). (gr. 3-7). pap. 6.99 *(978-0-545-16198-5(3)*, Scholastic Paperbacks) Scholastic, Inc.
—You Can't Scare Me! 2010. (Classic Goosebumps Ser.: 17). (ENG.). 160p. (J). (gr. 3-7). pap. 6.99 *(978-0-545-17796-2(0)*, Scholastic Paperbacks) Scholastic, Inc.
Stites, Theresa. The Orange Peel. 2007. 20p. per. 24.95 *(978-1-4241-8580-1(7))* America Star Bks.
Stocks, David. Moon Rabbit. 2008. 276p. pap. *(978-1-84747-838-2(7))* Chipmunkapublishing.
Stockton, Frank Richard. The Bee-Man of Orn & Other Fanciful Tales. 2005. 124p. per. 10.95 *(978-1-59818-695-6(7))* Aegypan.
—The Bee-Man of Orn & Other Fanciful Tales. 2007. (ENG.). 140p. pap. 18.99 *(978-1-4264-5788-3(X))*; 154p. pap. 21.99 *(978-1-4264-5848-4(7))* Creative Media Partners, LLC.
—The Bee-Man of Orn & Other Fanciful Tales. 2004. reprint ed. pap. 20.95 *(978-1-4191-5383-9(8))*; pap. 1.99 *(978-1-4192-5383-6(2))* Kessinger Publishing, LLC.
—John Gayther's Garden & the Stories Told Therein. 2008. 220p. pap. 15.95 *(978-1-60664-247-4(2))* Rodgers, Alan Bks.
Stoddard, Laura. The Dreamosphere. 2014. pap. 14.99 *(978-1-4621-1444-3(X))* Cedar Fort, Inc./CFI Distribution.
Stofko, Michael D. Has Anybody Seen Me? 2009. 24p. pap. 12.99 *(978-1-4389-9032-3(4))* AuthorHouse.
Stone, David Lee. The Shadewell Shenanigans. 2006. (Illus.). 308p. (J). *(978-1-4156-8147-3(3))* Hyperion Bks. for Children.
Stone, Kelsey. The Predahil Chronicles. 2005. (YA). per. 6.49 *(978-1-59196-995-2(6))* Instant Pub.
Storm, Jeff. No Return Land: You Are the Hero of This Book! Chan, Harvey, illus. 2015. (Determine Your Destiny Ser.: Vol. 2). (ENG.). 176p. (J). (gr. 4-7). pap. *(978-1-77143-247-4(0))* CCB Publishing.
Storrie, Paul. Perseus: The Hunt for Medusa's Head [A Greek Myth]. Yeates, Thomas, illus. 2009. (Graphic Myths & Legends Ser.). (ENG.). 48p. (gr. 4-8). pap. 8.95 *(978-1-58013-888-8(8))* Lerner Publishing Group.
Story And Pictures By Neenie. Rachel & the Rose Silk Unicorn. 2009. 24p. pap. 12.99 *(978-1-4389-7299-2(7))* AuthorHouse.
Stover, Anne Long. Cloudy. Spears, Ashley E., illus. 2005. 20p. (J). *(978-0-9762389-0-4(X))* Trent's Prints.
Straffi, Iginio. Winx Club: Magic Collection. 2014. (ENG.). 832p. (J). pap. 19.99 *(978-1-4215-7729-6(1))* Viz Media.
The Strange & Beautiful Sorrows of Ava Lavender. 2014. 320p. (J). (gr. 9). E-Book 8.99 *(978-0-7636-7034-4(0))* Candlewick Pr.
Stratton, Allan. The Grave Robber's Apprentice. 2012. 288p. (J). (gr. 5). 16.99 *(978-0-06-197608-7(3))* HarperCollins Pubs.
Strega Nona. 2005. (J). *(978-1-59564-834-1(8))* Steps To Literacy, LLC.
Strickland, AdriAnne. Lifeless. 2015. (ENG.). 312p. (YA). pap. 9.99 *(978-0-7387-4222-9(8)*, Flux) North Star Editions.
Strickland, Brad & Fuller, Thomas E. Missing! 2004. (Mars Year One Ser.: 2). (ENG., Illus.). 176p. (J). (gr. 3-7). pap. 9.99 *(978-0-689-86401-8(9)*, Aladdin) Simon & Schuster Children's Publishing.
Strickler, Ashley. Once upon A Time. 2007. 212p. pap. 12.95 *(978-1-4327-0207-6(6))* Outskirts Pr., Inc.
Strings Magazine Staff. The Wizard's Den: Spellbinding Stories of Magic & Magicians. Haining, Peter, ed. 2003. (ENG., Illus.). 320p. (J). (gr. 3-7). 22.95 *(978-0-285-63628-6(6))* Souvenir Pr. Ltd. GBR. Dist: Independent Pubs. Group.
Strobel-Cort, Joanne. Emillee Kart & the Seven Saving Signs: The Tale of Beasley's Bonnet. 2007. 204p. per. 24.95 *(978-1-4241-8597-9(1))* America Star Bks.
Strohm, Keith Francis. Bladesinger. 2006. (Fighters Ser.). (Illus.). 312p. *(978-1-4156-6627-2(X))* Wizards of the Coast.
Strong, Jeremy. Dinosaur Pox. Sharratt, Nick, illus. (ENG.). 128p. (J). 7.95 *(978-0-14-038979-1(2))* Penguin Bks., Ltd. GBR. Dist: Trafalgar Square Publishing.
—The Sneezles. Blundell, Tony, illus. 2005. (Collins Big Cat Ser.). (ENG.). 32p. (J). (gr. 1-3). pap. 7.99 *(978-0-00-718628-0(2))* HarperCollins Pubs. Ltd. GBR. Dist: Independent Pubs. Group.
Stroud, Jonathan. The Amulet of Samarkland. 2004. (Bartimaeus Novel Ser.). (ENG.). 480p. (J). (gr. 5-9). reprint ed. pap. 9.99 *(978-0-7868-5255-0(0))* Hyperion Pr.
—Ptolemy's Gate, Bk. 3. 3rd rev. ed. 2007. (Bartimaeus Novel Ser.). (ENG.). 512p. (J). (gr. 5-9). per. 9.99 *(978-0-7868-3868-4(X))* Hyperion Pr.
Strutz, Amuel U. Santa's New Reindeer Team. 2009. (Illus.). 60p. pap. 24.99 *(978-1-4389-6455-3(2))* AuthorHouse.
Stuart, Raff. A Roman Odyssey: Book One of the chronicles of Adam Black the Teenage Time Traveller. 2009. 228p. pap. 14.49 *(978-1-4389-7407-1(8))* AuthorHouse.
Stupniker, Yehudit. The Remarkable Invention That Saves Zion: A Tale of Triz. 2007. 292p. 18.95 *(978-1-932687-74-3(2)*, Devora Publishing) Simcha Media Group.
Sturm, Ilana. The 13th Moon. 2013. 92p. pap. *(978-1-936922-61-1(4))* Roxby Media Ltd.
Styczynski, Gary. The Animals of Greenback Valley: The Magic Card. 2009. 32p. pap. 24.95 *(978-1-59858-930-6(X))* Dog Ear Publishing, LLC.
Suarez de la Prida, Isabel. Los Diminutos. Bouchain, Nava, illus. 2003. (SPA.). 32p. (J). (gr. k-3). pap. 6.95 *(978-968-19-0631-3(4))* Santillana USA Publishing Co., Inc.
Sue, Grandma. The Zibbins: The Golden Necklace. 2011. 24p. (J). pap. 9.95 *(978-0-9846251-0-9(0))* Sea Keepers Publishing.
Suhay, Lisa. Our Fantasy Island: An Interactive Book. Hundley, Sam, illus. 2006. 30p. (J). pap. 8.00 *(978-0-9766628-0-8(9))* Fantasy Island Pr.
—There Goes a Mermaid - A NorFolktale. Sam, Hundley, illus. 2004. 32p. (J). pap. 7.95 *(978-0-9648308-2-0(5))* Virginian Pilot.
Suleyman, R. H. Tales Within. 2012. (Illus.). 130p. pap. *(978-1-78132-002-0(0))* SilverWood Bks.
Sullivan, Jenny. Nowhere Again. 2004. (ENG.). 230p. pap. 13.95 *(978-1-84323-297-1(9))* Beekman Bks., Inc.
Summerill, Erin. Ever the Hunted. 2016. (Clash of Kingdoms Novel Ser.). (ENG.). 400p. (YA). (gr. 7). 17.99 *(978-0-544-66445-6(0)*, HMH Books For Young Readers) Houghton Mifflin Harcourt Publishing Co.
Summers, Gillian. Into the Wildewood. 2008. (Faire Folk Saga Ser.: 2). (ENG.). 312p. (YA). (gr. 7-14). pap. 9.95 *(978-0-7387-1332-8(5)*, Flux) North Star Editions.
—The Secret of the Dread Forest: The Faire Folk Trilogy. 2009. (Faire Folk Saga Ser.: 3). (ENG.). 288p. (YA). pap. 9.95 *(978-0-7387-1411-0(9)*, Flux) North Star Editions.
Sumner, M. C. Deadly Secrets. 2013. (Extreme Zone Ser.: 4). (ENG., Illus.). 192p. (YA). (gr. 11). pap. 13.99 *(978-1-4814-2125-6(5)*, Simon Pulse) Simon Pulse.
Sunday, Bonnie. Sparkles, Dragons, & Dragonfly Land. 2012. 32p. pap. 19.99 *(978-1-4772-2914-9(0))* AuthorHouse.
Sundstrom, Dainel H. The Return of Oz. 2007. pap. 10.00 *(978-0-8059-8944-1(7))* Dorrance Publishing Co., Inc.
Suplicki, Mark J. Mirthburdz: The Discovery. 2004. (Illus.). 51p. (J). 19.95 *(978-0-9764385-0-2(X)*, 00B1) Jon'taar Graphxs.
Suritsch, Gina. Magical Tales from India: The Secret of the White Elephant & Mukti the Lion Finds Himself. 2013. 44p. pap. 22.99 *(978-1-4828-1435-4(8))* Partridge Pub.
Sussex, Lucy. The Revognase. 2005. (Illus.). 160p. pap. *(978-0-7344-0495-4(6)*, Lothian Children's Bks.) Hachette Australia.
Sutcliff, Rosemary. Beowulf, Dragon Slayer. 2017. (Puffin Book Ser.). (ENG., Illus.). 128p. (J). (gr. 4-6). pap. 8.99 ***(978-0-14-136869-6(1))*** Penguin Bks., Ltd. GBR. Dist: Independent Pubs. Group.
Sutherland, Jon, et al. The Emerald Pirate. 2005. (F. E. A. R. Adventures S. Ser.). (ENG., Illus.). 110p. (J). 8.00 *(978-1-84046-690-4(1)*, Wizard Books) Icon Bks., Ltd. GBR. Dist: Publishers Group Canada.
—The Spy Master. 2005. (F. E. A. R. Adventures S. Ser.). (ENG., Illus.). 128p. (J). 8.00 *(978-1-84046-692-8(8)*, Wizard Books) Icon Bks., Ltd. GBR. Dist: Publishers Group Canada.
Sutherland, Paul H. Finding Utopia. Gibbons, Timothy M., illus. 2006. 44p. (J). (gr. k-7). 20.00 *(978-0-9661060-4-6(0))* Utopia Pr.
Sutherland, Tui T. Against the Tide. 2014. (Spirit Animals Ser.: 5). (ENG.). 192p. (J). (gr. 3-7). 16.99 *(978-0-545-59975-7(X))*;Bk. 5. (Illus.). 12.99 *(978-0-545-52247-2(1))* Scholastic, Inc.
—The Brightest Night. (Wings of Fire Ser.: Bk. 5). (ENG.). 336p. (J). (gr. 3-7). 2015. pap. 6.99 *(978-0-545-34927-7(3)*, Scholastic Paperbacks) 2014. (Illus.). 16.99 *(978-0-545-34922-2(2)*, Scholastic Pr.) Scholastic, Inc.
—The Brightest Night. 2015. (Wings of Fire Ser.: 5). lib. bdg. 17.20 *(978-0-606-37017-2(X))* Turtleback Bks.
—The Dark Secret. 2013. (Wings of Fire Ser.: Bk. 4). (ENG., Illus.). 336p. (J). (gr. 3-7). 16.99 *(978-0-545-34921-5(4)*, Scholastic Pr.) Scholastic, Inc.
—Darkness of Dragons. 2017. (Wings of Fire Ser.: 10). (ENG.). 432p. (J). (gr. 3-7). 16.99 ***(978-0-545-68547-4(8)***, Scholastic Pr.) Scholastic, Inc.
—Darkstalker. 2016. (Wings of Fire Ser.). (ENG., Illus.). 400p. (J). (gr. 3-7). 17.99 *(978-1-338-05361-6(2)*, Scholastic Pr.) Scholastic, Inc.
—The Dragonet Prophecy. (Wings of Fire Ser.: 1). 2013. (ENG.). 336p. (J). (gr. 3-7). pap. 6.99 *(978-0-545-34923-9(0))* 2012. (ENG.). 336p. (J). (gr. 3-7). 16.99 *(978-0-545-34918-5(4))* 2012. (Illus.). 304p. pap. *(978-0-545-48603-3(3))* Scholastic, Inc. (Scholastic Pr.).
—The Dragonet Prophecy. 2013. (Wings of Fire Ser.: 1). lib. bdg. 17.20 *(978-0-606-31952-2(2)*, Turtleback) Turtleback Bks.
—The Hidden Kingdom. (Wings of Fire Ser.: 3). (ENG.). 336p. (J). (gr. 3-7). 2014. pap. 6.99 *(978-0-545-34925-3(7))* 2013. (Illus.). 16.99 *(978-0-545-34920-8(6)*, Scholastic Pr.) Scholastic, Inc.
—The Lost Heir. 2013. (Wings of Fire Ser.: 2). (ENG.). 336p. (J). (gr. 3-7). pap. 6.99 *(978-0-545-34924-6(9))*; 16.99 *(978-0-545-34919-2(2))* Scholastic, Inc. (Scholastic Pr.).
—The Lost Heir. 2013. (Wings of Fire Ser.: 2). lib. bdg. 17.20 *(978-0-606-32341-3(4)*, Turtleback) Turtleback Bks.
—Moon Rising. 2014. (Wings of Fire Ser.: Bk. 6). (ENG.). 336p. (J). (gr. 3-7). 16.99 *(978-0-545-68534-4(6)*, Scholastic Pr.) Scholastic, Inc.
—Moon Rising. 2016. (Wings of Fire Ser.: 6). lib. bdg. 17.20 *(978-0-606-38815-3(X))* Turtleback Bks.
—Winter Turning. 2015. (Wings of Fire Ser.: Bk. 7). (ENG., Illus.). 336p. (J). (gr. 3-7). 16.99 *(978-0-545-68537-5(0)*, Scholastic Pr.) Scholastic, Inc.
Sutherland, Tui T. & Sutherland, Kari. Dragon on Trial. 2014. (Menagerie Ser.: 2). (ENG.). 304p. (J). (gr. 3-7). 16.99 *(978-0-06-085143-9(0))* HarperCollins Pubs.
Sutliff, Jamie. The Elves of Owl's Head Mountain. Blumberg, Christine A., ed. Evens, Kevin C., illus. 2007. 276p. pap. 10.95 *(978-0-9712867-8-8(7))* Cold River Pubns.
—The Elves of Owl's Head Mountain. Blumberg, Christine A., ed. Evans, Kevin, illus. 2007. 280p. (gr. 8-12). 26.95 *(978-0-9712867-7-1(9))* Cold River Pubns.
—The Land of Nen-Us-Yok. Blumberg, Christine A., ed. Evans, Kevin C., illus. 2007. 256p. pap. 10.95 *(978-0-9712867-4-0(4))*; 26.95 *(978-0-9712867-6-4(0))* Cold River Pubns.
Sutton, Kelsey. Gardenia. 2017. (ENG.). 260p. pap. 13.99 *(978-1-62681-841-5(X))* Diversion Publishing Corp.
Sutton, S. A. A Hero for Quale. 2009. 72p. pap. 9.99 *(978-1-60860-189-9(7)*, Strategic Bk. Publishing) Strategic Book Publishing & Rights Agency (SBPRA).
Suzuki, Julia. The Gift of Charms. 2015. (Land of Dragor Ser.: 1). (ENG.). 190p. (J). (gr. 4-7). pap. 8.99 *(978-1-78219-924-3(1))* Blake, John Publishing, Ltd. GBR. Dist: Independent Pubs. Group.
Swainston, Jean. The Genie Family. 2015. (ENG.). 78p. (J). (gr. 2-3). pap. 10.95 *(978-1-84963-901-9(9)*, 0d77a881-d731-472e-91eb-840b25eb1350) Austin, Stan AUS. Dist: Bookmasters Distribution.
Swallow, Gerry. Blue in the Face: A Story of Risk, Rhyme, & Rebellion. Fabretti, Valerio, illus. (Magnificent Tales of Misadventure Ser.). (ENG.). (J). 2017. 336p. pap. 7.99 *(978-1-61963-489-3(9)*, 9781619634893) 2016. 320p. 16.99 *(978-1-61963-487-9(2)*, 9781619634879) Bloomsbury Publishing USA. (Bloomsbury USA Childrens).
—Long Live the Queen: A Blue in the Face Novel. Fabretti, Valerio, illus. 2017. (Magnificent Tales of Misadventure Ser.). (ENG.). 288p. (J). 16.99 *(978-1-61963-490-9(2)*, 9781619634909, Bloomsbury USA Childrens) Bloomsbury Publishing USA.
Swann, Linda. The Land of Watermelon Mountains: Destinations Thru Imaginations. 2008. 24p. 12.99 *(978-1-4389-2570-7(0))* AuthorHouse.
Swann, Mary. A Fearsome Day. Swann, Mary, illus. 2007. (Illus.). 56p. (J). (gr. 1-3). 19.95 *(978-0-932616-87-6(9))* BrickHouse Bks., Inc.
Swann, Stephen. The Magical TV. 2009. 43p. pap. 21.50 *(978-1-4452-3001-6(1))* Lulu Pr., Inc.
Swanson, David C. N. Tube World. Burke, Shane, illus. 2012. 158p. pap. 25.00 *(978-0-9830830-2-3(9))* Swanson, David.

Swanson, Stan. The Misadventures of Hobart Hucklebuck. 2007. (J). 16.95 *(978-0-9787925-3-4(X))*; per. 9.95 *(978-0-9787925-2-7(1))* Stony Meadow Publishing.

Swartz, Tracy. Blue for Me! 2008. 20p. 12.95 *(978-1-4357-1253-9(6))* Lulu Pr., Inc.

Sweet, Caitlin. Door in the Mountain. 2014. (ENG.). 280p. (J). (gr. 6). pap. 12.99 *(978-1-77148-191-5(9))* ChiZine Pubns. CAN. Dist: Consortium Bk. Sales & Distribution.

Swift, Jonathan. Gulliver's Travels. Akib, Jamel, illus. 2006. (Classic Starts(tm) Ser.). (ENG.). 160p. (J). (gr. 2-4). 6.95 *(978-1-4027-2662-0(7))* Sterling Publishing Co., Inc.

—Gulliver's Travels. Walker, John, illus. 2010. (Stepping Stone Book(TM) Ser.). (ENG.). 112p. (J). (gr. 1-4). 4.99 *(978-0-375-86569-5(1))*, Random Hse. Bks. for Young Readers) Random Hse. Children's Bks.

—Gulliver's Travels: And A Discussion of Tolerance. Clift, Eva, illus. 2003. (Values in Action Illustrated Classics Ser.). 191p. (J). *(978-1-59203-029-3(7))* Learning Challenge, Inc.

—Los Viajes de Gulliver. (SPA., Illus.). 144p. (YA). 14.95 *(978-84-7281-080-8(1))*, AF1080) Auriga, Ediciones S.A. ESP. Dist: Continental Bk. Co., Inc.

—Los Viajes de Gulliver. (Coleccion Clasicos de la Juventud). (SPA., Illus.). 204p. (J). 12.95 *(978-84-7189-062-7(3))*, ORT322) Ortells, Alfredo Editorial S.L. ESP. Dist: Continental Bk. Co., Inc.

—Viajes de Gulliver. 2003. (Advanced Reading Ser.). (SPA.). 344p. (J). 11.95 *(978-84-670-0095-5(3))* Espasa Calpe, S.A. ESP. Dist: Planeta Publishing Corp.

Swindells, Robert. In the Nick of Time. 2008. (ENG.). 224p. (YA). (gr. 7-18). 12.99 *(978-0-552-55585-2(1))* Transworld Publishers Ltd. GBR. Dist: Independent Pubs. Group.

Swindle, Stephanie. Pumpkin Pants. 2009. 32p. pap. 13.95 *(978-1-60860-461-6(6))*, Strategic Bk. Publishing) Strategic Book Publishing & Rights Agency (SBPRA).

Symon, Andrew. Jack Shian & the Destiny Stone: Book 3 in The Shian Quest Trilogy. 2014. (ENG., Illus.). 352p. (YA). (gr. 4). pap. 11.99 ***(978-1-84502-756-8(6))*** Black and White Publishing Ltd. GBR. Dist: Independent Pubs. Group.

—Jack Shian & the Mapa Mundi Bk. 2: In The Shian Quest Trilogy. 2014. (ENG.). 352p. (YA). (gr. 4). pap. 11.99 ***(978-1-84502-706-3(X))*** Black and White Publishing Ltd. GBR. Dist: Independent Pubs. Group.

Taaffe, Gary. Bullies: Billy's Gotta Survive the City. 2013. 130p. (YA). pap. *(978-0-9874937-1-2(X))* Bunya Publishing.

Taber, Kristen. Ærenden - the Child Returns. 2012. 382p. (YA). pap. 13.99 *(978-0-9851200-0-9(2))* Sean Tigh Pr.

Tabibzadeh, M. R. Angels' Whisper. Sholevar, Bahman, ed. 2009. (Literature-Fiction Ser.).Tr. of Najvaye Fereshteghan. (ITA & ENG.). 112p. pap. *(978-0-911323-23-8(6))* Concourse Pr.

Tabor, Stephen A. When I Wished ... Shamp, Danielle, illus. 2009. 31p. pap. 24.95 *(978-1-60836-086-4(5))* America Star Bks.

Taft, Christopher C. The Witch of Green Spring. 2013. 120p. pap. 11.00 *(978-1-61204-198-8(1))*, Strategic Bk. Publishing) Strategic Book Publishing & Rights Agency (SBPRA).

Tahir, Sabaa. An Ember in the Ashes. l.t. ed. 2016. (Ember in the Ashes Ser.: 1). (ENG.). 648p. 25.99 *(978-1-4104-8875-6(6))* Cengage Gale.

—An Ember in the Ashes. 2015. (ENG.). 464p. (YA). (gr. 9). 19.95 *(978-1-59514-803-2(5))*, Razorbill) Penguin Publishing Group.

—An Ember in the Ashes. 2016. (Ember in the Ashes Ser.: Bk. 1). (ENG.). 464p. (YA). (gr. 7). pap. 11.99 *(978-1-59514-804-9(3))*, Razorbill) Penguin Young Readers Group.

—An Ember in the Ashes. 2016. 464p. lib. bdg. 23.30 *(978-0-606-38848-1(6))* Turtleback Bks.

Tahir, Sabaa. A Torch Against the Night. (Ember in the Ashes Ser.: 2). (ENG.). (YA). (gr. 9). 2017. 480p. pap. 11.99 ***(978-1-101-99888-5(1))*** 2016. 464p. 19.95 *(978-1-101-99887-8(3))* Penguin Young Readers Group. (Razorbill).

—A Torch Against the Night. 2017. (Ember in the Ashes Ser.: 2). lib. bdg. 23.30 ***(978-0-606-40085-5(0))*** Turtleback Bks.

Taitano, Janice G. The Legend of Lutung. 2006. 260p. pap. 29.00 *(978-1-59752-482-7(4))*, Resource Pubns.(OR)) Wipf & Stock Pubs.

Takahashi, Rumiko. Inuyasha Vol. 19: Demon Box Set. 2004. (Inuyasha Ser.). (ENG., Illus.). 192p. pap. 24.99 *(978-1-59116-725-9(6))* Viz Media.

—Inuyasha Ani-Manga. (Inuyasha Ser.: 15). (ENG., Illus.). Vol. 15. 2006. 208p. pap. 11.99 *(978-1-4215-0482-7(0))* Vol. 20. 2007. 216p. pap. 11.99 *(978-1-4215-0904-4(0))* Viz Media.

—Inuyasha, Vol. 44. Set. Takahashi, Rumiko, illus. 2003. (Inuyasha Ser.). (ENG., Illus.). 200p. (YA). pap. 39.98 *(978-1-59116-235-3(1))*, Viz Comics) Viz Media.

—Mermaid Saga. Takahashi, Rumiko, illus. 2004. (Mermaid Saga Ser.). (ENG., Illus.). (YA). 3. 176p. pap. 9.99 *(978-1-59116-483-8(4))* Vol. 4. 2nd ed. 192p. pap. 9.99 *(978-1-59116-482-1(6))* Viz Media.

Takaya, Natsuki. Fruits Basket Collector's Edition, Vol. 11. 2017. (Fruits Basket Collector's Edition Ser.: 11). (ENG., Illus.). 384p. (gr. 8-17). pap. 20.00 *(978-0-316-50168-2(9))*, Yen Pr.) Orbit.

—Fruits Basket Collector's Edition, Vol. 7. 2016. (Fruits Basket Collector's Edition Ser.: 7). (ENG., Illus.). 384p. (gr. 8-17). pap. 20.00 *(978-0-316-36072-2(4))*, Yen Pr.) Orbit.

—Fruits Basket Collector's Edition, Vol. 8. 2016. (Fruits Basket Collector's Edition Ser.: 8). (ENG., Illus.). 384p. (gr. 8-17). pap. 20.00 *(978-0-316-36073-9(2))*, Yen Pr.) Orbit.

—Fruits Basket Collector's Edition, Vol. 9. 2017. (Fruits Basket Collector's Edition Ser.: 9). (ENG., Illus.). 384p. (gr. 8-17). pap. 20.00 *(978-0-316-50162-0(X))*, Yen Pr.) Orbit.

Tamura, Yumi. Wild Com. Tamura, Yumi, illus. 2004. (Wild Com Ser.). (ENG., Illus.). 192p. (YA). pap. 9.95 *(978-1-59116-559-0(8))* Viz Media.

Tanabe, Yellow. Kekkaishi, Vol. 23. Tanabe, Yellow, illus. 2010. (ENG., Illus.). 192p. pap. 9.99 *(978-1-4215-3200-4(X))* Viz Media.

—Kekkaishi, Vol. 6. Tanabe, Yellow, illus. 2006. (ENG., Illus.). 208p. pap. 9.99 *(978-1-4215-0487-2(1))* Viz Media.

Tanaka, Rika. Kilala Princess, Vol. 2. 2016. (ENG.). 208p. (J). pap. 10.99 *(978-1-4278-5663-0(X))*, 9781427856630) TOKYOPOP, Inc.

Taneja, Sweta. Krishna - Defender of Dharma. Nagulakonda, Rajesh, illus. 2013. (Campfire Graphic Novels Ser.). (ENG.). 152p. (YA). (gr. 5-12). pap. 14.99 *(978-93-80741-12-3(X))*, Campfire) Steerforth Pr.

Tanemura, Arina. O Sagashite Vol. 6, 7 vols. Tanemura, Arina, illus. 2006. (Full Moon Ser.: 6). (ENG., Illus.). 208p. pap. 8.99 *(978-1-4215-0397-4(2))* Viz Media.

Tanigawa, Nagaru. The Boredom of Haruhi Suzumiya. 2010. (Haruhi Suzumiya Ser.: 3). (ENG., Illus.). 224p. (YA). (gr. 10-17). 24.00 *(978-0-316-03886-7(5))*; pap. 18.00 *(978-0-316-03887-4(3))* Little, Brown Bks. for Young Readers.

—The Indignation of Haruhi Suzumiya. 2012. (Haruhi Suzumiya Ser.: 8). (ENG., Illus.). 224p. (YA). (gr. 10-17). 15.99 *(978-0-316-03900-0(4))*; pap. 18.00 *(978-0-316-03899-7(7))* Little, Brown Bks. for Young Readers.

Tanner, Lian. City of Lies. 2012. (Keepers Trilogy: Bk. 2). (ENG.). 288p. (J). (gr. 4-7). 6.99 *(978-0-375-85979-3(9))*, Yearling) Random Hse. Children's Bks.

—Museum of Thieves. (Keepers Ser.: Bk. 1). (ENG.). 320p. (J). (gr. 3-7). 2011. 8.99 *(978-0-375-85978-6(0))*, Yearling) 2010. 16.99 *(978-0-385-73905-4(2))*, Delacorte Bks. for Young Readers) Random Hse. Children's Bks.

—Path of Beasts. 2013. (Keepers Trilogy: Bk. 3). (ENG.). 352p. (J). (gr. 4-7). 8.99 *(978-0-375-85980-9(2))*, Yearling) Random Hse. Children's Bks.

Tanner, Matthew J. The Winds of Aragon. 2013. 40p. pap. 14.95 *(978-0-9885253-0-6(5))* Tanner, Matt J.

Tao, Teri. Cowherd Boy & Weaver Girl. 2008. (ENG.). 48p. pap. 5.99 *(978-1-930655-05-8(3))* Golden Peach Publishing.

Tarnowska, Wafa'. The Seven Wise Princesses: A Medieval Persian Epic. Nilesh, Misty, illus. 2008. (ENG.). 96p. (J). (gr. 5-9). 19.99 *(978-1-84686-250-2(7))* Barefoot Bks., Inc.

Tashlikowich, Natasha. The Secret of the Seven Stones. 2009. 117p. pap. 18.97 *(978-0-557-03747-6(6))* Lulu Pr., Inc.

Tatam, Michelle. Chameleon. 2014. (ENG.). 163p. (J). pap. *(978-0-9925742-1-5(8))* Solitary Cat Bks.

—The Midnight Running. 2014. (ENG.). 136p. (J). pap. *(978-0-9925742-0-8(X))* Solitary Cat Bks.

Tate, Bernice & Tate, Andrew. Zanzy's Purple Cheese & Orange Peas. 2010. 20p. 14.95 *(978-1-4490-9174-3(1))* AuthorHouse.

Taylor, C. J. Spirits, Fairies, & Merpeople: Native Stories of Other Worlds. 2009. (ENG., Illus.). 40p. (J). (gr. 2-4). 19.95 *(978-0-88776-872-9(5))*, Tundra Bks.) Tundra Bks. CAN. Dist: Penguin Random Hse. LLC.

Taylor, G. P. El Hechicero de las Sombras. Attrache, Ismael, tr. 2005. (SPA.). 328p. pap. 9.95 *(978-950-511-910-3(0))* Santillana USA Publishing Co., Inc.

—Shadowmancer: What Can Stand Against an Ancient Evil... 2004. (ENG., Illus.). 275p. 16.99 *(978-1-59185-613-9(2))*, Charisma Hse.) Charisma Media.

—The Shadowmancer Returns: The Curse of Salamander Street. 2008. (ENG.). 256p. (gr. 7-12). pap. 17.99 *(978-1-59979-084-8(X))*, Realms) Charisma Media.

—The Shadowmancer Returns: The Curse of Salamander Street. 2007. (Shadowmancer; 04 Ser.). 240p. (J). *(978-1-4287-4670-1(6))*, Putnam Juvenile) Penguin Publishing Group.

—The Tizzle Sisters & Erik. 2007. 188p. *(978-1-905692-22-4(6))* Markosia Enterprises, Ltd.

Taylor, Laini. Blackbringer. 2009. (Dreamdark Ser.: 1). (ENG., Illus.). 368p. (YA). (gr. 7-18). 9.99 *(978-0-14-241168-1(X))*, Firebird) Penguin Young Readers Group.

—Daughter of Smoke & Bone. 2011. (ENG.). 432p. (YA). (gr. 10-17). 20.00 *(978-0-316-13402-6(3))* Little Brown & Co.

—Days of Blood & Starlight. 2012. (ENG., (YA). (gr. 10-17). Illus.). 528p. 18.99 *(978-0-316-13397-5(3))*; 688p. 39.99 *(978-0-316-22433-8(2))* Little, Brown Bks. for Young Readers.

—Strange the Dreamer. 2017. 536p. (YA). ***(978-0-316-43120-0(6))*** Little Brown & Co.

—Strange the Dreamer. 2017. (ENG.). (J). 544p. (gr. 10-17). 18.99 *(978-0-316-34168-4(1))*; 704p. (gr. 9-17). 20.99 *(978-0-316-46427-7(9))* Little, Brown Bks. for Young Readers.

Taylor, Shane. The Magic of Mortals. 2006. (YA). pap. 11.95 *(978-1-58736-542-3(1))*, Starbound Bks.) Wheatmark, Inc.

Taylor, Stuart. Austin & the Lost Kingdom of Atlantis: The Austin Chronicles Volume Iii. 2013. 286p. pap. *(978-0-9560345-7-1(8))* Exciting Stories.

Taylor, Vacen. Starchild: The City of Souls. 2013. (ENG.). 176p. (J). pap. 13.95 *(978-1-922200-12-9(3))* Odyssey Bks. AUS. Dist: Lightning Source, Inc.

Taylor, Victoria. Caitlin's Wish. 2nd ed. 2012. (ENG.). 112p. pap. *(978-1-78088-101-0(0))* Troubador Publishing Ltd.

Teacher Created Resources Staff & Collins, Susan. A Guide for Using Time Soldiers in the Classroom. 2009. (ENG.). 48p. pap. 9.99 *(978-1-4206-2003-0(7))* Teacher Created Resources, Inc.

Teague, Victoria. Dragons, Demons, & Feathers. 2007. 48p. pap. 19.96 *(978-1-4357-0317-9(0))* Lulu Pr., Inc.

Teckentrup, Britta. Before I Wake Up..., 1 vol. 2016. (ENG., Illus.). 56p. (J). (gr. -1-3). 14.95 *(978-3-7913-7246-4(7))* Prestel Verlag GmbH & Co KG. DEU. Dist: Penguin Random Hse. LLC.

Ted's Red Ball: Set B Individual Title, 6 packs. (Supersonic Phonics Ser.). (gr. k-3). 29.00 *(978-0-7635-0538-7(2))* Rigby Education.

Teitelbaum, Michael. Tale of Zuko. Spaziante, Patrick, illus. 2008. (Avatar Ser.). (ENG.). 96p. (J). (gr. 2-6). pap. 5.99 *(978-1-4169-4984-8(4))*, Simon Spotlight/Nickelodeon) Simon Spotlight/Nickelodeon.

Teitelbaum, Michael & Golden Books Staff. Sleeping Beauty. DiCicco, Sue & Dias, Ron, illus. 2004. (Little Golden Book Ser.). (ENG.). 24p. (J). (gr. -1-k). 4.99 *(978-0-7364-2198-0(X))*, Golden/Disney) Random Hse. Children's Bks.

Telep, Trisha, ed. Kiss Me Deadly: 13 Tales of Paranormal Love. 2010. (ENG.). 432p. (YA). (gr. 9-17). pap. 9.95 *(978-0-7624-3949-2(1))* Running Pr. Bk. Pubs.

Telle, Nils. The Magical Forest. 2012. 76p. 37.37 *(978-1-4771-1927-3(2))*; pap. 18.68 *(978-1-4771-1926-6(4))* Xlibris Corp.

Tello, Jorge. Here Come the Blobbies. Tello, Jorge, illus. 2004. (Illus.). 32p. (J). pap. 15.89 incl. audio compact disk *(978-1-932179-32-3(1))* Pers Publishing.

Temple, Valerie. Mud Witch Boy of Ghost Canyon. 2009. 113p. pap. 21.95 *(978-1-4327-1133-7(4))* Outskirts Pr., Inc.

Tennant, Linda. Polly & Meril & the Wicked Spell. 2009. (Illus.). 20p. pap. 15.49 *(978-1-4389-7471-2(X))* AuthorHouse.

Tennapel, Doug. Ghostopolis. 2010. (ENG.). 272p. (J). (gr. 4-7). pap. 12.99 *(978-0-545-21028-7(3))*, Graphix) Scholastic, Inc.

Terpening, Lori. Hey! You Bug Me. 2012. 28p. pap. 21.99 *(978-1-4691-9529-2(1))* Xlibris Corp.

Terrell, Heather. Boundary. Cortes, Ricardo, illus. 2015. (ENG.). 276p. (YA). (gr. 9). pap. 10.99 *(978-1-61695-620-2(8))*, Soho Teen) Soho Pr., Inc.

—Relic: the Books of Eva 1. 2013. (ENG., Illus.). 280p. (YA). pap. *(978-1-61695-439-0(6))* Soho Pr., Inc.

—Relic (the Books of Eva I) Cortes, Ricardo, illus. 2014. (ENG.). 288p. (YA). (gr. 9). pap. 9.99 *(978-1-61695-406-2(X))*, Soho Teen) Soho Pr., Inc.

Tetlow, Karin. Harry the Carousel Horse. Guze, Tessa, illus. 2012. 32p. pap. 15.96 *(978-0-615-55671-0(X))* Juping Horse Pr.

Teves, Miles, illus. The Dragon Hunter's Handbook. 2008. (J). *(978-1-4351-0204-0(5))* Metro Bks.

Teys, Jo-Anne. I Wish I Was... Lahdensuo, Debbie, illus. 2005. 36p. (J). pap. *(978-0-9757001-1-2(1))* Love Song Publishing.

The Born Storytellers. Eye of the Tiger: A Born Storyteller Collection of Fantasy & Horror Stories. Price, Kevin, ed. 2013. (Illus.). 232p. (J). pap. *(978-0-9872559-7-6(5))* Logorythm.

Theodoridou, Despoina. Lola, the Lonely Doctor. 2012. (Illus.). 24p. pap. 15.99 *(978-1-4691-6637-7(2))* Xlibris Corp.

Thomas, Doris. Through the Eyes of the Orcas. 2010. 146p. pap. 14.90 *(978-3-8391-6582-9(2))* Bks. on Demand.

Thomas, Isabel. Hansel, Gretel, & the Pudding Plot. Carretero-Suarez, Mónica, illus. 2016. (Fairy Tales Today Ser.). (ENG.). 24p. (gr. 1-2). 9.95 *(978-1-4795-8748-3(6))* Picture Window Bks.

Thomas, Jane. Zioc Saves His Planet. 2009. (Illus.). 208p. pap. 14.49 *(978-1-4389-4930-7(8))* AuthorHouse.

Thomas, Jeanne Taylor. Kerry Mcdaniels & the Cave. 2012. (ENG.). 276p. pap. 18.95 *(978-1-4327-7296-3(1))* Outskirts Pr., Inc.

Thomas, John & Rowe, Susan. Mynydd y Brain. 2005. (WEL., Illus.). 32p. pap. *(978-1-85596-221-7(7))* Dref Wen.

Thomas, Marian. Fantasy Writer. (Illus.). (J). (gr. 3-6). pap. *(978-1-876367-11-4(3))* Wizard Bks.

Thomas, Michelle. Bubble World & the Enchanted Garden. 2010. (Illus.). 28p. pap. 12.49 *(978-1-4490-9088-3(5))* AuthorHouse.

—Bubble World & the Olympics. 2010. 28p. 12.49 *(978-1-4520-1682-5(8))* AuthorHouse.

Thomas, R. G. The Battle of Iron Gulch. 2017. (Town of Superstition Ser.: Vol. 3). (ENG., Illus.). (YA). pap. 14.99 ***(978-1-63533-244-5(3))***, Harmony Ink Pr.) Dreamspinner Pr.

Thomas, Rhiannon. Long May She Reign. 2017. 432p. (YA). (gr. 8). 17.99 *(978-0-06-241868-5(8))*, HarperTeen) HarperCollins Pubs.

Thomas, Rich. Thor: An Origin Story. Olliffe, Pat, illus. 2013. (Origin Story Ser.). (ENG.). 48p. (J). (gr. 1-3). 8.99 *(978-1-4231-7215-4(9))* Marvel Worldwide, Inc.

Thomas, Roy, text. Dracula. 2010. (ENG., Illus.). 208p. (gr. 10-17). 19.99 *(978-0-7851-4905-7(8))* Marvel Worldwide, Inc.

Thomas, Scarlett. Dragon's Green. 2017. (J). pap. ***(978-1-4814-9785-5(5))***, Simon & Schuster Bks. For Young Readers) Simon & Schuster Bks. For Young Readers.

Thomas, Shelley Moore. The Seven Tales of Trinket. 2014. (ENG., Illus.). 384p. (J). (gr. 3-7). pap. 11.99 *(978-1-250-03994-1(0))*, 9781250039941) Square Fish.

Thomas, Sherry. The Burning Sky. (Elemental Trilogy Ser.: 1). (ENG.). (YA). (gr. 9). 2014. 496p. pap. 9.99 *(978-0-06-220730-2(1))* 2013. 480p. 17.99 *(978-0-06-220729-6(6))* HarperCollins Pubs.

—The Immortal Heights. 2015. (Elemental Trilogy Ser.: 3). (ENG.). 448p. (YA). (gr. 9). 17.99 *(978-0-06-220735-7(0))* HarperCollins Pubs.

—The Perilous Sea. (Elemental Trilogy Ser.: 2). (ENG.). (YA). (gr. 9). 2015. 448p. pap. 9.99 *(978-0-06-220733-3(4))* 2014. 432p. 17.99 *(978-0-06-220732-6(6))* HarperCollins Pubs.

Thompson, Brian. Reject High. 2013. 270p. pap. 11.95 *(978-0-9891056-0-6(1))* Great Nation Publishing.

Thompson, Colin. Castles. Thompson, Colin, illus. 2007. (ENG., Illus.). 32p. (J). (gr. k-2). pap. 15.99 *(978-0-09-943942-4(5))*, Red Fox) Random House Children's Books GBR. Dist: Independent Pubs. Group.

Thompson, Jill. Magic Trixie. Thompson, Jill, illus. 2008. (ENG., Illus.). 96p. (J). (gr. 3-7). pap. 8.99 *(978-0-06-117045-4(3))* HarperCollins Pubs.

Thompson, Kate. The New Policeman. 2005. (Illus.). 416p. (J). *(978-0-370-32878-2(7))*; *(978-0-370-32823-2(X))* Random House Children's Books. (Bodley Head Childrens).

—The White Horse Trick. 2010. (New Policeman Trilogy Ser.: 3). (ENG.). 416p. (YA). (gr. 8-18). 17.99 *(978-0-06-200416-1(6))*, Greenwillow Bks.) HarperCollins Pubs.

Thompson, Kim. Shadow Wrack. 2016. (Eldritch Manor Ser.: 2). (ENG.). 168p. (J). pap. 12.99 *(978-1-4597-3205-6(7))* Dundurn CAN. Dist: Ingram Publisher Services.

Thompson, Mary G. Flicker & Mist. 2017. (ENG.). 384p. (YA). (gr. 7). 17.99 *(978-0-544-64840-1(4))*, Clarion Bks.) Houghton Mifflin Harcourt Trade & Reference Pubs.

—Wuftoom. 2013. (ENG.). 256p. (YA). (gr. 7). pap. 8.99 *(978-0-544-02247-8(5))* Houghton Mifflin Harcourt Publishing Co.

Thompson, Mike. Chicken Boy & the Wrath of Dr. Dimwad. Thompson, Mike, illus. 2008. (Illus.). 102p. (J). per. 9.95 *(978-0-9799216-0-5(0))* Thompson Original Productions LLC.

Thompson, Nina C. The Puzzle King. 2009. 56p. pap. 9.95 *(978-1-60860-149-3(8))*, Eloquent Bks.) Strategic Book Publishing & Rights Agency (SBPRA).

Thompson, Paul B. The Battle for the Brightstone: Book III of the Brightstone Saga. 2013. (Brightstone Saga Ser.). 176p. (J). 18.95 *(978-0-7660-3984-1(6))* Enslow Pubs., Inc.

—The Brightworking: Book I of the Brightstone Saga. 2013. (Brightstone Saga Ser.). 160p. (J). (gr. 5-12). pap. 10.95 *(978-1-4644-0169-5(1))* Enslow Pubs., Inc.

—The Fortune-Teller: Book II of the Brightstone Saga. 2013. (Brightstone Saga Ser.). 160p. (J). (gr. 5-12). pap. 10.95 *(978-1-4644-0265-4(5))*; 18.95 *(978-0-7660-3983-4(8))* Enslow Pubs., Inc.

Thompson, Ruth Plumly. The Enchanted Island of Oz. 2006. (J). 24.95 *(978-1-930764-10-1(3))* International Wizard of Oz Club, The.

—The Royal Book of Oz. 2004. reprint ed. pap. 1.99 *(978-1-4192-8123-5(2))*; pap. 20.95 *(978-1-4191-8123-8(8))* Kessinger Publishing, LLC.

—Sissajig & Other Surprises. 2003. 25.00 *(978-1-930764-05-7(7))*; pap. 12.00 *(978-1-930764-06-4(5))* International Wizard of Oz Club, The.

—The Wonder Book. 2006. (J). 24.95 *(978-1-930764-15-6(4))* International Wizard of Oz Club, The.

—Yankee in Oz. 2006. (J). 24.95 *(978-1-930764-13-2(8))* International Wizard of Oz Club, The.

Thompson, Ruth Plumly & Baum, L. Frank. The Silver Princess in Oz. Neill, John R., illus. 2011. 248p. 46.95 *(978-1-258-01166-6(2))* Literary Licensing, LLC.

Thompson-Swift, Joseph. The Adventures of Primrose Perfect. 2011. 248p. pap. *(978-1-907652-88-2(4))* Grosvenor Hse. Publishing Ltd.

Thomson, Bill. Fossil, 0 vols. Thomson, Bill, illus. 2013. (ENG., Illus.). 40p. (J). (gr. k-3). 17.99 *(978-1-4778-4700-8(6))*, 9781477847008, Amazon Children's Publishing) Amazon Publishing.

Thomson, Carly. Truth Seekers. 2013. 60p. pap. 9.99 *(978-1-62839-189-3(8))* Salem Author Services.

Thomson, John. A Small Boat at the Bottom of the Sea. 2005. (ENG., Illus.). (J). (gr. 4-7). 152p. 16.95 *(978-1-57131-657-8(4))*; 156p. per. 6.95 *(978-1-57131-656-1(6))* Milkweed Editions.

Thomson, Kate. Wild Blood. unabr. ed. 2004. (Switchers Ser.: Vol. 3). 240p. (J). (gr. 5-9). pap. 36.00 incl. audio *(978-0-8072-8853-5(5))*, LYA 276 SP, Listening Library) Random Hse. Audio Publishing Group.

Thomson, Rachel Starr. Theodore Pharris Saves the Universe. 2013. 176p. pap. *(978-1-927658-18-5(7))* Little Dozen Press.

Thomson, Sarah L. Dragon's Egg. 2007. (ENG.). 272p. (J). (gr. 3-7). 16.99 *(978-0-06-128848-7(9))*, Greenwillow Bks.) HarperCollins Pubs.

Thomson-Swift, Joe. The Monkeyboy & the Gruffits. 2011. (Illus.). 44p. pap. *(978-1-908105-63-9(1))* Grosvenor Hse. Publishing Ltd.

—The Twig People of Mossdown Woods. 2011. (Illus.). 36p. pap. *(978-1-908105-35-6(6))* Grosvenor Hse. Publishing Ltd.

Thorne, K. C. The Troll of MacKinac. Johnson, Vickie, illus. 2010. 32p. pap. 13.00 *(978-1-60911-178-6(8))*, Eloquent Bks.) Strategic Book Publishing & Rights Agency (SBPRA).

Thornewell, Danielle. The Mems. 2007. (ENG.). 52p. per. 16.95 *(978-1-4241-6106-5(1))* PublishAmerica, Inc.

Thornhill, Gail. The Secret Life of Truly Jones. 2003. 196p. (J). pap. 12.99 *(978-1-58832-081-0(2))* Unlimited Publishing LLC.

Thorpe, Kiki. A Dandelion Wish. Christy, Jana, illus. 2013. (Stepping Stone Book Series: No. 3). (ENG.). 128p. (J). (gr. 1-4). 5.99 *(978-0-7364-2796-8(1))*, RH/Disney) Random Hse. Children's Bks.

—A Dandelion Wish. Christy, Jana, illus. 2013. (Never Girls Ser.: 3). lib. bdg. 16.00 *(978-0-606-32199-0(3))*, Turtleback) Turtleback Bks.

—A Pinch of Magic. Christy, Jana, illus. 2014. (Never Girls Ser.: No. 7). (ENG.). 128p. (J). (gr. 1-4). 5.99 *(978-0-7364-3097-5(0))*, RH/Disney) Random Hse. Children's Bks.

—A Pinch of Magic. 2014. (Never Girls Ser.: 7). lib. bdg. 16.00 *(978-0-606-36008-1(5))* Turtleback Bks.

Through the Looking Glass. (Read-Along Ser.). (YA). pap., stu. ed. 34.95 incl. audio *(978-0-88432-971-8(2))*, S23946) Pavilion Pubs.

Thurber, James. The Wonderful O. Simont, Marc, illus. 2017. (Penguin Classics Deluxe Edition Ser.). (ENG.). 96p. pap. 17.00 ***(978-0-14-313042-0(0))***, Penguin Classics) Penguin Publishing Group.

Thurston, Alecia Frances. Shumalady's Butterfly Tree. 2010. 40p. pap. 18.49 *(978-1-4490-5609-4(1))* AuthorHouse.

Tibo, Gilles. Le Gardien du Sommeil. Jorisch, Stéphane, illus. 2004. (Mon Roman Ser.). (FRE.). 64p. (J). (gr. 2). pap. *(978-2-89021-691-4(8))* Diffusion du livre Mirabel (DLM).

—Noches de Papel. (Barril Sin Fondo Ser.). (SPA.). (J). (gr. 3-5). pap. *(978-968-6465-32-7(4))* Casa de Estudios de Literatura y Talleres Artisticos Amaquemecan A.C. MEX. Dist: Lectorum Pubns., Inc.

Tidball, Lee. Windfork Secrets. 2013. 256p. pap. *(978-1-927384-12-1(5))* Zeta Comics.

Tiernan, Cate. Book of Shadows, Bk. 1. 2007. (Sweep Ser.: 1). (ENG.). 192p. (YA). (gr. 7-18). pap. 7.99 *(978-0-14-240986-2(3))*, Speak) Penguin Young Readers Group.

—Changeling, Bk. 8. 2008. (Sweep Ser.: 8). (ENG.). 192p. (YA). (gr. 7-18). 7.99 *(978-0-14-241023-3(3))*, Speak) Penguin Young Readers Group.

—Darkness Falls. 2012. (Immortal Beloved Ser.: 2). (ENG.). 416p. (YA). (gr. 7-17). pap. 8.99 *(978-0-316-03594-1(7))*, Poppy) Little, Brown Bks. for Young Readers.

—Eternally Yours. 2013. (Immortal Beloved Ser.: 3). (ENG.). 464p. (YA). (gr. 7-17). pap. 10.00 *(978-0-316-03595-8(5))*, Poppy) Little, Brown Bks. for Young Readers.

—Spellbound. 2007. (Sweep Ser.: 6). (ENG.). 192p. (YA). (gr. 7-18). 7.99 *(978-0-14-241021-9(7))*, Speak) Penguin Young Readers Group.

Tiki Machine, LLC Staff, creator. Deus Libris: An Illustrated Collection. 2011. (Illus.). 58p. 19.99 *(978-0-615-49510-1(9))* Tiki Machine, LLC.

Tilley, Lawrence. Animal Retreat. 2004. 49p. pap. 16.95 *(978-1-4137-1136-3(7))* America Star Bks.

Tillis, Doris. Rudy the Rabbit. Tillis, Carrie, illus. 2005. 32p. per. 17.95 *(978-1-58961-410-9(0))* PageFree Publishing, Inc.

Tillman, Nancy. You & Me & the Wishing Tree. 2016. (ENG., Illus.). 32p. (J). 17.99 *(978-1-250-05629-0(2))*, 9781250056290) Feiwel & Friends.

Tillson, M. C. Secret of Bete Grise Bay: A Michigan Lighthouse Adventure. Bailey, Lisa, illus. 2008. (ENG.). (J). (gr. 1-5). pap. 9.95 *(978-0-9764824-2-0(8))* A & M Writing and Publishing,.

Tim Todd. The Town of Ill. 2009. 36p. pap. 18.99 *(978-1-4389-2778-7(9))* AuthorHouse.

Timroth, Stephen. Dreamhawk. 2009. 24p. pap. 12.00 (978-1-60860-501-9(9), Strategic Bk. Publishing) Strategic Book Publishing & Rights Agency (SBPRA).

Tintera, Amy. Avenged. (Ruined Ser.: 2). (YA). (gr. 8). 2018. (ENG.). 432p. pap. 9.99 **(978-0-06-239664-8(1))** 2017. 416p. 17.99 (978-0-06-239663-1(3)) HarperCollins Pubs. (HarperTeen).

Tintera, Amy. Ruined. (Ruined Ser.: 1). (YA). (gr. 8). 2017. 384p. pap. 9.99 (978-0-06-239661-7(7)) 2016. 368p. 17.99 (978-0-06-239660-0(9)) HarperCollins Pubs. (HarperTeen).

Tish, Aunty. Kiddiwink Kingdom. 2006. (Illus.). 58p. (J). per. 19.95 (978-1-59800-587-5(1)) Outskirts Pr., Inc.

Titan Comics Staff & Furman, Simon. Dangers of the Deep, Vol. 2. Max, Iman, illus. 2014. (Riders of Berk Ser.). (ENG.). 64p. (J). (gr. 3-7). pap. 6.99 (978-1-78276-077-1(6)) Titan Bks. Ltd. GBR. Dist: Penguin Random Hse. LLC.

—Dragon Down, Vol. 1. Nazif, Iwan, illus. 2014. (Riders of Berk Ser.). (ENG.). 64p. (J). (gr. 3-7). pap. 6.99 (978-1-78276-076-4(8)) Titan Bks. Ltd. GBR. Dist: Penguin Random Hse. LLC.

Titan Comics, Titan. The Ice Castle, Vol. 3. Lawrence, Jack, illus. 2015. (Riders of Berk Ser.). (ENG.). 64p. (J). (gr. 3-7). pap. 6.99 (978-1-78276-078-8(4)) Titan Bks. Ltd. GBR. Dist: Penguin Random Hse. LLC.

Titchenell, Elsa-Brita. Once Round the Sun. Gruelle, Justin C., illus. 2011. 62p. 36.95 (978-1-258-03323-1(2)) Literary Licensing, LLC.

Toby Forward Staff. Doubleborn. 2015. (Dragonborn Ser.: 3). (ENG.). 336p. (YA). (gr. 5-8). 16.99 (978-1-61963-528-9(3), 9781619635289, Bloomsbury USA Childrens) Bloomsbury Publishing USA.

Todd, Anne. Teddy Powers: The Stone Keepers. 2012. 394p. pap. 13.99 (978-1-938993-00-8(4)) Keogh, Anne.

Tokuda-Hall, Maggie. Also an Octopus. Davies, Benji, illus. 2016. (ENG.). 32p. (J). (gr. -1-2). 16.99 (978-0-7636-7084-9(7)) Candlewick Pr.

Tokyopop Staff, creator. Contents under Pressure, Vol. 3. 2005. (Lilo & Stitch Ser.). (Illus.). 89p. (gr. 3-7). pap. 14.99 (978-1-59532-069-8(5), Tokyopop Kids) TOKYOPOP, Inc.

Tokyopop Staff, illus. Rave Master: The Sound of Thunder, Vol. 3. 2005. 96p. (J). pap. 7.99 (978-1-59532-791-8(6)) TOKYOPOP, Inc.

Tolcser, Sarah. Song of the Current. 2017. (ENG.). 384p. (YA). 17.99 (978-1-68119-297-0(7), 9781681192970, Bloomsbury USA Childrens) Bloomsbury Publishing USA.

Toliver, Wendy. Once upon a Time: Red's Untold Tale. 2015. (ENG., Illus.). 410p. (YA). (gr. 7-12). 16.99 (978-1-4847-2746-1(0)) Hyperion Bks. for Children.

Tolkien, J. R. R. The Hobbit. Tolkien, J. R. R., illus. 75th anniv. ed. 2007. (ENG., Illus.). 320p. (gr. 7). 25.00 (978-0-618-96863-3(6)) Houghton Mifflin Harcourt Publishing Co.

—The Hobbit. movie tie-in ed. 2012. lib. bdg. 19.65 (978-0-606-26240-8(7), Turtleback) Turtleback Bks.

—Senhor dos Aneis. pap. 36.95 (978-85-336-1337-9(7)) Livraria Martins Editora BRA. Dist: Distribooks, Inc.

Tolkien, J. R. R. & Titley, Alan. An Hobad: Nó Anonn Agus Ar Ais Arís. 2012. (Illus.). 284p. (978-1-904808-90-9(5)) Evertype.

Tolkien, J. R. R., et al. An Hobad: Nó Anonn Agus Ar Ais Arís. 2013. (Illus.). 284p. pap. (978-1-78201-033-3(5)) Evertype.

Tolkien, Michael. Woodsy. 2014. 78p. pap. (978-1-910162-44-6(2)) Legend Pr.

Tomalin, Chris Fedorka. If I Had a Tail. 2017. (ENG., Illus.). (J). pap. 14.95 **(978-1-78629-411-1(7)**, 04f4f592-62c5-465b-9405-50ac16526c6b) Austin, Stan AUS. Dist: Bookmasters Distribution.

Tombo. The Magic Nickel: A Fable about an Unhappy Salesman, a Sad Retired Person, & an Invisible Monster. 2012. 26p. pap. 16.99 (978-1-4624-0280-9(1), Inspiring Voices) Author Solutions, Inc.

Tomita, Sukehiro. Young Love, Vol. 7. Yazawa, Nao, illus. 2004. (Wedding Peach Ser.). (ENG.). 200p. pap. 9.95 (978-1-59116-450-0(8)) Viz Media.

Tomizawa, Hitoshi. Alien Nine: Emulators. Pannone, Frank, ed. Jackson, Laura & Kobayashi, Yoko, trs. from JPN. Tomizawa, Hitoshi, illus. 2004. (Illus.). 248p. pap. 9.99 (978-1-58664-924-1(8), CMX 65004G, CPM Manga) Central Park Media Corp.

Tomos, Angharad. Cosyn. 2005. (WEL., Illus.). 24p. pap. (978-0-86243-566-0(8)) Y Lolfa.

Tooth, Lucy. Star the Tooth Fairy Haunted by Mr. Jack-O-Lantern in Pumpkinland! 2009. 36p. 16.95 (978-0-557-10300-3(2)) Lulu Pr., Inc.

—Star the Tooth Fairy Is Checking on You! 2009. 36p. 16.95 (978-0-557-07500-3(9)) Lulu Pr., Inc.

—Star the Tooth Fairy Wants to Know If You Need Braces? 2009. 36p. 16.95 (978-0-557-07542-3(4)) Lulu Pr., Inc.

Top That Publishing Editors, ed. Beastly Ballons. Dahl, Roald, illus. 2005. 24p. (J). pap. (978-1-905359-55-4(1)) Top That! Publishing PLC.

Torday, Piers. The Last Wild. 2014. (Last Wild Ser.: 1). (ENG., Illus.). 336p. (J). (gr. 3-7). 16.99 (978-0-670-01554-2(7), Viking Books for Young Readers) Penguin Young Readers Group.

Toreeva, Natalia G. The Battle on the Kalinov-Bridge: A Russian Fairy Tale. 2012. 48p. pap. 18.50 (978-1-61897-434-1(3), Strategic Bk. Publishing) Strategic Book Publishing & Rights Agency (SBPRA).

Toriyama, Akira. Dragon Ball (3-in-1 Edition), Vol. 4, 3 in 1 vols. 2014. (ENG., Illus.). 576p. (Orig.). pap. 14.99 (978-1-4215-5612-3(X)) Viz Media.

—Dragon Ball: Chapter Book, Vol. 9. Toriyama, Akira, illus. 2010. (ENG., Illus.). 80p. (J). pap. 4.99 (978-1-4215-3125-0(9)) Viz Media.

—Dragon Ball Full Color, Vol. 1. 2014. (ENG., Illus.). 248p. pap. 19.99 (978-1-4215-6592-7(7)) Viz Media.

—Dragon Ball Full Color, Vol. 2. 2014. (ENG., Illus.). 248p. pap. 19.99 (978-1-4215-6593-4(5)) Viz Media.

—Dragon Ball, Vol. 1. Toriyama, Akira, illus. 2nd ed. 2003. (ENG., Illus.). 192p. (Orig.). pap. 9.99 (978-1-56931-920-8(0)) Viz Media.

—Dragon Ball, Vol. 11. Morimoto, Mari, tr. from JPN. Toriyama, Akira, illus. 2003. (ENG., Illus.). 192p. (Orig.). pap. 9.99 (978-1-56931-919-2(7)) Viz Media.

—Dragon Ball, Vol. 2. Toriyama, Akira, illus. 2nd ed. 2003. (ENG., Illus.). 200p. (Orig.). pap. 9.99 (978-1-56931-921-5(9)) Viz Media.

—Dragon Ball, Vol. 3. Morimoto, Mari, tr. from JPN. Toriyama, Akira, illus. 2nd ed. 2003. (ENG., Illus.). 192p. (Orig.). pap. 9.99 (978-1-56931-922-2(7)) Viz Media.

—Dragon Ball, Vol. 4. Toriyama, Akira, illus. 2nd ed. 2003. (ENG., Illus.). 192p. (Orig.). pap. 9.99 (978-1-56931-923-9(5)) Viz Media.

—Dragon Ball, Vol. 5. Toriyama, Akira, illus. 2nd ed. 2003. (ENG., Illus.). 192p. (Orig.). pap. 9.99 (978-1-56931-924-6(3)) Viz Media.

—Dragon Ball, Vol. 6. Morimoto, Mari, tr. from JPN. Toriyama, Akira, illus. 2nd ed. 2003. (ENG., Illus.). 192p. (Orig.). pap. 9.99 (978-1-56931-925-3(1)) Viz Media.

—Dragon Ball, Vol. 7. Morimoto, Mari, tr. from JPN. Toriyama, Akira, illus. 2nd ed. 2003. (ENG., Illus.). 192p. (Orig.). pap. 9.99 (978-1-56931-926-0(X)) Viz Media.

—Dragon Ball, Vol. 8. Toriyama, Akira, illus. 2nd ed. 2003. (ENG., Illus.). 192p. (Orig.). pap. 9.99 (978-1-56931-927-7(8)) Viz Media.

—Dragon Ball, Vol. 9. Toriyama, Akira, illus. 2nd ed. 2003. (ENG., Illus.). 192p. (Orig.). pap. 9.99 (978-1-56931-928-4(6)) Viz Media.

—Fight to the Finish! Toriyama, Akira, illus. 2010. (Dragon Ball Ser.: 8). (ENG., Illus.). 80p. (J). pap. 4.99 (978-1-4215-3124-3(0)) Viz Media.

—Strongest under the Heavens. Toriyama, Akira, illus. 2010. (Dragon Ball Ser.: 10). (ENG., Illus.). 80p. (J). pap. 4.99 (978-1-4215-3126-7(7)) Viz Media.

Toufexis, George. Demonic Dragons Stickers. 2017. (Dover Stickers Ser.). (ENG., Illus.). 8p. pap. 1.99 (978-0-486-81563-3(3)) Dover Pubns., Inc.

Towbin, Meredith. Straightjacket. 2013. (ENG.). 272p. pap. 12.99 (978-1-939194-70-1(9)) Etopia Pr.

Town, Nathan. Ned Stapleton & the Wrath of the Death Gods. 2006. 174p. (YA). (978-0-9781040-0-9(5)) Emerald City Storytellers.

Townsan, Judy. The Wishing Flower, 1 vol. Rosado, Michael, illus. 2009. 13p. pap. 24.95 (978-1-61546-179-0(5)) America Star Bks.

Townsend, Charlene. The Trap & the Trip. 2013. 90p. pap. 8.99 (978-1-4808-0219-3(0)) Archway Publishing.

Townsend, Tamela Ann. Finding Pumpkin, 1 vol. 2010. 48p. pap. 16.95 (978-1-4489-5983-9(7)) America Star Bks.

ToyBox Innovations, creator. Disney's Instant Classics: Chicken Little/Lilo & Stitch/Brother Bear. unabr. abr. ed. 2005. (Disney's Read along Collection). (ENG., Illus.). (J). pap. (978-0-7634-1148-0(5)) Walt Disney Records.

Tracy, Judith. The Wildsidhe Chronicles Bk. 3: Dark Proposal. 2003. (J). pap. 7.99 (978-1-890096-15-1(6)) Padwolf Publishing, Inc.

The TrailFolk of Xunar-kun: Book Two in the Tellings of Xunar-kun. 2008. (YA). 30.95 (978-0-9768585-5-3(X)); pap. 16.95 (978-0-9768585-4-6(1)) Howe, Tina Field.

Travers, P. L. Mary Poppins. Shepard, Mary, illus. 2006. (Mary Poppins Ser.: No. 1). (ENG.). 224p. (J). (gr. 5-7). 16.99 (978-0-15-205810-4(9)) Houghton Mifflin Harcourt Publishing Co.

—Mary Poppins. (Mary Poppins Ser.: No. 1). 202p. (J). (gr. 3-5). pap. 6.00 (978-0-8072-1536-4(8), Listening Library) Random Hse. Audio Publishing Group.

—Mary Poppins: 80th Anniversary Collection. Shepard, Mary, illus. 2014. (ENG.). 1024p. (J). (gr. 5-7). 24.99 (978-0-544-34047-3(7), HMH Books For Young Readers) Houghton Mifflin Harcourt Publishing Co.

—Mary Poppins & Mary Poppins Comes Back. Shepard, Mary, illus. 2007. (Mary Poppins Ser.: No 1 and 2). (ENG.). 368p. (J). (gr. 5-7). 19.99 (978-0-15-205922-4(9)) Houghton Mifflin Harcourt Publishing Co.

—Mary Poppins Comes Back. Shepard, Mary, illus. 2006. (Mary Poppins Ser.: No. 2). (ENG.). 336p. (J). (gr. 5-7). 16.99 (978-0-15-205816-6(8)) Houghton Mifflin Harcourt Publishing Co.

—Mary Poppins from A to Z. Shepard, Mary, illus. 2006. (Mary Poppins Ser.). (ENG.). 64p. (J). (gr. 5-7). 16.99 (978-0-15-205834-0(6)) Houghton Mifflin Harcourt Publishing Co.

—Mary Poppins in the Park. Shepard, Mary, illus. 2006. (Mary Poppins Ser.: No. 4). (ENG.). 304p. (J). (gr. 5-7). 16.99 (978-0-15-205828-9(1)) Houghton Mifflin Harcourt Publishing Co.

—Mary Poppins Opens the Door. Sims, Agnes & Shepard, Mary, illus. 2006. (Mary Poppins Ser.: No. 3). (ENG.). 288p. (J). (gr. 5-7). 16.99 (978-0-15-205822-7(2)) Houghton Mifflin Harcourt Publishing Co.

—Mary Poppins Vintage Boxed Set: Three Enchanting Classics: Mary Poppins, Mary Poppins Comes Back, & Mary Poppins Opens the Door. 2007. (Illus.). (J). 38.85 (978-0-15-205858-6(3)) Harcourt Children's Bks.

Trayer, Edward. The Struggles of Felicity Brady. 2004. (YA). per. 14.95 (978-1-59571-043-7(4)) Word Association Pubs.

Trembath, Don. Hypnotized, 1 vol. 2007. (Orca Currents Ser.). (ENG.). (J). (gr. 5-9). 112p. lib. bdg. 14.95 (978-1-55143-707-1(4)); 128p. per. 9.95 (978-1-55143-705-7(8)) Orca Bk. Pubs. USA.

Trent, Tiffany. The Tinker King. 2014. (ENG., Illus.). 320p. (YA). (gr. 7). 17.99 (978-1-4424-5759-1(7), Simon & Schuster Bks. For Young Readers) Simon & Schuster Bks. For Young Readers.

—The Unnaturalists. (ENG., (YA). (gr. 7). 2013. Illus.). 336p. pap. 9.99 (978-1-4424-2207-0(6)) 2012. 320p. 16.99 (978-1-4424-2206-3(8)) Simon & Schuster Bks. For Young Readers. (Simon & Schuster Bks. For Young Readers).

Treskillard, Robert. Merlin's Nightmare, 1 vol. 2014. (Merlin Spiral Ser.). (ENG.). 432p. (YA). pap. 12.99 (978-0-310-73509-0(2)) Blink.

Trigg, Michael J. Greenwold & the Mystery Cave: Greenwold & the Minosaurs Story Books. 2013. 148p. pap. 12.97 (978-1-61897-466-2(1), Strategic Bk. Publishing) Strategic Book Publishing & Rights Agency (SBPRA).

Trigg, Roberta. Haworth Idyll: A Fantasy. Dashiell, Margaret, illus. 2012. 88p. 38.95 (978-1-258-23556-7(0)); pap. 23.95 (978-1-258-24510-8(8)) Literary Licensing, LLC.

Triton, Mathias & Martinez, Alitha. The Rise of el Diablo. 2015. (J). lib. bdg. 18.40 (978-0-606-36451-5(X)) Turtleback Bks.

Trivas, Tracy. The Wish Stealers. 2011. (ENG.). 288p. (J). (gr. 3-7). pap. 7.99 (978-1-4169-8726-0(6), Aladdin) Simon & Schuster Children's Publishing.

—The Wish Stealers. 2010. (ENG.). 288p. (J). (gr. 3-7). 17.99 (978-1-4169-8725-3(8), Simon & Schuster/Paula Wiseman Bks.) Simon & Schuster/Paula Wiseman Bks.

Trotter, Bob. The Curious Tale of Marmalade Tuttle. 2008. 116p. pap. 12.95 (978-1-60693-014-4(1), Eloquent Bks.) Strategic Book Publishing & Rights Agency (SBPRA).

—The Curious Tale of Marmalade Tuttle - Book Two Marmalade Tuttle & the Battle of Caldor. 2010. 122p. pap. 10.50 (978-1-60860-560-6(4), Eloquent Bks.) Strategic Book Publishing & Rights Agency (SBPRA).

Trottier, Doug. The Crow & His Boy. 2011. 382p. pap. 19.00 (978-1-60976-469-2(2), Eloquent Bks.) Strategic Book Publishing & Rights Agency (SBPRA).

Troughton, Ruth. The Invisible Ones. 2003. 88p. pap. 9.95 (978-0-595-29592-0(4)) iUniverse, Inc.

Troulis, Jennifer. Penelope & Priscilla & the City of the Banished. 2007. (J). per. 14.95 (978-0-9768602-1-1(X)) Twin Monkeys Pr.

Trout, Jenny. Such Sweet Sorrow. 2014. (Entangled Teen Ser.). (ENG.). 304p. (YA). (gr. 8-12). pap. 9.99 (978-1-62266-158-9(3), 9781622661589) Entangled Publishing, LLC.

Trowell, Michelle. Magical Mermaids. Top That Publishing Staff, ed. Richards, Kirsten, illus. 2008. (Magnetic Story & Play Scene Ser.). 9p. (J). (gr. -1). (978-1-84666-442-7(X), Tide Mill Pr.) Top That! Publishing PLC.

Troyer, Gloria Irene. Beatrice & the Snow People. 2013. 114p. pap. 14.95 (978-1-62646-481-0(2)) Booklocker.com, Inc.

Truehall, R. T. Not Dead. 2016. (ENG.). 234p. pap. 11.95 (978-1-78612-461-6(0), d64dc859-0642-417f-9111-bb57b730a206) Austin, Stan AUS. Dist: Bookmasters Distribution.

Trumbo, Stephen. Dreamers, Fantasies & Thrill Seekers. 2011. 26p. pap. 16.95 (978-1-4560-7319-0(2)) America Star Bks.

Trumbore, Cindy. The Genie in the Book. Alley, R. W., illus. 2004. (ENG.). 120p. (J). (gr. -1-7). 15.95 (978-1-59354-042-5(6), Handprint Bks.) Chronicle Bks. LLC.

Tucker, Peter E. Pumpkin Bunch. 2009. 36p. pap. 16.99 (978-1-4389-7883-3(9)) AuthorHouse.

Tucker, Sally A. Leo & Apollo: The Forbidden Land. 2012. 28p. pap. 15.00 (978-1-105-60121-7(8)) Lulu Pr., Inc.

Tull, Linda Handy. Fofo's Journey. 2012. 40p. pap. 24.95 (978-1-4626-7275-2(2)) America Star Bks.

Tullgren, Tom. Journey to Imagiland. 2012. 320p. pap. 17.95 (978-1-62141-272-4(5)) Booklocker.com, Inc.

Turcotte, Michael. Colours Made in Heaven, 1 vol. Turcotte, Derek, illus. 2009. 13p. pap. 24.95 (978-1-60836-316-2(3)) America Star Bks.

Turner, Deborah & Mohler, Diana. How Willy Got His Wings: The Continuing Adventures of Wheely Willy. Ahrends, Susan, illus. 2003. (ENG.). 32p. 15.95 (978-0-944875-88-9(2)) i-5 Publishing LLC.

Turner, Julie Anne. A Tale of Summerland. 2007. (Illus.). 72p. pap. (978-1-84401-902-1(0)) Athena Pr.

Turner, Mark. A Winter Tale: How Raven Gave Light to the World. Graves, Emily, illus. 2014. (ENG.). 48p. 20.00 (978-1-62288-032-4(3)) Austin, Stephen F. State Univ. Pr.

Turner, Max. End of Days. 2010. (Night Runner Novels Ser.: 2). (ENG.). 304p. (YA). (gr. 8-12). pap. 20.99 (978-0-312-59252-3(3), 9780312592523, St. Martin's Griffin) St. Martin's Pr.

Turner, Megan Whalen. The Queen of Attolia. (Queen's Thief Ser.: 2). (ENG.). (YA). (gr. 8). 2017. 416p. pap. 9.99 (978-0-06-264297-4(9)) 2006. 368p. pap. 6.99 (978-0-06-084182-9(6)) HarperCollins Pubs. (Greenwillow Bks.).

—The Queen of Attolia. 8 vols. (Attolia Ser.: 2). (J). 2013. 188.75 (978-1-4281-5237-3(7)) 2009. 73.75 (978-1-4361-6574-7(1)) 2008. 104.75 (978-1-4281-5236-6(9)) 2008. 75.75 (978-1-4281-5234-2(2)) 2007. 78.75 (978-1-4281-5232-8(6)) 2007. 162.75 (978-1-4281-5233-5(4)) 2007. 1.25 (978-1-4281-5229-8(6)) 2007. 101.75 (978-1-4281-5238-0(5)) Recorded Bks., Inc.

—The Queen of Attolia. 2017. (Queen's Thief Ser.: BK.2). (ENG.). (YA). lib. bdg. 20.85 **(978-0-606-40331-3(0))** Turtleback Bks.

Turner, Megan Whalen. Thick As Thieves. 2017. (Queen's Thief Ser.: 5). (ENG.). 352p. (YA). (gr. 8). 17.99 (978-0-06-256824-3(8), Greenwillow Bks.) HarperCollins Pubs.

Turner, Michael. Michael Turner's Soulfire, Vol. 1. 2012. (ENG., Illus.). 376p. (YA). pap. 39.99 (978-0-9823628-6-0(2), 9780982362860) Aspen MLT, Inc.

Turner, Patrenia. Barbie In The Queen Patrenialla Fairy - Tale. Turner, Keeng Troyius, ed. 2014. (Illus.). 31p. pap. (978-0-578-14812-0(9)) Patrenialla Turner, Queen .

Turner, Paul. ULYSSES: the Pegasi Incident. 2007. 216p. pap. 15.95 (978-1-84753-642-6(5)) Lulu Pr., Inc.

Turner, Tom. Sign of the Sandman. 2014. (ENG.). 320p. (J). 17.99 (978-1-938155-10-9(6)) Magic Factory, LLC, The.

Tyler, Jenny & Doherty, Gillian, eds. Usborne Stories for Little Girls. 2008. (Picture Books Ser.). (Illus.). 135p. (J). (gr. -1-3). 18.99 (978-0-7945-1974-2(1), Usborne) EDC Publishing.

Uahc, Ecarg. Adventures of I. Firebrace: The Battle in the Underground. 2011. 124p. pap. 10.95 (978-1-4502-9785-1(4)); (gr. 4-6). 20.95 (978-1-4502-9786-8(2)) iUniverse, Inc.

Udvari, Joseph G. Courage. 2012. 132p. pap. (978-1-84961-169-5(6)) RealTime Publishing.

Uehashi, Nahoko. Guardian of the Darkness. Hirano, Cathy, tr. Shimizu, Yuko, illus. 2009. (Moribito Ser.: 2). (ENG.). 272p. (J). (gr. 7-18). 17.99 (978-0-545-10295-7(2), Levine, Arthur A. Bks.) Scholastic, Inc.

Uehashi, Nahoko & Hirano, Cathy. Guardian of the Darkness. Shimizu, Yuko, illus. 2009. (Moribito Ser.: No. 2). (J). pap. (978-0-545-10874-4(8), Levine, Arthur A. Bks.) Scholastic, Inc.

Ueyama, Michiro. Chaotic Century. Ueyama, Michiro, illus. (Zoids Ser.). (ENG., Illus.). Vol. 11. 2004. 82p. pap. 5.95 (978-1-56931-858-4(1)) Vol. 12. 2003. 72p. pap. 5.95 (978-1-56931-867-6(0)) Viz Media.

Uncle Ernie's Tall Tales: Little Blue Guys. 2006. (Illus.). 110p. (YA). per. 7.95 (978-0-9760607-1-0(X), ON-E-1) Sanpitch Pr.

Underwood, Kim. The Wonderful World of Sparkle Girl & Doobins. Goldman, Garnet, illus. 2009. 48p. (J). pap. 16.95 (978-0-89587-373-6(7)) Blair, John F. Pub.

Ungerer, Tomi. El Hombre de la Luna. (SPA., Illus.). 40p. (J). (gr. k-2). 7.95 (978-84-204-3746-0(8), AF0456) Santillana USA Publishing Co., Inc.

—El Hombre de la Luna. Ungerer, Tomi, illus. 2003. (Picture Books Collection). (SPA., Illus.). 40p. (J). (gr. k-3). pap. 10.95 (978-968-19-0661-0(6)) Santillana USA Publishing Co., Inc.

Urban, Linda. Milo Speck, Accidental Agent. (ENG., Illus.). 272p. (J). (gr. 2-5). 2017. pap. 7.99 (978-0-544-93523-5(3)) 2015. 16.99 (978-0-544-41951-3(0)) Houghton Mifflin Harcourt Publishing Co. (HMH Books For Young Readers).

Urey, Gary. Pursued. 2017. (Secrets of the X-Point Ser.: 1). (ENG.). 288p. (J). (gr. 3-7). 16.99 (978-0-8075-6684-8(5)); pap. 9.99 **(978-0-8075-6686-2(1))** Whitman, Albert & Co.

Ursu, Anne. Breadcrumbs. McGuire, Erin, illus. 2013. (ENG.). 336p. (J). (gr. 3-7). pap. 6.99 (978-0-06-201506-8(0), Walden Pond Pr.) HarperCollins Pubs.

—Breadcrumbs. McGuire, Erin, illus. 2012. 320p. 55.00 (978-0-449-01400-4(2)) Random Hse., Inc.

—Breadcrumbs. 2013. (J). lib. bdg. 17.20 (978-0-606-27130-1(9), Turtleback) Turtleback Bks.

—The Immortal Fire. Fortune, Eric & Swaab, Neil, illus. 2009. (Cronus Chronicles Ser.: 3). (ENG.). 528p. (J). (gr. 3-7). 17.99 (978-1-4169-0591-2(X), Atheneum Bks. for Young Readers) Simon & Schuster Children's Publishing.

—The Real Boy. McGuire, Erin, illus. 2013. (ENG.). 352p. (J). (gr. 3-7). 16.99 (978-0-06-201507-5(9), Walden Pond Pr.) HarperCollins Pubs.

—The Shadow Thieves. Fortune, Eric, illus. (Cronus Chronicles Ser.: 1). (ENG.). 432p. (J). (gr. 3-7). 2007. pap. 8.99 (978-1-4169-0588-2(X)) 2006. 17.99 (978-1-4169-0587-5(1)) Simon & Schuster Children's Publishing. (Atheneum Bks. for Young Readers).

Uwuigiaren, Omoruyi. The Adventures of Nihu. Ayalomeh, Shedrach, illus. 2007. 158p. (J). (gr. 2-8). 16.95 (978-1-934138-15-1(0)) Bouncing Ball Bks., Inc.

Vajda, Tibor Timothy. The End of the World. 2008. 96p. pap. 9.95 (978-0-595-52914-8(3)) iUniverse, Inc.

Vakker, Hans Alric. The Riddle of the Jade Collar: A Twelve Cousins Book. 2013. 292p. 26.95 (978-1-4759-7522-2(8)); pap. 16.95 (978-1-4759-7521-5(X)) iUniverse, Inc.

Valente, Catherynne M. The Boy Who Lost Fairyland. Juan, Ana, illus. 2015. (Fairyland Ser.: 4). (ENG.). 240p. (YA). (gr. 5-9). 16.99 (978-1-250-02349-0(1), 9781250023490) Feiwel & Friends.

—The Girl Who Circumnavigated Fairyland in a Ship of Her Own Making. Juan, Ana, illus. 2011. (Fairyland Ser.: 1). (ENG.). 256p. (YA). (gr. 5-9). 16.99 (978-0-312-64961-6(4), 9780312649616) Feiwel & Friends.

—The Girl Who Circumnavigated Fairyland in a Ship of Her Own Making. 2012. (CHI & ENG., Illus.). 304p. (J). (gr. 5-8). pap. (978-986-6026-24-9(8)) Muses Publishing Hse.

—The Girl Who Circumnavigated Fairyland in a Ship of Her Own Making. Juan, Ana, illus. 2012. (Fairyland Ser.: 1). (ENG.). 288p. (YA). (gr. 5-9). pap. 7.99 (978-1-250-01019-3(5), 9781250010193) Square Fish.

—The Girl Who Fell Beneath Fairyland & Led the Revels There. Juan, Ana, illus. 2013. (Fairyland Ser.: 2). (ENG.). 304p. (YA). (gr. 5-9). pap. 7.99 (978-1-250-03412-0(4), 9781250034120) Square Fish.

—The Girl Who Soared over Fairyland & Cut the Moon in Two. Juan, Ana, illus. 2013. (Fairyland Ser.: 3). (ENG.). 256p. (YA). (gr. 5-9). 16.99 (978-1-250-02350-6(5), 9781250023506) Feiwel & Friends.

Valentino, Serena & Disney Book Group Staff. The Beast Within: A Tale of Beauty's Prince. Disney Storybook Artists Staff & Disney Storybook Art Team, illus. 2014. (Villains Ser.). (ENG.). 224p. (J). (gr. 5-9). 16.99 (978-1-4231-5912-4(8)) Disney Pr.

—Fairest of All: A Tale of the Wicked Queen. Disney Storybook Artists Staff, illus. 2009. (Villains Ser.: 1). (ENG.). 256p. (J). (gr. 5-9). 15.99 (978-1-4231-0629-6(6)) Disney Pr.

Van Allsburg, Chris. Jumanji. 30th anniv. ed. 2011. (ENG., Illus.). 32p. (J). (gr. 1-4). 18.99 (978-0-547-60838-9(1)) Houghton Mifflin Harcourt Publishing Co.

—The Wreck of the Zephyr. 30th anniv. ed. 2013. (ENG., Illus.). 32p. (J). (gr. -1-3). 18.99 (978-0-544-05005-1(3)) Houghton Mifflin Harcourt Publishing Co.

Van, Andi. Magic Fell. 2016. (ENG., Illus.). (YA). 24.99 **(978-1-63533-046-5(7))**; 190p. pap. 14.99 (978-1-63476-880-1(9)) Dreamspinner Pr. (Harmony Ink Pr.).

van Arsdale, Peternelle. The Beast Is an Animal. 2017. (ENG., Illus.). 352p. (YA). (gr. 9). 17.99 (978-1-4814-8841-9(4), McElderry, Margaret K. Bks.) McElderry, Margaret K. Bks.

van Diepen, Allison. The Vampire Stalker. 2011. (ENG.). 272p. (J). (gr. 7-7). 17.99 (978-0-545-28375-5(2)) Scholastic, Inc.

van Gosen, Ryan O'Dell, IV. Ray Conka & the Sortian Jewell. Maximilian Staff, ed. Walker, John, photos by. unabr. ed. 2004. (Illus.). 128p. (YA). lib. bdg. 12.50 (978-1-930211-55-1(4)) Maximilian Pr. Pubs.

Van Hamme, Jean. The Cage, Vol. 15. Rosinski, Grzegorz, illus. 2014. (Thorgal Ser.: 15). (ENG.). 48p. pap. 11.95 (978-1-84918-186-0(1)) CineBook GBR. Dist: National Bk. Network.

—The Invisible Fortress. Rosinski, Grzegorz, illus. 2012. (Thorgal Ser.: 11). (ENG.). 48p. (YA). (gr. 6-17). pap. 11.95 (978-1-84918-103-7(9)) CineBook GBR. Dist: National Bk. Network.

—Ogotai's Crown. Rosinski, Grzegorz, illus. 2013. (Thorgal Ser.: 13). (ENG.). 48p. pap. 11.95 (978-1-84918-142-6(X)) CineBook GBR. Dist: National Bk. Network.

Vanasse, Patricia. Resilient. Shalaby, Asharaf, illus. 2013. (ENG.). 328p. (YA). pap. 13.99 (978-0-9860373-2-0(X)) Pants On Fire Pr.

Vande Velde, Vivian. Dragon's Bait. 2003. (ENG., Illus.). 208p. (YA). (gr. 7-12). pap. 13.95 (978-0-15-216663-2(7)) Houghton Mifflin Harcourt Publishing Co.

—Now You See It ... 2006. (ENG., Illus.). 288p. (YA). (gr. 7-12). pap. 18.95 (978-0-15-205461-8(8)) Houghton Mifflin Harcourt Publishing Co.

—Smart Dog. 2007. (ENG., Illus.). 160p. (J). (gr. 5-7). pap. 7.99 (978-0-15-206172-2(X)) Houghton Mifflin Harcourt Publishing Co.

E
F
G

—A Well-Timed Enchantment. 2006. (ENG., Illus.). 240p. (J). (gr. 5-7). pap. 13.95 *(978-0-15-204919-5(3))* Houghton Mifflin Harcourt Publishing Co.
VanDerlinden, Jean A. The Family Tree: The Secret Door. 2013. 64p. pap. 24.99 *(978-1-4772-7941-0(5))* AuthorHouse.
Vanholme, Virginie. The Vampire from the Marshes. Mauricet, illus. 2008. (Scared to Death Ser.: 1). (ENG.). 46p. pap. 11.95 *(978-1-905460-47-2(3))* CineBook GBR. Dist: National Bk. Network.
Vann, Danielle A. The Whizbang Machine. 2016. (Whizbang Machine Ser.: 1). (ENG.). 404p. (J). pap. 14.95 *(978-1-943847-92-1(4),* 9781943847921) Waldorf Publishing.
Vargas, George. The Prophecy of the Ages: Of War & Choices. 2004. 458p. (YA). pap. 24.95 *(978-0-595-29607-1(6))* iUniverse, Inc.
Varma, Eric. The Orphaned Knight. 2004. (Caviant Ser.: Bk. 1). 200p. (YA). 24.95 *(978-0-595-66668-3(X))* iUniverse, Inc.
Varsell, Linda. Ends of Rainbow. Curtis, E., illus. 2003. 260p. (J). per. 8.00 *(978-0-9725479-5-6(9))* Rainbow Communications.
—The Humane Touch. Curtis, E., illus. 2003. 316p. per. 10.00 *(978-0-9728737-0-3(8))* Rainbow Communications.
—A Journey for Rainbows. Curtis, E., illus. 2003. 166p. (YA). per. 6.00 *(978-0-9725479-1-8(6))* Rainbow Communications.
—The Rainbow Breakers. Curtis, E., illus. 2003. 232p. per. 7.00 *(978-0-9725479-3-2(2))* Rainbow Communications.
—The Rainbow Circle. Curtis, E., illus. 2003. 428p. (J). per. 10.00 *(978-0-9725479-9-4(1))* Rainbow Communications.
—The Rainbow Dreamers. Curtis, E., illus. 2003. 262p. per. 8.00 *(978-0-9725479-4-9(0))* Rainbow Communications.
—The Rainbow Makers. Curtis, E., illus. 2003. 148p. per. 6.00 *(978-0-9725479-2-5(4))* Rainbow Communications.
—The Rainbow Planet. Curtis, E., illus. 2003. 162p. (J). per. 6.00 *(978-0-9725479-7-0(5))* Rainbow Communications.
—The Rainbow Remnants. Curtis, E., illus. 2003. 204p. (J). per. 7.00 *(978-0-9725479-8-7(3))* Rainbow Communications.
—The Rainbow Rescue. Curtis, E., illus. 2003. 200p. (J). per. 7.00 *(978-0-9725479-6-3(7))* Rainbow Communications.
—With a Human Touch. Curtis, E., illus. 2003. 178p. per. 6.00 *(978-0-9725479-0-1(8))* Rainbow Communications.
Vaughn, Carrie. Voices of Dragons. (ENG.). (YA). (gr. 8). 2011. 336p. pap. 8.99 *(978-0-06-154790-4(5))* 2010. 320p. 16.99 *(978-0-06-179894-8(0))* HarperCollins Pubs. (HarperTeen).
Vaughn, J. D. Second Guard. 2015. (Second Guard Novel Ser.). (ENG., Illus.). 424p. (J). (gr. 5-9). 16.99 *(978-1-4231-6909-3(3))* Disney Pr.
—The Shadow Guard. 2016. (Second Guard Novel Ser.). (ENG.). 320p. (J). (gr. 5-9). 16.99 *(978-1-4231-7097-6(0))* Hyperion Bks. for Children.
Vaughn, Richard. Rowena & the Magic Hawk, the First Adventure. 2009. 224p. pap. 14.95 *(978-1-60860-157-8(9),* Eloquent Bks.) Strategic Book Publishing & Rights Agency (SBPRA).
Vaught, S. R. & Redmond, J. B. A Prince among Killers, Pt. 2. 2009. (ENG.). 432p. (YA). (gr. 7-18). pap. 10.99 *(978-1-59990-376-7(8),* 9781599903767, Bloomsbury USA Childrens) Bloomsbury Publishing USA.
Vazov, George D. The Other Side of the Mushroom. 2006. 12.00 *(978-0-8059-9018-8(6))* Dorrance Publishing Co., Inc.
Veillon, A. M. Shelby & the Shifting Rings: Book One — -Defender of Time Series, 1. 2005. (Defender of Time Ser.: Bk. 1). (Illus.). 167p. (J). (gr. 5-7). 18.95 *(978-0-9762015-4-0(2))* Parity Pr.
—Shelby & the Shifting Rings Bk. 1: Defender of Time Series. 2005. (Illus.). 167p. (J). per. 9.95 *(978-0-9762015-5-7(0))* Parity Pr.
Velasquez, Crystal. Just Princesses. 2016. (ENG., Illus.). 160p. (J). (gr. 1-6). pap. 9.99 *(978-1-942275-34-3(X),* 9781942275343) Zenescope Entertainment.
Velvet, Black. The Adventures of Sam in Space: Planet of the Sweets. 2007. 32p. (J). pap. 8.00 *(978-0-8059-7367-9(2))* Dorrance Publishing Co., Inc.
Ventrillo, James & Ventrillo, Nick. Rick & Bobo: Two Brothers. One a Genius. One Not, 4 vols. Kunardi, Marco, illus. 2009. 332p. (YA). pap. 13.95 *(978-0-615-28865-9(0))* Vanir Bks.
Vermazen, Eve. Dogtales: Sebastian & the Destiny Stone. 2012. 36p. pap. 32.70 *(978-1-4797-4032-1(2))* Xlibris Corp.
Verne, Jules. Dick Sand. Munro, George, tr. 2008. 296p. pap. 15.95 *(978-1-60664-253-5(7))* Rodgers, Alan Bks.
Verne, Jules, illus. Viaje al Centro de la Tierra. Orig. Title: Journey to the Center of the Earth. (SPA.). 160p. (YA). 11.95 *(978-84-7281-084-6(4),* AF1084) Auriga, Ediciones S.A. ESP. Dist: Continental Bk. Co., Inc.
Verstraete, Majanka. Valentina & the Whackadoodle Witch: Valentina's Spooky Adventures. Giffin, Noelle, illus. l.t. ed. 2013. 2. (ENG.). 46p. (gr. k-4). pap. 10.95 *(978-1-62253-059-5(4))* Evolved Publishing.
Vevers, Rachel. Quest for the Unicorn. 2012. 222p. pap. *(978-1-78176-316-2(X))* FeedARead.com.
Viguié, Debbie. Midnight Pearls: A Retelling of the Little Mermaid. 2006. (Once upon a Time Ser.). (ENG., Illus.). 208p. (YA). (gr. 9-12). mass mkt. 6.99 *(978-1-4169-4016-6(2),* Simon Pulse) Simon Pulse.
—Scarlet Moon. 2004. (Once upon a Time Ser.). (ENG.). 176p. (YA). (gr. 9). mass mkt. 6.99 *(978-0-689-86716-3(6),* Simon Pulse) Simon Pulse.
Viknesh, R. My Fantasy Your Treat. 2012. 32p. pap. 28.55 *(978-1-4669-2733-9(X))* Trafford Publishing.
Virtue, Queen Petals De. Princess & the Rain. 2012. 28p. pap. 21.99 *(978-1-4691-2744-6(X))* Xlibris Corp.
Vision, Mutiya & Vision, David. The Land of Expression. Alcantara, Ignacio, illus. 2009. (ENG.). 48p. 15.00 *(978-0-9816254-0-9(1))* Von Curtis Publishing.
Vitale, Jill. Freddie: The Free-Range Chicken. 2007. (ENG., Illus.). 28p. (J). (gr. 1-2). 15.95 *(978-0-9767269-6-8(3))* WND Bks, Inc.
VIZ Media, . & Straffi, Iginio. WINX Club, Vol. 7. 2013. (ENG.). 96p. (J). pap. 6.99 *(978-1-4215-4204-1(8))* Viz Media.
VIZ Media Staff. WINX Club, Vol. 3. 2012. (ENG.). 96p. (J). pap. 6.99 *(978-1-4215-4161-7(0))* Viz Media.
VIZ Media Staff & Straffi, Iginio. WINX Club, Vol. 4. 2012. (ENG.). 96p. (J). pap. 6.99 *(978-1-4215-4162-4(9))* Viz Media.
—WINX Club, Vol. 6. 2013. (ENG.). 96p. (J). pap. 6.99 *(978-1-4215-4203-4(X))* Viz Media.
Vizzini, Ned. The Other Normals. 2012. (ENG.). 400p. (YA). (gr. 8). 17.99 *(978-0-06-207990-9(5))* HarperCollins Pubs.
Voigt, Brian Jeffrey. Guardian of the Zercons. 2003. (Illus.). 360p. (YA). 21.95 *(978-1-932545-18-0(2))* Blue Pig Productions.
Voigt, Cynthia. The Tale of Elske. 2015. (Tales of the Kingdom Ser.: 4). (ENG., Illus.). 368p. (YA). (gr. 7). 19.99 *(978-1-4814-2189-8(1),* Atheneum Bks. for Young Readers) Simon & Schuster Children's Publishing.
Voisin, Mandy Madson. Star of Deliverance. 2014. pap. 17.99 *(978-1-4621-1454-2(7))* Cedar Fort, Inc./CFI Distribution.
Voudrie, Krista. Sisters of Destiny. 2011. 96p. pap. 19.95 *(978-1-4560-5636-0(0))* America Star Bks.
Vyff, Shannon. 21st Century Kids. 2007. 280p. pap. 14.95 *(978-1-886057-00-5(1))* Warren Publishing, Inc.
Waddell, Barbara. If I Could Catch a Train. 2009. 20p. pap. 9.15 *(978-1-4251-8667-8(X))* Trafford Publishing.
Wade, Taylor. The Magical Well. 2008. 33p. pap. 12.95 *(978-1-4357-5175-0(2))* Lulu Pr., Inc.
Wagner, Hilary. Lords of Trillium: Book Iii of the Nightshade Chronicles. Rayyan, Omar, illus. 2014. (Nightshade Chronicles Ser.: 3). (ENG.). 224p. (J). (gr. 4). 17.95 *(978-0-8234-2413-9(8))* Holiday Hse., Inc.
—Nightshade City. Rayyan, Omar, illus. (Nightshade Chronicles Ser.: 1). (ENG.). 320p. (J). 2011. pap. 7.95 *(978-0-8234-2387-3(5))* 2010. (gr. 3-7). 17.95 *(978-0-8234-2285-2(2))* Holiday Hse., Inc.
—White Assassin. Rayyan, Omar, illus. 2011. (Nightshade Chronicles Ser.: 2). (ENG.). 304p. (J). (gr. 4). 17.95 *(978-0-8234-2333-0(6))* Holiday Hse., Inc.
—The White Assassin. 2012. (Nightshade Chronicles Ser.: 2). (ENG.). 304p. (J). (gr. 4). pap. 7.95 *(978-0-8234-2485-6(5))* Holiday Hse., Inc.
Wagner, Matt. The Demon - From the Darkness. 2014. (ENG., Illus.). 128p. pap. 14.99 *(978-1-4012-4250-3(2))* DC Comics.
Wagner, Mckenzie. The Amulet Chase. 2017. (ENG.). (J). pap. 10.99 ***(978-1-4621-1983-7(2),*** Sweetwater Bks.) Cedar Fort, Inc./CFI Distribution.
—Benotripia Trilogy. 2015. (J). pap. 17.99 *(978-1-4621-1751-2(1),* Horizon Pubs.) Cedar Fort, Inc./CFI Distribution.
—Casters of Doovik. 2015. 298p. (YA). pap. 17.99 *(978-1-4621-1757-4(0))* Cedar Fort, Inc./CFI Distribution.
—Keys to the Dream World. 2014. pap. 8.99 *(978-1-4621-1435-1(0))* Cedar Fort, Inc./CFI Distribution.
—The Rescue. 2012. pap. 8.99 *(978-1-4621-1014-8(2))* Cedar Fort, Inc./CFI Distribution.
Wagoner, Timothy Allen. The Adventures of Jacque & Wanderwan Bk. 1: Naoo. 2005. (J). pap. 14.99 *(978-0-9761739-2-2(1))* Grandoc Publishing.
Wakefield, Beth. The Cleaner. 2010. 151p. pap. 14.50 *(978-1-4457-6809-0(7))* Lulu Pr., Inc.
Waldegrave, Valerie. Arthur in the Land of Cats. 2016. (ENG.). 126p. (J). pap. 11.95 *(978-1-78554-538-2(8),* 06343282-0c38-464d-a861-f8df6ffbc6a3) Austin, Stan AUS. Dist: Bookmasters Distribution.
Waldman, Alan/A. Erica from America & the Start of the Gang of Four. Scobie, Andrea, illus. 2013. 44p. pap. *(978-0-9840514-2-7(2))* Roxby Media Ltd.
Wales, Amy S. Fiona & the Fiddle Tree. 2012. 32p. pap. 21.99 *(978-1-4691-5485-5(4))* Xlibris Corp.
Walker, Crystal. Maceys Magic Tree. 2009. 28p. pap. 12.49 *(978-1-4490-4916-4(8))* AuthorHouse.
Walker, Kagon. Amber Wings. 2009. 16p. pap. 9.99 *(978-1-4490-4266-0(X))* AuthorHouse.
Walker, Landry Q. Danger Club Vol. 1: Death. 2012. (ENG., Illus.). 102p. (YA). pap. 9.99 *(978-1-60706-634-7(3),* 9781607066347) Image Comics.
Walker, Lisa & Coyne, Adrian. The Boy Who Brought Thunder. 2012. (Illus.). 40p. pap. 12.95 *(978-9987-08-222-3(X))* Mkuki na Nyota Pubs. TZA. Dist: African Bks. Collective, Ltd.
Walker, Rachael. Angel Starlight & the Wish Book. 2006. 204p. per. *(978-1-905529-52-0(X))* Grosvenor Hse. Publishing Ltd.
Walker, Rysa. Timebound, 0 vols. 2014. (Chronos Files Ser.: 1). (ENG.). 374p. (YA). (gr. 7-12). pap. 14.95 *(978-1-4778-4815-9(0),* 9781477848159) Amazon Publishing.
—Time's Divide, 0 vols. 2015. (Chronos Files Ser.: 3). (ENG.). 543p. (YA). (gr. 7-12). pap. 12.95 *(978-1-5039-4658-3(4),* 9781503946583, Skyscape) Amazon Publishing.
Walker, Victoria. The Winter of Enchantment. 2007. (Illus.). 152p. (YA). (gr. 8-12). 18.95 *(978-1-930900-33-2(3))* Purple Hse. Pr.
Walkup, Jennifer. Second Verse. 2013. 270p. pap. 15.95 *(978-1-935462-87-3(3))* Luminis Bks., Inc.
Wallace, Barbara Brooks. The Interesting Thing That Happened at Perfect Acres, Inc. 2007. 148p. per. 11.95 *(978-0-595-45763-2(0),* Backinprint.com) iUniverse, Inc.
Wallace, Becky. The Skylighter. 2017. (Keepers' Chronicles Ser.). (ENG.). 432p. (YA). (gr. 9). pap. 11.99 *(978-1-4814-0569-0(1),* McElderry, Margaret K. Bks.) McElderry, Margaret K. Bks.
—The Storyspinner. 2015. (Keepers' Chronicles Ser.). (ENG., Illus.). 432p. (YA). (gr. 9). 17.99 *(978-1-4814-0565-2(9),* McElderry, Margaret K. Bks.) McElderry, Margaret K. Bks.
Wallace, Bonny. The Raymond Wikins' Adventures, Children of Straw. 2009. 70p. pap. 9.95 *(978-1-60860-699-3(6),* Eloquent Bks.) Strategic Book Publishing & Rights Agency (SBPRA).
Wallace Hunchak, Lisa. It Could Happen. 2013. 32p. pap. 17.25 *(978-1-4669-7130-1(4))* Trafford Publishing.
Wallace II, James C. & Wallace, Amanda D. The Emerald Slippers of Oz. 2013. 156p. pap. 14.99 *(978-0-578-12511-4(0))* Scientia Est Vox Pr.
Wallace, Kali. The Memory Trees. 2017. 432p. (YA). (gr. 9). 17.99 ***(978-0-06-236623-8(8),*** Tegen, Katherine Bks) HarperCollins Pubs.
Wallace, Paula S. Rick & Rocky. Fruisen, Catherine Myler, illus. 2004. 32p. (J). pap. *(978-1-893974-22-7(7),* Design Pr. Bks.) Savannah College of Art & Design Exhibitions.
Wallace, T. M. Under a Fairy Moon. 2012. 224p. pap. *(978-0-9868657-4-9(5))* Brownridge Publishing.
Walsh, Maria Elena. La Nube Traicionera. Fiorini, Nancy, illus. 2003. (SPA.). 88p. (YA). (gr. 5-8). 14.95 *(978-950-511-616-4(0))* Alfaguara S.A. de Ediciones ARG. Dist: Santillana USA Publishing Co., Inc.
Walsh, Patrick M., Jr. Who Says Timmy Can't Play: The Derby: A Timmy Wallings Story. McGriff, Aaron, ed. WFM Services, illus. 2011. 135p. (J). *(978-0-9842929-3-6(4))* Daddy Bean Bks.
Walter, Jackie. The Magic Porridge Pot. 2017. (Must Know Stories: Level 1 Ser.). (ENG., Illus.). 32p. (J). (gr. k-2). 4.99 *(978-1-4451-4450-4(6),* Franklin Watts) Hachette Children's Group GBR. Dist: Hachette Bk. Group.
Walters, Nicole Y. Charis: A Journey to Pandora's Jar. Conard, Vincent, illus. 2013. 214p. 32.95 *(978-1-62015-318-5(1),* Booktrope Editions) Booktrope.
—Charis: Journey to Pandora's Jar. 2013. 214p. pap. 14.95 *(978-1-62015-134-1(0),* Booktrope Editions) Booktrope.
Walton, Leslye. The Strange & Beautiful Sorrows of Ava Lavender. (ENG.). 320p. (YA). (gr. 9). 2015. pap. 8.99 *(978-0-7636-8027-5(3))* 2014. 17.99 *(978-0-7636-6566-1(5))* Candlewick Pr.
—The Strange & Beautiful Sorrows of Ava Lavender. 2015. lib. bdg. 19.65 *(978-0-606-36879-7(5))* Turtleback Bks.
Wandless, David. Natural Magic. 2010. 344p. pap. 27.50 *(978-1-4461-4163-2(2))* Lulu Pr., Inc.
Warburton, Ruth. Witch Finder. 2014. (ENG.). 384p. (J). (gr. 7). pap. 10.99 *(978-1-4449-1446-7(4))* Hodder & Stoughton GBR. Dist: Hachette Bk. Group.
Ward, James M. The Time Curse. 2007. (Paths of Doom Ser.). (Illus.). 128p. (J). per. 4.99 *(978-1-931567-72-5(7))* Margaret Weis Productions, Ltd.
Ward, M. P. Sam & the Sea Witch. 2013. 158p. pap. *(978-1-77127-397-8(6))* MuseItUp Publishing.
Ward, Nick. The Ice Child. Bailey, Peter, illus. 2004. 32p. (J). *(978-1-84458-038-5(5),* Pavilion Children's Books) Pavilion Bks.
Wardell, Joe. Doodey the Combat Camel. Bane, T. Glenn, illus. 2012. 20p. pap. 12.95 *(978-0-615-58866-7(2))* Little Clive Pr.
Warnasuriya, Chandrani. Spooky Tales from the Orient: Tales of Ogres, Demons, Ghosts, Spells, Charms & the Enchanted, 1 vol. 2009. 167p. pap. 24.95 *(978-1-61546-978-9(8))* America Star Bks.
Wartik, David J. The Vonnesta Project. 2006. 140p. (J). (gr. 3-6). pap. 12.95 *(978-1-59113-938-6(4))* Booklocker.com, Inc.
Washer, S. N. The Wingate Adventures: Our New Friends. 2006. 164p. pap. 11.95 *(978-1-59800-510-3(3))* Outskirts Pr., Inc.
Wasson, Christopher. Quest for Adlaremzee Molair Nopeeoh. 2003. 120p. pap. 19.95 *(978-1-4137-0117-3(5))* America Star Bks.
Watase, Yû. Imadoki!, Vol. 4: Nowadays, 5 vols. Watase, Yû, illus. 2004. (ENG., Illus.). 200p. pap. 9.95 *(978-1-59116-618-4(7))* Viz Media.
Watase, Yuu. Arata: The Legend, Vol. 17. Watase, Yuu, illus. 2014. (ENG., Illus.). 192p. pap. 9.99 *(978-1-4215-5876-9(9))* Viz Media.
—Fushigi Yûgi: Genbu Kaiden, Vol. 12. Watase, Yuu, illus. 2014. (ENG., Illus.). 192p. pap. 9.99 *(978-1-4215-6434-0(3))* Viz Media.
—Fushigi Yûgi: Genbu Kaiden, Vol. 4. Watase, Yuu, illus. 2006. (ENG., Illus.). 208p. pap. 8.99 *(978-1-4215-0579-4(7))* Viz Media.
—Imadoki!, Vol. 2, 5 vols. Watase, Yuu, illus. 2004. (ENG., Illus.). 200p. pap. 9.95 *(978-1-59116-469-2(9))* Viz Media.
—Imadoki!, Vol. 5, 5 vols. Watase, Yuu, illus. 2005. (ENG., Illus.). 200p. pap. 9.95 *(978-1-59116-619-1(5))* Viz Media.
Water, Charles. The Road to Iadorre. 2012. 48p. pap. 21.99 *(978-1-4772-4483-8(2))* AuthorHouse.
Waters, Fiona. Aesop's Forgotten Fables. Testa, Fulvio, illus. 2014. (ENG.). 96p. (J). (gr. 2-4). 24.99 *(978-1-84939-706-3(6))* Andersen Pr. GBR. Dist: Independent Pubs. Group.
Waters, Summer. River Rescue, 10. 2010. (Silver Dolphins Ser.: 10). (ENG.). 176p. (J). (gr. 2-4). pap. 7.99 *(978-0-00-736750-4(3),* HarperCollins Children's Bks.) HarperCollins Pubs. Ltd. GBR. Dist: HarperCollins Pubs.
Watkins, Dawn L. Shield. 2008. (J). 8.99 *(978-1-59166-833-6(6))* BJU Pr.
Watson-Dubisch, Carolyn. Andy! & the Magician's Horn, 1. l.t. ed. 2006. (Illus.). 32p. (J). per. 9.95 *(978-0-9779295-0-4(7))* Medusa Road Pr.
—Night of the Armadillos, 1. Watson-Dubisch, Carolyn, illus. l.t. ed. 2006. (Illus.). 32p. (J). per. 9.95 *(978-0-9779295-2-8(3))* Medusa Road Pr.
Watson, Heather M. J. L. Thistle Lodge: The Legendary Sidhe Saga. 2012. (ENG.). 224p. pap. *(978-1-78088-181-2(9))* Troubador Publishing Ltd.
Watson, J. R. Wizard down Under. 2009. 160p. 23.50 *(978-1-60860-138-7(2),* Eloquent Bks.) Strategic Book Publishing & Rights Agency (SBPRA).
Watts, Julia. Revived Spirits. 2011. (ENG.). 170p. (J). (gr. 7). pap. 8.95 *(978-0-9831032-2-6(4),* BeanPole Bks.) Harren Communications, LLC.
Waugh, Sandra. Lark Rising. 2015. (Guardians of Tarnec Ser.). (ENG.). 400p. (YA). (gr. 7). pap. 9.99 *(978-0-449-81751-3(2),* Ember) Random Hse. Children's Bks.
—Silver Eve. 2015. (Guardians of Tarnec Ser.). (ENG., Illus.). 384p. (YA). (gr. 7). 17.99 *(978-0-449-81752-0(0),* Random Hse. Bks. for Young Readers) Random Hse. Children's Bks.
Way, Daniel. Sabretooth: Open Season. Sears, Bart, illus. 2005. (Wolverine Ser.). 96p. pap. 9.99 *(978-0-7851-1507-6(2))* Marvel Worldwide, Inc.
Weatherbee, Tabatha. Dream Sharers: Love/Hate. 2013. 336p. (J). pap. 19.00 *(978-1-62212-978-2(4),* Strategic Bk. Publishing) Strategic Book Publishing & Rights Agency (SBPRA).
Weatherly, L. A. Angel Fever. 2013. (Angel Ser.: 3). (ENG.). 496p. (J). (gr. 9). 17.99 *(978-0-7636-5680-5(1))* Candlewick Pr.
Webb, Beth. Fleabag Trilogy. 2005. 640p. (J). pap. 14.00 *(978-0-7459-4977-2(0),* Lion Books) Lion Hudson PLC GBR. Dist: Trafalgar Square Publishing.
Webb, Holly. Lily & the Prisoner of Magic. 2012. (ENG.). 224p. (J). (gr. 2-4). pap. 8.99 *(978-1-4083-1351-0(0))* Hodder & Stoughton GBR. Dist: Hachette Bk. Group.
—Lily & the Shining Dragons. 2012. (ENG.). 256p. (J). (gr. 4-6). pap. 8.99 *(978-1-4083-1350-3(2))* Hodder & Stoughton GBR. Dist: Hachette Bk. Group.
Webb, M. St. John. Knock Three Times! 2003. (Children's Classics). (ENG.). 160p. (J). (gr. 3-6). pap. *(978-1-85326-132-9(7))* Wordsworth Editions, Ltd.
Webb, Mack Henry, Jr. Webb's Wondrous Tales Book 1. Webb, Celia, illus. 2006. 184p. (YA). per. 14.95 *(978-0-9779576-1-3(6))* Pilinut Pr., Inc.
Webb, Margot & Chorpash, Marci. My Grandmommy Is Shrinking. 2003. 60p. pap. 8.95 *(978-0-595-29143-4(0))* iUniverse, Inc.
Webb, Rita. Tears. 2012. 350p. pap. 12.99 *(978-0-615-51355-3(7))* Robot Playground, Inc.
Webster, Christy. Anna's Best Friends. 2014. (Disney Princess Step into Reading Ser.). lib. bdg. 13.55 *(978-0-606-35547-6(2))* Turtleback Bks.
—Bath Party! Random House Editors & VanTuyle, David, illus. 2015. (Step into Reading Ser.). (ENG.). 24p. (J). (gr. -1-1). pap. 4.99 *(978-0-385-38767-5(9),* Random Hse. Bks. for Young Readers) Random Hse. Children's Bks.
Webster, Clare L., retold by. The Elf, 1 vol. 2009. 27p. pap. 24.95 *(978-1-60836-775-7(4))* America Star Bks.
Weinbach, Shaindel. Shimmee & the Taste-Me Tree. Backman, Aidel, illus. Date not set. (J). (gr. -1-2). 2.95 *(978-0-87306-305-0(8))* Feldheim Pubs.
Weinberg, Jennifer Liberts. Pretty Pearl Mermaid. 2014. (Step into Reading Ser.). (ENG., Illus.). 32p. (J). (gr. -1-1). 3.99 *(978-0-385-37307-4(4),* Random Hse. Bks. for Young Readers) Random Hse. Children's Bks.
Weinshall Liberman, Judith. The Little Fairy. 2013. 32p. 21.99 *(978-1-4575-2351-9(5))* Dog Ear Publishing, LLC.
Weis, Claudia Brigitte. A B R A H A M: Bist du neugierig? 2010. 88p. pap. 17.90 *(978-3-8391-0698-3(2))* Bks. on Demand.
Weiss, Sonya. Rising. 2017. (ENG., Illus.). (YA). pap. 15.00 ***(978-1-5161-0028-6(X))*** Kensington Publishing Corp.
Weissmann, Joe, illus. The Gingerbread Man. 2005. (J). 7.95 *(978-0-9770473-0-7(X))* Heersink, Roland.
Welch, Julie. Happy Hearts, 1 vol. 2009. 52p. pap. 16.95 *(978-1-4489-1971-0(1))* America Star Bks.
Welles, Lee. Enter the Earth. Hameister, Ann, illus. 2007. (Gaia Girls Ser.: 1). (ENG.). 336p. (YA). (gr. 4-7). pap. 24.95 *(978-1-933609-01-0(X))* Chelsea Green Publishing.
—Gaia Girls: Way of Water. Coogan, Carol, illus. 2007. (Gaia Girls Ser.). (ENG.). 336p. (J). (gr. 4-7). 18.95 *(978-1-933609-02-7(8))* Chelsea Green Publishing.
Wells, Craig. Fangs for God: A Vampire Satire. 2011. 252p. pap. 16.95 *(978-1-4620-2136-9(0))* iUniverse, Inc.
Wells, J. & L. Antares & the Zodiac. 2012. (ENG.). 256p. pap. *(978-1-78088-294-9(7))* Troubador Publishing Ltd.
Wells, Shannon Nicole. Gold! A Tall Tale. 2009. (J). pap. 7.00 *(978-1-61623-111-8(4))* Independent Pub.
Wells, Susan. The Rainbow Dragon/ the Sorcerer's Race. 2004. (Illus.). 60p. (YA). 6.95 *(978-0-9741726-1-3(8))* Dreamtime Publishing.
—Rock Parables. 2004. (Illus.). 62p. (YA). 6.95 *(978-0-9741726-2-0(6))* Dreamtime Publishing.
Wenke, Christine. Willa's Secret. 2005. 160p. (Orig.). pap. *(978-0-7344-0675-0(4),* Lothian Children's Bks.) Hachette Australia.
Werner, Jane. Mad Hatter's Tea Party (Disney Alice in Wonderland) RH Disney, illus. 2016. (Little Golden Book Ser.). (ENG.). 24p. (J). (-k). 4.99 *(978-0-7364-3627-4(6),* Golden/Disney) Random Hse. Children's Bks.
Wert, Yijin, tr. The Little Monkey King's Journey: Retold in English & Chinese. Jian, Li, illus. 2012. (ENG & CHI.). 48p. (J). (gr. -1-3). 16.95 *(978-1-60220-981-7(2))* BetterLink Pr., Inc.
West, Alma Brown. Princess Logan & the Shy Spell. 2010. 54p. pap. 15.99 *(978-1-4535-3513-4(6))* Xlibris Corp.
West, Hannah. Kingdom of Ash & Briars. 2016. (ENG., Illus.). 368p. (YA). 17.95 *(978-0-8234-3651-4(9))* Holiday Hse., Inc.
West, Jacqueline. Spellbound. 2012. (Books of Elsewhere Ser.: 2). lib. bdg. 18.40 *(978-0-606-26082-4(X),* Turtleback) Turtleback Bks.
West, Paul & Denslow, W. W. The Pearl & the Pumpkin: A Classic Halloween Tale. Denslow, W. W., illus. 2009. (Dover Children's Classics Ser.). (ENG., Illus.). 264p. (J). (gr. 2-5). pap. 12.99 *(978-0-486-47031-3(8))* Dover Pubns., Inc.
West, Richard A. & Shortt, Yvonne M. Spell of the Iris. 2013. 42p. 27.95 *(978-0-9860691-0-9(8))* Industrial Gingerbread.
West, Robert. Attack of the Spider Bots, 1 vol. 2008. (Star-Fighters of Murphy Street Ser.). (ENG., Illus.). 160p. (J). (gr. 4-7). pap. 6.99 *(978-0-310-71426-2(5))* Zonderkidz.
—There's a Spaceship in My Tree!, 1 vol. 2008. (Star-Fighters of Murphy Street Ser.). (ENG., Illus.). 144p. (J). (gr. 4-7). pap. 6.99 *(978-0-310-71425-5(7))* Zonderkidz.
West, Steve, reader. Island of Legends. 2014. (Unwanteds Ser.: 4). (ENG., Illus.). 496p. (J). (gr. 3-7). 18.99 *(978-1-4424-9328-5(3),* Aladdin) Simon & Schuster Children's Publishing.
West, Tracey. More Monsters, More Problems. 2016. (LEGO NEXO Knights Ser.). (ENG.). 80p. (J). (gr. 2-5). pap. 4.99 *(978-1-338-03804-0(4))* Scholastic, Inc.
West, Tracey. Race to Danger (Pokémon: Chapter Book) 2017. (Pokémon Ser.). (ENG.). 96p. (J). (gr. 2-5). pap. 4.99 ***(978-1-338-17585-1(8))*** Scholastic, Inc.
Weston, Robert Paul. Prince Puggly of Spud & the Kingdom of Spiff. 2013. (ENG., Illus.). 224p. (J). (gr. 3-7). 15.99 *(978-1-59514-567-3(2),* Razorbill) Penguin Young Readers Group.
Weston Woods Staff, creator. Crictor. 2011. 18.95 *(978-0-545-23360-6(7));* 38.75 *(978-0-545-23361-3(5))* Weston Woods Studios, Inc.
—Dem Bones. 2004. 29.95 *(978-1-55592-702-8(5))* Weston Woods Studios, Inc.
—The Elves & the Shoemaker. 2004. 29.95 *(978-0-7882-0547-7(1))* Weston Woods Studios, Inc.
—Harold & the Purple Crayon. 2011. 18.95 *(978-0-439-72691-7(3));* 29.95 *(978-0-439-73474-5(6));* 38.75 *(978-0-439-72693-1(X))* Weston Woods Studios, Inc.
—In the Night Kitchen. 2011. 29.95 *(978-0-439-73480-6(0));* 18.95 *(978-0-439-72723-5(5));* 38.75 *(978-0-439-72728-0(6))* Weston Woods Studios, Inc.
—Petunia. 2011. 29.95 *(978-0-439-73509-4(2));* 38.75 *(978-0-439-72868-3(1));* 18.95 *(978-0-439-72867-6(3))* Weston Woods Studios, Inc.
—A Picture for Harold's Room. 2011. 18.95 *(978-0-439-72871-3(1));* 38.75 *(978-0-439-72872-0(X))* Weston Woods Studios, Inc.

Wewers, Jason. The Candy Bar Adventures: March of the Evil Mard. 2007. 156p. pap. 12.99 *(978-1-4357-0438-1(X))* Lulu Pr., Inc.

Wexler, Django. The Palace of Glass: The Forbidden Library: Volume 3. 2016. (Forbidden Library). (ENG., Illus.). 368p. (J). (gr. 5). 16.99 *(978-0-8037-3978-9(8),* Kathy Dawson Books) Penguin Young Readers Group.

Weyn, Suzanne. The Invisible World. 2012. (ENG.). 240p. (J). (gr. 9-9). 17.99 *(978-0-545-33486-0(1),* Scholastic Pr.) Scholastic, Inc.

Wheeldon, Shaun A. The Lost Kingdom of Fraydelore: A Long Journey. 2016. (ENG.). 241p. pap. 11.99 *(978-1-78612-375-6(4),* 9f7b5b22-b700-41a2-86e5-e0e15a0ad72f) Austin, Stan AUS. Dist: Bookmasters Distribution.

Whisp, Kennilworthy, pseud. Quidditch Through the Ages. 2017. (Harry Potter Ser.). (ENG.). 128p. (J). (gr. 3-3). 12.99 *(978-1-338-12574-0(5),* Levine, Arthur A. Bks.) Scholastic, Inc.

—Quidditch Through the Ages. 2017. (ENG.). (J). (gr. 3). lib. bdg. 24.50 ***(978-0-606-39694-3(2))*** Turtleback Bks.

White, Andrea. Radiant Girl. 2008. (ENG.). 256p. (J). (gr. 4-7). 19.95 *(978-1-933979-23-6(2),* 9781933979236) Bright Sky Pr.

White, Cecily. Conspiracy Boy. 2016. (ENG., Illus.). 280p. (YA). (gr. 7). pap. 14.99 *(978-1-68281-125-2(5))* Entangled Publishing, LLC.

White, Dorine. The Emerald Ring (Cleopatra's Legacy) 2013. 183p. (YA). pap. 13.99 *(978-1-4621-1133-6(5),* Horizon Pubs.) Cedar Fort, Inc./CFI Distribution.

White, E. B. La Telarana de Carlota, 1 vol. Williams, Garth, illus. 2005. (SPA.). 224p. (J). (gr. 3-7). pap. 7.99 *(978-0-06-075740-3(X))* HarperCollins Pubs.

—The Telarana of Carlota (La Telarana de Carlota) Williams, Garth, illus. 2005. (Charlotte's Web Ser.). (SPA.). 224p. (J). 16.99 *(978-0-06-075739-7(6),* Rayo) HarperCollins Pubs.

White, J. A. A Path Begins. Offermann, Andrea, illus. 2014. (Thickety Ser.: 1). (ENG.). 496p. (J). (gr. 5-7). 16.99 *(978-0-06-225724-6(2),* Tegen, Katherine Bks) HarperCollins Pubs.

—The Thickety: a Path Begins. Offermann, Andrea, illus. 2017. (Thickety Ser.: 4). 512p. (J). (gr. 5). 16.99 *(978-0-06-238139-2(3),* Tegen, Katherine Bks) HarperCollins Pubs.

—Well of Witches. Offermann, Andrea, illus. (Thickety Ser.: 3). (J). (gr. 5). 2017. 528p. pap. 7.99 *(978-0-06-225731-4(5))* 2016. 512p. 16.99 *(978-0-06-225732-1(3))* HarperCollins Pubs. (Tegen, Katherine Bks).

—The Whispering Trees. Offermann, Andrea, illus. 2015. (Thickety Ser.: 2). (ENG.). 528p. (J). (gr. 5). 16.99 *(978-0-06-225729-1(3),* Tegen, Katherine Bks) HarperCollins Pubs.

White, Kiersten. Illusions of Fate. 2014. (ENG.). 288p. (YA). (gr. 8). 17.99 *(978-0-06-213589-6(9),* HarperTeen) HarperCollins Pubs.

White, Kiersten. Now I Rise. 2017. (And I Darken Ser.: 2). (ENG.). 480p. (YA). (gr. 7). 18.99 ***(978-0-553-52235-8(3));*** lib. bdg. 21.99 ***(978-0-553-52236-5(1))*** Random Hse. Children's Bks. (Delacorte Pr.).

White, Mark. The Lion & the Mouse: A Retelling of Aesop's Fable, 1 vol. Pérez, Sara Rojo, illus. 2010. (My First Classic Story Ser.). (ENG.). 24p. (gr. k-3). pap. 7.10 *(978-1-4048-7365-0(1),* My First Classic Story) Picture Window Bks.

White, Mark & Aesop Enterprise Inc. Staff. The Ant & the Grasshopper: A Retelling of Aesop's Fable, 1 vol. Pérez, Sara Rojo, illus. 2011. (My First Classic Story Ser.). (ENG.). 24p. (gr. k-3). lib. bdg. 22.65 *(978-1-4048-6505-1(5),* My First Classic Story) Picture Window Bks.

—The Fox & the Grapes: A Retelling of Aesop's Fable, 1 vol. Pérez, Sara Rojo, illus. 2011. (My First Classic Story Ser.). (ENG.). 24p. (gr. k-3). lib. bdg. 22.65 *(978-1-4048-6508-2(X),* My First Classic Story) Picture Window Bks.

—The Wolf in Sheep's Clothing: A Retelling of Aesop's Fable, 1 vol. Pérez, Sara Rojo, illus. 2011. (My First Classic Story Ser.). (ENG.). 24p. (gr. k-3). lib. bdg. 22.65 *(978-1-4048-6509-9(8),* My First Classic Story) Picture Window Bks.

White, Wade Albert. The Adventurer's Guide to Dragons (and Why They Keep Biting Me) 2017. (Adventurer's Guide Ser.: 2). (ENG.). 384p. (J). (gr. 3-7). 16.99 ***(978-0-316-30531-0(6))*** Little, Brown Bks. for Young Readers.

White, Wade Albert. The Adventurer's Guide to Successful Escapes. (Adventurer's Guide Ser.: 1). (ENG.). (J). (gr. 3-7). 2017. 400p. pap. 6.99 ***(978-0-316-30526-6(X))*** 2016. (Illus.). 384p. 16.99 *(978-0-316-30528-0(6))* Little, Brown Bks. for Young Readers.

Whiteside, S. K. Inheritance. 2013. 320p. (YA). pap. 12.99 *(978-1-939769-27-5(2))* Crushing Hearts and Black Butterfly Publishing.

Whitesides, Tyler. Secrets of New Forest Academy. 2012. (Janitors Ser.: Bk. 2). 368p. (J). 18.99 *(978-1-60907-014-4(3))* Deseret Bk. Co.

Whitley, David. The Canticle of Whispers. 2013. (Agora Trilogy Ser.: 3). (ENG.). 400p. (J). (gr. 6-9). 17.99 *(978-1-59643-615-2(8),* 9781596436152) Roaring Brook Pr.

—The Midnight Charter. 2010. (Agora Trilogy Ser.: 1). (ENG.). 352p. (J). (gr. 6-9). pap. 19.99 *(978-0-312-62904-5(4),* 9780312629045) Square Fish.

Whitman, Emily. Radiant Darkness. 2009. (ENG.). 288p. (YA). (gr. 9-18). 16.99 *(978-0-06-172449-7(1),* Greenwillow Bks.) HarperCollins Pubs.

Whitmore, Andre. FunnyFruit. 2007. 42p. 19.50 *(978-0-615-16444-1(7))* American World Publishing.

Whitmore, Gary. Prince Luna & the Space Dreamers. 2011. (ENG.). 204p. pap. 8.50 *(978-1-4565-8438-2(3))* CreateSpace Independent Publishing Platform.

Whittaker, Liz. Manawi's Treasure. 2005. (ENG.). 190p. (J). pap. 11.95 *(978-0-86243-785-5(7))* Y Lolfa GBR. Dist: Dufour Editions, Inc.

Whyte, S. L. Finding Tir Na Nog: Finding Tir Na Nog. Ronsley, Jill, ed. Place, Konohiki, illus. 2013. (ENG.). 416p. (YA). pap. 12.99 *(978-0-9857523-0-9(0))* Fireglass Publishing.

Wick. Elfish Fantasy: The Great Chocolate Caper. 2003. 128p. (YA). pap. 11.95 *(978-0-595-29038-3(8))* iUniverse, Inc.

Wicke, Ed. The Muselings. Douglas, Janine, illus. 2012. 212p. pap. 9.99 *(978-0-9840718-8-3(1))* Blacknblue Pr.

—Wicked Tales. 2006. (ENG., Illus.). 156p. (J). per. 9.99 *(978-0-9677652-7-3(7),* BlacknBlue Pr. UK) Blacknblue Pr.

Wicks, Valerie. Seven Spectral: The Orange World Outlaw. Lang, Leslie, ed. Ingram, Charles, illus. 2013. 342p. pap. 12.99 *(978-0-9912594-0-3(8))* Wicks, Valerie.

Wiggin, Kate Douglas. The Bird's Christmas Carol. 2008. 88p. (gr. 4-7). pap. 8.95 *(978-1-60664-191-0(3))* Aegypan.

Wiggins, Bethany. The Dragon's Price (a Transference Novel) 2017. (Transference Trilogy Ser.: 1). (ENG.). 304p. (YA). (gr. 7). 17.99 *(978-0-399-54981-6(1),* Crown Books For Young Readers) Random Hse. Children's Bks.

Wilce, Ysabeau S. Flora's Dare: How a Girl of Spirit Gambles All to Expand Her Vocabulary, Confront a Bouncing Boy Terror, & Try to Save Califa from a Shaky Doom (Despite Being Confined to Her Room) 2010. (ENG.). 528p. (YA). (gr. 7). pap. 7.99 *(978-0-15-205403-8(0))* Houghton Mifflin Harcourt Publishing Co.

Wilcox, Jean A. Diary of Sir Winston Loki, 1 vol. 2010. 34p. 24.95 *(978-1-4512-1813-8(3))* PublishAmerica, Inc.

Wilkey, David. Through the Black Hole: The Incredible Adventures of Justin Hart. 2003. 154p. pap. 12.95 *(978-0-595-29497-8(9))* iUniverse, Inc.

Wilkinson, James H. Yang the Dragon Tells His Story, Halloween Train. Blake, Carol, illus. 2013. 32p. pap. 15.99 *(978-0-9886360-0-2(X))* Kids At Heart Publishing, LLC.

Willett, Edward. The Cave Beneath the Sea: The Shards of Excalibur Book 4, 1 vol. 2015. (Shards of Excalibur Ser.: 4). (ENG.). 224p. (YA). (gr. 7-9). pap. 14.95 *(978-1-55050-639-6(0))* Coteau Bks. CAN. Dist: Orca Bk. Pubs. USA.

William Elliot, Griffis. Dutch Fairy Tales for Young Folks. 2007. (ENG.). 140p. pap. 18.99 *(978-1-4264-3924-7(5))* Creative Media Partners, LLC.

Williams, Alan. Archy the Flying Dolphin & the Vampire's Curse. 2007. pap. 15.38 *(978-1-4251-3151-7(4))* Trafford Publishing.

Williams, Avery. The Impossibility of Tomorrow: An Incarnation Novel. 2013. (ENG., Illus.). 384p. (YA). (gr. 7). 16.99 *(978-1-4424-4319-8(7),* Simon & Schuster Bks. For Young Readers) Simon & Schuster Bks. For Young Readers.

Williams, Brenda & Lacombe, Benjamin. Lin Yi's Lantern. Lacombe, Benjamin, illus. 2012. (ENG., Illus.). 32p. (J). (gr. k-3). pap. 8.99 *(978-1-84686-793-4(2))* Barefoot Bks., Inc.

Williams, Brenda Gail. Little Mo Weep. 2004. (J). per. 7.95 *(978-1-59427-027-7(9))* Aglob Publishing.

Williams, C. B. Walkers. 2012. 118p. pap. 6.95 *(978-0-9881814-0-3(1))* BRYN WILLIAMS LLC.

Williams, David Morgan. Dragonrise. 2006. (ENG.). 96p. (J). pap. 11.95 *(978-0-86243-637-7(0))* Y Lolfa GBR. Dist: Dufour Editions, Inc.

—Xcalibur, Merlin & the Teeth of the Dragon. 2015. (ENG.). 160p. (J). pap. 13.00 *(978-1-84771-823-5(X))* Y Lolfa GBR. Dist: Dufour Editions, Inc.

Williams, John Joseph. The Frightened Garden. 2013. 98p. (J). pap. *(978-1-78299-167-0(0))* FeedARead.com.

Williams, Kristen. Sheepy Sue & the Bedtime Blues. 2012. 28p. pap. 12.95 *(978-1-105-48819-1(5))* Lulu.com GBR. Dist: Lulu Pr., Inc.

Williams, Margery. The Velveteen Rabbit: Or How Toys Become Real. Santore, Charles, illus. 2013. (Classic Edition Ser.). (ENG.). 48p. (J). 17.95 *(978-1-60433-277-3(8),* Applesauce Pr.) Cider Mill Pr. Bk. Pubs., LLC.

Williams, Rozanne Lanczak. The Purple Snerd. GrandPré, Mary, illus. 2003. (Green Light Readers Level 2 Ser.). (ENG.). 24p. (J). (gr. -1-3). pap. 3.95 *(978-0-15-204826-6(X))* Houghton Mifflin Harcourt Publishing Co.

Williamson, Joshua. Sketch Monsters Book 1: Escape of the Scribbles: Escape of the Scribbles. 2011. (ENG., Illus.). 40p. 12.99 *(978-1-934964-69-9(7),* 9781934964699) Oni Pr., Inc.

Williamson, Judithe Anne. Tiny with a Twist: Book 3 of the Tiny Village Series, 1 vol. 2010. 52p. pap. 16.95 *(978-1-4489-7247-0(7))* America Star Bks.

Willis, Jeanne & Ross, Melanie H. Dr Xargle's Book of Earth Hounds. 2003. (Illus.). 32p. (J). 9.95 *(978-0-86264-249-5(3))* Random Hse. GBR. Dist: Trafalgar Square Publishing.

Willow. Tirissa & the Necklace of Nulidor. 2009. 338p. pap. 17.95 *(978-1-4327-4013-9(X))* Outskirts Pr., Inc.

Willsea, Hedley. The Heath of the Graves. 2009. 371p. pap. 31.50 *(978-1-4092-2226-2(8))* Lulu Pr., Inc.

Wilson, Barbara Rogers. Deva & the Soul Snatcher an Environmental Fantasy. 2nd ed. 2013. 216p. pap. 11.95 *(978-0-9834956-9-7(6),* SpiritBooks) Portal Ctr. Pr.

Wilson, David Cramb. The Day that the Fairies stole Badger! 2008. 40p. pap. 9.95 *(978-0-557-00247-4(8))* Lulu Pr., Inc.

Wilson, Db. Teale Tales: Wyv Land of Magik. 2012. 266p. pap. *(978-1-78176-345-2(3))* FeedARead.com.

Wilson, Douglas, reader. What I Learned in Narnia. 2004. cd-rom 35.00 *(978-1-59128-438-3(4))* Canon Pr.

Wilson, Elaine Moody. Fisherman Jack Meets the River Creatures, 1 vol. Ducker Signs Plus, illus. 2009. 40p. pap. 24.95 *(978-1-60836-967-6(6))* PublishAmerica, Inc.

Wilson, Eva Adriana. My Power Ball. 2013. 48p. pap. 17.45 *(978-1-4525-7676-3(9),* Balboa Pr.) Author Solutions, Inc.

Wilson, Gerrard. Alice on Top of the World. 2009. 159p. pap. 17.50 *(978-0-9561553-0-6(8))* Wilson, Gerrard IRL. Dist: Lulu Pr., Inc.

Wilson, Mark A. The Amazing Gift from the Woods. 2008. 48p. pap. 16.95 *(978-1-60563-056-4(X))* America Star Bks.

—The Legend of Crawley Creek. 2008. 104p. pap. 9.95 *(978-1-60693-423-4(6),* Eloquent Bks.) Strategic Book Publishing & Rights Agency (SBPRA).

Wilson, N. D. Empire of Bones. (Ashtown Burials Ser.: Bk. 3). (ENG.). (J). (gr. 3-7). 2014. 464p. 7.99 *(978-0-375-86398-1(2),* Yearling) 2013. 352p. 16.99 *(978-0-375-86441-4(5),* Random Hse. Bks. for Young Readers) Random Hse. Children's Bks.

—Outlaws of Time: The Legend of Sam Miracle. 2016. (Outlaws of Time Ser.: 1). 336p. (J). (gr. 3-7). 16.99 *(978-0-06-232726-0(7),* Tegen, Katherine Bks) HarperCollins Pubs.

—The Song of Glory & Ghost. 2017. (Outlaws of Time Ser.: 2). 352p. (J). (gr. 3-7). 16.99 *(978-0-06-232729-1(1),* Tegen, Katherine Bks) HarperCollins Pubs.

Wilson, Robert. Pippy: The Miracle of A Dream. 2011. 136p. 21.95 *(978-1-4620-6634-6(8));* pap. 11.95 *(978-1-4620-6633-9(X))* iUniverse, Inc.

Wilson, W. Shane. Ryan of the Wildfire. 2009. 296p. pap. 19.75 *(978-0-557-14937-7(1))* Lulu Pr., Inc.

Windham, Ryder. Island of Lost Masks. Scholastic, Inc. Staff, illus. 2015. (LEGO Bionicle Ser.: 1). (ENG.). 128p. (J). (gr. 2-5). pap. 5.99 *(978-0-545-87325-3(8))* Scholastic, Inc.

—Island of Lost Masks. 2015. lib. bdg. 16.00 *(978-0-606-37793-5(X))* Turtleback Bks.

Winfield, A. C. The Star Pirate. 2013. (Illus.). 184p. pap. *(978-1-909202-11-5(8))* Little Acorns Publishing.

Winick, Judd. The Great Big Boom. 2017. (Hilo Ser.: 3). (ENG., Illus.). 208p. (J). (gr. 3-7). 13.99 *(978-0-385-38620-3(6));* lib. bdg. 16.99 *(978-0-385-38621-0(4))* Random Hse. Children's Bks. (Random Hse. Bks. for Young Readers).

Winkler, Ashley & Winkler, Michael. One Good Quest Deserves Another: A Crown of Amaranth Story. 2009. 292p. 28.95 *(978-0-595-71039-3(5));* pap. 18.95 *(978-0-595-47365-6(2))* iUniverse, Inc.

Winn, Christine M. & Walsh, David. Clover's Secret. Winn, Christine M., illus. 2004. (Illus.). 28p. (J). (gr. k-4). reprint ed. 15.00 *(978-0-7567-7653-4(8))* DIANE Publishing Co.

Winn, L. B. Butterpod Jerome & the Planet of Gabool. Winn, L. B., illus. 2007. (Illus.). (J). pap. 18.95 *(978-0-9791884-0-4(7))* Winn, Lynnette.

Winter, Barbara. The Golden Scarab. 2007. (Illus.). 48p. (J). lib. bdg. 15.00 *(978-1-4242-1617-8(6))* Dingles & Co.

Winter, Milo, illus. Aesop's Fables for Children. 2008. (Dover Read & Listen Ser.). (ENG.). 112p. (J). (gr. k-2). pap. 14.99 incl. cd-rom *(978-0-486-46770-2(8))* Dover Pubns., Inc.

Winter, P. K. Back at Eagle Lake: More Eagle Lake Giant Stories. Winter, P. K., illus. 2009. (Illus.). 182p. pap. 18.50 *(978-1-4251-8831-3(1))* Trafford Publishing.

Winters, Jeffrey. Mystic Uncle & the Magical Bridge. 2005. 116p. (J). (gr. 3-7). pap. 10.95 *(978-1-59526-167-0(2),* Llumina Pr.) Aeon Publishing Inc.

Winters, Kari-Lynn. Jeffrey & Sloth, 1 vol. Hodson, Ben, illus. 2008. (ENG.). 32p. (J). (gr. -1-3). per. 9.95 *(978-1-55143-974-7(3))* Orca Bk. Pubs. USA.

Winterson, Jeanette. The Battle of the Sun. 2010. (ENG.). 400p. (YA). 17.99 *(978-1-4088-0042-3(X),* 9781408800423, Bloomsbury USA Childrens) Bloomsbury Publishing USA.

Wiseman, Holly. Xavier & Lynx: And the Mean Trick. 2010. 32p. pap. 12.99 *(978-1-4520-1158-5(3))* AuthorHouse.

Wisher, Mark. Don't kiss the Prince. 2010. 33p. pap. 21.50 *(978-1-4457-7238-7(8))* Lulu Pr., Inc.

Wishinsky, Frieda. A Noodle up Your Nose, 1 vol. Laliberté, Louise-Andrée, illus. 2004. (Orca Echoes Ser.). (ENG.). 64p. (J). (gr. 2-3). pap. 6.95 *(978-1-55143-294-6(3))* Orca Bk. Pubs. USA.

Wissman, Celeste Farris. When I Teach My Monkey How to Dance. 2012. 24p. pap. 17.99 *(978-1-4772-6035-7(8))* AuthorHouse.

Wist, S. J. Whispering Stone. 2013. 342p. pap. *(978-0-9916914-0-1(7))* Infinity Dreamt.

Withaneye, Toni. Little Thunder's First Sound. 2012. 16p. pap. 10.00 *(978-1-4634-1576-1(1))* AuthorHouse.

Witschen, Kay. Clinker's Christmas Star. Witschen, Kay, illus. 2004. (Illus.). 24p. (J). 6.95 *(978-0-9741352-1-2(6))* Dwitt Publishing.

The Wizard of OZ. 2008. (Charm Book Classics Ser.). 32p. *(978-1-4075-1582-3(9))* Parragon, Inc.

Wizards of Waverly Place Insider's Guide. 2009. 128p. pap. 8.99 *(978-1-4231-2473-3(1))* Disney Pr.

Wohl, David, et al. Top Cow's Best of Michael Turner. 2006. (ENG., Illus.). 240p. (YA). pap. 24.99 *(978-1-58240-544-5(1),* 9781582405445) Image Comics.

Wolfe, Robert Hewitt. The Goblin Crown: Billy Smith & the Goblins, Book 1. 2016. (Billy Smith & the Goblins Ser.: 1). (ENG.). 336p. (J). pap. 16.95 *(978-1-68162-612-3(8))* Turner Publishing Co.

Wolfel, Ursula. Abecedario Fantastico. (SPA.). 128p. (YA). (gr. 5-8). *(978-84-279-3357-6(6),* NG3950) Noguer y Caralt Editores, S. A. ESP. Dist: Lectorum Pubns., Inc.

Wolverton, Barry. The Dragon's Gate. Stevenson, Dave, illus. 2016. (Chronicles of the Black Tulip Ser.: 2). 336p. (J). (gr. 3-7). 16.99 *(978-0-06-222193-3(0),* Walden Pond Pr.) HarperCollins Pubs.

Wong, Carmen L. F. Written By... 2013. 252p. (gr. 4-6). 33.25 *(978-1-4669-3179-4(5));* pap. 18.85 *(978-1-4669-3178-7(7))* Trafford Publishing.

Wong, Clarissa. S Is for Super Hero. Pierfederici, Mirco, illus. 2016. (ENG.). 26p. (J). (gr. -1-k). bds. 12.99 *(978-1-4847-2358-6(9),* Marvel Pr.) Disney Publishing Worldwide.

Wong, Clarissa S. World of Reading: Black Widow This Is Black Widow. Di Vito, Andrea, illus. 2015. (World of Reading Ser.). (ENG.). 32p. (J). (gr. 1-3). pap. 3.99 *(978-1-4847-2517-7(4),* Marvel Pr.) Disney Publishing Worldwide.

Wood, Audrey. Balloonia & Magic Shoelaces. (J). audio *(978-0-85953-373-7(5))* Child's Play International Ltd.

—Presto Change-O. Wood, Audrey, illus. 2005. (Child's Play Library). (ENG., Illus.). 32p. (J). pap. *(978-1-904550-52-5(5))* Child's Play International Ltd.

Wood, D. K. Nightmare at Indian Cave. 2006. pap. 10.00 *(978-1-4257-1640-0(7))* Xlibris Corp.

Wood, Dean. Michael Moon & the Curse of the Troll King. 2016. (ENG.). 240p. (J). pap. 11.95 *(978-1-78612-449-4(1),* 5266ffa9-8c46-48ba-83c7-12b771c9330f) Austin, Stan AUS. Dist: Bookmasters Distribution.

Wood, Francis. The SnowPeople. Larsen, Dan, illus. 2003. 96p. (YA). per. 14.95 *(978-0-9746372-0-4(3))* Tip-Of-The-Moon Publishing Co.

Wood, Francis Eugene. Return to Winterville. Pickett, Elizabeth & Dean, Tina, eds. Larsen, Dan, illus. 2004. 96p. (YA). per. 14.95 net. *(978-0-9746372-1-1(1))* Tip-Of-The-Moon Publishing Co.

Wood, Jacqui. Cliff Dreamers. 2017. (ENG.). 302p. (J). pap. 17.99 ***(978-1-78693-909-8(6),*** c6a96e5f-51f5-4a30-9049-4d533f30c109) Austin, Stan AUS. Dist: Bookmasters Distribution.

Wood, Jamie Robyn. Bearskin. 2015. 275p. (YA). pap. 17.99 *(978-1-4621-1716-1(3))* Cedar Fort, Inc./CFI Distribution.

Wood, Kate. Twinkle. 2013. (Illus.). 60p. (J). pap. 20.00 *(978-0-9837334-9-2(X))* Digi-Tall Media.

Wood, Maryrose. Why I Let My Hair Grow Out. 2007. (ENG.). 224p. (YA). (gr. 9). 11.00 *(978-0-425-21380-3(3),* Berkley) Penguin Publishing Group.

Woodell, Rejoice. Kohara, the White Veiled City. 2011. 138p. pap. 19.99 *(978-1-4568-7969-3(3))* Xlibris Corp.

Wooding, Chris. Havoc. 2010. (Malice Ser.: 2). (ENG., Illus.). 400p. (J). (gr. 3-7). 16.99 *(978-0-545-16045-2(6),* Scholastic Pr.) Scholastic, Inc.

—Malice, Bk. 1. Chernett, Dan, illus. 2009. (Malice Ser.: 1). (ENG.). 384p. (J). (gr. 7-12). 14.99 *(978-0-545-16043-8(X))* Scholastic, Inc.

—Malice #2: Havoc. 2012. (Malice Ser.: 2). (ENG.). 400p. (J). (gr. 3-7). pap. 9.99 *(978-0-545-16046-9(4),* Scholastic Pr.) Scholastic, Inc.

—Poison. 2006. 1.00 *(978-1-4237-9048-8(0))* Recorded Bks., Inc.

Woodruff, M. C. The Woods of Arreth. 2012. 248p. pap. 24.95 *(978-1-4626-8817-3(9))* America Star Bks.

Woodward, J. Howland. A Moment in Time. 2006. 55p. pap. 16.95 *(978-1-4241-1334-7(2))* America Star Bks.

Woon, Yvonne. Love Reborn. 2014. (Dead Beautiful Novel Ser.). (ENG., Illus.). 368p. (YA). (gr. 7-12). 16.99 *(978-1-4231-7120-1(9))* Hyperion Bks. for Children.

World of Fairy Tales. unabr. ed. 2004. (Chrysalis Childrens Classics Ser.). (Illus.). (YA). pap. *(978-1-84365-064-5(9),* Pavilion Children's Books) Pavilion Bks.

Worley, Roger A. 14 Wishes, 1 vol. 2009. 164p. pap. 24.95 *(978-1-61582-419-9(7))* America Star Bks.

Worth, K. D. The Grim Life. 2016. (ENG., Illus.). (J). 24.99 ***(978-1-63477-967-8(3),*** Harmony Ink Pr.) Dreamspinner Pr.

Wrecks, Billy. The Incredible Hulk (Marvel) Golden Books Staff & Spaziante, Patrick, illus. 2016. (Little Golden Book Ser.). (ENG.). 24p. (J). (gr. k-k). 4.99 *(978-0-307-93194-8(3),* Golden Bks.) Random Hse. Children's Bks.

Wrede, Patricia C. Across the Great Barrier. 2011. (Frontier Magic Ser.: 2). (ENG.). 352p. (J). (gr. 7-7). 16.99 *(978-0-545-03343-5(8),* Scholastic Pr.) Scholastic, Inc.

—Calling on Dragons. unabr. ed. 2004. (Enchanted Forest Chronicles: Bk. 3). 244p. (J). (gr. 6-18). pap. 38.00 incl. audio *(978-0-8072-0792-5(6),* LYA 347 SP, Listening Library) Random Hse. Audio Publishing Group.

—Calling on Dragons: The Enchanted Forest Chronicles, Book Three. 2015. (Enchanted Forest Chronicles Ser.: 3). (ENG.). 288p. (J). (gr. 5-7). pap. 7.99 *(978-0-544-54147-4(2),* HMH Books For Young Readers) Houghton Mifflin Harcourt Publishing Co.

—Dealing with Dragons: The Enchanted Forest Chronicles, Book One. 2015. (Enchanted Forest Chronicles Ser.: 1). (ENG., Illus.). 240p. (J). (gr. 5-7). pap. 7.99 *(978-0-544-54122-1(7),* HMH Books For Young Readers) Houghton Mifflin Harcourt Publishing Co.

—The Enchanted Forest Chronicles: [Boxed Set]. 2015. (Enchanted Forest Chronicles Ser.). (ENG.). 1120p. (J). (gr. 5-7). 31.99 *(978-0-544-54264-8(9),* HMH Books For Young Readers) Houghton Mifflin Harcourt Publishing Co.

—The Far West. 2012. (ENG.). 384p. (J). (gr. 7-7). 17.99 *(978-0-545-03344-2(6),* Scholastic Pr.) Scholastic, Inc.

—Searching for Dragons. unabr. ed. 2004. (Enchanted Forest Chronicles: Bk. 2). 242p. (J). (gr. 5-18). pap. 38.00 incl. audio *(978-0-8072-0670-6(9),* Listening Library) Random Hse. Audio Publishing Group.

—Searching for Dragons: The Enchanted Forest Chronicles, Book Two. 2015. (Enchanted Forest Chronicles Ser.: 2). (ENG., Illus.). 272p. (J). (gr. 5-7). pap. 7.99 *(978-0-544-54146-7(4),* HMH Books For Young Readers) Houghton Mifflin Harcourt Publishing Co.

—Snow White & Rose Red. 2009. (ENG.). 288p. (YA). (gr. 7-18). 8.99 *(978-0-14-241121-6(3),* Firebird) Penguin Young Readers Group.

—Talking to Dragons: The Enchanted Forest Chronicles, Book Four. 2015. (Enchanted Forest Chronicles Ser.: 4). (ENG.). 304p. (J). (gr. 5-7). pap. 7.99 *(978-0-544-54148-1(0),* HMH Books For Young Readers) Houghton Mifflin Harcourt Publishing Co.

Wrede, Patricia C. & Stevermer, Caroline. Sorcery & Cecelia or the Enchanted Chocolate Pot: Being the Correspondence of Two Young Ladies of Quality Regarding Various Magical Scandals in London & the Country. 2004. (ENG., Illus.). 336p. (YA). (gr. 7-12). pap. 7.99 *(978-0-15-205300-0(X))* Houghton Mifflin Harcourt Publishing Co.

Wrench, Peter. The Night of the Round Stable. Holland, Ruth, illus. 2012. 174p. pap. *(978-1-908895-49-3(7))* FeedARead.com.

Wright, Johnalan. Disco Danby. 2015. (ENG.). 163p. pap. 10.95 *(978-1-78455-192-6(9),* 6a8cf93f-5947-4b26-9e00-0eef9e57a984) Austin, Stan AUS. Dist: Bookmasters Distribution.

Wright, Marcus. Raincloud. 2007. 172p. pap. 9.88 *(978-0-615-15579-1(0))* Digitex-U Pubns.

Wyatt, Chris. World of Reading: Ant-Man This Is Ant-Man: Level 1. Lim, Ron & Rosenberg, Rachelle, illus. 2015. (World of Reading Ser.). (ENG.). 32p. (J). (gr. -1-k). pap. 3.99 *(978-1-4847-1455-3(5),* Marvel Pr.) Disney Publishing Worldwide.

Wyke-Smith, E. A. The Marvellous Land of Snergs. Morrow, George, illus. 2006. (Dover Children's Classics Ser.). (ENG.). 224p. (gr. 3-12). per. 11.95 *(978-0-486-45255-5(7))* Dover Pubns., Inc.

Wynn, Thad & Wynn, Juliette. The Tale of a Dragon. 2004. (Illus.). 85p. (gr. k-4). 15.95 *(978-1-57197-140-1(8))* Pentland Pr., Inc.

Wynne-Jones, Tim. I'll Make You Small. (J). pap. 15.95 *(978-0-88899-045-7(6));* pap. 4.95 *(978-0-88899-105-8(3))* Groundwood Bks. CAN. Dist: Publishers Group West (PGW).

—The Maestro, 1 vol. 2nd ed. 2004. (ENG.). 224p. (J). (gr. 5-9). pap. 8.95 *(978-0-88899-637-4(3))* Groundwood Bks. CAN. Dist: Publishers Group West (PGW).

—Zoom Upstream. (J). pap. 5.95 *(978-0-88899-188-1(6))* Groundwood Bks. CAN. Dist: Publishers Group West (PGW).

Wyss, Tyan. The Solitaire Prince. 2006. 168p. (YA). per. 12.95 *(978-1-58939-906-8(4))* Virtualbookworm.com Publishing, Inc.

X, Sulayman. King of Storms. 2016. (Five Kingdoms Ser.: Vol. 2). (ENG., Illus.). (YA). 29.99 ***(978-1-63533-038-0(6),*** Harmony Ink Pr.) Dreamspinner Pr.

Yagami, Yu & Yugami, Yu. Those Who Hunt Elves, Vol. 6. 2004. (Illus.). 202p. (YA). pap. 9.99 *(978-1-4139-0098-9(4))* ADV Manga.

Yakowicz, Susie. Fire Runner. 2004. (J). per. 12.95 *(978-0-9652546-3-2(1))* JESSPress/Susie Yakowicz.

Yamagata, Ishio. Rokka: Braves of the Six Flowers, Vol. 1 (light Novel) 2017. (Rokka: Braves of the Six Flowers (Light Novel) Ser.: 1). (ENG., Illus.). 224p. (gr. 8-17). pap. 14.00 *(978-0-316-50141-5(7)*, Yen Pr.) Orbit.

Yazawa, Nao. Moon & Blood, Vol. 1. 2011. (ENG., Illus.). 72p. (YA). pap. 6.95 *(978-1-56970-207-9(1)*, 9781569702079) Digital Manga Publishing.

Yelchin, Eugene & Kuryla, Mary. Heart of a Snowman. Yelchin, Eugene & Kuryla, Mary, illus. 2009. (ENG., Illus.). 40p. (J). (gr. -1-3). 16.99 *(978-0-06-125926-5(8))* HarperCollins Pubs.

Yep, Laurence. City of Death. 2013. (City Trilogy Ser.: 3). (ENG.). 384p. (J). (gr. 3-7). 17.99 *(978-0-7653-1926-5(8)*, 9780765319265, Starscape) Doherty, Tom Assocs., LLC.

Yolen, Jane. Centaur Rising. 2015. (J). lib. bdg. 18.40 *(978-0-606-37586-3(4))* Turtleback Bks.

—Curses! Foiled Again. Cavallaro, Mike, illus. 2013. (ENG.). 176p. (J). (gr. 6-9). pap. 15.99 *(978-1-59643-619-0(0)*, 9781596436190, First Second Bks.) Roaring Brook Pr.

—Dragon's Heart. Schmidt, Jonathon, ed. 2011. (Pit Dragon Chronicles Ser.: 4). (ENG.). 400p. (YA). (gr. 7). pap. 8.99 *(978-0-547-39862-4(X))* Houghton Mifflin Harcourt Publishing Co.

—Foiled. Cavallaro, Mike, illus. 2010. (ENG.). 160p. (J). (gr. 6-9). pap. 17.99 *(978-1-59643-279-6(9)*, 9781596432796, First Second Bks.) Roaring Brook Pr.

—Foiled. 2010. (J). lib. bdg. 30.60 *(978-0-606-14452-0(8)*, Turtleback) Turtleback Bks.

—Romping Monsters, Stomping Monsters. Murphy, Kelly, illus. 2013. (ENG.). 32p. (J). (gr. -1-2). 14.99 *(978-0-7636-5727-7(1))* Candlewick Pr.

—Wizard's Hall. 144p. (J). (gr. 3-5). pap. 6.00 *(978-0-8072-1544-9(9)*, Listening Library) Random Hse. Audio Publishing Group.

Yolen, Jane & Stemple, Adam. The Hostage Prince. 2014. (Seelie Wars Ser.). (ENG.). 256p. (J). (gr. 3-7). pap. 7.99 *(978-0-14-242234-2(7)*, Puffin Books) Penguin Young Readers Group.

—The Last Changeling. 2014. (Seelie Wars Ser.). (ENG.). 304p. (J). (gr. 3-7). 16.99 *(978-0-670-01435-4(4)*, Viking Books for Young Readers) Penguin Young Readers Group.

—The Seelie King's War. 2016. (Seelie Wars Ser.: 3). (ENG., Illus.). 336p. (J). (gr. 3-7). 17.99 *(978-0-670-01436-1(2)*, Viking Books for Young Readers) Penguin Young Readers Group.

Yorinks, Arthur. The Invisible Man. Date not set. (J). 14.99 *(978-0-06-205092-2(3))*; lib. bdg. 15.89 *(978-0-06-205093-9(1))* HarperCollins Pubs.

—The Nose. 2005. 64p. (J). pap. 5.99 *(978-0-7868-1342-1(3))* Hyperion Paperbacks for Children.

Yorke, Peter & Batley, Alan. Tales from Fidgety Forest. 2011. (Illus.). 80p. (gr. 1-2). pap. 12.52 *(978-1-4567-7961-0(3))* AuthorHouse.

Yoshikawa, Sachiko, illus. The Boy from the Dragon Palace: A Folktale from Japan. 2012. (J). *(978-1-61913-110-1(2))* Weigl Pubs., Inc.

Young, Ed. Seven Blind Mice. Young, Ed, illus. 2012. (ENG., Illus.). 36p. (J). (gr. -1 — 1). bds. 8.99 *(978-0-399-25742-1(X)*, Philomel Bks.) Penguin Young Readers Group.

Young, Julie. Dragon Stone: Dragon Cliff Trilogy Book Two. 2011. 160p. (gr. 4-6). pap. 12.95 *(978-1-4620-0682-3(5))* iUniverse, Inc.

Young, Katharine Anne. Grandmother Moon & Roy G Biv: A Colorful Bedtime Story for All Ages. EXPLORE the AMAZING SECRETS of COLOR. 2009. 72p. pap. 23.49 *(978-1-4389-7844-4(8))* AuthorHouse.

Young, Scott Alexander. The Wild Cats of Piran. Christe, Moreno, illus. 2014. (Young Europe Bks.). (ENG.). 124p. (YA). (gr. 5). pap. 10.99 *(978-0-9900043-0-1(9)*, Young Europe Bks.) Steerforth Pr.

Younge, Cathy. The Tale of Sidney Elderberry - an Ordinary Boy with Extraordinary Bowels. Taylor, Mark, illus. 2013. 32p. pap. *(978-1-78148-838-6(X))* Grosvenor Hse. Publishing Ltd.

Yovanoff, Brenna. The Space Between. 2012. (ENG., Illus.). 384p. (YA). (gr. 9). pap. 8.99 *(978-1-59514-483-6(8)*, Razorbill) Penguin Young Readers Group.

YoYo. Vermonia 7: Battle for the Turtle Realm, 1. 2014. (Vermonia Ser.). (ENG.). 208p. (J). (gr. 3-6). pap. 11.75 *(978-1-61533-651-7(6)*, Windmill Bks.) Rosen Publishing Group, Inc., The.

Yoyo Books Staff. Fantasy Stories: One Minute Goodnight Stories. 2004. 40p. bds. *(978-90-5843-581-1(4))* YoYo Bks.

Yu, Li, et al. The Holy Spark: Rogel & the Goddess of Liberty. 2006. (J). *(978-1-931907-42-2(0))* Homa & Sekey Bks.

Yuki, Kaori. Alice in Murderland, Vol. 5. 2017. (Alice in Murderland Ser.: 5). (ENG., Illus.). 176p. (gr. 11-17). 17.00 *(978-0-316-50279-5(0)*, Yen Pr.) Orbit.

—Demon from Afar. 2015. (Demon from Afar Ser.: 5). (ENG., Illus.). 176p. (gr. 11-17). 18.00 *(978-0-316-34579-8(2)*, Yen Pr.) Orbit.

Yun, Mi-Kyung. Bride of the Water God Volume 14. Simon, Philip, ed. Yun, Mi-Kyung, illus. 2013. (ENG., Illus.). 168p. pap. 9.99 *(978-1-61655-187-2(9))* Dark Horse Comics.

Yung, Kao & Liang, Kuan. Magic Lover's Tower, Vol. 2. 2008. (Magic Lover's Tower Ser.). (ENG., Illus.). 176p. (YA). (gr. 8). pap. 9.95 *(978-1-59796-154-7(X))* DrMaster Pubns. Inc.

Yzaguirre, Ricky. The Day I Turned into a Duck. 2012. 8p. pap. 15.99 *(978-1-4772-1275-2(2))* AuthorHouse.

Zahler, Diane. Baker's Magic. Price, Mina, illus. 2016. (Middle-Grade Novels Ser.). (ENG.). 336p. (gr. 4-7). lib. bdg. 26.65 *(978-1-4965-2724-0(0))* Stone Arch Bks.

—Princess of the Wild Swans. Gilbert, Yvonne, illus. 2013. (ENG.). 240p. (J). (gr. 3-7). pap. 6.99 *(978-0-06-200495-6(6))* HarperCollins Pubs.

—Sleeping Beauty's Daughters. 2013. (ENG.). 224p. (J). (gr. 3-7). 16.99 *(978-0-06-200496-3(4))* HarperCollins Pubs.

Zahler, Thomas F., et al. Pony Tales, Vol. 1. Curnow, Bobby, illus. 2013. (My Little Pony Ser.). (ENG.). 152p. pap. 19.99 *(978-1-61377-740-4(X)*, 9781613777404) Idea & Design Works, LLC.

Zahorak, Sarah. Candyland Forest. 2009. 24p. pap. 12.50 *(978-1-4343-9905-2(2))* AuthorHouse.

Zales, S. R. Jenny & the Hummingbird Faeries. 2012. 152p. pap. 14.95 *(978-1-4575-1330-5(7))* Dog Ear Publishing, LLC.

Zappa, Shana Muldoon & Zappa, Ahmet. Star Darlings Gemma & the Worst Wish Ever. Disney Storybook Art Team, illus. 2016. (Star Darlings Ser.: 12). (ENG.). 176p. (J). (gr. 3-7). pap. 6.99 *(978-1-4847-1431-7(8))* Disney Pr.

Zdenek, Joseph. Heart of Courage: The Narscix War. 2007. 372p. (gr. -1-7). per. 20.95 *(978-0-595-43187-8(9))* iUniverse, Inc.

Zeman, Ludmila, illus. & retold by. Sindbad: From the Tales of the Thousand & One Nights. Zeman, Ludmila, retold by. 2011. (ENG.). 32p. (J). (gr. 1-4). pap. 9.95 *(978-1-77049-264-6(X)*, Tundra Bks.) Tundra Bks. CAN. Dist: Penguin Random Hse. LLC.

—Sindbad in the Land of Giants: From the Tales of the Thousand & One Nights. Zeman, Ludmila, retold by. 2011. (ENG.). 32p. (J). (gr. 1-4). pap. 9.95 *(978-1-77049-266-0(6)*, Tundra Bks.) Tundra Bks. CAN. Dist: Penguin Random Hse. LLC.

—Sindbad's Secret: From the Tales of the Thousand & One Nights. Zeman, Ludmila, retold by. 2011. (ENG.). 32p. (J). (gr. 1-4). pap. 9.95 *(978-1-77049-265-3(8)*, Tundra Bks.) Tundra Bks. CAN. Dist: Penguin Random Hse. LLC.

Zenk, Molly. Hyperion Keats. 2013. 134p. pap. 5.49 *(978-0-9895262-5-8(9))* Highland Pr.

Zevgolis, Irene, illus. The Dreamer & the Moon: An Inspirational Story with a Ballet Theme. 2008. (J). *(978-0-615-17590-4(2))* E-City Publishing.

Zhang, Kat. Once We Were: The Hybrid Chronicles, Book 2. 2013. (Hybrid Chronicles Ser.: 2). (ENG.). 352p. (YA). (gr. 8). 17.99 *(978-0-06-211490-7(5))* HarperCollins Pubs.

Zimmerman, Diana S. Kandide & the Secret of the Mists. Gadd, Maxine, illus. 2008. (Calabiyau Chronicles Ser.: Bk. 1). 296p. (YA). (gr. 5-18). 17.99 *(978-0-9794328-3-5(9))* Noesis Publishing.

Zimmerman, W. Frederick. Unauthorized Harry Potter & the Alchemist's Cell News: Half-Blood Prince Analysis & Speculation. 2006. 160p. per. 14.94 *(978-0-9777424-7-9(4))* Nimble Bks. LLC.

—Unauthorized Harry Potter & the Chariots of Light News: Half-Blood Prince Analysis & Speculation. 2006. 160p. per. 14.94 *(978-0-9777424-8-6(2))* Nimble Bks. LLC.

Zimmermann, Andreas. Shard. 2012. 302p. 28.95 *(978-1-4620-8351-0(X))*; pap. 18.95 *(978-1-4620-8350-3(1))* iUniverse, Inc.

Zinn, Bridget. Poison. 2014. (ENG.). 288p. (YA). (gr. 7-12). pap. 9.99 *(978-1-4231-5330-6(8))* Hyperion Bks. for Children.

Zoe at the Fancy Dress Ball, 6 Packs. (Literatura 2000 Ser.). (gr. 2-3). 33.00 *(978-0-7578-5601-3(2))* Rigby Education.

Zoehfeld, Kathleen Weidner. Dolphin's First Day: The Story of a Bottlenose Dolphin. Petruccio, Steven James, illus. 2009. (Smithsonian Oceanic Collection). (J). 24.95 incl. audio compact disk *(978-1-59249-666-2(0))* Soundprints.

Zortman, Bruce. Eight Little Candles Plus: A Hanukkah Tale. 2011. (Illus.). 38p. pap. 14.50 *(978-1-60976-905-5(8)*, Eloquent Bks.) Strategic Book Publishing & Rights Agency (SBPRA).

Zug, Mark & Fan, Nancy Yi. Swordbird. Zug, Mark, illus. 2008. (Swordbird Ser.: 1). (ENG., Illus.). 256p. (J). (gr. 3-7). pap. 6.99 *(978-0-06-113101-1(6))* HarperCollins Pubs.

123 Sesame Street, ed. Abby in Wonderland. 2009. (ENG.). 20p. 16.99 *(978-1-59069-834-1(7))* Studio Mouse LLC.

FANTASY FICTION—HISTORY AND CRITICISM

Card, Orson Scott, et al. Great Snape Debate: Is Snape Innocent or Guilty? 2007. (ENG.). 192p. (J). (gr. 7). pap. *(978-1-933771-35-9(6))* BenBella Bks.

Cast, P. C., ed. Nyx in the House of Night: Mythology, Folklore & Religion in the PC & Kristin Cast Vampyre Series. 2011. (ENG., Illus.). 200p. (gr. 8-12). pap. 19.95 *(978-1-935618-55-3(5))* BenBella Bks.

Cast, P. C. & Doner, Kim. The Fledgling Handbook 101. 2010. (House of Night Novels Ser.). (ENG., Illus.). 176p. (YA). (gr. 7-12). pap. 14.99 *(978-0-312-59512-8(3)*, 9780312595128, St. Martin's Griffin) St. Martin's Pr.

Frost, Laurie. Philip Pullman's His Dark Materials: The Definitive Guide. 2006. (Illus.). 400p. (YA). 44.95 *(978-0-9759430-0-7(6))* Fell Pr., The.

Gillespie, Natalie. Believing in Narnia: A Kid's Guide to Unlocking the Secret Symbols of Faith in C. S. Lewis' the Chronicles of Narnia, 1 vol. 2008. (ENG., Illus.). 192p. (gr. 2-6). pap. 12.99 *(978-1-4003-1282-5(5))* Nelson, Thomas Inc.

Hamilton, John. Weapons of Fantasy & Folkore, 1 vol. 2006. (Fantasy & Folklore Ser.). (ENG., Illus.). 32p. (gr. 5-8). 27.07 *(978-1-59679-340-8(6)*, Abdo & Daughters) ABDO Publishing Co.

Kirk, E. J. Step into Narnia: A Journey Through the Lion, the Witch & the Wardrobe. 2005. (Chronicles of Narnia Ser.). (Illus.). 64p. (J). lib. bdg. 20.89 *(978-0-06-074234-8(8))* HarperCollins Pubs.

Maloof, Torrey & Hill, Christina. Yound Adult Literature: Magical Worlds. 2016. (Time for Kids Nonfiction Readers Ser.). (ENG.). (J). (gr. 5-8). lib. bdg. 20.85 ***(978-0-606-39533-5(4))*** Turtleback Bks.

Meyer, Stephenie. The Twilight Saga: The Official Illustrated Guide. (Twilight Saga Ser.). (ENG.). 560p. (YA). (gr. 7-17). 2013. pap. 17.99 *(978-0-316-24425-1(2))* 2011. (Illus.). 24.99 *(978-0-316-04312-0(5))* Little, Brown Bks. for Young Readers.

Mulhall, Jill K. Young Adult Literature: The Worlds Inside Us. 2016. (Time for Kids Nonfiction Readers Ser.). (ENG.). (J). (gr. 5-8). lib. bdg. 20.85 ***(978-0-606-39534-2(2))*** Turtleback Bks.

Nagle, Jeanne, ed. Great Authors of Science Fiction & Fantasy. 2013. (Essential Authors for Children & Teens Ser.). (Illus.). 175p. (YA). (gr. 7-12). 45.00 *(978-1-62275-090-0(X))* Rosen Publishing Group, Inc., The.

Riordan, Rick, ed. Demigods & Monsters: Your Favorite Authors on Rick Riordan's Percy Jackson & the Olympians Series. rev. ed. 2013. (ENG.). 288p. (J). (gr. 5). pap. 12.95 *(978-1-937856-36-6(4))* BenBella Bks.

Smith, Kiley E. Young Adult Literature: Dystopian Worlds. 2016. (Time for Kids Nonfiction Readers Ser.). (ENG.). (J). (gr. 5-8). lib. bdg. 20.85 ***(978-0-606-39535-9(0))*** Turtleback Bks.

Waters, Galadriel & Mithrandir, Astre. New Clues to Harry Potter: Hints from the Ultimate Unofficial Guide to the Mysteries of Harry Potter, Vol. 5. Waters, Galadriel, illus. 2015. (ENG., Illus.). 100p. (gr. 3-6). pap. 10.95 *(978-0-9723936-2-1(5)*, 1230146) Wizarding World Pr.

Westerfeld, Scott & Castro, Adam-Troy. Mind-Rain: Your Favorite Authors on Scott Westerfeld's Uglies Series. Westerfeld, Scott, ed. 2009. (ENG., Illus.). 224p. (J). (gr. 7-12). pap. 17.95 *(978-1-933771-34-2(8))* BenBella Bks.

Wheeler, Jill C. J. R. R. Tolkien, 1 vol. 2009. (Children's Authors Set 5 Ser.). (ENG.). 24p. (J). (gr. 2-5). 25.65 *(978-1-60453-080-3(4))* ABDO Publishing Co.

Willett, Edward. J. R. R. Tolkien: Master of Imaginary Worlds. 2004. (Authors Teens Love Ser.). (Illus.). 128p. (J). lib. bdg. 27.94 *(978-0-7660-2246-1(3))* Enslow Pubs., Inc.

FAR EAST

see East Asia

FARADAY, MICHAEL, 1791-1867

Bingham, Derick. Michael Faraday: Spiritual Dynamo. 2010. (Trailblazers Ser.). (ENG.). 176p. (J). pap. 8.99 *(978-1-84550-156-3(X)*, 6da8f6db-c74f-4245-818d-6fca339103d3) Christian Focus Pubns. GBR. Dist: Bookmasters Distribution.

Salzmann, Mary Elizabeth. Michael Faraday, 1 vol. 2016. (ENG., Illus.). 24p. (J). *(978-1-68078-156-4(1))* ABDO Publishing Co.

Zannos, Susan. Michael Faraday & the Discovery of Electromagnetism. 2004. (Uncharted, Unexplored, & Unexplained Ser.). (Illus.). 48p. (J). (gr. 4-8). lib. bdg. 29.95 *(978-1-58415-307-8(5))* Mitchell Lane Pubs., Inc.

FARALLON ISLANDS (CALIF.)—FICTION

Whitney, A. D. T. The Other Girls. l.t. ed. 2007. (ENG.). 398p. pap. 26.99 *(978-1-4346-0103-2(X))* Creative Media Partners, LLC.

FARM ANIMALS

see Domestic Animals; Livestock

FARM CROPS

see Farm Produce

FARM IMPLEMENTS

see Agricultural Machinery

FARM LABORERS

see Agricultural Laborers

FARM LIFE

see also Country Life; Ranch Life

ABDO Publishing Company Staff & Borth, Teddy. On the Farm. 2014. (On the Farm Ser.: 6). (ENG.). 24p. (J). (gr. 4-8). lib. bdg. 171.00 *(978-1-62970-049-6(5))* ABDO Publishing Co.

Alexander, Heather. Farm. Lozano, Andres, illus. 2017. (Life on Earth Ser.). (ENG.). 16p. (J). (gr. k-1). bds. 12.99 *(978-1-84780-905-6(7)*, Wide Eyed Editions) Quarto Publishing Group UK GBR. Dist: Hachette Bk. Group.

Allan, Delores. Magical Moments with Roy & Toni: Fun at the Fair. 2011. 28p. pap. 13.59 *(978-1-4634-1546-4(X))* AuthorHouse.

Andrews, Alexa. On a Farm. Keimig, Candice, illus. 2013. (Penguin Young Readers, Level 1 Ser.). (ENG.). 32p. (J). (gr. k-1). mass mkt. 3.99 *(978-0-448-46376-6(8)*, Penguin Young Readers) Penguin Young Readers Group.

Arlon, Penelope. La Granja. 2013. (Scholastic Explora Tu Mundo Ser.). (SPA.). 32p. (J). (gr. -1-3). 7.99 *(978-0-545-48874-7(5)*, Scholastic en Espanol) Scholastic, Inc.

Baggott, Stella, illus. Baby's Very First Noisy Book Farm. 2013. (Baby's Very First Noisy Book Ser.). (ENG.). 10p. (gr. -1). 15.99 *(978-0-7945-2703-7(5)*, Usborne) EDC Publishing.

Baginski, Deanna Fisher. Harvest Time at the Fisher Farms. 2011. 24p. pap. 12.79 *(978-1-4670-2643-7(3))* AuthorHouse.

Bannatyne-Cugnet, Jo. A Prairie Alphabet. Moore, Yvette, illus. 2009. (ABC Our Country Ser.). (ENG.). 32p. (J). (gr. 1-4). pap. 7.95 *(978-0-88776-937-5(3)*, Tundra Bks.) Tundra Bks. CAN. Dist: Penguin Random Hse. LLC.

Boom, Rosie. Where Lions Roar at Night. 2nd ed. 2013. (Illus.). 240p. *(978-1-921161-18-6(3))* Boom Tree Publishing.

Borth, Teddy. Farm Life on the Farm, 1 vol. 2014. (On the Farm Ser.). (ENG.). 24p. (J). (gr. 4-8). lib. bdg. 28.50 *(978-1-62970-053-3(3))* ABDO Publishing Co.

Borth, Teddy, et al. Vida en la Granja. 2015. (En la Granja Ser.). (SPA & ENG., Illus.). 24p. (gr. k-1). pap. 7.95 *(978-1-4966-0453-8(9))* Capstone Classroom.

Britto, Romero. Color Play! An Interactive Pop Art Book. Britto, Romero, illus. 2011. (ENG., Illus.). 12p. (J). (gr. -1-k). 10.99 *(978-1-4169-9622-4(2)*, Little Simon) Little Simon.

Brooks, Felicity. Farms lift & Look. Litchfield, Jo, illus. 2005. 12p. (J). 9.95 *(978-0-7945-0932-3(0)*, Usborne) EDC Publishing.

—Frank the Farmer. Litchfield, Jo, illus. 2005. (Jobs People Do Ser.). 23p. (J). (gr. -1-7). pap. 6.95 *(978-0-7945-0723-7(9)*, Usborne) EDC Publishing.

—La Granja Minilibros Usborne. Litchfield, Jo, illus. 2005. (SPA.). 10p. (J). 4.95 *(978-0-7460-6110-7(2)*, Usborne) EDC Publishing.

Brown, Don. The Great American Dust Bowl. 2017. (ENG., Illus.). 80p. (YA). (gr. 7). pap. 9.99 ***(978-1-328-74087-8(0)***, HMH Books For Young Readers) Houghton Mifflin Harcourt Publishing Co.

—The Great American Dust Bowl. Brown, Don, illus. 2013. (ENG., Illus.). 80p. (YA). (gr. 7). 18.99 *(978-0-547-81550-3(6))* Houghton Mifflin Harcourt Publishing Co.

Burton, Margie, et al. Life on a Farm. 2011. (Early Connections Ser.). (J). *(978-1-61672-258-6(4))* Benchmark Education Co.

—Living on the Farm. 2011. (Early Connections Ser.). (J). *(978-1-61672-297-5(5))* Benchmark Education Co.

Caballero, D., tr. La Granja. Ebert, Anne, illus. 2006. (Junior (Silver Dolphin) Ser.). (SPA.). 16p. (J). (gr. -1). 9.95 *(978-970-718-345-2(4))* Readerlink Distribution Services, LLC.

Chernesky, Felicia Sanzari. From Apple Trees to Cider, Please! Patton, Julia, illus. 2015. (ENG.). 32p. (J). (gr. -1-3). 16.99 *(978-0-8075-6513-1(X))* Whitman, Albert & Co.

Connell, Kate. Hoping for Rain: The Dust Bowl Adventures of Patty & Earl Buckler. 2004. (I Am American Ser.). (ENG., Illus.). 40p. (J). (gr. 3-7). pap. 6.99 *(978-0-7922-6903-8(9)*, National Geographic Children's Bks.) National Geographic Society.

Connell, Kate & National Geographic Learning Staff. Dust Bowl Days. 2007. (Reading Expeditions Ser.). (ENG., Illus.). 40p. (J). pap. 19.95 *(978-0-7922-4557-5(1))* CENGAGE Learning.

Dean, Carol. The Hen House: A True Story of Growing up on a Maine Farm. Dunn, Sandy, illus. 2003. (ENG.). 32p. (J). (gr. -1-17). 15.95 *(978-0-89272-609-7(1))* Down East Bks.

Diaz, Joanne Ruelos. Animals on the Farm, 1 vol. Mendez, Simon, illus. 2014. (Animals All Day! Ser.). (ENG.). 32p. (gr. k-2). 27.27 *(978-1-4795-5699-1(8))* Picture Window Bks.

Dickmann, Nancy. Las Estaciones en la Granja. 2011. (Mundo de la Granja Ser.). 24p. (gr. -1-1). (SPA & ENG.). 22.65 *(978-1-4329-5311-9(7))*; (ENG & SPA.). pap. 6.29 *(978-1-4329-5318-8(4))* Heinemann-Raintree. (Bellota).

—El Mundo de la Granja, 6 vols., Set. Incl. Alimentos de la Granja. pap. 6.29 *(978-1-4329-5315-7(X))*; Animales de la Granja. pap. 6.29 *(978-1-4329-5313-3(3))*; Estaciones en la Granja. pap. 6.29 *(978-1-4329-5318-8(4))*; Las Plantas de la Granja. (Illus.). pap. 6.29 *(978-1-4329-5317-1(6))*; Máquinas de la Granja. pap. 6.29 *(978-1-4329-5314-0(1))*; Trabajos en la Granja. pap. 6.29 *(978-1-4329-5316-4(8))*; (gr. -1-1). (Mundo de la Granja Ser.). (SPA.). 24p. 2011. Set pap. 35.94 *(978-1-4329-5319-5(2)*, Bellota) Heinemann-Raintree.

—Seasons on a Farm, 1 vol. 2010. (World of Farming Ser.). 24p. (ENG.). (gr. -1-1). pap. 6.29 *(978-1-4329-3953-3(X))*; pap. 32.35 *(978-1-4329-3944-1(0))* Heinemann-Raintree. (Acorn).

Donlon, Bridget. Got Milk? How? Chelsey, Emily, illus. 2012. 26p. (-18). 29.95 *(978-1-62709-613-3(2))* America Star Bks.

Dorling Kindersley Publishing Staff. Cock-a-Doodle-Doo! - Farm. 2014. (ENG.). 12p. (J). (gr. -1 — 1). bds. 14.99 *(978-1-4654-2469-3(5)*, DK Children) Dorling Kindersley Publishing, Inc.

—Farm. 2014. (ENG., Illus.). 10p. (J). (gr. -1 — 1). bds. 6.99 *(978-1-4654-1687-2(0)*, DK Children) Dorling Kindersley Publishing, Inc.

—My First Farm: Let's Get Working! 2009. (Tab Board Bks.). (ENG.). 28p. (J). (gr. -1 — 1). bds. 9.99 *(978-0-7566-5544-0(7)*, DK Children) Dorling Kindersley Publishing, Inc.

—Really Feely: Farm. 2017. (ENG., Illus.). 12p. (J). (— 1). bds. 6.99 *(978-1-4654-5517-8(5)*, DK Children) Dorling Kindersley Publishing, Inc.

Durden-Nelson, Mae. I Just Called Her Momma. 2003. (Illus.). xii, 162p. (J). 18.95 *(978-1-57168-714-2(9))* Eakin Pr.

Encyclopaedia Britannica, Inc. Staff, compiled by. Discover English with Ben & Bella: Series 5: on the Farm. 2010. 180.00 *(978-1-61535-352-1(6))* Encyclopaedia Britannica, Inc.

Farm Fun Crafts for Kids. 16.99 *(978-0-8307-2990-6(9)*, Gospel Light) Gospel Light Pubns.

Faulkner, Keith & Tyger, Rory. Time's Up! Faulkner, Keith & Tyger, Rory, illus. Lambert, Jonathan, illus. 2003. (J). *(978-0-439-56155-6(8))* Scholastic, Inc.

Flatt, Lizann. Life in a Farming Community. 2009. (Learn about Rural Life Ser.). (ENG., Illus.). 32p. (J). (gr. 3-6). pap. *(978-0-7787-5084-0(1))* Crabtree Publishing Co.

Fun Farm. (Flip Flap Fun Book Ser.). 10p. (J). bds. *(978-2-89393-819-6(1))* Phidal Publishing, Inc./Editions Phidal, Inc.

Galloway, Fhiona, illus. Look Through: Farm. 2016. (ENG.). 10p. (J). bds. 8.99 *(978-1-62686-580-8(9)*, Silver Dolphin Bks.) Readerlink Distribution Services, LLC.

Gillespie, Sarah. Diary of Sarah Gillespie: A Pioneer Farm Girl, 1 vol. 2014. (First-Person Histories Ser.). (ENG.). 32p. (gr. 3-4). lib. bdg. 27.32 *(978-1-4765-4194-5(9)*, Fact Finders) Capstone Press of Coughlan Cos.

Goldberg, Ella, ed. Farm Life. 2013. (Matching Pictures Ser.). (ENG.). 20p. (J). (gr. -1-k). bds. 5.95 *(978-1-61889-309-3(2))* AZ Bks. LLC.

Gordon, Sharon. At Home on the Farm. (Bookworms: at Home Ser.). (Illus.). (J). 2007. 31p. (gr. -1-3). pap. 6.99 *(978-0-7614-3308-8(2))* 2005. (SPA., 32p. (gr. 3-7). lib. bdg. *(978-0-7614-1958-7(6))* Marshall Cavendish Corp. (Benchmark Bks.).

—At Home on the Farm/Mi Casa en la Granja. 2006. (Bookworms Ser.). (ENG & SPA., Illus.). 32p. (gr. k-2). lib. bdg. 15.95 *(978-0-7614-2454-3(7))* Marshall Cavendish Corp.

—Mi Casa en la Granja. 2006. (Bookworms Ser.). (SPA & ENG., Illus.). 32p. (gr. k-2). lib. bdg. 15.95 *(978-0-7614-2375-1(3))* Marshall Cavendish Corp.

Guin, Valerie. In the Country. 2005. (One World (Smart Apple Media) Ser.). (Illus.). 30p. (J). (gr. 3-6). lib. bdg. 27.10 *(978-1-58340-695-3(6))* Black Rabbit Bks.

Hahn, Beverly. Twenty Acres of Love: Irrigation Time. Hahn, Beverly, illus. 2003. (Illus.). v, 65p. (J). (gr. -1-6). spiral bd. 12.95 *(978-0-9722494-0-9(0))* Hahn, Beverly.

—Twenty Acres of Love: Little Bit, 8 vols. Hahn, Beverly & Silva, Tom, illus. 2003. (J). (gr. k-6). 12.95 *(978-0-9722494-1-6(9))* Hahn, Beverly.

Hardy, Mary Smith. Uncle Hubbard & the Burlap Sack. 2012. 48p. (gr. 4-6). pap. 12.95 *(978-1-4759-0179-5(8))* iUniverse, Inc.

Henry, J. The Big Gray House II: More Adventures of Franklin Meyers. 2011. 112p. (gr. -1-2). pap. 12.06 *(978-1-4269-7337-6(3))* Trafford Publishing.

Highlights for Children Editorial Staff, creator. Farm Time. 2016. (Highlights(tm) Find & Color Hidden Pictures(r) Ser.). (ENG.). 32p. (J). (gr. -1-k). pap. 5.99 *(978-1-62979-715-1(4)*, Highlights) Boyds Mills Pr.

Hinds, Kathryn. The Countryside. 2007. (Life in Elizabethan England Ser.). (Illus.). 80p. (J). (gr. 4-7). lib. bdg. 32.79 *(978-0-7614-2543-4(8)*, Benchmark Bks.) Marshall Cavendish Corp.

Hinkler Books Staff. Farm Lift the Flap. Penton Overseas, Inc. Staff, ed. rev. ed. 2006. (ENG., Illus.). 10p. (J). (gr. 3-6). bds. 5.95 *(978-1-74157-932-1(5))* Hinkler Bks. Pty, Ltd. AUS. Dist: Penton Overseas, Inc.

Hodge, Deborah. Up We Grow! A Year in the Life of a Small, Local Farm. Harris, Brian, illus. 2010. (ENG.). 32p. (J). (gr. -1-2). 16.95 *(978-1-55453-561-3(1))* Kids Can Pr., Ltd. CAN. Dist: Hachette Bk. Group.

Holland, Gini. I Live in the Country. 2004. (Where I Live Ser.). (Illus.). 24p. (gr. k-3). lib. bdg. 22.00 *(978-0-8368-4079-7(8)*,

Weekly Reader Leveled Readers) Stevens, Gareth Publishing LLLP.
—I Live in the Country/Vivo en el Campo. Coffey, Colleen & Carrillo, Consuelo, trs. 2004. (Weekly Reader Early Learning Library). (SPA & ENG., Illus.). 24p. (gr. k-3). lib. bdg. 22.00 *(978-0-8368-4127-5(1)*, Weekly Reader Leveled Readers) Stevens, Gareth Publishing LLLP.
Hooks, Earnest. Let's go see Mother Wilkerson's Farm. 2011. 72p. pap. 27.08 *(978-1-4389-5072-3(1))* AuthorHouse.
Hopkins, Andrea. Viking Families & Farms. 2009. (Viking Library). 24p. (gr. 3-3). 42.50 *(978-1-60854-257-4(2)*, PowerKids Pr.) Rosen Publishing Group, Inc., The.
Hunt, Nancy Nye & Bradley, Nina Leopold. Aldo Leopold's Shack: Nina's Story. 2011. (Center for American Places - Center Books on American Places Ser.). (ENG., Illus.). 88p. 29.95 *(978-1-935195-17-7(4))* Ctr. for American Places, Inc.
Imperato, Teresa. On the Farm: A Barnyard Book. Rayner, Olivia, illus. 2005. 10p. (J). 7.95 *(978-1-58117-270-6(2)*, Intervisual/Piggy Toes) Bendon, Inc.
Jacobs, Jerry L. Adventures on the Farm. Conyers, Courtney, illus. 2012. 38p. pap. 10.99 *(978-0-9855202-6-7(4))* Kids At Heart Publishing, LLC.
Jensen, Stephanie L. The Purple Watermelon. 2010. 48p. 17.95 *(978-1-4520-1417-3(5))* AuthorHouse.
Katz, Jon. Lenore Finds a Friend: A True Story from Bedlam Farm. Katz, Jon, photos by. 2012. (My Readers Ser.). (ENG., Illus.). 32p. (J). (gr. -1-3). 15.99 *(978-0-8050-9220-2(X)*, 9780805092202, Holt, Henry & Co. Bks. For Young Readers) Holt, Henry & Co.
—Lenore Finds a Friend: A True Story from Bedlam Farm. Katz, Jon, photos by. 2014. (My Readers Ser.). (ENG., Illus.). 32p. (J). (gr. -1-3). 15.99 *(978-1-250-03432-8(9)*, 9781250034328) Square Fish.
—Meet the Dogs of Bedlam Farm. Katz, Jon, photos by. 2011. (ENG., Illus.). 32p. (J). (gr. -1-3). 17.99 *(978-0-8050-9219-6(6)*, 9780805092196, Holt, Henry & Co. Bks. For Young Readers) Holt, Henry & Co.
Kawa, Katie. My First Trip to the Farm. 2012. (My First Adventures Ser.). (Illus.). 24p. (gr. k-2). 69.20 *(978-1-4339-8050-3(9))*; (J). pap. 8.15 *(978-1-4339-7313-0(8))*; (J). lib. bdg. 22.60 *(978-1-4339-7312-3(X))* Stevens, Gareth Publishing LLLP.
—My First Trip to the Farm: Mi Primera Visita a una Granja. 2012. (My First Adventures / Mis primeras aventuras Ser.). (SPA & ENG., Illus.). 24p. (J). (gr. k-2). lib. bdg. 22.60 *(978-1-4339-7378-9(2))* Stevens, Gareth Publishing LLLP.
Kids Can Press Staff. This Is Daniel Cook at the Farm. 2006. (This Is Daniel Cook Ser.). (ENG., Illus.). 24p. (J). (gr. -1-1). 4.95 *(978-1-55453-078-6(4))* Kids Can Pr., Ltd. CAN. Dist: Hachette Bk. Group.
Kurtz, John. FLIP OUTS — Funny Farm: Color Your Own Cartoon! 2015. (ENG., Illus.). 64p. (J). (gr. k-3). pap. 1.99 *(978-0-486-79483-9(0))* Dover Pubns., Inc.
Litchfield, Jo. Farm. 2004. (Look & Say Board Books Ser.). (Illus.). 10p. (J). 7.95 *(978-0-7945-0702-2(6)*, Usborne) EDC Publishing.
Loggins, Trace. Farm Life, City Life. 2013. (Rosen Readers Ser.). (ENG.). 24p. (J). (gr. 2-3). pap. 49.50 *(978-1-4777-2249-7(1))*; pap. 8.25 *(978-1-4777-2248-0(3))* Rosen Publishing Group, Inc., The. (Rosen Classroom).
Look Who's Popping Up: On the Farm. 2003. (J). (gr. -1-k). 4.98 *(978-0-7525-8903-9(2))* Parragon, Inc.
Machell, Dawn & Illustrator, West Yorkshire, illus. 100 Farm Words. 2017. (ENG.). 24p. (J). bds. 6.99 ***(978-1-68412-040-6(3)***, Silver Dolphin Bks.) Readerlink Distribution Services, LLC.
Mack, Steve. Letters. Flash Kids Editors, ed. 2012. (Flash Kids Preschool Activity Bks.). (ENG., Illus.). 80p. (J). pap. 5.95 *(978-1-4114-5808-6(7)*, Spark Publishing Group) Sterling Publishing Co., Inc.
Mara, Wil. The Farmer. 2010. (Colonial People Ser.). 48p. (gr. 3-18). 29.93 *(978-0-7614-4797-9(0))* Marshall Cavendish Corp.
Mark R. Borene, R. Borene & Mark R Borene. Welcome to the Farm: Book 2 of Welcome to the World. 2009. (Illus.). 20p. pap. 10.49 *(978-1-4389-6549-9(4))* AuthorHouse.
Marks, Anthony. The Usborne Farmyard Tales Songbook. Tyler, Jenny, ed. Cartwright, Stephen, illus. 2005. 31p. (J). (gr. -1-7). per. 6.95 *(978-0-7945-0918-7(5)*, Usborne) EDC Publishing.
Marrin, Albert. Years of Dust: The Story of the Dust Bowl. 2009. (ENG., Illus.). 128p. (J). (gr. 5-18). 22.99 *(978-0-525-42077-4(0)*, Dutton Books for Young Readers) Penguin Young Readers Group.
Marshall, Natalie, illus. Farm Friends. 2017. (Touch & Learn Bks.). (ENG.). 12p. (J). (gr. -1 — 1). bds. 5.99 ***(978-1-4380-5002-7(X))*** Barron's Educational Series, Inc.
Marsico, Katie. What's It Like to Live Here? Farm. 2014. (Community Connections: What's It Like to Live Here? Ser.). (ENG., Illus.). 24p. (J). (gr. 2-5). 25.64 *(978-1-62431-569-5(0)*, 203264) Cherry Lake Publishing.
Mattern, Joanne. Farm Animals. 2017. (Readers Ser.). (ENG., Illus.). 48p. (J). (-k). pap. 4.99 *(978-1-4263-2687-5(4)*, National Geographic Children's Bks.) National Geographic Society.
McDowell, Pamela. Farm. 2015. (Illus.). 24p. (J). pap. *(978-1-4896-3602-7(1))* Weigl Pubs., Inc.
McGill, Jordan. Farm Life: Pioneers of Canada. 2011. 24p. (YA). (gr. 2-4). *(978-1-77071-679-7(3))*; pap. *(978-1-77071-683-4(1))* Weigl Educational Pubs. Ltd.
McKinley, Fred B. Chinqua Where? The Spirit of Rural America, 1947-1955. Blassingame, Calvin, illus. 2003. 319p. 24.95 *(978-0-9729655-0-7(5))* Willow Creel Publishing Co.
Meredith, Susan. Cows on the Farm. 2010. (Farm Animals Ser.). (Illus.). 24p. (J). (gr. k-3). 22.79 *(978-1-61590-265-1(1))* Rourke Educational Media.
Miedzybrodzka, Wiktoria. Farm. Fretczak-Rodak, Monika, illus. 2014. (Mommy & Me Bath Bks.). (ENG.). 6p. (J). (gr. -1 — 1). 4.99 *(978-1-4380-7484-9(0))* Barron's Educational Series, Inc.
Milbourne, Anna. Farmyard Tales Things to Make & Do. 2005. (Activity Books Ser.). 32p. (J). pap. 8.95 *(978-0-7945-0940-8(1)*, Usborne) EDC Publishing.
—On the Farm. Roberti, Alessandra, illus. 2006. 24p. (J). (gr. -1-3). 9.99 *(978-0-7945-1282-8(8)*, Usborne) EDC Publishing.
Miller, Jake. Who's Who in a Rural Community. (Communities at Work Ser.). 24p. (gr. 2-2). 2009. 42.50 *(978-1-61511-899-1(3))* 2005. (Illus.). (J). lib. bdg. 22.60 *(978-1-4042-2787-3(3))* Rosen Publishing Group, Inc., The. (PowerKids Pr.).
National Geographic Kids. National Geographic Kids on the Farm Sticker Activity Book: Over 1,000 Stickers! 2015. (NG Sticker Activity Bks.). (ENG.). 56p. (J). (gr. -1-3). pap. 6.99 *(978-1-4263-2057-6(4)*, National Geographic Children's Bks.) National Geographic Society.
Nikola-lisa, W. Till Year's Good End. Manson, Christopher, illus. 2009. (ENG.). 36p. (J). (gr. 1-4). 12.99 *(978-1-4424-0225-6(3)*, Atheneum Bks. for Young Readers) Simon & Schuster Children's Publishing.
Owen, Ruth. Bread! Life on a Wheat Farm. 2012. (Food from Farmers Ser.). (ENG.). 32p. (J). (gr. k-3). pap. 11.75 *(978-1-61533-544-2(7))*; lib. bdg. 26.50 *(978-1-61533-532-9(3))* Windmill Bks.
—Fruit! Life on an Apple Farm. 2012. (Food from Farmers Ser.). (Illus.). 32p. (J). (gr. k-3). pap. 11.75 *(978-1-61533-538-1(2))*; lib. bdg. 26.50 *(978-1-61533-530-5(7))* Windmill Bks.
—Vegetables! Life on a Produce Farm. 2012. (Food from Farmers Ser.). (Illus.). 32p. (J). (gr. k-3). pap. 11.75 *(978-1-61533-540-4(4))*; lib. bdg. 26.50 *(978-1-61533-531-2(5))* Windmill Bks.
Parker, Francis W. Uncle Robert's Geography (Uncle Robert's Visit, V. 3) 2006. 84p. pap. *(978-1-84702-205-9(7))* Echo Library.
Peterson, Cris. Century Farm: One Hundred Years on a Family Farm. Upitis, Alvis, photos by. 2009. (ENG., Illus.). 32p. (J). (gr. 2-4). pap. 12.95 *(978-1-59078-773-1(0))* Boyds Mills Pr.
Plourde, Lynn. Storytime Stickers: Farm Follies. Ferraro Close, Laura, illus. 2010. (Storytime Stickers Ser.). (ENG.). 16p. (J). (gr. k-2). pap. 5.95 *(978-1-4027-7127-9(4))* Sterling Publishing Co., Inc.
Priddy, Roger. Busy Farm Cloth Book. 2015. (My First Priddy Ser.). (ENG.). 6p. (J). (gr. -1 — 1). 10.99 *(978-0-312-51791-5(2)*, 9780312517915, Priddy Bks.) St. Martin's Pr.
—Lift-the-Flap Tab - Farm. 2014. (Lift-The-Flap Tab Bks.). (ENG.). 16p. (J). (gr. -1 — 1). bds. 8.99 *(978-0-312-51753-3(X)*, 9780312517533, Priddy Bks.) St. Martin's Pr.
—My Big Farm Book. 2011. (My Big Board Bks.). (ENG., Illus.). 12p. (J). (gr. -1 — 1). bds. 8.99 *(978-0-312-51082-4(9)*, 9780312510824, Priddy Bks.) St. Martin's Pr.
—Treasure Hunt: on the Farm. 2015. (Treasure Hunt Ser.). (ENG., Illus.). 10p. (J). (gr. -1 — 1). bds. 8.99 *(978-0-312-51796-0(3)*, 9780312517960, Priddy Bks.) St. Martin's Pr.
Remson, Billie. A Mississippi Summer on Bluebird Hill: A True Story about Our Little Farm in the Hills of Southern Mississippi. Garraway, Kym, illus. 2005. (J). pap. 12.95 *(978-1-59571-073-4(6))* Word Association Pubs.
Rettore. Farm. 2016. (Baby Sees Cloth Bks.). (ENG.). 6p. (J). (gr. -1 — 1). 10.99 *(978-1-4380-7760-4(2))* Barron's Educational Series, Inc.
Rice, D. M. A Visit to a Farm, 1 vol. 2nd rev. ed. 2014. (TIME for KIDS(r) Nonfiction Readers Ser.). (ENG., Illus.). 24p. (J). (gr. 2-2). pap. 23.96 *(978-1-4807-1035-1(0))* Shell Educational Publishing.
Rosen, Michael J. Our Farm: Four Seasons with Five Kids on One Family's Farm. 2008. 128p. (J). (gr. -1-3). 18.95 *(978-1-58196-067-9(0)*, Darby Creek) Lerner Publishing Group.
Roy, Jennifer Rozines & Roy, Gregory. Multiplication on the Farm. (Math All Around Ser.). (Illus.). 2007. 31p. (J). (gr. -1-3). pap. 6.99 *(978-0-7614-3386-6(4))* 2006. 32p. (gr. 2-7). lib. bdg. 29.93 *(978-0-7614-2268-6(4))* Marshall Cavendish Corp. (Benchmark Bks.).
Scarry, Huck. Life on a Farm: A Sketchbook. (J). 16.95 *(978-0-945912-32-3(3))* Pippin Pr.
Scholastic, Inc. Staff. Touch & Feel Farm. 2015. (Scholastic Early Learners Ser.). (ENG.). 14p. (J). (— 1). bds. 6.99 *(978-0-545-90321-9(1)*, Cartwheel Bks.) Scholastic, Inc.
Schomp, Virginia. The Countryside. 2010. (Life in Victorian England Ser.). 80p. (gr. 6). 34.21 *(978-1-60870-030-1(5))* Marshall Cavendish GBR. Dist: Marshall Cavendish Corp.
Sieling, Peter. Growing up on a Farm: Responsibilities & Issues. 2009. (Youth in Rural North America Ser.). (Illus.). 96p. (YA). (gr. 3-7). lib. bdg. 22.95 *(978-1-4222-0012-4(4))* Mason Crest.
Silver Dolphin Staff, ed. Peek-A-Boo Sliders: Farm. Choux, Nathalie, illus. 2016. (Peek-A-Boo Sliders Ser.). (ENG.). 10p. (J). bds. 8.99 *(978-1-62686-730-7(5)*, Silver Dolphin Bks.) Readerlink Distribution Services, LLC.
Smith, Alastair. On the Farm Lift-the-Flap. Torode, Justine, illus. 2004. (Luxury Lift-the-Flap Ser.). 16p. (J). (gr. 1-18). 11.95 *(978-0-7945-0508-0(2)*, Usborne) EDC Publishing.
Spurr, Elizabeth. The Farm Life. Björkman, Steve, illus. 2005. (ENG.). 32p. (J). (gr. k-3). tchr. ed. 16.95 *(978-0-8234-1777-3(8))* Holiday Hse., Inc.
Stanley, Mandy & Kingfisher Publications, Inc. Staff. Vamos a la Granja. 2003. (All Aboard Ser.). (SPA & ENG., Illus.). 12p. (J). (gr. -1-k). bds. 4.99 *(978-0-7534-5691-0(5)*, 9780753456910, Kingfisher) Roaring Brook Pr.
Steffora, Tracey. Math on the Farm, 1 vol. 2013. (Math on the Job Ser.). (ENG., Illus.). 24p. (gr. k-2). pap. 6.29 *(978-1-4329-7163-2(8))*; lib. bdg. 22.65 *(978-1-4329-7156-4(5))* Heinemann-Raintree. (Acorn).
Steinkraus, Kyla. Ducks on the Farm. 2010. (Farm Animals Ser.). (Illus.). 24p. (J). (gr. k-3). 22.79 *(978-1-61590-269-9(4))* Rourke Educational Media.
—Rabbits on the Farm. 2010. (Farm Animals Ser.). (Illus.). 24p. (J). (gr. k-3). 22.79 *(978-1-61590-268-2(6))* Rourke Educational Media.
Summers, Portia. My Rural Community. 2016. (Zoom in on Communities Ser.). 24p. (J). (gr. 2-2). pap. 9.35 *(978-0-7660-7815-4(9))* Enslow Pubs., Inc.
Thomas Nelson. Ultimate Sticker File Farm. 2016. (ENG.). 56p. (J). (gr. -1-7). pap. *(978-1-78598-487-7(X))* Make Believe Ideas.
Unstead, Sue. DK Readers L1: a Year on the Farm: A Year on the Farm. 2015. (DK Readers Ser.). (ENG., Illus.). 48p. (J). (gr. k-4). 14.99 *(978-1-4654-3576-7(X)*, DK Children) Dorling Kindersley Publishing, Inc.
Van Frankenhuyzen, Robbyn Smith. Itsy Bitsy & Teeny Weeny. van Frankenhuyzen, Gijsbert, illus. 2009. (Hazel Ridge Farm Stories Ser.). (ENG.). 48p. (J). (gr. 1-4). 16.95 *(978-1-58536-417-6(7)*, 202152) Sleeping Bear Pr.
Veitch, Catherine. Farms Around the World, 1 vol. 2011. (ENG.). 24p. (gr. -1-1). pap. 9.95 *(978-1-4329-5498-7(9))*; 25.99 *(978-1-4329-5353-9(2))* Heinemann-Raintree. (Acorn Read-Aloud).
Watt, Fiona. Farm. Wells, Rachel, illus. 2008. (Usborne Touchy-Feely Board Bks.). 8p. (J). (gr. -1-k). bds. 15.99 *(978-0-7945-1959-9(8)*, Usborne) EDC Publishing.
—Farm Fun. 2008. (Preschool Activities Ser.). 23p. (J). spiral bd. 12.99 *(978-0-7945-2080-9(4)*, Usborne) EDC Publishing.
Weeks, Sarah. Little Farmer. Date not set. 24p. (J). (gr. -1-18). 9.99 *(978-0-694-01203-9(3))* HarperCollins Pubs.
White, Joseph C. Forged in a Country Crucible. 2003. (Illus.). 278p. per. 19.95 *(978-0-9726095-1-7(2)*, FCC2003) Crossing Trails Pubns.
Wicks, Krista. Mazie Moo & Her Clever Clouds, Wonderful Water & Silly Sunshine. 2012. 24p. pap. 12.45 *(978-1-4497-6901-7(2)*, WestBow Pr.) Author Solutions, Inc.
Willard, Nancy. Cracked Corn & Snow Ice Cream: A Family Almanac. Dyer, Jane, illus. 2005. 56p. (YA). (gr. 4-8). 18.00 *(978-0-7567-8835-3(8))* DIANE Publishing Co.
Williams, Dave. Windgalore Farm. 2005. (Illus.). 182p. pap. 21.95 *(978-0-937921-56-2(4))* Acorn Publishing.
Wolfman, Judy. Life on a Cattle Farm. Winston, David Lorenz, photos by. 2005. (Life on a Farm Ser.). (Illus.). 48p. (gr. 2-5). lib. bdg. 23.93 *(978-1-57505-516-9(3))* Lerner Publishing Group.
—Life on a Chicken Farm. Winston, David Lorenz, illus. Winston, David Lorenz, photos by. 2004. (Life on a Farm Ser.). (ENG.). 48p. (gr. 2-5). lib. bdg. 23.93 *(978-1-57505-191-8(5))* Lerner Publishing Group.
—Life on a Dairy Farm. Winston, David Lorenz, illus. Winston, David Lorenz, photos by. 2004. (Life on a Farm Ser.). (ENG.). 48p. (gr. 2-5). lib. bdg. 23.93 *(978-1-57505-190-1(7))* Lerner Publishing Group.
—Life on a Sheep Farm. Winston, David Lorenz, illus. Winston, David Lorenz, photos by. 2004. (Life on a Farm Ser.). (ENG.). 48p. (gr. 2-5). lib. bdg. 23.93 *(978-1-57505-192-5(3))* Lerner Publishing Group.
—Life on an Apple Orchard. Winston, David Lorenz, illus. Winston, David Lorenz, photos by. 2004. (Life on a Farm Ser.). (ENG.). 48p. (gr. 2-5). lib. bdg. 23.93 *(978-1-57505-193-2(1))* Lerner Publishing Group.
Worek, Michael. What's on My Farm? 2013. (ENG., Illus.). 160p. (J). (gr. -1-k). 9.95 *(978-1-77085-236-5(0)*, 9781770852365) Firefly Bks., Ltd.

FARM LIFE—FICTION

Abbott, Jacob. Jonas on a Farm in Winter (Illustrated E. 2006. pap. *(978-1-4065-0358-6(4))* Dodo Pr.
—Rollo at Work. 2009. 148p. pap. 8.95 *(978-1-59915-342-1(4))* Yesterday's Classics.
—Rollo at Work & Rollo at Play. 2006. (Illus.). pap. 34.95 *(978-1-4286-4095-5(9))* Kessinger Publishing, LLC.
Abraham, Susan Gonzales & Abraham, Denise Gonzales. Cecilia's Year. 2007. (Latino Fiction for Young Adults Ser.). (ENG., Illus.). 210p. (J). (gr. 4-6). pap. 11.95 *(978-1-933693-02-6(9))* Cinco Puntos Pr.
—Surprising Cecilia. 2005. (Latino Fiction for Young Adults Ser.). (ENG., Illus.). 216p. (J). (gr. -1-7). 16.95 *(978-0-938317-96-8(2))* Cinco Puntos Pr.
Adams, Ben. Polly the Farm Puppy. Cameron, Craig, illus. 2013. (Googly Eyes Ser.). (ENG.). 12p. (J). (gr. -1-k). bds. 6.99 *(978-1-84322-319-1(8)*, Armadillo) Anness Publishing GBR. Dist: National Bk. Network.
Adams, Jesse. Farmer Dillo Paints His Barn. Speer, Julie & Davis, Christopher Owen, illus. 2007. 21p. (J). (gr. -1-1). *(978-1-59166-481-9(0))* BJU Pr.
—Farmer Dillo Shapes Things Up. Speer, Julie & Polhamus, Bruce, illus. 2009. 24p. (gr. -1-1). pap. 7.99 *(978-1-59166-865-7(4))* BJU Pr.
Adams, Leon. Mystic Lord. 2007. 181p. pap. 12.95 *(978-1-4357-0454-1(1))* Lulu Pr., Inc.
Adams, Pam, illus. Old Macdonald Had a Farm. 2003. (Classic Books with Holes 8x8 Ser.). (ENG.). 16p. (J). pap. *(978-0-85953-135-1(X))* Child's Play International Ltd.
Aigner-Clark, Julie. Baby Einstein: on the Farm. Zaidi, Nadeem, illus. 2007. (Baby Einstein Ser.). (ENG.). *(978-0-7634-2150-2(2))* Walt Disney Records.
Airgood, Ellen. Prairie Evers. (ENG.). 224p. (J). (gr. 3-7). 2014. pap. 7.99 *(978-0-14-242668-5(7)*, Puffin Books) 2012. 15.99 *(978-0-399-25691-2(1)*, Nancy Paulsen Books) Penguin Young Readers Group.
Aisha. Parsley, Sage, Rosemary & Thyme. 2012. 24p. 24.95 *(978-1-4626-5122-1(4))* America Star Bks.
Alborough, Jez. Six Little Chicks. 2013. (ENG.). 32p. (J). (gr. -1-1). pap. 6.99 *(978-1-4380-0181-4(9))* Barron's Educational Series, Inc.
Alger, Horatio. Frank's Campaign: Or, The Farm & the Camp. 2006. (ENG.). 196p. pap. 19.99 *(978-1-4264-0484-9(0))*; 188p. pap. 21.99 *(978-1-4264-0527-3(8))* Creative Media Partners, LLC.
—Frank's Campaign: Or, The Farm & the Camp. 2006. pap. *(978-1-4065-0705-8(9))* Dodo Pr.
Alger Jr. Horatio Staff. Frank's Campaign. rev. ed. 2006. 300p. 29.95 *(978-1-4218-1761-3(6))*; pap. 14.95 *(978-1-4218-1861-0(2))* 1st World Publishing, Inc. (1st World Library - Literary Society).
Allan, Delores. Magical Moments with Roy & Toni: Come on Lets Go. 2011. 24p. (gr. 1-2). pap. 12.79 *(978-1-4634-0950-0(8))* AuthorHouse.
Allbritton, Jan. Super Sweetie to the Rescue. 2008. 16p. pap. 10.95 *(978-1-4389-3803-5(9))* AuthorHouse.
Alvarez, Julia. Return to Sender. 2010. (ENG.). 352p. (J). (gr. 3-7). 6.99 *(978-0-375-85123-0(2)*, Yearling) Random Hse. Children's Bks.
Amado, Elisa. Why Are You Doing That?, 1 vol. Monroy, Manuel, illus. 2014. (ENG.). 28p. (J). (gr. -1-2). 16.95 *(978-1-55498-453-4(X))* Groundwood Bks. CAN. Dist: Publishers Group West (PGW).
Amery & Cartwright. Curly the Pig Kid Kit. 2007. (Kid Kits Ser.). (Illus.). 10p. (J). (gr. -1). bds. 12.99 *(978-1-60130-009-6(3)*, Usborne) EDC Publishing.
Amery, H. The Complete Book of Farmyard Tales. 2004. (Farmyard Tales Readers Ser.). 320p. (J). 24.95 *(978-0-7945-0902-6(9)*, Usborne) EDC Publishing.
—Where's Curly? Cartwright, Stephen, illus. 2004. (Treasury of Farmyard Tales Ser.). 16p. (J). (gr. 1-18). lib. bdg. 15.95 *(978-1-58086-563-0(1))* EDC Publishing.
Amery, Heather. Farmyard Tales Christmas Flap Bk And. 2006. 24p. 12.99 *(978-0-7945-0556-1(2)*, Usborne) EDC Publishing.
—Farmyard Tales Storybook. 2004. (Treasury of Farmyard Tales Ser.). (Illus.). 128p. (J). 7.95 *(978-0-7945-0270-6(9)*, Usborne) EDC Publishing.
—Farmyard Tales Treasury - Internet Referenced. Cartwright, Stephen, illus. 2007. 96p. (J). 19.99 *(978-0-7945-1440-2(5)*, Usborne) EDC Publishing.
—The Old Steam Train. Cartwright, Stephen, illus. rev. ed. 2007. (Farmyard Tales Readers Ser.). 16p. (J). (gr. -1-3). pap. 5.99 *(978-0-7945-0804-3(9)*, Usborne) EDC Publishing.
—The Old Steam Train Kid Kit. Cartwright, Stephen, illus. rev. ed. 2007. (Kid Kits Ser.). (J). 16p. 13.99 *(978-1-60130-038-6(7))*; 14p. pap. 13.99 *(978-1-60130-003-4(4))* EDC Publishing. (Usborne).
—Surprise Visitors. Cartwright, Stephen, illus. 2004. 16p. (J). pap. 5.95 *(978-0-7945-0784-8(0)*, Usborne) EDC Publishing.
—Where's Woolly? Tyler, Jenny, ed. Cartwright, Stephen, illus. 2006. (Treasury of Farmyard Tales Ser.). 16p. (J). (gr. -1-18). 15.95 *(978-1-58086-531-9(3))* EDC Publishing.
Amundson, Susan D. Three Little Lambs — Somewhere. Geiken, Brenda Joy, illus. 2006. 40p. (J). *(978-1-59984-002-4(2))* Bluedoor, llc.
Anderson, Jodi Lynn. Love & Peaches. 256p. (YA). 2009. (Peaches Ser.: 3). (ENG.). (gr. 8). pap. 8.99 *(978-0-06-073313-1(6))* 2008. (gr. 7-18). lib. bdg. 17.89 *(978-0-06-073312-4(8))* HarperCollins Pubs. (HarperTeen).
—Peaches. (ENG.). (YA). 2005. 320p. (gr. 7-12). 15.99 *(978-0-06-073305-6(5))* 2012. (Peaches Ser.: 1). 368p. (gr. 9-12). reprint ed. pap. 8.99 *(978-0-06-073307-0(1)*, HarperTeen) HarperCollins Pubs.
—The Secrets of Peaches. 2012. (Peaches Ser.: 2). (ENG.). 368p. (YA). (gr. 9-12). pap. 8.99 *(978-0-06-073310-0(1)*, HarperTeen) HarperCollins Pubs.
Anderson, Patricia. Tails of a Woodswoman. 2008. 72p. pap. 9.95 *(978-1-4327-2615-7(3))* Outskirts Pr., Inc.
Andrews, Charlie J. Tales of Animals on Farmer Brown's Farm: Children Stories. 2007. 60p. per. 10.95 *(978-1-4327-0138-3(X))* Outskirts Pr., Inc.
Andrews, Julie & Hamilton, Emma Walton. Dumpy to the Rescue! Walton, Tony, illus. 2004. 24p. (J). lib. bdg. 13.85 *(978-1-4242-0707-7(X))* Fitzgerald Bks.
Angelastro, Yvonne. The Four Lost Chicks. 2013. 28p. pap. 16.99 *(978-1-4808-0292-6(1))* Archway Publishing.
Annie Hamilton, Donnell. Three Young Knights & Miss Theodosia's Heartstrings. 2007. (ENG.). 142p. pap. 18.99 *(978-1-4346-1511-4(1))* Creative Media Partners, LLC.
Appleman, Pamela J. Copper Becomes a Farm Dog. 2013. 26p. pap. 9.99 *(978-0-9913190-4-6(4))* Mindstir Media.
Apps, Jerry. Stormy. Beatty-Anderson, Annika, illus. 2016. (ENG.). 32p. (J). (gr. 1-6). 10.00 *(978-1-930596-09-2(X))* Guest Cottage, Incorporated, The.
Arena, Felice & Kettle, Phil. Bull Riding. Cox, David, illus. 2004. (J). pap. *(978-1-59336-370-3(2))* Mondo Publishing.
—On the Farm/By Felice Arena & Phil Kettle; Illustrated by Susy Boyer. Boyer, Susy, illus. 2004. (J). pap. *(978-1-59336-363-5(X))* Mondo Publishing.
Aronson, Billy & Oxley, Jennifer. The Chicken Problem. 2012. (ENG., Illus.). 32p. (J). (gr. -1-2). 16.99 *(978-0-375-86989-1(1)*, Random Hse. Bks. for Young Readers) Random Hse. Children's Bks.
Artley, Bob. Christmas on the Farm, 1 vol. Artley, Bob, illus. 2003. (ENG., Illus.). 96p. 22.95 *(978-1-58980-108-0(3))* Pelican Publishing Co., Inc.
Artzi, Yocheved. Freedom Chickens: The Story of Lonely Chicken. 2011. 34p. pap. 13.50 *(978-1-61204-265-7(1)*, Strategic Bk. Publishing) Strategic Book Publishing & Rights Agency (SBPRA).
Aston, Dianna Hutts. The Moon over Star. Pinkney, Jerry, illus. 2008. (ENG.). 32p. (J). (gr. 1-3). 17.99 *(978-0-8037-3107-3(8)*, Dial Bks) Penguin Young Readers Group.
Averette, Sonya M. Aunt Ruby's Kisses, 1 vol. Proulx, Denis, illus. 2009. 35p. pap. 24.95 *(978-1-60749-045-6(5))* America Star Bks.
Avi. The Barn. 2014. (ENG.). 112p. (J). (gr. 3-7). pap. 6.99 *(978-0-545-60744-5(2)*, Scholastic Paperbacks) Scholastic, Inc.
Awdry, W. Thomas Scares the Crows (Thomas & Friends) 2016. (Pictureback(R) Ser.). (ENG.). 24p. (J). (gr. -1-2). 4.99 *(978-1-101-93831-7(5)*, Random Hse. Bks. for Young Readers) Random Hse. Children's Bks.
Aylesworth, Jim. Cock-a-Doodle-Doo, Creak, Pop-Pop, Moo. Sneed, Brad, illus. 2012. (ENG.). 32p. (J). 16.95 *(978-0-8234-2356-9(5))* Holiday Hse., Inc.
—Cock-a-Doodle Doo, Creak, Pop-Pop, Moo. Sneed, Brad, illus. 2013. (ENG.). 32p. (J). pap. 7.99 *(978-0-8234-2754-3(4))* Holiday Hse., Inc.
AZ Books, creator. Magic Farm. 2012. (Baby Book Ser.). (ENG., Illus.). 10p. (J). (gr. -1 — 1). bds. 4.95 *(978-1-61889-285-0(1))* AZ Bks. LLC.
AZ Books Staff. Horse's Farm. Potapenko, Olga, ed. 2012. (Talking Plush Animals Ser.). (ENG.). 10p. (J). (gr. -1-k). bds. 10.95 *(978-1-61889-112-9(X))* AZ Bks. LLC.
Azman, Hacer. God Loves Us All. 2011. (ENG.). 103p. 14.95 *(978-1-59784-233-4(8))* Tughra Bks.
Bader, Arlys Elaine. The Adventures of Garth & Cloey. 2008. 40p. pap. 16.99 *(978-1-4389-2472-4(0))* AuthorHouse.
Bailey, Arthur Scott. Sleepy-Time Tales: The Tale of Fatty Coo. 2006. pap. *(978-1-4065-0446-0(7))* Dodo Pr.
Bailey, Linda. The Farm Team. Slavin, Bill, illus. (ENG.). 32p. (J). (gr. -1-2). 2008. pap. 7.95 *(978-1-55453-317-6(1))* 2006. 16.95 *(978-1-55337-850-1(4))* Kids Can Pr., Ltd. CAN. Dist: Hachette Bk. Group.
Balian, Lorna. A Garden for a Groundhog, 1 vol. Balian, Lorna, illus. 2011. (ENG., Illus.). 32p. (J). pap. 6.95 *(978-1-59572-296-6(3))* Star Bright Bks., Inc.
—A Garden for a Groundhog, 1 vol. 2004. (ENG., Illus.). 32p. (J). 15.95 *(978-1-932065-38-1(5))* Star Bright Bks., Inc.

E
F
G

Banicki, Patsy & Staige, Pat. Farmer Carpenter's Barn & the Cow's Saturday Night Dance. Staige, Pat & Stanton, Janet, illus. Date not set. (Orig.). (J). (gr. k-4). pap. *(978-0-9641375-1-6(8))* Staige Productions.
Barnett, Wm. Billy's Wish. Kiste, Tori Lynn, illus. 2008. 28p. pap. 24.95 *(978-1-60563-330-5(5))* America Star Bks.
Barrett, Anna Pearl. Neecie & the Sparkling Spring. Weston, Eunice Guy, ed. Peguero, Phillip, illus. 2004. (Neecie Bks.: Vol. 5). 70p. (J). (gr. 1-6). 7.95 *(978-0-9661330-5-9(6))* Over the Rainbow Productions.
Barrows, Marjorie. Little Duck. Myers, Marie Honre, illus. 2011. 50p. 35.95 *(978-1-258-08897-2(5))* Literary Licensing, LLC.
Barth, Kathleen E. The Amazing Adventures of Quigley D Pigley & His Friends: How to Become an Astronaut. 2009. 16p. pap. 8.49 *(978-1-4389-8606-7(8))* AuthorHouse.
Base, Graeme. Little Elephants. 2012. (ENG., Illus.). 40p. (J). (gr. k-2). 17.95 *(978-1-4197-0463-5(X),* Abrams Bks. for Young Readers) Abrams, Inc.
Bateman, Teresa. April Foolishness. Westcott, Nadine Bernard, illus. 2004. (ENG.). 32p. (J). (gr. k-3). 6.99 *(978-0-8075-0405-5(X))* Whitman, Albert & Co.
—Job Wanted. Sheban, Chris, illus. 2015. (ENG.). 32p. (J). (gr. k-3). 16.95 *(978-0-8234-3391-9(9))* Holiday Hse., Inc.
Bates, Michelle. Strangers at the Stables. 2017. (Sandy Lane Stables Ser.). (ENG.). 128p. (YA). pap. 5.99 ***(978-0-7945-3916-0(5),*** Usborne) EDC Publishing.
Bauer, Joan. Peeled. 2009. (ENG.). 256p. (YA). (gr. 7-18). 8.99 *(978-0-14-241430-9(1),* Speak) Penguin Young Readers Group.
Bauer, Michael. The Adventures of Steel Wooly: And my Place on the Farm. 2012. (ENG.). 25p. (J). pap. 12.95 *(978-1-4327-8568-0(0))* Outskirts Pr., Inc.
Baxter, Nicola. My First Farmyard Tales: Eight Exciting Picture Stories for Little Ones. Lodge, Ali, illus. 2013. (ENG.). 16p. (J). (gr. -1-2). bds. 13.99 *(978-1-84322-990-2(0),* Armadillo) Anness Publishing GBR. Dist: National Bk. Network.
Bean, Margo Cronbaugh. Brutus the Bull. Perry, Aumi Kauffman, illus. 2013. 24p. 19.95 *(978-1-61633-373-7(1));* pap. 11.95 *(978-1-61633-374-4(X))* Guardian Angel Publishing, Inc.
—Buffaloed Badger. Perry, Aumi Kauffman, illus. 2012. 24p. 19.95 *(978-1-61633-239-6(5));* pap. 11.95 *(978-1-61633-240-2(9))* Guardian Angel Publishing, Inc.
Beauvais, Clémentine. Gargoyles Gone AWOL. Horne, Sarah, illus. 2015. (Sesame Seade Mystery Ser.: 2). (ENG.). 208p. (J). (gr. 2-6). 16.95 *(978-0-8234-3205-9(X))* Holiday Hse., Inc.
Beck, Sunny. In the Children's Meadow. 2004. (Illus.). (J). *(978-1-59404-013-9(3))* Peanut Butter Publishing.
Beckerman, Menucha. Friends on the Farm. 2004. (My Smiling World Ser.: No. 1). (Illus.). 32p. (J). 11.95 *(978-1-931681-53-7(8))* Israel Bookshop Pubns.
Beckhorn, Susan Williams. Moose Power! Muskeg Saves the Day. Huntington, Amy, illus. 2010. (ENG.). 40p. (J). (gr. -1-3). 16.95 *(978-0-89272-762-9(4))* Down East Bks.
Bee, William. Stanley the Farmer, 1 vol. Bee, William, illus. 2015. (Stanley Ser.). (ENG., Illus.). 32p. (J). (gr. 1-2). 14.95 *(978-1-56145-803-5(1))* Peachtree Pubs.
Beitler, Stacey Ann. Willy Goes to the Farm. 2009. 30p. pap. 14.50 *(978-1-60860-474-6(8),* Eloquent Bks.) Strategic Book Publishing & Rights Agency (SBPRA).
Belser, Maud Corier, illus. Grace & Marie's Little Farm on the Hill. 2007. 32p. (J). bds. 18.00 *(978-0-9791076-0-3(1))* WebbWorks.
Benavidez, Max. Historia de Carlito/ Carlito's Story. 2008. 121p. pap. 8.95 *(978-1-60448-004-7(1))* Lectura Bks.
Bender, Carrie. Hemlock Hill Hideaway: Whispering Brook Series #4. 2007. (Illus.). 168p. pap. 8.99 *(978-1-60126-022-2(9))* Masthof Pr.
—Summerville Days: Whispering Brook Series #2. 2007. (Illus.). 224p. pap. 8.99 *(978-1-60126-023-9(7))* Masthof Pr.
—Timber Lane Cove. 2003. (ENG.). 144p. (YA). pap. 8.99 *(978-0-8361-9202-5(8))* Herald Pr.
Benjamin, A. H. Baa! Moo! What Will We Do? Chapman, Jane, tr. Chapman, Jane, illus. 2003. 32p. (J). pap. 6.95 *(978-1-58925-381-0(7))* Tiger Tales.
Bentley, Sue. Muddy Paws, No. 2. Swan, Angela & Farley, Andrew, illus. 2009. (Magic Puppy Ser.: 2). (ENG.). 128p. (J). (gr. 1-3). pap. 5.99 *(978-0-448-45045-2(3),* Grosset & Dunlap) Penguin Young Readers Group.
—Muddy Paws. 2009. (Magic Puppy Ser.: 2). lib. bdg. 14.75 *(978-0-606-06021-9(9),* Turtleback) Turtleback Bks.
Berenstain, Stan & Berenstain, Jan. The Berenstain Bears down on the Farm. Berenstain, Stan & Berenstain, Jan, illus. 2006. (I Can Read Level 1 Ser.). (ENG., Illus.). 32p. (J). (gr. k-3). pap. 3.99 *(978-0-06-058351-4(7))* HarperCollins Pubs.
Berenstain, Stan, et al. The Berenstain Bears & the Haunted House. 2010. (Berenstain Bears Ser.). (ENG., Illus.). 16p. (J). (gr. -1-1). pap. 6.99 *(978-0-06-057426-0(7),* HarperFestival) HarperCollins Pubs.
Berne, Emma Carlson. Never Let You Go. 2012. (ENG.). 256p. (YA). (gr. 9). pap. 9.99 *(978-1-4424-4017-3(1),* Simon Pulse) Simon Pulse.
Beylon, Cathy. Old Macdonald's Farm. 2003. (Dover Coloring Bks.). (ENG., Illus.). 32p. (J). (gr. -1-2). pap. 3.99 *(978-0-486-43034-8(0))* Dover Pubns., Inc.
Bick, Ilsa J. The Sin-Eater's Confession. Elyum Studio, illus. 2014. (ENG.). 296p. (YA). (gr. 9-12). pap. 9.95 *(978-1-4677-3705-0(4),* Carolrhoda Lab™) Lerner Publishing Group.
—The Sin-Eater's Confession. 2013. (ENG.). 296p. (YA). (gr. 9-12). 17.95 *(978-0-7613-5687-5(8))* Lerner Publishing Group.
Billet, Marion, illus. Noisy Farm: My First Sound Book. 2017. (ENG.). 16p. (J). (— 1). 9.99 ***(978-1-338-13220-5(2),*** Cartwheel Bks.) Scholastic, Inc.
Björkman, Steve. Look Out, Mouse! Björkman, Steve, illus. 2015. (I Like to Read(r) Ser.). (ENG., Illus.). 24p. (J). (gr. -1-3). 6.99 *(978-0-8234-3397-1(8))* Holiday Hse., Inc.
Björkman, Steve, illus. Look Out, Mouse! 2015. (I Like to Read(r) Ser.). (ENG.). 24p. (J). (gr. -1-3). 14.95 *(978-0-8234-2953-0(9))* Holiday Hse., Inc.
Black, Michael Ian. Cock-a-Doodle-Doo-Bop. Myers, Matthew, illus. 2015. (ENG.). 40p. (J). (gr. -1-3). 17.99 *(978-1-4424-9510-4(3),* Simon & Schuster Bks. For Young Readers) Simon & Schuster Bks. For Young Readers.
Blais, Barb. Little Wally & the Skunk Family. 2008. 36p. pap. 15.68 *(978-1-4357-1256-0(0))* Lulu Pr., Inc.
Blevins, Wiley. Duck, Duck, Goose. Kreloff, Elliott, illus. 2016. (Basic Concepts Ser.). (ENG.). 24p. (J). (gr. -1-1). lib. bdg. 14.99 *(978-1-63440-084-8(4))* Red Chair Pr.
Blitz, Shmuel. The Adventures of Aliza & Dovid: Holidays at the Farm. Katz, Tova, illus. 2005. (ArtScroll Youth Ser.). 48p. (J). *(978-1-4226-0021-4(1))* Mesorah Pubns., Ltd.
Bloom, Suzanne. We Keep a Pig in the Parlor. 2004. (ENG., Illus.). 24p. (J). (gr. k-2). reprint ed. pap. 9.95 *(978-1-59078-084-8(1))* Boyds Mills Pr.
Bluecloud. A Space in Time. 2012. 24p. pap. 17.99 *(978-1-4685-6407-5(2))* AuthorHouse.
Bobeck, Jade. Paxton's Adventures: A Day on Grandpa's Farm. 2012. 24p. pap. 15.99 *(978-1-4797-4415-2(8))* Xlibris Corp.
Bobet, Leah. An Inheritance of Ashes. (ENG.). 400p. (YA). (gr. 7). 2016. pap. 9.99 *(978-0-544-81322-9(7),* HMH Books For Young Readers) 2015. 17.99 *(978-0-544-28111-0(X))* Houghton Mifflin Harcourt Publishing Co.
Bock, Lee. Oh, Crumps!Tr. of Ay, Caramba. (ENG.). 32p. (J). (gr. 4-7). 2010. pap. 7.95 *(978-1-934960-71-4(3))* 2009. 16.95 *(978-1-934960-70-7(5))* Continental Sales, Inc. (Raven Tree Pr.,Csi).
Boldt, Mike. The Gophers in Farmer Burrows' Field. 2009. (Illus.). 30p. (J). 15.99 *(978-0-88144-472-8(3))* Yorkshire Publishing Group.
Bond, Rebecca. Escape from Baxters' Barn. Bond, Rebecca, illus. 2017. (ENG., Illus.). 256p. (J). (gr. 2-5). pap. 7.99 ***(978-1-328-74093-9(5),*** HMH Books For Young Readers) Houghton Mifflin Harcourt Publishing Co.
—Escape from Baxters' Barn. 2015. (ENG., Illus.). 256p. (J). (gr. 2-5). 16.99 *(978-0-544-33217-1(2),* HMH Books For Young Readers) Houghton Mifflin Harcourt Publishing Co.
Booher, Brock. Healing Stone. 2014. pap. 15.99 *(978-1-4621-1394-1(X),* Horizon Pubs.) Cedar Fort, Inc./CFI Distribution.
Borgo, Lacy Finn. Big Mama's Baby. Cote, Nancy, illus. 2007. (ENG.). 32p. (J). (gr. k-2). 15.95 *(978-1-59078-187-6(2))* Boyds Mills Pr.
Brammer, Deb. Two Sides to Everything. 2003. (Illus.). 151p. (J). *(978-1-59166-166-5(8))* BJU Pr.
Brandeis, Batsheva. Faiga Finds the Way. Levitas, Alexander, illus. 2005. (Fun to Read Book Ser.). 120p. (J). pap. 9.95 *(978-1-929628-28-5(5))* Hachai Publishing.
Brenneman, Lynette Leaman, photos by. Susanna's Surprise: A Day at the Hans Herr House. 2012. (Illus.). 32p. (J). *(978-0-9859737-0-4(6))* Brenneman, Lynette.
Brett, Jan. Armadillo Rodeo. Brett, Jan, illus. 2004. (ENG., Illus.). 32p. (J). (gr. -1-3). pap. 6.99 *(978-0-14-240125-5(0),* Puffin Books) Penguin Young Readers Group.
Briers, Erica. Little Lamb to the Rescue. Boey, Stephanie, illus. 2004. (ENG.). 24p. (J). *(978-1-55168-257-0(5))* Fenn, H. B. & Co., Ltd.
—Runaway Chick. Boey, Stephanie, illus. 2006. (ENG.). 24p. (J). *(978-1-55168-314-0(8))* Fenn, H. B. & Co., Ltd.
Brookins, Cara. Doris Free. Barrow, Ann, illus. 2006. 127p. (J). pap. *(978-1-59336-333-8(8))* Mondo Publishing.
Brooks, Felicity. Frank the Farmer. Litchfield, Jo, illus. rev. ed. 2007. (Jobs People Do Ser.). 23p. (J). (gr. 4-7). pap. 6.99 *(978-0-7945-1621-5(1),* Usborne) EDC Publishing.
Brooks, Walter R. The Clockwork Twin: A Freddy the Pig Book on Everything. Wiese, Kurt, illus. 2013. (ENG.). 256p. (gr. 4-13). pap. 10.99 *(978-1-4683-0349-0(X),* 460349) Overlook Pr., The.
Brown, Celease N. & Mubarak, Enoch. The Color Orange. 2004. (Illus.). 32p. *(978-1-55306-742-9(8),* Guardian Bks.) Essence Publishing.
Brown, Irene Bennett. Before the Lark. 2011. (ENG.). 208p. (J). (gr. 4-7). pap. 18.95 *(978-0-89672-727-4(0))* Texas Tech Univ. Pr.
Brown, Margaret Wise. El Gran Granero Rojo, 1 vol. Bond, Felicia, illus. 2003.Tr. of Big Red Barn. (SPA.). 34p. (J). (gr. -1 — 1). 7.99 *(978-0-06-009107-1(X))* HarperCollins Pubs.
Brown, Ron. Three-Toes the Raccoon Visits the Farm. 2009. 24p. pap. 10.49 *(978-1-4389-9035-4(9))* AuthorHouse.
Brown, Ruth. The Big Sneeze. 2011. (ENG., Illus.). 32p. (J). (gr. k-k). pap. 9.99 *(978-1-84939-052-1(5))* Andersen Pr. GBR. Dist: Independent Pubs. Group.
Bruna, Dick. Farmer John's Seeds. 2004. (Illus.). 12p. pap. 5.99 *(978-1-59226-191-8(4))* Big Tent Entertainment, Inc.
Bruzzone, Catherine. Lucy the Cat at the Farm: Lucie le Chat a la Ferme. Beaton, Clare, illus. 2005. (Lucy Cat Ser.). (ENG & FRE.). 24p. (J). (gr. -1-1). pap. 7.99 *(978-1-902915-11-1(9))* B Small Publishing GBR. Dist: Independent Pubs. Group.
—Lucy the Cat in Town: Lucie le Chat en Ville. Beaton, Clare, illus. 2005. (Lucy Cat Ser.). (ENG & FRE.). 24p. (J). (gr. -1-1). pap. 7.99 *(978-1-902915-15-9(1))* B Small Publishing GBR. Dist: Independent Pubs. Group.
Buehner, Caralyn & Buehner, Mark. Fanny's Dream. Buehner, Caralyn & Buehner, Mark, illus. 2003. (ENG., Illus.). 32p. (J). (gr. k-3). 7.99 *(978-0-14-250060-6(7),* Puffin Books) Penguin Young Readers Group.
Butler, James L. The Cow-Pie Chronicles. Millsap, Lonnie, illus. 2013. (ENG.). 192p. (J). (gr. 2-4). pap. 9.95 *(978-1-938778-32-2(4))* Publishing Syndicate LLC.
The Butterfly Farm Burglar, 6 vols., Vol. 3. (Woodland Mysteriestm Ser.). 133p. (gr. 3-7). 42.50 *(978-0-322-02374-1(2))* Wright Group/McGraw-Hill.
Calhoun, Dia. After the River the Sun. Slater, Kate, illus. 2013. (ENG.). 368p. (J). (gr. 4-7). 16.99 *(978-1-4424-3985-6(8))* Simon & Schuster Children's Publishing.
—Eva of the Farm. Slater, Kate, illus. (ENG.). (J). (gr. 4-7). 2013. 272p. pap. 6.99 *(978-1-4424-1701-4(3))* 2012. 256p. 16.99 *(978-1-4424-1700-7(5))* Simon & Schuster Children's Publishing. (Atheneum Bks. for Young Readers).
Campbell, Nicola I. Grandpa's Girls, 1 vol. LaFave, Kim, illus. 2011. (ENG & SAL.). 32p. (J). (gr. -1-2). 16.95 *(978-1-55498-084-0(4))* Groundwood Bks. CAN. Dist: Publishers Group West (PGW).
Capucilli, Alyssa Satin. Biscuit Visits the Pumpkin Patch. Schories, Pat, illus. 2004. (Biscuit Ser.). (ENG.). 16p. (J). (gr. -1-3). bds. 4.99 *(978-0-06-009466-9(4),* HarperFestival) HarperCollins Pubs.
—Biscuit's Day at the Farm. Schories, Pat, illus. 2007. (My First I Can Read Ser.). (ENG.). 32p. (J). (gr. -1 — 1). pap. 3.99 *(978-0-06-074169-3(4));* 16.99 *(978-0-06-074167-9(8))* HarperCollins Pubs.
Carbonell-Matela, Anna. Whitaker Farm. 2012. 24p. pap. 15.99 *(978-1-4691-6352-9(7))* Xlibris Corp.
Carle, Eric. Dream Snow. Carle, Eric, illus. 2015. (ENG., Illus.). 22p. (J). (gr. -1 — 1). bds. 9.99 *(978-0-399-17314-1(5),* Philomel Bks.) Penguin Young Readers Group.
Carney, Larry, adapted by. Silly Farm. 2010. (ENG., Illus.). 24p. (J). pap. 6.95 *(978-1-60072-156-4(7))* PC Treasures, Inc.
Carolan, Joanna F. Old Makana Had a Taro Farm. Carolan, Joanna F., illus. 2008. (Illus.). 48p. 17.95 *(978-0-9715333-9-4(3))* Banana Patch Pr.
Carr, Debra. The Curry Comb Caper. Carr, Stephen, illus. 2006. 48p. per. 8.95 *(978-1-933912-59-2(6))* Westview Publishing Co., Inc.
Casad, Patricia E. Bubbykins: (Life on the Farm) 2008. 46p. pap. 24.95 *(978-1-4241-9140-6(8))* America Star Bks.
Castrataro, Kristen. Grandpa's Farm Has Lots of Saws. 2012. 32p. (-18). pap. 19.99 *(978-1-4772-8636-4(5))* AuthorHouse.
Cazet, Denys. Minnie & Moo: Hooves of Fire. Cazet, Denys, illus. 2014. (ENG., Illus.). 208p. (J). (gr. k-6). 15.95 *(978-1-939547-08-8(3))* Creston Bks.
—Minnie & Moo & the Haunted Sweater. Cazet, Denys, illus. 2007. (I Can Read Level 3 Ser.). (ENG., Illus.). 48p. (J). (gr. k-3). 16.99 *(978-0-06-073016-1(1))* HarperCollins Pubs.
—Minnie & Moo & the Seven Wonders of the World. Cazet, Denys, illus. 2003. (ENG., Illus.). 144p. (J). (gr. 2-5). 19.99 *(978-0-689-85330-2(0),* Atheneum/Richard Jackson Bks.) Simon & Schuster Children's Publishing.
Cazet, Denys, reader. Minnie & Moo: Will You Be My Valentine? 2004. (Read-Alongs for Beginning Readers Ser.). (Illus.). (J). (gr. -1-3). 25.95 incl. audio *(978-1-59112-892-2(7));* pap. 31.95 incl. audio compact disk *(978-1-59112-897-7(8));* pap. 29.95 incl. audio *(978-1-59112-893-9(5))* Live Oak Media.
Cecil, Randy. Duck. Cecil, Randy, illus. 2008. (ENG., Illus.). 40p. (J). (gr. -1-2). 15.99 *(978-0-7636-3072-0(1))* Candlewick Pr.
Chaconas, Dori. Coriander the Contrary Hen. Carrington, Marsha Gray, illus. 2007. (Carolrhoda Picture Bks.). (ENG.). 32p. (J). (gr. k-3). lib. bdg. 16.95 *(978-1-57505-749-1(2),* Carolrhoda Bks.) Lerner Publishing Group.
Chall, Marsha Wilson. A Secret Keeps. 2012. (Carolrhoda Picture Bks.). (ENG., Illus.). 32p. (J). (gr. k-3). lib. bdg. 16.95 *(978-0-7613-5593-9(6))* Lerner Publishing Group.
Chamberlin, Kate. Charles & David. Wroth, Dean, illus. 2010. 32p. (J). pap. 9.95 *(978-0-944727-37-9(9));* lib. bdg. 15.95 *(978-0-944727-36-2(0))* Jason & Nordic Pubs. (Turtle Bks.).
Charlesworth, Liza. Wake up, Rooster! An Animal Friends Reader. Smith, Ian, illus. 2015. 16p. (J). pap. ***(978-0-545-85971-4(9))*** Scholastic, Inc.
Chernesky, Felicia Sanzari. Pick a Circle, Gather Squares: A Fall Harvest of Shapes. Swan, Susan, illus. 2013. (ENG.). 32p. (J). (gr. -1-3). 16.99 *(978-0-8075-6538-4(5))* Whitman, Albert & Co.
—Sun above & Blooms Below: A Springtime of Opposites. Swan, Susan, illus. 2015. (ENG.). 32p. (J). (gr. -1-3). 16.99 *(978-0-8075-3632-2(6))* Whitman, Albert & Co.
Church, Caroline Jayne, illus. The Very Busy Farm. 2016. (ENG.). 10p. (J). (gr. -1-k). bds. 8.99 *(978-0-7944-3752-7(4),* Reader's Digest Children's Bks.) Studio Fun International.
Ciminera, Siobhan. Farm Animal Friends. Collection/Jupiterimages Unlimited, illus. 2009. (ENG.). 48p. (J). (gr. -1-2). 12.99 *(978-1-4169-6786-6(9),* Simon Scribbles) Simon Scribbles.
Civardi, Anna. Farm Magnet Book. Cartwright, Stephen, illus. 2009. (Magnet Bks). 10p. (J). bds. 19.99 *(978-0-7945-2231-5(9),* Usborne) EDC Publishing.
Clarissa - Evaluation Guide: Evaluation Guide. 2006. (J). *(978-1-55942-402-8(8))* Witcher Productions.
Clark, Eleanor. Eleanor Jo: The Farmer's Daughter. 2007. (Eleanor Ser.: Bk. 5). (Illus.). 193p. 14.99 *(978-0-9788726-1-8(4))* HonorNet.
Clarke, Jane. Old MacDonald's Things That Go. Blanco, Migy, illus. 2017. (ENG.). 32p. (J). (-k). 15.99 *(978-0-7636-9326-8(X),* Nosy Crow) Candlewick Pr.
Claus, Fred J. You're Too Small, 1 vol. Webb, Sarah, illus. 2009. 20p. pap. 24.95 *(978-1-60703-757-6(2))* America Star Bks.
Cleary, Beverly. Emily's Runaway Imagination. Krush, Beth et al, illus. 2008. (Cleary Reissue Ser.). (ENG.). 288p. (J). (gr. 3-7). pap. 6.99 *(978-0-380-70923-6(6))* HarperCollins Pubs.
—Emily's Runaway Imagination. 221p. (J). (gr. 2-4). pap. 4.95 *(978-0-8072-1416-9(7),* Listening Library) Random Hse. Audio Publishing Group.
Clement-Moore, Rosemary. Texas Gothic. 2012. (ENG.). 416p. (YA). (gr. 9). pap. 10.99 *(978-0-385-73694-7(0),* Ember) Random Hse. Children's Bks.
Clements, Andrew. Because Your Grandparents Love You. Alley, R. W., illus. 2015. (ENG.). 32p. (J). (gr. -1-3). 16.99 *(978-0-544-14854-3(1))* Houghton Mifflin Harcourt Publishing Co.
Cleveland, Rob. The Archer & the Sun: A Tale from China. Hoffmire, Baird, illus. 2007. (Story Cove Ser.). (ENG.). 24p. (J). (gr. -1-3). pap. 3.95 *(978-0-87483-878-7(9))* August Hse. Pubs., Inc.
Coatsworth, Elizabeth. Five Bushel Farm. Sewell, Helen, illus. 2004. 143p. (J). pap. 10.95 *(978-1-883937-84-3(1))* Bethlehem Bks.
Cochran, Jean M. Farmer Brown & His Little Red Truck. Enos, Daryl, illus. 2009. (ENG.). 32p. (J). (gr. -1-k). 16.95 *(978-0-9792035-0-3(3))* Pleasant St. Pr.
Cockey, Elizabeth J. & Cockey, Barton M. Drawn to the Land: The Romance of Farming. 2011. (Illus.). 40p. 18.95 *(978-0-9846473-2-3(5))* ThePaintedWord, Ltd.
Cole, Brock. The Money We'll Save. Cole, Brock, illus. 2011. (ENG., Illus.). 40p. (J). (gr. -1-3). 16.99 *(978-0-374-35011-6(6),* 9780374350116, Farrar, Straus & Giroux (BYR)) Farrar, Straus & Giroux.
Cole, Henry. Big Bug. Cole, Henry, illus. 2014. (ENG., Illus.). 32p. (J). (gr. -1-2). 14.99 *(978-1-4424-9897-6(8),* Little Simon) Little Simon.
Compestine, Ying. The Story of Kites: Amazing Chinese Inventions. Xuan, YongSheng, illus. 2016. (ENG & CHI.). 40p. (J). (gr. -1-3). 15.95 *(978-1-59702-122-7(9))* Immedium.
—The Story of Noodles: Amazing Chinese Inventions. Xuan, YongSheng, illus. 2016. (ENG & CHI.). 40p. (J). (gr. -1-3). 15.95 *(978-1-59702-121-0(0))* Immedium.
Conkling, Winifred. Sylvia & Aki. (ENG.). 160p. (J). 2013. (gr. 4-7). 6.99 *(978-1-58246-345-2(X),* Yearling) 2011. (Illus.). (gr. 3-7). 16.99 *(978-1-58246-337-7(9),* Tricycle Pr.) Random Hse. Children's Bks.
Cook, Teri Ann. The Adventures of Mrs. Patsy's Farm: A Gift! Is a Gift! Is a Gift!, 1 vol. 2009. 24p. pap. 24.95 *(978-1-60749-549-9(X))* America Star Bks.
Coomber, Suzanne. The Run Away Persimmon. 2009. 20p. pap. 12.49 *(978-1-4490-0911-3(5))* AuthorHouse.
Cooper, Elisha. Farm. 2010. (ENG.). 48p. (J). (gr. -1-3). 17.99 *(978-0-545-07075-1(9),* Orchard Bks.) Scholastic, Inc.
Cotton, Katie. And the Cow Said. Gausden, Vicki, illus. 2015. (ENG.). 24p. (J). (gr. -1-1). 12.99 *(978-1-4998-0101-9(7))* Little Bee Books Inc.
Courtin, Thierry. Decouvre les petits de la Ferme. 15.95 *(978-2-09-202273-3(3))* Nathan, Fernand FRA. Dist: Distribooks, Inc.
Cousins, Lucy. Maisy's Tractor. Cousins, Lucy, illus. 2015. (Maisy Ser.). (ENG., Illus.). 18p. (J). (— 1). bds. 5.99 *(978-0-7636-7305-5(6))* Candlewick Pr.
Cowley, Joy. Mrs. Wishy-Washy's Farm. Fuller, Elizabeth, illus. (ENG.). 32p. (J). (gr. -1-k). 2006. 5.99 *(978-0-14-240299-3(0),* Puffin Books) 2003. 16.99 *(978-0-399-23872-7(7),* Philomel Bks.) Penguin Young Readers Group.
Cox, Phil Roxbee. Curly's Friends. Cartwright, Stephen, illus. rev. ed. 2005. (Usborne Farmyard Tales Touchy-Feely Ser.). 10p. (J). (gr. -1-k). bds. 7.95 *(978-0-7945-1180-7(5),* Usborne) EDC Publishing.
Cox, Phil Roxbee & Cartwright, S. Wolly's Walk. 2004. (Farmyard Tales Touchy Feely Board Bks.). (ENG., Illus.). 1p. (J). bds. 7.95 *(978-0-7945-0039-9(0),* Usborne) EDC Publishing.
Coxon, Michele. Kitten's Adventure (Vietnamese/English), 1 vol. 2008. (ENG & VIE., Illus.). 32p. (J). (gr. -1-k). pap. 6.00 *(978-1-59572-157-0(6))* Star Bright Bks., Inc.
Crandall, Janet. Winter on the Farm. 2006. (J). per. 9.95 *(978-1-59872-612-1(9))* Instant Pub.
Cronin, Doreen. Dooby Dooby Moo. Lewin, Betsy, illus. 2010. (Click, Clack Book Ser.). (ENG.). 40p. (J). (gr. -1-k). bds. 7.99 *(978-1-4424-0890-6(1),* Little Simon) Little Simon.
—Dooby Dooby Moo. Lewin, Betsy, illus. 2006. (Click, Clack Book Ser.). (ENG.). 40p. (J). (gr. -1-3). 17.99 *(978-0-689-84507-9(3),* Atheneum Bks. for Young Readers) Simon & Schuster Children's Publishing.
—Dooby Dooby Moo, 1 vol. Lewin, Betsy, illus. 2008. (Doreen Cronin: Click-Clack & More Ser.). (ENG.). 40p. (gr. -1-3). lib. bdg. 24.21 *(978-1-59961-423-6(5))* Spotlight.
—Dooby Dooby Moo. Lewin, Betsy, illus. 2011. (J). (gr. -1-3). 29.95 *(978-0-545-04281-9(X))* Weston Woods Studios, Inc.
—Dubi Dubi Muu. Jimenez Rioja, Alberto, tr. from ENG. 2007.Tr. of Dooby Dooby Moo. (SPA., Illus.). 35p. (J). (gr. -1-1). 15.95 *(978-1-933032-33-7(2))* Lectorum Pubns., Inc.
Cronin, Doreen & Jiménez Rioja, Alberto. Pum, Cuac, Muu: Una Loca Aventura. Lewin, Betsy, illus. 2008. (SPA.). (J). pap. 5.99 *(978-1-933032-54-2(5))* Lectorum Pubns., Inc.
Crossley, David, illus. On the Farm. 2004. (Baby's First Learning Ser.). 12p. (J). bds. 4.99 *(978-1-85854-893-7(4))* Brimax Books Ltd. GBR. Dist: Byeway Bks.
Crownover, Rebecca. Texas Farm Girl. Daigle, Brian, illus. 2013. (ENG.). (J). (gr. -1-3). 14.95 *(978-1-62086-265-0(4))* Mascot Bks., Inc.
Crowson, Andrew. Flip Flap Farm. 2003. (Illus.). 12p. bds. *(978-1-85602-430-3(X),* Pavilion Children's Books) Pavilion Bks.
Crum, Shutta. My Mountain Song. 2007. (Illus.). 32p. (J). 16.00 *(978-1-4223-6590-8(5))* DIANE Publishing Co.
—Thunder-Boomer! Thompson, Carol, illus. 2009. (ENG.). 40p. (J). (gr. -1-3). 17.99 *(978-0-618-61865-1(1))* Houghton Mifflin Harcourt Publishing Co.
Cunningham, Terri Ann. Hillary Hind Hooth Lost Her Tooth. 2009. 28p. pap. 14.49 *(978-1-4389-3959-9(0))* AuthorHouse.
Cutler, Betty Jackson. The Flight of SaraJane, 1 vol. 2010. 30p. 24.95 *(978-1-4512-1018-7(3))* PublishAmerica, Inc.
Dahi, Khetam. The Mulberry Tree. 2013. 100p. (gr. -1). pap. 11.65 *(978-1-4669-8313-7(2))* Trafford Publishing.
Dale, Elizabeth. Little Red Hen's Great Escape. 2016. (ENG., Illus.). 32p. (J). *(978-0-7787-2461-2(1))* Crabtree Publishing Co.
Dale, Jenny. Bubble & Squeak. Hellard, Susan, illus. 2005. 60p. (J). *(978-0-439-79122-9(7))* Scholastic, Inc.
Dalton, Sherry A. A New Day - a New Beginning: All about a Day on the Farm. Whitlatch, Jessica A., illus. 2011. 40p. pap. 24.95 *(978-1-4560-7462-3(8))* America Star Bks.
Damron, Dugan. Old Shorty: Tales of a Midwestern Farm Boy, 1 vol. 2009. 51p. pap. 16.95 *(978-1-60813-651-3(5))* America Star Bks.
Danczyk, Kenneth. Grandpas Farm. 2008. 35p. pap. 16.00 *(978-1-4357-4021-1(1))* Lulu Pr., Inc.
Davies, Nicola. Escape from Silver Street Farm. McEwen, Katharine, illus. 2013. (Silver Street Farm Ser.). (ENG.). 80p. (J). (gr. 2-5). 12.99 *(978-0-7636-6133-5(3))* Candlewick Pr.
—Welcome to Silver Street Farm. McEwen, Katharine, illus. 2012. (Silver Street Farm Ser.). (ENG.). 80p. (J). (gr. 2-5). 12.99 *(978-0-7636-5831-1(6))* Candlewick Pr.
—Welcome to Silver Street Farm. McEwen, Katharine, illus. 2013. (Silver Street Farm Ser.). (ENG.). 80p. (J). (gr. 2-5). pap. 4.99 *(978-0-7636-6443-5(X))* Candlewick Pr.
Daviess, Maria Thompson. The Golden Bird. 2007. 92p. per. *(978-1-4068-1853-6(4))* Echo Library.
Davis, Caroline. Animals on the Farm. 2009. (My First Noisy Bath Bks.). (ENG.). 8p. (J). (gr. -1). 4.99 *(978-0-7641-9592-1(1))* Barron's Educational Series, Inc.
—Sparkly Farm. Davis, Caroline, illus. 2008. (Tiger Tales Ser.). (Illus.). 8p. (J). (gr. -1). bds. 6.95 *(978-1-58925-831-0(2))* Tiger Tales.
Davis, Lydia & Ollivant, Alfred. Alfred Ollivant's Bob, Son of Battle: The Last Gray Dog of Kenmuir. Kirmse, Marguerite, illus. 2014. (ENG.). 320p. (J). (gr. 3-7). 17.95 *(978-1-59017-729-7(0),* NYR Children's Collection) New York Review of Bks., Inc., The.
Davis, Peg. After the Storm: A Napoleon & Marigold Adventure. 2009. 40p. pap. 16.50 *(978-1-60860-222-3(2),*

Eloquent Bks.) Strategic Book Publishing & Rights Agency (SBPRA).

—Napoleon & Marigold. 2008. 24p. pap. 13.50 (978-1-60693-114-1(8), Eloquent Bks.) Strategic Book Publishing & Rights Agency (SBPRA).

Davis, Rebecca. Jake Riley: Irreparably Damaged. 2003. 240p. (J). 16.89 (978-0-06-051838-7(3)) HarperCollins Pubs.

Daynes, Katie. Enormous Turnip. Overwater, Georgien, illus. 2006. (First Reading Level 3 Ser.). 48p. (J). (gr. 1-4). 8.99 (978-0-7945-1376-4(X), Usborne) EDC Publishing.

Dayton, Dorothy. The Legend of Farmer Will. 2006. 70p. pap. 16.95 (978-1-4241-0985-2(X)) PublishAmerica, Inc.

de Brunhoff, Laurent. Babar et ses Amis a la Ferme. (Babar Ser.). (FRE., Illus.). 48p. (J). (gr. -1-3). 19.95 (978-0-7859-8805-2(X)) French & European Pubns., Inc.

de Las Casas, Dianne. The Gigantic Sweet Potato, 1 vol. Gentry, Marita, illus. 2010. (ENG.). 32p. (J). (gr. k-3). 16.99 (978-1-58980-755-6(3)) Pelican Publishing Co., Inc.

Dean, James. Old MacDonald Had a Farm. Dean, James, illus. 2014. (Pete the Cat Ser.). (ENG., Illus.). 32p. (J). (gr. -1-3). 9.99 (978-0-06-219873-0(4)) HarperCollins Pubs.

Debowksi, Sharon. The Grape Escape: Call 9-1-1, the Grapes Are on the Run! Fonseca-Hughes, Sarah, illus. 2007. 32p. (J). 14.95 (978-1-60227-472-3(X)) Above the Clouds Publishing.

Decola, Diane. Butterfly. 2008. 180p. pap. 15.99 (978-1-4389-0715-4(X)) AuthorHouse.

Deddens, Rachel Campbell. The Day the Calf Ate the Chocolate Cake. 2016. (ENG., Illus.). 28p. pap. 8.95 (978-1-63047-607-6(2)) Morgan James Publishing.

Defelice, Cynthia & DeFelice, Cynthia C. Under the Same Sky. 2005. (ENG.). 224p. (J). (gr. 5-9). pap. 9.99 (978-0-374-48065-3(6), 9780374480653) Square Fish.

Deiser, Donald. Egg Money. 2005. 112p. per. 12.95 (978-1-931195-76-8(5)) KiwE Publishing, Ltd.

Del Negro, Janice M. & Del Negro. Willa & the Wind, 1 vol. Solomon, Heather M., illus. 2005. (ENG.). 32p. (J). (gr. k-3). 16.95 (978-0-7614-5232-4(X)) Marshall Cavendish Corp.

Delena Deatherage. The Beginning of People's Chicken. Joe Kent, illus. 2009. 40p. pap. 18.95 (978-1-4208-9094-5(8)) AuthorHouse.

DePrisco, Dorothea. Pig-a-Boo! A Farmyard Peekaboo Book. Runnells, Patricia & Runnells, Treesha, illus. 2009. (ENG.). 14p. (J). (gr. -1-k). 9.99 (978-1-4169-7226-6(9), Little Simon) Little Simon.

Desisti, Sam F. The Paco & Angelina Stories, 1 vol. 2009. 48p. pap. 16.95 (978-1-61582-604-9(1)) America Star Bks.

Detlefsen, Lisl H. Time for Cranberries. Henry, Jed, illus. 2015. (ENG.). 32p. (J). (gr. -1-2). 17.99 (978-1-62672-098-5(3), 9781626720985) Roaring Brook Pr.

Dickson, Darnell G. Small Town, Big Dreams: A Dane Jordan Sports Novel. 2008. pap. 14.99 (978-1-59955-229-3(9)) Cedar Fort, Inc./CFI Distribution.

Disney Book Group. Disney Baby on the Farm. Disney Storybook Art Team, illus. 2017. (ENG.). 12p. (J). (gr. -1-k). bds. 8.99 (978-1-4847-8248-4(8)) Disney Pr.

DiTerlizzi, Tony. Kenny & the Dragon. 2008. (Playaway Children Ser.). (J). (gr. 3-7). 39.99 (978-1-60640-958-9(1)) Findaway World, LLC.

—Kenny & the Dragon. DiTerlizzi, Tony, illus. (ENG., Illus.). (J). (gr. 3-7). 2012. 176p. pap. 8.99 (978-1-4424-3651-0(4)) 2008. 160p. 17.99 (978-1-4169-3977-1(6)) Simon & Schuster Bks. For Young Readers. (Simon & Schuster Bks. For Young Readers).

—Kenny & the Dragon. DiTerlizzi, Tony, illus. 2008. (Illus.). 160p. (J). (gr. 3-7). 15.99 Simon & Schuster Children's Publishing.

Dixon, Franklin W. Farming Fear. 2005. (Hardy Boys II Ser.: No. 188). 154p. (J). lib. bdg. 15.00 (978-1-59054-839-4(6)) Fitzgerald Bks.

Dodds, Dayle Ann. Minnie's Diner: A Multiplying Menu. Manders, John, illus. 2007. (ENG.). 40p. (J). (gr. k-3). pap. 6.99 (978-0-7636-3313-4(5)) Candlewick Pr.

Donaldson, Julia. The Scarecrows' Wedding. Scheffler, Axel, illus. 2014. (ENG.). 32p. (J). (gr. -1-3). 17.99 (978-0-545-72606-1(9), Levine, Arthur A. Bks.) Scholastic, Inc.

Donnell, Annie Hamilton. Three Young Knights & Miss Theodosia's Heartstrings. l.t. ed. 2007. (ENG.). 156p. pap. 21.99 (978-1-4346-1605-0(3)) Creative Media Partners, LLC.

Donnelly, Jennifer. A Northern Light. 2004. (ENG.). 416p. (YA). (gr. 9-12). reprint ed. pap. 9.99 (978-0-15-205310-9(7)) Houghton Mifflin Harcourt Publishing Co.

—A Northern Light. 2004. 396p. (gr. 9-12). 20.00 (978-0-7569-3614-3(4)) Perfection Learning Corp.

Doodler, Todd H. Veggies with Wedgies. Doodler, Todd H., illus. 2014. (ENG., Illus.). 32p. (J). (gr. -1-k). 14.99 (978-1-4424-9340-7(2), Little Simon) Little Simon.

Dorling Kindersley Publishing Staff. Baby Cheep! Cheep! 2015. (ENG.). 14p. (J). (gr. -1 — 1). bds. 5.99 (978-1-4654-3184-4(5), DK Children) Dorling Kindersley Publishing, Inc.

Douglas, Erin. Get That Pest! Yee, Wong Herbert, illus. 2003. (Green Light Readers Level 2 Ser.). (ENG.). 24p. (J). (gr. -1-3). pap. 3.95 (978-0-15-204833-4(2)) Houghton Mifflin Harcourt Publishing Co.

—Get That Pest! / ¡Agarren a Ése! Campoy, F. Isabel & Flor Ada, Alma, trs. Yee, Wong Herbert, illus. 2008. (Green Light Readers Level 2 Ser.). (SPA & ENG.). 28p. (J). (gr. k-2). pap. 3.95 (978-0-15-206269-9(6)) Houghton Mifflin Harcourt Publishing Co.

Dowell, Frances O'Roark. Ten Miles Past Normal. (ENG., 224p. (YA). (gr. 7). 2012. Illus.). pap. 9.99 (978-1-4169-9586-9(2)) 2011. 16.99 (978-1-4169-9585-2(4)) Simon & Schuster Children's Publishing. (Atheneum Bks. for Young Readers).

Down on Piggy Farm. 2005. (J). bds. 12.95 (978-0-9764114-2-0(3)) Little People Bks.

Doyle, Eugenie. Sleep Tight Farms: A Farm Prepares for Winter. Stadtlander, Becca, illus. 2016. (ENG.). 36p. (J). (gr. -1-k). 16.99 (978-1-4521-2901-3(0)) Chronicle Bks. LLC.

Eaglehouse, Carolyn. The Magic of Milky Way Farm. l.t. ed. 2005. (Illus.). 24p. (J). pap. 10.00 (978-0-9773263-0-3(6)) Eaglehouse, Carolyn.

Edwards, Judith. Invasion on the Mountain: The Adventures of Will Ryan & the Civilian Conservation Corps 1933. 2011. (ENG., Illus.). 90p. (J). (gr. 3-7). pap. 12.50 (978-1-884592-55-3(4)) Images from the Past, Inc.

—Trouble on the Mountain: The Adventures of Will Ryan & the Civilian Conservation Corps, 1934-35. 2012. (ENG., Illus.). 118p. (J). (gr. 3-7). pap. 12.50 (978-1-884592-60-7(0)) Images from the Past, Inc.

Edwards, Pamela Duncan. McGillycuddy Could! Date not set. 32p. (J). (gr. -1-1). pap. 5.99 (978-0-06-443688-5(8)) HarperCollins Pubs.

—McGillycuddy Could! Porter, Sue, illus. 2005. 32p. (J). (gr. -1-1). 14.99 (978-0-06-029001-6(3)) HarperCollins Pubs.

Elliot, David. Henry's Map. Elliot, David, illus. 2013. (ENG., Illus.). 40p. (J). (gr. -1-3). 16.99 (978-0-399-16072-1(8), Philomel Bks.) Penguin Young Readers Group.

—Henry's Stars. Elliot, David, illus. 2015. (ENG., Illus.). 40p. (J). (gr. k-3). 16.99 (978-0-399-17116-1(9), Philomel Bks.) Penguin Young Readers Group.

Enright, Elizabeth. Thimble Summer. unabr. ed. 2004. 136p. (J). (gr. 3-7). pap. 36.00 incl. audio (978-0-8072-0671-3(7), Listening Library) Random Hse. Audio Publishing Group.

—Thimble Summer. 2006. 21.75 (978-0-8446-7281-6(5)) Smith, Peter Pub., Inc.

—Thimble Summer. Enright, Elizabeth, illus. 2008. (ENG., Illus.). 144p. (J). (gr. 3-7). pap. 6.99 (978-0-312-38002-1(X), 9780312380021) Square Fish.

Enriquez, Jose. Saving the Mango Farm. 2006. 23p. (J). 10.98 (978-1-4116-5917-9(1)) Lulu Pr., Inc.

Espluga, Maria. I, Farmer: Yo, Campesino. 2009. (SPA & ENG.). 28p. (J). 13.95 (978-1-931398-54-1(2)) Me+Mi Publishing.

Falango, Marcy. The Rescue. 2012. 24p. pap. 14.93 (978-1-4669-7094-6(4)) Trafford Publishing.

Falcone, Karen. Tales from Falmac Farm. Frake, Barbara, illus. 2005. (ENG.). 47p. (J). per. (978-1-933002-08-8(5)) PublishingWorks.

Falconer, Mary. The Spotted Sheep with the Worthless Wool. 2011. 24p. pap. 10.49 (978-1-4520-9636-0(8)) AuthorHouse.

The Farmer & the Clown. 2014. (ENG., Illus.). 32p. (J). (gr. -1-3). 17.99 (978-1-4424-9744-3(0), Beach Lane Bks.) Beach Lane Bks.

Farmer Says. 2005. (J). bds. (978-1-4194-0050-6(9)) Paradise Pr., Inc.

Farmyard Tales. 2017. (Farmyard Tales Ser.). 24p. (gr. 4-6). 70.80 **(978-1-5081-6179-0(8))**; pap. 24.75 **(978-1-5081-6181-3(X))** Rosen Publishing Group, Inc., The. (PowerKids Pr.).

Fass, Amanda L. Farm Friends. Swope, Brenda, illus. 2011. 28p. pap. 24.95 (978-1-4560-0894-9(3)) America Star Bks.

Feldman, Thea. Hello, Farm! 2015. (Flap Book Ser.: 3). (ENG.). 14p. (J). (gr. -1-k). 8.99 (978-0-7944-3298-0(0), Reader's Digest Children's Bks.) Studio Fun International.

—A Visit to the Farm. Trasler, Janee, illus. 2006. 3p. (J). (gr. -1-3). bds. 5.99 (978-1-932915-32-7(X)) Sandvik Publishing.

Fickey, Brenda. Beckoning Shadows, 1 vol. 2009. (ENG.). 179p. pap. 24.95 (978-1-61546-330-5(5)) America Star Bks.

Fleming, Candace. Emma's Circus. Davenier, Christine, illus. 2017. (ENG.). 40p. (J). 17.99 (978-0-374-39907-8(7), 9780374399078, Farrar, Straus & Giroux (BYR)) Farrar, Straus & Giroux.

—Go Sleep in Your Own Bed. Nichols, Lori, illus. 2017. (ENG.). 40p. (J). (gr. -1-2). 17.99 (978-0-375-86648-7(5), Schwartz & Wade Bks.) Random Hse. Children's Bks.

Fletcher, B. R. The Long Haired Yellow Bellies. 2008. 76p. pap. 24.99 (978-1-4389-1519-7(5)) AuthorHouse.

Fletcher, Corina. Playbook Farm. Teckentrup, Britta, illus. 2012. (ENG.). 12p. (J). (gr. -1-2). 24.00 (978-0-7636-6165-6(1), Nosy Crow) Candlewick Pr.

Florence Jahn Keller. Meet My Pets. 2009. 20p. pap. 10.49 (978-1-4389-5710-4(6)) AuthorHouse.

Flowers, Luke. Ninja on the Farm (Scholastic Reader, Level 1: Moby Shinobi) 2016. (Scholastic Reader, Level 1 Ser.). (ENG.). 32p. (J). (gr. -1-1). pap. 3.99 (978-0-545-93537-1(7)) Scholastic, Inc.

Folk Tale Staff. Gingerbread Man. Rodriguez, Beatrix, illus. 2012. (ENG.). 32p. (J). (gr. -1-3). 17.95 (978-0-7358-4086-7(5)) North-South Bks., Inc.

Forrester, Izola L. Kit of Greenacre Farm. 2007. (ENG.). 158p. pap. 19.99 (978-1-4264-8431-5(3)); 174p. pap. 21.99 (978-1-4264-8489-6(5)) Creative Media Partners, LLC.

Franco, Betsy. Going to Grandma's Farm. 2004. (Rookie Reader Español Ser.). (ENG., Illus.). 24p. (J). (gr. k-2). pap. 4.95 (978-0-516-27787-5(1), Children's Pr.) Scholastic Library Publishing.

Frazier, Laurence. Cranky the Rooster. 2011. 24p. pap. 12.79 (978-1-4567-6258-2(3)) AuthorHouse.

Frederick, Heather Vogel. Yours Truly. 2017. (Pumpkin Falls Mystery Ser.). (ENG., Illus.). 336p. (J). (gr. 5-9). 16.99 (978-1-4424-7186-3(7), Simon & Schuster Bks. For Young Readers) Simon & Schuster Bks. For Young Readers.

Freisinger, Vickie. Reno Does Chores, 1 vol. 2009. 36p. pap. 24.95 (978-1-60813-027-6(4)) America Star Bks.

Friend, R. Down on Friendly Acres Set 1: Books #1-4, 4. 2007. (Illus.). (J). (978-0-9743627-8-6(6)) Sunflower Seeds Pr.

Frillman, K. Country Stars: The Road Less Traveled. 2007. 348p. per. 21.95 (978-1-4303-1234-5(3)) Lulu Pr., Inc.

Froeb, Lori C. Let's Go to the Farm. 2016. (Fisher Price Lift the Flap Ser.). (ENG.). 10p. (J). (gr. -1-k). bds. 9.99 (978-0-7944-3832-6(6), Reader's Digest Children's Bks.) Studio Fun International.

Frueh, Pamela. Me & My Best Cousin Joy. 2007. 80p. pap. 8.95 (978-1-4303-2193-4(8)) Lulu Pr., Inc.

Fun on the Farm. 2014. (Happy Day Ser.). (ENG., Illus.). 16p. (J). pap. 2.49 (978-1-4143-9416-9(0)) Tyndale Hse. Pubs.

Galer, Chris. Ross Gang. 2006. 136p. per. (978-1-905529-84-1(8)) Grosvenor Hse. Publishing Ltd.

Galvin, Laura Gates. My First Trip to the Farm. Rabe, Tish, ed. rev. ed. 2007. (ENG., Illus.). 24p. (J). (gr. -1-3). 5.49 (978-1-59069-561-6(5)) Studio Mouse LLC.

Gamble, Adam & Kelly, Cooper. Good Night Farm. Kelly, Cooper, illus. 2009. (Good Night Our World Ser.). (ENG., Illus.). 28p. (J). (gr. k — 1). bds. 9.95 (978-1-60219-029-0(1)) Good Night Bks.

Gansle, Sherry. Oops, a Curious Horse Big Book. Light, Carol, illus. 2003. 56p. (J). (978-0-9745803-6-4(8)) Little Big Tomes.

—Oops, a Curious Horse Little Book. Light, Carol, illus. 2003. 52p. (J). (978-0-9745803-7-1(6)) Little Big Tomes.

—Oops, a Curious Horse Story Book Reader. Light, Carol, illus. 2003. 58p. (J). (978-0-9745803-5-7(X)) Little Big Tomes.

Gardam, Jane. The Hollow Land. 2015. (ENG.). 160p. (gr. 12). pap. 15.00 (978-1-60945-246-9(1)) Europa Editions, Inc.

Garis, Howard Roger. Uncle Wiggily on the Farm. Date not set. 192p. (J). 20.95 (978-0-8488-2275-0(7)) Amereon Ltd.

Garland, Michael. Grandpa's Tractor. Garland, Michael, illus. 2011. (ENG., Illus.). 32p. (J). (gr. k-1). 16.95 (978-1-59078-762-5(5)) Boyds Mills Pr.

Garson, Cindy. Welcome to Kristy's Farm: Book I (Black & White Version) 2007. (ENG.). 56p. per. 21.80 (978-1-84728-321-4(7)) Lulu Pr., Inc.

Geisert, Arthur, creator. Thunderstorm. (ENG., Illus.). (J). 2015. 34p. (gr. k). 60.00 (978-1-59270-170-4(1)) 2013. 32p. (gr. -1). 17.95 (978-1-59270-133-9(7)) Enchanted Lion Bks., LLC.

Gernhart, Cyndi. Gertrude Sees... On the Farm. Gernhart, Cyndi et al, illus. l.t. ed. 2006. 20p. (J). 8.00 (978-0-9778240-0-7(4)) Prairie Winds Publishing.

Gershator, Phillis. Who's in the Farmyard? McDonald, Jill, illus. 2012. (ENG.). 24p. (J). (gr. -1-k). bds. 14.99 (978-1-84686-574-9(3)) Barefoot Bks., Inc.

Ghigna, Charles. Lucy Goose. East, Jacqueline, illus. 2015. (Tiny Tales Ser.). (ENG.). 64p. (gr. -1-2). lib. bdg. 23.99 (978-1-4795-6529-0(6)) Tiny Tales.

Ghigna, Charles & Ghigna, Debra. Barn Storm. Greenseid, Diane, illus. 2010. (Step into Reading Ser.). (ENG.). 32p. (J). (gr. -1-1). pap. 3.99 (978-0-375-86114-7(9), Random Hse. Bks. for Young Readers) Random Hse. Children's Bks.

Gibbons, Faye. The Day the Picture Man Came. Meidell, Sherry, illus. 2003. (ENG.). 32p. (YA). (gr. k-2). 16.95 (978-1-56397-161-7(5)) Boyds Mills Pr.

Giff, Patricia Reilly. R My Name Is Rachel. 2012. (ENG.). 176p. (J). (gr. 4-7). pap. 6.99 (978-0-440-42176-4(4), Yearling) Random Hse. Children's Bks.

Gillam, David. Gingertown. Gilliam, David, illus. 2012. 216p. (J). 29.99 (978-1-60131-122-1(2)) Big Tent Bks.

Gilmore, Grace. The Big City. Brown, Petra, illus. 2015. (Tales from Maple Ridge Ser.: 3). (ENG.). 128p. (J). (gr. k-4). pap. 5.99 (978-1-4814-3006-7(8), Little Simon) Little Simon.

—Logan Pryce Makes a Mess. Brown, Petra, illus. 2015. (Tales from Maple Ridge Ser.: 1). (ENG.). 128p. (J). (gr. k-4). pap. 5.99 (978-1-4814-2624-4(9), Little Simon) Little Simon.

—The Lucky Wheel. Brown, Petra, illus. 2015. (Tales from Maple Ridge Ser.: 2). (ENG.). 128p. (J). (gr. k-4). pap. 5.99 (978-1-4814-2627-5(3), Little Simon) Little Simon.

Giulieri, Anne. Grandpa's Farm, 1 vol. Bailey, Martin, illus. 2012. (Engage Literacy Blue Ser.). (ENG.). 32p. (gr. k-2). pap. 5.99 (978-1-4296-8988-5(9), Engage Literacy) Capstone Press of Coughlan Cos.

Give & Take. 2014. (ENG., Illus.). 40p. (J). (gr. -1-3). 17.99 (978-1-4424-1655-0(6), Atheneum Bks. for Young Readers) Simon & Schuster Children's Publishing.

Glines, Abbi. While It Lasts. 2013. (Sea Breeze Ser.). (ENG., Illus.). 304p. (YA). (gr. 11). 18.99 (978-1-4424-8867-0(0)); pap. 9.99 (978-1-4424-8866-3(2)) Simon Pulse. (Simon Pulse).

Glover, Dennis W. The Goat Farm. 2009. 32p. pap. 12.99 (978-1-4490-1532-9(8)) AuthorHouse.

Golden Books Staff. Farm Tales. 2007. (Little Golden Book Treasury Ser.). (ENG., Illus.). 224p. (J). (gr. -1-2). 10.99 (978-0-375-83942-9(9), Golden Bks.) Random Hse. Children's Bks.

Good, Merle. Reuben & the Balloon. Moss, P. Buckley, illus. rev. ed. 2016. (ENG.). 32p. (J). (gr. -1-3). 16.99 (978-1-68099-149-9(3), Good Bks.) Skyhorse Publishing Co., Inc.

Goodell, Mary. The Chicken Pox Puppy: Kate & Jen's Daily Adventures. Goodell, Mary, illus. 2007. (Illus.). 29p. (J). per. 11.99 (978-1-59879-382-6(9)) Lifevest Publishing, Inc.

Goodspeed, Judy. Perky Turkey's Perfect Plan. 2007. (Illus.). 22p. (J). per. 11.99 (978-0-9797574-3-3(6)) Dragonfly Publishing, Inc.

Gourley, Robbin. Bring Me Some Apples & I'll Make You a Pie: A Story about Edna Lewis. (ENG., Illus.). 48p. (J). (gr. -1-3). 2016. pap. 6.99 (978-0-544-80901-7(7), HMH Books For Young Readers) 2008. 17.99 (978-0-618-15836-2(7)) Houghton Mifflin Harcourt Publishing Co.

Grant, Myrna. Ivan & the Hidden Bible. 2006. (Flamingo Fiction 9-13s Ser.). (ENG., Illus.). 144p. (J). (gr. 4-7). per. 6.99 (978-1-84550-133-4(0), 9394aef3-942b-4824-b0b8-0ae3449d32e0) Christian Focus Pubns. GBR. Dist: Bookmasters Distribution.

Gray, Dianne & Gray, Dianne E. Holding up the Earth. 2006. (ENG.). 210p. (J). (gr. 5-7). pap. 12.95 (978-0-618-73747-5(2)) Houghton Mifflin Harcourt Publishing Co.

Gray, Kes. Cluck O'Clock. McQuillan, Mary, tr. McQuillan, Mary, illus. 2004. (ENG.). 32p. (J). (gr. k-3). tchr. ed. 17.95 (978-0-8234-1809-1(X)) Holiday Hse., Inc.

Green, Ann L. Sgt. Dusty's New Home. 2006. (J). 15.95 (978-0-9795397-0-1(6)) Liferays Publishing.

Greenwell, Jessica. Farm Coloring Sticker Book. 2009. (Sticker Coloring Bks). 16p. (J). pap. 5.99 (978-0-7945-2512-5(1), Usborne) EDC Publishing.

Grogan, John. Farm Dog. Cowdrey, Richard, illus. 2011. (I Can Read Level 2 Ser.). (ENG.). 32p. (J). (gr. k-3). pap. 3.99 (978-0-06-198937-7(1)) HarperCollins Pubs.

Grosgebauer, Clare Ham. Snickerdoodle's Star-Spangled Fourth of July! Rissing, Karen, illus. 4th ed. 2005. 36p. (J). (gr. -1-3). 12.99 (978-0-9741888-6-7(7)) Small Wonders Enterprises.

Gross, S. D. Mugallumps. 2007. (Illus.). 32p. (J). per. 13.99 (978-1-59879-303-1(9)) Lifevest Publishing, Inc.

Gwaltney, Doris. Homefront. 2009. (ENG.). 320p. (J). (gr. 5-9). pap. 6.99 (978-1-4169-9572-2(2), Simon & Schuster Bks. For Young Readers) Simon & Schuster Bks. For Young Readers.

Hackett, J. J. Even Cows Wear Moo Moos. Pearn, Kayley, illus. 2013. 24p. pap. 14.95 (978-0-9897242-1-0(2), Over the Rainbow) Pearn & Assocs. Inc.

Haddix, Margaret Peterson. Takeoffs & Landings. 2004. 201p. (gr. 5-9). 17.00 (978-0-7569-4255-7(1)) Perfection Learning Corp.

Haesche, Richard Paul, Sr. My Pet Dinosaur. 2007. (ENG.). 60p. (J). 6.99 (978-0-9800552-0-7(2)) Kreative X-Pressions Pubns.

Haf, Eurgain & Wen, Dref. Fferm Ffion. 2005. (WEL., Illus.). 144p. pap. (978-1-85596-674-1(3)) Dref Wen.

Hagar, Erin. Doing Her Bit: A Story about the Women's Land Army of America. Hill, Jen, illus. 2016. (ENG.). 32p. (J). (gr. 1-4). lib. bdg. 16.95 (978-1-58089-646-7(4)) Charlesbridge Publishing, Inc.

Hall, Barbara. Dixie Storms. 2006. (ENG., Illus.). 224p. (YA). (gr. 7-12). pap. 12.95 (978-0-15-205756-5(0)) Houghton Mifflin Harcourt Publishing Co.

Hall, Donald. Lucy's Summer. McCurdy, Michael, illus. 2008. (ENG.). 40p. (J). (gr. 1-18). pap. 10.95 (978-1-56792-348-3(8)) Godine, David R. Pub.

Halse, Leif. The Boys from Vangen: Vangsgutane. Huntrods, Alexander Knud, tr. Nilssen, Jens R., illus. 2009. (ENG & NNO.). 176p. (J). 19.95 (978-0-9760541-5-3(9)) Astri My Astri Publishing.

Han, Xuemei. Brave Little Mongolian Sisters. Han, Xuemei, illus. 2007. (Illus.). (J). pap. 12.99 (978-0-9763168-7-9(0)) DigitalKu.

Hancock, Dennis. Goodnight on the Farm. Hancock, Uyen, illus. 2012. 28p. pap. 24.95 (978-1-4626-7233-2(7)) America Star Bks.

Hanson, Janell. I Will Help You. 2009. (J). (978-0-9662608-1-6(3)) Partae Pr.

Hapka, Catherine, pseud. Jingle Bells. Sanderson, Ruth, illus. 2014. (Horse Diaries). (ENG.). 208p. (J). (gr. 3-7). pap. 7.99 (978-0-385-38484-1(X), Random Hse. Bks. for Young Readers) Random Hse. Children's Bks.

—Jingle Bells. 2014. (Horse Diaries: 11). lib. bdg. 18.40 (978-0-606-36024-1(7)) Turtleback Bks.

Harlow, Joan Hiatt. Secret of the Night Ponies. (ENG.). (J). (gr. 3-7). 2010. 352p. pap. 7.99 (978-1-4169-0784-8(X)) 2009. 336p. 16.99 (978-1-4169-0783-1(1)) McElderry, Margaret K. Bks. (McElderry, Margaret K. Bks.).

Harris, Jane Ellen. Room for One More. Cole, Al, illus. 2007. 24p. (J). (gr. -1-3). pap. 11.98 (978-0-9800733-0-0(8), LSP) LSP Digital, LLC.

Harris, Nicholas. A Year at a Farm. (Time Goes By Ser.). (ENG.). 24p. (gr. k-3). 2009. pap. 6.95 (978-1-58013-798-0(9), First Avenue Editions) 2008. (Illus.). lib. bdg. 22.60 (978-1-58013-553-5(6)) Lerner Publishing Group.

Harris, Patricia. Everyone Has a Job on the Farm. 2017. (Farmyard Tales Ser.). 24p. (gr. 4-6). pap. 8.25 **(978-1-5383-2182-9(3)**, PowerKids Pr.) Rosen Publishing Group, Inc., The.

—A Visit to the Farm. 2017. (Farmyard Tales Ser.). 24p. (gr. 4-6). pap. 8.25 **(978-1-5383-2174-4(2)**, PowerKids Pr.) Rosen Publishing Group, Inc., The.

Harrison, Kenny. Hide & Seek Harry on the Farm. Harrison, Kenny, illus. 2015. (ENG., Illus.). 20p. (J). (-k). bds. 6.99 (978-0-7636-7370-3(6)) Candlewick Pr.

Harrison, Nicholas. A Year at a Farm. 2008. (Time Goes By Ser.). (ENG.). (gr. k-3). pap. 39.62 (978-0-7613-4713-2(5)) Lerner Publishing Group.

Harvey, Jacqueline. Clementine Rose & the Farm Fiasco. Yi, J., illus. 2015. (Clementine Rose Ser.: 4). (ENG.). 160p. (J). (gr. 2-4). 8.99 (978-1-74275-547-2(X)) Random Hse. Australia AUS. Dist: Independent Pubs. Group.

Harvey, Ruth S. The Farm of Barney B. Brown. 2012. 42p. pap. 16.95 (978-1-4575-1366-4(8)) Dog Ear Publishing, LLC.

Haseley, Dennis. The Old Banjo. Gammell, Stephen, illus. 2013. (ENG.). 32p. (J). (gr. -1-3). 16.99 (978-1-4424-8879-3(4), Simon & Schuster Bks. For Young Readers) Simon & Schuster Bks. For Young Readers.

Hawes, Alison. School Trip. Mould, Chris, illus. 2004. (ENG.). 24p. (J). lib. bdg. 23.65 (978-1-59646-694-4(4)) Dingles & Co.

Hawkins, Aaron. The Year Money Grew on Trees. 2011. (ENG.). 304p. (J). (gr. 5-7). pap. 6.99 (978-0-547-57716-6(8)) Houghton Mifflin Harcourt Publishing Co.

Hawksley, Gerald. Mommies & Babies on the Farm. Calitri, Susan, illus. 2004. (J). bds. 11.99 (978-1-890647-11-7(X)) TOMY International, Inc.

Haydon, Julie. Farm: Lift-A-Flap. (Illus.). 10p. (J). bds. (978-1-74121-413-0(0)) Hinkler Bks. Pty, Ltd.

Hazlett, V. Jake's Junction: Henry's Listening Ears. Tucker, E., illus. 2006. (ENG.). 28p. per. 11.95 (978-1-59800-628-5(2)) Outskirts Pr., Inc.

Hedderwick, Mairi. Walk with Grannie. 2003. (Illus.). 32p. (J). 19.99 (978-0-340-86642-9(X)) Hodder & Stoughton GBR. Dist: Trafalgar Square Publishing.

—A Walk with Grannie. Date not set. (ENG., Illus.). 32p. pap. (978-0-340-87353-3(1), Hodder Children's Books) Hachette Children's Group.

Hegarty, Patricia. Good Night Farm. Elliott, Thomas, illus. 2016. (ENG.). 18p. (J). (gr. -1-1). bds. 12.99 (978-1-58925-233-2(0)) Tiger Tales.

Heinz, Brian J. The Barnyard Cat. l.t. ed. 2003. (Illus.). 32p. (J). pap. 6.96 (978-0-936335-07-0(6)) Ballyhoo BookWorks, Inc.

—Red Fox at McCloskey's Farm. Sheban, Chris, illus. 2006. 32p. (J). (gr. -1-3). 17.95 (978-1-56846-195-3(X), Creative Editions) Creative Co., The.

Helakoski, Leslie. Big Chickens Fly the Coop. Cole, Henry, illus. 2010. (ENG.). 32p. (J). (gr. -1-k). pap. 6.99 (978-0-14-241464-4(6), Puffin Books) Penguin Young Readers Group.

Helquist, Brett. Grumpy Goat. Helquist, Brett, illus. 2013. (ENG., Illus.). 40p. (J). (gr. -1-3). 17.99 (978-0-06-113953-6(X)) HarperCollins Pubs.

Henning, Ann. Cow Patty Patti. 2004. 47p. pap. 24.95 (978-1-4137-3456-0(1)) PublishAmerica, Inc.

Hensel, Rita. Humble Stew in Going Country. 2008. 41p. pap. 24.95 (978-1-60563-219-3(8)) America Star Bks.

—Whooo's the Chicken Thief, a Humble Stew Book, 1 vol. 2010. 50p. pap. 16.95 (978-1-61546-640-5(1)) America Star Bks.

Hensler, K. Why Worry? The Adventures of Bay/Bob/A/Loo/Bop Everything in Moderation. 2008. 48p. pap. 24.95 (978-1-60610-813-0(1)) America Star Bks.

Henson, Heather. Dream of Night. 2010. (ENG.). 224p. (J). (gr. 3-7). 15.99 (978-1-4169-4899-5(6), Atheneum Bks. for Young Readers) Simon & Schuster Children's Publishing.

Henson, Heather. The Whole Sky. 2017. (ENG., Illus.). 256p. (J). (gr. 5-7). 16.99 **(978-1-4424-1405-1(7)**, Atheneum/Caitlyn Dlouhy Books) Simon & Schuster Children's Publishing.

Hernandez, Elaine. Welcome to Humming Meadow Ranch. Hernandez, Stacy, illus. 2005. 28p. (J). lib. bdg. 16.95 (978-0-9766431-0-4(3)) Humming Meadow Ranch.

Hesse, Karen. Out of the Dust. 240p. (YA). (gr. 5-18). pap. 4.99 (978-0-8072-1526-5(0), Listening Library) Random Hse. Audio Publishing Group.

—Out of the Dust. 2009. (gr. 5-8). 18.40 (978-0-613-11953-5(3), Turtleback) Turtleback Bks.

Heurtelou, Maude. Makso's Farm. Vilsaint, Fequiere, ed. Date not set. (ENG & CRP.). 20p. (J). (gr. 1-3). pap. 12.00 (978-1-881839-68-2(0)) Educa Vision Inc.

Hewitt, Hazel & Gillett, Chrissy. A Locust Ate My Daddy's Underwears. 2008. 24p. pap. 13.95 (978-1-84799-261-1(7)) Lulu Pr., Inc.

Hicks, Kelli. Field Trip Fiasco. 2015. (ENG.). 48p. (gr. k-3). 27.07 (978-1-63430-371-2(7)) Rourke Educational Media.

Higginson, Hadley. Keeker & the Springtime Surprise. Perrett, Lisa, illus. 2007. (Keeker & the Sneaky Pony Ser.: KEEK). (ENG.). 58p. (J). (gr. k-3). per. 4.99 (978-0-8118-5599-0(6)) Chronicle Bks. LLC.

Hill, Eric. Spot en la Granja. (SPA.). pap. 4.95 (978-950-07-1966-7(5)) Editorial Sudamericana S.A. ARG. Dist: Distribooks, Inc.

Hill, Janet Muirhead. Kyleah's Tree. Leonhard, Herb, illus. 2011. (J). pap. 12.00 (978-0-9827377-9-8(3)) Raven Publishing Inc. of Montana.

Hillenbrand, Will. Down by the Barn, 0 vols. 2014. (ENG.). 32p. (J). (gr. -1-k). 16.99 (978-1-4778-4731-2(6), 9781477847312, Amazon Children's Publishing) Amazon Publishing.

Hillert, Margaret. Dear Dragon Goes to Grandpa's Farm. Pullan, Jack, illus. 2014. (BeginningtoRead Ser.). (ENG.). 32p. (J). (gr. k-2). pap. 11.94 (978-1-60357-710-6(6)) Norwood Hse. Pr.

—Dragon Goes to the Farm: For the Earliest Reader. Starfall Education, illus. 2006. (ENG.). 32p. (J). (978-1-59577-032-5(1)); pap. (978-1-59577-034-9(8)) Starfall Education.

Himmelman, John. Cows to the Rescue. Himmelman, John, illus. 2011. (Barnyard Rescue Ser.). (ENG., Illus.). 32p. (J). (gr. -1-3). 17.99 (978-0-8050-9249-3(8), 9780805092493, Holt, Henry & Co. Bks. For Young Readers) Holt, Henry & Co.

—Duck to the Rescue. Himmelman, John, illus. 2014. (Barnyard Rescue Ser.). (ENG., Illus.). 32p. (J). (gr. -1-3). 16.99 (978-0-8050-9485-5(7), 9780805094855, Holt, Henry & Co. Bks. For Young Readers) Holt, Henry & Co.

—Pigs to the Rescue. Himmelman, John, illus. 2010. (ENG., Illus.). 32p. (J). (gr. -1-3). 17.99 (978-0-8050-8683-6(8), 9780805086836, Holt, Henry & Co. Bks. For Young Readers) Holt, Henry & Co.

Hinkler Editors, ed. On the Farm. 2009. 12p. 7.99 (978-1-74182-109-3(6), Ideal Pubns.) Worthy Publishing.

Hodges, Meredith. Jasper: The Story of a Mule. Shields, Bonnie, illus. 2003. 245p. (J). (gr. k-7). 39.95 (978-0-9702309-8-0(2)) Lucky 3 Ranch, Inc.

Hoffman, Emily Allen. A Friend of the Enemy. 2003. 108p. (J). pap. 7.95 (978-1-57249-312-4(7), White Mane Kids) White Mane Publishing Co., Inc.

Hoffmire, A. B., illus. & as told by. The Ogre Bully. Hoffmire, A. B., as told by. 2007. (Story Cove Ser.). (ENG.). 32p. (J). (gr. -1-3). 3.95 (978-0-87483-803-9(7)) August Hse. Pubs., Inc.

Holden, Pam. The Paper Trail, 6 pack. Hawley, Kelvin, illus. 2009. (Red Rocket Readers Ser.). (ENG.). 16p. (gr. 2-2). pap. (978-1-877363-69-6(3)) Flying Start Bks.

Hope, Laura Lee. Bunny Brown & His Sister Sue on Grandpa's Farm. 2007. (ENG.). 144p. pap. 18.99 (978-1-4346-3268-5(7)); 156p. pap. 21.99 (978-1-4346-3269-2(5)) Creative Media Partners, LLC.

—The Moving Picture Girls at Oak Farm. 2007. 180p. (gr. -1-7). 25.96 (978-1-4218-3890-8(7), 1st World Library - Literary Society) 1st World Publishing, Inc.

—The Moving Picture Girls at Oak Farm: Or, Queer Happenings While Taking Rural Plays. 2007. (ENG.). 140p. pap. 18.99 (978-1-4346-3488-7(4)); 154p. pap. 21.99 (978-1-4346-3489-4(2)) Creative Media Partners, LLC.

Hopgood, Sally. A Day on the Farm: A Pull-The-Tab Book. Hinton, Stephanie, illus. 2014. (J). (978-1-4351-5688-3(9)) Barnes & Noble, Inc.

Hopkins, William J. The Sandman: His Farm Stories (Yesterday's Classics) 2009. (Illus.). 132p. pap. 8.95 (978-1-59915-300-1(9)) Yesterday's Classics.

—The Sandman: More Farm Stories (Yesterday's Classics) Williamson, Ada Clendenin, illus. 2009. 150p. pap. 8.95 (978-1-59915-301-8(7)) Yesterday's Classics.

Housel, Debra. Charlotte's Web: An Instructional Guide for Literature. rev. ed. 2015. (Great Works). (ENG., Illus.). 72p. (gr. 3-5). pap. 9.99 (978-1-4807-6995-3(9)) Shell Educational Publishing.

Houts, Amy. Down on the Farm, 1 vol. Harpster, Steve, illus. 2011. (My First Graphic Novel Ser.). (ENG.). 32p. (gr. k-2). pap. 6.25 (978-1-4342-3063-8(5)); lib. bdg. 24.65 (978-1-4342-2516-0(X)) Stone Arch Bks. (My First Graphic Novel).

Houts, Michelle. The Beef Princess of Practical County. 2010. (ENG.). 240p. (J). (gr. 3-7). 7.99 (978-0-440-42270-9(1), Yearling) Random Hse. Children's Bks.

Howard, Ellen. Edith Herself. 2007. (ENG.). 144p. (J). (gr. 3-7). pap. 10.95 (978-1-4169-6454-4(1), Simon & Schuster/Paula Wiseman Bks.) Simon & Schuster/Paula Wiseman Bks.

Huggins, Peter. In the Company of Owls. Goodman Koz, Paula, illus. 2008. (ENG.). 96p. (J). 15.95 (978-1-58838-036-4(X), NewSouth Bks.) NewSouth, Inc.

Hughes, Dawn Marie. Oakley Farm Friends. 2006. 83p. pap. 16.95 (978-1-4241-2094-9(2)) PublishAmerica, Inc.

Hughes, Jenny. Dark Horse. 2014. (ENG.). 224p. (J). (gr. 3-7). pap. 9.95 (978-1-62124-010-5(X)) Breakaway Bks.

—A Horse by Any Other Name. 2014. (ENG.). 224p. (J). (gr. 3-7). pap. 9.95 (978-1-62124-009-9(6)) Breakaway Bks.

Huizenga, Nathaniel. Justice in Winter: Justice the Dog Series. 2009. 28p. pap. 13.99 (978-1-4389-7361-6(6)) AuthorHouse.

Hulst, W. G. van de & Hulst, Willem G. van de, illus. Herbie, the Runaway Duck. 2014. (J). (978-1-928136-19-4(2)) Inheritance Pubns.

Huneck, Stephen. Sally at the Farm. 2014. (Sally Board Bks.). (ENG., Illus.). 20p. (J). (gr. -1 — 1). bds. 7.95 (978-1-4197-1030-8(3), Abrams Appleseed) Abrams, Inc.

Hurst, Elva. The Pony Cart Adventure. 2014. (Farm Life Ser.). 64p. pap. 6.99 (978-0-7369-6089-2(9)) Harvest Hse. Pubs.

—The Pony Cart Adventure: A True Story. 2014. (Farm Life Ser.). (ENG., Illus.). 64p. (J). pap. 6.99 (978-0-7369-6088-5(0)) Harvest Hse. Pubs.

—Summer on the Farm. 2014. (Farm Life Ser.). 80p. pap. 6.99 (978-0-7369-6091-5(0)) Harvest Hse. Pubs.

—Summer on the Farm: A True Story. 2014. (Farm Life Ser.). (ENG., Illus.). 80p. (J). pap. 6.99 (978-0-7369-6090-8(2)) Harvest Hse. Pubs.

—When School Bells Call: Based on a True Story. 2015. (Farm Life Ser.). (ENG.). 80p. (J). pap. 6.99 (978-0-7369-6092-2(9)) Harvest Hse. Pubs.

Hysen, Sylvia. A Very Dairy Christmas. 2005. 290p. 24.95 (978-0-9763365-6-3(1)) 1st Impression Publishing.

Inthof, Marian. Our Friends at Farmer John's Meadow. 2008. 27p. pap. 24.95 (978-1-60441-286-4(0)) America Star Bks.

Ipcar, Dahlov. One Horse Farm, 1 vol. Ipcar, Dahlov, illus. 2011. (ENG., Illus.). 36p. (J). 17.95 (978-1-934031-39-1(9), 9c1cb594-de8e-4edf-b155-de5e1e50fbce) Islandport Pr., Inc.

Ippolito, Heidi. Bobo's New Home. 2009. 24p. pap. 11.50 (978-1-60860-220-9(6), Strategic Bk. Publishing) Strategic Book Publishing & Rights Agency (SBPRA).

Isaacs, Latricia. Mason & Hayden Visit Grandma. 2011. 16p. 8.32 (978-1-4567-0170-3(3)) AuthorHouse.

—Mason & Lilly Visit Grandpa. 2011. 16p. 8.32 (978-1-4567-2788-8(5)) AuthorHouse.

Ishwaran, Wobine. Shashi & Maya: A Life of Courage. 2009. 68p. pap. 12.25 (978-1-4269-0184-3(4)) Trafford Publishing.

J., Henry. The Big Gray House: The Adventures of Franklin Meyers. 2010. 96p. (gr. -1-2). pap. 12.00 (978-1-4269-4255-6(9)) Trafford Publishing.

Jacobs, Caroline E. The S. W. F. Club. 2007. (ENG.). 120p. pap. 18.99 (978-1-4346-2899-2(X)); 134p. pap. 19.99 (978-1-4346-2900-5(7)) Creative Media Partners, LLC.

Jahn-Clough, Lisa. Country Girl, City Girl. 2009. (ENG.). 192p. (YA). (gr. 7). pap. 12.95 (978-0-547-22322-3(6)) Houghton Mifflin Harcourt Publishing Co.

James, Scilla. Ponies at Owls' Wood. 2013. 112p. pap. (978-0-9568148-2-1(4)) Swift Publishing.

Jameson, Rosemary. Mortimer & Teasdale's Adventures. 2009. 44p. pap. 14.50 (978-1-60693-441-8(4), Eloquent Bks.) Strategic Book Publishing & Rights Agency (SBPRA).

Janney, Connie. The Most Extraordinary Farm. 2012. 30p. (-18). pap. 13.99 (978-1-4525-6213-1(X)) Balboa Pr.

Jean Emily Myers, Emily Myers & Jean Emily Myers. Mickey's Mini Farm. Tanner Voyles, illus. 2009. 32p. pap. 21.99 (978-1-4389-5544-5(8)) AuthorHouse.

Jennings, Patrick. The Ears of Corn: An Ike & Mem Story. Alter, Anna, illus. 2003. (ENG.). 56p. (J). (gr. k-3). tchr. ed. 15.95 (978-0-8234-1770-4(0)) Holiday Hse., Inc.

Jerry, Spinelli. Blue Ribbon Blues. 2014. (Stepping Stone Book Ser. Vol. 2 Ser.). (ENG.). 80p. (J). (gr. 7-12). 8.24 (978-1-63245-269-6(3)) Lectorum Pubns., Inc.

Johnson, D. B., illus. Four Legs Bad, Two Legs Good! 2007. (J). (978-1-4287-6423-1(2)) Houghton Mifflin Harcourt Publishing Co.

Johnston, Annie Fell. The Little Colonel. 2006. (Illus.). pap. (978-1-4065-1132-1(3)) Dodo Pr.

—The Little Colonel. 2005. reprint ed. pap. 21.95 (978-0-7661-9402-1(7)) Kessinger Publishing, LLC.

Jones, Connie. On the Farm with Kaden & Moxie. 2010. 20p. 12.49 (978-1-4490-8047-1(2)) AuthorHouse.

Jones, Karen. Stories from the Television Show Imagination Way. 2006. 10.00 (978-0-8059-8195-7(0)) Dorrance Publishing Co., Inc.

Jones, Kelly. Unusual Chickens for the Exceptional Poultry Farmer. Kath, Katie, illus. 2015. (ENG.). 224p. (J). (gr. 3-7). 16.99 (978-0-385-75552-8(X), Knopf Bks. for Young Readers) Random Hse. Children's Bks.

Jones, V. M. & Tulloch, Scott. Echo & Hush. 2008. (Illus.). 32p. pap. (978-1-86950-690-2(1)) HarperCollins Pubs. Australia.

Jordan, Apple. I Can Be a Farm Vet. 2016. (Barbie Step into Reading Level 2 Ser.). lib. bdg. 14.75 (978-0-606-38473-5(1)) Turtleback Bks.

Judson, Clara Ingram. Mary Jane - Her Visit. White, Frances, illus. 2008. 220p. 22.95 (978-1-934671-15-3(0)); per. 12.95 (978-1-934671-16-0(9)) Salem Ridge Press LLC.

Kadohata, Cynthia. The Thing about Luck. Kuo, Julia, illus. (ENG.). (J). (gr. 5-9). 2014. 304p. pap. 8.99 (978-1-4424-7465-9(3), Atheneum Bks. for Young Readers) 2013. 288p. 16.99 (978-1-4169-1882-0(5)) Simon & Schuster Children's Publishing.

—The Thing about Luck. 2014. lib. bdg. 18.40 (978-0-606-35798-2(X)) Turtleback Bks.

Karas, G. Brian. On the Farm & at the Market. Karas, G. Brian, illus. 2016. (ENG., Illus.). 40p. (J). 17.99 (978-0-8050-9372-8(9), 9780805093728, Holt, Henry & Co. Bks. For Young Readers) Holt, Henry & Co.

Keeley, Holly M. The Journey of a Grape. 2009. 20p. pap. 12.49 (978-1-4490-3060-5(2)) AuthorHouse.

Key, Watt. Fourmile, 1 vol. 2012. (ENG.). 240p. (J). (gr. 4-7). 24.99 (978-0-374-35095-6(7), 9780374350956, Farrar, Straus & Giroux (BYR)) Farrar, Straus & Giroux.

—Fourmile. 2014. (ENG.). 256p. (J). (gr. 4-7). pap. 8.99 (978-1-250-03995-8(9), 9781250039958) Square Fish.

Kinde, Christa. The Hidden Deep, 1 vol. 2013. (Threshold Ser.). (ENG.). 272p. (J). 14.99 (978-0-310-72489-6(9)) Zonderkidz.

King, Julia. Bingo Explores the Farm. (ENG., Illus.). 46p. (J). 2012. pap. 8.99 (978-0-9839827-1-5(6)) 2011. lib. bdg. 15.99 (978-0-9839827-0-8(8)) King, Julia.

King-smith, Dick. The Golden Goose. Kronheimer, Ann, illus. 2006. (ENG.). 128p. (J). (gr. 3-7). 5.99 (978-0-440-42030-9(X), Yearling) Random Hse. Children's Bks.

Kjellberg, B. Apple Acres: The Farm. 2006. (J). per. 7.95 (978-0-912868-10-3(4)) Kjellberg, Inc.

Kjellberg Publishers. Courtnee: A Farm Girl, 6 vols., bk. 1. 2nd ed. 2005. (ENG., Illus.). 84p. (J). 7.95 (978-0-912868-06-6(6), Kjellberg Pubs.) Kjellberg, Inc.

—Sandy: A City Girl, 6 bks., bk. 1. 2nd ed. 2005. (ENG., Illus.). 94p. (J). 7.95 (978-0-912868-08-0(2), 8080, Kjellberg Pubs.) Kjellberg, Inc.

Kjellberg Publishing. Abe: A Farm Boy, 6 vols., vol. 1. 2nd l.t. ed. 2006. (Illus.). 96p. (J). 7.95 (978-0-912868-07-3(4), Kjellberg Pubs.) Kjellberg, Inc.

Klein, Adria F. Max Goes to the Farm, 1 vol. Gallagher-Cole, Mernie, illus. 2007. (Read-It! Readers: the Life of Max Ser.). (ENG.). 24p. (gr. -1-2). lib. bdg. 21.32 (978-1-4048-3678-5(0), Easy Readers) Picture Window Bks.

Kneen, Maggie, illus. Some Pig! A Charlotte's Web Picture Book. 2006. (Charlotte's Web Ser.). 32p. (J). (gr. k-2). 17.89 (978-0-06-078162-0(9)) HarperCollins Pubs.

Koch, Dorothy Clarke. When the Cows Got Out. 2016. (Illus.). 32p. (J). **(978-0-7399-2535-5(0))** Rod & Staff Pubs., Inc.

Kormos, Lawrence. It Happened One Night in the Barn. Purdy, Joanne, illus. 2007. 24p. (978-1-55452-192-0(0)) Essence Publishing.

Krivinskas, Carol Italiano. Barnyard Babies to the Rescue. 2008. 20p. pap. 13.95 (978-1-4327-2183-1(6)) Outskirts Pr., Inc.

Krosoczka, Jarrett J. Punk Farm. (ENG.). 40p. (J). (gr. -1-2). 2010. pap. 7.99 (978-0-440-41793-4(7), Dragonfly Bks.) 2005. (Illus.). 15.95 (978-0-375-82429-6(4), Knopf Bks. for Young Readers) Random Hse. Children's Bks.

Kruse, Donald W. Where's the Gold. Shipman, Josie, illus. 2012. 50p. pap. 12.95 (978-1-59663-857-0(5), Castle Keep Pr.) Rock, James A. & Co. Pubs.

Kurtz, John & Kurtz, Sandrina. The Big & Little Farm Coloring Book: Featuring Romy the Cow. 2015. (ENG.). 32p. (J). (gr. -1-2). pap. 3.99 (978-0-486-78341-3(3)) Dover Pubns., Inc.

Kutner, Merrily. Down on the Farm. Hillenbrand, Will, illus. 2016. (ENG.). 24p. (J). (gr. -1 — 1). bds. 7.99 (978-0-8234-2177-0(5)) Holiday Hse., Inc.

La Valley, Josanne. The Vine Basket. 2015. (ENG.). 256p. (J). (gr. 5-7). pap. 7.99 (978-0-544-43939-9(2), HMH Books For Young Readers) Houghton Mifflin Harcourt Publishing Co.

Ladage, Cindy & Aumann, Jane. My Name Is Huber. (Illus.). (J). 2013. (ENG.). 24p. pap. 10.00 (978-1-61009-054-4(3)) 2012. (978-1-61009-050-6(0)) Oak Tree Publishing. (Acorn).

Laden, Nina. Peek-A Moo! 2017. (ENG., Illus.). 22p. (J). (gr. -1 — 1). bds. 6.99 **(978-1-4521-5474-9(0))** Chronicle Bks. LLC.

Lal, Neeta. The Whisker Cats: Life on the Farm. 2012. 16p. pap. 15.99 (978-1-4772-3706-9(2)) AuthorHouse.

Lambert, Megan Dowd. A Crow of His Own. Costello, David & Costello, David Hyde, illus. 2015. (ENG.). 32p. (J). (gr. -1-1). lib. bdg. 16.95 (978-1-58089-447-0(X)) Charlesbridge Publishing, Inc.

—A Crow of His Own. Costello, David, illus. 2014. (J). pap. (978-1-58089-448-7(8)) Charlesbridge Publishing, Inc.

Laminack, Lester. Three Hens & a Peacock, 1 vol. Cole, Henry, illus. 2014. (ENG.). 32p. (J). (gr. -1-3). pap. 7.95 (978-1-56145-726-7(4)) Peachtree Pubs.

Laminack, Lester L. Three Hens & a Peacock, 1 vol. Cole, Henry, illus. 2011. (ENG.). 32p. (J). (gr. -1-3). 15.95 (978-1-56145-564-5(4)) Peachtree Pubs.

Lange, Jessica. It's about a Little Bird. 2013. (ENG., Illus.). 40p. (J). (-3). 16.99 (978-1-4022-8526-4(4), 9781402285264, Sourcebooks Jabberwocky) Sourcebooks, Inc.

Lasky, Kathryn. Sugaring Time. 2003. (Illus.). 21.25 (978-0-8446-7248-9(3)) Smith, Peter Pub., Inc.

Laura Lee Hope. The Moving Picture Girls at Oak Farm. 2007. 180p. per. 11.95 (978-1-4218-3990-5(3), 1st World Library - Literary Society) 1st World Publishing, Inc.

Law, Jessica. A Farmer's Life for Me. McDonald, Jill, illus. 2013. (SPA.). 24p. (J). pap. 6.99 (978-1-78285-025-0(2)) Barefoot Bks., Inc.

Lawson-Goins, Helen. Surprise in the Garden. 2012. 40p. pap. 21.99 (978-1-4771-1258-8(8)) Xlibris Corp.

Layton, Roxanne A. Tommy's Happy Place. 2012. 28p. 24.95 (978-1-4626-6551-8(9)) America Star Bks.

Lean, Sarah. A Hundred Horses. 2014. (ENG.). 224p. (J). (gr. 3-7). 16.99 (978-0-06-212229-2(0), Tegen, Katherine Bks) HarperCollins Pubs.

Leatherman, Diane. Abigail Before the Revolution. 2005. (Illus.). 64p. (J). (978-0-9665861-2-1(3)) Bounty Project, The.

Lee, Mary Ellen. Danny & Life on Bluff Point: Blizzard of '95 revised Edition. 2009. 160p. (gr. 4-7). pap. 12.95 (978-0-595-53308-4(6)) iUniverse, Inc.

Leech, Carlyle & Leech, Thirma. Ha-Ha Farm. 2009. (ENG., Illus.). 24p. (J). (gr. -1-1). 14.95 (978-1-59583-396-9(X), 9781595833969, Green Tiger Pr.) Laughing Elephant.

Lemna, Don. When the Sergeant Came Marching Home. (ENG.). 208p. (J). (gr. 3-7). 2009. pap. 7.95 (978-0-8234-2211-1(9)) 2008. (Illus.). 17.95 (978-0-8234-2083-4(3)) Holiday Hse., Inc.

Lenski, Lois. Strawberry Girl. Lenski, Lois, illus. 60th anniv. ed. 2005. (ENG., Illus.). 208p. (J). (gr. 5-18). pap. 6.99 (978-0-06-440585-0(0)) HarperCollins Pubs.

Lewis, Alan K. I Grew up on a Farm. Fletcher, Bob, illus. 2005. (ENG.). 32p. (J). (gr. -1-3). 19.95 (978-0-9766805-2-9(1)) Keene Publishing.

Lewis, Gill. Wild Wings. Onoda, Yuta, illus. (ENG.). 304p. (J). (gr. 3-7). 2012. pap. 7.99 (978-1-4424-1446-4(4)) 2011. 18.99 (978-1-4424-1445-7(6)) Simon & Schuster Children's Publishing. (Atheneum Bks. for Young Readers).

Licata, Rosemarie & Reizer, Edwina. The Hare & the Hound. 2007. 17p. 14.95 (978-1-4357-0439-8(8)) Lulu Pr., Inc.

Light, Carol. Chickensing Big Book. Light, Carol, illus. 2003. (Illus.). (J). (978-0-9745803-2-6(5)) Little Big Tomes.

—Chickensing Little Book. Light, Carol, illus. 2003. (Illus.). 108p. (J). (978-0-9745803-3-3(3)) Little Big Tomes.

—Chickensing Story Book Reader. Light, Carol, illus. 2003. (Illus.). 60p. (J). (978-0-9745803-1-9(7)) Little Big Tomes.

Light, Carol, illus. Oops, a Curious Horse Story Telling Board. 2003. (J). (978-0-9745803-4-0(1)) Little Big Tomes.

Lindsey, Kathleen D. Sweet Potato Pie. Riley-Webb, Charlotte, illus. 2003. (J). 16.95 (978-1-58430-061-8(2)) Lee & Low Bks., Inc.

Linker, Julie. Disenchanted Princess. 2007. (ENG.). 240p. (YA). (gr. 9-18). pap. 11.99 (978-1-4169-3472-1(3), Simon Pulse) Simon Pulse.

Lionni, Leo. Six Crows. 2010. (ENG.). 32p. (J). (gr. -1-2). 16.99 (978-0-375-84550-5(X), Knopf Bks. for Young Readers) Random Hse. Children's Bks.

Little Engine- on the Farm. 2005. (J). (978-1-4194-0006-3(1)) Paradise Pr., Inc.

Little Engine AV on the Farm. 2005. (J). (978-1-4194-0009-4(6)) Paradise Pr., Inc.

Little Farm down the Lane, Bk. III. 2005. pap. 10.99 (978-1-59781-702-8(3)) Salem Author Services.

Lockhart, Barbara. Mosey's Field, 1 vol. Crow, Heather, illus. 2013. (ENG.). 32p. (J). 16.99 (978-0-7643-4388-9(2), 9780764343889) Schiffer Publishing, Ltd.

Lodge, Jo. Farm. 2014. (Touch & Feel Buggy Buddies Ser.). (ENG., Illus.). 10p. (J). (— 1). bds. 7.99 (978-1-4472-6800-0(8)) Pan Macmillan GBR. Dist: Independent Pubs. Group.

Loftin, Nancy. Sloppy Al. 2011. 24p. pap. 15.99 (978-1-4568-5595-6(6)) Xlibris Corp.

Long, Ethan & McPike, Elizabeth. In, over & on the Farm. Long, Ethan, illus. 2015. (ENG., Illus.). 40p. (J). (gr. -1-k). bds. 15.99 (978-0-399-16907-6(5), G.P. Putnam's Sons Books for Young Readers) Penguin Young Readers Group.

Long, Loren. Otis. Long, Loren, illus. (Otis Ser.). (Illus.). (J). (gr. -1-k). 2013. (SPA & ENG.). 40p. 7.99 (978-0-14-751124-9(0), Puffin Books) 2011. (ENG., 32p. bds. 8.99 (978-0-399-25600-4(8), Philomel Bks.) 2009. (ENG., 40p. 17.99 (978-0-399-25248-8(7), Philomel Bks.) Penguin Young Readers Group.

—Otis & the Kittens. Long, Loren, illus. 2016. (Otis Ser.). (ENG., Illus.). 40p. (J). (gr. -1-3). 17.99 (978-0-399-16398-2(0), Philomel Bks.) Penguin Young Readers Group.

—Otis & the Puppy. Long, Loren, illus. (Otis Ser.: 3). (ENG., Illus.). (J). (gr. -1-k). 2014. 38p. bds. 8.99 (978-0-399-17196-3(7)) 2013. 40p. 17.99 (978-0-399-25469-7(2)) Penguin Young Readers Group. (Philomel Bks.).

—Otis & the Scarecrow. Long, Loren, illus. 2014. (Otis Ser.). (ENG., Illus.). 40p. (J). (gr. k-3). 17.99 (978-0-399-16396-8(4), Philomel Bks.) Penguin Publishing Group.

—Otis & the Tornado. Long, Loren, illus. 2011. (Otis Ser.: 2). (ENG., Illus.). 40p. (J). (gr. -1-2). 17.99 (978-0-399-25477-2(3), Philomel Bks.) Penguin Young Readers Group.

—An Otis Christmas. Long, Loren, illus. 2013. (Otis Ser.: Bk. 4). (ENG., Illus.). 40p. (J). (gr. -1-2). 17.99 (978-0-399-16395-1(6), Philomel Bks.) Penguin Publishing Group.

—An Otis Christmas. Long, Loren, illus. 2016. (Otis Ser.). (ENG., Illus.). 38p. (J). (gr. -1-2). bds. 8.99 (978-0-399-54811-6(4), Philomel Bks.) Penguin Young Readers Group.

Loughead, Deb. Time & Again, 1 vol. 2005. (ENG.). 192p. (YA). (gr. 7-12). pap. (978-1-894549-39-4(2), Sumach Pr.) Canadian Scholars.

Lougher, Jenny. Ted & the Combine Harvester. Lewis, Wayne, illus. 2007. 23p. pap. (978-1-905553-27-3(7)) BookPublishingWorld.

Louise, Cristina & McIlroy, Michelle. Where Is Paco Now? Louise, Cristina & McIlroy, Michelle, illus. 2012. (SPA & ENG., Illus.). (J). (978-1-934370-26-1(6), Campanita Bks.) Editorial Campana.

Lyons, Fergus. Muckeen & the Big Freeze. 2012. (Pandas Ser.: 39). (ENG., Illus.). 64p. (J). pap. 9.95 (978-1-84717-243-3(1)) O'Brien Pr., Ltd., The IRL. Dist: Dufour Editions, Inc.

MacDonald, Betty Bard. Happy Birthday, Mrs. Piggle-Wiggle. Boiger, Alexandra, illus. 2007. (Mrs. Piggle-Wiggle Ser.). 193p. (J). (gr. 3-7). lib. bdg. 16.89 (978-0-06-072813-7(2)) HarperCollins Pubs.

—Hello, Mrs. Piggle-Wiggle. Knight, Hilary & Boiger, Alexandra, illus. 2007. (ENG.). 176p. (J). (gr. 3-7). 16.99 (978-0-397-31715-8(8)); pap. 5.99 (978-0-06-440149-4(9)) HarperCollins Pubs.

—Mrs. Piggle-Wiggle. Knight, Hilary & Boiger, Alexandra, illus. rev. ed. 2007. (ENG.). 144p. (J). (gr. 3-7). 16.99 (978-0-397-31712-7(3)) HarperCollins Pubs.

—Mrs. Piggle-Wiggle. Boiger, Alexandra, illus. rev. ed. 2007. (Trophy Bk.). (ENG.). 144p. (J). (gr. 3-7). pap. 5.99 (978-0-06-440148-7(0)) HarperCollins Pubs.

MacDonald, George. The Elect Lady. 2008. 148p. pap. 13.95 (978-1-60664-101-9(8)) Aegypan.

—Home Again. 2009. 124p. 22.95 (978-1-60664-613-7(3)); pap. 10.95 (978-1-60664-351-8(7)) Rodgers, Alan Bks.

MacDonald, Margaret Read & Macdonald, Margaret. Farmyard Jamboree. 2012. (978-1-84686-718-7(5)) Barefoot Bks., Ltd.

MacLachlan, Patricia. Kindred Souls. (J). (gr. 1-5). 2013. (ENG.). 144p. pap. 5.99 (978-0-06-052299-5(2)) 2012. (ENG.). 128p. 16.99 (978-0-06-052297-1(6)) 2012. 128p. lib. bdg. 17.89 (978-0-06-052298-8(4)) HarperCollins Pubs. (Tegen, Katherine Bks).

—Nora's Chicks. Brown, Kathryn, illus. 2013. (ENG.). 40p. (J). (gr. -1-2). 15.99 (978-0-7636-4753-7(5)) Candlewick Pr.

—Sarah, Plain & Tall: 30th Anniversary Edition. 2015. (J). lib. bdg. 17.20 (978-0-606-37247-3(4)) Turtleback Bks.

—The True Gift. Floca, Brian, illus. 2013. (ENG.). 112p. (J). (gr. 2-6). pap. 6.99 (978-1-4424-8858-8(1), Atheneum Bks. for Young Readers) Simon & Schuster Children's Publishing.

—The True Gift: A Christmas Story. Floca, Brian, illus. 2009. (ENG.). 96p. (J). (gr. 2-6). 14.99 (978-1-4169-9081-9(X), Atheneum Bks. for Young Readers) Simon & Schuster Children's Publishing.

—What You Know First. 2007. 17.00 (978-0-7569-7908-9(0)) Perfection Learning Corp.

MacNeil, Ben. The Farmer & His Animals. Smith, Charlie E. T., illus. 2013. 26p. pap. (978-1-927625-02-6(5)) Quarter Castle Publishing.

Madison, Mike. No Time to Nap. Peterson, Mary, illus. 2007. (J). (gr. -1-3). (978-1-59714-046-1(5)) Heyday.

Madou, Carol. When Pigs Can Fly! 2011. 40p. pap. 18.99 (978-1-4567-3534-0(9)) AuthorHouse.

Mae, Darcie. Sammy & Robert. 2008. 24p. pap. 24.95 (978-1-60474-811-6(7)) America Star Bks.

Malnor, Carol L. & Hunner, Trina L. Molly's Organic Farm. Hunner, Trina L., illus. 2012. (ENG., Illus.). 32p. (J). (gr. k-4).

16.95 *(978-1-58469-166-2(2))*; pap. 8.95 *(978-1-58469-167-9(0))* Dawn Pubns.
Mamburay, Yankuba & Mamburay, Khadijah. A Day at Grandma's Farm. 2011. 20p. pap. 24.95 *(978-1-4560-6707-6(9))* America Star Bks.
Marchini, Tracy. Chicken Wants a Nap. Felix, Monique, illus. 2017. (ENG.). 24p. (J). (gr. 1-3). 17.99 ***(978-1-56846-308-7(1)***, Creative Editions) Creative Co., The.
Marinaro, Stacy. Annabelle & the Meteor. 2008. 32p. pap. 8.95 *(978-1-4357-2841-7(6))* Lulu Pr., Inc.
Marsh, Scott. Hannah & the Golden Swan. 2011. 216p. pap. 24.95 *(978-1-4626-1084-6(6))* America Star Bks.
Marshall, Linda Elovitz. The Passover Lamb. Mai-Wyss, Tatjana, illus. 2013. (ENG.). 32p. (J). (gr. 1-4). 17.99 *(978-0-307-93177-1(3)*, Random Hse. Bks. for Young Readers) Random Hse. Children's Bks.
Martelli, Dawn. Like Me. Wharton, Jennifer Heyd, illus. 2004. (J). *(978-1-893516-01-4(6))* Our Child Pr.
Martin, Joanna F. Betsey's Wishes. 2010. (Illus.). 255p. (J). (gr. 3-6). 9.80 *(978-0-7399-2424-2(9))* Rod & Staff Pubs., Inc.
Mathews, Leslie. The Sheep Go on Strike. Dumont, Jean-françois, illus. 2014. (ENG.). 34p. (J). 16.00 *(978-0-8028-5470-4(2)*, Eerdmans Bks For Young Readers) Eerdmans, William B. Publishing Co.
Mathieson, Karen. Duel or Duet: Book Two of the Rosemary Ridge Trilogy. 2013. 160p. (J). pap. 7.99 *(978-1-940350-05-9(0))* Portable COO, The.
—Thirteen Times Three: Book One of the Rosemary Ridge Trilogy. 2013. 164p. (J). pap. 7.99 *(978-1-940350-02-8(6))* Portable COO, The.
May, Gary L. The Wilkins Family Farm, 1 vol. Monks, Christian, illus. 2009. 75p. pap. 19.95 *(978-1-4489-2605-3(X))* America Star Bks.
Mayer, Mercer. All That I Can Be. 2017. (Pictureback(R) Ser.). (ENG., Illus.). 48p. (J). (gr. -1-2). 5.99 ***(978-0-399-55377-6(0)***, Random Hse. Bks. for Young Readers) Random Hse. Children's Bks.
Mayr, Diane. Run, Turkey, Run! Rader, Laura, illus. 2009. (ENG.). 32p. (J). (gr. -1-2). pap. 7.99 *(978-0-8027-8481-0(X)*, 9780802784810, Bloomsbury USA Childrens) Bloomsbury Publishing USA.
McClurkan, Rob. What to Doodle? on the Farm. 2013. (ENG.). 64p. (J). (gr. k-3). pap. 1.50 *(978-0-486-49230-8(3))* Dover Pubns., Inc.
McConchie, Lyn. Autumn of the Wild Poney. 2012. (ENG.). 126p. (YA). pap. 12.00 *(978-1-936021-40-6(4)*, Banana Oil Bks.) Cyberwizard Productions.
—Winter of Waiting. 2015. (YA). (gr. 5-18). pap. 15.00 *(978-1-936021-55-0(2)*, Banana Oil Bks.) Cyberwizard Productions.
McConney, Aldith Olive. Stargazing in Autumn. 2013. 20p. pap. 17.99 *(978-1-4817-1040-4(0))* AuthorHouse.
McDougal-Littell Publishing Staff. Literature Connections English: Where the Red Fern Grows. 2004. (McDougal Littell Literature Connections Ser.). (ENG.). 328p. (gr. 7-7). 16.90 *(978-0-395-77528-8(0)*, 2-80097) Great Source Education Group, Inc.
McGougan, Kathy. Buddy on the Farm. 2010. (J). pap. 4.50 *(978-1-934887-23-3(4))* Buddy Bks. Publishing.
McKay, Sindy. We Read Phonics-the Garden Crew. Johnson, Meredith, illus. 2011. 32p. (J). 9.95 *(978-1-60115-345-6(7))*; pap. 4.99 *(978-1-60115-346-3(5))* Treasure Bay, Inc.
McMullan, Margaret. When I Crossed No-Bob. 2009. (ENG.). 224p. (J). (gr. 2-5). pap. 7.99 *(978-0-547-23763-3(4))* Houghton Mifflin Harcourt Publishing Co.
McOmber, Rachel B., ed. McOmber Phonics Storybooks: In the Dell. rev. ed. (Illus.). (J). *(978-0-944991-32-9(7))* Swift Learning Resources.
McQuinn, Anna. Colm's Lambs. Young, Paul, illus. 2014. (ENG.). 32p. (J). pap. 13.95 *(978-1-84717-339-3(X))* O'Brien Pr., Ltd., The IRL. Dist: Dufour Editions, Inc.
Meachen Rau, Dana. En la Granja. 2007. (¡A Divertirnos! Ser.). (SPA., Illus.). 24p. (gr. k-1). lib. bdg. 15.95 *(978-0-7614-2778-0(3)*, Benchmark Bks.) Marshall Cavendish Corp.
—On a Farm. 2007. (Fun Time Ser.). (Illus.). 24p. (gr. k-1). lib. bdg. 15.95 *(978-0-7614-2605-9(1)*, Benchmark Bks.) Marshall Cavendish Corp.
Mead, Jay. A Little Farm Story. 2010. 31p. pap. 10.00 *(978-0-9815560-4-8(3))* Harbor Mountain Pr.
Meddaugh, Susan. Martha Habla: Martha, la Perra Pastora/Martha Speaks: Farm Dog Martha (Bilingual Reader) 2016. (Martha Speaks Ser.). (ENG., Illus.). 24p. (J). (gr. -1-3). 12.99 *(978-0-544-64103-7(5)*, HMH Books For Young Readers) Houghton Mifflin Harcourt Publishing Co.
Meister, Victoria Buhlig. Our Playtime Friend. 2011. 28p. 13.59 *(978-1-4567-2883-0(0))* AuthorHouse.
Menix, Cinda. Tenbrook Farms. Menix, Cinda & McGuire, Bryan, illus. 2007. 67p. (J). (gr. 4-7). per. 23.99 *(978-1-59879-338-3(1))* Lifevest Publishing, Inc.
Mertz, Alyssa. The Lucky Farm Boy, 1 vol. Crum, A. M., illus. 2009. 28p. pap. 24.95 *(978-1-60813-892-0(5))* PublishAmerica, Inc.
Meyer, Linda. Jones & the Great Act. 2009. 118p. pap. 9.99 *(978-0-557-17339-6(6))* Lulu Pr., Inc.
Miller Cormier, Susan. Life on the Farm. 2007. (Illus.). 28p. (J). pap. 12.78 *(978-1-4251-1913-3(1))* Trafford Publishing.
Miller, Judith J. Just Too Little. Panse, Sonal, illus. 2013. 16p. pap. 9.95 *(978-1-61633-413-0(4))* Guardian Angel Publishing, Inc.
Mills, Judith Christine & Mills, Judith C. The Painted Chest. rev. ed. 2008. (ENG., Illus.). 32p. (J). (gr. k). *(978-1-55263-809-5(X))* Me to We.
Milord, Susan. The Ghost on the Hearth. Dabcovich, Lydia, illus. 2003. (Vermont Folklife Center Children's Book Ser.). (ENG.). 32p. (J). (gr. -1-3). 15.95 *(978-0-916718-18-3(2))* Vermont Folklife Ctr.
Mitter, Matt. Little People on the Farm. 2015. (ENG.). 16p. (J). (gr. -1-k). 12.99 *(978-0-7944-3322-2(7))* Reader's Digest Assn., Inc., The.
Molly's Magic: Evaluation Guide. 2006. (J). *(978-1-55942-417-2(6))* Witcher Productions.
Molski, Carol. Swimming Sal. DePalma, Mary Newell, illus. 2009. 36p. (J). (gr. -1-3). 17.00 *(978-0-8028-5327-1(7)*, Eerdmans Bks For Young Readers) Eerdmans, William B. Publishing Co.
Montanari, Susan McElroy. My Dog's a Chicken. Wilsdorf, Anne, illus. 2016. (ENG.). 40p. (J). (gr. -1-3). 16.99 *(978-0-385-38490-2(4)*, Schwartz & Wade Bks.) Random Hse. Children's Bks.
Moon, Jo, illus. Old MacDonald Had a Farm. 2016. (Carousel Bks.). (ENG.). 10p. (J). (gr. -1 — 1). bds. 8.99 *(978-0-7641-6859-8(2))* Barron's Educational Series, Inc.
Moore, Leslie. Guess What Ryan Saw at the Farm. 2008. 32p. pap. 19.50 *(978-1-4357-5024-1(1))* Lulu Pr., Inc.
Moreton, Clara. Frank & Fanny: A Rural Story. 2007. (ENG.). 66p. per. 16.99 *(978-1-4346-2717-9(9))*; per. 18.99 *(978-1-4346-2723-0(3))* Creative Media Partners, LLC.
Morpurgo, Michael. Farm Boy. Foreman, Michael, illus. 2007. (ENG.). 76p. (J). (gr. 4-7). pap. 15.99 *(978-1-84365-090-4(8))* Pavilion Bks. GBR. Dist: Independent Pubs. Group.
—Out of the Ashes. 1. unabr. ed. 2012. (ENG., Illus.). 128p. (J). (gr. 4-7). pap. 9.95 *(978-1-4472-0733-7(5))* Pan Macmillan GBR. Dist: Independent Pubs. Group.
Mosier, Pamela. Elizabeth, the Eastern Gray Squirrel. 2008. 44p. pap. 18.95 *(978-1-4357-5407-2(7))* Lulu Pr., Inc.
Moss, Marissa. Rose's Journal: The Story of a Girl in the Great Depression. 2003. (Young American Voices Ser.). (ENG., Illus.). 56p. (J). (gr. 2-5). pap. 7.99 *(978-0-15-204605-7(4))* Houghton Mifflin Harcourt Publishing Co.
—Rose's Journal: The Story of a Girl in the Great Depression. 2004. (Young American Voice Bks.). (Illus.). (gr. 3-7). 17.00 *(978-0-7569-4230-4(6))* Perfection Learning Corp.
Moulton, Mark Kimball. The Very Best Pumpkin. Good, Karen Hillard, illus. 2010. (ENG.). 32p. (J). (gr. -1-3). 12.99 *(978-1-4169-8288-3(4)*, Simon & Schuster/Paula Wiseman Bks.) Simon & Schuster/Paula Wiseman Bks.
Muhammad, Shahid. The Adventures of the Math Doctor: Book One: King Jafiz & the Evil Farmer Nimra. 2007. (J). per. 7.95 *(978-1-59872-778-4(8))* Instant Pub.
Mullendore, Bryan L. Scott's Many Adventures. 2010. 54p. pap. 22.95 *(978-0-557-63648-8(5))* Lulu Pr., Inc.
Mullican, Judy. Fall on the Farm. Gray, Stacy A., illus. l.t. ed. 2005. (Hrl Board Book Ser.). (J). (gr. -1-k). pap. 10.95 *(978-1-57332-323-9(3)*, HighReach Learning, Incorporated) Carson-Dellosa Publishing, LLC.
Mullins, Norman D. Mountain Boy: The Adventures of Orion Saddler. 2004. 104p. (YA). per. 9.95 *(978-0-9724867-4-3(7))* Woodland Pr., LLC.
Murdock, Catherine Gilbert. Dairy Queen. 2007. (ENG.). 304p. (YA). (gr. 7-12). pap. 9.99 *(978-0-618-86335-8(4))* Houghton Mifflin Harcourt Publishing Co.
—Front & Center. 2011. (ENG.). 288p. (YA). (gr. 7). pap. 8.99 *(978-0-547-40305-2(4))* Houghton Mifflin Harcourt Publishing Co.
—The off Season. 2011. (ENG.). 304p. (YA). (gr. 7). pap. 8.99 *(978-0-618-93493-5(6))* Houghton Mifflin Harcourt Publishing Co.
Murphy, Mary. How Kind! Murphy, Mary, illus. 2004. (ENG., Illus.). 24p. (J). (gr. k-k). bds. 6.99 *(978-0-7636-2307-4(5))* Candlewick Pr.
Murray, Alison. The House That Zack Built. Murray, Alison, illus. 2016. (ENG., Illus.). 32p. (J). (-k). 16.99 *(978-0-7636-7844-9(9))* Candlewick Pr.
Nash, Margaret. Hetty's New Hat. Impey, Martin, illus. 2005. (Reading Corner Ser.). 24p. (J). (gr. k-3). lib. bdg. 22.80 *(978-1-59771-007-7(5))* Sea-To-Sea Pubns.
Nast, Thomas, illus. The Fat Boy. 2011. (American Antiquarian Society Ser.). (ENG.). 24p. (gr. 1). 24.95 *(978-1-4290-9736-9(7))* Applewood Bks.
Nelson, Mary Beth & Linn, Laurent, illus. Elmo's Big Word Book/el Libro Grande de Palabras de Elmo. Barrett, John E., photos by. 2006. (Elmo's Big Word Book/el Libro Grande de Palabras de Elmo Ser.). (SPA, ENG, MUL & ANG.). 12p. (J). (gr. -1 — 1). bds. 8.95 *(978-0-87358-906-2(8))* Cooper Square Publishing Llc.
Newell, Stephanie Jordy. Nite, Nite Farm. 2009. 24p. pap. 12.98 *(978-1-4490-0170-4(X))* AuthorHouse.
Newman, Robin. A Wilcox & Griswold Mystery: the Case of the Missing Carrot Cake. Zemke, Deborah, illus. 2015. (Wilcox & Griswold Mystery Ser.). (ENG.). 40p. (J). (gr. -1-3). 15.95 *(978-1-939547-17-0(2))* Creston Bks.
Newton, Jill, illus. Crash Bang Donkey! 2015. 32p. (J). *(978-1-4896-3858-8(X))* Weigl Pubs., Inc.
Nickerson, Sara. The Secrets of Blueberries, Brothers, Moose & Me. 2015. (ENG.). 336p. (J). (gr. 5). 16.99 *(978-0-525-42654-7(X)*, Dutton Books for Young Readers) Penguin Young Readers Group.
Nicodemus, Laura Konger. Growing up on the Farm in The 1930s' 2011. 60p. pap. 24.20 *(978-1-4269-3201-4(4))* Trafford Publishing.
Night & Day Studios. Peekaboo Barn Farm Day. Night & Day Studios, illus. 2017. (Peekaboo Ser.). (ENG., Illus.). 20p. (J). (— 1). bds. 7.99 *(978-0-7636-7566-0(0)*, Candlewick Entertainment) Candlewick Pr.
Nobisso, Josephine. Francis Woke up Early. Hyde, Maureen, illus. 2011. (ENG.). 32p. (J). (gr. k-2). 17.95 *(978-0-940112-20-9(5))*; pap. 9.95 *(978-0-940112-22-3(1))* Gingerbread Hse.
Noble, Trinka Hakes. Apple Tree Christmas. Noble, Trinka Hakes, illus. 2005. (Holiday Ser.). (ENG., Illus.). 32p. (J). (gr. -1-3). 16.95 *(978-1-58536-270-7(0))* Sleeping Bear Pr.
Noisy Farm. (Push & Pop Ser.). 5p. bds. *(978-1-4054-8635-4(X))* Parragon, Inc.
Nordqvist, Sven. The Birthday Cake: The Adventures of Pettson & Findus. 2015. (Adventures of Pettson & Findus Ser.). (ENG., Illus.). 32p. (J). 17.95 *(978-0-7358-4203-8(5))* North-South Bks., Inc.
Northfield, Gary. Derek the Sheep. Northfield, Gary, illus. 2009. (ENG., Illus.). 64p. (J). (gr. k-2). 16.95 *(978-0-7475-9424-6(4))* Bloomsbury Publishing Plc GBR. Dist: Independent Pubs. Group.
Nosy Crow Staff. Bizzy Bear: Fun on the Farm. Davies, Benji, illus. 2011. (Bizzy Bear Ser.). (ENG.). 8p. (J). (gr. k — 1). bds. 6.99 *(978-0-7636-5879-3(0)*, Nosy Crow) Candlewick Pr.
—Cuddly Cow: A Farm Friends Sound Book. Scheffler, Axel, illus. 2017. (Farm Friends Sound Book Ser.). (ENG.). 12p. (J). (— 1). bds. 9.99 *(978-0-7636-9325-1(1)*, Nosy Crow) Candlewick Pr.
—Higgly Hen: A Farm Friends Sound Book. Scheffler, Axel, illus. 2017. (Farm Friends Sound Book Ser.). (ENG.). 12p. (J). (— 1). bds. 9.99 *(978-0-7636-9324-4(3)*, Nosy Crow) Candlewick Pr.
Oceanak, Karla. Cahoots. Spanjer, Kendra, illus. 2011. (Aldo Zelnick Comic Novel Ser.: 3). (ENG.). 151p. (J). (gr. 3-7). 12.95 *(978-1-934649-08-4(2))* Bailiwick Pr.
O'Donnell, Liam. Daisy on the Farm. 2005. (ENG., Illus.). 32p. (J). (gr. -1-2). 9.95 *(978-1-59249-452-1(8)*, 1B037) Soundprints.
—Daisy on the Farm. Hatala, Dan, illus. 2005. (Pet Tales Ser.). (ENG.). 32p. (J). (gr. -1-2). 2.95 *(978-1-59249-451-4(X)*, 1B036) Soundprints.
—Daisy the Farm Pony. Hatala, Dan, illus. 2005. (Pet Tales Ser.). (ENG.). 32p. (J). (gr. -1 — 1). 4.95 *(978-1-59249-450-7(1)*, 1B035) Soundprints.
Oja, L. G. Little Miss Izzy's Adventures - Miss Izzy & the Monsters. 2013. 24p. pap. *(978-1-4602-1421-3(8))* FriesenPress.
Old MacDonald's Farm. 2005. (J). bds. 6.99 *(978-0-9753127-6-6(6))* Family Bks. at Home.
Oldcome, Michelle. Landy Saves the Day. 2009. (Illus.). 32p. pap. 12.49 *(978-1-4490-0574-0(8))* AuthorHouse.
Oldfield, Jenny. Skye - The Champion, Bk. 13. (Illus.). 122p. (J). pap. 7.99 *(978-0-340-69985-0(X))* Hodder & Stoughton GBR. Dist: Trafalgar Square Publishing.
—Sorrel the Substitute, Bk. 12. (Illus.). 120p. (J). pap. 7.99 *(978-0-340-69984-3(1))* Hodder & Stoughton GBR. Dist: Trafalgar Square Publishing.
—Stevie the Rebel. (Home Farm Twins Ser.: Vol. 9). (Illus.). 128p. (J). pap. 7.99 *(978-0-340-68992-9(7))* Hodder & Stoughton GBR. Dist: Trafalgar Square Publishing.
—Sultan the Patient, Vol. 2. (Illus.). 119p. (J). pap. 7.99 *(978-0-340-69983-6(3))* Hodder & Stoughton GBR. Dist: Trafalgar Square Publishing.
Oliver, Andrew. Scrambled. 2007. 288p. (J). per. 12.95 *(978-0-9661009-8-3(0))* Adams-Pomeroy Pr.
Olson, John J. Wild Child & Annie. 2010. 44p. pap. 26.49 *(978-0-557-32534-4(X))* Lulu Pr., Inc.
On the Farm. 2004. (Out & about Ser.). 12p. (J). bds. 4.99 *(978-1-85997-805-4(3))* Byeway Bks.
Orzechowski, Shawneen. Sarah's Secret: Civil War Deserter at Fredericksburg. 2011. 104p. (J). pap. 8.95 *(978-1-57249-400-8(X)*, White Mane Kids) White Mane Publishing Co., Inc.
Oulton, Harry. Heather's Piglets. 2017. (Pig Called Heather Ser.: 3). (ENG., Illus.). 240p. (J). (gr. 4-7). pap. 8.99 ***(978-1-84812-479-0(1))*** Bonnier Publishing GBR. Dist: Independent Pubs. Group.
—A Pig Called Heather. 2015. (ENG.). 192p. (J). (gr. 3-7). 16.95 *(978-0-8234-3290-5(4))* Holiday Hse., Inc.
Oulton, Harry. The Return of a Pig Called Heather. 2017. (Pig Called Heather Ser.: 2). (ENG., Illus.). 192p. (J). (gr. 4-7). pap. 8.99 ***(978-1-84812-473-8(2))*** Bonnier Publishing GBR. Dist: Independent Pubs. Group.
Pakkala, Christine. Last-But-Not-Least Lola & the Wild Chicken. Hoppe, Paul, illus. 2014. (Last-But-Not-Least Lola Ser.). (ENG.). 216p. (J). (gr. 2-5). 15.95 *(978-1-59078-983-4(0))* Boyds Mills Pr.
Parker, Amy. Night Night, Farm, 1 vol. Allyn, Virginia, illus. 2016. (Night Night Ser.). (ENG.). 20p. (J). bds. 8.99 *(978-0-7180-8831-6(X))* Nelson, Thomas Inc.
Parker, Beth. Tom Turtle Visits Grandma's Farm. 2011. 28p. pap. 24.95 *(978-1-4560-1000-3(X))* America Star Bks.
Parker, Emma. At the Farm. 2010. (Illus.). pap. *(978-1-877547-94-2(8))* First Edition Ltd.
Parker, Gilles N. A Visit to the Farm: A Vet Makes New Friends. 2013. 24p. pap. 24.99 *(978-1-4669-3524-2(3))* Trafford Publishing.
Parks, Carmen. Farmers Market. Martinez, Edward, illus. 2003. (Green Light Readers Level 2 Ser.). (ENG.). 24p. (J). (gr. -1-3). pap. 3.95 *(978-0-15-204841-9(3))* Houghton Mifflin Harcourt Publishing Co.
—Farmers Market/Día de Mercado. Flor Ada, Alma & Campoy, F. Isabel, trs. from ENG. Martinez, Edward, illus. 2010. (Green Light Readers Level 2 Ser.). (SPA & ENG.). 28p. (J). (gr. -1-3). pap. 3.99 *(978-0-547-36900-6(X))* Houghton Mifflin Harcourt Publishing Co.
Parragon Publishing Staff. Busy Day at the Farm. (Busy Books Large Ser.). *(978-1-4054-7875-5(6))* Parragon, Inc.
Parramore, Helen. The Fragments of Fern Valley. 2009. 112p. pap. 10.95 *(978-1-4401-2943-8(6))* iUniverse, Inc.
Paulsen, Gary. Harris & Me. 2007. (ENG., Illus.). 176p. (J). (gr. 5-7). pap. 6.99 *(978-0-15-205880-7(X))* Houghton Mifflin Harcourt Publishing Co.
—Harris & Me. 2007. 157p. (gr. 5). 15.95 *(978-0-7569-7810-5(6))* Perfection Learning Corp.
—The Haymeadow. unabr. ed. 2004. 195p. (J). (gr. 5-9). pap. 36.00 incl. audio *(978-0-8072-0452-8(8)*, Listening Library) Random Hse. Audio Publishing Group.
—The Winter Room. l.t. ed. 2005. 105p. pap. 10.95 *(978-0-7862-7251-8(1)*, Large Print Pr.) Thorndike Pr.
Pellowski, Anne. First Farm in the Valley: Anna's Story. Sharpe, Roseanne, illus. 2008. 194p. (J). pap. 12.95 *(978-1-932350-24-1(1))* Bethlehem Bks.
—Stairstep Farm: Anna Roses's Story. Sharpe, Roseanne, illus. 2011. 182p. (J). pap. 12.95 *(978-1-932350-40-1(3))* Bethlehem Bks.
Persaud, Sandhya S. One Day. Ahmad, Maryam & Ramotar, Alexandra, illus. 2009. 12p. pap. 12.99 *(978-1-4389-4437-1(3))* AuthorHouse.
Peterson, Mary & Rofé, Jennifer. Piggies in the Pumpkin Patch. Peterson, Mary, illus. 2010. (ENG., Illus.). 28p. (J). (gr. -1-2). 16.95 *(978-1-57091-460-7(5))*; pap. 7.95 *(978-1-57091-461-4(3))* Charlesbridge Publishing, Inc.
Peterson, Shelley. Sundancer. Drake, Marybeth, illus. rev. ed. 2007. (ENG.). 264p. (YA). (gr. 7-12). pap. 7.95 *(978-1-55263-842-2(1))* Leaf Storm Pr.
Phanton, Richard G. Frankie. Baker, David, illus. 2012. 40p. 24.95 *(978-1-4560-3509-9(6))* America Star Bks.
Pienkowski, Jan. Ferme. (Folio Ser.). (FRE.). (J). 5.95 *(978-2-07-056307-4(3))* Schoenhof's Foreign Bks., Inc.
Pierre Brignaud, Pierre, illus. Baby Caillou: My Farm Friends: A Finger Fun Book. 2015. (Baby Caillou Ser.). (ENG.). 16p. (J). (— 1). bds. 6.99 *(978-2-89718-177-2(X))* Caillouet, Gerry.
Pigram, John. My Dog Jack. 2009. 20p. pap. 14.64 *(978-1-4269-2038-7(5))* Trafford Publishing.
Pitt, Sarah. Peek a Boo! Farm. 2009. (Little Peek a Boo Bks.). (Illus.). (J). bds. 9.99 *(978-1-934650-59-2(5))* Just For Kids Pr., LLC.
Plume, Ilse, illus. & adapted by. The Farmer in the Dell. Plume, Ilse, adapted by. 2010. (ENG.). 32p. pap. 8.95 *(978-1-56792-390-2(9))* Godine, David R. Pub.
Pochocki, Ethel. A Penny for a Hundred. Owens, Mary Beth, illus. 2005. 31p. (J). (gr. 2-5). pap. 9.95 *(978-1-883937-52-2(3))* Bethlehem Bks.
—A Penny for a Hundred. 2014. (ENG., Illus.). 32p. (J). (gr. -1-3). 15.95 *(978-1-60893-311-2(3))* Down East Bks.
Polk, Douglas. Marie's Home, 1 vol. 2009. 48p. pap. 16.95 *(978-1-60749-454-6(X))* America Star Bks.
Popper, Garry. High Noon in Didley Pidley. Forshaw, John, illus. 2004. (Bret the Vet Ser.). 40p. 7.00 *(978-1-84161-013-9(5))* Ravette Publishing, Ltd. GBR. Dist: Parkwest Pubns., Inc.
Porter, Pamela. The Crazy Man. 2013. 164p. pap. *(978-1-4596-6446-3(9))* ReadHowYouWant.com, Ltd.
Powers, Nelda Means & Terrell, Caitlyn. Puddle Puppy Goes to the Farm. 2012. 32p. pap. *(978-1-77067-628-2(7))* FriesenPress.
Pratta, Barbara. The Weeping Willow Tree. 2011. 344p. 28.95 *(978-1-4634-0762-9(9))*; pap. 17.99 *(978-1-4634-0763-6(7))* AuthorHouse.
Price, Bc. Mabel & Her Litter Of. 2008. 132p. pap. 12.00 *(978-0-615-20692-9(1))* BCP Pubns.
Priddy, Roger. Barnyard Fun! 2015. (Little Friends Ser.). (ENG., Illus.). 12p. (J). (gr. -1 — 1). bds. 8.99 *(978-0-312-51841-7(2)*, 9780312518417, Priddy Bks.) St. Martin's Pr.
—Farm. 2017. (Sticker Friends Ser.). (ENG., Illus.). 24p. (J). pap. 4.99 *(978-0-312-52155-4(3)*, 9780312521554, Priddy Bks.) St. Martin's Pr.
—Ten Barnyard Babies. 2009. (ENG.). 10p. (J). (gr. -1-k). bds. 15.99 *(978-0-312-50584-4(1)*, 9780312505844, Priddy Bks.) St. Martin's Pr.
—Toddler Town: Farm. 2014. (Toddler Town Ser.). (ENG.). 10p. (J). (gr. -1 — 1). bds. 7.99 *(978-0-312-51671-0(1)*, 9780312516710, Priddy Bks.) St. Martin's Pr.
Pringle, Cindy & Pringle, Kirby. Happy Tails: The Call of Nature. 2008. (ENG., Illus.). 32p. (J). (gr. 2-7). *(978-0-9777126-1-8(3))* Dogtown Artworks.
Prinz, Yvonne. All You Get Is Me. 2010. (ENG.). 288p. (YA). (gr. 9-18). 16.99 *(978-0-06-171580-8(8))* HarperCollins Pubs.
Provensen, Alice. A Day in the Life of Murphy. Provensen, Alice, illus. unabr. rev. ed. 2005. (Illus.). (J). (gr. -1-2). 28.95 incl. audio compact disk *(978-1-59519-538-8(6))* Live Oak Media.
—A Day in the Life of Murphy. Provensen, Alice, illus. 2003. (ENG., Illus.). 40p. (J). (gr. -1-3). 17.99 *(978-0-689-84884-1(6)*, Simon & Schuster Bks. For Young Readers) Simon & Schuster Bks. For Young Readers.
—A Day in the Life of Murphy. Provensen, Alice, illus. 2006. (ENG., Illus.). 40p. (J). (gr. -1-3). reprint ed. 7.99 *(978-1-4169-1800-4(0)*, Simon & Schuster/Paula Wiseman Bks.) Simon & Schuster/Paula Wiseman Bks.
Pryor, Bonnie. Greenbrook Farm. 2013. (ENG.). 36p. (J). (gr. -1-3). 14.99 *(978-1-4424-8873-1(5)*, Atheneum Bks. for Young Readers) Simon & Schuster Children's Publishing.
Puckett, Annie Marie. Pedro Learns about Salvation. 2006. 56p. per. 9.95 *(978-1-57258-453-2(X)*, 945-6314) TEACH Services, Inc.
Pyatt, K. C. Rebekah on the Farm. 2012. 132p. 29.99 *(978-1-4797-2188-7(3))*; pap. 19.99 *(978-1-4797-2187-0(5))* Xlibris Corp.
Quirk, Katie. A Girl Called Problem. 2013. (ENG., Illus.). 256p. (J). pap. 8.50 *(978-0-8028-5404-9(4)*, Eerdmans Bks For Young Readers) Eerdmans, William B. Publishing Co.
Randolph, Robert. Ben the Flying Cat, 1 vol. Sappington, Ray, illus. 2009. 30p. pap. 24.95 *(978-1-60749-088-3(9))* America Star Bks.
Random House. Bigfoot's Spring Break (Teenage Mutant Ninja Turtles) Spaziante, Patrick, illus. 2016. (Pictureback(R) Ser.). (ENG.). 16p. (J). (gr. -1-2). 4.99 *(978-1-101-93174-5(4)*, Random Hse. Bks. for Young Readers) Random Hse. Children's Bks.
Raschka, Chris. Farmy Farm. Raschka, Chris, illus. 2011. (ENG., Illus.). 8p. (J). (gr. -1 — 1). bds. 8.99 *(978-0-545-21981-5(7)*, Orchard Bks.) Scholastic, Inc.
Rau, Dana Meachen. Corn Aplenty. Iwai, Melissa, illus. 2009. (Step into Reading Ser.). (ENG.). 32p. (J). (gr. -1-1). 3.99 *(978-0-375-85575-7(0)*, Random Hse. Bks. for Young Readers) Random Hse. Children's Bks.
Rawlings, Marjorie Kinnan. The Yearling. Wyeth, N. C., illus. 2013. (Scribner Classics Ser.). (ENG.). 416p. (J). (gr. 5-9). 29.99 *(978-1-4424-8209-8(5)*, Atheneum Bks. for Young Readers) Simon & Schuster Children's Publishing.
Ray, Mary Lyn. Go to Sleep, Little Farm. Neal, Christopher Silas, illus. (ENG.). (J). 2015. 38p. (— 1). bds. 8.99 *(978-0-544-57916-3(X))* 2014. 40p. (gr. -1-3). 16.99 *(978-0-544-15014-0(7))* Houghton Mifflin Harcourt Publishing Co. (HMH Books For Young Readers).
Reader's Digest Editors. Talking Puzzles Sounds on the Farm. 2009. (ENG., Illus.). 10p. (J). (gr. -1). bds. 15.99 *(978-0-7944-1821-2(X))* Reader's Digest Assn., Inc., The.
Reasoner, Charles. A Day at the Farm. 2009. (Inside Outside Board Bks.). (Illus.). 10p. (J). bds. 10.99 *(978-1-934650-54-7(4))* Just For Kids Pr., LLC.
—Farm. 2009. (Learning Tab Board Bks.). (Illus.). 10p. (J). (gr. -1-k). bds. 9.99 *(978-1-934650-78-3(1))* Just For Kids Pr., LLC.
—Inside Old Mcdonald's Barn. Reasoner, Charles, illus. 2007. (Story Book Ser.). (Illus.). 12p. (J). (gr. k). bds. *(978-1-84666-287-4(7)*, Tide Mill Pr.) Top That! Publishing PLC.
Rebert, Brenda. Rooster Went A' Walkin' 2009. 28p. pap. 13.99 *(978-1-4389-3414-3(9))* AuthorHouse.
Reed, Amy. Over You. (ENG., Illus.). (YA). (gr. 9). 2014. 336p. pap. 9.99 *(978-1-4424-5697-6(3))* 2013. 320p. 16.99 *(978-1-4424-5696-9(5))* Simon Pulse. (Simon Pulse).
Reed, Jennifer. Time for a Trim. Mones, Marc, illus. 2012. (ENG.). 24p. (gr. 1-2). pap. 8.95 *(978-1-61810-319-2(9))* Rourke Educational Media.

EFG

Reely, Mary Katharine. The Blue Mittens. Wiese, Kurt, illus. 2011. 164p. 41.95 (978-1-258-10114-5(9)) Literary Licensing, LLC.

Reimiller, Diane L. A Duck Named Quackers, 1 vol. Jastrzebski, Brandy, illus. 2009. 12p. pap. 24.95 (978-1-60836-771-9(1)) America Star Bks.

Reynolds, Aaron. Chicks & Salsa. Bogan, Paulette, illus. 2007. (ENG.). 32p. (J). (gr. 1-3). pap. 7.99 (978-1-59990-099-5(8), 9781599900995, Bloomsbury USA Childrens) Bloomsbury Publishing USA.

Reynolds, Carl Stanley. The Turkey Mountain Gang: The Adventures Begin. 2009. 52p. pap. 22.50 (978-1-4389-7496-5(5)) AuthorHouse.

Rhodes, Carol. Gene the Pumpkin Man. 2008. 32p. pap. 16.95 (978-1-4327-1416-1(3)) Outskirts Pr., Inc.

Richards, Laura E. Marie. 2004. reprint ed. pap. 15.95 (978-1-4179-3794-3(7)) Kessinger Publishing, LLC.

Richards, Laura Elizabeth Howe. Queen Hildegarde. 2007. 92p. per. (978-1-4068-3867-1(5)) Echo Library.

Richardson, Steve. Billy's Mountain. Leonhard, Herb, illus. 2007. 52p. 14.95 (978-0-9786422-0-4(1)) Impossible Dreams Publishing Co.

Ridge, Yolanda. Road Block, 1 vol. 2012. (Orca Young Readers Ser.). (ENG.). 168p. (J). (gr. 3-6). pap. 7.95 (978-1-4598-0045-8(1)) Orca Bk. Pubs. USA.

Roberts, Pauline J. Girls Crying. 2007. 9.00 (978-0-8059-8863-5(7)) Dorrance Publishing Co., Inc.

Robertson, James & Fitt, Matthew. Katie's Ferm: A Hide-and-Seek Book for Wee Folk. Sutherland, Karen, illus. 2007. (ENG.). 18p. (J). (-k). bds. 10.99 (978-1-84502-149-8(5)) Black and White Publishing Ltd. GBR. Dist: Independent Pubs. Group.

Robinson, Michelle. Goodnight Tractor: The Perfect Bedtime Book! 2015. (Goodnight Ser.). (ENG., Illus.). 32p. (J). (gr. -1 — 1). pap. 7.99 (978-1-4380-0664-2(0)) Barron's Educational Series, Inc.

Roller, Ellen. Trading Places. Shea, Gary, illus. 2008. (J). pap. 11.95 (978-0-9792645-0-4(2)) Edgewood Publishing, LLC.

Root, Phyllis. Anywhere Farm. Karas, G. Brian, illus. 2017. (ENG.). 32p. (J). (-k). 16.99 (978-0-7636-7499-1(0)) Candlewick Pr.

—Snowy Sunday. Craig, Helen, illus. 2015. (ENG.). 24p. (J). (-k). 14.99 (978-0-7636-3627-2(4)) Candlewick Pr.

Rosa-Mendoza, Gladys. Animals at the Farm/Animales de la Granja. Wolff, Jason, illus. 2004. (English-Spanish Foundations Ser.). (SPA & ENG.). 20p. (J). (gr. -1). bds. 6.95 (978-1-931398-13-8(5)) Me+Mi Publishing.

Rosen, Michael. Farmyard Read & Play Set, 3 vols. Langley, Jonathan, illus. 2008. (ENG.). 96p. (J). (gr. -1-k). bds. 19.95 (978-0-00-725969-4(7)) HarperCollins Pubs. Ltd. GBR. Dist: Independent Pubs. Group.

—Running with Trains: A Novel in Poetry & Two Voices. 2012. (ENG.). 112p. (J). (gr. 5). 15.95 (978-1-59078-863-9(X), Wordsong) Boyds Mills Pr.

Rosen, Michael J. Don't Shoot! Chase R.'S Top Ten Reasons Not to Move to the Country. 2007. (ENG., Illus.). 160p. (YA). (gr. 7). per. 6.99 (978-0-7636-2088-2(2)) Candlewick Pr.

Rosoff, Meg. How I Live Now. 2006. (ENG.). 224p. (YA). (gr. 7-12). reprint ed. pap. 8.99 (978-0-553-37605-0(5), Lamb, Wendy Bks.) Random Hse. Children's Bks.

Rossing, Nina. Fjord Blue. 2016. (ENG., Illus.). (YA). 27.99 **(978-1-63533-016-8(5))**; 256p. (J). pap. 16.99 (978-1-63476-385-1(8)) Dreamspinner Pr. (Harmony Ink Pr.).

Rostoker-Gruber, Karen & Isaacs, Ronald H. Farmer Kobi's Hanukkah Match. Decker, C. B., illus. 2015. (J). (978-1-68115-501-2(X)); pap. (978-0-87441-924-5(7)) Behrman Hse., Inc.

Roy, Lillian Elizabeth. Little Woodcrafters' Fun on the Farm. Rogers, Walter S., illus. 2011. 232p. 46.95 (978-1-258-09314-3(6)) Literary Licensing, LLC.

Ruggiero, Wilma. The Orange Barnge. 2011. 40p. 24.00 (978-1-4520-9778-7(X)) AuthorHouse.

Ruiz, Joseph J. Manuel & the Magic Ring. 2003. (SPA & ENG., Illus.). 108p. (J). pap. 12.95 (978-0-86534-399-3(3)) Sunstone Pr.

Rylant, Cynthia. Henry & Mudge & the Wild Goose Chase. Bracken, Carolyn, illus. 2004. (Henry & Mudge Ser.). 40p. (gr. k-2). 14.00 (978-0-7569-3366-1(8)) Perfection Learning Corp.

—Henry & Mudge & the Wild Goose Chase. Bracken, Carolyn, illus. 2004. (Henry & Mudge Ready-To-Read Ser.: 26). 40p. (gr. k-2). lib. bdg. 13.55 (978-1-4176-4340-0(4), Turtleback) Turtleback Bks.

Rylant, Cynthia & Bracken, Carolyn. Henry & Mudge & the Wild Goose Chase. 2004. (Henry & Mudge Ser.: 23). (ENG., Illus.). 40p. (J). (gr. k-2). pap. 3.99 (978-0-689-83450-9(0), Simon Spotlight) Simon Spotlight.

—Henry & Mudge & the Wild Goose Chase. Bracken, Carolyn, illus. 2003. (Henry & Mudge Ser.: 23). (ENG., Illus.). 40p. (J). (gr. k-2). 16.99 (978-0-689-81172-2(1), Simon Spotlight) Simon Spotlight.

S., Lisa Hamilton Ed. From Plot to Plate: "a Story of Ambition & Dedication" 2012. 28p. pap. 15.99 (978-1-4691-4283-8(X)) Xlibris Corp.

Salway, Ruth. Through Rose Coloured Glasses. 2006. (Illus.). 252p. per. (978-1-905529-58-2(9)) Grosvenor Hse. Publishing Ltd.

Sammel, Rochelle. Tales of Two Mouse Brothers. 2008. 45p. pap. 24.95 (978-1-4241-9798-9(8)) America Star Bks.

Sandwall-Bergstrom, Martha. Goldie at the Farm. Stalsjo, Eva, illus. 24p. 17.95 (978-0-86315-485-0(9)) Floris Bks. GBR. Dist: SteinerBooks, Inc.

Sankey, Erica. Magic Dust. 2010. 32p. pap. 16.49 (978-1-4490-0893-2(3)) AuthorHouse.

Sanschagrin, Joceline. Caillou - A Day at the Farm. Brignaud, Pierre, illus. 2016. (Step by Step Ser.). (ENG.). 24p. (J). (gr. k-k). bds. 5.99 (978-2-89718-254-0(7)) Caillouet, Gerry.

Santa Claus & the Kids on the Farm. 2004. (J). per. 15.99 (978-0-9753533-0-1(6)) Golden Eagle Publishing Hse., Inc.

Santillo, LuAnn. Down on the Farm, 6 vols. Santillo, LuAnn, ed. 2003. (Half-Pint Kids Readers Ser.). (Illus.). 42p. (J). (gr. -1-1). pap. 6.95 (978-1-59256-056-1(3)) Half-Pint Kids, Inc.

—Six Jobs. Santillo, LuAnn, ed. 2003. (Half-Pint Kids Readers Ser.). (Illus.). 7p. (J). (gr. -1-1). pap. (978-1-59256-058-5(X)) Half-Pint Kids, Inc.

Santoro, Scott. Farm-Fresh Cats. 2006. (Illus.). 32p. (J). (gr. -1-2). 16.89 (978-0-06-078179-8(3)) HarperCollins Pubs.

Sargent, Dave & Sargent, David M., Jr. Speedy Roadrunner: Helping Others, 19 vols., Vol. 17. Lenoir, Jane, illus. 2003. (Feather Tales Ser.: 17). 42p. (J). pap. 10.95 (978-1-56763-752-6(3)) Ozark Publishing.

Sargent, Pat L. Jaguar #8 (PB), 6 vols. 2007. (Barney the Bear Killer Ser.: 8). (YA). pap. 9.95 (978-1-59381-425-0(9)) Ozark Publishing.

Schaefer, Lola M. Please Pass the Manners! Mealtime Tips for Everyone. Lewis, Kellie, illus. 2009. (ENG.). 12p. (J). (gr. -1-1). 7.99 (978-1-4169-4826-1(0), Little Simon) Little Simon.

Schantz, Sarah Elizabeth. Fig. 2016. (ENG.). 352p. (YA). (gr. 9). pap. 10.99 (978-1-4814-2359-5(2), McElderry, Margaret K. Bks.) McElderry, Margaret K. Bks.

Schertle, Alice. Little Blue Truck Farm Sticker Fun! McElmurry, Jill, illus. 2013. (Little Blue Truck Ser.). (ENG.). 24p. (J). (gr. -1-3). 5.99 (978-0-544-06687-8(1)) Houghton Mifflin Harcourt Publishing Co.

Schippers, Mary Kay. A Year on the Family Farm: And the Life Lessons Learned. 2013. 168p. pap. (978-1-4602-2597-4(X)) FriesenPress.

Schlitz, Laura Amy. The Hired Girl. 2015. (ENG., Illus.). 400p. (J). (gr. 7-10). 17.99 (978-0-7636-7818-0(X)) Candlewick Pr.

—The Hired Girl. 2018. lib. bdg. 22.10 **(978-0-606-40389-4(2))** Turtleback Bks.

Schmidt, Gary D. First Boy. 2007. (ENG.). 224p. (YA). (gr. 5-9). per. 10.99 (978-0-312-37149-4(7), 9780312371494) Square Fish.

Schneeberger, Thomas M. Catch the Wind & Spin, Spin, Spin, 1 vol. 2008. (ENG.). 23p. 24.95 (978-1-4241-8874-1(1)) America Star Bks.

Scholl, Jenny. Four Farm Boys: Turkey Times. Casto, Christina, illus. 2010. 36p. (J). pap. 13.95 (978-1-4327-5886-8(1)) Outskirts Pr., Inc.

Schories, Pat, illus. Biscuit Visits the Farm. 2012. (J). (978-1-4351-4383-8(3), HarperFestival) HarperCollins Pubs.

Schotter, Roni. Go, Little Green Truck! Kuo, Julia, illus. 2016. (ENG.). 32p. (J). 16.99 (978-0-374-30070-8(4), 9780374300708, Farrar, Straus & Giroux (BYR)) Farrar, Straus & Giroux.

Schrader, Margaret. Green Knee-High Farm. Schrader, Kimberly, illus. 2009. 28p. pap. 12.95 (978-1-60844-000-9(1)) Dog Ear Publishing, LLC.

Schröder, Monika. The Dog in the Wood. 2009. (ENG.). 168p. (J). (gr. 5-9). 17.95 (978-1-59078-701-4(3), Front Street) Boyds Mills Pr.

Schulz, Hal. Dak's Country Visit: The Painter & His Cat. 2011. 32p. pap. (978-1-4269-6743-6(8)) Trafford Publishing (UK) Ltd.

Seyfert, Ella Maie. Amish Moving Day. Jones, Henrietta, illus. 2011. 132p. 40.95 (978-1-258-01315-8(0)) Literary Licensing, LLC.

Shah, Idries. The Farmer's Wife. Santiago, Rose Mary, illus. 2005. 32p. (J). (gr. -1-3). pap., pap. 6.99 (978-1-883536-49-7(9), Hoopoe Bks.) I S H K.

—The Farmer's Wife (la Esposa Del Granjero) PB/CD Combo Bilingual. Santiago, Rose Mary, illus. 2005. (ENG & SPA.). (J). (gr. -1-18). pap. 18.95 incl. audio compact disk (978-1-883536-70-1(7), FAWCB4, Hoopoe Bks.) I S H K.

—The Farmer's Wife/la Esposa Del Granjero HB/CD Combo Bilingual. de Gonzales, Angelica Villagran, tr. Santiago, Rose Mary, illus. 2005. (ENG & SPA.). 32p. (J). (gr. 4-7). 28.95 incl. audio compact disk (978-1-883536-69-5(3), FAWCB3, Hoopoe Bks.) I S H K.

Shanks, Cindy. Emilia Camina la Vereda de Borregos. 2009. 48p. pap. 19.95 (978-1-4490-2388-1(6)) AuthorHouse.

Shannon, George. Wise Acres. Zemke, Deborah, illus. 2004. (ENG.). 40p. (J). (gr. -1-7). 15.95 (978-1-59354-041-8(8), Handprint Bks.) Chronicle Bks. LLC.

Sharkey-Wilmot. The Mysterious Golden Horse. 2007. 168p. 22.95 (978-0-595-69325-2(3)); per. 12.95 (978-0-595-45162-3(4)) iUniverse, Inc.

Sheehan, Peter. Willy Wagtail grows Up. 2010. 32p. pap. 19.99 (978-1-4461-3281-4(1)) Lulu Pr., Inc.

Siegrist, Bonnie. Little Farm down the Lane -Book IV. 2007. pap. 10.99 (978-1-60034-912-6(9)) Salem Author Services.

Siegrist, Bonnie Bedi. Little Farm down the Lane Book V. 2008. 124p. pap. 11.99 (978-1-60647-848-6(6)) Salem Author Services.

Silvano, Wendi. Turkey Trouble, 0 vols. 2009. (ENG., Illus.). 32p. (J). (gr. -1-2). 15.99 (978-0-7614-5529-5(9), 9780761455295, Two Lions) Amazon Publishing.

Silver Dolphin & Daly, Bob. Popposites - On the Farm. 2017. (Popposites! Ser.). (ENG., Illus.). 12p. (J). (gr. -1). 12.99 (978-1-62686-906-6(5), Silver Dolphin Bks.) Readerlink Distribution Services, LLC.

Silver Dolphin en Español Editors. Un Dia en la Granja. 2003. (SPA.). 60p. 9.95 (978-970-718-110-6(9), Silver Dolphin en Español) Advanced Marketing, S. de R. L. de C. V. MEX. Dist: Bilingual Pubns. Co., The.

Silver, Pattie, illus. Kitty's Barn. 2005. 12p. (J). bds. 9.95 (978-1-58117-385-7(7), Intervisual/Piggy Toes) Bendon, Inc.

Simmons, Lynn Sheffield. Sugar Lump, the Orphan Calf, 1 vol. 2003. (ENG., Illus.). 50p. (J). (gr. k-5). 12.95 (978-1-58980-216-2(0)) Pelican Publishing Co., Inc.

Sims, Nat. Peekaboo Barn. Tabor, Nathan, illus. 2014. (Peekaboo Ser.). (ENG.). 20p. (J). (— 1). bds. 7.99 (978-0-7636-7557-8(1), Candlewick Entertainment) Candlewick Pr.

Singhose, Rose. Granny's giggles book Two. 2010. 35p. pap. 16.95 (978-0-557-59182-4(1)) Lulu Pr., Inc.

Sipp, Leora Janson. Emma & Sara Learn about Harvest Time. 2008. 40p. pap. 14.95 (978-1-934925-01-0(2), Eloquent Bks.) Strategic Book Publishing & Rights Agency (SBPRA).

Sisco, Joann Ellen. Midnight at Faraway Farm. 2008. 79p. pap. 19.95 (978-1-60474-777-5(3)) America Star Bks.

Skyscrapers & Farms. 2005. (J). per. 5.00 (978-1-59872-020-4(1)) Instant Pub.

Smiley, Jeremy. The Flood of Mice City 2, 1 vol. 2010. 36p. 24.95 (978-1-4489-7617-1(0)) PublishAmerica, Inc.

Smith, Alex T. Claude in the Country, 1 vol. Smith, Alex T., illus. 2016. (Claude Ser.). (ENG., Illus.). 96p. (J). (gr. 1-3). 12.95 (978-1-56145-918-6(6)) Peachtree Pubs.

Smith, Debra West. Hattie Marshall & the Prowling Panther, 1 vol. 2005. (Hattie Marshall Ser.). (ENG.). 144p. (J). (gr. 4-6). pap. 7.95 (978-1-56554-940-1(6)) Pelican Publishing Co., Inc.

Smith, Sandra S. The Cost of Eggs: Hill House Farm Series. Mason, Turning Bear, illus. 2012. 24p. 24.95 (978-1-4626-4928-0(9)) America Star Bks.

Sommer, Carl. Your Job Is Easy. James, Kennon, illus. 2014. (J). pap. (978-1-57537-973-9(2)) Advance Publishing, Inc.

—Your Job Is Easy(Tu Trabajo Es Facil) James, Kennon, illus. 2009. (Another Sommer-Time Story Bilingual Ser.). (SPA & ENG.). 48p. (J). lib. bdg. 16.95 (978-1-57537-173-3(1)) Advance Publishing, Inc.

Spalding, Brenda M. Just Batty. Teagle, Caitlyn, illus. 2011. 26p. pap. 12.00 (978-1-61204-156-8(6), Strategic Bk. Publishing) Strategic Book Publishing & Rights Agency (SBPRA).

Spanabel, H. A. Skyler & the Skunks. 2009. 48p. pap. (978-1-84923-954-7(1)) YouWriteOn.

Spinelli, Jerry. Tooter Pepperday. 2004. (Stepping Stone Book Ser.). (ENG., Illus.). 96p. (J). (gr. 1-4). 3.99 (978-0-679-84702-1(2), Random Hse. Bks. for Young Readers) Random Hse. Children's Bks.

Stahler, David, Jr. Gathering of Shades. 2006. (ENG.). 256p. pap. (978-0-06-052296-4(8)) HarperCollins Canada, Ltd.

—A Gathering of Shades. 2005. (ENG.). 304p. (J). 15.99 (978-0-06-052294-0(1), HarperTeen) HarperCollins Pubs.

Stanek, Robert, pseud. The Bugville Critters Visit Garden Box Farms. (ENG.). (J). 2008. 28p. per. 10.99 (978-1-57545-147-3(6)) 2007. (Illus.). 52p. per. 19.95 (978-1-57545-124-4(7)) RP Media.

—Visit Garden Box Farms. 2008. (ENG., Illus.). 28p. (J). pap. 5.29 (978-1-57545-190-9(5)) RP Media.

Stansbie, Stephanie. Farm Fun: A Busy Sticker Activity Book. Nowowiejska, Kasia, illus. 2016. (Little Snappers Ser.). (ENG.). 96p. (J). (gr. -1-1). 9.99 (978-1-58925-318-6(3)) Tiger Tales.

Steele, Michael Anthony. Work This Farm! 2011. (Lego City Ser.). (ENG.). 24p. (J). (gr. -1-k). pap. 3.99 (978-0-545-29857-5(1)) Scholastic, Inc.

Steers, Billy. Lift-The-Flap Tab: Tractor Mac: Friends on the Farm. 2015. (Lift-The-Flap Tab Bks.). (ENG., Illus.). 16p. (J). (gr. -1-k). bds. 8.99 (978-0-374-30168-2(9), 9780374301682) Square Fish.

—Tractor Mac Arrives at the Farm. (Tractor Mac Ser.). (ENG., Illus.). (J). 2016. 24p. pap. 4.99 (978-0-374-30536-9(6), 9780374305369) 2015. 32p. (gr. -1-k). 8.99 (978-0-374-30102-6(6), 9780374301026) Farrar, Straus & Giroux. (Farrar, Straus & Giroux (BYR)).

—Tractor Mac Arrives at the Farm. 2016. (Tractor Mac Ser.). (ENG.). 24p. (J). (gr. -1-k). 14.75 (978-0-606-39287-7(4)) Turtleback Bks.

—Tractor Mac Builds a Barn. 2015. (Tractor Mac Ser.). (ENG., Illus.). 32p. (J). (gr. -1-2). 8.99 (978-0-374-30105-7(0), 9780374301057, Farrar, Straus & Giroux (BYR)) Farrar, Straus & Giroux.

—Tractor Mac Countdown to Christmas. 2016. (Tractor Mac Ser.). (ENG., Illus.). 16p. (J). bds. 6.99 (978-0-374-30120-0(4), 9780374301200, Farrar, Straus & Giroux (BYR)) Farrar, Straus & Giroux.

—Tractor Mac Farm Days. 2016. (Tractor Mac Ser.). (ENG., Illus.). 16p. (J). bds. 5.99 (978-0-374-30117-0(4), 9780374301170, Farrar, Straus & Giroux (BYR)) Farrar, Straus & Giroux.

—Tractor Mac Farmers' Market. 2015. (Tractor Mac Ser.). (ENG., Illus.). 32p. (J). (gr. -1-k). 8.99 (978-0-374-30107-1(7), 9780374301071, Farrar, Straus & Giroux (BYR)) Farrar, Straus & Giroux.

—Tractor Mac Farmers Market: Farmer's Market: Steers, Billy, illus. 2009. (ENG., Illus.). (J). 7.95 (978-0-9826870-1-7(X)) Tractor Mac Inc.

—Tractor Mac New Friend. 2015. (Tractor Mac Ser.). (ENG., Illus.). 32p. (J). (gr. -1-k). 8.99 (978-0-374-30110-1(7), 9780374301101, Farrar, Straus & Giroux (BYR)) Farrar, Straus & Giroux.

—Tractor Mac Teamwork. 2016. (Tractor Mac Ser.). (ENG., Illus.). 32p. (J). 8.99 (978-0-374-30113-2(1), 9780374301132, Farrar, Straus & Giroux (BYR)) Farrar, Straus & Giroux.

—Tractor Mac Worth the Wait. 2017. (Tractor Mac Ser.). (ENG., Illus.). 32p. (J). 8.99 (978-0-374-30115-6(8), 9780374301156, Farrar, Straus & Giroux (BYR)) Farrar, Straus & Giroux.

Steggall, Susan. Following the Tractor. 2015. (ENG., Illus.). 32p. (J). pap. 8.99 (978-1-84780-657-4(0), Frances Lincoln) Quarto Publishing Group UK GBR. Dist: Littlehampton Bk Services, Ltd.

Stephens, Charles Asbury. A Busy Year at the Old Squire's. 2007. 272p. pap. 21.99 (978-1-4346-3560-0(0)); (ENG.). 300p. pap. 23.99 (978-1-4346-3561-7(9)) Creative Media Partners, LLC.

Stewart, Grandmother. George the Rooster Goes to the Apple Orchard. 2007. (ENG., Illus.). 28p. (J). lib. bdg. 14.95 (978-0-9792135-0-2(9)) Rooster Pubns.

Stewart, Maria. An Omelet Fit for a King. Cost, Steve, illus. 2013. 24p. pap. 14.99 (978-1-936453-23-8(1)) Bezalel Bks.

Stine, R. L. Scarecrow Walks at Midnight. 2010. (Classic Goosebumps Ser.: 16). (ENG.). 160p. (J). (gr. 3-7). 6.99 (978-0-545-17801-3(0), Scholastic Paperbacks) Scholastic, Inc.

Stinson, Kathy. A Pocket Can Have a Treasure in It. Betteridge, Deirdre, illus. 2008. (ENG.). 32p. (J). (gr. -1-k). 18.95 (978-1-55451-126-6(7), 9781554511266); pap. 6.95 (978-1-55451-125-9(9), 9781554511259) Annick Pr., Ltd. CAN. Dist: Publishers Group West (PGW).

Stohner, Anu & Wilson, Henrike. Brave Charlotte. Wilson, Henrike, illus. 2005. (ENG., Illus.). 32p. (J). (gr. -1-3). 17.99 (978-1-58234-690-8(9), 9781582346908, Bloomsbury USA Childrens) Bloomsbury Publishing USA.

Stratton-Porter, Gene. At the Foot of the Rainbow. 2007. 180p. 18.95 (978-1-934169-52-0(8)); pap. 7.95 (978-1-934169-53-7(6)) Norilana Bks.

—A Daughter of the Land. 2008. pap. (978-1-84830-034-7(4), Wildhem Pr.) Echo Library.

—A Daughter of the Land. 2007. 340p. 22.95 (978-1-934169-46-9(3)); pap. 11.95 (978-1-934169-47-6(1)) Norilana Bks.

—The Strike at Shane's. 2006. 92p. per. (978-1-4067-9583-7(6), Pierides Pr.) Read Bks.

Stripland, Rubye Weldon. Lucy Bell, Queen of the Pasture Book Four. 2009. 94p. pap. 10.96 (978-1-4357-4742-5(9)) Lulu Pr., Inc.

Stuchner, Joan Betty. Can Hens Give Milk?, 1 vol. Weissmann, Joe, illus. 2013. (ENG.). 32p. (J). (gr. -1-3). 9.95 (978-1-4598-0427-2(9)) Orca Bk. Pubs. USA.

Summer of Dreaming. 2010. (Illus.). 157p. (YA). pap. (978-1-936021-22-2(6), Banana Oil Bks.) Cyberwizard Productions.

Swartz, Patricia. Pig-A-Poo Moves to the Zoo. 2009. (Illus.). 28p. pap. 14.99 (978-1-4490-4616-3(9)) AuthorHouse.

Swindle, Stephanie. Pumpkin Pants. 2009. 32p. pap. 13.95 (978-1-60860-461-6(6), Strategic Bk. Publishing) Strategic Book Publishing & Rights Agency (SBPRA).

Sykes, Julie. That Pesky Dragon. Williamson, Melanie, illus. 2007. 32p. (J). (gr. -1-3). 15.95 (978-1-58925-069-7(9)) Tiger Tales.

Symington, Martha M. Emily: Dream Believe Achieve. Nolan, Amanda M., illus. 2008. 36p. pap. (978-1-897435-21-2(5)) Agio Publishing Hse.

Tafuri, Nancy. Blue Goose. Tafuri, Nancy, illus. 2010. (Classic Board Bks.). (ENG., Illus.). 34p. (J). (gr. -1 — 1). bds. 7.99 (978-1-4169-2835-5(9), Little Simon) Little Simon.

—Blue Goose. Tafuri, Nancy, illus. 2008. (ENG., Illus.). 32p. (J). (gr. -1-3). 17.99 (978-1-4169-2834-8(0), Simon & Schuster Bks. For Young Readers) Simon & Schuster Bks. For Young Readers.

Tatsuyama, Sayuri. Happy Happy Clover, Vol. 2. Tatsuyama, Sayuri, illus. 2009. (ENG., Illus.). 192p. (J). pap. 9.99 (978-1-4215-2657-7(3)) Viz Media.

Taylor, Vernon T. Why Do Dogs Bark? 2012. 24p. pap. 24.95 (978-1-4626-5083-5(X)) America Star Bks.

Teal, Val. The Little Woman Wanted Noise. Lawson, Robert, illus. 2013. (ENG.). 48p. (J). (gr. -1-2). 14.95 (978-1-59017-711-2(8), NYR Children's Collection) New York Review of Bks., Inc., The.

Teckentrup, Britta, illus. Busy Bunny Days: In the Town, on the Farm & at the Port. 2014. (ENG.). 56p. (J). (gr. -1-3). 17.99 (978-1-4521-1700-3(4)) Chronicle Bks. LLC.

Terry-Todd, Terlene. Sweetie's Healthy Start. 2009. 28p. pap. 12.99 (978-1-60693-829-4(0), Strategic Bk. Publishing) Strategic Book Publishing & Rights Agency (SBPRA).

Thermes, Jennifer. Sam Bennett's New Shoes. 2006. (Illus.). (J). 15.95 (978-1-57505-822-1(7), Carolrhoda Bks.) Lerner Publishing Group.

Therriault - Bruder, Dovie G. Life on the Farm: Story One Adventure with the Chickens. 2011. 36p. pap. 15.14 (978-1-4670-3797-6(4)) AuthorHouse.

Theule, Larissa. Fat & Bones. Doyle, Adam S., illus. 2014. (ENG.). 112p. (J). (gr. 4-12). lib. bdg. 16.95 (978-1-4677-0825-8(9), Carolrhoda Bks.) Lerner Publishing Group.

Thomas, E. J. Brooster Rooster: King of the Farmyard, 1 vol. 2009. 22p. pap. 24.95 (978-1-60813-936-1(0)) America Star Bks.

Thomas Nelson. Babytown Noisy Farm. 2015. (ENG., Illus.). 14p. (gr. -1). bds. (978-1-78393-875-9(7)) Make Believe Ideas.

—My Awesome Farm. 2016. (ENG.). 30p. (gr. -1). bds. (978-1-78598-464-8(0)) Make Believe Ideas.

Thompson, Kim Mitzo. Old MacDonald Had a Farm. Girouard, Patrick, illus. 2010. (Padded Board Book W/CD Ser.). 8p. (J). (gr. k-2). bds. 10.99 incl. audio compact disk (978-1-59922-579-1(4)) Twin Sisters IP, LLC.

Thronson, Lloyd. Gomer the Goat & His New Home. 2011. 30p. pap. 16.95 (978-1-4626-1590-2(2)) America Star Bks.

Ticktock Media, Ltd. Staff. Farm. 2009. (Animal Fun Touch & Feel Ser.). (ENG.). 10p. (J). (gr. -1-k). bds. 4.95 (978-1-84696-827-3(5), TickTock Books) Octopus Publishing Group GBR. Dist: Independent Pubs. Group.

Tilson, Gina L. Patches: Adventures of a Country Cavalier. 2011. 48p. pap. 9.99 (978-1-4567-6386-2(5)) AuthorHouse.

Tomaselli, Doris. My Little People Farm (Mi Pequena Granja) Thompson Brothers Staff, illus. 2003. (Lift-The-Flap Ser.). (ENG & SPA.). 5p. (J). (gr. -1-k). bds. 8.99 (978-0-7944-0213-6(5)) Reader's Digest Assn., Inc., The.

Tompkins, Robyn Lee. Miss Molly's Adventure on the Farm: Another great adventure brought to you by Miss Molly & her dog Reyburn. Carson, Shawn, illus. 2006. (J). per. (978-0-9741647-7-9(1)) NRG Pubns.

Top That! Alphabet Farm (large Version) Parry, Jo, illus. 2007. 10p. (J). (gr. -1). (978-1-84666-553-0(1), Tide Mill Pr.) Top That! Publishing PLC.

Torres, J. Checkers & Dot on the Farm. Lum, J., illus. 2013. (Checkers & Dot Ser.). (ENG.). 16p. (J). (— 1). bds. 7.95 (978-1-77049-443-5(X), Tundra Bks.) Tundra Bks. CAN. Dist: Penguin Random Hse. LLC.

Tougas, Chris. Mechanimals, 1 vol. 2012. (ENG.). 32p. (J). (gr. -1-3). 9.95 (978-1-4598-0273-5(X)) Orca Bk. Pubs. USA.

Townsend, Una Belle. Grady's in the Silo, 1 vol. Artley, Bob, illus. 2003. (ENG.). 32p. (J). (gr. k-3). 16.99 (978-1-58980-098-4(2)) Pelican Publishing Co., Inc.

Trapani, Iza. Old Macdonald Had a... Zoo? Trapani, Iza, illus. 2017. (ENG., Illus.). 32p. (J). (-k). lib. bdg. 16.99 **(978-1-58089-729-7(0))** Charlesbridge Publishing, Inc.

Triplett, Annette. From the Farm to You Coloring Book. Vale, Joe, ed. Murphy, Dennis, illus. 2012. 28p. (J). (978-0-933842-34-2(1)) Univ. of Missouri, Extension.

Tub Tales: The Farm. 2003. (Illus.). 10p. (J). 6.00 (978-0-9713507-3-1(6), 844) Panline U.S.A., Inc.

Twohy, Mike. Wake up, Rupert! Twohy, Mike, illus. 2014. (ENG., Illus.). 32p. (J). (gr. -1-3). 16.99 (978-1-4424-5998-4(0), Simon & Schuster/Paula Wiseman Bks.) Simon & Schuster/Paula Wiseman Bks.

Uchida, Yoshiko. Samurai of Gold Hill. Forberg, Ati, illus. 2005. 119p. (J). (gr. 2). per. 8.95 (978-1-59714-015-7(5)) Heyday.

Van Dyne, Edith. Aunt Jane's Nieces at Millville. 2005. 204p. pap. 12.95 (978-1-4218-1126-0(X), 1st World Library - Literary Society) 1st World Publishing, Inc.

Van Frankenhuyzen, Robbyn Smith. Kelly of Hazel Ridge. van Frankenhuyzen, Gijsbert, illus. 3rd rev. ed. 2006. (Hazel Ridge Farm Stories Ser.). (ENG.). 32p. (J). (gr. k-5). 17.95 (978-1-58536-268-4(9)) Sleeping Bear Pr.

Van Leeuwen, Jean. Chicken Soup. Gavril, David, illus. 2009. (ENG.). 40p. (J). (gr. k-2). 16.95 (978-0-8109-8326-7(5), Abrams Bks. for Young Readers) Abrams, Inc.

Van Patter, Bruce. Tucker Took It! 2010. (ENG., Illus.). 32p. (J). (gr. k-2). 16.95 *(978-1-59078-698-7(X))* Boyds Mills Pr.
Villa, Ruben. Granola Farm. 2012. 34p. pap. 11.99 *(978-1-60820-708-4(0))* MLR Pr., LLC.
Vitale, Jill. Freddie: The Free-Range Chicken. 2007. (ENG., Illus.). 28p. (J). (gr. 1-2). 15.95 *(978-0-9767269-6-8(3))* WND Bks., Inc.
Voake, Steve. Daisy Dawson on the Farm. Meserve, Jessica, illus. 2012. (Daisy Dawson Ser.: 5). (ENG.). 96p. (J). (gr. 1-4). 14.99 *(978-0-7636-5882-3(0))* Candlewick Pr.
Voigt, Cynthia. Angus & Sadie. Leigh, Tom, illus. (ENG.). 208p. (J). (gr. 3-7). 2008. pap. 6.99 *(978-0-06-074584-4(3))* 2005. 16.99 *(978-0-06-074582-0(7))* HarperCollins Pubs.
Waddell, Martin. Farmer Duck. Oxenbury, Helen, illus. 2008. (Candlewick Storybook Animations Ser.). (ENG.). 40p. (J). (gr. -1-k). 14.99 *(978-0-7636-3512-1(X))* Candlewick Pr.
Wall, Laura. Goose on the Farm Board Book. Wall, Laura, illus. 2017. (Illus.). 36p. (J). (gr. -1 — 1). bds. 7.99 *(978-0-06-232440-5(3),* HarperFestival) HarperCollins Pubs.
Wallace, Bill. Beauty. 2007. (ENG.). 192p. (J). (gr. 3-7). pap. 6.99 *(978-1-4169-4942-8(9),* Simon & Schuster/Paula Wiseman Bks.) Simon & Schuster/Paula Wiseman Bks.
Wallace, Bonny. The Raymond Wikins' Adventures, Children of Straw. 2009. 70p. pap. 9.95 *(978-1-60860-699-3(6),* Eloquent Bks.) Strategic Book Publishing & Rights Agency (SBPRA).
Wallace, Sandra Neil. Little Joe. Elliott, Mark, illus. 2011. (ENG.). 192p. (J). (gr. 3-7). 6.99 *(978-0-375-85450-7(9),* Yearling) Random Hse. Children's Bks.
Waltz, Dan. Kornstalkers: Corn Maze Massacre. Waltz, Dan, illus. l.t. ed. 2005. (Chilled to the Bone! Ser.: No. 1). (Illus.). 120p. (J). per. 6.99 *(978-0-9741774-3-4(1))* D. W. Publishing.
Wangerin, Walter, Jr. I Am My Grandpa's Enkelin. Tate, Don, illus. 2008. 30p. (J). (gr. 3-7). 18.95 *(978-1-55725-468-9(0))* Paraclete Pr., Inc.
Warburton, Carol. Edge of Night: A Novel. 2004. (Illus.). 278p. pap. 14.95 *(978-1-59156-013-5(6))* Covenant Communications, Inc.
Ward, Joyce Claudine. Nanny the Goat. 2008. 22p. pap. 24.95 *(978-1-4241-9139-0(4))* America Star Bks.
Ward, Terri & Ward, Tom. Aunt Tami's Strawberry Farm. Kindt, Rita, illus. 2010. 38p. pap. 14.50 *(978-1-60693-935-2(1),* Eloquent Bks.) Strategic Book Publishing & Rights Agency (SBPRA).
Watson, Gayle. Catie Corn & the Corn Cops. Fautsch, Jackie, illus. l.t. ed. 22p. (J). 2006. 15.99 *(978-1-59879-098-6(6))* 2005. per. 9.99 *(978-1-59879-079-5(X))* Lifevest Publishing, Inc.
Watson, M. Veg Patch Gang. 2005. (Illus.). 40p. pap. *(978-1-84401-005-9(8))* Athena Pr.
Watson, Mary. The Paper Dragonfly. Watson, Mary, illus. 2007. (ENG., Illus.). 32p. (J). (gr. k-3). 15.95 *(978-0-9726614-3-0(3))* Shenanigan Bks.
Watt, Fiona. Children's Cookbook. Cartwright, Stephen & Sage, Molly, illus. 2006. (Usborne Farmyard Tales Ser.). (ENG.). 48p. (J). 6.99 *(978-0-7945-1418-1(9),* Usborne) EDC Publishing.
—Farm Stroller Book. Baggott, Stella, illus. 2010. 8p. (J). 7.99 *(978-0-7945-2811-9(2),* Usborne) EDC Publishing.
Wegman, William. Farm Days. Wegman, William, illus. 2014. (Penguin Young Readers, Level 2 Ser.). (ENG., Illus.). 32p. (J). (gr. 1-3). pap. 3.99 *(978-0-448-48230-9(4),* Penguin Young Readers) Penguin Young Readers Group.
Weidt, Maryann. Mama Loved to Worry. Balsaitis, Rachael, illus. 2016. (ENG.). 32p. (J). (gr. -1-1). 16.95 *(978-0-87351-994-6(9))* Minnesota Historical Society Pr.
Wellington, Monica. Ana Cultiva Manzanas/Apple Farmer Annie. Del Risco, Eida & del Risco, Eida, trs. from ENG. Wellington, Monica, illus. 2004. (ENG & SPA., Illus.). 32p. (J). (gr. -1-2). 16.99 *(978-0-525-47252-0(5),* Dutton Books for Young Readers) Penguin Young Readers Group.
—Apple Farmer Annie. Wellington, Monica, illus. 2004. (ENG., Illus.). 32p. (J). (gr. -1-2). pap. 6.99 *(978-0-14-240124-8(2),* Puffin Books) Penguin Young Readers Group.
—Apple Farmer Annie Board Book. Wellington, Monica, illus. 2012. (ENG., Illus.). 24p. (J). (gr. -1 — 1). bds. 5.99 *(978-0-8037-3888-1(9),* Dial Bks) Penguin Young Readers Group.
West, Lily June Wolford. A Trip to the Cellar. West, June & Wright, Shannon, illus. 2007. (J). (gr. -1-3). 16.99 *(978-1-59879-347-5(0))* Lifevest Publishing, Inc.
West, Stephen Earl. My Grandfather's Farm. Eller, Jerod R., illus. 2011. 20p. pap. 24.95 *(978-1-4560-6628-4(5))* America Star Bks.
Whelan, Gloria. Farewell to the Island. 2004. 200p. (J). (gr. 4-7). per. 7.95 *(978-1-882376-92-6(7))* Thunder Bay Pr.
—Friend on Freedom River. van Frankenhuyzen, Gijsbert, illus. 2004. (Tales of Young Americans Ser.). (ENG.). 32p. (J). 16.95 *(978-1-58536-222-6(0))* Sleeping Bear Pr.
Whitaker, Alecia. The Queen of Kentucky. 2013. (ENG.). 384p. (YA). (gr. 7-17). pap. 8.99 *(978-0-316-12494-2(X),* Poppy) Little, Brown Bks. for Young Readers.
White, E. B. Charlotte's Web. Williams, Garth, illus. 2005. (Charming Classics). 192p. (J). pap. 7.99 *(978-0-06-084594-0(5),* HarperFestival) HarperCollins Pubs.
—Charlotte's Web. movie tie-in ed. 2006. (Charlotte's Web Ser.). (ENG., Illus.). 192p. (J). (gr. 4-7). per. 7.99 *(978-0-06-112026-8(X))* HarperCollins Pubs.
—Charlotte's Web. Williams, Garth, illus. movie tie-in ed. 2006. (Charlotte's Web Ser.). (J). 192p. mass mkt. 7.99 *(978-0-06-122874-2(5),* Harper Trophy);Set. pap. 19.99 *(978-0-06-121502-5(3))* HarperCollins Pubs.
—Charlotte's Web. Williams, Garth, illus. 2004. (CHI.). 158p. (YA). pap. *(978-957-08-2568-8(5))* Linking Publishing Co., Ltd.
—Charlotte's Web. Williams, Garth, illus. 184p. (J). pap. 5.95 *(978-0-8072-8305-9(3),* Listening Library) Random Hse. Audio Publishing Group.
—Charlotte's Web. unabr. ed. 2004. 184p. (J). (gr. 3-7). pap. 36.00 incl. audio *(978-0-8072-8304-2(5),* YYA156SP, Listening Library) Random Hse. Audio Publishing Group.
—Charlotte's Web. 2012. (J). (gr. 3-6). 18.40 *(978-0-8085-3772-4(5),* Turtleback) Turtleback Bks.
—Wilbur's Adventure: A Charlotte's Web Picture Book. Kneen, Maggie, illus. 2008. (Charlotte's Web Ser.). 32p. (J). (gr. k-2). lib. bdg. 17.89 *(978-0-06-078165-1(3))* HarperCollins Pubs.
White, E. B. & DiCamillo, Kate. Charlotte's Web. Williams, Garth, illus. (ENG.). 192p. (J). (gr. 3-7). 2012. 16.99 *(978-0-06-026385-0(7))* 2012. 8.99 *(978-0-06-112495-2(8))* 2012. pap. 8.99 *(978-0-06-440055-8(7))* 2006. 16.99 *(978-0-06-088261-7(1))* HarperCollins Pubs.
White, Pam. Buddy's Trip to the Blueberry Farm. 2009. 16p. pap. 8.95 *(978-1-4389-7931-1(2))* AuthorHouse.
Whybrow, Ian. Faraway Farm. Ayliffe, Alex, illus. 2006. (ENG.). 32p. (J). (gr. -1-2). lib. bdg. 15.95 *(978-1-57505-938-9(X),* Carolrhoda Bks.) Lerner Publishing Group.
Wild, Margaret. Piglet & Granny. King, Stephen Michael, illus. 2009. (ENG.). 32p. (J). (gr. -1-k). 15.95 *(978-0-8109-4063-5(9),* Abrams Bks. for Young Readers) Abrams, Inc.
Wilder, Laura Ingalls. Farmer Boy. Williams, Garth, illus. 2008. (Little House Ser.: 2). (ENG.). 384p. (J). (gr. 3-7). pap. 7.99 *(978-0-06-440003-9(4))* HarperCollins Pubs.
—Farmer Boy. 2007. (Little House Ser.). 384p. (J). (gr. 3-7). pap., pap., pap. 6.99 *(978-0-06-088538-0(6),* Harper Trophy) HarperCollins Pubs.
—Farmer Boy. Williams, Garth, illus. 2004. (Little House Ser.: 2). (ENG.). 384p. (J). (gr. 3-7). pap. 8.99 *(978-0-06-058182-4(4))* HarperCollins Pubs.
—The First Four Years. Williams, Garth, illus. (Little House Ser.: 9). (ENG.). 160p. (J). (gr. 3-7). 2008. pap. 7.99 *(978-0-06-440031-2(X))* 2004. pap. 8.99 *(978-0-06-058188-6(3))* HarperCollins Pubs.
Will Mcallister. Sam Rivers & the Night Rustlers. 2009. 88p. pap. 9.95 *(978-0-595-46287-2(1))* iUniverse, Inc.
Williams, Billie A. Fourteen Is Too Many: The Survivors. 2013. 24p. pap. 24.95 *(978-1-63004-179-3(3))* America Star Bks.
—Haying Time: Fire. 2013. 24p. pap. 24.95 *(978-1-63004-305-6(2))* America Star Bks.
Williams, Heather. Farmer Boy Goes West. 2012. (Little House Sequel Ser.). (ENG.). 320p. (J). (gr. 3-7). 16.99 *(978-0-06-124251-9(9))* HarperCollins Pubs.
Williams, Jacklyn. Feliz Dia de Gracias, Gus!, 1 vol. Abello, Patricia, tr. from ENG. Cushman, Doug, illus. 2006. (Read-It! Readers en Español: Gus el Erizo Ser.). (SPA.). 32p. (gr. k-3). lib. bdg. 19.99 *(978-1-4048-2690-8(4),* Easy Readers) Picture Window Bks.
Williams, T. H. Jo's Bright New Day. 2008. 20p. pap. 24.95 *(978-1-60474-949-6(0))* America Star Bks.
Williamson, Sharon. Grandma Says, Don't Climb the Peach Tree. 2011. 18p. pap. 16.95 *(978-1-4560-8794-4(0))* America Star Bks.
Williamson, Stafford. Puppy Goes to Lambergarten. 2005. 11p. 11.18 *(978-1-4116-3854-9(9))* Lulu Pr., Inc.
Willis, Cynthia Chapman. Dog Gone. 2009. (ENG.). 240p. (J). (gr. 3-7). pap. 17.99 *(978-0-312-56113-0(X),* 9780312561130) Square Fish.
Wilson, Annette. K'Nyah's Big Celebration. 2012. 28p. pap. 24.95 *(978-1-4626-9925-4(1))* America Star Bks.
Wilson, Douglas. Maude, the Flop-Eared Mule. Fore, Elizabeth, illus. 2012. 38p. 24.95 *(978-1-4626-7455-8(0))* America Star Bks.
Wilson, Karma. Beautiful Babies. Wilson, Karma, photos by. 2009. (ENG., Illus.). 14p. (J). (gr. -1 — 1). bds. 6.99 *(978-1-4169-1908-7(2),* Little Simon) Little Simon.
Yocum, Randi. Cowpie Corgi: A Dog's Tale. Yocum, Sam, 2nd, photos by. 2007. (Illus.). 32p. (J). lib. bdg. 16.98 *(978-0-9663629-3-0(4))* By Grace Enterprises.
Yolen, Jane. Centaur Rising. 2014. (ENG.). 272p. (J). (gr. 3-7). 16.99 *(978-0-8050-9664-4(7),* 9780805096644, Holt, Henry & Co. Bks. For Young Readers) Holt, Henry & Co.
—The Scarecrow's Dance. Ibatoulline, Bagram, illus. 2009. (ENG.). 32p. (J). (gr. -1-3). 16.99 *(978-1-4169-3770-8(6),* Simon & Schuster Bks. For Young Readers) Simon & Schuster Bks. For Young Readers.
Yoon, Salina. Old MacDonald Had a Farm. 2008. (Salina Yoon Bks.). (ENG., Illus.). 12p. (J). (gr. -1-k). bds. 6.99 *(978-0-8431-2817-8(8),* Price Stern Sloan) Penguin Young Readers Group.
Yoon, Salina, illus. Pretend & Play: on the Farm. 2013. (Pretend & Play Ser.). (ENG.). 12p. (J). (gr. -1). bds. 12.95 *(978-1-60710-635-7(3),* Silver Dolphin Bks.) Readerlink Distribution Services, LLC.
Young, Pippa, illus. On the Farm. (Match & Twist Ser.). (J). 11.99 *(978-0-525-47054-0(9),* Dutton Juvenile) Penguin Publishing Group.
Yoyo Books Staff. On the Farm: Learning Words Series. 2005. 12p. bds. *(978-90-5843-605-4(5))* YoYo Bks.
—On the Farm: One Minute Goodnight Stories. 2004. 40p. bds. *(978-90-5843-580-4(6))* YoYo Bks.
Zarins, Kim. The Helpful Puppy. McCully, Emily Arnold, illus. 2012. (ENG.). 32p. (J). 16.95 *(978-0-8234-2318-7(2))* Holiday Hse., Inc.
—The Helpful Puppy. McCully, Emily Arnold, illus. 2013. (ENG.). 32p. (J). pap. 6.99 *(978-0-8234-2919-6(9))* Holiday Hse., Inc.
Zeeh, Shawn. Tucker Farm: Under the Big Top. 2012. 36p. pap. 21.99 *(978-1-4771-2685-1(6))* Xlibris Corp.
Zink, Michelle. A Walk in the Sun. 2016. 336p. (YA). (gr. 8). 17.99 *(978-0-06-243446-3(2),* HarperTeen) HarperCollins Pubs.
Zolan, Donald, illus. My Favorite Farm Animal Friends. 2010. (ENG.). 5p. (J). bds. 5.99 *(978-0-7369-2663-8(1))* Harvest Hse. Pubs.
Zwaid, John & DesRochers, Diane O. Mahmoud Meets Moses. Zwaid, John, illus. 2012. (Illus.). 26p. pap. 14.99 *(978-0-9838832-9-6(7))* WRB Pub.

FARM LIFE—POETRY

Riley, James Whitcomb. Riley Farm-Rhymes. Vawter, Will, ed. 2013. (Library of Indiana Classics Ser.). (ENG., Illus.). 192p. 18.00 *(978-0-253-00951-7(0),* 0253009510) Indiana Univ. Pr.

FARM MACHINERY

see Agricultural Machinery

FARM MANAGEMENT

Rudenko, Dennis. Planning My Farm: Reason with Shapes & Their Attributes. 2014. (Rosen Common Core Math Readers Ser.). (Illus.). 24p. (J). (gr. 2-3). (ENG.). pap. 8.25 *(978-1-4777-4887-9(3));* lib. bdg. 23.60 *(978-1-4777-6442-8(9))* Rosen Publishing Group, Inc., The. (PowerKids Pr.).

FARM MECHANICS

see Agricultural Machinery

FARM PRODUCE

Borth, Teddy. Crops on the Farm, 1 vol. 2014. (On the Farm Ser.). (ENG.). 24p. (J). (gr. 4-8). lib. bdg. 28.50 *(978-1-62970-052-6(5))* ABDO Publishing Co.
Borth, Teddy, et al. Cultivos de la Granja. 2015. (En la Granja Ser.). (SPA., Illus.). 24p. (gr. k-1). pap. 7.95 *(978-1-4966-0447-7(4))* Capstone Classroom.
Cornell, Kari. Plants We Eat & How They Grow. 2016. (Illus.). 32p. (J). pap. *(978-0-87659-710-1(X))* Gryphon Hse., Inc.
Dickmann, Nancy. El Mundo de la Granja, 6 vols., Set. Incl. Alimentos de la Granja. 22.65 *(978-1-4329-5308-9(7));* Animales de la Granja. 22.65 *(978-1-4329-5306-5(0));* Estaciones en la Granja. 22.65 *(978-1-4329-5311-9(7));* Las Plantas de la Granja. (Illus.). 22.65 *(978-1-4329-5310-2(9));* Máquinas de la Granja. 22.65 *(978-1-4329-5307-2(9));* Trabajos en la Granja. 22.65 *(978-1-4329-5309-6(5));* (gr. -1-1). (Mundo de la Granja Ser.). (SPA., Illus.). 24p. 2011. Set lib. bdg. 135.90 *(978-1-4329-5312-6(5),* Bellota) Heinemann-Raintree.
Lindeen, Mary. A Visit to the Market. 2015. (BeginningtoRead Ser.). (ENG.). 32p. (J). (gr. k-2). lib. bdg. 22.60 *(978-1-59953-692-7(7))* Norwood Hse. Pr.
Morgan, Sally. How We Use Plants for Making Everyday Things. 2009. (How We Use Plants Ser.). 32p. (gr. 2-5). pap. 10.60 *(978-1-4358-2614-4(0),* Rosen Classroom) Rosen Publishing Group, Inc., The.
—How We Use Plants to Make Everyday Things. 2008. (How We Use Plants Ser.). (Illus.). 32p. lib. bdg. 26.50 *(978-1-4042-4424-5(7),* PowerKids Pr.) Rosen Publishing Group, Inc., The.
Owen, Ruth. Vegetables! Life on a Produce Farm. 2012. (Food from Farmers Ser.). (Illus.). 32p. (J). (gr. k-3). pap. 11.75 *(978-1-61533-540-4(4));* lib. bdg. 26.50 *(978-1-61533-531-2(5))* Windmill Bks.
Peterson, Cris. Harvest Year. Upitis, Alvis, photos by. 2009. (ENG., Illus.). 32p. (J). pap. 10.95 *(978-1-59078-783-0(8))* Boyds Mills Pr.
Reader, Jack. A Trip to the Farmers' Market. 2016. (PowerKids Readers: My Community Ser.). 00024p. (J). (gr. k-k). pap. 8.25 *(978-1-4994-2779-0(4),* PowerKids Pr.) Rosen Publishing Group, Inc., The.
Regis, Natalie. Genetically Modified Crops & Food. 2015. (Biotechnology Revolution Ser.). (ENG., Illus.). 128p. (J). (gr. 10-10). 38.75 *(978-1-62275-578-3(2),* Britannica Educational Publishing) Rosen Publishing Group, Inc., The.
Sertori, Trisha. Fruits, Vegetables, & Legumes. 2008. (Body Fuel for Healthy Bodies Ser.). 32p. (gr. 4-18). lib. bdg. 18.56 *(978-0-7614-3799-4(1),* Benchmark Bks.) Marshall Cavendish Corp.
—Grains, Bread, Cereal & Pasta. 2008. (Body Fuel for Healthy Bodies Ser.). 32p. (gr. 4-18). lib. bdg. 18.56 *(978-0-7614-3800-7(9),* Benchmark Bks.) Marshall Cavendish Corp.
Smundak, Katharina. The Truth Behind GMOs. 2017. (J). pap. ***(978-1-4994-3927-4(X),*** Rosen Reference) Rosen Publishing Group, Inc., The.

FARM PRODUCE—MARKETING

Bowden, Rob. Food Industry. 2010. (Closer Look: Global Industries Ser.). (ENG., Illus.). 48p. (J). lib. bdg. 29.25 *(978-1-4358-9630-7(0),* Rosen Reference) Rosen Publishing Group, Inc., The.
Career Opportunities in the Food & Beverage Industry. 2010. (Career Opportunities Ser.). 320p. (C). (gr. 9-18). 49.50 *(978-0-8160-7612-3(X),* Ferguson Publishing Co.); pap. 18.95 *(978-0-8160-7613-0(8),* Checkmark Bks.) Facts On File, Inc.
Francis, Amy. The Local Food Movement. 2010. (At Issue Ser.). (ENG.). 128p. (gr. 10-12). 39.40 *(978-0-7377-4888-8(5));* pap. 27.80 *(978-0-7377-4889-5(3),* Greenhaven Pr., Inc.) Cengage Gale.
Graham, Ian. Food Technology. 2010. (New Technology Ser.). (ENG., Illus.). 48p. (J). 23.99 *(978-0-237-53425-7(8))* Evans Brothers, Ltd. GBR. Dist: Independent Pubs. Group.
Greathead, Helen. My Chocolate Bar & Other Foods. 2016. (Well Made, Fair Trade Ser.). (ENG., Illus.). 32p. (J). (gr. 5-8). *(978-0-7787-2714-9(9))* Crabtree Publishing Co.
Green, Sara. Kellogg's. 2015. (Brands We Know Ser.). (ENG., Illus.). 24p. (J). (gr. 3-8). lib. bdg. 25.95 *(978-1-62617-207-4(2),* Pilot Bks.) Bellwether Media.
Mason, Paul. How Big Is Your Food Footprint? 2009. (Environmental Footprints Ser.). 32p. (gr. 4). 28.50 *(978-0-7614-4413-8(0))* Marshall Cavendish Corp.
Senker, Cath. Heinz: The Story Behind the Iconic Business. 2016. (Big Business Ser.). (ENG., Illus.). 32p. (J). (gr. 4-6). pap. 11.99 *(978-0-7502-8952-8(X),* Wayland) Hachette Children's Group GBR. Dist: Hachette Bk. Group.
Sévigny, Eric, illus. Caillou: Fresh from the Farm. 2013. (Ecology Club Ser.). (ENG.). 24p. (J). (gr. -1-1). 5.99 *(978-2-89718-026-3(9))* Caillouet, Gerry.
Spilsbury, Richard & Spilsbury, Louise. From Farm to Table. 2010. (Food & Farming Ser.). (Illus.). 32p. (YA). (gr. 4-7). lib. bdg. 25.25 *(978-1-61532-580-1(8))* Rosen Publishing Group, Inc., The.
Wood, Alix. Food Design. 2017. (Design It! Ser.). 32p. (gr. 3-4). pap. 63.00 ***(978-1-5382-0782-6(6))*** Stevens, Gareth Publishing LLLP.

FARMING

see Agriculture

FARMS

Amery, Heather. The Farm. Cartwright, Stephen, illus. 2008. (Usborne Talkabout Bks.). 12p. (J). (gr. -1-3). bds. 8.99 *(978-0-7945-1795-3(1),* Usborne) EDC Publishing.
Andrews, Alexa. On a Farm. Keimig, Candice, illus. 2013. (Penguin Young Readers, Level 1 Ser.). (ENG.). 32p. (J). (gr. k-1). mass mkt. 3.99 *(978-0-448-46376-6(8),* Penguin Young Readers) Penguin Young Readers Group.
—On a Farm. 2013. (Penguin Young Readers Level 1 Ser.). lib. bdg. 13.55 *(978-0-606-28739-5(6),* Turtleback) Turtleback Bks.
Appleby, Alex. Dinosaurs on the Farm. 2013. (Dinosaur School Ser.). 24p. (J). (gr. k-1). pap. 8.15 *(978-1-4339-9058-8(X));* pap. 48.90 *(978-1-4339-9059-5(8));* (ENG., Illus.). lib. bdg. 22.60 *(978-1-4339-9057-1(1))* Stevens, Gareth Publishing LLLP.
Arlon, Penelope. La Granja. 2013. (Scholastic Explora Tu Mundo Ser.). (SPA.). 32p. (J). (gr. -1-3). 7.99 *(978-0-545-48874-7(5),* Scholastic en Espanol) Scholastic, Inc.
Arnold, Quinn M. Farmers. 2017. ***(978-1-60818-873-4(6),*** Creative Education) Creative Co., The.
—Seedlings: Farmers. 2017. (Seedlings Ser.). (ENG.). 24p. (J). (gr. -1-1). pap. 7.99 ***(978-1-62832-488-4(0),*** Creative Paperbacks) Creative Co., The.
AZ Books, creator. Walk Around a Farm. 2012. (Put Together Ser.). (ENG., Illus.). 16p. (J). (gr. -1-k). spiral bd. 6.95 *(978-1-61889-189-1(8))* AZ Bks. LLC.
AZ Books Staff. Making the Farm. Sisoj, Natalja, ed. 2012. (Modeling Clay Bks.). (ENG.). 12p. (J). (gr. -1-2). bds. 10.95 *(978-1-61889-197-6(9))* AZ Bks. LLC.
Bassler, Grace. It Comes from a Farm! 2009. (Real Life Readers Ser.). 16p. (gr. 2-3). pap. 7.05 *(978-1-4358-0109-7(1),* Rosen Classroom) Rosen Publishing Group, Inc., The.
Bauman, Amy. Farm Animal Sounds. 2010. 12p. (J). (gr. -1). 9.95 *(978-1-60747-708-2(4),* Pickwick Pr.) Phoenix Bks., Inc.
Bodden, Valerie. A Farming Town. (My First Look At Ser.). 24p. (J). 2011. (ENG.). (gr. 1-17). pap. 7.99 *(978-1-926722-30-6(2),* Creative Paperbacks) 2007. (Illus.). (gr. -1-3). lib. bdg. 24.25 *(978-1-58341-513-9(0),* Creative Education) Creative Co., The.
Bonnett, Rosaline. Very First Words on the Farm. 2011. (Very First Words Board Books Ser.). 12p. (J). ring bd. 6.99 *(978-0-7945-3042-6(7),* Usborne) EDC Publishing.
Borth, Teddy. Crops on the Farm, 1 vol. 2014. (On the Farm Ser.). (ENG.). 24p. (J). (gr. 4-8). lib. bdg. 28.50 *(978-1-62970-052-6(5))* ABDO Publishing Co.
Borth, Teddy, et al. Animales de la Granja. 2015. (En la Granja Ser.). (SPA., Illus.). 24p. (gr. k-1). pap. 7.95 *(978-1-4966-0443-9(1))* Capstone Classroom.
Braidich, S. Meet Me on the Farm: Learning the Long E Sound. 2009. (PowerPhonics Ser.). 24p. (gr. 1-1). 39.90 *(978-1-60851-458-8(7),* PowerKids Pr.) Rosen Publishing Group, Inc., The.
Brooks, Felicity. First Word Book on the Farm. 2015. (My First Word Bks.). (ENG.). 20p. (J). 9.99 *(978-0-7945-3445-5(7),* Usborne) EDC Publishing.
Byerly, Robbie. Work on the Farm. 2016. (1-3Y Jobs & Careers Ser.). (ENG., Illus.). 16p. (J). pap. 5.99 *(978-1-63437-477-4(0))* American Reading Co.
Color All About: A Giant Coloring Book about Work & Play on the Farm: the Farm. 2004. (SPA & ENG., Illus.). 36p. (J). *(978-1-59949-003-8(X))* Food Marketing Consultants, Inc.
Color All About: The Farm: A Giant Coloring Book about Having Fun on a Farm. 2004. (Illus.). (J). *(978-0-9763307-5-2(X))* Food Marketing Consultants, Inc.
Coppendale, Jean. Tractors & Farm Vehicles. 2010. (Mighty Machines Ser.). (ENG., Illus.). 24p. (J). (gr. -1-2). pap. 5.95 *(978-1-55407-620-8(X),* 9781554076208) Firefly Bks., Ltd.
Daynes, Katie. Look Inside a Farm. rev. ed. 2012. (Look Inside Board Bks). 13p. (J). ring bd. 15.99 *(978-0-7945-3249-9(7),* Usborne) EDC Publishing.
Deneux, Xavier. TouchThinkLearn: Farm. 2015. (ENG., Illus.). 22p. (J). (gr. -1 — 1). bds. 14.99 *(978-1-4521-4517-4(2))* Chronicle Bks. LLC.
Dickmann, Nancy. Los Alimentos de la Granja. 2011. (Mundo de la Granja Ser.). 24p. (gr. -1-1). (SPA & ENG.). 22.65 *(978-1-4329-5308-9(7));* (ENG & SPA.). pap. 6.29 *(978-1-4329-5315-7(X))* Heinemann-Raintree. (Bellota).
—Las Estaciones en la Granja. 2011. (Mundo de la Granja Ser.). 24p. (gr. -1-1). (SPA & ENG.). 22.65 *(978-1-4329-5311-9(7));* (ENG & SPA.). pap. 6.29 *(978-1-4329-5318-8(4))* Heinemann-Raintree. (Bellota).
—Food from Farms, 1 vol. 2010. (World of Farming Ser.). (ENG.). 24p. (gr. -1-k). pap. 6.29 *(978-1-4329-3943-4(2),* Acorn) Heinemann-Raintree.
—Jobs on a Farm, 1 vol. 2010. (World of Farming Ser.). (ENG., Illus.). 24p. (gr. -1-1). 22.65 *(978-1-4329-3937-3(8));* pap. 6.29 *(978-1-4329-3945-8(9))* Heinemann-Raintree. (Acorn).
—Las Plantas de la Granja, 1 vol. 2011. (Mundo de la Granja Ser.). (Illus.). 24p. (gr. -1-1). (SPA & ENG.). 22.65 *(978-1-4329-5310-2(9));* (ENG & SPA., pap. 6.29 *(978-1-4329-5317-1(6))* Heinemann-Raintree. (Bellota).
—El Mundo de la Granja, 6 vols., Set. Incl. Alimentos de la Granja. pap. 6.29 *(978-1-4329-5315-7(X));* Animales de la Granja. pap. 6.29 *(978-1-4329-5313-3(3));* Estaciones en la Granja. pap. 6.29 *(978-1-4329-5318-8(4));* Las Plantas de la Granja. (Illus.). pap. 6.29 *(978-1-4329-5317-1(6));* Máquinas de la Granja. pap. 6.29 *(978-1-4329-5314-0(1));* Trabajos en la Granja. pap. 6.29 *(978-1-4329-5316-4(8));* (gr. -1-1). (Mundo de la Granja Ser.). (SPA.). 24p. 2011. Set pap. 35.94 *(978-1-4329-5319-5(2));* Set lib. bdg. 135.90 *(978-1-4329-5312-6(5))* Heinemann-Raintree. (Bellota).
—Plants on a Farm, 1 vol. 2010. (World of Farming Ser.). (ENG.). 24p. (gr. -1-1). pap. 6.29 *(978-1-4329-3950-2(5),* Acorn) Heinemann-Raintree.
—Seasons on a Farm, 1 vol. 2010. (World of Farming Ser.). 24p. (ENG.). (gr. -1-1). pap. 6.29 *(978-1-4329-3953-3(X));* pap. 32.35 *(978-1-4329-3944-1(0))* Heinemann-Raintree. (Acorn).
—Los Trabajos en la Granja. 2011. (Mundo de la Granja Ser.). 24p. (gr. -1-1). (SPA & ENG.). 22.65 *(978-1-4329-5309-6(5));* (ENG & SPA.). pap. 6.29 *(978-1-4329-5316-4(8))* Heinemann-Raintree. (Bellota).
—World of Farming, 1 vol., Set. Incl. Farm Animals. pap. 6.29 *(978-1-4329-3941-0(6));* Farm Machines. pap. 6.29 *(978-1-4329-3942-7(4));* Food from Farms. pap. 6.29 *(978-1-4329-3943-4(2));* Jobs on a Farm. (Illus.). pap. 6.29 *(978-1-4329-3945-8(9));* Plants on a Farm. pap. 6.29 *(978-1-4329-3950-2(5));* Seasons on a Farm. pap. 6.29 *(978-1-4329-3953-3(X));* (gr. -1-1). (World of Farming Ser.). (ENG.). 24p. 2010. Set pap. 35.94 *(978-1-4329-3935-9(1),* Acorn) Heinemann-Raintree.
Dils, Tracey E. Down on the Farm 1,2,3: A Farm Counting Book. 2015. (1, 2, 3... Count with Me Ser.). (ENG., Illus.). 24p. (J). (gr. k-2). 19.95 *(978-1-60753-718-2(4))* Amicus Publishing.
Doherty, Gillian. 1001 Things to Spot on the Farm. 2009. (1001 Things to Spot Ser.). 32p. (J). 9.99 *(978-0-7945-2611-5(X),* Usborne) EDC Publishing.

EFG

Donahue, Peter. Farm & Zoo. 2010. (Dover Build a Poster Coloring Book Ser.). (ENG., Illus.). 48p. (J). (gr. 3-5). pap. 4.99 *(978-0-486-47947-7(1))* Dover Pubns., Inc.

Dorling Kindersley Publishing Staff. Farm. (Touch & Feel Ser.). (ENG.). (J). (gr. -1-k). 2011. 12p. bds. 6.99 *(978-0-7566-8989-6(9))* 2007. 16p. 9.99 *(978-0-7566-1971-8(8))* Dorling Kindersley Publishing, Inc. (DK Children).

—Ultimate Sticker Book: Farm. 2016. (Ultimate Sticker Bks.). (ENG.). 32p. (J). (gr. k-3). pap. 6.99 *(978-1-4654-4919-1(1),* DK Children) Dorling Kindersley Publishing, Inc.

Dorling Kindersley Publishing Staff, ed. Noisy Farm. 2005. (Fun Flaps Ser.). (ENG., Illus.). 14p. (J). (gr. -1-k). bds. 4.99 *(978-0-7566-0987-0(9),* DK Children) Dorling Kindersley Publishing, Inc.

Dunn, Mary. My Adventure at a Flower Farm. 2006. 44p. (J). 8.99 *(978-1-59092-262-0(X))* Blue Forge Pr.

Endres, Hollie J. The Farm, 6 vols., Set. 2004. (Letter Bks.). (ENG.). 8p. (gr. k-1). pap. 29.70 *(978-0-7368-4105-4(9),* Letter Bks.) Capstone Press of Coughlan Cos.

Farm. (Push & Pop Ser.). 5p. bds. *(978-1-4054-6892-3(0))* Parragon, Inc.

The Farm: Individual Title Six-Packs. (Literatura 2000 Ser.). (gr. -1-1). 28.00 *(978-0-7635-0004-7(6));* 16p. (gr. k-18). 27.00 *(978-0-7635-4389-1(6))* Rigby Education.

Farm (Gr. PreK-5) 2003. (J). *(978-1-58232-021-2(7))* ECS Learning Systems, Inc.

Felix, Rebecca. Are You a Ewe? 2015. (Hear Homophones Here Ser.). (Illus.). 16p. (J). 25.65 *(978-1-60753-568-3(8))* Amicus Publishing.

—Patterns on the Farm. 2015. (21st Century Basic Skills Library: Patterns All Around Ser.). (ENG., Illus.). 24p. (J). (gr. k-3). pap. 12.79 *(978-1-63188-939-4(7),* 206017) Cherry Lake Publishing.

Field Trips. 2005. (Transportation Ser.). (YA). (gr. k-3). 118.80 *(978-0-7368-4190-0(3),* Pebble Bks.) Capstone Press of Coughlan Cos.

Francis, Amy. The Local Food Movement. 2010. (At Issue Ser.). (ENG.). 128p. (gr. 10-12). 39.40 *(978-0-7377-4888-8(5));* pap. 27.80 *(978-0-7377-4889-5(3),* Greenhaven Pr., Inc.) Cengage Gale.

Fretland VanVoorst, Jenny. Las Formas en la Granja. 2015.Tr. of Shapes on the Farm. (SPA., Illus.). 24p. (J). lib. bdg. *(978-1-62031-247-6(6),* Bullfrog Bks.) Jump! Inc.

—Shapes on the Farm. 2015. 24p. (J). lib. bdg. *(978-1-62031-201-8(8),* Bullfrog Bks.) Jump! Inc.

From Farm to You. 2005. (From Farm to You Ser.). (Illus.). 32p. (gr. 4-6). 168.00 *(978-0-7910-7061-1(1),* Chelsea Hse.) Facts On File, Inc.

Fun on the Farm. 2016. (Fun on the Farm Ser.). 00024p. (J). lib. bdg. 135.60 ***(978-1-4824-5540-3(4))*** Stevens, Gareth Publishing LLLP.

Gaarder-Juntti, Oona. Shapes on a Farm, 1 vol. 2013. (Shapes Everywhere Ser.). (ENG.). 24p. (gr. k-4). lib. bdg. 25.65 *(978-1-61783-416-5(5),* Super SandCastle) ABDO Publishing Co.

Galvin, Laura Gates & Studio Mouse Staff. At the Farm. 2006. (ENG.). 80p. (J). 14.99 *(978-1-59069-484-8(8))* Studio Mouse LLC.

Geisert, Arthur. Country Road ABC: An Illustrated Journey Through America's Farmland. 2010. (ENG., Illus.). 64p. (J). (gr. -1-3). 17.00 *(978-0-547-19469-1(2))* Houghton Mifflin Harcourt Publishing Co.

Goodman, Polly. Food, Farming, & the Future. 2011. (Earth Alert! Ser.). 32p. (J). (gr. 3-6). lib. bdg. 26.60 *(978-1-4339-6005-5(2))* Stevens, Gareth Publishing LLLP.

Graham, Ian. On the Farm. 2007. (Qeb Machines at Work Ser.). (Illus.). 36p. (J). lib. bdg. 16.95 *(978-1-59566-189-0(1))* QEB Publishing Inc.

La Granja: Individual Title Six-Packs. (Chiquilibros Ser.). (SPA.). (gr. k-1). 23.00 *(978-0-7635-8591-4(2))* Rigby Education.

La Granja: Individual Title Two-Packs. (Chiquilibros Ser.). (SPA.). (gr. -1-1). 12.00 *(978-0-7635-8549-5(1))* Rigby Education.

Green, John, illus. Who Lives on the Farm? 2004. (Who Lives... Ser.). 12p. (J). bds. 4.99 *(978-1-85854-647-6(8))* Brimax Books Ltd. GBR. Dist: Byeway Bks.

Greenwell, Jessical. Farm Animals Lift & Look. 2010. (Lift & Look Board Bks). 12p. (J). bds. 9.99 *(978-0-7945-2612-2(8),* Usborne) EDC Publishing.

Gunzi, Christane. Farm. 2nd rev. ed. 2015. (ENG., Illus.). 34p. (J). 7.95 *(978-1-906572-28-0(3))* Award Pubns. Ltd. GBR. Dist: Parkwest Pubns., Inc.

Hamilton, Shawna. We Need Farms! 2017. (Text Connections Guided Close Reading Ser.). (J). (gr. k). *(978-1-4900-1772-3(0))* Benchmark Education Co.

Hanson-Harding, Brian. Dairy: From the Farm to Your Table. 2012. (Truth about the Food Supply Ser.). (ENG., Illus.). 48p. (J). (gr. 5-8). lib. bdg. 27.95 *(978-1-4488-6800-1(9),* Rosen Reference) Rosen Publishing Group, Inc., The.

Harkrader, Lisa. Fresh from the Farm. 2016. (Spring Forward Ser.). (J). (gr. 1). *(978-1-4900-9397-0(4))* Benchmark Education Co.

Hodge, Deborah. Up We Grow! A Year in the Life of a Small, Local Farm. Harris, Brian, illus. 2010. (ENG.). 32p. (J). (gr. -1-2). 16.95 *(978-1-55453-561-3(1))* Kids Can Pr., Ltd. CAN. Dist: Hachette Bk. Group.

Holloway, Jamie. I Help on Our Farm. 2015. (Rosen REAL Readers: STEM & STEAM Collection). (ENG.). 8p. pap. 5.46 *(978-1-4994-9662-8(1),* Rosen Classroom) Rosen Publishing Group, Inc., The.

Hutchings, Amy. What Happens at a Horse Farm? 2008. (Where People Work Ser.). 24p. (J). (gr. -1-3). lib. bdg. 22.00 *(978-0-8368-9274-1(7),* Weekly Reader Leveled Readers) Stevens, Gareth Publishing LLLP.

—What Happens at a Horse Farm? ¿Qué Pasa en una Granja de Caballos? 2008. (Where People Work Ser.). 24p. (gr. -1-3). pap. 8.15 *(978-0-8368-9373-1(5),* Weekly Reader Leveled Readers) Stevens, Gareth Publishing LLLP.

—What Happens at a Horse Farm? (¿Qué Pasa en una Granja de Caballos?) 2008. (Where People Work Ser.). (SPA & ENG.). 24p. (gr. -1-3). pap. 8.15 *(978-0-8368-9379-3(4),* Weekly Reader Leveled Readers) Stevens, Gareth Publishing LLLP.

—What Happens at a Horse Farm?/¿Qué Pasa en una Granja de Caballos? 2008. (Where People Work/Dónde Trabaja la Gente? Ser.). (ENG & SPA.). 24p. (J). (gr. -1-3). lib. bdg. 22.00 *(978-0-8368-9280-2(1),* Weekly Reader Leveled Readers) Stevens, Gareth Publishing LLLP.

Ipcar, Dahlov. Dahlov Ipcar's Farmyard Alphabet, 1 vol. 2010. (ENG., Illus.). 18p. (J). bds. 10.95 *(978-1-934031-43-8(7),* 322cba51-66de-4792-9574-ca10ba745057) Islandport Pr., Inc.

Jeffries, Joyce. Farmers, 01 vols., 1. 2016. (Hands-On Jobs Ser.). (ENG., Illus.). 24p. (J). pap. 8.25 *(978-1-5081-4359-8(5),* PowerKids Pr.) Rosen Publishing Group, Inc., The.

Kalz, Jill. Farm Adventure. Cerato, Mattia, illus. 2010. (A-MAZE-Ing Adventures Ser.). (ENG.). 32p. (gr. 1-2). lib. bdg. 26.65 *(978-1-4048-6038-4(X))* Picture Window Bks.

Kawa, Katie. My First Trip to the Farm. 2012. (My First Adventures Ser.). (Illus.). 24p. (gr. k-2). 69.20 *(978-1-4339-8050-3(9));* (J). pap. 8.15 *(978-1-4339-7313-0(8));* (J). lib. bdg. 22.60 *(978-1-4339-7312-3(X))* Stevens, Gareth Publishing LLLP.

—My First Trip to the Farm: Mi Primera Visita a una Granja. 2012. (My First Adventures / Mis primeras aventuras Ser.). (SPA & ENG., Illus.). 24p. (J). (gr. k-2). lib. bdg. 22.60 *(978-1-4339-7378-9(2))* Stevens, Gareth Publishing LLLP.

Keiser, Cody. We Live on a Farm, 01 vols., 1. 2016. (American Communities Ser.). (ENG., Illus.). 24p. (J). pap. 8.25 *(978-1-5081-4209-6(2),* PowerKids Pr.) Rosen Publishing Group, Inc., The.

Kids Can Press Staff. This Is Daniel Cook at the Farm. 2006. (This Is Daniel Cook Ser.). (ENG., Illus.). 24p. (J). (gr. -1-1). 4.95 *(978-1-55453-078-6(4))* Kids Can Pr., Ltd. CAN. Dist: Hachette Bk. Group.

Knapp, Andrew. Let's Find Momo! A Hide-And-Seek Board Book. 2017. (Find Momo Ser.). (ENG., Illus.). 24p. (J). (-k). bds. 9.99 *(978-1-59474-958-2(2))* Quirk Bks.

Ladybird. On the Farm. 2016. (Read It Yourself with Ladybird Ser.). (ENG., Illus.). 32p. (J). (gr. 2-4). 5.99 *(978-0-241-23731-1(9))* Penguin Bks., Ltd. GBR. Dist: Independent Pubs. Group.

—On the Farm, Level 2. 2016. (Read It Yourself with Ladybird Ser.). (ENG., Illus.). 32p. (J). pap. 9.99 *(978-0-241-23730-4(0))* Penguin Bks., Ltd. GBR. Dist: Independent Pubs. Group.

Laval, Thierry. Look & Find on the Farm. 2017. (Mini Look & Find Ser.). (ENG.). 14p. (J). 9.95 ***(978-0-531-23080-0(5),*** Children's Pr.) Scholastic Library Publishing.

Lindeen, Mary. A Visit to the Market. 2015. (BeginningtoRead Ser.). (ENG.). 32p. (J). (gr. k-2). lib. bdg. 22.60 *(978-1-59953-692-7(7))* Norwood Hse. Pr.

Litchfield, J. & Brooks, F. Farm. 2004. (Illus.). 10p. (J). 4.95 *(978-0-7945-0587-5(2))* EDC Publishing.

little bee books, little bee & Seal, Julia. Farm. 2016. (ENG., Illus.). 12p. (J). (gr. -1 — 1). bds. 6.99 *(978-1-4998-0260-3(9))* Little Bee Books Inc.

Machell, Dawn, illus. Super Sticker Activity: Farm. 2016. (Super Sticker Activity Ser.). (ENG.). 32p. (J). (gr. -1). 5.99 *(978-1-62686-647-8(3),* Silver Dolphin Bks.) Readerlink Distribution Services, LLC.

Markovics, Joyce L. Farm Colors: From Purple Plums to Pink Pigs. 2014. (Little Bits: Colors Tell a Story Ser.). (ENG.). 24p. (J). (gr. -1-3). lib. bdg. 23.93 *(978-1-62724-323-0(2))* Bearport Publishing Co., Inc.

—Los Colores de la Granja: De Las Ciruelas Moradas a Los Cerdos Rosados. 2014. (Los Colores Cuentan una Historia Ser.). (SPA.). 24p. (J). (gr. -1-3). lib. bdg. 23.93 *(978-1-62724-465-7(4))* Bearport Publishing Co., Inc.

Marsico, Katie. Working on a Farm. 2008. (21st Century Junior Library: Careers Ser.). (ENG.). 24p. (gr. 2-5). lib. bdg. 25.64 *(978-1-60279-271-5(2),* 200176) Cherry Lake Publishing.

Martin, John David. My Little Farm Book. 2007. (Illus.). 16p. (J). (gr. -1). pap. 1.90 *(978-0-7399-2399-3(4))* Rod & Staff Pubs., Inc.

McDowell, Pamela. Farm. 2015. (Illus.). 24p. (J). pap. *(978-1-4896-3602-7(1))* Weigl Pubs., Inc.

McFadden, Jesse. Franklin's Farm Stand: Understand Place Value. 2014. (Math Masters: Number & Operations in Base Ten Ser.). (Illus.). 24p. (J). 23.60 *(978-1-4777-6428-2(3));* (ENG., pap. 8.25 *(978-1-4777-4654-7(4))* Rosen Publishing Group, Inc., The. (Rosen Classroom).

Miller, Jonathan, illus. Farm Animals Fun Box. 2017. (ENG.). 24p. (J). (gr. -1-k). 7.99 *(978-2-9815807-2-6(8))* CrackBoom! Bks. CAN. Dist: Publishers Group West (PGW).

Moore, Elizabeth. Farms. 2011. (Wonder Readers Emergent Level Ser.). (ENG.). (gr. -1-1). 8p. pap. 35.94 *(978-1-4296-8230-5(2));* 32p. pap. 5.99 *(978-1-4296-7843-8(7))* Capstone Press of Coughlan Cos. (Wonder Readers).

Mortensen, Lori. Working on the Farm, 1 vol. Thompson, Jeffrey, illus. 2010. (First Graphics: My Community Ser.). (ENG.). 24p. (gr. 1-2). pap. 6.29 *(978-1-4296-5616-0(6));* pap. 35.70 *(978-1-4296-5617-7(4))* Capstone Press of Coughlan Cos.

Mumme, Sarah. Guess Who's on the Farm. Samuel, Janet, illus. 2015. (Guess Who's... Bks.). (ENG.). 10p. (J). (gr. -1 — 1). 5.99 *(978-0-7641-6802-4(9))* Barron's Educational Series, Inc.

Nelson, Kristin L. Farm Tractors on the Move. 2011. (Lightning Bolt Books Vroom-Vroom Ser.). 32p. pap. 45.32 *(978-0-7613-7617-0(8));* (ENG.). pap. 7.95 *(978-0-7613-7111-3(7));* (ENG.). lib. bdg. 26.60 *(978-0-7613-6025-4(5))* Lerner Publishing Group.

On the Farm: Individual Title Six-Packs. (Literatura 2000 Ser.). (gr. k-1). 28.00 *(978-0-7635-0010-8(0))* Rigby Education.

O'Toole, Janet. On the Farm: Lift the Flaps to Find Out about Farms! Adams, Ben, illus. 2013. (ENG.). 16p. bds. 6.99 *(978-1-84322-794-6(0),* Armadillo) Anness Publishing GBR. Dist: National Bk. Network.

Pendergast, George. At the Crop Farm. 2016. (Fun on the Farm Ser.). 00024p. (J). pap. 8.15 ***(978-1-4824-5512-0(9))*** Stevens, Gareth Publishing LLLP.

Pettiford, Rebecca. Farm. Fretland VanVoorst, Jenny, ed. 2016. (First Field Trips). 24p. (J). (gr. k-2). lib. bdg. 25.65 *(978-1-62031-295-7(6),* Bullfrog Bks.) Jump! Inc.

—La Granja. 2016. (Los Primeros Viajes Escolares (First Field Trips)).Tr. of Farm. (SPA.). 24p. (J). (gr. k-2). lib. bdg. 25.65 *(978-1-62031-330-5(8),* Bullfrog Bks.) Jump! Inc.

Priddy, Roger. Farm. 2016. (Playtown Ser.). (ENG., Illus.). 12p. (J). bds. 9.99 *(978-0-312-51959-9(1),* 9780312519599, Priddy Bks.) St. Martin's Pr.

—First Farm Words. 2017. (First 100 Ser.). (ENG.). 24p. (J). bds. 5.99 *(978-0-312-52283-4(5),* 9780312522834, Priddy Bks.) St. Martin's Pr.

—My Big Farm Book. 2011. (My Big Board Bks.). (ENG., Illus.). 12p. (J). (gr. -1 — 1). bds. 8.99 *(978-0-312-51082-4(9),* 9780312510824, Priddy Bks.) St. Martin's Pr.

Randall, Jory. My Day at the Farm. 2009. (Kid's Life! Ser.). 24p. (J). (ENG.). pap. 8.25 *(978-1-4358-2473-7(3));* (Illus.). lib. bdg. 22.60 *(978-1-4042-8077-9(4))* Rosen Publishing Group, Inc., The. (PowerKids Pr.).

Regan, Lisa. Farmyard Riddles. 2014. (Riddle Me This! Ser.). 32p. (J). (gr. 1-5). lib. bdg. 27.50 *(978-1-4777-9161-5(2))* Windmill Bks.

Rice, D. M. A Visit to a Farm, 1 vol. 2nd rev. ed. 2014. (TIME for KIDS(r) Nonfiction Readers Ser.). (ENG., Illus.). 24p. (J). (gr. 2-2). pap. 23.96 *(978-1-4807-1035-1(0))* Shell Educational Publishing.

—A Visit to a Farm, 1 vol. 2nd rev. ed. 2011. (Nonfiction Readers Ser.). (ENG.). 24p. (J). (gr. 2-2). pap. 6.99 *(978-1-4333-3608-9(1))* Teacher Created Materials, Inc.

Riggs, Kate. On the Farm. Dogi, Fiammetta & Kubinyi, Laszlo, illus. 2015. (ENG.). 14p. (J). (gr. -1 — 1). bds. 7.99 *(978-1-56846-272-1(7),* Creative Editions) Creative Co., The.

Rissman, Rebecca. Eddie & Ellie's Opposites at the Farm, 1 vol. 2013. (Eddie & Ellie's Opposites Ser.). (ENG.). 24p. (gr. -1-k). 22.65 *(978-1-4109-5343-8(2));* pap. 7.95 *(978-1-4109-5348-3(3))* Heinemann-Raintree. (NA-r).

—Going to a Farm, 1 vol. 2012. (World of Field Trips Ser.). (ENG.). 24p. (gr. -1-1). pap. 6.29 *(978-1-4329-6075-9(X));* lib. bdg. 22.65 *(978-1-4329-6066-7(0))* Heinemann-Raintree. (Acorn).

Rosen, Michael J. Our Farm: Four Seasons with Five Kids on One Family's Farm. 2008. 128p. (J). (gr. -1-3). 18.95 *(978-1-58196-067-9(0),* Darby Creek) Lerner Publishing Group.

Rotner, Shelley. Senses on the Farm. 2008. (Illus.). 32p. (J). (gr. -1-2). 23.93 *(978-0-8225-8623-4(1),* Millbrook Pr.) Lerner Publishing Group.

Rudenko, Dennis. Planning My Farm: Reason with Shapes & Their Attributes. 2014. (Rosen Common Core Math Readers Ser.). (ENG.). 24p. (J). (gr. 2-3). pap. 49.50 *(978-1-4777-4895-4(4),* Rosen Classroom) Rosen Publishing Group, Inc., The.

Rusling, Annette. Farm Sticker Activities. Cunliffe, Ian, illus. 2014. (My First Sticker Activity Book Ser.). (ENG.). 96p. (J). (gr. -1-3). pap. 9.99 *(978-1-58925-303-2(5))* Tiger Tales.

Samson, Tess. Animals on the Farm. 2010. (Sight Word Readers Ser.). (J). 3.49 *(978-1-60719-619-8(0))* Newmark Learning LLC.

Shepard, Daniel. All Kinds of Farms, 6 vols., Set. 2003. (Yellow Umbrella Early Level Ser.). (ENG.). 16p. (gr. k-1). pap. 35.70 *(978-0-7368-2989-2(X),* Yellow Umbrella Bks.) Capstone Press of Coughlan Cos.

Sloane, Eric. An Age of Barns: An Illustrated Review of Classic Barn Styles & Construction. Sloane, Eric, illus. rev. ed. 2005. (ENG., Illus.). 94p. (gr. 10-18). pap. 16.95 *(978-0-89658-565-2(4),* 0896585654, Voyageur Pr) Quarto Publishing Group USA.

Spilsbury, Louise & Spilsbury, Richard. A Nature Walk on the Farm, 1 vol. 2014. (Nature Walks Ser.). (ENG., Illus.). 24p. (gr. k-2). 23.32 *(978-1-4846-0402-1(4),* Heinemann Read & Learn) Heinemann-Raintree.

Steffora, Tracey. Math on the Farm, 1 vol. 2013. (Math on the Job Ser.). (ENG., Illus.). 24p. (gr. k-2). pap. 6.29 *(978-1-4329-7163-2(8));* lib. bdg. 22.65 *(978-1-4329-7156-4(5))* Heinemann-Raintree. (Acorn).

Sterling Children's, Sterling. A Day at the Farm: A Book of ABCs. 2016. (ENG., Illus.). 28p. (J). (— 1). bds. 6.95 *(978-1-4114-7587-8(9),* Spark Publishing Group) Sterling Publishing Co., Inc.

Tan, Richard. Farm Field Trip. 2015. (Rosen REAL Readers: STEM & STEAM Collection). (ENG.). 8p. pap. 5.46 *(978-1-4994-9589-8(7),* Rosen Classroom) Rosen Publishing Group, Inc., The.

Tatchell, Judy. On the Farm. Smith, Alastair, illus. 2004. (Lift-the-Flap Learners Ser.). (ENG.). 1p. (J). (gr. 1-18). pap. 8.95 *(978-0-7460-2775-2(3))* EDC Publishing.

Tiger Tales Staff, creator. Farm Puzzle + Book. 2014. (My First Puzzle Set Ser.). (ENG., Illus.). 26p. (J). (gr. -1-1). 9.99 *(978-1-58925-597-5(6))* Tiger Tales.

Top That Publishing Staff, ed. Alphabet Farm. Parry, Jo, illus. 2007. (Magnetic - Alphabet Ser.). 10p. (J). (gr. -1). bds. *(978-1-84666-272-0(9),* Tide Mill Pr.) Top That! Publishing PLC.

—Counting on the Farm. Sapp, Karen, illus. 2007. (Magnetic Fun Ser.). 16p. (J). (gr. -1). *(978-1-84666-270-6(2),* Tide Mill Pr.) Top That! Publishing PLC.

Top That!, creator. Old MacDonald's Farm. 2012. (Draw-on Wipe-off Doodle Storybook Ser.). (ENG., Illus.). 24p. (J). (gr. -1). *(978-1-84956-657-5(7))* Top That! Publishing PLC.

Unstead, Sue. DK Readers L1: a Year on the Farm: A Year on the Farm. 2015. (DK Readers Ser.). (ENG., Illus.). 48p. (J). (gr. k-4). 14.99 *(978-1-4654-3576-7(X),* DK Children) Dorling Kindersley Publishing, Inc.

Vogel, Julia. Save the Planet: Local Farms & Sustainable Foods. 2010. (Explorer Library: Language Arts Explorer Ser.). (ENG.). 32p. (gr. 4-8). pap. 14.21 *(978-1-60279-669-0(6),* 200916); lib. bdg. 28.50 *(978-1-60279-660-7(2),* 200353) Cherry Lake Publishing.

Watterson, Carol. The Edible Alphabet: 26 Reasons to Love the Farm. Sorrentino, Michela, illus. 2011. (ENG.). 48p. (J). (gr. k-3). 16.99 *(978-1-58246-421-3(9),* Tricycle Pr.) Random Hse. Children's Bks.

Wells, Rachel. Farm. 2011. (That's Not My... . Coloring Books Ser.). 32p. (J). pap. 4.99 *(978-0-7945-3011-2(7),* Usborne) EDC Publishing.

Welvaert, Scott R. Follow That Crop: From the Farmer's Field to Our Grocery Store. 2003. (From Here to There Ser.). (J). *(978-1-58417-194-2(4));* pap. *(978-1-58417-195-9(2))* Lake Street Pubs.

Workman Publishing Company Staff. The Horse Farm. Graham, Lindsay, illus. 2004. (ENG.). 18p. (J). (gr. -1). pap., tchr. ed. 7.95 *(978-1-58017-583-8(X),* 67583) Storey Publishing, LLC.

Zamosky, Lisa & National Geographic Learning Staff. Farmers Then & Now. 2010. (ENG., Illus.). 32p. (C). (gr. 2-2). pap. 14.95 *(978-0-7439-9377-7(2))* National Geographic School Publishing, Inc.

Zwemmer, Dominic, des. Farm. 2015. (ENG., Illus.). 16p. (J). pap. 7.99 *(978-1-907604-46-1(4))* Award Pubns. Ltd. GBR. Dist: Parkwest Pubns., Inc.

FARMS—POETRY

Andrews, Jackie. Old Macdonald on His Farm. Bennett, John, illus. 2012. (ENG.). 32p. pap. 6.50 *(978-1-84135-195-7(4))* Award Pubns. Ltd. GBR. Dist: Parkwest Pubns., Inc.

Weidner, Teri, illus. Sleep, Baby, Sleep. 2009. 20p. (J). (gr. -1-k). 8.95 *(978-1-58925-843-3(6))* Tiger Tales.

FARRAGUT, DAVID GLASGOW, 1801-1870

Dougherty, Terri. Admiral David Farragut: "Full Speed Ahead!" 2011. (J). *(978-1-59556-041-4(6));* pap. *(978-1-59556-047-6(5))* OTTN Publishing.

Stein, R. Conrad. David Farragut: First Admiral of the U. S. Navy. 2005. (Proud Heritage: the Hispanic Library). (ENG., Illus.). 40p. (J). (gr. 3-6). 29.93 *(978-1-59296-383-6(8),* 200005) Child's World, Inc., The.

FASCISM—GERMANY

see National Socialism

FASHION

see also Clothing and Dress; Costume; Dressmaking

Albee, Sarah. Why'd They Wear That? From Hair Shirts to Hoop Skirts, Platform Shoes to Tattoos, a Fashion History of the World. 2015. (ENG., Illus.). 192p. (J). (gr. 5-7). 19.99 *(978-1-4263-1919-8(3),* National Geographic Children's Bks.) National Geographic Society.

Aldridge, Rebecca. Stella Mccartney. 2011. (Famous Fashion Designers Ser.). (Illus.). 112p. (gr. 6-12). 35.00 *(978-1-60413-982-2(X),* Chelsea Hse.) Facts On File, Inc.

Anniss, Matt. Music, Fashion, & Style. 2015. (Music Scene Ser.). (J). lib. bdg. 37.10 *(978-1-59920-912-8(8))* Black Rabbit Bks.

Anniss, Matthew. Music, Fashion & Style. 2016. (ENG., Illus.). 48p. (J). (gr. 5-9). pap. 12.99 *(978-1-4451-3940-1(5),* Franklin Watts) Hachette Children's Group GBR. Dist: Hachette Bk. Group.

Barbo, Maria S. Fashionista! Gonzales, Chuck, illus. 2009. (ENG.). 128p. (J). (gr. 2-6). pap. 16.99 *(978-0-312-59607-1(3),* 9780312596071) Feiwel & Friends.

Barkan, Joanne. Looking Good. 2005. (Real Deal Ser.). (Illus.). 32p. (J). pap. *(978-0-7608-9634-1(8))* Sundance/Newbridge Educational Publishing.

Becker & Mayer, creator. Rock Fashion Design Studio. 2014. (SmartLAB Ser.). (ENG., Illus.). (J). (gr. 3). 19.99 *(978-1-60380-343-4(2))* becker&mayer! books.

Behnke, Alison. The Little Black Dress & Zoot Suits: Depression & Wartime Fashions from the 1930s to the 1950s. 2011. (Dressing a Nation: the History of U. S. Fashion Ser.). (ENG., Illus.). 64p. (gr. 5-12). lib. bdg. 31.93 *(978-0-7613-5892-3(7),* Twenty-First Century Bks.) Lerner Publishing Group.

Berman, Ron. Fashion. 2012. (Urban Entrepreneurs Ser.). (ENG., Illus.). 40p. (gr. 3-8). pap. 9.95 *(978-1-61570-516-0(3))* Scobre Pr. Corp.

Bernhardt, Carolyn. Duct Tape Fashion. 2017. (Create with Duct Tape Ser.). (ENG.). 32p. (J). (gr. 2-5). 12.99 ***(978-1-5124-3852-9(9),*** Lerner Pubns.); 39.99 ***(978-1-5124-2766-0(7),*** Lerner Pubns.); 39.99 ***(978-1-5124-3851-2(0),*** Lerner Pubns.); (Illus.). 26.65 *(978-1-5124-2669-4(5))* Lerner Publishing Group.

Boone, Mary & Jacobs, Marc. Marc Jacobs. 2011. (Famous Fashion Designers Ser.). (Illus.). 104p. (gr. 6-12). 35.00 *(978-1-60413-981-5(1),* Chelsea Hse.) Facts On File, Inc.

Branscomb, Leslie Wolf. Marc Jacobs. 2011. (Profiles in Fashion Ser.). (Illus.). 112p. 28.95 *(978-1-59935-153-7(6),* 1320457) Reynolds, Morgan Inc.

Bratz Fashion Funktivity Books. 2004. (J). 1.49 *(978-0-7666-1223-5(6),* 99215); 1.49 *(978-0-7666-1224-2(4),* 99215); 1.49 *(978-0-7666-1222-8(8),* 99215) Modern Publishing.

Brocklehurst, Ruth. Clothes & Fashion Sticker Book IR. Lardot, Christopher, illus. 2013. (Clothes & Fashion Sticker Book Ser.). 31p. (J). pap. 9.99 *(978-0-7945-3235-2(7),* Usborne) EDC Publishing.

Bugbird, T. Bff Fashion Boutique Designer. 2009. 48p. pap. *(978-1-84610-967-6(1))* Make Believe Ideas.

Butterfield, Moira. Wannabes Fashion Queen: For Girls Who Know What They Want to Be. 2004. (Illus.). 128p. (J). pap. *(978-1-84458-048-4(2),* Pavilion Children's Books) Pavilion Bks.

Calvin Klein. 2011. (Famous Fashion Designers Ser.). (Illus.). 136p. (gr. 6-12). 35.00 *(978-1-60413-979-2(X),* Chelsea Hse.) Facts On File, Inc.

Catwalk Fashion. 2013. (ENG.). 144p. (J). spiral bd. 10.95 *(978-1-84858-392-4(3))* Arcturus Publishing GBR. Dist: Bookmasters Distribution.

Catwalk Model: Clothes, Shoes & Accessories to Draw & Color. 2012. (ENG.). 144p. (J). spiral bd. 10.95 *(978-1-84837-916-9(1))* Arcturus Publishing GBR. Dist: Bookmasters Distribution.

Chu, Carol & Chang, Lulu. The Fashion Coloring Book. 2012. (ENG., Illus.). 128p. (YA). (gr. 7). pap. 14.99 *(978-0-547-55395-5(1))* Houghton Mifflin Harcourt Publishing Co.

Clerc, Lucille, illus. Flip Fashion. 2013. (ENG.). 44p. 14.95 *(978-1-85669-923-5(4))* King, Laurence Publishing GBR. Dist: Hachette Bk. Group.

Conrad, Lauren. Lauren Conrad Style. 2012. (ENG.). 240p. (YA). (gr. 8). pap. 12.99 *(978-0-06-198969-8(X))* HarperCollins Pubs.

Craats, Rennay. Fashion. 2008. (USA Past Present Future Ser.). (Illus.). 48p. (J). (gr. 4-6). pap. 10.95 *(978-1-59036-973-9(4));* lib. bdg. 29.05 *(978-1-59036-972-2(6))* Weigl Pubs., Inc.

Croll, Jennifer. Bad Girls of Fashion: Style Rebels Through the Ages. Buchholz, Ada, illus. 2016. (ENG.). 208p. (J). pap. 14.95 *(978-1-55451-785-5(0))* Annick Pr., Ltd. CAN. Dist: Publishers Group West (PGW).

Dakers, Diane. Calvin Klein: Fashion Design Superstar. 2010. (Crabtree Groundbreaker Biographies Ser.). (ENG., Illus.).

112p. (J). pap. *(978-0-7787-2543-5(X))*; (gr. 5-8). lib. bdg. *(978-0-7787-2534-3(0))* Crabtree Publishing Co.
—Vera Wang: A Passion for Bridal & Lifestyle Design. 2010. (Crabtree Groundbreaker Biographies Ser.). (ENG., Illus.). 112p. (J). pap. *(978-0-7787-2544-2(8))*; (gr. 5-8). lib. bdg. *(978-0-7787-2535-0(9))* Crabtree Publishing Co.
Daynes, Katie. Fabulous Story of Fashion. Mistry, Nilesh, illus. 2006. (Young Reading Series 2 Gift Bks.). 64p. (J). (gr. 2-5). 8.99 *(978-0-7945-1263-7(1)*, Usborne) EDC Publishing.
deCarufel, Laura. Learn to Speak Fashion: A Guide to Creating, Showcasing, & Promoting Your Style. Kulak, Jeff & Owlkids Books Inc. Staff, illus. 2012. (Learn to Speak Ser.). (ENG.). 96p. (J). (gr. 4-8). pap. 14.95 *(978-1-926973-42-5(9)*, Owlkids) Owlkids Bks. Inc. CAN. Dist: Publishers Group West (PGW).
Dorling Kindersley Publishing Staff. Fashion. 2014. (ENG.). 96p. (J). (gr. 2-4). pap. 12.99 *(978-1-4654-1653-7(6)*, DK Children) Dorling Kindersley Publishing, Inc.
—The Fashion Book. 2014. (ENG.). 160p. (YA). (gr. 8-12). 15.99 *(978-1-4654-2284-2(6)*, DK Children) Dorling Kindersley Publishing, Inc.
Downs, Alison. For People Who Are into Fashion. 2016. (Cool Careers Without College Ser.). 00104p. (J). (gr. 7-7). 38.45 *(978-1-5081-7278-9(1))* Rosen Publishing Group, Inc., The.
Erte. Erte Fashions Coloring Book. Noble, Marty, ed. 2003. (Dover Fashion Coloring Book Ser.). (ENG., Illus.). 32p. (gr. 6-8). pap. 4.99 *(978-0-486-43041-6(3))* Dover Pubns., Inc.
Espejo, Roman. Fashion Industry. 2010. (Opposing Viewpoints Ser.). (Illus.). 240p. (J). 42.95 *(978-0-7377-4512-2(6))*; pap. 29.45 *(978-0-7377-4513-9(4))* Cengage Gale.
Facts on File, Inc. Staff. Fashion. 2011. (Discovering Careers Ser.). (Illus.). 118p. (gr. 4-9). 24.95 *(978-0-8160-8056-4(9)*, Ferguson Publishing Co.) Facts On File, Inc.
Facts on File, Inc. Staff, ed. Fashions of a Decade, 8 Vols., Set. 2006. (Fashions of a Decade Ser.). (Illus.). 64p. (gr. 6-12). 280.00 *(978-0-8160-7059-6(8))* Facts On File, Inc.
Fashion. 2007. (What Can I Do Now? Ser.). (Illus.). 168p. (YA). (gr. 7-12). 32.95 *(978-0-8160-6029-0(0))* Facts On File, Inc.
Fashion Designer. 2008. (Cool Creations Style Folder Ser.). 32p. pap. *(978-1-4075-1651-6(5))* Parragon, Inc.
Fashion Fun: Let's go Shopping! (Girls' Activity Kit Ser.). (J). *(978-2-7643-0214-9(2))* Phidal Publishing, Inc./Editions Phidal, Inc.
Fashion Passion. 2004. (Bratz Krazy-Kool Sticker Blitz Bks.). (J). 2.99 *(978-0-7666-1229-7(5)*, 69580) Modern Publishing.
Focus on Fashion! 2004. (Bratz Ser.). (J). 1.49 *(978-0-7666-1225-9(2)*, 99215) Modern Publishing.
Freistadt, Margo. Kate Spade. 2011. (Profiles in Fashion Ser.). (Illus.). 112p. 28.95 *(978-1-59935-154-4(4))* Reynolds, Morgan Inc.
Friends & Trends. 2004. (Bratz). (J). 2.49 *(978-0-7666-1303-4(8)*, 49315) Modern Publishing.
Gardner, Jane P. Fashion Science, Vol. 11. Lewin, Russ, ed. 2015. (Science 24/7 Ser.). (Illus.). 48p. (J). (gr. 5). 20.95 *(978-1-4222-3409-9(6))* Mason Crest.
Gill, Mickey. Glam Slam! 2005. 100p. 12.95 *(978-1-892951-28-1(2))* Fine Print Publishing Co.
Gordon, Stephen G. Expressing the Inner Wild: Tattoos, Piercings, Jewelry, & Other Body Art. 2014. (Illus.). 56p. (J). (gr. 6-12). lib. bdg. 33.26 *(978-1-4677-1467-9(4)*, Twenty-First Century Bks.) Lerner Publishing Group.
Greathouse, Lisa. Backstage Pass: Fashion, 1 vol. 2nd rev. ed. 2014. (TIME for KIDS(r) Nonfiction Readers Ser.). (ENG., Illus.). 32p. (J). (gr. 3-3). pap. 25.96 *(978-1-4807-1076-4(8))* Shell Educational Publishing.
—Backstage Pass: Fashion, 1 vol. 2nd rev. ed. 2011. (TIME for KIDS(r) Nonfiction Readers Ser.). (ENG.). 32p. (J). (gr. 3-3). pap. 8.99 *(978-1-4333-3661-4(8))* Teacher Created Materials, Inc.
Greathouse, Lisa E. Todo Acceso: Una Casa de Modas. 2017. (TIME for Kids en Español - Level 3 Ser.). (SPA.). 32p. (gr. 3-3). lib. bdg. 31.99 ***(978-1-5157-5174-8(0))*** Time for Kids Inc AUS. Dist: Capstone Pub.
Hamilton Waxman, Laura & Waxman, Laura. Fabulous Fashion Inventions. 2013. (Awesome Inventions You Use Every Day Ser.). (ENG., Illus.). 32p. (gr. 3-6). lib. bdg. 26.60 *(978-1-4677-1093-0(8)*, Lerner Pubns.) Lerner Publishing Group.
Havelin, Kate. Hoopskirts, Union Blues, & Confederate Grays: Civil War Fashions from 1861 to 1865. 2011. (Dressing a Nation: the History of U. S. Fashion Ser.). (ENG., Illus.). 64p. (gr. 5-12). lib. bdg. 31.93 *(978-0-7613-5889-3(7)*, Twenty-First Century Bks.) Lerner Publishing Group.
Hibbert, Clare & Hachette Children's Group. Fashion Model: Find Out How the Top Fashion Models Made It! 2012. (Celeb Ser.). (Illus.). 32p. (gr. 4-6). lib. bdg. 28.50 *(978-1-59771-331-3(7))* Sea-To-Sea Pubns.
Hip-Hop World, 4 vols. 2010. (Hip-Hop World Ser.). (ENG.). 48p. (gr. 3-4). lib. bdg. 127.96 *(978-1-4296-4424-2(9))* Capstone Press of Coughlan Cos.
Hip-Hop World [Capstone Sole Source]. 2010. (Hip-Hop World Ser.). 48p. lib. bdg. 122.60 *(978-1-4296-5866-9(5))* Capstone Press of Coughlan Cos.
Hiton, Lisa. Inventions in Fashion: From Rawhide to Rayon. 2016. (Art & Invention Ser.). 112p. (YA). lib. bdg. 42.79 *(978-1-5026-2305-8(6))* Cavendish Square Publishing.
Hurley, Trish. The 10 Most Enduring Fashion Trends. 2008. (J). 14.99 *(978-1-55448-524-6(X))* Scholastic Library Publishing.
Ikids. Fashion Girls Around the World. 2010. (ENG., Illus.). 10p. (J). (gr. -1-1). 19.99 *(978-1-58476-960-6(2))* Innovative Kids.
Kelley, K. C. Fashion Design Secrets. 2016. 32p. (J). *(978-1-4896-4777-1(5))* Weigl Pubs., Inc.
Kenney, Karen Latchana. Boho Fashion. Kubley, Ashley Newsome, illus. 2014. (What's Your Style? Ser.). (ENG.). 48p. (gr. 5-8). lib. bdg. 30.60 *(978-1-4677-1470-9(4)*, Lerner Pubns.) Lerner Publishing Group.
Kimmel, Allison Crotzer. Prepped & Punked: Bringing 1980s & 1990s Flair to Your Wardrobe, 1 vol. 2014. (Fashion Forward Ser.). (ENG.). 64p. (gr. 4-5). lib. bdg. 34.65 *(978-1-4765-4000-9(4))* Capstone Press of Coughlan Cos.
Klutz Editors. My Fashion Portfolio. 2016. (ENG.). 60p. (J). (gr. 3-7). 21.99 *(978-0-545-90649-4(0))* Klutz.
Krohn, Katherine E. Calico Dresses & Buffalo Robes: American West Fashions from the 1840s to the 1890s. 2011. (Dressing a Nation: the History of U. S. Fashion Ser.). (ENG., Illus.). 64p. (gr. 5-12). lib. bdg. 31.93 *(978-0-7613-5890-9(0)*, Twenty-First Century Bks.) Lerner Publishing Group.
Lambert, Nancy. Accessories Designer: Cut, Color, Make & Create! Feyer, Diane Le, illus. 2017. (My Fashion Studio Ser.). (ENG.). 144p. (J). (gr. 3). pap. 12.99 *(978-1-78445-643-6(8))* Top That! Publishing PLC GBR. Dist: Independent Pubs. Group.
—Dress up Stylist: Cut, Color, Make & Create! Feyer, Diane Le, illus. 2016. (My Fashion Studio Ser.). (ENG.). 56p. (J). (gr. 3). pap. 9.99 *(978-1-78445-644-3(6))* Top That! Publishing PLC GBR. Dist: Independent Pubs. Group.
Langston-George, Rebecca. All Dolled Up: Bringing 1920s & 1930s Flair to Your Wardrobe, 1 vol. 2014. (Fashion Forward Ser.). (ENG.). 64p. (gr. 4-5). lib. bdg. 34.65 *(978-1-4765-3997-3(9))* Capstone Press of Coughlan Cos.
Langston-George, Rebecca, et al. Fashion Forward, 1 vol. 2014. (Fashion Forward Ser.). (ENG.). 64p. (gr. 4-5). lib. bdg. 138.60 *(978-1-4765-4659-9(2))* Capstone Press of Coughlan Cos.
Lardner, Dana. The International Fashionista's Lookbook Diary. Kei, Deanna, illus. 2016. (ENG.). (J). (gr. 3-6). pap. 14.99 ***(978-1-61984-577-0(6))*** Price World Publishing.
Levete, Sarah. Maker Projects for Kids Who Love Fashion. 2016. (ENG., Illus.). 32p. (J). *(978-0-7787-2246-5(5))* Crabtree Publishing Co.
—Stella McCartney Queen of the Catwalk! 2016. (Real-Life Stories Ser.). (ENG., Illus.). 32p. (J). (gr. 4-6). 17.99 *(978-0-7502-9052-4(8)*, Wayland) Hachette Children's Group GBR. Dist: Hachette Bk. Group.
Louie, Ai-Ling. Vera Wang Queen of Fashion; Amazing Chinese American: Biographies of Amazing Asian Americans. 2007. (Biographies of Amazing Asian Americans Ser.). (ENG., Illus.). 48p. (J). pap. 12.99 *(978-0-9787465-3-7(8))* Dragoneagle Pr.
Lundsten, Apryl. The Girls' Life Guide to Being a Style Superstar! Parett, Lisa, illus. 2004. 124p. (J). *(978-0-439-44984-7(7))* Scholastic, Inc.
Luster, Lori. Cool Cat: Bringing 1940s & 1950s Flair to Your Wardrobe, 1 vol. 2014. (Fashion Forward Ser.). (ENG., Illus.). 64p. (gr. 4-5). lib. bdg. 34.65 *(978-1-4765-3998-0(7))* Capstone Press of Coughlan Cos.
Luster, Lori, et al. Fashion Forward: Creating Your Look with the Best of Vintage Style, 1 vol. 2014. (Craft It Yourself Ser.). (ENG., Illus.). 208p. (gr. 3-4). pap. 14.95 *(978-1-62370-062-1(0))* Capstone Young Readers of Coughlan Cos.
Maggio, Viqui. Baby Tease. 2008. (ENG.). 16p. bds. 10.00 *(978-1-933572-08-6(6))* Centro Bks., LLC.
Mattern, Joanne. Ralph Lauren. 2011. (Famous Fashion Designers Ser.). (Illus.). 104p. (gr. 6-12). 35.00 *(978-1-60413-978-5(1)*, Chelsea Hse.) Facts On File, Inc.
McAlpine, Margaret. Working in the Fashion Industry. 2005. (My Future Career Ser.). (Illus.). 64p. (gr. 3-7). lib. bdg. 27.00 *(978-0-8368-4774-1(1)*, Gareth Stevens Learning Library) Stevens, Gareth Publishing LLLP.
Mihaly, Christy. Using Math in Fashion. 2017. (Math You Will Actually Use Ser.). 48p. (J). (gr. 10-10). pap. 11.75 ***(978-1-4994-3860-4(5)***, Rosen Central) Rosen Publishing Group, Inc., The.
Miller, Eileen Rudisill. Fashion Models Paper Dolls. 2013. (Dover Paper Dolls Ser.). (ENG.). 32p. (J). (gr. 2-5). pap. 7.99 *(978-0-486-48877-6(2))* Dover Pubns., Inc.
Miller, Shauna, creator. Penny Chic: How to Be Stylish on a Real Girl's Budget. 2014. (ENG., Illus.). 192p. (J). (gr. 7-17). 16.99 *(978-0-316-23656-0(X)*, Poppy) Little, Brown Bks. for Young Readers.
Mills, Clifford W. Isaac Mizrahi. 2011. (Famous Fashion Designers Ser.). (Illus.). 112p. (gr. 6-12). 35.00 *(978-1-60413-984-6(6)*, Chelsea Hse.) Facts On File, Inc.
Morley, Jacqueline. Fashion: The History of Clothes. 2014. (Illus.). 32p. (J). *(978-1-4351-5629-6(3))* Barnes & Noble, Inc.
Niven, Felicia Lowenstein. Fabulous Fashions of The 1920s. 2011. (Fabulous Fashions of the Decades Ser.). (Illus.). 48p. (J). (gr. 5-18). pap. 8.95 *(978-1-59845-275-4(4))*; lib. bdg. 25.27 *(978-0-7660-3551-5(4))* Enslow Pubs., Inc.
—Fabulous Fashions of The 1930s. 2011. (Fabulous Fashions of the Decades Ser.). (Illus.). 48p. (J). (gr. 5-18). pap. 8.95 *(978-1-59845-276-1(2))*; lib. bdg. 25.27 *(978-0-7660-3824-0(6))* Enslow Pubs., Inc.
—Fabulous Fashions of The 1940s. 2011. (Fabulous Fashions of the Decades Ser.). (Illus.). 48p. (J). (gr. 5-18). pap. 8.95 *(978-1-59845-277-8(0))*; lib. bdg. 25.27 *(978-0-7660-3552-2(2))* Enslow Pubs., Inc.
—Fabulous Fashions of The 1950s. 2011. (Fabulous Fashions of the Decades Ser.). (Illus.). 48p. (J). (gr. 5-18). pap. 8.95 *(978-1-59845-278-5(9))*; lib. bdg. 25.27 *(978-0-7660-3825-7(4))* Enslow Pubs., Inc.
—Fabulous Fashions of The 1960s. 2011. (Fabulous Fashions of the Decades Ser.). (Illus.). 48p. (J). (gr. 5-18). pap. 8.95 *(978-1-59845-279-2(7))*; lib. bdg. 25.27 *(978-0-7660-3553-9(0))* Enslow Pubs., Inc.
—Fabulous Fashions of The 1970s. 2011. (Fabulous Fashions of the Decades Ser.). (Illus.). 48p. (J). (gr. 5-18). pap. 8.95 *(978-1-59845-280-8(0))*; lib. bdg. 25.27 *(978-0-7660-3826-4(2))* Enslow Pubs., Inc.
—Fabulous Fashions of The 1980s. 2011. (Fabulous Fashions of the Decades Ser.). (Illus.). 48p. (J). (gr. 5-18). pap. 8.95 *(978-1-59845-281-5(9))*; lib. bdg. 25.27 *(978-0-7660-3554-6(9))* Enslow Pubs., Inc.
—Fabulous Fashions of The 1990s. 2011. (Fabulous Fashions of the Decades Ser.). (Illus.). 48p. (J). (gr. 5-18). pap. 8.95 *(978-1-59845-282-2(7))*; lib. bdg. 25.27 *(978-0-7660-3827-1(0))* Enslow Pubs., Inc.
Orme, David. Fashion. 2008. (Trailblazers Ser.). (ENG., Illus.). 36p. pap. *(978-1-84167-650-0(0))* Ransom Publishing Ltd.
Park, Louise. Extreme Fashions. 2013. (Discovery Education: Sensational True Stories Ser.). (ENG., Illus.). 32p. (J). (gr. 3-6). pap. 10.00 *(978-1-4777-0107-2(9))*; lib. bdg. 25.25 *(978-1-4777-0061-7(7))* Rosen Publishing Group, Inc., The.
Pease, Pamela. Design Dossier. 2011. (Design Dossiers Ser.). (ENG., Illus.). 96p. (J). (gr. 4). 24.00 *(978-0-9777905-1-7(7))* Paintbox Pr.
Petrillo, Lisa. Isaac Mizrahi. 2011. (Profiles in Fashion Ser.). (Illus.). 111p. 28.95 *(978-1-59935-152-0(8))* Reynolds, Morgan Inc.
—Vera Wang. 2011. (Profiles in Fashion Ser.). (Illus.). 112p. 28.95 *(978-1-59935-150-6(1))* Reynolds, Morgan Inc.
Phillips, Karen & Klutz Editors. My Fabulous Look Book: Fashion Drawing Made Easy. 2011. (ENG.). 114p. (J). 19.99 *(978-0-545-34620-7(7))* Klutz.
Platt, Richard. They Wore What?! The Weird History of Fashion & Beauty. 2007. (Weird History Ser.). (ENG.). 48p. (J). (gr. 3-6). 16.95 *(978-1-58728-582-0(7))*; pap. 9.95 *(978-1-58728-584-4(3))* Cooper Square Publishing Llc.
Pretty Fabulous: Fashion Show: Hundreds of Gorgeous Outfits to Draw & Color! 2012. (ENG.). 144p. (J). spiral bd. 9.95 *(978-1-84858-581-2(0))* Arcturus Publishing GBR. Dist: Bookmasters Distribution.
Project Runway. Project Runway Fashion Paper Doll Kit - African American Girl. 2008. (J). mass mkt. *(978-0-9819053-2-7(3))* Westrim Crafts.
—Project Runway Fashion Paper Doll Kit - Asian Girl. 2008. (J). mass mkt. 12.99 *(978-0-9819053-3-4(1))* Westrim Crafts.
—Project Runway Fashion Paper Doll Kit - Blonde Girl. 2008. (J). mass mkt. 12.99 *(978-0-9819053-6-5(6))* Westrim Crafts.
—Project Runway Fashion Paper Doll Kit - Brunette Girl. 2008. (J). mass mkt. 12.99 *(978-0-9819053-4-1(X))* Westrim Crafts.
—Project Runway Fashion Paper Doll Kit - Caucasian Girl. 2008. (J). mass mkt. 12.99 *(978-0-9819053-0-3(7))* Westrim Crafts.
—Project Runway Fashion Paper Doll Kit - Latina Girl. 2008. (J). mass mkt. 12.99 *(978-0-9819053-1-0(5))* Westrim Crafts.
Reid, Struan & Halstead, Rachel. Clothes: Discover How People Dressed Around the World With 30 Great Step-by-Step Projects. 2008. (ENG.). 64p. (J). (gr. 4-7). pap. 7.99 *(978-1-84476-523-2(7))* Anness Publishing GBR. Dist: National Bk. Network.
Reis, Ronald A. Valentino. 2011. (Famous Fashion Designers Ser.). (Illus.). 120p. (gr. 6-12). 35.00 *(978-1-60413-983-9(8)*, Chelsea Hse.) Facts On File, Inc.
Ridley, Sarah. Clothes. 2017. (Tell Me What You Remember Ser.). (ENG., Illus.). 24p. (J). (gr. k-2). 17.99 *(978-1-4451-3876-3(X)*, Franklin Watts) Hachette Children's Group GBR. Dist: Hachette Bk. Group.
Rissman, Rebecca. Fashion Hacks: Your Fashion Failures Solved! 2017. (Beauty Hacks Ser.). (ENG.). 48p. (gr. 4-5). lib. bdg. 31.32 ***(978-1-5157-6827-2(9))*** Capstone Press of Coughlan Cos.
Rissman, Rebecca. History of Fashion, 1 vol. 2014. (Essential Library of Cultural History Ser.). (ENG.). 112p. (J). (gr. 6-12). lib. bdg. 35.64 *(978-1-62403-553-1(1)*, Essential Library) ABDO Publishing Co.
Rubin, Susan Goldman. Hot Pink: The Life & Fashions of Elsa Schiaparelli. 2015. (ENG., Illus.). 56p. (J). (gr. 5-9). 21.95 *(978-1-4197-1642-3(5)*, Abrams Bks. for Young Readers) Abrams, Inc.
Ryan, Nellie. Fabulous Fashion. Ryan, Nellie, illus. 2014. (ENG., Illus.). 160p. (J). (gr. 3-7). pap. 12.99 *(978-1-907151-84-2(2))* O'Mara, Michael Bks., Ltd. GBR. Dist: Independent Pubs. Group.
Scott-Smith, Louise. Fashion Rebel Outfit Maker: Mix & Mismatch Styles. 2015. (ENG., Illus.). 100p. (J). (gr. 3-6). 17.95 *(978-0-500-65045-5(4)*, 565045) Thames & Hudson.
Simons, Rae. Fashion Math. 2013. (Math 24/7 Ser.: 10). 48p. (J). (gr. 5-18). 19.95 *(978-1-4222-2906-4(8))* Mason Crest.
Slee, Natasha. Design Line: History of Women's Fashion. Mander, Sanna, illus. 2015. (ENG.). 16p. (J). (gr. 5). 17.99 *(978-0-7636-7962-0(3)*, Big Picture Press) Candlewick Pr.
Smith, Kelly. Sticker Fashionista: A Year of Fashion. 2013. (ENG., Illus.). 44p. (J). (gr. 2-7). pap. 12.95 *(978-1-78067-113-0(X))* King, Laurence Publishing GBR. Dist: Hachette Bk. Group.
—Sticker Fashionista: Vintage Style. 2013. (ENG., Illus.). 44p. pap. 12.95 *(978-1-78067-303-5(5))* King, Laurence Publishing GBR. Dist: Hachette Bk. Group.
Song, Sok. Everyday Origami: A Foldable Fashion Guide. Song, Sok, illus. 2016. (Fashion Origami Ser.). (ENG., Illus.). 48p. (gr. 4-5). lib. bdg. 31.99 *(978-1-5157-1630-3(9))* Capstone Press of Coughlan Cos.
—Origami Accessories: A Foldable Fashion Guide. Song, Sok, illus. 2016. (Fashion Origami Ser.). (ENG., Illus.). 48p. (gr. 4-5). lib. bdg. 31.99 *(978-1-5157-1623-5(6))* Capstone Press of Coughlan Cos.
—Origami Outfits: A Foldable Fashion Guide. Song, Sok, illus. 2016. (Fashion Origami Ser.). (ENG., Illus.). 48p. (gr. 4-5). lib. bdg. 31.99 *(978-1-5157-1631-0(7))* Capstone Press of Coughlan Cos.
Sonneborn, Liz. Far Out Fashion: Bringing 1960s & 1970s Flair to Your Wardrobe, 1 vol. 2014. (Fashion Forward Ser.). (ENG., Illus.). 64p. (gr. 4-5). lib. bdg. 34.65 *(978-1-4765-3999-7(5))* Capstone Press of Coughlan Cos.
Spilsbury, Louise. The True Cost of Fashion. 2014. (ENG., Illus.). 48p. (J). *(978-0-7787-0483-6(1))*; pap. *(978-0-7787-0487-4(4))* Crabtree Publishing Co.
Stardoll. Stardoll: Sticker Red Carpet Dress Up. 2013. (Stardoll Ser.). (ENG.). 24p. (J). (gr. 2-4). pap. 6.99 *(978-0-85751-178-2(5))* Transworld Publishers Ltd. GBR. Dist: Independent Pubs. Group.
—Stardoll: Style Bible. 2014. (Stardoll Ser.). (ENG., Illus.). 304p. (J). (gr. 4-6). pap. 12.99 *(978-0-85751-101-0(7))* Transworld Publishers Ltd. GBR. Dist: Independent Pubs. Group.
—Sticker Catwalk Dress Up. 2013. (Stardoll Ser.). (ENG.). 24p. (J). (gr. 2-4). pap. 6.99 *(978-0-85751-176-8(9))* Transworld Publishers Ltd. GBR. Dist: Independent Pubs. Group.
—Sticker Holiday Dress Up. 2013. (Stardoll Ser.). (ENG.). 24p. (J). (gr. 2-4). pap. 6.99 *(978-0-85751-177-5(7))* Transworld Publishers Ltd. GBR. Dist: Independent Pubs. Group.
—Superstar Stylist. 2013. (Stardoll Ser.). (ENG., Illus.). 64p. (J). (gr. 4-6). 12.99 *(978-0-85751-082-2(7))* Transworld Publishers Ltd. GBR. Dist: Independent Pubs. Group.
Steadman, Barbara. Fairy Princess Sticker Paper Doll. 2008. (Dover Little Activity Books Paper Dolls Ser.). (ENG.). 4p. (J). (gr. k-3). pap. 1.50 *(978-0-486-46575-3(6))* Dover Pubns., Inc.
Steele-Saccio, Eva. Headbands & Hairstyles: Make & Wear Super Stylish Headbands. 2010. (ENG.). 60p. (J). (gr. 3-18). 19.99 *(978-1-59174-864-9(X))* Klutz.
Streissguth, Tom. Fashion & Dress Codes. 2011. (Life—a How-To Guide Ser.). (Illus.). 128p. (J). (gr. 6-18). pap. 10.95 *(978-1-59845-313-3(0))* Enslow Pubs., Inc.
—Fashion & Dress Codes: A How-to Guide. 2011. (Life—a How-To Guide Ser.). (Illus.). 128p. (J). lib. bdg. 33.27 *(978-0-7660-3444-0(5))* Enslow Pubs., Inc.
Sun, Jennie. Doodle Design & Draw ROCK STAR FASHIONS. 2012. (Dover Doodle Bks.). (ENG., Illus.). 64p. (J). (gr. 3-5). pap. 5.99 *(978-0-486-48703-8(2))* Dover Pubns., Inc.
—Fashion. 2011. (Dover Doodle Bks.). (ENG.). 64p. (J). (gr. 3-5). pap. 5.99 *(978-0-486-48050-3(X))* Dover Pubns., Inc.
Sun, Ming-Ju & Creative Haven Staff. Flower Fashion Fantasies. 2012. (Adult Coloring Ser.). (ENG., Illus.). 64p. (gr. 3). pap. 5.99 *(978-0-486-49863-8(8))* Dover Pubns., Inc.
Tierney, Tom. Cavalier & Puritan Fashions. 2005. (Dover Fashion Coloring Book Ser.). (ENG., Illus.). 48p. (J). (gr. 6-8). pap. 3.95 *(978-0-486-43655-5(1))* Dover Pubns., Inc.
—Fashions of the Roaring Twenties Coloring Book. 2013. (Dover Coloring Bks.). (ENG., Illus.). 32p. (gr. 3-12). pap. 3.99 *(978-0-486-49950-5(2))* Dover Pubns., Inc.
Ungs, Tim. Paul McCartney & Stella McCartney. 2004. (Famous Families Ser.). (Illus.). 48p. (J). lib. bdg. 29.25 *(978-1-4042-0263-4(3))* Rosen Publishing Group, Inc., The.
Vander Hook, Sue. Hip-Hop Fashion, 1 vol. 2010. (Hip-Hop World Ser.). (ENG.). 48p. (gr. 3-4). lib. bdg. 31.99 *(978-1-4296-4017-6(0))* Capstone Press of Coughlan Cos.
Voce, Karma. Forever Inspired Coloring Book: Paris Fashions. 2016. (ENG., Illus.). 96p. (J). (gr. 3-7). pap. 7.99 *(978-1-944686-60-4(6)*, Racehorse Publishing) Skyhorse Publishing Co., Inc.
—Forever Inspired Coloring Book: Tokyo Fashions. 2016. (ENG., Illus.). 96p. (J). (gr. 3-7). pap. 7.99 *(978-1-944686-61-1(4)*, Racehorse Publishing) Skyhorse Publishing Co., Inc.
Watson, Stephanie. Streetwear Fashion. Kubley, Ashley Newsome, illus. 2014. (What's Your Style? Ser.). (ENG.). 48p. (gr. 5-8). lib. bdg. 30.60 *(978-1-4677-1471-6(2)*, Lerner Pubns.) Lerner Publishing Group.
We are Photogirls Staff. DIY Fashion Shoot Book. 2014. (ENG., Illus.). 144p. 17.95 *(978-1-78067-299-1(3))* King, Laurence Publishing GBR. Dist: Hachette Bk. Group.
Weaver, Janice. From Head to Toe: Bound Feet, Bathing Suits, & Other Bizarre & Beautiful Things. Blake, Francis, illus. 2003. (ENG.). 80p. (J). (gr. 5-9). pap. 16.95 *(978-0-88776-654-1(4)*, Tundra Bks.) Tundra Bks. CAN. Dist: Penguin Random Hse. LLC.
Werle, Simone. 13 Fashion Styles Children Should Know. 2013. (ENG., Illus.). 48p. (J). (gr. 3-7). 14.95 *(978-3-7913-7134-4(7))* Prestel Verlag GmbH & Co KG. DEU. Dist: Penguin Random Hse. LLC.
Wilson, Rosie. Fashion Industry. 2010. (Closer Look: Global Industries Ser.). (ENG.). 48p. (YA). lib. bdg. 29.25 *(978-1-4358-9631-4(9)*, Rosen Reference) Rosen Publishing Group, Inc., The.

FASHION—FICTION

Anderson, Lynda & Bennett, Melanie. The Micro Meanies. 2008. 180p. pap. *(978-0-9783204-7-8(6))* Aaspirations.
Axelsson, Carina. Model Undercover: London. 2016. (Model Undercover Ser.: 3). (ENG.). 368p. (J). (gr. 5-8). pap. 6.99 *(978-1-4926-2088-4(2)*, Sourcebooks Jabberwocky) Sourcebooks, Inc.
—Model Undercover: New York. 2015. (Model Undercover Ser.: 2). (ENG.). 320p. (J). (gr. 4-8). pap. 6.99 *(978-1-4926-0785-4(1)*, Sourcebooks Jabberwocky) Sourcebooks, Inc.
—Paris. 2014. (Model Undercover Ser.: 1). (ENG.). 368p. (J). (gr. 4-7). pap. 6.99 *(978-1-4022-8587-5(6)*, Sourcebooks Jabberwocky) Sourcebooks, Inc.
AZ Books, creator. Fashion Collection. 2013. (My Workshop Ser.). (ENG., Illus.). 46p. (J). (gr. 1-3). spiral bd. 14.95 *(978-1-61889-073-3(5))* AZ Bks. LLC.
—My Favorite Pet. 2013. (Velvet Fantasy Ser.). (ENG., Illus.). 16p. (J). (gr. k-3). pap. 4.95 *(978-1-61889-293-5(2))* AZ Bks. LLC.
AZ Books Staff. Fashion Ideas. Batan, Natalia, ed. 2012. (Fashion Ideas Ser.). (ENG.). 60p. (J). bds. 15.95 *(978-1-61889-075-7(1))* AZ Bks. LLC.
Bateson, Maggie. My Fairy Fashion Show: A Pop-up & Play Book. Comfort, Louise, illus. 2008. (ENG.). 20p. (J). (gr. 4-8). 23.95 *(978-0-230-53035-5(4)*, Macmillan) Pan Macmillan GBR. Dist: Trans-Atlantic Pubns., Inc.
Benincasa, Sara. Great. 2014. (ENG.). 272p. (YA). (gr. 9). 17.99 *(978-0-06-222269-5(4)*, HarperTeen) HarperCollins Pubs.
Bennardo, Charlotte & Zaman, Natalie. Blonde Ops. 2014. (ENG.). 288p. (YA). (gr. 7). 17.99 *(978-1-250-03039-9(0)*, 9781250030399, St. Martin's Griffin) St. Martin's Pr.
—Sirenz. 2011. 270p. pap. 9.95 *(978-0-7387-2968-8(X))* Flux: Image Theory Group.
—Sirenz. 2011. (ENG.). 288p. (YA). (gr. 7-18). pap. 9.95 *(978-0-7387-2319-8(3)*, Flux) North Star Editions.
—Sirenz Back in Fashion. 2012. (ENG.). 288p. (YA). pap. 9.95 *(978-0-7387-3187-2(0)*, Flux) North Star Editions.
Bennett, Sophia. Sequins, Secrets, & Silver Linings. 2011. (ENG.). 304p. (J). (gr. 7-11). 16.99 *(978-0-545-24241-7(X)*, Chicken Hse., The) Scholastic, Inc.
Berk, Sheryl & Berk, Carrie. Designer Drama. 2016. (Fashion Academy Ser.: 3). (ENG.). 192p. (J). (gr. 5-8). pap. 7.99 *(978-1-4926-1353-4(3)*, 9781492613534, Sourcebooks Jabberwocky) Sourcebooks, Inc.
Black, Allyson. Fashion Face-off. Johnson, Shane L., illus. 2011. (Scarlett & Crimson Ser.). (ENG.). 112p. (J). (gr. 3-7). pap. 6.99 *(978-1-4169-5937-3(8)*, Simon Spotlight) Simon Spotlight.
Bradman, Tony. Happy Ever After, 1 vol. Warburton, Sarah, illus. 2009. (After Happily Ever After Ser.). (ENG.). 56p. (gr. 2-3). lib. bdg. 25.32 *(978-1-4342-1301-3(3)*, After Happily Ever After) Stone Arch Bks.
Bryant, Annie. Fashion Frenzy. 2006. (Beacon Street Girls Ser.: Vol. 9). (Illus.). 203p. (J). *(978-1-4156-9393-3(5))* B*tween Productions, Inc.
—Fashion Frenzy. 2009. (Beacon Street Girls Ser.: 9). (ENG.). 256p. (J). (gr. 4-8). pap. 7.99 *(978-1-4169-6439-1(8)*, Aladdin) Simon & Schuster Children's Publishing.
Carlson, Melody. Catwalk, 1 vol. 2014. (On the Runway Ser.). (ENG.). 224p. (YA). pap. 9.99 *(978-0-310-74810-6(0))* Zondervan.
—Ciao, 1 vol. 2014. (On the Runway Ser.). (ENG.). 208p. (YA). pap. 9.99 *(978-0-310-74843-4(7))* Zondervan.

—Glamour, 1 vol. 2014. (On the Runway Ser.). (ENG.). 224p. (YA). pap. 9.99 *(978-0-310-74887-8(9))* Zondervan.
—Premiere, 1 vol. 2014. (On the Runway Ser.). (ENG.). 224p. (YA). pap. 9.99 *(978-0-310-74728-4(7))* Zondervan.
—Rendezvous, 1 vol. 2014. (On the Runway Ser.). (ENG.). 224p. (YA). pap. 9.99 *(978-0-310-74861-8(5))* Zondervan.
Cross, Gillian. Where I Belong. 2011. (ENG., Illus.). 256p. (J). (gr. 5-18). 17.95 *(978-0-8234-2332-3(8))* Holiday Hse., Inc.
Dimopoulos, Elaine. Material Girls. (ENG.). 336p. (YA). (gr. 9). 2016. pap. 8.99 *(978-0-544-67173-7(2))* 2015. 17.99 *(978-0-544-38850-5(X))* Houghton Mifflin Harcourt Publishing Co. (HMH Books For Young Readers).
Disney Book Group. Descendants 2 Evie's Fashion Book. Disney Storybook Art Team, illus. 2017. (ENG.). 144p. (J). (gr. 3-7). 12.99 ***(978-1-368-00251-6(X))*** Disney Pr.
Disney Minnie, Disney. Disney Minnie - My Colorful Closet. 2014. (ENG.). 10p. (J). (gr. -1-1). 12.99 *(978-0-7944-3141-9(0))* Reader's Digest Assn., Inc., The.
Edwards, Mamie. Magical Mix-Ups: Friends & Fashion. Hodgkinson, Leigh, illus. 2012. (Magical Mix-Ups Ser.). (ENG.). 96p. (J). (gr. 2-5). pap. 6.99 *(978-0-7636-6166-3(X))*, Nosy Crow) Candlewick Pr.
Fowler, Elle & Fowler, Blair. Beneath the Glitter. 2013. (Sophia & Ava London Ser.: 1). (ENG.). 288p. (YA). (gr. 7). pap. 17.99 *(978-1-250-01715-4(7))*, 9781250017154, St. Martin's Griffin) St. Martin's Pr.
Get Together Girls - Fashion Show. 2005. (J). bds. *(978-1-4194-0086-5(X))* Paradise Pr., Inc.
Golden Books Staff. Barbie Loves Ballet/Fashion Show Fun!, 2 bks. in 1. Golden Books Staff, illus. 2009. (Pictureback(R) Ser.). (ENG., Illus.). 32p. (J). (gr. -1-2). pap. 4.99 *(978-0-375-85148-3(8))*, Golden Bks.) Random Hse. Children's Bks.
Gordon, Domenica More. Archie. 2012. (ENG., Illus.). 48p. (J). (gr. -1-1). 17.99 *(978-1-59990-936-3(7))*, 9781599909363, Bloomsbury USA Childrens) Bloomsbury Publishing USA.
Guillain, Adam & Guillain, Charlotte. The Three Frilly Goats Fluff. Littler, Phil, illus. 2015. (ENG.). 32p. (J). *(978-0-7787-1935-9(9))* Crabtree Publishing Co.
Gurevich, Margaret. All or Nothing. Hagel, Brooke, illus. 2016. (Chloe by Design Ser.). (ENG.). 96p. (gr. 5-8). lib. bdg. 25.32 *(978-1-4965-3263-3(5))* Stone Arch Bks.
—Back to Basics. Hagel, Brooke, illus. 2016. (Chloe by Design Ser.). (ENG.). 96p. (gr. 5-8). lib. bdg. 25.32 *(978-1-4965-3261-9(9))* Stone Arch Bks.
—Chloe by Design, 1 vol. Hagel, Brooke, illus. 2014. (Chloe by Design Ser.). (ENG.). 96p. (gr. 5-8). 101.28 *(978-1-4342-9379-4(3))* Stone Arch Bks.
—Chloe by Design: Making the Cut, 1 vol. Hagel, Brooke, illus. 2014. (Chloe by Design Ser.). (ENG.). 384p. (gr. 4-8). 14.95 *(978-1-62370-112-3(0))* Capstone Young Readers of Coughlan Cos.
—Chloe by Design: Measuring Up. Hagel, Brooke, illus. 2016. (Chloe by Design Ser.). (ENG.). 384p. (gr. 4-8). 14.95 *(978-1-62370-727-9(7))* Capstone Young Readers of Coughlan Cos.
—The Final Cut. Hagel, Brooke, illus. 2016. (Chloe by Design Ser.). (ENG.). 96p. (gr. 5-8). lib. bdg. 25.32 *(978-1-4965-3264-0(3))* Stone Arch Bks.
—Made to Measure. Hagel, Brooke, illus. 2016. (Chloe by Design Ser.). (ENG.). 96p. (gr. 5-8). lib. bdg. 25.32 *(978-1-4965-3262-6(7))* Stone Arch Bks.
Gutknecht, Allison. The Bling Queen. 2016. (Mix Ser.). (ENG., Illus.). 208p. (J). (gr. 4-8). pap. 7.99 *(978-1-4814-5308-0(4))*, Aladdin) Simon & Schuster Children's Publishing.
Hairston, Lisa Lee. Victoria Has A Secret. 2011. 36p. 23.00 *(978-1-4269-4994-4(4))* Trafford Publishing.
Harris, Tricia. Fairy Tales for Fashionistas. 2010. 57p. pap. 12.95 *(978-1-4457-2353-2(0))* Lulu Pr., Inc.
Hore, Rosie. Sticker Dolly Dressing Wartime Fashion IR. 2015. (Historical Sticker Dolly Dressing Ser.). (ENG.). 24+ 10p. (J). (gr. k-5). pap. 9.99 *(978-0-7945-3474-5(0))*, Usborne) EDC Publishing.
Jackson, Katy, illus. Pretty Fashions: Beautiful Fashions to Color! 2014. (ENG.). 96p. (J). (gr. -1-2). 7.99 *(978-1-4424-8386-6(5))*, Little Simon) Little Simon.
Jones, Jen. Ashley Goes Viral. Franco, Paula, illus. 2015. (Sleepover Girls Ser.). (ENG.). 128p. (gr. 3-5). pap. 6.95 *(978-1-62370-306-6(9))* Stone Arch Bks.
Juby, Susan. The Fashion Committee. 2017. (ENG.). 320p. (YA). (gr. 7). 18.99 *(978-0-451-46878-9(3))*, Viking Books for Young Readers) Penguin Young Readers Group.
Kann, Victoria. Fashion Fun. Kann, Victoria, illus. 2016. (Pinkalicious I Can Read Ser.). (ENG., Illus.). 32p. (J). (gr. -1-3). 13.55 *(978-0-606-39265-5(3))* Turtleback Bks.
Karasyov, Carrie & Kargman, Jill. Summer Intern. 2007. 184p. (YA). (gr. 7-18). lib. bdg. 17.89 *(978-0-06-115376-1(1))*, HarperTeen) HarperCollins Pubs.
Krosoczka, Jarrett J. Lunch Lady & the Picture Day Peril. 2012. (Lunch Lady Ser.). (ENG., Illus.). 96p. (J). (gr. 2-5). pap. 6.99 *(978-0-375-87035-4(0))*; lib. bdg. 12.99 *(978-0-375-97035-1(5))* Random Hse. Children's Bks. (Knopf Bks. for Young Readers).
—Lunch Lady & the Picture Day Peril. 2012. (Lunch Lady Ser.: 8). lib. bdg. 17.20 *(978-0-606-26811-0(1))*, Turtleback) Turtleback Bks.
Lenhard, Elizabeth. Drop-Dead Gorgeous. 2014. 186p. (J). pap. *(978-0-545-58951-2(7))* Scholastic, Inc.
Man-Kong, Mary. Barbie - Fashion Fairytale. Random House Value Publishing Staff, illus. 2010. (Step into Reading Ser.). (ENG.). 32p. (J). (gr. -1-1). pap. 3.99 *(978-0-375-86697-5(3))*, Random Hse. Bks. for Young Readers) Random Hse. Children's Bks.
Mattel Inc. Staff, illus. Barbie Always in Style. 2011. (Storybook & Playset Ser.). (ENG.). 24p. (J). (gr. -1-1). 19.99 *(978-0-7944-2316-2(7))* Reader's Digest Assn., Inc., The.
May, Kyla. Kiki: My Stylish Life. 2013. (Lotus Lane Ser.: 1). (ENG.). 96p. (J). (gr. 1-3). pap. 4.99 *(978-0-545-44512-2(4))* Scholastic, Inc.
—Kiki: My Stylish Life. 2013. (Lotus Lane Ser.: 1). lib. bdg. 14.75 *(978-0-606-31977-5(8))*, Turtleback) Turtleback Bks.
—Kiki Bk. 1: My Stylish Life. 2013. (Lotus Lane Ser.: 1). (ENG.). 96p. (J). (gr. 1-3). lib. bdg. 15.99 *(978-0-545-49613-1(6))* Scholastic, Inc.
McLoughlin, Coleen. Passion for Fashion. 2008. (Coleen Style Queen Ser.: 1). (ENG.). 160p. (J). pap. 7.99 *(978-0-00-727739-1(3))*, HarperCollins Children's Bks.) HarperCollins Pubs. Ltd. GBR. Dist: HarperCollins Pubs.
Meadows, Daisy. Alexa the Fashion Editor Fairy. 2013. (Rainbow Magic — the Fashion Fairies Ser.: 4). lib. bdg. 14.75 *(978-0-606-31994-2(8))*, Turtleback) Turtleback Bks.
Meister, Cari. The Fancy Octopus, 1 vol. Harpster, Steve, illus. 2011. (Ocean Tales Ser.). (ENG.). 32p. (gr. 2-3). pap. 6.25 *(978-1-4342-3392-9(8))*; lib. bdg. 22.65 *(978-1-4342-3201-4(8))* Stone Arch Bks.
Miller, Kirsten. The Eternal Ones: What If Love Refused to Die? 2011. (ENG.). 432p. (YA). (gr. 7-18). 9.99 *(978-1-59514-375-4(0))*, Razorbill) Penguin Young Readers Group.
More Gordon, Domenica. Archie. More Gordon, Domenica, illus. 2012. (ENG., Illus.). 48p. (J). (gr. -1-1). 18.89 *(978-1-59990-947-9(2))*, 9781599909479, Bloomsbury USA Childrens) Bloomsbury Publishing USA.
Moses, Jennifer Anne. Tales from My Closet. 2014. (J). 298p. pap. *(978-0-545-66811-8(5))*; (ENG.). 304p. (gr. 7-9). 17.99 *(978-0-545-51608-2(0))* Scholastic, Inc. (Scholastic Pr.).
O'Connor, Jane. Fancy Nancy Petite Library. Glasser, Robin Preiss, illus. 2010. (Fancy Nancy Ser.). (ENG.). 32p. (J). (gr. k-3). 14.99 *(978-0-06-191527-7(0))*, HarperFestival) HarperCollins Pubs.
—Fancy Nancy's Fashion Parade! Reusable Sticker Book. Glasser, Robin Preiss & Bracken, Carolyn, illus. 2008. (Fancy Nancy Ser.). (ENG.). 12p. (J). (gr. -1-2). pap. 6.99 *(978-0-06-123601-3(2))*, HarperFestival) HarperCollins Pubs.
—Fashionista. Glasser, Robin Preiss, illus. 2011. (Fancy Nancy Ser.). (ENG.). 32p. (J). (gr. -1-3). pap., act. bk. ed. 4.99 *(978-0-06-188266-1(6))*, HarperFestival) HarperCollins Pubs.
Oliver, Jasmine. Prada Princesses. 2007. (Project Fashion Ser.: 3). (ENG.). 192p. (YA). (gr. 9-12). pap. 9.99 *(978-1-4169-3812-5(5))*, Simon Pulse) Simon Pulse.
Paige, D. M. Size 0. 2015. (Opportunity Ser.). (ENG.). 120p. (YA). (gr. 6-12). 34.65 *(978-1-4677-6017-1(X))*, Lerner Digital) Lerner Publishing Group.
Palatini, Margie. Hogg, Hogg, & Hog. Palatini, Margie, illus. 2011. (ENG., Illus.). 32p. (J). (gr. -1-3). 15.99 *(978-1-4424-0322-2(5))*, Simon & Schuster Bks. For Young Readers) Simon & Schuster Bks. For Young Readers.
Perini, Mark & Cross, Julie. Halfway Perfect. 2015. (ENG.). 384p. (YA). (gr. 8-12). pap. 9.99 *(978-1-4022-9719-9(X))*, 9781402297199) Sourcebooks, Inc.
Perry, Brad Lee. Clumsy Claudia & the Gentle Forest Friends, 1 vol. Perry, Diana Tom, illus. 2010. 56p. pap. 16.95 *(978-1-4489-4633-4(6))* America Star Bks.
Peschke, Marci. Fashion Queen. Mourning, Tuesday, illus. 2015. (Kylie Jean Ser.). (ENG.). 112p. (gr. 2-3). 8.95 *(978-1-4795-5881-0(8))*, Kylie Jean) Picture Window Bks.
Pesson, Lauren. My Little Kappa Delta. 2006. (J). 15.00 *(978-0-9779594-0-2(6))* Lauren Elizabeth Design.
Random House Staff, illus. Barbie Fairytale Collection. 2011. (Step into Reading Ser.). (ENG.). 160p. (J). (gr. -1-1). pap. 7.99 *(978-0-375-87255-6(8))*, Random Hse. Bks. for Young Readers) Random Hse. Children's Bks.
Reader's Digest Staff. Disney Minnie - Take-Along Tunes; Music Player with 20 Tunes. 2013. (Take-Along Tunes Ser.). (ENG.). 32p. (J). (gr. -1-k). 19.99 *(978-0-7944-2553-1(4))* Reader's Digest Assn., Inc., The.
Reeve, Penny. The Back Leg of a Goat: A Tania Abbey Adventure. Apps, Fred, illus. 2008. (Tania Abbey Adventure Ser.). (ENG.). 96p. (J). pap. 6.99 *(978-1-84550-340-6(6))*, c8e23bb3-9904-4201-971e-e57faa66b8f3) Christian Focus Pubns. GBR. Dist: Bookmasters Distribution.
Robertson, Donald. Mitford at the Fashion Zoo. 2015. (ENG., Illus.). 40p. (J). (gr. -1-2). 17.99 *(978-0-451-47542-8(9))*, Viking Books for Young Readers) Penguin Young Readers Group.
—Mitford at the Hollywood Zoo. 2017. (ENG., Illus.). 40p. (J). (gr. -1-2). 17.99 *(978-0-451-47543-5(7))*, Viking Books for Young Readers) Penguin Young Readers Group.
Sauer, Tammi. Mary Had a Little Glam. Brantley-Newton, Vanessa, illus. 2016. (ENG.). 32p. (J). (gr. -1-2). 14.95 *(978-1-4549-1393-1(2))* Sterling Publishing Co., Inc.
Simon, Coco. Alexis: The Icing on the Cupcake. 2014. (Cupcake Diaries: 20). lib. bdg. 17.20 *(978-0-606-35786-9(6))* Turtleback Bks.
—Alexis the Icing on the Cupcake. 2014. (Cupcake Diaries: 20). (ENG., Illus.). 160p. (J). (gr. 3-7). pap. 6.99 *(978-1-4814-0468-6(7))*, Simon Spotlight) Simon Spotlight.
—Mia: A Matter of Taste. 2013. (Cupcake Diaries: 14). lib. bdg. 16.00 *(978-0-606-32042-9(3))*, Turtleback) Turtleback Bks.
—Mia: Fashion Plates & Cupcakes. 2014. (Cupcake Diaries: 18). lib. bdg. 16.00 *(978-0-606-35436-3(0))* Turtleback Bks.
—Mia a Matter of Taste. 2013. (Cupcake Diaries: 14). (ENG., Illus.). 160p. (J). (gr. 3-7). 15.99 *(978-1-4424-7480-2(7))*; pap. 6.99 *(978-1-4424-7435-2(1))* Simon Spotlight. (Simon Spotlight).
—Mia Fashion Plates & Cupcakes. 2014. (Cupcake Diaries: 18). (ENG., Illus.). 160p. (J). (gr. 3-7). pap. 5.99 *(978-1-4424-9790-0(4))*, Simon Spotlight) Simon Spotlight.
Smale, Holly. Geek Girl. 2015. (Geek Girl Ser.: 1). 384p. (YA). (gr. 8). 17.99 *(978-0-06-233357-5(7))*, HarperTeen) HarperCollins Pubs.
Sorrells, W. A. Florence Fiasco. Bancroft, Tom & Corley, Rob, illus. 2007. 136p. (J). *(978-0-9792912-2-7(4))* KidsGive, LLC.
Spaziante, Patrick, illus. OLIVIA & the Fashion Show. 2011. (Olivia TV Tie-In Ser.). (ENG.). 16p. (J). (gr. -1-1). pap. 5.99 *(978-1-4424-2028-1(6))*, Simon Spotlight) Simon Spotlight.
Steel, Danielle. Pretty Minnie in Hollywood. Valiant, Kristi, illus. 2016. (ENG.). 32p. (J). (gr. -1-2). 17.99 *(978-0-553-53755-0(5))*, Doubleday Bks. for Young Readers) Random Hse. Children's Bks.
Stern, A. J. Fashion Frenzy. Marts, Doreen Mulryan, illus. 2011. (Frankly, Frannie Ser.: 6). (ENG.). 128p. (J). (gr. 1-3). pap. 5.99 *(978-0-448-45544-0(7))*, Grosset & Dunlap) Penguin Young Readers Group.
Stilton, Geronimo & Stilton, Thea. Thea Stilton & the Mystery in Paris. 2010. (Thea Stilton Ser.: 5). (ENG.). 176p. (J). (gr. 2-5). pap. 8.99 *(978-0-545-22773-5(9))*, Scholastic Paperbacks) Scholastic, Inc.
Taylor, Chloe. Knot Too Shabby! Zhang, Nancy, illus. 2014. (Sew Zoey Ser.: 7). (ENG.). 176p. (J). (gr. 3-7). pap. 5.99 *(978-1-4814-1398-5(8))*, Simon Spotlight) Simon Spotlight.
—Ready to Wear. Christy, Jana & Zhang, Nancy, illus. 2013. (Sew Zoey Ser.: 1). (ENG.). 176p. (J). (gr. 3-7). pap. 6.99 *(978-1-4424-7933-3(7))*, Simon Spotlight) Simon Spotlight.
Taylor, Chloë. A Tangled Thread. Zhang, Nancy, illus. 2014. (Sew Zoey Ser.: 6). (ENG.). 176p. (J). (gr. 3-7). 16.99 *(978-1-4814-0444-0(X))*, Simon Spotlight) Simon Spotlight.
Taylor, Chloe. A Tangled Thread. Zhang, Nancy, illus. 2014. (Sew Zoey Ser.: 6). (ENG.). 176p. (J). (gr. 3-7). pap. 5.99 *(978-1-4814-0443-3(1))*, Simon Spotlight) Simon Spotlight.
Turetsky, Bianca. The Time-Traveling Fashionista at the Palace of Marie Antoinette. 2013. (Time-Traveling Fashionista Ser.: 2). (ENG., Illus.). 272p. (J). (gr. 3-7). pap. 9.00 *(978-0-316-10535-4(X))*, Poppy) Little, Brown Bks. for Young Readers.
Williams, Sean J. Fashion Fairies. 2012. 52p. pap. 37.37 *(978-1-4691-7600-0(9))* Xlibris Corp.
Young, Jessica. Fin-Tastic Fashion. Secheret, Jessica, illus. 2017. (Finley Flowers Ser.). (ENG.). 128p. (gr. 2-3). lib. bdg. 25.32 ***(978-1-4795-9804-5(6))***, Finley Flowers) Picture Window Bks.

FASHION—VOCATIONAL GUIDANCE

Beker, Jeanne. Passion for Fashion: Careers in Style. Dion, Nathalie, illus. 2008. (ENG.). 80p. (J). (gr. 5-9). pap. 18.95 *(978-0-88776-800-2(8))*, Tundra Bks.) Tundra Bks. CAN. Dist: Penguin Random Hse. LLC.
Brocklehurst, Ruth. Vintage Fashion Coloring Book IR. 2015. (Patterns to Color Ser.). (ENG.). 32p. (J). (gr. k-5). pap. 5.99 *(978-0-7945-3490-5(2))*, Usborne) EDC Publishing.
Dunn, Mary R. I Want to Be a Fashion Designer. 2009. (Dream Jobs Ser.). (Illus.). 24p. (YA). (gr. 2-5). lib. bdg. 22.60 *(978-1-4042-4472-6(7))* Rosen Publishing Group, Inc., The.
—Quiero Ser Diseñador de Modas. 2009.Tr. of I Want to Be a Fashion Designer. (SPA., Illus.). 24p. pap. 8.25 *(978-1-4358-3433-0(X))*, Editorial Buenas Letras) Rosen Publishing Group, Inc., The.
Fiscus, Jim. Careers in the Fashion Industry. rev. ed. 2005. (Career Resource Library). (Illus.). 192p. (YA). (gr. 7-12). lib. bdg. 34.60 *(978-0-8239-4082-0(9))* Rosen Publishing Group, Inc., The.
Freese, Susan M. Fashion, 1 vol. 2011. (Inside the Industry Ser.). (ENG., Illus.). 112p. (J). (gr. 6-12). lib. bdg. 35.64 *(978-1-61714-800-2(8))*, Essential Library) ABDO Publishing Co.
Giacobello, John. Careers in the Fashion Industry. 2009. (Career Resource Library). 192p. (gr. 7-12). 63.90 *(978-1-60853-405-0(7))* Rosen Publishing Group, Inc., The.
Giacobello, John. Choosing a Career in the Fashion Industry. 2005. (World of Work Ser.). (Illus.). 64p. (YA). (gr. 7-12). lib. bdg. 31.95 *(978-0-8239-3296-2(6))*, WWFASH) Rosen Publishing Group, Inc., The.
Henneberg, Susan. Behind-The-Scenes Fashion Careers. 2017. (Behind the Glamour Ser.). (ENG., Illus.). 64p. (gr. 4-5). lib. bdg. 31.32 *(978-1-5157-4897-7(9))* Capstone Press of Coughlan Cos.
Miller, Mirella S. Working in Fashion. 2018. (ENG.). 32p. (gr. 3-6). ***(978-1-63235-445-7(4))***, 12-Story Library) Pr. Room Editions LLC.
Mooney, Carla. STEM Jobs in Fashion & Beauty. 2014. (ENG., Illus.). 48p. (gr. 4-8). 35.64 *(978-1-62717-700-9(0))* Rourke Educational Media.
O'Donnell, Kerri. Careers in Modeling. (Career Resource Library). 192p. (gr. 7-12). 2009. 63.90 *(978-1-60853-400-5(6))* 2005. (Illus.). (YA). lib. bdg. 34.60 *(978-0-8239-3183-5(8))* Rosen Publishing Group, Inc., The.
So, You Want to Work in Fashion? How to Break into the World of Fashion & Design. 2014. (Be What You Want Ser.). (ENG., Illus.). 192p. (J). (gr. 3-7). pap. 11.99 *(978-1-58270-452-4(X))* Aladdin/Beyond Words.
Szumski, Bonnie. Careers in Fashion. 2014. (Exploring Careers). (ENG., Illus.). 80p. (J). lib. bdg. *(978-1-60152-704-2(7))* ReferencePoint Pr., Inc.
Thomas, Isabel. Being a Fashion Stylist. 2012. (On the Radar: Awesome Jobs Ser.). (ENG., Illus.). 32p. (gr. 4-8). lib. bdg. 26.60 *(978-0-7613-7778-8(6))*, Lerner Pubns.) Lerner Publishing Group.
Vescia, Monique. Fashion. 2010. (Career Launcher Ser.). (C). (gr. 9). 182p. 34.95 *(978-0-8160-7965-0(X))*, Ferguson Publishing Co.); 192p. pap. 14.95 *(978-0-8160-7987-2(0))*, Checkmark Bks.) Facts On File, Inc.

FASTS AND FEASTS

see also Christmas; Easter; Holidays

Addasi, Maha. The White Nights of Ramadan. Gannon, Ned, illus. 2008. (ENG.). 32p. (J). (gr. 2-4). 16.95 *(978-1-59078-523-2(1))* Boyds Mills Pr.
Allen, Katherine E., illus. Festival of Light: Deepavali Legends from Around India. 2005. 61p. (J). *(978-81-87111-70-2(4))* Vakils, Feffer & Simons, Ltd.
Aloian, Molly. Ramadan. 2008. (Celebrations in My World Ser.). (ENG., Illus.). 32p. (J). (gr. k-3). pap. *(978-0-7787-4303-3(9))*; lib. bdg. *(978-0-7787-4285-2(7))* Crabtree Publishing Co.
Amstutz, Lisa J. Ramadan. 2017. (Holidays Around the World Ser.). (ENG., Illus.). 24p. (gr. k-1). lib. bdg. 21.99 *(978-1-5157-4856-4(1))*, Pebble Bks.) Capstone Press of Coughlan Cos.
Anderson, Sheila. Ramadan, 1 vol. Conger, Holli, illus. 2009. (Cultural Holidays Ser.). (ENG.). 32p. (gr. -1-4). 28.50 *(978-1-60270-605-7(0))*, Looking Glass Library- Nonfiction) Magic Wagon.
Andrade, Mary J., photos by. Day of the Dead A Passion for Life: Día de los Muertos Pasión por la Vida. Andrade, Mary J., . 2nd ed. 2007. (SPA & ENG., Illus.). 200p. lib. bdg., stu. ed., tchr.'s training gde. ed. 29.95 *(978-0-9791624-0-4(8))* La Oferta Publishing Co.
Barner, Bob. The Day of the Dead (El Día de los Muerto) Mlawer, Teresa, tr. Barner, Bob, illus. 2011. (ENG., Illus.). 32p. (J). pap. 7.99 *(978-0-8234-2381-1(6))* Holiday Hse., Inc.
Bullard, Lisa. Rashad's Ramadan & Eid Al-Fitr. Conger, Holli, illus. 2012. (Holidays & Special Days Ser.). 24p. (J). (gr. k-2). pap. 39.62 *(978-0-7613-9250-7(5))*, Millbrook Pr.) Lerner Publishing Group.
—Rashad's Ramadan & Eid Al-Fitr. Conger, Holli, illus. 2012. (Cloverleaf Books — Holidays & Special Days Ser.). (ENG.). 24p. (J). (gr. k-2). lib. bdg. 23.93 *(978-0-7613-5079-8(9))* Lerner Publishing Group.
—Rashad's Ramadan & Eid Al-Fitr. Conger, Holli, illus. 2012. (Cloverleaf Books — Holidays & Special Days Ser.). (ENG.). 24p. (gr. k-2). pap. 6.95 *(978-0-7613-8583-7(5))*, Millbrook Pr.) Lerner Publishing Group.
Claybourne, Anna. Feasts in Ancient Times. 2011. (Big Picture: Food Ser.). (ENG.). 24p. (gr. 1-2). pap. 41.70 *(978-1-4296-6726-5(5))*, First Facts) Capstone Press of Coughlan Cos.
Dick, Judy. Sacred Time: The Jewish Calendar & Life Cycle. 2012. (J). *(978-0-87441-863-7(1))* Behrman Hse., Inc.
Dickmann, Nancy. Ramadan & Id-Ul-Fitr, 1 vol. 2010. (Holidays & Festivals Ser.). (ENG.). 24p. (gr. -1-1). pap. 6.29 *(978-1-4329-4068-3(6))*, Acorn) Heinemann-Raintree.
—Ramadán y el Eid Al-Fitr, 1 vol. 2011. (Fiestas Ser.). (SPA & ENG., Illus.). 24p. (gr. -1-1). 22.65 *(978-1-4329-5379-9(6))*; pap. 6.29 *(978-1-4329-5398-0(2))* Heinemann-Raintree. (Bellota).
Elayne. The Entrance of the Theotokos into the Temple. Gillis, Bonnie, illus. 2003. (Twelve Great Feasts for Children Ser.). (ENG.). 24p. (J). pap. 5.95 *(978-1-888212-40-2(3))* Ancient Faith Publishing.
Elliott, Lynne. Food & Feasts in the Middle Ages. 2004. (Medieval World Ser.). (ENG., Illus.). 32p. (J). pap. *(978-0-7787-1380-7(6))* Crabtree Publishing Co.
Foran, Jill. Buddha Day. 2003. (Celebrating Cultures Ser.). (Illus.). 24p. (J). lib. bdg. 24.45 *(978-1-59036-090-3(7))* Weigl Pubs., Inc.
Gallagher, Debbie. Family Meals. 2008. (Families Ser.). 32p. (gr. 1-2). lib. bdg. 18.56 *(978-0-7614-3138-1(1))*, Benchmark Bks.) Marshall Cavendish Corp.
Ganeri, Anita. Buddhist Festivals Through the Year. 2003. (Year of Festivals Ser.). 30p. (J). lib. bdg. 24.25 *(978-1-58340-375-4(2))* Black Rabbit Bks.
—Christian Festivals Through the Year. 2003. (Year of Festivals Ser.). 30p. (J). lib. bdg. 24.25 *(978-1-58340-370-9(1))* Black Rabbit Bks.
—Hindu Festivals Through the Year. 2003. (Year of Festivals Ser.). 30p. (J). lib. bdg. 24.25 *(978-1-58340-372-3(8))* Black Rabbit Bks.
—Muslim Festivals Through the Year. 2003. (Year of Festivals Ser.). 30p. (J). lib. bdg. 24.25 *(978-1-58340-371-6(X))* Black Rabbit Bks.
Gillespie, Katie. Passover. 2015. (Let's Celebrate American Holidays Ser.). (ENG.). (J). lib. bdg. 27.13 *(978-1-4896-3629-4(3))*, AV2 by Weigl) Weigl Pubs., Inc.
Gnojewski, Carol. Ramadan: A Muslim Time of Fasting, Prayer, & Celebration. 2004. (Finding Out about Holidays Ser.). (Illus.). 48p. (J). (gr. 2-5). lib. bdg. 25.27 *(978-0-7660-2275-1(7))* Enslow Pubs., Inc.
Grack, Rachel. Ramadan. 2017. (Ramadan Ser.). 24p. (J). (gr. k-3). pap. 6.99 ***(978-1-61891-276-3(3))***; (ENG., Illus.). lib. bdg. 25.95 *(978-1-62617-597-6(7))* Bellwether Media. (Blastoff! Readers).
Gunes, Aysenur. Ramadan & Fasting Activity Book. Polat, Ercan, illus. 2016. (Discover Islam Sticker Activity Bks.). (ENG.). 32p. (J). 5.95 *(978-0-86037-615-6(X))* Kube Publishing Ltd. GBR. Dist: Consortium Bk. Sales & Distribution.
Hackney Blackwell, Amy & Matters, Print. Ramadan. 2009. (Holidays & Celebration Ser.). (Illus.). 112p. (gr. 5-8). 40.00 *(978-1-60413-098-0(9))*, Chelsea Hse.) Facts On File, Inc.
Heiligman, Deborah. Celebrate Ramadan & Eid Al-Fitr: With Praying, Fasting, & Charity. 2006. (Holidays Around the World Ser.). (ENG., Illus.). 32p. (J). (gr. 1-4). lib. bdg. 23.90 *(978-0-7922-5927-5(0))*, National Geographic Children's Bks.) National Geographic Society.
Heiligman, Deborah & National Geographic Kids Staff. Celebrate Ramadan & Eid Al-Fitr: With Praying, Fasting, & Charity. 2006. (Holidays Around the World Ser.). (ENG., Illus.). 32p. (J). (gr. 1-4). 15.95 *(978-0-7922-5926-8(2))*, National Geographic Children's Bks.) National Geographic Society.
Hollihan, Kerrie Logan. Day of the Dead: Día de Los Muertos. 2010. (Latin American Celebrations & Festivals / Celebraciones y Festivales en Latinoamérica Ser.). (SPA & ENG., Illus.). 24p. (J). (gr. 2-5). lib. bdg. 22.60 *(978-1-4358-9363-4(8))* Rosen Publishing Group, Inc., The.
Jeffrey, Laura S. Celebrate Ramadan. 2007. (Celebrate Holidays Ser.). (Illus.). 112p. (J). (gr. 5-9). lib. bdg. 33.27 *(978-0-7660-2774-9(0))* Enslow Pubs., Inc.
MacMillan, Dianne M. Ramadan & Id Al-Fitr. rev. ed. 2008. (Best Holiday Bks.). (Illus.). 48p. (J). (gr. 3-7). lib. bdg. 25.27 *(978-0-7660-3045-9(8))* Enslow Pubs., Inc.
McKissack, Fredrick L. & McKissack, Lisa Beringer. Ramadan-Count & Celebrate! 2009. (Holidays—Count & Celebrate! Ser.). (Illus.). 32p. (J). (gr. k-3). lib. bdg. 23.94 *(978-0-7660-3100-5(4))* Enslow Pubs., Inc.
Mobin-Uddin, Asma. The Best Eid Ever. Jacobsen, Laura, illus. 2007. (ENG.). 32p. (J). (gr. 2-4). 16.95 *(978-1-59078-431-0(6))* Boyds Mills Pr.
—A Party in Ramadan. Jacobsen, Laura, illus. 2009. (ENG.). 34p. (J). (gr. 2-4). 16.95 *(978-1-59078-604-8(1))* Boyds Mills Pr.
Murray, Julie. Ramadan, 1 vol. 2011. (Holidays Set 3 Ser.). (ENG., Illus.). 24p. (J). (gr. 1-4). 25.65 *(978-1-61783-041-9(0))* ABDO Publishing Co.
Nason, Ruth. Celebrating Harvest. 2014. (Start up Religion Ser.). (ENG., Illus.). 32p. (J). (gr. -1-k). pap. 10.99 *(978-0-237-54373-0(7))* Evans Brothers, Ltd. GBR. Dist: Independent Pubs. Group.
O'Keefe, Kathy Della Torre. Child's Guide to the Holy Days. 2007. (Illus.). 32p. (J). (gr. k-4). 9.95 *(978-0-8091-6731-9(X))*, 6731-9) Paulist Pr.
Payne, Martyn. Footsteps to the Feast: 12 Two-Hour Children's Programmes for Christian Festivals & Special Times of the Year. 2007. (ENG., Illus.). 240p. pap. *(978-1-84101-464-7(8))*, Barnabas) Bible Reading Fellowship.
Pirotta, Saviour. Id-Ul-Fitr. 2007. (We Love Holidays Ser.). (Illus.). 24p. (J). (gr. 3-7). lib. bdg. 22.60 *(978-1-4042-3708-7(9))*, PowerKids Pr.) Rosen Publishing Group, Inc., The.
Ponto, Joanna & Gnojewski, Carol. Ramadan. 2016. (Story of Our Holidays Ser.). (Illus.). 32p. (J). pap. 10.52 *(978-0-7660-8350-9(0))* Enslow Pubs., Inc.
Ponto, Joanna & Parker-Rock, Michelle. Diwali. 2016. (Story of Our Holidays Ser.). (Illus.). 32p. (J). (gr. 3-3). pap. 10.52 *(978-0-7660-7646-4(6))* Enslow Pubs., Inc.

Rahim, Yasmeen. Hassan & Aneesa Love Ramadan. Burgess, Omar, illus. 2017. (Hassan & Aneesa Ser.). (ENG.). 24p. (J). pap. 5.99 *(978-0-86037-642-2(7))* Kube Publishing Ltd. GBR. Dist: Consortium Bk. Sales & Distribution.

Reynolds, Jan. Celebrate! Connections among Cultures, 1 vol. Reynolds, Jan, photos by. 2006. (ENG., Illus.). 32p. (J). pap. 9.95 *(978-1-60060-452-2(8))* Lee & Low Bks., Inc.

—Connections among Cultures. 2006. (ENG., Illus.). 32p. (J). (gr. k-4). 16.95 *(978-1-58430-253-7(4))* Lee & Low Bks., Inc.

Ring, Phyllis Edgerly. Jamila Does Not Want a Bat in Her House. Hosack, Leona, illus. 2016. 30p. (J). **(978-0-87743-718-5(1))** Baha'i Publishing Trust, U.S.

Robert, Na'ima B. Ramadan Moon. Adl, Shirin, illus. 2015. (ENG.). 32p. (J). (gr. -1-2). pap. 7.95 *(978-1-84780-206-4(0),* Frances Lincoln) Quarto Publishing Group UK GBR. Dist: Hachette Bk. Group.

Rocio, Mejia. Celebrando Dia de Muertos: Celebrating Day of the Dead. 2006. (SPA & ENG.). 8.00 *(978-0-9776332-6-5(8))* Salt City Books.

Sebra, Richard. It's Ramadan & Eid Al-Fitr! 2016. (Bumba Books (tm) — It's a Holiday! Ser.). (ENG., Illus.). 24p. (J). (gr. -1-1). 25.32 *(978-1-5124-1428-8(X))* Lerner Publishing Group.

Senker, Cath. My Buddhist Year. 2007. (Year of Religious Festivals Ser.). (Illus.). 32p. (J). (gr. 1-4). lib. bdg. 25.25 *(978-1-4042-3730-8(5))* Rosen Publishing Group, Inc., The.

—My Christian Year. 2007. (Year of Religious Festivals Ser.). (Illus.). 32p. (J). (gr. 4-7). lib. bdg. 23.95 *(978-1-4042-3729-2(1),* PowerKids Pr.) Rosen Publishing Group, Inc., The.

—My Hindu Year. 2007. (Year of Religious Festivals Ser.). (Illus.). 32p. (J). (gr. 1-4). lib. bdg. 25.25 *(978-1-4042-3731-5(3))* Rosen Publishing Group, Inc., The.

—My Muslim Year. 2007. (Year of Religious Festivals Ser.). (Illus.). 32p. (J). (gr. 4-7). lib. bdg. 23.95 *(978-1-4042-3728-5(3),* PowerKids Pr.) Rosen Publishing Group, Inc., The.

—My Sikh Year. 2007. (Year of Religious Festivals Ser.). (Illus.). 32p. (J). (gr. 1-4). lib. bdg. 25.25 *(978-1-4042-3733-9(X))* Rosen Publishing Group, Inc., The.

—A Year of Religious Festivals, 6 vols., Set. Incl. My Buddhist Year. (gr. 1-4). lib. bdg. 25.25 *(978-1-4042-3730-8(5));* My Christian Year. (gr. 4-7). lib. bdg. 23.95 *(978-1-4042-3729-2(1),* PowerKids Pr.); My Hindu Year. (gr. 1-4). lib. bdg. 25.25 *(978-1-4042-3731-5(3));* My Jewish Year. (gr. -1-3). lib. bdg. 23.95 *(978-1-4042-3732-2(1),* PowerKids Pr.); My Muslim Year. (gr. 4-7). lib. bdg. 23.95 *(978-1-4042-3728-5(3),* PowerKids Pr.); My Sikh Year. (gr. 1-4). lib. bdg. 25.25 *(978-1-4042-3733-9(X));* 32p. (J). 2007. 2008. Set lib. bdg. 143.70 *(978-1-4042-3891-6(3),* PowerKids Pr.) Rosen Publishing Group, Inc., The.

Spence, Kelly. Cultural Traditions in the Netherlands. 2016. (ENG., Illus.). 32p. (J). *(978-0-7787-8089-2(9))* Crabtree Publishing Co.

Tomljanovic, Tatiana. Ramadan. (American Celebrations (Weigl) Ser.). (Illus.). 24p. (J). (gr. 3-5). 2012. (ENG.). lib. bdg. 27.13 *(978-1-61913-865-0(4),* AV2 by Weigl) 2006. per. 8.95 *(978-1-59036-464-2(3))* 2006. lib. bdg. 24.45 *(978-1-59036-461-1(9))* Weigl Pubs., Inc.

—Ramadan with Code. 2012. (American Celebrations Ser.). (ENG., Illus.). 24p. (J). (gr. 3-5). pap. 12.95 *(978-1-61913-868-1(9),* AV2 by Weigl) Weigl Pubs., Inc.

Webb, Lois Sinaiko & Roten, Lindsay Grace. Holidays of the World Cookbook for Students, 1 vol. 2nd rev. ed. 2011. (C). 496p. pap. 36.00 *(978-0-313-39790-5(2),* A2878P); (Illus.). 442p. 105.00 *(978-0-313-38393-9(6),* A2878C) ABC-CLIO, LLC.

Whitman, Sylvia. Under the Ramadan Moon. Williams, Sue, illus. 2012. (J). 32.71 *(978-1-61913-151-4(X))* Weigl Pubs., Inc.

—Under the Ramadan Moon, 1 vol. Williams, Sue, illus. 2011. (ENG.). 24p. (J). (gr. -1-3). 6.99 *(978-0-8075-8305-0(7))* Whitman, Albert & Co.

World Book, Inc. Staff, contrib. by. Religious Celebrations. 2003. (World Book's Celebrations & Rituals Around the World Ser.). (Illus.). 46p. (J). *(978-0-7166-5015-7(0))* World Bk., Inc.

World Book, Inc Staff, contrib. by. Religious Celebrations. 2009. (Illus.). 46p. (J). *(978-0-7166-5049-2(5))* World Bk., Inc.

FASTS AND FEASTS—FICTION

Abdelsalam, Lisa. A Song for Me: A Muslim Holiday Story. Nielsen, Janet Marie, illus. 2006. 34p. (J). *(978-0-9755975-1-4(5))* Abdelsalam Corp.

Alvarez, Mrinali & Alvarez, Oneill J. Verde Navidad. 2006. (SPA.). 28p. 8.95 *(978-0-8477-1564-0(7))* Univ. of Puerto Rico Pr.

Blitz, Shmuel. The Adventures of Aliza & Dovid: Holidays at the Farm. Katz, Tova, illus. 2005. (ArtScroll Youth Ser.). 48p. (J). *(978-1-4226-0021-4(1))* Mesorah Pubns., Ltd.

Elissa, Barbara. The Remarkable Journey of Josh's Kippah. Zaman, Farida, illus. 2010. 32p. (J). (gr. -1-3). pap. 7.95 *(978-0-8225-9933-3(3),* Kar-Ben Publishing) Lerner Publishing Group.

Estrin, Leibel. Rabbi Riddle Says... Look Who Dropped in for Yom Tov. Sears, Dovid, illus. 2005. (J). 10.95 *(978-1-931681-74-2(0))* Israel Bookshop Pubns.

Falwell, Cathryn. Feast for 10. Falwell, Cathryn, illus. 2003. (ENG., Illus.). 28p. (J). (gr. -1 — 1). bds. 4.95 *(978-0-618-38226-2(7))* Houghton Mifflin Harcourt Publishing Co.

Faruqi, Reem & Lyon, Lea. Lailah's Lunchbox, 1 vol. 2015. (ENG., Illus.). 32p. (gr. 1-7). 16.95 *(978-0-88448-431-8(9),* 884431) Tilbury Hse. Pubs.

Gerstein, Mordicai. The White Ram: A Story of Abraham & Isaac. Gerstein, Mordicai, illus. 2006. (ENG., Illus.). 32p. (J). (gr. -1-3). 16.95 *(978-0-8234-1897-8(9))* Holiday Hse., Inc.

Gilani-Williams, Fawzia. The Lost Ring: An Eid Story. Burgess, Kulthum, illus. 2009. (ENG.). 29p. (J). (gr. 2-6). 6.95 *(978-0-86037-565-4(X))* Kube Publishing Ltd. GBR. Dist: Consortium Bk. Sales & Distribution.

Goldin, Barbara Diamond. Mountain of Blintzes, 0 vols. McGrory, Anik, illus. 2010. (ENG.). 32p. (J). (gr. -1-2). pap. 6.99 *(978-0-7614-5790-9(9),* 9780761457909, Amazon Children's Publishing) Amazon Publishing.

Grishaver, Joel Lurie. I Can Celebrate the Jewish Holidays. Bleicher, David, illus. 2010. 96p. (J). pap. 14.95 *(978-1-934527-33-7(5))* Torah Aura Productions.

Hamed, Maissa. The Last Night of Ramadan. El Wakil, Mohamed, illus. 2007. (J). (gr. -1-3). *(978-0-88010-586-6(0),* Bell Pond Bks.) SteinerBooks, Inc.

Jalali, Reza. Moon Watchers: Shirin's Ramadan Miraacle. 2017. lib. bdg. 19.60 **(978-0-606-40159-3(8))** Turtleback Bks.

Jalali, Reza. Moon Watchers: Shirin's Ramadan Miracle, 1 vol. Sibley O'Brien, Anne, illus. 2017. (ENG.). 32p. (gr. 1-7). pap. 8.95 *(978-0-88448-587-2(0),* 884587) Tilbury Hse. Pubs.

Khan, Hena. The Night of the Moon: A Muslim Holiday Story. Paschkis, Julie, illus. 2008. (ENG.). 32p. (J). (gr. -1-3). 16.99 *(978-0-8118-6062-8(0))* Chronicle Bks. LLC.

Kyrja. Rupert's Tales: The Wheel of the Year - Samhain, Yule, Imbolc, & Ostara, 1 vol. Osborn, Tonia Bennington, illus. 2012. (ENG.). 64p. (J). 19.99 *(978-0-7643-3987-5(7),* 9780764339875) Schiffer Publishing, Ltd.

—Rupert's Tales: The Wheel of the Year Activity Book, 1 vol. Osborn, Tonia Bennington, illus. 2012. (ENG.). 40p. (J). pap. 9.99 *(978-0-7643-4020-8(4),* 9780764340208) Schiffer Publishing, Ltd.

Kyrja, et al. Rupert's Tales: The Wheel of the Year Beltane, Litha, Lammas, & Mabon, 1 vol. 2011. (ENG., Illus.). 64p. (J). 19.99 *(978-0-7643-3689-8(4),* 9780764336898, Schiffer Publishing Ltd) Schiffer Publishing, Ltd.

Levy, Janice. I Remember Abuelito: A Day of the Dead Story. Arisa, Miguel, tr. Lopez, Loretta, illus. 2007.Tr. of Yo Recuerdo a Abuelito - Un Cuento del Dia de los Muertos. (SPA & ENG.). 32p. (J). (gr. -1-3). 6.99 *(978-0-8075-3517-2(6))* Whitman, Albert & Co.

McGinty, Alice B. Rabbi Benjamin's Buttons. Reinhardt, Jennifer Black, illus. (ENG.). 32p. (J). (gr. -1-3). 2017. pap. 7.99 *(978-1-58089-433-3(X))* 2014. lib. bdg. 17.95 *(978-1-58089-432-6(1))* Charlesbridge Publishing, Inc.

Mejuto, Eva. La Casa de la Mosca Fosca. Mora, Sergio, illus. 2017. (Libros para Soñar Ser.). (SPA.). 36p. (J). (gr. k-2). *(978-84-8464-143-8(0))* Kalandraka Ediciones Andalucía, S.L. ESP. Dist: Lectorum Pubns., Inc.

Park, Barbara. Turkeys We Have Loved & Eaten (And Other Thankful Stuff) Brunkus, Denise, illus. 2014. (Junie B. Jones Ser.). (ENG.). 144p. (J). (gr. 1-4). 4.99 *(978-0-375-87115-3(2),* Random Hse. Bks. for Young Readers) Random Hse. Children's Bks.

Pearl, Sydelle. Elijah's Tears: Stories for the Jewish Holidays, 1 vol. Skortcheva, Rossitza, illus. 2004. (ENG.). 80p. (J). (gr. 3-7). 14.95 *(978-1-58980-178-3(4))* Pelican Publishing Co., Inc.

Rafi, Natasha. The Jinni on the Roof: A Ramadan Story. Channa, Abdul Malik, illus. 2013. 40p. pap. 10.99 *(978-0-9888649-0-0(8))* Pamir LLC.

Reynolds, Aaron. The Pest Show on Earth, 1 vol. Lervold, Erik, illus. 2008. (Tiger Moth Ser.). (ENG.). 40p. (J). (gr. 1-3). lib. bdg. 23.99 *(978-1-4342-0454-7(5),* Graphic Sparks) Stone Arch Bks.

—The Pest Show on Earth: Tiger Moth, 1 vol. Lervold, Erik, illus. 2008. (Graphic Sparks Ser.). (ENG.). 40p. (J). (gr. 1-3). per. 5.95 *(978-1-4342-0504-9(5),* Graphic Sparks) Stone Arch Bks.

Rouss, Sylvia A. The Littlest Candlesticks. Hannon, Holly, illus. 2005. (Littlest Ser.). 32p. (J). 14.95 *(978-1-930143-48-7(6));* pap. 9.95 *(978-1-930143-49-4(4))* Simcha Media Group. (Devora Publishing).

Samira's Eid. 2004. (ENG & KUR.). (J). *(978-1-84444-667-4(0))* Mantra Lingua.

Savedoff, Barbara E. & Elissa, Barbara. The Remarkable Journey of Josh's Kippah. Jamana, Pharida & Zaman, Farida, illus. 2010. (ENG.). 24p. (J). (gr. -1-2). lib. bdg. 7.95 *(978-0-8225-9911-1(2),* Kar-Ben Publishing) Lerner Publishing Group.

Schotter, Roni. Purim Play, 0 vols. Hafner, Marylin, illus. 2010. (ENG.). 34p. (J). (gr. -1-2). pap. 6.99 *(978-0-7614-5800-5(X),* 9780761458005, Amazon Children's Publishing) Amazon Publishing.

Stein, Ethel. Jewish Holiday Adventures. Kaye, Donna M., illus. 2010. 52p. 25.00 *(978-1-4349-9618-3(2),* RoseDog Bks.) Dorrance Publishing Co., Inc.

Tremblay, Carole. Floop's Flowers. Beshwaty, Steve, illus. 2009. (Floop Ser.). 24p. (J). (gr. -1-k). 22.60 *(978-1-60754-344-2(3));* pap. 8.15 *(978-1-60754-346-6(X))* Windmill Bks.

Ulker, Munise. Little Batul's Eid Celebration: The Most Pleasant Festival of Sacrifice. 2013. (ENG., Illus.). 32p. (J). (gr. -1-3). pap. 6.95 *(978-1-59784-294-5(X))* Tughra Bks.

FASTS AND FEASTS—JUDAISM

see also names of individual fasts and feasts, e.g. Yom Kippur, etc.

Bar a Bat Mitzvah: Pecyn Gwybodaeth a Gweithgareddau (CA2) 2005. *(978-1-85357-093-3(1))* Welsh National Centre for Religious Education (Canolfan Genedlaethol Addysg Grefyddol).

Chanukah: Pecyn Gwybodaeth a Gweithgareddau (CA1/2) 2005. *(978-1-85357-094-0(X))* Welsh National Centre for Religious Education (Canolfan Genedlaethol Addysg Grefyddol).

Fishman, Cathy Goldberg. On Sukkot & Simchat Torah. Hall, Melanie, illus. 2006. (ENG.). 32p. (J). (gr. -1-4). lib. bdg. 17.95 *(978-1-58013-165-0(4),* Kar-Ben Publishing) Lerner Publishing Group.

Fun for Little Hands Series, 7 bks., Set. 2003. (Illus.). (J). 21.33 *(978-0-929371-92-4(5),* Kar-Ben Publishing) Lerner Publishing Group.

Ganeri, Anita. Jewish Festivals Through the Year. 2003. (Year of Festivals Ser.). 30p. (J). lib. bdg. 24.25 *(978-1-58340-373-0(6))* Black Rabbit Bks.

Gold-Vukson, Marji. The Shapes of My Jewish Year. Springer, Sally, illus. 2003. (Very First Board Bks.). (ENG.). 12p. (J). (gr. -1 — 1). 5.95 *(978-1-58013-049-3(6),* Kar-Ben Publishing) Lerner Publishing Group.

—The Sounds of My Jewish Year. Urban, Suzanne, illus. 2003. (Very First Board Bks.). (ENG.). 12p. (J). (gr. -1 — 1). 5.95 *(978-1-58013-047-9(X),* Kar-Ben Publishing) Lerner Publishing Group.

Gootel, Rifka. My First Learn & Do Jewish Holiday Book. Rosenberg, Amye, illus. 64p. (J). (gr. k-2). pap. 4.95 *(978-0-87441-475-2(X))* Behrman Hse., Inc.

Groffman, Simcha. Simcha's Kinder Torah Presents Awesome Days: Torah Stories & Thoughts for the Yomim Noraim & Succos to Enhance Your Yom Tov Table. 2004. (Illus.). 164p. (J). *(978-1-58330-709-0(5))* Feldheim Pubs.

Halper, Sharon D. Holy Days, Holy Ways. Rauchwerger, Lisa, illus. 2004. (gr. k-3). stu. ed. 8.95 *(978-0-8074-0793-6(3),* 102073) URJ Pr.

Koffsky, Ann D. My Jewish Holiday Fun Book. 2004. (Illus.). 32p. (gr. k-3). pap. 9.95 *(978-0-8074-0727-1(5),* 101983) URJ Pr.

Kress, Camille. The High Holy Days. Kress, Camille, illus. 2004. (Illus.). bds. 6.25 *(978-0-8074-0776-9(3),* 241856) URJ Pr.

—Purim! Kress, Camille, illus. 2004. (Illus.). 10p. (gr. -1-k). bds. 5.95 *(978-0-8074-0654-0(6),* 102555) URJ Pr.

—A Tree Trunk Seder. Kress, Camille, illus. 2004. (Camille Kress Library: Vol. 4). (Illus.). 7p. (gr. -1-k). bds. 6.25 *(978-0-8074-0735-6(6),* 101252) URJ Pr.

Kropf, Latifa Berry. It's Seder Time! Cohen, Tod, illus. Cohen, Tod, photos by. 2004. (ENG.). 24p. (J). (gr. -1-1). 12.95 *(978-1-58013-092-9(5),* Kar-Ben Publishing) Lerner Publishing Group.

Lewis, Jaime & Katz, Michelle V. Mahazor Katan: Machzor Katan: High Holiday Prayer Book for Families with Young Children. 2012. (ENG & HEB., Illus.). 11p. (J). *(978-0-87441-910-8(7))* Behrman Hse., Inc.

Michels, Dia L. Look What I See! Where Can I Be? At the Synagogue. Bowles, Michael J. N., photos by. 2005. (ENG., Illus.). 32p. (J). (gr. -1-3). 9.95 *(978-1-930775-16-9(4))* Platypus Media, L.L.C.

Newman, Lesléa. Here Is the World: A Year of Jewish Holidays. Gal, Susan, illus. 2014. (ENG.). 48p. (J). (gr. k-2). 18.95 *(978-1-4197-1185-5(7),* Abrams Bks. for Young Readers) Abrams, Inc.

Patz, Naomi. The Jewish Holiday Treasure Trail. 2009. (J). *(978-0-87441-833-0(X))* Behrman Hse., Inc.

Peppas, Lynn. Rosh Hashanah & Yom Kippur. 2009. (Celebrations in My World Ser.). (ENG., Illus.). 32p. (J). (gr. k-2). pap. *(978-0-7787-4775-8(1));* (gr. 1-3). *(978-0-7787-4757-4(3))* Crabtree Publishing Co.

Rauchwerger, Lisa. Chocolate Chip Challah: And Other Twists on the Jewish Holiday Table. Rauchwerger, Lisa, illus. 2004. (Illus.). 127p. (J). (gr. k-3). pap. 17.95 *(978-0-8074-0700-4(3),* 510606) URJ Pr.

—P: Winter, Spring & Summer Holidays. Rauchwerger, Lisa, illus. 2004. (Illus.). (gr. k-3). pap., act. bk. ed. 9.95 *(978-0-8074-0775-2(5),* 104036) URJ Pr.

Rosenberg, Tziporah. Round & Round the Jewish Year Vol. 1: Elul-Tishrei. Befus, Ruth, illus. 2009. 67p. (J). (gr. 3-6). 19.99 *(978-1-59826-376-3(5))* Feldheim Pubs.

Rouss, Sylvia A. Sammy Spider's First Book of Jewish Holidays. Kahn, Katherine, illus. 2013. (ENG.). 12p. (J). (gr. -1 — 1). 5.95 *(978-1-4677-1916-2(1),* Kar-Ben Publishing) Lerner Publishing Group.

Senker, Cath. My Jewish Year. 2007. (Year of Religious Festivals Ser.). (Illus.). 32p. (J). (gr. -1-3). lib. bdg. 23.95 *(978-1-4042-3732-2(1),* PowerKids Pr.) Rosen Publishing Group, Inc., The.

Sidon, Ephraim. The Animated Menorah: Travels on a Space Dreidel. Oren, Rony, illus. 2007. (Animated Holydays Ser.). 48p. 17.95 *(978-965-7108-80-2(2),* Lambda) Urim Pubns. ISR. Dist: Coronet Bks.

Sper, Emily. The Kids' Fun Book of Jewish Time. Sper, Emily, illus. 2006. (HEB & ENG., Illus.). 24p. (J). (gr. -1-1). 16.99 *(978-1-58023-311-8(2),* 1260461, Jewish Lights Publishing) LongHill Partners, Inc.

Wool, Danny & Yudin, Yefim (Chaim). The Animated Jewish Year. Portnoi, Jeremy, illus. 2006. 88p. 19.95 *(978-965-7108-79-6(9),* Lambda) Urim Pubns. ISR. Dist: Lambda Pubs., Inc.

FATHER AND CHILD

see also Fathers and Daughters; Fathers and Sons

Apel, Melanie Ann. Let's Talk about Living with Your Single Dad. 2009. (Let's Talk Library). 24p. (gr. 2-3). 42.50 *(978-1-60853-445-6(6),* PowerKids Pr.) Rosen Publishing Group, Inc., The.

Baron, L. A Day with My Dad: Learning the D Sound. 2009. (PowerPhonics Ser.). 24p. (gr. 1-1). 39.90 *(978-1-60851-429-8(3),* PowerKids Pr.) Rosen Publishing Group, Inc., The.

Berry, Joy. I Love Mommies & Daddies. Regan, Dana, illus. 2010. (Teach Me About Ser.). (ENG.). 20p. (J). (gr. k — 1). pap. 5.99 *(978-1-60577-001-7(9))* Berry, Joy Enterprises.

Chapman, Patricia. The Best Dad in the World. Chapman, Pat, illus. 2017. (ENG.). 32p. (J). (-k). 14.99 **(978-1-927262-74-0(7))** Upstart Pr. NZL. Dist: Independent Pubs. Group.

Dogan, Nakia C. My Daddy Is My Hero. 2012. 22p. pap. 16.95 *(978-1-4626-8981-1(7))* America Star Bks.

Haskins, Amanda. God Is My Daddy. I.t. ed. 2006. (Illus.). 26p. (J). per. 11.99 *(978-1-59879-279-9(2))* Lifevest Publishing, Inc.

Higgins, Melissa. The Night Dad Went to Jail: What to Expect When Someone You Love Goes to Jail, 1 vol. Kirwan, Wednesday, illus. 2011. (Life's Challenges Ser.). (ENG.). 24p. (gr. 2-3). lib. bdg. 25.99 *(978-1-4048-6679-9(5))* Picture Window Bks.

Howarth, Daniel, illus. Why I Love My Daddy. 2013. (ENG.). 32p. (J). pap. 6.99 *(978-0-00-750866-2(2),* HarperCollins Children's Bks.) HarperCollins Pubs. Ltd. GBR. Dist: HarperCollins Pubs.

Innes, Stephanie & Endrulat, Harry. A Bear in War, 1 vol. Deines, Brian, illus. 2013. (ENG.). 40p. (J). (gr. k-4). 19.95 *(978-1-927485-12-5(6))* Pajama Pr. CAN. Dist: Ingram Publisher Services.

Jenner, Caryn. My Dad. 2017. (Family World Ser.). (ENG., Illus.). 24p. (J). (gr. 1-3). pap. 9.99 **(978-1-4451-5222-6(3),** Franklin Watts) Hachette Children's Group GBR. Dist: Hachette Bk. Group.

L'Heureux, Christine. Play with Me! Brignaud, Pierre, illus. 2009. (Big Dipper Ser.). (ENG.). 24p. (J). (gr. -1-k). pap. 3.95 *(978-2-89450-679-0(1))* Caillouet, Gerry.

Liles, Rebecca. My Daddy's a Soldier, 2 bks. 2003. (Illus.). 16p. (J). 4.99 *(978-0-9744346-0-5(4))* Rebecca's Bks.

Mahtani, Nikhil & Mahtani, Sherina. What Do Dads Do? 2013. 24p. 22.99 *(978-1-4808-0167-7(4));* pap. 12.99 *(978-1-4808-0165-3(8))* Archway Publishing.

Parr, Todd. The Daddy Book. 2015. (ENG., Illus.). 20p. (J). (gr. -1 — 1). bds. 6.99 *(978-0-316-25784-8(2))* Little, Brown Bks. for Young Readers.

Saleh, Amal Kamal Ali. Guess Who My Best Friend Is. 2005. (Illus.). 15p. (J). 9.95 *(978-1-4120-6052-3(4))* Trafford Publishing.

Schaefer, Lola M. Fathers. Saunders-Smith, Gail, ed. rev. ed. 2008. (Families Ser.). (ENG., Illus.). 24p. (gr. k-1). per. 6.29 *(978-1-4296-1753-6(5),* Pebble Bks.) Capstone Press of Coughlan Cos.

Sebastian, Emily. My Dad. 2010. (My Family Ser.). (ENG.). 24p. (J). pap. 8.25 *(978-1-4488-1488-6(X));* lib. bdg. 22.60 *(978-1-4488-1461-9(8))* Rosen Publishing Group, Inc., The. (PowerKids Pr.).

—My Dad(Mi Papá) 2010. (My Family / Mi Familia Ser.). (SPA & ENG.). 24p. lib. bdg. 22.60 *(978-1-4488-0981-3(9),* Editorial Buenas Letras) Rosen Publishing Group, Inc., The.

Sharp, Zoe. I Help My Dad. 2007. (Windows on Literacy Ser.). (ENG., Illus.). 12p. pap. 10.95 *(978-0-7922-8464-2(X))* National Geographic School Publishing, Inc.

Thalhamer, Ellen Viola. I'm a Daddy: I Love to Pretend! 2010. 36p. pap. 16.49 *(978-1-4490-7489-0(8))* AuthorHouse.

FATHER AND CHILD—FICTION

Agnew, Kate. Dinosaur Disasters. Jones, Anna, illus. (Reading Ladder Ser.). (ENG.). 48p. (J). (gr. k-2). 2016. 7.99 *(978-1-4052-8228-4(2))* 2010. pap. 5.99 *(978-1-4052-4778-8(9))* Egmont Bks., Ltd. GBR. Dist: Independent Pubs. Group.

Allison, Catherine. Dear Daddy, I Love You. McNicholas, Shelagh, illus. 2014. (ENG.). (J). (gr. -1-3). *(978-1-74363-284-0(3))* Hinkler Bks. Pty, Ltd.

Andreasen, Dan. Saturday with Daddy. Andreasen, Dan, illus. (ENG., Illus.). (J). 2017. 26p. bds. 7.99 *(978-1-250-11265-1(6),* 9781250112651) 2013. 24p. (gr. -1-2). 12.99 *(978-0-8050-8687-4(0),* 9780805086874) Holt, Henry & Co. (Holt, Henry & Co. Bks. For Young Readers).

Avi. The Barn. 2014. (ENG.). 112p. (J). (gr. 3-7). pap. 6.99 *(978-0-545-60744-5(2),* Scholastic Paperbacks) Scholastic, Inc.

—The Traitors' Gate. Raude, Karina, illus. 2010. (ENG.). 368p. (J). (gr. 5-8). pap. 7.99 *(978-0-689-85336-4(X),* Atheneum Bks. for Young Readers) Simon & Schuster Children's Publishing.

Baker, Susan F. Don't Smoke, Daddy. 2008. 27p. 30.95 *(978-1-4357-2127-2(6))* Lulu Pr., Inc.

Barcelo, François. My Daddy's Footsteps. Mongeau, Marc, illus. 2009. (My First Stories Ser.). 24p. (J). (gr. -1-3). 22.60 *(978-1-60754-359-6(1));* pap. 8.15 *(978-1-60754-360-2(5))* Windmill Bks.

Bargach, Naim. Wolfen: Beware, even, of little Wolves... 2008. 56p. per. 8.95 *(978-1-4327-1802-2(9))* Outskirts Pr., Inc.

Basal, Patricia. Sammy Discovers Jesus. 2008. 28p. per. 24.95 *(978-1-4241-8400-2(2))* America Star Bks.

Bauer, Marion Dane. The Very Best Daddy of All. Wu, Leslie, illus. 2011. (Classic Board Bks.). (ENG.). 34p. (J). (gr. -1 — 1). bds. 7.99 *(978-1-4169-8517-4(4),* Little Simon) Little Simon.

—The Very Best Daddy of All. Wu, Leslie, illus. 2007. (ENG.). 40p. (J). (gr. -1-3). 6.99 *(978-1-4169-2736-5(0),* Simon & Schuster Bks. For Young Readers) Simon & Schuster Bks. For Young Readers.

Beam, Jon. Jardien's Dream, 1 vol. 2009. 185p. pap. 24.95 *(978-1-4489-2613-8(0))* America Star Bks.

Bedford, David. Daddy Does the Cha Cha Cha! Strevens-Marzo, Bridget, illus. 2010. (ENG.). 32p. (J). (gr. -1-k). pap. 8.99 *(978-1-921541-16-2(4))* Little Hare Bks. AUS. Dist: Independent Pubs. Group.

Bennett, Leonie. No Problem! Brown, Judy, illus. 2004. (ENG.). 16p. (J). lib. bdg. 23.65 *(978-1-59646-680-7(4))* Dingles & Co.

Bently, Peter & McPhillips, Robert, illus. Say Please, Little Bear. 2013. (J). *(978-1-4351-4727-0(8))* Barnes & Noble, Inc.

Berenstain, Jan & Berenstain, Mike. We Love Our Dad! 2013. (Berenstain Bears Ser.). (J). lib. bdg. 13.55 *(978-0-606-31785-6(6),* Turtleback) Turtleback Bks.

Berrios, Frank. Football with Dad. Biggs, Brian, illus. 2015. (Little Golden Book Ser.). (ENG.). 24p. (J). (-k). 4.99 *(978-0-385-37925-0(0),* Golden Bks.) Random Hse. Children's Bks.

Berry, Ron. Where Is Daddy? Smart Kids Publishing Staff, ed. 2009. (ENG.). 20p. (J). bds. 7.99 *(978-0-8249-1405-9(8),* Ideal Pubns.) Worthy Publishing.

Bland, Nick. Some Dads. 2017. (ENG., Illus.). 24p. (J). (gr. -1-1). 9.95 *(978-0-7624-6199-8(3),* Running Pr.) Running Pr. Bk. Pubs.

Buford, Stanley G. & Gillen, Rosemarie. Thanks Dad! 2012. 30p. pap. 9.99 *(978-1-61286-089-3(3))* Avid Readers Publishing Group.

Callahan, Sean. A Wild Day with Dad. Howarth, Daniel, illus. 2012. (ENG.). 18p. (J). (gr. -1 — 1). bds. 7.99 *(978-0-8075-2295-0(3))* Whitman, Albert & Co.

Carle, Eric. Mister Seahorse. Carle, Eric, illus. 2011. (ENG., Illus.). 64p. (J). (gr. -1 — 1). bds. 8.99 *(978-0-399-25490-1(0),* Philomel Bks.) Penguin Young Readers Group.

Cash, John Carter. Daddy Loves His Little Girl. Burckhardt, Marc, illus. 2010. (ENG.). 32p. (J). (gr. -1-3). 16.99 *(978-1-4169-7482-6(2),* Little Simon Inspirations) Little Simon Inspirations.

Catherine, Maria. Time Together, 1 vol. 2014. (Time Together Ser.). (ENG.). 32p. (gr. -1-2). pap. 15.90 *(978-1-4795-4822-4(7),* Fiction Picture Bks.) Picture Window Bks.

—Time Together: Me & Dad, 1 vol. Campion, Pascal, illus. 2014. (Time Together Ser.). (ENG.). 32p. (gr. -1-2). 8.95 *(978-1-4795-2253-8(8),* Fiction Picture Bks.) Picture Window Bks.

Chaud, Benjamin. The Bear's Sea Escape. 2014. (ENG., Illus.). 32p. (J). (gr. -1-k). 17.99 *(978-1-4521-2743-9(3))* Chronicle Bks. LLC.

Chering, Don. The Acorn That Doubted. 2008. 32p. pap. 14.49 *(978-1-4389-0493-1(2))* AuthorHouse.

Cleave, Brenda. The Money Tree. 2010. 40p. pap. 18.99 *(978-1-4490-7468-5(5))* AuthorHouse.

Climo, Liz. Rory the Dinosaur: Me & My Dad. 2015. (Illus.). 48p. (J). pap. *(978-0-316-26391-7(5))* Little Brown & Co.

EFG

Cohen, Miriam. Daddy's Busy Day, 1 vol. 2014. (ENG.). 32p. (J). bds. *(978-1-59572-668-1(3))* Star Bright Bks., Inc.
—Mine! (Spanish/English) A Backpack Baby Story, 1 vol. Fiol, Maria A., tr. 2005. (ENG & SPA., Illus.). 32p. (J). (gr. -1 — 1). bds. 5.95 *(978-1-59572-019-1(7))* Star Bright Bks., Inc.
Coleman-Veach, Marti. Balloons in Heaven. 2013. 32p. pap. *(978-1-4602-1826-6(4))* FriesenPress.
Cooper, Glenessa. Daddy's Number One Little Girl. Joseph, Patricia, illus. 2008. 10p. pap. 24.95 *(978-1-60563-983-3(4))* America Star Bks.
Costain, Meredith. Daddies Are Awesome. Lovsin, Polona, illus. 2017. (ENG.). 28p. (J). bds. 7.99 *(978-1-250-10720-6(2)*, 9781250107206, Holt, Henry & Co. Bks. For Young Readers) Holt, Henry & Co.
Daddy You're My Hero! 2005. (J). bds. 12.99 *(978-0-9729264-4-7(5)*, Books for Brats) Little Redhaired Girl Publishing, Inc.
Dalmatian Press Staff. Where's Daddy? 2008. (ENG.). 5p. bds. 4.95 *(978-1-58117-715-2(1)*, Intervisual/Piggy Toes) Bendon, Inc.
Davis, Terry. Camping with Dad: The Mystery of Valley Gulch. 2006. (ENG.). 148p. per. 24.95 *(978-1-4241-5659-7(9))* America Star Bks.
De Fombelle, Timothée. Toby Alone. Ardizzone, Sarah, tr. from FRE. Place, Francois, illus. 2009. (ENG.). 400p. (J). (gr. 4-7). 17.99 *(978-0-7636-4181-8(2))* Candlewick Pr.
DeClements, Barthe. Fourth Grade Wizards. 2008. (ENG.). 128p. (J). (gr. 3-7). 5.99 *(978-0-14-241348-7(8)*, Puffin Books) Penguin Young Readers Group.
Dickerson, Tim. Napping with Daddy. 2010. 24p. pap. 11.49 *(978-1-4490-4718-4(1))* AuthorHouse.
Dilz, Ric. My Dad Could Do Anything! (J). 2008. 14.95 *(978-0-9758704-4-0(0))* 2006. (Illus.). pap. 6.95 *(978-0-9758704-1-9(6))* Ric Design LLC.
Durango, Julia & Trupiano, Katie Belle. Dream Away. Goldstrom, Robert, illus. 2011. (ENG.). 32p. (J). (gr. -1-3). 16.99 *(978-1-4169-8702-4(9)*, Simon & Schuster Bks. For Young Readers) Simon & Schuster Bks. For Young Readers.
Easter, Julie. My Military Dad. 2004. (J). pap. 8.00 *(978-0-8059-6534-6(3))* Dorrance Publishing Co., Inc.
Eaton, Maxwell, III. I'm Awake! 2017. (ENG.). 32p. (J). (gr. k-3). 16.99 *(978-0-375-84575-8(5)*, Knopf Bks. for Young Readers) Random Hse. Children's Bks.
Fallon, Jimmy. Your Baby's First Word Will Be Dada. Ordóñez, Miguel, illus. 2015. (ENG.). (J). (gr. -1 — 1). 40p. 16.99 *(978-1-250-00934-0(0)*, 9781250009340); 16p. bds. 7.99 *(978-1-250-07181-1(X)*, 9781250071811) Feiwel & Friends.
Faulkerson, President & CEO Jeffery, Founder. IT's GOOD to BE GOLDEN: Golden Innovations. 2008. 30p. 14.95 *(978-0-615-19351-9(X))* PRACTICAL SOLUTIONS Writing, Editing, Consulting.
—IT's GOOD to BE GOLDEN: the Story of Henry the Heart. 2008. 19p. 14.95 *(978-0-615-19350-2(1))* PRACTICAL SOLUTIONS Writing, Editing, Consulting.
Finnemore, John. Jack Haydons Quest. 2006. pap. 15.95 *(978-0-8095-0116-8(3))* Wildside Pr., LLC.
Fliess, Sue. Let's Build!, 0 vols. 2014. (ENG.). 24p. (J). (gr. -1-3). 14.99 *(978-1-4778-4724-4(3)*, 9781477847244, Amazon Children's Publishing) Amazon Publishing.
Floyd, Gina. Can Daddy Stay Home & Play? Scott, Judy, illus. 2011. 28p. pap. 12.99 *(978-1-4567-1373-7(6))* AuthorHouse.
Foreman, Michael. I Love You, Too! Foreman, Michael, illus. 2014. (ENG., Illus.). 32p. (J). (gr. -1-3). 16.95 *(978-1-4677-3451-6(9))* Lerner Publishing Group.
Fox, Valerie P. Deefa: Seek the Vixen. 2008. 92p. pap. 10.49 *(978-1-4389-0723-9(0))* AuthorHouse.
Frederick, Heather Vogel. Hide-and-Squeak. Payne, C. F., illus. 2011. (ENG.). 32p. (J). (gr. -1-1). 16.99 *(978-0-689-85570-2(2)*, Simon & Schuster Bks. For Young Readers) Simon & Schuster Bks. For Young Readers.
Galante, Cecilia. Stealing Our Way Home. 2017. (ENG.). 304p. (J). (gr. 3-7). 17.99 ***(978-1-338-04296-2(3)***, Scholastic Pr.) Scholastic, Inc.
Ganzer, Diane & Swanson, Christopher. Called to Serve. 2008. 116p. pap. 9.99 *(978-1-935105-10-7(8))* Avid Readers Publishing Group.
Garis, Howard Roger. Daddy Takes Us Skating. 2007. 56p. per. *(978-1-4065-2765-0(3))* Dodo Pr.
—Daddy takes us to the Garden. 2005. 25.95 *(978-1-4218-1462-9(5))*; 124p. pap. 10.95 *(978-1-4218-1562-6(1))* 1st World Publishing, Inc. (1st World Library - Literary Society).
Griffith, Travis. Your Father Forever. Abreu, Raquel, illus. 2005. 32p. (J). (gr. -1-3). 15.95 *(978-0-9740190-3-1(8))* Illumination Arts Publishing Co., Inc.
Grimes, Nikki. Garvey's Choice. 2016. (ENG.). 120p. (J). (gr. 2-7). 16.95 *(978-1-62979-740-3(5)*, Wordsong) Boyds Mills Pr.
Grossmann-Hensel, Katharina. Papa is a Pirate. Grossmann-Hensel, Katharina, illus. 2009. (ENG., Illus.). 32p. (J). (gr. -1-3). 16.95 *(978-0-7358-2237-5(9))* North-South Bks., Inc.
Gutman, Anne & Hallensleben, Georg. Daddy Dreams. 2017. (ENG., Illus.). 14p. (J). (gr. -1 — 1). bds. 5.99 *(978-1-4521-5823-5(1))* Chronicle Bks. LLC.
Hallinan, P. K. My Daddy & I. 2005. (ENG., Illus.). 32p. (J). (gr. -1-k). pap. 3.95 *(978-0-8249-5521-2(8)*, Ideal Pubns.) Worthy Publishing.
Hardin, Melinda. Hero Dad, 0 vols. Langdo, Bryan, illus. 2010. (ENG.). 24p. (J). (gr. -1-3). 12.99 *(978-0-7614-5713-8(5)*, 9780761457138, Two Lions) Amazon Publishing.
Harker, Jillian. I Love You, Daddy. 2008. (I Love... Ser.). 32p. *(978-1-4075-0855-9(5))* Parragon, Inc.
Holsey, Chanda Nicole. Precious Pete, Will You Remember Me, When I Am Out to Sea? A Salute to All Navy Dads. 2011. 20p. 11.99 *(978-1-4520-9651-3(1))* AuthorHouse.
Holsey, Dr Chanda Nicole & Holsey, Chanda Nicole. Savvie Sunshine, Will You Remember Daddy When I Am Out to Sea? A Salute to All Navy Dads. 2010. 24p. pap. 13.50 *(978-1-4490-7729-7(3))* AuthorHouse.
Holub, Joan. Mighty Dads. Dean, James, illus. 2014. (ENG.). 40p. (J). (gr. -1-k). 16.99 *(978-0-545-60968-5(2)*, Scholastic Pr.) Scholastic, Inc.
Howard, Annabelle. A Father, His Son, & Their Donkey: An Aesop's Fable. 2006. (J). pap. *(978-1-4108-7154-1(1))* Benchmark Education Co.
Howard, Takesha. Where Are You Dad? 2011. 16p. pap. 10.75 *(978-1-4634-2964-5(9))* AuthorHouse.
Hubery, Julia. My Daddy. Elliot, Rebecca, illus. 2014. (J). *(978-1-4351-5507-7(6))* Barnes & Noble, Inc.
James, Suzi. Matilda Bear & Father Bear: I Love You Father Bear. 2012. (Illus.). 52p. pap. 23.95 *(978-1-4525-4822-7(6))* Balboa Pr.
Johnson, Angela. The First Part Last. (ENG.). 144p. (YA). (gr. 7). 2010. pap. 9.99 *(978-1-4424-0343-7(8))* 2003. (Illus.). 16.99 *(978-0-689-84922-0(2))* Simon & Schuster Bks. For Young Readers. (Simon & Schuster Bks. For Young Readers).
—The First Part Last. 2005. (ENG.). 144p. (YA). (gr. 7). reprint ed. pap. 7.99 *(978-0-689-84923-7(0)*, Simon Pulse) Simon Pulse.
—The First Part Last. l.t. ed. 2005. 241p. pap. 10.95 *(978-0-7862-7379-9(8)*, Large Print Pr.) Thorndike Pr.
Kaputa, Christine C. Jungle Gym Me & Him! 2008. 24p. pap. 10.95 *(978-1-59858-781-4(1))* Dog Ear Publishing, LLC.
Karapetkova, Holly & Robins, Maureen. Stop Arguing! Reese, Bob, illus. 2011. (ENG.). 24p. (gr. 2-3). pap. 8.95 *(978-1-61236-032-4(7))* Rourke Educational Media.
Katz, Karen. Daddy & Me. Katz, Karen, illus. 2003. (ENG., Illus.). 14p. (J). (gr. -1-k). bds. 6.99 *(978-0-689-84906-0(0)*, Little Simon) Little Simon.
—Daddy Hugs. Katz, Karen, illus. 2007. (Classic Board Bks.). (ENG., Illus.). 32p. (J). (gr. -1 — 1). bds. 7.99 *(978-1-4169-4120-0(7)*, Little Simon) Little Simon.
—Daddy Hugs 1 2 3. Katz, Karen, illus. 2005. (ENG., Illus.). 32p. (J). (gr. -1-1). 18.99 *(978-0-689-87771-1(4)*, McElderry, Margaret K. Bks.) McElderry, Margaret K. Bks.
Kelly, Kelley R. Sundays with Daddy. Cook, Jeffrey, illus. 2010. 32p. pap. 13.99 *(978-1-4490-6082-4(X))* AuthorHouse.
Kerner, Susan. Always by My Side, 1 vol. Haywood, Ian Benfold, illus. 2013. (ENG.). 32p. (J). pap. 6.99 *(978-1-59572-337-6(4))* Star Bright Bks., Inc.
Kimbrell, Lara. Where Does My Dadda Go? 2011. 36p. pap. 16.99 *(978-1-4634-2355-1(1))* AuthorHouse.
Kimura, Yasuko. You Look Yummy! 2015. (Tyrannosaurus Ser.). (ENG.). 40p. (J). (gr. k-2). 16.99 *(978-1-940842-06-6(9))* Museyon.
Kingsbury, Karen. Let's Have a Daddy Day, 1 vol. Andreasen, Dan, illus. 2010. (ENG.). 32p. (J). (gr. -1-2). 15.99 *(978-0-310-71215-2(7))* Zonderkidz.
Koehler, Fred. How to Cheer up Dad. 2014. (ENG.). 32p. (J). (gr. -1-k). 16.99 *(978-0-8037-3922-2(2)*, Dial Bks) Penguin Young Readers Group.
Kristina Learns about Fishing. 2007. (J). *(978-0-9792728-0-6(7))* Tracepaper Bks. Inc.
Lawson-Miller, Barb. I Love Daddy Because... 2004. (Illus.). 14p. bds. *(978-0-9688553-0-0(X))* Barbamel Bks., Inc.
Lee, Day's. The Fragrant Garden. Bellemare, Josee, illus. 2005. (ENG.). 32p. (J). (gr. -1-7). per. 11.95 *(978-1-894917-26-1(X)*, Napoleon & Co.) Dundurn CAN. Dist: Ingram Publisher Services.
Leland, Debbie. Daddy's Love. Rife, Ann Hollis, illus. 2006. (J). 15.95 *(978-0-9667086-4-6(4))* Wildflower Run.
L'Heureux, Christine. Moves Around. Brignaud, Pierre, illus. rev. ed. 2007. (First Word Bks.). (FRE & ENG.). 24p. (J). (gr. -1-k). bds. 7.95 *(978-2-89450-610-3(4))* Caillouet, Gerry.
Lies, Brian. Gator Dad. 2016. (ENG., Illus.). 32p. (J). (gr. -1-3). 17.99 *(978-0-544-53433-9(6)*, HMH Books For Young Readers) Houghton Mifflin Harcourt Publishing Co.
Litton, Jonathan. I Love My Daddy. Galloway, Fhiona, illus. 2016. (My Little World Ser.). (ENG.). 16p. (J). (gr. -1-k). bds. 7.99 *(978-1-58925-217-2(9))* Tiger Tales.
Lozano, Neal. Will You Bless Me? Hatke, Ben, illus. 2009. 32p. (J). lib. bdg. 16.95 *(978-1-883551-32-2(3)*, MCP-323, Maple Corners Press) Attic Studio Publishing Hse.
Ltd Daddy Kisses/Daddy Cuddles. 2005. (J). bds. 11.90 *(978-0-8118-9933-8(0))* Chronicle Bks. LLC.
MacDonald, George. The Elect Lady. 2008. 148p. pap. 13.95 *(978-1-60664-101-9(8))* Aegypan.
Manzanares, J. C. Have Sweet Dreams of Ice Cream. 2011. 24p. pap. 11.50 *(978-1-61204-481-1(6)*, Eloquent Bks.) Strategic Book Publishing & Rights Agency (SBPRA).
Marino, Gianna. Following Papa's Song. 2014. (ENG., Illus.). 40p. (J). (gr. -1-k). 16.99 *(978-0-670-01315-9(3)*, Viking Books for Young Readers) Penguin Young Readers Group.
Markell, Denis. Hush, Little Monster. Iwai, Melissa, illus. 2012. (ENG.). 32p. (J). (gr. -1-1). 9.99 *(978-1-4424-4195-8(X)*, Little Simon) Little Simon.
Maybank, Roger. The Sun Boat: A Fairytale. 2005. 324p. pap. 25.60 *(978-1-4120-6452-1(X))* Trafford Publishing.
Mayes, Kate. Daddy Cuddle. Acton, Sara, illus. 2017. (ENG.). 32p. (J). (gr. -1-3). 17.99 *(978-1-68152-193-0(8))* Amicus.
McBratney, Sam. Guess How Much I Love You: One More Tickle! Jeram, Anita, illus. 2016. (Guess How Much I Love You Ser.). (ENG.). (J). (gr. k-k). bds. 17.99 *(978-0-7636-8819-6(3))* Candlewick Pr.
—Guess How Much I Love You: One More Tickle! Tray, 3 vols. 2016. (ENG.). (J). bds. 53.97 *(978-0-7636-9127-1(5))* Candlewick Pr.
Melmed, Laura Krauss. My Love Will Be with You. Sorensen, Henri, illus. 2009. (ENG.). 24p. (J). (gr. -1-2). 17.99 *(978-0-06-155260-1(7))* HarperCollins Pubs.
Middleton, Julie. Are the Dinosaurs Dead, Dad?, 1 vol. Ayto, Russell, illus. 2013. (ENG.). 32p. (J). (gr. -1-3). pap. 16.95 *(978-1-56145-690-1(X))* Peachtree Pubs.
Mohamed, Abdullahi. The Forbidden Cake. 2013. 36p. pap. 22.88 *(978-1-4817-8266-1(5))* AuthorHouse.
Murguia, Bethanie Deeney. The Too-Scary Story. 2017. (ENG., Illus.). 40p. (J). (gr. -1-k). 16.99 *(978-0-545-73242-0(5))* Scholastic, Inc.
Murphy, Jill. Mr. Large in Charge. Murphy, Jill, illus. 2007. (ENG., Illus.). 40p. (J). (gr. -1-3). 16.99 *(978-0-7636-3504-6(9))* Candlewick Pr.
Musgrave, Sugin. Butterfly in the Sky: Daddy's Little Girl. 2008. 32p. 14.00 *(978-1-4389-2218-8(3))* AuthorHouse.
Nadel, Carolina. Daddy's Home. Nadel, Carolina, illus. 2012. (Illus.). 32p. 19.95 *(978-0-9792761-4-9(4))* Mookind Pr.
Nelid, Piper. Father's Day with My Forever Dad, 01 vols., 1. 2016. (Rosen REAL Readers: Social Studies Nonfiction / Fiction: Family, Community, & the World Ser.). (ENG.). 8p. (J). pap. 5.46 *(978-1-5081-1389-8(0)*, Rosen Classroom) Rosen Publishing Group, Inc., The.
North, Sherry. Because I Am Your Daddy. Hall, Marcellus, illus. 2010. (ENG.). 32p. (J). (gr. -1-1). 16.95 *(978-0-8109-8392-2(3)*, Abrams Bks. for Young Readers) Abrams, Inc.
O'Brien, Anne Sibley. In the Shadow of the Sun. 2017. (ENG.). 304p. (J). (gr. 3-7). 17.99 ***(978-0-545-90574-9(5))*** Scholastic, Inc.
Parker, Amy. Night Night, Daddy, 1 vol. 2016. (Night Night Ser.). (ENG., Illus.). 20p. (J). bds. 9.99 *(978-0-7180-4230-1(1))* Nelson, Thomas Inc.
Parry, Rosanne. Daddy's Home! Leonard, David, illus. 2009. (ENG.). 20p. (J). bds. 6.99 *(978-0-8249-1823-1(1)*, Ideal Pubns.) Worthy Publishing.
Perkins-Stell, Crystal. Never Knew a Father's Love. 2004. 256p. (YA). pap. 14.95 *(978-0-9740705-3-7(X))* Perkins-Stell, Crystal.
Peters, Andrew Fusek & Peters, Polly. The Color Thief. Littlewood, Karin, illus. 2015. (ENG.). 24p. (J). (gr. -1-3). 16.99 *(978-0-8075-1273-9(7))* Whitman, Albert & Co.
Poole, Philip. The Trouble with Time. 2012. (Illus.). 24p. pap. 19.82 *(978-1-4772-3459-4(4))* AuthorHouse.
Pope, Jerald. Madeleine Claire & the Dinosaur. 2006. (Illus.). (J). 16.00 *(978-0-9700125-6-2(X))* Brave Ulysses Bks.
Potvin, Amy K. I Miss Daddy. 2009. 28p. pap. 13.99 *(978-1-4259-1705-0(4))* AuthorHouse.
Powell, Luciana Navarro. My Dad Is the Best Playground. 2012. (ENG.). 26p. (J). (gr. k — 1). bds. 7.99 *(978-0-307-93090-3(4)*, Robin Corey Bks.) Random Hse. Children's Bks.
Price, Jesse. Dad. 2008. 28p. pap. 15.99 *(978-1-4363-1489-3(5))* Xlibris Corp.
Reynolds, Alison. Why I Love My Dad. Geddes, Serena, illus. 2015. (ENG.). 22p. (J). (gr. -1-1). 9.99 *(978-1-4998-0035-7(5))* Little Bee Books Inc.
Richards, Dawn. My Dad Is a Hero. 2014. (ENG., Illus.). 32p. (J). (gr. -1-k). 8.99 *(978-0-7641-6723-2(5))* Barron's Educational Series, Inc.
Robaard, Jedda, illus. A Little Book about Me & My Dad. 2014. (ENG.). 24p. (J). (gr. 1-5). 7.99 *(978-0-7641-6672-3(7))* Barron's Educational Series, Inc.
Romagnoli, L. M. The Worn-Out Backpack. Campbell, Lisa, illus. 2008. 15p. pap. 24.95 *(978-1-60563-934-5(6))* America Star Bks.
Ron, Berry. Daddy Do You Love Me. 2009. (ENG.). 20p. bds. 5.99 *(978-0-8249-1423-3(6)*, Ideal Pubns.) Worthy Publishing.
Roza, Greg. A Day for Dad. 2006. (Neighborhood Readers Ser.). (ENG.). 16p. (gr. 1-3). pap. 6.50 *(978-1-4042-7268-2(2)*, Rosen Classroom) Rosen Publishing Group, Inc., The.
Rylant, Cynthia. Herbert's First Halloween. Henry, Steven, illus. 2017. (ENG.). 36p. (J). (gr. -1 — 1). 15.99 *(978-1-4521-2533-6(3))* Chronicle Bks. LLC.
Sample, Matthew C. What a Day! 2010. 20p. pap. 12.49 *(978-1-4389-9853-4(8))* AuthorHouse.
Scoppettone, Carolyn Cory. Hold This, 1 vol. Alpaugh, Priscilla, illus. 2015. (ENG.). 32p. (J). 17.95 *(978-1-939017-68-0(8)*, 0746fc27-19be-4b00-8c9b-c95556c78519) Islandport Pr., Inc.
Seden, Paul. Crabbing with Dad. 2017. (ENG.). 32p. (J). (gr. k-3). pap. 15.99 *(978-1-925360-15-8(6))* Magabala Bks. AUS. Dist: Independent Pubs. Group.
Shapiro, Jane. Daddy, What Is Love? Robinson, Don, illus. 2008. (ENG.). 28p. (J). (gr. -1-3). *(978-1-59700-244-8(5))* Island Heritage Publishing.
Sharp, Lydia. Whenever I'm with You. 2017. (ENG.). 304p. (J). (gr. 7). 17.99 *(978-1-338-04749-3(3)*, Scholastic Pr.) Scholastic, Inc.
Sitomer, Alan Lawrence. Daddies Do It Different. Carter, Abby, illus. 2012. (ENG.). 40p. (J). (gr. -1 — 1). 16.99 *(978-1-4231-3315-5(3))* Hyperion Pr.
—Daddy's Back-To-School Shopping Adventure. Carter, Abby, illus. 2015. (ENG.). 40p. (J). (gr. -1-k). 16.99 *(978-1-4231-8421-8(1))* Hyperion Bks. for Children.
Skolmoski, Stephanie. A Paper Hug. Bennion, Anneliese, illus. 2006. 36p. (J). 6.95 *(978-0-9786425-0-1(3))* DesignAbility.
Smith, Icy. Daddy, My Favorite Guy. 2013. 28p. 16.95 *(978-0-9856237-9-1(9))* East West Discovery Pr.
Spinelli, Eileen. When Papa Comes Home Tonight. McPhail, David, illus. 2009. (ENG.). 32p. (J). (gr. -1-k). 16.99 *(978-1-4169-1028-2(X)*, Simon & Schuster Bks. For Young Readers) Simon & Schuster Bks. For Young Readers.
Stanley, Pauline. The Children & the Witches Magic. 2010. (Illus.). 48p. pap. 10.49 *(978-1-4490-9544-4(5))* AuthorHouse.
Stein, David Ezra. Tad & Dad. Stein, David Ezra, illus. 2015. (ENG., Illus.). 40p. (J). (gr. -1-k). 16.99 *(978-0-399-25671-4(7)*, Nancy Paulsen Books) Penguin Young Readers Group.
Stevenson, Robin. Hummingbird Heart, 1 vol. 2012. (ENG.). 280p. (YA). (gr. 8-12). pap. 12.95 *(978-1-55469-390-0(X))* Orca Bk. Pubs. USA.
Thompson, John & Thompson, Susan. The Lilychild. 2011. 256p. 35.95 *(978-1-4497-1331-7(9))*; pap. 19.95 *(978-1-4497-1330-0(0))* Author Solutions, Inc. (WestBow Pr.).
Thompson, Lauren. Mouse's First Snow. Erdogan, Buket, illus. 2011. (Classic Board Bks.). (ENG.). 34p. (J). (gr. -1 — 1). bds. 7.99 *(978-1-4424-2651-1(9)*, Little Simon) Little Simon.
Tran-Davies, N. Daddy Is a Conundrum! 2012. 40p. (-18). pap. *(978-1-4602-0043-8(8))* FriesenPress.
van Genechten, Guido. Daddies & Their Babies. 2012. (Black & White Ser.). (ENG.). 20p. (J). (gr. k — 1). bds. 9.95 *(978-1-60537-110-8(6))* Cobblestone Publishing Co.
Waite, Lance. A Day with Dad at the Beach. 2008. (J). 17.99 *(978-1-60131-016-3(1)*, Parents Publishing Group) Big Tent Bks.
—A Day with My Dad. Pentangelo, Manuela, illus. 2008. 24p. (J). (gr. -1-3). 17.99 *(978-1-60131-015-6(3)*, Parents Publishing Group) Big Tent Bks.
Walker, Anna. I Love My Dad. Walker, Anna, illus. 2010. (ENG., Illus.). 32p. (J). (gr. -1-1). 9.99 *(978-1-4169-8319-4(8)*, Simon & Schuster Bks. For Young Readers) Simon & Schuster Bks. For Young Readers.
Warnes, Tim. Daddy Hug. Chapman, Jane, illus. 2008. (ENG.). 32p. (J). (gr. -1-k). 17.99 *(978-0-06-058950-9(7))* HarperCollins Pubs.
Webb, Mack H., Jr. Danny & the Detention Demons. Espinola, Nicole & Nealon, Eve, illus. l.t. ed. 2007. 52p. (J). per. 15.95 *(978-0-9779576-2-0(4))* Pilinut Pr., Inc.
Wick, Michael J. I Love You All the Time. 2012. 24p. pap. 10.99 *(978-1-4624-0065-2(5)*, Inspiring Voices) Author Solutions, Inc.
Williams, Emma Louise. Daddy Loves You This Much. 2012. 24p. pap. 8.99 *(978-1-939076-03-8(X))* Wiggles, Piggy.
Wood, Douglas. When a Dad Says "I Love You" Bell, Jennifer A., illus. 2013. (ENG.). 32p. (J). (gr. -1-3). 17.99 *(978-0-689-87532-8(0)*, Simon & Schuster Bks. For Young Readers) Simon & Schuster Bks. For Young Readers.
Woodson, Jacqueline. Visiting Day. Ransome, James, illus. 2015. (ENG.). 32p. (J). (gr. k-2). 8.99 *(978-0-14-751608-4(0)*, Puffin Books) Penguin Young Readers Group.
Yaccarino, Dan. Every Friday. Yaccarino, Dan, illus. 2012. (ENG., Illus.). 32p. (J). (gr. -1-2). pap. 7.99 *(978-1-250-00473-4(X)*, 9781250004734) Square Fish.
—Every Friday. 2012. (J). lib. bdg. 18.40 *(978-0-606-26255-2(5)*, Turtleback) Turtleback Bks.
Yolen, Jane. My Father Knows the Names of Things. Jorisch, Stéphane, illus. 2010. (ENG.). 32p. (J). (gr. -1-3). 17.99 *(978-1-4169-4895-7(3)*, Simon & Schuster Bks. For Young Readers) Simon & Schuster Bks. For Young Readers.
Zappa, Ahmet. Because I'm Your Dad. Santat, Dan, illus. 2013. (ENG.). 32p. (J). (gr. -1-k). 15.99 *(978-1-4231-4774-9(X))* Disney Pr.
—Because I'm Your Dad. Santat, Dan, illus. 2016. (ENG.). 32p. (J). (gr. -1-k). bds. 7.99 *(978-1-4847-2661-7(8))* Hyperion Bks. for Children.

FATHERS

Arquette, Kerry. Daddy Promises. McCain, Kevin, illus. 2005. 32p. (J). pap. 7.49 *(978-0-7586-0905-2(1))* Concordia Publishing Hse.
Auld, Mary. Mi Papa. Carrillo, Consuelo & Coffey, Colleen, trs. from ENG. 2004. (Conoce la Familia Ser.). (SPA., Illus.). 24p. (gr. k-3). lib. bdg. 22.00 *(978-0-8368-3933-3(1)*, Gareth Stevens Learning Library) Stevens, Gareth Publishing LLLP.
—My Dad. 2004. (Meet the Family Ser.). (Illus.). 24p. (gr. k-3). lib. bdg. 22.00 *(978-0-8368-3925-8(0)*, Gareth Stevens Learning Library) Stevens, Gareth Publishing LLLP.
Ayer, Eleanor H. Todo lo que necesitas saber sobre la paternidad adolescente (Everything You Need to Know about Teen Fatherhood) 2009. (Todo lo que necesitas (the Need to Know Library) Ser.). (SPA.). 64p. (gr. 6-6). 58.50 *(978-1-60854-410-3(9)*, Editorial Buenas Letras) Rosen Publishing Group, Inc., The.
Baron, L. A Day with My Dad: Learning the D Sound. 2009. (PowerPhonics Ser.). 24p. (gr. 1-1). 39.90 *(978-1-60851-429-8(3)*, PowerKids Pr.) Rosen Publishing Group, Inc., The.
Brun-Cosme, Nadine, et al. Hoy lo Hace Papa! 2004. (SPA., Illus.). 32p. (J). (gr. -1-k). 13.99 *(978-84-8470-116-3(6))* Corimbo, Editorial S.L. ESP. Dist: Lectorum Pubns., Inc.
Chapman, Patricia. The Best Dad in the World. Chapman, Pat, illus. 2017. (ENG.). 32p. (J). (-k). 14.99 ***(978-1-927262-74-0(7))*** Upstart Pr. NZL. Dist: Independent Pubs. Group.
Hintze, Amy, illus. I'm So Glad When Daddy Comes Home. 2006. 16p. (J). 5.99 *(978-1-59156-562-8(6))* Covenant Communications, Inc.
Howarth, Daniel, illus. Why I Love My Daddy. 2013. (ENG.). 32p. (J). pap. 6.99 *(978-0-00-750866-2(2)*, HarperCollins Children's Bks.) HarperCollins Pubs. Ltd. GBR. Dist: HarperCollins Pubs.
Jenner, Caryn. My Dad. 2017. (Family World Ser.). (ENG., Illus.). 24p. (J). (gr. 1-3). pap. 9.99 ***(978-1-4451-5222-6(3)***, Franklin Watts) Hachette Children's Group GBR. Dist: Hachette Bk. Group.
Mahtani, Nikhil & Mahtani, Sherina. What Do Dads Do? 2013. 24p. 22.99 *(978-1-4808-0167-7(4))*; pap. 12.99 *(978-1-4808-0165-3(8))* Archway Publishing.
Numeroff, Laura Joffe. What Mommies Do Best; What Daddies Do Best. Munsinger, Lynn, illus. 2006. (ENG.). 40p. (J). (gr. -1-3). 4.99 *(978-0-689-84218-4(X)*, Simon & Schuster/Paula Wiseman Bks.) Simon & Schuster/Paula Wiseman Bks.
Parr, Todd. The Daddy Book. 2015. (ENG., Illus.). 20p. (J). (gr. -1 — 1). bds. 6.99 *(978-0-316-25784-8(2))* Little, Brown Bks. for Young Readers.
Powell, Jillian. My New Stepdad. 2012. (New Beginnings Ser.). (ENG., Illus.). 24p. (J). (gr. k-3). 21.25 *(978-1-4488-6635-9(9)*, PowerKids Pr.) Rosen Publishing Group, Inc., The.
Raatma, Lucia. Fathers Are Part of a Family. 2017. (Our Families Ser.). (ENG.). 24p. (gr. k-1). lib. bdg. 21.99 ***(978-1-5157-7463-1(5)***, Pebble Bks.) Capstone Press of Coughlan Cos.
Schaefer, Lola M. Fathers. Saunders-Smith, Gail, ed. rev. ed. 2008. (Families Ser.). (ENG., Illus.). 24p. (gr. k-1). per. 6.29 *(978-1-4296-1753-6(5)*, Pebble Bks.) Capstone Press of Coughlan Cos.
Sebastian, Emily. My Dad. 2010. (My Family Ser.). (ENG.). 24p. (J). pap. 8.25 *(978-1-4488-1488-6(X))*; lib. bdg. 22.60 *(978-1-4488-1461-9(8))* Rosen Publishing Group, Inc., The. (PowerKids Pr.).
—My Dad(Mi Papá) 2010. (My Family / Mi Familia Ser.). (SPA & ENG.). 24p. lib. bdg. 22.60 *(978-1-4488-0981-3(9)*, Editorial Buenas Letras) Rosen Publishing Group, Inc., The.
Sourcebooks. To the Best Dad Ever! 2016. (Sealed with a Kiss Ser.: 0). (ENG.). 48p. (J). (gr. 1-4). pap. 7.99 *(978-1-4926-3416-4(6))* Sourcebooks, Inc.
Stanley, Joseph & Jeffries, Joyce. I Learn from My Dad. 2016. (Things I Learn Ser.). (Illus.). 24p. (J). (gr. 1-1). pap. 8.25 *(978-1-4994-2342-6(X)*, PowerKids Pr.) Rosen Publishing Group, Inc., The.
Wilson, CeCe. Andre's Father Goes to School. 2015. (Rosen REAL Readers: STEM & STEAM Collection). (ENG.). 8p. pap. 5.46 *(978-1-4994-9695-6(8)*, Rosen Classroom) Rosen Publishing Group, Inc., The.

FATHERS—FICTION

Ashley-Hollinger, Mika. Precious Bones. 2013. (ENG.). 352p. (J). (gr. 4-7). 8.99 *(978-0-307-93070-5(X)*, Yearling) Random Hse. Children's Bks.
Avi. Poppy & Rye. Floca, Brian, illus. 2006. (Poppy Stories Ser.). (ENG.). 240p. (J). (gr. 3-7). pap. 6.99 *(978-0-380-79717-2(8))* HarperCollins Pubs.

—Poppy & Rye. Floca, Brian, illus. 2006. (Poppy Stories Ser.: 3). 182p. (J). (gr. 3-7). lib. bdg. 17.20 (978-0-613-17447-3(X), Turtleback) Turtleback Bks.

Banks, Steven. Pick a Dad, Any Dad! Moore, Harry, illus. 2005. (Fairly Odd Parents Ser.: 7). 24p. (J). lib. bdg. 15.00 (978-1-59054-804-2(3)) Fitzgerald Bks.

Barcelo, François. My Daddy's Footsteps. Mongeau, Marc, illus. 2009. (My First Stories Ser.). 24p. (J). (gr. -1-3). 22.60 (978-1-60754-359-6(1)); pap. 8.15 (978-1-60754-360-2(5)) Windmill Bks.

Barnaby, Hannah. Wonder Show. (ENG., 288p. (YA). (gr. 7). 2013. Illus.). pap. 8.99 (978-0-544-10483-9(8)) 2012. 16.99 (978-0-547-59980-9(3)) Houghton Mifflin Harcourt Publishing Co.

Barratt, Mark. The Wild Man. 2010. (ENG.). 352p. (YA). (gr. 6-18). pap. 9.00 (978-0-8028-5377-6(3), Eerdmans Bks For Young Readers) Eerdmans, William B. Publishing Co.

Barrow, Shelley. My Life: The Story of a NFL Child. 2007. (J). 16.99 (978-0-9792647-0-2(7)) Mikenzi's Kardz & Bks. Llc.

Beasley, Kama. Delaney's Journal: Dad Loses His Job. 2009. 48p. pap. 7.95 (978-1-936051-31-1(1)) Peppertree Pr., The.

Bently, Peter. Dustbin Dad. Ayto, Russell, illus. 2014. (ENG.). 32p. (J). 15.99 (978-1-84738-873-5(6)) Simon & Schuster, Ltd. GBR. Dist: Simon & Schuster, Inc.

Berenstain, Jan & Berenstain, Mike. We Love Our Dad! Berenstain, Jan & Berenstain, Mike, illus. 2013. (Berenstain Bears Ser.). (ENG., Illus.). 24p. (J). (gr. -1-3). pap. 3.99 (978-0-06-207551-2(9), HarperFestival) HarperCollins Pubs.

Berenstain, Stan & Berenstain, Jan. The Berenstain Bears & the Papa's Day Surprise. 2003. (First Time Books(R) Ser.). (ENG., Illus.). 32p. (J). (gr. -1-2). pap. 4.99 (978-0-375-81129-6(X), Random Hse. Bks. for Young Readers) Random Hse. Children's Bks.

Bevan, Lizzie. Never Far When in My Heart. 2013. (ENG., Illus.). 31p. (J). pap. 15.95 (978-1-4787-1027-1(6)) Outskirts Pr., Inc.

Bilen, Tracy. What She Left Behind. 2012. (ENG.). 256p. (YA). (gr. 9). pap. 9.99 (978-1-4424-3951-1(3), Simon Pulse) Simon Pulse.

Bland, Nick. Some Dads. 2017. (ENG., Illus.). 24p. (J). (gr. -1-1). 9.95 (978-0-7624-6199-8(3), Running Pr.) Running Pr. Bk. Pubs.

Bluemle, Elizabeth. My Father the Dog. Cecil, Randy, illus. (ENG.). 32p. (J). (gr. -1-3). 2008. pap. 6.99 (978-0-7636-3077-5(2)) 2006. 15.99 (978-0-7636-2222-0(2)) Candlewick Pr.

Blume, Judy. Tiger Eyes. 2014. (ENG., Illus.). 256p. (YA). (gr. 7). pap. 10.99 (978-1-4814-1387-9(2), Atheneum Bks. for Young Readers) Simon & Schuster Children's Publishing.

Bodeen, S. A. The Compound. 2008. (Compound Ser.: 1). (ENG.). 256p. (YA). (gr. 7-12). 18.99 (978-0-312-37015-2(6), 9780312370152) Feiwel & Friends.

—The Compound. 2011. 9.46 (978-0-7848-3490-9(3), Everbind) Marco Bk. Co.

—The Compound. 2009. (Compound Ser.: 1). (ENG.). 272p. (YA). (gr. 7-12). pap. 9.99 (978-0-312-57860-2(1), 9780312578602) Square Fish.

—The Gardener. 2011. (ENG.). 256p. (YA). (gr. 7-12). pap. 9.99 (978-0-312-65942-4(3), 9780312659424) Square Fish.

Braun, Sebastien. I Love My Daddy. Braun, Sebastien, illus. 2004. (ENG., Illus.). 32p. (J). (gr. -1-2). 12.99 (978-0-06-054311-2(6)) HarperCollins Pubs.

Briant, Ed. A Day at the Beach, No. 1. Briant, Ed, illus. 2006. (Illus.). 32p. (J). (gr. -1). 17.89 (978-0-06-079982-3(X)) HarperCollins Pubs.

Bridwell, Norman. Clifford's Day with Dad. Bridwell, Norman, illus. 2011. (Clifford 8x8 Ser.). (ENG., Illus.). 32p. (J). (gr. -1-k). pap. 3.99 (978-0-545-21593-0(5), Cartwheel Bks.) Scholastic, Inc.

Brown, Marc. Arthur & the 1,001 Dads, Bk. 28. Brown, Marc, illus. 2003. (ENG., Illus.). 64p. (J). (gr. 1-4). pap. 4.25 (978-0-316-12280-1(7)) Little, Brown Bks. for Young Readers.

Brown, Ruby. My Dad Is a Superhero. Vamos, Lesley, illus. 2014. (J). (978-1-4351-5488-9(6)) Barnes & Noble, Inc.

Bullard, Lisa. Turn Left at the Cow. 2013. (ENG.). 304p. (J). (gr. 5-7). 16.99 (978-0-544-02900-2(3)) Houghton Mifflin Harcourt Publishing Co.

Caletti, Deb. The Secret Life of Prince Charming. (ENG.). (YA). (gr. 7). 2010. 352p. pap. 11.99 (978-1-4169-5941-0(6)) 2009. 336p. 16.99 (978-1-4169-5940-3(8)) Simon Pulse. (Simon Pulse).

Calkin, Author & Calkin, Abigail B. The Carolyne Letters: A Story of Birth, Abortion & Adoption. 2013. (ENG., Illus.). 230p. (YA). pap. 14.95 (978-1-938301-15-5(3)) Familius LLC.

Carle, Eric. Mister Seahorse. Carle, Eric, illus. 2004. (ENG., Illus.). 32p. (J). (gr. -1-k). 18.99 (978-0-399-24269-4(4), Philomel Bks.) Penguin Young Readers Group.

Chronicle Books Staff. Papa Do You Love Me Teacher's. 2005. (J). pap. 0.01 (978-0-8118-9927-7(6)) Chronicle Bks. LLC.

Cohen, Miriam. Daddy's Busy Day, 1 vol. 2014. (ENG.). 32p. (J). bds. (978-1-59572-668-1(3)) Star Bright Bks., Inc.

Cole, Babette. The Trouble with Dad. 2005. (Illus.). 32p. (J). pap. 3.99 (978-1-4052-1122-2(9)) Egmont Bks., Ltd. GBR. Dist: Trafalgar Square Publishing.

Cooney, Doug. The Beloved Dearly. DiTerlizzi, Tony, illus. 2003. (ENG.). 192p. (J). (gr. 3-7). pap. 7.99 (978-0-689-86354-7(3), Simon & Schuster Bks. For Young Readers) Simon & Schuster Bks. For Young Readers.

Cooper, Glenessa. Daddy's Number One Little Girl. Joseph, Patricia, illus. 2008. 10p. pap. 24.95 (978-1-60563-983-3(4)) America Star Bks.

Costain, Meredith. Daddies Are Awesome. Lovsin, Polona, illus. 2016. (ENG.). 32p. (J). 16.99 (978-1-62779-452-7(2), 9781627794527, Holt, Henry & Co. Bks. For Young Readers) Holt, Henry & Co.

Crayon, Paula. An Angel in My Pocket. 2010. 44p. (J). pap. 17.99 (978-1-4490-9921-3(1)) AuthorHouse.

Cross, Julie & Perini, Mark. You Before Anyone Else. 2016. (ENG.). 400p. (YA). (gr. 8-12). pap. 10.99 (978-1-4926-0492-1(5), 9781492604921) Sourcebooks, Inc.

Croteau, Marie-Danielle. Le Tresor de Mon Pere. 2003. (Premier Roman Ser.). (FRE., Illus.). 64p. (J). (gr. 2-5). pap. (978-2-89021-246-6(7)) Diffusion du livre Mirabel (DLM).

Dad & Me: KinderConcepts, 6 Packs. (Kinderstarters Ser.). 8p. (gr. -1-1). 21.00 (978-0-7635-8735-2(4)) Rigby Education.

Dad cooks Breakfast: Individual Title Six-Packs. (gr. 1-2). 25.00 (978-0-7635-9135-9(1)) Rigby Education.

Daniels, Babygirl. Glitter. 2009. (ENG., Illus.). 208p. (YA). (gr. 9). pap. 9.95 (978-1-60162-198-6(1), Urban Renaissance) Kensington Publishing Corp.

Davies, Jacqueline. The Magic Trap. 2014. (Lemonade War Ser.: 5). (ENG., Illus.). 272p. (J). (gr. 2-5). 15.99 (978-0-544-05289-5(7), HMH Books For Young Readers) Houghton Mifflin Harcourt Publishing Co.

Davis, Adda Leah. Caleb's Song. l.t. ed. 2003. (Illus.). 56p. (J). (978-0-9747904-0-4(0)) Golden Harvest Publishing Co.

Davis, Tanita S. Happy Families. (ENG.). 240p. (YA). (gr. 7). 2013. pap. 9.99 (978-0-375-87170-2(5), Ember) 2012. 16.99 (978-0-375-86966-2(2), Knopf Bks. for Young Readers) Random Hse. Children's Bks.

Dean, James. Rock On, Mom & Dad! Dean, James, illus. 2015. (Pete the Cat Ser.). (ENG., Illus.). 24p. (J). (gr. -1-3). pap. 6.99 (978-0-06-230408-7(9), HarperFestival) HarperCollins Pubs.

—Rock on, Mom & Dad! Dean, James, illus. 2015. (Pete the Cat (HarperCollins) Ser.). (Illus.). (J). lib. bdg. 17.20 (978-0-606-36490-4(0)) Turtleback Bks.

DeStout, Carole. My Dad Wears Striped Pajamas. Heath, Paul Reaves, illus. 2003. (Children's Outreach Ser.). 38p. (J). pap. 5.00 (978-1-880994-83-2(6)) Mount Olive College Pr.

Deuker, Carl. High Heat. 2005. (ENG.). 352p. (J). (gr. 8-18). pap. 8.99 (978-0-06-057248-8(5), HarperTeen) HarperCollins Pubs.

Dowd, Siobhan. A Swift Pure Cry. 2008. (ENG.). 320p. (YA). (gr. 7). pap. 8.99 (978-0-440-42218-1(3)) Fickling, David Bks. GBR. Dist: Penguin Random Hse. LLC.

—A Swift Pure Cry. 2011. 10.54 (978-0-7848-3500-5(4), Everbind) Marco Bk. Co.

Dr. Seuss Enterprises Staff. Hop on Pop. 2004. (Bright & Early Board Books Ser.). (ENG., Illus.). 24p. (J). (gr. k-1). bds. 4.99 (978-0-375-82837-9(0), Random Hse. Bks. for Young Readers) Random Hse. Children's Bks.

Eddy, Daniel. Walter's Tours in the East: Walter in Je. 2005. pap. 16.95 (978-1-59605-437-0(9), Cosimo Classics) Cosimo, Inc.

Ehlert, Lois. Pie in the Sky. 2004. (ENG., Illus.). 40p. (J). (gr. -1-3). 17.99 (978-0-15-216584-0(3)) Houghton Mifflin Harcourt Publishing Co.

Eifrig, Kate. Scary Monster. Graves, Dennis, illus. 2003. (ENG.). 8p. (gr. k-1). pap. 7.95 (978-1-879835-29-0(0), Kaeden Bks.) Kaeden Corp.

Elmore, Wanda M. & Elmore, Wardon O. Mr. Fix, Design It, Carry It with You, My Dadee & Me. 2011. 30p. pap. 9.00 (978-1-4349-8601-6(2), RoseDog Bks.) Dorrance Publishing Co., Inc.

Encyclopaedia Britannica, Inc. Staff, compiled by. I Wish Daddy Didn't Drink So Much. 2008. 49.95 (978-1-59339-667-1(8)) Encyclopaedia Britannica, Inc.

Etshied, Karl Jeffrey. Eggplant Rufus: Amused Indifference on a Stupid Planet. 2008. 158p. pap. (978-0-9814627-3-8(1)) Great American Pr., The.

Fames, Catherine. The Slide. 2003. 128p. (J). 6.49 (978-1-57924-967-0(1)) BJU Pr.

Feiffer, Jules. The Daddy Mountain. 2004. (Illus.). 32p. (gr. -1-17). (978-0-7868-0912-7(4)) Hyperion Bks. for Children.

Fisher, Catherine. The Slanted Worlds. 2015. (Obsidian Mirror Ser.: 2). (ENG.). 384p. (YA). (gr. 7). pap. 9.99 (978-0-14-242678-4(4), Speak) Penguin Young Readers Group.

Fogg, K. L. Diamondback Cave: A Novel. 2008. 377p. (J). (978-1-59811-512-3(X)) Covenant Communications.

Fontes, Justine. Benito Runs. (Surviving Southside Ser.). (ENG.). 104p. (YA). (gr. 6-12). 2015. 34.65 (978-1-4677-6008-9(0), Lerner Digital) 2011. pap. 7.95 (978-0-7613-6165-7(0)) 2011. lib. bdg. 27.93 (978-0-7613-6151-0(0)) Lerner Publishing Group.

Frank, Janet & Golden Books Staff. Daddies. Gergely, Tibor, illus. 2011. (Little Golden Book Ser.). (ENG.). 24p. (J). (gr. -1-2). 4.99 (978-0-375-86130-7(0), Golden Bks.) Random Hse. Children's Bks.

Freeberg, Jane. The Scallop Christmas. Sheckels, Astrid, illus. 2011. (ENG.). 36p. (J). 16.95 (978-1-934031-25-4(9), 9781934031254) Islandport Pr., Inc.

Gaiman, NEil. The Day I Swapped My Dad for Two Goldfish. McKean, Dave, illus. 2004. (ENG.). 64p. (J). (gr. k). 17.99 (978-0-06-058701-7(6)) HarperCollins Pubs.

—Fortunately, the Milk. Young, Skottie, illus. (ENG.). 128p. (J). (gr. 3-7). 2014. pap. 5.99 (978-0-06-222408-8(5)) 2013. 14.99 (978-0-06-222407-1(7)) HarperCollins Pubs.

—Fortunately, the Milk. 2014. (J). lib. bdg. 16.00 (978-0-606-35965-8(6)) Turtleback Bks.

Gephart, Donna. Olivia Bean, Trivia Queen. (ENG.). 288p. (J). 2013. (gr. 4-7). 6.99 (978-0-375-87261-7(2), Yearling) 2012. (gr. 3-7). 16.99 (978-0-385-74052-4(2), Delacorte Bks. for Young Readers) Random Hse. Children's Bks.

Gikow, Louise. A Day with Daddy. Mazali, Gustavo, illus. 2004. (My First Reader Ser.). (ENG.). 32p. (J). (gr. k-1). pap. 3.95 (978-0-516-25501-9(0), Children's Pr.) Scholastic Library Publishing.

Glaze, Dave & Coteau Books Staff. Waiting for Pelly, 1 vol. 2003. (ENG., Illus.). 120p. (J). (gr. 3-6). pap. 7.95 (978-1-55050-228-2(X)) Coteau Bks. CAN. Dist: Orca Bk. Pubs. USA.

Goldstein, Bobby. The Story of the Pink Gorilla Monster. 2012. 40p. pap. 17.99 (978-1-4490-6377-1(2)) AuthorHouse.

Gonzalez, Genaro. A So-Called Vacation. 2009. 192p. (YA). (gr. 9-18). pap. 10.95 (978-1-55885-545-8(9), Piñata Books) Arte Publico Pr.

Gormley, Greg. Daddy's Day at Work. 2007. (Fantastic Phones Ser.). (ENG., Illus.). 12p. (J). (gr. k-k). bds. 9.99 (978-0-7475-8378-3(1)) Bloomsbury Publishing Plc GBR. Dist: Independent Pubs. Group.

Guest, Jacqueline & Leavey, Peggy Dymond. Growing up Ivy. 2010. (ENG.). 256p. (YA). (gr. 4-8). pap. 10.99 (978-1-55488-723-1(2)) Dundurn CAN. Dist: Ingram Publisher Services.

Gutman, Anne & Hallensleben, Georg. Daddy Kisses. 2003. (ENG., Illus.). 14p. (J). (gr. -1-7). bds. 5.99 (978-0-8118-3914-3(1)) Chronicle Bks. LLC.

Hallinan, P. K. We're Very Good Friends, My Father & I. 24p. (J). 5.95 (978-0-8249-5376-8(2)); 7.95 (978-0-8249-5375-1(4)) Worthy Publishing. (Ideal Pubns.).

Harkrader, L. D. Airball: My Life in Briefs. 2008. (ENG.). 208p. (J). (gr. 3-7). per. 9.99 (978-0-312-37382-5(1), 9780312373825) Square Fish.

Hiaasen, Carl. Flush. 2007. 263p. (gr. 5-9). 19.00 (978-0-7569-8192-1(1)) Perfection Learning Corp.

—Flush. (ENG.). 272p. (J). (gr. 5-6). 2010. 6.99 (978-0-375-86125-3(4), Yearling) 2007. pap. 8.99 (978-0-375-84185-9(7), Knopf Bks. for Young Readers) 2005. 16.95 (978-0-375-82182-0(1), Knopf Bks. for Young Readers) Random Hse. Children's Bks.

Higgins, Jack & Richards, Justin. Death Run. 2009. (Rich & Jade Ser.: Bk. 2). (ENG.). 288p. (YA). (gr. 7-18). 8.99 (978-0-14-241475-0(1), Speak) Penguin Young Readers Group.

—First Strike. 2011. (Rich & Jade Ser.: Bk. 4). (ENG.). 240p. (YA). (gr. 7-18). 8.99 (978-0-14-241909-0(5), Speak) Penguin Young Readers Group.

—Sharp Shot. 2010. (Rich & Jade Ser.: Bk. 3). (ENG.). 240p. (YA). (gr. 7-18). 8.99 (978-0-14-241730-0(0), Speak) Penguin Young Readers Group.

—Sure Fire. 2008. (Rich & Jade Ser.: Bk. 1). (ENG.). 272p. (YA). (gr. 7-18). 8.99 (978-0-14-241213-8(9), Speak) Penguin Young Readers Group.

Hill, Kirkpatrick. Bo at Ballard Creek. Pham, LeUyen, illus. 2013. (ENG.). 288p. (J). (gr. 3-7). 16.99 (978-0-8050-9351-3(6), 9780805093513, Holt, Henry & Co. Bks. For Young Readers) Holt, Henry & Co.

—Do Not Pass Go. 2011. (ENG.). 240p. (J). (gr. 4-9). pap. 6.99 (978-1-4424-2122-6(3), McElderry, Margaret K. Bks.) McElderry, Margaret K. Bks.

Hiris, Monica. Just Like Dad. Drzewiecki, Paul, illus. l.t. ed. 2003. (ENG.). 8p. (gr. k-1). pap. 7.95 (978-1-879835-76-4(2), Kaeden Bks.) Kaeden Corp.

Hoese, Ray. My Dad Is an Ironman. Steinbach, Coreen, illus. 2004. (ENG.). 32p. (J). 15.00 (978-1-891369-51-3(2)) Breakaway Bks.

How to Surprise a Dad. 2015. (ENG., Illus.). 32p. (J). (gr. k-3). 16.99 (978-0-553-49836-3(3), Knopf Bks. for Young Readers) Random Hse. Children's Bks.

Hunt, Leo. Eight Rivers of Shadow. 2016. (ENG.). 368p. (YA). (gr. 9). 17.99 (978-0-7636-8994-0(7)) Candlewick Pr.

Irene's Wish. 2014. (ENG., Illus.). 32p. (J). (gr. k-4). 17.99 (978-0-689-86300-4(4), Simon & Schuster/Paula Wiseman Bks.) Simon & Schuster/Paula Wiseman Bks.

Jacobs, Breena. Daddy's Girl. Austrew, Neva, illus. 2006. 32p. (J). (gr. -1-k). 15.95 (978-0-9749423-2-2(4)) Bookworm Bks.

Jobling, Curtis. My Daddy: My Daddy Is the Best in the Universe! 2006. (ENG., Illus.). 32p. (J). (gr. -1-k). pap. 8.99 (978-0-00-712255-4(1)) HarperCollins Pubs. Ltd. GBR. Dist: Independent Pubs. Group.

Johnson, Angela. The First Part Last. 2010. (ENG.). 144p. (YA). (gr. 7). pap. 9.99 (978-1-4424-0343-7(8), Simon & Schuster Bks. For Young Readers) Simon & Schuster Bks. For Young Readers.

Johnson, Craig Alan. Wave Watcher. 2005. viii, 139p. (J). pap. (978-0-87743-707-9(6)) Baha'i Publishing Trust, U.S.

Johnson, Vincent L. Daddy's Good Cookin' Pavlova, Vera, illus. 2006. 32p. (J). 16.95 (978-0-9657033-3-8(9)) Marzetta Bks.

Joosse, Barbara M. & Lavallee, Barbara. Papa, Do You Love Me? Lavallee, Barbara, illus. 2005. (Mama Ser.: MAMA). (ENG., Illus.). 36p. (J). (gr. -1-7). 15.99 (978-0-8118-4265-5(7)) Chronicle Bks. LLC.

Jougla, Frederic. Tricked on Halloween: Rina & Jax's Stories. Jougla, Karina, illus. l.t. ed. 2004. 36p. (J). bds. 14.99 (978-0-9754287-0-2(5)) Imagery Pr.

Kaaberbøl, Lene. The Serpent Gift. 3rd ed. 2007. (Shamer Chronicles Ser.: 3). Orig. Title: Slangens Gave. (ENG.). 384p. (J). (gr. 5-9). pap. 22.99 (978-0-8050-8655-3(2), 9780805086553, Holt, Henry & Co. Bks. For Young Readers) Holt, Henry & Co.

Kanevsky, Polly. Sleepy Boy. Anderson, Stephanie, illus. 2006. (ENG.). 32p. (J). (gr. -1-k). 16.99 (978-0-689-86735-4(2), Atheneum/Richard Jackson Bks.) Simon & Schuster Children's Publishing.

Kang, Hildi. Chengli & the Silk Road Caravan. 2012. (ENG.). 176p. (J). (gr. 2-7). pap. 8.95 (978-1-933718-78-1(1)) Tanglewood Pr.

Krensky, Stephen. Arthur & the 1,001 Dads. 2003. (Marc Brown Arthur Chapter Bks.). (Illus.). 57p. (J). (gr. 1-4). 11.90 (978-0-7569-1600-8(3)) Perfection Learning Corp.

Laínez, René Colato. Waiting for Papá/Esperando a Papá. Accardo, Anthony, illus.Tr. of Esperando a Papa. (ENG & SPA.). 32p. (gr. 1-3). 16.95 (978-1-55885-403-1(7), Piñata Books) Arte Publico Pr.

Levy, Janice. Alley Oops. Decker, C. B., illus. 2005. (ENG.). 32p. (J). (gr. k-3). 17.95 (978-0-9729225-4-8(7)) Flashlight Pr.

Logelin, Matthew & Jensen, Sara Bee. Be Glad Your Dad. Chapman, Jared, illus. 2016. (ENG.). 40p. (J). (gr. -1-3). 16.99 (978-0-316-25438-0(X)) Little Brown & Co.

Lowenstein, Sallie. Waiting for Eugene. Lowenstein, Sallie, illus. 2005. (Illus.). 208p. (J). 19.00 (978-0-9658486-5-7(5)) Lion Stone Bks.

Lowery, Linda. Truth & Salsa, 1 vol. (ENG.). 176p. (J). 2009. pap. 7.95 (978-1-56145-498-3(2)) 2006. (gr. 3-7). 15.95 (978-1-56145-366-5(8)) Peachtree Pubs.

Machajewski, Sarah. My Dad Is a Nurse. 2012. (InfoMax Readers Ser.). (ENG., Illus.). 24p. (J). (gr. 1-2). pap. 8.25 (978-1-4488-9001-9(2), Rosen Classroom) Rosen Publishing Group, Inc., The.

MacNeil, Stephen. Woolies & Worms. Sandford, John, illus. 2007. (ENG.). 192p. (J). (gr. 1-5). 16.95 (978-0-8126-2751-0(2)) Cricket Bks.

Madlener, Michael & Reeves, Patrick. Feed Your Fish. 2012. 40p. 24.95 (978-1-4626-6707-9(4)) PublishAmerica, Inc.

Maetani, Valynne E. Ink & Ashes. 2015. (ENG.). 368p. (YA). 19.95 (978-1-62014-211-0(2), Tu Bks.) Lee & Low Bks., Inc.

Marciniak, Christine. Reality Ali. 2012. (J). (978-1-61271-076-1(X)); (978-1-61271-075-4(1)); pap. 13.99 (978-1-61271-074-7(3)) Zumaya Pubns. LLC.

Matson, Morgan. Amy & Roger's Epic Detour. (ENG.). (YA). (gr. 7). 2011. 384p. pap. 10.99 (978-1-4169-9066-6(6)) 2010. 352p. 19.99 (978-1-4169-9065-9(8)) Simon & Schuster Bks. For Young Readers. (Simon & Schuster Bks. For Young Readers).

Mayfield, Sue. The Four Franks. 2005. (Blue Go Bananas Ser.). (ENG., Illus.). 48p. (J). (gr. 1-2). lib. bdg. (978-0-7787-2629-6(0)) Crabtree Publishing Co.

Maynard, Joyce. The Cloud Chamber. 2006. (ENG.). 288p. (YA). (gr. 7-7). pap. 13.99 (978-1-4169-2699-3(2), Simon Pulse) Simon Pulse.

Mazer, Norma Fox. Missing Pieces. 2007. (ENG., Illus.). 160p. (YA). (gr. 7-12). pap. 11.95 (978-0-15-206271-2(8)) Houghton Mifflin Harcourt Publishing Co.

McCarthy, Laura. My Daddy Can Too!!! 2011. 24p. pap. 28.03 (978-1-4568-3778-5(8)) Xlibris Corp.

McCormick, Wendy. Daniel & His Walking Stick, 1 vol. Bergum, Constance R., illus. 2005. (ENG.). 32p. (J). (gr. k-3). 15.95 (978-1-56145-330-6(7)) Peachtree Pubs.

McDonald, Abby. Jane Austen Goes to Hollywood. (ENG.). 336p. (YA). (gr. 9). 2015. pap. 8.99 (978-0-7636-7669-8(1)) 2013. 17.99 (978-0-7636-5508-2(2)) Candlewick Pr.

McKay, Hilary. Permanent Rose. 2006. (ENG.). 256p. (J). (gr. 3-7). reprint ed. per. 7.99 (978-1-4169-2804-1(9), McElderry, Margaret K. Bks.) McElderry, Margaret K. Bks.

McKinley, Robin. Shadows. 2013. 356p. (YA). (978-0-399-25625-7(3)) Penguin Publishing Group.

Miller, Marie. Party Time. 2006. (Neighborhood Readers Ser.). (ENG.). 8p. (gr. -1-3). pap. 5.15 (978-1-4042-6706-0(9), Rosen Classroom) Rosen Publishing Group, Inc., The.

Mitchell, Kathy. Daddy Got His Orders. Hergenroeder, Ernie, illus. 2004. 16p. (J). pap. 14.95 (978-0-9760811-0-4(5)) T.J. Publishing.

Montgomery Gibson, Jane. Daddy's Valentine. Montgomery Gibson, Jane, illus. 2005. (Illus.). (J). bds. 8.99 (978-1-4183-0046-3(2)) Christ Inspired, Inc.

Morrison, Kevin. Stitches. Nixon, John, illus. 2003. 32p. (J). 12.95 (978-1-929039-15-9(8)) Ambassador Bks., Inc.

Moss, Marissa. Amelia's Family Ties. Moss, Marissa, illus. 2013. (Amelia Ser.). (ENG., Illus.). (J). 5.99 (978-1-4169-1293-4(2), Simon & Schuster/Paula Wiseman Bks.) Simon & Schuster/Paula Wiseman Bks.

My Daddy Is a Giant. 2004. (J). (ENG & TUR.). (978-1-84444-522-6(4)); (ENG & URD.). (978-1-84444-523-3(2)); (ENG & POR.). (978-1-84444-517-2(8)); (ENG & POL.). (978-1-84444-516-5(X)); (ENG & PAN.). (978-1-84444-515-8(1)); (ENG & KUR.). (978-1-84444-514-1(3)); (ENG & JPN.). (978-1-84444-512-7(7)); (ENG & ITA.). (978-1-84444-511-0(9)); (ENG & HIN.). (978-1-84444-510-3(0)); (ENG & GUJ.). (978-1-84444-509-7(7)); (ENG & FRE.). (978-1-84444-507-3(0)); (ENG & PER.). (978-1-84444-506-6(2)); (CRO & ENG.). (978-1-84444-505-9(4)); (CHI & ENG.). (978-1-84444-504-2(6)); (ARA & ENG.). (978-1-84444-501-1(1)); (ALB & ENG.). (978-1-84444-499-1(6)); (ENG & SPA.). (978-1-84444-520-2(8)); (ENG & TAM.). (978-1-84444-521-9(6)); (ENG & TAG.). (978-1-84444-508-0(9)); (ENG & SOM.). (978-1-84444-519-6(4)) Mantra Lingua.

My Father the Mad Professor: Individual Title Six-Packs. (Action Packs Ser.). 120p. (gr. 3-5). 44.00 (978-0-7635-8424-5(X)) Rigby Education.

Nevin, Judy Carey. What Daddies Like. Six, Stephanie, illus. 2017. (ENG.). 32p. (J). (gr. -1-3). 16.99 (978-1-4998-0197-2(1)) Little Bee Books Inc.

Norac, Carl. My Daddy Is a Giant. 2005. (J). (CHI & ENG.). 16.95 (978-1-84444-503-5(8)); (ENG & RUS.). 16.95 (978-1-84444-518-9(6)); (ENG & VIE.). 16.95 (978-1-84444-524-0(0)); (BEN & ENG.). 16.95 (978-1-84444-502-8(X)); (ENG & KOR.). 16.95 (978-1-84444-513-4(5)) Mantra Lingua GBR. Dist: Chinasprout, Inc.

Osterlund, Anne. Academy 7. 2009. (ENG.). 272p. (YA). (gr. 7-18). pap. 8.99 (978-0-14-241437-8(9), Speak) Penguin Young Readers Group.

Papa Piccolo: Evaluation Guide. 2006. (J). 17.95 (978-1-55942-419-6(2)) Witcher Productions.

Parker, Amy. A Night Night Prayer, 1 vol. Pedler, Caroline, illus. 2014. (Night Night Ser.). (ENG.). 20p. (J). bds. 9.99 (978-1-4003-2431-6(9)) Nelson, Thomas Inc.

Parker, Marjorie Blain. When Dads Don't Grow Up. Alley, R. W., illus. 2012. (ENG.). 32p. (J). (gr. -1-k). 16.99 (978-0-8037-3717-4(3), Dial Bks) Penguin Young Readers Group.

Parr, Todd. The Daddy Book. 2010. (ENG., Illus.). 32p. (J). (gr. -1-1). pap. 7.99 (978-0-316-07039-3(4)) Little, Brown Bks. for Young Readers.

Pelton, Lisa. Logos & Obedience: Listening to His Father's Voice. 2009. 32p. pap. 13.99 (978-1-4389-5177-5(9)) AuthorHouse.

Pierce, Heather Vowell. What Does Your Daddy Do? Price, Dana, illus. 2010. 32p. pap. 16.49 (978-1-4520-1723-5(9)) AuthorHouse.

Pleau-Murissi, Marilyn. Caillou, Spends the Day with Daddy. CINAR Animation Staff, illus. 2004. (Clubhouse Usa Ser.). 24p. (J). (gr. -1-18). 3.95 (978-2-89450-523-6(X)) Ellipsis Pr.

Porter-Gaylord, Laurel. I Love My Daddy Because... Wolff, Ashley, illus. 2004. (ENG.). 20p. (J). (gr. -1 — 1). bds. 6.99 (978-0-525-47250-6(9), Dutton Books for Young Readers) Penguin Young Readers Group.

—I Love My Daddy Because... (Quiero a Mi Papa Porque...) Wolff, Ashley, illus. 2004. (ENG & SPA.). 22p. (J). (gr. -1 — 1). bds. 6.99 (978-0-525-47251-3(7), Dutton Books for Young Readers) Penguin Young Readers Group.

Portman, Frank. King Dork. 2007. 344p. 19.00 (978-0-7569-7950-8(1)) Perfection Learning Corp.

—King Dork. 2008. (ENG.). 368p. (YA). (gr. 9-12). pap. 9.99 (978-0-385-73450-9(6), Delacorte Bks. for Young Readers) Random Hse. Children's Bks.

Ramljak, Marijan. Where Is My Daddy? 2009. (Look for Me Bks.). (Illus.). (J). bds. 9.99 (978-1-934650-66-0(8)) Just For Kids Pr., LLC.

Random House. Ninja Dad! (Teenage Mutant Ninja Turtles) Johnson, Shane, illus. 2016. (Step into Reading Ser.). (ENG.). 24p. (J). (gr. -1-1). 4.99 (978-0-553-53937-0(X), Random Hse. Bks. for Young Readers) Random Hse. Children's Bks.

Reisfeld, Randi & Gilmour, H. B. What the Dog Said. 2012. (ENG.). 256p. (YA). (gr. 4-14). 16.99 (978-1-59990-702-4(X), 9781599907024, Bloomsbury USA Childrens) Bloomsbury Publishing USA.

Resau, Laura. Estrella en el Bosque (Star in the Forest) 2016. (ENG & SPA.). 160p. (J). (gr. 2-5). 18.40 (978-0-606-39132-0(0)) Turtleback Bks.

—The Indigo Notebook. 2010. (ENG.). 336p. (YA). (gr. 7). pap. 9.99 (978-0-375-84524-6(0), Ember) Random Hse. Children's Bks.

—Star in the Forest. 2012. (ENG.). 160p. (J). (gr. 2-5). 6.99 (978-0-375-85410-1(X), Yearling) Random Hse. Children's Bks.

Richards, Doyin. I Wonder: Celebrating Daddies Doin' Work. 2016. (ENG., Illus.). 32p. (J). 17.99 (978-1-250-07895-7(4), 9781250078957) Feiwel & Friends.

Rockwell, Anne F. Father's Day. Rockwell, Lizzy, illus. 2005. 40p. (J). (gr. -1-1). lib. bdg. 15.89 (978-0-06-051378-8(0)) HarperCollins Pubs.

Ryan, Darlene. Five Minutes More, 1 vol. 2009. (ENG.). 224p. (YA). (gr. 7-12). pap. 12.95 (978-1-55469-006-0(4)) Orca Bk. Pubs. USA.

Sáenz, Benjamin Alire. He Forgot to Say Goodbye. 2008. (ENG.). 336p. (YA). (gr. 7-12). 18.99 (978-1-4169-4963-3(1), Simon & Schuster Bks. For Young Readers) Simon & Schuster Bks. For Young Readers.

Salisbury, Graham. Calvin Coconut: Rocket Ride. Rogers, Jacqueline, illus. 2013. (Calvin Coconut Ser.). (ENG.). 160p. (J). (gr. 2-5). pap. 6.99 (978-0-375-86508-4(X), Yearling) Random Hse. Children's Bks.

Sanna, Francesca. The Journey. Sanna, Francesca, illus. 2016. (ENG., Illus.). 48p. (J). (gr. -1-2). 17.95 (978-1-909263-99-4(0)) Flying Eye Bks. GBR. Dist: Consortium Bk. Sales & Distribution.

Saudo, Coralie. My Dad at the Zoo. Di Giacomo, Kris, illus. 2016. (ENG.). 32p. (J). (gr. -1-2). 17.95 (978-1-59270-190-2(6)) Enchanted Lion Bks., LLC.

—My Dad Is Big & Strong, But... A Bedtime Story. Di Giacomo, Kris, illus. 2012. (ENG.). 32p. (J). (gr. -1-2). 16.95 (978-1-59270-122-3(1)) Enchanted Lion Bks., LLC.

Schiffer, Miriam B. Stella Brings the Family. Clifton-Brown, Holly, illus. 2015. (ENG.). 36p. (J). (gr. k-3). 16.99 (978-1-4521-1190-2(1)) Chronicle Bks. LLC.

Schmatz, Pat. Circle the Truth. 2007. (Exceptional Reading & Language Arts Titles for Intermediate Grades Ser.). (ENG.). 192p. (YA). (gr. 7-12). 16.95 (978-0-8225-7268-8(0)) Lerner Publishing Group.

Schmidt, Gary D. Orbiting Jupiter. 2015. (ENG.). 192p. (J). (gr. 7). 17.99 (978-0-544-46222-9(X), Clarion Bks.) Houghton Mifflin Harcourt Publishing Co.

—Orbiting Jupiter. 2017. (ENG.). (YA). (gr. 7). lib. bdg. 20.85 **(978-0-606-39818-3(X))** Turtleback Bks.

Schroeder, Lisa. Falling for You. 2013. (ENG., Illus.). 384p. (YA). (gr. 9). pap. 9.99 (978-1-4424-4400-3(2), Simon Pulse) Simon Pulse.

Scott, Kieran. This Is So Not Happening. 2013. (He's So/She's So Trilogy Ser.). (ENG., Illus.). 320p. (YA). (gr. 7). pap. 9.99 (978-1-4169-9956-0(6), Simon & Schuster Bks. For Young Readers) Simon & Schuster Bks. For Young Readers.

Sedgwick, Marcus. She Is Not Invisible. 2014. (ENG.). 224p. (YA). (gr. 7). 16.99 (978-1-59643-801-9(0), 9781596438019) Roaring Brook Pr.

—She Is Not Invisible. 2015. (ENG.). 240p. (YA). (gr. 7). pap. 9.99 (978-1-250-05698-6(5), 9781250056986) Square Fish.

Seskin, Steve & Shamblin, Allen. A Chance to Shine. Christie, R. & Christie, Gregory, illus. 2006. (ENG.). 30p. (J). (gr. -1-2). 16.99 (978-1-58246-167-0(8), Tricycle Pr.) Random Hse. Children's Bks.

Shamblin, Seskin & National Geographic Learning Staff. A Chance to Shine. Christie, R. Gregory, illus. 2008. (ENG.). 32p. (C). (gr. -1-2). pap. 12.95 (978-1-58246-304-9(2)) National Geographic School Publishing, Inc.

Sitomer, Alan Lawrence. Daddies Do It Different. Carter, Abby, illus. 2012. (ENG.). 40p. (J). (gr. -1 — 1). 16.99 (978-1-4231-3315-5(3)) Hyperion Pr.

Skuse, C. J. Pretty Bad Things. 2011. (ENG.). 256p. (J). (gr. 7-7). 17.99 (978-0-545-28973-3(4), Chicken Hse., The) Scholastic, Inc.

Smith, Hope Anita. Keeping the Night Watch. Lewis, E. B., illus. 2014. (ENG.). 80p. (J). (gr. 5-8). pap. 9.99 (978-0-312-65936-3(9), 9780312659363) Square Fish.

Spinelli, Eileen. A Big Boy Now. Lloyd, Megan, illus. 2012. (ENG.). 32p. (J). (gr. -1-3). 16.99 (978-0-06-008673-2(4)) HarperCollins Pubs.

Supplee, Audra. I Almost Love You, Eddie Clegg, 1 vol. 2004. (ENG.). 192p. (J). (gr. 3-7). 14.95 (978-1-56145-308-5(0)) Peachtree Pubs.

Swaby, Barbara. When Will Daddy Be Home? 2012. 32p. pap. 19.99 (978-1-4772-6439-3(6)) AuthorHouse.

Tattum, Stephan. Dad. 2005. (J). 4.95 (978-1-59792-002-5(9)) F.A.S.T. Learning LLC.

Terrell, Brandon. Second Chance Delivery. 2016. (Tartan House Ser.). (ENG., Illus.). 96p. (J). (gr. 5-12). pap. 9.95 (978-1-63235-205-7(2), 12-Story Library) Pr. Room Editions LLC.

Thome, Bella. Autumn Falls. 2014. (ENG.). 224p. (YA). (gr. 7). lib. bdg. 21.99 (978-0-375-99161-5(1), Delacorte Pr.) Random Hse. Children's Bks.

Turnage, Sheila. The Odds of Getting Even. 2015. (ENG., Illus.). 352p. (J). (gr. 5). 16.99 (978-0-8037-3961-1(3), Kathy Dawson Books) Penguin Young Readers Group.

Tyler, Amy J. & RH Disney Staff. Best Dad in the Sea. RH Disney Staff, illus. 2003. (Step into Reading Ser.). (ENG., Illus.). 32p. (J). (gr. k-3). pap. 3.99 (978-0-7364-2131-7(9), RH/Disney) Random Hse. Children's Bks.

Uhlberg, Myron. The Printer, 1 vol. Sørensen, Henri, illus. 2009. (ENG.). 32p. (J). (gr. -1-3). pap. 8.95 (978-1-56145-483-9(4)) Peachtree Pubs.

—The Printer, 1 vol. Sorensen, Henri, tr. Sorensen, Henri, illus. 2003. (ENG.). 32p. (J). (gr. k-3). 16.95 (978-1-56145-221-7(1)) Peachtree Pubs.

Ullman, Barb Bentler. Whistle Bright Magic: A Nutfolk Tale. 2010. 224p. (J). (gr. 3-7). 16.99 (978-0-06-188286-9(0)) HarperCollins Pubs.

Valentine, Jenny. Me, the Missing, & the Dead. 2010. 224p. (YA). (gr. 9). pap. 8.99 (978-0-06-085070-8(1), HarperTeen) HarperCollins Pubs.

Van Draanen, Wendelin. Sammy Keyes & the Showdown in Sin City. 2013. (Sammy Keyes Ser.: Bk. 16). (ENG.). 304p. (J). (gr. 5). pap. 7.99 (978-0-307-93061-3(0), Yearling) Random Hse. Children's Bks.

Van Slyke, Rebecca. Dad School. Burris, Priscilla, illus. 2016. (ENG.). 32p. (J). (gr. -1-2). 19.99 (978-0-385-38896-2(9), Doubleday Bks. for Young Readers) Random Hse. Children's Bks.

Vanderpool, Clare. Moon over Manifest. (ENG.). (J). (gr. 3-7). 2011. 384p. 7.99 (978-0-375-85829-1(6), Yearling) 2010. 368p. 16.99 (978-0-385-73883-5(8), Delacorte Bks. for Young Readers) Random Hse. Children's Bks.

—Moon over Manifest. l.t. ed. 2011. (ENG.). 452p. 23.99 (978-1-4104-3780-8(9)) Thorndike Pr.

—Moon over Manifest. 2011. lib. bdg. 18.40 (978-0-606-23875-5(1), Turtleback) Turtleback Bks.

Vision, David. Who's That Crying! Alcantara, Ignacio, illus. 2009. 64p. 17.00 (978-0-9659538-1-8(5)) Von Curtis Publishing.

Voigt, Cynthia. Sons from Afar. 2012. (Tillerman Cycle Ser.: 6). (ENG., Illus.). 288p. (YA). (gr. 7). 18.99 (978-1-4424-5065-3(7)); pap. 7.99 (978-1-4424-2883-6(X)) Simon & Schuster Children's Publishing. (Atheneum Bks. for Young Readers).

Wass, Eliza. The Cresswell Plot. 2016. (ENG., Illus.). 268p. (YA). (gr. 9-17). 17.99 (978-1-4847-3043-0(7)) Hyperion Bks. for Children.

Wennick, Elizabeth. Whatever Doesn't Kill You, 1 vol. 2013. (ENG.). 208p. (YA). (gr. 8-12). pap. 12.95 (978-1-4598-0083-0(4)) Orca Bk. Pubs. USA.

White & Hyatt, Sean. Naja vs P3OPLES Water Fight, 1 vol. 2009. 21p. pap. 24.95 (978-1-4489-0939-1(2)) America Star Bks.

Williams, Vicki & Williams, Kathy. Everybody Has a Daddy. Wood, Joe, illus. 2003. 16p. (J). 7.95 (978-0-9747597-0-8(8)) Self-Esteem Adventures Pr.

Wilson, John. Written in Blood, 1 vol. 2010. (Desert Legend Trilogy Ser.: 1). (ENG.). 176p. (YA). (gr. 8-12). pap. 12.95 (978-1-55469-270-5(9)) Orca Bk. Pubs. USA.

Wood, Douglas. What Dads Can't Do. 2004. (Illus.). (J). (gr. k-3). spiral bd. (978-0-616-07248-6(1)); spiral bd. (978-0-616-07247-9(3)) Canadian National Institute for the Blind/Institut National Canadien pour les Aveugles.

—When a Dad Says "I Love You" Bell, Jennifer A., illus. 2013. (ENG.). 32p. (J). (gr. -1-3). 17.99 (978-0-689-87532-8(0), Simon & Schuster Bks. For Young Readers) Simon & Schuster Bks. For Young Readers.

Yang, Gene Luen & Pham, Thien. Level Up. 2016. (YA). lib. bdg. 20.85 (978-0-606-38563-3(0)) Turtleback Bks.

Yee, Lisa. Absolutely Maybe. 2009. (ENG.). 288p. (J). (gr. 7-18). 16.99 (978-0-439-83844-3(4), Levine, Arthur A. Bks.) Scholastic, Inc.

Young, Janet Ruth. The Opposite of Music. 2008. (ENG.). 352p. (YA). (gr. 7-12). pap. 15.99 (978-1-4169-5823-9(1), Atheneum Bks. for Young Readers) Simon & Schuster Children's Publishing.

Zappa, Ahmet. Because I'm Your Dad. Santat, Dan, illus. 2013. (ENG.). 32p. (J). (gr. -1-k). 15.99 (978-1-4231-4774-9(X)) Disney Pr.

—Because I'm Your Dad. Santat, Dan, illus. 2016. (ENG.). 32p. (J). (gr. -1-k). bds. 7.99 (978-1-4847-2661-7(8)) Hyperion Bks. for Children.

FATHERS—POETRY

Cook, Annabel. Poems for Dad: A Collection of Poetry. 2005. (Illus.). 239p. (978-1-84602-213-5(4), Young Writers) Forward Pr.

Johnson, Angela. In Daddy's Arms, I Am Tall. 2004. (Illus.). (J). (gr. k-3). spiral bd. (978-0-616-03094-3(0)) Canadian National Institute for the Blind/Institut National Canadien pour les Aveugles.

FATHERS AND DAUGHTERS

Bates, Marni. Marni: My True Story of Stress, Hair-Pulling, & Other Obsessions. 2009. (Louder Than Words Ser.). (ENG.). 168p. (YA). (gr. 7-18). pap. 7.95 (978-0-7573-1412-4(0), HCI Teens) Health Communications, Inc.

Clark, Jeff. Dad's Masterpiece: The Patricia Masotto Story. 2009. 112p. 22.50 (978-1-60693-873-7(8), Strategic Bk. Publishing) Strategic Book Publishing & Rights Agency (SBPRA).

Farquharson, Jerome. Playtime to Bedtime: Memories That Last Forever... 2011. (Illus.). 24p. (J). pap. 10.95 (978-0-615-45886-1(6)) JFAR Bks.

Larsen, Carolyn. Little Girls Bible Storybook for Fathers & Daughters. Turk, Caron, illus. rev. ed. 2014. (ENG.). 288p. (J). 14.99 (978-0-8010-1549-6(9)) Baker Bks.

Linsley, Sonja Paschal. May I Have the First Dance? Linsley, Paul Adam, illus. 2005. 24p. (J). 19.95 net. (978-0-9766062-0-8(8)) Higher Ground Pr.

Morgan, Cindy. Dance Me, Daddy, 1 vol. O'Neill, Philomena, illus. 2009. (ENG.). 32p. (J). (gr. -1-2). 16.99 (978-0-310-71762-1(0)) Zonderkidz.

My Dad Is Great. 2008. (My Great Relatives... Ser.). 32p. (978-1-4075-0941-9(1)) Parragon, Inc.

Owenz, Roger. Mr Owenz Goes to School. 2009. 24p. pap. 12.99 (978-1-4490-2655-4(9)) AuthorHouse.

Perez-Fessenden, Lourdes. Daddy & I. Perez-Fessenden, Lourdes, illus. 2012. (Illus.). 34p. pap. (978-0-9840862-3-8(4)) Roxby Media Ltd.

Richardson, Jael Ealey. The Stone Thrower: A Daughter's Lessons, a Father's Life, 1 vol. James, Matt, illus. 2016. (ENG.). 32p. (J). (gr. k). 18.95 (978-1-55498-752-8(0)) Groundwood Bks. CAN. Dist: Publishers Group West (PGW).

Sharp, Zoe. I Help My Dad. 2007. (Windows on Literacy Ser.). (ENG., Illus.). 12p. pap. 10.95 (978-0-7922-8464-2(X)) National Geographic School Publishing, Inc.

Townsend, Sierra A. Dad & Me. 2007. (J). 7.95 (978-0-9796978-5-2(9)) G Publishing LLC.

Trosper, Chad. Apples in a Pail. 2011. 28p. pap. 12.50 (978-0-557-25147-6(8)) Lulu Pr., Inc.

FATHERS AND DAUGHTERS—FICTION

Abela, Deborah. Hollywood. O'Connor, George, illus. 2007. (Spy Force Ser.: 4). (ENG.). 240p. (J). (gr. 3-7). pap. 10.99 (978-1-4169-3969-6(5), Aladdin) Simon & Schuster Children's Publishing.

Abrams, Amir. Chasing Butterflies. 2016. (ENG.). 320p. (YA). (gr. 9). pap. 9.95 (978-0-7582-9482-1(4)) Kensington Publishing Corp.

Albuquerque, Jessica. Jessica & the Caramuri. 2012. 32p. pap. 19.99 (978-1-4772-7916-8(4)) AuthorHouse.

Alderman, Rusty. Daddy S Little Princess. 2013. 18p. pap. 9.99 (978-1-62697-788-4(7)) Salem Author Services.

Alexander, Lyndi. Windmills. 2013. 248p. (J). pap. 14.99 (978-1-61271-226-0(6)) Zumaya Pubns. LLC.

Alexander, R. C. Unfamiliar Magic. 2011. (ENG.). 368p. (J). (gr. 3-7). pap. 8.99 (978-0-375-85855-0(5), Yearling) Random Hse. Children's Bks.

Allen, Elanna. Itsy Mitsy Runs Away. Allen, Elanna, illus. 2011. (ENG., Illus.). 40p. (J). (gr. -1-2). 16.99 (978-1-4424-0671-1(2), Atheneum Bks. for Young Readers) Simon & Schuster Children's Publishing.

Allison, Jennifer. Gilda Joyce, Psychic Investigator. 2006. (Gilda Joyce Ser.). (ENG.). 336p. (J). (gr. 5-18). reprint ed. 8.99 (978-0-14-240698-4(8), Puffin Books) Penguin Young Readers Group.

Almond, David. My Dad's a Birdman. Dunbar, Polly, illus. 2008. (ENG.). 128p. (J). (gr. 3-7). 15.99 (978-0-7636-3667-8(3)) Candlewick Pr.

Alonso, Manuel L. Rumbo Sur. 2005. (978-84-263-5948-3(5)) Vives, Luis Editorial (Edelvives).

Amato, Mary. Get Happy. (ENG.). 244p. (gr. 7-12). 2016. pap. 9.99 (978-1-5124-2627-4(X), Carolrhoda Bks.) 2014. (J). 16.99 (978-1-60684-522-6(5), Carolrhoda Lab™) Lerner Publishing Group.

—The Naked Mole-Rat Letters. 2007. (ENG., Illus.). 208p. (J). (gr. 4-7). pap. 7.99 (978-0-8234-2098-8(1)) Holiday Hse., Inc.

Andersen, D. R. Why the Moon Changes in the Night Sky. 2005. (J). pap. (978-1-4108-4190-2(1)) Benchmark Education Co.

Anderson, Eric B. Alena & the Favorite Thing. Kuzma, Jakub, illus. 2008. 36p. (J). (ENG.). 18.95 (978-0-9798659-2-3(1)); pap. 13.95 (978-0-9798659-3-0(X)) Edgecliff Pr. LLC.

Anderson, Laurie Halse. The Impossible Knife of Memory. 2015. (ENG.). 416p. (YA). (gr. 7). pap. 9.99 (978-0-14-751072-3(4), Speak) Penguin Publishing Group.

—The Impossible Knife of Memory. 2014. (ENG.). 384p. (YA). (gr. 7). 18.99 (978-0-670-01209-1(2), Viking Books for Young Readers) Penguin Young Readers Group.

—The Impossible Knife of Memory. 2015. (ENG.). (YA). (gr. 7). lib. bdg. 20.60 **(978-1-68065-510-0(8))** Perfection Learning Corp.

—The Impossible Knife of Memory. 2015. lib. bdg. 20.85 (978-0-606-36798-1(5)) Turtleback Bks.

Anderson, T. N. Chiko & the Butterfly. 2009. 70p. pap. 7.00 (978-0-557-10395-9(9)) Lulu Pr., Inc.

Anderson, Vickie S. Pancakes for Supper. 2011. 24p. pap. 15.50 (978-1-4634-3846-3(X)) AuthorHouse.

Andracki, Andy. Dear Mother Teresa. 2005. 57p. pap. 16.95 (978-1-4137-7682-9(5)) America Star Bks.

Andreae, Giles. I Love My Daddy. Dodd, Emma, illus. 2014. (ENG.). 26p. (J). (gr. -1 — 1). bds. 6.99 (978-1-4231-9970-0(7)) Hyperion Bks. for Children.

Anglen, Becca. Nightmare in the Woods. McKeown, Christian, illus. 2007. 36p. (J). pap. 9.00 (978-0-8059-7655-7(8)) Dorrance Publishing Co., Inc.

Asim, Jabari. Girl of Mine. Pham, LeUyen, illus. 2010. (ENG.). 20p. (J). (gr. -1 — 1). bds. 6.99 (978-0-316-73578-0(7)) Little, Brown Bks. for Young Readers.

Aslan, Austin. The Islands at the End of the World. 2015. (ENG., Illus.). 384p. (YA). (gr. 7). pap. 9.99 (978-0-385-74403-4(X), Ember) Random Hse. Children's Bks.

Auerbach, Annie, adapted by. Despicable Me 2: The Junior Novel. movie tie-in ed. 2013. (ENG.). 144p. (J). (gr. 3-7). pap. 6.99 (978-0-316-23432-0(X)) Little, Brown Bks. for Young Readers.

Ayozie, Ben-EL. A Daddy's Princess. 2012. 16p. pap. 15.99 (978-1-4772-1296-7(5)) AuthorHouse.

Ayres, Katherine. Family Tree. 2012. 116p. pap. 7.99 (978-1-936495-21-4(X)) BookPartners, LLC.

Bacigalupi, Paolo. The Doubt Factory. 2014. (ENG.). 496p. (YA). (gr. 10-17). 18.00 (978-0-316-22075-0(2)) Little Brown & Co.

—The Doubt Factory. 2016. (ENG.). 512p. (YA). (gr. 10-17). pap. 12.99 (978-0-316-22076-7(0)) Little, Brown Bks. for Young Readers.

Bajaj, Varsha. Abby Spencer Goes to Bollywood. 2014. (ENG.). 256p. (J). (gr. 3-7). 16.99 (978-0-8075-6363-2(3)) Whitman, Albert & Co.

Baker, Andrea. Worlds Apart: Leah. 2013. 284p. pap. 14.99 (978-0-9892854-3-8(X)) Taylor Street Publishing LLC.

Baldwin, J. R. The Magic Jammies, 1 vol. 2010. 24p. 24.95 (978-1-4512-9442-2(5)) PublishAmerica, Inc.

Ballard, Lisa. A Moose for Mackenzie. Doucette, Constance, illus. 2008. 32p. pap. 24.95 (978-1-60610-123-0(4)) America Star Bks.

Balliett, Blue. Hold Fast. 2015. (ENG.). 288p. (J). (gr. 3-7). pap. 6.99 (978-0-545-29989-3(6), Scholastic Paperbacks) Scholastic, Inc.

Banting, Celia. I Only Said Yes So That They'd Like Me. 2006. (Illus.). 224p. (YA). per. 14.99 (978-0-9786648-1-7(7)) Wighita Pr.

Baptiste, Tracey. Angel's Grace. 2009. (ENG.). 176p. (YA). (gr. 7). pap. 9.99 (978-1-4169-9537-1(4), Simon & Schuster/Paula Wiseman Bks.) Simon & Schuster/Paula Wiseman Bks.

Barchers, Suzanne I. Rose & Dad, 1 vol. 2011. (Targeted Phonics Ser.). (ENG.). 16p. (J). (gr. k-2). pap. 5.99 (978-1-4333-2912-8(3)) Teacher Created Materials, Inc.

—The Tale of the Oki Islands: A Tale from Japan. Yokota, Hiromitsu, illus. 2013. (Tales of Honor Ser.). (ENG.). 32p. (gr. 1-3). pap. 8.95 (978-1-937529-62-8(2)) Red Chair Pr.

—What Can San Do?, 1 vol. 2011. (Targeted Phonics Ser.). (ENG., Illus.). 16p. (J). (gr. k-2). pap. 5.99 (978-1-4333-2408-6(3)) Teacher Created Materials, Inc.

Bartolome, Teresita Africano. We Lost Our House, 1 vol. 2010. 24p. 24.95 (978-1-4489-7338-5(4)) PublishAmerica, Inc.

Bash, Sarah E. My Daddy Is Strong, Handsome, & Tall. 2009. 32p. pap. 12.99 (978-1-4389-5470-7(0)) AuthorHouse.

Bateson, Catherine. Magenta Mcphee. 2010. (ENG.). 176p. (J). (gr. 3-7). pap. 16.95 (978-0-8234-2253-1(4)) Holiday Hse., Inc.

Bauer, Joan. Tell Me. (ENG.). (J). (gr. 5). 2015. 288p. 7.99 (978-0-14-751314-4(6), Puffin Books) 2014. 272p. 16.99 (978-0-451-47033-1(8), Viking Books for Young Readers) Penguin Young Readers Group.

Bauman, Beth Ann. Rosie & Skate. 2011. (ENG.). 224p. (YA). (gr. 9). pap. 8.99 (978-0-385-73736-4(X), Ember) Random Hse. Children's Bks.

Beard, Sarah. Porcelain Keys. 2014. pap. 15.99 (978-1-4621-1396-5(6), Horizon Pubs.) Cedar Fort, Inc./CFI Distribution.

Beasley, Kama. Delaney's Journal: Dad Loses His Job. 2009. 48p. pap. 7.95 (978-1-936051-31-1(1)) Peppertree Pr., The.

Because of Winn Dixie. 2011. 9.14 (978-0-7848-3659-0(0), Everbind) Marco Bk. Co.

Bemelmans, Ludwig. The Golden Basket. 2016. (ENG., Illus.). 96p. (J). (gr. 1-5). pap. 9.99 (978-0-486-80717-1(7)) Dover Pubns., Inc.

Bennett, Jenn. Alex, Approximately. 2017. (ENG., Illus.). 400p. (YA). (gr. 9). 17.99 (978-1-4814-7877-9(X), Simon Pulse) Simon Pulse.

Berry, Diane Lambright. Port City Pirates. 2008. 128p. pap. 12.95 (978-0-9815763-0-5(3)) Alabaster Bk. Pub.

Bibi, Zarina. The Bright Night Sky. 2012. 24p. pap. 15.49 (978-1-4685-4566-1(3)) AuthorHouse.

Billington, Rachel & Quarto Generic Staff. Poppy's Hero. 2012. (ENG.). 288p. (J). (gr. 4-7). pap. 8.99 (978-1-84780-192-0(7), Frances Lincoln) Quarto Publishing Group UK GBR. Dist: Hachette Bk. Group.

Birchall, Katy. The It Girl. 2016. (It Girl Ser.: 1). (ENG., Illus.). 352p. (J). (gr. 4-8). 16.99 (978-1-4814-6362-1(4), Aladdin) Simon & Schuster Children's Publishing.

Birdsall, Jeanne. The Penderwicks Paperback 4-Book Boxed Set, 4 vols. 2016. (ENG.). 270p. (J). (gr. 3-7). 31.96 (978-1-101-93760-0(2), Yearling) Random Hse. Children's Bks.

Birkett, Georgie, illus. Cook It!/¡A Cocinar! 2009. (Helping Hands English/Spanish Edition Ser.). (ENG & SPA.). 24p. (J). (gr. -1-k). pap. (978-1-84643-568-3(4)) Child's Play International Ltd.

Blair, Marion E. Just Beyond a Finger's Reach. 2013. (ENG.). 54p. (YA). pap. 21.95 (978-1-4787-1396-8(8)) Outskirts Pr., Inc.

Bledsoe, Josh. Hammer & Nails. Warrick, Jessica, illus. 2016. (ENG.). 32p. (J). (gr. k-2). 17.95 (978-1-936261-36-9(7)) Flashlight Pr.

Block, Francesca Lia. Pink Smog: Becoming Weetzie Bat. 2012. (Weetzie Bat Ser.: 6). (ENG.). 208p. (YA). (gr. 9). 17.99 (978-0-06-156598-4(9), HarperTeen) HarperCollins Pubs.

Blom, Jen K. Possum Summer. Rayyan, Omar, illus. 2011. (ENG.). 256p. (J). (gr. 3-7). 17.95 (978-0-8234-2331-6(X)) Holiday Hse., Inc.

Bloomer, Nancy Clark. Through the Glass Bottom Boat. 2012. 36p. pap. 18.60 (978-1-4772-4789-1(0)) AuthorHouse.

Blumenthal, Deborah. Mafia Girl. 2014. (ENG.). 272p. (YA). (gr. 8-12). 16.99 (978-0-8075-4911-7(8)) Whitman, Albert & Co.

Bolles, Joshua. Little Kitty in the City. 2008. 36p. 19.99 (978-0-578-00257-6(4)) Daven, Christian Publishing.

Bowe, Julie. Curve Ball. 2017. (Victoria Torres, Unfortunately Average Ser.). (ENG.). 160p. (gr. 4-4). pap. 5.95 (978-1-4965-3820-8(X)); lib. bdg. 26.65 (978-1-4965-3818-5(8)) Stone Arch Bks.

Broadhurst, Sherree. Bella Finds the Hidden Treasure. 2009. 28p. pap. 12.25 (978-1-60693-815-7(0), Eloquent Bks.) Strategic Book Publishing & Rights Agency (SBPRA).

Brody, Jessica. 52 Reasons to Hate My Father. 2013. (ENG.). 368p. (YA). (gr. 7-12). pap. 10.99 (978-1-250-02459-6(5), 9781250024596) Square Fish.

Brown, Allison. Perfection. 2010. 108p. pap. 8.52 (978-0-557-64243-4(4)) Lulu Pr., Inc.

Brown, Jocelyn. Mitochondrial Curiosities of Marcels 1 to 19. 2004. (ENG., Illus.). 180p. (J). (gr. 7-18). pap. 13.95 (978-1-55245-209-7(3)) Coach Hse. Bks. CAN. Dist: Consortium Bk. Sales & Distribution.

Brown, Petra, illus. Hush, Little Baby. 2007. (Padded Hardcover Ser.). 18p. (J). 8.95 (978-1-58925-819-8(3)) Tiger Tales.

Browne, Anthony. Gorilla. 30th anniv. ed. 2014. lib. bdg. 18.40 (978-0-606-35150-8(7)) Turtleback Bks.

Brun-Cosme, Nadine. With Dad, It's Like That. Huche, Magali Le, illus. 2016. (ENG.). 24p. (J). (gr. -1-3). 16.99 (978-0-8075-8731-7(1)) Whitman, Albert & Co.

Brust, Beth Wagner. The Great Tulip Trade. Mattheson, Jenny, illus. 2005. (Step into Reading Ser.). 48p. (J). (gr. 1-3). 11.65 (978-0-7569-5160-3(7)) Perfection Learning Corp.

Bryant, Annie. Freestyle with Avery. 2009. (Beacon Street Girls Ser.). (ENG.). 240p. (J). (gr. 4-8). pap. 8.99 (978-1-4169-6435-3(5), Aladdin) Simon & Schuster Children's Publishing.

Bryant, Jen. Pieces of Georgia. 2007. (ENG., Illus.). 176p. (J). (gr. 5-9). per. 6.99 (978-0-440-42055-2(5), Yearling) Random Hse. Children's Bks.

Bunting, Eve. The Pirate Captain's Daughter. 2011. (ENG.). 208p. (J). (gr. 6-18). pap. 8.95 (978-1-58536-525-8(4)); lib. bdg. 15.95 (978-1-58536-526-5(2)) Sleeping Bear Pr.

Burkinshaw, Kathleen. The Last Cherry Blossom. 2016. (J). **(978-1-63450-618-2(9))** Skyhorse Publishing Co., Inc.

Buske, Jody. Wilderness Awakening. 2006. 108p. pap. 19.95 (978-1-4241-2685-9(1)) PublishAmerica, Inc.

Butler, Terrold B. Sharing. 2010. 24p. 11.49 (978-1-4490-6890-5(1)) AuthorHouse.

Cabot, Meg. Journal d'une Princesse.Tr. of Princess Diaries. pap. 13.95 (978-2-01-321853-5(2)) Hachette Groupe Livre FRA. Dist: Distribooks, Inc.

—The Princess Diaries. 2008. (Princess Diaries: 1). (ENG.). 256p. (YA). (gr. 8). pap. 9.99 (978-0-06-147993-9(4))Vols. 1-3, Set. 2006. (Princess Diaries: Vol. I). (J). pap., pap. 19.99 (978-0-06-115389-1(3)) HarperCollins Pubs. (HarperTeen).

—The Princess Diaries. 2008. 20.00 (978-0-7569-8793-0(8)) Perfection Learning Corp.

—The Princess Diaries. unabr. ed. 2004. (Princess Diaries: Vol. I). 240p. (J). (gr. 7-18). pap. 38.00 incl. audio (978-0-8072-0669-0(5), Listening Library) Random Hse. Audio Publishing Group.

—The Princess Diaries. 2008. (Princess Diaries: 1). (YA). lib. bdg. 20.85 *(978-1-4178-2328-4(3)*, Turtleback) Turtleback Bks.

—The Princess Diaries Box Set: The Princess Diaries; Princess in the Spotlight; Princess in Love. 2003. (Princess Diaries). 304p. (gr. 7-18). pap. 19.99 *(978-0-06-058745-1(8))* HarperCollins Pubs.

Cadell, Ava. NeuroLoveology: The Power to Mindful Love & Sex. 2014. (ENG.). 310p. pap. 14.99 *(978-1-4976-6112-7(9))* Open Road Integrated Media, Inc.

Caletti, Deb. The Queen of Everything. Greenberg, Anne, ed. 2008. (ENG.). 352p. (YA). (gr. 7-12). pap. 8.99 *(978-1-4169-5781-2(2)*, Simon Pulse) Simon Pulse.

—Stay. (ENG.). (YA). (gr. 7). 2012. 336p. pap. 9.99 *(978-1-4424-0374-1(8))* 2011. 320p. 16.99 *(978-1-4424-0373-4(X))* Simon Pulse. (Simon Pulse).

Candelario, Margo. Looking to the Clouds for Daddy. Craft, Jerry, illus. 2009. (J). *(978-0-9820221-7-7(4))* Hunter, Karen Media.

The Captain, His Daughter, & Their Discovery. 2007. 48p. pap. 6.50 *(978-0-8341-2296-3(0)*, 083-412-2960) Beacon Hill Pr. of Kansas City.

Capucilli, Alyssa Satin. Katy Duck Goes to Work. Cole, Henry, illus. 2014. (Katy Duck Ser.). (ENG.). 24p. (J). (gr. -1-1). pap. 3.99 *(978-1-4424-7281-5(2)*, Simon Spotlight) Simon Spotlight.

—Katy Duck Goes to Work. 2014. (Simon & Schuster Ready-To-Read Level 1 Ser.). lib. bdg. 13.55 *(978-0-606-35455-4(7))* Turtleback Bks.

Carey, Benedict. Poison Most Vial: A Mystery. 2012. (ENG.). 240p. (J). (gr. 3-7). 17.95 *(978-1-4197-0031-6(6)*, Amulet Bks.) Abrams, Inc.

Carnes, Daphane. Grace. 2009. 48p. (J). pap. 12.95 *(978-1-4327-3380-3(X))* Outskirts Pr., Inc.

Casanova, Mary. When Eagles Fall. 2014. (Fesler-Lampert Minnesota Heritage Ser.). (ENG.). 160p. pap. 9.95 *(978-0-8166-9211-8(4))* Univ. of Minnesota Pr.

Casey, Sean. My Dad Cancelled Christmas! Casey, Quinn, illus. 2008. 25p. (J). 15.95 *(978-0-9797297-0-6(X))* Cool Kids Create.

Castellucci, Cecil. Beige. (ENG., 320p. (YA). 2009. Illus.). (gr. 9). pap. 8.99 *(978-0-7636-4232-7(0))* 2007. (Illus.). (gr. 9-18). 16.99 *(978-0-7636-3066-9(7))* 2007. 25.66 *(978-1-4287-4767-8(2))* Candlewick Pr.

Cavanaugh, Nancy J. This Journal Belongs to Ratchet. 2014. (ENG.). 320p. (J). (gr. 3-6). pap. 6.99 *(978-1-4926-0109-8(8)*, 9781492601098, Sourcebooks Jabberwocky) Sourcebooks, Inc.

Cerone, Diane. Lucy & the Red-Tailed Hawk. Auer, Lois, illus. 2007. 32p. (J). pap. 17.00 *(978-0-8059-7565-9(9))* Dorrance Publishing Co., Inc.

Cerullo, Jillian. The Danger of the River. 2005. 36p. pap. 14.99 *(978-1-4116-6988-8(6))* Lulu Pr., Inc.

Cervantes, Jennifer & Chronicle Books Staff. Tortilla Sun. 2010. (ENG.). 224p. (J). (gr. 4-7). 16.99 *(978-0-8118-7015-3(4))* Chronicle Bks. LLC.

Chapman, Steven Curtis. Cinderella: The Love of a Daddy & His Princess, 1 vol. 2008. (ENG., Illus.). 64p. 14.99 *(978-1-4041-0522-5(0))* Nelson, Thomas Inc.

Chatel, Kim. A Talent for Quiet. Chatel, Kim, photos by. 2009. (Illus.). 32p. pap. 10.95 *(978-1-935137-56-6(5))* Guardian Angel Publishing, Inc.

Choldenko, Gennifer. Chasing Secrets. 2015. (ENG.). 288p. (J). (gr. 4-7). lib. bdg. 19.99 *(978-0-375-99063-2(1)*, Lamb, Wendy Bks.) Random Hse. Children's Bks.

—Chasing Secrets. 2016. lib. bdg. 18.40 *(978-0-606-38879-5(6))* Turtleback Bks.

Christopher, Lucy. Flyaway. 2011. (ENG.). 336p. (J). (gr. 5-9). 16.99 *(978-0-545-31771-9(1)*, Chicken Hse., The) Scholastic, Inc.

Clark, Joan. Penny Nichols & the Knob Hill Mystery. 2012. 124p. pap. *(978-1-78139-157-0(2))* Benediction Classics.

—Penny Nichols Finds a Clue. 2012. 128p. pap. *(978-1-78139-154-9(8))* Benediction Classics.

—Penny Nichols Omnibus - Finds a Clue, Mystery of the Lost Key, Black Imp, & Knob Hill Mystery. 2012. 484p. *(978-1-78139-158-7(0))* Benediction Classics.

Cleary, Beverly. Ramona & Her Father. Tiegreen, Alan & Rogers, Jacqueline, illus. 2013. (Ramona Ser.: 4). (ENG.). 192p. (J). (gr. 3-7). pap. 6.99 *(978-0-380-70916-8(3))* HarperCollins Pubs.

—Ramona & Her Father. Tiegreen, Alan et al, illus. 2013. (Ramona Ser.: 4). (ENG.). 192p. (J). (gr. 3-7). 16.99 *(978-0-688-22114-0(9))* HarperCollins Pubs.

—Ramona & Her Father. 2009. 8.32 *(978-0-88483-705-3(X)*, Everbind) Marco Bk. Co.

—Ramona & Her Father. (Ramona Quimby Ser.). 186p. (J). (gr. 3-5). pap. 4.99 *(978-0-8072-1439-8(6)*, Listening Library) Random Hse. Audio Publishing Group.

—Ramona y Su Padre. 10th ed. 2003.Tr. of Ramona & Her Father. (SPA., Illus.). 136p. (J). (gr. 3-5). 15.95 *(978-84-239-9020-7(6)*, EC1443) Espasa Calpe, S.A. ESP. Dist: Lectorum Pubns., Inc., Distribooks, Inc.

Clements, Andrew. Because Your Daddy Loves You. Alley, R. W., illus. 2009. (ENG.). 32p. (J). (gr. -1-3). pap. 6.99 *(978-0-547-23764-0(2))* Houghton Mifflin Harcourt Publishing Co.

—Because Your Daddy Loves You. Alley, R. W., tr. Alley, R. W., illus. 2005. (ENG.). 32p. (J). (gr. -1-3). 16.99 *(978-0-618-00361-7(4))* Houghton Mifflin Harcourt Publishing Co.

Cocks, Heather & Morgan, Jessica. Spoiled. 2012. (ENG.). 384p. (YA). (gr. 10-17). pap. 10.00 *(978-0-316-09827-4(2)*, Poppy) Little, Brown Bks. for Young Readers.

Coe, Kimberly. My Dad Is A Marine. Coe, Kimberly, illus. 2007. (Illus.). 46p. (J). per. 12.00 *(978-0-9787113-1-3(9)*, Ithaca Pr.) Authors & Artists Publishers of New York, Inc.

Cohen, Lettie. Lila's New Pet. 2013. 20p. pap. 17.99 *(978-1-4817-0109-9(6))* AuthorHouse.

Cohlene, Terri. Won't Papa Be Surprised! Dooling, Michael & Sayles, Elizabeth, illus. 2003. 32p. (J). 16.89 *(978-0-688-13094-7(1))* HarperCollins Pubs.

Cohn, Edith. Spirit's Key. 2014. (ENG.). 320p. (J). (gr. 4-7). 16.99 *(978-0-374-30011-1(9)*, 9780374300111, Farrar, Straus & Giroux (BYR)) Farrar, Straus & Giroux.

Cohn, Scott M. Daddy Said a Word I Never Heard. 2015. (Daddy Ser.: 2). (ENG., Illus.). 32p. (J). (gr. -1-3). 15.00 *(978-0-316-40751-9(8))* Little Brown & Co.

Collins, Suzanne. Year of the Jungle. Proimos, James, illus. 2013. (ENG.). 40p. (J). (gr. -1-7). 17.99 *(978-0-545-42516-2(6)*, Scholastic Pr.) Scholastic, Inc.

Conyers, Miranda Parbhoo. Daddy Please Don't Cry. 2009. (J). *(978-1-61623-310-5(9))* Independent Pub.

Cook, Eileen. The Education of Hailey Kendrick. 2011. (ENG.). 288p. (YA). (gr. 9). pap. 9.99 *(978-1-4424-1326-9(3)*, Simon Pulse) Simon Pulse.

—Remember. 2015. (ENG., Illus.). 320p. (YA). (gr. 9). 17.99 *(978-1-4814-1696-2(0)*, Simon Pulse) Simon Pulse.

Cooley, Judy. I Love You More. (Illus.). (gr. -1-k). 2007. 32p. bds. 9.95 *(978-1-59038-758-0(9))* 2005. 29p. (J). 19.99 *(978-1-59038-432-9(6))* Shadow Mountain Publishing. (Shadow Mountain).

Cooper, Ilene. The Worst Noel: A Novel. 2006. 143p. (J). (gr. 4-8). reprint ed. pap. 4.00 *(978-1-4223-5411-7(3))* DIANE Publishing Co.

Corey, Shana. Milly & the Macy's Parade. Helquist, Brett, illus. 2006. (Scholastic Bookshelf Ser.). (ENG.). 40p. (J). (gr. -1-3). pap. 6.99 *(978-0-439-29755-4(9))* Scholastic, Inc.

Couloumbis, Audrey. Lexie. Denos, Julia, illus. 2012. (ENG.). 208p. (J). (gr. 3-7). pap. 6.99 *(978-0-375-85633-4(1)*, Yearling) Random Hse. Children's Bks.

Crompton, Laurie Boyle. Blaze (Or, Love in the Time of Supervillains) 2013. (ENG.). 320p. (YA). (gr. 7-12). pap. 8.99 *(978-1-4022-7343-8(6))* Sourcebooks, Inc.

Cross, Frances. Marty's Diary. 2008. (Cutting Edge Ser.). (ENG.). 160p. pap. *(978-1-84167-697-5(7))* Ransom Publishing Ltd.

Culbertson, Kim. The Possibility of Now. 2016. (Point Ser.). (ENG.). 304p. (J). (gr. 7). 17.99 *(978-0-545-73146-1(1))* Scholastic, Inc.

Cullen, Lyn. I Am Rembrandt's Daughter. 2011. 8.88 *(978-0-7848-3491-6(1)*, Everbind) Marco Bk. Co.

Curtis, Sarah. The Wondrous Flower. 2013. 36p. pap. 24.95 *(978-1-4626-9812-7(3))* America Star Bks.

Cushman, Karen. Alchemy & Meggy Swann. 2011. (ENG.). 176p. (J). (gr. 5-7). pap. 7.99 *(978-0-547-57712-8(5))* Houghton Mifflin Harcourt Publishing Co.

Daddy! 2005. (J). bds. *(978-0-9769910-6-9(3))* Terrific Twins LLC.

Daddy's Little Girl. (Daddy's / Mommy's Ser.). 32p. *(978-1-4054-9429-8(8))* Parragon, Inc.

Dakers, Diane. Homecoming, 1 vol. 2014. (Orca Soundings Ser.). (ENG.). 120p. (YA). (gr. 8-12). pap. 9.95 *(978-1-4598-0803-4(7))* Orca Bk. Pubs. USA.

Dale, Jay. Our Special Rock Pool, 1 vol. Everitt-Stewart, Andrew, illus. 2012. (Engage Literacy Green Ser.). (ENG.). 32p. (gr. k-2). pap. 5.99 *(978-1-4296-9009-6(7)*, Engage Literacy) Capstone Press of Coughlan Cos.

Danilo, Roberto. Mylene & the Moon. 2011. 24p. pap. 12.99 *(978-1-4634-1196-1(0))* AuthorHouse.

Danziger, Paula. Amber Brown Is Green with Envy. 2014. (Amber Brown Ser.: 9). (ENG., Illus.). 176p. (J). (gr. 2-5). pap. 5.99 *(978-0-14-242699-9(7)*, Puffin Books) Penguin Young Readers Group.

—Amber Brown Is Green with Envy. Ross, Tony, illus. 2004. (Amber Brown Ser.: No. 9). 151p. (J). (gr. 2-5). 12.65 *(978-0-7569-2978-7(4))* Perfection Learning Corp.

Darcy N. Carmichael. Ember's Rising. 2009. 104p. pap. 9.95 *(978-1-4401-6368-5(5))* iUniverse, Inc.

Davidson, Kayla Shurley. Daddy's Little Squirrel. 2010. 28p. pap. 12.49 *(978-1-4490-8474-5(5))* AuthorHouse.

Demas, Corinne. Returning to Shore. 2014. 208p. (YA). (gr. 6-12). 17.95 *(978-1-4677-1328-3(7)*, Carolrhoda Lab™) Lerner Publishing Group.

DeMatteis, J. M. Imaginalis. 2010. (ENG.). 256p. (J). (gr. 3-7). 16.99 *(978-0-06-173286-7(9)*, Tegen, Katherine Bks) HarperCollins Pubs.

Dempsey, Kristy. Surfer Chick. Cole, Henry, illus. 2012. (ENG.). 32p. (J). (gr. -1-k). 16.95 *(978-1-4197-0188-7(6)*, Abrams Bks. for Young Readers) Abrams, Inc.

dePaola, Tomie. Days of the Blackbird: A Tale of Northern Italy. dePaola, Tomie, illus. 2005. (Illus.). (J). 13.65 *(978-0-7569-5888-6(1))* Perfection Learning Corp.

Dessen, Sarah. The Moon & More. 2013. (ENG.). 384p. (J). (gr. 7). 19.99 *(978-0-670-78560-5(1)*, Viking Books for Young Readers) Penguin Young Readers Group.

DeStefano, Lauren. The Girl with the Ghost Machine. 2017. (ENG.). 224p. (J). 16.99 *(978-1-68119-444-8(9)*, 9781681194448, Bloomsbury USA Childrens) Bloomsbury Publishing USA.

Dewdney, Anna. Nelly Gnu & Daddy Too. (ENG., Illus.). (J). 2017. 36p. (-k). bds. 9.99 *(978-0-425-28977-8(X))* 2014. 40p. (gr. -1-k). 17.99 *(978-0-670-01227-5(0))* Penguin Young Readers Group. (Viking Books for Young Readers).

Dickens, Charles. A Tale of Two Cities: A Classic Retelling. 2006. (Classic Retelling Ser.). (Illus.). 240p. (YA). (gr. 8-12). *(978-0-618-03150-4(2)*, 2-00144) Holt McDougal.

Dickens, Charles & Hawksley, L. Dickens. A Tale of Two Cities. 2004. (Paperback Classics Ser.). 144p. (J). pap. 4.95 *(978-0-7945-0390-1(X))*; lib. bdg. 12.95 *(978-1-58086-515-9(1))* EDC Publishing.

Dickson, Julie A. Girl from the Shadows. 2011. 74p. pap. 19.95 *(978-1-4626-3473-6(7))* America Star Bks.

Dionne, Erin. Notes from an Accidental Band Geek. 2012. (ENG.). 304p. (J). (gr. 5). pap. 6.99 *(978-0-14-242247-2(9)*, Puffin Books) Penguin Young Readers Group.

Disney Book Group & Brody, Jessica. Freddie's Shadow Cards. No New Art Needed, illus. 2016. (School of Secrets Ser.: 2). (ENG.). 192p. (J). (gr. 3-7). 9.99 *(978-1-4847-7865-4(0))* Disney Pr.

Dixon, Heather. Entwined. (ENG.). 480p. (YA). (gr. 8). 2012. pap. 9.99 *(978-0-06-200104-7(3))* 2011. 17.99 *(978-0-06-200103-0(5))* HarperCollins Pubs. (Greenwillow Bks.).

Doller, Trish. The Devil You Know. (ENG.). 256p. (YA). 2016. pap. 9.99 *(978-1-68119-022-8(2)*, 9781681190228) 2015. (gr. 9). 17.99 *(978-1-61963-416-9(3)*, 9781619634169) Bloomsbury Publishing USA. (Bloomsbury USA Childrens).

Donnelly, Jennifer. These Shallow Graves. (ENG.). (YA). (gr. 7). 2016. 512p. pap. 10.99 *(978-0-385-73766-1(1)*, Ember) 2015. 496p. lib. bdg. 22.99 *(978-0-385-90679-1(X)*, Delacorte Pr.) 2015. (Illus.). 496p. 19.99 *(978-0-385-73765-4(3)*, Delacorte Pr.) Random Hse. Children's Bks.

—These Shallow Graves. 2016. (ENG.). 496p. (YA). (gr. 7). 22.10 *(978-0-606-39341-6(2))* Turtleback Bks.

Douglas, Eileen. Rachel & the Upside down Heart. 2006. (J). per. 14.95 *(978-0-9790041-0-0(1))* Dancing Magic Heart Bk.

Downer, Ann. Hatching Magic. Rayyan, Omar, illus. 2004. 242p. 16.00 *(978-0-7569-3481-1(8))* Perfection Learning Corp.

Doyle, Brian. Hey, Dad!, 1 vol. 3rd ed. 2006. (ENG.). 112p. (J). (gr. 4-8). pap. 6.95 *(978-0-88899-708-1(6))* Groundwood Bks. CAN. Dist: Publishers Group West (PGW).

Dubrule, Jackie. Kelli, God & New York. Baker, David, illus. 2013. 28p. pap. 24.95 *(978-1-4560-0969-4(9))* America Star Bks.

Dunbar, Fiona. The Truth Cookie. 2009. (Jinx,the Lulu Baker Trilogy Ser.: Bk. 1). (ENG.). 208p. (J). (gr. 4-6). pap. 9.99 *(978-1-4083-0744-1(8))* Hodder & Stoughton GBR. Dist: Hachette Bk. Group.

Dunham, Wendy. Hope Girl. 2016. (ENG.). 144p. (J). (gr. 2-7). pap. 7.99 *(978-0-7369-6495-1(9))* Harvest Hse. Pubs.

Eagland, Jane. Wild Song. 2013. (ENG.). 80p. (YA). (gr. 6-12). pap. 6.95 *(978-1-78112-182-5(6))*; lib. bdg. 22.60 *(978-1-78112-181-8(8))* Lerner Publishing Group.

Easley, Maryann. Warriors Daughter. 2007. 150p. pap. 24.95 *(978-1-4241-4875-2(8))* PublishAmerica, Inc.

Edison-Clark, Gina. Arrione's Daddies!, 1 vol. Newkirk, Errol Q., illus. 2010. 24p. pap. 24.95 *(978-1-4489-6511-3(X))* PublishAmerica, Inc.

—I Just Want My Daddy! Newkirk, Errol Q., illus. 2008. 13p. pap. 24.95 *(978-1-60672-026-4(0))* America Star Bks.

Ehrmantraut, Brenda. Hope Weavers. Magnuson, Diana, illus. 2009. (J). *(978-0-9729833-8-9(4))* Bubble Gum Pr.

Eliot, George. Silas Marner. 2008. (Bring the Classics to Life Ser.). (ENG., Illus.). 72p. (gr. 2-12). pap., act. bk. ed. 10.95 *(978-1-55576-356-5(1)*, EDCTR-209B) EDCON Publishing Group.

Elkeles, Simone. How to Ruin a Summer Vacation. 2006. (How to Ruin a Summer Vacation Novel Ser.: 1). (ENG.). 240p. (YA). (gr. 8-12). per. 9.95 *(978-0-7387-0961-1(1)*, Flux) North Star Editions.

—How to Ruin My Teenage Life. 2007. (How to Ruin a Summer Vacation Novel Ser.: 2). (ENG.). 288p. (YA). (gr. 7-12). per. 11.99 *(978-0-7387-1019-8(9)*, Flux) North Star Editions.

Ellis, Melody A. An Unexpected Hero. 2009. 48p. pap. 16.95 *(978-1-60749-834-6(0))* America Star Bks.

Ephron, Delia. Frannie in Pieces. Beckerman, Chad, illus. 2007. 374p. (YA). (gr. 7-12). lib. bdg. 17.89 *(978-0-06-074717-6(X)*, HarperTeen) HarperCollins Pubs.

Esham, Barbara. If You're So Smart, How Come You Can't Spell Mississippi? Esham, Barbara, illus. 2008. (Illus.). 32p. (J). (gr. k-18). 16.95 *(978-1-60336-448-5(X)*, Adventures of Everyday Geniuses, The) Mainstream Connections Publishing.

Etheridge, Judy. Olivia's Wish. 2009. 32p. pap. 21.99 *(978-1-4415-3915-1(8))* Xlibris Corp.

Evans, Richard. The Dance. Linton, Jonathan, illus. 2014. (ENG.). 32p. (J). 16.99 *(978-1-4814-3112-5(9)*, Simon & Schuster/Paula Wiseman Bks.) Simon & Schuster/Paula Wiseman Bks.

Evetts-Secker, Josephine. The Barefoot Book of Father & Daughter Tales. Cann, Helen, illus. 2012. (ENG.). 96p. (J). 23.99 *(978-1-84686-761-3(4))* Barefoot Bks., Inc.

Falls, Kat. Inhuman. 2015. (ENG.). 384p. (J). (gr. 7). pap. 9.99 *(978-0-545-37101-8(5)*, Scholastic Pr.) Scholastic, Inc.

Feiffer, Kate. My Mom Is Trying to Ruin My Life. Goode, Diane, illus. 2009. (ENG.). 32p. (J). (gr. -1-3). 18.99 *(978-1-4169-4100-2(2)*, Simon & Schuster/Paula Wiseman Bks.) Simon & Schuster/Paula Wiseman Bks.

—My Side of the Car. Feiffer, Jules, illus. 2011. (ENG.). 32p. (J). (gr. -1-3). 16.99 *(978-0-7636-4405-5(6))* Candlewick Pr.

Ferguson, Alane. The Christopher Killer. 2008. (Forensic Mystery Ser.). (ENG.). 288p. (YA). (gr. 7-18). 7.99 *(978-0-14-240811-7(5)*, Puffin Books) Penguin Young Readers Group.

—The Christopher Killer. 2008. (Forensic Mystery Ser.). 274p. (gr. 7-12). 17.00 *(978-0-7569-8930-9(2))* Perfection Learning Corp.

Feuti, Norm. The King of Kazoo. 2016. (ENG.). 208p. (J). (gr. 2-5). 22.99 *(978-0-545-77088-0(2)*, Graphix) Scholastic, Inc.

Fitzmaurice, Kathryn. The Year the Swallows Came Early. 2009. (ENG.). 288p. (J). (gr. 4-7). 16.99 *(978-0-06-162497-1(7))* HarperCollins Pubs.

Fitzpatrick, Becca. The Complete Hush, Hush Saga: Hush, Hush; Crescendo; Silence; Finale. 2012. (Hush, Hush Saga Ser.: Bks. 1-4). (ENG.). 1744p. (YA). (gr. 9). 74.99 *(978-1-4424-7372-0(X)*, Simon & Schuster Bks. For Young Readers) Simon & Schuster Bks. For Young Readers.

—Crescendo. 2011. (Hush, Hush Saga: Bk. 2). (SPA.). 408p. (YA). pap. 20.95 *(978-84-666-4639-0(6))* Ediciones B ESP. Dist: Spanish Pubs., LLC.

—Crescendo. (Hush, Hush Saga Ser.: Bk. 2). (ENG.). (YA). (gr. 9). 2012. 464p. pap. 12.99 *(978-1-4169-8944-8(7))* 2010. 432p. 18.99 *(978-1-4169-8943-1(9))* Simon & Schuster Bks. For Young Readers. (Simon & Schuster Bks. For Young Readers).

Flake, Sharon G. Begging for Change. rev. ed. 2007. (ENG.). 256p. (J). (gr. 7-12). pap. 7.99 *(978-1-4231-0384-4(X)*, Jump at the Sun) Hyperion Bks. for Children.

Fletcher, Donna. Sweet Baby Heather: Day at the Zoo. 2010. 24p. pap. 14.99 *(978-1-4520-2444-8(8))* AuthorHouse.

Flor Ada, Alma & Zubizarreta, Gabriel M. Dancing Home. (ENG., (J). (gr. 3-7). 2013. Illus.). 176p. pap. 7.99 *(978-1-4424-8175-6(7))* 2011. 160p. 15.99 *(978-1-4169-0088-7(8))* Simon & Schuster Children's Publishing. (Atheneum Bks. for Young Readers).

—Nacer Bailando (Dancing Home) 2011. (SPA.). 160p. (J). (gr. 3-7). lib. bdg. 16.99 *(978-1-4424-2061-8(8)*, Atheneum Bks. for Young Readers) Simon & Schuster Children's Publishing.

Forman, Gayle. Sisters in Sanity. (YA). 2016. (ENG.). 304p. (gr. 8). pap. 9.99 *(978-0-06-088749-0(4))* 2007. 290p. (gr. 7-12). lib. bdg. 17.89 *(978-0-06-088748-3(6))* 2007. (ENG.). 304p. (gr. 7-18). 16.99 *(978-0-06-088747-6(8))* HarperCollins Pubs. (HarperTeen).

Francis, Amy M. Why Is Daddy Different? Dealing with Huntington's Disease. 2011. 24p. pap. 11.50 *(978-1-4634-2792-4(1))* AuthorHouse.

Frazier, Angie. Everlasting. 2010. (ENG.). 336p. (J). (gr. 7-18). 17.99 *(978-0-545-11473-8(X)*, Scholastic Pr.) Scholastic, Inc.

Frederick, Heather Vogel. The Voyage of Patience Goodspeed. 2004. (Aladdin Historical Fiction Ser.). 219p. (J). (gr. 3-7). 13.65 *(978-0-7569-2943-5(1))* Perfection Learning Corp.

French, Jackie. Hitler's Daughter. 2003. (ENG.). 128p. (J). (gr. 3-7). 16.99 *(978-0-06-008652-7(1))* HarperCollins Pubs.

Friedman, Aimee. Two Summers. 2016. (ENG.). 368p. (J). (gr. 7). 17.99 *(978-0-545-51807-9(5))* Scholastic, Inc.

Fullwood, Millie. Daddy's Not Afraid of the Dark. 2008. 40p. 17.95 *(978-1-4357-0633-0(1))* Lulu Pr., Inc.

Funke, Cornelia. CORAZÓN DE TINTA. 2006. (SPA., Illus.). 598p. (J). *(978-84-7844-235-5(9))* Siruela, Ediciones S.A.

Furraway, Bec. Sarah Meets a Bully. 2008. 36p. pap. 18.50 *(978-1-60693-214-8(4)*, Eloquent Bks.) Strategic Book Publishing & Rights Agency (SBPRA).

Gaetz, Dayle Campbell. Spoiled Rotten. 2006. (Orca Currents Ser.). 103p. (gr. 5-9). 19.95 *(978-0-7569-6875-5(5))* Perfection Learning Corp.

Galbraith, Kathryn O. Arbor Day Square, 1 vol. Moore, Cyd, illus. 2016. (ENG.). 32p. (J). (gr. -1-3). pap. 7.95 *(978-1-56145-922-3(4))* Peachtree Pubs.

Galbraith, Kathryn Osebold. Arbor Day Square, 1 vol. Moore, Cyd, illus. 2010. (ENG.). 32p. (J). (gr. -1-3). 16.95 *(978-1-56145-517-1(2))* Peachtree Pubs.

Gallo, Tina. Po's Awesomely Perfect Present. 2015. (Kung Fu Panda 8x8 Ser.). lib. bdg. 13.55 *(978-0-606-37870-3(7))* Turtleback Bks.

Garlington, Shudonica. I'm the Princess & My Daddy's My King. 2012. 24p. pap. 15.99 *(978-1-4628-9885-5(8))* Xlibris Corp.

Gentry, Marley. Chase Learns to Ride. 2010. 24p. 14.99 *(978-1-4490-4640-8(1))* AuthorHouse.

Gibala-Broxholm, Scott. Maddie's Monster Dad, 0 vols. Gibala-Broxholm, Scott, illus. 2011. (ENG., Illus.). 40p. (J). (gr. -1-3). 16.99 *(978-0-7614-5846-3(8)*, 9780761458463, Amazon Children's Publishing) Amazon Publishing.

Giff, Patricia Reilly. Storyteller. 2011. (ENG.). 176p. (J). (gr. 3-7). pap. 6.99 *(978-0-440-42175-7(6)*, Yearling) Random Hse. Children's Bks.

A Gift for Roo. 2013. (Illus.). 24p. pap. 10.95 *(978-1-61633-441-3(X))* Guardian Angel Publishing, Inc.

Gilbert, Melissa. Daisy & Josephine. Kuo, Julia, illus. 2014. (ENG.). 32p. (J). (gr. -1-3). 17.99 *(978-1-4424-4578-9(5)*, Simon & Schuster/Paula Wiseman Bks.) Simon & Schuster/Paula Wiseman Bks.

Giles, Lamar. Overturned. 2017. (ENG.). 352p. (J). (gr. 7). 17.99 *(978-0-545-81250-4(X)*, Scholastic Pr.) Scholastic, Inc.

Gill, Nav K. Under the Moonlit Sky. 2010. (ENG.). 352p. (YA). pap. 15.95 *(978-1-894917-99-5(5)*, Napoleon & Co.) Dundurn CAN. Dist: Ingram Publisher Services.

Girard, Geoffrey. Truthers. 2017. (ENG.). 360p. (YA). (gr. 7-12). 17.99 *(978-1-5124-2779-0(9))* Lerner Publishing Group.

Golde, Justin F. Yes, My Dear, Alligators Do Belong on the Moon. 2012. 24p. pap. 11.50 *(978-1-62212-188-5(0)*, Strategic Bk. Publishing) Strategic Book Publishing & Rights Agency (SBPRA).

Golding, Julia. The Silver Sea, 0 vols. 2013. (ENG.). 352p. (YA). (gr. 7-11). pap. 9.99 *(978-1-4778-1598-4(8)*, 9781477815984, Amazon Children's Publishing) Amazon Publishing.

Gough, Erin. Get It Together, Delilah! 2017. (ENG., Illus.). 336p. (YA). 16.99 *(978-1-4521-5187-8(3))* Chronicle Bks. LLC.

Gownley, Jim. Amelia in Speak Softee to Me: #5, 1 vol. Gownley, Jim, illus. 2011. (Amelia Rules! Ser.). (ENG., Illus.). 36p. 24.21 *(978-1-59961-791-6(9))* Spotlight.

Gownley, Jimmy. Amelia in Joy & Wonder, 1 vol. 2013. (Amelia Rules! Set 2 Ser.). (ENG.). 36p. (J). (gr. 3-6). 24.21 *(978-1-61479-072-3(8))* Spotlight.

Grab, Daphne. Alive & Well in Prague, New York. 2008. (Laura Geringer Bks.). 247p. (YA). (gr. 7-18). lib. bdg. 17.89 *(978-0-06-125671-4(4)*, Geringer, Laura Book) HarperCollins Pubs.

Grainger, A. J. Captive. 2016. (ENG.). 272p. (YA). (gr. 7). pap. 11.99 *(978-1-4814-2904-7(3))* Simon & Schuster Children's Publishing.

GrandPré, Mary. Cleonardo, the Little Inventor. 2016. (ENG., Illus.). 48p. (J). (gr. -1-3). 18.99 *(978-0-439-35764-7(0))* Scholastic, Inc.

Grant, Alice. Dear Mr President, Please Send My Daddy Home. 2008. 23p. pap. 24.95 *(978-1-60441-293-2(3))* America Star Bks.

Green, Rich. Pearlsus. 2007. 140p. 20.95 *(978-0-595-91189-9(7))*; per. 10.95 *(978-0-595-45166-1(7))* iUniverse, Inc.

Greene, Carol. Buttons. 2007. 94p. (gr. 2-2). 24.99 *(978-1-4257-7420-2(2))*; per. 15.99 *(978-1-4257-7419-6(9))* Xlibris Corp.

Gregg, Stacy. The Princess & the Foal. 2015. (ENG.). 272p. (J). (gr. 5). pap. 7.99 *(978-0-14-751242-0(5)*, Puffin Books) Penguin Young Readers Group.

Grimm. Hija del molinero. 2005. incl. cd-rom *(978-84-494-2899-9(8))* Oceano Grupo Editoria, S.A.

Grimm, Jacob & Grimm, Wilhelm K. Doctor All-Knowing: A Folk Tale from the Brothers Grimm. Boiger, Alexandra, illus. 2008. (ENG.). 40p. (J). (gr. -1-1). 16.99 *(978-1-4169-1246-0(0)*, Atheneum/Richard Jackson Bks.) Simon & Schuster Children's Publishing.

Haddix, Margaret Peterson. Don't You Dare Read This, Mrs. Dunphrey. 2012. (ENG.). 128p. (YA). (gr. 7-7). pap. 9.99 *(978-1-4424-4315-0(4)*, Simon & Schuster Bks. For Young Readers) Simon & Schuster Bks. For Young Readers.

—Don't You Dare Read This, Mrs. Dunphrey. 2004. (ENG.). 128p. (YA). (gr. 7). mass mkt. 6.99 *(978-0-689-87102-3(3)*, Simon Pulse) Simon Pulse.

Hahn, Mary Downing. Witch Catcher. (ENG.). 240p. (J). (gr. 5-7). 2011. pap. 7.99 *(978-0-547-57714-2(1))* 2006. (Illus.). 16.00 *(978-0-618-50457-2(5))* Houghton Mifflin Harcourt Publishing Co.

Haines, Kathryn Miller. The Girl Is Trouble. 2012. (ENG.). 336p. (YA). (gr. 7-12). 17.99 *(978-1-59643-610-7(7))* Roaring Brook Pr.

Hamilton, Harriet. Ribbons of the Sun. 2006. 159p. (YA). (gr. 7-16). per. 8.95 *(978-0-9768126-2-3(2))* Brown Barn Bks.

Hamilton, Peter F. The Secret Throne. Eason, Rohan, illus. 2015. (Queen of Dreams Ser.: 1). (ENG.). 288p. (J). (gr. 4-7). pap. 11.99 *(978-1-4472-8865-7(3))* Pan Macmillan GBR. Dist: Independent Pubs. Group.

Hamilton, Virginia, et al. Plain City. (Barco de Vapor). (SPA.). 176p. (YA). (gr. 5-8). 6.95 *(978-84-348-4686-9(1)*, LEC6861) SM Ediciones ESP. Dist: Continental Bk. Co., Inc.

Hardy, Thomas. The Mayor of Casterbridge. Reed, Neil, illus. 2004. (Graphic Novels Ser.). (ENG.). 72p. (J). pap. 7.99 *(978-0-237-52314-5(0))* Evans Brothers, Ltd. GBR. Dist: Independent Pubs. Group.

—THE MAYOR OF CASTERBRIDGE LEVEL 5 UPPER-INTERMEDIATE. 2009. (ENG.). 112p. pap. 14.50 *(978-84-8323-560-7(9))* Cambridge Univ. Pr.

—THE MAYOR OF CASTERBRIDGE LEVEL 5 UPPER-INTERMEDIATE BOOK WITH CD-ROM AND AUDIO CDS (2) PACK, 1 vol. 2009. (ENG.). 112p. pap. 16.50 incl. cd-rom, audio compact disk *(978-84-8323-556-0(0))* Cambridge Univ. Pr.

Harmon, Michael. Brutal. 2011. (ENG.). 240p. (YA). (gr. 9). pap. 8.99 *(978-0-440-23995-6(8)*, Knopf Bks. for Young Readers) Random Hse. Children's Bks.

Harrington, Claudia. My Two Dads, 1 vol. Persico, Zoe, illus. 2016. (ENG.). 32p. (J). *(978-1-62402-108-4(5))* Magic Wagon.

Harris, M. S. Ed Rebecca a. & Harris, M. S. Ed. Megan's Monster. Lee, Joe, illus. 2009. 28p. pap. 15.00 *(978-1-4490-2822-0(5))* AuthorHouse.

Harrod-Eagles, Cynthia. The Changeling. 2010. 195p. pap. 18.50 *(978-1-4452-5850-8(1))* Lulu Pr., Inc.

Harvey, Matt. Shopping with Dad. Latimer, Miriam, illus. 2008. (ENG.). 32p. (J). (gr. -1-3). 16.99 *(978-1-84686-172-7(1))* Barefoot Bks., Inc.

Hastings, Brian. Song of the Deep. 2016. (ENG., Illus.). 176p. (J). (gr. 3-7). 12.95 *(978-1-4549-2096-0(3))* Sterling Publishing Co., Inc.

Hatton, L. J. Sing down the Stars, 0 vols. 2015. (Sing down the Stars Ser.: 1). (ENG.). 380p. (YA). (gr. 8-13). pap. 9.99 *(978-1-5039-4656-9(8)*, 9781503946569, Skyscape) Amazon Publishing.

Hawkins, Rachel. Demonglass. 2012. (ENG.). 384p. (YA). (gr. 6-17). pap. 8.99 *(978-1-4231-2844-1(3))* Hyperion Pr.

Heim, Alastair. Love You Too. Coburn, Alisa, illus. 2016. (ENG.). 32p. (J). (gr. -1-3). 16.99 *(978-1-4998-0174-3(2))* Little Bee Books Inc.

Henkes, Kevin. Protecting Marie. 2007. (ENG.). 224p. (J). (gr. 3-7). pap. 6.99 *(978-0-06-128876-0(4)*, Greenwillow Bks.) HarperCollins Pubs.

Henson, Heather. The Whole Sky. 2017. (ENG., Illus.). 256p. (J). (gr. 5-7). 16.99 ***(978-1-4424-1405-1(7)***, Atheneum/Caitlyn Dlouhy Books) Simon & Schuster Children's Publishing.

Herrick, Steven. The Wolf. 2007. (ENG.). 216p. (J). (gr. 7-18). 17.95 *(978-1-932425-75-8(6)*, Front Street) Boyds Mills Pr.

Hesse, Karen. Sable. Sewall, Marcia, illus. 2010. (ENG.). 96p. (J). (gr. 2-5). pap. 7.99 *(978-0-312-37610-9(3)*, 9780312376109) Square Fish.

Hill, Kirkpatrick. Bo at Ballard Creek. Pham, LeUyen, illus. 2014. (ENG.). 304p. (J). (gr. 3-7). pap. 7.99 *(978-1-250-04425-9(1)*, 9781250044259) Square Fish.

Hodder, Beth. The Ghost of Schafer Meadows. 2007. (J). per. 7.99 *(978-0-9793963-0-4(1))* Grizzly Ridge Publishing.

Hodgson, Miriam. Love from Dad: Stories about Fathers & Daughters. (ENG.). 160p. (J). pap. 8.99 *(978-0-7497-4330-7(1))* Egmont Bks., Ltd. GBR. Dist: Trafalgar Square Publishing.

Hof, Marjolijn. Against the Odds, 1 vol. Prins, Johanna, tr. 2011.Tr. of Een Kleine Kans. (ENG.). 128p. (J). (gr. 3-7). pap. 8.95 *(978-0-88899-950-4(X))* Groundwood Bks. CAN. Dist: Publishers Group West (PGW).

Hole, Stian. Anna's Heaven. 2014. (ENG., Illus.). 42p. (J). 17.00 *(978-0-8028-5441-4(9)*, Eerdmans Bks For Young Readers) Eerdmans, William B. Publishing Co.

Holmes, Sara. The Wolf Hour. 2017. (J). pap. ***(978-0-545-10798-3(9)***, Levine, Arthur A. Bks.) Scholastic, Inc.

Holmes, Sara Lewis. Letters from Rapunzel. 2007. 184p. (J). (gr. 3-7). lib. bdg. 16.89 *(978-0-06-078074-6(6))* HarperCollins Pubs.

Houts, Michelle. The Beef Princess of Practical County. 2010. (ENG.). 240p. (J). (gr. 3-7). 7.99 *(978-0-440-42270-9(1)*, Yearling) Random Hse. Children's Bks.

Howerton, James. The Blue River Valley. 2010. 304p. 28.95 *(978-1-4401-8317-1(1))*; pap. 18.95 *(978-1-4401-8319-5(8))* iUniverse, Inc.

Hoyle, K. B. The Six. 2016. (ENG., Illus.). (J). 29.99 ***(978-1-61213-396-6(7))*** 2012. 230p. pap. 22.50 *(978-1-61213-052-1(6))* Writer's Coffee Shop, The.

Hughes, Jenny. Audrey's Tree House. Bentley, Jonathan, illus. 2015. (J). pap. *(978-0-545-81405-8(7))*; (ENG.). 32p. (gr. -1-k). 17.99 *(978-0-545-81327-3(1))* Scholastic, Inc. (Scholastic Pr.).

Hulme, John & Wexler, Michael. The Lost Train of Thought, Bk. 3. 2009. (Seems Ser.). (ENG., Illus.). 304p. (YA). (gr. 3-6). 16.99 *(978-1-59990-131-2(5)*, 9781599901312, Bloomsbury USA Childrens) Bloomsbury Publishing USA.

Hunter, C. C. Eternal. 2014. (Shadow Falls: after Dark Ser.: 2). (ENG.). 400p. (YA). mass mkt. 9.99 *(978-1-250-07016-6(3)*, 9781250070166, St. Martin's Paperbacks); (gr. 7-12). 19.99 *(978-1-250-05630-6(6)*, St. Martin's Griffin) St. Martin's Pr.

—Eternal: Shadow Falls: After Dark. 2014. (Shadow Falls: after Dark Ser.: 2). (ENG.). 400p. (YA). (gr. 7-12). pap. 9.99 *(978-1-250-04461-7(8)*, 9781250044617, St. Martin's Griffin) St. Martin's Pr.

Hurst, Rich. The Goodnight Thing. Sprague, Lois Rosio, illus. 2006. 25p. (J). (gr. 4-7). 10.99 *(978-0-9763770-1-6(2))* Red Door Pr.

Hutchings, Harriet Anne. Amanda & the Angel. Cragg, Marcelyn Martin, illus. 2010. 24p. pap. 9.95 *(978-1-936051-81-6(8))* Peppertree Pr., The.

Hutton, Stacie Vaughn. Shovelful of Sunshine. Harness, Cheryl, illus. 2012. (ENG.). 32p. (J). 16.95 *(978-0-938467-39-7(5))* Headline Bks., Inc.

Impey, Rose. Introducing Scarlett Lee. 2008. (ENG.). 240p. (J). (gr. 4-6). pap. 8.99 *(978-1-84616-706-5(X))* Hodder & Stoughton GBR. Dist: Hachette Bk. Group.

Inches, Alison. I Love My Papi! (Dora the Explorer) Aikins, David, illus. 2014. (Step into Reading Ser.). (ENG.). 24p. (J). (gr. -1-1). 3.99 *(978-0-385-37459-0(3)*, Random Hse. Bks. for Young Readers) Random Hse. Children's Bks.

Irwin, Inez. Maida's Little Shop. 2006. 41.99 *(978-1-4219-7069-1(4))* IndyPublish.com.

James, Bethany & Shady, Leigh. Matilda Turnip's Endless Belly Button. 2010. (Illus.). 32p. (J). 12.99 *(978-1-60706-187-8(2))* Image Comics.

James, Brian. Zombie Blondes. 2009. (ENG.). 256p. (YA). (gr. 7-12). pap. 8.99 *(978-0-312-57375-1(8)*, 9780312573751) Square Fish.

Jayne, Hannah. The Escape. 2015. (ENG., Illus.). 256p. (YA). (gr. 8-12). pap. 9.99 *(978-1-4926-1654-2(0)*, 9781492616542) Sourcebooks, Inc.

Jeong, Gu-mi. Dad's Favorite Cookie: Japan. Cowley, Joy, ed. Joo, Soon-kyo, illus. 2015. (Global Kids Storybooks Ser.). (ENG.). 32p. (gr. 1-4). 7.99 *(978-1-925246-52-0(3))*; 26.65 *(978-1-925246-26-1(4))*; 26.65 *(978-1-925246-00-1(0))* ChoiceMaker Pty. Ltd., The AUS. (Big and SMALL). Dist: Lerner Publishing Group.

—Dad's Favorite Cookie: Japan. Cowley, Joy, ed. Joo, Soon-kyo, illus. 2015. (Global Kids Storybooks Ser.). (ENG.). 32p. (J). (gr. 1-4). pap. 7.99 *(978-1-925233-42-1(1))* Lerner Publishing Group.

Johansson, J. R. The Row. O'Malley, Janine, ed. 2016. (ENG.). 352p. (YA). 17.99 *(978-0-374-30025-8(9)*, 9780374300258, Farrar, Straus & Giroux (BYR)) Farrar, Straus & Giroux.

Johnson, Annabel. A Rock Candy Dream. 2009. 140p. 22.49 *(978-1-4389-4233-9(8))*; pap. 11.99 *(978-1-4389-4234-6(6))* AuthorHouse.

Johnson, Craig. Dance & Donuts with Dad. 2012. 24p. pap. 17.99 *(978-1-4772-9173-3(3))* AuthorHouse.

Johnson, Elana. Surrender. 2012. (ENG.). 480p. (YA). (gr. 9). 17.99 *(978-1-4424-4568-0(8)*, Simon Pulse) Simon Pulse.

—Surrender: A Possession Novel. 2013. (ENG.). 496p. (YA). (gr. 9). pap. 9.99 *(978-1-4424-4569-7(6)*, Simon Pulse) Simon Pulse.

Johnson, Maureen. Girl at Sea. 2008. (ENG., Illus.). 336p. (YA). (gr. 8-12). pap. 8.99 *(978-0-06-054146-0(6)*, HarperTeen) HarperCollins Pubs.

—The Key to the Golden Firebird. 2004. (ENG.). 304p. (J). (gr. 7-18). 15.99 *(978-0-06-054138-5(5))* HarperCollins Pubs.

Johnson, Rachel N. No Ordinary Princess. Hill, Jessie, illus. 2012. 32p. pap. 16.97 *(978-1-61204-993-9(1)*, Strategic Bk. Publishing) Strategic Book Publishing & Rights Agency (SBPRA).

Johnston, Kayla & Johnston, David. Butterflies in My Belly. 2010. 16p. pap. 10.99 *(978-1-4490-5339-0(4))* AuthorHouse.

Johnston, Tony. The Spoon in the Bathroom Wall. 2006. (ENG., Illus.). 144p. (J). (gr. 2-5). pap. 10.95 *(978-0-15-205625-4(4))* Houghton Mifflin Harcourt Publishing Co.

Jones, Katherine. The Forbidden Tree. 2013. 44p. pap. 19.57 *(978-1-4669-7447-0(8))* Trafford Publishing.

Jones, Patrick. Always Faithful. 2015. (ENG.). 112p. (YA). (gr. 6-12). lib. bdg. 27.99 *(978-1-4677-8052-0(9))*; 7.99 *(978-1-4677-9014-7(1))* Lerner Publishing Group. (Darby Creek).

Joseph, Danielle. Pure Red. 2011. (ENG.). 240p. (YA). pap. 9.95 *(978-0-7387-2743-1(1)*, Flux) North Star Editions.

Kadohata, Cynthia. Outside Beauty. (ENG.). (YA). (gr. 7). 2009. 288p. pap. 8.99 *(978-1-4169-9818-1(7))* 2008. (Illus.). 272p. 16.99 *(978-0-689-86575-6(9))* Simon & Schuster Children's Publishing. (Atheneum Bks. for Young Readers).

Karwoski, Gail Langer. Julie the Rockhound, 1 vol. Downey, Lisa, illus. 2007. (ENG.). 32p. (J). (gr. k-4). 15.95 *(978-0-9764943-7-9(X))* Arbordale Publishing.

Kelly, Jason. No Fish in My Dish. 2007. (Illus.). 30p. (J). pap. 9.95 *(978-0-9664387-1-0(X))* Kelly, Jason Pr.

Keplinger, Kody. A Midsummer's Nightmare. 2013. (ENG.). 304p. (YA). (gr. 10-17). pap. 9.99 *(978-0-316-08421-5(2)*, Poppy) Little, Brown Bks. for Young Readers.

Kerr, M. E., pseud. Someone Like Summer. 2007. (gr. 7-12). 272p. (J). lib. bdg. 17.89 *(978-0-06-114100-3(3))*; 208p. (YA). 16.99 *(978-0-06-114099-0(6))* HarperCollins Pubs. (HarperTeen).

Kidd, Ronald. Monkey Town: The Summer of the Scopes Trial. 2011. (ENG.). 288p. (YA). (gr. 7). pap. 13.99 *(978-1-4424-4211-5(5)*, Simon Pulse) Simon Pulse.

Kimmel, Elizabeth Cody. Legend of the Ghost Dog. 2012. (ENG.). 208p. (J). (gr. 3-7). 16.99 *(978-0-545-39127-6(X)*, Scholastic Pr.) Scholastic, Inc.

King, A. S. Glory O'Brien's History of the Future. 2014. (ENG.). 320p. (YA). (gr. 10-17). 18.00 *(978-0-316-22272-3(0))* Little, Brown Bks. for Young Readers.

King, M. C. Truth or Dare. 2nd ed. 2008. (Hannah Montana Ser.). (Illus.). 126p. (gr. 3-7). 15.00 *(978-0-7569-8336-9(3))* Perfection Learning Corp.

Kingsbury, Karen. Always Daddy's Princess, 1 vol. Docampo, Valeria, illus. rev. ed. 2013. (ENG.). 32p. (J). 15.99 *(978-0-310-71647-1(0))* Zonderkidz.

Kirby, Jessi. Moonglass. (ENG.). (YA). (gr. 7). 2012. 256p. pap. 9.99 *(978-1-4424-1695-6(5))* 2011. 240p. 16.99 *(978-1-4424-1694-9(7))* Simon & Schuster Bks. For Young Readers. (Simon & Schuster Bks. For Young Readers).

Klages, Ellen. The Green Glass Sea. 2008. (ENG.). 368p. (J). (gr. 3-7). 8.99 *(978-0-14-241149-0(3)*, Puffin Books) Penguin Young Readers Group.

—The Green Glass Sea. 2008. 321p. (gr. 4-7). 19.00 *(978-0-7569-8931-6(0))* Perfection Learning Corp.

Konigsburg, E. L. My Father's Daughter. 2nd ed. 2008. (ENG.). 144p. (J). (gr. 3-7). pap. 7.99 *(978-1-4169-5500-9(3)*, Atheneum Bks. for Young Readers) Simon & Schuster Children's Publishing.

Kosinski, Colleen Rowan, illus. Lilla's Sunflowers. 2016. (ENG.). 32p. (J). (gr. -1-k). 16.99 *(978-1-5107-0464-0(7)*, Sky Pony Pr.) Skyhorse Publishing Co., Inc.

Kovalkova-McKenna, Svetlana. Vasilisa & the Queen of Asps. 2009. 63p. pap. 8.02 *(978-0-557-05710-8(8))* Lulu Pr., Inc.

Krosoczka, Jarrett J. Naptastrophe! 2017. (ENG.). 40p. (J). (gr. -1-2). 17.99 ***(978-0-385-75483-5(3))***; lib. bdg. 20.99 ***(978-0-385-75484-2(1))*** Random Hse. Children's Bks. (Knopf Bks. for Young Readers).

Kula, Cheryl. Play Day with Daddy. Trolenberg, Karl, illus. 2013. 20p. pap. 6.95 *(978-1-4575-2336-6(1))* Dog Ear Publishing, LLC.

La Valley, Josanne. The Vine Basket. 2015. (ENG.). 256p. (J). (gr. 5-7). pap. 7.99 *(978-0-544-43939-9(2)*, HMH Books For Young Readers) Houghton Mifflin Harcourt Publishing Co.

LaFaye, A. Nissa's Place. 2010. (ENG.). 256p. (J). (gr. 2-8). pap. 8.00 *(978-1-57131-697-4(3))* Milkweed Editions.

LaFleur, John & Dubin, Shawn. Dreary & Naughty: The ABCs of Being Dead, 1 vol. 2013. (ENG., Illus.). 72p. (J). 14.99 *(978-0-7643-4496-1(X)*, 9780764344961) Schiffer Publishing, Ltd.

Lagercrantz, Rose. Life According to Dani. Eriksson, Eva, illus. 2016. (My Happy Life Ser.: 4). (ENG.). 108p. (gr. k-3). 16.99 *(978-1-77657-070-6(7))* Gecko Pr. NZL. Dist: Lerner Publishing Group.

Lake, Nick. Hostage Three. 2014. (ENG.). 400p. (YA). (gr. 7). pap. 9.99 *(978-1-61963-438-1(4)*, 9781619634381, Bloomsbury USA Childrens) 2013. (ENG.). 384p. (YA). (gr. 7). 17.99 *(978-1-61963-123-6(7)*, 9781619631236, Bloomsbury USA Childrens) 2013. 368p. 17.99 *(978-1-61963-149-6(0))* Bloomsbury Publishing USA.

Lallemand, Orianne & Strickland, Tessa. The Blue Bird's Palace. Hénaff, Carole, illus. 2016. (J). ***(978-1-78285-308-4(1))*** Barefoot Bks., Inc.

Lamb, Charles & Lamb, Mary. Tales from Shakespeare: "King Lear" Strang, Kay, ed. Andrews, Gary, illus. rev. ed. 2005. 35p. pap. 4.95 *(978-0-9542905-6-6(9))* Capercaillie Bks., Ltd GBR. Dist: Wilson & Assocs.

Larned, S. The Magic Muffin, 1 vol. Larned, Phillip, illus. 2010. 22p. pap. 24.95 *(978-1-4489-8138-0(7))* PublishAmerica, Inc.

Lawson, Jessica. Under the Bottle Bridge. 2017. (ENG., Illus.). 352p. (J). (gr. 3-7). 16.99 ***(978-1-4814-4842-0(0)***, Simon & Schuster Bks. For Young Readers) Simon & Schuster Bks. For Young Readers.

Lawson, JonArno & Smith, Sydney. Sidewalk Flowers, 1 vol. 2015. (ENG., Illus.). 32p. (J). (gr. -1-2). 16.95 *(978-1-55498-431-2(9))* Groundwood Bks. CAN. Dist: Publishers Group West (PGW).

Lawton, Wendy. A La Sombra de Su Mano, 1 vol. 2009. Orig. Title: Shadow of His Hand. (SPA.). 160p. pap. 4.99 *(978-0-8254-1379-7(6)*, Editorial Portavoz) Kregel Pubns.

Lee, Jc. Clara's Red Balloon. Park, Kathy, illus. 2011. 40p. pap. 24.95 *(978-1-4560-2491-8(4))* America Star Bks.

Legrand, Claire. The Year of Shadows. Kwasny, Karl, illus. 2013. (ENG.). 416p. (J). (gr. 3-7). 16.99 *(978-1-4424-4294-8(8)*, Simon & Schuster Bks. For Young Readers) Simon & Schuster Bks. For Young Readers.

L'Engle, Madeleine. A Wrinkle in Time. 2007. (Wrinkle in Time Quintet Ser.: 1). (ENG.). (J). (gr. 5-8). 224p. per. 6.99 *(978-0-312-36755-8(4)*, 9780312367558); 256p. per. 6.99 *(978-0-312-36754-1(6)*, 9780312367541) Square Fish.

Leonard, Marcia. El Hombre de Hojalata. Handelman, Dorothy, photos by. 2005. (ENG & SPA., Illus.). 32p. (J). (gr. -1-1). pap. 4.99 *(978-0-8225-3310-8(3))* Lerner Publishing Group.

Les Becquets, Diane. Season of Ice. 2008. (ENG.). 288p. (YA). (gr. 9-13). 16.95 *(978-1-59990-063-6(7)*, 9781599900636, Bloomsbury USA Childrens) Bloomsbury Publishing USA.

Lethcoe, Jason. The Capture of the Crimson Cape. Lethcoe, Jason, illus. 2006. (Amazing Adventures from Zoom's Academy Ser.). (ENG., Illus.). 144p. (J). (gr. 4-7). pap. 12.95 *(978-0-345-48356-0(1)*, Ballantine Bks.) Random House Publishing Group.

Levinson, Robin. Reyna & the Jade Star. 2006. (Illus.). (J). per. 12.00 *(978-0-9773673-1-3(2))* Gali Girls, Inc.

Lewis, J. M. The Adventures of Gabby & Coyote Girl. 2007. 64p. per. 7.95 *(978-1-4327-1511-3(9))* Outskirts Pr., Inc.

Lewis, Stewart. Stealing Candy. 2017. (ENG.). 288p. (YA). (gr. 8-12). pap. 10.99 *(978-1-4926-3888-9(9)*, 9781492638889) Sourcebooks, Inc.

Li-Qiong, Yu. A New Year's Reunion: A Chinese Story. Cheng-Liang, Zhu, illus. 2013. (ENG.). 40p. (J). (gr. -1-2). 6.99 *(978-0-7636-6748-1(X))* Candlewick Pr.

Liess, Claudia Schmidt. But Where Is Dad? 2007. 96p. per. 19.95 *(978-1-4241-6912-2(7))* America Star Bks.

Lindoff, Hannah. Mary's Wild Winter Feast. Koch, Nobu & Rizal, Clarissa, illus. 2014. 40p. pap. 14.95 *(978-1-60223-232-7(6))* Univ. of Alaska Pr.

Lindsay, Fitzroy A. My Daddy Came Home Long after the War. 2012. 28p. pap. 19.99 *(978-1-4685-6010-7(7))* AuthorHouse.

Lindy J. & Hubbard, Bobbie. The Story of Becky & Zippy. 2012. 32p. pap. 19.99 *(978-1-4772-6489-8(2))* AuthorHouse.

Lisle, Janet Taylor. The Crying Rocks. 2005. 281p. (YA). (gr. 7-12). 14.65 *(978-0-7569-5507-6(6))* Perfection Learning Corp.

Lively, Deborah Dreher. Vanishing Treasure of the Virungas. 2008. 88p. pap. 11.50 *(978-1-934925-54-6(3)*, Strategic Bk. Publishing) Strategic Book Publishing & Rights Agency (SBPRA).

Lois, Lowry. Crow Call. Ibatoulline, Bagram, illus. 2009. (ENG.). 32p. (J). (gr. 3-7). 19.99 *(978-0-545-03035-9(8)*, Scholastic Pr.) Scholastic, Inc.

—Crow Call. 2011. (J). (gr. -1-2). 29.95 incl. audio compact disk *(978-0-545-29674-8(9))* Weston Woods Studios, Inc.

Lollino, Jessica. Little Lily Mays & the Daddy Dilemma. Kendrick-TaZiyah, Brandi, illus. 2006. (Little Lily Mays Ser.: vol. 1). 32p. (J). per. 20.00 *(978-0-9712383-1-2(6))* Culturatti Ink.

Long, Sharon J. Let Me be Me. 2004. 137p. pap. 8.95 *(978-1-4116-1734-6(7))* Lulu Pr., Inc.

Lord, Cynthia. Half a Chance. 2014. (ENG.). 224p. (J). (gr. 3-7). 16.99 *(978-0-545-03533-0(3)*, Scholastic Pr.) Scholastic, Inc.

Lowenstein, Sallie Claire. Waiting for Eugene. 2006. (Illus.). 201p. (J). *(978-1-4156-6166-6(9))* Book Wholesalers, Inc.

Lupica, Mike. Miracle on 49th Street. 2007. (ENG.). 272p. (J). (gr. 5-18). 7.99 *(978-0-14-240942-8(1)*, Puffin Books) Penguin Young Readers Group.

—Miracle on 49th Street. 2007. 246p. (gr. 5-9). 18.00 *(978-0-7569-8157-0(3))* Perfection Learning Corp.

Lyons, Kelly Starling. One Million Men & Me. Ambush, Peter, illus. 2007. 32p. (J). (gr. -1-3). 16.95 *(978-1-933491-07-3(8))* Just Us Bks., Inc.

Mac & MAC. Anna Smudge: Professional Shrink. 2008. (Professionals Ser.: 1). (Illus.). 256p. (J). (gr. 14-18). pap. 9.99 *(978-1-934906-00-2(X))* Toasted Coconut Media LLC.

MacCready, Robin Merrow. Snapshot. 2017. (ENG.). 208p. (YA). 16.99 *(978-0-8050-9109-0(2)*, 9780805091090, Holt, Henry & Co. Bks. For Young Readers) Holt, Henry & Co.

MacDonald, George. The Elect Lady. 2008. 148p. 24.95 *(978-1-60664-792-9(X))* Aegypan.

Mack, Winnie. After All, You're Callie Boone. 2013. (ENG.). 192p. (J). (gr. 4-7). pap. 14.99 *(978-1-250-02735-1(7)*, 9781250027351) Square Fish.

MacPherson, M. j. The Magic Thread: Overcoming challenges during World War II, a young girl discovers secrets that change adversity into Adventure. 2009. 208p. pap. 17.95 *(978-0-595-52812-7(0))* iUniverse, Inc.

Maddox, Jake & Berne, Emma Carlson. Rebound Time, 1 vol. Wood, Katie, illus. 2013. (Jake Maddox Girl Sports Stories Ser.). (ENG.). 72p. (gr. 2-3). pap. 5.95 *(978-1-4342-4202-0(1))*; lib. bdg. 25.32 *(978-1-4342-4013-2(4))* Stone Arch Bks.

Madonia, Kristen-Paige. Fingerprints of You. 2013. (ENG., Illus.). 272p. (YA). (gr. 9). pap. 9.99 *(978-1-4424-2921-5(6)*, Simon & Schuster Bks. For Young Readers) Simon & Schuster Bks. For Young Readers.

—Fingerprints of You. Ribera, Terry, illus. 2012. (ENG.). 272p. (YA). (gr. 9). 16.99 *(978-1-4424-2920-8(8)*, Simon & Schuster Bks. For Young Readers) Simon & Schuster Bks. For Young Readers.

—Invisible Fault Lines. 2016. (ENG.). 320p. (YA). (gr. 7). 17.99 *(978-1-4814-3071-5(8)*, Simon & Schuster Bks. For Young Readers) Simon & Schuster Bks. For Young Readers.

Manzer, Jenny. Save Me, Kurt Cobain. 2016. (ENG.). 272p. (YA). (gr. 7). 17.99 *(978-0-553-52126-9(8)*, Delacorte Pr.) Random Hse. Children's Bks.

Marchetta, Melina. Looking for Alibrandi. 2006. (ENG.). 320p. (YA). (gr. 7-12). reprint ed. per. 9.99 *(978-0-375-83694-7(2)*, Knopf Bks. for Young Readers) Random Hse. Children's Bks.

Margolin, Phillip & Rome, Ami Margolin. Vanishing Acts. 2012. (ENG.). 176p. (J). (gr. 3-7). pap. 8.99 *(978-0-06-188558-7(4))* HarperCollins Pubs.

Marillier, Juliet. Cybele's Secret. 2011. (ENG.). 444p. (YA). (gr. 7). pap. 9.99 *(978-0-553-49486-0(4)*, Knopf Bks. for Young Readers) Random Hse. Children's Bks.

Marler, Jerilyn. Lily Hates Goodbyes. Stoltenberg, Nathan, illus. 2012. 32p. pap. 6.95 *(978-1-936214-78-5(4))* Wyatt-MacKenzie Publishing.

Marsh, Carole. The Secret of Skullcracker Swamp. 2006. (Pretty Darn Scary Mysteries Ser.). (Illus.). 113p. (YA). (gr. 7-14). 14.95 *(978-0-635-06238-3(0))*; (J). (gr. 3-5). per. 7.99 *(978-0-635-06234-5(8))* Gallopade International.

Martin, Ann M. The Long Way Home. 2013. (Family Tree Ser.: 2). (ENG.). 224p. (J). (gr. 3-7). 16.99 *(978-0-545-35943-6(0)*, Scholastic Pr.) Scholastic, Inc.

Martin, Laura. The Ark Plan. DesChamps, Eric, illus. 2017. (Edge of Extinction Ser.: 1). (ENG.). (J). (gr. 3-7). lib. bdg. 17.20 ***(978-0-606-40046-6(X))*** Turtleback Bks.

Matson, Morgan. The Unexpected Everything. 2016. (ENG.). (YA). (gr. 7). pap. 12.99 *(978-1-4814-8207-3(6))* Simon & Schuster.

—The Unexpected Everything. (ENG., Illus.). (YA). (gr. 7). 2017. 560p. pap. 9.99 *(978-1-4814-0455-6(5))* 2016. 528p. 17.99 *(978-1-4814-0454-9(7))* Simon & Schuster Bks. For Young Readers. (Simon & Schuster Bks. For Young Readers).

Maurer, Christine. Autumn Splendor. 2013. 28p. pap. 16.09 *(978-1-4669-9337-2(5))* Trafford Publishing.

Mayer, Mercer. Shibumi & the Kitemaker, 1 vol. 2003. (ENG., Illus.). 32p. (J). (gr. -1-3). pap. 5.95 *(978-0-7614-5145-7(5))* Marshall Cavendish Corp.

Maysonet, Melody. A Work of Art. 2015. (ENG.). 240p. (YA). 17.99 *(978-1-4405-8254-7(8)*, Simon Pulse) Simon Pulse.

Mazurick, Shannon K. Gemm: The Treasure Hunt with Griffin. 2012. 32p. pap. 19.99 *(978-1-4772-7740-9(4))* AuthorHouse.

Mazzucco, Melania G. The Story of King Lear. Jewiss, Virginia, tr. from ITA. Orciari, Emanuela, illus. 2016. (Save the Story Ser.). (ENG.). 104p. (J). (gr. 3-7). 19.95 *(978-1-78269-020-7(4)*, Pushkin Press) Steerforth Pr.

McCarthy, Andrew. Just Fly Away. 2017. (ENG.). 272p. (YA). (gr. 9-12). 17.95 *(978-1-61620-629-1(2))* Algonquin Bks. of Chapel Hill.

McClintock, Norah. Close to the Heel, 1 vol. 2012. (Seven (the Series) Ser.). (ENG., Illus.). 272p. (J). (gr. 5-10). pap. 9.95 *(978-1-55469-950-6(9))* Orca Bk. Pubs. USA.

McDaniel, Lurlene. Heart to Heart. 2012. (ENG.). 224p. (YA). (gr. 7). pap. 8.99 *(978-0-440-24017-4(4)*, Ember) Random Hse. Children's Bks.

—Somebody's Baby. 2017. (ENG.). 320p. (YA). (gr. 7). 17.99 *(978-0-385-74423-2(4)*, Delacorte Pr.) Random Hse. Children's Bks.

McDavid-Jones, Elizabeth. Mystery on Skull Island. 2009. (Mysteries Through Time Ser.). 192p. (YA). (gr. 4-8). 31.95 *(978-1-60754-286-5(2))*; pap. 15.25 *(978-1-60754-302-2(8))* Windmill Bks.

McDonald, John. The Tempest: The Graphic Novel. Gale Editor, ed. 2011. (Classic Graphic Novel Collection). (ENG.). 160p. (gr. 7-10). lib. bdg. 39.40 *(978-1-4205-0632-7(3))* Cengage Gale.

McDougall, Jill. Jinxed! 2008. (Lightning Strikes Ser.). 96p. (J). pap. *(978-1-921150-59-3(9))* Walker Bks. Australia Pty, Ltd.

McDuke, Doc. Emily, the Brave. Morse, Michelle, illus. 2010. 20p. pap. 10.95 *(978-1-61633-065-1(1))* Guardian Angel Publishing, Inc.

McElroy, Laurie, adapted by. Super Sneak. 2006. (Hannah Montana Ser.). (Illus.). 126p. (J). (gr. 3-7). 12.65 *(978-0-7569-8321-5(5))* Perfection Learning Corp.

McKay, Sindy. We Both Read Bilingual Edition-Museum Day/Dia Del Museo. Johnson, Meredith, illus. 2015.Tr. of Dia Del Museo. (ENG & SPA.). 44p. (J). (gr. k-1). pap. 4.99 *(978-1-60115-064-6(4))* Treasure Bay, Inc.

McMann, Lisa. Gone. (Wake Ser.: Bk. 3). (ENG.). (YA). (gr. 9). 2011. 240p. pap. 9.99 *(978-1-4169-7921-0(2))* 2010. 224p. 17.99 *(978-1-4169-7918-0(2))* Simon Pulse. (Simon Pulse).

McRee Turner, Amber. Sway. 2013. (ENG.). 320p. (J). (gr. 4-7). pap. 6.99 *(978-1-4231-3784-9(1))* Hyperion Pr.

McRitchie, Mike. Best Friends. 2009. 25p. 13.95 *(978-0-578-03644-1(4))* McRitchie, Mike.

Mead, Alice. Crossing the Starlight Bridge. 2008. (ENG.). 132p. (J). (gr. 4-6). pap. 7.99 *(978-1-4169-8964-6(1)*, Simon & Schuster Bks. For Young Readers) Simon & Schuster Bks. For Young Readers.

Meadows, Ashten. Heroes Never Die, 1 vol. 2010. 194p. pap. 24.95 *(978-1-4489-7273-9(6))* PublishAmerica, Inc.

Mechling, Lauren & Moser, Laura. All Q, No A: More Tales of a 10th-Grade Social Climber. 2006. (ENG.). 288p. (YA). (gr. 7-12). pap. 15.95 *(978-0-618-66378-1(9))* Houghton Mifflin Harcourt Publishing Co.

Metivier, Gary. Until Daddy Comes Home, 1 vol. Rath, Robert, illus. 2014. (ENG.). 32p. (J). (gr. k-3). 16.99 *(978-1-4556-1890-3(X))* Pelican Publishing Co., Inc.

Meyers, Ann Marie. Up in the Air. 2013. 244p. (J). 22.99 *(978-1-939967-03-9(1)*, Jolly Fish Pr.) North Star Editions.

Miceli, Mary Anne. Boston North Shore's Car Wash Squid. 2012. 44p. pap. 20.00 *(978-0-578-08747-4(2))* Miceli, Mary Anne.

Miko-Ray, Yours Truly. June's Scrapbook. 2009. 54p. pap. 16.95 *(978-1-61546-926-0(5))* America Star Bks.

Miller-Lachmann, Lyn. Surviving Santiago. 2015. (ENG.). 320p. (YA). (gr. 7). 16.95 *(978-0-7624-5633-8(7)*, Running Pr. Kids) Running Pr. Bk. Pubs.

Miller, Whitney A. The Violet Hour. 2014. (ENG.). 312p. (YA). pap. 9.99 *(978-0-7387-3721-8(6)*, Flux) North Star Editions.

Mitchell, Derrick Lee & Howard, Assuanta. Miyah & Koala's First Day. Mitchell, Derrick Lee, illus. 2012. (Illus.). 30p. 18.00 *(978-1-934947-69-2(5))* Asta Publications, LLC.

Miyazaki, Hayao. Ponyo Film Comic, Vol. 1. Miyazaki, Hayao, illus. movie tie-in ed. 2009. (ENG., Illus.). 172p. (J). pap. 9.99 *(978-1-4215-3077-2(5))* Viz Media.

—Ponyo Film Comic, Vol. 2. Miyazaki, Hayao, illus. movie tie-in ed. 2009. (ENG., Illus.). 172p. (J). pap. 9.99 *(978-1-4215-3078-9(3))* Viz Media.

—Ponyo Film Comic, Vol. 3. Miyazaki, Hayao, illus. movie tie-in ed. 2009. (ENG., Illus.). 172p. (J). pap. 9.99 *(978-1-4215-3079-6(1))* Viz Media.

—Ponyo Film Comic, Vol. 4. Miyazaki, Hayao, illus. movie tie-in ed. 2009. (ENG., Illus.). 172p. (J). pap. 9.99 *(978-1-4215-3080-2(5))* Viz Media.

Modiano, Patrick. Catherine Certitude. (FRE.). pap. 17.95 *(978-2-07-051608-7(3))* Gallimard, Editions FRA. Dist: Distribooks, Inc.

Moen, Ashley. Fantastic Journey: A Trip on a Raindrop. 2011. 12p. pap. 8.99 *(978-1-4634-0280-8(5))* AuthorHouse.

Monninger, Joseph. Whippoorwill. (ENG.). 288p. (YA). (gr. 7). 2016. pap. 9.99 *(978-0-544-81356-4(1))* 2015. 17.99 *(978-0-544-53123-9(X))* Houghton Mifflin Harcourt Publishing Co. (HMH Books For Young Readers).

Montgomery, L. M. Jane of Lantern Hill. 2014. (ENG.). 272p. (YA). (gr. 5-12). pap. 11.99 *(978-1-4022-8930-9(8))* Sourcebooks, Inc.

Morel, John Henry. Mary Winkle Umperdinck. 2009. 48p. pap. 22.99 *(978-1-935436-38-6(4))* Rodaian Pr.

Moreland, Karla Carter. Fishing with Daddy. 2008. (Illus.). 16p. 9.00 *(978-1-4120-4000-6(0))* Trafford Publishing.

Morgan, Melissa J. Natalie's Secret. 2005. (Camp Confidential Ser.: 1). (ENG.). 160p. (J). (gr. 3-7). 4.99 *(978-0-448-43737-8(6)*, Grosset & Dunlap) Penguin Young Readers Group.

Moriarty, Kathleen M. Wiil Waal: A Somali Folktale. Adam, Jamal, tr. Amir, Amin Abd al-Fattah Mahmud, illus. 2007. (SOM & ENG.). 32p. (J). (gr. -1-3). 15.95 *(978-1-931016-16-2(X))*; pap. 7.95 *(978-1-931016-17-9(8))* Minnesota Humanities Ctr.

Moroni, Lisa. Watch Out for the Crocodile. 2014. (Illus.). 32p. (J). (gr. -1-3). 17.95 *(978-1-877579-89-9(0))* Gecko Pr. NZL. Dist: Lerner Publishing Group.

Moss, Marissa. Amelia's Longest, Biggest, Most-Fights-Ever Family Reunion. Moss, Marissa, illus. 2006. (Amelia Ser.). (ENG., Illus.). 80p. (J). (gr. 4-7). 12.99 *(978-0-689-87447-5(2)*, Simon & Schuster/Paula Wiseman Bks.) Simon & Schuster/Paula Wiseman Bks.

—Amelia's Summer Survival Guide: Amelia's Longest, Biggest, Most-Fights-Ever Family Reunion; Amelia's Itchy-Twitchy, Lovey-Dovey Summer at Camp Mosquito. Moss, Marissa, illus. 2011. (Amelia Ser.). (ENG., Illus.). 160p. (J). (gr. 5-8). 12.99 *(978-1-4424-2331-2(5)*, Simon & Schuster/Paula Wiseman Bks.) Simon & Schuster/Paula Wiseman Bks.

Mueller, Laurie A. Eva's Day with Daddy. 2009. 36p. pap. 16.99 *(978-1-4343-2581-5(4))* AuthorHouse.

Nadin, Joanna. Wonderland. 2011. (ENG., Illus.). 224p. (YA). (gr. 9-18). 16.99 *(978-0-7636-4846-6(9))* Candlewick Pr.

Nash, J. Q. The Fishin' Hole. 2008. 48p. pap. 24.95 *(978-1-60563-621-4(5))* America Star Bks.

Nazarian, Leslie & Nazarian, George. Orelda & Corelda on Wall Street. 2007. 52p. (J). 14.94 *(978-1-4116-2302-6(9))* Lulu Pr., Inc.

Nelson, Theresa. Ruby Electric. 2004. 264p. (J). (gr. 5-7). 13.65 *(978-0-7569-3530-6(X))* Perfection Learning Corp.

Nelson, Theresa. The 25¢ Miracle. 2016. (ENG.). 144p. (J). (gr. 4-6). pap. 10.99 ***(978-1-5040-4072-3(4))*** Open Road Integrated Media, Inc.

Nibali, Ellen Cook. Secret of St. Nicholas. 2010. 32p. 16.95 *(978-0-9818154-1-1(3))* Fairland Bks.

Nicklas, James. Study Hall Story. 2008. 146p. pap. 8.84 *(978-1-4357-5691-5(6))* Lulu Pr., Inc.

Nord, Kristin Magnuson. Moosh & Grizzle. 2011. 28p. (gr. 1-2). 13.95 *(978-1-4269-6167-0(7))* Trafford Publishing.

North, Phoebe. Starglass. (Starglass Sequence Ser.). (ENG., Illus.). (YA). (gr. 7). 2014. 464p. pap. 9.99 *(978-1-4424-5954-0(9))* 2013. 448p. 17.99 *(978-1-4424-5953-3(0))* Simon & Schuster Bks. For Young Readers. (Simon & Schuster Bks. For Young Readers).

Oates, Joyce Carol. Freaky Green Eyes. 2005. 341p. (YA). 15.65 *(978-0-7569-6308-8(7))* Perfection Learning Corp.

O'Brien, Annemarie. Lara's Gift. 2014. (ENG.). 208p. (J). (gr. 5). 7.99 *(978-0-307-93175-7(7)*, Yearling) Random Hse. Children's Bks.

O'Connor, Jane. Fancy Nancy: Jojo & Daddy Bake a Cake. Glasser, Robin Preiss, illus. 2017. (My First I Can Read Ser.). 32p. (J). (gr. -1-3). pap. 3.99 ***(978-0-06-237801-9(5))*** HarperCollins Pubs.

O'Connor, Jane. Stellar Stargazer! Glasser, Robin Preiss, illus. 2011. (Fancy Nancy Ser.). (ENG.). 32p. (J). (gr. -1-2). 12.99 *(978-0-06-191523-9(8))* HarperCollins Pubs.

Odu, Nkemakolam. My Horrible Trip to New York. 2012. (Illus.). 74p. (gr. 4-6). pap. 13.66 *(978-1-4685-8217-8(8))* AuthorHouse.

Olasky, Susan. Annie Henry & the Birth of Liberty. 2011. (J). pap. *(978-1-59638-375-3(5))* P & R Publishing.

—Annie Henry & the Mysterious Stranger. 2011. (J). pap. *(978-1-59638-376-0(3))* P & R Publishing.

—Annie Henry & the Secret Mission. 2011. (J). pap. *(978-1-59638-374-6(7))* P & R Publishing.

Oliver, Jana. The Demon Trapper's Daughter. 2011. (Demon Trappers Ser.: 1). (ENG.). 368p. (YA). (gr. 7-18). pap. 9.99 *(978-0-312-61478-2(0)*, 9780312614782, St. Martin's Griffin) St. Martin's Pr.

O'Reilly, Jane. The Secret of Goldenrod. 2016. (ENG.). (gr. 3-6). 328p. (J). 17.99 *(978-1-5124-0135-6(8))*; 376p. 35.99 *(978-1-5124-0894-2(8))* Lerner Publishing Group. (Carolrhoda Bks.).

Orenstein, Denise Gosliner. Dirt. 2017. (J). pap. ***(978-0-545-92586-0(X)***, Scholastic Pr.) Scholastic, Inc.

Ormerod, Jan. Molly & Her Dad. Thompson, Carol, illus. 2008. 32p. *(978-1-921272-55-4(4))* Little Hare Bks. AUS. Dist: HarperCollins Pubs. Australia.

Orr, Wendy. Nim's Island. Millard, Kerry, illus. 2008. (ENG.). 128p. (J). (gr. 3-7). 6.99 *(978-0-385-73606-0(1)*, Yearling) Random Hse. Children's Bks.

Orrell, Brenda M. Eliza Blackbird. 2010. 256p. pap. 14.49 *(978-1-4520-8359-9(2))* AuthorHouse.

Osztian, Phillip J. Come off the Couch Daddy. 2012. 16p. pap. 15.99 *(978-1-4772-9566-3(6))* AuthorHouse.

Paradis, Susan. Snow Princess. 2005. (ENG., Illus.). 32p. (J). (gr. -1-3). 16.95 *(978-1-932425-31-4(4)*, Lemniscaat) Boyds Mills Pr.

Paratore, Coleen Murtagh. The Wedding Planner's Daughter. McGregor, Barbara, illus. 2006. (Wedding Planner's Daughter Ser.). (ENG.). 208p. (J). (gr. 3-8). reprint ed. pap. 6.99 *(978-1-4169-1854-7(X)*, Simon & Schuster Bks. For Young Readers) Simon & Schuster Bks. For Young Readers.

Patricelli, Leslie. Faster! Faster! Patricelli, Leslie, illus. (Leslie Patricelli Board Bks.). (ENG., Illus.). (J). (-k). 2013. 30p. bds. 6.99 *(978-0-7636-6222-6(4))* 2012. 32p. 15.99 *(978-0-7636-5473-3(6))* Candlewick Pr.

—Faster! Faster!/Mas Rapido! Mas Rapido! Patricelli, Leslie, illus. 2013. (Leslie Patricelli Board Bks.). (ENG., Illus.). 30p. (J). (-k). bds. 6.99 *(978-0-7636-6611-8(4))* Candlewick Pr.

Payne, Sandy. Find Your Magic. Goodpaster, Nancy, illus. 2013. 50p. pap. 12.95 *(978-1-937508-16-6(1))* Bearhead Publishing, LLC.

Pearce, Jackson. Purity. 2013. (ENG.). 224p. (YA). (gr. 10-17). pap. 9.00 *(978-0-316-18247-8(8))* Little, Brown Bks. for Young Readers.

Pearce, Jonathan. Nobody's Fault: Surprises from the Earth & the Heart. 2006. 234p. (J). per. *(978-0-9765479-3-8(7))* Balona Bks.

Pearce, Valarie. When Daddy Needs a Timeout. Johnson, Meredith, illus. 2012. 28p. pap. 10.99 *(978-0-9843111-4-9(9))* ImaRa Publishing.

Pérez, Alfredo. Sueno de Novela. (SPA.). (J). 8.95 *(978-958-04-6870-7(2))* Norma S.A. COL. Dist: Distribuidora Norma, Inc.

Pérez-Mercado, Mary Margaret. Splat! Torrey, Rich, illus. 2011. (Rookie Ready to Learn Ser.). 40p. (J). pap. 5.95 *(978-0-531-26678-6(8))*; (gr. -1-k). lib. bdg. 23.00 *(978-0-531-26373-0(8))* Scholastic Library Publishing. (Children's Pr.).

—¡Zas! Torrey, Richard L., illus. 2011. (Rookie Ready to Learn Español Ser.). (SPA.). 40p. (J). pap. 5.95 *(978-0-531-26788-2(1)*, Children's Pr.) Scholastic Library Publishing.

Pérez-Mercado, Mary Margaret & Torrey, Rich. ¡Zas! Torrey, Rich, illus. 2011. (Rookie Ready to Learn Español Ser.). (SPA., Illus.). 40p. (J). lib. bdg. 23.00 *(978-0-531-26120-0(4)*, Children's Pr.) Scholastic Library Publishing.

Perkins, Stephanie. Lola & the Boy Next Door. (ENG.). (YA). (gr. 9). 2013. 368p. pap. 10.99 *(978-0-14-242201-4(0)*, Speak) 2011. 352p. 16.99 *(978-0-525-42328-7(1)*, Dutton Books for Young Readers) Penguin Young Readers Group.

Perry, R. W. Kelly Mccabe in Slow Boat to Terror. 2003. 160p. (J). (gr. 3-6). pap. 11.95 *(978-0-9745522-0-0(8)*, Greenleaf Book Group Pr.) Greenleaf Book Group.

Petroff, Shani. Careful What You Wish For. McKenney, J. David, illus. 2010. (Bedeviled Ser.: 3). (ENG.). 240p. (J). (gr. 3-7). pap. 6.99 *(978-0-448-45113-8(1)*, Grosset & Dunlap) Penguin Young Readers Group.

—Daddy's Little Angel, No. 1. McKenney, J. David, illus. 2009. (Bedeviled Ser.: 1). (ENG.). 240p. (J). (gr. 5-7). pap. 7.99 *(978-0-448-45111-4(5)*, Grosset & Dunlap) Penguin Young Readers Group.

—The Good, the Bad, & the Ugly Dress. McKenney, J. David, illus. 2010. (Bedeviled Ser.: 2). (ENG.). 240p. (J). (gr. 5-7). pap. 6.99 *(978-0-448-45112-1(3)*, Grosset & Dunlap) Penguin Young Readers Group.

Petrucha, Stefan & Kinney, Sarah. Night of the Living Chatchke. 2009. (Nancy Drew Graphic Novels: Girl Detective Ser.). (ENG., Illus.). 96p. (J). (gr. 3-7). pap. 7.95 *(978-1-59707-143-7(9)*, 9781597071437) Papercutz.

—Night of the Living Chatchke. Murase, Sho, illus. 17th ed. 2009. (Nancy Drew Graphic Novels: Girl Detective Ser.: 17). (ENG.). 96p. (J). (gr. 3-7). 12.95 *(978-1-59707-144-4(7)*, 9781597071444) Papercutz.

Phelan, Matt. Druthers. Phelan, Matt, illus. 2014. (ENG., Illus.). 32p. (J). (-k). 15.99 *(978-0-7636-5955-4(X))* Candlewick Pr.

Philbin, Joanna. The Daughters Break the Rules. 2011. (Daughters Ser.: 2). (ENG.). 304p. (J). (gr. 7-17). pap., pap. 10.00 *(978-0-316-04905-4(0)*, Poppy) Little, Brown Bks. for Young Readers.

Phillips, Victoria. Why Is There a Raisin in My Meatloaf? 2013. 32p. pap. *(978-1-4602-1481-7(1))* FriesenPress.

Pincus, Donna & Kaplow, Julie. Samantha Jane's Missing Smile: A Story about Coping with the Loss of a Parent. Speigel, Beth, illus. 2007. 32p. (J). (gr. -1-3). 14.95 *(978-1-59147-808-9(1))*; per. 9.95 *(978-1-59147-809-6(X))* American Psychological Assn. (Magination Pr.).

Platt, Chris. Astra, 1 vol. 2010. (ENG.). 176p. (J). (gr. 3-7). 15.95 *(978-1-56145-541-6(5))* Peachtree Pubs.

Polk, Douglas. Marie's Home, 1 vol. 2009. 48p. pap. 16.95 *(978-1-60749-454-6(X))* America Star Bks.

Pon, Cindy. Silver Phoenix. (Silver Phoenix Ser.: 1). (ENG.). (YA). (gr. 9). 2011. 368p. pap. 8.99 *(978-0-06-173024-5(6))* 2009. 352p. 17.99 *(978-0-06-173021-4(1))* HarperCollins Pubs. (Greenwillow Bks.).

Porter, Pamela. The Crazy Man, 1 vol. 2006. (ENG.). 176p. (J). (gr. 3-7). pap. 8.95 *(978-0-88899-695-4(0))* Groundwood Bks. CAN. Dist: Publishers Group West (PGW).

Powell Sr., Liam Patrick. 1-2-3 Under-Dog! 2012. 24p. pap. 24.95 *(978-1-4626-8374-1(6))* America Star Bks.

Rahlens, Holly-Jane. Prince William, Maximilian Minsky, & Me. 2007. (ENG.). 320p. (YA). (gr. 7-11). per. 7.99 *(978-0-7636-3299-1(6))* Candlewick Pr.

Rajadel, Fernando López. False Love, True Love/Amor Falso, Amor Verdadero: The Alfambra Woman Buried Alive & the Lovers of Teruel. 2010.Tr. of Amor Falso, Amor Verdadero: La enterrada viva de Alfambra & Los amantes de Teruel. (SPA.). 164p. pap. 44.48 *(978-1-4251-8920-4(2))* Trafford Publishing.

Ransom, Candice. Finding Day's Bottom. 2006. 176p. (J). (gr. 3-7). lib. bdg. 15.95 *(978-1-57505-933-4(9)*, Carolrhoda Bks.) Lerner Publishing Group.

Raschka, Chris. Everyone Can Learn to Ride a Bicycle. Raschka, Chris, illus. 2013. (ENG., Illus.). 32p. (J). (gr. -1-3). 16.99 *(978-0-375-87007-1(5)*, Schwartz & Wade Bks.) Random Hse. Children's Bks.

Ray, Jane. The Dollhouse Fairy. Ray, Jane, illus. 2010. (ENG., Illus.). 32p. (J). (gr. -1-2). 16.99 *(978-0-7636-4411-6(0))* Candlewick Pr.

Reed, Tanya Jo. Daddy-O. 2012. 24p. pap. 15.99 *(978-1-4691-3757-5(7))* Xlibris Corp.

Reichs, Kathy. Code. 2013. (Virals Ser.: 3). (ENG.). 432p. (J). (gr. 5). pap. 8.99 *(978-1-59514-572-7(9)*, Puffin Books) Penguin Young Readers Group.

—Virals. 2014. lthr. 79.00 *(978-1-62715-582-3(1))* Leatherbound Bestsellers.

—Virals. (Virals Ser.: 1). (ENG.). (J). (gr. 5-18). 2011. 480p. 10.99 *(978-1-59514-426-3(9)*, Puffin Books) 2010. 464p. 17.99 *(978-1-59514-342-6(4)*, Razorbill) Penguin Young Readers Group.

—Virals. 2011. 20.00 *(978-1-61383-226-4(5))* Perfection Learning Corp.

Reichs, Kathy & Reichs, Brendan. Code. 2013. (Virals Ser.: 3). lib. bdg. 19.65 *(978-0-606-32140-2(3)*, Turtleback) Turtleback Bks.

—Terminal. 2015. (Virals Ser.: 5). (ENG.). 432p. (J). (gr. 5). 17.99 *(978-1-59514-528-4(1)*, G.P. Putnam's Sons Books for Young Readers) Penguin Young Readers Group.

—Virals. 2011. (Virals Ser.: 1). lib. bdg. 20.85 *(978-0-606-23069-8(6)*, Turtleback) Turtleback Bks.

Reinke, Beth Bence. Carla's Cloud Catastrophe. Nielson, Ginger, illus. 2011. 28p. pap. 14.99 *(978-0-9828346-0-2(8))* 4RV Publishing, LLC.

Remza, Freddie. Ride the Wave. 2011. 272p. pap. 16.95 *(978-1-4327-6642-9(2))* Outskirts Pr., Inc.

René, Richard. The Edge of Mysterion: Another Tale of Mysterion. 2011. (ENG.). 224p. (YA). pap. 14.95 *(978-1-936270-34-7(X))* Ancient Faith Publishing.

Renn, Diana. Tokyo Heist. 2013. (ENG.). 384p. (YA). (gr. 7). pap. 8.99 *(978-0-14-242654-8(7)*, Speak) Penguin Young Readers Group.

Rinaldi, Ann. Mutiny's Daughter. 2005. 218p. (J). (gr. 3-7). 13.65 *(978-0-7569-5602-8(1))* Perfection Learning Corp.

Robertson, John. My Mean Old Dad. 2009. 28p. pap. 12.25 *(978-1-60693-767-9(7)*, Strategic Bk. Publishing) Strategic Book Publishing & Rights Agency (SBPRA).

Robins, Eleanor. Be Fair, 1 vol. unabr. ed. 2011. (Carter High Senior Year Ser.). (ENG.). 49p. (YA). (gr. 9-12). pap. 7.95 *(978-1-61651-323-8(3))* Saddleback Educational Publishing, Inc.

Robinson, Jimmie. Evil & Malice - Save the World! 2009. (ENG., Illus.). 128p. (J). pap. 14.99 *(978-1-60706-091-8(4)*, 9781607060918) Image Comics.

Robinson, Nikia. The Lock-in. 2009. 38p. pap. 13.40 *(978-0-557-18567-2(X))* Lulu Pr., Inc.

Rohen, Sean. Unprincess Nermine. 2009. 84p. pap. 26.99 *(978-1-4490-3592-1(2))* AuthorHouse.

Romano, Juliana. Summer in the Invisible City. 2016. (ENG.). 320p. (YA). (gr. 9). 17.99 *(978-0-525-42917-3(4)*, Dial Bks) Penguin Young Readers Group.

Rorby, Ginny. How to Speak Dolphin. (ENG.). 272p. (J). (gr. 3-7). 2017. pap. 6.99 *(978-0-545-67607-6(X))* 2015. 16.99 *(978-0-545-67605-2(3))* Scholastic, Inc. (Scholastic Pr.).

Rose, Sandra. Doggone Grief. 2008. 20p. pap. 24.95 *(978-1-60474-623-5(8))* America Star Bks.

Rosner, Hannah. The Ambulance Club. 2005. 87p. pap. 19.95 *(978-1-4137-7492-4(X))* America Star Bks.

Rosoff, Meg. Picture Me Gone. 2013. (ENG.). 256p. (J). (gr. 7). 17.99 *(978-0-399-25765-0(9)*, G.P. Putnam's Sons Books for Young Readers) Penguin Young Readers Group.

Ross, Tony & Camp, Lindsay. Why? 2008. (ENG., Illus.). 32p. (J). (gr. -1-k). pap. 12.99 *(978-1-84270-607-7(1))* Andersen Pr. GBR. Dist: Independent Pubs. Group.

Rothberg, Kimmy. Saturdays with Daddy. 2010. 20p. 11.95 *(978-0-557-50036-9(2))* Lulu Pr., Inc.

Rotman, Risa. Azoi Vi Ess Past Fahr a Princessen (Fit for a Princess) Flohr, Perel, tr. Leff, Tova, illus. 2012.Tr. of Fit for a Princess. 32p. (J). 10.95 *(978-1-929628-66-7(8))* Hachai Publishing.

Rowley, Deborah Pace. My Wedding Day. Harmon, Glenn, illus. 2007. 24p. (J). (gr. -1-3). 15.99 *(978-1-59955-016-9(4))* Cedar Fort, Inc./CFI Distribution.

Rubin, Sarah. The Impossible Clue. 2017. (J). pap. ***(978-0-545-94272-0(1)***, Chicken Hse., The) Scholastic, Inc.

Rue, Nancy N. Motorcycles, Sushi & One Strange Book, 1 vol. 2010. (Real Life Ser.). (ENG.). 224p. (YA). (gr. 8-11). pap. 9.99 *(978-0-310-71484-2(2))* Zondervan.

Rush, Jennifer. Altered. 2013. (Altered Ser.: 1). (ENG.). (YA). (gr. 7-17). 352p. pap. 10.00 *(978-0-316-19709-0(2))*; 336p. 18.00 *(978-0-316-19708-3(4))* Little, Brown Bks. for Young Readers.

Ryder, Joanne. My Father's Hands. Graham, Mark, illus. 2014. 32p. pap. 8.00 *(978-1-61003-330-5(2))* Center for the Collaborative Classroom.

Rylant, Cynthia. Annie & Snowball & the Surprise Day. Stevenson, Suçie, illus. 2013. (Annie & Snowball Ser.: 11). (ENG.). 40p. (J). (gr. k-2). pap. 3.99 *(978-1-4169-3948-1(2)*, Simon Spotlight) Simon Spotlight.

—Annie & Snowball & the Wedding Day. Stevenson, Suçie, illus. 2014. (Annie & Snowball Ser.: 13). (ENG.). 40p. (J). (gr. k-2). 16.99 *(978-1-4169-7485-7(7)*, Simon Spotlight) Simon Spotlight.

—Annie & Snowball & the Wedding Day: The Thirteenth Book of Their Adventures. Stevenson, Suçie, illus. 2015. (Annie & Snowball Ser.: 13). (ENG.). 40p. (J). (gr. k-2). pap. 3.99 *(978-1-4169-7486-4(5)*, Simon Spotlight) Simon Spotlight.

Ryles, Donald. The Magic Holiday Forest. 2008. 40p. pap. 8.95 *(978-1-4357-4772-2(0))* Lulu Pr., Inc.

Salisbury, Linda G. No Sisters Sisters Club: A Bailey Fish Adventure. Grotke, Christopher A., illus. 2005. 188p. (J). per. 8.95 *(978-1-881539-40-7(7))* Tabby Hse. Bks.

Say, Allen. The Favorite Daughter. 2013. (J). pap. *(978-0-545-17663-7(8)*, Levine, Arthur A. Bks.) Scholastic, Inc.

—The Favorite Daughter. Say, Allen, illus. 2013. (ENG., Illus.). 32p. (J). (gr. -1-3). 17.99 *(978-0-545-17662-0(X)*, Levine, Arthur A. Bks.) Scholastic, Inc.

Sayer, Marjorie. The Girl Mechanic of Wanzhou. 2012. 186p. pap. 8.99 *(978-0-9882561-2-5(6))* Atelier Finwhale.

Scheffler, Stephanie. Elizabeth & the War of 1812. 2010. 292p. (YA). 28.95 *(978-1-4502-3539-6(5))*; (ENG.). pap. 18.95 *(978-1-4502-3540-2(9))* iUniverse, Inc.

Schepper, Denise Marie. My Dad the Navy Hero, 1 vol. 2008. (ENG.). 17p. 24.95 *(978-1-4241-9519-0(5))* America Star Bks.

Schulz, Heidi. Hook's Revenge. Hendrix, John, illus. (Hook's Revenge Ser.: Bk. 1). (ENG.). (J). (gr. 3-7). 2015. 310p. pap. 7.99 *(978-1-4847-1188-0(2))* 2014. 304p. 16.99 *(978-1-4231-9867-3(0))* Hyperion Bks. for Children.

Schusterman, Michelle. Dead Air #1. Olesh, Stephanie, illus. 2015. (Kat Sinclair Files Ser.: 1). (ENG.). 248p. (J). (gr. 3-7). 12.99 *(978-0-448-47980-4(X)*, Grosset & Dunlap) Penguin Young Readers Group.

Scott, Luke. Through a Crystal Doorknob. 2012. 88p. 24.95 *(978-1-4626-9420-4(9))* America Star Bks.

Scotton, Rob. Splat the Cat Makes Dad Glad. Scotton, Rob, illus. 2014. (I Can Read Level 1 Ser.). (ENG., Illus.). 32p. (J). (gr. -1-3). 16.99 *(978-0-06-211599-7(5))*; pap. 3.99 *(978-0-06-211597-3(9))* HarperCollins Pubs.

Seelen, Christopher. Daddy Is That the Best You Got? Moen, Tyler, illus. 2005. 36p. (J). pap. 8.99 *(978-0-9776385-0-5(2)*, Cotton Candy Pr.) Unveiled Media, LLC.

Sexton, Jessa Rose. Rose-Pie. Morozova, Anastasia, illus. 2011. 20p. pap. 6.00 *(978-0-9846244-0-9(6))* O'More Publishing.

Shaw, Natalie. A Special Day with Dad. Johnson, Shane L., illus. 2014. (Olivia TV Tie-In Ser.). (ENG.). 24p. (J). (gr. -1-2). pap. 4.99 *(978-1-4424-9751-1(3)*, Simon Spotlight) Simon Spotlight.

—A Special Day with Dad. 2014. (Olivia 8x8 Ser.). lib. bdg. 14.75 *(978-0-606-35460-8(3))* Turtleback Bks.

Shepherd, Megan. Her Dark Curiosity. 2014. (Madman's Daughter Ser.: 2). (ENG.). 432p. (YA). (gr. 8). 17.99 *(978-0-06-212805-8(1))* HarperCollins Pubs.

—The Madman's Daughter. 2013. (Madman's Daughter Ser.: 1). (ENG.). (YA). (gr. 8). 464p. pap. 9.99 *(978-0-06-212803-4(5))*; 432p. 17.99 *(978-0-06-212802-7(7))* HarperCollins Pubs.

Shevah, Emma. Dream on, Amber. Crawford-White, Helen, illus. (ENG.). (J). (gr. 3-7). 2016. 288p. pap. 7.99 *(978-1-4926-3592-5(8)*, 9781492635925) 2015. 272p. 12.99 *(978-1-4926-2250-5(8)*, 9781492622505) Sourcebooks, Inc. (Sourcebooks Jabberwocky).

Shvarts, Andrew. Royal Bastards. 2017. (Royal Bastards Ser.). (ENG.). 352p. (YA). (gr. 9-17). 18.99 ***(978-1-4847-6765-8(9))*** Hyperion Bks. for Children.

Siegel, Elizabeth. Taj. Toye, Derek, illus. 2007. 48p. (J). lib. bdg. 23.08 *(978-1-4242-1632-1(X))* Fitzgerald Bks.

Silver Phoenix Staff & Pon, Cindy. Fury of the Phoenix. 2011. (Silver Phoenix Ser.: 2). (ENG.). 368p. (YA). (gr. 9-18). 17.99 *(978-0-06-173025-2(4)*, Greenwillow Bks.) HarperCollins Pubs.

Slater, David Michael. Flour Girl: A Recipe for Disaster, 1 vol. Brooks, S. G., illus. 2007. (Missy Swiss & More Ser.). (ENG.). 32p. (gr. -1-4). 28.50 *(978-1-60270-009-3(5)*, Looking Glass Library) ABDO Publishing Co.

Sloan, L. Bridges. 2005. 164p. 22.99 *(978-1-58832-123-7(1))*; per. 12.99 *(978-1-58832-122-0(3))* Unlimited Publishing LLC.

Smith, Heather. Baygirl, 1 vol. 2013. (ENG.). 288p. (YA). (gr. 8-12). pap. 12.95 *(978-1-4598-0274-2(8))* Orca Bk. Pubs. USA.

Smith, Jennifer E. The Comeback Season. 2008. (ENG.). 256p. (YA). (gr. 8). 15.99 *(978-1-4169-3847-7(8)*, Simon & Schuster Bks. For Young Readers) Simon & Schuster Bks. For Young Readers.

Snelling, Lauraine. What about Cimmaron? 2008. (J). 8.99 *(978-1-59166-872-5(7))* BJU Pr.

Snowe, Olivia. The Glass Voice, 1 vol. Lamoreaux, Michelle, illus. 2014. (Twicetold Tales Ser.). (ENG.). 128p. (gr. 3-4). 25.32 *(978-1-4342-9148-6(0))* Stone Arch Bks.

Sones, Sonya. One of Those Hideous Books Where the Mother Dies. (ENG., (YA). (gr. 7). 2013. Illus.). 288p. pap. 9.99 *(978-1-4424-9383-4(6))* 2005. 272p. reprint ed. pap. 7.99 *(978-1-4169-0788-6(2))* Simon & Schuster Bks. For Young Readers. (Simon & Schuster Bks. For Young Readers).

Sonnenblick, Jordan. Falling over Sideways. (ENG.). 272p. (J). (gr. 7). 2017. pap. 9.99 ***(978-0-545-86325-4(2))*** 2016. 17.99 *(978-0-545-86324-7(4)*, Scholastic Pr.) Scholastic, Inc.

Sourcebooks. Twisted. 2016. (ENG.). 320p. (YA). (gr. 8-12). pap. 10.99 *(978-1-4926-3179-8(5)*, 9781492631798) Sourcebooks, Inc.

Sovern, Megan Jean. The Meaning of Maggie. 2015. (ENG.). 232p. (J). (gr. 3-7). pap. 6.99 *(978-1-4521-2876-4(6))* Chronicle Bks. LLC.

Spanabel, H. A. Skyler & the Skunks. 2009. 48p. pap. *(978-1-84923-954-7(1))* YouWriteOn.

Sparks, Megan. Boot Camp Blues, 1 vol. 2014. (Roller Girls Ser.). (ENG.). 256p. (gr. 8-10). 12.95 (978-1-62370-057-7(4)) Capstone Young Readers of Coughlan Cos.
—In a Jam, 1 vol. 2014. (Roller Girls Ser.). (ENG.). 256p. (gr. 8-10). 12.95 (978-1-62370-058-4(2)) Capstone Young Readers of Coughlan Cos.
Spencer, Mary A. Daddy's Girl. 2011. 24p. pap. 12.99 (978-1-4634-5256-8(X)) AuthorHouse.
Springer, Nancy. Somebody. 2009. (ENG.). 128p. (YA). (gr. 7-18). 16.95 (978-0-8234-2099-5(X)) Holiday Hse., Inc.
Springstubb, Tricia. What Happened on Fox Street. Ross, Heather, illus. 2011. (Fox Street Ser.: 1). (ENG.). 240p. (J). (gr. 3-7). pap. 6.99 (978-0-06-198636-9(4)) HarperCollins Pubs.
Staniszewski, Anna. The Gossip File. 2015. (Dirt Diary Ser.: 3). (ENG.). 224p. (J). (gr. 5-9). pap. 6.99 (978-1-4926-0463-1(1), 9781492604631, Sourcebooks Jabberwocky) Sourcebooks, Inc.
Stanton, Karen. Papi's Gift. Moreno, Rene King, illus. 2007. (ENG.). 32p. (J). (gr. 2-4). 16.95 (978-1-59078-422-8(7)) Boyds Mills Pr.
Stein, David Ezra. Interrupting Chicken. Stein, David Ezra, illus. (ENG., Illus.). 40p. (J). (gr. -1-3). 2016. 7.99 (978-0-7636-8903-2(3)) 2010. 16.99 (978-0-7636-4168-9(5)) Candlewick Pr.
—Interrupting Chicken. (J). 1.25 (978-1-4498-6832-1(0)); 2011. 37.75 (978-1-4498-6828-4(2)); 2011. 39.75 (978-1-4498-6829-1(0)); 2011. 37.75 (978-1-4498-6831-4(2)) Recorded Bks., Inc.
—Interrupting Chicken. Stein, David Ezra, illus. 2016. (ENG., Illus.). 40p. (J). (gr. -1-3). 18.40 (978-0-606-39099-6(5)) Turtleback Bks.
Stein, Mathilde. The Child Cruncher. Van Hout, Mies, illus. 2008. (ENG.). 32p. (J). (gr. -1-3). 16.95 (978-1-59078-635-2(1)) Lemniscaat USA.
Stentiford, Tyler Michael. A Darker Secret. 2009. (ENG.). 128p. (YA). pap. 9.99 (978-1-60138-315-0(0)) Atlantic Publishing Group, Inc.
Stevenson, Robin. Escape Velocity, 1 vol. 2011. (ENG.). 240p. (YA). (gr. 8-12). pap. 12.95 (978-1-55469-866-0(9)) Orca Bk. Pubs. USA.
Stewart, Maria. An Omelet Fit for a King. Cost, Steve, illus. 2013. 24p. pap. 14.99 (978-1-936453-23-8(1)) Bezalel Bks.
Stremanos, A. M., illus. Rosemary's Taken over My Potatoes. 2008. 20p. (J). 5.00 (978-0-9801372-0-0(9)) Benedetti, Jef.
Struyk-Bonn, Chris. Nice Girls Endure. 2016. (ENG.). 256p. (gr. 9-12). 16.95 (978-1-63079-047-9(8)) Switch Pr.
Stuchner, Joan Betty. Can Hens Give Milk?, 1 vol. Weissmann, Joe, illus. 2013. (ENG.). 32p. (J). (gr. -1-3). 9.95 (978-1-4598-0427-2(9)) Orca Bk. Pubs. USA.
Sullivan, Kiki. Midnight Dolls. 2015. (Dolls Ser.: 2). (ENG.). 336p. (YA). (gr. 8). pap. 9.99 (978-0-06-228150-0(X)) HarperCollins Pubs.
Sullivan, Mary M. If I Had a Daddy. Jane, Nance', illus. 2008. 28p. pap. 24.95 (978-1-60610-555-9(8)) America Star Bks.
Summers, Courtney. Fall for Anything. 2010. (ENG.). 240p. (YA). (gr. 7-18). pap. 15.99 (978-0-312-65673-7(4), 9780312656737, St. Martin's Griffin) St. Martin's Pr.
Summers, Gillian. Into the Wildewood. 2008. (Faire Folk Saga Ser.: 2). (ENG.). 312p. (YA). (gr. 7-14). pap. 9.95 (978-0-7387-1332-8(5), Flux) North Star Editions.
—The Tree Shepherd's Daughter. 2007. (Faire Folk Saga Ser.: 1). (ENG.). 336p. (YA). (gr. 7-12). per. 9.95 (978-0-7387-1081-5(4), Flux) North Star Editions.
Summy, Barrie. I So Don't Do Famous. 2012. (ENG.). 304p. (J). (gr. 5). 7.99 (978-0-385-73791-3(2), Yearling) Random Hse. Children's Bks.
Tal, Eve. Double Crossing: A Jewish Immigration Story. 2005. (ENG.). 216p. (J). (gr. 7-9). 16.95 (978-0-938317-94-4(6)) Cinco Puntos Pr.
Taylor, Mary Ann. Traitors: A Gander's Cove Mystery. Casteel, Kay, illus. 2006. (J). mass mkt. 5.99 (978-0-9753367-9-3(7)) Onstage Publishing, LLC.
Taylor, Sarah. Alison Learns to Deal with Her Dad's Ptsd. 2011. 24p. pap. 11.33 (978-1-4634-4050-3(2)) AuthorHouse.
The Series, Superdaddies. Superdaddies; the Series, Presents: Daddy, I Broke My Snowball! 2009. 32p. pap. 14.49 (978-1-4490-2632-5(X)) AuthorHouse.
Thomas, Shelley Moore. Secrets of Selkie Bay. 2015. (ENG.). 208p. (J). (gr. 3-7). 15.99 (978-0-374-36749-7(3), 9780374367497, Farrar, Straus & Giroux (BYR)) Farrar, Straus & Giroux.
Thompson, J. E. The Girl from Felony Bay. 2014. (Felony Bay Mysteries Ser.: 1). (ENG.). 400p. (J). (gr. 3-7). pap. 6.99 (978-0-06-210447-2(0), Waldon Pond Pr.) HarperCollins Pubs.
Thompson, Paul B. The Devil's Door: A Salem Witchcraft Story. 2010. (Historical Fiction Adventures (HFA) Ser.). (Illus.). 160p. (J). pap. 10.95 (978-1-59845-214-3(2)); (gr. 3-6). 29.27 (978-0-7660-3387-0(2)) Enslow Pubs., Inc.
Tiffany, Grace. Ariel. 2005. 240p. (J). 16.99 (978-0-06-075327-6(7)) HarperCollins Pubs.
Toon, Paige. The Accidental Life of Jessie Jefferson. 2016. (Jessie Jefferson Novels Ser.: 1). (ENG.). 336p. (J). pap. 9.99 (978-1-4711-4582-7(4), Simon & Schuster Children's) Simon & Schuster, Ltd. GBR. Dist: Simon & Schuster, Inc.
—I Knew You Were Trouble: A Jessie Jefferson Novel. 2016. (Jessie Jefferson Novels Ser.: 2). (ENG.). 336p. (J). pap. 9.99 (978-1-4711-1880-7(0), Simon & Schuster Children's) Simon & Schuster, Ltd. GBR. Dist: Simon & Schuster, Inc.
Top Secret Tiaras. 2009. (Princess Protection Program Ser.: No. 3). (ENG.). 144p. (gr. 3-7). pap. 4.99 (978-1-4231-2392-7(1)) Disney Pr.
Toten, Teresa. Better Than Blonde. 2007. (ENG.). 224p. (J). (gr. 3-7). pap. 11.99 (978-0-14-305314-9(0), Puffin Canada) Penguin Random House Canada Young Readers CAN. Dist: Penguin Random Hse. LLC.
Townsend, Tamela Ann. Finding Pumpkin, 1 vol. 2010. 48p. pap. 16.95 (978-1-4489-5983-9(7)) America Star Bks.
Townsend, Wendy. The Sundown Rule. 2011. (J). (gr. 5-9). 18.95 (978-1-60898-099-4(5)) namelos llc.
Treichel, Eliot. A Series of Small Maneuvers. 2015. (ENG.). 300p. (YA). pap. 14.95 (978-1-932010-79-4(3)) Ooligan Pr.
Tyrrell, Kevin. Froggy Kisses. Tyrrell, Kayla, illus. 2008. 22p. pap. 24.95 (978-1-60672-066-0(X)) America Star Bks.
Ungureanu, Dan. Nara & the Island. Ungureanu, Dan, illus. 2016. (ENG., Illus.). 32p. (gr. -1-3). 35.99 (978-1-5124-1794-4(7)) Lerner Publishing Group.
Van Draanen, Wendelin. Sammy Keyes & the Killer Cruise. (Sammy Keyes Ser.). (ENG.). (J). (gr. 5). 2014. 352p. 7.99 (978-0-307-93062-0(9), Yearling) 2013. 336p. 16.99 (978-0-375-87054-5(7), Knopf Bks. for Young Readers) Random Hse. Children's Bks.
Van Dyne, Edith. Aunt Jane's Nieces. 2005. 27.95 (978-1-4218-1025-6(5)); 228p. pap. 12.95 (978-1-4218-1125-3(1)) 1st World Publishing, Inc. (1st World Library - Literary Society).
van Leeuwen, Joke. The Day My Father Became a Bush. 2014. (ENG.). 104p. (978-1-877579-48-6(3)) Gecko Pr.
Verdi, Jessica. What You Left Behind. 2015. (ENG.). 368p. (YA). (gr. 8-12). pap. 9.99 (978-1-4926-0874-5(2)) Sourcebooks, Inc.
Vernick, Audrey. Water Balloon. 2011. (ENG.). 320p. (J). (gr. 5-7). 16.99 (978-0-547-59554-2(9), Clarion Bks.) Houghton Mifflin Harcourt Trade & Reference Pubs.
Vidal-Badalamenti, Nellian. Daddy's Little Girl: A Lullaby for Little Girls & Their Daddy. 2012. 24p. pap. 15.99 (978-1-4490-7430-2(8)) AuthorHouse.
Vision, David & Vision, Mutiya Sahar. Daddy Loves His Baby Girl. Vision, Mutiya Sahar, illus. 2009. (Illus.). 32p. 16.00 (978-0-9659538-7-0(4)) Visor Bks.
Waggoner, Sandra. Maggie's Treasure, 4 vols., Vol. 1. 2005. (Gatlin Fields Ser.: One). (ENG.). 108p. (J). per. 9.95 (978-0-9766823-0-1(3)) Sable Creek Pr. LLC.
Waldorf, Heather. Leftovers, 1 vol. 2009. (ENG.). 208p. (YA). (gr. 7-12). pap. 12.95 (978-1-55143-937-2(9)) Orca Bk. Pubs. USA.
Walsh, Ann. The Ghost of Soda Creek. 2009. (ENG.). 176p. (J). pap. 11.99 (978-1-55002-830-0(8), Sandcastle Bks.) Dundurn CAN. Dist: Ingram Publisher Services.
Wang, Jack, et al. Jane Austen's Emma. 2016. (ENG., Illus.). 24p. (J). (gr. -1 — 1). bds. 9.95 (978-1-4521-5255-4(1)) Chronicle Bks. LLC.
We Both Read-Museum Day. 2014. (Illus.). 44p. (J). 9.95 (978-1-60115-265-7(5)); pap. 4.99 (978-1-60115-266-4(3)) Treasure Bay, Inc.
Weatherly, Lee. Child X. 2004. 211p. 16.00 (978-0-7569-3211-4(4)) Perfection Learning Corp.
Weeks, Sarah. Honey. 2015. (ENG.). 160p. (J). (gr. 4-7). 16.99 (978-0-545-46557-1(5), Scholastic Pr.) Scholastic, Inc.
Welch, Jenna Evans. Love & Gelato. (ENG., Illus.). 400p. (YA). (gr. 7). 2017. pap. 10.99 **(978-1-4814-3255-9(9))** 2016. 17.99 (978-1-4814-3254-2(0)) Simon Pulse. (Simon Pulse).
Wells, Carolyn. Patty Fairfield. 2011. 166p. pap. 13.95 (978-1-60664-590-1(0)) Rodgers, Alan Bks.
Welty, Lauresta. The Best Place in the World, 1 vol. 2010. 40p. 24.95 (978-1-4512-9690-7(8)) PublishAmerica, Inc.
Weston Woods Staff, creator. Crow Call. 2011. 18.95 (978-0-545-37493-4(6)); 38.75 (978-0-545-37494-1(4)) Weston Woods Studios, Inc.
Whelan, Gloria. Parade of Shadows. 2007. 304p. (J). (gr. 5-18). lib. bdg. 16.89 (978-0-06-089029-2(0)) HarperCollins Pubs.
Whipple, Natalie. House of Ivy & Sorrow. 2014. (ENG.). 368p. (YA). (gr. 8). pap. 9.99 (978-0-06-212018-2(2), HarperTeen) HarperCollins Pubs.
White, Jennifer. Survival Strategies of the Almost Brave. 2015. (ENG.). 320p. (J). (gr. 3-7). 16.99 (978-0-374-30084-5(4), 9780374300845, Farrar, Straus & Giroux (BYR)) Farrar, Straus & Giroux.
Wick, Kimberly. Reaching for Heaven. 2009. 36p. pap. 16.99 (978-1-4389-2268-3(X)) AuthorHouse.
Willems, Mo. A Cautionary Tale. Willems, Mo, illus. 2011. (Illus.). 40p. (gr. -1-1). 19.99 (978-1-4231-4449-6(X)) Hyperion Pr.
—El Conejito Knuffle: Un Cuento Aleccionador. Willems, Mo, illus. rev. ed. 2007. (Knuffle Bunny Ser.). (ENG & SPA., Illus.). 40p. (J). (gr. -1-k). pap. 7.99 (978-1-4231-0567-1(2)) Hyperion Pr.
—Knuffle Bunny. 2014. 36p. pap. 8.00 (978-1-61003-228-5(4)) Center for the Collaborative Classroom.
—Knuffle Bunny: A Cautionary Tale. Willems, Mo, illus. unabr. ed. 2006. (Illus.). (J). (gr. -1-1). 29.95 (978-0-439-90583-1(4)) Weston Woods Studios, Inc.
—Knuffle Bunny Too: A Case of Mistaken Identity. Willems, Mo, illus. rev. ed. 2007. (Knuffle Bunny Ser.). (ENG., Illus.). 48p. (J). (gr. -1-k). 17.99 (978-1-4231-0299-1(1)) Hyperion Pr.
Willems, Mo & Willems, Trixie, narrated by. Knuffle Bunny Too: A Case of Mistaken Identity. 2011. (J). (gr. -1-2). 29.95 (978-0-545-13456-9(0)) Weston Woods Studios, Inc.
Williams, Joyce. A Daddy's Love Through a Girl's Eye. Petroff, Kathryn, illus. 2012. 58p. pap. 9.99 (978-0-9852729-3-7(7)) Faith Bks. & MORE.
Williams, Laura E. The Executioner's Daughter. 2007. (ENG.). 144p. (YA). (gr. 5-9). pap. 9.99 (978-0-8050-8186-2(0), 9780805081862, Holt, Henry & Co. Bks. For Young Readers) Holt, Henry & Co.
Williams, Sherri. My Daddy Is in the Army. 2011. 28p. pap. 15.25 (978-1-257-14167-8(8)) Lulu Pr., Inc.
Wilson, Angie. Dori's Gift. Teets, Ashley, illus. 2013. (ENG.). 32p. (J). (gr. -1-3). 16.95 (978-0-938467-85-4(9)) Headline Bks., Inc.
Wilson, Heather Gemmen. Lydia Barnes & the Blood Diamond Treasure. 2007. (Global Warning Ser.). 159p. (J). (gr. 3-7). per. 7.99 (978-0-89827-350-2(1)) Wesleyan Publishing Hse.
—Lydia Barnes & the Mystery of the Broken Cross. 2007. (Global Warning Ser.). 157p. (J). (gr. 3-7). per. 7.99 (978-0-89827-351-9(X)) Wesleyan Publishing Hse.
Wilson, Jacqueline. Candyfloss. Sharratt, Nick, illus. 2008. (ENG.). 352p. (J). (gr. 4-7). pap. 9.99 (978-0-312-38418-0(1), 9780312384180) Square Fish.
—Cookie. Sharratt, Nick, illus. 2010. (ENG.). 352p. (J). (gr. 4-7). pap. 11.99 (978-0-312-64290-7(3), 9780312642907) Square Fish.
Wilson, Rock. If I Had My Way — /By Rock S. Wilson; Illustrated by Carol Dixon. Dixon, Carol, illus. 2010. 32p. (J). (978-0-929915-44-9(5)) Headline Bks., Inc.
Wingard, Lucinda. The Turn-Around Bird. 2012. 296p. pap. 16.00 (978-0-9848400-1-4(X)) Plicata Pr. LLC.
Winters, Cat. The Cure for Dreaming. (ENG., Illus.). (YA). 2016. 384p. (gr. 8-17). pap. 9.95 (978-1-4197-1941-7(6)) 2014. 368p. (gr. 7-17). 17.95 (978-1-4197-1216-6(0)) Abrams, Inc. (Amulet Bks.).
Winters, Kari-Lynn. Good Pirate. Griffiths, Dean, illus. 2016. (ENG.). 32p. (J). (gr. k-3). 17.95 (978-1-927485-80-4(0)) Pajama Pr. CAN. Dist: Ingram Publisher Services.
Wisler, Joelle. Ariana Gold. 2016. (What's Your Dream? Ser.). (ENG., Illus.). 96p. (gr. 3-4). lib. bdg. 25.32 (978-1-4965-3442-2(5)) Capstone Press of Coughlan Cos.
Woltz, Anna. A Hundred Hours of Night. Watkinson, Laura, tr. from DUT. 2016. (ENG.). 256p. (YA). (gr. 9). 17.99 (978-0-545-84828-2(8), Levine, Arthur A. Bks.) Scholastic, Inc.
Woodson, Jacqueline. I Hadn't Meant to Tell You This. 2010. (ENG.). 160p. (YA). (gr. 7-18). 7.99 (978-0-14-241704-1(1), Puffin Books) Penguin Young Readers Group.
—I Hadn't Meant to Tell You This. 2006. 114p. (YA). (gr. 7-12). 13.65 (978-0-7569-6730-7(9)) Perfection Learning Corp.
Wynne-Jones, Tim. The Uninvited. 2009. (ENG., Illus.). 368p. (YA). (gr. 9). 16.99 (978-0-7636-3984-6(2)) Candlewick Pr.
Yokota, Hiromitsu, illus. The Tale of the Oki Islands: A Tale from Japan. 2013. (Tales of Honor (Red Chair Press) Ser.). (ENG.). 32p. (J). (gr. 1-4). lib. bdg. 26.60 (978-1-937529-78-9(9)) Red Chair Pr.
Yolen, Jane. The Emperor & the Kite. Young, Ed, illus. 2015. 32p. pap. 7.00 (978-1-61003-535-4(6)) Center for the Collaborative Classroom.
—Owl Moon. 2013. lib. bdg. 18.40 (978-0-606-36222-1(3)) Turtleback Bks.
Zahler, Diane. The Thirteenth Princess. 2011. (ENG.). 272p. (J). (gr. 3-7). pap. 6.99 (978-0-06-182500-2(X)) HarperCollins Pubs.
Zajac, Kristen. Chasing the Spirit of Service. Tucker, Julie, illus. 2013. 24p. 19.95 (978-1-61633-393-5(6)) Guardian Angel Publishing, Inc.
Zajac, Kristen J. Ebeneezer's Cousin. Houdeshell, Jennifer T., illus. 2010. 20p. pap. 10.95 (978-1-61633-045-3(7)) Guardian Angel Publishing, Inc.
Zajac, Kristen K. Ebeneezer's Cousin. Houdeshell, Jennifer Thomas, illus. 2013. 24p. 19.95 (978-1-61633-440-6(1)) Guardian Angel Publishing, Inc.

FATHERS AND SONS

Calixto, Melissa. This Father's Love. 2012. 20p. pap. 24.95 (978-1-4626-6005-6(3)) America Star Bks.
Christopher, Matt. On the Field With... Peyton & Eli Manning. 2008. (ENG.). 144p. (J). (gr. 3-7). pap. 5.99 (978-0-316-03696-2(X)) Little, Brown Bks. for Young Readers.
Desmet, Wendy. My Dad Is Different. 2012. (Illus.). 20p. pap. 19.82 (978-1-4678-9064-9(2)) AuthorHouse.
Francis, Elizabeth. Fishing on Father's Day. 2012. 16p. pap. 15.99 (978-1-4685-9554-3(7)) AuthorHouse.
Jenkins, Susan Padgett. Daddy Comes Back. 2011. 20p. pap. 24.95 (978-1-4626-2092-0(2)) America Star Bks.
McGehee, Claudia. My Wilderness: An Alaskan Adventure. 2015. (ENG., Illus.). 32p. (J). (gr. k-4). 16.99 (978-1-57061-950-2(6), Little Bigfoot) Sasquatch Bks.
Porterfield, Jason. Calvin Hill & Grant Hill: One Family's Legacy in Football & Basketball. 2010. (Sports Families Ser.). 48p. (YA). (gr. 5-8). lib. bdg., E-Book 53.00 (978-1-4488-0087-2(0)); (ENG., Illus.). (J). pap. 11.75 (978-1-4358-8516-5(3), Rosen Reference); (Illus.). (YA). (gr. 4-7). lib. bdg. 29.25 (978-1-4358-3549-8(2)) Rosen Publishing Group, Inc., The.
—Calvin Hill & Grant Hill: One Family's Legacy in Football & Basketball (Sports Families) l.t. ed. 2012. 96p. pap. (978-1-4596-3352-0(0)) ReadHowYouWant.com, Ltd.
Rabin, Staton. Mr. Lincoln's Boys. Ibatoulline, Bagram, illus. 2008. (ENG.). 36p. (J). (gr. k-3). 16.99 (978-0-670-06169-3(7), Viking Books for Young Readers) Penguin Young Readers Group.
Robertson, David Alexander. The Pact. Henderson, Scott B., illus. 2011. (7 Generations Ser.: 4). (ENG.). 32p. (YA). pap. (978-1-55379-230-7(0), 9781553792307, HighWater Pr.) Portage & Main Pr.
Sévigny, Eric, illus. Caillou & the Big Slide. 2012. (Clubhouse Ser.). (ENG.). 24p. (J). (gr. -1-1). pap. 3.99 (978-2-89450-867-1(0)) Caillouet, Gerry.
Worthington, Joe. The Mannings: Football's Famous Family. 2005. (High Five Reading - Blue Ser.). (ENG., Illus.). 48p. (gr. 3-4). per. 9.00 (978-0-7368-5741-3(9), High Five Reading (RBL)) Capstone Press of Coughlan Cos.

FATHERS AND SONS—FICTION

Abdo Publishing. The Mystical Pencil, 1 vol. 2013. (Mystical Pencil Ser.: 4). (ENG.). 32p. (J). (gr. 3-6). lib. bdg. 114.00 (978-1-61641-925-7(3), Graphic Planet) Magic Wagon.
Abdullah, Patricia Noor. Saving Daddy. Cabri, Alexandra, illus. 2006. 32p. (J). (gr. 2-5). 17.95 (978-1-933193-16-8(6)) EECI, Inc.
Acioli, Socorro. The Head of the Saint. Hahn, Daniel, tr. from POR. Snell, Alexis, illus. 2016. (ENG.). 192p. (YA). (gr. 7). 16.99 (978-0-553-53792-5(X), Delacorte Pr.) Random Hse. Children's Bks.
Adamson, Ged & Rylance, Ulrike. Elsie Clarke & the Vampire Hairdresser. Adamson, Ged, illus. 2013. (ENG., Illus.). 28p. (J). (gr. -1-1). 16.95 (978-1-62087-983-2(2), 620983, Sky Pony Pr.) Skyhorse Publishing Co., Inc.
Ailes, Mark Cusco. The Tree of No Boundaries: Book One. 2009. 196p. 24.95 (978-0-595-63594-8(6)) iUniverse, Inc.
Akins, Joni. Dean the Bean. 2007. 24p. per. 24.95 (978-1-4241-5015-1(9)) America Star Bks.
Alexander, Claire. The Best Part of Daddy's Day. 2016. (ENG., Illus.). 32p. (J). (gr. -1-3). 16.99 (978-1-4998-0196-5(3)) Little Bee Books Inc.
Alexander, Kwame. The Crossover. 2014. (ENG.). (J). (gr. 4-7). E-Book 16.99 (978-1-306-46985-2(6)) Harcourt Trade Pubs.
—The Crossover. 2014. (ENG.). 240p. (J). (gr. 4-7). 16.99 (978-0-544-10771-7(3), HMH Books For Young Readers) Houghton Mifflin Harcourt Publishing Co.
—The Crossover. 2014. lib. bdg. 29.40 (978-0-606-37975-5(4)) Turtleback Bks.
Almond, David. Slog's Dad. McKean, Dave, illus. 2011. (ENG.). 64p. (J). (gr. 5-18). 15.99 (978-0-7636-4940-1(6)) Candlewick Pr.
Alphin, Elaine Marie. Picture Perfect. 2003. (ENG., Illus.). 256p. (YA). (gr. 5-12). 15.95 (978-0-8225-0535-8(5)) Lerner Publishing Group.
Anderson, Peggy Perry. To the Tub. Anderson, Peggy Perry, illus. 2004. (Illus.). 52p. (gr. -1-3). 17.00 (978-0-7569-4258-8(6)) Perfection Learning Corp.
—To the Tub. 2012. (Green Light Readers — Level 1 Ser.). lib. bdg. 13.55 (978-0-606-26608-6(9), Turtleback) Turtleback Bks.
Angus, Sam. Soldier Dog. 2014. (ENG.). 272p. (J). (gr. 4-7). pap. 7.99 (978-1-250-04417-4(0), 9781250044174) Square Fish.
Appelt, Kathi. When Otis Courted Mama. Szekeres, Cyndy & McElmurry, Jill, illus. 2015. (ENG.). 40p. (J). (gr. -1-3). 16.99 (978-0-15-216688-5(2), HMH Books For Young Readers) Houghton Mifflin Harcourt Publishing Co.
Appleton, Victor. Into the Abyss. 2007. (Tom Swift, Young Inventor Ser.). (ENG.). 160p. (gr. 3-7). 27.07 (978-1-59961-350-5(6)) Spotlight.
Arceneaux, Kitty. If Daddy Can, I Can. Isaac, W. Smiley, illus. 2012. 24p. 24.95 (978-1-4626-4945-7(9)); pap. 12.99 (978-1-4626-7852-5(1)) America Star Bks.
Arnold, Ginger Fudge. Billy's Mountain Adventure, 1 vol. Almeyda, Tonito Avalon, illus. 2010. 32p. pap. 24.95 (978-1-4489-5582-4(3)) PublishAmerica, Inc.
—Two Tipsy Tots, 1 vol. Crème, Aurora C., illus. 2009. 32p. pap. 24.95 (978-1-4489-1891-1(X)) America Star Bks.
Asch, Frank. Just Like Daddy. Asch, Frank, illus. 2015. (Frank Asch Bear Book Ser.). (ENG., Illus.). 32p. (J). (gr. -1-3). 6.99 (978-1-4814-2207-9(3), Aladdin) Simon & Schuster Children's Publishing.
Aschermann, Kurt. Bj & the Amazing Doctor Directions. 2008. 172p. pap. 11.99 (978-1-4343-7708-1(3)) AuthorHouse.
Ashworth, Sherry. Close-Up. 2006. (ENG.). 256p. (J). (gr. 7). pap. 11.95 (978-1-4169-0474-8(3), Simon & Schuster Children's) Simon & Schuster, Ltd. GBR. Dist: Simon & Schuster, Inc.
Aunt Connye. Club House: Stories that Teach. 2012. 76p. pap. 28.99 (978-1-4670-4413-4(X)) AuthorHouse.
Avi. Wolf Rider. 2008. (ENG.). 208p. (YA). (gr. 7-12). mass mkt. 7.99 (978-1-4169-5444-6(9), Simon Pulse) Simon Pulse.
Award, Anna, et al. The Farmer & His Sons & the Donkey in the Lion's Den. 2014. (ENG.). 24p. (J). pap. 6.95 (978-1-84135-960-1(2)) Award Pubns. Ltd. GBR. Dist: Parkwest Pubns., Inc.
—The Fox & the Stork & the Man, His Son & the Donkey. 2014. (ENG.). 24p. (J). pap. 6.95 (978-1-84135-955-7(6)) Award Pubns. Ltd. GBR. Dist: Parkwest Pubns., Inc.
Baggott, Julianna. The Prince of Fenway Park. 2011. (ENG.). 352p. (J). (gr. 3-7). pap. 6.99 (978-0-06-087244-1(6)) HarperCollins Pubs.
Baker-Smith, Grahame. FArTHER. Baker-Smith, Grahame, illus. 2013. (ENG., Illus.). 40p. (J). (gr. k-3). 17.99 (978-0-7636-6370-4(0), Templar) Candlewick Pr.
Ball, S. N. Daddies Don't Get Snow Days. Howard, Ellie Nothaus, illus. 2013. (ENG.). 28p. (J). pap. 13.95 (978-1-4787-1188-9(4)) Outskirts Pr., Inc.
Baltazar, Armand. Diego & the Rangers of the Vastlantic. Baltazar, Armand, illus. 2017. (Timeless Ser.: 1). (Illus.). 624p. (J). (gr. 3-7). 19.99 (978-0-06-240236-3(6), Tegen, Katherine Bks) HarperCollins Pubs.
Bancks, Tristan. On the Run. 2015. (ENG.). 240p. (J). (gr. 5-7). 16.99 (978-0-374-30153-8(0), 9780374301538, Farrar, Straus & Giroux (BYR)) Farrar, Straus & Giroux.
Banks, Jane Whelen. Liam Wins the Game, Sometimes: A Story about Losing with Grace. 2008. (ENG., Illus.). 32p. 12.95 (978-1-84310-898-6(4), 5374) Kingsley, Jessica Pubs. GBR. Dist: Macmillan Distribution Ltd.
Banks, Kate. The Night Worker. Hallensleben, Georg, illus. 2007. (ENG.). 40p. (J). (gr. -1-1). 8.99 (978-0-374-40000-2(8), 9780374400002) Square Fish.
—Night Worker. 2014. 19.00 (978-1-63419-674-1(0)) Perfection Learning Corp.
Barbera, Anthony. Catching Baby Moses. 2009. (ENG.). 266p. pap. 12.95 (978-1-4196-7771-7(3)) CreateSpace Independent Publishing Platform.
Barchers, Suzanne I. Dad Wants a Nap, 1 vol. 2011. (Targeted Phonics Ser.). (ENG., Illus.). 16p. (J). (gr. k-2). pap. 5.99 (978-1-4333-2407-9(5)) Teacher Created Materials, Inc.
—Pack a Bag!, 1 vol. 2011. (Targeted Phonics Ser.). (ENG.). 16p. (J). (gr. k-2). pap. 5.99 (978-1-4333-2409-3(1)) Teacher Created Materials, Inc.
Barnes, Hannah. Rainbow Colored Skin a Father-Son Tattoo Tale. 2013. 28p. pap. 12.99 (978-1-300-77380-1(4)) Lulu Pr., Inc.
Barron, T. A. Doomraga's Revenge, 7 vols., Bk. 7. 2011. (Merlin Saga Ser.: 7). (ENG.). 272p. (J). (gr. 5-18). 8.99 (978-0-14-241925-0(7), Puffin Books) Penguin Young Readers Group.
Barry, Nick. Escape of the Terra-Cotta Soldiers: An Ethan Sparks Adventure. 2008. 180p. 23.95 (978-0-595-49365-4(3)); pap. 13.95 (978-0-595-45413-6(5)) iUniverse, Inc.
Barry, Rick. Kiriath's Quest. 2008. (J). 8.99 (978-1-59166-905-0(7)) BJU Pr.
Bartone, Elisa. Peppe the Lamplighter. Lewin, Ted, illus. 2015. 32p. pap. 7.00 (978-1-61003-612-2(3)) Center for the Collaborative Classroom.
Barwin, Steven. Rock Dogs, 1 vol. 2009. (Lorimer Sports Stories Ser.). (ENG.). 104p. (J). (gr. 4-8). 16.95 (978-1-55277-028-3(1), 9781552770283); 8.95 (978-1-55277-027-6(3), 9781552770276) Lorimer, James & Co., Ltd., Pubs. CAN. Dist: Casemate Pubs. & Bk. Distributors, LLC.
Beaty, Daniel. Knock Knock: My Dad's Dream for Me. 2013. (ENG.). 40p. (J). (gr. -1-3). 18.99 (978-0-316-20917-5(1)) Little, Brown Bks. for Young Readers.
Bergstrom, Gunilla. Good Night, Alfie Atkins. Dyssegaard, Elisabeth Kallick, tr. from SWE. Bergström, Gunilla, illus. 2005. 32p. (J). 15.00 (978-91-29-66154-5(4)) R & S Bks. SWE. Dist: Macmillan.
Berk, Ari. Death Watch. (Undertaken Trilogy Ser.: 1). (ENG.). (YA). (gr. 7). 2012. 560p. pap. 9.99 (978-1-4169-9116-8(6)) 2011. 544p. 17.99 (978-1-4169-9115-1(8)) Simon & Schuster Bks. For Young Readers. (Simon & Schuster Bks. For Young Readers).
Berryhill, Shane. Dragon Island. 2013. 216p. pap. 9.99 (978-1-937530-23-5(X)) Crossroad Pr.
Bets, Emily. The Shirt. 2012. 24p. pap. 14.93 (978-1-4669-0183-4(7)) Trafford Publishing.

Bianchini, Bob. Charlie Rides: Planes, Trains, Bikes, & More! 2017. (ENG., Illus.). 20p. (J). (gr. -1-k). bds. 8.95 *(978-1-4197-2292-9(1),* Abrams Appleseed) Abrams, Inc.

Bildner, Phil. The Greatest Game Ever Played. Pullen, Zachary, illus. 2015. (ENG.). 40p. (J). (gr. k-3). 8.99 *(978-0-14-751451-6(7),* Puffin Books) Penguin Young Readers Group.

Blackstone, Matt. Sorry You're Lost. 2014. (ENG.). 320p. (J). (gr. 5-9). 15.99 *(978-0-374-38065-6(1),* 9780374380656, Farrar, Straus & Giroux (BYR)) Farrar, Straus & Giroux.

Blair, Eric. Tom Thumb: A Retelling of the Grimm's Fairy Tale, 1 vol. Ouren, Todd, illus. 2013. (My First Classic Story Ser.). (ENG.). 32p. (gr. k-3). pap. 7.10 *(978-1-4795-1847-0(6),* My First Classic Story) Picture Window Bks.

Blount, Patty. Nothing Left to Burn. 2015. (ENG.). 368p. (YA). (gr. 8-12). pap. 9.99 *(978-1-4926-1329-9(0),* 9781492613299) Sourcebooks, Inc.

Blundell, Gerald Lee. Bunkalunken Goes to Washington & Other Stories, 1 vol. 2010. 138p. pap. 24.95 *(978-1-4489-5234-2(4))* America Star Bks.

Bonnell, Kris. Too Big to Play. 2006. (J). pap. 5.95 *(978-1-933727-35-6(7))* Reading Reading Bks., LLC.

Booth, Coe. Bronxwood. 2011. (ENG.). 336p. (J). (gr. 9). 17.99 *(978-0-439-92534-1(7),* PUSH) Scholastic, Inc.

Born to be a Tiger. 2004. (J). per. 18.50 net. *(978-0-615-12596-1(4))* Little Band Man Co., LLC, The.

Bowen, Fred. The Golden Glove, 1 vol. 2009. (Fred Bowen Sports Story Ser.). (ENG., Illus.). 112p. (J). (gr. 3). pap. 6.95 *(978-1-56145-505-8(9))* Peachtree Pubs.

Boykin, Antonee. Alex & Tony Learn to Be Gentlemen. 2011. 31p. (J). pap. 13.95 *(978-1-4327-5255-2(3))* Outskirts Pr., Inc.

Boyne, John. Stay Where You Are & Then Leave. Jeffers, Oliver, illus. 2014. (ENG.). 256p. (J). (gr. 4-7). 16.99 *(978-1-62779-031-4(4),* 9781627790314, Holt, Henry & Co. Bks. For Young Readers) Holt, Henry & Co.

Bradford, Quebe Merritt. In the Absence of My Father: Grief. Grit. Gangs. Guts. Grace. 2011. 188p. 24.79 *(978-1-4567-4026-9(1));* pap. 14.99 *(978-1-4567-3968-3(9))* AuthorHouse.

Bradford, William. Jeremy Mcbright Was Afraid of the Night. 2006. (Illus.). 36p. (J). lib. bdg. 13.95 *(978-0-9672585-2-2(9))* CyPress Pubns.

Brasch, Nicolas & Nickel, Adam. Dad & Dan Go Camping. 2008. (Rigby Focus Forward: Level G Ser.). (Illus.). 24p. (J). (gr. 4-7). pap. *(978-1-4190-3705-4(6),* Rigby) Pearson Education Australia.

—Dad & Dan Go Fishing. 2008. (Rigby Focus Forward: Level D Ser.). (Illus.). 16p. (J). (gr. 4-7). pap. *(978-1-4190-3668-2(8),* Rigby) Pearson Education Australia.

Breault, Christie Merriman. Logan West, Printer's Devil. Archambault, Matthew, illus. 2006. 142p. (J). pap. *(978-1-59336-762-6(7))* Mondo Publishing.

Brewer, Heather. The Chronicles of Vladimir Tod. 2011. (Chronicles of Vladimir Tod Ser.: 5). (ENG.). 336p. (YA). (gr. 7-18). 8.99 *(978-0-14-241752-2(1),* Speak) Penguin Young Readers Group.

—Twelfth Grade Kills. 5th ed. 2010. (Chronicles of Vladimir Tod Ser.: 5). (ENG.). 340p. (YA). (gr. 7-18). 16.99 *(978-0-525-42224-2(2),* Dutton Books for Young Readers) Penguin Young Readers Group.

Brisson, Pat. The Summer My Father Was Ten. Shine, Andrea, illus. 2014. 32p. pap. 8.00 *(978-1-61003-366-4(3))* Center for the Collaborative Classroom.

Brooke, Susan Rich, adapted by. The Lion King. 2003. (Illus.). (J). *(978-0-7853-9380-1(3))* Publications International, Ltd.

Brown, Marc. Arthur Jumps into Fall. 2006. (ENG., Illus.). 24p. (J). (gr. -1-1). pap. 3.99 *(978-0-316-05775-2(4))* Little, Brown Bks. for Young Readers.

Brown, Robert L. Daddy Grows Colors, 1 vol. 2010. 26p. 24.95 *(978-1-4512-1746-9(3))* PublishAmerica, Inc.

Bruchac, Joseph. Wolf Mark, 1 vol. 2013. (ENG.). 392p. (J). 17.95 *(978-1-60060-661-8(X),* Tu Bks.) Lee & Low Bks., Inc.

Bryce, Conor. Wesco P. Mcsnaffle & the Great Brave Quest. 2008. 127p. pap. 22.50 *(978-1-4092-1273-7(4))* Lulu Pr., Inc.

Buckley-Archer, Linda. The Time Travelers. 2012. (Gideon Trilogy Ser.: 1). (ENG.). 416p. (J). (gr. 5-9). 17.99 *(978-1-4424-6551-0(4),* Simon & Schuster Bks. For Young Readers) Simon & Schuster Bks. For Young Readers.

Bundy, John. Kimble's New Armor. 2011. 24p. (gr. 1-2). pap. 11.32 *(978-1-4567-6741-9(0))* AuthorHouse.

Bunting, Eve. My Red Balloon. Life, Kay, illus. 2005. (ENG.). 32p. (J). (gr. -1-2). 15.95 *(978-1-59078-263-7(1))* Boyds Mills Pr.

Burleigh, Robert. Good-Bye, Sheepie, 0 vols. Catalanotto, Peter, illus. 2010. (ENG.). 32p. (J). (gr. -1-k). 16.99 *(978-0-7614-5598-1(1),* 9780761455981, Amazon Children's Publishing) Amazon Publishing.

Burton, Jacky. The Other Stable. 2013. 32p. pap. 24.95 *(978-1-62709-371-2(0))* America Star Bks.

Burwick, Josh. Dad, I Wish I Was Your Age. Monroe, Dan, illus. 2012. 40p. (J). pap. 14.99 *(978-0-9852146-3-0(5))* AM Ink Publishing.

Busteed, Kerri J. Will's First Hunt. Byers, Leon, illus. 2010. 80p. pap. 21.50 *(978-1-60911-483-1(3),* Eloquent Bks.) Strategic Book Publishing & Rights Agency (SBPRA).

Byars, Betsy. Disappearing Acts. 2006. (Herculeah Jones Mystery Ser.). (ENG.). 144p. (J). (gr. 3-7). 6.99 *(978-0-14-240566-6(3),* Puffin Books) Penguin Young Readers Group.

Cafiero, Crystal. Gone Fishing, Just Daddy & Me. 2013. 24p. pap. 24.95 *(978-1-4241-1532-7(9))* America Star Bks.

Camacho, Hector, Jr. & Warburton, Dustin. Macho Dad. Monroe, Daniel, illus. 2014. (ENG.). (J). 19.99 *(978-0-9960374-3-3(8))* Dragonbrush Arts.

Campbell, Isaiah. The Struggles of Johnny Cannon. 2015. 322p. (J). pap. *(978-1-4814-2632-9(X),* Simon & Schuster Bks. For Young Readers) Simon & Schuster Bks. For Young Readers.

Campbell, L. A. Cartboy & the Time Capsule. (Cartboy Ser.: 1). (ENG.). 208p. (J). (gr. 3-7). 2015. pap. 6.99 *(978-0-7653-7844-6(2),* 9780765378446) 2013. (Illus.). 12.99 *(978-0-7653-3317-9(1),* 9780765333179) Doherty, Tom Assocs., LLC. (Starscape).

Campbell, Suzy. My Daddy Is a Soldier, 1 vol. 2009. 19p. pap. 24.95 *(978-1-61546-724-2(6))* America Star Bks.

—My Daddy Is a Soldier, 1 vol. 2010. 20p. 24.95 *(978-1-4512-1163-4(5))* PublishAmerica, Inc.

Campos, Tito. Muffler Man el Hombre Mofle. Alvarez, Lamberto, illus. 2009. 32p. (J). pap. 7.95 *(978-1-55885-557-1(2),* Piñata Books) Arte Publico Pr.

Capucilli, Alyssa Satin. My Dad & Me. Mitchell, Susan, illus. 2009. (ENG.). 16p. (J). (gr. -1-1). 7.99 *(978-1-4169-5828-4(2),* Little Simon) Little Simon.

Carroll, James Christopher. Papa's Backpack. Carroll, James Christopher, illus. 2015. (ENG., Illus.). 32p. (J). (gr. 1-3). pap. 15.99 *(978-1-58536-613-2(7),* 203942) Sleeping Bear Pr.

Carson, Jack. Swampland Slam. 2013. (ENG., Illus.). 128p. (J). pap. 7.99 *(978-0-85707-563-5(2),* Simon & Schuster Children's) Simon & Schuster, Ltd. GBR. Dist: Simon & Schuster, Inc.

Carter, Alden R. Walkaway. 2008. (ENG.). 192p. (YA). (gr. 7-18). 16.95 *(978-0-8234-2106-0(6))* Holiday Hse., Inc.

—Wart, Son of Toad, 0 vols. unabr. ed. 2013. (ENG.). 224p. (YA). (gr. 8-10). pap. 9.99 *(978-1-4778-1698-1(4),* 9781477816981, Amazon Children's Publishing) Amazon Publishing.

Carter, Scott William. Wooden Bones. (ENG., Illus.). 160p. (J). (gr. 3-7). 2013. pap. 6.99 *(978-1-4424-2752-5(3))* 2012. 15.99 *(978-1-4424-2751-8(5))* Simon & Schuster Bks. For Young Readers. (Simon & Schuster Bks. For Young Readers).

Casanova, Mary. Riot. 2014. (Fesler-Lampert Minnesota Heritage Ser.). (ENG.). 128p. pap. 9.95 *(978-0-8166-9209-5(2))* Univ. of Minnesota Pr.

Catanese, P. W. Donny's Inferno. 2016. (Donny's Inferno Ser.: 1). (ENG.). 320p. (J). (gr. 3-7). 16.99 *(978-1-4814-3800-1(X),* Aladdin) Simon & Schuster Children's Publishing.

Cervantes, Jennifer. Tortilla Sun. 2014. (ENG.). 224p. (J). (gr. 3-7). pap. 6.99 *(978-1-4521-3150-4(3))* Chronicle Bks. LLC.

Chaconas, Dori. Pennies in a Jar, 1 vol. Lewin, Ted, illus. 2007. (ENG.). 32p. (J). (gr. 1-5). 16.95 *(978-1-56145-422-8(2))* Peachtree Pubs.

Chalifour, Francis. After. 2005. (ENG.). 144p. (J). (gr. 7). pap. 7.95 *(978-0-88776-705-0(2),* Tundra Bks.) Tundra Bks. CAN. Dist: Penguin Random Hse. LLC.

CHARLES, A. M. A. N. & 1st World Publishing. Dad & Me Go to School. 2006. 24p. per. 9.95 *(978-1-4218-9924-4(8))* 1st World Publishing, Inc.

Chase, Scott J. What Should I Do When I Grow Up? 2011. (Illus.). 30p. pap. 12.95 *(978-1-4575-0472-3(3))* Dog Ear Publishing, LLC.

Chaud, Benjamin. The Bear's Sea Escape. 2014. (ENG., Illus.). 32p. (J). (gr. -1-k). 17.99 *(978-1-4521-2743-9(3))* Chronicle Bks. LLC.

—The Bear's Song. 2013. (ENG., Illus.). 32p. (J). (gr. -1-k). 17.99 *(978-1-4521-1424-8(2))* Chronicle Bks. LLC.

—The Bear's Surprise. 2015. (ENG., Illus.). 32p. (J). (gr. -1-k). 17.99 *(978-1-4521-4028-5(6))* Chronicle Bks. LLC.

Choldenko, Gennifer. Dad & the Dinosaur. Santat, Dan, illus. 2017. (ENG.). 40p. (J). (gr. k-3). 17.99 *(978-0-399-24353-0(4),* G.P. Putnam's Sons Books for Young Readers) Penguin Young Readers Group.

Chris, Crowe. Mississippi Trial 1955. 2014. (ENG.). 240p. (YA). (gr. 7-12). 10.24 *(978-1-63245-211-5(1))* Lectorum Pubns., Inc.

Christopher, Matt. Centerfield Ballhawk. Beier, Ellen, illus. 2009. (New Peach Street Mudders Sports Library). 64p. (J). (gr. 2-4). lib. bdg. 23.93 *(978-1-59953-317-9(0))* Norwood Hse. Pr.

Ciminelli, Marilyn Johnson. Where's My Father? Ciminelli, Matthew Joseph, illus. 2006. (ENG.). 24p. per. 12.99 *(978-1-59926-657-2(1))* Xlibris Corp.

Civitella, Mark. Angus the Angler: Snapper Surprise. 2012. (Illus.). 16p. pap. 18.30 *(978-1-4772-3951-3(0))* AuthorHouse.

Clark, Kristin Elizabeth. Jess, Chunk, & the Road Trip to Infinity. 2016. (ENG.). 272p. (YA). 17.99 *(978-0-374-38006-9(6),* 9780374380069, Farrar, Straus & Giroux (BYR)) Farrar, Straus & Giroux.

Clark, Marian. Benji's Sicarii Sword. 2007. 156p. per. 13.99 *(978-1-60266-022-9(0))* Salem Author Services.

Clement, Ben & LoPatin, Norman. Stone's Throw Away. 2011. (Illus.). 74p. pap. 21.50 *(978-1-60976-477-7(3),* Eloquent Bks.) Strategic Book Publishing & Rights Agency (SBPRA).

Clements, Andrew. Head of the Class: Frindle - The Landry News - The Janitor's Boy. Selznick, Brian, illus. 2007. (ENG.). 416p. (J). (gr. 3-7). pap. 20.99 *(978-1-4169-4974-9(7),* Atheneum Bks. for Young Readers) Simon & Schuster Children's Publishing.

Climo, Liz. Rory the Dinosaur: Me & My Dad. 2015. (ENG., Illus.). 40p. (J). (gr. -1-3). 17.00 *(978-0-316-27728-0(2))* Little Brown & Co.

Coates, Doug. Pitching for Success: Character Lessons, the Joe Nuxhall Way. 2014. (ENG.). 16.95 *(978-1-939710-09-3(X))* Orange Frazer Pr.

Cochrane, Mick. Fitz. (ENG.). 192p. (YA). (gr. 7). 2013. pap. 8.99 *(978-0-375-84611-3(5),* Ember) 2012. 16.99 *(978-0-375-85683-9(8),* Knopf Bks. for Young Readers) Random Hse. Children's Bks.

Cockcroft, Jason. Counter Clockwise. 2009. 208p. (J). lib. bdg. 16.89 *(978-0-06-125555-7(6));* (ENG., Illus.). (gr. 5-18). 15.99 *(978-0-06-125554-0(8))* HarperCollins Pubs. (Tegen, Katherine Bks).

Cole, Gina, illus. Adapt. 2005. 40p. (J). 17.00 *(978-0-9659538-3-2(1))* Soul Vision Works Publishing.

Cole, Steve. Z. Rex. (ENG.). 256p. (J). (gr. 5-18). 2010. 8.99 *(978-0-14-241712-6(2),* Puffin Books) 2009. 16.99 *(978-0-399-25253-2(3);* Philomel Bks.) Penguin Young Readers Group.

Colfer, Eoin. The Arctic Incident. 2009. (Artemis Fowl Ser.). (ENG.). 304p. (J). (gr. 5-9). pap. 8.99 *(978-1-4231-2454-2(5))* Hyperion Pr.

—The Arctic Incident. 2003. (Artemis Fowl Ser.: 2). 277p. (J). (gr. 5-7). lib. bdg. 19.65 *(978-0-613-62927-0(2),* Turtleback) Turtleback Bks.

—Encuentro en el Artico. 2013. (Vintage Espanol Ser.).Tr. of Arctic Incident. (SPA.). 320p. (YA). pap. 9.95 *(978-0-345-80535-5(6),* Vintage Espanol) Knopf Doubleday Publishing Group.

Collins, Pat Lowery. The Deer Watch. Slonim, David, illus. 2013. (ENG.). 32p. (J). (gr. -1-2). 15.99 *(978-0-7636-4890-9(6))* Candlewick Pr.

Colum, Padraic & Pogány, Willy. The Adventures of Odysseus & the Tale of Troy. 2008. 280p. per. 27.95 *(978-0-548-81877-0(0))* Kessinger Publishing, LLC.

Comora, Madeleine. Rembrandt & Titus: Artist & Son. Locker, Thomas, illus. 2005. (ENG.). 32p. (J). (gr. 3-5). 17.95 *(978-1-55591-490-5(X))* Fulcrum Publishing.

Costello, David Hyde. Little Pig Saves the Ship. Costello, David Hyde, illus. 2017. (ENG., Illus.). 32p. (J). (gr. -1-2). 14.99 *(978-1-58089-715-0(0))* Charlesbridge Publishing, Inc.

Cotter, Bill. Beard in a Box. 2016. (ENG., Illus.). 40p. (J). (gr. -1-3). 17.99 *(978-0-553-50835-2(0),* Knopf Bks. for Young Readers) Random Hse. Children's Bks.

Coulton, Mia. Danny & Dad Go Shopping. Coulton, Mia, photos by. 2003. (ENG., Illus.). pap. 5.35 *(978-0-9720295-4-4(0))* Maryruth Bks., Inc.

Cowley, Joy. Freddy Bear & the Beach. Webb, Philip, illus. 2016. (Freddy Bear Ser.). (ENG.). 20p. (J). (gr. -1-k). bds. 12.99 *(978-1-927262-56-6(9))* Upstart Pr. NZL. Dist: Independent Pubs. Group.

Coy, John. Crackback. 2007. 201p. (gr. 7-12). 17.00 *(978-0-7569-8274-4(X))* Perfection Learning Corp.

Cray, Jordan. Most Wanted. 2009. (Danger. com Ser.: 7). (ENG.). 240p. (YA). (gr. 7). pap. 11.99 *(978-1-4169-9851-8(9),* Simon Pulse) Simon Pulse.

Creech, Sharon. Fishing in the Air. Raschka, Chris, illus. 2003. pap. 9.95 incl. audio *(978-1-59112-223-4(6))* Live Oak Media.

—Replay. (J). (gr. 3-7). 2013. (ENG.). 224p. pap. 6.99 *(978-0-06-054021-0(4))* 2005. 240p. lib. bdg. 16.89 *(978-0-06-054020-3(6),* Cotler, Joanna Books) HarperCollins Pubs.

Crow, E. J. The Eye Pocket. 2006. (Fantastic Society of Peculiar Adventures Ser.). (ENG., Illus.). 48p. (J). (gr. 2-4). per. *(978-1-933255-17-0(X))* DNA Pr.

Crowe, Sara. Bone Jack. 2017. (ENG.). 256p. (J). (gr. 5). 16.99 *(978-0-399-17651-7(9),* Philomel Bks.) Penguin Young Readers Group.

Cruz, Wilfredo. Charlie's Box: A Story about a Boy & His Magical Box. 2013. 24p. pap. 24.95 *(978-1-63000-514-6(2))* America Star Bks.

Cumberland, Marcie Hoye. The Tree at the Top of the Hill. 2006. 80p. pap. 12.95 *(978-1-60145-019-7(2))* Booklocker.com, Inc.

Cummings, Priscilla. Autumn Journey, 1 vol. Ben-Ami, Doron, illus. 2009. (ENG.). 120p. (J). pap. 12.95 *(978-0-87033-606-5(1),* 9780870336065, Cornell Maritime Pr./Tidewater Pubs.) Schiffer Publishing, Ltd.

Curtis, Christopher Paul. Bud, Not Buddy. unabr. ed. 2004. 256p. (J). (gr. 4-7). pap. 36.00 incl. audio *(978-0-8072-8210-6(3),* LYA 140 S{, Listening Library) Random Hse. Audio Publishing Group.

—Bud, Not Buddy. 2004. (ENG., Illus.). 288p. (J). (gr. 3-7). mass mkt. 7.99 *(978-0-553-49410-5(4),* Laurel Leaf) Random Hse. Children's Bks.

Curtis, Gavin. The Bat Boy & His Violin. Lewis, E. B., illus. 2015. 32p. pap. 8.00 *(978-1-61003-618-4(2))* Center for the Collaborative Classroom.

Daddy's Little Boy. (Daddy's / Mommy's Ser.). 32p. *(978-1-4054-9428-1(X))* Parragon, Inc.

Dahl, Lisa. Gorm the Viking: The Lost Voyage. 2013. 282p. (gr. 4-6). 26.95 *(978-1-4759-5809-6(9));* pap. 16.95 *(978-1-4759-5807-2(2))* iUniverse, Inc.

Dahl, Roald. Danny the Champion of the World. Blake, Quentin, illus. 2007. (ENG.). 240p. (J). (gr. 3-7). 7.99 *(978-0-14-241033-2(0),* Puffin Books) Penguin Young Readers Group.

—Danny the Champion of the World. Blake, Quentin, illus. 2007. 205p. (gr. 4-7). 18.40 *(978-1-4177-8611-4(6),* Turtleback) Turtleback Bks.

Daudet, Alphonse. The Siege of Berlin & Other Stories. 2004. reprint ed. pap. 15.95 *(978-1-4191-8248-8(X));* pap. 1.99 *(978-1-4192-8248-5(4))* Kessinger Publishing, LLC.

Davies, Benji. The Storm Whale. Davies, Benji, illus. 2014. (ENG., Illus.). 32p. (J). (gr. -1-3). 17.99 *(978-0-8050-9967-6(0),* 9780805099676, Holt, Henry & Co. Bks. For Young Readers) Holt, Henry & Co.

De la Peña, Matt. Mexican WhiteBoy. 2010. (ENG.). 256p. (YA). (gr. 9). pap. 9.99 *(978-0-440-23938-3(9),* Ember) Random Hse. Children's Bks.

—Mexican WhiteBoy. 2010. lib. bdg. 20.85 *(978-0-606-12316-7(4),* Turtleback) Turtleback Bks.

De La Ramee, Louise & Ouida. Bimbi. 2007. 152p. per. 13.95 *(978-1-60312-344-0(X));* 24.95 *(978-1-60312-682-3(1))* Aegypan.

Deans, Sis Boulos. Racing the Past. 2005. 151p. (J). (gr. 5-9). 13.65 *(978-0-7569-5068-2(6))* Perfection Learning Corp.

DeCamp, Alison. My Near-Death Adventures: I Almost Died. Again. 2016. (ENG., Illus.). 288p. (J). (gr. 3-7). 16.99 *(978-0-385-39048-4(3),* Crown Books For Young Readers) Random Hse. Children's Bks.

Denslow, W. W., illus. & adapted by. Humpty Dumpty. Denslow, W. W., adapted by. 2007. (Rare Book Collections). (ENG.). 16p. (J). (gr. -1-3). 9.95 *(978-1-55709-077-5(7))* Applewood Bks.

Deuker, Carl. Gym Candy. 2008. (ENG.). 320p. (YA). (gr. 7). pap. 9.99 *(978-0-547-07631-7(2))* Houghton Mifflin Harcourt Publishing Co.

—Gym Candy. 2008. 313p. 19.00 *(978-1-60686-376-3(2))* Perfection Learning Corp.

Dilloway, Margaret. Momotaro Xander & the Lost Island of Monsters. Yung, Choong, illus. 2016. (Momotaro Ser.). (ENG.). 310p. (J). (gr. 3-7). 16.99 *(978-1-4847-2487-3(9))* Disney Publishing Worldwide.

—Momotaro Xander & the Lost Island of Monsters. Yoon, Choong, illus. 2017. (Momotaro Ser.). (ENG.). 336p. (J). (gr. 3-7). pap. 6.99 *(978-1-4847-4681-3(3))* Hyperion Bks. for Children.

—Xander & the Lost Island of Monsters. 2017. (J). lib. bdg. 17.20 *(978-0-606-39503-8(2))* Turtleback Bks.

Dingwell, Carson. Rory of Cain's Mountain. 2005. pap. 16.95 *(978-1-4137-8756-6(8))* America Star Bks.

Disney Book Group Staff. Finding Nemo. 2012. (Read-Along Storybook & CD Ser.). (ENG.). 912p. (J). (gr. -1 — 1). pap. 6.99 *(978-1-4231-6028-1(2))* Disney Pr.

Disney Storybook Artists Staff, illus. Finding Nemo. 2007. (Play-A-Sound Ser.). 15p. (J). (gr. -1-3). 15.98 *(978-1-4127-8754-3(8))* Publications International, Ltd.

Dixon, Heather. Illusionarium. 2015. (ENG.). 368p. (YA). (gr. 8). 17.99 *(978-0-06-200105-4(1),* Greenwillow Bks.) HarperCollins Pubs.

d'Lacey, Chris. A Crown of Dragons. 2016. (UFiles Ser.: 3). (ENG.). 320p. (J). (gr. 3-7). 16.99 *(978-0-545-60883-1(X),* Scholastic Pr.) Scholastic, Inc.

Dodds, Dayle Ann. Minnie's Diner: A Multiplying Menu. Manders, John, illus. 2007. (ENG.). 40p. (J). (gr. k-3). pap. 6.99 *(978-0-7636-3313-4(5))* Candlewick Pr.

Doherty, Berlie. Treason. 2012. (ENG.). 352p. (J). (gr. 4-7). pap. 12.99 *(978-1-84939-121-4(1))* Andersen Pr. GBR. Dist: Independent Pubs. Group.

Dohr, Robert. The Pumpkin Se. Dewyea, Glenn, illus. 2012. 32p. pap. 13.50 *(978-1-61204-337-1(2),* Strategic Bk. Publishing) Strategic Book Publishing & Rights Agency (SBPRA).

Dorros, Arthur. Papá & Me. Gutierrez, Rudy, illus. 2008. (ENG.). 32p. (J). (gr. -1-3). 16.99 *(978-0-06-058156-5(5),* Rayo) HarperCollins Pubs.

Downie, David. Horrible Stories My Dad Told Me. Tatsi, Andreanna, tr. Seroya, Tea, illus. 2012. 44p. pap. *(978-1-922159-95-3(6))* Blue Peg Publishing.

—Horrible Stories My Dad Told Me. Nanevich, Julia, tr. Seroya, Tea, illus. 2012. 44p. pap. *(978-1-922159-90-8(5))* Blue Peg Publishing.

—Horrible Stories My Dad Told Me. Ivanova, Kalina, tr. Seroya, Tea, illus. 2012. 42p. pap. *(978-1-922159-96-0(4))* Blue Peg Publishing.

—Horrible Stories My Dad Told Me. M, Akiko, tr. Seroya, Tea, illus. 2012. 44p. pap. *(978-1-922159-94-6(8))* Blue Peg Publishing.

Doyle, Brian. You Can Pick Me up at Peggy's Cove, 1 vol. 2nd ed. 2006. (ENG.). 104p. (J). (gr. 4-8). pap. 6.95 *(978-0-88899-709-8(4))* Groundwood Bks. CAN. Dist: Publishers Group West (PGW).

Dube, Pierrette. How to Become a Perfect Knight in Five Days. Hamel, Caroline, illus. 2009. (Rainy Day Readers Ser.). 32p. (J). (gr. -1-3). 22.60 *(978-1-60754-373-2(7));* pap. 10.55 *(978-1-60754-374-9(5))* Windmill Bks.

Dunbar, Helene. These Gentle Wounds. 2014. (ENG.). 312p. (YA). pap. 11.99 *(978-0-7387-4027-0(6),* Flux) North Star Editions.

Dunseith, Peter. Bird of Heaven: The Story of a Swazi Sangoma. 2010. 257p. pap. *(978-0-624-04557-1(9))* NB Pubs. Ltd.

Durand, Hallie. Mitchell's License. Fucile, Tony, illus. 2011. (ENG.). 40p. (J). (gr. -1-2). 15.99 *(978-0-7636-4496-3(X))* Candlewick Pr.

Durbin, William. Blackwater Ben. 2014. (Fesler-Lampert Minnesota Heritage Ser.). (ENG., Illus.). 216p. pap. 11.95 *(978-0-8166-9192-0(4))* Univ. of Minnesota Pr.

Eggleton, Jill. Tony's Dad. Hawley, Kelvin, illus. 2003. (Rigby Sails Sailing Solo Ser.). (ENG.). 24p. (gr. 1-2). pap. 9.05 *(978-0-7578-3975-7(4))* Rigby Education.

Ehrmantraut, Brenda. Night Catch. Wehrman, Vicki, illus. 2014. (J). pap. *(978-1-934617-28-1(8))* Elva Resa Publishing, LLC.

Eisenstein, Ann E. Hiding Carly, a Sean Gray Junior Special Agent Mystery. 2013. 162p. pap. 9.99 *(978-1-935711-27-8(X))* Peak City Publishing, LLC.

Elster, Jean Alicia. Who's Jim Hines? 2008. (Great Lakes Books Ser.). (ENG., Illus.). 146p. (J). pap. 14.99 *(978-0-8143-3402-7(4),* 2162) Wayne State Univ. Pr.

Emerson, Kevin. The Fellowship for Alien Detection. 2013. (ENG.). 432p. (J). (gr. 3-7). 16.99 *(978-0-06-207185-9(8),* Waldon Pond Pr.) HarperCollins Pubs.

Emond, Stephen. Bright Lights, Dark Nights. 2015. (ENG., Illus.). 384p. (YA). (gr. 7). 17.99 *(978-1-62672-206-4(4))* Roaring Brook Pr.

Enderle, Dotti. Crosswire. 2010. (ENG.). 144p. (J). (gr. 4-6). 17.95 *(978-1-59078-751-9(X),* Calkins Creek) Boyds Mills Pr.

Erickson, Patricia. The Little Christmas Tree. 2012. 24p. (-18). pap. 17.99 *(978-1-4772-8610-4(1))* AuthorHouse.

Ering, Timothy Basil. The Almost Fearless Hamilton Squidlegger. Ering, Timothy Basil, illus. 2014. (ENG., Illus.). 48p. (J). (gr. -1-2). 16.99 *(978-0-7636-2357-9(1))* Candlewick Pr.

Erskine, Kathryn. The Absolute Value of Mike. 2012. (ENG.). 272p. (J). (gr. 5-18). pap. 7.99 *(978-0-14-242101-7(4),* Puffin Books) Penguin Young Readers Group.

Fickey, Brenda. Whispering Darkness. 2007. (ENG.). 136p. per. 24.95 *(978-1-4241-6932-0(1))* America Star Bks.

Fine, Anne. Countdown. 2006. (Yellow Bananas Ser.). (ENG., Illus.). 48p. (J). (gr. -1-3). lib. bdg. *(978-0-7787-0958-9(2))* Crabtree Publishing Co.

Flake, Sharon G. Bang! 2007. (ENG., Illus.). 304p. (J). (gr. 5-9). pap. 9.99 *(978-0-7868-4955-0(X),* Jump at the Sun) Hyperion Bks. for Children.

Flannery, John. Beard Boy. Weinberg, Steven, illus. 2016. (ENG.). 32p. (J). (-k). 16.99 *(978-0-399-17336-3(6),* G.P. Putnam's Sons Books for Young Readers) Penguin Young Readers Group.

Fleischman, Paul. The Animal Hedge. Ibatoulline, Bagram, illus. 2008. (ENG.). 48p. (J). (gr. 1-4). pap. 8.99 *(978-0-7636-3842-9(0))* Candlewick Pr.

Fogelin, Adrian. The Real Question, 1 vol. (ENG.). 256p. (YA). 2009. pap. 7.95 *(978-1-56145-501-0(6))* 2006. (gr. 7-18). 15.95 *(978-1-56145-383-2(8))* Peachtree Pubs.

Forest, G. Daddy's Different: A Look at Brain Injury Through a Child's Eyes. 2013. 34p. 21.95 *(978-1-4575-1742-6(6))* Dog Ear Publishing, LLC.

Fraley, Patty. Fear at Night: To Matthew. 2011. 24p. (gr. -1). pap. 12.79 *(978-1-4567-5555-3(2))* AuthorHouse.

Frazier, Sundee T. Brendan Buckley's Sixth-Grade Experiment. 2013. (ENG.). 288p. (J). (gr. 4-7). 6.99 *(978-0-385-74051-7(4),* Yearling) Random Hse. Children's Bks.

Frederick, Heather Vogel. The Voyage of Patience Goodspeed. 2004. (Aladdin Historical Fiction Ser.). 219p. (J). (gr. 3-7). 13.65 *(978-0-7569-2943-5(1))* Perfection Learning Corp.

Freed, Crissy. The Child Within. 2008. 60p. pap. 12.99 *(978-1-4343-8478-2(0))* AuthorHouse.

E
F
G

Freely, Jessica. All the Colors of Love. 2016. (ENG., Illus.). (YA). (gr. 9-12). 24.99 ***(978-1-63477-932-6(0)***, Harmony Ink Pr.) Dreamspinner Pr.

French, Jackie. My Pa the Polar Bear. 2015. (Wacky Families Ser.: 08). 128p. 5.99 *(978-0-207-20078-6(5))* HarperCollins Pubs. Australia AUS. Dist: HarperCollins Pubs.

Friedman, Stanley. Quantum Outlaws. 2010. 210p. pap. 11.95 *(978-1-935630-09-8(1))* Bellissima Publishing, LLC.

Fruchter, Jason, illus. Big Enough to Help. 2015. (Daniel Tiger's Neighborhood Ser.). (ENG.). 24p. (J). (gr. -1-1). pap. 5.99 *(978-1-4814-2942-9(6)*, Simon Spotlight) Simon Spotlight.

—I Love You, Dad. 2015. (Daniel Tiger's Neighborhood Ser.). (ENG.). 26p. (J). (gr. -1-k). bds. 8.99 *(978-1-4814-5736-1(5)*, Simon Spotlight) Simon Spotlight.

Fry, Erin. Losing It, 0 vols. 2014. (ENG.). 274p. (J). (gr. 5-7). pap. 9.99 *(978-1-4778-1668-4(2)*, 9781477816684, Amazon Children's Publishing) Amazon Publishing.

Galvin, Laura Gates. I Love My Daddy. 2011. (I Love My... Ser.). (ENG., Illus.). 16p. (J). (gr. -1-k). 6.95 *(978-1-60727-346-2(2))* Soundprints.

Gantos, Jack. Joey Pigza Loses Control. braille ed. 2003. (Joey Pigza Ser.: Bk. 2). (J). (gr. 2). spiral bd. *(978-0-616-15268-3(X))* Canadian National Institute for the Blind/Institut National Canadien pour les Aveugles.

—Joey Pigza Loses Control. unabr. ed. 2004. (Joey Pigza Ser.: Bk. 2). 195p. (J). (gr. 5-9). pap. 36.00 incl. audio *(978-0-8072-8726-2(1)*, LyA 248 SP, Listening Library) Random Hse. Audio Publishing Group.

—Joey Pigza Loses Control. 2014. (Joey Pigza Ser.: 2). (J). lib. bdg. 18.40 *(978-0-606-36561-1(3))* Turtleback Bks.

Gavin, Rohan. Knightley & Son - K-9. 2015. (Knightley & Son Ser.: 2). (ENG., Illus.). 304p. (YA). (gr. 4-6). 16.99 *(978-1-61963-494-7(5)*, 9781619634947, Bloomsbury USA Childrens) Bloomsbury Publishing USA.

Gerald, A. I. Hathlin Behind the Gates of Hell. 2005. 104p. pap. 14.95 *(978-1-4208-5567-8(0))* AuthorHouse.

Germein, Katrina. My Dad Thinks He's Funny. Jellett, Tom, illus. 2013. (ENG.). 32p. (J). (gr. k-3). 14.99 *(978-0-7636-6522-7(3))* Candlewick Pr.

Gilbert, Kelly Loy. Conviction. 2015. (ENG.). 352p. (YA). (gr. 7-12). 17.99 *(978-1-4231-9738-6(0))* Hyperion Bks. for Children.

Ginn, Jennifer. My Father Flies, 1 vol. Kramer, David, illus. 2013. (ENG.). 32p. (J). 16.99 *(978-0-7643-4385-8(8)*, 9780764343858) Schiffer Publishing, Ltd.

Ginsberg, Mort. Ukey & His Magical Ukulele. 2008. 75p. pap. 19.95 *(978-1-60610-395-1(4))* America Star Bks.

Going, K. L. King of the Screwups. 2010. (ENG., Illus.). 320p. (YA). (gr. 7). pap. 9.99 *(978-0-547-33166-9(5))* Houghton Mifflin Harcourt Publishing Co.

Golden Books. Race Against Time (Mr. Peabody & Sherman) Fransisco, Tina, illus. 2014. (Super Color with Stickers Ser.). (ENG.). 96p. (J). (gr. -1-2). pap. 3.99 *(978-0-385-37151-3(9)*, Golden Bks.) Random Hse. Children's Bks.

Gomes, Barbara K. Esau at the Big House. 2006. 76p. pap. 19.95 *(978-1-4241-2288-2(0))* America Star Bks.

Goode, John. Going the Distance. (YA). 2016. (ENG., Illus.). (gr. 8-12). 24.99 ***(978-1-63533-020-5(3)***, Harmony Ink Pr.) 2015. lib. bdg. *(978-1-63216-620-3(8))* Dreamspinner Pr.

Gordon, Amy. The Shadow Collector's Apprentice. 2012. (ENG.). 208p. (J). 16.95 *(978-0-8234-2359-0(X))* Holiday Hse., Inc.

Gould, Robert. Father & Son Read-Aloud Stories. Gurin, Lara, illus. 2006. (ENG.). 56p. (J). (gr. -1-k). 12.95 *(978-1-929945-67-2(1))* Big Guy Bks., Inc.

Grandfeather Press. Roly Poly Napoleon Discovers Colors. 2011. (ENG., Illus.). 36p. (J). pap. 6.99 *(978-0-9832355-0-7(3))* Grandfeather Pr.

Grant, Jacob. Little Bird's Bad Word. 2015. (ENG., Illus.). 32p. (J). (gr. -1-2). 16.99 *(978-1-250-05149-3(5)*, 9781250051493) Feiwel & Friends.

Gratz, Alan. Samurai Shortstop. 2008. (ENG.). 288p. (YA). (gr. 7-18). 7.99 *(978-0-14-241099-8(3)*, Speak) Penguin Young Readers Group.

Gray, Stephen J. For the Love of a Cloud Maker. 2013. 28p. pap. 13.55 *(978-1-4669-8004-4(4))* Trafford Publishing.

Green, Sally. Half Bad. (ENG.). (YA). 2015. (Half Bad Trilogy Ser.: 1). 432p. (gr. 7). pap. 9.99 *(978-0-14-751146-1(1)*, Speak) 2014. (Half Bad Trilogy Ser.: 1). 416p. (gr. 7). 18.99 *(978-0-670-01678-5(0)*, Viking Books for Young Readers)Pack. 2015. pap. 89.91 *(978-0-14-751591-9(2)*, Speak) Penguin Young Readers Group.

—Half Wild. 2015. (Half Bad Trilogy Ser.: 2). (ENG.). 432p. (YA). (gr. 7). 18.99 *(978-0-670-01713-3(2)*, Viking Books for Young Readers) Penguin Young Readers Group.

Green, Tim. Baseball Great. (Baseball Great Ser.: 1). (ENG.). (J). (gr. 3-7). 2010. 272p. pap. 6.99 *(978-0-06-162688-3(0))* 2009. 256p. 16.99 *(978-0-06-162686-9(4))* HarperCollins Pubs.

—Baseball Great. 2010. (Baseball Great Ser.: 1). (J). lib. bdg. 17.20 *(978-0-606-10356-5(2)*, Turtleback) Turtleback Bks.

—The Big Time. (Football Genius Ser.: 4). (ENG.). (J). (gr. 3-7). 2011. 304p. pap. 6.99 *(978-0-06-168621-4(2))* 2010. 288p. 16.99 *(978-0-06-168619-1(0))* HarperCollins Pubs.

—First Team. 2015. (ENG.). 352p. (J). (gr. 3-7). pap. 6.99 *(978-0-06-220876-7(4))* HarperCollins Pubs.

—First Team. 2014. (ENG.). 336p. (J). (gr. 3-7). 16.99 *(978-0-06-220875-0(6))* HarperCollins Pubs.

—First Team. 2015. (J). lib. bdg. 17.20 *(978-0-606-37616-7(X))* Turtleback Bks.

—Kid Owner. (J). (gr. 3-7). 2016. 352p. pap. 6.99 *(978-0-06-229380-0(X))* 2015. (ENG.). 336p. 16.99 *(978-0-06-229379-4(6))* HarperCollins Pubs.

—Lost Boy. (J). (gr. 3-7). 2016. 320p. pap. 6.99 *(978-0-06-231709-4(1))* 2015. (ENG.). 304p. 16.99 *(978-0-06-231708-7(3))* HarperCollins Pubs.

—New Kid. (ENG.). (J). (gr. 3-7). 2015. 336p. pap. 6.99 *(978-0-06-220873-6(X))* 2014. 320p. 16.99 *(978-0-06-220872-9(1))* HarperCollins Pubs.

—Rivals: A Baseball Great Novel. (Baseball Great Ser.: 2). (ENG.). (J). (gr. 3-7). 2011. 288p. pap. 6.99 *(978-0-06-162694-4(5))* 2010. 272p. 16.99 *(978-0-06-162692-0(9))* HarperCollins Pubs.

Guerra, S. F. Billy the Kid Is Not Crazy, 0 vols. 2013. (ENG.). 224p. (J). (gr. 4-6). 16.99 *(978-1-4778-1732-2(8)*, 9781477817322, Amazon Children's Publishing) Amazon Publishing.

Haig, Matt. To Be a Cat. Curtis, Stacy, illus. (ENG.). 304p. (J). (gr. 3-7). 2014. pap. 8.99 *(978-1-4424-5406-4(7))* 2013. 16.99 *(978-1-4424-5405-7(9))* Simon & Schuster Children's Publishing.

Hale, Marian. Dark Water Rising. 2010. (ENG.). 256p. (J). (gr. 5-9). pap. 7.99 *(978-0-312-62908-3(7)*, 9780312629083) Square Fish.

Hale, Nick. The Edge. 2012. (Striker Ser.: 3). (ENG.). 224p. (J). (gr. 5-7). pap. 7.99 *(978-1-4052-5685-8(0))* Egmont Bks., Ltd. GBR. Dist: Independent Pubs. Group.

Hall, Mary Lou. Wirewalker. 2016. (ENG.). 304p. (YA). (gr. 7). 17.99 *(978-0-670-01646-4(2)*, Viking Books for Young Readers) Penguin Young Readers Group.

Halls, Kelly Milner. Dive into Danger. Parks, Phil, illus. 2016. (Animal Rescues Ser.: 2). (ENG.). 88p. (J). (gr. 4-8). lib. bdg. 25.32 *(978-1-4677-7220-4(8)*, Darby Creek) Lerner Publishing Group.

Harmon, Michael. Stick. 2015. (ENG.). 240p. (YA). (gr. 9). 17.99 *(978-0-385-75436-1(1))*; lib. bdg. 20.99 *(978-0-385-75437-8(X))* Random Hse. Children's Bks. (Knopf Bks. for Young Readers).

Harper, Lee. Snow! Snow! Snow! Harper, Lee, illus. 2009. (ENG., Illus.). 40p. (J). (gr. -1-3). 14.99 *(978-1-4169-8454-2(2)*, Simon & Schuster/Paula Wiseman Bks.) Simon & Schuster/Paula Wiseman Bks.

Harrar, Frank W. Wee Dragonslayers. Galan-Robles, Francisco, illus. 2008. 45p. pap. 24.95 *(978-1-60610-851-2(4))* America Star Bks.

Harrar, George. The Trouble with Jeremy Chance. Thayer, Elizabeth, illus. 2007. (Historical Fiction for Young Readers Ser.). (ENG.). 168p. (J). (gr. 2-8). per. 6.95 *(978-1-57131-669-1(8))* Milkweed Editions.

Harris, Kandi. Prince, the Future King: A Father's Example Wyman, M. C. & Anderson, Bill, illus. 2005. 32p. (J). bds. 19.95 *(978-0-9770331-0-2(4))* Harris, K Publishing, Inc.

Hartman, Brett. Cadillac Chronicles. 2012. (ENG.). 304p. (J). (gr. 10). 16.95 *(978-1-935955-41-2(1))* Cinco Puntos Pr.

Haseley, Dennis. My Father Doesn't Know about the Woods & Me. 2013. (ENG., Illus.). 32p. (J). (gr. -1-3). 16.99 *(978-1-4814-0159-3(9)*, Atheneum Bks. for Young Readers) Simon & Schuster Children's Publishing.

Hawke, Rosanne. The Keeper. (Illus.). 164p. (J). pap. *(978-0-7344-0068-0(3)*, Lothian Children's Bks.) Hachette Australia.

Healy, Tim. The Birthday Chronicles: Volume I. 2013. 36p. pap. 15.99 *(978-1-4624-0628-9(9)*, Inspiring Voices) Author Solutions, Inc.

Helland, Jenna. The August 5. 2015. (ENG., Illus.). 320p. (YA). (gr. 7). 16.99 *(978-0-374-38264-3(6)*, 9780374382643, Farrar, Straus & Giroux (BYR)) Farrar, Straus & Giroux.

Hemmerle, Jamie. The Lost & Found Summer. 2010. (Illus.). 312p. pap. 15.95 *(978-1-4327-6268-1(0))* Outskirts Pr., Inc.

Hemphill, Helen. Long Gone Daddy. (ENG.). 176p. 2014. (YA). (gr. 6). pap. 8.95 *(978-1-62091-737-4(8))* 2006. (J). (gr. 8-12). 16.95 *(978-1-932425-38-3(1)*, Lemniscaat) Boyds Mills Pr.

Hemyng, Bracebridge. Jack Harkaway & His Son's Escape from the Brigand's of Greece. 2007. (ENG.). 342p. pap. 23.99 *(978-1-4264-2290-4(3))*; 386p. pap. 26.99 *(978-1-4264-2325-3(X))* Creative Media Partners, LLC.

—Jack Harkaway & His Son's Escape from the Brigands of Greece. 2004. reprint ed. pap. 1.99 *(978-1-4192-2705-9(X))* Kessinger Publishing, LLC.

Henighan, Tom. Demon in My View. 2007. (ENG.). 176p. (J). (gr. 4). pap. 12.99 *(978-1-55002-656-6(9)*, Boardwalk Bks.) Dundurn CAN. Dist: Ingram Publisher Services.

Henry, April. Girl, Stolen. 2010. (Girl, Stolen Ser.). (ENG.). 224p. (YA). (gr. 7-12). 18.99 *(978-0-8050-9005-5(3)*, 9780805090055, Holt, Henry & Co. Bks. For Young Readers) Holt, Henry & Co.

Herlong, M. H. The Great Wide Sea. 2010. (ENG.). 288p. (YA). (gr. 7-18). 8.99 *(978-0-14-241670-9(3)*, Puffin Books) Penguin Young Readers Group.

Hernandez, David. Suckerpunch. 2007. (ENG.). 224p. (YA). (gr. 9-18). 17.99 *(978-0-06-117330-1(4)*, HarperTeen) HarperCollins Pubs.

Herrick, Steven. Cold Skin. 2009. (ENG.). 279p. (YA). (gr. 9-18). 18.95 *(978-1-59078-572-0(X)*, Front Street) Boyds Mills Pr.

Hibbitts, Mark. Alfie Potts: Alfie & the Mind Virus. Purchase, Brendan, illus. 2011. (ENG.). 40p. (J). *(978-1-907498-60-2(5)*, Book Shaker) Lean Marketing Pr.

—Alfie Potts: Alfie & the Seminar. Purchase, Brendan, illus. 2011. (ENG.). 40p. pap. *(978-1-907498-75-6(3)*, Book Shaker) Lean Marketing Pr.

Hillert, Margaret. Dear Dragon's Day with Father. Schimmell, David, illus. 2008. (BeginningtoRead Ser.). 32p. (J). (-2). (ENG.). pap. 11.94 ***(978-1-68404-010-0(8))***; lib. bdg. 22.60 *(978-1-59953-162-5(3))* Norwood Hse. Pr.

Hillert, Margaret. Dear Dragon's Day with Father (Querido Dragon Pasa el Dia con Papa) Del Risco, Eida, tr. from ENG. Schimmell, David, illus. 2010. (BeginningtoRead Ser.). (SPA & ENG.). 32p. (J). (gr. k-2). lib. bdg. 22.60 *(978-1-59953-360-5(X))* Norwood Hse. Pr.

Hippie Bob. Robbie & the Magic Mirror: Who Do You See? 2009. 28p. pap. 14.99 *(978-1-4490-0437-8(7))* AuthorHouse.

Holmberg, Bo R. A Day with Dad. Eriksson, Eva, illus. 2008. (ENG.). 32p. (J). (gr. -1-3). 15.99 *(978-0-7636-3221-2(X))* Candlewick Pr.

Holt, Sharon & Proudfoot, Dean. Don't Embarrass Me, Dad! 2008. (Rigby Focus Forward: Level H Ser.). (Illus.). 24p. (J). (gr. 4-7). pap. *(978-1-4190-3735-1(8)*, Rigby) Pearson Education Australia.

Horn, Peter. When I Grow Up... Kadmon, Cristina, illus. 2014. 32p. pap. 8.00 *(978-1-61003-370-1(1))* Center for the Collaborative Classroom.

Howe, James. Also Known As Elvis. (Misfits Ser.). (ENG., Illus.). (J). (gr. 5-9). 2015. 304p. pap. 7.99 *(978-1-4424-4511-6(4))* 2014. 288p. 16.99 *(978-1-4424-4510-9(6)*, Atheneum Bks. for Young Readers) Simon & Schuster Children's Publishing.

Howland, Leila. Nantucket Summer [Nantucket Blue & Nantucket Red Bind-Up]. 2017. (Nantucket Blue Ser.). (ENG.). 608p. (YA). (gr. 9-17). pap. 11.99 *(978-1-368-00212-7(9))* Hyperion Bks. for Children.

Hueller, Andy. Skipping Stones at the Center of the Earth: A Middle Grade Novel. 2011. (J). pap. 8.99 *(978-1-59955-488-4(7)*, Bonneville Bks.) Cedar Fort, Inc./CFI Distribution.

Hughes, Monica. The Golden Aquarians. 2009. (ENG.). 192p. (YA). (gr. 7-7). pap. 9.99 *(978-1-4424-0223-2(7)*, Simon & Schuster Bks. For Young Readers) Simon & Schuster Bks. For Young Readers.

Hughes, V. I. Aziz the Story Teller. Czernecki, Stefan, illus. 2006. 29p. (J). (gr. k-4). reprint ed. 17.00 *(978-1-4223-5298-4(6))* DIANE Publishing Co.

Hunter, Muata. Check Up. 2009. 94p. pap. 24.99 *(978-0-557-04443-6(X))* Lulu Pr., Inc.

Huppert, Susan. The Perfect Gift. White, Rachel, illus. 2007. 24p. (J). per. *(978-0-9799635-0-6(8))* Homegrown Pubns.,LLC.

Hutchinson, Wanda Phillips. The Bee Man. 2009. 24p. pap. 14.49 *(978-1-4490-3596-9(5))* AuthorHouse.

James, Dalton. The Sneakiest Pirates. 2008. 20p. pap. 10.95 *(978-1-4327-2477-1(0))* Outskirts Pr., Inc.

Jang, Ji-yun. Father's Road novel. Jun, Tan, illus. 2016. (J). 10.00 *(978-0-8028-5472-8(9)*, Eerdmans Bks For Young Readers) Eerdmans, William B. Publishing Co.

Jarmes, Jon Jeffery. Jason Post: Magic at the Downs. 2006. (YA). 19.95 *(978-0-9770483-0-4(6))* Speech Publishing Hse.

The Jesus Jeepney. 2007. 32p. pap. 4.50 *(978-0-8341-2276-5(6)*, 083-412-2766) Beacon Hill Pr. of Kansas City.

Jeter, Derek. Change Up. 2016. (Jeter Publishing Ser.). (ENG., Illus.). 176p. (J). (gr. 3-7). 16.99 *(978-1-4814-6445-1(0)*, Simon & Schuster/Paula Wiseman Bks.) Simon & Schuster/Paula Wiseman Bks.

Jiang, Ji-Li. Red Kite, Blue Kite. Ruth, Greg, illus. 2013. (ENG.). 32p. (J). (gr. 1-3). 17.99 *(978-1-4231-2753-6(6))* Hyperion Pr.

Johnson, Peter. What Happened. 2007. (ENG.). 136p. (J). (gr. 8-18). 16.95 *(978-1-932425-67-3(5)*, Front Street) Boyds Mills Pr.

Johnston, Tony. Bone by Bone by Bone. 2007. (ENG.). 192p. (YA). (gr. 7-12). 29.99 *(978-1-59643-113-3(X)*, 9781596431133) Roaring Brook Pr.

Johri, Subia Ali. The Snackman & His Son, 1 vol. Johri, Shaan Mohammad, illus. 2010. 28p. 24.95 *(978-1-4512-0978-5(9))* America Star Bks.

Jones, F. Thomas. Backstep Forward. 2011. 184p. 24.59 *(978-1-4520-8441-1(6))*; pap. 14.03 *(978-1-4520-8440-4(8))* AuthorHouse.

Jones, Patrick. Combat Zone. 2015. (ENG.). 96p. (YA). (gr. 6-12). pap. 7.99 *(978-1-4677-8094-0(4))* Lerner Publishing Group.

—Doing Right. 2015. (J). 27.99 *(978-1-4677-7691-2(2))*; (ENG.). 104p. (gr. 6-12). lib. bdg. 27.99 *(978-1-4677-5803-1(5))* Lerner Publishing Group.

—Out of the Tunnel. 2014. (Red Zone Ser.: 1). (ENG.). 104p. (YA). (gr. 6-12). pap. 7.95 *(978-1-4677-4471-3(9)*, Darby Creek); lib. bdg. 27.93 *(978-1-4677-2126-4(3))* Lerner Publishing Group.

—Returning to Normal. 2015. (J). 104p. 9.99 *(978-1-4677-7700-1(5))*; (ENG.). 112p. (gr. 6-12). lib. bdg. 27.99 *(978-1-4677-5799-7(3))* Lerner Publishing Group.

—Taking Sides. 2015. (J). 97p. 9.99 *(978-1-4677-7703-2(X))*; (ENG.). 104p. (gr. 6-12). lib. bdg. 27.99 *(978-1-4677-5800-0(0))* Lerner Publishing Group.

—Triangle Choke. 2013. (Dojo Ser.). (ENG.). 136p. (YA). (gr. 6-12). pap. 7.95 *(978-1-4677-1487-7(9))*; lib. bdg. 27.93 *(978-1-4677-0630-8(2))* Lerner Publishing Group. (Darby Creek).

Jones, Patrick & Chartier, Brent. Collateral Damage. 2015. (ENG.). 128p. (YA). (gr. 6-12). pap. 7.99 *(978-1-4677-8091-9(X))* Lerner Publishing Group.

Jones, V. M. Out of Reach, 0 vols. unabr. ed. 2013. (ENG.). 272p. (J). (gr. 7-9). pap. 9.99 *(978-1-4778-1705-6(0)*, 9781477817056, Amazon Children's Publishing) Amazon Publishing.

Jordan, Terry W. Carson Goes to Work with Dad. 2012. 28p. pap. 24.95 *(978-1-4626-8892-0(6))* America Star Bks.

Jules, Jacqueline. Never Say a Mean Word Again: A Tale from Medieval Spain. Bernhard, Durga Yael, illus. 2014. (ENG.). 32p. (J). (gr. -1-3). 16.95 *(978-1-937786-20-5(X)*, Wisdom Tales) World Wisdom, Inc.

Jury, Walter & Fine, Sarah. Burn. 2015. (ENG.). 352p. (YA). (gr. 7). bds. 17.99 *(978-0-399-16068-4(X)*, G.P. Putnam's Sons Books for Young Readers) Penguin Young Readers Group.

Kaulen, Diane Bouman. In the Wake of Suicide: A Child's Journey. McAdoo, Grami & McAdoo, O'Pa, illus. 2008. (J). (gr. 3-5). 14.95 *(978-0-9764026-5-7(3))* Longhorn Creek Pr.

Kehret, Peg. Abduction! 2006. (ENG.). 224p. (J). (gr. 5-18). 6.99 *(978-0-14-240617-5(1)*, Puffin Books) Penguin Young Readers Group.

—Abduction! 2007. 215p. (gr. 3-7). 17.00 *(978-0-7569-8282-9(0))* Perfection Learning Corp.

Kendall, Christine. Riding Chance. 2016. (ENG.). 224p. (J). (gr. 5-9). 16.99 *(978-0-545-92404-7(9)*, Scholastic Pr.) Scholastic, Inc.

Kennedy Tosten, S. Troy's Amazing Universe: A for Aliens. 2005. 124p. pap. 13.95 *(978-1-59113-672-9(5))* Booklocker.com, Inc.

Kerr, M. E., pseud. If I Love You, Am I Trapped Forever?, 0 vols. 2011. (ENG.). 192p. (J). (gr. 7-9). pap. 9.99 *(978-0-7614-5839-5(5)*, 9780761458395, Amazon Children's Publishing) Amazon Publishing.

Kerr, P. B., pseud. One Small Step. 2009. (ENG.). 320p. (J). (gr. 3-9). pap. 8.99 *(978-1-4169-4214-6(9)*, McElderry, Margaret K. Bks.) McElderry, Margaret K. Bks.

Key, Watt. Dirt Road Home. 2011. (Alabama Moon Ser.: 2). (ENG.). 240p. (J). (gr. 5-9). pap. 8.99 *(978-0-312-67435-9(X)*, 9780312674359) Square Fish.

King, J. Eric & Graham, Greg. Byron Carmichael Book One: The Human Corpse Trade. Mizer, Lindsay, ed. Warner, Michael, illus. 2008. (ENG.). 408p. (gr. 8-12). 18.95 *(978-0-615-15770-2(X))* G & K Publishing.

Kirk, Connie Ann. Sky Dancers, 1 vol. Hale, Christy, illus. 2013. (ENG.). 32p. (J). (gr. 2-4). pap. 8.95 *(978-1-62014-147-2(7))* Lee & Low Bks., Inc.

Klass, David. Grandmaster. 2014. (ENG.). 240p. (YA). (gr. 7). 16.99 *(978-0-374-32771-2(8)*, 9780374327712, Farrar, Straus & Giroux (BYR)) Farrar, Straus & Giroux.

Klise, Kate. Homesick. 2012. (ENG.). 192p. (J). (gr. 5-9). 16.99 *(978-1-250-00842-8(5)*, 9781250008428) Feiwel & Friends.

Konigsberg, Bill. Honestly Ben. 2017. (ENG.). 336p. (J). (gr. 9). 17.99 *(978-0-545-85826-7(7))* Scholastic, Inc.

Konigsburg, E. L. Journey to an 800 Number. 2008. (ENG.). 160p. (J). (gr. 4-8). pap. 6.99 *(978-1-4169-5875-8(4)*, Atheneum Bks. for Young Readers) Simon & Schuster Children's Publishing.

Korman, Gordon. Born to Rock. 2008. (ENG.). 272p. (J). (gr. 7-17). per. 8.99 *(978-0-7868-0921-9(3))* Hyperion Pr.

—Born to Rock. 2011. 10.36 *(978-0-7848-3479-4(2)*, Everbind) Marco Bk. Co.

Korman, Gordon. Born to Rock (repackage) 2017. (ENG.). 240p. (J). (gr. 5-9). pap. 8.99 ***(978-1-4847-9841-6(4))*** Hyperion Bks. for Children.

Kraus, Daniel. Rotters. 2012. (ENG.). 464p. (YA). (gr. 9). pap. 10.99 *(978-0-385-73858-3(7)*, Ember) Random Hse. Children's Bks.

Kraus, Robert. Daddy Long Ears' Halloween. 2014. (ENG., Illus.). 32p. (J). (gr. -1-3). 13.99 *(978-1-4814-3108-8(0)*, Simon & Schuster/Paula Wiseman Bks.) Simon & Schuster/Paula Wiseman Bks.

Krebs, Patricia, illus. On Your Mark, Get Set, Go! 2009. 32p. (J). 16.95 *(978-0-9796380-1-5(1))* Three Wishes Publishing Co.

Kuhlman, Evan. The Last Invisible Boy. Coovert, J. P., illus. (ENG.). 240p. (J). (gr. 5-9). 2010. pap. 6.99 *(978-1-4169-6089-8(9))* 2008. 16.99 *(978-1-4169-5797-3(9))* Simon & Schuster Children's Publishing. (Atheneum Bks. for Young Readers).

Kwaymullina, Ezekiel. My Amazing Dad. Jellett, Tom, illus. 2016. (ENG.). 24p. (J). (gr. -1-k). 16.99 *(978-1-5107-0584-5(8)*, Sky Pony Pr.) Skyhorse Publishing Co., Inc.

LaFaye, A. Worth. unabr. ed. 2006. (Live Oak Histories Ser.). (J). (gr. 3-6). pap. 28.95 incl. audio compact disk *(978-1-59519-767-2(2))*; pap. 24.95 incl. audio *(978-1-59519-766-5(4))* Live Oak Media.

—Worth. 2006. 144p. (J). (gr. 4-7). 13.65 *(978-0-7569-6614-0(0))* Perfection Learning Corp.

—Worth. 2006. (ENG.). 160p. (J). (gr. 4-7). reprint ed. pap. 7.99 *(978-1-4169-1624-6(5)*, Simon & Schuster Bks. For Young Readers) Simon & Schuster Bks. For Young Readers.

LaFevers, R. L. The Forging of the Blade. 2006. (ENG.). 144p. (J). (gr. 3-7). 5.99 *(978-0-14-240557-4(4)*, Puffin Books) Penguin Young Readers Group.

Laínez, René Colato. My Shoes & I. Broeck, Fabricio Vanden, illus. 2010. (ENG.). 32p. (J). (gr. 2-4). 16.95 *(978-1-59078-385-6(9))* Boyds Mills Pr.

Laird, Elizabeth. Jake's Tower. 2017. (ENG.). 160p. (J). (gr. 3-8). pap. 9.99 ***(978-1-5098-2671-1(8))*** Pan Macmillan GBR. Dist: Independent Pubs. Group.

Lamkin, Robert J. Tommy's Train. 2008. 44p. pap. 24.95 *(978-1-60672-147-6(X))* America Star Bks.

Laurence, Yep. Dragonwings. 25th rev. ed. 2014. (Golden Mountain Chronicles Ser.). (ENG.). 336p. (J). (gr. 12-12). 11.24 *(978-1-63245-143-9(3))* Lectorum Pubns., Inc.

Lawlor, Laurie. He Will Go Fearless. (ENG.). 224p. (J). (gr. 5-9). 2012. pap. 10.99 *(978-0-689-86580-0(5))* 2006. 15.95 *(978-0-689-86579-4(1))* Simon & Schuster Bks. For Young Readers. (Simon & Schuster Bks. For Young Readers).

Leblanc, A. J. Donnie & His First Surf Lesson. 2012. 20p. pap. 24.95 *(978-1-4626-8646-9(X))* PublishAmerica, Inc.

Lee, Ingrid. Cat Found. 2013. (ENG.). 176p. (J). (gr. 3-7). pap. 6.99 *(978-0-545-35108-9(1)*, Chicken Hse., The) Scholastic, Inc.

Leighfield, D. K. Abel's Song. 2013. 132p. (gr. 2-4). pap. 11.95 *(978-1-4908-1327-1(6)*, WestBow Pr.) Author Solutions, Inc.

Lemieux, Jean. Toby Shoots for Infinity. Cummins, Sarah, tr. from FRE. Casson, Sophie, illus. 2005. (Formac First Novels Ser.: 55). (ENG.). 64p. (J). (gr. 2-5). 14.95 *(978-0-88780-685-8(6)*, 9780887806858) Formac Publishing Co., Ltd. CAN. Dist: Casemate Pubs. & Bk. Distributors, LLC.

—Toby Shoots for Infinity, 1 vol. Cummins, Sarah, tr. from FRE. Casson, Sophie, illus. 2005. (Formac First Novels Ser.: 55). (ENG.). 64p. (J). (gr. 2-5). 4.95 *(978-0-88780-684-1(8)*, 9780887806841) Formac Publishing Co., Ltd. CAN. Dist: Casemate Pubs. & Bk. Distributors, LLC.

Leno, Jay. If Roast Beef Could Fly. Whitehead, S. B., illus. 2005. 30p. (J). (gr. k-4). 18.00 *(978-0-7567-9365-4(3))* DIANE Publishing Co.

Leonard, M. G. Beetle Boy. (ENG.). (J). (gr. 3-7). 2017. 304p. pap. 6.99 ***(978-0-545-85347-7(8))*** 2016. 288p. 16.99 *(978-0-545-85346-0(X))* Scholastic, Inc. (Chicken Hse., The).

Leonard, Niall. Crusher. 2013. (ENG.). 368p. (YA). (gr. 9). pap. 9.99 *(978-0-385-74362-4(9)*, Ember) Random Hse. Children's Bks.

LeTourneau, Marie & Baty, Danielle Reed. The Mice of Bistrot des Sept Frères. LeTourneau, Marie, illus. 2006. (ENG., Illus.). 32p. (J). (gr. -1-3). 15.95 *(978-0-9749303-6-7(9))* Tanglewood Pr.

Lewman, David & Gomez, Yuliana. Batter up!/¡a Batear!(SpongeBob SquarePants) Random House, illus. 2014. (Pictureback Ser.). (ENG.). 24p. (J). (gr. -1-2). 3.99 *(978-0-385-38436-0(X)*, Random Hse. Bks. for Young Readers) Random Hse. Children's Bks.

Lignell, Kirk. Listen to the Raindrops: Featuring the Storm Song. Lignell, Brent, illus. 2007. 32p. (J). (gr. -1-3). 17.95 *(978-1-932399-15-8(1))* Huron River Pr.

Lindgren, Astrid. Mio, My Son. Morgan, Jill, tr. from SWE. Wikland, Ilon, illus. 2015.Tr. of Mio, Min Mio. (ENG.). 184p. (J). (gr. 3-7). 16.95 *(978-1-59017-870-6(X)*, NYR Children's Collection) New York Review of Bks., Inc., The.

Llanes, Adrian & Llanes, Christi. There's a Monster in My Closet. 2011. 28p. pap. 12.03 *(978-1-4634-4054-1(5))* AuthorHouse.

Lloyd-Jones, Sally. Just Because You're Mine. Endersby, Frank, illus. 2011. (ENG.). 32p. (J). (gr. -1-2). 16.99 *(978-0-06-201476-4(5))* HarperCollins Pubs.

Lo, Rich. Father's Chinese Opera. Lo, Rich, illus. 2014. (ENG., Illus.). 40p. (J). (gr. -1-k). 16.95 *(978-1-62873-610-6(0)*, Sky Pony Pr.) Skyhorse Publishing Co., Inc.

Loever, Charmaine. David's Big Break. Bohman, Natasha, illus. 2008. 52p. pap. 22.99 *(978-1-4389-3173-9(5))* AuthorHouse.

Lomp, Stephan. Papasaurus. 2017. (ENG., Illus.). 40p. (J). 16.99 *(978-1-4521-4425-2(7))* Chronicle Bks. LLC.

London, Jonathan. Froggy's Day with Dad. Remkiewicz, Frank, illus. 2006. (Froggy Ser.). (ENG.). 32p. (J). (gr. -1-k). pap. 6.99 *(978-0-14-240634-2(1)*, Puffin Books) Penguin Young Readers Group.

—Giving Thanks. Manchess, Gregory, illus. 2011. (ENG.). 32p. (J). (gr. -1-2). pap. 6.99 *(978-0-7636-5594-5(5))* Candlewick Pr.

—Grizzly Peak. London, Sean, illus. 2017. (Aaron's Wilderness Ser.). (ENG.). 174p. (YA). pap. 12.99 *(978-1-943328-77-2(3)*, West Winds Pr.) Graphic Arts Ctr. Publishing Co.

Lorenzi, Natalie Dias. A Long Pitch Home. 2016. (ENG.). 256p. (J). (gr. 4-7). lib. bdg. 16.95 *(978-1-58089-713-6(4))* Charlesbridge Publishing, Inc.

Lubar, David. Character, Driven: A Novel. 2016. (ENG.). 304p. (YA). 17.99 *(978-0-7653-1633-2(1)*, 9780765316332, Tor Teen) Doherty, Tom Assocs., LLC.

Lunde, Stein Erik. My Father's Arms Are a Boat. Dickson, Kari, tr. from NOR. Torseter, Øyvind, illus. 2013. (ENG.). 40p. (J). (gr. -1). 15.95 *(978-1-59270-124-7(8))* Enchanted Lion Bks., LLC.

Luper, Eric. Seth Baumgartner's Love Manifesto. 2010. (ENG.). 304p. (YA). (gr. 8-18). 16.99 *(978-0-06-182753-2(3))* HarperCollins Pubs.

Lupica, Mike. The Big Field. 2009. (ENG.). 272p. (J). (gr. 3-7). 7.99 *(978-0-14-241910-6(9)*, Puffin Books) Penguin Young Readers Group.

—The Extra Yard. 2016. (Home Team Ser.). (ENG., Illus.). 304p. (J). (gr. 3-7). 17.99 *(978-1-4814-1000-7(8)*, Simon & Schuster Bks. For Young Readers) Simon & Schuster Bks. For Young Readers.

—Game Changers. (Game Changers Ser.: 1). (ENG.). 224p. (J). (gr. 3-7). 2013. pap. 6.99 *(978-0-545-38179-6(7))*Bk. 1. 2012. 16.99 *(978-0-545-38182-6(7))* Scholastic, Inc. (Scholastic Pr.).

—Hero. (ENG.). 304p. (J). (gr. 5-18). 2011. 7.99 *(978-0-14-241960-1(5)*, Puffin Books) 2010. 17.99 *(978-0-399-25283-9(5)*, Philomel Bks.) Penguin Young Readers Group.

—Hero. 2011. lib. bdg. 18.40 *(978-0-606-23142-8(0)*, Turtleback) Turtleback Bks.

—Hot Hand, 1 vol. 2012. (Comeback Kids Ser.). (ENG.). 176p. (J). (gr. 4-8). lib. bdg. 27.07 *(978-1-59961-175-4(9))* Spotlight.

—Last Man Out. (ENG.). (J). (gr. 5). 2017. 272p. 8.99 ***(978-0-14-751491-2(6)***, Puffin Books) 2016. 256p. 17.99 *(978-0-399-17279-3(3)*, Philomel Bks.) Penguin Young Readers Group.

—Qb 1. 2013. (ENG.). 272p. (J). (gr. 5). 17.99 *(978-0-399-25228-0(2)*, Philomel Bks.) Penguin Publishing Group.

—Qb 1. 2014. (ENG.). 288p. (J). (gr. 5). pap. 7.99 *(978-0-14-751152-2(6)*, Puffin Books) Penguin Young Readers Group.

—Travel Team. l.t. ed. 2005. (Thorndike Literacy Bridge Ser.). 400p. (J). (gr. 4-7). lib. bdg. 23.95 *(978-0-7862-7415-4(8))* Thorndike Pr.

—Travel Team & the Big Field. 2011. (ENG.). 544p. (J). (gr. 5-18). 8.99 *(978-0-14-241984-7(2)*, Puffin Books) Penguin Young Readers Group.

Luthardt, Kevin. Flying!, 1 vol. Luthardt, Kevin, illus. (ENG., Illus.). 32p. (J). (gr. -1-1). 2013. 7.95 *(978-1-56145-724-3(8))* 2009. 15.95 *(978-1-56145-430-3(3))* Peachtree Pubs.

Lyga, Barry. Blood of My Blood. 2014. (ENG.). 480p. (YA). (gr. 10-17). 18.00 *(978-0-316-19870-7(6))* Little, Brown Bks. for Young Readers.

—I Hunt Killers. (ENG.). (YA). (gr. 10-17). 2014. 464p. mass mkt. 8.00 *(978-0-316-28363-2(0))* 2013. 384p. pap. 10.00 *(978-0-316-12583-3(0))* Little, Brown Bks. for Young Readers.

Lynch, Chris. Hothouse. 2010. (ENG.). 208p. (YA). (gr. 8-18). 16.99 *(978-0-06-167379-5(X)*, HarperTeen) HarperCollins Pubs.

—Irreversible. 2016. (ENG., Illus.). 352p. (YA). (gr. 7). 17.99 *(978-1-4814-2985-6(X)*, Simon & Schuster Bks. For Young Readers) Simon & Schuster Bks. For Young Readers.

—Killing Time in Crystal City. 2015. (ENG., Illus.). 240p. (YA). (gr. 7). 17.99 *(978-1-4424-4011-1(2)*, Simon & Schuster Bks. For Young Readers) Simon & Schuster Bks. For Young Readers.

—Shadow Boxer. 2013. (ENG.). 176p. (YA). (gr. 7). 16.99 *(978-1-4424-5811-6(9)*, Simon & Schuster Bks. For Young Readers) Simon & Schuster Bks. For Young Readers.

Lynch, F. Michael. I Will Always Need You. 2008. 24p. pap. 14.50 *(978-1-60693-141-7(5)*, Eloquent Bks.) Strategic Book Publishing & Rights Agency (SBPRA).

MacDonald, George. Malcolm. 2008. 232p. 29.95 *(978-1-60664-853-7(5))*; pap. 15.95 *(978-1-60664-099-9(2))* Aegypan.

MacDonald, Tom. Secret of the Tree: Marcus Speer's Ecosentinel. Stieber, Joel, illus. 2009. 300p. pap. 18.95 *(978-0-595-52402-0(8))* iUniverse, Inc.

Mack, Jeff. Duck in the Fridge, 0 vols. 2014. (ENG.). 40p. (J). (gr. 1-3). 16.99 *(978-1-4778-4776-3(6)*, 9781477847763, Amazon Children's Publishing) Amazon Publishing.

Maddox, Jake. Behind the Plate, 1 vol. Tiffany, Sean, illus. 2012. (Jake Maddox Sports Stories Ser.). (ENG.). 72p. (gr. 2-3). pap. 5.95 *(978-1-4342-4205-1(6))*; lib. bdg. 25.32 *(978-1-4342-4010-1(X))* Stone Arch Bks.

Magenta, Emma. Orlando on a Thursday. Magenta, Emma, illus. 2010. (ENG., Illus.). 32p. (J). (gr. -1-2). 15.99 *(978-0-7636-4560-1(5))* Candlewick Pr.

Maier, Inger M. When Fuzzy Was Afraid of Big & Loud Things. Candon, Jennifer, illus. 2005. (Fuzzy the Little Sheep Ser.). (J). (gr. -1-3). 32p. 14.95 *(978-1-59147-322-0(5))*; 30p. per. 9.95 *(978-1-59147-323-7(3))* American Psychological Assn. (Magination Pr.).

Mankell, Henning. A Bridge to the Stars. 2009. (Joel Gustafson Stories Ser.: No. 1). (ENG.). 180p. (YA). (gr. 7). pap. 7.99 *(978-0-440-24042-6(5)*, Delacorte Bks. for Young Readers) Random Hse. Children's Bks.

—Journey to the End of the World. 2011. (Joel Gustafson Stories Ser.: No. 4). (ENG.). 208p. (YA). (gr. 7). pap. 7.99 *(978-0-385-73498-1(0)*, Delacorte Bks. for Young Readers) Random Hse. Children's Bks.

—Shadows in the Twilight. 2010. (Joel Gustafson Stories Ser.: No. 2). (ENG.). 208p. (YA). (gr. 7). pap. 7.99 *(978-0-440-24043-3(3)*, Delacorte Bks. for Young Readers) Random Hse. Children's Bks.

—When the Snow Fell. 2011. (Joel Gustafson Stories Ser.: No. 3). (ENG.). 256p. (YA). (gr. 7). pap. 8.99 *(978-0-440-24044-0(1)*, Delacorte Bks. for Young Readers) Random Hse. Children's Bks.

Manning, Peyton, et al. Family Huddle. Madsen, Jim, illus. 2009. (J). *(978-0-545-21351-6(7)*, Scholastic Pr.) Scholastic, Inc.

Manson, Mary K. I Love You More. 2012. 24p. pap. 15.99 *(978-1-4691-6318-5(7))* Xlibris Corp.

Marcotte, Jennifer. Noah's Star. 2009. 24p. pap. 14.99 *(978-1-4490-0743-0(0))* AuthorHouse.

Marsh, Barry. Good Harbor Bay. 2009. (J). 14.95 *(978-0-9767268-1-4(5))* Crofton Creek Pr.

Mass, Wendy. Jeremy Fink & the Meaning of Life. 2008. (ENG.). 304p. (J). (gr. 3-7). per. 8.99 *(978-0-316-05849-0(1))* Little, Brown Bks. for Young Readers.

Mass, Wendy & Brawer, Michael. B. U. R. P. Strikes Back. 2017. (Space Taxi Ser.: 5). (ENG., Illus.). 144p. (J). (gr. 1-5). pap. 5.99 *(978-0-316-30840-3(4))* Little, Brown Bks. for Young Readers.

—B. U. R. P. Strikes Back. 2017. (Space Taxi Ser.: 5). (J). lib. bdg. 16.00 ***(978-0-606-40226-2(8))*** Turtleback Bks.

—The Galactic B. U. R. P. 2016. (Space Taxi Ser.: 4). (ENG., Illus.). 128p. (J). (gr. 1-5). 14.99 *(978-0-316-24331-5(0))* Little, Brown Bks. for Young Readers.

—Space Taxi: Aliens on Earth. 2017. (Space Taxi Ser.: 6). (ENG., Illus.). 128p. (J). (gr. 1-5). 15.99 *(978-0-316-30842-7(0))* Little, Brown Bks. for Young Readers.

—Water Planet Rescue. 2014. (Space Taxi Ser.: 2). (ENG., Illus.). 128p. (J). (gr. 1-5). 15.00 *(978-0-316-24323-0(X))* Little, Brown Bks. for Young Readers.

Maxwell, Calvin. American Pool Player. 2012. 168p. 22.99 *(978-1-62230-142-3(0))* Salem Author Services.

MaxwellJr, Calvin. American Pool Player. 2012. 168p. pap. 14.99 *(978-1-62230-141-6(2))* Salem Author Services.

Mayer, Kirsten & Auerbach, Annie, texts. Hop: The Chapter Book. 2011. (Hop Ser.). (ENG.). 80p. (J). (gr. 3-7). pap. 4.99 *(978-0-316-12900-8(3))* Little, Brown Bks. for Young Readers.

Mayer, Mercer. Just a Special Day. 2014. (Little Critter: I Can Read! Ser.). (J). lib. bdg. 13.55 *(978-0-606-35961-0(3))* Turtleback Bks.

—Just an Adventure at Sea. 2017. (Little Critter: I Can Read! Ser.). lib. bdg. 13.55 ***(978-0-606-40062-6(1))*** Turtleback Bks.

—Just Helping My Dad. Mayer, Mercer, illus. 2011. (My First I Can Read Ser.). (ENG., Illus.). 32p. (J). (gr. -1-3). pap. 3.99 *(978-0-06-083563-7(X))* HarperCollins Pubs.

—Just Helping My Dad. 2011. (Little Critter: I Can Read! Ser.). (J). lib. bdg. 13.55 *(978-0-606-23023-0(8)*, Turtleback) Turtleback Bks.

—Just Me & My Mom. 2014. (Little Critter Ser.). lib. bdg. 14.75 *(978-0-606-35555-1(3))* Turtleback Bks.

—Little Critter - Just a Special Day. Mayer, Mercer, illus. 2014. (My First I Can Read Ser.). (ENG., Illus.). 32p. (J). (gr. -1-3). pap. 3.99 *(978-0-06-147817-8(2))* HarperCollins Pubs.

—Little Critter: 5-Minute Little Critter Stories. Mayer, Mercer, illus. 2017. (Little Critter Ser.). (Illus.). 192p. (J). (gr. -1-3). 12.99 ***(978-0-06-265525-7(6)***, HarperFestival) HarperCollins Pubs.

Mayer, Mercer. Little Critter: Just an Adventure at Sea. Mayer, Mercer, illus. 2017. (My First I Can Read Ser.). (Illus.). 32p. (J). (gr. -1-3). pap. 3.99 *(978-0-06-243140-0(4))* HarperCollins Pubs.

Mayfield, Jamie. Determination. 2016. (ENG., Illus.). (J). 29.99 ***(978-1-63533-001-4(7)***, Harmony Ink Pr.) 2013. 336p. pap. 17.99 *(978-1-62798-009-8(1))* Dreamspinner Pr.

Mayhar, Ardath. Medicine Walk. 2007. (ENG.). 96p. (YA). (gr. 9). pap. 7.95 *(978-1-4169-6846-7(6)*, Simon Pulse) Simon Pulse.

McAllister, Cameron. The Tin Snail. Usher, Sam, illus. 2016. (ENG.). 288p. (J). (gr. 4-7). 16.99 *(978-0-553-53638-6(9)*, Delacorte Bks. for Young Readers) Random Hse. Children's Bks.

McBratney, Sam. Guess How Much I Love You. Jeram, Anita, illus. 2005. 34p. (J). bds. 19.95 *(978-0-9769313-1-7(1))* BrailleInk.

—Guess How Much I Love You. Jeram, Anita, illus. (Guess How Much I Love You Ser.). (J). 2014. (ENG.). 30p. (gr. k-4). 9.99 *(978-0-7636-7446-5(X))* 2011. (ENG.). 16p. (gr. -1-2). 19.99 *(978-0-7636-5378-1(0))* 2011. (ENG.). (gr. -1-k). bds. 9.99 *(978-0-7636-4976-0(7))* 2006. 32p. (gr. -1-3). 15.99 *(978-0-7636-3503-9(0))* Candlewick Pr.

—Guess How Much I Love You 20th Anniversary Edition. Jeram, Anita, illus. 2014. (Guess How Much I Love You Ser.). (ENG.). 40p. (J). (gr. k-12). 16.99 *(978-0-7636-7448-9(6))* Candlewick Pr.

—Guess How Much I Love You All Year Round. Jeram, Anita, illus. 2010. (Guess How Much I Love You Ser.). (ENG.). 72p. (J). (gr. -1-2). 16.99 *(978-0-7636-4654-7(7))* Candlewick Pr.

—There, There. Bates, Ivan, illus. 2015. (ENG.). 32p. (J). (-k). bds. 7.99 *(978-0-7636-7565-3(2)*, Templar) Candlewick Pr.

—Tomhais Méid Mo Ghrá Duit (Guess How Much I Love You in Irish) Jeram, Anita, illus. 2013. (Guess How Much I Love You Ser.). (ENG & GLE.). 32p. (J). (gr. -1-2). 9.99 *(978-0-7636-6570-8(3))* Candlewick Pr.

McCleery, William. Wolf Story. Chappell, Warren, illus. 2012. (ENG.). 88p. (J). (gr. k-4). 15.95 *(978-1-59017-589-7(1)*, NYR Children's Collection) New York Review of Bks., Inc., The.

McCormick, Wilfred. The Three-Two Pitch: A Bronc Burnett Story. 2011. 192p. 42.95 *(978-1-258-10008-7(8))* Literary Licensing, LLC.

McDaniel, Lurlene. Losing Gabriel: a Love Story. 2017. (ENG.). 336p. (YA). (gr. 7). pap. 9.99 ***(978-0-385-74422-5(6)***, Ember) Random Hse. Children's Bks.

McDaniel, Lurlene. Prey. 2010. (ENG.). 208p. (YA). (gr. 7). mass mkt. 7.99 *(978-0-440-24015-0(8)*, Laurel Leaf) Random Hse. Children's Bks.

Mcghee, Alison. Little Boy. Reynolds, Peter H., illus. 2008. (ENG.). 40p. (J). (gr. -1-3). 16.99 *(978-1-4169-5872-7(X)*, Atheneum Bks. for Young Readers) Simon & Schuster Children's Publishing.

McKee, Brett. The Tickle Ghost. McKee, David, illus. 2011. (ENG.). 32p. (J). (gr. k-2). 19.99 *(978-1-84939-246-4(3))* Andersen Pr. GBR. Dist: Independent Pubs. Group.

McQuinn, Anna. Colm's Lambs. Young, Paul, illus. 2014. (ENG.). 32p. (J). pap. 13.95 *(978-1-84717-339-3(X))* O'Brien Pr., Ltd., The IRL. Dist: Dufour Editions, Inc.

—Leo Can Swim. Hearson, Ruth, illus. 2016. (ENG.). 24p. (J). (— 1). lib. bdg. 9.95 *(978-1-58089-725-9(8))* Charlesbridge Publishing, Inc.

McSpadden, Judy. Heart for Thunder. 2010. 148p. 22.95 *(978-1-4401-9487-0(4))*; pap. 12.95 *(978-1-4401-9489-4(0))* iUniverse, Inc.

Melling, David. Dont Worry Douglas. Melling, David, illus. 2011. (ENG., Illus.). 32p. 12.95 *(978-1-58925-106-9(7))* Tiger Tales.

Melton, Marcia. Joe Henry's Journey. 2014. (Illus.). 169p. (J). pap. 12.00 *(978-1-937849-20-7(1))* Raven Publishing Inc. of Montana.

Mercier, Deborah. The Captain's Hat. Mills, Faythe, illus. 2007. 32p. (J). 17.99 *(978-0-9799410-0-9(8))* Minnewaska Pr.

Merritt, Virginia. A Ram for Isaac. 2009. (J). *(978-1-59166-983-8(9))* BJU Pr.

Michael, Jan. Just Joshua. 2003. (ENG.). 192p. (J). pap. 10.95 *(978-0-86278-818-6(8))* O'Brien Pr., Ltd., The IRL. Dist: Dufour Editions, Inc.

Miklowitz, Gloria. Camouflage. 2015. (ENG.). 176p. (YA). (gr. 7). pap. 8.99 *(978-0-544-33614-8(3)*, HMH Books For Young Readers) Houghton Mifflin Harcourt Publishing Co.

Miles, Ryan. The Picnic Nightmare. 2012. 24p. pap. 24.95 *(978-1-4512-7153-9(0))* America Star Bks.

Miller-Lachmann, Lyn. Gringolandia. 2009. (ENG.). 288p. (YA). (gr. 9-18). 18.95 *(978-1-931896-49-8(6))* Curbstone Pr.

Millman, Selena. The Prince & Me. 2006. 146p. (YA). per. 11.20 *(978-1-4243-2353-1(3))* Independent Publisher Services.

Mims-Word, Marsha. The Great Vacation. 2011. 36p. pap. 21.99 *(978-1-4568-9675-1(X))* Xlibris Corp.

Moeri, Louise. The Devil in Ol' Rosie. 2009. (ENG.). 208p. (J). (gr. 3-6). pap. 10.99 *(978-1-4424-0202-7(4)*, Atheneum Bks. for Young Readers) Simon & Schuster Children's Publishing.

Montanari, Eva. Go-Cart Number 1. 2005. (Picture Books/Quality Time Ser.). (Illus.). 32p. (gr. k-3). lib. bdg. 26.00 *(978-0-8368-4478-8(5)*, Gareth Stevens Learning Library) Stevens, Gareth Publishing LLLP.

Morpurgo, Michael. Listen to the Moon. 2015. (ENG.). 352p. (J). (gr. 5-9). 16.99 *(978-1-250-04204-0(6)*, 9781250042040) Feiwel & Friends.

Mors, Peter D. & Mors, Terry M. L D the Littlest Dragster. Weiss, Tracy, illus. 2009. 36p. pap. 16.99 *(978-1-4389-7445-3(0))* AuthorHouse.

Morton, Scott. An Encyclopedia for My Son, 1 vol. 2010. 46p. 24.95 *(978-1-4489-4748-5(0))* PublishAmerica, Inc.

Morton-Shaw, Christine. The Hunt for the Seventh. 2009. (ENG.). 288p. (J). (gr. 5). pap. 7.99 *(978-0-06-072824-3(8)*, Tegen, Katherine Bks) HarperCollins Pubs.

Murphy, Barbara Beasley. Ace Flies Like an Eagle. 2003. (Can't Stop Ace Ser.: No. 3). 180p. (J). pap. 16.95 *(978-0-86534-409-9(4))* Sunstone Pr.

Murphy, Brendan. Ready for School, Murphy? Murphy, Brendan, illus. 2015. (ENG., Illus.). 40p. (J). (gr. -1-k). 16.99 *(978-1-4847-0740-1(0))* Disney Publishing Worldwide.

Myers, Jason. Blazed. 2014. (ENG., Illus.). 528p. (YA). (gr. 11-11). pap. 11.99 *(978-1-4424-8721-5(6)*, Simon Pulse) Simon Pulse.

Myers, Walter Dean. The Dream Bearer. 2004. 16.00 *(978-0-7569-3242-8(4))* Perfection Learning Corp.

—It Ain't All for Nothin' 2003. 226p. (gr. 7-12). 17.00 *(978-0-7569-1460-8(4))* Perfection Learning Corp.

—Somewhere in the Darkness. 2008. 18.00 *(978-0-7569-9060-2(2))* Perfection Learning Corp.

—Somewhere in the Darkness. 2008. (ENG., Illus.). 192p. (J). (gr. 7). pap. 8.99 *(978-0-545-05577-2(6)*, Scholastic Paperbacks) Scholastic, Inc.

Nedelcu, Ovi. Just Like Daddy. 2015. (ENG., Illus.). 32p. (J). (gr. -1-2). 17.95 *(978-1-57687-756-2(6)*, powerHouse Bks.) powerHouse Cultural Entertainment, Inc.

Neeman, Sylvie. Something Big. Godon, Ingrid, illus. 2013. (ENG.). 40p. (J). (gr. -1-3). 16.95 *(978-1-59270-140-7(X))* Enchanted Lion Bks., LLC.

Neff, Fred. The Memory Tree. Montmeat, Jack, illus. 2008. 36p. pap. 14.99 *(978-1-59858-854-5(0))* Dog Ear Publishing, LLC.

Neff, Henry H. The Hound of Rowan. 2008. (Tapestry Ser.: 1). (ENG., Illus.). 448p. (J). (gr. 3-7). 7.99 *(978-0-375-83895-8(3)*, Yearling) Random Hse. Children's Bks.

Neil Wallace, Sandra. Muckers. 2013. (ENG.). 288p. (YA). (gr. 7). 16.99 *(978-0-375-86754-5(6)*, Knopf Bks. for Young Readers) Random Hse. Children's Bks.

Nelson, Marilyn. American Ace. 2016. (ENG.). 128p. (YA). (gr. 7). 17.99 *(978-0-8037-3305-3(4)*, Dial Bks) Penguin Young Readers Group.

Neri, G. Ghetto Cowboy. Watson, Jesse Joshua, illus. 2013. (ENG.). 224p. (J). (gr. 5). pap. 6.99 *(978-0-7636-6453-4(7))* Candlewick Pr.

Nesbit, E. Harding's Luck. 2006. 164p. (gr. 4-7). per. 13.95 *(978-1-59818-878-3(X))*; 25.95 *(978-1-59818-170-8(X))* Aegypan.

Nichele, Neika. Tayance, a Young Sioux Indian. Bright, Phyllis, illus. 2008. 47p. pap. 24.95 *(978-1-60703-606-7(1))* America Star Bks.

Niemann, Christoph. Subway. Niemann, Christoph, illus. 2010. (Illus.). 40p. (J). (gr. -1-k). (ENG.). 16.99 *(978-0-06-157779-6(0))*; lib. bdg. 17.89 *(978-0-06-157780-2(4))* HarperCollins Pubs. (Greenwillow Bks.).

Nimmo, Jenny & Keating, John. The Snow Spider. 2006. (Magician Trilogy Ser.: Bk. 1). (ENG.). (J). (gr. 3-7). audio compact disk 39.95 *(978-0-439-89844-7(7))* Scholastic, Inc.

Nolan, Han. Crazy. 2010. (ENG.). 352p. (YA). (gr. 7-18). 17.00 *(978-0-15-205109-9(0))* Houghton Mifflin Harcourt Publishing Co.

Norac, Carl. My Daddy Is a Giant: For Everyone Who Has the Best Daddy in the World. Godon, Ingrid, illus. 2004. (ENG & GLE.). 32p. (J). pap. *(978-1-84444-719-0(7))* Mantra Lingua.

—My Daddy Is a Giant: For Everyone Who Has the Best Daddy in the World. 2004. (ENG., Illus.). 32p. (J). *(978-1-4050-2167-8(5)*, Macmillan Children's Bks.) Pan Macmillan.

—My Daddy Is a Giant: For Everyone Who Has the Best Daddy in the World. Godon, Ingrid, illus. 2005. (ENG.). 32p. (J). pap. 14.95 *(978-1-4050-2168-5(3)*, Macmillan Children's Bks.) Pan Macmillan GBR. Dist: Trans-Atlantic Pubns., Inc.

Nuño, Fran. Fairground Lights. 2013. (ENG., Illus.). 24p. (J). (gr. k-2). 16.95 *(978-84-15784-20-3(1))* Eastern National.

Nussbaum, Ben. Take Me Out to the Ballgame. Studio Mouse Staff, ed. rev. ed. 2007. (ENG.). 24p. 4.99 *(978-1-59069-603-3(4))* Studio Mouse LLC.

O'Callaghan, G. Slave Prince. 2007. 172p. per. *(978-1-84693-031-7(6))* Best Global Publishing Ltd.

Odom, Mel. The Mystery Unravels. 2013. (Hunter's League Ser.: 2). (ENG.). 256p. (YA). (gr. 7). pap. 16.99 *(978-1-4814-0154-8(8)*, Simon Pulse) Simon Pulse.

Oliver, Merlin. John Laughinghouse. 2007. 20.00 *(978-0-8059-7333-4(8))* Dorrance Publishing Co., Inc.

Oppel, Kenneth. Sunwing. 2008. (Silverwing Trilogy Ser.). (ENG.). 336p. (J). (gr. 3-7). pap. 7.99 *(978-1-4169-4997-8(6)*, Simon & Schuster Bks. For Young Readers) Simon & Schuster Bks. For Young Readers.

Orshoski, Paul. We Read Phonics-Dad Does It All. Ebbeler, Jeffrey, illus. 2011. 32p. (J). 9.95 *(978-1-60115-341-8(4))*; (YA). pap. 4.99 *(978-1-60115-342-5(2))* Treasure Bay, Inc.

Osborn, Kelly. The Green Knight. 2006. 64p. pap. 19.95 *(978-1-4241-1741-3(0))* America Star Bks.

Ostrovski, Emil. The Paradox of Vertical Flight. 2014. (ENG.). 272p. (YA). (gr. 9). pap. 9.99 *(978-0-06-223853-5(1)*, Greenwillow Bks.) HarperCollins Pubs.

Out of the Blue. 2014. (J). pap. *(978-0-8163-5016-2(7))* Pacific Pr. Publishing Assn.

Park, Linda Sue. The Third Gift. Ibatoulline, Bagram, illus. 2011. (ENG.). 32p. (J). (gr. 1-4). 16.99 *(978-0-547-20195-5(8))* Houghton Mifflin Harcourt Publishing Co.

Parsons, Ash. Still Waters. 2015. (ENG.). 320p. (YA). (gr. 9). 17.99 *(978-0-399-16847-5(8)*, Philomel Bks.) Penguin Young Readers Group.

Pass, Erica. Hooray for Dads! 2014. (SpongeBob Squarepants 8X8 Ser.). lib. bdg. 14.75 *(978-0-606-35560-5(X))* Turtleback Bks.

Paterson, Katherine. Marvin One Too Many. Clark Brown, Jane, illus. 2003. 28.95 incl. audio compact disk *(978-1-59112-635-5(5))*; 25.95 incl. audio *(978-1-59112-254-8(6))*; 28.95 incl. audio compact disk *(978-1-59112-635-5(5))*; pap. 31.95 incl. audio compact disk *(978-1-59112-636-2(3))* Live Oak Media.

—Preacher's Boy. 2013. (ENG.). 176p. (J). (gr. 5-7). pap. 7.99 *(978-0-544-10490-7(0))* Houghton Mifflin Harcourt Publishing Co.

Paulsen, Gary. The Tent: A Parable in One Sitting. 2006. (ENG., Illus.). 96p. (YA). (gr. 7-12). pap. 7.95 *(978-0-15-205833-3(8))* Houghton Mifflin Harcourt Publishing Co.

—The Tent: A Parable in One Sitting. 2006. 86p. (gr. 7-12). 15.95 *(978-0-7569-6891-5(7))* Perfection Learning Corp.

Paulsen, Gary & Paulsen, Jim. Field Trip. 2015. (ENG.). 128p. (J). (gr. 5). 12.99 *(978-0-553-49674-1(3)*, Lamb, Wendy Bks.) Random Hse. Children's Bks.

—Road Trip. 2014. (ENG.). 128p. (J). (gr. 5). pap. 6.99 *(978-0-307-93086-6(5)*, Yearling) Random Hse. Children's Bks.

Paxton, Tom. The Marvelous Toy. Cox, Steve, illus. 2014. (ENG.). 22p. (J). (gr. -1-2). bds. 7.95 *(978-1-62354-043-2(7))* Charlesbridge Publishing, Inc.

Pearsall, Shelley. All Shook Up. 2009. (ENG.). 272p. (J). (gr. 3-7). 6.99 *(978-0-440-42139-9(X)*, Yearling) Random Hse. Children's Bks.

—Jump into the Sky. (ENG.). 352p. (J). 2013. (gr. 4-7). pap. 7.99 *(978-0-440-42140-5(3)*, Yearling) 2012. (gr. 5). 16.99 *(978-0-375-83699-2(3)*, Knopf Bks. for Young Readers) Random Hse. Children's Bks.

Peck, Dale. Sprout. 2009. (ENG.). 288p. (YA). (gr. 9-12). 16.99 *(978-1-59990-160-2(9)*, 9781599901602, Bloomsbury USA Childrens) Bloomsbury Publishing USA.

Peet, Mal & Graham, Elspeth. Night Sky Dragons. Benson, Patrick, illus. 2014. (ENG.). 64p. (J). (gr. -1-3). 15.99 *(978-0-7636-6144-1(9))* Candlewick Pr.

Petrucha, Stefan. Ripper. 2013. (ENG.). 432p. (YA). (gr. 7). pap. 9.99 *(978-0-14-242418-6(8)*, Speak) Penguin Young Readers Group.

Petrucha, Stefan & Kinney, Sarah. City under the Basement. Murase, Sho, illus. 2009. (Nancy Drew Graphic Novels: Girl Detective Ser.: 18). (ENG.). 96p. (J). (gr. 3-7). pap. 7.95 *(978-1-59707-154-3(4)*, 9781597071543); 18th ed. 12.95 *(978-1-59707-155-0(2)*, 9781597071550) Papercutz.

Phi, Bao. A Different Pond. Bui, Thi, illus. 2017. (Fiction Picture Bks.). (ENG.). 32p. (gr. 2-3). lib. bdg. 23.32 ***(978-1-4795-9746-8(5)***, Fiction Picture Bks.) Picture Window Bks.

Philbrick, Rodman & Philbrick, W. R. The Young Man & the Sea. 2005. 192p. (gr. 4-7). 17.00 *(978-0-7569-4899-3(1))* Perfection Learning Corp.

Pincus, Gregory K. The 14 Fibs of Gregory K. 2013. (J). pap. *(978-0-439-91300-3(4))*; (ENG.). 240p. (gr. 3-7). 17.99 *(978-0-439-91299-0(7))* Scholastic, Inc. (Levine, Arthur A. Bks.).

Ploof, Douglas. Weekend at Dad's. 2012. 32p. pap. 24.95 *(978-1-4626-7597-5(2))* America Star Bks.

—Weekend at Dad's: The Campout. 2013. 24p. pap. 24.95 *(978-1-4626-9896-7(4))* America Star Bks.

Polacco, Patricia. Christmas Tapestry. 2008. (ENG.). 48p. (J). (gr. 1-4). pap. 7.99 *(978-0-14-241165-0(5)*, Puffin Books) Penguin Young Readers Group.

Polak, Monique. Finding Elmo, 1 vol. 2007. (Orca Currents Ser.). (ENG.). (J). (gr. 5-9). 112p. lib. bdg. 14.95 *(978-1-55143-688-3(4))*; 128p. per. 9.95 *(978-1-55143-686-9(8))* Orca Bk. Pubs. USA.

Polisner, Gae. The Pull of Gravity. 2013. (ENG.). 224p. (YA). (gr. 7). pap. 10.99 (978-1-250-01933-2(8), 9781250019332) Square Fish.

Pope, Cody/Louis Ray. Andy & the Dragons. 2008. (Illus.). 48p. (J). per. (978-0-9798792-1-0(3)) Scavenger's Pubns.

Posada, Jorge. Play Ball! Colón, Raúl, illus. 2010. (ENG.). 32p. (J). (gr. 1-5). 6.99 (978-1-4169-9825-9(X), Simon & Schuster/Paula Wiseman Bks.) Simon & Schuster/Paula Wiseman Bks.

—Sí, Puedes. Colón, Raúl, illus. 2010.Tr. of Play Ball! (SPA.). 32p. (J). (gr. 1-5). 6.99 (978-1-4169-9826-6(8), Simon & Schuster/Paula Wiseman Bks.) Simon & Schuster/Paula Wiseman Bks.

Poulsen, David A. Old Man. 2013. (ENG.). 224p. (YA). pap. 12.99 (978-1-4597-0547-0(5)) Dundurn CAN. Dist: Ingram Publisher Services.

—Old Man. 2013. 276p. pap. (978-1-4596-6325-1(X)) ReadHowYouWant.com, Ltd.

Preller, James. The Courage Test. 2016. (ENG.). 224p. (J). 16.99 (978-1-250-09391-2(0), 9781250093912) Feiwel & Friends.

Proimos, James. 12 Things to Do Before You Crash & Burn. 2011. (ENG.). 128p. (YA). (gr. 9-13). 14.99 (978-1-59643-595-7(X)) Roaring Brook Pr.

Publications International Ltd. Staff, ed. Finding Nemo. 2007. (J). 9.98 (978-1-4127-6516-9(1)) Publications International, Ltd.

Pyke, Helen Godfrey. Pinch River: Growing up Hard & Fast on the Michigan Frontier. 2008. (J). pap. 7.97 (978-0-8163-2250-3(3)) Pacific Pr. Publishing Assn.

Quartz, Jane & Quartz, Oliver. How Much Are We Alike? 2009. (Illus.). 40p. (J). 17.95 (978-0-9816641-1-8(3)) Forks Pr.

Quirby, A. Leigh. Every Other Weekend. 2008. (Illus.). (J). (978-1-4243-2537-5(4)) Independent Publisher Services.

Raisner Glass, Beth. Blue-Ribbon Dad. Moore, Margie, illus. 2011. (ENG.). 32p. (J). (gr. k-2). 15.95 (978-0-8109-9727-1(4), Abrams Bks. for Young Readers) Abrams, Inc.

Random House. Hooray for Dads! (SpongeBob SquarePants) Random House, illus. 2014. (Pictureback(R) Ser.). (ENG., Illus.). 24p. (J). (gr. -1-2). 4.99 (978-0-385-37607-5(3), Random Hse. Bks. for Young Readers) Random Hse. Children's Bks.

Raschke, Erik. The Book of Samuel: A Novel. 2009. (ENG.). 256p. (YA). (gr. 4-7). pap. 18.99 (978-0-312-37969-8(2), 9780312379698, St. Martin's Griffin) St. Martin's Pr.

Readler, Blaine C. Under the Radar: The Spy Drone Adventure. 2006. (ENG.). 248p. (J). (gr. 7-12). per. (978-1-933255-18-7(8)) DNA Pr.

Reid, Roger. Space. 2008. (ENG.). 160p. (J). 19.95 (978-1-58838-230-6(3), NewSouth Bks.) NewSouth, Inc.

Reilly, Carmel & Orsini, Cheryl. Everything Is Changing. 2008. (Rigby Focus Forward: Level I Ser.). (Illus.). 24p. (J). (gr. 4-7). pap. (978-1-4190-3753-5(6), Rigby) Pearson Education Australia.

Revell, Mike. Stormwalker. 2016. (ENG.). 304p. (J). (gr. 5-9). 16.99 (978-1-68144-493-2(3)) Quercus NA.

Reynolds, Luke. Bedtime Blast-Off! Yamada, Mike, illus. 2016. (ENG.). 40p. (J). (gr. -1-1). 16.99 (978-0-545-77855-8(7), Orchard Bks.) Scholastic, Inc.

—If My Love Were a Fire Truck. Mack, Jeff, illus. 2017. (ENG.). 32p. (J). (gr. -1-2). 16.99 (978-1-101-93740-2(8), Doubleday Bks. for Young Readers) Random Hse. Children's Bks.

Riley-Collins, Jennifer. Daddy God. 2007. (J). pap. (978-0-9791374-1-9(1)) Favored Publishing, Inc.

Riley, Zach. Down for the Count. Ricci, Andrés, illus. 2012. (Zach Riley Ser.). 80p. (J). (gr. 3-6). lib. bdg. 27.07 (978-1-61783-533-9(1)) Magic Wagon.

Rio, Adam del & Noel III. Teo & the Brick. Rio, Adam del & Noel III, illus. 2006. (SPA & ENG., Illus.). 28p. (978-0-9772852-4-2(3)); (978-0-9772852-5-9(1)) Lectura Bks.

Riordan, Rick. The Lightning Thief. (Percy Jackson & the Olympians Ser.: Bk. 1). (ENG.). (J). (gr. 5-9). 2005. 384p. 17.99 (978-0-7868-5629-9(7))Bk. 1. 2006. 416p. reprint ed. per. 7.99 (978-0-7868-3865-3(5)) Disney Publishing Worldwide.

—The Lightning Thief. 2008. (J). 54.99 (978-0-7393-7113-8(4)) Findaway World, LLC.

—The Lightning Thief. 2006. (Percy Jackson & the Olympians Ser.: Bk. 1). 377p. (J). (gr. 5-12). 15.65 (978-0-7569-6603-4(5)) Perfection Learning Corp.

—The Lightning Thief. rev. l.t. ed. 2006. (Percy Jackson & the Olympians Ser.: 1). (ENG.). 483p. (gr. 5-18). 22.95 (978-0-7862-8225-8(8)) Thorndike Pr.

—The Lightning Thief. 2006. (Percy Jackson & the Olympians Ser.: 1). (J). lib. bdg. 18.40 (978-1-4177-3247-0(4), Turtleback) Turtleback Bks.

—The Sea of Monsters, Bk. 2. Tk, illus. 2nd rev. ed. 2007. (Percy Jackson & the Olympians Ser.: Bk. 2). (ENG.). 320p. (J). (gr. 5-9). pap. 7.99 (978-1-4231-0334-9(3)) Disney Publishing Worldwide.

—The Sea of Monsters. 2011. 9.68 (978-0-7848-3440-4(7), Everbind) Marco Bk. Co.

—The Sea of Monsters. l.t. ed. 2006. (Percy Jackson & the Olympians Ser.: Bk. 2). 361p. (J). (gr. 5-9). 22.95 (978-0-7862-9074-1(9)) Thorndike Pr.

—The Sea of Monsters. 2007. (Percy Jackson & the Olympians Ser.: 2). 279p. (J). (gr. 4-7). lib. bdg. 18.40 (978-1-4177-7612-2(9), Turtleback) Turtleback Bks.

Riordan, Rick & Venditti, Robert. The Lightning Thief. Futaki, Attila & Villarrubia, Jose, illus. 2010. (Percy Jackson & the Olympians Ser.). (ENG.). 128p. (J). (gr. 5-9). 21.99 (978-1-4231-1696-7(8)); pap. 12.99 (978-1-4231-1710-0(7)) Hyperion Pr.

—The Sea of Monsters. Futaki, Attila & Gaspar, Tamas, illus. 2013. (Percy Jackson & the Olympians Ser.). (ENG.). 128p. (J). (gr. 5-9). 19.99 (978-1-4231-4529-5(1)); pap. 12.99 (978-1-4231-4550-9(X)) Hyperion Pr.

Ripken, Cal. Cal Ripken, Jr.'s All-Stars Squeeze Play. 2015. (Cal Ripken, Jr.'s All Stars Ser.). (ENG.). 224p. (J). (gr. 3-7). pap. 6.99 (978-1-4231-9465-1(9)) Hyperion Bks. for Children.

Ritchie, Alison. Me & My Dad! Edgson, Alison, illus. 2007. (J). pap. (978-0-545-02064-0(6)) Scholastic, Inc.

Ritter, John H. Choosing up Sides. 2004. 166p. (gr. 5-9). 16.00 (978-0-7569-4094-2(X)) Perfection Learning Corp.

Rivera, Rafael, et al. Baseball on Mars/Béisbol en Marte. Rivera, Rafael et al, illus. 2009.Tr. of Béisbol en Marte. (SPA & ENG.). 32p. (J). (gr. -1-3). 16.95 (978-1-55885-521-2(1)) Arte Publico Pr.

Rivers, Karen. Before We Go Extinct: A Novel. 2016. (ENG.). 256p. (YA). 17.99 (978-0-374-30240-5(5), 9780374302405, Farrar, Straus & Giroux (BYR)) Farrar, Straus & Giroux.

—What Is Real. 1 vol. 2011. (ENG.). 304p. (YA). (gr. 7-12). pap. 12.95 (978-1-55469-356-6(X)) Orca Bk. Pubs. USA.

Roadbloc. Vending MacHine Lunch. 2012. 172p. pap. (978-0-9570633-4-1(2)) Fragged Publishing.

Robertson, Jacob Ryan. Far Away. 2012. 50p. (-18). pap. 15.99 (978-1-4797-4679-8(7)) Xlibris Corp.

Rocco, John & Primiano, Jay. Swim That Rock. Rocco, John, illus. 2014. (ENG., Illus.). 304p. (YA). (gr. 7). 16.99 (978-0-7636-6905-8(9)) Candlewick Pr.

Rodriguez, Bobbie. How I Love My Dad. 2013. 40p. 22.99 (978-1-62697-112-7(9)); pap. 11.99 (978-1-62509-995-2(9)) Salem Author Services.

Rodriguez, Felix Manuel. Dad, Me, & Muhammad Ali: A Father-and-Son Story. 2011. 108p. (gr. -1). pap. 9.95 (978-1-936236-53-4(2)) iUniverse, Inc.

Roehm, R. Curtis. My Dad's Gto. 2011. 36p. pap. 18.99 (978-1-4634-4379-5(X)) AuthorHouse.

Rogers, Don. The Adventures of Shawn & Jeremy. 2011. 20p. pap. 24.95 (978-1-4626-3674-7(8)) America Star Bks.

Romagnoli, L. M. Memories of Me, 1 vol. 2009. 22p. pap. 24.95 (978-1-60836-084-0(9)) America Star Bks.

Rose, Caroline Starr. Jasper & the Riddle of Riley's Mine. 2017. (ENG.). 288p. (J). (gr. 5). 16.99 (978-0-399-16811-6(7), G.P. Putnam's Sons Books for Young Readers) Penguin Young Readers Group.

Rosen, Michael. Michael Rosen's Sad Book. Blake, Quentin, illus. 2005. (ENG.). 32p. (J). (gr. k-12). 16.99 (978-0-7636-2597-9(3)) Candlewick Pr.

Roth, Adam J. Checking up on Daddy! 2010. 36p. pap. 10.95 (978-1-60844-547-9(X)) Dog Ear Publishing, LLC.

Roxy. The Adventure of Benny Franklin: A Boy Tale. 2012. 26p. 19.95 (978-1-4626-7972-0(2)) America Star Bks.

Roy, Deryl. Just Like Dad. 2011. 20p. pap. 24.95 (978-1-4626-3793-5(0)) America Star Bks.

Rubens, Michael. The Bad Decisions Playlist. (ENG.). 304p. (YA). (gr. 9). 2017. pap. 9.99 (978-1-328-74208-7(3), HMH Books For Young Readers) 2016. 17.99 (978-0-544-09667-7(3)) Houghton Mifflin Harcourt Publishing Co.

Rushdie, Salman. Luka & the Fire of Life. 2009. 14.75 (978-0-7848-3731-3(7), Everbind) Marco Bk. Co.

—Luka & the Fire of Life. 2011. (ENG.). 240p. (J). (gr. 7). pap. 17.00 (978-0-679-78347-3(4), Random Hse. Trade Paperbacks) Random House Publishing Group.

Rylant, Cynthia. Henry & Mudge & the Funny Lunch. Bracken, Carolyn, illus. 2005. (Henry & Mudge Ready-To-Read Ser.: 24). 40p. (gr. k-2). lib. bdg. 13.55 (978-1-4176-7107-6(6), Turtleback) Turtleback Bks.

Sagar, Marie. Cuddly Sam. 2009. 24p. pap. 12.99 (978-1-4389-9334-8(X)) AuthorHouse.

Saldana, Rene, Jr. The Jumping Tree. 2008. 181p. (gr. 5-7). 16.50 (978-0-7569-8950-7(7)) Perfection Learning Corp.

Saldana, Rene. The Whole Sky Full of Stars. 2008. (ENG.). 144p. (YA). (gr. 7-11). mass mkt. 5.99 (978-0-440-23791-4(2), Laurel Leaf) Random Hse. Children's Bks.

Salkey, Andrew. Riot. 2011. (Caribbean Modern Classics Ser.). (ENG., Illus.). 176p. (J). (gr. 7). pap. 14.95 (978-1-84523-181-1(3)) Peepal Tree Pr., Ltd. GBR. Dist: Independent Pubs. Group.

Sassoli de Bianchi, Massimiliano. What weighs more: 1 kg of iron or 1 kg of Feathers? 2010. 164p. pap. 19.50 (978-1-4452-9957-0(7)) Lulu Pr., Inc.

Schmidt, Gary D. Anson's Way. 2009. (ENG.). 224p. (J). (gr. 2-5). pap. 15.95 (978-0-547-23761-9(8)) Houghton Mifflin Harcourt Publishing Co.

Schneider, Josh. Tales for Very Picky Eaters. Schneider, Josh, illus. 2011. (ENG., Illus.). 48p. (J). (gr. 1-4). 15.99 (978-0-547-14956-1(5)) Houghton Mifflin Harcourt Publishing Co.

Schraff, Anne. The Shadow Man. 2008. (Passages Ser.). 134p. (YA). (gr. 7-9). lib. bdg. 13.95 (978-0-7569-8382-6(7)) Perfection Learning Corp.

—To Be Somebody. 2008. (Passages Ser.). 120p. (J). (gr. 4-6). lib. bdg. 13.95 (978-0-7569-8390-1(8)) Perfection Learning Corp.

Scotton, Rob. Splat the Cat: Twice the Mice. Scotton, Rob, illus. 2015. (I Can Read Level 1 Ser.). (ENG., Illus.). 32p. (J). (gr. -1-3). pap. 3.99 (978-0-06-229421-0(0)) HarperCollins Pubs.

—Splat the Cat - Twice the Mice. Scotton, Rob, illus. 2015. (I Can Read Level 1 Ser.). (ENG., Illus.). 32p. (J). (gr. -1-3). 16.99 (978-0-06-229422-7(9)) HarperCollins Pubs.

—Splat the Cat Makes Dad Glad. 2014. (Splat the Cat: I Can Read Ser.). (J). lib. bdg. 13.55 (978-0-606-35475-2(1)) Turtleback Bks.

The Secret Life of Jack O' Lanterns. 2004. 32p. 15.00 (978-1-883211-35-6(2)) Laughing Elephant.

Service, Pamela F. Alien Encounter. Gorman, Mike, illus. (Alien Agent Ser.: 4). (ENG.). 152p. (J). (gr. 4-6). 2011. pap. 5.95 (978-0-7613-5248-8(1)) 2010. 16.95 (978-0-8225-8873-3(0), Carolrhoda Bks.) Lerner Publishing Group.

—#4 Alien Encounter. Gorman, Mike, illus. 2011. (Alien Agent Ser.). 152p. (J). pap. 33.92 (978-0-7613-7608-8(9), Darby Creek) Lerner Publishing Group.

Shahan, Sherry. That's Not How You Play Soccer, Daddy!, 1 vol. Mai-Wyss, Tatjana, illus. 2007. (ENG.). 32p. (J). (gr. -1-3). 15.95 (978-1-56145-416-7(6), Peachtree Junior) Peachtree Pubs.

Shaw, Marilyn Bishop. Solomon. 2006. (Florida Historical Fiction for Youth Ser.). (ENG.). 204p. (J). (gr. 4-9). 14.95 (978-1-56164-349-3(1)) Pineapple Pr., Inc.

Shea, Bob. Oh, Daddy! Shea, Bob, illus. 2010. (ENG., Illus.). 40p. (J). (gr. -1-1). 16.99 (978-0-06-173080-1(7)) HarperCollins Pubs.

Shearer, Alex. A Message to the Sea. 2016. (ENG.). 224p. (J). (gr. 4-7). pap. 8.99 (978-1-84812-569-8(0)) Bonnier Publishing GBR. Dist: Independent Pubs. Group.

Shephard, H. Ferebee. Dad's Birthday Present. 2010. 24p. pap. 15.99 (978-1-4535-3496-0(2)) Xlibris Corp.

Sherrard, Brent R. Wasted, 1 vol. 2009. (Lorimer SideStreets Ser.). (ENG.). 144p. (YA). (gr. 9-12). 16.95 (978-1-55277-420-5(1), 9781552774205); 9.95 (978-1-55277-419-9(8), 9781552774199) Lorimer, James & Co., Ltd., Pubs. CAN. Dist: Casemate Pubs. & Bk. Distributors, LLC.

Shulman, Mark. Gorilla Garage, 0 vols. Nguyen, Vincent, illus. 2013. (ENG.). 42p. (J). (gr. -1-3). pap. 9.99 (978-1-4778-1663-9(1), 9781477816639, Amazon Children's Publishing) Amazon Publishing.

Shusterman, Neal. Chasing Forgiveness. 2015. (ENG., Illus.). 240p. (YA). (gr. 7). pap. 9.99 (978-1-4814-2991-7(4)) Simon & Schuster Children's Publishing.

Simmons, Michael. Pool Boy. 2005. 164p. (gr. 7). 17.95 (978-0-7569-5064-4(3)) Perfection Learning Corp.

Sitomer, Alan Lawrence. Caged Warrior. 2014. (ENG., Illus.). 224p. (YA). (gr. 7-12). 16.99 (978-1-4231-7124-9(1)) Disney Pr.

—Caged Warrior. 2015. (Caged Warrior Ser.). (ENG., Illus.). 240p. (YA). (gr. 7-12). pap. 8.99 (978-1-4847-2280-0(9)) Hyperion Bks. for Children.

Skidmore, Marlene. In Trouble Again! 2010. 24p. pap. 9.99 (978-0-9845208-9-3(9)) Faithful Life Pubs.

Sklar, David. A Day at the Zoo with My Daddy. 2013. 24p. pap. 17.99 (978-1-4817-0152-5(5)) AuthorHouse.

Slater, David Michael. Comin' Through, 1 vol. Rooney, Ronnie, illus. 2007. (Missy Swiss & More Ser.). (ENG.). 32p. (gr. -1-4). 28.50 (978-1-60270-008-6(7), Looking Glass Library) ABDO Publishing Co.

Slavin, John Mark. My Friend Dad. 2010. 14p. 10.49 (978-0-557-61038-9(9)) Lulu Pr., Inc.

Sloan, Holly Goldberg. I'll Be There. (ENG.). (YA). (gr. 7-17). 2012. 416p. pap. 11.99 (978-0-316-12276-4(9)) 2011. (Illus.). 400p. 18.00 (978-0-316-12279-5(3)) Little, Brown Bks. for Young Readers.

Smelcer, John. Edge of Nowhere. 2014. (ENG.). 194p. (J). (gr. 6). pap. 9.99 (978-1-935248-57-6(X)) Leapfrog Pr.

—Savage Mountain. 2015. (ENG., Illus.). 160p. (J). (gr. 6). pap. 12.00 (978-1-935248-65-1(0)) Leapfrog Pr.

Smith, Andrew. 100 Sideways Miles. 2014. (ENG., Illus.). 288p. (YA). (gr. 9). 17.99 (978-1-4424-4495-9(9), Simon & Schuster Bks. For Young Readers) Simon & Schuster Bks. For Young Readers.

Smith, Margaret Ann. A New Kind of Life for Eddie Eagle. 2008. 36p. pap. 24.95 (978-1-60441-168-3(6)) America Star Bks.

Smith, Roland. Eruption. 2012. (Storm Runners Ser.: 3). (ENG.). 160p. (J). (gr. 3-7). 16.99 (978-0-545-08174-0(2), Scholastic Pr.) Scholastic, Inc.

—Storm Runners. (Storm Runners Ser.: Bk. 1). (ENG.). 160p. (J). (gr. 3-7). 2012. pap. 5.99 (978-0-545-08177-1(7), Scholastic Pr.) 2011. 16.99 (978-0-545-08175-7(0)) Scholastic, Inc.

Snowden, Gary. The Lost Treasure of Hawkins Cave. Pierce Clark, Donna, illus. 2013. 112p. pap. 7.99 (978-1-938768-10-1(8)) Gypsy Pubns.

Sobol, Donald J. Encyclopedia Brown Finds the Clues. Shortall, Leonard W., illus. 2008. (Encyclopedia Brown Ser.). 96p. (gr. 4-7). 15.00 (978-0-7569-8846-3(2)) Perfection Learning Corp.

Sorrells, Walter. First Shot. 2009. (ENG.). 288p. (YA). (gr. 7-18). 8.99 (978-0-14-241421-7(2), Puffin Books) Penguin Young Readers Group.

Spain, Susan. The Deep Cut, 0 vols. 2014. (ENG.). 228p. pap. 9.99 (978-1-4778-4768-8(5), 9781477847688, Amazon Children's Publishing) Amazon Publishing.

Spain, Susan Rosson. The Deep Cut, 1 vol. 2006. (ENG., Illus.). 224p. (J). (gr. 5-9). 16.99 (978-0-7614-5316-1(4)) Marshall Cavendish Corp.

Sperring, Mark. How Many Sleeps 'til Christmas? Braun, Sebastien, illus. 2014. (ENG.). 32p. (J). (gr. -1-3). 16.99 (978-1-58925-160-1(1)) Tiger Tales.

—How Many Sleeps 'Til My Birthday? Braun, Sebastien, illus. 2016. (ENG.). 32p. (J). (gr. -1-2). 16.99 (978-1-68010-009-9(2)) Tiger Tales.

Spillebeen, Geert. Kipling's Choice. Edelstein, Terese, tr. 2007. (ENG.). 160p. (YA). (gr. 7-9). pap. 12.95 (978-0-618-80035-3(2)) Houghton Mifflin Harcourt Publishing Co.

—Kipling's Choice. Edelstein, Terese, tr. 2007. 147p. (YA). (gr. 7-9). 15.65 (978-0-7569-8061-0(5)) Perfection Learning Corp.

Spinelli, Eileen. Boy, Can He Dance! Yalowitz, Paul, illus. 2012. (ENG.). 32p. (J). (gr. -1-3). 16.99 (978-1-4424-7441-3(6), Simon & Schuster Bks. For Young Readers) Simon & Schuster Bks. For Young Readers.

Spinelli, Jami. David's Tractor. Margolis, Lois, illus. l.t. ed. 2006. (J). 32p. 20.99 (978-1-59879-242-3(3)); 27p. (gr. -1-3). per. 11.99 (978-1-59879-241-6(5)) Lifevest Publishing, Inc.

Spinelli, Jerry. My Daddy & Me. Chwast, Seymour, illus. 2006. (ENG.). 40p. (J). (gr. -1-2). pap. 6.99 (978-0-553-11303-7(8), Dragonfly Bks.) Random Hse. Children's Bks.

Springer, Nancy. Wild Boy. 2005. (Tales of Rowan Hood Ser.). 115p. (J). (gr. 3). 13.65 (978-0-7569-5490-1(8)) Perfection Learning Corp.

Springer, T. S. Tyler Builds a Birdhouse. 2012. 28p. pap. 24.95 (978-1-4626-9972-8(3)) America Star Bks.

Spurr, Elizabeth. In the Woods, 1 vol. Oliphant, Manelle, illus. 2012. (ENG.). 22p. (J). bds. 6.95 (978-1-56145-582-9(2)) Peachtree Pubs.

Sretaw. Homonym Hunt. 2010. 24p. pap. 28.03 (978-1-4500-5228-3(2)) Xlibris Corp.

Stanley, Shalanda. Drowning Is Inevitable. 2015. (ENG.). 288p. (YA). (gr. 9). 17.99 (978-0-553-50828-4(8), Knopf Bks. for Young Readers) Random Hse. Children's Bks.

Stark, Ulf. When Dad Showed Me the Universe. Eriksson, Eva, illus. 2015.Tr. of Nar Pappa Visade Mej Varldsalltet. (ENG.). 32p. (J). (gr. 2-4). 16.99 (978-1-927271-81-0(9)) Gecko Pr. NZL. Dist: Lerner Publishing Group.

Stevens, Eric. The Classic: '69 Chevy Camaro. 2013. (Turbocharged Ser.). (ENG.). 96p. (gr. 6-12). pap. 7.95 (978-1-4677-1479-2(8)); lib. bdg. 27.93 (978-1-4677-1247-7(7)) Lerner Publishing Group. (Darby Creek).

Stewart, Martin. Riverkeep. (ENG.). 416p. (YA). (gr. 7). 2017. pap. 10.99 (978-1-101-99831-1(8), Speak) 2016. (Illus.). 17.99 (978-1-101-99829-8(6), Viking Books for Young Readers) Penguin Young Readers Group.

Stewart, Paul. In the Dark of the Night. Vyner, Tim, illus. 2009. (ENG.). 40p. (J). (gr. -1-2). (978-1-84507-764-8(4)) Rough Guides, Ltd.

Stewart, Paul & Riddell, Chris. Stormchaser. 2008. (Edge Chronicles Ser.: Bk. 2). (ENG., Illus.). 400p. (J). (gr. 3-7). 8.99 (978-0-440-42088-0(1), Yearling) Random Hse. Children's Bks.

Stier, Roy E. Son of Bunyan & the Sacred Moonstone. 2003. (Illus.). 158p. (J). per. 15.95 (978-1-892264-10-7(2)) Timeless Voyager Pr.

Stoudemire, Amar'e. Home Court. 2012. (STAT: Standing Tall & Talented Ser.: 1). lib. bdg. 16.00 (978-0-606-26169-2(9), Turtleback) Turtleback Bks.

Strasser, Todd. Slide or Die. Phillips, Craig, illus. 2006. (DriftX Ser.: 1). (ENG.). 224p. (YA). (gr. 9-18). pap. 10.99 (978-1-4169-0581-3(2), Aladdin) Simon & Schuster Children's Publishing.

Stratford, Anne Margaret. My Daddy Is A Soldier. 2008. (Illus.). 40p. (J). 17.99 (978-0-9817938-0-1(0)) Diamond Fly Publishing, Inc.

Stratton, Allan. Borderline. (ENG.). (YA). (gr. 8). 2012. 320p. pap. 9.99 (978-0-06-145113-3(4)) 2010. (Illus.). 304p. 16.99 (978-0-06-145111-9(8)) HarperCollins Pubs. (HarperTeen).

Streeter, Lord Ronald. Grumpy Brother Christmas. 2008. 28p. pap. 16.50 (978-1-60693-566-8(6), Strategic Bk. Publishing) Strategic Book Publishing & Rights Agency (SBPRA).

Sullivan, Derek E. Biggie. 2015. (ENG.). 272p. (YA). (gr. 8-12). 16.99 (978-0-8075-0727-8(X)) Whitman, Albert & Co.

Swartout, Jenny. The Little One Behind the Badge. 2017. (ENG., Illus.). (J). (gr. -1-3). pap. 7.99 (978-1-935666-95-0(9)) Nodin Pr.

Taback, Simms. Postcards from Camp. Taback, Simms, illus. 2011. (ENG., Illus.). 40p. (J). (gr. -1-3). 17.99 (978-0-399-23973-1(1), Nancy Paulsen Books) Penguin Young Readers Group.

Tarpley, Natasha Anastasia. Bippity Bop Barbershop. Lewis, E. B., illus. 2009. (ENG.). 32p. (gr. -1-3). pap. 7.99 (978-0-316-03382-4(0)) Little, Brown Bks. for Young Readers.

Taylor, L. D. Motive Games. 2012. (ENG.). 192p. pap. (978-1-921632-25-9(9)) Wombat Bks.

Taylor, Sean. Small Bad Wolf. Lewis, Jan, illus. 2004. (I Am Reading Ser.). 45p. (J). (gr. -1-3). 11.60 (978-0-7569-5400-0(2)) Perfection Learning Corp.

Terrell, Brandon. Daydream Receiver. 2017. (Jake Maddox Graphic Novels Ser.). (ENG., Illus.). 72p. (gr. 2-5). lib. bdg. 26.65 (978-1-4965-3702-7(5)) Stone Arch Bks.

—Double Scribble. 2017. (Jake Maddox Graphic Novels Ser.). (ENG., Illus.). 72p. (gr. 2-5). lib. bdg. 26.65 (978-1-4965-3701-0(7)) Stone Arch Bks.

Theurer, Harold, Jr. Hey Dad, Let's Have a Catch! 2006. 32p. (J). 16.95 (978-0-9786584-0-3(X)) Column Hall Concepts, LLC.

Thomas, Patricia. Red Sled. Demarest, Chris L., illus. (ENG.). 32p. (J). (gr. -1-1). 2013. pap. 6.95 (978-1-62091-592-9(8)) 2008. 16.95 (978-1-59078-559-1(2)) Boyds Mills Pr.

Thomas, Rob. Rats Saw God. 2009. 9.00 (978-0-7848-2881-6(4), Everbind) Marco Bk. Co.

—Rats Saw God. 2010. (ENG.). 202p. 17.10 (978-0-7569-8366-6(5)) Perfection Learning Corp.

—Rats Saw God. 2013. (ENG.). 224p. (YA). (gr. 7). 16.99 (978-1-4424-5976-2(X)); (Illus.). pap. 10.99 (978-1-4424-5738-6(4)) Simon & Schuster Bks. For Young Readers. (Simon & Schuster Bks. For Young Readers).

Tong, Kevin. The Earth Machine. Tong, Kevin, illus. 2007. (Illus.). 32p. (J). (gr. -1-3). 15.95 (978-1-60108-001-1(8)) Red Cygnet Pr.

Tooke, Wes. King of the Mound: My Summer with Satchel Paige. (ENG.). 160p. (J). (gr. 3-7). 2013. pap. 7.99 (978-1-4424-3347-2(7)) 2012. (Illus.). 17.99 (978-1-4424-3346-5(9)) Simon & Schuster Bks. For Young Readers. (Simon & Schuster Bks. For Young Readers).

Townley, Roderick. Sky. 2010. (ENG.). 272p. (YA). (gr. 7). pap. 12.99 (978-1-4423-3973-6(X), Atheneum Bks. for Young Readers) Simon & Schuster Children's Publishing.

Townsend, Una Belle. The Oklahoma Land Run, 1 vol. Henriquez, Emile, illus. 2008. (ENG.). 32p. (J). (gr. k-3). 16.99 (978-1-58980-566-8(6)) Pelican Publishing Co., Inc.

Trevor, Simeon. I'm Going to Fly SomeDay. 2004. 36p. spiral bd. 13.93 (978-1-4116-2072-8(0)) Lulu Pr., Inc.

The Troubles of Johnny Cannon. 2014. (ENG., Illus.). 304p. (J). (gr. 3-7). 16.99 (978-1-4814-0003-9(7), Simon & Schuster Bks. For Young Readers) Simon & Schuster Bks. For Young Readers.

Trueman, Terry. No Right Turn. 2009. (ENG.). 176p. (YA). (gr. 9). pap. 8.99 (978-0-06-057493-2(3), HarperTeen) HarperCollins Pubs.

Ungerer, Tomi. The Mellops Go Spelunking. 2015. (ENG., Illus.). 32p. (gr. -1-k). 14.95 (978-0-7148-6971-1(6)) Phaidon Pr., Inc.

U'Nique, Mystique Ann. Reg, Dave & Zach. 2013. 24p. pap. 24.95 (978-1-62709-972-1(7)) PublishAmerica, Inc.

Urban, Linda. Milo Speck, Accidental Agent. (ENG., Illus.). 272p. (J). (gr. 2-5). 2017. pap. 7.99 (978-0-544-93523-5(3)) 2015. 16.99 (978-0-544-41951-3(0)) Houghton Mifflin Harcourt Publishing Co. (HMH Books For Young Readers).

—Weekends with Max & His Dad. Kath, Katie, illus. 2016. (ENG.). 160p. (J). (gr. 2-5). 16.99 (978-0-544-59817-1(2), HMH Books For Young Readers) Houghton Mifflin Harcourt Publishing Co.

van Genechten, Guido & Paradise, Susan. My Daddy. 2011. (ENG.). 20p. (J). (gr. k — 1). bds. 12.95 (978-1-60537-098-9(3)) Cobblestone Publishing Co.

Van Tol, Alex. Food Freak. 2017. (Orca Currents Ser.). lib. bdg. 20.80 (978-0-606-40452-5(X)) Turtleback Bks.

Veldkamp, Tjibbe. Tom the Tamer. Hopman, Philip, illus. 2011. (ENG.). 32p. (J). (gr. -1). 16.95 (978-1-935954-05-7(9), 9781935954057) Lemniscaat USA.

Venditti, Robert & Riordan, Rick. The Sea of Monsters. 2013. (Percy Jackson & the Olympians Graphic Novels Ser.: 2). (J). lib. bdg. 24.50 (978-0-606-23611-9(2), Turtleback) Turtleback Bks.

Venning, Edward W. The Truck & a Boy: The Truck with a big Heart. 2007. 48p. (YA). per. 15.95 (978-1-4327-0738-5(8)) Outskirts Pr., Inc.

Vernick, Audrey. Screaming at the Ump. 2014. (ENG.). 272p. (J). (gr. 5-7). 16.99 (978-0-544-25208-0(X), Clarion Bks.) Houghton Mifflin Harcourt Trade & Reference Pubs.

Vilchez, Deann. The Boy Who Loved His Dad. 2012. 32p. pap. 14.62 (978-1-4251-3109-8(3)) Trafford Publishing.

Villareal, Ray. Body Slammed! 2012. (YA). pap. 11.95 (978-1-55885-749-0(4), Piñata Books) Arte Publico Pr.

Villasenor, Victor. Goodnight, Papito Dios/Buenos Noches, Papito Dios. Villarroel, Carolina, tr. Ramirez, Jose, illus. 2007. (SPA & ENG.). 32p. (J). (gr. -1-2). 16.95 (978-1-55885-467-3(3), Piñata Books) Arte Publico Pr.

Voigt, Cynthia. A Solitary Blue. 2012. (Tillerman Cycle Ser.: 3). (ENG., Illus.). 256p. (YA). (gr. 7). 18.99 (978-1-4424-5062-2(2)); pap. 8.99 (978-1-4424-2880-5(5)) Simon & Schuster Children's Publishing. (Atheneum Bks. for Young Readers).

—A Solitary Blue. l.t. ed. 2005. (Tillerman Cycle Ser.: Bk. 3). 359p. (J). pap. 10.95 (978-0-7862-7912-8(5)) Thorndike Pr.

Volponi, Paul. Game Seven. 2016. lib. bdg. 20.85 (978-0-606-38392-9(1)) Turtleback Bks.

—Homestretch. 2009. (ENG.). 160p. (YA). (gr. 7-18). 16.99 (978-1-4169-3987-0(3), Atheneum Bks. for Young Readers) Simon & Schuster Children's Publishing.

—Hurricane Song. 2009. (ENG.). 160p. (YA). (gr. 7-18). 6.99 (978-0-14-241418-7(2), Speak) Penguin Young Readers Group.

Volponi, Paul & Wells, Rosemary. Game Seven. 2015. (ENG.). 256p. (YA). (gr. 7). bds. 17.99 (978-0-670-78518-6(0), Viking Books for Young Readers) Penguin Young Readers Group.

Wainscott, Bud. The Wounded Hawk. 2012. 48p. pap. 11.95 (978-1-4772-5354-0(8)) AuthorHouse.

Walker, John Anthony. Frel. 2009. 32p. pap. 12.99 (978-1-935436-15-7(5)) Rodaian Pr.

Walker, Lane. Terror at Deadwood Lake. 2014. (Hometown Hunters Collection: Vol. 3). (ENG.). 137p. (YA). (gr. 7-13). pap. 9.99 (978-1-58169-519-9(5), Evergreen Pr.) Genesis Communications, Inc.

Wallace, Bill. Skinny-Dipping at Monster Lake. 2004. 212p. (gr. 3-7). 16.00 (978-0-7569-3486-6(9)) Perfection Learning Corp.

Wallace, Rich. Southpaw. 2006. 105p. (J). lib. bdg. 15.38 (978-1-4242-2166-0(8)) Fitzgerald Bks.

—Southpaw. 6th ed. 2007. (Winning Season Ser.). (ENG.). 128p. (J). (gr. 3-7). 5.99 (978-0-14-240785-1(2), Puffin Books) Penguin Young Readers Group.

—War & Watermelon. 2012. (ENG.). 192p. (J). (gr. 5-18). pap. 6.99 (978-0-14-242138-3(3), Puffin Books) Penguin Young Readers Group.

Walsh, Patrick M., Jr. Who Says Timmy Can't Play: The Derby: A Timmy Wallings Story. McGriff, Aaron, ed. WFM Services, illus. 2011. 135p. (J). (978-0-9842929-3-6(4)) Daddy Bean Bks.

Walter, Aaron T. Mr Lincoln's Hat. 2008. 75p. pap. 16.95 (978-1-60672-852-9(0)) PublishAmerica, Inc.

Walters, Virginia. Are We There Yet, Daddy? Schindler, S. D., illus. 2005. 27p. (J). (gr. k-4). reprint ed. 16.00 (978-0-7567-9708-9(X)) DIANE Publishing Co.

Warwick, J. M. An Open Vein. 2007. (YA). per. 12.95 (978-1-933963-96-9(4)) Grove Creek Publishing, LLC.

Watley, Maylin. Malachi Goes Fishing with His Pap. 2012. 20p. pap. 15.99 (978-1-4685-7320-6(9)) AuthorHouse.

Watson, Cristy. Living Rough, 1 vol. 2011. (Orca Currents Ser.). (ENG.). 128p. (J). (gr. 5-9). 9.95 (978-1-55469-434-1(5)); lib. bdg. 16.95 (978-1-55469-888-2(X)) Orca Bk. Pubs. USA.

Watson, Mary. The Paper Dragonfly. Watson, Mary, illus. 2007. (ENG., Illus.). 32p. (J). (gr. k-3). 15.95 (978-0-9726614-3-0(3)) Shenanigan Bks.

Welford, Ross. Time Traveling with a Hamster. 2016. (ENG.). 432p. (J). (gr. 3-7). 16.99 (978-0-399-55149-9(2), Schwartz & Wade Bks.) Random Hse. Children's Bks.

Wells, Eva. Wishing I Was Fishing. 2006. 32p. lib. bdg. 16.95 (978-1-59298-168-7(2)) Beaver's Pond Pr., Inc.

Weulersse, Odile & Merz, Kathleen. Nasreddine. Dautremer, Rebecca, illus. 2013. (ENG.). 34p. (J). 17.00 (978-0-8028-5416-2(8), Eerdmans Bks For Young Readers) Eerdmans, William B. Publishing Co.

Whelan, Gloria. Mackinac Bridge: The Story of the Five-Mile Poem. van Frankenhuyzen, Gijsbert, illus. 2006. (Tales of Young Americans Ser.). (ENG.). 32p. (J). 17.95 (978-1-58536-283-7(2)) Sleeping Bear Pr.

Wibberley, Leonard. Peter Treegate's War. 2009. 134p. (YA). pap. 12.95 (978-1-932350-21-0(7)) Bethlehem Bks.

Wilkinson, Carole. Buried at Sea. 2007. 96p. (YA). pap. (978-1-4207-0738-0(8)) Sundance/Newbridge Educational Publishing.

Williams, Karen Lynn. A Beach Tail. Cooper, Floyd, illus. 2010. (ENG.). 32p. (J). (gr. -1-2). 17.95 (978-1-59078-712-0(9)) Boyds Mills Pr.

Williams, Stanley. Willie's Dad. 2008. 26p. 14.95 (978-0-615-19121-8(5)) Williamspublishing.

Williams, Vera B. Home at Last. Raschka, Chris, illus. 2016. 40p. (J). (gr. -1-3). 17.99 (978-0-06-134973-7(9), Greenwillow Bks.) HarperCollins Pubs.

Willis, Janet, illus. A Dad's Delight. 2006. (978-0-9785077-0-1(3)); pap. (978-0-9785077-1-8(1)) Khesed Foundation.

Winfield, Arthur M. The Rover Boys in New York. 2007. 268p. 26.95 (978-1-4218-4133-5(9)); per. 11.95 (978-1-4218-4231-8(9)) 1st World Publishing, Inc. (1st World Library - Literary Society).

—The Rover Boys in New York or Saving the. 2004. reprint ed. pap. 22.95 (978-1-4191-8117-7(3)) Kessinger Publishing, LLC.

Winfield, Arthur M. The Rover Boys in New York or Saving Their Father's Honor. 2004. reprint ed. pap. 1.99 (978-1-4192-8117-4(8)) Kessinger Publishing, LLC.

Winmilawe. Shango's Son. Melchishua, Tewodross, illus. 2012. 20p. pap. 9.95 (978-0-9839318-0-5(1)) Gazing In Publishing.

Wohnoutka, Mike. Dad's First Day. Wohnoutka, Mike, illus. 2015. (ENG., Illus.). 40p. (J). (gr. -1-3). 16.99 (978-1-61963-473-2(2), 9781619634732, Bloomsbury USA Childrens) Bloomsbury Publishing USA.

Wojciechowska, Maia. Shadow of a Bull. 2011. 8.32 (978-0-7848-3457-2(1), Everbind) Marco Bk. Co.

Wood, Cary D. Davis & Pop Go Hiking. Turner, Cecilia, illus. 2014. (ENG.). 30p. (gr. -1-4). 34.95 (978-1-63047-217-7(4)) Morgan James Publishing.

Wooten, Laura. With My Little Box of Crayons. Pennington, Kelly, illus. 2008. 50p. pap. 18.95 (978-1-4251-7103-2(6)) Trafford Publishing.

Wurge, B. B. The Last Notebook of Leonardo. 2010. (LeapKids Ser.). (ENG., Illus.). 154p. (J). (gr. 1-7). pap. 9.95 (978-1-935248-14-9(6)) Leapfrog Pr.

Wyley, Enda. The Silver Notebook. 2007. (ENG.). 208p. (J). pap. 12.95 (978-1-84717-020-0(X)) O'Brien Pr., Ltd., The IRL. Dist: Dufour Editions, Inc.

Wynne-Jones, Tim. The Maestro. l.t. ed. 2013. 304p. pap. (978-1-4596-6503-3(1)) ReadHowYouWant.com, Ltd.

Yee, Lisa. Bobby the Brave (Sometimes) Santat, Dan, illus. 2012. (ENG.). 160p. (J). (gr. 2-5). pap. 5.99 (978-0-545-05595-6(4), Levine, Arthur A. Bks.) Scholastic, Inc.

—Stanford Wong Flunks Big-Time. 2007. (Apple Signature Edition Ser.). (ENG., Illus.). 320p. (J). (gr. 3-7). per. 6.99 (978-0-439-62248-6(4), Levine, Arthur A. Bks.) Scholastic, Inc.

Yee, Paul. Money Boy. 2013. 192p. pap. (978-1-4596-6450-0(7)) ReadHowYouWant.com, Ltd.

Yelchin, Eugene. Breaking Stalin's Nose. Yelchin, Eugene, illus. 2011. (ENG., Illus.). 160p. (J). (gr. 4-7). 15.99 (978-0-8050-9216-5(1), 9780805092165, Holt, Henry & Co. Bks. For Young Readers) Holt, Henry & Co.

—Breaking Stalin's Nose. Yelchin, Eugene, illus. 2013. (ENG., Illus.). 176p. (J). (gr. 4-7). pap. 7.99 (978-1-250-03410-6(8), 9781250034106) Square Fish.

—Breaking Stalin's Nose. 2013. (J). lib. bdg. 18.40 (978-0-606-32308-6(2), Turtleback) Turtleback Bks.

Yep, Laurence & Yep, Kathleen S. The Dragon's Child: A Story of Angel Island. 2011. (ENG.). 160p. (J). (gr. 3-7). pap. 5.99 (978-0-06-201815-1(9)) HarperCollins Pubs.

Young, Janet Ruth. My Beautiful Failure. (ENG., Illus.). 320p. (YA). (gr. 7). 2013. pap. 9.99 (978-1-4424-8269-2(9)) 2012. 16.99 (978-1-4169-5489-7(9)) Simon & Schuster Children's Publishing. (Atheneum Bks. for Young Readers).

Young, Jessica. Spy Guy: The Not-So-Secret Agent. Santoso, Charles, illus. 2015. (ENG.). 40p. (J). (gr. -1-3). 16.99 (978-0-544-20859-9(5), HMH Books For Young Readers) Houghton Mifflin Harcourt Publishing Co.

Young, Judy. Promise. 2016. (ENG.). 368p. (J). (gr. 4-6). pap. 8.99 (978-1-58536-915-7(2), 204079) Sleeping Bear Pr.

—Tuki & Moka: A Tale of Two Tamarins. Madsen, Jim, illus. 2013. (ENG.). 32p. 16.99 (978-1-58536-795-5(8)) Sleeping Bear Pr.

Young, Ned. Zoomer. Young, Ned, illus. 2010. (ENG., Illus.). 32p. (J). (gr. -1-2). 16.99 (978-0-06-170088-0(6)) HarperCollins Pubs.

Zerbe, Tim. The King of Pumpkin Ridge. 2012. 28p. pap. 9.95 (978-1-937600-80-8(7)) Salem Author Services.

Zwald, John & DesRochers, Diane O. Mahmoud Meets Moses. Zwald, John, illus. 2012. (Illus.). 26p. pap. 14.99 (978-0-9838832-9-6(7)) WRB Pub.

FAULKNER, WILLIAM, 1897-1962

Mcarthur, Debra. Reading & Interpreting the Works of William Faulkner. 2016. (Lit Crit Guides). (ENG., Illus.). 160p. (J). (gr. 8-8). lib. bdg. 39.93 (978-0-7660-7354-8(8)) Enslow Pubs., Inc.

McArthur, Debra. A Student's Guide to William Faulkner. 2009. (Understanding Literature Ser.). (Illus.). 160p. (YA). (gr. 9-12). lib. bdg. 29.27 (978-0-7660-2885-2(2)) Enslow Pubs., Inc.

FAUNA

see Animals; Zoology

FAWKES, GUY, 1570-1606

Ashworth, Leon. Guy Fawkes. (Illus.). 32p. (978-0-7451-5288-2(0)) Cherrytree Bks.

Howell, Izzi. Guy Fawkes & the Gunpowder Plot. 2016. (Why Do We Remember? Ser.). (ENG., Illus.). 32p. (J). (gr. 1-3). 17.99 (978-1-4451-4850-2(1), Franklin Watts) Hachette Children's Group GBR. Dist: Hachette Bk. Group.

Malam, John. Gunpowder Plot. 2007. (Dates with History Ser.). (ENG., Illus.). 48p. (J). pap. 9.99 (978-1-84234-536-8(2)) Evans Brothers, Ltd. GBR. Dist: Independent Pubs. Group.

White-Thomson, Stephen. Guy Fawkes. 2017. (Popcorn: People in History Ser.). (ENG., Illus.). 24p. (J). (gr. 4-6). pap. 10.99 (978-0-7502-8372-4(6), Wayland) Hachette Children's Group GBR. Dist: Hachette Bk. Group.

FEAR

see also Courage

Aboff, Marcie. Everyone Feels Scared Sometimes, 1 vol. Ward, Damian, illus. 2010. (Everyone Has Feelings Ser.). (ENG.). 24p. (gr. k-2). lib. bdg. 25.99 (978-1-4048-5756-8(7)) Picture Window Bks.

Adams, Carol J. God Listens When You're Afraid: Prayers for When Animals Scare You. 2006. (God Listens Ser.). 48p. (J). (gr. -1). per. (978-0-8298-1741-6(7)) Pilgrim Pr., The/United Church Pr.

Annunziata, Jane & Nemiroff, Marc. Sometimes I'm Scared. Langdo, Bryan, illus. 2009. 32p. pap. 9.95 (978-1-4338-0550-9(2)); (J). (gr. -1-3). 14.95 (978-1-4338-0449-6(2)) American Psychological Assn. (Magination Pr.).

Amaldo, Monica. The Little Book of Big Fears. 2015. (ENG., Illus.). 40p. (J). (gr. k-4). 16.95 (978-1-77147-047-6(X), Owlkids) Owlkids Bks. Inc. CAN. Dist: Publishers Group West (PGW).

Aunt Darla. There's a Monster under the Captain's Bed!!! Erik's Monster. Petersen, Darla & Shields, Erik P., illus. Date not set. 32p. 16.00 (978-0-9658926-1-2(1)) Poet Tree Pubns.

Berry, Joy. Fear. 2005. (Winning skills series, get over It! Ser.). (ENG., Illus.). 48p. (J). pap. 3.95 (978-1-57687-275-8(0), PowerHouse Kids) powerHouse Cultural Entertainment, Inc.

—Feeling Afraid. 2009. (ENG.). 40p. (J). (gr. -1-k). pap. 7.95 (978-1-60577-201-1(1)) Berry, Joy Enterprises.

—Let's Talk about Feeling Afraid. Smith, Maggie, illus. 2010. (Let's Talk About Ser.). (ENG.). 32p. (J). (gr. -1-k). pap. 4.99 (978-1-60577-205-9(4)) Berry, Joy Enterprises.

Bingham, Jane. Everybody Feels Scared. 2008. (Everybody Feels Ser.). (ENG., Illus.). 24p. (J). pap. (978-0-7787-4067-4(6)) Crabtree Publishing Co.

Brignaud, Pierre, illus. Caillou: Good Night! Sleep Well: Nighttime. 2017. (Caillou's Essentials Ser.). (ENG.). 24p. (J). (gr. -1-k). bds. 7.99 (978-2-89718-357-8(8)) Caillouet, Gerry.

Broadbent, Paul. What Are You Scared Of? 2007. (Trackers-Math Ser.). (gr. 2-5). pap. 5.00 (978-1-59055-928-4(2)) Pacific Learning, Inc.

Cantor, Joanne. Teddy's TV Troubles. Lowes, Tom, illus. 2004. 36p. (J). mass mkt. 16.95 (978-0-9647663-7-2(X)) HenschelHAUS Publishing.

Chong, Elaine S. & Hovanec, Erin. Phobias. 2011. (Understanding Brain Diseases & Disorders Ser.). (ENG.). 64p. (YA). (gr. 7-12). lib. bdg. 31.95 (978-1-4488-5541-4(1)) Rosen Publishing Group, Inc., The.

Clark, Rosalyn. Feeling Scared. 2017. (Bumba Books (tm) — Feelings Matter Ser.). (ENG.). (J). (gr. -1-1). pap. 6.99 **(978-1-5124-5548-9(2))**; (Illus.). lib. bdg. 25.32 **(978-1-5124-3369-2(1))** Lerner Publishing Group.

Crist, James J. What to Do When You're Scared & Worried: A Guide for Kids. 2004. (ENG., Illus.). 128p. (YA). (gr. 4-8). pap. 10.99 (978-1-57542-153-7(4)) Free Spirit Publishing, Inc.

Egar, Joann. Caillou: Sometimes Moms Get Angry. Brignaud, Pierre, illus. 2014. (ENG.). 24p. (J). (gr. -1-k). 5.99 (978-2-89718-116-1(8)) Caillouet, Gerry.

Etingoff, Kim. Fear & Anxiety. Croft, Cindy, ed. 2014. (Causes & Effects of Emotions Ser.: 13). 64p. (J). (gr. 7-18). 23.95 (978-1-4222-3073-2(2)) Mason Crest.

Franzen, Lenore. Fear. 2004. (My Feelings Ser.). (Illus.). 24p. (J). lib. bdg. 15.95 (978-1-58341-319-7(7), Creative Education) Creative Co., The.

Graves, Sue. Take a Deep Breath. Guicciardini, Desideria, illus. 2013. (Our Emotions & Behavior Ser.). (ENG.). 32p. (J). (gr. -1-3). 12.99 (978-1-57542-446-0(0)) Free Spirit Publishing, Inc.

Hadi, Aryo. Fall, Learn, Rise. 2011. (JPN & ENG., Illus.). 140p. 29.66 (978-1-4567-7512-4(X)); pap. 16.52 (978-1-4567-7511-7(1)) AuthorHouse.

Harpster, Steve, illus. Catherine Finds Her Courage: An Emotional Literacy Book. 2004. (Emotional Literacy Ser.). 44p. (J). (gr. 2-18). 14.95 (978-0-9747789-2-1(3), 67314) CTC Publishing.

Iorizzo, Carrie. Anxiety & Phobias. 2013. (ENG., Illus.). 48p. (J). (978-0-7787-0082-1(8)); pap. (978-0-7787-0088-3(7)) Crabtree Publishing Co.

Johnson, Marion. Caillou, What's That Noise. CINAR Corporation Staff, illus. 2004. (Clubhouse Usa Ser.). (ENG.). 24p. (J). pap. 3.95 (978-2-89450-489-5(6)) Ellipsis Pr.

Kahn, Ada P. & Doctor, Ronald M. Phobias. 2003. (Life Balance Ser.). (ENG., Illus.). 80p. (J). 20.50 (978-0-531-12256-3(5), Watts, Franklin) Scholastic Library Publishing.

Knutson, Eric. I Never Get Scared. Stensen, Cindy, illus. 2010. (J). (978-1-930596-99-3(5)) Amherst Pr.

Kreiner, Anna. Being Afraid. 2004. (Let's Talk Library). (Illus.). 24p. (J). 22.60 (978-0-8239-6930-2(4), PowerKids Pr.) Rosen Publishing Group, Inc., The.

—Let's Talk about Being Afraid. 2009. (Let's Talk Library). 24p. (gr. 2-3). 42.50 (978-1-60853-450-0(2), PowerKids Pr.) Rosen Publishing Group, Inc., The.

Larsen, Carolyn. Being Brave: A Book about Being Afraid. O'Connor, Tim, illus. 2017. (Growing God's Kids Ser.). (ENG.). 32p. (J). pap. 4.99 (978-0-8010-0974-7(X)) Baker Bks.

Leblanc, Catherine. My Monster-Mashing. Garrigue, Roland, illus. 2016. (ENG.). 80p. (J). (gr. -1). pap., act. bk. ed. 14.99 (978-1-60887-710-2(8)) Insight Editions.

Leonard, Marcia. I Feel Scared. Bartholomew, illus. 2003. 24p. (J). bds. 2.95 (978-0-8249-6525-9(6), Ideal Pubns.) Worthy Publishing.

MacKay, Jennifer. Phobias. 2009. (Diseases & Disorders Ser.). (ENG., Illus.). 128p. (gr. 7-10). lib. bdg. 39.90 (978-1-4205-0103-2(8), LML02109-244486, Lucent Bks.) Cengage Gale.

Meiners, Cheri J. When I Feel Afraid. 2003. (Learning to Get Along(r) Ser.). (ENG., Illus.). 40p. (J). (gr. -1-3). pap. 10.95 (978-1-57542-138-4(0)) Free Spirit Publishing, Inc.

Moses, Melissa. Alex & the Scary Things: A Story for Children Who Have Experienced Scary Things. MacEachern, Alison, illus. 2015. (ENG.). 40p. (J). 17.95 (978-1-84905-793-6(1), 4189) Kingsley, Jessica Pubs. GBR. Dist: Macmillan Distribution Ltd.

Mundy, Michaelene. Sometimes I'm Afraid: A Book about Fear... Just for Me! Fitzgerald, Anne, illus. 2012. 32p. (J). pap. 7.95 (978-0-87029-500-3(4)) Abbey Pr.

Naish, Sarah & Jefferies, Rosie. William Wobbly & the Mysterious Holey Jumper: A Story about Fear & Coping. Evans, Megan, illus. 2017. (Therapeutic Parenting Bks.). (ENG.). 32p. (J). pap. 14.95 **(978-1-78592-281-7(5)**, 9201) Kingsley, Jessica Pubs. GBR. Dist: Macmillan Distribution Ltd.

Nichols, Cheyenne. Miedo Es... Strictly Spanish Translation Services Staff, tr. from ENG. 2013. (Reconoce Tus Emociones/Know Your Emotions Ser.).Tr. of Scared Is.... (ENG, SPA & MUL.). 24p. (gr. 1-2). lib. bdg. 27.32 (978-1-62065-153-7(X)) Capstone Press of Coughlan Cos.

La Nueva Maestra. (Coleccion Chiquilines). (SPA., Illus.). 24p. (J). 8.50 (978-950-11-0066-2(9), SGM066) Sigmar ARG. Dist: Continental Bk. Co., Inc.

Orme, David. Fear. 2011. (Fact to Fiction Grafx Ser.). (ENG., Illus.). 36p. (J). (gr. 4-7). lib. bdg. 17.45 (978-1-61384-018-4(7)) Perfection Learning Corp.

Orr, Tamra B. Fear. 2016. (21st Century Basic Skills Library: Feelings Ser.). (ENG., Illus.). 24p. (J). (gr. k-3). 24.21 (978-1-63471-046-6(0), 208264) Cherry Lake Publishing.

Peters, Daniel B., et al. The Warrior Workbook: A Guide for Conquering Your Worry Monster. 2017. (Illus.). vii, 96p. (J). pap. 16.95 (978-1-935067-44-3(3)) Great Potential Pr., Inc.

Priddy, Roger. The Talent Show. Crimi-Trent, Ellen, illus. 2014. (Schoolies Ser.). (ENG.). 28p. (J). (gr. -1-1). 4.99 (978-0-312-51664-2(9), 9780312516642, Priddy Bks.) St. Martin's Pr.

El Primer Dia De Clases. (Coleccion Chiquilines). (SPA.). 24p. (J). 8.50 (978-950-11-0359-5(5), SGM359) Sigmar ARG. Dist: Continental Bk. Co., Inc.

Salas, Laura Purdie & Nichols, Cheyenne. Scared Is... 2011. (Know Your Emotions Ser.). (ENG.). 24p. (gr. 1-2). lib. bdg. 27.32 (978-1-4296-6045-7(7), Aplus Bks.) Capstone Press of Coughlan Cos.

Sévigny, Eric, illus. Caillou & the Big Slide. 2012. (Clubhouse Ser.). (ENG.). 24p. (J). (gr. -1-1). pap. 3.99 (978-2-89450-867-1(0)) Caillouet, Gerry.

—The Missing Sock. rev. ed. 2003. (Clubhouse Ser.). (ENG.). 24p. (J). (gr. -1-1). pap. 3.99 (978-2-89450-445-1(4)) Caillouet, Gerry.

Shepherd, Joanne. What I Look Like When I Am Scared. (Let's Look at Feelings Ser.). 24p. 2009. (gr. k-1). 42.50 (978-1-61514-242-2(8)) 2004. (Illus.). (gr. -1-1). 22.60 (978-1-4042-2509-1(9)) Rosen Publishing Group, Inc., The. (PowerKids Pr.).

—What I Look Like When I Am Scared: Como Me Veo Cuando Estoy Asustado. 2004. (Let's Look at Feelings / un Vistazo a Los Sentimientos Ser.). (ENG., Illus.). 24p. (J). (gr. -1-1). lib. bdg. 22.60 (978-1-4042-7509-6(6), Editorial Buenas Letras) Rosen Publishing Group, Inc., The.

—What I Look Like When I am Scared / Cómo me veo cuando estoy Asustado. 2009. (Let's Look at Feelings / un vistazo a los sentimientos Ser.). (ENG & SPA.). 24p. (gr. k-1). 42.50 (978-1-61514-248-4(7), Editorial Buenas Letras) Rosen Publishing Group, Inc., The.

Shuman, Carol. Jenny Is Scared! When Sad Things Happen in the World. Pillo, Cary, tr. Pillo, Cary, illus. 2003. 32p. (J). (gr. k-3). pap. 9.95 (978-1-59147-003-8(X)); 14.95 (978-1-59147-002-1(1)) American Psychological Assn. (Magination Pr.).

Smith, Paula. Phobias & Other Anxiety Disorders. 2013. 48p. (J). (978-0-7787-0856-8(X)); (Illus.). pap. (978-0-7787-0862-9(4)) Crabtree Publishing Co.

Sunderland, Margot & Hancock, Nicky. Helping Children with Fear: A Guidebook, 2 vols. Armstrong, Nicky, tr. 2012. (Helping Children with Feelings Ser.). (ENG., Illus.). 140p. (C). pap. 34.95 (978-0-86388-464-1(4), Y329801, Routledge) Taylor & Francis Group GBR. Dist: Taylor & Francis Group.

Thaler, Mike. The Class Trip from the Black Lagoon, 1 vol. Lee, Jared, illus. 2011. (Black Lagoon Adventures Ser.: No. 1). (ENG.). 64p. (gr. 3-6). 24.21 (978-1-59961-811-1(7)) Spotlight.

Umbach, Andrea. Conquer Your Fears & Phobias for Teens: How to Overcome Scary Situations & Increase Your Freedom. 2015. (ENG.). 240p. (YA). (gr. 6-12). pap. 17.95 (978-1-62625-145-8(2)) New Harbinger Pubns.

Ward, Damian, illus. Everyone Has Feelings, 4 vols., Set. Incl. Everyone Feels Angry Sometimes. Meister, Cari. lib. bdg. 25.99 (978-1-4048-5753-7(2)); Everyone Feels Happy Sometimes. Meister, Cari. lib. bdg. 25.99 (978-1-4048-5754-4(0)); Everyone Feels Sad Sometimes. Aboff, Marcie. lib. bdg. 25.99 (978-1-4048-5755-1(9)); Everyone Feels Scared Sometimes. Aboff, Marcie. lib. bdg. 25.99 (978-1-4048-5756-8(7)); (Illus.). (gr. k-2). (Everyone Has Feelings Ser.). (ENG.). 24p. 2010. Set lib. bdg. 103.96 (978-1-4048-6001-8(0)) Picture Window Bks.

FEAR—FICTION

The Acorn Story: An Adventure about Change. 2005. (J). 12.95 (978-0-9767769-0-1(1)) Rutigliano, Joe.

Adams, Michelle M. I Will Not Be Afraid. Tugeau, Jeremy, illus. 2008. 32p. (J). (gr. -1-3). 14.99 (978-0-7586-1335-6(0)) Concordia Publishing Hse.

Adams, William J. Hate that Thunder. Stiglich, Tom, illus. 2005. 24p. (J). pap. 8.95 (978-0-9772757-0-0(1)) Mandy & Andy Bks., Inc.

Adamson, Ged & Rylance, Ulrike. Elsie Clarke & the Vampire Hairdresser. Adamson, Ged, illus. 2013. (ENG., Illus.). 28p. (J). (gr. -1-1). 16.95 (978-1-62087-983-2(2), 620983, Sky Pony Pr.) Skyhorse Publishing Co., Inc.

Alberts, Katharine O. Boo on the Loose. 2006. (J). 14.00 (978-0-8059-7071-5(1)) Dorrance Publishing Co., Inc.

Alexander, Louise. My Little Pony: Happy Haunting. 2016. (ENG.). 24p. (J). (gr. -1-3). 8.99 (978-0-316-36150-7(X)) Little, Brown Bks. for Young Readers.

Anderson, Laurie Halse. Storm Rescue. 2008. (Vet Volunteers Ser.: 6). (ENG.). 144p. (J). (gr. 3-7). 6.99 (978-0-14-241101-8(9), Puffin Books) Penguin Young Readers Group.

Applegate, Katherine. The Buffalo Storm. Ormerod, Jan, illus. 2014. (ENG.). 32p. (J). (gr. -1-3). pap. 7.99 (978-0-544-33921-7(5), HMH Books For Young Readers) Houghton Mifflin Harcourt Publishing Co.

Appleton, Nancy. The Rescue: Cecelia's Story. 2012. 24p. 24.95 (978-1-4626-6713-0(9)) America Star Bks.

Arnno, Nancy. A Friend for Mole, 1 vol. Arnno, Nancy, illus. 2016. (ENG., Illus.). 32p. (J). (gr. -1-k). 16.95 (978-1-56145-865-3(1)) Peachtree Pubs.

Auntie Nana. Falling off My Bike. 2013. pap. 15.95 (978-0-7414-8280-8(0)) Infinity Publishing.

—Falling off My Bike with Cd. 2013. pap. 20.95 (978-0-7414-8281-5(9)) Infinity Publishing.

Baghdasaryan, Rouzanna. The Dark. Morchiladze, Manana, illus. 2007. 32p. (J). (POL & ENG.). pap. 12.95 (978-1-60195-096-3(9)); (ARA & ENG.). pap. 12.95 (978-1-60195-086-4(1)) International Step by Step Assn.

Baguley, Elizabeth. Ready, Steady, Ghost! Lindsay, Marion, illus. 2014. (ENG.). 32p. (J). (gr. -1-k). 16.99 (978-1-4231-8039-5(9)) Hyperion Bks. for Children.

Bailey, Kevin. Anthony Meets the Playground Bully. 2009. 20p. pap. 13.50 (978-1-60860-072-4(6), Eloquent Bks.) Strategic Book Publishing & Rights Agency (SBPRA).

Baisden, Crystal. Carlie's New Friend. 2012. 24p. pap. 24.95 (978-1-4626-8405-2(X)) America Star Bks.

Baldwin, Kevin. Beetle Dan & the Big Purple Slide: A Beetle Dan Story. 2006. (Beetle Dan Story Ser.). (ENG., Illus.). 32p. (J). (gr. -1-2). 14.99 (978-1-59185-921-5(2), Creation Hse.) Charisma Media.

Balmes, Santi. I Will Fight Monsters for You. Lyona, illus. 2015. (ENG.). 32p. (J). (gr. -1-3). 16.99 (978-0-8075-9056-0(8)) Whitman, Albert & Co.

Banks, Steven. The Big Halloween Scare. Martinez, Heather, illus. 2003. (SpongeBob SquarePants Ser.: Vol. 1). (ENG.). 32p. (J). (gr. k-2). pap. 3.99 (978-0-689-84196-5(5), Simon Spotlight/Nickelodeon) Simon Spotlight/Nickelodeon.

—Spongebob Goes to the Doctor. Saunders, Zina, illus. 2005. 22p. (J). lib. bdg. 15.00 (978-1-4242-0976-7(5)) Fitzgerald Bks.

Bardhan-Quallen, Sudipta. Purrmaids #1: the Scaredy Cat. 2017. (Purrmaids Ser.: 1). (ENG.). 96p. (J). (gr. 1-4). lib. bdg. 12.99 **(978-1-5247-0162-8(9))**; (Illus.). 4.99 **(978-1-5247-0161-1(0))** Random Hse. Children's Bks. (Random Hse. Bks. for Young Readers).

Barickman, Traci. Cooper's Adventures: Facing Our Fears. 2010. 24p. 11.49 (978-1-4520-0326-9(2)) AuthorHouse.

Bauer, Joan. Tell Me. (ENG.). (J). (gr. 5). 2015. 288p. 7.99 (978-0-14-751314-4(6), Puffin Books) 2014. 272p. 16.99 (978-0-451-47033-1(8), Viking Books for Young Readers) Penguin Young Readers Group.

Beck, Patricia. Princess Feldings & the Academy of Queens. 2010. 28p. 13.99 (978-1-4490-1376-9(7)) AuthorHouse.

Beckman, Chris & Beckman, Kelly. It's Not Scary You See... 2012. (ENG.). (J). pap. (978-1-4675-3871-8(X)) Independent Pub.

Bee, Clair. Ten Seconds to Play: A Chip Hilton Sports Story. 2011. 222p. (gr. 8-12). 44.95 (978-1-258-09715-8(X)) Literary Licensing, LLC.

Bee, Nanny. William. 2012. 52p. (-18). pap. 16.95 (978-1-4626-9765-6(8)) America Star Bks.

Benoist, Cathy & Gilmore, Cathy. El Conejito de Pascua: El Cuento de un Dia Extraordinario. Sundy, Jonathan, illus. 2014. (SPA.). 40p. (J). (gr. 4-7). 16.99 (978-0-7648-2456-2(2), Libros Liguori) Liguori Pubns.

Bently, Peter. Charlie & the Banana Monster: A Lift-the-Flap Story about Chimpanzees. 2013. (ENG.). 20p. (J). (gr. -1-2). bds. 9.99 (978-1-4263-1097-3(8), National Geographic Children's Bks.) National Geographic Society.

—King Jack & the Dragon. Oxenbury, Helen, illus. 2011. (ENG.). 32p. (J). (gr. -1-k). 17.99 (978-0-8037-3698-6(3), Dial Bks) Penguin Young Readers Group.

Berenstain, Stan & Berenstain, Jan. The Berenstain Bears & the Bad Dream. 2004. (Berenstain Bears First Time Bks.). (J). (gr. -1-2). spiral bd. (978-0-616-01555-1(0)); spiral bd. (978-0-616-01556-8(9)) Canadian National Institute for the Blind/Institut National Canadien pour les Aveugles.

Berenstain, Stan, et al. Do Not Fear, God Is Near, 1 vol. 2013. (I Can Read! / Berenstain Bears / Living Lights Ser.). (ENG.). 32p. (J). pap. 3.99 (978-0-310-72511-4(9)) Zonderkidz.

Bergman, Mara. Snip Snap! What's That? Maland, Nick, illus. 2005. (ENG.). 32p. (J). (gr. -1-3). 16.99 (978-0-06-077754-8(0), Greenwillow Bks.) HarperCollins Pubs.

Berneger, Marcia. Buster the Little Garbage Truck. Zimmer, Kevin, illus. 2015. (ENG.). 32p. (J). (gr. -1-1). 14.99 (978-1-58536-894-5(6), 203814) Sleeping Bear Pr.

Bertagnolli, Daniel. Whooo Turned Out the Lights? Bertagnolli, Daniel, illus. 2009. (Illus.). 20p. pap. 9.14 (978-1-4269-0590-2(4)) Trafford Publishing.

Berube, Kate. Hannah & Sugar. 2016. (ENG., Illus.). 32p. (J). (gr. k-2). 16.95 (978-1-4197-1890-8(8), Abrams Bks. for Young Readers) Abrams, Inc.

Best-Everette, Shabarbara. Will You Be My Friend? 2010. 32p. pap. 17.25 (978-1-4269-4186-3(2)) Trafford Publishing.

Binch, Caroline. The Princess & the Castle. Binch, Caroline, illus. 2005. (ENG., Illus.). 32p. (J). (gr. k-2). 8.99 (978-0-09-943236-4(6), Red Fox) Random House Children's Books GBR. Dist: Independent Pubs. Group.

Birney, Betty G. Humphrey's Creepy-Crawly Camping Adventure. Burris, Priscilla, illus. 2015. (Humphrey's Tiny Tales Ser.: 3). (ENG.). 96p. (J). (gr. k-3). 14.99 (978-0-399-17227-4(0), G.P. Putnam's Sons Books for Young Readers) Penguin Young Readers Group.

Blackman, Christy. Mr. Thunder Is Here, but There's No Reason to Fear. 2008. 36p. pap. 24.95 (978-1-60441-695-4(5)) America Star Bks.

Blegvad, Lenore. Ana Banana y Yo. Puncel, María & Blegvad, Erik, trs. Blegvad, Erik, illus. 2003.Tr. of Anna Banana & Me. (SPA.). 56p. (J). (gr. k-3). pap. 9.95 (978-84-204-4375-1(1)) Santillana USA Publishing Co., Inc.

—Ana Banana y Yo. Blegvad, Erik, illus. 14th ed. 2003.Tr. of Anna Banana & Me. (SPA.). 56p. (gr. k-3). pap. 10.95 (978-84-204-0083-9(1), Alfaguara) Santillana USA Publishing Co., Inc.

BMI Staff, compiled by. Fear Street Collection - Set, 98 vols. 2009. (YA). 114.81 (978-1-60884-415-9(3)) BMI Educational Services.

Bogel, Rachel Anne. A Ride on the Monster's Back. Greenfelder, Jill, illus. 2008. 28p. pap. 15.99 (978-1-59858-752-4(8)) Dog Ear Publishing, LLC.

Bond, Felicia. Poinsettia & the Firefighters. Bond, Felicia, illus. 2003. (Illus.). (J). (978-0-06-056871-9(2)) HarperCollins Pubs.

Bondor-Stone, Annabeth & White, Connor. The Shivering. Holden, Anthony, illus. 2016. (Shivers! Ser.: 2). 208p. (J). (gr. 3-7). 12.99 (978-0-06-231389-8(4)) HarperCollins Pubs.

—Shivers! - The Pirate Who's Afraid of Everything. Holden, Anthony, illus. 2015. (Shivers! Ser.: 1). (ENG.). 192p. (J). (gr. 3-7). 12.99 (978-0-06-231387-4(8)) HarperCollins Pubs.

Bowman, Chaliece. Sarah's Camping Trip. 2012. 20p. pap. 17.99 (978-1-4772-5531-5(1)) AuthorHouse.

Bowman, Crystal. Jake's Brave Night, 1 vol. Maizel, Karen, illus. 2007. (I Can Read! / the Jake Ser.). (ENG.). 32p. (J). (gr. -1-3). pap. 3.99 (978-0-310-71456-9(7)) Zonderkidz.

Bracegirdle, P. J. The Dead Family Diaz. Bernatene, Poly, illus. 2012. (ENG.). 40p. (J). (gr. 1-4). 16.99 (978-0-8037-3326-8(7), Dial Bks) Penguin Young Readers Group.

Bradford, Karleen. Ghost Wolf. Cormack, Allan & Drew-Brook, Deborah, illus. 2005. 59p. (J). lib. bdg. 20.00 (978-1-4242-1254-5(5)) Fitzgerald Bks.

Bradford, William. Jeremy Mcbright Was Afraid of the Night. 2006. (Illus.). 36p. (J). lib. bdg. 13.95 (978-0-9672585-2-2(9)) CyPress Pubns.

Brand, Brandon. Lily Is... Wide Awake. 2008. 32p. (J). 16.00 (978-0-9802329-0-5(2)) Upside Down Tree Publishing.

Brandy. COULD & COULDN't Are Not Afraid of the Dark: Big Life Lessons for Little Kids. 2017. (ENG., Illus.). 40p. 10.00 **(978-981-4771-30-6(9))** Marshall Cavendish International (Asia) Private Ltd. SGP. Dist: National Bk. Network.

Brendler, Carol. Not Very Scary. Pizzoli, Greg, illus. 2014. (ENG.). 40p. (J). (gr. -1-1). 12.99 (978-0-374-35547-0(9), 9780374355470, Farrar, Straus & Giroux (BYR)) Farrar, Straus & Giroux.

Brice, Ginny. Princess Maddy & Her Blankie. Gary Ripper, illus. 2011. 20p. pap. 24.95 (978-1-4560-7745-7(7)) America Star Bks.

Bright, J. E. Scarecrow's Nightmare Maze. Vecchio, Luciano, illus. 2016. (Batman & Robin Adventures Ser.). (ENG.). 88p. (gr. 2-3). lib. bdg. 26.65 (978-1-4965-2537-6(X), DC Super Heroes) Stone Arch Bks.

Brooke, Samantha. Star of the Show. 2014. lib. bdg. 13.55 (978-0-606-35857-6(9)) Turtleback Bks.

Brown, J. A. Scaredy Duck. Knight, Paula, illus. 2004. (Funny Faces Ser.). 10p. (J). 3.95 (978-1-58925-716-0(2)) Tiger Tales.

Bruchac, Joseph. Whisper in the Dark. Comport, Sally Wern, illus. 2009. (ENG.). 192p. (J). (gr. 5). pap. 6.99 (978-0-06-058089-6(5)) HarperCollins Pubs.

Bruel, Nick. Bad Kitty Scaredy-Cat. 2016. (Bad Kitty Ser.). (ENG., Illus.). 32p. (J). 16.99 (978-1-59643-978-8(5), 9781596439788) Roaring Brook Pr.

Brugger, Ruth L. Count Candy Corn. 2013. 32p. pap. 13.99 (978-1-4808-0190-5(9)) Archway Publishing.

Bryan, Ashley. Can't Scare Me! Bryan, Ashley, illus. 2013. (ENG., Illus.). 40p. (J). (gr. -1-3). 16.99 (978-1-4424-7657-8(5), Atheneum Bks. for Young Readers) Simon & Schuster Children's Publishing.

Buchanan, Nelda. The Hall Closet Light. 2009. 36p. (J). pap. 13.95 (978-1-4327-4584-4(0)) Outskirts Pr., Inc.

Bunting, Eve. Snowboarding on Monster Mountain. Ritz, Karen, illus. 2003. (ENG.). 64p. (J). 15.95 (978-0-8126-2704-6(0)) Cricket Bks.

Bush, Maureen. Cursed!, 1 vol. 2010. (Orca Young Readers Ser.). (ENG., Illus.). 128p. (J). (gr. 3-6). pap. 7.95 (978-1-55469-286-6(5)) Orca Bk. Pubs. USA.

Buxton, W. J. Winkiedoub Twinkletoe: Upon the Window Ledge. 2012. 36p. pap. 20.99 (978-1-4685-3050-6(X)) AuthorHouse.

Cairo, Anna. The Spider in My Shower. 2012. 28p. pap. 16.99 (978-1-4634-8768-3(1)) AuthorHouse.

Caldwell, Daisy L. Sarah the Oh So Silly, but Shy Stegosaurus, 1 vol. 2009. 24p. pap. 24.95 (978-1-61546-319-0(4)) America Star Bks.

Capdevila, Roser & Vendrell, Maria Martinez. El Agua Inquieta. 2003.Tr. of Rough Water. (SPA.). 24p. (J). 7.95 (978-84-233-1742-4(0)) Ediciones Destino ESP. Dist: Planeta Publishing Corp.

Carlow, Emma & Bradman, Tony. Flora the Fairy. Carlow, Emma, illus. 2005. (Green Bananas Ser.). (ENG., Illus.). 48p. (J). lib. bdg. (978-0-7787-1022-6(X)) Crabtree Publishing Co.

Carlson, Nancy. Harriet's Recital. 2006. (Illus.). (J). 15.95 (978-1-57505-898-6(7), Carolrhoda Bks.); (ENG., 32p. per. 9.95 (978-1-57505-929-7(0), First Avenue Editions) Lerner Publishing Group.

Carlstrom, Nancy White. What a Scare, Jesse Bear. Degen, Bruce, illus. 2012. (ENG.). 32p. (J). (gr. -1-1). 16.99 (978-0-689-85190-2(1), Simon & Schuster/Paula Wiseman Bks.) Simon & Schuster/Paula Wiseman Bks.

Carman, Patrick. Eve of Destruction. Arrasmith, Patrick, illus. 2012. (Dark Eden Ser.: 2). (ENG.). 288p. (YA). (gr. 8). 17.99 (978-0-06-210182-2(X), Tegen, Katherine Bks) HarperCollins Pubs.

Carmona, Adela. The Boy Who Could See. Chapman, Robert E., illus. 2008. 32p. pap. 24.95 (978-1-60672-697-6(8)) PublishAmerica, Inc.

Castro, Edmund Lee. Crystal & the Not-So-Scary Night. 2008. 36p. pap. 24.95 (978-1-60672-236-7(0)) America Star Bks.

Chaconas, Dori. Pennies in a Jar, 1 vol. Lewin, Ted, illus. 2007. (ENG.). 32p. (J). (gr. 1-5). 16.95 (978-1-56145-422-8(2)) Peachtree Pubs.

Chandler, Terry Ann. Miss Beula Helps Libby. 2010. 32p. pap. 21.99 (978-1-4500-9584-6(4)) Xlibris Corp.

Chapman, Kelly. A Warrior Prince for God. Ebbeler, Jeff, illus. 2010. (ENG.). 32p. (J). (gr. -1-4). 14.99 (978-0-7369-2895-3(2)) Harvest Hse. Pubs.

—A Warrior Prince for God Curriculum Leader's Guide. Ebbeler, Jeff, illus. 2009. pap. 12.99 (978-0-7369-2899-1(5)) Harvest Hse. Pubs.

Charlie Bumpers vs. the Squeaking Skull, 1 vol. 2014. (Charlie Bumpers Ser.). (ENG., Illus.). (J). (gr. 2-4). 10p. 16.95 (978-1-56145-809-7(0)); 160p. 13.95 (978-1-56145-808-0(2)) Peachtree Pubs.

Childress, H. Lee. The Cane. 2007. pap. 9.00 (978-0-8059-8453-8(4)) Dorrance Publishing Co., Inc.

Choldenko, Gennifer. Dad & the Dinosaur. Santat, Dan, illus. 2017. (ENG.). 40p. (J). (gr. k-3). 17.99 (978-0-399-24353-0(4), G.P. Putnam's Sons Books for Young Readers) Penguin Young Readers Group.

Christopher, Lawrence. The Tickle Fingers: Where Is Pinky? Christopher, Lawrence, illus. 2006. (ENG., Illus.). 24p. (J). (gr. -1-18). 9.95 (978-0-9712278-3-5(7)) MF Unlimited.

Christopher, Matt. Rock On. Koelsch, Michael, illus. 5th ed. 2004. (ENG.). 64p. (J). (gr. 1-4). pap. 13.99 (978-0-316-76265-6(2)) Little, Brown Bks. for Young Readers.

Churchman, Jennifer & Churchman, John. Brave Little Finn. 2016. (Sweet Pea & Friends Ser.). (ENG., Illus.). 40p. (J). (gr. -1-3). 17.99 (978-0-316-27359-6(7)) Little, Brown Bks. for Young Readers.

Clayton, Dallas. Lily the Unicorn. Clayton, Dallas, illus. 2014. (ENG., Illus.). 48p. (J). (gr. -1-3). 17.99 (978-0-06-211668-0(1)) HarperCollins Pubs.

Clegg, Maryanne & Bester, Maryanne. Why Dog Is Afraid of Storms. Bester, Shayle, illus. 2012. (ENG.). 32p. (J). (gr. -1-k). pap. 12.95 (978-1-4314-0219-9(2)) Jacana Media ZAF. Dist: Independent Pubs. Group.

Clements, Andrew. Fear Itself. Stower, Adam, illus. 2011. (Benjamin Pratt & the Keepers of the School Ser.: 2). (ENG.). 224p. (J). (gr. 2-5). 16.99 (978-1-4169-3887-3(7), Atheneum Bks. for Young Readers) Simon & Schuster Children's Publishing.

Cochran, Jean M. On a Dark, Dark Night. Morris, Jennifer E., illus. 2009. (ENG.). 32p. (J). (gr. k-2). 16.95 (978-1-935025-00-9(7)) Pleasant St. Pr.

Cohen, Deborah Bodin. Nachshon, Who Was Afraid to Swim: A Passover Story. Jago, illus. (Passover Ser.). (ENG.). 32p. (J). (gr. -1-2). 2009. pap. 8.95 (978-0-8225-8765-1(3)) 2008. 17.95 (978-0-8225-8764-4(5)) Lerner Publishing Group. (Kar-Ben Publishing).

Coleman, K. R. Truth or Dare. 2017. (Midnight Ser.). (ENG.). 104p. (YA). (gr. 6-12). lib. bdg. 26.65 (978-1-5124-2768-4(3)); 12.99 **(978-1-5124-3495-8(7))**; 39.99 **(978-1-5124-2788-2(8))**; 39.99 **(978-1-5124-3494-1(9))** Lerner Publishing Group. (Darby Creek).

Collingridge, Richard. Lionheart. 2016. (ENG., Illus.). 32p. (J). (gr. -1-k). 17.99 (978-0-545-83321-9(3)) Scholastic, Inc.

Collins, Nafessa. Mrs. Precious & the Possum. 2012. 56p. (gr. -1). pap. 8.95 (978-1-4759-1273-9(0)) iUniverse, Inc.

Cook, Jacqueline. The Little Bear Who Worried Too Much: Suzie Bear & the Music Festival. 2010. 32p. pap. 13.00 (978-1-60860-529-3(9), Strategic Bk. Publishing) Strategic Book Publishing & Rights Agency (SBPRA).

Corbett, CeCe. Please Turn on the Lights! 2008. 21p. pap. 24.95 (978-1-60672-029-5(5)) America Star Bks.

Cordell, Ray. Airborne Bunny. 2013. (ENG.). 30p. (J). pap. 13.95 (978-1-4787-1072-1(1)) Outskirts Pr., Inc.

cordone-warner, debra. Starzzee & A Day of Play. 2010. 40p. pap. 18.99 (978-0-557-54780-7(6)) Lulu Pr., Inc.

Cowell, Cressida. How to Be a Viking. 2014. (ENG.). 32p. (J). (gr. -1-3). 15.00 (978-0-316-28635-0(4)) Little, Brown Bks. for Young Readers.

Craig, Joni. A Bad Night's Sleep. ALDEN, B. E. A., illus. 2013. 46p. 16.95 (978-1-940224-11-4(X)) Taylor and Seale Publishing, LLC.

Crawford, Deborah. Tyler the Turtle Is Afraid of the Dark. Balzer, Jeremy, illus. 2006. 32p. (J). 14.95 (978-0-9770516-1-8(7)) Laffin Minor Pr.

Crespo, Ana. JP & the Giant Octopus: Feeling Afraid. Sirotich, Erica, illus. 2015. (My Emotions & Me Ser.). (ENG.). 32p. (J). (gr. -1-3). 16.99 (978-0-8075-3975-0(9)) Whitman, Albert & Co.

Crimi, Carolyn. Where's My Mummy? Manders, John, illus. 2008. (ENG.). 32p. (J). (gr. -1-3). 15.99 (978-0-7636-3196-3(5)) Candlewick Pr.

Crites, Elisa Maria. Secrets under the Midnight Sun. 2010. 108p. 28.95 (978-1-4497-0603-6(7)); pap. 11.95 (978-1-4497-0602-9(9)) Author Solutions, Inc. (WestBow Pr.).

Cunningham, Laura Shaine & Cunningham, Laura S. The Midnight Diary of Zoya Blume. 2005. 176p. (J). (gr. 3-18). 15.99 (978-0-06-072259-3(2), Geringer, Laura Book) HarperCollins Pubs.

D'Agata, Tabatha Jean. Storm Tunes: Yes, I Can Read! Nature Series, Book 2. Lineberger, Judy, illus. 2006. (Yes, I Can Read! Ser.: Bk. 2). 30p. (J). pap. 6.95 (978-1-934138-02-1(9)) Bouncing Ball Bks., Inc.

Dahl, Michael. Cold Feet, 1 vol. Ornia-Blanco, Miguel, illus. 2010. (Monster Street Ser.). (ENG.). 32p. (gr. 1-3). lib. bdg. 23.99 (978-1-4048-6070-4(3), Monster Street) Picture Window Bks.

—Frightmares: A Creepy Collection of Scary Stories. Bonet, Xavier, illus. 2015. (Michael Dahl's Really Scary Stories Ser.). (ENG.). 224p. (gr. 2-3). pap. 8.95 (978-1-4965-0598-9(0)) Stone Arch Bks.

—Frightmares 2: More Scary Stories for the Fearless Reader. Bonet, Xavier, illus. 2016. (Michael Dahl's Really Scary Stories Ser.). (ENG.). 224p. (gr. 2-3). pap. 8.95 (978-1-4965-4136-9(7)) Stone Arch Bks.

—Frightmares 3: Even More Scary Stories to Read If You Dare. Bonet, Xavier, illus. 2017. (Michael Dahl's Really Scary Stories Ser.). (ENG.). 224p. (gr. 2-3). pap. 8.95 **(978-1-4965-4915-0(5))** Stone Arch Bks.

—Igor S Lab of Fear, 8 vols. Catling, Andy, illus. 2016. (Igor's Lab of Fear Ser.). (ENG.). 40p. (gr. 1-3). 191.92 (978-1-4965-3542-9(1)) Stone Arch Bks.

—The Stranger on the Stairs: And Other Scary Tales. Bonet, Xavier, illus. 2015. (Michael Dahl's Really Scary Stories Ser.). (ENG.). 72p. (gr. 2-3). lib. bdg. 25.32 (978-1-4965-0594-1(8)) Stone Arch Bks.

—The Voice in the Boys' Room & Other Scary Tales. Bonet, Xavier, illus. 2015. (Michael Dahl's Really Scary Stories Ser.). (ENG.). 72p. (gr. 2-3). lib. bdg. 25.32 (978-1-4965-0596-5(4)) Stone Arch Bks.

Daneshvari, Gitty. The Final Exam. 2012. (School of Fear Ser.: 3). (ENG.). 352p. (J). (gr. 3-7). pap. 8.99 (978-0-316-18285-0(0)) Little, Brown Bks. for Young Readers.

—School of Fear. 2010. (School of Fear Ser.: 1). (ENG., Illus.). 368p. (J). (gr. 3-7). pap. 8.99 (978-0-316-03327-5(8)) Little, Brown Bks. for Young Readers.

Danielson, Diane K. There Is a Mouse That Is Haunting Our House. 2012. (ENG.). 28p. (J). pap. 14.99 (978-0-9885157-0-3(9)) SDP Publishing.

Davis, Helen J. Good Times with Gregory: Airplanes: A Visit to A 747. Davis, Robyn L., illus. 2008. (Good Times with Gregory Ser.). 37p. (J). (gr. -1-4). 12.95 (978-1-935122-11-8(8)) K&B Products.

Davis, Jacky & Soman, David. Ladybug Girl at the Beach. Soman, David, illus. 2010. (Ladybug Girl Ser.). (ENG., Illus.). 36p. (J). (gr. -1-k). 17.99 (978-0-8037-3416-6(6), Dial Bks) Penguin Young Readers Group.

Davis, Jon. Small Blue & the Deep Dark Night. 2014. (ENG., Illus.). 40p. (J). (gr. -1-3). 16.99 (978-0-544-16466-6(0), HMH Books For Young Readers) Houghton Mifflin Harcourt Publishing Co.

Day, Nancy Raines. On a Windy Night. Bates, George, illus. 2010. (ENG.). 40p. (J). (gr. k-2). 16.95 (978-0-8109-3900-4(2), Abrams Bks. for Young Readers) Abrams, Inc.

Denucci, Sharon. Grammie & the Gecko. DeNucci, Corinne, illus. 2008. 40p. pap. 16.99 (978-1-4389-1790-0(2)) AuthorHouse.

Derrick, David G., Jr., illus. I'm the Scariest Thing in the Jungle! 2013. (ENG.). 36p. (J). (gr. -1-3). 15.95 (978-1-59702-087-9(7)) Immedium.

Derubertis, Barbara. Victor Vicuna's Volcano Vacation. Alley, R. W., illus. 2011. (Animal Antics A to Z Set III Ser.). pap. 45.32 (978-0-7613-8431-1(6)) Kane Press, Inc.

deRubertis, Barbara. Victor Vicuna's Volcano Vacation. Alley, R. W., illus. 2011. (Animal Antics A to Z Ser.). 32p. (J). (ENG.). pap. 7.95 (978-1-57565-347-1(8)); lib. bdg. 22.60 (978-1-57565-355-6(9)) Kane Press, Inc.

deRubertis, Barbara & DeRubertis, Barbara. Victor Vicuna's Volcano Vacation. Alley, R. W., illus. 2012. (Animal Antics A to Z Ser.). 32p. (J). (gr. 2 — 1). cd-rom 7.95 (978-1-57565-415-7(6)) Kane Press, Inc.

Desir, C. & Perry, Jolene. Love Blind. 2016. (ENG., Illus.). 320p. (YA). (gr. 9). 17.99 (978-1-4814-1693-1(6), Simon Pulse) Simon Pulse.

Desmet, Sara. Scared Silly. Desmet, Sara, illus. 2006. (Illus.). 32p. (J). (gr. -1-3). 15.95 (978-1-60108-009-7(3)) Red Cygnet Pr.

Destiny, A. & Kahler, A. R. Love Is in the Air. 2015. 221p. (YA). (978-1-4814-2377-9(0), Simon Pulse) Simon Pulse.

Deuker, Carl. Gutless. (ENG.). 336p. (YA). (gr. 7). 2017. pap. 9.99 **(978-1-328-74206-3(7))** 2016. 17.99 (978-0-544-64961-3(3)) Houghton Mifflin Harcourt Publishing Co. (HMH Books For Young Readers).

Deutsch, Neil. Rose & the Pelican. 2013. 32p. pap. 19.99 (978-1-4817-0947-7(X)) AuthorHouse.

Dharma Publishing Staff. The Rabbit Who Overcame Fear: A Story about Wise Action. 2nd ed. 2013. (ENG.). 36p. (gr. -1-7). pap. 8.95 (978-0-89800-492-2(6)) Dharma Publishing.

DiCamillo, Kate. Francine Poulet Meets the Ghost Raccoon. Van Dusen, Chris, illus. 2015. (Tales from Deckawoo Drive Ser.: Vol. 2). (ENG.). 112p. (J). (gr. 1-4). 12.99 (978-0-7636-6886-0(9)) Candlewick Pr.

Dickinson, Peter. Chuck & Danielle. 115p. (J). (gr. 3-5). pap. 3.99 (978-0-8072-1504-3(X), Listening Library) Random Hse. Audio Publishing Group.

Diesen, Deborah. The Pout-Pout Fish in the Big-Big Dark. Hanna, Dan, illus. (Pout-Pout Fish Adventure Ser.: 2). (ENG.). (J). (gr. -1-1). 2015. 34p. bds. 7.99 (978-0-374-30189-7(1), 9780374301897) 2010. 32p. 16.99 (978-0-374-30798-1(9), 9780374307981) Farrar, Straus & Giroux. (Farrar, Straus & Giroux (BYR)).

Diggle, David Mark. Sally: And Her Singing Stage Debut. Preuss, Sarah Louise, illus. 2011. 24p. (J). pap. (978-0-9871658-6-2(0)) Diggle de Doo Productions Pty, Ltd.

Dongweck, James. The Dragon Cant. Baker, Joe, illus. 2004. 32p. (J). per. 16.95 (978-0-9719632-0-7(7)) Golden Monkey Publishing, LLC.

Donovan, Anna. Emma Says Boo. Fox, Woody, illus. 2003. (Panda Cubs Ser.: 03). (ENG.). 48p. (J). pap. 9.95 (978-0-86278-795-0(5)) O'Brien Pr., Ltd., The IRL. Dist: Dufour Editions, Inc.

Drouin, Véronique. L'Île D'Aurélie. 2004. (Mon Roman Ser.). (FRE.). 304p. (J). (gr. 2). pap. (978-2-89021-690-7(X)) Diffusion du livre Mirabel (DLM).

Dubosarsky, Ursula. The Terrible Plop. Joyner, Andrew, illus. 2009. (ENG.). 40p. (J). (gr. -1-1). 17.99 (978-0-374-37428-0(7), 9780374374280, Farrar, Straus & Giroux (BYR)) Farrar, Straus & Giroux.

Dumas, Kim Foster. Gator Gets a Nose Bleed. 2012. 24p. 24.95 (978-1-4626-4239-7(X)) America Star Bks.

Dusablon, David. The Dentist, 1 vol. Spoerl, Amber, illus. 2009. 11p. pap. 24.95 (978-1-60836-186-1(1)) America Star Bks.

Dyan, Penelope. I Can't Stand the Rain! Dyan, Penelope, illus. 2012. (Illus.). 34p. pap. 11.95 (978-1-61477-040-4(9)) Bellissima Publishing, LLC.

—Out of Deepest Africa — -Another of Ben's Big Adventures — -for Boys Only (r). Dyan, Penelope, illus. 2010. (Illus.). 34p. pap. 11.95 (978-1-935630-13-5(X)) Bellissima Publishing, LLC.

Eaton, Deborah. Canciones de Monstruos. Translations.com Staff, tr. from ENG. Handelman, Dorothy, photos by. 2007. (Lecturas para niños de verdad - Nivel 2 (Real Kids Readers - Level 2) Ser.).Tr. of Monster Songs. (SPA., Illus.). 32p. (gr. k-3). per. 5.95 (978-0-8225-7803-1(4)) Lerner Publishing Group.

Eboch, M. M. Monster Island. 2015. (ENG.). 96p. (gr. 3-6). 31.36 (978-1-63430-394-1(6)) Rourke Educational Media.

Elkins, Stephen. Know God, No Fear. Reisch, Jessie, illus. 2003. 32p. (J). (gr. k-5). 14.99 (978-0-8054-2658-8(2)) B&H Publishing Group.

Engelbreit, Mary. Queen of Halloween. Engelbreit, Mary, illus. 2008. (Illus.). 32p. (J). (gr. -1-3). lib. bdg. 17.89 (978-0-06-008191-1(0)); (ENG., 16.99 (978-0-06-008190-4(2)) HarperCollins Pubs.

Esbaum, Jill. I Am Cow, Hear Me Moo! Gordon, Gus, illus. 2014. (ENG.). 32p. (J). (gr. -1-k). 16.99 (978-0-8037-3524-8(3), Dial Bks) Penguin Young Readers Group.

Experiences of Terror. Date not set. (Nelson Readers Ser.: 5). (J). pap. (978-0-17-557038-6(8)) Addison-Wesley Longman, Inc.

The Fearful Fairy. 2007. (ENG., Illus.). 39p. (J). 16.95 (978-0-9793823-0-7(0)) StonesThrow Publishing, LLC.

Fears & Phantoms. 2006. (J). (978-1-933343-20-4(6)) Stabenfeldt Inc.

Fenton, Joe. What's under the Bed? Fenton, Joe, illus. 2008. (ENG., Illus.). 32p. (J). (gr. -1-2). 15.99 (978-1-4169-4943-5(7), Simon & Schuster Bks. For Young Readers) Simon & Schuster Bks. For Young Readers.

Fischer, Scott M. Jump! Fischer, Scott M., illus. 2010. (ENG., Illus.). 32p. (J). (gr. -1-3). 15.99 (978-1-4169-7884-8(4), Simon & Schuster Bks. For Young Readers) Simon & Schuster Bks. For Young Readers.

Fleming, Chula. Spooky Old Tree, 1 vol. 2010. 26p. pap. 24.95 (978-1-4489-9166-2(8)) PublishAmerica, Inc.

Foley, Greg. Willoughby & the Moon. Foley, Greg, illus. 2010. (ENG., Illus.). 40p. (J). (gr. -1-2). 18.99 (978-0-06-154753-9(0)) HarperCollins Pubs.

Foltz, Joanna "Gwen". The Owl Tree. 2011. 28p. pap. 13.59 (978-1-4634-1199-2(5)) AuthorHouse.

Fontaine, Renee. Boy in the Hoodie. Margolis, Al, illus. 2012. 34p. (J). 19.95 (978-1-61863-105-3(5)) Bookstand Publishing.

Fox, Jennifer. Teen Titans Go! - Boys Versus Girls. 2015. (Passport to Reading Level 2 Ser.). (ENG., Illus.). 32p. (J). (gr. -1-3). pap. 4.99 (978-0-316-37727-0(9)) Little, Brown Bks. for Young Readers.

Fox, Laura. Stan the Timid Turtle: Helping Children Cope with Fears about School Violence. DuFalla, Anita, illus. 2014. (ENG.). 48p. (J). (gr. -1-2). 9.95 (978-0-88282-466-6(X)) New Horizon Pr. Pubs., Inc.

Fox, Sabrina. Who Can Help Me Sleep? Rothan, Ann, illus. 2004. 32p. (gr. -1-3). 16.95 (978-1-885394-36-1(5)) Amber Lotus Publishing.

Freedman, Deborah. Shy. 2016. (ENG., Illus.). 40p. (J). (-k). 17.99 *(978-0-451-47496-4(1),* Viking Books for Young Readers) Penguin Young Readers Group.

Friedman, Laurie. I'm Not Afraid of This Haunted House. Murfin, Teresa, illus. 2005. (ENG.). 32p. (J). (gr. k-3). 16.95 *(978-1-57505-751-4(4),* Carolrhoda Bks.) Lerner Publishing Group.

Froeber, Sarah & Mosher, Kim. Pelican & Pelicant. 2003. (Illus.). 36p. (J). 17.99 *(978-0-9744926-0-5(4))* Toucan Pr., Inc.

Fruchter, Jason, illus. Daniel Gets Scared. 2015. (Daniel Tiger's Neighborhood Ser.). (ENG.). 32p. (J). (gr. -1-k). pap. 3.99 *(978-1-4814-5257-1(6),* Simon Spotlight) Simon Spotlight.

Fuchs-Rice, Dwayne. Troika. 2007. 248p. per. 16.95 *(978-0-595-45834-9(3))* iUniverse, Inc.

Fuks, Menuhah & Tager, Gavriella. Smile with Avigayil #2: Avigayil & the Black Cat. Haas, Esti, illus. 2006. (ENG.). 64p. (J). 12.95 *(978-1-932443-58-5(4))* Judaica Pr., Inc., The.

Fuqua, Jonathon Scott. The Reappearance of Sam Webber. 2010. (ENG.). 250p. pap. 12.95 *(978-1-890862-60-2(6))* Bancroft Pr.

Gackenbach, Dick. Harry & the Terrible Whatzit. 2014. 40p. pap. 8.00 *(978-1-61003-378-7(7))* Center for the Collaborative Classroom.

Galante, Cecilia. Be Brave, Willa Bean! Valiant, Kristi, illus. 2011. (Little Wings Ser.: 2). (ENG.). 112p. (J). (gr. 1-4). 4.99 *(978-0-375-86948-8(4),* Random Hse. Bks. for Young Readers) Random Hse. Children's Bks.

Galbraith, Kathryn O. Boo, Bunny! Mack, Jeff, illus. 2008. (ENG.). 40p. (J). (gr. -1-2). 16.00 *(978-0-15-216246-7(1))* Houghton Mifflin Harcourt Publishing Co.

—Boo, Bunny! Board Book. Mack, Jeff, illus. 2012. (ENG.). 32p. (J). (gr. -1 — 1). bds. 5.99 *(978-0-547-81850-4(5))* Houghton Mifflin Harcourt Publishing Co.

Galloway, Shannon. The Little Pig That Was Afraid of the Mud. Woodard, Dana, illus. 2007. (J). (gr. -1-3). per. 12.99 *(978-1-59879-244-7(X))* Lifevest Publishing, Inc.

Gardner, Alecia. Peachy Penelope. 2010. 44p. pap. 19.99 *(978-1-4490-0419-4(9))* AuthorHouse.

Garrott, Dawn E. How Riley Tamed the Invisible Monster. 2008. (J). pap. *(978-0-87743-709-3(2))* Baha'i Publishing Trust, U.S.

Gehl, Laura. I'm Not Hatching. Wan, Joyce, illus. 2016. (Peep & Egg Ser.). (ENG.). 40p. (J). 16.99 *(978-0-374-30121-7(2),* 9780374301217, Farrar, Straus & Giroux (BYR)) Farrar, Straus & Giroux.

—I'm Not Trick-Or-Treating. Wan, Joyce, illus. 2016. (Peep & Egg Ser.). (ENG.). 40p. (J). 16.99 *(978-0-374-30122-4(0),* 9780374301224, Farrar, Straus & Giroux (BYR)) Farrar, Straus & Giroux.

Gehring, Lisa B. Emily Grace & the What Ifs: A Story for Children about Nighttime Fears. Flath, Regina, illus. 2016. 32p. (J). *(978-1-4338-2106-6(0),* Magination Pr.) American Psychological Assn.

Gentry, Marley. Chase Learns to Ride. 2010. 24p. 14.99 *(978-1-4490-4640-8(1))* AuthorHouse.

Geoghegan, Adrienne. There's a Wardrobe in My Monster! Johnson, Adrian, illus. 2003. (Picture Bks.). 32p. (J). (gr. -1-3). 15.95 *(978-1-57505-414-8(0),* Carolrhoda Bks.) Lerner Publishing Group.

George, Olivia. The Bravest Girls in the World. DuBurke, Randy, illus. 2004. 32p. (J). lib. bdg. 15.00 *(978-1-4242-0241-6(8))* Fitzgerald Bks.

Gerard, Justin, illus. The Lightlings. 2006. 40p. (J). (gr. -1-3). lib. bdg. *(978-1-56769-078-1(5))* Reformation Pubs.

Giff, Patricia Reilly. Bears Beware. Bright, Alasdair, illus. 2012. (Zigzag Kids Ser.). (ENG.). 80p. (J). (gr. 1-4). pap. 4.99 *(978-0-375-85913-7(6),* Yearling) Random Hse. Children's Bks.

Giles, Polly. Have You Ever Been Afraid of Animals? 2012. 28p. pap. 15.99 *(978-1-4691-2517-6(X))* Xlibris Corp.

Gilmore, Cathy & Benoist, Carol. Easter Bunny's AMAZING Day. Sundy, Jonathan, illus. 2011. (ENG.). 40p. (J). 15.99 *(978-0-9847656-1-4(1))* I.H.S. Pubs.

Goldin, Barbara Diamond. Night Lights: A Sukkot Story. Carmi, Giora, illus. 2004. (gr. k-3). 13.95 *(978-0-8074-0803-2(4),* 142687) URJ Pr.

Goldthorpe, Jake. Mommy! Daddy! Help! There's a Monster in My Room! 2008. 28p. pap. 15.99 *(978-1-4363-7114-8(7))* Xlibris Corp.

Gollub, Matthew. The Twenty-Five Mixtec Cats. Martinez, Leovigildo, illus. 2004. 32p. (J). pap. 6.95 *(978-1-889910-29-1(5))* Tortuga Pr.

Gollub, Matthew W. The Twenty-five Mixtec Cats. Martinez, Leovigildo, illus. rev. ed. 2004. 32p. (J). 15.95 *(978-1-889910-28-4(7))* Tortuga Pr.

Goodman, Jill. Mustang, the Little Dog Who Was Afraid to Go to School. 2004. (Illus.). (J). pap. *(978-1-889636-63-4(0))* Youthlight, Inc.

Gorbachev, Valeri. When Someone Is Afraid, 1 vol. Gorbachev, Kostya, illus. (ENG.). 32p. (J). 2012. pap. 6.95 *(978-1-59572-344-4(7))* 2005. (gr. -1-2). 15.95 *(978-1-932065-99-2(7))* Star Bright Bks., Inc.

Goss, Leon. By the Light of the Moon. Luo, Shiyin Sean, illus. 2005. (J). pap. *(978-1-933156-12-5(0),* VisionQuest Kids) GSVQ Publishing.

Gosselin, Jake & Gosselin, Laura. The Pinkaboos: Belladonna & the Nightmare Academy. 2016. (Pinkaboos Ser.: 2). (ENG.). 96p. (J). pap. 7.99 *(978-1-4494-7832-2(8))* Andrews McMeel Publishing.

Graber, Lois, illus. A Song in the Storm. 2012. 32p. (J). *(978-0-7399-2445-7(1))* Rod & Staff Pubs., Inc.

Grant, Michael. Fear. 2012. (Gone Ser.: 5). (ENG.). 528p. (YA). (gr. 9). 17.99 *(978-0-06-144915-4(6),* Tegen, Katherine Bks) HarperCollins Pubs.

—Light. 2013. (Gone Ser.: 6). 432p. (YA). (gr. 9). (ENG.). 18.99 *(978-0-06-144918-5(0));* lib. bdg. 19.89 *(978-0-06-144919-2(9))* HarperCollins Pubs. (Tegen, Katherine Bks).

—Messenger of Fear. 2014. (Messenger of Fear Ser.: 1). (ENG.). 272p. (YA). (gr. 9). 17.99 *(978-0-06-220740-1(7),* Tegen, Katherine Bks) HarperCollins Pubs.

—The Tattooed Heart. 2015. (Messenger of Fear Ser.: 2). (ENG.). 400p. (YA). (gr. 9). 17.99 *(978-0-06-220743-2(1))* HarperCollins Pubs.

Grant, Vicki. Un Trabajo Sin Futuro, 1 vol. 2008. (Spanish Soundings Ser.). (SPA.). 128p. (YA). (gr. 8-12). pap. 9.95 *(978-1-55469-051-0(X))* Orca Bk. Pubs. USA.

Gravett, Emily. Little Mouse's Big Book of Fears. Gravett, Emily, illus. 2nd rev. ed. 2007. (ENG., Illus.). 32p. (J). (gr. k-4). *(978-1-4050-8948-7(2),* Macmillan Children's Bks.) Pan Macmillan.

—Little Mouse's Big Book of Fears. Gravett, Emily, illus. 2008. (ENG., Illus.). 32p. (J). (gr. -1-3). 19.99 *(978-1-4169-5930-4(0),* Simon & Schuster Bks. For Young Readers) Simon & Schuster Bks. For Young Readers.

Gravett, Emily, illus. Little Mouse's Big Book of Beasts. 2016. (ENG.). 32p. (J). (gr. -1-3). 17.99 *(978-1-4814-3929-9(4),* Simon & Schuster Bks. For Young Readers) Simon & Schuster Bks. For Young Readers.

Green, Alison. The Fox in the Dark. Allwright, Deborah, illus. (ENG.). 32p. (J). (gr. -1-1). 2012. pap. 7.95 *(978-1-58925-437-4(6))* 2010. 15.95 *(978-1-58925-091-8(5))* Tiger Tales.

Green, Poppy. The Emerald Berries. Bell, Jennifer A., illus. 2015. (Adventures of Sophie Mouse Ser.: 2). (ENG.). 128p. (J). (gr. k-4). pap. 5.99 *(978-1-4814-2835-4(7),* Little Simon) Little Simon.

Greene, Stephanie. Princess Posey & the First Grade Parade, Bk. 1. Sisson, Stéphanie Roth, illus. 2010. (Princess Posey, First Grader Ser.: 1). (ENG.). 96p. (J). (gr. k-3). 12.99 *(978-0-399-25167-2(7),* G.P. Putnam's Sons Books for Young Readers) Penguin Young Readers Group.

—Princess Posey & the First Grade Parade, Bk. 1. Sisson, Stéphanie Roth, illus. 2011. (Princess Posey, First Grader Ser.: 1). (ENG.). 96p. (J). (gr. k-3). 5.99 *(978-0-14-241827-7(7),* Puffin Books) Penguin Young Readers Group.

—Princess Posey & the Next-Door Dog, 3 vols. Sisson, Stéphanie Roth, illus. 2011. (Princess Posey, First Grader Ser.: 3). (ENG.). 96p. (J). (gr. k-3). 5.99 *(978-0-14-241939-7(7),* Puffin Books); 12.99 *(978-0-399-25463-5(3),* G.P. Putnam's Sons Books for Young Readers) Penguin Young Readers Group.

Griffin, Michele. It's Haircut Time! How one little boy overcame his fear of haircut Day. 2012. (ENG., Illus.). 32p. pap. 9.95 *(978-1-935567-33-2(0))* Sensory Resources.

Guilloppe, Antoine. One Scary Night. 2005. (Illus.). 32p. (J). 15.95 *(978-0-689-04636-0(7),* Milk & Cookies) ibooks, Inc.

Hadfield, Chris. The Darkest Dark. Fan, Eric et al, illus. 2016. (ENG.). 48p. (J). (gr. -1-3). 17.99 *(978-0-316-39472-7(6))* Little, Brown Bks. for Young Readers.

Hale, Bruce. Afraid of the Dark. Francis, Guy, illus. 2015. (Clark the Shark Ser.). (ENG.). 32p. (J). (gr. -1-3). 17.99 *(978-0-06-237450-9(8))* HarperCollins Pubs.

—Clark the Shark. 2016. (Clark the Shark: I Can Read Level 1 Ser.). (J). lib. bdg. 13.55 *(978-0-606-38774-3(9))* Turtleback Bks.

—Clark the Shark - Tooth Trouble. Francis, Guy, illus. 2014. (I Can Read Level 1 Ser.). (ENG.). 32p. (J). (gr. -1-3). 16.99 *(978-0-06-227908-8(4))* HarperCollins Pubs.

Hall, Kirsten. I'm Not Scared. Holub, Joan, illus. 2003. (My First Reader Ser.). (ENG.). 32p. (J). 18.50 *(978-0-516-22929-4(X),* Children's Pr.) Scholastic Library Publishing.

Hapka, Catherine, pseud. Moonlight Mile. 2015. (Marguerite Henry's Ponies of Chincoteague Ser.: 4). (ENG., Illus.). 192p. (J). (gr. 3-7). pap. 6.99 *(978-1-4814-0345-0(1),* Aladdin) Simon & Schuster Children's Publishing.

Harastová, Helena. I'm Not Afraid of the Dark. Cenkl, Jakub, illus. 2017. (ENG.). 14p. (J). (gr. -1-3). 14.95 *(978-1-4549-2170-7(6))* Sterling Publishing Co., Inc.

Hardwell, Gary D. A Boo Bears' Story: Stormy Night. 2007. (Illus.). 36p. per. 10.00 *(978-0-9792016-9-1(1))* Professional Publishing Hse. LLC.

Harimann, Sierra. Water Pups. 2013. (Illus.). 30p. (J). *(978-0-545-47235-7(0))* Scholastic, Inc.

Harley, Bill. Charlie Bumpers vs. the Squeaking Skull, 1 vol. Gustavson, Adam, illus. 2015. (Charlie Bumpers Ser.). (ENG.). 176p. (J). (gr. 2-4). pap. 6.95 *(978-1-56145-888-2(0))* Peachtree Pubs.

Harper, Charise Mericle. Just Grace & the Super Sleepover. 2014. (Just Grace Ser.: 11). (ENG., Illus.). 208p. (J). (gr. 1-4). 15.99 *(978-0-544-04584-2(X))* Houghton Mifflin Harcourt Publishing Co.

Harper, Jamie. Miss Mingo & the Fire Drill. Harper, Jamie, illus. 2012. (ENG., Illus.). 40p. (J). (gr. -1-3). pap. 6.99 *(978-0-7636-6086-4(8))* Candlewick Pr.

Harris, Philip. Inky Pinky. 2013. 20p. pap. 13.77 *(978-1-4669-9937-4(3))* Trafford Publishing.

Harris, Robie H. When Lions Roar. Raschka, Chris, illus. 2013. (ENG.). 32p. (J). (gr. -1-k). 16.99 *(978-0-545-11283-3(4),* Orchard Bks.) Scholastic, Inc.

Harrison, David L. A Monster Is Coming! Wilhelm, Hans, illus. 2011. (Step into Reading Ser.). (ENG.). 32p. (J). (gr. -1-1). pap. 3.99 *(978-0-375-86677-7(9),* Random Hse. Bks. for Young Readers) Random Hse. Children's Bks.

Hawthorne, Rachel. The Crocodile Who Was Afraid of the Water. 2009. (Illus.). 16p. pap. 8.49 *(978-1-4389-9674-5(8))* AuthorHouse.

Heide, Florence Parry. Some Things Are Scary. Feiffer, Jules, illus. 2011. (ENG.). 40p. (J). (gr. -1-2). pap. 7.99 *(978-0-7636-5590-7(2))* Candlewick Pr.

Helakoski, Leslie. Big Chickens. Cole, Henry, illus. 2008. (J). (gr. -1-3). lib. bdg. 14.65 *(978-0-7569-8913-2(2))* Perfection Learning Corp.

—Big Chickens Fly the Coop. Cole, Henry, illus. 2010. (ENG.). 32p. (J). (gr. -1-k). pap. 6.99 *(978-0-14-241464-4(6),* Puffin Books) Penguin Young Readers Group.

Hembree, G. Wil. The Willisby Orphans: In the Keys to the Bottomless Pit. 2011. 552p. (gr. -1 — 1). 44.95 *(978-1-4497-2366-8(7));* pap. 34.95 *(978-1-4497-2365-1(9))* Author Solutions, Inc. (WestBow Pr.).

Hendry, Diana. The Very Snowy Christmas. Chapman, Jane, illus. (J). 2013. (ENG.). 16p. (gr. -1). bds. 8.95 *(978-1-58925-617-0(4))* 2007. 32p. pap. 6.95 *(978-1-58925-406-0(6))* 2005. 32p. (gr. -1-2). 15.95 *(978-1-58925-051-2(6))* Tiger Tales.

Henkes, Kevin. Words of Stone. 2005. (ENG.). 160p. (J). (gr. 3-7). reprint ed. pap. 6.99 *(978-0-06-078230-6(7),* Greenwillow Bks.) HarperCollins Pubs.

Hernandez, Christopher. Scaredycrow. 2013. lib. bdg. 14.75 *(978-0-606-31953-9(0),* Turtleback) Turtleback Bks.

Hersh, Kristin. Toby Snax. 2016. (ENG., Illus.). 40p. (J). 14.95 *(978-1-4773-1127-1(0))* Univ. of Texas Pr.

Hiti, Samuel. Waga's Big Scare. Hiti, Samuel, illus. 2012. (Carolrhoda Picture Bks.). (ENG., Illus.). 32p. (J). (gr. k-3). lib. bdg. 16.95 *(978-0-7613-5622-6(3))* Lerner Publishing Group.

Hole, Stian. Garmann's Summer. Bartlett, Don, tr. from NOR. Hole, Stian, illus. 2008. (ENG., Illus.). 42p. (J). (gr. k-3). 17.50 *(978-0-8028-5339-4(0),* Eerdmans Bks For Young Readers) Eerdmans, William B. Publishing Co.

Holm, Jennifer L. The Creek. 2003. 240p. (J). (gr. 7-18). 16.89 *(978-0-06-000134-6(8));* 15.99 *(978-0-06-000133-9(X))* HarperCollins Pubs.

Holm, Jennifer L. & Holm, Matthew. Fear the Amoeba. Holm, Jennifer L. & Holm, Matthew, illus. 2014. (Squish Ser.: No. 6). (ENG., Illus.). 96p. (J). (gr. 2-5). 12.99 *(978-0-307-98303-9(X));* No. 6. pap. 6.99 *(978-0-307-98302-2(1))* Random Hse. Children's Bks. (Random Hse. Bks. for Young Readers).

—Fear the Amoeba. 2014. (Squish Ser.: 6). lib. bdg. 17.20 *(978-0-606-36025-8(5))* Turtleback Bks.

—Our Hero. 2005. (Babymouse Ser.: 2). (ENG., Illus.). 96p. (J). (gr. 2-5). pap. 6.99 *(978-0-375-83230-7(0));* lib. bdg. 12.99 *(978-0-375-93230-4(5))* Random Hse. Children's Bks. (Random Hse. Bks. for Young Readers).

Holt, Simon. The Devouring #2: Soulstice. 2010. (Devouring: Book 2 Ser.). (ENG.). 288p. (YA). (gr. 7-17). pap. 19.99 *(978-0-316-03574-3(2))* Little, Brown Bks. for Young Readers.

Holt, Theresa. What If I Wet My Pants. 2011. 28p. pap. 15.99 *(978-1-4628-5319-9(6))* Xlibris Corp.

Holub, Joan. Scaredy-Pants! A Halloween Story. Terry, Will, illus. 2007. (Ant Hill Ser.). (ENG.). 24p. (J). (gr. -1-k). pap. 3.99 *(978-1-4169-0956-9(7),* Simon Spotlight/Nickelodeon) Simon Spotlight/Nickelodeon.

Hooton, David James. It Circled Twice. 2011. 32p. pap. 24.95 *(978-1-4137-6130-6(5))* America Star Bks.

Hornsby, Ashley. Pretty Little Lilly & the Magical Light. Couch, Greg, illus. 2007. 32p. (J). 15.95 *(978-0-9777241-0-9(7))* Cepia LLC.

Hornsby, Ashley Brooke. Pretty Little Lilly & the Magical Night (paperback) 2006. (Illus.). (J). *(978-0-9777241-1-6(5))* Cepia LLC.

Hughes, Cheryl. Jackson, the Pigeon Who Was Afraid of Heights. 2008. 44p. pap. 16.99 *(978-1-4389-2143-3(8))* AuthorHouse.

Hughes, Patricia A. Tommy Learns It's Not So Scary. 2012. 48p. pap. 18.41 *(978-1-4669-7044-1(8))* Trafford Publishing.

Hulme, Joy N. Eerie Feary Feeling: A Hairy Scary Pop-up Book. Ely, Paul & Dudley, Dick, illus. 2006. 12p. (J). (gr. k-4). reprint ed. 14.00 *(978-1-4223-5171-0(8))* DIANE Publishing Co.

Hulst, W. G. van de & Hulst, Willem G. van de. Three Foolish Sisters. 2014. (J). *(978-1-928136-15-6(X))* Inheritance Pubns.

Hunter, Tammy. Tede's Search for his Mom. 2004. 27p. pap. 24.95 *(978-1-4137-2854-5(5))* PublishAmerica, Inc.

Hutton, Stacie Vaughn. Shoveful of Sunshine. Harness, Cheryl, illus. 2012. (ENG.). 32p. (J). 16.95 *(978-0-938467-39-7(5))* Headline Bks., Inc.

It's Dark! 2005. (J). bds. *(978-0-9769910-1-4(2))* Terrific Twins LLC.

Jacqueline, Thomas. Birthday Picnic. 2010. 24p. pap. 9.99 *(978-0-88144-493-3(6))* Yorkshire Publishing Group.

Jahangiri, Holly. Trockle. 2008. (Illus.). 32p. (J). 18.99 *(978-0-9797513-2-5(2))* 4RV Publishing, LLC.

James, Richard E., III. Adventures of the Elements Vol. 3: Dangerous Games. Lyle, Maryann, ed. Welch, Chad, illus. 2004. 169p. (YA). (gr. 3-12). pap. 5.95 *(978-0-9675901-2-7(4))* Alchemy Creative, Inc.

Jazynka, Kitson. Boys Camp: Nate's Story. Orback, Craig, illus. 2015. (ENG.). 144p. (J). (gr. 1-5). pap. 9.95 *(978-1-62914-806-9(7),* Sky Pony Pr.) Skyhorse Publishing Co., Inc.

—Nate's Story, Bk. 2. Orback, Craig, illus. 2013. (ENG.). 144p. (J). (gr. 2-5). 14.95 *(978-1-62087-981-8(6),* 620981, Sky Pony Pr.) Skyhorse Publishing Co., Inc.

Jensen, Patricia. I Am Sick. Hantel, Johanna, illus. (My First Reader Ser.). (ENG.). 32p. (J). (gr. k-1). 2006. per. 3.95 *(978-0-516-24970-4(3))* 2005. lib. bdg. 18.50 *(978-0-516-24878-3(2))* Scholastic Library Publishing. (Children's Pr.).

Jepsen, D. R. Fabulous Fred Gets the Cheese. 2007. 16p. per. 24.95 *(978-1-4241-8456-9(8))* America Star Bks.

JiSeung, Kook. Ouch! It Stings! JiSeung, Kook, illus. rev. ed. 2014. (MySELF Bookshelf Ser.). (ENG., Illus.). 32p. (J). (gr. k-2). pap. 11.94 *(978-1-60357-653-6(3));* lib. bdg. 25.27 *(978-1-59953-644-6(7))* Norwood Hse. Pr.

Jo, Kami. Toby Learns to Fly. 2010. 36p. pap. 15.49 *(978-1-4269-3964-8(7))* Trafford Publishing.

Joe, Anna Rose. The Common Snipe. Afcan, Paschal, ed. Afcan, Paschal, tr. Chikoyak, Andrew J., illus. 2004. (J). pap. 7.50 *(978-1-58084-224-2(0))* Lower Kuskokwim Schl. District.

Johnson, Grace. The Little Fish Who Was Afraid to Swim. 2008. 36p. pap. 15.49 *(978-1-4389-2262-1(0))* AuthorHouse.

Jonas. Three's a Crowd. 6th ed. 2010. 128p. pap. 4.99 *(978-1-4231-2282-1(8))* Disney Pr.

Jones, Elisabeth & Jones, Lis. A Walk in the Wild Woods. Coplestone, Jim, illus. 2010. (ENG.). 32p. (J). (gr. -1-1). 16.95 *(978-1-84507-956-7(6),* Frances Lincoln) Quarto Publishing Group UK GBR. Dist: Hachette Bk. Group.

Jordan, Mark. Courage the Monkey. 2006. (Illus.). 40p. (J). 13.95 *(978-0-9717013-7-3(7))* Decere Publishing.

Karapetkova, Holly. Las Serpientes en el Tercer Grado. 2012.Tr. of Snakes in Third Grade. (SPA & ENG.). 24p. (gr. 2-3). pap. 8.95 *(978-1-61810-545-5(0))* Rourke Educational Media.

Kear, Nicole C. The Fix-It Friends: Have No Fear! Dockray, Tracy, illus. 2017. (Fix-It Friends Ser.). (ENG.). 144p. (J). 16.99 *(978-1-250-11577-5(9),* 9781250115775) Imprint IND. Dist: Macmillan.

Keep, Richard. A Thump from Upstairs: Starring Mr. Boo & Max, 1 vol. Keep, Richard, illus. 2005. (ENG., Illus.). 36p. (J). (gr. -1-3). 15.95 *(978-1-56145-348-1(X))* Peachtree Pubs.

Keller, Holly. Help! A Story of Friendship. Keller, Holly, illus. 2007. (ENG., Illus.). 40p. (J). (gr. -1-3). 16.99 *(978-0-06-123913-7(5),* Greenwillow Bks.) HarperCollins Pubs.

—Sophie's Window. Keller, Holly, illus. 2005. (Illus.). 32p. (J). 16.89 *(978-0-06-056283-0(8))* HarperCollins Pubs.

Keyes, Eric, 3rd, et al. The Light in the Dark, 1. Marie, Paula Braxton, illus. l.t. ed. 2004. (ENG.). 40p. (J). pap. 14.99 *(978-0-9722795-5-0(5),* Highest Good Pubns.) EbonyEnergy Publishing, Inc.

Khan, Sharaz. Zambo & the Haunted House. 2008. 47p. pap. 9.99 *(978-1-4357-3928-4(0))* Lulu Pr., Inc.

Kidd, Ronald. The Year of the Bomb. 2009. (ENG.). 208p. (YA). (gr. 7). pap. 5.99 *(978-1-4169-9625-5(7));* 16.99 *(978-1-4169-5892-5(4))* Simon & Schuster Bks. For Young Readers. (Simon & Schuster Bks. For Young Readers).

—Year of the Bomb. 2009. 208p. 5.99 *(978-1-4169-9504-3(8))* Studio Fun International.

Kilgore, Mary & Kilgore, Mitchell. Where Is My Mommy? Coping When a Parent Leaves (and Doesn't Come Back) Pillo, Cary, illus. 2010. (ENG.). 32p. (J). (gr. -1-4). pap. 12.95 *(978-1-884734-46-5(4))* Parenting Pr., Inc.

A Kiss for Jake. 2008. (Jake Flocked Board Ser.). 8p. bds. *(978-1-4075-1816-9(X))* Parragon, Inc.

Klein, Abby. Camping Catastrophe! McKinley, John, illus. 2008. (Ready, Freddy! Ser.: 14). (ENG.). 96p. (J). (gr. -1-3). 5.99 *(978-0-439-89594-1(4),* Blue Sky Pr., The) Scholastic, Inc.

Kline, Suzy. Horrible Harry on the Ropes. Remkiewicz, Frank & Wummer, Amy, illus. 2011. (Horrible Harry Ser.). (ENG.). 80p. (J). (gr. 2-4). 4.99 *(978-0-14-241695-2(9),* Puffin Books) Penguin Young Readers Group.

—Horrible Harry on the Ropes, 24 vols. Wummer, Amy, illus. 2009. (Horrible Harry Ser.: 24). (ENG.). 80p. (J). (gr. 2-4). 14.99 *(978-0-670-01097-4(9),* Viking Books for Young Readers) Penguin Young Readers Group.

Knowles, Alison. Ollie & His Super Powers. Wiltshire, Sophie, illus. 2016. (Ollie & His Superpowers Ser.). (ENG.). 32p. (J). 15.95 *(978-1-78592-049-3(9),* 8455) Kingsley, Jessica Pubs. GBR. Dist: Macmillan Distribution Ltd.

Koller, Jackie French. No Such Thing. Lewin, Betsy, illus. 2012. (ENG.). 32p. (J). (gr. k-2). pap. 7.95 *(978-1-59078-911-7(3))* Boyds Mills Pr.

Kopp, Megan. Scary Folktales, 1 vol. 2010. (Scary Stories Ser.). (ENG.). 32p. (gr. 3-4). lib. bdg. 27.99 *(978-1-4296-4571-3(7),* Edge Bks.) Capstone Press of Coughlan Cos.

Korngold, Jamie. Sadie, Ori, & Nuggles Go to Camp. Fortenberry, Julie, illus. 2014. (ENG.). 24p. (J). (gr. -1-1). 17.95 *(978-1-4677-0424-3(5),* Kar-Ben Publishing) Lerner Publishing Group.

Kredensor, Diane. Ollie & Moon: Aloha! 2013. (Step into Reading Ser.). (ENG., Illus.). 48p. (J). (gr. 1-4). 3.99 *(978-0-307-97950-6(4),* Random Hse. Bks. for Young Readers) Random Hse. Children's Bks.

LaFaye, A. Water Steps. 2009. (ENG., Illus.). 208p. (J). (gr. 2-7). 16.95 *(978-1-57131-687-5(6));* pap. 6.95 *(978-1-57131-686-8(8))* Milkweed Editions.

Lamb, Lenny. Facing Your Fears: Greener Grass Volume 4. 2012. 48p. pap. 24.95 *(978-1-4626-5398-0(7))* America Star Bks.

Landgraf, James, Jr. Monsters Monsters Go Away. Warrick, Jessica, illus. 2008. 40p. (J). 8.99 *(978-0-9819283-0-2(7))* Makdan Publishing.

Larcombe, Jennifer Rees. The Terrible Giant. Björkman, Steve, illus. 2004. (Best Bible Stories Ser.). 24p. (gr. -1-3). 2.99 *(978-1-58134-054-9(0))* Crossway.

Lascurain, Guadalupe Aleman. La Domadora de Miedos. Arte y Cultura, A.C Staff, illus. rev. ed. 2006. (Castillo de la Lectura Roja Ser.). (SPA & ENG.). 232p. (YA). (gr. 7). pap. 8.95 *(978-970-20-0182-9(X))* Castillo, Ediciones, S. A. de C. V. MEX. Dist: Macmillan.

Lavoie, Jennifer. Meeting Chance. 2013. (ENG.). 264p. (gr. 7). pap. 11.95 *(978-1-60282-952-7(7))* Bold Strokes Bks.

Layne, Steven L. My Brother Dan's Delicious, 1 vol. Galey, Chuck, illus. 2003. (ENG.). 32p. (J). (gr. k-3). 16.99 *(978-1-58980-071-7(0))* Pelican Publishing Co., Inc.

Leblanc, A. J. Donnie the Little Knee Boarder. 2012. 28p. pap. 24.95 *(978-1-4626-8313-0(4))* PublishAmerica, Inc.

Lemieux, Jean. Toby Shoots for Infinity. Casson, Sophie, illus. 2005. 61p. (J). lib. bdg. 12.00 *(978-1-4242-1201-9(4))* Fitzgerald Bks.

Lester, Helen. Tacky & the Haunted Igloo. Munsinger, Lynn, illus. 2015. (Tacky the Penguin Ser.). (ENG.). 32p. (J). 16.99 *(978-0-544-33994-1(0),* HMH Books For Young Readers) Houghton Mifflin Harcourt Publishing Co.

Liautaud, Judy. Lulu Turns on the Night Light. Liautaud, Judy, illus. 2013. (Illus.). 24p. pap. 12.95 *(978-1-883841-19-5(4))* City Creek Pr., Inc.

Lignell, Kirk. Listen to the Raindrops: Featuring the Storm Song. Lignell, Brent, illus. 2007. 32p. (J). (gr. -1-3). 17.95 *(978-1-932399-15-8(1))* Huron River Pr.

Liniers & Lindgren, Barbro. What There Is Before There Is Anything There: A Scary Story, 1 vol. Amado, Elisa, tr. from SPA. 2014. (ENG., Illus.). 24p. (J). (gr. -1-2). 18.95 *(978-1-55498-385-8(1))* Groundwood Bks. CAN. Dist: Publishers Group West (PGW).

Lionni, Leo. Swimmy. 2013. (ENG., Illus.). 32p. (J). (gr. -1-2). 17.99 *(978-0-385-75358-6(6));* lib. bdg. 20.99 *(978-0-385-75366-1(7))* Random Hse. Children's Bks. (Knopf Bks. for Young Readers).

Listening with Zachary. (J). pap. 13.75 *(978-0-8136-4655-8(3))* Modern Curriculum Pr.

Little Is Big. 2006. (Illus.). (J). *(978-1-882601-58-5(0))* See-More's Workshop.

Loggins, Thelma Puckett. Little Moo Moo's Afraid. 2011. 52p. (gr. -1). pap. 11.49 *(978-1-4389-7080-6(3))* AuthorHouse.

Look, Lenore. Alvin Ho: Allergic to Babies, Burglars, & Other Bumps in the Night. Pham, LeUyen, illus. 2013. (Alvin Ho Ser.). (ENG.). 192p. (J). (gr. 1-4). 15.99 *(978-0-375-87033-0(4),* Schwartz & Wade Bks.) Random Hse. Children's Bks.

—Alvin Ho: Allergic to Birthday Parties, Science Projects, & Other Man-Made Catastrophes. Pham, LeUyen, illus. 2011. (Alvin Ho Ser.). (ENG.). 192p. (J). (gr. 1-4). 6.99 *(978-0-375-87369-0(4),* Yearling) Random Hse. Children's Bks.

—Alvin Ho: Allergic to Camping, Hiking, & Other Natural Disasters. Pham, LeUyen, illus. 2010. (Alvin Ho Ser.). (ENG.). 192p. (J). (gr. 1-4). 6.99 (978-0-375-85750-8(8), Yearling) Random Hse. Children's Bks.

—Alvin Ho: Allergic to the Great Wall, the Forbidden Palace, & Other Tourist Attractions. Pham, LeUyen, illus. 2014. (Alvin Ho Ser.). (ENG.). 176p. (J). (gr. 1-4). 15.99 (978-0-385-36972-5(7), Schwartz & Wade Bks.) Random Hse. Children's Bks.

—Alvin Ho: Allergic to Babies, Burglars, & Other Bumps in the Night. Pham, LeUyen, illus. 2014. (Alvin Ho Ser.). (ENG.). 192p. (J). (gr. 1-4). 6.99 (978-0-385-38600-5(1), Yearling) Random Hse. Children's Bks.

—Alvin Ho: Allergic to Dead Bodies, Funerals, & Other Fatal Circumstances. Pham, LeUyen, illus. 2012. (Alvin Ho Ser.). (ENG.). 208p. (J). (gr. 1-4). 6.99 (978-0-307-97695-6(5), Yearling) Random Hse. Children's Bks.

Lorimer, Janet. Ring of Fear, 1 vol. unabr. ed. 2010. (Q Reads Ser.). (ENG.). 32p. (YA). (gr. 9-12). pap. 6.95 (978-1-61651-194-4(X)) Saddleback Educational Publishing, Inc.

Low, J. H. Night in the Gardens. 2017. (ENG.). 40p. 10.00 (978-981-4751-42-1(1)) Marshall Cavendish International (Asia) Private Ltd. SGP. Dist: National Bk. Network.

Lozano, Neal. Can God See Me in the Dark? Hatke, Ben, illus. 2007. (ENG.). 32p. (J). 16.95 (978-1-883551-45-2(5), Maple Corners Press) Attic Studio Publishing Hse.

Lucado, Max & Schmidt, Troy. Webster, the Scaredy Spider. 2005. 32p. (J). pap. 3.99 (978-1-4003-0665-7(5)) Nelson, Thomas Inc.

Lyssenko, Taras. Wendy's Fear of Heights. 2003. 14p. (J). (978-0-9740542-0-9(8)) Prairie Shore Creative, Inc.

MacDonald, Alan. Scaredy Mouse. Warnes, Tim, illus. 2007. (Storytime Board Bks.). 16p. (J). (gr. -1-k). bds. 6.95 (978-1-58925-827-3(4)) Tiger Tales.

Mackall, Dandi Daley. Natalie: School's First Day of Me, 1 vol. Blakeslee, Lys, illus. 2009. (That's Nat! Ser.). (ENG.). 96p. (J). (gr. 1-4). pap. 4.99 (978-0-310-71568-9(7)) Zonderkidz.

—No, No Noah!, 1 vol. Kucharik, Elena, illus. 2007. (ENG.). 26p. (gr. -1-k). bds. 6.99 (978-1-4003-1007-4(5)) Nelson, Thomas Inc.

MacLeod, Doug. Heather Fell in the Water. Smith, Craig, illus. 2013. (ENG.). 32p. (J). (gr. -1-k). 19.99 (978-1-74237-648-6(7)) Allen & Unwin AUS. Dist: Independent Pubs. Group.

Maddox, Jake. Cowboy Up, 1 vol. Tiffany, Sean, illus. 2011. (Jake Maddox Sports Stories Ser.). (ENG.). 72p. (gr. 2-3). pap. 5.95 (978-1-4342-3425-4(8)); lib. bdg. 25.32 (978-1-4342-2989-2(0)) Stone Arch Bks.

—Double-Axel Doubt, 1 vol. 2011. (Jake Maddox Girl Sports Stories Ser.). (ENG.). 72p. (gr. 2-3). lib. bdg. 25.32 (978-1-4342-2499-6(6)) Stone Arch Bks.

Maddox, Jake & Berne, Emma Carlson. Running Scared, 1 vol. Wood, Katie, illus. 2013. (Jake Maddox Girl Sports Stories Ser.). (ENG.). 72p. (gr. 2-3). pap. 5.95 (978-1-4342-4203-7(X)); lib. bdg. 25.32 (978-1-4342-4015-6(0)) Stone Arch Bks.

Maggiore, Lisa. Ava the Monster Slayer. Felten, Ross, illus. 2015. (ENG.). 32p. (J). (gr. -1-k). 16.99 (978-1-63450-151-4(9), Sky Pony Pr.) Skyhorse Publishing Co., Inc.

Mahoney, Tammy. Eddie the Eagle Learns to Fly. 2012. 24p. pap. 19.99 (978-1-4772-1747-4(9)) AuthorHouse.

Maier, Inger M. When Fuzzy Was Afraid of Big & Loud Things. Candon, Jennifer, illus. 2005. (Fuzzy the Little Sheep Ser.). (J). (gr. -1-3). 32p. 14.95 (978-1-59147-322-0(5)); 30p. per. 9.95 (978-1-59147-323-7(3)) American Psychological Assn. (Magination Pr.).

Malaspina, Ann. The Mouse & the Wizard: A Hindu Folktale. Sylvaine, Jenny, illus. 2013. (Folktales from Around the World Ser.). (ENG.). 24p. (J). (gr. k-3). 28.50 (978-1-62323-633-5(9), 206384) Child's World, Inc., The.

Maltby, Robert I. My Money Got Gobbled, 1 vol. 2010. 36p. 24.95 (978-1-4489-6407-9(5)) PublishAmerica, Inc.

Manceau, Édouard, illus. Tickle Monster. 2015. (ENG.). 32p. (J). (gr. -1-k). 14.95 (978-1-4197-1731-4(6)) Abrams, Inc.

Manning, Matthew K. Batman & the Flock of Fear. Vecchio, Luciano, illus. 2013. (Dark Knight Ser.). (ENG.). 88p. (gr. 2-3). pap. 5.95 (978-1-4342-4217-4(X)) Stone Arch Bks.

—Scarecrow's Flock of Fear, 1 vol. Vecchio, Luciano, illus. 2012. (Dark Knight Ser.). (ENG.). 88p. (gr. 2-3). lib. bdg. 26.65 (978-1-4342-4090-3(8)) Stone Arch Bks.

—Superman Battles the Billionaire Bully. Beavers, Ethen, illus. 2017. (DC Super Hero Stories Ser.). (ENG.). 56p. (gr. 1-3). lib. bdg. 25.32 (978-1-4965-4634-0(2), DC Super Heroes) Stone Arch Bks.

Manushkin, Fran. Katie Goes Camping, 1 vol. Lyon, Tammie, illus. 2010. (Katie Woo Ser.). (ENG.). 32p. (gr. k-2). lib. bdg. 21.32 (978-1-4048-5731-5(1)) Picture Window Bks.

Martín Anguita, Carmen & Carmen, Martín Anguita. Cuando Llega la Noche. Cortazar, Alicia Canas, illus. 2008. (SPA.). 32p. (J). 10.99 (978-84-241-5400-4(2)) Everest Editora ESP. Dist: Lectorum Pubns., Inc.

Martin, C. L. Ducky Goes to the Dentist. 2013. 16p. pap. 24.95 (978-1-62709-742-0(2)) America Star Bks.

Martin, Molly. Princess Sophia Gets Scared, 1 vol. Florian, Mélanie, illus. 2013. (Princess Heart Ser.). (ENG.). 24p. (gr. -1-1). 6.95 (978-1-4048-8110-5(7)); lib. bdg. 22.65 (978-1-4048-7854-9(8)) Picture Window Bks.

Martone, Ginny. Trouble at Big Bear Falls. 2011. 90p. pap. 19.95 (978-1-4626-2558-1(4)) America Star Bks.

Marts, Doreen Mulryan, illus. Even Monsters Say Good Night. 2015. (ENG.). 32p. (gr. -1-2). 14.95 (978-1-62370-256-4(9)) Capstone Young Readers of Coughlan Cos.

Maynor, Megan. Ella & Penguin Stick Together. Bonnet, Rosalinde, illus. 2016. 32p. (J). (gr. -1-3). 17.99 (978-0-06-233088-8(8)) HarperCollins Pubs.

McCarthy, Jenna. Poppy Louise Is Not Afraid of Anything. Idle, Molly, illus. 2017. (ENG.). 40p. (J). (gr. -1-2). lib. bdg. 19.99 (978-0-375-97356-7(7), Random Hse. Bks. for Young Readers) Random Hse. Children's Bks.

McClure, Kim. Edgar the Seagull who was Afraid to Fly. 2009. 34p. pap. 16.70 (978-0-557-05920-1(8)) Lulu Pr., Inc.

McDonald, Kirsten. The Nighttime Noise, 1 vol. Meza, Erika, illus. 2016. (Carlos & Carmen Ser.). (ENG.). 32p. (J). (gr. k-3). 27.07 (978-1-62402-139-8(5)) Magic Wagon.

Mcghee, Alison. Countdown to Kindergarten. Bliss, Harry, illus. 2006. (ENG.). 32p. (J). (gr. -1-3). reprint ed. pap. 6.99 (978-0-15-205586-8(X)) Houghton Mifflin Harcourt Publishing Co.

—Countdown to Kindergarten. Bliss, Harry, illus. pap. incl. audio compact disk (978-1-59112-469-6(7)); pap. 39.95 incl. audio (978-1-59112-929-5(X)) Live Oak Media.

—Julia Gillian - And the Art of Knowing. Kozjan, Drazen, illus. 2009. (Julia Gillian Ser.). (ENG.). 304p. (J). (gr. 3-7). 6.99 (978-0-545-03349-7(7), Scholastic Paperbacks) Scholastic, Inc.

McGinty, Alice B. Eliza's Kindergarten Pet, 0 vols. Speir, Nancy, illus. 2010. (ENG.). 32p. (J). (gr. k-3). 15.99 (978-0-7614-5702-2(X), 9780761457022, Amazon Children's Publishing) Amazon Publishing.

McKee, David. Elmer & the Monster. McKee, David, illus. 2014. (Illus.). 32p. (J). (gr. -1-3). 16.95 (978-1-4677-4200-9(7)) Lerner Publishing Group.

McKelvey, Lonnie. Benny the Brave. Wooten, Neal, illus. 2008. 28p. (J). pap. 7.99 (978-0-9817521-3-6(6)) Mirror Publishing.

McMahon, Kara. Friday the Scaredy Cat. McClellan, Maddy, illus. 2011. (Friday the Scaredy Cat Ser.). (ENG.). 24p. (J). (gr. -1-1). 15.99 (978-1-4424-3612-1(3)); pap. 3.99 (978-1-4424-2293-3(9)) Simon Spotlight. (Simon Spotlight).

—Playdates Are Not Scary! McClellan, Maddy, illus. 2015. (Friday the Scaredy Cat Ser.). (ENG.). 24p. (J). (gr. -1-1). pap. 3.99 (978-1-4814-3591-8(4), Simon Spotlight) Simon Spotlight.

—The Scariest Day Ever ... So Far. McClellan, Maddy, illus. 2013. (Friday the Scaredy Cat Ser.). (ENG.). 24p. (J). (gr. -1-1). 16.99 (978-1-4424-6694-4(4), Simon Spotlight) Simon Spotlight.

—The Scariest Day Ever... So Far. McClellan, Maddy, illus. 2013. (Friday the Scaredy Cat Ser.). (ENG.). 24p. (J). (gr. -1-1). pap. 3.99 (978-1-4424-6693-7(6), Simon Spotlight) Simon Spotlight.

McMurtrie, Kevin. Succotash Pudding. 2013. 16p. pap. 12.70 (978-1-4669-7682-5(9)) Trafford Publishing.

McNamara, Margaret. First-Grade Bunny. Gordon, Mike, illus. 2005. (Robin Hill School Ser.). (ENG.). 32p. (J). (gr. -1-1). pap. 3.99 (978-0-689-86427-8(2), Simon Spotlight) Simon Spotlight.

—Halloween Fun. Gordon, Mike, illus. 2008. (Robin Hill School Ser.). (ENG.). 32p. (J). (gr. -1-1). pap. 3.99 (978-1-4169-3496-7(0), Simon Spotlight) Simon Spotlight.

—Snow Day. Gordon, Mike, illus. 2007. (Robin Hill School Ser.). (ENG.). 32p. (J). (gr. -1-1). pap. 3.99 (978-1-4169-3493-6(6), Simon Spotlight) Simon Spotlight.

McPhail, David. The Blue Door. Ellis, Sarah, ed. O'Connor, John, illus. 2003. (ENG.). 32p. pap. (978-1-55041-802-6(5)) Fitzhenry & Whiteside, Ltd.

Mcwherter, Barbara. Oliver & His Mountain Climbing Adventures. McWherter, Shelley, illus. 2012. 34p. 24.95 (978-1-4626-7601-9(4)) America Star Bks.

Mehnert, Robert. Spelunkers. 2012. 108p. pap. 19.95 (978-1-62709-036-0(3)) America Star Bks.

Meister, Cari. The Brave Puffer Fish, 1 vol. Harpster, Steve, illus. 2011. (Ocean Tales Ser.). (ENG.). 32p. (gr. 2-3). pap. 6.25 (978-1-4342-3389-9(8)) Stone Arch Bks.

Merkel, Tara & Monahan, Ryan. The Thunderstorm. 2007. 20p. per. 11.00 (978-1-4343-0585-5(6)) AuthorHouse.

Meserve, Jessica. Bedtime Without Arthur. Meserve, Jessica, illus. 2010. (ENG., Illus.). 32p. (J). (gr. -1-3). 16.95 (978-0-7613-5497-0(2)) Lerner Publishing Group.

Meunier, Sylvain & Lapierre, Steeve. Graindsel et Bretel. Fil et, Julie, illus. 2004. (était une Fois Ser.). (FRE.). 24p. (J). (gr. -1). pap. (978-2-89021-699-0(3)) Diffusion du livre Mirabel (DLM).

Meyer, Linda. The Kid in My Closet. Roberts, Miranda, illus. 2008. (ENG.). 32p. (J). pap. 12.95 (978-1-887542-94-4(9)) Book Pubs. Network.

Meyer, Susan. Matthew & Tall Rabbit Go Camping. Huntington, Amy, illus. 2008. (ENG.). 32p. (J). (gr. -1-3). 15.95 (978-0-89272-769-8(1)) Down East Bks.

Miceli, Mary Anne. Boston North Shore's Car Wash Squid. 2012. 44p. pap. 20.00 (978-0-578-08747-4(2)) Miceli, Mary Anne.

—How 'Pilly-Pine', the Alpaca, Lost His Quills. Terry, Roger, illus. 2012. 44p. pap. 20.00 (978-0-578-10145-3(9)) Miceli, Mary Anne.

Miranda, Megan. The Safest Lies. (ENG.). 368p. (YA). (gr. 9). 2017. pap. 9.99 (978-0-553-53754-3(7), Ember) 2016. 17.99 (978-0-553-53751-2(2), Crown Books For Young Readers) Random Hse. Children's Bks.

Modarressi, Mitra. Owlet's First Flight. Modarressi, Mitra, illus. 2012. (ENG., Illus.). 32p. (J). (gr. -1-k). 16.99 (978-0-399-25526-7(5), G.P. Putnam's Sons Books for Young Readers) Penguin Young Readers Group.

Montes, Hugo & Montes, Michelle. Young Eagles Armor Academy: Fear of Flying, V01. 2010. 76p. (J). pap. 5.99 (978-1-60683-021-5(X)) Harrison House Pubs.

Moore, Steve. King of the Bench: Control Freak. Moore, Steve, illus. 2017. (King of the Bench Ser.: 2). (Illus.). 224p. (J). (gr. 3-7). 13.99 (978-0-06-220332-8(0)) HarperCollins Pubs.

Morris, Richard & Morris, Winifred. What If the Shark Wears Tennis Shoes? 2007. (ENG.). 36p. (J). (gr. k-3). 11.99 (978-1-4169-6726-2(5), Simon & Schuster/Paula Wiseman Bks.) Simon & Schuster/Paula Wiseman Bks.

Morrison, Daequan T. What's the Spook? 2011. 28p. pap. 18.62 (978-1-4670-3887-4(3)) AuthorHouse.

Morrison, Toni & Morrison, Slade. Please, Louise. Strickland, Shadra, illus. 2014. (ENG.). 32p. (J). (gr. -1-3). 17.99 (978-1-4169-8338-5(4), Simon & Schuster Bks. For Young Readers) Simon & Schuster Bks. For Young Readers.

Mortensen, Lori. Bree's Bike Jump, 1 vol. Sullivan, Mary, illus. 2009. (My First Graphic Novel Ser.). (ENG.). 32p. (gr. k-2). 24.65 (978-1-4342-1620-5(9), My First Graphic Novel) Stone Arch Bks.

—Chicken Lily. Crittenden, Nina Victor, illus. 2016. (ENG.). 40p. (J). 16.99 (978-1-62779-120-5(5), 9781627791205, Holt, Henry & Co. Bks. For Young Readers) Holt, Henry & Co.

Moss, Miriam. Wiley & Jasper. Bucker, Jutta, tr. Bucker, Jutta, illus. 2003. (J). 25p. pap. (978-1-59336-061-0(4)); 32p. 15.95 (978-1-59336-060-3(6)) Mondo Publishing.

Murphy, Anne. Animal Island. 2009. 44p. pap. 16.99 (978-1-4389-4263-6(X)) AuthorHouse.

Murphy, Steve & Murphy, Sonia. The Secret. Ostrom, Bob, illus. 2004. (Teenage Mutant Ninja Turtles Ser.). 32p. (J). (gr. k-2). 11.65 (978-0-7569-5401-7(0)) Perfection Learning Corp.

Musco, Rance K. The Legend of Sabor. 2009. 52p. pap. 22.50 (978-1-4389-4573-6(6)) AuthorHouse.

Naylor, Phyllis Reynolds. Alice the Brave. (Alice Ser.: 7). (ENG., (J). 2011. Illus.). 176p. (gr. 5-9). pap. 7.99 (978-1-4424-2851-5(1), Atheneum Bks. for Young Readers) 2009. 160p. (gr. 4-8). pap. 7.99 (978-1-4169-7542-7(X), Aladdin) Simon & Schuster Children's Publishing.

Nelson, Connie. The Lizard's Secret Door. Waller, Joyce, illus. 2014. 32p. (J). 19.95 (978-1-59298-933-1(0)) Beaver's Pond Pr., Inc.

Nelson, Sheila K. The Backpack Bears' Adventure: Friendship. 2009. 24p. pap. 16.50 (978-1-4490-0554-2(3)) AuthorHouse.

Newmark, Rachel J. Fearless Faith: And the New School. Specialty Publishing Company, illus. 2006. (J). pap. 7.95 (978-0-9755199-4-3(8)) Specialty Publishing Co.

Nicholson, David L. Little Johnny's First Day of School, 1 vol. 2009. 32p. pap. 24.95 (978-1-60813-611-7(6)) America Star Bks.

Nickel, Scott. Curse of the Red Scorpion, 1 vol. Harpster, Steve, illus. 2006. (Graphic Sparks Ser.). (ENG.). 40p. (gr. 1-3). 23.99 (978-1-59889-034-1(4), Graphic Sparks) Stone Arch Bks.

Nielsen, Susin. Optimists Die First. 2017. (ENG.). 240p. (YA). (gr. 7). 17.99 (978-0-553-49690-1(5), Lamb, Wendy Bks.) Random Hse. Children's Bks.

Night, P. J. The Terror Behind the Mask. 2014. (You're Invited to a Creepover Ser.: 19). (ENG., Illus.). 160p. (J). (gr. 3-7). pap. 6.99 (978-1-4814-0460-0(1), Simon Spotlight) Simon Spotlight.

—The Terror Behind the Mask. 2014. (Creepover Ser.: 19). lib. bdg. 17.20 (978-0-606-35797-5(1)) Turtleback Bks.

Noël, Alyson. Dreamland. 2011. (Riley Bloom Book Ser.: 3). (ENG.). 224p. (J). (gr. 4-7). pap. 7.99 (978-0-312-56375-2(2), 9780312563752) Square Fish.

Northrop, Michael. Plunked. 2014. (ENG.). 256p. (J). (gr. 3-7). pap. 7.99 (978-0-545-29715-8(X), Scholastic Paperbacks) Scholastic, Inc.

Novotny-Hunter, Jana. A Bear Hug at Bedtime. Widdowson, Kay, illus. 2017. (Child's Play Library). (ENG.). 32p. (J). pap. (978-1-84643-988-9(4)) Child's Play International Ltd.

Nutt, Robert. Amy's Light. Nutt, Robert, illus. 2010. (Illus.). 44p. (J). (gr. -1-3). 16.95 (978-1-58469-128-0(X)); (ENG., pap. 8.95 (978-1-58469-129-7(8)) Dawn Pubns.

Odgers, Darrel & Odgers, Sally. The Awful Pawful. Dawson, Janine, illus. 2007. (Jack Russell: Dog Detective Ser.: 5). 96p. (J). (gr. 1-6). pap. 4.99 (978-1-933605-53-1(7)) Kane Miller.

Oelschlager, Vanita. Let Me Bee. Blackwood, Kristin, illus. 2008. (ENG.). 42p. (J). (gr. -1-3). 17.95 (978-0-9800162-1-5(5)) VanitaBooks.

Oliver, Lin, et al. There's a Zombie in My Bathtub #5. Garrett, Scott, illus. 2015. (Here's Hank Ser.: 5). (ENG.). 128p. (J). (gr. 1-3). bds. 5.99 (978-0-448-48512-6(5), Grosset & Dunlap) Penguin Young Readers Group.

Ørbeck-Nilssen, Constance. I'm Right Here. Düzakin, Akin, illus. 2015. (ENG.). 28p. (J). 16.00 (978-0-8028-5455-1(9), Eerdmans Bks For Young Readers) Eerdmans, William B. Publishing Co.

O'Reilly, Sean. Lost in Spooky Forest, 1 vol. 2010. (Mighty Mighty Monsters Ser.). (ENG.). 48p. (gr. 2-3). lib. bdg. 23.99 (978-1-4342-2149-0(0)) Stone Arch Bks.

Orr, Wendy. The Princess & Her Panther. Stringer, Lauren, illus. 2010. (ENG.). 40p. (J). (gr. -1-3). 16.99 (978-1-4169-9780-1(6), Beach Lane Bks.) Beach Lane Bks.

Ortiz, Raquel M. & Ventura, Gabriela Baeza. Sofi & the Magic Musical Mural. Dominguez, Maria, illus. 2015. (SPA & ENG.). (J). 17.95 (978-1-55885-803-9(2), Piñata Books) Arte Publico Pr.

O'Ryan, Ray. Drake Makes a Splash! Jack, Colin, illus. 2014. (Galaxy Zack Ser.: 8). (ENG.). 128p. (J). (gr. k-2). pap. 5.99 (978-1-4424-9360-5(7), Little Simon) Little Simon.

Ostow, Micol. Louise Trapeze Is Totally 100% Fearless. Barrager, Brigette, illus. 2015. (Louise Trapeze Ser.: 1). (ENG.). 112p. (J). (gr. 1-4). 14.99 (978-0-553-49739-7(1), Random Hse. Bks. for Young Readers) Random Hse. Children's Bks.

Padur, Simone. Things That Go Bump in the Night. 2012. 20p. pap. 19.99 (978-0-9847831-7-5(2)) Big Country Publishing, LLC.

Palmer, Bernard. Danny & Ron Orlis in the Sacred Cave. 2011. 130p. 40.95 (978-1-258-08134-8(2)) Literary Licensing, LLC.

Park, Barbara. Boo... & I Mean It! Brunkus, Denise, illus. 2005. (Junie B. Jones Ser.: Bk. 7). 86p. (gr. 1-4). 15.00 (978-0-7569-4783-5(9)) Perfection Learning Corp.

—Junie B., First Grader - Boo...and I Mean It! Brunkus, Denise, illus. 2005. (Junie B. Jones Ser.: No. 7). (ENG.). 96p. (J). (gr. 1-4). 4.99 (978-0-375-82807-2(9), Random Hse. Bks. for Young Readers) Random Hse. Children's Bks.

Parker, Danny. Parachute. Ottley, Matt, illus. 2016. (ENG.). 32p. (J). 16.00 (978-0-8028-5469-8(9), Eerdmans Bks For Young Readers) Eerdmans, William B. Publishing Co.

Parr, Todd. The I'm Not Scared Book. 2011. (ENG., Illus.). 32p. (J). (gr. -1-1). 11.99 (978-0-316-08445-1(X)) Little Brown & Co.

—The I'm NOT SCARED Book. 2017. (ENG., Illus.). 32p. (J). (gr. -1-1). 7.99 (978-0-316-43198-9(2)) Little, Brown Bks. for Young Readers.

—The I'm Not Scared Book. 2017. (J). lib. bdg. 18.40 (978-0-606-40224-8(1)) Turtleback Bks.

Parrott, Matt. Daniel & the Dark. 2011. 24p. 16.99 (978-1-4520-8830-3(6)) AuthorHouse.

Pascal, Francine. Betrayed. 2011. (Fearless Ser.: 24). (ENG.). 256p. (YA). (gr. 11). pap. 12.99 (978-1-4424-3108-9(3), Simon Pulse) Simon Pulse.

—Fearless: Fearless; Sam; Run. 2012. (Fearless Ser.). (ENG.). 608p. (YA). (gr. 9). pap. 12.99 (978-1-4424-4631-1(5), Simon Pulse) Simon Pulse.

Patricelli, Leslie. The Patterson Puppies & the Midnight Monster Party. Patricelli, Leslie, illus. 2010. (ENG., Illus.). 32p. (J). (gr. -1-k). 14.99 (978-0-7636-3243-4(0)) Candlewick Pr.

Penn, Audrey. Chester the Brave. Gibson, Barbara Leonard, illus. 2012. (Kissing Hand Ser.). (ENG.). 32p. (J). (gr. -1-3). 16.95 (978-1-933718-79-8(X)) Tanglewood Pr.

Petersen, Pat. The Turtle Who Couldn't Swim. Pham, Xuan, illus. 2012. 28p. pap. 24.95 (978-1-4626-4847-4(9)) America Star Bks.

Peterson, Doug & Kenney, Cindy. Lost in Place: A Lesson in Overcoming Fear, 1 vol. Big Idea Productions Staff, illus. 2005. (Big Idea Books / VeggieTown Values Ser.: Bk. 4). (ENG.). 32p. (J). pap. 3.99 (978-0-310-70629-8(7)) Zonderkidz.

Philips, Dixie. Whistling Dixie. Caponigro, Laureen, illus. 2012. 16p. pap. 9.95 (978-1-61633-272-3(7)) Guardian Angel Publishing, Inc.

Phillips, Linda. My Bus Adventure: My Bus Ride. 2009. 24p. pap. 11.49 (978-1-4490-1675-3(8)) AuthorHouse.

Pierce, Stacey C. Kenny's Summer Fun. 2008. 40p. pap. 24.95 (978-1-60703-625-8(8)) America Star Bks.

Pinfold, Levi. Black Dog. Pinfold, Levi, illus. 2012. (ENG., Illus.). 32p. (J). (gr. -1-3). 15.99 (978-0-7636-6097-0(3), Templar) Candlewick Pr.

Poblocki, Dan. The Nightmarys. 2011. (ENG.). 336p. (J). (gr. 3-7). pap. 7.99 (978-0-375-84257-3(8), Yearling) Random Hse. Children's Bks.

Polacco, Patricia. Thunder Cake. 2015. 32p. pap. 8.00 (978-1-61003-536-1(4)) Center for the Collaborative Classroom.

Porter, Rhonda. Brody Meets a Bully. 2008. 16p. pap. 24.95 (978-1-60610-311-1(3)) America Star Bks.

Potter, Alicia. Miss Hazeltine's Home for Shy & Fearful Cats. Sif, Birgitta, illus. 2015. (ENG.). 40p. (J). (gr. k-3). 16.99 (978-0-385-75334-0(9)); lib. bdg. 19.99 (978-0-385-75335-7(7)) Random Hse. Children's Bks. (Knopf Bks. for Young Readers).

Pottie, Marjolein & Auzary-Luton, Sylvie. Going Batty! Special Glow-in-the-Dark Surprise Pictures. Auzary-Luton, Sylvie, illus. 2005. (Illus.). 32p. (J). 15.95 (978-0-689-04635-3(9), Milk & Cookies) ibooks, Inc.

Powell-Tuck, Maudie. Pirates Aren't Afraid of the Dark! Edgson, Alison, illus. 2014. (ENG.). 32p. (J). (gr. -1-3). 16.99 (978-1-58925-165-6(2)) Tiger Tales.

Price, Jesse. Dad. 2008. 28p. pap. 15.99 (978-1-4363-1489-3(5)) Xlibris Corp.

Puckett, Kelley. Batman's Dark Secret. Muth, Jon J., illus. 2015. (ENG.). 32p. (J). (gr. k-2). 17.99 (978-0-545-86755-9(X), Scholastic Pr.) Scholastic, Inc.

Pumphrey, W. Jerome. Creepy Things Are Scaring Me! (Illus.). 32p. (J). (gr. -1-3). 5.99 (978-0-06-443680-9(2)) HarperCollins Pubs.

Punter, Russell. Scaredy Cat. 2009. 48p. 19.99 (978-0-7945-2281-0(5)) EDC Publishing.

Purdy, Rebekah L. The Winter People. 2014. (Entangled Teen Ser.). (ENG.). 320p. (YA). (gr. 7-12). 16.99 (978-1-62266-368-2(3), 9781622663682) Entangled Publishing, LLC.

Quinton, Sasha. Florabelle. Barrager, Brigette & Tcherevkoff, Michel, illus. 2015. (ENG.). 40p. (J). (gr. -1-3). 15.99 (978-0-06-229182-0(3)) HarperCollins Pubs.

Ramon, Elisa. Aquello Que Tanto Queria Susana. Lavarello, Jose Maria, illus. 2004.Tr. of What Susana Loved Dearly. (SPA.). (J). pap. 7.99 (978-84-236-6702-4(2)) Edebé ESP. Dist: Lectorum Pubns., Inc.

Ransom, Candice. Seeing Sky-Blue Pink. 2007. (Exceptional Reading & Language Arts Titles for Intermediate Grades Ser.). 122p. (J). (gr. 4-7). 16.95 (978-0-8225-7142-1(0), Carolrhoda Bks.) Lerner Publishing Group.

Rash, Andy. Archie the Daredevil Penguin. Rash, Andy, illus. 2015. (ENG., Illus.). 34p. (J). (gr. -1-3). 16.99 (978-0-451-47123-9(7), Viking Books for Young Readers) Penguin Young Readers Group.

Raye, Varuna. Frederick & the Scaries. 2009. 32p. pap. 15.50 (978-0-557-11104-6(8)) Lulu Pr., Inc.

Reh, Rusalka. The Secret of the Water Knight, 0 vols. Derbyshire, Katy, tr. unabr. ed. 2011. (ENG.). 100p. (J). (gr. 4-7). pap. 9.95 (978-1-61109-006-2(7), 9781611090062) Amazon Publishing.

Reichardt, Marisa. Underwater. 2016. (ENG.). 288p. (YA). 17.99 (978-0-374-36886-9(4), 9780374368869, Farrar, Straus & Giroux (BYR)) Farrar, Straus & Giroux.

Reilly, Carmel & Miesen, Christina. The Call of the Wolf. 2008. (Rigby Focus Forward: Level H Ser.). (Illus.). 24p. (J). (gr. 4-7). pap. (978-1-4190-3722-1(6), Rigby) Pearson Education Australia.

Reis, Jason & Hurley, Meagan. The Adventures of Burt: Burt & the Big Race. 2012. 28p. pap. 19.99 (978-1-4634-4126-5(6)) AuthorHouse.

Remkiewicz, Frank. Gus Gets Scared. 2011. (Scholastic Reader Pre-Level 1 Ser.). (ENG., Illus.). 24p. (J). (gr. k-1). pap. 3.99 (978-0-545-24471-8(4), Cartwheel Bks.) Scholastic, Inc.

Reynolds, Aaron. Creepy Pair of Underwear! Brown, Peter, illus. 2017. (ENG.). 48p. (J). (gr. -1-3). 17.99 (978-1-4424-0298-0(9), Simon & Schuster Bks. For Young Readers) Simon & Schuster Bks. For Young Readers.

—Sea Monkey & Bob. Ohi, Debbie Ridpath, illus. 2017. (ENG.). 40p. (J). (gr. -1-3). 17.99 (978-1-4814-0676-5(0), Simon & Schuster Bks. For Young Readers) Simon & Schuster Bks. For Young Readers.

Riad, Hala. Twinkie Has a New Home. 2011. 24p. pap. 14.93 (978-1-4269-7120-4(6)) Trafford Publishing.

Richards, Dan. The Problem with Not Being Scared of Monsters. Neubecker, Robert, illus. 2014. (ENG.). 32p. (J). (gr. -1-3). 15.95 (978-1-62091-024-5(1)) Boyds Mills Pr.

Rippin, Sally. The Midnight Feast. Fukuoka, Aki, illus. 2012. 44p. (J). (978-1-61067-134-7(1)) Kane Miller.

River Runners: Individual Title Six-Packs. (Action Packs Ser.). 120p. (gr. 3-5). 44.00 (978-0-7635-8398-9(7)) Rigby Education.

Rivers, Karen. The Girl in the Well Is Me. (ENG.). 224p. (J). (gr. 5-8). 2017. pap. 6.95 (978-1-61620-696-3(9)) 2016. 16.95 (978-1-61620-569-0(5)) Algonquin Bks. of Chapel Hill.

Rix, James. Panda Panic. 2013. (Awesome Animals Ser.). (ENG., Illus.). 192p. (J). (gr. 2-7). pap. 6.99 (978-1-4380-0304-7(8)) Barron's Educational Series, Inc.

Roberts, Gaylia. Giant Feathered Monsters. 2008. 20p. pap. 24.95 (978-1-60441-582-7(7)) America Star Bks.

Rockwell, Anne F. Katie Catz Makes a Splash. Meisel, Paul, illus. 2003. (Good Sports Ser.). 40p. (J). (gr. -1-1). 15.99 *(978-0-06-028441-1(2))* HarperCollins Pubs.

Rosen, Devora. Mystery in Spain. 2009. 250p. 19.99 *(978-1-59826-327-5(7))* Feldheim Pubs.

Rosenthal, Eileen. I'll Save You Bobo! Rosenthal, Marc, illus. 2012. (ENG.). 40p. (J). (gr. -1-1). 14.99 *(978-1-4424-0378-9(0)*, Atheneum Bks. for Young Readers) Simon & Schuster Children's Publishing.

Ross, Dev. We Both Read-Frank & the Giant (Picture Book) Reinhart, Larry, illus. 2007. (We Both Read Ser.). 44p. (J). (gr. -1-2). lib. bdg. 14.95 *(978-1-60115-006-6(7))* Treasure Bay, Inc.

Ross, Jeff. The Drop, 1 vol. 2011. (Orca Sports Ser.). (ENG.). 168p. (YA). (gr. 6-10). pap. 9.95 *(978-1-55469-392-4(6))* Orca Bk. Pubs. USA.

Roy, Philip. Mouse Tales. Torrey Balsara, Andrea, illus. 2014. (ENG.). 32p. pap. 9.95 *(978-1-55380-262-4(4))* Ronsdale Pr. CAN. Dist: SPD-Small Pr. Distribution.

Rubin, Adam. Big Bad Bubble. Salmieri, Daniel, illus. (ENG.). 40p. (J). (gr. -1-3). 2017. pap. 7.99 *(978-0-544-92782-7(6)*, HMH Books For Young Readers) 2014. 16.99 *(978-0-544-04549-1(1))* Houghton Mifflin Harcourt Publishing Co.

Ruelle, Karen Gray. The Monster in Harry's Backyard. Ruelle, Karen Gray, illus. 2003. (Holiday House Readers Ser.). (ENG., Illus.). 32p. (J). (gr. k-3). 4.95 *(978-0-8234-1783-4(2))* Holiday Hse., Inc.

Runnells, Treesha. Afraid of the Dark? Runnells, Treesha, illus. 2005. (Stories to Share Ser.). (Illus.). 14p. (J). (gr. -1-2). 10.95 *(978-1-58117-107-5(2)*, Intervisual/Piggy Toes) Bendon, Inc.

Russ, Tim & Roskilly, Jedda. Bugsters! 2008. (Illus.). 32p. (J). 16.95 *(978-0-9795131-7-6(0))* Woods N' Water Pr., Inc.

Russell, Natalie. Hamish the Highland Cow. 2003. (J). 7.99 *(978-1-58234-818-6(9))* Bloomsbury Publishing USA.

Russell, Shane. Phloomp! 2010. (ENG.). 158p. pap. *(978-1-84748-759-9(9))* Athena Pr.

Russo, Mary. The Adventures of Wizahickon. 2010. 28p. pap. 13.99 *(978-1-4520-1831-7(6))* AuthorHouse.

Rylant, Cynthia. Annie & Snowball & the Shining Star. Stevenson, Suçie, illus. 2010. (Annie & Snowball Ser.: 6). (ENG.). 40p. (J). (gr. k-2). pap. 3.99 *(978-1-4169-3950-4(4)*, Simon Spotlight) Simon Spotlight.

Sachar, Louis. Super Fast, Out of Control. Record, Adam, illus. 2015. (Marvin Redpost Ser.: 7). (ENG.). 96p. (J). (gr. 1-4). lib. bdg. 12.99 *(978-0-553-53545-7(5)*, Random Hse. Bks. for Young Readers) Random Hse. Children's Bks.

Saito, Ryusuke & Takidaira, Jiro. The Tree of Courage. Laughlin, Sako, tr. 2008. (Illus.). 32p. (J). 14.95 incl. audio compact disk *(978-1-74126-442-5(1))* R.I.C. Pubns. AUS. Dist: SCB Distributors.

Salley, Coleen. Epossumondas Plays Possum. Stevens, Janet, illus. 2009. (ENG.). 40p. (J). (gr. -1-3). 17.99 *(978-0-15-206420-4(6))* Houghton Mifflin Harcourt Publishing Co.

Santat, Dan. After the Fall (How Humpty Dumpty Got Back up Again) Santat, Dan, illus. 2017. (ENG., Illus.). 40p. (J). 17.99 ***(978-1-62672-682-6(5)**, 9781626726826)* Roaring Brook Pr.

Sateren, Shelley Swanson. Fearless Freddie. Melmon, Deborah, illus. 2015. (Adventures at Hound Hotel Ser.). (ENG.). 72p. (gr. 2-3). lib. bdg. 25.32 *(978-1-4795-5898-8(2)*, Adventures at Hound Hotel) Picture Window Bks.

Schmid, Paul. Oliver & His Alligator. Schmid, Paul, illus. 2013. (ENG., Illus.). 40p. (J). (gr. -1-k). 15.99 *(978-1-4231-7437-0(2))* Disney Pr.

Schneider, Richard H. The Lighthouse Boy: A Story about Courage. Petrov, Anton, illus. 2007. (ENG.). 32p. (J). (gr. -1-3). pap. 8.99 *(978-0-8249-5557-1(9)*, Ideal Pubns.) Worthy Publishing.

Schnitzlein, Danny. Trick or Treat on Monster Street, 1 vol. Faulkner, Matt, illus. 2008. (ENG.). 32p. (J). (gr. k-3). 16.95 *(978-1-56145-465-5(6))* Peachtree Pubs.

Schwarz, Viviane. Shark & Lobster's Amazing Undersea Adventure. Stewart, Joel, illus. 2006. 34p. (J). *(978-1-4156-8140-4(6))* Candlewick Pr.

Scotton, Rob. Splish, Splash, Splat! Scotton, Rob, illus. 2011. (Splat the Cat Ser.). (ENG., Illus.). 40p. (J). (gr. -1-3). 16.99 *(978-0-06-197868-5(X))* HarperCollins Pubs.

Scripture Teachers: Solomon & Friends Learn about Trusting God. 2003. pap. *(978-0-9712894-2-0(5))* Lighthouse Christian Products Co.

Seeger, Laura Vaccaro. I Used to Be Afraid. 2015. (ENG., Illus.). 40p. (J). (gr. -1-3). 17.99 *(978-1-59643-631-2(X)*, 9781596436312) Roaring Brook Pr.

Segel, Jason & Miller, Kirsten. Nightmares! Kwasny, Karl, illus. (Nightmares! Ser.). (ENG.). (J). (gr. 3-7). 2015. 400p. 7.99 *(978-0-385-74426-3(9)*, Yearling) 2014. 368p. 16.99 *(978-0-385-74425-6(0)*, Delacorte Bks. for Young Readers) 2014. 368p. lib. bdg. 19.99 *(978-0-375-99157-8(3)*, Delacorte Bks. for Young Readers) Random Hse. Children's Bks.

Seuss, Dr. What Was I Scared Of? A Glow-in-the-Dark Encounter. 2009. (Classic Seuss Ser.). (ENG., Illus.). 32p. (J). (gr. k-4). 12.99 *(978-0-375-85342-5(1)*, Random Hse. Bks. for Young Readers) Random Hse. Children's Bks.

Sharp, Stephanie. The Bird That Couldn't. 2008. 44p. per. 24.95 *(978-1-4241-8250-3(6))* America Star Bks.

Shea, Bob. I'm a Shark. Shea, Bob, illus. 2011. (ENG., Illus.). 40p. (J). (gr. -1-1). 16.99 *(978-0-06-199846-1(X))* HarperCollins Pubs.

Shea, Bob. The Scariest Book Ever. Shea, Bob, illus. 2017. (ENG., Illus.). 40p. (J). (gr. 1-3). 16.99 ***(978-1-4847-3046-1(1))*** Hyperion Bks. for Children.

Sheinmel, Courtney. Scaredy Cat. Bell, Jennifer A., illus. 2016. (Stella Batts Ser.). (ENG.). 160p. (J). (gr. 1-3). 9.99 *(978-1-58536-919-5(5)*, 204026) Sleeping Bear Pr.

Sher, Emil. Young Man with Camera. Wyman, David, photos by. 2015. (ENG., Illus.). 240p. (J). (gr. 7). 17.99 *(978-0-545-54131-2(X)*, Levine, Arthur A. Bks.) Scholastic, Inc.

Sherry, Kevin. I'm the Scariest Thing in the Castle. 2011. (ENG.). 28p. (J). (gr. -1 — 1). bds. 6.99 *(978-0-8037-3390-9(9)*, Dial Bks) Penguin Young Readers Group.

Shoemaker, Tim. Below the Surface, 1 vol. 2015. (Code of Silence Novel Ser.). (ENG.). 416p. (J). pap. 9.99 *(978-0-310-73765-0(6))* Zonderkidz.

Shughart-Knecht, Kimberly. Princess Kiali & the Purple Box. 2010. 32p. pap. 12.99 *(978-1-4490-0913-7(1))* AuthorHouse.

Shum, Benson. Holly's Day at the Pool: A Walt Disney Animation Studios Artist Showcase. Shum, Benson, illus. 2017. (Walt Disney Animation Studios Artist Showcase Ser.). (ENG., Illus.). 40p. (J). (gr. -1-k). 16.99 *(978-1-4847-0938-2(1))* Disney Pr.

Shusterman, Neal. Dread Locks. 2006. (Dark Fusion Ser.: 1). (ENG.). 176p. (YA). (gr. 7-18). 7.99 *(978-0-14-240599-4(X)*, Speak) Penguin Young Readers Group.

Siems, Dorthy R. A Fairy's Wings: Set 1. 2007. (Illus.). 50p. (J). spiral bd. 15.00 net. *(978-0-9794483-3-1(6))* Siems, D.R.

Sill, Cathryn. About Mollusks: A Guide for Children, 1 vol. Sill, John, illus. 2008. (About... Ser.). (ENG.). 40p. (J). (gr. k-3). pap. 7.95 *(978-1-56145-406-8(0))* Peachtree Pubs.

Slater, Teddy. Tim Feels Scared. Rescek, Sanja, illus. 2011. (J). *(978-0-545-35179-9(0))* Scholastic, Inc.

Small, Lily. Kylie the Kitten. 2017. (Fairy Animals of Misty Wood Ser.). (ENG., Illus.). 144p. (J). pap. 5.99 ***(978-1-250-12698-6(3)**, 9781250126986*, Holt, Henry & Co. Bks. For Young Readers) Holt, Henry & Co.

Snicket, Lemony, pseud. The Dark. Klassen, Jon, illus. 2013. (ENG.). 40p. (J). (gr. -1-3). 16.99 *(978-0-316-18748-0(8))* Little, Brown Bks. for Young Readers.

Snyder, Maria V. Storm Watcher. 2013. 228p. (gr. 4-8). pap. 9.99 *(978-1-61603-033-9(X))* Leap Bks.

Spelman, Cornelia. When I Feel Scared. Parkinson, Kathy, illus. 2012. (J). *(978-1-61913-141-5(2))* Weigl Pubs., Inc.

Spelman, Cornelia Maude. When I Feel Scared. Parkinson, Kathy, illus. 2010. (ENG.). 16p. (J). (gr. -1 — 1). bds. 7.99 *(978-0-8075-8905-2(5))* Whitman, Albert & Co.

Spruill, Patricia Thomas. Josie Is Afraid. 2008. 32p. pap. 14.49 *(978-1-4343-7898-9(5))* AuthorHouse.

Stack, David Martin. Good Morning Captain. 2009. 58p. pap. 10.99 *(978-0-557-06575-2(5))* Lulu Pr., Inc.

Stalling-Patton, Deborah. Shypoodie: Getting to Know You. 2009. 40p. pap. 17.99 *(978-1-4389-3899-8(3))* AuthorHouse.

Steele, Giselle. The off-Limits Watermelon Patch. 2006. (Illus.). 35p. (J). per. 12.95 *(978-0-9769949-0-9(9))* Stuart & Weitz Publishing Group.

Stein, Mathilde. Brave Ben. Van Hout, Mies, illus. 2006. (ENG.). 32p. (J). (gr. 2-6). 15.95 *(978-1-932425-64-2(0)*, Lemniscaat) Boyds Mills Pr.

Steinkraus, Kyla. Vamos a Acampar. 2012. (SPA & ENG.). 24p. (gr. 2-3). pap. 8.95 *(978-1-61810-549-3(3))* Rourke Educational Media.

Stephens, Sarah Hines. Night of the Scaredy Crows, 1 vol. Baltazar, Art, illus. 2012. (DC Super-Pets Ser.). (ENG.). 56p. (gr. 2-2). pap. 4.95 *(978-1-4048-7663-7(4))*; lib. bdg. 23.99 *(978-1-4048-6492-4(X))* Picture Window Bks. (DC Super-Pets).

Stevens, Elizabeth. Mister D. Frongia, Daniela, illus. 2012. 24p. (J). 16.95 *(978-1-60131-114-6(1))* Big Tent Bks.

Stewart, Dianne. Who's Afraid of the Dark? Rankin, Joan, illus. 2012. (ENG.). 32p. (J). (gr. k-2). pap. 6.95 *(978-1-4314-0118-5(8))* Jacana Media ZAF. Dist: Independent Pubs. Group.

Stilton, Geronimo, et al. Robot Attack. Usai, Luca & Verzini, Daniele, illus. 2015. 117p. (J). *(978-0-545-86796-2(7))* Scholastic, Inc.

Stine, R. L. Darkest Dawn. 2005. (Fear Street Nights Ser.: No. 3). 182p. (YA). lib. bdg. 20.00 *(978-1-4242-0994-1(3))* Fitzgerald Bks.

—Darkest Dawn. 2012. (Fear Street Nights Ser.: 3). (ENG.). 192p. (YA). (gr. 7). pap. 9.99 *(978-1-4424-6058-4(X)*, Simon Pulse) Simon Pulse.

—Don't Scream! 2012. (J). 137p. *(978-0-545-48408-4(1))*; (Goosebumps Hall of Horrors Ser.: 5). (ENG.). 160p. (gr. 3-7). pap. 6.99 *(978-0-545-28937-5(8)*, Scholastic Paperbacks) Scholastic, Inc.

—Don't Scream! 2012. (Goosebumps HorrorLand: Hall of Horrors Ser.: 5). lib. bdg. 17.20 *(978-0-606-23727-7(5)*, Turtleback) Turtleback Bks.

—Fright Knight & the Ooze: Twice Terrifying Tales. 2010. (R. L. Stine's Ghosts of Fear Street Ser.). (ENG.). 240p. (J). (gr. 3-7). pap. 6.99 *(978-1-4169-9135-9(2)*, Aladdin) Simon & Schuster Children's Publishing.

—Monstruos en el Campamento. (Fantasmas de Fear Street Coleccion). (SPA.). (YA). (gr. 5-8). pap. 7.95 *(978-950-04-1871-3(1)*, EM10012) Emecé Editores S.A. ARG. Dist: Planeta Publishing Corp., Lectorum Pubns., Inc.

—A Night in Terror Tower. 2009. (Classic Goosebumps Ser.: 12). (ENG.). 160p. (J). (gr. 3-7). 6.99 *(978-0-545-15887-9(7)*, Scholastic Paperbacks) Scholastic, Inc.

—Stay Away from the Tree House & Eye of the Fortuneteller: Twice Terrifying Tales. 2009. (R. L. Stine's Ghosts of Fear Street Ser.). (ENG., Illus.). 224p. (J). (gr. 3-7). pap. 7.99 *(978-1-4169-9137-3(9)*, Aladdin) Simon & Schuster Children's Publishing.

Stine, R. L., ed. Fear: 13 Stories of Suspense & Horror. 2010. (ENG.). 320p. (YA). (gr. 7-18). 7.99 *(978-0-14-241774-4(2)*, Speak) Penguin Young Readers Group.

Stockton, Frank Richard, et al. Simply Suspense. 2nd ed. 2008. (ENG., Illus.). 56p. pap. 11.99 *(978-1-4058-6948-5(8))* Pearson Education.

A Stormy Adventure: Facing the Fear of Storms. 2004. (J). 6.99 *(978-0-9753870-3-0(0))* Write On!

Suen, Anastasia. La Noche de Terror. Heck, Claudia M., tr. from ENG. Laughead, Mike, illus. 2012. (Robot y Rico/Robot & Rico Ser.).Tr. of Scary Night. (MUL, SPA & ENG.). 32p. (gr. 1-2). pap. 5.05 *(978-1-4342-3918-1(7))*; lib. bdg. 22.65 *(978-1-4342-3779-8(6))* Stone Arch Bks. (Bilingual Stone Arch Readers).

Sunderland, Margot & Hancock, Nicky. Teenie Weenie in a Too Big World, 2 vols. Armstrong, Nicky, tr. Armstrong, Nicky, illus. (ENG.). 32p. pap. *(978-0-86388-460-3(1)*, 002-5144, Routledge) Taylor & Francis Group.

Swanson Sateren, Shelley. Adventures of Hound Hotel. Melmon, Deborah, illus. 2015. (Adventures at Hound Hotel Ser.). (ENG.). 72p. (gr. 2-3). 101.28 *(978-1-4795-6291-6(2)*, Adventures at Hound Hotel) Picture Window Bks.

Sweet, Susan D. & Miles, Brenda. Jacqueline & the Beanstalk: A Tale of Facing Giant Fears. Docampo, Valeria, illus. 2017. 32p. (J). 15.95 ***(978-1-4338-2682-5(8)**,* Magination Pr.) American Psychological Assn.

TerKeurst, Lysa. It Will Be Okay: Trusting God Through Fear & Change, 1 vol. 2014. (ENG., Illus.). 32p. (J). 14.99 *(978-1-4003-2419-4(X))* Nelson, Thomas Inc.

Testa, Maggie. Daniel Gets Scared. 2015. (Daniel Tiger's Neighborhood Ready-To-Read Ser.). lib. bdg. 13.55 *(978-0-606-38243-4(7))* Turtleback Bks.

Thaler, Mike. Black Lagoon, 6 vols., Set. Lee, Jared, illus. Incl. Gym Teacher from the Black Lagoon. lib. bdg. 24.21 *(978-1-59961-794-7(3))*; Librarian from the Black Lagoon. lib. bdg. 24.21 *(978-1-59961-795-4(1))*; Music Teacher from the Black Lagoon. lib. bdg. 24.21 *(978-1-59961-796-1(X))*; Principal from the Black Lagoon. lib. bdg. 24.21 *(978-1-59961-797-8(8))*; School Nurse from the Black Lagoon. lib. bdg. 24.21 *(978-1-59961-798-5(6))*; Teacher from the Black Lagoon. lib. bdg. 24.21 *(978-1-59961-799-2(4))*; (gr. -1-2). (Black Lagoon Set 1 Ser.: 6). (ENG., Illus.). 32p. 2011. Set lib. bdg. 145.26 *(978-1-59961-793-0(5))* Spotlight.

—The Bully from the Black Lagoon. Lee, Jared, illus. 2008. (From the Black Lagoon Ser.). (gr. -1-3). 14.00 *(978-0-7569-8834-0(9))* Perfection Learning Corp.

—The Bully from the Black Lagoon. Lee, Jared, illus. (J). 2008. (ENG.). 32p. (gr. -1-3). pap. 3.99 *(978-0-545-06521-4(6)*, Cartwheel Bks.) 2004. *(978-0-439-68072-1(7))* Scholastic, Inc.

—The Bully from the Black Lagoon, 1 vol. Lee, Jared, illus. 2012. (Black Lagoon Set 2 Ser.: No. 2). (ENG.). 32p. (J). (gr. 1-4). lib. bdg. 24.21 *(978-1-59961-953-8(9))* Spotlight.

—The Custodian from the Black Lagoon, 1 vol. 2014. (From the Black Lagoon Ser.). (ENG., Illus.). 32p. (J). (gr. 1-4). lib. bdg. 24.21 *(978-1-61479-196-6(1))* Spotlight.

—The Field Day from the Black Lagoon. Lee, Jared, illus. 2008. (From the Black Lagoon Ser.). 64p. (gr. 2-5). 14.00 *(978-0-7569-8801-2(2))* Perfection Learning Corp.

—The Field Day from the Black Lagoon. Lee, Jared, illus. 2008. (Black Lagoon Adventures Ser.: 6). (ENG.). 64p. (J). (gr. 2-5). pap. 4.99 *(978-0-439-68076-9(X))* Scholastic, Inc.

—The Field Day from the Black Lagoon, 1 vol. Lee, Jared, illus. 2011. (Black Lagoon Adventures Ser.: No. 1). (ENG.). 64p. (gr. 3-6). 24.21 *(978-1-59961-812-8(5))* Spotlight.

Theys, Erchen. Birdie Hop: The True Story. 2011. (Illus.). 28p. 12.19 *(978-1-4567-7522-3(7))* AuthorHouse.

Thomas, Jan. The Doghouse. 2008. (ENG., Illus.). 40p. (J). (gr. -1-k). 12.95 *(978-0-15-206533-1(4))* Houghton Mifflin Harcourt Publishing Co.

Tolle, Eckhart & Friedman, Robert S. Milton's Secret: An Adventure of Discovery Through Then, When & the Power of Now. Riccio, Frank, illus. 2008. (ENG.). 40p. (J). (gr. 3-7). 18.95 *(978-1-57174-577-4(7))* Hampton Roads Publishing Co., Inc.

Tomlinson, Jill. Owl Who Was Afraid of the Dark. (Illus.). 95p. (J). pap. 6.99 *(978-0-7497-0795-8(X))* Egmont Bks., Ltd. GBR. Dist: Trafalgar Square Publishing.

—The Owl Who Was Afraid of the Dark. Pack, Set. Howard, Paul, illus. 2015. (ENG.). 32p. (J). (gr. -1-2). 22.99 *(978-1-4052-7554-5(5))* Egmont Bks., Ltd. GBR. Dist: Independent Pubs. Group.

Trapani, Iza. Gabe & Goon. Trapani, Iza, illus. 2016. (ENG., Illus.). 32p. (J). (gr. -1-1). lib. bdg. 16.95 *(978-1-58089-640-5(5))* Charlesbridge Publishing, Inc.

Treanor, H. T. The Sun Stone. Tarnowski, Mark, illus. 2012. 16p. pap. 10.00 *(978-1-60976-125-7(1)*, Strategic Bk. Publishing) Strategic Book Publishing & Rights Agency (SBPRA).

Tremblay, Carole. Floop in the Dark. Beshwaty, Steve, illus. 2009. (Floop Ser.). 24p. (J). (gr. -1-k). 22.60 *(978-1-60754-341-1(9))* Windmill Bks.

Trigueros, Nury. I Don't Like to Be Afraid. 2010. 24p. pap. 16.99 *(978-1-4490-7287-2(9))* AuthorHouse.

Trivette, Donna K. Ringo & Girl. 2011. 40p. pap. 24.95 *(978-1-4626-1369-4(1))* America Star Bks.

Trueit, Trudi. Mom, There's a Dinosaur in Beeson's Lake. Paillot, Jim, illus. 2011. (Secrets of a Lab Rat Ser.). (ENG.). 160p. (J). (gr. 3-7). pap. 5.99 *(978-1-4169-6112-3(7)*, Aladdin) Simon & Schuster Children's Publishing.

Trueit, Trudi Strain. Mom, There's a Dinosaur in Beeson's Lake. Paillot, Jim, illus. 2010. (Secrets of a Lab Rat Ser.). (ENG.). 160p. (J). (gr. 3-7). 14.99 *(978-1-4169-7593-9(4)*, Simon & Schuster/Paula Wiseman Bks.) Simon & Schuster/Paula Wiseman Bks.

Tyler, Sandy. Herkimer's Big Day: Herkimer the Police Horse Meets a Young Girl Named Sammy. Williams, Brian, illus. 2012. (ENG.). 22p. (J). pap. 20.95 *(978-1-4327-9005-9(6))* Outskirts Pr., Inc.

Upjohn, Rebecca. The Last Loon, 1 vol. 2010. (Orca Young Readers Ser.). (ENG., Illus.). 144p. (J). (gr. 3-6). pap. 7.95 *(978-1-55469-292-7(X))* Orca Bk. Pubs. USA.

Uttley, Tracy. Molly Mcsholly Conquers Kindergarten. 2004. 32p. (J). bds. 15.95 *(978-1-59298-077-2(5))* Beaver's Pond Pr., Inc.

Valentine, Madeline. George in the Dark. 2014. (ENG., Illus.). 40p. (J). (gr. -1-2). 16.99 *(978-0-449-81334-8(7))*; lib. bdg. 19.99 *(978-0-449-81335-5(5))* Random Hse. Children's Bks. (Knopf Bks. for Young Readers).

van Genechten, Guido. Floppy in the Dark. 2004. (Illus.). (J). 25p. *(978-1-85269-244-5(8))*; 25p. *(978-1-85269-247-6(2))*; 25p. *(978-1-85269-241-4(3))*; 25p. *(978-1-85269-249-0(9))*; 25p. *(978-1-85269-250-6(2))*; 25p. *(978-1-85269-251-3(0))*; 25p. *(978-1-85269-278-0(2))*; 25p. *(978-1-85269-282-7(0))*; (ENG & PAN., 28p. pap. *(978-1-85269-245-2(6))*; (ENG & BEN., 28p. pap. *(978-1-85269-238-4(3))*; (POR & ENG., 28p. pap. *(978-1-85269-246-9(4))*; (ENG & URD., 28p. pap. *(978-1-85269-252-0(9))* Mantra Lingua.

—Ricky Is Brave. van Genechten, Guido, illus. 2011. (Ricky Ser.). (ENG., Illus.). 32p. (J). (gr. -1-k). 16.95 *(978-1-60537-097-2(5))* Cobblestone Publishing Co.

van Genechten, Guido, tr. from DUT. Floppy in the Dark: Veshllapushi Ne Erresire. 2004. (Illus.). 25p. (J). *(978-1-85269-234-6(0))* Mantra Lingua.

Vandepeer, Helen. Gifts. 2008. 76p. pap. 35.80 *(978-0-557-03191-7(5))* Lulu Pr., Inc.

Vermeulen, Thomas. Gabangani Guinea Fowl & Huzu the Bird Eating Spider. 2009. 50p. pap. 19.50 *(978-1-60693-741-9(3)*, Eloquent Bks.) Strategic Book Publishing & Rights Agency (SBPRA).

Viorst, Judith. And Two Boys Booed. Blackall, Sophie, illus. 2014. (ENG.). 32p. (J). (gr. -1-3). 16.99 *(978-0-374-30302-0(9)*, 9780374303020, Farrar, Straus & Giroux (BYR)) Farrar, Straus & Giroux.

Vogel, Vin. Bedtime for Yeti. 2016. (ENG., Illus.). 32p. (J). (-k). 16.99 *(978-1-101-99431-3(2)*, Dial Bks) Penguin Young Readers Group.

Wagner, Linda. Lady Flatterley. 2008. 44p. pap. 22.95 *(978-1-4327-3233-2(1))* Outskirts Pr., Inc.

Walter, Chris. Tell Your Dreams to Me. 2008. 32p. pap. 14.95 *(978-1-4389-0162-6(3))* AuthorHouse.

Wan Aisyah, Aisyah & Wan Aisyah. The Potty Monster. 2010. 32p. pap. *(978-1-4269-3019-5(4))* Trafford Publishing (UK) Ltd.

Wargin, Kathy-jo. Frank & Beans & the Scary Campout, 1 vol. Lewis, Anthony, illus. 2010. (I Can Read! / Frank & Beans Ser.). (ENG.). 32p. (J). pap. 3.99 *(978-0-310-71850-5(3))* Zonderkidz.

Waters-Porter, Amber Rae. Rachael's Auntie Is Bald-Headed. 2010. (ENG.). 16p. pap. 9.49 *(978-1-4490-7755-6(2))* AuthorHouse.

Watt, Fiona. Complete Book of First Experiences. rev. ed. 2011. (First Experiences Ser.). 144p. (J). ring bd. 19.99 *(978-0-7945-2948-2(8)*, Usborne) EDC Publishing.

Watt, Mélanie. Scaredy Squirrel. Watt, Mélanie, illus. 2008. (ENG., Illus.). 40p. (J). (gr. -1-3). pap. 7.95 *(978-1-55453-023-6(7))* Kids Can Pr., Ltd. CAN. Dist: Hachette Bk. Group.

—Scaredy Squirrel. 2011. (J). (gr. -1-3). 18.95 *(978-0-545-32752-7(0))*; 29.95 *(978-0-545-32740-4(7))*;Set. 38.75 *(978-0-545-32759-6(8))* Weston Woods Studios, Inc.

—Scaredy Squirrel at Night. Watt, Mélanie, illus. 2009. (ENG., Illus.). 32p. (J). (gr. -1-3). 16.95 *(978-1-55453-288-9(4))* Kids Can Pr., Ltd. CAN. Dist: Hachette Bk. Group.

—Scaredy Squirrel at the Beach. Watt, Mélanie, illus. 2008. (ENG., Illus.). 32p. (J). (gr. -1-3). 15.95 *(978-1-55453-225-4(6))* Kids Can Pr., Ltd. CAN. Dist: Hachette Bk. Group.

Weitzman, Jacqueline Preiss. Superhero Joe. Barrett, Ron, illus. 2011. (ENG.). 32p. (J). (gr. -1-3). 16.99 *(978-1-4169-9157-1(3)*, Simon & Schuster/Paula Wiseman Bks.) Simon & Schuster/Paula Wiseman Bks.

—Superhero Joe & the Creature Next Door. Barrett, Ron, illus. 2013. (ENG.). 32p. (J). (gr. -1-3). 16.99 *(978-1-4424-1268-2(2)*, Simon & Schuster Bks. For Young Readers) Simon & Schuster Bks. For Young Readers.

Welch, Eric. Jimmy the Gnome Won't Leave His Home, 1 vol. Natelli, Kenny, illus. 2009. 17p. pap. 24.95 *(978-1-60836-679-8(0))* America Star Bks.

West, Tracey. Song of the Poison Dragon: a Branches Book (Dragon Masters #5) Jones, Damien, illus. 2016. (Dragon Masters Ser.: 5). (ENG.). 96p. (J). (gr. 1-3). pap. 4.99 *(978-0-545-91387-4(X))* Scholastic, Inc.

Westheimer, Ruth K. Leopold. (ENG., Illus.). 2017. 36p. pap. 11.99 ***(978-1-68336-709-3(X))*** 2015. 34p. (J). 23.99 *(978-1-63026-918-0(2))* Turner Publishing Co.

Weston Woods Staff, creator. The Little Old Lady Who Was Not Afraid of Anything. 2011. 18.95 *(978-0-545-37419-4(7))*; 38.75 *(978-0-545-37497-2(9))* Weston Woods Studios, Inc.

Wheatonnovember. The Little Hermit Ant. 2011. 28p. pap. 24.95 *(978-1-4626-3805-5(8))* America Star Bks.

Wheeler, Lisa. One Dark Night. Bates, Ivan, illus. 2006. (ENG.). 32p. (J). (gr. -1-3). reprint ed. pap. 6.99 *(978-0-15-205888-3(5))* Houghton Mifflin Harcourt Publishing Co.

Wigger, Sherry. Scary Stories for Brave Kids, 1 vol. 2009. 73p. pap. 16.95 *(978-1-61582-308-6(5))* PublishAmerica, Inc.

Wiles, Deborah. Countdown. 2010. (Sixties Ser.). (ENG.). 400p. (J). (gr. 4-7). 19.99 *(978-0-545-10605-4(2)*, Scholastic Pr.) Scholastic, Inc.

Willems, Mo. Sam, the Most Scaredy-Cat Kid in the Whole World. Willems, Mo, illus. 2017. (ENG., Illus.). 48p. (J). (gr. -1-k). 17.99 ***(978-1-368-00214-1(5))*** Hyperion Bks. for Children.

Williams, Amy. Gertrude the Silly Puppy. 2011. 28p. pap. 24.95 *(978-1-4626-2603-8(3))* America Star Bks.

Williams, C. E. Cj's World: My First Day of Second Grade. 2012. 28p. pap. 24.95 *(978-1-4626-6249-4(8))* America Star Bks.

Williams, Simon. The Kite Who Was Scared of Heights. Papaleo, Antonio, illus. 2013. 38p. pap. *(978-1-910053-36-2(8))* Legend Pr.

Willis, Jeanne. La Tormenta Monstruosa. (Cotton Cloud Ser.). (SPA.). (J). (gr. 1-3). pap. *(978-84-480-0180-3(X))* Timun Mas, Editorial S.A. ESP. Dist: Lectorum Pubns., Inc.

Wilson, Angela. Tara the Terrified Turtle. Basta, Stormie, illus. 2012. 28p. pap. 24.95 *(978-1-4626-7454-1(2))* America Star Bks.

Wilson, Budge. The Fear of Angelina Domino. 2004. (Illus.). (J). (gr. k-3). spiral bd. *(978-0-616-07246-2(5))* Canadian National Institute for the Blind/Institut National Canadien pour les Aveugles.

Wilson, Karma. Bear Feels Scared. Chapman, Jane, illus. 2011. (Bear Bks.). (ENG.). 34p. (J). (gr. -1 — 1). bds. 7.99 *(978-1-4424-2755-6(8)*, Little Simon) Little Simon.

—Bear Feels Scared. Chapman, Jane, illus. 2008. (Bear Bks.). (ENG.). 40p. (J). (gr. -1-3). 17.99 *(978-0-689-85986-1(4)*, McElderry, Margaret K. Bks.) McElderry, Margaret K. Bks.

—Don't Be Afraid, Little Pip. Chapman, Jane, illus. 2009. (ENG.). 40p. (J). (gr. -1-2). 16.99 *(978-0-689-85987-8(2)*, McElderry, Margaret K. Bks.) McElderry, Margaret K. Bks.

—Who Goes There? Currey, Anna, illus. 2013. (ENG.). 40p. (J). (gr. -1-3). 16.99 *(978-1-4169-8002-5(4)*, McElderry, Margaret K. Bks.) McElderry, Margaret K. Bks.

Winnick, Karen B. Lucy's Cave: A Story of Vicksburg 1863. 2008. (ENG.). 32p. (J). (gr. 4-6). 16.95 *(978-1-59078-194-4(5))* Boyds Mills Pr.

Winton, Tim. The Deep. Louise, Karen, illus. 32p. (YA). pap. 13.95 *(978-1-86368-210-7(4))* Fremantle Pr. AUS. Dist: Independent Pubs. Group.

Wishinsky, Frieda. Nothing Scares Us. Layton, Neal, illus. (Carolrhoda Picture Books Ser.). 32p. (J). 2004. (gr. 1-4). pap. 6.25 *(978-1-57505-669-2(0))* 2003. (gr. -1-3). 15.95 *(978-1-57505-490-2(6)*, Carolrhoda Bks.) Lerner Publishing Group.

E
F
G

Witek, Jo. Brave as Can Be: A Book of Courage. Roussey, Christine, illus. 2015. (Growing Hearts Ser.). (ENG.). 32p. (J). (gr. -1 — 1). 16.95 *(978-1-4197-1923-3(8)*, Abrams Appleseed) Abrams, Inc.

Wittinger, Ellen. This Means War! 2010. (ENG.). 224p. (J). (gr. 5-9). 16.99 *(978-1-4169-7101-6(7)*, Simon & Schuster Bks. For Young Readers) Simon & Schuster Bks. For Young Readers.

Wittman, Patricia. Scrabble Creek. 2013. (ENG., Illus.). 32p. (J). (gr. -1-3). 16.99 *(978-1-4814-2145-4(X)*, Simon & Schuster Bks. For Young Readers) Simon & Schuster Bks. For Young Readers.

Wolkstein, Diane. The Banza: A Haitian Story. Brown, Marc, illus. 33p. (J). (gr. k-2). pap. 5.99 *(978-0-8072-1268-4(7)*, Listening Library) Random Hse. Audio Publishing Group.

Woman, Magpie Sleeping. Big Eyes: The Keeper of the Night. 2013. 24p. pap. 24.95 *(978-1-4626-9569-0(8))* America Star Bks.

Woodward, Caroline. Singing Away the Dark. Morstad, Julie, illus. 2011. (ENG.). 36p. (J). (gr. -1-3). 16.95 *(978-1-897476-41-3(8))* Simply Read Bks. CAN. Dist: Ingram Publisher Services.

Wormell, Chris. Molly & the Night Monster. Wormell, Chris, illus. 2011. (ENG., Illus.). 32p. (J). (gr. -1-k). pap. 9.99 *(978-1-86230-185-6(9)*, Red Fox) Random House Children's Books GBR. Dist: Independent Pubs. Group.

Yoon, Salina. Stormy Night. (ENG., Illus.). (J). 2016. 32p. bds. 7.99 *(978-1-68119-165-2(2)*, 9781681191652) 2015. 40p. (gr. -1-1). 14.99 *(978-0-8027-3780-9(3)*, 9780802737809) Bloomsbury Publishing USA. (Bloomsbury USA Childrens).

Zaibak, Bushra. I am Not Afraid. 2007. (Illus.). 37p. (J). mass mkt. *(978-0-9787849-7-3(9))* Lucent Interpretations, LLC.

Zimmerman, Erik. Booga-Boo - Coloring Book. 2005. (Illus.). 32p. (J). per. 7.99 *(978-1-59879-009-2(9))* Lifevest Publishing, Inc.

Zoller, Elisabeth & Kolloch, Brigitte. Antonia & the Big Competition: The Rosenburg Riding Stables, Volume 2. Gotzen-Beek, Betina, illus. 2014. (ENG.). 92p. (J). (gr. 2-7). 9.95 *(978-1-62873-597-0(X)*, Sky Pony Pr.) Skyhorse Publishing Co., Inc.

FEASTS

see Fasts and Feasts

FEDERATION, INTERNATIONAL

see International Organization

FEELING

see Perception; Touch

FEELINGS

see Emotions

FEET

see Foot

FELIDAE

see Cat Family (Mammals)

FELIX THE CAT (FICTITIOUS CHARACTER)—FICTION

The Comic Adventures of Felix the Cat. 2004. (Illus.). 128p. (YA). per. 12.95 *(978-0-615-12660-9(X))* Felix Comics, Inc.

Yoe, Craig, et al. Felix the Cat Paintings. Ollerenshaw, Rod, ed. 2014. (ENG., Illus.). 168p. 34.99 *(978-1-61377-839-5(2)*, 9781613778395) Idea & Design Works, LLC.

FELLOWSHIPS

see Scholarships

FELONY

see Crime

FEMINISM

see also Women's Rights

Adhikary, Qiron. Feminist Folktales from India. 2003. (Illus.). 97p. (YA). per. 9.95 *(978-0-9714127-3-6(1))* Masalai Pr.

Anderson, Jennifer Joline. Women's Rights Movement, 1 vol. 2013. (Essential Library of Social Change Ser.). (ENG.). 112p. (J). (gr. 6-12). lib. bdg. 35.64 *(978-1-61783-889-7(6)*, Essential Library) ABDO Publishing Co.

Archer, Jules. The Feminist Revolution: A Story of the Three Most Inspiring & Empowering Women in American History: Susan B. Anthony, Margaret Sanger, & Betty Friedan. rev. ed. 2015. (Jules Archer History for Young Readers Ser.). (ENG., Illus.). 200p. (J). (gr. 6). 16.99 *(978-1-63220-603-9(X)*, Sky Pony Pr.) Skyhorse Publishing Co., Inc.

Bailey Association Staff & Gorman, Jacqueline Laks. The Modern Feminist Movement. 2011. (Cultural History of Women in America Ser.). (Illus.). 64p. (gr. 6-12). 35.00 *(978-1-60413-935-8(8)*, Chelsea Hse.) Facts On File, Inc.

Bailey Association Staff & Senker, Cath. Strength in Numbers. 2011. (Cultural History of Women in America Ser.). (Illus.). 64p. (gr. 6-12). 35.00 *(978-1-60413-931-0(5)*, Chelsea Hse.) Facts On File, Inc.

—Women Claim the Vote. 2011. (Cultural History of Women in America Ser.). (Illus.). 64p. (gr. 6-12). 35.00 *(978-1-60413-930-3(7)*, Chelsea Hse.) Facts On File, Inc.

Bailey Association Staff, et al. Women of Today. 2011. (Cultural History of Women in America Ser.). (Illus.). 64p. (gr. 6-12). 35.00 *(978-1-60413-936-5(6)*, Chelsea Hse.) Facts On File, Inc.

Bakshi, Kelly. Perspectives on the Women's Rights Movement. 2018. (ENG.). 32p. (gr. 3-6). ***(978-1-63235-405-1(5)***, 12-Story Library) Pr. Room Editions LLC.

Bohannon, Lisa Frederiksen. Woman's Work: The Story of Betty Friedan. 2004. (Illus.). 144p. (YA). (gr. 6-12). 23.95 *(978-1-931798-41-9(9))* Reynolds, Morgan Inc.

Coster, Patience & Walker, Pamela. A New Deal for Women. 2011. (Cultural History of Women in America Ser.). (Illus.). 64p. (gr. 6-12). 35.00 *(978-1-60413-934-1(X)*, Chelsea Hse.) Facts On File, Inc.

Cunningham, Anne C. Critical Perspectives on Feminism. 2017. (Analyzing the Issues Ser.). 208p. (J). (gr. 8-8). lib. bdg. 47.93 ***(978-0-7660-8481-0(7))*** Enslow Pubs., Inc.

Gelletly, LeeAnne. The Equal Rights Amendment. 2012. (J). pap. *(978-1-4222-2361-1(2))* Mason Crest.

—The Equal Rights Amendment. Harrington, A. Page, ed. 2012. (Finding a Voice: Women's Fight for Equality in U. S. Society Ser.). 64p. (J). (gr. 5). 22.95 *(978-1-4222-2351-2(5))* Mason Crest.

—Origins of the Women's Rights Movement. 2012. (Illus.). 64p. (J). pap. *(978-1-4222-2363-5(9))* Mason Crest.

—Origins of the Women's Rights Movement. Harrington, A. Page, ed. 2012. (Finding a Voice: Women's Fight for Equality in U. S. Society Ser.). (Illus.). 64p. (J). (gr. 5). 22.95 *(978-1-4222-2353-6(1))* Mason Crest.

Gordon, Minette, et al. Understanding Women's Rights. 2011. (Personal Freedom & Civic Duty Ser.). (J). lib. bdg. 35.95 *(978-1-4488-4671-9(4))* Rosen Publishing Group, Inc., The.

Hanson-Harding, Alexandra. Activism: Taking on Women's Issues. 2012. (Young Woman's Guide to Contemporary Issues Ser.). (ENG., Illus.). 112p. (YA). (gr. 9-12). lib. bdg. 34.60 *(978-1-4488-8401-8(2))* Rosen Publishing Group, Inc., The.

Higgins, Nadia Abushanab. Feminism: Reinventing the F-Word. 2016. (ENG., Illus.). 112p. (YA). (gr. 7-12). 53.32 *(978-1-4677-9578-4(X)*, Twenty-First Century Bks.) Lerner Publishing Group.

—Feminism 3.0: Reinventing the F Word. 2016. (Nonfiction - Young Adult Ser.). (ENG., Illus.). 112p. (J). (gr. 7-12). 35.99 *(978-1-4677-6147-5(8)*, Twenty-First Century Bks.) Lerner Publishing Group.

Humphrey, Elizabeth King. The Feminist Movement Today. 2012. (J). pap. *(978-1-4222-2362-8(0))* Mason Crest.

—The Feminist Movement Today. Harrington, A. Page, ed. 2012. (Finding a Voice: Women's Fight for Equality in U. S. Society Ser.). 64p. (J). (gr. 5). 22.95 *(978-1-4222-2352-9(3))* Mason Crest.

Jennings, Terry Catasús. The Women's Liberation Movement, 1960-1990. 2012. (J). pap. *(978-1-4222-2368-0(X))* Mason Crest.

—The Women's Liberation Movement, 1960-1990. Harrington, A. Page, ed. 2012. (Finding a Voice: Women's Fight for Equality in U. S. Society Ser.). 64p. (J). (gr. 5). 22.95 *(978-1-4222-2358-1(2))* Mason Crest.

Jensen, Kelly, ed. Here We Are: Feminism for the Real World. 2017. (ENG., Illus.). 240p. (YA). (gr. 9-12). pap. 16.95 *(978-1-61620-586-7(5))* Algonquin Bks. of Chapel Hill.

Kendall, Martha E. Failure Is Impossible! The History of American Women's Rights. 3rd ed. 2005. (People's History Ser.). (Illus.). 96p. (gr. 6-12). lib. bdg. 26.60 *(978-0-8225-1744-3(2))* Lerner Publishing Group.

Kent, Deborah. The Seneca Falls Convention: Working to Expand Women's Rights. 2016. (Heroes of the Women's Suffrage Movement Ser.). (Illus.). 128p. (J). (gr. 6-6). 37.27 *(978-0-7660-7892-5(2))* Enslow Pubs., Inc.

Lowery, Zoe & Mills, J. Elizabeth. Social Roles & Stereotypes. 2017. (Women in the World Ser.). 112p. (gr. 12-11). 37.10 ***(978-1-5081-7441-7(5)***, Rosen Young Adult) Rosen Publishing Group, Inc., The.

McIntosh, Kenneth R. Women & Religion: Reinterpreting Scriptures to Find the Sacred Feminine. 2007. (Religion & Modern Culture Ser.). (Illus.). 112p. (YA). (gr. 3-7). lib. bdg. 22.95 *(978-1-59084-977-4(9))* Mason Crest.

Meade, Marion. Free Woman: The Life & Times of Victoria Woodhull. 2011. 176p. pap. 15.95 *(978-1-61756-052-1(9))* Open Road Integrated Media, Inc.

Phelps, Ethel Johnston, ed. Kamala: Feminist Folktales from Around the World. Boynton, Suki, illus. 2016. (Feminist Folktales Ser.: 2). (ENG.). 120p. (J). (gr. 2-7). pap. 14.95 *(978-1-55861-940-1(2))* Feminist Pr. at The City Univ. of New York.

—Sea Girl: Feminist Folktales from Around the World. Boynton, Suki, illus. 2017. (Feminist Folktales Ser.: 3). (ENG.). 200p. (J). (gr. 2-7). pap. 14.95 *(978-1-55861-418-5(4))* Feminist Pr. at The City Univ. of New York.

Pitman, Gayle E. Feminism from A to Z. 2017. (J). pap. ***(978-1-4338-2721-1(2)***, Magination Pr.) American Psychological Assn.

Schomp, Virginia. American Voices from the Women's Movement. 2006. (American Voices Ser.). (Illus.). 128p. (gr. 6-7). lib. bdg. 26.95 *(978-0-7614-2171-9(8)*, Benchmark Bks.) Marshall Cavendish Corp.

Stoinich, Elisabetta, illus. Good Night Stories for Rebel Girls: Coloring Book. 2016. (ENG.). pap. 9.00 ***(978-0-9978958-0-3(2))*** Timbuktu Labs, inc.

Tewa, Rev. Bagan. Man at the Cross. 2012. 352p. pap. 19.99 *(978-1-4771-5081-8(1))* Xlibris Corp.

Turner, Cherie. Everything You Need to Know about the Riot Grrrl Movement: The Feminism of a New Generation. 2009. (Need to Know Library). 64p. (gr. 5-5). 58.50 *(978-1-60854-095-2(2))* Rosen Publishing Group, Inc., The.

Weidt, Maryann N. Fighting for Equal Rights: A Story about Susan B. Anthony. Sartor, Amanda, tr. Sartor, Amanda, illus. (Creative Minds Biography Ser.). 64p. 2004. (J). 22.60 *(978-1-57505-181-9(8)*, Carolrhoda Bks.) 2003. (ENG.). (gr. 4-8). pap. 8.95 *(978-1-57505-609-8(7))* Lerner Publishing Group.

Wheaton, Elizabeth. Ms. The Story of Gloria Steinem. 2004. (Feminist Voices Ser.). (Illus.). 112p. (YA). (gr. 6-12). 23.95 *(978-1-883846-82-4(X)*, First Biographies) Reynolds, Morgan Inc.

Willis, Laurie. The Culture of Beauty. 2010. (Global Viewpoints Ser.). (ENG.). 224p. 40.45 *(978-0-7377-4929-8(6))*; pap. 27.95 *(978-0-7377-4930-4(X))* Cengage Gale. (Greenhaven Pr., Inc.).

Wittekind, Erika. Gloria Steinem: Women's Liberation Leader, 1 vol. 2011. (Essential Lives Set 7 Ser.). (ENG., Illus.). 112p. (J). (gr. 6-12). lib. bdg. 35.64 *(978-1-61783-007-5(0))* ABDO Publishing Co.

FENCING

Doeden, Matt. Combat Sports. 2015. (Summer Olympic Sports Ser.). (ENG., Illus.). 32p. (J). (gr. 2-4). 19.95 *(978-1-60753-807-3(5))* Amicus Publishing.

FERMI, ENRICO, 1901-1954

Stux, Erica. Enrico Fermi: Trailblazer in Nuclear Physics. 2004. (Nobel Prize-Winning Scientists Ser.). (Illus.). 128p. (J). lib. bdg. 27.94 *(978-0-7660-2177-8(7))* Enslow Pubs., Inc.

FERNS

Owens, L. L. The Life Cycle of a Fern. 2011. (Life Cycles Ser.). (ENG., Illus.). 32p. (J). (gr. k-3). lib. bdg. 29.93 *(978-1-60973-149-6(2)*, 201172) Child's World, Inc., The.

FERRIES

Hilton, George Woodman. The Great Lakes Car Ferries. 2003. (Illus.). 240p. lib. bdg. 39.95 net. *(978-0-9658624-3-1(7))* Montevallo Historical Pr., Inc.

Peters, Elisa. Let's Take the Ferry! 2014. (Public Transportation Ser.). 24p. (J). (gr. k-2). pap. 49.50 *(978-1-4777-6515-9(8)*, PowerKids Pr.) Rosen Publishing Group, Inc., The.

—¡Vamos a Tomar el Transbordador! / Let's Take the Ferry! de la Vega, Eida, ed. 2014. (Transporte Público / Public Transportation Ser.). (SPA & ENG.). 24p. (J). (gr. k-2). 23.60 *(978-1-4777-6783-2(5)*, PowerKids Pr.) Rosen Publishing Group, Inc., The.

Zimmermann, Karl. Steamboats: The Story of Lakers, Ferries, & Majestic Paddle-Wheelers. Zimmermann, Karl, photos by. 2007. (ENG., Illus.). 48p. (J). (gr. 4-9). 19.95 *(978-1-59078-434-1(0))* Boyds Mills Pr.

FERRIES—FICTION

Bohrer, Maddie. Penny's Penny Puzzle. 2010. 24p. pap. 11.49 *(978-1-4490-6477-8(9))* AuthorHouse.

Briggs, Martha Wren. The Little Ferry Travels with Virginia Bk. 6: The Little Ferry Goes to Yorktown. Starbuck-McMillan, Elizabeth, illus. 2007. (The Little Ferry Travels with Virginia Ser.: Vol. 6). 30p. (YA). (gr. 5-8). pap. 6.95 *(978-0-9633240-8-5(X))* Dory Pr.

Dale, Jay. Captain Ross & the Old Sea Ferry, 1 vol. Smith, Graham, illus. 2012. (Engage Literacy Green Ser.). (ENG.). 32p. (gr. k-2). pap. 5.99 *(978-1-4296-9016-4(X)*, Engage Literacy) Capstone Press of Coughlan Cos.

Fuller, Harvey. Tommy & the Island. Fuller, Harvey, illus. 2007. (Illus.). (J). pap. 18.95 *(978-0-9773725-7-7(X))* Flat Hammock Pr.

Kenah, Katharine. Ferry Tail. Wong, Nicole, illus. 2014. (ENG.). 32p. (J). (gr. k-3). 16.99 *(978-1-58536-829-7(6)*, 203011) Sleeping Bear Pr.

Montgomery, Anson. Paying the Ferryman. 2009. 196p. (J). (gr. 4-7). 11.99 *(978-1-933390-83-3(2))* Chooseco LLC.

Optic, Oliver, pseud. Haste & Waste; or, the Young Pilot of Lake Champlain. 2007. 112p. (gr. 4-7). per. *(978-1-4068-3636-3(2))* Echo Library.

St Jean, Catherine Avery. A Staten Island Ferry Tale. Frahm, Paul, illus. 2006. 32p. (J). per. 26.99 *(978-1-4134-0262-9(3))* Xlibris Corp.

FERTILIZERS AND MANURES

Barker, David. Save the Planet: Compost It. 2010. (Explorer Library: Language Arts Explorer Ser.). (ENG.). 32p. (gr. 4-8). pap. 14.21 *(978-1-60279-665-2(3)*, 200912); lib. bdg. 28.50 *(978-1-60279-656-0(4)*, 200349) Cherry Lake Publishing.

Glaser, Linda. Garbage Helps Our Garden Grow: A Compost Story. Rotner, Shelley, photos by. 2010. (ENG., Illus.). 32p. (gr. k-3). lib. bdg. 25.26 *(978-0-7613-4911-2(1))* Lerner Publishing Group.

Hicks, Dwayne. Composting. 2015. (Garden Squad! Ser.). (ENG.). 24p. (J). (gr. 3-4). 23.60 *(978-1-4994-1010-5(7)*, PowerKids Pr.) Rosen Publishing Group, Inc., The.

Koontz, Robin Michal. Composting: Nature's Recyclers, 1 vol. Harrad, Matthew, illus. 2006. (Amazing Science Ser.). (ENG.). 24p. (gr. k-4). per. 8.95 *(978-1-4048-2200-9(3))* Picture Window Bks.

Lay, Richard & Zarrinnaal, Laura Nienhaus. A Green Kid's Guide to Composting, 1 vol. 2013. (Green Kid's Guide to Gardening! Ser.). (ENG.). 24p. (J). (gr. -1-4). 27.07 *(978-1-61641-943-1(1))* Magic Wagon.

—A Green Kid's Guide to Organic Fertilizers, 1 vol. 2013. (Green Kid's Guide to Gardening! Ser.). (ENG.). 24p. (J). (gr. -1-4). 27.07 *(978-1-61641-945-5(8))* Magic Wagon.

Mangor, Jodie. Really Rotten Truth about Composting. 2016. (Let's Explore Science Ser.). (ENG., Illus.). 48p. (gr. 5-8). 35.64 *(978-1-68191-392-6(5))* Rourke Educational Media.

Pettiford, Rebecca. Composting. Fretland VanVoorst, Jenny, ed. 2015. (J). lib. bdg. 25.65 *(978-1-62031-229-2(8))* Jump! Inc.

Schwartz, Tom. How Mother Nature Flowered the Fields. 2007. 152p. (J). (gr. -1-3). per. 9.99 *(978-1-57545-142-8(5))* RP Media.

Sévigny, Eric, illus. Caillou: The Magic of Compost. 2011. (Ecology Club Ser.). (ENG.). 24p. (J). (gr. -1-1). pap. 5.95 *(978-2-89450-773-5(9))* Caillouet, Gerry.

FESTIVALS

see also Fasts and Feasts; Holidays

Aloian, Molly. Cultural Traditions in Australia. 2012. (ENG.). 32p. (J). *(978-0-7787-7516-4(X))*; (Illus.). pap. *(978-0-7787-7521-8(6))* Crabtree Publishing Co.

—Cultural Traditions in Brazil. 2012. (ENG.). 32p. (J). lib. bdg. *(978-0-7787-7583-6(6))*; (Illus.). pap. *(978-0-7787-7590-4(9))* Crabtree Publishing Co.

—Cultural Traditions in Canada. 2014. (ENG., Illus.). 32p. (J). *(978-0-7787-0297-9(9))* Crabtree Publishing Co.

—Cultural Traditions in Israel. 2014. (ENG., Illus.). 32p. (J). *(978-0-7787-0303-7(7))* Crabtree Publishing Co.

—Cultural Traditions in Russia. 2012. (ENG.). 32p. (J). pap. *(978-0-7787-7595-9(X))*; lib. bdg. *(978-0-7787-7588-1(7))* Crabtree Publishing Co.

—Cultural Traditions in Thailand. 2012. (ENG.). 32p. (J). *(978-0-7787-7519-5(4))*; (Illus.). pap. *(978-0-7787-7524-9(0))* Crabtree Publishing Co.

—Cultural Traditions in the United States. 2014. (ENG., Illus.). 32p. (J). *(978-0-7787-0305-1(3))* Crabtree Publishing Co.

—Mardi Gras & Carnival. 2009. (Celebrations in My World Ser.). (ENG., Illus.). 32p. (J). (gr. k-2). pap. *(978-0-7787-4773-4(5))*; (gr. 1-3). *(978-0-7787-4755-0(7))* Crabtree Publishing Co.

Aloian, Molly & Peppas, Lynn. Cultural Traditions in Mexico. 2012. (ENG.). 32p. (J). lib. bdg. *(978-0-7787-7587-4(9))* Crabtree Publishing Co.

Aloian, Molly & Peppas, Lynne. Cultural Traditions in Mexico. 2012. (ENG.). 32p. (J). pap. *(978-0-7787-7594-2(1))* Crabtree Publishing Co.

Ancona, George. Mis Fiestas: My Celebrations. 2005. (Somos Latinos (We Are Latinos) Ser.).Tr. of My Celebrations. (ENG & SPA., Illus.). 32p. (J). (gr. 1-3). lib. bdg. 21.00 *(978-0-516-25290-2(9))* Scholastic Library Publishing.

Anderson, Gennifer. Celebrations! Baity, Susan, illus. 2013. 38p. pap. 16.95 *(978-1-57258-905-6(1))* TEACH Services, Inc.

Barghoorn, Linda. Cultural Traditions in Poland. 2017. 32p. (J). ***(978-0-7787-8098-4(8))*** Crabtree Publishing Co.

Barlas, Robert & Tompsett, Norm. Canada. 2010. (Festivals of the World Ser.). 32p. (gr. 3). 28.50 *(978-1-60870-095-0(X))* Marshall Cavendish Corp.

Baumbusch, Brigitte. Festivals in Art. 2005. (What Makes A Masterpiece? Ser.). (Illus.). 32p. (gr. 1-4). lib. bdg. 23.00 *(978-0-8368-4781-9(4)*, Gareth Stevens Learning Library) Stevens, Gareth Publishing LLLP.

Bentley, Joyce. Happy Divali: The Festival of Lights. 2016. (ENG., Illus.). 24p. (J). (gr. k-2). 16.99 *(978-0-7502-9566-6(X)*, Wayland) Hachette Children's Group GBR. Dist: Hachette Bk. Group.

Berendes, Mary. Holidays & Celebrations (Los Días de Fiestas y Las Celebraciones) Petelinsek, Kathleen, illus. 2008. (WordBooks/Libros de Palabras Ser.). (SPA & ENG.). 24p. (J). (gr. k-3). 25.64 *(978-1-59296-991-3(7)*, 201093) Child's World, Inc., The.

Berg, Elizabeth. Egypt. 2010. (Festivals of the World Ser.). 32p. (gr. 3). 28.50 *(978-1-60870-097-4(6))* Marshall Cavendish Corp.

—Mexico. 2010. (Festivals of the World Ser.). 32p. (gr. 3). 28.50 *(978-1-60870-104-9(2))* Marshall Cavendish GBR. Dist: Marshall Cavendish Corp.

—The United States. 2010. (Festivals of the World Ser.). 32p. (gr. 3). 28.50 *(978-1-60870-106-3(9))* Marshall Cavendish GBR. Dist: Marshall Cavendish Corp.

Burns, Kylie. Cultural Traditions in Cuba. 2017. 32p. (J). ***(978-0-7787-8094-6(5))*** Crabtree Publishing Co.

Burton, Margie, et al. Celebrations Around the World. 2011. (Early Connections Ser.). (J). *(978-1-61672-516-7(8))* Benchmark Education Co.

Carnaval! 2004. (YA). tchr. ed. 75.00 incl. VHS *(978-1-56290-327-5(6))* Crystal Productions.

Celebrations & Rituals Around the World Set, 5 vol. set. 2003. (gr. 4-8). 154.00 *(978-0-7166-5020-1(7))* World Bk., Inc.

Chan, Arlene. The Moon Festival: A Chinese Mid-Autumn Celebration. 2004. (J). (gr. k-3). spiral bd. *(978-0-616-01615-2(8))* Canadian National Institute for the Blind/Institut National Canadien pour les Aveugles.

Cheong, Colin. China. 2010. (Festivals of the World Ser.). 32p. (gr. 3). 28.50 *(978-1-60870-096-7(8))* Marshall Cavendish Corp.

Conklin, Wendy. Fun & Games: Clockwork Carnival: Measuring Time (Grade 3) 2017. (Mathematics Readers Ser.). (Illus.). 32p. (gr. 3-3). 8.99 ***(978-1-4807-5805-6(1))*** Teacher Created Materials, Inc.

Coppendale, Jean. Family Festivals. 2006. (Illus.). 32p. (YA). (gr. 1-18). lib. bdg. 27.10 *(978-1-931983-96-9(8))* Chrysalis Education.

—Party Time. 2006. (Illus.). 32p. (YA). (gr. 1-18). lib. bdg. 27.10 *(978-1-931983-97-6(6))* Chrysalis Education.

—Special Holidays. 2006. (Illus.). 32p. (YA). (gr. 1-18). lib. bdg. 27.10 *(978-1-931983-98-3(4))* Chrysalis Education.

Dawson, Emily C. Holidays & Celebrations. 2010. (Special Days Ser.). 24p. 25.65 *(978-1-60753-030-5(9))* Amicus Publishing.

Dickmann, Nancy. Diwali, 1 vol. 2010. (Holidays & Festivals Ser.). (ENG., Illus.). 24p. (gr. -1-1). 22.65 *(978-1-4329-4051-5(1))*; pap. 6.29 *(978-1-4329-4070-6(8))* Heinemann-Raintree. (Acorn).

Doney, Meryl. Festivals. 2004. (Crafts from Many Cultures Ser.). (Illus.). 32p. (gr. 2-5). lib. bdg. 26.00 *(978-0-8368-4043-8(7)*, Gareth Stevens Learning Library) Stevens, Gareth Publishing LLLP.

Dworkin, Motoko. A Year in Japan: Folktales, Songs & Art for the Classroom. 2nd ed. 2012. (Illus.). 151p. pap. 26.95 *(978-0-9836716-1-9(3))* Paradise Copies, Inc.

Flood Williams, Colleen Madonna, et al. The Festivals of Mexico. 2009. (Mexico: Beautiful Land, Diverse People Ser.). (Illus.). 64p. (YA). (gr. 7-12). 21.95 *(978-1-4222-0657-7(2))* Mason Crest.

Flynn, Claire E. Running with the Bulls. 2014. (Illus.). 32p. (J). *(978-1-4824-0169-1(X))* Stevens, Gareth Publishing LLLP.

Foran, Jill. Mardi Gras. 2003. (Celebrating Cultures Ser.). (Illus.). 24p. (J). lib. bdg. 24.45 *(978-1-59036-093-4(1))* Weigl Pubs., Inc.

—Oktoberfest. 2003. (Celebrating Cultures Ser.). (Illus.). 24p. (J). lib. bdg. 24.45 *(978-1-59036-094-1(X))* Weigl Pubs., Inc.

—Powwow. 2003. (Celebrating Cultures Ser.). (Illus.). 24p. (J). lib. bdg. 24.45 *(978-1-59036-095-8(8))* Weigl Pubs., Inc.

Foy, Don. Israel. 2010. (Festivals of the World Ser.). 32p. (gr. 3). 28.50 *(978-1-60870-102-5(6))* Marshall Cavendish Corp.

Fuller, Rachel. All Kinds of Festivals. 2012. (All Kinds Of Ser.). (ENG., Illus.). 16p. (J). (gr. -1-k). 12.99 *(978-1-85707-801-5(2))* Tango Bks. GBR. Dist: Independent Pubs. Group.

Galat, Joan Marie. Cultural Traditions in Ghana. 2017. 32p. (J). ***(978-0-7787-8095-3(3))*** Crabtree Publishing Co.

—Cultural Traditions in Turkey. 2017. 32p. (J). ***(978-0-7787-8100-4(3))*** Crabtree Publishing Co.

Gallagher, Debbie. Family Celebrations. 2008. (Families Ser.). 32p. (gr. 1-2). lib. bdg. 18.56 *(978-0-7614-3133-6(0)*, Benchmark Bks.) Marshall Cavendish Corp.

—Family Stories. 2008. (Families Ser.). 32p. (gr. 1-2). lib. bdg. 18.56 *(978-0-7614-3142-8(X)*, Benchmark Bks.) Marshall Cavendish Corp.

Ganeri, Anita. The Divali Story. 2003. (Festival Stories Ser.). (Illus.). 24p. (YA). pap. *(978-0-237-52471-5(6))* Evans Brothers, Ltd.

Gerace, Frank E. & Leslie, Clare Walker. The Ancient Celtic Festivals: And How We Celebrate Them Today. 2nd ed. 2008. (ENG., Illus.). 64p. (J). (gr. 4-7). pap. 12.95 *(978-1-59477-256-6(8))* Inner Traditions International, Ltd.

Gilchrist, Cherry. A Calendar of Festivals. Cann, Helen, illus. 2006. 79p. (J). (gr. 4-8). reprint ed. pap. 10.00 *(978-1-4223-5551-0(9))* DIANE Publishing Co.

Gilchrist, Cherry & Cann, Helen. A Calendar of Festivals: Celebrations from Around the World. Mistry, Nilesh, illus. 2005. (ENG.). 80p. (J). pap. 12.99 *(978-1-84148-970-4(0))* Barefoot Bks., Inc.

Glupker, Dianne. Great Tastes of Michigan. Delsi, Dawna, illus. 2006. (J). per. 9.95 *(978-0-9769846-1-0(X))* Harambee Pr.

Grack, Rachel. Diwali. 2017. (Diwali Ser.). 24p. (J). (gr. k-3). pap. 6.99 ***(978-1-61891-272-5(0)***, Blastoff! Readers) Bellwether Media.

Grack, Rachel. Ramadan. 2017. (Celebrating Holidays! Ser.). (ENG., Illus.). 24p. (J). (gr. k-3). lib. bdg. 25.95 *(978-1-62617-597-6(7)*, Blastoff! Readers) Bellwether Media.

Greathouse, Lisa. Count Me In! School Carnival, 1 vol. 2nd rev. ed. 2011. (TIME for KIDS(r) Nonfiction Readers Ser.). (ENG.). 28p. (J). (gr. 2-2). pap. 6.99 *(978-1-4333-3637-9(5))* Teacher Created Materials, Inc.

Grolier Educational Staff, contrib. by. Argentina. 2003. (Illus.). 32p. (J). 309.00 *(978-0-7172-5788-1(6)*, Grolier) Scholastic Library Publishing.

Head, Honor. Celebrating Harvest Festivals Around the World. 2009. (We Love Holidays Ser.). 24p. (J). (gr. k-5). (ENG., Illus.). pap. 8.25 (978-1-4358-2904-6(2)); lib. bdg. 22.60 (978-1-4358-2844-5(5)) Rosen Publishing Group, Inc., The. (PowerKids Pr.).

Heaney, Shane. Food from Around the World: Represent & Solve Problems Involving Division. 2014. (Rosen Common Core Math Readers Ser.). (Illus.). 24p. (J). (gr. 3-4). (ENG.). pap. 8.25 (978-1-4777-4977-7(2)); lib. bdg. 23.60 (978-1-4777-6446-6(1)) Rosen Publishing Group, Inc., The. (PowerKids Pr.).

Heiligman, Deborah. Celebrate Diwali: With Sweets, Lights, & Fireworks. 2006. (Holidays Around the World Ser.). (ENG., Illus.). 32p. (J). (gr. 1-4). 15.95 (978-0-7922-5922-0(X)); lib. bdg. 23.90 (978-0-7922-5923-7(8)) National Geographic Society. (National Geographic Children's Bks.).

Hill, Z. B. Art Festivals & Galleries: The Art of Selling Art. 2014. (Art Today! Ser.: 10). 64p. (J). (gr. 7-18). 23.95 (978-1-4222-3169-2(0)) Mason Crest.

Hinman, Bonnie. Thanksgiving/Accion de Gracias. de la Vega, Eida, tr. from ENG. 2010. (Celebrate with Me/Celebra Conmigo Ser.). (ENG & SPA., Illus.). 32p. (J). (gr. -1-2). lib. bdg. 25.70 (978-1-58415-861-5(1)) Mitchell Lane Pubs., Inc.

Holidays & Celebrations, Vol. 2. 2005. (One World, Many Cultures Ser.). (YA). (gr. k-3). 356.40 (978-0-7368-4194-8(6), Pebble Bks.) Capstone Press of Coughlan Cos.

Holidays & Festivals, 1 vol., Set. Incl. Chinese New Year. Dickmann, Nancy. (Illus.). pap. 6.29 (978-1-4329-4069-0(4)); Christmas. Dickmann, Nancy. pap. 6.29 (978-1-4329-4066-9(X)); Diwali. Dickmann, Nancy. (Illus.). pap. 6.29 (978-1-4329-4070-6(8)); Easter. Dickmann, Nancy. (Illus.). pap. 6.29 (978-1-4329-4067-6(8)); Election Day. Rissman, Rebecca. pap. 6.29 (978-1-4329-4082-9(1)); Hanukkah. Dickmann, Nancy. (Illus.). pap. 6.29 (978-1-4329-4071-3(6)); Ramadan & Id-Ul-Fitr. Dickmann, Nancy. pap. 6.29 (978-1-4329-4068-3(6)); (gr. -1-1). (Holidays & Festivals Ser.). (ENG.). 24p. 2010. Set pap. 107.10 o.p. (978-1-4329-4084-3(8), Acorn) Heinemann-Raintree.

Hollihan, Kerrie Logan. Carnival in Latin America: Carnaval en Latinoamérica. Sanz, Ma Pilar, tr. 2010. (Latin American Celebrations & Festivals / Celebraciones y Festivales en Latinoamérica Ser.). (SPA & ENG., Illus.). 24p. (J). (gr. 2-5). lib. bdg. 22.60 (978-1-4358-9366-5(2)) Rosen Publishing Group, Inc., The.

Hyde, Katherine. Lucia: Saint of Light. 2009. 32p. 18.50 (978-0-9822770-4-1(0)) Ancient Faith Publishing.

Hyde, Natalie. Cultural Traditions in Sweden. 2015. (ENG., Illus.). 32p. (J). (978-0-7787-8064-9(3)) Crabtree Publishing Co.

Kagda, Falaq. India. 2010. (Festivals of the World Ser.). 32p. (gr. 3). 28.50 (978-1-60870-101-8(8)) Marshall Cavendish Corp.

Kindersley, Barnabas & Kindersley, Anabel, photos by. Celebraciones. 2005.Tr. of Celebrations. (SPA., Illus.). (J). (gr. 1-4). 18.95 (978-0-9628720-5-1(9)) Iaconi, Mariuccia Bk. Imports.

Krebs, Laurie. Sube y Baja Por Los Andes: Un Cuento de un Festival Peruano. Fronty, Aurélia, illus. 2011. (SPA.). 32p. (J). (gr. 1-6). pap. 7.99 (978-1-84686-548-0(4)) Barefoot Bks., Inc.

—Up & down the Andes. Fronty, Aurélia, illus. 2011. (ENG.). 32p. (J). (gr. k-1). pap. 8.99 (978-1-84686-468-1(2)) Barefoot Bks., Inc.

—Up & down the Andes: A Peruvian Festival Tale. Fronty, Aurélia, illus. 2008. (ENG.). 32p. (J). (gr. -1-5). 16.99 (978-1-84686-203-8(5)) Barefoot Bks., Inc.

Kumar, Monica & Kumar, Manisha. Diwali: A Festival of Lights & Fun. Sona & Jacob, illus. 2006.Tr. of Diwali: Khushiyon Ka Tyohaar. (ENG & HIN.). 32p. (J). 11.00 (978-0-9773645-7-2(7)) MeeraMasi, Inc.

Kummer, Patricia K. The Food of Thailand. 2011. (Flavors of the World Ser.). (ENG., Illus.). 64p. (J). (gr. 4-6). lib. bdg. 31.36 (978-1-60870-238-1(3), Cavendish Children's Bks.) Marshall Cavendish Corp.

Labrie, Julia. Cultural Traditions in Vietnam. 2017. 32p. (J). **(978-0-7787-8101-1(1))** Crabtree Publishing Co.

Lee, Michelle. Mardi Gras. 2016. (World's Greatest Celebrations Ser.). (ENG., Illus.). 32p. (gr. 3-8). 27.99 (978-1-62920-569-4(9)) Scobre Pr. Corp.

—Running of the Bulls. 2016. (World's Greatest Celebrations Ser.). (ENG., Illus.). 32p. (gr. 3-8). 27.99 (978-1-62920-575-5(3)) Scobre Pr. Corp.

Liao, Yan. Food & Festivals of China. Wang, Jianwei, ed. 2012. (China: the Emerging Superpower Ser.). 120p. (J). (gr. 7). 24.95 (978-1-4222-2159-4(8)) Mason Crest.

Loh-Hagan, Virginia. Craft Fair. 2017. (D. I. Y. Make It Happen Ser.). (ENG.). 32p. (J). (gr. 4-8). 29.93 (978-1-63472-143-1(8), 209144, 45th Parallel Press) Cherry Lake Publishing.

Lord, Richard. Germany. 2010. (Festivals of the World Ser.). 32p. (gr. 3). 28.50 (978-1-60870-100-1(X)) Marshall Cavendish GBR. Dist: Marshall Cavendish Corp.

Loughran, Donna. Carnival Coins: How Will We Count Our Money? 2013. (IMath Ser.). (Illus.). 24p. (J). (gr. k-2). pap. 11.94 (978-1-60357-491-4(3)); lib. bdg. 21.27 (978-1-59953-552-4(1)) Norwood Hse. Pr.

MacMillan, Dianne M. Diwali - Hindu Festival of Lights. rev. ed. 2008. (Best Holiday Bks.). (Illus.). 48p. (J). (gr. 1-4). lib. bdg. 25.27 (978-0-7660-3060-2(1)) Enslow Pubs., Inc.

—Mardi Gras. rev. ed. 2008. (Best Holiday Bks.). (Illus.). 48p. (J). (gr. 3-4). lib. bdg. 25.27 (978-0-7660-3062-6(8)) Enslow Pubs., Inc.

Maile, Ruby. Why Are You Having A Party? 2014. (Little Books of Answers: Level B Ser.). (Illus.). 16p. (gr. k-2). pap. 7.95 (978-1-927136-10-2(5)) Three Crows Media NZL. Dist: RiverStream Publishing.

Manderly, Lorin. Lilith Celebrates Lammas. Drewes, Dan, illus. 2010. 36p. pap. 15.50 (978-1-4520-2689-3(0)) AuthorHouse.

Matters, Print & Morrill, Ann. Easter, Passover, & Other Spring Festivals. 2009. (Holidays & Celebration Ser.). (Illus.). 112p. (gr. 5-8). 40.00 (978-1-60413-099-7(7), Chelsea Hse.) Facts On File, Inc.

McGee, Randel. Paper Crafts for Mardi Gras. 2011. (Paper Craft Fun for Holidays Ser.). (Illus.). 48p. (J). (gr. 3-18). pap. 8.95 (978-1-59845-334-8(3), Enslow Elementary) Enslow Pubs., Inc.

McKay, Susan. France. 2010. (Festivals of the World Ser.). 32p. (gr. 3). 28.50 (978-1-60870-099-8(2)) Marshall Cavendish Corp.

—Japan. 2010. (Festivals of the World Ser.). 32p. (gr. 3). 28.50 (978-1-60870-103-2(4)) Marshall Cavendish Corp.

McNeil, Niki, et al. HOCPP 1108 Harvest Festival. 2006. spiral bd. 14.00 (978-1-60308-108-5(9)) In the Hands of a Child.

Meekins, Katrina L. Deep Blue Year of Festivals: Intergenerational Celebrations. 2016. (Deep Blue Ser.). 48p. pap. 12.99 (978-1-5018-2033-5(8)) Abingdon Pr.

Menon, Sujatha. Celebrating Holi: A Hindu Celebration of Spring. 2009. (We Love Holidays Ser.). 24p. (J). (gr. k-5). (ENG., Illus.). pap. 8.25 (978-1-4358-2903-9(4), 1291608); lib. bdg. 22.60 (978-1-4358-2843-8(7)) Rosen Publishing Group, Inc., The. (PowerKids Pr.).

Miteff, Deb & Falk, Cathy. The un-Halloween Book: A Complete Fall Festival for Children's Ministry. 2004. (Illus.). 248p. (J). pap. 16.99 (978-1-885358-74-5(1), Legacy Pr.) Rainbow Pubs. & Legacy Pr.

MoonRattles. Heritage Holiday Activity Guide: Mid Autumn Festival. 2007. (Illus.). 52p. (J). spiral bd. (978-0-9790920-8-4(6)) MoonRattles.

MoonRattles, compiled by. Heritage Holiday Activity Guide: Dragon Boat Festival. 2007. 52p. (J). spiral bd. 12.00 (978-0-9790920-4-6(3)) MoonRattles.

Morey, Allan. Diwali. Sorrentino, Flavia, illus. 2017. (Holidays in Rhythm & Rhyme Ser.). (ENG.). 24p. (gr. 1-3). 33.99 **(978-1-68410-021-7(6))** Cantata Learning.

Morganelli, Adrianna. Cultural Traditions in Argentina. 2016. (ENG., Illus.). 32p. (J). lib. bdg. (978-0-7787-8086-1(4)) Crabtree Publishing Co.

—Cultural Traditions in Italy. 2016. (ENG., Illus.). 32p. (J). (978-0-7787-8087-8(2)) Crabtree Publishing Co.

Murphy, Charles. Celebrations Around the World. 2016. (Adventures in Culture Ser.). 00024p. (J). pap. 8.15 **(978-1-4824-5575-5(7))** Stevens, Gareth Publishing LLLP.

My Puptatl Book. 2006. (J). spiral bd. 8.00 (978-0-9786947-0-8(8)) Puptattle Pr., Inc.

My Puptatl Youth Book. 2006. (J). spiral bd. 8.00 (978-0-9786947-1-5(6)) Puptattle Pr., Inc.

O'Brien, Cynthia. Cultural Traditions in Iceland. 2017. 32p. (J). **(978-0-7787-8097-7(X))** Crabtree Publishing Co.

—Cultural Traditions in Sri Lanka. 2017. 32p. (J). **(978-0-7787-8099-1(6))** Crabtree Publishing Co.

Orr, Tamra. The Food of China. 2011. (Flavors of the World Ser.). 64p. (gr. 4). 31.36 (978-1-60870-234-3(0)) Marshall Cavendish Corp.

—The Food of Greece. 2011. (Flavors of the World Ser.). (Illus.). 64p. (J). (gr. 4). 31.36 (978-1-60870-235-0(9)) Marshall Cavendish GBR. Dist: Marshall Cavendish Corp.

Otto, Carolyn. Celebrate Chinese New Year: With Fireworks, Dragons, & Lanterns. 2009. (Holidays Around the World Ser.). (ENG., Illus.). 32p. (J). (gr. 1-4). lib. bdg. 23.90 (978-1-4263-0382-1(3), National Geographic Children's Bks.) National Geographic Society.

Otto, Carolyn & National Geographic Kids Staff. Celebrate Chinese New Year: With Fireworks, Dragons, & Lanterns. 2009. (Holidays Around the World Ser.). (ENG., Illus.). 32p. (J). (gr. 1-4). 15.95 (978-1-4263-0381-4(5), National Geographic Children's Bks.) National Geographic Society.

Payne, Martyn. Footsteps to the Feast: 12 Two-Hour Children's Programmes for Christian Festivals & Special Times of the Year. 2007. (ENG., Illus.). 240p. pap. (978-1-84101-464-7(8), Barnabas) Bible Reading Fellowship.

Peppas, Lynn. Cultural Traditions in China. 2012. (ENG.). 32p. (J). pap. (978-0-7787-7591-1(7)); lib. bdg. (978-0-7787-7584-3(4)) Crabtree Publishing Co.

—Cultural Traditions in Egypt. 2012. (ENG., Illus.). 32p. (J). pap. (978-0-7787-7522-5(4)) Crabtree Publishing Co.

—Cultural Traditions in France. 2014. (ENG., Illus.). 32p. (J). (978-0-7787-0302-0(9)) Crabtree Publishing Co.

—Cultural Traditions in Greece. 2012. (ENG.). 32p. (J). (978-0-7787-7518-8(6)); (Illus.). pap. (978-0-7787-7523-2(2)) Crabtree Publishing Co.

—Cultural Traditions in Japan. 2012. (ENG.). 32p. (J). pap. (978-0-7787-7593-5(3)); lib. bdg. (978-0-7787-7586-7(0)) Crabtree Publishing Co.

—Cultural Traditions in the United Kingdom. 2014. (ENG., Illus.). 32p. (J). (978-0-7787-0301-3(0)) Crabtree Publishing Co.

—Holi. 2009. (Celebrations in My World Ser.). (ENG., Illus.). 32p. (J). (gr. k-2). pap. (978-0-7787-4771-0(9)); (gr. 1-3). (978-0-7787-4753-6(0)) Crabtree Publishing Co.

Peppas, Lynn & Aloian, Molly. Cultural Traditions in India. 2012. (ENG.). 32p. (J). pap. (978-0-7787-7592-8(5)); lib. bdg. (978-0-7787-7585-0(2)) Crabtree Publishing Co.

Pfeffer, Wendy. The Shortest Day: Celebrating the Winter Solstice. Reisch, Jesse, illus. 2003. (ENG.). 40p. (J). (gr. 1-4). 17.99 (978-0-525-46968-1(0), Dutton Books for Young Readers) Penguin Young Readers Group.

Pirotta, Saviour. Divali. 2007. (We Love Holidays Ser.). (Illus.). 24p. (J). (gr. 3-7). lib. bdg. 22.60 (978-1-4042-3706-3(2), PowerKids Pr.) Rosen Publishing Group, Inc., The.

Plum-Ucci, Carol. Celebrate Diwali. 2007. (Celebrate Holidays Ser.). (Illus.). 128p. (J). (gr. 3-7). lib. bdg. 33.27 (978-0-7660-2778-7(3)) Enslow Pubs., Inc.

Ponto, Joanna. Mardi Gras. 2016. (Illus.). 32p. (J). pap. (978-0-7600-7472-5(0)); (ENG., (gr. 3-3). 25.27 (978-0-7660-7460-6(9)) Enslow Pubs., Inc.

Powell, Jillian. Caribbean Carnival. 2016. (ENG., Illus.). 32p. (J). (gr. 2-3). pap. 8.95 (978-0-00-816383-9(9)) HarperCollins Pubs. Ltd. GBR. Dist: Independent Pubs. Group.

Rajczak, Kristen. Renaissance Fairs, 01 vols., 1. 2016. (Role-Playing for Fun & Profit Ser.). (ENG.). 48p. (J). pap. 11.75 (978-1-4994-3720-1(X), Rosen Reference) Rosen Publishing Group, Inc., The.

Reynolds, Jan. Celebrate! Connections among Cultures, 1 vol. Reynolds, Jan, photos by. 2006. (ENG., Illus.). 32p. (J). pap. 9.95 (978-1-60060-452-2(8)) Lee & Low Bks., Inc.

—Connections among Cultures. 2006. (ENG., Illus.). 32p. (J). (gr. k-4). 16.95 (978-1-58430-253-7(4)) Lee & Low Bks., Inc.

Rissman, Rebecca. Festivals, 1 vol. 2013. (Picture This! Ser.). (ENG.). 24p. (gr. -1-k). pap. 9.95 (978-1-4109-5260-8(6), NA-r) Heinemann-Raintree.

Robison, Greg. Christian Rock Festivals. 2009. (Monster Music Festivals Ser.). 48p. (gr. 5-8). (Illus.). pap. 11.75 (978-1-4358-5122-1(6)); 53.00 (978-1-61514-650-5(4)) Rosen Publishing Group, Inc., The. (Rosen Reference).

—Coachella. 2009. (Monster Music Festivals Ser.). 48p. (gr. 5-6). 53.00 (978-1-61514-653-6(9), Rosen Reference) Rosen Publishing Group, Inc., The.

—Ozzfest. (Monster Music Festivals Ser.). 48p. 2009. (gr. 5-8). pap. 11.75 (978-1-4358-5121-4(8), Rosen Classroom) 2008. (Illus.). (J). lib. bdg. 29.25 (978-1-4042-1756-0(8)) Rosen Publishing Group, Inc., The.

Rohr, Ian. Children's Celebrations. 2011. (Celebrations Ser.). (Illus.). 32p. (J). lib. bdg. 28.50 (978-1-59920-535-9(1)) Black Rabbit Bks.

—Indigenous Celebrations. 2011. (Celebrations Ser.). (Illus.). 32p. (J). lib. bdg. 28.50 (978-1-59920-537-3(8)) Black Rabbit Bks.

—National & Global Celebrations. 2011. (Celebrations Ser.). (Illus.). 32p. (J). lib. bdg. 28.50 (978-1-59920-538-0(6)) Black Rabbit Bks.

Romulo, Liana. Filipino Celebrations: A Treasury of Feasts & Festivals. Dandan-Albano, Corazon, illus. 2012. (ENG.). 48p. (J). (gr. k-4). 16.95 (978-0-8048-3821-4(6)) Tuttle Publishing.

Rondina, Catherine. Lighting Our World: A Year of Celebrations. Oakley, Jacqui, illus. 2012. (ENG.). 32p. (J). (gr. 2-5). 17.95 (978-1-55453-594-1(8)) Kids Can Pr., Ltd. CAN. Dist: Hachette Bk. Group.

Russell, Ching Yeung & Boyds Mills Press Staff. Moon Festival. Zhang, Christopher Zhong-Yuan, illus. 2003. (ENG.). 32p. (J). (gr. 2-4). pap. 9.95 (978-1-59078-079-4(5)) Boyds Mills Pr.

Safran, Sheri. All Kinds of Festivals. Fuller, Rachel, illus. 2012. (ENG.). 12p. (J). (gr. -1). 12.99 (978-1-60887-162-9(2)) Insight Editions.

Sanna, Ellyn. Folk Festivals. 2004. (North American Folklore Ser.). (Illus.). 112p. (J). (gr. 7-18). lib. bdg. 22.95 (978-1-59084-340-6(1)) Mason Crest.

Sebra, Richard. It's Diwali! 2017. (Bumba Books (tm) — It's a Holiday! Ser.). (ENG.). 24p. (J). (gr. -1-1). 12.99 **(978-1-5124-3696-9(8)**, Lerner Pubns.); 38.65 **(978-1-5124-3695-2(X)**, Lerner Pubns.); 38.65 **(978-1-5124-2742-4(X)**, Lerner Pubns.); (Illus.). 25.32 (978-1-5124-2563-5(X)) Lerner Publishing Group.

Selwyn, Josephine. What Holidays Do You Have? 2014. (Little Books of Answers: Level d Ser.). (Illus.). 16p. (gr. k-2). pap. 7.95 (978-1-927136-30-0(X)) Three Crows Media NZL. Dist: RiverStream Publishing.

Shafto, Daniel & Matters, Print. Carnival. 2009. (Holidays & Celebration Ser.). (Illus.). 96p. (gr. 5-8). 40.00 (978-1-60413-095-9(4), Chelsea Hse.) Facts On File, Inc.

Shahan, Sherry. Fiesta! A Celebration of Latino Festivals. Barragán, Paula, illus. 2008. (ENG.). 32p. (J). (gr. -1-3). 16.95 (978-0-87483-861-9(4)) August Hse. Pubs., Inc.

Singh, Rina. Diwali: Festival of Lights, 1 vol. 2016. (Orca Origins Ser.). (ENG.). 96p. (J). (gr. 3-7). 24.95 (978-1-4598-1007-5(4)) Orca Bk. Pubs. USA.

Sjonger, Rebecca. Cultural Traditions in Honduras. 2017. 32p. (J). **(978-0-7787-8096-0(1))** Crabtree Publishing Co.

Swazinski, Ed. At the Carnival: Understand & Apply Properties of Operations. 2013. (Rosen Math Readers Ser.). (ENG.). 24p. (J). (gr. 1-2). pap. 49.50 (978-1-4777-2059-2(6)); (Illus.). pap. 8.25 (978-1-4777-2058-5(8)) Rosen Publishing Group, Inc., The. (Rosen Classroom).

Tabor, Nancy Maria Grande. Celebraciones: Dias Feriados de los Estados Unidos y Mexico. Tabor, Nancy Maria Grande, illus. 2004.Tr. of Celebrations - Holidays of the United States of America & Mexico. (SPA & ENG., Illus.). 32p. (J). (gr. -1-2). pap. 7.95 (978-1-57091-550-5(4)) Charlesbridge Publishing, Inc.

Tang, Sanmu. Celebrating Chinese Festivals: A Collection of Holiday Tales, Poems & Activities. 2012. (ENG., Illus.). 72p. (J). (gr. -1-3). 16.95 (978-1-60220-961-9(8)) BetterLink Pr., Inc.

—Celebrating the Dragon Boat Festival. Tenison, Mina, tr. from CHI. 2010. (Chinese Festivals Ser.). (ENG., Illus.). 32p. (J). (gr. -1-3). pap. 4.95 (978-1-60220-968-8(5)) BetterLink Pr., Inc.

—Celebrating the Mid-Autumn Festival. Tenison, Mina, tr. from CHI. 2010. (Chinese Festivals Ser.). (ENG., Illus.). 32p. (J). (gr. -1-3). pap. 4.95 (978-1-60220-969-5(3)) BetterLink Pr., Inc.

Torpie, Kate. Diwali. 2008. (Celebrations in My World Ser.). (ENG., Illus.). 32p. (J). (gr. k-3). pap. (978-0-7787-4300-2(4)) Crabtree Publishing Co.

The Whole World Loves Festivals, 6 vols. (Book2WebTM Ser.). (gr. 4-8). 36.50 (978-0-322-02990-3(2)) Wright Group/McGraw-Hill.

Whyte, Harlinah. England. 2010. (Festivals of the World Ser.). 32p. (gr. 3). 28.50 (978-1-60870-098-1(4)) Marshall Cavendish GBR. Dist: Marshall Cavendish Corp.

World Book, Inc Staff, contrib. by. Harvest Celebrations. 2009. (Illus.). 46p. (J). (978-0-7166-5041-6(X)) World Bk., Inc.

—National Celebrations. 2009. (Illus.). 46p. (J). (978-0-7166-5043-0(6)) World Bk., Inc.

—New Year's Celebrations. 2009. (Illus.). 46p. (J). (978-0-7166-5040-9(1)) World Bk., Inc.

World Book, Inc. Staff, contrib. by. Religious Celebrations. 2003. (World Book's Celebrations & Rituals Around the World Ser.). (Illus.). 46p. (J). (978-0-7166-5015-7(0)) World Bk., Inc.

World Book, Inc Staff, contrib. by. Religious Celebrations. 2009. (Illus.). 46p. (J). (978-0-7166-5049-2(5)) World Bk., Inc.

—Spring Celebrations. 2009. (Illus.). 46p. (J). (978-0-7166-5042-3(8)) World Bk., Inc.

World Book, Inc. Staff, contrib. by. Winter Celebrations. 2003. (World Book's Celebrations & Rituals Around the World Ser.). (Illus.). 46p. (J). (978-0-7166-5013-3(4)) World Bk., Inc.

World Book, Inc Staff, contrib. by. Winter Celebrations. 2009. (Illus.). 46p. (J). (978-0-7166-5047-8(9)) World Bk., Inc.

Zocchi, Judy. On Halloween Night. Wallis, Rebecca, illus. 2005. (Holiday Happenings Ser.). (ENG.). 32p. (J). lib. bdg. 21.65 (978-1-891997-77-8(7)) Dingles & Co.

FESTIVALS—FICTION

Alderson, Lisa, illus. The Snow Family: A Winter's Tale. 2005. (ENG.). 12p. (J). 12.95 (978-1-58117-233-1(8), Intervisual/Piggy Toes) Bendon, Inc.

Ancona, George. Fiesta Fireworks. 2007. (Illus.). 28p. (YA). (gr. 4-8). reprint ed. 16.00 (978-1-4223-6257-0(4)) DIANE Publishing Co.

Bellingham, Brenda. Lilly & the Hullabaloo, 1 vol. MacDonald, Clarke, illus. 2008. (Formac First Novels Ser.). (ENG.). 64p. (gr. 2-5). (J). 5.95 (978-0-88780-752-7(6), 9780887807527); (YA). 14.95 (978-0-88780-754-1(2), 9780887807541) Formac Publishing Co., Ltd. CAN. Dist: Casemate Pubs. & Bk. Distributors, LLC.

Berger, Samantha. Snoozefest. Litten, Kristyna, illus. 2015. (ENG.). 34p. (J). (gr. -1-k). 16.99 (978-0-8037-4046-4(8), Dial Bks) Penguin Young Readers Group.

Biedrzycki, David. Breaking News: Bear Alert. Biedrzycki, David, illus. 2016. (Breaking News Ser.). (ENG., Illus.). 32p. (J). (gr. -1-3). lib. bdg. 17.95 (978-1-58089-624-5(3)) Charlesbridge Publishing, Inc.

Biz, Jen. The Terrible Noise. 2012. 16p. pap. 24.95 (978-1-4626-9619-2(8)) America Star Bks.

Brallier, Max. Galactic Hot Dogs 2: The Wiener Strikes Back. Maguire, Rachel & Kelley, Nichole, illus. 2016. (Galactic Hot Dogs Ser.: 2). (ENG.). 288p. (J). (gr. 3-7). 13.99 (978-1-4814-2496-7(3), Aladdin) Simon & Schuster Children's Publishing.

Brown, Tricia. Charlie & the Blanket Toss. Martinsen, Sarah, illus. 2015. (ENG.). 32p. (J). pap. 10.99 (978-1-941821-66-4(9), Alaska Northwest Bks.) Graphic Arts Ctr. Publishing Co.

Browne, Susan Chalker. Hey Freddy, It's Canada's Birthday!, 1 vol. Rose, Hilda, illus. 2009. (ENG.). 32p. (J). (gr. k-5). 10.95 (978-1-897174-39-5(X), Tuckamore Bks) Creative Bk. Publishing CAN. Dist: Orca Bk. Pubs. USA.

Cassidy, Cathy. Dizzy. 2005. (ENG.). 272p. (J). (gr. 3-7). 6.99 (978-0-14-240474-4(8), Puffin Books) Penguin Young Readers Group.

Cohn, Diana. Crane Boy. 2015. (ENG., Illus.). 40p. (J). (gr. 2-5). 17.95 (978-1-941026-16-8(8)) Cinco Puntos Pr.

Cook, Jacqueline. The Little Bear Who Worried Too Much: Suzie Bear & the Music Festival. 2010. 32p. pap. 13.00 (978-1-60860-529-3(9), Strategic Bk. Publishing) Strategic Book Publishing & Rights Agency (SBPRA).

Cronin, Doreen. Thump, Quack, Moo: A Whacky Adventure. Lewin, Betsy, illus. 2008. (Click, Clack Book Ser.). (ENG.). 42p. (J). (gr. -1-2). 16.99 (978-1-4169-1630-7(X), Atheneum Bks. for Young Readers) Simon & Schuster Children's Publishing.

Cronin, Doreen & Jiménez Rioja, Alberto. Pum, Cuac, Muu: Una Loca Aventura. Lewin, Betsy, illus. 2008. (SPA.). (J). pap. 5.99 (978-1-933032-54-2(5)); 36p. 16.99 (978-1-933032-53-5(7)) Lectorum Pubns., Inc.

Curato, Mike. Little Elliot, Big Fun. Curato, Mike, illus. 2016. (Little Elliot Ser.). (ENG., Illus.). 40p. (J). 17.99 (978-0-8050-9827-3(5), 9780805098273, Holt, Henry & Co. Bks. For Young Readers) Holt, Henry & Co.

D'Amico, Carmela & D'Amico, Steven. Ella Sets Sail. 2008. (J). (978-0-439-83156-7(3), Levine, Arthur A. Bks.) Scholastic, Inc.

Damschroder, Scott. The Crazy Carnival Clown We Call Croc. 2006. (Illus.). 40p. (J). lib. bdg. 19.95 (978-0-9754728-1-1(X)) Big Ransom Studio.

David, Lawrence. The Terror of the Pink Dodo Balloons. Gott, Barry, illus. 2003. (Horace Splattly Ser.). 153p. (J). (gr. 4-7). 12.65 (978-0-7569-2816-2(8)) Perfection Learning Corp.

Dawson, Keila. The King Cake Baby, 1 vol. Smith, Vernon, illus. 2015. (ENG.). 32p. (J). (gr. k-3). 8.99 (978-1-4556-2013-5(0)) Pelican Publishing Co., Inc.

de Las Casas, Dianne. Dinosaur Mardi Gras, 1 vol. Gentry, Marita, illus. 2011. (ENG.). 32p. (J). (gr. k-3). 16.99 (978-1-58980-966-6(1)) Pelican Publishing Co., Inc.

De Laurentiis, Giada, et al. Rio de Janeiro! #5. Gambatesa, Francesca, illus. 2015. (Recipe for Adventure Ser.: 5). (ENG.). 160p. (J). (gr. 2-4). bds. 6.99 (978-0-448-48204-0(5), Grosset & Dunlap) Penguin Young Readers Group.

Delacre, Lulu. Rafi y Rosi ¡Carnaval!, 1 vol. 2016. (Rafi & Rosi Ser.).Tr. of Rafi & Rosi Carnival. (SPA & ENG., Illus.). 64p. (J). pap. 8.95 (978-0-89239-380-0(7)) Lee & Low Bks., Inc.

Delawrence, T. M. Millie: M. C. E. (Mail Carrier Extraordinaire) In. 2012. 28p. pap. 24.95 (978-1-4626-6057-5(6)) America Star Bks.

Disney Book Group. Elena of Avalor un Dia para Recordar (Spanish Edition) Disney Storybook Art Team, illus. 2017. (ENG.). 24p. (J). (gr. 1-3). pap. 5.99 **(978-1-368-00110-6(6))** Disney Pr.

Disney Book Group & Rogers, Tom. Elena of Avalor a Day to Remember. Disney Storybook Art Team, illus. 2017. (ENG.). 24p. (J). (gr. 1-3). pap. 5.99 **(978-1-4847-4791-9(7))** Disney Pr.

Disney Editors. Cinderella Takes the Stage. 2017. (Disney Princess Beginnings Ser.). lib. bdg. 17.20 **(978-0-606-39857-2(0))** Turtleback Bks.

Dole, Mayra L. Drum, Chavi, Drum! Tonel, illus. 2013.Tr. of ¡Toca, Chavi, Toca! (ENG & SPA.). 32p. (J). pap. 9.95 (978-0-89239-302-2(5), Children's Book Press) Lee & Low Bks., Inc.

—Toca, Chavi, Toca! Tonel, illus. 2003.Tr. of Drum, Chavi, Drum! (ENG & SPA.). 32p. (J). 16.95 (978-0-89239-186-8(3)) Lee & Low Bks., Inc.

Dunseith, Peter. Bird of Heaven: The Story of a Swazi Sangoma. 2010. 257p. pap. (978-0-624-04557-1(9)) NB Pubs. Ltd.

Earhart, Kristin. Roscoe & the Pony Parade. Gurney, John Steven, illus. 2008. (Little Apple Ser.). 88p. (J). (978-0-545-08094-1(0)) Scholastic, Inc.

Ediger, Max. Caleb & Shalev. 2010. 36p. pap. 13.95 (978-1-60860-808-9(5), Eloquent Bks.) Strategic Book Publishing & Rights Agency (SBPRA).

Elliott, Rebecca. Eva's Treetop Festival, Bk. 1. Elliott, Rebecca, illus. 2015. (Owl Diaries: 1). (ENG., Illus.). 80p. (J). (gr. k-2). pap. 4.99 (978-0-545-68362-3(9)) Scholastic, Inc.

Esquivel, Eric. Carnival Capers! 2016. (LEGO DC Super Heroes Ser.). lib. bdg. 13.55 (978-0-606-38829-0(X)) Turtleback Bks.

Evans, Clay Bonnyman. The Winter Witch. Bender, Robert, illus. 2005. (ENG.). 32p. (J). (gr. -1-3). 16.95 *(978-0-8234-1615-8(1))* Holiday Hse., Inc.

Everett, Reese. Charlie's Big Break. 2015. (ENG.). 48p. (gr. k-3). 27.07 *(978-1-63430-376-7(8))* Rourke Educational Media.

Fellers, Tina. Toby & the Alien: In the Adventures of the Unusual Toys, 1 vol. Fellers, Cody, illus. 2009. 28p. pap. 24.95 *(978-1-60672-195-7(X))* America Star Bks.

Fraser, Mary Ann. Heebie-Jeebie Jamboree. 2011. (ENG.). 32p. (J). (gr. -1-2). 15.95 *(978-1-59078-857-8(5))* Boyds Mills Pr.

Freeman, Martha. Who Stole New Year's Eve? 2013. (Chickadee Court Mystery Ser.). (ENG.). 224p. (J). (gr. 2-7). 16.95 *(978-0-8234-2750-5(1))* Holiday Hse., Inc.

Fusco, Kimberly Newton. Beholding Bee. 2015. (ENG.). 336p. (J). (gr. 3-7). 7.99 *(978-0-375-86808-5(9)*, Yearling) Random Hse. Children's Bks.

Gallo, Tina. Where's My Valentine? 2009. (Yo Gabba Gabba! Ser.). (ENG.). 12p. (J). (gr. -1-k). 7.99 *(978-1-4169-9063-5(1)*, Simon Spotlight) Simon Spotlight.

Gantos, Jack. Practice Makes Perfect for Rotten Ralph. Rubel, Nicole, illus. 2009. (Rotten Ralph Rotten Readers Ser.: 2). (ENG.). 48p. (J). (gr. 1-3). pap. 8.99 *(978-0-374-40002-6(4)*, 9780374400026) Square Fish.

Garber, Stephanie. Caraval. 2017. (SPA.). 432p. pap. 16.95 ***(978-607-07-4044-2(0))*** Editorial Planeta, S. A. ESP. Dist: Two Rivers Distribution.

—Caraval. 2017. (Caraval Ser.). (ENG.). (YA). 416p. 18.99 *(978-1-250-09525-1(5)*, 9781250095251); (gr. 8-12). pap. 11.99 ***(978-1-250-14149-1(4))*** Flatiron Bks.

Golden Books Staff, et al. Christmas Favorites. Catusanu, Mircea & Wilkin, Eloise, illus. 2009. (Little Golden Book Favorites Ser.). (ENG.). 80p. (J). (gr. -1-2). 6.99 *(978-0-375-85778-2(8)*, Golden Bks.) Random Hse. Children's Bks.

Gorman, Carol. A Midsummer Night's Dork. 2004. (ENG.). 224p. (J). 15.99 *(978-0-06-050718-3(7))* HarperCollins Pubs.

Green, Poppy. The Maple Festival. Bell, Jennifer A., illus. 2015. (Adventures of Sophie Mouse Ser.: 5). (ENG.). 128p. (J). (gr. k-4). pap. 5.99 *(978-1-4814-4196-4(5)*, Little Simon) Little Simon.

Gutman, Dan. Ms. Sue Has No Clue! 2013. (My Weirder School Ser.: 9). (J). lib. bdg. 14.75 *(978-0-606-32173-0(X)*, Turtleback) Turtleback Bks.

Guy, Ginger Foglesong & Guy, Ginger F. Fiesta! Board Book. Moreno, Rene King, illus. 2003. (SPA & ENG.). 34p. (J). (gr. -1-3). bds. 7.99 *(978-0-06-009263-4(7)*, Greenwillow Bks.) HarperCollins Pubs.

Halstead, Stefanie Merie. The Night of the Festival. 2008. 36p. pap. 24.95 *(978-1-60703-697-5(5))* America Star Bks.

Heidi Heckelbeck Gets the Sniffles. 2014. (Heidi Heckelbeck Ser.: 12). (ENG., Illus.). 128p. (J). (gr. k-4). pap. 5.99 *(978-1-4814-1362-6(7)*, Little Simon) Little Simon.

Hobden, Helen. Be in the Place. 2006. (ENG.). 198p. (YA). (gr. 7). pap. 9.99 *(978-1-84270-460-8(5))* Andersen Pr. GBR. Dist: Independent Pubs. Group.

Hoover, Leighnne W. Festus & his Fest Favorites. 2010. pap. 11.99 *(978-0-578-05051-5(X))* Word of Mouth Pr.

Ip, Ivy S. Clues at the Carnival, 1 vol. 2013. (Scooby-Doo! Picture Clue Bks.). (ENG.). 24p. (J). (gr. -1-1). lib. bdg. 24.21 *(978-1-61479-036-5(1)*, Essential Library) ABDO Publishing Co.

Islam, Hina. An Eid for Everyone. 2009. 16p. pap. 9.99 *(978-1-4389-4845-4(X))* AuthorHouse.

Kann, Victoria. Cherry Blossom. Kann, Victoria, illus. 2015. (I Can Read Level 1 Ser.). (ENG., Illus.). 32p. (J). (gr. -1-3). 16.99 *(978-0-06-224593-9(7))* HarperCollins Pubs.

Keene, Carolyn. The Apple Bandit. Jones, Jan Naimo, illus. 2005. (Nancy Drew Notebooks). 74p. (J). (gr. 1-4). 11.65 *(978-0-7569-6505-1(5))* Perfection Learning Corp.

—Sabotage Surrender: Book Three in the Sabotage Mystery Trilogy. 2011. (Nancy Drew (All New) Girl Detective Ser.: 44). (ENG.). 128p. (J). (gr. 3-7). pap. 6.99 *(978-1-4169-9071-0(2)*, Aladdin) Simon & Schuster Children's Publishing.

—Secret Sabotage, Bk. 1. 2010. (Nancy Drew (All New) Girl Detective Ser.: 42). (ENG.). 144p. (J). (gr. 3-7). pap. 5.99 *(978-1-4169-9069-7(0)*, Aladdin) Simon & Schuster Children's Publishing.

Kelsey, Marybeth. A Recipe for Robbery. 2009. (ENG.). 288p. (J). (gr. 3-7). 16.99 *(978-0-06-128843-2(8)*, Greenwillow Bks.) HarperCollins Pubs.

Kenah, Katharine. Scholastic Reader Level 1: the Saturday Triplets #2: the Pumpkin Fair Problem. Lyon, Tammie, illus. 2013. (Scholastic Reader Level 1 Ser.). (ENG.). 32p. (J). (gr. -1-2). pap. 3.99 *(978-0-545-48144-1(9))* Scholastic, Inc.

Kertell, Lynn Maslen. Buddy to the Rescue. Hendra, Sue, illus. 2012. (Scholastic Reader Level 1 Ser.). (ENG.). 32p. (J). (gr. -1-2). pap. 3.99 *(978-0-545-38273-1(4))* Scholastic, Inc.

—Buddy to the Rescue. 2012. (BOB Books: Scholastic Readers Level 1 Ser.: 6). lib. bdg. 13.55 *(978-0-606-26753-3(0)*, Turtleback) Turtleback Bks.

Khan, Rukhsana. King for a Day, 1 vol. Krömer, Christiane, illus. 2014. (ENG.). 32p. (J). 17.95 *(978-1-60060-659-5(8))* Lee & Low Bks., Inc.

Kittscher, Kristen. The Tiara on the Terrace. 2016. 400p. (J). (gr. 3-7). 16.99 *(978-0-06-222798-0(X))* HarperCollins Pubs.

Kontis, Alethea. AlphaOops! H Is for Halloween. Kolar, Bob, illus. 2010. (ENG.). 40p. (J). (gr. -1-3). 15.99 *(978-0-7636-3966-2(4))* Candlewick Pr.

Landen, Cynthia & Phillips, Lorrie. The Elson Readers, Primer. 2005. (ENG.). 120p. (J). (gr. -1-12). pap., tchr. ed. 14.95 *(978-1-890623-24-1(5))* Lost Classic Bks.

Lightburn, Sandra. Pumpkin People, 1 vol. Lightburn, Ron, illus. 2009. (ENG.). 32p. (J). (gr. -1-5). 17.95 *(978-1-55109-681-0(1))* Nimbus Publishing, Ltd. CAN. Dist: Orca Bk. Pubs. USA.

Lin, Grace. Thanking the Moon: Celebrating the Mid-Autumn Moon Festival. 2010. (ENG.). 32p. (J). (gr. -1-2). 16.99 *(978-0-375-86101-7(7)*, Knopf Bks. for Young Readers) Random Hse. Children's Bks.

Luciani, Brigitte. The Carnival. Tharlet, Eve, illus. 2014. (ENG.). 32p. (J). pap. 6.95 *(978-1-4677-4204-7(X))*; lib. bdg. 25.26 *(978-1-4677-4203-0(1)*, Graphic Universe™) Lerner Publishing Group.

Mair, J. Samia. Amira's Totally Chocolate World. 2010. (ENG., Illus.). 29p. (J). (gr. k-3). 8.95 *(978-0-86037-408-4(4))* Kube Publishing Ltd. GBR. Dist: Consortium Bk. Sales & Distribution.

Martin, W. Lyon. Aidan's First Full Moon Circle: A Magical Child Story. Martin, W. Lyon, illus. 2008. (Illus.). 32p. (J). (gr. -1-1). lib. bdg. 16.95 *(978-0-9796834-4-2(0))* Shades of White.

Mayer, Mercer. The Fall Festival. 2012. (Illus.). 32p. (J). *(978-1-4351-4384-5(1))*; *(978-0-06-222992-2(3))* HarperCollins Pubs.

—Little Critter Fall Storybook Collection. Mayer, Mercer, illus. 2015. (Little Critter Ser.). (ENG., Illus.). 192p. (J). (gr. -1-3). 11.99 *(978-0-06-238032-6(X))* HarperCollins Pubs.

McAllister, Margaret. The Octave of Angels. 2004. 128p. (J). pap. 8.00 *(978-0-8028-5240-3(8))* Eerdmans, William B. Publishing Co.

McConduit, Alexander Brian. Snoballs for All, 1 vol. Ganucheau, Paulina, illus. 2015. (ENG.). 32p. (J). (gr. k-3). pap. 8.99 *(978-1-4556-2002-9(5))* Pelican Publishing Co., Inc.

McConnie Zapater, Beatriz. Fiesta. Ortega, Jose, illus. 2005. (Multicultural Celebrations Ser.). 32p. (J). 4.95 *(978-1-59373-009-3(8))* Bunker Hill Publishing, Inc.

Mills, Claudia. Annika Riz, Math Whiz. Shepperson, Rob, illus. 2014. (Franklin School Friends Ser.: 2). (ENG.). 128p. (J). (gr. 2-5). 15.99 *(978-0-374-30335-8(5)*, 9780374303358, Farrar, Straus & Giroux (BYR)) Farrar, Straus & Giroux.

Morrel Disbrow, Corlyss. Ran's Upside-Down Day. 2012. 20p. pap. 24.95 *(978-1-4626-8368-0(1))* America Star Bks.

Murrell, Belinda. Lulu Bell's Best Friends Ever. 2017. (Lulu Bell Ser.). (ENG.). 384p. (J). (gr. 1-4). 16.99 ***(978-0-14-378257-5(6))*** Random Hse. Australia AUS. Dist: Independent Pubs. Group.

Neuschwander, Cindy. Sir Cumference & the off-The-Charts Dessert. Geehan, Wayne, illus. 2013. (ENG.). 32p. (J). (gr. 3-7). pap. 7.95 *(978-1-57091-199-6(1))* Charlesbridge Publishing, Inc.

—Sir Cumference & the off-The-Charts Dessert. 2013. (Sir Cumference Ser.). lib. bdg. 18.40 *(978-0-606-34743-3(7)*, Turtleback) Turtleback Bks.

Night, P. J. The Ride of Your Life. 2014. (You're Invited to a Creepover Ser.: 18). (ENG., Illus.). 160p. (J). (gr. 3-7). pap. 6.99 *(978-1-4424-9729-0(7)*, Simon Spotlight) Simon Spotlight.

—The Ride of Your Life. 2014. (Creepover Ser.: 18). lib. bdg. 17.20 *(978-0-606-35431-8(X))* Turtleback Bks.

Peschke, Marci. Daisy's Fall Festival, 1 vol., Bk. 4. Pilz, M. H., illus. 2011. (Growing up Daisy Ser.). (ENG.). 80p. (gr. 3-8). 27.07 *(978-1-61641-117-6(1)*, Calico Chapter Bks) Magic Wagon.

Pinkwater, Daniel M. Irving & Muktuk: Two Bad Bears. 2004. (Illus.). (J). (gr. k-3). spiral bd. *(978-0-616-11136-9(3))*; spiral bd. *(978-0-616-11137-6(1))* Canadian National Institute for the Blind/Institut National Canadien pour les Aveugles.

Pratt, Non. Remix. 2017. (ENG.). 320p. (YA). (gr. 9). pap. 10.99 *(978-1-4424-9776-4(9))* Simon & Schuster Children's Publishing.

Prochovnic, Dawn Babb. A to Z Sign with Me: Sign Language for the Alphabet, 1 vol. Bauer, Stephanie, illus. 2012. (ENG.). 32p. 28.50 *(978-1-61641-835-9(4)*, Looking Glass Library) Magic Wagon.

Q., Bev. When the Carnival Comes to Town. Thomas, Lillie Michelle, illus. 2009. 28p. pap. 24.95 *(978-1-60749-682-3(8))* America Star Bks.

Random House Staff. Riddle Me This! Random House Staff, illus. 2010. (Pictureback(R) Ser.). (ENG., Illus.). 24p. (J). (gr. -1-2). pap. 3.99 *(978-0-375-84747-9(2)*, Random Hse. Bks. for Young Readers) Random Hse. Children's Bks.

Richardson, Bill. I Would Have Gone to Woodstock. 2007. 28p. (YA). per. 12.95 *(978-1-4327-1256-3(X))* Outskirts Pr., Inc.

Rosen, Michael. Bear Flies High. Reynolds, Adrian, illus. 2009. (ENG.). 32p. (J). (gr. -1-1). 16.99 *(978-1-59990-386-6(5)*, 9781599903866, Bloomsbury USA Childrens) Bloomsbury Publishing USA.

Roy Shah, Amita. It's Time for Holi! Lucas, Diane, illus. 2011. 24p. pap. 13.95 *(978-1-60844-943-9(2))* Dog Ear Publishing, LLC.

Ryles, Donald. The Magic Holiday Forest. 2008. 40p. pap. 8.95 *(978-1-4357-4772-2(0))* Lulu Pr., Inc.

Santomero, Angela C. Daniel Goes to the Carnival. 2017. (Daniel Tiger's Neighborhood 8X8 Ser.). lib. bdg. 13.55 ***(978-0-606-40216-3(0))*** Turtleback Bks.

Sazaklis, John. The Hopping Hero, 1 vol. Baltazar, Art, illus. 2011. (DC Super-Pets Ser.). (ENG.). 56p. (gr. 2-2). pap. 4.95 *(978-1-4048-6843-4(7))*; lib. bdg. 23.99 *(978-1-4048-6477-1(6))* Picture Window Bks. (DC Super-Pets).

Smith, Icy. Mystery of the Giant Mask of Sanxingdui. Roski, Gayle Garner, illus. 2015. (J). *(978-0-9913454-8-9(7))* East West Discovery Pr.

Soares, Valérie I. O. Lily & Kayden's 1969 Woodstock Adventure. Tzekov, Jack, illus. 2014. pap. *(978-1-927032-12-1(1))* Petra Bks.

Steers, Billy. Tractor Mac Harvest Time. 2015. (Tractor Mac Ser.). (ENG., Illus.). 32p. (J). (gr. -1-2). 8.99 *(978-0-374-30111-8(5)*, 9780374301118, Farrar, Straus & Giroux (BYR)) Farrar, Straus & Giroux.

Stephens, Monique Z. Fantastic Four: The Fantastic Four Versus Doctor Doom. 2005. (Festival Reader Ser.). (Illus.). 32p. (J). (gr. -1-2). 14.99 *(978-0-06-082245-3(7)*, HarperFestival) HarperCollins Pubs.

Stevenson, Steve. The Crown of Venice, No. 7. Turconi, Stefano, illus. 2014. (Agatha: Girl of Mystery Ser.: 7). (ENG.). 144p. (J). (gr. 2-5). 5.99 *(978-0-448-46225-7(7)*, Grosset & Dunlap) Penguin Young Readers Group.

—The Crown of Venice. 2014. (Agatha Girl of Mystery Ser.: 7). lib. bdg. 16.00 *(978-0-606-36164-4(2))* Turtleback Bks.

Stewart, Whitney. A Catfish Tale: A Bayou Story of the Fisherman & His Wife. Guerlais, Gérald, illus. 2014. (ENG.). 32p. (J). (gr. -1-3). 16.99 *(978-0-8075-1098-8(X))* Whitman, Albert & Co.

Tatulli, Mark. Desmond Pucket & the Cloverfield Junior High Carnival of Horrors. 2016. (Desmond Pucket Ser.: 3). (ENG., Illus.). 240p. (J). 13.99 *(978-1-4494-6628-2(1))* Andrews McMeel Publishing.

Verma, Jatinder. The Story of Divaali. Mistry, Nilesh, illus. 2007. (ENG.). 40p. (J). (gr. -1-3). pap. 7.99 *(978-1-84686-131-4(4))* Barefoot Bks., Inc.

Vrettos, Adrienne Maria. Best Friends for Never. 2016. (ENG.). 240p. (J). (gr. 3-7). 16.99 *(978-0-545-56149-5(3)*, Scholastic Pr.) Scholastic, Inc.

Walters, Eric. Splat!, 1 vol. 2008. (Orca Currents Ser.). (ENG.). (J). (gr. 5-9). 128p. pap. 9.95 *(978-1-55143-986-0(7))*; 112p. lib. bdg. 16.95 *(978-1-55143-988-4(3))* Orca Bk. Pubs. USA.

Wang, Ruowen. To Share One Moon. Xu, Wei & Zheng, Xiaoyan, illus. 2008. 32p. (J). (gr. 2-4). *(978-0-9738799-5-7(5))* Kevin & Robin Bks., Ltd.

Weeks, Sarah. The Cake Lady. (Growing Tree Ser.). 24p. (J). (gr. -1-18). 9.99 *(978-0-694-01074-5(X)*, Geringer, Laura Book) HarperCollins Pubs.

Wharton, Laura Spanton, et al. Mystery at the Phoenix Festival. 2012. 140p. pap. 9.99 *(978-0-9837148-8-0(6))* Broad Creek Pr.

Williams, Brenda. Lin Yi's Lantern: A Moon Festival Tale. Lacombe, Benjamin, illus. 2009. (ENG.). 32p. (J). (gr. -1-5). 16.99 *(978-1-84686-147-5(0))* Barefoot Bks., Inc.

—Lin Yi's Lantern: A Moon Festival Tale. Tavares, Victor, illus. 2008. 32p. (J). *(978-1-84686-148-2(9))* Barefoot Bks., Inc.

Wolek, Guy, illus. OLIVIA & the School Carnival. 2010. (Olivia TV Tie-In Ser.). (ENG.). 24p. (J). (gr. -1-2). pap. 3.99 *(978-1-4424-0870-8(7)*, Simon Spotlight) Simon Spotlight.

Wolf, Gita. Visit the Bhil Carnival. Amaliyar, Subhash, illus. 2015. (ENG.). 24p. (J). (gr. k). 19.95 *(978-93-83145-11-9(0))* Tara Books Agency IND. Dist: Publishers Group West (PGW).

Yoon, Salina. My Chanukah Playbook. Yoon, Salina, illus. 2009. (ENG., Illus.). 10p. (J). (gr. -1-k). 10.99 *(978-1-4169-8957-8(9)*, Little Simon) Little Simon.

Ziglar, Christy. Whatever Wanda. Billin-Frye, Paige, illus. 2015. (J). *(978-0-8249-5668-4(0)*, Ideal Pubns.) Worthy Publishing.

Zucker, Jonny. Lighting a Lamp: A Diwali Story. Cohen, Jan Barger, illus. 2004. (Festival Time Ser.). (ENG.). 24p. (J). pap. 8.99 *(978-0-7641-2670-3(9))* Barron's Educational Series, Inc.

FESTIVALS—JEWS

see Fasts and Feasts—Judaism

FETT, BOBA (FICTITIOUS CHARACTER)—FICTION

Barlow, Jeremy. Star Wars Adventures: Boba Fett & the Ship of Fear, 1 vol. 2013. (Star Wars Digests Set 2 Ser.). (ENG.). 80p. (J). (gr. 4-8). lib. bdg. 27.07 *(978-1-61479-056-3(6)*, Essential Library) ABDO Publishing Co.

Dorling Kindersley Publishing Staff & Hibbert, Clare. Boba Fett Jedi Hunter, Level 2. 2011. (DK Readers Ser.). (ENG.). 32p. (J). (gr. 1-3). 3.99 *(978-0-7566-8281-1(9)*, DK Children) Dorling Kindersley Publishing, Inc.

Hand, Elizabeth. A New Threat. 2004. (Star Wars Ser.: Vol. 5). 139p. (J). lib. bdg. 20.00 *(978-1-4242-0781-7(9))* Fitzgerald Bks.

FEUDALISM

see also Chivalry; Middle Ages; Peasants

Davenport, John. The Age of Feudalism. 2007. (World History Ser.). (ENG., Illus.). 104p. (J). (gr. 7-10). lib. bdg. 34.95 *(978-1-59018-649-7(4)*, Lucent Bks.) Cengage Gale.

Macdonald, Fiona. The Medieval Chronicles: Vikings, Knights, & Castles. Antram, David, illus. 2013. 92p. (J). *(978-1-4351-5067-6(8))* Barnes & Noble, Inc.

Nagle, Jeanne, ed. Feudalism, Monarchies, & Nobility. 2014. (Political & Economic Systems Ser.). 312p. (J). (gr. 9-12). 45.00 *(978-1-62275-347-5(X))* Rosen Publishing Group, Inc., The.

O'Brian, Pliny. Feudalism in Medieval Europe. 2015. (Exploring the Ancient & Medieval Worlds Ser.). (ENG., Illus.). 160p. (J). (gr. 8-8). lib. bdg. 45.64 *(978-1-5026-0681-5(X))* Cavendish Square Publishing.

Padrino, Mercedes. Feudalism & Village Life in the Middle Ages. 2005. (World Almanac Library of the Middle Ages). (Illus.). 48p. (gr. 5-12). lib. bdg. 31.00 *(978-0-8368-5894-5(8)*, Gareth Stevens Secondary Library) Stevens, Gareth Publishing LLLP.

Watson, Danielle. The Castle in Medieval Europe. 2016. (Life in Medieval Europe Ser.). (Illus.). 80p. (J). (gr. 6-6). 35.64 *(978-1-5026-1878-8(8))* Cavendish Square Publishing.

Woog, Adam. The Early Middle Ages. 2011. (Understanding World History Ser.). (ENG., Illus.). 96p. (YA). (gr. 7-12). lib. bdg. 27.95 *(978-1-60152-151-4(0))* ReferencePoint Pr., Inc.

FEVER

Calamandrei, Camilla. Fever. 2008. (Health Alert Ser.). 64p. (gr. 4-18). lib. bdg. 32.79 *(978-0-7614-2915-9(8)*, Benchmark Bks.) Marshall Cavendish Corp.

Caper, William. Typhoid Fever: Dirty Food, Dirty Water! 2010. (Nightmare Plagues Ser.). 32p. (YA). (gr. 4-9). lib. bdg. 25.27 *(978-1-936088-04-1(5))* Bearport Publishing Co., Inc.

Hecht, Alan & Yannielli, Len. Lyme Disease. 2nd rev. ed. 2011. (Deadly Diseases & Epidemics Ser.). 116p. (C). (gr. 9). 34.95 *(978-1-61753-018-0(2)*, Chelsea Hse.) Facts On File, Inc.

Jarrow, Gail. Fatal Fever: Tracking down Typhoid Mary. 2015. (ENG., Illus.). 192p. (J). (gr. 4). 17.95 *(978-1-62091-597-4(9)*, Calkins Creek) Boyds Mills Pr.

Kalman, Bobbie. Warm-Blooded or Cold-Blooded? 2008. (Big Science Ideas Ser.). (ENG., Illus.). 32p. (J). (gr. 1-4). lib. bdg. *(978-0-7787-3281-5(9))* Crabtree Publishing Co.

Landau, Elaine. Fever. 2009. (Head-to Toe Health 2 Ser.). 32p. (gr. 2). 28.50 *(978-0-7614-3499-3(2))* Marshall Cavendish GBR. Dist: Marshall Cavendish Corp.

Lew, Kristi. Mosquito-Borne Illnesses. 2009. (Health Alert 6 Ser.). 64p. (gr. 4). 32.79 *(978-0-7614-3980-6(3))* Marshall Cavendish GBR. Dist: Marshall Cavendish Corp.

Walker, David H. Rocky Mountain Spotted Fever. Alcamo, I. Edward, ed. 2007. (Deadly Diseases & Epidemics Ser.). (Illus.). 95p. (YA). (gr. 9-12). lib. bdg. 34.95 *(978-0-7910-8678-0(X))* Facts On File, Inc.

FIAT MONEY

see Paper Money

FIBERS

see also Cotton; Paper; Silk

Alford, Douglas. Cozy Clozy: From Fibers to Fabrics. Hayes, Betsy, illus. 2004. (J). 6.96 net. *(978-0-9762208-0-0(6))* Mfg Application Konsulting Engineering.

Centore, Michael. Fiber. 2017. (J). ***(978-1-4222-3735-9(4))*** Mason Crest.

Fibers from Plants: 6 Each of 1 Student Book, 6 vols. (Sunshinetm Science Ser.). 24p. (gr. 1-2). 41.95 *(978-0-7802-1431-6(5))* Wright Group/McGraw-Hill.

Fibers from Plants: Big Book. (Sunshinetm Science Ser.). 24p. (gr. 1-2). 37.50 *(978-0-7802-1432-3(3))* Wright Group/McGraw-Hill.

Fibers Made by People, 6 vols. (Sunshinetm Science Ser.). 24p. (gr. 1-2). 41.95 *(978-0-7802-1437-8(4))* Wright Group/McGraw-Hill.

Rainis, Kenneth G. Hair, Clothing, & Tire Track Evidence: Crime-Solving Science Experiments. 2006. (Forensic Science Projects Ser.). (Illus.). 128p. (J). (gr. 5-18). lib. bdg. 33.27 *(978-0-7660-2729-9(5))* Enslow Pubs., Inc.

FICTION—HISTORY AND CRITICISM

Bitetto, Marco A. V. Corrections to Article Inaccuracy. l.t. ed. 2003. (Illus.). 120p. (YA). reprint ed. pap. 2.50 *(978-1-58578-487-5(7))* Institute of Cybernetics Research, Inc.

—Theme Stream Vol. 11: Helicopters. l.t. ed. 2003. (Illus.). 120p. (YA). pap. 2.50 *(978-1-58578-484-4(2))* Institute of Cybernetics Research, Inc.

—Theme Stream Vol. 13: Helicopters. l.t. ed. 2003. (Illus.). 120p. (YA). pap. 10.00 *(978-1-58578-485-1(0))* Institute of Cybernetics Research, Inc.

Bloom, Harold. Charlotte Brontë's Jane Eyre. annot. ed. 2007. (Bloom's Guides). 100p. (YA). (gr. 9-12). lib. bdg. 30.00 *(978-0-7910-9362-7(X))* Facts On File, Inc.

—Novelists & Novels: A Collection of Critical Essays. 2007. (Bloom's 20th Anniversary Collection Ser.). 200p. (C). (gr. 9). per. 21.95 *(978-0-7910-9727-4(7)*, Checkmark Bks.) Facts On File, Inc.

Bodden, Valerie. Romance. 2013. 48p. (J). 35.65 *(978-1-60818-179-7(0)*, Creative Education) Creative Co., The.

Guillain, Charlotte. What Is a Novel? 2015. (Connect with Text Ser.). (ENG.). 32p. (gr. 2-4). 30.65 *(978-1-4109-6826-5(X)*, Raintree Perspectives) Heinemann-Raintree.

Hamilton, Sue L. Masters of Horror, 1 vol. 2007. (World of Horror Ser.). (ENG.). 32p. (gr. 4-8). 27.07 *(978-1-59928-770-6(6)*, Abdo & Daughters) ABDO Publishing Co.

Lusted, Marcia Amidon. How to Analyze the Works of Stephen King, 1 vol. 2010. (Essential Critiques Set 1 Ser.). (ENG.). 112p. (J). (gr. 6-12). lib. bdg. 35.64 *(978-1-61613-536-2(0)*, Essential Library) ABDO Publishing Co.

Notes York Staff. The Color Purple. McEwan, Neil, ed. 2003. (ENG.). 120p. pap. 20.00 *(978-0-582-78434-5(4))* Pearson Education, Ltd. GBR. Dist: Trans-Atlantic Pubns., Inc.

Roza, Greg. What Is Fiction?, 1 vol. 2015. (ENG., Illus.). 32p. (J). 23.45 *(978-1-62275-660-5(6)*, Britannica Educational Publishing) Rosen Publishing Group, Inc., The.

Segall, Miriam. Career Building Through Fan Fiction Writing: New Work Based on Favorite Fiction. 2009. (Digital Career Building Ser.). 64p. (gr. 6-6). 58.50 *(978-1-61512-166-3(8))* Rosen Publishing Group, Inc., The.

—Fan Fiction Writing: New Work Based on Favorite Fiction. 2008. (Digital Career Building Ser.). (Illus.). 64p. (YA). (gr. 8-12). lib. bdg. 31.95 *(978-1-4042-1356-2(2)*, 1277017) Rosen Publishing Group, Inc., The.

Thomas, Helen. Caryl Phillips. 2006. (ENG.). 112p. (C). pap. 19.95 *(978-0-7463-0956-8(2))* Northcote Hse. Publishers, Ltd. GBR. Dist: Casemate Academic.

Wade, Mary Dodson. Joan Lowery Nixon: Masterful Mystery Writer. 2004. (Authors Teens Love Ser.). (Illus.). 128p. (J). lib. bdg. 27.94 *(978-0-7660-2194-5(7))* Enslow Pubs., Inc.

FICTION—TECHNIQUE

Anderson, Jennifer Joline. Writing Fantastic Fiction. 2015. (ENG., Illus.). 56p. (gr. 6-8). 33.32 *(978-1-4677-7908-1(3)*, Lerner Pubns.) Lerner Publishing Group.

Bodden, Valerie. Dialogue & Characterization. 2016. (Illus.). 80p. (J). *(978-1-60818-727-0(6)*, Creative Education) Creative Co., The.

—Imagery & Description. 2016. (Illus.). 80p. (J). *(978-1-60818-728-7(4)*, Creative Education) Creative Co., The.

—Narration & Point of View. 2016. (Illus.). 80p. *(978-1-60818-729-4(2)*, Creative Education) Creative Co., The.

—What Are Fiction Genres? 2014. (Name That Text Type! Ser.). (Illus.). 32p. (gr. 2-4). pap. 7.95 *(978-1-4677-4516-1(2))*; (ENG., lib. bdg. 26.60 *(978-1-4677-3664-0(3)*, Lerner Pubns.) Lerner Publishing Group.

Farrell, Tish. Be a Creative Writer. 2010. (ENG.). 96p. (J). (gr. 4-7). pap. 9.95 *(978-1-84696-209-7(9)*, TickTock Books) Octopus Publishing Group GBR. Dist: Independent Pubs. Group.

Giff, Patricia Reilly. Writing with Rosie: You Can Write a Story Too. 2016. (ENG.). 80p. (J). (gr. 3-6). 15.95 *(978-0-8234-3656-9(X))* Holiday Hse., Inc.

Hamilton, John. You Write It! Mystery. 2009. (You Write It! Ser.). (Illus.). 32p. (gr. 5-8). 27.07 *(978-1-60453-507-5(5)*, Abdo & Daughters) ABDO Publishing Co.

Lynette, Rachel. Frank & Fiona Build a Fictional Story. Lieffering, Jan, illus. 2014. (Writing Builders Ser.). (ENG.). 32p. (J). (gr. 2-4). pap. 11.94 *(978-1-60357-561-4(8))*; lib. bdg. 25.27 *(978-1-59953-587-6(4))* Norwood Hse. Pr.

Shipp, Catherine Elisabeth. 12 Great Tips on Writing Fiction. 2017. (Great Tips on Writing Ser.). (ENG.). 32p. (J). (gr. 3-6). 21.95 *(978-1-63235-274-3(5))* Pr. Room Editions LLC.

FICTITIOUS ANIMALS

see Animals, Mythical

FIEFS

see Feudalism

FIELD ATHLETICS

see Track and Field

FIELD SPORTS

see Hunting; Sports

FIGHTER PLANES

Alpert, Barbara. U. S. Military Fighter Planes, 1 vol. 2012. (U. S. Military Technology Ser.). (ENG., Illus.). 32p. (gr. 1-2). 26.65 *(978-1-4296-8439-2(9))* Capstone Press of Coughlan Cos.

Alvarez, Carlos. F-35 Lightning IIs. 2010. (Military Machines Ser.). (ENG., Illus.). 24p. (J). (gr. 3-7). lib. bdg. 25.95 *(978-1-60014-332-8(6))* Bellwether Media.

—F/a-18E/F Super Hornets. 2009. (Military Machines Ser.). (ENG., Illus.). 24p. (J). (gr. 3-7). lib. bdg. 25.95 *(978-1-60014-285-7(0))* Bellwether Media.

Bledsoe, Karen & Bledsoe, Glen. Fighter Planes: Fearless Fliers. 2006. (Mighty Military Machines Ser.). (Illus.). 48p. (J). (gr. 4-10). lib. bdg. 25.27 *(978-0-7660-2660-5(4))* Enslow Pubs., Inc.

Bodden, Valerie. Built for Battle: Fighter Jets. 2012. (Built for Battle Ser.). (ENG., Illus.). 24p. (J). (gr. 1-3). pap. 7.99 *(978-0-89812-701-0(7)*, Creative Paperbacks) Creative Co., The.

—Fighter Jets. 2012. (J). 25.65 *(978-1-60818-126-1(X)*, Creative Education) Creative Co., The.

Combat Aircraft. 2003. (Illus.). 32p. (YA). pap. *(978-1-904516-32-3(7)*, Pavilion Children's Books) Pavilion Bks.

Cooke, Tim. Fighter Planes. 2012. (Ultimate Military Machines Ser.). (Illus.). 32p. (gr. 4-7). lib. bdg. 31.35 *(978-1-59920-820-6(2))* Black Rabbit Bks.

Dartford, Mark. Fighter Planes. 2003. (Military Hardware in Action Ser.). (ENG., Illus.). 48p. (gr. 5-9). lib. bdg. 25.26 *(978-0-8225-4706-8(6))* Lerner Publishing Group.

David, Jack. F-14 Tomcats. 2008. (Military Machines Ser.). (ENG., Illus.). 24p. (YA). (gr. 3-7). lib. bdg. 25.95 *(978-1-60014-202-4(8))* Bellwether Media.

—F-15 Eagles. 2008. (Military Machines Ser.). (ENG., Illus.). 24p. (J). (gr. 3-7). lib. bdg. 25.95 *(978-1-60014-203-1(6))* Bellwether Media.

Doeden, Matt. Fighter Planes, 1 vol. 2005. (Mighty Machines Ser.). (ENG., Illus.). 24p. (gr. k-1). 24.65 *(978-0-7368-3657-9(8)*, Pebble Plus) Capstone Press of Coughlan Cos.

Ertle-Rickard, Stephen. Fighter Pilot. 2008. (321 Go! Ser.). (ENG., Illus.). 36p. pap. *(978-1-84167-758-3(2))* Ransom Publishing Ltd.

Finn, Denny Von. F-14 Tomcats. 2013. (Military Vehicles Ser.). (ENG., Illus.). 24p. (J). (gr. 3-7). lib. bdg. 25.95 *(978-1-60014-941-2(3)*, Epic Bks.) Bellwether Media.

—F-15 Eagles. 2013. (Military Vehicles Ser.). (ENG., Illus.). 24p. (J). (gr. 3-7). lib. bdg. 25.95 *(978-1-60014-942-9(1)*, Epic Bks.) Bellwether Media.

—F-22 Raptors. 2012. (Military Vehicles Ser.). (ENG., Illus.). 24p. (J). (gr. 3-7). lib. bdg. 25.95 *(978-1-60014-817-0(4)*, Epic Bks.) Bellwether Media.

—F-35 Lightning IIs. 2013. (Military Vehicles Ser.). (ENG., Illus.). 24p. (J). (gr. 3-7). lib. bdg. 25.95 *(978-1-60014-885-9(9)*, Epic Bks.) Bellwether Media.

—F/a-18E/F Super Hornets. 2012. (Military Vehicles Ser.). (ENG., Illus.). 24p. (J). (gr. 3-7). lib. bdg. 25.95 *(978-1-60014-818-7(2)*, Epic Bks.) Bellwether Media.

Gardner, Adrian. The F-14 Tomcat. (U. S. Warplanes Ser.). 48p. (gr. 5-8). 2009. 53.00 *(978-1-60854-597-1(0)*, Rosen Reference) 2005. (Illus.). (YA). lib. bdg. 29.25 *(978-0-8239-3870-4(0))* Rosen Publishing Group, Inc., The.

Jackson, Robert. 101 Great Fighters. 2010. (101 Greatest Weapons of All Times Ser.). (Illus.). 112p. (YA). (gr. 9-12). lib. bdg. 34.60 *(978-1-4358-3597-9(2))* Rosen Publishing Group, Inc., The.

Kennedy, Robert. Would You Dare Fly a Fighter Jet? 2016. (Would You Dare? Ser.). 00032p. (J). pap. 10.50 ***(978-1-4824-5810-7(1))***; lib. bdg. 26.60 ***(978-1-4824-5812-1(8))*** Stevens, Gareth Publishing LLLP.

Kiland, Taylor Baldwin, et al. Fighter Planes: Masters of the Sky. 2015. (Military Engineering in Action Ser.). (ENG.). 48p. (J). (gr. 6-6). 27.93 *(978-0-7660-6910-7(9))*; pap. 11.70 *(978-0-7660-7061-5(1))* Enslow Pubs., Inc.

Mairi, Mackinnon. Fighter Planes. 2012. (Discovery Adventures Ser.). 80p. (J). pap. 8.99 *(978-0-7945-3124-9(5)*, Usborne) EDC Publishing.

Mullins, Matt. How Does It Fly? Fighter Plane. 2011. (Community Connections: How Does It Fly? Ser.). (ENG.). 24p. (gr. 2-5). lib. bdg. 25.64 *(978-1-61080-066-2(4)*, 201058) Cherry Lake Publishing.

Murray, Laura K. Fighter Jets. 2016. (Seedlings Ser.). (Illus.). 24p. (J). (gr. k-2). (ENG.). pap. 7.99 *(978-1-62832-248-4(9))*; 28.50 *(978-1-60818-663-1(6))* Creative Co., The. (Creative Education).

Oxlade, Chris. Inside Fighter Planes. 2017. (Inside Military Machines Ser.). (ENG., Illus.). 32p. (J). (gr. 3-6). 26.65 ***(978-1-5124-3227-5(X)***, Hungry Tomato (r)) Lerner Publishing Group.

Peppas, Lynn. Fighter Jets: Defending the Skies. 2011. (ENG.). 32p. (J). pap. *(978-0-7787-2753-8(X))*; lib. bdg. *(978-0-7787-2748-4(3))* Crabtree Publishing Co.

Portman, Michael. Fighter Jets. 2013. (Military Machines Ser.). (Illus.). 32p. (J). (gr. 3-6). pap. 10.50 *(978-1-4339-8463-1(6))*; lib. bdg. 26.60 *(978-1-4339-8462-4(8))* Stevens, Gareth Publishing LLLP.

Seidman, David. The F/A-18 Hornet. (U. S. Warplanes Ser.). 48p. (gr. 5-8). 2009. 53.00 *(978-1-60854-596-4(2)*, Rosen Reference) 2005. (Illus.). (YA). lib. bdg. 29.25 *(978-0-8239-3874-2(3))* Rosen Publishing Group, Inc., The.

Von Finn, Denny. Jet Fighters. 2010. (World's Fastest Ser.). (ENG., Illus.). 24p. (J). (gr. 3-7). lib. bdg. 25.95 *(978-1-60014-335-9(0))* Bellwether Media.

West, David. Fighter Pilots. 2009. (Graphic Careers Ser.). (ENG.). 48p. (YA). (gr. 5-5). 58.50 *(978-1-61512-880-8(8)*, Rosen Reference) Rosen Publishing Group, Inc., The.

—Fighter Pilots. Field, James, illus. 2008. (Graphic Careers Ser.). (ENG.). 48p. (gr. 5-8). per. 14.05 *(978-1-4042-1456-9(9))*; (YA). lib. bdg. 31.95 *(978-1-4042-1455-2(0))* Rosen Publishing Group, Inc., The.

Winchester, Jim. Jet Fighters: Inside & Out. 2011. (Weapons of War Ser.). (ENG.). 160p. (YA). (gr. 9-12). lib. bdg. 42.60 *(978-1-4488-5982-5(4))* Rosen Publishing Group, Inc., The.

Zobel, Derek. A-10 Thunderbolts. 2008. (Military Machines Ser.). (ENG., Illus.). 24p. (J). (gr. 3-7). lib. bdg. 25.95 *(978-1-60014-201-7(X))* Bellwether Media.

—F-117A Nighthawks. 2008. (Military Machines Ser.). (ENG., Illus.). 24p. (J). (gr. 3-7). lib. bdg. 25.95 *(978-1-60014-221-5(4))* Bellwether Media.

—F-22 Raptors. 2008. (Military Machines Ser.). (ENG., Illus.). 24p. (YA). (gr. 3-7). lib. bdg. 25.95 *(978-1-60014-204-8(4))* Bellwether Media.

Zuehlke, Jeffrey. Fighter Planes. 2005. (Pull Ahead Books-Mighty Movers Ser.). (ENG., Illus.). 32p. (J). (gr. k-3). lib. bdg. 22.60 *(978-0-8225-2667-4(0)*, Lerner Pubns.) Lerner Publishing Group.

FIGHTING

see Battles; Boxing; Fencing; Naval Art and Science; Self-Defense; War

FIGURE DRAWING

Bergin, Mark. Action Fighting Figures. 2012. (How to Draw Ser.). (ENG.). 32p. (J). (gr. 4-6). pap. 11.75 *(978-1-4488-6475-1(5))*; lib. bdg. 26.50 *(978-1-4488-6464-5(X))* Rosen Publishing Group, Inc., The. (PowerKids Pr.).

—How to Draw Comic Book Heroes. 2010. (How to Draw Ser.). (Illus.). 32p. (YA). (gr. 6-18). pap. 11.75 *(978-1-4488-1604-0(1))*; lib. bdg. 26.50 *(978-1-4488-1579-1(7))* Rosen Publishing Group, Inc., The. (PowerKids Pr.).

Boothroyd, Jennifer. Facial Features: Freckles, Earlobes, Noses, & More. 2012. (Lightning Bolt Books (tm) — What Traits Are in Your Genes? Ser.). (ENG., Illus.). 32p. (gr. k-2). lib. bdg. 26.60 *(978-0-7613-8939-2(3)*, Lerner Pubns.) Lerner Publishing Group.

Gray, Peter. Male Action Figures. 2009. (Drawing Manga Ser.). 32p. (gr. 4-4). 50.50 *(978-1-61512-199-1(4))* Rosen Publishing Group, Inc., The.

Gray, Peter C. Male Action Figures. 2006. (Drawing Manga Ser.). (Illus.). 32p. (YA). (gr. 3-6). lib. bdg. 26.50 *(978-1-4042-3328-7(8))* Rosen Publishing Group, Inc., The.

Green, John & Drawing Staff. How to Draw Horses. 2009. (Dover How to Draw Ser.). (ENG., Illus.). 64p. (J). (gr. 1-4). pap. 4.99 *(978-0-486-46759-7(7))* Dover Pubns., Inc.

Hosley, Maria. People, 1 vol. 2007. (First Drawings Ser.). (ENG., Illus.). 24p. (gr. -1-3). 25.65 *(978-1-59679-812-0(2)*, Buddy Bks.) ABDO Publishing Co.

Kaufman Yaun, Debra. Drawing - Faces & Features: Learn to Draw Step by Step. 2006. (How to Draw & Paint Ser.). (ENG., Illus.). 32p. pap. 8.95 *(978-1-56010-965-5(3)*, 1560109653) Quarto Publishing Group USA.

LaBaff, Stephanie. Draw Superheroes in 4 Easy Steps: Then Write a Story. LaBaff, Tom, illus. 2012. (Drawing in 4 Easy Steps Ser.). 48p. (J). (gr. 3-18). pap. 8.95 *(978-1-4644-0015-5(6)*, Enslow Elementary); 25.27 *(978-0-7660-3842-4(4))* Enslow Pubs., Inc.

Lee, Frank. Drawing Action in Your Graphic Novel. 2012. (How to Draw Your Own Graphic Novel Ser.). (ENG.). 32p. (J). (gr. 4-6). pap. 12.30 *(978-1-4488-6451-5(8))*; lib. bdg. 26.50 *(978-1-4488-6477-5(1))* Rosen Publishing Group, Inc., The. (PowerKids Pr.).

—Drawing the Heroes in Your Graphic Novel. 2012. (How to Draw Your Own Graphic Novel Ser.). (ENG.). 32p. (J). (gr. 4-6). pap. 12.30 *(978-1-4488-6447-8(X))*; lib. bdg. 26.50 *(978-1-4488-6432-4(1))* Rosen Publishing Group, Inc., The. (PowerKids Pr.).

—Drawing the Villains in Your Graphic. 2012. (How to Draw Your Own Graphic Novel Ser.). (ENG.). 32p. (J). (gr. 4-6). pap. 12.30 *(978-1-4488-6449-2(6))*; lib. bdg. 26.50 *(978-1-4488-6433-1(X))* Rosen Publishing Group, Inc., The. (PowerKids Pr.).

Levy, Barbara Soloff & Drawing Staff. ART START Funny Characters: How to Draw with Simple Shapes. 2010. (Dover How to Draw Ser.). (ENG., Illus.). 64p. (J). (gr. k-3). pap. 4.99 *(978-0-486-47679-7(0))* Dover Pubns., Inc.

—How to Draw Princesses & Other Fairy Tale Pictures. 2008. (Dover How to Draw Ser.). (ENG., Illus.). 64p. (J). (gr. 1-5). pap. 4.99 *(978-0-486-46813-6(5))* Dover Pubns., Inc.

Raczka, Bob. Action Figures: Paintings of Fun, Daring, & Adventure. (Bob Raczka's Art Adventures Ser.). (ENG.). 32p. (gr. -1-3). 2010. pap. 9.95 *(978-0-7613-4172-7(2)*, First Avenue Editions) 2009. 25.26 *(978-0-7613-4140-6(4)*, Millbrook Pr.) Lerner Publishing Group.

Scrace, Carolyn. Drawing Monsters. 2016. (Art Works). 32p. (gr. 2-6). 31.35 *(978-1-62588-346-9(3)*, Smart Apple Media) Black Rabbit Bks.

—Drawing Robots. 2016. (Art Works). 32p. (gr. 2-6). 31.35 *(978-1-62588-347-6(1)*, Smart Apple Media) Black Rabbit Bks.

Tonatiuh, Duncan. Funny Bones: Posada & His Day of the Dead Calaveras. 2015. (ENG., Illus.). 40p. (J). (gr. 1-5). 18.95 *(978-1-4197-1647-8(6)*, Abrams Bks. for Young Readers) Abrams, Inc.

FIGURE SKATING

see Skating

FIJI

NgCheong-Lum, Roseline. Fiji. 2nd rev. ed. 2010. (Cultures of the World 20 Ser.). 144p. (gr. 6). 42.79 *(978-1-60870-022-6(4))* Marshall Cavendish Corp.

FIJI—FICTION

Prasad, Sunayna. Alyssa Mccarthy's Magical Missions: Book 1. 2013. 216p. pap. *(978-1-4602-0701-7(7))* FriesenPress.

Soisson, Chelsea. Tate's Wayward Voyage. 2012. (ENG.). (J). pap. 17.99 *(978-1-4675-2650-0(9))*; pap. 17.99 *(978-1-4675-2651-7(7))* Independent Pub.

FINANCE

see also Bankruptcy; Banks and Banking; Bonds; Commerce; Credit; Finance, Personal; Income; Insurance; Investments; Money; Paper Money; Stock Exchanges

Bailey, Gerry & Law, Felicia. World Money. Beech, Mark, illus. 2015. (How Money Works). (ENG.). 64p. (J). (gr. 4-6). lib. bdg. 29.27 *(978-1-59953-720-7(6))* Norwood Hse. Pr.

Barrington, Richard. Using Math in Finance. 2017. (Math You Will Actually Use Ser.). 48p. (gr. 10-10). pap. 11.75 ***(978-1-4994-3864-2(8)***, Rosen Central) Rosen Publishing Group, Inc., The.

Bell, N. Wayne. Childrens' Economics: A Book on Money & Finance. Lt. ed. 2004. (Illus.). 32p. (J). per. *(978-0-9729753-5-3(7))* Really Big Coloring Bks., Inc.

Berlatsky, Noah, ed. Inflation. 2012. (Opposing Viewpoints Ser.). (ENG., Illus.). 240p. (gr. 10-12). pap. 29.45 *(978-0-7377-6427-7(9))*; lib. bdg. 42.95 *(978-0-7377-6426-0(0))* Cengage Gale. (Greenhaven Pr., Inc.).

Bonnice, Sherry. Financial Advisor. Riggs, Ernestine G. & Gholar, Cheryl, eds. 2013. (Careers with Character Ser.: 18). 96p. (J). (gr. 7-18). 22.95 *(978-1-4222-2755-8(3))* Mason Crest.

Brezina, Corona. How Deflation Works. 2010. (Real World Economics Ser.). (Illus.). 80p. (YA). (gr. 7-18). lib. bdg. 33.25 *(978-1-4358-9465-5(0))* Rosen Publishing Group, Inc., The.

Cassedy, Patrice, tr. Finance. 2003. (Careers for the Twenty-First-Century Ser.). (ENG., Illus.). 112p. (J). 30.85 *(978-1-59018-520-9(X)*, Lucent Bks.) Cengage Gale.

Catalano, Angela. Community Plans: Making Choices about Money in Communities. 2005. (Communities at Work Ser.). (Illus.). 24p. (J). (gr. 1-4). lib. bdg. 22.60 *(978-1-4042-2779-8(2))* Rosen Publishing Group, Inc., The.

Connolly, Sean & Claybourne, Anna. Insurance. 2011. (On the Edge Ser.). 32p. (YA). (gr. 3-6). 28.50 *(978-1-59920-519-9(X))* Black Rabbit Bks.

Connolly, Sean & Morgan, Sally. International Aid & Loans. 2011. (Earth Cycles Ser.). 32p. (YA). (gr. 3-6). lib. bdg. 28.50 *(978-1-59920-521-2(1))* Black Rabbit Bks.

Connolly, Sean & Pipe, Jim. Banks & Banking. 2011. (On the Edge Ser.). 32p. (YA). (gr. 3-6). 28.50 *(978-1-59920-517-5(3))* Black Rabbit Bks.

Crayton, Lisa A. & Furang, Kathy. The Stock Market: What It Is & How It Works. 2016. (Economics in the 21st Century Ser.). (ENG.). 96p. (J). (gr. 8-8). 34.60 *(978-0-7660-7384-5(X))* Enslow Pubs., Inc.

Crayton, Lisa A. & Hart, Joyce. Inflation: What It Is & How It Works. 2016. (Economics in the 21st Century Ser.). (ENG.). 96p. (J). (gr. 8-8). 34.60 *(978-0-7660-7248-0(7))* Enslow Pubs., Inc.

Fisanick, Christina. Debt. 2009. (Opposing Viewpoints Ser.). (ENG.). 240p. (J). (gr. 10-12). 29.45 *(978-0-7377-4203-9(8)*, Greenhaven Pr., Inc.) Cengage Gale.

Fischer, James. The Power to Do Good: Money & Charity. 2010. (Junior Library of Money). 64p. (YA). (gr. 7-18). pap. 9.95 *(978-1-4222-1888-4(0))*; lib. bdg. 22.95 *(978-1-4222-1769-6(8))* Mason Crest.

Foran, Racquel. Developing Nations' Debt, 1 vol. 2011. (Essential Issues Set 3 Ser.). (ENG., Illus.). 112p. (J). (gr. 6-12). lib. bdg. 35.64 *(978-1-61783-132-4(8))* ABDO Publishing Co.

Hall, Alvin. Show Me the Money. 2016. (Big Questions Ser.). (ENG., Illus.). 96p. (J). (gr. 3-7). pap. 9.99 *(978-1-4654-4000-6(3)*, DK Children) Dorling Kindersley Publishing, Inc.

Hart, Joyce. How Inflation Works. 2009. (Real World Economics Ser.). (Illus.). 80p. (YA). (gr. 7-12). lib. bdg. 33.25 *(978-1-4358-5320-1(2))* Rosen Publishing Group, Inc., The.

—How Inflation Works (Real World Economics) Lt. ed. 2012. 142p. pap. *(978-1-4596-3375-9(X))* ReadHowYouWant.com, Ltd.

Hatton, Fran. Learning about Earning. 2015. (First-Glance Finance Ser.). (ENG.). 48p. (J). (gr. 4-4). 31.36 *(978-1-5026-0094-3(3))* Cavendish Square Publishing.

Hiber, Amanda. Alternative Lending. 2010. (Opposing Viewpoints Ser.). (Illus.). 240p. (J). 42.95 *(978-0-7377-4753-9(6))*; pap. 29.45 *(978-0-7377-4754-6(4))* Cengage Gale. (Greenhaven Pr., Inc.).

Hocking, Justin. Taking Action: How to Get Your City to Build a Public Skatepark. 2004. (Skateboarder's Guide to Skate Parks, Half-Pipes, Bowls, & Obstacles Ser.). (Illus.). 48p. (J). lib. bdg. 29.25 *(978-1-4042-0341-9(9))* Rosen Publishing Group, Inc., The.

Hollander, Barbara. How Currency Devaluation Works. 2011. (Real World Economics Ser.). (ENG.). 80p. (YA). lib. bdg. 33.25 *(978-1-4488-1270-7(4))* Rosen Publishing Group, Inc., The.

Hunnicutt, Susan C. The Federal Budget Deficit. 2010. (At Issue Ser.). (Illus.). 128p. pap. 24.45 *(978-0-7377-4686-0(6)*, Greenhaven Pr., Inc.) Cengage Gale.

January, Brendan. Globalize It! The Stories of the IMF, the World Bank, the WTO - And Those Who Protest. 2003. (Single Titles Ser.). (Illus.). 144p. (gr. 7-18). 26.90 *(978-0-7613-2417-1(8)*, Twenty-First Century Bks.) Lerner Publishing Group.

Junior Library of Money, 14 vols., Set. Incl. All about Money: The History, Culture, & Meaning of Modern Finance. Simons, Rae. lib. bdg. 22.95 *(978-1-4222-1760-3(4))*; Banking Basics. Fischer, James. lib. bdg. 22.95 *(978-1-4222-1761-0(2))*; Cost of Living. Thompson, Helen. lib. bdg. 22.95 *(978-1-4222-1762-7(0))*; Earning Money: Jobs. Fischer, James. lib. bdg. 22.95 *(978-1-4222-1763-4(9))*; Entrepreneurship. Simons, Rae. lib. bdg. 22.95 *(978-1-4222-1764-1(7))*; Guide to Teaching Young Adults about Money. Simons, Rae. lib. bdg. 22.95 *(978-1-4222-1765-8(5))*; Investing Money. Thompson, Helen. lib. bdg. 22.95 *(978-1-4222-1766-5(3))*; Money & Relationships. Simons, Rae. lib. bdg. 22.95 *(978-1-4222-1767-2(1))*; Planning for Your Education. Fischer, James. lib. bdg. 22.95 *(978-1-4222-1768-9(X))*; Power to Do Good: Money & Charity. Fischer, James. lib. bdg. 22.95 *(978-1-4222-1769-6(8))*; Spending Money. Simons, Rae. lib. bdg. 22.95 *(978-1-4222-1770-2(1))*; Sustainable Lifestyles in a Changing Economy. Simons, Rae. lib. bdg. 22.95 *(978-1-4222-1771-9(X))*; Understanding Credit. Thompson, Helen. lib. bdg. 22.95 *(978-1-4222-1772-6(8))*; Understanding the Stock Market. Thompson, Helen. lib. bdg. 22.95 *(978-1-4222-1773-3(6))*; (YA). (gr. 7-18). 2010. (Illus.). 64p. 2011. Set lib. bdg. 321.30 *(978-1-4222-1759-7(0))* Mason Crest.

La Bella, Laura. World Financial Meltdown. 2010. (Doomsday Scenarios: Separating Fact from Fiction Ser.). 64p. (YA). (gr. 5-8). E-Book 58.50 *(978-1-4488-1209-7(7))* Rosen Publishing Group, Inc., The.

Levete, Sarah. The Race to Fix the Global Economy. 2014. (World in Crisis Ser.). (Illus.). 48p. (J). (gr. 5-8). 30.25 *(978-1-4777-7844-9(6))* Rosen Publishing Group, Inc., The.

Mapua, Jeff. Making the Most of Crowdfunding, 1 vol. 2015. (ENG.). 48p. (YA). 30.25 *(978-1-4777-7942-2(6)*, Rosen Reference) Rosen Publishing Group, Inc., The.

Mattern, Joanne. Careers in Finance. 2015. (ENG., Illus.). 80p. (J). lib. bdg. *(978-1-60152-810-0(8))* ReferencePoint Pr., Inc.

Maybury, Richard J. Uncle Eric Talks about Personal, Career, & Financial Security. Williams, Jane A. & Daniels, Kathryn, eds. 2nd ed. 2004. ("Uncle Eric" Bk.: 1). (ENG., Illus.). 187p. pap. 14.95 *(978-0-942617-38-2(X))* Bluestocking Pr.

McAlpine, Margaret. Working in Banking & Finance. 2005. (My Future Career Ser.). (Illus.). 64p. (J). (gr. 3-7). lib. bdg. 27.00 *(978-0-8368-4772-7(5)*, Gareth Stevens Learning Library) Stevens, Gareth Publishing LLLP.

Mooney, Carla. Using Computer Science in Fintech Careers. 2017. (Coding Your Passion Ser.). 80p. (J). (gr. 12-12). 35.75 ***(978-1-5081-7513-1(6)***, Rosen Young Adult) Rosen Publishing Group, Inc., The.

Morrison, Jessica. Saving. 2017. (J). ***(978-1-5105-1947-3(5))*** SmartBook Media, Inc.

Seuling, Barbara. There Are Millions of Millionaires: And Other Freaky Facts About Earning, Saving, & Spending. Haugen, Ryan, illus. 2010. (Freaky Facts Ser.). 40p. pap. 0.35 *(978-1-4048-6550-1(0)*, Nonfiction Picture Bks.) Picture Window Bks.

Spath, Carolyn E. W. Making a Budget. 2015. (J). lib. bdg. *(978-1-62713-389-0(5))*; (ENG., Illus.). 48p. (gr. 4-4). 31.36 *(978-1-5026-0099-8(4))* Cavendish Square Publishing.

—Savvy Saving. 2015. (J). lib. bdg. *(978-1-62713-304-3(6))*; (ENG.). 48p. (gr. 4-4). 31.36 *(978-1-5026-0096-7(X))* Cavendish Square Publishing.

Spath, Carolyn E. W., et al. Plants. 2016. (Know It All Ser.). (ENG., Illus.). 32p. (J). (gr. 5-5). lib. bdg. 28.50 *(978-1-5026-0896-3(0)*, 1398905) Cavendish Square Publishing.

Spilsbury, Richard. Global Economy, 1 vol. 2012. (Hot Topics Ser.). (ENG.). 64p. (gr. 7-8). 34.65 *(978-1-4329-6038-4(5)*, NA-h) Heinemann-Raintree.

Stinson, Paul. Sales, Marketing, Business & Finance. 2008. (Great Careers with a High School Diploma Ser.). 110p. (C). (gr. 9). 32.95 *(978-0-8160-7051-0(2)*, Ferguson Publishing Co.) Facts On File, Inc.

Trembinsky, Laverne Gray. A Friend Sent from Heaven for Andrew: A Little Boy Finds His Self Experiencing Loneliness Because His Family Had to Move Because of Financial Hardsh. 2009. 45p. (J). pap. 10.95 *(978-1-4327-3458-9(X))* Outskirts Pr., Inc.

Uhler, Matt. The Right to a Living Wage. 2017. (J). pap. ***(978-1-5345-0080-8(4))*** Greenhaven Publishing LLC.

What Can I Do Now: Business & Finance. 2010. (What Can I Do Now? Ser.). 240p. (gr. 6-12). 32.95 *(978-0-8160-8081-6(X))* Facts On File, Inc.

Wiseman, Blaine. Budgeting. 2017. (J). ***(978-1-5105-1943-5(2))*** SmartBook Media, Inc.

FINANCE, PERSONAL

see also Home Economics—Accounting; Insurance; Investments

Anderson, Marjorie L. The Key: Wise Money Choices for Teens. 2013. 88p. pap. 15.99 *(978-1-4797-8102-7(9))* Xlibris Corp.

Andrade, J. Jack. Mom, Dad, Tell Me about Money: A Primer. 2004. 68p. (YA). per. 19.95 *(978-0-9759494-0-5(3)*, 2004-money01) Thundermist Consulting and Research Co.

Bailey, Diane. Top 10 Secrets for Creating & Sticking to a Budget Successfully. 2013. (Illus.). 64p. (YA). (gr. 7-12). 31.95 *(978-1-4488-9360-7(7))*; pap. 12.95 *(978-1-4488-9369-0(0))*; pap. 77.70 *(978-1-4488-9370-6(4))* Rosen Publishing Group, Inc., The.

Bailey, Gerry & Law, Felicia. Your Money. Beech, Mark, illus. 2015. (How Money Works). (ENG.). 64p. (J). (gr. 4-6). lib. bdg. 29.27 *(978-1-59953-718-4(4))* Norwood Hse. Pr.

Bateman, Katherine R. The Young Investor: Projects & Activities for Making Your Money Grow. 2nd ed. 2010. (ENG., Illus.). 144p. (J). (gr. 4). pap. 14.95 *(978-1-56976-546-3(4))* Chicago Review Pr., Inc.

Beaton, Kathryn. Payday! 2015. (21st Century Skills Library: Real World Math Ser.). (ENG., Illus.). 32p. (J). (gr. 4-7). 29.93 *(978-1-63362-573-0(7)*, 206476) Cherry Lake Publishing.

Berg, David W. & Green, Meg. Savings & Investments. 2011. (J). 77.70 *(978-1-4488-4754-9(0)*, Rosen Reference); (J). pap. 12.95 *(978-1-4488-4722-8(2)*, Rosen Reference); (YA). (gr. 5-9). lib. bdg. 31.95 *(978-1-4488-4712-9(5))* Rosen Publishing Group, Inc., The.

Best, B. J. Investing Your Money. 2015. (J). lib. bdg. *(978-1-62713-391-3(7))*; (ENG.). 48p. (gr. 4-4). 31.36 *(978-1-5026-0103-2(6))* Cavendish Square Publishing.

Bickerstaff, Linda. Smart Strategies for Saving & Building Wealth. 2014. (Financial Security & Life Success for Teens Ser.). (Illus.). 80p. (J). (gr. 7-12). pap. 84.90 *(978-1-4777-7629-2(X))* Rosen Publishing Group, Inc., The.

Blohm, Craig E. Teen Guide to Credit & Debt. 2016. (ENG.). 64p. (J). (gr. 5-12). lib. bdg. *(978-1-68282-080-3(7))* ReferencePoint Pr., Inc.

Bochner, Arthur, et al. The New Totally Awesome Money Book for Kids. 3rd rev. ed. 2007. (New Totally Awesome Ser.: 1). (ENG., Illus.). 192p. (gr. 7-9). per. 11.99 *(978-1-55704-738-0(3)*, William Morrow Paperbacks) HarperCollins Pubs.

Bradley, Kathleen E. Making Money Grow, 1 vol. 2nd rev. ed. 2013. (Nonfiction Readers Ser.). (ENG.). 64p. (J). (gr. 5-5). pap. 10.99 *(978-1-4333-4908-9(6))*; (Illus.). (J). 31.96 *(978-1-4333-7431-9(5))* Teacher Created Materials, Inc.

Braun, Eric & Donovan, Sandy. The Survival Guide for Money Smarts: Earn, Save, Spend, Give. 2016. (ENG., Illus.). 128p. (J). (gr. 3-9). pap. 13.99 *(978-1-63198-028-2(9))* Free Spirit Publishing, Inc.

Brooks, Yvonne. Kids Finance 101: A Guide to Financial Success for Parents & their Children. 2007. 208p. per. 17.95 *(978-0-595-45962-9(5))* iUniverse, Inc.

Bullard, Lisa. Brody Borrows Money. Byrne, Mike, illus. 2013. (Cloverleaf Books — Money Basics Ser.). (ENG.). 24p. (gr. k-2). pap. 6.95 *(978-1-4677-1508-9(5))*; lib. bdg. 23.93 *(978-1-4677-0763-3(5))* Lerner Publishing Group. (Millbrook Pr.).

—Ella Earns Her Own Money. Moran, Mike, illus. 2013. (Cloverleaf Books — Money Basics Ser.). (ENG.). 24p. (gr. k-2). pap. 6.95 *(978-1-4677-1511-9(5)*, Millbrook Pr.) Lerner Publishing Group.

—Ella Earns Her Own Money. Moran, Michael, illus. 2013. (Cloverleaf Books — Money Basics Ser.). (ENG.). 24p. (gr. k-2). lib. bdg. 23.93 *(978-1-4677-0761-9(9)*, Millbrook Pr.) Lerner Publishing Group.

—Lily Learns about Wants & Needs. Schneider, Christine M., illus. 2013. (Cloverleaf Books — Money Basics Ser.). (ENG.). 24p. (gr. k-2). pap. 6.95 *(978-1-4677-1509-6(3))*; lib. bdg. 23.93 *(978-1-4677-0764-0(3))* Lerner Publishing Group. (Millbrook Pr.).

—Shanti Saves Her Money. Schneider, Christine M., illus. 2013. (Cloverleaf Books — Money Basics Ser.). (ENG.).

24p. (gr. k-2). pap. 6.95 *(978-1-4677-1513-3(1))*; lib. bdg. 23.93 *(978-1-4677-0765-7(1))* Lerner Publishing Group. (Millbrook Pr.).

Burncrot, Curt. Personal Finance Packet. Zyp, Nicole, ed. 2005. 41p. (YA). (gr. 10-12). pap. 15.00 *(978-1-888786-46-0(9))* Basic Skills Assessment & Educational Services.

Bundlie, Mike, et al. Make More Than Your Parents: Your Guide to Financial Freedom. 2003. (ENG., Illus.). 144p. (J). pap. 16.95 *(978-0-7573-0122-3(3))* Health Communications, Inc.

Burstein, John. Dollars & Sense: Developing Good Money Habits. 2010. (ENG., Illus.). 32p. (J). pap. *(978-0-7787-4810-6(3))*; lib. bdg. *(978-0-7787-4794-9(8))* Crabtree Publishing Co.

Burton, Margie, et al. Travel Money, U. S. A. 2011. (Early Connections Ser.). (J). *(978-1-61672-508-2(7))* Benchmark Education Co.

Canetti, Yanitzia. En Tiempos Difíciles. Willy, Romont, illus. 2010. (SPA & ENG.). 32p. (J). (gr. k-2). pap. 8.99 *(978-1-59835-102-6(8)*, BrickHouse Education) Cambridge BrickHouse, Inc.

—When Times Are Tough. Keating, Alison, tr. Willy, Romont, illus. 2009. 32p. (J). (gr. k-2). 8.99 *(978-1-59835-103-3(6))* Cambridge BrickHouse, Inc.

Challen, Paul & Cipriano, Jeri. How Do Mortgages, Loans, & Credit Work? 2009. (Economics in Action Ser.). (ENG., Illus.). 32p. (J). (gr. 3-7). pap. *(978-0-7787-4456-6(6))* Crabtree Publishing Co.

Chambers, Don. The Entitlement Trap: Families & Money. 2010. (ENG.). *(978-0-9722071-1-9(2))* Healthy Wealth.

—Money Basics for Young Adults: College Edition. 2010. (C). *(978-0-9722071-2-6(0))* Healthy Wealth.

Chariot, F. Home Allowance & Chore Kit. 2004. (Christian Financial Concept Ser.). 17.99 *(978-983-45-0258-4(3)*, 9834502583) Cook, David C.

Chatzky, Jean. Not Your Parents' Money Book: Making, Saving, & Spending Your Own Money. Jenkins, Ward & Haya, Erwin, illus. 2010. (ENG.). 176p. (J). (gr. 5-9). pap. 12.99 *(978-1-4169-9472-5(6)*, Simon & Schuster Bks. For Young Readers) Simon & Schuster Bks. For Young Readers.

The Chavo Cuentos of Zito & Lilis: The Importance of Savings. 2004. (J). pap. 2.50 *(978-0-9770312-0-7(9))* Itiya Publishing, Inc.

A Child's Guide to Money. 2007. (YA). per. *(978-1-59916-190-7(7))* Printing Systems.

Collins, Robyn, et al. Prepare to Be a Teen Millionaire: Detailed Examples & Step-By-Step Instructions from Self-Made Millionaires. 2008. (ENG., Illus.). 304p. (gr. 8-18). pap. 16.95 *(978-0-7573-0723-2(X))* Health Communications, Inc.

Croke, Liam & Naik, Anita. I'm Broke! The Money Handbook. 2009. (Really Useful Handbooks Ser.). (ENG., Illus.). 48p. (J). (gr. 5-11). pap. *(978-0-7787-4402-3(7))*; lib. bdg. *(978-0-7787-4389-7(6))* Crabtree Publishing Co.

Currie, Stephen. Teen Guide to Saving & Investing. 2016. (ENG.). 64p. (J). (gr. 5-12). lib. bdg. *(978-1-68282-086-5(6))* ReferencePoint Pr., Inc.

Dakers, Diane. The Bottom Line: Money Basics. 2017. (Financial Literacy for Life Ser.). (ENG.). 48p. (J). ***(978-0-7787-3095-8(6))***; pap. ***(978-0-7787-3104-7(9))*** Crabtree Publishing Co.

—Getting Your Money's Worth: Making Smart Financial Choices. 2017. (Financial Literacy for Life Ser.). (ENG.). 48p. (J). ***(978-0-7787-3097-2(2))***; pap. ***(978-0-7787-3106-1(5))*** Crabtree Publishing Co.

—It Doesn't Grow on Trees: Sources of Income. 2017. (Financial Literacy for Life Ser.). (ENG.). 48p. (J). ***(978-0-7787-3096-5(4))***; pap. ***(978-0-7787-3105-4(7))*** Crabtree Publishing Co.

—Money for Your Life: Invest in Your Financial Future. 2017. (Financial Literacy for Life Ser.). (ENG.). 48p. (J). ***(978-0-7787-3098-9(0))***; pap. ***(978-0-7787-3107-8(3))*** Crabtree Publishing Co.

DaSilva-Gordon, Maria. Top 10 Secrets for Making Money & Even More Money. 2013. 64p. (YA). (gr. 7-12). 31.95 *(978-1-4488-9359-1(3))*; pap. 12.95 *(978-1-4488-9373-7(9))*; pap. 77.70 *(978-1-4488-9374-4(7))* Rosen Publishing Group, Inc., The.

Dayton, Howard & Dayton, Beverly. The ABC's of Handling Money God's Way. Davenport, Andy, illus. 2003. (ENG.). 96p. (J). pap., tchr. ed. 11.99 *(978-0-8024-3151-6(8))* Moody Pubs.

—The Secret of Handling Money God's Way. 2003. (Leading Young Hearts & Minds to God Ser.). (ENG.). 112p. (J). pap. 14.99 *(978-0-8024-3154-7(2))* Moody Pubs.

Divorce & Your Family. 2016. (Divorce & Your Family Ser.). 64p. (gr. 7-7). 206.70 *(978-1-4777-8546-1(9)*, Rosen Young Adult) Rosen Publishing Group, Inc., The.

Donovan, Sandra. Budgeting Smarts: How to Set Goals, Save Money, Spend Wisely, & More. 2012. (USA TODAY Teen Wise Guides: Time, Money, & Relationships Ser.). (ENG.). 64p. (gr. 8-12). lib. bdg. 31.93 *(978-0-7613-7016-1(1))* Lerner Publishing Group.

Donovan, Sandy. Budgeting. 2005. (How Economics Works). (ENG., Illus.). 48p. (gr. 4-6). lib. bdg. 25.26 *(978-0-8225-2665-0(4)*, Lerner Pubns.) Lerner Publishing Group.

—USA TODAY(r) Teen Wise Guides: Time, Money, & Relationships: Spring 2012 New Releases. 2012. (USA TODAY Teen Wise Guides: Time, Money, & Relationships Ser.). (ENG.). 64p. (gr. 8-12). lib. bdg. 191.58 *(978-0-7613-7014-7(5)*, Twenty-First Century Bks.) Lerner Publishing Group.

Dugan, Christine. From Rags to Riches, 1 vol. 2nd rev. ed. 2013. (Nonfiction Readers Ser.). (ENG.). 64p. (J). (gr. 5-5). pap. 10.99 *(978-1-4333-4910-2(8))*; (Illus.). pap. 31.96 *(978-1-4333-7433-3(1))* Teacher Created Materials, Inc.

—Where Does Your Money Go?, 1 vol. 2nd rev. ed. 2013. (Nonfiction Readers Ser.). (ENG.). 64p. (J). (gr. 5-5). pap. 10.99 *(978-1-4333-4909-6(4))*; (Illus.). pap. 31.96 *(978-1-4333-7432-6(3))* Teacher Created Materials, Inc.

Eagen, Rachel. Learning about Earning. 2016. (Money Sense: an Introduction to Financial Literacy Ser.). (ENG., Illus.). 24p. (J). (gr. 1-4). *(978-0-7787-2665-4(7))* Crabtree Publishing Co.

—What Do I Want? What Do I Need? 2016. (Money Sense: an Introduction to Financial Literacy Ser.). (ENG., Illus.). 24p. (J). (gr. 1-4). *(978-0-7787-2664-7(9))* Crabtree Publishing Co.

—Why Does Money Matter? 2016. (Money Sense: an Introduction to Financial Literacy Ser.). (ENG., Illus.). 24p. (J). (gr. 1-4). *(978-0-7787-2666-1(5))* Crabtree Publishing Co.

—Why Should I Save for a Rainy Day? 2016. (Money Sense: an Introduction to Financial Literacy Ser.). (ENG., Illus.). 24p. (J). (gr. 1-4). *(978-0-7787-2663-0(0))* Crabtree Publishing Co.

Edelstein, Judy & Howe, Katherine. Money Matters: How to Become a Smart Consumer. 2005. (ENG.). 48p. pap. 14.95 *(978-1-59363-108-6(1))* Prufrock Pr.

Einspruch, Andrew. Managing Money. 2012. (Money Sense Ser.). (Illus.). 32p. (gr. 4-6). lib. bdg. 28.50 *(978-1-59920-432-1(0))* Black Rabbit Bks.

Elias, Keith James. The Friendly Dragons & the Secrets of K-star: Kids Learning the Wisdom of Money Management. 2003. (J). per. 12.95 *(978-0-9726247-0-1(8))* Elias Pubns., LLC.

Fay, Gail. Using Money, 1 vol. 2011. (Understanding Money Ser.). (ENG.). 48p. (gr. 3-5). pap. 9.95 *(978-1-4329-4641-8(2))*; 33.32 *(978-1-4329-4634-0(X))* Heinemann-Raintree. (Heinemann InfoSearch).

Feldman, Jean R. & Karapetkova, Holly. Found a Penny (Tune, Found a Peanut) Lap Book. 2010. (ENG., Illus.). 16p. (gr. -1-k). 9.95 *(978-1-61590-204-0(X))* Rourke Educational Media.

Financial Security & Life Success for Teens. 2014. (Financial Security & Life Success for Teens Ser.). 80p. (YA). (gr. 7-12). 205.50 *(978-1-4777-7638-4(9))*; pap. 84.90 *(978-1-4777-8110-4(2))* Rosen Publishing Group, Inc., The.

Flatt, Andy. Penny Wise Finds Out about Borrowing - Pupil's Book: Penny Is Ten & Wants to Know What Money Is All about & Why Grown-Ups Make Such a Fuss about It. 2014. (ENG.). 24p. (C). pap. 4.50 *(978-1-85741-102-7(1))* Parkwest Pubns., Inc.

Ford, Brian. Marshmallows & Bikes: Teaching Children (and Adults) Personal Finance. 2007. (Illus.). 36p. (J). 13.95 *(978-0-9798854-0-2(X))* Mainstay, LLC.

Fradin, Dennis B. & Fradin, Judith Bloom. Saving. 2010. (Money Smart Ser.). 64p. (gr. 4). 32.79 *(978-1-60870-125-4(5))* Marshall Cavendish GBR. Dist: Marshall Cavendish Corp.

Fradin, Dennis Brindell & Fradin, Judith Bloom. Borrowing. 2010. (Money Smart Ser.). 64p. (gr. 4). 32.79 *(978-1-60870-122-3(0))* Marshall Cavendish Corp.

—Investing. 2010. (Money Smart Ser.). 64p. (gr. 4). 32.79 *(978-1-60870-124-7(7))* Marshall Cavendish Corp.

—Spending. 2010. (Money Smart Ser.). 64p. (gr. 4). 32.79 *(978-1-60870-126-1(3))* Marshall Cavendish Corp.

Gagne, Tammy. A Dividend Stock Strategy for Teens. 2013. (Illus.). 48p. (gr. 4-8). lib. bdg. 29.95 *(978-1-61228-426-2(4))* Mitchell Lane Pubs., Inc.

—Investment Options for Teens. 2013. (ENG., Illus.). 48p. (gr. 4-8). lib. bdg. 29.95 *(978-1-61228-540-5(6))* Mitchell Lane Pubs., Inc.

—A Teen Guide to Buying Bonds. 2013. (ENG., Illus.). 48p. (gr. 4-8). lib. bdg. 29.95 *(978-1-61228-424-8(8))* Mitchell Lane Pubs., Inc.

—Teen Guide to Earning Income. 2014. (ENG., Illus.). 48p. (gr. 4-6). lib. bdg. 29.95 *(978-1-61228-470-5(1))* Mitchell Lane Pubs., Inc.

—A Teen Guide to Safe-Haven Savings. 2013. (Illus.). 48p. (gr. 4-8). lib. bdg. 29.95 *(978-1-61228-428-6(0))* Mitchell Lane Pubs., Inc.

—Teen Guide to Saving & Investing. 2014. (Illus.). 48p. (gr. 4-8). lib. bdg. 29.95 *(978-1-61228-471-2(X))* Mitchell Lane Pubs., Inc.

Gale, ed. U-X-L Money: Making Sense of Economics & Personal Finance, Teacher's Guide. 2015. (U-X-L Money Ser.). (ENG.). 5.00 *(978-1-4103-3437-4(6)*, UXL) Cengage Gale.

Garbus, Julia. UXL Money: Making Sense of Economics & Personal Finance. 2015. (Illus.). (J). *(978-1-57302-980-3(7))* Cengage Gale.

Garman, E. Thomas & Forgue, Raymond E. Personal Finance Handbook: A Guide to Securing Your Financial Future. 9th ed. 2003. (ENG.). 128p. (C). pap. 24.95 *(978-0-618-37231-7(8)*, 345462) Cengage South-Western.

Gerber, Larry. Top 10 Tips for Developing Money Management Skills. 2012. (Tips for Success Ser.). (ENG., Illus.). 64p. (J). (gr. 7-12). 31.95 *(978-1-4488-6862-9(9))* Rosen Publishing Group, Inc., The.

Gordon, Sherri Mabry. Be Smart about Money: Money Management & Budgeting. 2014. (Be Smart about Money & Financial Literacy Ser.). 48p. (J). lib. bdg. 22.60 *(978-0-7660-4292-6(8))* Enslow Pubs., Inc.

Graham, Amy. Be Smart about Your Career: College, Income, & Careers. 2014. (Be Smart about Money & Financial Literacy Ser.). 48p. (J). lib. bdg. 22.60 *(978-0-7660-4286-5(3))* Enslow Pubs., Inc.

Green, Meg. Everything You Need to Know about Credit Cards & Fiscal Responsibility. 2009. (Need to Know Library). 64p. (gr. 5-5). 58.50 *(978-1-60854-060-0(X))* Rosen Publishing Group, Inc., The.

Guy, Pauline. Let's Count. 2004. 24p. (J). (gr. -1). 15.99 *(978-0-9744205-6-1(5))* Golden Eagle Publishing Hse., Inc.

Hall, Alvin. Show Me the Money. 2016. (Big Questions Ser.). (ENG., Illus.). 96p. (J). (gr. 3-7). pap. 9.99 *(978-1-4654-4000-6(3)*, DK Children) Dorling Kindersley Publishing, Inc.

Hansen, Mark & Ferber, Kevin S. Success 101 for Teens: Dollars & Sense for a Winning Financial Life. 2012. (ENG.). 176p. pap. 12.95 *(978-1-55778-901-3(0)*, 4580c8ac-14b2-4d64-ae8a-be308d9302c6) Paragon Hse. Pubs.

Harmon, Daniel E. First Job Smarts. 2009. (J). 77.70 *(978-1-4358-5543-4(4))*; pap. 12.95 *(978-1-4358-5542-7(6))*; (Illus.). 64p. (gr. 7-12). lib. bdg. 31.95 *(978-1-4358-5268-6(0))* Rosen Publishing Group, Inc., The.

Heckman, Philip. Saving Money. 2005. (How Economics Works). (ENG., Illus.). 48p. (gr. 4-6). lib. bdg. 25.26 *(978-0-8225-2664-3(6)*, Lerner Pubns.) Lerner Publishing Group.

Hendricks, Tim. The Mentor: The True Story of an Hourly Factory Employee who Became Financially Independent. 2005. 240p. per. 16.99 *(978-1-933215-09-9(7))* Music City Publishing.

Hill, Christina. Georgia: Money & Me. 2016. (Primary Source Readers Ser.). 32p. (gr. 2-2). 8.99 *(978-1-4938-2562-2(3))* Teacher Created Materials, Inc.

Hill, Mary. Spending & Saving. 2005. (Welcome Bks.). (ENG., Illus.). 24p. (J). (gr. -1-2). 19.00 *(978-0-516-25059-5(0)*, Children's Pr.) Scholastic Library Publishing.

Hollander, Barbara. Top 10 Secrets for Investing Successfully. 2013. (Student's Guide to Financial Empowerment Ser.). (Illus.). 64p. (YA). (gr. 7-12). pap. 12.95 *(978-1-4488-9371-3(2))* Rosen Publishing Group, Inc., The.

—Top 10 Secrets for Spending Your Money Wisely. 2013. (Student's Guide to Financial Empowerment Ser.). (Illus.). 64p. (YA). (gr. 7-12). pap. 77.70 *(978-1-4488-9381-2(X))*; pap. 12.95 *(978-1-4488-9380-5(1))* Rosen Publishing Group, Inc., The.

Hollander, Barbara & Gottfried Hollander, Barbara. Top 10 Secrets for Investing Successfully. 2013. (Illus.). 64p. (YA). (gr. 7-12). 31.95 *(978-1-4488-9357-7(7))* Rosen Publishing Group, Inc., The.

—Top 10 Secrets for Spending Your Money Wisely. 2013. (Illus.). 64p. (YA). (gr. 7-12). 31.95 *(978-1-4488-9361-4(5))* Rosen Publishing Group, Inc., The.

Houghton, Gillian. Creating a Budget. 2009. (Invest Kids Ser.). 24p. (gr. 2-5). (ENG., Illus.). (J). pap. 8.25 *(978-1-4358-3209-1(4))*; 42.50 *(978-1-61513-614-8(2))*; (Illus.). (J). lib. bdg. 22.60 *(978-1-4358-2774-5(0))* Rosen Publishing Group, Inc., The. (PowerKids Pr.).

Ink, Oliver. My Allowance. 2013. (InfoMax Readers Ser.). (ENG.). 24p. (J). (gr. 3-4). pap. 49.50 *(978-1-4777-2525-2(3))*; (Illus.). pap. 8.25 *(978-1-4777-2524-5(5))* Rosen Publishing Group, Inc., The. (Rosen Classroom).

Israel-Clark, Anani. 7 Spiritual Laws of Money. 2007. 108p. per. 12.95 *(978-1-933912-06-6(5))* Westview Publishing Co., Inc.

Jaffe, Max. My Money, Myself: Lessons on Keeping More of What You Make. 2003. (Illus.). 128p. (YA). pap. 12.95 *(978-0-9729732-0-5(6))* Spending Solutions Pr.

Kamberg, Mary-Lane. Frequently Asked Questions about Financial Literacy. 2011. (FAQ: Teen Life Ser.). (ENG.). 64p. (YA). lib. bdg. 31.95 *(978-1-4488-1327-8(1))* Rosen Publishing Group, Inc., The.

Keller, Ellen & Schifini, Alfredo. Kids Manage Money. 2007. (Rise & Shine Ser.). (ENG., Illus.). 32p. (J). pap. 17.95 *(978-0-7922-8694-3(4))* CENGAGE Learning.

Kemper, Bitsy. Budgeting, Spending & Saving. 2015. (Searchlight Books (tm) — How Do We Use Money? Ser.). (ENG., Illus.). 40p. (J). (gr. 3-5). pap. 8.99 *(978-1-4677-6105-5(2))*; lib. bdg. 27.99 *(978-1-4677-5228-2(2))* Lerner Publishing Group. (Lerner Pubns.).

—Budgeting, Spending, & Saving. 2015. (Searchlight Books (tm) — How Do We Use Money? Ser.). (ENG., Illus.). 40p. (gr. 3-5). 39.99 *(978-1-4677-8914-1(3)*, Lerner Digital) Lerner Publishing Group.

—Growing Your Money. 2015. (Searchlight Books (tm) — How Do We Use Money? Ser.). (ENG., Illus.). 40p. (gr. 3-5). 39.99 *(978-1-4677-8916-5(X)*, Lerner Digital); (J). pap. 8.99 *(978-1-4677-6108-6(7)*, Lerner Pubns.); (J). lib. bdg. 27.99 *(978-1-4677-5230-5(4)*, Lerner Pubns.) Lerner Publishing Group.

Kiyosaki, Robert. Wisdom from Rich Dad, Poor Dad for Teens: The Secrets about Money — That You Don't Learn in School! 2016. (Miniature Editions Ser.). (ENG.). 128p. (YA). (gr. 8-17). 5.95 *(978-0-7624-6100-4(4)*, Running Pr. Minature Editions) Running Pr. Bk. Pubs.

Kiyosaki, Robert T. Rich Dad Poor Dad for Teens. 2011. 14.44 *(978-0-7848-3384-1(2)*, Everbind) Marco Bk. Co.

—Rich Dad's Escape from the Rat Race: How to Become a Rich Kid by Following Rich Dad's Advice. 2013. (ENG.). 64p. (J). pap. 12.95 *(978-1-61268-055-2(0))* Plata Publishing.

Kiyosaki, Robert T. & Lechter, Sharon L. Rich Dad's Escape from the Rat Race: How to Become a Rich Kid by Following Rich Dad's Advice. Hoseley, Rantz, illus. 2005. (ENG.). 64p. (J). (gr. 3-7). pap. 9.99 *(978-0-316-00047-5(7))* Little, Brown Bks. for Young Readers.

—The Secrets about Money: That You Don't Learn in School! 2004. (ENG.). 160p. (J). (gr. 7-17). pap. 14.99 *(978-0-446-69321-9(9))* Little, Brown Bks. for Young Readers.

Kjelle, Marylou Morano. A Teen Guide to Buying Mutual Funds. 2013. (Illus.). 48p. (gr. 4-8). lib. bdg. 29.95 *(978-1-61228-427-9(2))* Mitchell Lane Pubs., Inc.

Kowalski, Kathiann M. Be Smart about Credit: Credit & Debt Management. 2014. (Be Smart about Money & Financial Literacy Ser.). 48p. (J). lib. bdg. 22.60 *(978-0-7660-4282-7(0))* Enslow Pubs., Inc.

—Be Smart about Investing: Planning, Saving, & the Stock Market. 2014. (Be Smart about Money & Financial Literacy Ser.). 48p. (J). lib. bdg. 22.60 *(978-0-7660-4281-0(2))* Enslow Pubs., Inc.

Kulp, Donald. Money Puppies: America's #1 Money Management Book for Kids. 2010. 36p. pap. 14.99 *(978-1-4490-8977-1(1))* AuthorHouse.

La Bella, Laura. How Consumer Credit & Debt Work. 2012. (Real World Economics Ser.). (ENG., Illus.). 80p. (J). (gr. 7-12). 33.25 *(978-1-4488-6785-1(1))* Rosen Publishing Group, Inc., The.

Larson, Jennifer S. Do I Need It? or Do I Want It? Making Budget Choices. 2010. (Lightning Bolt Books — Exploring Economics Ser.). (ENG., Illus.). 32p. (gr. k-2). pap. 7.95 *(978-0-7613-5664-6(9))*; lib. bdg. 26.60 *(978-0-7613-3914-4(0))* Lerner Publishing Group.

Lawrence, Lane & Ridgway, Tom. Buying Goods & Services. 2011. (J). 77.70 *(978-1-4488-4751-8(6)*, Rosen Reference); (J). pap. 12.95 *(978-1-4488-4719-8(2)*, Rosen Reference); (YA). (gr. 5-9). lib. bdg. 31.95 *(978-1-4488-4715-0(X))* Rosen Publishing Group, Inc., The.

Linde, Barbara. Managing Your Money: Understanding Math Operations Involving Decimals & Integers. 2009. (PowerMath: Advanced Proficiency Plus Ser.). 32p. (gr. 5-5). 47.90 *(978-1-60851-361-1(0)*, PowerKids Pr.) Rosen Publishing Group, Inc., The.

Linde, Barbara M. Managing Your Money: Understanding Math Operations Involving Decimals & Integers. (Math for the Real World Ser.). (Illus.). 32p. 2009. (ENG.). (gr. 6-7). pap. 10.00 *(978-1-4042-6091-7(9))* 2006. (YA). (gr. 5-9). lib. bdg. 25.25 *(978-1-4042-3369-0(5))* Rosen Publishing Group, Inc., The.

Lindeen, Mary. Saving Money. 2015. (BeginningtoRead Ser.). (ENG.). 32p. (J). (gr. k-2). lib. bdg. 22.60 *(978-1-59953-699-6(4))*; (Illus.). pap. 11.94 *(978-1-60357-759-5(9))* Norwood Hse. Pr.

Llewellyn, Claire. Saving My Money. Gordon, Mike, illus. 2016. (Your Money Ser.). 00024p. (J). (gr. 1-1). pap. 8.25 *(978-1-4994-8194-5(2)*, Windmill Bks.) Rosen Publishing Group, Inc., The.

—Spending My Money. Gordon, Mike, illus. 2016. (Your Money Ser.). 00024p. (J). (gr. 1-1). pap. 8.25 *(978-1-4994-8197-6(7)*, Windmill Bks.) Rosen Publishing Group, Inc., The.

—What Is Money? Gordon, Mike, illus. 2016. (Your Money Ser.). 00024p. (J). (gr. 1-1). pap. 8.25 *(978-1-4994-8200-3(0)*, Windmill Bks.) Rosen Publishing Group, Inc., The.

Loewen, Nancy. Save, Spend, or Donate? A Book about Managing Money. Fitzpatrick, Brad & Jensen, Brian, illus. 2005. (Money Matters Ser.). (ENG.). 24p. (gr. 1-3). 25.99 *(978-1-4048-0952-9(X)*, Nonfiction Picture Bks.) Picture Window Bks.

Lynette, Rachel. Let's Work It Out: What to Do When Your Family Has to Cut Costs. 2010. (Let's Work It Out Ser.). (ENG.). 24p. (J). pap. 8.25 *(978-1-4358-9768-7(4)*, PowerKids Pr.) Rosen Publishing Group, Inc., The.

—What to Do When Your Family Has to Cut Costs. 2010. (Let's Work It Out Ser.). (Illus.). 24p. (J). (gr. 2-5). lib. bdg. 22.60 *(978-1-4358-9340-5(9))* Rosen Publishing Group, Inc., The.

MacKenzie, Catherine. George Müller: Does Money Grow on Trees? 2012. (Little Lights Ser.). (ENG., Illus.). 24p. (J). (gr. -1-3). 7.99 *(978-1-84550-110-5(1)*, af11d222-af25-41e4-93d0-1d014d537a0d) Christian Focus Pubns. GBR. Dist: Bookmasters Distribution.

Make Money Now! 2013. (Make Money Now! Ser.). 80p. (YA). (gr. 7-12). 232.75 *(978-1-4488-9396-6(8))* Rosen Publishing Group, Inc., The.

Maloof, Torrey. Money Matters: What's It Worth? Financial Literacy (Grade 3) 2017. (Mathematics Readers Ser.). (Illus.). 32p. (gr. 3-3). 8.99 ***(978-1-4807-5806-3(X))*** Teacher Created Materials, Inc.

Marsico, Katie. Investing: Making Your Money Work for You. 2015. (21st Century Skills Library: Real World Math Ser.). (ENG., Illus.). 32p. (J). (gr. 4-7). 29.93 *(978-1-63362-571-6(0)*, 206468) Cherry Lake Publishing.

—Understanding Taxes. 2015. (21st Century Skills Library: Real World Math Ser.). (ENG., Illus.). 32p. (J). (gr. 4-7). 29.93 *(978-1-63362-577-8(X)*, 206492) Cherry Lake Publishing.

—Using Credit Wisely. 2015. (21st Century Skills Library: Real World Math Ser.). (ENG., Illus.). 32p. (J). (gr. 4-7). 29.93 *(978-1-63362-578-5(8)*, 206496) Cherry Lake Publishing.

—What Is Money? 2015. (21st Century Skills Library: Real World Math Ser.). (ENG., Illus.). 32p. (J). (gr. 4-7). 29.93 *(978-1-63362-579-2(6)*, 206500) Cherry Lake Publishing.

Matheson, Murdoch H. Building Wealth for Teens: Answers to Questions Teens Care About. 2007. 116p. 24.65 *(978-1-4251-2358-1(9))* Trafford Publishing.

Maybury, Richard J. Uncle Eric Talks about Personal, Career, & Financial Security. Williams, Jane A. & Daniels, Kathryn, eds. 2nd ed. 2004. ("Uncle Eric" Bk.: 1). (ENG., Illus.). 187p. pap. 14.95 *(978-0-942617-38-2(X))* Bluestocking Pr.

McGillian, Jamie Kyle. The Kids' Money Book. Phillips, Ian, illus. 2006. 96p. (J). (gr. 4-8). reprint ed. 18.00 *(978-0-7567-9900-7(7))* DIANE Publishing Co.

—The Kids' Money Book: Earning, Saving, Spending, Investing, Donating. 2016. (ENG., Illus.). 112p. (J). (gr. 3-7). pap. 7.95 *(978-1-4549-1977-3(9))* Sterling Publishing Co., Inc.

McGuire, Kara. Cover Your Assets: The Teens' Guide to Protecting Their Money, Their Stuff, & Themselves, 1 vol. 2014. (Financial Literacy for Teens Ser.). (ENG.). 64p. (gr. 6-7). lib. bdg. 33.99 *(978-0-7565-4921-3(3))* Compass Point Bks.

—Financial Literacy for Teens, 1 vol. 2014. (Financial Literacy for Teens Ser.). (ENG.). 64p. (gr. 6-7). 135.96 *(978-0-7565-4924-4(8)*, CPB Grades 4-8) Compass Point Bks.

—Making Money Work: A Teen's Guide to Saving, Investing, & Building Wealth, 1 vol. 2014. (Financial Literacy for Teens Ser.). (ENG.). 64p. (gr. 6-7). lib. bdg. 33.99 *(978-0-7565-4922-0(1)*, CPB Grades 4-8) Compass Point Bks.

—Smart Spending: The Teens' Guide to Cash, Credit, & Life's Costs, 1 vol. 2014. (Financial Literacy for Teens Ser.). (ENG.). 64p. (gr. 6-7). lib. bdg. 33.99 *(978-0-7565-4923-7(X)*, CPB Grades 4-8) Compass Point Bks.

—The Teen Money Manual: A Guide to Cash, Credit, Spending, Saving, Work, Wealth, & More, 1 vol. 2014. (ENG., Illus.). 208p. (gr. 6-7). pap. 9.95 *(978-1-62370-135-2(X))* Capstone Young Readers of Coughlan Cos.

Mckenna, James & Glista, Jeannine. How to Turn $100 Into $1,000,000: Earn! Invest! Save! 2016. lib. bdg. 24.45 *(978-0-606-37953-3(3))* Turtleback Bks.

McKenna, James, et al. How to Turn $100 Into $1,000,000: A Kid's Guide to Earning, Saving, & Investing. 2016. (ENG., Illus.). 144p. (J). (gr. 4-8). pap. 12.95 *(978-0-7611-8080-7(X))* Workman Publishing Co., Inc.

McManus, Madelyn. Britney Makes a Budget. 2013. (Rosen Readers Ser.). (ENG.). 24p. (J). (gr. 3-4). pap. 8.25 *(978-1-4777-2528-3(8))*; pap. 49.50 *(978-1-4777-2529-0(6))* Rosen Publishing Group, Inc., The. (Rosen Classroom).

Meachen Rau, Dana. Gastando el dinero (Spending Money) 2010. (Dinero y los Bancos (Money & Banks) Ser.). (SPA., Illus.). 24p. (gr. 2-5). pap. 8.15 *(978-1-4339-3724-8(7))* Stevens, Gareth Publishing LLLP.

—Saving Money. 2010. (Money & Banks Ser.). (Illus.). 24p. (gr. 2-5). pap. 8.15 *(978-1-4339-3387-5(X))* Stevens, Gareth Publishing LLLP.

—Spending Money. 2010. (Money & Banks Ser.). (Illus.). 24p. (gr. 2-5). pap. 8.15 (978-1-4339-3390-5(X)) Stevens, Gareth Publishing LLLP.

Minden, Cecilia. Giving Back. 2009. (21st Century Skills Library: Real World Math Ser.). (ENG.). 32p. (gr. 4-8). lib. bdg. 28.50 (978-1-60279-314-9(X), 200210) Cherry Lake Publishing.

—Investing: Making Your Money Work for You. 2007. (21st Century Skills Library: Real World Math Ser.). (ENG., Illus.). 32p. (gr. 4-8). lib. bdg. 28.50 (978-1-60279-003-2(5), 200069) Cherry Lake Publishing.

—Living on a Budget. (21st Century Skills Library: Real World Math Ser.). (ENG., Illus.). 32p. (gr. 4-7). 2015. (J). 29.93 (978-1-63362-572-3(9), 206472) 2007. lib. bdg. 28.50 (978-1-60279-004-9(3), 200070) Cherry Lake Publishing.

—Payday! 2007. (21st Century Skills Library: Real World Math Ser.). (ENG., Illus.). 32p. (gr. 4-8). lib. bdg. 28.50 (978-1-60279-000-1(0), 200071) Cherry Lake Publishing.

—Saving for the Future. (21st Century Skills Library: Real World Math Ser.). (ENG., Illus.). 32p. (gr. 4-7). 2015. (J). 29.93 (978-1-63362-574-7(5), 206480) 2007. lib. bdg. 28.50 (978-1-60279-001-8(9), 200072) Cherry Lake Publishing.

—Smart Shopping. 2015. (21st Century Skills Library: Real World Math Ser.). (ENG., Illus.). 32p. (J). (gr. 4-7). 29.93 (978-1-63362-575-4(3), 206484) Cherry Lake Publishing.

—Using Credit Wisely. 2007. (21st Century Skills Library: Real World Math Ser.). (ENG., Illus.). 32p. (gr. 4-8). lib. bdg. 28.50 (978-1-60279-002-5(7), 200074) Cherry Lake Publishing.

Money Matters: A Kid's Guide to Money, 6 vols., Set. 2010. (J). (gr. 3-6). lib. bdg. 179.70 (978-1-58415-835-6(2)) Mitchell Lane Pubs., Inc.

Monroe Peterson, Judy. Smart Strategies for Investing Wisely & Successfully. 2014. (Financial Security & Life Success for Teens Ser.). 80p. (J). (gr. 7-12). pap. 84.90 (978-1-4777-7621-6(4)) Rosen Publishing Group, Inc., The.

Monteverde, Matt. Frequently Asked Questions about Budgeting & Money Management. 2009. (FAQ: Teen Life Ser.). 64p. (gr. 5-6). 58.50 (978-1-61512-569-2(8)) Rosen Publishing Group, Inc., The.

Monteverde, Matthew. Frequently Asked Questions about Budgeting & Money Management. 2008. (FAQ: Teen Life Ser.). (Illus.). 64p. (YA). (gr. 7-12). lib. bdg. 31.95 (978-1-4042-1804-8(1)) Rosen Publishing Group, Inc., The.

Mototsune, Kat. Money: Deal with It or Pay the Price, 1 vol. Geoffroi, Remie, illus. 2007. (Lorimer Deal with It Ser.). (ENG.). 32p. (J). (gr. 4-6). pap. 12.95 (978-1-55028-958-9(6), 9781550289589) Lorimer, James & Co., Ltd., Pubs. CAN. Dist: Casemate Pubs. & Bk. Distributors, LLC.

Murphy, Stuart J. Less Than Zero. Remkiewicz, Frank, illus. 2003. (MathStart 3 Ser.: Vol. 49). (ENG.). 40p. (J). (gr. 2-18). pap. 5.99 (978-0-06-000126-1(7)) HarperCollins Pubs.

—Less Than Zero. 2003. (MathStart Level 3 Ser.). (J). (gr. k-3). lib. bdg. 16.00 (978-0-613-68443-9(5), Turtleback) Turtleback Bks.

My Money, 6 vols., Set. 2006. (My Money Ser.). (ENG., Illus.). 24p. (gr. 4-6). 122.60 (978-0-7565-1699-4(4)) Compass Point Bks.

North, Charles & Caes, Charles J. The Stock Market. 2011. (J). 77.70 (978-1-4488-4755-6(9)); (J). pap. 12.95 (978-1-4488-4723-5(0)); (YA). (gr. 5-9). lib. bdg. 31.95 (978-1-4488-4717-4(6)) Rosen Publishing Group, Inc., The.

O'Neal, Claire. A Teen Guide to Buying Stocks. 2013. (ENG., Illus.). 48p. (gr. 4-8). lib. bdg. 29.95 (978-1-61228-425-5(6)) Mitchell Lane Pubs., Inc.

Orr, Tamra. Budgeting Tips for Kids. 2008. (Money Matters Ser.). (Illus.). 48p. (YA). (gr. 3-6). lib. bdg. 29.95 (978-1-58415-644-4(9)) Mitchell Lane Pubs., Inc.

—A Kid's Guide to Earning Money. 2008. (Money Matters Ser.). (Illus.). 48p. (YA). (gr. 3-6). lib. bdg. 29.95 (978-1-58415-643-7(0)) Mitchell Lane Pubs., Inc.

—Money Matters: A Kid's Guide to Money, 5 vols., Set. Incl. Budgeting Tips for Kids. lib. bdg. 29.95 (978-1-58415-644-4(9)); Coins & Other Currency. lib. bdg. 29.95 (978-1-58415-640-6(6)); Kid's Guide to Earning Money. lib. bdg. 29.95 (978-1-58415-643-7(0)); Kid's Guide to Stock Market Investing. lib. bdg. 29.95 (978-1-58415-642-0(2)); Savings Tips for Kids. lib. bdg. 29.95 (978-1-58415-641-3(4)); (Illus.). 48p. (YA). (gr. 3-6). 2008. 2008. Set lib. bdg. 149.75 (978-1-58415-645-1(7)) Mitchell Lane Pubs., Inc.

—Savings Tips for Kids. 2008. (Money Matters Ser.). (Illus.). 48p. (YA). (gr. 3-6). lib. bdg. 29.95 (978-1-58415-641-3(4)) Mitchell Lane Pubs., Inc.

Pellegrini, Mary Ellen. Managing Money: Spending & Saving Wisely. 2007. (J). pap. (978-1-58760-040-1(4)) Child Welfare League of America, Inc.

Pellittiere II, Michael. GROW MONEY - A Kid's Guide to Saving & Investing. 2007. 60p. (YA). pap. 10.40 (978-0-615-14589-1(2)) Dakota Assocs., Inc.

—GROW MONEY II - A Teenager's Guide to Saving & Investing. 2008. 118p. (YA). pap. 11.42 (978-0-615-18343-5(3)) Dakota Assocs., Inc.

The Penny Project. 2005. (YA). (978-0-88441-693-7(3)) Girl Scouts of the USA.

Peterson, Judy Monroe. First Budget Smarts. 2009. (J). 77.70 (978-1-4358-5553-3(1)); pap. 12.95 (978-1-4358-5552-6(3)); (Illus.). 64p. (gr. 7-12). lib. bdg. 31.95 (978-1-4358-5273-0(7)) Rosen Publishing Group, Inc., The.

Prindle, Twyla. Can I Have Some Money Please? Hansen, Lorie Miller, illus. 2005. (J). (gr. -1-3). 14.95 (978-0-9759527-3-3(0), Prindle House Publishing Co.) Prindle Hse. Publishing Co.

—Where Is My Money? Jennings, Randy, illus. 2007. (J). bds. 14.95 (978-0-9759527-8-8(1), 1000, Prindle House Publishing Co.) Prindle Hse. Publishing Co.

Ramsey, Dave. The Super Red Racer: Junior Discovers Work. 2003. (Illus.). 26p. (J). 7.95 (978-0-9726323-0-0(1)) Ramsey Pr.

Randolph, Ryan. How to Spend Smart. 2013. (Smart Kid's Guide to Personal Finance Ser.). (ENG., Illus.). 24p. (J). (gr. 3-6). lib. bdg. 22.60 (978-1-4777-0746-3(8), PowerKids Pr.) Rosen Publishing Group, Inc., The.

Randolph, Ryan P. How to Earn Money. 2013. (Smart Kid's Guide to Personal Finance Ser.). 24p. (J). (gr. 3-6). 22.60 (978-1-4777-0741-8(7)); pap. 8.25 (978-1-4777-0823-1(5)); pap. 49.50 (978-1-4777-0824-8(3)) Rosen Publishing Group, Inc., The. (PowerKids Pr.).

—How to Make a Budget. 2013. (Smart Kid's Guide to Personal Finance Ser.). 24p. (J). (gr. 3-6). pap. 49.50 (978-1-4777-0828-6(6)); (ENG., Illus.). pap. 8.25 (978-1-4777-0827-9(8)); (ENG., Illus.). lib. bdg. 22.60 (978-1-4777-0743-2(3)) Rosen Publishing Group, Inc., The. (PowerKids Pr.).

—How to Manage Risk. 2013. (Smart Kid's Guide to Personal Finance Ser.). 24p. (J). (gr. 3-6). 22.60 (978-1-4777-0745-6(X)); pap. 49.50 (978-1-4777-0832-3(4)); pap. 8.25 (978-1-4777-0831-6(6)) Rosen Publishing Group, Inc., The. (PowerKids Pr.).

—How to Spend Smart. 2013. (Smart Kid's Guide to Personal Finance Ser.). 24p. (J). (gr. 3-6). pap. 49.50 (978-1-4777-0834-7(0)); pap. 8.25 (978-1-4777-0833-0(2)) Rosen Publishing Group, Inc., The. (PowerKids Pr.).

Rau, Dana Meachen. Gastar el Dinero. 2010. (Dinero y los Bancos Ser.). (SPA., Illus.). 24p. (J). (gr. 2-5). lib. bdg. 22.00 (978-1-4339-3723-1(9)) Stevens, Gareth Publishing LLLP.

—Saving Money. 2010. (Money & Banks Ser.). (Illus.). 24p. (J). (gr. 2-5). lib. bdg. 22.00 (978-1-4339-3386-8(1)) Stevens, Gareth Publishing LLLP.

—Spending Money. 2010. (Money & Banks Ser.). (Illus.). 24p. (J). (gr. 2-5). lib. bdg. 22.00 (978-1-4339-3389-9(6)) Stevens, Gareth Publishing LLLP.

Rauf, Don. Social Network-Powered Investing & Saving Opportunities. 2013. (Teen's Guide to the Power of Social Networking Ser.). 80p. (YA). (gr. 7-12). 33.25 (978-1-4777-1684-7(X)); pap. 14.15 (978-1-4777-1917-6(2)) Rosen Publishing Group, Inc., The.

Reina, Mary. Save Money. 2015. (Money & You Ser.). (ENG.). 24p. (gr. k-1). lib. bdg. 21.99 (978-1-4914-2083-6(9), Pebble Bks.) Capstone Press of Coughlan Cos.

Reynolds, Mattie. Kids Making Money: An Introduction to Financial Literacy. 2013. (Start Smart: Money Ser.). (Illus.). 24p. (gr. k-2). (J). lib. bdg. 17.95 net. (978-1-937529-41-3(X)); (ENG., pap. 5.95 (978-1-937529-37-6(1)) Red Chair Pr.

—Saving for the Future: An Introduction to Financial Literacy. 2013. (Start Smart: Money Ser.). (Illus.). 24p. (gr. k-2). (J). lib. bdg. 17.95 net. (978-1-937529-42-0(8)); (ENG., pap. 5.95 (978-1-937529-38-3(X)) Red Chair Pr.

—Sharing with Others: An Introduction to Financial Literacy. 2013. (Start Smart: Money Ser.). (Illus.). 24p. (J). (gr. k-2). (ENG.). pap. 5.95 (978-1-937529-40-6(1)); lib. bdg. 23.93 (978-1-937529-44-4(4)) Red Chair Pr.

—Super-Smart Shopping: An Introduction to Financial Literacy. 2013. (Start Smart: Money Ser.). (Illus.). 24p. (gr. k-2). (J). lib. bdg. 17.95 net. (978-1-937529-43-7(6)); (ENG., pap. 5.95 (978-1-937529-39-0(8)) Red Chair Pr.

Richter, Abigail. Money: Saving & Spending. 2008. (Real Readers - Upper Emergent Ser.). (ENG., Illus.). 12p. (gr. 1-2). pap. 5.90 (978-0-8239-8194-6(0)) Rosen Publishing Group, Inc., The.

Roderick, Stacey & Warwick, Ellen. Centsibility: The Planet Girl Guide to Money. Melnychuk, Monika, illus. 2008. (Planet Girl Ser.). (ENG.). 80p. (J). (gr. 5-9). 12.95 (978-1-55453-208-7(6)) Kids Can Pr., Ltd. CAN. Dist: Hachette Bk. Group.

Rumsch, BreAnn. Saving & Investing, 1 vol. 2012. (Economy in Action! Ser.). (ENG.). 32p. (J). (gr. 3-6). lib. bdg. 27.07 (978-1-61783-490-5(4), Checkerboard Library) ABDO Publishing Co.

Sapara, Jim. Money Freedom: Achieve the Millionaire Lifestyle of Your Dreams. 2004. per. 19.95 (978-0-9755681-1-8(6)) Quantum One Publishing.

Scheunemann, Pam. Cool Jobs for Handy Helpers: Ways to Make Money Doing Home Services, 1 vol. 2011. (Cool Kid Jobs Ser.). (ENG.). 32p. (gr. 3-6). 28.50 (978-1-61613-195-1(0), Checkerboard Library) ABDO Publishing Co.

—Cool Jobs for Kids Who Like Kids: Ways to Make Money Working with Children, 1 vol. 2011. (Cool Kid Jobs Ser.). (ENG.). 32p. (gr. 3-6). 28.50 (978-1-61613-196-8(9), Checkerboard Library) ABDO Publishing Co.

—Cool Jobs for Yard-Working Kids: Ways to Make Money Doing Yard Work, 1 vol. 2011. (Cool Kid Jobs Ser.). (ENG.). 32p. (gr. 3-6). 28.50 (978-1-61613-198-2(5), Checkerboard Library) ABDO Publishing Co.

—Cool Jobs for Young Entertainers: Ways to Make Money Putting on an Event, 1 vol. 2011. (Cool Kid Jobs Ser.). (ENG.). 32p. (gr. 3-6). 28.50 (978-1-61613-199-9(3), Checkerboard Library) ABDO Publishing Co.

—Cool Jobs for Young Pet Lovers: Ways to Make Money Caring for Pets, 1 vol. 2011. (Cool Kid Jobs Ser.). (ENG.). 32p. (gr. 3-6). 28.50 (978-1-61613-200-2(0), Checkerboard Library) ABDO Publishing Co.

Schuh, Mari. Saving Money. 2015. (Money Matters Ser.). (ENG., Illus.). 24p. (J). (gr. k-3). lib. bdg. 25.95 (978-1-62617-247-0(1), Blastoff! Readers) Bellwether Media.

—Spending Money. 2015. (Money Matters Ser.). (ENG., Illus.). 24p. (J). (gr. k-3). lib. bdg. 25.95 (978-1-62617-248-7(X), Blastoff! Readers) Bellwether Media.

Schwartz, Heather E. Bank Wisely. 2015. (Money Smarts Ser.). (ENG., Illus.). 32p. (J). (gr. 2-4). 19.95 (978-1-60753-792-2(3)) Amicus Publishing.

—Save Wisely. 2015. (Money Smarts Ser.). (ENG., Illus.). 32p. (J). (gr. 2-4). 19.95 (978-1-60753-794-6(X)) Amicus Publishing.

Seba, Jaime A. Smashing the Stereotypes: What Does It Mean to Be Gay, Lesbian, Bisexual, or Transgender? 2009. (Gallup's Guide to Modern Gay, Lesbian, & Transgender Lifestyle Ser.). 64p. (YA). (gr. 7-18). pap. 9.95 (978-1-4222-1874-7(0)) Mason Crest.

Shea, Therese. Top 10 Secrets for Managing Credit Cards & Paying Bills Successfully. 2013. (Student's Guide to Financial Empowerment Ser.). (ENG., Illus.). 64p. (YA). (gr. 7-12). pap. 12.95 (978-1-4488-9376-8(3)); lib. bdg. 31.95 (978-1-4488-9358-4(5)) Rosen Publishing Group, Inc., The. (Rosen Classroom).

Sieplinga, Drew. Paint Your Own Piggy Bank. 2007. (Illus.). 32p. (J). (978-0-545-02112-8(X)) Scholastic, Inc.

Simon, Les. How To: Have Money & Avoid & Dump Debt. 2004. (SPA.). 110p. (YA). pap. 10.00 (978-0-9761914-0-7(7)) Simon, Les.

Simons, Rae. A Guide to Teaching Young Adults about Money. 2010. (Junior Library of Money). 64p. (YA). (gr. 7-18). pap. 9.95 (978-1-4222-1884-6(8)); lib. bdg. 22.95 (978-1-4222-1765-8(5)) Mason Crest.

—Spending Money. 2010. (Junior Library of Money). 64p. (YA). (gr. 7-18). lib. bdg. 22.95 (978-1-4222-1770-2(1)) Mason Crest.

A Smart Kid's Guide to Personal Finance. 2013. (Smart Kid's Guide to Personal Finance Ser.). 24p. (J). (gr. 3-6). 135.60 (978-1-4777-1139-2(2)); pap. 297.00 (978-1-4777-1252-8(6)); pap. 49.50 (978-1-4777-1251-1(8)) Rosen Publishing Group, Inc., The. (PowerKids Pr.).

The SmartiPantz Money Organizer Child Workbook. 2004. (J). spiral bd. (978-0-9747563-0-1(X)) SmartiPantz Publishing.

Social Network-Powered Investing & Saving Opportunities. 2013. (Teen's Guide to the Power of Social Networking Ser.). 80p. (YA). (gr. 7-12). pap. 84.90 (978-1-4777-1918-3(0)) Rosen Publishing Group, Inc., The.

Spath, Carolyn E. W. Making a Budget. 2015. (J). lib. bdg. (978-1-62713-389-0(5)) Cavendish Square Publishing.

St. Germain, Mark. Tres Tazas. Willy, April, illus. 2010.Tr. of Three Cups. (SPA.). 24p. (J). (978-0-9794563-1-2(2)) Three Cups, LLC.

Stahl, Michael. Early to Rise: A Young Adult's Guide to Investing... & Financial Decisions That Can Shape Your Life. 2nd ed. 2005. 240p. 14.95 (978-1-56343-791-5(0)) Silver Lake Publishing.

Stefoff, Rebecca. Smart Spending. 2015. (J). lib. bdg. (978-1-62713-387-6(9)); (ENG., Illus.). 48p. (gr. 4-4). 31.36 (978-1-5026-0281-7(4)) Cavendish Square Publishing.

Sundance/Newbridge LLC Staff. Wants & Needs. 2004. (Reading PowerWorks Ser.). (gr. 1-3). 37.50 (978-0-7608-9819-2(7)); pap. 6.10 (978-0-7608-9820-8(0)) Sundance/Newbridge Educational Publishing.

Swanson, Jennifer A. Top 10 Secrets for Saving Successfully. 2013. (Student's Guide to Financial Empowerment Ser.). 64p. (YA). (gr. 7-12). 31.95 (978-1-4488-9356-0(9)); pap. 77.70 (978-1-4488-9379-9(8)); (ENG., Illus.). pap. 12.95 (978-1-4488-9378-2(X), Rosen Classroom) Rosen Publishing Group, Inc., The.

Symonds, Doris. How I Saved $10,500 with Only 4 Quarters a Day. 2003. (YA). spiral bd. 14.95 (978-0-9741182-0-8(6), 2500) TALK.

Thomas, Keltie. The Kids Guide to Money Cent$ MacEachern, Stephen, tr. MacEachern, Stephen, illus. 2004. (ENG.). 56p. (J). 8.95 (978-1-55337-391-9(X)); (gr. 4-6). 8.95 (978-1-55337-390-2(1)) Kids Can Pr., Ltd. CAN. Dist: Hachette Bk. Group.

Thompson, Helen. Banking Math. 2013. (Math 24/7 Ser.: 10). 48p. (J). (gr. 5-18). 19.95 (978-1-4222-2902-6(5)) Mason Crest.

—Cost of Living. 2010. (Junior Library of Money). 64p. (YA). (gr. 7-18). lib. bdg. 22.95 (978-1-4222-1762-7(0)) Mason Crest.

—Investing Money. 2010. (Junior Library of Money). 64p. (YA). (gr. 7-18). pap. 9.95 (978-1-4222-1885-3(6)); lib. bdg. 22.95 (978-1-4222-1766-5(3)) Mason Crest.

Thornton, J. D. How to Make Money. 2006. (Illus.). 92p. (J). pap. (978-0-545-07195-6(X)) Scholastic, Inc.

Thouin, Juanita. Get Your Wallet On: The Money Quiz for High School Grads. 2003. 97p. (YA). per. 6.49 (978-0-9740641-0-9(6)) Daisy Publishing.

Titus, Julia. Claudia's Pink Piggy Bank: Saving. 2013. (ENG.). 25p. (J). pap. 12.95 (978-1-4787-1459-0(X)) Outskirts Pr., Inc.

Top 10 Secrets for Managing Credit Cards & Paying Bills Successfully. 2013. (Student's Guide to Financial Empowerment Ser.). 64p. (YA). (gr. 7-12). pap. 77.70 (978-1-4488-9377-5(1)) Rosen Publishing Group, Inc., The.

U X L, ed. UXL Money, Banking & Trading, 3 vols. 2015. (ENG., Illus.). (J). 286.00 (978-1-57302-979-7(3), UXL) Cengage Gale.

UC Publishing Staff & Murphy, Sally. Action Numeracy: Who Wants to be a Millionaire? 2008. (Action Numeracy Upper Primary Ser.). 32p. pap. 9.95 (978-0-86431-791-9(3)) ACER Pr. AUS. Dist: ISBS Publisher Services.

Vickers, Rebecca. 101 Ways to Be Smart about Money. 2011. (101 Ser.). (ENG.). 56p. (gr. 5-9). pap. 9.95 (978-1-4109-4382-8(8), NA-r) Heinemann-Raintree.

Weston Woods Staff, creator. If You Made a Million. 2011. 38.75 (978-0-439-84579-3(3)) Weston Woods Studios, Inc.

Whitehead, William. Family Money. Beech, Mark, illus. 2015. (How Money Works). (ENG.). 64p. (J). (gr. 4-6). lib. bdg. 29.27 (978-1-59953-717-7(6)); pap. 15.93 **(978-1-68404-070-4(1))** Norwood Hse. Pr.

Williams, Anna Graf, et al. The Family Guide to the American Workplace. Williams, Anna Graf, ed. 2003. (Illus.). 272p. per. 31.00 (978-0-9705790-4-1(7), 866/332-5905) Learnovation, LLC.

FINANCE, PERSONAL—FICTION

Abbruzzi, Danielle. Penelope's Piggies. Sampson, Kathleen, illus. 2012. 42p. 24.95 (978-1-4626-6264-7(1)) America Star Bks.

Benton, Jim. Dumbness Is a Dish Best Served Cold. Benton, Jim, illus. 2016. (Dear Dumb Diary Ser.). (ENG., Illus.). 224p. (J). (gr. 3-7). 12.99 (978-0-545-93228-8(9), Scholastic Pr.) Scholastic, Inc.

D'Arruda, Kim. A Day to Play. 2007. (Illus.). 32p. (J). 14.95 (978-0-9777993-2-9(8)) Financial Safari Pr.

Dussling, Jennifer. Fair Is Fair! Palmisciano, Diane, illus. 2003. (Math Matters Ser.). (ENG.). 32p. (J). (gr. 1-3). pap. 5.95 (978-1-57565-131-6(9)) Kane Press, Inc.

—Lo Justo Es Justo; Fair Is Fair. 2008. pap. 34.95 (978-1-58013-785-0(7)) Kane Press, Inc.

Dussling, Jennifer A. Lo Justo Es Justo! Palmisciano, Diane, illus. 2008. (Math Matters en Espanol Ser.). (SPA.). 32p. (J). (gr. -1-3). pap. 5.95 (978-1-57565-269-6(2)) Kane Press, Inc.

Harris, Trudy. Jenny Found a Penny. Hovell, John, illus. 2007. (Math Is Fun! Ser.). (ENG.). 32p. (gr. k-3). lib. bdg. 23.93 (978-0-8225-6725-7(3), Millbrook Pr.) Lerner Publishing Group.

Hyde, Natalie. I Owe You One, 1 vol. 2011. (Orca Young Readers Ser.). (ENG.). 136p. (J). (gr. 3-6). pap. 7.95 (978-1-55469-414-3(0)) Orca Bk. Pubs. USA.

Nourigat, Paul. Debt Dangers: A Book in the Series Marvels of Money ... for Kids. Nourigat, Natalie, illus. 2012. (Marvels of Money for Kids Ser.: 4). (ENG.). 38p. (J). lib. bdg. 12.29 (978-1-936872-03-9(X)) FarBeyond Publishing LLC.

—Earning Excitement: a book in the series Marvels of Money ... for Kids. Nourigat, Natalie, illus. 2014. (Marvels of Money for Kids Ser.: 1). 38p. (J). pap. 9.29 (978-1-936872-21-3(8)) FarBeyond Publishing LLC.

—Earning Excitement: A Book in the Series Marvels of Money ... for Kids. Nourigat, Natalie, illus. l.t. ed. 2012. (Marvels of Money for Kids Ser.: 1). (ENG.). 38p. (J). 12.29 (978-1-936872-01-5(3)) FarBeyond Publishing LLC.

—Giving Greatness: A Book in the Series Marvels of Money ... for Kids. 2014. (Marvels of Money for Kids Ser.: 3). (Illus.). 38p. (J). pap. 9.29 (978-1-936872-24-4(2)) FarBeyond Publishing LLC.

—Giving Greatness: A Book in the Series Marvels of Money ... for Kids. Nourigat, Natalie, illus. 2012. (Marvels of Money for Kids Ser.: 3). (ENG.). 38p. (J). lib. bdg. 12.29 (978-1-936872-04-6(8)) FarBeyond Publishing LLC.

—Spending Success: A Book in the Series Marvels of Money ... for Kids. Nourigat, Natalie, illus. 2014. (Marvels of Money for Kids Ser.: 2). 38p. (J). pap. (978-1-936872-22-0(6)) FarBeyond Publishing LLC.

—Spending Success: A Book in the Series Marvels of Money for Kids. l.t. ed. 2012. (Marvels of Money for Kids Ser.: 2). (ENG., Illus.). 38p. (J). lib. bdg. 12.29 (978-1-936872-02-2(1)) FarBeyond Publishing LLC.

—Terrific Tools for Money: A Book in the Series Marvels of Money ... for Kids. 2014. (Marvels of Money for Kids Ser.: 5). (Illus.). 38p. (J). pap. 9.29 (978-1-936872-25-1(0)) FarBeyond Publishing LLC.

—Terrific Tools for Money: A Book in the Series Marvels of Money ... for Kids. Nourigat, Natalie, illus. 2012. (Marvels of Money for Kids Ser.: 5). (ENG.). 38p. (J). lib. bdg. 12.89 (978-1-936872-05-3(6)) FarBeyond Publishing LLC.

Reitz, Theresa, et al. The Money Tree: A Financial Book for Children. 2009. (Illus.). 52p. pap. 22.95 (978-1-4327-3653-8(1)) Outskirts Pr., Inc.

Rogers, Ramona. Buck & Penny. 2013. 26p. pap. 9.99 (978-0-9894748-9-4(5)) Mindstir Media.

Shinno, Stephanie. Syler & the Sandpaper Towel. Douglas, Vannick, illus. 2012. 32p. 24.95 (978-1-4626-6677-5(9)) America Star Bks.

Sparks, Candi. Max Gets It!, 4 vols. William, Graf, illus. 2008. (Can I Have Some Money? Ser.: Vol. 3). (ENG.). 32p. (J). pap. (978-0-9789445-1-3(8)) Sparks Fly.

—Of Course You Can! Educating Children about Money. Graf, William, illus. 2006. (Can I Have Some Money? Ser.). pap. 11.99 (978-0-9789445-0-6(X)) Sparks Fly.

Sparks, Candi & Sparks, Kelvin. Lemonade Sold Out: Can I Have Some Money? (No. 5) 2015. (Can I Have Some Money? Ser.: 5). (ENG., Illus.). 34p. (J). (gr. 1-8). pap. 12.98 (978-0-9789445-9-9(3)) Sparks Fly.

Sparks, Candi, et al. Nacho Money. Bill, Graf, illus. 2012. (Can I Have Some Money? Ser.). 36p. pap. 11.99 (978-0-9789445-6-8(9)) Sparks Fly.

FINANCE, PUBLIC

Catalano, Angela. Community Plans: Choices about Money Making in Communities. 2009. (Communities at Work Ser.). 24p. (gr. 2-2). 42.50 (978-1-61511-890-8(X), PowerKids Pr.) Rosen Publishing Group, Inc., The.

Ruffin, David C. The Duties & Responsibilities of the Secretary of the Treasury. (Your Government in Action Ser.). 32p. (gr. 3-3). 2009. 43.90 (978-1-60854-920-7(8)) 2005. (Illus.). (J). lib. bdg. 23.95 (978-1-4042-2690-6(7)) Rosen Publishing Group, Inc., The. (PowerKids Pr.).

Wiseman, Blaine. Budgeting. 2009. (Everyday Economics Ser.). (Illus.). 32p. (J). (gr. 4-6). pap. 9.95 (978-1-60596-644-1(4)); lib. bdg. 26.00 (978-1-60596-643-4(6)) Weigl Pubs., Inc.

FINANCE—UNITED STATES

Freedman, Jeri. The U.S. Auto Industry: American Carmakers & the Economic Crisis. 2010. (In the News Ser.). (ENG.). 64p. (YA). pap. 12.95 (978-1-4488-1680-4(7)); (gr. 7-12). lib. bdg. 31.95 (978-1-4358-9448-8(0)) Rosen Publishing Group, Inc., The.

Furgang, Kathy & Furgang, Adam. Understanding Budget Deficits & the National Debt. 2011. (Real World Economics Ser.). (ENG.). 80p. (YA). (gr. 7-12). lib. bdg. 33.25 (978-1-4488-5570-4(5)) Rosen Publishing Group, Inc., The.

Hocking, Justin. Taking Action: How to Get Your City to Build a Public Skate Park. 2009. (Skateboarder's Guide to Skate Parks, Half-Pipes, Bowls, & Obstacles Ser.). 48p. (gr. 5-8). 53.00 (978-1-60854-234-5(3), Rosen Reference) Rosen Publishing Group, Inc., The.

Hunnicutt, Susan C. The Federal Budget Deficit. 2010. (At Issue Ser.). (Illus.). 128p. 34.45 (978-0-7377-4685-3(8), Greenhaven Pr., Inc.) Cengage Gale.

Ruffin, David C. The Duties & Responsibilities of the Secretary of the Treasury. (Your Government in Action Ser.). 32p. (gr. 3-3). 2009. 43.90 (978-1-60854-920-7(8)) 2005. (Illus.). (J). lib. bdg. 23.95 (978-1-4042-2690-6(7)) Rosen Publishing Group, Inc., The. (PowerKids Pr.).

FINANCIERS

see Capitalists and Financiers

FINGER PAINTING

Deuchars, Marion. Let's Make Some Great Fingerprint Art. 2012. (ENG., Illus.). 128p. (J). (gr. 1-6). pap. 14.95 (978-1-78067-015-7(X)) King, Laurence Publishing GBR. Dist: Hachette Bk. Group.

Emberley, Ed. Ed Emberley's Fingerprint Drawing Book. Emberley, Ed, illus. 2005. (ENG., Illus.). 48p. (J). (gr. 2-17). pap., pap. 7.99 (978-0-316-78969-1(0)) Little, Brown Bks. for Young Readers.

Wilson, CeCe. Painting with My Fingers. 2015. (Rosen REAL Readers: STEM & STEAM Collection). (ENG.). 8p. pap. 5.46 (978-1-4994-9720-5(2), Rosen Classroom) Rosen Publishing Group, Inc., The.

FINGER PLAY

Astacio, Mrinali Alvarez, illus. Pon, Pon: A Jugar con el Bebé! 2007. (SPA.). 28p. 14.95 (978-0-8477-1575-6(2)) Univ. of Puerto Rico Pr.

Close, Laura Ferraro. Grey Squirrel. 2009. (Favorite Children's Songs Ser.). (ENG., Illus.). 16p. (J). (gr. -1-2). 25.64 (978-1-60253-189-5(7), 200102) Child's World, Inc., The.

Collier-Morales, Roberta. Where Is Thumbkin? 2009. (Favorite Children's Songs Ser.). (ENG., Illus.). 16p. (J). (gr. -1-2).

25.64 (978-1-60253-196-3(X), 200109) Child's World, Inc., The.

Delacre, Lulu, illus. & compiled by. Arrorro Mi Nino: Latino Lullabies & Gentle Games, 1 vol. Delacre, Lulu, compiled by. 2004. (ENG & SPA.). 32p. (J). 16.95 (978-1-58430-159-2(7)) Lee & Low Bks., Inc.

Dowell, Ruth I. Move over, Mother Goose! Finger Plays, Action Verses & Funny Rhymes. Charner, Kathleen, ed. Scott, Concetta C., illus. 2004. 126p. (Orig.). (gr. -1-1). pap. 12.95 (978-0-87659-113-0(6), 10006) Gryphon Hse., Inc.

Itsy Bitsy Spider. 2004. (J). per. (978-1-57657-427-0(X)) Paradise Pr., Inc.

Juego de Dedos. 2004. (SPA.). 12p. (J). (978-968-494-161-8(7)) Centro de Informacion y Desarrollo de la Comunicacion y la Literatura MEX. Dist: AIMS International Bks., Inc.

Kemp, Moira. Pat-a-Cake, Pat-a-Cake. Kemp, Moira, illus. 2009. (Favorite Children's Songs Ser.). (ENG., Illus.). 16p. (J). (gr. -1-2). 25.64 (978-1-60253-194-9(3), 200105) Child's World, Inc., The.

—Round & Round the Garden. Kemp, Moira, illus. 2009. (Favorite Children's Songs Ser.). (ENG., Illus.). 16p. (J). (gr. -1-2). 25.64 (978-1-60253-195-6(1), 200106) Child's World, Inc., The.

MansBach, Sara. Round & Round the Garden, Finger Games in English & Spanish. Arroyave, Heidy, tr. Landau, Donna, illus. 2007. 42p. spiral bd. (978-0-9785477-2-1(1)) BladeRunner Publishing.

FINGERPRINTS

Ahouse, Jeremy John & Barber, Jacqueline. Fingerprinting. Bevilacqua, Carol & Klofkorn, Lisa, illus. Hoyt, Richard, photos by. 2006. (Great Explorations in Math & Science Ser.). 72p. (J). 10.50 (978-1-931542-06-7(6), GEMS) Univ. of California, Berkeley, Lawrence Hall of Science.

Beres, D. B. Sticky Evidence: Burglar Caught on Tape. 2011. (J). pap. (978-0-545-32803-6(9)) Scholastic, Inc.

Beres, D. B. & Franklin, Watts. Dusted & Busted! The Science of Fingerprinting. 2007. (24/7: Science Behind the Scenes Ser.). (ENG., Illus.). 64p. (YA). (gr. 9-12). 29.00 (978-0-531-11822-1(3), Watts, Franklin) Scholastic Library Publishing.

Gardner, Robert. Whose Fingerprints Are These? Crime-Solving Science Projects. 2010. (Who Dunnit? Forensic Science Experiments Ser.). (Illus.). 48p. (J). (gr. 2-5). 25.27 (978-0-7660-3245-3(0)) Enslow Pubs., Inc.

Hamilton, Sue L. Fingerprint Analysis: Hints from Prints, 1 vol. 2008. (Crime Scene Investigation Ser.). (ENG.). 32p. (gr. 4-8). 27.07 (978-1-59928-988-5(1), Abdo & Daughters) ABDO Publishing Co.

Holzer, David. Prime Suspect: Suspect Identification System. 2004. (Illus.). 48p. (J). pap. (978-0-439-68027-1(1)) Scholastic, Inc.

Jeffrey, Gary. Solving Crimes with Trace Evidence. 2009. (Graphic Forensic Science Ser.). (ENG.). 48p. (YA). (gr. 5-5). 58.50 (978-1-61512-955-3(3), Rosen Reference) Rosen Publishing Group, Inc., The.

—Solving Crimes with Trace Evidence. Richardson, Peter, illus. 2008. (Graphic Forensic Science Ser.). (ENG.). 48p. (gr. 5-8). per. 14.05 (978-1-4042-1432-3(1)); (YA). lib. bdg. 31.95 (978-1-4042-1431-6(3)) Rosen Publishing Group, Inc., The.

Libal, Angela. Fingerprints, Bite Marks, Ear Prints. Noziglia, Carla Miller & Siegel, Jay A., eds. 2013. (Solving Crimes with Science: Forensics Ser.: 12). (Illus.). 112p. (J). (gr. 7-18). 22.95 (978-1-4222-2868-5(1)) Mason Crest.

Lunis, Natalie. Fun with Fingerprints. 2011. (Early Connections Ser.). (J). (978-1-61672-610-2(5)) Benchmark Education Co.

MacKay, Jenny. Fingerprints & Impression Evidence. 2007. (Crime Scene Investigations Ser.). (ENG., Illus.). 128p. (gr. 3-7). lib. bdg. 40.40 (978-1-4205-0037-0(6), Lucent Bks.) Cengage Gale.

Molnar, Ilona, et al. Fingerprint Princesses & Fairies. 2016. (Fingerprint Art Ser.). (ENG., Illus.). 160p. (J). (gr. 3-7). pap. 14.99 (978-1-63159-142-6(8), Quarry Bks.) Quarto Publishing Group USA.

Murray, Hallie & Stiefel, Chana. Investigating Fingerprints. 2017. (J). **(978-0-7660-9185-6(6))** Enslow Pubs., Inc.

Rainis, Kenneth G. Fingerprints: Crime-Solving Science Experiments. 2006. (Forensic Science Projects Ser.). (Illus.). 128p. (J). (gr. 5-18). lib. bdg. 33.27 (978-0-7660-1960-7(8)) Enslow Pubs., Inc.

Sawyer, Sarah. Careers in DNA Analysis. 2008. (Careers in Forensics Ser.). (Illus.). 64p. (J). (gr. 3-7). lib. bdg. 31.95 (978-1-4042-1343-2(0)) Rosen Publishing Group, Inc., The.

Spaulding, Jeffrey. Careers in Fingerprint & Trace Analysis. 2009. (Careers in Forensics Ser.). 64p. (gr. 5-5). 58.50 (978-1-61511-804-5(7), Rosen Reference) Rosen Publishing Group, Inc., The.

Stiefel, Chana. Fingerprints: Dead People Do Tell Tales. 2011. (True Forensic Crime Stories Ser.). (Illus.). 104p. (J). (gr. 5-18). pap. 10.95 (978-1-59845-364-5(5)); (gr. 7-12). lib. bdg. 33.27 (978-0-7660-3689-5(8)) Enslow Pubs., Inc.

Watt, Fiona. Fingerprint Activities. 2015. (Fingerprint Activities Ser.). (ENG.). 64p. (J). (gr. k-5). 15.99 (978-0-7945-3475-2(9), Usborne) EDC Publishing.

FINK, MIKE, 1770-1823?

Krensky, Stephen. Mike Fink. 2008. pap. 40.95 (978-0-8225-9294-5(0)) Lerner Publishing Group.

FINLAND

Borgert-Spaniol, Megan. Finland. 2014. (Exploring Countries Ser.). (ENG., Illus.). 32p. (J). (gr. 3-7). lib. bdg. 26.95 (978-1-62617-066-7(5), Blastoff! Readers) Bellwether Media.

Clark, Geri. Finland - Enchantment of the World. 2008. (Enchantment of the World Ser.). (ENG., Illus.). 144p. (J). (gr. 5-9). 40.00 (978-0-531-12098-9(8)) Scholastic Library Publishing.

De Capua, Sarah & DiPiazza, Francesca. Finland in Pictures. 2010. (Visual Geography Series, Second Ser.). (ENG., Illus.). 80p. (J). (gr. 5-12). lib. bdg. 31.93 (978-0-7613-4626-5(0)) Lerner Publishing Group.

Dyan, Penelope. Reindeer & Mermaids, a Kid's Guide to Helsinki Finland. Weigand, John D., photos by. 2011. (Illus.). 34p. pap. 11.95 (978-1-61477-000-8(X)) Bellissima Publishing, LLC.

McKenna, Amy, ed. Denmark, Finland, & Sweden. 2013. (Britannica Guide to Countries of the European Union Ser.). (ENG., Illus.). 256p. (YA). (gr. 9-12). lib. bdg. 53.00 (978-1-61530-969-6(1)) Rosen Publishing Group, Inc., The.

Phillips, Douglas A. Finland. 2008. (Modern World Nations Ser.). 120p. (gr. 6-12). 35.00 (978-0-7910-9671-0(8), Chelsea Hse.) Facts On File, Inc.

Schmermund, Elizabeth & Tan, Chung Lee. Finland. 3rd enl. ed. 2016. (Cultures of the World (Third Edition) (r) Ser.). 144p. (J). lib. bdg. 47.07 (978-1-5026-2227-3(0)) Cavendish Square Publishing.

Sia, Nicole. Finland. 2007. (European Union Ser.). (Illus.). 88p. (YA). (gr. 3-7). lib. bdg. 21.95 (978-1-4222-0046-9(9), 1247998) Mason Crest.

Sia, Nicole & Indovino, Shaina Carmel. Finland. 2012. (J). (978-1-4222-2241-6(1)); pap. (978-1-4222-2272-0(1)) Mason Crest.

Tan, Chung Lee. Finland. 2nd rev. ed. 2006. (Cultures of the World Ser.). (Illus.). 144p. (gr. 6-7). lib. bdg. 42.79 (978-0-7614-2073-6(8), Benchmark Bks.) Marshall Cavendish Corp.

FINLAND—FICTION

Bowman, James Cloyd, et al. Tales from a Finnish Tupa. Kolehmainen, Aili, tr. Bannon, Laura, illus. 2009. (ENG.). 288p. pap. 15.95 (978-0-8166-6768-0(3)) Univ. of Minnesota Pr.

Brooks, Kaarina, tr. from FIN. & illus. Peikko, the Foolish Ogre. Brooks, Kaarina, illus. 2003. (Aspasia Children's Bks.). (ENG.). 61p. pap. 12.00 (978-0-9731053-2-2(1)) Aspasia Bks. CAN. Dist: Univ. of Toronto Pr.

Gerber, Linda. The Finnish Line. 2007. (S. A. S. S. Ser.). (ENG.). 224p. (YA). (gr. 7-18). 7.99 (978-0-14-240916-9(2), Speak) Penguin Young Readers Group.

Lukkarinen, Ritva. Amy. Vainio, Pirkko, illus. 2009. (ENG.). 30p. (J). (gr. -1-k). 16.95 (978-1-60537-058-3(4)) Cobblestone Publishing Co.

Yates, Alexander. The Winter Place. 2015. (ENG., Illus.). 448p. (YA). (gr. 9). 17.99 (978-1-4814-1981-9(1)) Simon & Schuster Children's Publishing.

FINN, HUCKLEBERRY (FICTITIOUS CHARACTER)—DRAMA

Twain, Mark, pseud. Huckleberry Finn. 2009. (Foundation Classics Ser.). (Illus.). 56p. (J). (gr. 5-9). lib. bdg. 27.95 (978-1-60754-541-5(1)) Windmill Bks.

FINN, HUCKLEBERRY (FICTITIOUS CHARACTER)—FICTION

Adams, Jennifer. The Adventures of Huckleberry Finn: A Camping Primer, 1 vol. Oliver, Alison, illus. 2014. (ENG.). 22p. (J). (gr. k-1). bds. 9.99 (978-1-4236-3622-9(8)) Gibbs Smith, Publisher.

Hepfler, Caroline Ann. Huckleberrys Hiccups. 2009. 20p. pap. 11.25 (978-1-60693-917-8(3), Strategic Bk. Publishing) Strategic Book Publishing & Rights Agency (SBPRA).

Moliken, Paul, ed. The Adventures of Huckleberry Finn. 2005. 280p. per. 4.99 (978-1-58049-583-7(4), 200053) Prestwick Hse., Inc.

Twain, Mark, pseud. Adventures of Huckleberry Finn. Powell, Eric, illus. 2012. (ENG.). 276p. 19.99 (978-1-61377-086-3(3), 9781613770863) Idea & Design Works, LLC.

—The Adventures of Huckleberry Finn. 2008. (Bring the Classics to Life Ser.). (Illus.). 72p. (gr. 1-12). pap., act. bk. ed. 10.95 (978-1-55576-088-5(0), EDCTR-105B) EDCON Publishing Group.

—The Adventures of Huckleberry Finn. (Coleccion Clasicos de la Juventud). (SPA., Illus.). 192p. (J). 12.95 (978-84-7189-027-6(5), ORT313) Ortells, Alfredo Editorial S.L. ESP. Dist: Continental Bk. Co., Inc.

—The Adventures of Huckleberry Finn. Andreasen, Dan, illus. 2010. (Classic Starts(tm) Ser.). (ENG.). 160p. (J). (gr. 2-4). cd-rom 9.95 (978-1-4027-7355-6(2)) Sterling Publishing Co., Inc.

—The Adventures of Huckleberry Finn. McKowen, Scott, illus. 2006. (Sterling Unabridged Classics Ser.). (ENG.). 320p. (J). (gr. 5-7). 14.95 (978-1-4027-2600-2(7)) Sterling Publishing Co., Inc.

—The Adventures of Huckleberry Finn. 2008. (Puffin Classics Ser.). 386p. (gr. 3-7). lib. bdg. 16.00 (978-0-613-63913-2(8), Turtleback) Turtleback Bks.

—Las Aventuras de Huckleberry Finn. de Atauri, Ines & de Atauri, Juan Diaz, eds. 2006. (Clasicos Juveniles Ser.).Tr. of Adventures of Huckleberry Finn. (SPA., Illus.). 359p. pap. 17.95 (978-84-263-5252-1(9)) Vives, Luis Editorial (Edelvives) ESP. Dist: Lectorum Pubns., Inc.

—Las Aventuras de Tom Sawyer. 2003. (Advanced Reading Ser.).Tr. of Adventures of Tom Sawyer. (SPA.). 124p. (J). 11.95 (978-84-239-9045-0(1)) Espasa Calpe, S.A. ESP. Dist: Planeta Publishing Corp.

Vizoso Veiga, Xoán Antón. The READING LESSON: Adventures of Huckleberry Finn. 2008. 72p. pap. 13.50 (978-1-4092-0361-2(1)) Lulu Pr., Inc.

FIRE

see also Fires; Fuel; Heat; Heating

Bair, Carolyn. Fireman Dave Goes to School. 2012. 16p. pap. 13.99 (978-1-4685-4194-6(3)) AuthorHouse.

Bell, Samantha S. Detecting Wildfires. 2017. (Detecting Disasters (paperback) Ser.). (ENG., Illus.). 32p. (J). (gr. 4-7). pap. 9.95 **(978-1-63517-063-4(X)**, Focus Readers) North Star Editions.

Donahue, Jill Urban. Cómo Contener el Fuego. Masheris, Bob, illus. 2011. (Cómo Mantenemos Seguros/How to Be Safe Ser.).Tr. of Contain the Flame. (SPA, ENG & MUL.). 24p. (gr. k-2). 26.65 (978-1-4048-6887-8(9)) Picture Window Bks.

Dugan, Christine. Struggle for Survival: Fire. 2016. (Time for Kids Nonfiction Readers Ser.). (ENG.). (J). (gr. 5-8). lib. bdg. 20.85 **(978-0-606-39541-0(5))** Turtleback Bks.

Feuer: Freund Oder Feind?Tr. of Fire: Friend or Enemy? (GER., Illus.). (YA). 31.95 (978-3-411-09031-0(6), MY9031E) Bibliographisches Institut & F. A. Brockhaus AG DEU. Dist: Continental Bk. Co., Inc.

Fire. 2014. (Four Elements Ser.). (Illus.). 32p. (J). (gr. k-3). pap. 60.00 (978-1-4777-9269-8(4)) Windmill Bks.

Fire Administration (U.S.) & Federal Emergency Management Agency (U.S.), United States Fire Administrati. Let's Have Fun with Fire Safety. 2016. (ENG.). 12p. (J). (gr. -1-3). 6.00 **(978-0-16-093444-5(3)**, Federal Emergency Management Agency) United States Government Printing Office.

Fire! Fire! 6 Each of 1 Anthology, 6 vols. (Wildcats Ser.). 32p. (gr. 2-8). (978-0-322-00581-5(7)) Wright Group/McGraw-Hill.

Herweck, Diana. Un día en la Vida de un Bombero. 2017. (TIME for Kids en Español - Level 3 Ser.). (SPA.). 32p. (gr. 3-3). lib. bdg. 31.99 **(978-1-5157-5163-2(5))** Time for Kids Inc AUS. Dist: Capstone Pub.

Katirgis, Jane & Droham, Michele Ingber. Fearsome Forest Fires. 2015. (Earth's Natural Disasters Ser.). (ENG., Illus.). 32p. (J). (gr. 3-4). 25.27 (978-0-7660-6811-7(0)) Enslow Pubs., Inc.

Kyi, Tanya Lloyd. 50 Burning Questions: A Sizzling History of Fire. Kinnaird, Ross, illus. 2010. (50 Questions Ser.). (ENG.). 104p. (J). (gr. 3-18). 21.95 (978-1-55451-221-8(2), 9781554512218); pap. 12.95 (978-1-55451-220-1(4), 9781554512201) Annick Pr., Ltd. CAN. Dist: Publishers Group West (PGW).

Laplante, Walter. What Makes Fire Burn? 2016. (Everyday Mysteries Ser.). (ENG.). 24p. (J). (gr. 1-2). pap. 8.15 (978-1-4824-3844-4(5)) Stevens, Gareth Publishing LLLP.

Lindeen, Mary & Kesselring, Susan. Being Safe with Fire. McGeehan, Dan & Moore, David, illus. 2011. (Be Safe Ser.). (ENG.). 24p. (J). (gr. k-3). lib. bdg. 27.07 (978-1-60954-372-3(6), 200083) Child's World, Inc., The.

MacDonald, Margaret. Fire. 2011. (Learn-Abouts Ser.). (Illus.). 16p. (J). pap. 7.95 (978-1-59920-618-9(8)) Black Rabbit Bks.

Open Court Staff. Fire Fire. (J). pap. (978-0-8126-1012-3(1), 61012) Open Court Publishing Co.

Peluso, Beth A. The Charcoal Forest: How Fire Helps Animals & Plants. Peluso, Beth A., illus. 2007. (Illus.). 56p. (J). (gr. -1-3). pap. 12.00 (978-0-87842-532-7(2)) Mountain Pr. Publishing Co., Inc.

Raum, Elizabeth. Wildfire! 2016. (Natural Disasters Ser.). (ENG., Illus.). 32p. (J). (gr. k-3). 20.95 (978-1-60753-993-3(4)) Amicus Publishing.

Rice, Dona Herweck. First Fire. 2015. (Building Fluency Through Reader's Theater Ser.). (ENG., Illus.). 32p. (gr. 4-4). pap. 7.99 (978-1-4938-1291-2(2)) Teacher Created Materials, Inc.

Spilsbury, Richard. Chemical Reactions: Investigating an Industrial Accident, 1 vol. 2013. (Anatomy of an Investigation Ser.). (ENG.). 56p. (gr. 7-8). 34.65 (978-1-4329-7600-2(1)); pap. 9.95 (978-1-4329-7606-4(0)) Heinemann-Raintree.

Stein, R. Conrad. The Great Chicago Fire. 2005. (Cornerstones of Freedom Ser.). (ENG., Illus.). 48p. (J). 26.00 (978-0-516-23640-7(7), Children's Pr.) Scholastic Library Publishing.

Willett, Edward. Fires & Wildfires: A Practical Survival Guide. 2009. (Library of Emergency Preparedness Ser.). 64p. (gr. 6-6). 58.50 (978-1-60853-594-1(0), Rosen Reference) Rosen Publishing Group, Inc., The.

Woolf, Alex. You Wouldn't Want to Live Without Fire! 2015. (You Wouldn't Want to Live Without Ser.). lib. bdg. 20.80 (978-0-606-36712-7(8)) Turtleback Bks.

FIRE—FICTION

Adams, Peter. Why Rain & Fire Are Enemies. 2009. 28p. pap. 21.99 (978-1-4415-4317-2(1)) Xlibris Corp.

Allison, Samuel Buel. An American Robinson Crusoe. 2006. pap. (978-1-4065-0803-1(9)) Dodo Pr.

Awdry, Wilbert V. Flynn Saves the Day. Courtney, Richard, illus. 2011. (Step into Reading Ser.). (ENG.). 32p. (J). (gr. -1-1). pap. 3.99 (978-0-375-86935-8(2), Random Hse. Bks. for Young Readers) Random Hse. Children's Bks.

Baez, Debra. C a F a S Caring about Fire & Safety. 2011. 32p. pap. 24.95 (978-1-4137-5779-8(0)) America Star Bks.

Blazin' Hot: Coloring/Activity Book (English) 2005. (Illus.). (J). 2.99 (978-0-9770455-0-1(1)) Mighty Kids Media.

Blazin' Hot: Picture Book (English) 8x8. 2006. (J). 5.99 (978-1-933934-29-7(8)) Mighty Kids Media.

Blazin' Hot Picture Book (English) 2005. (Illus.). (J). 5.99 (978-0-9765953-9-7(7)) Mighty Kids Media.

BlueWolf, James Don. Speaking for Fire. Greenlee, Carolyn Wing, illus. 2007. (ENG.). 44p. (gr. 2-7). per. 12.95 (978-1-887400-31-2(1)) Earthen Vessel Production, Inc.

Bridwell, Norman. Clifford the Firehouse Dog. Bridwell, Norman, illus. 2010. (Clifford 8x8 Ser.).Tr. of Clifford the Firehouse Dog. (ENG., Illus.). 32p. (J). (gr. -1-3). pap. 3.99 (978-0-545-21580-0(3), Cartwheel Bks.) Scholastic, Inc.

Brozman, Dave. The Littlest Smoke Detector. Roguez, Jesus, illus. 2006. (ENG.). 32p. per. 21.99 (978-1-4259-6096-4(0)) AuthorHouse.

Claybourne, Anna, retold by. Jane Eyre. 2004. (Paperback Classics Ser.). 144p. (J). lib. bdg. 12.95 (978-1-58086-639-2(5), Usborne) EDC Publishing.

Confederated Salish and Kootenai Tribes Staff. Beaver Steals Fire: A Salish Coyote Story. Sandoval, Sam, illus. 2008. (ENG.). 64p. (YA). (gr. k-3). pap. 14.95 (978-0-8032-1640-2(8), Bison Bks.) Univ. of Nebraska Pr.

Daher, Anita. Two Foot Punch, 1 vol. 2007. (Orca Sports Ser.). (ENG., Illus.). 176p. (YA). (gr. 6-10). per. 9.95 (978-1-55143-876-4(3)) Orca Bk. Pubs. USA.

Del Amo, Montserrat. El Fuego y el Oro. (SPA.). 112p. (YA). (gr. 5-8). (978-84-279-3150-3(6), NG3976) Noguer y Caralt Editores, S. A. ESP. Dist: Lectorum Pubns., Inc.

Eden, Alexandra. Holy Smoke: A Bones & the Duchess Mystery. 2004. (ENG., Illus.). 117p. (J). 16.00 (978-1-888310-46-7(4)) Knoll, Allen A. Pubs.

Educational Adventures, creator. Blazin' Hot: Picture Book (Spanish) 9x9. 2006. (SPA., Illus.). (J). 5.99 (978-0-9770455-4-9(4)) Mighty Kids Media.

Edwards, Lori. Fire Fawn. 2013. 58p. pap. 8.99 (978-1-4525-7703-6(X), Balboa Pr.) Author Solutions, Inc.

Eggleton, Jill. The Fire. Pye, Trevor, illus. 2003. (Rigby Sails Early Ser.). (ENG.). 16p. (gr. 1-2). pap. 6.95 (978-0-7578-8663-8(9)) Houghton Mifflin Harcourt Publishing Co.

Elfgren, Sara B. & Strandberg, Mats. Fire: The Engelsfors Trilogy Book II. 2014. (Engelsfors Trilogy Ser.: 2). (ENG.). 704p. (gr. 9-13). 18.99 (978-1-4683-0672-9(3), 460672) Overlook Pr., The.

Fire! Individual Title Six-Packs. (Bookweb Ser.). 32p. (gr. 4-18). 34.00 (978-0-7635-3739-5(X)) Rigby Education.

Fire at Fry's Farm. 2004. (J). lib. bdg. (978-0-9727273-2-7(9)) Green Owl, Inc.

Forward, Toby. Fireborn. 2015. (Dragonborn Ser.: 2). (ENG.). 448p. (YA). (gr. 5-8). pap. 8.99 (978-1-61963-439-8(2), 9781619634398, Bloomsbury USA Childrens) Bloomsbury Publishing USA.

Good, Merle. Reuben & the Fire. Moss, P. Buckley, illus. rev. ed. 2016. (ENG.). 32p. (J). (gr. -1-3). 16.99 (978-1-68099-153-6(1), Good Bks.) Skyhorse Publishing Co., Inc.

Guy, Glen. The Adventure Fire: Adventures of Dusty Sourdough. 2003. (YA). pap. 9.95 (978-1-59433-006-3(9)) Publication Consultants.

Hale, Shannon. Enna Burning. 2004. (Books of Bayern Ser.: No. 2). (ENG., Illus.). 300p. (YA). 18.99 (978-1-58234-889-6(8), 9781582348896, Bloomsbury USA Childrens) Bloomsbury Publishing USA.

Hate Fighters. (Good News Club Ser.). (J). (gr. 4-9). pap. 4.99 (978-1-55976-492-6(9)) CEF Pr.

Heidari, Mahdi. Little Red Fire. Taylor, Adam, illus. 2012. 40p. (J). pap. 12.99 (978-0-9838321-8-8(8)) Higher Ground Pr.

Hill, Stuart. Blade of Fire. 2007. 574p. (J). pap. (978-0-545-01969-9(9)) Scholastic, Inc.

Hillyer, Lexa. Spindle Fire. 2017. (Spindle Fire Ser.: 1). 368p. (YA). (gr. 9). 17.99 (978-0-06-244087-7(X), HarperTeen) HarperCollins Pubs.

Holden, Pam. Fire in the Jungle, 6 pack. Hatam, Samer, illus. 2009. (Red Rocket Readers Ser.). (ENG.). 16p. (gr. 2-2). pap. (978-1-877363-73-3(1)) Flying Start Bks.

Hooker, Lou. The Year of the Fire. l.t. ed. 2004. (Illus.). 102p. (J). pap. 8.95 (978-0-9755106-0-5(6)) Hooker, Lou.

Hunter, Erin. Fire in the Sky. 2010. (Seekers Ser.: 5). (ENG.). 272p. (J). (gr. 3-7). 16.99 (978-0-06-087134-5(2)) HarperCollins Pubs.

Kaufman, Jeanne. Young Henry & the Dragon. Tessler, Daria, illus. 2011. (J). (978-1-934860-11-3(5)) Shenanigan Bks.

Kizer, Linda M. Plug, the Lonely Little Fire Hydrant. 2009. 60p. pap. 26.99 (978-1-4490-2873-2(X)) AuthorHouse.

Matheny, Bill, et al. The Batman Is on Fire!, 1 vol. 2014. (Batman Strikes! Ser.). (ENG., Illus.). 32p. (gr. 2-3). 22.60 (978-1-4342-9229-2(0)) Stone Arch Bks.

McBride, Lish. Pyromantic. 2017. (Firebug Ser.). (ENG.). 336p. (YA). (gr. 9-17). 18.99 (978-0-8050-9863-1(1), 9780805098631, Holt, Henry & Co. Bks. For Young Readers) Holt, Henry & Co.

McFarlane, Brian. Fire in the North. 2007. (ENG.). 220p. (J). (gr. 2-7). pap. (978-1-55168-243-3(5)) Magma.

McKinley, Robin & Dickinson, Peter. Fire: Tales of Elemental Spirits. 2010. (ENG.). 304p. (gr. 12). 15.00 (978-0-441-01919-9(6), Ace Bks.) Penguin Publishing Group.

—Fire: Tales of Elemental Spirits. 2011. (ENG.). 320p. (YA). (gr. 7-18). 9.99 (978-0-14-241945-8(1), Firebird) Penguin Young Readers Group.

Nez, John. One Smart Cookie. Nez, John, illus. 2006. (ENG., Illus.). 32p. (J). (gr. k-3). lib. bdg. 16.99 (978-0-8075-6099-0(5)) Whitman, Albert & Co.

O'Donnell, Liam. Duncan: A Brave Rescue. Hynes, Robert, illus. 2004. (ENG.). 32p. (J). (gr. -1-2). 9.95 (978-1-59249-317-3(3), 1B004) Soundprints.

Park, Linda Sue. The Firekeeper's Son. Downing, Julie, illus. 2009. (ENG.). 40p. (J). (gr. -1-3). pap. 7.99 (978-0-547-23769-5(3)) Houghton Mifflin Harcourt Publishing Co.

Ratcliffe, Linda. Lindylou Starts a Fire. 2012. 32p. pap. 8.99 (978-1-62419-875-5(9)) Salem Author Services.

Richey, Denise. Four in a Fire. 2011. 28p. (gr. -1). pap. 12.03 (978-1-4520-6142-9(4)) AuthorHouse.

Sargent, Dave & Sargent, Pat. The Fire: A Second Chance, 10 vols., Vol. 10. Lenoir, Jane, illus. 2005. (Colorado Cowboys Ser.: 10). 32p. (J). pap. 10.95 (978-1-59381-105-1(5)) Ozark Publishing.

Urrea, Lourdes, et al. Si Juegas Con Fuego. 2005. (Ediciones Castillo Castillo Del Terror Ser.).Tr. of If You Play with Fire. (SPA.). (J). (gr. 2-6). pap. 7.95 (978-970-20-0394-6(6)) Castillo, Ediciones, S. A. de C. V. MEX. Dist: Iaconi, Mariuccia Bk. Imports.

Vasiliu, Michelle & Orsini, Cheryl. Fire Ready. 2008. (Rigby Focus Forward: Level P Ser.). (Illus.). 24p. (J). (gr. 4-7). pap. (978-1-4190-3855-6(9), Rigby) Pearson Education Australia.

Wallace, Rich. Phantom Flames. Volpari, Daniela, illus. 2016. 48p. (J). (978-1-62402-150-3(6)) Magic Wagon.

Whitney, Daisy. The Fire Artist. 2014. (ENG.). 288p. (YA). (gr. 7). 17.99 (978-1-61963-132-8(6), 9781619631328, Bloomsbury USA Childrens) Bloomsbury Publishing USA.

Wood, Gail Ann. Lizzie & the Prairie Fire: Girl Pioneer in the American Midwest. 2006. (American Frontier Story Ser.). (Illus.). 115p. (YA). (gr. 8-12). per. 7.95 (978-1-57249-381-0(X), White Mane Kids) White Mane Publishing Co., Inc.

Zephaniah, Benjamin. Face. 2004. (ENG.). 208p. (YA). (gr. 7). reprint ed. pap. 9.99 (978-1-58234-921-3(5), 9781582349213, Bloomsbury USA Childrens) Bloomsbury Publishing USA.

FIRE BALLS

see Meteors

FIRE DEPARTMENTS

Armentrout, David & Armentrout, Patricia. The Fire Department. 2008. (Illus.). 24p. (J). 22.79 (978-1-60472-336-6(X)) Rourke Educational Media.

Behrman, Carol H. Thomas Jefferson. 2005. (Just the Facts Biographies Ser.). (ENG., Illus.). 112p. (gr. 5-12). lib. bdg. 27.93 (978-0-8225-2645-2(X), Lerner Pubns.) Lerner Publishing Group.

Butler, Dori Hillestad. F Is for Firefighting, 1 vol. Waites, Joan C., illus. 2007. (ENG.). 32p. (J). (gr. k-3). 16.99 (978-1-58980-420-3(1)) Pelican Publishing Co., Inc.

Caballero, D., tr. Los Bomberos. Metzger, Wolfgang, illus. 2006. (Junior (Silver Dolphin) Ser.). (SPA.). 16p. (J). (gr. 5). 9.95 (978-970-718-344-5(6)) Readerlink Distribution Services, LLC.

Carr, Aaron. The Fire Station. 2013. (J). (978-1-62127-344-8(X)); pap. (978-1-62127-349-3(0)) Weigl Pubs., Inc.

Clark, Rosalyn. A Visit to the Fire Station. 2017. (Bumba Books (tm) — Places We Go Ser.). (ENG.). 24p. (J). (gr. -1-1). 25.32 **(978-1-5124-3372-2(1))** Lerner Publishing Group.

Gordon, Sharon. What's Inside a Firehouse/Que Hay Dentro de un Cuartel de Bomberos? 2006. (Bookworms Ser.). (ENG & SPA., Illus.). 32p. (gr. 1-2). lib. bdg. 15.95 (978-0-7614-2473-4(3)) Marshall Cavendish Corp.

Gordon, Sharon, ed. Que Hay Dentro de un Cuartel de Bomberos? 2006. (Bookworms Ser.). (SPA., Illus.). 32p. (gr. 1-2). lib. bdg. 15.95 (978-0-7614-2393-5(1)) Marshall Cavendish Corp.

Gorman, Jacqueline Laks & Laks Gorman, Jacqueline. Firefighters. Andersen, Gregg, photos by. 2010. (People in My Community Ser.). (Illus.). 24p. (gr. k-3). 22.60 *(978-1-4339-3338-7(1))* Stevens, Gareth Publishing LLLP.

Kawa, Katie. My First Trip to the Fire Station. 2012. (My First Adventures Ser.). (Illus.). 24p. (gr. k-2). 69.20 *(978-1-4339-8051-0(7))*; (J). pap. 8.15 *(978-1-4339-7317-8(0))*; (J). lib. bdg. 22.60 *(978-1-4339-7316-1(2))* Stevens, Gareth Publishing LLLP.

—My First Trip to the Fire Station /Mi Primera Visita A la EstaciÓN de Bomberos. 2012. (My First Adventures / Mis primeras aventuras Ser.). (SPA & ENG., Illus.). 24p. (J). (gr. k-2). 22.60 *(978-1-4339-7380-2(4))* Stevens, Gareth Publishing LLLP.

Kids Can Press Staff. This Is Daniel Cook at the Fire Station. Li, Karen, ed. 2006. (This Is Daniel Cook Ser.). (ENG., Illus.). 24p. (J). (gr. -1-1). 4.95 *(978-1-55453-076-2(8))* Kids Can Pr., Ltd. CAN. Dist: Hachette Bk. Group.

Lindeen, Mary. A Visit to the Fire Station. 2015. (BeginningtoRead Ser.). (ENG., Illus.). 32p. (J). (gr. k-2). lib. bdg. 22.60 *(978-1-59953-693-4(5))* Norwood Hse. Pr.

Mortensen, Lori. A Day at the Fire Station. Thompson, Jeffrey, illus. 2010. (First Graphics: My Community Ser.). (ENG.). 24p. (gr. 1-2). pap. 35.70 *(978-1-4296-5613-9(1))* Capstone Press of Coughlan Cos.

Rucker, Jeffrey A. A Trip to the Fire Station. (Rosen Real Readers: Upper Emergent Ser.). (ENG., Illus.). 12p. (gr. 1-2). 2008. pap. 5.90 *(978-0-8239-8131-1(2))* 2006. 33.50 *(978-1-4042-6216-4(4))* Rosen Publishing Group, Inc., The.

Santora, Maureen Crethan. The Day the Towers Fell: The Story of September 11, 2001. Santora, Maureen Crethan, illus. 2008. (Illus.). 32p. (J). 31.99 *(978-1-4257-7872-9(0))* Xlibris Corp.

—My Son Christopher: A 9/11 Mother's Tale of Remembrance. 2008. 36p. 31.99 *(978-1-4363-3044-2(0))* Xlibris Corp.

Torr, James D. Responding to Attack: Firefighters & Police. 2003. (Lucent Library of Homeland Security). (Illus.). 112p. (J). 30.85 *(978-1-59018-375-5(4)*, Lucent Bks.) Cengage Gale.

Troupe, Thomas Kingsley. If I Were a Firefighter, 1 vol. Reid, Mick, illus. 2010. (Dream Big! Ser.). (ENG.). 24p. (gr. k-3). lib. bdg. 26.65 *(978-1-4048-5535-9(1))* Picture Window Bks.

FIRE DEPARTMENTS—FICTION

Allen, Kenny. Jose Visits the Fire Station. 2012. (InfoMax Readers Ser.). (ENG., Illus.). 16 pp.p. (J). (gr. k-1). pap. 7.00 *(978-1-4488-8920-4(0)*, Rosen Classroom) Rosen Publishing Group, Inc., The.

Chandler, Jeff. The Fire Dog Champ. 2008. 28p. pap. 24.95 *(978-1-4241-8615-0(3))* America Star Bks.

Crews, Donald, illus. Fire! 2016. (J). *(978-0-06-237349-6(8)*, Greenwillow Bks.) HarperCollins Pubs.

DiCamillo, Kate. Mercy Watson to the Rescue. DiCamillo, Kate & Van Dusen, Chris, illus. 2009. (Mercy Watson Ser.: 1). (ENG.). 80p. (J). (gr. 1-4). pap. 5.99 *(978-0-7636-4504-5(4))* Candlewick Pr.

—Mercy Watson to the Rescue. Van Dusen, Chris, illus. 2005. (Mercy Watson Ser.: 1). (ENG.). 80p. (J). (gr. k-4). 14.99 *(978-0-7636-2270-1(2))* Candlewick Pr.

—Mercy Watson to the Rescue. 2009. (Mercy Watson Ser.: Bk. 1). lib. bdg. 16.00 *(978-0-606-06704-1(3)*, Turtleback) Turtleback Bks.

Finn, Rebecca, illus. Busy Fire Station. 2016. (Busy Bks.). (ENG.). 10p. (J). (gr. -1). bds. 8.95 *(978-1-4549-1942-1(6))* Sterling Publishing Co., Inc.

Garces Iii, Joseph Louis. Garrett the Firefighter. Abercrombie, Bethaney, illus. 2008. 24p. pap. 12.99 *(978-1-59858-716-6(1))* Dog Ear Publishing, LLC.

Gershenson, Harold P. The Kindertown Fire Brigade. Mills, Christopher, illus. 2006. (J). *(978-1-58987-019-2(0))* Kindermusik International.

Gutman, Dan. Mrs. Meyer Is on Fire! 2016. (My Weirdest School Ser.: 4). (J). lib. bdg. 14.75 *(978-0-606-38154-3(6))* Turtleback Bks.

Hillert, Margaret. Dear Dragon Goes to the Firehouse. Schimmell, David, illus. 2010. (BeginningtoRead Ser.). 32p. (J). (gr. k-2). lib. bdg. 22.60 *(978-1-59953-375-9(8))* Norwood Hse. Pr.

—Querido Dragón Va a la Estación de Bomberos/Dear Dragon Goes to the Firehouse. de', Eida, tr. Schimmell, David, illus. 2011. (BeginningtoRead Ser.). 32p. (J). (-2). pap. 11.94 *(978-1-60357-552-2(9))* Norwood Hse. Pr.

—Querido Dragón Va Al Cuartel de Bomberos/Dear Dragon Goes to the Firehouse. del Risco, Eida, tr. from ENG. Schimmell, David, illus. 2011. (BeginningtoRead Ser.). 32p. (J). (gr. k-2). lib. bdg. 22.60 *(978-1-59953-468-8(1))* Norwood Hse. Pr.

Houran, Lori Haskins. Flat Stanley & the Firehouse. Pamintuan, Macky, illus. 2013. 32p. (J). *(978-1-4351-5055-3(4))* Barnes & Noble, Inc.

Klein, Adria F. Max Goes to the Fire Station, 1 vol. Gallagher-Cole, Mernie, illus. 2009. (Read-It! Readers: the Life of Max Ser.). (ENG.). 24p. (gr. -1-2). 21.32 *(978-1-4048-5266-2(2)*, Easy Readers) Picture Window Bks.

Munsch, Robert. The Fire Station. Martchenko, Michael, illus. 5th ed. 2012. (ENG.). 24p. (J). (gr. -1-k). bds. 7.99 *(978-1-55451-423-6(1)*, 9781554514236) Annick Pr., Ltd. CAN. Dist: Publishers Group West (PGW).

Murray, Laura. The Gingerbread Man Loose on the Fire Truck. Lowery, Mike, illus. 2013. (ENG.). 32p. (J). (gr. k-3). 16.99 *(978-0-399-25779-7(9)*, G.P. Putnam's Sons Books for Young Readers) Penguin Young Readers Group.

Rey, H. A., et al. Curious George & the Firefighters. 2007. (Curious George Ser.). (ENG., Illus.). 24p. (J). (gr. -1-3). bds. 11.99 *(978-0-618-89194-8(3))* Houghton Mifflin Harcourt Publishing Co.

Rockwell, Anne F. At the Firehouse. Rockwell, Anne F., illus. 2003. (Illus.). 40p. (J). (gr. -1-1). 16.89 *(978-0-06-029816-6(2))* HarperCollins Pubs.

Scarry, Richard & Scarry, Huck. A Day at the Fire Station. 2003. (Pictureback(R) Ser.). (ENG., Illus.). 24p. (J). (gr. -1-2). pap. 4.99 *(978-0-307-10545-5(8)*, Random Hse. Bks. for Young Readers) Random Hse. Children's Bks.

Slater, Jean M. At the Fire Station: An Interactive Book. 2nd ed. 2003. (Illus.). 13p. (J). bds. *(978-0-9743149-0-7(0))* Slater Software. Inc.

Teague, Mark. Firehouse! Teague, Mark, illus. (StoryPlay Ser.). (ENG., Illus.). (J). (gr. -1-k). 2017. 40p. 5.99 *(978-1-338-18159-3(9))* 2013. 32p. bds. 6.99 *(978-0-545-49215-7(7))* Scholastic, Inc. (Cartwheel Bks.).

A Visit to the Fire Station. 2003. (J). per. *(978-1-57657-900-8(X))* Paradise Pr., Inc.

FIRE ENGINES

Abbot, Henry. I Want to Drive a Fire Truck. 2016. (At the Wheel Ser.). 00024p. (J). (gr. 1-1). pap. 8.25 *(978-1-4994-2660-1(7)*, PowerKids Pr.) Rosen Publishing Group, Inc., The.

Aloian, Molly. Les Camions de Pompiers. 2013. (FRE.). 32p. (J). pap. 9.95 *(978-2-89579-488-2(X))* Bayard Canada Livres CAN. Dist: Crabtree Publishing Co.

—Fire Trucks: Racing to the Scene. 2010. (Vehicles on the Move Ser.). (ENG.). 32p. (J). (gr. k-3). lib. bdg. *(978-0-7787-3046-0(8))* Crabtree Publishing Co.

Becker, Ann. Fire Engines. 2009. (Amazing Machines Ser.). 32p. (gr. 2). 28.50 *(978-0-7614-4403-9(3))* Marshall Cavendish Corp.

Best, B. J. Fire Trucks. 2017. (J). ***(978-1-5026-2554-0(7))*** Cavendish Square Publishing.

—Fireboats. 2017. (J). ***(978-1-5026-2557-1(1))*** Cavendish Square Publishing.

Big Fire Engine. 2008. (Vehicle Board Ser.). 6p. bds. *(978-1-4054-9868-5(4))* Parragon, Inc.

Bodden, Valerie. Fire Trucks. (J). 2014. pap. *(978-1-62832-065-7(6)*, Creative Paperbacks) 2011. (ENG.). 24p. (gr. 1-3). pap. 7.99 *(978-0-89812-577-1(4)*, Creative Paperbacks) 2011. 24p. (gr. k-2). 16.95 *(978-1-60818-006-6(9))* Creative Co., The.

Bowman, Chris. Fire Trucks. 2017. (Mighty Machines in Action Ser.). (ENG., Illus.). 24p. (J). (gr. k-3). lib. bdg. 25.95 *(978-1-62617-604-1(3)*, Blastoff! Readers) Bellwether Media.

Bridges, Sarah. I Drive a Fire Engine, 1 vol. Muehlenhardt, Amy Bailey, illus. 2006. (Working Wheels Ser.). (ENG.). 24p. (gr. -1-2). 26.65 *(978-1-4048-1606-0(2))* Picture Window Bks.

Carr, Aaron. Fire Trucks. 2014. (Illus.). 24p. (J). *(978-1-4896-3220-3(4))* Weigl Pubs., Inc.

Chancellor, Deborah. Fire Rescue. 2013. (Emergency Vehicles Ser.). 24p. (gr. k-3). 28.50 *(978-1-59920-889-3(X))* Black Rabbit Bks.

Coppendale, Jean. Fire Trucks & Rescue Vehicles. 2010. (Mighty Machines Ser.). (ENG., Illus.). 24p. (J). (gr. -1-2). pap. 5.95 *(978-1-55407-621-5(8)*, 9781554076215) Firefly Bks., Ltd.

Dorling Kindersley Publishing Staff. Fire Engine. 2011. (Touch & Feel Ser.). (ENG.). 12p. (J). (gr. -1-k). bds. 6.99 *(978-0-7566-8992-6(9)*, DK Children) Dorling Kindersley Publishing, Inc.

—Fire Truck. (ENG.). (J). (gr. -1-k). 2009. 10p. bds. 7.99 *(978-0-7566-5228-9(6))* 2003. (Illus.). 12p. bds. 6.99 *(978-0-7894-9712-3(3))* Dorling Kindersley Publishing, Inc. (DK Children).

—Noisy Fire Engine Peekaboo! 2016. (ENG., Illus.). 12p. (J). (— 1). bds. 12.99 *(978-1-4654-5422-5(5)*, DK Children) Dorling Kindersley Publishing, Inc.

Fortuna, Lois. Fire Trucks. 2016. (To the Rescue! Ser.). 24p. (J). (gr. k-k). 22.60 *(978-1-4824-4660-9(X))* Stevens, Gareth Publishing LLLP.

Freeman, Marcia S. Fire Engines [Scholastic]. 2009. (Community Vehicles Ser.). 24p. (gr. k-1). pap. 0.36 *(978-1-4296-4243-9(2)*, Pebble Bks.) Capstone Press of Coughlan Cos.

Gordon, Sharon. Que Hay Dentro de un Camion de Bomberos? 2006. (Bookworms Ser.). (SPA., Illus.). 32p. (gr. 1-2). lib. bdg. 15.95 *(978-0-7614-2391-1(5))* Marshall Cavendish Corp.

—Whats Inside a Fire Truck? (¿Qué Hay Dentro de un Camión de Bomberos?) 2006. (Bookworms Ser.). (ENG & SPA., Illus.). 32p. (gr. 1-2). lib. bdg. 15.95 *(978-0-7614-2472-7(5))* Marshall Cavendish Corp.

Graubart, Norman D. Fire Trucks, 1 vol. 2015. (ENG.). 24p. (J). lib. bdg. 23.60 *(978-1-4994-0105-9(1)*, PowerKids Pr.) Rosen Publishing Group, Inc., The.

Gregory, Josh. What Does It Do? Fire Truck. 2011. (Community Connections: What Does It Do? Ser.). (ENG.). 24p. (gr. 2-5). lib. bdg. 25.64 *(978-1-60279-971-4(7)*, 200964) Cherry Lake Publishing.

Hanson, Anne E. Fire Trucks in Action, 1 vol. 2011. (Transportation Zone Ser.). (ENG.). 24p. (gr. 1-2). lib. bdg. 25.32 *(978-1-4296-6824-8(5)*, First Facts) Capstone Press of Coughlan Cos.

Jango-Cohen, Judith. Fire Trucks on the Move. 2010. pap. 45.32 *(978-0-7613-6940-0(6))*; (ENG., Illus.). 32p. lib. bdg. 26.60 *(978-0-7613-6023-0(9))* Lerner Publishing Group.

LaFontaine, Bruce. Shiny Fire Engines Stickers. 2006. (Dover Little Activity Books Stickers Ser.). (ENG., Illus.). 2p. (J). (gr. -1-5). 1.50 *(978-0-486-44826-8(6))* Dover Pubns., Inc.

Lindeen, Mary. Fire Trucks. 2007. (Mighty Machines Ser.). (ENG., Illus.). 24p. (J). (gr. k-3). lib. bdg. 25.95 *(978-1-60014-059-4(9))* Bellwether Media.

Mattern, Joanne. Fire Trucks. 2015. (Rookie Read-About(tm) Science: How Things Work Ser.). (ENG.). 32p. (J). lib. bdg. 25.00 *(978-0-531-21373-5(0)*, Children's Pr.) Scholastic Library Publishing.

Mitton, Tony. Flashing Fire Engines. Parker, Ant, illus. 2016. (Amazing Machines Ser.). (ENG.). 24p. pap., act. bk. ed. 4.99 *(978-0-7534-7256-9(2)*, 9780753472569, Kingfisher) Roaring Brook Pr.

Page, Josephine. I Am a Fire Truck. Migliari, Paola, illus. 2007. (ENG.). 4p. (J). (gr. -1 — 1). bds. 4.99 *(978-0-439-91618-9(6))* Scholastic, Inc.

Randolph, Joanne. Fire Trucks. (To the Rescue! Ser.). 24p. 2009. (gr. 1-1). 42.50 *(978-1-60854-397-7(8))* 2008. (Illus.). (J). (gr. 4-7). lib. bdg. 22.60 *(978-1-4042-4149-7(3))* Rosen Publishing Group, Inc., The. (PowerKids Pr.).

—Fire Trucks/Caminones de Bomberos. Alaman, Eduardo, tr. from ENG. 2008. (To the Rescue! / ¡Al Rescate! Ser.). (Illus.). 24p. (J). (gr. -1-3). lib. bdg. 22.60 *(978-1-4042-7673-4(4)*, Editorial Buenas Letras) Rosen Publishing Group, Inc., The.

—Fire Trucks/Camiones de Bomberos. 2009. (To the Rescue! / ¡Al rescate! Ser.). (ENG & SPA.). 24p. (gr. 1-1). 42.50 *(978-1-60854-403-5(6)*, Editorial Buenas Letras) Rosen Publishing Group, Inc., The.

—Let's Draw a Fire Truck with Shapes: Vamos a Dibujar un Camion de Bomberos Usando Figuras. Muschinske, Emily, illus. 2005. (Let's Draw with Shapes / Vamos a Dibujar con Figuras Ser.). (ENG & SPA.). (J). 22.60 *(978-1-4042-7556-0(8)*, PowerKids Pr.) Rosen Publishing Group, Inc., The.

Riggs, Kate. Fire Trucks. 2015. (Illus.). 24p. (J). *(978-1-60818-581-8(8)*, Creative Education) Creative Co., The.

—Fire Trucks: Seedlings. 2016. (Seedlings Ser.). (ENG.). 24p. (J). (gr. k-2). pap. 7.99 *(978-1-62832-186-9(5)*, Creative Paperbacks) Creative Co., The.

Schmidt, Maria T. Fire Trucks. 2012. (ENG., Illus.). 24p. (J). lib. bdg. 25.65 *(978-1-62031-020-5(1))* Jump! Inc.

Silverman, Buffy. How Do Fire Trucks Work? 2016. (Lightning Bolt Books (tm) — How Vehicles Work Ser.). (ENG., Illus.). 32p. (J). (gr. 1-3). lib. bdg. 26.65 *(978-1-4677-9504-3(6))* Lerner Publishing Group.

Sís, Peter. Fire Truck. Sís, Peter, illus. 2004. (ENG., Illus.). 28p. (J). (gr. -1-1). bds. 6.99 *(978-0-06-056259-5(5)*, Greenwillow Bks.) HarperCollins Pubs.

Tieck, Sarah. Fire Trucks. 2005. (Buddy Book Ser.). (Illus.). 24p. (gr. k-4). 25.65 *(978-1-59197-828-2(9)*, Buddy Bks.) ABDO Publishing Co.

Tourville, Amanda Doering. Fire Trucks, 1 vol. Trover, Zachary, illus. 2009. (Mighty Machines Ser.). (ENG.). 32p. (J). (gr. -1-3). 28.50 *(978-1-60270-624-8(7))* Magic Wagon.

FIRE ENGINES—FICTION

Armstrong, Jennifer. Magnus at the Fire. Smith, Owen, illus. 2005. (ENG.). 32p. (J). (gr. k-3). 18.99 *(978-0-689-83922-1(7)*, Simon & Schuster Bks. For Young Readers) Simon & Schuster Bks. For Young Readers.

Austin, Mike. Fire Engine No. 9. 2015. (ENG., Illus.). 40p. (J). (gr. -1-2). 19.99 *(978-0-375-97428-1(8)*, Random Hse. Bks. for Young Readers) Random Hse. Children's Bks.

Awdry, W. Thomas & Fire Engine Flynn Book & CD (Thomas & Friends) 2016. (Pictureback(R) Ser.). (ENG., Illus.). 24p. (J). (gr. -1-2). pap. 6.99 *(978-1-101-93829-4(3)*, Random Hse. Bks. for Young Readers) Random Hse. Children's Bks.

Awdry, Wilbert V. Thomas & the Big, Big Bridge. 2003. (Little Golden Book Ser.). (ENG., Illus.). 24p. (J). (gr. -1-2). 4.99 *(978-0-307-10335-2(8)*, Golden Bks.) Random Hse. Children's Bks.

Baczynski, Jolanta & Baczynski, Olga. Freddie & Jet. 2013. 36p. pap. *(978-0-9918166-4-4(1))* Flower Pr.

Barthelme, Donald. The Slightly Irregular Fire Engine. 2006. (ENG., Illus.). 32p. (J). (gr. 4-13). 19.95 *(978-1-58567-828-0(7)*, 856828) Overlook Pr., The.

Beck, Andrea. Elliot's Fire Truck, 1 vol. Beck, Andrea, illus. 2010. (ENG., Illus.). 32p. (J). (gr. -1-3). 19.95 *(978-1-55469-143-2(5))* Orca Bk. Pubs. USA.

Billet, Marion. My First Fire Engine. Billet, Marion, illus. 2015. (Whizzy Wheels Ser.). (ENG., Illus.). 10p. (J). (gr. -1-k). bds. 11.99 *(978-1-4472-7698-2(1))* Pan Macmillan GBR. Dist: Independent Pubs. Group.

Brooke, Samantha. Fire in the Forest! Kiernan, Kenny, illus. 2012. 31p. (J). *(978-1-4242-5340-1(3))* Scholastic, Inc.

Brooke, Samantha & Scholastic, Inc. Staff. Fire in the Forest! 2012. (Lego City Ser.). (ENG., Illus.). 32p. (J). (gr. -1-k). pap. 3.99 *(978-0-545-36992-3(4))* Scholastic, Inc.

Cowley, Joy. Miss Doll & Friends: Where Is Fire Engine? Bordicchia, Gaia, illus. 2014. (ENG.). 8p. pap. *(978-0-927244-57-2(8)*, Joy Cowley Club) Flying Start Bks.

Crow, Melinda Melton. Brave Fire Truck, 1 vol. Thompson, Chad, illus. 2011. (Wonder Wheels Ser.). (ENG.). 32p. (gr. -1-1). pap. 6.25 *(978-1-4342-3384-4(7))*; lib. bdg. 22.65 *(978-1-4342-3029-4(5))* Stone Arch Bks.

de Sève, Randall. A Fire Truck Named Red. Staake, Bob, illus. 2016. (ENG.). 40p. (J). 16.99 *(978-0-374-30073-9(9)*, 9780374300739, Farrar, Straus & Giroux (BYR)) Farrar, Straus & Giroux.

Estes, Don. Willy: The Little Jeep Who Wanted to Be a Fire Truck. Garrison, Sue, illus. 2003. 46p. (J). lib. bdg. 14.95 *(978-1-883551-47-6(1)*, ASP-471, Attic Studio Pr.) Attic Studio Publishing Hse.

—Willy & Friends traveling through the Seasons: The continuing story of Willy the little fire jeep. Glass, Eric, illus. 2006. (J). *(978-1-883551-75-9(7)*, Maple Corners Press) Attic Studio Publishing Hse.

Flory, Jane & dePaola, Tomie. The Too Little Fire Engine. Flory, Jane, illus. 2015. (G&d Vintage Ser.). (ENG., Illus.). 24p. (J). (gr. -1-k). bds. 7.99 *(978-0-448-48217-0(7)*, Grosset & Dunlap) Penguin Young Readers Group.

Golden Books. The Fire Engine Book. Gergely, Tibor, illus. 2015. (Little Golden Board Book Ser.). (ENG.). 26p. (J). (-k). bds. 7.99 *(978-0-553-52224-2(8)*, Golden Bks.) Random Hse. Children's Bks.

Jackson, Alisha. Noah's Fire Engine. 2011. 16p. 9.00 *(978-1-4567-2977-6(2))* AuthorHouse.

Jiang, Eva. Eric Loved Fire Trucks. 2013. 28p. pap. 16.09 *(978-1-4669-7117-2(7))* Trafford Publishing.

Kuphal, Shirley M. Flavor's Wild Wish. 2008. 36p. pap. 21.99 *(978-1-4363-0656-0(6))* Xlibris Corp.

Lenski, Lois. The Little Fire Engine. 2017. (Lois Lenski Bks.). (ENG., Illus.). 32p. (J). (gr. k — 1). bds. 7.99 *(978-0-375-82263-6(1)*, Random Hse. Bks. for Young Readers) Random Hse. Children's Bks.

McMahon, Susan. Billy Mcgee. 2008. 24p. pap. 12.99 *(978-1-4389-2041-2(5))* AuthorHouse.

Penn, Audrey. Kai to the Rescue. Yamada, Mike, illus. 2016. (ENG.). 40p. (J). (gr. -1-k). 17.99 *(978-0-545-81636-6(X))* Scholastic, Inc.

Rey, H. A. Curious George's Fire Truck. 2014. (Curious George Ser.). (ENG., Illus.). 12p. (J). (— 1). bds. 8.99 *(978-0-544-14709-6(X)*, HMH Books For Young Readers) Houghton Mifflin Harcourt Publishing Co.

Roberts, Ken. The Thumb in the Box. 2013. 56p. pap. *(978-1-4596-6500-2(7))* ReadHowYouWant.com, Ltd.

Rockwell, Anne F. At the Firehouse. Rockwell, Anne F., illus. 2003. (Illus.). 40p. (J). (gr. -1-1). 16.89 *(978-0-06-029816-6(2))* HarperCollins Pubs.

Sander, Sonia. Fire Truck to the Rescue! 2009. (LEGO City Adventures Scholastic Readers Level 1 Ser.: 1). lib. bdg. 13.55 *(978-0-606-05872-8(9)*, Turtleback) Turtleback Bks.

—LEGO City Reader Collection: LEGO City Emergency. 2012. (Illus.). 127p. (J). *(978-1-4351-3985-5(2))* Scholastic, Inc.

Scholastic, Inc. Staff, contrib. by. Trucks Around the City. 2011. (Lego City Ser.). (ENG.). 14p. (J). (gr. -1-k). bds. 7.99 *(978-0-545-35629-9(6))* Scholastic, Inc.

Shea, Lisa. Meet Heatwave the Fire-Bot. 2013. (Transformers Passport to Reading Ser.). (J). lib. bdg. 14.75 *(978-0-606-31737-5(6)*, Turtleback) Turtleback Bks.

Tango Books Staff. Noisy Pops - Fire Engine. Abbott, Simon, illus. 2011. (Noisy Pops! Ser.). (ENG.). 10p. (J). (gr. -1-k). bds. 11.99 *(978-1-85707-710-0(5))* Tango Bks. GBR. Dist: Independent Pubs. Group.

Watanabe, Shigeo. Jeeper the Fire Engine. Yamamoto, Tadayoshi, illus. 2005. 28p. (J). 11.95 *(978-4-902216-14-1(0))* R.I.C. Publications Asia Co, Inc. JPN. Dist: Continental Enterprises Group, Inc. (CEG).

Wojtowycz, David. Fizz the Fire Engine! 2003. (Illus.). (J). pap. *(978-0-439-82852-9(X))* Scholastic, Inc.

Wood, Audrey. Alphabet Rescue. Wood, Bruce, illus. 2006. (ENG.). 40p. (J). (gr. -1-k). 17.99 *(978-0-439-85316-3(8)*, Blue Sky Pr., The) Scholastic, Inc.

Wood, Audrey & Wood, Bruce Robert, illus. Alphabet Rescue. 2006. (J). *(978-0-439-88927-8(8))* Scholastic, Inc.

FIRE EXTINCTION

see also Fire Engines

Aloian, Molly. Fire Trucks: Racing to the Scene. 2010. (Vehicles on the Move Ser.). (ENG.). 32p. (J). (gr. k-3). lib. bdg. *(978-0-7787-3046-0(8))* Crabtree Publishing Co.

Ames, Michelle. Firefighters in Our Community. 2009. (J). 49.50 *(978-1-4358-2463-8(6))*; (ENG.). 24p. pap. 8.25 *(978-1-4358-2455-3(5))*; (ENG., Illus.). 24p. lib. bdg. 22.60 *(978-1-4042-8058-8(8)*, 1300570) Rosen Publishing Group, Inc., The. (PowerKids Pr.).

Anderson, Sheila. Fire Station. 2008. pap. 22.95 *(978-0-8225-9371-3(8))*; (ENG., Illus.). 8p. (gr. -1-1). pap. 4.95 *(978-0-8225-8841-2(2))* Lerner Publishing Group.

Apps, Roy. Smoke Flame Fire! A History of Firefighting. 2017. (ENG., Illus.). 32p. (J). (gr. 2-4). 16.99 ***(978-0-7502-9796-7(4)**, Wayland)* Hachette Children's Group GBR. Dist: Hachette Bk. Group.

Arkham, Thomas. Sirens & Smoke: Firefighters Folklore. Jabbour, Alan, ed. 2012. (North American Folklore for Youth Ser.). (Illus.). 48p. (J). (gr. 4). 19.95 *(978-1-4222-2489-2(9))* Mason Crest.

Battistoni, I. I Fight Fires: Learning the Long I Sound. 2009. (PowerPhonics Ser.). 24p. (gr. 1-1). 39.90 *(978-1-60851-447-2(1)*, PowerKids Pr.) Rosen Publishing Group, Inc., The.

Behrman, Carol H. Thomas Jefferson. 2005. (Just the Facts Biographies Ser.). (ENG., Illus.). 112p. (gr. 5-12). lib. bdg. 27.93 *(978-0-8225-2645-2(X)*, Lerner Pubns.) Lerner Publishing Group.

Best, B. J. Fire Trucks. 2017. (J). ***(978-1-5026-2554-0(7))*** Cavendish Square Publishing.

—Fireboats. 2017. (J). ***(978-1-5026-2557-1(1))*** Cavendish Square Publishing.

Bodden, Valerie. Fire Trucks. 2014. (J). pap. *(978-1-62832-065-7(6)*, Creative Paperbacks) Creative Co., The.

Bowman, Chris. Firefighter. 2014. (Dangerous Jobs Ser.). (ENG., Illus.). 24p. (J). (gr. 3-7). lib. bdg. 25.95 *(978-1-62617-110-7(6)*, Torque Bks.) Bellwether Media.

Bowman-Kruhm, Mary. A Day in the Life of a Firefighter. 2009. (Kids' Career Library). 24p. (gr. 3-3). 42.50 *(978-1-60853-437-1(5)*, PowerKids Pr.) Rosen Publishing Group, Inc., The.

Bridges, Sarah. I Drive a Fire Engine, 1 vol. Muehlenhardt, Amy Bailey, illus. 2006. (Working Wheels Ser.). (ENG.). 24p. (gr. -1-2). 26.65 *(978-1-4048-1606-0(2))* Picture Window Bks.

Brooks, Felicity. Fred the Firefighter. Litchfield, Jo, illus. rev. ed. 2006. (Jobs People Do Ser.). 23p. (J). (gr. -1). pap. 6.99 *(978-0-7945-1496-9(0)*, Usborne) EDC Publishing.

Carr, Aaron. The Fire Station. 2013. (J). *(978-1-62127-344-8(X))*; (J). pap. *(978-1-62127-349-3(0))*; 24p. pap. 12.95 *(978-1-4896-1667-8(5))* Weigl Pubs., Inc.

Christy, Lee Louis. I Go to Work as a Firefighter. 2003. (I Go to Work As Ser.). (Illus.). (J). *(978-1-58417-039-6(5))* Lake Street Pubs.

Clark, Rosalyn. A Visit to the Fire Station. 2017. (Bumba Books (tm) — Places We Go Ser.). (ENG.). 24p. (J). (gr. -1-1). 25.32 ***(978-1-5124-3372-2(1))*** Lerner Publishing Group.

Cooper, Michael L. Fighting Fire! Ten of the Deadliest Fires in American History & How We Fought Them. 2014. (ENG., Illus.). 224p. (J). (gr. 5-9). 19.99 *(978-0-8050-9714-6(7)*, 9780805097146, Holt, Henry & Co. Bks. For Young Readers) Holt, Henry & Co.

Crabtree, Marc. Meet My Neighbor, the Firefighter. 2013. (ENG., Illus.). 24p. (J). *(978-0-7787-0872-8(1))*; pap. *(978-0-7787-0876-6(4))* Crabtree Publishing Co.

Daynes Katie, et al. Firefighters. Fox, Christyan, illus. 2006. (Usborne Beginners Ser.). 32p. (J). *(978-0-439-88992-6(8))* Scholastic, Inc.

Demarest, Chris L. Firefighters A to Z. Demarest, Chris L., illus. 2003. (ENG., Illus.). 32p. (J). (gr. -1-3). 7.99 *(978-0-689-85999-1(6)*, McElderry, Margaret K. Bks.) McElderry, Margaret K. Bks.

Eliason, Mike & Kelley, K. C. Firefighter, Vol. 12. 2015. (On a Mission Ser.). (Illus.). 48p. (J). (gr. 5). 20.95 *(978-1-4222-3396-2(0))* Mason Crest.

Fitzgerald, Lee. Firefighters on the Job. 2017. (J). (gr. 1-1). 24p. 24.60 ***(978-1-5345-2143-8(7)**, KidHaven Publishing)*; 24p. pap. 8.25 ***(978-1-5345-2141-4(0))***; pap. 49.50 ***(978-1-5345-2142-1(9))*** Cengage Gale.

Fortuna, Lois. Fire Trucks. 2016. (To the Rescue! Ser.). 24p. (J). (gr. k-k). 22.60 *(978-1-4824-4660-9(X))* Stevens, Gareth Publishing LLLP.

Goldish, Meish. Firefighters to the Rescue. 2011. (Work of Heroes: First Responders in Action Ser.). 32p. (YA). (gr. 1-4). lib. bdg. 25.27 *(978-1-61772-284-4(7))* Bearport Publishing Co., Inc.

Gordon, Sharon. Que Hay Dentro de un Camion de Bomberos? 2006. (Bookworms Ser.). (SPA., Illus.). 32p. (gr. 1-2). lib. bdg. 15.95 *(978-0-7614-2391-1(5))* Marshall Cavendish Corp.

—Whats Inside a Fire Truck? (¿Qué Hay Dentro de un Camión de Bomberos?) 2006. (Bookworms Ser.). (ENG & SPA., Illus.). 32p. (gr. 1-2). lib. bdg. 15.95 *(978-0-7614-2472-7(5))* Marshall Cavendish Corp.

Gregory, Helen. A Firefighter's Day. 2011. (Wonder Readers Early Level Ser.). (ENG.). (gr. -1-1). 16p. pap. 35.94 *(978-1-4296-8062-2(8))*; 32p. pap. 5.99

E
F
G

(978-1-4296-7793-6(7)) Capstone Press of Coughlan Cos. (Wonder Readers).

Greve, Tom. Firefighters: Battling Smoke & Flames. 2014. (ENG., Illus.). 32p. (J). (gr. 4-8). 32.79 (978-1-62717-652-1(7)) Rourke Educational Media.

Hanson, Anne E. Fire Trucks in Action, 1 vol. 2011. (Transportation Zone Ser.). (ENG.). 24p. (gr. 1-2). lib. bdg. 25.32 (978-1-4296-6824-8(5), First Facts) Capstone Press of Coughlan Cos.

Hayward, Katherine. Fire Extinguisher Training. 2004. (Illus.). 40p. 5.95 (978-0-9740473-1-7(7)) Pivotal Force.

Herweck, Dona. A Day in the Life of a Firefighter, 1 vol. 2nd rev. ed. 2014. (TIME for KIDS(r) Nonfiction Readers Ser.). (ENG., Illus.). 28p. (J). (gr. 3-3). pap. 25.96 (978-1-4807-1066-5(0)) Shell Educational Publishing.

Hirsch, Judd, reader. Fireboat: The Heroic Adventures of the John J. Harvey. (Illus.). (J). 2006. pap. incl. audio (978-1-59112-985-1(0)) 2004. pap. 39.95 incl. audio compact disk (978-1-59112-989-9(3)) Live Oak Media.

Jeffries, Joyce. Meet the Fireman. 2012. (People Around Town Ser.). (Illus.). 24p. (J). (gr. k-2). 69.20 (978-1-4339-8060-2(6)); (J). 22.60 (978-1-4339-7328-4(6)); (J). pap. 8.15 (978-1-4339-7329-1(4)) Stevens, Gareth Publishing LLLP.

—Meet the Fireman / Te Presento A Los Bomberos. 2012. (People Around Town / Gente de mi ciudad Ser.). (SPA & ENG., Illus.). 24p. (J). (gr. k-2). 22.60 (978-1-4339-7386-4(3)) Stevens, Gareth Publishing LLLP.

Kalman, Bobbie. Bomberos Al Rescate. 2006. (Mi Communidad y Quienes Contribuyen a Ella Ser.). (ENG & SPA., Illus.). 32p. (J). (gr. 3-7). pap. (978-0-7787-8442-5(8)); lib. bdg. (978-0-7787-8428-9(2)) Crabtree Publishing Co.

—Firefighters to the Rescue! 2004. (My Community & Its Helpers Ser.). (ENG., Illus.). 32p. (J). pap. (978-0-7787-2124-6(8)) Crabtree Publishing Co.

Kalman, Maira. Fireboat: The Heroic Adventures of the John J. Harvey. Kalman, Maira, illus. 2005. (ENG., Illus.). 48p. (J). (gr. -1-3). reprint ed. pap. 6.99 (978-0-14-240362-4(8), Puffin Books) Penguin Young Readers Group.

Kalz, Jill. A Fire Station. 2003. 24p. (J). lib. bdg. 14.95 (978-1-58340-326-6(4)) Black Rabbit Bks.

Kenan, Tessa. Hooray for Firefighters! 2017. (Bumba Books (tm) — Hooray for Community Helpers! Ser.). (ENG.). 24p. (J). (gr. -1-1). lib. bdg. 25.32 **(978-1-5124-3349-4(7))** Lerner Publishing Group.

Laks Gorman, Jacqueline. Firefighters / Bomberos. Andersen, Gregg, photos by. 2010. (People in My Community / Mi comunidad Ser.). (SPA., Illus.). 24p. (gr. k-3). pap. 8.15 (978-1-4339-3757-6(3)) Stevens, Gareth Publishing LLLP.

Lewis, Brenda Ralph. Firefighters. 2004. (Rescue & Prevention Ser.). (Illus.). 96p. (YA). (gr. 7-18). lib. bdg. 22.95 (978-1-59084-402-1(5)) Mason Crest.

Lewis, Brenda Ralph. Putting Out Fires: Firefighters. 2017. (J). **(978-1-4222-3769-4(9))** Mason Crest.

Lindeen, Mary. A Visit to the Firehouse. 2015. (BeginningtoRead Ser.). (ENG.). 32p. (J). (gr. k-2). pap. 11.94 (978-1-60357-753-3(X)); (Illus.). lib. bdg. 22.60 (978-1-59953-693-4(5)) Norwood Hse. Pr.

McKinney, Devon. A Firefighter's Tools. 2015. (Community Helpers & Their Tools Ser.). (ENG.). 24p. (J). (gr. 2-3). 23.60 (978-1-4994-0897-3(8), PowerKids Pr.) Rosen Publishing Group, Inc., The.

Meachen Rau, Dana. Un Bombero. 2007. (En el Trabajo Ser.). (SPA., Illus.). 24p. (gr. k-1). lib. bdg. 15.95 (978-0-7614-2782-7(1), Benchmark Bks.) Marshall Cavendish Corp.

—Firefighter. 2007. (Jobs in Town Ser.). (SPA., Illus.). 24p. (gr. k-1). lib. bdg. 15.95 (978-0-7614-2617-2(5), Benchmark Bks.) Marshall Cavendish Corp.

Miller, Connie Colwell. I'll Be a Firefighter. Baroncelli, Silvia, illus. 2016. (When I Grow Up Ser.). (ENG.). 24p. (J). (gr. k-3). 20.95 (978-1-60753-761-8(3)) Amicus Publishing.

Minden, Cecilia. Firefighters. 2014. (People in Our Community Ser.). (ENG.). 24p. (J). (gr. k-3). 27.07 (978-1-62687-013-0(6), 206803) Child's World, Inc., The.

Murray, Aaron R. Firefighters Help Us. 2012. (All about Community Helpers Ser.). (Illus.). 24p. (J). pap. 7.95 (978-1-4644-0053-7(9)); (gr. -1-1). 22.60 (978-0-7660-4047-2(X)) Enslow Pubs., Inc. (Enslow Elementary).

Murray, Julie. Bomberos. 2016. (Trabajos en Mi Comunidad Ser.). (SPA.). 24p. (J). (gr. k-5). pap. 7.95 (978-1-4966-0719-5(8)) Capstone Classroom.

Nolan, Janet. The Firehouse Light. Lafrance, Marie, illus. 2010. (ENG.). 32p. (J). (gr. k-3). 15.99 (978-1-58246-298-1(4), Tricycle Pr.) Random Hse. Children's Bks.

Olsen, Alana. Firefighters to the Rescue. 2016. (Community Helpers Ser.). 00024p. (J). (gr. 1-1). pap. 8.25 (978-1-4994-2702-8(6), PowerKids Pr.) Rosen Publishing Group, Inc., The.

Pohl, Kathleen. What Happens at a Firehouse? (¿Qué pasa en una estación de Bomberos?) 2006. (Where People Work/Dónde Trabaja la Gente? Ser.). (ENG & SPA., Illus.). 24p. (gr. -1-3). pap. 8.15 (978-0-8368-7395-5(5), Weekly Reader Leveled Readers) Stevens, Gareth Publishing LLLP.

Ready, Dee. Firefighters Help. 2013. (Our Community Helpers Ser.). (ENG.). 24p. (gr. k-1). pap. 35.70 (978-1-62065-846-8(1)); pap. 6.29 (978-1-62065-845-1(3)); lib. bdg. 21.99 (978-1-62065-082-0(7)) Capstone Press of Coughlan Cos. (Pebble Bks.).

Riddle, John & Simons, Rae. Firefighter. Riggs, Ernestine G. & Gholar, Cheryl, eds. 2013. (Careers with Character Ser.: 18). 96p. (J). (gr. 7-18). 22.95 (978-1-4222-2756-5(1)) Mason Crest.

Rivera, Sheila. Firefighter. Behrman, Carol H., ed. 2005. (First Step Nonfiction - Work People Do Ser.). (ENG.). 8p. (gr. -1-1). pap. 4.95 (978-0-8225-5358-8(9), Lerner Pubns.) Lerner Publishing Group.

Royston, Angela. Fire Fighter! 2011. (DK Readers Ser.). (ENG.). 32p. (J). (gr. 1-3). 3.99 (978-0-7566-7589-9(8), DK Children) Dorling Kindersley Publishing, Inc.

Schmidt, Erin. Lo Que Hacen los Bomberos. 2007. (What Does a Community Helper Do? Bilingual Ser.).Tr. of What Firefighters Do. (ENG & SPA., Illus.). 24p. (J). (gr. 1-3). lib. bdg. 22.60 (978-0-7660-2826-5(7), Enslow Elementary) Enslow Pubs., Inc.

—What Does a Firefighter Do? 2005. (What Does a Community Helper Do? Ser.). (Illus.). 24p. (J). lib. bdg. 22.60 (978-0-7660-2539-4(X), Enslow Elementary) Enslow Pubs., Inc.

Shepherd, Jodie. A Day with Firefighters. 2012. (ENG., Illus.). 32p. (J). lib. bdg. 23.00 (978-0-531-28951-8(6)) Scholastic Library Publishing.

Siemens, Jared. Firefighters. 2016. (J). **(978-1-5105-2105-6(4))** SmartBook Media, Inc.

—Firefighters. 2015. (Illus.). 24p. (J). (978-1-4896-3645-4(5)) Weigl Pubs., Inc.

Staniford, Linda. Firefighters to the Rescue Around the World. 2016. (To the Rescue! Ser.). (ENG.). 24p. (gr. k-2). lib. bdg. 23.32 (978-1-4846-2751-8(2), Heinemann Read & Learn) Heinemann-Raintree.

Tourville, Amanda Doering. Fire Trucks, 1 vol. Trover, Zachary, illus. 2009. (Mighty Machines Ser.). (ENG.). 32p. (J). (gr. -1-3). 28.50 (978-1-60270-624-8(7)) Magic Wagon.

Troupe, Thomas Kingsley. Fighting a Fire, Step by Step, 1 vol. 2011. (Step-By-Step Stories Ser.). (ENG.). 32p. (gr. 1-2). lib. bdg. 27.32 (978-1-4296-6025-9(2), Aplus Bks.) Capstone Press of Coughlan Cos.

Wheeler, Jill C. Firefighters, 1 vol. 2003. (Everyday Heroes Ser.). (ENG., Illus.). 32p. (gr. k-6). 27.07 (978-1-57765-855-9(8), Checkerboard Library) ABDO Publishing Co.

Willett, Edward. Fires & Wildfires: A Practical Survival Guide. (Library of Emergency Preparedness Ser.). 64p. 2009. (gr. 6-6). 58.50 (978-1-60853-594-1(0), Rosen Reference) 2005. (Illus.). (YA). (gr. 5-9). lib. bdg. 31.95 (978-1-4042-0532-1(2)) Rosen Publishing Group, Inc., The.

FIRE EXTINCTION—VOCATIONAL GUIDANCE

Beyer, Mark. Smokejumpers: Life Fighting Fires. 2005. (Extreme Careers Ser.). (Illus.). 64p. (YA). (gr. 5-8). 31.95 (978-0-8239-3370-9(9)) Rosen Publishing Group, Inc., The.

Kenney, Karen L. Firefighters at Work, 1 vol. Dumm, Brian Caleb, illus. 2009. (Meet Your Community Workers Ser.). (ENG.). 32p. (J). (gr. -1-2). 28.50 (978-1-60270-648-4(4)) Magic Wagon.

Parks, Peggy J. Firefighter. 2004. (EXPLORING CAREERS Ser.). (ENG., Illus.). 48p. (J). 27.50 (978-0-7377-2066-2(2), Greenhaven Pr., Inc.) Cengage Gale.

Reeves, Diane Lindsey. Firefighter. 2008. (Virtual Apprentice Ser.). (Illus.). 64p. (gr. 4-9). per. 9.95 (978-0-8160-7551-5(4), Checkmark Bks.) Facts On File, Inc.

Thomas, William David. Forest Firefighter. 2008. (Cool Careers: Adventure Careers Ser.). (Illus.). 32p. (gr. 5-8). pap. 10.50 (978-0-8368-8889-8(8)); lib. bdg. 26.00 (978-0-8368-8882-9(0)) Stevens, Gareth Publishing LLLP.

Zeiger, Jennifer. What Do They Do? Firefighters. 2010. (Community Connections: What Do They Do? Ser.). (ENG.). 24p. (gr. 2-5). lib. bdg. 25.64 (978-1-60279-804-5(4), 200498) Cherry Lake Publishing.

FIRE FIGHTERS

ABDO Publishing Company Staff. Emergency Workers. 2012. (Emergency Workers Ser.: 6). (ENG.). 32p. (J). (gr. 5-9). lib. bdg. 162.42 (978-1-61783-511-7(0), Abdo & Daughters) ABDO Publishing Co.

Ames, Michelle. Firefighters in Our Community. 2009. (J). 49.50 (978-1-4358-2463-8(6)); (ENG.). 24p. pap. 8.25 (978-1-4358-2455-3(5)); (ENG., Illus.). 24p. lib. bdg. 22.60 (978-1-4042-8058-8(8), 1300570) Rosen Publishing Group, Inc., The. (PowerKids Pr.).

Apps, Roy. Smoke Flame Fire! A History of Firefighting. 2017. (ENG., Illus.). 32p. (J). (gr. 2-4). 16.99 **(978-0-7502-9796-7(4)**, Wayland) Hachette Children's Group GBR. Dist: Hachette Bk. Group.

Arkham, Thomas. Sirens & Smoke: Firefighters Folklore. Jabbour, Alan, ed. 2012. (North American Folklore for Youth Ser.). (Illus.). 48p. (J). (gr. 4). 19.95 (978-1-4222-2489-2(9)) Mason Crest.

Arlon, Penelope. Emergency! (LEGO Nonfiction) 2017. (Lego Ser.). (ENG.). 32p. (J). (gr. -1-3). pap. 4.99 **(978-1-338-14914-2(8))** Scholastic, Inc.

Arnold, Tedd. Firefighters. Arnold, Tedd, illus. 2014. (Fly Guy Presents Ser.). (ENG., Illus.). 32p. (J). (gr. k-2). pap. 3.99 (978-0-545-63160-0(2), Scholastic Reference) Scholastic, Inc.

Askew, Amanda & Crowson, Andrew. Firefighter. 2012. (Illus.). 24p. (gr. 1-3). pap. 7.95 (978-1-926853-48-2(2)) Saunders Bk. Co. CAN. Dist: RiverStream Publishing.

Battistoni, I. I Fight Fires: Learning the Long I Sound. 2009. (PowerPhonics Ser.). 24p. (gr. 1-1). 39.90 (978-1-60851-447-2(1), PowerKids Pr.) Rosen Publishing Group, Inc., The.

Behnke, Alison & Markle, Sandra. Firefighters. 2005. (Pull Ahead Bks.). (Illus.). 32p. (J). lib. bdg. 22.60 (978-0-8225-0063-6(9)) Lerner Publishing Group.

Behrman, Carol H. Thomas Jefferson. 2005. (Just the Facts Biographies Ser.). (ENG., Illus.). 112p. (gr. 5-12). lib. bdg. 27.93 (978-0-8225-2645-2(X), Lerner Pubns.) Lerner Publishing Group.

Bellisario, Gina. Let's Meet a Firefighter. Myer, Ed, illus. 2013. (Cloverleaf Books — Community Helpers Ser.). (ENG.). 24p. (gr. k-2). pap. 6.95 (978-1-4677-0802-9(X)); lib. bdg. 23.93 (978-0-7613-9025-1(1)) Lerner Publishing Group. (Millbrook Pr.).

Beyer, Mark. Smokejumpers: Life Fighting Fires. 2009. (Extreme Careers Ser.). 64p. (gr. 5-5). 58.50 (978-1-61512-408-4(X), Rosen Reference) Rosen Publishing Group, Inc., The.

Bourgeois, Paulette. Firefighters. LaFave, Kim, illus. 2005. (Kids Can Read Ser.). (ENG.). 32p. (J). (gr. 1-3). 3.95 (978-1-55337-751-1(6)) Kids Can Pr., Ltd. CAN. Dist: Hachette Bk. Group.

Bow, James. Rescue Missions. 2008. (Science Solves It Ser.). (ENG., Illus.). 32p. (J). (gr. 3-7). pap. (978-0-7787-4176-3(1), 1286290); lib. bdg. (978-0-7787-4169-5(9), 1286290) Crabtree Publishing Co.

Bowman, Chris. Firefighter. 2014. (Dangerous Jobs Ser.). (ENG., Illus.). 24p. (J). (gr. 3-7). lib. bdg. 25.95 (978-1-62617-110-7(6), Torque Bks.) Bellwether Media.

Bowman-Kruhm, Mary. A Day in the Life of a Firefighter. 2009. (Kids' Career Library). 24p. (gr. 3-3). 42.50 (978-1-60853-437-1(5), PowerKids Pr.) Rosen Publishing Group, Inc., The.

Bowman-Kruhm, Mary & Wirths, Claudine G. A Day in the Life of a Firefighter. 2004. (Kids' Career Library). (Illus.). 24p. (J). lib. bdg. 22.60 (978-0-8239-6809-1(X), PowerKids Pr.) Rosen Publishing Group, Inc., The.

Bridges, Sarah. I Drive a Fire Engine, 1 vol. Muehlenhardt, Amy Bailey, illus. 2006. (Working Wheels Ser.). (ENG.). 24p. (gr. -1-2). 26.65 (978-1-4048-1606-0(2)) Picture Window Bks.

Brooks, Felicity. Fred the Firefighter. Litchfield, Jo, illus. (Jobs People Do Ser.). (J). 2004. (ENG.). 24p. pap. 6.95 (978-0-7945-0725-1(5)) 2006. 23p. (gr. -1). pap. 6.99 (978-0-7945-1496-9(0)) EDC Publishing. (Usborne).

Brown, Don. America Is under Attack: September 11, 2001: the Day the Towers Fell. 2014. (Actual Times Ser.: 4). (ENG., Illus.). 64p. (J). (gr. 1-5). pap. 9.99 (978-1-250-04415-0(4), 9781250044150) Square Fish.

Brown, Mike. Rescue Services. 2004. (Twentieth-Century Developments in Fashion & Costume Ser.). (Illus.). 64p. (YA). (gr. 7-18). lib. bdg. 19.95 (978-1-59084-428-1(9)) Mason Crest.

Carr, Aaron. The Fire Station. 2013. (J). (978-1-62127-344-8(X)); (J). pap. (978-1-62127-349-3(0)); 24p. pap. 12.95 (978-1-4896-1667-8(5)) Weigl Pubs., Inc.

Charles, Audrey. I Can Be a Firefighter. 2017. (I Can Be Anything! Ser.). 24p. (gr. k-k). pap. 8.15 **(978-1-4824-6321-7(0))** Stevens, Gareth Publishing LLLP.

Christy, Lee Louis. I Go to Work as a Firefighter. 2003. (I Go to Work As Ser.). (Illus.). (J). (978-1-58417-039-6(5)) Lake Street Pubs.

Clemson, Wendy & Clemson, David. Firefighters to the Rescue. 2007. (Math Adventures Ser.). (Illus.). 32p. (gr. 1-4). pap. 10.50 (978-0-8368-8138-7(9)); lib. bdg. 26.00 (978-0-8368-7839-4(6)) Stevens, Gareth Publishing LLLP. (Gareth Stevens Learning Library).

Coan, Sharon. Trabajadores Que Me Cuidan (Workers Who Take Care of Me) 2016. (TIME for KIDS(r) Nonfiction Readers Ser.). (SPA.). 12p. (J). (gr. k-k). 4.99 (978-1-4938-3028-2(7)) Teacher Created Materials, Inc.

Crabtree, Marc. Meet My Neighbor, the Firefighter. 2013. (ENG., Illus.). 24p. (J). (978-0-7787-0872-8(1)); pap. (978-0-7787-0876-6(4)) Crabtree Publishing Co.

Daynes, Katie. Firefighters. Fox, Christyan, illus. 2007. (Beginners Social Studies). 32p. (J). (gr. -1-3). 4.99 (978-0-7945-1658-1(0), Usborne) EDC Publishing.

Daynes Katie, et al. Firefighters. Fox, Christyan, illus. 2006. (Usborne Beginners Ser.). 32p. (J). (978-0-439-88992-6(8)) Scholastic, Inc.

Demarest, Chris L. Firefighters A to Z. Demarest, Chris L., illus. 2003. (ENG., Illus.). 32p. (J). (gr. -1-3). 7.99 (978-0-689-85999-1(6), McElderry, Margaret K. Bks.) McElderry, Margaret K. Bks.

Dorling Kindersley Publishing Staff & Gersh, Camilla. Emergency Rescuers & Crime Fighters. 2016. (DK Readers Ser.). (ENG., Illus.). 64p. (J). (gr. 2-4). 14.99 (978-1-4654-4500-1(5), DK Children) Dorling Kindersley Publishing, Inc.

Eliason, Mike & Kelley, K. C. Firefighter, Vol. 12. 2015. (On a Mission Ser.). (Illus.). 48p. (J). (gr. 5). 20.95 (978-1-4222-3396-2(0)) Mason Crest.

Entin, Cindy. My First Counting Book: Firefighters. Boldman, Craig, illus. 2014. (ENG.). 10p. (J). bds. 5.99 (978-1-60433-470-8(3), Applesauce Pr.) Cider Mill Pr. Bk. Pubs., LLC.

Fitzgerald, Lee. Firefighters on the Job. 2017. (J). (gr. 1-1). 24p. 24.60 **(978-1-5345-2143-8(7)**, KidHaven Publishing); pap. 49.50 **(978-1-5345-2142-1(9))**; 24p. pap. 8.25 **(978-1-5345-2141-4(0))** Cengage Gale.

Forgotten Heroes of Ground Zero. 2005. (J). per. (978-1-59872-131-7(3)) Instant Pub.

Furgang, Kathy. National Geographic Readers: Wildfires. 2015. (Readers Ser.). (ENG., Illus.). 48p. (J). (gr. 1-4). pap. 3.99 (978-1-4263-2133-7(3), National Geographic Children's Bks.) National Geographic Society.

Gersh, Camilla. Emergency Rescue. 2016. (Illus.). 64p. (J). **(978-1-4806-9867-3(9))** Dorling Kindersley Publishing, Inc.

Gibson, Tim. We Are Firefighters. 2017. (Text Connections Guided Close Reading Ser.). (J). (gr. k). (978-1-4900-1781-5(X)) Benchmark Education Co.

Gigliotti, Jim. Smoke Jumpers. 2006. (Reading Rocks! Ser.). (ENG., Illus.). 32p. (J). (gr. 2-5). 28.50 (978-1-59296-735-3(3), 200721) Child's World, Inc., The.

Goldish, Meish. City Firefighters. 2014. (Fire Fight! the Bravest Ser.). 32p. (J). (gr. 2-7). lib. bdg. 26.60 (978-1-62724-097-0(7)) Bearport Publishing Co., Inc.

—Firefighters to the Rescue. 2011. (Work of Heroes: First Responders in Action Ser.). 32p. (YA). (gr. 1-4). lib. bdg. 25.27 (978-1-61772-284-4(7)) Bearport Publishing Co., Inc.

—Marine Firefighters. 2014. (Fire Fight! the Bravest Ser.). 32p. (J). (gr. 2-7). lib. bdg. 26.60 (978-1-62724-098-7(5)) Bearport Publishing Co., Inc.

—Smokejumpers. 2014. (Fire Fight! the Bravest Ser.). 32p. (J). (gr. 2-7). lib. bdg. 26.60 (978-1-62724-100-7(0)) Bearport Publishing Co., Inc.

Gordon, Nick. Smoke Jumper. 2012. (Dangerous Jobs Ser.). (ENG., Illus.). 24p. (J). (gr. 3-7). lib. bdg. 25.95 (978-1-60014-781-4(X), Torque Bks.) Bellwether Media.

Gorman, Jacqueline Laks. Firefighters. Andersen, Gregg, photos by. 2010. (People in My Community Ser.). (Illus.). 24p. (gr. k-3). pap. 8.15 (978-1-4339-3339-4(X)) Stevens, Gareth Publishing LLLP.

Gregory, Helen. A Firefighter's Day. 2011. (Wonder Readers Early Level Ser.). (ENG.). (gr. -1-1). 16p. pap. 35.94 (978-1-4296-8062-2(8)); 32p. pap. 5.99 (978-1-4296-7793-6(7)) Capstone Press of Coughlan Cos. (Wonder Readers).

Greve, Tom. Firefighters: Battling Smoke & Flames. 2014. (ENG., Illus.). 32p. (J). (gr. 4-8). 32.79 (978-1-62717-652-1(7)) Rourke Educational Media.

Herweck, Dona. A Day in the Life of a Firefighter, 1 vol. 2nd rev. ed. 2014. (TIME for KIDS(r) Nonfiction Readers Ser.). (ENG., Illus.). 28p. (J). (gr. 3-3). pap. 25.96 (978-1-4807-1066-5(0)) Shell Educational Publishing.

—A Day in the Life of a Firefighter, 1 vol. 2nd rev. ed. 2011. (Nonfiction Readers Ser.). (ENG.). 28p. (J). (gr. 3-3). pap. 8.99 (978-1-4333-3651-5(0)) Teacher Created Materials, Inc.

Jeffries, Joyce. Meet the Fireman. 2012. (People Around Town Ser.). (Illus.). 24p. (gr. k-2). 69.20 (978-1-4339-8060-2(6)); (J). 22.60 (978-1-4339-7328-4(6)); (J). pap. 8.15 (978-1-4339-7329-1(4)) Stevens, Gareth Publishing LLLP.

—Meet the Fireman / Te Presento A Los Bomberos. 2012. (People Around Town / Gente de mi ciudad Ser.). (SPA & ENG., Illus.). 24p. (J). (gr. k-2). 22.60 (978-1-4339-7386-4(3)) Stevens, Gareth Publishing LLLP.

Kalman, Bobbie. Bomberos Al Rescate. 2006. (Mi Communidad y Quienes Contribuyen a Ella Ser.). (ENG & SPA., Illus.). 32p. (J). (gr. 3-7). pap. (978-0-7787-8442-5(8)); lib. bdg. (978-0-7787-8428-9(2)) Crabtree Publishing Co.

—Emergency Workers Are on Their Way! 2004. (My Community & Its Helpers Ser.). (ENG., Illus.). 32p. (J). pap. (978-0-7787-2122-2(1)); lib. bdg. (978-0-7787-2094-2(2)) Crabtree Publishing Co.

—Firefighters to the Rescue! 2004. (My Community & Its Helpers Ser.). (ENG., Illus.). 32p. (J). pap. (978-0-7787-2124-6(8)) Crabtree Publishing Co.

Kenan, Tessa. Hooray for Firefighters! 2017. (Bumba Books (tm) — Hooray for Community Helpers! Ser.). (ENG.). 24p. (J). (gr. -1-1). lib. bdg. 25.32 **(978-1-5124-3349-4(7))** Lerner Publishing Group.

Kenney, Karen L. Firefighters at Work, 1 vol. Dumm, Brian Caleb, illus. 2009. (Meet Your Community Workers Ser.). (ENG.). 32p. (J). (gr. -1-2). 28.50 (978-1-60270-648-4(4)) Magic Wagon.

Keogh, Josie. A Trip to the Firehouse. 2012. (PowerKids Readers: My Community Ser.). (ENG., Illus.). 24p. (J). (gr. k-2). pap. 8.25 (978-1-4488-7485-9(8)); lib. bdg. 22.60 (978-1-4488-7406-4(8)) Rosen Publishing Group, Inc., The. (PowerKids Pr.).

—A Trip to the Firehouse: De Visita en la Estación de Bomberos. 2012. (PowerKids Readers: My Community / Mi comunidad Ser.). (SPA & ENG., Illus.). 24p. (J). (gr. k-2). lib. bdg. 22.60 (978-1-4488-7830-7(6), PowerKids Pr.) Rosen Publishing Group, Inc., The.

Keman, Elizabeth. Meet Firefighter Jen. 2008. (Rosen Real Readers: Upper Emergent Ser.). (ENG., Illus.). 12p. (gr. 1-2). pap. 5.90 (978-0-8239-8127-4(4)) Rosen Publishing Group, Inc., The.

Laks Gorman, Jacqueline. Firefighters / Bomberos. Andersen, Gregg, photos by. 2010. (People in My Community / Mi comunidad Ser.). (SPA., Illus.). 24p. (gr. k-3). pap. 8.15 (978-1-4339-3757-6(3)) Stevens, Gareth Publishing LLLP.

Lewis, Brenda Ralph. Firefighters. 2004. (Rescue & Prevention Ser.). (Illus.). 96p. (YA). (gr. 7-18). lib. bdg. 22.95 (978-1-59084-402-1(5)) Mason Crest.

Lewis, Brenda Ralph. Putting Out Fires: Firefighters. 2017. (J). **(978-1-4222-3769-4(9))** Mason Crest.

Lidner, D. B. The A,B, C's of Firefighting & Fire Safety. 2009. pap. 3.95 (978-1-61584-189-9(X)) Independent Pub.

Liebman, Dan. Bombero. 2003. (Quiero Ser.).Tr. of I Want to Be a Firefighter. (SPA., Illus.). 24p. (J). (gr. -1-2). pap. 5.99 (978-1-55297-743-9(9), 9781552977439) Firefly Bks., Ltd.

—Pompier. Lior, Tsipora, tr. from ENG. 2006. (Je Veux Etre Ser.). (FRE., Illus.). 24p. (J). (gr. -1-2). pap. 5.95 (978-1-55407-104-3(6), 9781554071043) Firefly Bks., Ltd.

Lindeen, Mary. A Visit to the Firehouse. 2015. (BeginningtoRead Ser.). (ENG.). 32p. (J). (gr. k-2). pap. 11.94 (978-1-60357-753-3(X)); (Illus.). lib. bdg. 22.60 (978-1-59953-693-4(5)) Norwood Hse. Pr.

Mara, Wil. Smokejumper. 2015. (21st Century Skills Library: Cool STEAM Careers Ser.). (ENG.). 32p. (J). (gr. 4-7). 29.93 (978-1-63362-007-0(7), 205940) Cherry Lake Publishing.

Martin, Isabel. A Fire Station Field Trip. 2015. (Let's Take a Field Trip Ser.). (ENG.). 24p. (J). pap. 6.95 (978-1-4914-2314-1(5), Pebble Plus) Capstone Press of Coughlan Cos.

Mattern, Joanne. Brigadas Aereas Contraincendios. 2004. (Trabajo en Grupo (Working Together) Ser.). (SPA & ENG., Illus.). 24p. (J). (gr. 1-4). lib. bdg. 22.60 (978-0-8239-6844-2(8)) Rosen Publishing Group, Inc., The.

—Brigadas aéreas contraincendios (Smoke Jumpers) 2009. (Trabajo en grupo (Working Together) Ser.). (SPA.). 24p. (gr. 1-2). 42.50 (978-1-60854-575-9(X), Editorial Buenas Letras) Rosen Publishing Group, Inc., The.

—Smoke Jumpers. 2009. (Working Together Ser.). 24p. (gr. 1-2). 42.50 (978-1-60854-833-0(3), PowerKids Pr.) Rosen Publishing Group, Inc., The.

McKinney, Devon. A Firefighter's Tools. 2015. (Community Helpers & Their Tools Ser.). (ENG.). 24p. (J). (gr. 2-3). 23.60 (978-1-4994-0897-3(8), PowerKids Pr.) Rosen Publishing Group, Inc., The.

Meachen Rau, Dana. Un Bombero. 2007. (En el Trabajo Ser.). (SPA., Illus.). 24p. (gr. k-1). lib. bdg. 15.95 (978-0-7614-2782-7(1), Benchmark Bks.) Marshall Cavendish Corp.

—Firefighter. 2007. (Jobs in Town Ser.). (SPA., Illus.). 24p. (gr. k-1). lib. bdg. 15.95 (978-0-7614-2617-2(5), Benchmark Bks.) Marshall Cavendish Corp.

Michele, Tracey. What Do Firefighters Do? 2011. (Learn-Abouts Ser.). (Illus.). 16p. (J). pap. 7.95 (978-1-59920-592-2(0)) Black Rabbit Bks.

Miller, Connie Colwell. I'll Be a Firefighter. Baroncelli, Silvia, illus. 2016. (When I Grow Up Ser.). (ENG.). 24p. (J). (gr. k-3). 20.95 (978-1-60753-761-8(3)) Amicus Publishing.

Mills, Nathan & Roza, Greg. Firefighters Help Us. 2012. (Rosen Readers Ser.). (ENG., Illus.). 16p. (J). (gr. k-1). pap. 7.00 (978-1-4488-8701-9(1), Rosen Classroom) Rosen Publishing Group, Inc., The.

Minden, Cecilia. Firefighters. 2014. (People in Our Community Ser.). (ENG.). 24p. (J). (gr. k-3). 27.07 (978-1-62687-013-0(6), 206803) Child's World, Inc., The.

Murray, Aaron R. Firefighters Help Us. 2012. (All about Community Helpers Ser.). (Illus.). 24p. (J). pap. 7.95 (978-1-4644-0053-7(9)); (gr. -1-1). 22.60 (978-0-7660-4047-2(X)) Enslow Pubs., Inc. (Enslow Elementary).

Murray, Julie. Bomberos. 2016. (Trabajos en Mi Comunidad Ser.). (SPA.). 24p. (J). (gr. k-5). pap. 7.95 (978-1-4966-0719-5(8)) Capstone Classroom.

—Fire Fighters, 1 vol. 2015. (ENG., Illus.). 24p. (J). 27.07 (978-1-62970-913-0(1)) ABDO Publishing Co.

Neiman, Tommy & Reynolds, Sue. Sirens for the Cross for the Rookie Rescuer. Reynolds, Sue & Hygh, Angela, eds. 2003. (J). per. 14.95 (978-0-9668878-2-2(4)) Embrace Communications.

Ochiltree, Dianne. Molly, by Golly! The Legend of Molly Williams, America's First Female Firefighter. Kemly,

Kathleen, illus. 2012. (ENG.). 32p. (J). (gr. 2-4). 16.95 *(978-1-59078-721-2(8)*, Calkins Creek) Boyds Mills Pr.

Ollhoff, Jim. Firefighter. 2012. (Emergency Workers Ser.). 32p. (J). (gr. 5-9). lib. bdg. 27.07 *(978-1-61783-513-1(7)*, Abdo & Daughters) ABDO Publishing Co.

Olsen, Alana. Firefighters to the Rescue. 2016. (Community Helpers Ser.). 00024p. (J). (gr. 1-1). pap. 8.25 *(978-1-4994-2702-8(6)*, PowerKids Pr.) Rosen Publishing Group, Inc., The.

Owen, Ann. Protecting Your Home: A Book about Firefighters, 1 vol. Thomas, Eric, illus. 2003. (Community Workers Ser.). (ENG.). 24p. (gr. -1-3). per. 8.95 *(978-1-4048-0482-1(X))* Picture Window Bks.

Oxlade, Chris & Feldman, Thea. Kingfisher Readers L3: Firefighters. 2014. (Kingfisher Readers Ser.). (ENG., Illus.). 32p. (J). (gr. k-3). 12.99 *(978-0-7534-7122-7(1)*, 9780753471227, Kingfisher) Roaring Brook Pr.

Petersen, Justin. Smokejumpers: Fighting Fires from the Sky. 2016. (Emergency! Ser.). (ENG., Illus.). 32p. (gr. 3-4). lib. bdg. 27.99 *(978-1-4914-8030-4(0)*, Edge Bks.) Capstone Press of Coughlan Cos.

Pohl, Kathleen. What Happens at a Firehouse? (¿Qué pasa en una estación de Bomberos?) 2006. (Where People Work/Dónde Trabaja la Gente? Ser.). (ENG & SPA., Illus.). 24p. (gr. -1-3). pap. 8.15 *(978-0-8368-7395-5(5)*, Weekly Reader Leveled Readers) Stevens, Gareth Publishing LLLP.

Ready, Dee. Firefighters Help. 2013. (Our Community Helpers Ser.). (ENG.). 24p. (gr. k-1). pap. 35.70 *(978-1-62065-846-8(1))*; pap. 6.29 *(978-1-62065-845-1(3))*; lib. bdg. 21.99 *(978-1-62065-082-0(7))* Capstone Press of Coughlan Cos. (Pebble Bks.).

Riddle, John & Simons, Rae. Firefighter. Riggs, Ernestine G. & Gholar, Cheryl, eds. 2013. (Careers with Character Ser.: 18). 96p. (J). (gr. 7-18). 22.95 *(978-1-4222-2756-5(1))* Mason Crest.

Rivera, Sheila. Firefighter. Behrman, Carol H., ed. 2005. (First Step Nonfiction - Work People Do Ser.). (ENG.). 8p. (gr. -1-1). pap. 4.95 *(978-0-8225-5358-8(9)*, Lerner Pubns.) Lerner Publishing Group.

Rogers, Amy B. Que Hacen Los Bomberos? / What Do Firefighters Do? 2015. (Ayudantes de la Comunidad / Helping the Community Ser.). (ENG & SPA.). 24p. (J). (gr. 1-1). 23.60 *(978-1-4994-0639-9(8)*, PowerKids Pr.) Rosen Publishing Group, Inc., The.

—What Do Firefighters Do? 2015. (Helping the Community Ser.). (ENG., Illus.). 24p. (J). (gr. 1-1). 23.60 *(978-1-4994-0628-3(2)*, PowerKids Pr.) Rosen Publishing Group, Inc., The.

Royston, Angela. Diary of a Firefighter, 1 vol. 2013. (Diary of A... Ser.). (ENG.). 32p. (gr. 1-3). 27.32 *(978-1-4329-7583-8(8))*; pap. 8.95 *(978-1-4329-7590-6(0))* Heinemann-Raintree. (Heinemann First Library).

—Fire Fighter! 2011. (DK Readers Ser.). (ENG.). 32p. (J). (gr. 1-3). 3.99 *(978-0-7566-7589-9(8)*, DK Children) Dorling Kindersley Publishing, Inc.

—Fire Fighter! 2011. (DK Reader Level 2 Ser.). (gr. k-3). lib. bdg. 13.55 *(978-0-613-07767-5(9)*, Turtleback) Turtleback Bks.

Sanna, Ellyn. Firefighters' Folklore. 2004. (North American Folklore Ser.). (Illus.). 112p. (YA). (gr. 7-18). lib. bdg. 22.95 *(978-1-59084-334-5(7))* Mason Crest.

Santora, Maureen Crethan. My Son Christopher: A 9/11 Mother's Tale of Remembrance. 2008. 36p. 31.99 *(978-1-4363-3044-2(0))* Xlibris Corp.

Santos, Penelope. A Fireman & Fire. 2015. (Rosen REAL Readers: STEM & STEAM Collection). (ENG.). 12p. (gr. 1-2). pap. 6.33 *(978-1-4994-9741-0(5)*, Rosen Classroom) Rosen Publishing Group, Inc., The.

Scarry, Richard. A Day at the Fire Station. 2003. (gr. k-3). 14.75 *(978-0-613-83879-5(3)*, Turtleback) Turtleback Bks.

Schmidt, Erin. Lo Que Hacen los Bomberos. 2007. (What Does a Community Helper Do? Bilingual Ser.).Tr. of What Firefighters Do. (ENG & SPA., Illus.). 24p. (J). (gr. 1-3). lib. bdg. 22.60 *(978-0-7660-2826-5(7)*, Enslow Elementary) Enslow Pubs., Inc.

—What Does a Firefighter Do? 2005. (What Does a Community Helper Do? Ser.). (Illus.). 24p. (J). lib. bdg. 22.60 *(978-0-7660-2539-4(X)*, Enslow Elementary) Enslow Pubs., Inc.

Settle, Melissa A. Firefighters Then & Now, 1 vol. 2006. (Primary Source Readers Ser.). (ENG.). 32p. (J). (gr. 1-1). pap. 8.99 *(978-0-7439-9371-5(3))* Shell Educational Publishing.

Sévigny, Eric, illus. Caillou - The Firefighter. 2013. (Playtime Ser.). (ENG.). 24p. (J). (gr. -1-1). 4.99 *(978-2-89450-861-9(1))* Caillouet, Gerry.

Shepherd, Jodie. A Day with Firefighters. 2012. (Rookie Read-About Community Ser.). (ENG., Illus.). 32p. (J). pap. 5.95 *(978-0-531-29251-8(7))*; lib. bdg. 23.00 *(978-0-531-28951-8(6))* Scholastic Library Publishing.

Siemens, Jared. Firefighters. 2016. (J). ***(978-1-5105-2105-6(4))*** SmartBook Media, Inc.

—Firefighters. 2015. (Illus.). 24p. (J). *(978-1-4896-3645-4(5))* Weigl Pubs., Inc.

Thiessen, Mark. Extreme Wildfire: Smoke Jumpers, High-Tech Gear, Survival Tactics, & the Extraordinary Science of Fire. 2016. (ENG., Illus.). 112p. (J). (gr. 3-7). pap. 12.99 *(978-1-4263-2530-4(4)*, National Geographic Children's Bks.) National Geographic Society.

Thomas, William David. Forest Firefighter. 2008. (Cool Careers: Adventure Careers Ser.). (Illus.). 32p. (gr. 5-8). pap. 10.50 *(978-0-8368-8889-8(8))*; lib. bdg. 26.00 *(978-0-8368-8882-9(0))* Stevens, Gareth Publishing LLLP.

Tieck, Sarah. Smoke Jumpers, 1 vol. 2011. (Extreme Jobs Ser.). (ENG., Illus.). 32p. (J). (gr. 2-5). 28.50 *(978-1-61783-027-3(5))* ABDO Publishing Co.

Troupe, Thomas Kingsley. Fighting a Fire, Step by Step, 1 vol. 2011. (Step-By-Step Stories Ser.). (ENG.). 32p. (gr. 1-2). lib. bdg. 27.32 *(978-1-4296-6025-9(2)*, Aplus Bks.) Capstone Press of Coughlan Cos.

—If I Were a Firefighter, 1 vol. Reid, Mick, illus. 2010. (Dream Big! Ser.). (ENG.). 24p. (gr. k-3). lib. bdg. 26.65 *(978-1-4048-5535-9(1))* Picture Window Bks.

Westmark, Jon. Smoke Jumpers in Action. 2017. (Dangerous Jobs in Action Ser.). (ENG.). 32p. (J). (gr. 3-6). lib. bdg. 27.07 *(978-1-5038-1632-9(X)*, 211148) Child's World, Inc., The.

Wheeler, Jill C. Firefighters, 1 vol. 2003. (Everyday Heroes Ser.). (ENG., Illus.). 32p. (gr. k-6). 27.07 *(978-1-57765-855-9(8)*, Checkerboard Library) ABDO Publishing Co.

White, Nancy. Aviation Firefighters. 2014. (Fire Fight! the Bravest Ser.). 32p. (J). (gr. 2-7). lib. bdg. 26.60 *(978-1-62724-096-3(9))* Bearport Publishing Co., Inc.

Zeiger, Jennifer. What Do They Do? Firefighters. 2010. (Community Connections: What Do They Do? Ser.). (ENG.). 24p. (gr. 2-5). lib. bdg. 25.64 *(978-1-60279-804-5(4)*, 200498) Cherry Lake Publishing.

FIRE FIGHTERS—FICTION

Andrews, Julie & Hamilton, Emma Walton. Dumpy & the Firefighters. Walton, Tony, illus. 2003. (Julie Andrews Collection). (ENG.). 32p. (J). (gr. -1-2). 15.99 *(978-0-06-052681-8(5)*, Julie Andrews Collection) HarperCollins Pubs.

Appleton, Victor. Tom Swift among the Fire Fighters: Or Battling with Flames from the Air. l.t. ed. 2007. (ENG.). 154p. pap. 21.99 *(978-1-4346-1583-1(9))* Creative Media Partners, LLC.

—Tom Swift among the Fire Fighters or Bat. 2006. pap. *(978-1-4065-0893-2(4))* Dodo Pr.

Austin, Mike. Fire Engine No. 9. 2015. (ENG., Illus.). 40p. (J). (gr. -1-2). 19.99 *(978-0-375-97428-1(8)*, Random Hse. Bks. for Young Readers) Random Hse. Children's Bks.

Ballantyne, Robert Michael. Life in the Red Brigade: London Fire Brigade. l.t. ed. 2007. 98p. pap. 18.99 *(978-1-4346-3772-7(7))* Creative Media Partners, LLC.

Beaty, Andrea. Firefighter Ted. Lemaître, Pascal, illus. 2009. (ENG.). 32p. (J). (gr. -1-3). 17.99 *(978-1-4169-2821-8(9)*, McElderry, Margaret K. Bks.) McElderry, Margaret K. Bks.

Beck, Andrea. Elliot's Fire Truck, 1 vol. Beck, Andrea, illus. 2010. (ENG., Illus.). 32p. (J). (gr. -1-3). 19.95 *(978-1-55469-143-2(5))* Orca Bk. Pubs. USA.

Berenstain, Mike. The Berenstain Bears Visit the Firehouse. 2016. (Berenstain Bears Ser.). (J). lib. bdg. 13.55 *(978-0-606-38771-2(4))* Turtleback Bks.

Berenstain, Mike, et al. The Berenstain Bears(r) Visit the Firehouse. 2016. (Illus.). (J). ***(978-1-5182-1125-6(9))*** Baker & Taylor, CATS.

Biggs, Brian. I'm a Firefighter. 2016. (Tinyville Town Ser.). (ENG., Illus.). 22p. (J). (gr. -1 — 1). bds. 7.95 *(978-1-4197-2134-2(8)*, Abrams Appleseed) Abrams, Inc.

Blount, Patty. Nothing Left to Burn. 2015. (ENG.). 368p. (YA). (gr. 8-12). pap. 9.99 *(978-1-4926-1329-9(0)*, 9781492613299) Sourcebooks, Inc.

Bourgeois, Paulette. Fire Fighters. LaFave, Kim, illus. 2005. 32p. (J). lib. bdg. 15.38 *(978-1-4242-1189-0(1))* Fitzgerald Bks.

Bowen, Carl. Back Burn. Lee, Marc, illus. 2016. (Firestormers Ser.). (ENG.). 112p. (gr. 4-8). lib. bdg. 26.65 *(978-1-4965-3305-0(4))* Stone Arch Bks.

—Bone Yard. Lee, Marc, illus. 2016. (Firestormers Ser.). (ENG.). 112p. (gr. 4-8). lib. bdg. 26.65 *(978-1-4965-3306-7(2))* Stone Arch Bks.

—Fire Front. Lee, Marc, illus. 2016. (Firestormers Ser.). (ENG.). 112p. (gr. 4-8). lib. bdg. 26.65 *(978-1-4965-3308-1(9))* Stone Arch Bks.

—Firestormers, 4 vols. Lee, Marc, illus. 2016. (Firestormers Ser.). (ENG.). 112p. (gr. 4-8). 106.60 *(978-1-4965-3321-0(6))* Stone Arch Bks.

—Firestormers: Elite Firefighting Crew. Lee, Marc, illus. 2016. (ENG.). 224p. (gr. 4-8). pap. 8.95 *(978-1-62370-756-9(0))* Capstone Young Readers of Coughlan Cos.

—Hot Spot. Lee, Marc, illus. 2016. (Firestormers Ser.). (ENG.). 112p. (gr. 4-8). lib. bdg. 26.65 *(978-1-4965-3307-4(0))* Stone Arch Bks.

Brewster, James Burd. Uncle Rocky, Fireman: Fire! Barley-Cohrs, Dayna, illus. 2013. 34p. pap. 11.49 *(978-0-9911994-1-9(3))* J2B Publishing LLC.

—Uncle Rocky, Fireman: Something's Missing. Barley-Cohrs, Dayna, illus. 2013. 34p. pap. 11.49 *(978-0-9911994-2-6(1))* J2B Publishing LLC.

Brooke, Samantha. Fire in the Forest! 2012. (LEGO City Scholastic Readers Level 1 Ser.). (Illus.). 31p. (J). lib. bdg. 13.55 *(978-0-606-23730-7(5)*, Turtleback) Turtleback Bks.

Brooke, Samantha & Scholastic, Inc. Staff. Fire in the Forest! 2012. (Lego City Ser.). (ENG., Illus.). 32p. (J). (gr. -1-k). pap. 3.99 *(978-0-545-36992-3(4))* Scholastic, Inc.

Carbone, Courtney. Rescue Buddies! (Disney Planes: Fire & Rescue) Random House Disney Staff, illus. 2015. (Friendship Box Ser.). (ENG.). 48p. (J). (-k). bds. 10.99 *(978-0-7364-3333-4(3)*, RH/Disney) Random Hse. Children's Bks.

Caviezel, Giovanni & Mesturini, Cristina. Fireman. 2009. (Mini People Shape Bks.). (ENG., Illus.). 10p. (J). (gr. -1-2). bds. 5.99 *(978-0-7641-6220-6(9))* Barron's Educational Series, Inc.

Chandler, Jeff. The Fire Dog Champ. 2008. 28p. pap. 24.95 *(978-1-4241-8615-0(3))* America Star Bks.

Clemesha, David & Zimmerman, Andrea. Fire Engine Man. Clemesha, David & Zimmerman, Andrea, illus. 2007. (ENG., Illus.). 32p. (J). (gr. -1-k). 17.99 *(978-0-8050-7905-0(X)*, 9780805079050, Holt, Henry & Co. Bks. For Young Readers) Holt, Henry & Co.

Coffin, Rebecca, et al. Binkie & the Firemen: A Lost Puppy Rescued in A Basement Fire Becomes the Firemen's Pet. 2011. 50p. 35.95 *(978-1-258-06785-4(4))* Literary Licensing, LLC.

Cohen, Alana. Heroes! White, David A., illus. 2011. (Lego City Ser.). (ENG.). 10p. (J). (gr. -1-k). bds. 9.99 *(978-0-545-27439-5(7))* Scholastic, Inc.

Coll-Seck, Jayden. The Fire & the Firefighter, 01 vols., 1. 2016. (Rosen REAL Readers: Social Studies Nonfiction / Fiction: Family, Community, & the World Ser.). (ENG.). 12p. (J). pap. 6.33 *(978-1-5081-1946-3(5)*, Rosen Classroom) Rosen Publishing Group, Inc., The.

Cousins, Lucy. Maisy's Fire Engine. Cousins, Lucy, illus. 2009. (Maisy Ser.). (ENG., Illus.). 16p. (J). (gr. k-k). bds. 5.99 *(978-0-7636-4252-5(5))* Candlewick Pr.

Davies, Beth & Ripley, Esther. DK Readers L2: LEGO City: Heroes to the Rescue. 2016. (DK Readers Ser.). (ENG., Illus.). 48p. (J). (gr. k-2). pap. 3.99 *(978-1-4654-5189-7(7)*, DK Children) Dorling Kindersley Publishing, Inc.

Disney. Dusty to the Rescue. 2014. lib. bdg. 14.75 *(978-0-606-35999-3(0))* Turtleback Bks.

Disney Editors. Brave Firefighters. 2014. (Step into Reading Level 2 Ser.). lib. bdg. 13.55 *(978-0-606-36000-5(X))* Turtleback Bks.

Dormer, Frank W. Firefighter Duckies! Dormer, Frank W., illus. 2017. (ENG., Illus.). 40p. (J). (gr. -1-3). 17.99 *(978-1-4814-6090-3(0)*, Atheneum Bks. for Young Readers) Simon & Schuster Children's Publishing.

Durden, Angela K. Heroes Need Practice, Too! Hohn, Tracy, illus. 2006. (J). 11.95 *(978-0-9701356-1-2(0))* WRITER for HIRE!

Elya, Susan Middleton. Fire! Fuego! Brave Bomberos. Santat, Dan, illus. 2012. (ENG & SPA.). 40p. (J). (gr. -1-1). lib. bdg. 17.89 *(978-1-59990-759-8(3)*, 9781599907598, Bloomsbury USA Childrens) Bloomsbury Publishing USA.

—Fire! ¡Fuego! Brave Bomberos. Dantat, Dan & Santat, Dan, illus. 2012. (ENG & SPA.). 40p. (J). (gr. -1-1). 16.99 *(978-1-59990-461-0(6)*, 9781599904610, Bloomsbury USA Childrens) Bloomsbury Publishing USA.

Filmer, Mary, et al. Farmer Frank: Educational Fire Safety, Poetry & Story Colouring Book. 2010. 50p. pap. 9.99 *(978-1-60911-721-4(2)*, Eloquent Bks.) Strategic Book Publishing & Rights Agency (SBPRA).

Fireman Sam Pocket Library, 6 vols. 2010. (Illus.). 10p. bds. *(978-1-4052-4987-4(0))* Egmont Bks., Ltd.

Giff, Patricia Reilly. Winter Sky. 2014. (ENG.). 160p. (J). (gr. 3-7). 15.99 *(978-0-375-83892-7(9)*, Lamb, Wendy Bks.) Random Hse. Children's Bks.

Godwin, Laura. This Is the Firefighter [Board Book]. Hector, Julian, illus. 2015. (ENG.). 24p. (J). (gr. -1 — 1). bds. 6.99 *(978-1-4847-0733-3(8))* Hyperion Bks. for Children.

Goebel, Jenny & dePaola, Tomie. The Firefighter. Psacharopulo, Alessandra, illus. 2015. (ENG.). 32p. (J). (gr. -1-k). bds. 3.99 *(978-0-448-48101-2(4)*, Grosset & Dunlap) Penguin Young Readers Group.

Golden Books. The Fire Engine Book. Gergely, Tibor, illus. 2015. (Little Golden Board Book Ser.). (ENG.). 26p. (J). (-k). bds. 7.99 *(978-0-553-52224-2(8)*, Golden Bks.) Random Hse. Children's Bks.

Greene, Rhonda Gowler. Firebears, the Rescue Team. Andreasen, Dan, illus. 2015. (ENG.). 30p. (J). (gr. -1 — 1). bds. 7.99 *(978-1-62779-240-0(6)*, 9781627792400, Holt, Henry & Co. Bks. For Young Readers) Holt, Henry & Co.

Gross, S. D. Freddie, Fireman Mike. 2007. (Illus.). 24p. (J). (gr. -1-3). per. 12.99 *(978-1-59879-343-7(8))* Lifevest Publishing, Inc.

Haley, Patty. Firefighter Fred's Busy Day. Karactaz, illus. 2010. (ENG.). 24p. (gr. 1-2). pap. 8.95 *(978-1-61181-071-4(X)*, Kaeden Bks.) Kaeden Corp.

—Firefighter Fred's Busy Day (6 Pack) Karactaz, illus. 2010. (ENG.). 24p. (gr. 1-2). pap. *(978-1-61181-072-1(8)*, Kaeden Bks.) Kaeden Corp.

Hasbro Editors. Training Academy: Firefighters. 2016. (Transformers Passport to Reading Ser.). (J). lib. bdg. 13.55 *(978-0-606-38321-9(2))* Turtleback Bks.

Hawes, Rachelle. Dan the Rescue Man: Fire at Farmer Dave's. 2013. 24p. pap. 10.95 *(978-1-4525-1161-0(6)*, Balboa Pr.) Author Solutions, Inc.

Hegarty, Pat. If I Were a... Firefighter. Pope, Liz & Pope, Kate, illus. 2008. 12p. (J). (gr. -1). bds. 6.95 *(978-1-58925-839-6(8))* Tiger Tales.

Hicks, John B. The Ghost of Fire Company 18. 2005. 149p. (J). per. 6.50 *(978-0-9742829-2-3(8))* Quiet Man Publishing.

Hubbell, Patricia. Firefighters! Speeding! Spraying! Saving!, 0 vols. Garofoli, Viviana, illus. 2012. (ENG.). 32p. (J). (gr. -1-2). pap. 7.99 *(978-0-7614-6245-3(7)*, 9780761462453, Amazon Children's Publishing) Amazon Publishing.

—Firefighters! Speeing! Spraying! Saving!, 0 vols. Garofoli, Viviana, illus. 2009. (ENG.). 32p. (J). (gr. -1-2). bds. 7.99 *(978-0-7614-5615-5(5)*, 9780761456155, Amazon Children's Publishing) Amazon Publishing.

Johnson, Stephen T. My Little Red Fire Truck. Johnson, Stephen T., illus. 2009. (ENG., Illus.). 16p. (J). (gr. -1-2). 24.99 *(978-1-4169-2522-4(8)*, Simon & Schuster/Paula Wiseman Bks.) Simon & Schuster/Paula Wiseman Bks.

Kavanagh, Charlene Kate. Going Home: The Lost Story of Chief the Fire Dog. 2007. 116p. 20.95 *(978-0-595-88236-6(6))*; 112p. (gr. 10-12). per. 10.95 *(978-0-595-40946-4(6))* iUniverse, Inc.

King, Trey. Firefighter Rescue. Kiernan, Kenny, illus. 2015. (Lego City Ser.). (ENG.). 32p. (J). (gr. -1-3). pap. 3.99 *(978-0-545-82555-9(5))* Scholastic, Inc.

—Firefighter Rescue. 2015. (LEGO City Scholastic Readers Level 1 Ser.). lib. bdg. 13.55 *(978-0-606-37795-9(6))* Turtleback Bks.

—Halloween Rescue! Wang, Sean, illus. 2013. (Lego City Ser.). (ENG.). 24p. (J). (gr. -1-3). 4.99 *(978-0-545-51572-6(6))* Scholastic, Inc.

Klein, Marissa. Rosie Wants to Be a Fireman. Hagel, Brooke, illus. 2013. 30p. (J). 19.95 *(978-0-9894933-3-8(4))* Rissylyn.

Klimo, Kate. Sparky. Jessell, Tim, illus. 2016. (Dog Diaries: 9). (ENG.). 160p. (J). (gr. 2-5). pap. 7.99 *(978-0-553-53493-1(9)*, Random Hse. Bks. for Young Readers) Random Hse. Children's Bks.

Lego, et al. Fire Truck to the Rescue!, No. 1. 2009. (Lego City Ser.). (ENG.). 32p. (J). (gr. -1-k). pap. 3.99 *(978-0-545-11543-8(4))* Scholastic, Inc.

Lenahan, Joe. Fire House. 2013. 28p. pap. 16.10 *(978-1-4669-7105-9(3))* Trafford Publishing.

London, Jonathan. Here Comes Firefighter Hippo. Eduar, Gilles, illus. 2013. (Little Hippo Ser.). (ENG.). 32p. (J). (gr. -1-1). 15.95 *(978-1-59078-968-1(7))* Boyds Mills Pr.

Long, Loren. Otis & the Kittens. Long, Loren, illus. 2016. (Otis Ser.). (ENG., Illus.). 40p. (J). (gr. -1-3). 17.99 *(978-0-399-16398-2(0)*, Philomel Bks.) Penguin Young Readers Group.

Lupica, Mike. Last Man Out. (ENG.). (J). (gr. 5). 2017. 272p. 8.99 ***(978-0-14-751491-2(6)***, Puffin Books) 2016. 256p. 17.99 *(978-0-399-17279-3(3)*, Philomel Bks.) Penguin Young Readers Group.

Lynch, Chris. Hothouse. 2010. (ENG.). 208p. (YA). (gr. 8-18). 16.99 *(978-0-06-167379-5(X)*, HarperTeen) HarperCollins Pubs.

Mammano, Julie. Rhinos Who Rescue. 2007. (Rhinos Ser.: RHIN). (ENG., Illus.). 32p. (J). (gr. -1-1). 13.95 *(978-0-8118-5419-1(1))* Chronicle Bks. LLC.

Marsh, Carole. The Adventure Diaries of Felipe, the Fearless Firefighter!, 12 vols. 2003. 48p. (J). (gr. 1-4). pap. 5.95 *(978-0-635-01096-4(8))* Gallopade International.

Mayer, Mercer. Little Critter Collection. Mayer, Mercer, illus. 2012. (My First I Can Read Ser.). (ENG., Illus.). 96p. (J). (gr. -1 — 1). pap. 11.99 *(978-0-06-207567-3(5))* HarperCollins Pubs.

—Little Critter Fall Storybook Collection. Mayer, Mercer, illus. 2015. (Little Critter Ser.). (ENG., Illus.). 192p. (J). (gr. -1-3). 11.99 *(978-0-06-238032-6(X))* HarperCollins Pubs.

McLaren-Tishler, Sylvia. Finn the Fireman. 2008. 33p. pap. 16.95 *(978-0-557-02552-7(4))* Lulu Pr., Inc.

McMahon, Susan. Billy Mogee. 2008. 24p. pap. 12.99 *(978-1-4389-2041-2(5))* AuthorHouse.

Metaxas, Eric. Mose the Fireman, 1 vol. Peck, Everett, illus. 2004. (Rabbit Ears-A Classic Tale Ser.). (ENG.). 40p. (gr. k-5). 25.65 *(978-1-59197-766-7(5))* Spotlight.

Morgan, Allen. Matthew & the Midnight Firefighters. 2004. (Illus.). (J). (gr. k-3). spiral bd. *(978-0-616-07242-4(2))* Canadian National Institute for the Blind/Institut National Canadien pour les Aveugles.

Nosy Crow Staff. Fire Rescue! Davies, Benji, illus. 2013. (Bizzy Bear Ser.). (ENG.). 8p. (J). (— 1). bds. 6.99 *(978-0-7636-6518-0(5)*, Nosy Crow) Candlewick Pr.

O'Donnell, Liam & O'Donnell, Laura. Duncan: A Brave Rescue. Hynes, Robert, illus. 2004. (Pet Tales Ser.). (ENG.). 32p. (J). (gr. -1-3). 4.95 *(978-1-59249-291-6(6)*, 1B001) Soundprints.

—Duncan: A Brave Rescue. Hynes, Robert, illus. 2005. (Pet Tales Ser.). (ENG.). 32p. (J). (gr. -1-2). 2.95 *(978-1-59249-292-3(4)*, 1B003) Soundprints.

Osborne, Mary Pope & National Geographic Learning Staff. New York's Bravest. Johnson, Steve & Fancher, Lou, illus. 2006. (ENG.). 32p. (J). (gr. -1-2). 7.99 *(978-0-375-83841-5(4)*, Dragonfly Bks.) Random Hse. Children's Bks.

Rabley, Stephen. The Fireboy. Date not set. (Illus.). 16p. pap. 73.13 *(978-0-582-06072-2(9))* Addison-Wesley Longman, Ltd. GBR. Dist: Trans-Atlantic Pubns., Inc.

Random House Disney Staff. Brave Firefighters (Disney Planes: Fire & Rescue) Random House Disney Staff, illus. 2014. (Step into Reading Ser.). (ENG., Illus.). 32p. (J). (gr. -1-1). 3.99 *(978-0-7364-3240-5(X)*, RH/Disney) Random Hse. Children's Bks.

Reed, Lynn Rowe. Fireman Fred. Reed, Lynn Rowe, illus. 2014. (I Like to Read(r) Ser.). (ENG., Illus.). 24p. (J). (gr. -1-3). pap. 6.99 *(978-0-8234-3182-3(7))* Holiday Hse., Inc.

—Fireman Jack. 2013. (I Like to Read(r) Ser.). (ENG., Illus.). 24p. (J). (gr. -1-3). 14.95 *(978-0-8234-2658-4(0))* Holiday Hse., Inc.

Rey, H. A., et al. Curious George & the Firefighters. (Curious George Ser.). (ENG., Illus.). 24p. (J). (gr. -1-3). 2007. bds. 11.99 *(978-0-618-89194-8(3))* 2004. 4.99 *(978-0-618-49496-5(0))* 2004. 14.99 *(978-0-618-49497-2(9))* Houghton Mifflin Harcourt Publishing Co.

Rockwell, Anne F. At the Firehouse. Rockwell, Anne F., illus. 2003. (Illus.). 40p. (J). (gr. -1-1). 16.89 *(978-0-06-029816-6(2))* HarperCollins Pubs.

Salmassian, Jennifer. Sally the Firefighter. 2007. (J). per. 0.01 net. *(978-1-60402-164-6(0))* Independent Pub.

Sander, Sonia. Fire Truck to the Rescue! 2009. (LEGO City Adventures Scholastic Readers Level 1 Ser.: 1). lib. bdg. 13.55 *(978-0-606-05872-8(9)*, Turtleback) Turtleback Bks.

—LEGO City Reader Collection: LEGO City Emergency. 2012. (Illus.). 127p. (J). *(978-1-4351-3985-5(2))* Scholastic, Inc.

Santillo, LuAnn. The Fire Fighter. Santillo, LuAnn, ed. 2003. (Half-Pint Kids Readers Ser.). (Illus.). 7p. (J). (gr. -1-1). pap. 1.00 *(978-1-59256-124-7(1))* Half-Pint Kids, Inc.

Scarry, Richard. Richard Scarry's Smokey the Fireman. Scarry, Richard, illus. 2015. (Step into Reading Ser.). (ENG., Illus.). 32p. (J). (gr. -1-1). 12.99 *(978-0-375-97363-5(X)*, Random Hse. Bks. for Young Readers) Random Hse. Children's Bks.

Searcy, Doc. Jimmy Jack & Jilly Jan, the Fireman. 2005. 33p. (J). 10.73 *(978-1-4116-2564-8(1))* Lulu Pr., Inc.

Soda, Masahito. Firefighter! Vol. 10: Daigo of Fire Company M. Soda, Masahito, illus. 2005. (Firefighter Ser.: Vol. 10). (ENG., Illus.). 208p. pap. 9.95 *(978-1-59116-635-1(7))* Viz Media.

—Firefighter! Vol. 14. 2006. (Firefighter Ser.). (ENG., Illus.). 208p. pap. 9.95 *(978-1-4215-0318-9(2))* Viz Media.

Steele, Michael Anthony. Fight This Fire! 2011. (Lego City Ser.). (ENG.). 24p. (J). (gr. -1-k). pap. 3.99 *(978-0-545-31759-7(2))* Scholastic, Inc.

Teague, Mark. Firehouse! Teague, Mark, illus. (StoryPlay Ser.). (ENG., Illus.). (J). (gr. -1-k). 2017. 40p. 5.99 ***(978-1-338-18159-3(9))*** 2013. 32p. bds. 6.99 *(978-0-545-49215-7(7))* Scholastic, Inc. (Cartwheel Bks.).

Theiss, Lewis E. The Young Wireless Operator-As a Fire Patrol: The Story of a Young Wireless Amateur Who Made Goo. 2006. (ENG.). 234p. pap. 20.99 *(978-1-4264-6428-7(2))*; 256p. pap. 23.99 *(978-1-4264-6502-4(5))* Creative Media Partners, LLC.

Tierney, John. Jack, Tommy & the Phoenix Street Firefighters. Algar, James, illus. 2012. 70p. pap. 11.99 *(978-1-78035-416-3(9)*, Fastprint Publishing) Upfront Publishing Ltd. GBR. Dist: Printondemand-worldwide.com.

Tillworth, Mary. Firefighter Gil! (Bubble Guppies) Nunn, Paul, illus. 2013. (Pictureback(R) Ser.). (ENG.). 24p. (J). (gr. -1-2). 4.99 *(978-0-449-81770-4(9)*, Random Hse. Bks. for Young Readers) Random Hse. Children's Bks.

Tilthem, Sam. Pete Plan Pup. 2013. 20p. (J). pap. 24.95 *(978-1-4626-9947-6(2))* America Star Bks.

Tuchman, Lauryn & Silverhardt, Lauryn. A Visit to the Firehouse. Craig, Karen, illus. 2009. (Blue's Clues Ser.). (ENG.). 24p. (J). (gr. -1-2). pap. 3.99 *(978-1-4169-7193-1(9)*, Simon Spotlight/Nickelodeon) Simon Spotlight/Nickelodeon.

Van Dusen, Ross, illus. Lyle Got Stuck in a Tree & Became an Honorary Fireman. 2015. (J). *(978-1-936744-45-9(7)*, Rio Grande Bks.) LPD Pr.

Van Straaten, Harmen. Little trunk Late. 2008. (ENG.). 32p. (J). (gr. 1-7). 12.95 *(978-1-60136-004-5(5))* Audio Holdings, LLC.

Victor, Appleton. Tom Swift among the Fire Fighters: Or Battling with Flames from the Air. 2007. (ENG.). 136p. pap. 18.99 *(978-1-4346-1489-6(1))* Creative Media Partners, LLC.

Weissman, Steven. The Kid Firechief. 2004. (ENG., Illus.). 96p. pap. 12.95 *(978-1-56097-596-0(2))* Fantagraphics Bks.

EFG

Wellington, Monica. Firefighter Frank. 2011. (ENG.). 26p. (J). (gr. -1 — 1). bds. 5.99 *(978-0-525-42373-7(7),* Dutton Books for Young Readers) Penguin Young Readers Group.

Weston Woods Staff, creator. Dot the Fire Dog. 2004. (J). (gr. -1-2). 29.95 *(978-1-55592-623-6(1))* Weston Woods Studios, Inc.

Williams, Allen. Claude the Backward Jumping Bullfrog - Firefighter: Buster's Great Adventure. 2009. 36p. pap. 16.99 *(978-1-4389-7817-8(0))* AuthorHouse.

Wojtowycz, David, illus. Elephant Joe, Brave Firefighter! 2015. (Step into Reading Ser.). (ENG.). 32p. (J). (gr. -1-1). 12.99 *(978-0-375-97203-4(X),* Random Hse. Bks. for Young Readers) Random Hse. Children's Bks.

Zimmerman, Andrea & Clemesha, David. Fire Engine Man. Zimmerman, Andrea & Clemesha, David, illus. 2016. (ENG., Illus.). 30p. (J). bds. 7.99 *(978-1-62779-503-6(0),* 9781627795036, Holt, Henry & Co. Bks. For Young Readers) Holt, Henry & Co.

FIRE PREVENTION

see also Fire Extinction

also names of cities with the subdivision Fires and Fire Prevention, e.g. Chicago—Fires and Fire Prevention, etc.

Beeping Ben Fire Safety Rules for the Whole. (J). 29.50 *(978-1-56230-327-3(9))* Syndistar, Inc.

Fire!Fire! Level K, 6 vols. 128p. (gr. 2-3). 40.50 *(978-0-7699-0997-4(3))* Shortland Pubns. (U. S. A.) Inc.

Ghigna, Charles. Dial 911! Thomas, Glenn, illus. 2017. (Fire Safety Ser.). (ENG.). 24p. (gr. k-2). 33.99 ***(978-1-68410-019-4(4))*** Cantata Learning.

Guard, Anara. What If There Is a Fire?, 1 vol. Pfleegor, Gina, illus. 2011. (Danger Zone Ser.). (ENG.). 24p. (gr. 1-2). lib. bdg. 25.99 *(978-1-4048-6685-0(X))* Picture Window Bks.

Heos, Bridget. Be Safe Around Fire. Baroncelli, Silvia, illus. 2015. (Be Safe! Ser.). 24p. (J). 25.65 *(978-1-60753-444-0(4))* Amicus Publishing.

Herrington, Lisa M. Fire Safety. 2012. (Rookie Read-About(tm) Safety Ser.). (ENG., Illus.). 32p. (J). lib. bdg. 25.00 *(978-0-531-28970-9(2));* (gr. -1-1). pap. 5.95 *(978-0-531-29272-3(X))* Scholastic Library Publishing.

I Don't Play with Matches. (J). 29.50 *(978-1-56230-054-8(7))* Syndistar, Inc.

Johnson, Sandi. Red Hot Dot's Fire Safety Book: Fire Safety. Durant, Sybrina, ed. Vu, Thi, illus. I.t. ed. 2014. 44p. (J). (gr. k-5). pap. 12.99 *(978-1-929063-86-4(5),* 279) Moons & Stars Publishing For Children.

Kids Can Press Staff. This Is Daniel Cook at the Fire Station. Li, Karen, ed. 2006. (This Is Daniel Cook Ser.). (ENG., Illus.). 24p. (J). (gr. -1-1). 16.95 *(978-1-55453-076-2(8))* Kids Can Pr., Ltd. CAN. Dist: Hachette Bk. Group.

Lidner, D. B. The A,B, C's of Firefighting & Fire Safety. 2009. pap. 3.95 *(978-1-61584-189-9(X))* Independent Pub.

Lindeen, Mary & Kesselring, Susan. Being Safe with Fire. McGeehan, Dan & Moore, David, illus. 2011. (Be Safe Ser.). (ENG.). 24p. (J). (gr. k-3). lib. bdg. 27.07 *(978-1-60954-372-3(6),* 200083) Child's World, Inc., The.

Mara, Wil. What Should I Do? If There Is a Fire. 2011. (Community Connections: What Should I Do? Ser.). (ENG.). 24p. (gr. 2-5). lib. bdg. 25.64 *(978-1-61080-053-2(2),* 201048) Cherry Lake Publishing.

Miller, Edward. Fireboy to the Rescue! A Fire Safety Book. Miller, Edward, illus. (ENG., Illus.). 32p. (J). 2011. pap. 7.95 *(978-0-8234-2344-6(1))* 2010. (gr. -1-3). 17.95 *(978-0-8234-2222-7(4))* Holiday Hse., Inc.

Pendziwol, Jean E. No Dragons for Tea. 2004. (Illus.). (J). (gr. k-3). spiral bd. *(978-0-616-01756-2(1));* spiral bd. *(978-0-616-01755-5(3))* Canadian National Institute for the Blind/Institut National Canadien pour les Aveugles.

Person, Stephen. Struck by Lightning! 2010. (Disaster Survivors Ser.). (Illus.). 32p. (YA). (gr. 4-7). lib. bdg. 25.27 *(978-1-936087-47-1(2))* Bearport Publishing Co., Inc.

Pohl, Kathleen. What Happens at a Firehouse? 2006. (Where People Work Ser.). (Illus.). 24p. (gr. -1-3). pap. 8.15 *(978-0-8368-6894-4(3));* lib. bdg. 22.00 *(978-0-8368-6887-6(0))* Stevens, Gareth Publishing LLLP. (Weekly Reader Leveled Readers).

Raatma, Lucia. Staying Safe Around Fire. 2011. (Staying Safe Ser.). (ENG.). 24p. (gr. 1-2). pap. 41.70 *(978-1-4296-7194-1(7));* lib. bdg. 25.32 *(978-1-4296-6820-0(2))* Capstone Press of Coughlan Cos. (First Facts).

Rau, Dana Meachen. Fire Safety: Seguridad en Caso de Incendio. 2009. (Bookworms — Bilingual Editions: Safe Kids/Ninos Seguros Ser.). (SPA & ENG.). 32p. (gr. k-2). lib. bdg. 15.95 *(978-0-7614-4784-9(9))* Marshall Cavendish Corp.

Rau, Dana Meachen & Meachen Rau, Dana. Fire Safety: Seguridad en Caso de Incendio. 2009. (Bookworms: Safe Kids Ser.). (SPA & ENG.). 32p. (gr. k-2). 15.95 *(978-0-7614-4091-8(7))* Marshall Cavendish Corp.

Rivera, Sheila. Fire Safety. 2007. (First Step Nonfiction - Safety Ser.). (ENG.). 8p. (gr. -1-1). pap. 4.95 *(978-0-8225-6820-9(9))* Lerner Publishing Group.

Safety & Security. 2nd rev. ed. 2007. (What Can I Do Now? Ser.). 200p. (YA). (gr. 7-12). 32.95 *(978-0-8160-6030-6(4))* Facts On File, Inc.

Scarry, Richard. A Day at the Fire Station. 2003. (gr. k-3). 14.75 *(978-0-613-83879-5(3),* Turtleback) Turtleback Bks.

Sévigny, Eric, illus. Caillou - The Firefighter. 2013. (Playtime Ser.). (ENG.). 24p. (J). (gr. -1-1). 4.99 *(978-2-89450-861-9(1))* Caillouet, Gerry.

FIRE PREVENTION—FICTION

Cruz, Sarah, et al. Bernie Burn: A Storybook about Burn Injury Prevention & Safety in the Home. 2004. (Illus.). 38p. (J). 3.50 *(978-0-9767230-0-4(X))* Little Boots Publishing.

Cuyler, Margery. Stop Drop & Roll. Howard, Arthur, illus. 28.95 incl. audio compact disk *(978-1-59112-980-6(X));* 25.95 incl. audio *(978-1-59112-976-9(1));* pap. 18.95 incl. audio compact disk *(978-1-59112-979-0(6));* pap. 16.95 incl. audio *(978-1-59112-975-2(3));* pap. incl. audio *(978-1-59112-977-6(X));* pap. incl. audio compact disk *(978-1-59112-981-3(8))* Live Oak Media.

Filmer, Mary, et al. Farmer Frank: Educational Fire Safety, Poetry & Story Colouring Book. 2010. 50p. pap. 9.99 *(978-1-60911-721-4(2),* Eloquent Bks.) Strategic Book Publishing & Rights Agency (SBPRA).

Gutman, Dan. Mrs. Meyer Is on Fire! Paillot, Jim, illus. 2016. 105p. (J). ***(978-1-4806-9926-7(8))*** Harper & Row Ltd.

Hawes, Rachelle. Dan the Rescue Man: Fire at Farmer Dave's. 2013. 24p. pap. 10.95 *(978-1-4525-1161-0(6),* Balboa Pr.) Author Solutions, Inc.

Montgomery, R. A. Smoke Jumpers. Peguy, Laurence, illus. 2009. (Choose Your Own Adventure Ser.: No. 29). 144p. (J). (gr. 2-7). pap. 6.99 *(978-1-933390-29-1(8))* Chooseco LLC.

Slater, Teddy. Fire Prevention. Lewis, Anthony, illus. 2010. 16p. (J). *(978-0-545-24603-3(2))* Scholastic, Inc.

Wasserman, Shannon & Wasserman, Curt. The Adventures of Ruff-N-Rescue: Adventures with the Heroes of New Barker Island. Wasserman, Curt et al, illus. 2006. 40p. (J). (gr. -1-3). 16.95 *(978-1-931643-87-0(3))* Seven Locks Pr.

FIREARMS

see also Gun Control; Ordnance; Rifles

Annie Oakley. 2009. 48p. pap. 8.95 *(978-0-8225-5788-3(6))* Lerner Publishing Group.

Apel, Lorelei. Dealing with Weapons at School & at Home. (Conflict Resolution Library). 24p. 2009. (gr. 2-3). 42.50 *(978-1-60853-411-1(1))* 2004. (Illus.). (J). 22.60 *(978-0-8239-6932-6(0))* Rosen Publishing Group, Inc., The. (PowerKids Pr.).

Becnel, Barbara, ed. Gangs & Weapons: Stanley Tookie Williams Street Peace Series, 8 bks., Vol. 1, Bk. 3. 2008. 24p. (J). *(978-0-9753584-3-6(X))* Damamli Publishing Co.

Blumenthal, Karen. Tommy: The Gun That Changed America. 2015. (ENG., Illus.). 240p. (YA). (gr. 5-9). 19.99 *(978-1-62672-084-8(3),* 9781626720848) Roaring Brook Pr.

Brownell, Frank R., 3rd. Gunsmith's Firearms Repair Log, 1. 2004. (Illus.). 48p. 3.00 *(978-0-9767409-8-8(2))* Brownell, F. & Son, Pubs.

Broyles, Janell. Careers in Ballistics Investigation. 2009. (Careers in Forensics Ser.). 64p. (gr. 5-5). 58.50 *(978-1-61511-800-7(4),* Rosen Reference) Rosen Publishing Group, Inc., The.

Cashin, John. Firearms Safety. 2014. (J). 33.95 *(978-1-61900-048-3(2))* Eldorado Ink.

Croft, Jennifer. Everything You Need to Know about Guns in Your Home. 2005. (Need to Know Library). (Illus.). 64p. (YA). (gr. 7-12). lib. bdg. 31.95 *(978-0-8239-3162-0(5),* NTGUHO) Rosen Publishing Group, Inc., The.

Doeden, Matt. Gun Control: Preventing Violence or Crushing Constitutional Rights? 2011. (USA TODAY's Debate: Voices & Perspectives Ser.). (ENG., Illus.). 128p. (gr. 9-12). lib. bdg. 35.93 *(978-0-7613-6433-7(1),* Twenty-First Century Bks.) Lerner Publishing Group.

Dougherty, Martin. The Most Amazing Weapons of War. 2010. (Extreme! Ser.). (ENG.). 32p. (gr. 3-4). pap. 47.70 *(978-1-4296-5133-2(4),* Fact Finders) Capstone Press of Coughlan Cos.

Ferguson, John E., et al. Gun Control. 2nd rev. ed. 2011. (Point/Counterpoint Ser.). 120p. (C). (gr. 9). 35.00 *(978-1-60413-905-1(6),* Chelsea Hse.) Facts On File, Inc.

Fischer, Rusty. Weapons of the West. 2004. (History of the Old West Ser.). (Illus.). 64p. (YA). (gr. 5-18). lib. bdg. 19.95 *(978-1-59084-066-5(6))* Mason Crest.

Greenhaven Press Editors & MacKay, Jennifer, eds. Gun Control. 2013. (Hot Topics Ser.). (ENG., Illus.). 128p. (gr. 7-10). lib. bdg. 33.95 *(978-1-4205-0815-4(6),* Lucent Bks.) Cengage Gale.

Gunston, Bill Tudor & Guy, John. Battle Machines. 2009. (ENG.). 112p. (J). (gr. 4-7). pap. 12.95 *(978-1-84696-201-1(3),* TickTock Books) Octopus Publishing Group GBR. Dist: Independent Pubs. Group.

Hamilton, John. Weapons of World War I, 1 vol. 2004. (World War I Ser.). (ENG.). 32p. (gr. 4-8). 27.07 *(978-1-57765-917-4(1),* Abdo & Daughters) ABDO Publishing Co.

Hamilton, Sue L. Forensic Ballistics: Styles of Projectiles, 1 vol. 2008. (Crime Scene Investigation Ser.). (ENG.). 32p. (gr. 4-8). 27.07 *(978-1-59928-990-8(3),* Abdo & Daughters) ABDO Publishing Co.

Harmon, Daniel E. Chemical & Biological Weapons: Agents of War & Terror. 2009. (Science & Society Ser.). (Illus.). 64p. (YA). (gr. 7-12). lib. bdg. 31.95 *(978-1-4358-5023-1(8))* Rosen Publishing Group, Inc., The.

Hemstock, Annie Wendt. Hunting Laws & Safety. 2014. (Open Season Ser.). 32p. (J). (gr. 4-6). lib. bdg. 26.25 *(978-1-4777-6725-2(8),* PowerKids Pr.) Rosen Publishing Group, Inc., The.

—Hunting with Shotguns. 2014. (Open Season Ser.). (Illus.). 32p. (J). (gr. 4-6). lib. bdg. 26.25 *(978-1-4777-6705-4(3),* PowerKids Pr.) Rosen Publishing Group, Inc., The.

Herbst, Judith. The History of Weapons. 2005. (Major Inventions Through History Ser.). (ENG., Illus.). 56p. (gr. 5-8). lib. bdg. 26.60 *(978-0-8225-3805-9(9),* Twenty-First Century Bks.) Lerner Publishing Group.

Houser, Aimee. Tragedy in Tucson: The Arizona Shooting Rampage, 1 vol. 2012. (Essential Events Set 8 Ser.). (ENG.). 112p. (J). (gr. 6-12). lib. bdg. 35.64 *(978-1-61783-312-0(6))* ABDO Publishing Co.

Ives, Rob. Ready, Aim, Launch! Make Your Own Small Launchers. Paul de Quay, John, illus. 2016. (Tabletop Wars Ser.). (ENG.). 32p. (J). (gr. 3-6). lib. bdg. 26.65 *(978-1-5124-0636-8(8))* Lerner Publishing Group.

Joyce, Jaime. Bullet Proof! The Evidence That Guns Leave Behind. 2007. (24/7: Science Behind the Scenes Ser.). (ENG., Illus.). 64p. (YA). (gr. 9-12). 29.00 *(978-0-531-11820-7(7),* Watts, Franklin) Scholastic Library Publishing.

—Going Ballistic: Who Pulled the Trigger in a Gangland Massacre? 2011. (J). pap. *(978-0-545-32801-2(2))* Scholastic, Inc.

Kevin, Brian. Gun Safety, 1 vol. 2012. (Gun Education & Safety Ser.). (ENG.). 32p. 27.07 *(978-1-61783-316-8(9),* Checkerboard Library) ABDO Publishing Co.

—Guns & Ammunition, 1 vol. 2012. (Gun Education & Safety Ser.). (ENG.). 32p. 27.07 *(978-1-61783-318-2(5),* Checkerboard Library) ABDO Publishing Co.

—Guns & Special Weapons, 1 vol. 2012. (Gun Education & Safety Ser.). (ENG., Illus.). 32p. (J). 27.07 *(978-1-61783-319-9(3),* Checkerboard Library) ABDO Publishing Co.

Laidacker, John S. Engraved Handguns of . 22 Calibre, 1855-1885, 1 vol. 2003. (ENG., Illus.). 168p. (gr. 10-13). 69.95 *(978-0-7643-1683-8(4),* 9780764316838) Schiffer Publishing, Ltd.

Lankford, Ronnie D. Gun Violence. 2010. (Social Issues Firsthand Ser.). (Illus.). 192p. (J). 33.75 *(978-0-7377-4797-3(8),* Greenhaven Pr., Inc.) Cengage Gale.

Magoon, Kekla. Gun Control, 1 vol. 2007. (Essential Viewpoints Set 1 Ser.). (ENG., Illus.). 112p. (J). (gr. 6-12). lib. bdg. 35.64 *(978-1-59928-860-4(5))* ABDO Publishing Co.

Mara, Wil. The Gunsmith. 2013. (Colonial People 3 Ser.). 48p. (J). (gr. 4-8). pap. 12.93 *(978-1-62712-046-3(7))* Cavendish Square Publishing.

Mitchell, Barbara. Maker of Machines: A Story about Eli Whitney. Jones, Jan Naimo, tr. Jones, Jan Naimo, illus. 2004. (Creative Minds Biographies Ser.). (ENG.). 64p. (gr. 4-8). 22.60 *(978-1-57505-603-6(8),* Carolrhoda Bks.); pap. 8.95 *(978-1-57505-634-0(8))* Lerner Publishing Group.

Moe, Barbara A. The Search for Weapons of Mass Destruction in Iraq. 2004. (Library of Weapons of Mass Destruction Ser.). (Illus.). 64p. (J). lib. bdg. 31.95 *(978-1-4042-0295-5(1))* Rosen Publishing Group, Inc., The.

Murray, Hallie. The Right to Bear Arms: The Second Amendment. 2017. (Bill of Rights Ser.). 48p. (J). (gr. 5-6). lib. bdg. 27.93 ***(978-0-7660-8551-0(1))*** Enslow Pubs., Inc.

Oxlade, Chris. Gunpowder, 1 vol. 2011. (Tales of Invention Ser.). (ENG.). 32p. (gr. 3-5). pap. 8.95 *(978-1-4329-5458-1(X));* 30.65 *(978-1-4329-5444-4(X))* Heinemann-Raintree. (NA-h).

Royston, Angela. Gun Crimes. 2010. (Solve It with Science Ser.). (Illus.). 48p. (YA). (gr. 5-9). lib. bdg. 34.25 *(978-1-59920-330-0(8))* Black Rabbit Bks.

Schleifer, Jay. Everything You Need to Know about Weapons in School & at Home. rev. ed. 2005. (Need to Know Library). (Illus.). 64p. (YA). (gr. 7-12). lib. bdg. 31.95 *(978-0-8239-3315-0(6))* Rosen Publishing Group, Inc., The.

Wolny, Philip. Avoiding Danger on the Hunt. 2012. (Hunting: Pursuing Wild Game! Ser.). (ENG., Illus.). 64p. (YA). (gr. 5-8). pap. 12.95 *(978-1-4488-8283-0(4));* lib. bdg. 31.95 *(978-1-4488-8278-6(8))* Rosen Publishing Group, Inc., The. (Rosen Reference).

World Book, Inc Staff, contrib. by. Warfare. 2009. (J). *(978-0-7166-0388-7(8))* World Bk., Inc.

Wright, Susan. Weapons of Mass Destruction: Illicit Trade & Trafficking. 2004. (Library of Weapons of Mass Destruction Ser.). (Illus.). 64p. (J). lib. bdg. 31.95 *(978-1-4042-0297-9(8))* Rosen Publishing Group, Inc., The.

Wyckoff, Edwin Brit. The Man Behind the Gun: Samuel Colt & His Revolver. 2010. (Genius at Work! Great Inventor Biographies Ser.). (Illus.). 32p. (J). 23.94 *(978-0-7660-3446-4(1))* Enslow Pubs., Inc.

FIREARMS—HISTORY

Atkin, S. Beth. Gunstories: Life-Changing Experiences with Guns. Atkin, S. Beth, illus. 2007. (ENG., Illus.). 256p. (YA). (gr. 8-12). per. 8.99 *(978-0-06-052661-0(0),* Tegen, Katherine Bks) HarperCollins Pubs.

Kevin, Brian. Gun History & Development, 1 vol. 2012. (Gun Education & Safety Ser.). (ENG.). 32p. 27.07 *(978-1-61783-314-4(2),* Checkerboard Library) ABDO Publishing Co.

FIREARMS—LAW AND LEGISLATION

Here are entered works on the legal aspects of gun control. General and non-legal works on the control of guns are entered under Gun Control.

Bjorklund, Ruth. Gun Control. 2012. (J). 32.79 *(978-0-7614-4974-4(4))* Marshall Cavendish Corp.

—Gun Control. 2014. (Illus.). 80p. (J). *(978-1-62712-416-4(0))* Musa Publishing.

Everything You Need to Know about (Legally) Carrying a Handgun in Missouri. 2nd unabr. ed. 2004. per. 24.95 *(978-0-9741480-1-4(6),* 18) Certified Firearms Instructors, LLC.

Furgang, Adam. Everything You Need to Know about Gun Violence. 2017. (Need to Know Library). 64p. (J). (gr. 12-11). pap. 12.95 ***(978-1-5081-7402-8(4),*** Rosen Young Adult) Rosen Publishing Group, Inc., The.

Gerber, Larry. Second Amendment: The Right to Bear Arms. 2011. (Amendments to the United States Constitution: the Bill of Rights Ser.). (ENG., Illus.). 64p. (J). pap. 12.95 *(978-1-4488-2303-1(X),* Rosen Reference) Rosen Publishing Group, Inc., The.

—The Second Amendment: The Right to Bear Arms. 2011. (Amendments to the United States Constitution: the Bill of Rights Ser.). (Illus.). 64p. (YA). (gr. 5-9). lib. bdg. 31.95 *(978-1-4488-1253-0(4))* Rosen Publishing Group, Inc., The.

Gonzales, Doreen. A Look at the Second Amendment: To Keep & Bear Arms. 2007. (Constitution of the United States Ser.). (Illus.). 128p. (J). (gr. 5). lib. bdg. 34.60 *(978-1-59845-061-3(1),* MyReportLinks.com Bks.) Enslow Pubs., Inc.

Kevin, Brian. Gun Rights & Responsibilities, 1 vol. 2012. (Gun Education & Safety Ser.). (ENG.). 32p. 27.07 *(978-1-61783-315-1(0),* Checkerboard Library) ABDO Publishing Co.

Larson, Kirsten W. The Second Amendment: The Right to Bear Arms. 2017. (Cause & Effect: the Bill of Rights Ser.). (ENG.). 32p. (gr. 3-4). lib. bdg. 27.32 ***(978-1-5157-7165-4(2),*** Fact Finders) Capstone Press of Coughlan Cos.

Murray, Hallie. The Right to Bear Arms: The Second Amendment. 2017. (Bill of Rights Ser.). 48p. (J). (gr. 5-6). pap. 11.70 ***(978-0-7660-8729-3(8))*** Enslow Pubs., Inc.

Smith, Rich. Second & Third Amendments: The Right to Security, 1 vol. 2007. (Bill of Rights Ser.). (ENG.). 32p. (gr. 3-7). 27.07 *(978-1-59928-915-1(6),* Abdo & Daughters) ABDO Publishing Co.

Streissguth, Tom. District of Columbia V. Heller: The Right to Bear Arms Case. 2010. (Landmark Supreme Court Cases, Gold Edition Ser.). (Illus.). 112p. (J). (gr. 7-12). 33.27 *(978-0-7660-3430-3(5))* Enslow Pubs., Inc.

Wolny, Philip. Gun Rights: Interpreting the Constitution. 2014. (Understanding the United States Constitution Ser.). (Illus.). 112p. (J). (gr. 7-12). 35.60 *(978-1-4777-7516-5(1))* Rosen Publishing Group, Inc., The.

Ziff, John. Gun Laws. 2014. (J). *(978-1-61900-055-1(5));* 33.95 *(978-1-61900-049-0(0))* Eldorado Ink.

FIREBOATS

Best, B. J. Fireboats. 2017. (J). ***(978-1-5026-2557-1(1))*** Cavendish Square Publishing.

Chancellor, Deborah. Fire Rescue. 2013. (Emergency Vehicles Ser.). 24p. (gr. k-3). 28.50 *(978-1-59920-889-3(X))* Black Rabbit Bks.

Kalman, Maira. Fireboat: The Heroic Adventures of John J. Harvey. 2004. (Illus.). (J). 28.95 incl. audio compact disk *(978-1-59112-988-2(5))* Live Oak Media.

FIREFLIES

Allyn, Daisy & Flynn, Michael. Glowworms Are Not Worms! 2014. (Confusing Creature Names Ser.). 24p. (J). (gr. 1-3). 22.60 *(978-1-4824-0941-3(0))* Stevens, Gareth Publishing LLLP.

Ashley, Susan. Fireflies. (Incredible World of Insects Ser.). (Illus.). 24p. 2011. (J). (gr. 1-3). pap. 8.15 *(978-1-4339-4584-7(3))* 2011. (J). (gr. 1-3). lib. bdg. 22.60 *(978-1-4339-4583-0(5))* 2004. (gr. k-3). lib. bdg. 22.00 *(978-0-8368-4053-7(4),* Weekly Reader Leveled Readers) Stevens, Gareth Publishing LLLP.

Beck, W. H. Glow: Animals with Their Own Night-Lights. 2015. (ENG., Illus.). 32p. (J). (gr. -1-3). 17.99 *(978-0-544-41666-6(X),* HMH Books For Young Readers) Houghton Mifflin Harcourt Publishing Co.

Dunn, Mary R. Fireflies, 1 vol. 2011. (Nocturnal Animals Ser.). (ENG.). 24p. (gr. k-1). pap. 7.29 *(978-1-4296-7120-0(3));* pap. 41.70 *(978-1-4296-7121-7(1));* lib. bdg. 26.65 *(978-1-4296-6649-7(8))* Capstone Press of Coughlan Cos. (Pebble Plus).

Fascinating Firefly. 2004. (Illus.). 10p. (J). *(978-1-59340-144-3(2))* Grandreams Bks., Inc.

Heiget, Nicole. Fireflies. 2007. (Bugbooks Ser.). (Illus.). 24p. (J). (gr. -1-3). lib. bdg. 24.25 *(978-1-58341-542-9(4),* Creative Education) Creative Co., The.

Howell, Sara. Fireflies, 1 vol. 2015. (ENG.). 24p. (J). lib. bdg. 23.60 *(978-1-4994-0114-1(0),* PowerKids Pr.) Rosen Publishing Group, Inc., The.

Kenney, Karen Latchana. Hunt with the Fireflies, 1 vol. Hedicker, Lisa, illus. 2010. (Bug's World Ser.). (ENG.). 32p. 28.50 *(978-1-60270-787-0(1),* Looking Glass Library-Nonfiction) Magic Wagon.

Kuntz, Lynn. Firefly. 2004. (Bugs Ser.). (ENG., Illus.). 32p. (J). (gr. 4-8). lib. bdg. 26.20 *(978-0-7377-3132-3(X),* Greenhaven Pr., Inc.) Cengage Gale.

Leaf, Christina. Fireflies. 2017. (Insects up Close Ser.). (ENG., Illus.). 24p. (J). (gr. k-3). lib. bdg. 25.95 ***(978-1-62617-664-5(7),*** Blastoff! Readers) Bellwether Media.

Loewen, Nancy. Living Lights: Fireflies in Your Backyard. Reibeling, Brandon, illus. 2003. (Backyard Bugs Ser.). (ENG.). 24p. (gr. -1-3). per. 8.95 *(978-1-4048-0447-0(1))* Picture Window Bks.

McLaughlin, Kari Massie. My Adventure with Flamingos. 2009. 44p. (J). 8.99 *(978-1-59092-454-9(1))* Blue Forge Pr.

Meachen Rau, Dana. Brilla Luciérnaga, Brilla! 2007. (¡Vamos Criaturita, Vamos! Ser.). (SPA & ENG., Illus.). 24p. (gr. k-1). lib. bdg. 15.95 *(978-0-7614-2792-6(9),* Benchmark Bks.) Marshall Cavendish Corp.

—Flash, Firefly, Flash! 2007. (Go, Critter, Go! Ser.). (SPA & ENG., Illus.). 24p. (gr. k-1). lib. bdg. 15.95 *(978-0-7614-2651-6(5),* Benchmark Bks.) Marshall Cavendish Corp.

—Flash, Firefly, Flash!/Brilla Luciérnaga, Brilla! 2007. (Go, Critter, Go!/¡Vamos Criaturita, Vamos! Ser.). (SPA & ENG., Illus.). 24p. (gr. k-1). lib. bdg. 15.95 *(978-0-7614-2816-9(X),* Benchmark Bks.) Marshall Cavendish Corp.

Morgan, Emily R. Next Time You See a Firefly. 2013. (Next Time You See Ser.). (ENG.). 32p. (J). (gr. k-5). lib. bdg. 18.95 *(978-1-938946-16-5(2));* (Illus.). pap. 12.95 *(978-1-936959-18-1(6))* National Science Teachers Assn.

Murray, Julie. Fireflies, 1 vol. 2010. (Big Buddy Bks.). (ENG.). 32p. (J). (gr. 2-5). 28.50 *(978-1-61613-485-3(2))* ABDO Publishing Co.

Otfinoski, Steven. Fireflies. 2014. 32p. 28.50 *(978-1-62712-307-5(5))* Cavendish Square Publishing.

Schuh, Mari. Fireflies. 2014. (Illus.). 24p. (J). lib. bdg. 25.65 *(978-1-62031-084-7(8),* Bullfrog Bks.) Jump! Inc.

Stewart, Melissa. Zoom in on Fireflies. 2014. (Zoom in on Insects! Ser.). 24p. (J). 22.60 *(978-0-7660-4213-1(8));* pap. 7.95 *(978-1-4644-0369-9(4),* Enslow Elementary) Enslow Pubs., Inc.

Troupe, Thomas Kingsley. Glowing with Electricity: Science Adventures with Glenda the Origami Firefly, 1 vol. Christoph, Jamey, illus. 2014. (Origami Science Adventures Ser.). (ENG.). 24p. (gr. 3-4). lib. bdg. 27.32 *(978-1-4795-2189-0(2))* Picture Window Bks.

Walker, Sally M. Fireflies. 2003. (Early Bird Nature Bks.). 48p. (J). 6.95 *(978-0-8225-0025-4(6),* Carolrhoda Bks.) Lerner Publishing Group.

Waxman, Laura Hamilton. Flashing Fireflies. 2016. (First Step Nonfiction — Backyard Critters Ser.). (ENG.). 24p. (J). (gr. k-2). 23.99 *(978-1-5124-0882-9(4))* Lerner Publishing Group.

FIREFLIES—FICTION

Alborozo, Gabriel. Good Night, Firefly. Alborozo, Gabriel, illus. 2015. (ENG., Illus.). 32p. (J). (gr. -1-2). 16.99 *(978-1-62779-222-6(8),* 9781627792226, Holt, Henry & Co. Bks. For Young Readers) Holt, Henry & Co.

Angelo, Tony. Go-bez Nibe: Very Clever Firefly, 1 vol. Lubitsky, Maribeth Jenkins, illus. 2010. 48p. 24.95 *(978-1-4489-5184-0(4))* PublishAmerica, Inc.

Bailey, Arthur Scott. The Tale of Freddie Firefly. 2004. reprint ed. pap. 15.95 *(978-1-4191-8478-9(4));* pap. 1.99 *(978-1-4192-8478-6(9))* Kessinger Publishing, LLC.

—Tuck-Me-in Tales: The Tale of Freddie Fi. 2006. pap. *(978-1-4065-0449-1(1))* Dodo Pr.

Basha, Irena Canaj. The Birthday Party, It Was Saturday... 2013. 16p. pap. 24.95 *(978-1-62709-182-4(3))* America Star Bks.

Bedford, William. Glow-Worm Who Lost Her Glow. Joyce, Sophie, illus. 2004. (Blue Bananas Ser.). (ENG.). 48p. (J). (gr. k-2). pap. 5.99 *(978-1-4052-0976-2(3))* Egmont Bks., Ltd. GBR. Dist: Independent Pubs. Group.

—The Glowworm Who Lost Her Glow. Joyce, Sophie, illus. 2005. (Blue Go Bananas Ser.). (ENG.). 48p. (J). (gr. 1-2). lib. bdg. *(978-0-7787-2630-2(4))* Crabtree Publishing Co.

Black, Cassandra. Twinkle: A Chapter Book. 2003. 113p. (J). 7.99 *(978-0-9742739-0-7(2))* Lavender Bks.

—Twinkle: The Only Firefly Who Couldn't Light Up. Kirk, Tim, illus. 3rd ed. 2012. (ENG.). 111p. (J). (gr. 4-7). pap. 12.99 *(978-0-9742739-3-8(7))* Lavender Bks.

Blair, Liza Sparks. Fairy Firefly. 2008. 28p. pap. 24.95 *(978-1-4241-9598-5(5))* America Star Bks.

Brown, Elizabeth. Aristotle: the Firefly's Message. Schuna, Ramona, illus. 2007. (ENG.). 40p. per. 19.95 *(978-1-59800-557-8(X))* Outskirts Pr., Inc.

Brummett, Charlotte K. Doozy, the Lonely Firefly. 2006. (Illus.). 24p. (J). (gr. -1-3). per. 16.00 *(978-1-58961-464-2(X))* PageFree Publishing, Inc.

Burries-Hall, Tracy. Honey the Firefly: Honey the Firefly & the Cub Scout. 2010. 28p. 13.99 *(978-1-4520-2550-6(9))* AuthorHouse.

Carle, Eric. My Own Very Lonely Firefly Coloring Book. Carle, Eric, illus. 2006. (ENG., Illus.). 32p. (J). (gr. -1-k). 5.99 *(978-0-399-24646-3(0),* Philomel Bks.) Penguin Young Readers Group.

—Shine with the Very Lonely Firefly. Carle, Eric, illus. 2006. (World of Eric Carle Ser.). (ENG., Illus.). 16p. (J). (gr. -1-k). pap. 5.99 *(978-0-448-44422-2(4),* Grosset & Dunlap) Penguin Young Readers Group.

—The Very Lonely Firefly. 2012. (Penguin Young Readers, Level 2 Ser.). (ENG.). 32p. (J). (gr. 1-2). 14.99 *(978-0-448-45851-9(9));* pap. 3.99 *(978-0-448-45850-2(0))* Penguin Young Readers Group. (Penguin Young Readers).

—The Very Lonely Firefly. 2012. (Penguin Young Readers Level 2 Ser.). lib. bdg. 13.55 *(978-0-606-26069-5(2),* Turtleback) Turtleback Bks.

Connelly, Wendy. Fiona the Firefly! 2003. (Illus.). (J). 12.95 *(978-1-929039-16-6(6))* Ambassador Bks., Inc.

Cummings, Troy. Charge of the Lightning Bugs. Cummings, Troy, illus. 2015. (Notebook of Doom Ser.: 8). (ENG., Illus.). 96p. (J). (gr. 1-3). 15.99 *(978-0-545-79554-8(0));* pap. 4.99 *(978-0-545-79555-5(9))* Scholastic, Inc.

De Sena, Joseph. The Love Bug & the Light of Love. 2007. 64p. per. 19.95 *(978-1-4327-0737-8(X))* Outskirts Pr., Inc.

Drachman, Eric. Leo the Lightning Bug. Muscarello, James, illus. l.t. ed. 2005. (ENG.). 32p. (J). (gr. -1-2). 18.95 incl. audio compact disk *(978-0-9703809-0-6(9))* Kidwick Bks.

Friedman, Becky. Daniel's First Fireworks. 2016. (Daniel Tiger's Neighborhood 8X8 Ser.). lib. bdg. 13.55 *(978-0-606-38990-7(3))* Turtleback Bks.

Fruchter, Jason, illus. Daniel's First Fireworks. 2016. (Daniel Tiger's Neighborhood Ser.). (ENG.). 24p. (J). (gr. -1-2). pap. 3.99 *(978-1-4814-6053-8(6),* Simon Spotlight) Simon Spotlight.

Garis, Howard R. The Curlytops on Star Island. 2009. 120p. 22.95 *(978-1-60664-611-3(7));* pap. 10.95 *(978-1-60664-343-3(6))* Rodgers, Alan Bks.

Glasgow, Yvonne M. Frankie the Firefly Belongs. 2008. 20p. per. 24.95 *(978-1-4241-9424-7(5))* America Star Bks.

Jaklich, Brian. The Fireflies' Christmas. 2010. 24p. pap. 11.32 *(978-1-4567-0075-1(8))* AuthorHouse.

Jennings, Patrick. The Lightning Bugs. Alter, Anna, illus. 2003. (ENG.). 56p. (J). (gr. k-3). tchr. ed. 15.95 *(978-0-8234-1673-8(9))* Holiday Hse., Inc.

Joiner, D. Wayne, Sr. Dudley Gloworm & the Saving Light. Joiner, D. Wayne, Sr., illus. 2006. (Illus.). (J). 25.00 *(978-0-9785103-0-5(5))* Willy Waw wees, LLC.

Ketch, Ann. Lightning Bugs. Hood, Joyce, illus. 2003. (ENG.). 12p. (gr. k-1). pap. 7.95 *(978-1-57874-038-3(X),* Kaeden Bks.) Kaeden Corp.

Lewandowski, Lisa & Trost, Shannon. Darcy Daisy & the Firefly Festival: Learning about Bipolar Disorder & Community. Shaw-Peterson, Kimberly, illus. 2005. 32p. (J). (gr. -1-9). pap. 9.95 *(978-0-9785075-2-7(5),* Ferne Pr.) Nelson Publishing & Marketing.

Lott, Cheryl Lynn. My Firefly Friends. 2003. 32p. (J). pap. 10.00 *(978-0-8059-5533-0(X))* Dorrance Publishing Co., Inc.

Martin, Bill, Jr., et al. The Little Squeegy Bug. 0 vols. Corrigan, Patrick, illus. 2005. (ENG.). 32p. (J). (gr. -1-2). reprint ed. pap. 9.99 *(978-0-7614-5243-0(5),* 9780761452430, Amazon Children's Publishing) Amazon Publishing.

Mattucci, Sandra. Levi the Lightning Bug's Amazing Discovery. Mattucci, Sandra, illus. 2012. (Illus.). 36p. 19.99 *(978-1-936453-08-5(8))* Bezalel Bks.

Mcghee, Alison. Firefly Hollow. Denise, Christopher, illus. (ENG.). 304p. (J). (gr. 3-7). 2016. pap. 9.99 *(978-1-4424-2337-4(4),* Atheneum/Caitlyn Dlouhy Books) 2015. 16.99 *(978-1-4424-2336-7(6),* Atheneum Bks. for Young Readers) Simon & Schuster Children's Publishing.

Moore, Carol Hair. Busy Bumble Bee Rides the Waves. Harrell, Michael, illus. 2009. (I Wish You Ice Cream & Cake Ser.: 2). (ENG.). 32p. (J). lib. bdg. 15.95 *(978-1-935083-06-1(6))* CyPress Pubns.

Nutt, Robert. Amy's Light. Nutt, Robert, illus. 2010. (Illus.). 44p. (J). (gr. -1-3). 16.95 *(978-1-58469-128-0(X));* (ENG., pap. 8.95 *(978-1-58469-129-7(8))* Dawn Pubns.

Orsi, Tea. Tinker Bell & the Legend of the NeverBeast. 2015. (Disney Fairies Graphic Novels Ser.: 17). (J). lib. bdg. 18.40 *(978-0-606-37295-4(4))* Turtleback Bks.

Pfeffer, Wendy. Firefly at Stony Brook Farm. Mikec, Larry, illus. 2005. (Smithsonian's Backyard Ser.). (ENG.). 32p. (J). (gr. -1-2). 15.95 *(978-1-59249-282-4(7),* B5026) Soundprints.

—Firefly at Stonybrook Farm. Mikec, Larry, illus. 2004. (Smithsonian's Backyard Ser.). (ENG.). 32p. (J). (gr. 2-2). 4.99 *(978-1-59249-283-1(5),* B5076) Soundprints.

Porter, Todd. Firefly Fred. Patenaude, Brian, illus. 2004. (ENG.). 36p. (J). (gr. -1-3). 19.95 *(978-1-932278-00-2(1))* Mayhaven Publishing, Inc.

Raye, Donna. Edison the Firefly & Sierra the Special Spider. 2013. 28p. pap. 9.99 *(978-0-9910324-9-5(7))* Mindstir Media.

—Edison the Firefly & the Invention of the Light Bulb. Balsano, Sean, illus. 2012. (POR, SPA & ENG.). 28p. pap. 9.99 *(978-0-9836771-0-9(7))* Mindstir Media.

Ross, Katharine. Twinkle, Twinkle, Little Bug. Cooke, Tom & Brannon, Tom, illus. 2014. (Step into Reading Ser.). (ENG.). 32p. (J). (gr. -1-1). pap. 3.99 *(978-0-679-87666-3(9),* Random Hse. Bks. for Young Readers) Random Hse. Children's Bks.

Sadar, Albin. Hamster Holmes, on the Right Track. Fabbretti, Valerio, illus. 2016. (Hamster Holmes Ser.). (ENG.). 32p. (J). (gr. k-2). pap. 3.99 *(978-1-4814-2042-6(9),* Simon Spotlight) Simon Spotlight.

—Hamster Holmes, on the Right Track. 2016. (Simon & Schuster Ready-To-Read Level 2 Ser.). lib. bdg. 13.55 *(978-0-606-38245-8(3))* Turtleback Bks.

Sargent, Dave & Sargent, Pat. Lizzy Lightning Bug. 10 vols., Vol. 17. Robinson, Laura, illus. 2004. (Learn to Read Ser.: 10). 18p. (J). lib. bdg. 10.95 *(978-1-56763-830-1(9));* lib. bdg. 20.95 *(978-1-56763-829-5(5))* Ozark Publishing.

—Lizzy Lightning Bug/Lizzy la Luciérnaga. 10 vols. Robinson, Laura, illus. 2004. (Learn to Read Ser.: 10). (ENG & SPA.). 18p. (J). pap. 10.95 *(978-1-56763-994-0(1))* Ozark Publishing.

Scoggins, Terry. Electric Ellie & Lightning Lucy: Firefly Friends Forever. 2008. 16p. pap. 8.99 *(978-1-4389-1254-7(4))* AuthorHouse.

Sudduth, Brent H. Buster. Spengler, Kenneth J., illus. 2003. 32p. (J). 15.95 *(978-1-59034-478-1(2))* Mondo Publishing.

Tarver, Monroe S. Little Light Shine Bright. Tarver, Monroe S., illus. l.t. ed. 2004. (Illus.). 32p. (J). 6.99 *(978-0-9743568-4-6(0))* Tarver, Monroe.

Thomas, Patricia. Firefly Mountain. 1 vol. Sylvada, Peter, illus. 2007. (ENG.). 32p. (J). (gr. 1-5). 16.95 *(978-1-56145-360-3(9))* Peachtree Pubs.

FIREMEN

see Fire Fighters

FIRES

see also Fire Extinction; Fire Prevention; Forest Fires

Alagna, Magdalena. The Great Fire of London Of 1666. 2009. (Tragic Fires Throughout History Ser.). 48p. (gr. 5-8). 53.00 *(978-1-60854-583-4(0),* Rosen Reference) Rosen Publishing Group, Inc., The.

Armentrout, David & Armentrout, Patricia. Fires. 2006. (Earth's Power Ser.). (Illus.). 32p. (YA). (gr. 2-5). lib. bdg. 28.50 *(978-1-60044-231-5(5))* Rourke Educational Media.

Bath, Louella. Making Fire in the Wild. 01 vols., 1. 2016. (Wilderness Survival Skills Ser.). (ENG., Illus.). 24p. (J). pap. 8.25 *(978-1-5081-4320-8(X),* PowerKids Pr.) Rosen Publishing Group, Inc., The.

Bennie, Paul. The Great Chicago Fire Of 1871. 2008. (Great Historic Disasters Ser.). (Illus.). 128p. (gr. 5-8). lib. bdg. 35.00 *(978-0-7910-9638-3(6),* Chelsea Hse.) Facts On File, Inc.

Cleland, JoAnn. Surviving the Great Chicago Fire. 2009. (ENG., Illus.). 32p. (gr. 4-8). pap. 9.95 *(978-1-60694-549-0(1))* Rourke Educational Media.

Collard, Sneed B., III. Fire Birds. 2015. (Illus.). 48p. (J). *(978-0-9844460-7-0(9))* Bucking Horse Bks.

Curtis, Jennifer Keats. La Camada con Suerte: Cachorros de Lobo Rescatados de un Incendio Forestal. 1 vol. Gomes, John, illus. 2015. (ENG & SPA.). 32p. (J). (gr. 2-5). pap. 9.95 *(978-1-62855-720-6(6))* Arbordale Publishing.

—The Lucky Litter: Wolf Pups Rescued from Wildfire. 1 vol. Gomes, John, illus. 2015. (ENG.). 32p. (J). (gr. 2-5). 17.95 *(978-1-62855-718-3(4))* Arbordale Publishing.

Farndon, John. Extreme Fires & Floods. 2017. (When Nature Attacks Ser.). (ENG., Illus.). 32p. (J). (gr. 3-6). 26.65 ***(978-1-5124-3221-3(0),*** Hungry Tomato (r)) Lerner Publishing Group.

Ford, Jean. Explosives & Arson Investigation. Noziglia, Carla Miller & Siegel, Jay A., eds. 2013. (Solving Crimes with Science: Forensics Ser.: 12). (Illus.). 112p. (J). (gr. 7-18). 22.95 *(978-1-4222-2867-8(3))* Mason Crest.

Friddell, Claudia. Goliath: Hero of the Great Baltimore Fire. Howell, Troy, illus. 2010. (True Stories Ser.). (ENG.). 32p. (J). (gr. 1-4). 17.95 *(978-1-58536-455-8(X),* 202179) Sleeping Bear Pr.

Furgang, Kathy. National Geographic Readers: Wildfires. 2015. (Readers Ser.). (ENG., Illus.). 48p. (J). (gr. 1-4). pap. 3.99 *(978-1-4263-2133-7(3),* National Geographic Children's Bks.) National Geographic Society.

Ghigna, Charles. Dial 911! Thomas, Glenn, illus. 2017. (Fire Safety Ser.). (ENG.). 24p. (gr. k-2). 33.99 ***(978-1-68410-019-4(4))*** Cantata Learning.

—Get Out. Stay Out! Thomas, Glenn, illus. 2017. (Fire Safety Ser.). (ENG.). 24p. (gr. k-2). 33.99 ***(978-1-68410-029-3(1))*** Cantata Learning.

—Plan & Prepare! Thomas, Glenn, illus. 2017. (Fire Safety Ser.). (ENG.). 24p. (gr. k-2). 33.99 ***(978-1-68410-045-3(3))*** Cantata Learning.

Huey, Lois Miner. Floodwaters & Flames: The 1913 Disaster in Dayton, Ohio. 2016. (ENG., Illus.). 56p. (gr. 4-8). (J). lib. bdg. 33.32 *(978-1-4677-9432-9(5));* 50.65 *(978-1-4677-9728-3(6))* Lerner Publishing Group. (Millbrook Pr.).

Hunter, Nick. Fighting Fires. 1 vol. 2012. (Heroic Jobs Ser.). (ENG., Illus.). 32p. (gr. 1-2). lib. bdg. 29.99 *(978-1-4109-4356-9(9),* Read Me!) Heinemann-Raintree.

Johnson, Robin. The Great Chicago Fire. 2016. (ENG., Illus.). 48p. (J). pap. *(978-0-7787-2235-9(X))* Crabtree Publishing Co.

Knickelbine, Scott. The Great Peshtigo Fire: Stories & Science from America's Deadliest Fire. 2012. (ENG., Illus.). 88p. (J). pap. 15.95 *(978-0-87020-499-9(8))* Wisconsin Historical Society.

Levy, Janey. World's Worst Fires. 2009. (Deadly Disasters Ser.). 24p. (gr. 2-6). pap. 9.40 *(978-1-4042-4539-6(1),* Rosen Classroom); 42.50 *(978-1-61512-139-7(0),* PowerKids Pr.) Rosen Publishing Group, Inc., The.

Lewis, Brenda Ralph. Putting Out Fires: Firefighters. 2017. (J). ***(978-1-4222-3769-4(9))*** Mason Crest.

Libretto, Ellen V. The General Slocum Steamboat Fire of 1904. 2004. (Tragic Fires Throughout History Ser.). (Illus.). 48p. (J). (gr. 5-8). lib. bdg. 29.25 *(978-0-8239-4486-6(7),* Rosen Reference) Rosen Publishing Group, Inc., The.

—The General Slocum Steamboat Fire Of 1904. 2009. (Tragic Fires Throughout History Ser.). 48p. (gr. 5-8). 53.00 *(978-1-60854-581-0(4),* Rosen Reference) Rosen Publishing Group, Inc., The.

Lieurance, Suzanne. The Triangle Shirtwaist Fire & Sweatshop Reform in American History. 2003. (In American History Ser.). (Illus.). 128p. (J). (gr. 5-12). lib. bdg. 27.94 *(978-0-7660-1839-6(3))* Enslow Pubs., Inc.

Marsico, Katie. The Triangle Shirtwaist Factory Fire: Its Legacy of Labor Rights. 2009. (Perspectives Ser.). 112p. (gr. 7-18). 39.93 *(978-0-7614-4027-7(5))* Marshall Cavendish Corp.

Marx, Christy. The Great Chicago Fire Of 1871. 2009. (Tragic Fires Throughout History Ser.). 48p. (gr. 5-8). 53.00 *(978-1-60854-582-7(2),* Rosen Reference) Rosen Publishing Group, Inc., The.

Mason, Paul. Wildfires. 2012. (Disaster Watch! Ser.). (Illus.). 32p. (gr. 4-6). lib. bdg. 28.50 *(978-1-59920-428-4(2))* Black Rabbit Bks.

McDougall, Chros. San Francisco Earthquake & Fire. 1 vol. 2013. (History's Greatest Disasters Ser.). (ENG.). 48p. (J). (gr. 3-6). lib. bdg. 32.79 *(978-1-61783-959-7(0))* ABDO Publishing Co.

McDougall, Chrs. San Francisco Earthquake & Fire Paperback. 2013. (J). pap. 15.64 *(978-1-62403-024-6(6),* Core Library) ABDO Publishing Co.

McDowell, Pamela. Wildfires. 2016. (J). ***(978-1-5105-2081-3(3))*** SmartBook Media, Inc.

McHugh, Janet. The Great Chicago Fire. 2007. (Code Red Ser.). (Illus.). 32p. (YA). (gr. 2-5). lib. bdg. 25.27 *(978-1-59716-360-6(0))* Bearport Publishing Co., Inc.

Murphy, Jim. The Great Fire. 2006. (Illus.). 144p. (gr. 4-7). 23.00 *(978-0-7569-6632-4(9))* Perfection Learning Corp.

—The Great Fire. 2006. (ENG., Illus.). 144p. (J). (gr. 4-7). pap. 12.99 *(978-0-439-20307-4(X),* Scholastic Paperbacks) Scholastic, Inc.

Owens, L. L. The Great Chicago Fire. 1 vol. 2007. (Essential Events Set 1 Ser.). (ENG., Illus.). 112p. (J). (gr. 6-12). lib. bdg. 35.64 *(978-1-59928-851-2(6))* ABDO Publishing Co.

Pascal, Janet. What Was the Great Chicago Fire? 2016. (What Was? Ser.). (ENG., Illus.). 112p. (J). (gr. 3-7). 5.99 *(978-0-399-54158-2(6),* Penguin Workshop); lib. bdg. 15.99 *(978-0-399-54238-1(8),* Grosset & Dunlap) Penguin Young Readers Group.

Rau, Dana Meachen. Fire Safety: Seguridad en Caso de Incendio. 2009. (Bookworms — Bilingual Editions: Safe Kids/Ninos Seguros Ser.). (SPA & ENG.). 32p. (gr. k-2). lib. bdg. 15.95 *(978-0-7614-4784-9(9))* Marshall Cavendish Corp.

Raum, Elizabeth. Wildfire! 2017. (Natural Disasters Ser.). (ENG., Illus.). 32p. (J). (gr. 1-3). pap. 9.99 *(978-1-68152-086-5(9))* Amicus.

Regan, Michael. The Great Chicago Fire: A Cause-And-Effect Investigation. 2016. (Cause-And-Effect Disasters Ser.). (ENG., Illus.). 40p. (J). (gr. 4-6). 30.65 *(978-1-5124-1120-1(5));* 46.65 *(978-1-5124-1130-0(2),* Lerner Pubns.) Lerner Publishing Group.

Rice, Dona Herweck. You Are There! London 1666. 2017. (Time for Kids Nonfiction Readers Ser.). lib. bdg. 19.65 ***(978-0-606-40263-7(2))*** Turtleback Bks.

Rice, William B. Los Incendios. 1 vol. rev. ed. 2010. (Science Readers: a Closer Look Ser.). (SPA., Illus.). 32p. (J). (gr. 2-3). pap. 8.99 *(978-1-4333-2158-0(0))* Shell Educational Publishing.

Schaefer, A. R. & Schaefer, Adam R. The Triangle Shirtwaist Factory Fire. 2003. (Landmark Events in American History Ser.). (Illus.). 48p. (gr. 5-12). pap. 14.05 *(978-0-8368-5411-4(X),* Gareth Stevens Secondary Library) Stevens, Gareth Publishing LLLP.

Scher, Linda. The Texas City Disaster. 2007. (Code Red Ser.). (Illus.). 32p. (YA). (gr. 2-5). lib. bdg. 25.27 *(978-1-59716-363-7(5))* Bearport Publishing Co., Inc.

Shea, Therese. The Texas Wildfires. 2007. (Nature in the News Ser.: Vol. 2). (Illus.). 32p. (YA). (gr. 2-5). lib. bdg. 23.95 *(978-1-4042-3540-3(X))* Rosen Publishing Group, Inc., The.

Silverstein, Alvin, et al. Wildfires: The Science Behind Raging Infernos. 2009. (Science Behind Natural Disasters Ser.). (Illus.). 48p. (J). (gr. 5-9). lib. bdg. 25.27 *(978-0-7660-2973-6(5))* Enslow Pubs., Inc.

Simon, Seymour. Wildfires. 2016. (Illus.). 32p. (J). (gr. 1-5). 17.99 *(978-0-06-234502-8(8))* HarperCollins Pubs.

Spilsbury, Louise & Spilsbury, Richard. Top 10 Worst Wildfires. 2016. (Nature's Ultimate Disasters Ser.). 00032p. (J). (gr. 3-4). pap. 10.00 *(978-1-4994-3069-1(8),* PowerKids Pr.) Rosen Publishing Group, Inc., The.

Steele, Philip, et al. Extreme Planet. 2014. (Illus.). 128p. (J). *(978-1-4351-5523-7(8))* Barnes & Noble, Inc.

Tanaka, Shelley. Earthquake! A Day That Changed America. Craig, David, illus. 2006. 48p. (J). (gr. 4-8). reprint ed. 17.00 *(978-1-4223-5635-7(3))* DIANE Publishing Co.

Trammel, Howard K. Wildfires. 2009. (True Book(tm), a — Earth Science Ser.). (ENG.). 48p. (J). (gr. 2-5). 31.00 *(978-0-531-16887-5(5))* Scholastic Library Publishing.

Walsh, Kenneth C. H. You Are There! San Francisco 1906. 2017. (J). pap. 8.97 *(978-1-4938-3617-8(X))* Teacher Created Materials, Inc.

Willett, Edward. Fires & Wildfires: A Practical Survival Guide. 2005. (Library of Emergency Preparedness Ser.). (Illus.). 64p. (YA). (gr. 5-9). lib. bdg. 31.95 *(978-1-4042-0532-1(2))* Rosen Publishing Group, Inc., The.

Woods, Michael & Woods, Mary B. Fires. 2006. (Disasters up Close Ser.). (ENG., Illus.). 64p. (J). (gr. 4-8). lib. bdg. 27.93 *(978-0-8225-4713-6(9),* Lerner Pubns.) Lerner Publishing Group.

Woollett, Laura A. Big Top Burning: The True Story of an Arsonist, a Missing Girl, & the Greatest Show on Earth. 2015. (ENG.). 176p. (J). (gr. 5). 18.95 *(978-1-61373-114-7(0))* Chicago Review Pr., Inc.

FIRES—FICTION

Bestul, Nancy M. The Final Clue: An Historical Novel. 2014. (Illus.). 150p. (J). pap. 12.99 *(978-1-4951-1481-6(3))* Independent Pub.

Blazin' Hot: Coloring/Activity Book (English) Incl. Stickers. 2007. (J). 2.99 *(978-1-933934-51-8(4))* Mighty Kids Media.

Blazin' Hot: Picture Book (English) NL 9x9 with Snipe. 2007. (J). 5.99 *(978-1-933934-46-4(8))* Mighty Kids Media.

Bowen, Carl. Back Burn. Lee, Marc, illus. 2016. (Firestormers Ser.). (ENG.). 112p. (gr. 4-8). lib. bdg. 26.65 *(978-1-4965-3305-0(4))* Stone Arch Bks.

—Bone Yard. Lee, Marc, illus. 2016. (Firestormers Ser.). (ENG.). 112p. (gr. 4-8). lib. bdg. 26.65 *(978-1-4965-3306-7(2))* Stone Arch Bks.

—Fire Front. Lee, Marc, illus. 2016. (Firestormers Ser.). (ENG.). 112p. (gr. 4-8). lib. bdg. 26.65 *(978-1-4965-3308-1(9))* Stone Arch Bks.

—Firestormers: Elite Firefighting Crew. Lee, Marc, illus. 2016. (ENG.). 224p. (gr. 4-8). pap. 8.95 *(978-1-62370-756-9(0))* Capstone Young Readers of Coughlan Cos.

—Hot Spot. Lee, Marc, illus. 2016. (Firestormers Ser.). (ENG.). 112p. (gr. 4-8). lib. bdg. 26.65 *(978-1-4965-3307-4(0))* Stone Arch Bks.

Choldenko, Gennifer. Al Capone Does My Homework. 2014. (ENG.). 240p. (J). (gr. 5). pap. 7.99 *(978-0-14-242522-0(2),* Puffin Books) Penguin Young Readers Group.

—Al Capone Does My Homework. 2014. (Tale from Alcatraz (Al Capone) Ser.: 3). lib. bdg. 18.40 *(978-0-606-35714-2(9))* Turtleback Bks.

Clover, Peter. Rescue Riders: Fire Alert. l.t. ed. 2007. 108p. per. *(978-1-905665-30-3(X))* Pollinger In Print.

Deen, Natasha. Burned. 1 vol. 2015. (Retribution Ser.). (ENG.). 168p. (YA). (gr. 8-12). pap. 9.95 *(978-1-4598-0726-6(X))* Orca Bk. Pubs. USA.

Duey, Kathleen & Bale, Karen A. Fire: Chicago 1871. 2014. (Survivors Ser.). (ENG., Illus.). 176p. (J). (gr. 3-7). pap. 6.99 *(978-1-4424-9054-3(3),* Aladdin) Simon & Schuster Children's Publishing.

—Fire: Chicago 1871. 2014. (Survivors Ser.). (ENG., Illus.). 176p. (J). (gr. 3-7). 16.99 *(978-1-4424-9055-0(1),* Simon & Schuster/Paula Wiseman Bks.) Simon & Schuster/Paula Wiseman Bks.

Erickson, John R. The Case of the Blazing Sky. Holmes, Gerald L., illus. 2011. (Hank the Cowdog Ser.). (ENG.). 129p. (J). (gr. 3-6). pap. 5.99 *(978-1-59188-151-3(X))* Maverick Bks., Inc.

Gunnery, Sylvia. Out of Bounds. 2004. (Sports Stories Ser.). (ENG.). 104p. (J). (gr. 3-8). *(978-1-55028-827-8(X))* Lorimer, James & Co., Ltd., Pubs. CAN. Dist: Casemate Pubs. & Bk. Distributors, LLC.

Hart, Alison. Emma's River. 1 vol. Bachem, Paul, illus. 2010. (ENG.). 160p. (J). (gr. 2-5). 12.95 *(978-1-56145-524-9(5),* Peachtree Junior) Peachtree Pubs.

Hopkinson, Deborah. Into the Firestorm: A Novel of San Francisco 1906. 2008. (Yearling Bks.). (ENG.). 208p. (J). (gr. 3-7). per. 6.99 *(978-0-440-42129-0(2),* Yearling) Random Hse. Children's Bks.

Hughes, Shirley. Daisy Saves the Day. Hughes, Shirley, illus. 2015. (ENG., Illus.). 32p. (J). (gr. k-4). 16.99 *(978-0-7636-7323-9(4))* Candlewick Pr.

Kertell, Lynn Maslen. Buddy to the Rescue. 2012. (BOB Books: Scholastic Readers Level 1 Ser.: 6). lib. bdg. 13.55 *(978-0-606-26753-3(0),* Turtleback) Turtleback Bks.

Li, Judith L. & Herring, M. L. Ricky's Atlas: Mapping a Land on Fire. 2016. (ENG., Illus.). 128p. (J). (gr. 3-6). pap. 17.95 *(978-0-87071-842-7(8))* Oregon State Univ. Pr.

Long, Loren. Otis & the Kittens. Long, Loren, illus. 2016. (Otis Ser.). (ENG., Illus.). 40p. (J). (gr. -1-3). 17.99 *(978-0-399-16398-2(0),* Philomel Bks.) Penguin Young Readers Group.

McCalla Njee, Lena. Ivan Consigue la Casa de Sus Suenos. Urruela, Maria Cristina, tr. 2013. 46p. pap. 13.99 *(978-976-95510-3-9(1))* Minna Pr.

McMullin, Neridah & McLean, Andrew. Fabish: The Horse That Braved a Bushfire. 2016. (ENG.). 32p. (J). (gr. 1-4). 18.99 *(978-1-925266-86-3(9))* Allen & Unwin AUS. Dist: Independent Pubs. Group.

Montgomery, R. A. Fire! 2015. (ENG.). 80p. (Orig.). (J). pap. 7.99 *(978-1-937133-49-8(4))* Chooseco LLC.

Night, P. J. Home, Sweet Haunt. 2013. (Creepover Ser.: 15). lib. bdg. 16.00 *(978-0-606-32047-4(4),* Turtleback) Turtleback Bks.

Ross, Jill. The Real Nitty-Gritty. Pruitt, Gwendolyn, illus. 2010. (ENG.). 60p. (J). (gr. 3-7). pap. 9.95 *(978-1-59825-949-0(0))* Shenanigans Series.

Saddleback Educational Publishing Staff, ed. Camp. 1 vol. unabr. ed. 2011. (Heights Ser.). (ENG.). 50p. (gr. 5-8). pap. 7.95 *(978-1-61651-284-2(9))* Saddleback Educational Publishing, Inc.

Sander, Sonia. LEGO City Reader Collection: LEGO City Emergency. 2012. (Illus.). 127p. (J). *(978-1-4351-3985-5(2))* Scholastic, Inc.

Schultz, Jan Neubert. Firestorm. 2003. (Adventures in Time Ser.). 204p. (YA). (gr. 4-7). 15.95 *(978-0-87614-276-9(5),* Carolrhoda Bks.) Lerner Publishing Group.

Shaw, Susan. One of the Survivors. (ENG.). 208p. (J). (gr. 5-9). 2011. pap. 6.99 *(978-1-4169-6389-9(8))* 2009. 15.99 *(978-1-4169-6129-1(1))* McElderry, Margaret K. Bks. (McElderry, Margaret K. Bks.).

Spinelli, Eileen. Hero Cat. 0 vols. Stammen, Jo Ellen McAllister, illus. 2011. (ENG.). 32p. (J). (gr. -1-3). pap. 9.99 *(978-0-7614-5837-1(9),* 9780761458371, Amazon Children's Publishing) Amazon Publishing.

Stockland, Patricia M. Stop the Grassfires!. 1 vol. Haugen, Ryan, illus. 2008. (Safari Friends Ser.). (ENG.). 32p. (gr. -1-3). 28.50 *(978-1-60270-086-4(9),* Looking Glass Library) ABDO Publishing Co.

Tarshis, Lauren. I Survived the Great Chicago Fire 1871. 2015. (I Survived Ser.: 11). (ENG., Illus.). 112p. (J). (gr. 2-5). pap. 4.99 *(978-0-545-65846-1(2))* Scholastic, Inc.

Welling, Peter J. Darlene Halloween & the Great Chicago Fire. 1 vol. Welling, Peter J., illus. 2007. (ENG., Illus.). 32p. (J). (gr. k-3). 16.99 *(978-1-58980-479-1(1))* Pelican Publishing Co., Inc.

Wellington, Monica. Firefighter Frank. 2011. (ENG.). 26p. (J). (gr. -1 — 1). bds. 5.99 *(978-0-525-42373-7(7),* Dutton Books for Young Readers) Penguin Young Readers Group.

FIREWORKS

Cobb, Vicki. Fireworks. 2008. pap. 52.95 *(978-0-8225-9449-9(8))* Lerner Publishing Group.

—Fireworks. Gold, Michael, photos by. 2005. (Where's the Science Here? Ser.). (Illus.). 48p. (J). (gr. 3-7). lib. bdg. 23.93 *(978-0-7613-2771-4(1),* Millbrook Pr.) Lerner Publishing Group.

Einhorn, Kama. The Explosive Story of Fireworks! Guidera, Daniel, illus. 2015. (History of Fun Stuff Ser.). (ENG.). 48p. (J). (gr. 1-3). 16.99 *(978-1-4814-3848-3(4))* Simon & Schuster Children's Publishing.

Firestone, Mary. Pyrotechnician. 2005. (Weird Careers in Science Ser.). (Illus.). 72p. (gr. 5-8). lib. bdg. 25.00 *(978-0-7910-8703-9(4),* Chelsea Hse.) Facts On File, Inc.

Merrick, Patrick. Fourth of July Fireworks. 2015. (Our Holiday Symbols Ser.). (ENG.). 24p. (J). (gr. 1-4). 25.64 *(978-1-63143-744-1(5),* 208553) Child's World, Inc., The.

Rau, Dana Meachen. Fireworks. 2010. (Bookworms Chapter Books: Surprising Science Ser.). 24p. (gr. 2-3). 22.79 *(978-0-7614-4868-6(3))* Marshall Cavendish Corp.

Rocker, Megan. How It Happens at the Fireworks Factory. Wolfe, Bob & Wolfe, Diane, photos by. 2004. (How It

Happens Ser.). (Illus.). 32p. (J). (gr. 2-5). lib. bdg. 19.95 *(978-1-881508-97-7(8))* Oliver Pr., Inc.

Wood, Alix. Explosives Expert, 1 vol., 1. 2014. (World's Coolest Jobs Ser.). (ENG.). 32p. (J). (gr. 3-6). pap. 10.00 *(978-1-4777-6012-3(1))*; lib. bdg. 26.25 *(978-1-4777-6011-6(3))* Rosen Publishing Group, Inc., The. (PowerKids Pr.).

FIREWORKS—FICTION

Clark, Karen. Flash, Bang, Wheee! White, Ian, illus. 2004. 24p. (J). *(978-1-85269-280-3(4))*; *(978-1-85269-430-2(0))*; *(978-1-85269-374-9(6))*; *(978-1-85269-433-3(5))*; *(978-1-85269-434-0(3))*; *(978-1-85269-438-8(6))*; *(978-1-85269-437-1(8))*; *(978-1-85269-435-7(1))*; *(978-1-85269-432-6(7))*; *(978-1-85269-350-3(9))*; *(978-1-85269-353-4(3))*; *(978-1-85269-355-8(X))*; *(978-1-85269-356-5(8))* Mantra Lingua.

—Flash Bang Wheee! White, Ian, illus. 2004. (J). *(978-1-85269-678-8(8))* Mantra Lingua.

—Flash Bang Wheee! White, Ian, illus. 2004. (ENG & VIE.). (J). pap. 12.95 *(978-1-85269-808-9(X))* Mantra Lingua GBR. Dist: Chinasprout, Inc.

Clark, Karen & White, Ian, illus. Flash, Bang, Wheee! Bing, Bang, Boum! 2004. 24p. (J). *(978-1-85269-354-1(1))* Mantra Lingua.

—Flash, Bang, Wheee! Shkreptime, Gjemim Dhe Vershellime! 2004. 24p. (J). *(978-1-85269-349-7(5))* Mantra Lingua.

Dowling, Paul. The Night Journey. 2003. 12p. (J). 9.95 *(978-1-57717-290-1(6))* New Line Bks.

Falconer, Ian. Olivia Forma una Banda. Mlawer, Teresa, tr. from ENG. Falconer, Ian, illus. 2007. (SPA., Illus.). 39p. (J). (gr. -1-3). 17.99 *(978-1-933032-23-8(5))* Lectorum Pubns., Inc.

—Olivia Forms a Band. Falconer, Ian, illus. 2009. (ENG., Illus.). 50p. (J). (gr. -1-3). 12.99 *(978-1-4169-8037-7(7)*, Atheneum Bks. for Young Readers) Simon & Schuster Children's Publishing.

Friedman, Becky. Daniel's First Fireworks. 2016. (Daniel Tiger's Neighborhood 8X8 Ser.). lib. bdg. 13.55 *(978-0-606-38990-7(3))* Turtleback Bks.

Fruchter, Jason, illus. Daniel's First Fireworks. 2016. (Daniel Tiger's Neighborhood Ser.). (ENG.). 24p. (J). (gr. -1-2). pap. 3.99 *(978-1-4814-6053-8(6)*, Simon Spotlight) Simon Spotlight.

Gentry, Jennifer Mills. Maria's 4th of July. 2011. 32p. pap. 24.95 *(978-1-4560-7300-8(1))* America Star Bks.

Iggulden, Conn & Duncan, Lizzy. Tollins 2: Dynamite Tales, Vol. 2. 2012. (Tollins Ser.: 2). (Illus.). 192p. (J). 16.99 *(978-0-06-173101-3(3))* HarperCollins Pubs.

Jane, Hale. Boomland. 2003. (Land Ser.: 4). 240p. (J). per. 12.95 *(978-0-934426-20-6(1))* NAPSAC Reproductions.

McDonald, Kirsten. The Sparkly Night. 2016. (Carlos & Carmen Set 3 Ser.). (ENG., Illus.). (J). (gr. -1-3). lib. bdg. 27.07 ***(978-1-62402-185-5(9))*** ABDO Publishing Co.

Meddaugh, Susan. Fireworks for All. 2011. (Martha Speaks Ser.). (Illus.). 24p. (J). (gr. -1-3). (ENG.). pap. 3.99 *(978-0-547-42892-5(8))*; (SPA & ENG., pap. 3.99 *(978-0-547-55620-8(9))* Houghton Mifflin Harcourt Publishing Co.

Nallam, Stu. Freddie, the Unhappy Firecracker, 1 vol. 2009. 21p. pap. 24.95 *(978-1-61546-373-2(9))* America Star Bks.

Particular, Nowen N. Boomtown, 1 vol. 2010. (ENG.). 320p. pap. 9.99 *(978-1-4003-1553-6(0))* Nelson, Thomas Inc.

Shea, Therese. Flags & Fireworks. 2006. (Neighborhood Readers Ser.). (ENG.). 8p. (gr. -1-3). pap. 5.15 *(978-1-4042-5726-9(8)*, Rosen Classroom) Rosen Publishing Group, Inc., The.

Wilde, Oscar. El Famoso Cohete. Zwerger, Lisbeth, illus. (SPA.). 72p. (J). *(978-84-392-8693-6(7))* Gaviota Ediciones ESP. Dist: Lectorum Pubns., Inc.

FIRST AID

Aretha, David. Top 10 Worst Injuries in Football. 2016. (Sports Greats Ser.). 48p. (J). pap. 11.70 *(978-0-7660-8300-4(4))* Enslow Pubs., Inc.

Bell-Rehwoldt, Sheri. The Kids' Guide to Duct Tape Projects, 1 vol. 2011. (Kids' Guides). (ENG.). 32p. (gr. 3-4). 27.99 *(978-1-4296-6010-5(4)*, Edge Bks.) Capstone Press of Coughlan Cos.

Boelts, Maribeth & Boelts, Darwin. Kids to the Rescue! First Aid Techniques for Kids. Megale, Marina, illus. rev. ed. 2003. (ENG.). 72p. (J). (gr. -1-7). pap. 9.95 *(978-1-884734-78-6(2))* Parenting Pr., Inc.

Cobb, Vicki. Your Body Battles A Skinned Knee. 2009. pap. 40.95 *(978-0-7613-4620-3(1))* Lerner Publishing Group.

Edwards, Erika. What If I Get a Sprain? 2016. (Benched: Dealing with Sports Injuries Ser.). 24p. (J). (gr. 3-2). 22.60 *(978-1-4824-4889-4(0))* Stevens, Gareth Publishing LLLP.

Evans, Michael. The Adventures of Medical Man: Kids' Illnesses & Injuries Explained. Williams, Gareth, illus. 2010. (ENG.). 72p. (J). (gr. 3-5). 21.95 *(978-1-55451-263-8(8)*, 9781554512638); pap. 12.95 *(978-1-55451-262-1(X)*, 9781554512621) Annick Pr., Ltd. CAN. Dist: Publishers Group West (PGW).

First Aid & Home Safety. (YA). (gr. 6-12). pap. 10.95 *(978-0-8224-4366-7(X))* Globe Fearon Educational Publishing.

Frick, Gary. How Do Cuts & Bruises Heal?, Vol. 1. 2014. (My Body Does Strange Stuff! Ser.). (ENG., Illus.). 24p. (J). (gr. 1-2). 22.60 *(978-1-4824-0234-6(3))* Stevens, Gareth Publishing LLLP.

Furgang, Kathy. Frequently Asked Questions about Sports Injuries. 2007. (FAQ: Teen Life Ser.). (Illus.). 64p. (YA). (gr. 7-12). lib. bdg. 31.95 *(978-1-4042-1933-5(1))* Rosen Publishing Group, Inc., The.

Greathouse, Lisa. Emergency! Be Prepared, 1 vol. 2011. (Science Readers: a Closer Look Ser.). (ENG., Illus.). 32p. (J). (gr. 2-2). pap. 8.99 *(978-1-4333-3092-6(X))* Teacher Created Materials, Inc.

Green, M. I. Primeros Auxilios para Ninos (First Aid for Children) (SPA., Illus.). 192p. (J). pap. 9.95 *(978-968-416-411-6(4)*, FN4114) Fernandez USA Publishing.

Hayes, Amy. What If I Feel Faint? 2016. (Benched: Dealing with Sports Injuries Ser.). 24p. (J). (gr. 3-2). 22.60 *(978-1-4824-4887-0(4))* Stevens, Gareth Publishing LLLP.

Hewitt, Sally. Happy Doctor. Cameron, Craig, illus. 2003. 14p. (J). pap. 10.95 *(978-1-57145-734-9(8)*, Silver Dolphin Bks.) Readerlink Distribution Services, LLC.

Johansson, Philip. What You Can Do about Carpal Tunnel Syndrome & Other Repetitive Strain Injuries. 2015. (Contemporary Diseases & Disorders Ser.). (ENG., Illus.). 128p. (J). (gr. 7-7). 37.27 *(978-0-7660-7034-9(4))* Enslow Pubs., Inc.

Kamberg, Mary-Lane. Sports Concussions. 2011. (Headlines! Ser.). (ENG.). 64p. (YA). lib. bdg. 31.95 *(978-1-4488-1289-9(5))* Rosen Publishing Group, Inc., The.

Landau, Elaine. Sprains & Strains. 2010. (Head-to Toe Health 3 Ser.). 32p. (gr. 2). 28.50 *(978-0-7614-4833-4(0))* Marshall Cavendish GBR. Dist: Marshall Cavendish Corp.

Langwith, Jacqueline. Sports Injuries. Greenhaven Press Editors & Gale, A. G., eds. 2014. (Perspectives on Diseases & Disorders Ser.). (ENG., Illus.). 144p. (gr. 10-12). lib. bdg. 44.30 *(978-0-7377-6358-4(2)*, Greenhaven Pr., Inc.) Cengage Gale.

Lew, Kristi. Clot & Scab: Gross Stuff about Your Scrapes, Bumps, & Bruises. Slack, Michael H., illus. 2009. (Gross Body Science Ser.). (ENG.). 48p. (gr. 3-5). lib. bdg. 29.27 *(978-0-8225-8965-5(6))* Lerner Publishing Group.

Longnecker, Steve. Steve Longenecker's Wilderness Emergency Medical Aid Book for Kids & Their Adults. Lee, Frank, illus. 2005. 176p. (YA). (gr. 5-18). pap. 16.95 *(978-1-889596-18-1(3))* Milestone Pr., Inc.

MacNab, Chris. Weight Training. 2005. (Sports Injuries Ser.). (Illus.). 64p. (YA). lib. bdg. 19.95 *(978-1-59084-641-4(9))* Mason Crest.

Markle, Sandra. Bad Burns. 2010. (Powerful Medicine Ser.). (ENG.). 48p. (gr. 5-8). lib. bdg. 27.93 *(978-0-8225-8702-6(5))* Lerner Publishing Group.

Mattern, Joanne. I Have Cuts & Scrapes. 2016. (Rookie Read-About Health Ser.). (ENG., Illus.). 32p. (J). pap. 5.95 *(978-0-531-22581-3(X)*, Children's Pr.) Scholastic Library Publishing.

McClafferty, Carla Killough. Fourth down & Inches: Concussions & Football's Make-or-Break Moment. 2013. (ENG., Illus.). 96p. (gr. 6-12). 20.95 *(978-1-4677-1067-1(9)*, Carolrhoda Bks.) Lerner Publishing Group.

McCoy, Lisa. Cheerleading. 2005. (Sports Injuries Ser.). (Illus.). 64p. (YA). lib. bdg. 19.95 *(978-1-59084-628-5(1))* Mason Crest.

Nelson, Kristen Rajczak. What If I Break a Bone? 2016. (Benched: Dealing with Sports Injuries Ser.). 24p. (J). (gr. 3-2). 22.60 *(978-1-4824-4885-6(8))* Stevens, Gareth Publishing LLLP.

Randolph, Joanne. Ambulances. 2009. (To the Rescue! Ser.). 24p. (gr. 1-1). 42.50 *(978-1-60854-394-6(3)*, PowerKids Pr.) Rosen Publishing Group, Inc., The.

—Ambulances/Ambulancias. 2009. (To the Rescue! / ¡Al rescate! Ser.). 24p. (gr. 1-1). 42.50 *(978-1-60854-400-4(1)*, Editorial Buenas Letras) Rosen Publishing Group, Inc., The.

Royston, Angela. Cuts, Bruises, & Breaks. 2009. (How's Your Health? Ser.). (J). (gr. 1-4). 28.50 *(978-1-59920-222-8(0))* Black Rabbit Bks.

Roza, Greg. Disaster Relief Workers. 2009. (Extreme Careers Ser.). 64p. (gr. 5-5). 58.50 *(978-1-61512-391-9(1)*, Rosen Reference) Rosen Publishing Group, Inc., The.

—Frequently Asked Questions about Emergency Lifesaving Techniques. 2009. (FAQ: Teen Life Ser.). (Illus.). 64p. (J). (gr. 5-6). lib. bdg. 31.95 *(978-1-4358-5327-0(X))* Rosen Publishing Group, Inc., The.

Schnapp, Eric Cesar, et al. First Aid Clueless: An Emergency Guide for Young People. 2003. (YA). per. 8.95 *(978-0-9719337-3-6(1))* Elma Colletes & Sons.

Shea, Therese. What If I Need Stitches? 2016. (Benched: Dealing with Sports Injuries Ser.). 24p. (J). (gr. 3-2). 22.60 *(978-1-4824-4890-0(4))* Stevens, Gareth Publishing LLLP.

Streeter, Michael. Ice Skating. 2005. (Sports Injuries Ser.). (Illus.). 64p. (YA). lib. bdg. 19.95 *(978-1-59084-635-3(4))* Mason Crest.

Torrisi, Cathy. I Know First Aid. 2011. pap. 39.95 *(978-0-7664-3749-4(3))* Abrams & Co. Pubs., Inc.

Weber, Rebecca. First Aid Basics. 2012. (Health & Your Body Ser.). (ENG.). 24p. (gr. k-1). pap. 41.70 *(978-1-4296-8345-6(7))*; (Illus.). lib. bdg. 26.65 *(978-1-4296-7695-3(7))* Capstone Press of Coughlan Cos. (Pebble Plus).

Wilson, Patrick. Survival First Aid. Carney, John, ed. 2014. (Extreme Survival in the Military Ser.: 12). (Illus.). 64p. (J). (gr. 7-18). lib. bdg. 23.95 *(978-1-4222-3086-2(4))* Mason Crest.

Wright, John. Baseball. 2005. (Sports Injuries Ser.). (Illus.). 64p. (YA). lib. bdg. 19.95 *(978-1-59084-626-1(5))* Mason Crest.

—Basketball. 2005. (Sports Injuries Ser.). (Illus.). 64p. (YA). lib. bdg. 19.95 *(978-1-59084-627-8(3))* Mason Crest.

—Equestrian Sport. 2005. (Sports Injuries Ser.). (Illus.). 64p. (YA). lib. bdg. 19.95 *(978-1-59084-629-2(X))* Mason Crest.

—Hockey. 2005. (Sports Injuries Ser.). (Illus.). 64p. (YA). lib. bdg. 19.95 *(978-1-59084-634-6(6))* Mason Crest.

FIRST AID—FICTION

Carey, Becky. Wilma Goes to the Hospital. 2007. (Illus.). (J). 9.95 *(978-0-9791331-0-7(6))* Carey, Rebecca.

Fretz, Denette. Conrad & the Cowgirl Next Door, 1 vol. Barretta, Gene, illus. 2014. (Next Door Ser.). (ENG.). 40p. (J). 12.99 *(978-0-310-72349-3(3))* Zonderkidz.

Fryer, Jane Eayre. The Mary Frances First Aid Book 100th Anniversary Edition: A Childrens Story-Instruction First Aid Book with Home Remedies Plus Bonus Patterns for Child's Nurse Cap & Apron. 2011. (ENG., Illus.). 110p. (J). pap. 19.95 *(978-1-937564-04-9(5)*, Classic Bookwrights) Lindaloo Enterprises.

Guy, Belinda. A First Aid Manual for Children: In the Form of Three Short Stories. 2012. (Illus.). 28p. pap. 21.35 *(978-1-4772-2671-1(0))* AuthorHouse.

Hoblin, Paul & Hueller, Patrick. The Beast. 2013. (Counterattack Ser.). (ENG.). 112p. (YA). (gr. 6-12). pap. 7.95 *(978-1-4677-0716-9(3))* Lerner Publishing Group.

Manushkin, Fran. Ready, Set, Oops! 2008. pap. 34.95 *(978-1-58013-762-1(8))* Kane Press, Inc.

Marsh, Carole. The Adventure Diaries of Li, the Excellent EMT!, 7 vols. 2004. 48p. (J). (gr. 1-4). pap. 5.95 *(978-0-635-01145-9(X))* Gallopade International.

Patton, Katherine. Bam Bam the Bandage. 2010. 16p. pap. 10.99 *(978-1-4343-4967-5(5))* AuthorHouse.

Walder, Lysa. Katie the Paramedic. 2009. (Illus.). 28p. pap. 12.49 *(978-1-4389-7134-6(6))* AuthorHouse.

FIRST DAY OF SCHOOL

Barber, Nicola. First Day of School. 2009. (Big Day! Ser.). 24p. (J). (gr. k-2). (ENG., Illus.). pap. 8.25 *(978-1-4358-2895-7(X)*, 1291894); lib. bdg. 22.60 *(978-1-4358-2839-1(9))* Rosen Publishing Group, Inc., The. (PowerKids Pr.).

Bullard, Lisa. Sofia's First Day of School. Sakamoto, Miki, illus. 2017. (Cloverleaf Books (tm) — off to School Ser.). (ENG.). (J). (gr. k-2). pap. 7.99 ***(978-1-5124-5579-3(2))***; lib. bdg. 25.32 ***(978-1-5124-3936-6(3))*** Lerner Publishing Group. (Millbrook Pr.).

Busic, Valerie. Jason's First Day. OI Foundation, ed. Meyers, Jeff, illus. l.t. ed. 2004. 48p. per. 8.50 *(978-0-9642189-4-9(1))* Osteogenesis Imperfecta Foundation.

Civardi, Anne. Going to School. Cartwright, Stephen, illus. 2005. 16p. (J). pap. 4.95 *(978-0-7945-1008-4(6)*, Usborne) EDC Publishing.

Codell, Esmé Raji. It's Time for Preschool! Ramá, Sue, illus. 2012. 40p. (J). (gr. -1-k). (ENG.). 15.99 *(978-0-06-145518-6(0))*; lib. bdg. 16.89 *(978-0-06-145519-3(9))* HarperCollins Pubs. (Greenwillow Bks.).

Gray, Kes. First Day. Paul, Korky, illus. 2007. (Collins Big Cat Ser.). (ENG.). 152p. (J). (gr. 1-2). pap. 6.99 *(978-0-00-718666-2(5))* HarperCollins Pubs. Ltd. GBR. Dist: Independent Pubs. Group.

Guillain, Charlotte. My First Day at a New School, 1 vol. 2011. (Growing Up Ser.). (ENG.). 24p. (gr. k-2). 23.32 *(978-1-4329-4796-5(6)*, Heinemann Read & Learn) Heinemann-Raintree.

Hamilton, Lily & Myers, Barbara. Lily Goes to School. Sellaro, Brendan, illus. 2012. (ENG.). 32p. (J). 17.95 *(978-0-938467-59-5(X))* Headline Bks., Inc.

Jackson, Ellen B. It's Back to School We Go! First Day Stories Fro Around the World. Ellis, Jan Davey, illus. 2003. 32p. lib. bdg. 23.90 *(978-0-7613-2562-8(X)*, Millbrook Pr.) Lerner Publishing Group.

—It's Back to School We Go! First Day Stories from Around the World. Ellis, Jan Davey, illus. 2003. (ENG.). 32p. (J). (gr. k-3). 17.99 *(978-0-7613-1948-1(4)*, Millbrook Pr.) Lerner Publishing Group.

Medcalf, Carol & Hempstock, Becky. Letts Monster Practice e Starting School Age 4-5. 2014. (Letts Monster Practice Ser.). (ENG.). 32p. (J). (gr. -1-k). pap. 6.99 *(978-1-84419-773-6(5))* HarperCollins Pubs. Ltd. GBR. Dist: Independent Pubs. Group.

Meyer, Terry. Navigating a New School. 2012. (Middle School Survival Handbook Ser.). (ENG., Illus.). 64p. (YA). (gr. 5-8). lib. bdg. 31.95 *(978-1-4488-8312-7(1)*, Rosen Reference) Rosen Publishing Group, Inc., The.

Meyer, Terry Teague. Navigating a New School. 2012. (Middle School Survival Handbook Ser.). (ENG., Illus.). 64p. (YA). (gr. 5-8). pap. 12.95 *(978-1-4488-8319-6(9)*, Rosen Reference) Rosen Publishing Group, Inc., The.

RIGBY. The First Day of School: Kindergarten Big Books. 2003. (Rigby on Our Way to English Ser.). (ENG.). 16p. (gr. k-k). pap. 50.70 *(978-0-7578-1614-7(2))* Rigby Education.

Usborne Books Staff. Going to School Kid Kit. 2005. (Usborne First Experiences Ser.). 16p. (J). pap. 9.99 *(978-1-58086-846-4(0)*, Usborne) EDC Publishing.

FIRST DAY OF SCHOOL—FICTION

Adkins, Ryan. Dream Catcher. 2013. 28p. pap. 16.99 *(978-1-4808-0326-8(X))* Archway Publishing.

Ain, Beth. Izzy Kline Has Butterflies. 2017. (ENG.). 176p. (J). (gr. 3-7). 16.99 *(978-0-399-55080-5(1)*, Random Hse. Bks. for Young Readers) Random Hse. Children's Bks.

Alexandria, Shalayne. Nyville High No. 1: Welcome to Nyville. 2007. 124p. (YA). per. 10.00 *(978-0-9786180-1-8(7))* 5 Muses Publishing.

Allen, Richard L. Kindergarteners on Their First School Bus. 2012. 34p. pap. 9.95 *(978-1-60414-636-3(2))* Fideli Publishing, Inc.

Allyson, Libby. Scottie Rides the Bus. 2004. 27p. pap. 24.95 *(978-1-4137-3298-6(4))* PublishAmerica, Inc.

Andrews, Cynthia. Molly Goes to Preschool. 2012. 16p. pap. 15.99 *(978-1-4772-7894-9(X))* AuthorHouse.

Anholt, Laurence. Billy & the Big New School. Anholt, Catherine, illus. 2015. (Kipper Ser.). (ENG.). 32p. (J). (gr. -1-k). pap. 10.99 *(978-1-4083-3979-4(X))* Hodder & Stoughton GBR. Dist: Hachette Bk. Group.

Argueta, Jorge. Moony Luna. Gómez, Elizabeth, illus. 2013.Tr. of Luna, Lunita Lunera. (ENG & SPA.). 32p. (J). pap. 9.95 *(978-0-89239-306-0(8)*, Children's Book Press) Lee & Low Bks., Inc.

Ashburn, Boni. The Class. Gee, Kimberly, illus. 2016. (ENG.). 40p. (J). (gr. -1-3). 17.99 *(978-1-4424-2248-3(3)*, Beach Lane Bks.) Beach Lane Bks.

Asher, Penny & Booker, Ricki. My First Day of School. Kassab, Selena, illus. 2006. 32p. (J). 12.95 *(978-0-9755902-2-5(7))* Change Is Strange, Inc.

Auerbach, Adam. Edda: A Little Valkyrie's First Day of School. Auerbach, Adam, illus. 2014. (ENG., Illus.). 40p. (J). (gr. -1-3). 16.99 *(978-0-8050-9703-0(1)*, 9780805097030, Holt, Henry & Co. Bks. For Young Readers) Holt, Henry & Co.

Bailey, Tressie. Sebatian's First Day at School. 2009. 35p. pap. 21.50 *(978-0-557-03113-9(3))* Lulu Pr., Inc.

Balardo, Sharon. I Am Abel. 2012. 24p. pap. 17.99 *(978-1-4772-7798-0(6))* AuthorHouse.

Barr, Barbara Jean. My Mom Inside My Pocket, 1 vol. Stutz, Chris, illus. 2010. 16p. 24.95 *(978-1-4489-5704-0(4))* America Star Bks.

Benn, Iris H. Penelope's Big Day: Early Childhood Life Lesson. 2012. (ENG.). 34p. (J). 29.95 *(978-1-4327-6373-2(3))* Outskirts Pr., Inc.

Bertrand, Diane Gonzales, et al. Adelita & the Veggie Cousins / Adelita y las primas Verduritas. Rodriguez, Tina, illus. 2011. (SPA.). (J). 16.95 *(978-1-55885-699-8(4)*, Piñata Books) Arte Publico Pr.

Bhuyan, Sangeetha. Kukola's First School Day. 2011. 20p. pap. 11.99 *(978-1-4634-4414-3(1))* AuthorHouse.

Bienvenido a nuestra escuela y el primer día de escuela de Katy: Teacher's Guide. 2004. (SPA.). instr.'s gde. ed. *(978-1-4108-2370-0(9))* Benchmark Education Co.

The Big Race, Level 2. 2016. (Ladybird Readers Ser.). (ENG.). 16p. (J). pap., act. bk. ed. 5.99 *(978-0-241-25456-1(6))* Penguin Bks., Ltd. GBR. Dist: Independent Pubs. Group.

Bise, Sharon. Jay's First Day at School. 2013. 24p. pap. 14.93 *(978-1-4669-8304-5(3))* Trafford Publishing.

Blabey, Aaron. Sunday Chutney. Blabey, Aaron, illus. 2009. (ENG., Illus.). 32p. (J). (gr. -1-k). 16.95 *(978-1-59078-597-3(5)*, Front Street) Boyds Mills Pr.

Boldt, Mike. A Tiger Tail; (or What Happened to Anya on Her First Day of School) Boldt, Mike, illus. 2016. (ENG., Illus.). 40p. (J). (gr. -1-3). 17.99 *(978-1-4814-4885-7(4))* Simon & Schuster, Inc.

Borden, Louise. Off to First Grade. Schindler, S. D. et al, illus. 2008. (ENG.). 40p. (J). (gr. -1-3). 17.99 *(978-0-689-87395-9(6)*, McElderry, Margaret K. Bks.) McElderry, Margaret K. Bks.

Boucha, Becky. Kayla Nicole Goes to School: Kayla Nicole Series. 2009. 24p. pap. 12.99 *(978-1-4389-6535-2(4))* AuthorHouse.

Bouldin, Anthony Roth & Bouldin, Morshica. Tag along with Momo & Jojo: You're IT! Series #1 Jojo's 1st day of School. 2011. 16p. 14.95 *(978-1-4567-2077-3(5))* AuthorHouse.

Bourke, Debra. First Day at Bouddi School. Cowley, Ray B., illus. 2012. 32p. pap. 18.00 *(978-1-4349-8469-2(9)*, RoseDog Bks.) Dorrance Publishing Co., Inc.

Brexel, Bernadette. First Grade Fun. 2015. (Rosen REAL Readers: STEM & STEAM Collection). (ENG.). 8p. pap. 5.46 *(978-1-4994-9592-8(7)*, Rosen Classroom) Rosen Publishing Group, Inc., The.

Bridwell, Norman. Clifford Goes to Kindergarten. 2015. (Clifford Ser.). (ENG., Illus.). 32p. (J). (gr. -1-k). pap. 3.99 *(978-0-545-82335-7(8))* Scholastic, Inc.

Brink Hull, Amanda. Maslyn: A Different Kind of Name for a Delightful Little Girl. 2009. (Illus.). 36p. pap. 16.99 *(978-1-4389-9338-6(2))* AuthorHouse.

Brokamp, Elizabeth. Back to School, Picky Little Witch!, 1 vol. Welling, Peter, illus. 2014. (ENG.). 32p. (J). (gr. k-3). 16.99 *(978-1-4556-1887-3(X))* Pelican Publishing Co., Inc.

Bronstein, Christine. Starts School. Young, Karen L., illus. 2014. (Stewie BOOM! Ser.). (ENG.). 48p. (J). (gr. -1-3). 17.99 *(978-0-9904652-0-1(9))* Nothing But The Truth, LLC.

—Stewie BOOM! Starts School. Young, Karen L., illus. 2014. (Stewie BOOM! Ser.). (ENG.). 48p. (gr. -1-3). pap. 9.99 *(978-0-9883754-9-9(4))* Nothing But The Truth, LLC.

Brooks, Felicity. Max & Millie Start School. Guicciardini, Desideria, illus. 2013. (Toddler Bks.). (ENG.). 23p. (gr. -1). 7.99 *(978-0-7945-3302-1(7)*, Usborne) EDC Publishing.

Brown, Courtney Allison. BJ Goes to School. 2008. 36p. per. 24.95 *(978-1-4241-9724-8(4))* America Star Bks.

Brown, Marc. Monkey: Not Ready for Kindergarten. 2015. (ENG., Illus.). 32p. (J). (gr. -1-2). 12.99 *(978-0-553-49658-1(1)*, Knopf Bks. for Young Readers) Random Hse. Children's Bks.

Brown Sr., David F. Tabby Goes to School: The First in the Tabatha Adventures Series, 1 vol. Brown Jr., David F., illus. 2009. 20p. pap. 24.95 *(978-1-60836-181-6(0))* America Star Bks.

Buzzeo, Toni. Adventure Annie Goes to Kindergarten. Wummer, Amy, illus. 2013. (ENG.). 32p. (J). (gr. -1-k). mass mkt. 7.99 *(978-0-14-242695-1(4)*, Puffin Books) Penguin Young Readers Group.

Cameron, Wade. Melvin the Mischievious Mongoose First Day of School. 2012. 28p. pap. 18.65 *(978-1-4797-0270-1(6))* Xlibris Corp.

Capucilli, Alyssa Satin. Not This Bear: A First Day of School Story. Hussey, Lorna, illus. 2015. (ENG.). 32p. (J). (gr. -1-1). 16.99 *(978-0-8050-9896-9(8)*, 9780805098969, Holt, Henry & Co. Bks. For Young Readers) Holt, Henry & Co.

Cardoza, Kristina. Pinky Bunny's First Day of Kindergarten. 2011. 16p. pap. 8.75 *(978-1-4634-8753-9(3))* AuthorHouse.

Carlson, Nancy. First Grade, Here I Come! 2006. (Illus.). (J). *(978-1-4156-8114-5(7)*, Viking Adult) Penguin Publishing Group.

Carlstrom, Nancy White. It's Your First Day of School, Annie Claire. Moore, Margie, illus. 2009. (ENG.). 32p. (J). (gr. k-2). 16.95 *(978-0-8109-4057-4(4)*, Abrams Bks. for Young Readers) Abrams, Inc.

Carroll, Michael Shane. Brewster's New School. Carroll, Katie, illus. 2012. 24p. pap. 5.00 *(978-1-937260-13-2(5))* Sleepytown Pr.

—Bye-Bye Brewster. Carroll, Katie, illus. 2012. 20p. pap. 5.00 *(978-1-937260-14-9(3))* Sleepytown Pr.

Cerullo, Claudio V. Isabella Goes to Kindergarden, 1 vol. 2010. 24p. 24.95 *(978-1-4489-2455-4(3))* PublishAmerica, Inc.

Chapman, Jared. Steve, Raised by Wolves. 2015. (ENG., Illus.). 40p. (J). (gr. -1-3). 17.00 *(978-0-316-25390-1(1))* Little Brown & Co.

Chast, Roz. Marco Goes to School. Chast, Roz, illus. 2012. (ENG., Illus.). 32p. (J). (gr. -1-3). 16.99 *(978-1-4169-8475-7(5)*, Atheneum Bks. for Young Readers) Simon & Schuster Children's Publishing.

Child, Lauren. I Am Too Absolutely Small for School. Child, Lauren, illus. (Charlie & Lola Ser.). (ENG., Illus.). 32p. (J). (gr. -1-2). 2004. 16.99 *(978-0-7636-2403-3(9))* 2005. reprint ed. per. 8.99 *(978-0-7636-2887-1(5))* Candlewick Pr.

—I Am Too Absolutely Small for School. 2007. (Charlie & Lola (Shang Yi Publishing) Ser.). (CHI., Illus.). (J). *(978-957-762-437-6(5))* Hsin Yi Pubns.

—I Am Too Absolutely Small for School. Child, Lauren, illus. 2005. (ENG., Illus.). (J). (gr. -1-1). lib. bdg. 14.65 *(978-0-7569-6495-5(4))* Perfection Learning Corp.

Christie, Douglas, Jr. Dougie Goes to School. 2009. 32p. (J). pap. 16.50 *(978-0-9794827-7-9(1))* Infinite Love Publishing.

Christopher, Kathleen. Janie's First Day of School. 2012. 32p. pap. 24.95 *(978-1-62709-914-1(X))* America Star Bks.

Cocca-Leffler, Maryann. Jack's Talent. Cocca-Leffler, Maryann, illus. 2007. (ENG., Illus.). 32p. (J). (gr. -1-3). 17.99 *(978-0-374-33681-3(4)*, 9780374336813, Farrar, Straus & Giroux (BYR)) Farrar, Straus & Giroux.

Cohen, Jeff. Eva & Sadie & the Best Classroom Ever! Allen, Elanna, illus. 2015. (ENG.). 32p. (J). (gr. -1-3). 17.99 *(978-0-06-224938-8(X))* HarperCollins Pubs.

Colandro, Lucille. There Was an Old Lady Who Swallowed Some Books! Lee, Jared D., illus. 2012. (J). *(978-0-545-48186-1(4))* Scholastic, Inc.

Collicott, Sharleen. Mildred & Sam & Their Babies. Collicott, Sharleen, illus. 2005. (I Can Read Bks.). (Illus.). 48p. (J). (gr. -1-2). 15.99 *(978-0-06-058111-4(5)*, Geringer, Laura Book) HarperCollins Pubs.

Coven, Wanda. The Heidi Heckelbeck Collection: A Bewitching Four-Book Boxed Set: Heidi Hecklebeck Has a Secret; Heidi Hecklebeck Casts a Spell; Heidi Hecklebeck & the Cookie

Contest; Heidi Hecklebeck in Disguise. Burris, Priscilla, illus. 2013. (Heidi Heckelbeck Ser.). (ENG.). 512p. (J). (gr. k-4). pap. 23.99 (978-1-4424-8976-9(6), Little Simon) Little Simon.

—Heidi Heckelbeck Has a Secret. Burris, Priscilla, illus. 2012. (Heidi Heckelbeck Ser.: 1). (ENG.). 128p. (J). (gr. k-4). 16.99 (978-1-4424-4087-6(2)); pap. 5.99 (978-1-4424-3565-0(8)) Little Simon. (Little Simon).

—Heidi Heckelbeck Has a Secret. 2012. (Heidi Heckelbeck Ser.: 1). lib. bdg. 16.00 (978-0-606-26326-9(8), Turtleback) Turtleback Bks.

Crow, Melinda Melton. Little Lizard's First Day, 1 vol. Rowland, Andrew, illus. 2010. (Little Lizards Ser.). (ENG.). 32p. (gr. -1-1). lib. bdg. 22.65 (978-1-4342-2005-9(2)) Stone Arch Bks.

—Little Lizard's First Day. Rowland, Andrew & Rowlands, Andy, illus. 2010. (Little Lizards Ser.). (ENG.). 32p. (gr. -1-1). pap. 6.25 (978-1-4342-2789-8(8)) Stone Arch Bks.

—Lucky School Bus, 1 vol. Thompson, Chad, illus. 2011. (Wonder Wheels Ser.). (ENG.). 32p. (gr. -1-1). pap. 6.25 (978-1-4342-3381-3(2)); lib. bdg. 22.65 (978-1-4342-3026-3(0)) Stone Arch Bks.

Crow, P. For the Love of Miss Bard. 2010. 222p. pap. 18.00 (978-0-9802257-9-2(5)) Peddlers Group.

Danziger, Paula. Get Ready for Second Grade, Amber Brown. Ross, Tony, illus. 2003. (Is for Amber Ser.). (ENG.). 48p. (J). (gr. 1-3). mass mkt. 3.99 (978-0-14-250081-1(X), Penguin Young Readers) Penguin Young Readers Group.

—Get Ready for Second Grade, Amber Brown. Ross, Tony, illus. 2004. (A Is for Amber Ser.). 48p. (gr. k-2). 14.00 (978-0-7569-2177-4(5)) Perfection Learning Corp.

Danzinger, Paula. Get Ready for Second Grade, Amber Brown. Ross, Tony, illus. 2003. pap. 31.95 incl. audio compact disk (978-1-59112-562-4(6)); (J). 25.95 incl. audio (978-1-59112-234-0(1)); (J). pap. 29.95 incl. audio (978-1-59112-235-7(X)) Live Oak Media.

Davis, Katie. Kindergarten Rocks! (ENG., Illus.). 32p. (J). (gr. -1-3). 2008. pap. 7.99 (978-0-15-206468-6(0)) 2005. 16.99 (978-0-15-204932-4(0)) Houghton Mifflin Harcourt Publishing Co.

Davis, Melissa. Remy's First Day of School. Kalpart, illus. 2013. 20p. pap. 10.95 (978-1-62212-480-0(4), Strategic Bk. Publishing) Strategic Book Publishing & Rights Agency (SBPRA).

Davison, Roz & Laird, Elizabeth. Jungle School. Sims, David, illus. 2nd ed. 2016. (Reading Ladder Ser.). (ENG.). 48p. (J). (gr. k-2). pap. 7.99 (978-1-4052-8226-0(6)) Egmont Bks., Ltd. GBR. Dist: Independent Pubs. Group.

Dean, James. Too Cool for School. 2014. (Pete the Cat I Can Read Ser.). (J). lib. bdg. 13.55 (978-0-606-35062-4(4), Turtleback) Turtleback Bks.

Debra Maymon. Debra Meets Her Best Friend in Kindergarten. Richa Kinra, illus. 2009. 36p. pap. 15.49 (978-1-4389-6261-0(4)) AuthorHouse.

The Deer Report. 2005. (The Fawn Chapter Ser.). (J). 7.67 (978-1-58453-311-5(0)) Pioneer Valley Bks.

deGroat, Diane. Brand-New Pencils, Brand-New Books. deGroat, Diane, illus. (ENG., Illus.). 32p. (J). (gr. -1-3). 2007. pap. 6.99 (978-0-06-072616-4(4)) 2005. 15.99 (978-0-06-072613-3(X)) HarperCollins Pubs.

—Brand-New Pencils, Brand-New Books. deGroat, Diane, illus. 2007. (Gilbert & Friends Ser.). (Illus.). (J). (gr. -1-3). 14.65 (978-0-7569-8087-0(9)) Perfection Learning Corp.

dePaola, Tomie. Meet the Barkers: Morgan & Moffat Go to School. dePaola, Tomie, illus. 2003. (Barker Twins Ser.). (ENG., Illus.). 32p. (J). (gr. -1-3). 6.99 (978-0-14-250083-5(6), Puffin Books) Penguin Young Readers Group.

—Meet the Barkers: Morgan & Moffat Go to School. 2005. (J). (gr. k-3). pap. 17.95 incl. audio (978-0-8045-6934-7(7), SAC6934) Spoken Arts, Inc.

deRubertis, Barbara. Nina Nandu's Nervous Noggin. Alley, R. W., illus. 2011. (Animal Antics A to Z Ser.). 32p. (J). pap. 45.32 (978-0-7613-7660-6(7)); (ENG.). lib. bdg. 22.60 (978-1-57565-335-8(4)); (gr. -1-3). pap. 7.95 (978-1-57565-326-6(5)) Kane Press, Inc.

deRubertis, Barbara & DeRubertis, Barbara. Nina Nandu's Nervous Noggin. Alley, R. W., illus. 2012. (Animal Antics A to Z Ser.). 32p. (J). (gr. 2 — 1). cd-rom 7.95 (978-1-57565-407-2(5)) Kane Press, Inc.

DeVillers, Julia. New Girl in Town. Pooler, Paige, illus. 2011. (Liberty Porter, First Daughter Ser.: 2). (ENG.). 224p. (J). (gr. 3-7). pap. 6.99 (978-1-4169-9129-8(8), Simon & Schuster/Paula Wiseman Bks.) Simon & Schuster/Paula Wiseman Bks.

Diesen, Deborah. The Pout-Pout Fish Goes to School. Hanna, Dan, illus. 2014. (Pout-Pout Fish Adventure Ser.). (ENG.). 32p. (J). (gr. -1-k). 16.99 (978-0-374-36095-5(2), 9780374360955, Farrar, Straus & Giroux (BYR)) Farrar, Straus & Giroux.

Dodd, Emma. Foxy. Dodd, Emma, illus. 2012. (ENG., Illus.). 40p. (J). (gr. -1-2). 14.99 (978-0-06-201419-1(6)) HarperCollins Pubs.

Durst, Sarah Beth. Roar & Sparkles Go to School. Whitehouse, Ben, illus. 2017. (ENG.). 40p. (J). (gr. -1-1). 16.99 **(978-0-7624-5986-5(7)**, Running Pr.) Running Pr. Bk. Pubs.

Dyan, Penelope. Off to School. Dyan, Penelope, illus. 2010. (Illus.). 34p. pap. 11.95 (978-1-935630-21-0(0)) Bellissima Publishing, LLC.

Edwards, Becky. My First Day at Nursery School. Flintoft, Anthony, illus. 2004. (ENG.). 32p. (J). (gr. -1-1). pap. 7.99 (978-1-58234-909-1(6), 9781582349091, Bloomsbury USA Childrens) Bloomsbury Publishing USA.

Ellerson, Terryann. The Rappin' Tappin Alphabet. 2011. 24p. pap. 11.99 (978-1-4567-6733-4(X)) AuthorHouse.

Elwood, Danielle. I Love Me, I Love You. 2009. 20p. pap. 10.49 (978-1-4490-2409-3(2)) AuthorHouse.

Emerson, Carl. Monster Boy's First Day of School, 1 vol. Levin, Lon, illus. 2008. (Monster Boy Ser.). (ENG.). 32p. (gr. -1-4). 28.50 (978-1-60270-237-0(3), Looking Glass Library) ABDO Publishing Co.

Erickson, Mary Ellen. First Day of School. 2004. pap. 5.00 (978-0-9765453-0-9(6)) Dr. Mary's Bks.

Eugster, Rachel. The Pocket Mommy. Goldsmith, Tom, illus. 2013. (ENG.). 32p. (J). (gr. -1-1). 16.95 (978-1-77049-300-1(X), Tundra Bks.) Tundra Bks. CAN. Dist: Penguin Random Hse. LLC.

Fakhouri, Shoua. Omar's First Day at School Pink B Band. Pérez, Moni, illus. 2016. (Cambridge Reading Adventures Ser.). (ENG.). 16p. pap. 6.56 (978-1-316-60811-1(5)) Cambridge Univ. Pr.

Friedman, Laurie. Back to School, Mallory. Schmitz, Tamara, illus. (Mallory Ser.: 2). (ENG.). 176p. (J). (gr. 2-5). 2005. per. 5.95 (978-1-57505-865-8(0)) 2004. 15.95 (978-1-57505-658-6(5)) Lerner Publishing Group.

—A Clases Otra Vez, Mallory. Anaya, Josefina, tr. from ENG. Schmitz, Tamara, illus. 2008. (Mallory en español (Mallory in Spanish) Ser.).Tr. of Back to School, Mallory. (SPA & ENG.). 176p. (J). (gr. 2-5). pap. 5.95 (978-0-7613-3904-5(3)) Lerner Publishing Group.

Gaiman, NEil. Chu's First Day of School. Rex, Adam, illus. 2014. (ENG.). 32p. (J). (gr. -1-3). 17.99 (978-0-06-222397-5(6)) HarperCollins Pubs.

—Chu's First Day of School Board Book. Rex, Adam, illus. 2015. (ENG.). 36p. (J). (gr. -1 — 1). bds. 7.99 (978-0-06-237149-2(5), HarperFestival) HarperCollins Pubs.

Gall, Chris. Dinotrux Go to School. 2014. (Passport to Reading Level 1 Ser.). (ENG., Illus.). 32p. (J). (gr. -1-3). 3.99 (978-0-316-40061-9(0)) Little, Brown Bks. for Young Readers.

Ganz-Schmitt, Sue. Planet Kindergarten. Prigmore, Shane, illus. 2014. (ENG.). 40p. (J). (gr. -1-k). 16.99 (978-1-4521-1893-2(0)) Chronicle Bks. LLC.

—Planet Kindergarten. Prigmore, Shane, illus. 2014. 37.75 (978-1-4906-3417-3(7)); 1.25 (978-1-4906-3415-9(0)); 39.75 (978-1-4906-3418-0(5)) Recorded Bks., Inc.

Gaydos, Nora. Now I'm Growing! - First Day of School. Gutierrez, Akemi, illus. 2011. (ENG.). 30p. (J). (gr. -1-17). 8.99 (978-1-60169-152-1(1)) Innovative Kids.

George, Lucy M. Back to School Tortoise. Eyckerman, Merel, illus. 2011. (ENG.). 24p. (J). (gr. -1-3). 15.99 (978-0-8075-0510-6(2)) Whitman, Albert & Co.

Giordano, Paula J. The Honey Bees Going to a New School. 2012. 30p. 29.99 (978-1-61996-501-0(1)); pap. 19.99 (978-1-61996-500-3(3)) Salem Author Services.

Goldfinger, Jennifer P. Hello, My Name Is Tiger. Goldfinger, Jennifer P., illus. 2016. (Illus.). 40p. (J). (gr. -1-3). 17.99 (978-0-06-239951-9(9)) HarperCollins Pubs.

Grandits, John. Ten Rules You Absolutely Must Not Break If You Want to Survive the School Bus. Austin, Michael Allen, illus. 2011. (ENG.). 32p. (J). (gr. 1-4). 16.99 (978-0-618-78822-4(0)) Houghton Mifflin Harcourt Publishing Co.

Greene, Marjorie. Cassie's Big Day. 2003. (Illus.). (J). 16.95 (978-0-9741764-0-6(0)) Greene, Marjorie A.

Greene, Stephanie. Princess Posey & the First Grade Parade, Bk. 1. Sisson, Stéphanie Roth, illus. 2010. (Princess Posey, First Grader Ser.: 1). (ENG.). 96p. (J). (gr. k-3). 12.99 (978-0-399-25167-2(7), G.P. Putnam's Sons Books for Young Readers) Penguin Young Readers Group.

—Princess Posey & the First Grade Parade, Bk. 1. Sisson, Stéphanie Roth, illus. 2011. (Princess Posey, First Grader Ser.: 1). (ENG.). 96p. (J). (gr. k-3). 5.99 (978-0-14-241827-7(7), Puffin Books) Penguin Young Readers Group.

Greenfield, Eloise. Me & Neesie. Gilchrist, Jan Spivey, illus. anniv. ed. 2005. (Amistad Ser.). 32p. (J). (gr. -1-3). 15.99 (978-0-06-000701-0(X), Amistad) HarperCollins Pubs.

Grogan, John. Marley Goes to School. Cowdrey, Richard, illus. (Marley Ser.). 40p. (J). (gr. -1-3). 2012. (ENG.). 9.99 (978-0-06-211366-5(6)) 2009. (ENG.). 17.99 (978-0-06-156151-1(7)) 2009. lib. bdg. 18.89 (978-0-06-156152-8(5)) HarperCollins Pubs.

Gutman, Dan. Rappy Goes to School. Bowers, Tim, illus. 2016. 40p. (J). (gr. -1-3). 17.99 (978-0-06-229181-3(5)) HarperCollins Pubs.

Gutta, Razeena. Faatimah & Ahmed - We're Little Muslims. 2015. (ENG., Illus.). 34p. (J). pap. (978-1-925209-24-2(5)) Vivid Publishing.

Hackett, J. J. Even Cows Wear Moo Moos. Pearn, Kayley, illus. 2013. 24p. pap. 14.95 (978-0-9897242-1-0(2), Over the Rainbow) Pearn & Assocs. Inc.

Hamilton, Laura, reader. Vera's First Day of School. unabr. ed. 2006. (Picture Book Readalong Ser.). (Illus.). (J). (gr. -1-3). 25.95 incl. audio (978-1-59519-662-0(5)); pap. 39.95 incl. audio compact disk (978-1-59519-661-3(7));Set. pap. 37.95 incl. audio (978-1-59519-660-6(9)) Live Oak Media.

Hapka, Cathy, pseud & Titlebaum, Ellen. How Not to Start Third Grade. Palen, Debbie, illus. 2007. (Step into Reading Ser.). (ENG.). 48p. (J). (gr. 2-4). pap. 3.99 (978-0-375-83904-7(6), Random Hse. Bks. for Young Readers) Random Hse. Children's Bks.

Hardgrave, Gayle. Daniel Goes to Pre-K. 2009. 32p. pap. 12.99 (978-1-4389-7090-5(0)) AuthorHouse.

Harewood, Sean C. It's Only the First Day. 2008. 48p. pap. 19.49 (978-1-4343-7367-0(3)) AuthorHouse.

Harper, Jamie. Miss Mingo & the First Day of School. 2006. (Illus.). 26p. (J). (978-1-4156-9174-8(6)) Candlewick Pr.

Harris, Robie H. I Am Not Going to School Today! Ormerod, Jan, illus. 2003. (ENG.). 32p. (J). (gr. -1-3). 17.99 (978-0-689-83913-9(8), McElderry, Margaret K. Bks.) McElderry, Margaret K. Bks.

Hartshorne, Holly L. School Time for the Three Little Fish, 1 vol. 2009. 12p. pap. 24.95 (978-1-60749-404-1(3)) America Star Bks.

Hartt-Sussman, Heather. Noni Is Nervous. Côté, Geneviève, illus. 2013. (ENG.). 24p. (J). (gr. -1-2). 17.95 (978-1-77049-323-0(9), Tundra Bks.) Tundra Bks. CAN. Dist: Penguin Random Hse. LLC.

Hayes, Carolyn. School Starts Today: The Mccool School Series. 2011. 28p. pap. 13.59 (978-1-4520-6747-6(3)) AuthorHouse.

Hays, Anna Jane. Kindergarten Countdown. Davick, Linda, illus. 2013. (ENG.). 24p. (J). (gr. -1-2). 6.99 (978-0-385-75371-5(3), Dragonfly Bks.) Random Hse. Children's Bks.

—Ready, Set, Preschool! Kelley, True, illus. 2016. (ENG.). 40p. (J). (gr. -1-2). 7.99 (978-1-101-94024-2(7), Dragonfly Bks.) Random Hse. Children's Bks.

Heller, Maryellen. My Big Sister's First Day of School. Soman, David, illus. 2009. (J). (978-0-8037-3246-9(5), Dial) Penguin Publishing Group.

Henkes, Kevin. Prudencia Se Preocupa. 2017.Tr. of Wemberly Worried. (SPA.). (J). pap. **(978-1-63245-666-3(4))** Lectorum Pubns., Inc.

Henkes, Kevin. Wemberly Worried. Henkes, Kevin, illus. 2010. (ENG., Illus.). 32p. (J). (gr. -1-4). pap. 6.99 (978-0-06-185776-8(9), Greenwillow Bks.) HarperCollins Pubs.

—Wemberly Worried. Henkes, Kevin, illus. (Illus.). pap. incl. audio (978-0-87499-808-5(5)); pap. 39.95 incl. audio compact disk (978-1-59112-561-7(8)); pap. 18.95 incl. audio compact disk (978-1-59112-359-0(3)); pap. 16.95 incl. audio (978-0-87499-806-1(9)) Live Oak Media.

Hennessy, B. G. Mr. Ouchy's First Day. Meisel, Paul, illus. 2007. (J). (gr. k-3). 27.95 incl. audio (978-0-8045-6946-0(0)); 29.95 incl. audio compact disk (978-0-8045-4160-2(4)) Spoken Arts, Inc.

Hill, Eric. Spot Goes to School. Hill, Eric, illus. 2004. (Spot Ser.). (ENG., Illus.). 24p. (J). (gr. -1-k). 6.99 (978-0-14-240167-5(6), Warne) Penguin Young Readers Group.

—Spot Loves School. Hill, Eric, illus. 2015. (Spot Ser.). (ENG., Illus.). 10p. (J). (gr. -1-k). bds. 5.99 (978-0-14-135654-9(5), Warne) Penguin Publishing Group.

Himle, Lisa. Hands as Warm as Toast. Langton, Bruce, illus. 2006. 32p. (J). (gr. -1-3). 17.95 (978-1-58726-298-2(3), Mitten Pr.) Ann Arbor Editions LLC.

Hodgkinson, Jo. A Big Day for Migs. Hodgkinson, Jo, illus. 2014. (ENG., Illus.). 32p. (J). (gr. -1-3). 16.95 (978-1-4677-5014-1(X)) Lerner Publishing Group.

Hodgson, Christy. Debra's First Day of School. 2011. 40p. pap. 19.95 (978-1-4567-3260-8(9)) AuthorHouse.

Holabird, Katherine. Twinkle. Warburton, Sarah, illus. 2014. (J). (978-1-4351-5628-9(5)) Barnes & Noble, Inc.

Horse, Harry. Little Rabbit Goes to School. Horse, Harry, illus. (Little Rabbit Ser.). (Illus.). 32p. (J). 2011. (gr. -1-1). pap. 7.95 (978-1-56145-574-4(1)) 2004. (ENG., (gr. k-1). 15.95 (978-1-56145-320-7(X)) Peachtree Pubs.

Hudson, Lisa. Meet Lisa Jo: First Day of School & Words Can Hurt. 2013. 42p. pap. 17.45 (978-1-4497-8463-8(1), WestBow Pr.) Author Solutions, Inc.

Husband, Amy. Dear Teacher. 2010. (ENG.). 24p. (J). (gr. 1-3). pap. 9.99 (978-1-4022-4268-7(9), Sourcebooks Jabberwocky) Sourcebooks, Inc.

Imam, Seema & Imam, Ibrahim. I am Listening. 2007. (I Am Good Ser.). (Illus.). 32p. (J). mass mkt. (978-0-9787849-8-0(7)) Lucent Interpretations, LLC.

Irick, Angela. Ashley Wins the First Day of School. 2012. 16p. pap. 15.99 (978-1-4772-7182-7(1)) AuthorHouse.

Izzo, Donna. Mischievous Michael's 1st Day of School. 2011. 28p. pap. 15.99 (978-1-4568-5531-4(X)) Xlibris Corp.

Jakubowski, Michele. Sidney & Sydney. 2013. (Sidney & Sydney Ser.). (ENG.). 128p. (gr. 1-3). 50.64 (978-1-4795-1696-4(1)) Picture Window Bks.

—Third Grade Mix-Up. Montalto, Luisa, illus. (Sidney & Sydney Ser.). (ENG.). 128p. (gr. 1-3). 2015. pap. 7.15 (978-1-4795-6754-6(X)) 2013. 8.95 (978-1-4048-8104-4(2)) 2013. lib. bdg. 25.32 (978-1-4048-8001-6(1)) Picture Window Bks.

Janousky, Peggy Robbins. Move It, Miss Macintosh! Lands, Meghan, illus. 2016. (ENG.). 32p. (J). (gr. -1-2). 17.95 (978-1-55451-863-0(6)) Annick Pr., Ltd. CAN. Dist: Publishers Group West (PGW).

—Move It, Miss Macintosh! Lands, Meghan, illus. 2016. (ENG.). 32p. (J). (gr. -1-2). 9.95 (978-1-55451-862-3(8)) Annick Pr., Ltd. CAN. Dist: Publishers Group West (PGW).

Johnson, Jacquitta. My First Day of School. 2007. 16p. per. 10.95 (978-1-4327-0707-1(8)) Outskirts Pr., Inc.

Jones, Tammy & Smith, Carrie. Katy's First Day of School. 2004. (Shared Connections Ser.). (J). pap. (978-1-4108-1625-2(7)); instr.'s gde. ed. 27.00 (978-1-4108-1601-6(X)) Benchmark Education Co.

Julie, Danneberg. First Day Jitters. 2014. (Mrs. Hartwell's Class Adventures Ser.). (ENG.). 32p. (J). (gr. k-3). 11.20 (978-1-63245-322-8(3)) Lectorum Pubns., Inc.

Juncar, Nicola. The Legend of Thornton Wood. 2012. 238p. pap. (978-1-78176-184-7(1)) FeedARead.com.

Karlik, Danielle. The Kaylee Chronicles: First Day Fright. 2007. 20p. per. 24.95 (978-1-4241-8346-3(4)) America Star Bks.

Katz, Karen. Rosie Goes to Preschool. 2015. (ENG., Illus.). 40p. (J). (-k). 16.99 (978-0-385-37917-5(X), Schwartz & Wade Bks.) Random Hse. Children's Bks.

Kaufmann, Nancy. Bye, Bye! Spetter, Jung-Hee, illus. 2004. (ENG.). 32p. (J). (gr. -1-1). 14.95 (978-1-886910-95-9(2), Lemniscaat) Boyds Mills Pr.

Keane, Dave. First Day Frights. Keane, Dave, illus. 2012. (I Can Read Level 2 Ser.). (ENG., Illus.). 32p. (J). (gr. -1-3). pap. 3.99 (978-0-06-085475-1(8)) HarperCollins Pubs.

—Monster School: First Day Frights. Keane, Dave, illus. 2012. (I Can Read Level 2 Ser.). (ENG., Illus.). 32p. (J). (gr. -1-3). 16.99 (978-0-06-085476-8(6)) HarperCollins Pubs.

Krumwiede, Lana. Just Itzy. Pizzoli, Greg, illus. 2015. (ENG.). 40p. (J). (-k). 15.99 (978-0-7636-5811-3(1)) Candlewick Pr.

Lawlor, Ashley. Ashley & the First Day of School. 2012. 24p. pap. 24.95 (978-1-4626-6518-1(7)) America Star Bks.

Lee, Janice. Ethan's First Day of School. 2013. 20p. pap. 24.95 (978-1-62709-501-3(2)) America Star Bks.

Lehrhaupt, Adam. Chicken in School. Kober, Shahar, illus. 2017. 40p. (J). (gr. -1-3). 17.99 (978-0-06-236413-5(8)) HarperCollins Pubs.

Lette, Lauren Britt. Kiwi's First Day of School. 2008. 32p. pap. 24.95 (978-1-60441-418-9(9)) America Star Bks.

Lillian's First Day. 2003. (J). 12.00 (978-0-9724442-3-1(8)) LightHouse Pr.

Livingston, A. A. B. Bear & Lolly: Off to School. Chou, Joey, illus. 2014. (ENG.). 32p. (J). (gr. -1-3). 15.99 (978-0-06-219788-7(6)) HarperCollins Pubs.

Liz Collard. Jeremiah, the Schoolhouse Dog. 2009. 28p. pap. 12.79 (978-1-4269-0990-0(X)) Trafford Publishing.

Lobo, Chris. Brand New Day: (of School) 2008. 36p. pap. 24.95 (978-1-60441-973-3(3)) America Star Bks.

Lorenz, Albert. The Exceptionally, Extraordinarily Ordinary First Day of School. 2010. (ENG., Illus.). 32p. (J). (gr. 1-4). 15.95 (978-0-8109-8960-3(3), Abrams Bks. for Young Readers) Abrams, Inc.

Lovell, Brandy. Crazy Colours. Mitchell, Tina, illus. 2011. 42p. pap. (978-0-9867761-0-6(6)) Bing Long Bks.

Lynch, F. Michael. I Will Always Need You. 2008. 24p. pap. 14.50 (978-1-60693-141-7(5), Eloquent Bks.) Strategic Book Publishing & Rights Agency (SBPRA).

MacDowell, Maureen. Tomorrow Is the First Day of School. Hergenrother, Max, illus. 2007. 32p. (J). 15.95 (978-0-9791463-0-5(5)) Wading River Bks., LLC.

Mackall, Dandi Daley. Natalie: School's First Day of Me, 1 vol. Blakeslee, Lys, illus. 2009. (That's Nat! Ser.). (ENG.). 96p. (J). (gr. 1-4). pap. 4.99 (978-0-310-71568-9(7)) Zonderkidz.

Mackintosh, David. Marshall Armstrong Is New to Our School. 2011. (ENG., Illus.). 32p. (J). (gr. k-2). 17.95 (978-1-4197-0036-1(7), Abrams Bks. for Young Readers) Abrams, Inc.

Manell, Keane. Hall Pass to the Tenth Dimension. 2009. 56p. pap. 10.95 (978-1-4389-7401-9(9)) AuthorHouse.

Mangieri, Catherine. A Funny First Day. 2006. (Neighborhood Readers Ser.). (ENG., Illus.). 12p. (gr. 1-3). pap. 5.90 (978-1-4042-6839-5(1), Rosen Classroom) Rosen Publishing Group, Inc., The.

Marshall, Linda Elovitz. Kindergarten Is Cool! Chatterton, Chris, illus. 2016. (ENG.). 32p. (J). (gr. -1-1). 8.99 (978-0-545-65266-7(9), Cartwheel Bks.) Scholastic, Inc.

Martin, Abigail M. Welcome to Applewood Place. 2008. 24p. pap. 24.95 (978-1-60441-167-6(8)) America Star Bks.

Martín Anguita, Carmen & Carmen, Martín Anguita. El Primer Día de Colegio de David. Cortazar, Alicia Canas, illus. 2008. (SPA.). 32p. (J). 10.99 (978-84-241-5790-6(7)) Everest Editora ESP. Dist: Lectorum Pubns., Inc.

May, Eleanor. Albert Starts School. Melmon, Deborah, illus. 2015. (Mouse Math (r) Ser.). (ENG.). 32p. (J). (gr. -1-1). 22.60 (978-1-57565-741-7(4)) Kane Press, Inc.

McCarthy, Jenna. Lola Knows a Lot. Palacios, Sara, illus. 2016. 32p. (J). (gr. -1-3). 17.99 (978-0-06-225017-9(5)) HarperCollins Pubs.

McCarty, Peter. Henry in Love. McCarty, Peter, illus. 2009. (ENG., Illus.). 48p. (J). (gr. -1-1). 16.99 (978-0-06-114288-8(3)) HarperCollins Pubs.

McDonald, Megan. The Holly Joliday. Reynolds, Peter H., illus. 2008. (Judy Moody Ser.: No. 1). (ENG.). 96p. (J). (gr. k-3). pap. 7.99 (978-0-7636-4113-9(8)) Candlewick Pr.

—Judy Moody. 2010. (Judy Moody Ser.: 1). lib. bdg. 16.00 (978-0-606-12330-3(X), Turtleback) Turtleback Bks.

—Was in a Mood. Reynolds, Peter H., illus. 2010. (Judy Moody Ser.: 1). (ENG.). 160p. (J). (gr. 1-4). 15.99 (978-0-7636-4850-3(7)) Candlewick Pr.

Mcghee, Alison. Countdown to Kindergarten. Bliss, Harry, illus. 2006. (ENG.). 32p. (J). (gr. -1-3). reprint ed. pap. 6.99 (978-0-15-205586-8(X)) Houghton Mifflin Harcourt Publishing Co.

—Countdown to Kindergarten. Bliss, Harry, illus. pap. 39.95 incl. audio (978-1-59112-929-5(X)); pap. incl. audio compact disk (978-1-59112-469-6(7)) Live Oak Media.

—Mrs. Watson Wants Your Teeth. Bliss, Harry, illus. 2007. 32p. (J). reprint ed. 16.00 (978-1-4223-6777-3(0)) DIANE Publishing Co.

—Mrs. Watson Wants Your Teeth. Bliss, Harry, illus. 2008. (ENG.). 36p. (J). (gr. -1-3). pap. 6.00 (978-0-15-206348-1(X)) Houghton Mifflin Harcourt Publishing Co.

—Mrs. Watson Wants Your Teeth. Bliss, Harry, illus. unabr. ed. 2007. (Picture Book Readalong Ser.). (J). (gr. -1-2). 28.95 incl. audio compact disk (978-1-59519-902-7(0)) Live Oak Media.

McGinty, Alice B. Eliza's Kindergarten Surprise, 0 vols. Speir, Nancy, illus. 2013. (ENG.). 34p. (J). (gr. k-3). pap. 9.99 (978-1-4778-1683-7(6), 9781477816837, Amazon Children's Publishing) Amazon Publishing.

McMullan, Kate. A Fine Start Bk. 3: Meg's Prairie Diary. 2003. (My America Ser.). (ENG.). 112p. (J). 12.95 (978-0-439-37061-5(2)) Scholastic, Inc.

—The New Kid at School, 1 vol. Basso, Bill, illus. 2006. (Dragon Slayers' Academy Ser.: No. 1). (ENG.). 112p. (gr. 1-7). 24.21 (978-1-59961-126-6(0)) Spotlight.

McNamara, Margaret. The First Day of School. Gordon, Mike, illus. 2008. (Robin Hill School Ser.). (J). (gr. -1-3). pap. 16.95 (978-1-4301-0604-3(2)) Live Oak Media.

—The First Day of School. Gordon, Mike, illus. 2005. (Robin Hill School Ser.). (ENG.). 32p. (J). (gr. -1-1). pap. 3.99 (978-0-689-86914-3(2), Simon Spotlight) Simon Spotlight.

Messner, Kate. Sea Monster's First Day. Rash, Andy, illus. 2011. (ENG.). 36p. (J). (gr. -1-3). 16.99 (978-0-8118-7564-6(4)) Chronicle Bks. LLC.

Miller, Pat Zietlow. Sophie's Squash Go to School. Wilsdorf, Anne, illus. 2016. (ENG.). 40p. (J). (gr. -1-2). 17.99 (978-0-553-50944-1(6), Schwartz & Wade Bks.) Random Hse. Children's Bks.

Mills, David. Sam's First Day. Finlay, Lizzie, illus. 2004. 24p. (J). (PER & ENG.). (978-1-85269-634-4(6)); (978-1-85269-630-6(3)); (978-1-85269-635-1(4)); (978-1-85269-637-5(0)); (978-1-85269-639-9(7)); (978-1-85269-636-8(2)); (978-1-84444-166-2(0)); (TUR & ENG.). (978-1-85269-644-3(3)); (978-1-85269-640-5(0)); (978-1-85269-642-9(7)); (978-1-85269-643-6(5)); (978-1-85269-645-0(1)); (978-1-85269-646-7(X)); (978-1-85269-702-0(4)) Mantra Lingua.

Mills, David & Finlay, Lizzie. Sam's First Day. 2004. (Illus.). 24p. (J). (978-1-85269-641-2(9)) Mantra Lingua.

Milot, Carryanne. Austin & the Bully. Proulx, Denis, illus. 2012. 40p. pap. (978-1-77097-970-3(0)) FriesenPress.

Minuto, Kristin. My First Day of Kindergarten. 2011. 28p. pap. 21.99 (978-1-4568-6470-5(X)) Xlibris Corp.

Mitchell, Dennis. First Day of School: A Day in the Life of Noah. 2009. 36p. pap. 16.99 (978-1-4389-9198-6(3)) AuthorHouse.

Moreillon, Judi. Ready & Waiting for You. Stock, Catherine, illus. 2013. (ENG.). 32p. (J). 17.00 (978-0-8028-5355-4(2), Eerdmans Bks For Young Readers) Eerdmans, William B. Publishing Co.

Morello, Jill. Lily Goes to School. 2010. 28p. pap. 13.99 (978-1-4490-6218-7(0)) AuthorHouse.

Mortensen, Lori. First Day, No Way!, 1 vol. Simard, Remy, illus. (My First Graphic Novel Ser.). (ENG.). 32p. (gr. k-2). 2011. pap. 6.25 (978-1-4342-3102-4(X)) 2010. 24.65 (978-1-4342-2015-8(X)) Stone Arch Bks. (My First Graphic Novel).

Moss, Marissa. The Name Game! Moss, Marissa, illus. 2011. (Daphne's Diary of Daily Disasters Ser.). (ENG., Illus.). 80p. (J). (gr. 2-5). pap. 5.99 (978-1-4424-1738-0(2)); lib. bdg. 9.99

(978-1-4424-2676-4(4)) Simon & Schuster/Paula Wiseman Bks. (Simon & Schuster/Paula Wiseman Bks.).

Murray, Martine. Henrietta & the Perfect Night. 2017. (Henrietta Ser.). (ENG.). 96p. (J). (gr. k-2). 12.99 ***(978-1-76029-024-5(6))*** Allen & Unwin AUS. Dist: Independent Pubs. Group.

Myracle, Lauren. The Fashion Disaster That Changed My Life. 2008. (ENG.). 160p. (J). (gr. 5-18). 6.99 *(978-0-14-240717-2(8),* Puffin Books) Penguin Young Readers Group.

Napolitano, Gretchen. Christopher Lee & Bozzie Bear's First Day of School. 2012. (ENG.). 56p. 27.95 *(978-1-4327-9443-9(4));* pap. 20.95 *(978-1-4327-8487-4(0))* Outskirts Pr., Inc.

Neubecker, Robert. Fall Is for School. Neubecker, Robert, illus. 2017. (ENG., Illus.). 32p. (J). (gr. -1-k). 17.99 ***(978-1-4847-3254-0(5))*** Disney Pr.

Nicholson, David L. Little Johnny's First Day of School, 1 vol. 2009. 32p. pap. 24.95 *(978-1-60813-611-7(6))* America Star Bks.

The Night Before Kindergarten. 2014. (Night Before Ser.). (ENG.). 32p. (J). (gr. 7-12). 8.24 *(978-1-63245-263-4(4))* Lectorum Pubns., Inc.

O'Brien, Gerry. Bubba Begonia, You'll Be Sorry. Jones, Brenda, illus. 2006. (SBPRA). (ENG.). 80p. (J). per. 6.95 *(978-1-894838-23-8(8))* Acorn Pr., The CAN. Dist: Univ. of Toronto Pr.

Oh, Jiwon. Mr. Monkey's Classroom. Oh, Jiwon, illus. 2005. (Illus.). 32p. (J). (gr. -1-2). lib. bdg. 15.89 *(978-0-06-055722-5(2))* HarperCollins Pubs.

Omara, Charlotte. My Scary First Day of School. 2012. 26p. 24.95 *(978-1-4626-7652-1(9))* America Star Bks.

Onyefulu, Ifeoma. Deron Goes to Nursery School. Onyefulu, Ifeoma, photos by. 2010. (First Experiences Ser.). (ENG., Illus.). 32p. (J). (gr. -1-2). 17.95 *(978-1-84507-864-5(0),* Frances Lincoln) Quarto Publishing Group UK GBR. Dist: Hachette Bk. Group.

Ormerod, Jan. When an Elephant Comes to School. 2005. (ENG., Illus.). 32p. (J). (gr. -1-1). pap. 8.99 *(978-1-84507-431-9(9),* Frances Lincoln) Quarto Publishing Group UK GBR. Dist: Hachette Bk. Group.

Paner, Amy & Fisher, Stacey. Nutty Scurries to School. 2008. 25p. 14.95 *(978-0-615-23931-6(5))* Fisher-Paner Publishing.

Paquette, Heather. Kammy the Chameleon Goes to School. Paquette Jr., Edward D., illus. 2012. 24p. pap. 24.95 *(978-1-62709-765-9(1))* America Star Bks.

Parish, Herman. Amelia Bedelia Storybook Treasury: Amelia Bedelia's First Day of School; Amelia Bedelia's First Field Trip; Amelia Bedelia Makes a Friend; Amelia Bedelia Sleeps over; Amelia Bedelia Hits the Trail. Avril, Lynne, illus. 2013. (ENG.). 192p. (J). (gr. -1-3). 11.99 *(978-0-06-228714-4(1),* Greenwillow Bks.) HarperCollins Pubs.

—Amelia Bedelia's First Day of School. Avril, Lynne, illus. (Amelia Bedelia Ser.). (ENG.). 32p. (J). (gr. -1-3). 2015. pap. 6.99 *(978-0-06-154457-6(4))* 2011. 9.99 *(978-0-06-203274-4(7))* 2009. 16.99 *(978-0-06-154455-2(8))* HarperCollins Pubs. (Greenwillow Bks.).

Park, Barbara. Junie B. Jones & the Stupid Smelly Bus. unabr. ed. 2004. (Junie B. Jones Ser.: Vol. 1). 69p. (J). (gr. k-3). pap. 17.00 incl. audio *(978-0-8072-0778-9(0),* LFTR 237 SP, Listening Library) Random Hse. Audio Publishing Group.

Parr, Todd. Otto Goes to School. 2013. (Passport to Reading Level 1 Ser.). (ENG., Illus.). 32p. (J). (gr. -1-1). 4.99 *(978-0-316-22931-9(8))* Little, Brown Bks. for Young Readers.

—Otto Goes to School. 2013. (Passport to Reading Level 1 Ser.). (J). lib. bdg. 14.75 *(978-0-606-31740-5(6),* Turtleback) Turtleback Bks.

Pedraza, M. Eugenia Rueda. Nico's Voyage. 2013. 32p. pap. *(978-1-4602-2360-4(8))* FriesenPress.

Pennypacker, Sara. Stuart Goes to School. Matje, Martin, illus. 2005. (ENG.). 64p. (J). (gr. -1-3). reprint ed. per. 5.99 *(978-0-439-30183-1(1),* Scholastic Paperbacks) Scholastic, Inc.

Perrine, David L. Birdie School Days: The First Day of School. Perry, Margie, illus. 2005. (J). pap. 15.00 *(978-0-8059-6699-2(4))* Dorrance Publishing Co., Inc.

Plourde, Lynn. You're Wearing That to School?! Cornelison, Sue, illus. 2013. (ENG.). 32p. (J). (gr. -1-3). 16.99 *(978-1-4231-5510-2(6))* Disney Pr.

Preller, James. A Pirate's Guide to First Grade. Ruth, Greg, illus. 2013. (ENG.). 48p. (J). (gr. -1-1). 7.99 *(978-1-250-02721-4(7),* 9781250027214) Square Fish.

Priddy, Roger & Crimi-Trent, Ellen. My First Day at School. 2013. (Schoolies Ser.). (ENG., Illus.). 28p. (J). (gr. -1-1). 4.99 *(978-0-312-51612-3(6),* 9780312516123, Priddy Bks.) St. Martin's Pr.

Puttock, Simon. You're Too Big. 2003. (Illus.). 32p. (J). 19.99 *(978-0-385-60432-1(7),* Doubleday Children's) Random House Children's Books GBR. Dist: Trafalgar Square Publishing.

Quivers, Anthony S. Lil' Johnny's First Day of School. 2010. 24p. 13.99 *(978-1-4520-4149-0(0))* AuthorHouse.

Rainey. School Is Cool. Huggens, Karin, illus. 2004. (J). *(978-0-9666199-9-7(4))* DreamDog Pr.

Random House. Dora Goes to School/Dora Va a la Escuela (Dora the Explorer) MJ Illustrations, illus. 2014. (Pictureback(R) Ser.). (ENG.). 24p. (J). (gr. -1-2). 3.99 *(978-0-385-37496-5(8),* Random Hse. Bks. for Young Readers) Random Hse. Children's Bks.

Randy. The Adventures of Rico. 2010. 28p. pap. 13.79 *(978-1-4490-8353-3(6))* AuthorHouse.

Rankin, Joan E. First Day. Rankin, Joan E., illus. 2007. (ENG., Illus.). 32p. (J). (gr. -1-2). 10.99 *(978-1-4169-6848-1(2),* Simon & Schuster/Paula Wiseman Bks.) Simon & Schuster/Paula Wiseman Bks.

Ransom, Candice. Amanda Panda Quits Kindergarten. Grove, Christine, illus. 2017. (ENG.). 32p. (J). (gr. -1-2). 17.99 *(978-0-399-55455-1(6),* Doubleday Bks. for Young Readers) Random Hse. Children's Bks.

Recorvits, Helen. My Name Is Yoon. Swiatkowska, Gabi, illus. 2003. (ENG.). 32p. (J). (gr. -1-3). 17.99 *(978-0-374-35114-4(7),* 9780374351144, Farrar, Straus & Giroux (BYR)) Farrar, Straus & Giroux.

—My Name Is Yoon. Swiatkowska, Gabi, illus. 2014. (ENG.). 32p. (J). (gr. -1-3). 6.99 *(978-1-250-05711-2(6),* 9781250057112) Square Fish.

Rex, Adam. School's First Day of School. Robinson, Christian, illus. 2016. (ENG.). 40p. (J). (gr. -1-3). 17.99 *(978-1-59643-964-1(5),* 9781596439641) Roaring Brook Pr.

Rhodes, Terry. Marley's Big Day. 2008. 16p. pap. 24.95 *(978-1-60474-947-2(4))* America Star Bks.

Rim, Sujean. Birdie's First Day of School. 2015. (ENG., Illus.). 40p. (J). (gr. -1-3). 17.00 *(978-0-316-40745-8(3))* Little Brown & Co.

Rivers, Phoebe. Haunted Memories. 2012. (Saranormal Ser.: 2). (ENG.). 176p. (J). (gr. 3-7). 15.99 *(978-1-4424-5381-4(8));* pap. 5.99 *(978-1-4424-4040-1(6))* Simon Spotlight. (Simon Spotlight).

Rockwell, Anne F. First Day of School. Rockwell, Lizzy, illus. 2013. (ENG.). 40p. (J). (gr. -1-3). pap. 6.99 *(978-0-06-050193-8(6))* HarperCollins Pubs.

Rodman, Mary Ann. First Grade Stinks!, 1 vol. Spiegel, Beth, illus. (ENG.). 32p. (J). (gr. k-3). 2008. pap. 8.95 *(978-1-56145-462-1(1))* 2006. 15.95 *(978-1-56145-377-1(3))* Peachtree Pubs.

Rodriguez, Marisela. Violet's Sweater. 2012. (ENG.). 27p. (J). pap. 12.95 *(978-1-4787-1806-2(4))* Outskirts Pr., Inc.

Rooney, Sean. Paddy's First Day at Hilltop School. 2010. (Illus.). 28p. pap. 12.50 *(978-1-60860-115-8(3),* Strategic Bk. Publishing) Strategic Book Publishing & Rights Agency (SBPRA).

Rose Salih, Sara. Tales of a Sevie. 2013. 160p. pap. 14.99 *(978-0-9853466-0-7(4))* Harlan Rose Publishing.

Rozelaar, Angie, illus. Hello School. 2016. (Hello! Ser.). (ENG.). 10p. (J). (gr. -1-k). 15.99 *(978-1-4472-6693-8(5))* Pan Macmillan GBR. Dist: Independent Pubs. Group.

Rusackas, Francesca. I Love You All Day Long. Burris, Priscilla, illus. 2004. (ENG.). 32p. (J). (gr. -1-k). reprint ed. pap. 6.99 *(978-0-06-050278-2(9))* HarperCollins Pubs.

Rusu, Meredith. Peppa's School Day. Eone, illus. 2016. (Peppa Pig Ser.). (ENG.). 32p. (J). (gr. -1-k). pap. 3.99 *(978-0-545-92547-1(9))* Scholastic, Inc.

Rutland, Mirium. Miss Pistachios Big Day. 2007. (Illus.). 48p. pap. *(978-1-58690-063-2(3))* Mould, Paul Publishing.

Ryan, Karlene Kay. Genevieve Goes to School. Johnson, Meredith, illus. 2013. 34p. pap. 9.99 *(978-0-9888843-2-8(1))* Ryan, Karlene Kay Author.

Ryan, Pam Muñoz. Tony Baloney: School Rules. Fotheringham, Edwin, illus. (J). (gr. k-2). 2013. (ENG.). 40p. 6.99 *(978-0-545-48166-3(X))* 2012. pap. *(978-0-545-48167-0(8))* Scholastic, Inc.

Sanders, Rob. Ruby Rose: Off to School She Goes! Ohi, Debbie Ridpath, illus. 2016. 32p. (J). (gr. -1-3). 15.99 *(978-0-06-223569-5(9))* HarperCollins Pubs.

Schaefer, Lola M. Frankie Stein Starts School, 0 vols. Atteberry, Kevan, illus. 2010. (ENG.). 32p. (J). (gr. k-3). 15.99 *(978-0-7614-5656-8(2),* 9780761456568, Amazon Children's Publishing) Amazon Publishing.

Scotton, Rob. The Name of the Game. Scotton, Rob, illus. 2012. (I Can Read Level 1 Ser.). (ENG., Illus.). 32p. (J). (gr. -1-3). 16.99 *(978-0-06-209015-7(1))* HarperCollins Pubs.

—On with the Snow. 2013. (Splat the Cat 8X8 Ser.). (J). lib. bdg. 13.55 *(978-0-606-27152-3(X),* Turtleback) Turtleback Bks.

—Splat the Cat. Scotton, Rob, illus. 2008. (Splat the Cat Ser.). (Illus.). 40p. (J). (gr. -1-3). (ENG.). 17.99 *(978-0-06-083154-7(5));* lib. bdg. 17.89 *(978-0-06-083155-4(3))* HarperCollins Pubs.

—Splat the Cat. 2011. (J). (gr. -1-2). 29.95 *(978-0-545-23794-9(7))* Weston Woods Studios, Inc.

—Splat the Cat: Big Reading Collection. Scotton, Rob, illus. 2012. (I Can Read Level 1 Ser.). (ENG., Illus.). 100p. (J). (gr. k-3). pap. 16.99 *(978-0-06-209029-4(1))* HarperCollins Pubs.

—Up in the Air at the Fair. 2014. (Splat the Cat: I Can Read Ser.). (J). lib. bdg. 13.55 *(978-0-606-35059-4(4),* Turtleback) Turtleback Bks.

Sesame Workshop. Off to School! 2015. (Sesame Street Scribbles Elmo Ser.: 0). (ENG.). 32p. (J). (-3). 10.99 *(978-1-4022-9745-8(9),* Sourcebooks Jabberwocky) Sourcebooks, Inc.

Shahbaz, Zak Iman. Ameerah & the Missing Lunchbox. 2012. (ENG.). (J). pap. 8.95 *(978-1-4675-2268-7(6))* Independent Pub.

—Ameerah's First Day. 2012. (ENG.). (J). pap. 8.95 *(978-1-4675-2269-4(4))* Independent Pub.

Shells, B. Malone. Henry Has a Head Cold. 2010. 32p. 17.00 *(978-1-4389-5326-7(7))* AuthorHouse.

Sierra, Judy. We Love Our School! Davick, Linda, illus. 2016. (ENG.). 24p. (J). (gr. -1-2). 6.99 *(978-1-101-94025-9(5),* Dragonfly Bks.) Random Hse. Children's Bks.

—We Love Our School! A Read-Together Rebus Story. Davick, Linda, illus. 2011. (ENG.). 24p. (J). (gr. -1-2). 7.99 *(978-0-375-86728-6(7),* Knopf Bks. for Young Readers) Random Hse. Children's Bks.

Silverman, Erica. School Days. Lewin, Betsy, illus. 2008. (Cowgirl Kate & Cocoa Ser.). (ENG.). 48p. (J). (gr. 1-4). pap. 5.95 *(978-0-15-206130-2(4))* Houghton Mifflin Harcourt Publishing Co.

Simpson, Rodney. Frannie Fern Goes to Kindergarten. 2011. 52p. pap. 20.26 *(978-1-4490-5455-7(2))* AuthorHouse.

Sisler, Stephanie. One Bright Monster. Holcomb, Nicholas, illus. 2012. 36p. pap. 12.95 *(978-1-61493-124-9(0))* Peppertree Pr., The.

Sixtus, Albert. Rabbit School: A Light-Hearted Tale. Freischlad, Roland, tr. from GER. Koch-Gotha, Fritz, illus. 2009. (ENG.). 32p. (J). (gr. -1-2). 14.95 *(978-1-56792-383-4(6))* Godine, David R. Pub.

Skarmeas, Nancy. My First Day of School. 2nd ed. 2010. (Illus.). 32p. (J). (gr. -1-1). 8.99 *(978-0-8249-5622-6(2),* Ideal Pubns.) Worthy Publishing.

Smith, Jane. It's the First Day of Preschool, Chloe Zoe! Smith, Jane, illus. 2016. (Chloe Zoe Ser.). (ENG., Illus.). 32p. (J). (gr. -1-3). 12.99 *(978-0-8075-2456-5(5))* Whitman, Albert & Co.

Smith, Latisha. Mama Always Knows Best. 2009. 28p. pap. 12.49 *(978-1-4389-9951-7(8))* AuthorHouse.

Sorenson, Margo. Aloha for Carol Ann. Burris, Priscilla, illus. 2011. 32p. (J). (gr. -1-3). pap. 8.95 *(978-0-60349-027-6(2),* Marimba Bks.) Hudson Publishing Group, The.

Sparrow, Leilani. My First Day. Taylor, Dan, illus. 2015. (ENG.). 32p. (J). (gr. -1-k). 16.99 *(978-1-4998-0111-8(4))* Little Bee Books Inc.

Staub, Leslie. Time for (Earth) School, Dewey Dew. Mack, Jeff, illus. 2016. (ENG.). 32p. (J). (gr. -1-3). 16.95 *(978-1-59078-958-2(X))* Boyds Mills Pr.

Stiles, Norman. On My Very First School Day I Met... Mayer, Bill, illus. 2005. (ENG.). 32p. (J). (gr. -1-3). 9.95 *(978-1-59687-182-3(2))* IBks., Inc.

—On My Very First School Day I Met... Mayer, Bill, illus. 2005. 32p. (J). (gr. -1). 9.95 *(978-0-689-03924-9(7),* Milk & Cookies) ibooks, Inc.

Strickland, Sharon. Even Though: A Story about Being Different, 1 vol. 2009. 15p. pap. 24.95 *(978-1-60813-821-0(6))* PublishAmerica, Inc.

Stuve-Bodeen, Stephanie. La Escuela de Elizabeti. Sarfatti, Esther, tr. from ENG. Hale, Christy, illus. 2007. (SPA.). 32p. (J). (gr. -1-2). pap. 9.95 *(978-1-60060-235-1(5))* Lee & Low Bks., Inc.

Style Guide, Style, illus. School Is Awesome! 2014. (Yo Gabba Gabba! Ser.). (ENG.). 24p. (J). (gr. -1-1). pap. 3.99 *(978-1-4814-0930-8(1),* Simon Spotlight) Simon Spotlight.

Swain, Cynthia. Bill's First Day. 2006. (Early Explorers Ser.). (J). pap. *(978-1-4108-6033-0(7))* Benchmark Education Co.

Symes, Ruth Louise. Mondays at Monster School. Reeve, Rosie, illus. 2009. (ENG.). 32p. (J). (gr. -1-k). pap. 11.99 *(978-1-84255-536-1(7),* Orion Children's Bks.) Hachette Children's Group GBR. Dist: Independent Pubs. Group.

Thaler, Mike. Back-to-School Fright from the Black Lagoon, 1 vol. Lee, Jared, illus. 2012. (Black Lagoon Adventures Ser.: No. 2). (ENG.). 64p. (J). (gr. 2-5). 24.21 *(978-1-59961-961-3(X))* Spotlight.

Thompson, Lauren. Mouse's First Day of School. Erdogan, Buket, illus. 2010. (Mouse Ser.). (ENG.). 34p. (J). (gr. -1 — 1). bds. 7.99 *(978-1-4169-9476-3(9),* Little Simon) Little Simon.

Thompson, Lauren & Jackson, Livia. Mouse's First Day of School. Erdogan, Buket, illus. 2003. (Mouse Ser.). (ENG.). 32p. (J). (gr. -1-3). 15.99 *(978-0-689-84727-1(0),* Simon & Schuster Bks. For Young Readers) Simon & Schuster Bks. For Young Readers.

Thorpe, Kiki. Before the Bell. RH Disney Staff & Christy, Jana, illus. 2015. (Never Girls Ser.: 9). (ENG.). 128p. (J). (gr. 1-4). lib. bdg. 12.99 *(978-0-7364-8167-0(2),* RH/Disney) Random Hse. Children's Bks.

—Before the Bell. RH Disney Staff, illus. 2015. (Never Girls Ser.: No. 9). (ENG.). 128p. (J). (gr. 1-4). 5.99 *(978-0-7364-3304-4(X),* RH/Disney) Random Hse. Children's Bks.

—Before the Bell. 2015. (Never Girls Ser.: 9). lib. bdg. 16.00 *(978-0-606-36385-3(8))* Turtleback Bks.

Timmis, Jeff. You'd Have Wings If You'd Just Said No. 2012. 28p. pap. 19.99 *(978-1-4772-7604-4(1))* AuthorHouse.

Torrey, Richard. Ally-Saurus & the First Day of School. 2015. (Ally-Saurus Ser.). (ENG., Illus.). 40p. (J). (gr. -1-2). 14.95 *(978-1-4549-1179-1(4))* Sterling Publishing Co., Inc.

Tuminelly, Nancy. Horse Shoes. Nobens, C. A., illus. 2006. (Fact & Fiction Ser.). 24p. (J). pap. 48.42 *(978-1-59679-944-8(7))* ABDO Publishing Co.

—Los Zapatos de la Potranca, 1 vol. Nobens, C. A., illus. 2007. (Cuentos de Animales Ser.). (SPA & ENG.). 24p. (J). (gr. k-3). lib. bdg. 24.21 *(978-1-59928-677-8(7),* SandCastle) ABDO Publishing Co.

Underwood, Deborah. Super Saurus Saves Kindergarten. Young, Ned, illus. 2017. (ENG.). 40p. (J). (gr. -1-k). 16.99 *(978-1-4231-7568-1(9))* Disney Pr.

Urdahl, Catherine. Polka-Dot Fixes Kindergarten. Kemble, Mai S., illus. 2011. (ENG.). 32p. (J). (gr. -1-3). 16.95 *(978-1-57091-737-0(X));* pap. 7.95 *(978-1-57091-738-7(8))* Charlesbridge Publishing, Inc.

Van Kersen, Elizabeth. Whos' Riley? Stevens, Debra, illus. l.t. ed. 2006. 23p. (J). 15.99 *(978-1-59879-173-0(7))* Lifevest Publishing, Inc.

Ventura, Marne. Nervous Nellie Fights First-Day Frenzy. Trinidad, Leo, illus. 2016. (Worry Warriors Ser.). (ENG.). 96p. (gr. 2-4). lib. bdg. 25.99 *(978-1-4965-3613-6(4))* Stone Arch Bks.

Vernick, Audrey. Second Grade Holdout. Cordell, Matthew, illus. 2017. (ENG.). 32p. (J). (gr. -1-3). 16.99 *(978-0-544-87681-1(4),* Clarion Bks.) Houghton Mifflin Harcourt Trade & Reference Pubs.

Vulliamy, Clara. Martha Bunny Loves School. Vulliamy, Clara, illus. 2013. (ENG., Illus.). 32p. (J). (gr. -1-3). 16.99 *(978-0-8075-4976-6(2))* Whitman, Albert & Co.

Walker, Charmaine. Jon & Alex: Goes to School. 2012. 34p. pap. *(978-1-105-62383-7(1))* Lulu.com.

Weiss, Ellen. I Don't Want to Go to School! A Fold-Out Surprise Book. Bennett, Andy, illus. 2006. (PBS Kids Ser.). 12p. (J). 6.95 *(978-1-57791-313-9(2))* Brighter Minds Children's Publishing.

Wells, Rosemary. Emily's First 100 Days of School. Wells, Rosemary, illus. 2005. (ENG., Illus.). 64p. (J). (gr. -1-1). pap. 9.99 *(978-0-7868-1354-4(7))* Hyperion Pr.

—Emily's First 100 Days of School. 2006. (Illus.). (J). (gr. -1-4). 18.95 *(978-0-439-84903-6(9),* WPCD654) Weston Woods Studios, Inc.

West, C. The Adventures of Ice Cream & Honey Buns: Ready to Learn. 2012. 28p. pap. 16.09 *(978-1-4669-4739-9(X))* Trafford Publishing.

Weston Woods Staff, creator. Emily's First 100 Days of School. 2011. 38.75 *(978-0-439-84892-3(X))* Weston Woods Studios, Inc.

—Will I Have a Friend? 2011. 38.75 *(978-0-439-72970-3(X))* Weston Woods Studios, Inc.

Wick, Kimberly. Katie's First Day of School: The Adventures of Mrs. Swirlie. 2009. 36p. pap. 15.49 *(978-1-4389-2257-7(4))* AuthorHouse.

Wilhelm, Hans. I Love School! Wilhelm, Hans, illus. 2010. (Scholastic Reader Level 1 Ser.). (ENG., Illus.). 32p. (J). (gr. -1-k). pap. 3.99 *(978-0-545-13474-3(9),* Cartwheel Bks.) Scholastic, Inc.

Williams, Bonnie. Meet Teddy Rex! Gordon, John, illus. 2012. (Dino School Ser.). (ENG.). 24p. (J). (gr. -1-1). 15.99 *(978-1-4424-4996-1(9));* pap. 3.99 *(978-1-4424-4995-4(0))* Simon Spotlight. (Simon Spotlight).

Williams, T. E. Fluffy!! 2011. 24p. 16.25 *(978-1-4520-3743-1(4))* AuthorHouse.

Willis, Jeanne. Be Gentle, Python! Birchall, Mark, illus. 2005. (Picture Bks.). 28p. (J). (gr. k-2). 7.95 *(978-1-57505-508-4(2))* Lerner Publishing Group.

—Be Quiet, Parrot! Birchall, Mark, illus. 2005. (Picture Bks.). 32p. (J). (gr. k-2). 7.25 *(978-1-57505-492-6(2))* Lerner Publishing Group.

—Take Turns, Penguin! Birchall, Mark, illus. 2003. (Picture Bks.). 32p. (J). (gr. -1-3). 7.95 *(978-1-57505-493-3(0),* Carolrhoda Bks.) Lerner Publishing Group.

Wing, Natasha. The Night Before First Grade. Zemke, Deborah, illus. (Night Before Ser.). (ENG.). 32p. (J). (gr. k-1). 2014. 12.99 *(978-0-448-48256-9(8))* 2005. pap. 4.99 *(978-0-448-43747-7(3))* Penguin Young Readers Group. (Grosset & Dunlap).

—The Night Before Kindergarten. Durrell, Julie, illus. 2014. (Night Before Ser.). (ENG.). 32p. (J). (gr. -1-k). 12.99 *(978-0-448-48255-2(X),* Grosset & Dunlap) Penguin Young Readers Group.

—The Night Before Preschool. Wummer, Amy, illus. (Night Before Ser.). (ENG.). 32p. (J). (gr. -1-k). 2014. 12.99 *(978-0-448-48254-5(1))* 2011. pap. 4.99 *(978-0-448-45451-1(3))* Penguin Young Readers Group. (Grosset & Dunlap).

Winget, Susan. Tucker's Four-Carrot School Day. Winget, Susan, illus. 2005. (ENG., Illus.). 40p. (J). (gr. -1-k). 12.99 *(978-0-06-054642-7(5))* HarperCollins Pubs.

Winters, Kay. This School Year Will Be the Best! Andriani, Renee, illus. 2010. (ENG.). 32p. (J). (gr. 1-3). 16.99 *(978-0-525-42275-4(7),* Dutton Books for Young Readers) Penguin Young Readers Group.

—This School Year Will Be the Best! Andriani, Renee, illus. 2013. (ENG.). 32p. (J). (gr. 1-3). mass mkt. 6.99 *(978-0-14-242696-8(2),* Puffin Books) Penguin Young Readers Group.

Wohnoutka, Mike. Dad's First Day. Wohnoutka, Mike, illus. 2015. (ENG., Illus.). 40p. (J). (gr. -1-3). 16.99 *(978-1-61963-473-2(2),* 9781619634732, Bloomsbury USA Childrens) Bloomsbury Publishing USA.

Yoon, Salina. Bear's Big Day. 2017. (ENG., Illus.). 32p. (J). bds. 7.99 *(978-1-68119-436-3(8),* 9781681194363, Bloomsbury USA Childrens) Bloomsbury Publishing USA.

Yum, Hyewon. Mom, It's My First Day of Kindergarten!, 1 vol. Yum, Hyewon, illus. 2012. (ENG., Illus.). 36p. (J). (gr. -1-2). 16.99 *(978-0-374-35004-8(3),* 9780374350048, Farrar, Straus & Giroux (BYR)) Farrar, Straus & Giroux.

Zadunajsky, Donna M. Tayla's First Day of School. Bicking, Judith, illus. 2013. (ENG.). 26p. pap. 9.15 *(978-1-938037-35-1(9))* Zadunajsky, Donna M.

Zakatchenko, Lilian. Girls from Brazil, 1 vol. 2010. 16p. 24.95 *(978-1-4489-3834-6(1))* PublishAmerica, Inc.

FISH

see Fishes

FISH CULTURE

Etingoff, Kim. Farmed Fish. 2013. (Feeding the World Ser.: 8). (Illus.). 48p. (J). (gr. 4-18). 19.95 *(978-1-4222-2745-9(6))* Mason Crest.

Somervill, Barbara A. Producing Fish, 1 vol. 2012. (Technology of Farming Ser.). (ENG.). 48p. (gr. 4-6). lib. bdg. 33.32 *(978-1-4329-6405-4(4),* Heinemann InfoSearch) Heinemann-Raintree.

Squire, Ann O. Seafood. 2017. (True Book(tm), a — Farm to Table Ser.). (ENG., Illus.). 48p. (J). lib. bdg. 31.00 *(978-0-531-22935-4(1),* Children's Pr.) Scholastic Library Publishing.

FISHERIES

Here are entered works on the fishing industry.

see also Fishes

Bliss, John. Catching & Raising Seafood, 1 vol. 2011. (Ethics of Food Ser.). (ENG.). 56p. (gr. 6-6). 34.65 *(978-1-4329-5102-3(5))* Heinemann-Raintree.

Bocknek, Jonathan & Piddock, Charles. Sustainable Fishery. 2017. (J). ***(978-1-5105-2205-3(0))*** SmartBook Media, Inc.

Boudreau, Hélène. Life in a Fishing Community. 2009. (Learn about Rural Life Ser.). (ENG., Illus.). 32p. (J). (gr. 3-6). pap. *(978-0-7787-5085-7(X))* Crabtree Publishing Co.

Branse, J. L. A Day in the Life of a Colonial Sea Captain. 2009. (Library of Living & Working in Colonial Times Ser.). 24p. (gr. 3-3). 42.50 *(978-1-60853-737-2(4),* PowerKids Pr.) Rosen Publishing Group, Inc., The.

Johanson, Paula. Fish: From the Catch to Your Table. 2012. (Truth about the Food Supply Ser.). (ENG.). 48p. (YA). (gr. 5-8). 27.95 *(978-1-4488-6801-8(7),* Rosen Reference) Rosen Publishing Group, Inc., The.

Kurlansky, Mark. The Cod's Tale. Schindler, S. D., illus. 2014. (ENG.). 48p. (J). (gr. 2-5). 8.99 *(978-0-14-751277-2(8),* Puffin Books) Penguin Young Readers Group.

—World Without Fish. Stockton, Frank, illus. 2014. (ENG.). 208p. (J). (gr. 5). pap. 14.95 *(978-0-7611-8500-0(3))* Workman Publishing Co., Inc.

Labrecque, Ellen. Commercial Fisherman. 2016. (21st Century Skills Library: Cool Vocational Careers Ser.). (ENG., Illus.). 32p. (J). (gr. 4-7). 29.93 *(978-1-63471-061-9(4),* 208324) Cherry Lake Publishing.

Lukidas, Lydia. Fisheries. 2017. ***(978-1-5105-1933-6(5))*** SmartBook Media, Inc.

Navarre, Gabrielle. Cool Careers Without College for People Who Love Nature. 2013. (New Cool Careers Without College Ser.). (Illus.). 144p. (J). (gr. 7-12). 35.95 *(978-1-4777-1821-6(4))* Rosen Publishing Group, Inc., The.

Rose, Simon. Fisher. 2014. (Illus.). 24p. (J). *(978-1-4896-2986-9(6))* Weigl Pubs., Inc.

Royston, Angela. What Happens If We Overfish the Oceans? 2015. (Unstable Earth Ser.). (Illus.). 32p. (J). 31.35 *(978-1-62588-162-5(2))* Black Rabbit Bks.

Shea, Therese. Overfishing. 2014. (Illus.). 32p. (J). lib. bdg. *(978-1-4339-9925-3(0))* Stevens, Gareth Publishing LLLP.

Somervill, Barbara. Commercial Fisher. 2011. (21st Century Skills Library: Cool Careers Ser.). (ENG.). 32p. (gr. 4-8). lib. bdg. 28.50 *(978-1-60279-986-8(5),* 200980) Cherry Lake Publishing.

Squire, Ann O. Seafood. 2017. (True Book(tm), a — Farm to Table Ser.). (ENG., Illus.). 48p. (J). lib. bdg. 31.00 *(978-0-531-22935-4(1),* Children's Pr.) Scholastic Library Publishing.

Sylvester, Oscar. Life on a Commercial Fishing Boat. 2013. (Extreme Jobs in Extreme Places Ser.). (Illus.). 32p. (J). (gr. 3-6). pap. 10.50 *(978-1-4339-8488-4(1));* lib. bdg. 26.60 *(978-1-4339-8487-7(3))* Stevens, Gareth Publishing LLLP.

Thomas, William. Deep Sea Fisher. 2010. (Benchmark Rockets: Dirty & Dangerous Jobs Ser.). 32p. (J). (gr. 3-6). 28.50 (978-1-60870-171-1(9)) Marshall Cavendish GBR. Dist: Marshall Cavendish Corp.

Thomas, William David. Deep-Sea Fishing. 2008. (Cool Careers: Adventure Careers Ser.). 32p. (gr. 5-8). pap. 10.50 (978-0-8368-8888-1(X)); (Illus.). lib. bdg. 26.00 (978-0-8368-8881-2(2)) Stevens, Gareth Publishing LLLP.

Tieck, Sarah. Commercial Fishermen, 1 vol. 2011. (Extreme Jobs Ser.). (ENG., Illus.). 32p. (J). (gr. 2-5). 28.50 (978-1-61783-025-9(9)) ABDO Publishing Co.

Winters, Adam. Choosing a Career in the Fishing Industry. (World of Work Ser.). 64p. 2009. (gr. 5-5). 58.50 (978-1-60854-337-3(4)) 2005. (Illus.). (YA). (gr. 7-12). lib. bdg. 31.95 (978-0-8239-3330-3(X)) Rosen Publishing Group, Inc., The.

FISHERIES—FICTION

Buklis, Lawrence S. Mysteries from the Yukon: Three Fisheries Adventures for Students. 2003. 217p. (J). pap. 21.00 (978-1-888569-52-0(2)) American Fisheries Society.

Deas, Mike, illus. Dalen & Gole: Scandal in Port Angus, 1 vol. 2011. (ENG.). 128p. (J). (gr. 3-6). pap. 9.95 (978-1-55469-800-4(6)) Orca Bk. Pubs. USA.

Freeberg, Jane. The Scallop Christmas. Sheckels, Astrid, illus. 2011. (ENG.). 36p. (J). 16.95 (978-1-934031-25-4(9), 9781934031254) Islandport Pr., Inc.

Kipling, Rudyard. Captains Courageous. 2008. (Bring the Classics to Life Ser.). (ENG., Illus.). 72p. (gr. 4-12). pap., act. bk. ed. 10.95 (978-0-931334-66-5(7), EDCTR-401B) EDCON Publishing Group.

FISHERMEN

see Fishers

FISHERS

Boudreau, Hélène. Life in a Fishing Community. 2009. (Learn about Rural Life Ser.). (ENG., Illus.). 32p. (J). (gr. 3-6). pap. (978-0-7787-5085-7(X)) Crabtree Publishing Co.

Gordon, Nick. Deep Sea Fisherman. 2012. (Dangerous Jobs Ser.). (ENG., Illus.). 24p. (J). (gr. 3-7). lib. bdg. 25.95 (978-1-60014-779-1(8), Torque Bks.) Bellwether Media.

Johnson, Janet. Life on the Water: A Commercial Fishermen's Tale on Lake Superior. 2012. 44p. pap. 21.99 (978-1-4653-3800-6(4)) Xlibris Corp.

Jones, Emma. Fishermen & Fisherwomen, 01 vols., 1. 2016. (Hands-On Jobs Ser.). (ENG., Illus.). 24p. (J). pap. 8.25 (978-1-5081-4363-5(3), PowerKids Pr.) Rosen Publishing Group, Inc., The.

Kuligowski, Stephanie & Rice, Katelyn. Dangerous Catch! - Deep Sea Fishers, 1 vol. 2nd rev. ed. 2013. (Nonfiction Readers Ser.). (ENG., Illus.). 64p. (J). (gr. 5-5). pap. 31.96 (978-1-4333-7442-5(0)) Teacher Created Materials, Inc.

Labrecque, Ellen. Commercial Fisherman. 2016. (21st Century Skills Library: Cool Vocational Careers Ser.). (ENG., Illus.). 32p. (J). (gr. 4-7). 29.93 (978-1-63471-061-9(4), 208324) Cherry Lake Publishing.

Pallotta, Jerry. Going Lobstering. Bolster, Rob, illus. 2008. (ENG.). 20p. (J). (gr. -1-3). bds. 7.95 (978-1-57091-623-6(3)) Charlesbridge Publishing, Inc.

Rose, Simon. Fisher. 2014. (Illus.). 24p. (J). (978-1-4896-2986-9(6)) Weigl Pubs., Inc.

Rotner, Shelley. Grow! Raise! Catch! How We Get Our Food. (ENG.). 32p. (J). 2017. 7.99 **(978-0-8234-3884-6(8))** 2016. (Illus.). 16.95 (978-0-8234-3643-9(8)) Holiday Hse., Inc.

Somervill, Barbara. Commercial Fisher. 2011. (21st Century Skills Library: Cool Careers Ser.). (ENG.). 32p. (gr. 4-8). lib. bdg. 28.50 (978-1-60279-986-8(5), 200980) Cherry Lake Publishing.

Sylvester, Oscar. Life on a Commercial Fishing Boat. 2013. (Extreme Jobs in Extreme Places Ser.). (Illus.). 32p. (J). (gr. 3-6). pap. 10.50 (978-1-4339-8488-4(1)); lib. bdg. 26.60 (978-1-4339-8487-7(3)) Stevens, Gareth Publishing LLLP.

Tieck, Sarah. Commercial Fishermen, 1 vol. 2011. (Extreme Jobs Ser.). (ENG., Illus.). 32p. (J). (gr. 2-5). 28.50 (978-1-61783-025-9(9)) ABDO Publishing Co.

Zamosky, Lisa. Fishers Then & Now, 1 vol. 2006. (Primary Source Readers Ser.). (ENG.). 32p. (J). (gr. 1-1). pap. 8.99 (978-0-7439-9378-4(0)) Shell Educational Publishing.

FISHERS—FICTION

Award, Anna, et al. Monkey & the Fishermen & the Donkey in the Pond. 2014. (ENG.). 24p. (J). pap. 6.95 (978-1-84135-956-4(4)) Award Pubns. Ltd. GBR. Dist: Parkwest Pubns., Inc.

Ballantyne, R. M. The Young Trawler. 2011. 250p. 27.95 (978-1-4638-9496-2(1)) Rodgers, Alan Bks.

Boyd, Roland. The Fisherman & His Wife. Wright, Carol, ed. Zarvatski, Derek, illus. rev. ed. 20p. (J). (gr. 1-2). pap. 6.95 (978-0-9701573-0-0(4)) Chameleon Designs.

Burggraaf, Deborah. Crow No More. Lumsden, Matt, illus. 2011. 28p. (J). pap. 10.95 (978-0-9845161-8-6(2)) Protective Hands Communications.

Cameron, Sam. Mystery of the Tempest: A Fisher Key Adventure. 2011. (ENG.). 288p. (J). (gr. 7). pap. 13.95 (978-1-60282-579-6(3)) Bold Strokes Bks.

Dahl, Michael. Wings above the Waves, 1 vol. Piatti, Federico, illus. 2010. (Dragonblood Ser.). (ENG.). 40p. (gr. 1-3). lib. bdg. 23.99 (978-1-4342-1924-4(0), Zone Bks.) Stone Arch Bks.

Dateno, Maria Grace. Danger at Sea. Cunningham, Paul, illus. 2013. 80p. (J). pap. 5.95 (978-0-8198-1891-1(7)) Pauline Bks. & Media.

Duncan, Daniel. South. 2017. (ENG., Illus.). 40p. (J). (gr. k-2). 17.95 (978-1-4197-2299-8(9), Abrams Bks. for Young Readers) Abrams, Inc.

Eiseman, Joan. Ricardo & the Fisherman. Eiseman, Joan, illus. 2007. (Illus.). 32p. (J). per. 12.95 (978-0-9786745-4-0(5)) Marble Hse. Editions.

Ferrari, G. m. Lake, Sky, Dragonfly. 2009. 44p. pap. 16.99 (978-1-4490-2895-4(0)) AuthorHouse.

The Fisherman. 2013. (Illus.). 16p. pap. 9.95 (978-1-61633-446-8(0)) Guardian Angel Publishing, Inc.

Gooderham, Chris. Wicked Rhymes. 2008. 68p. pap. 13.95 (978-1-4092-1662-9(4)) Lulu Pr., Inc.

Lamana, Julie T. Three Little Bayou Fishermen. 2010. 28p. (J). pap. 17.95 (978-1-4327-2056-8(2)) Outskirts Pr., Inc.

Marsden, Carolyn & Niem, Thay. The Buddha's Diamonds. 2010. (ENG., Illus.). 112p. (J). (gr. 3-7). pap. 5.99 (978-0-7636-4828-2(0)) Candlewick Pr.

Rodriguez, AJ. A Cajun Crawfish Tale. 2009. 20p. pap. 12.49 (978-1-4389-5529-2(4)) AuthorHouse.

Rogers, Anne. CAPTAIN DAN & SAILOR SAM. 2008. 37p. pap. 24.95 (978-1-4092-1029-0(4)) Lulu Pr., Inc.

San Souci, Robert D. Six Foolish Fishermen, 1 vol. Kennedy, Doug, illus. 2011. (ENG.). 32p. (J). (gr. k-3). 16.99 (978-1-4556-1473-8(4)) Pelican Publishing Co., Inc.

Smart, Andy. Bob'n Joe Book One: Lunch Time. Smart, Andy, illus. 2013. (Illus.). 42p. (J). pap. (978-0-9919196-1-1(0)) Beckon Creative.

Stewart, Whitney. A Catfish Tale: A Bayou Story of the Fisherman & His Wife. Guerlais, Gérald, illus. 2014. (ENG.). 32p. (J). (gr. -1-3). 16.99 (978-0-8075-1098-8(X)) Whitman, Albert & Co.

Wilson, Elaine Moody. Fisherman Jack Meets the River Creatures, 1 vol. Ducker Signs Plus, illus. 2009. 40p. pap. 24.95 (978-1-60836-967-6(6)) PublishAmerica, Inc.

FISHES

see also Aquariums; Fish Culture; Fisheries; Fishing also names of fishes, e.g. Salmon, etc.

ABDO Publishing Company. Xtreme Fish. 2014. (Xtreme Fish Ser.: 6). (ENG.). 32p. (gr. 8-15). lib. bdg. 162.42 (978-1-62403-445-9(4), A&D Xtreme) ABDO Publishing Co.

ABDO Publishing Company Staff. Fish & Game. 2014. (Fish & Game Ser.: 6). (ENG.). 32p. (gr. 3-6). lib. bdg. 162.42 (978-1-62403-105-2(6), Checkerboard Library) ABDO Publishing Co.

—Underwater World, 1 vol. 2007. (Underwater World Ser.). (ENG.). 32p. 324.84 (978-1-59928-809-3(5), Buddy Bks.) ABDO Publishing Co.

Amstutz, Lisa J. Fish. 2017. (My First Animal Kingdom Encyclopedias Ser.). (ENG., Illus.). 32p. (gr. 1-2). lib. bdg. 27.32 (978-1-5157-3929-6(5), Aplus Bks.) Capstone Press of Coughlan Cos.

Andrews, Alexa. At the Beach. Keimig, Candice, illus. 2013. (Penguin Young Readers, Level 1 Ser.). (ENG.). 32p. (J). (gr. k-1). 14.99 (978-0-448-46570-8(1)); pap. 3.99 (978-0-448-46471-8(3)) Penguin Young Readers Group. (Penguin Young Readers).

Antill, Sara. Stonefish. 2010. (Unusual Animals Ser.). (Illus.). 24p. (J). (gr. k-3). (ENG.). pap. 8.15 (978-1-60754-999-4(9)); lib. bdg. 22.60 (978-1-60754-992-5(1)) Windmill Bks.

Bailey, Gerry. Tylosaurus. Carr, Karen, illus. 2011. (Smithsonian Prehistoric Zone Ser.). (ENG.). 32p. (J). (gr. k-3). (978-0-7787-1805-5(0)); pap. (978-0-7787-1818-5(2)) Crabtree Publishing Co.

Baker, Robin J. & Baker, Kelly A. 3-D Coloring Book — Fish Frenzy! 2012. (Dover 3-D Coloring Book Ser.). (ENG., Illus.). 32p. (J). (gr. 2-6). pap. 5.99 (978-0-486-49011-3(4)) Dover Pubns., Inc.

Barnard, Edward S. Fishes. 2009. (Amazing Animals Ser.). 48p. (gr. 2-6). pap. 10.50 (978-1-4339-2023-3(9), Gareth Stevens Learning Library); (YA). (gr. 3-6). lib. bdg. 28.00 (978-0-8368-9106-5(6)) Stevens, Gareth Publishing LLLP.

—Fishes. 2007. (J). (978-1-59939-136-6(8), Reader's Digest Young Families, Inc.) Studio Fun International.

Baumbusch, Brigitte. Fish in Art. 2005. (What Makes a Masterpiece? Ser.). (Illus.). 32p. (gr. 1-4). lib. bdg. 23.00 (978-0-8368-4446-7(7), Gareth Stevens Learning Library) Stevens, Gareth Publishing LLLP.

Beck, Angela. Fish: Keeping & Caring for Your Pet. 2013. (Keeping & Caring for Your Pet Ser.). 72p. (J). lib. bdg. 29.27 (978-0-7660-4185-1(9)); (gr. 6-12). pap. 8.95 (978-1-4644-0301-9(5)) Enslow Pubs., Inc.

Bedry, Christa. Fish. 2004. (Prehistoric Life Ser.). (J). pap. 9.95 (978-1-59036-172-6(5)); (Illus.). 32p. lib. bdg. 26.00 (978-1-59036-112-2(1)) Weigl Pubs., Inc.

Bell, Samantha. Boxfish. 2014. (21st Century Skills Library: Exploring Our Oceans Ser.). (ENG.). 32p. (J). (gr. 3-6). 28.50 (978-1-63188-017-9(9), 205475) Cherry Lake Publishing.

—Cuttlefish. 2014. (21st Century Skills Library: Exploring Our Oceans Ser.). (ENG., Illus.). 32p. (J). (gr. 3-6). 28.50 (978-1-63188-018-6(7), 205479) Cherry Lake Publishing.

Berendes, Mary. Piranhas. 2015. (Animals of the Rain Forest Ser.). (ENG.). 24p. (J). (gr. 2-5). 27.07 (978-1-63143-750-2(X), 208579) Child's World, Inc., The.

Biard, Philippe, et al. Fish. Krawczyk, Sabine, illus. 2006. (ENG.). 36p. (J). (gr. k-3). pap. 11.99 (978-1-85103-365-2(3)) Moonlight Publishing, Ltd. GBR. Dist: Independent Pubs. Group.

Bodden, Valerie. Fish. 2009. (My First Look at: Pets Ser.). (J). (gr. 1-5). 24.25 (978-1-58341-722-5(2), Creative Education) Creative Co., The.

Bonner, Hannah. When Fish Got Feet, When Bugs Were Big, & When Dinos Dawned: A Cartoon Prehistory of Life on Earth. 2015. (ENG., Illus.). 128p. (J). (gr. 3-7). pap. 12.99 (978-1-4263-2104-7(X), National Geographic Children's Bks.) National Geographic Society.

Boothroyd, Jennifer. Endangered & Extinct Fish. 2014. (Lightning Bolt Books Animals in Danger Ser.). (ENG., Illus.). 32p. (gr. k-2). lib. bdg. 26.60 (978-1-4677-1331-3(7), Lerner Pubns.) Lerner Publishing Group.

—Scales. 2011. (First Step Nonfiction / Body Coverings Ser.). pap. 33.92 (978-0-7613-8609-4(2)); (ENG.). 24p. pap. 6.95 (978-0-7613-7829-7(4)); (ENG., Illus.). 24p. lib. bdg. 23.93 (978-0-7613-5787-2(4)) Lerner Publishing Group.

—Shells. 2011. (First Step Nonfiction / Body Coverings Ser.). (ENG.). 24p. (gr. k-2). pap. 6.95 (978-0-7613-7830-3(8)) Lerner Publishing Group.

Bozzo, Linda. Mi Primer Pez. 2008. (My First Pet Bilingual Library from the American Humane Association Ser.).Tr. of My First Fish. (ENG & SPA., Illus.). 32p. (J). (gr. 1-3). lib. bdg. 23.94 (978-0-7660-3036-7(9)) Enslow Pubs., Inc.

—My First Fish. 2007. (My First Pet Library from the American Humane Association Ser.). (Illus.). 32p. (J). (gr. 1-2). lib. bdg. 23.94 (978-0-7660-2751-0(1), Enslow Elementary) Enslow Pubs., Inc.

Buckmaster, Marjorie L. Freshwater Fishes. 2007. (Great Pets Ser.). (Illus.). 48p. (gr. 3-7). lib. bdg. 29.93 (978-0-7614-2712-4(0), Benchmark Bks.) Marshall Cavendish Corp.

Calmenson, Stephanie. Look! Fish! Pinillos, Puy, illus. 2016. (Look! Ser.). (ENG.). 24p. (J). (gr. -1-1). 7.99 (978-1-4998-0166-8(1)) Little Bee Books Inc.

Caputo, Christine A. Fish. 2012. (Illus.). 32p. (J). pap. (978-0-545-46700-1(4)) Scholastic, Inc.

Carpenter, Tom. Freshwater Fishing: Bass, Trout, Walleye, Catfish, & More. 2012. (Great Outdoors Sports Zone Ser.). (ENG., Illus.). 32p. (gr. 4-8). lib. bdg. 26.60 (978-1-4677-0219-5(6), Lerner Pubns.) Lerner Publishing Group.

—Saltwater Fishing: Snapper, Mackerel, Bluefish, Tuna, & More. 2012. (Great Outdoors Sports Zone Ser.). (ENG., Illus.). 32p. (gr. 4-8). lib. bdg. 26.60 (978-1-4677-0220-1(X), Lerner Pubns.) Lerner Publishing Group.

Carson-Dellosa Publishing Staff. Go Fish. 2006. (ENG., Illus.). 54p. (gr. -1-2). 2.99 (978-0-7696-4839-2(8), Brighter Child) Carson-Dellosa Publishing, LLC.

Cavell-Clarke, Steffi. Fish. 2017. (Animal Classification Ser.). (J). (gr. 3-4). pap. 63.00 **(978-1-5345-2010-3(4))**; 32p. pap. 10.50 **(978-1-5345-2009-7(0))**; 32p. lib. bdg. 27.25 **(978-1-5345-2011-0(2))** Greenhaven Publishing LLC. (KidHaven Publishing).

Cerullo, Mary M. City Fish Country Fish CL: How Fish Adapt to Tropical Seas & Cold Oceans, 1 vol. Rotman, Jeffrey L., photos by. 2nd ed. 2017. (How Nature Works: 0). (ENG., Illus.). 40p. (gr. 3-7). 17.95 (978-0-88448-529-2(3), 884529) Tilbury Hse. Pubs.

Cerullo, Mary M. & Rotman, Jeffrey L. City Fish, Country Fish, 1 vol. 2012. (ENG., Illus.). 32p. (gr. 3-7). 16.95 (978-0-88448-323-6(1), 884323) Tilbury Hse. Pubs.

Chancellor, Deborah. Piranhas. 2009. (Extreme Pets Ser.). (YA). (gr. 4-7). 28.50 (978-1-59920-237-2(9)) Black Rabbit Bks.

Ciletti, Barbara. Northern Snakeheads. 2017. (Invasive Species Takeover Ser.). (ENG., Illus.). 32p. (J). (gr. 3-7). 31.35 **(978-1-68072-016-7(3)**, Bolt) Black Rabbit Bks.

Ciletti, Barbara J. Asian Carp. 2017. (Invasive Species Takeover Ser.). (ENG., Illus.). 32p. (J). (gr. 3-7). 31.35 **(978-1-68072-013-6(9))** Black Rabbit Bks.

Cleary, Brian P. Catfish, Cod, Salmon, & Scrod: What Is a Fish? Goneau, Martin, illus. 2012. (Animal Groups Are CATegorical (tm) Ser.). (ENG.). 32p. (gr. k-3). (J). lib. bdg. 26.60 (978-0-7613-6211-1(8)); pap. 7.95 (978-1-4677-0337-6(0)) Lerner Publishing Group. (Millbrook Pr.).

Clish, Marian L. Fish Don't Swim in a Tree. Clish, Lori, illus. (J). (gr. k-3). pap. 7.95 (978-1-928632-12-2(2)) Writers Marketplace:Consulting, Critiquing & Publishing.

Coldiron, Deborah. Anglerfish, 1 vol. 2007. (Underwater World Ser.). (ENG.). 32p. (gr. 3-7). 27.07 (978-1-59928-819-2(2), Buddy Bks.) ABDO Publishing Co.

—Barracuda, 1 vol. 2008. (Underwater World Set II Ser.). (ENG.). 32p. (gr. k-4). 27.07 (978-1-60453-129-9(0), Buddy Bks.) ABDO Publishing Co.

—Clownfish, 1 vol. 2008. (Underwater World Set II Ser.). (ENG.). 32p. (gr. k-4). 27.07 (978-1-60453-130-5(4), Buddy Bks.) ABDO Publishing Co.

—Crayfish, 1 vol. 2008. (Underwater World Set II Ser.). (ENG.). 32p. (gr. k-4). 27.07 (978-1-60453-131-2(2), Buddy Bks.) ABDO Publishing Co.

—Cuttlefish, 1 vol. 2008. (Underwater World Set II Ser.). (ENG.). 32p. (gr. k-4). 27.07 (978-1-60453-132-9(0), Buddy Bks.) ABDO Publishing Co.

—Eels, 1 vol. 2007. (Underwater World Ser.). (ENG.). 32p. (gr. 3-7). 27.07 (978-1-59928-818-5(4), Buddy Bks.) ABDO Publishing Co.

—Ocean Sunfish, 1 vol. 2008. (Underwater World Set II Ser.). (ENG.). 32p. (gr. k-4). 27.07 (978-1-60453-135-0(5), Buddy Bks.) ABDO Publishing Co.

—Piranhas, 1 vol. 2008. (Underwater World Set II Ser.). (ENG.). 32p. (gr. k-4). 27.07 (978-1-60453-136-7(3), Buddy Bks.) ABDO Publishing Co.

—Sea Urchins, 1 vol. 2008. (Underwater World Set II Ser.). (ENG.). 32p. (gr. k-4). 27.07 (978-1-60453-137-4(1), Buddy Bks.) ABDO Publishing Co.

—Stingrays, 1 vol. 2007. (Underwater World Ser.). (ENG.). 32p. (gr. 3-7). 27.07 (978-1-59928-817-8(6), Buddy Bks.) ABDO Publishing Co.

—Swordfish, 1 vol. 2007. (Underwater World Ser.). (ENG.). 32p. (gr. 3-7). 27.07 (978-1-59928-820-8(6), Buddy Bks.) ABDO Publishing Co.

—Tuna, 1 vol. 2008. (Underwater World Set II Ser.). (ENG.). 32p. (gr. k-4). 27.07 (978-1-60453-140-4(1), Buddy Bks.) ABDO Publishing Co.

Coleman, Miriam. Bass Eat Their Own Young!, 1 vol., 1. 2014. (Disgusting Animal Dinners Ser.). (ENG.). 24p. (J). (gr. k-5). 23.60 (978-1-4777-2887-1(2), PowerKids Pr.) Rosen Publishing Group, Inc., The.

Connors, Kathleen. Sea Creature Fossils. 2012. (Fossilized! Ser.). (Illus.). 24p. (J). (gr. 2-5). pap. 8.15 (978-1-4339-6430-5(9)); lib. bdg. 22.60 (978-1-4339-6428-2(7)) Stevens, Gareth Publishing LLLP.

Davies, Caroline, illus. Fish. 2013. (Shake & Play Bath Bks.). (ENG.). 8p. (J). (gr. -1 — 1). 5.99 (978-1-4380-7340-8(2)) Barron's Educational Series, Inc.

de Hugo, Pierre. Fish Underwater. de Hugo, Pierre, illus. 2012. (ENG., Illus.). 36p. (J). (gr. -1-k). spiral bd. 12.99 (978-1-85103-409-3(9)) Moonlight Publishing, Ltd. GBR. Dist: Independent Pubs. Group.

Deboo, Ana. Clownfish & Other Saltwater Aquarium Fish. 2009. (J). (978-0-7166-1374-9(3)) World Bk., Inc.

Dellaccio, Tanya. Frogfish. 2017. (Freaky Fish Ser.). 24p. (J). (gr. 2-3). pap. 48.90 **(978-1-5382-0247-0(6))** Stevens, Gareth Publishing LLLP.

Dessen, Maci. Let's Go Snorkeling! Use Place Value Understanding. 2014. (Rosen Common Core Math Readers Ser.). (ENG.). 24p. (J). (gr. 3-4). pap. 8.25 (978-1-4777-4938-8(1), Rosen Classroom) Rosen Publishing Group, Inc., The.

Didier, Dominique A. Moray Eel. 2014. (21st Century Skills Library: Exploring Our Oceans Ser.). (ENG., Illus.). 32p. (J). (gr. 3-6). 28.50 (978-1-63188-020-9(9), 205487) Cherry Lake Publishing.

Dorling Kindersley Publishing Staff & Parker, Steve. DK Eyewitness Books - Fish. 2005. (DK Eyewitness Bks.). (ENG.). 72p. (J). (gr. 3-7). 16.99 (978-0-7566-1073-9(7), DK Children) Dorling Kindersley Publishing, Inc.

Dunn, Mary R. Piranhas, 1 vol. 2012. (South American Animals Ser.). (ENG.). 24p. (gr. k-1). lib. bdg. 26.65 (978-1-4296-7586-4(1), Pebble Plus) Capstone Press of Coughlan Cos.

Encyclopaedia Britannica, Inc. Staff, compiled by. Britannica Illustrated Science Library: Fish & Amphibians, 16 vols. 2008. (Illus.). (J). 29.95 (978-1-59339-389-2(X)) Encyclopaedia Britannica, Inc.

Farrington, S. Kip, Jr. Bill, the Broadbill Swordfish. Date not set. lib. bdg. 16.95 (978-0-8488-1855-5(5)) Amereon Ltd.

Fish: Level E. (Wonder Worldtm Ser.). 16p. 26.50 (978-0-7802-7004-6(5)); 29.95 (978-0-7802-1994-6(5)) Wright Group/McGraw-Hill.

Fish: The Complete Fish & Seafood Companion. 2007. (Illus.). (J). cd-rom 9.99 (978-0-9795190-4-8(7)) Color & Learn.

Fish: The Complete Fish & Seafood Companion. 2004. (J). per. (978-1-57657-355-6(9)) Paradise Pr., Inc.

Fish Sets: 1 Each of 3 Big Books. (Sunshinetm Science Ser.). (gr. 1-2). 111.50 (978-0-7802-1447-7(1)) Wright Group/McGraw-Hill.

Fletcher, Patricia. Why Do Mudskippers Walk? And Other Curious Fish Adaptations. 2017. (Odd Adaptations Ser.). 32p. (J). (gr. 3-4). pap. 10.50 **(978-1-5382-0393-4(6))** Stevens, Gareth Publishing LLLP.

Fractions with Fish. 2013. (Animal Math Ser.). 24p. (J). (gr. 1-3). pap. 48.90 (978-1-4339-9310-7(4)) Stevens, Gareth Publishing LLLP.

Freaky Fish. 2017. (Freaky Fish Ser.). 24p. (gr. 2-3). pap. 48.90 **(978-1-5382-0483-2(5))**; lib. bdg. 135.60 **(978-1-5382-0468-9(1))** Stevens, Gareth Publishing LLLP.

Ganeri, Anita. Piranha, 1 vol. 2010. (Day in the Life: Rain Forest Animals Ser.). (ENG., Illus.). 24p. (gr. k-2). 23.32 (978-1-4329-4108-6(9), Heinemann Read & Learn) Heinemann-Raintree.

Gerber, Carole. Stingrays! Underwater Fliers. Mones, Isidre, illus. 2015. (Step into Reading Ser.). (ENG.). 48p. (J). (gr. k-3). 12.99 (978-0-375-97153-2(X), Random Hse. Bks. for Young Readers) Random Hse. Children's Bks.

Gibbs, Maddie. Clownfish. 2013. (PowerKids Readers: Fun Fish Ser.). 24p. (J). (gr. k-2). 22.60 (978-1-4777-0757-9(3)); pap. 49.50 (978-1-4777-0848-4(0)); pap. 8.25 (978-1-4777-0847-7(2)) Rosen Publishing Group, Inc., The. (PowerKids Pr.).

—Clownfish / Los Peces Payaso. De La Vega, Eida, ed. 2013. (PowerKids Readers: Fun Fish / Peces Divertidos Ser.). (ENG & SPA.). 24p. (J). (gr. k-2). 22.60 (978-1-4777-1215-3(1), PowerKids Pr.) Rosen Publishing Group, Inc., The.

—Rays. 2013. (PowerKids Readers: Fun Fish Ser.). 24p. (J). (gr. k-2). 22.60 (978-1-4777-0762-3(X)); pap. 8.25 (978-1-4777-0857-6(X)); pap. 49.50 (978-1-4777-0858-3(8)) Rosen Publishing Group, Inc., The. (PowerKids Pr.).

—Rays / Las Rayas. De La Vega, Eida, ed. 2013. (PowerKids Readers: Fun Fish / Peces Divertidos Ser.). (ENG & SPA.). 24p. (J). (gr. k-2). 22.60 (978-1-4777-1220-7(8), PowerKids Pr.) Rosen Publishing Group, Inc., The.

Gish, Melissa. Living Wild: Piranhas. 2013. (Living Wild Ser.). (ENG., Illus.). 48p. (J). (gr. 4-7). pap. 12.00 (978-0-89812-775-1(0), Creative Paperbacks) Creative Co., The.

—Piranhas. (J). 2017. **(978-1-60818-820-8(5))** 2012. (Illus.). 48p. (gr. 5-12). 23.95 (978-1-60818-168-1(5)) Creative Co., The. (Creative Education).

Gish, Melissa. Rays. (Living Wild Ser.). (Illus.). (J). 2017. (ENG.). 48p. (gr. 4-7). pap. 12.00 (978-1-62832-304-7(3), Creative Paperbacks) 2016. 46p. (978-1-60818-708-9(X), Creative Education) Creative Co., The.

Glaser, Rebecca. Fish Swim. 2017. (Amicus Ink Board Bks.). (ENG., Illus.). 14p. (J). (gr. -1 — 1). bds. 7.99 **(978-1-68152-198-5(9))** Amicus.

Goldish, Meish. Disgusting Hagfish. 2008. (Gross-Out Defenses Ser.). (Illus.). 24p. (J). (gr. k-3). lib. bdg. 21.28 (978-1-59716-719-2(3), 1284313) Bearport Publishing Co., Inc.

—Moray Eel: Dangerous Teeth. 2009. (Afraid of the Water Ser.). (Illus.). 24p. (YA). (gr. 2-5). lib. bdg. 22.61 (978-1-59716-941-7(2)) Bearport Publishing Co., Inc.

—Stonefish: Needles of Pain. 2009. (Afraid of the Water Ser.). (Illus.). 24p. (YA). (gr. 2-5). lib. bdg. 22.61 (978-1-59716-943-1(9)) Bearport Publishing Co., Inc.

Goldsworthy, Kaite. Fish. 2016. (J). (978-1-5105-1112-5(1)) SmartBook Media, Inc.

Graubart, Norman D. Mi Pez / My Fish, 1 vol., 1. Green, Christina, ed. 2014. (¡Las Mascotas Son Geniales! / Pets Are Awesome! Ser.). (SPA & BYN.). 24p. (J). (gr. k-2). 23.60 (978-1-4777-3307-3(8), PowerKids Pr.) Rosen Publishing Group, Inc., The.

—My Fish, 1 vol., 1. 2014. (Pets Are Awesome! Ser.). (ENG.). 24p. (J). (gr. k-2). 23.60 (978-1-4777-2866-6(X), PowerKids Pr.) Rosen Publishing Group, Inc., The.

Gray, Susan H. Discover Rays. 2015. (21st Century Basic Skills Library: Splash! Ser.). (ENG., Illus.). 24p. (J). (gr. 2-4). 24.21 (978-1-63362-604-1(0), 206600) Cherry Lake Publishing.

—Lionfish. 2014. (21st Century Skills Library: Exploring Our Oceans Ser.). (ENG., Illus.). 32p. (J). (gr. 3-6). 28.50 (978-1-63188-019-3(5), 205483) Cherry Lake Publishing.

—Rays. 2014. (21st Century Skills Library: Exploring Our Oceans Ser.). (ENG., Illus.). 32p. (J). (gr. 3-6). 28.50 (978-1-62431-599-2(2), 203180) Cherry Lake Publishing.

—Walking Catfish. 2008. (21st Century Skills Library: Animal Invaders Ser.). (ENG., Illus.). 32p. (gr. 4-8). lib. bdg. 28.50 (978-1-60279-242-5(9), 200117) Cherry Lake Publishing.

Green, Jen. Moray Eel. 2013. (Science Slam: the Deep End-Animal Life Underwater Ser.). 24p. (J). (gr. -1-3). lib. bdg. 23.93 (978-1-61772-921-8(3)) Bearport Publishing Co., Inc.

Green, Sara. Freshwater Fishing. 2012. (Outdoor Adventures Ser.). (ENG., Illus.). 24p. (J). (gr. 3-8). lib. bdg. 25.95 (978-1-60014-799-9(2), Pilot Bks.) Bellwether Media.

Greve, Tom. Freshwater Fish. 2011. (ENG., Illus.). 24p. (gr. 2-5). pap. 8.95 (978-1-61741-979-9(6)) Rourke Educational Media.

Gross, Miriam J. The Jellyfish. 2006. (Weird Sea Creatures Ser.). (Illus.). 24p. (J). (gr. 3-7). lib. bdg. 22.60 (978-1-4042-3192-4(7), PowerKids Pr.) Rosen Publishing Group, Inc., The.

—The Moray Eel. 2009. (Weird Sea Creatures Ser.). 24p. (gr. 3-3). 42.50 (978-1-60854-752-4(3), PowerKids Pr.) Rosen Publishing Group, Inc., The.

—The Sea Dragon. (Weird Sea Creatures Ser.). 24p. (gr. 3-3). 2009. 42.50 (978-1-60854-756-2(6)) 2006. (Illus.). (J). lib. bdg. 22.60 (978-1-4042-3193-1(5)) Rosen Publishing Group, Inc., The. (PowerKids Pr.).

—The Stingray. 2009. (Weird Sea Creatures Ser.). 24p. (gr. 3-3). 42.50 (978-1-60854-758-6(2), PowerKids Pr.) Rosen Publishing Group, Inc., The.

Hamilton, Lynn. Caring for Your Fish. 2005. (Caring for Your Pet Ser.). (Illus.). 32p. (J). (gr. 4-7). lib. bdg. 26.00 (978-1-59036-035-4(4)) Weigl Pubs., Inc.

—Fish. 2008. (My Pet Ser.). (Illus.). 32p. (J). (gr. 3-5). pap. 9.95 (978-1-59036-905-0(X)); lib. bdg. 26.00 (978-1-59036-904-3(1)) Weigl Pubs., Inc.

Hamilton, Lynn A. Caring for Your Fish. Kissock, Heather & Marshall, Diana, eds. 2003. (Caring for Your Pet Ser.). (Illus.). 32p. (J). pap. 9.95 (978-1-59036-065-1(6)) Weigl Pubs., Inc.

Hamilton, S. L. Barracuda. 2014. (Xtreme Fish Ser.). (ENG.). 32p. (gr. 8-15). lib. bdg. 27.07 (978-1-62403-446-6(2), A&D Xtreme) ABDO Publishing Co.

—Catfish. 2014. (Xtreme Fish Ser.). (ENG., Illus.). 32p. (J). (gr. 8-15). lib. bdg. 27.07 (978-1-62403-447-3(0), A&D Xtreme) ABDO Publishing Co.

—Eels. 2014. (Xtreme Fish Ser.). (ENG.). 32p. (gr. 8-15). lib. bdg. 27.07 (978-1-62403-448-0(9), A&D Xtreme) ABDO Publishing Co.

—Fish. 2013. (Xtreme Pets Ser.). (Illus.). 32p. (J). (gr. 3-9). lib. bdg. 27.07 (978-1-61783-973-3(6), Abdo & Daughters) ABDO Publishing Co.

—Marlin. 2014. (Xtreme Fish Ser.). (ENG.). 32p. (gr. 8-15). lib. bdg. 27.07 (978-1-62403-449-7(7), A&D Xtreme) ABDO Publishing Co.

—Piranha. 2014. (Xtreme Fish Ser.). (ENG., Illus.). 32p. (J). (gr. 8-15). lib. bdg. 27.07 (978-1-62403-450-3(0), A&D Xtreme) ABDO Publishing Co.

—Sturgeon. 2014. (Xtreme Fish Ser.). (ENG., Illus.). 32p. (J). (gr. 8-15). lib. bdg. 27.07 (978-1-62403-451-0(9), A&D Xtreme) ABDO Publishing Co.

Hand, Carol. Dead Zones. 2016. (Nonfiction - Young Adult Ser.). (ENG., Illus.). 80p. (J). (gr. 7-12). 35.99 (978-1-4677-7573-1(8), Twenty-First Century Bks.) Lerner Publishing Group.

—Dead Zones: Why Earth's Waters Are Losing Oxygen. 2016. (ENG., Illus.). 80p. (YA). (gr. 7-12). 53.32 (978-1-4677-9575-3(5), Twenty-First Century Bks.) Lerner Publishing Group.

Hansen, Grace. Tropical Fish, 1 vol. 2014. (Ocean Life Ser.). (ENG.). 24p. (J). (gr. 2-4). lib. bdg. 28.50 (978-1-62970-712-9(0)) ABDO Publishing Co.

Harris, Tim, ed. Fish. 2011. (FAYFT: Endangered Animals Ser.). 64p. (gr. 4-10). lib. bdg. 39.95 (978-1-936333-32-5(5)) Brown Bear Bks.

Harrub, Brad. God Made Fish. 2007. (ENG., Illus.). (J). 3.00 (978-0-932859-87-7(9)) Apologetics Pr., Inc.

Harvey, Bev. Fish. (Eyes on Nature Ser.). (J). (gr. 1). 32p. pap. (978-1-882210-53-4(0)); 36p. pap. (978-1-882210-06-0(9)) Action Publishing, Inc.

Hayashi, Leslie Ann. A Fishy Alphabet in Hawaii. Bishop, Kathleen Wong, illus. 2007. (J). 13.95 (978-1-56647-830-4(8)) Mutual Publishing LLC.

Head, Honor. Amazing Fish. 2008. (Amazing Life Cycles Ser.). (Illus.). 32p. (gr. 2-6). lib. bdg. 26.00 (978-0-8368-8895-9(2), Gareth Stevens Learning Library) Stevens, Gareth Publishing LLLP.

Hegarty, Patricia. The River. Clulow, Hanako, illus. 2016. (J). 12.99 (978-1-61067-468-3(5)) Kane Miller.

Herrington, Lisa M. Freaky Fish. 2016. (Rookie Read-About Science(tm): Strange Animals Ser.). (ENG., Illus.). 32p. (J). lib. bdg. 25.00 (978-0-531-22601-8(8), Children's Pr.) Scholastic Library Publishing.

Holt, Rinehart and Winston Staff. Holt Science & Technology Chapter 16: Life Science: Fishes, Amphibians, & Reptiles. 5th ed. 2004. (Illus.). pap. 12.86 (978-0-03-030221-3(8)) Holt McDougal.

How do Fish Live? 6 Each of 1 Student Book, 6 vols. (Sunshinetm Science Ser.). 24p. (gr. 1-2). 41.95 (978-0-7802-1425-5(0)) Wright Group/McGraw-Hill.

How do Fish Live? Big Book. (Sunshinetm Science Ser.). 24p. (gr. 1-2). 37.50 (978-0-7802-1426-2(9)) Wright Group/McGraw-Hill.

Howard, Melanie A. Freshwater Fishing for Kids, 1 vol. 2012. (Into the Great Outdoors Ser.). (ENG., Illus.). 32p. (gr. 3-4). pap. 7.95 (978-1-4296-9269-4(3)); lib. bdg. 27.99 (978-1-4296-8422-4(4)) Capstone Press of Coughlan Cos.

Howell, Izzi. Fish. 2017. (Fact Finders: Animals Ser.). 24p. (gr. 7-7). 24.60 **(978-1-4994-8302-4(3)**, Windmill Bks.) Rosen Publishing Group, Inc., The.

Howell, Sara. Lantern Fish, 1 vol. 2015. (ENG., Illus.). 24p. (J). lib. bdg. 23.60 (978-1-4994-0147-9(7), PowerKids Pr.) Rosen Publishing Group, Inc., The.

Hudak, Heather C. Fish. (Animal Facts Ser.). (Illus.). 24p. (J). 2005. per. 8.95 (978-1-59036-243-3(8)) 2004. lib. bdg. 24.45 (978-1-59036-202-0(0)) Weigl Pubs., Inc.

Hunt, Santana. Attack of the Asian Carp! 2016. (Animal Invaders: Destroying Native Habitats Ser.). 00024p. (J). pap. 8.15 (978-1-4824-5655-4(9)) Stevens, Gareth Publishing LLLP.

—Name That Fish! 2016. (Guess That Animal! Ser.). 24p. (J). (gr. 2-1). lib. bdg. 22.60 (978-1-4824-4745-3(2)) Stevens, Gareth Publishing LLLP.

Ingalls, Ann. Piranha, 1 vol. 2013. (Great Predators Ser.). (ENG., Illus.). 48p. (J). (gr. 3-6). lib. bdg. 32.79 (978-1-61783-951-1(5)) ABDO Publishing Co.

—Piranha Paperback. 2013. (Illus.). 48p. (J). pap. 15.64 (978-1-62403-016-1(5), Core Library) ABDO Publishing Co.

Innovative Kids Staff, creator. Soft Shapes Photo Books: Tropical Fish. 2012. (ENG., Illus.). 8p. (J). (gr. -1 — 1). 10.99 (978-1-60169-225-2(0)) Innovative Kids.

Jacobs, Pat. Why Do Fish Have Gills? And Other Questions about Evolution & Classification. 2016. (Wildlife Wonders Ser.). 00032p. (J). (gr. 3-3). pap. 10.00 (978-1-4994-3206-0(2), PowerKids Pr.) Rosen Publishing Group, Inc., The.

Jeffrey, Laura S. Choosing a Fish: How to Choose & Care for a Fish. 2013. (American Humane Association Pet Care Ser.). 48p. (J). (gr. 3-18). lib. bdg. 25.27 (978-0-7660-4081-6(X)); pap. 8.95 (978-1-4644-0216-6(7), Enslow Elementary) Enslow Pubs., Inc.

—Fish: How to Choose & Care for a Fish. 2004. (American Humane Pet Care Library). (Illus.). 48p. (J). lib. bdg. 25.27 (978-0-7660-2517-2(9)) Enslow Pubs., Inc.

Kalman, Bobbie & Sjonger, Rebecca. Les écrevisses. 2011. (Petit Monde Vivant (Small Living World) Ser.: No. 73). (FRE., Illus.). 32p. (J). pap. 9.95 (978-2-89579-365-6(4)) Bayard Canada Livres CAN. Dist: Crabtree Publishing Co.

—The Life Cycle of a Crayfish. 2006. (Life Cycle Ser.). (ENG., Illus.). 32p. (J). (gr. -1-3). pap. (978-0-7787-0703-5(2)) Crabtree Publishing Co.

Kaspar, Anna. What's a Fish? 2012. (All about Animals Ser.). (ENG., Illus.). 24p. (J). (gr. k-3). pap. 8.25 (978-1-4488-6228-3(0)); lib. bdg. 22.60 (978-1-4488-6135-4(7)) Rosen Publishing Group, Inc., The. (PowerKids Pr.).

—What's a Fish? Qué Es un Pez? 2012. (All about Animals / Todo sobre los animales Ser.). (SPA & ENG., Illus.). 24p. (J). (gr. k-3). lib. bdg. 22.60 (978-1-4488-6701-1(0), PowerKids Pr.) Rosen Publishing Group, Inc., The.

Keating, Jess. Shark Lady: The Daring Tale of How Eugenie Clark Dove into History. Alvarez Miguens, Marta, illus. 2017. (ENG.). 40p. (J). (-4). 17.99 (978-1-4926-4204-6(5), Sourcebooks Jabberwocky) Sourcebooks, Inc.

Kenan, Tessa. Look, a Clown Fish! 2016. (Bumba Books (tm) — I See Ocean Animals Ser.). (ENG., Illus.). 24p. (J). (gr. -1-1). 25.32 (978-1-5124-1422-6(0)) Lerner Publishing Group.

—Look, a Ray! 2016. (Bumba Books (tm) — I See Ocean Animals Ser.). (ENG., Illus.). 24p. (J). (gr. -1-1). 25.32 (978-1-5124-1420-2(4)) Lerner Publishing Group.

—¡Mira, un Pez Payaso! (Look, a Clown Fish!) 2017. (Bumba Books (tm) en Español — Veo Animales Marinos (I See Ocean Animals) Ser.). (SPA., Illus.). 24p. (J). (gr. -1-1). 25.32 (978-1-5124-2864-3(7)) Lerner Publishing Group.

—¡Mira, una Raya! (Look, a Ray!) 2017. (Bumba Books (tm) en Español — Veo Animales Marinos (I See Ocean Animals) Ser.). (SPA., Illus.). 24p. (J). (gr. -1-1). 25.32 (978-1-5124-2867-4(1)) Lerner Publishing Group.

Keppeler, Jill. Leafy Sea Dragons. 2017. (Freaky Fish Ser.). 24p. (J). (gr. 2-3). pap. 48.90 **(978-1-5382-0248-7(4))** Stevens, Gareth Publishing LLLP.

Kids: Fish & Fishing. 2003. (J). 1.00 (978-1-888631-30-2(9)) Project WET Foundation.

Klepeis, Alicia. The Pufferfish. 2017. (J). **(978-1-5026-2582-3(2))** Cavendish Square Publishing.

Kralovansky, Susan. Whale or Fish?, 1 vol. 2014. (This or That? Ser.). (ENG.). 24p. (J). (gr. 5-10). lib. bdg. 25.65 (978-1-62403-290-5(7), Super SandCastle) ABDO Publishing Co.

Kurlansky, Mark. The Cod's Tale. Schindler, S. D., illus. 2014. (ENG.). 48p. (J). (gr. 2-5). 8.99 (978-0-14-751277-2(8), Puffin Books) Penguin Young Readers Group.

—World Without Fish. Stockton, Frank, illus. 2014. (ENG.). 208p. (J). (gr. 5). pap. 14.95 (978-0-7611-8500-0(3)) Workman Publishing Co., Inc.

Larson, Jennifer S. Guppies. 2008. (J). lib. bdg. 25.26 (978-0-8225-7902-1(2), Lerner Pubns.) Lerner Publishing Group.

Laughlin, Kara L. Clownfish. 2017. (In the Deep Blue Sea Ser.). (ENG.). 24p. (J). (gr. k-3). lib. bdg. 27.07 (978-1-5038-1684-8(2), 211518) Child's World, Inc., The.

Lawrence, Ellen. Arapaima. 2017. (Apex Predators of the Amazon Rain Forest Ser.). (ENG., Illus.). 24p. (J). (gr. -1-3). 17.95 **(978-1-68402-033-1(6))** Bearport Publishing Co., Inc.

Leaf, Christina. Anglerfish. 2014. (Extremely Weird Animals Ser.). (ENG., Illus.). 24p. (J). (gr. 3-8). lib. bdg. 25.95 (978-1-62617-072-8(X), Pilot Bks.) Bellwether Media.

Lechner, Judith. Our New Fish Tank: Learning to Estimate & Round Numbers to the Nearest Ones, Tens, & Hundreds Places. 2009. (Math for the REAL World Ser.). 16p. (gr. 2-3). pap. 7.05 (978-0-8239-8881-5(3), Rosen Classroom) Rosen Publishing Group, Inc., The.

Let's Make a Fish with Everyday Materials. 2006. (Let's Do Arts & Crafts Ser.). (Illus.). 24p. (J). (gr. -1-3). lib. bdg. 22.60 (978-1-4042-3062-0(9)) Rosen Publishing Group, Inc., The.

Levesque, Haude. Fish Tricks: The Wild & Wacky World of Fish. 2016. (ENG., Illus.). 80p. (J). (gr. 3-7). 14.95 (978-1-63322-114-7(8), Moondance) Quarto Publishing Group USA.

Levine, Michelle. Fish. 2015. (Illus.). 32p. (J). lib. bdg. 28.50 (978-1-60753-473-0(8)) Amicus Publishing.

Lewis, Clare. Fish Body Parts. 2015. (Animal Body Parts Ser.). (ENG., Illus.). 24p. (gr. k-2). 23.32 (978-1-4846-2556-9(0)) Heinemann-Raintree.

Lindeen, Carol K. Clown Fish. 2016. (Under the Sea Ser.). (ENG.). 24p. (gr. k-1). pap. 7.29 (978-1-5157-5969-0(5), Pebble Plus) Capstone Press of Coughlan Cos.

Litton, Jonathan. Big Fish Little Fish. Galloway, Fhiona, illus. 2016. (My Little World Ser.). (ENG.). 16p. (J). (gr. -1-k). bds. 7.99 (978-1-58925-215-8(2)) Tiger Tales.

Lugtu, Carol J. Clown Fish [Scholastic]. 2011. (Under the Sea Ser.). 24p. pap. 0.50 (978-1-4296-6303-8(0), Pebble Plus) Capstone Press of Coughlan Cos.

Lumpy, Alex. Itty Bitty Guppies, Vol. 1. 2014. (Itty Bitty Animals Ser.). (ENG.). 24p. (J). (gr. k-k). 22.60 (978-1-4339-9882-9(3)) Stevens, Gareth Publishing LLLP.

Lundblad, Kristina & Kalman, Bobbie. Animales llamados Peces. 2006. (?Qui Tipo de Animal Es? Ser.). (SPA., Illus.). 32p. (J). (gr. 3-7). pap. (978-0-7787-8869-0(5)); lib. bdg. (978-0-7787-8833-1(4)) Crabtree Publishing Co.

—Animals Called Fish. 2005. (What Kind of Animal Is It? Ser.). (ENG., Illus.). 32p. (J). lib. bdg. (978-0-7787-2161-1(2)); pap. (978-0-7787-2219-9(8)) Crabtree Publishing Co.

Lunis, Natalie. Electric Animals. 2011. (Animals with Super Powers Ser.). 24p. (YA). (gr. 2-5). lib. bdg. 22.61 (978-1-61772-121-2(2)) Bearport Publishing Co., Inc.

Lynette, Rachel. Deep-Sea Anglerfish & Other Fearsome Fish, 1 vol. 2011. (Creatures of the Deep Ser.). (ENG., Illus.). 32p. (gr. 3-5). pap. 8.95 (978-1-4109-4202-9(3), NA-r) Heinemann-Raintree.

—Piranhas. 2013. (Monsters of the Animal Kingdom Ser.). (ENG., Illus.). 24p. (J). (gr. k-5). pap. 8.25 (978-1-4488-9723-0(8)); lib. bdg. 22.60 (978-1-4488-9634-9(7)) Rosen Publishing Group, Inc., The. (PowerKids Pr.).

MacCallum, Jess. Swimming with the Fishes. 5th rev. ed. 2004. per. 5.95 (978-0-9749673-0-1(0)) In Ardua Tendit Pr.

Mannion, Mary. The Boy & the Fish. Fitzgerald, Brian, illus. 2010. 52p. pap. (978-1-907276-62-0(9)) Lapwing Pubns.

Mara, Wil. From Sharks to... Swimsuits. 2012. (21st Century Skills Innovation Library: Innovations from Nature Ser.). (ENG.). 32p. (gr. 4-8). 28.50 (978-1-61080-499-8(6), 202109); pap. 14.21 (978-1-61080-673-2(5), 202283) Cherry Lake Publishing.

Markovics, Joyce L. Pufferfish. 2016. (Weird but Cute Ser.). (ENG., Illus.). 24p. (J). (gr. -1-3). lib. bdg. 17.95 (978-1-62724-850-1(1)) Bearport Publishing Co., Inc.

Martin, Bobi. What Are Fish? 2016. (Let's Find Out! Marine Life Ser.). 00032p. (J). (gr. 2-3). 24.45 (978-1-5081-0383-7(6), Britannica Educational Publishing) Rosen Publishing Group, Inc., The.

—What Are Fish? 2016. (J). lib. bdg. (978-1-5081-0458-2(1)) Windmill Bks.

Martin, Isabel. Fish: A Question & Answer Book, 1 vol. 2014. (Animal Kingdom Questions & Answers Ser.). (ENG., Illus.). 24p. (gr. k-1). pap. 6.95 (978-1-4914-0631-1(3), Pebble Plus) Capstone Press of Coughlan Cos.

Martineau, Susan & James, Hel. Meat, Fish, & Eggs. 2012. (Healthy Eating Ser.). (Illus.). 32p. (gr. 2-6). pap. 8.95 (978-1-59920-244-0(1)) Black Rabbit Bks.

Martinneau, Susan & James, Hel. Meat Fish & Eggs. 2006. (Healthy Eating Ser.). (Illus.). 32p. (YA). (gr. 1-4). lib. bdg. 28.50 (978-1-58340-893-3(2), 1262657) Black Rabbit Bks.

Maydak, Michael S., illus. Wild Stickers - Sharks & Rays. 2003. 4p. (J). 2.50 (978-0-941042-34-5(0)) Dog-Eared Pubns.

Mazurkiewicz, Jessica & Coloring Books Staff. Creatures of the Deep Stained Glass Coloring Book. 2012. (Dover Stained Glass Coloring Book Ser.). (ENG., Illus.). 32p. (J). (gr. 3-5). pap. 6.99 (978-0-486-48523-2(4)) Dover Pubns., Inc.

McCall, Gerrie. Weird & Wonderful Fish. 2006. (Nature's Monsters: Water Creatures Ser.). (Illus.). 32p. (gr. 2-6). lib. bdg. 26.00 (978-0-8368-6179-2(5), Gareth Stevens Learning Library) Stevens, Gareth Publishing LLLP.

McCloskey, Kevin. Something's Fishy: TOON Level 1. 2017. (Giggle & Learn Ser.). (ENG., Illus.). 40p. (J). (gr. -1-3). 12.95 (978-1-943145-15-7(6)) TOON Books / RAW Junior, LLC.

McDowell, Pamela. Clownfish. 2011. (J). (gr. 2-4). pap. 12.95 (978-1-61690-696-2(0), AV2 by Weigl); (Illus.). 24p. (gr. 3-6). 27.13 (978-1-61690-692-4(8)) Weigl Pubs., Inc.

—Sea Dragons. 2011. (Ocean Life Ser.). (Illus.). 24p. (J). (gr. 3-6). 27.13 (978-1-61690-831-7(9)) Weigl Pubs., Inc.

McFee, Shane. Deadly Fish. 2009. (Poison! Ser.). 24p. (gr. 2-3). 42.50 (978-1-60851-321-5(1), PowerKids Pr.) Rosen Publishing Group, Inc., The.

—Stingrays. 2009. (Poison! Ser.). 24p. (gr. 2-3). 42.50 (978-1-60851-326-0(2), PowerKids Pr.) Rosen Publishing Group, Inc., The.

Meachen Rau, Dana. Top 10 Fish for Kids. 2008. (Top Pets for Kids with American Humane Ser.). (Illus.). 48p. (J). (gr. 2-5). lib. bdg. 25.27 (978-0-7660-3073-2(3)) Enslow Pubs., Inc.

Meinking, Mary. Dolphin vs. Fish, 1 vol. 2011. (Predator vs. Prey Ser.). (ENG., Illus.). 32p. (gr. 1-2). 29.99 (978-1-4109-3940-1(5)); pap. 8.29 (978-1-4109-3949-4(9)) Heinemann-Raintree. (Read Me!).

Meister, Cari. Clownfish. 2013. 24p. (J). lib. bdg. (978-1-62031-030-4(9)) Jump! Inc.

—Eels. 2014. (Illus.). 24p. (J). lib. bdg. 25.65 (978-1-62031-097-7(X), Bullfrog Bks.) Jump! Inc.

—Fish. 2014. (Illus.). 24p. (J). lib. bdg. 25.65 (978-1-62031-123-3(2), Bullfrog Bks.) Jump! Inc.

—Parrotfish. 2014. (Illus.). 24p. (J). lib. bdg. 25.65 (978-1-62031-100-4(3), Bullfrog Bks.) Jump! Inc.

—Stingrays. 2014. (Illus.). 24p. (J). lib. bdg. 25.65 (978-1-62031-102-8(X), Bullfrog Bks.) Jump! Inc.

Meredith, Susan Markowitz. Hiding in the Sea. 2011. (Early Connections Ser.). (J). (978-1-61672-581-5(8)) Benchmark Education Co.

Miller, Tori. Eels. 2009. (Freaky Fish Ser.). 24p. (gr. 2-5). (Illus.). (J). pap. 8.25 (978-1-4358-3170-4(5), 1291798); 42.50 (978-1-61512-636-1(8)) Rosen Publishing Group, Inc., The. (PowerKids Pr.).

—Manta Rays. 2009. (Freaky Fish Ser.). (Illus.). 24p. (J). (gr. 2-5). pap. 8.25 (978-1-4358-3169-8(1), 1291796, PowerKids Pr.); 24p. (gr. 2-3). 42.50 (978-1-61512-637-8(6), PowerKids Pr.); (J). (gr. 1-4). lib. bdg. 22.60 (978-1-4358-2753-0(8)) Rosen Publishing Group, Inc., The.

—Pufferfish. 2009. (Freaky Fish Ser.). 24p. (ENG., Illus.). (J). (gr. 2-5). pap. 8.25 (978-1-4358-3171-1(3), 1291799, PowerKids Pr.); (gr. 2-3). 42.50 (978-1-61512-643-9(0), PowerKids Pr.); (J). (gr. 1-4). lib. bdg. 22.60 (978-1-4358-2818-6(6)) Rosen Publishing Group, Inc., The.

—Scorpion Fish. 2009. (Freaky Fish Ser.). (ENG., Illus.). 24p. (J). (gr. 2-5). pap. 8.25 (978-1-4358-3172-8(1), 1291801, PowerKids Pr.); 24p. (gr. 2-3). 42.50 (978-1-61512-646-0(5), PowerKids Pr.); (J). (gr. 1-4). lib. bdg. 22.60 (978-1-4358-2755-4(4)) Rosen Publishing Group, Inc., The.

Montgomery, Kelly & Creative Haven Staff. Sea Life Designs Coloring Book. 2012. (Adult Coloring Ser.). (ENG., Illus.). 64p. (gr. 3). pap. 5.99 (978-0-486-49088-5(2)) Dover Pubns., Inc.

Morey, Allan. Freshwater Fishing. 2017. (Great Outdoors Ser.). (ENG., Illus.). 32p. (J). (gr. 1-3). pap. 9.99 (978-1-68152-078-0(8)) Amicus.

—Freshwater Fishing. 2016. (Great Outdoors Ser.). (ENG., Illus.). 32p. (J). (gr. 1-4). 20.95 (978-1-60753-799-1(0)) Amicus Publishing.

Morgan, Sally. Encyclopedia of Ocean Life. 2012. (Illus.). 224p. (J). (978-1-4351-4351-7(5)) Barnes & Noble, Inc.

—Fish. 2007. (QEB Down on the Farm Ser.). (Illus.). 24p. (J). (gr. -1-3). lib. bdg. 15.95 (978-1-59566-388-7(6)) QEB Publishing Inc.

Murphy, Julie. Anglerfish. 2014. (21st Century Skills Library: Exploring Our Oceans Ser.). (ENG.). 32p. (J). (gr. 3-6). 28.50 (978-1-63188-024-7(1), 205503) Cherry Lake Publishing.

Murray, Julie. Fish, 1 vol. 2015. (ENG., Illus.). 24p. (J). 27.07 (978-1-62970-901-7(8), 1391171) ABDO Publishing Co.

Nagelhout, Ryan. Bloodsucking Lampreys. 2016. (Real-Life Vampires Ser.). (ENG., Illus.). 24p. (J). (gr. 2-3). pap. 8.15 (978-1-4824-3947-2(6)) Stevens, Gareth Publishing LLLP.

—Clownfish / Peces Payaso. 2013. (Underwater World / el Mundo Submarino Ser.). (ENG & SPA., Illus.). 24p. (gr. k-2). 22.60 (978-1-4339-8778-6(3)) Stevens, Gareth Publishing LLLP.

National Geographic Kids & Hogan, Zeb. Monster Fish: True Stories of Adventures with Animals. 2017. (NGK Chapters Ser.). (ENG., Illus.). 112p. (J). (gr. 2-5). pap. 5.99 (978-1-4263-2703-2(X), National Geographic Children's Bks.) National Geographic Society.

Neuman, Susan B. Swim Fish! Explore the Coral Reef. 2014. (Readers Ser.). (ENG.). 24p. (J). (-k). pap. 3.99 (978-1-4263-1510-7(4), National Geographic Children's Bks.) National Geographic Society.

Niven, Felicia Lowenstein. Learning to Care for Fish. 2010. (Beginning Pet Care with American Humane Ser.). 48p. (J). 25.27 (978-0-7660-3193-7(4), Enslow Elementary) Enslow Pubs., Inc.

Niver, Heather Moore. 20 Fun Facts about Anglerfish. 2012. (Fun Fact File: Fierce Fish! Ser.). (Illus.). 32p. (J). (gr. 2-5). pap. 10.50 (978-1-4339-6972-0(6)); lib. bdg. 25.25 (978-1-4339-6971-3(8)) Stevens, Gareth Publishing LLLP.

—20 Fun Facts about Barracudas. 2012. (Fun Fact File: Fierce Fish! Ser.). (Illus.). 32p. (J). (gr. 2-5). pap. 10.50 (978-1-4339-6976-8(9)); lib. bdg. 25.25 (978-1-4339-6975-1(0)) Stevens, Gareth Publishing LLLP.

—20 Fun Facts about Lionfish. 2012. (Fun Fact File: Fierce Fish! Ser.). (Illus.). 32p. (J). (gr. 2-5). pap. 10.50 (978-1-4339-6980-5(7)); lib. bdg. 25.25 (978-1-4339-6979-9(3)) Stevens, Gareth Publishing LLLP.

—20 Fun Facts about Piranhas. 2012. (Fun Fact File: Fierce Fish! Ser.). (Illus.). 32p. (J). (gr. 2-5). 25.25 (978-1-4339-6987-4(4)); pap. 10.50 (978-1-4339-6988-1(2)) Stevens, Gareth Publishing LLLP. (Gareth Stevens Learning Library).

—20 Fun Facts about Stingrays. 2012. (Fun Fact File: Fierce Fish! Ser.). (Illus.). 32p. (J). (gr. 2-5). 25.25 (978-1-4339-6991-1(2)); pap. 10.50 (978-1-4339-6992-8(0)) Stevens, Gareth Publishing LLLP. (Gareth Stevens Learning Library).

Nugent, Samantha. Meat & Fish. 2015. (Let's Learn about Food Ser.). (ENG.). (J). lib. bdg. 27.13 (978-1-4896-3999-8(3), AV2 by Weigl) Weigl Pubs., Inc.

O'Hare, Ted. Fish. 2005. (What Is an Animal Ser.). (Illus.). 24p. (J). (gr. 1-4). lib. bdg. 22.79 (978-1-59515-417-0(5)) Rourke Educational Media.

Orr, Tamra. Piranhas. 2003. (Animal Attacks Ser.). (Illus.). 48p. (J). 23.70 (978-0-7377-1888-1(9), Greenhaven Pr., Inc.) Cengage Gale.

Owen, Ruth. Angler Fish, 1 vol., 1. 2014. (Real Life Sea Monsters Ser.). (ENG.). 32p. (J). (gr. k-5). 26.25 (978-1-4777-6257-8(4), PowerKids Pr.) Rosen Publishing Group, Inc., The.

—Moray Eels, 1 vol., 1. 2014. (Real Life Sea Monsters Ser.). (ENG.). 32p. (J). (gr. k-5). 26.25 (978-1-4777-6253-0(1), PowerKids Pr.) Rosen Publishing Group, Inc., The.

—Stingrays, 1 vol., 1. 2014. (Real Life Sea Monsters Ser.). (ENG.). 32p. (J). (gr. k-5). 26.25 (978-1-4777-6265-3(5), PowerKids Pr.) Rosen Publishing Group, Inc., The.

Owens, L. L. The Life Cycle of a Clown Fish. 2011. (Life Cycles Ser.). (ENG., Illus.). 32p. (J). (gr. k-3). lib. bdg. 29.93 (978-1-60973-145-8(X), 201170) Child's World, Inc., The.

Patterson, Caroline. Fish Do WHAT in the Water? The Secret Lives of Marine Animals. Rath, Robert, illus. 2012. 48p. (J). 14.95 (978-1-56037-519-7(1)) Farcountry Pr.

Pettiford, Rebecca. Puffer Fish. 2017. (Ocean Life up Close Ser.). (ENG., Illus.). 24p. (J). (gr. k-3). lib. bdg. 25.95 (978-1-62617-572-3(1), Blastoff! Readers) Bellwether Media.

—Stingrays. 2016. (Ocean Life up Close Ser.). (ENG., Illus.). 24p. (J). (gr. k-3). 25.95 (978-1-62617-423-8(7), Blastoff! Readers) Bellwether Media.

Pfeffer, Wendy. What's It Like to Be a Fish? Keller, Holly, illus. 2015. (Let's-Read-And-Find-Out Science 1 Ser.). (ENG.). 32p. (J). (gr. -1-3). pap. 6.99 (978-0-06-238199-6(7)) HarperCollins Pubs.

Piehl, Janet. Pinching Crayfish. 2008. pap. 40.95 (978-0-8225-9319-5(X)) 2007. (Illus.). 32p. (J). lib. bdg. 22.60 (978-0-8225-5931-3(5), Lerner Pubns.) 2007. (Illus.). 32p. (J). (gr. -1-3). per. 6.95 (978-0-8225-6706-6(7), First Avenue Editions) Lerner Publishing Group.

Polydoros, Lori. Piranhas: On the Hunt. 2016. (Killer Animals Ser.). (ENG.). 32p. (gr. 1-2). pap. 7.95 (978-1-5157-6243-0(2), Blazers) Capstone Press of Coughlan Cos.

Powerkids Readers: Fun Fish. 2013. (PowerKids Readers: Fun Fish Ser.). 24p. (J). (gr. k-2). 135.60 (978-1-4777-1141-5(4)); pap. 49.50 (978-1-4777-2676-1(4)); pap. 297.00 (978-1-4777-2677-8(2)) Rosen Publishing Group, Inc., The. (PowerKids Pr.).

Powerkids Readers: Fun Fish / Peces Divertidos. 2013. (PowerKids Readers: Fun Fish / Peces Divertidos Ser.). (ENG & SPA.). 24p. (J). (gr. k-2). 135.60 (978-1-4777-1238-2(0), PowerKids Pr.) Rosen Publishing Group, Inc., The.

Pratt Serafini, Kristin Joy, illus. A Swim Through the Sea, 1 vol. 2006. (Simply Nature Bks.). (ENG.). 26p. (J). (gr. -1). bds. 7.95 (978-1-58469-080-1(1)) Dawn Pubns.

Rajczak Nelson, Kristen. Fangtooth Fish. 2017. (Freaky Fish Ser.). 24p. (J). (gr. 2-3). pap. 48.90 **(978-1-5382-0246-3(8))** Stevens, Gareth Publishing LLLP.

Rake, Jody S. Sea Dragons. 2017. (Real-Life Dragons Ser.). (ENG., Illus.). 32p. (gr. 3-4). lib. bdg. 27.99 (978-1-5157-5072-7(8), Edge Bks.) Capstone Press of Coughlan Cos.

Rake, Jody Sullivan. Mudskippers & Other Extreme Fish Adaptations, 1 vol. 2014. (Extreme Adaptations Ser.). (ENG.). 32p. (gr. 3-4). lib. bdg. 27.32 (978-1-4914-0165-1(6)) Capstone Press of Coughlan Cos.

Rand, Casey. Giant Morays & Other Extraordinary Eels, 1 vol. 2011. (Creatures of the Deep Ser.). (ENG., Illus.). 32p. (gr. 3-5). pap. 8.95 (978-1-4109-4204-3(X)); 30.65 (978-1-4109-4197-8(3)) Heinemann-Raintree. (NA-r).

Randolph, Joanne. Fish. (Classroom Pets Ser.). 24p. 2009. (gr. 2-3). 42.50 (978-1-61511-856-4(X)) 2007. (Illus.). (J). (gr. 3-7). lib. bdg. 22.60 (978-1-4042-3681-3(3), 1266091) Rosen Publishing Group, Inc., The. (PowerKids Pr.).

Rau, Dana Meachen. Kids Top 10 Pet Fish. 2015. (American Humane Association Top 10 Pets for Kids Ser.). 48p. (J). (gr. 3-4). 25.27 (978-0-7660-6640-3(1)) Enslow Pubs., Inc.

Raum, Elizabeth. Stingrays. 2015. (Poisonous Animals Ser.). (ENG., Illus.). 32p. (J). (gr. 2-4). 19.95 *(978-1-60753-789-2(3))* Amicus Publishing.
—Stonefish. 2015. (Poisonous Animals Ser.). (ENG., Illus.). 32p. (J). (gr. 2-4). 19.95 *(978-1-60753-790-8(7))* Amicus Publishing.
Reher, Matt. Are You a Fish? 2016. (1G Marine Life Ser.). (ENG., Illus.). 28p. (J). pap. 5.99 ***(978-1-63437-604-4(8))*** American Reading Co.
—Fish Eggs. 2016. (1G Marine Life Ser.). (ENG., Illus.). 28p. (J). pap. 5.99 ***(978-1-63437-672-3(2))*** American Reading Co.
—Fish Teeth. 2016. (1G Marine Life Ser.). (ENG., Illus.). 24p. (J). pap. 5.99 ***(978-1-63437-680-8(3))*** American Reading Co.
Reinhart, Robin. Fierce Freshwater Fish: Measure Lengths in Standard Units. 2014. (Math Masters: Measurement & Data Ser.). (Illus.). 24p. (J). (gr. 2-3). 23.60 *(978-1-4777-6404-6(6))*; (ENG., pap. 8.25 *(978-1-4777-4804-6(0))* Rosen Publishing Group, Inc., The. (Rosen Classroom).
Rice, Katie. ¡Capturas Peligrosas! Pescadores de Alta Mar. 2016. (TIME for Kids en Español - Level 5 Ser.). (SPA.). 64p. (gr. 5-5). lib. bdg. 31.99 *(978-1-5157-2944-0(3))* Time for Kids Inc AUS. Dist: Capstone Pub.
Richardson, Joy. Fish. 2005. (Variety of Life Ser.). (Illus.). 32p. (gr. 1-4). lib. bdg. 26.00 *(978-0-8368-4503-7(X))*, Gareth Stevens Learning Library) Stevens, Gareth Publishing LLLP.
Rodríguez, Ana María. Secret of the Suffocating Slime Trap... & More! 2008. (Animal Secrets Revealed! Ser.). (Illus.). 48p. (J). (gr. 5-9). lib. bdg. 25.27 *(978-0-7660-2954-5(9))* Enslow Pubs., Inc.
Rodríguez, Ana María. The Shocking Secret of the Electric Eel... & More! 2017. (Animal Secrets Revealed! Ser.). 48p. (J). (gr. 4-4). lib. bdg. 27.93 ***(978-0-7660-8726-2(3))*** Enslow Pubs., Inc.
Rosen, Michael J. Fresh Fish. 2017. (Illus.). 32p. (J). *(978-1-60818-771-3(3)*, Creative Education) Creative Co., The.
Rosen, Michael J. Reel Time: Fresh Fish. 2017. (Reel Time Ser.). (ENG., Illus.). 32p. (J). (gr. 2-5). pap. 9.99 ***(978-1-62832-379-5(5)**, Creative Paperbacks)* Creative Co., The.
Royston, Angela. Fish. (Illus.). 32p. (YA). (gr. 2-18). lib. bdg. 27.10 *(978-1-932333-35-0(5))* Chrysalis Education.
—Fish. 2015. (Animal Classifications Ser.). (ENG., Illus.). 32p. (gr. 1-3). 27.32 *(978-1-4846-0751-0(1)*, Heinemann First Library) Heinemann-Raintree.
—What Happens If We Overfish the Oceans? 2015. (Unstable Earth Ser.). (Illus.). 32p. (J). 31.35 *(978-1-62588-162-5(2))* Black Rabbit Bks.
Roza, Greg. Deadly Pufferfish. 2011. (Small but Deadly Ser.). 24p. (J). (gr. 2-5). pap. 8.15 *(978-1-4339-5748-2(5))*; lib. bdg. 22.60 *(978-1-4339-5746-8(9))* Stevens, Gareth Publishing LLLP. (Gareth Stevens Learning Library).
—Zap! The Electric Eel & Other Electric Animals. 2011. (Armed & Dangerous Ser.). (Illus.). 24p. (J). pap. 8.25 *(978-1-4488-2678-0(0)*, PowerKids Pr.); (YA). (gr. 1-4). 22.60 *(978-1-4488-2547-9(4))* Rosen Publishing Group, Inc., The.
Rudenko, Dennis. Look Out for the Pufferfish! 2015. (Surprisingly Scary! Ser.). (ENG., Illus.). 24p. (J). (gr. 2-3). pap. 8.25 *(978-1-4994-0881-2(1)*, PowerKids Pr.) Rosen Publishing Group, Inc., The.
Rudolph, Jessica. MIS Dientes Son Agudos y Afilados (Sawfish) 2016. (Pistas de Animales 2 Ser.). (SPA.). 24p. (J). (gr. -1-3). 17.95 *(978-1-944102-74-6(4))* Bearport Publishing Co., Inc.
—My Body Is Striped & Leafy (Leafy Sea Dragon) 2014. (Zoo Clues Ser.). 24p. (J). (gr. -1-3). lib. bdg. 23.93 *(978-1-62724-112-0(4))* Bearport Publishing Co., Inc.
—My Teeth Are Sharp & Pointy. 2016. (Zoo Clues 2 Ser.). (ENG.). 24p. (J). (gr. -1-3). lib. bdg. 17.95 *(978-1-944102-56-2(6))* Bearport Publishing Co., Inc.
Rupp, Kristina. You Are a Fish. 2015. (1-3Y Wild Animals Ser.). (ENG., Illus.). 24p. (J). pap. 5.99 *(978-1-63437-146-9(1))* American Reading Co.
Rustad, Martha E. Rays [Scholastic]. 2009. (Ocean Life Ser.). 24p. (gr. k-1). pap. 2.99 *(978-1-4296-3677-3(7)*, Pebble Bks.) Capstone Press of Coughlan Cos.
Rustad, Martha E. H. Clown Fish & Sea Anemones Work Together, 1 vol. (Animals Working Together Ser.). (ENG., 24p. (gr. k-1). 2011. Illus.). pap. 7.29 *(978-1-4296-6198-0(4))* 2011. pap. 41.70 *(978-1-4296-6367-0(7))* 2010. lib. bdg. 26.65 *(978-1-4296-5297-1(7))* Capstone Press of Coughlan Cos. (Pebble Plus).
—Parrotfish. 2007. (Oceans Alive Ser.). (ENG., Illus.). 24p. (J). (gr. k-3). lib. bdg. 25.95 *(978-1-60014-079-2(3))* Bellwether Media.
—A Saltwater Stumper: A Zoo Animal Mystery, 1 vol. 2010. (Zoo Animal Mysteries Ser.). (ENG.). 24p. (gr. k-1). lib. bdg. 26.65 *(978-1-4296-4496-9(6)*, Pebble Plus) Capstone Press of Coughlan Cos.
Sadorus, Lauri. Pacific Halibut Flat or Fiction?, 1. Soderlund, Birgit, illus. 2005. 24p. (J). per. *(978-0-9776931-0-8(4))* International Pacific Halibut Commission.
Salzmann, Mary Elizabeth. Flashy Fish, 1 vol. Craig, Diane, ed. 2007. (Perfect Pets Ser.). (ENG., Illus.). 24p. (J). (gr. k-3). lib. bdg. 24.21 *(978-1-59928-747-8(1)*, SandCastle) ABDO Publishing Co.
—What Has Scales?, 1 vol. 2007. (Creature Features Ser.). (ENG., Illus.). 24p. (gr. -1-3). 25.65 *(978-1-59928-870-3(2)*, Super SandCastle) ABDO Publishing Co.
Savage, Stephen. Focus on Fish. 2011. (Animal Watch Ser.). 32p. (YA). (gr. 3-6). lib. bdg. 26.60 *(978-1-4339-5984-4(4))* Stevens, Gareth Publishing LLLP.
Sayre, April Pulley. Trout, Trout, Trout! 2004. (American City Ser.). (ENG., Illus.). 32p. (J). (gr. k-3). 15.95 *(978-1-55971-889-9(7))* Cooper Square Publishing Llc.
—Trout, Trout, Trout: (A Fish Chant) Park, Trip, illus. 2007. (American City Ser.). (ENG.). 32p. (J). (gr. k-3). pap. 8.95 *(978-1-55971-979-7(6))* Cooper Square Publishing Llc.
Schleichert, Elizabeth. Peces. 2008. (Descubre la Naturaleza Ser.). (SPA., Illus.). 60p. (J). (gr. 4-7). 12.95 *(978-1-58087-129-7(1))* National Geographic Society.
Schuetz, Kari. Caring for Your Fish. 2010. (Pet Care Library). (ENG., Illus.). 24p. (J). (gr. 2-5). lib. bdg. 25.95 *(978-1-60014-467-7(5)*, Blastoff! Readers) Bellwether Media.
—Clownfish. (Clownfish Ser.). 24p. (J). (gr. k-3). 2017. pap. 6.99 ***(978-1-61891-280-0(1))*** 2016. (ENG., Illus.). 25.95 *(978-1-62617-414-6(8))* Bellwether Media. (Blastoff! Readers).
Schuetz, Kari. Fish. 2012. (Animal Classes Ser.). (ENG., Illus.). 24p. (J). (gr. k-3). lib. bdg. 25.95 *(978-1-60014-773-9(9)*, Blastoff! Readers) Bellwether Media.
Schuh, Mari. Parrotfish. 2017. (Ocean Life up Close Ser.). (ENG., Illus.). 24p. (J). (gr. k-3). lib. bdg. 25.95 *(978-1-62617-571-6(3)*, Blastoff! Readers) Bellwether Media.
—Pufferfish. 2015. (Illus.). 24p. (J). lib. bdg. *(978-1-62031-190-5(9)*, Bullfrog Bks.) Jump! Inc.
—The World's Biggest Fish. 2015. (Illus.). 24p. (J). lib. bdg. 25.65 *(978-1-62031-207-0(7))* Jump! Inc.
Schuh, Mari C. Clown Fish. 2015. (Sea Life Ser.). (ENG., Illus.). 24p. (gr. k-1). lib. bdg. 26.65 *(978-1-4914-6042-9(3))* Capstone Press of Coughlan Cos.
—Regal Tangs. 2015. (Sea Life Ser.). (ENG., Illus.). 24p. (gr. k-1). lib. bdg. 26.65 *(978-1-4914-6041-2(5))* Capstone Press of Coughlan Cos.
Schulte, Mary. Piranhas & Other Fish. 2005. (Scholastic News Nonfiction Readers Ser.). (Illus.). 24p. (J). pap. *(978-0-516-24791-5(3))* Children's Pr., Ltd.
Schwartz, David M. Fighting Fish. Kuhn, Dwight, photos by. (Life Cycles Ser.). (Illus.). 16p. (J). (gr. 1-3). pap. 2.99 *(978-1-57471-560-6(7)*, 3070) Creative Teaching Pr., Inc.
Sexton, Colleen. Angelfish. 2009. (Oceans Alive Ser.). (ENG., Illus.). 24p. (J). (gr. k-3). lib. bdg. 25.95 *(978-1-60014-248-2(6))* Bellwether Media.
—Angelfish. 2009. (Blastoff! Readers Ser.). (ENG., Illus.). 24p. (J). (gr. k-3). 20.00 *(978-0-531-21711-5(6)*, Children's Pr.) Scholastic Library Publishing.
—Barracudas. 2009. (Oceans Alive Ser.). (ENG., Illus.). 24p. (J). (gr. k-3). lib. bdg. 25.95 *(978-1-60014-270-3(2))* Bellwether Media.
—Frogfish. 2009. (Oceans Alive Ser.). (ENG., Illus.). 24p. (J). (gr. k-3). lib. bdg. 25.95 *(978-1-60014-249-9(4))* Bellwether Media.
—Frogfish. 2009. (Blastoff! Readers Ser.). (ENG., Illus.). 24p. (J). (gr. k-3). 20.00 *(978-0-531-21712-2(4)*, Children's Pr.) Scholastic Library Publishing.
—Lionfish. 2009. (Blastoff! Readers Ser.). (ENG., Illus.). 24p. (J). (gr. k-3). 20.00 *(978-0-531-21713-9(2)*, Children's Pr.) Scholastic Library Publishing.
—Manta Rays. 2009. (Oceans Alive Ser.). (ENG., Illus.). 24p. (J). (gr. k-3). lib. bdg. 25.95 *(978-1-60014-267-3(2))* Bellwether Media.
—Puffer Fish. 2008. (Oceans Alive Ser.). (ENG., Illus.). 24p. (J). (gr. k-3). lib. bdg. 25.95 *(978-1-60014-173-7(0))* Bellwether Media.
—Swordfish. 2009. (Oceans Alive Ser.). (ENG., Illus.). 24p. (J). (gr. k-3). lib. bdg. 25.95 *(978-1-60014-253-6(2))* Bellwether Media.
—Swordfish. 2009. (Blastoff! Readers Ser.). (ENG., Illus.). 24p. (J). (gr. k-3). 20.00 *(978-0-531-21715-3(9)*, Children's Pr.) Scholastic Library Publishing.
Shaw, Daniel. Southwest Aquatic Habitats: On the Trail of Fish in a Desert. 2013. (Barbara Guth Worlds of Wonder Science Series for Young Readers Ser.). (ENG., Illus.). 112p. (J). 34.95 *(978-0-8263-5309-2(6))* Univ. of New Mexico Pr.
Shaw-Russell, Susan. Under the Sea Party Sticker Activity Book. 2011. (Dover Little Activity Books Stickers Ser.). (ENG., Illus.). 4p. (J). (gr. k-3). 1.99 *(978-0-486-47535-6(2))* Dover Pubns., Inc.
Shea, Therese. Pufferfish. 2017. (Freaky Fish Ser.). 24p. (J). (gr. 2-3). pap. 48.90 ***(978-1-5382-0249-4(2))*** Stevens, Gareth Publishing LLLP.
Shetterly, Susan Hand. Swimming Home. Raye, Rebekah, illus. 2014. (Tilbury House Nature Book Ser.: 0). (ENG.). 32p. (gr. 1-6). 16.95 *(978-0-88448-354-0(1)*, 884354) Tilbury Hse. Pubs.
Shone, Rob. Ichthyosaurus: The Fish Lizard. 2012. (Illus.). 32p. (J). 73.80 *(978-1-4488-5251-2(X))*; pap. 12.30 *(978-1-4488-5250-5(1))*; lib. bdg. 26.50 *(978-1-4488-5206-2(4))* Rosen Publishing Group, Inc., The. (PowerKids Pr.).
Shusterman, Danielle. I Am a Pufferfish. 2016. (1-3Y Marine Life Ser.). (ENG., Illus.). 16p. (J). pap. 5.99 ***(978-1-63437-571-9(8))*** American Reading Co.
Sill, Cathryn. About Fish: A Guide for Children, 1 vol. Sill, John, illus. rev. ed. 2017. (About... Ser.). (ENG.). 48p. (J). (gr. -1-2). pap. 7.95 ***(978-1-56145-988-9(7))*** Peachtree Pubs.
Sill, Cathryn & De la Torre, Cristina. About Fish: A Guide for Children = Sobre los Peces: Una Guia para Niños, 1 vol. Sill, Cathryn P., illus. 2017. (About... Ser.). (SPA & ENG.). 48p. (J). (gr. -1-2). pap. 8.95 ***(978-1-56145-989-6(5))*** Peachtree Pubs.
Sill, Cathryn & Sill, William. About Fish: A Guide for Children, 1 vol. Sill, John, illus. rev. ed. 2017. (About... Ser.). (ENG.). 48p. (J). (gr. -1-2). 16.95 ***(978-1-56145-987-2(9))*** Peachtree Pubs.
Silverman, Buffy. Do You Know about Fish? 2009. (Lightning Bolt Bks.). 32p. (gr. k-2). (J). 25.26 *(978-0-8225-7540-5(X)*, Lerner Pubns.); (ENG., Illus.). pap. 7.95 *(978-1-58013-858-1(6))* Lerner Publishing Group.
—¿Sabes Algo Sobre Peces? (Do You Know about Fish?) 2012. (Libros Rayo — Conoce Los Grupos de Animales (Lightning Bolt Books — Meet the Animal Groups) Ser.). (Illus.). 32p. (gr. k-2). (ENG & SPA.). pap. 7.95 *(978-0-7613-9369-6(2))*; (SPA., lib. bdg. 26.60 *(978-0-7613-9194-4(0))* Lerner Publishing Group. (Ediciones Lerner).
Silverstein, Alvin, et al. Fabulous Fish. 2003. (What a Pet! Ser.). (ENG., Illus.). 48p. (gr. 3-6). lib. bdg. 23.93 *(978-0-7613-2514-7(X)*, Millbrook Pr.) Lerner Publishing Group.
Sisk, Maeve T. Fractions with Fish. 2013. (Animal Math Ser.). 24p. (J). (gr. 1-3). 22.60 *(978-1-4339-9308-4(2))*; pap. 8.15 *(978-1-4339-9309-1(0))* Stevens, Gareth Publishing LLLP.
Sjonger, Rebecca. Les Raies. 2009. (Petit Monde Vivant Ser.). (FRE., Illus.). 32p. (J). pap. 9.95 *(978-2-89579-227-7(5))* Bayard Canada Livres CAN. Dist: Crabtree Publishing Co.
Sjonger, Rebecca & Kalman, Bobbie. Skates & Rays. 2005. (Living Ocean Ser.). (ENG., Illus.). 32p. (J). (gr. 3-4). lib. bdg. *(978-0-7787-1303-6(2))* Crabtree Publishing Co.
Smalley, Carol. A Project Guide to Fishes & Amphibians. 2010. (Life Science Projects for Kids Ser.). (Illus.). 48p. (J). (gr. 4-8). lib. bdg. 29.95 *(978-1-58415-873-8(5))* Mitchell Lane Pubs., Inc.
Snedden, Robert. Fish. (Living Things Ser.). (Illus.). 32p. 2009. (J). (gr. -1-3). pap. 7.95 *(978-1-59920-194-8(1))* 2007. (YA). (gr. 3-6). lib. bdg. 28.50 *(978-1-59920-077-4(5))* Black Rabbit Bks.
Somervill, Barbara. Asian Carp. 2008. (21st Century Skills Library: Animal Invaders Ser.). (ENG.). 32p. (gr. 4-8). lib. bdg. 28.50 *(978-1-60279-118-3(X)*, 200093) Cherry Lake Publishing.
—Sea Lamprey. 2008. (21st Century Skills Library: Animal Invaders Ser.). (ENG., Illus.). 32p. (gr. 4-8). lib. bdg. 28.50 *(978-1-60279-240-1(2)*, 200116) Cherry Lake Publishing.
Spunter, Bill. Fish from Head to Tail. 2016. (Animals from Head to Tail Ser.). 24p. (J). (gr. k-k). lib. bdg. 22.60 *(978-1-4824-4538-1(7))* Stevens, Gareth Publishing LLLP.
Stefoff, Rebecca. The Fish Classes. 2008. (Family Trees Ser.). (Illus.). 96p. (gr. 6-7). lib. bdg. 34.21 *(978-0-7614-2695-0(7)*, Benchmark Bks.) Marshall Cavendish Corp.
Stevens, Kathryn. Fish. 2015. (Pet Care Ser.). (ENG.). 24p. (J). (gr. -1-2). 25.64 *(978-1-63143-732-8(1)*, 208545) Child's World, Inc., The.
Stewart, Melissa. A Place for Fish, 1 vol. Bond, Higgins, illus. 2011. (ENG.). 32p. (J). (gr. 1-5). 16.95 *(978-1-56145-562-1(8))* Peachtree Pubs.
Stille, Darlene R. The Life Cycle of Fish, 1 vol. 2011. (Life Cycles Ser.). (ENG.). 48p. (gr. 3-5). pap. 9.95 *(978-1-4329-4987-7(X)*, Heinemann InfoSearch) Heinemann-Raintree.
Stockdale, Susan. Fabulous Fishes, 1 vol. Stockdale, Susan, illus. 2008. (ENG., Illus.). 32p. (J). (gr. k-1). 15.95 *(978-1-56145-429-7(X))* Peachtree Pubs.
Stoltman, Joan. My First Fish. 2017. (Let's Get a Pet! Ser.). 24p. (J). (gr. 1-2). pap. 8.15 ***(978-1-4824-6453-5(5))*** Stevens, Gareth Publishing LLLP.
Storad, Conrad J. Piranhas. 2009. (Early Bird Nature Bks.). (ENG.). 48p. (gr. 2-5). 26.60 *(978-0-8225-9433-8(1)*, Lerner Pubns.) Lerner Publishing Group.
Superstar Fish. 2014. (Nature's Got Talent Ser.). (Illus.). 32p. (J). (gr. k-3). lib. bdg. 26.25 *(978-1-4777-7068-9(2)*, PowerKids Pr.) Rosen Publishing Group, Inc., The.
The Survival of Fish, 6 vols. (Sunshinetm Science Ser.). 24p. (gr. 1-2). 37.50 *(978-0-7802-1423-1(4))*; 41.95 *(978-0-7802-1422-4(6))* Wright Group/McGraw-Hill.
Swinney, Geoff. Fish Facts, 1 vol. Mason, Janeen, illus. 2011. (ENG.). 48p. (J). (gr. k-3). 17.99 *(978-1-58980-908-6(4))* Pelican Publishing Co., Inc.
Taylor-Butler, Christine. Fish. 2013. (True Book(tm), a — Animal Kingdom Ser.). (ENG.). 48p. (J). 31.00 *(978-0-531-21752-8(3))*; pap. 6.95 *(978-0-531-22337-6(X))* Scholastic Library Publishing.
Taylor, Leighton. Anemone Fish. 2007. (Early Bird Nature Bks.). (ENG., Illus.). 48p. (gr. 2-5). lib. bdg. 26.60 *(978-0-8225-6467-6(X)*, Lerner Pubns.) Lerner Publishing Group.
Thomas, Isabel. Fantastic Fish, 1 vol. 2012. (Extreme Animals Ser.). (ENG.). 32p. (gr. 1-3). pap. 8.29 *(978-1-4109-4686-7(X)*, Read Me!) Heinemann-Raintree.
Torckler, Gillian & Torckler, Darryl. Life-Size Guide to New Zealand Fish. 2003. (Illus.). 4p. (J). pap. *(978-1-86941-586-0(8))* Random Hse. New Zealand.
Van Dyck, Sara. Electric Eels. 2008. (Early Bird Nature Bks.). (ENG., Illus.). 48p. (gr. 2-5). lib. bdg. 26.60 *(978-0-8225-7886-4(7))* Lerner Publishing Group.
Veitch, Catherine. Fish Babies, 1 vol. 2013. (Animal Babies Ser.). (ENG.). 24p. (gr. -1-1). 22.65 *(978-1-4329-7493-0(9))*; pap. 6.95 *(978-1-4329-8418-2(7))*; pap. 35.94 *(978-1-4329-8425-0(X))* Heinemann-Raintree. (Acorn).
Visca, Curt. How to Draw Cartoon Fish. 2003. (Kid's Guide to Drawing Ser.). (Illus.). 24p. (J). lib. bdg. 25.25 *(978-0-8239-6159-7(1)*, PowerKids Pr.) Rosen Publishing Group, Inc., The.
Visca, Kelly. How to Draw Cartoon Fish. 2009. (Kid's Guide to Drawing Ser.). 24p. (gr. 3-3). 47.90 *(978-1-61511-014-8(3)*, PowerKids Pr.) Rosen Publishing Group, Inc., The.
Vogel, Julia. Are You My Fish?, 1 vol. Williams, Matthew, illus. 2008. (Are You My Pet? Ser.). (ENG.). 32p. (J). (gr. 1-4). 28.50 *(978-1-60270-244-8(6))* Magic Wagon.
Walker, Sally M. Mystery Fish. Gould, Shawn, illus. 2006. (On My Own Science Ser.). 47p. (J). pap. 6.95 *(978-1-57505-850-4(2)*, First Avenue Editions) Lerner Publishing Group.
—Mystery Fish: Secrets of the Coelacanth. 2005. (On My Own Science Ser.). (Illus.). 48p. (J). (gr. 3-7). lib. bdg. 25.26 *(978-1-57505-638-8(0))* Lerner Publishing Group.
Wallace, Karen. Think of an Eel Big Book. Bostock, Mike, illus. 2004. (Read & Wonder Ser.). (ENG.). 32p. (J). (gr. -1-2). pap. 24.99 *(978-0-7636-2470-5(5))* Candlewick Pr.
Wearing, Judy. Manta Rays. 2009. (World of Wonder Ser.). (Illus.). 24p. (J). (gr. 2-4). lib. bdg. 24.45 *(978-1-60596-104-0(3))* Weigl Pubs., Inc.
—Manta Rays: World of Wonder: Underwater Life. 2009. (Illus.). 24p. (J). pap. 8.95 *(978-1-60596-105-7(1))* Weigl Pubs., Inc.
Weber, Valerie J. Anglerfish. 2005. (Weird Wonders of the Deep Ser.). (Illus.). 24p. (gr. 1-4). lib. bdg. 23.00 *(978-0-8368-4560-0(9)*, Gareth Stevens Learning Library) Stevens, Gareth Publishing LLLP.
—Coelacanth: The Living Fossil. 2005. (Weird Wonders of the Deep Ser.). (Illus.). 24p. (gr. 1-4). lib. bdg. 23.00 *(978-0-8368-4561-7(7)*, Gareth Stevens Learning Library) Stevens, Gareth Publishing LLLP.
Weekly, Ellen M. Do Pigfish Really Oink? 2011. 28p. pap. 21.99 *(978-1-4568-9909-7(0))* Xlibris Corp.
Whelan, Piper. Clown Fish. 2016. (J). ***(978-1-4896-5372-7(4))*** Weigl Pubs., Inc.
William H. Sadlier Staff. Felix, the Very Hungry Fish. 2005. (Emergent Library: Vol. 2). (gr. -1-1). 24.00 net. *(978-0-8215-8920-5(2))* Sadlier, William H. Inc.
Williams, Zella. Piranhas & Other Creatures of the Amazon: Pirañas y Otros Animales de la Selva Amazónica. 2009. (Animals of Latin America / Animales de Latinoamérica Ser.). (SPA & ENG., Illus.). 24p. pap. 8.25 *(978-1-4358-3386-9(4))*; lib. bdg. 22.60 *(978-1-4042-8147-9(9))* Rosen Publishing Group, Inc., The. (PowerKids Pr.).
Willis, John. Piranha. 2015. (Illus.). 24p. (J). *(978-1-4896-4121-2(1))* Weigl Pubs., Inc.
Windsor, Jo. Animal Lights: Early Level Satellite Individual Title Six-Packs. (Sails Literacy Ser.). 16p. (gr. 1-2). 27.00 *(978-0-7578-2938-3(4))* Rigby Education.
Winkelman, Barbara Gaines. Puffer's Surprise. Petruccio, Steven James, illus. (Smithsonian Oceanic Collection). (ENG.). 32p. (J). (gr. -1-2). 2005. 15.95 *(978-1-59249-032-5(8)*, B4024) 2003. 19.95 *(978-1-59249-035-6(2)*, BC4024) 2003. 9.95 *(978-1-59249-038-7(7)*, PB4074) 2003. 4.95 *(978-1-59249-033-2(6)*, B4074) 2003. 6.95 *(978-1-59249-034-9(4)*, S4024) Soundprints.
Wood, Selina. Fish. 2008. (Owning a Pet Ser.). (Illus.). 32p. (YA). (gr. 2-5). lib. bdg. 28.50 *(978-1-59771-057-2(1))* Sea-To-Sea Pubns.
World Book, Inc Staff, contrib. by. Fish. 2009. (Illus.). 48p. (J). *(978-0-7166-0404-4(3))* World Bk., Inc.
Yasuda, Anita. Giant Moray Eel. 2014. (J). *(978-1-4896-1090-4(1))* Weigl Pubs., Inc.
Yin, Robert, illus. & photos by. Sharks & Rays. Yin, Robert, photos by. 2004. (ENG.). 24p. (J). (gr. 1-2). pap. 7.47 net. *(978-0-7685-0357-9(4)*, Dominie Elementary) Pearson Schl.
Zobel, Derek. Eels. 2008. (Oceans Alive Ser.). (ENG., Illus.). 24p. (J). (gr. k-3). lib. bdg. 25.95 *(978-1-60014-172-0(2))* Bellwether Media.
Zoller, Arthur David. Fish Colors. 2004. 14p. (J). (gr. -1-k). bds. 6.95 *(978-0-88106-073-7(9))* Charlesbridge Publishing, Inc.

FISHES—FICTION

Aardvark, D. The Congraduation Fish. Aardvark, D., illus. l.t. ed. 2005. (Illus.). 48p. (J). per. 12.95 *(978-0-9755567-1-9(1))* Aardvark's Weedpatch Pr.
Aguilar, Gaby. Guspar the Fish: A Story of Perseverance. 2013. 40p. 25.99 *(978-1-4582-1002-9(2))*; pap. 16.99 *(978-1-4582-1003-6(0))* Author Solutions, Inc. (Abbott Pr.).
Allen, Elanna. Poor Little Guy. 2016. (ENG., Illus.). 40p. (J). (-k). 16.99 *(978-0-525-42825-1(9)*, Dial Bks) Penguin Young Readers Group.
Allen, Nancy Kelly. Trouble in Troublesome Creek: A Troublesome Creek Kids Story. Crawford, K. Michael, illus. 2010. (ENG.). 32p. (J). (gr. -1-3). 16.95 *(978-1-933176-32-1(6))* Red Rock Pr., Inc.
Almond, David. The Boy Who Swam with Piranhas. Jeffers, Oliver, illus. 2013. (ENG.). 256p. (J). (gr. 4-7). 15.99 *(978-0-7636-6169-4(4))* Candlewick Pr.
Aloha Potter! Evaluation Guide: Evaluation Guide. 2006. (J). *(978-1-55942-397-7(8))* Witcher Productions.
Amon, Ras Ran. Gerald, Fish of the Spirit! A Caribbean Tale of Fortune & Greed. Betiku, Olatukunbo, illus. 2006. Orig. Title: Gerald, Fish of the Spirit! A Caribbean Tale of Fortune & Greed. (ENG.). (J). 7.99 *(978-0-9776603-0-8(3))* One Love Assn. Bks.
—Gerald Fish of the Spirit! Activity Book. 2006. (J). act. bk. ed. 3.99 *(978-0-9776603-2-2(X))* One Love Assn. Bks.
Amon, Ras Ran, adapted by. Gerald, Fish of the Spirit! A Caribbean Tale of Fortune & Greed. 2005. Orig. Title: Gerald, Fish of the Spirit! A Caribbean Tale of Fortune & Greed. (J). cd-rom 5.99 *(978-0-9776603-1-5(1))* One Love Assn. Bks.
Anderson - Hutchison, Laura M. Toby & Talula Trout. 2012. 20p. pap. 17.99 *(978-1-4772-3711-3(9))* AuthorHouse.
Andrew, Joe. The Three Lady Fish: A Friend in Need. Andrew, Joe, illus. 2007. (Illus.). (J). (gr. -1-3). pap. 9.95 *(978-0-9787995-6-4(9))* High-Pitched Hum Inc.
Anita D Martinez. Worm Imposters. 2009. 32p. pap. 14.49 *(978-1-4389-2605-6(7))* AuthorHouse.
Ann, Melissa. Redfish, Goldfish. 2012. 24p. 24.95 *(978-1-4626-5772-8(9))* America Star Bks.
Arena, Felice & Kettle, Phil. Crawfish Hunt. Vane, Mitch, illus. 2004. (J). pap. *(978-1-59336-358-1(3))* Mondo Publishing.
Arends, Donald L. Grandpa Grouper, the Fish with Glasses. 2006. (J). *(978-0-9768880-0-0(9))* Mission Manuscripts, Inc.
Arruda, Diane. The Ancient One, Book II in the Dream River Adventure. 2009. 56p. pap. 12.95 *(978-1-60860-397-8(0)*, Eloquent Bks.) Strategic Book Publishing & Rights Agency (SBPRA).
—The Undiscovered River: Golden Fish & a True Dream. 2008. 60p. pap. 12.95 *(978-1-60693-399-2(X)*, Eloquent Bks.) Strategic Book Publishing & Rights Agency (SBPRA).
Asani, Samantha. Everyone Is Special: A Lesson in Teamwork. 2012. 28p. pap. 19.99 *(978-1-4685-5320-8(8))* AuthorHouse.
Avi. What Do Fish Have to Do with Anything? 2004. (ENG., Illus.). 208p. (J). (gr. 5-9). reprint ed. 6.99 *(978-0-7636-2319-7(9))* Candlewick Pr.
Babin, Claire. Gus Is a Fish. Bedrick, Claudia Z., tr. from FRE. Tallec, Olivier & Sorman, Joy, illus. 2008. (ENG.). 32p. (J). (gr. -1-2). 14.95 *(978-1-59270-101-8(9))* Enchanted Lion Bks., LLC.
Bailey, Lin. The Search for Tommy's Shell. 2013. 36p. pap. *(978-1-910053-32-4(5))* Legend Pr.
Baines, Andy. I Know a Goldfish That Can't Swim. 2012. 72p. (-18). pap. *(978-1-909395-50-3(1))* Legend Pr.
Barroux. Starfish, Where Are You? 2016. (ENG., Illus.). 40p. (J). (gr. -1-1). 17.99 *(978-1-4998-0258-0(7))* Little Bee Books Inc.
Barroux, Stephane, illus. My Goldfish. 2009. 36p. (J). (gr. -1-2). 15.00 *(978-0-8028-5334-9(X)*, Eerdmans Bks For Young Readers) Eerdmans, William B. Publishing Co.
Batson, Susann. Gilly the Seasick Fish. l.t. ed. 2006. (Illus.). (J). 28p. 15.99 *(978-1-933090-22-1(7))*; 32p. E-Book 5.00 incl. cd-rom *(978-1-933090-37-5(5))* Guardian Angel Publishing, Inc.
Bauer, Tiffany Jamie. Swim Little Swimmy, 1 vol. 2009. 25p. pap. 24.95 *(978-1-60813-520-2(9))* America Star Bks.
Baxter, Nicola & Adams, Ben. Freddie the Fish, Star of the Show. Cameron, Craig, illus. 2013. (Googly Eyes Ser.). (ENG.). 12p. (J). (gr. -1-k). bds. 6.99 *(978-1-84322-621-5(9)*, Armadillo) Anness Publishing GBR. Dist: National Bk. Network.
Beck, Sharon. The Fish in Our Class. 2011. (Randy's Corner Ser.). (Illus.). 32p. (J). (gr. -1-2). lib. bdg. 25.70 *(978-1-58415-978-0(2))* Mitchell Lane Pubs., Inc.
Beckenstein, Cara. The True Story of Federico Fish & Ana Alligator. Tanchak, Diane, illus. 2003. 32p. 11.95 *(978-0-9726699-0-0(6))* Laughing Gull Pr.
Beh-Rang, Samad. The Little Black Fish. Emam, Ruby, tr. 2008. 32p. pap. 13.25 *(978-1-4389-1399-5(0))* AuthorHouse.

E
F
G

Benjamin, Ali. The Thing about Jellyfish. (ENG.). 352p. (J). (gr. 5-17). 2017. pap. 8.99 *(978-0-316-38084-3(9))* 2015. 17.99 *(978-0-316-38086-7(5))* Little, Brown Bks. for Young Readers.

—The Thing about Jellyfish. 2017. (J). lib. bdg. 19.65 ***(978-0-606-40218-7(7))*** Turtleback Bks.

Bennett, Eric. Noodles & Albie. Bannish, Liz, illus. 2014. (ENG.). (J). 17.95 *(978-1-937650-40-7(5))* Small Batch Bks.

Bennett, Kelly. Not Norman: A Goldfish Story. Jones, Noah Z., illus. 2008. (ENG.). 32p. (J). (gr. -1-3). pap. 6.99 *(978-0-7636-2763-8(1))* Candlewick Pr.

Bentley, Tadgh. Samson: The Piranha Who Went to Dinner. Bentley, Tadgh, illus. 2017. (Illus.). 40p. (J). (gr. -1-3). 17.99 *(978-0-06-233537-1(5))* HarperCollins Pubs.

Berkes, Marianne. Over in the Ocean: In a Coral Reef. 1 vol. Canyon, Jeanette, illus. 2004. 36p. (J). (gr. -1-2). (ENG.). 16.95 *(978-1-58469-063-4(1))*; pap. 8.95 *(978-1-58469-062-7(3))* Dawn Pubns.

Blair, Eric. El Pescador y Su Mujer: Versión del Cuento de los Hermanos Grimm. Abello, Patricia, tr. Ouren, Todd, illus. 2006. (Read-It! Readers en Español: Cuentos de Hadas Ser.). (SPA.). 32p. (gr. k-3). 21.32 *(978-1-4048-1630-5(5),* Easy Readers) Picture Window Bks.

Blevins, Wiley. Max Has a Fish. Clanton, Ben, illus. 2012. (Penguin Young Readers, Level 1 Ser.). (ENG.). 32p. (J). (gr. k-1). pap. 3.99 *(978-0-448-46158-8(7),* Penguin Young Readers) Penguin Young Readers Group.

—Max Has a Fish. 2012. (Penguin Young Readers Level 1 Ser.). lib. bdg. 13.55 *(978-0-606-26640-6(2),* Turtleback) Turtleback Bks.

Boen, Sherry. The Fish Who Made a Magical Wish. 1 vol. 2009. 21p. pap. 24.95 *(978-1-61582-726-8(9))* America Star Bks.

Boniface, William. The Adventures of Max the Minnow. Sullivan, Don, illus. 2015. (ENG.). 26p. (J). bds. 9.99 *(978-1-4494-6490-5(4))* Andrews McMeel Publishing.

Bonnell, Kris. A Friend for Jellyfish. 2006. (J). pap. 3.95 *(978-1-933727-28-8(4))* Reading Reading Bks., LLC.

Books, Appleknobb. Charlie's Monster. Books, Appleknobb, illus. 2013. (Illus.). 26p. (J). pap. 13.95 *(978-0-9890903-0-8(2))* Happy Apple Bks.

Boucher, Julie. Small Fry on the Magnetawan. 2009. 24p. pap. 14.95 *(978-0-9819727-4-9(8))* Fiction Publishing, Inc.

Bright, Paul. Fidgety Fish & Friends. Galloway, Ruth, illus. 2008. (Tiger Tales Ser.). 24p. (J). (gr. -1-2). pap. 6.95 *(978-1-58925-409-1(0))* Tiger Tales.

Britland, Jan. The Adventures of Rodger Dodger Dog. Swaim, Michael, illus. 2009. 40p. pap. 15.95 *(978-1-936051-23-6(0))* Peppertree Pr., The.

Brothers Grimm & Isadora, Rachel. The Fisherman & His Wife. Isadora, Rachel, illus. 2008. (ENG., Illus.). 32p. (J). (gr. -1-3). 16.99 *(978-0-399-24771-2(8),* G.P. Putnam's Sons Books for Young Readers) Penguin Young Readers Group.

Buckeridge, Anthony. Jennings & Darbishire. 2008. (Jennings Ser.: 4). (ENG.). 210p. (J). (gr. -1-12). pap. 12.95 *(978-0-7551-0153-5(7))* House of Stratus, Inc. GBR. Dist: Gardners Bks. Ltd.

Buckingham, Matt. Bright Stanley. 2006. (Illus.). 32p. (J). (gr. -1-3). 15.95 *(978-1-58925-059-8(1))* Tiger Tales.

Bunting, Eve. Finn McCool & the Great Fish. Pullen, Zachary, illus. 2010. (ENG.). 38p. (J). (gr. k-6). 16.95 *(978-1-58536-366-7(9))* Sleeping Bear Pr.

—Gleam & Glow. Sylvada, Peter, illus. 2005. (ENG.). 32p. (J). (gr. -1-3). reprint ed. pap. 7.99 *(978-0-15-205380-2(8))* Houghton Mifflin Harcourt Publishing Co.

Butterfield, Moira. Found You, Magic Fish! Child, Jeremy, illus. 2010. (Magic Bath Bks.). (ENG.). 8p. (J). (gr. -1-k). 5.99 *(978-0-7641-9791-8(6))* Barron's Educational Series, Inc.

Callahan, Ann Marie. The Sun Tea Fish. Sponheimer, Katheryne, illus. 2008. 16p. pap. 24.95 *(978-1-60672-160-5(7))* America Star Bks.

Cannon, A. E. Sophie's Fish. White, Lee, illus. 2012. (ENG.). 32p. (J). (gr. -1-k). 15.99 *(978-0-670-01291-6(2),* Viking Books for Young Readers) Penguin Young Readers Group.

Carle, Eric. Mister Seahorse. Carle, Eric, illus. (ENG., Illus.). (J). (gr. -1 — 1). 2011. 64p. bds. 8.99 *(978-0-399-25490-1(0))* 2004. 32p. 18.99 *(978-0-399-24269-4(4))* Penguin Young Readers Group. (Philomel Bks.).

—Rooster Is off to See the World. 2013. (Eric Carle Ready-To-Read Ser.). lib. bdg. 13.55 *(978-0-606-32063-4(6),* Turtleback) Turtleback Bks.

Carlos, Tio. My Fish Trish. 2008. 16p. pap. 8.49 *(978-1-4343-7960-3(4))* AuthorHouse.

Cassels, Rosemary Van Liew. Rainbow Fish. 1 vol. 2010. 28p. pap. 24.95 *(978-1-4489-9021-4(1))* PublishAmerica, Inc.

Charlesworth, Liza. Fish School: An Animal Friends Reader. Smith, Ian, illus. 2015. 16p. (J). pap. ***(978-0-545-85963-9(8))*** Scholastic, Inc.

Cheek, Stephen. Catfish Cowboy & Mr. Turtle. 2008. 35p. pap. 21.80 *(978-0-557-02684-5(9))* Lulu Pr., Inc.

Cheng, Andrea. Goldfish & Chrysanthemums. Chang, Michelle, illus. 2003. (ENG.). 32p. (J). 16.95 *(978-1-58430-057-1(4))*; pap. 8.95 *(978-1-60060-889-6(2))* Lee & Low Bks., Inc.

Clar, David Austin, illus. Follow the Leader. 2003. (Rainbow Fish & Friends Ser.). (ENG.). 24p. (J). (gr. -1-2). 3.99 *(978-1-59014-106-9(7))* North-South Bks., Inc.

Clar, David Austin & David Austin Clar Studio Staff, illus. Surprise Party. 2003. (Rainbow Fish & Friends Ser.). (ENG.). 24p. (J). (gr. -1-2). 9.95 *(978-1-59014-114-4(8))* North-South Bks., Inc.

Clarke, Jane & Fuge, Charles. Gilbert the Great. 2016. (ENG., Illus.). 32p. (J). (gr. -1-2). 6.95 *(978-1-4549-1912-4(4))* Sterling Publishing Co., Inc.

Clements, Andrew. Big Al. Yoshi, illus. 2015. 32p. pap. 8.00 *(978-1-61003-598-9(4))* Center for the Collaborative Classroom.

—Big Al & Shrimpy. Kogo, Yoshi, illus. 2005. (ENG.). 40p. (J). (gr. -1-3). reprint ed. 7.99 *(978-1-4169-0366-6(6),* Atheneum Bks. for Young Readers) Simon & Schuster Children's Publishing.

Clish, Marian L. I Wonder What a Fish Would Wish For? Swaim, Mike, illus. 2009. 29p. pap. 24.95 *(978-1-60836-289-9(2))* America Star Bks.

Clough, Julie, illus. The Starfish. 2008. (Seaside Bath Bks.). (ENG.). 6p. (J). (gr. -1-k). 6.99 *(978-0-7641-9533-4(6))* Barron's Educational Series, Inc.

Cohen, Barbara. The Carp in the Bathtub. 48p. (J). (gr. 2-4). pap. 5.95 *(978-0-8072-1332-2(2),* Listening Library) Random Hse. Audio Publishing Group.

Cohen, Santiago, illus. The Yiddish Fish. 2014. (ENG.). 32p. (J). (gr. -1-k). 16.95 *(978-1-62914-633-1(1),* Sky Pony Pr.) Skyhorse Publishing Co., Inc.

Collier, Kevin Scott. Hope, the Angelfish. Collier, Kevin Scott, illus. 2008. (Illus.). 24p. pap. 10.95 *(978-1-933090-17-7(0))* Guardian Angel Publishing, Inc.

—Journeys of Hope, a Star Shall Lead Them. 2005. (Illus.). 32p. (J). E-Book 6.00 incl. cd-rom *(978-1-933090-28-3(6))* Guardian Angel Publishing, Inc.

Collier, Kristen. Joy the Jellyfish. 2007. (Illus.). 24p. (J). per. *(978-0-9797574-7-1(9))*; *(978-0-9797574-6-4(0))* Dragonfly Publishing, Inc.

Collins, Terry. Spongebob NaturePants, Vol. 7. 2004. 64p. (J). (gr. 2-5). pap. 17.00 incl. audio *(978-1-4000-8630-6(2),* Listening Library) Random Hse. Audio Publishing Group.

Conejito Azul: Salva a los Peces.Tr. of Bunny Rabbit Saves the Fish. (SPA.). (J). 2.98 *(978-970-22-0021-5(0))* Larousse, Ediciones, S. A. de C. V. MEX. Dist: Continental Bk. Co., Inc.

Cook, Bernadine. The Little Fish That Got Away. Johnson, Crockett, illus. 2005. 64p. (J). (gr. -1-3). lib. bdg. 15.89 *(978-0-06-055714-0(1))* HarperCollins Pubs.

Cooper, Jason. Gilbert the Great Fish. 2011. 28p. pap. 14.99 *(978-1-4670-4289-5(7))* AuthorHouse.

Cooper, Ross Gordon. Clarence the Catfish. 2010. 32p. pap. 21.95 *(978-0-557-30913-9(1))* Lulu Pr., Inc.

Copeland, Cynthia L. & Lewis, Alexandra P. Splashy Fins, Flashy Skins: Deep-Sea Rhymes to Make You Grin. 2003. (Silly Millies Ser.: 4). (Illus.). 32p. lib. bdg. 17.90 *(978-0-7613-2906-0(4),* Millbrook Pr.) Lerner Publishing Group.

Coulton, Mia. Circus Fish. Coulton, Mia, photos by. 2008. (ENG., Illus.). pap. 5.35 *(978-1-933624-29-7(9))* Maryruth Bks., Inc.

—A New Home for Fish. Coulton, Mia, photos by. 2007. (ENG., Illus.). pap. 5.35 *(978-1-933624-14-3(0))* Maryruth Bks., Inc.

—Pirate Fish. Coulton, Mia, photos by. 2007. (ENG., Illus.). pap. 5.35 *(978-1-933624-15-0(9))* Maryruth Bks., Inc.

Cousins, Lucy. Hooray for Fish! Cousins, Lucy, illus. (ENG., Illus.). (J). (— 1). 2017. 34p. bds. 8.99 *(978-0-7636-9352-7(9))* 2008. 34p. bds. 8.99 *(978-0-7636-3918-1(4))* 2005. 40p. 16.99 *(978-0-7636-2741-6(0))* Candlewick Pr.

Craig, Joni. The Fish from the Cherryville Grill. 2013. 30p. pap. 13.95 *(978-1-940224-02-2(0))* Taylor and Seale Publishing, LLC.

Crisp, Lisa. Stewart & His Fish Tank. 2011. 28p. pap. 24.95 *(978-1-4560-1007-2(7))* America Star Bks.

Crownberry, Ethan. A Fish with a Wish. 2013. 52p. 17.95 *(978-0-9898533-0-9(6))* Jetpack Publishing.

—A Fish with a Wish. 2012. 84p. pap. 8.95 *(978-1-105-84560-4(5))* Lulu Pr., Inc.

Cuasay, Alison Taimanglo. Tasi & Matina: The Story of the First Clown Fish. 2010. 28p. pap. 12.99 *(978-1-4520-6672-1(8))* AuthorHouse.

Cummings, Troy. Day of the Night Crawlers. 2013. (Notebook of Doom Ser.: 2). (ENG.). 96p. (J). (gr. 1-3). 15.99 *(978-0-545-49324-6(2))*; pap. 4.99 *(978-0-545-49325-3(0))*; E-Book *(978-0-545-49327-7(7))* Scholastic, Inc.

—Day of the Night Crawlers. 2013. (Notebook of Doom Ser.: 2). lib. bdg. 14.75 *(978-0-606-32368-0(6),* Turtleback) Turtleback Bks.

Daigle, Damien. The Fish That Went Roar. Daigle, Casie, illus. 2011. 28p. pap. 24.95 *(978-1-4560-5080-1(X))* America Star Bks.

David Austin Clar Studio Staff, illus. Surprise Party. 2003. (Rainbow Fish & Friends Ser.). (ENG.). 24p. (J). (gr. -1). 3.99 *(978-1-59014-107-6(5))* North-South Bks., Inc.

De Matos, Isabel Freire. El Pececito Magico. Torres, Walter, illus. 2004. (SPA.). 22p. (J). pap. 6.95 *(978-1-57581-578-7(8))* Santillana USA Publishing Co., Inc.

de Vries, Maggie. Fraser Bear: A Cub's Life. Benoit, Renné, illus. 2012. (ENG.). 48p. (J). (gr. k-4). pap. 10.95 *(978-1-926812-95-3(6))* Greystone Books Ltd. CAN. Dist: Publishers Group West (PGW).

—Tale of a Great White Fish: A Sturgeon Story. Benoit, Renné, illus. 2010. (ENG.). 48p. (J). (gr. k-4). pap. 10.95 *(978-1-55365-303-5(3))* Greystone Books Ltd. CAN. Dist: Publishers Group West (PGW).

Debruzzi, Jeremy. A Minnesota Fish Tail. 2012. 48p. 24.99 *(978-1-4628-8580-0(2))*; pap. 15.99 *(978-1-4628-8579-4(9))* Xlibris Corp.

Depken, Kristen L. Wisdom to Remember: Life Advice from a Forgetful Fish. Random House Disney Staff, illus. 2016. (Official Guide Ser.). (ENG.). 80p. (J). (gr. -1-2). 9.99 *(978-0-7364-3710-3(X),* RH/Disney) Random Hse. Children's Bks.

DePrisco, Dorothea. Little School of Fish. Gévry, Claudine, illus. 2006. 12p. (gr. -1-k). 10.95 *(978-1-58117-485-4(3),* Intervisual/Piggy Toes) Bendon, Inc.

Dharma Publishing Staff. The Fish King: A Story about the Power of Goodness. 2nd ed. 2013. (ENG.). 36p. (gr. -1-7). pap. 8.95 *(978-0-89800-491-5(8))* Dharma Publishing.

Diamond, Charlotte. Slippery Fish in Hawaii. Aardema, John, illus. 2013. (ENG.). 16p. (J). (gr. -1-1). bds. 7.95 *(978-1-933067-57-5(8))* Beachhouse Publishing, LLC.

DiBenedetto, Salvatore. Christian the Fish: Who am I? 2011. 44p. pap. 20.45 *(978-1-4497-0600-5(2),* WestBow Pr.) Author Solutions, Inc.

Dicmas, Courtney. The Great Googly Moogly. Dicmas, Courtney, illus. 2014. (Child's Play Library). (ENG., Illus.). 32p. (J). *(978-1-84643-640-6(0))* Child's Play International Ltd.

Diesen, Deborah. Happy Easter, Pout-Pout Fish. Hanna, Dan, illus. 2017. (Pout-Pout Fish Mini Adventure Ser.). (ENG.). 12p. (J). bds. 5.99 *(978-0-374-30400-3(9),* 9780374304003, Farrar, Straus & Giroux (BYR)) Farrar, Straus & Giroux.

—Kiss, Kiss, Pout-Pout Fish. Hanna, Dan, illus. 2015. (Pout-Pout Fish Mini Adventure Ser.). (ENG.). 14p. (J). (gr. -1 — 1). 5.99 *(978-0-374-30190-3(5),* 9780374301903, Farrar, Straus & Giroux (BYR)) Farrar, Straus & Giroux.

—The Not Very Merry Pout-Pout Fish. Hanna, Dan, illus. (Pout-Pout Fish Adventure Ser.). (ENG.). (J). 2017. 34p. bds. 7.99 *(978-0-374-30459-1(9),* 9780374304591) 2015. 32p. (gr. -1-1). 16.99 *(978-0-374-35549-4(5),* 9780374355494) Farrar, Straus & Giroux. (Farrar, Straus & Giroux (BYR)).

—The Pout-Pout Fish. Hanna, Dan, illus. (Pout-Pout Fish Adventure Ser.: 1). (ENG.). (J). (gr. -1 — 1). 2013. 36p. bds. 7.99 *(978-0-374-36097-9(9),* 9780374360979) 2008. 32p. 16.99 *(978-0-374-36096-2(0),* 9780374360962) Farrar, Straus & Giroux. (Farrar, Straus & Giroux (BYR)).

—The Pout-Pout Fish & the Bully-Bully Shark. Hanna, Dan, illus. 2017. (Pout-Pout Fish Adventure Ser.). (ENG.). 32p. (J). 16.99 ***(978-0-374-30402-7(5),*** 9780374304027, Farrar, Straus & Giroux (BYR)) Farrar, Straus & Giroux.

—The Pout-Pout Fish Book & CD Storytime Set. unabr. ed. 2013. (ENG.). (J). (gr. -1-1). 12.99 *(978-1-4272-3176-5(1),* 9781427231765) Macmillan Audio.

—The Pout-Pout Fish, Far, Far from Home. Hanna, Dan, illus. 2017. (Pout-Pout Fish Adventure Ser.). (ENG.). 32p. (J). 16.99 *(978-0-374-30194-1(8),* 9780374301941, Farrar, Straus & Giroux (BYR)) Farrar, Straus & Giroux.

—The Pout-Pout Fish Goes to School. Hanna, Dan, illus. 2014. (Pout-Pout Fish Adventure Ser.). (ENG.). 32p. (J). (gr. -1-k). 16.99 *(978-0-374-36095-5(2),* 9780374360955, Farrar, Straus & Giroux (BYR)) Farrar, Straus & Giroux.

—The Pout-Pout Fish in the Big-Big Dark. Hanna, Dan, illus. 2015. (Pout-Pout Fish Adventure Ser.: 2). (ENG.). 34p. (J). (gr. -1-1). bds. 7.99 *(978-0-374-30189-7(1),* 9780374301897, Farrar, Straus & Giroux (BYR)) Farrar, Straus & Giroux.

—The Pout-Pout Fish Undersea Alphabet: Touch & Feel. Hanna, Dan, illus. 2016. (Pout-Pout Fish Novelty Ser.). (ENG.). 20p. (J). bds. 12.99 *(978-1-250-06392-2(2),* 9781250063922, Farrar, Straus & Giroux (BYR)) Farrar, Straus & Giroux.

—Smile, Pout-Pout Fish. Hanna, Dan, illus. 2014. (Pout-Pout Fish Mini Adventure Ser.). (ENG.). 12p. (J). (gr. -1 — 1). bds. 5.99 *(978-0-374-37084-8(2),* 9780374370848, Farrar, Straus & Giroux (BYR)) Farrar, Straus & Giroux.

—Trick or Treat, Pout-Pout Fish. Hanna, Dan, illus. 2016. (Pout-Pout Fish Mini Adventure Ser.). (ENG.). 12p. (J). bds. 5.99 *(978-0-374-30191-0(3),* 9780374301910, Farrar, Straus & Giroux (BYR)) Farrar, Straus & Giroux.

Dipucchio, Kelly. Gilbert Goldfish Wants a Pet. Shea, Bob, illus. 2011. (ENG.). 32p. (J). (gr. -1-k). 16.99 *(978-0-8037-3394-7(1),* Dial Bks) Penguin Young Readers Group.

Disney & Disney / LeapFrog. Disney Princess: Les aventures D'Ariel. 2008. (J). 20.79 *(978-1-59319-944-9(9))* LeapFrog Enterprises, Inc.

Disney & Pixar Animators. Disney-Pixar Finding Dory Cinestory. 2016. (J). lib. bdg. 26.95 *(978-0-606-38729-3(3))* Turtleback Bks.

Disney & Scollon, Bill. Disney*Pixar Finding Dory - Follow Me. 2016. (ENG.). 10p. (J). (gr. -1-k). bds. 9.99 *(978-0-7944-3669-8(2))* Studio Fun International.

Disney Book Group. Finding Dory Middle Grade Novel. 2016. (ENG., Illus.). 128p. (J). (gr. 3-7). 10.99 *(978-1-4847-4871-8(9))* Disney Pr.

—Finding Dory Novelty. 2016. (ENG.). 10p. (J). (gr. -1-k). bds. 9.99 *(978-1-4847-2592-4(1))* Disney Pr.

—Finding Dory (Picture Book) 2016. (ENG.). 40p. (J). (gr. 1-3). 16.99 *(978-1-4847-2585-6(9))* Disney Pr.

Disney Book Group Staff. Finding Nemo. 2012. (Read-Along Storybook & CD Ser.). (ENG.). 912p. (J). (gr. -1 — 1). pap. 6.99 *(978-1-4231-6028-1(2))* Disney Pr.

Disney Editors. Disney-Pixar Finding Nemo Cinestory Comic. 2016. (J). lib. bdg. 26.95 *(978-0-606-38732-3(3))* Turtleback Bks.

—Dory's Story. 2016. (Step into Reading Level 2 Ser.). lib. bdg. 14.75 *(978-0-606-38891-7(5))* Turtleback Bks.

—Finding Dory Junior Novelization. 2016. lib. bdg. 17.20 *(978-0-606-38893-1(1))* Turtleback Bks.

—Hank the Septopus. 2016. (Disney/Pixar Finding Dory 8x8 Ser.). lib. bdg. 14.75 *(978-0-606-38894-8(X))* Turtleback Bks.

Disney Pixar Editors. Disney Pixar Finding Dory Comics Collection. 2016. (J). lib. bdg. 20.85 *(978-0-606-39074-3(X))* Turtleback Bks.

Disney Pixar Staff. Nemo's Big Race. 2013. (Countdown Ser.: 1). (ENG.). 18p. (J). (gr. -1-k). 12.99 *(978-0-7944-2817-4(7),* Reader's Digest Children's Bks.) Studio Fun International.

Disney Storybook Art Team, illus. Finding Dory (Read-Along Storybook & CD) 2016. (Disney Storybook & CD Ser.). (ENG.). 32p. (J). (gr. 1-3). pap. 6.99 *(978-1-4847-2586-3(7))* Disney Pr.

Disney Storybook Artists Staff, illus. Finding Nemo. 2007. (Play-A-Sound Ser.). 15p. (J). (gr. -1-3). 15.98 *(978-1-4127-8754-3(8))* Publications International, Ltd.

DiTerlizzi, Tony & DiTerlizzi, Angela. Big Fun! DiTerlizzi, Tony, illus. 2009. (Adventure of Meno Ser.: 1). (ENG., Illus.). 48p. (J). (gr. -1-k). 9.99 *(978-1-4169-7148-1(3),* Simon & Schuster Bks. For Young Readers) Simon & Schuster Bks. For Young Readers.

—Uh-Oh Sick! DiTerlizzi, Tony, illus. 2010. (Adventure of Meno Ser.: 4). (ENG., Illus.). 52p. (J). (gr. -1-k). 9.99 *(978-1-4169-7153-5(X),* Simon & Schuster Bks. For Young Readers) Simon & Schuster Bks. For Young Readers.

—Wet Friend! DiTerlizzi, Tony, illus. 2009. (Adventure of Meno Ser.: 2). (ENG., Illus.). 48p. (J). (gr. -1-k). 9.99 *(978-1-4169-7149-8(1),* Simon & Schuster Bks. For Young Readers) Simon & Schuster Bks. For Young Readers.

—Yummy Trip! DiTerlizzi, Tony, illus. 2010. (Adventure of Meno Ser.: 3). (ENG., Illus.). 48p. (J). (gr. -1-k). 9.99 *(978-1-4169-7150-4(5),* Simon & Schuster Bks. For Young Readers) Simon & Schuster Bks. For Young Readers.

Donaldson, Julia. The Fish Who Cried Wolf. Scheffler, Axel, illus. (J). 2017. (ENG.). 40p. (gr. -1-k). 17.99 *(978-0-439-92825-0(7))* 2008. pap. *(978-0-545-03454-8(X))* Scholastic, Inc. (Levine, Arthur A. Bks.).

—Wrong Kind of Bark. Parsons, Garry, illus. 2004. (Red Bananas Ser.). (ENG.). 48p. (J). (gr. k-2). pap. 5.99 *(978-1-4052-1062-1(1))* Egmont Bks., Ltd. GBR. Dist: Independent Pubs. Group.

Donovan, Gail. 100th Day Fun. Clar, David Austin, illus. 2003. (Rainbow Fish & Friends Ser.). 24p. (J). lib. bdg. 9.95 *(978-1-59014-141-0(5))* Night Sky Bks.

Dorling Kindersley Publishing Staff. Finding Nemo. 2003. (Ultimate Sticker Bks.). (ENG., Illus.). 16p. (J). (gr. k-3). pap. 6.99 *(978-0-7894-9245-6(8),* DK Children) Dorling Kindersley Publishing, Inc.

Doudna, Kelly. Jellyfish Role. 1 vol. Chawla, Neena, illus. 2007. (Critter Chronicles Ser.). (ENG.). 24p. (J). (gr. k-3). lib. bdg. 24.21 *(978-1-59928-446-0(4),* SandCastle) ABDO Publishing Co.

Douglas, Babette. Squirt: The Magic Cuddlefish. Williams, Ted, illus. 2006. (Kiss a Me Teacher Creature Stories Ser.). (J). (gr. -1-3). 9.99 *(978-1-890343-47-7(1))* Kiss A Me Productions, Inc.

Dubovoy, Silvia. Turquesita. (SPA.). (J). pap. *(978-968-6465-18-1(9))* Casa de Estudios de Literatura y Talleres Artisticos Amaquemecan A.C. MEX. Dist: Lectorum Pubns., Inc.

Dubuc, Marianne. The Sea. 2012. (ENG., Illus.). 92p. 19.95 *(978-88-89854-85-3(5))* Officina Libraria srl ITA. Dist: National Bk. Network.

Ealy, Gerald & Ealy, Gerald. I Made a Wish to Be a Fish. 2012. 32p. pap. 9.95 *(978-0-9843837-5-7(1))* G340 Publishing.

Ehlert, Lois. Rain Fish. Ehlert, Lois, illus. 2016. (ENG., Illus.). 40p. (J). (gr. -1-3). 17.99 *(978-1-4814-6152-8(4),* Beach Lane Bks.) Beach Lane Bks.

Engler, Zoe. The Lonely Starfish. 1 vol. 2010. 26p. 24.95 *(978-1-4489-2929-0(6))* PublishAmerica, Inc.

Espinoza, Olivia G. Jay-Dylan's Cat & Fish. 2011. 24p. (gr. -1). pap. 14.39 *(978-1-4567-5119-7(0))* AuthorHouse.

Fair, Chuck. Steven Sockeye Salmon. 2005. 106p. pap. 10.95 *(978-1-4116-4780-0(7))* Lulu Pr., Inc.

Fardell, John. Jeremiah Jellyfish Flies High! Fardell, John, illus. 2011. (ENG., Illus.). 32p. (J). (gr. -1-k). pap. 13.99 *(978-1-84939-147-4(5))* Andersen Pr. GBR. Dist: Independent Pubs. Group.

Fay, Nancy Cartnick. I Wanted a Puppy - Not Fish! 2012. 24p. pap. 15.99 *(978-1-4691-7535-5(5))* Xlibris Corp.

Fenske, Jonathan. Barnacle Is Bored. 2016. (ENG.). 40p. (J). (gr. -1-k). 14.99 *(978-0-545-86504-3(2),* Scholastic Pr.) Scholastic, Inc.

—Guppy Up! 2013. (Penguin Young Readers Level 1 Ser.). lib. bdg. 13.55 *(978-0-606-28736-4(1),* Turtleback) Turtleback Bks.

Ferrier, Charlotte. A Home for Little Fish. Hirashima, Jean, illus. 2005. (J). *(978-1-890647-16-2(0))* TOMY International, Inc.

Fischer, JoAnn. Our Teacher Is A Fish! 2008. (ENG.). 34p. pap. 10.00 *(978-1-4196-7477-8(3))* CreateSpace Independent Publishing Platform.

The Fish That Made A Wish. 2005. (J). 15.95 *(978-0-9762835-0-8(6))* Shooting Star Publishing.

Follow the Fish. 2005. (J). bds. 6.66 *(978-0-9753127-4-2(X))* Family Bks. at Home.

Fontenot, Mary Alice. Clovis Crawfish & Echo Gecko. 1 vol. Buckner, Julie Dupre, illus. 2003. (Clovis Crawfish Ser.). (ENG.). 32p. (J). (gr. k-3). 16.99 *(978-1-56554-708-7(X))* Pelican Publishing Co., Inc.

—Clovis Crawfish & His Friends. 1 vol. Graves, Keith, illus. 2009. (Clovis Crawfish Ser.). (ENG.). 32p. (J). (gr. k-3). 16.99 *(978-1-58980-762-4(6))* Pelican Publishing Co., Inc.

Ford, Carole S. Timothy Turtle & Sammy Scallop. Edwin, Kimberly, illus. 30p. (J). (gr. -1-k). pap. 4.95 *(978-1-891533-02-0(9))* Calvin Partnership, LLC.

Foreman, Michael. Friends. Foreman, Michael, illus. 2012. (Andersen Press Picture Bks). (ENG., Illus.). 32p. (J). (gr. -1-3). 16.95 *(978-1-4677-0317-8(6))* Lerner Publishing Group.

Fossey, Robert. Little Armstrong. 2009. (Illus.). 20p. pap. 12.49 *(978-1-4389-5206-2(6))* AuthorHouse.

Fraser, Jennifer. Scott the Starfish - an Unexpected Adventure! Eastley, Melanie, illus. 2012. 32p. pap. *(978-0-9868776-4-3(6))* MW Bk. Pubs.

Frazier, Craig. Stanley Goes Fishing. 2006. (Stanley Ser.: STAN). (ENG., Illus.). 40p. (J). (gr. -1-7). 15.95 *(978-0-8118-5244-9(X))* Chronicle Bks. LLC.

Freedman, Deborah. The Story of Fish & Snail. 3rd ed. 2013. (ENG., Illus.). 40p. (J). (gr. -1-k). 16.99 *(978-0-670-78489-9(3),* Viking Books for Young Readers) Penguin Young Readers Group.

Fulton, Kelly. Larry the Lonely Lionfish. 2013. 20p. pap. 11.95 *(978-1-4787-1391-3(7))* Outskirts Pr., Inc.

Furuya, Michael, illus. Keoni's Special Gift. 2009. (J). *(978-1-56647-915-8(0))* Mutual Publishing LLC.

Galjanic, Lisa. When Fish Are Mean. Hope, Michelle, illus. 2007. (J). 9.95 *(978-1-933532-01-1(7))* LSG Pubns.

—When Series 6 Volume Set, 6, 6. 2007. (Illus.). 100p. (J). 34.95 *(978-1-933532-06-6(8))* LSG Pubns.

Galloway, Ruth. Fidgety Fish. Galloway, Ruth, illus. (Ocean Adventures Ser.). (Illus.). (J). 2017. (ENG.). 32p. (gr. -1-2). 23.99 ***(978-1-68010-055-6(6))*** 2006. 16p. bds. 6.95 *(978-1-58925-772-6(3))* 2003. 32p. pap. 6.95 *(978-1-58925-377-3(9))* Tiger Tales.

Galloway, Ruth. The Very Fidgety Fish. Galloway, Ruth, illus. 2014. (My First Storybook Ser.). (ENG., Illus.). 32p. (J). (gr. -1-1). 6.99 *(978-1-58925-509-8(7))* Tiger Tales.

Garland, Michael. Fish Had a Wish. Garland, Michael, illus. (I Like to Read(r) Ser.). (ENG., Illus.). 24p. (J). 2013. pap. 6.99 *(978-0-8234-2757-4(9))* 2012. 14.95 *(978-0-8234-2394-1(8))* Holiday Hse., Inc.

Garrett, Lyn. Horatio & the Sea Tornado. 2012. 28p. (-18). pap. 12.50 *(978-1-62212-615-6(7),* Strategic Bk. Publishing) Strategic Book Publishing & Rights Agency (SBPRA).

Gay, Marie-Louise. Estela, la Estrella del Mar. (Buenas Noches Ser.). (SPA.). (J). 8.95 *(978-958-04-5628-5(3))* Norma S.A. COL. Dist: Distribuidora Norma, Inc., Lectorum Pubns., Inc.

Gee, Randi. Goldfish & Poodle. 2010. 32p. pap. 15.50 *(978-0-557-52979-7(4))* Lulu Pr., Inc.

Geist, Ken. The Three Little Fish & the Big Bad Shark. Gorton, Julia, illus. 2007. (ENG.). 32p. (J). (gr. -1-3). 7.99 *(978-0-439-71962-9(3))* Scholastic, Inc.

—The Three Little Fish & the Big Bad Shark - A Board Book. Gorton, Julia, illus. 2016. (ENG.). 22p. (J). (gr. -1 — 1). bds. 6.99 *(978-0-545-94483-0(X),* Cartwheel Bks.) Scholastic, Inc.

Gesser, Bernadette. The Adventures of Rocky, Croaker & Spot. Mavronis, Michelle, illus. 2008. 20p. pap. 24.95 *(978-1-60703-178-9(7))* America Star Bks.

Glori, Debi. Little Bear & the Wish Fish. (Illus.). 32p. (J). (gr. -1-2). pap. *(978-0-7112-0986-2(3))* ReiseArt Buchhandlung GmbH.

Goldfish. 2004. (J). per. *(978-1-57657-399-0(0))* Paradise Pr., Inc.

Gonzalez, Noni. Kubla, a Koi Story. Gonzalez, Tom, illus. 2013. (ENG.). 38p. (J). pap. 9.99 *(978-1-939337-68-9(2))*; 14.99 *(978-1-939337-72-6(0))* Telemachus Pr., LLC.

Gordon, Mike, illus. The Wish Fish. 2007. (First Reading Level 1 Ser.). 32p. (J). (gr. -1-3). 8.99 *(978-0-7945-1697-0(1)*, Usborne) EDC Publishing.

Gorski, Grzegorz. Bajka o Rybaku i Prawie Zöotej Rybce. 2005. 28p. 11.99 *(978-1-4116-2826-7(8))* Lulu Pr., Inc.

Grant, Joan. Cat & Fish. Curtis, Neil, illus. 2005. (ENG.). 32p. (J). (gr. k-3). 16.95 *(978-1-894965-14-9(0))* Simply Read Bks. CAN. Dist: Ingram Publisher Services.

—Cat & Fish Go to See. Curtis, Neil, illus. 2006. (ENG.). 32p. (J). (gr. -1-3). 16.95 *(978-1-894965-39-2(6))* Simply Read Bks. CAN. Dist: Ingram Publisher Services.

Greenwood, Dwayne. The Tales of Wally the Whale & Sammy the Salmon. 2006. 17.00 *(978-0-8059-9074-4(7))* Dorrance Publishing Co., Inc.

Gregory, Manju. The Dragon's Tears. Le, Guo, illus. 2004. (ENG & JPN.). 24p. (J). pap. *(978-1-85269-810-2(1))*; pap. *(978-1-85269-805-8(5))*; pap. *(978-1-85269-787-7(3))*; pap. *(978-1-85269-699-3(0))*; pap. *(978-1-85269-698-6(2))*; pap. *(978-1-85269-697-9(4))*; pap. *(978-1-85269-696-2(6))*; pap. *(978-1-85269-695-5(8))*; pap. *(978-1-85269-694-8(X))*; pap. *(978-1-85269-692-4(3))*; pap. *(978-1-85269-691-7(5))*; pap. *(978-1-85269-688-7(5))*; pap. *(978-1-85269-687-0(7))*; pap. *(978-1-85269-686-3(9))* Mantra Lingua.

Griffiths, Andy. Killer Koalas from Outer Space & Lots of Other Very Bad Stuff That Will Make Your Brain Explode! Denton, Terry, illus. 2012. (ENG.). 192p. (J). (gr. 3-7). pap. 7.99 *(978-1-250-01017-9(9)*, 9781250010179) Square Fish.

Grimm, Jacob & Grimm, Wilhelm K. The Fisherman & His Wife/ El Pescador y Su Esposa. 2004. (Illus.). (J). *(978-1-933530-20-8(0))* Bingo Bks., Inc.

Grimm, Kristi. Mommy, Tell Me a Story about a Fish. 2013. (Illus.). 34p. pap. 13.99 *(978-0-9899001-3-3(4))* Richer Life, LLC.

Gritton, Steve. Plain Fish. 2007. (Illus.). (J). 17.95 *(978-0-9795361-2-0(X))* Bad Frog Art/SMG Bks.

Gummelt, Donna & Melchiorre, Dondino. Do Fish Kiss? Wall, Randy Hugh, ed. Varela, Juan D., illus. I.t. ed. 2006.Tr. of Los peces Besan. (SPA.). 32p. (J). 14.95 *(978-0-9764798-0-2(X))* Story Store Collection Publishing.

Gundaya, Asela Hazel Z. Butete: The Sotry of a Remarkable Fish. Estoquia, Jonathan T., illus. 2009. 45p. (J). *(978-1-4415-4909-9(9))* Xlibris Corp.

Guzman, Stephanie. The Adventures of Oliver the Clownfish: Acting Cool. 2008. (Illus.). 32p. (J). (ENG.). *(978-1-59664-002-3(2))*; pap. *(978-1-59664-003-0(0))* R J Communications, LLC.

—Oliver the Clownfish: The Invitation Slip-up. 2008. (ENG., Illus.). (J). 14.95 *(978-1-59664-001-6(4))* R J Communications, LLC.

Hanson, Anders. Lone Shark, 1 vol. Haberstroh, Anne, illus. 2007. (Critter Chronicles Ser.). (ENG.). 24p. (J). (gr. k-3). lib. bdg. 24.21 *(978-1-59928-452-1(9)*, SandCastle) ABDO Publishing Co.

Harrington, Claudia. Book 3: Yum-Yum the Very Spoiled Fish. 2016. (Hank the Pet Sitter Ser.). (ENG.). (gr. -1-3). lib. bdg. 27.07 ***(978-1-62402-189-3(1))*** ABDO Publishing Co.

Hartshorne, Holly L. School Time for the Three Little Fish, 1 vol. 2009. 12p. pap. 24.95 *(978-1-60749-404-1(3))* America Star Bks.

Hawk, J. L. If I Were a Creature under the Seaà. 2008. 12p. pap. 24.95 *(978-1-60703-378-3(X))* America Star Bks.

Hawkins, June Morris. When Tony Caught a Fish. 2011. 28p. (gr. 1-2). 12.03 *(978-1-4567-5249-1(9))* AuthorHouse.

Hay, Sam. Goldfish from Beyond the Grave. 2015. (Undead Pets Ser.: 4). lib. bdg. 16.00 *(978-0-606-36220-7(7))* Turtleback Bks.

—Goldfish from Beyond the Grave #4. Cooper, Simon, illus. 2015. (Undead Pets Ser.: 4). (ENG.). 112p. (J). (gr. 1-3). 5.99 *(978-0-448-47798-5(X)*, Grosset & Dunlap) Penguin Young Readers Group.

—Wish Fish. May, Kate, illus. 2011. (My Phonics Readers: Level 2 Ser.). 24p. (J). (gr. -1-1). 24.25 *(978-1-84898-508-7(8))* Sea-To-Sea Pubns.

Hayes, Denis. Silly Fishy Stories for Kids. 2014. 56p. pap. 30.00 *(978-1-4828-9439-4(4))* Partridge Pub.

Hayward, Allan J. The Lost Little Fish. 2003. pap. 9.00 *(978-0-8059-6284-0(0))* Dorrance Publishing Co., Inc.

Hecke, Stephanie. Fishy Dreams. 2011. 28p. pap. 15.99 *(978-1-4628-5907-8(0))* Xlibris Corp.

Hendra, Sue. Barry the Fish with Fingers. 2010. (Illus.). 32p. *(978-1-84738-920-6(1))* Simon & Schuster, Ltd.

—Barry the Fish with Fingers & the Hairy Scary Monster. 2011. 32p. *(978-1-74276-025-4(2)*, Koala Books) Scholastic Australia.

Henry, Kristina, et al. The Fish Tank, 1 vol. 2011. (ENG., Illus.). 48p. (J). 16.99 *(978-0-7643-3706-2(8)*, 9780764337062, Schiffer Publishing Ltd) Schiffer Publishing, Ltd.

Hesse, Diane. Charlie Catfish & the Big Mistake. 2011. 24p. pap. 24.95 *(978-1-4626-4084-3(2))* America Star Bks.

Hill, James. Larry the Lunker. 2004. 35p. pap. 24.95 *(978-1-4137-2972-6(X))* PublishAmerica, Inc.

Hinkler Books Staff, ed. Funny Fish. 2009. (ENG.). 12p. (J). bds. 7.99 *(978-1-74182-110-9(X)*, Ideal Pubns.) Worthy Publishing.

Hofmeister, Alan, et al. The Fun Fish. (Reading for All Learners Ser.). (Illus.). (J). pap. *(978-1-56861-121-1(6))* Swift Learning Resources.

Holding, James Malcolm, 3rd, et al. The Mullet Masters. 2007. pap. 8.00 *(978-0-8059-7147-7(5))* Dorrance Publishing Co., Inc.

Holloway, Jamie. Jimmy Is Not a Fish. 2015. (Rosen REAL Readers: STEM & STEAM Collection). (ENG.). 12p. (gr. 1-2). pap. 6.33 *(978-1-4994-9514-0(5)*, Rosen Classroom) Rosen Publishing Group, Inc., The.

Hoobler, David. Zonk & the Secret Lagoon: The Further Adventures of Zonk the Dreaming Tortoise. Hoobler, David, illus. I.t. ed. 2005. (Illus.). 32p. (J). lib. bdg. 18.95 *(978-0-9706537-1-0(9))* Zonk Galleries and Pubns.

Hopgood, Sally. Five Little Fishes. Piwowarski, Marcin & Marcin, Piwowarski, illus. 2012. (Five Little Counting Bks.). (ENG.). 10p. (J). (gr. -1). 7.99 *(978-1-84956-659-9(3))* Top That! Publishing PLC GBR. Dist: Independent Pubs. Group.

Hoshino, Ryuichi. Finding Nemo Manga Collection. 2016. lib. bdg. 28.15 *(978-0-606-38899-3(0))* Turtleback Bks.

Howarth, Kylie. Fish Jam. 2015. (ENG., Illus.). 40p. (J). (gr. -1-2). 16.99 *(978-1-4998-0098-2(3))* Little Bee Books Inc.

Howe, James. Otter & Odder: A Love Story. Raschka, Chris, illus. 2012. (ENG.). 40p. (J). (gr. 1-4). 14.00 *(978-0-7636-4174-0(X))* Candlewick Pr.

Huang, Yu-Hsuan, illus. Baby Fish: Finger Puppet Book. 2017. (ENG.). 12p. (J). bds. 6.99 *(978-1-4521-5610-1(7))* Chronicle Bks. LLC.

Humu the Little Fish Who Wished Away His Colors. 2003. (J). 10.99 *(978-0-89610-548-5(2))* Island Heritage Publishing.

If I Were a Fish. (J). 26.20 *(978-0-8136-8443-7(9))*; (gr. -1-3). 59.50 *(978-0-8136-8008-8(5))* Modern Curriculum Pr.

ImageBooks Staff & Chronicle Books Staff. Little Fish Finger Puppet Book. 2010. (Little Finger Puppet Board Bks.). (ENG., Illus.). 12p. (J). (gr. -1 — 1). bds. 6.99 *(978-0-8118-7344-4(7))* Chronicle Bks. LLC.

Inglis, Lillian. The One That Caught Away. 2012. 52p. pap. 31.99 *(978-1-4691-8622-1(5))* Xlibris Corp.

Isaacs, Latricia. Mason & Lilly Visit Grandpa. 2011. 16p. 8.32 *(978-1-4567-2788-8(5))* AuthorHouse.

Jacobsen, Annie. Ole Mackerel. Everson, Mya, illus. 2012. 32p. (J). 9.98 *(978-0-9778276-5-7(8))* Pickled Herring Pr.

Jacques, Florence Page. There Once Was a Puffin. Halpern, Shari, illus. 2016. (ENG.). 32p. (J). 15.95 *(978-0-7358-4245-8(0))* North-South Bks., Inc.

Jaimungal, Richard Neal. The Hungry Bird & the Lonely Fish. 2011. 16p. pap. 11.32 *(978-1-4634-3136-5(8))* AuthorHouse.

Janow, Jody. Eddie's Great Escape. 2010. 44p. pap. 19.99 *(978-1-4520-1764-8(6))* AuthorHouse.

Johnson, Carl & Johnson, Gwen. Diggin' the Big'un. Johnson, Gwen, illus. 2007. (Illus.). 16p. (YA). 14.95 *(978-0-9795860-1-9(1))* Fish Tales Publishing.

Johnson, David. Toby the Blow Fish: A Fish on A Quest & Learns A Life Lesson. 2011. (ENG.). 16p. pap. 9.95 *(978-1-4327-6680-1(5))* Outskirts Pr., Inc.

Johnson, Grace. The Little Fish Who Was Afraid to Swim. 2008. 36p. pap. 15.49 *(978-1-4389-2262-1(0))* AuthorHouse.

Johnson, Mark. Little Fish Lou. 2008. 28p. pap. 17.95 *(978-1-4327-2934-9(9))* Outskirts Pr., Inc.

Johnson, Rebecca. Clown Fish Finds a Friend. Parish, Steve, illus. 2005. (Animal Storybooks Ser.). 24p. (gr. k-3). lib. bdg. 22.00 *(978-0-8368-5969-0(3)*, Gareth Stevens Learning Library) Stevens, Gareth Publishing LLLP.

Julie, Aunt. State Symbols of Texas - Paddleduck #8. 2012. 50p. pap. 5.95 *(978-1-105-91163-7(2))* Lulu Pr., Inc.

Kalar, Bonnie. Josh & the Fish. Spreen, Kathe, illus. Date not set. 8p. (J). (gr. -1-2). pap. *(978-1-891619-14-4(4))* Corona Pr.

Kelly, David A. The Missing Marlin. Meyers, Mark, illus. 2014. (Ballpark Mysteries Ser.: Bk. 8). (ENG.). 112p. (J). (gr. 1-4). 4.99 *(978-0-307-97782-3(X)*, Random Hse. Bks. for Young Readers) Random Hse. Children's Bks.

—The Missing Marlin. 2014. (Ballpark Mysteries Ser.: Bk. 8). lib. bdg. 14.75 *(978-0-606-35565-0(0))* Turtleback Bks.

Keyser-Rogers, Marianne. Lighthouse Neighbors Are Coral Reefs. 2012. 40p. 24.95 *(978-1-4626-4898-6(3))* America Star Bks.

KING, R. O. N. S. The Soul-pearl. 2010. 169p. pap. 11.50 *(978-1-4457-5542-7(4))* Lulu Pr., Inc.

Kirker, Solveig. The Florida Pod. 2009. 32p. pap. 12.99 *(978-1-4389-3137-1(9))* AuthorHouse.

Kitamura, Satoshi. El Pecezito Juega a las Escondidas. (Buenas Noches Ser.). (SPA.). (J). pap. 7.95 *(978-958-04-5089-4(7))* Norma S.A. COL. Dist: Distribuidora Norma, Inc.

Klassen, Jon. This Is Not My Hat. Klassen, Jon, illus. 2012. (ENG., Illus.). 40p. (J). (gr. -1-3). 16.99 *(978-0-7636-5599-0(6))* Candlewick Pr.

Klett, David. The Adventures of Willy & Billy Bk. 1: The Lake Lure Chronicles - Book 1. Lang, Carole, illus. I.t. ed. 2006. 32p. (J). lib. bdg. 17.95 *(978-0-9779325-0-4(8))* Five Oaks Pr.

Knudsen, Michelle. Fish & Frog: Brand New Readers. Petrone, Valeria, illus. 2005. (Brand New Readers Ser.). (ENG.). 8p. (J). (gr. -1-3). pap. 5.99 *(978-0-7636-2457-6(8))* Candlewick Pr.

—Fish & Frog Big Book: Brand New Readers. Petrone, Valeria, illus. 2010. (Brand New Readers Ser.). (ENG.). 48p. (J). (gr. -1-3). pap. 24.99 *(978-0-7636-4810-7(8))* Candlewick Pr.

Koppens, Judith. Good-Bye, Fish. van Lindenhuizen, Eline, illus. 2013. (Animal Square Ser.). (ENG.). 32p. (J). (gr. -1-k). 13.95 *(978-1-60537-153-5(X))* Cobblestone Publishing Co.

Kor, Paul. Flash the Fish. Kor, Paul, illus. 2017. (ENG., Illus.). 32p. (J). (-k). 16.99 *(978-0-7352-2746-0(2)*, Dial Bks) Penguin Young Readers Group.

Korda, Lerryn. Into the Wild. Korda, Lerryn, illus. 2010. (Playtime with Little Nye Ser.). (ENG., Illus.). 26p. (J). (gr. -1 — 1). 8.99 *(978-0-7636-4812-1(4))* Candlewick Pr.

Korman, Susan. Swordfish Returns. Stegos, Daniel J., illus. 2011. (Smithsonian Oceanic Collection Ser.). (ENG.). 32p. (J). (gr. -1-3). 8.95 *(978-1-60727-666-1(6))*; 19.95 *(978-1-60727-665-4(8))* Soundprints.

—Swordfish Returns. Stegos, Daniel, illus. (ENG.). 32p. (J). 2005. (gr. -1-2). 9.95 *(978-1-59249-132-2(4)*, PB4075) 2005. (gr. -1-2). 4.95 *(978-1-59249-126-1(X)*, B4075) 2004. (gr. 2-2). pap. 6.95 *(978-1-59249-127-8(8)*, S4025) 2003. (gr. -1-2). 19.95 *(978-1-59249-128-5(6)*, BC4025) 2003. (gr. -1-2). 8.95 *(978-1-59249-129-2(4)*, SC4025) Soundprints.

—Swordfish Returns. Stegos, Daniel J., illus. 2003. (Smithsonian Oceanic Collection). (ENG.). 32p. (J). (gr. 2-2). 15.95 *(978-1-59249-125-4(1)*, B4025) Soundprints.

Kralapp, Karl E. Fish Food. Kralapp, Karl E., illus. 2013. (Illus.). 28p. pap. 9.99 *(978-1-937165-62-8(0))* Orange Hat Publishing.

Kranz, Linda. Only One You. Mlawer, Teresa, tr. from ENG. 2014. (ENG & SPA., Illus.). 32p. (J). (gr. -1-1). 12.95 *(978-1-63076-023-6(4))* Taylor Trade Publishing.

—You Be You. Mlawer, Teresa, tr. from ENG. 2014. (ENG & SPA., Illus.). 32p. (J). (gr. -1-1). 12.95 *(978-1-63076-021-2(8))* Taylor Trade Publishing.

—You Be You. (J). 2011. *(978-1-58979-667-6(5))* 2011. (ENG., Illus.). 32p. (gr. -1-1). 12.95 *(978-1-58979-666-9(7))* Vol. 2013. (ENG., Illus.). 32p. (gr. -1 — 1). 7.95 *(978-1-58979-747-5(7))* Taylor Trade Publishing.

Kristina Learns about Fishing. 2007. (J). *(978-0-9792728-0-6(7))* Tracepaper Bks. Inc.

Krohn, Gretchen & Johnson, John Norton. The Scales of the Silver Fish. Haring, Mary, illus. 2011. 238p. 46.95 *(978-1-258-08176-8(8))* Literary Licensing, LLC.

Krulik, Nancy. Something's Fishy, No. 26. John and Wendy Staff, illus. 2007. (Katie Kazoo, Switcheroo Ser.: 26). (ENG.). 80p. (J). (gr. 2-4). pap. 4.99 *(978-0-448-44442-0(9)*, Grosset & Dunlap) Penguin Young Readers Group.

Krulik, Nancy E. Something's Fishy. John & Wendy, illus. 2008. (Katie Kazoo, Switcheroo Ser.). 76p. 14.00 *(978-0-7569-8348-2(7))* Perfection Learning Corp.

Krykorka, Ian. Carl the Christmas Carp, 1 vol. Krykorka, Vladyana, illus. 2016. (ENG.). 32p. (J). (gr. -1-3). 15.95 *(978-1-4598-1377-9(4))* Orca Bk. Pubs. USA.

Kurlander, Keith. Tommy the Fishboy. Belomlinsky, Alex, illus. 2012. 34p. 24.95 *(978-1-4626-4527-5(5))* America Star Bks.

La Coccinella. Look & See: Mommy, Where Are You? 2014. (Look & See! Ser.). (ENG., Illus.). 24p. (J). (gr. -1 — 1). bds. 6.95 *(978-1-4549-0615-5(4))* Sterling Publishing Co., Inc.

Laboy, Gloria J. Freddie Learns Obedience. 2008. 24p. pap. 13.95 *(978-1-4327-1906-7(8))* Outskirts Pr., Inc.

—Sally Learns Honesty. 2008. 20p. pap. 13.95 *(978-1-4327-2553-2(X))* Outskirts Pr., Inc.

Lagonegro, Melissa & RH Disney Staff. Just Keep Swimming. Harchy, Atelier Philippe, illus. 2005. (Step into Reading Ser.). (ENG.). 32p. (J). (gr. k-3). pap. 3.99 *(978-0-7364-2319-9(2)*, RH/Disney) Random Hse. Children's Bks.

Lamb, Rosy. Paul Meets Bernadette. Lamb, Rosy, illus. 2013. (ENG., Illus.). 40p. (J). (gr. -1-3). 14.00 *(978-0-7636-6130-4(9))* Candlewick Pr.

Landman, Yael & Hill, Barbara. Fred's Wish for Fish. Stein, Laurie, illus. 2009. 8p. (J). *(978-0-545-16144-2(4))* Scholastic, Inc.

Landrón, Rafael & Landrón, José Rafael. Beba y la Isla Nena: Beba & the Little Island. Ordóñez, María Antonia, illus. 2010. (SPA & ENG.). 32p. (J). *(978-1-934370-05-6(3)*, Campanita Bks.) Editorial Campana.

LaReau, Kara. Ugly Fish. Magoon, Scott, illus. 2006. (ENG.). 40p. (J). (gr. -1-3). 16.99 *(978-0-15-205082-5(5))* Houghton Mifflin Harcourt Publishing Co.

Larsen, Dean. Fish Dreams. 2006. 32p. (J). 14.25 *(978-1-4116-7783-8(8))* Lulu Pr., Inc.

Lavi, Yifat. Fish Also Fade: Illustrated by: Oren Somech. 2011. (Illus.). 32p. pap. 14.58 *(978-1-4520-9084-9(X))* AuthorHouse.

Le, Guo, illus. The Dragon's Tears. 2004. (ENG & POR.). 24p. (J). pap. *(978-1-85269-693-1(1))*; pap. *(978-1-85269-700-6(8))* Mantra Lingua.

Lee, Sharon. The Tale of the Selfish Shellfish. 2011. (Illus.). 36p. pap. 15.31 *(978-1-4567-7697-8(5))* AuthorHouse.

Leon, Georgina Lazaro. La Niña y la Estrella. Perez-Moliere, Mamie, illus. 2003. (Yellow Ser.). (SPA.). 31p. (gr. k-3). pap. 7.95 *(978-1-57581-436-0(6))* Santillana USA Publishing Co., Inc.

Lesley, Sharon. The Red Scarf & Other Stories. 2010. 165p. pap. 14.95 *(978-1-4457-6720-8(1))* Lulu Pr., Inc.

Libby, Lori Ann. The Adventures of Henry Hamper & the Flying Fish. Lee, Tricia Ting, illus. 2010. 34p. pap. 13.95 *(978-1-60911-493-0(0)*, Eloquent Bks.) Strategic Book Publishing & Rights Agency (SBPRA).

Lim, Charlotte. Attack of the Swordfish & Other Singapore Tales: Text by Charlotte Lim: Illustrations by Alicia Tan Yen Ping: Creative Directing by Ruby Lim-Yang. 2005. (Illus.). 48p. *(978-981-05-3215-4(6))* National Heritage Board.

Lima, Rick. Redd: The Beta Fish. 2009. 28p. pap. 12.49 *(978-1-4389-4320-6(2))* AuthorHouse.

Lionni, Leo. Fish Is Fish. 2015. (Step into Reading Ser.). (ENG., Illus.). 40p. (J). (gr. -1-2). 3.99 *(978-0-553-52218-1(3)*, Random Hse. Bks. for Young Readers) Random Hse. Children's Bks.

—Nadarín. Mlawer, Teresa, tr. from SPA. 2005. (SPA., Illus.). 24p. (J). (gr. -1-3). per. 6.99 *(978-1-930332-80-5(7))* Lectorum Pubns., Inc.

—Swimmy. 2013. (ENG., Illus.). 32p. (J). (gr. -1-2). 17.99 *(978-0-385-75358-6(6))*; lib. bdg. 20.99 *(978-0-385-75366-1(7))* Random Hse. Children's Bks. (Knopf Bks. for Young Readers).

little bee books, little bee. Dive into the Sea! Llewhellin, Gareth, illus. 2016. (ENG.). 12p. (J). (gr. -1 — 1). bds. 7.99 *(978-1-4998-0297-9(8))* Little Bee Books Inc.

Little Fish Christmas Merchandiser. (J). 128.16 *(978-0-8307-2909-8(7)*, Gospel Light) Gospel Light Pubns.

Little Fish Easter Merchandiser. (J). 128.16 *(978-0-8307-2908-1(9)*, Gospel Light) Gospel Light Pubns.

Little Fish Jesus Merchandiser. (J). 128.16 *(978-0-8307-2907-4(0)*, Gospel Light) Gospel Light Pubns.

Little Is Big. 2006. (Illus.). (J). *(978-1-882601-58-5(0))* See-More's Workshop.

Lloyd-Jones, Sally. Poor Doreen: a Fishy Tale. Boiger, Alexandra, illus. 2014. (ENG.). 40p. (J). (gr. -1-3). 17.99 *(978-0-375-86918-1(2)*, Schwartz & Wade Bks.) Random Hse. Children's Bks.

Louise, Kate. The Upside-Down Fish. Matine, Laura, illus. 2015. (ENG.). 32p. (J). (gr. -1-k). 16.95 *(978-1-62914-628-7(5)*, Sky Pony Pr.) Skyhorse Publishing Co., Inc.

Lumry, Amanda & Hurwitz, Laura. Survival of the Salmon. 2006. (Adventures of Riley (Unnumbered) Ser.). (Illus.). 34p. (J). (gr. -1-3). 15.95 *(978-0-9748411-3-7(7))* Eaglemont Pr.

Lyle-Soffe, Shari. On the Go with Rooter & Snuffle. Collier, Kevin Scott, illus. 2008. 20p. pap. 9.95 *(978-1-933090-96-2(0))* Guardian Angel Publishing, Inc.

Malouf, Ranya. Blue Fish's Secret Wish. 2011. 32p. pap. *(978-9963-610-72-3(2))* Rimal Pubns.

Mansfield, Andy. Fish Food. Lohlein, Henning, illus. 2015. (ENG.). 14p. (J). (gr. -1-k). 9.99 *(978-1-4998-0044-9(4))* Little Bee Books Inc.

—One Lonely Fish. Flintham, Thomas & Mansfield, Andy, illus. 2017. (ENG.). 22p. (J). 15.99 *(978-1-68119-201-7(2)*, 9781681192017, Bloomsbury USA Childrens) Bloomsbury Publishing USA.

Marchetti, Dave. Steve the Stickleback. 2011. 28p. pap. 13.99 *(978-1-4634-2038-3(2))* AuthorHouse.

Marin, Cheech. Captain Cheech. Ramirez, Orlando L., illus. 2008. 32p. (J). (gr. -1-3). lib. bdg. 17.89 *(978-0-06-113208-7(X))* HarperCollins Pubs.

Marino, Gianna. Splotch. 2017. (ENG., Illus.). 40p. (J). (gr. -1-1). 17.99 *(978-0-451-46957-1(7)*, Viking Books for Young Readers) Penguin Young Readers Group.

Marsh, Carole. The Awesome Aquarium Mystery. 2006. (Awesome Mystery Ser.). (Illus.). 104p. (J). (gr. 7-14). 14.95 *(978-0-635-06227-7(5))* Gallopade International.

Marston, Hope Irvin. My Little Book of Manatees. Mirocha, Stephanie, illus. 2007. 32p. (J). (gr. k-5). pap. 7.95 *(978-0-89317-065-3(8)*, Windward Publishing) Finney Co., Inc.

Martin, Brenda Darnley. Freddie, Hector & Tish: The Treasure-Hunt Fish. 2008. 36p. per. 24.95 *(978-1-60441-109-6(0))* America Star Bks.

—The Treasure Hunt Fish & Miss Bernadette's Wish. Ramos, Amy Jones, illus. 2009. 40p. pap. 14.95 *(978-0-9841074-1-4(X))* Jimsam Inc. Publishing.

Matthews, L. S. Fish. 2006. (ENG.). 192p. (J). (gr. 3-7). reprint ed. 6.99 *(978-0-440-42021-7(0)*, Yearling) Random Hse. Children's Bks.

Mayo, Jason. Do Witches Make Fishes? 2010. 36p. pap. 16.99 *(978-1-4520-6944-9(1))* AuthorHouse.

McAllister O'Connell, Andrea. Jackson, Josie, & the (almost) Free Lunch. 2010. (J). 16.95 *(978-1-59298-300-1(6))* Beaver's Pond Pr., Inc.

McBride, Anthony. The Fish That Was Afraid to Swim. 2013. 52p. pap. 21.88 *(978-1-4669-9388-4(X))* Trafford Publishing.

McDonnell, Patrick. Shine! 2017. (ENG., Illus.). 40p. (J). (gr. -1-3). 16.99 *(978-0-316-26278-1(1))* Little Brown & Co.

McGowan, Kim. A Fish Tale. 2010. 24p. 12.95 *(978-1-4520-2089-1(2))* AuthorHouse.

McKinney, Frank & Mason, Kate. Dead Fred, Flying Lunchboxes & the Good Luck Circle. 2009. (ENG.). 336p. (J). (gr. 4-8). 18.95 *(978-0-7573-1382-0(5))* Health Communications, Inc.

McOmber, Rachel B., ed. McOmber Phonics Storybooks. rev. ed. (Illus.). (J). *(978-0-944991-72-5(6))* Swift Learning Resources.

Meadows, Daisy. Courtney the Clownfish Fairy. 2011. (Illus.). 62p. (J). *(978-0-545-28877-4(0))* Scholastic, Inc.

—Stephanie the Starfish Fairy. 2011. (Illus.). 65p. (J). *(978-0-545-28875-0(4))* Scholastic, Inc.

Meister, Cari. The Brave Puffer Fish, 1 vol. Harpster, Steve, illus. 2011. (Ocean Tales Ser.). (ENG.). 32p. (gr. 2-3). pap. 6.25 *(978-1-4342-3389-9(8))* Stone Arch Bks.

—The Hiding Eel, 1 vol. Harpster, Steve, illus. 2011. (Ocean Tales Ser.). (ENG.). 32p. (gr. 2-3). pap. 6.25 *(978-1-4342-3390-5(1))*; lib. bdg. 22.65 *(978-1-4342-3199-4(2))* Stone Arch Bks.

Mellon, Gray. The Weird Worlds of Willoughby Wren Wren & the Pigeons. 2010. 196p. pap. *(978-1-907652-06-6(X))* Grosvenor Hse. Publishing Ltd.

Meomi (Firm) Staff. The Octonauts & the Frown Fish. 2008. (Octonauts Ser.). (ENG., Illus.). 36p. (J). (gr. -1-3). 15.95 *(978-1-59702-014-5(1))* Immedium.

Messner, Kate. Sea Monster & the Bossy Fish. Rash, Andy, illus. 2013. (ENG.). 40p. (J). (gr. -1-k). 16.99 *(978-1-4521-1253-4(3))* Chronicle Bks. LLC.

—Sea Monster's First Day. Rash, Andy, illus. 2011. (ENG.). 36p. (J). (gr. -1-3). 16.99 *(978-0-8118-7564-6(4))* Chronicle Bks. LLC.

—The Seventh Wish. 2017. (ENG.). 256p. (J). pap. 7.99 *(978-1-68119-431-8(7)*, 9781681194318, Bloomsbury USA Childrens) Bloomsbury Publishing USA.

Metaxas, Eric. Princess Scargo & the Birthday Pumpkin, 1 vol. Barbour, Karen, illus. 2004. (Rabbit Ears-A Classic Tale Ser.). (ENG.). 40p. (gr. k-5). 25.65 *(978-1-59197-769-8(X))* Spotlight.

Meyers, Tim. Let's Call Him Lau-Wiliwili-Humuhumu-Nukunuku-Nukunuku-Apua'a-Oi'oi. 2005. (Illus.). 24p. (J). 16.95 incl. audio compact disk *(978-1-57306-252-7(9))* Bess Pr., Inc.

Miller, Alex. Beyond the River, 1 vol. Miller, Caroline, illus. 2011. (ENG.). 64p. (J). 16.99 *(978-0-7643-3741-3(6)*, 9780764337413, Schiffer Publishing Ltd) Schiffer Publishing, Ltd.

Miller, Jay. Sal & Sally. 2008. 52p. pap. 20.49 *(978-1-935028-13-0(8))* AuthorHouse.

Milton, Cathlene. The Wonders of Billy Sniggles: Billy Sniggles & the Dead Fish. 2013. 18p. pap. 9.99 *(978-1-62509-780-4(8))* Salem Author Services.

Mitchell, Laurence. Fish with Feet: From the Travels of Guppy Flynn, Book # 3. 2009. 32p. pap. 12.99 *(978-1-4389-5300-7(3))* AuthorHouse.

Mitchell, Mary Esther. The Adventures of Timmy Gills. 2005. (J). pap. 20.00 *(978-0-8059-9660-9(5)*, RoseDog Bks.) Dorrance Publishing Co., Inc.

Miyazaki, Hayao. Ponyo Film Comic, Vol. 1. Miyazaki, Hayao, illus. movie tie-in ed. 2009. (ENG., Illus.). 172p. (J). pap. 9.99 *(978-1-4215-3077-2(5))* Viz Media.

—Ponyo Film Comic, Vol. 2. Miyazaki, Hayao, illus. movie tie-in ed. 2009. (ENG., Illus.). 172p. (J). pap. 9.99 *(978-1-4215-3078-9(3))* Viz Media.

—Ponyo Film Comic, Vol. 3. Miyazaki, Hayao, illus. movie tie-in ed. 2009. (ENG., Illus.). 172p. (J). pap. 9.99 *(978-1-4215-3079-6(1))* Viz Media.

—Ponyo Film Comic, Vol. 4. Miyazaki, Hayao, illus. movie tie-in ed. 2009. (ENG., Illus.). 172p. (J). pap. 9.99 *(978-1-4215-3080-2(5))* Viz Media.

—Ponyo Picture Book, Vol. 1. Miyazaki, Hayao, illus. 2009. (ENG., Illus.). 152p. (J). (gr. 2-7). 19.99 *(978-1-4215-3065-9(1))* Viz Media.

Monsell, Mary Elise. A Fish Named Yum: Vol. IV. 2016. (ENG.). 68p. pap. 8.99 *(978-1-5040-2967-4(4))* Open Road Integrated Media, Inc.

Morgan, Roxy. Melvin the Moose & Mr. Bluefish. 2007. (Illus.). 35p. (J). lib. bdg. 18.95 *(978-0-9768052-4-3(3))* New Century Publishing, LLC.

Mullarkey, Lisa. TJ Zaps the Freeze Out: Stopping the Silent Treatment #3, 1 vol. LaCoste, Gary, illus. 2012. (TJ Trapper, Bully Zapper Ser.). (ENG.). 80p. (J). (gr. 2-5). lib. bdg. 27.07 *(978-1-61641-907-3(5)*, Calico Chapter Bks) Magic Wagon.

My Fish. (Early Intervention Levels Ser.). 21.30 *(978-0-7362-0359-3(1))* CENGAGE Learning.

E
F
G

My Fish Are Fine with Me, 6 vols., Pack. (gr. -1-2). 27.00 (978-0-7635-9465-7(2)) Rigby Education.
Nam, Jongpil. A Fish. 2012. 116p. pap. 15.18 (978-1-4772-1886-0(6)) AuthorHouse.
Nestell, Mark. Gordon & the Magic Fishbowl, 1 vol. Daley-Prado, M. J., illus. 2010. 26p. pap. 24.95 (978-1-4489-8495-4(5)) America Star Bks.
Nickelodeon Staff & Nickelodeon / LeapFrog. Go Diego Go! Underwater Mystery. 2008. (J). 13.99 (978-1-59319-925-8(2)) LeapFrog Enterprises, Inc.
Nicola, Robbin. Fighter Joe: The Fish of Which Dreams Are Made. Wolf, Claudia, illus. 2006. 24p. (J). per. 2.99 (978-1-59958-001-2(2)) Journey Stone Creations, LLC.
Nix, Jonathan J. Egghead: The Story of One Small Trout. 2008. 24p. pap. 24.95 (978-1-60474-955-7(5)) America Star Bks.
Nordling, Lee. Fishfishfish. Bosch, Meritxell, illus. 2015. (Three-Story Bks.). (ENG.). 32p. (J). (gr. k-3). lib. bdg. 25.26 (978-1-4677-4575-8(8), Graphic Universe™) Lerner Publishing Group.
—FishFishFish. Bosch, Meritxell, illus. 2015. (Three-Story Bks.). (ENG.). 32p. (J). (gr. k-3). pap. 6.95 (978-1-4677-4576-5(6), Graphic Universe™) Lerner Publishing Group.
O'Connor, Jane. Peanut Butter & Jellyfish. Glasser, Robin Preiss, illus. 2015. (I Can Read Level 1 Ser.). (ENG.). 32p. (J). (gr. -1-3). pap. 3.99 (978-0-06-226975-1(5)) HarperCollins Pubs.
—Peanut Butter & Jellyfish. 2015. (Fancy Nancy - I Can Read! Ser.). (J). lib. bdg. 13.55 (978-0-606-36479-9(X)) Turtleback Bks.
Oe, Patricia Daly. Where Are My Stripes? Oe, Patricia Daly, illus. 2007. (R. I. C. Story Chest Ser.). (Illus.). 20p. (J). (gr. -1-k). 11.95 incl. audio compact disk (978-1-74126-438-8(3)) R.I.C. Pubns. AUS. Dist: SCB Distributors.
Oh, DaYun. We Are Brothers. Godeassi, Anna, illus. 2014. (MySELF Bookshelf Ser.). (ENG.). 32p. (J). (gr. k-2). pap. 11.94 (978-1-60357-692-5(4)) Norwood Hse. Pr.
O'Hara, Mo. Any Fin Is Possible. Jagucki, Marek, illus. 2016. (My Big Fat Zombie Goldfish Ser.: 4). (ENG.). 224p. (J). (gr. 3-5). 12.99 (978-1-250-06353-3(1), 9781250063533) Feiwel & Friends.
—The Fin-Tastic Fish-Sitter. Jagucki, Marek, illus. 2016. (My Big Fat Zombie Goldfish Ser.). (ENG.). 40p. (J). (gr. -1-2). 16.99 (978-1-250-06523-0(2), 9781250065230) Feiwel & Friends.
—Fins of Fury. Jagucki, Marek, illus. 2015. (My Big Fat Zombie Goldfish Ser.: Bk. 3). (ENG.). 224p. (J). (gr. 2-5). 12.99 (978-1-250-02921-8(X), 9781250029218) Feiwel & Friends.
—Jurassic Carp. Jagucki, Marek, illus. 2017. (My Big Fat Zombie Goldfish Ser.: 6). (ENG.). 224p. (J). 12.99 (978-1-250-06357-1(4), 9781250063571) Feiwel & Friends.
—My Big Fat Zombie Goldfish. 2013. (My Big Fat Zombie Goldfish Ser.: Bk. 1). (ENG., Illus.). 192p. (J). (gr. 2-5). 12.99 (978-1-250-02919-5(8), 9781250029195) Feiwel & Friends.
—My Big Fat Zombie Goldfish. Jagucki, Marek, illus. 2014. (My Big Fat Zombie Goldfish Ser.: 1). (ENG.). 208p. (J). (gr. 2-5). pap. 6.99 (978-1-250-05215-5(7), 9781250052155) Square Fish.
—The SeaQuel. Jagucki, Marek, illus. 2014. (My Big Fat Zombie Goldfish Ser.: 2). (ENG.). 208p. (J). (gr. 2-5). 12.99 (978-1-250-02920-1(1), 9781250029201) Feiwel & Friends.
Olien, Jessica. The Blobfish Book. Olien, Jessica, illus. 2016. (Illus.). 40p. (J). (gr. -1-3). 17.99 (978-0-06-239415-6(0)) HarperCollins Pubs.
Oliver the Clownfish: The Invitation Slip-up. 2006. (J). 5.95 (978-1-59664-000-9(6)) R J Communications, LLC.
O'Neill, Michael Patrick. Fishy Friends: A Journey Through the Coral Kingdom. O'Neill, Michael Patrick, photos by. 2003. (Illus.). 64p. (J). 19.95 (978-0-9728653-0-2(6)) Batfish Bks.
Orford, Margie. The Magic Fish. Littlewort, Lizza, illus. 2012. (Best Loved Tales for Africa Ser.). (ENG.). 32p. (J). (gr. k-2). pap. 9.95 (978-1-77009-822-0(4)) Jacana Media ZAF. Dist: Independent Pubs. Group.
Origlio, Peter, illus. Charlie & Albert. 2007. 22p. (J). pap. 12.95 (978-0-9801329-0-8(8)) Charlie & Albert.
Page, Nick & Page, Claire. The Loaves & Fishes. Shimmen, Cathy, illus. 2006. (Read with Me (Make Believe Ideas) Ser.). 30p. (J). (gr. k-2). (978-1-84610-175-5(1)) Make Believe Ideas.
Park, Barbara. Junie B. Jones Smells Something Fishy. unabr. ed. 2004. (Junie B. Jones Ser.: No. 12). 66p. (J). (gr. k-3). pap. 17.00 incl. audio (978-0-8072-0533-4(8), Listening Library) Random Hse. Audio Publishing Group.
Parker, Emma. Davey Dory. 2010. (Illus.). 20p. pap. (978-1-877561-58-0(4)) First Edition Ltd.
—How Many Fish? 2010. (Illus.). pap. (978-1-877561-10-8(X)) First Edition Ltd.
Parker, Vic, compiled by. The Fish & the Hare & Other Silly Stories. 2016. (Silly Stories Ser.). (ENG.). 40p. (J). (gr. 2-3). pap. 14.05 (978-1-4824-4199-4(3)) Stevens, Gareth Publishing LLLP.
Parsons, Leif. Only Fish Fall from the Sky. 2015. (ENG., Illus.). 32p. (J). (gr. -1-2). 17.95 (978-1-57687-757-9(4), powerHouse Bks.) powerHouse Cultural Entertainment, Inc.
Pati, Geeta. Finny's Voyage Through the Universe: Nebula, Supernova, Open Star Cluster. 2007. 100p. per. 11.95 (978-1-59526-422-0(1), Llumina Pr.) Aeon Publishing Inc.
Paul Ahrens-Gray & Ericka Grogan. Fish. 2005. (Illus.). 60p. (J). pap., act. bk. ed. 4.95 (978-1-59867-001-1(8)) Global Learning, Inc.
Paul, Miranda. Blobfish Throws a Party. Caton, Maggie, illus. 2017. (ENG.). 32p. (J). (gr. -1-3). 16.99 **(978-1-4998-0422-5(9))** Little Bee Books Inc.
Pelosi, Vincent L. The Magical Underwater Kingdom of Balenarium. 2012. 200p. 46.72 (978-1-4797-1951-8(X)); pap. 28.03 (978-1-4797-1950-1(1)) Xlibris Corp.
Percy, Graham. The Heron & the Fish. Percy, Graham, illus. 2009. (Aesop's Fables Ser.). (ENG., Illus.). 32p. (J). (gr. k-3). 28.50 (978-1-60253-202-1(8), 200037) Child's World, Inc., The.
Petreman, Gwen. A Wish for Haidan. 2011. 24p. (gr. -1). 12.56 (978-1-4269-5739-0(4)) Trafford Publishing.
Pfister, Marcus. The Adventures of Rainbow Fish. 2014. (Rainbow Fish Ser.). (ENG., Illus.). 144p. (J). 19.95 (978-0-7358-4185-7(3)) North-South Bks., Inc.
—Good Night, Little Rainbow Fish. 2012. (Rainbow Fish Ser.). (ENG., Illus.). 32p. (J). (gr. -1-3). 18.95 (978-0-7358-4082-9(2)) North-South Bks., Inc.
—Rainbow Fish / Perz Arco Iris. 2015. (Rainbow Fish Ser.). (ENG & SPA., Illus.). 32p. (J). 9.95 (978-0-7358-4197-0(7)) North-South Bks., Inc.
—The Rainbow Fish Anniversary Edition. 2017. (ENG., Illus.). 32p. (J). (gr. -1-3). 25.00 **(978-0-7358-4284-7(1))** North-South Bks., Inc.
—Rainbow Fish Colors. 2013. (Rainbow Fish Ser.). (ENG., Illus.). 12p. (J). (gr. 1-1). bds. 7.95 (978-0-7358-4147-5(0)) North-South Bks., Inc.
—Rainbow Fish Deep Sea Adventure Sticker & Coloring Storybook. 2010. (Rainbow Fish Ser.). (ENG.). 24p. (gr. -1-2). 5.95 (978-0-7358-2318-1(9)) North-South Bks., Inc.
—Rainbow Fish Finds His Way. James, J. Alison, tr. from GER. Pfister, Marcus, illus. 2006. (Rainbow Fish Ser.). (ENG., Illus.). 32p. (J). (gr. k-3). 18.95 (978-0-7358-2084-5(8)) North-South Bks., Inc.
—Rainbow Fish Opposites. 2013. (Rainbow Fish Ser.). (ENG., Illus.). 12p. (J). (gr. 1-1). bds. 7.95 (978-0-7358-4146-8(2)) North-South Bks., Inc.
—Rainbow Fish Puzzle Book. 2012. (Rainbow Fish Ser.). (ENG., Illus.). 16p. (J). (gr. -1-3). bds. 9.95 (978-0-7358-4096-6(2)) North-South Bks., Inc.
—Rainbow Fish to the Rescue! 2015. (Rainbow Fish Ser.).Tr. of Regenbogenfisch, Komm Hilf Mir! (ENG., Illus.). 32p. (J). pap. 9.95 (978-3-314-01574-8(7)) North-South Bks., Inc.
Pfister, Marcus. You Can't Win Them All, Rainbow Fish. 2017. (ENG., Illus.). 32p. (J). (gr. -1-3). 18.95 **(978-0-7358-4287-8(6))** North-South Bks., Inc.
Philpot, Graham, illus. The Fish That Talked. 2008. (Usborne First Reading: Level 3 Ser.). 48p. (J). 8.99 (978-0-7945-1945-2(8), Usborne) EDC Publishing.
Popsicle, Patty. Crack-a-Doodle Horse Tales: A Tale about Biting. 2011. 24p. (gr. -1). pap. 12.99 (978-1-4343-5157-9(2)) AuthorHouse.
Potter, Beatrix. The Classic Tale of Mr. Jeremy Fisher. Santore, Charles, illus. 2015. (ENG.). 22p. (J). bds. 8.95 (978-1-60433-548-4(3), Applesauce Pr.) Cider Mill Pr. Bk. Pubs., LLC.
Poydar, Nancy. Fish School. 2009. (ENG., Illus.). 32p. (J). (gr. -1-3). 16.95 (978-0-8234-2140-4(6)) Holiday Hse., Inc.
Procter, Diann. It Happened in the Goldfish Bowl. Procter, Bill, illus. 2007. 28p. pap. 24.95 (978-1-4241-8357-9(X)) America Star Bks.
Publications International Ltd. Staff. My 1St Look & Find Disney Pixar Friends & Heroes. 2007. 18p. (J). 9.98 (978-1-4127-6848-1(9), PIL Kids) Publications International, Ltd.
—Nemo First Look & Find. 2007. 18p. (J). 9.98 (978-1-4127-6838-2(1)) Phoenix International Publications, Inc.
Publications International Ltd. Staff, creator. Jellyfish Jam: Pop-up Songbook. 2005. (Play-A-Song Ser.). (Illus.). 12p. (J). (gr. -1-k). 16.98 (978-1-4127-3293-2(X), 7243700) Publications International, Ltd.
Publications International Ltd. Staff, ed. Finding Nemo. 2007. (J). 9.98 (978-1-4127-6516-9(1)) Publications International, Ltd.
—Finding Nemo: A Party for Nemo. 2009. 9p. (J). bds. 4.50 (978-1-4127-2926-0(2), PIL Kids) Publications International, Ltd.
—Finding Nemo: Let's Go to School. 2009. 18p. (J). bds. 10.98 (978-1-4127-1733-5(7), PIL Kids) Publications International, Ltd.
—Finding Nemo - Let's Go to School. 2011. 12p. (J). bds. (978-1-4508-0510-0(8)) Publications International, Ltd.
—Finding Nemo: Hide & Seek: Book & Plush. 2010. 8p. (J). bds. 11.98 (978-1-60553-599-9(0)) Publications International, Ltd.
—What's Different Finding Nemo. 2009. 24p. (J). 9.98 (978-1-4127-7769-8(0), PIL Kids) Publications International, Ltd.
Puffy. 2006. (J). (978-0-9779521-0-6(X)) City on a Hill, Inc.
Punter, Russell. There Was a Crooked Man. Semple, David, illus. 2010. (First Reading Level 2 Ser.). 32p. (J). 6.99 (978-0-7945-2682-5(9), Usborne) EDC Publishing.
Pursh, Eric. I Sette Pesci: The Seven Fishes. Lucot, Erica, illus. 2005. (J). per. (978-0-9727319-3-5(8), Blacktypewriter Pr.) Pittsburgh Literary Arts Network LLC.
Rabe, Tish. The Thinga-Ma-Jigger Is Coming Today! Moroney, Christopher, illus. 2010. (Little Golden Book Ser.). (ENG.). 24p. (J). (gr. -1-2). 4.99 (978-0-375-85927-4(6), Golden Bks.) Random Hse. Children's Bks.
Rain Fish & Big Blue Whale Readers Guide. 2005. (J). pap. (978-0-7358-1174-4(1)) North-South Bks., Inc.
Rainbow Fish Readers Guide. 2005. (J). pap. (978-0-7358-1172-0(5)) North-South Bks., Inc.
Rainbow Fish to Rescue Reader Guide. 2005. (J). pap. (978-0-7358-1173-7(3)) North-South Bks., Inc.
Rand, Johnathan. American Chillers #22 Nuclear Jelly Fish of New Jersey. 2007. 208p. (J). pap. 5.99 (978-1-893699-93-9(5)) AudioCraft Publishing, Inc.
Random House. Big Fish, Little Fish: a Book of Opposites (Bubble Guppies) Random House, illus. 2015. (Board Book Ser.). (ENG., Illus.). 24p. (J). (-k). bds. 4.99 (978-0-385-38442-1(4), Random Hse. Bks. for Young Readers) Random Hse. Children's Bks.
Random House Disney & Webster, Christy. Finding Dory: Big Fish, Little Fish. Random House Disney & The Disney Storybook Art Team, illus. 2016. (Step into Reading Level 1 Ser.). (ENG.). 24p. (J). (gr. -1-1). 14.75 (978-0-606-39353-9(6)) Turtleback Bks.
Random House Disney Staff. Finding Nemo. 2004. (Read-Aloud Board Book Ser.). (ENG., Illus.). 24p. (J). (gr. k — 1). bds. 4.99 (978-0-7364-2249-9(8), RH/Disney) Random Hse. Children's Bks.
Razilov, Evelyn. The Beautiful Fish. 2012. 20p. pap. 13.77 (978-1-4669-4032-1(8)) Trafford Publishing.
Ready Reader Staff. I Got a Goldfish: Hard & Soft G, 6 bks., set. Level B. 2003. (J). (gr. -1-3). 24.50 (978-0-8136-2040-4(6)) Modern Curriculum Pr.
Reasoner, Charles. I'm Just a Fish. 2008. (Googley-Eye Bks.). (ENG.). 12p. (J). (gr. -1). 7.99 (978-1-84666-155-6(2)) Top That! Publishing PLC GBR. Dist: Independent Pubs. Group.
Reiter, Naomi. Sandy the Stingray. 2007. 24p. per. 24.95 (978-1-4241-8619-8(6)) America Star Bks.
Reynolds, Aaron. Sea Monkey & Bob. Ohi, Debbie Ridpath, illus. 2017. (ENG.). 40p. (J). (gr. -1-3). 17.99 (978-1-4814-0676-5(0), Simon & Schuster Bks. For Young Readers) Simon & Schuster Bks. For Young Readers.
RH Disney. Dory's Sea of Wonders. RH Disney, illus. 2016. (Pictureback(R) Ser.). (ENG., Illus.). 24p. (J). (gr. -1-2). 4.99 (978-0-7364-3507-9(7), RH/Disney) Random Hse. Children's Bks.
—Dory's Story. RH Disney, illus. 2016. (Step into Reading Ser.). (ENG., Illus.). 24p. (J). (gr. -1-1). 4.99 (978-0-7364-3498-0(4), RH/Disney) Random Hse. Children's Bks.
—Finding Dory. RH Disney, illus. 2016. (Junior Novel Ser.). (ENG., Illus.). 144p. (J). (gr. 2-5). 6.99 (978-0-7364-3486-7(0), RH/Disney) Random Hse. Children's Bks.
—Finding Dory Big Golden Book (Disney/Pixar Finding Dory) RH Disney, illus. 2016. (Big Golden Book Ser.). (ENG., Illus.). 48p. (J). (gr. -1-2). 9.99 (978-0-7364-3506-2(9), Golden/Disney) Random Hse. Children's Bks.
—Finding Dory Deluxe Step into Reading (Disney/Pixar Finding Dory) RH Disney, illus. 2016. (Step into Reading Ser.). (ENG., Illus.). 24p. (J). (gr. -1-1). pap. 4.99 (978-0-7364-3704-2(5)); lib. bdg. 12.99 (978-0-7364-8188-5(5)) Random Hse. Children's Bks. (RH/Disney).
—Finding Dory Little Golden Book (Disney/Pixar Finding Dory) RH Disney, illus. 2016. (Little Golden Book Ser.). (ENG., Illus.). 24p. (J). (-k). 4.99 (978-0-7364-3511-6(5), Golden/Disney) Random Hse. Children's Bks.
—Finding Dory Pictureback with Stickers (Disney/Pixar Finding Dory) RH Disney, illus. 2016. (Pictureback(R) Ser.). (ENG., Illus.). 24p. (J). (gr. -1-2). pap. 4.99 (978-0-7364-3708-0(8), RH/Disney) Random Hse. Children's Bks.
—Finding Dory: the Deluxe Junior Novelization (Disney/Pixar Finding Dory) RH Disney, illus. 2016. (Deluxe Junior Novel Ser.). (ENG., Illus.). 144p. (J). (gr. 2-5). 9.99 (978-0-7364-3573-4(5), RH/Disney) Random Hse. Children's Bks.
—Hank the Septopus. RH Disney, illus. deluxe ed. 2016. (Pictureback(R) Ser.). (ENG., Illus.). 24p. (J). (gr. -1-2). 4.99 (978-0-7364-3510-9(7), RH/Disney) Random Hse. Children's Bks.
—Hello, Dory! RH Disney, illus. 2016. (Tabbed Board Book Ser.). (ENG., Illus.). 16p. (J). (— 1). bds. 7.99 (978-0-7364-3625-0(1), RH/Disney) Random Hse. Children's Bks.
RH Disney Staff & Disney Enterprises Inc. Staff. Best Dad in the Sea. 2003. (Step into Reading Level 1 Ser.). (gr. k-3). lib. bdg. 13.55 (978-0-613-73685-5(0), Turtleback) Turtleback Bks.
RH Disney Staff & Scollon, Bill. Ocean of Color. RH Disney Staff & The Disney Storybook Art Team, illus. 2016. (Step into Reading Ser.). (ENG.). 24p. (J). (gr. -1-1). 4.99 (978-0-7364-3519-2(0), RH/Disney) Random Hse. Children's Bks.
Richards, Kitty. SpongeBob AirPants: The Lost Episode, Vol. 8. 2004. 64p. (J). (gr. 2-5). pap. 17.00 incl. audio (978-1-4000-8631-3(0), Listening Library) Random Hse. Audio Publishing Group.
Richards, Lucy & Finn, Rebecca, illus. Silly Sea (W/Hang Tag) 2004. (Cuddly Cuffs Ser.: No. 8). 10p. (J). tchr. ed. 5.95 (978-1-58925-728-3(6)) Tiger Tales.
—Silly Sea (W/Header Card) 2004. (Cuddly Cuffs Ser.: 8). 10p. (J). tchr. ed. 5.95 (978-1-58925-732-0(4)) Tiger Tales.
Richmond, Marianne. Friendly Floppy Fishie, What Do Wish For? 2009. (Beginner Boards Ser.). (ENG., Illus.). 14p. (gr. -1-k). bds. 7.95 (978-1-934082-52-2(X), Marianne Richmond Studios, Inc.) Sourcebooks, Inc.
Riley, Brad. Timothy: A Little Fish with a Big Purpose! Goodale, Krystahl, illus. 2013. 30p. 22.95 (978-1-62015-341-3(6)); pap. 14.95 (978-1-62015-148-8(0)) Booktrope. (Vox Dei).
Roach. Night of the Zombie Goldfish. 2013. (Monstrous Stories Ser.: 1). lib. bdg. 14.75 (978-0-606-31523-4(3), Turtleback) Turtleback Bks.
Roberts, Melva J. Mrs Moon's Pond. 2011. 28p. pap. 21.99 (978-1-4628-4613-9(0)) Xlibris Corp.
Roberts, Rachel. The Fish & the Fisherman. 2012. 28p. pap. 32.70 (978-1-4797-1459-9(3)) Xlibris Corp.
Robertson, Elysia Hill. Do Fish Cry ? Robertson, Elysia Hill, illus. 2005. (Illus.). 116p. (J). per. 12.95 (978-0-9764444-1-1(0), EJWV-002) E. J. Publishing.
Robinson, Fay. Fish Wish. 2005. (Illus.). 32p. (J). (978-1-84011-605-2(6)) Templar Publishing.
Robinson, Virginia. The Squid Kids. Doery, Marya, illus. 2008. 44p. pap. 24.95 (978-1-4241-9901-3(8)) America Star Bks.
Robles, Anthony. Lakas & the Manilatown Fish. Angel, Carl, illus. 2015. (ENG & TGL.). 32p. (J). pap. 9.95 (978-0-89239-211-7(8), Children's Book Press) Lee & Low Bks., Inc.
Robles, Anthony D. & Children's Book Press Staff. Lakas & the Manilatown Fish (Si Lakas at Ang Isdang Manilatown) de Jesus, Eloisa D. & de Guzman, Magdalena, trs. Angel, Carl, illus. 2003.Tr. of Si Lakas at Ang Isdang Manilatown. (ENG & TAG.). 32p. (J). 16.95 (978-0-89239-182-0(0)) Lee & Low Bks., Inc.
Rodriguez, AJ. A Cajun Crawfish Tale. 2009. 20p. pap. 12.49 (978-1-4389-5529-2(4)) AuthorHouse.
Rogers, Anne. CAPTAIN DAN & SAILOR SAM. 2008. 37p. pap. 24.95 (978-1-4092-1029-0(4)) Lulu Pr., Inc.
Rosario, Joann. Joey & His Famous Fish! Rosario, Joann, illus. 2004. (Illus.). 20p. (J). (gr. -1-5). pap. 10.00 (978-0-9758746-2-2(4), 1246169) J.G.R. Enterprises.
Rosen, Lucy. Justice League: Meet the Justice League. Gordon, Eric A. & Gordon, Steven E., illus. 2013. (I Can Read Level 2 Ser.). (ENG.). 32p. (J). (gr. -1-3). pap. 3.99 (978-0-06-221002-9(5)) HarperCollins Pubs.
Rouss, Sylvia & Avalone, C. The Littlest Fish. 2008. 32p. 12.95 (978-1-934440-53-7(1), Pitspopany Pr.) Simcha Media Group.
Roy, James. Chaz at the Fish Market. Gorissen, Dean, illus. 2015. (J). pap. (978-1-4966-0251-0(X)) Capstone Classroom.
—The Legend of Big Red. Dale, Rae, illus. 2005. (UQP Children's Fiction Ser.). 96p. (J). pap. (978-0-7022-3528-3(8)) Univ. of Queensland Pr.
Rylant, Cynthia. Mr. Putter & Tabby Feed the Fish. Howard, Arthur, illus. 2007. (Mr. Putter & Tabby Ser.). pap. 7.93 (978-1-4189-5238-9(9)) Houghton Mifflin Harcourt Supplemental Pubs.
Salvati, Elizabeth A. Tony Trout of the Toccoa River. 2011. 44p. pap. 16.95 (978-1-4567-5817-2(9)) AuthorHouse.
Salzmann, Mary Elizabeth. Goldfish Bowl, 1 vol. Chawla, Neena, illus. 2006. (Animal Tales Ser.). (ENG.). 24p. (J). (gr. k-3). lib. bdg. 24.21 (978-1-59679-939-4(0), SandCastle) ABDO Publishing Co.
—Goldfish Bowl (6-pack) Chawla, Neena, illus. 2006. (Fact & Fiction Ser.). 24p. (J). pap. 59.57 (978-1-59679-940-0(4)) ABDO Publishing Co.
Sampson, Brent. One Wacky Wasp: The Perfect Children's Book for Kids Ages 3-6 Who Are Learning to Read. 2010. 24p. (J). 14.95 (978-1-4327-6217-9(6)); pap. 9.95 (978-1-4327-0465-0(6)) Outskirts Pr., Inc.
Sauer, Tammi. Nugget & Fang. 2015. lib. bdg. 17.20 (978-0-606-36825-4(6)) Turtleback Bks.
—Nugget & Fang: Friends Forever - Or Snack Time? Slack, Michael, illus. 2013. (ENG.). 40p. (J). (gr. -1-3). 16.99 (978-0-547-85285-0(1)) Houghton Mifflin Harcourt Publishing Co.
—Nugget & Fang: Friends Forever — Or Snack Time? Slack, Michael, illus. 2015. (ENG.). 40p. (J). (gr. -1-3). 6.99 (978-0-544-48171-8(2), HMH Books For Young Readers) Houghton Mifflin Harcourt Publishing Co.
Savage, Derek. Cool Cat Loves Baseball. 2010. (Trolly the Trout Ser.: Vol. 1).Tr. of Cool Cat le gusta Beisbol. (ENG & SPA., Illus.). 32p. (J). pap. 7.95 (978-0-9673000-0-9(2)) Blue Thunder Bks.
—Cool Cat Loves Wrestling. 2010. (Trolly the Trout Ser.: Vol. 2).Tr. of Cool Cat le gusta Lucha Libre. (ENG & SPA., Illus.). 32p. (J). pap. 7.95 (978-0-9673000-1-6(0)) Blue Thunder Bks.
Scanlon, Jody. The Lonely Little Fish. 2008. 24p. pap. 24.95 (978-1-60672-554-2(8)) America Star Bks.
Schroder, Jennifer Michaels. Fish Food: Skimmer Catches His Spirit. 2010. 24p. pap. 14.49 (978-1-4490-4784-9(X)) AuthorHouse.
Schwartz, Betty & Seresin, Lynn. You're It, Little Red Fish! A Back-And-Forth Color Book. Powell, Luciana Navarro, illus. 2015. (J). (978-1-62370-235-9(6)) Capstone Young Readers of Coughlan Cos.
Scillian, Devin. Memoirs of a Goldfish. Bowers, Tim, illus. 2010. (ENG.). 32p. (J). (gr. -1-3). 15.95 (978-1-58536-507-4(6)) Sleeping Bear Pr.
Scollon, Bill. Disney*Pixar Finding Dory: Friends Forever. 2016. (ENG.). 12p. (J). (gr. -1-k). 8.99 (978-0-7944-3670-4(6), Reader's Digest Children's Bks.) Studio Fun International.
—Let's Keep Swimming. 2016. (ENG.). 32p. (J). (gr. -1-2). 17.99 (978-0-7944-3674-2(9)) Studio Fun International.
Scotton, Rob. Fishy Tales. Scotton, Rob, illus. 2012. (Splat the Cat Ser.). (ENG., Illus.). 24p. (J). (gr. -1-3). pap. 3.99 (978-0-06-197852-4(3), HarperFestival) HarperCollins Pubs.
Sesso, Karen A. Off They Swam, 1 vol. 2009. 37p. pap. 19.95 (978-1-61546-453-1(0)) PublishAmerica, Inc.
Seuling, Barbara. How Does a Fish Take a Bath? 2008. (ENG., Illus.). 32p. 16.00 (978-0-15-216654-0(8), Houghton Mifflin Bks. for Children) Houghton Mifflin Harcourt Trade & Reference Pubs.
Seuss, Dr. One Fish, Two Fish, Red Fish, Blue Fish Book & CD, 1 vol. 2005. (Book & CD Ser.). (ENG., Illus.). 64p. (J). (gr. -1-2). 9.95 (978-0-375-83497-4(4), Random Hse. Bks. for Young Readers) Random Hse. Children's Bks.
—One Fish, Two Fish, Three, Four, Five Fish. 2005. (Dr. Seuss Nursery Collection). (ENG., Illus.). 12p. (J). (— 1). bds. 8.99 (978-0-375-83387-8(0), Random Hse. Bks. for Young Readers) Random Hse. Children's Bks.
Seuss, Dr., illus. Poisson Un - Poisson Deux - Poisson Rouge - Poisson Bleu. 2011. (FRE & ENG.). 64p. (J). (gr. -1-3). 12.95 (978-1-61243-029-4(5)) Ulysses Pr.
Sexton, Bethany. Big Dog, Little Dog, Fish. Briggs Johnson, Chloe, illus. 2015. (ENG.). 17.95 (978-1-59298-862-4(8)) Beaver's Pond Pr., Inc.
Shannon, David. Jangles: A Big Fish Story. Shannon, David, illus. 2012. (ENG., Illus.). 32p. (J). (gr. -1-3). 17.99 (978-0-545-14312-7(8), Blue Sky Pr., The) Scholastic, Inc.
Shaw, Chrysie. The Cat & the Goldfish. 2013. 20p. pap. 9.99 (978-1-4575-2451-6(1)) Dog Ear Publishing, LLC.
Shields, Gillian. DogFish. Taylor, Dan, illus. 2008. (ENG.). 32p. (J). (gr. -1-2). 16.99 (978-1-4169-7127-6(0), Atheneum Bks. for Young Readers) Simon & Schuster Children's Publishing.
Shoemaker, E. W. Mother Nature & the Tales of North Fork. 2009. 220p. pap. 18.75 (978-1-4389-8604-3(1)) AuthorHouse.
Shutt, Susan R. Four Seasons in the Spring House: Book 1. 2012. 16p. pap. 15.99 (978-1-4772-7493-4(6)) AuthorHouse.
Siegel, R. V. The Seagull & the Starfish. 2005. 38p. 11.23 (978-1-4116-3283-7(4)); 48p. pap. 16.73 (978-1-4116-3505-0(1)) Lulu Pr., Inc.
Simpkins, Debra Burke. The Luna Tuna. 2010. 32p. 12.99 (978-1-4520-0213-2(4)) AuthorHouse.
Smith, Danna. Swallow the Leader. Sherry, Kevin, illus. 2016. (ENG.). 32p. (J). (gr. -1-3). 16.99 (978-0-544-10518-8(4), Clarion Bks.) Houghton Mifflin Harcourt Trade & Reference Pubs.
Smith, Iain. Angel Fish: A Pull & Lift Book. Smith, Iain, illus. 2005. (Stories to Share Ser.). (Illus.). 12p. (J). 10.95 (978-1-58117-084-9(X), Intervisual/Piggy Toes) Bendon, Inc.
Smith, R. Cadwallader. Within the Deep. 2004. reprint ed. pap. 1.99 (978-1-4192-9456-3(3)) Kessinger Publishing, LLC.
Smithrud, Norma. The Mucky Yucky Swamp. Miles, Peregrine B., illus. 2011. 28p. pap. 24.95 (978-1-4560-8790-6(8)) America Star Bks.
Snicket, Lemony, pseud. Goldfish Ghost. Brown, Lisa, illus. 2017. (ENG.). 40p. (J). 17.99 (978-1-62672-507-2(1), 9781626725072) Roaring Brook Pr.
Soundprints Staff. Smithsonian Oceanic Collection Micro 4 Book Set. 2007. (ENG.). 32p. 14.95 (978-1-59249-748-5(9)); 14.95 (978-1-59249-749-2(7)) Soundprints.

Stanley, Jan. If I Could Breathe Like Fishes Do, 11 vols. Wennekes, Ron, illus. 2006. 25p. (J). bds. 12.99 (978-0-9776893-0-9(1)) Midwest Graphics, Inc.
Starboortz Fish. 2007. (Illus.). 32p. (J). 18.95 (978-0-9792946-0-0(6)) Starlit Publishing LLC.
Stead, Philip C. Creamed Tuna Fish & Peas on Toast. Stead, Philip C., illus. 2009. (ENG., Illus.). 32p. (J). (gr. -1-1). 16.99 (978-1-59643-401-1(5), 9781596434011) Roaring Brook Pr.
—The Only Fish in the Sea. Cordell, Matthew, illus. 2017. (ENG.). 40p. (J). 17.99 (978-1-62672-282-8(X), 9781626722828) Roaring Brook Pr.
Steinkraus, Kyla. The Trouble with Trading. Reese, Bob, illus. 2011. (ENG.). 24p. (gr. 2-3). pap. 8.95 (978-1-61236-034-8(3)) Rourke Educational Media.
Stender, Joshua. Na Makana a Na I'a: The Fish & Their Gifts. 2004. (Pauahi Readers Ser.). (HAW & ENG., Illus.). 52p. (J). 15.95 (978-0-87336-081-4(8)) Kamehameha Publishing.
Stone Arch Readers, Set of 71. 2013. (Stone Arch Readers Ser.). (ENG.). 32p. lib. bdg. 1585.50 (978-1-4342-4848-0(8)) Stone Arch Bks.
Strow, Lorie. The Shimmers. 2011. 32p. pap. 21.99 (978-1-4568-8133-7(7)) Xlibris Corp.
Stuart, Wrigley. Who'd Have Thunk It? 2014. (Amazing World of Gumball Ser.). (ENG., Illus.). 208p. (J). (gr. 3-7). pap. 9.99 (978-0-8431-8106-7(0), Price Stern Sloan) Penguin Young Readers Group.
Sullivan, Tom. I Used to Be a Fish. Sullivan, Tom, illus. 2016. (Illus.). 48p. (J). (gr. -1-3). 17.99 (978-0-06-245198-9(7)) HarperCollins Pubs.
Sweet Dreams, Pout-Pout Fish. 2015. (Pout-Pout Fish Mini Adventure Ser.). (ENG., Illus.). 12p. (J). (gr. -1 — 1). bds. 5.99 (978-0-374-38010-6(4), 9780374380106, Farrar, Straus & Giroux (BYR)) Farrar, Straus & Giroux.
Swift, Austin Christopher. A Mako Meets a Puffer: A Reel Fish Story. Breeden, Don, illus. 2004. (J). per. 10.95 (978-0-9764208-0-4(5)) Austin Christopher Swift.
Tait, Barbara. Timothy Toot... Goes Fishing. Margolis, Al, illus. 2011. 28p. (J). 24.95 (978-1-58909-879-4(X)) Bookstand Publishing.
Talley, Linda. Aloha Potter! - hardcover Book. Chase, Andra, illus. 2004. 30p. (J). (978-1-55942-200-0(9)) Witcher Productions.
Tate, Suzanne. Rosie Ray: A Tale of Watery Wings. Melvin, James, illus. 2003. (Suzanne Tate's Nature Ser.: No. 25). 28p. (J). (gr. -1-3). pap. 4.95 (978-1-878405-40-1(3)) Nags Head Art, Inc.
Tegan-Olsen, Sandra, illus. Joey's adventures by the Sea: Jellyfish Everywhere! 2008. 20p. (J). per. 9.95 (978-0-9801527-0-8(4)) Freefox Publishing.
Thiele, Colin. Speedy. (Illus.). 112p. pap. (978-0-7344-0404-6(2), Lothian Children's Bks.) Hachette Australia.
Thorpe, Kiki. Into the Waves. Christy, Jana, illus. 2016. (Never Girls Ser.: 11). (ENG.). 128p. (J). (gr. 1-4). 5.99 (978-0-7364-3525-3(5), RH/Disney) Random Hse. Children's Bks.
Tickle, Jack. Fish on a Dish! Tickle, Jack, illus. 2015. (ENG., Illus.). 24p. (J). (gr. -1-3). 16.99 (978-1-58925-191-5(1)) Tiger Tales.
Ticulous, Maurice. Herbert the Turbot. 2009. 127p. pap. 10.50 (978-1-4092-7079-9(3)) Lulu Pr., Inc.
Tombio, Penelope. Never Get Too Close to a Fish. 2011. 24p. pap. 12.56 (978-1-4269-5724-6(6)) Trafford Publishing.
ToyBox Innovations, creator. Disney's Finding Nemo Read-along. 2006. (Disney's Read Along Ser.). (ENG., Illus.). 24p. (J). pap. (978-0-7634-2172-4(3)) Walt Disney Records.
—Disney's the Little Mermaid. abr. ed. 2006. (Disney's Read along Collection). (ENG.). (J). (gr. -1-3). pap. (978-0-7634-2184-7(7)) Walt Disney Records.
Trussell-Cullen, Alan. The Seagull & the Fish. Teo, Ali, illus. 2010. (ENG.). 16p. (gr. k-2). pap. 7.95 (978-1-61181-039-4(6), Kaeden Bks.) Kaeden Corp.
—The Seagull & the Fish (6 Packs) Teo, Ali, illus. 2010. (ENG.). 16p. (gr. k-2). pap. (978-1-61181-040-0(X), Kaeden Bks.) Kaeden Corp.
Tyler, Amy J. & RH Disney Staff. Best Dad in the Sea. RH Disney Staff, illus. 2003. (Step into Reading Ser.). (ENG., Illus.). 32p. (J). (gr. k-3). pap. 3.99 (978-0-7364-2131-7(9), RH/Disney) Random Hse. Children's Bks.
Tyler, Craig, illus. A Fine Kettle of Fish. adapted ed. 2005. 42p. (J). lib. bdg. 16.95 (978-0-9761953-0-6(5)) Stairway Publishing.
Velez, Edia L. Jessica's Summer Vacation - Las Vacaciones de Verano de Jéssic. 2011. 44p. pap. 18.49 (978-1-4490-2301-0(0)) AuthorHouse.
Walker, Sally M. Seahorse Reef: A Story of the South Pacific. Petruccio, Steven James, illus. 2005. (Smithsonian Oceanic Collection: No. 20). (ENG.). 32p. (J). (gr. -1-2). 15.95 (978-1-56899-869-5(4), B4020) Soundprints.
Walt Disney Company Staff & Pixar Animation Studios Staff, contrib. by. Finding Nemo: Fish in a Box. 2003. (Illus.). (978-0-7364-2157-7(2)); (978-0-7364-2156-0(4)); (978-0-7364-2155-3(6)); (978-0-7364-2158-4(0)) Random Hse., Inc.
Walthers, Joanie. The Fish Smuggler. Walthers, Don, illus. 2013. (ENG.). 24p. (J). 19.95 (978-1-4787-1167-4(1)) Outskirts Pr., Inc.
Watson, Leilani. Sina & the Eel: A Tale from Samoa. Cooper, Jenny, illus. 2016. 24p. (J). pap. (978-1-927244-56-2(0)) Flying Start Bks.
—Sina & the Eel (Big Book Edition) A Tale from Samoa. Cooper, Jenny, illus. 2016. 24p. (J). pap. (978-1-927244-66-1(8)) Flying Start Bks.
Watt, Fiona. Baby's Very First Slide & See under the Sea. 2015. (Baby's Very First Slide & See Board Bks.). (ENG.). 10p. (J). 14.99 (978-0-7945-3482-0(1), Usborne) EDC Publishing.
Webster, Christy. Big Fish, Little Fish. 2016. (Illus.). 24p. (J). E-Book **(978-0-7364-3705-9(3))** Random Hse., Inc.
Weeks, Timothy. The Wise Mullet of Cook Bayou. Jeanne, Miss, illus. rev. ed. 2006. 48p. (J). per. 14.99 (978-0-9779928-0-5(2)) Foolosophy Media.
Weeks, Timothy A. Ol' Middler Saves the Day: A Mullet Buddy Homecoming. 2006. (Illus.). 48p. (J). (gr. -1-3). per. 14.99 (978-0-9779928-1-2(0)) Foolosophy Media.
Weston, Martha. Cats Are Like That. Weston, Martha, illus. (Holiday House Reader Ser.). (ENG., Illus.). 32p. (J). (gr. k-3). tchr. ed. 15.95 (978-0-8234-1419-2(1)) Holiday Hse., Inc.
Wethington, Constance. The Adventures of One-Eyed Jack. 2012. 28p. pap. 24.95 (978-1-4626-8286-7(3)) America Star Bks.
Wheelie, P. The Fishing Trip: The tales of Tommy the tortoise & Friends. 2009. (Illus.). 32p. pap. 12.99 (978-1-4389-6414-0(5)) AuthorHouse.
White, Marco. Freddy's Fishbowl. 2006. (Neighborhood Readers Ser.). (ENG.). 8p. (gr. -1-3). pap. 5.15 (978-1-4042-6702-2(6), Rosen Classroom) Rosen Publishing Group, Inc., The.
Whiteley, Jason. Tales from the Tacklebox: Escape from the Crooked Tree. 2012. 48p. 23.99 (978-1-4575-1152-3(5)); pap. 14.99 (978-1-4575-1150-9(9)) Dog Ear Publishing, LLC.
Williams, Brenda May. The Unusual Pet Shop. Williams, Raymond, illus. 2012. 24p. pap. 11.50 (978-1-61897-798-4(9), Strategic Bk. Publishing) Strategic Book Publishing & Rights Agency (SBPRA).
Williams, Greg. Cuddie the Cut Throat Trout. 2011. 28p. pap. 19.00 (978-1-60746-981-0(2)) FastPrncil, Inc.
Williams, Howard. Salmon Sam's Great Salmon Run. 2011. 36p. pap. 16.99 (978-1-4567-1831-2(2)) AuthorHouse.
Williamson, Stafford. Puppyfish. 2005. 48p. (J). pap. 18.49 (978-1-4116-3836-5(0)) Lulu Pr., Inc.
Winkelman, Barbara Gaines. Puffer's Surprise. Petruccio, Steven James, illus. 2011. (Smithsonian Oceanic Collection Ser.). (ENG.). 32p. (J). (gr. -1-3). 19.95 (978-1-60727-658-6(5)); 8.95 (978-1-60727-659-3(3)) Soundprints.
Wise, William. Ten Sly Piranhas: A Counting Story in Reverse (A Tale of Wickedness - And Worse!) Chess, Victoria, illus. 2004. (ENG.). 32p. (J). (gr. -1-k). pap. 5.99 (978-0-14-240074-6(2), Puffin Books) Penguin Young Readers Group.
The Wish Fish: Individual Title Six-Packs. (Action Packs Ser.). 104p. (gr. 3-5). 44.00 (978-0-7635-8411-5(8)) Rigby Education.
Wodarski, Loran. If a Dolphin Were a Fish, 1 vol. Klein, Laurie Allen, illus. 2006. (ENG.). 32p. (J). (gr. -1-2). 15.95 (978-0-9768823-2-9(9)) Arbordale Publishing.
Wood, Audrey. Ten Little Fish. Wood, Bruce, illus. 2004. (ENG.). 40p. (J). (gr. -1-k). 17.99 (978-0-439-63569-1(1), Blue Sky Pr., The) Scholastic, Inc.
Woods, Linda J. The Gift of the Jumping Goldfish (A True Story) 2011. 48p. (gr. 1-2). pap. 19.46 (978-1-4567-5796-0(2)) AuthorHouse.
Wrecks, Billy. Nemo's Big Adventure (Disney/Pixar Finding Nemo) RH Disney Staff, illus. 2012. (Pictureback(R) Ser.). (ENG.). 16p. (J). (gr. -1-2). pap. 4.99 (978-0-7364-2968-9(9), RH/Disney) Random Hse. Children's Bks.
Yerushalmi, Miriam. Gedalia the Goldfish Who Wanted Be Just Like the King. Weinberg, Devorah, illus. 2007. 26p. (J). (gr. -1-3). 16.50 (978-0-911643-36-7(2)) Aura Printing, Inc.
Yoo, Tae-Eun. The Little Red Fish. 2007. (Illus.). (J). (978-1-4287-3601-6(8), Dial) Penguin Publishing Group.
Zmelman, Nathan. A Fishy Story. O'Malley, Kathleen, illus. 2003. (Books for Young Learners). (ENG.). 16p. (J). pap. 5.75 (978-1-57274-538-4(X), 2453, Bks. for Young Learners) Owen, Richard C. Pubs., Inc.

FISHING

Bailey, Diane. Discovering Nature. 2017. (Illus.). 48p. (J). (978-1-4222-3565-2(3)) Mason Crest.
Befus, Tyler. A Kid's Guide to Fly Tying. 2008. 128p. (J). pap. 16.00 (978-1-55566-425-1(3), Johnson Bks.) Bower Hse.
—A Kid's Guide to Flyfishing: It's More Than Catching Fish. 2006. (Illus.). 95p. (J). (gr. 4-7). per. 16.00 (978-1-55566-394-0(X), Johnson Bks.) Bower Hse.
—The ORVIS Kids' Guide to Beginning Fly Fishing: Tips for the Absolute Beginner. 2016. (ENG., Illus.). 96p. (J). (gr. 2). pap. 14.99 (978-1-63450-338-9(4), Sky Pony Pr.) Skyhorse Publishing Co., Inc.
Benjamin, Tina. Let's Go Fishing. 2015. (Let's Go Outdoors! Ser.). (ENG., Illus.). 24p. (J). (gr. k-k). pap. 8.15 (978-1-4824-2621-2(8)) Stevens, Gareth Publishing LLLP.
Burlingame, Jeff. How to Freshwater Fish Like a Pro. 2014. (Outdoor Sports Skills Ser.). (Illus.). 48p. (J). (gr. 4-10). 14.95 (978-1-62285-224-6(9)) Enslow Pubs., Inc.
Carpenter, Tom. Freshwater Fishing: Bass, Trout, Walleye, Catfish, & More. 2012. (Great Outdoors Sports Zone Ser.). (ENG., Illus.). 32p. (gr. 4-8). lib. bdg. 26.60 (978-1-4677-0219-5(6), Lerner Pubns.) Lerner Publishing Group.
—Saltwater Fishing: Snapper, Mackerel, Bluefish, Tuna, & More. 2012. (Great Outdoors Sports Zone Ser.). (ENG., Illus.). 32p. (gr. 4-8). lib. bdg. 26.60 (978-1-4677-0220-1(X), Lerner Pubns.) Lerner Publishing Group.
Cermele, Joe. Field & Stream's Guide to Catching Bass. The Editors of Field & Stream, ed. 2015. (Field & Stream's Guide to the Outdoors Ser.). (ENG., Illus.). 96p. (J). (gr. 6-8). lib. bdg. 35.95 (978-1-4824-3185-8(8)) Stevens, Gareth Publishing LLLP.
Cohen, Robert Z. Catfish Fishing. 2011. (J). 77.70 (978-1-4488-4736-5(2)); pap. 12.95 (978-1-4488-4605-4(6)); lib. bdg. 31.95 (978-1-4488-4602-3(1)) Rosen Publishing Group, Inc., The. (Rosen Reference).
Complete Guide to Fishing, 7 vols., Set. (Illus.). 64,144p. (YA). (gr. 7-18). lib. bdg. (978-1-59084-492-2(0)) Mason Crest.
Crockett, Sally. Fly Fishing. 2011. (J). 77.70 (978-1-4488-4737-2(0)); pap. 12.95 (978-1-4488-4606-1(4)); lib. bdg. 31.95 (978-1-4488-4601-6(3)) Rosen Publishing Group, Inc., The. (Rosen Reference).
Davis, James (Jim) W. Out-takes of 55 Years of Camping 2004. (Illus.). 168p. (YA). per. 5.95 (978-0-9760960-0-9(5)) Davis, James (Jim).
Destination Disaster: Individual Title Six-Packs. (Action Packs Ser.). 104p. (gr. 3-5). 44.00 (978-0-7635-3300-7(9)) Rigby Education.
Un dia de Pesca, 6 packs. (Literatura 2000 Ser.). (SPA.). (gr. 2-3). 33.00 (978-0-7635-1260-6(5)) Rigby Education.
Dorman, Clive & Dorman, Helen. Okomi Goes Fishing, Vol. 7. Hutchings, Tony, illus. 2004. (Okomi Stories Ser.). 24p. (J). pap. 4.95 (978-1-58469-057-3(7)) Dawn Pubns.
Dyer, Hadley & Kalman, Bobbie. Fishing in Action. 2005. (Sports in Action Ser.). (ENG., Illus.). 32p. (J). (gr. 2-3). pap. (978-0-7787-0363-1(0)); lib. bdg. (978-0-7787-0343-3(6)) Crabtree Publishing Co.
Early Bird Books Staff. Going Fishing: Step 2, Level C. Date not set. (J). (gr. 2). 1.95 (978-0-394-86705-2(X), Random Hse. Bks. for Young Readers) Random Hse. Children's Bks.
Fishing. 2013. (Adventures in the Great Outdoors Ser.). 32p. (J). (gr. 3-6). pap. 70.50 (978-1-61533-816-0(0), PowerKids Pr.) Rosen Publishing Group, Inc., The.
Fishing: Level F, 6 vols. (Wonder Worldtm Ser.). 16p. 29.95 (978-0-7802-1996-0(1)) Wright Group/McGraw-Hill.
Fishing: Tips & Techniques: Set 2. 2013. (Fishing: Tips & Techniques Ser.). 64p. (J). (gr. 5-8). 191.70 (978-1-4488-9499-4(9)) Rosen Publishing Group, Inc., The.
Fishing: Tips & Techniques: Sets 1 - 2. 2013. (Fishing: Tips & Techniques Ser.). 64p. (J). (gr. 5-8). 383.40 (978-1-4777-0616-9(X)); pap. 155.40 (978-1-4777-2669-3(1)); pap. 932.40 (978-1-4777-2670-9(5)) Rosen Publishing Group, Inc., The.
Fishing the Flats. 2013. (Fishing: Tips & Techniques Ser.). 64p. (J). (gr. 5-8). pap. 77.70 (978-1-4488-9505-2(7)) Rosen Publishing Group, Inc., The.
Fitzsimmons, Kakie. Bur Bur's Fishing Adventure: An Exciting Fishing Adventure. VanDeWeghe, Lindsay & Bohnet, Christopher, illus. 2007. (Bur Bur & Friends Ser.). 32p. (J). (gr. -1-3). lib. bdg. (978-0-9777121-3-7(3)) IGI Pr.
Ford, Martin. Fishing. 2010. (Master This! Ser.). (ENG.). 32p. (J). lib. bdg. 25.25 (978-1-61532-598-6(0), PowerKids Pr.) Rosen Publishing Group, Inc., The.
Frazel, Ellen. Deep Sea Fishing. 2013. (Outdoor Adventures Ser.). (ENG., Illus.). 24p. (J). (gr. 3-8). lib. bdg. 25.95 (978-1-60014-890-3(5), Pilot Bks.) Bellwether Media.
Freshwater Fishing Magazine Staff, et al. Trout Fishing Tactics. 2006. (Illus.). 96p. 19.99 (978-1-86513-080-4(X)) Australian Fishing Network AUS. Dist: Cardinal Pubs. Group.
Friesen, Helen Lepp. Fishing. (J). 2016. **(978-1-4896-5719-0(3))** 2012. (978-1-61913-503-1(5)) 2012. pap. 27.13 (978-1-61913-507-9(8)) Weigl Pubs., Inc.
Gibbons, Gail. Surrounded by Sea: Life on a New England Fishing Island. Gibbons, Gail, illus. 2006. (ENG., Illus.). 32p. (J). (gr. -1-3). 17.95 (978-0-8234-1941-8(X)); 6.95 (978-0-8234-2021-6(3)) Holiday Hse., Inc.
Goosley, Stephen M. Fishing with Steve. 2010. 76p. pap. 24.99 (978-1-4520-3342-6(0)) AuthorHouse.
Gordon, Nick. Deep Sea Fisherman. 2012. (Dangerous Jobs Ser.). (ENG., Illus.). 24p. (J). (gr. 3-7). lib. bdg. 25.95 (978-1-60014-779-1(8), Torque Bks.) Bellwether Media.
Green, Sara. Freshwater Fishing. 2012. (Outdoor Adventures Ser.). (ENG., Illus.). 24p. (J). (gr. 3-8). lib. bdg. 25.95 (978-1-60014-799-9(2), Pilot Bks.) Bellwether Media.
—Ice Fishing. 2014. (Outdoor Adventures Ser.). (ENG., Illus.). 24p. (J). (gr. 3-8). lib. bdg. 25.95 (978-1-62617-085-8(1), Pilot Bks.) Bellwether Media.
Hamilton, S. L. Big Game Fishing. 2014. (Xtreme Fishing Ser.). (ENG.). 32p. (gr. 3-9). lib. bdg. 27.07 (978-1-62403-679-8(1), Abdo & Daughters) ABDO Publishing Co.
—Fly Fishing. 2014. (Xtreme Fishing Ser.). (ENG.). 32p. (gr. 3-9). lib. bdg. 27.07 (978-1-62403-680-4(5), Abdo & Daughters) ABDO Publishing Co.
—Freshwater Fishing, 1 vol. 2014. (Xtreme Fishing Ser.). (ENG.). 32p. (gr. 3-9). lib. bdg. 27.07 (978-1-62403-681-1(3), Abdo & Daughters) ABDO Publishing Co.
—Ice Fishing. 2014. (Xtreme Fishing Ser.). (ENG.). 32p. (gr. 3-9). lib. bdg. 27.07 (978-1-62403-682-8(1), Abdo & Daughters) ABDO Publishing Co.
—Saltwater Fishing. 2014. (Xtreme Fishing Ser.). (ENG.). 32p. (gr. 3-9). lib. bdg. 27.07 (978-1-62403-683-5(X), Abdo & Daughters) ABDO Publishing Co.
—Spearfishing. 2014. (Xtreme Fishing Ser.). (ENG., Illus.). 32p. (gr. 3-9). lib. bdg. 27.07 (978-1-62403-684-2(8), 1382631, Abdo & Daughters) ABDO Publishing Co.
—Xtreme Fishing. 2014. (Xtreme Fishing Ser.: 6). (ENG.). 32p. (gr. 3-9). lib. bdg. 162.42 (978-1-62403-678-1(3), Abdo & Daughters) ABDO Publishing Co.
Hardyman, Robyn. Fishing. 2013. (Adventures in the Great Outdoors Ser.). 32p. (J). (gr. 3-6). 26.50 (978-1-61533-749-1(0)); (ENG., Illus.). pap. 11.75 (978-1-61533-815-3(2)) Rosen Publishing Group, Inc., The. (PowerKids Pr.).
Heidtke, John. Hey! Take Me Fishing, Again. 2008. 124p. pap. 12.95 (978-0-9792739-3-3(5)) Ajoyin Publishing, Inc.
Heos, Bridget. Ice Fishing. 2011. (J). pap. 12.95 (978-1-4488-4607-8(2)); lib. bdg. 31.95 (978-1-4488-4600-9(5)) Rosen Publishing Group, Inc., The. (Rosen Reference).
Howard, Melanie A. Freshwater Fishing for Kids, 1 vol. 2012. (Into the Great Outdoors Ser.). (ENG., Illus.). 32p. (gr. 3-4). pap. 7.95 (978-1-4296-9926-4(3)); lib. bdg. 27.99 (978-1-4296-8422-4(4)) Capstone Press of Coughlan Cos.
Hunt, Chris. Stream Dreams: A Fly Fisher's Guide to Eastern Idaho's Small Water 2004. (Illus.). 120p. per. 17.95 net. (978-0-9749865-0-0(X)) Idaho State Journal.
Hunting & Fishing: A Kid's Guide. 2016. (Hunting & Fishing: a Kid's Guide Ser.). 00032p. (J). (gr. 3-3). 157.50 (978-1-4994-2648-9(8), PowerKids Pr.) Rosen Publishing Group, Inc., The.
Ireland, Kevin. How to Catch a Fish. 6th ed. 2005. (Ginger Ser.). (ENG., Illus.). 128p. pap. 14.95 (978-0-9582538-6-4(2)) Awa Pr. NZL. Dist: Independent Pubs. Group.
James, Martin & Newman, Gary. Fishing. 2008. (ENG., Illus.). 32p. (J). (gr. 5-9). lib. bdg. (978-0-7787-3769-8(1)) Crabtree Publishing Co.
Jenson-Elliott, Cindy. Fly Fishing, 1 vol. 2011. (Wild Outdoors Ser.). (ENG.). 32p. (gr. 1-2). lib. bdg. 26.65 (978-1-4296-4811-0(2), Blazers) Capstone Press of Coughlan Cos.
Kamberg, Mary-Lane. Saltwater Fishing. 2011. (Illus.). 64p. (J). 77.70 (978-1-4488-4739-6(7)); pap. 12.95 (978-1-4488-4608-5(0)); lib. bdg. 31.95 (978-1-4488-4599-6(8)) Rosen Publishing Group, Inc., The. (Rosen Reference).
Kennedy, Nia. We're Going Ice Fishing. 2016. (Hunting & Fishing: a Kid's Guide Ser.). 00032p. (J). (gr. 3-3). pap. 10.00 (978-1-4994-2748-6(4), PowerKids Pr.) Rosen Publishing Group, Inc., The.
Kids: Fish & Fishing. 2003. (J). 1.00 (978-1-888631-30-2(9)) Project WET Foundation.
Kihm, Steve. The Lost Candy Bar. 2004. (J). mass mkt. 6.95 (978-0-9786794-0-8(7)) Lost Candy Bar Pr., LLC.
Klein, Adam G. Fishing, 1 vol. 2008. (Outdoor Adventure! Ser.). (ENG., Illus.). 32p. (gr. k-6). 27.07 (978-1-59928-958-8(X), Checkerboard Library) ABDO Publishing Co.
Kuligowski, Stephanie & Rice, Katelyn. Dangerous Catch! - Deep Sea Fishers, 1 vol. 2nd rev. ed. 2013. (Nonfiction Readers Ser.). (ENG., Illus.). 64p. (J). (gr. 5-5). pap. 31.96 (978-1-4333-7442-5(0)) Teacher Created Materials, Inc.
Kurlansky, Mark. World Without Fish. Stockton, Frank, illus. 2014. (ENG.). 208p. (J). (gr. 5). pap. 14.95 (978-0-7611-8500-0(3)) Workman Publishing Co., Inc.
Labignan, Italo. Hook, Line & Sinker: Everything Kids Want to Know about Fishing! MacRae, Jock, illus. rev. ed. 2007. (ENG.). 48p. (J). (gr. 2-7). pap. 14.95 (978-1-55263-549-0(X)) Leaf Storm Pr.
Laughlin, Kara L. Ice Fishing. 2016. (Beginning Sports Ser.). (ENG.). 24p. (J). (gr. k-3). 27.07 (978-1-5038-0778-5(9), 210606) Child's World, Inc., The.
Lew, Kristi. Fishing the Flats. 2013. (Fishing: Tips & Techniques Ser.). 64p. (J). (gr. 5-8). 31.95 (978-1-4488-9487-1(5)); (ENG., Illus.). pap. 12.95 (978-1-4488-9504-5(9), Rosen Reference) Rosen Publishing Group, Inc., The.
Love, Ann. Fishing. 2004. (Illus.). (J). (gr. k-3). spiral bd. (978-0-616-00141-7(X)) Canadian National Institute for the Blind/Institut National Canadien pour les Aveugles.
Lyon, Harold C., Jr. Angling in the Smile of the Great Spirit: Six Centuries of Wisdom from the Master Anglers of Lake Winnipesaukee 2004. (Illus.). 304p. per. 24.95 (978-0-9748171-1-8(2)) Deep Waters Pr.
Marie, June. Harry the Plum Island Fisherman. 2012. 24p. pap. 15.99 (978-1-4797-0009-7(6)) Xlibris Corp.
Marsico, Katie. What's It Like to Live Here? Fishing Village. 2014. (Community Connections: What's It Like to Live Here? Ser.). (ENG., Illus.). 24p. (J). (gr. 2-5). 25.64 (978-1-62431-565-7(8), 203248) Cherry Lake Publishing.
Martin, Ashley P. & Walker, Andrew D. How to Improve at Fishing. 2009. (How to Improve at... Ser.). (ENG., Illus.). 48p. (J). (gr. 3-9). pap. (978-0-7787-3594-6(X)) Crabtree Publishing Co.
Mason, Paul. Fishing: The World's Greatest Fishing Spots & Techniques, 1 vol. 2011. (Passport to World Sports Ser.). (ENG.). 32p. (gr. 3-4). lib. bdg. 27.99 (978-1-4296-6864-4(4), Edge Bks.) Capstone Press of Coughlan Cos.
Mebane, Jeanie. Ice Fishing, 1 vol. 2011. (Wild Outdoors Ser.). (ENG.). 32p. (gr. 1-2). lib. bdg. 26.65 (978-1-4296-6006-8(6), Blazers) Capstone Press of Coughlan Cos.
Monroe Peterson, Judy. Trout Fishing. 2013. (Fishing: Tips & Techniques Ser.). 64p. (J). (gr. 5-8). pap. 77.70 (978-1-4488-9509-0(X)) Rosen Publishing Group, Inc., The.
—Walleye Fishing. 2013. (Fishing: Tips & Techniques Ser.). 64p. (J). (gr. 5-8). 31.95 (978-1-4488-9491-8(3)); pap. 77.70 (978-1-4488-9511-3(1)); pap. 12.95 (978-1-4488-9510-6(3)) Rosen Publishing Group, Inc., The.
Morey, Allan. Freshwater Fishing. 2017. (Great Outdoors Ser.). (ENG., Illus.). 32p. (J). (gr. 1-3). pap. 9.99 (978-1-68152-078-0(8)) Amicus.
—Freshwater Fishing. 2016. (Great Outdoors Ser.). (ENG., Illus.). 32p. (J). (gr. 1-4). 20.95 (978-1-60753-799-1(0)) Amicus Publishing.
Mozer, Mindy. Pier Fishing. 2013. (Fishing: Tips & Techniques Ser.). 64p. (J). (gr. 5-8). 31.95 (978-1-4488-9488-8(3)); pap. 77.70 (978-1-4488-9507-6(3)); (ENG., Illus.). pap. 12.95 (978-1-4488-9506-9(5), Rosen Classroom) Rosen Publishing Group, Inc., The.
Nickens, T. Eward. Field & Stream's Guide to Fishing. 2015. (Field & Stream's Guide to the Outdoors Ser.). (ENG., Illus.). 96p. (J). (gr. 6-8). 35.95 (978-1-4824-2300-6(6)) Stevens, Gareth Publishing LLLP.
Nordin, Hans. Ice Fishing. 2004. (Complete Guide to Fishing Ser.). (Illus.). 96p. (YA). (gr. 7-18). lib. bdg. 24.95 (978-1-59084-497-7(1)) Mason Crest.
Omoth, Tyler. Deep-Sea Fishermen in Action. 2017. (Dangerous Jobs in Action Ser.). (ENG.). 32p. (J). (gr. 3-6). lib. bdg. 27.07 (978-1-5038-1628-2(1), 211144) Child's World, Inc., The.
—Fly Fishing for Kids, 1 vol. 2013. (Into the Great Outdoors Ser.). (ENG., Illus.). 32p. (gr. 3-4). pap. 7.95 (978-1-62065-694-5(9)); lib. bdg. 27.99 (978-1-4296-9902-0(7)) Capstone Press of Coughlan Cos.
Omoth, Tyler & Bihrle, Craig. Ice Fishing for Kids, 1 vol. 2013. (Into the Great Outdoors Ser.). (ENG.). 32p. (gr. 3-4). pap. 7.95 (978-1-62065-695-2(7)); lib. bdg. 27.99 (978-1-4296-9903-7(5)) Capstone Press of Coughlan Cos.
Orsi, Leo N., Jr. Striper Chronicles: East Coast Surf Fishing Legends & Adventures, 1. 2004. (Illus.). 180p. 24.95 (978-0-9745952-9-0(2), 888-792-1414) AKMO Pubs.
Outdoor Adventure. 2014. (Outdoor Adventure Ser.). 32p. (J). (gr. 3-6). pap. 63.00 (978-1-4824-1579-7(8)) Stevens, Gareth Publishing LLLP.
The Outdoor Youth Adventures Bass Fishing Coloring Book. 2003. (J). pap. (978-0-9745863-4-2(X)) Cypress Knees Publishing.
The Outdoor Youth Adventures Freshwater Fishing Coloring & Activity Book. 2004. (J). pap. (978-0-9745863-7-3(4)) Cypress Knees Publishing.
The Outdoor Youth Adventures Saltwater Fishing Activity & Coloring Book. 2003. (J). pap. (978-0-9745863-2-8(3)) Cypress Knees Publishing.
The Outdoor Youth Adventures Trout Fishing Activity & Coloring Book. 2003. (J). pap. (978-0-9745863-5-9(8)) Cypress Knees Publishing.
Palmer, Andrea. We're Going Freshwater Fishing. 2016. (Hunting & Fishing: a Kid's Guide Ser.). 00032p. (J). (gr. 3-3). pap. 10.00 (978-1-4994-2749-3(2), PowerKids Pr.) Rosen Publishing Group, Inc., The.
Patchett, Fiona. Starting Fishing: Internet-Linked. 2004. (First Skills Ser.). 32p. (J). lthr. 12.95 (978-1-58086-643-9(3), Usborne) EDC Publishing.
—Starting Fishing - Internet Linked. Venus, Joanna, illus. rev. ed. 2004. (First Skills Ser.). 32p. (J). pap. 4.95 (978-0-7945-0672-8(0), Usborne) EDC Publishing.
Payment, Simone. Bass Fishing. 2011. (J). 77.70 (978-1-4488-4735-8(4)); pap. 12.95 (978-1-4488-4604-7(8)); lib. bdg. 31.95 (978-1-4488-4598-9(X)) Rosen Publishing Group, Inc., The. (Rosen Reference).

E F G

Pendergast, George. Deep-Sea Fishing. 2014. (Outdoor Adventure Ser.). 32p. (J). (gr. 3-6). pap. 63.00 *(978-1-4824-1235-2(7))* Stevens, Gareth Publishing LLLP.

—Fly Fishing. 2014. (Outdoor Adventure Ser.). (Illus.). 32p. (J). (gr. 3-6). pap. 10.50 *(978-1-4824-1229-1(2),* 1376453) Stevens, Gareth Publishing LLLP.

—Freshwater Fishing. 2014. (Outdoor Adventure Ser.). 32p. (J). (gr. 3-6). pap. 10.50 *(978-1-4824-1231-4(4))* Stevens, Gareth Publishing LLLP.

Perritano, John. Fishing, Vol. 10. 2016. (Great Outdoors! Ser.: Vol. 10). (ENG., Illus.). 48p. (J). (gr. 5-8). 20.95 *(978-1-4222-3568-3(8))* Mason Crest.

Peterson, Judy Monroe. Fishing in Lakes & Ponds. 2011. (Illus.). 62p. (J). 77.70 *(978-1-4488-4734-1(6));* pap. 12.95 *(978-1-4488-4603-0(X));* lib. bdg. 31.95 *(978-1-4488-4597-2(1))* Rosen Publishing Group, Inc., The. (Rosen Reference).

—Trout Fishing. 2013. (Fishing: Tips & Techniques Ser.). (ENG., Illus.). 64p. (J). (gr. 5-8). pap. 12.95 *(978-1-4488-9508-3(1),* Rosen Classroom); lib. bdg. 31.95 *(978-1-4488-9490-1(5),* Rosen Reference) Rosen Publishing Group, Inc., The.

Poolos, Christine. Deep-Sea Fishing. 2013. (Fishing: Tips & Techniques Ser.). 64p. (J). (gr. 5-8). 31.95 *(978-1-4488-9486-4(7));* pap. 77.70 *(978-1-4488-9503-8(0));* (ENG., Illus.). pap. 12.95 *(978-1-4488-9502-1(2),* Rosen Classroom) Rosen Publishing Group, Inc., The.

Porterfield, Jason. Bowfishing. 2013. (Fishing: Tips & Techniques Ser.). 64p. (J). (gr. 5-8). 31.95 *(978-1-4488-9489-5(1));* (ENG., Illus.). pap. 12.95 *(978-1-4488-9500-7(6),* Rosen Classroom) Rosen Publishing Group, Inc., The.

Pound, Blake. Fly Fishing. 2012. (Outdoor Adventures Ser.). (ENG., Illus.). 24p. (J). (gr. 3-8). lib. bdg. 25.95 *(978-1-60014-798-2(4),* Pilot Bks.) Bellwether Media.

Puccinelli, Marie. Catch a Fish. 2014. (ENG.). 48p. (J). (gr. -1-3). 13.99 *(978-1-4814-2964-1(7),* Atheneum Bks. for Young Readers) Simon & Schuster Children's Publishing.

Rice, Katelyn & Kuligowski, Stephanie. Dangerous Catch! Deep Sea Fishers, 1 vol. 2nd rev. ed. 2013. (Nonfiction Readers Ser.). (ENG.). 64p. (J). (gr. 5-5). pap. 10.99 *(978-1-4333-4943-0(4))* Teacher Created Materials, Inc.

Rice, Katie. ¡Capturas Peligrosas! Pescadores de Alta Mar. 2016. (TIME for Kids en Español - Level 5 Ser.). (SPA.). 64p. (gr. 5-5). lib. bdg. 31.99 *(978-1-5157-2944-0(3))* Time for Kids Inc AUS. Dist: Capstone Pub.

Ringstad, Arnold. Fishing. 2014. (Great Outdoors Ser.). (ENG.). 24p. (J). (gr. 2-5). 28.50 *(978-1-62687-329-2(1),* 207169) Child's World, Inc., The.

Ritchie, Scot. P'ésk'a & the First Salmon Ceremony, 1 vol. 2015. (ENG., Illus.). 32p. (J). (gr. -1-2). 18.95 *(978-1-55498-718-4(0))* Groundwood Bks. CAN. Dist: Publishers Group West (PGW).

Rosen, Michael J. Gone Fishing. 2017. (Illus.). 32p. (J). *(978-1-60818-772-0(1),* Creative Education) Creative Co., The.

—The Perfect Spot. 2017. (Illus.). 32p. (J). *(978-1-60818-774-4(8),* Creative Education) Creative Co., The.

—Reel Time: Gone Fishing. 2017. (Reel Time Ser.). (ENG., Illus.). 32p. (J). (gr. 2-5). pap. 9.99 ***(978-1-62832-380-1(9),*** Creative Paperbacks) Creative Co., The.

—Reel Time: Take the Bait. 2017. (Reel Time Ser.). (ENG., Illus.). 32p. (J). (gr. 2-5). pap. 9.99 ***(978-1-62832-383-2(3),*** Creative Paperbacks) Creative Co., The.

—Reel Time: the Perfect Spot. 2017. (Reel Time Ser.). (ENG., Illus.). 32p. (J). (gr. 2-5). pap. 9.99 ***(978-1-62832-382-5(5),*** Creative Paperbacks) Creative Co., The.

—Tackling the Box. 2017. (Illus.). 32p. (J). *(978-1-60818-776-8(4),* Creative Education) Creative Co., The.

—Take the Bait. 2017. (Illus.). 32p. (J). *(978-1-60818-775-1(6),* Creative Education) Creative Co., The.

Ross, Nick. Fishing. 2009. (Get Outdoors Ser.). (Illus.). 32p. (ENG.). (J). pap. 10.00 *(978-1-4358-3050-9(4),* PowerKids Pr.); (YA). (gr. 4-7). lib. bdg. 25.25 *(978-1-4358-3042-4(3))* Rosen Publishing Group, Inc., The.

The Saltwater Game Fish Coloring Book. 2005. (J). mass mkt. *(978-0-9763757-1-5(0))* Cypress Knees Publishing.

Schuh, Mari C. Going Ice Fishing: Lever vs. Screw. 2015. (ENG., Illus.). 24p. (J). (gr. k-2). 23.99 *(978-1-4677-8029-2(4),* Lerner Pubns.) Lerner Publishing Group.

Schwartz, Tina P. Bass Fishing. 2012. (Reel It in Ser.). (ENG., Illus.). 24p. (J). (gr. 3-6). pap. 8.25 *(978-1-4488-6361-7(9));* lib. bdg. 22.60 *(978-1-4488-6201-6(9))* Rosen Publishing Group, Inc., The. (PowerKids Pr.).

—Deep-Sea Fishing. 2012. (Reel It in Ser.). (ENG.). 24p. (J). (gr. 3-6). pap. 8.25 *(978-1-4488-6353-2(8));* lib. bdg. 22.60 *(978-1-4488-6197-2(7))* Rosen Publishing Group, Inc., The. (PowerKids Pr.).

—Fly-Fishing. 2012. (Reel It in Ser.). (ENG.). 24p. (J). (gr. 3-6). pap. 8.25 *(978-1-4488-6355-6(4));* lib. bdg. 22.60 *(978-1-4488-6198-9(5))* Rosen Publishing Group, Inc., The. (PowerKids Pr.).

—Freshwater Fishing. 2012. (Reel It in Ser.). (ENG., Illus.). 24p. (J). (gr. 3-6). pap. 8.25 *(978-1-4488-6357-0(0));* lib. bdg. 22.60 *(978-1-4488-6199-6(3))* Rosen Publishing Group, Inc., The. (PowerKids Pr.).

—Ice Fishing. 2012. (Reel It in Ser.). (ENG.). 24p. (J). (gr. 3-6). pap. 8.25 *(978-1-4488-6359-4(7));* lib. bdg. 22.60 *(978-1-4488-6200-9(0))* Rosen Publishing Group, Inc., The. (PowerKids Pr.).

—Salmon Fishing. 2012. (Reel It in Ser.). (ENG.). 24p. (J). (gr. 3-6). pap. 8.25 *(978-1-4488-6351-8(1));* lib. bdg. 22.60 *(978-1-4488-6196-5(9))* Rosen Publishing Group, Inc., The. (PowerKids Pr.).

Shea, Therese. Overfishing. 2014. (Illus.). 32p. (J). lib. bdg. *(978-1-4339-9925-3(0))* Stevens, Gareth Publishing LLLP.

Slade, Suzanne. Let's Go Fishing. (Adventures Outdoors Ser.). 32p. 2009. (gr. 4-5). 47.90 *(978-1-61511-269-2(3))* 2007. (Illus.). (J). (gr. 3-7). lib. bdg. 25.25 *(978-1-4042-3647-9(3))* Rosen Publishing Group, Inc., The. (PowerKids Pr.).

Somervill, Barbara A. Producing Fish, 1 vol. 2012. (Technology of Farming Ser.). (ENG.). 48p. (J). (gr. 4-6). lib. bdg. 33.32 *(978-1-4329-6405-4(4),* Heinemann InfoSearch) Heinemann-Raintree.

Thomas, William. Deep Sea Fisher. 2010. (Benchmark Rockets: Dirty & Dangerous Jobs Ser.). 32p. (J). (gr. 3-6). 28.50 *(978-1-60870-171-1(9))* Marshall Cavendish GBR. Dist: Marshall Cavendish Corp.

Walke, Ted, illus. & compiled by. Boating Safety Sidekicks Color a Fish: Freshwater Fish Coloring Book. Walke, Ted, compiled by. 2008. 28p. (J). *(978-0-9718864-4-5(X))* Within Reach, Inc.

Walter Foster Creative Team & Maas, Dave. Kids' Guide to Fishing: The Young Angler's Guide to Catching More & Bigger Fish. 2017. (Ranger Rick Kids' Guides). (ENG., Illus.). 96p. (J). (gr. 3-7). 14.95 ***(978-1-63322-382-0(5),*** Walter Foster Jr) Quarto Publishing Group USA.

Weingarten, E. T. Fishing. 2012. (Great Outdoors Ser.). (Illus.). 24p. (J). (gr. 2-5). pap. 8.15 *(978-1-4339-7096-2(1));* lib. bdg. 22.60 *(978-1-4339-7095-5(3))* Stevens, Gareth Publishing LLLP.

Whiting, Jim. Deep-Sea Fishing. 2017. (J). ***(978-1-60818-687-7(3),*** Creative Education) Creative Co., The.

Wolny, Philip & Solomon, Dane. Fishing, 01 vols., 1. 2016. (Outdoor Life Ser.). (ENG., Illus.). 64p. (YA). 32.95 *(978-1-4994-6225-8(5),* 1398929, Rosen Young Adult) Rosen Publishing Group, Inc., The.

Young, Judy. H Is for Hook: A Fishing Alphabet. Palmer, Gary, illus. 2008. (Sports Alphabet Ser.). (ENG.). 40p. (J). (gr. 1-4). 17.95 *(978-1-58536-347-6(2),* 202305) Sleeping Bear Pr.

—H Is for Hook: A Fishing Alphabet. Palmer, Gary, illus. 2015. (Av2 Fiction Readalong 2016 Ser.). (ENG.). (J). (gr. 1-4). lib. bdg. 34.28 *(978-1-4896-3747-5(8),* AV2 by Weigl) Weigl Pubs., Inc.

Zobel, Derek. Fishing. 2011. (My First Sports Ser.). (ENG., Illus.). 24p. (J). (gr. 2-5). lib. bdg. 25.95 *(978-1-60014-569-8(8),* Blastoff! Readers) Bellwether Media.

—Fishing. 2011. pap. *(978-0-531-20635-5(1))* Grolier Publishing.

FISHING—EQUIPMENT AND SUPPLIES

Rosen, Michael J. Fishing Gear. 2017. (Illus.). 32p. (J). *(978-1-60818-773-7(X),* Creative Education) Creative Co., The.

—Reel Time: Fishing Gear. 2017. (Reel Time Ser.). (ENG., Illus.). 32p. (J). (gr. 2-5). pap. 9.99 ***(978-1-62832-381-8(7),*** Creative Paperbacks) Creative Co., The.

—Reel Time: Tackling the Box. 2017. (Reel Time Ser.). (ENG., Illus.). 32p. (J). (gr. 2-5). pap. 9.99 ***(978-1-62832-384-9(1),*** Creative Paperbacks) Creative Co., The.

Wessman, Bo. Building Your Own Rod. 2004. (Complete Guide to Fishing Ser.). (Illus.). 72p. (YA). (gr. 7-18). lib. bdg. 19.95 *(978-1-59084-550-9(1))* Mason Crest.

FISHING—FICTION

Adams, Julie. Kem's Adventures: The Fishing Trip. 2009. 40p. pap. 16.99 *(978-1-4389-8458-2(8))* AuthorHouse.

Akinje, Wale. The Adventures of Imhotep. Young, Craig, illus. 2006. (J). *(978-0-9768485-0-9(3))* Nile Publishing.

Anderson, Max Elliot. North Woods Poachers. 2004. 144p. pap. 10.95 *(978-0-9729256-8-6(6),* Tweener Pr.) Baker Trittin Pr.

Arena, Felice & Kettle, Phil. Crawfish Hunt. Vane, Mitch, illus. 2004. (J). pap. *(978-1-59336-358-1(3))* Mondo Publishing.

—Gone Fishing. Boyer, Susy, illus. 2004. (J). pap. *(978-1-59336-359-8(1))* Mondo Publishing.

Arnold, Ginger Fudge. Two Tipsy Tots, 1 vol. Crème, Aurora C., illus. 2009. 32p. pap. 24.95 *(978-1-4489-1891-1(X))* America Star Bks.

Arrington, Linda. Ugly Trees. Arrington, Linda, photos by. 2012. (Illus.). 24p. pap. 24.95 *(978-1-4626-8925-5(6))* America Star Bks.

Aruego, Jose & Dewey, Ariane. Splash! 2003. (Green Light Readers Level 2 Ser.). (ENG., Illus.). 32p. (J). (gr. -1-3). pap. 3.95 *(978-0-15-204832-7(4))* Houghton Mifflin Harcourt Publishing Co.

Awdry, W. Thomas Goes Fishing. Courtney, Richard, illus. 2005. (Step into Reading Ser.). (ENG.). 32p. (J). (gr. -1-1). pap. 3.99 *(978-0-375-83118-8(5),* Random Hse. Bks. for Young Readers) Random Hse. Children's Bks.

Baker, Keith. More Mr. & Mrs. Green, 1 vol. Baker, Keith, illus. 2007. (Mr. & Mrs. Green Ser.). (ENG., Illus.). 68p. (gr. 2-4). 27.07 *(978-1-59961-302-4(6))* Spotlight.

Ballantyne, Robert Michael. The Lighthouse. 2007. (ENG.). 256p. pap. 21.99 *(978-1-4264-9381-2(9));* 286p. pap. 23.99 *(978-1-4264-9762-9(8))* Creative Media Partners, LLC.

Bell, Leann. Ed & Alma Go Fishing. 2010. 28p. pap. 15.99 *(978-1-4535-3023-8(1))* Xlibris Corp.

Belmudes, Bonnie. The Adventures of Gus & Gunther: How They Met. 2012. 44p. pap. 21.99 *(978-1-4772-5350-2(5))* AuthorHouse.

Berenstain, Mike. The Berenstain Bears: Gone Fishin'! Berenstain, Mike, illus. 2014. (I Can Read Level 1 Ser.). (ENG., Illus.). 32p. (J). (gr. -1-3). pap. 3.99 *(978-0-06-207559-8(4))* HarperCollins Pubs.

—The Berenstain Bears - Gone Fishin'! Berenstain, Mike, illus. 2014. (I Can Read Level 1 Ser.). (ENG., Illus.). 32p. (J). (gr. -1-3). 16.99 *(978-0-06-207560-4(8))* HarperCollins Pubs.

—Gone Fishin'! 2014. (Berenstain Bears: I Can Read! Ser.). (J). lib. bdg. 13.55 *(978-0-606-35476-9(X))* Turtleback Bks.

The Big Catch: Individual Title Six-Packs. (Literatura 2000 Ser.). (gr. 2-3). 33.00 *(978-0-7635-0253-9(7))* Rigby Education.

Bonehill, Ralph. Young Hunters of the Lake. rev. ed. 2006. 212p. 27.95 *(978-1-4218-1805-4(1));* pap. 12.95 *(978-1-4218-1905-1(8))* 1st World Publishing, Inc. (1st World Library - Literary Society).

Bootman, Colin. Fish for the Grand Lady. Bootman, Colin, illus. 2006. (ENG., Illus.). 32p. (J). (gr. -1-3). 16.95 *(978-0-8234-1898-5(7))* Holiday Hse., Inc.

Bozanich, Tony L. & Wight, Joe. Nazi Zombies. Isaksen, Patricia, ed. Isaksen, Lisa A., illus. 2013. (ENG.). 112p. (gr. -1-4). pap. 14.95 *(978-0-930655-00-6(1),* 9780930655006) Antarctic Pr., Inc.

Brasch, Nicolas & Nickel, Adam. Dad & Dan Go Fishing. 2008. (Rigby Focus Forward: Level D Ser.). (Illus.). 16p. (J). (gr. 4-7). pap. *(978-1-4190-3668-2(8),* Rigby) Pearson Education Australia.

Brooks, Bertha. The Big Fishing Trip. 2004. (Illus.). 32p. (J). 12.00 *(978-1-58374-086-6(4))* Chicago Spectrum Pr.

Cafiero, Crystal. Gone Fishing, Just Daddy & Me. 2013. 24p. pap. 24.95 *(978-1-4241-1532-7(9))* America Star Bks.

Caldas, Iara. The Fisherman Collection: The Fishery. 2013. (ENG.). 35p. (J). pap. 13.95 *(978-1-4327-9406-4(X))* Outskirts Pr., Inc.

Carlson, Nancy. Loudmouth George & the Fishing Trip. 2nd rev. ed. 2005. (ENG., Illus.). 32p. (J). (gr. k-2). pap. 9.95 *(978-1-57505-733-0(6),* First Avenue Editions) Lerner Publishing Group.

Chapman, Charlotte. The Adventures of Little Payton. 2008. 24p. pap. 14.49 *(978-1-4343-9598-6(7))* AuthorHouse.

Chronicle Books Staff. Stanley Goes Fishing Hc (French) 2006. (J). 15.95 *(978-92-0-195244-8(9))* Chronicle Bks. LLC.

Civitella, Mark. Angus the Angler: Snapper Surprise. 2012. (Illus.). 16p. pap. 18.30 *(978-1-4772-3951-3(0))* AuthorHouse.

Creech, Sharon. Fishing in the Air. Raschka, Chris, illus. 2003. (ENG.). 32p. (J). (gr. -1-3). pap. 6.99 *(978-0-06-051606-2(2))* HarperCollins Pubs.

—Fishing in the Air. Raschka, Chris, illus. 2003. pap. 9.95 incl. audio *(978-1-59112-223-4(6));* (J). 25.95 incl. audio *(978-1-59112-225-8(2));* (J). pap. 39.95 incl. audio compact disk *(978-1-59112-521-1(9));* (J). pap. 37.95 incl. audio *(978-1-59112-226-5(0))* Live Oak Media.

—Fishing in the Air. 2003. (J). (gr. k-3). 17.20 *(978-0-613-66967-2(3),* Turtleback) Turtleback Bks.

Criss, Lisa. You Can't Teach a Doll How to Fish! 2008. 36p. per. 24.95 *(978-1-4241-9359-2(1))* America Star Bks.

Cronin, Doreen. Clic, Clac, Plif, Plaf: Una Aventura de Contar. Lewin, Betsy, illus. 2006. (J). (gr. -1-k). per. 6.99 *(978-1-933032-03-0(0))* Lectorum Pubns., Inc.

—Clic, Clac, Plif, Plaf: Una Aventura de Contar. Rioja, Alberto Jimenez, tr. from ENG. Lewin, Betsy, illus. 2006. (J). (gr. 5-6). 12.99 *(978-1-933032-11-5(1))* Lectorum Pubns., Inc.

—Click, Clack, Splish, Splash: A Counting Adventure. Lewin, Betsy, illus. 2006. (Click, Clack Book Ser.). (ENG.). 24p. (J). (gr. -1-3). 17.99 *(978-0-689-87716-2(1),* Atheneum Bks. for Young Readers) Simon & Schuster Children's Publishing.

Cronin, Doreen & Lewin, Betsy. Click, Clack, Splish, Splash: A Counting Adventure, 1 vol. 2006. (Doreen Cronin: Click-Clack & More Ser.). (ENG.). 24p. (gr. -1-3). lib. bdg. 24.21 *(978-1-59961-090-0(6))* Spotlight.

Dail, Ernestine. A Voice in the Night. Gillen, Rosemarie, illus. 2012. 46p. pap. 9.99 *(978-1-61286-099-2(0))* Avid Readers Publishing Group.

Damitz, Charlie. Diving for el Corazon. Diefendorf, Cathy, illus. 2007. (ENG.). 101p. (J). pap. 7.95 *(978-0-9744446-3-5(4))* All About Kids Publishing.

Daniel, David A. Gone Ice Cream Fishing. 2012. 32p. pap. 21.99 *(978-1-4691-9383-0(3))* Xlibris Corp.

Davies, Lewis. Tai & the Tremorfa Troll. Acreman, Hayley, illus. 2007. (ENG.). 20p. (J). pap. 7.95 *(978-1-905762-48-4(8))* Parthian Bks. GBR. Dist: Independent Pubs. Group.

De felice, Cynthia. Devil's Bridge. 2008. (ENG.). 96p. (YA). (gr. 7). pap. 9.99 *(978-1-4169-8307-1(4),* Atheneum Bks. for Young Readers) Simon & Schuster Children's Publishing.

DeFelice, Cynthia C. The Missing Manatee. 2008. (ENG.). 192p. (J). (gr. 3-7). pap. 8.99 *(978-0-374-40020-0(2),* 9780374400200) Square Fish.

Dewey, Ariane & Aruego, Jose. Splash! 2003. (Green Light Readers Level 2 Ser.). (Illus.). (J). (gr. k-2). 11.60 *(978-0-7569-0534-7(6))* Perfection Learning Corp.

Un dia de Pesca, 6 packs. (Literatura 2000 Ser.). (SPA.). (gr. 2-3). 33.00 *(978-0-7635-1260-6(5))* Rigby Education.

DiLorenzo, Michael & Julich, Jennifer. Adventures with Jonny: Ice Fishing! The Coolest Sport on Earth - A Parent & Child Ice Fishing Adventure & Guide. 2009. (Illus.). 76p. (J). (gr. -1). 17.95 *(978-0-9777210-1-6(9))* Running Moose Publications.

Dion. Fishing with Balloons. 2004. (Illus.). 57p. (J). pap. 4.95 *(978-1-881929-34-5(5))* Oxton Hse., Pubs.

Dwyer, Mindy. The Salmon Princess: An Alaska Cinderella Story. 2004. (Paws IV Ser.). (ENG., Illus.). 32p. (J). (gr. -1-2). pap. 10.99 *(978-1-57061-355-5(9),* Little Bigfoot) Sasquatch Bks.

Dyan, Penelope. The Fish That Got Away — -for Boys Only(r). Dyan, Penelope, illus. 2010. (Illus.). 34p. pap. 11.95 *(978-1-935630-29-6(6))* Bellissima Publishing, LLC.

Farish, Terry. Either the Beginning or the End of the World. 2015. (ENG.). 200p. (YA). (gr. 8-12). 18.99 *(978-1-4677-8813-7(9),* Carolrhoda Lab™) Lerner Publishing Group.

Farrell, Bill. Walter's Pond: The True Story of Three Brothers Who Went Fishing for Trouble. Julich, Jenniffer, illus. 2008. 16p. 8.95 *(978-0-9797790-0-8(6))* Lower Lane Publishing LLC.

Fishing: KinderReaders Individual Title Six-Packs. (Kinderstarters Ser.). 8p. (gr. -1-1). 21.00 *(978-0-7635-8665-2(X))* Rigby Education.

Fleming, David. Charlie Blue Berry Fipple Berry. 2012. 88p. 19.95 *(978-1-4759-1945-5(X));* pap. 9.95 *(978-1-4759-1944-8(1))* iUniverse, Inc.

Fox, Valerie P. Deefa: Seek the Vixen. 2008. 92p. pap. 10.49 *(978-1-4389-0723-9(0))* AuthorHouse.

Frazier, Craig. Stanley Goes Fishing. 2006. (Stanley Ser.: STAN). (ENG., Illus.). 40p. (J). (gr. -1-7). 15.95 *(978-0-8118-5244-9(X))* Chronicle Bks. LLC.

Freeman, Marcia S. Catfish & Spaghetti. Stock, Rose, illus. 2013. (Maupin House Ser.). (ENG.). 48p. (gr. 3-5). pap. 4.50 *(978-0-929895-21-5(5))* Maupin Hse. Publishing.

Ganzer, Diane. Summer School Blues. 2008. 124p. pap. 9.99 *(978-1-935105-19-0(1))* Avid Readers Publishing Group.

Gogarty, Brian. Shamrock Sean Goes Fishing. Burchartz, Roxanne, illus. 2007. (ENG.). 12p. (J). pap. 7.95 *(978-0-86278-968-8(0))* O'Brien Pr., Ltd., The IRL. Dist: Dufour Editions, Inc.

Gordon, Marie Elaina. My Grand-Mom Told Me-down by the Sea. 2008. 108p. pap. 19.95 *(978-1-4241-9095-9(9))* America Star Bks.

Gott, Ricky. I Wish, I Wish... I Wish to Fish / IT. 2011. (Illus.). 80p. (J). pap. 24.95 *(978-0-9837334-1-6(4))* Digi-Tall Media.

Grandma Janet Mary. Grandpa's Fishin' Friend. Pennington, Craig, illus. 2nd ed. 2007. (Grandma Janet Mary Ser.). 28p. (J). 16.95 *(978-0-9742732-7-3(9))* My Grandma & Me Pubs.

Gravett, Emily. Bear & Hare Go Fishing. Gravett, Emily, illus. 2015. (Bear & Hare Ser.). (ENG., Illus.). 32p. (J). (gr. -1-3). 15.99 *(978-1-4814-2289-5(8),* Simon & Schuster Bks. For Young Readers) Simon & Schuster Bks. For Young Readers.

Gray, Kes. Daisy & the Trouble with Maggots, No. 6. Sharratt, Nick & Parsons, Garry, illus. 2010. (Daisy Ser.: 6). (ENG.). 240p. (J). (gr. 2-4). pap. 8.99 *(978-1-86230-846-6(2),* Red Fox) Random House Children's Books GBR. Dist: Independent Pubs. Group.

Guest, Elissa Haden. Iris & Walter & Cousin Howie. Davenier, Christine, illus. alt. ed. 2012. (Green Light Readers Level 3 Ser.). (ENG.). 44p. (J). (gr. 1-4). pap. 3.99 *(978-0-547-85068-9(9))* Houghton Mifflin Harcourt Publishing Co.

Hancock, H. Irving. The High School Boys' Fishing Trip. rev. ed. 2006. 216p. 27.95 *(978-1-4218-1749-1(7));* pap. 12.95 *(978-1-4218-1849-8(3))* 1st World Publishing, Inc. (1st World Library - Literary Society).

—The High School Boys' Fishing Trip. 2007. 180p. per. *(978-1-4065-1984-6(7))* Dodo Pr.

Heible, Beverly. A River Row: Andrew & Luke Fishing with Grandpa. 2012. 24p. 24.95 *(978-1-4626-6648-5(5))* America Star Bks.

Hobbs, Will. Leaving Protection. 2005. 178p. (gr. 5-9). 19.00 *(978-0-7569-5121-4(6))* Perfection Learning Corp.

Holland, Diane. Sally Butterfield Goes Fishing! 2005. 49p. pap. 16.95 *(978-1-4137-9767-1(9))* America Star Bks.

Holubitsky, Katherine. The Big Snapper, 1 vol. 2006. (Orca Young Readers Ser.). (ENG., Illus.). 144p. (J). (gr. 3-5). per. 6.95 *(978-1-55143-563-3(2))* Orca Bk. Pubs. USA.

Houseman, D. L. Harvey & His Friends Great Fishing Adventure. 2010. pap. 18.95 *(978-0-578-05355-4(1))* Stuff on Paper.

Howell, Gill. Selkie Child. Keen, Sophie, illus. 2005. (ENG.). 24p. (J). lib. bdg. 23.65 *(978-1-59646-750-7(9))* Dingles & Co.

Hunger, Chrissy. Kuna Caught a Tun. 2012. 36p. pap. 20.99 *(978-1-4772-6125-5(7))* AuthorHouse.

Immi's Gift, 1 vol. 2014. (ENG., Illus.). 32p. (J). (gr. -1-3). 7.95 *(978-1-56145-813-4(9))* Peachtree Pubs.

Ingle, L. G. Little Willy Wiggle & Johnny Amigo. 2012. 40p. pap. *(978-1-77097-479-1(2))* FriesenPress.

Iwamura, Kazuo. Seven Little Mice Have Fun on the Ice. 2011. (ENG., Illus.). 32p. (J). (gr. -1-2). 16.95 *(978-0-7358-4048-5(2))* North-South Bks., Inc.

Johnston, Shawn. A Tale from the Forest of Fairshaw: The Big Fish Story. 2012. 24p. 24.95 *(978-1-4626-6830-4(5))* America Star Bks.

Jones, C. B. Sleeping with the Fishes. Green, Chris, illus. 2017. (Bog Hollow Boys Ser.). (ENG.). 72p. (gr. 4-5). lib. bdg. 25.32 *(978-1-4965-4055-3(7))* Stone Arch Bks.

Just One Fish Would Do: Individual Title Six-Packs. (gr. k-1). 23.00 *(978-0-7635-8847-2(4))* Rigby Education.

Kapai, Tommy. Cuzzies Meet the Motuhoa Shark. Henry, Mike, illus. 2006. (Cuzzies Adventures Ser.). (MAO & ENG.). 32p. (J). (gr. -1-3). pap. 9.00 *(978-1-86969-100-4(8))* Huia Pubs. NZL. Dist: Univ. of Hawaii Pr.

Kelly, Jason. No Fish in My Dish. 2007. (Illus.). 30p. (J). pap. 9.95 *(978-0-9664387-1-0(X))* Kelly, Jason Pr.

Kelsey, Linda J. Big Fish. Kelsey-Livin, Barbara, illus. 2012. 28p. pap. 24.95 *(978-1-4626-6887-8(9))* America Star Bks.

Kipling, Rudyard. Captains Courageous. 2006. (Classics Ser.). (Illus.). 48p. (YA). per. 17.95 *(978-1-56254-869-8(7));* 80p. (J). (gr. 4-7). per. *(978-1-56254-868-1(9))* Saddleback Educational Publishing, Inc.

Knight, Richard, et al. Finn at Clee Point. Hurst, Oliver, illus. 2012. (ENG.). 128p. (J). pap. 12.99 *(978-1-84686-401-8(1))* Barefoot Bks., Inc.

Kristina Learns about Fishing. 2007. (J). *(978-0-9792728-0-6(7))* Tracepaper Bks. Inc.

Lamkin, Robert J. Tommy's Train. 2008. 44p. pap. 24.95 *(978-1-60672-147-6(X))* America Star Bks.

Lane, Deborah. Fishing with Mom. 2003. pap. 9.00 *(978-0-8059-6321-2(9))* Dorrance Publishing Co., Inc.

Larson, Deborah Jo. One Frozen Lake. Johnson, Steve & Fancher, Lou, illus. 2012. (ENG.). 32p. (J). 16.95 *(978-0-87351-866-6(7))* Minnesota Historical Society Pr.

LeBox, Annette. Salmon Creek, 1 vol. Reczuch, Karen, illus. 2005. (ENG.). 32p. (J). pap. 12.95 *(978-0-88899-644-2(6))* Groundwood Bks. CAN. Dist: Publishers Group West (PGW).

Lingle, Lise. One for You & One for Me. 2012. 20p. pap. 17.99 *(978-1-4772-1702-3(9))* AuthorHouse.

Littlewood, Karin. Immi's Gift, 1 vol. Littlewood, Karin, illus. 2010. (ENG., Illus.). 32p. (J). (gr. -1-3). 15.95 *(978-1-56145-545-4(8))* Peachtree Pubs.

Llewellyn, Claire. Splash!, 1 vol. Beard, Lauren, illus. 2013. (Start Reading Ser.). (ENG.). 24p. (gr. k-1). pap. 7.95 *(978-1-4765-3186-1(2));* pap. 41.94 *(978-1-4765-3232-5(X))* Capstone Press of Coughlan Cos.

Lovett, Darrell F. Darrell's Lake Franklin. 2007. 13.00 *(978-0-8059-8807-9(6))* Dorrance Publishing Co., Inc.

Lyall, Maureen. Magus & the Blue Fairy. 2012. 20p. pap. 17.99 *(978-1-4772-6562-8(7))* AuthorHouse.

Maccarone, Grace. The Gingerbread Family: A Scratch-and-Sniff Book. Gardner, Louise, illus. 2010. (ENG.). 14p. (J). (gr. -1-k). bds. 7.99 *(978-1-4424-0678-0(X),* Little Simon) Little Simon.

Maddox, Jake. Legend of the Lure, 1 vol. Tiffany, Sean, illus. 2008. (Jake Maddox Sports Stories Ser.). (ENG.). 72p. (gr. 2-3). 25.32 *(978-1-4342-0783-8(8));* pap. 5.95 *(978-1-4342-0879-8(6))* Stone Arch Bks.

Maddox, Tony & Wen, Dref. Ffred Ar y Môr: Cyfres Ffred Ci'r Fferm. 2005. (WEL., Illus.). 32p. pap. *(978-1-85596-666-6(2))* Dref Wen.

Massey, Ed. Jedlo, Defender of the Deep. 2005. (J). 17.95 *(978-0-9766799-0-5(6))* Moombaya Bks.

Matthews, Curtis. Boots Meets the Grizzly Bears. 2007. 164p. per. 13.95 *(978-1-4343-3372-8(8))* AuthorHouse.

Mayer, Mercer & Mayer, Gina. Just Fishing with Grandma. 2015. (Little Critter Ser.). (J). lib. bdg. 13.55 *(978-0-606-36492-8(7))* Turtleback Bks.

McDonald, Rae A. A Fishing Surprise. Kemly, Kathleen, illus. 2007. (ENG.). 32p. (J). (gr. -1-3). 16.95 *(978-1-55971-977-3(X))* Cooper Square Publishing Llc.

McKenzie, Precious. Fishing for Danger. 2015. (ENG.). 96p. (gr. 3-6). 31.36 *(978-1-63430-392-7(X))* Rourke Educational Media.

McKissack, Patricia C. A Million Fish... More or Less. Schutzer, Dena, illus. 2016. (ENG.). 32p. (J). (gr. -1-2). 17.99

(978-0-679-80692-9(X), Knopf Bks. for Young Readers) Random Hse. Children's Bks.

McMillan, Dawn. Catch of the Day! Vignolo, Enrique, illus. 2013. (ENG.). 24p. (gr. 3-3). pap. *(978-1-927197-70-7(8)*, Red Rocket Readers) Flying Start Bks.

Miller, Jay. Bingo the Banjo Picking Bear. 2007. 40p. (YA). per. 14.95 *(978-1-4327-0739-2(6))* Outskirts Pr., Inc.

Miller, Jennifer. Run, Rasputin, Run! Trials & Friendships (Book 2) 2006. (ENG., Illus.). 172p. per. 14.85 *(978-1-4120-8494-9(6))* Trafford Publishing.

Moreland, Karla Carter. Fishing with Daddy. 2008. (Illus.). 16p. 9.00 *(978-1-4120-4000-6(0))* Trafford Publishing.

Muluka, B. Kandu & the Lake. 2004. (Illus.). 44p. pap. *(978-9966-25-165-7(0))* Heinemann Kenya, Limited (East African Educational Publishers Ltd E.A.E.P.) KEN. Dist: Michigan State Univ. Pr.

Newberry, Geoffrey C. The Cape Don Adventure. 2011. 48p. pap. 6.99 *(978-1-61667-262-1(5))* Raider Publishing International.

Ninnes, Jay. Smelly Footed Toad. 2009. (Illus.). 40p. pap. 16.99 *(978-1-4343-9418-7(2))* AuthorHouse.

O'Brien, Richard. Christopher & Joshua Go Fishing. 2012. (Illus.). 38p. pap. 11.00 *(978-1-78035-257-2(3)*, Fastprint Publishing) Upfront Publishing Ltd. GBR. Dist: Printondemand-worldwide.com.

O'Connor, Miles. The Tree That Moved. 2012. (ENG.). pap. 3.99 *(978-1-4675-1647-1(3))* Independent Pub.

Oelschlager, Vanita. A Tale of Two Mommies. Blanc, Mike, illus. 2011. (ENG.). 40p. (J). (gr. -1-3). 15.95 *(978-0-9826366-6-4(0))*; pap. 8.95 *(978-0-9826366-7-1(9))* VanitaBooks.

Olds, Helen Diehl. Fisherman Jody. Gotlieb, Jules, illus. 2011. 64p. 36.95 *(978-1-258-07129-5(0))* Literary Licensing, LLC.

Olsen, Sylvia. Catching Spring, 1 vol. 2004. (Orca Young Readers Ser.). (ENG., Illus.). 128p. (J). (gr. 3-6). pap. 7.95 *(978-1-55143-298-4(6)*, 1234542) Orca Bk. Pubs. USA.

Oppel, Kenneth. Peg & the Whale. 2004. (Illus.). (J). (gr. k-3). spiral bd. *(978-0-616-07245-5(7))* Canadian National Institute for the Blind/Institut National Canadien pour les Aveugles.

Parker, Beth. Tom Turtle's Fishing Tail, 1 vol. 2010. 26p. 24.95 *(978-1-4489-4134-6(2))* America Star Bks.

Peppers, F. J. That's not a Fish! 2011. 24p. pap. 12.55 *(978-1-4567-6423-4(3))* AuthorHouse.

Peschke, Marci. Fishing Queen. Mourning, Tuesday, illus. 2017. (Kylie Jean Ser.). (ENG.). 112p. (gr. 2-3). lib. bdg. 22.65 ***(978-1-4795-9900-4(X)***, Kylie Jean) Picture Window Bks.

Petreman, Gwen. A Wish for Haidan. 2011. 24p. (gr. -1). 12.56 *(978-1-4269-5739-0(4))* Trafford Publishing.

Phelps, Elizabeth Stuart. Jack the Fisherman. Reed, C. W., illus. 2005. reprint ed. pap. 15.95 *(978-1-4179-3778-3(5))* Kessinger Publishing, LLC.

Phi, Bao. A Different Pond. Bui, Thi, illus. 2017. (Fiction Picture Bks.). (ENG.). 32p. (gr. 2-3). lib. bdg. 23.32 ***(978-1-4795-9746-8(5)***, Fiction Picture Bks.) Picture Window Bks.

Philbrick, Rodman & Philbrick, W. R. The Young Man & the Sea. 2005. 192p. (gr. 4-7). 17.00 *(978-0-7569-4899-3(1))* Perfection Learning Corp.

Potter, Beatrix. The Tale of Mr. Jeremy Fisher. (Beatrix Potter Bookmark Board Book Ser.). (Illus.). 6p. (J). bds. 3.95 *(978-1-58989-202-6(X))* Thurman Hse., LLC.

Price, J. M. Patience, 1 vol. Bullard, Joyce, illus. 2010. 16p. pap. 24.95 *(978-1-4489-6233-4(1))* PublishAmerica, Inc.

Pritchett, Susan & Wetterwald, Florence. Sardine Goes Fishing (a Blabla Book) 2017. (ENG., Illus.). 24p. (J). (— 1). bds. 7.99 ***(978-0-553-52052-1(0)***, Random Hse. Bks. for Young Readers) Random Hse. Children's Bks.

Prosek, James. The Day My Mother Left. Prosek, James, illus. 2009. (ENG., Illus.). 304p. (J). (gr. 4-7). pap. 7.99 *(978-1-4169-0771-8(8)*, Simon & Schuster Bks. For Young Readers) Simon & Schuster Bks. For Young Readers.

—A Good Day's Fishing. Prosek, James, illus. 2004. (ENG., Illus.). 40p. (J). (gr. 1-5). 17.99 *(978-0-689-85327-2(0)*, Simon & Schuster Bks. For Young Readers) Simon & Schuster Bks. For Young Readers.

Raheb, Donna. The Adventures of Henrietta Ham: Gone Fishing. 2008. 36p. pap. 14.95 *(978-1-4327-2565-5(3))* Outskirts Pr., Inc.

Rand, Johnathan. American Chillers #25 Mississippi Megalodon. 2008. 208p. (J). pap. 5.99 *(978-1-893699-33-5(1))* AudioCraft Publishing, Inc.

Rawlings, Marjorie Kinnan. The Secret River. Dillon, Leo & Dillon, Diane, illus. 2011. (ENG.). 56p. (J). (gr. -1-3). 19.99 *(978-1-4169-1179-1(0)*, Atheneum Bks. for Young Readers) Simon & Schuster Children's Publishing.

Rey, H. A. C. G. Fish, Rides. (ENG., Illus.). bds., bds., bds. 95.20 *(978-0-618-13189-1(2))* Houghton Mifflin Harcourt Publishing Co.

Rhyne, Nancy. The Crab Boys. 2007. (J). pap. 6.95 *(978-0-87844-183-9(2))* Sandlapper Publishing Co., Inc.

Richards, Sonja. Comet Kid. 2007. 31p. pap. 8.95 *(978-0-9794935-0-8(1))* Olde Towne Publishing.

Richter, Jutta. The Summer of the Pike. Brailovsky, Anna, tr. from GER. Buchholz, Quint, illus. 2006. (ENG.). 132p. (J). (gr. 2-8). 16.95 *(978-1-57131-671-4(X))*; (gr. 8-12). per. 6.95 *(978-1-57131-672-1(8))* Milkweed Editions.

Robbins, Maureen. Cuentos de Pesca. 2012. (SPA & ENG.). 24p. (gr. 2-3). pap. 8.95 *(978-1-61810-548-6(5))* Rourke Educational Media.

Robbins, Neal. The Crimson Fish. Eisenfeld, Candice, illus. 58p. (Orig.). (J). (gr. 1-18). pap. 4.00 *(978-1-884993-02-2(8))* Koldarana Pubns.

Roberson, T. S. Riley's Race. 2012. 24p. pap. 15.99 *(978-1-4691-6428-1(0))* Xlibris Corp.

Robinson, Hilary. A Croc Shock! Gordon, Mike, illus. 2009. (Get Set Readers Ser.). 32p. (J). (gr. -1-2). lib. bdg. 22.60 *(978-1-60754-265-0(X))* Windmill Bks.

Roddy-Worsham, Clara. Bear Baby Goes Fishing. 2013. 24p. 24.95 *(978-1-63004-070-3(3))* America Star Bks.

Saddleback Educational Publishing Staff, ed. Neptune, 1 vol. unabr. ed. 2011. (Heights Ser.). (ENG.). 50p. (gr. 5-8). pap. 7.95 *(978-1-61651-285-9(7))* Saddleback Educational Publishing, Inc.

Salisbury, Graham. Calvin Coconut: Man Trip. Rogers, Jacqueline, illus. 2013. (Calvin Coconut Ser.). (ENG.). 144p. (J). (gr. 2-5). pap. 6.99 *(978-0-375-86507-7(1)*, Yearling) Random Hse. Children's Bks.

—Lord of the Deep. braille ed. 2003. (J). (gr. 2). spiral bd. *(978-0-616-15872-2(6))* Canadian National Institute for the Blind/Institut National Canadien pour les Aveugles.

—Lord of the Deep. 2003. 182p. (J). (gr. 5-9). 13.65 *(978-0-7569-1455-4(8))* Perfection Learning Corp.

—Lord of the Deep. 2003. (ENG.). 192p. (YA). (gr. 7). mass mkt. 6.99 *(978-0-440-22911-7(1)*, Laurel Leaf) Random Hse. Children's Bks.

—Lord of the Deep: A Novel. 2006. 182p. (J). (gr. 6-10). reprint ed. 16.00 *(978-1-4223-5841-2(0))* DIANE Publishing Co.

Sanders, Addie Meyer. I Don't Want to Go. l.t. ed. 2012. 43p. (J). pap. *(978-1-4596-3449-7(7))* ReadHowYouWant.com, Ltd.

Santillo, LuAnn. Fishing. Santillo, LuAnn, ed. 2003. (Half-Pint Kids Readers Ser.). (Illus.). 7p. (J). (gr. -1-1). pap. 1.00 *(978-1-59256-093-6(8))* Half-Pint Kids, Inc.

Saviola, Erin. The Biggest Fish. 2006. (Neighborhood Readers Ser.). (ENG.). 8p. (gr. -1-3). pap. 5.15 *(978-1-4042-6453-3(1)*, Rosen Classroom) Rosen Publishing Group, Inc., The.

Schlosser, Jeffrey A. Little Jacky Yooper: Kid Fisherman. 2011. (Illus.). 20p. pap. 8.50 *(978-1-4567-5163-0(8))* AuthorHouse.

Singhose, Rose & StGermain, Annetta. Gramma's Sure Fire Cure for Insomnia in the Very Young. 2010. 67p. pap. 27.50 *(978-0-557-08697-9(3))* Lulu Pr., Inc.

Smiley, Lucy Ireland. Bass-Fishing Bears. 2006. (J). pap. 8.00 *(978-0-8059-7017-3(7))* Dorrance Publishing Co., Inc.

Stanley, Andy. Go Fish: Because of What's on the Line. 2005. (North Point Resources Ser.). (ENG.). 96p. stu. ed., per., pupil's gde. ed. 9.99 *(978-1-59052-548-7(5)*, Multnomah Bks.) Crown Publishing Group.

Stanley, Dan. Danny the Fisherman, 1 vol. LaRue, Athena Mariah, illus. 2010. 46p. 24.95 *(978-1-4512-9695-2(9))* PublishAmerica, Inc.

Sterer, Gideon. Skyfishing. Bernatene, Poly, illus. 2017. (ENG.). 40p. (J). (gr. -1-3). 17.95 *(978-1-4197-1911-0(4)*, Abrams Bks. for Young Readers) Abrams, Inc.

Stone, Charlene. The Greatest Fishing Adventure of a Lifetime: American Kids Greatest Adventures. 2004. 47p. pap. 24.95 *(978-1-4137-2862-0(6))* PublishAmerica, Inc.

Suen, Anastasia. The Big Catch: A Robot & Rico Story, 1 vol. Laughead, Mike, illus. 2009. (Robot & Rico Ser.). (ENG.). 32p. (gr. 1-2). 22.65 *(978-1-4342-1626-7(8))*; pap. 6.25 *(978-1-4342-1751-6(5))* Stone Arch Bks.

Suen, Anastasia & Heck, Claudia M. La Gran Pesca. Laughead, Mike, illus. 2012. (Robot y Rico/Robot & Rico Ser.).Tr. of Big Catch. (MUL, SPA & ENG.). 32p. (gr. 1-2). pap. 5.05 *(978-1-4342-3920-4(9))*; lib. bdg. 22.65 *(978-1-4342-3781-1(8))* Stone Arch Bks. (Bilingual Stone Arch Readers).

Tait, Barbara. Timothy Toot... Goes Fishing. Margolis, Al, illus. 2011. 28p. (J). 24.95 *(978-1-58909-879-4(X))* Bookstand Publishing.

Tangerine, Tracey. Buddy Zooka: In the French Quarter & Beyond. 2010. (ENG.). 201p. (J). (gr. 7-12). pap. 16.00 *(978-0-9741995-8-0(3))* Chin Music Pr.

Tegan-Olsen, Sandra, illus. Joey's adventures by the Sea: Jellyfish Everywhere! 2008. 20p. (J). per. 9.95 *(978-0-9801527-0-8(4))* Freefox Publishing.

Thelen, Bob. Adventures with Grandpa: The Fishing Trip. 2010. 28p. pap. 12.99 *(978-1-4520-2255-0(0))* AuthorHouse.

Trout Fishing in America Staff, et al. My Name Is Chicken Joe. Jorisch, Stéphane, illus. 2009. (ENG.). 50p. (J). (gr. -1-2). 16.95 *(978-2-923163-49-9(4))* La Montagne Secrete CAN. Dist: Independent Pubs. Group.

Tulik, Alice, et al. Fishing Adventures. Tulik, Alice et al, illus. 2006. (Adventure Story Collection Ser.). 36p. (J). (gr. 2-6). pap. 12.00 *(978-1-58084-248-8(8))* Lower Kuskokwim Schl. District.

Tullson, Diane. Sea Change, 1 vol. 2010. (Orca Soundings Ser.). (ENG.). 128p. (YA). (gr. 8-12). pap. 9.95 *(978-1-55469-332-0(2))* Orca Bk. Pubs. USA.

Van Scoyoc, Pam. I Could Catch a Whale/ Yo Podria Pescar una Ballena. Santillan-Cruz, Sylvia R., tr. Lewis, R. J., illus. l.t. ed. 2005. (ENG & SPA.). 32p. (J). (gr. k-2). lib. bdg. 16.98 *(978-0-9663629-5-4(0))* By Grace Enterprises.

Varner, Carla. Theodore Goes Fishing. 2003. (J). 11.95 *(978-0-9745787-2-9(X))* I Can Do All Things Productions.

Vento, Anthony. Holes Are Us: A Worm's Tale about Friendship & Trust. 2009. 40p. pap. 21.99 *(978-1-4415-3446-0(6))* Xlibris Corp.

Wall, Layton E. Rat Fishin' with Ralphie Rat: A Bully Learns a Lesson. 2010. 28p. pap. 12.85 *(978-1-4520-4960-1(2))* AuthorHouse.

Walsh, Liam Francis. Fish. 2016. (ENG., Illus.). 32p. (J). 17.99 *(978-1-62672-333-7(8)*, 9781626723337) Roaring Brook Pr.

Ward, Ian. Bobby Blah Blah & the Mystery of the U F O in Sniggery Woods. 2009. (Illus.). 84p. pap. 10.49 *(978-1-4389-7963-2(0))* AuthorHouse.

Ward, Kari. Marley & Maverick Go Fishing. 2012. 26p. pap. *(978-1-897512-54-8(6))* Saga Bks.

Waterton, Betty. A Salmon for Simon, 1 vol. Blades, Ann, illus. 35th ed. 2013. (ENG.). 32p. (J). (gr. -1-k). 14.95 *(978-1-55498-392-6(4))* Groundwood Bks. CAN. Dist: Publishers Group West (PGW).

Watley, Maylin. Malachi Goes Fishing with His Pap. 2012. 20p. pap. 15.99 *(978-1-4685-7320-6(9))* AuthorHouse.

Weaver, Joyce A. Mckissick. Chubby Bear & His Two Brothers. 2008. 28p. per. 24.95 *(978-1-4241-9047-8(9))* America Star Bks.

Wells, Eva. Wishing I Was Fishing. 2006. 32p. lib. bdg. 16.95 *(978-1-59298-168-7(2))* Beaver's Pond Pr., Inc.

White, James C. David Goes Fishing. Chapin, Patrick, illus. 2003. 32p. (J). 6.95 *(978-0-9747752-0-3(7))* White, James C.

Wilson, Elaine. Fisherman Jack's Secret. 2007. 25p. pap. 24.95 *(978-1-4241-9163-5(7))* PublishAmerica, Inc.

Wissinger, Tamera Will & Long, Earlene R. Gone Fishing: A Novel. Cordell, Matthew & Brown, Richard, illus. (ENG.). 128p. (J). 2015. (gr. 5-7). pap. 6.99 *(978-0-544-43931-3(7)*, HMH Books For Young Readers) 2013. (gr. 1-4). 15.99 *(978-0-547-82011-8(9))* Houghton Mifflin Harcourt Publishing Co.

Woodsonrick. Poodles in Space. 2012. 24p. 24.95 *(978-1-4626-5333-1(2))* America Star Bks.

Woolston, Blythe. Troutzilla. 2012. (Carolrhoda YA Ser.). (ENG.). 216p. (YA). (gr. 9-12). 17.95 *(978-0-7613-7755-9(7)*, Carolrhoda Lab™) Lerner Publishing Group.

FISHING INDUSTRY

see Fisheries

FISHING TACKLE

see Fishing—Equipment and Supplies

FITZGERALD, F. SCOTT (FRANCIS SCOTT), 1896-1940

Bankston, John. F. Scott Fitzgerald. 2004. (Classic Storytellers Ser.). (Illus.). 48p. (J). (gr. 4-8). lib. bdg. 29.95 *(978-1-58415-249-1(4))* Mitchell Lane Pubs., Inc.

Becnel, Kim E. Bloom's How to Write about F. Scott Fitzgerald. 2007. (Bloom's How to Write about Literature Ser.). 232p. (C). (gr. 9-18). 45.00 *(978-0-7910-9482-2(0)*, Chelsea Hse.) Facts On File, Inc.

Bloom, Harold, ed. F. Scott Fitzgerald. 2nd rev. ed. 2006. (Bloom's Modern Critical Views Ser.). 261p. (C). (gr. 9). lib. bdg. 45.00 *(978-0-7910-8570-7(8)*, Chelsea Hse.) Facts On File, Inc.

Brackett, Virginia R. F. Scott Fitzgerald: Writer of the Jazz Age. 2004. (World Writers Ser.). (Illus.). 128p. (YA). (gr. 6-12). 23.95 *(978-1-883846-90-9(0)*, First Biographies) Reynolds, Morgan Inc.

Combs, Maggie. How to Analyze the Works of F. Scott Fitzgerald, 1 vol. 2011. (Essential Critiques Set 2 Ser.). (ENG., Illus.). 112p. (J). (gr. 6-12). lib. bdg. 35.64 *(978-1-61783-092-1(5))* ABDO Publishing Co.

Fitzgerald, F. Scott. The Great Gatsby. Bloom, Harold Ron, ed. 2006. (Bloom's Guides). 80p. (YA). (gr. 9-12). lib. bdg. 30.00 *(978-0-7910-8580-6(5))* Facts On File, Inc.

Newman, Gerald & Newman Layfield, Eleanor. Reading & Interpreting the Works of F. Scott Fitzgerald. 2016. (Lit Crit Guides). (ENG., Illus.). 160p. (J). (gr. 8-8). lib. bdg. 39.93 *(978-0-7660-7346-3(7))* Enslow Pubs., Inc.

Weisbrod, Eva. A Student's Guide to F. Scott Fitzgerald. 2004. (Understanding Literature Ser.). (Illus.). 160p. (YA). lib. bdg. 29.27 *(978-0-7660-2202-7(1))* Enslow Pubs., Inc.

FLAG DAY

Bennett, Kelly. Flag Day. 2003. (Rookie Read-About Holidays Ser.). (ENG., Illus.). 32p. (J). (gr. 1-2). pap. 5.95 *(978-0-516-27755-4(3)*, Children's Pr.) Scholastic Library Publishing.

Dean, Sheri. Flag Day. 2010. (Our Country's Holidays Ser.). (ENG.). 24p. (J). (gr. k-3). pap. 8.15 *(978-1-4339-3912-9(6))*; lib. bdg. 22.60 *(978-1-4339-3911-2(8))* Stevens, Gareth Publishing LLLP.

—Flag Day (Día de la Bandera) 2006. (Our Country's Holidays/ Las fiestas de nuestra nacion Ser.). (ENG & SPA., Illus.). 24p. (gr. k-3). lib. bdg. 22.00 *(978-0-8368-6518-9(9)*, Weekly Reader Leveled Readers) Stevens, Gareth Publishing LLLP.

—Flag Day (Dia de la Bandera) 2006. (Our Country's Holidays/ Las fiestas de nuestra nacion Ser.). (ENG & SPA., Illus.). 24p. (gr. k-3). pap. 8.15 *(978-0-8368-6525-7(1)*, Weekly Reader Leveled Readers) Stevens, Gareth Publishing LLLP.

Gaspar, Joe. The Flag. 2013. (PowerKids Readers: American Symbols Ser.). (Illus.). 24p. (J). (gr. k-2). pap. 49.50 *(978-1-4777-0814-9(6))*; pap. 8.25 *(978-1-4777-0813-2(8))*; lib. bdg. 22.60 *(978-1-4777-0736-4(0))* Rosen Publishing Group, Inc., The. (PowerKids Pr.).

—The Flag / la Bandera. Alamn, Eduardo, ed. 2013. (PowerKids Readers: American Symbols / Smbolos de Amrica Ser.). (ENG & SPA.). 24p. (J). (gr. k-2). 22.60 *(978-1-4777-1204-7(6)*, PowerKids Pr.) Rosen Publishing Group, Inc., The.

Kaplan, Leslie C. Flag Day. (Library of Holidays Ser.). 24p. 2009. (gr. 2-3). 42.50 *(978-1-60853-710-5(2))* 2004. (Illus.). (J). lib. bdg. 22.60 *(978-0-8239-6659-2(3))* Rosen Publishing Group, Inc., The. (PowerKids Pr.).

Nelson, Robin. Flag Day. 2009. (First Step Nonfiction - American Holidays Ser.). (ENG.). 24p. (gr. k-2). 23.93 *(978-0-7613-4932-7(4))* Lerner Publishing Group.

Walker, Robert. Flag Day. 2012. (ENG.). 32p. (J). *(978-0-7787-4087-2(0))*; pap. *(978-0-7787-4092-6(7))* Crabtree Publishing Co.

FLAGS

see also Signals and Signaling

Allen, Patrick. The History of the American Flag. 2009. (Real Life Readers Ser.). 16p. (gr. 2-3). pap. 7.05 *(978-1-4358-0081-6(8)*, Rosen Classroom) Rosen Publishing Group, Inc., The.

Applesauce Press Staff. My First American Flag, Kit. 2015. (ENG.). 96p. (J). pap. 16.95 *(978-1-60433-466-1(5)*, Applesauce Pr.) Cider Mill Pr. Bk. Pubs., LLC.

Autumn Publishing Staff, illus. World of Flags. 2004. (Wall Charts Ser.). (J). pap. 4.99 *(978-1-85997-277-9(2))* Byeway Bks.

Baker, Karle Wilson. Texas Flag Primer. 2005. reprint ed. pap. 20.95 *(978-0-7661-9572-1(4))* Kessinger Publishing, LLC.

Banting, Erinn. Flags & Seals. 2004. (American Symbols Ser.). (Illus.). 24p. (J). (gr. 4-7). per. 8.95 *(978-1-59036-176-4(8))*; (gr. 1-3). lib. bdg. 24.45 *(978-1-59036-130-6(X))* Weigl Pubs., Inc.

Bartoletti, Susan Campbell. The Flag Maker: A Story of the Star-Spangled Banner. Nivola, Claire A., illus. 2007. (ENG.). 32p. (J). (gr. 2-5). 7.99 *(978-0-618-80911-0(2))* Houghton Mifflin Harcourt Publishing Co.

Beatrice, Paul & Rodhe, Paul. The Nifty Fifty State Flags. 2008. (ENG.). 16p. (J). (gr. 3). pap. 14.95 *(978-1-933662-99-2(9)*, Applesauce Pr.) Cider Mill Pr. Bk. Pubs., LLC.

Bednar, Sylvie. Flags of the World. Daneshjoo, Gita, tr. from FRE. 2009. (ENG., Illus.). 192p. (J). (gr. 3-7). 21.95 *(978-0-8109-8010-5(X)*, Abrams Bks. for Young Readers) Abrams, Inc.

Behrens, Janice. What Is the Story of Our Flag? 2009. (Scholastic News Nonfiction Readers Ser.). (ENG.). 24p. (J). (gr. 1-2). pap. 6.95 *(978-0-531-22430-4(9))* Scholastic Library Publishing.

Bennet, Janice. Flag Fractions! Develop Understanding of Fractions & Numbers. 2014. (Rosen Common Core Math Readers Ser.). (ENG.). 24p. (J). (gr. 3-4). pap. 8.25 *(978-1-4777-4924-1(1)*, PowerKids Pr.) Rosen Publishing Group, Inc., The.

Brannon, Cecelia H. Zoom in on the US Flag. 2016. (Zoom in on American Symbols Ser.). (Illus.). 24p. (J). pap. 9.35 *(978-0-7660-8458-2(2))* Enslow Pubs., Inc.

Buckley, James, Jr. Who Was Betsy Ross? O'brien, John & Harrison, Nancy, illus. 2014. (Who Was? Ser.). (ENG.). 112p. (J). (gr. 3-7). 5.99 *(978-0-448-48243-9(6)*, Grosset & Dunlap) Penguin Young Readers Group.

Buckley, James. Who Was Betsy Ross? 2014. (Who Was... ? Ser.). lib. bdg. 16.00 *(978-0-606-36181-1(2))* Turtleback Bks.

Carr, Aaron. American Flag. 2013. (J). *(978-1-62127-203-8(6))*; pap. *(978-1-62127-207-6(9))* Weigl Pubs., Inc.

—The Great Seal. 2013. (J). *(978-1-62127-204-5(4))*; pap. *(978-1-62127-208-3(7))* Weigl Pubs., Inc.

—Pledge of Allegiance. 2014. (J). *(978-1-4896-2902-9(5))* Weigl Pubs., Inc.

Clay, Kathryn. The Pledge of Allegiance: Introducing Primary Sources. 2016. (Introducing Primary Sources Ser.). (ENG., Illus.). 32p. (gr. 1-2). lib. bdg. 27.99 *(978-1-4914-8227-8(3))* Capstone Press of Coughlan Cos.

—The U. S. Flag: Introducing Primary Sources. 2016. (Introducing Primary Sources Ser.). (ENG., Illus.). 32p. (gr. 1-2). lib. bdg. 27.99 *(978-1-4914-8222-3(2))* Capstone Press of Coughlan Cos.

Congress (U.S.), Joint Committee on Printing Staff, compiled by. Our Flag. rev. ed. 2007. (ENG., Illus.). 52p. pap. 4.50 *(978-0-16-076598-8(6)*, Joint Committee on Printing) United States Government Printing Office.

Cox, Vicki. Betsy Ross: Flag for a New Nation. 2005. (Leaders of the American Revolution Ser.). (Illus.). 100p. (gr. 5-8). lib. bdg. 30.00 *(978-0-7910-8618-6(6))* Facts On File, Inc.

Crampton, W. Flags of the World. 2004. (Spotter's Guides). 64p. (J). pap. 5.95 *(978-0-7945-0450-2(7))* EDC Publishing.

Crampton, William. Spotter's Guide to Flags of the World. 2006. (Spotter's Guides). (Illus.). 64p. (J). (gr. 2). lib. bdg. 13.95 *(978-1-58086-530-2(5))* EDC Publishing.

Craven, Tracy Leininger. Our Flag Was Still There: The Story of the Star-Spangled Banner. Farnsworth, Bill, illus. 2004. (J). *(978-0-9724287-3-6(9))* Vision Forum, Inc., The.

Crewe, Sabrina & Ingram, Scott. The Writing of "The Star-Spangled Banner" 2004. (Events That Shaped America Ser.). (Illus.). 32p. (gr. 3-6). lib. bdg. 26.00 *(978-0-8368-3409-3(7)*, Gareth Stevens Learning Library) Stevens, Gareth Publishing LLLP.

Damanda, Lori. The Story of the "Star-Spangled Banner" 2009. (Real Life Readers Ser.). 32p. (J). (ENG., Illus.). (gr. 5-6). pap. 10.00 *(978-1-4358-0205-6(5))*; (gr. 4-6). lib. bdg. 25.25 *(978-1-4358-3015-8(6))* Rosen Publishing Group, Inc., The. (PowerKids Pr.).

—The Story of the Star-Spangled Banner. 2009. (American History Milestones Ser.). 32p. (gr. 5-5). 47.90 *(978-1-61511-375-0(4)*, PowerKids Pr.) Rosen Publishing Group, Inc., The.

Depue, Anne. We See the Flag. 2016. (Spring Forward Ser.). (J). (gr. k). *(978-1-4900-3733-2(0))* Benchmark Education Co.

Diemer, Lauren. Flags. 2008. (U. S. Sites & Symbols Ser.). (Illus.). 48p. (J). (gr. 3-5). pap. 10.95 *(978-1-59036-887-9(8))*; lib. bdg. 29.05 *(978-1-59036-886-2(X))* Weigl Pubs., Inc.

Doering Tourville, Amanda. The Pledge of Allegiance, 1 vol. Ouren, Todd, illus. 2008. (Our Nation's Pride Ser.). (ENG.). 32p. (gr. -1-3). 28.50 *(978-1-60270-114-4(8)*, Looking Glass Library- Nonfiction) Magic Wagon.

—The United States Flag, 1 vol. Ouren, Todd, illus. 2008. (Our Nation's Pride Ser.). (ENG.). 32p. (gr. -1-3). 28.50 *(978-1-60270-116-8(4)*, Looking Glass Library- Nonfiction) Magic Wagon.

Dorling Kindersley Publishing Staff. Ultimate Sticker Book: Flags Around the World. 2017. (Ultimate Sticker Bks.). (ENG.). 32p. (J). (gr. k-2). pap. 6.99 *(978-1-4654-6201-5(5)*, DK Children) Dorling Kindersley Publishing, Inc.

Douglas, Lloyd G. The American Flag. 2003. (Welcome Bks.). (ENG., Illus.). 24p. (J). (gr. -1-2). pap. 4.95 *(978-0-516-27873-5(8)*, Children's Pr.) Scholastic Library Publishing.

Eldridge, Alison & Eldridge, Stephen. The American Flag: An American Symbol. 2012. (All about American Symbols Ser.). 24p. (J). (gr. -1-1). (Illus.). pap. 7.95 *(978-1-4644-0046-9(6))*; 22.60 *(978-0-7660-4057-1(7))* Enslow Pubs., Inc. (Enslow Elementary).

Fata, Heather. The Pledge of Allegiance. 2009. (Primary Source Library of American Citizenship Ser.). 32p. (gr. 5-5). 47.90 *(978-1-61511-228-9(6)*, Rosen Reference) Rosen Publishing Group, Inc., The.

Ferry, Joseph. American Flag: The Story of Old Glory. Moreno, Barry, ed. 2014. (Patriotic Symbols of America Ser.: 20). 48p. (J). (gr. 4-18). 20.95 *(978-1-4222-3119-7(4))* Mason Crest.

—The Star-Spangled Banner: Story of Our National Anthem. Moreno, Barry, ed. 2014. (Patriotic Symbols of America Ser.: 20). 48p. (J). (gr. 4-18). 20.95 *(978-1-4222-3132-6(1))* Mason Crest.

Firestone, Mary. Our American Flag, 1 vol. Skeens, Matthew, illus. 2006. (American Symbols Ser.). (ENG.). 24p. (gr. 1-2). 9.95 *(978-1-4048-2218-4(6)*, 1258436) Picture Window Bks.

Flags: Individual Title Six-Packs. (Action Packs Ser.). 104p. (gr. 3-5). 44.00 *(978-0-7635-8413-9(4))* Rigby Education.

Flags of the World Sticker Book. 2012. (J). 5.95 *(978-0-8437-0984-1(7))* Hammond World Atlas Corp.

Flags over Corydon Coloring Book. 2005. (J). 4.95 *(978-0-9769829-1-3(9))* Dorcas Pubns., LLC.

Fontes, Justine. The Pledge of Allegiance. 2014. (Rookie Read-About(r) American Symbols Ser.). (ENG.). 32p. (J). pap. 5.95 *(978-0-531-21843-3(0))*; lib. bdg. 25.00 *(978-0-531-21570-8(9))* Scholastic Library Publishing.

Frenetti, Jackson. Flags of the World: Develop Understanding of Fractions & Numbers, 1 vol. 2015. (InfoMax Common Core Math Readers Ser.). (ENG.). 24p. (J). pap. 8.25 *(978-1-4777-4615-8(3)*, Rosen Classroom) Rosen Publishing Group, Inc., The.

Gaddi, Rosalie. I Wave the American Flag. 2016. (Symbols of Our Country Ser.). 00024p. (J). (gr. 1-1). pap. 8.25 *(978-1-4994-2735-6(2)*, PowerKids Pr.) Rosen Publishing Group, Inc., The.

Gaspar, Joe. The Flag. 2013. (PowerKids Readers: American Symbols Ser.). (Illus.). 24p. (J). (gr. k-2). pap. 8.25 *(978-1-4777-0813-2(8))*; pap. 49.50 *(978-1-4777-0814-9(6))*;

lib. bdg. 22.60 (978-1-4777-0736-4(0)) Rosen Publishing Group, Inc., The. (PowerKids Pr.).
—The Flag / la Bandera. Alamn, Eduardo, ed. 2013. (PowerKids Readers: American Symbols / Smbolos de Amrica Ser.). (ENG & SPA.). 24p. (J). (gr. k-2). 22.60 (978-1-4777-1204-7(6), PowerKids Pr.) Rosen Publishing Group, Inc., The.
—The National Anthem. 2013. (PowerKids Readers: American Symbols Ser.). 24p. (J). (gr. k-2). 22.60 (978-1-4777-0740-1(9)); (ENG., Illus.). pap. 8.25 (978-1-4777-0821-7(9)) Rosen Publishing Group, Inc., The. (PowerKids Pr.).
—The National Anthem / el Himno Nacional. Alamn, Eduardo, ed. 2013. (PowerKids Readers: American Symbols / Smbolos de Amrica Ser.). (ENG & SPA.). 24p. (J). (gr. k-2). 22.60 (978-1-4777-1208-5(9), PowerKids Pr.) Rosen Publishing Group, Inc., The.
Girard, Robert. The American Flag: Learning to Identify Two-Digit Numbers up To 50. 2004. (Math Big Bookstm Ser.). (ENG.). 12p. (gr. 1-2). 33.50 (978-0-8239-7632-4(7)) Rosen Publishing Group, Inc., The.
—The American Flag: Learning to Identify Two-Digit Numbers up to 50. 2009. (Math for the REAL World Ser.). 12p. (gr. 1-2). pap. 5.90 (978-0-8239-8888-4(0), Rosen Classroom) Rosen Publishing Group, Inc., The.
Gold, Susan Dudley. Saluting the Flag: West Virginia State Board of Education V. Barnette. 2014. lib. bdg. (978-1-62712-396-9(2)) Cavendish Square Publishing.
—Saluting the Flag: West Virginia State Board of Education V. Barnette. 2012. (J). 42.79 (978-1-60870-911-3(6)) Marshall Cavendish Corp.
Gregoire, Maryellen. La Bandera (the Flag) 2012. (Wonder Readers Spanish Emergent Ser.). (SPA.). (gr. -1-1). pap. 35.94 (978-1-62065-568-9(3)) Capstone Press of Coughlan Cos.
—The Flag, 1 vol. 2012. (Wonder Readers Emergent Level Ser.). (ENG.). (gr. -1-1). 32p. pap. 5.99 (978-1-4296-9192-5(1)); 16p. pap. 35.94 (978-1-4296-9202-1(2)) Capstone Press of Coughlan Cos. (Wonder Readers).
Harness, Cheryl. Flags over America: A Star-Spangled Story. Harness, Cheryl, illus. 2014. (ENG., Illus.). 32p. (J). (gr. 2-3). 16.99 (978-0-8075-2470-1(0)) Whitman, Albert & Co.
Harris, Nancy. The National Anthem. 2016. (Patriotic Symbols Ser.). (ENG.). 24p. (gr. -1-1). pap. 6.29 (978-1-4846-3811-8(5), Acorn) Heinemann-Raintree.
Healy, Nick. The American Flag. 2003. (J). pap. (978-1-58417-116-4(2)); lib. bdg. (978-1-58417-053-2(0)) Lake Street Pubs.
—The Star-Spangled Banner. 2003. (J). (978-1-58417-055-6(7)); pap. (978-1-58417-118-8(9)) Lake Street Pubs.
Herrington, Lisa M. The American Flag. 2014. (Rookie Read-About(r) American Symbols Ser.). (ENG., Illus.). 32p. (J). pap. 5.95 (978-0-531-21839-6(2)); lib. bdg. (978-0-531-21566-1(0)) Scholastic Library Publishing.
Hess, Deborah. The American Flag. 2007. (J). pap. 6.99 (978-0-7614-3389-7(9)) Marshall Cavendish Corp.
Hicks, Terry Allan. The Pledge of Allegiance. 2006. (Symbols of America Ser.). (Illus.). 40p. (gr. 3-7). lib. bdg. 20.95 (978-0-7614-2136-8(X), Benchmark Bks.) Marshall Cavendish Corp.
—Symbols of America Group 2, 6 bks., Set. Incl. Bald Eagle. (J). lib. bdg. 28.50 (978-0-7614-2133-7(5)); Capitol. lib. bdg. 20.95 (978-0-7614-2132-0(7)); Declaration of Independence. lib. bdg. 20.95 (978-0-7614-2135-1(1)); Ellis Island. lib. bdg. 20.95 (978-0-7614-2134-4(3)); Pledge of Allegiance. lib. bdg. 20.95 (978-0-7614-2136-8(X)); Uncle Sam. lib. bdg. 20.95 (978-0-7614-2137-5(8)); (Illus.). 40p. (gr. 3-7). 2006. 2007. Set lib. bdg. 171.00 (978-0-7614-2130-6(0), Benchmark Bks.) Marshall Cavendish Corp.
Hotchkins, Dewayne. The U. S. Flag. 2016. (Rosen REAL Readers: Social Studies Nonfiction / Fiction: Family, Community, & the World Ser.). 8p. (gr. 1-k). pap. 5.46 (978-1-5081-2257-9(1), Rosen Classroom) Rosen Publishing Group, Inc., The.
Howard, Rebecca. Flagtastic Flags. 2006. (ENG., Illus.). 32p. (J). (gr. -1-3). 14.95 (978-0-7145-3305-6(X)) Boyars, Marion Pubs., Ltd. GBR. Dist: Consortium Bk. Sales & Distribution.
Ingram, Scott. The Writing of The Star-Spangled Banner. 2004. (Landmark Events in American History Ser.). (Illus.). 48p. (gr. 5-12). pap. 14.05 (978-0-8368-5418-3(7), Gareth Stevens Secondary Library) Stevens, Gareth Publishing LLLP.
Jacobson, Ryan. The Story of the Star-Spangled Banner, 1 vol. Martin, Cynthia & Beatty, Terry, illus. 2006. (Graphic History Ser.). (ENG.). 32p. (gr. 3-4). 30.65 (978-0-7368-5493-1(2), Graphic Library) Capstone Press of Coughlan Cos.
Jango-Cohen, Judith. The American Flag. 2003. (Pull Ahead Books-American Symbols Ser.). (ENG.). 32p. (gr. k-3). pap. 7.95 (978-0-8225-3753-3(2)); (Illus.). lib. bdg. 22.60 (978-0-8225-3804-2(0)) Lerner Publishing Group.
—La Bandera Estadounidense. Translations.com Staff, tr. from ENG. 2005. (Libros para Avanzar-Simbolos Estadounidenses(Pull Ahead Books-American Symbols) Ser.). (SPA., Illus.). 32p. (gr. k-3). per. 7.95 (978-0-8225-3133-3(X), Ediciones Lerner) Lerner Publishing Group.
Jeffries, Corina. My Class Makes a Flag: Breaking down the Problem. 2017. (Computer Science for the Real World Ser.). 8p. (gr. 5-6). pap. 6.20 **(978-1-5383-5036-2(X)**, Rosen Classroom) Rosen Publishing Group, Inc., The.
Jones, Rebecca C. The Biggest (And Best) Flag That Ever Flew, 1 vol. Geer, Charles, illus. 2009. (ENG.). 30p. (J). (gr. -1-3). 8.99 (978-0-87033-440-5(9), 9780870334405, Cornell Maritime Pr./Tidewater Pubs.) Schiffer Publishing, Ltd.
Jordan, Shirley. The American Flag: Moments in History. 2003. (Cover-To-Cover Books). (Illus.). 72p. pap. 8.95 (978-0-7891-5917-5(1)); (J). (gr. 4-7). lib. bdg. 17.95 (978-0-7569-1185-0(0)) Perfection Learning Corp.
Kallio, Jamie. 12 Questions about "The Star-Spangled Banner" 2017. (Examining Primary Sources Ser.). (ENG., Illus.). 32p. (J). (gr. 3-6). 21.95 (978-1-63235-288-0(5)) Pr. Room Editions LLC.
Kozleski, Lisa. The Pledge of Allegiance: Story of One Indivisible Nation. Moreno, Barry, ed. 2014. (Patriotic Symbols of America Ser.: 20). 48p. (J). (gr. 4-18). lib. bdg. 20.95 (978-1-4222-3131-9(3)) Mason Crest.
Kulling, Monica. Francis Scott Key's Star-Spangled Banner. 2012. (Step into Reading Level 3 Ser.). lib. bdg. 13.55 (978-0-606-23857-1(3), Turtleback) Turtleback Bks.
Lambert, Nancy. The Star-Spangled Banner. 2016. (Smithsonian Ser.). (ENG., Illus.). 48p. (J). (gr. 3-4). pap. 3.99 (978-1-101-99607-2(2), Penguin Young Readers) Penguin Young Readers Group.
Landau, Elaine. The American Flag. 2008. (True Bks.). (ENG., Illus.). 48p. (J). (gr. 3-5). pap. 6.95 (978-0-531-14775-7(4), Children's Pr.) Scholastic Library Publishing.
Mara, Wil. Betsy Ross. 2006. (Rookie Biographies Ser.). (ENG., Illus.). 32p. (J). (gr. 1-2). per. 4.95 (978-0-516-25369-5(7), Children's Pr.) Scholastic Library Publishing.
Marcovitz, Hal. Confederate Flag: Controversial Symbol of the South. Moreno, Barry, ed. 2014. (Patriotic Symbols of America Ser.: 20). 48p. (J). (gr. 4-18). 20.95 (978-1-4222-3121-0(6)) Mason Crest.
Marcovitz, Hal & Ferry, Joseph. The American Flag. 2004. (American Symbols & Their Meanings Ser.). (Illus.). 48p. (J). (gr. 4-18). lib. bdg. 19.95 (978-1-59084-026-9(7)) Mason Crest.
McKinney, Devon. I Sing the Star-Spangled Banner. 2016. (Symbols of Our Country Ser.). 00024p. (J). (gr. 1-1). 23.60 (978-1-4994-2730-1(1)); pap. 8.25 (978-1-4994-2729-5(8)) Rosen Publishing Group, Inc., The. (PowerKids Pr.).
Memling, Carl. Our Flag. 2011. (Little Golden Book Ser.). (ENG., Illus.). 24p. (J). (gr. -1-2). 4.99 (978-0-375-86524-4(1), Golden Bks.) Random Hse. Children's Bks.
Miles, Lisa. Flags Sticker Book. rev. ed. 2008. (Spotter's Guides Sticker Books - New Format Ser.). (Illus.). 24p. (J). pap. 8.99 (978-0-7945-1360-3(3), Usborne) EDC Publishing.
—Libro de Pegatinas Banderas Todos los Paises del Mundo. 2004. (Spotter's Guides Sticker Bks.). (SPA., Illus.). 23p. (J). (gr. 2-18). pap. 7.95 (978-0-7460-3644-0(2), EDC6442) EDC Publishing.
Monroe, Tyler. American Flag. 2013. (U. S. Symbols Ser.). (ENG.). 24p. (gr. k-1). 26.65 (978-1-4765-3085-7(8)); pap. 7.95 (978-1-4765-3534-0(5)) Capstone Press of Coughlan Cos. (Pebble Plus).
—Pledge of Allegiance. 2013. (U. S. Symbols Ser.). (ENG.). 24p. (gr. k-1). 26.65 (978-1-4765-3090-1(4)); pap. 7.95 (978-1-4765-3539-5(6)) Capstone Press of Coughlan Cos. (Pebble Plus).
My Red, White & Blue. (Illus.). (J). bds. 5.00 net. (978-1-56021-388-8(4)) W.J. Fantasy, Inc.
The National Anthem. 2013. (PowerKids Readers: American Symbols Ser.). 24p. (J). (gr. k-2). pap. 49.50 (978-1-4777-0822-4(7), PowerKids Pr.) Rosen Publishing Group, Inc., The.
Nelson, Maria. The National Anthem. 2015. (Symbols of America Ser.). (ENG.). 24p. (J). (gr. 1-2). 22.60 (978-1-4824-1874-3(6)) Stevens, Gareth Publishing LLLP.
—20 Fun Facts about the US Flag. 2013. (Fun Fact File: US History! Ser.). 32p. (J). (gr. 3-6). pap. 63.00 (978-1-4339-9195-0(0)); pap. 10.50 (978-1-4339-9194-3(2)) Stevens, Gareth Publishing LLLP.
Ogden, Lesley Evans. Canada's Flag. 2011. 24p. (YA). (gr. 2-4). (978-1-77071-663-6(7)); pap. (978-1-77071-669-8(6)) Weigl Educational Pubs. Ltd.
Olson, Kay Melchisedech. Betsy Ross & the American Flag, 1 vol. Cool, Anna Maria et al, illus. 2005. (Graphic History Ser.). (ENG.). 32p. (gr. 3-4). 30.65 (978-0-7368-4962-3(9), Graphic Library) Capstone Press of Coughlan Cos.
Orr, Tamra B. The Star-Spangled Banner: Introducing Primary Sources. 2016. (Introducing Primary Sources Ser.). (ENG., Illus.). 32p. (gr. 1-2). lib. bdg. 27.99 (978-1-4914-8226-1(5)) Capstone Press of Coughlan Cos.
Owens, Ann-Maureen & Yealland, Jane. Our Flag: The Story of Canada's Maple Leaf. Slavin, Bill & Melo, Esperança, illus. 2014. (ENG.). 32p. (J). (gr. 2-5). 17.95 (978-1-77138-111-6(6)); pap. 9.95 (978-1-77138-112-3(4)) Kids Can Pr., Ltd. CAN. Dist: Hachette Bk. Group.
Owens, Tom. The Star-Spangled Banner: The Flag & Its Anthem. 2003. (Illus.). 48p. (J). pap. (978-0-7891-5890-1(6)) Perfection Learning Corp.
Palazzo-Craig, Janet. The Making of the American Flag: Betsy Ross & George Washington. 2009. (Great Moments in American History Ser.). 32p. (gr. 3-3). 47.90 (978-1-61513-155-6(8)) Rosen Publishing Group, Inc., The.
Patrick, Joseph. Our National Symbols. 2009. (Real Life Readers Ser.). 16p. (gr. 2-3). pap. 7.05 (978-1-4358-0049-6(4), Rosen Classroom) Rosen Publishing Group, Inc., The.
Pearl, Norman. Our National Anthem. Skeens, Matthew, illus. 2006. (American Symbols Ser.). (ENG.). 24p. (gr. 1-2). lib. bdg. 26.65 (978-1-4048-2215-3(1)) Picture Window Bks.
—Our National Anthem, 1 vol. Skeens, Matthew, illus. 2006. (American Symbols Ser.). (ENG.). 24p. (gr. 1-2). 9.95 (978-1-4048-2221-4(6)) Picture Window Bks.
—The Pledge of Allegiance, 1 vol. Skeens, Matthew, illus. 2007. (American Symbols Ser.). (ENG.). 24p. (gr. 1-2). 9.95 (978-1-4048-2647-2(5)) Picture Window Bks.
Pearl, Norman & Picture Window Books Staff. The Pledge of Allegiance, 1 vol. Skeens, Matthew, illus. 2007. (American Symbols Ser.). (ENG.). 24p. (gr. 1-2). 26.65 (978-1-4048-2644-1(0)) Picture Window Bks.
Pingry, Patricia A. The Story of the Star-Spangled Banner. Munger, Nancy, illus. 2014. (Story of Ser.). 24p. (J). bds. 6.99 (978-0-8249-1930-6(0), Ideal Pubns.) Worthy Publishing.
Poolos, Christine. The American Flag. 2009. (Primary Source Library of American Citizenship Ser.). 32p. (gr. 5-5). 47.90 (978-1-61511-220-3(0), Rosen Reference) Rosen Publishing Group, Inc., The.
Purcell, John M. American City Flags Vols. 9&10: 146 Flags from Akron to Yonkers. Kaye, Edward B., ed. l.t. ed. 2004. (Illus.). 400p. per. 35.00 (978-0-9747728-0-6(1), 48) North American Vexillological Assoc. (NAVA).
Randolph, Ryan. Betsy Ross: The American Flag, & Life in a Young America. 2009. (Library of American Lives & Times Ser.). 112p. (gr. 5-5). 69.20 (978-1-60853-473-9(1)) Rosen Publishing Group, Inc., The.
Randolph, Ryan P. Betsy Ross: The American Flag & Life in Young America. 2005. (Library of American Lives & Times). (Illus.). 112p. (J). (gr. 4-8). lib. bdg. 34.60 (978-0-8239-5730-9(6)) Rosen Publishing Group, Inc., The.
Richards, Jon & Colson, Rob. The Book of Flags. 2017. (ENG., Illus.). 64p. (J). (gr. 4-6). pap. 9.99 **(978-0-7502-9828-5(6)**, Wayland) Hachette Children's Group GBR. Dist: Hachette Bk. Group.
Rubin, Susan Goldman. The Flag with Fifty-Six Stars: A Gift from the Survivors of Mauthausen. Farnsworth, Bill, illus. 2005. (ENG.). 40p. (J). (gr. 1-5). 17.95 (978-0-8234-1653-0(4)) Holiday Hse., Inc.
Rustad, Martha. Why Are There Stripes on the American Flag? Poling, Kyle, illus. 2014. (Cloverleaf Books — Our American Symbols Ser.). 24p. (gr. k-2). (J). lib. bdg. 23.93 (978-1-4677-2140-0(9)); pap. 6.95 (978-1-4677-4465-2(4)) Lerner Publishing Group. (Millbrook Pr.).
Ryan, Pam Muñoz. The Flag We Love. Masiello, Ralph, illus. 10th anniv. ed. 2006. (ENG.). 32p. (J). (gr. k-3). 17.95 (978-1-57091-707-3(8)) Charlesbridge Publishing, Inc.
Schwaeber, Barbie. The Star-Spangled Banner. 2006. (American Favorites Ser.). (ENG., Illus.). 32p. (J). (gr. 3-7). 9.85 (978-1-59249-652-5(0)) Soundprints.
Silate, Jennifer. The American Flag. (Primary Sources of American Symbols Ser.). 24p. (gr. 3-3). 2009. 42.50 (978-1-60851-507-3(9), PowerKids Pr.) 2006. (Illus.). (J). lib. bdg. 22.60 (978-1-4042-2686-9(9)) Rosen Publishing Group, Inc., The.
—Betsy Ross. 2004. (Famous People in American History Ser.). (ENG., Illus.). 32p. (gr. 4-8). pap. 10.00 (978-0-8239-4176-6(0)) Rosen Publishing Group, Inc., The.
—Betsy Ross: Creadora de la bandera estadounidense. 2004. (Grandes personajes en la historia de los Estados Unidos Ser.). (SPA.). 32p. (gr. 3-6). pap. 10.00 (978-0-8239-4222-0(8), Rosen Classroom) Rosen Publishing Group, Inc., The.
—Betsy Ross: Creadora de la bandera estadounidense (Betsy Ross: Creator of the American Flag) 2009. (Grandes personajes en la historia de los Estados Unidos (Famous People in American History) Ser.). (SPA.). 32p. (gr. 2-3). 47.90 (978-1-61512-791-7(7), Editorial Buenas Letras) Rosen Publishing Group, Inc., The.
—Betsy Ross: Creator of the American Flag. 2009. (Primary Sources of Famous People in American History Ser.). 32p. (gr. 2-3). 47.90 (978-1-60851-657-5(1)) Rosen Publishing Group, Inc., The.
—Betsy Ross: Creator of the American Flag / Creadora de la bandera Estadounidense. 2009. (Famous People in American History/Grandes personajes en la historia de los Estados Unidos Ser.). (ENG & SPA.). 32p. (gr. 2-3). 47.90 (978-1-61512-539-5(6), Editorial Buenas Letras) Rosen Publishing Group, Inc., The.
Smith, Whitney. Flag Lore of All Nations. 2003. (Illus.). 112p. (J). (gr. 3-6). pap. 12.95 (978-0-7613-1899-6(2), Millbrook Pr.) Lerner Publishing Group.
Sonneborn, Liz. The Pledge of Allegiance: The Story Behind Our Patriotic Promise. 2003. (America in Words & Song Ser.). (Illus.). 32p. (gr. 4-6). 23.00 (978-0-7910-7336-0(X), Chelsea Hse.) Facts On File, Inc.
—The Star-Spangled Banner: The Story Behind Our National Anthem. 2003. (America in Words & Song Ser.). (Illus.). 32p. (gr. 4-6). 23.00 (978-0-7910-7337-7(8), Chelsea Hse.) Facts On File, Inc.
Sturm, Jeanne. The American Flag. 2014. (ENG., Illus.). 32p. (gr. 3-6). 32.79 (978-1-62717-735-1(3)) Rourke Educational Media.
Thomson, Sarah L. American Flag Q & A. Collins Staff, illus. 2008. 48p. (J). (gr. k-4). 16.99 (978-0-06-089959-2(X), Collins) HarperCollins Pubs.
Top That!, creator. Flags Sticker Book. 2004. (Stickertastic Ser.). (Illus.). 24p. (J). (gr. 2). pap. (978-1-84510-118-3(9)) Top That! Publishing PLC.
The United States & Its Flag, 6 bks., Set. (Illus.). (J). (gr. 3-12). lib. bdg. 109.70 (978-1-56674-913-8(1)) Forest Hse. Publishing Co., Inc.
Urwin, Kirsten. Betsy Ross & the Creation of the American Flag. 2015. (Spotlight on American History Ser.). (ENG., Illus.). 24p. (J). (gr. 4-6). pap. 10.00 (978-1-4994-1789-0(6), PowerKids Pr.) Rosen Publishing Group, Inc., The.
von Zumbusch, Amelie. The True Story of the American Flag. 2009. (What Really Happened? Ser.). 24p. (gr. 2-3). 42.50 (978-1-60854-766-1(3), PowerKids Pr.) Rosen Publishing Group, Inc., The.
Walker, Robert. Flag Day. 2012. (ENG.). 32p. (J). (978-0-7787-4087-2(0)); pap. (978-0-7787-4092-6(7)) Crabtree Publishing Co.
Welch, Catherine A. La Bandera de Estrellas Centelleantes: El Himno Nacional. Translations.com Staff, tr. from ENG. Warwick, Carrie H., illus. 2005. (Yo Solo - Historia (on My Own - History) Ser.).Tr. of Star-Spangled Banner. (SPA.). 48p. (gr. 2-4). lib. bdg. 25.26 (978-0-8225-3114-2(3)) Lerner Publishing Group.
—La Bandera de Estrellas Centelleantes; the Star-Spangled Banner. 2008. pap. 40.95 (978-0-7613-3867-3(5)) Lerner Publishing Group.
—The Star-Spangled Banner. Warwick, Carrie, illus. 2004. (On My Own History Ser.). 48p. (J). (gr. 1-3). pap. 6.95 (978-1-57505-697-5(6)); (ENG.). (gr. 2-4). 25.26 (978-1-57505-590-9(2)) Lerner Publishing Group.
Zumbusch, Amelie von. The True Story of the American Flag. 2009. (What Really Happened? Ser.). (Illus.). 24p. (YA). (gr. 3-6). lib. bdg. 22.60 (978-1-4042-4478-8(6)) Rosen Publishing Group, Inc., The.

FLATS

see Apartment Houses

FLEAS

Bodden, Valerie. Creepy Creatures: Fleas. 2014. (Creepy Creatures Ser.). (ENG.). 24p. (J). (gr. 1-3). pap. 7.99 (978-0-89812-934-2(6), Creative Paperbacks) Creative Co., The.
—Fleas. 2014. (J). (Illus.). 24p. (978-1-60818-355-5(6)); (978-1-60818-354-8(8)) Creative Co., The. (Creative Education).
Honders, Christine. Bloodsucking Fleas & Ticks. 2016. (Real-Life Vampires Ser.). (ENG., Illus.). 24p. (J). (gr. 2-3). pap. 8.15 (978-1-4824-3943-4(3)) Stevens, Gareth Publishing LLLP.
Keiser, Cody. Fleas. 2015. (Freaky Freeloaders: Bugs That Feed on People Ser.). (ENG.). 24p. (J). (gr. 2-3). 23.60 (978-1-4994-0753-2(X), PowerKids Pr.) Rosen Publishing Group, Inc., The.
Petrie, Kristin. Fleas, 1 vol. 2009. (Bugs! Ser.). (ENG.). 32p. (gr. 3-6). 27.07 (978-1-60453-067-4(7), Checkerboard Library) ABDO Publishing Co.
Silverman, Buffy. Fleas. 2004. (Parasites Ser.). 32p. (J). (gr. 4-7). 22.45 (978-0-7377-2632-9(6), Greenhaven Pr., Inc.) Cengage Gale.
Somervill, Barbara A. Fleas: Feasting on Blood. (Bloodsuckers Ser.). 24p. (gr. 2-3). 2009. 42.50 (978-1-61511-632-4(X), PowerKids Pr.) 2007. (Illus.). (YA). lib. bdg. 22.60 (978-1-4042-3805-3(0), 1270722) Rosen Publishing Group, Inc., The.

FLEAS—FICTION

Bond, Jameselle. Poka Dot Fle. 2011. 36p. pap. 24.95 (978-1-4560-6750-2(8)) America Star Bks.
Britland, Jan. The Adventures of Rodger Dodger Dog. Swaim, Michael, illus. 2009. 40p. pap. 15.95 (978-1-936051-23-6(0)) Peppertree Pr., The.
Carretero, Mónica. FLEA CIRCUS. 2011. (Mini-Animalist Ser.). (ENG., Illus.). 32p. (J). (gr. k-2). (978-84-938240-0-6(3)) D P & G Military Pubs.
Cohen, Laurie. The Flea, 0 vols. Owlkids Books Inc. Staff & Quinn, Sarah, trs. Béal, Marjorie, illus. 2014. (ENG & FRE.). 32p. (J). (gr. -1-2). 16.95 (978-1-77147-056-8(9), Owlkids) Owlkids Bks. Inc. CAN. Dist: Publishers Group West (PGW).
Connolly, C J. The Boomerang. 2010. (Illus.). 32p. (J). 16.95 (978-0-9825559-1-0(1)) Crosswinds Pr., Inc.
—Wil, Fitz, & a Flea Named T. 2009. (Illus.). 32p. (J). 16.95 (978-0-9825559-0-3(3)) Crosswinds Pr., Inc.
Dixon, Ronald. The Adventures of Nip & Dip, on a Dog Named Duffy. 2010. 28p. 13.99 (978-1-4490-7533-0(9)) AuthorHouse.
Doodler, Todd H. Super Fly vs. Furious Flea! 2016. (Super Fly Ser.). (ENG., Illus.). 128p. (J). pap. 6.99 (978-1-61963-384-1(1), 9781619633841, Bloomsbury USA Childrens) Bloomsbury Publishing USA.
—Super Fly vs. Furious Flea! 2016. (Super Fly Ser.: 3). (J). lib. bdg. 17.20 (978-0-606-39556-4(3)) Turtleback Bks.
Downey, Lynn. The Flea's Sneeze. Firehammer, Karla, illus. 2005. (ENG.). 32p. (J). (gr. -1-1). reprint ed. pap. 8.99 (978-0-8050-7756-8(1), 9780805077568) Square Fish.
Dyan, Penelope. There's a Flea in My Te. Dyan, Penelope, illus. 2012. (Illus.). 34p. pap. 11.95 (978-1-61477-047-3(6)) Bellissima Publishing, LLC.
Eggleton, Jill. Flea & Big Bill. Matijasevich, Astrid, illus. 2003. (Rigby Sails Early Ser.). (ENG.). 16p. (gr. 1-2). pap. 6.95 (978-0-7578-8722-2(8)) Houghton Mifflin Harcourt Publishing Co.
—Flea Goes Out! Matijasevich, Astrid, illus. 2003. (Rigby Sails Early Ser.). (ENG.). 16p. (gr. 1-2). pap. 6.95 (978-0-7578-8737-6(6)) Houghton Mifflin Harcourt Publishing Co.
Evans, Sarah. The Moose, the Flea, the Fly. 2007. 16p. pap. 24.95 (978-1-4241-8533-7(5)) America Star Bks.
Kruse, Donald W. Fleas, Please. Crank, Donny, illus. 2012. 48p. pap. 12.95 (978-1-59663-858-7(3), Castle Keep Pr.) Rock, James A. & Co. Pubs.
Lee, Hoseok M. A Different Kind of Fle. 2009. 28p. pap. 12.49 (978-1-4490-1545-9(X)) AuthorHouse.
Levy, Elizabeth. A Hare-Raising Tale. Gerstein, Mordicai, illus. unabr. ed. 2006. (First Chapter Bks.). (J). (gr. 2-4). pap. 17.95 incl. audio (978-1-59519-704-7(4)); pap. 20.95 incl. audio compact disk (978-1-59519-705-4(2)) Live Oak Media.
—The Mixed-Up Mask Mystery: A Fletcher Mystery. Gerstein, Mordicai, illus. unabr. ed. 2006. (First Chapter Bks.). (J). (gr. 2-4). pap. 17.95 incl. audio (978-1-59519-710-8(9)); pap. 20.95 incl. audio compact disk (978-1-59519-711-5(7)) Live Oak Media.
MacDonald, Alan. Fleas!, 1 vol. Roberts, David, illus. 2013. (Dirty Bertie Ser.). (ENG.). 112p. (gr. 1-3). pap. 4.95 (978-1-4342-4822-0(4)); lib. bdg. 25.32 (978-1-4342-4618-9(3)) Stone Arch Bks.
McCaffery, William, illus. The Flea Circus. 2013. (J). (978-0-307-97997-1(0)); lib. bdg. (978-0-375-97132-7(7)) Random Hse. Children's Bks.
Shreeve, Elizabeth. Hector Springs Loose. Levy, Pamela R., illus. 2004. (Ready-For-Chapters Ser.). (ENG.). 80p. (J). (gr. 1-4). pap. 3.99 (978-0-689-86414-8(0), Simon & Schuster/Paula Wiseman Bks.) Simon & Schuster/Paula Wiseman Bks.
Talbot Healy, John Adrian. The Flea & the Cauliflower. 2009. (Illus.). 92p. pap. 30.49 (978-1-4490-1360-8(0)) AuthorHouse.
Weston Woods Staff, creator. The Napping House. 2011. 29.95 (978-0-439-72863-8(0)) Weston Woods Studios, Inc.
Wood, Audrey. The Napping House. Wood, Audrey & Wood, Don, illus. 25th ed. 2009. (ENG.). 32p. (J). (gr. -1-3). 18.99 (978-0-15-256708-8(9)) Houghton Mifflin Harcourt Publishing Co.
—Napping House / La Casa Adormecida. Wood, Don, illus. 2012. (ENG & SPA.). 32p. (J). (gr. -1 — 1). bds. 6.99 (978-0-547-71920-7(5)) Houghton Mifflin Harcourt Publishing Co.

FLEMING, ALEXANDER, SIR, 1881-1955

Rooney, Anne. Alexander Fleming & the Discovery of Penicillin. 2012. (Miracle Makers Ser.). (ENG., Illus.). 48p. (YA). (gr. 5-8). 27.95 (978-1-4488-6035-7(0), Rosen Reference) Rosen Publishing Group, Inc., The.

FLIES

Arnold, Tedd. Sharks. Arnold, Tedd, illus. 2013. (Fly Guy Ser.). (ENG., Illus.). 32p. (J). (gr. -1-3). pap. 3.99 (978-0-545-50771-4(5), Scholastic Reference) Scholastic, Inc.
Berger, Melvin & Berger, Gilda. Flies. 2011. (Illus.). 16p. (J). pap. (978-0-545-24446-6(3)) Scholastic, Inc.
Black, Nessa. Flies. 2017. (Spot Creepy Crawlies Ser.). (ENG.). 16p. (gr. k-3). 17.95 **(978-1-68151-108-5(8))** Amicus Publishing.
Coleman, Miriam. Flies Eat Poop!, 1 vol., 1. 2014. (Disgusting Animal Dinners Ser.). (ENG.). 24p. (J). (gr. k-5). 23.60 (978-1-4777-2885-7(6), PowerKids Pr.) Rosen Publishing Group, Inc., The.
Eggs, Larvae, & Flies: Big Book. (Sunshinetm Science Ser.). 24p. (gr. 1-2). 37.50 (978-0-7802-1389-0(0)) Wright Group/McGraw-Hill.

Eggs, Larve, & Flies: 6 Each of 1 Student Book, 6 vols. (Sunshinetm Science Ser.). 24p. (gr. 1-2). 41.95 *(978-0-7802-1388-3(2))* Wright Group/McGraw-Hill.

Flies Sets: 1 Each of 3 Big Books. (Sunshinetm Science Ser.). (gr. 1-2). 111.50 *(978-0-7802-1448-4(X))* Wright Group/McGraw-Hill.

Flies Sets: 1 Each of 3 Student Books. (Sunshinetm Science Ser.). (gr. 1-2). 20.95 *(978-0-7802-1750-8(0))* Wright Group/McGraw-Hill.

Gallagher, Debbie. Flies. 2011. (Mighty Minibeasts Ser.). 32p. (gr. 2). 28.50 *(978-1-60870-545-0(5))* Marshall Cavendish Corp.

Gravel, Élise. The Fly. (Disgusting Critters Ser.). (ENG., Illus.). 32p. (J). (gr. 1-4). 2016. pap. 5.99 *(978-1-101-91840-1(3))* 2014. 10.99 *(978-1-77049-636-1(X))* Tundra Bks. CAN. (Tundra Bks.). Dist: Penguin Random Hse. LLC.

Hamilton, S. L. Flies. 2014. (Xtreme Insects Ser.). (ENG.). 32p. (gr. 3-9). lib. bdg. 27.07 *(978-1-62403-689-7(9),* Abdo & Daughters) ABDO Publishing Co.

Hayes, Amy. A Larva Becomes a Fly. 2016. (Transformations in Nature Ser.). (ENG.). 24p. (J). (gr. 1-1). pap. 8.22 *(978-1-5026-0830-7(8))* Cavendish Square Publishing.

Heos, Bridget. I, Fly. Plecas, Jennifer, illus. 2015. (ENG.). 48p. (J). (gr. -1-3). 17.99 *(978-0-8050-9469-5(5),* 9780805094695, Holt, Henry & Co. Bks. For Young Readers) Holt, Henry & Co.

How Flies Live. (Sunshinetm Science Ser.). 24p. (gr. 1-2). 37.50 *(978-0-7802-1386-9(6))* Wright Group/McGraw-Hill.

How Flies Live: 6 Each of 1 Student Book, 6 vols. (Sunshinetm Science Ser.). 24p. (gr. 1-2). 41.95 *(978-0-7802-1385-2(8))* Wright Group/McGraw-Hill.

Hudak, Heather C. Fireflies. 2008. (World of Wonder Ser.). (Illus.). 24p. (J). (gr. k-3). pap. 8.95 *(978-1-59036-869-5(X));* lib. bdg. 24.45 *(978-1-59036-868-8(1))* Weigl Pubs., Inc.

I Can Fly: Big Book: Level A. Group 1. (Sunshine Ser.). 8p. 20.95 *(978-0-7802-5709-2(X))* Wright Group/McGraw-Hill.

Lockwood, Sophie. Flies. 2007. (World of Insects Ser.). (ENG., Illus.). 40p. (J). (gr. 3-6). 31.36 *(978-1-59296-822-0(8),* 200975) Child's World, Inc., The.

Petrie, Kristin. Flies, 1 vol. 2009. (Bugs! Ser.). (ENG.). 32p. (gr. 3-6). 27.07 *(978-1-60453-068-1(5),* Checkerboard Library) ABDO Publishing Co.

Rockwood, Leigh. Flies & Maggots Are Gross! 2010. (Creepy Crawlies Ser.). (Illus.). 24p. (J). (gr. k-2). lib. bdg. 22.60 *(978-1-4488-0703-1(4));* pap. 8.25 *(978-1-4488-1367-4(0),* PowerKids Pr.) Rosen Publishing Group, Inc., The.

Roza, Greg. Freaky Flies. 2011. (World of Bugs Ser.). (Illus.). 24p. (gr. k-2). 69.20 *(978-1-4339-6147-2(4));* (J). (gr. -1-2). lib. bdg. 22.60 *(978-1-4339-4595-3(9));* (J). (gr. k-2). pap. 8.15 *(978-1-4339-4596-0(7))* Stevens, Gareth Publishing LLLP.

Rupp, Kristina. Flies Eat What?! 2015. (1G Bugs Ser.). (ENG., Illus.). 24p. (J). pap. 5.99 *(978-1-63437-110-0(0))* American Reading Co.

Smith, Sian. Flies, 1 vol. 2012. (Creepy Critters Ser.). (ENG.). 24p. (gr. -1-k). pap. 8.95 *(978-1-4109-4820-5(X));* lib. bdg. 25.32 *(978-1-4109-4807-6(2))* Heinemann-Raintree.

Trapani, Iza. Shoo Fly! Trapani, Iza, illus. 2007. (ENG., Illus.). 32p. (J). (gr. k-3). per. 7.95 *(978-1-58089-076-2(8))* Charlesbridge Publishing, Inc.

Washington, Joi. Robber Flies. 2011. (Predator Bugs Ser.). 16p. pap. 39.62 *(978-1-61541-296-9(4))* American Reading Co.

Washington, Joi & Dibble, Traci. Robber Flies. Dibble, Traci, illus. 2010. (1-3Y Bugs Ser.). (ENG., Illus.). 16p. (J). (gr. k-2). pap. 5.99 *(978-1-61541-294-5(8))* American Reading Co.

Washington, Joi, et al. Moscas Predadoras. 2011. (2Y Bichos Depredadores Ser.).Tr. of Robber Flies. (SPA.). 16p. (J). (gr. k-2). pap. 6.99 *(978-1-61541-295-2(6))* American Reading Co.

What Is a Fly?, 6 vols. (Sunshinetm Science Ser.). 24p. (gr. 1-2). 37.50 *(978-0-7802-1383-8(1));* 41.95 *(978-0-7802-1382-1(3))* Wright Group/McGraw-Hill.

FLIGHT

see also Aeronautics

Bailey, Gerry. Flight. 2009. (Simply Science Ser.). (Illus.). 32p. (YA). (gr. 3-6). lib. bdg. 26.00 *(978-1-4339-0032-7(7))* Stevens, Gareth Publishing LLLP.

Bailey, Jacqui. What Happens When You Move? (gr. k-5). 2009. 32p. pap. 10.60 *(978-1-4358-2617-5(5),* Rosen Classroom) 2008. (Illus.). 30p. (J). lib. bdg. 26.50 *(978-1-4042-4426-9(3),* PowerKids Pr.) Rosen Publishing Group, Inc., The.

Bledsoe, Karen E. Daredevils of the Air: Thrilling Tales of Pioneer Aviators. 2003. (Avisson Young Adult Ser.). (Illus.). 155p. (J). pap. 19.95 *(978-1-888105-58-2(5))* Avisson Pr., Inc.

Brasch, Nicholas. Conquering the Sky. 2013. (Discovery Education: Discoveries & Inventions Ser.). 32p. (J). (gr. 3-6). pap. 60.00 *(978-1-4777-1505-5(3),* PowerKids Pr.) Rosen Publishing Group, Inc., The.

Brasch, Nicolas. Conquering the Sky. 2013. (Discovery Education: Discoveries & Inventions Ser.). (ENG., Illus.). 32p. (J). (gr. 3-6). pap. 10.00 *(978-1-4777-1504-8(5));* lib. bdg. 25.25 *(978-1-4777-1331-0(X))* Rosen Publishing Group, Inc., The. (PowerKids Pr.).

Brown, Jordan. How Airplanes Get from Here... to There! Borgions, Mark, illus. 2016. 48p. (J). ***(978-1-5182-1871-2(7),*** Simon Spotlight) Simon Spotlight.

Brown, Jordan D. How Airplanes Get from Here ... to There! Borgions, Mark, illus. 2016. (Science of Fun Stuff Ser.). (ENG.). 48p. (J). (gr. 1-3). pap. 3.99 *(978-1-4814-6164-1(8),* Simon Spotlight) Simon Spotlight.

Brown, Ruth Tepper. Smithsonian Discover: Flight. 2014. (Smithsonian Discover Ser.). (ENG., Illus.). 64p. (J). (gr. 2). spiral bd. 16.95 *(978-1-62686-162-6(5),* Silver Dolphin Bks.) Readerlink Distribution Services, LLC.

Candlewick Press, Candlewick. The Story of Flight: Panorama Pops. Holcroft, John, illus. 2015. (ENG.). 30p. (J). (gr. k-4). 8.99 *(978-0-7636-7700-8(0))* Candlewick Pr.

Crabtree Staff & Rooney, Anne. Aerospace Engineering & the Principles of Flight. 2012. (ENG., Illus.). 32p. (J). pap. *(978-0-7787-7500-3(3))* Crabtree Publishing Co.

Dibben, Colin. Flight. 2006. (Illus.). 48p. (J). lib. bdg. 29.95 *(978-1-60044-259-9(5))* Rourke Educational Media.

Downey, Glen R. & Cond, Sandie. The 10 Coolest Flying Machines. 2008. 14.99 *(978-1-55448-530-7(4))* Scholastic Library Publishing.

Enz, Tammy. The Science Behind Superman's Flight. 2017. (Science Behind Superman Ser.). (ENG., Illus.). 24p. (gr. 1-2). lib. bdg. 25.32 *(978-1-5157-5097-0(3),* DC Super Heroes) Stone Arch Bks.

—Soaring the Skies: Superman & the Science of Flight. 2016. (Superman Science Ser.). (ENG., Illus.). 32p. (gr. 3-4). lib. bdg. 27.32 *(978-1-5157-0913-8(2),* DC Super Heroes) Stone Arch Bks.

Evans, David & Williams, Claudette. Air & Flying. (Let's Explore Science Ser.). (Illus.). (J). 12.95 *(978-0-590-74943-5(9))* Scholastic, Inc.

Feathers & Flight: 6 Each of 1 Student Book, 6 vols. (Sunshinetm Science Ser.). 24p. (gr. 1-2). 41.95 *(978-0-7802-1395-1(5))* Wright Group/McGraw-Hill.

Feathers & Flight: Big Book. (Sunshinetm Science Ser.). 24p. (gr. 1-2). 37.50 *(978-0-7802-1396-8(3))* Wright Group/McGraw-Hill.

A Fifty Year Affair: Living with Light Planes. I.t. ed. 2004. (Illus.). 208p. (YA). pap. 18.95 *(978-0-9746564-0-3(2))* Julson, D. K.

Fight Deck: Level D, 6 vols. (Wonder Worldtm Ser.). 16p. 24.95 *(978-0-7802-1203-9(7))* Wright Group/McGraw-Hill.

Flight. (Make It Work Ser.). 42p. (J). (gr. 4-8). pap. *(978-1-882210-47-3(6))* Action Publishing, Inc.

Flight. (J). 41.95 *(978-0-382-40669-0(9))* Cobblestone Publishing Co.

Flight Sets: 1 Each of 3 Big Books. (Sunshinetm Science Ser.). (gr. 1-2). 111.50 *(978-0-7802-2816-0(2))* Wright Group/McGraw-Hill.

Flight Sets: 1 Each of 3 Student Books. (Sunshinetm Science Ser.). (gr. 1-2). 20.95 *(978-0-7802-2817-7(0))* Wright Group/McGraw-Hill.

Flying Without an Engine: 6 Each of 1 Student Book, 6 vols. (Sunshinetm Science Ser.). 24p. (gr. 1-2). 41.95 *(978-0-7802-2712-5(3))* Wright Group/McGraw-Hill.

Flying Without an Engine: Big Book. (Sunshinetm Science Ser.). 24p. (gr. 1-2). 37.50 *(978-0-7802-2790-3(5))* Wright Group/McGraw-Hill.

Flying Without Wings: 6 Each of 1 Student Book, 6 vols. (Sunshinetm Science Ser.). 24p. (gr. 1-2). 41.95 *(978-0-7802-2714-9(X))* Wright Group/McGraw-Hill.

Flying Without Wings: Big Book. (Sunshinetm Science Ser.). 24p. (gr. 1-2). 37.50 *(978-0-7802-2791-0(3))* Wright Group/McGraw-Hill.

Glass, Andrew. Flying Cars: The True Story. 2015. (ENG., Illus.). 128p. (J). (gr. 5-7). 17.99 *(978-0-618-98482-4(8))* Houghton Mifflin Harcourt Publishing Co.

Goldstone, Lawrence. Higher, Steeper, Faster: The Daredevils Who Conquered the Skies. 2017. (ENG., Illus.). 256p. (J). (gr. 3-7). 18.99 *(978-0-316-35023-5(0))* Little Brown & Co.

Green, Jen. Flying High. 2016. (Collins Big Cat Ser.). (ENG.). 24p. (J). (gr. 2-2). pap. 7.99 *(978-0-00-759120-6(9))* HarperCollins Pubs. Ltd. GBR. Dist: Independent Pubs. Group.

Grist, Julie. Flying: Just Plane Fun. Grist, Julie, illus. 2006. (ENG., Illus.). 24p. (J). (gr. k-7). pap. 8.95 *(978-0-9725750-2-7(2))* Spoonbender Bks.

Gunston, Bill, et al. The World of Flight. 2012. (ENG., Illus.). 48p. 15.00 *(978-1-899762-89-7(2))* Award Pubns. Ltd. GBR. Dist: Parkwest Pubns., Inc.

Hansen, Ole Steen. The Story of Flight. 2003. (Illus.). 190p. (J). *(978-0-7787-1212-1(5))* Crabtree Publishing Co.

—The Story of Flight, 12 bks. Incl. Amazing Flights: The Golden Age. (gr. 4). 2002. lib. bdg. *(978-0-7787-1202-2(8));* Commercial Aviation. (gr. 4). 2002. lib. bdg. *(978-0-7787-1205-3(2));* Flying for Fun. (gr. 4). 2003. lib. bdg. *(978-0-7787-1211-4(7));* Military Aircraft of WWI. (gr. 4). 2002. lib. bdg. *(978-0-7787-1201-5(X));* Modern Military Aircraft. (gr. 4). 2002. lib. bdg. *(978-0-7787-1204-6(4));* Seaplanes & Naval Aviation. (gr. 4). 2003. lib. bdg. *(978-0-7787-1209-1(5));* Space Flight. (gr. 2-9). 2003. lib. bdg. *(978-0-7787-1207-7(9));* Weird & Wonderful Aircraft. (gr. 4). 2003. lib. bdg. *(978-0-7787-1210-7(9));* Wright Brothers & Other Pioneers of Flight. (gr. 4). 2002. lib. bdg. *(978-0-7787-1200-8(1));* 32p. (J). (Illus.). 2003. *(978-0-7787-1198-8(6));* Set pap. *(978-0-7787-1214-5(1))* Crabtree Publishing Co.

Hanson-Harding, Alexandra & Benchmark Education Co. Staff. The Science of Flight. 2014. (Text Connections Ser.). (J). (gr. 6). *(978-1-4900-1535-4(3))* Benchmark Education Co.

Haslam, Andrew, et al. Flight. (Make It Work! Ser.). (Illus.). 48p. (J). pap. 7.99 *(978-0-590-24687-3(9))* Scholastic, Inc.

Hay DeSimone, Corkey. Air & Space Activity & Coloring Book: An Early Introduction to the History of Flight. Hay DeSimone, Corkey, illus. 2006. (Illus.). (J). 7.95 *(978-0-9747921-4-9(4))* Gentle Giraffe Pr.

Hicks, Kelli. Airplanes. 2014. (ENG.). 24p. (gr. k-3). 28.50 *(978-1-62717-649-1(7))* Rourke Educational Media.

Hodgkins, Fran. How People Learned to Fly. 2006. lib. bdg. *(978-0-06-029599-8(6))* HarperCollins Canada, Ltd.

—How People Learned to Fly. Kelley, True, illus. 2007. (Let's-Read-And-Find-Out Science 2 Ser.). (ENG.). 40p. (J). (gr. k-4). pap. 5.99 *(978-0-06-445221-2(2))* HarperCollins Pubs.

—How People Learned to Fly. Kelley, True, illus. 2007. (Let's-Read-and-Find-Out Science Ser.). 33p. (gr. k-4). 16.00 *(978-0-7569-8101-3(8))* Perfection Learning Corp.

Hodgkins, Fran & Hodgkins. How People Learned to Fly. Kelley, True, illus. 2007. (Let's-Read-And-Find-Out Science 2 Ser.). (ENG.). 40p. (J). (gr. k-4). 16.99 *(978-0-06-029558-5(9),* Collins) HarperCollins Pubs.

Holzweiss, Kristina. Amazing MakerSpace DIY Fliers. 2017. (True Book — MakerSpace Projects Ser.). (ENG.). 48p. (J). lib. bdg. 31.00 ***(978-0-531-23846-2(6),*** Children's Pr.) Scholastic Library Publishing.

Holzweiss, Kristina A. Fliers. 2017. (True Book — MakerSpace Projects Ser.). (ENG.). 48p. (J). pap. 7.95 ***(978-0-531-24097-7(5),*** Children's Pr.) Scholastic Library Publishing.

Jeffrey, Gary. The History of Flight. (Graphic Discoveries Ser.). (ENG.). 48p. 2009. (YA). (gr. 5-5). 58.50 *(978-1-61512-938-6(3),* Rosen Reference) 2008. (gr. 3-8). pap. 14.05 *(978-1-4042-9589-6(5))* 2008. (Illus.). (J). (gr. 5-9). lib. bdg. 31.95 *(978-1-4042-1087-5(3))* Rosen Publishing Group, Inc., The.

Kids Can Press Staff. This Is Daniel Cook on a Plane. 2006. (This Is Daniel Cook Ser.). (ENG., Illus.). 24p. (J). (gr. -1-1). 4.95 *(978-1-55453-082-3(2))* Kids Can Pr., Ltd. CAN. Dist: Hachette Bk. Group.

Lunis, Natalie. Gravity-Defying Animals. 2014. (Animals with Super Powers Ser.). 24p. (J). (gr. 1-6). lib. bdg. 22.61 *(978-1-62724-080-2(2))* Bearport Publishing Co., Inc.

Madgwick, Wendy. Up in the Air: 17 Easy-to-Follow Experiments for Learning Fun - Find Out about Flight & How Weather Works! 2014. (ENG., Illus.). 270p. (J). (gr. -1-12). 8.99 *(978-1-86147-350-9(8),* Armadillo) Anness Publishing GBR. Dist: National Bk. Network.

Mellett, Peter. Find Out about Flight: With 18 Projects & More Than 240 Pictures. 2013. (ENG., Illus.). 64p. (J). (gr. 3-7). 9.99 *(978-1-84322-869-1(6))* Anness Publishing GBR. Dist: National Bk. Network.

Mellett, Peter, et al. What Is Flight? Birds; Planes; Kites; Balloons. 2015. (ENG., Illus.). 64p. (J). (gr. k-6). 12.99 *(978-1-86147-401-8(6),* Armadillo) Anness Publishing GBR. Dist: National Bk. Network.

Moore, Rob. Why Do Airplanes Fly? 2010. (Solving Science Mysteries Ser.). (Illus.). 24p. (J). pap. 8.25 *(978-1-61531-912-1(3),* PowerKids Pr.); (YA). (gr. 3-6). lib. bdg. 22.60 *(978-1-61531-890-2(9))* Rosen Publishing Group, Inc., The.

—Why Do Airplanes Fly? All about Flight. 2010. 24p. (J). 49.50 *(978-1-61531-923-7(9),* PowerKids Pr.) Rosen Publishing Group, Inc., The.

O'Brien, Patrick. Fantastic Flights: One Hundred Years of Flying on the Edge. 2003. (Illus.). 40p. (J). 18.85 *(978-0-8027-8881-8(5))* Walker & Co.

Page, Robin & Jenkins, Steve. Animals in Flight. Jenkins, Steve, illus. 2005. (ENG., Illus.). 32p. (J). (gr. -1-3). pap. 6.99 *(978-0-618-54882-8(3))* Houghton Mifflin Harcourt Publishing Co.

Parker, Steve. Tabletop Scientist — the Science of Air: Projects & Experiments with Air & Flight. 2013. (ENG., Illus.). 32p. (J). (gr. 3-8). pap. 6.99 *(978-0-486-49265-0(6))* Dover Pubns., Inc.

Las Plumas y el Vuelo, 6 vols. (Explorers: Exploradores Nonfiction Sets Ser.). (SPA.). 32p. (gr. 3-6). 44.95 *(978-0-7699-0633-1(8))* Shortland Pubns. (U. S. A.) Inc.

Rees, Peter. How Does It Fly? The Science of Flight. 2007. (Shockwave: Technology & Manufacturing Ser.). (ENG., Illus.). 36p. (J). (gr. 4-6). lib. bdg. 25.00 *(978-0-531-17587-3(1),* Children's Pr.) Scholastic Library Publishing.

Richards, Jon. Air & Flight. (Science Factory Ser.). 32p. (gr. 4-5). 2009. 50.50 *(978-1-60853-018-2(3),* PowerKids Pr.) 2008. (Illus.). (YA). lib. bdg. 26.50 *(978-1-4042-3907-4(3))* Rosen Publishing Group, Inc., The.

Rieger, Linda. Flying Animals. Bianchi, John, illus. 2006. 20p. (J). *(978-0-9779427-1-8(6))* Pathways into Science.

Rooney, Anne. Aerospace Engineering & the Principles of Flight. 2012. (ENG.). 32p. (J). *(978-0-7787-7495-2(3))* Crabtree Publishing Co.

Sarver, Amy. Science at the Airport. 2007. (Reading Expeditions Ser.). (ENG., Illus.). 24p. (J). pap. 14.95 *(978-0-7922-4568-1(7))* CENGAGE Learning.

Sian revision flightgliders to Jets. 2004. (Science in A Nutshell Ser.). (J). *(978-1-59242-028-5(1))* Delta Education, LLC.

Solway, Andrew. Secrets of Flight. 2010. (Science Secrets Ser.). 32p. (gr. 4). 28.50 *(978-1-60870-136-0(0))* Marshall Cavendish Corp.

Spilsbury, Louise. Flight, 1 vol. 2012. (Science Behind Ser.). (ENG.). 32p. (gr. 3-3). pap. 8.29 *(978-1-4109-4502-0(2));* lib. bdg. 30.65 *(978-1-4109-4491-7(3))* Heinemann-Raintree. (Raintree Perspectives).

Taylor, Kim. Flight. (Illus.). 32p. (YA). (gr. 3-18). lib. bdg. 27.10 *(978-1-931983-74-7(7))* Chrysalis Education.

Top That Publishing Staff, ed. Flight. 2005. (Illus.). 24p. pap. *(978-1-84510-158-9(8))* Top That! Publishing PLC.

Der Traum Von Fliegen.Tr. of Dream of Flying. (GER.). (YA). 31.95 *(978-3-411-09091-4(X))* Bibliographisches Institut & F. A. Brockhaus AG DEU. Dist: Continental Bk. Co., Inc.

Upgrade kit dsm-3 Flight&rocketry. (J). 2004. *(978-1-59242-530-3(5))* 2003. *(978-1-59242-413-9(9))* Delta Education, LLC.

Vargus, Nanci R. Flying. 2006. (On the Move Ser.). (Illus.). 24p. (gr. k-1). lib. bdg. 15.95 *(978-0-7614-2319-5(2),* Benchmark Bks.) Marshall Cavendish Corp.

—A Volar! 2006. (En Movimiento Ser.). (SPA & ENG., Illus.). 24p. (gr. k-1). lib. bdg. 15.95 *(978-0-7614-2425-3(3),* Benchmark Bks.) Marshall Cavendish Corp.

Veitch, Catherine. Big Machines Fly!, 1 vol. 2014. (Big Machines Ser.). (ENG.). 24p. (gr. k-1). 23.32 *(978-1-4846-0586-8(1),* Heinemann Read & Learn) Heinemann-Raintree.

Vuelo en Las Alturas, 6 vols., Vol. 2. (Explorers. Exploradores Nonfiction Sets Ser.). (SPA.). 32p. (gr. 3-6). 44.95 *(978-0-7699-0643-0(5))* Shortland Pubns. (U. S. A.) Inc.

Watton, Ross, illus. Too Close to the Sun: The Story of Daedalus & Icarus: A Greek Legend. 2004. (ENG.). 20p. (J). (gr. 3-3). pap. 6.47 net. *(978-0-7685-2121-4(1),* Dominie Elementary) Pearson Schl.

World Book, Inc Staff, contrib. by. A Dream Takes Flight: A Supplement to Childcraft, the How & Why Library. 2013. (Illus.). 26p. (J). *(978-0-7166-0629-1(1))* World Bk., Inc.

FLIGHT—FICTION

Almond, David. My Dad's a Birdman. Dunbar, Polly, illus. 2008. (ENG.). 128p. (J). (gr. 3-7). 15.99 *(978-0-7636-3667-8(3))* Candlewick Pr.

Andersen, David W. Tell Us a Story about Flying. 2012. 28p. pap. 24.95 *(978-1-4626-8081-8(X))* America Star Bks.

Anderson, David. Charlie Sparrow & the Secret of Flight. Anderson, David, illus. 2013. (Illus.). 98p. pap. *(978-0-9918003-2-2(X))* Underdog Bks.

Anholt, Laurence. Leonardo & the Flying Boy. 2007. (Anholt's Artists Books for Children Ser.). (ENG., Illus.). 36p. (J). (gr. -1-3). 8.99 *(978-0-7641-3851-5(0))* Barron's Educational Series, Inc.

Baker-Smith, Grahame. FArTHER. Baker-Smith, Grahame, illus. 2013. (ENG., Illus.). 40p. (J). (gr. k-3). 17.99 *(978-0-7636-6370-4(0),* Templar) Candlewick Pr.

Bancks, Tristan. Noob, the Boy Who Could Fly. Gorissen, Dean, illus. 2015. (Legends in Their Own Lunchbox Ser.). (ENG.). 56p. (gr. 2-3). pap. 7.99 *(978-1-4966-0259-6(5),* Legends in Their Own Lunchbox) Capstone Classroom.

Beach, Charles Amory. Air Service Boys over the Atlantic, or, the Longest Flight on Record. 2007. 144p. per. *(978-1-4065-3676-8(8))* Dodo Pr.

Biddulph, Rob. Blown Away. Biddulph, Rob, illus. 2015. (ENG., Illus.). 40p. (J). (gr. -1-3). 17.99 *(978-0-06-236724-2(2))* HarperCollins Pubs.

Bildner, Phil. The Hallelujah Flight. Holyfield, John, illus. 2010. (ENG.). 32p. (J). (gr. k-3). 16.99 *(978-0-399-24789-7(0),* G.P. Putnam's Sons Books for Young Readers) Penguin Young Readers Group.

Bloncourt, Nelson & Botero, Fernando. Botero: Paintings & Works on Paper. Polyansky, Nikita, illus. 2013. (ENG.). 252p. 125.00 *(978-0-9881745-1-1(0))* Glitterati, Inc.

Bloom, Suzanne, illus. Bear Can Dance! 2015. (Goose & Bear Stories Ser.). (ENG.). 40p. (J). (-k). 16.95 *(978-1-62979-442-6(2))* Boyds Mills Pr.

Boonen, Stefan. When Pigs Fly! Loufane, illus. 2004. 32p. (J). 6.95 *(978-1-58925-384-1(1))* Tiger Tales.

Brill, Calista. Little Wing Learns to Fly. Bell, Jennifer A., illus. 2016. (Little Wing Ser.). 32p. (J). (gr. -1-3). 17.99 *(978-0-06-236033-5(7))* HarperCollins Pubs.

Brock, Betty. No Flying in the House. 2005. (J). (gr. 3-6). 16.00 *(978-0-613-08451-2(9),* Turtleback) Turtleback Bks.

Brock, Betty & Brock. No Flying in the House. Tripp, Wallace, illus. 2005. (Harper Trophy Bks.). (ENG.). 144p. (J). (gr. 2-6). pap. 5.99 *(978-0-06-440130-2(8))* HarperCollins Pubs.

Brooke, Samantha. Star of the Show. 2014. lib. bdg. 13.55 *(978-0-606-35857-6(9))* Turtleback Bks.

Brooks, Walter R. Freddy the Pilot. Wiese, Kurt, tr. 2012. (ENG., Illus.). 256p. (gr. 4-13). pap. 10.99 *(978-1-59020-867-0(6),* 902867) Overlook Pr., The.

Brown, Peter. Flight of the Dodo. 2010. (ENG., Illus.). 32p. (J). (gr. -1-3). pap. 7.99 *(978-0-316-08339-3(9))* Little, Brown Bks. for Young Readers.

Cain, Sheridan. The Crunching Munching Caterpillar. Tickle, Jack, illus. 2013. (ENG.). 20p. (J). (gr. -1). 9.99 *(978-1-58925-616-3(6))* Tiger Tales.

—Crunching Munching Caterpillar. Tickle, Jack, illus. 2003. 32p. (J). tchr. ed. 15.95 *(978-1-58925-025-3(7))* Tiger Tales.

Church, Caroline Jayne. Ping Pong Pig. Church, Caroline Jayne, illus. 2008. (ENG., Illus.). 32p. (J). (gr. -1-1). 16.95 *(978-0-8234-2176-3(7))* Holiday Hse., Inc.

Clark, Leslie Ann. Peepsqueak! Clark, Leslie Ann, illus. 2012. (ENG., Illus.). 32p. (J). (gr. -1-k). 12.99 *(978-0-06-207801-8(1))* HarperCollins Pubs.

Clarke, Covington. For Valor & Desert Wings. 2005. reprint ed. pap. 42.95 *(978-0-7661-9827-2(8))* Kessinger Publishing, LLC.

Colfer, Eoin. Airman. 2009. (ENG.). 416p. (J). (gr. 5-9). pap. 8.99 *(978-1-4231-0751-4(9))* Hyperion Pr.

—Airman. 2009. (J). lib. bdg. 19.65 *(978-0-606-12534-5(5),* Turtleback) Turtleback Bks.

Cosby, Bill. Friends of a Feather: One of Life's Little Fables. Cosby, Erika, illus. 2003. (ENG.). 64p. (gr. k-3). 16.95 *(978-0-06-009147-7(9))* HarperCollins Pubs.

Cotter, Bill. Hello, Airplane! 2014. (ENG., Illus.). 32p. (J). (-3). 16.99 *(978-1-4926-0353-5(8),* Sourcebooks Jabberwocky) Sourcebooks, Inc.

Coulman, Valerie. When Pigs Fly. I.t. ed. 2012. 63p. (J). pap. *(978-1-4596-3455-8(1))* ReadHowYouWant.com, Ltd.

Courtney, Suzanne Gene. Florence Flies Alone: An Alliterative Airline Adventure. 2013. 24p. pap. 13.50 *(978-1-62212-902-7(4),* Strategic Bk. Publishing) Strategic Book Publishing & Rights Agency (SBPRA).

Dalmatian Press Staff. Star Light, Star Bright. 2008. (ENG.). 6p. bds. 4.95 *(978-1-58117-723-7(2),* Intervisual/Piggy Toes) Bendon, Inc.

Davies, Gill. Brave Little Owl. Twinney, Dick, illus. 2006. (ENG.). 24p. (J). *(978-1-55168-279-2(6))* Fenn, H. B. & Co., Ltd.

de Beer, Hans, pseud. Little Polar Bear & the Big Balloon. Lanning, Rosemary, tr. from GER. 2006. (Illus.). 22p. (J). (gr. k-4). reprint ed. 16.00 *(978-0-7567-9875-8(2))* DIANE Publishing Co.

Dixon, Tiffany. Everyone Is Special. 2008. 16p. per. 24.95 *(978-1-60441-231-4(3))* America Star Bks.

Doudna, Kelly. Goose Down, 1 vol. Haberstroh, Anne, illus. 2006. (Animal Tales Ser.). 24p. (J). (gr. k-3). (ENG.). lib. bdg. 24.21 *(978-1-59679-941-7(2),* SandCastle); pap. 48.42 *(978-1-59679-942-4(0))* ABDO Publishing Co.

Draper, Rochelle. The Stone Wall Dragon. Draper, Rochelle, illus. 2007. (ENG., Illus.). 32p. (J). (gr. 1-17). 15.95 *(978-0-89272-690-5(3))* Down East Bks.

Drawson, Blair. Flying Dimitri, 1 vol. (ENG., Illus.). 32p. (J). 16.95 *(978-0-88899-284-0(X))* Groundwood Bks. CAN. Dist: Publishers Group West (PGW).

Duble, Kathleen Benner. Bravo Zulu, Samantha!, 1 vol. 2007. (ENG.). 144p. (J). (gr. 3-7). 14.95 *(978-1-56145-401-3(X))* Peachtree Pubs.

Dudley, Rebecca. Hank Has a Dream. Dudley, Rebecca, photos by. 2014. (ENG., Illus.). 32p. (J). 16.99 *(978-1-4413-1572-4(1),* 9781441315724) Peter Pauper Pr. Inc.

Dychtwald, Ken, et al. Gideon's Dream: A Tale of New Beginnings. Zaboski, Dave, illus. 2008. 40p. (J). (gr. -1-3). lib. bdg. 17.89 *(978-0-06-143498-3(1))* HarperCollins Pubs.

Echols, Jennifer. Such a Rush. 2012. (ENG.). 336p. pap. 20.99 *(978-1-4516-5802-6(8),* Gallery Bks.) Gallery Bks.

Ericks, Leonard. The Red Dragon Ryan Learns How to Fly. 2010. 24p. pap. 12.25 *(978-1-60911-201-1(6),* Eloquent Bks.) Strategic Book Publishing & Rights Agency (SBPRA).

Ferrari, Michael. Born to Fly. 2011. (ENG.). 224p. (J). (gr. 3-7). 6.99 *(978-0-375-84607-6(7),* Yearling) Random Hse. Children's Bks.

Forester, Victoria. The Girl Who Could Fly. 2008. (ENG.). 336p. (J). (gr. 4-7). 16.95 *(978-0-312-37462-4(3),* 9780312374624) Feiwel & Friends.

—The Girl Who Could Fly. Barcellona, Christine, ed. 2015. (ENG.). 352p. (J). (gr. 4-7). pap. 7.99 *(978-1-250-07246-7(8),* 9781250072467) Square Fish.

French, Vivian. Pig in Love. Archbold, Tim, illus. 2005. 32p. (J). lib. bdg. 9.00 *(978-1-4242-0889-0(0))* Fitzgerald Bks.

EFG

Furuya, Michael, illus. Keoni's Special Gift. 2009. (J). (978-1-56647-915-8(0)) Mutual Publishing LLC.

Ganges, Montse. Cooper, Flying Dog. Urberuaga, Emilio, illus. 2009. (Cooper Ser.). 24p. (J). (gr. -1-3). 22.60 (978-1-60754-239-1(0)); pap. 8.15 (978-1-60754-240-7(4)) Windmill Bks.

Garis, Howard Roger. Dick Hamiltons Airship. 2005. 28.95 (978-1-4218-1463-6(3)); 260p. pap. 13.95 (978-1-4218-1563-3(X)) 1st World Publishing, Inc. (1st World Library - Literary Society).

—Uncle Wiggily's Airship. Date not set. 192p. (J). 20.95 (978-0-8488-2277-4(3)) Amereon Ltd.

Gay, Marie-Louise. Caramba & Henry. 2011. (ENG., Illus.). 40p. (J). (gr. k-k). 17.95 (978-1-55498-097-0(6)) Groundwood Bks. CAN. Dist: Publishers Group West (PGW).

Gigi, Jessy. The Sky Ride of Jimmy & Friends. 2011. 20p. pap. 24.95 (978-1-4626-2723-3(4)) America Star Bks.

Glass, Andrew. The Wondrous Whirligig: The Wright Brothers¿ First Flying Machine. Glass, Andrew, illus. 2007. (Illus.). 30p. (J). reprint ed. 17.00 (978-1-4223-6765-0(7)) DIANE Publishing Co.

Gober, Thomas. Dandylion the Duck. Gillen, Rosemarie, illus. 2012. 26p. (J). 16.95 (978-1-60131-126-9(5), Castlebridge Bks.) Big Tent Bks.

Goldfrap, John Henry. The Boy Aviators' Polar Dash: Or Facing Death in the Antarctic. 2007. (ENG.). 180p. pap. 19.99 (978-1-4264-5072-3(9)); 200p. pap. 21.99 (978-1-4264-5373-1(6)) Creative Media Partners, LLC.

Graves, Jonathan. Isabella Propeller & the Magic Beanie. Haley, Gail E., illus. 2011. (J). 15.95 (978-1-933251-74-5(3)) Parkway Pubs., Inc.

Griffin, Wiley Chase. Chase the Shark: Flies Like a Bird. 2010. 28p. pap. 12.50 (978-1-4520-5173-4(9)) AuthorHouse.

Gutman, Dan. Race for the Sky: The Kitty Hawk Diaries of Johnny Moore. 2003. (ENG., Illus.). 192p. (J). (gr. 5-9). 19.99 (978-0-689-84554-3(5), Simon & Schuster Bks. For Young Readers) Simon & Schuster Bks. For Young Readers.

Harley, Bill. The Amazing Flight of Darius Frobisher, 1 vol. 2006. (ENG., Illus.). 160p. (J). (gr. 3-7). 14.95 (978-1-56145-381-8(1)) Peachtree Pubs.

Henry, Heather French. Flying Away. Henry, Heather French, illus. 2004. (Claire's Everyday Adventures Ser.). (Illus.). 32p. (J). (gr. k-4). pap. 8.95 (978-0-9706341-8-4(8), 1231610); (ENG., 15.95 (978-0-9706341-4-6(5), 1231610) Cubbie Blue Publishing.

Herodotus. The Wright Brothers Adventure. 2005. (Illus.). (J). (978-0-9762509-1-3(8)) Society For The Understanding Of Early Child Development.

Hill, Susanna Leonard. Airplane Flight! Larrañaga, Ana Martín, illus. 2009. (ENG.). 12p. (J). (gr. -1-k). bds. 7.99 (978-1-4169-7832-9(1), Little Simon) Little Simon.

Hillert, Margaret. The Funny Ride. Selivanova, Elena, illus. 2016. (BeginningtoRead Ser.). (ENG.). 32p. (J). (gr. -1-2). pap. 11.94 (978-1-60357-978-0(8)); (gr. k-2). 22.60 (978-1-59953-816-7(4)) Norwood Hse. Pr.

Holden, Pam. Paulo the Pilot, 6 pack. Whimp, Pauline, illus. 2009. (Red Rocket Readers Ser.). (ENG.). 16p. (gr. 2-2). pap. (978-1-877363-67-2(7), Red Rocket Readers) Flying Start Bks.

Holtei, Christa. Nanuk Flies Home. Vohwinkel, Astrid, illus. 2008. 26p. (J). (gr. 4-7). 16.00 (978-0-8028-5342-4(0)) Eerdmans, William B. Publishing Co.

Homan, Lynn M. & Reilly, Thomas. Girls Fly!, 1 vol. Shepherd, Rosalie M., tr. Shepherd, Rosalie M., illus. 2003. (ENG.). 32p. (J). (gr. k-3). 16.99 (978-1-58980-154-7(7)) Pelican Publishing Co., Inc.

Hooray for Boys & Girls! 2006. (J). 15.95 (978-0-9776837-0-3(2)) West Woods Pr.

Hulin, Rachel, photos by. Flying Henry. 2013. (ENG., Illus.). 40p. (J). (-k). 12.95 (978-1-57687-626-8(8), powerHouse Bks.) powerHouse Cultural Entertainment, Inc.

I Wish I Could Fly: Lonely Caterpillar/the Lonely Butterfly. l.t. ed. 2006. (Illus.). 60p. (J). (gr. -1-3). per. 17.99 (978-1-59879-196-9(6)) Lifevest Publishing, Inc.

James, J. Alison. Eucalyptus Wings. Demi, illus. 2012. (ENG.). 36p. (J). (gr. k-3). 17.99 (978-1-4424-7484-0(X), Atheneum Bks. for Young Readers) Simon & Schuster Children's Publishing.

James, Simon. George Flies South. 2011. (ENG., Illus.). 40p. (J). (gr. -1-2). 16.99 (978-0-7636-5724-6(7)) Candlewick Pr.

Jeffers, Oliver. Up & Down. Jeffers, Oliver, illus. 2010. (ENG., Illus.). 40p. (J). (gr. -1-2). 17.99 (978-0-399-25545-8(1), Philomel Bks.) Penguin Young Readers Group.

Judge, Lita. Flight School. Judge, Lita, illus. 2014. (ENG., Illus.). 40p. (J). (gr. -1-3). 17.99 (978-1-4424-8177-0(3), Atheneum Bks. for Young Readers) Simon & Schuster Children's Publishing.

Kinerk, Robert. Clorinda Takes Flight. Kellogg, Steven, illus. 2007. (ENG.). 40p. (J). (gr. -1-3). 17.99 (978-0-689-86864-1(2), Simon & Schuster/Paula Wiseman Bks.) Simon & Schuster/Paula Wiseman Bks.

Kroll, Steven. Super-Dragon, 0 vols. Holgate, Doug, illus. 2011. (ENG.). 32p. (J). (gr. -1-2). 16.99 (978-0-7614-5819-7(0), 9780761458197, Amazon Children's Publishing) Amazon Publishing.

Kuhlmann, Torben. Lindbergh: The Tale of a Flying Mouse. 2014. (ENG., Illus.). 96p. (J). (gr. k-k). 19.95 (978-0-7358-4167-3(5)) North-South Bks., Inc.

Langen, Annette. Felix & the Flying Suitcase Adventure. Droop, Constanza, illus. 2003. 47p. (J). 14.99 (978-1-59384-035-8(7)) Parklane Publishing.

Leavitt, Lindsey. Have a Mice Flight! Ford, A. G., illus. 2016. (Commander in Cheese Ser.: 3). (ENG.). 112p. (J). (gr. 2-5). 4.99 (978-1-101-93118-9(3), Random Hse. Bks. for Young Readers) Random Hse. Children's Bks.

Leiter, Richard & Kober, Shahar. The Flying Hand of Marco B. 2015. (ENG., Illus.). 24p. (J). (gr. k-2). 15.99 (978-1-58536-888-4(1), 203813) Sleeping Bear Pr.

Lethem, Mara. The Highest Mountain of Books in the World. Bonilla, Rocio, illus. 2016. (J). (978-1-4413-1999-9(9)) Peter Pauper Pr. Inc.

Light, Steve. Zephyr Takes Flight. Light, Steve, illus. 2012. (ENG., Illus.). 40p. (J). (gr. -1-3). 16.99 (978-0-7636-5695-9(X)) Candlewick Pr.

Linkowski, Tami Leli. Lynn Can Fly, 1 vol. Selover, Lisa & Selover, Arthur, illus. 2009. 15p. pap. 24.95 (978-1-60749-611-3(9)) America Star Bks.

Loux, Lynn Crosbie. The Day I Could Fly. Porfirio, Guy, illus. 2003. (ENG.). 32p. (J). (gr. k-3). 15.95 (978-1-55971-866-0(8)) Cooper Square Publishing Llc.

Luthardt, Kevin. Flying!, 1 vol. Luthardt, Kevin, illus. (ENG., Illus.). 32p. (J). (gr. -1-1). 2013. 7.95 (978-1-56145-724-3(8)) 2009. 15.95 (978-1-56145-430-3(3)) Peachtree Pubs.

Malaspina, Ann. The People Could Fly: An African-American Folktale. Otero, Sole, illus. 2013. (Folktales from Around the World Ser.). (ENG.). 24p. (J). (gr. k-3). 28.50 (978-1-62323-617-5(7), 206385) Child's World, Inc., The.

Malepart, Celine, illus. When Pigs Fly: A Piggy Pop-up Book! 2008. (ENG.). 12p. 16.95 (978-1-58117-671-1(6), Intervisual/Piggy Toes) Bendon, Inc.

Marcero, Deborah, illus. Ursa's Light. 2016. (J). (978-1-4413-1881-7(X)) Peter Pauper Pr. Inc.

Mason, David. Davey McGravy. Silverstein, Grant, illus. 2015. (ENG.). 120p. (J). (gr. k). pap. 14.95 (978-1-58988-099-3(4)) Dry, Paul Bks., Inc.

Matte, Johane, et al. Flight Explorer, Vol. 1. Kibuishi, Kazu, ed. Armstrong, Matthew S., illus. 2008. (ENG.). 112p. (YA). pap. 16.00 (978-0-345-50313-8(9), Villard Bks.) Random House Publishing Group.

McCaffrey, Laura Williams. Marked. 2016. (ENG.). 368p. (YA). (gr. 7-9). 17.99 (978-0-547-23556-1(9), Clarion Bks.) Houghton Mifflin Harcourt Trade & Reference Pubs.

McCarty, Peter. Moon Plane. McCarty, Peter, illus. 2006. (ENG., Illus.). 40p. (J). (gr. -1-1). 18.99 (978-0-8050-7943-2(2), 9780805079432, Holt, Henry & Co. Bks. For Young Readers) Holt, Henry & Co.

Mcghee, Alison. Only a Witch Can Fly. Yoo, Taeeun, illus. movie tie-in ed. 2009. (ENG.). 32p. (J). (gr. -1-3). 16.99 (978-0-312-37503-4(4), 9780312375034) Feiwel & Friends.

Mckenzie, Precious. Disaster Day. Mones, Marc, illus. 2012. (ENG.). 24p. (gr. 2-3). pap. 8.95 (978-1-61810-331-4(8)) Rourke Educational Media.

Meade, Holly. If I Never Forever Endeavor. Meade, Holly, illus. 2011. (ENG., Illus.). 32p. (J). (gr. -1-3). 16.99 (978-0-7636-4071-2(9)) Candlewick Pr.

Meyers, Ann Marie. Up in the Air. 2013. 244p. (J). 22.99 (978-1-939967-03-9(1), Jolly Fish Pr.) North Star Editions.

Meza, Martin. Martin Mezas Story Time Three Short Stories, Vol. 1. 2007. 64p. pap. 14.21 (978-1-4116-8486-7(9)) Lulu Pr., Inc.

Miceli, Mary Anne. Boston North Shore's... Mouse Tales of Early Salem. 2013. 44p. pap. 20.00 (978-0-9888654-1-9(6)) Miceli, Mary Anne.

Misty. Tristan, the Youngest Blue Jay. 2012. 24p. 24.95 (978-1-4626-5184-9(4)) America Star Bks.

Modarressi, Mitra. Owlet's First Flight. Modarressi, Mitra, illus. 2012. (ENG., Illus.). 32p. (J). (gr. -1-k). 16.99 (978-0-399-25526-7(5), G.P. Putnam's Sons Books for Young Readers) Penguin Young Readers Group.

Morgan, Michelle. Colorsaurus. 2009. 32p. pap. 18.00 (978-0-557-06120-4(2)) Lulu Pr., Inc.

Nettrour, Nelani. Dragonfly Flight. Lesnick, Tina, illus. l.t. ed. 2003. 62p. (J). pap. 11.94 (978-1-932657-02-9(9)) Third Millennium Pubns.

Neumeier, Rachel. The Floating Islands. 2012. (ENG.). 400p. (YA). (gr. 7). pap. 9.99 (978-0-440-24060-0(3)) Random Hse. Children's Bks.

Newcomer, Carolyn. Barf's First Flight. Raschke, Andrea, illus. 2009. 40p. (J). 14.95 (978-0-9792583-8-1(3)) White Stag Pr.

Okorafor-Mbachu, Nnedi. Zahrah the Windseeker. 2008. (ENG., Illus.). 320p. (J). (gr. 5-7). pap. 8.99 (978-0-547-02028-0(7)) Houghton Mifflin Harcourt Publishing Co.

Olshan, Matthew. A Voyage in the Clouds: The (Mostly) True Story of the First International Flight by Balloon in 1785. Blackall, Sophie, illus. 2016. (ENG.). 40p. (J). 17.99 (978-0-374-32954-9(0), 9780374329549, Farrar, Straus & Giroux (BYR)) Farrar, Straus & Giroux.

O'Neal, Kerry. I Wish I Could Fly/I Can Fly! The Lonely Caterpillar BOOK I & the Lonely Butterfly BOOK II. O'Neal, Kerry, illus. l.t. ed. 2006. (Illus.). 60p. (J). 29.99 (978-1-59879-197-6(4)) Lifevest Publishing, Inc.

Otten, Charlotte. The Flying Mouse. Crawford, Greg, illus. 2014. (ENG.). 32p. (J). 17.95 (978-1-59373-152-6(3)) Bunker Hill Publishing, Inc.

Pacovskà, Kveta. Flying. Pacovskà, Kveta, illus. 2005.Tr. of Turme. (Illus.). 39p. (J). reprint ed. 20.00 (978-0-7567-8532-1(4)) DIANE Publishing Co.

Parker, A. J. The Table of Shadows. 2007. 273p. pap. 16.95 (978-1-84753-762-1(6)) Lulu Pr., Inc.

Parker, Emma. Captain Gold. 2010. (Illus.). pap. (978-1-877561-26-9(6)) First Edition Ltd.

Pérez-Foncea, Juan Antonio & Caro, Stephen. Ivan of Aldenuri: The Forest of the Taurocs. 2007. (J). (978-1-59835-058-6(7)) Cambridge BrickHouse, Inc.

Peyo. Sky-High Smurf. Peyo, illus. 2014. (Smurfs Classic Ser.). (ENG., Illus.). 16p. (J). (gr. -1-3). 5.99 (978-1-4424-9740-5(8), Simon Spotlight) Simon Spotlight.

Plourde, Paulette. I Can Fly. l.t. ed. 2005. (Illus.). 40p. (J). per. 9.95 (978-1-59879-012-2(9)) Lifevest Publishing, Inc.

Raymond, Jeanpaul. The Kids That Could. 2009. 40p. pap. 17.99 (978-1-4389-5585-8(5)) AuthorHouse.

Reeve, Philip. Fever Crumb: a Web of Air. 2013. (Fever Crumb Ser.). (ENG.). 304p. (J). (gr. 7-7). pap. 9.99 (978-0-545-22217-4(6), Scholastic Pr.) Scholastic, Inc.

—A Web of Air. 2011. (Fever Crumb Ser.). (ENG.). 304p. (J). (gr. 7-7). 17.99 (978-0-545-22216-7(8)) Scholastic, Inc.

Richards, Dan. Can One Balloon Make an Elephant Fly? Newman, Jeff, illus. 2016. (ENG.). 40p. (J). (gr. -1-3). 17.99 (978-1-4424-5215-2(3)) Simon & Schuster Bks. For Young Readers.

Rigsby, Annelle & Raffa, Edwina. Race to Kitty Hawk. 2003. (Adventures in America Ser.). (Illus.). 84p. (gr. 4). 14.95 (978-1-893110-33-5(8)) Silver Moon Pr.

Ringgold, Faith. Tar Beach. 2014. 32p. pap. 7.00 (978-1-61003-377-0(9)) Center for the Collaborative Classroom.

Rosen, Michael. Bear Flies High. Reynolds, Adrian, illus. 2009. (ENG.). 32p. (J). (gr. -1-1). 16.99 (978-1-59990-386-6(5), 9781599903866, Bloomsbury USA Childrens) Bloomsbury Publishing USA.

Russell, James. The Dragon Riders. Choi, Link, illus. 2017. (Dragon Brothers Ser.: 3). (ENG.). 32p. (J). (-4). 16.99 **(978-1-4926-4867-3(1)**, Sourcebooks Jabberwocky) Sourcebooks, Inc.

Ryan, Candace. Ewe & Aye. Ruble, Stephanie, illus. 2014. (ENG.). 40p. (J). (gr. -1-k). 17.99 (978-1-4231-7591-9(3)) Hyperion Bks. for Children.

Spinelli, Eileen. Buzz. Nguyen, Vincent, illus. 2010. (ENG.). 32p. (J). (gr. -1-3). 17.99 (978-1-4169-4925-1(9), Simon & Schuster Bks. For Young Readers) Simon & Schuster Bks. For Young Readers.

Stamp, Jørgen & Buckley, William F., Jr. Flying High. 2009. (ENG., Illus.). 32p. (J). (gr. -1-2). 16.95 (978-1-59270-089-9(6)) Enchanted Lion Bks., LLC.

Steers, Billy. Tractor Mac Learns to Fly. (Tractor Mac Ser.). (ENG., Illus.). (J). 2016. 24p. pap. 4.99 (978-0-374-30537-6(4), 9780374305376) 2015. 32p. (gr. -1-2). 8.99 (978-0-374-30103-3(4), 9780374301033) Farrar, Straus & Giroux. (Farrar, Straus & Giroux (BYR)).

—Tractor Mac Learns to Fly. 2016. (Tractor Mac Ser.). (J). lib. bdg. 14.75 (978-0-606-39558-8(X)) Turtleback Bks.

Stephas, Kristi. Flying Solo Smith, Rachael, illus. 2005. 40p. (J). 16.95 (978-0-9764983-2-2(4)) Toy Truck Publishing.

Stoeke, Janet Morgan. The Loopy Coop Hens. Stoeke, Janet Morgan, illus. 2013. (Loopy Coop Hens Ser.). (ENG., Illus.). 32p. (J). (gr. 1-2). mass mkt. 3.99 (978-0-448-46272-1(9), Penguin Young Readers) Penguin Young Readers Group.

Stoltz, Donald R. The Bubble Flight. Wiesner, Al, illus. 2008. 26p. pap. 24.95 (978-1-60672-994-6(2)) America Star Bks.

Sutton, Felix. We Were There at the First Airplane Flight. Matulay, Laszlo, illus. 2013. (ENG.). 192p. (J). (gr. 3-8). pap. 6.99 (978-0-486-49258-2(3)) Dover Pubns., Inc.

Tanaka, Shinsuke, illus. Wings. 2006. (ENG.). 80p. (J). (gr. -1). 14.95 (978-1-933327-19-8(7)) Purple Bear Bks., Inc.

Taylor, Theodore. The Boy Who Could Fly Without a Motor. 2004. (ENG., Illus.). 168p. (J). (gr. 2-5). pap. 11.95 (978-0-15-204767-2(0)) Houghton Mifflin Harcourt Publishing Co.

Terri, Branson. Brother Dragon. l.t. ed. 2007. (ENG., Illus.). 24p. (J). 14.99 (978-0-9787421-9-5(2)) Dragonfly Publishing, Inc.

Todd, Barbara. Edward & the Eureka Lucky Wish Company. Storms, Patricia, illus. 2009. (ENG.). 32p. (J). (gr. -1-2). 16.95 (978-1-55453-264-3(7)) Kids Can Pr., Ltd. CAN. Dist: Hachette Bk. Group.

Trent, Sandy Chase. Tommy's Amazing Journey: The Cat that Could Fly. 2011. 16p. pap. 24.95 (978-1-4626-2363-1(8)) America Star Bks.

Uhlberg, Myron. Flying over Brooklyn, 1 vol. Fitzgerald, Gerald, illus. 2003. (ENG.). 32p. (J). (gr. k-3). pap. 7.95 (978-1-56145-294-1(7)) Peachtree Pubs.

Walters, Eric. Skye Above, 1 vol. Parkins, David, illus. 2014. (Orca Echoes Ser.). (ENG.). 64p. (J). (gr. 2-3). pap. 6.95 (978-1-4598-0701-3(4)) Orca Bk. Pubs. USA.

Webb, Ramona. Tee & Tye Learn to Fly. Webb, Terris, illus. 2008. 20p. pap. 24.95 (978-1-60703-729-3(7)) America Star Bks.

Weinberg, Jennifer Liberts. Fly, Dumbo, Fly! Kurtz, John & Lo Raso, Carlo, illus. 2012. (Step into Reading Ser.). (ENG.). 32p. (J). (gr. -1-1). pap. 3.99 (978-0-7364-2044-0(4), RH/Disney) Random Hse. Children's Bks.

Wells, Helen. Cherry Ames, Flight Nurse. 2006. (Cherry Ames Nurse Stories Ser.). 224p. (J). (gr. 3-7). 14.95 (978-0-8261-0397-0(9)) Springer Publishing Co., Inc.

Willems, Mo. Let's Say Hi to Friends Who Fly! Willems, Mo, illus. 2010. (Illus.). 32p. (J). (gr. -1-3). (ENG.). 10.99 (978-0-06-172842-6(X)); lib. bdg. 14.89 (978-0-06-172846-4(2)) HarperCollins Pubs.

Willis, Ben. Ben's Flight South. 2010. 40p. pap. 16.99 (978-1-4520-4633-4(6)) AuthorHouse.

Willis, Jeanne. Fly, Chick, Fly! Ross, Tony, illus. 2012. (Andersen Press Picture Bks). (ENG.). 32p. (J). (gr. -1-3). 16.95 (978-1-4677-0314-7(1)) Lerner Publishing Group.

Wishinsky, Frieda. Flying High! Griffiths, Dean & Owlkids Books Inc. Staff, illus. 2007. (Canadian Flyer Adventures Ser.: 5). (ENG.). 96p. (J). (gr. 1-4). per. 7.95 (978-1-897066-99-7(6), Owlkids) Owlkids Bks. Inc. CAN. Dist: Publishers Group West (PGW).

Yeoman, John. Up with Birds! 2013. (ENG., Illus.). 32p. (J). (gr. k-2). pap. 11.99 (978-1-84939-651-6(5)) Andersen Pr. GBR. Dist: Independent Pubs. Group.

Zullo, Germano. Little Bird. Albertine, illus. 2012. (ENG.). 72p. (J). (gr. k). 16.95 (978-1-59270-118-6(3)) Enchanted Lion Bks., LLC.

FLIGHT ATTENDANTS

Thomas, William David. Flight Attendant. 2009. (Cool Careers: on the Go Ser.). 32p. (gr. 5-8). (J). pap. 10.50 (978-1-4339-0167-6(6)); (YA). lib. bdg. 26.00 (978-1-4339-0003-7(3)) Stevens, Gareth Publishing LLLP.

FLIGHT TO THE MOON

see Space Flight to the Moon

FLIGHT TRAINING

see Airplanes—Piloting

FLIGHTS AROUND THE WORLD

see Aeronautics—Flights

FLOATS (PARADES)

see Parades

FLOODS

see also Reclamation of Land; Rivers

Baker, John R. The World's Worst Floods. 2016. (World's Worst Natural Disasters Ser.). (ENG., Illus.). 32p. (gr. 1-2). lib. bdg. 26.65 (978-1-5157-1787-4(9)) Capstone Press of Coughlan Cos.

Barber, Nicola, et al. Inside Fires & Floods. 2006. (Inside Nature's Disasters Ser.). (Illus.). 36p. (gr. 3-7). lib. bdg. 26.00 (978-0-8368-7248-4(7), Gareth Stevens Learning Library) Stevens, Gareth Publishing LLLP.

Bauer, Marion Dane. Flood! Wallace, John, illus. 2008. (Natural Disasters Ser.). (ENG.). 32p. (J). (gr. -1-1). pap. 3.99 (978-1-4169-2553-8(8), Simon Spotlight) Simon Spotlight.

Brimner, Larry Dane. The Rain Wizard: The Amazing, Mysterious, True Life of Charles Mallory Hatfield. 2015. (ENG., Illus.). 80p. (J). (gr. 3-7). 16.95 (978-1-59078-990-2(3), Calkins Creek) Boyds Mills Pr.

Ceban, Bonnie J. Floods & Mudslides: Disaster & Survival. 2005. (Deadly Disasters Ser.). (Illus.). 48p. (J). (gr. 4-10). lib. bdg. 25.27 (978-0-7660-2389-5(3)) Enslow Pubs., Inc.

Coster, Patience. Rain & Floods. 2010. (Weatherwise Ser.). 32p. (ENG.). (J). pap. 10.60 (978-1-61532-274-9(4), PowerKids Pr.); (Illus.). (YA). (gr. 3-6). lib. bdg. 26.50 (978-1-61532-261-9(2)) Rosen Publishing Group, Inc., The.

Cox Cannons, Helen. Rain, 1 vol. 2014. (Weather Wise Ser.). (ENG., Illus.). 24p. (gr. -1-1). pap. 5.99 (978-1-4846-0555-4(1), Acorn) Heinemann-Raintree.

Davis, Graeme. Floods. 2012. (21st Century Skills Library: Real World Math Ser.). (ENG., Illus.). 32p. (J). (gr. 4-8). pap. 14.21 (978-1-61080-409-7(0), 201341); lib. bdg. 28.50 (978-1-61080-324-3(8), 201304) Cherry Lake Publishing.

Doeden, Matt. Inundaciones/Floods, 1 vol. 2010. (Tierra en Acción/Earth in Action Ser.). (MUL, SPA & ENG.). 24p. (gr. k-1). lib. bdg. 26.65 (978-1-4296-6121-8(6)) Capstone Press of Coughlan Cos.

Donnelly, Karen. Floods of the Past & the Future. 2009. (Earth's Changing Weather & Climate Ser.). 24p. (gr. 4-4). 42.50 (978-1-61512-245-5(1), PowerKids Pr.) Rosen Publishing Group, Inc., The.

Donnelly, Karen J. Floods of the Past & Future. 2003. (Earth's Changing Weather & Climate Ser.). (Illus.). 24p. (J). lib. bdg. 22.60 (978-0-8239-6218-1(0)) Rosen Publishing Group, Inc., The.

Dougherty, Terri. Anatomy of a Flood. 2011. (Disasters Ser.). (ENG.). 48p. (gr. 3-4). pap. 59.70 (978-1-4296-7356-3(7)); lib. bdg. 31.99 (978-1-4296-6021-1(X)) Capstone Press of Coughlan Cos.

Dougherty, Terri & Wacholtz, Anthony. The Worst Floods of All Time, 1 vol. 2012. (Epic Disasters Ser.). (ENG., Illus.). 32p. (gr. 3-4). lib. bdg. 27.99 (978-1-4296-8415-6(1)) Capstone Press of Coughlan Cos.

Dougherty, Terri, et al. Sports Debate: A Rip-Roaring Game of Either-Or Questions. 2012. (This or That? Ser.). (ENG., Illus.). 32p. (gr. 3-4). pap. 8.29 (978-1-4296-9276-2(6)) Capstone Press of Coughlan Cos.

Draper, Penny. Red River Raging, 1 vol. 2014. (Disaster Strikes! Ser.: 8). (ENG.). 168p. (J). (gr. 5-8). pap. 8.95 (978-1-55050-584-9(X)) Coteau Bks. CAN. Dist: Orca Bk. Pubs. USA.

Dwyer, Helen. Floods. 2010. (Eyewitness Disaster Ser.). 32p. (J). (gr. 2-5). 28.50 (978-1-60870-002-8(X)) Marshall Cavendish GBR. Dist: Marshall Cavendish Corp.

Eagen, Rachel. Flood & Monsoon Alert! 3rd rev. ed. 2011. (ENG., Illus.). 32p. (J). pap. (978-0-7787-1624-2(4)) Crabtree Publishing Co.

Elkins, Elizabeth. Investigating Floods. 2017. (Investigating Natural Disasters Ser.). (ENG., Illus.). 32p. (gr. 3-4). lib. bdg. 27.99 (978-1-5157-4040-7(4), Edge Bks.) Capstone Press of Coughlan Cos.

Farndon, John. Extreme Fires & Floods. 2017. (When Nature Attacks Ser.). (ENG., Illus.). 32p. (J). (gr. 3-6). 26.65 **(978-1-5124-3221-3(0)**, Hungry Tomato (r)) Lerner Publishing Group.

Ganeri, Anita. Rain. 2004. (Weather Around You Ser.). (Illus.). 24p. (gr. 1-4). pap. 8.15 (978-0-8368-4304-0(5)); lib. bdg. 22.00 (978-0-8368-4299-9(5)) Stevens, Gareth Publishing LLLP. (Weekly Reader Leveled Readers).

Gonzales, Doreen. Floods & Tsunamis. 2012. (Killer Disasters Ser.). (ENG., Illus.). 24p. (J). (gr. 3-6). pap. 8.25 (978-1-4488-7511-5(0)); lib. bdg. 22.60 (978-1-4488-7438-5(6)) Rosen Publishing Group, Inc., The. (PowerKids Pr.).

Gray-Wilburn, Renée & Kalz, Jill. Floods: Be Aware & Prepare, 1 vol. 2014. (Weather Aware Ser.). (ENG.). 32p. (gr. 1-2). lib. bdg. 27.32 (978-1-4765-9904-5(1)) Capstone Press of Coughlan Cos.

Green, Jen. 1993 Mississippi River Floods. 2005. (Disasters Ser.). (Illus.). 32p. (gr. 2-6). lib. bdg. 26.00 (978-0-8368-4495-5(5), Gareth Stevens Learning Library) Stevens, Gareth Publishing LLLP.

Greenlaw, M. Jean. Flood. 2014. (It's a Disaster! Ser.). 24p. (J). (gr. -1-3). lib. bdg. 23.93 (978-1-62724-129-8(9)) Bearport Publishing Co., Inc.

—Inundacion. 2014. (Pedacitos Primeros Lectores: Que Desastre! Ser.). (SPA., Illus.). 24p. (J). (gr. -1-2). lib. bdg. 23.93 (978-1-62724-250-9(3)) Bearport Publishing Co., Inc.

Hamilton, S. L. Floods. 2012. 32p. 27.07 (978-1-61783-260-4(X), Abdo & Daughters) ABDO Publishing Co.

Howse, Jennifer. Floods. 2016. (J). **(978-1-5105-2075-2(9))** SmartBook Media, Inc.

Huey, Lois Miner. Floodwaters & Flames: The 1913 Disaster in Dayton, Ohio. 2016. (ENG., Illus.). 56p. (gr. 4-8). (J). lib. bdg. 33.32 (978-1-4677-9432-9(5)); 50.65 (978-1-4677-9728-3(6)) Lerner Publishing Group. (Millbrook Pr.).

Jeffrey, Gary. Tsunamis & Floods. 2009. (Graphic Natural Disasters Ser.). (ENG.). 48p. (YA). (gr. 5-5). 58.50 (978-1-61513-005-4(5), Rosen Reference) Rosen Publishing Group, Inc., The.

Jeffrey, Gary, illus. Tsunamis & Floods. 2007. (Graphic Natural Disasters Ser.). (ENG.). 48p. (J). (gr. 5-9). lib. bdg. 31.95 (978-1-4042-1990-8(0)) Rosen Publishing Group, Inc., The.

Johnson, Robin. What Is a Flood? 2016. (ENG., Illus.). 24p. (J). (978-0-7787-2396-7(8)) Crabtree Publishing Co.

Katirgis, Jane & Drohan, Michele Ingber. Frightening Floods. 2015. (Earth's Natural Disasters Ser.). (ENG., Illus.). 32p. (J). (gr. 3-4). 25.27 (978-0-7660-6799-8(8)) Enslow Pubs., Inc.

Katirgis, Jane & Ingber Drohan, Michele. Frightening Floods. 2015. (Earth's Natural Disasters Ser.). (ENG.). 32p. (J). (gr. 3-4). pap. 10.52 (978-0-7660-6797-4(1)) Enslow Pubs., Inc.

Kenah, Katharine. Flood Warning. Schimler-Safford, Amy, illus. 2016. (Let's-Read-And-Find-Out Science 2 Ser.). 40p. (J). (gr. -1-3). pap. 6.99 (978-0-06-238661-8(1)) HarperCollins Pubs.

Kline, Lisa Williams. Floods. 2004. (J). 27.45 (978-1-59018-132-4(8), Lucent Bks.) Cengage Gale.

Knox, Barbara. Flood! The 1993 Midwest Downpours. 2006. (X-Treme Disasters That Changed America Ser.). (Illus.). 32p. (J). (gr. 2-5). lib. bdg. 25.27 (978-1-59716-172-5(1)) Bearport Publishing Co., Inc.

Koponen, Libby. Floods. 2009. (True Book(tm), a — Earth Science Ser.). (ENG.). 48p. (J). (gr. 2-5). 31.00

(978-0-531-16883-7(2)); pap. 6.95 (978-0-531-21351-3(X), Children's Pr.) Scholastic Library Publishing.

Kops, Deborah. The Great Molasses Flood. 2015. (ENG.). 112p. (J). (gr. 4-7). pap. 11.95 (978-1-58089-349-7(X)) Charlesbridge Publishing, Inc.

—The Great Molasses Flood: Boston 1919. 2015. lib. bdg. 23.25 (978-0-606-36650-2(4)) Turtleback Bks.

Kusky, Timothy. Floods: Hazards of Surface & Groundwater Systems. 2008. (Hazardous Earth Ser.). (Illus.). 144p. (gr. 6-12). 39.50 (978-0-8160-6468-7(7)) Facts On File, Inc.

Lay, Kathryn. Attack of the Giant Flood, 1 vol., Vol. 5. Wolff, Jason, illus. 2011. (Wendy's Weather Warriors Ser.). (ENG.). 80p. (gr. 2-5). 27.07 (978-1-60270-758-0(8), Calico Chapter Bks) Magic Wagon.

Levy, Janey. World's Worst Floods. 2009. (Deadly Disasters Ser.). 24p. (gr. 2-6). pap. 9.40 (978-1-4042-4540-2(5), Rosen Classroom); (gr. 2-3). 42.50 (978-1-61512-140-3(4), PowerKids Pr.); (Illus.). (J). lib. bdg. 22.60 (978-1-4042-4516-7(2), PowerKids Pr.) Rosen Publishing Group, Inc., The.

Linde, Barbara M. When Floods Flow. 2015. (Eye on the Sky Ser.). (ENG., Illus.). 32p. (J). (gr. 3-4). pap. 10.50 (978-1-4824-2880-3(6)) Stevens, Gareth Publishing LLLP.

Markle, Sandra. Thirsty, Thirsty Elephants. Vanden Broeck, Fabricio, illus. 2017. (ENG.). 32p. (J). (gr. -1-2). lib. bdg. 16.99 (978-1-58089-634-4(0)) Charlesbridge Publishing, Inc.

Marquardt, Meg. The Science of a Flood. 2015. (21st Century Skills Library: Disaster Science Ser.). (ENG., Illus.). 32p. (J). (gr. 4-8). 29.93 (978-1-63362-479-5(X), 206824) Cherry Lake Publishing.

Marsico, Katie. The Wettest & the Driest. 2015. (True Book(tm), a — Extreme Places Ser.). (ENG., Illus.). 48p. (J). lib. bdg. 31.00 (978-0-531-21847-1(3), Children's Pr.) Scholastic Library Publishing.

Mattern, Joanne. Floods. 2015. (ENG.). 48p. (gr. 3-6). 35.64 (978-1-63430-427-6(6)) Rourke Educational Media.

—Floods, Dams, & Levees. 2011. (ENG., Illus.). 48p. (J). (gr. 4-6). pap. 10.95 (978-1-61741-988-1(5)) Rourke Educational Media.

McElligott, Matthew. Mad Scientist Academy: the Weather Disaster. 2016. (Mad Scientist Academy Ser.: 2). (ENG., Illus.). 40p. (J). (gr. k-3). 17.99 (978-0-553-52376-8(7), Crown Books For Young Readers) Random Hse. Children's Bks.

Menon, Sujatha. Fire & Flood. 2007. (Wild Nature Ser.). (Illus.). 48p. (YA). (gr. 3-6). lib. bdg. 29.25 (978-1-4042-3899-2(9)) Rosen Publishing Group, Inc., The.

—Fire & Floods. 2009. (Wild Nature Ser.). 48p. (gr. 4-5). 53.00 (978-1-60854-793-7(0), PowerKids Pr.) Rosen Publishing Group, Inc., The.

Michele, Tracey. When Can A Flood Happen? 2014. (Little Books of Answers: Level d Ser.). (Illus.). 16p. (gr. k-2). pap. 7.95 (978-1-927136-35-5(0)) Three Crows Media NZL. Dist: RiverStream Publishing.

Miller, Petra. Floods. 2015. lib. bdg. (978-1-62713-523-8(5)) Cavendish Square Publishing.

Minden, Cecilia. Floods! 2010. (21st Century Basic Skills Library: Natural Disasters Ser.). (ENG.). 24p. (gr. k-3). lib. bdg. 22.79 (978-1-60279-866-3(4), 200598) Cherry Lake Publishing.

Murray, Peter. Floods. 2015. (Forces of Nature Ser.). (ENG.). 24p. (J). (gr. 2-5). 27.07 (978-1-63143-765-6(8), 208605) Child's World, Inc., The.

Orr, Tamra B. Forecasting a Flood. 2014. (Explorer Library: Follow the Clues Ser.). (ENG.). 32p. (J). (gr. 4-8). 28.50 (978-1-62431-778-1(2), 203308) Cherry Lake Publishing.

Oxlade, Chris. Floods in Action. (Natural Disasters in Action Ser.). (Illus.). 48p. 2009. (ENG.). (gr. 5-8). pap. 11.75 (978-1-4358-5137-5(4), Rosen Reference) 2008. (J). lib. bdg. 29.25 (978-1-4042-1867-3(X)) Rosen Publishing Group, Inc., The.

Perish, Patrick. Survive a Flood. 2016. (Survival Zone Ser.). (ENG., Illus.). 24p. (J). (gr. 3-7). 25.95 (978-1-62617-442-9(3), Torque Bks.) Bellwether Media.

Portman, Michael. Deadly Floods. 2012. (Angry Earth Ser.). (ENG.). 32p. (gr. 3-6). (J). pap. 10.50 (978-1-4339-6535-7(6), Gareth Stevens Learning Library); (YA). lib. bdg. 26.60 (978-1-4339-6533-3(X)) Stevens, Gareth Publishing LLLP.

Pratt, Mary K. Hurricane Katrina & the Flooding of New Orleans: A Cause-And-Effect Investigation. 2016. (Cause-And-Effect Disasters Ser.). (ENG., Illus.). 40p. (J). (gr. 4-6). lib. bdg. 30.65 (978-1-5124-1117-1(5)); 46.65 (978-1-5124-1128-7(0), Lerner Pubns.) Lerner Publishing Group.

Prentzas, G. S. Floods, Flash Floods, & Mudslides: A Practical Survival Guide. 2005. (Library of Emergency Preparedness Ser.). (Illus.). 64p. (YA). (gr. 5-9). lib. bdg. 31.95 (978-1-4042-0534-5(9)) Rosen Publishing Group, Inc., The.

Prokos, Anna & Keedle, Jayne. Tsunamis & Floods. 2008. (Ultimate 10 Ser.). (Illus.). 48p. (J). (gr. 5-9). lib. bdg. 31.00 (978-0-8368-9154-6(6)) Stevens, Gareth Publishing LLLP.

Raum, Elizabeth. Flood! 2016. (Natural Disasters Ser.). (ENG., Illus.). 32p. (J). (gr. k-3). 20.95 (978-1-60753-990-2(X)) Amicus Publishing.

—Surviving Floods, 1 vol. 2011. (Children's True Stories: Natural Disasters Ser.). (ENG.). 32p. (gr. 3-3). pap. 8.29 (978-1-4109-4098-8(5)); 30.65 (978-1-4109-4091-9(8)) Heinemann-Raintree. (Raintree Perspectives).

Reher, Matt. Beware of Floods. 2016. (2R Science Ser.). (ENG., Illus.). 28p. (J). pap. 5.99 **(978-1-63437-722-5(2))** American Reading Co.

Rice, William B. Las Inundaciones y las Ventiscas, 1 vol. rev. ed. 2010. (Science Readers: a Closer Look Ser.).Tr. of Floods & Blizzards. (SPA., Illus.). 32p. (J). (gr. 2-3). pap. 8.99 (978-1-4333-2157-3(2)) Shell Educational Publishing.

Richards, Marlee. The Johnstown Flood: Core Events of Deadly Disaster, 1 vol. 2014. (What Went Wrong? Ser.). (ENG.). 32p. (gr. 3-4). pap. 7.95 (978-1-4765-5131-9(6)); lib. bdg. 27.32 (978-1-4765-4182-2(5)) Capstone Press of Coughlan Cos. (Fact Finders).

Sepahban, Lois. Floods. 2013. (Illus.). 48p. (J). pap. 15.64 (978-1-62403-003-1(3)); (ENG., (gr. 3-6). lib. bdg. 32.79 (978-1-61783-938-2(8)) ABDO Publishing Co.

Shulman, Mark. Super Storms That Rocked the World: Hurricanes, Tsunamis, & Other Disasters. 2007. (Illus.). 40p. (J). (978-0-696-23702-7(4)) Meredith Bks.

Silverstein, Alvin, et al. Floods: The Science Behind Raging Waters & Mudslides. 2009. (Science Behind Natural Disasters Ser.). (Illus.). 48p. (J). (gr. 5-9). lib. bdg. 25.27 (978-0-7660-2974-3(3)) Enslow Pubs., Inc.

Spilsbury, Louise & Spilsbury, Richard. Raging Floods, 1 vol. 2nd ed. 2010. (Awesome Forces of Nature Ser.). (ENG., Illus.). 32p. (gr. 3-6). 33.32 (978-1-4329-3782-9(0)); pap. 8.29 (978-1-4329-3789-8(8)) Heinemann-Raintree. (Heinemann InfoSearch).

—Top 10 Worst Floods. 2016. (Nature's Ultimate Disasters Ser.). 00032p. (J). (gr. 3-4). pap. 10.00 (978-1-4994-3073-8(6), PowerKids Pr.) Rosen Publishing Group, Inc., The.

Steele, Philip, et al. Extreme Planet. 2014. (Illus.). 128p. (J). (978-1-4351-5523-7(8)) Barnes & Noble, Inc.

Stein, Paul. Floods of the Future. 2009. (Library of Future Weather & Climate Ser.). 64p. (gr. 5-5). 58.50 (978-1-60853-645-0(9)) Rosen Publishing Group, Inc., The.

Ventura, Marne. Detecting Floods. 2017. (Detecting Disasters (paperback) Ser.). (ENG., Illus.). 32p. (J). (gr. 4-7). pap. 9.95 **(978-1-63517-058-0(3)**, Focus Readers) North Star Editions.

Ventura, Marne. How to Survive a Flood. 2015. (Survival Guides). (ENG.). 24p. (J). (gr. 2-5). 27.07 (978-1-60973-158-8(1), 208791) Child's World, Inc., The.

Villa, Alvaro F., illus. Flood. 1 vol. 2013. (ENG.). 32p. (gr. 1-3). 15.95 (978-1-62370-001-0(9)) Capstone Press of Coughlan Cos.

Winget, Mary. Floods. 2009. pap. 40.95 (978-0-7613-4768-2(2)) 2008. (ENG.). 32p. 22.60 (978-0-8225-8830-6(7), Lerner Pubns.) Lerner Publishing Group.

Woods, Michael & Woods, Mary B. Floods. 2007. (Disasters up Close Ser.). (ENG., Illus.). 64p. (gr. 4-8). lib. bdg. 27.93 (978-0-8225-4712-9(0), Lerner Pubns.) Lerner Publishing Group.

World Book, Inc Staff, contrib. by. Floods. (J). 2007. (978-0-7166-9805-0(6)) 2nd ed. 2009. (Illus.). 47p. (978-0-7166-9821-0(8)) World Bk., Inc.

Yasuda, Anita. Yu the Great Conquers the Flood: A Chinese Nature Myth. 2014. (Short Tales Chinese Myths Ser.). 32p. (J). (gr. 3-6). lib. bdg. 24.21 (978-1-62402-035-3(6), Short Tales) Magic Wagon.

FLOODS—FICTION

Anderson, T. Neill. City of the Dead: Galveston Hurricane 1900. 2013. (J). pap. 16.95 (978-1-58089-515-6(8)); (ENG., Illus.). 144p. (YA). (gr. 7). 16.95 (978-1-58089-514-9(X)) Charlesbridge Publishing, Inc.

Bates, Sonya. Thunder Creek Ranch, 1 vol. Charko, Kasia, illus. 2013. (Orca Echoes Ser.). (ENG.). 64p. (J). (gr. 2-3). pap. 6.95 (978-1-4598-0112-7(1)) Orca Bk. Pubs. USA.

Bentley, Sue. Friendship Forever. 2013. (Magic Puppy Ser.: 10). lib. bdg. 14.75 (978-0-606-32123-5(3), Turtleback) Turtleback Bks.

—Friendship Forever #10. Swan, Angela, illus. 2013. (Magic Puppy Ser.: 10). (ENG.). 128p. (J). (gr. 1-3). 5.99 (978-0-448-46733-7(X), Grosset & Dunlap) Penguin Young Readers Group.

Bird, Benjamin. Bubble Trouble! Levins, Tim, illus. 2015. (Amazing Adventures of Superman! Ser.). (ENG.). 32p. (gr. k-2). pap. 3.95 (978-1-4795-6524-5(5), DC Super Heroes) Stone Arch Bks.

Boeve, Eunice. The Summer of the Crow. 2013. 306p. pap. 14.95 (978-1-939054-06-7(0)) Rowe Publishing and Design.

Capstone Press Staff. Flood, 1 vol. Vila, Alvaro F., illus. 2013. (Fiction Picture Bks.). (ENG.). 32p. (gr. 1-3). 22.60 (978-1-4048-8006-1(2), Fiction Picture Bks.) Picture Window Bks.

Coleman, Claudia. Yo Yo & the Great Flood. 2008. 100p. pap. 22.95 (978-1-60145-606-9(9)) Booklocker.com, Inc.

Collier, Kristen & Collier, Kevin. Natalie's Ark. 2009. 84p. pap. 8.95 (978-1-61633-007-1(4)) Guardian Angel Publishing, Inc.

Coughlin, Shirley. Beyond the Flood. 2011. 68p. pap. 12.50 (978-1-60976-710-5(1), Eloquent Bks.) Strategic Book Publishing & Rights Agency (SBPRA).

Cowley, Joy. Big Bear & Little Bear: Puddle. Lam, Amy, illus. 2013. (ENG.). 8p. pap. (978-1-927186-34-3(X), Joy Cowley Club) Flying Start Bks.

Duey, Kathleen & Bale, Karen A. Flood: Mississippi 1927. 2015. (Survivors Ser.). (ENG., Illus.). 176p. (J). (gr. 3-7). pap. 6.99 (978-1-4814-1642-9(1), Aladdin) Simon & Schuster Children's Publishing.

Flaherty, Mildred. The Great Saint Patrick's Day Flood. 2004. (Illus.). 104p. (J). pap. (978-0-9711835-8-2(9)) Local History Co., The.

Gilliland, C., compiled by. The Great Flood. 2007. 108p. pap. 10.95 (978-0-89992-168-6(X)) Council for Indian Education.

Gottesfeld, Jeff. Killer Flood, 1 vol. 2014. (Red Rhino Ser.). (ENG.). 64p. (J). (gr. 4-6). pap. 7.95 (978-1-62250-946-1(3)) Saddleback Educational Publishing, Inc.

Greene, Janice. The Eye of the Hurricane, 1 vol. unabr. ed. 2010. (Q Reads Ser.). (ENG.). 32p. (YA). (gr. 9-12). pap. 6.95 (978-1-61651-191-3(5)) Saddleback Educational Publishing, Inc.

Hanson, Bonnie Compton. A Stormy Spring. 2004. (Ponytail Girls Ser.). (Illus.). 192p. (J). pap. 7.99 (978-1-58411-032-3(5), Legacy Pr.) Rainbow Pubs. & Legacy Pr.

Johnson, Rebecca. Big Flood. 2017. (Juliet, Nearly a Vet Ser.: 11). (ENG.). 96p. (J). (gr. 3-5). 8.99 **(978-0-14-350703-1(6))** Random Hse. Australia AUS. Dist: Independent Pubs. Group.

Karwoski, Gail Langer. When Hurricane Katrina Hit Home. Marshall, Julia, illus. 2013. Orig. Title: When Hurricane Katrina Hit Home. (ENG.). 192p. (gr. 4-7). 15.99 (978-1-62619-083-2(6), History Pr., The) Arcadia Publishing.

Kehret, Peg. Flood Disaster. 2008. (ENG.). 160p. (J). (gr. 3-7). pap. 8.99 (978-1-4169-9109-0(3), Simon & Schuster/Paula Wiseman Bks.) Simon & Schuster/Paula Wiseman Bks.

Kurtz, Jane. River Friendly, River Wild. Brennan, Neil, illus. 2007. (ENG.). 40p. (J). (gr. -1-3). 7.99 (978-1-4169-3487-5(1), Simon & Schuster/Paula Wiseman Bks.) Simon & Schuster/Paula Wiseman Bks.

MacLachlan, Patricia. Fly Away. 2014. (ENG., Illus.). 128p. (J). (gr. 2). 15.99 (978-1-4424-6008-9(3), McElderry, Margaret K. Bks.) McElderry, Margaret K. Bks.

Manos, John. Big Ben Helps the Town. 2006. (Early Explorers Ser.). (J). pap. (978-1-4108-6119-1(8)) Benchmark Education Co.

Manushkin, Fran. Too Much Rain, 1 vol. Lyon, Tammie, illus. 2009. (Katie Woo Ser.). (ENG.). 32p. (gr. k-2). 21.32 (978-1-4048-5494-9(0)) Picture Window Bks.

Maria, Miss Yvonne. Beautiful Black Mermaids of the Bayou, 1 vol. 2009. 48p. pap. 16.95 (978-1-60836-236-3(1)) America Star Bks.

McKee, David. Elmer & the Flood. McKee, David, illus. 2015. (ENG., Illus.). 32p. (J). (gr. -1-3). 17.99 (978-1-4677-9314-8(0)); 17.99 (978-1-4677-9312-4(4)) Lerner Publishing Group.

Monninger, Joseph. Flood. 2014. (Stay Alive Ser.: 4). lib. bdg. 16.00 (978-0-606-36065-4(4)) Turtleback Bks.

Mullarkey, John & Mullarkey, Lisa. Johnstown Flood: An Up2U Historical Fiction Adventure, 1 vol. Martin, Dana, illus. 2013. (Up2U Adventures Ser.). (ENG.). 80p. (J). (gr. 2-5). lib. bdg. 27.07 (978-1-61641-967-7(9), Calico Chapter Bks) Magic Wagon.

Nowra, Louis. Into That Forest. 2013. 162p. 16.99 (978-1-4778-6725-9(2)) Amazon Publishing.

O'Ryan, Ellie, adapted by. Ice Age 2: The Meltdown: Join the Pack! 2006. (I Can Read Bks.). (Illus.). 31p. (J). (978-1-4156-5155-1(8)) HarperCollins Pubs.

Pearce, Jacqueline. Flood Warning, 1 vol. Franson, Leanne, illus. 2012. (Orca Echoes Ser.). (ENG.). 64p. (J). (gr. 2-3). pap. 6.95 (978-1-4598-0068-7(0)) Orca Bk. Pubs. USA.

Richards, Jame. Three Rivers Rising. 2011. (ENG.). 306p. (YA). (gr. 7). pap. 8.99 (978-0-375-85369-2(3), Ember) Random Hse. Children's Bks.

Rosenberg, Aaron. Flood: Race Against Time. 2016. (S. T. E. M. Squad Ser.). (ENG.). 224p. (J). (gr. 3-10). pap. 7.99 (978-1-4380-0805-9(8)) Barron's Educational Series, Inc.

Smiley, Jeremy. The Flood of Mice City 2, 1 vol. 2010. 36p. 24.95 (978-1-4489-7617-1(0)) PublishAmerica, Inc.

Sutton, Sally. Farmer John's Tractor. Belton, Robyn, illus. 2013. (ENG.). 32p. (J). (gr. -1-2). 15.99 (978-0-7636-6430-5(8)) Candlewick Pr.

Tarshis, Lauren. I Survived Hurricane Katrina 2005. 2011. (I Survived Ser.: 3). (ENG.). 112p. (J). (gr. 3-7). pap. 4.99 (978-0-545-20696-9(0), Scholastic Paperbacks) Scholastic, Inc.

—I Survived Hurricane Katrina 2005. 2011. (I Survived ... Ser.: No. 3). lib. bdg. 14.75 (978-0-606-23743-7(7), Turtleback) Turtleback Bks.

Tomos, Angharad. Stremplan. 2005. (WEL., Illus.). 48p. pap. (978-0-86243-127-3(1)) Y Lolfa.

Uhlberg, Myron. A Storm Called Katrina, 1 vol. Bootman, Colin, illus. 2015. (ENG.). 40p. (J). (gr. 2-4). pap. 8.95 (978-1-56145-887-5(2)) Peachtree Pubs.

—A Storm Called Katrina. 2015. lib. bdg. 19.60 (978-0-606-37467-5(1)) Turtleback Bks.

Villa, Alvaro F., illus. Flood. 2013. (Fiction Picture Bks.). (ENG.). 32p. (gr. 1-3). 9.95 (978-1-4795-2256-9(2), Fiction Picture Bks.) Picture Window Bks.

Vivian, Siobhan. The Last Boy & Girl in the World. 2016. (ENG., Illus.). 432p. (YA). (gr. 9). 17.99 (978-1-4814-5229-8(0), Simon & Schuster Bks. For Young Readers) Simon & Schuster Bks. For Young Readers.

Woods, Brenda. Saint Louis Armstrong Beach. 2012. lib. bdg. 16.00 (978-0-606-26661-1(5), Turtleback) Turtleback Bks.

Yeoman, John. Mr. Nodd's Ark. Blake, Quentin, illus. 2016. (ENG.). 32p. (J). (-k). pap. 9.99 (978-1-78344-374-1(X)) Andersen Pr. GBR. Dist: Independent Pubs. Group.

FLOODS—PENNSYLVANIA—JOHNSTOWN (CAMBRIA COUNTY)

Gow, Mary. Johnstown Flood: The Day the Dam Burst. 2003. (American Disasters Ser.). (Illus.). 48p. (J). (gr. 4-10). lib. bdg. 25.27 (978-0-7660-2109-9(2)) Enslow Pubs., Inc.

Koestler-Grack, Rachel A. The Johnstown Flood Of 1889. 2008. (Great Historic Disasters Ser.). (Illus.). 104p. (gr. 5-8). 35.00 (978-0-7910-9763-2(3), Chelsea Hse.) Facts On File, Inc.

Leathers, Daniel. The Johnstown Flood 1889. 2007. (Natural Disasters Ser.). (Illus.). 32p. (J). (gr. 1-4). lib. bdg. 25.70 (978-1-58415-570-6(1)) Mitchell Lane Pubs., Inc.

FLORA

see Botany; Plants

FLORAL DECORATION

see Flower Arrangement

FLORAL DESIGN

see Design, Decorative

FLORENCE (ITALY)

Dyan, Penelope. Walk the Renaissance Walk — -A Kid's Guide to Florence, Italy. Weigand, John D., photos by. 2009. (Illus.). 42p. pap. 11.95 (978-1-935118-70-1(6)) Bellissima Publishing, LLC.

Ford, Nick. Niccolò Machiavelli: Florentine Statesman, Playwright, & Poet. 2009. (Rulers, Scholars, & Artists of the Renaissance Ser.). 112p. (gr. 5-8). 66.50 (978-1-60852-943-8(6), Rosen Reference) Rosen Publishing Group, Inc., The.

Hancock, Lee. Lorenzo de' Medici: Florence's Great Leader & Patron of the Arts. 2009. (Rulers, Scholars, & Artists of the Renaissance Ser.). 112p. (gr. 5-8). 66.50 (978-1-60852-942-1(8), Rosen Reference) Rosen Publishing Group, Inc., The.

Kids Go Europe: Treasure Hunt Florence. 2006. (J). spiral bd. 9.95 (978-0-9772699-1-4(4)) Kids Go Europe, Inc.

Rossi, Renzo. In Renaissance Florence with Leonardo. Baldanzi, Alessandro, illus. 2008. (Come See My City Ser.). 48p. (gr. 4-8). lib. bdg. 28.50 (978-0-7614-4329-2(0), Benchmark Bks.) Marshall Cavendish Corp.

Wagner, Heather Lehr. Machiavelli: Renaissance Political Analyst & Author. 2005. (Makers of the Middle Ages & Renaissance Ser.). (Illus.). 136p. (gr. 5-8). lib. bdg. 32.95 (978-0-7910-8629-2(1), Chelsea Hse.) Facts On File, Inc.

—The Medicis: A Ruling Dynasty. 2005. (Makers of the Middle Ages & Renaissance Ser.). (Illus.). 168p. (gr. 5-8). lib. bdg. 32.95 (978-0-7910-8630-8(5), Chelsea Hse.) Facts On File, Inc.

FLORENCE (ITALY)—FICTION

Fern, Tracey E. Pippo the Fool. Estrada, Pau, illus. (ENG.). 48p. (J). (gr. k-3). 2011. pap. 7.95 (978-1-57091-793-6(0)) 2009. 15.95 (978-1-57091-655-7(1)) Charlesbridge Publishing, Inc.

Friedlander, Mark P., Jr. Innovators in Action! Leonardo Da Vinci Gets a Do-Over. Sakprayoonpong, Worachet Boon, illus. 2014. (Innovators in Action Ser.: 1). (ENG.). 208p. (J). (gr. 5-9). pap. 12.95 (978-0-9678020-6-0(7)) Science, Naturally!

Hopkins, Cathy. Mates, Dates, & Great Escapes. 2011. (Mates, Dates Ser.). (ENG.). 224p. (YA). (gr. 7). pap. 10.99 (978-1-4424-3080-8(X), Simon Pulse) Simon Pulse.

Hughes, Shirley. Hero on a Bicycle. 2013. (ENG., Illus.). 224p. (J). (gr. 5-9). 16.99 (978-0-7636-6037-6(X)) Candlewick Pr.

Kephart, Beth. One Thing Stolen. (ENG.). (YA). 2016. 296p. pap. 9.99 (978-1-4521-5213-4(6)) 2015. 272p. (gr. 7-12). 17.99 (978-1-4521-2831-3(6)) Chronicle Bks. LLC.

Lindner, April. Love, Lucy. (ENG.). 304p. (YA). (gr. 10-17). 2016. pap. 9.99 (978-0-316-40068-8(8)) 2015. 18.00 (978-0-316-40069-5(6)) Little, Brown Bks. for Young Readers. (Poppy).

Napoli, Donna Jo. The Smile. 2009. (ENG.). 272p. (YA). (gr. 7-18). 7.99 (978-0-14-241492-7(1), Speak) Penguin Young Readers Group.

Osborne, Mary A. Nonna's Book of Mysteries. 2010. (ENG., Illus.). 352p. (gr. 8-17). pap. 16.95 (978-1-936181-16-2(9)) Lake Street Pr.

Osborne, Mary Pope. Monday with a Mad Genius. Murdocca, Sal, illus. (Magic Tree House Merlin Mission Ser.: 10). (ENG.). (J). (gr. 2-5). 2009. 144p. 5.99 (978-0-375-83730-2(2)) 2007. 128p. 11.99 (978-0-375-83729-6(9)) Random Hse. Children's Bks. (Random Hse. Bks. for Young Readers).

—Monday with a Mad Genius. 2009. (Magic Tree House Merlin Missions Ser.: 10). lib. bdg. 16.00 (978-0-606-01777-0(1), Turtleback) Turtleback Bks.

Sabuda, Robert. Uh-Oh, Leonardo! The Adventures of Providence Traveler. Sabuda, Robert, illus. 2007. (ENG., Illus.). 48p. (J). (gr. k-3). 12.99 (978-1-4169-6164-2(X), Aladdin) Simon & Schuster Children's Publishing.

Sorrells, W. A. Florence Fiasco. Bancroft, Tom & Corley, Rob, illus. 2007. 136p. (J). (978-0-9792912-2-7(4)) KidsGive, LLC.

FLORICULTURE

see Flower Gardening

FLORIDA

Avery, Sherrie. Miami Metrozoo. 2003. (Great Zoos of the United States Ser.). (Illus.). 24p. (J). lib. bdg. 22.60 (978-0-8239-6316-4(0), PowerKids Pr.) Rosen Publishing Group, Inc., The.

Bredeson, Carmen. Florida. 2005. (Rookie Espanol: Geografia Ser.). (SPA., Illus.). 32p. (J). (gr. k-2). pap. 5.95 (978-0-516-25514-9(2), Children's Pr.) Scholastic Library Publishing.

—Florida. Risco, Eida del, tr. from ENG. Ancona, George, photos by. 2004. (Rookie Readers Spanish Ser.). (SPA., Illus.). 32p. (J). 19.50 (978-0-516-25108-0(2), Watts, Franklin) Scholastic Library Publishing.

Brown, Robin C. The Crafts of Florida's First People. 2003. (ENG., Illus.). 63p. (J). pap. 9.95 (978-1-56164-282-3(7)) Pineapple Pr., Inc.

Bruun, Erik. Florida. Peterson, Rick, illus. 2006. (ENG.). 48p. (J). (gr. -1-17). 9.95 (978-1-57912-231-7(0), 81231, Black Dog & Leventhal Pubs. Inc.) Hachette Bks.

Chui, Patricia. Florida. Porras, Carlos & D'Andrea, Patricia, trs. from ENG. 2003. (World Almanac Biblioteca de los Estados). (SPA., Illus.). 48p. (gr. 4-9). lib. bdg. 31.00 (978-0-8368-5543-2(4), Gareth Stevens Learning Library) Stevens, Gareth Publishing LLLP.

Costello, Emily. Realm of the Panther: A Story of South Florida's Forests. 2005. (Habitat Ser.). (ENG., Illus.). 32p. (J). (gr. 1-4). 19.95 (978-1-56899-849-7(X)) Soundprints.

—Realm of the Panther: A Story of South Florida's Forests. Siegrist, Wes, illus. 2005. (Habitat Ser.). (ENG.). 32p. (J). (gr. 1-4). 15.95 (978-1-56899-847-3(3)); pap. 6.95 (978-1-56899-848-0(1)) Soundprints.

Downey, Tika. Florida: The Sunshine State. (Illus.). 24p. (J). 2010. pap. 8.25 (978-1-4358-3338-8(4), 1300526) 2009. lib. bdg. 22.60 (978-1-4042-8109-7(6), 1300526) Rosen Publishing Group, Inc., The. (PowerKids Pr.).

Duling, Jean Saunders. Marco Island A-Z: A Coloring Book for You. Duling, Jean Saunders, ed. 2003. (Illus.). 36p. (J). (gr. -1-6). pap. 5.95 (978-0-9743445-0-8(8)) Duling Designs.

Feinstein, Stephen. Florida: A MyReportLinks.com Book. 2003. (States Ser.). (Illus.). 48p. (J). (gr. 4-10). lib. bdg. 25.26 (978-0-7660-5027-3(0), MyReportLinks.com Bks.) Enslow Pubs., Inc.

Gamble, Adam & Jasper, Mark. Count to Sleep Florida. Veno, Joe, illus. 2014. (Count to Sleep Ser.). (ENG.). 20p. (J). (— 1). bds. 7.95 (978-1-60219-202-7(2)) Good Night Bks.

Hart, Joyce & Chang, Perry. Florida. 2nd rev. ed. 2006. (Celebrate the States Ser.). (Illus.). 144p. (gr. 6-7). lib. bdg. 42.79 (978-0-7614-2348-5(6), Benchmark Bks.) Marshall Cavendish Corp.

Hicks, Rob & Hicks, Kim. Amelia, A to Z. Bolton-Eells, Sharon, illus. 2011. (J). (978-0-9829908-0-3(4)) Island Media Publishing, LLC.

Johnson, Annie P. & Johnson, Russell. My Florida Alphabet. Hume, John, illus. 2014. (ENG.). 64p. (J). pap. 15.95 (978-1-56164-729-3(2)) Pineapple Pr., Inc.

Johnson, Russell W. & Johnson, Annie P. My Florida Facts. Swing, Michael, illus. 2009. (ENG.). 64p. (J). (gr. 3-7). 14.95 (978-1-56164-430-8(7)) Pineapple Pr., Inc.

Knowles, Elizabeth & Smith, Martha. Discovering Florida Through Literature. 2003. 112p. pap. 14.95 (978-0-929895-54-3(1)) Maupin Hse. Publishing.

Marsh, Carole. Florida Current Events Projects: 30 Cool, Activities, Crafts, Experiments & More for Kids to Do to Learn about Your State! 2003. (Florida Experience Ser.). 32p. (gr. k-5). pap. 5.95 (978-0-635-02028-4(9), Marsh, Carole Bks.) Gallopade International.

—The Florida Experience Pocket Guide. 2004. (Florida Experience! Ser.). (Illus.). 96p. (J). (gr. 3-8). pap. 6.95 (978-0-7933-9448-7(1)) Gallopade International.

—Florida Geography Projects: 30 Cool, Activities, Crafts, Experiments & More for Kids to Do to Learn about Your State! 2003. (Florida Experience Ser.). 32p. (gr. k-5). pap. 5.95 (978-0-635-01828-1(4), Marsh, Carole Bks.) Gallopade International.

—Florida Government Projects: 30 Cool, Activities, Crafts, Experiments & More for Kids to Do to Learn about Your State! 2003. (Florida Experience Ser.). 32p. (gr. k-5). pap. 5.95 *(978-0-635-01928-8(0),* Marsh, Carole Bks.) Gallopade International.

—Florida People Projects: 30 Cool, Activities, Crafts, Experiments & More for Kids to Do to Learn about Your State! 2003. (Florida Experience Ser.). 32p. (gr. k-5). pap. 5.95 *(978-0-635-01978-3(7),* Marsh, Carole Bks.) Gallopade International.

—Florida Symbols & Facts Projects: 30 Cool, Activities, Crafts, Experiments & More for Kids to Do to Learn about Your State! 2003. (Florida Experience Ser.). 32p. (gr. k-5). pap. 5.95 *(978-0-635-01878-6(0),* Marsh, Carole Bks.) Gallopade International.

McNamara, Connie. My First Florida State Words. 2004. (J). bds. 11.95 *(978-0-9743244-7-0(7))* Shamrock Publishing, Inc.

—My First University of Florida Words. 2004. (J). bds. 11.95 *(978-0-9743244-4-9(2))* Shamrock Publishing, Inc.

McNeil, Niki, et al. HOCPP 1075 Florida. 2006. spiral bd. 24.00 *(978-1-60308-075-0(9))* In the Hands of a Child.

Murray, Julie. Florida, 1 vol. 2006. (Buddy Book Ser.). (ENG., Illus.). 32p. (gr. 2-4). 27.07 *(978-1-59197-668-4(5),* Buddy Bks.) ABDO Publishing Co.

Obregon, Jose Maria. Florida. 2005. (Bilingual Library of the United States of America Ser.: Set 1). (ENG & SPA., Illus.). 32p. (J). (gr. 3-6). lib. bdg. 25.25 *(978-1-4042-3074-3(2))* Rosen Publishing Group, Inc., The.

Obregón, José María. Florida. 2009. (Bilingual Library of the United States of America Ser.). (ENG & SPA.). 32p. (gr. 2-2). 47.90 *(978-1-60853-352-7(2),* Editorial Buenas Letras) Rosen Publishing Group, Inc., The.

Ocala National Forest Staff, prod. Exploring Ocala National Forest & Central Florida's Parks. 2007. (Illus.). 52p. 5.95 *(978-1-888213-67-6(1))* Eastern National.

Ollhoff, Jim. Florida, 1 vol. 2009. (United States Ser.). (ENG., Illus.). 48p. (YA). (gr. 2-5). 27.07 *(978-1-60453-644-7(6))* ABDO Publishing Co.

Orr, Tamra. Florida. 2017. (True Book — My United States Ser.). (ENG.). 48p. (J). pap. 7.95 ***(978-0-531-23284-2(0),*** Children's Pr.) Scholastic Library Publishing.

Orr, Tamra B. Florida. 144p. (J). 2014. (America the Beautiful Ser.: 3). (ENG.). lib. bdg. 40.00 *(978-0-531-24880-5(1))* 2011. (America the Beautiful, Third Ser.). (Illus.). pap. 12.95 *(978-0-531-22922-4(X),* Children's Pr.) Scholastic Library Publishing.

Quasha, Jennifer. How to Draw Florida's Sights & Symbols. 2009. (Kid's Guide to Drawing America Ser.). 32p. (gr. k-k). 50.50 *(978-1-61511-054-4(2),* PowerKids Pr.) Rosen Publishing Group, Inc., The.

Rudy, Carol-Ann. Coral Gables, Gateway to the Sun. George, Paul S., ed. Date not set. (Hometown Heritage Ser.). (Illus.). 32p. (Orig.). (J). (gr. 2-4). pap. 3.50 *(978-1-889300-03-0(9))* Dormouse Productions, Inc.

—Crossing to Freedom. George, Paul S., ed. Rudy, Carol-Ann, illus. Date not set. (Hometown Heritage Ser.). (Illus.). 48p. (Orig.). (J). (gr. 2-4). pap. 4.95 *(978-1-889300-02-3(0))* Dormouse Productions, Inc.

Sawyer, Sarah. Florida: Past & Present. 2009. (Illus.). 48p. (J). 70.50 *(978-1-4358-5575-5(2));* pap. 11.75 *(978-1-4358-5574-8(4));* (ENG., lib. bdg. 29.25 *(978-1-4358-5288-4(5))* Rosen Publishing Group, Inc., The. (Rosen Reference).

Segal, Robin. ABC in Miami: And the Beaches. 2008. (All 'Bout Cities Ser.). (ENG & SPA.). 32p. (J). (gr. -1-k). *(978-0-9719697-2-8(8))* Murray Hill Bks., LLC.

Sirvaitis, Karen. Florida. (J). 2012. lib. bdg. 25.26 *(978-0-7613-4527-5(2),* Lerner Pubns.) 2nd rev. exp. ed. 2003. (Illus.). 84p. (gr. 3-6). pap. 6.95 *(978-0-8225-4144-8(0))* Lerner Publishing Group.

Somervill, Barbara A. Florida. 2008. (From Sea to Shining Sea, Second Ser.). (ENG., Illus.). 80p. (J). (gr. 3-7). pap. 7.95 *(978-0-531-18802-6(7),* Children's Pr.) Scholastic Library Publishing.

Sullivan, E. J. F Is for Florida. Eldredge, Ernie, illus. 2006. (State Alphabet Bks.). 24p. (J). *(978-1-58173-525-3(1))* Sweetwater Pr.

Thorpe, Sandy. Sand in Their Shoes. 2004. (Illus.). 192p. per. *(978-0-9764147-0-4(8))* Thorpe, Sandy.

Wimmer, Teresa. Florida. 2008. (This Land Called America Ser.). 32p. (YA). (gr. 3-6). lib. bdg. 22.95 *(978-1-58341-634-1(X))* Creative Co., The.

Young, Claiborne. Cruising Guide to Eastern Florida, 1 vol. Nudelman, Edward, ed. 5th ed. 2004. (Cruising Guide Ser.). (ENG., Illus.). 560p. pap. 34.95 *(978-1-58980-255-1(1))* Pelican Publishing Co., Inc.

FLORIDA—FICTION

The Airs of Tillie. 2004. 150p. pap. 12.95 *(978-1-932162-24-0(0))* Benoy Publishing.

Alexander, Goldie. Body & Soul. 2003. 236p. pap. *(978-0-9578735-9-9(X))* IAD Pr.

Allen, Quinc. The Outdoor Chums on the Gulf. 2006. pap. *(978-1-4065-0781-2(4))* Dodo Pr.

Alten, Steve. Sharkman. 2014. (ENG.). 272p. 22.95 *(978-1-63076-019-6(5))* Taylor Trade Publishing.

Anderson, Laurie Halse. Manatee Blues, No. 4. 2008. (Vet Volunteers Ser.: 4). (ENG.). 144p. (J). (gr. 3-7). 7.99 *(978-0-14-241084-4(5),* Puffin Books) Penguin Young Readers Group.

Anderson, Patricia. Tails of a Woodswoman. 2008. 72p. pap. 9.95 *(978-1-4327-2615-7(3))* Outskirts Pr., Inc.

Ann. My Name Is Oak... Daytona Oak. 2013. 28p. pap. 24.95 *(978-1-63004-172-4(6))* America Star Bks.

Applegate, Katherine. Spring Break. 2010. (Summer Ser.). (ENG., Illus.). 240p. (YA). (gr. 9-18). pap. 8.99 *(978-1-4169-9094-9(1),* Simon Pulse) Simon Pulse.

Arnosky, Jim. The Pirates of Crocodile Swamp. 2009. (ENG.). 240p. (J). (gr. 4-7). 15.99 *(978-0-399-25068-2(9),* G.P. Putnam's Sons Books for Young Readers) Penguin Young Readers Group.

Arthur, Peggy Ann. Come & Look in Grandma's Garden. 2012. 26p. 24.95 *(978-1-4560-3988-2(1))* America Star Bks.

Ashkenas, Bruce. Auntie's Ghost. 2007. 108p. 34.50 *(978-1-4303-1929-0(1))* Lulu Pr., Inc.

August, Elaine. Southern Mischief. 2012. 80p. 21.95 *(978-1-61582-082-5(5))* America Star Bks.

August, Elaine Schiller. Southern Mischief. 2005. 78p. pap. 19.95 *(978-1-4137-7893-9(3))* America Star Bks.

Baglio, Ben M. Vanishing Point. Ettlinger, Doris, illus. 2007. 158p. (J). pap. *(978-0-439-87145-7(X))* Scholastic, Inc.

Banks, Anna. Of Poseidon, 1 vol. 2012. 59.95 *(978-0-7927-9019-8(7),* Sound Library) AudioGO.

Banks, Piper. Geek Abroad, 2 vols. 2008. (Geek High Ser.: 2). (ENG.). 256p. (YA). (gr. 9-18). 9.99 *(978-0-451-22393-7(4),* Berkley) Penguin Publishing Group.

—Revenge of the Geek. 2010. (Geek High Ser.: 4). (ENG.). 256p. (gr. 12-18). 9.99 *(978-0-451-23134-5(1),* Berkley) Penguin Publishing Group.

—Summer of the Geek. 2010. (Geek High Ser.: 3). (ENG.). 256p. (YA). (gr. 5-18). 9.99 *(978-0-451-22984-7(3),* Berkley) Penguin Publishing Group.

Barkley, Brad & Hepler, Heather. Dream Factory. 2009. (ENG.). 272p. (YA). (gr. 7-18). 8.99 *(978-0-14-241298-5(8),* Speak) Penguin Young Readers Group.

Barnhart, Judy. Sand Angels in the Snow. 2007. 68p. per. 8.95 *(978-0-595-45154-8(3))* iUniverse, Inc.

Barth, Kathleen E. The Amazing Adventures of Quigley D Pigley & His Friends. 2009. 16p. pap. 8.49 *(978-1-4389-8322-6(0))* AuthorHouse.

—The Amazing Adventures of Quigley D Pigley & His Friends: How to Become an Astronaut. 2009. 16p. pap. 8.49 *(978-1-4389-8606-7(8))* AuthorHouse.

Beard, Robert W. A Boy Named Shawn. 2009. (A Shawn Barton Adventure Ser.). 116p. (J). pap. 12.95 *(978-1-935083-07-8(X))* CyPress Pubns.

—Halcyon. 2009. (J). pap. *(978-1-935083-08-5(2))* CyPress Pubns.

Because of Winn Dixie. 2011. 9.14 *(978-0-7848-3659-0(0),* Everbind) Marco Bk. Co.

Bell, Rebecca. Message from Miami: The Adventures of Sharp-Eye, Book 2. Bell, Rebecca, illus. 2005. (Adventures of Sharp-Eye). (Illus.). 30p. (J). 9.95 *(978-1-934138-09-0(6))* Bouncing Ball Bks., Inc.

Benedict, Norma. Grammy Hits the Road. 2009. 40p. pap. 16.99 *(978-1-4490-0905-2(0))* AuthorHouse.

Berard, Robin M. King Tut & the Girl Who Loved Him: The Strange Adventures of Johanna Wilson. 2007. 212p. per. 12.95 *(978-1-58348-477-7(9),* iUniverse Star) iUniverse, Inc.

Bhakta, Sanjini. My Life as a Dollar Bill. 2010. 28p. pap. 12.95 *(978-1-4520-6152-8(1))* AuthorHouse.

Bloor, Edward. Tangerine. (ENG.). 320p. (J). (gr. 5-7). 2007. 18.00 *(978-0-15-201246-5(X))* 2006. (Illus.). pap. 8.99 *(978-0-15-205780-0(3))* Houghton Mifflin Harcourt Publishing Co.

—Tangerine Spanish Edition. de la Vega, Pablo, tr. 2014. (ENG.). 384p. (J). (gr. 5-7). 16.99 *(978-0-544-33611-7(9),* HMH Books For Young Readers) Houghton Mifflin Harcourt Publishing Co.

Blume, Judy. Starring Sally J. Freedman As Herself. 2014. (ENG., Illus.). (J). (gr. 3-7). 384p. 17.99 *(978-1-4814-1437-1(2));* 400p. pap. 7.99 *(978-1-4814-1355-8(4))* Simon & Schuster Children's Publishing. (Atheneum Bks. for Young Readers).

Blundell, Judy. What I Saw & How I Lied. (ENG.). 288p. (J). (gr. 7-12). 2010. 9.99 *(978-0-439-90348-6(3),* Scholastic Paperbacks) 2008. 16.99 *(978-0-439-90346-2(7),* Scholastic Pr.) Scholastic, Inc.

Bond, Victoria & Simon, T. R. Zora & Me. (Zora & Me Ser.). (ENG., Illus.). 192p. (J). (gr. 5). 2011. pap. 7.99 *(978-0-7636-5814-4(6))* 2010. 16.99 *(978-0-7636-4300-3(9))* Candlewick Pr.

Bonner, Anne. Intrigue at Pine Haven: Civil War in Florida. Akridge, Bill, illus. 2006. 220p. (YA). 12.95 net. *(978-1-878398-76-5(8),* Blue Note Bks.) Blue Note Pubns.

Brazina, Rhonda & Margolis, Ida R. Carrots for Charlie. 2012. 42p. pap. 9.95 *(978-0-9851184-6-4(6))* Barringer Publishing.

Brooks, Walter R. Freddy Goes to Florida. Wiese, Kurt, illus. 2012. (ENG.). 224p. (gr. 4-13). 10.99 *(978-1-59020-741-3(6),* 902741) Overlook Pr., The.

Brouwer, Sigmund. Hurricane Power, 1 vol. 2007. (Orca Sports Ser.). (ENG.). 176p. (YA). (gr. 6-10). per. 9.95 *(978-1-55143-865-8(8))* Orca Bk. Pubs. USA.

Burton, Hallie. For a Price. 2016. (ENG., Illus.). (J). 24.99 ***(978-1-63533-017-5(3),*** Harmony Ink Pr.) Dreamspinner Pr.

Cabot, Meg. Abandon. 2011. (ENG.). 320p. (J). (gr. 9-18). 17.99 *(978-0-545-28410-3(4))* Scholastic, Inc.

—Awaken. 2013. (ENG.). 336p. (J). (gr. 9). 17.99 *(978-0-545-28412-7(0))* Scholastic, Inc.

—Underworld. 2012. (Abandon Ser.). (ENG.). 336p. (J). (gr. 9). 17.99 *(978-0-545-28411-0(2))* Scholastic, Inc.

Cameron, Sam. The Missing Juliet: a Fisher Key Adventure. 2013. (ENG.). 264p. (gr. 7). pap. 11.95 *(978-1-60282-959-6(4))* Bold Strokes Bks.

—Mystery of the Tempest: A Fisher Key Adventure. 2011. (ENG.). 288p. (J). (gr. 7). pap. 13.95 *(978-1-60282-579-6(3))* Bold Strokes Bks.

Carlson, Melody. Spring Breakdown, 1 vol. 2014. (Carter House Girls Ser.). (ENG.). 208p. (YA). pap. 9.99 *(978-0-310-74809-0(7))* Zondervan.

Cartaya, Pablo. The Epic Fail of Arturo Zamora. 2017. (ENG.). 256p. (J). (gr. 5). 16.99 *(978-1-101-99723-9(0),* Viking Books for Young Readers) Penguin Young Readers Group.

Christy Mahler Mills. No Regrets. 2010. 180p. 23.95 *(978-1-4401-9740-6(7));* pap. 13.95 *(978-1-4401-9738-3(5))* iUniverse, Inc.

Cola, Arthur. Papa & the Gingerbread Man. 2006. 14.95 *(978-0-9789423-0-4(2))* Cola, Arthur.

Cole, Bob. Charging Forward: Heart, Team & Eight Seconds, the Boys that Refuse to Lose, 1 vol. 2009. 149p. pap. 24.95 *(978-1-61546-775-4(0))* America Star Bks.

Colhoun, Sheelah. Elric's Florida Holiday. Cotton, Sue Lynn, illus. 2012. 20p. pap. 13.95 *(978-1-61493-110-2(0))* Peppertree Pr., The.

Corbett, Sue. Free Baseball. 2008. (ENG.). 160p. (J). (gr. 3-7). 6.99 *(978-0-14-241080-6(2),* Puffin Books) Penguin Young Readers Group.

Counts, Monika, illus. Florida Countdown to Touchdown. 2010. (Countdown to Touchdown Ser.). 20p. 14.95 *(978-1-61524-082-1(9),* Intervisual/Piggy Toes) Bendon, Inc.

Cray, Jordan. Firestorm. 2009. (Danger. com Ser.: 2). (ENG.). 208p. (YA). (gr. 7). pap. 9.99 *(978-1-4169-9846-4(2),* Simon Pulse) Simon Pulse.

Crocker, Carter & Snyder, Carrie A. The Tale of the Swamp Rat. 2005. (ENG.). 240p. (J). (gr. 3-7). reprint ed. 6.99 *(978-0-14-240314-3(8),* Puffin Books) Penguin Young Readers Group.

Crowley-Ranelli, D. Holiday Island: Santa in a Bathing Suit? 2009. 56p. pap. 9.95 *(978-1-60860-268-1(0),* Eloquent Bks.) Strategic Book Publishing & Rights Agency (SBPRA).

Dabrio-Martinez, Mutzai. The Day the Dinosaurs Came to St. Andrew. 2013. 112p. pap. 10.95 *(978-1-4759-6077-8(8))* iUniverse, Inc.

Dalton, Michelle. Pulled Under. 2014. (Sixteenth Summer Ser.). (ENG., Illus.). 288p. (YA). (gr. 7). pap. 9.99 *(978-1-4814-0700-7(7),* Simon Pulse) Simon Pulse.

Danticat, Edwidge. Untwine: A Novel. 2015. (ENG.). 320p. (J). (gr. 7). 16.99 *(978-0-545-42303-8(1),* Scholastic Pr.) Scholastic, Inc.

Darling, Angela. Isabella's Spring Break Crush. 2014. (Crush Ser.: 6). (ENG., Illus.). 160p. (J). (gr. 3-7). pap. 5.99 *(978-1-4814-0493-8(8),* Simon Spotlight) Simon Spotlight.

Davis, Carol Marie. The Adventures of Moon Spirit, a Girl from Florida's Past. Davis, Carol Marie, illus. 2008. (Illus.). 60p. pap. 8.95 *(978-0-9821654-2-3(0))* Peppertree Pr., The.

Day, Jan. Kissimmee Pete & the Hurricane, 1 vol. Mason, Janeen, illus. 2008. (ENG.). 32p. (J). (gr. 1-3). 16.99 *(978-1-58980-544-6(5))* Pelican Publishing Co., Inc.

—Kissimmee Pete, Cracker Cow Hunter, 1 vol. Mason, Janeen, illus. 2005. (ENG.). 32p. (J). (gr. k-3). 16.99 *(978-1-58980-325-1(6))* Pelican Publishing Co., Inc.

De Laurentiis, Giada, et al. Miami! #7. Gambatesa, Francesca, illus. 2015. (Recipe for Adventure Ser.: 7). (ENG.). 160p. (J). (gr. 2-4). bds. 6.99 *(978-0-448-48393-1(9),* Grosset & Dunlap) Penguin Young Readers Group.

De Palma, Toni. Under the Banyan Tree. 2007. (ENG.). 192p. (YA). (gr. 7-18). 16.95 *(978-0-8234-1965-4(7))* Holiday Hse., Inc.

DeFelice, Cynthia C. The Missing Manatee. 2008. (ENG.). 192p. (J). (gr. 3-7). pap. 8.99 *(978-0-374-40020-0(2),* 9780374400200) Square Fish.

DiCamillo, Kate. Because of Winn-Dixie. movie tie-in ed. 2004. (Because of Winn-Dixie Ser.). (ENG., Illus.). 192p. (J). (gr. 3-7). mass mkt. 6.99 *(978-0-7636-2558-0(2))* Candlewick Pr.

—The Tiger Rising. (ENG.). (J). (gr. 5). 2015. 144p. pap. 6.99 *(978-0-7636-8087-9(7))* 2011. (Illus.). 128p. 15.99 *(978-0-7636-5270-8(9))* Candlewick Pr.

—The Tiger Rising. Sheban, Chris, illus. 2006. 144p. (J). (gr. 5). pap. 5.99 *(978-0-7636-2916-8(2))* Candlewick Pr.

—The Tiger Rising. aut. ed. 2011. (ENG., Illus.). 128p. (J). (gr. 5). 50.00 *(978-0-7636-5383-5(7))* Candlewick Pr.

—The Tiger Rising. unabr. ed. 2004. (Middle Grade Cassette Librariestm Ser.). 128p. (J). (gr. 5-9). pap. 29.00 incl. audio *(978-0-8072-0998-1(8),* S YA 285 SP, Listening Library) Random Hse. Audio Publishing Group.

Dillon, Doug. Stepping off a Cliff [the St. Augustine Trilogy: The St. Augustine Trilogy: Book II. 2013. (ENG., Illus.). 394p. (YA). pap. 13.99 *(978-0-9833684-3-4(0))* Old St. Augustine Pubns.

Dimarcello, Pete. Panic at the Pool. Harpan, Gaile, ed. Baker, Edmund, illus. 2013. 20p. pap. 12.95 *(978-1-61493-169-0(0))* Peppertree Pr., The.

DiTerlizzi, Tony & Black, Holly. The Nixies Song - A Giant Problem - The Wyrm King Set. Set. DiTerlizzi, Tony, illus. 2009. (Beyond the Spiderwick Chronicles Ser.: Nos. 1-3). (ENG., Illus.). 528p. (J). (gr. 2-5). 33.99 *(978-1-4169-9011-6(9),* Simon & Schuster Bks. For Young Readers) Simon & Schuster Bks. For Young Readers.

Doerr, Bonnie J. Kenzie's Key. Aberle, Xylena Apotheloz, illus. 2003. 211p. (J). 16.95 *(978-0-9619155-6-8(0))* Laurel & Herbert, Inc.

—Stakeout. Edwards, Laurie J. & Britt, Joanna, illus. 2011. 310p. pap. 12.99 *(978-1-61603-007-0(0))* Leap Bks.

Dole, Mayra L. Drum, Chavi, Drum! Tonel, illus. 2013.Tr. of ¡Toca, Chavi, Toca! (ENG & SPA.). 32p. (J). pap. 9.95 *(978-0-89239-302-2(5),* Children's Book Press) Lee & Low Bks., Inc.

—Toca, Chavi, Toca! Tonel, illus. 2003.Tr. of Drum, Chavi, Drum! (ENG & SPA.). 32p. (J). 16.95 *(978-0-89239-186-8(3))* Lee & Low Bks., Inc.

Doller, Trish. The Devil You Know. (ENG.). 256p. (YA). 2016. pap. 9.99 *(978-1-68119-022-8(2),* 9781681190228) 2015. (gr. 9). 17.99 *(978-1-61963-416-9(3),* 9781619634169) Bloomsbury Publishing USA. (Bloomsbury USA Childrens).

—Where the Stars Still Shine. 2013. (ENG.). 352p. (YA). (gr. 9). 17.99 *(978-1-61963-144-1(X),* 9781619631441, Bloomsbury USA Childrens); 256p. 17.99 *(978-1-61963-145-8(8))* Bloomsbury Publishing USA.

Doty, Mariel. A Different Kind of Princess: Pictures of You. 2010. 260p. 26.50 *(978-1-60911-318-6(7),* Eloquent Bks.) Strategic Book Publishing & Rights Agency (SBPRA).

Douglas, Marjory Stoneman & Milkweed Editions Staff. Alligator Crossing. Nicholson, Trudy, illus. 2003. (ENG.). 192p. (J). (gr. 3-8). pap. 7.95 *(978-1-57131-644-8(2))* Milkweed Editions.

Draper, Sharon M. Copper Sun. 2014. (ENG.). 336p. (YA). 14.24 *(978-1-63245-110-1(7))* Lectorum Pubns., Inc.

—Copper Sun. 2011. 11.04 *(978-0-7848-3373-5(7),* Everbind) Marco Bk. Co.

—Copper Sun. (ENG.). (YA). 2008. 336p. (gr. 9-12). pap. 10.99 *(978-1-4169-5348-7(5))* 2006. 320p. (gr. 8-18). 19.99 *(978-0-689-82181-3(6))* Simon & Schuster Children's Publishing. (Atheneum Bks. for Young Readers).

—Copper Sun. l.t. ed. 2006. 358p. (YA). (gr. 8-18). 22.95 *(978-0-7862-8948-6(1))* Thorndike Pr.

—Copper Sun. 2008. lib. bdg. 22.10 *(978-1-4177-9702-8(9),* Turtleback) Turtleback Bks.

Echols, Jennifer. Biggest Flirts. 2014. (Superlatives Ser.). (ENG., Illus.). 336p. (YA). (gr. 9). pap. 9.99 *(978-1-4424-7445-1(9),* Simon Pulse) Simon Pulse.

—Perfect Couple. 2015. (Superlatives Ser.). (ENG., Illus.). 336p. (YA). (gr. 9). pap. 10.99 *(978-1-4424-7448-2(3),* Simon Pulse) Simon Pulse.

Enriquez, Jose. Saving the Mango Farm. 2006. 23p. (J). 10.98 *(978-1-4116-5917-9(1))* Lulu Pr., Inc.

Estergren, Fred B. Tale of a Dog Called Sunshine, 1 vol. 2009. 201p. pap. 24.95 *(978-1-4489-2575-9(4))* America Star Bks.

Everett, Reese. Jayla's Jitters. 2015. (ENG.). 48p. (gr. k-3). 27.07 *(978-1-63430-374-3(1))* Rourke Educational Media.

Famularo, Joe. Taco/Fatso: The Story of a Fat Dog, Too Fat to Fly. 2013. 32p. pap. 17.25 *(978-1-4669-4926-3(0))* Trafford Publishing.

Feathers at Las Flores - Evaluation Guide: Evaluation Guide. 2006. (J). *(978-1-55942-405-9(2))* Witcher Productions.

Fields, Jan. Search for Bigfoot, 1 vol. Brundage, Scott, illus. 2014. (Monster Hunters Ser.). (ENG.). 80p. (J). (gr. 8-12). 27.07 *(978-1-62402-046-9(1))* Magic Wagon.

Fields, Trisha A. Eggbert, the Hero. 2012. 44p. pap. 21.99 *(978-1-4771-3548-8(0))* Xlibris Corp.

Finotti, M. C. Paintbrushes & Arrows. 2016. 113p. (J). ***(978-1-56164-968-6(6))*** Pineapple Pr., Inc.

—Paintbrushes & Arrows: A Story of St. Augustine. 2016. (ENG.). 112p. (J). pap. 9.95 *(978-1-56164-963-1(5))* Pineapple Pr., Inc.

—The Treasure of Amelia Island. 2008. (Florida Historical Fiction for Youth Ser.). (ENG., Illus.). 97p. (J). (gr. 3-7). 14.95 *(978-1-56164-416-2(1))* Pineapple Pr., Inc.

Finotti, M. C. & National Geographic Learning Staff. The Treasure of Amelia Island. 2012. (ENG.). 108p. (C). pap. 14.95 *(978-1-56164-536-7(2))* National Geographic School Publishing, Inc.

Flinn, Alex. Cloaked. (YA). 2012. (ENG.). 368p. (gr. 8). pap. 9.99 *(978-0-06-087424-7(4))* 2011. 341p. lib. bdg. 17.89 *(978-0-06-087423-0(6))* 2011. (ENG.). 352p. (gr. 8-18). 16.99 *(978-0-06-087422-3(8))* HarperCollins Pubs. (HarperTeen).

—Diva. 2013. (ENG.). 304p. (YA). (gr. 9). pap. 9.99 *(978-0-06-212434-0(X))* HarperCollins Pubs.

—A Kiss in Time. (ENG.). (YA). (gr. 8-18). 2010. 400p. pap. 9.99 *(978-0-06-087421-6(X))* 2009. 384p. 17.99 *(978-0-06-087419-3(8))* HarperCollins Pubs. (HarperTeen).

—Nothing to Lose. 2004. 288p. (J). 16.99 *(978-0-06-051750-2(6),* HarperTeen) HarperCollins Pubs.

Flores-Galbis, Enrique. 90 Miles to Havana. 2012. (ENG.). 304p. (J). (gr. 4-7). pap. 7.99 *(978-1-250-00559-5(0),* 9781250005595) Square Fish.

Fogelin, Adrian. Anna Casey's Place in the World. 2003. (ENG.). 224p. (J). (gr. 3-7). pap. 7.95 *(978-1-56145-295-8(5),* Q32694) Peachtree Pubs.

—The Big Nothing. (ENG.). 224p. (J). (gr. 3-7). 2006. pap. 7.95 *(978-1-56145-388-7(9))* 2004. 15.95 *(978-1-56145-326-9(9))* Peachtree Pubs.

—My Brother's Hero, 1 vol. 2005. (ENG.). 224p. (J). (gr. 3-7). reprint ed. pap. 7.95 *(978-1-56145-352-8(8))* Peachtree Pubs.

—The Real Question, 1 vol. (ENG.). 256p. (YA). 2009. pap. 7.95 *(978-1-56145-501-0(6))* 2006. (gr. 7-18). 15.95 *(978-1-56145-383-2(8))* Peachtree Pubs.

—The Sorta Sisters, 1 vol. 2007. (ENG., Illus.). 224p. (J). (gr. 3-7). 15.95 *(978-1-56145-424-2(9))* Peachtree Pubs.

—Sorta Sisters, 1 vol. Fogelin, Adrian, illus. 2011. (ENG., Illus.). 288p. pap. 7.95 *(978-1-56145-592-8(X),* Peachtree Junior) Peachtree Pubs.

Gamble, Adam & Jasper, Mark. Buenas Noches, Florida. 2013. (Buenas Noches Ser.). (SPA & ENG., Illus.). 20p. (J). (— 1). bds. 9.95 *(978-1-60219-092-4(5))* Good Night Bks.

—Good Night Florida. Veno, Joe & Hansen, Red, illus. 2nd ed. 2010. (Good Night Our World Ser.). (ENG.). 20p. (J). (gr. k — 1). bds. 9.95 *(978-1-60219-045-0(3))* Good Night Bks.

Gantos, Jack. The Follower. 2015. (ENG.). 224p. (YA). (gr. 7-10). 17.99 *(978-0-374-37995-7(5),* 9780374379957, Farrar, Straus & Giroux (BYR)) Farrar, Straus & Giroux.

Gantos, Jack. The Trouble in Me. 2017. (YA). lib. bdg. 20.85 ***(978-0-606-39592-2(X))*** Turtleback Bks.

Gephart, Donna. Lily & Dunkin. 2016. (ENG.). 352p. (J). (gr. 5). 16.99 *(978-0-553-53674-4(5),* Delacorte Bks. for Young Readers) Random Hse. Children's Bks.

Gibaldi, Lauren. The Night We Said Yes. 2015. (ENG.). 304p. (YA). (gr. 9). 17.99 *(978-0-06-230219-9(1),* HarperTeen) HarperCollins Pubs.

Gillespie, Gary Franklin. Storytime with Grandp. 2011. 60p. pap. 31.99 *(978-1-4653-3598-2(6))* Xlibris Corp.

Gioia, Robyn. Under Siege! 2016. (ENG., Illus.). 192p. (J). pap. 12.95 *(978-1-56164-964-8(3))* Pineapple Pr., Inc.

Gonzalez, Gabriela & Triana, Gaby. Backstage Pass. 2004. (Illus.). 224p. (J). (gr. 7-18). 15.99 *(978-0-06-056017-1(7));* lib. bdg. 16.89 *(978-0-06-056018-8(5))* HarperCollins Pubs.

Gosule, Bette & Longmire, Lynda. Sneakers Hangs Out. Dewitt, Kenny, illus. 2012. 26p. (J). 14.95 *(978-1-60131-129-0(X),* Castlebridge Bks.) Big Tent Bks.

Graffius, Richard. The Great Groundhog Caper. 2007. pap. 9.00 *(978-0-8059-8423-1(2))* Dorrance Publishing Co., Inc.

Grandpa Casey. Another Mush-Mice Adventure. Brennan, Lisa, illus. 2012. 48p. 24.95 *(978-1-4626-9379-5(2))* America Star Bks.

—Another Mush-Mice Adventure: Florida Vacation, 1 vol. Brennan, Lisa, illus. 2009. 45p. pap. 24.95 *(978-1-60813-329-1(X))* America Star Bks.

Green, John. Paper Towns. 2011. 11.04 *(978-0-7848-3497-8(0),* Everbind) Marco Bk. Co.

—Paper Towns. movie tie-in ed. 2015. (ENG.). 336p. (YA). (gr. 9). pap. 10.99 *(978-0-14-751765-4(6),* Penguin Books) Penguin Publishing Group.

—Paper Towns. (ENG.). (YA). (gr. 9-18). 2009. 336p. 10.99 *(978-0-14-241493-4(X),* Speak) 2008. 320p. 18.99 *(978-0-525-47818-8(3),* Dutton Books for Young Readers) Penguin Young Readers Group.

—Paper Towns. 2010. (ENG., Illus.). 305p. (gr. 9-12). 20.00 *(978-1-60686-913-0(2))* Perfection Learning Corp.

—Paper Towns. 2009. lib. bdg. 20.85 *(978-0-606-10658-0(8),* Turtleback) Turtleback Bks.

Green, Tim. Deep Zone. 2012. (Football Genius Ser.: 5). (J). lib. bdg. 17.20 *(978-0-606-26854-7(5),* Turtleback) Turtleback Bks.

Greene, Janice. The Eye of the Hurricane, 1 vol. unabr. ed. 2010. (Q Reads Ser.). (ENG.). 32p. (YA). (gr. 9-12). pap. 6.95 *(978-1-61651-191-3(5))* Saddleback Educational Publishing, Inc.

Grover, Lorie Ann. Hold Me Tight. 2007. (ENG.). 352p. (J). (gr. 5-9). pap. 16.95 *(978-1-4169-6753-8(2),* McElderry, Margaret K. Bks.) McElderry, Margaret K. Bks.

Haddix, Margaret Peterson. The House on the Gulf. (ENG., Illus.). 208p. (J). (gr. 3-7). 2006. pap. 7.99 *(978-1-4169-1406-8(4))* 2004. 17.99 *(978-0-689-85422-4(6))* Simon & Schuster Bks. For Young Readers. (Simon & Schuster Bks. For Young Readers).

Hale, Nick. The Edge. 2012. (Striker Ser.: 3). (ENG.). 224p. (J). (gr. 5-7). pap. 7.99 *(978-1-4052-5685-8(0))* Egmont Bks., Ltd. GBR. Dist: Independent Pubs. Group.
Hall, Angela Marie. Priscilla Pennybrook: Hello World, I Have Arrived!, 1 vol. 2009. 55p. pap. 16.95 *(978-1-61582-899-9(0))* America Star Bks.
Hall, Natalie Susan. Andy Anole's Adventure, 1 vol. 2009. 26p. pap. 24.95 *(978-1-60813-350-5(8))* America Star Bks.
Hammond, Meredith. The World According to Tiffany: The Airplane Trip. 2011. 28p. (gr. -1). pap. 12.03 *(978-1-4567-3150-2(5))* AuthorHouse.
Hanson, Ed. Danger at 20 Fathoms. 2003. (Barclay Family Adventure Ser.: Bk. 2). (Illus.). 64p. (J). (gr. k-6). per. 3.95 *(978-1-56254-551-2(5),* SP 5515) Saddleback Educational Publishing, Inc.
Happel-Holtz, Ruby H. Kool Kat Charlie of Cocoa Beach. 2011. 72p. pap. *(978-1-4269-9484-5(2))* Trafford Publishing (UK) Ltd.
Harlow, Joan Hiatt. Blown Away! (ENG.). 272p. (J). (gr. 4-7). 2008. pap. 7.99 *(978-1-4169-0782-4(3))* 2007. 16.99 *(978-1-4169-0781-7(5))* McElderry, Margaret K. Bks. (McElderry, Margaret K. Bks.).
Harmon, Victoria Marie. Say Hello to My Little Green Friend Tiki. 2013. 20p. pap. 24.95 *(978-1-63004-192-2(0))* America Star Bks.
Harris, Donna. Ruff Life. 2011. 240p. pap. 17.99 *(978-1-4567-5081-7(X))* AuthorHouse.
Harris, Loretta. Hard Life. 2007. 25p. (YA). 1.99 *(978-0-9786681-2-9(X))* Triumphant Living Enterprises, Inc.
Harrison, Lisi. Charmed & Dangerous: The Clique Prequel. 2012. (Clique Ser.). (ENG.). 208p. (YA). (gr. 7-17). pap. 8.99 *(978-0-316-05536-9(0),* Poppy) Little, Brown Bks. for Young Readers.
Hartman, Brett. Cadillac Chronicles. 2012. (ENG.). 304p. (J). (gr. 10). 16.95 *(978-1-935955-41-2(1))* Cinco Puntos Pr.
Heard, Foreman. Tales of Pinkie Posie. 2008. 76p. pap. 15.90 *(978-1-4357-3292-6(8))* Lulu Pr., Inc.
Heck, C. S. Memory-Kisses. 2007. 104p. per. 9.95 *(978-0-595-41514-4(8))* iUniverse, Inc.
Henkes, Kevin. Junonia. Henkes, Kevin, illus. 2011. (Illus.). 192p. (J). (gr. 3-7). (ENG.). 15.99 *(978-0-06-196417-6(4));* lib. bdg. 16.89 *(978-0-06-196418-3(2))* HarperCollins Pubs. (Greenwillow Bks.).
Herbach, Geoff. Nothing Special. 2012. (Felton Reinstein Trilogy Ser.: 2). (ENG., Illus.). 304p. (YA). (gr. 7-12). pap. 12.99 *(978-1-4022-6507-5(7))* Sourcebooks, Inc.
Hiaasen, Carl. Chomp. (ENG.). 304p. (J). (gr. 5). 2013. pap. 8.99 *(978-0-375-86827-6(5),* Ember) 2012. 16.99 *(978-0-375-86842-9(9),* Knopf Bks. for Young Readers) Random Hse. Children's Bks.
—Chomp. l.t. ed. 2012. (ENG.). 364p. 23.99 *(978-1-4104-5101-9(1))* Thorndike Pr.
—Chomp. 2013. lib. bdg. 19.65 *(978-0-606-27006-9(X),* Turtleback) Turtleback Bks.
—Flush. 2007. 263p. (gr. 5-9). 19.00 *(978-0-7569-8192-1(1))* Perfection Learning Corp.
—Flush. (ENG.). 272p. (J). (gr. 5-6). 2010. 6.99 *(978-0-375-86125-3(4),* Yearling) 2007. pap. 8.99 *(978-0-375-84185-9(7),* Knopf Bks. for Young Readers) 2005. 16.95 *(978-0-375-82182-0(1),* Knopf Bks. for Young Readers) Random Hse. Children's Bks.
—Hoot. (ENG.). 304p. 2005. (J). (gr. 5-7). 6.99 *(978-0-440-41939-6(5),* Yearling) 2004. (YA). (gr. 7). reprint ed. pap. 8.99 *(978-0-375-82916-1(4),* Ember) Random Hse. Children's Bks.
—Scat. 2011. 10.54 *(978-0-7848-3574-6(8),* Everbind) Marco Bk. Co.
—Scat. (ENG.). (J). (gr. 5). 2012. 400p. 7.99 *(978-0-440-42104-7(7),* Yearling) 2010. 384p. pap. 8.99 *(978-0-375-83487-5(7),* Ember) 2009. 384p. 16.99 *(978-0-375-83486-8(9),* Knopf Bks. for Young Readers) Random Hse. Children's Bks.
—Scat. 2012. lib. bdg. 18.40 *(978-0-606-26532-4(5),* Turtleback) Turtleback Bks.
—Skink - No Surrender. (ENG.). 288p. (gr. 7). 2015. (YA). pap. 9.99 *(978-0-307-93059-0(9),* Ember) 2014. (J). 18.99 *(978-0-375-87051-4(2),* Knopf Bks. for Young Readers) Random Hse. Children's Bks.
Higgins, Jim. The Enchanted Nursery: Heather & Hamish, Fun in Florida, Reggie Rabbit at the Seaside, Percy Penguin's Friends. 2009. (Illus.). 36p. pap. 15.49 *(978-1-4389-9904-3(6))* AuthorHouse.
Hiiasen, Carl. Hoot. 2014. 17.00 *(978-1-63419-707-6(0))* Perfection Learning Corp.
Hilbum, Dora. Between. 2015. 247p. (YA). pap. *(978-1-56825-175-2(0))* Rainbow Bks., Inc.
Hillyer, Brenda L. Mystery in the Marsh. 2008. 48p. pap. 16.95 *(978-1-60703-784-2(X))* America Star Bks.
Hodkin, Michelle. The Evolution of Mara Dyer. (Mara Dyer Trilogy Ser.: 2). (ENG., Illus.). (YA). (gr. 9). 2013. 560p. pap. 12.99 *(978-1-4424-2180-6(0))* 2012. 544p. 19.99 *(978-1-4424-2179-0(7))* Simon & Schuster Bks. For Young Readers. (Simon & Schuster Bks. For Young Readers).
—The Unbecoming of Mara Dyer. (Mara Dyer Trilogy Ser.: 1). (ENG., Illus.). (YA). (gr. 9). 2012. 480p. pap. 12.99 *(978-1-4424-2177-6(0))* 2011. 464p. 21.99 *(978-1-4424-2176-9(2))* Simon & Schuster Bks. For Young Readers. (Simon & Schuster Bks. For Young Readers).
Holm, Jennifer L. Full of Beans. 2016. (ENG.). 208p. (J). (gr. 3-7). 16.99 *(978-0-553-51036-2(3));* lib. bdg. 19.99 *(978-0-553-51037-9(1))* Random Hse. Children's Bks. (Random Hse. Bks. for Young Readers).
—Sunny Side Up. Holm, Matthew, illus. 2015. (ENG.). 224p. (J). (gr. 3-7). 23.99 *(978-0-545-74165-1(3));* pap. 12.99 *(978-0-545-74166-8(1))* Scholastic, Inc. (Graphix).
—Turtle in Paradise. 2012. (CHI.). 187p. (J). (gr. 3-7). pap. *(978-7-221-10316-1(X))* Guizhou People's Publishing Hse.
—Turtle in Paradise. 2009. 9.14 *(978-0-7848-3781-8(3),* Everbind) Marco Bk. Co.
—Turtle in Paradise. 2011. (ENG.). 224p. (J). (gr. 3-7). pap. 7.99 *(978-0-375-83690-9(X),* Yearling) Random Hse. Children's Bks.
—Turtle in Paradise. 2011. lib. bdg. 18.40 *(978-0-606-23877-9(8),* Turtleback) Turtleback Bks.
Holm, Jennifer L., et al. Sunny Side Up. 2015. (Illus.). 216p. (J). ***(978-0-545-89934-5(6),*** Graphix) Scholastic, Inc.
Holt, Kimberly Willis. Piper Reed, Campfire Girl. Davenier, Christine, illus. 2010. (Piper Reed Ser.: 4). (ENG.). 160p. (J). (gr. 3-6). 15.99 *(978-0-8050-9006-2(1),* 9780805090062, Holt, Henry & Co. Bks. For Young Readers) Holt, Henry & Co.
—Piper Reed, Campfire Girl. Davenier, Christine, illus. 2011. (Piper Reed Ser.: 4). (ENG.). 176p. (J). (gr. 3-6). pap. 6.99 *(978-0-312-67482-3(1),* 9780312674823) Square Fish.
—Piper Reed, Clubhouse Queen. Davenier, Christine, illus. 2011. (Piper Reed Ser.: 2). (ENG.). 160p. (J). (gr. 3-6). 15.99 *(978-0-8050-9431-2(8),* 9780805094312, Holt, Henry & Co. Bks. For Young Readers) Holt, Henry & Co.
—Piper Reed Gets a Job. Davenier, Christine, illus. 2009. (Piper Reed Ser.: 3). (ENG.). 160p. (J). (gr. 3-6). 14.99 *(978-0-8050-8199-2(2),* 9780805081992, Holt, Henry & Co. Bks. For Young Readers) Holt, Henry & Co.
Hope, Laura Lee. The Moving Picture Girls under the Palms: Or Lost in the Wilds of Florida. 2007. 140p. pap. 18.99 *(978-1-4346-0717-1(8));* (ENG.). 158p. pap. 21.99 *(978-1-4346-0777-5(1))* Creative Media Partners, LLC.
—Outdoor Girls in Florida. 2006. 26.95 *(978-1-4218-2982-1(7));* pap. 11.95 *(978-1-4218-3082-7(5))* 1st World Publishing, Inc.
—The Outdoor Girls in Florida: Or Wintering in the Sunny South. 2007. 130p. pap. 18.99 *(978-1-4264-9645-5(1));* 144p. pap. 19.99 *(978-1-4264-4927-7(5))* Creative Media Partners, LLC.
Howard, J. J. That Time I Joined the Circus. 2013. (ENG.). 272p. (J). (gr. 7). 17.99 *(978-0-545-43381-5(9))* Scholastic, Inc.
Hutchinson, Shaun David. Deathday Letter. 2010. (ENG.). 256p. (YA). (gr. 9-18). pap. 9.99 *(978-1-4169-9608-8(7),* Simon Pulse) Simon Pulse.
Jacobs, Lily. The Littlest Bunny in Florida: An Easter Adventure. Dunn, Robert, illus. 2015. (ENG.). 32p. (J). (-3). 9.99 *(978-1-4926-1069-4(0),* Sourcebooks Jabberwocky) Sourcebooks, Inc.
—The Littlest Bunny in Tampa Bay: An Easter Adventure. Dunn, Robert, illus. 2015. (ENG.). 32p. (J). (-3). 9.99 *(978-1-4926-1204-9(9),* Sourcebooks Jabberwocky) Sourcebooks, Inc.
Jacobson, Ryan. The Case of the Florida Freeze, 1 vol. Beikholm, Erica, illus. l.t. ed. 2005. (Santa Claus: Super Spy Ser.). (ENG.). 80p. (J). per. 4.99 *(978-0-9774122-0-4(2),* Getchu Bks.) Lake 7 Creative, LLC.
James, Eric. A Halloween Scare in Florida. Le Ray, Marina, illus. 2014. (ENG.). 32p. (J). (-5). 9.99 *(978-1-4926-0585-0(9),* 9781492605850, Sourcebooks Jabberwocky) Sourcebooks, Inc.
—A Halloween Scare in Tampa Bay. Le Ray, Marina, illus. 2015. (ENG.). 32p. (J). (-5). 9.99 *(978-1-4926-2402-8(0),* 9781492624028, Sourcebooks Jabberwocky) Sourcebooks, Inc.
—Santa's Sleigh Is on Its Way to Florida. Dunn, Robert, illus. 2015. (ENG.). 32p. (J). (-2). 12.99 *(978-1-4926-2743-2(7),* Sourcebooks Jabberwocky) Sourcebooks, Inc.
—Santa's Sleigh Is on Its Way to Tampa Bay: A Christmas Adventure. Dunn, Robert, illus. 2016. (ENG.). 32p. (J). (-2). 12.99 *(978-1-4926-4357-9(2),* 9781492643579, Sourcebooks Jabberwocky) Sourcebooks, Inc.
Jasper, Mark. Good Night Florida Keys. Rosen, Anne, illus. 2008. (Good Night Our World Ser.). (ENG.). 20p. (J). (gr. k — 1). bds. 9.95 *(978-1-60219-020-7(8))* Good Night Bks.
Jordan, L. W. Santa Heads South: Casey's Christmas Surprise. Lasson, Matt, illus. 2008. 40p. per. 24.95 *(978-1-60441-374-8(3))* America Star Bks.
Jordan, Rosa. The Goatnappers. 2007. (ENG.). 224p. (J). (gr. 3-7). 14.95 *(978-1-56145-400-6(1))* Peachtree Pubs.
—The Last Wild Place, 1 vol. 2008. (ENG.). 256p. (J). (gr. 3-7). 15.95 *(978-1-56145-458-7(3),* Peachtree Junior) Peachtree Pubs.
Joseph, Danielle. Shrinking Violet. 2009. (ENG.). 320p. pap. 19.99 *(978-1-4165-9696-7(8),* MTV Bks.) MTV Books.
Kaminski, Tom. Miss Olivia, the Little Red Poodle: Her First Big Adventure. Fallon, Lisa, illus. 2006. (J). pap. 16.00 *(978-0-8059-7253-5(6))* Dorrance Publishing Co., Inc.
Katschke, Judy, et al. Shore Thing. 2003. (ENG., Illus.). 112p. *(978-0-00-714464-8(4),* HarperCollins Children's Bks.) HarperCollins Pubs. Ltd.
Kelly, David A. The Missing Marlin. Meyers, Mark, illus. 2014. (Ballpark Mysteries Ser.: Bk. 8). (ENG.). 112p. (J). (gr. 1-4). 4.99 *(978-0-307-97782-3(X),* Random Hse. Bks. for Young Readers) Random Hse. Children's Bks.
—The Missing Marlin. 2014. (Ballpark Mysteries Ser.: Bk. 8). lib. bdg. 14.75 *(978-0-606-35565-0(0))* Turtleback Bks.
Kirker, Solveig. The Florida Pod. 2009. 32p. pap. 12.99 *(978-1-4389-3137-1(9))* AuthorHouse.
Knight, Karsten. Embers & Echoes. (ENG., (YA). (gr. 9). 2013. Illus.). 496p. pap. 9.99 *(978-1-4424-5035-6(5))* 2012. 480p. 16.99 *(978-1-4424-5030-1(4))* Simon & Schuster Bks. For Young Readers. (Simon & Schuster Bks. For Young Readers).
Konigsburg, E. L. The Mysterious Edge of the Heroic World. 2007. (ENG., Illus.). 256p. (J). (gr. 4-8). 16.99 *(978-1-4169-4972-5(0),* Atheneum Bks. for Young Readers) Simon & Schuster Children's Publishing.
—T-Backs, T-Shirts, Coat, & Suit. 2008. (ENG.). 192p. (J). (gr. 4-8). pap. 6.99 *(978-1-4169-5877-2(0),* Atheneum Bks. for Young Readers) Simon & Schuster Children's Publishing.
Kropp, Joseph. Bowlegs' Bounty. 2005. 192p. (J). pap. 9.95 *(978-1-890905-24-8(0))* Day to Day Enterprises.
Kuehnel, Judy Lyons. Archie & Abigail. 2008. 64p. per. 17.95 *(978-1-4327-0565-7(2))* Outskirts Pr., Inc.
Lasky, Kathryn. Shadows in the Water. 2008. (ENG., Illus.). 224p. (J). (gr. 2-5). pap. 14.95 *(978-0-15-205874-6(5))* Houghton Mifflin Harcourt Publishing Co.
Lease, Janice. Pellina the Pelican. 2008. 48p. pap. 19.95 *(978-0-9800762-1-9(8))* Cinnamon Ridge Publishing.
Lockhart, E., et al. How to Be Bad. 2008. 325p. (YA). (gr. 9-12). lib. bdg. 17.89 *(978-0-06-128423-6(8),* HarperTeen) HarperCollins Pubs.
Lopez, David Mark. Walk Like an Egyptian. 2006. (J). (gr. 3-7). *(978-0-9744097-0-2(7))* Lopez, David.
Lucero, Len & Tracy, Kristina. Woo-Hoo ... Chris P. Is 2! Weber, Penny, illus. 2015. (ENG.). 32p. 14.99 *(978-1-4019-4441-4(8),* Hay Hse. Lifestyles) Hay Hse., Inc.
Ludwig, Sabine, tr. WINN-DIXIE. (GER.). pap. 17.95 *(978-3-423-70771-8(2))* Deutscher Taschenbuch Verlag GmbH & Co KG DEU. Dist: Distribooks, Inc.
A Manatee Christmas. 2007. (Illus.). 32p. (J). lib. bdg. 15.99 *(978-0-9771059-7-7(0))* Thomas Expressions, LLC.
Manatee Moon. 2006. (J). per. 9.95 *(978-0-9766620-3-7(5))* Avery Goode-Reid Pubs.
Mann's Miracles, creator. When the Hurricane Blew. 2005. (Illus.). 34p. (J). (gr. 3-7). per. *(978-0-9773569-0-4(6))* Clear Horizon.
Marsh, Carole. The Mystery at Disney World. (Real Kids, Real Places Ser.). (Illus.). 146p. (J). 2009. lib. bdg. 18.99 *(978-0-635-06990-0(3),* Marsh, Carole Mysteries) 2003. (gr. 2-8). lib. bdg. 14.95 *(978-0-635-02105-2(6))* Gallopade International.
Martinez, Lisa Bolivar, et al. Good Night Miami. 2011. (Good Night Our World Ser.). (ENG.). 20p. (J). (gr. k — 1). bds. 9.95 *(978-1-60219-051-1(8))* Good Night Bks.
Mass, Wendy. Leap Day. 2006. (ENG.). 208p. (YA). (gr. 7-17). per. 10.99 *(978-0-316-05828-5(9))* Little, Brown Bks. for Young Readers.
Matson, Laurie. Jaz-O & 'G' in Key West. Matson, Laurie, illus. l.t. ed. 2003. (Illus.). (J). 4.95 *(978-0-9673704-5-3(0))* Seastory Pr.
McDaniel, Lurlene. Raina's Story. 2006. (Angels in Pink Ser.). (ENG.). 208p. (YA). (gr. 7-12). mass mkt. 6.99 *(978-0-440-23866-9(8),* Laurel Leaf) Random Hse. Children's Bks.
Means-Dallas, Anastasia. Fourth Street. 2012. 24p. pap. 17.99 *(978-1-4772-0900-4(X))* AuthorHouse.
Meyer, Kim Shapiro. The Journey of the Coconut. Shapiro, Pepper, illus. 2012. 34p. 24.95 *(978-1-4626-5576-2(9));* 36p. pap. 24.95 *(978-1-4626-8641-4(9))* America Star Bks.
Mikaelsen, Ben. Stranded. 2010. (ENG.). 288p. (J). (gr. 3-7). pap. 5.99 *(978-1-4231-3362-9(5))* Hyperion Pr.
Miller, Janet. Little House on the Highway - a Story of a Homeless Family & School Bullying. 2011. 200p. pap. 19.95 *(978-1-257-83540-9(8))* Lulu Pr., Inc.
Mills, Emma. First & Then. 2015. (ENG.). 272p. (YA). (gr. 9-12). 17.99 *(978-1-62779-235-6(X),* 9781627792356, Holt, Henry & Co. Bks. For Young Readers) Holt, Henry & Co.
—This Adventure Ends. 2016. (ENG.). 320p. (YA). 17.99 *(978-1-62779-935-5(4),* 9781627799355, Holt, Henry & Co. Bks. For Young Readers) Holt, Henry & Co.
Miner, Ann. Polly Possum's Wandering Path. Farmer, Libby, illus. 2013. 20p. (J). pap. 12.95 *(978-1-4575-1849-2(X))* Dog Ear Publishing, LLC.
Moore, Carol Hair. Busy Bumble Bee Rides the Waves. Harrell, Michael, illus. 2009. (I Wish You Ice Cream & Cake Ser.: 2). (ENG.). 32p. (J). lib. bdg. 15.95 *(978-1-935083-06-1(6))* CyPress Pubns.
Moore, Stephanie Perry & Moody Publishing Staff. Finding Your Faith 2009. (Yasmin Peace Ser.: 1). (ENG.). 176p. (gr. 7-10). pap. 7.99 *(978-0-8024-8602-8(9),* Lift Every Voice) Moody Pubs.
Mortensen, Carl. Flea & Gang & the Tube Dogs. Mortensen, Carl, illus. 2009. (Illus.). 16p. pap. 11.95 *(978-1-4251-8657-9(2))* Trafford Publishing.
Moulder, Holly. Eyes of the Calusa. 2007. 111p. (J). pap. 8.95 *(978-0-9790405-0-4(7))* White Pelican Pr.
Munroe, Kirk. Flamingo Feather. 2006. pap. 27.95 *(978-1-4304-4189-2(5))* Kessinger Publishing, LLC.
Murphy, Thomas. Island Boy. 2007. 124p. per. 19.95 *(978-1-4241-7940-4(8))* America Star Bks.
My First Seminoles Book. 2004. (J). bds. 8.95 *(978-0-9754317-1-9(4))* JEM Bks., Inc.
Nelson, N. A. Bringing the Boy Home. 2008. (ENG.). 224p. (J). (gr. 3-7). 16.99 *(978-0-06-088698-1(6))* HarperCollins Pubs.
Northrop, Michael. Surrounded by Sharks. 2014. (ENG.). 224p. (J). (gr. 4-7). 17.99 *(978-0-545-61545-7(3),* Scholastic Pr.) Scholastic, Inc.
Olin, Sean. Wicked Games. 2014. (Wicked Games Ser.: 1). (ENG.). 352p. (YA). (gr. 9). 17.99 *(978-0-06-219237-0(X),* Tegen, Katherine Bks) HarperCollins Pubs.
O'Malley Cerra, Kerry. Just a Drop of Water. (ENG.). 320p. (J). (gr. 2-7). 2016. pap. 7.99 *(978-1-5107-1234-8(8))* 2014. 14.95 *(978-1-62914-613-3(7))* Skyhorse Publishing Co., Inc. (Sky Pony Pr.).
Pallas-Luke, Barbara. Cryptic Society. 2005. (YA). 5.00 *(978-0-9765637-0-9(3))* Iris Pallas-Luke E-Writings/E-Literature.
Palmer, Robin. Little Miss Red. 2010. (ENG.). 320p. (YA). (gr. 7-18). 9.99 *(978-0-14-241123-0(X),* Speak) Penguin Young Readers Group.
Parramore, Helen. Maudie's Promise: A Girl on the Florida Frontier. 2008. 36p. pap. 20.99 *(978-1-4389-0226-5(3))* AuthorHouse.
Parsons, Pateh. Lickitysplit, the Handicapped Horse. 2008. 36p. pap. 24.95 *(978-1-60563-933-8(8))* America Star Bks.
Pastis, Stephan. Timmy Failure: the Cat Stole My Pants. Pastis, Stephan, illus. 2017. (Timmy Failure Ser.: 6). (ENG., Illus.). 288p. (J). (gr. 3-7). 14.99 *(978-0-7636-9733-4(8))* Candlewick Pr.
Pearson, Ridley. Dark Passage. 2014. (Kingdom Keepers Ser.). (ENG., Illus.). 256p. (J). (gr. 5-9). pap. 8.99 *(978-1-4231-6523-1(3))* Hyperion Bks. for Children.
—Dark Passage. 2013. (Kingdom Keepers Ser.: Bk. 6). (ENG.). 448p. (YA). (gr. 5-9). 17.99 *(978-1-4231-6489-0(X))* Hyperion Pr.
—Dark Passage. 2014. (Kingdom Keepers Ser.: 6). (J). lib. bdg. 19.65 *(978-0-606-35254-3(6))* Turtleback Bks.
—Disney after Dark. 2005. (Kingdom Keepers Ser.: Bk. 1). 324p. *(978-1-4156-2836-2(X))* Disney Pr.
—Disney after Dark. Elwell, Tristan, illus. 2009. (Kingdom Keepers Ser.: Bk. 1). (ENG.). 336p. (J). (gr. 5-9). pap. 8.99 *(978-1-4231-2311-8(5))* Hyperion Pr.
—Disney at Dawn. Elwell, Tristan, illus. 2009. (Kingdom Keepers Ser.: Bk. 2). (ENG.). 384p. (J). (gr. 5-9). pap. 8.99 *(978-1-4231-0708-8(X))* Hyperion Pr.
—Disney in Shadow. Elwell, Tristan, illus. 2011. (Kingdom Keepers Ser.: Bk. 3). (ENG.). 576p. (J). (gr. 5-17). pap. 8.99 *(978-1-4231-3856-3(2))* Hyperion Pr.
—Disney Lands. 2015. (Kingdom Keepers: Bk. 1). (ENG., Illus.). 352p. (J). (gr. 4-7). 17.99 *(978-1-4231-8431-7(9))* Hyperion Bks. for Children.
—The Insider. (Kingdom Keepers Ser.). (ENG., Illus.). (J). (gr. 5-9). 2015. 626p. pap. 9.99 *(978-1-4231-6524-8(1))* 2014. 614p. 17.99 *(978-1-4231-6490-6(3))* Hyperion Bks. for Children.
—Kingdom Keepers Boxed Set. 2014. (Kingdom Keepers Ser.). (ENG., Illus.). 1296p. (J). (gr. 3-7). pap. 25.99 *(978-1-4847-0402-8(9))* Hyperion Bks. for Children.
—Power Play. Elwell, Tristan, illus. 2011. (Kingdom Keepers Ser.: Bk. 4). (ENG.). 448p. (J). (gr. 5-9). 17.99 *(978-1-4231-3857-0(0))* Hyperion Pr.
—Power Play. 2012. (Kingdom Keepers Ser.: 4). (J). lib. bdg. 19.65 *(978-0-606-23613-3(9),* Turtleback) Turtleback Bks.
—Shell Game. 2013. (Kingdom Keepers Ser.: Bk. 5). (ENG.). 560p. (J). (gr. 5-9). pap. 8.99 *(978-1-4231-7195-9(0))* Hyperion Pr.
—Shell Game. 2013. (Kingdom Keepers Ser.: 5). (J). lib. bdg. 19.65 *(978-0-606-27067-0(1),* Turtleback) Turtleback Bks.
—The Syndrome. 2015. (Kingdom Keepers Ser.). (ENG., Illus.). 300p. (J). (gr. 5-9). 12.99 *(978-1-4847-2408-8(9))* Hyperion Bks. for Children.
Peck, Robert Newton. Bro. 2004. (ENG.). 160p. (J). (gr. 7-18). 16.99 *(978-0-06-052974-1(1))* HarperCollins Pubs.
—Horse Thief. 2003. 277p. (YA). (gr. 7). 13.65 *(978-0-7569-1461-5(2))* Perfection Learning Corp.
Pescatore, Faith. A Bell for Justin. 2009. 56p. pap. 10.99 *(978-1-4389-6821-6(3))* AuthorHouse.
Pons, Lele & De la Cruz, Melissa. Surviving High School: Do It for the Vine: A Novel. 2017. (ENG.). 272p. (gr. 8). pap. 11.99 *(978-1-5011-2054-1(9),* Gallery Bks.) Gallery Bks.
Prager, Ellen. The Shark Rider. Caparo, Antonio Javier, illus. 2015. (Tristan Hunt & the Sea Guardians Ser.: 2). (ENG.). 326p. (J). (gr. 3-7). pap. 9.95 *(978-1-938063-51-0(1),* Mighty Media Junior Readers) Mighty Media Pr.
—The Shark Whisperer. Caparo, Antonio Javier, illus. 2014. (Tristan Hunt & the Sea Guardians Ser.). (ENG.). 288p. (J). (gr. 3-7). pap. 9.95 *(978-1-938063-44-2(9),* Mighty Media Junior Readers) Mighty Media Pr.
Price, M. J. Momot. Grandma & Grandpa Are Retiring. 2013. 32p. pap. 24.95 *(978-1-63000-966-3(0))* America Star Bks.
Princesa Stephanie. 2005. (SPA.). (YA). per. 9.95 *(978-0-9764982-8-5(6))* Legacy Publishing Services, Inc.
Raffa, Edwina & Rigsby, Annelle. Kidnapped in Key West. (Florida Historical Fiction for Youth Ser.). (ENG.). (J). 2012. 138p. pap. 9.95 *(978-1-56164-537-4(0))* 2008. (Illus.). 127p. (gr. 3-7). 14.95 *(978-1-56164-413-1(7))* Pineapple Pr., Inc.
Raffensperger. The Eagle Tree. 2013. 60p. (J). pap. 14.95 *(978-0-9896338-6-4(1))* Barringer Publishing.
Rawlings, Marjorie Kinnan. The Secret River. Dillon, Leo & Dillon, Diane, illus. 2011. (ENG.). 56p. (J). (gr. -1-3). 19.99 *(978-1-4169-1179-1(0),* Atheneum Bks. for Young Readers) Simon & Schuster Children's Publishing.
—The Yearling. Wyeth, N. C., illus. 2013. (Scribner Classics Ser.). (ENG.). 416p. (J). (gr. 5-9). 29.99 *(978-1-4424-8209-8(5),* Atheneum Bks. for Young Readers) Simon & Schuster Children's Publishing.
Remkiewicz, Frank, illus. The Twelve Days of Christmas in Florida. (Twelve Days of Christmas in America Ser.). (ENG.). (J). (— 1). 2017. 22p. bds. 7.95 ***(978-1-4549-2283-4(4))*** 2008. 40p. 12.95 *(978-1-4027-3817-3(X))* Sterling Publishing Co., Inc.
Renfroe, Marjorie. The Doll Safari. 2009. 28p. pap. 15.49 *(978-1-4389-5130-0(2))* AuthorHouse.
Richardson, D. L. Feedback. 2013. 254p. pap. 11.99 *(978-1-939194-83-1(0))* Etopia Pr.
Richburg, Sheila. The Story of Panhandle Pete Part One. 2010. 19p. 16.95 *(978-0-557-15382-4(4))* Lulu Pr., Inc.
Ripley's Believe It or Not Editors & Ripley's Believe It Or Not! Staff. A Scaly Tale. 2010. (Rbi Ser.: 1). (ENG.). 128p. (J). pap. 4.99 *(978-1-893951-52-5(9))* Ripley Entertainment, Inc.
Roger, Moore & Ron, Kurtz. Arfie Plays Pirates. 2007. 40p. 17.95 *(978-0-9710343-5-8(4))* Photographs Naturally, Inc.
Roop, James Q. Billy Brahman: The Story of A Calf. Pomerantz, Norman, illus. 2011. 28p. 35.95 *(978-1-258-01757-6(1))* Literary Licensing, LLC.
Rorby, Ginny. How to Speak Dolphin. (ENG.). 272p. (J). (gr. 3-7). 2017. pap. 6.99 *(978-0-545-67607-6(X))* 2015. 16.99 *(978-0-545-67605-2(3))* Scholastic, Inc. (Scholastic Pr.).
Rose, Andrea. A Home for Abby. 2011. 24p. pap. 12.79 *(978-1-4634-2121-2(4))* AuthorHouse.
Rue, Nancy N. Motorcycles, Sushi & One Strange Book, 1 vol. 2010. (Real Life Ser.). (ENG.). 224p. (YA). (gr. 8-11). pap. 9.99 *(978-0-310-71484-2(2))* Zondervan.
Russell, Krista. The Other Side of Free, 1 vol. 2013. (ENG.). 256p. (J). (gr. 5-9). 16.95 *(978-1-56145-710-6(8))* Peachtree Pubs.
Rutley, Erika L. Adventures in Pup-A-Dupping. 2012. 36p. pap. 24.95 *(978-1-62709-710-9(4))* America Star Bks.
Sabina, C. Frosted August. 2007. 128p. (YA). per. 10.95 *(978-0-595-44636-0(1))* iUniverse, Inc.
Sacre, Antonio. La Noche Buena: A Christmas Story. Dominguez, Angela, illus. 2010. (ENG.). 32p. (J). (gr. k-2). 17.95 *(978-0-8109-8967-2(0),* Abrams Bks. for Young Readers) Abrams, Inc.
Saddleback Educational Publishing Staff, ed. Dive, 1 vol. unabr. ed. 2011. (Heights Ser.). (ENG.). 50p. (gr. 5-8). pap. 7.95 *(978-1-61651-282-8(2))* Saddleback Educational Publishing, Inc.
Saunders, Harry M. Teenagers on an Adventure: Journey of Two Boys & a Girl. 2013. 168p. pap. 19.95 *(978-1-62709-466-5(0))* America Star Bks.
Scattergood, Augusta. The Way to Stay in Destiny. 2015. (ENG.). 192p. (J). (gr. 3-7). 16.99 *(978-0-545-53824-4(6),* Scholastic Pr.) Scholastic, Inc.
Schraff, Anne. Sounds of Terror, 1 vol. unabr. ed. 2010. (Q Reads Ser.). (ENG.). 32p. (YA). (gr. 9-12). pap. 6.95 *(978-1-61651-206-4(7))* Saddleback Educational Publishing, Inc.
Scott, Kieran. I Was a Non-Blonde Cheerleader. 2007. (ENG.). 272p. (YA). (gr. 7-18). 8.99 *(978-0-14-240910-7(3),* Speak) Penguin Young Readers Group.
Scott, Kieran & Scott, Kiernan. Brunettes Strike Back. 2007. (ENG.). 272p. (YA). (gr. 7-18). 8.99 *(978-0-14-240778-3(X),* Speak) Penguin Young Readers Group.
Seabrooke, Brenda. Cemetery Street. 2008. 144p. (J). (gr. 3-7). 16.95 *(978-0-8234-2115-2(5))* Holiday Hse., Inc.
Secrets at Pine Haven: Civil War Comes to Florida. 2006. (Illus.). 180p. (J). per. 12.95 *(978-1-878398-75-8(X),* Blue Note Bks.) Blue Note Pubns.

E
F
G

Self, Jeffery. Drag Teen. (ENG.). 272p. (gr. 9). 2017. (J). pap. 9.99 (978-1-338-16063-5(X)) 2016. (YA). 17.99 (978-0-545-82993-9(3)) Scholastic, Inc. (PUSH).

Shankman, Ed. My Grandma Lives in Florida. O'Neill, Dave, illus. 2013. (Shankman & O'Neill Ser.). (ENG.). 32p. (J). (gr. -1-3). 14.95 (978-1-933212-35-7(7), Commonwealth Editions) Applewood Bks.

Shaw, J. M. Molly's Stallion. 2010. (J). pap. (978-0-88092-769-7(0)) Royal Fireworks Publishing Co.

Shaw, Marilyn Bishop. Solomon. 2006. (Florida Historical Fiction for Youth Ser.). (ENG.). 204p. (J). (gr. 4-9). 14.95 (978-1-56164-349-3(1)) Pineapple Pr., Inc.

Shearin, Effie Mae. Pedro Menendez: The Adelantado of Florida. 2005. (Illus.). pap. 7.95 (978-0-9773506-0-5(6)) Dolly Dimple Ink Children's Bks.

Shepperson, Jacqueline. Martins of the Everglades. 2007. (ENG.). 152p. per. 24.95 (978-1-4241-5446-3(4)) America Star Bks.

Silvano, Wendi. Love Is All Around Florida. Czernichowska, Joanna, illus. 2016. (ENG.). 32p. (J). (-6). 12.99 (978-1-4926-2918-4(9), Sourcebooks Jabberwocky) Sourcebooks, Inc.

—Love Is All Around Tampa Bay. Czernichowska, Joanna, illus. 2016. (ENG.). 32p. (J). (-6). 12.99 (978-1-4926-2963-4(4), Sourcebooks Jabberwocky) Sourcebooks, Inc.

Skelton, Vonda Skinner. Bitsy & the Mystery at Amelia Island. 2005. (Bitsy Burroughs Mysteries Ser.). (ENG.). 183p. (J). 15.95 (978-1-57072-306-3(0), Silver Dagger Mysteries) Overmountain Pr.

Smallman, Steve. Santa Is Coming to Florida. Dunn, Robert, illus. 2012. (ENG.). 32p. (J). (-3). 9.99 (978-1-4022-7527-2(7), Sourcebooks Jabberwocky) Sourcebooks, Inc.

—Santa Is Coming to Jacksonville. Dunn, Robert, illus. 2015. (ENG.). 32p. (J). (-3). 9.99 (978-1-4926-2635-0(X), Sourcebooks Jabberwocky) Sourcebooks, Inc.

—Santa Is Coming to Miami. Dunn, Robert, illus. 2013. (ENG.). 32p. (J). (-3). 9.99 (978-1-4022-9051-0(9), Sourcebooks Jabberwocky) Sourcebooks, Inc.

—Santa Is Coming to Orlando. Dunn, Robert, illus. 2015. (ENG.). 32p. (J). (-3). 9.99 (978-1-4926-2633-6(3), Sourcebooks Jabberwocky) Sourcebooks, Inc.

—Santa Is Coming to Tampa Bay & St. Petersburg. Dunn, Robert, illus. 2013. (ENG.). 32p. (J). (-3). 9.99 (978-1-4022-9054-1(3), Sourcebooks Jabberwocky) Sourcebooks, Inc.

Smith, Roland. Storm Runners. (Storm Runners Ser.: Bk. 1). (ENG.). 160p. (J). (gr. 3-7). 2012. pap. 5.99 (978-0-545-08177-1(7), Scholastic Pr.) 2011. 16.99 (978-0-545-08175-7(0)) Scholastic, Inc.

—The Surge. 2011. (Storm Runners Ser.: 2). (J). (ENG.). 144p. (gr. 3-7). 16.99 (978-0-545-08179-5(3)); 133p. pap. (978-0-545-39462-8(7)) Scholastic, Inc. (Scholastic Pr.).

Snadowsky, Daria. Anatomy of a Boyfriend. 2008. (ENG.). 272p. (YA). (gr. 9). pap. 8.99 (978-0-440-23944-4(3), Ember) Random Hse. Children's Bks.

Sonneborn, Scott. No Guts, No Gloria. Banks, Timothy, illus. 2015. (Frankenstein Journals). (ENG.). 80p. (gr. 2-3). 22.65 (978-1-4965-0221-6(3)) Stone Arch Bks.

Spears, Jr. Derek's Dilemm. 2009. 148p. pap. 24.95 (978-1-60836-387-2(2)) America Star Bks.

Spradlin, Michael P. Killer Species #4: Ultimate Attack. 2014. (Killer Species Ser.: 4). (ENG.). 192p. (J). (gr. 3-7). pap. 5.99 (978-0-545-50678-6(6), Scholastic Paperbacks) Scholastic, Inc.

Stern, A. J. Funny Business, 4 vols. Marts, Doreen Mulryan, illus. 2011. (Frankly, Frannie Ser.: 4). (ENG.). 128p. (J). (gr. 1-3). pap. 5.99 (978-0-448-45540-2(4), Grosset & Dunlap) Penguin Young Readers Group.

Stewart, Kiera. The Summer of Bad Ideas. 2017. 304p. (J). (gr. 3-7). 16.99 (978-0-06-236021-2(3)) HarperCollins Pubs.

Strand, Jeff. Stranger Things Have Happened. 2017. (ENG., Illus.). (YA). (gr. 7-12). 23.99 **(978-1-4926-6234-1(8))** Sourcebooks, Inc.

Sullivan, R. J. Tales of a Florida Boyhood. Voldseth, Beverly & Sullivan, Myra L., eds. rev. ed. Orig. Title: Tales of Boyhood RJL 1892-1907. (Illus.). 122p. (YA). (gr. 5-18). pap. 12.00 (978-1-887649-20-9(4)) Black Hat Pr.

Sully, Katherine. Night-Night Florida. Kolanovic, Dubravka & Poole, Helen, illus. 2016. (ENG.). 20p. (J). (-1). bds. 9.99 (978-1-4926-4218-3(5), 9781492642183, Sourcebooks Jabberwocky) Sourcebooks, Inc.

Sweeney, Joyce. Waiting for June, 0 vols. 2006. (ENG.). 158p. (YA). (gr. 10-12). pap. 7.99 (978-0-7614-5329-1(6), 9780761453291, Amazon Children's Publishing) Amazon Publishing.

Swoboda, Lois. Old Neb & the Ghost Ship. Wallace, Leslie, illus. 2015. (Old Neb Ser.). (ENG.). 126p. (J). pap. 10.95 (978-1-56164-797-2(7)) Pineapple Pr., Inc.

—Old Neb & the Lighthouse Treasure. Wallace, Leslie, illus. 2015. (Old Neb Ser.). (ENG.). 125p. (J). pap. 10.95 (978-1-56164-787-3(X)) Pineapple Pr., Inc.

Taylor, Pearl Fleming. Snowbird Weenie, 1 vol. 2009. 59p. pap. 16.95 (978-1-60836-745-0(2)) America Star Bks.

Thompson, Aiyana M. Miranda Fishhook: Makes a New Friend. 2010. 24p. 16.00 (978-1-4520-2364-9(6)) AuthorHouse.

Tomblin, Marian Strong. The Mystery at Hotel Ormond 2004. (Illus.). 142p. (J). per. 9.95 (978-0-9766620-0-6(0)) Avery Goode-Reid Pubs.

—Where's Capone's Cash? 2005. (Illus.). 232p. (J). per. 9.95 (978-0-9766620-1-3(9)) Avery Goode-Reid Pubs.

Torricelli, Dr Richard & Torricelli, Richard. A Tale of a Schnauzer. 2011. 44p. pap. 14.95 (978-1-936343-77-5(0)) Peppertree Pr., The.

Tozier, Christopher. Olivia Brophie & the Pearl of Tagelus. 2012. (ENG.). 208p. (J). pap. 12.95 (978-1-56164-519-0(2)) Pineapple Pr., Inc.

—Olivia Brophie & the Sky Island. 2014. (ENG.). 304p. (J). pap. 12.95 (978-1-56164-680-7(6)) Pineapple Pr., Inc.

Triana, Gaby. Summer of Yesterday. 2014. (ENG., Illus.). 272p. (YA). (gr. 9). pap. 9.99 (978-1-4814-0130-2(0), Simon Pulse) Simon Pulse.

Trinidad Joe. Santa's Key West Vacation. 2007. (Illus.). 80p. per. 12.95 (978-0-9799474-0-7(5)) Seastory Pr.

Tsang, Evonne. I Love Him to Pieces. Görrissen, Janina, illus. 2011. (My Boyfriend Is a Monster Ser.: 1). (ENG.). 128p. (YA). (gr. 7-12). 29.27 (978-0-7613-6004-9(2)) Lerner Publishing Group.

—#01 I Love Him to Pieces. Görrissen, Janina, illus. 2011. (My Boyfriend Is a Monster Ser.). 128p. (YA). pap. 56.72 (978-0-7613-7602-6(X), Graphic Universe™) Lerner Publishing Group.

van Diepen, Allison. Light of Day. 2015. (ENG.). 320p. (YA). (gr. 9). 17.99 (978-0-06-230347-9(3)) HarperCollins Pubs.

Viehl, Lynn. Dead of Night. 2012. (Youngbloods Ser.: 2). (ENG.). 312p. (YA). pap. 9.95 (978-0-7387-2646-5(X), Flux) North Star Editions.

Waters, Zack C. Blood Moon Rider. 2006. (Florida Historical Fiction for Youth Ser.). (ENG.). 126p. (J). (gr. 4-9). 13.95 (978-1-56164-350-9(5)) Pineapple Pr., Inc.

Watkins, Steve. Down Sand Mountain. (ENG., Illus.). 336p. (YA). (gr. 7). 2011. pap. 7.99 (978-0-7636-4835-0(3)) 2008. 16.99 (978-0-7636-3839-9(0)) Candlewick Pr.

Webb, Sarah. Summer Secrets. 2011. (Ask Amy Green Ser.: 2). (ENG., Illus.). 288p. (YA). (gr. 7-18). 16.99 (978-0-7636-5071-1(4)) Candlewick Pr.

Weeks, Timothy. The Wise Mullet of Cook Bayou. Jeanne, Miss, illus. rev. ed. 2006. 48p. (J). per. 14.99 (978-0-9779928-0-5(2)) Foolosophy Media.

Weltman, June. Mystery of the Missing Candlestick. 2004. (ENG.). 216p. (J). (gr. 4-7). 23.95 (978-1-878044-98-3(2)) Mayhaven Publishing, Inc.

Whispers from the Bay. 2008. 224p. (YA). 22.95 (978-0-9794454-0-8(X)) Tkac, John Enterprises LLC.

Whitaker, Nathan. Snap Decision, 1 vol. 2015. (Game Face Ser.). (ENG.). 272p. (J). pap. 8.99 (978-0-310-73703-2(6)) Zonderkidz.

Williams, Geoffrey T. Manatees & Mermaids. 2010. (ENG., Illus.). 64p. (J). (gr. 3-7). 8.95 (978-0-9800444-3-0(X)) Save Our Seas, Ltd.

Wilsdon, Christina. An Alligator Adventure in Florida. Mayo, Frank, illus. 2006. 26p. (J). 7.99 (978-1-59939-010-9(8)) Cornerstone Pr.

Wilson, Debra. 65 Mustang: A Novel. 2011. 300p. pap. (978-1-934922-47-7(1)) IBJ Custom Publishing.

Wood, Jane R. Adventures on Amelia Island: A Pirate, a Princess, & Buried Treasure. Blacker, Elizabeth A., illus. Wood, Jane R., photos by. 2007. (ENG.). 132p. (J). (gr. 3-8). pap. 8.99 (978-0-9792304-0-0(3)) Florida Kids Pr., Inc.

Woods, Brenda. My Name Is Sally Little Song. 2007. (ENG.). 192p. (J). (gr. 3-7). 7.99 (978-0-14-240943-5(X), Puffin Books) Penguin Young Readers Group.

—My Name Is Sally Little Song. 2007. (Illus.). 182p. (gr. 2-7). 17.00 (978-0-7569-8156-3(5)) Perfection Learning Corp.

Young, Ann Eastman. Once Blue. 2011. 108p. pap. 15.00 (978-0-557-71193-2(2)) Lulu Pr., Inc.

Zinner, Gennieve. The UFB's of Bugsville, Florida USA, 1 vol. Ballinger, Carolyn, illus. 2010. 48p. pap. 24.95 (978-1-4489-7977-6(3)) PublishAmerica, Inc.

FLORIDA—HISTORY

Addario, Yvonne. Treasure Diving with Captain Dom - Special Archival Section: Special Archival Section. 2007. (ENG., Illus.). 56p. (YA). per. 15.99 (978-0-9743414-1-5(X)) Adventure in Discovery.

Ancona, George. Mi Familia. 2004. (Somos Latino (We Are Latinos) Ser.).Tr. of My Family. 21.00 (978-0-516-23687-2(3), Watts, Franklin) Scholastic Library Publishing.

Aronson, Virginia & Szejko, Allyn. Iguana Invasion! Exotic Pets Gone Wild in Florida. 2010. (ENG.). 69p. (YA). (gr. 7-18). 16.95 (978-1-56164-468-1(4)) Pineapple Pr., Inc.

Baloyra, Patricia. Goodnight Miami. Knotz, Sarah, illus. 2012. (ENG.). 28p. (J). (gr. -1-3). 17.95 (978-1-4507-9592-0(7)) Ampersand, Inc.

Bauer, Marion Dane. Celebrating Florida: 50 States to Celebrate. Canga, C. B., illus. 2013. (Green Light Readers Level 3 Ser.). (ENG.). 40p. (J). (gr. 1-4). 12.99 (978-0-547-89699-1(9)); pap. 3.99 (978-0-547-89698-4(0)) Houghton Mifflin Harcourt Publishing Co.

Bodden, Valerie. Florida. 2010. (Let's Explore America Ser.). 24p. (J). (gr. k-2). 19.95 (978-1-58341-833-8(4)) Creative Co., The.

Boehm Jerome, Kate. Jacksonville & the State of Florida: Cool Stuff Every Kid Should Know. 2011. (Arcadia Kids Ser.). (ENG., Illus.). 48p. (J). (gr. 3-6). pap. 9.99 (978-1-4396-0092-4(9)) Arcadia Publishing.

—Orlando, Fl: Cool Stuff Every Kid Should Know. 2010. (Arcadia Kids Ser.). (ENG., Illus.). 48p. (J). (gr. 3-6). pap. 9.99 (978-1-4396-0064-1(3)) Arcadia Publishing.

Bredeson, Carmen. Florida. 2003. (Rookie Read-about Science Ser.). (Illus.). 31p. (J). (gr. -1-3). 13.60 (978-0-7569-7143-4(8)) Perfection Learning Corp.

Brown, Jonatha A. Florida. 2005. (Portraits of the States Ser.). (Illus.). 32p. (gr. 2-6). pap. 10.50 (978-0-8368-4641-6(9)); lib. bdg. 26.00 (978-0-8368-4622-5(2)) Stevens, Gareth Publishing LLLP. (Gareth Stevens Learning Library).

Brown, Rachel K. Daily Life in a Southern Colonial Town: St. Augustine. 2003. (J). (978-1-58417-014-3(X)); pap. (978-1-58417-077-8(8)) Lake Street Pubs.

Calfee, Susan. St. Augustine a to Z: A Young Reader's Guide to America's Oldest City. Senn, Oscar, illus. 2016. (ENG.). (J). pap. 12.95 (978-0-9895487-1-7(6)) Wordwhittler Bks.

Cannavale, Matthew C. Florida, 1513-1821. 2006. (National Geographic Voices from ColonialAmerica Ser.). (ENG., Illus.). 112p. (J). (gr. 5-9). 21.95 (978-0-7922-6409-5(6)); lib. bdg. 32.90 (978-0-7922-6866-6(0)) National Geographic Society. (National Geographic Children's Bks.).

Cerulean, Susan I., et al, eds. Between Two Rivers: Stories from the Red Hills to the Gulf. Meyer, Nancy, illus. 2004. 352p. (YA). per. 21.95 (978-0-9759339-0-9(6)) Red Hills Writers Project.

Coetzee, Mark M., et al. Where Art Is Happening - Artcenter/South Florida. 2003. (Illus.). 120p. (YA). (gr. 7-12). 200.00 (978-0-9719492-1-8(2)); pap. 30.00 (978-0-9719492-0-1(4)); lthr. 500.00 (978-0-9719492-2-5(0)) South Florida Art Ctr., Inc.

Conklin, Wendy. Finding Florida: Exploration & Its Legacy. 2016. (Primary Source Readers Ser.). 32p. (J). (gr. 4-4). pap. 8.99 (978-1-4938-3536-2(X)) Teacher Created Materials, Inc.

Crane, Carol. Little Florida. Monroe, Michael Glenn, illus. 2010. (My Little State Ser.). (ENG.). 22p. (J). 9.95 (978-1-58536-487-9(8)) Sleeping Bear Pr.

Crewe, Sabrina. La colonia de San Agustín. 2006. (Hitos de la historia de Estados Unidos (Landmark Events in American History) Ser.). (SPA.). 48p. (gr. 5-12). pap. 11.70 (978-0-8368-7472-3(2), Gareth Stevens Learning Library) Stevens, Gareth Publishing LLLP.

Crewe, Sabrina & Riehecky, Janet. La Colonia de San Agustin. 2006. (Hitos de la historia de Estados Unidos (Landmark Events in American History) Ser.).Tr. of Settling of St. Augustine. (SPA., Illus.). 48p. (gr. 5-12). lib. bdg. 27.00 (978-0-8368-7465-5(X), Gareth Stevens Secondary Library) Stevens, Gareth Publishing LLLP.

DeGraaf, Rob L. Fat Tire Favorites: South Florida off-Road Bicycling. DeGraaf, Rob L. & DeGraaf, Rebecca L., eds. DeGraaf, Rebecca L., photos by. 2003. Orig. Title: Guide to South Florida off-Road Bicycling. (Illus.). 111p. per. 12.95 (978-0-9678385-2-6(5)) DeGraaf Publishing.

Dillon, Doug. St. Augustine. 2010. (Class Trip Ser.). (Illus.). 48p. (J). (gr. 2-5). lib. bdg. 29.95 (978-1-58415-882-0(4)) Mitchell Lane Pubs., Inc.

Dippold-Brady, Melissa. Florida Fossils for Kids. 2009. pap. (978-1-61584-678-8(6)) Independent Pub.

Dittmer, Lori. The Story of the Orlando Magic. 2010. (NBA — A History of Hoops Ser.). 48p. (YA). (gr. 5-18). 23.95 (978-1-58341-956-4(X), Creative Education) Creative Co., The.

Durrie, Karen. Florida: The Sunshine State. 2012. (J). (978-1-61913-339-6(3)); pap. (978-1-61913-340-2(7)) Weigl Pubs., Inc.

Fairbanks, George R. Rainsford. History of Florida from Its Discovery by Ponce de Leon, in 1512, to the Close of the Florida War, In 1842, 5 vols. 2006. (ENG., Illus.). (YA). (gr. 4-12). act. bk. ed. incl. cd-rom (978-1-892824-22-6(1)) AFCHRON.

Florida's Women's Heritage Trail. (Heritage Trail Ser.). (J). (gr. -1-7). pap. 2.40 (978-1-889030-19-7(8)) Florida Div. of Historical Resources.

Flynn, Jim. Tampa Bay Buccaneers, 1 vol. 2010. (Inside the NFL Ser.). (ENG.). 48p. (YA). (gr. 3-6). lib. bdg. 32.79 (978-1-61714-030-3(9)) ABDO Publishing Co.

Francis, Peter, illus. God Bless Florida, 1 vol. 2016. (Land That I Love Book Ser.). (ENG.). 18p. (J). bds. 9.99 (978-0-310-75348-3(1)) Zonderkidz.

Harmon, Daniel E. Lower Atlantic: Florida, Georgia, South Carolina, Vol. 19. 2015. (Let's Explore the States Ser.). (Illus.). 64p. (J). (gr. 5). 23.95 (978-1-4222-3325-2(1)) Mason Crest.

Hemmel, David Lee & Knutson, Janette C. Alexis' Island: Growing up in the Tropical Paradise of Key West. 2006. (J). per. 14.95 (978-0-9745637-2-5(2)) Duval Publishing.

Hess, Debra & Wiesenfeld, Lori P. Florida. 2014. (J). pap. (978-1-62712-738-7(0)) Cavendish Square Publishing.

—Florida. 2nd rev. ed. 2010. (It's My State! Ser.). 80p. (gr. 3-18). lib. bdg. 31.36 (978-1-60870-049-3(6)) Marshall Cavendish Corp.

Housel, Debra J. Controlling Florida: Colonization to Statehood. 2016. (Primary Source Readers Ser.). 32p. (J). (gr. 4-4). pap. 8.99 (978-1-4938-3537-9(8)) Teacher Created Materials, Inc.

Jenkins, Lizzie L. P. R. The Real Rosewood. 2003. per. 24.95 (978-0-9724926-3-8(1), 0-9724926-3-1) Bookends Pr.

Jerome, Kate B. Lucky to Live in Florida. 2017. (Arcadia Kids Ser.). (ENG., Illus.). 32p. (J). 16.99 **(978-0-7385-2771-0(8))** Arcadia Publishing.

Jerome, Kate Boehm. Tampa, Fl: Cool Stuff Every Kid Should Know. 2010. (Arcadia Kids Ser.). (ENG., Illus.). 48p. (J). (gr. 3-6). pap. 9.99 (978-1-4396-0065-8(1)) Arcadia Publishing.

Johnson, Robin. Everglades Research Journal. 2017. (Illus.). 32p. (J). **(978-0-7787-3469-7(2))**; pap. **(978-0-7787-3494-9(3))** Crabtree Publishing Co.

Kenney, Karen Latchana. The Sunshine Champs: A Story about Florida, 1 vol. 2008. (Fact & Fable: State Stories Ser.). (ENG., Illus.). 24p. (J). (gr. -1-2). 25.65 (978-1-60453-187-9(8)) ABDO Publishing Co.

Kirchner, Jason. Florida. 2016. (States Ser.). (ENG., Illus.). 32p. (gr. 3-4). lib. bdg. 27.32 (978-1-5157-0395-2(9)) Next Page Pr., The.

Lantz, Peggy Sias & Hale, Wendy A. The Oceans of Florida. 2014. (Florida Water Story Ser.). (ENG., Illus.). 34p. (J). (gr. 4). pap. 6.95 (978-1-56164-704-0(7)) Pineapple Pr., Inc.

Latina, Paul A. The Places You'll Go: While at the University of Florida. 2012. 20p. pap. 16.50 (978-1-61204-831-4(5), Strategic Bk. Publishing) Strategic Book Publishing & Rights Agency (SBPRA).

Lewis, Anne Margaret. What Am I? Florida. Mills, Tom, illus. 2012. (ENG.). 24p. (J). (gr. -1 — 1). 9.99 (978-0-8075-8966-3(7)) Whitman, Albert & Co.

Mac, Janie. The Moon over Florida. 2013. 20p. pap. 13.77 (978-1-4669-9692-2(7)) Trafford Publishing.

Marsh, Carole. The Big Florida Reproducible Activity Book! 2004. (Florida Experience Ser.). (Illus.). 96p. pap. 12.95 (978-0-635-06408-0(1)) Gallopade International.

—Exploring Florida Through Project-Based Learning. 2016. (Florida Experience Ser.). (ENG.). (J). pap. 9.99 (978-0-635-12333-6(9)) Gallopade International.

—Florida History Projects: 30 Cool, Activities, Crafts, Experiments & More for Kids to Do to Learn about Your State! 2003. (Florida Experience Ser.). 32p. (gr. k-5). pap. 5.95 (978-0-635-01778-9(4), Marsh, Carole Bks.) Gallopade International.

—Let's Discover Florida! 2004. (J). (gr. 2-8). cd-rom 14.95 (978-0-7933-9487-6(2)) Gallopade International.

Marx, Trish. Everglades Forever: Restoring America's Great Wetland, 1 vol. Karp, Cindy, illus. Karp, Cindy, photos by. 2004. (ENG.). 40p. (J). 17.95 (978-1-58430-164-6(3)) Lee & Low Bks., Inc.

Mattern, Joanne. Exploring Florida's Geography, Culture, & Climate. 2016. (Primary Source Readers Ser.). 32p. (J). (gr. 4-4). pap. 8.99 (978-1-4938-3547-8(5)) Teacher Created Materials, Inc.

Maynard, Charles W. Castillo de San Marcos. 2009. (Famous Forts Throughout American History Ser.). 24p. (gr. 3-4). 42.50 (978-1-61512-514-2(0), PowerKids Pr.) Rosen Publishing Group, Inc., The.

Meinking, Mary. What's Great about Florida? 2014. (Our Great States Ser.). (ENG., Illus.). 32p. (gr. 2-5). pap. 7.95 (978-1-4677-4541-3(3)); lib. bdg. 26.60 (978-1-4677-3391-5(1), Lerner Pubns.) Lerner Publishing Group.

Mountjoy, Shane. St. Augustine. 2007. (Colonial Settlements in America Ser.). (Illus.). 104p. (YA). (gr. 5-9). lib. bdg. 30.00 (978-0-7910-9337-5(9)) Facts On File, Inc.

National Geographic Learning. From Cuba to the United States. 2009. (Inside the USA Ser.). (ENG., Illus.). 16p. (C). pap. 13.95 (978-0-7362-7056-4(6)) CENGAGE Learning.

O'Brien, Cynthia. Explore with Ponce de León. 2014. (ENG., Illus.). 32p. (J). (978-0-7787-1429-3(2)) Crabtree Publishing Co.

Paris, Stephanie Herweck. Jonathan Clarkson Gibbs: Reconstruction Revolutionary. 2016. (Primary Source Readers Ser.). 32p. (J). (gr. 4-4). pap. 8.99 (978-1-4938-3540-9(8)) Teacher Created Materials, Inc.

Publications International Ltd. Staff. Yesterday & Today Football Universary of Florida. 2009. 144p. 9.95 (978-1-4127-6111-6(5)) Publications International, Ltd.

Quinby, Michelle. Wars at Home: America Forms an Identity (1812-1820) 2012. (J). pap. (978-1-4222-2415-1(5)) Mason Crest.

—Wars at Home: America Forms an Identity (1812-1820) Rakove, Jack N., ed. 2012. (How America Became America Ser.). 48p. (J). (gr. 3-4). 19.95 (978-1-4222-2401-4(5)) Mason Crest.

Rey, Carol. Iris Wall, Cracker Cowgirl, 1 vol. Lux, Eldon, illus. 2012. (ENG.). 32p. (J). (gr. k-3). 16.99 (978-1-4556-1525-4(0)) Pelican Publishing Co., Inc.

Rice, Katelyn. Florida in the Early 20th Century: Boom & Bust. 2016. (Primary Source Readers Ser.). 32p. (J). (gr. 4-4). pap. 8.99 (978-1-4938-3542-3(4)) Teacher Created Materials, Inc.

Richter, Allen. America's Oldest Colony: The Story of St. Augustine. 2009. (Real Life Readers Ser.). 24p. (gr. 3-5). pap. 8.25 (978-1-4358-0228-5(4), Rosen Classroom) Rosen Publishing Group, Inc., The.

Riehecky, Janet. The Settling of St. Augustine. 2003. (Landmark Events in American History Ser.). (Illus.). 48p. (gr. 5-12). pap. 14.05 (978-0-8368-5404-6(7)); lib. bdg. 31.00 (978-0-8368-5376-6(8)) Stevens, Gareth Publishing LLLP. (Gareth Stevens Secondary Library).

Rodgers, Kelly. Florida's Fight for Equality. 2016. (Primary Source Readers Ser.). 32p. (J). (gr. 4-4). pap. 8.99 (978-1-4938-3544-7(0)) Teacher Created Materials, Inc.

Ruffin, Frances E. St. Augustine. 2006. (Places in American History Ser.). (Illus.). 24p. (gr. 1-4). lib. bdg. 22.00 (978-0-8368-6412-0(3), Weekly Reader Leveled Readers) Stevens, Gareth Publishing LLLP.

Ryan, Susan Jane & Tomatore, Carol. Florida a to Z. 2014. (ENG., Illus.). 64p. (J). (gr. 6). pap. 18.95 (978-1-56164-610-4(5)) Pineapple Pr., Inc.

Sammons, Sandra Wallus. Henry Flagler, Builder of Florida. 2010. (Pineapple Press Biography Ser.). (ENG.). 64p. (J). (gr. 4-7). pap. 8.95 (978-1-56164-467-4(6)) Pineapple Pr., Inc.

—Ponce de Leon & the Discovery of Florida. 2013. (ENG., Illus.). 72p. (J). (gr. 4-6). 12.95 (978-1-56164-592-3(3)); pap. 9.95 (978-1-56164-593-0(1)) Pineapple Pr., Inc.

Schwartz, Heather E. Florida's Government: Power, Purpose, & People. 2016. (Primary Source Readers Ser.). 32p. (J). (gr. 4-4). pap. 8.99 (978-1-4938-3546-1(7)) Teacher Created Materials, Inc.

—Growth of Florida: Pioneers & Technological Advances. 2016. (Primary Source Readers Ser.). 32p. (J). (gr. 4-4). pap. 8.99 (978-1-4938-3538-6(6)) Teacher Created Materials, Inc.

Sipperley, Keli. The Old Fort at St. Augustine. 2015. (ENG.). 32p. (gr. 3-6). 32.79 (978-1-63430-041-4(6)) Rourke Educational Media.

Sonneborn, Liz. The Acquisition of Florida: America's Twenty-Seventh State. 2009. (Milestones in American History Ser.). (Illus.). 120p. (gr. 6-12). 35.00 (978-1-60413-054-6(7), Chelsea Hse.) Facts On File, Inc.

Suben, Eric. The Spanish Missions of Florida. 2010. (True Book(tm), a — Spanish Missions Ser.). 48p. (J). (gr. 2-5). 31.00 (978-0-531-20578-5(9)); (gr. 3-5). pap. 6.95 (978-0-531-21241-7(6)) Scholastic Library Publishing.

Sullivan, Ann. Florida. 2011. (Guide to American States Ser.). (Illus.). 48p. (YA). (gr. 3-6). 29.99 (978-1-61690-781-5(9)) Weigl Pubs., Inc.

Sullivan, Ann. Florida: The Sunshine State. 2016. (J). **(978-1-5105-2087-5(2))** SmartBook Media, Inc.

—Florida: The Sunshine State. 2016. (J). (978-1-4896-4842-6(9)) Weigl Pubs., Inc.

Sutcliffe, Jane. Juan Ponce de Leon. 2005. (History Maker Bios Ser.). (Illus.). 48p. (J). (gr. 3-7). lib. bdg. 26.60 (978-0-8225-2944-6(0), Lerner Pubns.) Lerner Publishing Group.

Tieck, Sarah. Florida, 1 vol. 2012. (Explore the United States Ser.). (ENG.). 32p. (J). (gr. 2-5). 28.50 (978-1-61783-347-2(9)) ABDO Publishing Co.

Turner, Glennette Tilley. Fort Mosé: And the Story of the Man Who Built the First Free Black Settlement in Colonial America. 2010. (ENG., Illus.). 48p. (J). (gr. 3-7). 18.95 (978-0-8109-4056-7(6), Abrams Bks. for Young Readers) Abrams, Inc.

Ward, Jill. St. Marys River. 2009. (J). (978-1-935077-59-6(7)); pap. (978-1-935077-66-4(X)) State Standards Publishing, LLC.

Waxler, Melanie. Orlando. 2016. (Dropping in On Ser.). (ENG., Illus.). 32p. (gr. 2-4). 32.79 (978-1-68191-402-2(6)) Rourke Educational Media.

Williams, Dinah. Secrets of Walt Disney World: Weird & Wonderful Facts about the Most Magical Place on Earth. 2013. (ENG., Illus.). 160p. (J). (gr. 2-4). 8.95 (978-1-4549-0814-2(9)) Sterling Publishing Co., Inc.

Zschock, Martha Day. Hello, Florida! 2013. (Hello! Ser.). (ENG., Illus.). 16p. (J). (gr. -1-k). bds. 9.95 (978-1-933212-32-6(2), Commonwealth Editions) Applewood Bks.

FLORIDA MARLINS (BASEBALL TEAM)

Frisch, Aaron. Florida Marlins. 2009. (World Series Champions Ser.). (Illus.). 23p. (J). (gr. 2-3). 24.25 (978-1-58341-691-4(9), Creative Education) Creative Co., The.

Gilbert, Sara. Miami Marlins. 2012. (J). 25.65 *(978-1-60818-264-0(9),* Creative Education) Creative Co., The.

—The Story of the Florida Marlins. 2011. (Illus.). 48p. (J). 35.65 *(978-1-60818-041-7(7),* Creative Education) Creative Co., The.

Peterson, Sheryl. The Story of the Florida Marlins. 2007. (Baseball, the Great American Game Ser.). (Illus.). 48p. (YA). (gr. 4-7). lib. bdg. 32.80 *(978-1-58341-488-0(6))* Creative Co., The.

Sandler, Michael. Josh Beckett & the Florida Marlins: 2003 World Series. 2008. (World Series Superstars). (Illus.). 24p. (J). (gr. 1-4). lib. bdg. 22.61 *(978-1-59716-639-3(1))* Bearport Publishing Co., Inc.

Smolka, Bo. Florida Marlins. 2011. (Inside MLB Ser.). (Illus.). 48p. (YA). (gr. 3-6). 31.35 *(978-1-61714-044-0(9))* ABDO Publishing Co.

—Miami Marlins. 2012. (Inside MLB Ser.). (ENG., Illus.). 48p. (J). 32.79 *(978-1-61783-551-3(X))* ABDO Publishing Co.

Stewart, Mark. The Miami Marlins. 2012. (Team Spirit Ser.). 48p. (J). (gr. 3-6). lib. bdg. 29.27 *(978-1-59953-482-4(7))* Norwood Hse. Pr.

FLORISTS DESIGNS

see Flower Arrangement

FLOWER ARRANGEMENT

Fairies: Petal People You Make Yourself. 2009. (ENG.). 38p. (J). (gr. 3). spiral bd. 16.95 *(978-1-59174-802-1(X))* Klutz.

Sato, Shozo & Sato, Alice Ogura. Ikebana: Create Beautiful Flower Arrangements with This Traditional Japanese Art. 2004. (Asian Arts & Crafts for Creative Kids Ser.). (ENG., Illus.). 64p. (J). (gr. 2-6). 15.95 *(978-0-8048-3502-2(0))* Tuttle Publishing.

Tarbox, Charlene. Creative Haven Beautiful Flower Arrangements Coloring Book. 2013. (Adult Coloring Ser.). (ENG., Illus.). 64p. (gr. 3). pap. 5.99 *(978-0-486-49345-9(8))* Dover Pubns., Inc.

FLOWER GARDENING

Here are entered works on the cultivation of flowering plants for either commercial or private purposes.

see also Flowers; Plant Breeding; Plant Propagation

Decker, William. Growing Flowers. 2015. (Garden Squad! Ser.). (ENG.). 24p. (J). (gr. 3-4). 23.60 *(978-1-4994-1012-9(3),* PowerKids Pr.) Rosen Publishing Group, Inc., The.

The Flower Garden: Individual Title Two-Packs. (Chiquilibros Ser.). (gr. -1-1). 12.00 *(978-0-7635-8530-3(0))* Rigby Education.

El Jardin de Flores: Individual Title, 2 Packs. (Chiquilibros Ser.). (SPA.). (gr. -1-1). 12.00 *(978-0-7635-8550-1(5))* Rigby Education.

Leavitt, Amie Jane. A Backyard Flower Garden for Kids. 2008. (Gardening for Kids Ser.). (Illus.). 48p. (YA). (gr. 1-4). lib. bdg. 29.95 *(978-1-58415-633-8(3))* Mitchell Lane Pubs., Inc.

Lounsberry, Alice. The Garden Book for Young People. 2008. (Gardening in America Ser.). (ENG., Illus.). 404p. (J). (gr. 4-7). pap. 24.95 *(978-1-4290-1407-6(5))* Applewood Bks.

Wellington, Monica. Color & Garden FLOWERS. 2011. (Dover Coloring Bks.). (ENG., Illus.). 32p. (J). (gr. -1-3). pap. 4.99 *(978-0-486-47860-9(2))* Dover Pubns., Inc.

FLOWER PAINTING AND ILLUSTRATION

Ames, Lee J. Draw 50 Flowers, Trees, & Other Plants. 2012. (Draw 50 Ser.). lib. bdg. 20.85 *(978-0-606-26437-2(X),* Turtleback) Turtleback Bks.

Ames, Lee J. & Ames, P. Lee. Draw 50 Flowers, Trees, & Other Plants: The Step-by-Step Way to Draw Orchids, Weeping Willows, Prickly Pears, Pineapples, & Many More... 2012. (ENG., Illus.). 64p. pap. 9.99 *(978-0-8230-8579-8(1),* Watson-Guptill) Potter/TenSpeed/Harmony.

Baker, Robin J. & McElwain, Kelly A. 3-D Coloring Book — Flower Power! 2nd ed. 2012. (Dover 3-D Coloring Book Ser.). (ENG., Illus.). 32p. (J). (gr. 2-6). pap. 5.99 *(978-0-486-49012-0(2))* Dover Pubns., Inc.

Baumbusch, Brigitte. Flowers in Art. 2005. (What Makes a Masterpiece? Ser.). (Illus.). 32p. (gr. 1-4). lib. bdg. 23.00 *(978-0-8368-4447-4(5),* Gareth Stevens Learning Library) Stevens, Gareth Publishing LLLP.

Noble, Marty. Color Your Own Great Flower Paintings. 2004. (Dover Art Coloring Book Ser.). (ENG., Illus.). 32p. (gr. 3-8). pap., spiral bd. 4.99 *(978-0-486-43335-6(8))* Dover Pubns., Inc.

—Floral Mandalas Stained Glass Coloring Book. 2011. (Dover Design Stained Glass Coloring Book Ser.). (ENG., Illus.). 32p. (gr. 3-5). pap. 7.99 *(978-0-486-48312-2(6))* Dover Pubns., Inc.

Swanson, Maggie. Floral Fantasies Stained Glass Coloring Book. 2013. (Dover Stained Glass Coloring Book Ser.). (ENG., Illus.). 32p. (gr. 3-8). pap. 7.99 *(978-0-486-49807-2(7))* Dover Pubns., Inc.

Tarbox, Charlene. Floral Beauty Coloring Book. 2006. (Dover Nature Coloring Book Ser.). (ENG., Illus.). 96p. (J). (gr. 3-8). 7.95 *(978-0-486-45922-6(5))* Dover Pubns., Inc.

FLOWERS

see also Flower Arrangement; Flower Gardening; Flower Painting and Illustration; Plants; State Flowers; Wild Flowers

Aloian, Molly & Kalman, Bobbie. El Ciclo de Vida de la Flor. 2006. (Ciclos de Vida Ser.). (SPA., Illus.). 32p. (J). (gr. 3-7). pap. *(978-0-7787-8717-4(6))*; lib. bdg. *(978-0-7787-8671-9(4))* Crabtree Publishing Co.

—Les Fleurs. 2011. (Petit Monde Vivant (Small Living World) Ser.: No. 74). (FRE., Illus.). 32p. (J). pap. 9.95 *(978-2-89579-366-3(2))* Bayard Canada Livres CAN. Dist: Crabtree Publishing Co.

—The Life Cycle of a Flower. 2003. (Life Cycle Ser.). (ENG., Illus.). 32p. (J). pap. *(978-0-7787-0697-7(4))* Crabtree Publishing Co.

arsEdition. Sea of Flowers. 2017. (Mini Pads of Color Ser.). (ENG., Illus.). 80p. pap. 5.99 *(978-1-4380-1012-0(5))* Barron's Educational Series, Inc.

Bishop, Celeste. ¿Por Qué Las Plantas Tienen Flores? / Why Do Plants Have Flowers?, 01 vols., 1. 2016. (Partes de la Planta / Plant Parts Ser.). (ENG & SPA., Illus.). 24p. (J). 23.60 *(978-1-5081-4739-8(6),* PowerKids Pr.) Rosen Publishing Group, Inc., The.

—Why Do Plants Have Flowers?, 01 vols., 1. 2016. (Plant Parts Ser.). (ENG., Illus.). 24p. (J). pap. 8.25 *(978-1-5081-4213-3(0),* PowerKids Pr.) Rosen Publishing Group, Inc., The.

Blackaby, Susan. Buds & Blossoms: A Book about Flowers, 1 vol. DeLage, Charlene, illus. 2003. (Growing Things Ser.). (ENG.). 24p. (gr. -1-2). per. 8.95 *(978-1-4048-0388-6(2))* Picture Window Bks.

Bodach, Vijaya K. Flowers [Scholastic]. 2010. (Plant Parts Ser.). 24p. pap. 0.52 *(978-1-4296-5057-1(5),* Pebble Plus) Capstone Press of Coughlan Cos.

Bodach, Vijaya Khisty. Flowers. 2016. (Plant Parts Ser.). (ENG.). 24p. (gr. k-1). pap. 7.29 *(978-1-5157-4243-2(1),* Pebble Plus) Capstone Press of Coughlan Cos.

Boothroyd, Jennifer. Animal Pollinators. 2015. (First Step Nonfiction - Pollination Ser.). (ENG., Illus.). 24p. (gr. k-2). 39.99 *(978-1-4677-8904-2(6),* Lerner Digital); pap. 6.99 *(978-1-4677-6069-0(2),* Lerner Pubns.) Lerner Publishing Group.

—Cross-Pollination. 2015. (First Step Nonfiction - Pollination Ser.). (ENG., Illus.). 24p. (gr. k-2). 39.99 *(978-1-4677-8905-9(4),* Lerner Digital) Lerner Publishing Group.

—Insect Pollinators. 2015. (First Step Nonfiction - Pollination Ser.). (ENG., Illus.). 24p. (gr. k-2). pap. 6.99 *(978-1-4677-6068-3(4),* Lerner Pubns.) Lerner Publishing Group.

—Self-Pollination. 2015. (First Step Nonfiction - Pollination Ser.). (ENG.). 24p. (gr. k-2). pap. 6.99 *(978-1-4677-6071-3(4),* Lerner Pubns.) Lerner Publishing Group.

Bredeson, Carmen & Cousins, Lindsey. Can You Find These Flowers? 2012. (All about Nature Ser.). (Illus.). 24p. (J). (gr. -1-1). pap. 7.95 *(978-1-4644-0067-4(9),* Enslow Elementary) Enslow Pubs., Inc.

Calmenson, Stephanie. Look! Flowers! Pinillos, Puy, illus. 2016. (Look! Ser.). (ENG.). 24p. (J). (gr. -1-1). 7.99 *(978-1-4998-0115-6(7))* Little Bee Books Inc.

Clay, Kathryn. Flowers. 2016. (Celebrate Spring Ser.). (ENG., Illus.). 24p. (gr. k-1). lib. bdg. 21.99 *(978-1-4914-8304-6(0),* Pebble Bks.) Capstone Press of Coughlan Cos.

Colby, Jennifer. Flowers. 2014. (21st Century Junior Library: Plants Ser.). (ENG., Illus.). 24p. (J). (gr. 2-5). 25.64 *(978-1-63188-035-3(7),* 205547) Cherry Lake Publishing.

Collinson, Clare. British Trees & Flowers. 2017. (Nature in Your Neighbourhood Ser.). (ENG., Illus.). 32p. (J). (gr. 2-4). 17.99 *(978-1-4451-3641-7(4),* Franklin Watts) Hachette Children's Group GBR. Dist: Hachette Bk. Group.

¿Como Crecen las Flores? (Coleccion Primeros Pasos en la Ciencia). (SPA.). (J). (gr. 1-3). 3.16 *(978-950-724-014-0(4),* LMA8216) Lumen ARG. Dist: Lectorum Pubns., Inc.

Corwin, Judith Hoffman. Bright Yellow Flower. 2003. (Illus.). (J). *(978-0-439-44162-9(5))* Scholastic, Inc.

Cunningham, Kevin. Bees & Flowers. 2016. (21st Century Junior Library: Better Together Ser.). (ENG., Illus.). 24p. (J). (gr. 2-5). 27.07 *(978-1-63471-083-1(5),* 208411) Cherry Lake Publishing.

Decker, William. Growing Flowers. 2015. (Garden Squad! Ser.). (ENG.). 24p. (J). (gr. 3-4). 23.60 *(978-1-4994-1012-9(3),* PowerKids Pr.) Rosen Publishing Group, Inc., The.

Edwards, Nicola. Flowers. 2007. (See How Plants Grow Ser.). (Illus.). 24p. (J). (gr. 4-7). lib. bdg. 22.60 *(978-1-4042-3699-8(6))* Rosen Publishing Group, Inc., The.

Farndon, John. Flowers. (World of Plants (Blackbirch) Ser.). 24p. (J). (gr. 2-4). 2006. (ENG., Illus.). lib. bdg. 26.65 *(978-1-4103-0423-0(X))* 2005. pap. 22.45 *(978-1-4103-0517-6(1))* Cengage Gale. (Blackbirch Pr., Inc.).

La Flor. 2003. 23.95 *(978-0-673-77772-0(3))* Celebration Pr.

Flowers: 6 Each of 1 Student Book, 6 vols. (Sunshinetm Science Ser.). 24p. (gr. 1-2). 41.95 *(978-0-7802-2684-5(4))* Wright Group/McGraw-Hill.

Flowers: Big Book. (Sunshinetm Science Ser.). 24p. (gr. 1-2). 37.50 *(978-0-7802-2776-7(X))* Wright Group/McGraw-Hill.

Flowers & Fruit Sets: 1 Each of 3 Big Books. (Sunshinetm Science Ser.). (gr. 1-2). 111.50 *(978-0-7802-2818-4(9))* Wright Group/McGraw-Hill.

Flowers & Fruit Sets: 1 Each of 3 Student Books. (Sunshinetm Science Ser.). (gr. 1-2). 20.95 *(978-0-7802-2819-1(7))* Wright Group/McGraw-Hill.

Flowers, Pam. Douggie: The Playful Pup Who Became a Sled Dog Hero. Van Zyle, Jon, illus. 2008. (ENG.). 32p. (J). (gr. k-5). pap. 10.99 *(978-0-88240-655-8(8),* Alaska Northwest Bks.) Graphic Arts Ctr. Publishing Co.

Fox, Frances Margaret. Flowers & Their Travels. Funk, Clotilde Embree, illus. 2011. 230p. 46.95 *(978-1-258-07400-5(1))* Literary Licensing, LLC.

Fretland VanVoorst, Jenny & Pettiford, Rebecca. Flowers. 2015. (J). lib. bdg. 25.65 *(978-1-62031-231-5(X))* Jump! Inc.

Gerber, Carole. Spring Blossoms. Evans, Leslie, illus. (ENG.). 32p. (J). (gr. -1-3). 2015. pap. 7.95 *(978-1-58089-413-5(5))* 2013. lib. bdg. 16.95 *(978-1-58089-412-8(7))* Charlesbridge Publishing, Inc.

Glaser, Rebecca. Flowers. 2012. (ENG., Illus.). 24p. (J). lib. bdg. 25.65 *(978-1-62031-024-3(4))* Jump! Inc.

Gleisner, Jenna Lee. What Blossoms in Spring? 2014. (21st Century Basic Skills Library: Let's Look at Spring Ser.). (ENG.). 24p. (J). (gr. k-3). 22.79 *(978-1-62431-659-3(X),* 203148); pap. 12.79 *(978-1-62431-686-9(7),* 203149) Cherry Lake Publishing.

Goryl, Madeline, illus. The Garden Flowers Coloring Book. 2015. (Creative Stress Relieving Adult Coloring Book Ser.). (ENG.). 80p. (J). (gr. -1). pap. 5.99 *(978-1-63220-524-7(6),* Sky Pony Pr.) Skyhorse Publishing Co., Inc.

Gray, Rita. Flowers Are Calling. Pak, Kenard, illus. 2015. (ENG.). 32p. (J). (gr. -1-3). 16.99 *(978-0-544-34012-1(4),* HMH Books For Young Readers) Houghton Mifflin Harcourt Publishing Co.

Green, John. The Language of Flowers Coloring Book, 2 vols. 2004. (Dover Nature Coloring Book Ser.). (ENG., Illus.). 32p. (gr. 6-8). pap. 3.99 *(978-0-486-43035-5(9))* Dover Pubns., Inc.

Helbrough, Emma. How Flowers Grow. Silver, Maggie & Mayer, Uwe, illus. (Beginners Nature Ser.). 32p. (J). 2007. (gr. -1-3). 4.99 *(978-0-7945-1340-5(9),* Usborne) 2006. (gr. 4-7). lib. bdg. 12.95 *(978-1-58086-508-1(9))* EDC Publishing.

—How Flowers Grow. 2004. (Beginners Ser.). (ENG.). 32p. (J). (gr. 1-18). pap. 4.95 *(978-0-7945-0382-6(9))* EDC Publishing.

Heller, Ruth. Motivo de una Flor (Reason for a Flower) (SPA.). (J). 8.95 *(978-968-419-959-0(7))* Grijalbo, Editorial MEX. Dist: AIMS International Bks., Inc.

—The Reason for a Flower. (FRE.). (J). 6.99 *(978-0-590-71999-5(8))* Scholastic, Inc.

Higgins, Nadia. Experiment with Pollination. 2015. (Lightning Bolt Books (tm) — Plant Experiments Ser.). (ENG., Illus.). 32p. (gr. k-2). lib. bdg. 26.65 *(978-1-4677-5734-8(9),* Lerner Pubns.) Lerner Publishing Group.

Hoffmann, Sara. Kinds of Flowers. 2012. (First Step Nonfiction - Kinds of Plants Ser.). (ENG., Illus.). 8p. (gr. -1-1). pap. 4.95 *(978-1-4677-0500-4(4),* Lerner Pubns.) Lerner Publishing Group.

Hollow, Stanley. First Spring Flowers. 2016. (We Love Spring! Ser.). 00024p. (J). pap. 8.15 ***(978-1-4824-5489-5(0))*** Stevens, Gareth Publishing LLLP.

Horstschäfer, Felicitas. Flowers: Make Your Own Mobile Inspired by Emil Nolde. 2014. (ENG., Illus.). 16p. (J). (gr. 1-4). pap. 9.95 *(978-3-7913-7188-7(6))* Prestel Verlag GmbH & Co KG. DEU. Dist: Penguin Random Hse. LLC.

Houbre, Gilbert. Light. Houbre, Gilbert, illus. 2012. (ENG., Illus.). 36p. (J). (gr. -1-k). 12.99 *(978-1-85103-405-5(6))* Moonlight Publishing, Ltd. GBR. Dist: Independent Pubs. Group.

Huseby, Victoria. Daisy. 2008. (J). 25.65 *(978-1-59920-179-5(8))* Black Rabbit Bks.

Hutchinson, Alberta & Creative Haven Staff. Lotus Designs. 2012. (Adult Coloring Ser.). (ENG., Illus.). 64p. (gr. 3). pap. 5.99 *(978-0-486-49089-2(0))* Dover Pubns., Inc.

Jacobs, Pat. Why Do Plants Have Flowers? And Other Questions about Evolution & Classification. 2016. (Wildlife Wonders Ser.). 00032p. (J). (gr. 3-3). 26.25 *(978-1-4994-3273-2(9),* PowerKids Pr.) Rosen Publishing Group, Inc., The.

Jennings, Dorothy. Our Flower Garden. 2017. (Plants in My World Ser.). 24p. (gr. 4-6). pap. 8.25 ***(978-1-5383-2117-1(3),*** PowerKids Pr.) Rosen Publishing Group, Inc., The.

Jensen, Karl, et al. Flowers for Grandma. 2007. (Windows on Literacy Ser.). (ENG., Illus.). 12p. (J). pap. 10.95 *(978-0-7922-8457-4(7))* CENGAGE Learning.

Kababik, Dana. From Bulb to Flower. 2003. (Grow up! Ser.). (J). *(978-1-58417-175-1(8))* Lake Street Pubs.

—From Seed to Flower. 2003. (Grow up! Ser.). (J). *(978-1-58417-170-6(7))*; pap. *(978-1-58417-176-8(6))* Lake Street Pubs.

Kalman, Bobbie. What Is Pollination? 2010. (Big Science Ideas Ser.). (ENG.). 32p. (J). (gr. k-3). pap. *(978-0-7787-3306-5(8))* Crabtree Publishing Co.

Keyes, Daniel. Flores para Algernon. (SPA.). 98p. (J). 11.95 *(978-84-348-5274-7(8))* SM Ediciones ESP. Dist: AIMS International Bks., Inc.

Konicek-Moran, Richard. From Flower to Fruit. Konicek-Moran, Kathleen, illus. 2017. (ENG.). 30p. (J). (gr. k-2). pap. 11.95 *(978-1-941316-34-4(4))* National Science Teachers Assn.

MacAulay, Kelley. What Are Flowers? 2013. (ENG., Illus.). 24p. (J). *(978-0-7787-1286-2(9))*; pap. *(978-0-7787-0016-6(X))* Crabtree Publishing Co.

Masters, Nancy Robinson. Flowers Bloom. 2015. (Tell Me Why Library). (ENG., Illus.). 24p. (J). (gr. 2-5). 27.07 *(978-1-63362-610-2(5),* 206624) Cherry Lake Publishing.

Mattern, Joanne. How Tulips Grow. 2006. (How Plants Grow Ser.). (Illus.). 24p. (gr. k-2). pap. 8.15 *(978-0-8368-6341-3(0))*; lib. bdg. 22.00 *(978-0-8368-6334-5(8))* Stevens, Gareth Publishing LLLP. (Weekly Reader Leveled Readers).

—How Tulips Grow (Cómo crecen los Tulipanes) 2006. (How Plants Grow/ Como crecen las plantas Ser.). (ENG & SPA., Illus.). 24p. (gr. k-3). pap. 8.15 *(978-0-8368-6472-4(7))*; lib. bdg. 22.00 *(978-0-8368-6465-6(4))* Stevens, Gareth Publishing LLLP. (Weekly Reader Leveled Readers).

Mazurkiewicz, Jessica, et al. Floral Designs. 2012. (Adult Coloring Ser.). (ENG., Illus.). 32p. (gr. 1). pap. 5.99 *(978-0-486-47245-4(0))* Dover Pubns., Inc.

Meredith, Susan. Flowers to Color. Cooper, Jenny, illus. 2013. (Nature Coloring Bks). 32p. (J). pap. 5.99 *(978-0-7945-3058-7(3),* Usborne) EDC Publishing.

Mettler, Ren'e & Mettler, René. La Flor. (Coleccion Mundo Maravilloso). (SPA., Illus.). 40p. (J). *(978-84-348-3537-5(1),* FL9916) SM Ediciones.

Michaels, Eric. Flowers, 6 vols. 2004. (Phonics Readers Books 37-72 Ser.). (ENG.). 8p. (gr. k-1). pap. 35.70 *(978-0-7368-4077-4(X),* Phonics Readers) Capstone Press of Coughlan Cos.

Miller, Eileen Rudisill. True Love Stained Glass Coloring Book. 2011. (Dover Stained Glass Coloring Book Ser.). (ENG., Illus.). 32p. (gr. 3-8). pap. 6.99 *(978-0-486-47835-7(1))* Dover Pubns., Inc.

Mitchell, Melanie S. Flowers. 2004. (First Step Nonfiction - Parts of Plants Ser.). (ENG., Illus.). 8p. (gr. -1-1). pap. 4.95 *(978-0-8225-3917-9(9),* Lerner Pubns.) Lerner Publishing Group.

—Tulips. (First Step Nonfiction Ser.). (Illus.). (gr. k-2). 2005. 24p. lib. bdg. 17.27 *(978-0-8225-4614-6(0))* 2003. 23p. (J). pap. 5.95 *(978-0-8225-4615-3(9),* Lerner Pubns.) Lerner Publishing Group.

Morgan, Sally. Flowers, Fruits & Seeds. (Looking at Plants Ser.). (Illus.). 32p. (J). lib. bdg. 24.25 *(978-1-931983-10-5(0))* Chrysalis Education.

Owen, Ruth. What Do Roots, Stems, Leaves, & Flowers Do? 2014. (World of Plants Ser.). 32p. (J). (gr. 2-5). lib. bdg. 26.25 *(978-1-4777-7137-2(9),* PowerKids Pr.) Rosen Publishing Group, Inc., The.

Owens, L. L. The Life Cycle of a Daisy. 2011. (Life Cycles Ser.). (ENG., Illus.). 32p. (J). (gr. k-3). lib. bdg. 29.93 *(978-1-60973-146-5(8),* 201171) Child's World, Inc., The.

Owings, Lisa. From Bulb to Tulip. 2015. (Start to Finish, Second Ser.). (ENG., Illus.). 24p. (gr. k-3). pap. 6.95 *(978-1-4677-6109-3(5))*; lib. bdg. 23.93 *(978-1-4677-6021-8(8))* Lerner Publishing Group. (Lerner Pubns.).

Paine, Penelope C. Gift of Flowers. Maeno, Itoko, illus. 2006. 24p. per. 5.95 *(978-0-9707944-5-1(2))* Paper Posie.

Pascoe, Elaine. Flowers. 2003. (Illus.). 48p. (J). 24.95 *(978-1-56711-432-4(6),* Blackbirch Pr., Inc.) Cengage Gale.

Petersen, Christine. Flowers. 2008. (21st Century Junior Library: Plants Ser.). (ENG.). 24p. (gr. 2-5). lib. bdg. 25.64 *(978-1-60279-275-3(5),* 200180) Cherry Lake Publishing.

Plants & Flowers of Desert. (Butterfly Bks.). (ARA., Illus.). 32p. (J). (gr. 3-5). 8.95 *(978-0-86685-402-3(9),* LDL252) International Bk. Ctr., Inc.

Porter, Matthew. Flowers. 2010. (ENG., Illus.). 28p. (J). (gr. -1-k). bds. 8.95 *(978-1-897476-13-0(2))* Simply Read Bks. CAN. Dist: Ingram Publisher Services.

Rajczak, Kristen. Watch Tulips Grow. 2011. (Watch Plants Grow! Ser.). 24p. (gr. k-2). 69.20 *(978-1-4339-6159-5(8))*; (Illus.). (J). pap. 8.15 *(978-1-4339-4846-6(X))*; (Illus.). (J). lib. bdg. 22.60 *(978-1-4339-4845-9(1))* Stevens, Gareth Publishing LLLP.

—Watch Tulips Grow / ¡Mira cómo crecen los Tulipanes! 2011. (Watch Plants Grow! / ¡Mira cómo crecen las plantas! Ser.). (ENG & SPA., Illus.). 24p. (J). (gr. -1-2). 22.60 *(978-1-4339-4849-7(4))* Stevens, Gareth Publishing LLLP.

Ransom, Candice. Cross-Pollination. 2015. (First Step Nonfiction - Pollination Ser.). (ENG., Illus.). 24p. (gr. k-2). pap. 6.99 *(978-1-4677-6067-6(6),* Lerner Pubns.) Lerner Publishing Group.

—Parts of a Flower. 2015. (First Step Nonfiction - Pollination Ser.). (ENG.). 24p. (gr. k-2). (J). lib. bdg. 23.99 *(978-1-4677-5739-3(X),* Lerner Pubns.); (Illus.). pap. 6.99 *(978-1-4677-6070-6(6))* Lerner Publishing Group.

Relf, Patricia. Magic School Plants Seeds. 2014. 14.00 *(978-1-63419-672-7(4))* Perfection Learning Corp.

René, Ellen. Investigating How Flowers Grow. 2009. (Science Detectives Ser.). 24p. (gr. 2-3). 42.50 *(978-1-60853-012-0(4),* PowerKids Pr.); (Illus.). (J). lib. bdg. 22.60 *(978-1-4042-4484-9(0))* Rosen Publishing Group, Inc., The.

Richardson, Joy. Flowers. 2005. (Variety of Life Ser.). (Illus.). 32p. (gr. 1-4). lib. bdg. 26.00 *(978-0-8368-4504-4(8),* Gareth Stevens Learning Library) Stevens, Gareth Publishing LLLP.

Robson, Kirsteen. Mosaic Sticker Flowers. 2015. (Mosaic Sticker Bks.). (ENG.). 20+10p. (J). (gr. k-5). pap. 9.99 *(978-0-7945-3545-2(3),* Usborne) EDC Publishing.

Rod and Staff Publishers Staff, contrib. by. My Little Flower Book. 2012. (Illus.). 24p. (J). pap. *(978-0-7399-2454-9(0))* Rod & Staff Pubs., Inc.

Rohrer, Martha. Flowers, Flowers, Flowers. 2004. (Illus.). 32p. (gr. -1-5). 1.70 *(978-0-7399-2350-4(1),* 2952) Rod & Staff Pubs., Inc.

Royston, Angela. Flowers. (Illus.). 32p. (YA). (gr. 2-18). lib. bdg. 27.10 *(978-1-932333-39-8(8))* Chrysalis Education.

Schaefer, Lola M. Pick, Pull, Snap! Where Once a Flower Bloomed. George, Lindsay Barrett, illus. 2003. (ENG.). 32p. (J). (gr. k-5). 17.99 *(978-0-688-17834-5(0),* Greenwillow Bks.) HarperCollins Pubs.

Schaub, Michelle. Honeybees Help Flowers. 2006. (Early Explorers Ser.). (J). pap. *(978-1-4108-6122-1(8))* Benchmark Education Co.

Schwartz, Tom. How Mother Nature Flowered the Fields. 2007. 152p. (J). (gr. -1-3). per. 9.99 *(978-1-57545-142-8(5))* RP Media.

Senker, Cath. Garden Flowers, 01 vols., 1. 2016. (Adventures in Nature Ser.). (ENG.). 32p. (J). pap. 10.00 *(978-1-5081-4583-7(0),* PowerKids Pr.) Rosen Publishing Group, Inc., The.

Shapiro, David R. Flowers by Number. Vair, Hayley, illus. 2013. (Little Naturalist Ser.). (ENG.). 32p. (J). 14.99 *(978-0-9844422-8-7(6))* Craigmore Creations.

Sian Flowering Plants. 2004. (J). *(978-1-59242-030-8(3))* Delta Education, LLC.

Snedden, Robert. Flowers. (Living Things Ser.). (Illus.). 32p. 2009. (J). (gr. -1-3). pap. 7.95 *(978-1-59920-195-5(X))* 2007. (YA). (gr. 3-6). lib. bdg. 28.50 *(978-1-59920-078-1(3))* Black Rabbit Bks.

Soffer, Ruth. Butterflies & Flowers to Paint or Color. 2005. (Dover Art Coloring Book Ser.). (ENG., Illus.). 48p. (gr. 3-8). per. 5.99 *(978-0-486-44496-3(1))* Dover Pubns., Inc.

—The Flower Garden Coloring Book. 2005. (Dover Nature Coloring Book Ser.). (ENG., Illus.). 32p. (gr. 3-8). 3.99 *(978-0-486-44497-0(X))* Dover Pubns., Inc.

Sterling, Kristin. Exploring Flowers. 2011. (First Step Nonfiction / Let's Look at Plants Ser.). pap. 33.92 *(978-0-7613-8614-8(9))*; (ENG.). 24p. pap. 6.95 *(978-0-7613-7832-7(4))*; (ENG.). 24p. lib. bdg. 23.93 *(978-0-7613-5779-7(3))* Lerner Publishing Group.

Stockdale, Susan, illus. Fantastic Flowers, 1 vol. 2017. (ENG.). 32p. (J). (gr. -1-1). 16.95 *(978-1-56145-952-0(6))* Peachtree Pubs.

Stone, Lynn. Flowers. 2007. (Plant Parts Ser.). (Illus.). 24p. per. 7.95 *(978-1-60044-691-7(4))* Rourke Educational Media.

Stoutland, Allison. Take a Deep Breath: Little Lessons from Flowers for a Happier World. Hofner, Cathy, illus. I.t. ed. 2003. 32p. 14.95 *(978-0-9670941-2-0(7))* Inch By Inch Pubns., LLC.

Stuart, Carrie. How Flowers Grow. 2008. (Rosen Real Readers: Upper Emergent Ser.). (ENG., Illus.). 12p. (gr. 1-2). pap. 5.90 *(978-0-8239-8129-8(0))* Rosen Publishing Group, Inc., The.

Swanson, Maggie. Spark - Flower Fun Coloring Book. 2016. (ENG., Illus.). 64p. (J). (gr. k-3). pap. 5.99 *(978-0-486-80215-2(9))* Dover Pubns., Inc.

Throp, Claire. All about Flowers. (All about Plants Ser.). (ENG.). 24p. (gr. -1-1). 2016. pap. 5.99 *(978-1-4846-3846-0(8))* 2014. 22.65 *(978-1-4846-0506-6(3))* Heinemann-Raintree. (Acorn).

Toole, Spencer. Flowers Need Sun: If... Then. 2017. (Computer Science for the Real World Ser.). 8p. (gr. 5-6). pap. 6.20 ***(978-1-5383-5107-9(2),*** Rosen Classroom) Rosen Publishing Group, Inc., The.

Utarid, Anjana. Count Me In. 2008. 24p. pap. 12.95 *(978-1-60264-281-2(8))* Virtualbookworm.com Publishing, Inc.

Wade, Mary Dodson. Flowers Bloom! 2009. (I Like Plants! Ser.). (Illus.). 24p. (J). (gr. k-3). lib. bdg. 22.60 *(978-0-7660-3157-9(8))* Enslow Pubs., Inc.

Waldron, Melanie. Flowers, 1 vol. 2014. (Plant Parts Ser.). (ENG.). 32p. (gr. 2-4). lib. bdg. 30.65 *(978-1-4109-5420-6(X),* Raintree Perspectives) Heinemann-Raintree.

Whitehouse, Patricia. Las Flores, 1 vol. 2nd ed. 2010. (Las Plantas Ser.). (ENG & SPA.). 24p. (gr. k-2). 23.32 *(978-1-4329-4186-4(0))*; pap. 6.79 *(978-1-4329-4191-8(7))* Heinemann-Raintree.

Whitman, Nancy C. Counting Petals. 2009. 36p. pap. 21.99 *(978-1-4363-8561-9(X))* Xlibris Corp.

EFG

—Counting Petals: Using Flowers of Hawaii. Chong, Luther, photos by. 2009. (Illus.). 31p. (J). *(978-1-4363-8562-6(8))* Xlibris Corp.

Williams, Angela Claudette. The Wonderful Things about a Flower. 2008. 17p. 14.50 *(978-0-615-16052-8(2))* Williams, Angela Claudette.

Wolf, Helmut, photos by. Flowers of India. 2010. (ENG., Illus.). 24p. (J). (gr. k — 1). bds. *(978-81-907546-7-5(X))* Tara Publishing.

Wolfsgruber, Linda. A Daisy Is a Daisy Is a Daisy (Except When It's Girl's Name), 1 vol. 2011. (ENG., Illus.). 32p. (J). (gr. -1). 16.95 *(978-1-55498-099-4(2))* Groundwood Bks. CAN. Dist: Publishers Group West (PGW).

Young, Jessica. Finley Flowers. 2015. (Finley Flowers Ser.). (ENG.). 128p. (gr. 2-3). 101.28 *(978-1-4795-7922-8(X),* Finley Flowers) Picture Window Bks.

FLOWERS—ARRANGEMENT

see Flower Arrangement

FLOWERS, ARTIFICIAL

see Artificial Flowers

FLOWERS—FICTION

Akley, Jason. Sweet Pea & the Bumblebee. 2007. (ENG.). 36p. (J). per. 16.95 *(978-1-4327-0341-7(2))* Outskirts Pr., Inc.

Alcott, Louisa May. Flower Fables. 2005. (ENG., Illus.). 224p. (gr. 4-7). 15.95 *(978-1-55709-954-9(5))* Applewood Bks.

Allaway, Al. Laughing Flowers & Blooming Animals. 2009. 32p. pap. 17.95 *(978-0-557-04195-4(3))* Lulu Pr., Inc.

Anaya, Rudolfo. How Hollyhocks Came to New Mexico. Garcia, Nasario, tr. Otéro, Nicolas, illus. 2012. 48p. 24.95 *(978-1-936744-12-1(0),* Rio Grande Bks.) LPD Pr.

Arroyo, Andrea, illus. The Legend of the Lady Slipper. 2004. (ENG.). 32p. (J). (gr. -1-3). reprint ed. pap. 6.99 *(978-0-618-43231-8(0))* Houghton Mifflin Harcourt Publishing Co.

Aulbach, Kathy. Flower Sprouts: Let's have a Fest! 2009. 29p. 15.95 *(978-0-615-21683-6(8))* Flower Sprouts.

—Meet the Flowers. 2009. 31p. 15.95 *(978-0-615-21179-4(8))* Flower Sprouts.

Badu. Learning with the Flowerrrs: Vol. -1 Hospital Visit. 2011. 40p. pap. 21.67 *(978-1-4634-1878-6(7))* AuthorHouse.

Ballard, George Anne. Flowers along the Way. Ballard, George Anne & Bolton, Georgia Helen, illus. 2012. 26p. pap. 12.00 *(978-0-9855312-2-5(3))* Bolton Publishing LLC.

Baniti, Nailah. Nia's Dream the Talking Tulips. Bayramoglu, Hatice, illus. 2nd ed. 2013. 24p. pap. 7.99 *(978-0-9853574-5-0(2))* Mountan Creek Pubns.

Barker, Cicely Mary. Magical Doors: Discover the Doors to Fairyopolis. 2009. (Flower Fairies Ser.). (ENG.). 16p. (J). (gr. k-4). 22.99 *(978-0-7232-6351-7(5),* Warne) Penguin Young Readers Group.

Baxter, David. The Tournesol Twins. 2006. 68p. pap. *(978-1-84401-901-4(2))* Athena Pr.

Beamer, Winona Desha & Beamer-Trapp, Kaliko. Pua Polu: The Pretty Blue Hawaiian Flower. Loebel-Fried, Caren Keala, illus. 2005. (HAW & ENG.). 36p. (J). audio compact disk 14.95 *(978-1-58178-041-3(9))* Bishop Museum Pr.

Berkove, Lawrence I. How Butterflies Got Colored Wings. Barshishat, Malka Michaela, illus. 2017. (J). pap. ***(978-1-5011-4872-9(9))*** Meadowbrook Pr.

Bickel, Karla. Lilac Rose: A Flower's Lifetime. Bickel, Karla, illus. l.t. ed. 2004. (Illus.). 16p. (J). (gr. -1-6). pap. 5.00 *(978-1-891452-10-9(X),* 8) Heart Arbor Bks.

Bonnell, Kris. A Flower for a Bee. 2006. (J). pap. 3.95 *(978-1-933727-23-3(3))* Reading Reading Bks., LLC.

—The Little Sprout. 2007. (J). pap. 5.95 *(978-1-933727-54-7(3))* Reading Reading Bks., LLC.

—Yellow Flowers. 2006. (J). pap. 5.95 *(978-1-933727-36-3(5))* Reading Reading Bks., LLC.

Boynton, Cara. Sam's Secret World. 2006. (ENG.). 48p. per. 16.95 *(978-1-4241-4529-4(5))* PublishAmerica, Inc.

Burnett, Frances Hodgson. The Land of Blue Flower. 2007. 76p. pap. 14.45 *(978-1-59462-742-2(8),* Book Jungle) Standard Pubns., Inc.

—The Land of the Blue Flower. 2007. 76p. per. 9.45 *(978-1-59462-779-8(7),* Book Jungle) Standard Pubns., Inc.

Burrowes, Adjoa J. Grandma's Purple Flowers. 2004. (J). (gr. k-3). spiral bd. *(978-0-616-07252-3(X));* spiral bd. *(978-0-616-08496-0(X))* Canadian National Institute for the Blind/Institut National Canadien pour les Aveugles.

Byars, Betsy. Wanted... Mud Blossom. (Blossom Family Ser.: Bk. 5). 148p. (J). (gr. 4-6). pap. 4.99 *(978-0-8072-1470-1(1),* Listening Library) Random Hse. Audio Publishing Group.

Cabral, Jeane. Just One Flower. 2009. (Jeane Cabral Bks.). (Illus.). (J). bds. 12.99 *(978-1-934650-07-3(2))* Just For Kids Pr., LLC.

Cafege, Adam. Of Petals & Hope: Sunny Sunflower Triumphs over Bullying. Calindas, Marconi, illus. 2013. 36p. pap. 24.95 *(978-0-9840204-4-7(6))* Pacific Raven Pr.

Calarco, Donald Charles. In a Dandelion's World: A Small Book with a Big Story! 2009. 40p. pap. 17.95 *(978-1-4327-1167-2(9))* Outskirts Pr., Inc.

Canetti, Yanitzia. ABC's of Plants. 2010. (ENG.). 40p. (J). pap. 8.99 *(978-1-59835-118-7(4),* BrickHouse Education) Cambridge BrickHouse, Inc.

—Abecedario de Plantas. 2010. (SPA.). 40p. (J). pap. 8.99 *(978-1-59835-119-4(2),* BrickHouse Education) Cambridge BrickHouse, Inc.

Carle, Eric. The Tiny Seed. Carle, Eric, illus. 2005. (World of Eric Carle Ser.). (ENG., Illus.). 34p. (J). (gr. -1-k). bds. 8.99 *(978-0-689-87149-8(X),* Little Simon) Little Simon.

Carriger, Candace. Inside My Garden. Allen, Cassandra, illus. 2011. 46p. (J). pap. 11.95 *(978-0-9816047-5-6(7))* Sadie Bks.

Cheng, Andrea. Goldfish & Chrysanthemums. Chang, Michelle, illus. 2003. (ENG.). 32p. (J). 16.95 *(978-1-58430-057-1(4));* pap. 8.95 *(978-1-60060-889-6(2))* Lee & Low Bks., Inc.

Clark, Danell. Daisy. Irwin, April, illus. 2008. 28p. pap. 11.95 *(978-1-59858-642-8(4))* Dog Ear Publishing, LLC.

Coates, Theresa. Imaginary Time of Life. 2007. 102p. pap. 10.95 *(978-0-7414-4067-9(9))* Infinity Publishing.

Colburn, Cherie Foster. Bloomin' Tales: Legends of Seven Favorite Texas Wildflowers. Hein, Joy Fisher, illus. 2012. (ENG.). 64p. (J). (gr. 4-4). 24.95 *(978-1-936474-18-9(2),* 91c14e7a-1c5d-4381-b022-da21965048db) Bright Sky Pr.

Cook, Julia. The Judgmental Flower. DuFalla, Anita, illus. 2016. (ENG.). 32p. (J). pap. 10.95 *(978-1-944882-05-1(7))* Boys Town Pr.

Corderoy, Tracey. Flower in the Snow. Allsopp, Sophie, illus. 2012. (ENG.). 32p. (J). (-3). 16.99 *(978-1-4022-7740-5(7),* 1350490, Sourcebooks Jabberwocky) Sourcebooks, Inc.

Coughlin, Denise & Pappas, Maria. Petal Pals. 2008. 32p. 14.95 *(978-0-9705100-7-5(1))* NK Pubns.

Cowsar, Susan. The Magic Flower. 2013. 58p. pap. 10.99 *(978-1-62697-943-7(X))* Salem Author Services.

Crawford, K. Michael, illus. The Munched-up Flower Garden. 2006. (Troublesome Creek Kids Story Ser.). (ENG.). 32p. (J). (gr. -1-3). 16.95 *(978-1-933176-04-8(0));* pap. 10.95 *(978-1-933176-06-2(7))* Red Rock Pr., Inc.

Curtis, Sarah. The Wondrous Flower. 2013. 36p. pap. 24.95 *(978-1-4626-9812-7(3))* America Star Bks.

Dale, Jay. Pippa & the Flowers, 1 vol. Draycott, Michelle, illus. 2012. (Wonder Words Ser.). (ENG.). 32p. (gr. k-2). pap. 5.99 *(978-1-4296-8908-3(0),* Engage Literacy) Capstone Press of Coughlan Cos.

Daly, Catherine R. Too Many Blooms. 2011. (Petal Pushers Ser.: 1). (ENG.). 192p. (J). (gr. 3-7). pap. 5.99 *(978-0-545-21450-6(5),* Scholastic Paperbacks) Scholastic, Inc.

De Sena, Joseph. Mrs. Mouse & the Golden Flower. 2007. 56p. per. 19.95 *(978-1-4327-1525-0(9))* Outskirts Pr., Inc.

Deluca, Laura. Flora & the Silver Coins. Manni, Mia (Maio), illus. 2011. 40p. pap. 24.95 *(978-1-4560-7752-5(X))* America Star Bks.

DiCamillo, Kate. Mercy Watson Thinks Like a Pig. Van Dusen, Chris, illus. (Mercy Watson Ser.: 5). (ENG.). 80p. (J). (gr. 1-4). 2011. pap. 5.99 *(978-0-7636-5231-9(8))* 2008. 12.99 *(978-0-7636-3265-6(1))* Candlewick Pr.

Diederich, Ellen Jean. Where's Petunia? 2003. (Illus.). 32p. (J). per. 18.99 *(978-0-9728654-0-1(3))* Givinity Pr.

Dompierre, Judith E. Wow, What's That? 2012. 48p. pap. 24.95 *(978-1-4626-9332-0(6))* America Star Bks.

Donaldson, Julia. Wrong Kind of Bark. Parsons, Garry, illus. 2004. (Red Bananas Ser.). (ENG.). 48p. (J). (gr. k-2). pap. 5.99 *(978-1-4052-1062-1(1))* Egmont Bks., Ltd. GBR. Dist: Independent Pubs. Group.

Don't Eat the Bluebonnets. 2006. (J). lib. bdg. 17.95 *(978-0-9645493-3-3(6))* Bluebonnets, Boots & Bks. Pr.

Ehlert, Lois. Planting a Rainbow. Ehlert, Lois, illus. 2003. (ENG., Illus.). 32p. (J). (gr. k — 1). bds. 7.99 *(978-0-15-204633-0(X))* Houghton Mifflin Harcourt Publishing Co.

—Planting a Rainbow: Lap-Sized Board Book. 2008. (ENG., Illus.). 32p. (J). (gr. -1 — 1). bds. 11.99 *(978-0-15-206304-7(8))* Houghton Mifflin Harcourt Publishing Co.

Eisele, Barbara. Miss Thistle & Friends. 2009. 48p. pap. 12.99 *(978-1-4490-2007-1(0))* AuthorHouse.

Ellison, Penny. Daisy the Dancing Flower. 2006. (J). 15.95 *(978-0-9771121-2-8(8))* Ellison, Penny.

Ergün, Erol. The Generous Bestower. 2011. (ENG., Illus.). 176p. pap. 9.95 *(978-1-59784-258-7(3))* Tughra Bks.

Ernst, Cindy Kathleen. Sunny the Sunflower. 2012. 32p. pap. *(978-1-4602-0276-0(7))* FriesenPress.

Fairy-Tale Flowers: Individual Title, 6 pack. (Story Steps Ser.). (gr. k-2). 23.00 *(978-0-7635-9842-6(9))* Rigby Education.

Farley, Jan. Fleur, a Lonely Pocket Mouse. 2011. 32p. pap. 16.95 *(978-1-4560-4073-4(1))* America Star Bks.

Fernandez, Martina. Jellybean: Jellybean Finds a Home. 2012. 28p. pap. 19.99 *(978-1-4772-7237-4(2))* AuthorHouse.

Flaherty, Finn. The Flowerpot. 2006. (Neighborhood Readers Ser.). (ENG.). 16p. (gr. 1-3). pap. 6.50 *(978-1-4042-7224-8(0),* Rosen Classroom) Rosen Publishing Group, Inc., The.

The Flower Child. 2013. (Illus.). 28p. 17.99 *(978-0-9891510-1-6(8))* Zebra Ginkgo.

Floyd, Jamie. The Spring Flower. 2008. 17p. pap. 24.95 *(978-1-60610-810-9(7))* America Star Bks.

Foster Colburn, Cherie. Bloomin' Tales: Seven Favorite Wildflower Legends. Fisher Hein, Joy, illus. 2012. (ENG.). 64p. (J). pap. 9.95 *(978-1-936474-36-3(0),* 1987c76b-83d5-44af-9831-cd68dda6cbfd) Bright Sky Pr.

Frommer, Julia. Happiness Is Yours. 2007. 24p. 13.95 *(978-1-4303-1176-8(2))* Lulu Pr., Inc.

Fry, Debbie, illus. Donkeywise & Otherwise: The Story of Daisy Doo & Dudley Duz. 2004. 44p. (J). *(978-0-9759647-0-5(4),* 1238040) Fry, Debbie.

Galjanic, Lisa. When Flowers Dance. Hope, Michelle, illus. 2007. (J). 9.95 *(978-1-933532-05-9(X))* LSG Pubns.

—When Series 6 Volume Set, 6, 6. 2007. (Illus.). 100p. (J). 34.95 *(978-1-933532-06-6(8))* LSG Pubns.

Gallacher, Marcie. Amaryllis Lilies. 148p. (YA). pap. 7.95 *(978-1-56236-451-9(0))* Aspen Bks.

Garland, Sherry. The Lotus Seed. Kiuchi, Tatsuro, illus. 2014. 32p. pap. 7.00 *(978-1-61003-219-3(5))* Center for the Collaborative Classroom.

Giles, Mike, illus. Spring Showers Bring Flowers. 2014. (Yo Gabba Gabba! Ser.). (ENG.). 12p. (J). (gr. -1-k). bds. 5.99 *(978-1-4424-9572-2(3),* Simon Spotlight) Simon Spotlight.

Glover, Dennis W. The Talking Flower. 2010. 32p. pap. 12.99 *(978-1-4490-5599-8(0))* AuthorHouse.

Gulino, ViTina Corso. Peter Rabbit & My Tulips. Murariu, Lorraine, illus. 2012. 26p. (J). pap. 9.95 *(978-1-61863-275-3(2))* Bookstand Publishing.

Gunn, Barbara & Dunn, Richard. Flowers: Read Well Level K Unit 9 Storybook. Nolte, Larry, illus. 2004. (Read Well Level K Ser.). 20p. (J). *(978-1-57035-680-3(7))* Cambium Education, Inc.

Gutierrez, Debbi Miller. Cactus Factory. 2007. (J). pap. 5.99 *(978-0-9740173-4-1(5))* Prints By Mail.

Hahn, Rebecca. A Creature of Moonlight. 2014. (ENG.). 224p. (YA). (gr. 7-12). 17.99 *(978-0-544-10935-3(X),* HMH Books For Young Readers) Houghton Mifflin Harcourt Publishing Co.

Hamilton, George. Seeing Red: Story Seeds Vol 1. Hazel, Andrew, illus. 2008. 20p. pap. 13.99 *(978-1-4343-8004-3(1))* AuthorHouse.

Harris, Tammy. Fairy Flower Alphabet. 2011. 32p. pap. 12.77 *(978-1-4389-3169-2(7))* AuthorHouse.

Hearn, Diane Dawson. Anna in the Garden. 2006. (Illus.). 29p. (J). (gr. k-4). reprint ed. 15.00 *(978-1-4223-5087-4(8))* DIANE Publishing Co.

Henkes, Kevin. A Box Full of Lilly: Lilly's Big Day. Henkes, Kevin, illus. 2006. (Illus.). (J). (gr. -1-4). 27.99 *(978-0-06-112852-3(X),* Greenwillow Bks.) HarperCollins Pubs.

—So Happy! Lobel, Anita, illus. 2005. (ENG.). 32p. (J). (gr. -1-3). 16.99 *(978-0-06-056483-4(0),* Greenwillow Bks.) HarperCollins Pubs.

Hill, Susanna Leonard. No Sword Fighting in the House. Kelley, True, illus. (Holiday House Reader Ser.: Level 2). (ENG.). 32p. (J). (gr. k-3). 14.95 *(978-0-8234-1916-6(9))* Holiday Hse., Inc.

Hix, Melvin. The Magic Speech Flower: Or Little Luke & His Animal Friends. 2007. (ENG.). 110p. pap. 18.99 *(978-1-4346-0790-4(9));* 114p. pap. 19.99 *(978-1-4346-0797-3(6))* Creative Media Partners, LLC.

Höhn, Jessica. Please Don't Pick the Flowers I Am Watching You. 2012. 24p. pap. 17.99 *(978-1-4685-9573-4(3))* AuthorHouse.

Hoke, Jeehyun. Boy & the Little Violet Flower. 2012. (ENG.). (J). pap. 10.99 *(978-1-4675-2921-1(4))* Independent Pub.

Holland-Davis, Tami. The Purple Tulip. 2011. 24p. pap. 15.99 *(978-1-4628-9378-2(3))* Xlibris Corp.

Holmes-Merritt, Angela. LINK Fairflies & Fairies. 2008. 36p. 17.50 *(978-0-615-17415-0(9))* AngiesInk.

Hooser, Betty J. Kids with Large Insects & Flowers & Unusual Things. 2012. 32p. 24.95 *(978-1-4626-4784-2(7))* America Star Bks.

Hopkins, Joseph. Lydia Greenfingers. 2016. (ENG.). 29p. (J). pap. 13.95 *(978-1-78554-949-6(9),* 6aec58fe-f008-4877-af7f-60d9415b2ffa) Austin, Stan AUS. Dist: Bookmasters Distribution.

Isaacs, Latricia. Mason & Baylee Learn to Count. 2011. 16p. (gr. -1). pap. 8.32 *(978-1-4634-0442-0(5))* AuthorHouse.

James, Hartwell. The Enchanted Castle. 2011. 44p. 13.95 *(978-1-4638-9769-7(3));* pap. 8.95 *(978-1-4638-0103-8(3))* Rodgers, Alan Bks.

Jane, Sarah. Hope's Garden. Ferrigno, Angela, illus. 2008. (ENG.). 32p. (J). (gr. -1-2). lib. bdg. 16.95 *(978-0-9790962-0-4(0))* Tri Valley Children's Publishing.

Jenks, Patricia. I'm Only a Little Bunny. Lehto, Christine, illus. 2013. 34p. 15.99 *(978-1-937165-48-2(5))* Orange Hat Publishing.

Jenn, Lady. Talking Flower Garden: A Series of Ricky's Secret Friends, 6, vol. 5. Jenn, Lady, illus. 2016. (Ricky's Secret Friends Picturebook Ser.). (ENG & CHI., Illus.). (gr. 1-4). 29.95 *(978-0-9787591-1-7(7))* Direct World Publishing.

Kann, Victoria. Flower Girl. 2013. (Pinkalicious Ser.). (J). lib. bdg. 13.55 *(978-0-606-27143-1(0),* Turtleback) Turtleback Bks.

Kennedy, Hugh J. The Flowers & the Fairies. 2009. 32p. pap. 18.97 *(978-1-4490-0265-7(X))* AuthorHouse.

Kleven, Elisa. Glasswings: A Butterfly's Story. 2013. (ENG., Illus.). 32p. (J). (gr. -1-k). 16.99 *(978-0-8037-3742-6(4),* Dial Bks) Penguin Young Readers Group.

Kline, Trish & Donev, Mary. Where Can Lost Bee Be? KA Reader 6. 2007. (Illus.). 32p. (J). per. 20.00 *(978-0-9717234-9-4(4))* Ghost Hunter Productions.

Knoll, Amos. The Flower That Could Not Talk. 2010. 64p. pap. 28.99 *(978-1-4490-7590-3(8))* AuthorHouse.

The Land of the Blue Flower. 2006. 76p. pap. 7.45 *(978-1-59462-377-6(5),* 413, Book Jungle) Standard Pubns., Inc.

Landreth, Christina. Tommy Picks Flowers. 2004. 27p. pap. 24.95 *(978-1-4137-3943-5(1))* PublishAmerica, Inc.

Lawson, JonArno & Smith, Sydney. Sidewalk Flowers, 1 vol. 2015. (ENG., Illus.). 32p. (J). (gr. -1-2). 16.95 *(978-1-55498-431-2(9))* Groundwood Bks. CAN. Dist: Publishers Group West (PGW).

Lease, Janice. Marigold Little Squirrel in a Cactus Patch. 2008. 48p. pap. 19.95 *(978-0-9800762-0-2(X))* Cinnamon Ridge Publishing.

Leone, Dee. Bizz & Buzz Make Honey Buns. Maritie, illus. 2014. (Penguin Core Concepts Ser.). (ENG.). 32p. (J). (gr. -1-k). 3.99 *(978-0-448-47927-9(3),* Grosset & Dunlap) Penguin Young Readers Group.

Lewis, Bisa, as told by. How Flowers Get Their Colors. 2005. (J). *(978-0-9745469-9-5(2))* Ashley & Taylor Publishing, Co.

Light, John. The Flower. Evans, Lisa, illus. (Child's Play Library). (ENG.). 32p. (J). 2011. *(978-1-84643-070-1(4))* 2007. (gr. 1-2). *(978-1-84643-072-5(0))* Child's Play International Ltd.

—The Flower. 2005. (Illus.). 26p. *(978-1-897968-17-8(5))* Photon Pr.

Long, Robert. Inside the Chrysanthemum: New Japanese Fables. 2007. 156p. pap. 53.30 *(978-1-4303-0543-9(6))* Lulu Pr., Inc.

Louie, Therese On & Wang, Suling. Raymond's Perfect Present, 1 vol. 2015. (ENG.). 32p. (J). pap. 9.95 *(978-1-62014-229-5(5))* Lee & Low Bks., Inc.

Maher, Liam. Golden Daffodils. Movshina, Marina, illus. 2010. 20p. pap. 10.95 *(978-1-61633-073-6(2))* Guardian Angel Publishing, Inc.

Make Believe Ideas. Flower Friends Daisy's First Words. 2013. (ENG.). 10p. (J). bds. 6.99 *(978-1-78235-604-2(5))* Make Believe Ideas GBR. Dist: Nelson, Thomas Inc.

—Flower Friends Primrose's Counting. 2013. (ENG.). 10p. (J). bds. 6.99 *(978-1-78235-602-8(9))* Make Believe Ideas GBR. Dist: Nelson, Thomas Inc.

—Flower Friends Rosie's Colors. 2013. (ENG.). 10p. (J). bds. 6.99 *(978-1-78235-605-9(3))* Make Believe Ideas GBR. Dist: Nelson, Thomas Inc.

Mancil, Arlene. The Garden Fairy. 2008. 32p. pap. 24.95 *(978-1-60441-735-7(8))* PublishAmerica, Inc.

Mannering, Rose. The Spotty Dotty Daffodil. Straker, Bethany, illus. 2014. (ENG.). 32p. (J). (gr. -1-k). 16.95 *(978-1-62636-346-5(3),* Sky Pony Pr.) Skyhorse Publishing Co., Inc.

Mannone, Christine. Flowers for Pudding Street. Carolan, Christine, illus. 2009. (ENG.). 32p. (J). 15.95 *(978-1-934860-02-1(6))* Shenanigan Bks.

Marshall, Denise. The Adventures of Hip Hop: Hip Hop & the Yellow Hat. Schley, Cheri & Champagne, Heather, illus. 2011. 36p. pap. 14.75 *(978-1-60976-342-8(4),* Eloquent Bks.) Strategic Book Publishing & Rights Agency (SBPRA).

Marsoli, Lisa Ann. Leaping Lily: A Ballet Story. Leijten, Aileen, illus. 2005. (J). bds. 14.99 *(978-0-9767325-3-2(X))* Toy Quest.

Marzollo, Jean. I'm a Seed. Moffatt, Judith, illus. 2010. (Rise & Shine Ser.: Level 1). (ENG.). 32p. (C). (gr. -1-1). pap. 10.95 *(978-0-590-26586-7(5))* National Geographic School Publishing, Inc.

Matsuura, Richard & Matsuura, Ruth. Fruit, the Tree & the Flower. (J). 8.95 *(978-1-887916-02-8(4))* Orchid Isle Publishing Co.

McCabe, Jane. The Remarkable Story of the Very First Flower: And How She Changed the World. 2010. 56p. pap. 24.99 *(978-1-4490-8361-8(7))* AuthorHouse.

McCumbers, Jaime. Don't Step on the Flowers! 2008. 12p. per. 24.95 *(978-1-4241-9092-8(4))* America Star Bks.

McKelvey, Katrina. Dandelions. Lonergan, Kirrili, illus. 2015. (ENG.). 32p. (J). (gr. -1-4). 17.99 *(978-1-921966-82-8(3))* Exisle Publishing Pty Ltd. AUS. Dist: Hachette Bk. Group.

Meadows, Daisy. Louise the Lily Fairy. 2009. (Petal Fairies Ser.: 3). (ENG., Illus.). 80p. (J). (gr. 2-5). pap. 4.99 *(978-0-545-07092-8(9),* Scholastic Paperbacks) Scholastic, Inc.

Menconi, James Pasqual. Queen Mariella & the Fable of the Peony. 2011. 24p. (gr. -1). pap. 13.50 *(978-1-4567-3934-8(4))* AuthorHouse.

Miller, Victoria, illus. Flowers for Mami Unicorn! 2010. (Dora the Explorer Ser.). (ENG.). 24p. (J). (gr. -1-2). pap. 3.99 *(978-1-4169-9064-2(X),* Simon Spotlight/Nickelodeon) Simon Spotlight/Nickelodeon.

Morris, Ann. Surprise in Auntie's Garden! Varkarotas, Heather, illus. 2013. (ENG.). (J). (gr. -1-3). 14.95 *(978-1-62086-224-7(7))* Mascot Bks., Inc.

!Myster?Ous M! & Courageous $Oul. The Lonely Flower. Courageous $oul, illus. 2011. 20p. pap. 24.95 *(978-1-4560-6950-6(0))* America Star Bks.

Nolen, Jerdine. Bradford Street Buddies: Springtime Blossoms. Henninger, Michelle, illus. 2017. (Green Light Readers Level 3 Ser.). (ENG.). 48p. (J). (gr. 1-4). pap. 3.99 *(978-0-544-87390-2(4),* HMH Books For Young Readers) Houghton Mifflin Harcourt Publishing Co.

Ott, Karen. The Foolish Dandelion. 2012. 28p. pap. 13.99 *(978-1-4525-6277-3(6))* Balboa Pr.

Pandelis, Bloomin' Harmony Judy E. Bloomin' Harmony. 2010. 32p. pap. 18.00 *(978-0-557-32902-1(7))* Lulu Pr., Inc.

Pin, Isabel. Bumblebee Blues. James, J. Alison, tr. from GER. 2003. (Illus.). 32p. (J). (gr. k-3). 15.95 *(978-0-7358-1813-2(4));* lib. bdg. 16.50 *(978-0-7358-1814-9(2))* North-South Bks., Inc. (Michael Neugebauer Bks.).

Powell, Kathy Bingham. Save the Seeds. 2010. (Illus.). 24p. pap. 14.99 *(978-1-4490-5936-1(8))* AuthorHouse.

Ramsey, Marcy Dunn. Rosie's Posies, 1 vol. Ramsey, Marcy Dunn, illus. 2009. (ENG., Illus.). 34p. (J). (gr. -1-3). 14.95 *(978-0-87033-472-6(7),* 9780870334726, Cornell Maritime Pr./Tidewater Pubs.) Schiffer Publishing, Ltd.

Randolph, Joanne. Rose: A Flower's Story. 2009. (Nature Stories Ser.). (Illus.). 24p. (J). (gr. -1-2). pap. 8.15 *(978-1-60754-102-8(5));* lib. bdg. 22.60 *(978-1-60754-101-1(7))* Windmill Bks.

Rawlinson, Julia. Fletcher & the Springtime Blossoms. Beeke, Tiphanie, illus. 2009. (ENG.). 32p. (J). (gr. -1-2). 17.99 *(978-0-06-168855-3(X),* Greenwillow Bks.) HarperCollins Pubs.

—Fletcher & the Springtime Blossoms. 2011. (J). (gr. -1-2). 29.95 *(978-0-545-32738-1(5))* Weston Woods Studios, Inc.

Ray, Miasyn Summer. One Lucky Petal. 2005. (Illus.). 36p. (J). per. *(978-0-9761844-3-0(5))* South Hadley Publishing.

Reed, Jennifer. The Falling Flowers. Cole, Dick, illus. 2005. (Falling Flowers Ser.). 32p. (J). (gr. -1-3). 16.95 *(978-1-885008-28-2(7),* Shen's Bks.) Lee & Low Bks., Inc.

Rey, H. A. Curious George at the Park. Meyer, Emily, ed. 2010. (Curious George Ser.). (ENG., Illus.). 10p. (J). (gr. -1 — 1). bds. 6.99 *(978-0-547-24300-9(6))* Houghton Mifflin Harcourt Publishing Co.

Reynolds, Peter H. Rose's Garden. Reynolds, Peter H., illus. 2009. (ENG., Illus.). 40p. (J). (gr. k-12). 15.99 *(978-0-7636-4641-7(5))* Candlewick Pr.

Ridley, Sharon, illus. My Wildflower Friends. Phillips, Marilyn, photos by. 2006. (J). *(978-0-9786168-0-9(4))* Rio Wildflower Pubns.

Riveros, Gabriela. El Encargo de Fernanda. Castillo, Jesus, illus. rev. ed. 2006. (Castillo de la Lectura Blanca Ser.). (SPA & ENG.). 64p. (J). (gr. k-2). pap. 6.95 *(978-970-20-0126-3(9))* Castillo, Ediciones, S. A. de C. V. MEX. Dist: Macmillan.

Rodda, Emily. The Rainbow Wand. Vitale, Raoul, illus. 2007. (Fairy Realm Ser.). 116p. (gr. 3-7). 25.65 *(978-1-59961-332-1(8))* Spotlight.

Rose, Naomi C. Tashi & the Tibetan Flower Cure. 2016. (ENG.). 40p. (J). (gr. 1-6). pap. 10.95 ***(978-1-62014-318-6(6))*** Lee & Low Bks., Inc.

Rushton, Jenna. A Simple Flower. 2012. 24p. pap. 14.50 *(978-1-4772-0295-1(1))* AuthorHouse.

Sansone, V. K. Heavenly Hannah's Little Black Hat. 2009. 32p. pap. 14.98 *(978-0-557-07065-7(1))* Lulu Pr., Inc.

Scheunemann, Pam. Spelling Bee, 1 vol. 2007. (Critter Chronicles Ser.). (ENG., Illus.). 24p. (J). (gr. k-3). lib. bdg. 24.21 *(978-1-59928-472-9(3),* SandCastle) ABDO Publishing Co.

Schubert, Jan. The Sun Seed. Schubert, Jan, illus. 2007. (Illus.). 28p. (J). (gr. -1-k). lib. bdg. *(978-0-88010-585-9(2),* Bell Pond Bks.) SteinerBooks, Inc.

Schwartz, Suzanne & Schwartz, Robert. The Christmas Palm Tree: A Storybook to Color. Schwartz, Suzanne & Schwartz, Robert, illus. l.t. ed. 2005. (Illus.). 22p. (J). spiral bd. 3.99 *(978-0-9764152-3-7(2))* Seascay Productions.

Seuss, Dr. Daisy-Head Mayzie. 2016. (Classic Seuss Ser.). (ENG., Illus.). 64p. (J). (gr. k-4). 17.99 *(978-0-553-53900-4(0));* lib. bdg. 20.99 *(978-0-553-53906-6(X))* Random Hse. Children's Bks. (Random Hse. Bks. for Young Readers).

Shats, Marina. Nature Knows (Paperback) 2010. 24p. 21.50 *(978-0-557-32587-0(0))* Lulu Pr., Inc.

Siegel, Rv. A Bee Called Kangaroo. 2005. 81p. pap. 9.16 *(978-1-4116-2890-8(X))* Lulu Pr., Inc.

Sloniker, Phyllis. The Quest for the Golden Flower. 2005. 11.00 *(978-0-8059-9399-8(1))* Dorrance Publishing Co., Inc.

Smith, Shelli. Grammy Goes Green. 2012. 24p. pap. 12.45 *(978-1-4624-0104-8(X),* Inspiring Voices) Author Solutions, Inc.

Somerville, Mary Ann. The Traveler & the Flower. 2012. 40p. pap. 21.99 *(978-1-4691-6115-0(X))* Xlibris Corp.
Sommer, Cindy. Salvando Las Flores de Camelia, 1 vol. Klein, Laurie Allen, illus. 2016. (SPA.). 32p. (J). (gr. k-3). pap. 9.95 *(978-1-62855-872-2(5))* Arbordale Publishing.
—Saving Kate's Flowers, 1 vol. Klein, Laurie Allen, illus. 2016. (ENG & SPA.). 32p. (J). (gr. k-3). 17.95 *(978-1-62855-870-8(9))* Arbordale Publishing.
Steadman, Ralph. Flowers for the Moon. 2004. (Illus.). 42p. 100.00 *(978-0-9760742-0-5(6))* Sylph Pubns.
Stefanescu, Estera. Megan's Great Day. 2009. 20p. pap. 15.99 *(978-1-4389-6318-1(1))* AuthorHouse.
Stilton, Thea. Thea Stilton & the Great Tulip Heist. 2014. (Thea Stilton Ser.: 18). lib. bdg. 19.65 *(978-0-606-35386-1(0))* Turtleback Bks.
Surber, Shawn-Michelle. Hope, 1. Surber, Shawn-Michelle, illus. collector's ed. 2007. (Illus.). 35p. (J). 19.99 *(978-0-9763534-0-9(7)*, Mornin'Light Media) Mornin' Light Media.
Tagg, Christine. Cinderlily: A Floral Fairy Tale. Ellwand, David, ed. Ellwand, David, photos by. 2006. (Illus.). 26p. (J). (gr. k-4). reprint ed. 17.00 *(978-1-4223-5558-9(6))* DIANE Publishing Co.
Taylor-Butler, Christine. Step-by-Step. Miller, Susan, illus. 2005. (My First Reader Ser.). (ENG.). 32p. (J). (gr. k-1). lib. bdg. 18.50 *(978-0-516-24875-2(8)*, Children's Pr.) Scholastic Library Publishing.
Taylor, Sean. Huck Runs Amuck! Reynolds, Peter, illus. 2011. (ENG.). 48p. (J). (gr. k-3). 16.99 *(978-0-8037-3261-2(9)*, Dial Bks) Penguin Young Readers Group.
Thomas, Glenn. Little Flowers Can't Talk. 2012. 40p. pap. 32.70 *(978-1-4691-6004-7(8))* Xlibris Corp.
Thompson, Gareth. Sunshine to the Sunless. 2008. (ENG.). 256p. (YA). (gr. 7). pap. 11.99 *(978-1-86230-467-3(X))* Transworld Publishers Ltd. GBR. Dist: Independent Pubs. Group.
Thomson, Sarah L. Deadly Flowers: A Ninja's Tale. 2016. (Ninja's Journey Ser.). (ENG., Illus.). 272p. (J). (gr. 4-9). 17.95 *(978-1-62979-214-9(4)*, 1402729) Boyds Mills Pr.
Thurman, Carol. Molly's Field of Dreams. 2011. 24p. pap. 11.99 *(978-1-4567-3101-4(7))* AuthorHouse.
Townsan, Judy. The Wishing Flower, 1 vol. Rosado, Michael, illus. 2009. 13p. pap. 24.95 *(978-1-61546-179-0(5))* America Star Bks.
Tremblay, Carole. Floop's Flowers. Beshwaty, Steve, illus. 2009. (Floop Ser.). 24p. (J). (gr. -1-k). 22.60 *(978-1-60754-344-2(3))*; pap. 8.15 *(978-1-60754-346-6(X))* Windmill Bks.
Trotman, Althea. How the East Pond Got Its Flowers. Sasso, illus. Date not set. 88p. (J). (gr. 3-7). pap. *(978-0-920813-85-0(2))* Sister Vision Pr.
Ure, Jean. The Flower Power Collection: Passion Flower, Shrinking Violet & Pumpkin Pie. 2011. (ENG., Illus.). 544p. (J). (gr. 4-7). pap. 16.99 *(978-0-00-720155-6(9)*, HarperCollins Children's Bks.) HarperCollins Pubs. Ltd. GBR. Dist: HarperCollins Pubs.
Van Winkle, Amy. The Flower Fairy, 1 vol. 2010. 13p. pap. 24.95 *(978-1-61582-729-9(3))* PublishAmerica, Inc.
Waddell, Martin. Something So Big. Canty, Charlotte, illus. 2004. (ENG.). 24p. (J). lib. bdg. 23.65 *(978-1-59646-706-4(1))* Dingles & Co.
Walsh, Roger L. When Dandelions Fly. 2010. 26p. pap. 15.99 *(978-1-4535-0871-8(6))* Xlibris Corp.
Warren, Jill. Bizzy Bee & the Flowers. 2012. (ENG.). 31p. (J). pap. 16.95 *(978-1-4327-8239-9(8))* Outskirts Pr., Inc.
Watts, Irene N. Flower. 2005. (ENG.). 192p. (J). (gr. 4-7). pap. 8.95 *(978-0-88776-710-4(9)*, Tundra Bks.) Tundra Bks. CAN. Dist: Penguin Random Hse. LLC.
Weston Woods Staff, creator. Planting a Rainbow. 2011. 29.95 *(978-0-439-80436-3(1))*; 38.75 *(978-0-439-80645-9(3))*; 18.95 *(978-0-439-80643-5(7))* Weston Woods Studios, Inc.
Wheeler, Christine. Bella's Marigold Cake. 2008. 20p. pap. 18.50 *(978-1-60693-100-4(8)*, Eloquent Bks.) Strategic Book Publishing & Rights Agency (SBPRA).
White, Amy Brecount. Forget-Her-Nots. 2010. (ENG.). 384p. (YA). (gr. 8-18). 16.99 *(978-0-06-167298-9(X)*, Greenwillow Bks.) HarperCollins Pubs.
Williams, Jill Ann. Listen to the Flowers: Ten Flower Stories for Children. 2006. pap. 8.00 *(978-0-8059-7198-9(X))* Dorrance Publishing Co., Inc.
Williams, Nate & Snow, Virginia Brimhall. Spring Walk, 1 vol. 2015. (ENG., Illus.). 32p. (J). (gr. 2-3). 16.99 *(978-1-4236-3879-7(4))* Gibbs Smith, Publisher.
Williams, T. D. Happy Village. 2010. 24p. 13.99 *(978-1-4269-3492-6(0))* Trafford Publishing.
Willis, Wren. The Flower I Met in My Garden. 2004. 116p. per. 6.85 *(978-1-4116-1783-4(5))* Lulu Pr., Inc.
Wojtowicz, Jen. The Boy Who Grew Flowers. Adams, Steve, illus. 2012. (ENG.). 32p. (J). (gr. k-5). 8.99 *(978-1-84686-749-1(5))* Barefoot Bks., Inc.
Wojtowicz, Jen & Wojzowitz, Jen. The Boy Who Grew Flowers. Adams, Steve, illus. 2005. (ENG.). 32p. (J). (gr. -1-3). 16.99 *(978-1-84148-686-4(8))* Barefoot Bks., Inc.
Zerza, Safoora Z. Sophia V. Is Flower Girl. 2012. 24p. pap. 17.99 *(978-1-4685-5136-5(1))* AuthorHouse.
Zintel, Kristian. Frank Flower & Willie Weed. 2011. 28p. pap. 17.32 *(978-1-4568-5038-8(5))* Xlibris Corp.
Zupsic, Kelly. Mrs. Sneeze & the Three Legged Goat. 2013. 28p. pap. 24.95 *(978-1-62709-791-8(0))* America Star Bks.

FLOWERS, STATE

see State Flowers

FLOWERS, WILD

see Wild Flowers

FLOWERS IN ART

see Design, Decorative; Flower Painting and Illustration

FLY

see Flies

FLYING

see Flight

FLYING BOMBS

see Guided Missiles

FLYING SAUCERS

see Unidentified Flying Objects

FOG

Doudna, Kelly & Craig, Diane. Cloud or Fog?, 1 vol. 2016. (This or That? Weather Ser.). (ENG., Illus.). 24p. (J). (gr. k-4). 25.65 *(978-1-62403-953-9(7))* ABDO Publishing Co.
Lawrence, Ellen. Fog, Mist, or Haze? 2015. (Weather Wise Ser.). (ENG., Illus.). 24p. (J). (gr. -1-3). lib. bdg. 23.93 *(978-1-62724-864-8(1))* Bearport Publishing Co., Inc.
Masters, Nancy Robinson. It Gets Foggy. 2015. (Tell Me Why Library). (ENG., Illus.). 24p. (J). (gr. 2-5). 27.07 *(978-1-63362-614-0(8)*, 206640) Cherry Lake Publishing.
Pope, Kristen. What Is the Difference Between Clouds & Fog? 2016. (Everyday Earth Science Ser.). (ENG.). 24p. (J). (gr. k-3). 27.07 *(978-1-5038-0794-5(0)*, 210629) Child's World, Inc., The.
Schuetz, Kristin. Cloud Cover. 2015. (Understanding Weather Ser.). (ENG., Illus.). 24p. (J). (gr. k-3). lib. bdg. 25.95 *(978-1-62617-250-0(1)*, Blastoff! Readers) Bellwether Media.

FOG—FICTION

Elliott, Alan. Willy the Texas Longhorn, 1 vol. Ford, Stephanie, illus. 2013. (ENG.). 32p. (J). (gr. k-3). 16.99 *(978-1-4556-1870-5(5))* Pelican Publishing Co., Inc.
Manning, Matthew K. Mystery of the Mist Monster. Neely, Scott, illus. 2016. (Scooby-Doo Comic Chapter Bks.). (ENG.). 88p. (gr. 3-7). pap. 5.95 *(978-1-4965-3590-0(1))* Capstone Press of Coughlan Cos.
Robinson, Keith. Chamber of Ghosts. 2013. 222p. pap. *(978-0-9843906-5-6(0))* Roxby Media Ltd.
Steedman, Judith & Mitchell-Cranfield, Robin. Foggy. 2008. (Windy Ser.). (ENG., Illus.). 32p. (J). (gr. -1-3). 15.95 *(978-1-894965-96-5(5))* Simply Read Bks. CAN. Dist: Ingram Publisher Services.
Thorpe, Kiki. From the Mist. Christy, Jana, illus. 2013. (Stepping Stone Book Series: No. 4). (ENG.). 128p. (J). (gr. 1-4). 5.99 *(978-0-7364-2797-5(X)*, RH/Disney) Random Hse. Children's Bks.
Via, Jennifer Welsh. The Foggy Meadow Discovery. 2007. 216p. per. 14.95 *(978-0-595-44680-3(9))* iUniverse, Inc.

FOG SIGNALS

see Signals and Signaling

FOLIAGE

see Leaves

FOLK ART

Here are entered general and historical works on peasant and popular art in the fields of decorative arts, music, dancing, theater, etc.

see also Art, Primitive; Art Industries and Trade

Bogart, Jo Ellen. Capturing Joy: The Story of Maud Lewis. Lang, Mark, illus. 2011. (ENG.). 32p. (J). (gr. 3-7). pap. 8.95 *(978-1-77049-262-2(3)*, Tundra Bks.) Tundra Bks. CAN. Dist: Penguin Random Hse. LLC.
Bonnice, Sherry. Folk Arts & Crafts. 2004. (North American Folklore Ser.). (Illus.). 112p. (J). (gr. 7-18). lib. bdg. 22.95 *(978-1-59084-335-2(5))* Mason Crest.
Jabbour, Alan, ed. Folk Speech, 21 vols., Set. 2003. (North American Folklore Ser.). (Illus.). 112p. (J). (gr. 7-18). lib. bdg. *(978-1-59084-328-4(2))* Mason Crest.
Kafka, Tina. Folk Art. 2007. (Eye on Art Ser.). (ENG., Illus.). 128p. (gr. 4-7). lib. bdg. 39.40 *(978-1-59018-960-3(4)*, Lucent Bks.) Cengage Gale.
Ketchum, Jr. American Folk Art. 2017. (Art Collections: Vol. 7). (ENG., Illus.). (YA). (gr. 9-12). 26.95 ***(978-1-4222-3932-2(2))*** Mason Crest.
Madden-Lunsford, Kerry. Nothing Fancy about Kathryn & Charlie. Madden-Lunsford, Lucy, illus. 2013. (ENG.). 36p. (J). pap. 14.95 *(978-0-9828528-0-4(0))* Mockingbird Publishing.
Michaels, Alexandra. The Kids' Multicultural Art Book: Art & Craft Experiences from Around the World. 2008. (ENG., Illus.). 160p. (gr. 1-2). pap. 14.29 *(978-0-8249-6808-3(5)*, Ideal Pubns.) Worthy Publishing.
Mooney, Carla. Amazing Africa Projects. Stems, Megan, illus. 2010. (Build It Yourself Ser.). (ENG.). 128p. (J). (gr. 3-7). pap. 15.95 *(978-1-934670-41-5(3))* Octavio Publishing.
Mooney, Carla & Stearns, Megan. Amazing Africa Projects. 2010. (Build It Yourself Ser.). (ENG., Illus.). 128p. (J). (gr. 3-7). 21.95 *(978-1-934670-42-2(1))* Octavio Publishing.
Panchyk, Richard & Ketchum, William C., Jr. American Folk Art for Kids: With 21 Activities. 2004. (For Kids Ser.). (ENG., Illus.). 128p. (J). (gr. 4). pap. 16.95 *(978-1-55652-499-8(4))* Chicago Review Pr., Inc.
Snedeker, Gus. Quilts, Rag Dolls, & Rocking Chairs: Folk Arts & Crafts. 2013. (Illus.). 48p. (J). pap. *(978-1-4222-2501-1(1))* Mason Crest.
—Quilts, Rag Dolls, & Rocking Chairs: Folk Arts & Crafts. Jabbour, Alan, ed. 2012. (North American Folklore for Youth Ser.). (Illus.). 48p. (J). (gr. 4). 19.95 *(978-1-4222-2490-8(2))* Mason Crest.
Terzian, Alexandria M. The Kids Multicultural Art Book. Terzian, Alexandria M., illus. 2007. (ENG., Illus.). 160p. (gr. 1-2). 16.99 *(978-0-8249-6807-6(7)*, Ideal Pubns.) Worthy Publishing.
Weill, Cynthia. ABeCedarios: Mexican Folk Art ABCs in English & Spanish. Basseches, K. B., photos by. 2008. (First Concepts in Mexican Folk Art Ser.). (SPA & ENG., Illus.). 32p. (J). (gr. k — 1). 14.95 *(978-1-933693-13-2(4))* Cinco Puntos Pr.
—ABeCedarios - Mexican Folk Art ABCs in English & Spanish. Basseches, K. B., photos by. 2017. (First Concepts in Mexican Folk Art Ser.). (ENG., Illus.). 32p. (J). (— 1). bds. 9.95 *(978-1-941026-66-3(4))* Cinco Puntos Pr.
—Animal Talk. 2017. (First Concepts in Mexican Folk Art Ser.). (ENG.). 32p. (J). (— 1). bds. 9.95 *(978-1-941026-69-4(9))* Cinco Puntos Pr.
—Colores de la Vida. 2017. (First Concepts in Mexican Folk Art Ser.). (ENG.). 32p. (J). (— 1). bds. 9.95 *(978-1-941026-67-0(2))* Cinco Puntos Pr.
—Count Me In! 2017. (First Concepts in Mexican Folk Art Ser.). (ENG.). 32p. (J). (— 1). bds. 9.95 *(978-1-941026-70-0(2))* Cinco Puntos Pr.
—My Skeleton Family. de Oaxaco, Jesus & Zarate, Jesus, illus. 2013. (First Concepts in Mexican Folk Art Ser.). (ENG & SPA.). 32p. (J). (-k). 14.95 *(978-1-935955-50-4(0))* Cinco Puntos Pr.
—Opuestos. 2017. (First Concepts in Mexican Folk Art Ser.). (ENG.). 32p. (J). (— 1). bds. 9.95 *(978-1-941026-68-7(0))* Cinco Puntos Pr.
—Opuestos: Mexican Folk Art Opposites in English & Spanish. 2009. (First Concepts in Mexican Folk Art Ser.). (SPA & ENG., Illus.). 32p. (J). (gr. -1-1). 14.95 *(978-1-933693-56-9(8))* Cinco Puntos Pr.
Weill, Cynthia & Cinco Puntos Press Staff. Colores de la Vida: Mexican Folk Art Colors in English & Spanish. 2011. (First Concepts in Mexican Folk Art Ser.). (SPA & ENG., Illus.). 32p. (J). (gr. -1-k). 14.95 *(978-1-933693-82-8(7))* Cinco Puntos Pr.
Youngs, Clare & Young, Clare. Explorar y Crear. 2012. (SPA.). 128p. (gr. 13-13). pap. 20.99 *(978-84-261-3887-3(X))* Juventud, Editorial ESP. Dist: Lectorum Pubns., Inc.

FOLK DANCING

Bonnice, Sherry. Folk Dance. 2004. (North American Folklore Ser.). (Illus.). 112p. (YA). (gr. 7-18). lib. bdg. 22.95 *(978-1-59084-337-6(1))* Mason Crest.
Feierabend, John M. The Book of Song Dances. 2015. (First Steps in Music Ser.). (ENG., Illus.). 122p. (J). (gr. 2-4). pap. 17.95 *(978-1-62277-086-1(2))* G I A Pubns., Inc.
Miller, Randy & Perron, Jack. New England Fiddler's Repertoire: A Source Book of Established Contra Dance Music Bley-Vroman, Robert, ed. 2nd rev. ed. 2003. (Illus.). 96p. spiral bd. 20.00 *(978-0-9770530-0-1(8))* Miller, Randy.
Storey, Rita. Irish Dancing: And Other National Dances. 2007. (Get Dancing Ser.). (Illus.). 32p. (J). lib. bdg. 28.50 *(978-1-59771-050-3(4))* Sea-To-Sea Pubns.
Will, Heidi. The Ghillie Girls: Irish Dance Pals. Will, Heidi, illus. 2008. (Illus.). 24p. (J). pap. 9.99 *(978-0-9821065-0-1(5))* Cinealta Pr.

FOLK LORE

see Folklore

FOLK MUSIC

see Folk Songs

FOLK SONGS

see also Ballads; Carols; Folklore; National Songs

Adams, Pam, illus. There Was an Old Lady Who Swallowed the Sea. 2006. (Classic Books with Holes Soft Cover with CD Ser.). (ENG.). 16p. (J). (gr. -1-k). pap. incl. audio compact disk *(978-1-84643-035-0(6))* Child's Play International Ltd.
—This Old Man. 2007. (Classic Books with Holes 8x8 with CD Ser.). (ENG.). 16p. (J). (gr. -1-1). pap. incl. audio compact disk *(978-1-904550-63-1(0))* Child's Play International Ltd.
Andreasen, Dan, illus. The Twelve Days of Christmas. 2012. (ENG.). 32p. (J). (gr. k-2). 14.99 *(978-1-58536-834-1(2)*, 202344) Sleeping Bear Pr.
Arkham, Thomas. Sirens & Smoke: Firefighters Folklore. 2013. (Illus.). 48p. (J). *(978-1-4222-2486-1(4))*; *(978-1-4222-2497-7(X))*; pap. *(978-1-4222-2500-4(3))* Mason Crest.
Bladey, Conrad, ed. A Beuk of the Sangs of Tommy Armstrong the Pitman's Poet. 2003. (Illus.). 90p. *(978-0-9702386-8-9(1))* Hutman Productions.
Cauthen, Joyce, prod. Bullfrog Jumped: Children's Folksongs from the Byron Arnold Collection. 2006. (J). 17.00 incl. audio compact disk *(978-0-9672672-9-6(3))* Alabama Folklife Assn.
Choi, Robert. Korean Folks Songs: Stars in the Sky & Dreams in Our Hearts. Back, Samee, illus. 2014. (ENG & KOR.). 32p. (J). (gr. -1-3). 15.95 *(978-0-8048-4468-0(2))* Tuttle Publishing.
Downing, Johnette, illus. & adapted by. There Was an Old Lady Who Swallowed Some Bugs, 1 vol. Downing, Johnette, adapted by. 2010. (ENG.). 32p. (J). (gr. k-3). 16.99 *(978-1-58980-858-4(4))* Pelican Publishing Co., Inc.
Ellwand, David, photos by. Old MacDonald Had a Farm. 2016. (Teddy Bear Sing-Along Ser.). (ENG., Illus.). 14p. (J). bds. 14.99 *(978-1-62686-653-9(8)*, Silver Dolphin Bks.) Readerlink Distribution Services, LLC.
Engel, Christiane. Knick Knack Paddy Whack. Engels, Christiane, illus. 2008. (ENG.). 24p. (J). (gr. -1-k). 16.99 *(978-1-84686-144-4(6))* Barefoot Bks., Inc.
Engel, Christiane & Songs, Steve. Knick Knack Paddy Whack. Engel, Christiane, illus. 2011. (ENG., Illus.). 24p. (J). (gr. -1-2). 9.99 *(978-1-84686-659-3(6))* Barefoot Bks., Inc.
Feierabend, John M. The Book of Call & Response. Caton, Tim, illus. 2003. (First Steps in Music Ser.). (ENG.). 88p. (J). (gr. -1-2). pap. 14.95 *(978-1-57999-215-6(3))* G I A Pubns., Inc.
—The Book of Children's Song Tales. Caton, Tim, illus. 2003. (First Steps in Music Ser.). (ENG.). 104p. (J). (gr. -1-2). pap. 14.95 *(978-1-57999-213-2(7))* G I A Pubns., Inc.
—The Book of Echo Songs. Caton, Tim, illus. 2003. (First Steps in Music Ser.). (ENG.). 88p. (J). (gr. -1-2). pap. 14.95 *(978-1-57999-214-9(5))* G I A Pubns., Inc.
Handyside, Chris. A History of Folk. 2006. (J). *(978-1-4109-1813-0(0))* Steck-Vaughn.
Isadora, Rachel. Old Mikamba Had a Farm. Isadora, Rachel, illus. 2013. (ENG., Illus.). 40p. (J). (gr. -1-k). 17.99 *(978-0-399-25740-7(3)*, Nancy Paulsen Books) Penguin Young Readers Group.
Julian, Alison, illus. The 12 Days of Christmas. 2005. (J). *(978-1-74157-281-0(9))* Hinkler Bks. Pty, Ltd.
Kadair, Deborah Ousley, illus. Today Is Monday in Texas, 1 vol. 2010. (ENG.). 32p. (J). (gr. k-k). 16.99 *(978-1-58980-701-3(4))* Pelican Publishing Co., Inc.
Katz, Karen. The Babies on the Bus. Katz, Karen, illus. (ENG., Illus.). (J). (gr. -1-k). 2013. 28p. bds. 7.99 *(978-0-8050-9779-5(1)*, 9780805097795) 2011. 32p. 14.99 *(978-0-8050-9011-6(8)*, 9780805090116) Holt, Henry & Co. (Holt, Henry & Co. Bks. For Young Readers).
Kralovansky, Susan Holt. There Was a Tall Texan Who Swallowed a Flea, 1 vol. Kadair, Deborah Ousley, illus. 2013. (ENG.). 32p. (J). (gr. -1-k). 16.99 *(978-1-4556-1717-3(2))* Pelican Publishing Co., Inc.
McNicholas, Shelagh, illus. This Little Light of Mine. 2013. (ENG.). 12p. (J). (gr. -1-k). bds. 6.99 *(978-0-545-47768-0(9)*, Little Shepherd) Scholastic, Inc.
Ochs, Bill. The Clarke Tin Whistle. deluxe ed. 2006. (ENG.). 80p. 19.99 *(978-0-9623456-7-8(9))* Pennywhistler's Pr.
Quattlebaum, Mary. Jo MacDonald Saw a Pond. Bryant, Laura J., illus. 2011. 32p. (J). 16.95 *(978-1-58469-150-1(6))* Dawn Pubns.
Riggs, Kate. Folk Music. 2008. (World of Music Ser.). (Illus.). 24p. (J). (gr. -1). lib. bdg. 24.25 *(978-1-58341-566-5(1)*, Creative Education) Creative Co., The.
Snedeker, Gus. Campfire Songs, Ballads, & Lullabies: Folk Music. 2013. (Illus.). 48p. (J). pap. *(978-1-4222-2503-5(8))* Mason Crest.
—Campfire Songs, Ballads, & Lullabies: Folk Music. Jabbour, Alan, ed. 2012. (North American Folklore for Youth Ser.). (Illus.). 48p. (J). (gr. 4). 19.95 *(978-1-4222-2492-2(9))* Mason Crest.
Spirin, Gennady. The Twelve Days of Christmas, 0 vols. Spirin, Gennady, illus. 2009. (ENG., Illus.). 32p. (J). (gr. -1-3). 16.99 *(978-0-7614-5551-6(5)*, 9780761455516, Amazon Children's Publishing) Amazon Publishing.
Twinn, M. Old MacDonald Had a Farm. Adams, Pam, illus. 2007. (Classic Books with Holes 8x8 with CD Ser.). (ENG.). 16p. (J). (gr. -1-1). pap. incl. audio compact disk *(978-1-904550-64-8(9))* Child's Play International Ltd.
—There Was an Old Lady Who Swallowed a Fly. Adams, Pam, illus. 2007. (Classic Books with Holes 8x8 with CD Ser.). (ENG.). 16p. (J). (gr. -1-1). pap. incl. audio compact disk *(978-1-904550-62-4(2))* Child's Play International Ltd.
Vilsaint, Fequiere. Children Songs from Haiti: Chante Timoun Ayiti. Date not set. 28p. (J). (gr. 1-5). wbk. ed. 25.00 *(978-1-881839-55-2(9))* Educa Vision Inc.
Ward, Jennifer. There Was an Odd Princess Who Swallowed a Pea, 0 vols. Calderon, Lee, illus. 2011. (ENG.). 32p. (J). (gr. -1-3). 16.99 *(978-0-7614-5822-7(0)*, 9780761458227, Amazon Children's Publishing) Amazon Publishing.
Weston Woods Staff, creator. Drummer Hoff. 2004. 29.95 *(978-1-55592-407-2(7))* Weston Woods Studios, Inc.
—Frog Went A-Courtin' 2011. 29.95 *(978-0-545-23379-8(8))*; 18.95 *(978-0-545-23380-4(1))*; 38.75 *(978-0-545-23381-1(X))* Weston Woods Studios, Inc.

FOLK SONGS, AMERICAN

see Folk Songs—United States

FOLK SONGS, ENGLISH

Austin, Michael Allen. London Bridge Is Falling Down. Austin, Michael Allen, illus. 2011. (Favorite Children's Songs Ser.). (ENG., Illus.). 16p. (J). (gr. -1-2). lib. bdg. 25.64 *(978-1-60954-292-4(4)*, 200096) Child's World, Inc., The.
Cannon, Nick & Carey, Mariah. Roc & Roe's Twelve Days of Christmas. Ford, A. G., illus. 2014. (ENG.). 32p. (J). (gr. -1-k). 17.99 *(978-0-545-51950-2(0)*, Orchard Bks.) Scholastic, Inc.
Childrens Press Staff. Everywhere a Moo, Moo. 2009. (Rookie Toddler: Sing along Toddler Ser.). (ENG.). 12p. (J). (gr. -1). bds. 6.95 *(978-0-531-24548-4(9))* Scholastic Library Publishing.
Colandro, Lucille. There Was an Old Lady Who Swallowed a Fly! Lee, Jared D., illus. 2014. (There Was an Old Lad Ser.). (ENG.). 32p. (J). (gr. -1-1). 6.99 *(978-0-545-68292-3(4)*, Cartwheel Bks.) Scholastic, Inc.
—There Was an Old Lady Who Swallowed a Rose! Lee, Jared, illus. 2012. (There Was an Old Lady Ser.). lib. bdg. 17.20 *(978-0-606-26734-2(4)*, Turtleback) Turtleback Bks.
—There Was an Old Lady Who Swallowed a Shell! Lee, Jared, illus. 2006. (J). *(978-0-439-81536-9(3))* Scholastic, Inc.
Cornelison, Sue. Down by the Bay. 2011. (ENG.). 32p. (J). (gr. k-5). 17.95 *(978-1-60727-199-4(0))* Soundprints.
Dalmatian Press Staff. I Know an Old Lady Who Swallow. 2008. (ENG.). 12p. (J). bds. 4.95 *(978-1-58117-710-7(0)*, Intervisual/Piggy Toes) Bendon, Inc.
Davis, Jimmie. The More We Get Together. Church, Caroline Jayne, illus. 2011. (ENG.). 12p. (J). (— 1). bds. 6.99 *(978-0-545-28146-1(6)*, Cartwheel Bks.) Scholastic, Inc.
Emberley, Rebecca & Emberley, Adrian. There Was an Old Monster! Emberley, Ed, illus. 2009. (ENG.). 32p. (J). (gr. -1-k). 17.99 *(978-0-545-10145-5(X)*, Orchard Bks.) Scholastic, Inc.
Feierabend, John M. The Book of Song Dances. 2015. (First Steps in Music Ser.). (ENG., Illus.). 122p. (J). (gr. 2-4). pap. 17.95 *(978-1-62277-086-1(2))* G I A Pubns., Inc.
—The Book of Song Tales for Upper Grades. 2015. (First Steps in Music Ser.). (ENG., Illus.). 144p. (J). (gr. 4-7). pap. 18.95 *(978-1-62277-087-8(0))* G I A Pubns., Inc.
Ferraro Close, Laura. The Farmer in the Dell. 2011. (Favorite Children's Songs Ser.). (ENG., Illus.). 16p. (J). (gr. -1-2). lib. bdg. 25.64 *(978-1-60954-296-2(7)*, 200100) Child's World, Inc., The.
Golden Books Staff. The Twelve Days of Christmas: A Christmas Carol. Beckett, Sheilah, illus. 2015. (Little Golden Book Ser.). (ENG.). 24p. (J). (gr. k-k). 4.99 *(978-0-307-00149-8(0)*, Golden Bks.) Random Hse. Children's Bks.
Kadair, Deborah, illus. Today Is Monday in Kentucky, 1 vol. 2012. (ENG.). 32p. (J). (gr. k-k). 16.99 *(978-1-4556-1533-9(1))* Pelican Publishing Co., Inc.
Ketteman, Helen. There Once Was a Cowpoke Who Swallowed an Ant. Terry, Will, illus. 2014. (ENG.). 32p. (J). (gr. -1-3). 16.99 *(978-0-8075-7850-6(9))* Whitman, Albert & Co.
Long, Laurel. The Twelve Days of Christmas. 2011. (ENG.). 32p. (J). (gr. -1-2). 16.99 *(978-0-8037-3357-2(7)*, Dial Bks) Penguin Young Readers Group.
Pizzoli, Greg. The Twelve Days of Christmas. Pizzoli, Greg, illus. 2017. (ENG., Illus.). 56p. (J). (gr. -1-k). 16.99 ***(978-1-4847-5031-5(4))*** Hyperion Bks. for Children.
Plume, Ilse. The Farmer in the Dell. 2004. (ENG., Illus.). 32p. (J). 17.95 *(978-1-56792-270-7(8))* Godine, David R. Pub.
Quattlebaum, Mary. Jo MacDonald Saw a Pond, 1 vol. Bryant, Laura J., illus. 2011. (ENG.). 32p. (J). pap. 8.95 *(978-1-58469-151-8(4))* Dawn Pubns.
Ray, Jane. The Twelve Days of Christmas. 2011. (ENG., Illus.). 32p. (J). (gr. -1-2). 16.99 *(978-0-7636-5735-2(2))* Candlewick Pr.
Roitman, Tanya, illus. The More We Are Together. 2009. (Rookie Toddler: Sing along Toddler Ser.). (ENG.). 12p. (J). (gr. -1). bds. 6.95 *(978-0-531-24547-7(0))* Scholastic Library Publishing.
Seeger, Pete. One Grain of Sand: A Lullaby. Wingerter, Linda, illus. 2005. 30p. (J). (gr. -1-4). reprint ed. 16.00 *(978-0-7567-8586-4(3))* DIANE Publishing Co.
Simpson, Steve, illus. The Farmer in the Dell. 2009. (J). *(978-0-545-06702-7(2))* Scholastic, Inc.
Spier, Peter. The Fox Went Out on a Chilly Night: An Old Song. 2014. (ENG., Illus.). 48p. (J). (gr. -1-2). 17.99 *(978-0-385-37616-7(2))*; lib. bdg. 20.99 *(978-0-375-97207-2(2))* Random Hse. Children's Bks. (Doubleday Bks. for Young Readers).

EFG

Spier, Peter, illus. The Fox Went Out on a Chilly Night: An Old Song. unabr. ed. 2006. (J). (gr. -1-3). pap. 16.95 incl. audio *(978-1-59112-440-5(9))*;Set. pap. 39.95 incl. audio compact disk *(978-1-59112-443-6(3))*;Set. pap. 37.95 incl. audio *(978-1-59112-442-9(5))* Live Oak Media.

St. James, Rebecca. Friendly Beasts: An Old English Christmas Carol, 1 vol. Vojtech, Anna, illus. 2012. (ENG.). 32p. (J). 16.99 *(978-0-310-72012-6(5))* Zonderkidz.

Trapani, Iza. Froggie Went A-Courtin' Trapani, Iza, illus. 2006. (ENG., Illus.). 32p. (J). (gr. 2-k). pap. 7.95 *(978-1-58089-029-8(6))* Charlesbridge Publishing, Inc.

Westcott, Nadine Bernard. I Know an Old Lady Who Swallowed a Fly, 3 vols. 2003. (ENG., Illus.). 11p. (J). (gr. -1 — 1). bds. 6.99 *(978-0-316-93084-0(9)*, Tingley, Megan Bks.) Little, Brown Bks. for Young Readers.

Yacowitz, Caryn. I Know an Old Lady Who Swallowed a Dreidel. Slonim, David, illus. 2014. (ENG.). 32p. (J). (gr. -1-3). 17.99 *(978-0-439-91530-4(9)*, Levine, Arthur A. Bks.) Scholastic, Inc.

Yarrow, Peter, et al. I'm in Love with a Big Blue Frog. Brunet, Joshua S., illus. 2013. (ENG.). 28p. (J). (gr. -1-3). 17.95 *(978-1-936140-37-4(3))* Charlesbridge Publishing, Inc.

FOLK SONGS—UNITED STATES

Beaky, Suzanne, illus. She'll Be Comin' Round the Mountain. rev. ed. 2007. (ENG.). 24p. (J). (gr. -1-k). 4.99 *(978-1-59069-604-0(2))* Studio Mouse LLC.

Bissex, Rachel. Dancing With My Mother. Passman, Emily, illus. 2003. 14p. (J). spiral bd. 10.00 *(978-0-9742516-0-8(7))* Minimal Pr., The.

Carlin, Richard. Folk. 2007. (American Popular Music Ser.). (Illus.). 304p. (gr. 6-12). per. 21.95 *(978-0-8160-7340-5(6)*, Checkmark Bks.) Facts On File, Inc.

Childrens Press Staff. Everywhere a Moo, Moo. 2009. (Rookie Toddler: Sing along Toddler Ser.). (ENG.). 12p. (J). (gr. -1). bds. 6.95 *(978-0-531-24548-4(9))* Scholastic Library Publishing.

Downing, Johnette, illus. & adapted by. My Aunt Came Back from Louisiane, 1 vol. Downing, Johnette, adapted by. 2008. (ENG.). 32p. (J). (gr. 1-3). 16.99 *(978-1-58980-607-8(7))* Pelican Publishing Co., Inc.

Erdei, Peter, ed. 150 American Folk Songs to Sing Read & Play. 2004. (ENG.). 136p. (gr. k-6). pap. 22.99 *(978-0-913932-04-9(3)*, 0913932043) Boosey & Hawkes, Inc.

Kadair, Deborah, illus. Today Is Monday in Kentucky, 1 vol. 2012. (ENG.). 32p. (J). (gr. k-k). 16.99 *(978-1-4556-1533-9(1))* Pelican Publishing Co., Inc.

Quattlebaum, Mary. Jo MacDonald Had a Garden. Bryant, Laura J., illus. 2013. (ENG.). 26p. (J). (gr. -1 — 1). bds. 7.95 *(978-1-58469-225-6(1))* Dawn Pubns.

Sieling, Peter. Folk Music. 2004. (North American Folklore Ser.). (Illus.). 112p. (YA). (gr. 7-18). lib. bdg. 22.95 *(978-1-59084-342-0(8))* Mason Crest.

—Folk Songs. 2004. (North American Folklore Ser.). (Illus.). 112p. (YA). (gr. 7-18). lib. bdg. 22.95 *(978-1-59084-344-4(4))* Mason Crest.

FOLK TALES

see Folklore

FOLKLORE

see also Fairies; Grail; Monsters; Mythology; Superstition

Aardema, Verna. Who's in Rabbit's House? 2004. 38.75 *(978-1-55592-489-8(1))*; (J). 18.95 *(978-1-55592-488-1(3))* Weston Woods Studios, Inc.

Aesop. Bat's Big Game. Nobati, Eugenia, illus. 2012. (J). 34.28 *(978-1-61913-131-6(5))* Weigl Pubs., Inc.

—Belling the Cat. 2014. (J). *(978-1-4896-2431-4(7))* Weigl Pubs., Inc.

—The Brazier & His Dog. 2014. (J). *(978-1-4896-2449-9(X))* Weigl Pubs., Inc.

—The Lion, the Wolf, & the Fox. 2014. (J). *(978-1-4896-2446-8(5))* Weigl Pubs., Inc.

—Mercury & the Workmen. 2014. (J). *(978-1-4896-2434-5(1))* Weigl Pubs., Inc.

—The Peasant & the Eagle. 2014. (J). *(978-1-4896-2437-6(6))* Weigl Pubs., Inc.

—The Swollen Fox. 2014. (J). *(978-1-4896-2443-7(0))* Weigl Pubs., Inc.

—The Thief & the Housedog. 2015. (J). *(978-1-4896-2428-4(7))* Weigl Pubs., Inc.

—The Two Goats. 2014. (J). *(978-1-4896-2440-6(6))* Weigl Pubs., Inc.

Afanasyev, Alexander. Russian Fairy Tales. Bilibin, Ivan, illus. 2012. 90p. (-18). pap. *(978-1-908478-68-9(3))* Planet, The.

Amery, Heather. Stories from Around the World. Edwards, Linda, illus. 2004. (Stories for Young Children Ser.). (SPA.). 128p. (J). (gr. -1-3). lib. bdg. 24.95 *(978-1-58086-330-8(2))* EDC Publishing.

Anaya, Rudolfo A. La Llorona: The Crying Woman. Lamadrid, Enrique R., tr. Córdova, Amy, illus. 2011. (SPA & ENG.). 40p. (J). 19.95 *(978-0-8263-4460-1(7))* Univ. of New Mexico Pr.

Arai, Shizuko. The Turtle & the Warrior. Maeda, Matsuo, illus. 2014. (J). 8.95 *(978-1-935523-69-7(4))* World Tribune Pr.

Arengo, Sue. The Shoemaker & the Elves. 2nd ed. 2011. (ENG., Illus.). 24p. pap. 7.94 *(978-0-19-423882-3(2))* Oxford Univ. Pr., Inc.

Ariel, A. D., retold by. The Girl Made of Snow a Russian Folktale. 2016. (Spring Forward Ser.). (J). (gr. 2). *(978-1-4900-9461-8(X))* Benchmark Education Co.

Arkhurst, Joyce Cooper. The Further Adventures of Spider: West African Folktales. Pinkney, Jerry, illus. 2012. (Passport to Reading Level 4 Ser.). (ENG.). 32p. (J). (gr. -1-3). pap. 4.99 *(978-0-316-20345-6(9))* Little, Brown Bks. for Young Readers.

Artell, Mike. Jacques & de Beanstalk. Harris, Jim, illus. 2010. (ENG.). 32p. (J). (gr. k-3). 18.99 *(978-0-8037-2816-5(6)*, Dial Bks) Penguin Young Readers Group.

Atwater-Rhodes, Amelia. Hawksong. 2004. (Kiesha'ra Ser.: Bk. 1). (ENG.). 256p. (YA). (gr. 7). reprint ed. mass mkt. 7.99 *(978-0-440-23803-4(X)*, Laurel Leaf) Random Hse. Children's Bks.

Babbitt, Ellen C. More Jataka Tales. Young, Ellsworth, illus. 2006. pap. *(978-1-4065-0347-0(9))* Dodo Pr.

—More Jataka Tales. 2004. reprint ed. pap. 1.99 *(978-1-4192-3522-1(2))* Kessinger Publishing, LLC.

Baia, Edward. Aikanana. 2013. 30p. pap. *(978-9980-86-490-1(7))* University of Papua New Guinea Press.

—Isokau Akuaku: A Traditional Story from Central Province. Mape, Michael & Ella, Peter Leo, illus. 2013. 30p. pap. *(978-9980-86-494-9(X))* University of Papua New Guinea Press.

Baldursson, Halldór, illus. Egil's Saga: The Story of Egil Skallagrimsson: an Icelandic Classic. 2016. (ENG.). 64p. pap. 6.95 *(978-1-906230-87-6(0))* Real Reads Ltd. GBR. Dist: Casemate Pubs. & Bk. Distributors, LLC.

Barchers, Suzanne. Bunyip in the Moon: A Tale from Australia. Clarke, Peter, illus. 2015. (Tales of Honor Ser.). (ENG.). 32p. (gr. 1-3). lib. bdg. 26.60 *(978-1-939656-77-3(X))* Red Chair Pr.

Barclay, Aegea & Barclay, Katrina. The Hand of Zeus. 2004. 48p. 16.95 *(978-0-9758803-6-4(5))* Aegean Design.

Barker, Geoff. What Is a Folktale?, 1 vol., 1. 2014. (Britannica Common Core Library). (ENG.). 32p. (gr. 2-5). pap. 12.90 *(978-1-62275-213-3(9))*; lib. bdg. 23.45 *(978-1-62275-210-2(4))* Rosen Publishing Group, Inc., The.

Barkow, Henriette. The Giant Turnip. Johnson, Richard, illus. 2004. 32p. (J). (ENG & BEN.). pap. *(978-1-85269-734-1(2))*; (ENG & PAN.). pap. *(978-1-85269-742-6(3))*; (POL & ENG.). pap. *(978-1-85269-743-3(1))*; (ENG & POR.). pap. *(978-1-85269-744-0(X))*; (ENG & URD.). pap. *(978-1-85269-750-1(4))* Mantra Lingua.

Batt, Tanya Robyn. The Faerie's Gift. Ceccoli, Nicoletta, illus. 2003. 32p. (J). (gr. -1-3). 16.99 *(978-1-84148-998-8(0))* Barefoot Bks., Inc.

Bechstein, Ludwig. The Rabbit Catcher & Other Fairy Tales. Jarrell, Randall, tr. Fontana, Ugo, illus. 2011. 42p. 35.95 *(978-1-258-08375-5(2))* Literary Licensing, LLC.

Besant, Annie W. Legends & Tales Lotus Leaves for the Y. 2006. pap. 19.95 *(978-1-4286-2494-8(5))* Kessinger Publishing, LLC.

Between the Lions - Early Literacy Kit - Oh, Yes, It Can!, 1 cass., 1 bk. 2005. (Between the Lions Ser.). 36p. (J). VHS 29.95 *(978-1-59375-286-6(5)*, WG38643) WGBH Boston Video.

Bingham, Jane & Sansom, Fiona. Chinese Myths. Kennedy, Graham, illus. 2009. (Myths from Many Lands Ser.). 48p. (YA). (gr. 2-6). pap. 12.85 *(978-1-60754-219-3(6))* Windmill Bks.

Blair, Eric. Annie Oakley, 1 vol. Silverman, Dianne, illus. 2013. (My First Classic Story Ser.). (ENG.). 32p. (gr. k-3). pap. 7.10 *(978-1-4795-1846-3(8)*, My First Classic Story) Picture Window Bks.

—The Country Mouse & the City Mouse: A Retelling of Aesop's Fable, 1 vol. Silverman, Dianne, illus. 2013. (My First Classic Story Ser.). (ENG.). 24p. (gr. k-3). pap. 7.10 *(978-1-4795-1858-6(1)*, My First Classic Story) Picture Window Bks.

—The Donkey in the Lion's Skin: A Retelling of Aesop's Fable, 1 vol. Silverman, Dianne, illus. 2013. (My First Classic Story Ser.). (ENG.). 24p. (gr. k-3). pap. 7.10 *(978-1-4795-1855-5(7)*, My First Classic Story) Picture Window Bks.

—Pecos Bill, 1 vol. Chambers-Goldberg, Micah, illus. 2013. (My First Classic Story Ser.).Tr. of Pecos Bill. (ENG.). 32p. (gr. k-3). pap. 7.10 *(978-1-4795-1860-9(3)*, My First Classic Story) Picture Window Bks.

Bonnice, Sherry. Christmas & Santa Claus Folklore. 2004. (North American Folklore Ser.). (Illus.). 112p. (J). (gr. 7-18). lib. bdg. 22.95 *(978-1-59084-330-7(4))* Mason Crest.

—Folk Fashion. 2004. (North American Folklore Ser.). (Illus.). 112p. (YA). (gr. 7-18). lib. bdg. 22.95 *(978-1-59084-338-3(X))* Mason Crest.

Boston, David, illus. Wonder Tales from Around the World. 2006. (World Storytelling from August House Ser.). (ENG.). 158p. (J). (gr. 3-7). pap. 19.95 *(978-0-87483-422-2(8)*, AH228) August Hse. Pubs., Inc.

Brabourne, Edward Hugessen Knatchbull-Hugessen. River Legends of the Thames & Rhine. Doré, Gustave, illus. 2005. (J). pap. *(978-0-486-44372-0(8))* Dover Pubns., Inc.

Bradman, Tony. Happy Ever After. Warburton, Sarah, illus. 2014. (After Happily Ever After Ser.). (ENG.). 56p. (gr. 2-3). pap. 5.05 *(978-1-4342-7960-6(X)*, After Happily Ever After) Stone Arch Bks.

Brinkerhoff, Shirley. Family Folklore. 2004. (North American Folklore Ser.). (Illus.). 112p. (YA). (gr. 7-18). lib. bdg. 22.95 *(978-1-59084-333-8(9))* Mason Crest.

Bukiet, Suzanne. Scripts of the World. 2nd ed. (Illus.). 91p. (YA). reprint ed. 19.95 *(978-0-9656274-1-2(1))* Another Language Pr.

Byrd, Robert. Brave Chicken Little. Byrd, Robert, illus. 2014. (ENG., Illus.). 40p. (J). (gr. -1-3). 17.99 *(978-0-670-78616-9(0)*, Viking Books for Young Readers) Penguin Young Readers Group.

Canton, William. A Child's Book of Warriors. Cole, Herbert, illus. 2012. 290p. pap. 12.75 *(978-1-936639-21-2(1))* St. Augustine Academy Pr.

Chifamba-Barnes, Sarudzayi Elizabeth. The Village Story-Teller: Zimbabwean Folktales. 2009. (Illus.). 100p. (gr. 3-7). pap. *(978-0-9558082-1-0(9))* Lion Pr. Ltd., The.

Clay, Kathryn & Vonne, Mira. Top 10 Urban Legends, 1 vol. 2012. (Top 10 Unexplained Ser.). (ENG.). 32p. (gr. 1-2). 26.65 *(978-1-4296-7638-0(8)*, Blazers) Capstone Press of Coughlan Cos.

Coleman, Melvin. B. C. & Phoenicia: A Traditional Folktale. 2004. (Illus.). 201p. 25.00 *(978-0-9764065-0-1(0))* Gestalt Pubns.

Colfer, Chris. The Land of Stories: A Treasury of Classic Fairy Tales. Dorman, Brandon, illus. 2016. 323p. (J). ***(978-0-316-55193-9(7))*** Little Brown & Co.

Colum, Padraic. The Adventures of Odysseus & the Tale of Troy. Pogány, Willy, illus. 2008. 164p. pap. *(978-1-4068-2730-9(4))* Echo Library.

Colum, Padraic & Pogány, Willy. The Adventures of Odysseus & the Tale of Troy. 2008. 280p. 42.95 *(978-1-4366-0896-1(1))* Kessinger Publishing, LLC.

Cross, Luther. Ogres. 2015. (Creatures of Fantasy Ser.). (ENG., Illus.). 64p. (J). (gr. 5-5). 34.21 *(978-1-5026-0504-7(X)*, Exhibit A) Cavendish Square Publishing.

Crow, Kristyn & Aesop. The Really Groovy Story of the Tortoise & the Hare. Forshay, Christina, illus. 2012. (J). *(978-1-61913-128-6(5))* Weigl Pubs., Inc.

Daning, Tom. Chinese Mythology: The Four Dragons. 2007. (Jr. Graphic Mythologies Ser.). (ENG., Illus.). 24p. (J). (gr. 2-5). lib. bdg. 25.25 *(978-1-4042-3400-0(4))* Rosen Publishing Group, Inc., The.

—The Four Dragons: A Chinese Myth. 2007. (Graphic Myths (New York, N.Y.) Ser.). (ENG., Illus.). 24p. (gr. 3-8). pap. 10.60 *(978-1-4042-2153-6(0)*, PowerKids Pr.) Rosen Publishing Group, Inc., The.

Darmani, L. Stories from Africa, Vol. 3. 2003. (Illus.). 48p. pap. *(978-9964-87-854-2(0))* African Christian Pr. GHA. Dist: Michigan State Univ. Pr.

Davila, Andrew. Prophecies of the Ancient. 2003. 110p. (YA). pap. 9.95 *(978-0-595-26851-1(X))* iUniverse, Inc.

Davis, David. Fandango Stew. Galbraith, Ben, illus. 2015. (ENG.). 32p. (J). (gr. -1-3). pap. 6.95 *(978-1-4549-1680-2(X))* Sterling Publishing Co., Inc.

de Las Casas, Dianne. The Little Read Hen, 1 vol. Stone-Barker, Holly, illus. 2013. (ENG.). 32p. (J). (gr. -1-k). 16.99 *(978-1-4556-1702-9(4))* Pelican Publishing Co., Inc.

dePaola, Tomie & Airgood, Ellen. The Magical World of Strega Nona: A Treasury. dePaola, Tomie, illus. 2015. (ENG., Illus.). 224p. (J). (gr. k-3). 40.00 *(978-0-399-17345-5(5)*, Nancy Paulsen Books) Penguin Young Readers Group.

DeSpain, Pleasant. Tales of Cats, Vol. 9. Bell, Don, tr. Bell, Don, illus. 2005. (ENG.). 80p. (J). (gr. 3-6). 14.95 *(978-0-87483-713-1(8))* August Hse. Pubs., Inc.

—Tales of Enchantment, Vol. 7. Bell, Don, tr. Bell, Don, illus. 2005. (ENG.). 80p. (J). (gr. 3-6). 14.95 *(978-0-87483-711-7(1))* August Hse. Pubs., Inc.

—Tales of Heroes, Vol. 4. Bell, Don, illus. 2005. (Books of Nine Lives: Vol. 4). (ENG.). 80p. (J). (gr. 3-6). 14.95 *(978-0-87483-666-0(2))* August Hse. Pubs., Inc.

—Tales of Holidays, Vol. 5. Bell, Don, illus. 2005. (Books of Nine Lives: Vol. 5). (ENG.). 80p. (J). (gr. 3-6). 14.95 *(978-0-87483-667-7(0))* August Hse. Pubs., Inc.

—Tales of Insects, Vol. 6. Bell, Don, illus. 2005. (Books of Nine Lives: Vol. 6). (ENG.). 80p. (J). (gr. 3-6). 14.95 *(978-0-87483-668-4(9))* August Hse. Pubs., Inc.

—Tales of Nonsense & Tomfoolery. Bell, Don, illus. (ENG.). 80p. (J). (gr. 3-6). 2006. pap. 9.95 *(978-0-87483-645-5(X))* Vol. 2. 2005. (Books of Nine Lives: Vol. 2). 14.95 *(978-0-87483-670-7(0))* August Hse. Pubs., Inc.

—Tales of Tricksters. Bell, Don, illus. 2005. (Books of Nine Lives: Vol. 1). (ENG.). 80p. (J). (gr. -1-12). 14.95 *(978-0-87483-669-1(7))* August Hse. Pubs., Inc.

—Tales of Tricksters: Books of Nine Lives, Vol. 1. Bell, Don, illus. 2006. (ENG.). 80p. (J). (gr. 3-6). pap. 9.95 *(978-0-87483-644-8(1))* August Hse. Pubs., Inc.

—Tales of Wisdom & Justice, Vol. 3. Bell, Don, illus. 2005. (Books of Nine Lives: Vol. 3). (ENG.). 80p. (J). (gr. 3-6). 14.95 *(978-0-87483-671-4(9))* August Hse. Pubs., Inc.

—Tales of Wisdom & Justice: Books of Nine Lives. Bell, Don, illus. 2006. (Books of Nine Lives: Vol. 3). (ENG.). 80p. (J). (gr. 3-6). pap. 9.95 *(978-0-87483-646-2(8))* August Hse. Pubs., Inc.

—Tales to Frighten & Delight, Vol. 8. Bell, Don, tr. Bell, Don, illus. 2005. (ENG.). 80p. (J). (gr. -1-12). 14.95 *(978-0-87483-712-4(X))* August Hse. Pubs., Inc.

Dijkstra, Lida. Little Mouse. Grobler, Piet, illus. 2004. (ENG.). 32p. (J). 15.95 *(978-1-932425-06-2(3)*, Lemniscaat) Boyds Mills Pr.

Diouf, Sylvianne. Bintou's Braids. Evans, Shane, illus. 2004. (ENG.). 40p. (J). (gr. -1-7). pap. 6.99 *(978-0-8118-4629-5(6))* Chronicle Bks. LLC.

Disney Princess Enchanted Character Guide. 2014. (ENG., Illus.). 144p. (J). (gr. 2-5). 16.99 *(978-1-4654-1569-1(6)*, DK Children) Dorling Kindersley Publishing, Inc.

Disney Staff, creator. Chicken Little, Vol. 1. 2005. (Illus.). 96p. pap. 14.99 *(978-1-59532-724-6(X)*, Tokyopop Kids) TOKYOPOP, Inc.

Doolittle, Eva M. Old Fairy Tales Anew. Telielska, M. Magdalena, illus. 2008. 88p. (J). *(978-0-9791065-0-7(8))* Vesta Bks., LLC.

Downie, Mary Alice & Zola, Mequido. How the Devil Got His Cat & Other Multicultural Folktales for Children. Gilliland, Jillian Hulme, illus. 144p. (J). pap. 16.95 *(978-1-55082-100-0(8))* Quarry Pr. CAN. Dist: LPC/InBook.

Doyle, Malachy & Sharkey, Niamh. Tales from Old Ireland. 2017. (Illus.). 96p. 16.99 ***(978-1-78285-358-9(8))*** Barefoot Bks., Inc.

East, Helen & Maddern, Eric. Spirit of the Forest: Tree Tales from Around the World. Marks, Alan, illus. 2003. 48p. (J). pap. *(978-0-7112-1879-6(X))* ReiseArt Buchhandlung GmbH.

East, Jacqueline, illus. Beauty & the Beast. 2015. (J). *(978-1-4723-3133-5(8))* Parragon Bk. Service Ltd.

Egelberg, Arlene & Clark, Raymond C. How & Why Folktales: From Around the World. Braun, Chuck, illus. 2004. 106p. (gr. 6-12). pap., stu. ed. 15.00 *(978-0-86647-180-0(4))* Pro Lingua Assocs., Inc.

Emberley, Ed & Emberley, Rebecca. Chicken Little. Emberley, Ed, illus. 2009. (ENG., Illus.). 34p. (J). (gr. -1-2). 18.99 *(978-1-59643-464-6(3)*, 9781596434646) Roaring Brook Pr.

Evetts-Secker, Josephine. Mother & Daughter Tales. Cann, Helen, illus. 2011. (ENG.). 40p. (J). 21.99 *(978-1-84686-572-5(7))* Barefoot Bks., Inc.

Ferrin, Wendy Wakefield. Grandmother's Alligator: Burukenge Wa Nyanya. Mwangi, Simmon, tr. Broyles, Beverly Ashley, illus. 2003. (SWA & ENG.). 56p. (J). (gr. 1-18). 17.95 *(978-0-9703632-3-7(0))* Wakefield Connection, The.

Finch, Mary. The Little Red Hen & the Ear of Wheat. 2011. (J). *(978-1-84686-576-3(X))* Barefoot Bks., Inc.

Flor Ada, Alma. With Love, Little Red Hen. Tryon, Leslie, illus. 2004. (ENG.). 40p. (J). (gr. k-3). 7.99 *(978-0-689-87061-3(2)*, Atheneum Bks. for Young Readers) Simon & Schuster Children's Publishing.

Floyd, Lucy. Rabbit & Turtle Go to School. Denise, Christopher, illus. 2003. (Green Light Readers Level 1 Ser.). (ENG.). 24p. (J). (gr. -1-3). pap. 3.95 *(978-0-15-204851-8(0))* Houghton Mifflin Harcourt Publishing Co.

—Rabbit & Turtle Go to School. 2003. (Green Light Readers — Level 1 Ser.). (gr. k-3). lib. bdg. 13.50 *(978-0-613-63339-0(3)*, Turtleback) Turtleback Bks.

Forest, Heather. Ancient & Epic Tales: From Around the World. 2016. (ENG.). 175p. (J). (gr. 3-5). pap. 17.95 *(978-1-939160-87-4(1))* August Hse. Pubs., Inc.

—Stone Soup. 2005. (ENG., Illus.). 32p. (J). (gr. -1-2). pap. 8.95 *(978-0-87483-602-8(6))* August Hse. Pubs., Inc.

—Wisdom Tales from Around the World. 2005. (ENG.). 160p. (J). (gr. 3-7). pap. 19.95 *(978-0-87483-479-6(1)*, AH4791) August Hse. Pubs., Inc.

Gág, Wanda. Gone Is Gone: Or the Story of a Man Who Wanted to Do Housework. Gág, Wanda, illus. 2003. (Fesler-Lampert Minnesota Heritage Ser.). (Illus.). 64p. 14.95 *(978-0-8166-4243-4(5))* Univ. of Minnesota Pr.

Galdone, Paul. The Folk Tale Classics Heirloom Library. 2012. (Folk Tale Classics Ser.). (ENG., Illus.). 176p. (J). (gr. -1-3). 19.99 *(978-0-547-85276-8(2))* Houghton Mifflin Harcourt Publishing Co.

Galdone, Paul, illus. The Three Bears. 2011. (J). pap. ***(978-0-547-86831-8(6))*** Harcourt.

Gehl, Laura & Aesop. Hare & Tortoise Race Across Israel. Goodreau, Sarah, illus. 2015. (ENG.). 32p. (J). (gr. -1-1). lib. bdg. 17.95 *(978-1-4677-2199-8(9)*, Kar-Ben Publishing) Lerner Publishing Group.

Ghose, Sudhindra Nath. The Flame of the Forest. 2003. 288p. pap. 29.00 *(978-0-7581-9376-6(9))* Textbook Pubs.

Giles, Bridget. West African Myths. 2010. (Myths from Around the World Ser.). 48p. (gr. 6-8). (YA). lib. bdg. 31.00 *(978-1-4339-3536-7(8))*; (Illus.). (J). pap. 14.05 *(978-1-4339-3537-4(6))* Stevens, Gareth Publishing LLLP. (Gareth Stevens Secondary Library).

Glaser, Linda. Stone Soup with Matzoh Balls: A Passover Tale in Chelm. Tabatabaei, Maryam, illus. 2014. (ENG.). 32p. (J). (gr. -1-2). 16.99 *(978-0-8075-7620-5(4))* Whitman, Albert & Co.

Goble, Paul. Walking Along: Plains Indian Trickster Stories. Goble, Paul, illus. 2011. (Illus.). (J). 19.95 *(978-0-9845041-5-2(X)*, South Dakota State Historical Society Pr.) South Dakota State Historical Society Pr.

Goldsworthy, Steve. Zombies: The Truth Behind History's Terrifying Flesh-Eaters. 2015. (Monster Handbooks Ser.). (ENG., Illus.). 32p. (gr. 3-4). lib. bdg. 27.99 *(978-1-4914-4252-4(2))* Capstone Press of Coughlan Cos.

Gray, Luli. Ant & Grasshopper. Ferri, Giuliano, illus. 2011. (ENG.). 32p. (J). (gr. -1-2). 17.99 *(978-1-4169-5140-7(7)*, McElderry, Margaret K. Bks.) McElderry, Margaret K. Bks.

Great Books Foundation Staff, contrib. by. Junior Great Books. 2011. (J). *(978-1-933147-00-0(8))* Great Bks. Foundation.

Grimm, Jacob. MÄRCHEN DER BRÜDER GRIMM. (GER.). pap. 29.95 *(978-3-257-00866-1(X))* Diogenes Verlag AG CHE. Dist: Distribooks, Inc.

Guillain, Charlotte. Finn MacCool & the Giant's Causeway: An Irish Folk Tale, 1 vol. Dorado, Steve, illus. 2014. (Folk Tales from Around the World Ser.). (ENG.). 24p. (gr. 1-3). pap. 6.95 *(978-1-4109-6699-5(2)*, NA-r) Heinemann-Raintree.

—Folk Tales from Around the World, 1 vol. Dorado, Steve, illus. 2014. (Folk Tales from Around the World Ser.). (ENG.). 24p. (gr. 1-3). pap. 41.70 *(978-1-4109-6702-2(6)*, NA-r) Heinemann-Raintree.

—The Foolish, Timid Rabbit: An Indian Folk Tale, 1 vol. Dorado, Steve, illus. 2014. (Folk Tales from Around the World Ser.). (ENG.). 24p. (gr. 1-3). pap. 6.95 *(978-1-4109-6700-8(X)*, NA-r) Heinemann-Raintree.

—The Tree of Life: An Amazonian Folk Tale, 1 vol. Dorado, Steve, illus. 2014. (Folk Tales from Around the World Ser.). (ENG.). 24p. (gr. 1-3). pap. 6.95 *(978-1-4109-6698-8(4)*, NA-r) Heinemann-Raintree.

—The Unhappy Stonecutter: A Japanese Folk Tale, 1 vol. Dorado, Steve, illus. 2014. (Folk Tales from Around the World Ser.). (ENG.). 24p. (gr. 1-3). pap. 6.95 *(978-1-4109-6696-4(8)*, NA-r) Heinemann-Raintree.

—Why the Spider Has Long Legs: An African Folk Tale, 1 vol. Dorado, Steve, illus. 2014. (Folk Tales from Around the World Ser.). (ENG.). 24p. (gr. 1-3). pap. 6.95 *(978-1-4109-6701-5(8)*, NA-r) Heinemann-Raintree.

Hall, Amanda. The Stolen Sun. Hall, Amanda, illus. 2004. (Illus.). 32p. (J). (gr. 10-18). 17.00 *(978-0-8028-5225-0(4))* Eerdmans, William B. Publishing Co.

Hamilton, John. Fantasy & Folklore Set II. 2006. (Fantasy & Folkore Set 2 Ser.). (gr. 4-8). 162.42 *(978-1-59679-334-7(1)*, Abdo & Daughters) ABDO Publishing Co.

—Magic Rings & Other Magical Things, 1 vol. 2006. (Fantasy & Folklore Ser.). (ENG., Illus.). 32p. (gr. 5-8). 27.07 *(978-1-59679-337-8(6)*, Abdo & Daughters) ABDO Publishing Co.

—Weapons of Fantasy & Folkore, 1 vol. 2006. (Fantasy & Folklore Ser.). (ENG., Illus.). 32p. (gr. 5-8). 27.07 *(978-1-59679-340-8(6)*, Abdo & Daughters) ABDO Publishing Co.

Hamilton, Martha & Weiss, Mitch. Noodlehead Stories: World Tales Kids Can Read & Tell. Elsammak, Ariane, illus. 2006. (ENG.). 96p. (J). (gr. 1-6). 24.95 *(978-0-87483-584-7(4))* August Hse. Pubs., Inc.

—Through the Grapevine: World Tales Kids Can Read & Tell. Lyon, Carol, illus. (ENG.). 128p. (J). (gr. 1-6). 2006. pap. 15.95 *(978-0-87483-624-0(7))* 2005. 24.95 *(978-0-87483-625-7(5))* August Hse. Pubs., Inc.

Hamilton, Martha, et al. Noodlehead Stories: World Tales Kids Can Read & Tell. 2006. (ENG., Illus.). 96p. (J). (gr. 1-6). pap. 14.95 *(978-0-87483-585-4(2))* August Hse. Pubs., Inc.

Hamilton, S. L. Zombies. 2010. (Xtreme Monsters Ser.). 32p. (gr. 3-9). 27.07 *(978-1-61613-472-3(0)*, A&D Xtreme) ABDO Publishing Co.

Hamilton, Sue L. Zombies, 1 vol. 2007. (World of Horror Ser.). (ENG., Illus.). 32p. (J). (gr. 4-8). lib. bdg. 27.07 *(978-1-59928-777-5(3)*, Abdo & Daughter) ABDO Publishing Co.

Hansen, Doug & Aesop. Aesop in California. 2013. (J). 16.95 *(978-1-59714-235-9(2))* Heyday.

Harris, Joel Chandler, et al. The Tar Baby & Other Rhymes of Uncle Remus. 2005. (ENG., Illus.). 208p. (gr. -1). pap. 15.95 *(978-1-55709-489-6(6))* Applewood Bks.

Hartman, Bob. The Lion Storyteller Bedtime Book. Nagy, Krisztina Kállai, illus. 2015. (ENG.). 128p. (J). (gr. k-2). pap. 16.99 *(978-0-7459-6494-2(X))* Lion Hudson PLC GBR. Dist: Independent Pubs. Group.

Hartman, Bob & Hudson, Brett. Polly & the Frog: And Other Folk Tales. 2004. (Storyteller Tales Ser.). (ENG., Illus.). 64p.

(J). (gr. k-4). pap. 7.99 *(978-0-7459-4698-6(4))* Lion Hudson PLC GBR. Dist: Independent Pubs. Group.

Hillert, Margaret. The Boy & the Goats. Szulyovszky, Sarolta, illus. 2016. (BeginningtoRead Ser.). (ENG.). 32p. (J). (-2). lib. bdg. 22.60 *(978-1-59953-777-1(X))* Norwood Hse. Pr.

—La Galletita. Jack Pullan & Petruccio, Steven James, illus. 2017. (BeginningtoRead Ser.).Tr. of Little Cookie. (ENG & SPA.). 32p. (J). (-2). 22.60 ***(978-1-59953-845-7(8))*** Norwood Hse. Pr.

—The Little Cookie. Petruccio, Steven James, illus. 2016. (BeginningtoRead Ser.). (ENG.). 32p. (J). (-2). lib. bdg. 22.60 *(978-1-59953-782-5(6))* Norwood Hse. Pr.

—Little Red Riding Hood. Barnum-Newman, Winifred, illus. 2016. (BeginningtoRead Ser.). (ENG.). 32p. (J). (-2). pap. 11.94 *(978-1-60357-909-4(5))*; lib. bdg. 22.60 *(978-1-59953-783-2(4))* Norwood Hse. Pr.

—The Magic Beans. Jamana, Pharida & Zaman, Farida, illus. 2016. (BeginningtoRead Ser.). (ENG.). 32p. (J). (-2). lib. bdg. 22.60 *(978-1-59953-784-9(2))* Norwood Hse. Pr.

—El Niño y los Chivos. Jack Pullan & Szulyovszky, Sarolta, illus. 2017. (BeginningtoRead Ser.).Tr. of Boy & the Goats. (ENG & SPA.). 32p. (J). (-2). 22.60 ***(978-1-59953-840-2(7))*** Norwood Hse. Pr.

—Not I, Not I. Dodson, Bert, illus. 2016. (BeginningtoRead Ser.). (ENG.). 32p. (J). (-2). lib. bdg. 22.60 *(978-1-59953-785-6(0))* Norwood Hse. Pr.

—The Three Bears. Undercuffler, Gary, illus. 2016. (BeginningtoRead Ser.). (ENG.). 32p. (J). (-2). lib. bdg. 22.60 *(978-1-59953-787-0(7))* Norwood Hse. Pr.

—The Three Little Pigs. Dorenkamp, Michelle, illus. 2016. (BeginningtoRead Ser.). (ENG.). 32p. (J). (-2). lib. bdg. 22.60 *(978-1-59953-789-4(3))* Norwood Hse. Pr.

—Los Tres Chivos. Jack Pullan & Banks, Timothy, illus. 2017. (BeginningtoRead Ser.).Tr. of Three Goats. (ENG & SPA.). 32p. (J). (-2). 22.60 ***(978-1-59953-851-8(2))*** Norwood Hse. Pr.

—Los Tres Osos. Jack Pullan & Undercuffler, Gary, illus. 2017. (BeginningtoRead Ser.).Tr. of Three Bears. (ENG & SPA.). 32p. (J). (-2). 22.60 ***(978-1-59953-850-1(4))*** Norwood Hse. Pr.

—Yo No, Yo No. Jack Pullan & Dodson, Bert, illus. 2017. (BeginningtoRead Ser.).Tr. of Not I, Not I. (ENG & SPA.). 32p. (J). (-2). 22.60 ***(978-1-59953-848-8(2))*** Norwood Hse. Pr.

Hockerman, Dennis, et al, illus. Folktales from Ecosystems Around the World. 2009. (Steck-Vaughn Pair-It Books Proficiency Stage 6 Ser.). (ENG.). 48p. (gr. 5-5). pap. 9.65 *(978-0-7398-6171-4(9))* Houghton Mifflin Harcourt Publishing Co.

Holt, David & Mooney, Bill, eds. Ready-to-Tell Tales: Sure-Fire Stories from America's Favorite Storytellers. 2005. (American Storytelling Ser.). (ENG., Illus.). 224p. (gr. 7-17). pap. 19.95 *(978-0-87483-381-2(7))* August Hse. Pubs., Inc.

Hopkins, Jackie Mims. La Gallinita de la Pradera, 1 vol. Cole, Henry, illus. 2015. (SPA & ENG.). 32p. (J). (gr. 1-3). 17.95 *(978-1-56145-841-7(4))* Peachtree Pubs.

Hunter, Llyn. A Little Book of Magical Beings. Hunter, Llyn, illus. 2008. (Illus.). 32p. (J). 7.95 *(978-0-9776419-1-8(0))* Bobcat Publishing.

—A Little Book of Monsters. Hunter, Llyn, illus. 2007. (Illus.). 32p. (J). 7.95 *(978-0-9776419-0-1(2))*, 0-9776419-0-2) Bobcat Publishing.

Hyman, Trina Schart, illus. The Kitchen Knight: A Tale of King Arthur. 2007. (ENG.). 32p. (J). (gr. 1-4). 7.99 *(978-0-8234-1063-7(3))* Holiday Hse., Inc.

Ifans, Rhiannon. Magic of the Mabinogion. Holmes, Helen, illus. 2006. (ENG.). 112p. (J). pap. 9.95 *(978-0-86243-174-7(3))* Y Lolfa GBR. Dist: Dufour Editions, Inc.

—Tales from Wales. Holmes, Helen, illus. 2009. (ENG.). 112p. (J). pap. 8.95 *(978-0-86243-182-2(4))* Y Lolfa GBR. Dist: Dufour Editions, Inc.

Ingham, Donna. Tales with a Texas Twist: Original Stories & Enduring Folklore from the Lone Star State. Hoffman, Paul G., illus. 2005. (ENG.). 160p. (gr. -1-7). per. 12.95 *(978-0-7627-3899-1(5))* Globe Pequot Pr., The.

Jacobs, Kim, illus. & retold by. Princess Sophie & the Six Swans: A Tale from the Brothers Grimm. Jacobs, Kim, retold by. 2017. (ENG.). 40p. (J). (gr. k-3). 16.95 *(978-1-937786-67-0(6)*, Wisdom Tales) World Wisdom, Inc.

Johnson, Richard, illus. The Giant Turnip. 2004. (J). 24p. *(978-1-85269-748-8(2))*; 24p. *(978-1-85269-747-1(4))*; 24p. *(978-1-85269-746-4(6))*; 24p. *(978-1-85269-745-7(8))*; 24p. *(978-1-85269-749-5(0))*; 24p. *(978-1-85269-789-1(X))*; 24p. *(978-1-85269-733-4(4))*; 24p. *(978-1-85269-735-8(0))*; 24p. *(978-1-85269-736-5(9))*; 24p. *(978-1-85269-737-2(7))*; 24p. *(978-1-85269-739-6(3))*; 24p. *(978-1-85269-740-2(7))*; 24p. *(978-1-85269-741-9(5))*; (ENG & RUS.). 32p. pap. *(978-1-85269-788-4(1))* Mantra Lingua.

Jones, Christianne C. Beauty & the Beast, 1 vol. Muehlenhardt, Amy Bailey, illus. 2013. (My First Classic Story Ser.). (ENG.). 32p. (gr. k-3). pap. 7.10 *(978-1-4795-1851-7(4)*, My First Classic Story) Picture Window Bks.

—John Henry, 1 vol. Peterson, Ben, illus. 2013. (My First Classic Story Ser.).Tr. of John Henry. (ENG.). 32p. (gr. k-3). pap. 7.10 *(978-1-4795-1861-6(1)*, My First Classic Story) Picture Window Bks.

—Rapunzel: A Retelling of the Grimms' Fairy Tale, 1 vol. Muehlenhardt, Amy Bailey, illus. 2013. (My First Classic Story Ser.). (ENG.). 32p. (gr. k-3). pap. 7.10 *(978-1-4795-1852-4(2)*, My First Classic Story) Picture Window Bks.

Jorgensen, David, illus. The Three Little Pigs, 1 vol. 2005. (Rabbit Ears-A Classic Tale Set 2 Ser.). (ENG.). 28p. (gr. k-5). 25.65 *(978-1-59197-755-1(X))* Spotlight.

Kann, Alice G. Tales from Time & Beyond the Stars, Vol. 1. Date not set. (Illus.). 50p. (J). (gr. -1-6). 16.95 *(978-0-9654522-1-2(2))* Metapublishing.

Ketteman, Helen. Armadilly Chili. Terry, Will, illus. 2012. (J). *(978-1-61913-143-9(9))* Weigl Pubs., Inc.

Kimmel, Eric A. Joseph & the Sabbath Fish. Peluso, Martina, illus. 2011. (Shabbat Ser.). (ENG.). 32p. (J). (gr. k-3). pap. 7.95 *(978-0-7613-5909-8(5)*, Kar-Ben Publishing) Lerner Publishing Group.

Kirkwood, Neville A. Jungle Heroes. 2011. 138p. pap. 11.50 *(978-1-60976-267-4(3)*, Eloquent Bks.) Strategic Book Publishing & Rights Agency (SBPRA).

Korty, Carol. Silly Soup. Landes, William-Alan, ed. Colombo, David, illus. Helms, Tina, photos by. 2003. (Plays & Play Collections). 128p. (Orig.). (J). (gr. k-6). pap. 17.00 *(978-0-88734-679-8(0))* Players Pr., Inc.

Krensky, Stephen. On My Own Folklore: Classroom Set. 2008. pap. 40.95 *(978-0-8225-9127-6(8))* Lerner Publishing Group.

—On My Own Folklore: Complete Set. 2008. pap. 244.95 *(978-0-8225-9121-4(9))* Lerner Publishing Group.

—Zombies. 2008. pap. 52.95 *(978-0-8225-9893-0(0))* Lerner Publishing Group.

Kung, Annie, tr. Auntie Tigress & Other Favorite Chinese Folk Tales. Wang, Eva, illus. 2006. (ENG.). 48p. (J). (gr. -1). lib. bdg. 16.50 *(978-1-933327-29-7(4))* Purple Bear Bks., Inc.

Lagonegro, Melissa. A Dream for a Princess (Disney Princess) Saichann, Alberto & Estudio, Pulsar, illus. 2016. (Step into Reading Ser.). (ENG.). 24p. (J). (gr. -1-1). pap. 4.99 *(978-0-7364-3668-7(5)*, RH/Disney) Random Hse. Children's Bks.

Lang, Andrew. The Green Fairy Book. 2004. reprint ed. pap. 1.99 *(978-1-4192-6492-4(3))*; pap. 28.95 *(978-1-4191-6492-7(9))* Kessinger Publishing, LLC.

—The Red Fairy Book. 2007. 444p. per. 18.95 *(978-1-4218-3926-4(1)*, 1st World Library - Literary Society) 1st World Publishing, Inc.

Lang, Andrew, ed. The Crimson Fairy Book. (Twelve-Point Ser.). 2003. lib. bdg. 25.00 *(978-1-58287-205-6(8))* 2004. 455p. 26.00 *(978-1-58287-689-4(4))* North Bks.

Lasky, Kathryn. Shadow Wolf. 2010. (Wolves of the Beyond Ser.: 2). (ENG.). 272p. (J). (gr. 3-7). 17.99 *(978-0-545-09312-5(0)*, Scholastic Pr.) Scholastic, Inc.

Lauture, Mireille B. Bobo, Chen Odasye A / Bobo, the Sneaky Dog: Mancy's Haitian Folktale Collection. Minckler, Kathleen L., illus. 2010. 28p. pap. 12.49 *(978-1-4520-6173-3(4))* AuthorHouse.

Layne, Deborah & Layne, Steven. P Is for Princess: A Royal Alphabet. Papp, Robert & Papp, Lisa, illus. rev. ed. 2007. (ENG.). 40p. (J). (gr. k-6). 17.95 *(978-1-58536-306-3(5))* Sleeping Bear Pr.

Lessing, Edeltraut B. Amber & Flax. 2009. *(978-1-61623-777-6(5))* Independent Pub.

Li, Yiyun. The Story of Gilgamesh. 2016. (Save the Story Ser.). (ENG., Illus.). 104p. (J). (gr. 3-7). 19.95 *(978-1-78269-023-8(9)*, Pushkin Press) Steerforth Pr.

The Lion & the Hare: [an East African Folktale]. 2009. (On My Own Folklore Ser.). (gr. 3-5). pap. 6.95 *(978-1-58013-849-9(7)*, First Avenue Editions) Lerner Publishing Group.

Lively, Joe. Notes of a Time Traveler: Our Forgotten Folk Heritage. 2nd ed. (Illus.). 260p. (YA). (gr. 6-18). reprint ed. 28.95 *(978-0-9656688-2-8(7))* ABM Enterprises, Inc.

Loebel-Fried, Caren, retold by. Hawaiian Legends of Dreams. 2005. (Latitude 20 Bks.). (Illus.). 146p. (J). (gr. 4-7). 21.99 *(978-0-8248-2961-2(1))* Univ. of Hawaii Pr.

Loh-Hagan, Virginia. Zombies: Magic, Myth, & Mystery. 2016. (Magic, Myth, & Mystery Ser.). (ENG., Illus.). 32p. (J). (gr. 4-8). 29.93 *(978-1-63471-111-1(4)*, 208555, 45th Parallel Press) Cherry Lake Publishing.

Lottridge, Celia Barker & Chan, Harvey. Music for the Tsar of the Sea. 2006. (Illus.). 30p. (J). (gr. k-4). reprint ed. 17.00 *(978-0-7567-9931-1(7))* DIANE Publishing Co.

Lowell, Susan. Dusty Locks & the Three Bears. Cecil, Randy, illus. rev. ed. 2004. (ENG.). 32p. (J). (gr. -1-3). pap. 8.99 *(978-0-8050-7534-2(8)*, 9780805075342) Square Fish.

Lundbergh, Holger, tr. from SWE. Swedish Folk Tales, 1 vol. Bauer, John, illus. 2004. (ENG.). 240p. (J). 28.00 *(978-0-86315-457-7(3))* Floris Bks. GBR. Dist: SteinerBooks, Inc.

Lunge-Larsen, Lise. Adventures of Thor the Thunder God. Madsen, Jim, illus. 2007. (ENG.). 80p. (gr. 5-7). 19.95 *(978-0-618-47301-4(7))* Houghton Mifflin Harcourt Publishing Co.

Lupton, Hugh. The Story Tree. Fatus, Sophie, illus. 2009. (ENG.). 64p. (J). 19.99 *(978-1-84686-301-1(5))* Barefoot Bks., Inc.

—The Story Tree: Tales to Read Aloud. Fatus, Sophie, illus. 2005. (ENG.). 64p. (J). (gr. -1-2). 16.99 *(978-1-905236-13-8(1))* Barefoot Bks., Inc.

Lutz, A. Fowler. Stories of the Child Jesus from Many Lands. 2003. (Illus.). viii, 175p. (J). pap. 10.95 *(978-1-928832-96-6(2))* Sophia Institute Pr.

Lynette, Rachel. Urban Legends. 2008. (Mysterious Encounters Ser.). (ENG., Illus.). 48p. (gr. 4-8). lib. bdg. 33.60 *(978-0-7377-4049-3(3)*, LML02109-240016, Kidhaven) Cengage Gale.

MacDonald, Margaret Read. Conejito: A Folktale from Panama. Valério, Geraldo, illus. 2015. (ENG.). 32p. (J). (gr. -1-3). pap. 8.95 *(978-1-939160-96-6(0))* August Hse. Pubs., Inc.

—Give up, Gecko!, 0 vols. Melmon, Deborah, illus. unabr. ed. 2013. (ENG.). 32p. (J). (gr. k-3). 16.99 *(978-1-4778-1635-6(6)*, 9781477816356, Amazon Children's Publishing) Amazon Publishing.

—Tuck-Me-In Tales: Bedtime Stories from Around the World. 2005. (ENG., Illus.). 64p. (J). (gr. -1-2). pap. 9.95 *(978-0-87483-622-6(0))* August Hse. Pubs., Inc.

—Tuck-Me-In Tales: Bedtime Stories from Around the World. Davis, Yvonne, illus. 2005. (ENG.). 64p. (J). (gr. -1-2). 19.95 *(978-0-87483-461-1(9))* August Hse. Pubs., Inc.

MacDonald, Margaret Read & Taibah, Nadia Jameel. How Many Donkeys? An Arabic Counting Tale. Liddiment, Carol, illus. 2012. (J). 34.28 *(978-1-61913-148-4(X))* Weigl Pubs., Inc.

Mackall, Dandi Daley. The Legend of Ohio. LaFever, Greg, illus. 2005. (Legend Ser.). (ENG.). 40p. (J). (gr. k-5). 17.95 *(978-1-58536-244-8(1))* Sleeping Bear Pr.

MacLaren, Dorothy H. Esopus Hodie, Aesop Today, Vol. 1. (ENG & LAT.). 64p. (YA). (gr. 9-12). 9.75 *(978-0-939507-06-1(4)*, B20) American Classical League, The.

Maggi, María Elena. The Great Canoe: A Karina Legend. 2004. (Illus.). (J). (gr. -1-18). spiral bd. *(978-0-616-14620-0(5))*; spiral bd. *(978-0-616-14621-7(3))* Canadian National Institute for the Blind/Institut National Canadien pour les Aveugles.

Malaspina, Ann. The Hunting of the Great Bear: A Native American Folktale. Maiborada, Tanya, illus. 2013. (Folktales from Around the World Ser.). (ENG.). 24p. (J). (gr. k-3). 28.50 *(978-1-62323-616-8(9)*, 206383) Child's World, Inc., The.

—The Mouse & the Wizard: A Hindu Folktale. Sylvaine, Jenny, illus. 2013. (Folktales from Around the World Ser.). (ENG.). 24p. (J). (gr. k-3). 28.50 *(978-1-62323-633-5(9)*, 206384) Child's World, Inc., The.

—The People Could Fly: An African-American Folktale. Otero, Sole, illus. 2013. (Folktales from Around the World Ser.). (ENG.). 24p. (J). (gr. k-3). 28.50 *(978-1-62323-617-5(7)*, 206385) Child's World, Inc., The.

Martin, John, et al. Aesop's Fables in Rhyme for Little Philosophers. 2014. (ENG., Illus.). 96p. (J). (gr. 1-5). pap. 12.99 *(978-0-486-78180-8(1))* Dover Pubns., Inc.

Matthews, John. The Barefoot Book of Giants, Ghosts, & Goblins. Manna, Giovanni, illus. 2008. (ENG.). 80p. (J). 21.99 *(978-1-84686-235-9(3))* Barefoot Bks., Inc.

McCaughrean, Geraldine. The Wish-Bringer. Diemberger, Jana, illus. 2014. (Monacello Trilogy Ser.). (ENG.). 56p. (J). (gr. 4-7). pap. 12.99 *(978-1-907912-06-1(1))* Phoenix Yard Bks. GBR. Dist: Independent Pubs. Group.

McCullough, Joseph A. Hunting Zombies. 2016. (Monster Hunting Ser.). 00088p. (YA). (gr. 8-8). 37.10 *(978-1-4994-6532-7(7)*, Rosen Young Adult) Rosen Publishing Group, Inc., The.

McCullum, Kenya. 12 Creepy Urban Legends. 2017. (Scary & Spooky Ser.). (ENG., Illus.). 32p. (J). (gr. 3-6). 21.95 *(978-1-63235-292-7(3))* Pr. Room Editions LLC.

McDonnell, Julia. The Legend of Robin Hood. 2015. (Famous Legends Ser.). (ENG., Illus.). 32p. (J). (gr. 2-3). pap. 10.50 *(978-1-4824-2748-6(6))* Stevens, Gareth Publishing LLLP.

McGovern, Ann. Aesop's Fables. Tercio, Ricardo, illus. 2013. (ENG.). 80p. (J). (gr. 2-5). pap. 4.99 *(978-0-545-46722-3(5))* Scholastic, Inc.

McGrath, Barbara Barbieri. The Little Gray Bunny. Kim, Violet, illus. 2013. (ENG.). 32p. (J). (gr. -1-2). 16.95 *(978-1-58089-394-7(5))*; pap. 7.95 *(978-1-58089-395-4(3))* Charlesbridge Publishing, Inc.

—The Little Green Witch. Alexander, Martha, illus. 2005. (ENG.). 32p. (J). (gr. -1-2). 15.95 *(978-1-58089-042-7(3))* Charlesbridge Publishing, Inc.

Meadows, Daisy. Pet Parade. 2013. (Rainbow Magic — Scholastic Reader Ser.). lib. bdg. 13.55 *(978-0-606-31973-7(5)*, Turtleback) Turtleback Bks.

Miller, Bobbi. Miss Sally Ann & the Panther. Lloyd, Megan, illus. 2012. (ENG.). 32p. (J). 16.95 *(978-0-8234-1833-6(2))* Holiday Hse., Inc.

Miller, Raymond H. Vampires. 2004. (Monsters (Kidhaven Press) Ser.). (ENG., Illus.). 48p. (J). (gr. 4-7). lib. bdg. 27.50 *(978-0-7377-2619-0(9)*, Greenhaven Pr., Inc.) Cengage Gale.

Miller, Reagan & Alexander, Carol. How to Tell a Folktale. Crabtree Publishing Staff, ed. 2011. (Text Styles Ser.: No. 2). (ENG.). 32p. (J). (gr. 3-6). pap. *(978-0-7787-1636-5(8))* Crabtree Publishing Co.

—How to Tell a Folktale. 2011. (Text Styles Ser.). (ENG.). 32p. (J). (gr. 3-6). *(978-0-7787-1631-0(7))* Crabtree Publishing Co.

Milord, Susan. Tales Alive! Donato, Michael A., illus. 2007. (ENG.). 128p. 16.99 *(978-0-8249-6804-5(2)*, Ideal Pubns.) Worthy Publishing.

Monsters in Myth, 8 vols., Set. Incl. Cerberus. Tracy, Kathleen. lib. bdg. 29.95 *(978-1-58415-924-7(3))*; Chimaera. LaRoche, Amy. lib. bdg. 29.95 *(978-1-58415-925-4(1))*; Cyclopes. Roberts, Russell. lib. bdg. 29.95 *(978-1-58415-926-1(X))*; Medusa. Tracy, Kathleen. lib. bdg. 29.95 *(978-1-58415-928-5(6))*; Minotaur. Roberts, Russell. lib. bdg. 29.95 *(978-1-58415-929-2(4))*; Monsters of Hercules. Orr, Tamra. lib. bdg. 29.95 *(978-1-58415-927-8(8))*; Sirens. Orr, Tamra. lib. bdg. 29.95 *(978-1-58415-930-8(8))*; Sphinx. DiPrimio, Pete. lib. bdg. 29.95 *(978-1-58415-931-5(6))*; (Illus.). 48p. (J). (gr. 4-7). 2010. 239.60 *(978-1-58415-932-2(4))* Mitchell Lane Pubs., Inc.

Moore, Elizabeth & Couvillon, Alice. How the Gods Created the Finger People, 1 vol. Lopez, Luz-Maria, illus. 2011. (ENG & SPA.). 32p. (J). (gr. k-3). 18.99 *(978-1-58980-889-8(4))* Pelican Publishing Co., Inc.

Morgan, Connie & Morgan, Connie Collins. The Runaway Beignet, 1 vol. Leonhard, Herb, illus. 2014. (ENG.). 32p. (J). (gr. k-3). 16.99 *(978-1-4556-1912-2(4))* Pelican Publishing Co., Inc.

Morley, Jacqueline & Salariya, David. World of Myths & Legends. Franklin, Carolyn, illus. 2013. (Mythology Ser.). 64p. (gr. 3-6). 41.35 ***(978-1-908973-93-1(5))*** Book Hse. GBR. Dist: Black Rabbit Bks.

Mott, A. S. Fireside Ghost Stories, 1 vol., Vol. 1. Kubish, Shelagh, ed. rev. ed. 2003. (Ghost Stories Ser.). (ENG.). 216p. (gr. 4). pap. 12.95 *(978-1-894877-40-4(3)*, 1894877403, Ghost Hse. Bks.) Lone Pine Publishing USA.

Muten, Burleigh. Grandfather Mountain: Stories of Gods & Heroes from Many Cultures. Bailey, Sian, illus. 2004. (ENG.). 80p. (J). (gr. 3-6). 19.99 *(978-1-84148-789-2(9))* Barefoot Bks., Inc.

Muth, Jon J. Stone Soup. Muth, Jon J., illus. 2011. (ENG., Illus.). (J). (gr. -1-3). 9.99 *(978-0-545-35394-6(7))* Scholastic, Inc.

Myths & Legends. pap. *(978-1-84458-374-4(0)*, Pavilion Children's Books) Pavilion Bks.

Nagle, Frances. Zombies. 2016. (Monsters! Ser.). (Illus.). 32p. (J). (gr. 2-1). pap. 10.50 *(978-1-4824-4876-4(9))* Stevens, Gareth Publishing LLLP.

Namm, Diane. The Gingerbread Boy. Wakefield, Scott J., illus. 2013. (J). *(978-1-4027-8431-6(7))* Sterling Publishing Co., Inc.

Nanji, Shenaaz. Indian Tales. 2017. (ENG., Illus.). 96p. (J). (gr. 1-4). 16.99 ***(978-1-78285-357-2(X))*** Barefoot Bks., Inc.

Newman, Paul. Ambrose the Whale: A Novel for Children & Adults. 2003. 108p. pap. 9.95 *(978-0-595-27091-0(3)*, Writers Club Pr.) iUniverse, Inc.

O'Hearn, Kate. The Runaway. 2017. (Valkyrie Ser.: 2). (ENG., Illus.). 368p. (J). (gr. 4-8). 17.99 *(978-1-4814-4740-9(8)*, Simon & Schuster/Paula Wiseman Bks.) Simon & Schuster/Paula Wiseman Bks.

O'Leary-Coggins, Annette. The Rescueteers' Christmas Mission: Book 2. 2010. 168p. 22.95 *(978-1-4502-3085-8(7))*; pap. 12.95 *(978-1-4502-3087-2(3))* iUniverse, Inc.

Olmstead, Kathleen. The Lion & the Mouse. Wakefield, Scott, illus. 2014. (Silver Penny Stories Ser.). (ENG.). 48p. (J). (gr. -1-1). 4.95 *(978-1-4027-8347-0(7))* Sterling Publishing Co., Inc.

Onajin, Alaba. The Adventures of Atioro: the Rainmaker of Aramada (Colour Edition) 2010. 78p. pap. 37.95 *(978-0-557-34753-7(X))* Lulu Pr., Inc.

O'Shei, Tim. Creepy Urban Legends, 1 vol. 2010. (Scary Stories Ser.). (ENG.). 32p. (gr. 3-4). lib. bdg. 27.99 *(978-1-4296-4572-0(5)*, Edge Bks.) Capstone Press of Coughlan Cos.

Owings, Lisa. What Are Legends, Folktales, & Other Classic Stories? 2014. (Name That Text Type! Ser.). (Illus.). 32p. (gr. 2-4). pap. 7.95 *(978-1-4677-4518-5(9))*; lib. bdg. 26.60 *(978-1-4677-4061-6(6)*, Lerner Pubns.) Lerner Publishing Group.

Palermo, Miguel Angel. Lo Que Cuentan los Guaranies. (Cuentamerica Ser.). (SPA.). (YA). (gr. 4-18). pap. *(978-950-07-1337-5(3)*, SA30062) Editorial Sudamericana S.A. ARG. Dist: Lectorum Pubns., Inc.

Parnell, Fran. The Abominable Snowman: A Story from Nepal. Fatus, Sophie, illus. 2011. (Monster Stories Ser.). (ENG.). 48p. (J). (gr. 1-5). pap. 8.99 *(978-1-84686-558-9(1))* Barefoot Bks., Inc.

Parnell, Fran & Fatus, Sophie. Rona Long-Teeth: A Story from Tahiti. Fatus, Sophie, illus. 2013. (Monster Stories Ser.: 5). (ENG., Illus.). 48p. (J). (gr. 1-5). pap. 8.99 *(978-1-84686-908-2(0))* Barefoot Bks., Inc.

Paterson, Katherine. The Tale of the Mandarin Ducks. 2009. 9.00 *(978-0-7848-3652-1(3)*, Everbind) Marco Bk. Co.

Patterson, Irania & McElvane, Catherine. Wings & Dreams (Alas y Suenos) The Legend of Angel Falls (La Leyenda del Salto Angel) 2010. (ENG & SPA.). 40p. (J). (gr. 1-3). 19.95 *(978-0-9815192-4-1(5))* Novello Festival Pr.

Paul Bunyan: 6 Small Books. (gr. k-2). 23.00 *(978-0-7635-8508-2(4))* Rigby Education.

Paul, John. Porcupine. (Illus.). (J). pap. 3.00 *(978-1-55500-072-1(X))* Alaska Native Language Ctr.

Peck, Jan. Giant Peach Yodel, 1 vol. Root, Barry, illus. 2012. (ENG.). 32p. (J). (gr. k-3). 16.99 *(978-1-58980-980-2(7))* Pelican Publishing Co., Inc.

Pellowski, Anne. Storytelling Handbook. 2008. (ENG.). 128p. (YA). (gr. 7). pap. 7.99 *(978-1-4169-7598-4(5)*, Simon & Schuster/Paula Wiseman Bks.) Simon & Schuster/Paula Wiseman Bks.

The People Could Fly: American Black Folktales / Frederick Douglass in His Own Words Paired Set. 2016. (LitLinks Ser.). (gr. 5-3). 61.27 *(978-1-4824-5376-8(2))* Stevens, Gareth Publishing LLLP.

The People Could Fly: American Black Folktales / Frederick Douglass in His Own Words Reader Resource Guide. 2016. (LitLinks Ser.). (gr. 5-3). pap. *(978-1-4824-5430-7(0))* Stevens, Gareth Publishing LLLP.

Percy, Graham, illus. Tales from the Arabian Nights. 2011. (10-Minute Bedtime Stories Ser.). (ENG.). 64p. (J). (gr. k-4). 14.99 *(978-1-84365-144-4(0)*, Pavilion Children's Books) Pavilion Bks. GBR. Dist: Independent Pubs. Group.

Perrault, Charles. Puss in Boots (El Gato Con Botas) Merino, Jose Luis, illus. 2004. (Bilingual Fairy Tales Ser.: BILI). (ENG & SPA.). 32p. (J). (gr. -1-7). pap. 6.99 *(978-0-8118-3924-2(9))* Chronicle Bks. LLC.

Phelps, Ethel Johnston, ed. Kamala: Feminist Folktales from Around the World. Boynton, Suki, illus. 2016. (Feminist Folktales Ser.: 2). (ENG.). 120p. (J). (gr. 2-7). pap. 14.95 *(978-1-55861-940-1(2))* Feminist Pr. at The City Univ. of New York.

—Tatterhood: Feminist Folktales from Around the World. Boynton, Suki, illus. 2016. (Feminist Folktales Ser.: 1). (ENG.). 120p. (J). (gr. k). 14.95 *(978-1-55861-929-6(1))* Feminist Pr. at The City Univ. of New York.

Pinkney, Jerry. The Lion & the Mouse. 2009. (ENG., Illus.). 40p. (J). (gr. -1-3). 18.00 *(978-0-316-01356-7(0))* Little, Brown Bks. for Young Readers.

—The Lion & the Mouse. 2011. 29.95 *(978-0-545-29677-9(3))* Weston Woods Studios, Inc.

—The Tortoise & the Hare. 2013. (ENG., Illus.). 40p. (J). (gr. -1-3). 18.00 *(978-0-316-18356-7(3))* Little, Brown Bks. for Young Readers.

Piper, Sophie. The Lion Book of Nursery Fables. Kolanovic, Dubravka, illus. 2014. (ENG.). 128p. (J). (gr. -1 — 1). 17.99 *(978-0-7459-6466-9(4))* Lion Hudson PLC GBR. Dist: Independent Pubs. Group.

Powell, Patricia Hruby. Zinnia: How the Corn Was Saved. Ruffenach, Jessie, ed. Thomas, Peter, tr. from NAV. Benally, Kendrick, illus. 2004. (ENG & NAV.). 32p. (J). (gr. -1-3). 17.95 *(978-1-893354-38-8(5))* Salina Bookshelf Inc.

Puerto, Carlos. La Luna en Sus Manos. 2003. (Disney Collection). (SPA.). 96p. (J). 6.95 *(978-84-670-0304-8(9))* Espasa Calpe, S.A. ESP. Dist: Planeta Publishing Corp.

QEB Start Reading & Writing National Book Stores Edition: Little Red Riding Hood. 2006. (J). per. *(978-1-59566-267-5(7))* QEB Publishing Inc.

Ren, Rongrong. Chinese Folk Tales. 2016. (J). *(978-1-62246-025-0(1))* Homa & Sekey Bks.

Retana, Maria Luisa. Tanili: An Afrocuban Folktale. 2004. 36p. 17.95 *(978-0-9652920-1-6(0))* High Desert Productions.

Rice, Clay. Mama, Let's Make a Moon. 2013. 32p. 16.95 *(978-1-938301-05-6(6))* Familius LLC.

Ripley's Believe It or Not Editors. The Remarkable Revealed: Unusual Tales. (Ripley's Remarkable & Unexpected Ser.). 36p. (J). (gr. 3-18). 2010. lib. bdg. 19.95 *(978-1-4222-2028-3(1))* 2009. pap. 8.95 *(978-1-4222-2062-7(1))* Mason Crest.

Roberts, Tom. Goldilocks, 1 vol. Kubinyi, Laszlo, illus. 2005. (Rabbit Ears: A Classic Tale Ser.). (ENG.). 28p. (gr. 2-7). 25.65 *(978-1-59197-748-3(7))* Spotlight.

Rodriguez, Ed. Kiki Koki: La Leyenda Encantada del Coquí. 2015.Tr. of Kiki Koki - The Enchanted Legend of the Coqui Frog. (SPA & ENG., Illus.). 40p. (J). (gr. -1-3). 17.99 *(978-1-62672-104-3(1)*, 9781626721043) Roaring Brook Pr.

—Kiki Koki: La Leyenda Encantada Del Coquí (Kiki Koki: the Enchanted Legend of the Coquí Frog) 2015. (SPA., Illus.). 40p. (J). (gr. -1-3). 8.99 *(978-1-62672-132-6(7)*, 9781626721326) Roaring Brook Pr.

E
F
G

Roy, Tamba. A Gift for Anansi. 2010. (Illus.). 36p. pap. *(978-1-907211-96-6(9))* Grosvenor Hse. Publishing Ltd.

Rustad, Martha E. H. Learning about Folktales, Fables, & Fairy Tales, 1 vol. 2014. (Language Arts Ser.). (ENG.). 24p. (gr. k-1). 26.65 *(978-1-4914-0577-2(5)*, Pebble Plus) Capstone Press of Coughlan Cos.

Ryan, Patrick. Shakespeare's Storybook: Folk Tales That Inspired the Bard. Mayhew, James, illus. 2009. (ENG.). (J). 21.99 *(978-1-84686-271-7(X))* Barefoot Bks., Inc.

San Souci, Robert D. Cut from the Same Cloth: American Women of Myth, Legend, & Tall Tale. Pinkney, Brian, illus. 2005. 140p. 17.00 *(978-0-7569-6284-5(6))* Perfection Learning Corp.

Sanderson, Ruth. The Golden Mare, the Firebird, & the Magic Ring. 2016. (ENG., Illus.). 32p. (J). 17.95 *(978-1-56656-079-5(9)*, Crocodile Bks.) Interlink Publishing Group, Inc.

Sanna, Ellyn. Firefighters' Folklore. 2004. (North American Folklore Ser.). (Illus.). 112p. (YA). (gr. 7-18). lib. bdg. 22.95 *(978-1-59084-334-5(7))* Mason Crest.

Sastrias, Martha. El Uso Del Folklore Para Motivar a los Ninos a Leer y Escribir. 2005. (SPA & ENG., Illus.). 238p. (gr. k-2). pap. 18.00 *(978-968-860-532-5(8))* Editorial Pax MEX. Dist: Independent Pubs. Group.

Savory, Phyllis. The Best of African Folklore. 2015. (ENG., Illus.). 128p. pap. 12.00 *(978-1-4323-0342-6(2))* Penguin Random House Grupo Editorial ESP. Dist: Casemate Pubs. & Bk. Distributors, LLC.

Sayler, Machelle, illus. Folkeminnevitskap II. 2004. 144p. *(978-0-9744422-1-1(6))* Erickson, Rakel L.

Schwartz, Alvin. More Scary Stories to Tell in the Dark. 2010. (Scary Stories Ser.: 2). (J). lib. bdg. 16.00 *(978-0-606-14981-5(3)*, Turtleback) Turtleback Bks.

Schwartz, Alvin. More Scary Stories to Tell in the Dark. Gammell, Stephen, illus. 2017. (Scary Stories Ser.: 2). 112p. (J). (gr. 3-7). pap. 6.99 ***(978-0-06-268285-7(7))*** HarperCollins Pubs.

Scieszka, Jon, et al. Guys Read: True Stories. 2014. (Guys Read Ser.: 5). (ENG.). 272p. (J). (gr. 3-7). pap. 7.99 *(978-0-06-196381-0(X)*, Walden Pond Pr.) HarperCollins Pubs.

Sellier, Marie. What the Rat Told Me. Louis, Catherine, illus. 2014. (ENG.). 32p. (J). (gr. k-3). 7.95 *(978-0-7358-4158-1(6))* North-South Bks., Inc.

Shah, Idries. The Boy Without a Name. Caron, Mona, illus. 2007. 32p. (J). pap. 7.99 *(978-1-883536-94-7(4)*, Hoopoe Bks.) I S H K.

—The Boy Without a Name / el Nino Sin Nombre. Wirkala, Rita, tr. Caron, Mona, illus. 2007. 32p. (J). 18.00 *(978-1-883536-92-3(8))*; pap. 7.99 *(978-1-883536-93-0(6))* I S H K. (Hoopoe Bks.).

—The Farmer's Wife HB/CD Combo English. Santiago, Rose Mary, illus. 2005. (Sounds of Afghanistan Ser.). 32p. (J). (gr. -1-3). 28.95 incl. audio compact disk *(978-1-883536-67-1(7)*, FAWCB1, Hoopoe Bks.) I S H K.

—The Farmer's Wife/la Esposa Del Granjero. Santiago, Rose Mary, illus. 2003. (SPA & ENG.). (J). 18.00 *(978-1-883536-33-6(2)*, FAWI2, Hoopoe Bks.) I S H K.

—The Lion Who Saw Himself in the Water HB/CD Combo English. Rodriguez, Ingrid, illus. 2005. (Sounds of Afghanistan Ser.). (J). (gr. -1-3). 28.95 incl. audio compact disk *(978-1-883536-71-8(5)*, LIWCB1, Hoopoe Bks.) I S H K.

—The Lion Who Saw Himself in the Water/el Leon Que Se Vio en el Aqua. Rodriguez, Ingrid, illus. 2003. (SPA & ENG.). (J). 6.95 *(978-1-883536-32-9(4)*, LIWS4); 18.00 *(978-1-883536-31-2(6)*, LIWS3) I S H K. (Hoopoe Bks.).

—The Man & the Fox. Mallam, Sally, illus. 2006. 32p. (J). (gr. -1). 18.00 *(978-1-883536-43-5(X))*; pap. 7.99 *(978-1-883536-60-2(X))* I S H K. (Hoopoe Bks.).

Sharkey, Niamh, illus. Tales of Wisdom & Wonder. 2005. 64p. (J). *(978-1-84148-231-6(5))* Barefoot Bks., Inc.

Shephard, Esther. Paul Bunyan. Kent, Rockwell, illus. 2006. (ENG.). 256p. (J). (gr. 5-7). pap. 15.95 *(978-0-15-205857-9(5))* Houghton Mifflin Harcourt Publishing Co.

Shepherd, J. A., illus. Old Hendrik's Tales - 13 South African Folk Tales. 2013. 198p. pap. *(978-1-909302-15-0(5))* Abela Publishing.

Sherman, Josepha. Magic Hoofbeats: Horse Tales from Many Lands. Wingerter, Linda, illus. 2004. (ENG.). 80p. (J). 19.99 *(978-1-84148-091-6(6))* Barefoot Bks., Inc.

Sieling, Peter. Folk Medicine. 2004. (North American Folklore Ser.). (Illus.). 112p. (YA). (gr. 7-18). lib. bdg. 22.95 *(978-1-59084-341-3(X))* Mason Crest.

Singh, Rina. A Forest of Stories: Magical Tree Tales from Around the World. Cann, Helen, illus. 2003. 64p. (J). 19.99 *(978-1-84148-963-6(8))* Barefoot Bks., Inc.

Skillen, Roy. The Three Wise Men. 2010. 24p. pap. 11.50 *(978-1-60911-107-6(9)*, Eloquent Bks.) Strategic Book Publishing & Rights Agency (SBPRA).

Smith, Andrea P. Paul Bunyan. 2012. (Illus.). 24p. (J). 63.60 *(978-1-4488-5221-5(8))*; pap. 10.60 *(978-1-4488-5220-8(X))*; lib. bdg. 25.25 *(978-1-4488-5191-1(2))* Rosen Publishing Group, Inc., The. (PowerKids Pr.).

Sommer, Carl. Three Little Pigs. 2003. (Another Sommer-Time Story Ser.). (Illus.). 48p. (J). (gr. 1-4). 16.95 incl. audio compact disk *(978-1-57537-511-3(7))*; 16.95 incl. audio *(978-1-57537-560-1(5))* Advance Publishing, Inc.

Sommer, Carl & Aesop. Divide to Conquer(Divide y Venceras) Mercado, Jorge, illus. 2009. (Quest for Success Bilingual Ser.). (ENG & SPA.). 72p. (YA). lib. bdg. 14.95 *(978-1-57537-225-9(8))* Advance Publishing, Inc.

—The Silent Scream(El Grito Silencioso) Bogdan, Enache, illus. 2009. (Quest for Success Bilingual Ser.). (SPA & ENG.). 72p. (YA). lib. bdg. 14.95 *(978-1-57537-235-8(5))* Advance Publishing, Inc.

—Tiny Giant(La Gigante Pequeña) Mercado, Jorge, illus. 2009. (Quest for Success Bilingual Ser.). (ENG & SPA.). 72p. (YA). lib. bdg. 14.95 *(978-1-57537-236-5(3))* Advance Publishing, Inc.

Souhami, Jessica, illus. King Pom & the Fox. 2009. (ENG.). 36p. (J). (gr. -1-2). pap. 7.95 *(978-1-84507-365-7(7)*, Frances Lincoln) Quarto Publishing Group UK GBR. Dist: Hachette Bk. Group.

Sperling, Thomas, illus. Stone Cheese. 2005. (J). *(978-0-7664-1053-4(6))* Abrams, Inc.

Sperry, Armstrong. Call It Courage. 2008. 17.20 *(978-1-4178-1178-6(1)*, Turtleback) Turtleback Bks.

stewart, gail. Urban Legends. 2011. (Mysterious & Unknown Ser.). (Illus.). 80p. (YA). (gr. 7-12). lib. bdg. 27.95 *(978-1-60152-185-9(5))* ReferencePoint Pr., Inc.

Storrie, Paul D. Robin Hood: Outlaw of Sherwood Forest. Yeates, Thomas, illus. 2007. (Graphic Myths & Legends Ser.). (ENG.). 48p. (J). (gr. 4-8). lib. bdg. 27.93 *(978-0-8225-5964-1(1))* Lerner Publishing Group.

Stott, Jon C. A Book of Tricksters: Tales from Many Lands, 1 vol. Dombrowski, Theo, illus. 2010. (ENG.). 144p. (J). (gr. 4-7). pap. 12.95 *(978-1-926613-69-7(4))* Heritage Hse. CAN. Dist: Orca Bk. Pubs. USA.

Subramaniam, Manasi. The Story & the Song. Sankaranarayanan, Ayswarya, illus. 2013. (ENG.). 32p. (J). (gr. k). pap. 9.95 *(978-81-8190-273-3(4))* Karadi Tales Co. Pvt. Ltd. IND. Dist: Consortium Bk. Sales & Distribution.

Surviving Zombie Warfare. 2016. (Surviving Zombie Warfare Ser.). 48p. (gr. 7-7). pap. 35.25 *(978-1-5081-7167-6(X)*, Rosen Young Adult); (ENG., Illus.). (J). lib. bdg. 95.25 *(978-1-4994-6379-8(0))* Rosen Publishing Group, Inc., The.

Susaeta, Equipo. Leo y Veo, las Hadas.Tr. of I Read & See, the Fairies. (SPA.). 24p. (J). 3.48 *(978-84-305-9408-5(6))* Susaeta Ediciones, S.A. ESP. Dist: AIMS International Bks., Inc.

Szarka, Balazs. European Folk Tales. 2009. 60p. pap. 22.00 *(978-1-60860-432-6(2)*, Eloquent Bks.) Strategic Book Publishing & Rights Agency (SBPRA).

Tallec, Olivier. Louis I, King of the Sheep. 2015. (ENG., Illus.). 40p. (J). (gr. k-4). 17.95 *(978-1-59270-185-8(X))* Enchanted Lion Bks., LLC.

Taplin, Sam. Sleeping Beauty. 2008. (First Fairytales Look & Say Ser.). 12p. (J). (gr. -1). bds. 9.99 *(978-0-7945-2200-1(9)*, Usborne) EDC Publishing.

Terry, Will, illus. Little Rooster's Diamond Button. 2012. (J). *(978-1-61913-156-9(0))* Weigl Pubs., Inc.

Thompson, Susan Conklin, et al, eds. Mayan Folktales: Cuentos Folklóricos Mayas, 1 vol. 2007. (World Folklore Ser.). (SPA & ENG., Illus.). 236p. (C). 40.00 *(978-1-59158-138-3(9)*, LU1389, Libraries Unlimited) ABC-CLIO, LLC.

Three Folk Tales. Date not set. (Nelson Readers Ser.). (J). pap. *(978-0-17-557041-6(8))* Addison-Wesley Longman, Inc.

Tieck, Sarah. Zombies, 1 vol. 2016. (ENG., Illus.). 32p. (J). *(978-1-62403-770-2(4))* ABDO Publishing Co.

Treasury of Virtues for Children. 2012. (Illus.). 159p. (J). *(978-1-4508-3590-9(2))* Publications International, Ltd.

Ungar, Richard. Rachel's Gift. 2003. (ENG., Illus.). 32p. (J). (gr. 2-5). 16.95 *(978-0-88776-616-9(1)*, Tundra Bks.) Tundra Bks. CAN. Dist: Penguin Random Hse. LLC.

—Rachel's Library. 2004. (ENG.). 32p. (J). (gr. 2-5). 15.95 *(978-0-88776-678-7(1)*, Tundra Bks.) Tundra Bks. CAN. Dist: Penguin Random Hse. LLC.

Vagnozzi, Barbara, illus. Sleeping Beauty. 2007. (First Fairy Tales Ser.). 32p. (J). (gr. -1-3). lib. bdg. 28.50 *(978-1-59771-073-2(3))* Sea-To-Sea Pubns.

Verrett, Michael. The White Alligator Crown Quatro. 2010. 147p. pap. 13.95 *(978-0-557-58121-4(4))* Lulu Pr., Inc.

Von Wielligh, G. R. Animal Tales, Vol. 1. Bankenaar, Dale, illus. 2012. (ENG.). 93p. pap. 12.00 *(978-1-86919-433-8(0))* Protea Boekhuis ZAF. Dist: Casemate Pubs. & Bk. Distributors, LLC.

—Animal Tales, Vol. 2. Bankenaar, Dale, illus. 2012. (ENG.). 93p. pap. 12.00 *(978-1-86919-504-5(3))* Protea Boekhuis ZAF. Dist: Casemate Pubs. & Bk. Distributors, LLC.

Wade, Mary Dodson. No Year of the Cat. 2012. (ENG., Illus.). 32p. (J). (gr. 1-5). 16.95 *(978-1-58536-785-6(0))* Sleeping Bear Pr.

Wallace, Ian. The Man Who Walked the Earth, 1 vol. 2003. (ENG., Illus.). 32p. (J). 16.95 *(978-0-88899-545-2(8))* Groundwood Bks. CAN. Dist: Publishers Group West (PGW).

Walluk, Wilbur, illus. The Alaskan Ten-Footed Bear & Other Legends. 2013. 44p. pap. 9.95 *(978-1-61646-201-7(9))* Coachwhip Pubns.

Wang, Eva, illus. Auntie Tigress & Other Favorite Chinese Folk Tales. 2006. (ENG.). 48p. (J). 15.95 *(978-1-933327-28-0(6))* Purple Bear Bks., Inc.

Weston Woods Staff, creator. Arrow to the Sun. 2004. (J). 38.75 *(978-1-55592-373-0(9))*; 18.95 *(978-1-55592-371-6(2))* Weston Woods Studios, Inc.

—Drummer Hoff. 2004. (J). 38.75 *(978-1-55592-406-5(9))* Weston Woods Studios, Inc.

—The Funny Little Woman. 2004. 38.75 *(978-1-55592-416-4(6))*; 18.95 *(978-1-55592-415-7(8))* Weston Woods Studios, Inc.

—Joseph Had a Little Overcoat. 2004. 29.95 *(978-1-55592-109-5(4))* Weston Woods Studios, Inc.

—The Little Red Hen. 2004. 38.75 *(978-1-55592-757-8(2))*; 29.95 *(978-1-55592-823-0(4))*; 18.95 *(978-1-55592-807-0(2))* Weston Woods Studios, Inc.

—Rapunzel. 2004. 18.95 *(978-1-55592-744-8(0))*; 38.75 *(978-1-55592-752-3(1))*; 29.95 *(978-1-55592-738-7(6))* Weston Woods Studios, Inc.

Wildish, Lee, illus. The Boy Who Cried Wolf. 2008. (I'm Going to Read(r) Ser.). (ENG.). 32p. (J). (gr. 1-2). pap. 3.95 *(978-1-4027-5546-0(5))* Sterling Publishing Co., Inc.

Wilhelm, Hans. All for the Best! The Secret to Happiness. 2003. (ENG., Illus.). 32p. (gr. -1-3). 16.95 *(978-1-57174-344-2(8))* Hampton Roads Publishing Co., Inc.

Wilson, Barbara Ker & So, Meilo. Wishbones: A Folk Tale from China. (Illus.). 32p. (J). (gr. -1-2). pap. *(978-0-7112-1415-6(8))* ReiseArt Buchhandlung GmbH.

Winslade, Jayn E. Emily & Jen Dance for Deeron. 2010. 352p. pap. *(978-1-907211-48-5(9))* Grosvenor Hse. Publishing Ltd.

Winter, Milo, illus. Aesops Fables for Children. 2012. 294p. pap. *(978-1-907256-72-1(5))* Abela Publishing.

The Wizard of Oz. 2013. (Wizard of Oz Ser.). (ENG.). 24p. (gr. 1-2). 111.96 *(978-1-4765-3786-3(0))* Capstone Press of Coughlan Cos.

Wolf, Linda Little. The Great Spirit Horse, 1 vol. 2nd ed. 2003. (ENG., Illus.). 152p. (J). (gr. 3-6). pap. 10.95 *(978-1-58980-123-3(7))* Pelican Publishing Co., Inc.

Woog, Adam. Giants. 2011. 80p. (YA). lib. bdg. 37.27 *(978-1-60152-224-5(X))* ReferencePoint Pr., Inc.

Woollvin, Bethan. Little Red, 1 vol. Woollvin, Bethan, illus. 2016. (ENG., Illus.). 32p. (J). (gr. k-4). 16.95 *(978-1-56145-917-9(8))* Peachtree Pubs.

World Book, Inc Staff, contrib. by. Tales Through Time: A Supplement to Childcraft-The How & Why Library. 2009. (Illus.). 204p. (J). *(978-0-7166-0622-2(4))* World Bk., Inc.

Young, Ed. Lon Po Po: A Red-Riding Hood Story from China. unabr. ed. 2006. (J). (gr. k-4). 18.95 *(978-0-439-87366-6(5)*, WPCD690); (Illus.). 29.95 *(978-0-439-87367-3(3)*, WHCD690) Weston Woods Studios, Inc.

FOLKLORE—AFRICA

Aardema, Verna. Koi & the Kola Nuts: A Tale from Liberia. Cepeda, Joe, illus. rev. ed. 2003. (ENG.). 32p. (J). (gr. k-3). 16.99 *(978-0-689-85677-8(6)*, Simon & Schuster/Paula Wiseman Bks.) Simon & Schuster/Paula Wiseman Bks.

African Tales & Myths, 6 bks., Set. (Illus.). (J). (gr. 2-5). lib. bdg. 159.60 *(978-1-57103-242-3(8))* Rourke Educational Media.

Bryan, Ashley. Beautiful Blackbird. Bryan, Ashley, illus. 2003. (ENG., Illus.). 40p. (J). (gr. -1-3). 19.99 *(978-0-689-84731-8(9)*, Atheneum Bks. for Young Readers) Simon & Schuster Children's Publishing.

Cabral, Len. La Cinturita de Anansi, Level 3. Flor Ada, Alma, tr. Diaz, David, illus. 3rd ed. 2003. (Dejame Leer Ser.). (SPA.). 16p. (J). (gr. -1-3). 6.50 *(978-0-673-36294-0(9)*, Good Year Bks.) Celebration Pr.

Eisner, Will. Sundiata: A Legend of Africa. 2003. (ENG., Illus.). 32p. pap. 7.95 *(978-1-56163-340-1(2))* NBM Publishing Co.

Eisner, Will, illus. & retold by. Sundiata: A Legend of Africa. Eisner, Will, retold by. 2003. (ENG.). 32p. (gr. k-3). 15.95 *(978-1-56163-332-6(1))* NBM Publishing Co.

Herdling, Glenn. African Mythology: Anansi. 2009. (Jr. Graphic Mythologies Ser.). (ENG.). 24p. (J). (gr. 2-3). 47.90 *(978-1-61513-855-5(2)*, PowerKids Pr.) Rosen Publishing Group, Inc., The.

Jeffrey, Gary. African Myths. 2009. (Graphic Mythology Ser.). (ENG.). 48p. (YA). (gr. 4-5). 58.50 *(978-1-61512-976-8(6)*, Rosen Reference) Rosen Publishing Group, Inc., The.

Mandela, Nelson. Favorite African Folktales. 2004. (ENG., Illus.). 192p. pap. 13.95 *(978-0-393-32624-6(1)*, 32624) Norton, W. W. & Co., Inc.

Mankell, Henning. Secrets in the Fire. Stuksrud, Anne Connie, tr. from SWE. 4th ed. 2003.Tr. of Eldens Hemlighet. (ENG.). 176p. (YA). (gr. 6-12). 19.95 *(978-1-55037-801-6(5)*, 9781550378016); pap. 11.95 *(978-1-55037-800-9(7)*, 9781550378009) Annick Pr., Ltd. CAN. Dist: Publishers Group West (PGW).

Mbanze, Dinah M. & Daly, Niki. The Berry Basket: Three African Folktales. 2010. (ENG., Illus.). 48p. *(978-0-7957-0100-9(4))* NB Pubs. Ltd.

Morris, Neil. African Myths. Kennedy, Graham, illus. 2009. (Myths from Many Lands Ser.). 48p. (YA). (gr. 2-6). pap. 12.85 *(978-1-60754-216-2(1))* Windmill Bks.

Weston Woods Staff, creator. Anansi the Spider. 2011. 18.95 *(978-0-439-88174-6(9))*; 38.75 *(978-0-439-84573-1(4))* Weston Woods Studios, Inc.

—A Story-A Story. 2011. 29.95 *(978-0-439-73521-6(1))*; 18.95 *(978-0-439-72891-1(6))* Weston Woods Studios, Inc.

—A Story-Astory. 2011. 38.75 *(978-0-439-72892-8(4))* Weston Woods Studios, Inc.

FOLKLORE—AFRICA, SOUTHERN

Brett, Jan. The 3 Little Dassies. Brett, Jan, illus. 2010. (ENG., Illus.). 32p. (J). (gr. -1-k). 17.99 *(978-0-399-25499-4(4)*, G.P. Putnam's Sons Books for Young Readers) Penguin Young Readers Group.

Seeger, Pete & Jacobs, Paul DuBois. Abiyoyo Returns. Hays, Michael, illus. 2004. (ENG.). 40p. (J). (gr. -1-3). 8.99 *(978-0-689-87054-5(X)*, Aladdin) Simon & Schuster Children's Publishing.

FOLKLORE—AFRICA, WEST

Hoffmire, Baird, illus. Anansi & the Tug O' War. 2007. (Story Cove Ser.). (ENG.). 32p. (J). (gr. -1-3). pap. 4.95 *(978-0-87483-825-1(8))* August Hse. Pubs., Inc.

Offodile, Buchi. The Orphan Girl & Other Stories: West African Folk Tales. 2004. (International Folk Tales Ser.). (ENG., Illus.). 272p. pap. 15.00 *(978-1-56656-375-8(5))* Interlink Publishing Group, Inc.

Souhami, Jessica. The Leopard's Drum: An Asante Tale from West Africa. Souhami, Jessica, illus. 2006. (ENG., Illus.). 36p. (J). (gr. -1-2). pap. 8.99 *(978-1-84507-506-4(4)*, Frances Lincoln) Quarto Publishing Group UK GBR. Dist: Hachette Bk. Group.

Vernon-Jackson, Hugh. West African Folk Tales. Wright, Patricia, illus. 2003. (African American Ser.). (ENG.). 144p. pap. 8.95 *(978-0-486-42764-5(1))* Dover Pubns., Inc.

Wrenn, Tom, illus. The Clever Monkey Rides Again. 2007. (Story Cove Ser.). (ENG.). 32p. (J). (gr. -1-3). pap. 3.95 *(978-0-87483-828-2(2))* August Hse. Pubs., Inc.

FOLKLORE, AFRICAN AMERICAN

see African Americans—Folklore

FOLKLORE—ARAB COUNTRIES

Ali Baba & the Forty Thieves. 2004. (J). (ARA & ENG.). *(978-1-84444-527-1(5))*; (ENG & GUJ.). *(978-1-84444-646-9(8))*; (ENG & SPA.). *(978-1-84444-542-4(9))*; (ENG & SOM.). *(978-1-84444-541-7(0))*; (ENG & POL.). *(978-1-84444-538-7(0))*; (ENG & PAN.). *(978-1-84444-537-0(2))*; (ENG & ITA.). *(978-1-84444-535-6(6))* Mantra Lingua.

Ali BabaForty Thieves. 2004. (J). cd-rom *(978-1-84444-452-6(X))* Mantra Lingua.

Attard, Ebenor. Ali Baba & the Forty Thieves. 2004. (J). (ENG & VIE.). pap. 16.95 *(978-1-84444-547-9(X))*; (ENG & URD.). pap. 15.24 *(978-1-84444-546-2(1))*; (BEN & ENG.). pap. 15.24 *(978-1-84444-528-8(3))*; (CHI & ENG.). pap. 16.95 *(978-1-84444-529-5(1))* Mantra Lingua GBR. Dist: Chinasprout, Inc.

Attard, Enebor. Ali Baba & the Forty Thieves. Holland, Richard, illus. 32p. (J). 2005. pap. *(978-1-84444-526-4(7))* 2004. (CHI & ENG.). bds. *(978-1-84444-530-1(5))* Mantra Lingua.

Auerbach, Annie. Sinbad: Legend of the Seven Seas Pop-up. McMahon, Brad, illus. 2003. (Media Favorites!! Ser.). 10p. (J). 9.95 *(978-1-58117-171-6(4)*, Intervisual/Piggy Toes) Bendon, Inc.

Barkow, Henriette. Ali Baba & the Forty Thieves. Brazell, Derek, illus. 2004. 28p. (J). (ENG & SWE.). pap. *(978-1-84444-539-4(9))*; (ENG, RUS, SWE & SOM.). pap. *(978-1-84444-540-0(2))*; (POL & ENG.). pap. *(978-1-84444-545-5(3))* Mantra Lingua.

Clynes, Kate & Anstey, David. Ali Baba & the Forty Thieves. 2005. (Illus.). 32p. (J). pap. *(978-1-84444-407-6(4))*; (ENG & FRE., pap. *(978-1-84444-408-3(2))*; pap. *(978-1-84444-409-0(0))*; pap. *(978-1-84444-410-6(4))*; (ITA & ENG., pap. *(978-1-84444-412-0(0))*; pap. *(978-1-84444-413-7(9))*; (POR & ENG., pap. *(978-1-84444-416-8(3))*; (RUS & ENG., pap. *(978-1-84444-417-5(1))*; (ENG & SHO., pap. *(978-1-84444-418-2(X))*; (SOM & ENG., pap. *(978-1-84444-419-9(8))*; (ENG & SPA., pap. *(978-1-84444-420-5(1))*; (TUR & ENG., pap. *(978-1-84444-422-9(8))*; (ENG & TAM., pap. *(978-1-84444-421-2(X))*; (ALB & ENG., pap. *(978-1-84444-400-7(7))*; pap. *(978-1-84444-401-4(5))*; pap. *(978-1-84444-403-8(1))*; pap. *(978-1-84444-404-5(X))*; (CHI & ENG., pap. *(978-1-84444-405-2(8))*; (SER & ENG., pap. *(978-1-84444-406-9(6))*; pap. *(978-1-84444-425-0(2))*; (RUM & ENG., pap. *(978-1-84444-427-4(9))* Mantra Lingua.

Clynes, Kate, et al. Ali Baba & the Forty Thieves. Holland, Richard, illus. 2005. (ENG & POL.). 32p. (J). pap. *(978-1-84444-415-1(5))*; pap. *(978-1-84444-414-4(7))*; pap. *(978-1-84444-424-3(4))*; pap. *(978-1-84444-411-3(2))*; pap. *(978-1-84444-402-1(3))* Mantra Lingua.

Comelles, Salvador. Cuentame un Cuento, Vol. 5. Decis, Anne, illus. 2003. (SPA.). 96p. *(978-84-480-1674-6(2)*, TM30559) Timun Mas, Editorial S.A. ESP. Dist: Lectorum Pubns., Inc.

Gregory, Manju. Ali Baba & the Forty Thieves. Jago, illus. 2004. (J). *(978-1-84444-544-8(5))* Mantra Lingua.

Jago, illus. Ali Baba & the Forty Thieves. 2004. (ITA & ENG.). 31p. (J). *(978-1-84444-543-1(7))* Mantra Lingua.

Kubler, Annie. The Wheels on the Bus, 15 vols. Kubler, Annie, illus. (Illus.). 14p. (J). 2005. (SWA, ENG & MUL.). bds. *(978-1-84444-533-2(X))* 2005. (ENG, PER & MUL., bds. *(978-1-84444-532-5(1))* 2004. (ENG, TGL & MUL., bds. *(978-1-84444-534-9(8))* Mantra Lingua.

Lodge, Jo. Ali Baba & the Forty Thieves. 2004. (Illus.). 10p. (J). *(978-1-84444-531-8(3))* Mantra Lingua.

Vera, Luisa, illus. Ali Baba & the Forty Thieves. 2004. 63p. (J). *(978-1-84444-536-3(4))* Mantra Lingua.

Yeoman, John. The Seven Voyages of Sinbad the Sailor. Blake, Quentin, illus. 2003. (Chrysalis Childrens Classics Ser.). (YA). pap. *(978-1-84365-040-9(1)*, Pavilion Children's Books) Pavilion Bks.

FOLKLORE—ASIA

Dutta-Yean, Tutu & Maire, Lucy Bedoya. Twelve Treasures of the East: Legends & Folk Tales from Asia. Dutta-Yean, Tutu, ed. Konatich, James, illus. 2005. (J). per. *(978-0-9768436-0-3(9)*, 20) Maire, Lucy Bedoya.

Lyons, Kay. Malaysian Children's Favourite Stories. Loh, Martin, illus. 2014. (ENG.). 64p. (J). (gr. 2-6). pap. 12.95 *(978-0-8048-4401-7(1))* Tuttle Publishing.

Shah, Idries. The Man with Bad Manners. Santiago, Rose Mary, tr. Santiago, Rose Mary, illus. 2003. 32p. (J). 18.00 *(978-1-883536-30-5(8)*, MABM1, Hoopoe Bks.) I S H K.

—The Man with Bad Manners HB/CD Combo English. Santiago, Rose Mary, illus. 2005. (Sounds of Afghanistan Ser.). (J). (gr. -1-3). 28.95 incl. audio compact disk *(978-1-883536-75-6(8)*, Hoopoe Bks.) I S H K.

—The Old Woman & the Eagle. Delmar, Natasha, illus. 32p. (J). 2005. (gr. -1-3). pap., pap. 6.99 *(978-1-883536-28-2(6))* 2003. 18.00 *(978-1-883536-27-5(8)*, OLWE1) I S H K. (Hoopoe Bks.).

—The Old Woman & the Eagle HB/CD English. Delmar, Natasha, illus. 2005. (Sounds of Afghanistan Ser.). (J). (gr. -1-3). 28.95 incl. audio compact disk *(978-1-883536-77-0(4)*, Hoopoe Bks.) I S H K.

FOLKLORE—AUSTRALIA

Jones, Penny & Norris, Aaron, illus. Bangu the Flying Fox: A Dreamtime Story of the Yuin People of Wallaga Lake. 2nd ed. 2011. (ENG.). 24p. (J). (gr. -1-k). pap. 17.95 *(978-0-85575-700-7(0))* Aboriginal Studies Pr. AUS. Dist: Independent Pubs. Group.

FOLKLORE—BRAZIL

DeSpain, Pleasant. Dancing Turtle: A Folktale from Brazil. Boston, David, illus. 2005. (ENG.). 32p. (J). (gr. -1-2). 15.95 *(978-0-87483-502-1(X))* August Hse. Pubs., Inc.

FOLKLORE—CANADA

Craigan, Charles J., illus. Mayuk the Grizzly Bear: A Legend of the Sechelt People. braille ed. 2004. (J). (gr. k-3). spiral bd. *(978-0-616-07562-3(6))* Canadian National Institute for the Blind/Institut National Canadien pour les Aveugles.

Finnigan, Joan. Witches, Ghosts & Loups-Garous. (Illus.). 96p. (J). pap. 10.95 *(978-1-55082-086-7(9))* Quarry Pr. CAN. Dist: LPC/InBook.

Souci, Justin San, illus. The Flying Canoe: A Christmas Story. 2011. (ENG.). 32p. (J). 16.95 *(978-0-8234-1730-8(1))* Holiday Hse., Inc.

Vitale, Ann E. Regional Folklore. 2004. (North American Folklore Ser.). (Illus.). 112p. (YA). (gr. 7-18). lib. bdg. 22.95 *(978-1-59084-349-9(5))* Mason Crest.

FOLKLORE—CARIBBEAN AREA

Keens-Douglas, Richardo & Tradewind Books Staff. Mama God, Papa God: A Caribbean Tale, 1 vol. Czernecki, Stefan, illus. 2016. (ENG.). 32p. (J). (gr. k-2). 16.95 *(978-1-896580-16-6(5))* Tradewind Bks. CAN. Dist: Orca Bk. Pubs. USA.

San Souci, Robert D. The Twins & the Bird of Darkness: A Hero Tale from the Caribbean. Widener, Terry, illus. 2004. (J). (gr. k-3). spiral bd. *(978-0-616-14625-5(6))* Canadian National Institute for the Blind/Institut National Canadien pour les Aveugles.

FOLKLORE, CELTIC

see Celts—Folklore

FOLKLORE—CHINA

ABDO Publishing Company Staff. Short Tales Chinese Myths. 2014. (Short Tales Chinese Myths Ser.: 6). 32p. (J). (gr. 3-6). lib. bdg. 145.26 *(978-1-62402-029-2(1)*, Short Tales) Magic Wagon.

Bingham, Jane & Sansom, Fiona. Chinese Myths. Kennedy, Graham, illus. 2009. (Myths from Many Lands Ser.). 48p. (YA). (gr. 4-7). 29.25 *(978-1-60754-218-6(8))* Windmill Bks.

Brennan, Sarah. The Tale of Sybil Snake. Harrison, Harry, illus. 2012. (ENG.). 32p. (J). *(978-1-937160-53-1(X))* Auspicious Times.

Carpenter, Frances. Tales of a Chinese Grandmother. 293p. (J). (gr. 5-6). reprint ed. lib. bdg. 24.95 *(978-0-89190-481-6(6),* Rivercity Pr.) Amereon Ltd.

Chan, Arlene. The Moon Festival: A Chinese Mid-Autumn Celebration. 2004. (J). (gr. k-3). spiral bd. *(978-0-616-01615-2(8))* Canadian National Institute for the Blind/Institut National Canadien pour les Aveugles.

Compestine, Ying Chang. The Real Story of Stone Soup. Jorisch, Stéphane, illus. 2007. (ENG.). 32p. (J). (gr. k-3). 16.99 *(978-0-525-47493-7(5),* Dutton Books for Young Readers) Penguin Young Readers Group.

Daning, Tom. Chinese Mythology: The Four Dragons. 2009. (Jr. Graphic Mythologies Ser.). (ENG.). 24p. (J). (gr. 2-3). 47.90 *(978-1-61513-858-6(7),* PowerKids Pr.) Rosen Publishing Group, Inc., The.

—Mitología China: Los Cuatro Dragones. 2009. (Historietas Juveniles: Mitologías (Jr. Graphic Mythologies) Ser.). (SPA., Illus.). 24p. (gr. 3-8). pap. 10.60 *(978-1-4358-3326-5(0))* Rosen Publishing Group, Inc., The.

DeSpain, Pleasant. The Magic Pot: Story Cove. Wrenn, Tom, illus. 2007. (Story Cove Ser.). (ENG.). 32p. (J). (gr. -1-3). pap. 3.95 *(978-0-87483-827-5(4))* August Hse. Pubs., Inc.

Ge, Tang, illus. The Dragon Emperor: A Chinese Folktale. 2007. (On My Own Folklore Ser.). (ENG.). 48p. (gr. 2-4). lib. bdg. 25.26 *(978-0-8225-6740-0(7),* Millbrook Pr.) Lerner Publishing Group.

Granfield, Linda. The Legend of the Panda. braille ed. 2004. (Illus.). (J). (gr. k-3). spiral bd. *(978-0-616-01343-4(4))* Canadian National Institute for the Blind/Institut National Canadien pour les Aveugles.

Guillain, Charlotte. The Empty Pot: A Chinese Folk Tale, 1 vol. Dorado, Steve, illus. 2014. (Folk Tales from Around the World Ser.). (ENG.). 24p. (gr. 1-3). pap. 6.95 *(978-1-4109-6697-1(6),* NA-r) Heinemann-Raintree.

Jones, Teresa Chin. Tales of the Monkey King. Harris, Miki, illus. 2008. (J). *(978-1-881896-30-2(7))* Pacific View Pr.

Kendall, Carol & Li, Yao-Wen. Sweet & Sour: Tales from China. Felts, Shirley, illus. 2007. (ENG.). 114p. (J). (gr. 5-7). per. 8.95 *(978-0-618-75245-4(5))* Houghton Mifflin Harcourt Publishing Co.

Leo, Veronica, illus. & retold by. The Three Silver Coins: A Story from Tibet. Leo, Veronica, trans. 2nd ed. 2011. (ENG.). 32p. (J). (gr. -1-3). pap. 14.95 *(978-1-55939-372-0(6),* Snow Lion Publications, Inc.) Shambhala Pubns., Inc.

Leonard, Scott A. Myths & Legends of China. 2015. (Illus.). 64p. (J). *(978-0-7166-2632-9(2))* World Bk., Inc.

Mosel, Arlene. Tikki Tikki Tembo. Lent, Blair, illus. 2007. (ENG.). 48p. (J). (gr. -1-3). 8.99 *(978-0-312-36748-0(1),* 9780312367480) Square Fish.

Pfeffer, Wendy. Mysterious Spinners. Kim, Julie J., illus. 2005. 48p. (J). *(978-1-59336-315-4(X));* pap. *(978-1-59336-316-1(8))* Mondo Publishing.

Rose, Naomi. Tibetan Tales for Little Buddhas. 2003. (TIB & ENG., Illus.). 64p. (J). pap. 16.95 *(978-1-57416-081-9(8))* Clear Light Pubs.

Rose, Naomi C. Tibetan Tales from the Top of the World. 2006. (ENG & TIB., Illus.). 64p. (J). (gr. 1-7). pap. 16.95 *(978-1-57416-089-5(3))* Clear Light Pubs.

Storrie, Paul D. Yu the Great. 2008. pap. 52.95 *(978-0-8225-9464-2(1))* Lerner Publishing Group.

—Yu the Great: Conquering the Flood. Carruthers, Sandy, illus. 2007. (Graphic Myths & Legends Ser.). (ENG.). 48p. (gr. 4-8). lib. bdg. 27.93 *(978-0-8225-3088-6(0))* Lerner Publishing Group.

—Yu the Great: Conquering the Flood - A Chinese Legend. Carruthers, Sandy, illus. 2008. (Graphic Myths & Legends Ser.). (ENG.). 48p. (gr. 4-8). per. 8.95 *(978-0-8225-6562-8(5))* Lerner Publishing Group.

Tang, Youshan, illus. The Magical Monkey King: Mischief in Heaven. 2004. (J). (gr. 2-5). 113p. 14.95 *(978-1-885008-24-4(4));* 32p. per. 8.95 *(978-1-885008-25-1(2))* Lee & Low Bks., Inc. (Shen's Bks.).

Wang, Ping. The Dragon Emperor. Tang, Ge, illus. 2007. (J). lib. bdg. 6.95 *(978-0-8225-6744-8(X),* Millbrook Pr.) Lerner Publishing Group.

Weston Woods Staff, creator. Lon Po Po. 2011. 38.75 *(978-0-439-87369-7(X))* Weston Woods Studios, Inc.

—Tikki Tikki Tembo. 2004. 38.75 *(978-1-55592-762-2(9));* 29.95 *(978-1-55592-854-4(4));* 18.95 *(978-1-55592-812-4(9))* Weston Woods Studios, Inc.

Wilson, Barbara Ker & So, Meilo. Wishbones: A Folk Tale from China. (Illus.). 32p. (J). (gr. -1-2). pap. *(978-0-7112-1415-6(8))* ReiseArt Buchhandlung GmbH.

Yasuda, Anita. Monkey King: A Chinese Monkey Spirit Myth. 2014. (Short Tales Chinese Myths Ser.). 32p. (J). (gr. 3-6). lib. bdg. 24.21 *(978-1-62402-032-2(1),* Short Tales) Magic Wagon.

—N Gua Mends the Sky: A Chinese Flood Myth. 2014. (Short Tales Chinese Myths Ser.). 32p. (J). (gr. 3-6). lib. bdg. 24.21 *(978-1-62402-033-9(X),* Short Tales) Magic Wagon.

—Pangu Separates the Sky from the Earth: A Chinese Creation Myth. 2014. (Short Tales Chinese Myths Ser.). (Illus.). 32p. (J). (gr. 3-6). lib. bdg. 24.21 *(978-1-62402-034-6(8),* Short Tales) Magic Wagon.

—Yu the Great Conquers the Flood: A Chinese Nature Myth. 2014. (Short Tales Chinese Myths Ser.). 32p. (J). (gr. 3-6). lib. bdg. 24.21 *(978-1-62402-035-3(6),* Short Tales) Magic Wagon.

Young, Ed. The Sons of the Dragon King: A Chinese Legend. Young, Ed, illus. 2004. (ENG., Illus.). 32p. (J). (gr. -1-3). 19.99 *(978-0-689-85184-1(7),* Atheneum Bks. for Young Readers) Simon & Schuster Children's Publishing.

Zhang, Song Nan. A Time of Golden Dragons. 2004. (J). (gr. 3-5). spiral bd. *(978-0-616-07258-5(9))* Canadian National Institute for the Blind/Institut National Canadien pour les Aveugles.

Zhang, Song Nan & Zhang, Hao Yu. A Time of Golden Dragons. Zhang, Song Nan, illus. 2006. (ENG., Illus.). 24p. (J). (gr. 4-7). pap. 11.95 *(978-0-88776-791-3(5),* Tundra Bks.) Tundra Bks. CAN. Dist: Penguin Random Hse. LLC.

FOLKLORE—CHINA—TIBET AUTONOMOUS REGION

Rose, Naomi C. Tibetan Tales from the Top of the World. 2006. (ENG & TIB., Illus.). 64p. (J). (gr. 1-7). pap. 16.95 *(978-1-57416-089-5(3))* Clear Light Pubs.

FOLKLORE—DENMARK

Andersen, Hans Christian. The Little Match Girl. unabr. ed. (World of Words Ser.). (J). (gr. k-3). pap. 10.00 incl. audio Spoken Arts, Inc.

—Thumbelina. Lai, Hsin-Shih, illus. 2008.Tr. of Tommelise. 56p. (J). 19.95 *(978-0-88010-592-7(5),* Bell Pond Bks.) SteinerBooks, Inc.

MacDonald, Margaret Read. Fat Cat: A Danish Folktale. Paschkis, Julie, illus. 2005. (ENG.). 32p. (J). (gr. -1-2). pap. 8.95 *(978-0-87483-765-0(0))* August Hse. Pubs., Inc.

FOLKLORE—EAST ASIA

Bosco, Don. Island of Legends. 2016. (ENG., Illus.). 96p. pap. 12.99 *(978-981-4751-36-0(7))* Marshall Cavendish International (Asia) Private Ltd. SGP. Dist: National Bk. Network.

FOLKLORE—ENGLAND

Creswick, Paul & Wyeth, N. C. Robin Hood. 2003. (Scribner Storybook Classics Ser.: Vol. 4). (ENG., Illus.). 64p. (J). (gr. 3-7). 19.99 *(978-0-689-85467-5(6),* Atheneum Bks. for Young Readers) Simon & Schuster Children's Publishing.

Folklore. Jack & the Robbers. (J). pap. 2.99 *(978-0-8136-2417-4(7))* Modern Curriculum Pr.

Johnson, Richard, tr. & illus. Jack & the Beanstalk. Johnson, Richard, illus. 2004. 31p. (J). *(978-1-84444-108-2(3))* Mantra Lingua.

Limke, Jeff. El Rey Arturo: La Espada Excalibur Desenvainada; King Arthur: Excalibur Unsheathed. 2008. pap. 52.95 *(978-0-8225-9636-3(9))* Lerner Publishing Group.

McSpadden, J. Walker. Robin Hood. 2004. reprint ed. pap. 22.95 *(978-1-4191-4516-2(9));* pap. 1.99 *(978-1-4192-4516-9(3))* Kessinger Publishing, LLC.

Osborne, Mary Pope. Kate & the Beanstalk. Potter, Giselle, illus. 2005. (ENG.). 40p. (J). (gr. -1-3). reprint ed. 8.99 *(978-1-4169-0818-0(8),* Aladdin) Simon & Schuster Children's Publishing.

Potter, Melisande, illus. Dick Whittington & His Cat. 2006. (ENG.). 32p. (J). (gr. -1-3). 16.95 *(978-0-8234-1987-6(8))* Holiday Hse., Inc.

Pye, Ken. More Merseyside Tales. 2017. (ENG., Illus.). 192p. 17.95 **(978-0-7509-7052-5(9))** History Pr. Ltd.,The GBR. Dist: Independent Pubs. Group.

Pyle, Howard. The Adventures of Robin Hood. Corvino, Lucy, illus. 2005. (Classic Starts(tm) Ser.). (ENG.). 160p. (J). (gr. 2-4). 6.95 *(978-1-4027-1257-9(X))* Sterling Publishing Co., Inc.

—The Merry Adventures of Robin Hood. (Young Collector's Illustrated Classics Ser.). (Illus.). 192p. (J). (gr. 3-7). 9.95 *(978-1-56156-454-5(0))* Kidsbooks, LLC.

—The Merry Adventures of Robin Hood. l.t. ed. 2004. (Large Print Ser.). 518p. 26.00 *(978-1-58287-684-9(3))* North Bks.

—The Story of Sir Lancelot & His Companions. 2004. reprint ed. pap. 27.95 *(978-1-4179-5609-8(7))* Kessinger Publishing, LLC.

Spong, Clive, illus. King Arthur & the Magic Sword: An English Legend. 2004. (ENG.). 24p. (J). (gr. 3-3). pap. 6.47 net. *(978-0-7685-2123-8(8),* Dominie Elementary) Pearson Schl.

Thomas, Taffy. Lakeland Folk Tales for Children. 2017. (Folk Tales for Children Ser.). (ENG., Illus.). 192p. (J). (gr. 2-4). pap. 16.99 **(978-0-7509-6611-5(4))** History Pr. Ltd.,The GBR. Dist: Independent Pubs. Group.

Wahl, Jan. Little Johnny Buttermilk: After an Old English Folktale. Mazzucco, Jennifer, illus. 2005. (ENG.). 32p. (J). (gr. -1-3). 15.95 *(978-0-87483-559-5(3))* August Hse. Pubs., Inc.

FOLKLORE, ESKIMO

see Eskimos—Folklore

FOLKLORE—EUROPE

Andersen, Hans Christian. El Patito Feo. (Mi Primeros Cuentos Ser.). (SPA & ENG., Illus.). (J). (gr. -1-3). pap. 5.95 incl. audio compact disk *(978-88-8148-251-1(7))* EMC/Paradigm Publishing.

Andrews, Jackie. Henny Penny. Taylor, Lawrie, illus. 2012. (ENG.). 32p. (J). pap. 6.50 *(978-1-84135-194-0(6))* Award Pubns. Ltd. GBR. Dist: Parkwest Pubns., Inc.

Aylesworth, Jim. My Grandfather's Coat. McClintock, Barbara, illus. 2014. (ENG.). 32p. (J). (gr. -1-3). 17.99 *(978-0-439-92545-7(2),* Scholastic Pr.) Scholastic, Inc.

Barber, Antonia & Quarto Generic Staff. Hidden Tales from Eastern Europe. Guild, Shena, ed. Hess, Paul, illus. 2004. (ENG.). 48p. (J). (gr. 2-17). 9.99 *(978-1-84507-147-9(6),* Frances Lincoln) Quarto Publishing Group UK GBR. Dist: Hachette Bk. Group.

Forest, Heather. A Big Quiet House: A Yiddish Folktale from Eastern Europe. Greenstein, Susan, illus. 2005. (ENG.). 32p. (J). (gr. k-3). 15.95 *(978-0-87483-462-8(7))* August Hse. Pubs., Inc.

Keding, Dan. Stories of Hope & Spirit: Folktales from Eastern Europe. 2005. (ENG., Illus.). 112p. (J). (gr. 3-7). 18.95 *(978-0-87483-727-8(8))* August Hse. Pubs., Inc.

Rogasky, Barbara & Fisher, Leonard Everett. The Dybbuk: A Version. 2005. (ENG., Illus.). 64p. (J). (gr. 5-9). 16.95 *(978-0-8234-1616-5(X))* Holiday Hse., Inc.

Trembinski, Donna. Medieval Myths, Legends, & Songs. 2005. (Medieval World Ser.). (ENG., Illus.). 32p. (J). (gr. 5-9). lib. bdg. *(978-0-7787-1359-3(8))* Crabtree Publishing Co.

Umansky, Kaye. The Emperor's New Clothes. 2003. (Curtain Up Ser.: Vol. 6). (ENG., Illus.). 48p. (J). (gr. 1-4). pap. *(978-0-7136-4624-5(1),* A&C Black) Bloomsbury Publishing Plc.

FOLKLORE—FRANCE

Beauty & the Beast. unabr. ed. (Read-Along Ser.). (J). 7.99 incl. audio *(978-1-55723-252-6(0))* Walt Disney Records.

Disney Staff. Beauty & the Beast. 2004. (J). (gr. -1-2). spiral bd. *(978-0-616-01630-5(1))* Canadian National Institute for the Blind/Institut National Canadien pour les Aveugles.

—Beauty & the Beast. (FRE.). 96p. (J). (gr. k-5). pap. 9.95 *(978-0-7859-8844-1(0))* French & European Pubns., Inc.

Findlay, Lisa. Puss in Boots. Bowers, Tim, illus. 2008. (Step into Reading Ser.). (ENG.). 48p. (J). (gr. k-3). pap. 3.99 *(978-0-375-84671-7(9),* Random Hse. Bks. for Young Readers) Random Hse. Children's Bks.

LeapFrog Staff. Disney Princess Stories - France. 2003. (Illus.). spiral bd. 14.99 *(978-1-59319-005-7(0))* LeapFrog Enterprises, Inc.

Leprince de Beaumont, Marie & Perrault, Charles. Beauty & the Beast & Other Fairy Tales. 2011. (Dover Children's Thrift Classics Ser.). (ENG., Illus.). 96p. (Orig.). (J). (gr. 3-8). pap. 3.00 *(978-0-486-28032-5(2))* Dover Pubns., Inc.

Muth, Jon J. Stone Soup. Muth, Jon J., illus. 2003. (ENG., Illus.). 32p. (J). (gr. -1-3). 18.99 *(978-0-439-33909-4(X),* Scholastic Pr.) Scholastic, Inc.

Perrault, Charles. Puss in Boots. Bell, Anthea, tr. Lunelli, Giuliano, illus. 2003. 24p. (J). (gr. 3-5). reprint ed. 18.00 *(978-0-7567-6600-9(1))* DIANE Publishing Co.

Le Petit Chaperon Rouge.Tr. of Little Red Riding Hood. (FRE.). 48p. (J). pap. 12.95 incl. audio compact disk *(978-2-89558-051-5(0))* Coffragants CAN. Dist: Penton Overseas, Inc.

Le Petit Chaperon Rouge. (Musicontes Ser.).Tr. of Little Red Riding Hood. (FRE.). (J). 24.95 incl. audio *(978-2-09-230468-6(2))* Nathan, Fernand FRA. Dist: Distribooks, Inc.

RH Disney Staff. Cinderella. RH Disney Staff, tr. (FRE.). 96p. (J). (gr. k-5). pap. 9.95 *(978-0-7859-8855-7(6))* French & European Pubns., Inc.

Souvestre, Emile. Peronnik: A French Fairy Tale of the Grail Quest. 2003. (ENG., Illus.). 1p. (gr. 1-5). 9.95 *(978-0-89281-061-1(0),* Healing Arts Pr.) Inner Traditions International, Ltd.

Stockham, Jess, illus. Stone Soup. 2007. (Flip-Up Fairy Tales Ser.). (ENG.). 24p. (J). (gr. -1-2). audio compact disk *(978-1-84643-094-7(1))* Child's Play International Ltd.

FOLKLORE—GERMANY

Arisman, Marshall. The Cat Who Invented Bebop. Arisman, Marshall, illus. 2008. (ENG., Illus.). 32p. (J). (gr. 1-3). 17.95 *(978-1-56846-152-6(6))* Creative Co., The.

La Belle au Bois Dormant. (FRE.). 48p. pap. 12.95 incl. audio compact disk *(978-2-89558-067-6(7))* Coffragants CAN. Dist: Penton Overseas, Inc.

Buskers of Bremen. 2004. (J). E-Book incl. cd-rom *(978-1-84444-455-7(4))* Mantra Lingua.

Ceccoli, Nicoletta, illus. Little Red Riding Hood. 2004. 32p. (J). 16.99 *(978-1-84148-621-5(3))* Barefoot Bks., Inc.

Costa, Jana, illus. Sleeping Beauty. 2007. (Usborne Young Reading: Series One Ser.). 48p. (J). 8.99 *(978-0-7945-1458-7(8),* Usborne) EDC Publishing.

Disney Staff. Snow White & the Seven Dwarfs. 2004. (J). (gr. -1-2). spiral bd. *(978-0-616-01633-6(6));* spiral bd. *(978-0-616-01632-9(8))* Canadian National Institute for the Blind/Institut National Canadien pour les Aveugles.

—Snow White & the Seven Dwarfs. (FRE.). 96p. (J). (gr. k-5). pap. 9.95 *(978-0-7859-8853-3(X))* French & European Pubns., Inc.

Dry, Roland, illus. Pied Piper. 2004. (J). E-Book incl. cd-rom *(978-1-84444-466-3(X))* Mantra Lingua.

Gaiman, NEil. Hansel & Gretel. Mattotti, Lorenzo, illus. 2014. (ENG.). (J). (gr. 2-7). 56p. 16.95 *(978-1-935179-62-7(4));* 60p. 29.95 *(978-1-935179-65-8(9))* TOON Books / RAW Junior, LLC.

Gay, Marie-Louise. Rumpelstiltskin. 2004. (J). (gr. -1-2). spiral bd. *(978-0-616-01348-9(5));* spiral bd. *(978-0-616-01646-6(8))* Canadian National Institute for the Blind/Institut National Canadien pour les Aveugles.

Grimm, Jacob. The Elves & the Shoemaker. 2004. (Treasure Tree Ser.). (Illus.). 32p. (J). *(978-0-7166-1600-9(9))* World Bk., Inc.

Grimm, Jacob & Grimm, Wilhelm. Sleeping Beauty & Other Fairy Tales. 2011. (Dover Children's Thrift Classics Ser.). (ENG., Illus.). 96p. (Orig.). (J). (gr. 3-6). pap. 4.00 *(978-0-486-27084-5(X))* Dover Pubns., Inc.

Grimm, Jacob & Grimm, Wilhelm K. The Brave Little Tailor. 2005. (SPA.). 12p. (J). pap. *(978-958-30-1783-4(3))* Panamericana Editorial.

—Grandpa Mouse & Little Mouse: A Tale about Respect for Elders. Lonaytis, Olga, illus. 2006. (J). *(978-1-59939-088-8(4),* Reader's Digest Young Families, Inc.) Studio Fun International.

—Sleeping Beauty. 2005. (SPA.). 12p. (J). pap. *(978-958-30-1781-0(7))* Panamericana Editorial.

—Snow White. 2005. (SPA.). 12p. (J). pap. *(978-958-30-1777-3(9))* Panamericana Editorial.

Grimm, Jacob, et al. The Elves & the Shoemaker: A Grimm Graphic Novel, 1 vol. Rodriquez, Pedro, illus. 2011. (Graphic Spin Ser.). (ENG.). 40p. (gr. 1-3). lib. bdg. 25.32 *(978-1-4342-2553-5(4),* Graphic Revolve) Stone Arch Bks.

Guicciardini, Desideria, illus. Rumpelstiltskin. 2007. (Young Reading Series 1 Gift Bks.). 47p. (J). (gr. -1-3). 8.99 *(978-0-7945-1446-4(4),* Usborne) EDC Publishing.

Hansel & Gretel. Date not set. (J). 4.99 *(978-0-7214-5406-1(2))* Nickel Pr.

Hansel et Gretel.Tr. of Hansel & Gretel. (FRE.). 48p. pap. 12.95 incl. audio compact disk *(978-2-89558-055-3(3))* Coffragants CAN. Dist: Penton Overseas, Inc.

Holden, Robert. The Pied Piper of Hamelin. Zak, Drahos, illus. 2004. 28p. (J). (gr. k-4). reprint ed. 15.00 *(978-0-7567-7686-2(4))* DIANE Publishing Co.

LaMarche, Jim. The Elves & the Shoemaker. 2003. (ENG., Illus.). 32p. (J). (gr. -1-7). 16.99 *(978-0-8118-3477-3(8))* Chronicle Bks. LLC.

Page, Nick & Claire. Elves & the Shoemaker. 2006. (Read with Me (Make Believe Ideas) Ser.). (Illus.). 32p. (J). (gr. k-2). *(978-1-84610-161-8(1))* Make Believe Ideas.

Pied Piper. 2004. (J). *(978-1-84444-299-7(3))* Mantra Lingua.

Random House Disney Staff. Snow White & the Seven Dwarfs. Random House Disney Staff, illus. 2003. (Little Golden Book Ser.). (ENG., Illus.). 24p. (J). (gr. -1-2). 4.99 *(978-0-7364-2186-7(6),* Golden/Disney) Random Hse. Children's Bks.

Reed, Nathan, illus. Buskers of Bremen: Big Book English Only. 2004. (BEN & ENG.). (J). *(978-1-84444-301-7(9))* Mantra Lingua.

Ros, Roser. The Musicians of Bremen/Los Musicos de Bremen. Montserrat, Pep, illus. 2005. (Bilingual Fairy Tales Ser.: BILI). (ENG & SPA.). 32p. (J). (gr. -1-3). 6.99 *(978-0-8118-4796-4(9))* Chronicle Bks. LLC.

Sanderson, Ruth. Rose Red & Snow White. 2013. (ENG., Illus.). 32p. (J). 16.95 *(978-1-56656-910-1(9),* Crocodile Bks.) Interlink Publishing Group, Inc.

Stewart, Whitney. A Catfish Tale: A Bayou Story of the Fisherman & His Wife. Guerlais, Gérald, illus. 2014. (ENG.). 32p. (J). (gr. -1-3). 16.99 *(978-0-8075-1098-8(X))* Whitman, Albert & Co.

Stockham, Jess, illus. Little Red Riding Hood. 2007. (Flip-Up Fairy Tales Ser.). (ENG.). 24p. (J). (gr. -1-2). audio compact disk *(978-1-84643-088-6(7))* Child's Play International Ltd.

Tan, Shaun. The Singing Bones. Tan, Shaun, illus. 2016. (ENG., Illus.). 192p. (J). (gr. 7). 24.99 *(978-0-545-94612-4(3),* Levine, Arthur A. Bks.) Scholastic, Inc.

Wilhelm, Hans, retold by. Los Musicos de Bremen. (SPA.). (J). pap. 4.80 net. *(978-0-439-17707-8(3),* SO30111) Scholastic, Inc.

FOLKLORE—GREAT BRITAIN

Hodges, Margaret & Malory, Sir Thomas. Merlin & the Making of the King. Hyman, Trina Schart, tr. Hyman, Trina Schart, illus. 2004. (ENG.). 40p. (J). (gr. 4-6). tchr. ed. 16.95 *(978-0-8234-1647-9(X))* Holiday Hse., Inc.

MacDonald, Margaret Read. The Old Woman Who Lived in a Vinegar Bottle. 2005. (ENG., Illus.). 32p. (J). (gr. -1-3). pap. 8.95 *(978-0-87483-723-0(5))* August Hse. Pubs., Inc.

O'Leary, Michael. Hampshire Folk Tales for Children. 2016. (Folk Tales for Children Ser.). (ENG., Illus.). 192p. (J). (gr. 2-4). pap. 16.99 **(978-0-7509-6484-5(7))** History Pr. Ltd.,The GBR. Dist: Independent Pubs. Group.

FOLKLORE—GREECE

James Baldwin. Fifty Famous Stories Retold. 2009. (Illus.). 132p. pap. 5.95 *(978-1-60386-206-6(4),* Merchant Bks.) Rough Draft Printing.

Morpurgo, Michael & Aesop. The McElderry Book of Aesop's Fables. Chichester Clark, Emma, illus. 2005. (ENG.). 96p. (J). (gr. 1-5). 24.99 *(978-1-4169-0290-4(2),* McElderry, Margaret K. Bks.) McElderry, Margaret K. Bks.

FOLKLORE—HAITI

Di Benedetto, Angelo, illus. How the Donkeys Came to Haiti & Other Folk Tales. 124p. (J). (gr. 4-9). 12.95 *(978-0-8159-5706-5(8))* Devin-Adair Pubs., Inc.

FOLKLORE—HAWAII

Au, May Parker. Princess Huilua & Kamapuaa. 2007.Tr. of Ke Kamalii Wahine o Huilua a me Kamapuaa. (ENG & HAW.). (J). lib. bdg. *(978-0-9773495-4-8(3))* Na Kamalei Koolauloa Early Education Program.

Ehlers, Sabine. Hawaiian Stories for Boys & Girls. (J). pap. 4.95 *(978-0-681-26583-7(3))* Booklines Hawaii, Ltd.

Lum, Leimomi o. Kamahae Kuamoo Mookini. The Legend of Kuamo'o Mo'okini & Hamumu the Great Whale. Kam, Kathleen, illus. 2004. 24p. (J). 12.95 *(978-1-58178-036-9(2))* Bishop Museum Pr.

Nordenstrom, Michael, illus. & adapted by. Hina & the Sea of Stars. Nordenstrom, Michael, adapted by. 2003. 32p. 10.95 *(978-1-57306-167-4(0))* Bess Pr., Inc.

Two Tales of Hawaii. 2003. (J). 10.99 *(978-0-89610-923-0(2))* Island Heritage Publishing.

Varez, Dietrich. The Legend of La'ieikawai. 2004. (Latitude 20 Bks.). (Illus.). 88p. 14.99 *(978-0-8248-2839-4(9))* Univ. of Hawaii Pr.

FOLKLORE—INDIA

Adhikary, Qiron. Feminist Folktales from India. 2003. (Illus.). 97p. (YA). per. 9.95 *(978-0-9714127-3-6(1))* Masalai Pr.

Buri & the Marrow. 2004. (J). (ENG & HIN.). *(978-1-84444-668-1(9));* cd-rom *(978-1-84444-454-0(6))* Mantra Lingua.

Cleveland, Rob. The Drum: A Folktale from India. Wrenn, Tom, illus. 2006. (Story Cove Ser.). (ENG.). 32p. (J). (gr. -1-3). pap. 4.95 *(978-0-87483-802-2(9))* August Hse. Pubs., Inc.

Divakaruni, Chitra Banerjee. Grandma & the Great Gourd: A Bengali Folktale. Waters, Susy Pilgrim, illus. 2013. (ENG.). 32p. (J). (gr. 1-3). 18.99 *(978-1-59643-378-6(7),* 9781596433786) Roaring Brook Pr.

Hausman, Gerald. The Otter, the Spotted Frog & the Great Flood: A Creek Indian Story. Shiloh, Ramon, illus. 2013. (ENG.). 36p. (J). (gr. k-3). 17.95 *(978-1-937786-12-0(9),* Wisdom Tales) World Wisdom, Inc.

Jacobs, Joseph. Indian Fairy Tales. Batten, John D., illus. 2011. (Dover Children's Classics Ser.). (ENG.). 255p. (J). (gr. 2-5). reprint ed. pap. 19.95 *(978-0-486-21828-1(7))* Dover Pubns., Inc.

Johari, Harish & Sperling, Vatsala. How Ganesh Got His Elephant Head. Weltevrede, Pieter, illus. 2003. (ENG.). 32p. (J). (gr. -1-6). 15.95 *(978-1-59143-021-6(6))* Bear & Co.

Leonard, Scott A. Myths & Legends of South Asia & Southeast Asia. 2015. (Illus.). 64p. (J). *(978-0-7166-2630-5(6))* World Bk., Inc.

Novesky, Amy. The Elephant Prince: The Story of Ganesh. Wedman, Belgin K., illus. 2004. (ENG.). 32p. 16.95 *(978-1-886069-16-9(6),* BK2304HB) Insight Editions.

Novesky, Amy & Wedman, Belgin K. The Elephant Prince: The Story of Ganesh. 2005. (Illus.). 32p. (J). 16.95 *(978-1-932771-16-9(6))* Mandala Publishing.

Peters, Andrew & Fusek Peters, Andrew. Monkey's Clever Tale. Montgomery-Higham, Amanda, illus. 2003. (Traditional Tales with a Twist Ser.). (ENG.). 32p. (J). (gr. 2-3). *(978-0-85953-051-4(5))* Child's Play International Ltd.

Sehgal, Kabir & Sehgal, Surishtha. A Bucket of Blessings. Tsong, Jing Jing, illus. 2014. (ENG.). 32p. (J). (gr. -1-3). 17.99 *(978-1-4424-5870-3(4),* Beach Lane Bks.) Beach Lane Bks.

Souhami, Jessica. Rama & the de Mon King: An Ancient Tale from India. 2006. (Illus.). 30p. (J). (gr. k-4). reprint ed. 15.00 *(978-0-7567-9813-0(2))* DIANE Publishing Co.

Young, Ed. Seven Blind Mice. Young, Ed, illus. 2007. (Illus.). pap. 14.95 incl. audio *(978-0-439-02784-7(5));* (J). 24.95 incl. audio *(978-0-439-02782-3(9))* Scholastic, Inc.

—Seven Blind Mice. Young, Ed, illus. 2011. (Illus.). 18.95 *(978-0-439-02785-4(3));* (J). 29.95 *(978-0-439-02783-0(7))* Weston Woods Studios, Inc.

FOLKLORE, INDIAN

see Indians of North America—Folklore

FOLKLORE—INDONESIA

Suyenaga, Joan. Indonesian Children's Favorite Stories. Martowiredjo, Salim, illus. 2015. (ENG.). 64p. (J). (gr. k-8). pap. 11.95 *(978-0-8048-4511-3(5))* Tuttle Publishing.

FOLKLORE, JEWISH

see Jews—Folklore

E
F
G

FOLKLORE—IRAQ

McCaughrean, Geraldine. Gilgamesh the Hero. Parkins, David, illus. 2003. (ENG.). 96p. (J). (gr. 6-9). 20.00 *(978-0-8028-5262-5(9))* Eerdmans, William B. Publishing Co.

FOLKLORE—IRELAND

Children of Lir. 2004. (J). cd-rom *(978-1-84444-456-4(2))* Mantra Lingua.

Crosbie, Duncan. A Claddagh Ring for Nuala, 1 vol. Rutherford, Peter, illus. gif. ed. 2003. (ENG.). 16p. (J). (gr. k-3). 7.95 *(978-1-58980-175-2(X))* Pelican Publishing Co., Inc.

Doyle, Malachy & Sharkey, Niamh. Tales from Old Ireland. 2006. (ENG., Illus.). 96p. (J). (gr. 2-6). 16.99 *(978-1-905236-32-9(8))* Barefoot Bks., Inc.

Gleeson, Brian. Finn McCoul, 1 vol. de Sève, Peter, illus. 2005. (Rabbit Ears Ser.). (ENG.). 36p. (gr. k-5). 25.65 *(978-1-59679-223-4(X))* Spotlight.

Milligan, Bryce. Brigid's Cloak: An Ancient Irish Story. Cann, Helen, illus. 32p. (J). (gr. k-17). 2005. (ENG.). 9.00 *(978-0-8028-5297-7(1),* Eerdmans Bks For Young Readers) 2004. 16.00 *(978-0-8028-5224-3(6))* Eerdmans, William B. Publishing Co.

Mortensen, Lori. Leprechauns. 2007. (Mysterious Encounters Ser.). (ENG., Illus.). 48p. (J). (gr. 3-5). 29.00 *(978-0-7377-3663-2(1),* Kidhaven) Cengage Gale.

Mullins, Tom, ed. Irish Stories for Children. 2010. (ENG.). 112p. (J). (gr. 5-18). pap. 12.95 *(978-1-85635-027-3(4))* Mercier Pr., Ltd., The IRL. Dist: Dufour Editions, Inc.

Osborne, Mary Pope & Boyce, Natalie Pope. Leprechauns & Irish Folklore: A Nonfiction Companion to Leprechaun in Late Winter. Murdocca, Sal, illus. 2010. (Magic Tree House - Fact Tracker Ser.: 21). (ENG.). 128p. (J). (gr. 2-5). 6.99 *(978-0-375-86009-6(6),* Random Hse. Bks. for Young Readers) Random Hse. Children's Bks.

—Leprechauns & Irish Folklore: A Nonfiction Companion to Leprechaun in Late Winter. 2010. (Magic Tree House Fact Tracker Ser.: 21). lib. bdg. 17.20 *(978-0-606-07030-0(3),* Turtleback) Turtleback Bks.

FOLKLORE—ITALY

Carsey, Alice, illus. Pinocchio. 2005.Tr. of Avventure di Pinocchio. (ENG.). 136p. (J). (gr. 2-5). 19.95 *(978-1-933327-00-6(6))* Purple Bear Bks., Inc.

Kunhardt, Dorothy, ed. Pinocchio. (FRE.). 96p. (J). (gr. k-5). pap. 9.95 *(978-0-7859-8845-8(9))* French & European Pubns., Inc.

FOLKLORE—JAPAN

Hearn, Lafcadio, et al. The Boy Who Drew Cats & Other Japanese Fairy Tales. Green, Yuko, illus. 2012. (Dover Children's Thrift Classics Ser.). (ENG.). 64p. (J). (gr. 3-8). pap. 3.00 *(978-0-486-40348-9(3))* Dover Pubns., Inc.

Ikeda, Daisaku. The Snow Country Prince. McCaughrean, Geraldine, tr. from JPN. Wildsmith, Brian, illus. 2013. 6.95 *(978-1-935523-60-4(0))* World Tribune Pr.

Manley, Curtis. The Crane Girl: A Japanese Folktale. Wang, Lin, illus. 2017. (ENG.). 40p. (J). 18.95 *(978-1-885008-57-2(0))* Lee & Low Bks., Inc.

Metaxas, Eric. Peachboy, 1 vol. Smith, Jeffrey, illus. 2005. (Rabbit Ears Ser.). (ENG.). 36p. (gr. k-6). 25.65 *(978-1-59679-227-2(2))* Spotlight.

Paterson, Katherine. The Tale of the Mandarin Ducks. Dillon, Leo & Dillon, Diane, illus. 2004. 32p. (J). (gr. k-4). reprint ed. 15.00 *(978-0-7567-7698-5(8))* DIANE Publishing Co.

Sakade, Florence. More Japanese Children's Favorite Stories. Hayashi, Yoshio, illus. anniv. ed. 2014. (ENG.). 96p. (J). (gr. 3-11). 17.95 *(978-4-8053-1265-0(3))* Tuttle Publishing.

Urashima Taro. 2003. (J). 11.95 *(978-0-89610-639-0(X))* Island Heritage Publishing.

Wells, Ruth. Farmer & the Poor God. 2008. (ENG.). 40p. (J). (gr. -1-3). 10.99 *(978-1-4169-8967-7(6),* Simon & Schuster Bks. For Young Readers) Simon & Schuster Bks. For Young Readers.

Weston Woods Staff, creator. The Tale of the Mandarin Ducks. 2004. 18.95 *(978-1-55592-742-4(4));* 38.75 *(978-1-55592-750-9(5))* Weston Woods Studios, Inc.

Yoshikawa, Sachiko, illus. The Boy from the Dragon Palace. 2011. (ENG.). 32p. (J). (gr. -1-3). 16.99 *(978-0-8075-7513-0(5))* Whitman, Albert & Co.

FOLKLORE—KOREA

Kang, Mi-Sun, illus. The Lazy Man/the Spring of Youth. 2008. (Korean Folk Tales for Children Ser.: Vol. 3). (ENG & KOR.). 44p. (J). (gr. 2-5). lib. bdg. 14.50 *(978-0-930878-73-3(6))* Hollym International Corp.

—The Snail Lady/the Magic Vase. 2008. (Korean Folk Tales for Children Ser.: Vol. 6). (ENG & KOR.). 44p. (J). (gr. 2-5). lib. bdg. 14.50 *(978-0-930878-89-4(2))* Hollym International Corp.

Kang, Mi-Sun & Kim, Yon-Kyong, illus. Brave Hong Gil-Dong/the Man Who Bought the Shade of a Tree. 2008. (Korean Folk Tales for Children Ser.: Vol. 8). (ENG & KOR.). 44p. (J). (gr. 2-5). lib. bdg. 14.50 *(978-0-930878-91-7(4))* Hollym International Corp.

—The Faithful Daughter Sim Cheong/the Little Frog Who Never Listened. 2008. (Korean Folk Tales for Children Ser.: Vol. 9). (ENG & KOR.). 44p. (J). (gr. 2-5). lib. bdg. 14.50 *(978-0-930878-92-4(2))* Hollym International Corp.

Kim, Yon-Kyong, illus. Mr. Moon & Miss Sun/the Herdsman & the Weaver. 2008. (Korean Folk Tales for Children Ser.: Vol. 2). (ENG & KOR.). 44p. (J). (gr. 2-5). lib. bdg. 14.50 *(978-0-930878-72-6(8))* Hollym International Corp.

—The Ogres' Magic Clubs - the Tiger & the Dried Persimmons. 2008. (Korean Folk Tales for Children Ser.: Vol. 5). (ENG & KOR.). 44p. (J). (gr. 2-5). lib. bdg. 14.50 *(978-0-930878-88-7(4))* Hollym International Corp.

—The Woodcutter & the Heavenly Maiden & the Fire Dogs. 2008. (Korean Folk Tales for Children Ser.: 1). (ENG & KOR.). 44p. (J). (gr. 2-5). lib. bdg. 18.50 *(978-0-930878-71-9(X))* Hollym International Corp.

Kim, Yon-Kyong & Kang, Mi-Sun, illus. The Son of the Cinnamon Tree/the Donkey's Egg. 2006. (Korean Folk Tales for Children Ser.: Vol. 10). (ENG.). 44p. (J). (gr. 2-5). lib. bdg. 14.50 *(978-0-930878-93-1(0))* Hollym International Corp.

Korean Folk Tales for Children, 10 vols. 2008. (Illus.). 450p. (J). (gr. 2-5). lib. bdg. 145.00 *(978-0-930878-05-4(1))* Hollym International Corp.

Pak, Mi-Son, illus. The Seven Brothers & the Big Dipper/Heungbu, Nolbu & the Magic Gourds. 2008. (Korean Folk Tales for Children Ser.: Vol. 4). (ENG & KOR.). 44p. (J). (gr. 2-5). lib. bdg. 14.50 *(978-0-930878-74-0(4))* Hollym International Corp.

Pak, Mi-Son & Kim, Yon-Kyong, illus. The Greedy Princess/the Rabbit & the Tiger, vols. 10, vol. 7. 2008. (Korean Folk Tales for Children Ser.: 7). (ENG & KOR.). 44p. (J). (gr. 2-5). lib. bdg. 19.50 *(978-0-930878-90-0(6))* Hollym International Corp.

Park, Janie Jaehyun. The Tiger & the Persimmon. 2004. (Illus.). (J). (gr. -1-18). spiral bd. *(978-0-616-14623-1(X));* spiral bd. *(978-0-616-14622-4(1))* Canadian National Institute for the Blind/Institut National Canadien pour les Aveugles.

Rojo, Sara, illus. Why the Sea Is Salty. 2009. (First Reading Level 4 Ser.). 48p. (J). 6.99 *(978-0-7945-2308-4(0),* Usborne) EDC Publishing.

So-un, Kim. Korean Children's Favorite Stories. 2004. (Illus.). 96p. (YA). 16.95 *(978-0-7946-0170-6(7),* PeriplusEdition) Tuttle Publishing.

So-Un, Kim & Kyoung-Sim, Jeong. Korean Children's Favorite Stories. 2004. (ENG., Illus.). 96p. (J). (gr. k-8). 18.95 *(978-0-8048-3591-6(8))* Tuttle Publishing.

FOLKLORE—LATIN AMERICA

Flor Ada, Alma & Campoy, F. Isabel. Tales Our Abuelitas Told: A Hispanic Folktale Collection. Davalos, Felipe et al, illus. 2006. (ENG.). 128p. (J). (gr. k-5). 19.95 *(978-0-689-82583-5(8),* Atheneum Bks. for Young Readers) Simon & Schuster Children's Publishing.

FOLKLORE—LIBERIA

Paye, Won-Ldy & Lippert, Margaret H. Head, Body, Legs: A Story from Liberia. Paschkis, Julie, illus. 2005. (ENG.). 32p. (J). (gr. -1-3). pap. 8.99 *(978-0-8050-7890-9(8),* 9780805078909) Square Fish.

FOLKLORE, MAORI

see Maori (New Zealand People)—Folklore

FOLKLORE—MEXICO

Eckhardt, Jason C., illus. The Legend of the China Poblana. 2003. (J). 10.95 *(978-1-57168-731-9(9),* Eakin Pr.) Eakin Pr.

Gerson, Mary-Joan. Fiesta Femenina. Gonzalez, Maya Christina, illus. 2003. (SPA & ENG.). 64p. (J). 19.99 *(978-1-84148-964-3(6))* Barefoot Bks., Inc.

Gollub, Matthew. Uncle Snake. Martinez, Leovigildo, illus. 2004. (J). *(978-1-889910-31-4(7));* pap. *(978-1-889910-32-1(5))* Tortuga Pr.

Hayes, Joe. ¡El Cucuy! A Bogeyman Cuento in English & Spanish. Robledo, Honorio, illus. 2003. (ENG & SPA.). 40p. (J). (gr. k-2). pap. 7.95 *(978-0-938317-78-4(4))* Cinco Puntos Pr.

—La Llorona - The Weeping Woman: An Hispanic Legend Told in Spanish & English. Hill, Vicki Trego & Pennypacker, Mona, illus. 3rd ed. 2004. (ENG & SPA.). 32p. (J). (gr. 4-6). 16.95 *(978-0-938317-86-9(5))* Cinco Puntos Pr.

Lopez, Victoria. The Little King: An Aztec Tale. 2011. (Illus.). 84p. (YA). 14.95 *(978-1-890379-21-6(2))* Randall, Charles Inc.

Marcos, Subcomandante. The Story of Colors (La Historia de los Colores) A Bilingual Folktale from the Jungles of Chiapas. Din, Anne Bar, tr. Dominguez, Domitila, illus. 2003. (ENG & SPA.). 40p. (J). (gr. 4-6). pap. 8.95 *(978-0-938317-71-5(7))* Cinco Puntos Pr.

Morales, Yuyi. Just a Minute: A Trickster Tale & Counting Book. 2003. (SPA & ENG., Illus.). 36p. (J). (gr. -1-7). 15.99 *(978-0-8118-3758-3(0))* Chronicle Bks. LLC.

Tonatiuh, Duncan. The Princess & the Warrior: A Tale of Two Volcanoes. 2016. (ENG., Illus.). 40p. (J). (gr. 1-4). 16.95 *(978-1-4197-2130-4(5),* Abrams Bks. for Young Readers) Abrams, Inc.

Villaseñor, Victor. Frog & His Friends Save Humanity/la Rana y Sus Amigos Salvan ALA Humanidad. Ochoa, Edna, tr. Ramirez, Jose, illus. 2005. (ENG & SPA.). 32p. (J). (gr. -1). 16.95 *(978-1-55885-429-1(0),* Piñata Books) Arte Publico Pr.

—Mother Fox & Mr. Coyote / Mamá Zorra y Don Coyote. Turcios, Guadalupe Vanessa, tr. Ugalde Alcantara, Felipe, illus. (ENG & SPA.). 32p. (gr. 2-4). 16.95 *(978-1-55885-428-4(2),* Piñata Books) Arte Publico Pr.

FOLKLORE—NEAR EAST

see Folklore—Asia

FOLKLORE, NEGRO

see African Americans—Folklore

FOLKLORE—NIGERIA

Baumann, Margaret. Ajapa the Tortoise: A Book of Nigerian Folk Tales. unabr. ed. 2003. (Dover Children's Classics Ser.). (ENG., Illus.). 112p. (J). (gr. 3-8). pap. 7.95 *(978-0-486-42361-6(1))* Dover Pubns., Inc.

FOLKLORE—NORTH AMERICA

Bonnice, Sherry. Children's Folklore. 2004. (North American Folklore Ser.). (Illus.). 112p. (YA). (gr. 7-18). lib. bdg. 22.95 *(978-1-59084-329-1(0))* Mason Crest.

Brinkerhoff, Shirley. Contemporary Folklore. 2004. (North American Folklore Ser.). (Illus.). 112p. (J). (gr. 7-18). lib. bdg. 22.95 *(978-1-59084-331-4(2))* Mason Crest.

Bruchac, Joseph. The Boy Who Lived with the Bears: And Other Iroquois Stories. Jacob, Murv, illus. 2003. (Storytime Ser.). 63p. (J). (gr. k-5). pap. 11.95 *(978-0-930407-61-2(X))* Parabola Bks.

Goble, Paul. The Earth Made New: Plains Indian Stories of Creation. 2009. (ENG.). 40p. (J). (gr. 4-7). 17.95 *(978-1-933316-67-3(5))* World Wisdom, Inc.

Sanna, Ellyn. Ethnic Folklore. 2004. (North American Folklore Ser.). (Illus.). 112p. (YA). (gr. 7-18). lib. bdg. 22.95 *(978-1-59084-332-1(0))* Mason Crest.

—Folk Customs. 2004. (North American Folklore Ser.). (Illus.). 112p. (YA). (gr. 7-18). lib. bdg. 22.95 *(978-1-59084-336-9(3))* Mason Crest.

—Folk Religion. 2004. (North American Folklore Ser.). (Illus.). 112p. (YA). (gr. 7-18). lib. bdg. 22.95 *(978-1-59084-348-2(7))* Mason Crest.

—Folk Tales & Legends. 2004. (North American Folklore Ser.). (Illus.). 112p. (J). (gr. 7-18). lib. bdg. 22.95 *(978-1-59084-346-8(0))* Mason Crest.

—Food Folklore. 2004. (North American Folklore Ser.). (Illus.). 112p. (YA). (gr. 7-18). lib. bdg. 22.95 *(978-1-59084-347-5(9))* Mason Crest.

FOLKLORE—NORWAY

Appleby, Ellen. The Three Billy Goats Gruff. (FRE.). (J). 6.99 *(978-0-590-71770-0(7))* Scholastic, Inc.

—Les Trois Barbichu, Big Bk. I.t. ed. (FRE.). (J). ring bd. 29.99 *(978-0-590-71769-4(3))* Scholastic, Inc.

Arenson, Roberta & Finch, Mary. The Three Billy Goats Gruff. Arenson, Roberta & Asbjørnsen, Peter Christen, illus. 2003. (ENG.). 32p. (J). pap. 7.99 *(978-1-84148-351-1(6))* Barefoot Bks., Inc.

Batt, Tanya Robyn. The Princess & the White Bear King. Ceccoli, Nicoletta, illus. 2004. 40p. (J). 16.99 *(978-1-84148-339-9(7))* Barefoot Bks., Inc.

D'Aulaire, Ingri & D'Aulaire, Edgar Parin. D' Aulaires' Book of Trolls. 2006. (New York Review Children's Collection Ser.). (ENG., Illus.). 76p. (J). (gr. k-4). 19.95 *(978-1-59017-217-9(5),* NYR Children's Collection) New York Review of Bks., Inc., The.

Mayer, Mercer. East of the Sun & West of the Moon. Mayer, Mercer, illus. 2017. (ENG., Illus.). 32p. (J). (gr. k-3). 13.99 ***(978-1-5344-1240-8(9),*** Aladdin) Simon & Schuster Children's Publishing.

FOLKLORE—POLYNESIA

Sperry, Armstrong. Call It Courage. unabr. ed. 2004. 95p. (J). (gr. 5-9). pap. 29.00 incl. audio *(978-0-8072-8685-2(0),* YA235SP, Listening Library) Random Hse. Audio Publishing Group.

FOLKLORE—PUERTO RICO

Bernier-Grand, Carmen T. Shake It, Morena! And Other Folklore from Puerto Rico. Delacre, Lulu, illus. 2007. 48p. (J). (gr. -1-3). per. 6.95 *(978-0-8225-7026-4(2),* First Avenue Editions) Lerner Publishing Group.

Jaffe, Nina. The Golden Flower: A Taino Myth from Puerto Rico. Sanchez, Enrique O., illus. 2005. 32p. (J). (gr. -1-3). 16.95 *(978-1-55885-452-9(5),* Piñata Books) Arte Publico Pr.

FOLKLORE—ROMANIA

Cohen, Robert Z. Transylvania: Birthplace of Vampires. 2011. (J). 77.70 *(978-1-4488-2234-8(3),* Rosen Reference); (J). pap. 12.95 *(978-1-4488-2231-7(9),* Rosen Reference); (YA). (gr. 5-9). lib. bdg. 31.95 *(978-1-4488-1228-8(3))* Rosen Publishing Group, Inc., The.

FOLKLORE—RUSSIA (FEDERATION)

Corr, Christopher. Deep in the Woods. 2017. (ENG., Illus.). 32p. (J). (gr. -1-1). 17.99 *(978-1-84780-726-7(7),* Frances Lincoln Children's Bks.) Quarto Publishing Group UK GBR. Dist: Hachette Bk. Group.

Johnson, Richard, illus. Giant Turnip. 2004. (J). E-Book incl. cd-rom *(978-1-84444-459-5(7))* Mantra Lingua.

McCaughrean, Geraldine. Grandma Chickenlegs. Kemp, Moira, illus. 2003. (Picture Bks.). 32p. (J). (gr. -1-3). 15.95 *(978-1-57505-415-5(9));* pap. 6.95 *(978-0-87614-908-9(5),* Carolrhoda Bks.) Lerner Publishing Group.

Olmstead, Kathleen. The Enormous Turnip. Olafsdottir, Linda, illus. 2013. (J). *(978-1-4027-8344-9(2))* Sterling Publishing Co., Inc.

Pogorelsky, Antony & Spirin, Gennady. The Little Black Hen. 2003. (ENG., Illus.). 32p. (J). (gr. k-4). 16.95 *(978-1-894965-03-3(5))* Simply Read Bks. CAN. Dist: Ingram Publisher Services.

Ransome, Arthur. Favorite Russian Fairy Tales. Galkin, Simon, illus. 2011. (Dover Children's Thrift Classics Ser.). (ENG.). 96p. (J). (gr. 3-8). pap. 4.00 *(978-0-486-28632-7(0))* Dover Pubns., Inc.

Stihler, Cherie. The Giant Cabbage: An Alaska Folktale. Trammell, Jeremiah, illus. 2003. (Paws IV Ser.). (ENG.). 32p. (J). (gr. -1-2). pap. 10.99 *(978-1-57061-357-9(5),* Little Bigfoot) Sasquatch Bks.

Yolen, Jane. Baba Yaga. Date not set. 32p. (J). (gr. -1-1). pap. 5.99 *(978-0-06-443599-4(7))* HarperCollins Pubs.

—The Flying Witch. Vagin, Vladimir, illus. 2003. 40p. (J). (gr. -1-1). 15.99 *(978-0-06-028536-4(2))* HarperCollins Pubs.

FOLKLORE—SCANDINAVIA

Leonard, Scott A. Myths & Legends of Scandinavia. 2015. (Illus.). 63p. (J). *(978-0-7166-2636-7(5))* World Bk., Inc.

FOLKLORE—SCOTLAND

Lupton, Hugh. Pirican Pic & Pirican Mor. Heo, Yumi, illus. 2003. (ENG.). 40p. (J). (gr. 1-3). 16.99 *(978-1-84148-070-1(3))* Barefoot Bks., Inc.

MacKenzie, Donald A. Scottish Fairy Tales. Green, John, illus. 2011. (Dover Children's Thrift Classics Ser.). (ENG.). 96p. (J). (gr. 3-8). pap. 4.50 *(978-0-486-29900-6(7))* Dover Pubns., Inc.

FOLKLORE—SLAVIC COUNTRIES

Bateson Hill, Margaret. Masha & the Firebird. Wilson, Anne, illus. 2005. (Folk Tales Ser.: 1). (RUS & ENG.). 32p. (J). pap. *(978-1-84089-201-7(3))* Zero to Ten, Ltd.

FOLKLORE—SOUTH AMERICA

Croy, Anita. Myths & Legends of Central & South America. 2015. (Illus.). 64p. (J). *(978-0-7166-2628-2(4))* World Bk., Inc.

Ehlert, Lois. Un Lazo a la Luna. Prince, Amy, tr. 2003.Tr. of Moon Rope. (ENG & SPA., Illus.). 36p. (J). (gr. -1 — 1). pap. 7.99 *(978-0-15-201702-6(X))* Houghton Mifflin Harcourt Publishing Co.

Ehlert, Lois, et al. Un Lazo a la Luna: Una Leyenda Peruana. Prince, Amy, tr. abr. ed. 2003. (Avenues Ser.).Tr. of Moon Rope - A Peruvian Folktale. (SPA & ENG., Illus.). 32p. (C). (gr. -1 — 1). pap. 22.95 *(978-0-15-255343-2(6))* National Geographic School Publishing, Inc.

Fatus, Sophie, illus. A Hen, a Chick & a String Guitar. 2005. 32p. (J). 17.99 incl. audio compact disk *(978-1-84148-796-0(1))* Barefoot Bks., Inc.

Knutson, Barbara. Love & Roast Chicken: A Trickster Tale from the Andes Mountains. Knutson, Barbara, illus. 2004. (Carolrhoda Picture Books Ser.). (ENG., Illus.). 40p. (J). (gr. k-3). 17.95 *(978-1-57505-657-9(7))* Lerner Publishing Group.

Pitcher, Caroline. Mariana & the Merchild. Morris, Jackie, illus. 2004. 32p. (J). (gr. -1-7). 17.00 *(978-0-8028-5204-5(1))* Eerdmans, William B. Publishing Co.

FOLKLORE—SOUTHEAST ASIA

Leonard, Scott A. Myths & Legends of South Asia & Southeast Asia. 2015. (Illus.). 64p. (J). *(978-0-7166-2630-5(6))* World Bk., Inc.

Spagnoli, Cathy. Nine-In-One:Grr! Grr! Hom, Nancy, illus. 2013. (ENG.). 32p. (J). (gr. -1-5). pap. 9.95 *(978-0-89239-048-9(4))* Lee & Low Bks., Inc.

FOLKLORE—TURKEY

Brett, Jan. The Mitten. Brett, Jan, illus. 20th anniv. ed. 2009. (ENG., Illus.). 32p. (J). (gr. -1-k). 17.99 *(978-0-399-25296-9(7),* G.P. Putnam's Sons Books for Young Readers) Penguin Young Readers Group.

Demi. The Hungry Coat: A Tale from Turkey. Demi, illus. 2004. (ENG., Illus.). 40p. (J). (gr. 1-5). 21.99 *(978-0-689-84680-9(0),* McElderry, Margaret K. Bks.) McElderry, Margaret K. Bks.

Singh, Rina. Nearly Nonsense: Hoja Tales from Turkey. Zaman, Farida, illus. 2011. (ENG.). 48p. (J). (gr. k-3). 17.95 *(978-0-88776-974-0(8),* Tundra Bks.) Tundra Bks. CAN. Dist: Penguin Random Hse. LLC.

FOLKLORE—UKRAINE

Kimmel, Eric A. The Castle of Cats: A Story from Ukraine. Krenina, Katya, illus. 2004. (ENG.). 32p. (J). (gr. k-3). tchr. ed. 16.95 *(978-0-8234-1565-6(1))* Holiday Hse., Inc.

Krenina, Katya, illus. The Birds' Gift: A Ukrainian Easter Story. 32p. (J). (gr. k-3). tchr. ed. 16.95 *(978-0-8234-1384-3(5))* Holiday Hse., Inc.

—The Spider's Gift: A Ukrainian Christmas Story. 2005. (ENG.). 32p. (J). (gr. -1-3). 16.95 *(978-0-8234-1743-8(3))* Holiday Hse., Inc.

Noble, Trinka Hakes. The Christmas Spider's Miracle. Costanza, Stephen, illus. 2011. (ENG.). 32p. (YA). (gr. k-3). 16.95 *(978-1-58536-602-6(1))* Sleeping Bear Pr.

FOLKLORE—UNITED STATES

Alvarez O'Neill, Juan, illus. Grano a grano... Refranes Populares. 2005. (SPA.). (J). 8.95 *(978-0-8477-1554-1(X))* Univ. of Puerto Rico Pr.

American Mythology. 2013. (Mythology & Culture Worldwide Ser.). (ENG., Illus.). 128p. (J). (gr. 7-10). lib. bdg. 34.45 *(978-1-4205-0904-5(7),* Lucent Bks.) Cengage Gale.

Becker, Sandra. Paul Bunyan. 2003. (Folk Heroes Ser.). (Illus.). 24p. (J). lib. bdg. 24.45 *(978-1-59036-076-7(1))* Weigl Pubs., Inc.

Birenbaum, Barbara. Groundhog Phil's Message: Groundhog Legends & Lore. 2004. (Story Within a Story Ser.). (ENG., Illus.). 48p. (J). 21.00 *(978-0-935343-69-4(5))* Peartree (r).

Chase, Richard. Grandfather Tales: American-English Folk Tales. 2003. (ENG., Illus.). 240p. (J). (gr. 5-7). pap. 8.95 *(978-0-618-34690-5(2))* Houghton Mifflin Harcourt Publishing Co.

—The Jack Tales: Folk Tales from the Southern Appalachians. 2003. (ENG., Illus.). 240p. (J). (gr. 5-7). pap. 7.95 *(978-0-618-34692-9(9))* Houghton Mifflin Harcourt Publishing Co.

Davis, Donald. The Pig Who Went Home on Sunday: An Appalachian Folktale. Mazzucco, Jennifer, illus. 2005. (ENG.). 40p. (J). (gr. -1-3). 16.95 *(978-0-87483-571-7(2))* August Hse. Pubs., Inc.

—Southern Jack Tales. 2005. (ENG.). 217p. (J). (gr. 5-17). pap. 13.95 *(978-0-87483-500-7(3))* August Hse. Pubs., Inc.

DeSpain, Pleasant. Sweet Land of Story: Thirty-Six American Tales to Tell. (ENG., Illus.). 176p. (J). (gr. 3-7). 2006. 19.95 *(978-0-87483-569-4(0))* 2005. pap. 12.95 *(978-0-87483-600-4(X))* August Hse. Pubs., Inc.

Donohoe, Kitty & Warstler, Pasqua Cekola. Bunyan & Banjoes: Michigan Songs & Stories. Warstler, Pasqua Cekola, illus. 2004. (Illus.). 48p. (J). pap. 19.95 incl. audio compact disk *(978-1-882376-58-2(7))* Thunder Bay Pr.

Duvall, Deborah L. How Rabbit Lost His Tail: A Traditional Cherokee Legend. Jacob, Murv, illus. 2003. (Grandmother Stories Ser.: Vol. 3). (ENG.). 32p. (J). 16.95 *(978-0-8263-3010-9(X))* Univ. of New Mexico Pr.

Flood, Nancy Bo. The Navajo Year, Walk Through Many Seasons. Whitethorne, Billy, illus. 2006. (ENG.). 32p. (J). (gr. 4-7). 17.95 *(978-1-893354-06-7(7))* Salina Bookshelf Inc.

—The Navajo Year, Walk Through Many Seasons: Activities for Learning & Exploring. Ruffenach, Jessie E., ed. Whitethorne, Billy & Whitethorne, Bahe, Jr., illus. 2006. (ENG.). 48p. (J). (gr. 4-7). pap. 7.95 *(978-1-893354-98-2(9))* Salina Bookshelf Inc.

Garcia, Nasario. The Talking Lizard: New Mexico's Magic & Mystery. Montoya, Jeremy, illus. 2014. (SPA & ENG.). (J). pap. *(978-1-936744-36-7(8),* Rio Grande Bks.) LPD Pr.

Gleeson, Brian. Paul Bunyan, 1 vol. Meyerowitz, Rick, illus. 2004. (Rabbit Ears-A Classic Tale Ser.). (ENG.). 40p. (gr. k-5). 25.65 *(978-1-59197-767-4(3))* Spotlight.

—Pecos Bill, 1 vol. Raglin, Tim, illus. 2004. (Rabbit Ears-A Classic Tale Ser.). (ENG.). 36p. (gr. k-5). 25.65 *(978-1-59197-768-1(1))* Spotlight.

Gould, Jane H. John Henry. 2014. (Jr. Graphic American Legends Ser.). (Illus.). 24p. (J). (gr. 3-6). lib. bdg. 26.25 *(978-1-4777-7197-6(2),* PowerKids Pr.) Rosen Publishing Group, Inc., The.

Hamilton, Martha & Weiss, Mitch. The Hidden Feast: A Folktale from the American South. Tate, Don, illus. 2006. (ENG.). 32p. (J). (gr. k-3). 16.95 *(978-0-87483-758-2(8))* August Hse. Pubs., Inc.

Hamilton, Virginia. The People Could Fly: American Black Folktales. Dillon, Leo & Dillon, Diane, illus. 2009. (American Black Folktales Ser.). (ENG.). 192p. (J). (gr. k-12). 24.99 *(978-0-394-86925-4(7),* Knopf Bks. for Young Readers) Random Hse. Children's Bks.

—The People Could Fly: The Picture Book. Dillon, Leo & Dillon, Diane, illus. movie tie-in ed. 2004. (ENG.). 32p. (J). (gr. k-12). 16.95 *(978-0-375-82405-0(7),* Knopf Bks. for Young Readers) Random Hse. Children's Bks.

Harris, Joel Chandler. The Story of Brer Rabbit & the Wonderful Tar Baby, 1 vol. Drescher, Henrik, illus. 2004. (Rabbit Ears-A Classic Tale Ser.). (ENG.). 40p. (gr. k-5). 25.65 *(978-1-59197-761-2(4))* Spotlight.

Hurston, Zora Neale & Thomas, Joyce Carol. Lies & Other Tall Tales. Myers, Christopher, illus. 2005. (ENG.). 40p. (J). (gr. 1-5). 17.99 *(978-0-06-000655-6(2))* HarperCollins Pubs.

Ippisch, Hanneke. Spotted Bear: A Rocky Mountain Folktale. Ort, Kathleen, ed. Rappe-Flowers, Hedvig, illus. rev. ed. 49p. (J). (gr. 3-4). *(978-0-87842-387-3(7),* 326) Mountain Pr. Publishing Co., Inc.

Johnston, Marianne. Paul Bunyan. 2009. (American Legends Ser.). 24p. (gr. 3-3). 42.50 *(978-1-61511-385-9(1),* PowerKids Pr.) Rosen Publishing Group, Inc., The.

Keats, Ezra Jack. John Henry: An American Legend. 50th anniv. ed. 2014. (ENG., Illus.). 32p. (J). (gr. -1-2). 17.99 *(978-0-553-51307-3(9),* Knopf Bks. for Young Readers) Random Hse. Children's Bks.

—John Henry: an American Legend 50th Anniversary Edition. 2014. (ENG.). 32p. (J). (gr. -1-2). lib. bdg. 20.99 (978-0-553-51308-0(7), Knopf Bks. for Young Readers) Random Hse. Children's Bks.

Kellogg, Steven. Paul Bunyan. Kellogg, Steven, illus. 20th anniv. ed. 2004. (ENG., Illus.). 48p. (J). (gr. -1-3). pap. 6.99 (978-0-688-05800-5(0)) HarperCollins Pubs.

—Paul Bunyan. 2004. (J). (gr. k-3). 17.20 (978-0-8085-6790-5(X), Turtleback) Turtleback Bks.

Kessler, Brad. John Henry. Jackson, Barry, illus. 2005. (Rabbit Ears-A Classic Tale Ser.). 36p. (J). (gr. k-5). 25.65 (978-1-59197-764-3(9)) Spotlight.

Kessler, Brad & Harris, Joel Chandler. Brer Rabbit & Boss Lion. 1 vol. Mayer, Bill, illus. 2004. (Rabbit Ears-A Classic Tale Ser.). (ENG.). 40p. (gr. k-5). 25.65 (978-1-59197-760-5(6)) Spotlight.

Krensky, Stephen. John Henry. Oldroyd, Mark, illus. 2006. (On My Own Folklore Ser.). (ENG.). 48p. (gr. 2-4). lib. bdg. 25.26 (978-1-57505-887-0(1), Millbrook Pr.) Lerner Publishing Group.

—Mike Fink. 2008. pap. 40.95 (978-0-8225-9294-5(0)) Lerner Publishing Group.

—Paul Bunyan. 2008. pap. 40.95 (978-0-8225-9295-2(9)) Lerner Publishing Group.

—Pecos Bill. 2008. pap. 40.95 (978-0-8225-9296-9(7)) Lerner Publishing Group.

Lester, Julius. The Tales of Uncle Remus: The Adventures of Brer Rabbit. Pinkney, Jerry, illus. 2006. (Puffin Modern Classics Ser.). (ENG.). 160p. (J). (gr. 3-7). 7.99 (978-0-14-240720-2(8), Puffin Books) Penguin Young Readers Group.

McGill, Alice. Way up & over Everything. Daly, Jude, illus. 2008. (ENG.). 32p. (J). (gr. 2-5). 16.00 (978-0-618-38796-0(X)) Houghton Mifflin Harcourt Publishing Co.

Metaxas, Eric. Stormalong, 1 vol. Vanderbeek, Don, illus. 2004. (Rabbit Ears-A Classic Tale Ser.). (ENG.). 36p. (gr. k-5). 25.65 (978-1-59197-772-8(X)) Spotlight.

Moreno-Hinojosa, Hernan. The Ghostly Rider & Other Chilling Tales. 2003. 96p. (J). pap. 9.95 (978-1-55885-400-0(2), Piñata Books) Arte Publico Pr.

Petruccio, Steven James. American Legends & Tall Tales. 2011. (Dover Classic Stories Coloring Book Ser.). (ENG., Illus.). 32p. (J). (gr. 3-6). pap. 3.99 (978-0-486-47786-2(X)) Dover Pubns., Inc.

Reneaux, J. J. Cajun Folktales. 2005. (American Storytelling Ser.). (ENG.). 176p. (J). (gr. 4-17). pap. 12.95 (978-0-87483-282-2(9)) August Hse. Pubs., Inc.

Rigby Education Staff. Paul Bunyan: Jumbled Tumble. (gr. k-2). 21.00 (978-0-7635-2425-8(5)) Rigby Education.

Schomp, Virginia & Harris, Joel Chandler. Brer Rabbit & the Number-Nine Shoes. 2013. (Illus.). 32p. (J). (gr. 6-9). 28.50 (978-1-60870-439-2(4)) Cavendish Square Publishing.

Stoutenburg, Adrien. American Tall Tales. 2009. 9.00 (978-0-7848-0115-4(0), Everbind) Marco Bk. Co.

Sundance/Newbridge LLC Staff. Our American Folklore. 2004. (Reading PowerWorks Ser.). (gr. 1-3). 37.50 (978-0-7608-9795-9(6)); pap. 6.10 (978-0-7608-9796-6(4)) Sundance/Newbridge Educational Publishing.

Vitale, Ann E. Regional Folklore. 2004. (North American Folklore Ser.). (Illus.). 112p. (YA). (gr. 7-18). lib. bdg. 22.95 (978-1-59084-349-9(5)) Mason Crest.

Willey, Margaret. Clever Beatrice. Solomon, Heather M., illus. 2004. (ENG.). 40p. (J). (gr. -1-3). reprint ed. 7.99 (978-0-689-87068-2(X), Atheneum Bks. for Young Readers) Simon & Schuster Children's Publishing.

—Clever Beatrice & the Best Little Pony. Solomon, Heather M., illus. 2004. (ENG.). 40p. (J). (gr. -1-3). 18.99 (978-0-689-85339-5(4), Atheneum Bks. for Young Readers) Simon & Schuster Children's Publishing.

FOLKLORE—WALES

Jones, Jac, et al. Dianc. 2005. (WEL., Illus.). 40p. pap. 5.99 (978-1-84323-372-5(X)) Gomer Pr. GBR. Dist: Gomer Pr.

FOLKLORE—WEST INDIES

Weiss, Mitch & Hamilton, Martha. Rooster's Night Out. Hoffmire, Baird, illus. 2007. (Story Cove Ser.). (ENG.). 32p. (J). (gr. -1-3). pap. 3.95 (978-0-87483-826-8(6)) August Hse. Pubs., Inc.

FOLKWAYS

see Manners and Customs

FOOD

see also Beverages; Cooking; Diet; Farm Produce; Fruit; Markets; Nutrition; Nuts; Poultry; Vegetables; Vegetarianism; Vitamins

also names of foods, e.g. Bread, etc.

Aboff, Marcie & Lee, Sally. First Graphics: Myplate & Healthy Eating. Poling, Kyle & Swift, Gary, illus. 2011. (First Graphics: Myplate & Healthy Eating Ser.). (ENG.). 24p. (gr. 1-2). pap. 12.58 (978-1-4296-7171-2(8)); lib. bdg. 119.95 (978-1-4296-6094-5(5)); pap. 214.20 (978-1-4296-7172-9(6)) Capstone Press of Coughlan Cos.

Abrams, Pam. Now I Eat My ABC's. Wolf, Bruce, illus. 2004. (ENG.). 8p. (J). (gr. k — 1). bds. 7.99 (978-0-439-64942-1(0), Cartwheel Bks.) Scholastic, Inc.

Alexander's Enrichment Activties. 2006. (J). pap. 5.95 (978-0-9742806-6-0(6)) Heart to Heart Publishing, Inc.

All about Food Crops. 2017. (All about Food Crops Ser.). 24p. (gr. k-1). pap. 56.10 **(978-0-7660-8888-7(X))**; lib. bdg. 135.60 **(978-0-7660-8600-5(3))** Enslow Pubs., Inc.

Allman, Toney. Food in Schools. rev. ed. 2014. (Matters of Opinion Ser.). (ENG.). 64p. (J). (gr. 4-6). pap. 14.60 (978-1-60357-584-3(7)); lib. bdg. 27.93 (978-1-59953-604-0(8)) Norwood Hse. Pr.

Allsop, Marcus. We Like to Help Cook: Nos Gusta Ayudar a Cocinar. Iverson, Diane, illus. 2015. (ENG.). 32p. (J). (gr. -1-1). pap. 9.95 (978-1-890772-70-3(4)) Hohm Pr.

—We Like to Help Cook: Nos Gusta Ayudar a Cocinar. Iverson, Diane, illus. (We Like To Ser.). 32p. 2011. (SPA & ENG.). pap. 10.95 (978-1-935826-00-2(X)) 2011th alt. ed. 2012. (ENG.). pap. 9.95 (978-1-935826-05-7(0)) Kalindi Pr.

Allsop, Marcus & Iverson, Diane. Nos Gusta Ayudar a Cocinar: We Like to Help Cook. Iverson, Diane, illus. 2009. (SPA & ENG., Illus.). (J). pap. (978-1-890772-97-0(6)) Hohm Pr.

Aloian, Molly. Eating Green. 2013. (ENG., Illus.). 24p. (J). (978-0-7787-0263-4(4)); pap. (978-0-7787-0277-1(4)) Crabtree Publishing Co.

Apte, Sunita. Eating Green. 2009. (Going Green Ser.). (Illus.). 32p. (YA). (gr. 3-6). lib. bdg. 25.27 (978-1-59716-965-3(X)) Bearport Publishing Co., Inc.

Ayer, Paula. Foodprints: The Story of What We Eat. 2015. (ENG., Illus.). 208p. (YA). (gr. 6-12). pap. 16.95 (978-1-55451-718-3(4), 9781554517183) Annick Pr., Ltd. CAN. Dist: Publishers Group West (PGW).

Ayer, Paula & Banyard, Antonia. Eat Up! An Infographic Exploration of Food. Wuthrich, Belle, illus. 2017. (Visual Exploration Ser.). (ENG.). 72p. (gr. 3-7). 22.95 (978-1-55451-884-5(9)) Annick Pr., Ltd. CAN. Dist: Publishers Group West (PGW).

—Eat Up! An Infographic Exploration of Food. Wuthrich, Belle, illus. 2017. (Visual Exploration Ser.). (ENG.). 72p. (gr. 3-7). pap. 12.95 (978-1-55451-883-8(0)) Annick Pr., Ltd. CAN. Dist: Publishers Group West (PGW).

AZ Books Staff. What Do I Eat? Sisoj, Natalja, ed. 2012. (Peek-A-Boo Ser.). (ENG.). 10p. (J). (— 1). bds. 10.95 (978-1-61889-115-0(4)) AZ Bks. LLC.

Ball, Jacqueline A. Food Creations: From Hot Dogs to Ice Cream Cones. 2006. (Which Came First? Ser.). (Illus.). 32p. (YA). (gr. 3-6). lib. bdg. 25.27 (978-1-59716-130-5(6)) Bearport Publishing Co., Inc.

Ballard, Carol. Food Safety. 2009. (What If We Do Nothing? Ser.). 48p. (YA). (gr. 4-7). lib. bdg. 31.00 (978-1-4339-1982-4(6)) Stevens, Gareth Publishing LLLP.

Banzoff, Chris. Critical World Issues: Food Technology. Vol. 16. 2016. (Critical World Issues Ser.: Vol. 16). (ENG., Illus.). 112p. (J). (gr. 7-12). 25.95 (978-1-4222-3654-3(4)) Mason Crest.

Barker, David M. Organic Foods. 2016. (Growing Green Ser.). (ENG., Illus.). 64p. (J). (gr. 6-8). lib. bdg. 34.65 (978-1-4677-9391-9(4)); 51.99 (978-1-4677-9712-2(X), Lerner Pubns.) Lerner Publishing Group.

Bartos, Judeen. Food Safety. 2011. (At Issue Ser.). (ENG.). 128p. (gr. 12-12). lib. bdg. 39.40 (978-0-7377-5149-9(5)); pap. 27.80 (978-0-7377-5150-5(9)) Cengage Gale. (Greenhaven Pr., Inc.).

BeachHouse Publishing. Noodles for Baby. Jamie, Meckel, illus. 2011. (ENG.). 16p. (J). (gr. -1-1). bds. 7.95 (978-1-933067-40-7(3)) Beachhouse Publishing, LLC.

Beaver, Simon. Slice by Slice: The Story of Pizza. 2014. (ENG.). 24p. (J). pap. 9.50 (978-1-107-65037-4(2)) Cambridge Univ. Pr.

Benduhn, Tea. Meat & Beans. 2007. (Find Out about Food Ser.). 24p. (gr. k-3). pap. 8.15 (978-0-8368-8259-9(8)); (Illus.). lib. bdg. 22.00 (978-0-8368-8252-0(0)) Stevens, Gareth Publishing LLLP. (Weekly Reader Leveled Readers).

—Meat & Beans (Carne y Frijoles) 2007. (Find Out about Food/ Conoce la comida Ser.). (SPA & ENG.). 24p. (gr. k-3). pap. 8.15 (978-0-8368-8463-0(9), Weekly Reader Leveled Readers) Stevens, Gareth Publishing LLLP.

—Meat & Beans/Carne y Legumbres. 2007. (Find Out about Food/Conoce la Comida Ser.). (SPA & ENG., Illus.). 24p. (gr. k-3). lib. bdg. 22.00 (978-0-8368-8456-2(6), Weekly Reader Leveled Readers) Stevens, Gareth Publishing LLLP.

—Oils (Aceites) 2007. (Find Out about Food/ Conoce la comida Ser.). (SPA & ENG.). 24p. (gr. k-3). pap. 8.15 (978-0-8368-8465-4(5), Weekly Reader Leveled Readers) Stevens, Gareth Publishing LLLP.

—Oils/Aceites. 2007. (Find Out about Food/Conoce la Comida Ser.). (SPA & ENG., Illus.). 24p. (gr. k-3). lib. bdg. 22.00 (978-0-8368-8458-6(2), Weekly Reader Leveled Readers) Stevens, Gareth Publishing LLLP.

Berendes, Mary. Food/la Comida. Petelinsek, Kathleen, illus. 2007. (WordBooks/Libros de Palabras Ser.). (SPA & ENG.). 24p. (J). (gr. k-3). 25.64 (978-1-59296-798-8(1), 201092) Child's World, Inc., The.

Berger, Melvin & Berger, Gilda. Healthy Eating. 2007. (Now I Know Ser.). (Illus.). 32p. (J). (978-0-439-02446-4(3)) Scholastic, Inc.

Berman, Ron. Food. 2012. (Urban Entrepreneurs Ser.). (ENG., Illus.). 40p. (gr. 3-8). pap. 9.95 (978-1-61570-517-7(1)) Scobre Pr. Corp.

Best, B. J. Flour to Pasta. 2016. (How It Is Made Ser.). 24p. (J). pap. 8.22 (978-1-5026-2126-9(6)) Cavendish Square Publishing.

Bickerstaff, Linda. Nutrition Sense: Counting Calories, Figuring Out Fats, & Eating Balanced Meals. (Library of Nutrition Ser.). 48p. 2009. (gr. 5-8). 53.00 (978-1-60853-773-0(0), Rosen Reference) 2008. (Illus.). (YA). (gr. 8-12). lib. bdg. 26.50 (978-1-4042-1872-7(6), Rosen Reference) 2008. (ENG., Illus.). (gr. 5-8). per. 11.75 (978-1-4042-1636-5(7)) 2004. (Illus.). (J). lib. bdg. 26.50 (978-1-4042-0299-3(4)) Rosen Publishing Group, Inc., The.

The Big Picture: Food. 2011. (Big Picture: Food Ser.). (ENG.). 24p. (gr. 1-2). pap. 166.80 (978-1-4296-6736-4(2), First Facts) Capstone Press of Coughlan Cos.

Blaxland, Wendy. French Food. 2011. (I Can Cook ! Ser.). 32p. (YA). (gr. 2-5). 28.50 (978-1-59920-669-2(2)) Black Rabbit Bks.

—Mexican Food. 2011. (I Can Cook ! Ser.). 32p. (YA). (gr. 2-5). 28.50 (978-1-59920-668-4(4)) Black Rabbit Bks.

—Middle-Eastern Food. 2011. (I Can Cook ! Ser.). 32p. (YA). (gr. 2-5). 28.50 (978-1-59920-672-1(2)) Black Rabbit Bks.

Bledsoe, Michele. Kitty Treats Cookbook. Rupert, Chris et al, illus. 2010. (ENG.). 15p. (gr. 6). bds. 10.95 (978-0-9753883-8-9(X)) Come & Get It Publishing.

Bolchazy, Marie Carducci. Quis Me Amat?/Who Loves Me? 2003. (I Am Reading Latin Ser.). (ENG & LAT., Illus.). 64p. (J). (gr. k-3). 10.00 (978-0-86516-541-0(6)) Bolchazy-Carducci Pubs.

Bone, Emily. Look Inside Food IR. 2015. (Look Inside Board Bks.). (ENG.). 14p. (J). (gr. k-5). 14.99 (978-0-7945-3498-1(8), Usborne) EDC Publishing.

Boothroyd, Jennifer. Foods. 2006. (First Step Nonfiction Ser.). (Illus.). 8p. (J). pap. 3.95 (978-0-8225-5727-2(4), Lerner Pubns.) Lerner Publishing Group.

—What's on My Plate? 2016. (Lightning Bolt Books — Healthy Eating Ser.). (ENG., Illus.). 32p. (J). (gr. 1-3). 26.65 (978-1-4677-9470-1(8), Lerner Pubns.) Lerner Publishing Group.

—What's on My Plate? Choosing from the Five Food Groups. 2016. (Lightning Bolt Books — Healthy Eating Ser.). (ENG., Illus.). 32p. (gr. 1-3). 39.99 (978-1-5124-1669-5(X), Lerner Digital); (J). (gr. 2-3). E-Book 39.99 (978-1-4677-9672-9(7), 9781467796729, Lerner Pubns.) Lerner Publishing Group.

Botnick, Julie & Linden, Becca. Min Ha'aretz: Making Meaning from Our Food. 2016. (978-0-87441-938-2(7)) Behrman Hse., Inc.

Brasch, Nicolas. The Foods We Eat. 2010. (Science Behind Ser.). 32p. lib. bdg. 28.50 (978-1-59920-560-1(2)) Black Rabbit Bks.

Brash, Lorna. Professor Cook's Dynamite Dinners. 2013. (Professor Cook's... Ser.). 32p. (J). (gr. 4-12). pap. 7.95 (978-1-4644-0547-1(6)); (Illus.). lib. bdg. 23.94 (978-0-7660-4301-5(0)) Enslow Pubs., Inc.

—Professor Cook's Mind-Blowing Baking. 2013. (Professor Cook's... Ser.). (Illus.). 32p. (J). lib. bdg. 23.94 (978-0-7660-4303-9(7)) Enslow Pubs., Inc.

—Professor Cook's Smashing Snacks. 2013. (Professor Cook's... Ser.). 32p. (J). lib. bdg. 23.94 (978-0-7660-4304-6(5)); (gr. 4-12). pap. 7.95 (978-1-4644-0553-2(0)) Enslow Pubs., Inc.

Bredeson, Carmen. Weird but True Food. 2011. (Weird but True Science Ser.). (Illus.). 24p. (J). (gr. k-18). pap. 7.95 (978-1-59845-367-6(X), Enslow Elementary); (gr. 5-9). lib. bdg. 22.60 (978-0-7660-3866-0(1)) Enslow Pubs., Inc.

Bright, Michael. From Field to Plate. 2016. (Source to Resource Ser.). (ENG., Illus.). 32p. (J). (gr. 3-6). (978-0-7787-2705-7(X)) Crabtree Publishing Co.

Bullard, Lisa. Brown Food Fun [Ars Scribendi (Netherlands)]. 2010. (Eat Your Colors Ser.). 32p. lib. bdg. 2.50 (978-1-4296-5231-5(4), Aplus Bks.) Capstone Press of Coughlan Cos.

—Green Food Fun [Ars Scribendi (Netherlands)]. 2010. (Eat Your Colors Ser.). 32p. lib. bdg. 2.50 (978-1-4296-5232-2(2), Aplus Bks.) Capstone Press of Coughlan Cos.

—My Food, Your Food. Schneider, Christine, illus. 2015. (Cloverleaf Books (tm) — Alike & Different Ser.). (ENG.). 24p. (gr. k-2). (J). lib. bdg. 23.99 (978-1-4677-4903-9(6)); pap. 6.99 (978-1-4677-6031-7(5)) Lerner Publishing Group. (Millbrook Pr.).

—Orange Food Fun [Ars Scribendi (Netherlands)]. 2010. (Eat Your Colors Ser.). 32p. lib. bdg. 2.50 (978-1-4296-5233-9(0), Aplus Bks.) Capstone Press of Coughlan Cos.

—Red Food Fun, 1 vol. 2006. (Eat Your Colors Ser.). (ENG., Illus.). 32p. (gr. 1-2). 27.32 (978-0-7368-5383-5(9), Aplus Bks.) Capstone Press of Coughlan Cos.

—Red Food Fun [Ars Scribendi (Netherlands)]. 2010. (Eat Your Colors Ser.). 32p. lib. bdg. 2.50 (978-1-4296-5234-6(9), Aplus Bks.) Capstone Press of Coughlan Cos.

—White Food Fun [Ars Scribendi (Netherlands)]. 2010. (Eat Your Colors Ser.). 32p. lib. bdg. 2.50 (978-1-4296-5235-3(7), Aplus Bks.) Capstone Press of Coughlan Cos.

—Yellow Food Fun [Ars Scribendi (Netherlands)]. 2010. (Eat Your Colors Ser.). 32p. lib. bdg. 2.50 (978-1-4296-5236-0(5), Aplus Bks.) Capstone Press of Coughlan Cos.

Burgan, Michael & Bliss, John. Processing Your Food, 1 vol. 2011. (Ethics of Food Ser.). (ENG.). 56p. (gr. 6-6). 34.65 (978-1-4329-5103-0(3)) Heinemann-Raintree.

Butler, Daphne. What Happens When Food Cooks? 2004. (Illus.). 31p. (J). (gr. k-4). reprint ed. 10.00 (978-0-7567-7561-2(2)) DIANE Publishing Co.

Butterfield, Moira. Food Around the World. 2016. (Children Like Us Ser.). (ENG., Illus.). 32p. (J). (gr. 3-3). pap. 10.58 (978-1-5026-0838-3(3)) Cavendish Square Publishing.

Butterworth, Chris. How Did That Get in My Lunchbox? The Story of Food. Gaggiotti, Lucia, illus. 2013. (Exploring the Everyday Ser.). (ENG.). 32p. (J). (gr. k-3). 5.99 (978-0-7636-6503-6(7)) Candlewick Pr.

Butterworth, Christine. How Did That Get in My Lunchbox? The Story of Food. Gaggiotti, Lucia, illus. 2011. (ENG.). 32p. (J). (gr. k-3). 12.99 (978-0-7636-5005-6(6)) Candlewick Pr.

Byers, Ann. Fruits & Vegetables: From the Garden to Your Table. 2012. (Truth about the Food Supply Ser.). (ENG., Illus.). 48p. (J). (gr. 5-8). lib. bdg. 27.95 (978-1-4488-6799-8(1), Rosen Reference) Rosen Publishing Group, Inc., The.

Cain, Marie Mowery. Something to Snack On. 2013. (Big Books, Blue Ser.). (ENG & SPA., Illus.). 16p. pap. 33.00 (978-1-59246-023-6(2)) Big Books, by George!

Caldicott, Chris. World Food Alphabet. 2015. (ENG., Illus.). 32p. (J). (gr. k-3). pap. 9.99 (978-1-84780-653-6(8), Frances Lincoln) Quarto Publishing Group UK GBR. Dist: Hachette Bk. Group.

Canetti, Yanitzia. Tasty Colors/Colores de Sabores: A World of Color. 2010. (SPA & ENG.). 24p. (J). pap. 6.99 (978-1-59835-270-2(9), BrickHouse Education) Cambridge BrickHouse, Inc.

Cardenas, Ernesto A. I Will Grow Strong & Healthy! 2009. 19.95 (978-1-60698-008-8(4)); pap. 3.95 (978-1-60698-006-4(8)) Milo Educational Bks. & Resources.

Carle, Eric. My Very First Book of Food. Carle, Eric, illus. 2007. (ENG., Illus.). 18p. (J). (gr. -1 — 1). bds. 5.99 (978-0-399-24747-7(5), Philomel Bks.) Penguin Young Readers Group.

Centore, Michael. Fiber. 2017. (J). **(978-1-4222-3735-9(4))** Mason Crest.

—Organic Foods. 2017. (J). **(978-1-4222-3740-3(0))** Mason Crest.

—Protein. 2017. (J). **(978-1-4222-3741-0(9))** Mason Crest.

—Salt. 2017. (J). **(978-1-4222-3742-7(7))** Mason Crest.

Cesa, Irene, ed. Chemistry of Food, 28 vols. 2003. (ChemTopic Labs Ser.: 23). (Illus.). 96p. (YA). pap. 11.95 (978-1-877991-91-2(0)) Flinn Scientific, Inc.

Clark, Katie. Balanced Meals. 2013. (Healthy Eating with Myplate Ser.). (ENG.). 24p. (J). (gr. 1-4). 28.50 (978-1-62323-599-4(5), 206401) Child's World, Inc., The.

Cleary, Brian P. Black Beans & Lamb, Poached Eggs & Ham: What Is in the Meat & Beans Group? Goneau, Martin, illus. 2011. (Food Is CATegorical Ser.). (ENG.). 32p. (gr. k-3). pap. 7.95 (978-0-7613-6387-3(4)) Lerner Publishing Group.

—Macaroni & Rice & Bread by the Slice: What Is in the Grains Group? Goneau, Martin, illus. 2011. (Food Is CATegorical Ser.). (ENG.). 32p. (gr. k-3). pap. 7.95 (978-0-7613-6386-6(6)) Lerner Publishing Group.

Cleary, Brian P. & Goneau, Martin. Black Beans & Lamb, Poached Eggs & Ham: What Is in the Meat & Beans Group? 2011. (Food Is CATegorical Ser.). pap. 45.32 (978-0-7613-8349-9(2), Millbrook Pr.) Lerner Publishing Group.

—Macaroni & Rice & Bread by the Slice: What Is in the Grains Group? 2011. (Food Is CATegorical Ser.). pap. 45.32 (978-0-7613-8351-2(4), Millbrook Pr.) Lerner Publishing Group.

Cleary, Brian P. & Nelson, Jennifer K. Black Beans & Lamb, Poached Eggs & Ham: What Is in the Meat & Beans Group? Goneau, Martin, illus. 2010. (Food Is CATegorical Ser.). (ENG.). 32p. (gr. k-3). lib. bdg. 25.26 (978-1-58013-591-7(9)) Lerner Publishing Group.

Clissold, Caroline. Food Around the World. 2007. (Trackers-Math Ser.). (gr. 2-5). pap. 5.00 (978-1-59055-910-9(X)) Pacific Learning, Inc.

Cobb, Vicki. Junk Food. 2008. pap. 52.95 (978-0-8225-9448-2(X)) Lerner Publishing Group.

—Junk Food. Gold, Michael, photos by. 2005. (Where's the Science Here? Ser.). (ENG., Illus.). 48p. (gr. 3-5). 23.93 (978-0-7613-2773-8(8), Millbrook Pr.) Lerner Publishing Group.

—Science Experiments You Can Eat. Carpenter, Tad, illus. 2016. 256p. (J). (gr. 3-7). pap. 9.99 (978-0-06-237729-6(9)) HarperCollins Pubs.

Collins, Stan. Food Signs. 2003. (ENG.). 10p. (gr. k-2). spiral bd. 19.95 (978-1-930820-36-4(4)) Garlic Pr.

Community Connections: How Do We Live Together?, 8 vols. Incl. How Do We Live Together? Coyotes. Marsico, Katie. lib. bdg. 25.64 (978-1-60279-621-8(1), 200325); How Do We Live Together? Deer. Raatma, Lucia. lib. bdg. 25.64 (978-1-60279-618-8(1), 200326); How Do We Live Together? Hawks. Marsico, Katie. lib. bdg. 25.64 (978-1-60279-624-9(6), 200327); How Do We Live Together? Mountain Lions. Raatma, Lucia. lib. bdg. 25.64 (978-1-60279-625-6(4), 200328); How Do We Live Together? Rabbits. Marsico, Katie. lib. bdg. 25.64 (978-1-60279-622-5(X), 200329); How Do We Live Together? Raccoons. Raatma, Lucia. lib. bdg. 25.64 (978-1-60279-619-5(X), 200330); How Do We Live Together? Snakes. Raatma, Lucia. lib. bdg. 25.64 (978-1-60279-620-1(3), 200331); How Do We Live Together? Turtles. Marsico, Katie. lib. bdg. 25.64 (978-1-60279-623-2(8), 200332); (gr. 2-5). 24p. 2010. Set lib. bdg. 143.60 (978-1-60279-617-1(3), 200357) Cherry Lake Publishing.

CQ Products Staff. Fake-Out Food: Wacky Treats to Fool Your Friends! 2010. (ENG.). 64p. spiral bd. 12.00 (978-1-56383-383-0(2)) G & R Publishing.

Crawford, Greg. Super Hero Foods & the Abc's of Nutrition. 2013. 108p. pap. 21.95 (978-0-9890227-0-5(6)) It's a Lifestyle Fitness.

Crewe, Sabrina. In Your Food. 2010. (Under the Microscope Ser.). 32p. (gr. 2-4). 30.00 (978-1-60413-824-5(6), Chelsea Clubhouse) Facts On File, Inc.

Crockett, Kyle A. Navigating Your School Cafeteria & Convenience Store. Borus, Joshua, ed. 2013. (Understanding Nutrition: a Gateway to Physical & Mental Health Ser.: 11). (Illus.). 48p. (J). (gr. 5-18). 19.95 (978-1-4222-2882-1(7)) Mason Crest.

—The Numbers: Calories, BMI, & Portion Sizes. Borus, Joshua, ed. 2013. (Understanding Nutrition: a Gateway to Physical & Mental Health Ser.: 11). (Illus.). 48p. (J). (gr. 5-18). 19.95 (978-1-4222-2883-8(5)) Mason Crest.

Currie, Stephen. Junk Food. 2008. (21st Century Skills Library: Health at Risk Ser.). (ENG., Illus.). 32p. (gr. 4-8). lib. bdg. 28.50 (978-1-60279-284-5(4), 200133) Cherry Lake Publishing.

Daste, Larry. Fast Food Stickers. 2004. (Dover Little Activity Books Stickers Ser.). (ENG., Illus.). 4p. (J). (gr. -1-5). pap. 1.50 (978-0-486-43307-3(2)) Dover Pubns., Inc.

Davies, Monika. Surprising Things We Eat. 2017. (J). pap. 10.99 **(978-1-4938-3637-6(4))** Teacher Created Materials, Inc.

Dawson, Emily C. Cooking. 2010. (Everyday Science Ser.). 24p. (J). (gr. k-3). 25.65 (978-1-60753-020-6(1)) Amicus Publishing.

A Day at the Playground. 2004. (J). pap. 12.95 (978-1-59526-606-4(2)) Aeon Publishing Inc.

DePietro, Frank. Latino American Cuisine. 2012. (Illus.). 64p. (J). pap. (978-1-4222-2337-6(X)) Mason Crest.

—Latino American Cuisine. Limón, José E., ed. 2012. (Hispanic Americans: Major Minority Ser.). (Illus.). 64p. (J). (gr. 4). 22.95 (978-1-4222-2320-8(5)) Mason Crest.

Desrocher, Jack, illus. Health Zone, 6 vols., Set. Incl. Eat Right! How You Can Make Good Food Choices. Doeden, Matt. lib. bdg. 30.60 (978-0-8225-7552-8(3)); Keep Your Cool! What You Should Know about Stress. Leder, Jane Mersky & Donovan, Sandy. lib. bdg. 30.60 (978-0-8225-7555-9(8)); Stay Clear! What You Should Know about Skin Care. Donovan, Sandy. lib. bdg. 30.60 (978-0-8225-7550-4(7)); Stay Fit! How You Can Get in Shape. Doeden, Matt. (YA). lib. bdg. 30.60 (978-0-8225-7553-5(1)); Stay Safe! How You Can Keep Out of Harm's Way. Nelson, Sara Kirsten. lib. bdg. 30.60 (978-0-8225-7551-1(5)); Take a Stand! What You Can Do about Bullying. Golus, Carrie. (YA). lib. bdg. 30.60 (978-0-8225-7554-2(X)); (Illus.). 64p. (gr. 4-7). 2008. 2008. Set lib. bdg. 183.60 (978-0-8225-7549-8(3)) Lerner Publishing Group.

Dickmann, Nancy. Los Alimentos de la Granja. 2011. (Mundo de la Granja Ser.). 24p. (gr. -1-1). (SPA & ENG.). 22.65 (978-1-4329-5308-9(7)); (ENG & SPA.). pap. 6.29 (978-1-4329-5315-7(X)) Heinemann-Raintree. (Bellota).

—Food from Farms, 1 vol. 2010. (World of Farming Ser.). (ENG.). 24p. (gr. -1-k). pap. 6.29 (978-1-4329-3943-4(2), Acorn) Heinemann-Raintree.

Dingles, Molly. Crescent Kitchen. Brodie, Neale, illus. 2006. (Community of Shapes Ser.). (J). (978-1-59646-049-2(0)) Dingles & Co.

Dinner: KinderWords Individual Title, 6 packs. (Kinderstarters Ser.). 8p. (gr. -1-1). 21.00 (978-0-7635-8702-4(8)) Rigby Education.

Dolbear, Emily. How Did That Get to My Table? Pumpkin Pie. 2009. (Community Connections: How Did That Get to My Table? Ser.). (ENG.). 24p. (gr. 2-5). lib. bdg. 25.64 (978-1-60279-472-6(3), 200268) Cherry Lake Publishing.

Dorling Kindersley Publishing Staff. Mealtime. 2012. (Baby Touch & Feel Ser.). (ENG.). 14p. (J). (gr. -1 — 1). bds. 5.99 (978-1-4654-0161-8(X), DK Children) Dorling Kindersley Publishing, Inc.

Dosier, Susan & Gunderson, Mary. Exploring History Through Food. 2016. (Exploring History Through Food Ser.). (ENG.).

EFG

32p. (gr. 3-4). 109.28 (978-1-5157-2369-1(0), Fact Finders) Capstone Press of Coughlan Cos.
Dunn-Georgiou, Elisha. Everything You Need to Know about Organic Foods. (Need to Know Library). 64p. 2009. (gr. 5-5). 58.50 (978-1-60854-079-2(0)) 2005. (Illus.). (YA). (gr. 4-6). lib. bdg. 31.95 (978-0-8239-3551-2(5)) Rosen Publishing Group, Inc., The.
Dyson, Nikki, illus. 1,000 Things to Eat. 2015. (1,000 Pictures Ser.). (ENG.). 34p. (J). (gr. k-5). 14.99 (978-0-7945-3406-6(6), Usborne) EDC Publishing.
Eamer, Claire. The World in Your Lunch Box: The Wacky History & Weird Science of Everyday Foods. Boothroyd, Sa, illus. 2012. (ENG.). 128p. (J). (gr. 2-18). 3rd ed. 22.95 (978-1-55451-393-2(6), 9781554513932) 4th ed. pap. 14.95 (978-1-55451-392-5(8), 9781554513925) Annick Pr., Ltd. CAN. Dist: Publishers Group West (PGW).
Eck, Kristin. Hide-and-Seek Food. 2004. (Hide-And-Seek Books). (Illus.). 16p. (J). lib. bdg. 21.25 (978-1-4042-2703-3(2), PowerKids Pr.) Rosen Publishing Group, Inc., The.
—Hide & Seek Food. 2009. (Tough Toddler Bks). 16p. (gr. k-k). 42.50 (978-1-60854-570-4(9), PowerKids Pr.) Rosen Publishing Group, Inc., The.
Elton, Sarah. Starting from Scratch: What You Should Know about Food & Cooking, 0 vols. Kulak, Jeff & Owlkids Books Inc. Staff, illus. 2014. (ENG.). 96p. (J). (gr. 4-6). 18.95 (978-1-926973-96-8(8), Owlkids) Owlkids Bks. Inc. CAN. Dist: Publishers Group West (PGW).
Endres, Hollie J. Healthy Foods, 6 vols., Set. 2004. (Letter Bks.). (ENG.). 8p. (gr. k-1). pap. 29.70 (978-0-7368-4115-3(6), Letter Bks.) Capstone Press of Coughlan Cos.
—The Letter Cc Set: Food, 6 vols. 2004. (Letter Bks.). (ENG.). 8p. (gr. k-1). pap. 29.70 (978-0-7368-4102-3(4), Letter Bks.) Capstone Press of Coughlan Cos.
Etingoff, Kim. Decisions, Decisions: Vegetarianism, Breakfasts, & Beyond. Borus, Joshua, ed. 2013. (Understanding Nutrition: a Gateway to Physical & Mental Health Ser.: 11). (Illus.). 48p. (J). (gr. 5-18). 19.95 (978-1-4222-2875-3(4)) Mason Crest.
—Healthy Fast Foods. Borus, Joshua, ed. 2013. (Understanding Nutrition: a Gateway to Physical & Mental Health Ser.). (Illus.). 48p. (J). (gr. 5-18). pap. 9.95 (978-1-4222-2988-0(2)) Mason Crest.
—How to Read Food Product Labels. Borus, Joshua, ed. 2013. (Illus.). 48p. (J). (gr. 5-18). pap. 9.95 (978-1-4222-2993-4(9)); (Understanding Nutrition: a Gateway to Physical & Mental Health Ser.: 11). 19.95 (978-1-4222-2880-7(0)) Mason Crest.
Falk, Laine. This Is the Way We Eat Our Food. 2010. (Rise & Shine Ser.). (ENG.). 24p. (C). (gr. 1-2). pap. 11.95 (978-0-531-21439-8(7)) National Geographic School Publishing, Inc.
—This Is the Way We Eat Our Food. 2009. (Scholastic News Nonfiction Readers Ser.). (ENG.). 24p. (J). (gr. 1-2). lib. bdg. 22.00 (978-0-531-21339-1(0)) Scholastic Library Publishing.
Fandel, Jennifer, et al. Louis Pasteur & Pasteurization. Wilson, Keith, illus. 2007. (Inventions & Discovery Ser.). (ENG.). 32p. (gr. 3-4). pap. 8.10 (978-0-7368-7896-8(3), Graphic Library) Capstone Press of Coughlan Cos.
—Louis Pasteur & Pasteurization, 1 vol. Wilson, Keith et al, illus. 2007. (Inventions & Discovery Ser.). (ENG.). 32p. (gr. 3-4). 30.65 (978-0-7368-6844-0(5), Graphic Library) Capstone Press of Coughlan Cos.
Feldman, Jean R. & Karapetkova, Holly. Fraction Pizza (Tune, He's Got the Whole World in His Hands) 2010. (ENG., Illus.). 12p. (gr. -1-k). 9.95 (978-1-61590-222-4(8)) Rourke Educational Media.
Felix, Rebecca. Patterns in Food. 2015. (21st Century Basic Skills Library: Patterns All Around Ser.). (ENG., Illus.). 24p. (J). (gr. k-3). pap. 12.79 (978-1-63188-936-3(2), 206005) Cherry Lake Publishing.
Field, Jon Eben. Kitchen Chemistry. 2011. (Chemtastrophe! Ser.). (ENG.). 32p. (J). (gr. 5-8). pap. (978-0-7787-5303-2(4)); lib. bdg. (978-0-7787-5286-8(0)) Crabtree Publishing Co.
Fiol, Maria A., tr. Eating the Rainbow (Spanish/English), 1 vol. 2010. (Libro de Comidas de Colores/Colorful Food Bks.). (ENG., Illus.). 16p. (J). bds. 6.95 (978-1-59572-203-4(3)) Star Bright Bks., Inc.
—Que Sabroso Arco Iris!, 1 vol. 2010. (Libro de Comidas de Colores Ser.).Tr. of Eating the Rainbow. (SPA., Illus.). 32p. (J). bds. 6.95 (978-1-59572-225-6(4)) Star Bright Bks., Inc.
Flaherty, Liz. Cooking up a Storm. 2007. (Action Numeracy Middle Primary Ser.). 32p. pap. 9.95 (978-0-86431-670-7(4)) ACER Pr. AUS. Dist: ISBS Publisher Services.
Fleisher, Paul. Forest Food Webs. 2007. (Early Bird Food Webs Ser.). (Illus.). 48p. (J). (gr. 2-5). lib. bdg. 26.60 (978-0-8225-6729-5(6), Lerner Pubns.) Lerner Publishing Group.
Fletcher, Patricia. Kelp: The Underwater Forest! 2016. (World's Weirdest Plants Ser.). 00024p. (J). pap. 8.15 **(978-1-4824-5614-1(1))** Stevens, Gareth Publishing LLLP.
Fontes, Ron. Proteins. 2005. (Rookie Read-About Health Ser.). (ENG., Illus.). 32p. (J). (gr. k-2). lib. bdg. 20.50 (978-0-516-23647-6(4), Children's Pr.) Scholastic Library Publishing.
Food. 2010. (Experimenting with Everyday Science Ser.). (Illus.). 168p. (gr. 6-12). 35.00 (978-1-60413-173-4(X), Chelsea Hse.) Facts On File, Inc.
Food - Set1: Outside-Inside-Name. 2004. (J). spiral bd. 23.40 (978-0-9770248-1-0(4)) Sidedoor Publishing LLC.
Food Fit for a King: 3-in-1 Package. (Sails Literacy Ser.). 24p. (gr. 2-18). 57.00 (978-0-7578-3215-4(6)) Rigby Education.
Food Fit for a King: Big Book Only. (Sails Literacy Ser.). 24p. (gr. 2-18). 27.00 (978-0-7635-6997-6(6)) Rigby Education.
Food Friends: How to Make Friends Out of Food. 2016. (J). (978-0-87659-713-2(4)) Gryphon Hse., Inc.
Food Groups. 2004. (Illus.). lib. bdg. 7.95 (978-0-8225-4787-7(2)) Lerner Publishing Group.
The Food Journey: Individual Title Six-Packs. (gr. k-1). 23.00 (978-0-7635-9045-1(2)) Rigby Education.
Foods of the World, 6 vols. (Book2WebTM Ser.). (gr. 4-8). 36.50 (978-0-322-02985-9(6)) Wright Group/McGraw-Hill.
Forman, Lillian E. Genetically Modified Foods, 1 vol. 2009. (Essential Viewpoints Set 4 Ser.). (ENG., Illus.). 112p. (J). (gr. 6-12). lib. bdg. 35.64 (978-1-60453-531-0(8)) ABDO Publishing Co.
Franchino, Vicky. Genetically Modified Foods. 2008. (21st Century Skills Library: Global Perspectives Ser.). (ENG.). 32p. (gr. 4-8). lib. bdg. 28.50 (978-1-60279-132-9(5), 200098) Cherry Lake Publishing.
Freedman, Jeri. Genetically Modified Food: How Biotechnology Is Changing What We Eat. 2009. (Science & Society Ser.). 64p. (gr. 5-6). 58.50 (978-1-60853-008-3(6)); (Illus.). (YA). (gr. 7-12). lib. bdg. 31.95 (978-1-4358-5025-5(4)) Rosen Publishing Group, Inc., The.
Fun Food Trivia. 2013. (Ultimate Trivia Challenge Ser.). 32p. (J). (gr. 2-5). pap. 63.00 (978-1-4339-8294-1(3)) Stevens, Gareth Publishing LLLP.
Fun Foods for Cool Cooks. 2016. (Fun Foods for Cool Cooks Ser.). (ENG.). 32p. (gr. 3-4). lib. bdg. 139.95 (978-1-5157-4031-5(5), Snap Bks.) Capstone Press of Coughlan Cos.
Furgang, Adam. Salty & Sugary Snacks: The Incredibly Disgusting Story. 2011. (Incredibly Disgusting Food Ser.). (Illus.). 48p. (YA). pap. 11.75 (978-1-4488-2283-6(1), Rosen Reference); (gr. 5-9). lib. bdg. 29.25 (978-1-4488-1267-7(4)) Rosen Publishing Group, Inc., The.
Gaarder-Juntti, Oona. Shapes in Food, 1 vol. 2013. (Shapes Everywhere Ser.). (ENG.). 24p. (gr. k-4). lib. bdg. 25.65 (978-1-61783-413-4(0), Super SandCastle) ABDO Publishing Co.
—What in the World Is Green Food?, 1 vol. 2010. (Super SandCastle Ser.). (ENG.). 24p. 25.65 (978-1-61613-192-0(6), Super SandCastle) ABDO Publishing Co.
Galė. Junior Worldmark Encyclopedia of Foods & Recipes of the World, 4 vols. 2nd ed. 2012. (Junior Worldmark Encyclopedia of Foods & Recipes of the World Ser.). (ENG., Illus.). 800p. lib. bdg. 372.00 (978-1-4144-9071-7(2), UXL) Cengage Gale.
Gall, Susan B. & Edgar, Kathleen J. Junior Worldmark Encyclopedia of Foods & Recipes of the World, 4 vols. 2nd ed. 2012. (Illus.). (978-1-4144-9073-1(9)); (978-1-4144-9075-5(5)); (978-1-4144-9074-8(7)); (978-1-4144-9072-4(0)) Cengage Gale. (UXL).
Gardner, Jane P. Food Science, Vol. 11. Lewin, Russ, ed. 2015. (Science 24/7 Ser.). (Illus.). 48p. (J). (gr. 5). 20.95 (978-1-4222-3410-5(X)) Mason Crest.
Gardner, Robert, et al. Ace Your Food Science Project: Great Science Fair Ideas. 2009. (Ace Your Science Project Ser.). (Illus.). 128p. (J). (gr. 5-9). lib. bdg. 33.27 (978-0-7660-3228-6(0)) Enslow Pubs., Inc.
Gifford, Clive. Food Technology. 2004. (World Issues Ser.). (J). lib. bdg. 28.50 (978-1-59389-152-7(0)) Chrysalis Education.
Gilbert, Sara. American Food. 2015. (J). (978-1-60818-500-9(1), Creative Education) Creative Co., The.
—Chinese Food. 2015. (J). (978-1-60818-501-6(X), Creative Education) Creative Co., The.
—Cooking School: American Food. 2015. (Cooking School Ser.). (ENG.). 24p. (J). (gr. 1-3). pap. 9.99 (978-1-62832-094-7(X), Creative Paperbacks) Creative Co., The.
—Cooking School: Chinese Food. 2015. (Cooking School Ser.). (ENG.). 24p. (J). (gr. 1-3). pap. 9.99 (978-1-62832-095-4(8), Creative Paperbacks) Creative Co., The.
—Cooking School: French Food. 2015. (Cooking School Ser.). (ENG.). 24p. (J). (gr. 1-3). pap. 9.99 (978-1-62832-096-1(6), Creative Paperbacks) Creative Co., The.
—Cooking School: Italian Food. 2015. (Cooking School Ser.). (ENG.). 24p. (J). (gr. 1-3). pap. 9.99 (978-1-62832-097-8(4), Creative Paperbacks) Creative Co., The.
—Cooking School: Mexican Food. 2015. (Cooking School Ser.). (ENG.). 24p. (J). (gr. 1-3). pap. 9.99 (978-1-62832-098-5(2), Creative Paperbacks) Creative Co., The.
—Cooking School: Middle-Eastern Food. 2015. (Cooking School Ser.). (ENG.). 24p. (J). (gr. 1-3). pap. 9.99 (978-1-62832-099-2(0), Creative Paperbacks) Creative Co., The.
—French Food. 2015. (J). (978-1-60818-502-3(8), Creative Education) Creative Co., The.
—Italian Food. 2015. (J). (978-1-60818-503-0(6), Creative Education) Creative Co., The.
—Mexican Food. 2015. (J). (978-1-60818-504-7(4), Creative Education) Creative Co., The.
—Middle Eastern Food. 2015. (J). (978-1-60818-505-4(2), Creative Education) Creative Co., The.
Gleisner, Jenna Lee. My Body Needs Food. 2015. (Healthy Me Ser.). (Illus.). 24p. (J). 27.10 (978-1-60753-587-4(4)) Amicus Publishing.
Goldsmith, Connie. Dietary Supplements: Harmless, Helpful, or Hurtful? 2015. (ENG., Illus.). 96p. (gr. 7-12). 34.65 (978-1-4677-8801-4(5), Twenty-First Century Bks.) Lerner Publishing Group.
Goodbody, Slim & Burstein, John. Big Fat Lies: Advertising Tricks. 2008. (Slim Goodbody's Lighten Up! Ser.). (ENG., Illus.). 32p. (J). (gr. 3-7). pap. (978-0-7787-3931-9(7)); lib. bdg. (978-0-7787-3913-5(9)) Crabtree Publishing Co.
—Fast Food: Slowing Us All Down. 2008. (Slim Goodbody's Lighten Up! Ser.). (ENG., Illus.). 32p. (J). (gr. 3-7). pap. (978-0-7787-3933-3(3)); lib. bdg. (978-0-7787-3915-9(5)) Crabtree Publishing Co.
—Looking at Labels: The Inside Story. 2008. (Slim Goodbody's Lighten Up! Ser.). (ENG., Illus.). 32p. (J). (gr. 3-7). pap. (978-0-7787-3935-7(X)); lib. bdg. (978-0-7787-3917-3(1)) Crabtree Publishing Co.
—The Shape of Good Nutrition: The Food Pyramid. 2008. (Slim Goodbody's Lighten Up! Ser.). (ENG., Illus.). 32p. (J). (gr. 3-7). pap. (978-0-7787-3937-1(6)) Crabtree Publishing Co.
—Snack Attack: Unhealthy Treats. 2008. (Slim Goodbody's Lighten Up! Ser.). (ENG., Illus.). 32p. (J). (gr. 3-7). pap. (978-0-7787-3936-4(8)); lib. bdg. (978-0-7787-3918-0(X)) Crabtree Publishing Co.
Gordon, Sherri Mabry. Peanut Butter, Milk, & Other Deadly Threats: What You Should Know about Food Allergies. 2006. (Issues in Focus Today Ser.). (Illus.). 112p. (J). (gr. 6-12). lib. bdg. 33.27 (978-0-7660-2529-5(2)) Enslow Pubs., Inc.
Greathouse, Lisa. Count Me In! What's for Lunch?, 1 vol. 2nd rev. ed. 2014. (TIME for KIDS(r) Nonfiction Readers Ser.). (ENG., Illus.). 28p. (J). (gr. 2-2). pap. 23.96 (978-1-4807-1060-3(1)) Shell Educational Publishing.
—Eat Healthy, 1 vol. 2011. (Science Readers: a Closer Look Ser.). (ENG., Illus.). 32p. (J). (gr. 3-3). pap. 8.99 (978-1-4333-3087-2(3)) Teacher Created Materials, Inc.
—Sweet: Inside a Bakery, 1 vol. 2nd rev. ed. 2014. (TIME for KIDS(r) Nonfiction Readers Ser.). (ENG., Illus.). 32p. (J). (gr. 3-3). pap. 25.96 (978-1-4807-1078-8(4)) Shell Educational Publishing.
Green, Emily K. Meat & Beans. 2011. (Blastoff! Readers: New Food Guide Pyramid Ser.). (Illus.). 24p. (J). pap. 5.95 (978-0-531-25854-5(8), Children's Pr.) Scholastic Library Publishing.
Greenhaven Press Editors & Busby, Barbara Sheen. Foods of Indonesia. 2012. (Taste of Culture Ser.). (ENG., Illus.). 64p. (gr. 3-6). lib. bdg. 35.20 (978-0-7377-5950-1(X), Kidhaven) Cengage Gale.
Gritzner, Charles F. Feeding a Hungry World. 2009. (Global Connections Ser.). (Illus.). 120p. (gr. 5-8). 35.00 (978-1-60413-290-8(6), Chelsea Hse.) Facts On File, Inc.
Grossman, Rena. Eating the Rainbow, 1 vol. 2009. (ENG.). 32p. (J). (gr. -1). bds. 6.95 (978-1-59572-174-7(6)) Star Bright Bks., Inc.
Group/McGraw-Hill, Wright. Set 1: Los Alimentos, 6 vols. (First Explorers. Primeros Exploradores Nonfiction Sets Ser.). (SPA.). (gr. 1-2). 29.95 (978-0-7699-1469-5(1)) Shortland Pubns. (U. S. A.) Inc.
Gutiérrez, Elisa & Owlkids Books Inc. Staff. Letter Lunch, 0 vols. 2014. (ENG., Illus.). 32p. (J). (gr. -1-2). 16.95 (978-1-77147-000-1(3), Owlkids) Owlkids Bks. Inc. CAN. Dist: Publishers Group West (PGW).
Harmon, Daniel E. Fish, Meat, & Poultry: Dangers in the Food Supply. (What's in Your Food? Recipe for Disaster Ser.). 48p. (gr. 5-5). 2009. 53.00 (978-1-60854-772-2(8), Rosen Reference) 2008. (Illus.). (YA). lib. bdg. 29.25 (978-1-4042-1419-4(4)) Rosen Publishing Group, Inc., The.
—Poultry: From the Farm to Your Table. 2012. (Truth about the Food Supply Ser.). (ENG., Illus.). 48p. (J). (gr. 5-8). lib. bdg. 27.95 (978-1-4488-6798-1(3), Rosen Reference) Rosen Publishing Group, Inc., The.
Harris, Brooke. Healthy Snacks: Lap Book. 2009. (My First Reader's Theater Set B Ser.). (J). 28.00 (978-1-4108-8545-6(3)) Benchmark Education Co.
Harvey, Joanna & Crabtree, Marc. Meet My Neighbor, the Restaurant Owner. 2010. (ENG., Illus.). 24p. (J). pap. (978-0-7787-4586-0(4)); lib. bdg. (978-0-7787-4576-1(7)) Crabtree Publishing Co.
Hassan, Masood. Madeline & Friends: Fruits & Veggies vs Candy. Lady Josephine, illus. 2010. (978-0-9812600-6-8(3)) Sapphira Pubns.
Haugen, David M. Food/the Food Industry in Eric Schlosser's Fast Food Nation. 2012. (Social Issues in Literature Ser.). (ENG., Illus.). 224p. (gr. 10-12). lib. bdg. 46.40 (978-0-7377-6381-2(7), Greenhaven Pr., Inc.) Cengage Gale.
Haugen, David M., ed. Food/the Food Industry in Eric Schlosser's Fast Food Nation. 2012. (Social Issues in Literature Ser.). (ENG., Illus.). 224p. (gr. 10-12). pap. 28.45 (978-0-7377-6382-9(5), Greenhaven Pr., Inc.) Cengage Gale.
Hawley, Ella. Exploring Food & Nutrition. 2012. (Let's Explore Life Science Ser.). (ENG., Illus.). 24p. (J). (gr. 3-6). pap. 8.25 (978-1-4488-6310-5(4)); lib. bdg. 22.60 (978-1-4488-6176-7(4)) Rosen Publishing Group, Inc., The. (PowerKids Pr.).
Hayhurst, Chris. Everything You Need to Know about Food Additives. (Need to Know Library). 64p. 2009. (gr. 5-5). 58.50 (978-1-60854-068-6(5)) 2005. (Illus.). (YA). (gr. 4-6). lib. bdg. 31.95 (978-0-8239-3548-2(5)) Rosen Publishing Group, Inc., The.
Hazan, Maurice, creator. Resto Presto. (SPA.). (J). 169.95 (978-1-932770-42-1(9), SG3) Symtalk, Inc.
Heos, Bridget. So You Want to Grow a Pizza? Fabbri, Daniele, illus. 2015. (Grow Your Food Ser.). (ENG.). 24p. (gr. 1-3). 19.95 (978-1-60753-740-3(0)) Amicus Publishing.
—So You Want to Grow a Salad? Fabbri, Daniele, illus. 2015. (Grow Your Food Ser.). (ENG.). 24p. (gr. 1-3). 19.95 (978-1-60753-741-0(9)) Amicus Publishing.
Herrington, Lisa M. Tomatoes to Ketchup. 2013. (Rookie Read-About(r) Science Ser.). (ENG.). 32p. (J). pap. 5.95 (978-0-531-24709-9(0), Children's Pr.); lib. bdg. 23.00 (978-0-531-24743-3(0)) Scholastic Library Publishing.
Hewitt, Sally. Grains & Cereals. 2008. (Good for Me Ser.). (Illus.). 24p. (J). (gr. -1-3). lib. bdg. 22.60 (978-1-4042-4270-8(8), PowerKids Pr.) Rosen Publishing Group, Inc., The.
—Meat & Fish. 2008. (Good for Me Ser.). (Illus.). 24p. (J). (gr. -1-3). lib. bdg. 22.60 (978-1-4042-4266-1(X), PowerKids Pr.) Rosen Publishing Group, Inc., The.
—Your Food. 2008. (Green Team Ser.). (ENG., Illus.). 32p. (J). (gr. 3-7). pap. (978-0-7787-4106-0(0)) Crabtree Publishing Co.
Higgins, Nadia. Fun Food Inventions. 2013. (Awesome Inventions You Use Every Day Ser.). (ENG., Illus.). 32p. (gr. 3-6). lib. bdg. 26.60 (978-1-4677-1091-6(1), Lerner Pubns.) Lerner Publishing Group.
Hillstrom, Laurie, ed. Food Regulation & Safety. 2012. (Nutrition & Health Ser.). (ENG., Illus.). 80p. (J). (gr. 7-10). lib. bdg. 30.95 (978-1-4205-0721-8(4), Lucent Bks.) Cengage Gale.
Hnatov, Catherine. Yum, Yum (Spanish/English), 1 vol. 2011. (ENG., Illus.). 32p. (J). bds. 5.95 (978-1-59572-276-8(9)) Star Bright Bks., Inc.
Holden, Pam. Are You Hungry?, 6 pack. Hawley, Kelvin, illus. 2009. (Red Rocket Readers Ser.). (ENG.). 16p. (gr. -1-1). pap. (978-1-877363-23-8(5), Red Rocket Readers) Flying Start Bks.
Holt, Rinehart and Winston Staff. Environmental Science Chptr. 15: Food & Agriculture. 4th ed. Date not set. pap. 11.20 (978-0-03-068076-2(X)) Holt McDougal.
Hughes, Meredith Sayles. Flavor Foods: Spices & Herbs. 2005. (Plants We Eat Ser.). (Illus.). 104p. (gr. 6-9). 26.60 (978-0-8225-2835-7(5)) Lerner Publishing Group.
Hunnicutt, Susan C., ed. Is the Western Diet Making the World Sick? 2012. (At Issue Ser.). (ENG.). 128p. (gr. 10-12). lib. bdg. 39.40 (978-0-7377-6191-7(1), Greenhaven Pr., Inc.) Cengage Gale.
Hunter, Nick. Louis Pasteur, 1 vol. 2014. (Science Biographies Ser.). (ENG.). 32p. (gr. 2-4). lib. bdg. 30.65 (978-1-4109-6236-2(9), Raintree Perspectives) Heinemann-Raintree.
Hunter, William. Nature & Nurture: The Causes of Obesity. 2015. (Illus.). 104p. (YA). (978-1-4222-3056-5(2)) Mason Crest.
Icibaci, Neusa, tr. Eating the Rainbow (Portuguese/English), 1 vol. 2010. (Um Colorido Livro de Alimentos/Colorful Food Bks.). (ENG., Illus.). 20p. (J). 6.95 (978-1-59572-204-1(1)) Star Bright Bks., Inc.
Idee, Ari. What's Your Snack? 2013. 28p. pap. 9.49 (978-0-9798991-2-6(5)) Technology & Imagination Pr.
Incredibly Disgusting Food, 4 vols., Set. Incl. Carbonated Beverages: The Incredibly Disgusting Story. Furgang, Adam. (YA). lib. bdg. 29.25 (978-1-4488-1266-0(6)); Fake Foods: Fried, Fast, & Processed: The Incredibly Disgusting Story. Johanson, Paula. (YA). lib. bdg. 29.25 (978-1-4488-1269-1(0)); Mystery Meat: Hot Dogs, Sausages, & Lunch Meats. Watson, Stephanie. (J). lib. bdg. 29.25 (978-1-4488-1268-4(2), 1323609); Salty & Sugary Snacks: The Incredibly Disgusting Story. Furgang, Adam. (YA). lib. bdg. 29.25 (978-1-4488-1267-7(4)); (gr. 5-9). 2011. (Incredibly Disgusting Food Ser.). (Illus.). 48p. 2011. Set lib. bdg. 106.00 (978-1-4488-1390-2(5), Rosen Reference) Rosen Publishing Group, Inc., The.
Innovative Kids Staff. In the Garden. Phillips, Jillian, illus. 2009. (ENG.). 20p. (J). (gr. -1-1). 8.99 (978-1-58476-810-4(X)) Innovative Kids.
Ipcizade, Catherine. Favorite Food Facts. 2011. (Favorite Food Facts Ser.). (ENG.). 24p. (gr. k-1). lib. bdg. 53.30 (978-1-4296-6512-4(2), Pebble Plus) Capstone Press of Coughlan Cos.
Jacobson, Ryan. What Eats That? Tekiela, Stan, photos by. 2017. (Wildlife Picture Bks.). (ENG., Illus.). 32p. (J). (gr. -1-3). 14.95 **(978-1-59193-749-4(3))** Adventure Pubns.
Jenkins, Steve & Page, Robin. Time to Eat. Jenkins, Steve, illus. 2014. (ENG., Illus.). 24p. (J). (gr. -1-3). 26.99 (978-0-544-23753-7(6), HMH Books For Young Readers) Houghton Mifflin Harcourt Publishing Co.
Johansen, Heidi Leigh. My Food. 2008. (Board Bks.). (Illus.). 16p. (J). (gr. -1-k). bds. 11.95 (978-1-4042-2802-3(0), PowerKids Pr.) Rosen Publishing Group, Inc., The.
Johanson, Paula. Fake Foods: Fried, Fast, & Processed: The Incredibly Disgusting Story. 2011. (Incredibly Disgusting Food Ser.). (Illus.). 48p. (YA). pap. 11.75 (978-1-4488-2285-0(8)); (gr. 5-9). lib. bdg. 29.25 (978-1-4488-1269-1(0)) Rosen Publishing Group, Inc., The.
—What's in Your Food? Fast Food. 2009. (Health & Your Body Ser.). 48p. (gr. 5-8). pap. 11.75 (978-1-4358-5162-7(5), Rosen Classroom) Rosen Publishing Group, Inc., The.
Jorgensen, Katrina. Food, Football, & Fun! Sports Illustrated Kids' Football Recipes. 2015. (Sports Illustrated Kids Ser.). (ENG., Illus.). 144p. (gr. 3-6). pap. 15.95 (978-1-62370-230-4(5)) Capstone Press of Coughlan Cos.
—Football Party Recipes: Delicious Ideas for the Big Event. 2015. (Football Cookbooks Ser.). (ENG.). 48p. (gr. 3-6). lib. bdg. 31.32 (978-1-4914-2136-9(3)) Capstone Press of Coughlan Cos.
Kalman, Bobbie. Food & Farming Then & Now. 2013. (ENG., Illus.). 24p. (J). (978-0-7787-0126-2(3)); pap. (978-0-7787-0208-5(1)) Crabtree Publishing Co.
—Food Chains & You. 2004. (Food Chains Ser.). (ENG., Illus.). 32p. (J). lib. bdg. (978-0-7787-1942-7(1)) Crabtree Publishing Co.
—Forest Food Chains. 2004. (Food Chains Ser.). (ENG., Illus.). 32p. (J). lib. bdg. (978-0-7787-1943-4(X)) Crabtree Publishing Co.
—How Do Living Things Find Food? 2010. (Introducing Living Things Ser.). (ENG.). 24p. (J). (gr. 1-4). pap. (978-0-7787-3258-7(4)); lib. bdg. (978-0-7787-3234-1(7)) Crabtree Publishing Co.
—I Eat a Rainbow: Me Como un Arco Iris. 2010. (SPA, ENG & MUL.). 16p. (J). pap. (978-0-7787-8263-6(8)); lib. bdg. (978-0-7787-8270-4(0)) Crabtree Publishing Co.
—Me Como un Arco Iris. 2010. (SPA.). 16p. (J). pap. (978-0-7787-8578-1(5)); lib. bdg. (978-0-7787-8552-1(1)) Crabtree Publishing Co.
—Multicultural Meals: Step-by-Step Healthy Recipes for Kids. 2003. (Kid Power Ser.). (ENG., Illus.). 32p. (J). (gr. 3). lib. bdg. (978-0-7787-1255-8(9)) Crabtree Publishing Co.
—Super Snacks: Step-by-Step Recipes. 2003. (Kid Power Ser.). (ENG., Illus.). 32p. (J). (gr. 3). pap. (978-0-7787-1274-9(5)) Crabtree Publishing Co.
—La Toundra. 2011. (FRE., Illus.). 32p. (J). pap. 10.95 (978-2-89579-396-0(4)) Bayard Canada CAN. Dist: Crabtree Publishing Co.
Kalman, Bobbie & MacAulay, Kelley. Desert Food Chains. 2004. (Food Chains Ser.). (ENG., Illus.). 32p. (J). pap. (978-0-7787-1990-8(1)) Crabtree Publishing Co.
Katirgis, Jane. STEM Jobs in Food & Nutrition. 2014. (ENG., Illus.). 48p. (gr. 4-8). 35.64 (978-1-62717-703-0(5)) Rourke Educational Media.
Katzen, Mollie. Honest Pretzels: And 64 Other Amazing Recipes for Kids Who Love to Cook. 2009. (ENG., Illus.). 192p. (J). (gr. 3-7). pap. 17.99 (978-1-58246-305-6(0), Tricycle Pr.) Random Hse. Children's Bks.
Keoke, Emory Dean & Porterfield, Kay Marie. Food, Farming, & Hunting. 2005. (American Indian Contributions to the World Ser.). (Illus.). 160p. (gr. 5-8). 35.00 (978-0-8160-5393-3(6)) Facts On File, Inc.
Kessler, David A. Your Food Is Fooling You: How Your Brain Is Hijacked by Sugar, Fat, & Salt. 2012. (ENG., Illus.). 192p. (YA). (gr. 7-12). pap. 10.99 (978-1-59643-831-6(2), 9781596438316) Roaring Brook Pr.
Koellhoffer, Tara, ed. Food & Nutrition. 2006. (Science News for Kids Ser.). (Illus.). 128p. (gr. 4-6). lib. bdg. 30.00 (978-0-7910-9121-0(X), Chelsea Clubhouse) Facts On File, Inc.
Kompelien, Tracy. Ahi to Ziti: Food from A to Z, 1 vol. 2007. (Let's See A to Z Ser.). (ENG., Illus.). 32p. (gr. -1-3). 27.07 (978-1-59928-880-2(X), Super SandCastle) ABDO Publishing Co.
Kops, Deborah. Were Potato Chips Really Invented by an Angry Chef? And Other Questions about Food. 2011. (Is

That a Fact? Ser.). (ENG.). 40p. (gr. 4-6). 26.60 *(978-0-7613-6099-5(9))* Lerner Publishing Group.

Krensky, Stephen. The Deep Dish on Pizza! Guidera, Daniel, illus. 2014. (History of Fun Stuff Ser.). (ENG.). 48p. (J). (gr. 1-3). pap. 3.99 *(978-1-4814-2055-6(0),* Simon Spotlight) Simon Spotlight.

Kronheimer, Ann. Delicious Doodles: Super Sweet Designs to Complete & Create. 2014. (ENG., Illus.). 160p. (J). (gr. -1-17). pap. 12.95 *(978-0-7624-5480-8(6),* Running Pr. Kids) Running Pr. Bk. Pubs.

Kuskowski, Alex. Cool Healthy Muffins: Fun & Easy Baking Recipes for Kids!, 1 vol. 2014. (Cool Cupcakes & Muffins Ser.). (ENG.). 32p. (gr. 8-12). 28.50 *(978-1-62403-302-5(4))* ABDO Publishing Co.

—Cool Savory Muffins: Fun & Easy Baking Recipes for Kids!, 1 vol. 2014. (Cool Cupcakes & Muffins Ser.). (ENG.). 32p. (gr. 8-12). 28.50 *(978-1-62403-303-2(2))* ABDO Publishing Co.

—Cool Sweet Muffins: Fun & Easy Baking Recipes for Kids!, 1 vol. 2014. (Cool Cupcakes & Muffins Ser.). (ENG.). 32p. (gr. 8-12). 28.50 *(978-1-62403-304-9(0))* ABDO Publishing Co.

La Bella, Laura. Safety & the Food Supply. 2009. (In the News Ser.). (ENG., Illus.). 64p. (J). (gr. 7-12). pap. 12.95 *(978-1-4358-5364-5(4));* 64p. (gr. 6-6). 58.50 *(978-1-61513-486-1(7));* (YA). (gr. 7-12). lib. bdg. 31.95 *(978-1-4358-5036-1(X))* Rosen Publishing Group, Inc., The.

Labat, Yancey C., illus. Pizza-Zazz & Lotsa Pasta. 2006. 56p. (J). *(978-0-439-83187-1(3))* Scholastic, Inc.

—Rise & Shine! It's Breakfast Time! 2006. 56p. (J). *(978-0-439-83223-6(3))* Scholastic, Inc.

Lacey, Saskia. Foods for the Future. 2015. (Building Fluency Through Reader's Theater Ser.). (ENG., Illus.). 32p. (gr. 5-5). pap. 7.99 *(978-1-4938-1295-0(5))* Teacher Created Materials, Inc.

Lake, G. G. Take Your Pick of Disgusting Foods. 2017. (Take Your (Equally Horrible) Pick! Ser.). (ENG., Illus.). 32p. (gr. 1-2). lib. bdg. 26.65 *(978-1-5157-4470-2(1),* Blazers) Capstone Press of Coughlan Cos.

Landau, Elaine. A Healthy Diet. 2003. (Watts Library). (ENG., Illus.). 64p. (J). 25.50 *(978-0-531-12027-9(9),* Watts, Franklin) Scholastic Library Publishing.

Lankford, Ronnie D. Junk Food. 2010. (Issues That Concern You Ser.). (ENG.). 144p. 36.95 *(978-0-7377-4954-0(7))* Cengage Gale.

Lanser, Amanda. Food Science: You Are What You Eat, 1 vol. 2014. (History of Science Ser.). (ENG.). 112p. (J). (gr. 6-12). lib. bdg. 35.64 *(978-1-62403-560-9(4),* Essential Library) ABDO Publishing Co.

—School Lunches: Healthy Choices vs. Crowd Pleasers. 2015. (Perspectives Flip Books: Issues Ser.). (ENG.). 64p. (gr. 5-6). 33.99 *(978-0-7565-4993-0(0))* Compass Point Bks.

Lanz, Helen. What Shall We Eat? 2012. (Go Green Ser.). 32p. (gr. 3-6). lib. bdg. 28.50 *(978-1-59771-305-4(8))* Sea-To-Sea Pubns.

LaPenta, Marilyn. Artful Snacks. 2011. (Yummy Tummy Recipes Ser.). 24p. (J). (gr. 1-4). lib. bdg. 22.61 *(978-1-61772-307-0(X))* Bearport Publishing Co., Inc.

Lappi, Megan. Decomposers. 2006. (Nature's Food Chain Ser.). (Illus.). 24p. (J). (gr. -1-3). lib. bdg. 24.45 *(978-1-59036-239-6(X))* Weigl Pubs., Inc.

Larrew, Brekka Hervey. Banana-Berry Smoothies & Other Breakfast Recipes, 1 vol. 2008. (Fun Foods for Cool Cooks Ser.). (ENG.). 32p. (gr. 3-4). 27.99 *(978-1-4296-2015-4(3),* Snap Bks.) Capstone Press of Coughlan Cos.

Lawrence, Ellen. The Food We Eat. 2015. (My World Your World Ser.). (ENG.). 24p. (J). (gr. -1-3). lib. bdg. 23.93 *(978-1-910549-10-0(X))* Bearport Publishing Co., Inc.

LeBoutillier, Linda. Food Long Ago & Today, 1 vol. 2014. (Long Ago & Today Ser.). (ENG.). 24p. (gr. 1-2). 25.32 *(978-1-4914-0297-9(0));* pap. 6.95 *(978-1-4914-0305-1(5))* Capstone Press of Coughlan Cos. (First Facts).

Lee, Sally. Food Safety, 1 vol. 2012. (Staying Safe Ser.). (ENG.). 24p. (gr. 1-2). pap. 7.29 *(978-1-4296-7958-9(1));* lib. bdg. 25.32 *(978-1-4296-7618-2(3));*Set pap. 41.70 *(978-1-4296-8388-3(0))* Capstone Press of Coughlan Cos. (First Facts).

—Healthy Snacks, Healthy You!, 1 vol. Swift, Gary, illus. 2011. (First Graphics: Myplate & Healthy Eating Ser.). (ENG.). 24p. (gr. 1-2). pap. 6.29 *(978-1-4296-7162-0(9));* pap. 35.70 *(978-1-4296-7168-2(8))* Capstone Press of Coughlan Cos.

—Healthy Snacks, Healthy You! [Scholastic]. Swift, Gary, illus. 2013. (First Graphics: Myplate & Healthy Eating Ser.). (ENG.). (gr. 1-2). pap. 0.50 *(978-1-4765-3129-8(3))* Capstone Press of Coughlan Cos.

—The Powerful Protein Group. Swift, Gary, illus. 2011. (First Graphics: Myplate & Healthy Eating Ser.). (ENG.). 24p. (gr. 1-2). pap. 35.70 *(978-1-4296-7170-5(X))* Capstone Press of Coughlan Cos.

Lennon, Liz. What I Like - My Food. 2017. (Little Stars Ser.). (ENG., Illus.). 24p. (J). (gr. -1-k). pap. 6.99 *(978-1-4451-4768-0(8),* Franklin Watts) Hachette Children's Group GBR. Dist: Hachette Bk. Group.

Levete, Sarah. Food Around the World. 2011. (Big Picture: Food Ser.). (ENG.). 24p. (gr. 1-2). pap. 41.70 *(978-1-4296-6727-2(3),* First Facts) Capstone Press of Coughlan Cos.

—Toxins in the Food Chain. 2010. (Protecting Our Planet Ser.). (ENG., Illus.). 32p. (J). (gr. 3-6). *(978-0-7787-5215-8(1));* pap. *(978-0-7787-5232-5(1))* Crabtree Publishing Co.

Liao, Yan. Food & Festivals of China. Wang, Jianwei, ed. 2012. (China: the Emerging Superpower Ser.). 120p. (J). (gr. 7). 24.95 *(978-1-4222-2159-4(8))* Mason Crest.

Libal, Autumn. Fast Food & the Obesity Epidemic. Garcia, Victor, ed. 2014. (Understanding Obesity Ser.: 10). 104p. (J). (gr. 7-18). lib. bdg. 24.95 *(978-1-4222-3061-9(9))* Mason Crest.

Lift-The-Flap Questions & Answers about Food IR. 2017. (Lift-The-Flap Questions & Answers Ser.). (ENG.). (J). bds. 14.99 ***(978-0-7945-3927-6(0),*** Usborne) EDC Publishing.

Lin, Grace & McKneally, Ranida T. Our Food. Zong, Grace, illus. 2016. (ENG.). 40p. (J). (gr. k-3). lib. bdg. 16.95 *(978-1-58089-590-3(5))* Charlesbridge Publishing, Inc.

Litchfield, J. My Food. 2004. (Rattle Books). 16p. (J). 4.95 *(978-0-7945-0053-5(6),* Usborne) EDC Publishing.

Llewellyn, Claire. Your Food. 2008. (Look after Yourself Ser.). (Illus.). 30p. (J). (gr. 1-4). lib. bdg. 28.50 *(978-1-59771-098-5(9))* Sea-To-Sea Pubns.

Logue, Damien. Favorite Foods: Classify & Count Objects in Each Category. 2013. (Rosen Math Readers Ser.). (ENG.). 16p. (J). (gr. k-1). pap. 42.00 *(978-1-4777-1654-0(8));* (Illus.). pap. 7.00 *(978-1-4777-1653-3(X))* Rosen Publishing Group, Inc., The. (Rosen Classroom).

Lundgren, Julie K. What's on the Food Chain Menu? 2011. (ENG., Illus.). 24p. (gr. 2-3). pap. 8.95 *(978-1-61741-947-8(8))* Rourke Educational Media.

Lynette, Rachel. Mountain Food Chains, 1 vol. 2010. (Protecting Food Chains Ser.). (ENG.). 48p. (gr. 3-6). 33.32 *(978-1-4329-3858-1(4));* pap. 9.95 *(978-1-4329-3865-9(7))* Heinemann-Raintree. (Heinemann InfoSearch).

Macdonald, Margaret. Where Can You Eat This Food? 2014. (Little Books of Answers: Level F Ser.). (Illus.). 16p. (gr. k-2). pap. 7.95 *(978-1-927136-50-8(4))* Three Crows Media NZL. Dist: RiverStream Publishing.

Malerba, Giulia. Food Atlas: Discover All the Delicious Foods of the World. Sillani, Febe, illus. 2017. (ENG.). 72p. (J). (gr. 3-12). 19.95 ***(978-1-77085-952-4(7),*** 9781770859524) Firefly Bks., Ltd.

Markovics, Joyce L. Food Colors: From Blueberries to Beets. 2014. (Little Bits: Colors Tell a Story Ser.). (ENG.). 24p. (J). (gr. -1-3). lib. bdg. 23.93 *(978-1-62724-324-7(0))* Bearport Publishing Co., Inc.

—Los Colores de Los Alimentos: De Los Arándanos a la Remolacha. 2014. (Los Colores Cuentan una Historia Ser.). (SPA., Illus.). 24p. (J). (gr. -1-3). lib. bdg. 23.93 *(978-1-62724-466-4(2))* Bearport Publishing Co., Inc.

Marshall Cavendish. The Cooking of Brazil. 2nd rev. ed. 2011. (Superchef, Second Edition Ser.). (Illus.). 96p. (J). (gr. 6). 35.64 *(978-1-60870-549-8(8))* Marshall Cavendish Corp.

—The Cooking of China. 2nd rev. ed. 2011. (Superchef, Second Edition Ser.). (Illus.). 96p. (J). (gr. 6). 35.64 *(978-1-60870-550-4(1))* Marshall Cavendish Corp.

Marsico, Katie. Your Healthy Plate - Oils & Fats. 2012. (21st Century Basic Skills Library: Your Healthy Plate Ser.). (ENG., Illus.). 24p. (J). (gr. k-3). lib. bdg. 22.79 *(978-1-61080-351-9(5),* 201296) Cherry Lake Publishing.

—Your Healthy Plate - Protein. 2012. (21st Century Basic Skills Library: Your Healthy Plate Ser.). (ENG., Illus.). 24p. (J). (gr. k-3). lib. bdg. 22.79 *(978-1-61080-349-6(3),* 201298) Cherry Lake Publishing.

—Your Healthy Plate: Oils & Fats. 2012. (21st Century Basic Skills Library: Your Healthy Plate Ser.). (ENG., Illus.). 24p. (J). (gr. k-3). pap. 12.79 *(978-1-61080-402-8(3),* 201337) Cherry Lake Publishing.

Martin, Jacqueline Briggs. Alice Waters & the Trip to Delicious. 2014. pap. 31.95 *(978-1-4301-1781-0(8))* Live Oak Media.

—Alice Waters & the Trip to Delicious. Choi, Hayelin, illus. 2014. (ENG.). 32p. (J). (gr. k). 18.95 *(978-0-9836615-6-6(1))* READERS to EATERS.

Martineau, Susan. Fizz in the Kitchen. Noyes, Leighton, illus. 2011. (Everyday Science Experiments Ser.). (ENG.). 24p. (J). (gr. 3-6). pap. 10.60 *(978-1-61533-411-7(4),* 1328714); lib. bdg. 25.25 *(978-1-61533-373-8(8),* 1328714) Windmill Bks.

Martineau, Susan & James, Hel. Meat, Fish, & Eggs. 2012. (Healthy Eating Ser.). (Illus.). 32p. (gr. 2-6). pap. 8.95 *(978-1-59920-244-0(1))* Black Rabbit Bks.

Martinneau, Susan & James, Hel. Meat Fish & Eggs. 2006. (Healthy Eating Ser.). (Illus.). 32p. (YA). (gr. 1-4). lib. bdg. 28.50 *(978-1-58340-893-3(2),* 1262657) Black Rabbit Bks.

Mason, Tom & Danko, Dan. Food Magic: How to Do Amazing Tricks with Ordinary Food! 2007. (Illus.). 48p. (J). *(978-0-439-90715-6(2))* Scholastic, Inc.

Mattern, Joanne. Eating Lunch at School. 2006. (My Day at School Ser.). 24p. (gr. k-3). pap. 8.15 *(978-0-8368-6791-6(2));* (Illus.). lib. bdg. 22.00 *(978-0-8368-6784-8(X))* Stevens, Gareth Publishing LLLP. (Weekly Reader Leveled Readers).

—How Peas Grow. 2006. (How Plants Grow Ser.). (Illus.). 24p. (gr. k-2). pap. 8.15 *(978-0-8368-6339-0(9));* lib. bdg. 22.00 *(978-0-8368-6332-1(1))* Stevens, Gareth Publishing LLLP. (Weekly Reader Leveled Readers).

Mayo Clinic Center for Social Media Staff. Mayo Clinic Kids' 50 Favorite Recipes for Fun & Healthy Eating. 2012. (ENG., Illus.). 128p. (gr. -1-7). 19.95 *(978-1-56148-751-6(1),* Da Capo Lifelong) Da Capo Pr., Inc.

Mayo, Gretchen Will. Cereal. 2004. (Where Does Our Food Come From? Ser.). (Illus.). 24p. (gr. 1-4). lib. bdg. 21.00 *(978-0-8368-4065-0(8),* Weekly Reader Leveled Readers) Stevens, Gareth Publishing LLLP.

—Where Does Our Food Come From?, 6 bks. Incl. Applesauce. lib. bdg. 21.00 *(978-0-8368-4064-3(X));* Cereal. lib. bdg. 21.00 *(978-0-8368-4065-0(8));* (gr. 1-4)., Weekly Reader Leveled Readers (Where Does Our Food Come from? Ser.). (Illus.). 24p. 2004. 119.58 o.p. *(978-0-8368-4063-6(1),* Weekly Reader) Stevens, Gareth Publishing LLLP.

McCallum, Ann. Eat Your Science Homework: Recipes for Inquiring Minds. Hernandez, Leeza, illus. 2014. (Eat Your Homework Ser.). (ENG.). 48p. (J). (gr. 2-5). 16.95 *(978-1-57091-298-6(X))* Charlesbridge Publishing, Inc.

McCarthy, Rose. Food Labels: Using Nutrition Information to Create a Healthy Diet. 2008. (Library of Nutrition Ser.). (ENG., Illus.). 48p. (gr. 5-8). per. 11.75 *(978-1-4042-1633-4(2))* Rosen Publishing Group, Inc., The.

—Food Labels: Using Nutritional Information to Create a Healthy Diet. 2004. (Library of Nutrition). (Illus.). 48p. (J). lib. bdg. 26.50 *(978-1-4042-0300-6(1))* Rosen Publishing Group, Inc., The.

McConnell, S. Let's Bring Mom Breakfast: Learning the BR Sound. 2009. (PowerPhonics Ser.). 24p. (gr. 1-1). 39.90 *(978-1-60851-455-7(2),* PowerKids Pr.) Rosen Publishing Group, Inc., The.

Meachen Rau, Dana. La Comida y la Cocina: en la historia de América. 2006. (Como era la vida en America (How People Lived in America) Ser.). (SPA., Illus.). 24p. (gr. 1-4). lib. bdg. 22.00 *(978-0-8368-7430-3(7),* Weekly Reader Leveled Readers) Stevens, Gareth Publishing LLLP.

—La Comida y la Cocina en la Historia de América. 2006. (Como era la vida en America (How People Lived in America) Ser.). (SPA., Illus.). 24p. (gr. 1-4). pap. 8.15 *(978-0-8368-7437-2(4),* Weekly Reader Leveled Readers) Stevens, Gareth Publishing LLLP.

—Food & Cooking in American History. 2006. (How People Lived in America Ser.). (Illus.). 24p. (gr. 1-4). lib. bdg. 22.00 *(978-0-8368-7206-4(1),* Weekly Reader Leveled Readers) Stevens, Gareth Publishing LLLP.

—Food & Cooking in American History. 2006. (How People Lived in America Ser.). (Illus.). 24p. (gr. 1-4). pap. 8.15 *(978-0-8368-7213-2(4),* Weekly Reader Leveled Readers) Stevens, Gareth Publishing LLLP.

—Pizza. 2008. (What's Cooking? Ser.). 24p. (gr. k-1). lib. bdg. 15.95 *(978-0-7614-2891-6(7));* (SPA.). lib. bdg. 15.95 *(978-0-7614-3437-5(2))* Marshall Cavendish Corp. (Benchmark Bks.).

Merino, Noel. Genetic Engineering. 2013. (Opposing Viewpoints Ser.). (ENG., Illus.). 224p. (gr. 10-12). pap. 33.80 *(978-0-7377-6425-3(2),* Greenhaven Pr., Inc.) Cengage Gale.

Merino, No'l, ed. Genetic Engineering. 2013. (Opposing Viewpoints Ser.). (ENG., Illus.). 224p. (gr. 10-12). lib. bdg. 48.80 *(978-0-7377-6424-6(4),* Greenhaven Pr., Inc.) Cengage Gale.

Michalek, Erin. Fun Food Trivia. 2013. 32p. (J). (gr. 2-5). 25.25 *(978-1-4339-8292-7(7));* pap. 10.50 *(978-1-4339-8293-4(5))* Stevens, Gareth Publishing LLLP.

Miller, Connie Colwell. Disgusting Foods. 2016. (That's Disgusting! Ser.). (ENG.). 32p. pap. 7.95 *(978-1-5157-6280-5(7),* Blazers) Capstone Press of Coughlan Cos.

—Disgusting Foods [Scholastic]. 2011. (That's Disgusting! Ser.). 32p. pap. 1.00 *(978-1-4296-6485-1(1),* Blazers) Capstone Press of Coughlan Cos.

Miller, Debra A. Organic Foods. 2007. (Hot Topics Ser.). (ENG., Illus.). 111p. (J). (gr. 3-7). lib. bdg. 33.95 *(978-1-59018-994-8(9),* Lucent Bks.) Cengage Gale.

Miller, Jeanne. Food Science. 2008. (Cool Science Ser.). (ENG.). 48p. (gr. 4-8). 27.93 *(978-0-8225-7589-4(2))* Lerner Publishing Group.

Minden, Cecilia. Breakfast by the Numbers. 2007. (21st Century Skills Library: Real World Math Ser.). (ENG., Illus.). 32p. (gr. 4-8). lib. bdg. 28.50 *(978-1-60279-011-7(6),* 200060) Cherry Lake Publishing.

—Restaurants by the Numbers. 2007. (21st Century Skills Library: Real World Math Ser.). (ENG.). 32p. (gr. 4-8). lib. bdg. 28.50 *(978-1-60279-009-4(4),* 200067) Cherry Lake Publishing.

Mommy & Me Start Cooking. 2014. (ENG.). 80p. (J). (gr. k-4). 15.99 *(978-1-4654-1690-2(0),* DK Children) Dorling Kindersley Publishing, Inc.

Mommy, Is it safe to Eat? 2006. (YA). per. *(978-1-59872-386-1(3))* Instant Pub.

Moore, Heidi. Ocean Food Chains, 1 vol. 2010. (Protecting Food Chains Ser.). (ENG., Illus.). 48p. (gr. 3-6). 33.32 *(978-1-4329-3859-8(2));* pap. 9.95 *(978-1-4329-3866-6(5))* Heinemann-Raintree. (Heinemann InfoSearch).

—Rain Forest Food Chains, 1 vol. 2010. (Protecting Food Chains Ser.). (ENG., Illus.). 48p. (gr. 3-6). 33.32 *(978-1-4329-3860-4(6));* pap. 9.95 *(978-1-4329-3867-3(3))* Heinemann-Raintree. (Heinemann InfoSearch).

Moore, Hugh. Food Jokes, 1 vol. 2005. (More Jokes! Ser.). (ENG., Illus.). 24p. (gr. k-4). 25.65 *(978-1-59197-871-8(8),* Buddy Bks.) ABDO Publishing Co.

Morgan, Sally. How We Use Plants: For Food. (How We Use Plants Ser.). 32p. 2009. (gr. 2-5). pap. 10.60 *(978-1-4358-2611-3(6),* Rosen Classroom) 2008. (Illus.). (J). lib. bdg. 26.50 *(978-1-4042-4421-4(2),* PowerKids Pr.) Rosen Publishing Group, Inc., The.

Morrison, Lillian. I Scream, You Scream: A Feast of Food Rhymes. Dunaway, Nancy, illus. 2005. (Story Cove Ser.). (ENG.). 96p. (J). (gr. -1-3). 12.95 *(978-0-87483-495-6(3))* August Hse. Pubs., Inc.

Murphy, Charles. Food Around the World. 2016. (Adventures in Culture Ser.). 00024p. (J). pap. 8.15 ***(978-1-4824-5582-3(X))*** Stevens, Gareth Publishing LLLP.

Murphy, Frank. Thomas Jefferson's Feast. Walz, Richard, illus. 2004. (Step into Reading Ser.). 48p. 14.00 *(978-0-7569-3235-0(1))* Perfection Learning Corp.

—Thomas Jefferson's Feast. Walz, Richard, illus. 2003. (Step into Reading Ser.). (ENG.). 48p. (J). (gr. 2-4). pap. 3.99 *(978-0-375-82289-6(5),* Random Hse. Bks. for Young Readers) Random Hse. Children's Bks.

Nadeau, Nicole. Caillou: I'm Not Hungry! Brignaud, Pierre, illus. 2011. (Hand in Hand Ser.). (ENG.). 24p. (J). (gr. -1-k). 5.95 *(978-2-89450-829-9(8))* Caillouet, Gerry.

National Geographic Kids Staff & Beer, Julie. Food: 300 Bite-Size Facts about Incredible Edibles. 2015. (Weird but True Ser.). (ENG., Illus.). 208p. (J). (gr. 3-7). pap. 7.99 *(978-1-4263-1871-9(5),* National Geographic Children's Bks.) National Geographic Society.

—300 Bite-Size Facts about Incredible Edibles! 2015. (Weird but True Ser.). (ENG., Illus.). 208p. (J). (gr. 3-7). lib. bdg. 16.90 *(978-1-4263-1872-6(3),* National Geographic Children's Bks.) National Geographic Society.

Nelson, Maria. I'm Allergic to Peanuts. 2014. (I'm Allergic Ser.). 24p. (J). (gr. 1-3). 22.60 *(978-1-4824-0974-1(7))* Stevens, Gareth Publishing LLLP.

Nelson, Robin. Las Carnes y las Proteinas. Castañer, Mercedes P. & Fitzpatrick, Julia, trs. 2003. (Mi Primer Paso Al Mundo Real - Los Grupos de Alimentos (First Step Nonfiction - Food Groups) Ser.). (SPA., Illus.). 24p. (gr. k-2). lib. bdg. 23.93 *(978-0-8225-5064-8(4))* Lerner Publishing Group.

—Las Grasas, los Aceites, y los Dulces. Castañer, Mercedes P. & Fitzpatrick, Julia, trs. 2003. (Mi Primer Paso Al Mundo Real - Los Grupos de Alimentos (First Step Nonfiction - Food Groups) Ser.).Tr. of Fats, Oils, & Sweets. (SPA., Illus.). 24p. (gr. k-2). lib. bdg. 23.93 *(978-0-8225-5061-7(X))* Lerner Publishing Group.

Nicole, Heather. What Is a Food Chain? 2006. (Science Leveled Readers Ser.). (ENG., Illus.). 8p. (gr. k-k). pap. 5.40 *(978-0-15-365337-7(X))* Harcourt Schl. Pubs.

Nsrc. Science & Technology for Children Books: Food Chemistry. 2004. (Illus.). 64p. (J). *(978-1-933008-06-6(7))* Smithsonian Science Education Ctr. (SSEC).

O'Donnell, Liam & Anderson, Bill. The World of Food Chains with Max Axiom, Super Scientist. Martin, Cynthia, illus. 2016. (Graphic Science Ser.). (ENG.). 32p. (gr. 3-4). lib. bdg. 30.65 *(978-1-5157-4648-5(8),* Graphic Library) Capstone Press of Coughlan Cos.

Oelschlager, Vanita. Life Is a Bowl Full of Cherries. 2011. (ENG., Illus.). 40p. (J). (gr. -1-3). 15.95 *(978-0-9826366-3-3(6));* pap. 8.95 *(978-0-9826366-2-6(8))* VanitaBooks.

Olson, Gillia M. MyPlate & You, 1 vol. 2011. (Health & Your Body Ser.). (ENG.). 24p. (gr. k-1). pap. 7.29 *(978-1-4296-7129-3(7));* lib. bdg. 26.65 *(978-1-4296-6809-5(1));* pap. 41.70 *(978-1-4296-7135-4(1))* Capstone Press of Coughlan Cos. (Pebble Plus).

Orme, Helen. Healthy Eating. 2010. (Science Everywhere! Ser.). 24p. 24.25 *(978-1-84898-289-5(5))* Black Rabbit Bks.

Pallotta, Jerry. Pizza Fractions. Bolster, Rob, illus. 2007. 32p. (J). pap. *(978-0-545-00687-3(2))* Scholastic, Inc.

Paré, Jean. Kitchen Fun for Kids. 2011. (2-In-1 Cookbook Collection). (ENG.). 256p. (J). spiral bd. 19.99 *(978-1-897069-85-1(5),* 9781897069851) Company's Coming Publishing, Ltd. CAN. Dist: Lone Pine Publishing USA.

Paris, Stephanie. Hablemos Claro: la Verdad Sobre la Comida. 2017. (TIME for Kids en Español - Level 4 Ser.).Tr. of Straight Talk - The Truth about Food. (SPA., Illus.). 48p. (gr. 4-4). lib. bdg. 31.99 *(978-1-5157-5138-0(4))* Time for Kids Inc AUS. Dist: Capstone Pub.

—Straight Talk: The Truth about Food, 1 vol. 2nd rev. ed. 2013. (Nonfiction Readers Ser.). (ENG., Illus.). 48p. (J). (gr. 4-4). pap. 29.96 *(978-1-4807-1109-9(8))* Shell Educational Publishing.

—Straight Talk - The Truth about Food , 1 vol. 2nd rev. ed. 2012. (Nonfiction Readers Ser.). (ENG.). 48p. (J). (gr. 4-4). pap. 9.99 *(978-1-4333-4857-0(8))* Teacher Created Materials, Inc.

Parker, Vic. Snacks: Healthy Food Choices, 1 vol. 2014. (Healthy Food Choices Ser.). (ENG.). 32p. (gr. 1-3). lib. bdg. 27.32 *(978-1-4329-9119-7(1),* Heinemann First Library) Heinemann-Raintree.

Perdew, Laura. Eating Local. 2016. (Growing Green Ser.). (ENG., Illus.). 64p. (J). (gr. 6-8). lib. bdg. 34.65 *(978-1-4677-9388-9(4))* Lerner Publishing Group.

Perish, Patrick. Disgusting Foods. 2014. (Totally Disgusting Ser.). (ENG.). 24p. (J). (gr. 3-7). 25.95 *(978-1-62617-130-5(0),* Epic Bks.) Bellwether Media.

Perritano, John. Flavorings, Colorings, & Preservatives. 2017. (J). ***(978-1-4222-3736-6(2))*** Mason Crest.

—The Most Disgusting Foods on the Planet, 1 vol. 2012. (Disgusting Stuff Ser.). (ENG.). 48p. (gr. 3-4). lib. bdg. 31.99 *(978-1-4296-7534-5(9))* Capstone Press of Coughlan Cos.

—Starch & Other Carbohydrates. 2017. (J). ***(978-1-4222-3743-4(5))*** Mason Crest.

—Sugar & Sweeteners. 2017. (J). ***(978-1-4222-3744-1(3))*** Mason Crest.

Peters, Celeste A. Food. 2009. (Science Q & A Ser.). (Illus.). 48p. (YA). (gr. 5-8). pap. 10.95 *(978-1-60596-075-3(6));* lib. bdg. 29.05 *(978-1-60596-074-6(8))* Weigl Pubs., Inc.

—Food Q & A. 2014. (Science Discovery Ser.). (ENG., Illus.). 48p. (J). (gr. 5-8). pap. 13.95 *(978-1-4896-0689-1(0),* AV2 by Weigl) Weigl Pubs., Inc.

Petrie, Kristin. Food Options: Following Special Diets, 1 vol. 2012. (Mission: Nutrition Ser.). (ENG., Illus.). 32p. (YA). (gr. 3-6). 27.07 *(978-1-61783-084-6(4))* ABDO Publishing Co.

—Food Safety: Avoiding Hidden Dangers, 1 vol. 2012. (Mission: Nutrition Ser.). (ENG., Illus.). 32p. (YA). (gr. 3-6). 27.07 *(978-1-61783-085-3(2))* ABDO Publishing Co.

Pizza: KinderFacts Individual Title Six-Packs. (Kinderstarters Ser.). 8p. (gr. -1-1). 21.00 *(978-0-7635-8748-2(6))* Rigby Education.

Plews, Sue, et al. Dylunio a Thechnoleg, Cwrs Sylfaen Bwyd. Williams, Janice, tr. from ENG. 2005. (WEL., Illus.). 96p. pap. *(978-1-85644-603-7(4))* CAA.

¿Por Que Come la Gente? (Coleccion Primeros Pasos en la Ciencia). (SPA., Illus.). (J). (gr. 1-3). pap. *(978-950-724-487-2(5),* LMA8228) Lumen ARG. Dist: Lectorum Pubns., Inc.

Priddy, Roger. Mealtime - A High Contrast High Chair Book. 2013. (Hello Baby Ser.). (ENG., Illus.). 8p. (J). (gr. -1 — 1). bds. 5.99 *(978-0-312-51602-4(9),* 9780312516024, Priddy Bks.) St. Martin's Pr.

—Picture Play: Mealtime. 2016. (Picture Play Ser.). (ENG., Illus.). 10p. (J). bds. 5.99 *(978-0-312-51961-2(3),* 9780312519612, Priddy Bks.) St. Martin's Pr.

Processed Food: Level G, 6 vols. (Wonder Worldtm Ser.). 16p. 29.95 *(978-0-7802-2022-5(6))* Wright Group/McGraw-Hill.

Puck. My Foodie ABC: A Little Gourmet's Guide. Lemay, Violet, illus. 2010. (ENG.). 22p. (J). (gr. -1-k). bds. 8.95 *(978-0-9825295-2-2(X))* Duo Pr. LLC.

Quinlan, Julia J. & Furgang, Adam. The Truth Behind Snack Foods. 2017. (J). pap. ***(978-1-4994-3934-2(2),*** Rosen Reference) Rosen Publishing Group, Inc., The.

—The Truth Behind Soft Drinks. 2017. (J). ***(978-1-4777-8992-6(8))*** Rosen Publishing Group, Inc., The.

Quinlan, Julia J. & Johanson, Paula. The Truth Behind Factory Foods. 2017. (J). pap. ***(978-1-4994-3923-6(7),*** Rosen Reference) Rosen Publishing Group, Inc., The.

Quinlan, Julia J. & Watson, Stephanie. The Truth Behind Manufactured Meats. 2017. (J). pap. ***(978-1-4777-8994-0(4),*** Rosen Reference) Rosen Publishing Group, Inc., The.

Rand, Casey. Food, 1 vol. 2012. (Science Behind Ser.). (ENG.). 32p. (gr. 3-3). pap. 8.29 *(978-1-4109-4497-9(2));* lib. bdg. 30.65 *(978-1-4109-4486-3(7))* Heinemann-Raintree. (Raintree Perspectives).

Randall, Ronne. Where Food Comes From. 2010. (Science Everywhere! Ser.). 24p. 24.25 *(978-1-84898-294-9(1))* Black Rabbit Bks.

Rau, Dana Meachen. Food Safety: Seguridad de Los Alimentos. 2009. (Bookworms — Bilingual Editions: Safe Kids/Ninos Seguros Ser.). (SPA & ENG.). 32p. (gr. k-2). lib. bdg. 15.95 *(978-0-7614-4777-1(6))* Marshall Cavendish Corp.

Rau, Dana Meachen & Meachen Rau, Dana. Food Safety: Seguridad de Los Alimentos. 2009. (Bookworms: Safe Kids Ser.). (SPA & ENG.). 32p. (gr. k-2). 15.95 *(978-0-7614-4087-1(9))* Marshall Cavendish GBR. Dist: Marshall Cavendish Corp.

Rebvik. A-Z of Dangerous Food. 2012. (ENG., Illus.). 56p. pap. 10.95 *(978-1-84976-016-4(0))* Tate Publishing, Ltd. GBR. Dist: Abrams, Inc.

Reeves, Diane Lindsey. Food & Natural Resources. 2017. (Bright Futures Press: World of Work Ser.). (ENG., Illus.). 32p. (J). (gr. 4-7). lib. bdg. 29.93 *(978-1-63472-622-1(7),* 209522) Cherry Lake Publishing.

EFG

Regis, Natalie. Genetically Modified Crops & Food. 2015. (Biotechnology Revolution Ser.). (ENG., Illus.). 128p. (J). (gr. 10-10). 38.75 *(978-1-62275-578-3(2),* Britannica Educational Publishing) Rosen Publishing Group, Inc., The.

Reinke, Beth Bence. Healthy Snacks. 2013. (Healthy Eating with Myplate Ser.). (ENG.). 24p. (J). (gr. 1-4). 28.50 *(978-1-62323-600-7(2),* 206402) Child's World, Inc., The.

Reino, Jessica. Food Allergies: The Ultimate Teen Guide. 2015. (It Happened to Me Ser.: 45). (ENG., Illus.). 182p. (J). 45.00 *(978-1-4422-3573-1(X))* Rowman & Littlefield Publishers, Inc.

Reitmeyer, Hans. What People Eat. 2009. (Real Life Readers Ser.). 8p. (gr. k-1). pap. 5.15 *(978-1-4042-8010-6(3),* Rosen Classroom) Rosen Publishing Group, Inc., The.

Ribke, Simone T. The Shapes We Eat. 2004. (Rookie Read-About Math Ser.). (J). 20.50 *(978-0-516-24431-0(0),* Children's Pr.) Scholastic Library Publishing.

Rice, Dona Herweck. Comer Bien, 1 vol. 2nd rev. ed. 2012. (Nonfiction Readers Ser.). (SPA.). 20p. (J). (gr. 1-1). pap. 4.99 *(978-1-4333-4430-5(0))* Teacher Created Materials, Inc.

—Delicious & Nutritious, 1 vol. 2011. (Early Childhood Themes Ser.). (ENG.). 16p. (J). (gr. -1-2). pap. 19.99 *(978-1-4333-2370-6(2));* pap. 6.99 *(978-1-4333-2369-0(9))* Teacher Created Materials, Inc.

—Eating Right, 1 vol. 2nd rev. ed. 2014. (TIME for KIDS(r) Nonfiction Readers Ser.). (ENG., Illus.). 20p. (J). (gr. 1-1). pap. 19.96 *(978-1-4807-1030-6(X))* Shell Educational Publishing.

Rice, Dona Herwick. Eating Right, 1 vol. 2nd rev. ed. 2011. (Nonfiction Readers Ser.). (ENG.). 20p. (J). (gr. 1-1). pap. 4.99 *(978-1-4333-3597-6(2))* Teacher Created Materials, Inc.

Ridley, Sarah. Food. 2017. (Tell Me What You Remember Ser.). (ENG., Illus.). 24p. (J). (gr. k-2). 17.99 *(978-1-4451-3986-9(3),* Franklin Watts) Hachette Children's Group GBR. Dist: Hachette Bk. Group.

Rissman, Rebecca. Eat, 1 vol. 2013. (Say What You See Ser.). (ENG.). 24p. (gr. -1-1). 22.65 *(978-1-4109-5047-5(6));* pap. 7.10 *(978-1-4109-5052-9(2))* Heinemann-Raintree.

Ritchie, Scot. See What We Eat! A First Book of Healthy Eating. Ritchie, Scot, illus. 2017. (ENG., Illus.). 32p. (J). (gr. -1-2). 16.99 ***(978-1-77138-618-0(5))*** Kids Can Pr., Ltd. CAN. Dist: Hachette Bk. Group.

Rockwell, Lizzy. Good Enough to Eat: A Kid's Guide to Food & Nutrition. Rockwell, Lizzy, illus. 2009. (ENG., Illus.). 40p. (J). (gr. k-4). pap. 6.99 *(978-0-06-445174-1(7))* HarperCollins Pubs.

Rodger, Ellen. Reducing Your Foodprint: Farming, Cooking, & Eating for a Healthy Planet. 2010. (ENG., Illus.). 32p. (J). pap. *(978-0-7787-2936-5(2))* Crabtree Publishing Co.

Rose, Elizabeth. Food & Nutrition. 24p. 2009. (Illus.). (J). (gr. 3-6). pap. 8.25 *(978-1-4358-3264-0(7))* 2009. (gr. 3-4). 42.50 *(978-1-60854-001-3(4))* 2006. (Illus.). (J). (gr. -1-3). lib. bdg. 21.25 *(978-1-4042-2821-4(7))* Rosen Publishing Group, Inc., The. (PowerKids Pr.).

Rosen, Lynn. Tomorrow's Vision. 2010. 56p. pap. 12.99 *(978-1-4520-1602-3(X))* AuthorHouse.

Rosenberg, Pam. How Did That Get to My Table? Cereal. 2009. (Community Connections: How Did That Get to My Table? Ser.). (ENG.). 24p. (gr. 2-5). lib. bdg. 25.64 *(978-1-60279-466-5(9),* 200261) Cherry Lake Publishing.

Rotner, Shelley. Grow! Raise! Catch! How We Get Our Food. (ENG.). 32p. (J). 2017. 7.99 ***(978-0-8234-3884-6(8))*** 2016. (Illus.). 16.95 *(978-0-8234-3643-9(6))* Holiday Hse., Inc.

Rotner, Shelley & Goss, Gary. Where Does Food Come From? 2006. (Illus.). 32p. (J). (gr. -1-2). 22.60 *(978-0-7613-2935-0(8))* Lerner Publishing Group.

Rotner, Shelley & Kelly, Sheila M. Yummy! Rotner, Shelley, photos by. 2013. (ENG., Illus.). 32p. (J). (gr. -1-1). 16.95 *(978-0-8234-2426-9(X))* Holiday Hse., Inc.

Rustad, Martha E. H. Colorful Foods. 2016. (Colorful Foods Ser.). (ENG.). 24p. (gr. k-1). 87.96 *(978-1-5157-2390-5(9),* Pebble Bks.) Capstone Press of Coughlan Cos.

—Green Foods. 2016. (Colorful Foods Ser.). (ENG.). 24p. (gr. k-1). lib. bdg. 21.99 *(978-1-5157-2372-1(0),* Pebble Bks.) Capstone Press of Coughlan Cos.

—Orange Foods. 2016. (Colorful Foods Ser.). (ENG.). 24p. (gr. k-1). lib. bdg. 21.99 *(978-1-5157-2370-7(4),* Pebble Bks.) Capstone Press of Coughlan Cos.

—Red Foods. 2016. (Colorful Foods Ser.). (ENG.). 24p. (gr. k-1). lib. bdg. 21.99 *(978-1-5157-2373-8(9),* Pebble Bks.) Capstone Press of Coughlan Cos.

—Yellow Foods. 2016. (Colorful Foods Ser.). (ENG.). 24p. (gr. k-1). lib. bdg. 21.99 *(978-1-5157-2371-4(2),* Pebble Bks.) Capstone Press of Coughlan Cos.

Ryall, Jeanette. Food Art. 2012. (Awesome Art Ser.). (ENG., Illus.). 32p. (J). (gr. 3-6). 26.50 *(978-1-4488-8086-7(6));* pap. 11.75 *(978-1-4488-8139-0(0))* Windmill Bks.

Sachse, Dina, illus. My Food: 12 Lift-N-Learn Flashcards about Food!, 26 vols. 2013. (Early Start Singles Ser.). (ENG.). 12p. (J). *(978-1-77132-102-0(4))* SpiceBox Products Ltd.

Salzmann, Mary Elizabeth. Know Your Numbers: Food, 1 vol. 2014. (Numbers 1-20 Ser.). (ENG.). 24p. (J). (gr. k-3). lib. bdg. 24.21 *(978-1-62403-265-3(6),* SandCastle) ABDO Publishing Co.

—Money for Food, 1 vol. 2010. (Your Piggy Bank: A Guide to Spending & Saving for Kids! Ser.). (ENG.). 24p. (J). (gr. k-3). 27.07 *(978-1-61641-029-2(9))* Magic Wagon.

Samson, Tess. Snack Time. 2010. (Sight Word Readers Ser.). (J). 3.49 *(978-1-60719-618-1(2))* Newmark Learning LLC.

Scherer, Lauri S. Fast Food. Greenhaven Press Editors, ed. 2013. (Introducing Issues with Opposing Viewpoints Ser.). (ENG.). 144p. (gr. 10-12). lib. bdg. 42.00 *(978-0-7377-6922-7(X),* Greenhaven Pr., Inc.) Cengage Gale.

Schrier, Allyson Valentine. Eat Right: Your Guide to Maintaining a Healthy Diet. 2011. (Healthy Me Ser.). (ENG.). 32p. (gr. 3-4). pap. 47.70 *(978-1-4296-7292-4(7));* lib. bdg. 27.99 *(978-1-4296-6544-5(0))* Capstone Press of Coughlan Cos. (Snap Bks.).

Schuette, Sarah L. A Ballerina Cookbook: Simple Recipes for Kids, 1 vol. 2012. (First Cookbooks Ser.). (ENG.). 24p. (gr. 1-2). lib. bdg. 25.32 *(978-1-4296-7622-9(1),* First Facts) Capstone Press of Coughlan Cos.

—First Cookbooks. 2011. (First Cookbooks Ser.). (ENG.). 24p. (gr. 1-2). lib. bdg. 50.64 *(978-1-4296-6134-8(8),* First Facts) Capstone Press of Coughlan Cos.

—First Cookbooks, 6 vols., Set. Incl. Christmas Cookbook: Simple Recipes for Kids. 2011. lib. bdg. 25.32 *(978-1-4296-5999-4(8));* Princess Cookbook: Simple Recipes for Kids. 2010. lib. bdg. 25.32 *(978-1-4296-5374-9(4));* Superhero Cookbook: Simple Recipes for Kids. 2011. lib. bdg. 25.32 *(978-1-4296-5998-7(X));* (gr. 1-2). (First Cookbooks Ser.). (ENG.). 24p. 2011. Set lib. bdg. 75.96 *(978-1-4296-6135-5(6),* First Facts) Capstone Press of Coughlan Cos.

—A Football Cookbook: Simple Recipes for Kids, 1 vol. 2012. (First Cookbooks Ser.). (ENG.). 24p. (gr. 1-2). lib. bdg. 25.32 *(978-1-4296-7620-5(5),* First Facts) Capstone Press of Coughlan Cos.

Schuh, Mari. Ants. 2013. (ENG., Illus.). 24p. (J). lib. bdg. 25.65 *(978-1-62031-050-2(3))* Jump! Inc.

—Butterflies. 2013. (ENG., Illus.). 24p. (J). lib. bdg. 25.65 *(978-1-62031-053-3(8))* Jump! Inc.

—Dairy on Myplate. 2012. (What's on Myplate? Ser.). (ENG.). 24p. (gr. k-1). pap. 41.70 *(978-1-4296-9411-7(4),* Pebble Plus) Capstone Press of Coughlan Cos.

—Healthy Snacks on Myplate, 1 vol. 2012. (What's on Myplate? Ser.). (ENG., Illus.). 24p. (gr. k-1). pap. 7.29 *(978-1-4296-9418-6(1),* Pebble Plus) Capstone Press of Coughlan Cos.

Schuh, Mari C. Healthy Snacks on Myplate, 1 vol. 2012. (What's on Myplate? Ser.). (ENG., Illus.). 24p. (gr. k-1). lib. bdg. 26.65 *(978-1-4296-8748-5(7),* Pebble Plus) Capstone Press of Coughlan Cos.

—Proteínas en MiPlato. Strictly Spanish LLC. Staff, tr. 2013. (¿Qué Hay en MiPlato?/What's on My Plate? Ser.).Tr. of Protein on MyPlate. (SPA, ENG & MUL.). 24p. (gr. k-1). lib. bdg. 26.65 *(978-1-62065-945-8(X))* Capstone Press of Coughlan Cos.

—Snacks for Healthy Teeth, 1 vol. Saunders-Smith, Gail, ed. 2008. (Healthy Teeth Ser.). (ENG., Illus.). 24p. (gr. k-1). pap. 7.29 *(978-1-4296-1785-7(3),* Pebble Plus) Capstone Press of Coughlan Cos.

Science & Technology for Children Books, Food Chemistry Set, 8 vols. 2004. (Illus.). 64p. (J). *(978-1-933008-18-9(0))* Smithsonian Science Education Ctr. (SSEC).

Scratch N Sniff Staff. Scratch N Sniff Food. 2005. 12p. 6.95 *(978-0-9762524-6-7(5))* Gimme Gimme Toys & Games, Inc.

Seaborn, Ron. The Children's Health Food Book. rev. ed. 2006. 40p. 16.95 *(978-0-9647089-2-1(2))* Life Line, Inc.

Segarra, Mercedes. Yummy Snacks: Little Chef Recipes. 2013. (Little Chef Ser.). 36p. (J). lib. bdg. 23.94 *(978-0-7660-4264-3(2),* Enslow Elementary) Enslow Pubs., Inc.

Senker, Cath. McDonald's: The Business Behind the Golden Arches. 2016. (Big Brands Ser.). (ENG., Illus.). 32p. (J). (gr. 4-6). 26.65 *(978-1-5124-0590-3(6))* Lerner Publishing Group.

Sertori, Trisha. Meats, Fish, Eggs, Nuts, & Beans. 2008. (Body Fuel for Healthy Bodies Ser.). 32p. (gr. 4-18). lib. bdg. 18.56 *(978-0-7614-3801-4(7),* Benchmark Bks.) Marshall Cavendish Corp.

Sesame Workshop, Sesame & McQuillan, Susan. Sesame Street Let's Cook! 2015. (Sesame Street Ser.). (ENG., Illus.). 128p. (gr. -1-k). spiral bd. 17.99 *(978-0-544-45436-1(7))* Houghton Mifflin Harcourt Publishing Co.

Sévigny, Eric, illus. Caillou: Fresh from the Farm. 2013. (Ecology Club Ser.). (ENG.). 24p. (J). (gr. -1-1). 5.99 *(978-2-89718-026-3(9))* Caillouet, Gerry.

—Caillou Makes a Meal: Includes a Simple Pizza Recipe. 2016. (Clubhouse Ser.). (ENG.). 24p. (J). (gr. -1 — 1). pap. 3.99 *(978-2-89718-258-8(X))* Caillouet, Gerry.

Shaw-Russell, Susan. Build Your Own Breakfast Sticker Activity Book. 2011. (Dover Little Activity Books Stickers Ser.). (ENG., Illus.). 4p. (J). (gr. k-3). pap. 1.99 *(978-0-486-48182-1(4))* Dover Pubns., Inc.

Sheen, Barbara. Peru. 2010. (Taste of Culture Ser.). 64p. lib. bdg. 30.45 *(978-0-7377-5346-2(3),* Kidhaven) Cengage Gale.

Sheen, Barbara, ed. Foods of Colombia. 2012. (Taste of Culture Ser.). (ENG., Illus.). 64p. (J). (gr. 3-6). lib. bdg. 30.45 *(978-0-7377-5948-8(8),* Kidhaven) Cengage Gale.

—Foods of Ghana. 2012. (Taste of Culture Ser.). (ENG., Illus.). 64p. (gr. 3-6). lib. bdg. 35.20 *(978-0-7377-5949-5(6),* Kidhaven) Cengage Gale.

—Foods of South Africa. 2012. (Taste of Culture Ser.). (ENG., Illus.). 64p. (gr. 3-6). lib. bdg. 30.45 *(978-0-7377-5952-5(6),* Kidhaven) Cengage Gale.

Sherrow, Victoria. Food Safety. 2008. (Point/Counterpoint Ser.). (Illus.). 168p. (YA). (gr. 9-12). lib. bdg. 35.00 *(978-0-7910-9269-7(5))* Facts On File, Inc.

Shofner, Shawndra. How It Happens at the Pizza Company. Wolfe, Bob & Wolfe, Diane, photos by. 2006. (How It Happens Ser.). (Illus.). 32p. (J). (gr. 2-5). lib. bdg. 19.95 *(978-1-881508-98-4(6))* Oliver Pr., Inc.

Shores, Erika L. How Food Gets from Farms to Store Shelves. 2016. (Here to There Ser.). (ENG.). 24p. (gr. k-1). lib. bdg. 26.65 *(978-1-4914-8428-9(4),* Pebble Plus) Capstone Press of Coughlan Cos.

Shryer, Donna. Body Fuel: A Guide to Good Nutrition. 2007. (Food & Fitness Ser.). (Illus.). 128p. (YA). (gr. 7-12). lib. bdg. 38.50 *(978-0-7614-2552-6(7))* Marshall Cavendish Corp.

Silate, Jennifer. Planning & Preparing Healthy Meals & Snacks: A Day-to-Day Guide to a Healthier Diet. 2008. (Library of Nutrition Ser.). (ENG., Illus.). 48p. (gr. 5-8). per. 11.75 *(978-1-4042-1634-1(0))* Rosen Publishing Group, Inc., The.

Slade, Suzanne. What Do You Know about Food Chains & Food Webs? 2009. (20 Questions: Science Ser.). 24p. (gr. 2-3). 42.50 *(978-1-60854-962-7(3),* PowerKids Pr.) Rosen Publishing Group, Inc., The.

Smallwood, Sally. Cool as a Cucumber. 2005. (Things I Eat Ser.: 1). (ENG., Illus.). 24p. (J). (gr. -1-k). *(978-1-84089-418-9(0))* Zero to Ten, Ltd.

—Sweet as a Strawberry. Smallwood, Sally, illus. 2005. (Things I Eat Ser.: 1). (ENG., Illus.). 24p. (J). (gr. -1-k). *(978-1-84089-419-6(9))* Zero to Ten, Ltd.

Smith, Andrea Claire Harte. Food Safety & Farming. 2003. (In the News Ser.). (J). lib. bdg. 24.25 *(978-1-58340-394-5(9))* Black Rabbit Bks.

Smith, Paula. Foods in Different Places. 2015. (Learning about Our Global Community Ser.). (ENG., Illus.). 24p. (J). *(978-0-7787-2009-6(8))* Crabtree Publishing Co.

Sohn, Emily & Bair, Diane. Food & Nutrition: Eating to Win. 2011. (IScience Readers Ser.). 48p. (J). (gr. 5-6). lib. bdg. 23.94 *(978-1-59953-424-4(X))* Norwood Hse. Pr.

Solway, Andrew. Food Chains & Webs, 1 vol. 2012. (Web of Life Ser.). (ENG.). 48p. (gr. 3-3). pap. 9.49 *(978-1-4109-4431-3(X),* Raintree Freestyle Express) Heinemann-Raintree.

Somervill, Barbara. Food Scientist. 2009. (21st Century Skills Library: Cool Science Careers Ser.). (ENG.). 32p. (gr. 4-8). lib. bdg. 28.50 *(978-1-60279-505-1(3),* 200305) Cherry Lake Publishing.

Squire, Ann O. Seafood. 2017. (True Book(tm), a — Farm to Table Ser.). (ENG., Illus.). 48p. (J). lib. bdg. 31.00 *(978-0-531-22935-4(1),* Children's Pr.) Scholastic Library Publishing.

Staniford, Linda. Food & Drink. 2015. (Wants vs Needs Ser.). (ENG., Illus.). 24p. (gr. k-2). 23.32 *(978-1-4846-0943-9(3),* Heinemann Read & Learn) Heinemann-Raintree.

—How Do Animals Give Us Food? 2016. (From Farm to Fork: Where Does My Food Come From? Ser.). (ENG.). 24p. (gr. k-2). lib. bdg. 23.99 *(978-1-4846-3350-2(4),* Heinemann Read & Learn) Heinemann-Raintree.

Star Bright Books, creator. Eating the Rainbow (Vietnamese/English), 1 vol. 2010. (Sach Ve Thuc Pham Day Mau Sac/Eating the Rainbow Ser.). (VIE & ENG., Illus.). 20p. (J). 6.95 *(978-1-59572-219-5(X))* Star Bright Bks., Inc.

Stein, Joshua David. Can I Eat That? 2016. (ENG., Illus.). 40p. 16.95 *(978-0-7148-7110-3(9))* Phaidon Pr., Inc.

Stephens, William R. Finding Food in the Wild. 2003. (Extreme Animals Ser.). (J). pap. *(978-1-58417-247-5(9));* lib. bdg. *(978-1-58417-246-8(0))* Lake Street Pubs.

Sterling Children's, Sterling. Food/Los Alimentos. 2016. (Say & Play Ser.). (ENG., Illus.). 28p. (J). (— 1). bds. 4.95 *(978-1-4549-1998-8(1))* Sterling Publishing Co., Inc.

Sterling Publishing Co., Inc. Food. 2016. (Say & Play Ser.). (ENG., Illus.). 28p. (J). (— 1). bds. 4.95 *(978-1-4549-1973-5(6))* Sterling Publishing Co., Inc.

Stille, Darlene R. Good Food, Good for Earth. 2011. (Go Green! Ser.). (ENG., Illus.). 32p. (J). (gr. 1-4). lib. bdg. 28.50 *(978-1-60973-173-1(5),* 201152) Child's World, Inc., The.

—Lunch Lady Science: Understanding the Food That Goes in Your Body, 1 vol. 2011. (Everyday Science Ser.). (ENG.). 64p. (gr. 5-7). pap. 9.10 *(978-0-7565-4502-4(1),* CPB Grades 4-8) Compass Point Bks.

Stilwell, Debra. Where Does Our Food Come From? 2012. (Everyday Mysteries Ser.). (ENG., Illus.). 24p. (J). (gr. 2-4). pap. 8.15 *(978-1-4339-6319-3(1));* lib. bdg. 22.60 *(978-1-4339-6317-9(5))* Stevens, Gareth Publishing LLLP.

Stones, Brenda & Feldman, Thea. Kingfisher Readers L2 What We Eat. 2014. (Kingfisher Readers Ser.). (ENG., Illus.). 32p. (J). (gr. 1-3). 12.99 *(978-0-7534-7120-3(5),* 9780753471203, Kingfisher) Roaring Brook Pr.

Storper, Barbara. Janey Junkfood's Fresh Adventure! Making Good Eating Great Fun! Schneid, Frances E., illus. 2008. 32p. (J). (gr. 3-7). 15.95 *(978-0-9642858-5-9(1))* FoodPlay Productions.

Sullivan, Jaclyn. What's in Your Chicken Nugget? 2012. (What's in Your Fast Food Ser.). (ENG., Illus.). 24p. (J). (gr. 2-5). pap. 8.25 *(978-1-4488-6375-4(9),* PowerKids Pr.); lib. bdg. 22.60 *(978-1-4488-6208-5(6))* Rosen Publishing Group, Inc., The.

Sundance/Newbridge LLC Staff. Make Mine Ice Cream. 2007. (Early Science Ser.). (gr. k-3). pap. 6.10 *(978-1-4007-6518-8(8))* Sundance/Newbridge Educational Publishing.

—Pasta, Please! 2007. (Early Science Ser.). (gr. k-3). 18.95 *(978-1-4007-6332-0(0));* pap. 6.10 *(978-1-4007-6328-3(2))* Sundance/Newbridge Educational Publishing.

—You Are What You Eat. 2007. (Early Science Ser.). (gr. k-3). 18.95 *(978-1-4007-6432-7(7));* pap. 6.10 *(978-1-4007-6428-0(9))* Sundance/Newbridge Educational Publishing.

Sylver, Adrienne. Hot Diggity Dog: The History of the Hot Dog. Smith, Elwood, illus. 2015. (ENG.). 32p. (J). (gr. k-3). 8.99 *(978-0-14-751578-0(5),* Puffin Books) Penguin Young Readers Group.

Tarbox, A. D. An Arctic Tundra Food Chain. 2011. (Nature's Bounty Ser.). (ENG., Illus.). 48p. (J). (gr. 5-17). pap. 9.99 *(978-1-897563-08-3(6),* Creative Paperbacks) Creative Co., The.

—An Arctic Tundra Food Chain: Odysseys in Nature. 2016. (Odysseys in Nature Ser.). (ENG.). 80p. (J). (gr. 7-10). pap. 14.99 *(978-1-62832-139-5(3),* Creative Paperbacks) Creative Co., The.

—An Ocean Food Chain: Odysseys in Nature. 2016. (Odysseys in Nature Ser.). (ENG.). 80p. (J). (gr. 7-10). pap. 14.99 *(978-1-62832-142-5(3),* Creative Paperbacks) Creative Co., The.

—A Prairie Food Chain: Odysseys in Nature. 2016. (Odysseys in Nature Ser.). (ENG.). 80p. (J). (gr. 7-10). pap. 14.99 *(978-1-62832-143-2(1),* Creative Paperbacks) Creative Co., The.

—A Rainforest Food Chain: Odysseys in Nature. 2016. (Odysseys in Nature Ser.). (ENG.). 80p. (J). (gr. 7-10). pap. 14.99 *(978-1-62832-144-9(X),* Creative Paperbacks) Creative Co., The.

Taste Bud Travels: Individual Title Six-Packs. (Bookweb Ser.). 32p. (gr. 4-18). 34.00 *(978-0-7635-3742-5(X))* Rigby Education.

Tasty Treats, 6 bks., Set. (J). (gr. 1-4). lib. bdg. 143.58 *(978-1-57103-334-5(3))* Rourke Educational Media.

Thomas, Ann. Food Series, 6 vols., Set. 2005. (Food Ser.). (Illus.). 32p. (gr. 2-4). 92.00 *(978-0-7910-7052-9(2),* Chelsea Hse.) Facts On File, Inc.

Thompson, Tamara. Fast Food. Greenhaven Press Staff, ed. 2015. (At Issue Ser.). (ENG.). 128p. (gr. 10-12). lib. bdg. 39.40 *(978-0-7377-7165-7(8),* Greenhaven Pr., Inc.) Cengage Gale.

Thornborough, Kathy. Food. Petelinsek, Kathleen, illus. 2014. (Talking Hands Ser.). (ENG.). 24p. (J). (gr. k-3). 25.64 *(978-1-62687-319-3(4),* 207159) Child's World, Inc., The.

Ticktock Media, Ltd. Staff. Favorite Foods: Colors & Shapes. 2008. (Tab Bks.). (ENG.). 10p. (J). (gr. -1-k). bds. 4.95 *(978-1-84696-821-1(6),* TickTock Books) Octopus Publishing Group GBR. Dist: Independent Pubs. Group.

Tomczyk, Tara & Smith, Terry L. Nutrition & Food Safety. 2010. (Healthy Eating: A Guide to Nutrition Ser.). 184p. (C). (gr. 9). 35.00 *(978-1-60413-776-7(2),* Chelsea Hse.) Facts On File, Inc.

Top of the Food Chain. 2013. (Top of the Food Chain Ser.). 32p. (J). (gr. k-5). 151.50 *(978-1-4777-1544-4(4))* Windmill Bks.

Traini, Agostino, illus. Chef Foody's Field Trip. 2015. (ENG.). 40p. (J). (gr. -1-2). 14.95 *(978-0-7892-1241-2(2),* Abbeville Kids) Abbeville Pr., Inc.

Tripp, Natalie. We Care! Making Care Packages: Understand the Relationship Between Multiplication & Division. 2014. (Rosen Common Core Math Readers Ser.). (ENG., Illus.). 24p. (J). (gr. 3-4). pap. 8.25 *(978-1-4777-4955-5(1),* PowerKids Pr.) Rosen Publishing Group, Inc., The.

Tuminelly, Nancy. Cool Cake & Cupcake Food Art: Easy Recipes That Make Food Fun to Eat!, 1 vol. 2011. (Cool Food Art Ser.). (ENG.). 32p. (gr. 3-6). 28.50 *(978-1-61613-362-7(7),* Checkerboard Library) ABDO Publishing Co.

—Cool Creepy Food Art: Easy Recipes That Make Food Fun to Eat!, 1 vol. 2011. (Cool Food Art Ser.). (ENG.). 32p. (gr. 3-6). 28.50 *(978-1-61613-363-4(5),* Checkerboard Library) ABDO Publishing Co.

—Cool Fruit & Veggie Food Art: Easy Recipes That Make Food Fun to Eat!, 1 vol. 2011. (Cool Food Art Ser.). (ENG.). 32p. (gr. 3-6). 28.50 *(978-1-61613-364-1(3),* Checkerboard Library) ABDO Publishing Co.

—Cool Holiday Food Art: Easy Recipes That Make Food Fun to Eat!, 1 vol. 2011. (Cool Food Art Ser.). (ENG., Illus.). 32p. (J). (gr. 3-6). 28.50 *(978-1-61613-365-8(1),* Checkerboard Library) ABDO Publishing Co.

—Cool Sandwich Food Art: Easy Recipes That Make Food Fun to Eat!, 1 vol. 2011. (Cool Food Art Ser.). (ENG., Illus.). 32p. (gr. 3-6). 28.50 *(978-1-61613-366-5(X),* Checkerboard Library) ABDO Publishing Co.

—Cool Snack Food Art: Easy Recipes That Make Food Fun to Eat!, 1 vol. 2011. (Cool Food Art Ser.). (ENG.). 32p. (gr. 3-6). 28.50 *(978-1-61613-367-2(8),* Checkerboard Library) ABDO Publishing Co.

—Super Simple Breakfasts: Easy No-Bake Recipes for Kids, 1 vol. 2010. (Super Simple Cooking Ser.). (ENG.). 32p. (gr. k-4). 27.07 *(978-1-61613-383-2(X),* Super SandCastle) ABDO Publishing Co.

—Super Simple Snacks: Easy No-Bake Recipes for Kids, 1 vol. 2010. (Super Simple Cooking Ser.). (ENG.). 32p. (gr. k-4). 27.07 *(978-1-61613-388-7(0),* Super SandCastle) ABDO Publishing Co.

Turnbull, Stephanie. Fabulous Food. 2016. (Sleepover Secrets Ser.). 24p. (gr. 2-6). 28.50 *(978-1-62588-379-7(X),* Smart Apple Media) Black Rabbit Bks.

—Why Do We Eat? Haggerty, Tim, illus. 2006. (Beginners Science: Level 2 Ser.). 32p. (J). (gr. 1-3). 4.99 *(978-0-7945-1333-7(6));* (gr. 4-7). lib. bdg. 12.99 *(978-1-58086-933-1(5))* EDC Publishing. (Usborne).

Twin Sisters(r) Staff. Gruesome Grub. 2009. 16p. 4.99 *(978-1-59922-418-3(6))* Twin Sisters IP, LLC.

Tyler, Jenny. Baby's Very First Mealtime Book. 2009. (Baby's Very First Board Bks). 10p. (J). (gr. -1). bds. 6.99 *(978-0-7945-2607-8(1),* Usborne) EDC Publishing.

Vander Klipp, Michael. God Made Food, 1 vol. 2008. (God Made... Ser.). 14p. (J). bds. 3.99 *(978-0-8254-3913-1(2))* Kregel Pubns.

Vaughn, Inés. Chiles. 2009. (Native Foods of Latin America / Alimentos Indígenas de Latinoamérica Ser.). (SPA & ENG.). (J). 22.60 *(978-1-4358-2725-7(2),* PowerKids Pr.) Rosen Publishing Group, Inc., The.

Ventura, Marne. The 12 Biggest Breakthroughs in Food Technology. 2014. (ENG.). 32p. (J). *(978-1-63235-014-5(9))* Pr. Room Editions LLC.

Verdick, Elizabeth. Mealtime. Heinlen, Marieka, illus. 2011. (Toddler Tools Ser.). (ENG.). 24p. (J). (gr. k — 1). 7.95 *(978-1-57542-366-1(9))* Free Spirit Publishing, Inc.

Vogel, Julia. Deciduous Forest Food Chains, 1 vol. Adams, Hazel, illus. 2010. (Fascinating Food Chains Ser.). (ENG.). 32p. 28.50 *(978-1-60270-792-4(8),* Looking Glass Library-Nonfiction) Magic Wagon.

Waldron, Kevin. Harold's Hungry Eyes. 2016. (ENG., Illus.). 32p. (gr. -1-1). 16.95 *(978-0-7148-7124-0(9))* Phaidon Pr., Inc.

Walters, Peter. The Hungriest Mouth in the Sea, 1 vol. 2015. (ENG., Illus.). 32p. (J). (gr. k-3). pap. 9.95 *(978-1-62855-636-0(6))* Arbordale Publishing.

Watson, Stephanie. Mystery Meat: Hot Dogs, Sausages, & Lunch Meats. 2011. (Incredibly Disgusting Food Ser.). (Illus.). 48p. (J). pap. 11.75 *(978-1-4488-2284-3(X),* 1323609); (gr. 5-9). lib. bdg. 29.25 *(978-1-4488-1268-4(2),* 1323609) Rosen Publishing Group, Inc., The.

—What's in Your Food? Processed Food. 2009. (Health & Your Body Ser.). 48p. (gr. 5-8). pap. 11.75 *(978-1-4358-5163-4(3),* Rosen Classroom) Rosen Publishing Group, Inc., The.

Watt, F. Vamos a Comer! 2004.Tr. of Baby's Mealtime. (SPA., Illus.). 16p. (J). (gr. -1). pap. 4.95 *(978-0-7460-4540-4(9))* EDC Publishing.

Weekly Reader Editorial Staff. Las Cosas Que Como. 2006. (Things in My World/ Las cosas de mi mundo Ser.). (SPA., Illus.). 16p. (gr. -1-2). lib. bdg. 19.00 *(978-0-8368-7222-4(3),* Weekly Reader Leveled Readers) Stevens, Gareth Publishing LLLP.

—Things I Eat. 2006. (Things in My World Ser.). (Illus.). 16p. (gr. -1-2). lib. bdg. 19.00 *(978-0-8368-6810-4(2),* Weekly Reader Leveled Readers) Stevens, Gareth Publishing LLLP.

Weekly Reader Editorial Staff, contrib. by. Things I Eat/las Cosas Que Como. 2006. (Things in My World/ Las cosas de mi mundo Ser.). (ENG & SPA.). 16p. (gr. -1-2). pap. 5.30 *(978-0-8368-7229-3(0),* Weekly Reader Leveled Readers) Stevens, Gareth Publishing LLLP.

What Is Delicious?, 6, Pack. (gr. 1-2). 22.00 *(978-0-7635-9091-8(6))* Rigby Education.

William H. Sadlier Staff. Good Food. 2005. (Emergent (Prek-2) Health Package Ser.). 12p. (gr. -1-1). 25.20 *(978-0-8215-7847-6(2))* Sadlier, William H. Inc.

Williams, Kara. Frequently Asked Questions about My Pyramid: Eating Right. 2009. (FAQ: Teen Life Ser.). 64p. (gr.

5-6). 58.50 *(978-1-61512-583-8(3))* Rosen Publishing Group, Inc., The.

—Mypyramid: Eating Right. 2007. (FAQ: Teen Life Ser.). (Illus.). 64p. (YA). (gr. 7-12). lib. bdg. 31.95 *(978-1-4042-1974-8(9))* Rosen Publishing Group, Inc., The.

wintranslation.com, tr. Eating the Rainbow (French/English). 1 vol. 2010. (Livre D'Aliments Colores/Colorful Food Bks.). (ENG & FRE., Illus.). 20p. (J). 6.95 *(978-1-59572-218-8(1))* Star Bright Bks., Inc.

Woods, Michael & Woods, Mary B. Ancient Agricultural Technology: From Sickles to Plows. 2011. (Technology in Ancient Cultures Ser.). (ENG.). 96p. (gr. 6-12). lib. bdg. 31.93 *(978-0-7613-6526-6(5))* Lerner Publishing Group.

World Book, Inc Staff, contrib. by. Good Food for You. 2010. (J). *(978-0-7166-7739-0(3))* World Bk., Inc.

Wroble, Lisa A. & Library. Food for a Greener Planet: What You Can Do. 2010. (Green Issues in Focus Ser.). (Illus.). 112p. (J). (gr. 7-12). lib. bdg. 33.27 *(978-0-7660-3349-8(X))* Enslow Pubs., Inc.

Yasuda, Anita. Eating Green. 2016. (J). ***(978-1-5105-2213-8(1))*** SmartBook Media, Inc.

Yerdon, Joe. America's Oddest Foods. 2016. (Weird America Ser.). (ENG., Illus.). 32p. (J). (gr. 3-4). pap. 10.50 *(978-1-4824-4012-6(1))* Stevens, Gareth Publishing LLLP.

Ziefert, Harriet. One Red Apple. Gudeon, Karla, illus. 2009. 36p. (J). 15.99 *(978-1-934706-46-6(9))* Blue Apple Bks.

Zoehfeld, Kathleen Weidner. Secrets of the Garden: Food Chains & the Food Web in Our Backyard. Lamont, Priscilla, illus. 2012. (ENG.). 40p. (J). (gr. k-4). 16.99 *(978-0-517-70990-0(2),* Knopf Bks. for Young Readers) Random Hse. Children's Bks.

Zurakowski, Michele. Evening Meals Around the World, 1 vol. Yesh, Jeff, illus. 2004. (Meals Around the World Ser.). (ENG.). 24p. (gr. k-4). per. 8.95 *(978-1-4048-1132-4(X))* Picture Window Bks.

FOOD—FICTION

Adler, David A. Bones & the Cupcake Mystery, No. 3. Newman, Barbara Johansen, illus. 2008. (Bones Ser.: 3). (ENG.). 32p. (J). (gr. 1-3). mass mkt. 3.99 *(978-0-14-241147-6(7),* Penguin Young Readers) Penguin Young Readers Group.

Adler, Karen A. Maybe Donna Wants a Cheeseburger! 2004. (Illus.). 32p. (J). 16.95 *(978-0-9679772-2-5(3))* Adler, Karen.

The Adventures of Molly. 2004. pap. 13.95 *(978-1-59526-180-9(X))* Aeon Publishing Inc.

Ahlberg, Allan. Hooray for Bread. Ingman, Bruce, illus. 2013. (ENG.). 32p. (J). (gr. -1-2). 15.99 *(978-0-7636-6311-7(5))* Candlewick Pr.

Albee, Sarah, retold by. Stone Soup. 2006. (J). per. 6.99 *(978-1-59939-037-6(X))* Cornerstone Pr.

Alexander Enjoys His Fruits & Vegetables. 2006. (J). 14.99 *(978-0-9742806-4-6(X))* Heart to Heart Publishing, Inc.

Alexander's First Babysitter. 2004. (J). 5.00 *(978-1-882541-38-6(3))* Food Allergy & Anaphylaxis Network.

Aliki. Quiet in the Garden. Aliki, illus. 2009. (ENG., Illus.). 32p. (J). (gr. -1-2). 17.99 *(978-0-06-155207-6(0),* Greenwillow Bks.) HarperCollins Pubs.

Allison, Ray. Where Did They Go? Allison, Ralph, illus. 2013. 36p. pap. 14.95 *(978-1-61493-191-1(7))* Peppertree Pr., The.

Amitzahandreanias. Weebles & the Cake Walk, 1 vol. 2010. 20p. 24.95 *(978-1-4489-4180-3(6))* PublishAmerica, Inc.

Anderson, Derek. Gladys Goes Out to Lunch. Anderson, Derek, illus. 2005.Tr. of Signed in American Sign Language. (ENG., Illus.). 40p. (J). (gr. -1-3). 17.99 *(978-0-689-85688-4(1),* Simon & Schuster Bks. For Young Readers) Simon & Schuster Bks. For Young Readers.

—Ten Hungry Pigs: An Epic Lunch Adventure. Anderson, Derek, illus. 2016. (ENG., Illus.). 40p. (J). (gr. -1-k). 16.99 *(978-0-545-16848-9(1))* Scholastic, Inc.

Andrews, Jennifer M. The Good Stuff Is Always on the Inside. 2011. 32p. pap. 13.00 *(978-1-4567-2989-9(6))* AuthorHouse.

Anna's Sandwich 6 Packs: Individual Title. (gr. 1-2). 22.00 *(978-0-7635-9176-2(9))* Rigby Education.

Anthony, David & David, Charles. Heroes A2Z #1: (Heroes a to Z): Alien Ice Cream. Blakeslee, Lys, illus. 2007. 128p. (J). pap. 4.99 *(978-0-9728461-8-9(2))* Sigil Publishing.

Armenteros, Sarah. Emma & the Mashed Potato Monster. 2009. (ENG., Illus.). 44p. (J). 18.99 *(978-1-59092-384-9(7))* Blue Forge Pr.

Armour, Peter. Stop That Pickle! Shachat, Andrew, illus. 2005. (ENG.). 32p. (J). (gr. -1-3). 6.99 *(978-0-618-54889-7(0))* Houghton Mifflin Harcourt Publishing Co.

Aronson, Emme & Aronson, Phillip. What Are You Hungry For? Feed Your Tummy & Your Heart. Brooks, Erik, illus. 2007. 32p. (J). (gr. -1-3). lib. bdg. 16.89 *(978-0-06-054308-2(6))* HarperCollins Pubs.

Aros, Angela. Aunt Emma's Secret Recipe, 1 vol. 2009. 15p. pap. 19.95 *(978-1-60813-862-3(3))* PublishAmerica, Inc.

Asch, Frank. Milk & Cookies. 2015. lib. bdg. 18.40 *(978-0-606-36292-4(4))* Turtleback Bks.

—Pizza. Asch, Frank, illus. 2015. (Frank Asch Bear Book Ser.). (ENG., Illus.). 32p. (J). (gr. -1-3). 16.99 *(978-1-4424-6675-3(8),* Aladdin) Simon & Schuster Children's Publishing.

—Popcorn. Asch, Frank, illus. 2015. (Frank Asch Bear Book Ser.). (ENG., Illus.). 40p. (J). (gr. -1-3). 16.99 *(978-1-4424-6662-3(6),* Aladdin) Simon & Schuster Children's Publishing.

Asselin, Kristine Carlson. Worst Case of Pasketti-Itis. Luisa, Gioffre-Suzuki, illus. 2013. 24p. pap. 12.99 *(978-0-9889617-0-8(9))* 4RV Publishing, LLC.

Aston, Dianna Hutts. An Orange in January. Maren, Julie, illus. 2007. (ENG.). 32p. (J). (gr. -1-3). 17.99 *(978-0-8037-3146-2(9),* Dial Bks) Penguin Young Readers Group.

Athey, Victoria. No Peas, Please! Delaney, Molly, illus. 2005. (ENG.). 20p. (gr. k-2). pap. 8.95 *(978-1-57874-087-1(8),* Kaeden Bks.) Kaeden Corp.

Auerbach, Andrea. Dinnertime. 2012. 28p. pap. 19.99 *(978-1-4772-7169-8(4))* AuthorHouse.

Baca, Ana. Benito's Sopaipillas/Las Sopaipillas de Benito. Villarroel, Carolina, tr. Accardo, Anthony, illus. 2007. (ENG & SPA.). 32p. (J). (gr. -1-2). 16.95 *(978-1-55885-370-6(7),* Piñata Books) Arte Publico Pr.

Badoe, Adwoa A. Crabs for Dinner. 2004. (J). (gr. k-3). spiral bd. *(978-0-616-01533-9(X));* spiral bd. *(978-0-616-01534-6(8))* Canadian National Institute for the Blind/Institut National Canadien pour les Aveugles.

Bailey, Linda. Toads on Toast. Jack, Colin, illus. 2012. (ENG.). 32p. (J). (gr. -1-2). 16.95 *(978-1-55453-662-7(6))* Kids Can Pr., Ltd. CAN. Dist: Hachette Bk. Group.

Baker, Amanda, illus. The Cheesehead Night Before Christmas. 2007. 40p. (J). per. 19.95 *(978-0-9797781-0-0(7))* Dreams 2 Wings LLC.

Baker, Keith. Little Green Peas: A Big Book of Colors. Baker, Keith, illus. 2014. (Peas Ser.). (ENG., Illus.). 40p. (J). (gr. -1-3). 17.99 *(978-1-4424-7660-8(5),* Beach Lane Bks.) Beach Lane Bks.

—On the Go with Mr. & Mrs. Green, 1 vol. Baker, Keith, illus. 2007. (Mr. & Mrs. Green Ser.). (ENG., Illus.). 72p. (gr. 2-4). 27.07 *(978-1-59961-303-1(4))* Spotlight.

Baker, Mary. Amy's Apple Butter Granny. 2009. 48p. pap. 16.95 *(978-1-61582-032-0(9))* America Star Bks.

Balmer, Fred. Festus & the Missing Bag of Feed. Newcomb, Kristene, illus. 2004. 26p. (J). per. 7.00 *(978-0-9760790-0-2(3))* Folsom Fallies Pr.

Barchers, Suzanne I. Green Peas in Cream, 1 vol. 2011. (Targeted Phonics Ser.). (ENG.). 16p. (J). (gr. k-2). pap. 5.99 *(978-1-4333-2916-6(6))* Teacher Created Materials, Inc.

Barrett, Judi. Cloudy with a Chance of Meatballs. Barrett, Ronald, illus. 2012. (ENG.). 32p. (J). (gr. -1-3). pap. 9.99 *(978-1-4424-4337-2(5),* Little Simon) Little Simon.

—Cloudy with a Chance of Meatballs. Barrett, Ron, illus. 2011. (Classic Board Bks.). (ENG.). 34p. (J). (gr. -1-k). bds. 7.99 *(978-1-4424-3023-5(0),* Little Simon) Little Simon.

—Cloudy with a Chance of Meatballs. Barrett, Ron, illus. 2009. 9.00 *(978-1-55744-455-4(2),* Everbind) Marco Bk. Co.

—Cloudy with a Chance of Meatballs 3: Planet of the Pies. Mones, Isidre, illus. 2013. (ENG.). 32p. (J). (gr. -1-3). 17.99 *(978-1-4424-9027-7(6),* Atheneum Bks. for Young Readers) Simon & Schuster Children's Publishing.

—Cloudy with a Chance of Meatballs Collection: Cloudy with a Chance of Meatballs; Pickles to Pittsburgh - Cloudy with a Chance of Meatballs 3. Barrett, Ron, illus. 2016. (ENG.). 96p. (J). (gr. -1-3). 53.99 *(978-1-4814-9890-6(8),* Atheneum/Caitlyn Dlouhy Books) Simon & Schuster Children's Publishing.

—Pickles to Pittsburgh: Cloudy with a Chance of Meatballs 2. Barrett, Ronald, illus. (Classic Board Bks.). (ENG.). (J). (gr. -1-k). 2013. 34p. bds. 7.99 *(978-1-4424-6493-3(3))* 2012. 32p. pap. 9.99 *(978-1-4424-4459-1(2))* Little Simon. (Little Simon).

—Pickles to Pittsburgh: The Sequel to Cloudy with a Chance of Meatballs. Barrett, Ron, illus. 2004. 26p. (gr. -1-3). 17.00 *(978-0-7569-4215-1(2))* Perfection Learning Corp.

Bassett, Madge A. At Bumblebee Farm. Bassett, Madge A., illus. 2009. (Illus.). 20p. pap. 13.46 *(978-1-4251-9230-3(0))* Trafford Publishing.

Beale, Madeline. Sarah's Favourite Food. Goh, Douglas, illus. 2017. (ENG.). 24p. 10.00 *(978-981-4751-85-8(5))* Marshall Cavendish International (Asia) Private Ltd. SGP. Dist: National Bk. Network.

Beall, Kirsten. Jake & the Big Cake Mistake. Desmond, Hillary, illus. 2011. 36p. pap. 24.95 *(978-1-4626-4524-4(0))* America Star Bks.

Beckerman, Menucha. The Candy Kids. 2004. (My Smiling World Ser.: No. 3). (Illus.). 32p. (J). 11.95 *(978-1-931681-54-4(6))* Israel Bookshop Pubns.

Beckstrand, Karl. Crumbs on the Stairs - Migas en Las Escaleras: A Mystery. Beckstrand, Karl, illus. 2011. (Mini-Mysteries for Minors Ser.: 2).Tr. of Migas en Las Escaleras. (ENG & SPA., Illus.). 24p. (J). pap. 14.95 *(978-0-9776065-9-7(7),* Gozo Bks.) Premio Publishing & Gozo Bks., LLC.

Beeke, Joel R. & Kleyn, Diana. How God Sent a Dog to Save a Family. Anderson, Jeff, illus. 2008. (Building on the Rock Ser.). (ENG.). 176p. (J). pap. 8.99 *(978-1-85792-819-8(9),* 9781857928198, CF4Kids) Christian Focus Pubns. GBR. Dist: Bookmasters Distribution.

Bell, Julia. Massive. 2006. (ENG., Illus.). 272p. (YA). (gr. 7-18). pap. 8.99 *(978-1-4169-0207-2(4),* Simon Pulse) Simon Pulse.

Benchmark Education Co., LLC. Strawberry Girl Big Book. 2014. (Shared Reading Foundations Ser.). (J). (gr. -1). *(978-1-4509-9448-4(2))* Benchmark Education Co.

Bender, Carol. Picky Eater, That Peter. 2011. 25p. (J). 24.95 *(978-1-4327-7055-6(1))* Outskirts Pr., Inc.

Benhamu, Margaret. Pizza Friday. Salanitro, Robert, illus. 2009. (Slide-Out Book Ser.). 9p. (J). 7.99 *(978-1-60436-025-7(9))* Educational Publishing LLC.

Bently, Peter. Dustbin Dad. Ayto, Russell, illus. 2014. (ENG.). 32p. (J). 15.99 *(978-1-84738-873-5(6))* Simon & Schuster, Ltd. GBR. Dist: Simon & Schuster, Inc.

Bertrand, Diane Gonzales. Sip, Slurp, Soup, Soup/Caldo, Caldo, Caldo. Castilla, Julia Mercedes, tr. Delange, Alex Pardo, illus. 2008. (SPA & ENG.). 32p. (J). (gr. -1-2). pap. 7.95 *(978-1-55885-241-9(7),* Piñata Books) Arte Publico Pr.

Biers-Ariel, Matt. The Seven Species. Goodman, Tama, illus. 2003. 48p. 19.95 *(978-0-8074-0852-0(2),* 161902) URJ Pr.

Bird, Benjamin. Scooby-Doo's 1-2-3 Mystery. 2015. (Scooby-Doo! Little Mysteries Ser.). (ENG., Illus.). 20p. (gr. -1 — 1). bds. 7.99 *(978-1-62370-177-2(5))* Capstone Press of Coughlan Cos.

Birkett, Georgie, illus. Cook It!/¡A Cocinar! 2009. (Helping Hands English/Spanish Edition Ser.). (ENG & SPA.). 24p. (J). (gr. -1-k). pap. *(978-1-84643-568-3(4))* Child's Play International Ltd.

Black, Holly. The Poison Eaters: And Other Stories. Black, Theo, illus. 2011. (ENG.). 224p. (YA). (gr. 9). pap. 9.99 *(978-1-4424-1232-3(1),* McElderry, Margaret K. Bks.) McElderry, Margaret K. Bks.

Blackwell-Burke, Melissa & Kunkel, Kristen. Pizza Pie Pizzazz. 2003. (J). spiral bd. 14.95 *(978-1-58605-957-6(2),* LeapFrog Schl. Hse.) LeapFrog Enterprises, Inc.

Blake, Colleen H. Robley. Don't You Wish Your Momma Could Cook Like Mine? Jennings, Randy, illus. 2012. 40p. pap. 16.97 *(978-1-61204-876-5(5),* Strategic Bk. Publishing) Strategic Book Publishing & Rights Agency (SBPRA).

Bloom, C. P. The Monkey Goes Bananas. Raymundo, Peter, illus. 2014. (Monkey Goes Bananas Ser.). (ENG.). 40p. (J). (gr. k-2). 14.95 *(978-1-4197-0885-5(6),* Abrams Bks. for Young Readers) Abrams, Inc.

Bloze, Eden. Banana Beach. 2008. 12p. pap. 24.95 *(978-1-60610-033-2(5))* America Star Bks.

Bodden, Michelle, adapted by. Obara & the Merchants. 2004. (Illus.). 32p. (J). 14.95 *(978-0-9753089-0-5(4))* Water Daughter Publishing.

Bonnell, Kris. The Big Hungry Cat. 2006. (J). pap. 5.95 *(978-1-933727-33-2(0))* Reading Reading Bks., LLC.

—Lemonade. 2006. (J). pap. 5.95 *(978-1-933727-31-8(4))* Reading Reading Bks., LLC.

—Mmm, Apples. 2006. (J). pap. 3.95 *(978-1-933727-22-6(5))* Reading Reading Bks., LLC.

—Pizza for Carl. 2006. (J). pap. 3.95 *(978-1-933727-27-1(6))* Reading Reading Bks., LLC.

—Red Apples for Me. 2007. (J). pap. 5.95 *(978-1-933727-52-3(7))* Reading Reading Bks., LLC.

Border, Terry. Peanut Butter & Cupcake. Border, Terry, illus. 2014. (ENG., Illus.). 32p. (J). (gr. -1-2). 17.99 *(978-0-399-16773-7(0),* Philomel Bks.) Penguin Publishing Group.

—Peanut Butter's Yummy Numbers. Border, Terry, illus. 2016. (ENG., Illus.). 20p. (J). (— 1). bds. 6.99 *(978-0-399-54665-5(0),* Philomel Bks.) Penguin Young Readers Group.

Border, Terry & Mack, Jeff. Happy Birthday, Cupcake! Border, Terry, illus. 2015. (ENG., Illus.). 32p. (J). (gr. k-3). bds. 17.99 *(978-0-399-17160-4(6),* Philomel Bks.) Penguin Young Readers Group.

Boucher, Paul. A Stickeee & Gooweee Week of Fun. 2012. 16p. pap. 15.99 *(978-1-4772-7289-3(5))* AuthorHouse.

Boutenko, Victoria. Green Smoothie Magic. Korobkina, Katya, illus. 2013. (ENG.). 56p. (J). (gr. -1-3). 12.95 *(978-1-58394-601-5(2))* North Atlantic Bks.

Boyes, Alison. What Charlotte Ate: The Story of a Naughty Dog Who Loved to Eat. Boyes, Faye, illus. 2012. 28p. (J). pap. *(978-0-9808685-7-9(2))* Mono Unlimited.

Boza, Eduardo Robles. Mi Amiga No Quiere Comer.Tr. of My Friend Doesn't Want to Eat. (SPA.). (J). 4.95 *(978-968-419-873-9(6))* Grijalbo, Editorial MEX. Dist: AIMS International Bks., Inc.

Brave M.A., Kathryn A. & Lavin, Paul J. A Fit ting Fairy Tale. 2006. 60p. pap. 16.95 *(978-1-4241-2992-8(3))* PublishAmerica, Inc.

Brennan, Frank. Tasty Tales Level 4, 1 vol. 2009. (ENG.). 96p. pap. 16.50 incl. audio compact disk *(978-84-8323-545-4(5))* Cambridge Univ. Pr.

Brett, Jan. Gingerbread Friends. Brett, Jan, illus. 2008. (ENG., Illus.). 32p. (J). (gr. -1-k). 17.99 *(978-0-399-25161-0(8),* G.P. Putnam's Sons Books for Young Readers) Penguin Young Readers Group.

Brisson, Pat. Before We Eat: From Farm to Table, 1 vol. Azarian, Mary, illus. 2014. (ENG.). 32p. (gr. k-3). 16.95 *(978-0-88448-352-6(5),* 884352) Tilbury Hse. Pubs.

Brody, Leslie. The Bouncing Worry Ball & Mighty Mitt. 2012. 68p. pap. 15.50 *(978-1-105-48841-2(1))* Lulu Pr., Inc.

Brown, Jeff. Flat Stanley & the Very Big Cookie. Pamintuan, Macky, illus. 2015. (I Can Read Level 2 Ser.). (ENG.). 32p. (J). (gr. -1-3). 16.99 *(978-0-06-218979-0(4));* pap. 3.99 *(978-0-06-218978-3(6))* HarperCollins Pubs.

Brown-Wood, Janay & Burris, Priscilla. Grandma's Tiny House. 2017. (ENG., Illus.). 32p. (J). (-k). lib. bdg. 16.99 *(978-1-58089-712-9(6))* Charlesbridge Publishing, Inc.

Bruel, Nick. Bad Kitty. Bruel, Nick, illus. 2nd ed. 2007. (Bad Kitty Ser.). (ENG., Illus.). 40p. (J). (gr. -1-3). 17.99 *(978-1-59643-299-4(3),* 9781596432994) Roaring Brook Pr.

Bruna, Dick. The Apple. 2013. (ENG., Illus.). 28p. (J). (gr. -1-1). 7.95 *(978-1-84976-214-4(7))* Tate Publishing, Ltd. GBR. Dist: Abrams, Inc.

Bruton, Seth. I'm So Cute, You Can't Be Mad. Hicks, Kaylee, illus. 2012. 24p. pap. 13.97 *(978-1-61204-897-0(8),* Strategic Bk. Publishing) Strategic Book Publishing & Rights Agency (SBPRA).

The Bubble Gum Contest. 2007. (Spaceboy Chapter Ser.). (J). per. 7.67 *(978-1-932570-62-5(4))* Pioneer Valley Bks.

Buckley, Charlie. Show Jo How to Make a Sandwich. 2007. (Show Jo Language Development Ser.). (Illus.). 16p. (J). (gr. -1-1). per., bds. 14.95 *(978-1-933669-08-3(X))* Literary Architects, LLC.

Bug, June. The Legend of the Wooden Bowl. 2013. 44p. pap. 20.45 *(978-1-4624-0688-3(2),* Inspiring Voices) Author Solutions, Inc.

Burgess, Lisa Maria. Juma Cooks Chapati. Gugu, Abdul M., illus. 2013. 32p. 19.95 *(978-1-939604-08-8(7));* pap. 9.99 *(978-1-939604-04-0(4))* Barranca Pr.

Burke, Linda. Knood the Cat. 2008. 24p. pap. 13.50 *(978-1-60693-449-4(X),* Eloquent Bks.) Strategic Book Publishing & Rights Agency (SBPRA).

Burroway, Janet & Lord, John Vernon. The Giant Jam Sandwich. Lord, John Vernon, illus. 2009. (ENG., Illus.). 28p. (J). (gr. -1-3). bds. 7.99 *(978-0-547-15077-2(6))* Houghton Mifflin Harcourt Publishing Co.

The Cake: Individual Title Six-Packs. (Story Steps Ser.). (gr. k-2). 29.00 *(978-0-7635-9601-9(9))* Rigby Education.

Candlewick Press, Candlewick. Nelly Nitpick, Kid Food Critic. Lunch Lab LLC, Lunch Lab, illus. 2015. (Fizzy's Lunch Lab Ser.). (ENG.). 48p. (J). (gr. 1-4). pap. 5.99 *(978-0-7636-6885-3(0),* Candlewick Entertainment) Candlewick Pr.

Capone, Deb. Dumplings Are Delicious. Jaskiel, Stan, illus. 2006. 24p. (J). (gr. -1-3). 14.95 *(978-0-9728666-4-4(7))* As Simple As That Publishing.

Carbone, Courtney. Food Fight! Random House Editors & Aikins, Dave, illus. 2015. (Step into Reading Ser.). (ENG.). 24p. (J). (gr. -1-1). pap. 4.99 *(978-0-385-38773-6(3),* Random Hse. Bks. for Young Readers) Random Hse. Children's Bks.

Carle, Eric. Eric Carle Classics: The Tiny Seed - Pancakes, Pancakes! - Walter the Baker. Carle, Eric, illus. 2011. (World of Eric Carle Ser.). (ENG., Illus.). 112p. (J). (gr. -1-2). 19.99 *(978-1-4424-3988-7(2),* Simon & Schuster Bks. For Young Readers) Simon & Schuster Bks. For Young Readers.

—Walter the Baker. Carle, Eric, illus. 2014. (World of Eric Carle Ser.). (ENG., Illus.). 32p. (J). (gr. -1-2). pap. 3.99 *(978-1-4814-0917-9(4),* Simon Spotlight) Simon Spotlight.

Carry-out Food: 6 Small Books. (gr. k-3). 24.00 *(978-0-7635-6234-2(3))* Rigby Education.

Cesler, Margaret E. The Bread Book. 2013. 12p. pap. 10.97 *(978-1-62212-527-2(4),* Strategic Bk. Publishing) Strategic Book Publishing & Rights Agency (SBPRA).

Chabot, Jacob & Mcginty, Ian. Delicious! 2014. (Hello Kitty Graphic Novel Ser.). lib. bdg. 18.40 *(978-0-606-35470-7(0))* Turtleback Bks.

Charlesworth, Liza. Pig Wants a Peach: An Animal Friends Reader. Smith, Ian, illus. 2015. 16p. (J). pap. ***(978-0-545-85965-3(4))*** Scholastic, Inc.

Charlesworth, Liza & Scholastic, Inc. Staff. Monkey's Missing Bananas. Sexton, Brenda, illus. 2005. (Number Tales Ser.). (ENG.). 16p. (J). (gr. -1-1). pap. 2.99 *(978-0-439-69032-4(3))* Scholastic, Inc.

Chaudhary, Shahida. Sammy's Midnight Hunger. Mikle, Toby, illus. 2012. 38p. pap. 14.50 *(978-1-61897-255-2(3),* Strategic Bk. Publishing) Strategic Book Publishing & Rights Agency (SBPRA).

Child, Lauren, et al. Fydda i Byth Bythoedd yn Bwyta Tomato. 2005. (WEL., Illus.). 32p. pap. *(978-1-85596-668-0(9))* Dref Wen.

The Chocolate Moose. 2007. (Illus.). 48p. (J). per. 13.00 *(978-0-9767189-5-6(2))* Better Day Publishing LLC.

Cochran, Jean M. Your Tummy's Talking! Gullens, Lee M., illus. 2008. (ENG.). 32p. (J). (gr. -1-k). 16.95 *(978-0-9792035-3-4(8))* Pleasant St. Pr.

Codor, Richard. Too Many Latkes! Codor, Richard, illus. 2011. (ENG., Illus.). 44p. (J). (gr. -1-3). pap. 9.95 *(978-0-87441-882-8(8))* Behrman Hse., Inc.

Cohen, Milly. La Dulceria de Don Tono. Velazquez, Jose Luis Reyes & Velazquez, Jose Luis Reye, illus. rev. ed. 2006. (Castillo de la Lectura Verde Ser.). (SPA & ENG.). 112p. (J). (gr. 2-4). pap. 7.95 *(978-970-20-0198-0(6))* Castillo, Ediciones, S. A. de C. V. MEX. Dist: Macmillan.

Collins, Izola. Pip, Squeak, & Zoom. 2009. 68p. pap. 23.49 *(978-1-4490-0717-1(1))* AuthorHouse.

Concrafter. Minecraft: An Unofficial Guide with New Facts & Commands. 2016. (J). lib. bdg. 24.50 *(978-0-606-38433-9(2))* Turtleback Bks.

Cone-Watson, Arianna. Fooey Fruits & Fickle Foods. 2009. 20p. pap. 10.99 *(978-1-4490-1563-3(8))* AuthorHouse.

Connolly, Megan B. Mommy, Mommy! Is This for Me? Mundy, Jen, illus. 2013. (ENG.). (J). 14.95 *(978-1-62086-356-5(1))* Mascot Bks., Inc.

Conrad, Perrin Cothran. The Ballad of the Shirley T & Other Stories. 2011. 80p. pap. 8.95 *(978-1-4620-5671-2(7))* iUniverse, Inc.

Consiglio, Joe. Big Billy & the Ice Cream Truck That Wouldn't Stop, 1 vol. Simko, Joe, illus. 2012. (ENG.). 48p. (J). 16.99 *(978-0-7643-4067-3(0),* 9780764340673) Schiffer Publishing, Ltd.

Cooke, Brandy. Cupcakes! A Sweet Treat with More Than 200 Stickers. Kramer, Connie, photos by. 2011. (ENG., Illus.). 18p. (J). (gr. -1-k). bds. 6.99 *(978-1-4424-2825-6(2),* Little Simon) Little Simon.

Cookies for Santa. 2006. (Little Elf Set 1 Ser.). (J). 7.33 *(978-1-932570-75-5(6))* Pioneer Valley Bks.

Cooper, Helen S. & Butterworth, Ian. Pinsiaid o Bupur. Williams, Dylan, tr. from ENG. 2005. (WEL., Illus.). 36p. *(978-1-84512-022-1(1))* Cymdeithas Lyfrau Ceredigion.

Cooperman, Ben. Cereal for Breakfast Cereal for Lunch. Dishaw, Karen, illus. 2013. 42p. pap. *(978-0-9919356-0-4(8))* Teacherben Publishing.

Coplans, Peta. Spaghetti for Suzy. 2003. (Illus.). 32p. (J). pap. 6.95 *(978-1-84270-100-3(2))* Andersen Pr. GBR. Dist: Trafalgar Square Publishing.

Corbett, Robyn. Kokoye Kiko Yo: Kiko's Coconuts. 2013. (ENG.). 44p. (J). pap. 18.95 *(978-1-4787-1533-7(2))* Outskirts Pr., Inc.

Cordsen, Carol Foskett. The Milkman. Jones, Douglas B., illus. 2007. (gr. -1-3). 17.00 *(978-0-7569-8148-8(4))* Perfection Learning Corp.

Cormier, Robert. Guerra Dei Cioccolatini. pap. 19.95 *(978-88-451-2161-6(5))* Fabbri Editori - RCS Libri ITA. Dist: Distribooks, Inc.

—La Guerra del Chocolate. 2003.Tr. of Chocolate War. (SPA.). 258p. (J). (gr. 5-8). 11.95 *(978-1-56014-666-7(4))* Santillana USA Publishing Co., Inc.

Cotter, Amelia. Breakfast with Bigfoot. Swinford, Charles, illus. 2013. 30p. pap. 11.95 *(978-1-61876-017-3(3))* Black Oak Media, Inc.

Cousins, Lucy. Los Alimentos de Maisy. Cousins, Lucy, illus. 2009. (Maisy Ser.). (SPA & ENG., Illus.). 16p. (J). (gr. -1-2). bds. 5.99 *(978-0-7636-4519-9(2))* Candlewick Pr.

—Maisy's First Colors: A Maisy Concept Book. Cousins, Lucy, illus. 2013. (Maisy Ser.). (ENG., Illus.). 14p. (J). (-k). bds. 6.99 *(978-0-7636-6804-4(4))* Candlewick Pr.

—Maisy's Placemat Doodle Book. Cousins, Lucy, illus. 2014. (Maisy Ser.). (ENG., Illus.). 104p. (J). (-k). pap. 11.99 *(978-0-7636-7108-2(8))* Candlewick Pr.

Cowley, Joy. Those Yucky Meanies. 2009. pap. 8.25 *(978-1-60559-098-1(3))* Hameray Publishing Group, Inc.

Cox, Miss Karin & Cox, Karin. Pancakes on Sunday. Acar, Sinan, illus. 2012. 26p. pap. *(978-0-9873602-2-9(1))* Indelible Ink Pr.

Craddock, Erik. Ninja Slice. Craddock, Erik, illus. 2010. (Stone Rabbit Ser.: No. 5). (ENG., Illus.). 96p. (J). (gr. 3-7). pap. 6.99 *(978-0-375-86723-1(6),* Random Hse. Bks. for Young Readers) Random Hse. Children's Bks.

Crear, Williadean. Anika & Her New Body. 2011. 28p. pap. 21.99 *(978-1-4568-9480-1(3))* Xlibris Corp.

Crummel, Susan Stevens. Sherlock Bones & the Missing Cheese, 0 vols. Donohue, Dorothy, illus. 2012. (ENG.). 40p. (J). (gr. k-3). 17.99 *(978-0-7614-6186-9(8),* 9780761461869, Amazon Children's Publishing) Amazon Publishing.

Cullimore, Stan. Alien Swap. Schon, Nick, illus. 2005. (ENG.). 24p. (J). lib. bdg. 23.65 *(978-1-59646-744-6(4))* Dingles & Co.

Cusack, Bob. The Squirming Squirrel. 2009. 16p. pap. 12.99 *(978-1-4389-5551-3(0))* AuthorHouse.

Dad's Turkey Sandwich. 2003. (Mom & Dad Ser.). (J). 7.33 *(978-1-58453-255-2(6))* Pioneer Valley Bks.

Dahl, Michael. Snack Time for Cow, 1 vol. Vidal, Oriol, illus. 2011. (Hello Genius Ser.). (ENG.). 20p. (gr. 1-2). bds. 7.99 *(978-1-4048-6496-2(2))* Picture Window Bks.

Daisy, April. The Crazy 8 Diner. 2004. (Illus.). 28p. (J). per. 7.95 *(978-1-59466-023-8(9),* Little Ones) Port Town Publishing.

EFG

Dale, Jay. Bananas in My Tummy, 1 vol. Hancock, Anna, illus. 2012. (Engage Literacy Yellow Ser.). (ENG.). 32p. (gr. k-2). pap. 5.99 *(978-1-4296-8835-2(1))*, Engage Literacy) Capstone Press of Coughlan Cos.

—A Big Box of Bananas, 1 vol. Diggory, Nick, illus. 2012. (Engage Literacy Blue Ser.). (ENG.). 16p. (gr. k-2). pap. 5.99 *(978-1-4296-8980-9(3)*, Engage Literacy) Capstone Press of Coughlan Cos.

Dale, Katie. Rub-A-dub-dub: Three Men & a Pancake. 2016. (ENG., Illus.). 32p. (J). *(978-0-7787-2463-6(8))* Crabtree Publishing Co.

Dalmatian Press Staff. Pizza! Pizza! Pizza! 2008. (ENG.). 6p. (J). bds. 4.95 *(978-1-58117-721-3(6)*, Intervisual/Piggy Toes) Bendon, Inc.

Dalton, Sherry A. Do Indians Eat Soup? 2011. 32p. pap. 24.95 *(978-1-4560-7463-0(6))* America Star Bks.

Daly, Kathleen N. The Good Humor Man. Gergely, Tibor, illus. 2016. (Little Golden Book Ser.). (ENG.). 24p. (J). (gr. k-k). 4.99 *(978-0-307-96029-0(3)*, Golden Bks.) Random Hse. Children's Bks.

Damon, Matt. The Fall of General Custard, or the Overthrow of a Leftover. Kendall, Gideon, illus. 2016. (HumanKIND Project Ser.). (ENG.). 32p. (J). (gr. k-6). 17.95 *(978-1-940468-33-4(7))* White Cloud Pr.

Daniels, Kristine. Floyd & the Irresistible Cookie. 2009. 32p. pap. 18.00 *(978-1-60844-276-8(4))* Dog Ear Publishing, LLC.

Davey, Owen, illus. Foxly's Feast. 2014. (ENG.). 32p. (J). (-k). 14.95 *(978-1-62914-608-9(0)*, Sky Pony Pr.) Skyhorse Publishing Co., Inc.

Davies, Jacqueline. The Lemonade War. 2007. (Lemonade War Ser.: 1). (ENG., Illus.). 192p. (J). (gr. 2-5). 16.99 *(978-0-618-75043-6(6))* Houghton Mifflin Harcourt Publishing Co.

Davis, Aubrey. Bagels from Benny. Petricic, Dusan, illus. 2005. (ENG.). 32p. (J). (gr. -1-3). 7.95 *(978-1-55337-749-8(4))* Kids Can Pr., Ltd. CAN. Dist: Hachette Bk. Group.

De Boer, Joan. THE SULTAN AND THE MICE. 2007. (ENG., Illus.). 36p. (J). 18.95 *(978-84-96788-84-8(9))* OQO, Editora ESP. Dist: Baker & Taylor Bks.

De Laurentiis, Giada. Hong Kong! #3. Gambatesa, Francesca, illus. 2014. (Recipe for Adventure Ser.: 3). (ENG.). 144p. (J). (gr. 2-5). 6.99 *(978-0-448-46258-5(3))*; 16.99 *(978-0-448-48040-4(9))* Penguin Young Readers Group. (Grosset & Dunlap).

De Regniers, Beatrice Schenk. What Did You Put in Your Pocket? Date not set. 32p. (J). (gr. -1-1). pap. 5.95 *(978-0-06-443700-4(0))* HarperCollins Pubs.

Dean, James. Pete's Big Lunch. Dean, James, illus. 2013. (My First I Can Read Ser.). (ENG., Illus.). 32p. (J). (gr. -1-3). 16.99 *(978-0-06-211070-1(5))* HarperCollins Pubs.

Dean, James & Dean, Kimberly. Pete the Cat & the Missing Cupcakes. Dean, James, illus. 2016. (Pete the Cat Ser.). (Illus.). 40p. (J). (gr. -1-3). 17.99 *(978-0-06-230434-6(8))*; lib. bdg. 18.89 *(978-0-06-230435-3(6))* HarperCollins Pubs.

Dent, Josh. Hot Chips & Sauce. 2011. 40p. pap. 32.70 *(978-1-4628-7132-2(1))* Xlibris Corp.

dePaola, Tomie. Jamie O'Rourke & the Big Potato. 2009. (ENG.). 14p. (J). (gr. -1-k). bds. 5.99 *(978-0-448-45090-2(9)*, Grosset & Dunlap) Penguin Young Readers Group.

Deutsch, Stacia, adapted by. Cloudy with a Chance of Meatballs 2 Movie Novelization. 2013. (Cloudy with a Chance of Meatballs Movie Ser.). (ENG., Illus.). 128p. (J). (gr. 3-7). pap. 5.99 *(978-1-4424-9551-7(0)*, Simon Spotlight) Simon Spotlight.

Dhami, Narinder. Samosa Thief. Blundell, Tony, illus. 2005. (ENG.). 24p. (J). lib. bdg. 23.65 *(978-1-59646-708-8(8))* Dingles & Co.

Diehl, Bill. The Hungry Bunny. 2010. 28p. 12.59 *(978-1-4389-5107-2(8))* AuthorHouse.

Diggle, David Mark. Brian: Eats Himself Smarter. Diggle, Daniel James, illus. 2011. 24p. (J). pap. *(978-0-9871657-4-9(7))* Diggle de Doo Productions Pty, Ltd.

Dinner: Individual Title Six-Packs. (Sails Literacy Ser.). 16p. (gr. k-18). 27.00 *(978-0-7635-4445-4(0))* Rigby Education.

Dinnertime. 2003. (J). per. *(978-1-57657-965-7(4))* Paradise Pr., Inc.

Dipucchio, Kelly. Everyone Loves Bacon. Wight, Eric, illus. 2015. (ENG.). 40p. (J). (gr. -1-1). 17.99 *(978-0-374-30052-4(6)*, 9780374300524, Farrar, Straus & Giroux (BYR)) Farrar, Straus & Giroux.

Dobkin, Bonnie. Crazy Pizza Day. Dey, Romi, illus. 2010. (J). *(978-1-60617-150-9(X))* Teaching Strategies, LLC.

Dodds, Dayle Ann. Full House: An Invitation to Fractions. Carter, Abby, illus. 2009. (ENG.). 32p. (J). (gr. 1-4). pap. 6.99 *(978-0-7636-4130-6(8))* Candlewick Pr.

Dogiakis, Helen. Captain Terry the Pirate Cow's Adventure to Greece. 2012. 24p. pap. 17.99 *(978-1-4685-9403-4(6))* AuthorHouse.

Donovan, Anna. Emma Says Oops! Fox, Woody, illus. 2004. (Panda Cubs Ser.: 04). (ENG.). 48p. (J). pap. 9.95 *(978-0-86278-902-2(8))* O'Brien Pr., Ltd., The IRL. Dist: Dufour Editions, Inc.

Duncan, Billy. A Haunting Good Time, 1 vol. 2009. 48p. pap. 16.95 *(978-1-60836-120-5(9))* America Star Bks.

Dungy, Tony & Dungy, Lauren. The Missing Cupcake Mystery. 2013. (Simon & Schuster Ready-To-Read Level 2 Ser.). lib. bdg. 13.55 *(978-0-606-27055-7(8)*, Turtleback) Turtleback Bks.

Durand, Hallie. Dessert First. Davenier, Christine, illus. 2009. (ENG.). 160p. (J). (gr. 2-5). 14.99 *(978-1-4169-6385-1(5)*, Atheneum Bks. for Young Readers) Simon & Schuster Children's Publishing.

Dyan, Penelope. Who Deserves a Giant Chocolate Chip Cookie? Dyan, Penelope, illus. 2009. (Illus.). 44p. pap. 11.95 *(978-1-935118-56-5(0))* Bellissima Publishing, LLC.

Earl, Cheri Pray & Williams, Carol Lynch. Secret in Pennsylvania. 2009. (J). *(978-1-56145-477-8(X)*, Peachtree Junior) Peachtree Pubs.

Ebel, Sherry. Cassie's Magic Doors. 2008. 28p. pap. 15.99 *(978-1-4363-2970-5(1))* Xlibris Corp.

Eiseman, Joan. Ricardo & the Fisherman. Eiseman, Joan, illus. 2007. (Illus.). 32p. (J). per. 12.95 *(978-0-9786745-4-0(5))* Marble Hse. Editions.

Elgar, Rebecca. Where's My Dinner? 2003. (ENG., Illus.). 12p. (J). bds. 9.99 *(978-1-4052-0451-4(6))* Egmont Bks., Ltd. GBR. Dist: Trafalgar Square Publishing.

Eliopoulos, Chris. Okie Dokie Donuts: Open for Business! Open for Business! 2011. (ENG., Illus.). 48p. (J). (gr. 2-5). 9.95 *(978-1-60309-068-1(1)*, 9781603090681) Top Shelf Productions.

Elliott, Stacey "Sissy". What Kind of Bread Does a Monkey Eat ? 2011. 28p. pap. 15.99 *(978-1-4628-5921-4(6))* Xlibris Corp.

Erlandson, Nick. Duncan & the Bone Tree, 1 vol. 2009. 40p. pap. 24.95 *(978-1-60813-864-7(X))* America Star Bks.

Erlich, Arty. A Vegie Adventure. 2011. 24p. pap. *(978-1-4269-7427-4(2))* Trafford Publishing (UK) Ltd.

Esparza-Vela, Mary. Bearly Learning about Water. Morris, Alexander, illus. 2012. 16p. pap. 9.95 *(978-1-61633-288-4(3))* Guardian Angel Publishing, Inc.

Evans, Cambria. Bone Soup. 2016. (ENG., Illus.). 32p. (J). (gr. 2-5). 7.99 *(978-0-544-66836-2(7)*, HMH Books For Young Readers) Houghton Mifflin Harcourt Publishing Co.

Everett, F. The Burglar's Breakfast. 2004. (Young Reading Ser.: Vol. 1). (Illus.). 48p. (J). (gr. 2-18). pap. 5.95 *(978-0-7945-0221-8(0)*, Usborne) EDC Publishing.

Farnworth, Michael M. The Sinister Mr. Pickle & the Fickle He Got the Mcwickles Into. 2008. 40p. per. 24.95 *(978-1-60441-285-7(2))* America Star Bks.

Fast Food Felicity: Individual Title Six-Packs. (Bookweb Ser.). 32p. (gr. 3-18). 34.00 *(978-0-7635-3933-7(3))* Rigby Education.

Fearnley, Jan. Mr Wolf's Pancakes. 2008. (ENG., Illus.). 32p. (J). (gr. -1-2). 12.95 *(978-1-4052-3872-4(0))* Egmont Bks., Ltd. GBR. Dist: Independent Pubs. Group.

Fields, Terri. Burro's Tortillas, 1 vol. Rogers, Sherry, illus. 2007. (ENG.). 32p. (J). (gr. -1-3). 15.95 *(978-0-9768823-9-8(6))* Arbordale Publishing.

Fillion, Susan. Pizza in Pienza. Fillion, Susan, illus. 2013. (ENG & ITA., Illus.). 32p. (J). 17.95 *(978-1-56792-459-6(X))* Godine, David R. Pub.

Fleming, Candace. A Big Cheese for the White House: The True Tale of a Tremendous Cheddar. Schindler, S. D., illus. 2004. (ENG.). 32p. (J). (gr. -1-3). reprint ed. pap. 8.99 *(978-0-374-40627-1(8)*, 9780374406271) Square Fish.

Fleming, Maria. Five Shiny Apples. Sexton, Brenda, illus. 2005. (Number Tales Ser.). (ENG.). 16p. (J). (gr. -1-1). pap. 2.99 *(978-0-439-69014-0(5))* Scholastic, Inc.

Fragasso, Ruth Ann (Reichner). The Little Boy Who Ate Like a Bird. 2011. 16p. (gr. -1). 12.68 *(978-1-4269-6287-5(8))* Trafford Publishing.

Franco, Betsy. Pond Circle. Vitale, Stefano, illus. 2009. (ENG.). 32p. (J). (gr. -1-3). 17.99 *(978-1-4169-4021-0(9)*, McElderry, Margaret K. Bks.) McElderry, Margaret K. Bks.

French, Jackie. Too Many Pears! (Japanese/English), 1 vol. Whatley, Bruce, illus. 2007. (JPN & ENG.). 32p. (J). (gr. -1). pap. 5.95 *(978-1-59572-112-9(6))* Star Bright Bks., Inc.

Friedman, Becky. Daniel Tries a New Food. 2015. (Daniel Tiger's Neighborhood 8X8 Ser.). lib. bdg. 13.55 *(978-0-606-37874-1(X))* Turtleback Bks.

Friesen, Ray. Yarg! & Other Stories. 2006. (Lookit! Ser.). (ENG., Illus.). 104p. (gr. 3-6). per. 11.95 *(978-0-9728177-9-0(4))* Don't Eat Any Bugs Productions.

Fyne, Olga. Jerry & Sherry. 2008. (Illus.). 24p. pap. 12.99 *(978-1-4389-3672-7(9))* AuthorHouse.

—Squirrel Race. 2009. 28p. pap. 13.99 *(978-1-4389-3676-5(1))* AuthorHouse.

Gabriel, Nat. Bubble Trouble. Nez, John, illus. 2004. 32p. (J). lib. bdg. 20.00 *(978-1-4242-1085-5(2))* Fitzgerald Bks.

—Bubble Trouble. Nez, John, illus. 2004. (Science Solves It Ser.). 32p. (gr. -1-3). 15.00 *(978-0-7569-4286-1(1))* Perfection Learning Corp.

Galindo, Mary Sue. Icy Watermelon/Sandia Fria. Rodriguez Howard, Pauline & Howard, Pauline Rodriguez, illus. 2008. (J). (gr. -1-2). pap. 7.95 *(978-1-55885-307-2(3)*, Piñata Books) Arte Publico Pr.

Gamblin, Rose Tooley & Hernández, Oscar. Bill's Lunch: El Almuerzo de Bill. 2010. (ENG & SPA., Illus.). 32p. (J). *(978-0-8127-0472-3(X))* Review & Herald Publishing Assn.

Gaven, Jim. Friends Find Fun for Food: All about Alliterations. 2013. 28p. pap. 24.95 *(978-1-63000-140-7(6))* America Star Bks.

Gee, Randi. Smart Cookie. 2010. 32p. pap. 15.50 *(978-0-557-52976-6(X))* Lulu Pr., Inc.

Genhart, Michael. Peanut Butter & Jellyous: ...sometimes Friendships Get Sticky. Mack, Steve, illus. 2017. (J). ***(978-1-4338-2337-4(3)***, Magination Pr.) American Psychological Assn.

George, Lynn. The Super Sandwich. 2006. (Neighborhood Readers Ser.). (ENG.). 16p. (gr. 1-3). pap. 6.50 *(978-1-4042-7240-8(2)*, Rosen Classroom) Rosen Publishing Group, Inc., The.

Gibbons, Teresa Dominguez. Pancakes Every Morning. 2008. 24p. per. 24.95 *(978-1-60441-065-5(5))* America Star Bks.

Giff, Patricia Reilly. All the Way Home. 2003. (ENG., Illus.). 176p. (J). (gr. 3-7). pap. 7.99 *(978-0-440-41182-6(3)*, Yearling) Random Hse. Children's Bks.

Gilman, Grace. Dixie & the Class Treat. Rogers, Jacqueline, illus. 2012. (I Can Read Level 1 Ser.). (ENG.). 32p. (J). (gr. -1-3). 16.99 *(978-0-06-208606-8(5))*; pap. 3.99 *(978-0-06-208605-1(7))* HarperCollins Pubs.

—Dixie & the School Trip. McConnell, Sarah, illus. 2012. (I Can Read Level 1 Ser.). (ENG.). 32p. (J). (gr. -1-3). 16.99 *(978-0-06-208609-9(X))*; pap. 3.99 *(978-0-06-208608-2(1))* HarperCollins Pubs.

Giulieri, Anne. Little Sea Horse & the Big Crab, 1 vol. Aranda, Omar, illus. 2012. (Engage Literacy Yellow Ser.). (ENG.). 32p. (gr. k-2). pap. 5.99 *(978-1-4296-8968-7(4)*, Engage Literacy) Capstone Press of Coughlan Cos.

Glass, Susan. The Great Eggscape, 1 vol. Van Wright, Cornelius, illus. 2011. 32p. (J). (gr. k-5). (ENG.). 16.95 *(978-1-59572-261-4(0))*; pap. 6.95 *(978-1-59572-253-9(X))* Star Bright Bks., Inc.

Glazer, Tom. On Top of Spaghetti. 32p. (J). pap. 4.95 *(978-0-06-443547-5(4))* HarperCollins Pubs.

Glesener, Loretta. Bringing Back Dinner Time. 2011. 40p. pap. 24.95 *(978-1-4560-4221-9(1))* America Star Bks.

Golden Books Staff. Triceratops for Lunch. Meurer, Caleb, illus. 2010. (Little Golden Book Ser.). (ENG.). 24p. (J). (gr. -1-2). 4.99 *(978-0-375-86151-2(3)*, Golden Bks.) Random Hse. Children's Bks.

Gonzalez, Rafael. Cookie Boy! 2011. 20p. pap. 11.99 *(978-1-4634-0324-9(0))* AuthorHouse.

Goodin, Carolyn M. Candy Land. Goodin, Carolyn M., illus. 2007. (Illus.). 38p. (J). per. 14.99 *(978-0-9797879-1-1(2))* Family Legacy Ministries.

Gowar, Mick. The Pie-Eating Contest. Hall, Francois, illus. 2013. (Start Reading Ser.). (ENG.). 24p. (gr. k-1). pap. 7.95 *(978-1-4765-4127-3(2))* Capstone Press of Coughlan Cos.

Graham, Elspeth. Sandwich that Jack Made. Mould, Chris, illus. 2004. (ENG.). 24p. (J). lib. bdg. 23.65 *(978-1-59646-698-2(7))* Dingles & Co.

Graux, Amélie. I Love to Eat. Graux, Amélie, illus. deluxe ed. 2012. (ENG, SPA & FRE., Illus.). 12p. (J). (gr. k — 1). bds. 9.99 *(978-0-547-84842-6(0))* Houghton Mifflin Harcourt Publishing Co.

Greenwald, Marni Leigh. What Kind of Bagel Am I? 2005. (Illus.). 34p. per. 8.99 *(978-1-932338-46-1(2))* Lifevest Publishing, Inc.

Grimm, Jacob & Grimm, Wilhelm K. Doctor All-Knowing: A Folk Tale from the Brothers Grimm. Boiger, Alexandra, illus. 2008. (ENG.). 40p. (J). (gr. -1-1). 16.99 *(978-1-4169-1246-0(0)*, Atheneum/Richard Jackson Bks.) Simon & Schuster Children's Publishing.

Groves. Tea Break. Date not set. (Illus.). 16p. pap. 129.15 *(978-0-582-18297-4(2))* Addison-Wesley Longman, Ltd. GBR. Dist: Trans-Atlantic Pubns., Inc.

Gudule. Nouille Vivante. pap. 15.95 *(978-2-09-250239-6(5))* Nathan, Fernand FRA. Dist: Distribooks, Inc.

Guest, Elissa Haden. Who's My Cupcake? Fedotova, Marina, illus. 2011. (ENG.). 16p. (J). (gr. -1 — 1). bds. 6.99 *(978-1-4424-2051-9(0)*, Little Simon) Little Simon.

Gutierrez, Rochelle. Melvin Munch Wants My Lunch. 2010. 20p. pap. 12.49 *(978-1-4490-7996-3(2))* AuthorHouse.

Gutman, Dan. Funny Boy Takes on the Chit-Chatting Cheeses from Chattanooga. Dietz, Mike, illus. 2012. (Funny Boy Ser.). (ENG.). 138p. (J). (gr. 2-5). pap. 10.99 *(978-1-4532-9530-4(5))* Open Road Integrated Media, Inc.

Gym Shoe Salad. 2007. (J). pap. 15.00 *(978-0-9779207-7-8(1))* Text 4m Publishing.

H & T Imaginations Unlimited, Inc. Professor Woodpecker's Strawberry Patch! Wholesome, Fun children's story with Professor Woodpecker. 2008. 20p. pap. 12.49 *(978-1-4389-1304-9(4))* AuthorHouse.

Hafer, Tom. The Lemonade Crash. Terry, Brian, illus. 2010. 24p. 16.95 *(978-1-4520-1439-5(6))* AuthorHouse.

Hale, Natalie. Spaghetti! Date not set. (Illus.). 32p. (J). (gr. -1-3). pap. 14.95 *(978-0-9702698-0-5(3))* Special Reads for Special Needs.

Hall, Bureda Ann Greathouse. Stories of My Little Blue Monkey. 2007. (Illus.). 32p. (J). pap. 15.00 *(978-0-8059-7397-6(4))* Dorrance Publishing Co., Inc.

Hammelef, Danielle S. The Mystery of the Missing Cookies. 2006. (Early Explorers Ser.). (J). pap. *(978-1-4108-6131-3(7))* Benchmark Education Co.

Hansen, Jeanne. Wow! an Upside down Cake Birthday Party! 2011. 24p. pap. 15.99 *(978-1-4653-6016-8(6))* Xlibris Corp.

Harper, Charise Mericle. Cupcake. Harper, Charise Mericle, illus. 2010. (ENG., Illus.). 32p. (J). (gr. -1-1). 14.99 *(978-1-4231-1897-8(9))* Hyperion Pr.

Harris, Missy. I'm Allergic. 2008. 16p. pap. 12.99 *(978-1-4343-9421-7(2))* AuthorHouse.

Harris, Patricia. Raven & the Farmer. 2017. (Raven's Orchard Ser.). 24p. (gr. 4-6). pap. 8.25 ***(978-1-5081-6143-1(7)***, PowerKids Pr.) Rosen Publishing Group, Inc., The.

Harris, Robie H. What's So Yummy? All about Eating Well & Feeling Good. Westcott, Nadine Bernard, illus. 2014. (Let's Talk about You & Me Ser.). (ENG.). 40p. (J). (-k). 15.99 *(978-0-7636-3632-6(0))* Candlewick Pr.

Harrison, Paul. Yummy in My Tummy! Worsley, Belinda, illus. 2009. (Get Ready (Windmill Books) Ser.). 32p. (J). (gr. k-2). lib. bdg. 22.60 *(978-1-60754-263-6(3))* Windmill Bks.

Hartley Bellows, Carol. Icabog Bear. 2009. 24p. pap. 15.50 *(978-1-4389-3856-1(X))* AuthorHouse.

Hartman, Bob. The Wolf Who Cried Boy. Raglin, Tim, illus. 2004. (ENG.). 32p. (J). (gr. k-3). pap. 7.99 *(978-0-14-240159-0(5)*, Puffin Books) Penguin Young Readers Group.

—The Wolf Who Cried Boy. Raglin, Tim, illus. 2004. (Picture Puffins Ser.). (gr. k-3). 17.00 *(978-0-7569-2950-3(4))* Perfection Learning Corp.

Hemingway, Edward. Bad Apple's Perfect Day. Hemingway, Edward, illus. 2014. (ENG., Illus.). 32p. (J). (gr. -1-k). 16.99 *(978-0-399-16036-3(1)*, G.P. Putnam's Sons Books for Young Readers) Penguin Young Readers Group.

Henkes, Kevin. A Box of Treats: Five Little Picture Books about Lilly & Her Friends. Henkes, Kevin, illus. 2004. (ENG., Illus.). (J). (gr. -1-k). pap. 14.99 *(978-0-06-073211-0(3)*, Greenwillow Bks.) HarperCollins Pubs.

Hepler, Heather. The Cupcake Queen. 2010. (ENG.). 256p. (YA). (gr. 7-18). 7.99 *(978-0-14-241668-6(1)*, Speak) Penguin Young Readers Group.

Herman, Debbie. Carla's Sandwich. Bailey, Sheila, illus. 2004. (ENG.). 32p. (J). (gr. k-3). 17.95 *(978-0-9729225-2-4(0))* Flashlight Pr.

Herman, Emmi S. We All Fall for Apples. Kennedy, Annie, illus. 2003. (Hello Reader Ser.). 32p. (J). pap. *(978-0-439-57396-2(3))* Scholastic, Inc.

Heyliger, William. Hot Dog Partners. Hastings, Howard L., illus. 2011. 216p. 44.95 *(978-1-258-08024-2(9))* Literary Licensing, LLC.

Hillert, Margaret. Dear Dragon Eats Out. Schimmell, David, illus. rev. ed. 2014. (BeginningtoRead Ser.). (ENG.). 32p. (J). (gr. k-2). pap. 11.94 *(978-1-60357-637-6(1))*; lib. bdg. 22.60 *(978-1-59953-629-3(3))* Norwood Hse. Pr.

Hills, Ian. The Toxic Toadburger Conspiracy. 2005. (ENG.). 366p. (J). (gr. 4-6). per. 8.95 *(978-1-84046-564-8(6)*, Wizard Books) Icon Bks., Ltd. GBR. Dist: Publishers Group Canada.

Hiranandani, Veera. Lunch Will Never Be the Same! Dreidemy, Joëlle, illus. 2014. (Phoebe G. Green Ser.: 1). (ENG.). 96p. (J). (gr. 1-3). pap. 4.99 *(978-0-448-46695-8(3)*, Grosset & Dunlap) Penguin Young Readers Group.

Hiss, Jill. Peppeto's Magic Jelly Bean. 2005. 19.00 *(978-0-8059-9893-1(4))* Dorrance Publishing Co., Inc.

Hoenecke, Karen. What's for Dinner? Biddle, Bruce, illus. 2006. (Bridging School to Home Series B). (ENG.). 8p. (gr. k-1). pap. 7.95 *(978-1-879835-36-8(3)*, Kaeden Bks.) Kaeden Corp.

Hoffman, Mary Ann. Bananas for Breakfast! 2006. (Neighborhood Readers Ser.). (ENG.). 16p. (gr. 1-3). pap. 6.50 *(978-1-4042-7034-3(5)*, Rosen Classroom) Rosen Publishing Group, Inc., The.

Holaves, Chris. Even the Dead Get up for Milk. Goomas, John, illus. 2008.Tr. of Hasta los muertos se levantan por Leche. (ENG & SPA.). 64p. (J). lib. bdg. 15.95 *(978-0-9792991-0-0(1))* Astakos Publishing.

Holden, Pam. Magic Stone Soup - BIG BOOK. Hawley, Kelvin, illus. 2016. (ENG.). 16p. (-1). Beta *(978-1-77654-164-5(2)*, Red Rocket Readers) Flying Start Bks.

Holt, Jeri. Little Sugar Cube. 2011. 28p. pap. 15.99 *(978-1-4568-9577-8(X))* Xlibris Corp.

Hooton, David James. Carrots in Candy Land. 2008. 25p. pap. 24.95 *(978-1-60672-828-4(8))* America Star Bks.

Howe, James. Horace & Morris Say Cheese (Which Makes Dolores Sneeze!) Walrod, Amy, illus. 2010. (ENG.). 32p. (J). (gr. -1-3). 7.99 *(978-0-689-87177-1(5)*, Atheneum Bks. for Young Readers) Simon & Schuster Children's Publishing.

Hsia, Pei Chen. The Little Dumpling. 2012. 82p. pap. 19.95 *(978-1-4626-8041-2(0))* America Star Bks.

Hubbard, Sharron/Y. Link & Rosie Pick Berries. Schleihs, Krostin, illus. 2007. (J). bds. 7.95 *(978-0-9762434-2-7(3))* Link & Rosie Pr.

Huiner, Jacque. Anna Ate. 2009. 36p. pap. 21.99 *(978-1-4389-1765-8(1))* AuthorHouse.

Hulme, Joy N. Mary Clare Likes to Share: A Math Reader. Rockwell, Lizzy, illus. 2006. (Step into Reading Ser.: Vol. 2). (ENG.). 32p. (J). (gr. -1-1). pap. 3.99 *(978-0-375-83421-9(4)*, Random Hse. Bks. for Young Readers) Random Hse. Children's Bks.

The Hungry Giant's Lunch: Level H. Group 1. (Story Box Ser.). 16p. 31.50 *(978-0-7802-9371-7(1))* Wright Group/McGraw-Hill.

Hunt, Debbie Colleen. The Dinosaur Who Loved to Bake & Eat Cakes. Hunt, Craig J. S., illus. 2012. 32p. 24.95 *(978-1-4626-3213-8(0))* America Star Bks.

Husar, Stephane. Cat & Mouse Eat Good Food! Mehee, Loic, illus. 2015. (Av2 Fiction Readalong 2016 Ser.). (ENG.). (J). lib. bdg. 34.28 *(978-1-4896-3807-6(5)*, AV2 by Weigl) Weigl Pubs., Inc.

Hutchings, Paul. Don't Eat That! Rhyming Words. 2012. 24p. pap. 24.95 *(978-1-4626-6228-9(5))* America Star Bks.

Hutchins, Pat. The Doorbell Rang. 2004. (Illus.). 24p. (J). (gr. -1-2). 28.95 incl. audio compact disk *(978-1-59112-713-0(0))* Live Oak Media.

Hyman, Teisha Lashe'. Uh Oh! a Human. 2011. 16p. pap. 15.99 *(978-1-4634-3019-1(1))* AuthorHouse.

Ice Cream for Breakfast. 2006. (J). 10.00 *(978-0-9785002-0-7(2))* Johnson, Colleen.

The Ice cream Truck. 2004. (J). per. 15.95 *(978-0-9778937-4-4(X))* Priceless Ink Publishing Co., Inc.

Ingalls, Ann. Ice Cream Soup. 2013. (Penguin Young Readers Level 1 Ser.). lib. bdg. 13.55 *(978-0-606-31704-7(X)*, Turtleback) Turtleback Bks.

Ingman, Bruce & Ahlberg, Allan. The Runaway Dinner. Ingman, Bruce, illus. 2008. (ENG., Illus.). 40p. (J). (gr. -1-3). pap. 6.99 *(978-0-7636-3893-1(5))* Candlewick Pr.

Irbinskas, Heather. Pauly the Adventurous Pallid Bat. Anthis, Brian, illus. Tuttle, Merlin D., photos by. 2003. 32p. (J). pap. 7.95 *(978-1-58369-032-1(8))* Western National Parks Assn.

Jackson, Armitra L. Eating Safe with Ace & Mace! 2007. 44p. per. 15.95 *(978-1-4327-1255-6(1))* Outskirts Pr., Inc.

James, Anne. ¡ataque de Las Hormigas! (Ant Attack!) 2009. (SPA.). pap. 34.95 *(978-0-7613-4802-3(6))* Lerner Publishing Group.

Jarrell, Pamela R. A Nice Cool Drink. Teeple, Jackie, illus. l.t. ed. 2005. (J). (gr. -1-k). pap. 10.95 *(978-1-57332-341-3(1))*; pap. 10.95 *(978-1-57332-340-6(3))* Carson-Dellosa Publishing, LLC. (HighReach Learning, Incorporated).

Jeffers, Oliver. The Incredible Book Eating Boy. Jeffers, Oliver, illus. (ENG., Illus.). 32p. pap. *(978-0-00-718231-2(7)*, HarperCollins Children's Bks.) HarperCollins Pubs. Ltd.

Jenkins, Emily. A Fine Dessert: Four Centuries, Four Families, One Delicious Treat. Blackall, Sophie, illus. 2015. (ENG.). 44p. (J). (gr. -1-3). 17.99 *(978-0-375-86832-0(1))*; 20.99 *(978-0-375-96832-7(6))* Random Hse. Children's Bks. (Schwartz & Wade Bks.).

Jennings, Sharon. Franklin & the Cookies. Gagnon, Celeste et al, illus. 2005. 32p. (J). lib. bdg. 15.38 *(978-1-4242-1167-8(0))* Fitzgerald Bks.

Jepsen, D. R. Fabulous Fred Gets the Cheese. 2007. 16p. per. 24.95 *(978-1-4241-8456-9(8))* America Star Bks.

Joe's Pizza Parlor: Individual Title, 6 Packs. (gr. -1-2). 27.00 *(978-0-7635-9455-8(5))* Rigby Education.

Johns, Linda. Crazy Fruit Salad. 2004. (Shared Connections Ser.). (J). pap. 27.00 *(978-1-4108-1648-1(6))*; instr.'s gde. ed. 27.00 *(978-1-4108-1624-5(9))* Benchmark Education Co.

Johnston, Jack. The Ice Cream Hotel. 2012. 32p. (J). 17.95 *(978-0-9852869-0-3(3))* Norwen Pubns.

Johnston, Tony & National Geographic Learning Staff. Big Red Apple. Corwin, Judith Hoffman, illus. 2010. (Rise & Shine Ser.: Level 1). (ENG.). 32p. (C). (gr. -1-3). pap. 6.95 *(978-0-439-09860-1(2))* National Geographic School Publishing, Inc.

Jones, A. Not One, Not Two, Not Even a Few. 2011. 36p. pap. 24.95 *(978-1-4626-1744-9(1))* America Star Bks.

Jones, Callie Carol Rodgers. Sweet Potato Pie. 2012. 20p. pap. 17.99 *(978-1-4685-6114-2(6))* AuthorHouse.

Jones, Nick. Food-head Makes a Pie. 2008. 28p. pap. 24.95 *(978-1-60610-225-1(7))* America Star Bks.

Jones, Noah Z. Jack & the Snackstalk. Jones, Noah Z., illus. 2016. (ENG., Illus.). 80p. (J). (gr. k-2). 15.99 *(978-0-545-84862-6(8))* Scholastic, Inc.

Jordan, Pasquel. Little Edward Pumpernickel. Johnson, Elijah, illus. 2007. (J). *(978-0-9795586-0-3(3))* Journique Publishing Group, Inc.

Judge for a Day. (Greetings Ser.: Vol. 1). 32p. (gr. 3-5). 31.00 *(978-0-7635-3173-7(1))* Rigby Education.

Judge for a Day: 6 Small Books. (Greetings Ser.: Vol. 1). 32p. (gr. 3-5). 31.00 *(978-0-7635-1795-3(X))* Rigby Education.

The Junk-Food Files. 2003. (Illus.). pap. 5.60 *(978-0-7398-7513-1(2))* Steck-Vaughn.

Junk Food June. 2006. (J). 7.95 *(978-0-9788536-3-1(6))* G Publishing LLC.

Justice, Robert H. Rainbow Chicken Feed. 2012. 32p. pap. *(978-1-77097-121-9(1))* FriesenPress.

Kadono, Eiko. Grandpa's Soup. Ichikawa, Santomi, illus. 2009. (ENG.). 40p. (J). (gr. -1-3). pap. 9.00 *(978-0-8028-5347-9(1)*,

Eerdmans Bks For Young Readers) Eerdmans, William B. Publishing Co.

Kajikawa, Kimiko, et al. Yoshi's Feast. Heo, Yumi, illus. 2003. (Avenues Ser.). (ENG.). 32p. (C). (gr. -1-3). pap. 21.95 *(978-0-7894-2607-9(2))* National Geographic School Publishing, Inc.

Kamau, G. How Porcupine Got His Spines. 2004. (Illus.). 26p. pap. *(978-9966-25-168-8(5))* Heinemann Kenya, Limited (East African Educational Publishers Ltd E.A.E.P.) KEN. Dist: Michigan State Univ. Pr.

Kariya, Tetsu. Oishinbo: Izakaya — Pub Food, Vol. 7. Hanasaki, Akira, illus. 2010. (ENG.). 276p. pap. 12.99 *(978-1-4215-2145-9(8))* Viz Media.

Kasza, Keiko. Badger's Fancy Meal. 2009. (ENG.). 32p. (J). (gr. -1-3). pap. 6.99 *(978-0-14-241271-8(6),* Puffin Books) Penguin Young Readers Group.

Katz, Karen. Where Is Baby's Birthday Cake? Katz, Karen, illus. 2008. (ENG., Illus.). 14p. (J). (gr. -1 — 1). bds. 6.99 *(978-1-4169-5817-8(7),* Little Simon) Little Simon.

Keenan, Penny. Cooking with Ginger: Ginger Gets Lost Book I. Murray, Carol, illus. 2005. (J). per. 19.95 *(978-1-932604-23-8(5))* Tennessee Valley Publishing.

Keene, Carolyn. The Apple Bandit. Jones, Jan Naimo, illus. 2005. (Nancy Drew Notebooks). 74p. (J). (gr. 1-4). 11.65 *(978-0-7569-6505-1(5))* Perfection Learning Corp.

—Cupcake Chaos. Pamintuan, Macky, illus. 2013. (Nancy Drew & the Clue Crew Ser.: 34). (ENG.). 96p. (J). (gr. 1-4). pap. 5.99 *(978-1-4424-5351-7(6),* Aladdin) Simon & Schuster Children's Publishing.

Kelley, True. School Lunch. Kelley, True, illus. 2005. (ENG., Illus.). 32p. (J). (gr. -1-3). 16.95 *(978-0-8234-1894-7(4))* Holiday Hse., Inc.

Kelly, Katy. Melonhead & the Vegalicious Disaster. Johnson, Gillian, illus. 2013. (Melonhead Ser.). (ENG.). 224p. (J). (gr. 3-7). 6.99 *(978-0-307-92969-3(8),* Yearling) Random Hse. Children's Bks.

Kendall, Jack. The Magic Apple Tree. Bostrom, Sally, illus. l.t. ed. 2006. (ENG.). 48p. (J). per. 9.95 *(978-0-9787740-4-2(3))* Peppertree Pr., The.

Keman, Elizabeth. Fred's Bread. 2006. (Neighborhood Readers Ser.). (ENG., Illus.). 16p. (gr. 1-3). pap. 6.50 *(978-1-4042-7010-7(8),* Rosen Classroom) Rosen Publishing Group, Inc., The.

Kerr, Judith. The Tiger Who Came to Tea. Kerr, Judith, illus. 2009. (ENG., Illus.). 32p. (J). (gr. -1-2). 17.99 *(978-0-7636-4563-2(X))* Candlewick Pr.

Kertell, Lynn Maslen. Cupcake Surprise! 2012. (BOB Books: Scholastic Readers Level 1 Ser.). lib. bdg. 13.55 *(978-0-606-23910-3(3),* Turtleback) Turtleback Bks.

King, Zelda. The Lemonade Stand. 2006. (Neighborhood Readers Ser.). (ENG.). 12p. (gr. -1-3). pap. 5.90 *(978-1-4042-6722-0(0),* Rosen Classroom) Rosen Publishing Group, Inc., The.

—Let's Bake a Cake. 2006. (Neighborhood Readers Ser.). (ENG.). 16p. (gr. 1-3). pap. 6.50 *(978-1-4042-7260-6(7),* Rosen Classroom) Rosen Publishing Group, Inc., The.

Kingfisher, Rupert. Madame Pamplemousse & Her Incredible Edibles. Hellard, Sue, illus. 2008. (ENG.). 144p. (YA). (gr. 3-6). 15.99 *(978-1-59990-306-4(7),* 9781599903064, Bloomsbury USA Childrens) Bloomsbury Publishing USA.

Kingsley, Salome. Two Wishes for Natty's Birthday. 2007. (Illus.). 54p. (J). pap. 15.00 *(978-0-8059-7391-4(5))* Dorrance Publishing Co., Inc.

Kittinger, Jo S. A Lunch with Punch. 2004. (Rookie Reader Español Ser.). (ENG., Illus.). 32p. (J). (gr. k-2). pap. 4.95 *(978-0-516-27785-1(5),* Children's Pr.) Scholastic Library Publishing.

Kladstrup, Kristin. The Gingerbread Pirates. Tavares, Matt, illus. 2009. (ENG.). 32p. (J). (gr. -1-3). 16.99 *(978-0-7636-3223-6(6))* Candlewick Pr.

Klein, Zoë. The Goblins of Knottingham: A History of Challah. Bogert, Beth, illus. 2017. (J). ***(978-1-68115-526-5(5))*** Behrman Hse., Inc.

Kline, Suzy. Horrible Harry Takes the Cake. Remkiewicz, Frank, illus. 2007. (Horrible Harry Ser.). (ENG.). 64p. (J). (gr. 2-4). 4.99 *(978-0-14-240939-8(1),* Puffin Books) Penguin Young Readers Group.

Kochalka, James. The Glorkian Warrior Delivers a Pizza. Kochalka, James, illus. 2014. (Glorkian Warrior Ser.: 1). (ENG., Illus.). 112p. (J). (gr. k-4). pap. 12.99 *(978-1-59643-917-7(3),* 9781596439177, First Second Bks.) Roaring Brook Pr.

—The Happy Apples, Bk. 3. 2009. (Johnny Boo Ser.: 3). (ENG., Illus.). 40p. (J). (gr. 2-5). 9.95 *(978-1-60309-041-4(X),* 9781603090414) Top Shelf Productions.

Komura, Ayumi. Mixed Vegetables, Vol. 8. Komura, Ayumi, illus. 2010. (Mixed Vegetables Ser.: 8). (ENG., Illus.). 208p. pap. 9.99 *(978-1-4215-3235-6(2))* Viz Media.

Kralapp, Karl E. Fish Food. Kralapp, Karl E., illus. 2013. (Illus.). 28p. pap. 9.99 *(978-1-937165-62-8(0))* Orange Hat Publishing.

Krall, Dan. The Great Lollipop Caper. Krall, Dan, illus. 2013. (ENG., Illus.). 48p. (J). (gr. -1-3). 16.99 *(978-1-4424-4460-7(6),* Simon & Schuster Bks. For Young Readers) Simon & Schuster Bks. For Young Readers.

Krichilsky, Lauren. The Great Hunger. Madden, Colleen, illus. 2017. (Text Connections Guided Close Reading Ser.). (J). (gr. 2). *(978-1-4900-1862-1(X))* Benchmark Education Co.

Krosoczka, Jarrett J. Lunch Lady & the Cyborg Substitute. 2009. (Lunch Lady Ser.). (ENG.). 96p. (J). (gr. 3-7). lib. bdg. 12.99 *(978-0-375-94683-7(7),* Knopf Bks. for Young Readers) Random Hse. Children's Bks.

Krulik, Nancy. Any Way You Slice It. John and Wendy Staff, illus. 9th ed. 2003. (Katie Kazoo, Switcheroo Ser.: 9). (ENG.). 80p. (J). (gr. 2-4). pap. 4.99 *(978-0-448-43204-5(8),* Grosset & Dunlap) Penguin Young Readers Group.

Kuo, Julia. Everyone Eats. Kuo, Julia, illus. 2012. (ENG., Illus.). 22p. (J). (gr. -1). 9.95 *(978-1-897476-74-1(4))* Simply Read Bks. CAN. Dist: Ingram Publisher Services.

Kurup, Sindhu. Baby Bear's Favorite Food Pyramid. 2011. 28p. pap. 11.99 *(978-1-935268-91-8(0))* Halo Publishing International.

Kyle, Tracey C. Gazpacho for Nacho, 0 vols. 2014. (ENG.). 32p. (J). (gr. 1-3). 16.99 *(978-1-4778-1727-8(1),* 9781477817278, Amazon Children's Publishing) Amazon Publishing.

Labatt, Mary. Pizza for Sam. Sarrazin, Marisol, illus. 2003. (Kids Can Read Ser.). (ENG.). 32p. (J). (gr. k-1). 3.95 *(978-1-55337-331-5(6));* 14.95 *(978-1-55337-329-2(4))* Kids Can Pr., Ltd. CAN. Dist: Hachette Bk. Group.

Lankford, T. R. Sweet Te. 2011. 28p. pap. 15.99 *(978-1-4628-5501-8(6))* Xlibris Corp.

Laurentine, Florianne Daphne. The Mystery Chronicles: The Amazing Chocolate Mystery & the Case of the Phantom Cat. 2008. 100p. pap. 8.99 *(978-1-934360-61-3(9))* Raider Publishing International.

LeBaron, Cecilia. Nat & Tab. 2007. (Illus.). 16p. (J). 5.95 *(978-0-9798869-0-4(2))* Crush Publishing.

LeBlanc, Ellen Lieb. Tea & Cookie. Pape, Wendy Fehrle, illus. 2005. (J). bds. *(978-0-9773010-0-3(1))* Talmage Publishing.

Lederer, Ryan. The Adventures of Captain Candy. 2007. (Illus.). 48p. (J). (gr. 4-7). 15.95 *(978-0-9795852-1-0(X))* Seven Locks Pr.

Leigh, Autumn. The Apple Tree. (Neighborhood Readers Ser.). (ENG.). 16p. 2007. 33.50 *(978-1-4042-7328-3(X))* 2006. (gr. 1-3). pap. 6.50 *(978-1-4042-7128-9(7))* Rosen Publishing Group, Inc., The. (Rosen Classroom).

—El manzano (the Apple Tree) 2007. (Lecturas del barrio (Neighborhood Readers) Ser.). (SPA.). 16p. 33.50 *(978-1-4042-7329-0(8),* Rosen Classroom) Rosen Publishing Group, Inc., The.

Leighton, Davis L. & Strickland, Karen L. The Three Little Dinosaurs. 2010. (Illus.). 16p. (J). pap. 13.95 *(978-1-4327-5064-0(X))* Outskirts Pr., Inc.

Lenny Learns about Food Labels. 2004. (J). 5.00 *(978-1-882541-39-3(1))* Food Allergy & Anaphylaxis Network.

LeTourneau, Marie & Baty, Danielle Reed. The Mice of Bistrot des Sept Frères. 2008. (ENG & FRE.). 32p. (J). (gr. -1-3). pap. 7.95 *(978-1-933718-18-7(8))* Tanglewood Pr.

Levy, Janey. Edwin Visits Earth. 2006. (Neighborhood Readers Ser.). (ENG.). 16p. (gr. 1-3). pap. 6.50 *(978-1-4042-7160-9(0),* Rosen Classroom) Rosen Publishing Group, Inc., The.

Lieberman, Sylvia. Archibald's Swiss Cheese Mountain. Wendell, Jeremy, illus. 2007. 44p. (J). (gr. k-2). 17.95 *(978-0-9795852-5-8(2))* Seven Locks Pr.

Lin, Grace. Thanking the Moon: Celebrating the Mid-Autumn Moon Festival. 2010. (ENG.). 32p. (J). (gr. -1-2). 16.99 *(978-0-375-86101-7(7),* Knopf Bks. for Young Readers) Random Hse. Children's Bks.

Lindsay, Norman. The Magic Pudding. Lindsay, Norman, illus. 2016. (ENG., Illus.). 184p. (J). (gr. 4-7). pap. 9.99 *(978-1-59017-994-9(3),* NYRB Kids) New York Review of Bks., Inc., The.

Little, Robert. Grandma's Biscuits. Richmond, Jamea, illus. 2004. 32p. (J). (gr. -1-7). 15.95 *(978-0-9701863-5-5(5))* Relde Publishing.

Loccisano, Rina Fuda. Meatball 1 & Meatball 2. 2012. 56p. *(978-1-77097-770-9(8));* pap. *(978-1-77097-771-6(6))* FriesenPress.

Louise, Cristina & McIlroy, Michelle. Where Is Paco Now? Louise, Cristina & McIlroy, Michelle, illus. 2012. (SPA & ENG., Illus.). (J). *(978-1-934370-26-1(6),* Campanita Bks.) Editorial Campana.

Lovelace, Kelley. Ready Set Go Organic. 2006. 7.99 *(978-0-9791029-0-5(1))* KelleyGreenworks Publishing.

Lowell, Jax Peters. No More Cupcakes & Tummy Aches. 2004. (Illus.). 38p. (J). 22.99 *(978-1-4134-6255-5(3))* Xlibris Corp.

Lucas, Ian & Medoza, Chris. The Million Year Meal. Cruz, Cheryl, illus. 2012. 32p. (J). 19.95 *(978-1-60131-099-6(4))* Big Tent Bks.

Lukeman, Noah. It's Ice Cream Time! 2015. (ENG., Illus.). 20p. (J). pap. 5.99 *(978-1-63291-452-1(2))* Morgan Rice Bks.

Lutz, Nancie Anne. Patsy & Freckles Make Christmas Cookies. Lutz, Nancie Anne, illus. 2005. (Illus.). 25p. (J). *(978-0-9760064-1-1(3))* Dollworks.

Lyons, Theresa. Eating My ABC's. 2008. 18p. pap. 24.95 *(978-1-60474-946-5(6))* America Star Bks.

MacDonald, Alysha. Noodles - a Lunchtime Adventure. Swaim, Mike, illus. 2012. 28p. pap. *(978-0-9735526-8-3(9))* Cold Rock Publishing.

MacDonald, Margaret Read. Pickin' Peas. Cummings, Pat, illus. 2014. (ENG.). 32p. pap. 8.95 *(978-1-939160-83-6(9))* August Hse. Pubs., Inc.

MacGregor, Helen. Gnasher, Delta & the Biscuits. 2009. 48p. pap. 10.49 *(978-1-4389-1367-4(2))* AuthorHouse.

Mackall, Dandi Daley. The Legend of the Christmas Cookie, 1 vol. Cowdrey, Richard, illus. 2015. (ENG.). 32p. (J). 16.99 *(978-0-310-74767-3(8))* Zonderkidz.

Majid, Ellisha. A Sausage Went for a Walk. Kendall, Peter, illus. 2008. 20p. (J). bds. 12.95 *(978-1-921361-38-8(7))* Fremantle Pr. AUS. Dist: Independent Pubs. Group.

Major, Roberta Olsen. The Ice Cream Crone. 2007. (Royal Pains Ser.: 5). (YA). pap. 11.95 *(978-1-59705-801-8(7))* Wings ePress, Inc.

Mandel, Peter. Bun, Onion, Burger. Eliopoulos, Chris, illus. 2010. (ENG.). 40p. (J). (gr. -1-1). 12.99 *(978-1-4169-2466-1(3),* Simon & Schuster Bks. For Young Readers) Simon & Schuster Bks. For Young Readers.

Mankita, Jay. Elar. 2013. (Illus.). 38p. (J). pap. 9.95 *(978-1-935734-49-9(0))* Kitanie Bks.

Manzanares, J. C. Have Sweet Dreams of Ice Cream. 2011. 24p. pap. 11.50 *(978-1-61204-481-1(6),* Eloquent Bks.) Strategic Book Publishing & Rights Agency (SBPRA).

Marchon, Benoit. Spoonful: A Peek-A-Boo Book. Bravi, Soledad, illus. 2013. (ENG.). 38p. (J). (gr. k — 1). bds. 7.99 *(978-0-547-89313-6(2))* Houghton Mifflin Harcourt Publishing Co.

Mardinly, Berdan. Fresh Tarhana Soup: Story in English & in Turkish. 2008. (ENG & TUR., Illus.). 24p. (J). 8.75 *(978-0-9801675-4-2(X))* Robertson Publishing.

—Fresh Tarhana Soup - English. Mardinly, Berdan, illus. 2008. (ENG., Illus.). 16p. (J). pap. 5.50 *(978-1-935125-05-1(2))* Robertson Publishing.

Marko, Cyndi. Let's Get Cracking! Marko, Cyndi, illus. 2014. (Kung Pow Chicken Ser.: 1). (ENG., Illus.). 80p. (J). (gr. k-2). 15.99 *(978-0-545-61062-9(1));* pap. 4.99 *(978-0-545-61061-2(3))* Scholastic, Inc.

Marquez, Sofia. Pepe Perez Mexican Mouse: Pepe Perez Comes to the United States: Book 1, 1 vol. Marquez, Sofia, illus. 2009. (Illus.). 20p. pap. 24.95 *(978-1-61546-496-8(4))* America Star Bks.

Martinez, Rocio, illus. The Fox & the Crow. 2007. (First Reading Level 1 Ser.). 32p. (J). (gr. -1-3). 8.99 *(978-0-7945-1813-4(3),* Usborne) EDC Publishing.

Mason, Cherie. Everybody's Somebody's Lunch, 1 vol. Moore, Gustav, illus. 2005. (ENG.). 40p. (J). (gr. 3-6). 7.95 *(978-0-88448-200-0(6))* Tilbury Hse. Pubs.

Mass, Wendy. The Candymakers & the Great Chocolate Chase. (ENG.). (J). (gr. 3-7). 2017. 560p. pap. 8.99 ***(978-0-316-08918-0(4))*** 2016. 544p. 18.99 *(978-0-316-08919-7(2))* Little, Brown Bks. for Young Readers.

Matthews, Trisha. I Smell Pancakes! 2006. (Neighborhood Readers Ser.). (ENG., Illus.). 16p. (gr. 1-3). pap. 6.50 *(978-1-4042-7188-3(0),* Rosen Classroom) Rosen Publishing Group, Inc., The.

Mauldin, Mary. What a Carrot-Astrophy! 2011. 32p. pap. 14.99 *(978-1-4634-3366-6(2))* AuthorHouse.

Maverick, Peter. The Old Man & the Peach. 2008. 20p. pap. 24.95 *(978-1-60474-331-9(X))* America Star Bks.

May, Eleanor. Mac & Cheese, Pleeeeeeze! 2008. pap. 34.95 *(978-1-58013-780-5(6))* Kane Press, Inc.

—Mac & Cheese, Pleeeeze! Palmisciano, Diane, illus. 2008. (Math Matters Ser.). (ENG.). 32p. (J). (gr. -1-3). pap. 5.95 *(978-1-57565-260-3(9))* Kane Press, Inc.

Mayer, Mercer. Snowball Soup. Mayer, Mercer, illus. 2007. (My First I Can Read Bks.). (ENG., Illus.). 32p. (J). (gr. -1-k). 16.99 *(978-0-06-083544-6(3));* pap. 3.99 *(978-0-06-083543-9(5))* HarperCollins Pubs.

Mayfield, Marilee Joy. Chef Etouffee & the Great Gumbo Day. 2005. 64p. (J). lib. bdg. 19.95 *(978-0-9659222-6-5(X))* Leaping Antelope Productions.

Mazer, Anne. That's the Way the Cookie Crumbles. 2005. (Amazing Days of Abby Hayes Ser.: Bk. 16). (Illus.). 119p. (J). (gr. 3-7). 12.65 *(978-0-7569-6480-1(6))* Perfection Learning Corp.

Mbe na Nkita: The Tortoise & the Dog. 2008. (YOR & ENG., Illus.). 36p. 16.00 *(978-0-9801243-1-6(X))* Blazing Ideas Ltd.

Mcandrew, Maria. The Invasion of the Evil Chocolate Chips. 2013. 24p. pap. 24.95 *(978-1-63004-186-1(6))* America Star Bks.

McClure, Brian D. The Meal. Plumlee, Buddy, illus. 2009. (Brian D. Mcclure Childrens Book Collection). 59p. (J). (gr. -1-3). 16.95 *(978-1-933426-04-4(7))* Universal Flag Publishing.

McClure, Nikki. Apple. 2012. (ENG., Illus.). 40p. (J). (gr. -1-k). 13.95 *(978-1-4197-0378-2(1),* Abrams Appleseed) Abrams, Inc.

McClure, Wendy. The Princess & the Peanut Allergy, 1 vol. Lyon, Tammie, illus. 2009. (ENG.). 32p. (J). (gr. 1-3). 16.99 *(978-0-8075-6623-7(3))* Whitman, Albert & Co.

McCurry, Miya. The Foods Return. 2005. (J). per. 8.99 *(978-0-9764690-3-2(0))* Professional Publishing Hse. LLC.

McDonald, Megan. Beetle Mcgrady Eats Bugs! Manning, Jane K., illus. 2005. (ENG.). 32p. (J). (gr. k-5). 17.99 *(978-0-06-001354-7(0),* Greenwillow Bks.) HarperCollins Pubs.

McDonald, Rae A. A Fishing Surprise. Kemly, Kathleen, illus. 2007. (ENG.). 32p. (J). (gr. -1-3). 16.95 *(978-1-55971-977-3(X))* Cooper Square Publishing Llc.

Mcevoy, Ariane. Little Monkey Learns to Share. 2012. 28p. pap. 15.99 *(978-1-4691-5830-3(2))* Xlibris Corp.

Mcghee, Alison. The Case of the Missing Donut. Roxas, Isabel, illus. 2013. (ENG.). 32p. (J). (gr. -1-k). 16.99 *(978-0-8037-3925-3(7),* Dial Bks) Penguin Young Readers Group.

McGoldrick, Bernita. Pretty Pretty Picky Penelope. McGoldrick, Bernita, illus. 2010. (Illus.). 32p. pap. 12.95 *(978-1-935268-49-9(X))* Halo Publishing International.

McGregor, Melissa Lee. Ainsley & Owen: An Unexpected Friendship. 2013. 40p. pap. *(978-1-4602-0111-4(6))* FriesenPress.

McIntyre, Sarah & O'Connell, David. Jampires. 2015. (ENG., Illus.). 32p. (J). (gr. -1-k). 16.99 *(978-0-545-81663-2(7))* Scholastic, Inc.

McKnight, Alex. Waiting for Ding. Tellekamp, Lynda, illus. 2013. 20p. pap. 24.95 *(978-1-62709-362-0(1))* America Star Bks.

McNamara, Margaret. The Apple Orchard Riddle. Karas, G. Brian, illus. 2013. (Mr. Tiffin's Classroom Ser.). (ENG.). 40p. (J). (gr. -1-3). 17.99 *(978-0-375-84744-8(8),* Schwartz & Wade Bks.) Random Hse. Children's Bks.

—Picking Apples. Gordon, Mike, illus. 2009. (Robin Hill School Ser.). (ENG.). 32p. (J). (gr. -1-1). pap. 3.99 *(978-1-4169-5539-9(9),* Simon Spotlight) Simon Spotlight.

McTrustry, Chris. Red Goes Green, 1 vol. rev. ed. 2013. (Fiction Readers Ser.). (ENG., Illus.). 32p. (J). (gr. 3-3). pap. 8.99 *(978-1-4333-5641-4(4))* Shell Educational Publishing.

Meadows, Daisy. The Rainbow Fairies. 2010. (Scholastic Reader Level 2 Ser.). (ENG.). 32p. (J). (gr. 1-3). pap. 3.99 *(978-0-545-22291-4(5),* Cartwheel Bks.) Scholastic, Inc.

Medina, Jamie B. Juan Carlos & the Hairy-Chested Chili Pepper. 2008. 28p. pap. 24.95 *(978-1-4241-9869-6(0))* America Star Bks.

Medina, Juana. 1 Big Salad: A Delicious Counting Book. 2016. (ENG., Illus.). 32p. (J). (— 1). 17.99 *(978-1-101-99974-5(8),* Viking Books for Young Readers) Penguin Young Readers Group.

Metz, Melinda. S. M. A. R. T. S. & the Poison Plates. McKenzie, Heath, illus. 2015. (S. M. A. R. T. S. Ser.). (ENG.). 128p. (gr. 3-6). 22.65 *(978-1-4965-0464-7(X))* S.M.A.R.T.S. Learning System.

Metzger, Steve. Ice Cream King. Downing, Julie, illus. 2011. (ENG.). 32p. (J). (gr. -1-2). 15.95 *(978-1-58925-096-3(6));* pap. 7.95 *(978-1-58925-427-5(9))* Tiger Tales.

Meyer, Jane G. & Gannon, Ned. The Woman & the Wheat. Meyer, Jane G. & Gannon, Ned, illus. 2009. (Illus.). 32p. (J). 18.00 *(978-0-88141-059-4(4))* St. Vladimir's Seminary Pr.

Meza, Martin. Martin Mezas Story Time Three Short Stories, Vol. 1. 2007. 64p. pap. 14.21 *(978-1-4116-8486-7(9))* Lulu Pr., Inc.

Middleton, Shawn. Sam & the Peanut Butter Crackers. 2009. 32p. pap. 12.99 *(978-1-4389-3400-6(9))* AuthorHouse.

Miller, Margaret. Baby Food. Miller, Margaret, photos by. 2009. (Look Baby! Bks.). (ENG., Illus.). 14p. (J). (gr. -1 — 1). bds. 4.99 *(978-1-4169-8996-7(X),* Little Simon) Little Simon.

Miller, Sara F. Pooh's Honey Trouble. 2012. (ENG.). 16p. (J). (gr. -1-1). bds. 6.99 *(978-1-4231-3579-1(2))* Disney Pr.

Mills, David. Lima's Red Hot Chilli. Brazell, Derek, illus. 2004. (J). 24p. *(978-1-85269-504-0(8));* 24p. *(978-1-85269-505-7(6));* 24p. *(978-1-85269-429-6(7));* 24p. *(978-1-85269-534-7(X));* 24p. *(978-1-85269-468-5(8));* 24p. *(978-1-85269-467-8(X));* (ENG & KOR.). 32p. pap. *(978-1-85269-543-9(9));* (ENG & FRE.). 32p. pap. *(978-1-85269-533-0(1));* (ENG & PER.). 32p. pap. *(978-1-85269-506-4(4));* (ENG & TAM.). 32p. pap. *(978-1-85269-469-2(6));* (ENG & GRE.). 32p. pap. *(978-1-85269-466-1(1));* (ENG & KHM.). 32p. pap. *(978-1-85269-542-2(0));* (ENG & URD.). 32p. pap. *(978-1-85269-427-2(0));* (ENG & TUR.). 32p. pap. *(978-1-85269-426-5(2));* (ENG & SOM.). 32p. pap. *(978-1-85269-425-8(4));* (ENG & POR.). 32p. pap. *(978-1-85269-424-1(6));* (ENG & GUJ.). 32p. pap. *(978-1-85269-423-4(8));* (ENG & BEN.). 32p. pap. *(978-1-85269-421-0(1));* (ENG & ARA.). 32p. pap. *(978-1-85269-420-3(3));* (ENG & ALB.). 32p. pap. *(978-1-85269-465-4(3))* Mantra Lingua.

Mire, Sahra. Too Many Sweets. 2011. (Illus.). 28p. pap. 15.66 *(978-1-4567-8416-4(1))* AuthorHouse.

Mitchell, Shirley Lipscomb. The Legend of the Sweet Potato Pie. Tombers, Monica, ed. Stafford, Jordan, illus. 2012. 40p. (-18). pap. 12.95 *(978-0-9851996-0-9(1))* HMSI, Inc.

Mohamed, Abdullahi. The Forbidden Cake. 2013. 36p. pap. 22.88 *(978-1-4817-8266-1(5))* AuthorHouse.

Monk, Isabell. Family. Porter, Janice Lee, illus. (Carolrhoda Picture Bks.). 32p. (J). 2005. (ENG.). (gr. k-4). per. 10.95 *(978-1-57505-917-4(7))* 2003. (gr. -1-3). 15.95 *(978-1-57505-485-8(X),* Carolrhoda Bks.) Lerner Publishing Group.

Monroe, Gregory. It's Chili & I Don't Like It! 2012. 28p. pap. 21.99 *(978-1-4691-8429-6(X))* Xlibris Corp.

Moran, Alex. Popcorn. Everitt, Betsy, illus. 2003. (Green Light Readers Level 1 Ser.). (ENG.). 24p. (J). (gr. -1-3). pap. 3.95 *(978-0-15-204861-7(8))* Houghton Mifflin Harcourt Publishing Co.

—Popcorn. 2003. (Green Light Readers — Level 1 Ser.). (gr. k-3). 13.50 *(978-0-613-66372-4(1),* Turtleback) Turtleback Bks.

Morden, Daniel. So Hungry. Carpenter, Suzanne, illus. 2004. (ENG.). 32p. pap. 29.95 *(978-1-84323-455-5(6))* Beekman Bks., Inc.

Morgan, Mary Sue. Swifty. 2008. 24p. pap. 24.95 *(978-1-60441-579-7(7))* America Star Bks.

Morgan, Ruth. Batter Splatter! Mikhail, Jess, illus. 2005. (ENG.). 24p. (J). lib. bdg. 23.65 *(978-1-59646-704-0(5))* Dingles & Co.

Moroney, Trace. Dinnertime: Baxter Bear Chubby. Moroney, Trace, illus. 2008. (Illus.). 10p. (J). (gr. -1-1). bds. 5.99 *(978-1-86463-174-6(0))* Gardner Pubns.

Moskowitz, Hannah. Break. 2009. (ENG.). 272p. (YA). (gr. 9-18). pap. 10.99 *(978-1-4169-8275-3(2),* Simon Pulse) Simon Pulse.

Mourabiti, Hassan & Rosen, Lynn. Once upon a Time in Hunger Land. 2012. 48p. pap. 11.95 *(978-1-4772-0819-9(4))* AuthorHouse.

Mulder, Michelle. Maggie & the Chocolate War, 1 vol. 2008. (Kids' Power Book Ser.). (ENG., Illus.). 94p. (J). (gr. 4-8). pap. 14.95 *(978-1-897187-27-2(0))* Second Story Pr. CAN. Dist: Orca Bk. Pubs. USA.

Muldrow, Diane. Chocolate Cakes & Cookie Bakes! Swanson, Maggie, illus. 2009. (Storytime Stickers Ser.). (ENG.). 16p. (J). (gr. -1-1). pap. 5.95 *(978-1-4027-6128-7(1))* Sterling Publishing Co., Inc.

Mull, Brandon. The Candy Shop War. 2011. E-Book 6.64 *(978-1-60641-649-5(9))* Deseret Bk. Co.

—The Candy Shop War. (Candy Shop War Ser.: Bk. 1). 2008. 368p. pap. 6.99 *(978-1-59038-970-6(0))* 2007. (Illus.). 409p. (J). (gr. 3-7). 19.99 *(978-1-59038-783-2(X))* Shadow Mountain Publishing. (Shadow Mountain).

Munch. 2015. (ENG., Illus.). 24p. (J). (gr. k-4). 7.99 *(978-1-85733-731-0(X));* 19.99 *(978-1-85733-732-7(8))* Lerner Publishing Group.

Munsch, Robert. More Pies. Martchenko, Michael, illus. 2004. (J). (gr. k-3). spiral bd. *(978-0-616-14590-6(X))* Canadian National Institute for the Blind/Institut National Canadien pour les Aveugles.

—Une Tonne de Tartes! 2004. (FRE., Illus.). (J). (gr. k-3). spiral bd. *(978-0-616-14602-6(7))* Canadian National Institute for the Blind/Institut National Canadien pour les Aveugles.

Mure, Nancy. Massimo's Meatballs. Miller, Margot, illus. 2015. (ENG.). 40p. (J). pap. 9.98 *(978-0-7443-2196-8(4))* SynergEbks.

Murray, Brian Robert. Belle Curve: In Lemonade into Lemons. 2007. (ENG.). 52p. per. 24.95 *(978-1-4241-8370-8(7))* America Star Bks.

Murray, Laura. The Gingerbread Man Loose on the Fire Truck. Lowery, Mike, illus. 2013. (ENG.). 32p. (J). (gr. k-3). 16.99 *(978-0-399-25779-7(9),* G.P. Putnam's Sons Books for Young Readers) Penguin Young Readers Group.

Murray, Laura & McPike, Elizabeth. The Gingerbread Man Loose at Christmas. Lowery, Mike, illus. 2015. (ENG.). 32p. (J). (gr. k-k). 16.99 *(978-0-399-16866-6(4),* G.P. Putnam's Sons Books for Young Readers) Penguin Young Readers Group.

Nakagawa, Chihiro. Who Made This Cake? Koyose, Junji, illus. 2008. (ENG.). 32p. (J). (gr. -1-2). 16.95 *(978-1-59078-595-9(9),* Front Street) Boyds Mills Pr.

Nast, Thomas, illus. The Fat Boy. 2011. (American Antiquarian Society Ser.). (ENG.). 24p. (gr. 1). 24.95 *(978-1-4290-9736-9(1))* Applewood Bks.

Nazareth, Melanie. Can I Have Some Cake Too? Lehner-Rhoades, Shirley, illus. 2013. 32p. (J). pap. 14.95 *(978-1-935914-28-0(6))* River Sanctuary Publishing.

Neill, Joan Walmer. The Amazing Tale of Bub the Trier. 2012. 36p. pap. 20.00 *(978-1-4772-6240-5(7))* AuthorHouse.

Neuschwander, Cindy. Sir Cumference & the off-The-Charts Dessert. 2013. (Sir Cumference Ser.). lib. bdg. 18.40 *(978-0-606-34743-3(7),* Turtleback) Turtleback Bks.

Newbigging, Robert Delford. Robert Rat Has A Problem: A Tale of Broccoli. 2010. 44p. pap. 16.99 *(978-1-4520-2134-8(1))* AuthorHouse.

Newman, Robin. A Wilcox & Griswold Mystery: the Case of the Missing Carrot Cake. Zemke, Deborah, illus. 2015. (Wilcox &

Griswold Mystery Ser.). (ENG.). 40p. (J). (gr. -1-3). 15.95 (978-1-939547-17-0(2)) Creston Bks.

Newth, Rebecca. Tinkum's Dog. Primm, Thomas, illus. 2005. 32p. (J). 15.00 (978-0-9630310-7-5(4)) Will Hall Bks.

Norfolk, Bobby & Norfolk, Sherry. Anansi Goes to Lunch. Hoffmire, Baird, illus. 2007. (Story Cove Ser.). (ENG.). 32p. (J). (gr. -1-3). pap. 4.95 (978-0-87483-852-7(5)) August Hse. Pubs., Inc.

North, Laura. The Boy with the Pudding Touch. Chapman, Neil, illus. 2014. (ENG.). 32p. (J). pap. (978-0-7787-1364-7(4)) Crabtree Publishing Co.

North, Merry. All Gone. Woolf, Julia, illus. 2005. (J). (978-1-57151-753-1(7)) Playhouse Publishing.

Numeroff, Laura Joffe. If You Give a Cat a Cupcake. Bond, Felicia, illus. 2008. (If You Give... Ser.). 32p. (J). (gr. -1-3). lib. bdg. 17.89 (978-0-06-028325-4(4)) HarperCollins Pubs.

—If You Give a Cat a Cupcake. Bond, Felicia, illus. 2008. (If You Give... Ser.). (ENG.). 32p. (J). (gr. -1-3). 17.99 (978-0-06-028324-7(6)) HarperCollins Pubs.

—If You Give a Dog a Donut. Bond, Felicia, illus. 2011. (If You Give... Ser.). 32p. (J). (gr. -1-3). 17.89 (978-0-06-026684-4(8)); (ENG.). 17.99 (978-0-06-026683-7(X)) HarperCollins Pubs.

—If You Give a Mouse a Brownie. Bond, Felicia, illus. 2016. (If You Give... Ser.). (ENG.). 32p. (J). (gr. -1-3). 17.99 (978-0-06-027571-6(5)) HarperCollins Pubs.

—If You Give a Mouse a Cookie. 2004. (Illus.). (J). (gr. k-3). spiral bd. (978-0-616-01751-7(0)); spiral bd. (978-0-616-01752-4(9)) Canadian National Institute for the Blind/Institut National Canadien pour les Aveugles.

—If You Give a Mouse a Cookie. Bond, Felicia, illus. Date not set. 32p. (J). (gr. -1-2). 4.95 (978-0-06-443166-8(5)) HarperCollins Pubs.

—If You Give a Pig a Pancake Big Book. braille ed. 2004. (Illus.). (J). (gr. k-3). spiral bd. (978-0-616-07243-1(0)); spiral bd. (978-0-616-07244-8(9)) Canadian National Institute for the Blind/Institut National Canadien pour les Aveugles.

Nutrition Adventures with the Nutri Gang, Race Day, Issue #1: The Nutri Gang. 2007. (J). 2.99 (978-0-9792383-0-7(7)) KJ Pubns.

Nyika, Tendayi R. The Disappearance of the Any Flavor Cake. 2011. 44p. pap. 21.99 (978-1-4628-7096-7(1)) Xlibris Corp.

Oceanak, Karla. Finicky. Spanjer, Kendra, illus. 2012. (Aldo Zelnick Comic Novel Ser.: 6). (ENG.). 160p. (J). (gr. 3-7). 12.95 (978-1-934649-24-4(4)) Bailiwick Pr.

O'Donnell, Liam. Food Fight, 1 vol. Deas, Mike, illus. 2010. (Graphic Guides). (ENG.). 64p. (J). (gr. 3-7). pap. 9.95 (978-1-55469-067-1(6)) Orca Bk. Pubs. USA.

Okaty, Nicole. Orange Blossom's Fruity Fun Book: A Juicy Orange Adventure. 2004. (Illus.). 39p. (978-0-439-70466-3(9)) Scholastic, Inc.

Olson, Denise. P Is for Picky. 2011. 16p. 13.99 (978-1-4567-5837-0(3)) AuthorHouse.

Ormond, Jennifer. DJ's Allergies. Walstead, Curt, illus. 2011. 16p. (gr. -1-k). bds. 8.95 (978-0-9792010-1-1(2)) Ormond, Jennifer.

Otitoloju/Blazing Ideas Ltd, Ololade/Adewunmi, retold by. Kunkuru Da Kare: The Tortoise & the Dog. 2008. (YOR & ENG., Illus.). 36p. 16.00 (978-0-9801243-6-1(0)) Blazing Ideas Ltd.

Oxenbury, Helen. It's My Birthday. Oxenbury, Helen, illus. 2010. (ENG., Illus.). 24p. (J). (gr. -1-k). bds. 8.99 (978-0-7636-4970-8(8)) Candlewick Pr.

Oxley, Jennifer & Aronson, Billy. Peg + Cat: The Pizza Problem. 2016. (Peg + Cat Ser.). (ENG., Illus.). (J). (gr. -1-2). 12.99 (978-0-7636-7559-2(8), Candlewick Entertainment) Candlewick Pr.

—Peg + Cat: the Pizza Problem. 2017. (Peg + Cat Ser.). (ENG.). 32p. (J). (gr. -1-2). 5.99 (978-0-7636-9246-9(8), Candlewick Entertainment) Candlewick Pr.

Pace, Dianne. Odel's Diner. 2007. (J). per. 12.95 (978-0-89315-419-6(9)) Lambert Bk. Hse., Inc.

Page, Nick & Page, Claire. Read with Me Gingerbread Fred: Sticker Activity Book. Baker, Sara, illus. 2006. (Read with Me (Make Believe Ideas) Ser.). 12p. (J). (gr. k-2). pap. (978-1-84610-178-6(6)) Make Believe Ideas.

Paikai, Tammy. Too Many Mangos. Robinson, Don, illus. 2009. 28p. (J). (gr. -1). 11.95 (978-1-59700-758-0(7)) Island Heritage Publishing.

Palatini, Margie. Bad Boys Get Cookie! 2007. (J). (gr. k-3). 29.95 incl. audio compact disk (978-0-8045-4180-0(9)); 27.95 incl. audio compact disk (978-0-8045-6957-6(6)) Spoken Arts, Inc.

Palmer, Catherine. Fatal Harvest. l.t. ed. 2004. (Matthew 25 Ser.). 496p. (YA). 28.95 (978-0-7862-6259-5(1)) Thorndike Pr.

Pangan, Catherine Hagerman. No Peanuts for Me! Warf, Gracie, illus. 2013. (ENG.). 30p. (J). (gr. -1-3). 14.95 (978-1-62086-433-3(9)) Mascot Bks., Inc.

Parish, Herman. Amelia Bedelia Takes the Cake. Avril, Lynne, illus. 2016. (I Can Read Level 1 Ser.). 32p. (J). (gr. -1-3). pap. 3.99 (978-0-06-233430-5(1), Greenwillow Bks.) HarperCollins Pubs.

Park, Barbara. Junie B. Jones & the Yucky Blucky Fruitcake. unabr. ed. 2004. (Junie B. Jones Ser.: No. 5). 71p. (J). (gr. k-3). pap. 17.00 incl. audio (978-0-8072-0641-6(5), Listening Library) Random Hse. Audio Publishing Group.

—Turkeys We Have Loved & Eaten (And Other Thankful Stuff) Brunkus, Denise, illus. 2014. (Junie B. Jones Ser.). (ENG.). 144p. (J). (gr. 1-4). 4.99 (978-0-375-87115-3(2), Random Hse. Bks. for Young Readers) Random Hse. Children's Bks.

Patterson, Irania. Chipi Chipis, Small Shells of the Sea. McElvane, Catherine, illus. 2005.Tr. of Chipi Chipis, Caracolitos del Mar. (SPA.). 44p. (J). per. 12.99 (978-1-59494-006-4(1)) CPCC Pr.

Patterson, Trina Dawkins. A Tale of Two Cookies: A Message of Kindness & Acceptance. Wilson, Bonnita, illus. 2011. (ENG.). 32p. (J). (gr. -1-3). pap. 10.99 (978-0-9819860-9-8(9)) Amber Skye Publishing LLC.

Pau Pau. The Princess' Adventure. 2007. 52p. pap. 16.95 (978-1-60441-069-3(8)) America Star Bks.

Paul, Ruth. Red Panda's Candy Apples. Paul, Ruth, illus. 2014. (ENG., Illus.). 32p. (J). (gr. -1-2). 14.99 (978-0-7636-6758-0(7)) Candlewick Pr.

Penner, Evelyn. The Kid Who Ate Dog Food. Chullabrahm, T. M., illus. 2008. 32p. (J). 15.99 (978-0-9796500-0-0(3)) Peppernut Publishing.

Penovi, Celina. Alboroto a la Hora Del Desayuno / Scrambled Breakfast. 2009. 20p. pap. 14.99 (978-1-4490-2743-8(1)) AuthorHouse.

Perelman, Helen. Caramel Moon. Waters, Erica-Jane, illus. 2010. (Candy Fairies Ser.: 3). (ENG.). 128p. (J). (gr. 2-5). pap. 5.99 (978-1-4169-9456-5(4), Aladdin) Simon & Schuster Children's Publishing.

—Chocolate Dreams. Waters, Erica-Jane, illus. 2012. (Candy Fairies Ser.: 1). (ENG.). 128p. (J). (gr. 2-5). 15.99 (978-1-4424-5775-1(9), Simon & Schuster/Paula Wiseman Bks.) Simon & Schuster/Paula Wiseman Bks.

—Jelly Bean Jumble. Waters, Erica-Jane, illus. 2013. (Candy Fairies Ser.: 10). (ENG.). 128p. (J). (gr. 2-5). pap. 5.99 (978-1-4424-5297-8(8), Aladdin) Simon & Schuster Children's Publishing.

—Jelly Bean Jumble. Waters, Erica-Jane, illus. 2013. (Candy Fairies Ser.: 10). (ENG.). 128p. (J). (gr. 2-5). 15.99 (978-1-4424-6000-3(8), Simon & Schuster/Paula Wiseman Bks.) Simon & Schuster/Paula Wiseman Bks.

Pérez-Mercado, Mary Margaret. ¡Zas! Torrey, Richard L., illus. 2011. (Rookie Ready to Learn Español Ser.). (SPA.). 40p. (J). pap. 5.95 (978-0-531-26788-2(1), Children's Pr.) Scholastic Library Publishing.

Pérez-Mercado, Mary Margaret & Torrey, Rich. ¡Zas! Torrey, Rich, illus. 2011. (Rookie Ready to Learn Español Ser.). (SPA., Illus.). 40p. (J). lib. bdg. 23.00 (978-0-531-26120-0(4), Children's Pr.) Scholastic Library Publishing.

Peterson, Cris. Extra Cheese, Please! Mozzarella's Journey from Cow to Pizza. Upitis, Alvis, photos by. 2003. (ENG., Illus.). 32p. (J). (gr. -1-3). pap. 10.95 (978-1-59078-246-0(1)) Boyds Mills Pr.

Phipps, Dorothy. Chocolate Milk & White Milk. 2011. 28p. pap. 15.99 (978-1-4568-9036-0(0)) Xlibris Corp.

Pilkey, Dav. A Friend for Dragon. 2008. (Dragon Tales Ser.). (Illus.). (gr. -1-3). 16.00 (978-0-7569-8299-7(5)) Perfection Learning Corp.

Plant, David J. Hungry Roscoe. 2015. (ENG., Illus.). 40p. (J). (gr. -1-2). 17.95 (978-1-909263-53-6(2)) Flying Eye Bks. GBR. Dist: Consortium Bk. Sales & Distribution.

Postgate, Daniel, illus. Rumpled Stilton Skin. 2015. (ENG.). 32p. (J). (978-0-7787-1930-4(8)) Crabtree Publishing Co.

The Power of Chocolate. 2005. (YA). (978-0-9771020-0-6(9)) Savas, Bachtsoglou.

Prichard, Diana. The Cow in Patrick O'Shanahan's Kitchen. Knopf, Heather, illus. 2013. (ENG.). 32p. (J). (gr. -1-3). 17.95 (978-1-939775-01-6(9)) March 4th, Inc.

Prochovnic, Dawn Babb. The Big Blue Bowl: Sign Language for Food, 1 vol. Bauer, Stephanie, illus. 2009. (Story Time with Signs & Rhymes Ser.). (ENG.). 32p. (gr. -1-3). 28.50 (978-1-60270-668-2(9), Looking Glass Library) ABDO Publishing Co.

Pugliano-Martin, Carol. The Day I Followed the Pickle. Beckes, Shirley, illus. 2004. (Reader's Theater Ser.). (J). pap. (978-1-4108-2297-0(4), A22974) Benchmark Education Co.

The Queen of Hearts: 6 Small Books. (gr. k-2). 23.00 (978-0-7635-8494-8(0)) Rigby Education.

Quest, Stacy. Sad Sam & the Magic Cookies. Wertheimer, Beverly & Ronsley, Jill, eds. Morris, Michael, illus. 2006. (ENG.). (J). 16.95 (978-1-932367-01-0(2)) BookBound Publishing.

Quinlivan, Ada. Mealtime. 2016. (It's Time Ser.). 24p. (gr. 1-1). pap. 8.25 (978-1-4994-2280-1(6), PowerKids Pr.) Rosen Publishing Group, Inc., The.

Rabei, Carolina. Crunch! Rabei, Carolina, illus. 2016. (Child's Play Library). (ENG., Illus.). 36p. (J). (978-1-84643-733-5(4)) Child's Play International Ltd.

Rader, Josh. Detective Stephy Wephy Holmes in the Missing Cake. Meyer, Sarah, illus. 2007. 36p. (J). (gr. -1-3). per. 14.99 (978-1-59879-399-4(3)) Lifevest Publishing, Inc.

Radlauer. Breakfast by Molly. 2007. (ENG.). 32p. (J). (gr. -1-2). 8.99 (978-1-4169-6837-5(7), Simon & Schuster/Paula Wiseman Bks.) Simon & Schuster/Paula Wiseman Bks.

Ramsay, Mark. The Good Neighbors' Cheese Feast: A Cheesy Mouse Tale of Subtraction with Regrouping. Robinson, Susan G., illus. 2010. (ENG.). 32p. (J). pap. 9.95 (978-0-9842863-1-7(4)) Strategic Educational Tools.

Real, F. A. Casey & the Car Wash. 2008. 20p. pap. 24.95 (978-1-4241-9091-1(6)) America Star Bks.

Reasoner, Charles. Color Crunch! 2009. (Bite Bks.). (Illus.). (J). bds. 7.99 (978-1-934650-15-8(3)) Just For Kids Pr., LLC.

—Shapes for Lunch! 2009. (Bite Bks.). (Illus.). (J). bds. 7.99 (978-1-934650-16-5(1)) Just For Kids Pr., LLC.

Rebecca, Amy. Healthy Habits: The Rainbow Food. 2013. 28p. pap. 24.95 (978-1-63004-021-5(5)) America Star Bks.

Reberg, Evelyne. Roi des de la Tambouille. pap. 21.95 (978-2-227-73104-2(4)) Bayard Editions FRA. Dist: Distribooks, Inc.

Redhead, Janet S. & Dale, Christine. The Big Block of Chocolate. (Illus.). (J). pap. (978-0-908643-75-2(6)) Scholastic New Zealand Ltd.

Reid Banks, Lynne & Stephenson, Omri. The Spice Rack. 2010. 40p. pap. 23.50 (978-1-4461-3229-6(3)) Lulu Pr., Inc.

Renee, Lindsey. What Kind of Fairy Is Merry Berry? 2010. (ENG., Illus.). 36p. (J). (gr. -1-1). 12.99 (978-0-8118-7685-8(3)) Chronicle Bks. LLC.

Renfroe, Ann. The Living Ice Cream Guys. Wilson, Alonza S., illus. 2012. 34p. pap. 13.95 (978-0-9858398-9-5(9)) Mindstir Media.

Rey. Panique a la Chocolaterie. 16.95 (978-2-09-250165-8(8)) Nathan, Fernand FRA. Dist: Distribooks, Inc.

Rey, H. A. Curious George Farm to Table (CGTV 8x8) 2016. (Curious George Ser.). (ENG., Illus.). 24p. (J). (gr. -1-3). 12.99 (978-0-544-65220-0(7), HMH Books For Young Readers) Houghton Mifflin Harcourt Publishing Co.

Rey, H. A. & Rey, Margret. Curious George & the Pizza Party. 2013. (Curious George Ser.). (ENG., Illus.). 24p. (J). (gr. -1-3). pap. 4.99 (978-0-544-10988-9(0)) Houghton Mifflin Harcourt Publishing Co.

—Curious George & the Pizza Party. Shalleck, Alan J., ed. 2010. (Curious George Ser.). (ENG., Illus.). 24p. (J). (gr. -1-3). 13.99 (978-0-547-23211-9(X)) Houghton Mifflin Harcourt Publishing Co.

Rey, Margret & Rey, H. A. Makes Pancakes. 2008. (Curious George Ser.). (ENG., Illus.). 24p. (J). (gr. -1-3). audio compact disk 10.95 (978-0-618-99727-5(X)) Houghton Mifflin Harcourt Publishing Co.

Ricci, Christine. Dora's Rainbow Picnic. Mangano, Tom et al, illus. 2007. (J). pap. (978-1-4127-8927-1(3)) Publications International, Ltd.

Rie, Jannie. The Community Food Tree. 2012. (ENG.). (J). pap. (978-1-4675-5240-0(2)) Independent Pub.

Robey, Stephanie. My Favorite Food. Loeffelholz, Sarah, illus. 2006. (J). 14.95 (978-0-9786850-0-3(8)) Overdue Bks.

Rog&eacute. The French Fry King. Rog&eacute, illus. 2012. (ENG., Illus.). 32p. (J). (gr. -1-1). 17.95 (978-1-77049-350-6(6), Tundra Bks.) Tundra Bks. CAN. Dist: Penguin Random Hse. LLC.

Rogers, Anne. PRINCE & the APPLE TREE. 2008. 32p. pap. 23.50 (978-1-4092-1035-1(9)) Lulu Pr., Inc.

Rompella, Natalie. Edgar, Allan, & Poe, & the Tell-Tale Beets. l.t. ed. 2012. 63p. (J). pap. (978-1-4596-3447-3(0)) ReadHowYouWant.com, Ltd.

Rosa-Casanova, Sylvia. Mama Provi & the Pot of Rice. 2004. (Illus.). (J). (gr. k-3). spiral bd. (978-0-616-07257-8(0)) Canadian National Institute for the Blind/Institut National Canadien pour les Aveugles.

Rosenfeld, Dina. A Chanukah Story for Night Number Three. 2009. (Illus.). 32p. (J). 12.95 (978-1-929628-54-4(4)) Hachai Publishing.

Rosenthal, Amy Krouse. Cookies: Bite-Size Life Lessons. Dyer, Jane, illus. 2016. 36p. (J). (gr. -1 — 1). bds. 7.99 (978-0-06-242739-7(3), HarperFestival) HarperCollins Pubs.

—Sugar Cookies: Sweet Little Lessons on Love. Dyer, Jane & Dyer, Brooke, illus. 2009. (ENG.). 40p. (J). (gr. k-5). 12.99 (978-0-06-174072-5(1)) HarperCollins Pubs.

Roth, Anthony H. Little Anthony Doesn't Want to Eat His Dinner. 2012. 26p. 24.95 (978-1-4626-5776-6(1)) America Star Bks.

Rothenberg, Joan. Matzah Ball Soup. Rothenberg, Joan, illus. 2005. (Illus.). 29p. (J). (gr. -1-2). reprint ed. 15.00 (978-0-7567-8930-5(3)) DIANE Publishing Co.

Rouss, Sylvia A. & Rouss, Shannan. A Watermelon in the Sukkah. Iosa, Ann, illus. 2013. (Sukkot & Simchat Torah Ser.). (ENG.). 24p. (J). (gr. -1-2). 7.95 (978-0-7613-8119-8(8)); 16.95 (978-0-7613-8118-1(X)) Lerner Publishing Group. (Kar-Ben Publishing).

Roza, Greg. Lucy's Lunch. 2006. (Neighborhood Readers Ser.). (ENG.). 16p. (gr. -1-3). pap. 5.15 (978-1-4042-5649-1(0), Rosen Classroom) Rosen Publishing Group, Inc., The.

—Where's the Spaghetti? 2006. (Neighborhood Readers Ser.). (ENG.). 8p. (gr. -1-3). pap. 5.15 (978-1-4042-5655-2(5), Rosen Classroom) Rosen Publishing Group, Inc., The.

Rubin, Adam. Fiesta Secreta de Pizza. Salmieri, Daniel, illus. 2015. (ENG & SPA.). 40p. (J). (gr. -1-k). 8.99 (978-0-14-751560-5(2), Puffin Books) Penguin Young Readers Group.

Ruelle, Karen Gray. Easy As Apple Pie: A Harry & Emily Adventure. 2003. (Holiday House Readers Ser.). (ENG., Illus.). 32p. (J). (gr. k-3). 4.95 (978-0-8234-1800-8(6)) Holiday Hse., Inc.

Running Press Staff. Berry Best Friends. 2009. (Miniature Editions Ser.). (ENG.). 128p. 5.95 (978-0-7624-3589-0(5), Running Pr.) Running Pr. Bk. Pubs.

Running Press Staff & Parker, Amy. Tiny Blessings: for Mealtime. Walsh, Sarah, illus. 2016. (ENG.). 10p. (J). (gr. -1-17). bds. 7.95 (978-0-7624-6096-0(2), Running Pr. Kids) Running Pr. Bk. Pubs.

Rusu, Meredith. A Piece of Cake. 2017. (Shopkins: Shoppies Ser.). (ENG.). 32p. (J). (gr. -1-3). pap. 3.99 **(978-1-338-13558-9(9))** Scholastic, Inc.

Rylant, Cynthia. Annie & Snowball & the Teacup Club. Stevenson, Suçie, illus. 2009. (Annie & Snowball Ser.: 3). (ENG.). 40p. (J). (gr. k-2). pap. 3.99 (978-1-4169-1461-7(7), Simon Spotlight) Simon Spotlight.

—Henry & Mudge & the Funny Lunch. Bracken, Carolyn, illus. 2005. (Henry & Mudge Ready-To-Read Ser.: 24). 40p. (gr. k-2). lib. bdg. 13.55 (978-1-4176-7107-6(6), Turtleback) Turtleback Bks.

—Mr. Putter & Tabby Stir the Soup. Howard, Arthur, illus. 2004. (Mr. Putter & Tabby Ser.). (gr. 1-4). 16.00 (978-0-7569-3915-1(1)) Perfection Learning Corp.

—Puppy Mudge Has a Snack. Mones, Isidre, illus. 2005. (Puppy Mudge Ser.). (gr. -1-k). 14.00 (978-0-7569-5764-3(8)) Perfection Learning Corp.

—Puppy Mudge Has a Snack. Mones, Isidre, illus. 2003. (Puppy Mudge Ser.). (ENG.). 32p. (J). (gr. -1-k). 16.99 (978-0-689-83981-8(2), Simon Spotlight) Simon Spotlight.

Rylant, Cynthia & Bracken, Carolyn. Henry & Mudge & the Funny Lunch. Bracken, Carolyn, illus. 2004. (Henry & Mudge Ser.: 24). (ENG., Illus.). 40p. (J). (gr. k-2). 16.99 (978-0-689-81178-4(0), Simon Spotlight) Simon Spotlight.

Saddler-Reed, Gloria. Dewan!! "Ooh,Nuts" 2011. 24p. pap. 15.99 (978-1-4653-4587-5(6)) Xlibris Corp.

Salzman, Jeremiah. The Day of the Sandwich. Smith, Stephan, illus. 2010. (Very Small Adventures of Daisie Pup! Ser.). 48p. (J). pap. 8.99 (978-0-9842632-8-8(4)) Scandora.

Sam, 6 Packs. (Kinderstarters Ser.). 8p. (gr. -1-1). 21.00 (978-0-7635-8657-7(9)) Rigby Education.

Sanger, Rick. No Eat Not Food: The Search for Intelligent Food on Planet Earth. Russell, Carol, illus. l.t. ed. 2006. 48p. (J). 15.95 (978-0-9653149-2-3(8)) Mountain Path Pr.

Santillo, LuAnn. Good Food. Santillo, LuAnn, ed. 2003. (Half-Pint Kids Readers Ser.). (Illus.). 7p. (J). (gr. -1-1). pap. 1.00 (978-1-59256-118-6(7)) Half-Pint Kids, Inc.

Sarcone-Roach, Julia. The Bear Ate Your Sandwich. 2015. (ENG., Illus.). 40p. (J). (gr. -1-2). 16.99 (978-0-375-85860-4(1)); lib. bdg. 19.99 (978-0-375-95860-1(6)) Random Hse. Children's Bks. (Knopf Bks. for Young Readers).

Sattler, Jennifer. Sylvie. 2013. (ENG., Illus.). 40p. (J). (gr. -1-2). 7.99 (978-0-449-81072-9(0), Dragonfly Bks.) Random Hse. Children's Bks.

Sattler, Jennifer Gordon. Sylvie. 2009. (ENG., Illus.). 40p. (J). (gr. -1-2). 15.99 (978-0-375-85708-9(7), Random Hse. Bks. for Young Readers) Random Hse. Children's Bks.

Sauvageau-Smestad, Sheila. Cassie's Creepy Candy Store. Berg, Kelly, illus. 2006. 35p. (J). per. 17.95 (978-0-9767732-2-1(8)) Black Jackal Bks. Ltd.

Sazaklis, John. Jumping for Junk Food. Robinson, Lee, illus. 2016. (Billy Burger, Model Citizen Ser.). (ENG.). 96p. (gr. 2-3). lib. bdg. 22.65 (978-1-4965-2586-4(8)) Stone Arch Bks.

Scelsa, Greg. Muffin Man. Faulkner, Stacey, ed. Allen, Joy, illus. 2006. (J). pap. 2.99 (978-1-59198-321-7(5)) Creative Teaching Pr., Inc.

Schmid, Teresa Anne Marie. Teresa & the Bananas. 2013. (ENG.). 24p. (J). pap. 8.95 (978-1-4787-0238-2(9)) Outskirts Pr., Inc.

Schmidt, Kristina Edelkamp. Miss Flavia & the Cookie Cottage. Cologne, Starla, illus. 2009. 28p. pap. 7.99 (978-1-935125-61-7(3)) Robertson Publishing.

Schram, Peninnah. The Magic Pomegranate. Hall, Melanie, illus. (On My Own Folklore Ser.). 48p. 2008. (ENG.). (gr. 2-4). pap. 6.95 (978-0-8225-6746-2(6), First Avenue Editions) 2007. (J). lib. bdg. 17.95 (978-0-8225-8856-6(0), Kar-Ben Publishing) Lerner Publishing Group.

Schulz. Tutti qui Biscotti. pap. 19.95 (978-88-451-2810-3(5)) Fabbri Editori - RCS Libri ITA. Dist: Distribooks, Inc.

Schwartz, Joanne. Our Corner Grocery Store. Beingessner, Laura, illus. 2009. (ENG.). 32p. (J). (gr. -1-2). 19.95 (978-0-88776-868-2(7), Tundra Bks.) Tundra Bks. CAN. Dist: Penguin Random Hse. LLC.

Scott, Sally. Time for Tea. 2006. (Neighborhood Readers Ser.). (ENG.). 12p. (gr. 1-3). pap. 5.90 (978-1-4042-6867-8(7), Rosen Classroom) Rosen Publishing Group, Inc., The.

Scott, Stephen K. Grunions with Onions: A Children's Food Fantasy. 2011. 36p. pap. 16.99 (978-1-4634-4550-8(4)) AuthorHouse.

Scotton, Rob. Splat the Cat Takes the Cake. Scotton, Rob, illus. 2012. (I Can Read Level 1 Ser.). (ENG., Illus.). 32p. (J). (gr. k-3). 16.99 (978-0-06-197860-9(4)); pap. 3.99 (978-0-06-197859-3(0)) HarperCollins Pubs.

—Splat the Cat Takes the Cake. 2012. (Splat the Cat: I Can Read Ser.). (J). lib. bdg. 13.55 (978-0-606-23582-2(5), Turtleback) Turtleback Bks.

Scraper, Katherine. Garden Lunch. 2006. (Early Explorers Ser.). (J). pap. (978-1-4108-6027-9(2)) Benchmark Education Co.

Sendak, Maurice. La Cocina de Noche. Sendak, Maurice, illus. 2003. (Picture Books Collection). (SPA., Illus.). 40p. (J). (gr. k-3). 10.95 (978-84-204-4570-0(3)) Ediciones Alfaguara ESP. Dist: Santillana USA Publishing Co., Inc.

Seuss, Dr. Green Eggs & Ham, 1 vol. 2005. (Book & CD Ser.). (ENG., Illus.). 64p. (J). (gr. -1-2). 9.95 (978-0-375-83495-0(8), Random Hse. Bks. for Young Readers) Random Hse. Children's Bks.

—Les Oeufs Verts Au Jambon: The French Edition of Green Eggs & Ham. 2009. (FRE & ENG., Illus.). 64p. (J). (gr. -1-3). 12.95 (978-1-56975-688-1(0)) Ulysses Pr.

Seymour, Kristen. No Thank You, I'm Allergic: A Story Agout Food Allergy Awareness. 2011. 27p. (J). pap. 12.95 (978-1-4327-3293-6(5)) Outskirts Pr., Inc.

Shasha, Mark. Night of the Moonjellies: 15th Anniversary Edition. 2007. (Illus.). 32p. (J). (gr. -1-2). 12.95 (978-1-930900-34-9(1)) Purple Hse. Pr.

Shaw, Dana Alton, III. My Friend Zundel. 2006. per. (978-0-9791091-0-2(8)) Shaw, Dana.

Shaw, Natalie. Snack Attack! Style Guide Staff, illus. 2013. (Cloudy with a Chance of Meatballs Movie Ser.). (ENG.). 16p. (J). (gr. -1-2). pap. 5.99 (978-1-4424-9737-5(8), Simon Spotlight) Simon Spotlight.

Shea, Therese. The Lunch Bunch. (Neighborhood Readers Ser.). (ENG.). 12p. 2007. 33.50 (978-1-4042-7322-1(0)) 2006. (Illus.). (gr. 1-3). pap. 5.90 (978-1-4042-7038-1(8)) Rosen Publishing Group, Inc., The. (Rosen Classroom).

—Un lunch muy especial (the Lunch Bunch) 2007. (Lecturas del barrio (Neighborhood Readers) Ser.). (SPA.). 12p. 33.50 (978-1-4042-7323-8(9), Rosen Classroom) Rosen Publishing Group, Inc., The.

Sheils, Christine M. Owen Has Burgers & Drum: Helping to Understand & Befriend Kids with Asperger's Syndrome. DuFalla, Anita, illus. 2013. (Let's Talk Ser.). (ENG.). 48p. (J). (gr. -1-2). 9.95 (978-0-88282-434-5(1)) New Horizon Pr. Pubs., Inc.

Shepherd, Donna J. Chizzy's Topsy Tale. Collier, Kevin Scott, illus. 2008. 20p. pap. 10.95 (978-1-935137-10-8(7)) Guardian Angel Publishing, Inc.

Shiring, Jeff. Pizza by the Numbers. 2008. 32p. pap. 17.49 (978-1-4363-0289-0(7)) Xlibris Corp.

Shivers, Juliette. Brenda Doesn't Like Broccoli. 2006.Tr. of Brenda no le Gusta Bróculi. (SPA.). (J). 6.50 (978-0-9769379-1-3(3)) Ingram's Nutrition Consultations.

Simon, Coco. Emma Raining Cats & Dogs ... & Cupcakes! 2016. (Cupcake Diaries: 27). (ENG., Illus.). 160p. (J). (gr. 3-7). pap. 6.99 (978-1-4814-5524-4(9), Simon Spotlight) Simon Spotlight.

—Emma Raining Cats & Dogs... & Cupcakes! 2016. (Cupcake Diaries: 27). lib. bdg. 17.20 (978-0-606-38251-9(8)) Turtleback Bks.

—Katie: Just Desserts. 2016. (Cupcake Diaries: 29). (ENG.). 160p. (J). (gr. 3-7). 17.20 (978-0-606-39235-8(1)) Turtleback Bks.

Sinclair, Nicholas, et al. The Cookie Story. Wall, Randy Hugh, ed. Varela, Juan D., tr. Varela, Juan D., illus. l.t. ed. 2005.Tr. of Cuent de Galletas. (SPA.). 33p. (J). 14.95 (978-0-9764798-1-9(8)) Story Store Collection Publishing.

Sipp, Leora Janson. Emma & Sara Learn about Harvest Time. 2008. 40p. pap. 14.95 (978-1-934925-01-0(2), Eloquent Bks.) Strategic Book Publishing & Rights Agency (SBPRA).

Sís, Peter. Ice Cream Summer. 2015. (ENG., Illus.). 40p. (J). (gr. k-3). 17.99 (978-0-545-73161-4(5), Scholastic Pr.) Scholastic, Inc.

Skene, Pat. Monster Lunch, 1 vol. Ross, Graham T., illus. 2008. (Orca Echoes Ser.). (ENG.). 64p. (J). (gr. 2-3). pap. 6.95 (978-1-55143-941-9(7)) Orca Bk. Pubs. USA.

Skinner, J. C. Ringo & the Fruit Tree. 2008. 24p. pap. 24.95 (978-1-60441-028-0(0)) America Star Bks.

Slater, David Michael. Missy Swiss, 1 vol. Reibeling, Brandon, illus. 2007. (Missy Swiss & More Ser.). (ENG.). 32p. (gr. -1-4). 28.50 (978-1-60270-010-9(9), Looking Glass Library) ABDO Publishing Co.

Slegers, Liesbet. Eating. 2010. (Clavis Toddler: Daily Life Ser.). (ENG.). 12p. (J). (gr. k — 1). bds. 5.95 (978-1-60537-067-5(3)) Cobblestone Publishing Co.

Slippery, Sloppery Spaghetti: Individual Title Six-Packs. (gr. k-1). 23.00 (978-0-7635-9025-3(8)) Rigby Education.

Sloat, Teri & Huffmon, Betty. Berry Magic. 2004. (ENG., Illus.). 32p. (J). pap. 11.99 (978-0-88240-576-6(4)) Graphic Arts Ctr. Publishing Co.

Slonim, David. Oh, Ducky! A Chocolate Calamity. Slonim, David, illus. 2006. (Illus.). 28p. (J). (gr. k-4). 16.00 *(978-1-4223-5259-5(5))* DIANE Publishing Co.

Smedstad, Shannon. Tomorrow Is My Birthday. 2009. 24p. pap. 11.99 *(978-1-4389-9881-7(3))* AuthorHouse.

Smith, Doris Buchanan & Smith. A Taste of Blackberries. Wimmer, Michael, illus. 2004. (Trophy Bk.). (ENG.). 96p. (J). (gr. 3-7). reprint ed. pap. 5.99 *(978-0-06-440238-5(X))* HarperCollins Pubs.

Smith, Nicole. Chad the Allergic Chipmunk: A Children's Story of Nut Allergies. 2006. (Illus.). (J). per. 11.95 *(978-1-58628-054-3(6))* Allergic Child Publishing Group.

Smith, Robert Kimmel. Chocolate Fever. Fiammenghi, Gioia, illus. 2006. (ENG.). 96p. (J). (gr. 3-7). 5.99 *(978-0-14-240595-6(7),* Puffin Books) Penguin Young Readers Group.

—Chocolate Fever. 93p. (J). (gr. 2-4). pap. 3.99 *(978-0-8072-1405-3(1));* pap. 4.50 *(978-0-8072-1500-5(7))* Random Hse. Audio Publishing Group. (Listening Library).

Smith, Robert Kimmel, ed. Chocolate Fever. unabr. ed. 2004. (Middle Grade Cassette Librariestm Ser.). 93p. (J). (gr. 2-4). pap. 29.00 incl. audio *(978-0-8072-7785-0(1),* S YA 917 SP, Listening Library) Random Hse. Audio Publishing Group.

Smith-Rogers & Smith, Brady A. The Culinary Capers of Canon & Lily: Canon Grows a Garden. 2009. 20p. pap. 11.49 *(978-1-4490-1305-9(8))* AuthorHouse.

Snow, Pegeen. Eat Your Peas, Louise! Venezia, Mike, illus. 2011. (Rookie Ready to Learn Ser.). 40p. (J). (ENG.). pap. 5.95 *(978-0-531-26709-7(1));* (gr. -1-k). lib. bdg. 23.00 *(978-0-531-26527-7(7))* Scholastic Library Publishing. (Children's Pr.).

Snyder, Laurel. Baxter, the Pig Who Wanted to Be Kosher. 2010. (J). pap. 2.46 *(978-1-58246-373-5(5),* Tricycle Pr.) Ten Speed Pr.

Solomon, Michelle & Pereira, Lavinia. Cow Cake. Faust, Laurie A., illus. 2009. 24p. pap. 10.96 *(978-1-4251-8951-8(2))* Trafford Publishing.

St. John, Justine. Wilbur the Zucchini-Eating Dragon. 2012. (ENG., Illus.). 24p. (J). pap. 9.99 *(978-0-9829256-3-8(8))* SDP Publishing.

Staake, Bob. The Donut Chef. Staake, Bob, illus. 2013. (ENG., Illus.). 40p. (J). (gr. -1-2). 7.99 *(978-0-385-36992-3(1),* Dragonfly Bks.) Random Hse. Children's Bks.

Stanton, Andy. What's for Dinner, Mr Gum? Tazzyman, David, illus. 2015. (Mr Gum Ser.: 6). (ENG.). 256p. (J). (gr. 2-4). pap. 8.99 *(978-1-4052-7497-5(2))* Egmont Bks., Ltd. GBR. Dist: Independent Pubs. Group.

Star, Ian. Breakfast at the Farm. 2006. (Neighborhood Readers Ser.). (ENG.). 12p. (gr. -1-3). pap. 5.90 *(978-1-4042-6473-1(6),* Rosen Classroom) Rosen Publishing Group, Inc., The.

Steers, Billy. Tractor Mac Farmers' Market. 2015. (Tractor Mac Ser.). (ENG., Illus.). 32p. (J). (gr. -1-k). 8.99 *(978-0-374-30107-1(7),* 9780374301071, Farrar, Straus & Giroux (BYR)) Farrar, Straus & Giroux.

—Tractor Mac Farmers Market: Farmer's Market. Steers, Billy, illus. 2009. (ENG., Illus.). (J). 7.95 *(978-0-9826870-1-7(X))* Tractor Mac Inc.

Steig, William. Pete's a Pizza. 2004. (Illus.). 32p. (J). (gr. -1-2). 28.95 incl. audio compact disk *(978-1-59112-740-6(8))* Live Oak Media.

Steiner, Lana. Thor's Tummy. 2011. 28p. pap. 15.99 *(978-1-4628-7546-7(7))* Xlibris Corp.

Stephens, Ann Marie. Stella Eats Out. Bolan, Michael, illus. 2004. 32p. (J). per. 12.95 *(978-0-9729285-2-6(9),* 2-9) Kinkachoo Pr., The.

Sterling, Christina. What Makes a Sandwich... 2006. 15.50 *(978-0-8059-9954-9(X))* Dorrance Publishing Co., Inc.

Stihler, Chérie B. The Sourdough Man: An Alaska Folktale. Lavallee, Barbara, illus. 2010. (Paws IV Ser.). (ENG.). 32p. (J). (gr. -1-2). pap. 10.99 *(978-1-57061-594-8(2),* Little Bigfoot) Sasquatch Bks.

Stilton, Geronimo. The Mysterious Cheese Thief. 2007. (Geronimo Stilton Ser.). (Illus.). 111p. (J). (gr. 2-5). 14.65 *(978-0-7569-8303-1(7))* Perfection Learning Corp.

—The Mysterious Cheese Thief. 2007. (Geronimo Stilton Ser.: 31). (Illus.). 111p. (J). (gr. 4-7). 18.40 *(978-1-4177-9646-5(4),* Turtleback) Turtleback Bks.

Stine, R. L. The Big Blueberry Barf-Off! Park, Trip, illus. 2005. (Rotten School Ser.: No. 1). 128p. (J). lib. bdg. 14.89 *(978-0-06-078587-1(X))* HarperCollins Pubs.

—The Boy Who Ate Fear Street. 2011. (R. L. Stine's Ghosts of Fear Street Ser.). (ENG.). 128p. (J). (gr. 3-7). pap. 5.99 *(978-1-4424-1719-9(6),* Aladdin) Simon & Schuster Children's Publishing.

Stoll, Scott. The Cupcake Boy. Amy Belle Elementary School, illus. 2012. 108p. pap. 7.95 *(978-0-9827842-4-2(4))* Argonauts, The.

Stoll, Scott & Stoll, Kristen. God's Garden Friends. 2012. (ENG.). pap. *(978-1-4675-2486-5(7))* Independent Pub.

String Food: Individual Title Six-Packs. (gr. k-1). 23.00 *(978-0-7635-9023-9(1))* Rigby Education.

Su'a, Melissa L. What Animals Eat Can Be My Healthy Treat. 2010. 24p. pap. 11.49 *(978-1-4389-9078-1(2))* AuthorHouse.

Super Kids Nutrition, creator. Super Baby Abigail's Lunch Time Adventure. 2008. (Illus.). 30p. (J). *(978-0-9801148-0-5(2))* SuperKids Nutrition Inc.

Susie's Sister Has Food Allergy. 2004. (J). 5.00 *(978-1-882541-36-2(7))* Food Allergy & Anaphylaxis Network.

Swain, H. A. Hungry. 2014. (ENG.). 384p. (YA). (gr. 8). 16.99 *(978-1-250-02829-7(9),* 9781250028297) Feiwel & Friends.

Swarbrick, David E. Twenty Goofy Gumballs: Counting Made Fun. 2012. 26p. 24.95 *(978-1-4626-6248-7(X))* America Star Bks.

Tait, Elena. The Day My Peanut Butter Lost Its Stick. Lee, Joe, illus. 2008. 24p. pap. 12.99 *(978-1-4389-1936-2(0))* AuthorHouse.

Tango-Hampton, Doreen. I Like Gum. Pfleegor, Gina, illus. 2007. (ENG.). 32p. (J). (gr. -1-3). 15.95 *(978-0-9726614-2-3(5))* Shenanigan Bks.

Taylor, Gaylia. George Crum & the Saratoga Chip, 1 vol. Morrison, Frank, illus. 2006. (ENG.). 32p. (J). (gr. 1-5). 16.95 *(978-1-58430-255-1(0))* Lee & Low Bks., Inc.

Taylor, Gaylia & Morrison, Frank. George Crum & the Saratoga Chip. 2006. (ENG., Illus.). 32p. (J). pap. 9.95 *(978-1-60060-656-4(3))* Lee & Low Bks., Inc.

A Teeny Tiny Taste: Individual Title Six-Packs. (gr. -1-2). 27.00 *(978-0-7635-9478-7(4))* Rigby Education.

Tennsiwood, Mark. Thank You God for Onions. Motz, Mike, illus. 2006. (J). 14.95 *(978-1-60131-003-3(X))* Big Tent Bks.

Terry-Todd, Terlene. Sweetie's Healthy Start. 2009. 28p. pap. 12.99 *(978-1-60693-829-4(0),* Strategic Bk. Publishing) Strategic Book Publishing & Rights Agency (SBPRA).

Thaler, Mike. The Cafeteria Lady from the Black Lagoon, 1 vol. Lee, Jared, illus. 2012. (Black Lagoon Set 2 Ser.: No. 2). (ENG.). 32p. (J). (gr. 1-4). lib. bdg. 24.21 *(978-1-59961-954-5(7))* Spotlight.

Thomas, Chandler Turner. Fundays Food Dilemm. 2011. 32p. pap. 24.95 *(978-1-4626-0679-5(2))* America Star Bks.

Thomas, Tim, illus. Fruitman. 2007. 32p. (J). *(978-0-9790487-0-8(2))* J & K Publishing.

Thompson, Heather M. If the World Were Made of Chocolate, 1 vol. 2009. 36p. pap. 24.95 *(978-1-61546-965-9(6))* America Star Bks.

Thompson, Lauren. The Apple Pie That Papa Baked. Bean, Jonathan, illus. 2007. (ENG.). 32p. (J). (gr. k-3). 17.99 *(978-1-4169-1240-8(1),* Simon & Schuster Bks. For Young Readers) Simon & Schuster Bks. For Young Readers.

Titus, Eve. Anatole. 2010. (ENG., Illus.). 32p. (J). (gr. k-3). pap. 7.99 *(978-0-375-85546-7(7),* Dragonfly Bks.) Random Hse. Children's Bks.

—Anatole & the Cat. 2010. (ENG., Illus.). 32p. (J). (gr. k-3). pap. 7.99 *(978-0-375-85547-4(5),* Dragonfly Bks.) Random Hse. Children's Bks.

Todd, Mark. Food Trucks! 2014. (ENG., Illus.). 32p. (J). (gr. -1-3). 16.99 *(978-0-544-15784-2(2),* HMH Books For Young Readers) Houghton Mifflin Harcourt Publishing Co.

Tolstoy, Alexei. The Enormous Turnip. Goto, Scott, illus. 2003. (Green Light Readers Level 2 Ser.). (ENG.). 24p. (J). (gr. -1-3). pap. 3.95 *(978-0-15-204843-3(X))* Houghton Mifflin Harcourt Publishing Co.

Tomlinson, Mark K. Share the Grain. 2010. 12p. pap. 8.49 *(978-1-4490-6059-6(5))* AuthorHouse.

Too Much. 2008. (Illus.). 24p. (J). 9.95 *(978-0-9798189-0-5(7));* 12.95 *(978-0-9798189-2-9(3))* Little Britches Childrens Bks.

Tort, Pep & Josep, Tort. El Rey Ignacio. Duran, Teresa, illus. 2006. (Montana Encantada Ser.). (SPA.). 47p. (J). per. *(978-84-241-8558-9(7))* Everest Editora.

Townsend, Amber C. The Hungry Chickens. 2007. (Illus.). (J). per. 7.95 *(978-0-9801297-4-8(5))* G Publishing LLC.

—Once upon a Time. 2007. (J). 7.95 *(978-0-9796978-6-9(7))* G Publishing LLC.

Train, Alan Mark. Strawberry Fairchild & the Green Flame: A Fable by Alan Mark Train. 2012. 32p. pap. 21.99 *(978-1-4771-2451-2(9))* Xlibris Corp.

Trini Torres Carrion. The Magic of a Strawberry Lollipop. 2009. 16p. pap. 8.49 *(978-1-4389-7900-7(2))* AuthorHouse.

Tritt, Adam Byrn. Bud the Spud. Goldacker, "Java John", illus. 2012. (ENG.). 52p. (J). (gr. 3-7). 16.95 *(978-1-60419-062-5(0))* Axios Pr.

Tulani, K. Todd & Ricca: The Pepperoni Pizza. 2011. 24p. 11.32 *(978-1-4567-0188-8(6))* AuthorHouse.

Tuzee, John, creator. What A Grape Can Be. 2007. (Illus.). 32p. (J). 9.95 *(978-0-9755348-3-0(1))* Kids Life Pr.

U. S. National Geographic Society Staff. The Great Cheese Chase. 2008. (Toot & Puddle Ser.). (ENG., Illus.). 24p. (J). (gr. -1-2). lib. bdg. 11.90 *(978-1-4263-0371-5(8),* National Geographic Children's Bks.) National Geographic Society.

Ungor, Rita. No Nana's for Hannah. 2006. 16p. per. 8.95 *(978-1-59526-441-1(8),* Llumina Kids) Aeon Publishing Inc.

Van Wemmer, Deby. Wishes & Walnuts. 2009. 28p. pap. 14.50 *(978-1-60860-723-5(2),* Eloquent Bks.) Strategic Book Publishing & Rights Agency (SBPRA).

Vandervelde, Mark. Pizza for Everyone. 2010. 32p. 17.25 *(978-1-4269-2916-8(1))* Trafford Publishing.

Varon, Sara. Bake Sale. Varon, Sara, illus. 2011. (ENG., Illus.). 160p. (J). (gr. 3-7). 19.99 *(978-1-59643-740-1(5),* 9781596437401); pap. 17.99 *(978-1-59643-419-6(8),* 9781596434196) Roaring Brook Pr. (First Second Bks.).

Velvet, Black. The Adventures of Sam in Space: Planet of the Sweets. 2007. 32p. (J). pap. 8.00 *(978-0-8059-7367-9(2))* Dorrance Publishing Co., Inc.

Vere, Ed. Everyone's Hungry. 2003. (ENG., Illus.). 12p. (J). 6.95 *(978-0-333-78041-1(8))* Macmillan Pubs., Ltd. GBR. Dist: Trafalgar Square Publishing.

Vernon, Ursula. Curse of the Were-Wiener. 3rd ed. 2010. (Dragonbreath Ser.: 3). (ENG.). 208p. (J). (gr. 3-7). 12.99 *(978-0-8037-3469-2(7),* Dial Bks) Penguin Young Readers Group.

Vevaina, Coomi S. Bernice Banan. 2011. (Illus.). 12p. pap. 8.43 *(978-1-4567-8897-1(3))* AuthorHouse.

Voorheis, Tracy. Nibbles... a strawberry Tale. Voorheis, Tracy, illus. 2007. (Illus.). 60p. (J). per. 19.00 *(978-0-9787113-0-6(0),* Ithaca Pr.) Authors & Artists Publishers of New York, Inc.

Vote for Us! Individual Title Six-Packs. (Bookweb Ser.). 32p. (gr. 6-18). 34.00 *(978-0-7578-0907-1(3))* Rigby Education.

Walde, Christine. The Candy Darlings. 2006. (ENG.). 310p. (YA). (gr. 9-12). per. 18.95 *(978-0-618-58969-2(4))* Houghton Mifflin Harcourt Publishing Co.

Walker, Nan. The Yum-Yum House. Pilz, M. H., illus. 2009. (Math Matters Complete Set Ser.). 32p. (J). (gr. 3-5). pap. 5.95 *(978-1-57565-290-0(0))* Kane Press, Inc.

Wall, Julia & Nickel, Adam. Bruno's Tea. 2008. (Rigby Focus Forward: Level N Ser.). (Illus.). 24p. (J). (gr. 4-7). pap. *(978-1-4190-3833-4(8),* Rigby) Pearson Education Australia.

Wallace, Nancy Elizabeth. Apples, Apples, Apples, 0 vols. 2004. (ENG., Illus.). 32p. (J). (gr. -1-3). pap. 5.95 *(978-0-7614-5181-5(1),* 9780761451815, Amazon Children's Publishing) Amazon Publishing.

Wan, Joyce. You Are My Cupcake. Wan, Joyce, illus. 2011. (ENG., Illus.). 14p. (J). (gr. k — 1). bds. 6.99 *(978-0-545-30741-3(4))* Scholastic, Inc.

—You Are My Cupcake: a Cloth Book. 2016. (ENG.). 6p. (J). (— 1). 12.99 *(978-1-338-02921-5(5),* Cartwheel Bks.) Scholastic, Inc.

Wang, Margaret. Who Stole the Cookie from the Cookie Jar? Schneider, Christine, illus. 2006. (ENG.). (J). 22p. bds. 10.95 *(978-1-58117-383-3(0));* 12p. (gr. -1-3). 4.95 *(978-1-58117-429-8(2))* Bendon, Inc. (Intervisual/Piggy Toes).

Ward Appleton's Pancakes a Special Way. 2005. 10.95 *(978-0-9754779-6-0(X))* Chosen Word Publishing.

Warnack, Rhonda. Kelsey's Candy World Adventure. 2009. 48p. pap. 17.49 *(978-1-4490-4438-1(7))* AuthorHouse.

Warner, Carl. A World of Food: Discover Magical Lands Made of Things You Can Eat! 2012. (ENG., Illus.). 32p. (J). (gr. k-2). 18.95 *(978-1-4197-0162-7(2),* Abrams Bks. for Young Readers) Abrams, Inc.

Warner, Cheryl Ware. Chunkerella. 2006. (J). pap. 8.00 *(978-0-8059-7060-9(6))* Dorrance Publishing Co., Inc.

Warren, Wendy Ann. Potato Chip, an Irish Tale. 2008. 28p. pap. 15.99 *(978-1-4363-0551-8(9))* Xlibris Corp.

Watson, Tom. Stick Dog Chases a Pizza. 2014. (Stick Dog Ser.: 3). (ENG.). 208p. (J). (gr. 3-7). 12.99 *(978-0-06-227805-0(3))* HarperCollins Pubs.

Watt, Fiona & Watt, F. Baby's Mealtime. 2004. (Baby's World Bathbooks Ser.). (ENG., Illus.). 1p. (YA). (gr. -1-k). 7.95 *(978-0-7460-4176-5(4))* EDC Publishing.

Weigl Publishers, creator. The Milk Woman & Her Pail: What Happens If You Count on Getting Something Before You Have It? 2013. (AV2 Animated Storytime Ser.: Vol. 17). (ENG., Illus.). 32p. (J). (gr. -1-3). lib. bdg. 29.99 *(978-1-62127-921-1(9),* AV2 by Weigl) Weigl Pubs., Inc.

Weiss, Ellen. Fruit Salad: A Touch-and-Learn Book. Bennett, Andy, illus. 2006. (PBS Kids Ser.). 8p. (J). (gr. -1-k). bds. 6.95 *(978-1-57791-314-6(0))* Brighter Minds Children's Publishing.

Wellington, Monica. Mr. Cookie Baker. Wellington, Monica, illus. 2006. (ENG., Illus.). 32p. (J). (gr. -1-k). 16.99 *(978-0-525-47763-1(2),* Dutton Books for Young Readers) Penguin Young Readers Group.

Wells, Rosemary. Bunny Cakes. Wells, Rosemary, illus. 2014. (Max & Ruby Ser.). (ENG & SPA., Illus.). 32p. (J). (gr. -1-k). 7.99 *(978-0-14-751586-5(6),* Puffin Books) Penguin Young Readers Group.

—Yoko. Wells, Rosemary, illus. 2009. (ENG., Illus.). 32p. (J). (gr. -1-1). pap. 6.99 *(978-1-4231-1983-6(5))* Hyperion Pr.

Welsh, Karen Leis. Eh, Spaghetti You Say? 2012. 36p. pap. 20.99 *(978-1-4772-0473-3(3))* AuthorHouse.

West, C. The Adventures of Ice Cream & Honey Buns: What Time Is It? 2013. 28p. pap. 16.09 *(978-1-4669-5671-1(2))* Trafford Publishing.

Weston Woods Staff, creator. Hansel & Gretel. 2011. 38.75 *(978-0-439-80425-7(6))* Weston Woods Studios, Inc.

—In the Night Kitchen. 2011. 29.95 *(978-0-439-73480-6(0));* 18.95 *(978-0-439-72723-5(5));* 38.75 *(978-0-439-72728-0(6))* Weston Woods Studios, Inc.

—Pete's a Pizza. 2011. 29.95 *(978-0-439-74519-2(5))* Weston Woods Studios, Inc.

—Stone Soup. 2011. 38.75 *(978-0-439-84572-4(6));* 29.95 *(978-0-439-74595-6(0))* Weston Woods Studios, Inc.

Wheat, Valerie A. The Kid Who Loved Mac & Cheese. 2013. 40p. pap. *(978-1-4602-2516-5(2))* FriesenPress.

Wherry, Alwyn. The Hungry Little Mouse. 2006. 17p. (J). 12.08 *(978-1-4116-8056-2(1))* Lulu Pr., Inc.

White, Cal. The Apple Tree. Boyne, Linda, illus. 2008. 48p. pap. 24.95 *(978-1-4241-8636-5(6))* America Star Bks.

Whitehouse, Elizabeth. Sushi for Lunch. 2005. (J). pap. 5.95 *(978-1-933031-82-8(4))* Whitehouse Publishing.

Wilks, Peter. The Foragers. 2006. (ENG., Illus.). 166p. *(978-1-905886-07-4(1))* Troubador Publishing Ltd.

Willard, Nancy. The Three Mouths of Little Tom Drum. Hawkes, Kevin, illus. 2015. (ENG.). 48p. (J). (gr. -1-3). 16.99 *(978-0-7636-5476-4(0))* Candlewick Pr.

Willems, Mo. Should I Share My Ice Cream? Willems, Mo, illus. 2011. (Elephant & Piggie Book Ser.). (ENG., Illus.). 64p. (J). (gr. -1-k). 9.99 *(978-1-4231-4343-7(4))* Hyperion Pr.

—That Is Not a Good Idea! Willems, Mo, illus. 2013. (ENG., Illus.). 48p. (J). (gr. k-3). 17.99 *(978-0-06-220309-0(6))* HarperCollins Pubs.

Willems, Mo & Campoy, F. Isabel. ¿Debo Compartir Mi Helado? Willems, Mo, illus. 2015. (Elephant & Piggie Book Ser.). (SPA., Illus.). 64p. (J). (gr. -1-k). 9.99 *(978-1-4847-2291-6(4))* Disney Publishing Worldwide.

Willis, Jeanne. Mammoth Pie. Ross, Tony, illus. 2008. (ENG.). 32p. (J). (gr. -1-k). 19.99 *(978-1-84270-659-6(4))* Andersen Pr. GBR. Dist: Independent Pubs. Group.

Willis, Lisa M. The Bug's Picnic. 2008. 28p. pap. 24.95 *(978-1-60563-389-3(5))* America Star Bks.

Wilson, Karma. Bear Wants More. Chapman, Jane, illus. 2008. (Bear Bks.). (ENG.). 34p. (J). (gr. -1-2). bds. 7.99 *(978-1-4169-4922-0(4),* Little Simon) Little Simon.

—Bear Wants More. Chapman, Jane, illus. 2003. (Bear Bks.). (ENG.). 40p. (J). (gr. -1-3). 17.99 *(978-0-689-84509-3(X),* McElderry, Margaret K. Bks.) McElderry, Margaret K. Bks.

Wilson, Mary. Mark & the Mega Buffet. 2005. 37p. (J). pap. 15.58 *(978-1-4116-4172-3(8))* Lulu Pr., Inc.

Winkler, Henry & Oliver, Lin. Always Watch Out for the Flying Potato Salad! 2017. (Here's Hank Ser.: 9). lib. bdg. 16.00 ***(978-0-606-40339-9(6))*** Turtleback Bks.

Wise-Douglas, Terri. The Wonderful World of Cupcakes. Duckworth, Jeffrey, illus. 2011. 28p. pap. 24.95 *(978-1-4626-3570-2(9))* America Star Bks.

Wismer, C. L. The Missing Chocolate Chip Oatmeal Peanut Butter Raisin Cookie. 2011. 28p. pap. 24.95 *(978-1-4626-3395-1(1))* America Star Bks.

Wolff, Virginia Euwer. Make Lemonade. unabr. ed. 2004. (Make Lemonade Trilogy: No. 1). 200p. (J). (gr. 7-18). pap. 36.00 incl. audio *(978-0-8072-0793-2(4),* S YA 348 SP, Listening Library) Random Hse. Audio Publishing Group.

Womack, Rowena. Popcorn. Archer, Angela, illus. 2013. 26p. (J). 16.99 *(978-1-61160-595-2(4))* Whiskey Creek Restorations.

Wood, Audrey & Wood, Don. The Little Mouse, the Red Ripe Strawberry, & the Big Hungry Bear. Wood, Don, illus. 2007. (Child's Play Library). (ENG., Illus.). 32p. (J). audio compact disk *(978-1-84643-050-3(X))* Child's Play International Ltd.

Woomer, Lisa. Cookie. 2009. 25p. (J). pap. 17.95 *(978-1-4327-3020-8(7))* Outskirts Pr., Inc.

Wynne-Jones, Tim. Lord of the Fries. (Illus.). pap. 6.95 *(978-0-88899-384-7(6))* Groundwood Bks. CAN. Dist: Publishers Group West (PGW).

Yaccarino, Dan. Zorgoochi Intergalactic Pizza. 2016. (J). lib. bdg. 18.40 *(978-0-606-38434-6(0))* Turtleback Bks.

Yaldezian, Lisa M. 500 Presents for Penelope Potts. Seltzer, Jerry, illus. 2006. (J). 16.95 *(978-1-60131-005-7(6))* Big Tent Bks.

Yanisko, Thomas. What You Eat It's up to You. Hoyes, Kerry, illus. 2012. 36p. pap. 9.99 *(978-1-937260-26-2(7))* Sleepytown Pr.

Yee, Wong Herbert. Hamburger Heaven. 2005. (ENG., Illus.). 32p. (J). (gr. -1-3). reprint ed. 5.95 *(978-0-618-54885-9(8))* Houghton Mifflin Harcourt Publishing Co.

Young, Cybèle. A Few Bites, 1 vol. 2012. (ENG., Illus.). 48p. (J). (gr. -1-2). 18.95 *(978-1-55498-295-0(2))* Groundwood Bks. CAN. Dist: Publishers Group West (PGW).

Young, Eugene Randolph, illus. & des. The Food Convention. Young, Eugene Randolph, des. l.t. ed. 2006. 32p. (J). 16.95 *(978-0-9792000-0-7(8))* Les Lum Pubs.

Young, Shelley. Doc Broc's Cave Adventure. Young, Shelley, illus. 2005. (Illus.). 44p. 19.95 *(978-1-58054-406-1(1))* Woodland Publishing, Inc.

Yoyo Books Staff. Food: Mini Baby's First Library. 2005. 42p. bds. *(978-90-5843-829-4(5))* YoYo Bks.

Zafra, Jose. Historias de Sergio. (SPA.). 160p. (J). *(978-84-216-2870-6(4),* BU6937) Bruño, Editorial ESP. Dist: Lectorum Pubns., Inc.

Zana, Brian. Maurice Tries New Foods. 2012. 24p. pap. 15.99 *(978-1-4797-1430-8(5))* Xlibris Corp.

Zeller, Penny. Hollyhocks. 2004. (Illus.). 44p. (gr. -1-7). per. 14.95 *(978-0-9760836-0-3(4))* Booklocker.com, Inc.

Zenker, Marlene M. The Empty Bowl. 2012. 44p. pap. 21.99 *(978-1-4685-2307-2(4))* AuthorHouse.

Zimmerman, Michael. The Mouse & the Acorn. 2007. 32p. per. 11.95 *(978-1-4327-0462-9(1))* Outskirts Pr., Inc.

FOOD—PRESERVATION

see also Canning and Preserving

Graham, Ian. From Crude Oil to Fast Food Snacks: An Energy Journey Through the World of Heat. 2015. (Energy Journeys Ser.). (ENG., Illus.). 48p. (gr. 3-6). 33.32 *(978-1-4846-0885-2(2),* Heinemann InfoSearch) Heinemann-Raintree.

Harmon, Daniel E. Fish, Meat, & Poultry: Dangers in the Food Supply. 2009. (What's in Your Food? Recipe for Disaster Ser.). 48p. (gr. 5-5). 53.00 *(978-1-60854-772-2(8),* Rosen Reference) Rosen Publishing Group, Inc., The.

Jango-Cohen, Judith. The History of Food. 2005. (Major Inventions Through History Ser.). (ENG., Illus.). 56p. (gr. 5-8). lib. bdg. 26.60 *(978-0-8225-2484-7(8),* Twenty-First Century Bks.) Lerner Publishing Group.

Loh-Hagan, Virginia. Food Stylist. 2016. (Odd Jobs Ser.). (ENG., Illus.). 32p. (J). (gr. 4-8). 29.93 *(978-1-63471-095-4(9),* 208491, 45th Parallel Press) Cherry Lake Publishing.

Mecozzi, Maureen. The Uncanny Can. 2007. (Shockwave: Science in Practice Ser.). (ENG., Illus.). 36p. (J). (gr. 3-5). 25.00 *(978-0-531-17584-2(7),* Children's Pr.) Scholastic Library Publishing.

Proudfit, Benjamin. Why Does Food Go Bad? 2016. (Everyday Mysteries Ser.). (ENG., Illus.). 24p. (J). (gr. 1-2). pap. 8.15 *(978-1-4824-3848-2(8))* Stevens, Gareth Publishing LLLP.

Sarver, Amy. Science at the Grocery. 2007. (Reading Expeditions Ser.). (ENG., Illus.). 24p. (J). pap. 14.95 *(978-0-7922-4567-4(9))* CENGAGE Learning.

FOOD CONTROL

see Food Supply

FOOD HABITS

ABDO Publishing Company Staff. Food Dudes Set 2. 2014. (Food Dudes Set 2 Ser.: 6). (ENG.). 32p. (gr. 8-12). lib. bdg. 162.42 *(978-1-62403-313-1(X),* Checkerboard Library) ABDO Publishing Co.

Ancona, George. Come & Eat! Ancona, George, photos by. 2011. (ENG., Illus.). 48p. (J). (gr. k-3). 16.95 *(978-1-58089-366-4(X));* pap. 7.95 *(978-1-58089-367-1(8))* Charlesbridge Publishing, Inc.

—Let's Eat. 2003. (J). *(978-0-7636-1805-6(5))* Candlewick Pr.

Augustin, Byron. The Food of Mexico. 2011. (Flavors of the World Ser.). 64p. (gr. 4). 31.36 *(978-1-60870-237-4(5))* Marshall Cavendish Corp.

Azima, Cricket. Everybody Eats Lunch. Thomas, Titus V., illus. 2008. (ENG.). 16p. (J). (gr. -1-3). 16.00 *(978-0-9793384-4-1(1))* Glitterati, Inc.

Barker, Geoff. The World of Food - Mexico. 2010. (World of Food Ser.). 32p. (YA). (gr. 4-7). lib. bdg. 24.95 *(978-1-934545-13-3(9))* Oliver Pr., Inc.

Batmanglij, Najmieh. Happy Nowruz: Cooking with Children to Celebrate the Persian New Year. 2008. (ENG., Illus.). 120p. spiral bd. 40.00 *(978-1-933823-16-4(X))* Mage Pubs., Inc.

Bellisario, Gina. Choose Good Food! My Eating Tips. Conger, Holli, illus. 2014. (Cloverleaf Books — My Healthy Habits Ser.). (ENG.). 24p. (gr. k-2). lib. bdg. 23.93 *(978-1-4677-1350-4(3),* Millbrook Pr.) Lerner Publishing Group.

Berry, Joy. I Love Mealtime. Regan, Dana, illus. 2010. (Teach Me About Ser.). (ENG.). 20p. (J). (gr. k — 1). pap. 5.99 *(978-1-60577-006-2(X))* Berry, Joy Enterprises.

—Teach Me about Mealtime. 2009. (ENG.). 40p. (J). (gr. k — 1). bds. 7.95 *(978-1-60577-007-9(8))* Berry, Joy Enterprises.

Bibbo, Molly. The Hidden World of Edible Insects: Comparing Fractions (Grade 4) 2017. (Mathematics Readers Ser.). (Illus.). 32p. (gr. 4-4). pap. 9.99 ***(978-1-4258-5553-6(9))*** Teacher Created Materials, Inc.

Bullard, Lisa. My Food, Your Food. Schneider, Christine, illus. 2015. (Cloverleaf Books (tm) — Alike & Different Ser.). (ENG.). 24p. (J). (gr. k-2). lib. bdg. 23.99 *(978-1-4677-4903-9(6),* Millbrook Pr.) Lerner Publishing Group.

Caldicott, Chris. World Food Alphabet. 2015. (ENG., Illus.). 32p. (J). (gr. k-3). pap. 9.99 *(978-1-84780-653-6(8),* Frances Lincoln) Quarto Publishing Group UK GBR. Dist: Hachette Bk. Group.

Carole, Bonnie. Junk Food, Yes or No. 2015. (ENG.). 24p. (gr. k-3). 28.50 *(978-1-63430-350-7(4))* Rourke Educational Media.

Claybourne, Anna. Feasts in Ancient Times. 2011. (Big Picture: Food Ser.). (ENG.). 24p. (gr. 1-2). pap. 41.70 *(978-1-4296-6726-5(5),* First Facts) Capstone Press of Coughlan Cos.

Cleland, Jo. Fabulous Food. 2012. (ENG.). 24p. (gr. k-2). pap. 8.95 *(978-1-61810-217-1(6))* Rourke Educational Media.

Clissold, Caroline. Food Around the World. 2007. (Trackers-Math Ser.). (gr. 2-5). pap. 5.00 *(978-1-59055-910-9(X))* Pacific Learning, Inc.

EFG

Davies, Monika. Surprising Things We Eat. 2017. (Time for Kids Nonfiction Readers Ser.). lib. bdg. 22.10 **(978-0-606-40273-6(X))** Turtleback Bks.

Davis, Caroline. Yum Yum! Davis, Caroline, illus. 2010. (ENG., Illus.). 20p. (J). bds. *(978-1-4083-0787-8(1))*, Orchard Bks.) Hachette Children's Group GBR. Dist: Hachette Bk. Group.

Dawson, Imogen. Food & Feasts with the Aztecs. 2004. (Illus.). 32p. (J). (gr. 4-8). reprint ed. 14.00 *(978-0-7567-7143-0(9))* DIANE Publishing Co.

DePietro, Frank. Latino American Cuisine. 2012. (Illus.). 64p. (J). pap. *(978-1-4222-2337-6(X))* Mason Crest.

—Latino American Cuisine. Limón, José E., ed. 2012. (Hispanic Americans: Major Minority Ser.). (Illus.). 64p. (J). (gr. 4). 22.95 *(978-1-4222-2320-8(5))* Mason Crest.

Dorling Kindersley Publishing Staff. Are You What You Eat? 2015. (ENG.). 96p. (J). (gr. 3-7). 16.99 *(978-1-4654-2944-5(1))*, DK Children) Dorling Kindersley Publishing, Inc.

Dosier, Susan. Civil War Cooking: The Confederacy. 2016. (Exploring History Through Food Ser.). (ENG., Illus.). 32p. (gr. 3-4). lib. bdg. 27.32 *(978-1-5157-2354-7(2))* Capstone Press of Coughlan Cos.

—Civil War Cooking: The Union. 2016. (Exploring History Through Food Ser.). (ENG., Illus.). 32p. (gr. 3-4). lib. bdg. 27.32 *(978-1-5157-2353-0(4))* Capstone Press of Coughlan Cos.

—Colonial Cooking. 2016. (Exploring History Through Food Ser.). (ENG., Illus.). 32p. (gr. 3-4). lib. bdg. 27.32 *(978-1-5157-2356-1(9))* Capstone Press of Coughlan Cos.

Elgin, Kathy. France. 2010. (World of Food Ser.). 32p. (YA). (gr. 4-7). lib. bdg. 24.95 *(978-1-934545-10-2(4))* Oliver Pr., Inc.

Etingoff, Kim. Building a Healthy Diet with the 5 Food Groups. Prock, Lisa Albers, ed. 2014. (On My Plate Ser.: 6). 48p. (J). (gr. 5-18). 20.95 *(978-1-4222-3095-4(3))* Mason Crest.

Fajardo, Anika. The Dish on Food & Farming in Colonial America. (Life in the American Colonies Ser.). (ENG.). 32p. (gr. 3-4). 2017. pap. 8.10 **(978-1-5157-9748-7(1))** 2011. pap. 8.10 *(978-1-4296-7217-7(X))* 2011. pap. 47.70 *(978-1-4296-7218-4(8))* Capstone Press of Coughlan Cos. (Fact Finders).

Falk, Laine. This Is the Way We Eat Our Food. 2010. (Rise & Shine Ser.). (ENG.). 24p. (C). (gr. 1-2). pap. 11.95 *(978-0-531-21439-8(7))* National Geographic School Publishing, Inc.

—This Is the Way We Eat Our Food. 2009. (Scholastic News Nonfiction Readers Ser.). (ENG.). 24p. (J). (gr. 1-2). lib. bdg. 22.00 *(978-0-531-21339-1(0))* Scholastic Library Publishing.

Feldman, Jean R. & Karapetkova, Holly. Eat Green! (Lap Book) 2010. (ENG., Illus.). 12p. (gr. -1-k). 9.95 *(978-1-61590-188-3(4))* Rourke Educational Media.

Florence, Sarah. Pilgrim Foods & Recipes. 2009. (Reading Room Collection 2 Ser.). 24p. (gr. 3-4). 42.50 *(978-1-60851-983-5(X))*, PowerKids Pr.) Rosen Publishing Group, Inc., The.

Foy, Debbie. Spoon, Cup, Dinner's Up! 2017. (All by Myself Ser.). (ENG., Illus.). 20p. (J). (gr. -1-k). pap. 6.99 *(978-0-7502-9621-2(6))*, Wayland) Hachette Children's Group GBR. Dist: Hachette Bk. Group.

Franklin, E. Joan. I Eat & I Grow. 2009. 26p. pap. 13.25 *(978-1-60693-713-6(8))*, Eloquent Bks.) Strategic Book Publishing & Rights Agency (SBPRA).

Fulcher, Roz. Be Good to Your Body: Healthy Eating & Fun Recipes. 2012. (Dover Children's Activity Bks.). (ENG.). 80p. (J). (gr. 3-5). pap. 6.99 *(978-0-486-48643-7(5))* Dover Pubns., Inc.

Fun Food: Individual Title Six-Packs. (gr. -1-2). 23.00 *(978-0-7635-8995-0(0))* Rigby Education.

Gay, Kathlyn. Do You Know What to Eat? 2015. (Got Issues? Ser.). (ENG., Illus.). 128p. (J). (gr. 7-7). 37.27 *(978-0-7660-6987-9(7))* Enslow Pubs., Inc.

Gifford, Clive. Food & Cooking in Ancient Egypt. 2010. (Cooking in World Cultures Ser.). (Illus.). 32p. (J). (ENG.). pap. 10.60 *(978-1-61532-359-3(7))*; (gr. 3-5). lib. bdg. 26.50 *(978-1-61532-337-1(6))* Rosen Publishing Group, Inc., The. (PowerKids Pr.).

—Food & Cooking in Ancient Greece. 2010. (Cooking in World Cultures Ser.). (Illus.). 32p. (J). (ENG.). pap. 10.60 *(978-1-61532-361-6(9))*; (gr. 3-5). lib. bdg. 26.50 *(978-1-61532-338-8(4))* Rosen Publishing Group, Inc., The. (PowerKids Pr.).

—Food & Cooking in Ancient Rome. 2010. (Cooking in World Cultures Ser.). (Illus.). 32p. (J). (ENG.). pap. 10.60 *(978-1-61532-363-0(5))*; (gr. 3-5). lib. bdg. 26.50 *(978-1-61532-339-5(2))* Rosen Publishing Group, Inc., The. (PowerKids Pr.).

Gioffrè, Rosalba. Fun with French Cooking. 2009. (Let's Get Cooking! Ser.). (Illus.). 32p. (J). (ENG.). pap. 11.75 *(978-1-4358-3473-6(9))*; (gr. 3-6). lib. bdg. 26.50 *(978-1-4358-3454-5(2))* Rosen Publishing Group, Inc., The. (PowerKids Pr.).

—Fun with Italian Cooking. 2009. (Let's Get Cooking! Ser.). (Illus.). 32p. (J). (ENG.). pap. 11.75 *(978-1-4358-3489-7(5))*; (gr. 3-6). lib. bdg. 26.50 *(978-1-4358-3451-4(8))* Rosen Publishing Group, Inc., The. (PowerKids Pr.).

Goodman, Polly. Food in China. 2008. (Food Around the World Ser.). (Illus.). 30p. (J). (gr. 3-7). lib. bdg. 25.25 *(978-1-4042-4297-5(X))*, PowerKids Pr.) Rosen Publishing Group, Inc., The.

—Food in India. 2008. (Food Around the World Ser.). (Illus.). 30p. (J). (gr. 3-7). lib. bdg. 25.25 *(978-1-4042-4296-8(1))*, PowerKids Pr.) Rosen Publishing Group, Inc., The.

—Food in Italy. 2008. (Food Around the World Ser.). (Illus.). 30p. (J). (gr. 3-7). lib. bdg. 25.25 *(978-1-4042-4298-2(8))*, PowerKids Pr.) Rosen Publishing Group, Inc., The.

—Food in the Carribbean. 2008. (Food Around the World Ser.). (Illus.). 30p. (J). (gr. 3-7). lib. bdg. 25.25 *(978-1-4042-4299-9(6))*, PowerKids Pr.) Rosen Publishing Group, Inc., The.

Green, Jen. The Caribbean. 2010. (World of Food Ser.). 32p. (YA). (gr. 4-7). lib. bdg. 24.95 *(978-1-934545-15-7(5))* Oliver Pr., Inc.

Gregoire, Maryellen. Morning Meals Around the World, 1 vol. Yesh, Jeff, illus. 2004. (Meals Around the World Ser.). (ENG.). 24p. (gr. k-4). per. 8.95 *(978-1-4048-1130-0(3))* Picture Window Bks.

Gunderson, Jessica & Gunderson, Mary. Pioneer Farm Cooking. 2016. (Exploring History Through Food Ser.). (ENG., Illus.). 32p. (gr. 3-4). lib. bdg. 27.32 *(978-1-5157-2355-4(0))* Capstone Press of Coughlan Cos.

Hibbert, Clare. China. 2010. (World of Food Ser.). 32p. (YA). (gr. 4-7). lib. bdg. 24.95 *(978-1-934545-09-6(0))* Oliver Pr., Inc.

Hill, Z. B. Eating Right & Additional Supplements for Fitness. Hart, Diane H., ed. 2014. (Integrated Life of Fitness Ser.). 64p. (J). (gr. 7-18). pap. 11.95 *(978-1-4222-3197-5(6))* Mason Crest.

Hollyer, Beatrice. Let's Eat: What Children Eat Around the World. rev. ed. 2004. (ENG., Illus.). 48p. (J). (gr. k-4). 18.99 *(978-0-8050-7322-5(1))*, 9780805073225, Holt, Henry & Co. Bks. For Young Readers) Holt, Henry & Co.

Houts, Amy. Cooking Around the Country with Kids: USA Regional Recipes & Fun Activities. 2009. (J). 19.95 *(978-0-930643-20-1(8))* Images Unlimited Publishing.

Ingredients for a Healthy Life. 2014. (Ingredients for a Healthy Life Ser.). 24p. (J). (gr. 2-5). pap. 48.90 *(978-1-4824-1543-8(7))* Stevens, Gareth Publishing LLLP.

Jones, Susan Smith & Warren, Dianne. Vegetable Soup - The Fruit Bowl. Lindman, Amy Sorvaag, illus. rev. ed. 2006. 64p. (J). (gr. -1-3). per. 14.95 *(978-0-9652736-0-2(1))* Oasis Pubns.

Kadair, Deborah, illus. Today Is Monday in Kentucky, 1 vol. 2012. (ENG.). 32p. (J). (gr. k-k). 16.99 *(978-1-4556-1539-9(1))* Pelican Publishing Co., Inc.

Kallen, Stuart A. Medieval Food & Customs. 2014. (The Library of Medieval Times Ser). (ENG., Illus.). 80p. (J). lib. bdg. *(978-1-60152-718-9(7))* ReferencePoint Pr., Inc.

Kalman, Bobbie. Lunch Munch: Step-by-Step Recipes. 2003. (Kid Power Ser.). (ENG., Illus.). 32p. (J). (gr. 3). pap. *(978-0-7787-1273-2(7))*; lib. bdg. *(978-0-7787-1251-0(6))* Crabtree Publishing Co.

Kawa, Katie. Recipes of the Westward Expansion. 2017. (Cooking Your Way Through American History Ser.). (J). (gr. 3-3). pap. 63.60 **(978-1-5345-2101-8(1))**; 24p. pap. 10.60 **(978-1-5345-2100-1(3))**; 24p. lib. bdg. 27.25 **(978-1-5345-2102-5(X))** Greenhaven Publishing LLC. (KidHaven Publishing).

Klepeis, Alicia Z. The World's Strangest Foods. 2015. (Library of Weird Ser.). (ENG., Illus.). 32p. (gr. 3-4). lib. bdg. 27.99 *(978-1-4914-2017-1(0))* Capstone Press of Coughlan Cos.

KociendaGenevieve. SUSHI NATION LOW INTERMEDIATE BOOK WITH ONLINE ACCESS. 2014. (ENG., Illus.). 28p. (J). pap. 9.50 *(978-1-107-63147-2(5))* Cambridge Univ. Pr.

Kummer, Patricia K. The Food of Thailand. 2011. (Flavors of the World Ser.). (ENG., Illus.). 64p. (J). (gr. 4-6). lib. bdg. 31.36 *(978-1-60870-238-1(3))*, Cavendish Children's Bks.) Marshall Cavendish Corp.

La Coccinella. Look & See: What Do I Eat? 2008. (Look & See! Ser.). (ENG., Illus.). 26p. (J). (gr. -1-1). bds. 6.95 *(978-1-4027-5827-0(8))* Sterling Publishing Co., Inc.

Lake, G. G. Take Your Pick of Disgusting Foods. 2017. (Take Your (Equally Horrible) Pick! Ser.). (ENG., Illus.). 32p. (gr. 1-2). lib. bdg. 26.65 *(978-1-5157-4470-2(1))*, Blazers) Capstone Press of Coughlan Cos.

Lauber, Patricia. What You Never Knew about Fingers, Forks, & Chopsticks. Manders, John, illus. 2009. (ENG.). 36p. (J). (gr. 1-5). pap. 12.99 *(978-1-4424-0937-8(1))*, Simon & Schuster Bks. For Young Readers) Simon & Schuster Bks. For Young Readers.

Leavitt, Amie Jane. Bizarre Things We've Eaten. 2015. (History of the Bizarre Ser.). (ENG., Illus.). 32p. (gr. 3-4). pap. 7.95 *(978-1-4914-4345-3(6))* Capstone Press of Coughlan Cos.

Lee, Frances. Fun with Chinese Cooking. 2009. (Let's Get Cooking! Ser.). (Illus.). 32p. (J). (ENG.). pap. 11.75 *(978-1-4358-3475-0(5))*; (gr. 3-6). lib. bdg. 26.50 *(978-1-4358-3453-8(4))* Rosen Publishing Group, Inc., The. (PowerKids Pr.).

Lee, Hope H. What Colors Did You Eat Today? 2012. 16p. pap. 10.00 *(978-1-4120-7674-6(9))* Trafford Publishing.

Levete, Sarah. Food Around the World. 2011. (Big Picture: Food Ser.). (ENG.). 24p. (gr. 1-2). pap. 41.70 *(978-1-4296-6727-2(3))*, First Facts) Capstone Press of Coughlan Cos.

Lewis, Carole. First Place Food Exchange Pocket Guide. 2004. 72p. mass mkt. 5.99 *(978-0-8307-3232-6(2))*, Gospel Light) Gospel Light Pubns.

Locricchio, Matthew. The Cooking of Italy. 2nd rev. ed. 2011. (Superchef, Second Edition Ser.). (Illus.). 96p. (J). (gr. 6). 35.64 *(978-1-60870-554-2(4))* Marshall Cavendish GBR. Dist: Marshall Cavendish Corp.

—The Cooking of Thailand. 2004. (Superchef Ser.). (Illus.). 80p. (J). 29.93 *(978-0-7614-1731-6(1))*, Benchmark Bks.) Marshall Cavendish Corp.

Loewen, Nancy & Skelley, Paula. Food of the World. 2015. (Go Go Global Ser.). (ENG., Illus.). 32p. (gr. 1-2). lib. bdg. 27.32 *(978-1-4914-3918-0(1))* Capstone Press of Coughlan Cos.

Macdonald, Margaret. Where Can You Eat This Food? 2014. (Little Books of Answers: Level F Ser.). (Illus.). 16p. (gr. k-2). pap. 7.95 *(978-1-927136-50-8(4))* Three Crows Media NZL. Dist: RiverStream Publishing.

Maher, Erin. Chinese Foods & Recipes. 2009. (Reading Room Collection 2 Ser.). 24p. (gr. 3-4). 42.50 *(978-1-60851-961-3(9))*, PowerKids Pr.) Rosen Publishing Group, Inc., The.

Malerba, Giulia. Food Atlas: Discover All the Delicious Foods of the World. Sillani, Febe, illus. 2017. (ENG.). 72p. (J). (gr. 3-12). 19.95 **(978-1-77085-952-4(7))**, 9781770859524) Firefly Bks., Ltd.

Marshall Cavendish. The Cooking of Greece. 2nd rev. ed. 2011. (Superchef, Second Edition Ser.). (Illus.). 96p. (J). (gr. 6). 35.64 *(978-1-60870-552-8(8))* Marshall Cavendish Corp.

Marshall Cavendish Benchmark Staff. The Cooking of France. 2nd rev. ed. 2011. (Superchef, Second Edition Ser.). (Illus.). 96p. (gr. 6). 35.64 *(978-1-60870-551-1(X))* Marshall Cavendish Corp.

Martin, Priscilla. The Big Fat Hare. 2011. 24p. pap. 24.95 *(978-1-4626-3649-5(7))* America Star Bks.

Matthew, John. Foods of Italy. 2011. (Culture in the Kitchen Ser.). 24p. (J). (gr. 2-5). pap. 8.15 *(978-1-4339-5712-3(4))*; lib. bdg. 22.60 *(978-1-4339-5710-9(8))* Stevens, Gareth Publishing LLLP. (Gareth Stevens Learning Library).

McDaniel, Jan. The Food of Mexico. 2009. (Mexico: Beautiful Land, Diverse People Ser.). (Illus.). 64p. (YA). (gr. 7-12). 21.95 *(978-1-4222-0655-3(6))* Mason Crest.

Mihailescu, Maureen. Fruits & Veggies Are Really Great! 2012. 24p. pap. 8.00 *(978-1-936509-18-8(0))* Windsurf Publishing LLC.

Milet Limited Publishing Staff & Swain, Gwenyth. Eating. 2005. (Small World Ser.). (PAN & ENG., Illus.). 24p. (J). pap. 9.95 *(978-1-84059-142-2(0))* Milet Publishing.

Murphy, Charles. Food Around the World. 2016. (Adventures in Culture Ser.). 00024p. (J). pap. 8.15 **(978-1-4824-5582-3(X))** Stevens, Gareth Publishing LLLP.

Nelson, Robin. Food. 2004. (First Step Nonfiction - Basic Human Needs Ser.). (ENG., Illus.). 8p. (gr. -1-1). pap. 4.95 *(978-0-8225-3928-5(4))*, Lerner Pubns.) Lerner Publishing Group.

Olson, Karen. Eat, Run & Live Healthy. Hamelin, Marie-Micheline, illus. 2nd rev. ed. 2009. (Caring for Me Ser.). (ENG.). 20p. (J). pap. 9.95 *(978-1-894778-50-3(2))* Theytus Bks., Ltd. CAN. Dist: Univ. of Toronto Pr.

Orr, Tamra. The Food of China. 2011. (Flavors of the World Ser.). (Illus.). 64p. (J). (gr. 4). 31.36 *(978-1-60870-234-3(0))* Marshall Cavendish Corp.

—The Food of Greece. 2011. (Flavors of the World Ser.). (Illus.). 64p. (J). (gr. 4). 31.36 *(978-1-60870-235-0(9))* Marshall Cavendish GBR. Dist: Marshall Cavendish Corp.

Pearce, Kevin. Foods of Mexico. 2011. (Culture in the Kitchen Ser.). 24p. (J). (gr. 2-5). pap. 8.15 *(978-1-4339-5716-1(7))*; lib. bdg. 22.60 *(978-1-4339-5714-7(0))* Stevens, Gareth Publishing LLLP. (Gareth Stevens Learning Library).

Person, Naomi, et al. Sow What? Hooper, Hadley & Stryk, Suzanne, illus. 2009. 94p. (YA). pap. *(978-0-88441-735-4(2))* Girl Scouts of the USA.

Petrie, Kristin. The Food Pyramid. 2004. (Nutrition Ser.). (Illus.). 32p. (J). (gr. k-6). lib. bdg. 22.78 *(978-1-59197-403-1(8))* ABDO Publishing Co.

Priddy, Roger. Mealtime - A High Contrast High Chair Book. 2013. (Hello Baby Ser.). (ENG., Illus.). 8p. (J). (gr. -1 — 1). bds. 5.99 *(978-0-312-51602-4(9))*, 9780312516024, Priddy Bks.) St. Martin's Pr.

Rebvik. A-Z of Dangerous Food. 2012. (ENG., Illus.). 56p. pap. 10.95 *(978-1-84976-016-4(0))* Tate Publishing, Ltd. GBR. Dist: Abrams, Inc.

Ridley, Sarah. Food. 2017. (Tell Me What You Remember Ser.). (ENG., Illus.). 24p. (J). (gr. k-2). 17.99 *(978-1-4451-3986-9(3))*, Franklin Watts) Hachette Children's Group GBR. Dist: Hachette Bk. Group.

Ring, Susan. Places We Live. 2005. (Yellow Umbrella Fluent Level Ser.). (ENG.). 16p. (gr. k-1). pap. 35.70 *(978-0-7368-5316-3(2))*, Yellow Umbrella Bks.) Capstone Press of Coughlan Cos.

Ripley's Believe It Or Not! Staff. Eating Habits. 2012. (Ripley's Disbelief & Shock Ser.). 36p. (J). (gr. 3-4). 19.95 *(978-1-4222-2567-7(4))* Mason Crest.

Rissman, Rebecca. Cooking & Eating: Comparing Past & Present, 1 vol. 2014. (Comparing Past & Present Ser.). (ENG.). 24p. (gr. -1-1). lib. bdg. 22.65 *(978-1-4329-8990-3(1))*, Acorn) Heinemann-Raintree.

Roholt, Christine VeLure. Foods of Brazil. 2014. (Cook with Me Ser.). (ENG., Illus.). 24p. (J). (gr. 3-7). lib. bdg. 25.95 *(978-1-62617-115-2(7))*, Express Bks.) Bellwether Media.

—Foods of China. 2014. (Cook with Me Ser.). (ENG., Illus.). 24p. (J). (gr. 3-7). lib. bdg. 25.95 *(978-1-62617-116-9(5))*, Express Bks.) Bellwether Media.

—Foods of France. 2014. (Cook with Me Ser.). (ENG., Illus.). 24p. (J). (gr. 3-7). lib. bdg. 25.95 *(978-1-62617-117-6(3))*, Express Bks.) Bellwether Media.

—Foods of India. 2014. (Cook with Me Ser.). (ENG., Illus.). 24p. (J). (gr. 3-7). lib. bdg. 25.95 *(978-1-62617-118-3(1))*, Express Bks.) Bellwether Media.

—Foods of Italy. 2014. (Cook with Me Ser.). (ENG.). 24p. (J). (gr. 3-7). lib. bdg. 25.95 *(978-1-62617-119-0(X))*, Express Bks.) Bellwether Media.

—Foods of Japan. 2014. (Cook with Me Ser.). (ENG.). 24p. (J). (gr. 3-7). 25.95 *(978-1-62617-120-6(3))*, Express Bks.) Bellwether Media.

—Foods of Mexico. 2014. (Cook with Me Ser.). (ENG.). 24p. (J). (gr. 3-7). 25.95 *(978-1-62617-121-3(1))*, Express Bks.) Bellwether Media.

—Foods of Thailand. 2014. (Cook with Me Ser.). (ENG.). 24p. (J). (gr. 3-7). 25.95 *(978-1-62617-122-0(X))*, Express Bks.) Bellwether Media.

Rose, Elizabeth. Food & Nutrition. (Life Science Library). 24p. 2009. (gr. 3-4). 42.50 *(978-1-60854-001-3(4))* 2006. (Illus.). (J). (gr. -1-3). lib. bdg. 21.25 *(978-1-4042-2821-4(7))* Rosen Publishing Group, Inc., The. (PowerKids Pr.).

Rosen, Michael J. & Kassoy, Ben. Strange Foods. Jones, Doug, illus. 2013. (No Way! Ser.). (ENG.). 32p. (J). (gr. 3-5). lib. bdg. 26.60 *(978-0-7613-8984-2(9))*, Millbrook Pr.) Lerner Publishing Group.

Roten, Lindsay Grace & Webb, Lois Sinaiko. The Multicultural Cookbook for Students. 2nd rev. ed. 2009. (Illus.). 354p. (C). (gr. 6-18). 94.00 *(978-0-313-37558-3(5))*, GR7558, Greenwood) ABC-CLIO, LLC.

Schlosser, Eric. Chew on This: Everything You Don't Want to Know about Fast Food. 2007. lib. bdg. 20.85 *(978-1-4177-7657-3(9))*, Turtleback) Turtleback Bks.

Schlosser, Eric & Wilson, Charles. Chew on This: Everything You Don't Want to Know about Fast Food. 2007. (ENG., Illus.). 336p. (YA). (gr. 7). pap. 9.99 *(978-0-618-59394-1(2))* Houghton Mifflin Harcourt Publishing Co.

Senker, Cath. Lebanon. 2010. (World of Food Ser.). 32p. (YA). (gr. 4-7). lib. bdg. 24.95 *(978-1-934545-12-6(0))* Oliver Pr., Inc.

Shea, Mary Molly. Foods of India. 2011. (Culture in the Kitchen Ser.). 24p. (J). (gr. 2-5). pap. 8.15 *(978-1-4339-5708-6(6))*; lib. bdg. 22.60 *(978-1-4339-5706-2(X))* Stevens, Gareth Publishing LLLP. (Gareth Stevens Learning Library).

Shea, Therese. Foods of China. 2011. (Culture in the Kitchen Ser.). 24p. (J). (gr. 2-5). pap. 8.15 *(978-1-4339-5704-8(3))*; lib. bdg. 22.60 *(978-1-4339-5702-4(7))* Stevens, Gareth Publishing LLLP. (Gareth Stevens Learning Library).

Sheen, Barbara. Peru. 2010. (Taste of Culture Ser.). 64p. lib. bdg. 30.45 *(978-0-7377-5346-2(3))*, Kidhaven) Cengage Gale.

Sheen, Barbara, ed. Foods of Canada. 2012. (Taste of Culture Ser.). (ENG., Illus.). 64p. (J). (gr. 3-6). lib. bdg. 30.45 *(978-0-7377-5947-1(X))*, Kidhaven) Cengage Gale.

—Foods of England. 2011. (Taste of Culture Ser.). (ENG.). 64p. (J). (gr. 3-6). 30.45 *(978-0-7377-5881-8(3))*, Kidhaven) Cengage Gale.

Silverstein, Alvin, et al. Chocolate Ants, Maggot Cheese, & More: The Yucky Food Book. Kelley, Gerald, illus. 2010. (Yucky Science Ser.). 48p. (J). (gr. 5-9). 25.27 *(978-0-7660-3315-3(5))* Enslow Pubs., Inc.

Simons, Rae. Bigger Isn't Always Better: Choosing Your Portions. 2010. (Kids & Obesity Ser.). (Illus.). 48p. (YA). lib. bdg. 19.95 *(978-1-4222-1706-1(X))* Mason Crest.

Smith, Paula. Foods in Different Places. 2015. (Learning about Our Global Community Ser.). (ENG., Illus.). 24p. (J). *(978-0-7787-2009-6(8))* Crabtree Publishing Co.

Stiefel, Chana. There's a Rat in My Soup: Could You Survive Medieval Food? Kelley, Gerald, illus. 2011. (Ye Yucky Middle Ages Ser.). 48p. (J). (gr. 5-18). pap. 8.95 *(978-1-59845-375-1(0))*; (gr. 7-12). lib. bdg. 25.27 *(978-0-7660-3785-4(1))* Enslow Pubs., Inc.

Tarbox, A. D. A Mountain Food Chain: Odysseys in Nature. 2016. (Odysseys in Nature Ser.). (ENG.). 80p. (J). (gr. 7-10). pap. 14.99 *(978-1-62832-141-8(5))*, Creative Paperbacks) Creative Co., The.

Taylor, Dereen. The World of Food - Nigeria. 2010. (World of Food Ser.). 32p. (YA). (gr. 4-7). lib. bdg. 24.95 *(978-1-934545-14-0(7))* Oliver Pr., Inc.

Time for Dinner: Individual Title Six-Packs. (Chiquilibros Ser.). (gr. k-1). 23.00 *(978-0-7635-0414-4(9))* Rigby Education.

Torrisi, Cathy. Eat All Your Colors. 2011. pap. 39.95 *(978-0-7664-3747-0(7))* Abrams & Co. Pubs., Inc.

WalkerTheo. EAT UP! BEGINNING BOOK WITH ONLINE ACCESS. 2014. (ENG.). 24p. (J). pap. 9.50 *(978-1-107-68962-6(7))* Cambridge Univ. Pr.

Walton, Adrienne. Food. 2004. (Activities for 3-5 Year Olds Ser.). (Illus.). 32p. pap. 11.00 *(978-1-897675-57-1(7))* Brilliant Pubns. GBR. Dist: Parkwest Pubns., Inc.

Ward, Karen. Fun with Mexican Cooking. 2009. (Let's Get Cooking! Ser.). (Illus.). 32p. (J). (ENG.). pap. 11.75 *(978-1-4358-3477-4(1))*; (gr. 3-6). lib. bdg. 26.50 *(978-1-4358-3452-1(6))* Rosen Publishing Group, Inc., The. (PowerKids Pr.).

Whittaker, Helen. Food. 2011. (Living Green Ser.). 32p. (gr. 3). 28.50 *(978-1-60870-574-0(9))* Marshall Cavendish GBR. Dist: Marshall Cavendish Corp.

Wood, Ira. A Mexican Feast: The Foods & Recipes of Mexico. 2009. (Reading Room Collection 2 Ser.). 24p. (gr. 3-4). 42.50 *(978-1-60851-953-8(8))*, PowerKids Pr.) Rosen Publishing Group, Inc., The.

FOOD HABITS—FICTION

Adams, Jean Ekman. Clarence & the Purple Horse Bounce into Town. Adams, Jean Ekman, illus. 2003. (Illus.). 32p. (J). (gr. -1-3). 15.95 *(978-0-87358-826-3(6))*, Rising Moon Bks. for Young Readers) Northland Publishing.

Aguirre, Zuriñe. Sardines of Love. Aguirre, Zuriñe, illus. 2015. (Child's Play Library). (ENG., Illus.). 36p. (J). *(978-1-84643-726-7(1))* Child's Play International Ltd.

Alfaro, Manuel. Griego el Magnífico y la Gotita Verde Golosa Pegajos. Harrington, David, illus. 2007. (SPA.). 36p. per. 15.50 *(978-1-59858-337-3(9))* Dog Ear Publishing, LLC.

Allan, Jo. Hungry Hettie, 1 vol. 2010. (ENG., Illus.). 24p. (J). (gr. -1-1). 11.95 *(978-0-86315-779-0(3))* Floris Bks. GBR. Dist: SteinerBooks, Inc.

Allen, Nancy. Everyone Eats. 2015. (ENG.). 24p. (gr. k-3). 28.50 *(978-1-63430-363-7(6))* Rourke Educational Media.

Amore, Joanne. Joe's Fruit Store, 1 vol. 2009. 19p. pap. 24.95 *(978-1-60749-331-0(4))* America Star Bks.

Anonymous. Letting Ana Go. 2013. (ENG.). 304p. (YA). (gr. 9). 17.99 *(978-1-4424-7223-5(5))*; (Illus.). pap. 10.99 *(978-1-4424-7213-6(8))* Simon Pulse. (Simon Pulse).

Backer, Marni. Food Allergy Friends. 2012. (ENG.). pap. 14.99 *(978-1-4675-4513-6(9))* Independent Pub.

Bardhan-Quallen, Sudipta. Hampire! Fine, Howard, illus. 2011. (ENG.). 32p. (J). (gr. -1-3). 16.99 *(978-0-06-114239-0(5))* HarperCollins Pubs.

Barry, Debra R. Brady Pickles. 2011. 32p. pap. 24.95 *(978-1-4626-3716-4(7))* America Star Bks.

Breen, Steve. Woodpecker Wants Waffles. Breen, Steve, illus. 2016. (Illus.). 32p. (J). (gr. -1-3). 17.99 *(978-0-06-234257-7(6))* HarperCollins Pubs.

Brennan-Nelson, Denise. Leopold the Lion. Barshaw, Ruth McNally, illus. 2015. (ENG.). 32p. (J). (gr. 1-3). 16.99 *(978-1-58536-828-0(8))*, 203951) Sleeping Bear Pr.

Brokamp, Elizabeth. The Picky Little Witch, 1 vol. Riti, Marsha, illus. 2011. (ENG.). 32p. (J). (gr. k-3). 16.99 *(978-1-58980-882-9(7))* Pelican Publishing Co., Inc.

Brouwer, Sigmund. Mommy Ant, Eat Your Vegetables. 2004. (Bug's-Eye View Bks.). (ENG., Illus.). 18p. (J). pap. 4.99 *(978-0-8499-7756-5(8))* Nelson, Thomas Inc.

Brown, Marc. D. W. la Quisquillosa. Sarfatti, Esther, tr. from ENG. 2003.Tr. of D. W. the Picky Eater. (SPA.). (J). (gr. k-2). pap. 6.95 *(978-1-930332-42-3(4))* Lectorum Pubns., Inc.

Bruel, Nick. Bad Kitty Does Not Like Candy. 2015. (Bad Kitty Ser.). (ENG., Illus.). 24p. (J). (gr. -1-k). 4.99 *(978-1-62672-230-9(7))*, 9781626722309) Square Fish.

—Bad Kitty Does Not Like Candy. 2015. (Bad Kitty Picture Bks.). (J). lib. bdg. 14.75 *(978-0-606-37274-9(1))* Turtleback Bks.

Buckley, Richard. The Foolish Tortoise. Carle, Eric, illus. 2013. (World of Eric Carle Ser.). (ENG.). 24p. (J). (gr. -1-3). pap. 9.99 *(978-1-4424-6638-8(3))*, Little Simon) Little Simon.

—The Greedy Python. Carle, Eric, illus. 2012. (World of Eric Carle Ser.). (ENG.). 24p. (J). (gr. -1-1). 16.99 *(978-1-4424-4577-2(7))*; pap. 3.99 *(978-1-4424-4576-5(9))* Simon Spotlight. (Simon Spotlight).

—The Greedy Python. 2012. (Eric Carle Ready-To-Read Ser.). lib. bdg. 13.55 *(978-0-606-26357-3(8))*, Turtleback) Turtleback Bks.

—The Greedy Python: Lap Edition. Carle, Eric, illus. 2013. (World of Eric Carle Ser.). (ENG.). 24p. (J). (gr. -1-k). bds. 12.99 *(978-1-4424-8991-2(X))*, Little Simon) Little Simon.

Bug, June. The Legend of the Wooden Bowl. 2013. 44p. pap. 20.45 *(978-1-4624-0688-3(2))*, Inspiring Voices) Author Solutions, Inc.

Butler, M. Christina. Who's Been Eating My Porridge? Howarth, Daniel, illus. 2004. 32p. (J). (gr. -1). tchr. ed. 15.95 *(978-1-58925-040-6(0))* Tiger Tales.

Canetti, Yanitzia. Abecedario Nutritivo. 2009. (SPA.). 40p. (J). pap. 8.99 *(978-1-59835-115-6(X)*, BrickHouse Education) Cambridge BrickHouse, Inc.

—Yummy ABC's. 2010. (ENG.). 40p. (J). pap. 8.99 *(978-1-59835-114-9(1)*, BrickHouse Education) Cambridge BrickHouse, Inc.

Chandler, Susan. What I Do with Vegetable Glue. Odriozola, Elena, illus. 2012. (ENG.). 24p. (J). (gr. k-3). 16.95 *(978-1-61608-661-9(0)*, 608661, Sky Pony Pr.) Skyhorse Publishing Co., Inc.

Child, Lauren. I Will Never Not Ever Eat a Tomato. Child, Lauren, illus. 2003. (Charlie & Lola Ser.). (ENG., Illus.). 32p. (J). (gr. -1-3). reprint ed. 8.99 *(978-0-7636-2180-3(3))* Candlewick Pr.

—I Will Never Not Ever Eat a Tomato. 2004. (Charlie & Lola Ser.). (Illus.). (gr. -1-3). 17.00 *(978-0-7569-3178-0(9))* Perfection Learning Corp.

—I Will Never Not Ever Eat a Tomato. 2003. (Charlie & Lola Ser.). lib. bdg. 19.65 *(978-0-613-69403-2(1)*, Turtleback) Turtleback Bks.

Ciccone, Tizania & Linardi, Franca. The Pancake Princess. Bucci, Gino, illus. 2012. 36p. pap. 13.95 *(978-1-61897-720-5(2)*, Strategic Bk. Publishing) Strategic Book Publishing & Rights Agency (SBPRA).

Ciccone, Tiziana & Linardi, Franca. No More Peanut Butter, Daniel! Bucci, Gino, illus. 2012. 36p. pap. 13.95 *(978-1-61897-718-2(0)*, Strategic Bk. Publishing) Strategic Book Publishing & Rights Agency (SBPRA).

Colossal, Eric. Feasts of Fury. 2016. (Rutabaga the Adventure Chef Ser.: 2). (J). lib. bdg. 20.80 *(978-0-606-38205-2(4))* Turtleback Bks.

Crangle, Claudine, illus. Woolfred Does Not Eat Dandelions. 2014. (J). *(978-1-4338-1672-7(5))*; pap. *(978-1-4338-1673-4(3))* American Psychological Assn. (Magination Pr.).

Dahl, Michael. Bunny Eats Lunch, 1 vol. Vidal, Oriol, illus. 2010. (Hello Genius Ser.). (ENG.). 20p. (gr. 1-2). bds. 7.99 *(978-1-4048-5728-5(1))* Picture Window Bks.

Davies, Kate, ed. Old Woman Who Swallowed a Fly. Home, Sarah, illus. 2009. (First Reading Level 3 Ser.). 48p. (J). (gr. 2). 6.99 *(978-0-7945-2267-4(X)*, Usborne) EDC Publishing.

De Anda, Diane. A Day without Sugar / un día sin Azúcar. Baeza Ventura, Gabriela, tr. Montecalvo, Janet, illus. 2012. (SPA & ENG.). (J). 17.95 *(978-1-55885-702-5(8)*, Piñata Books) Arte Publico Pr.

Derubertis, Barbara. Zachary Zebra's Zippity Zooming. Alley, R. W., illus. 2011. (Animal Antics A to Z Set III Ser.). pap. 45.32 *(978-0-7613-8435-9(9))* Kane Press, Inc.

deRubertis, Barbara. Zachary Zebra's Zippity Zooming. Alley, R. W., illus. 2011. (Animal Antics A to Z Ser.). 32p. (J). pap. 7.95 *(978-1-57565-351-8(6))*; lib. bdg. 22.60 *(978-1-57565-359-4(1))* Kane Press, Inc.

deRubertis, Barbara & DeRubertis, Barbara. Zachary Zebra's Zippity Zooming. Alley, R. W., illus. 2012. (Animal Antics A to Z Ser.). 32p. (J). (gr. 2 — 1). cd-rom 7.95 *(978-1-57565-419-5(9))* Kane Press, Inc.

Dimari. I See a Healthy Me! 2013. 16p. pap. 7.95 *(978-1-4525-8414-0(1)*, Balboa Pr.) Author Solutions, Inc.

Donnio, Sylviane. I'd Really Like to Eat a Child. 2012. (ENG., Illus.). 32p. (J). (gr. -1-2). pap. 7.99 *(978-0-307-93008-8(4)*, Dragonfly Bks.) Random Hse. Children's Bks.

—I'd Really Like to Eat a Child. 2012. lib. bdg. 18.40 *(978-0-606-23845-8(X)*, Turtleback) Turtleback Bks.

Downing, Johnette. Today Is Monday in Louisiana, 1 vol. Kadair, Deborah Ousley, illus. 2006. (ENG.). 32p. (J). (gr. k-k). 16.99 *(978-1-58980-406-7(6))* Pelican Publishing Co., Inc.

Dussling, Jennifer. Picky Peggy. Adams, Lynn, tr. Adams, Lynn, illus. 2004. (Science Solves It! Ser.). 32p. (J). pap. 5.95 *(978-1-57565-138-5(6))* Kane Press, Inc.

Emerson, Carl. Monster Boy's School Lunch, 1 vol. Levin, Lon, illus. 2008. (Monster Boy Ser.). (ENG.). 32p. (gr. -1-4). 28.50 *(978-1-60270-238-7(1)*, Looking Glass Library) ABDO Publishing Co.

Falk, Kristi & Falk, Daniel. Eartha Gets Well. Peters, Rob, illus. 2012. (ENG.). 30p. (J). 24.95 *(978-1-937084-27-1(2)*, BQB Publishing) Boutique of Quality Books Publishing Co., Inc.

Fell, Amy. Two Terrible Eaters. 2012. 72p. pap. *(978-1-105-43640-6(3))* Lulu.com.

Fine, Karen. Veggiesaurus Lex. 2009. 24p. pap. 12.99 *(978-1-4490-0290-9(0))* AuthorHouse.

Fischer, Ellen. If an Armadillo Went to a Restaurant. Wood, Laura, illus. 2014. (ENG.). 32p. (J). (-2). 14.95 *(978-1-938063-39-8(2)*, Mighty Media Kids) Mighty Media Pr.

Fleming, Denise. Lunch. 2014. 32p. pap. 8.00 *(978-1-61003-225-4(X))* Center for the Collaborative Classroom.

Freedman, Claire. Spider Sandwiches. Hendra, Sue, illus. 2014. (ENG.). 32p. (J). (gr. k-3). 14.99 *(978-1-61963-364-3(7)*, 9781619633643, Bloomsbury USA Childrens) Bloomsbury Publishing USA.

Gantos, Jack. Rotten Ralph Feels Rotten. Rubel, Nicole, tr. Rubel, Nicole, illus. 2004. (Rotten Ralph Rotten Readers Ser.: 3). (ENG.). 48p. (J). (gr. 1-3). 16.99 *(978-0-374-36357-4(9)*, 9780374363574, Farrar, Straus & Giroux (BYR)) Farrar, Straus & Giroux.

—Rotten Ralph Feels Rotten. Rubel, Nicole, illus. 2007. (Rotten Ralph Ser.). (J). (gr. -1-3). 28.95 incl. audio compact disk *(978-1-4301-0098-0(2))* Live Oak Media.

Gavin, Ciara. Bear Likes Jam. 2017. (ENG., Illus.). 32p. (J). (gr. -1-2). 16.99 *(978-0-399-55179-6(4)*, Knopf Bks. for Young Readers) Random Hse. Children's Bks.

Geis, Patricia. Let's Eat! Folch, Sergio, illus. 2009. (Good Habits with Coco & Tula Ser.). 16p. (J). (gr. -1-k). bds. 11.40 *(978-1-60754-411-1(3))* Windmill Bks.

Gonzales Bertrand, Diane. Sofia & the Purple Dress / Sofia y el Vestido Morado. Baeza Ventura, Gabriela, tr. Fields, Lisa, illus. 2012. (SPA & ENG.). (J). 17.95 *(978-1-55885-701-8(X)*, Piñata Books) Arte Publico Pr.

Gutman, Dan. Ms. Leakey Is Freaky! Paillot, Jim, illus. 2011. (My Weird School Daze Ser.: 12). 112p. (J). (gr. 1-5). lib. bdg. 15.89 *(978-0-06-170403-1(2))* HarperCollins Pubs.

—Ms. Leakey Is Freaky! No. 12. Paillot, Jim, illus. 2011. (My Weird School Daze Ser.: 12). (ENG.). 112p. (J). (gr. 1-5). pap. 4.99 *(978-0-06-170402-4(4))* HarperCollins Pubs.

Hamilton, Mimi. Kevin & Tak. 2012. 24p. pap. 15.99 *(978-1-4653-9957-1(7))* Xlibris Corp.

Harper, Charise Mericle. Just Grace & the Snack Attack. 2010. (Just Grace Ser.: 5). (ENG., Illus.). 176p. (J). (gr. 1-4). pap. 5.99 *(978-0-547-40629-9(0))* Houghton Mifflin Harcourt Publishing Co.

Harrison, David L. A Monster Is Coming! Wilhelm, Hans, illus. 2011. (Step into Reading Ser.). (ENG.). 32p. (J). (gr. -1-1). pap. 3.99 *(978-0-375-86677-7(9)*, Random Hse. Bks. for Young Readers) Random Hse. Children's Bks.

Heller, Donna & Payne, James. The Enchanted Tree. Zamboni, David, illus. 2007. 44p. per. 14.95 *(978-1-934246-72-6(7))* Peppertree Pr., The.

Hicks, Barbara Jean. Monsters Don't Eat Broccoli. Hendra, Sue, illus. (ENG.). 40p. (J). (gr. -1-2). 2014. 7.99 *(978-0-385-75521-4(X)*, Dragonfly Bks.) 2009. 16.99 *(978-0-375-85686-0(2)*, Knopf Bks. for Young Readers) Random Hse. Children's Bks.

Hoban, Russell. Bread & Jam for Frances. Hoban, Lillian, illus. 2008. (I Can Read Level 2 Ser.). (ENG.). 48p. (J). (gr. k-3). 16.99 *(978-0-06-083798-3(5))*; pap. 3.99 *(978-0-06-083800-3(0))* HarperCollins Pubs.

Hoberman, Mary Ann. The Seven Silly Eaters. Frazee, Marla, illus. 2004. (J). (gr. k-3). spiral bd. *(978-0-616-14576-0(4))* Canadian National Institute for the Blind/Institut National Canadien pour les Aveugles.

Hoyes, Amy & Reimann, A. J. Happy the Hippo: Eats Healthy Food. Stewart, K. L., illus. 2013. 24p. pap. 9.99 *(978-1-938743-08-5(3))* Reimann Bks.

Ide, Laurie Shimizu. Okazu at the Zoo. Kanekuni, Daniel, illus. 2006. (J). *(978-1-56647-776-5(X))* Mutual Publishing LLC.

Jeffers, Oliver. The Incredible Book Eating Boy. Jeffers, Oliver, illus. 2007. (ENG., Illus.). 32p. (J). (gr. -1-3). 17.99 *(978-0-399-24749-1(1)*, Philomel Bks.) Penguin Young Readers Group.

Jensen, Joel, et al. Tiny Hamster Is a Giant Monster. 2015. (ENG., Illus.). 32p. (J). (gr. -1-3). 17.99 *(978-1-4814-5110-9(3)*, Simon & Schuster Bks. For Young Readers) Simon & Schuster Bks. For Young Readers.

Jensen, Patricia & Demar, Regier. Good Food. Clar, David Austin & Hantel, Johanna, illus. 2006. (My First Reader Ser.). (ENG.). 32p. (J). (gr. k-1). per. 3.95 *(978-0-516-24969-8(X)*, Children's Pr.) Scholastic Library Publishing.

Jones, Christianne C. Pruebalo, 1 vol. Ruiz, Carlos, tr. Yi, Hye Won, illus. 2006. (Read-It! Readers en Español: Story Collection).Tr. of Just Try it. (SPA.). 24p. (gr. -1-3). 21.32 *(978-1-4048-1692-3(5)*, Easy Readers) Picture Window Bks.

Jones, Nathan Smith. The Boy Who Ate America. Nelson, Casey, illus. 2007. 32p. (J). (gr. -1-3). 16.95 *(978-1-59038-814-3(3)*, Shadow Mountain) Shadow Mountain Publishing.

Kann, Victoria. Love, Pinkalicious. Kann, Victoria, illus. 2009. (Pinkalicious Ser.). (ENG., Illus.). 12p. (J). (gr. -1-2). pap. 6.99 *(978-0-06-192731-7(7)*, HarperFestival) HarperCollins Pubs.

—Pinkalicious. Kann, Victoria, illus. 2013. (Pinkalicious Ser.). (ENG., Illus.). 192p. (J). (gr. -1-3). 11.99 *(978-0-06-218800-7(3))* HarperCollins Pubs.

—Pinkalicious: School Rules! Kann, Victoria, illus. 2010. (I Can Read Level 1 Ser.). (ENG., Illus.). 32p. (J). (gr. -1-3). 16.99 *(978-0-06-192886-4(0))* HarperCollins Pubs.

—Pinkalicious - Soccer Star. Kann, Victoria, illus. 2012. (I Can Read Level 1 Ser.). (ENG., Illus.). 32p. (J). (gr. -1-3). pap. 3.99 *(978-0-06-198964-3(9))* HarperCollins Pubs.

—Pinkalicious & the Pink Drink. Kann, Victoria, illus. 2010. (Pinkalicious Ser.). (ENG., Illus.). 24p. (J). (gr. -1-3). pap. 3.99 *(978-0-06-192732-4(5)*, HarperFestival) HarperCollins Pubs.

—Pinkalicious & the Pink Drink. 2010. (Pinkalicious Ser.). (J). lib. bdg. 13.55 *(978-0-606-14868-9(X)*, Turtleback) Turtleback Bks.

—The Pinkalicious Take-Along Storybook Set. Kann, Victoria, illus. 2015. (Pinkalicious Ser.). (ENG., Illus.). 120p. (J). (gr. -1-3). pap. 11.99 *(978-0-06-241080-1(6)*, HarperFestival) HarperCollins Pubs.

—School Rules! Kann, Victoria, illus. 2010. (I Can Read Level 1 Ser.). (ENG., Illus.). 32p. (J). (gr. -1-3). pap. 3.99 *(978-0-06-192885-7(2))* HarperCollins Pubs.

Kann, Victoria & Kann, Elizabeth. Pinkalicious. Kann, Victoria, illus. (Pinkalicious Ser.). (Illus.). 40p. (J). 2016. (ENG.). (gr. -1-3). 17.99 *(978-0-06-077639-8(0))* 2011. (SPA., (gr. k-3). 17.99 *(978-0-06-179959-4(9))* 2006. (gr. -1-3). lib. bdg. 17.89 *(978-0-06-077640-4(4))* HarperCollins Pubs.

Kaplan, Michael B. Betty Bunny Loves Chocolate Cake. Jorisch, Stéphane, illus. 2011. (Betty Bunny Ser.). (ENG.). 36p. (J). (gr. -1-k). 17.99 *(978-0-8037-3407-4(7)*, Dial Bks) Penguin Young Readers Group.

Karnosh, Ami. Let's Eat: A Book about Food. 2008. 28p. pap. 24.95 *(978-1-60563-377-0(1))* PublishAmerica, Inc.

Kompelien, Tracy. Fly Paper, 1 vol. Haberstroh, Anne, illus. 2007. (Critter Chronicles Ser.). (ENG.). 24p. (J). (gr. k-3). lib. bdg. 24.21 *(978-1-59928-438-5(3)*, SandCastle) ABDO Publishing Co.

Krulik, Nancy. Free the Worms! John and Wendy Staff, illus. 2008. (Katie Kazoo, Switcheroo Ser.: 28). (ENG.). 80p. (J). (gr. 2-4). pap. 3.99 *(978-0-448-44675-2(8)*, Grosset & Dunlap) Penguin Young Readers Group.

—Free the Worms! John & Wendy, illus. 2008. (Katie Kazoo, Switcheroo Ser.). 78p. (J). 11.65 *(978-0-7569-8807-4(1))* Perfection Learning Corp.

Landry, Leo. Eat Your Peas, Ivy Louise! 2005. (J). (gr. -1-k). 12.00 *(978-0-618-58112-2(X))* Houghton Mifflin Harcourt Trade & Reference Pubs.

LaRochelle, David. How Martha Saved Her Parents from Green Beans. Fearing, Mark, illus. 2013. (ENG.). 32p. (J). (gr. k-3). 16.99 *(978-0-8037-3766-2(1)*, Dial Bks) Penguin Young Readers Group.

Leedy, Loreen. Jack & the Hungry Giant: Eat Right with Myplate. 2013. (ENG., Illus.). 32p. (J). 17.95 *(978-0-8234-2602-7(5))* Holiday Hse., Inc.

Leedy, Loreen & Leedy, Loreen. Jack & the Hungry Giant: Eat Right with Myplate. 2015. (ENG.). 32p. (J). (gr. -1-3). 7.99 *(978-0-8234-3308-7(0))* Holiday Hse., Inc.

Levinson, Lara. Zachary's Dinnertime, 1 vol. Van Wright, Cornelius, illus. 2012. (ENG.). 32p. (J). 16.95 *(978-1-59572-329-1(3))*; pap. 6.95 *(978-1-59572-330-7(7))* Star Bright Bks., Inc.

Manning, Mick & Granström, Brita. Chomp, Chomp! 2003. (Mick Manning & Brita Granstrom Ser.). (SPA., Illus.). (J). *(978-970-690-586-4(3))* Planeta Mexicana Editorial S. A. de C. V.

Martín Anguita, Carmen & Carmen, Martín Anguita. Cuéntame un Cuento, Que Voy a Comer. Cortazar, Alicia Canas, illus. 2008. (SPA.). 32p. (J). 10.99 *(978-84-241-5752-4(4))* Everest Editora ESP. Dist: Lectorum Pubns., Inc.

McClements, George. Night of the Veggie Monster. McClements, George, illus. (ENG., Illus.). 32p. (J). (gr. -1-1). 2014. 7.99 *(978-1-61963-180-9(6)*, 9781619631809) 2008. 16.99 *(978-1-59990-061-2(0)*, 9781599900612) Bloomsbury Publishing USA. (Bloomsbury USA Childrens).

McCully, Emily Arnold. Pete Won't Eat. McCully, Emily Arnold, illus. 2014. (I Like to Read(r) Ser.). (ENG., Illus.). 24p. (J). (gr. -1-3). pap. 6.99 *(978-0-8234-3183-0(5))* Holiday Hse., Inc.

—Pete Won't Eat. 2013. (I Like to Read(r) Ser.). (ENG., Illus.). 24p. (J). (gr. -1-3). 14.95 *(978-0-8234-2853-3(2))* Holiday Hse., Inc.

McGee, Joe. Peanut Butter & Aliens: A Zombie Culinary Tale. Santoso, Charles, illus. 2017. (ENG.). 32p. (J). (gr. -1-2). 16.95 ***(978-1-4197-2530-2(0)***, Abrams Bks. for Young Readers) Abrams, Inc.

McGee, Joe. Peanut Butter & Brains. Santoso, Charles, illus. 2015. (ENG.). 32p. (J). (gr. -1-3). 16.95 *(978-1-4197-1247-0(0)*, Abrams Bks. for Young Readers) Abrams, Inc.

McQueen, Todd. Bob & Rob & Corn on the Cob. McQueen, Todd, illus. 2014. (ENG., Illus.). 32p. (J). (gr. -1-k). 16.95 *(978-1-62873-591-8(0)*, Sky Pony Pr.) Skyhorse Publishing Co., Inc.

Miller, Deborah U. & Ostrove, Karen. Fins & Scales: A Kosher Tale. Ostrove, Karen, illus. 2004. (Israel Ser.). (Illus.). 32p. (J). (gr. 1-3). pap. 4.95 *(978-0-929371-25-2(9)*, Kar-Ben Publishing) Lerner Publishing Group.

Moerder, Lynne. Things That Go Burp! in the Night. Moerder, Lynne, illus. 2015. (ENG., Illus.). 32p. (J). (gr. -1-k). 16.99 *(978-1-4847-1669-4(8))* Hyperion Bks. for Children.

Namm, Diane. Little Bear. McCue, Lisa, illus. 2003. (My First Reader Ser.). (ENG.). 32p. (J). 18.50 *(978-0-516-22931-7(1)*, Children's Pr.) Scholastic Library Publishing.

Nelligan, Patty. Peppy Up: Eat Your Best, Be Your Best! Ocello, Salvatore & Nelligan, Kevin, illus. 2013. 32p. pap. 12.95 *(978-1-939418-41-8(0))* Writer of the Round Table Pr.

Nobleman, Marc Tyler. The Chupacabra Ate the Candelabra. Aranda, Ana, illus. 2017. (ENG.). 32p. (J). (gr. k-3). 17.99 *(978-0-399-17443-8(5)*, Nancy Paulsen Books) Penguin Young Readers Group.

Nogarr, Ilona. Lola & the Apple. 2012. 16p. pap. 24.95 *(978-1-4626-7273-8(6))* America Star Bks.

North, Laura. Hansel & Gretel & the Green Witch. Jevons, Chris, illus. 2015. (ENG.). 32p. (J). *(978-0-7787-1928-1(6))* Crabtree Publishing Co.

Olson, Denise. P Is for Picky. 2011. 16p. 13.99 *(978-1-4567-5837-0(3))* AuthorHouse.

Oppel, Kenneth. The King's Taster. Johnson, Steve & Fancher, Lou, illus. 2009. 32p. (J). (gr. -1-1). (ENG.). 17.99 *(978-0-06-075372-6(2))*; lib. bdg. 18.89 *(978-0-06-075373-3(0))* HarperCollins Pubs.

Oppenheim, Joanne F. & Barefoot Books Staff. The Prince's Breakfast. Latimer, Miriam, illus. 2014. 32p. (J). (gr. -1-2). 9.99 *(978-1-78285-075-5(9))*; 16.99 *(978-1-78285-074-8(0))* Barefoot Bks., Inc.

Palatini, Margie & Davis, Jack E. Sweet Tooth. Davis, Jack E., illus. 2004. (ENG., Illus.). 40p. (J). (gr. -1-3). 18.99 *(978-0-689-85159-9(6)*, Simon & Schuster Bks. For Young Readers) Simon & Schuster Bks. For Young Readers.

Pearce, Tracy. How to Eat Fried Worms. 2015. (Great Works). (ENG., Illus.). 72p. (gr. 3-5). pap. 9.99 *(978-1-4807-6994-6(0))* Shell Educational Publishing.

Pitzer, Marjorie W. I Like Berries, Do You? Pitzer, Marjorie W., photos by. 2013. (ENG., Illus.). 14p. (J). 11.95 *(978-1-60613-183-1(4))* Woodbine Hse.

Queen Rania of Jordan Al Abdullah Staff, et al. The Sandwich Swap. Tusa, Tricia, illus. 2010. (ENG.). 32p. (J). (gr. -1-2). 16.99 *(978-1-4231-2484-9(7))* Hyperion Pr.

Radford, Sheri. Penelope & the Humongous Burp. Lt. ed. 2012. 64p. (J). pap. *(978-1-4596-3451-0(9))* ReadHowYouWant.com, Ltd.

Radlauer. Breakfast by Molly. 2007. (ENG.). 32p. (J). (gr. -1-2). 8.99 *(978-1-4169-6837-5(7)*, Simon & Schuster/Paula Wiseman Bks.) Simon & Schuster/Paula Wiseman Bks.

Rebein, Alyssa Chase & Chase, Andra. Stanley's "This Is the Life!" Chase, Andra, illus. 2008. (Illus.). (J). *(978-1-55942-570-4(9))* Witcher Productions.

Reich, Susanna. Minette's Feast: The Delicious Story of Julia Child & Her Cat. Bates, Amy, illus. 2012. (ENG.). 40p. (J). (gr. -1-k). 17.95 *(978-1-4197-0177-1(0)*, Abrams Bks. for Young Readers) Abrams, Inc.

Reidy, Jean. Too Pickley! Leloup, Geneviève, illus. (Too! Bks.). (ENG.). (J). (gr. -1 — 1). 2012. 26p. bds. 7.99 *(978-1-59990-680-5(5)*, 9781599906805) 2010. 32p. 11.99 *(978-1-59990-309-5(1)*, 9781599903095) Bloomsbury Publishing USA. (Bloomsbury USA Childrens).

Robertson, Jean. How Many Bites? Dufalla, Anita, illus. 2011. (ENG.). 24p. (gr. k-1). pap. 8.95 *(978-1-61236-005-8(X))* Rourke Educational Media.

Rompella, Natalie. Edgar, Allan, & Poe, & the Tell-Tale Beets. Lt. ed. 2012. 63p. (J). pap. *(978-1-4596-3447-3(0))* ReadHowYouWant.com, Ltd.

Rosenthal, Amy Krouse. Little Pea. Corace, Jen, illus. (ENG.). (J). (gr. -1-k). 2015. 32p. bds. 7.99 *(978-1-4521-4289-0(0))* 2005. 36p. 15.99 *(978-0-8118-4658-5(X))* Chronicle Bks. LLC.

Rosenthal, Betsy R. Porcupine's Picnic: Who Eats What? Capizzi, Giusi, illus. 2017. (ENG.). 32p. (gr. -1-2). 19.99 *(978-1-4677-9519-7(4)*, Millbrook Pr.) Lerner Publishing Group.

Rubin, Adam. Dragons Love Tacos. Salmieri, Daniel, illus. 2012. (ENG.). 40p. (J). (gr. -1-2). 16.99 *(978-0-8037-3680-1(0)*, Dial Bks) Penguin Young Readers Group.

—Dragons Love Tacos 2: The Sequel. Salmieri, Daniel, illus. 2017. (ENG.). 48p. (J). (-k). 18.99 *(978-0-525-42888-6(7)*, Dial Bks) Penguin Young Readers Group.

Rubin, Adam & Salmieri, Daniel. Dragons Love Tacos. 2016. (ENG., Illus.). 40p. (J). (gr. -1-2). 17.99 *(978-0-7352-2823-8(X)*, Dial Bks) Penguin Young Readers Group.

Rylant, Cynthia. Brownie & Pearl Grab a Bite. Biggs, Brian, illus. 2011. (Brownie & Pearl Ser.). (ENG.). 24p. (J). (gr. -1-k). 13.99 *(978-1-4169-8634-8(0)*, Beach Lane Bks.) Beach Lane Bks.

—Brownie & Pearl Grab a Bite. Biggs, Brian, illus. 2014. (Brownie & Pearl Ser.). (ENG.). 24p. (J). (gr. -1-k). 16.99 *(978-1-4814-1717-4(7))*; pap. 3.99 *(978-1-4814-1715-0(0))* Simon Spotlight. (Simon Spotlight).

Salvatore, Wilsin. Picky Joshy. 2007. 20p. per. 24.95 *(978-1-4137-2554-4(6))* America Star Bks.

Schneider, David. Dillan Mcmillan, Please Eat Your Peas. Shelly, Jeff, Sr., illus. 2016. (ENG.). 36p. (J). 16.95 *(978-0-9744446-4-2(2))* All About Kids Publishing.

Schneider, Josh. Tales for Very Picky Eaters. Schneider, Josh, illus. 2011. (ENG., Illus.). 48p. (J). (gr. 1-4). 15.99 *(978-0-547-14956-1(5))* Houghton Mifflin Harcourt Publishing Co.

Schnitzlein, Danny. The Monster Who Ate My Peas, 1 vol. Faulkner, Matt, illus. 2010. (ENG.). 32p. (J). pap. 7.95 *(978-1-56145-533-1(4))* Peachtree Pubs.

Shear, Dani. The Foodie Club. Weinstein, Holly, illus. 2013. (ENG.). 50p. (J). 16.99 *(978-1-61053-027-9(6))* Blackbird Bks.

Shipton, Paul. What's for Breakfast? Stuart, Jon, illus. 2006. (Collins Big Cat Ser.). (ENG.). 16p. (J). (gr. -1-k). pap. 5.99 *(978-0-00-718668-6(1))* HarperCollins Pubs. Ltd. GBR. Dist: Independent Pubs. Group.

Snow, Pegeen. Eat Your Peas, Louise! Venezia, Mike, illus. 2011. (Rookie Ready to Learn Ser.). 40p. (J). (ENG.). pap. 5.95 *(978-0-531-26709-7(1))*; (gr. -1-k). lib. bdg. 23.00 *(978-0-531-26527-7(7))* Scholastic Library Publishing. (Children's Pr.).

Snyder, Casey. Adventures of Food. 2013. 24p. pap. 24.95 *(978-1-4626-8661-2(3))* America Star Bks.

Spinelli, Eileen. Miss Fox's Class Shapes Up. Kennedy, Anne, illus. 2011. (ENG.). 32p. (J). (gr. 1-3). 16.99 *(978-0-8075-5171-4(6))* Whitman, Albert & Co.

Steers, Billy. Tractor Mac Farmers' Market. 2015. (Tractor Mac Ser.). (ENG., Illus.). 32p. (J). (gr. -1-k). 8.99 *(978-0-374-30107-1(7)*, 9780374301071, Farrar, Straus & Giroux (BYR)) Farrar, Straus & Giroux.

—Tractor Mac Farmers Market: Farmer's Market. Steers, Billy, illus. 2009. (ENG., Illus.). (J). 7.95 *(978-0-9826870-1-7(X))* Tractor Mac Inc.

Stonesifer, Gertrude. The Peanut Butter Kid. Rogers, Denny, illus. 2003. (ENG.). 32p. (J). (gr. 1-4). pap. 9.95 *(978-1-878044-44-0(3))* Mayhaven Publishing, Inc.

Sweet, Susan D. & Miles, Brenda. Princess Penelopea Hates Peas: A Tale of Picky Eating & Avoiding Catastropeas. 2016. (Illus.). 32p. (J). *(978-1-4338-2046-5(3)*, Magination Pr.) American Psychological Assn.

Swindells, Pat. Junk Food Hero. 2010. (ENG., Illus.). 280p. (J). (gr. 6). pap. 18.95 *(978-1-906582-02-9(5))* Aurora Metro Pubns. Ltd. GBR. Dist: Consortium Bk. Sales & Distribution.

Tel-Or, Nava. Tristan & the Magical Vegetable Stew. 2011. (Illus.). 36p. (gr. -1). pap. 22.24 *(978-1-4567-7024-2(1))* AuthorHouse.

Thompson, Lauren. Chew, Chew, Gulp! Krosoczka, Jarrett J., illus. 2011. (ENG.). 32p. (J). (gr. -1-k). 14.99 *(978-1-4169-9744-3(X)*, McElderry, Margaret K. Bks.) McElderry, Margaret K. Bks.

Too Much. 2008. (Illus.). 24p. (J). 9.95 *(978-0-9798189-0-5(7))*; 12.95 *(978-0-9798189-2-9(3))* Little Britches Childrens Bks.

Van Fleet, Matthew. Monday the Bullfrog. Van Fleet, Matthew, illus. 2010. (ENG., Illus.). 20p. (J). (gr. -1). 24.99 *(978-1-4424-0958-3(4)*, Simon & Schuster/Paula Wiseman Bks.) Simon & Schuster/Paula Wiseman Bks.

Van Patter, Bruce. Tucker Took It! 2010. (ENG., Illus.). 32p. (J). (gr. k-2). 16.95 *(978-1-59078-698-7(X))* Boyds Mills Pr.

Walton, Rick. Bullfrog Pops!, 1 vol. McAllister, Chris, illus. 2005. (ENG.). 32p. (J). (gr. 3-3). pap. 7.99 *(978-1-58685-840-7(8))* Gibbs Smith, Publisher.

Whelen-Banks, Jane. Liam Goes Poo in the Toilet: A Story about Trouble with Toilet Training. 2008. (ENG., Illus.). 32p. 12.95 *(978-1-84310-900-6(X)*, 5371) Kingsley, Jessica Pubs. GBR. Dist: Macmillan Distribution Ltd.

Willard, Nancy. The Three Mouths of Little Tom Drum. Hawkes, Kevin, illus. 2015. (ENG.). 48p. (J). (gr. -1-3). 16.99 *(978-0-7636-5476-4(0))* Candlewick Pr.

Willems, Mo. I Really Like Slop! Willems, Mo, illus. 2015. (Elephant & Piggie Book Ser.). (ENG., Illus.). 64p. (J). (gr. 1-3). 9.99 *(978-1-4847-2262-6(0))* Hyperion Bks. for Children.

Williams, Hal G. Qudola's Quest. 2011. 48p. pap. 16.95 *(978-1-4560-5167-9(9))* America Star Bks.

Willis, Jeanne. Flabby Cat & Slobby Dog. Ross, Tony, illus. 2009. (Andersen Press Picture Bks). (ENG.). 32p. (J). (gr. -1-3). 16.95 *(978-0-7613-5151-1(5)*, Carolrhoda Bks.) Lerner Publishing Group.

Yee, Wong Herbert. Hamburger Heaven. 2005. (ENG., Illus.). 32p. (J). (gr. -1-3). reprint ed. 5.95 *(978-0-618-54885-9(8))* Houghton Mifflin Harcourt Publishing Co.

FOOD INDUSTRY AND TRADE—VOCATIONAL GUIDANCE

Aaseng, Nathan. Business Builders in Sweets & Treats. 2005. (Business Builders Ser.: Vol. 9). (Illus.). 160p. (J). (gr. 5-18). lib. bdg. 24.95 *(978-1-881508-84-7(6))* Oliver Pr., Inc.

Ayer, Paula & Banyard, Antonia. Eat Up! An Infographic Exploration of Food. Wuthrich, Belle, illus. 2017. (Visual Exploration Ser.). (ENG.). 72p. (gr. 3-7). 22.95 *(978-1-55451-884-5(9))* Annick Pr., Ltd. CAN. Dist: Publishers Group West (PGW).

—Eat Up! An Infographic Exploration of Food. Wuthrich, Belle, illus. 2017. (Visual Exploration Ser.). (ENG.). 72p. (gr. 3-7). pap. 12.95 *(978-1-55451-883-8(0))* Annick Pr., Ltd. CAN. Dist: Publishers Group West (PGW).

Burgan, Michael. Food Engineering: From Concept to Consumer. 2015. (ENG.). 64p. (J). lib. bdg. *(978-0-531-21898-3(8)*, Orchard Bks.) Scholastic, Inc.

Cooper, Sharon Katz. Milton Hershey's Sweet Idea: A Chocolate Kingdom. Lokus, Rex & Sánchez, Alvaro Iglesias, illus. 2015. (Story Behind the Name Ser.). (ENG.). 32p. (gr. 2-3). lib. bdg. 28.65 *(978-1-4795-7137-6(7))* Picture Window Bks.

Ferguson Publishing Staff, creator. Food. 3rd rev. ed. 2007. (Careers in Focus Ser.). (Illus.). 192p. (gr. 6-12). 32.95 *(978-0-8160-6591-2(8)*, Ferguson Publishing Co.) Facts On File, Inc.

Green, Sara. General Mills. 2017. (Brands We Know Ser.). (ENG., Illus.). 24p. (J). (gr. 3-8). lib. bdg. 25.95 ***(978-1-62617-652-2(3)***, Pilot Bks.) Bellwether Media.

Harmon, Daniel E. Fish, Meat, & Poultry: Dangers in the Food Supply. 2009. (What's in Your Food? Recipe for Disaster Ser.). 48p. (gr. 5-5). 53.00 *(978-1-60854-772-2(8)*, Rosen Reference) Rosen Publishing Group, Inc., The.

Hobbs, Mike. Food & Drink. 2013. (Young Entrepreneurs' Club Ser.). (Illus.). 48p. (gr. 5-11). lib. bdg. 37.10 *(978-1-59920-923-4(3))* Black Rabbit Bks.

Hubbard, Rita & Hubbard, Rita Lorraine. Getting a Job in the Food Industry. 2013. 80p. (YA). (gr. 9-12). 33.25 *(978-1-4488-9606-6(1))* Rosen Publishing Group, Inc., The.

Kalman, Bobbie. Where Does Our Food Come From? 2011. (ENG.). 24p. (J). *(978-0-7787-9565-0(9))*; (My World Ser.: No. 61). pap. *(978-0-7787-9590-2(X))* Crabtree Publishing Co.

Loh-Hagan, Virginia. Food Stylist. 2016. (Odd Jobs Ser.). (ENG., Illus.). 32p. (J). (gr. 4-8). 29.93 *(978-1-63471-095-4(9)*, 208491, 45th Parallel Press) Cherry Lake Publishing.

McAlpine, Margaret. Working in the Food Industry. 2005. (My Future Career Ser.). (Illus.). 64p. (gr. 3-7). lib. bdg. 27.00 *(978-0-8368-4776-5(8)*, Gareth Stevens Learning Library) Stevens, Gareth Publishing LLLP.

Miller, Jeanne. Food Science. 2009. pap. 52.95 *(978-0-7613-4783-5(6))* Lerner Publishing Group.

The Exploratorium, The. Exploring - Kitchen Science. 2015. (ENG.). 112p. (J). 14.95 *(978-1-61628-800-6(0))* Weldon Owen, Inc.

FOOD PLANTS

see Plants, Edible

FOOD POISONING

Faulk, Michelle. The Case of the Undercooked Burger: Annie Biotica Solves Digestive System Disease Crimes. 2013. (Body System Disease Investigations Ser.). 48p. (J). (gr. 5-12). pap. 8.95 *(978-1-4644-0229-6(9))*; lib. bdg. 25.27 *(978-0-7660-3947-6(1))* Enslow Pubs., Inc.

Isle, Mick. Everything You Need to Know about Food Poisoning. 2009. (Need to Know Library). 64p. (gr. 5-5). 58.50 *(978-1-60854-069-3(3))* Rosen Publishing Group, Inc., The.

Landau, Elaine. Food Poisoning & Foodborne Diseases. 2010. (USA TODAY Health Reports: Diseases & Disorders Ser.). (ENG., Illus.). 128p. (gr. 6-12). lib. bdg. 34.60 *(978-0-8225-7290-9(7))* Lerner Publishing Group.

Rauf, Don, et al. What You Can Do About Food Poisoning. 2015. (Contemporary Diseases & Disorders Ser.). (ENG., Illus.). 128p. (J). (gr. 7-7). 37.27 *(978-0-7660-7038-7(7))* Enslow Pubs., Inc.

Rosaler, Maxine. Botulism. (Epidemics Ser.). 64p. 2009. (gr. 5-5). 58.50 *(978-1-61512-274-5(5))* 2004. (Illus.). (YA). (gr. 7-12). lib. bdg. 31.95 *(978-0-8239-4197-1(3))* Rosen Publishing Group, Inc., The.

—Listeriosis. (Epidemics Ser.). 64p. (gr. 5-5). 2009. 58.50 *(978-1-61512-291-2(5))* 2004. (Illus.). lib. bdg. 31.95 *(978-0-8239-4202-2(3))* Rosen Publishing Group, Inc., The.

Silverstein, Alvin, et al. The Food Poisoning Update. 2007. (Disease Update Ser.). (Illus.). 128p. (J). (gr. 3-7). lib. bdg. 33.27 *(978-0-7660-2748-0(1))* Enslow Pubs., Inc.

Taylor-Butler, Christine. Food Safety. 2008. (True Bks.). (ENG.). 48p. (J). pap. 6.95 *(978-0-531-20734-5(X)*, Children's Pr.) Scholastic Library Publishing.

FOOD PRESERVATION

see Food—Preservation

FOOD SERVICE—VOCATIONAL GUIDANCE

Brefere, Lisa M., et al. So You Want to Be a Chef? Your Guide to Culinary Careers. 2nd ed. 2008. (ENG., Illus.). 252p. pap. 46.95 *(978-0-470-08856-2(7)*, Wiley) Wiley, John & Sons, Inc.

Ferguson Publishing Staff, creator. Food. 3rd rev. ed. 2007. (Careers in Focus Ser.). (Illus.). 192p. (gr. 6-12). 32.95 *(978-0-8160-6591-2(8)*, Ferguson Publishing Co.) Facts On File, Inc.

Hubbard, Rita & Hubbard, Rita Lorraine. Getting a Job in the Food Industry. 2013. 80p. (YA). (gr. 9-12). 33.25 *(978-1-4488-9606-6(1))* Rosen Publishing Group, Inc., The.

Machajewski, Sarah. Cool Careers Without College for People Who Love to Cook & Eat. 2013. (New Cool Careers Without College Ser.). (Illus.). 144p. (J). (gr. 7-12). 35.95 *(978-1-4777-1820-9(6))* Rosen Publishing Group, Inc., The.

FOOD SUPPLY

see also Food—Preservation; Meat Industry and Trade

Bailey, Gerry. Farming for the Future. 2011. (Planet SOS Ser.). (Illus.). 48p. (J). (gr. 3-6). pap. 14.05 *(978-1-4339-4967-8(9))*; lib. bdg. 31.95 *(978-1-4339-4966-1(0))* Stevens, Gareth Publishing LLLP. (Gareth Stevens Learning Library).

Baines, John. Food for Life. 2006. (Sustainable Futures Ser.). (Illus.). 48p. (YA). (gr. 5-9). lib. bdg. 32.80 *(978-1-58340-978-7(5)*, 1262622) Black Rabbit Bks.

Baines, John D. Food & Farming. 2009. (J). 32.80 *(978-1-59920-103-0(8))* Black Rabbit Bks.

Barker, Geoff. Hunger. 2010. (Voices Ser.). (YA). (gr. 5-9). 34.25 *(978-1-59920-281-5(6))* Black Rabbit Bks.

Bontempo, Nancy Rogers. Word of Mouth: The Food You Eat. 2011. (Second Nature Ser.). 48p. (J). (gr. 5-8). 26.60 *(978-1-59953-449-7(5))* Norwood Hse. Pr.

Bowden, Rob. Food & Water. 2010. (Development Without Damage Ser.). (YA). (gr. 5-9). 34.25 *(978-1-59920-248-8(4))* Black Rabbit Bks.

Burgan, Michael. Farming Vegetables & Grains, 1 vol. 2011. (Ethics of Food Ser.). (ENG.). 56p. (gr. 6-6). 34.65 *(978-1-4329-5100-9(9))*; pap. 9.99 *(978-1-4329-6190-9(X))* Heinemann-Raintree.

—Making Food Choices, 1 vol. 2011. (Ethics of Food Ser.). (ENG.). 56p. (gr. 6-6). pap. 10.95 *(978-1-4329-6194-7(2))* Heinemann-Raintree.

Chancellor, Deborah. Food Waste. 2010. (Reduce, Reuse, Recycle! Ser.). 32p. (J). (ENG.). pap. 10.60 *(978-1-61532-240-4(X)*, PowerKids Pr.); (gr. 1-5). E-Book 50.50 *(978-1-4488-0363-7(2))*; (Illus.). (gr. 2-5). lib. bdg. 26.50 *(978-1-61532-233-6(7))* Rosen Publishing Group, Inc., The.

Colson, Mary. The Race to Feed the Hungry. 2014. (World in Crisis Ser.). (Illus.). 48p. (J). (gr. 5-8). 30.25 *(978-1-4777-7846-3(2))* Rosen Publishing Group, Inc., The.

Cunningham, Kevin. Surviving Droughts & Famines, 1 vol. 2011. (Children's True Stories: Natural Disasters Ser.). (ENG.). 32p. (gr. 3-3). pap. 8.29 *(978-1-4109-4101-5(9))*; 30.65 *(978-1-4109-4094-0(2))* Heinemann-Raintree. (Raintree Perspectives).

Etingoff, Kim. Corn. 2013. (Feeding the World Ser.: 8). (Illus.). 48p. (J). (gr. 4-18). 19.95 *(978-1-4222-2742-8(1))* Mason Crest.

—Dairy Products. 2013. (J). *(978-1-4222-2741-1(3))*; (Feeding the World Ser.: 8). (Illus.). 48p. (gr. 4-18). 19.95 *(978-1-4222-2743-5(X))* Mason Crest.

—Eggs. 2013. (Feeding the World Ser.: 8). (Illus.). 48p. (J). (gr. 4-18). 19.95 *(978-1-4222-2744-2(8))* Mason Crest.

—Farmed Fish. 2013. (Feeding the World Ser.: 8). (Illus.). 48p. (J). (gr. 4-18). 19.95 *(978-1-4222-2745-9(6))* Mason Crest.

Food Services. 2010. (Career Launcher Ser.). 176p. (C). (gr. 9-18). 34.95 *(978-0-8160-7967-4(6)*, Ferguson Publishing Co.) Facts On File, Inc.

Fridell, Ron. The War on Hunger: Dealing with Dictators, Deserts, & Debt. 2003. (In a Perfect World Ser.). (Illus.). 80p. (gr. 5-8). lib. bdg. 26.90 *(978-0-7613-2650-2(2)*, Twenty-First Century Bks.) Lerner Publishing Group.

Gay, Kathlyn. Food: The New Gold. (ENG., Illus.). 96p. (gr. 6-12). 2015. 34.65 *(978-1-4677-5993-9(7)*, Lerner Digital) 2012. lib. bdg. 31.93 *(978-0-7613-4607-4(4))* Lerner Publishing Group.

Goodman, Polly. Food, Farming, & the Future. 2011. (Earth Alert! Ser.). 32p. (J). (gr. 3-6). lib. bdg. 26.60 *(978-1-4339-6005-5(2))* Stevens, Gareth Publishing LLLP.

Graham, Ian. Farming & the Future. 2010. (Food & Farming Ser.). (Illus.). 32p. (YA). (gr. 4-7). lib. bdg. 25.25 *(978-1-61532-578-8(6))* Rosen Publishing Group, Inc., The.

—Food Technology. 2009. (New Technology Ser.). (YA). (gr. 7-12). 34.25 *(978-1-59920-162-7(3))* Black Rabbit Bks.

Green, Jen. Food & Farming, 1 vol. 2012. (Impact of Environmentalism Ser.). (ENG.). 64p. (gr. 6-10). pap. 10.95 *(978-1-4329-6523-5(9))*; lib. bdg. 35.99 *(978-1-4329-6517-4(4))* Heinemann-Raintree.

Gritzner, Charles F. Feeding a Hungry World. 2009. (Global Connections Ser.). (Illus.). 120p. (gr. 5-8). 35.00 *(978-1-60413-290-8(6)*, Chelsea Hse.) Facts On File, Inc.

Hunnicutt, Susan C. World Hunger. 2006. (At Issue Ser.). (ENG., Illus.). 128p. (gr. 10-12). 39.40 *(978-0-7377-2761-6(6)*, Greenhaven Pr., Inc.) Cengage Gale.

Hunnicutt, Susan C., ed. World Hunger. 2006. (At Issue Ser.). (ENG., Illus.). 91p. (gr. 3-7). pap. 24.45 *(978-0-7377-2762-3(4)*, Greenhaven Pr., Inc.) Cengage Gale.

Jakab, Cheryl. Food Supplies. 2010. (Environment in Focus Ser.). 32p. (gr. 4). 28.50 *(978-1-60870-090-5(9))* Marshall Cavendish Corp.

Kerr, J. B. Food - Ethical Debates in What We Eat. 2008. (Dilemmas in Modern Science Ser.). (ENG., Illus.). 48p. (J). 23.99 *(978-0-237-53367-0(7))* Evans Brothers, Ltd. GBR. Dist: Independent Pubs. Group.

Kukathas, Uma. The Global Food Crisis. 2009. (Current Controversies Ser.). (ENG.). (gr. 10-12). 240p. (J). pap. 40.95 *(978-0-7377-4613-6(0))*; 224p. pap. 32.00 *(978-0-7377-4612-9(2))* Cengage Gale. (Greenhaven Pr., Inc.).

La Bella, Laura. Safety & the Food Supply. 2009. (In the News Ser.). (ENG., Illus.). 64p. (J). (gr. 7-12). pap. 12.95 *(978-1-4358-5364-5(4))*; 64p. (gr. 6-6). 58.50 *(978-1-61513-486-1(7))*; (YA). (gr. 7-12). lib. bdg. 31.95 *(978-1-4358-5036-1(X))* Rosen Publishing Group, Inc., The.

Lanz, Helen. What Shall We Eat? 2012. (Go Green Ser.). 32p. (gr. 3-6). lib. bdg. 28.50 *(978-1-59771-305-4(8))* Sea-To-Sea Pubns.

Lassieur, Allison. Grains. 2015. (Illus.). 32p. (J). lib. bdg. 28.50 *(978-1-60753-497-6(5))* Amicus Publishing.

Macken, JoAnn Early. Take a Closer Look at Bees. 2016. (Core Content Science — Take a Closer Look Ser.). (ENG., Illus.). 40p. (J). (gr. 2-4). lib. bdg. 26.65 *(978-1-63440-052-7(6))* Red Chair Pr.

Maddocks, Steven. World Hunger. 2004. (21st Century Issues Ser.). (Illus.). 48p. (gr. 5-12). lib. bdg. 31.00 *(978-0-8368-5646-0(5)*, Gareth Stevens Secondary Library) Stevens, Gareth Publishing LLLP.

O'Neill, Joseph R. The Irish Potato Famine, 1 vol. 2009. (Essential Events Set 3 Ser.). (ENG., Illus.). 112p. (J). (gr. 6-12). lib. bdg. 35.64 *(978-1-60453-514-3(8))* ABDO Publishing Co.

Peacock, Kathy Wilson & Hendrickson, Mary K. Food Security. 2011. (Global Issues Ser.). (Illus.). 400p. (C). (gr. 9). 45.00 *(978-0-8160-8203-2(0))* Facts On File, Inc.

Perdew, Laura. Eating Local. 2016. (Growing Green Ser.). (ENG., Illus.). 64p. (J). (gr. 6-8). 51.99 *(978-1-4677-9711-5(1)*, Lerner Pubns.) Lerner Publishing Group.

Pollan, Michael. The Omnivore's Dilemma: The Secrets Behind What You Eat. 2015. (ENG., Illus.). 400p. (J). (gr. 5). 18.99 *(978-1-101-99382-8(0))*; pap. 9.99 *(978-1-101-99383-5(9))* Penguin Young Readers Group. (Dial Bks).

Rooney, Anne. Feeding the World. 2010. (World at Risk Ser.). (YA). (gr. 5-9). 34.25 *(978-1-59920-377-5(4))* Black Rabbit Bks.

Singer, Jane E. Meat. 2013. (Feeding the World Ser.: 8). (Illus.). 48p. (J). (gr. 4-18). 19.95 *(978-1-4222-2746-6(4))* Mason Crest.

—Rice. 2013. (Feeding the World Ser.: 8). (Illus.). 48p. (J). (gr. 4-18). 19.95 *(978-1-4222-2747-3(2))* Mason Crest.

—Soybeans. 2013. (Feeding the World Ser.: 8). (Illus.). 48p. (J). (gr. 4-18). 19.95 *(978-1-4222-2748-0(0))* Mason Crest.

—Wheat. 2013. (Feeding the World Ser.: 8). (Illus.). 48p. (J). (gr. 4-18). 19.95 *(978-1-4222-2749-7(9))* Mason Crest.

Solway, Andrew. Cadenas y Redes Alimentarias. 2012. (SPA & ENG.). 48p. (gr. 4-8). pap. 10.95 *(978-1-61810-467-0(5))* Rourke Educational Media.

Sonneborn, Liz. The Great Irish Famine. 2011. (Milestones in Modern World History Ser.). (Illus.). 124p. (C). (gr. 9). 35.00 *(978-1-60413-918-1(8)*, Chelsea Hse.) Facts On File, Inc.

Spilsbury, Richard & Spilsbury, Louise. Feeding the World. 2010. (Food & Farming Ser.). (Illus.). 32p. (YA). (gr. 4-7). lib. bdg. 25.25 *(978-1-61532-579-5(4))* Rosen Publishing Group, Inc., The.

—From Farm to Table. 2010. (Food & Farming Ser.). (Illus.). 32p. (YA). (gr. 4-7). lib. bdg. 25.25 *(978-1-61532-580-1(8))* Rosen Publishing Group, Inc., The.

Stagliano, Katie. Katie's Cabbage. Heid, Karen, illus. 2014. (Young Palmetto Bks.). (ENG.). 40p. 19.95 *(978-1-61117-504-2(6))* Univ. of South Carolina Pr.

Stradling, Jan. Food for All: Level I, 6 vols. (First Explorers Ser.). 24p. (gr. 1-2). 29.95 *(978-0-7699-1445-9(4))* Shortland Pubns. (U. S. A.) Inc.

Tate, Nikki. Down to Earth: How Kids Help Feed the World, 1 vol. (Orca Footprints Ser.). (ENG., Illus.). 48p. (J). (gr. 3-7). 2017. pap. 12.95 *(978-1-4598-1412-7(6))* 2013. 19.95 *(978-1-4598-0423-4(6))* Orca Bk. Pubs. USA.

Top of the Food Chain. 2013. (Top of the Food Chain Ser.). 32p. (J). (gr. k-5). pap. 360.00 *(978-1-61533-881-8(0))*; pap. 60.00 *(978-1-61533-880-1(2))* Windmill Bks.

The True Cost of Food. 2014. (ENG., Illus.). 48p. (J). *(978-0-7787-0484-3(X))* Crabtree Publishing Co.

Veness, Kimberley. Let's Eat: Sustainable Food for a Hungry Planet, 1 vol. 2017. (Orca Footprints Ser.). (ENG., Illus.). 48p. (J). (gr. 3-7). 19.95 *(978-1-4598-0939-0(4))* Orca Bk. Pubs. USA.

Wilson, Michael R. Hunger: Food Insecurity in America. 2009. (In the News Ser.). (Illus.). 64p. (YA). (gr. 7-12). lib. bdg. 31.95 *(978-1-4358-5278-5(8))* Rosen Publishing Group, Inc., The.

—Hunger: Food Insecurity in the United States. 2009. (In the News Ser.). (Illus.). 64p. (J). 77.70 *(978-1-4358-5563-2(9))*; (ENG., (YA). pap. 12.95 *(978-1-4358-5562-5(0))* Rosen Publishing Group, Inc., The.

World Book, Inc. Staff, contrib. by. Food, Water, & Climate Change. 2015. (Illus.). 48p. (J). *(978-0-7166-2712-8(4))* World Bk., Inc.

—Foraging to Supermarkets: A Timeline of Food. 2016. (J). *(978-0-7166-3547-5(X))* World Bk., Inc.

Wroble, Lisa A. Starving: Can We Feed Everyone? 2016. (End of Life As We Know It Ser.). (ENG.). 128p. (J). (gr. 7-8). 37.27 *(978-0-7660-7374-6(2))* Enslow Pubs., Inc.

FOOD TRADE

see Farm Produce—Marketing

FOOLS AND JESTERS—FICTION

Arnold, Tedd, et al. Noodleheads Nightmares. Arnold, Tedd, illus. 2016. (ENG., Illus.). 48p. (J). (gr. 1-5). 15.95 *(978-0-8234-3566-1(0))* Holiday Hse., Inc.

—Noodleheads See the Future. Arnold, Tedd, illus. 2017. (ENG., Illus.). 48p. (J). (gr. 1-5). 15.95 *(978-0-8234-3673-6(X))* Holiday Hse., Inc.

Herbert, Bethany Zohner. The Perfect Fool. 2015. 279p. (YA). pap. 17.99 *(978-1-4621-1620-1(5))* Cedar Fort, Inc./CFI Distribution.

Santillo, LuAnn. Stop Hopping. Santillo, LuAnn, ed. 2003. (Half-Pint Kids Readers Ser.). (Illus.). 7p. (J). (gr. -1-1). pap. 1.00 *(978-1-59256-054-7(7))* Half-Pint Kids, Inc.

Spinner, Stephanie. Damosel: In Which the Lady of the Lake Renders a Frank & Often Startling Account of Her Wondrous Life & Times. 2010. (ENG.). 208p. (YA). (gr. 7). pap. 8.99 *(978-0-553-49511-9(9)*, Knopf Bks. for Young Readers) Random Hse. Children's Bks.

FOOT

Andrus, Aubre. Lotions, Potions, & Polish: DIY Crafts & Recipes for Hands, Nails, & Feet. 2017. (DIY Day Spa Ser.). (ENG., Illus.). 48p. (gr. 4-5). lib. bdg. 31.32 *(978-1-5157-3445-1(5))* Capstone Press of Coughlan Cos.

Arndt, Ingo. Best Foot Forward: Exploring Feet, Flippers, & Claws. Arndt, Ingo, photos by. 2014. (ENG., Illus.). 36p. (J). (gr. k-3). 6.99 *(978-0-8234-3185-4(1))* Holiday Hse., Inc.

Bokhari, Raana. Allah Gave Me Two Hands & Feet. Clarke, Asiya, illus. 2015. (ENG.). 32p. (J). 8.95 *(978-0-86037-348-3(7))* Kube Publishing Ltd. GBR. Dist: Consortium Bk. Sales & Distribution.

Bozzo, Linda. Amazing Animal Feet. (Creature Features Ser.). 24p. 2009. (gr. 2-3). 42.50 *(978-1-61512-066-6(1))* 2008. (Illus.). (J). (gr. 3-7). lib. bdg. 22.60 *(978-1-4042-4167-1(1))* Rosen Publishing Group, Inc., The. (PowerKids Pr.).

Brown, Jonatha A. Animal Feet & Legs. 2006. (Why Animals Look Different Ser.). (Illus.). 24p. (gr. 1-4). lib. bdg. 22.00 *(978-0-8368-6860-9(9)*, Weekly Reader Leveled Readers) Stevens, Gareth Publishing LLLP.

—Las patas y los pies de los animales. 2006. (En que se diferencian los animales (Why Animals Look Different) Ser.). (SPA., Illus.). 24p. (J). (gr. 1-4). lib. bdg. 22.00 *(978-0-8368-7414-3(5)*, Weekly Reader Leveled Readers) Stevens, Gareth Publishing LLLP.

Douglas, Lloyd G. My Legs & Feet. 2004. (Welcome Bks.). (ENG.). 24p. (J). (gr. -1-2). pap. 4.95 *(978-0-516-22130-4(2)*, Children's Pr.) Scholastic Library Publishing.

Enslow, Brian. My Hands & Feet. 2010. (All about My Body Ser.). (Illus.). 24p. (J). 22.60 *(978-0-7660-3816-5(5))*; pap. 7.95 *(978-1-59845-173-3(1))* Enslow Pubs., Inc. (Enslow Elementary).

Hess, Nina. Whose Feet? Kanzler, John, tr. Kanzler, John, illus. 2004. (Step into Reading Ser.). (ENG.). 32p. (J). (gr. -1-1). pap. 3.99 *(978-0-375-82623-8(8)*, Random Hse. Bks. for Young Readers) Random Hse. Children's Bks.

Hulbert, Laura. Who Has These Feet? Brooks, Erik, illus. 2011. (ENG.). 44p. (J). (gr. -1-2). 16.99 *(978-0-8050-8907-3(1)*, 9780805089073, Holt, Henry & Co. Bks. For Young Readers) Holt, Henry & Co.

Hunt, Connie. Hooray for Feet! Melmon, Deborah, illus. 2008. (J). *(978-1-58728-699-5(8)*, Two-Can Publishing) T&N Children's Publishing.

Klingel, Cynthia & Noyed, Robert B. Feet. 2010. (Let's Read about Our Bodies Ser.). (Illus.). 24p. (gr. k-3). pap. 8.15 *(978-1-4339-3360-8(8))*; (J). lib. bdg. 22.00 *(978-1-4339-3359-2(4))* Stevens, Gareth Publishing LLLP.

—Feet / Los Pies. 2010. (Let's Read about Our Bodies / Hablemos del cuerpo humano Ser.). (SPA., Illus.). 24p. (gr. k-3). pap. 8.15 *(978-1-4339-3736-1(0))* Stevens, Gareth Publishing LLLP.

—Feet/Los Pies. 2010. (Let's Read about Our Bodies / Hablemos del cuerpo humano Ser.). (SPA., Illus.). 24p. (J). (gr. k-3). lib. bdg. 22.00 *(978-1-4339-3735-4(2))* Stevens, Gareth Publishing LLLP.

Markle, Sandra. What If You Had Animal Feet? McWilliam, Howard, illus. 2015. (ENG.). 32p. (J). (gr. k-3). pap. 4.99 *(978-0-545-73312-0(X)*, Scholastic Paperbacks) Scholastic, Inc.

Miller, Sara Swan. All Kinds of Feet. 2007. (All Kinds Of Ser.). (Illus.). 48p. (gr. 3-3). lib. bdg. 29.93 *(978-0-7614-2520-5(9))* Marshall Cavendish Corp.

Mitchell, Melanie S. Feet. 2004. (First Step Nonfiction - Animal Traits Ser.). (ENG., Illus.). 8p. (gr. -1-1). pap. 4.95 *(978-0-8225-3912-4(8)*, Lerner Pubns.) Lerner Publishing Group.

Murphy, Julie. I've Got Feet!: Fantastical Feet of the Animal World. Tolson, Hannah, illus. 2017. (ENG.). 32p. (J). (gr. -1-1). 17.99 ***(978-1-68152-195-4(4))*** Amicus.

Prostova, Elena & Shaw, Cathleen. Toe-rrific: A Simple Guide to Creating Healthy & Beautiful Feet. 2005. (Illus.). 72p. pap. 24.95 *(978-0-9745627-0-4(X)*, 1234067) Happy Women Publishing Co.

Randolph, Joanne. Whose Toes Are Those? 2009. (Animal Clues Ser.). 24p. (gr. 1-1). 42.50 *(978-1-61511-435-1(1))*; (Illus.). (J). lib. bdg. 22.60 *(978-1-4042-4452-8(2))* Rosen Publishing Group, Inc., The. (PowerKids Pr.).

—Whose Toes Are Those? De Quién Son Estas Patas? 2009. (Animal Clues / ¿Adivina de Quién Es? Ser.). (ENG & SPA., Illus.). 24p. (J). lib. bdg. 22.60 *(978-1-4358-2529-1(2)*, PowerKids Pr.) Rosen Publishing Group, Inc., The.

—Whose Toes Are Those? / ¿de quién son estas Patas? 2009. (Animal Clues / ¿Adivina de Quién Es? Ser.). (ENG & SPA.). 24p. (gr. 1-1). 42.50 *(978-1-61511-441-2(6)*, Editorial Buenas Letras) Rosen Publishing Group, Inc., The.

Rice, Dona. Marvelous Me: My Feet. 2015. (TIME for KIDS(r) Nonfiction Readers Ser.). (ENG., Illus.). 12p. (gr. k-k). 4.99 *(978-1-4938-2149-5(0))* Teacher Created Materials, Inc.

—Soy Maravilloso. 2016. (Nonfiction Readers Ser.). (SPA., Illus.). 12p. (J). (gr. k-k). pap. 4.99 *(978-1-4938-3030-5(9))* Teacher Created Materials, Inc.

Roza, Greg. Gross Things under Your Feet. 2012. (That's Gross! Ser.). (Illus.). 24p. (J). (gr. 2-5). 22.60 *(978-1-4339-7131-0(3))*; pap. 8.15 *(978-1-4339-7132-7(1))* Stevens, Gareth Publishing LLLP. (Gareth Stevens Learning Library).

Salzmann, Mary Elizabeth. What Has Paws?, 1 vol. 2007. (Creature Features Ser.). (ENG., Illus.). 24p. (gr. -1-3). 25.65 *(978-1-59928-869-7(9)*, Super SandCastle) ABDO Publishing Co.

—What Has Webbed Feet?, 1 vol. 2007. (Creature Features Ser.). (ENG., Illus.). 24p. (gr. -1-3). 25.65 *(978-1-59928-875-8(3)*, Super SandCastle) ABDO Publishing Co.

Souza, Dorothy M. Look What Feet Can Do. 2006. (Look What Animals Can Do Ser.). (Illus.). 48p. (J). (gr. 3-7). lib. bdg. 22.60 *(978-0-7613-9460-0(5)*, Lerner Pubns.) Lerner Publishing Group.

Stewart, Melissa. Fantastic Feet up Close. 2012. (Animal Bodies up Close Ser.). 24p. (J). (gr. k-3). (Illus.). pap. 7.95 *(978-1-4644-0084-1(9))*; 22.60 *(978-0-7660-3890-5(4))* Enslow Pubs., Inc. (Enslow Elementary).

—Give Me a Hand: The Secrets of Hands, Feet, Arms, & Legs. Hamlin, Janet, illus. 2010. (Gross & Goofy Body 2 Ser.). 48p. (gr. 3). lib. bdg. 29.93 *(978-0-7614-4158-8(1))* Marshall Cavendish Corp.

Taylor, Kelda. Look at My Feet Feet Go!, 1 vol. 2009. 15p. pap. 24.95 *(978-1-60749-046-3(3))* America Star Bks.

Tekiela, Stan. Paws & Claws, 1 vol. 2013. (Adventure Boardbook Ser.). (ENG.). 22p. (J). (gr. -1-k). bds. 6.95 *(978-1-59193-425-7(7))* Adventure Pubns.

Terry, Donna. Whose Toes Are Those? 2009. 24p. pap. 11.99 *(978-1-4490-0009-7(6))* AuthorHouse.

Verdick, Elizabeth. Feet Are Not for Kicking. Heinlen, Marieka, illus. 2004. (Best Behavior Ser.). (ENG.). 24p. (J). 7.95 *(978-1-57542-158-2(5))* Free Spirit Publishing, Inc.

Verdick, Elizabeth. Feet Are Not for Kicking / los Pies No Son para Patear. Heinlen, Marieka, illus. 2017. (Best Behavior Ser.). (ENG & SPA.). 24p. (J). (— 1). bds. 7.95 ***(978-1-63198-197-5(8))*** Free Spirit Publishing, Inc.

FOOTBALL

see also Rugby Football; Soccer

The ABC's of Oklahoma Sooner Football. 2003. (Illus.). 32p. (J). *(978-0-9747689-0-8(1))* Little Scribblers Bks., LLC.

Abdo Publishing. Inside College Football Set 2, 1 vol. 2013. (Inside College Football Set 2 Ser.: 8). (ENG.). 48p. (J). (gr. 3-6). lib. bdg. 262.32 *(978-1-61783-650-3(8)*, SportsZone) ABDO Publishing Co.

Anastasio, Dina. What Is the Super Bowl? 2015. (What Is... ? Ser.). lib. bdg. 16.00 *(978-0-606-37549-8(X))* Turtleback Bks.

Anastasio, Dina & dePaola, Tomie. What Is the Super Bowl? Groff, David & McVeigh, Kevin, illus. 2015. (What Was? Ser.). (ENG.). 112p. (J). (gr. 3-7). 5.99 *(978-0-448-48695-6(4)*, Grosset & Dunlap) Penguin Young Readers Group.

Appleby, Alex. Puedo Ser un Jugador de Fútbol / I Can Be a Football Player. 2014. (Cuando Sea Grande / When I Grow Up Ser.). (SPA.). 24p. (J). (gr. k-2). 22.60 *(978-1-4824-0859-1(7))* Stevens, Gareth Publishing LLLP.

, Arsenal Football Club PLC, Arsenal Football Club Plc. The Official Arsenal Ultimate Young Gunners' Book: The Ultimate Guide for the Ultimate Fan! 2014. (ENG., Illus.). 96p. (J). (gr. 1-4). 16.99 *(978-1-78312-007-9(X))* Carlton Bks., Ltd. GBR. Dist: Independent Pubs. Group.

At the Game, 6, Packs. (gr. -1-2). 27.00 *(978-0-7635-9436-7(9))* Rigby Education.

Barber, Phil. Football & Player Safety, Vol. 10. 2016. (All about Professional Football Ser.: Vol. 10). (ENG., Illus.). 64p. (J). (gr. 7-12). 23.95 *(978-1-4222-3578-2(5))* Mason Crest.

Barber, Tiki. Tiki: My Life in the Game & Beyond. 2008. (ENG.). 240p. pap. 15.99 *(978-1-4169-5564-1(X)*, Gallery Bks.) Gallery Bks.

Bethea, Nikole Brooks. The Science of Football with Max Axiom, Super Scientist. 2015. (Science of Sports with Max

Axiom Ser.). (ENG., Illus.). 32p. (gr. 3-4). lib. bdg. 30.65 (978-1-4914-6085-6(7)) Capstone Press of Coughlan Cos.
—The Science of Football with Max Axiom, Super Scientist. Cacau, Caio, illus. 2015. (Science of Sports with Max Axiom Ser.). (ENG.). 32p. (gr. 3-4). pap. 7.95 (978-1-4914-6089-4(X), Graphic Library) Capstone Press of Coughlan Cos.
Bianchi, Mike & Novak, Marisol. Swampmeet: A Gator Counting Book. Marlette, Andy, illus. 2004. 32p. (J). (gr. -1-k). 6.95 (978-1-58261-780-0(5)) Sports Publishing, LLC.
Biskup, Agnieszka. Football: How It Works. 2010. (Science of Sports (Sports Illustrated for Kids) Ser.). (ENG.). 48p. (gr. 3-4). pap. 59.70 (978-1-4296-5108-0(3)) Capstone Press of Coughlan Cos.
Blaine, Richard. Cups, Bowls, & Other Football Championships. 2016. (ENG., Illus.). 32p. (J). (978-0-7787-2293-9(7)) Crabtree Publishing Co.
Bodden, Valerie. Robert Griffin III. 2013. 21p. 23.09 (978-1-60818-475-0(7)) Creative Co., The.
Booth, Tanis. Football. 2009. (In the Zone Ser.). 24p. (J). (gr. 3-5). pap. 8.95 (978-1-60596-127-9(2)); (Illus.). lib. bdg. 24.45 (978-1-60596-126-2(4)) Weigl Pubs., Inc.
Bowker, Paul. Playing Pro Football. 2014. (Playing Pro Sports Ser.). (ENG.). 64p. (gr. 4-8). lib. bdg. 26.60 (978-1-4677-3844-6(1), Lerner Pubns.) Lerner Publishing Group.
Bradley, Michael. Donovan McNabb. 2004. (Benchmark All-Stars 2 Ser.). (Illus.). 48p. (gr. 4). 21.95 (978-0-7614-1756-9(7), Benchmark Bks.) Marshall Cavendish Corp.
Brady, Tom, et al. Tom Brady. 2015. (Quotes from the Greatest Athletes Ser.). (ENG., Illus.). 24p. (J). lib. bdg. 12.95 (978-1-4896-3381-1(2), AV2 by Weigl) Weigl Pubs., Inc.
Bratton, Deboral B. & Bratton, Ashley A. Record-a-Sport Football Sport Organizer. Bratton, Deboral B. & Bratton, Ashley A., eds. Bratton, Ashley A., illus. 2003. (Illus.). (gr. 1-18). 18.95 (978-1-931746-05-2(2)) Sport Your Stuff Corp.
Braun, Eric. Football's Greatest, 1 vol. 2014. (Football's Greatest Ser.). (ENG.). 32p. (gr. 3-9). 111.96 (978-1-4914-0762-2(X)) Capstone Press of Coughlan Cos.
—Super Bowl Surprises. 2016. (Everything Super Bowl Ser.). (ENG.). 32p. (gr. 3-4). lib. bdg. 27.99 (978-1-5157-2634-0(7)) Capstone Press of Coughlan Cos.
—Super Football Infographics. 2015. (Super Sports Infographics Ser.). (ENG., Illus.). 32p. (J). (gr. 3-5). pap. 8.99 (978-1-4677-7576-2(2)); lib. bdg. 26.65 (978-1-4677-5231-2(2)) Lerner Publishing Group. (Lerner Pubns.).
Brock, Ted. Inside Pro Football Media, Vol. 10. 2016. (All about Professional Football Ser.: Vol. 10). (ENG., Illus.). 64p. (J). (gr. 7-12). 23.95 (978-1-4222-3581-2(5)) Mason Crest.
Brown, Jonatha A. Football. 2004. (My Favorite Sport Ser.). (Illus.). 24p. (gr. 1-4). pap. 8.15 (978-0-8368-4346-0(0)); lib. bdg. 22.00 (978-0-8368-4339-2(8)) Stevens, Gareth Publishing LLLP. (Weekly Reader Leveled Readers).
Buckley, James, Jr. Fantasy Football, Vol. 10. 2016. (All about Professional Football Ser.: Vol. 10). (ENG.). 64p. (J). (gr. 7-12). 23.95 (978-1-4222-3577-5(7)) Mason Crest.
Burgess, Zack. Meet the Carolina Panthers. 2016. (Big Picture Sports Ser.). (ENG., Illus.). 24p. (J). (gr. k-3). lib. bdg. 22.60 (978-1-59953-741-2(9)) Norwood Hse. Pr.
Byerly, Robbie. Football (2Y) Byerly, Robbie, illus. 2010. (1-3Y Sports Ser.). (ENG., Illus.). 16p. (J). pap. 5.99 (978-1-61541-520-5(3)) American Reading Co.
Campbell, Dave. Story of the Orange Bowl, 1 vol. 2016. (ENG., Illus.). 48p. (J). **(978-1-62403-889-1(1)**, SportsZone) ABDO Publishing Co.
Challen, Paul. What Does a Defensive Back Do? 2014. (Football Smarts Ser.). 32p. (J). (gr. 3-6). 26.25 (978-1-4777-6990-4(0), PowerKids Pr.) Rosen Publishing Group, Inc., The.
—What Does a Running Back Do? 2014. (Football Smarts Ser.). (Illus.). 32p. (J). (gr. 3-6). 26.25 (978-1-4777-6994-2(3), PowerKids Pr.) Rosen Publishing Group, Inc., The.
Challen, Paul C. What Does a Linebacker Do? 2014. (Football Smarts Ser.). (Illus.). 32p. (J). (gr. 3-6). lib. bdg. 26.25 (978-1-4777-7006-1(2), PowerKids Pr.) Rosen Publishing Group, Inc., The.
—What Does a Quarterback Do? 2014. (Football Smarts Ser.). (Illus.). 32p. (J). (gr. 3-6). lib. bdg. 26.25 (978-1-4777-6986-7(2), PowerKids Pr.) Rosen Publishing Group, Inc., The.
Clay, Kathryn. Cool Football Facts. 2011. (Cool Sports Facts Ser.). (ENG.). 24p. (gr. k-1). pap. 41.70 (978-1-4296-7385-3(0), Pebble Plus) Capstone Press of Coughlan Cos.
—Cool Football Facts (Datos Geniales Sobre Fútbol Americano) Strictly Spanish LLC. Staff, tr. from SPA. 2012. (Datos Geniales Sobre Deportes/Cool Sports Facts Ser.). (ENG & MUL., Illus.). 24p. (gr. k-1). lib. bdg. 26.65 (978-1-4296-9214-4(6)) Capstone Press of Coughlan Cos.
Corporate Contributor Staff & Flatt, Lizann. The Economics of the Super Bowl. 2013. (ENG.). 48p. (J). (978-0-7787-7972-8(6)); pap. (978-0-7787-7977-3(7)) Crabtree Publishing Co.
Crosby, Jim. Devotions for the Armchair Quarterback. 2004. 109p. per. 12.95 (978-1-932338-33-1(0)) Lifevest Publishing, Inc.
Crossingham, John. Football in Action. 2008. (FRE., Illus.). 32p. (J). pap. 9.95 (978-2-89579-206-2(2)) Bayard Canada Livres CAN. Dist: Crabtree Publishing Co.
—Futbol Americano en Accion. 2005. (Deportes en Accion Ser.). (SPA., Illus.). 32p. (J). (gr. 6-9). pap. (978-0-7787-8619-1(6)) Crabtree Publishing Co.
Crumley, Daniel Wade. 4 -0n- 4 Flag Football Training Manual: Flag Football. 2005. spiral bd. 19.99 (978-0-9772203-0-4(3)) Go Flag Football.
Diemer, Lauren. Rose Bowl. 2009. (Sporting Championships Ser.). 32p. (gr. 4-6). (J). pap. 8.95 (978-1-60596-639-7(8)); (Illus.). (YA). lib. bdg. 26.00 (978-1-60596-638-0(X)) Weigl Pubs., Inc.
Doeden, Matt. All about Football. 2015. (All about Sports Ser.). (ENG.). 32p. (gr. 1-2). lib. bdg. 27.32 (978-1-4914-1995-3(4)) Capstone Press of Coughlan Cos.
—Fantasy Football Math: Using Stats to Score Big in Your League. 2016. (Fantasy Sports Math Ser.). (ENG., Illus.). 32p. (gr. 3-4). lib. bdg. 27.99 (978-1-5157-2168-0(X)) Capstone Press of Coughlan Cos.
—Play Football Like a Pro: Key Skills & Tips. 2010. (Play Like the Pros (Sports Illustrated for Kids) Ser.). (ENG.). 32p. (gr. 3-4). pap. 7.19 (978-1-4296-5646-7(8)); pap. 41.70 (978-1-4296-5959-8(9)); lib. bdg. 26.65 (978-1-4296-4825-7(2)) Capstone Press of Coughlan Cos.
Doeden, Matt & Stewart, Mark. Peyton Manning. 2009. (Sports Heroes & Legends Ser.). (ENG.). (gr. 5-12). pap. 56.72 (978-0-7613-4809-2(3)) Lerner Publishing Group.
Douglas, Peter. Football: Toughness on the Gridiron. 2017. (Preparing for Game Day Ser.: Vol. 10). (ENG.). (YA). (gr. 7-12). 24.95 **(978-1-4222-3917-9(9))** Mason Crest.
Durrie, Karen. Football. 2011. (J). 27.13 (978-1-61690-939-0(0)) Weigl Pubs., Inc.
—El Fútbol Americano. 2012. (J). (978-1-61913-200-9(1)) Weigl Pubs., Inc.
Edwards, Ethan. Meet LaDainian Tomlinson: Football's Fastest Running Back. 2009. (All-Star Players Ser.). (Illus.). 32p. (YA). (gr. 4-7). lib. bdg. 25.25 (978-1-4042-4491-7(3)) Rosen Publishing Group, Inc., The.
Ellenport, Craig. The Super Bowl: More Than a Game, Vol. 10. 2016. (All about Professional Football Ser.). (Illus.). 64p. (J). (gr. 7). 23.95 (978-1-4222-3586-7(6)) Mason Crest.
Fantasy Chronicles, 5 vols., Set. Incl. Fairies & Elves. Knudsen, Shannon. lib. bdg. 27.93 (978-0-8225-9979-1(1)); Fantastical Creatures & Magical Beasts. Knudsen, Shannon. (Illus.). lib. bdg. 27.93 (978-0-8225-9987-6(2)); Giants, Trolls, & Ogres. Knudsen, Shannon. (Illus.). lib. bdg. 27.93 (978-0-8225-9985-2(6)); Mermaids & Mermen. Knudsen, Shannon. lib. bdg. 27.93 (978-0-8225-9981-4(3)); Wizards & Witches. Kerns, Ann. (Illus.). lib. bdg. 27.93 (978-0-8225-9983-8(X)); 48p. (gr. 4-7). 2009. Set lib. bdg. 139.65 (978-0-8225-9977-7(5), Lerner Pubns.) Lerner Publishing Group.
Flynn, Brendan. Football Time! 2016. (Bumba Books (tm) — Sports Time! Ser.). (ENG., Illus.). 24p. (J). (gr. -1-1). 25.32 (978-1-5124-1433-2(6)) Lerner Publishing Group.
—¡Hora de Fútbol Americano! 2017. (Bumba Books (tm) en Español — ¡Hora de Deportes! (Sports Time!) Ser.). (SPA., Illus.). 24p. (J). (gr. -1-1). 25.32 (978-1-5124-2872-8(8)) Lerner Publishing Group.
Football Smarts. 2014. (Football Smarts Ser.). 32p. (J). (gr. 3-6). 157.50 (978-1-4777-7010-8(0), PowerKids Pr.) Rosen Publishing Group, Inc., The.
Frederick, Shane. The Best of Everything Football Book, 1 vol. 2010. (All-Time Best of Sports Ser.). (ENG.). 64p. (gr. 3-4). lib. bdg. 34.65 (978-1-4296-5466-1(X)) Capstone Press of Coughlan Cos.
—Football: The Math of the Game, 1 vol. 2011. (Sports Math Ser.). (ENG.). 48p. (gr. 5-6). pap. 8.19 (978-1-4296-7319-8(2)); pap. 47.70 (978-1-4296-7320-4(6)); lib. bdg. 31.99 (978-1-4296-6567-4(X)) Capstone Press of Coughlan Cos.
—The Technology of Football, 1 vol. 2013. (High-Tech Sports Ser.). (ENG.). 48p. (gr. 3-9). pap. 8.95 (978-1-62065-910-6(7)); pap. 53.70 (978-1-62065-911-3(5)); lib. bdg. 31.99 (978-1-4296-9953-2(1)) Capstone Press of Coughlan Cos.
—The Ultimate Collection of Pro Football Records. 2012. (For the Record Ser.). (ENG.). 64p. (gr. 4-6). pap. 53.70 (978-1-4296-9433-9(5)); lib. bdg. 34.65 (978-1-4296-8578-8(6)) Capstone Press of Coughlan Cos.
—Wacky Football Trivia: Fun Facts for Every Fan. 2016. (Wacky Sports Trivia Ser.). (ENG., Illus.). 32p. (gr. 3-4). lib. bdg. 27.99 (978-1-5157-1993-9(6)) Capstone Press of Coughlan Cos.
Frisch, Aaron. St. Louis Rams. 2011. (Super Bowl Champions Ser.). (J). (gr. 1-3). 24.25 (978-1-60818-027-1(1)) Creative Co., The.
—Tampa Bay Buccaneers. 2011. (Super Bowl Champions Ser.). (J). (gr. 1-3). 24.25 (978-1-60818-029-5(8)) Creative Co., The.
Gibson, Karen. Adrian Peterson. 2011. (Robbie Reader Ser.). (Illus.). 32p. (J). (gr. 2-5). lib. bdg. 25.70 (978-1-61228-060-8(9)) Mitchell Lane Pubs., Inc.
Gifford, Clive. Football. 2009. (Tell Me about Sports Ser.). 32p. (gr. 3-18). 28.50 (978-0-7614-4456-5(4)) Marshall Cavendish Corp.
Gigliotti, Jim. Football. 2008. (21st Century Skills Innovation Library: Innovation in Sports Ser.). (ENG., Illus.). 32p. (gr. 4-8). lib. bdg. 28.50 (978-1-60279-257-9(7), 200126) Cherry Lake Publishing.
Gilbert, Sara. The Story of the NFL. 2011. (Built for Success Ser.). (Illus.). (J). (gr. 5-9). 34.25 (978-1-60818-063-9(8)) Creative Co., The.
Gitlin, Martin. Football Skills: How to Play Like a Pro. 2008. (How to Play Like a Pro Ser.). (Illus.). 48p. (J). (gr. 3-6). lib. bdg. 25.27 (978-0-7660-3203-3(5)) Enslow Pubs., Inc.
Glaser, Jason. Tom Brady. 2008. (Sports Idols Ser.). (Illus.). 24p. (J). (gr. 2-5). lib. bdg. 22.60 (978-1-4042-4184-8(1)) Rosen Publishing Group, Inc., The.
Goldsworthy, Kaite. Grey Cup. 2011. 24p. (YA). (gr. 2-4). (978-1-77071-664-3(5)); pap. (978-1-77071-670-4(X)) Weigl Educational Pubs. Ltd.
Graves, Will. Best NFL Defenses of All Time, 1 vol. 2013. (NFL's Best Ever Ser.). (ENG., Illus.). 64p. (J). (gr. 3-6). lib. bdg. 32.79 (978-1-61783-907-8(8), SportsZone) ABDO Publishing Co.
—Best NFL Offenses of All Time, 1 vol. 2013. (NFL's Best Ever Ser.). (ENG., Illus.). 64p. (J). (gr. 3-6). lib. bdg. 32.79 (978-1-61783-909-2(4), SportsZone) ABDO Publishing Co.
Greenhaven Press Staff. Professional Football. 2015. (Current Controversies Ser.). (ENG.). 224p. (gr. 10-12). pap. 32.00 (978-0-7377-7425-2(8), Greenhaven Pr., Inc.) Cengage Gale.
Greve, Tom. Linebackers. 2009. (Illus.). 24p. (J). pap. 7.95 (978-1-60694-826-2(1)) Rourke Educational Media.
Guess McKerley, Jennifer, ed. Football. 2011. (Science Behind Sports Ser.). (Illus.). 128p. (YA). (gr. 9-12). lib. bdg. 34.45 (978-1-4205-0594-8(7)) Cengage Gale.
Hantula, Richard. Science at Work in Football. 2011. (Benchmark Rockets: Sports Science Ser.). 32p. (gr. 4). 28.50 (978-0-7614-4456-5(4)) Marshall Cavendish Corp.
Herzog, Brad. Little Football. Bowles, Doug, illus. 2011. (Little Sports Ser.). (ENG.). 22p. (J). 7.95 (978-1-58536-546-3(7)) Sleeping Bear Pr.
—T Is for Touchdown: A Football Alphabet. Braught, Mark, illus. 2006. (Sports Alphabet Ser.). (ENG.). 40p. (J). (gr. 1-4). pap. 7.95 (978-1-58536-337-7(5), 202300) Sleeping Bear Pr.
—T Is for Touchdown: A Football Alphabet. Stacy, Alan & Braught, Mark, illus. 2004. (Sports Ser.). (ENG.). 40p. (J). (gr. -1-5). 16.95 (978-1-58536-233-2(6)) Sleeping Bear Pr.
Hetrick, Hans. Football's Record Breakers. 2017. (Record Breakers Ser.). (ENG., Illus.). 32p. (gr. 3-4). lib. bdg. 27.32 (978-1-5157-3761-2(6)) Capstone Press of Coughlan Cos.
Hetrick, Hans, et al. Winner Takes All. 2012. (Winner Takes All Ser.). (ENG.). 32p. (gr. 3-4). pap. 166.80 (978-1-4296-9447-6(5)) Capstone Press of Coughlan Cos.
Hill, Bert & Watterson, Steve. Conditioning: How to Get in Football Shape. 2007. (Illus.). 136p. (YA). pap. 20.00 (978-1-4223-6674-5(X)) DIANE Publishing Co.
Hoena, Blake. Football. 2015. (J). lib. bdg. 25.65 (978-1-62031-178-3(X), Bullfrog Bks.) Jump! Inc.
Howell, Brian. Football, 1 vol. 2012. (ENG.). 64p. 32.79 (978-1-61783-142-3(5), SportsZone) ABDO Publishing Co.
Hurley, Michael. Football, 1 vol. 2013. (Fantastic Sports Facts Ser.). (ENG.). 32p. (gr. 1-3). pap. 8.29 (978-1-4109-5115-1(4)); lib. bdg. 29.99 (978-1-4109-5108-3(1)) Heinemann-Raintree. (Read Me!).
In the Zone, 6 vols., Set. Incl. Baseball. Craats, Rennay. (gr. 3-5). lib. bdg. 24.45 (978-1-60596-122-4(1)); Basketball. Craats, Rennay. (gr. 3-5). lib. bdg. 24.45 (978-1-60596-128-6(0)); Football. Booth, Tanis. (gr. 3-5). lib. bdg. 24.45 (978-1-60596-126-2(4)); Hockey. Johnstone, Robb. (gr. 3-5). lib. bdg. 24.45 (978-1-60596-130-9(2)); Skateboarding. Craats, Rennay. (gr. 3-5). lib. bdg. 24.45 (978-1-60596-120-0(5)); Soccer. Rediger, Pat. lib. bdg. 24.45 (978-1-60596-124-8(8)); (Illus.). 24p. (J). 2009. 2010. Set lib. bdg. 146.70 (978-1-60596-670-0(3)) Weigl Pubs., Inc.
Jacobs, Greg. Kids' Football Book: The All-Time Greats, Legendary Teams, Today's Superstars & Tips on Playing Like a Pro. 2008. (Everything(r) Kids Ser.). (ENG., Illus.). 144p. (J). pap. 8.99 (978-1-59869-565-6(7)) Adams Media Corp.
Kalman, Bobbie & Crossingham, John. Huddle up Football. 2007. (Sports Starters Ser.). (ENG., Illus.). 32p. (J). (gr. 3-7). lib. bdg. (978-0-7787-3137-5(5)); (gr. 1-5). pap. (978-0-7787-3169-6(3)) Crabtree Publishing Co.
—Trabajo en Equipo en el Fútbol Americano. 2008. (SPA.). 32p. (J). pap. (978-0-7787-8648-1(X)); lib. bdg. (978-0-7787-8639-9(0)) Crabtree Publishing Co.
Kelley, K. C. Football's No. 1s! 2016. (ENG.). 32p. (J). (gr. 2-5). pap. 3.99 (978-1-338-03274-1(7)) Scholastic, Inc.
Kennedy, Mike. Football. 2003. (Watts Library). (Illus.). 64p. (J). 25.50 (978-0-531-12272-3(7), Watts, Franklin) Scholastic Library Publishing.
Koestler-Grack, Rachel A. Tom Brady. 2008. (Football Superstars Ser.). (Illus.). 151p. (YA). (gr. 7-12). lib. bdg. 30.00 (978-0-7910-9689-5(0)) Facts On File, Inc.
Kopp, Megan. Football. 2011. (J). (gr. 4-6). pap. 13.95 (978-1-61690-705-1(3), AV2 by Weigl); (Illus.). 32p. (YA). (gr. 2-5). 28.55 (978-1-61690-700-6(2)) Weigl Pubs., Inc.
Kortemeier, Tom. Pro Football by the Numbers. 2016. (Pro Sports by the Numbers Ser.). (ENG., Illus.). 32p. (gr. 3-4). lib. bdg. 27.99 (978-1-4914-9060-0(8), Edge Bks.) Capstone Press of Coughlan Cos.
Kristof-Mohn, Beti. The First Football ABC Pretzel Book. 2004. (J). spiral bd. 9.95 net. (978-0-9717148-0-9(0)) Hardway Pr.
Laínez, René Colato. Juguemos Al Futbol y Al Football!/Let's Play Futbol & Football! 2014. (ENG & SPA., Illus.). 31p. (J). (gr. -1-2). 16.00 (978-0-88272-328-0(6), Alfaguara) Santillana USA Publishing Co., Inc.
Latimer, Clay. VIP Pass to a Pro Football Game Day: From the Locker Room to the Press Box (and Everything in Between), 1 vol. 2011. (Game Day (Sports Illustrated for Kids) Ser.). (ENG.). 32p. (gr. 3-4). pap. 8.19 (978-1-4296-6285-7(9)); pap. 47.70 (978-1-4296-6449-3(5)) Capstone Press of Coughlan Cos.
Laughlin, Kara L. Flag Football. 2016. (Beginning Sports Ser.). (ENG.). 24p. (J). (gr. k-3). 27.07 (978-1-5038-0775-4(4), 210603) Child's World, Inc., The.
Layden, Joe & Preller, James. NFL: Super Bowl - Behind the Scenes. 2004. (ENG., Illus.). 32p. (J). pap. 5.99 (978-0-439-69178-9(8)) Scholastic, Inc.
Lindeen, Mary. Let's Play Football! 2015. (BeginningtoRead Ser.). (ENG., Illus.). 32p. (J). (gr. k-2). lib. bdg. 22.60 (978-1-59953-684-2(6)) Norwood Hse. Pr.
—Let's Play Football. 2015. (BeginningtoRead Ser.). (ENG., Illus.). 32p. (J). (gr. k-2). pap. 11.94 (978-1-60357-744-1(0)) Norwood Hse. Pr.
Liverpool Football Club Staff. The Official Liverpool FC Ultimate Junior Reds' Book. 2014. (ENG., Illus.). 96p. (J). (gr. -1-3). pap. 16.99 (978-1-78312-008-6(8)) Carlton Bks., Ltd. GBR. Dist: Independent Pubs. Group.
Loh-Hagan, Virginia. Fantasy Football League. 2016. (D. I. Y. Make It Happen Ser.). (ENG., Illus.). 32p. (J). (gr. 4-8). 29.93 (978-1-63470-499-1(1), 207727) Cherry Lake Publishing.
Lourdes-Pitt, H. H. Brett Favre. 2009. (Superstars of Pro Football Ser.). 64p. (YA). (gr. 5-18). pap. 9.95 (978-1-4222-1982-9(8)) Mason Crest.
Lynette, Rachel. Footballs. 2016. (J). (978-1-4896-4531-9(4)) Weigl Pubs., Inc.
—Footballs Before the Store. McGeehan, Dan, illus. 2012. (Before the Store Ser.). (ENG.). 32p. (J). (gr. 2-5). lib. bdg. 29.93 (978-1-60973-675-0(3), 201251) Child's World, Inc., The.
Macmillan Children's Books Staff & Pan Macmillan Limited Staff. Match! Euro Diary 2016: Record Every Game of Your Euro Journey! 2016. (ENG.). 32p. (J). (gr. 2-9). 9.99 (978-1-5098-2473-1(1)) Pan Macmillan GBR. Dist: Independent Pubs. Group.
Mahaney, Ian F. The Math of Football. 2011. (J). 49.50 (978-1-4488-2691-9(8), PowerKids Pr.); (J). pap. 8.25 (978-1-4488-2690-2(X), PowerKids Pr.); (YA). (gr. 2-5). lib. bdg. 22.60 (978-1-4488-2553-0(9)) Rosen Publishing Group, Inc., The.
Malloy, Devin. FootballTalk: Conversation Cards for the Entire Family. 2008. (Tabletalk Conversation Cards Ser.). (Illus.). (J). (gr. 4-7). 6.00 (978-1-57281-630-5(9)) U.S. Games Systems, Inc.
Manning, Peyton, et al. Peyton Manning. 2015. (Quotes from the Greatest Athletes Ser.). (ENG., Illus.). 24p. (J). lib. bdg. 12.95 (978-1-4896-3373-6(1), AV2 by Weigl) Weigl Pubs., Inc.
Marshall, Sarah. Learning Football with the Hokie Bird. 2011. 32p. 14.95 (978-0-9844399-0-4(0)) Mascot Bks., Inc.
Marsico, Katie. Football. 2008. (21st Century Skills Library: Real World Math Ser.). (ENG., Illus.). 32p. (gr. 4-8). lib. bdg. 28.50 (978-1-60279-247-0(X), 200198) Cherry Lake Publishing.
Mason, Tyler. Story of the Rose Bowl, 1 vol. 2016. (ENG., Illus.). 48p. (J). **(978-1-62403-890-7(5)**, 1391405, SportsZone) ABDO Publishing Co.
Mattern, Joanne. At the Football Game. 2006. (Rosen Publishing Group's Reading Room Collection). (Illus.). 16p. (J). (gr. 3-7). lib. bdg. 18.75 (978-1-4042-3339-3(3), PowerKids Pr.) Rosen Publishing Group, Inc., The.
—At the Football Game: Learning the Symbols , And = 2009. (Math for the REAL World Ser.). 16p. (gr. 2-3). pap. 7.05 (978-0-8239-8875-4(9), Rosen Classroom); 37.50 (978-1-60851-372-7(6), PowerKids Pr.) Rosen Publishing Group, Inc., The.
—I Know Football. 2013. (21st Century Basic Skills Library: I Know Sports Ser.). (ENG., Illus.). 24p. (J). (gr. k-3). 22.79 (978-1-62431-399-8(X), 202716); pap. 12.79 (978-1-62431-475-9(9), 202718) Cherry Lake Publishing.
McClellan, Ray. Football. 2009. (My First Sports Ser.). (ENG., Illus.). 24p. (J). (gr. 2-5). lib. bdg. 25.95 (978-1-60014-194-2(3), Blastoff! Readers) Bellwether Media.
McFee, Shane. Let's Play Football. (Let's Get Active Ser.). 24p. 2009. (gr. 2-3). 42.50 (978-1-61514-253-8(3)) 2008. (Illus.). (J). (gr. 3-7). lib. bdg. 22.60 (978-1-4042-4192-3(2)) Rosen Publishing Group, Inc., The. (PowerKids Pr.).
McIntosh, J. S. Football. 2010. (Getting the Edge Ser.). 96p. (YA). lib. bdg. 24.95 (978-1-4222-1733-7(7)) Mason Crest.
Murray, Stuart A. P. Score with Football Math. 2013. (Score with Sports Math Ser.). 48p. (J). lib. bdg. 25.27 (978-0-7660-4173-8(5)); (gr. 3-4). pap. 8.95 (978-1-4644-0285-2(X)) Enslow Pubs., Inc. (Enslow Elementary).
Nagelhout, Ryan. Aaron Rodgers, Vol. 1. 2014. (Today's Great Quarterbacks Ser.). (ENG.). 32p. (J). (gr. 1-1). pap. 10.50 (978-1-4824-0120-2(7)) Stevens, Gareth Publishing LLLP.
—Becoming a Pro Football Player. 2015. (Going Pro Ser.). (ENG., Illus.). 32p. (J). (gr. 3-4). pap. 10.50 (978-1-4824-2062-3(7)) Stevens, Gareth Publishing LLLP.
—Football: Who Does What? 2017. (Sports: What's Your Position? Ser.). 32p. (J). (gr. 3-4). pap. 63.00 **(978-1-5382-0425-2(8))**; pap. 10.50 **(978-1-5382-0424-5(X))** Stevens, Gareth Publishing LLLP.
—Football's Greatest Records, 1 vol. 2015. (ENG., Illus.). 32p. (J). lib. bdg. 26.25 (978-1-4994-0231-5(7), PowerKids Pr.) Rosen Publishing Group, Inc., The.
—Me Encanta el Fútbol Americano / I Love Football. 2014. (My Favorite Sports Ser.). (SPA.). 24p. (J). (gr. k-2). 22.60 (978-1-4824-0850-8(3)) Stevens, Gareth Publishing LLLP.
—Robert Griffin III, Vol. 1. 2014. (Today's Great Quarterbacks Ser.). (ENG.). 32p. (J). (gr. 1-1). pap. 10.50 (978-1-4824-0484-5(2)) Stevens, Gareth Publishing LLLP.
—The Science of Football. 2015. (Sports Science Ser.). (ENG.). 32p. (J). (gr. 4-5). 26.25 (978-1-4994-1132-4(4)); pap. 10.00 (978-1-4994-1066-2(2)) Rosen Publishing Group, Inc., The. (PowerKids Pr.).
—Talk Like a Football Player. 2016. (Let's Talk Sports! Ser.). 00032p. (J). pap. 10.50 **(978-1-4824-5700-1(8))** Stevens, Gareth Publishing LLLP.
Nagelhout, Ryan. 20 Fun Facts about Football. 2016. (Fun Fact File: Sports! Ser.). (ENG.). 32p. (J). (gr. 2-3). pap. 10.50 (978-1-4824-3974-8(3)) Stevens, Gareth Publishing LLLP.
Nelson, Robin. Football Is Fun! 2013. (First Step Nonfiction - Sports Are Fun! Ser.). (ENG., Illus.). 24p. (J). (gr. k-2). pap. 6.95 (978-1-4677-1537-9(9)); lib. bdg. 23.93 (978-1-4677-1103-6(9), Lerner Pubns.) Lerner Publishing Group.
—From Leather to Football. 2014. (Start to Finish: Sports Gear Ser.). (Illus.). 24p. (gr. k-3). lib. bdg. 23.93 (978-1-4677-3890-3(5), Lerner Pubns.) Lerner Publishing Group.
Newman, Elizabeth. Instant Replay. Goehner, Amy Lennard, ed. (Illus.). 32p. (J). (gr. 2-8). pap. 3.99 (978-1-886749-79-5(5)) Sports Illustrated For Kids.
Nicolai, Gregory. The Science of Football: The Top Ten Ways Science Affects the Game. 2016. (Top 10 Science Ser.). (ENG.). 32p. (gr. 3-4). lib. bdg. 27.99 (978-1-4914-8219-3(2)) Capstone Press of Coughlan Cos.
Omoth, Tyler. First Source to Football: Rules, Equipment, & Key Playing Tips. 2016. (First Sports Source Ser.). (ENG., Illus.). 24p. (gr. 1-2). lib. bdg. 25.32 (978-1-4914-8421-0(7), First Facts) Capstone Press of Coughlan Cos.
Orr, Tamra. Chris Johnson. 2011. (Robbie Reader Ser.). (Illus.). 32p. (J). (gr. 2-5). lib. bdg. 25.70 (978-1-61228-064-6(1)) Mitchell Lane Pubs., Inc.
Perritano, John. Football Numbers: Graphing Data. 2013. (IMath Ser.). 32p. (J). (gr. 3-4). lib. bdg. 22.60 (978-1-59953-566-1(1)) Norwood Hse. Pr.
—Football Numbers: Graphing Numbers. 2013. (IMath Ser.). (Illus.). 32p. (J). (gr. 3-4). pap. 11.94 (978-1-60357-505-8(7)) Norwood Hse. Pr.
Peterson, Brian C. Pro Football Players in the News: Two Sides of the Story, Vol. 10. 2016. (All about Professional Football Ser.: Vol. 10). (ENG., Illus.). 64p. (J). (gr. 7-12). 23.95 (978-1-4222-3584-3(X)) Mason Crest.
Rappoport, Ken. Tim Tebow: A Football Star Who Cares. 2013. (Sports Stars Who Care Ser.). 48p. (J). 25.27 (978-0-7660-4297-1(9)) Enslow Pubs., Inc.
Rustad, Martha E. H. Down the Field 10, 20, 30: A Football Counting by Tens Book. 2017. (1, 2, 3 Count with Me Ser.). (ENG., Illus.). 24p. (J). (gr. k-2). pap. 8.99 (978-1-68152-112-1(1)) Amicus.
—Down the Field 10, 20, 30: A Football Counting by Tens Book. 2016. (1, 2, 3 Count with Me Ser.). (ENG., Illus.). 24p. (J). (gr. k-3). 20.95 (978-1-60753-921-6(7), Amicus Readers) Amicus Publishing.
Salzmann, Mary Elizabeth. Football by the Numbers, 1 vol. 2010. (Team Sports by the Numbers Ser.). (ENG.). 24p. (J). (gr. k-3). lib. bdg. 24.21 (978-1-60453-769-7(8), SandCastle) ABDO Publishing Co.
Savage, Jeff. Adrian Peterson. 2010. pap. 39.62 (978-0-7613-6964-6(3)) Lerner Publishing Group.

—Drew Brees. 2010. pap. 39.62 *(978-0-7613-6967-7(8))* Lerner Publishing Group.

—Football Super Stats. 2017. (Pro Sports Stats Ser.). (ENG., Illus.). (J). (gr. 3-6). lib. bdg. 27.99 ***(978-1-5124-3408-8(6))*** Lerner Publishing Group.

—Michael Vick. 2005. (Amazing Athletes Ser.). (Illus.). 32p. (J). (gr. 3-7). pap. 6.95 *(978-0-8225-2955-2(6))* Lerner Publishing Group.

—Tom Brady. 2005. (Amazing Athletes Ser.). (Illus.). 32p. (J). (gr. 4-7). per. 5.95 *(978-0-8225-2956-9(4))* Lerner Publishing Group.

—Tony Romo. 2010. pap. 39.62 *(978-0-7613-6971-4(6))* Lerner Publishing Group.

Savage, Jeff, photos by. Play-by-Play Football. 2005. (Play-by-Play Ser.). (Illus.). 80p. (gr. 4-8). lib. bdg. 23.93 *(978-0-8225-3935-3(7))* Lerner Publishing Group.

Scheff, Matt. Amazing NFL Stories: 12 Highlights from NFL History. 2015. (NFL at a Glance Ser.). (ENG., Illus.). 32p. (gr. 3-5). *(978-1-63235-151-7(X)*, 12-Story Library) Pr. Room Editions LLC.

—Best NFL Quarterbacks of All Time, 1 vol. 2013. (NFL's Best Ever Ser.). (ENG., Illus.). 64p. (J). (gr. 3-6). lib. bdg. 32.79 *(978-1-61783-910-8(8)*, SportsZone) ABDO Publishing Co.

—Best NFL Running Backs of All Time, 1 vol. 2013. (NFL's Best Ever Ser.). (ENG., Illus.). 64p. (J). (gr. 3-6). lib. bdg. 32.79 *(978-1-61783-912-2(4)*, SportsZone) ABDO Publishing Co.

—Classic NFL Games: 12 Thrillers from NFL History. 2015. (NFL at a Glance Ser.). (ENG., Illus.). 32p. (gr. 3-5). *(978-1-63235-154-8(4)*, 12-Story Library) Pr. Room Editions LLC.

—Incredible Football Records. 2016. (Incredible Sports Records Ser.). (ENG.). 24p. (J). (gr. 2-5). 28.50 *(978-1-5038-0888-1(2)*, 210677) Child's World, Inc., The.

Schuette, Sarah L. A Football Cookbook: Simple Recipes for Kids, 1 vol. 2012. (First Cookbooks Ser.). (ENG.). 24p. (gr. 1-2). lib. bdg. 25.32 *(978-1-4296-7620-5(5)*, First Facts) Capstone Press of Coughlan Cos.

—Football Frenzy: A Spot-It Challenge, 1 vol. 2013. (Spot It Ser.). (ENG.). 32p. (gr. 1-2). lib. bdg. 27.32 *(978-1-62065-062-2(2)*, Aplus Bks.) Capstone Press of Coughlan Cos.

Schuh, Mari C. Football. 2017. (Spot Sports Ser.). (ENG.). 16p. (gr. k-3). 17.95 ***(978-1-68151-086-6(3))*** Amicus Publishing.

Sheinkin, Steve. Undefeated: Jim Thorpe & the Carlisle Indian School Football Team. Hsu, Connie, ed. 2017. (ENG., Illus.). 288p. (J). 19.99 *(978-1-59643-954-2(8)*, 9781596439542) Roaring Brook Pr.

Smith, Brenda. A Football Goalpost Killed My Son. 2008. 76p. pap. *(978-1-84747-679-1(1))* Chipmunkapublishing.

Sommers, Michael. Football in the Big 12. 2009. (Inside College Football Ser.). 48p. (gr. 5-6). 53.00 *(978-1-61513-520-2(0)*, Rosen Reference) Rosen Publishing Group, Inc., The.

—The NFL: Steroids & Human Growth Hormone. 2009. (Disgraced! the Dirty History of Performance-Enhancing Drugs in Sports Ser.). (Illus.). 48p. (YA). (gr. 5-9). 29.25 *(978-1-4358-5304-1(0)*, 1300477) Rosen Publishing Group, Inc., The.

Sterling Children's, Sterling. My First Football Book. 2015. (First Sports Ser.). (ENG., Illus.). 22p. (J). (— 1). bds. 6.95 *(978-1-4549-1488-4(2))* Sterling Publishing Co., Inc.

Stewart, Mark. Football. 2009. (Ultimate 10: Sports Ser.). 48p. (ENG.). (J). (gr. 4-8). pap. 10.50 *(978-1-4339-2207-7(X))*; (YA). (gr. 5-9). lib. bdg. 31.00 *(978-0-8368-9159-1(7))* Stevens, Gareth Publishing LLLP.

Stewart, Mark & Kennedy, Mike. Touchdown: The Power & Precision of Football's Perfect Play. 2009. (Spectacular Sports Ser.). (ENG.). 64p. (gr. 5-12). 33.27 *(978-0-8225-8751-4(3))* Lerner Publishing Group.

Storden, Thom. Amazing Football Records, 1 vol. 2014. (Epic Sports Records Ser.). (ENG.). 32p. (gr. 1-2). lib. bdg. 26.65 *(978-1-4914-0743-1(3))* Capstone Press of Coughlan Cos.

Stuckey, Rachel. Be a Force on the Field: Skills, Drills, & Plays. 2016. (ENG., Illus.). 32p. (J). *(978-0-7787-2291-5(0))* Crabtree Publishing Co.

Suen, Anastasia. La Historia Del Futbol Americano. 2004. (Historia de Los Deportes (Sports History) Ser.). (SPA & ENG., Illus.). 24p. (J). (gr. 3-6). lib. bdg. 22.60 *(978-0-8239-6869-5(3)*, Editorial Buenas Letras) Rosen Publishing Group, Inc., The.

Sweeny, Sheila. Wacky Football Facts to Kick Around. Safro, Jill, ed. Haggerty, Tim, illus. Date not set. 32p. (Orig.). (J). (gr. k-3). pap. *(978-1-886749-17-7(5))* Sports Illustrated For Kids.

Swope, Bob. Teach'n Beginning Defensive Football Drills, Plays, & Games Free Flow Handbook. 2013. 84p. pap. 19.95 *(978-0-9860361-1-8(0))* Jacobob Pr., LLC.

Temple, Ramey. Tampa Bay Buccaneers. 2015. (Illus.). 32p. (J). pap. *(978-1-4896-0899-4(0))* Weigl Pubs., Inc.

The Editors of Sports Illustrated Kids. My First Book of Football: A Rookie Book. 2015. (Sports Illustrated Kids Rookie Bks.). (ENG., Illus.). 48p. (J). (gr. -1-17). 11.99 *(978-1-61893-151-1(2))* Time Inc. Bks.

Torres, John Albert. Top 25 Football Skills, Tips, & Tricks. 2011. (Top 25 Sports Skills, Tips, & Tricks Ser.). (Illus.). 48p. (J). (gr. 2-5). lib. bdg. 25.27 *(978-0-7660-3858-5(0))*; (gr. 4-18). pap. 8.95 *(978-1-59845-355-3(6))* Enslow Pubs., Inc.

Tustison, Matt. Awesome NFL Records: 12 Hard-to-Reach Marks. 2015. (NFL at a Glance Ser.). (ENG., Illus.). 32p. (J). (gr. 3-5). *(978-1-63235-156-2(0)*, 12-Story Library) Pr. Room Editions LLC.

Van Pelt, Don & Wingate, Brian. An Insider's Guide to Football. 2014. (Sports Tips, Techniques, & Strategies Ser.). (Illus.). 48p. (J). (gr. 5-8). pap. 11.75 *(978-1-4777-8600-0(7)*, Rosen Reference) Rosen Publishing Group, Inc., The.

Wacholtz, Anthony. Picture a Touchdown: A Football Drawing Book, 1 vol. Ray, Mike, illus. 2013. (Drawing with Sports Illustrated Kids Ser.). (ENG.). 64p. (gr. 5-7). 33.99 *(978-1-4765-3104-5(8))* Capstone Press of Coughlan Cos.

Walters, John. Inside College Football: Preparing for the Pros, Vol. 10. 2016. (All about Professional Football Ser.: Vol. 10). (ENG., Illus.). 64p. (J). (gr. 7-12). 23.95 *(978-1-4222-3579-9(3))* Mason Crest.

—Inside High School Football: A Changing Tradition, Vol. 10. 2016. (All about Professional Football Ser.: Vol. 10). (ENG., Illus.). 64p. (J). (gr. 7-12). 23.95 *(978-1-4222-3580-5(7))* Mason Crest.

Weakland, Mark. Fast, Strong, Fearless: Football Adjectives. 2015. (Football Words Ser.). (ENG., Illus.). 32p. (gr. 2-4). lib. bdg. 27.32 *(978-1-62065-175-9(0))* Capstone Press of Coughlan Cos.

—Football ABC, 1 vol. 2013. (SI Kids Rookie Bks.). (ENG.). (gr. 1-2). 20p. bds. 7.95 *(978-1-4296-9965-5(5))*; (Illus.). 32p. lib. bdg. 27.32 *(978-1-4296-9958-7(2))* Capstone Press of Coughlan Cos.

—Football Colors, 1 vol. 2013. (SI Kids Rookie Bks.). (ENG.). (gr. 1-2). 20p. bds. 7.95 *(978-1-4296-9966-2(3))*; 32p. lib. bdg. 27.32 *(978-1-4296-9959-4(0))* Capstone Press of Coughlan Cos.

—Football Opposites, 1 vol. 2013. (SI Kids Rookie Bks.). (ENG., (gr. 1-2). Illus.). 20p. bds. 7.95 *(978-1-4296-9967-9(1))*; 32p. lib. bdg. 27.32 *(978-1-4296-9960-0(4))* Capstone Press of Coughlan Cos.

—Football Words. 2015. (Football Words Ser.). (ENG.). 32p. (gr. 2-4). 109.28 *(978-1-4914-6962-0(5))* Capstone Press of Coughlan Cos.

—Pass, Catch, Tackle: Football Verbs. 2015. (Football Words Ser.). (ENG., Illus.). 32p. (gr. 2-4). lib. bdg. 27.32 *(978-1-62065-159-9(9))* Capstone Press of Coughlan Cos.

—SI Kids Rookie Books: Football. 2013. (SI Kids Rookie Bks.). (ENG.). (gr. 1-2). 20p. bds. 23.85 *(978-1-4296-9969-3(8))*; 32p. lib. bdg. 81.96 *(978-1-4296-9961-7(2))* Capstone Press of Coughlan Cos.

—SI Kids Rookie Books: Football & Hockey. 2013. (SI Kids Rookie Bks.). (ENG.). (gr. 1-2). 32p. lib. bdg. 163.92 *(978-1-4765-3744-3(5))*; 20p. bds. 39.75 *(978-1-4765-3743-6(7))* Capstone Press of Coughlan Cos.

—Stadium, Jersey, Player: Football Nouns. 2015. (Football Words Ser.). (ENG., Illus.). 32p. (gr. 2-4). lib. bdg. 27.32 *(978-1-62065-174-2(2))* Capstone Press of Coughlan Cos.

What Does a Lineman Do? 2014. (Football Smarts Ser.). (Illus.). 32p. (J). (gr. 3-6). lib. bdg. 26.25 *(978-1-4777-6998-0(6)*, PowerKids Pr.) Rosen Publishing Group, Inc., The.

What Does a Receiver Do? 2014. (Football Smarts Ser.). (Illus.). 32p. (J). (gr. 3-6). lib. bdg. 26.25 *(978-1-4777-7002-3(X)*, PowerKids Pr.) Rosen Publishing Group, Inc., The.

Whiting, Jim. Liverpool FC. 2016. (Illus.). 24p. (J). *(978-1-60818-802-4(7)*, Creative Education) Creative Co., The.

—Real Madrid. 2016. (Illus.). 24p. (J). *(978-1-60818-804-8(3)*, Creative Education) Creative Co., The.

Wilner, Barry. Best NFL Defensive Players of All Time, 1 vol. 2013. (NFL's Best Ever Ser.). (ENG., Illus.). 64p. (J). (gr. 3-6). lib. bdg. 32.79 *(978-1-61783-908-5(6)*, SportsZone) ABDO Publishing Co.

—Best NFL Receivers of All Time, 1 vol. 2013. (NFL's Best Ever Ser.). (ENG., Illus.). 64p. (J). (gr. 3-6). lib. bdg. 32.79 *(978-1-61783-911-5(6)*, SportsZone) ABDO Publishing Co.

Wilson, Danny. Lots & Lots of Orange: A Trip to Neyland Stadium. Wilson, Danny, illus. 2003. (Illus.). 24p. (J). 8.95 *(978-0-9743968-0-4(X))* Satellite Studio.

Wingate, Brian. Football: Rules, Tips, Strategy, & Safety. (Sports from Coast to Coast Ser.). 48p. 2009. (gr. 6-6). 53.00 *(978-1-60853-124-0(4)*, Rosen Reference) 2007. (Illus.). (J). (gr. 3-7). lib. bdg. 29.25 *(978-1-4042-0993-0(X))* Rosen Publishing Group, Inc., The.

Wiseman, Blaine. Football. 2010. (Record Breakers Ser.). (Illus.). 24p. (YA). (gr. 3-6). lib. bdg. 27.13 *(978-1-61690-103-5(9))*; (J). (gr. 4-6). pap. 12.95 *(978-1-61690-104-2(7))* Weigl Pubs., Inc.

Wood, Kristen. Find Albert Alberta Too. 2009. 36p. 19.95 *(978-1-935159-11-7(9))* My Campus Adventure, Inc.

—Find Reveille. 2009. 36p. 19.95 *(978-1-935159-08-7(9))* My Campus Adventure, Inc.

—Find Uga Hairy Dawg Too. 2009. 36p. 19.95 *(978-1-935159-09-4(7))* My Campus Adventure, Inc.

World of Football. 2012. (Collins Big Cat Ser.). (ENG.). 16p. (J). pap., wbk. ed. 4.99 *(978-0-00-747286-4(2))* HarperCollins Pubs. Ltd. GBR. Dist: Independent Pubs. Group.

Wright, John D. Football. 2005. (Sports Injuries Ser.). (Illus.). 64p. (YA). lib. bdg. 19.95 *(978-1-59084-632-2(X))* Mason Crest.

Wyatt, James. Football. 2012. (On the Team Ser.). (ENG.). 24p. (J). (gr. 2-5). pap. 8.15 *(978-1-4339-6442-8(2))*; lib. bdg. 22.60 *(978-1-4339-6440-4(6))* Stevens, Gareth Publishing LLLP. (Gareth Stevens Learning Library).

Yomtov, Nel. The Science of a Spiral. 2015. (21st Century Skills Library: Full-Speed Sports Ser.). (ENG., Illus.). 32p. (J). (gr. 4-7). 29.93 *(978-1-63362-585-3(0)*, 206524) Cherry Lake Publishing.

Yuen, Kevin. The 10 Most Intense College Football Rivalries. 2008. 14.99 *(978-1-55448-545-1(2))* Scholastic Library Publishing.

FOOTBALL—BIOGRAPHY

Abdo Publishing, creator. Football's Greatest Stars. 2015. (Football's Greatest Stars Ser.: Vol. 6). (ENG.). 32p. (J). (gr. 4-7). lib. bdg. 162.42 *(978-1-62403-823-5(9))* ABDO Publishing Co.

Alexander, Markus. Mesut Özil Superstar. 2012. 74p. pap. *(978-3-942654-37-1(7))* Baltic Sea Pr.

Anderson, Jameson. Aaron Rodgers, 1 vol. 2014. (Awesome Athletes Ser.). (ENG.). 32p. (gr. 8-12). 27.07 *(978-1-62403-335-3(0))* ABDO Publishing Co.

—Clay Matthews, 1 vol. 2014. (Awesome Athletes Ser.). (ENG.). 32p. (gr. 8-12). 27.07 *(978-1-62403-334-6(2))* ABDO Publishing Co.

—Colin Kaepernick, 1 vol. 2014. (Awesome Athletes Ser.). (ENG.). 32p. (gr. 8-12). 27.07 *(978-1-62403-331-5(8))* ABDO Publishing Co.

—Johnny Manziel, 1 vol. 2014. (Awesome Athletes Ser.). (ENG.). 32p. (J). (gr. 8-12). lib. bdg. 27.07 *(978-1-62403-333-9(4)*, Checkerboard Library) ABDO Publishing Co.

—Peyton Manning, 1 vol. 2014. (Awesome Athletes Ser.). (ENG., Illus.). 32p. (gr. 8-12). 27.07 *(978-1-62403-332-2(6))* ABDO Publishing Co.

—Russell Wilson, 1 vol. 2014. (Awesome Athletes Ser.). (ENG.). 32p. (J). (gr. 8-12). lib. bdg. 27.07 *(978-1-62403-337-7(7)*, Checkerboard Library) ABDO Publishing Co.

Anderson, Michael. Football & Its Greatest Players. 2011. (J). lib. bdg. 31.70 *(978-1-61530-511-7(4))* Rosen Publishing Group, Inc., The.

Angst, Frank. Chad Johnson. 2009. (Superstars of Pro Football Ser.). (Illus.). 64p. (YA). (gr. 5-18). lib. bdg. 22.95 *(978-1-4222-0556-3(8))* Mason Crest.

Anniss, Matt. Peyton & Eli Manning in the Community, 1 vol., 1. 2014. (Making a Difference: Athletes Who Are Changing the World Ser.). (ENG.). 48p. (J). (gr. 5-8). 25.85 *(978-1-62275-165-5(5))* Rosen Publishing Group, Inc., The.

—Robert Griffin III in the Community, 1 vol., 1. 2014. (Making a Difference: Athletes Who Are Changing the World Ser.). (ENG.). 48p. (J). (gr. 5-8). 25.85 *(978-1-62275-175-4(2))* Rosen Publishing Group, Inc., The.

Appleby, Alex. I Can Be a Football Player. 2014. (When I Grow Up Ser.). 24p. (J). (gr. k-2). 22.60 *(978-1-4824-0748-8(5))* Stevens, Gareth Publishing LLLP.

Aretha, David. Aaron Rodgers: Champion Football Star. 2017. (Sports Star Champions Ser.). 48p. (J). (gr. 5-6). lib. bdg. 27.93 ***(978-0-7660-8716-3(6))*** Enslow Pubs., Inc.

—Colin Kaepernick. 2015. (Football Heroes Making a Difference Ser.). (ENG.). 24p. (J). (gr. 1-6). lib. bdg. 22.61 *(978-1-62724-544-9(8))* Bearport Publishing Co., Inc.

—Joe Flacco. 2015. (Football Heroes Making a Difference Ser.). (ENG.). 24p. (J). (gr. 1-6). lib. bdg. 22.61 *(978-1-62724-545-6(6))* Bearport Publishing Co., Inc.

—Top 10 Quarterbacks in Football. 2016. (Sports Greats Ser.). (Illus.). 48p. (J). pap. 11.70 *(978-0-7660-8316-5(0))* Enslow Pubs., Inc.

Aretha, David A. Tiki Barber. 2008. (Football Superstars Ser.). (Illus.). 136p. (YA). (gr. 7-12). 30.00 *(978-0-7910-9836-3(2))* Facts On File, Inc.

Artell, Mike. Drew Brees: Football Superstar, 1 vol. 2011. (Superstar Athletes Ser.). (ENG.). 24p. (gr. 1-2). lib. bdg. 25.32 *(978-1-4296-6565-0(3))* Capstone Press of Coughlan Cos.

—Peyton Manning: Football Superstar, 1 vol. 2011. (Superstar Athletes Ser.). (ENG.). 24p. (gr. 1-2). pap. 7.29 *(978-1-4296-7311-2(7))*; pap. 41.70 *(978-1-4296-7312-9(5))*; lib. bdg. 25.32 *(978-1-4296-6564-3(5))* Capstone Press of Coughlan Cos.

Barber, Ronde & Barber, Tiki. Go Long! 2008. (Barber Game Time Bks.). (ENG.). 160p. (J). (gr. 3-7). 15.99 *(978-1-4169-3619-0(X)*, Simon & Schuster/Paula Wiseman Bks.) Simon & Schuster/Paula Wiseman Bks.

Barber, Tiki & Barber, Ronde. By My Brother's Side. Root, Barry, illus. 2004. (ENG.). 32p. (J). (gr. 1-5). 17.99 *(978-0-689-86559-6(7)*, Simon & Schuster/Paula Wiseman Bks.) Simon & Schuster/Paula Wiseman Bks.

—Game Day. Root, Barry, illus. 2005. (ENG.). 32p. (J). (gr. k-5). 17.99 *(978-1-4169-0093-1(4)*, Simon & Schuster/Paula Wiseman Bks.) Simon & Schuster/Paula Wiseman Bks.

—Kickoff! 2008. (Barber Game Time Bks.). (ENG.). 176p. (J). (gr. 3-7). pap. 7.99 *(978-1-4169-7080-4(0)*, Simon & Schuster/Paula Wiseman Bks.) Simon & Schuster/Paula Wiseman Bks.

—Teammates. Root, Barry, illus. (ENG.). 32p. (J). (gr. 1-5). 2011. 7.99 *(978-1-4424-1262-0(3))* 2006. 16.95 *(978-1-4169-2489-0(2))* Simon & Schuster/Paula Wiseman Bks. (Simon & Schuster/Paula Wiseman Bks.).

Barrington, Richard. Tom Brady: Super Bowl Champion. 2015. (Living Legends of Sports Ser.). (ENG.). 48p. (J). (gr. 5-6). pap. 14.05 *(978-1-68048-120-4(7))*; (Illus.). 25.85 *(978-1-68048-119-8(3))* Rosen Publishing Group, Inc., The. (Britannica Educational Publishing).

Bednar, Chuck. Tony Romo. 2013. (J). *(978-1-4222-2726-8(X))* 2007. (YA). (gr. 5-18). pap. 9.95 *(978-1-4222-0835-9(4))* Mason Crest.

Berman, Ron & McFadden, Stephen. T-Lloyd: In the Trenches. 2013. (Av2 Audio Chapter Bks.). (ENG., Illus.). 69p. (J). (gr. 4-7). lib. bdg. 27.13 *(978-1-62127-991-4(X)*, AV2 by Weigl) Weigl Pubs., Inc.

Bernstein, Ross. Sports Great Daunte Culpepper. 2003. (Sports Great Bks.). (Illus.). 64p. (J). lib. bdg. 23.94 *(978-0-7660-2037-5(1))* Enslow Pubs., Inc.

Bodden, Valerie. The Big Time - Calvin Johnson. 2014. (Big Time Ser.). (ENG., Illus.). 24p. (J). (gr. 1-3). pap. 9.99 *(978-1-62832-076-3(1)*, Creative Paperbacks) Creative Co., The.

—Calvin Johnson. 2015. (J). *(978-1-60818-494-1(3)*, Creative Education) Creative Co., The.

Bradley, Michael. Pro Football's Underdogs: Players & Teams Who Shocked the Football World. 2017. (Sports Shockers! Ser.). (ENG.). 32p. (gr. 3-4). lib. bdg. 27.99 ***(978-1-5157-8048-9(1))*** Capstone Press of Coughlan Cos.

Brady, Tom, et al. Tom Brady. 2015. (Quotes from the Greatest Athletes Ser.). (ENG., Illus.). 24p. (J). lib. bdg. 28.55 *(978-1-4896-3380-4(4)*, AV2 by Weigl) Weigl Pubs., Inc.

Braun, Eric. Football's Greatest Receivers, 1 vol. 2014. (Football's Greatest Ser.). (ENG.). 32p. (gr. 3-4). 27.99 *(978-1-4914-0760-8(3))* Capstone Press of Coughlan Cos.

—Football's Greatest Running Backs, 1 vol. 2014. (Football's Greatest Ser.). (ENG.). 32p. (gr. 3-4). lib. bdg. 27.99 *(978-1-4914-0759-2(X))* Capstone Press of Coughlan Cos.

—Super Bowl Records. 2016. (Everything Super Bowl Ser.). (ENG., Illus.). 32p. (gr. 3-4). lib. bdg. 27.99 *(978-1-5157-2636-4(3))* Capstone Press of Coughlan Cos.

—Tom Brady. 2017. (Sports All-Stars Ser.). (ENG.). 32p. (J). (gr. 2-5). 12.99 ***(978-1-5124-3798-0(0)***, Lerner Pubns.); 39.99 ***(978-1-5124-2830-8(2)***, Lerner Pubns.); 39.99 ***(978-1-5124-3797-3(2)***, Lerner Pubns.); (Illus.). 26.65 *(978-1-5124-2579-6(6))* Lerner Publishing Group.

Brian Urlacher. 2009. (Amazing Athletes Ser.). (gr. 4-7). pap. 6.95 *(978-1-58013-791-1(1)*, First Avenue Editions) Lerner Publishing Group.

Brignall, Richard. China Clipper: Pro Football's First Chinese-Canadian Player, Normie Kwong, 1 vol. 2010. (Lorimer Recordbooks Ser.). (ENG., Illus.). 152p. (YA). (gr. 7-12). mass mkt. 9.95 *(978-1-55277-527-1(5)*, 9781552775271) Lorimer, James & Co., Ltd., Pubs. CAN. Dist: Casemate Pubs. & Bk. Distributors, LLC.

Brignall, Richard & Sherrard, Brent. China Clipper: Pro Football's First Chinese-Canadian Player, Normie Kwong, 1 vol. 2010. (Lorimer Recordbooks Ser.). (ENG., Illus.). 152p. (YA). (gr. 7-12). lib. bdg. 16.95 *(978-1-55277-528-8(3)*, 9781552775288) Lorimer, James & Co., Ltd., Pubs. CAN. Dist: Casemate Pubs. & Bk. Distributors, LLC.

Bryant, Howard. Legends: The Best Players, Games, & Teams in Football. 2016. (ENG., Illus.). 320p. (J). (gr. 3-7). 8.99 *(978-0-14-751256-7(5)*, Puffin Books) Penguin Young Readers Group.

Buckley, Jim. Von Miller & the Denver Broncos: Super Bowl 50. 2016. (Super Bowl Superstars Ser.). (ENG.). 24p. (J). (gr. 1-6). 16.96 *(978-1-944102-96-8(5))* Bearport Publishing Co., Inc.

Carlisle, Brady. Tony Dungy. (Sharing the American Dream Ser.). 64p. (YA). (gr. 7-12). 2009. (Illus.). 22.95 *(978-1-4222-0588-4(6))* 2007. pap. 9.95 *(978-1-4222-0743-7(9))* Mason Crest.

Chatlien, Michael. Donovan McNabb. (Superstars of Pro Football Ser.). (Illus.). 64p. (YA). 2009. (gr. 7-12). lib. bdg. 22.95 *(978-1-4222-0559-4(2))* 2007. (gr. 5-18). pap. 9.95 *(978-1-4222-0829-8(X))* Mason Crest.

Christopher, Matt. Drew Brees. 2015. (Great Americans in Sports Ser.). (J). lib. bdg. 16.00 *(978-0-606-37525-2(2))* Turtleback Bks.

—Great Americans in Sports: Drew Brees. 2015. (ENG., Illus.). 160p. (J). (gr. 3-7). pap. 5.99 *(978-0-316-29666-3(X))* Little, Brown Bks. for Young Readers.

—On the Field With... Peyton & Eli Manning. 2008. (ENG.). 144p. (J). (gr. 3-7). pap. 5.99 *(978-0-316-03696-2(X))* Little, Brown Bks. for Young Readers.

Colin Kaepernick. 2014. (Amazing Athletes Ser.). (ENG., Illus.). 32p. (J). (gr. 2-5). lib. bdg. 25.26 *(978-1-4677-3674-9(0)*, Lerner Pubns.) Lerner Publishing Group.

Collie, Ashley Jude. Gridiron Greats: 8 of Today's Hottest NFL Stars. (Sports Illustrated for Kids Bks). 176p. (gr. 7-12). 2009. 63.90 *(978-1-60853-147-9(3))* 2005. (Illus.). (YA). lib. bdg. 33.25 *(978-0-8239-3691-5(0))* Rosen Publishing Group, Inc., The.

Corporate Contributor. Drew Brees. 2012. (ENG.). 32p. (J). *(978-0-7787-7616-1(6))*; pap. *(978-0-7787-7629-1(8))* Crabtree Publishing Co.

Crompton, Samuel Willard. John Elway. 2008. (Football Superstars Ser.). (Illus.). 152p. (J). (gr. 7-12). lib. bdg. 30.00 *(978-0-7910-9604-8(1))* Facts On File, Inc.

—Peyton Manning. 2008. (Football Superstars Ser.). (Illus.). 152p. (J). (gr. 6-12). 30.00 *(978-0-7910-9605-5(X)*, Chelsea Hse.) Facts On File, Inc.

Currie, Stephen. Adrian Peterson. 2012. (Superstars of Pro Football Ser.). 64p. (J). 22.95 *(978-1-4222-2724-4(3))* Mason Crest.

Danakas, John. Choice of Colours: The Pioneering African-American Quarterbacks Who Changed the Face of Football. 2007. (Lorimer Recordbooks Ser.). (ENG., Illus.). (YA). 120p. (gr. 4-9). 16.95 *(978-1-55028-993-0(4)*, 9781550289930); 128p. (gr. 7-12). 9.95 *(978-1-55028-991-6(8)*, 9781550289916) Lorimer, James & Co., Ltd., Pubs. CAN. Dist: Casemate Pubs. & Bk. Distributors, LLC.

DeMarco, Tony. Ed McCaffrey: Catching a Star. 2003. (SuperStar Ser.: Vol. 1). 96p. (gr. 4-7). 4.95 *(978-1-58261-170-9(X))* Sports Publishing, LLC.

DiPrimio, Pete. Drew Brees. 2010. (Blue Banner Biography Ser.). (Illus.). 32p. (YA). (gr. 4-7). lib. bdg. 25.70 *(978-1-58415-911-7(1))* Mitchell Lane Pubs., Inc.

—Eli Manning. 2008. (Robbie Reader Ser.). (Illus.). 32p. (YA). (gr. 2-5). lib. bdg. 25.70 *(978-1-58415-726-7(7))* Mitchell Lane Pubs., Inc.

—Peyton Manning. 2015. (ENG., Illus.). 32p. (J). 26.50 *(978-1-62469-092-1(0))* Purple Toad Publishing, Inc.

—Tom Brady. 2008. (Robbie Reader Ser.). (Illus.). 32p. (YA). (gr. 2-5). lib. bdg. 25.70 *(978-1-58415-718-2(6))* Mitchell Lane Pubs., Inc.

Doeden, Matt. Doug Flutie. 2008. pap. 58.95 *(978-0-8225-9398-0(X))* Lerner Publishing Group.

—Doug Flutie. 2007. (Sports Heroes & Legends Ser.). (Illus.). 106p. (YA). (gr. 7-12). lib. bdg. 30.60 *(978-0-8225-7162-9(5))* Twenty First Century Bks.

—Eli Manning: Sports Heroes & Legends. 2008. (Sports Heroes & Legends Ser.). (YA). (gr. 7-12). 29.27 *(978-0-7613-4171-0(4))* Lerner Publishing Group.

—Football Legends in the Making, 1 vol. 2014. (Legends in the Making Ser.). (ENG.). 32p. (gr. 3-4). lib. bdg. 27.99 *(978-1-4765-4064-1(0))* Capstone Press of Coughlan Cos.

—Football's Greatest Defenders, 1 vol. 2014. (Football's Greatest Ser.). (ENG.). 32p. (gr. 3-4). lib. bdg. 27.99 *(978-1-4914-0761-5(1))* Capstone Press of Coughlan Cos.

—Football's Greatest Quarterbacks, 1 vol. 2014. (Football's Greatest Ser.). (ENG.). 32p. (gr. 3-4). lib. bdg. 27.99 *(978-1-4914-0758-5(1))* Capstone Press of Coughlan Cos.

—Luke Kuechly. 2017. (Sports All-Stars Ser.). (ENG.). 32p. (J). (gr. 2-5). 12.99 ***(978-1-5124-3789-8(1)***, Lerner Pubns.); 39.99 ***(978-1-5124-2829-2(9)***, Lerner Pubns.); 39.99 ***(978-1-5124-3788-1(3)***, Lerner Pubns.); (Illus.). 26.65 *(978-1-5124-2584-0(2))* Lerner Publishing Group.

—Peyton Manning. 2008. (Sports Heroes & Legends Ser.). (YA). (gr. 7-12). lib. bdg. 30.60 *(978-0-8225-9041-5(7))* Twenty First Century Bks.

—Tim Tebow: Football Superstar. 2012. (Superstar Athletes Ser.). (ENG.). 24p. (gr. 1-2). pap. 41.70 *(978-1-62065-625-9(6))*; (Illus.). pap. 7.29 *(978-1-62065-624-2(8))* Capstone Press of Coughlan Cos.

—Tom Brady. 2009. (Sports Heroes & Legends Ser.). (ENG.). 120p. (gr. 5-12). 30.60 *(978-0-7613-4226-7(5))* Lerner Publishing Group.

—Tom Brady: Unlikely Champion. 2011. (USA TODAY Lifeline Biographies Ser.). (ENG.). 112p. (gr. 6-12). lib. bdg. 34.60 *(978-0-7613-6423-8(4))* Lerner Publishing Group.

—Tony Dungy. 2009. (Sports Heroes & Legends Ser.). (ENG.). 120p. (gr. 5-12). 30.60 *(978-0-7613-4225-0(7))* Lerner Publishing Group.

—The World's Greatest Football Players, 1 vol. 2010. (World's Greatest Sports Stars (Sports Illustrated for Kids) Ser.). (ENG.). 32p. (gr. 2-3). pap. 8.95 *(978-1-4296-4871-4(6))*; pap. 53.70 *(978-1-4296-5104-2(0))*; lib. bdg. 27.99 *(978-1-4296-3924-8(5))* Capstone Press of Coughlan Cos.

Doeden, Matt & Savage, Jeff. Eli Manning. 2009. (Sports Heroes & Legends Ser.). (ENG.). (gr. 5-12). pap. 56.72 *(978-0-7613-4808-5(5))* Lerner Publishing Group.

Donnelly, Karen. Deacon Jones. (Football Hall of Famers Ser.). 112p. (gr. 5-8). 2009. 63.90 *(978-1-61512-624-8(4))* 2003. (Illus.). (YA). lib. bdg. 34.60 *(978-0-8239-3606-9(6))* Rosen Publishing Group, Inc., The. (Rosen Reference).

Dougherty, Denis. Michael Vick. 2003. (Awesome Athletes Ser.). (J). 22.78 *(978-1-59197-487-1(9))* ABDO Publishing Co.

Dougherty, Terri & Hillstrom, Kevin. Brett Favre. 2008. (People in the News Ser.). (ENG., Illus.). 128p. (gr. 7-12). lib. bdg. 39.40 *(978-1-4205-0124-7(0)*, LML02109-245438) Cengage Gale.

Dunn, Jeremy K. Ray Lewis. 2013. (J). *(978-1-4222-2722-0(7))* Mason Crest.

Edwards, Ethan. Arian Foster: Football's Ultimate Rusher, 1 vol., 1. 2014. (All-Star Players Ser.). (ENG.). 32p. (J). (gr. 3-6). 26.25 *(978-1-4777-2916-8(X)*, PowerKids Pr.) Rosen Publishing Group, Inc., The.

—Calvin Johnson: Football's Megatron. 2014. (All-Star Players Ser.). (ENG.). 32p. (J). (gr. 3-6). 26.25 *(978-1-4777-2917-5(8)*, PowerKids Pr.) Rosen Publishing Group, Inc., The.

—Meet Ladainian Tomlinson: Football's Fastest Running Back. 2009. (All-Star Players Ser.). 32p. (gr. 4-5). 47.90 *(978-1-61511-288-3(X)*, PowerKids Pr.) Rosen Publishing Group, Inc., The.

—Meet Tom Brady: Football's Famous Quarterback. 2009. (All-Star Players Ser.). 32p. (gr. 4-5). 47.90 *(978-1-61511-296-8(0)*, PowerKids Pr.); (Illus.). (YA). lib. bdg. 25.25 *(978-1-4042-4492-4(1))* Rosen Publishing Group, Inc., The.

Ellenport, Craig. Ladainian Tomlinson: All-Pro on & off the Field. 2006. (Sports Stars with Heart Ser.). (Illus.). 128p. (J). (gr. 5-9). lib. bdg. 33.27 *(978-0-7660-2820-3(8))* Enslow Pubs., Inc.

Fishman, Jon. Colin Kaepernick. 2014. (Amazing Athletes Ser.). (ENG., Illus.). 32p. (gr. 2-5). pap. 7.95 *(978-1-4677-4491-1(3))* Lerner Publishing Group.

—Rob Gronkowski. 2017. (Sports All-Stars Ser.). (ENG.). (J). (gr. 2-5). 32p. pap. 8.99 ***(978-1-5124-5619-6(5))***; (Illus.). lib. bdg. 26.65 ***(978-1-5124-3924-3(X))*** Lerner Publishing Group.

—Russell Wilson. 2014. (Amazing Athletes Ser.). (ENG., Illus.). 32p. (gr. 2-5). pap. 7.95 *(978-1-4677-4492-8(1))* Lerner Publishing Group.

Fishman, Jon. Von Miller. 2017. (Sports All-Stars Ser.). (ENG., Illus.). 32p. (J). (gr. 2-5). pap. 8.99 ***(978-1-5124-5620-2(9))*** Lerner Publishing Group.

Fishman, Jon M. Andrew Luck. 2013. (Amazing Athletes Ser.). (ENG., Illus.). 32p. (gr. 2-5). pap. 7.95 *(978-1-4677-1888-2(2))*; lib. bdg. 25.26 *(978-1-4677-1879-0(3)*, Lerner Pubns.) Lerner Publishing Group.

—Dez Bryant. 2015. (ENG., Illus.). 32p. (J). (gr. 2-5). 26.65 *(978-1-4677-7919-7(9))* Lerner Publishing Group.

—Lesean McCoy. 2015. (Amazing Athletes Ser.). (ENG., Illus.). 32p. (gr. 2-5). pap. 7.95 *(978-1-4677-8111-4(8)*, Lerner Pubns.) Lerner Publishing Group.

—Odell Beckham Jr. 2016. (Amazing Athletes Ser.). (ENG., Illus.). 32p. (J). (gr. 2-5). 26.65 *(978-1-5124-1335-9(6))* Lerner Publishing Group.

—Robert Griffin III. 2013. (Amazing Athletes Ser.). (ENG., Illus.). 32p. (gr. 2-5). pap. 7.95 *(978-1-4677-1894-3(7))*; lib. bdg. 25.26 *(978-1-4677-1878-3(5)*, Lerner Pubns.) Lerner Publishing Group.

—Russell Wilson. 2014. (Amazing Athletes Ser.). (ENG.). 32p. (gr. 2-5). lib. bdg. 25.26 *(978-1-4677-3675-6(9)*, Lerner Pubns.) Lerner Publishing Group.

Fishman, Jon M. Von Miller. 2017. (Sports All-Stars Ser.). (ENG., Illus.). 32p. (J). (gr. 2-5). 26.65 ***(978-1-5124-3455-2(8)***, Lerner Pubns.) Lerner Publishing Group.

Football Smarts. 2014. (Football Smarts Ser.). 32p. (J). (gr. 3-6). pap. 60.00 *(978-1-4777-7219-5(7)*, PowerKids Pr.) Rosen Publishing Group, Inc., The.

Frederick, Shane. Side-By-Side Football Stars: Comparing Pro Football's Greatest Players, 1 vol. 2014. (Side-By-Side Sports Ser.). (ENG., Illus.). 48p. (gr. 4-6). lib. bdg. 27.99 *(978-1-4765-6165-3(6))* Capstone Press of Coughlan Cos.

—Stars of the Super Bowl. 2016. (Everything Super Bowl Ser.). (ENG., Illus.). 32p. (gr. 3-4). lib. bdg. 27.99 *(978-1-5157-2635-7(5))* Capstone Press of Coughlan Cos.

—The Super Bowl's Greatest Plays. 2016. (Everything Super Bowl Ser.). (ENG., Illus.). 32p. (gr. 3-4). lib. bdg. 27.99 *(978-1-5157-2633-3(9))* Capstone Press of Coughlan Cos.

Frederick, Shane & Braun, Eric. Everything Super Bowl. 2016. (Everything Super Bowl Ser.). (ENG.). 32p. (gr. 3-4). 111.96 *(978-1-5157-2649-4(5))* Capstone Press of Coughlan Cos.

Frisaro, Joe. Peyton Manning: Passing Legacy. 2003. (SuperStar Ser.: Vol. 3). (Illus.). 96p. (gr. 4-7). 4.95 *(978-1-58261-164-8(5))* Sports Publishing, LLC.

Frisch, Aaron. Adrian Peterson. 2013. (Illus.). 24 p.p. (J). 25.65 *(978-1-60818-335-7(1)*, Creative Education) Creative Co., The.

—St. Louis Rams. 2014. (Illus.). 24p. (J). *(978-1-60818-386-9(6)*, Creative Education) Creative Co., The.

Frisch, Aaron & Bodden, Valerie. The Big Time: Aaron Rodgers. 2014. (Big Time Ser.). (ENG.). 24p. (J). (gr. 1-3). pap. 9.99 *(978-1-62832-059-6(1)*, Creative Paperbacks) Creative Co., The.

—The Big Time: Adrian Peterson. 2014. (Big Time Ser.). (ENG.). 24p. (J). (gr. 1-3). pap. 9.99 *(978-1-62832-060-2(5)*, Creative Paperbacks) Creative Co., The.

Gagne, Tammy. Aaron Rodgers. 2012. (Illus.). 32p. (J). lib. bdg. 25.70 *(978-1-61228-330-2(6))* Mitchell Lane Pubs., Inc.

—Colin Kaepernick. 2014. (J). (gr. 1-4). 25.70 *(978-1-61228-637-2(2))* Mitchell Lane Pubs., Inc.

—What It's Like to Be Pele. de la Vega, Eida, tr. 2011. (What It's Like to Be... = Que Se Sienta Al Ser... Ser.). (ENG & SPA., Illus.). 32p. (J). (gr. -1-2). lib. bdg. 25.70 *(978-1-58415-993-3(6))* Mitchell Lane Pubs., Inc.

Gatto, Kimberly. Tom Brady: Never-Quit Quarterback. 2005. (Sports Leaders Ser.). (Illus.). 104p. (J). (gr. 5-9). lib. bdg. 27.94 *(978-0-7660-2475-5(X))* Enslow Pubs., Inc.

Gigliotti, Jim. Defensive Backs. 2009. (Game Day: Football Ser.). (ENG.). 48p. (YA). (gr. 5-9). lib. bdg. 31.00 *(978-1-4339-1964-0(8))* Stevens, Gareth Publishing LLLP.

—Eli Manning. 2016. (Football Heroes Making a Difference Ser.). (ENG.). 24p. (J). (gr. 1-6). 16.96 *(978-1-943553-40-2(8))* Bearport Publishing Co., Inc.

—Linebackers. 2009. (Game Day: Football Ser.). (ENG.). 48p. (YA). (gr. 5-9). lib. bdg. 31.00 *(978-1-4339-1959-6(1))* Stevens, Gareth Publishing LLLP.

—Linemen. 2009. (Game Day: Football Ser.). (ENG.). 48p. (YA). (gr. 5-9). lib. bdg. 31.00 *(978-1-4339-1960-2(5))* Stevens, Gareth Publishing LLLP.

—Philip Rivers. 2016. (Football Heroes Making a Difference Ser.). (ENG., Illus.). 24p. (J). (gr. 1-6). 16.96 *(978-1-943553-41-9(6))* Bearport Publishing Co., Inc.

—Receivers. 2009. (Game Day: Football Ser.). (ENG.). 48p. (J). (gr. 5-9). lib. bdg. 31.00 *(978-1-4339-1962-6(1))* Stevens, Gareth Publishing LLLP.

Gimpel, Diane Marczely. Terrell Owens. 2007. (Superstars of Pro Football Ser.). 64p. (YA). (gr. 7-18). pap. 9.95 *(978-1-4222-0831-1(1))* Mason Crest.

Gitlin, Martin. Adrian Peterson: Record-Setting Running Back, 1 vol. 2012. (Playmakers Ser.). (ENG.). 32p. (J). (gr. 3-6). 27.07 *(978-1-61783-293-2(6))* ABDO Publishing Co.

—Drew Brees: Super Bowl Champ, 1 vol. 2011. (Playmakers Ser.). (ENG., Illus.). 32p. (YA). (gr. 3-6). 27.07 *(978-1-61714-743-2(5))* ABDO Publishing Co.

—Joe Flacco: Super Bowl MVP, 1 vol. 2013. (Playmakers Set 4 Ser.). (ENG.). 32p. (gr. 2-6). lib. bdg. 27.07 *(978-1-61783-699-2(0)*, SportsZone) ABDO Publishing Co.

—Peyton Manning: Superstar Quarterback, 1 vol. 2011. (Playmakers Ser.). (ENG., Illus.). 32p. (YA). (gr. 3-6). 27.07 *(978-1-61714-748-7(6))* ABDO Publishing Co.

—Tom Brady: Super Bowl Quarterback, 1 vol. 2012. (Playmakers Ser.). (ENG.). 32p. (J). (gr. 3-6). 27.07 *(978-1-61783-290-1(1))* ABDO Publishing Co.

Gitlin, Marty. Odell Beckham Jr: Football Star. 2017. (Biggest Names in Sports (hardcover) Ser.). (ENG., Illus.). 32p. (J). (gr. 4-7). lib. bdg. 28.50 ***(978-1-63517-038-2(9)***, Focus Readers) North Star Editions.

—Von Miller: Football Star. 2017. (Biggest Names in Sports (paperback) Ser.). (ENG.). 32p. (J). (gr. 4-7). pap. 9.95 ***(978-1-63517-099-3(0)***, Focus Readers) North Star Editions.

Glaser, Jason. Peyton Manning. 2011. (Today's Sports Greats Ser.). 32p. (gr. 4-6). (J). pap. 10.50 *(978-1-4339-5868-7(6)*, Gareth Stevens Learning Library); (YA). lib. bdg. 26.60 *(978-1-4339-5866-3(X))* Stevens, Gareth Publishing LLLP.

—Tom Brady. 2009. (Sports Idols Ser.). 24p. (gr. 2-3). 42.50 *(978-1-60853-145-5(7)*, PowerKids Pr.) Rosen Publishing Group, Inc., The.

—Tom Brady. 2011. (Today's Sports Greats Ser.). (Illus.). 32p. (gr. 4-6). (J). pap. 10.50 *(978-1-4339-5884-7(8)*, Gareth Stevens Learning Library); (YA). 26.60 *(978-1-4339-5882-3(1))* Stevens, Gareth Publishing LLLP.

Glave, Tom. Baltimore Ravens. 2015. (Insider's Guide to Pro Football Ser.). (ENG.). 32p. (J). (gr. k-3). 28.50 *(978-1-63143-991-9(X)*, 208826) Child's World, Inc., The.

Gordon, Nick. Tom Brady, 1 vol. 2016. (ENG., Illus.). 32p. (J). *(978-1-62403-824-2(7))* ABDO Publishing Co.

Gordon, Stephen G. Tim Tebow: Quarterback with Conviction. 2013. (USA TODAY Lifeline Biographies Ser.). (ENG.). 112p. (gr. 6-12). lib. bdg. 34.60 *(978-1-4677-0809-8(7))* Lerner Publishing Group.

Grabowski, John F. Larry Fitzgerald. 2010. (Superstars of Pro Football Ser.). 64p. (J). 22.95 *(978-1-4222-2721-3(9))* Mason Crest.

Graves, Will. Robert Griffin III: NFL Sensation: RGIII, 1 vol. 2013. (Playmakers Set 4 Ser.). (ENG.). 32p. (gr. 2-6). lib. bdg. 27.07 *(978-1-61783-700-5(8)*, SportsZone) ABDO Publishing Co.

Gray, Aaron Jonathan. Football Record Breakers, 1 vol. 2016. (ENG., Illus.). 48p. (J). ***(978-1-62403-847-1(6)***, SportsZone) ABDO Publishing Co.

Grayson, Robert. Plaxico Burress. 2009. (Superstars of Pro Football Ser.). (Illus.). 64p. (YA). (gr. 7-12). lib. bdg. 22.95 *(978-1-4222-0552-5(5))* Mason Crest.

Gregory, Josh. Andrew Luck. 2014. (Football Stars up Close Ser.). 24p. (J). (gr. 1-6). lib. bdg. 23.93 *(978-1-62724-084-0(5))* Bearport Publishing Co., Inc.

Gregory, Josh & Wilner, Barry. Peyton Manning. 2015. (Football Stars up Close Ser.). (ENG.). 24p. (J). (gr. k-5). lib. bdg. 23.93 *(978-1-62724-543-2(X))* Bearport Publishing Co., Inc.

Hammer, Maxwell. Peyton Manning: NFL MVP & Champion. 2015. (Today's MVPs & Champions Ser.). (ENG.). 24p. (J). (gr. 2-5). 27.07 *(978-1-63143-738-0(0)*, 208573) Child's World, Inc., The.

Hasday, Judy L. & Crompton, Samuel Willard. Barry Sanders. 2008. (Football Superstars Ser.). (Illus.). 120p. (J). (gr. 7-12). 30.00 *(978-0-7910-9667-3(X))* Facts On File, Inc.

Hasday, Judy L. & Worth, Richard. Donovan Mcnabb. 2008. (Football Superstars Ser.). (Illus.). 128p. (YA). (gr. 7-12). 30.00 *(978-0-7910-9668-0(8))* Facts On File, Inc.

Helts, Rudolph T. Ben Roethlisberger. 2010. (Superstars of Pro Football Ser.). 64p. (YA). (gr. 5-18). lib. bdg. 22.95 *(978-1-4222-1664-4(0))* Mason Crest.

—Ben Rothlisberger. 2009. (Superstars of Pro Football Ser.). 64p. (YA). (gr. 5-18). pap. 9.95 *(978-1-4222-1984-3(4))* Mason Crest.

—DeMarcus Ware. 2010. (Superstars of Pro Football Ser.). 64p. (YA). (gr. 5-18). lib. bdg. 22.95 *(978-1-4222-1665-1(9))* Mason Crest.

Heos, Bridget. Ronde & Tiki Barber: Football Stars. 2010. (Sports Families Ser.). 48p. (YA). (gr. 5-8). lib. bdg., E-Book 53.00 *(978-1-4488-0123-7(0))*; (ENG., Illus.). (J). pap. 11.75 *(978-1-4358-8510-3(4)*, Rosen Reference); (Illus.). (YA). (gr. 4-7). lib. bdg. 29.25 *(978-1-4358-3553-5(0))* Rosen Publishing Group, Inc., The.

—Ronde & Tiki Barber: Football Stars (Sports Families) l.t. ed. 2012. 96p. pap. *(978-1-4596-3354-4(7))* ReadHowYouWant.com, Ltd.

Herzog, Brad. T Is for Touchdown: A Football Alphabet. Braught, Mark, illus. 2015. (Av2 Fiction Readalong 2016 Ser.). (ENG.). (J). (gr. 1-4). lib. bdg. 34.28 *(978-1-4896-3765-9(6)*, AV2 by Weigl) Weigl Pubs., Inc.

Hetrick, Hans. Six Degrees of Peyton Manning: Connecting Football Stars. 2015. (Six Degrees of Sports Ser.). (ENG.). 48p. (gr. 3-4). lib. bdg. 31.99 *(978-1-4914-2145-1(2))* Capstone Press of Coughlan Cos.

Hoblin, Paul. Aaron Rodgers: Super Bowl MVP, 1 vol. 2012. (Playmakers Ser.). (ENG.). 32p. (J). (gr. 3-6). 27.07 *(978-1-61783-295-6(2))* ABDO Publishing Co.

—Andrew Luck: Rising NFL Star, 1 vol. 2013. (Playmakers Set 4 Ser.). (ENG.). 32p. (gr. 2-6). lib. bdg. 27.07 *(978-1-61783-702-9(4)*, SportsZone) ABDO Publishing Co.

—Colin Kaepernick: NFL Phenom, 1 vol. 2013. (Playmakers Set 4 Ser.). (ENG.). 32p. (gr. 2-6). lib. bdg. 27.07 *(978-1-61783-701-2(6)*, SportsZone) ABDO Publishing Co.

Hoffman, Mary Ann. Peyton Manning: Football Star. (Sports Superstars Ser.). 24p. (gr. 1-1). 2009. 42.50 *(978-1-60853-181-3(3)*, PowerKids Pr.) 2007. (Illus.). (J). lib. bdg. 22.60 *(978-1-4042-3531-1(0))* Rosen Publishing Group, Inc., The.

—Peyton Manning: Football Star/Estrella del Futbol Americano. Alaman, Eduardo, tr. 2007. (Amazing Athletes/Atletas increibles Ser.). (SPA., Illus.). 24p. (J). (gr. 2-5). lib. bdg. 22.60 *(978-1-4042-7601-7(7))* Rosen Publishing Group, Inc., The.

—Shaun Alexander: Football Star. (Sports Superstars Ser.). 24p. (gr. 1-1). 2009. 42.50 *(978-1-60853-182-0(1)*, PowerKids Pr.) 2007. (Illus.). (J). lib. bdg. 22.60 *(978-1-4042-3532-8(9))* Rosen Publishing Group, Inc., The.

—Shaun Alexander: Football Star/Estrella del futbol Americano. 2009. (Amazing Athletes/Atletas increibles Ser.). 24p. (gr. 1-2). 42.50 *(978-1-61511-308-8(8)*, Editorial Buenas Letras) Rosen Publishing Group, Inc., The.

—Shaun Alexander: Football Star/Estrella del Futbol Americano. Alaman, Eduardo, tr. 2007. (Amazing Athletes/Atletas increibles Ser.). (SPA., Illus.). 24p. (J). (gr. 2-5). lib. bdg. 22.60 *(978-1-4042-7603-1(3))* Rosen Publishing Group, Inc., The.

Holmes, Parker. Tim Tebow. 2012. (Football's Rising Stars Ser.). (ENG., Illus.). 24p. (J). (gr. 2-5). 23.95 *(978-1-4488-9191-7(4))*; pap. 10.60 *(978-1-4488-9206-8(6))* Rosen Publishing Group, Inc., The. (PowerKids Pr.).

Horn, Geoffrey M. Peyton Manning. 2006. (Today's Superstars). (Illus.). 32p. (gr. 5-8). lib. bdg. 31.95 *(978-0-8368-6183-9(3))* Stevens, Gareth Publishing LLLP.

Hunter, Amy N. Tony Gonzalez. 2009. (Superstars of Pro Football Ser.). (Illus.). 64p. (YA). (gr. 7-12). lib. bdg. 22.95 *(978-1-4222-0541-9(X))* Mason Crest.

Kelley, K. C. Football Superstars 2015. 2015. (ENG., Illus.). 32p. (J). (gr. 2-5). pap. 5.99 *(978-0-545-82642-6(X)*, Scholastic Paperbacks) Scholastic, Inc.

—Football Superstars 2016. 2016. (ENG.). 32p. (J). (gr. 2-5). pap. 5.99 *(978-1-338-03275-8(5))* Scholastic, Inc.

—J. J. Watt. 2016. (Football Stars up Close Ser.). (ENG., Illus.). 24p. (J). (gr. k-5). 17.95 *(978-1-943553-37-2(8))* Bearport Publishing Co., Inc.

—Odell Beckham Jr. 2016. (Football Stars up Close Ser.). (ENG., Illus.). 24p. (J). (gr. k-5). 17.95 *(978-1-943553-38-9(6))* Bearport Publishing Co., Inc.

—Quarterback Superstars 2015. 2015. (Illus.). 32p. (J). *(978-0-545-88736-6(4))* Scholastic, Inc.

—Quarterbacks. 2009. (Game Day: Football Ser.). (ENG.). 48p. (J). (gr. 5-9). lib. bdg. 31.00 *(978-1-4339-1961-9(3))* Stevens, Gareth Publishing LLLP.

—Rob Gronkowski. 2016. (Football Stars up Close Ser.). (ENG., Illus.). 24p. (J). (gr. k-5). 17.95 *(978-1-943553-39-6(4))* Bearport Publishing Co., Inc.

—Running Backs. 2009. (Game Day: Football Ser.). (ENG.). 48p. (J). (gr. 5-9). lib. bdg. 31.00 *(978-1-4339-1963-3(X))* Stevens, Gareth Publishing LLLP.

Kimmich, Ian. Antonio Gates. 2009. (Superstars of Pro Football Ser.). (Illus.). 64p. (YA). (gr. 7-12). lib. bdg. 22.95 *(978-1-4222-0553-2(3))* Mason Crest.

Kirkpatrick, Rob. Doug Flutie: Estrella Internacional de Fútbol Americano (International Football Star) 2009. (Deportistas de Poder (Power Players) Ser.). (SPA.). 24p. (gr. 1-1). 42.50 *(978-1-61512-156-4(0)*, Editorial Buenas Letras) Rosen Publishing Group, Inc., The.

—Doug Flutie: International Football Star. 2009. (Power Players Ser.). 24p. (gr. 1-1). 42.50 *(978-1-60851-327-7(0)*, PowerKids Pr.) Rosen Publishing Group, Inc., The.

—Terrell Davis: Corredor de Superbowl (Super Bowl Running Back) 2009. (Deportistas de Poder (Power Players) Ser.). 24p. (gr. 1-1). 42.50 *(978-1-61512-161-8(7)*, Editorial Buenas Letras) Rosen Publishing Group, Inc., The.

Koestler-Grack, Rachel A. Brett Favre. 2008. (Football Superstars Ser.). (Illus.). 144p. (gr. 6-12). lib. bdg. 30.00 *(978-0-7910-9690-1(4)*, Chelsea Hse.) Facts On File, Inc.

Krumenauer, Heidi. Brett Favre. 2008. (Blue Banner Biography Ser.). (Illus.). 32p. (YA). (gr. 4-7). lib. bdg. 25.70 *(978-1-58415-670-3(8))* Mitchell Lane Pubs., Inc.

—Joe Flacco. 2009. (Blue Banner Biography Ser.). (Illus.). 32p. (YA). (gr. 4-7). lib. bdg. 25.70 *(978-1-58415-771-7(2))* Mitchell Lane Pubs., Inc.

—Michael Strahan. 2012. (J). lib. bdg. 25.70 *(978-1-61228-331-9(4))* Mitchell Lane Pubs., Inc.

Lace, William W. LaDanian Tomlinson. 2009. (Superstars of Pro Football Ser.). (Illus.). 64p. (YA). (gr. 7-12). lib. bdg. 22.95 *(978-1-4222-0546-4(0))* Mason Crest.

Layden, Joseph. Rising Stars, NFL. 2005. (Illus.). 32p. (J). pap. *(978-0-439-80247-5(4))* Scholastic, Inc.

LeGrand, Eric & Yorkey, Mike. Believe: The Victorious Story of Eric LeGrand. 2012. (ENG., Illus.). 224p. (J). (gr. 3-7). 16.99 *(978-0-06-222582-5(0)*, Collins) HarperCollins Pubs.

Leventhal, Josh. Defensive Linemen. 2017. (Football's All-Time Greats Ser.). (ENG., Illus.). 32p. (J). (gr. 3-7). 31.35 ***(978-1-68072-038-9(4)***, Bolt) Black Rabbit Bks.

—Head Coaches. 2017. (Football's All-Time Greats Ser.). (ENG., Illus.). 32p. (J). (gr. 3-7). 31.35 ***(978-1-68072-039-6(2)***, Bolt) Black Rabbit Bks.

—Linebackers. 2017. (Football's All-Time Greats Ser.). (ENG., Illus.). 32p. (J). (gr. 3-7). 31.35 ***(978-1-68072-040-2(6)***, Bolt) Black Rabbit Bks.

—Quarterbacks. 2017. (Football's All-Time Greats Ser.). (ENG.). 32p. (gr. 3-7). 31.35 ***(978-1-68072-041-9(4)***, Bolt) Black Rabbit Bks.

—Receivers. 2017. (Football's All-Time Greats Ser.). (ENG.). 32p. (gr. 3-7). 31.35 ***(978-1-68072-042-6(2)***, Bolt) Black Rabbit Bks.

—Running Backs. 2017. (Football's All-Time Greats Ser.). (ENG., Illus.). 32p. (J). (gr. 3-7). 31.35 ***(978-1-68072-043-3(0)***, Bolt) Black Rabbit Bks.

Lourdes-Pitt, H. H. Brett Favre. 2010. (Superstars of Pro Football Ser.). 64p. (YA). (gr. 5-18). lib. bdg. 22.95 *(978-1-4222-1662-0(4))* Mason Crest.

Mack, Larry. The Atlanta Falcons Story. 2016. (NFL Teams Ser.). (ENG., Illus.). 32p. (J). (gr. 3-7). lib. bdg. 26.95 *(978-1-62617-356-9(7)*, Torque Bks.) Bellwether Media.

MacKay, Jennifer. Tim Tebow. Greenhaven Press Editors, ed. 2013. (People in the News Ser.). (ENG., Illus.). 128p. (gr. 7-10). lib. bdg. 39.40 *(978-1-4205-0893-2(8)*, Lucent Bks.) Cengage Gale.

Macnow, Glen. Deion Sanders: Hall of Fame Football Superstar. (Hall of Fame Sports Greats Ser.). 64p. (J). (gr. 4-9). 2014. pap. 9.95 *(978-1-62285-046-4(7))* 2013. 15.95 *(978-1-62285-045-7(9))* Enslow Pubs., Inc.

—Troy Aikman: Hall of Fame Football Superstar. (Hall of Fame Sports Greats Ser.). 64p. (J). (gr. 4-9). 2014. pap. 9.95 *(978-1-62285-041-9(6))* 2013. 15.95 *(978-1-62285-040-2(8))* Enslow Pubs., Inc.

MacRae, Sloan. Aaron Rodgers. 2012. (Sports Heroes Ser.). (ENG., Illus.). 24p. (J). (gr. 3-6). pap. 8.25 *(978-1-4488-6280-1(9))*; lib. bdg. 22.60 *(978-1-4488-6161-3(6))* Rosen Publishing Group, Inc., The. (PowerKids Pr.).

—Chad Ochocinco. 2012. (Sports Heroes Ser.). (ENG., Illus.). 24p. (J). (gr. 3-6). pap. 8.25 *(978-1-4488-6282-5(5))*; lib. bdg. 22.60 *(978-1-4488-6162-0(4))* Rosen Publishing Group, Inc., The. (PowerKids Pr.).

—Meet Ben Roethlisberger: Football's Big Ben. 2009. (All-Star Players Ser.). 32p. (Illus.). (J). (gr. 4-6). pap. 10.00 *(978-1-4358-3098-1(9))*; (gr. 4-5). 47.90 *(978-1-61511-275-3(8))*; (J). lib. bdg. 25.25 *(978-1-4358-2706-6(6))* Rosen Publishing Group, Inc., The. (PowerKids Pr.).

—Meet Eli Manning: Football's Unstoppable Quarterback. 2009. (All-Star Players Ser.). 32p. (Illus.). (J). (gr. 4-6). pap. 10.00 *(978-1-4358-3097-4(0))*; (gr. 4-5). 47.90 *(978-1-61511-284-5(7))*; (J). lib. bdg. 25.25 *(978-1-4358-2705-9(8))* Rosen Publishing Group, Inc., The. (PowerKids Pr.).

Manning, Peyton, et al. Peyton Manning. 2015. (Quotes from the Greatest Athletes Ser.). (ENG., Illus.). 24p. (J). lib. bdg. 28.55 *(978-1-4896-3372-9(3)*, AV2 by Weigl) Weigl Pubs., Inc.

Marcovitz, Hal. The Manning Brothers. 2013. (J). *(978-1-4222-2723-7(5))* 2013. (J). pap. *(978-1-4222-9094-1(8))* 2009. (Illus.). 64p. (YA). (gr. 7-12). lib. bdg. 22.95 *(978-1-4222-0543-3(6)*, 1291172) Mason Crest.

Mattern, Joanne. Dak Prescott. 2017. lib. bdg. 25.70 ***(978-1-68020-127-7(1))*** Mitchell Lane Pubs., Inc.

—Donovan Mcnabb. 2004. (Robbie Reader Ser.). (Illus.). 32p. (J). (gr. 1-4). lib. bdg. 25.70 *(978-1-58415-294-1(X))* Mitchell Lane Pubs., Inc.

—Peyton Manning: Indianapolis Colts Star Quarterback. 2006. (Blue Banner Biography Ser.). (Illus.). 32p. (YA). (gr. 4-7). lib. bdg. 25.70 *(978-1-58415-506-5(X))* Mitchell Lane Pubs., Inc.

—Tiki Barber: Star NY Giants Running Back. 2006. (Robbie Reader Ser.). (Illus.). 32p. (J). (gr. 2-5). lib. bdg. 25.70 *(978-1-58415-522-5(1))* Mitchell Lane Pubs., Inc.

Maurer, Tracy Nelson. Aaron Rodgers. 2015. (Famous Athletes Ser.). (ENG., Illus.). 24p. (gr. k-1). lib. bdg. 26.65 *(978-1-4914-6234-8(5))* Capstone Press of Coughlan Cos.

Miller, Calvin Craig. Tom Brady. 2013. (J). *(978-1-4222-2719-0(7))* Mason Crest.

Mills, Cliff. Tony Romo. 2011. (Football Superstars Ser.). (Illus.). 128p. (gr. 6-12). 30.00 *(978-1-60413-754-5(1))* Facts On File, Inc.

Mills, Clifford W. Adrian Peterson. 2011. (Football Superstars Ser.). (Illus.). 120p. (J). (gr. 6-12). 30.00 *(978-1-60413-755-2(X))* Facts On File, Inc.

Monnig, Alex. Carolina Panthers. 2015. (Insider's Guide to Pro Football Ser.). (ENG.). 32p. (J). (gr. k-3). 28.50 *(978-1-63407-012-6(7)*, 208847) Child's World, Inc., The.

—Eli Manning: Super Bowl Hero, 1 vol. 2012. (Playmakers Set 3 Ser.). (ENG.). 32p. (J). (gr. 2-6). lib. bdg. 27.07 *(978-1-61783-549-0(8)*, SportsZone) ABDO Publishing Co.

—Tim Tebow: Quarterback Sensation, 1 vol. 2012. (Playmakers Set 3 Ser.). (ENG., Illus.). 32p. (J). (gr. 2-6). lib. bdg. 27.07 *(978-1-61783-550-6(1)*, SportsZone) ABDO Publishing Co.

Murray, Laura K. Andrew Luck. 2016. (Illus.). 21p. (J). *(978-1-60818-668-6(7)*, Creative Education) Creative Co., The.

Murray, Laura K. & Bodden, Valerie. The Arab Spring. 2017. (Turning Points Ser.). (ENG., Illus.). 48p. (J). (gr. 7-12). pap. 12.00 *(978-1-62832-341-2(8)*, Creative Paperbacks) Creative Co., The.

Nagelhout, Ryan. Aaron Rodgers, Vol. 1. 2014. (Today's Great Quarterbacks Ser.). 32p. (J). (gr. 3-6). 25.25 *(978-1-4824-0117-2(7))* Stevens, Gareth Publishing LLLP.

—Andrew Luck, Vol. 1. 2014. (Today's Great Quarterbacks Ser.). (ENG.). 32p. (J). (gr. 1-1). 25.25 *(978-1-4824-0124-0(X))* Stevens, Gareth Publishing LLLP.

—Joe Flacco, Vol. 1. 2014. (Today's Great Quarterbacks Ser.). 32p. (J). (ENG.). (gr. 1-1). pap. 10.50 *(978-1-4824-0145-5(2))*; (gr. 3-6). 25.25 *(978-1-4824-0143-1(6))* Stevens, Gareth Publishing LLLP.

—Peyton Manning, Vol. 1. 2014. (Today's Great Quarterbacks Ser.). 32p. (J). (ENG.). (gr. 1-1). pap. 10.50 *(978-1-4824-0480-7(X))*; (gr. 3-6). 25.25 *(978-1-4824-0478-4(8))* Stevens, Gareth Publishing LLLP.

—Robert Griffin III, Vol. 1. 2014. (Today's Great Quarterbacks Ser.). 32p. (J). (gr. 3-6). 25.25 *(978-1-4824-0482-1(6))* Stevens, Gareth Publishing LLLP.

—Tom Brady, Vol. 1. 2014. (Today's Great Quarterbacks Ser.). (ENG.). 32p. (J). (gr. 1-1). 25.25 *(978-1-4824-0148-6(7))* Stevens, Gareth Publishing LLLP.

Needham, Tom. Tiki Barber: All-Pro on & off the Field. 2007. (Sports Stars with Heart Ser.). (Illus.). 128p. (J). (gr. 5-9). lib. bdg. 33.27 *(978-0-7660-2865-4(8))* Enslow Pubs., Inc.

O'Day, John. Reggie Bush: Superstar on Offense. 2010. (Inspiring Lives Ser.). 32p. (J). (gr. 5-8). lib. bdg. 25.25 *(978-1-4339-3646-3(1))*; (Illus.). pap. 10.50 *(978-1-4339-3647-0(X))* Stevens, Gareth Publishing LLLP.

O'Neal, Claire. Andrew Luck. 2013. (ENG.). (J). (gr. 1-4). lib. bdg. 25.70 *(978-1-61228-460-6(4))* Mitchell Lane Pubs., Inc.

Paprocki, Ray. Eli Manning. 2011. (Football Superstars Ser.). (Illus.). 109p. (gr. 6-12). 30.00 *(978-1-60413-753-8(3))* Facts On File, Inc.

Polzer, Tim. Peyton Manning: Leader on & off the Field. 2006. (Sports Stars with Heart Ser.). (Illus.). 128p. (J). (gr. 5-9). lib. bdg. 33.27 *(978-0-7660-2822-7(4))* Enslow Pubs., Inc.

—Tim Tebow: Always a Hero. 2012. (ENG.). 48p. (J). (gr. -1-3). pap. 3.99 *(978-0-545-48595-1(9))* Scholastic, Inc.

Porterfield, Jason. Calvin Hill & Grant Hill: One Family's Legacy in Football & Basketball. 2010. (Sports Families Ser.). (Illus.). 48p. (ENG.). (J). pap. 11.75 *(978-1-4358-8516-5(3)*, Rosen Reference); (YA). (gr. 4-7). lib. bdg. 29.25 *(978-1-4358-3549-8(2))* Rosen Publishing Group, Inc., The.

—Calvin Hill & Grant Hill: One Family's Legacy in Football & Basketball (Sports Families) l.t. ed. 2012. 96p. pap. *(978-1-4596-3352-0(0))* ReadHowYouWant.com, Ltd.

Portman, Michael. Drew Brees. 2010. (Today's Superstars Ser.). (Illus.). 48p. (gr. 5-8). 31.95 *(978-1-4339-3992-1(4))*; pap. 14.05 *(978-1-4339-3993-8(2))* Stevens, Gareth Publishing LLLP.

Prisco, Pete. Mark Brunnell: Super Southpaw. 2003. (SuperStar Ser.: Vol. 5). (Illus.). 96p. (J). (gr. 4-7). 4.95 *(978-1-58261-166-2(1))* Sports Publishing, LLC.

Publishers, Chelsea House, creator. Football Superstars Set, 12-Volumes. 2008. (Football Superstars Ser.). (gr. 6-12). 360.00 *(978-0-7910-9886-8(9)*, Chelsea Hse.) Facts On File, Inc.

Pulditor, Seth H. DeSean Jackson. 2010. (Superstars of Pro Football Ser.). 64p. (YA). (gr. 5-18). lib. bdg. 22.95 *(978-1-4222-1663-7(2))* Mason Crest.

—Drew Brees. 2013. (J). *(978-1-4222-2720-6(0))* Mason Crest.

Rains, Rob. Marshall Faulk: Rushing to Glory. 2003. (SuperStar Ser.: Vol. 8). (Illus.). 96p. (J). pap. 4.95 *(978-1-58261-191-4(2))* Sports Publishing, LLC.

Rappoport, Ken. Peyton Manning: Champion Football Star. 2012. (Sports Star Champions Ser.). (Illus.). 48p. (J). (gr. 5-18). lib. bdg. 25.27 *(978-0-7660-4027-4(5))* Enslow Pubs., Inc.

—Richard Sherman. 2015. (Football Stars up Close Ser.). (ENG.). 24p. (J). (gr. k-5). lib. bdg. 23.93 *(978-1-62724-542-5(1))* Bearport Publishing Co., Inc.

—Russell Wilson. 2015. (Football Stars up Close Ser.). (ENG.). 24p. (J). (gr. k-5). lib. bdg. 23.93 *(978-1-62724-541-8(3))* Bearport Publishing Co., Inc.

—Super Sports Star Jerome Bettis. 2003. (Super Sports Star Ser.). (Illus.). 48p. (J). (gr. 1-4). lib. bdg. 25.27 *(978-0-7660-2053-5(3))* Enslow Pubs., Inc.

—Super Sports Star Peyton Manning. 2003. (Super Sports Star Ser.). (Illus.). 48p. (J). lib. bdg. 25.27 *(978-0-7660-2079-5(7))* Enslow Pubs., Inc.

—Tim Tebow: A Football Star Who Cares. 2013. (Sports Stars Who Care Ser.). 48p. (J). (gr. 3-4). pap. 8.95 *(978-1-4644-0539-6(5)*, Enslow Elementary) Enslow Pubs., Inc.

Raum, Elizabeth. Cam Newton. 2017. (Pro Sports Biographies Ser.). (ENG.). 24p. (J). (gr. 1-4). 20.95 ***(978-1-68151-137-5(1)**, Amicus High Interest)* Amicus Publishing.

—J. J. Watt. 2017. (Pro Sports Biographies Ser.). (ENG.). 24p. (J). (gr. 1-4). 20.95 ***(978-1-68151-136-8(3)**, Amicus High Interest)* Amicus Publishing.

—Pro Sports Biographies: J. J. Watt. 2017. (Pro Sports Biographies Ser.). (ENG.). 24p. (J). (gr. 1-3). pap. 8.99 ***(978-1-68152-167-1(9))*** Amicus.

Regard, Jady. Born to be an Aggie. 2007. 32p. 19.95 *(978-0-9789475-1-4(7))* Slice of Lime Publishing.

Rekela, George R. Sports Great Kurt Warner. 2003. (Sports Great Bks.). (Illus.). 64p. (J). (gr. 4-10). lib. bdg. 22.60 *(978-0-7660-2034-4(7))* Enslow Pubs., Inc.

Richardson, Jael Ealey. The Stone Thrower: A Daughter's Lessons, a Father's Life, 1 vol. James, Matt, illus. 2016. (ENG.). 32p. (J). (gr. k). 18.95 *(978-1-55498-752-8(0))* Groundwood Bks. CAN. Dist: Publishers Group West (PGW).

Rivkin, Jennifer. Gridiron Greats: Heroes of Football. 2016. (ENG., Illus.). 32p. (J). *(978-0-7787-2295-3(3))* Crabtree Publishing Co.

Roberts, Russell. Larry Fitzgerald. 2010. (Robbie Reader Ser.). (Illus.). 32p. (J). (gr. 2-5). lib. bdg. 25.70 *(978-1-58415-899-8(9))* Mitchell Lane Pubs., Inc.

Robinson, Tom. Ben Roethlisberger: Gifted & Giving Football Star. 2010. (Sports Stars Who Give Back Ser.). (Illus.). 128p. (J). (gr. 5-9). lib. bdg. 33.27 *(978-0-7660-3590-4(5))* Enslow Pubs., Inc.

—Donovan Mcnabb: Leader on & off the Field. 2007. (Sports Stars with Heart Ser.). (Illus.). 128p. (J). (gr. 5-9). lib. bdg. 33.27 *(978-0-7660-2864-7(X))* Enslow Pubs., Inc.

—Today's 12 Hottest NFL Superstars. 2015. (ENG., Illus.). 32p. (J). *(978-1-63235-022-0(X))* Pr. Room Editions LLC.

Robson, David. Randy Moss. (Superstars of Pro Football Ser.). 64p. (YA). (gr. 7-12). 2009. (Illus.). lib. bdg. 22.95 *(978-1-4222-0550-1(9))* 2007. pap. 9.95 *(978-1-4222-0830-4(3))* Mason Crest.

Rogers, Andy. Who's Who of Pro Football: A Guide to the Game's Greatest Players. 2015. (Who's Who of Pro Sports Ser.). (ENG., Illus.). 32p. (gr. 3-4). lib. bdg. 27.99 *(978-1-4765-5715-1(2))* Capstone Press of Coughlan Cos.

Ryan, Mike. Amazing Football: Stars, Stats & Facts. 2016. (ENG., Illus.). 64p. (J). (gr. 5-10). pap. 9.95 *(978-1-77085-777-3(X)*, 9781770857773) Firefly Bks., Ltd.

Sandler, Michael. Aaron Rodgers & the Green Bay Packers: Super Bowl XLV. 2011. (Super Bowl Superstars Ser.). 24p. (YA). (gr. k-3). lib. bdg. 22.61 *(978-1-61772-309-4(6))* Bearport Publishing Co., Inc.

—Adrian Peterson. 2010. (Football Heroes Making a Difference Ser.). (Illus.). 24p. (YA). (gr. 2-5). lib. bdg. 22.61 *(978-1-936087-59-4(6))* Bearport Publishing Co., Inc.

—Ben Roethlisberger. 2009. (Football Heroes Making a Difference Ser.). (Illus.). 24p. (J). (gr. 2-5). lib. bdg. 22.61 *(978-1-59716-770-3(3))* Bearport Publishing Co., Inc.

—Brett Favre. 2009. (Football Heroes Making a Difference Ser.). (Illus.). 24p. (YA). (gr. 2-5). lib. bdg. 22.61 *(978-1-59716-771-0(1))* Bearport Publishing Co., Inc.

—Brian Urlacher. 2009. (Football Heroes Making a Difference Ser.). (Illus.). 24p. (J). (gr. 2-5). lib. bdg. 22.61 *(978-1-59716-775-8(4))* Bearport Publishing Co., Inc.

—Donovan Mcnabb. 2009. (Football Heroes Making a Difference Ser.). (Illus.). 24p. (YA). (gr. 2-5). lib. bdg. 22.61 *(978-1-59716-772-7(X))* Bearport Publishing Co., Inc.

—Drew Brees & the New Orleans Saints. 2010. (Super Bowl Superstars Ser.). 24p. (YA). (gr. k-3). lib. bdg. 22.61 *(978-1-936088-27-0(4))* Bearport Publishing Co., Inc.

—Eli Manning & the New York Giants: Super Bowl Xlvi. 2012. (Super Bowl Superstars Ser.). (Illus.). 24p. (J). (gr. 1-6). lib. bdg. 22.61 *(978-1-61772-578-4(1))* Bearport Publishing Co., Inc.

—Hines Ward & the Pittsburgh Steelers. 2007. (Super Bowl Superstars Ser.). (Illus.). 24p. (J). (gr. k-3). lib. bdg. 22.61 *(978-1-59716-538-9(7))* Bearport Publishing Co., Inc.

—Joe Flacco & the Baltimore Ravens: Super Bowl XLVII. 2013. (Super Bowl Superstars Ser.). 24p. (J). (gr. 1-6). lib. bdg. 22.61 *(978-1-61772-933-1(7))* Bearport Publishing Co., Inc.

—Joe Montana & the San Fransisco 49ers. 2008. (Super Bowl Superstars Ser.). (Illus.). 24p. (J). (gr. k-3). lib. bdg. 22.61 *(978-1-59716-738-3(X))* Bearport Publishing Co., Inc.

—John Elway & the Denver Broncos. 2007. (Super Bowl Superstars Ser.). (Illus.). 24p. (J). (gr. k-3). lib. bdg. 22.61 *(978-1-59716-536-5(0))* Bearport Publishing Co., Inc.

—Kurt Warner & the St. Louis Rams. 2007. (Super Bowl Superstars Ser.). (Illus.). 24p. (J). (gr. k-3). lib. bdg. 22.61 *(978-1-59716-539-6(5))* Bearport Publishing Co., Inc.

—Ladainian Tomlinson. 2009. (Football Heroes Making a Difference Ser.). (Illus.). 24p. (J). (gr. 2-5). lib. bdg. 22.61 *(978-1-59716-774-1(6))* Bearport Publishing Co., Inc.

—Larry Fitzgerald. 2010. (Football Heroes Making a Difference Ser.). (Illus.). 24p. (YA). (gr. 2-5). lib. bdg. 22.61 *(978-1-936087-58-7(8))* Bearport Publishing Co., Inc.

—Malcolm Smith & the Seattle Seahawks: Super Bowl XLVIII. 2015. (Illus.). 24p. (J). lib. bdg. *(978-1-62724-295-0(3))* Bearport Publishing Co., Inc.

—Mark Sanchez. 2011. (Football Heroes Making a Difference Ser.). 24p. (YA). (gr. 2-5). lib. bdg. 22.61 *(978-1-61772-310-0(X))* Bearport Publishing Co., Inc.

—Matt Hasselbeck. 2009. (Football Heroes Making a Difference Ser.). (Illus.). 24p. (J). (gr. 2-5). lib. bdg. 22.61 *(978-1-59716-773-4(8))* Bearport Publishing Co., Inc.

—Most Spectacular Quarterbacks. 2010. (Football-O-Rama Ser.). 24p. (YA). (gr. 3-6). lib. bdg. 22.61 *(978-1-936088-23-2(1))* Bearport Publishing Co., Inc.

—Peyton Manning. 2011. (Football Heroes Making a Difference Ser.). 24p. (YA). (gr. 2-5). lib. bdg. 22.61 *(978-1-61772-311-7(8))* Bearport Publishing Co., Inc.

—Peyton Manning & the Indianapolis Colts. 2007. (Super Bowl Superstars Ser.). (Illus.). 24p. (J). (gr. k-3). lib. bdg. 22.61 *(978-1-59716-540-2(9))* Bearport Publishing Co., Inc.

—Tim Tebow. 2012. (Football Heroes Making a Difference Ser.). (Illus.). 24p. (J). (gr. 1-6). lib. bdg. 22.61 *(978-1-61772-607-1(9))* Bearport Publishing Co., Inc.

—Tom Brady & the New England Patriots. 2007. (Super Bowl Superstars Ser.). (Illus.). 24p. (J). (gr. k-3). lib. bdg. 22.61 *(978-1-59716-535-8(2))* Bearport Publishing Co., Inc.

—Tony Gonzalez. 2010. (Football Heroes Making a Difference Ser.). (Illus.). 24p. (YA). (gr. 2-5). lib. bdg. 22.61 *(978-1-936087-61-7(8))* Bearport Publishing Co., Inc.

—Tony Romo. 2010. (Football Heroes Making a Difference Ser.). (Illus.). 24p. (YA). (gr. 2-5). lib. bdg. 22.61 *(978-1-936087-60-0(X))* Bearport Publishing Co., Inc.

—Troy Aikman & the Dallas Cowboys. 2008. (Super Bowl Superstars Ser.). (Illus.). 24p. (J). (gr. k-3). lib. bdg. 22.61 *(978-1-59716-737-6(1))* Bearport Publishing Co., Inc.

—Troy Polamalu. 2011. (Football Heroes Making a Difference Ser.). 24p. (YA). (gr. 2-5). lib. bdg. 22.61 *(978-1-61772-312-4(6))* Bearport Publishing Co., Inc.

Savage, Jeff. Aaron Rodgers. 2011. (Amazing Athletes Set VIII Ser.). pap. 45.32 *(978-0-7613-8600-1(9))*; (ENG.). 32p. (gr. 2-5). pap. 7.95 *(978-0-7613-8224-9(0))*; (ENG., Illus.). 32p. (gr. 2-5). lib. bdg. 25.26 *(978-0-7613-8223-2(2))* Lerner Publishing Group.

—Adrian Peterson. 2010. (Amazing Athletes Ser.). (ENG.). 32p. (gr. 2-5). 25.26 *(978-0-7613-5746-9(7))*; pap. 7.95 *(978-0-7613-5758-2(0))* Lerner Publishing Group.

—Brett Favre. 2010. (Amazing Athletes Ser.). (ENG.). 32p. (gr. 2-5). 25.26 *(978-0-7613-6651-5(2))*; pap. 7.95 *(978-0-7613-6653-9(9))* Lerner Publishing Group.

—Brian Urlacher. 2009. (Amazing Athletes Ser.). (ENG.). 32p. (gr. 2-5). 25.26 *(978-0-8225-9991-3(0))* Lerner Publishing Group.

—Clay Matthews. 2012. (Amazing Athletes Ser.). (ENG., Illus.). 32p. (gr. 2-5). pap. 7.95 *(978-1-4677-0308-6(7))*; lib. bdg. 25.26 *(978-1-4677-0307-9(9)*, Lerner Pubns.) Lerner Publishing Group.

—Drew Brees. 2012. (J). lib. bdg. 25.26 *(978-1-4677-0276-8(5)*, Lerner Pubns.) 2010. 32p. (J). (gr. 2-5). 25.26 *(978-0-7613-6652-2(0))* 2010. (ENG.). 32p. (gr. 2-5). pap. 7.95 *(978-0-7613-6654-6(7))* Lerner Publishing Group.

—Eli Manning. (Amazing Athletes Ser.). 2009. (J). (gr. 2-5). 23.93 *(978-0-7613-3984-7(1))* 2009. pap. 40.95 *(978-0-7613-4776-7(3))* 2012. (ENG., Illus.). 32p. (gr. 2-5). pap. 7.95 *(978-0-7613-7684-2(4))* 2012. (ENG., Illus.). 32p. (gr. 2-5). lib. bdg. 25.26 *(978-1-4677-0873-9(9))* Lerner Publishing Group.

—LaDainian Tomlinson. 2009. (Amazing Athletes Ser.). (ENG.). 32p. (gr. 2-5). 25.26 *(978-0-8225-9989-0(9))*; pap. 7.95 *(978-1-58013-792-8(X)*, First Avenue Editions) Lerner Publishing Group.

—Mark Sanchez. 2011. (Amazing Athletes Set VIII Ser.). pap. 45.32 *(978-0-7613-8603-2(3))*; (ENG.). 32p. (gr. 2-5). pap. 7.95 *(978-0-7613-7820-4(0))*; (ENG., Illus.). 32p. (gr. 2-5). lib. bdg. 25.26 *(978-0-7613-7673-6(9))* Lerner Publishing Group.

—Michael Vick. (Amazing Athletes Ser.). 32p. (gr. 2-5). 2005. (Illus.). (J). lib. bdg. 23.93 *(978-0-8225-2430-4(9))* 2011. (ENG.). pap. 7.95 *(978-0-7613-8129-7(5))* Lerner Publishing Group.

—Michael Vick (Revised Edition) 2011. (Amazing Athletes Set VIII Ser.). pap. 45.32 *(978-0-7613-8604-9(1))* Lerner Publishing Group.

—Peyton Manning. (Amazing Athletes Ser.). (Illus.). 32p. 2007. (J). (gr. 2-5). lib. bdg. 23.93 *(978-0-8225-6445-4(9))* 2007. (J). (gr. 2-6). per. 7.95 *(978-0-8225-6446-1(7))* 2005. (J). (gr. 3-4). lib. bdg. 23.93 *(978-0-8225-4034-2(7))* 2nd rev. ed. 2012. (ENG., (gr. 2-5). pap. 7.95 *(978-1-4677-0875-3(5))* 2nd rev. ed. 2012. (ENG., (gr. 2-5). lib. bdg. 25.26 *(978-1-4677-0874-6(7))* Lerner Publishing Group.

—Peyton Manning: Precision Passer. (Sports Achievers Biographies Ser.). (Illus.). 2005. 80p. (gr. 7-12). lib. bdg. 22.60 *(978-0-8225-3683-3(8))* 2003. 64p. (YA). (gr. 4-9). pap. 5.95 *(978-0-8225-9865-7(5))* Lerner Publishing Group.

—Tim Tebow. 2012. (Amazing Athletes Ser.). (ENG., Illus.). 32p. (gr. 2-5). pap. 7.95 *(978-1-4677-0334-5(6))* Lerner Publishing Group.

—Tom Brady. 32p. 2008. (Illus.). (J). pap. 7.95 *(978-0-7613-4215-1(X))* 2005. (Illus.). (J). (gr. 3-7). lib. bdg. 23.93 *(978-0-8225-2948-4(3))* 2nd rev. ed. 2014. (ENG.). (gr. 2-5). pap. 7.95 *(978-1-4677-4582-6(0))* Lerner Publishing Group. (Lerner Pubns.).

—Tom Brady (Revised Edition) 2009. pap. 40.95 *(978-0-7613-4898-6(0))* Lerner Publishing Group.

—Tony Romo. 2010. (Amazing Athletes Ser.). (ENG.). 32p. (gr. 2-5). 25.26 *(978-0-7613-5744-5(0))*; pap. 7.95 *(978-0-7613-5754-4(8))* Lerner Publishing Group.

Schauer, Pete. Russell Wilson: Super Bowl Sensation. 2015. (Living Legends of Sports Ser.). (ENG.). 48p. (J). (gr. 5-6). pap. 14.05 *(978-1-68048-115-0(0)*, Britannica Educational Publishing) Rosen Publishing Group, Inc., The.

Schauer, Peter J. Russell Wilson: Super Bowl Sensation. 2015. (Living Legends of Sports Ser.). (ENG., Illus.). 48p. (J). (gr. 5-6). 25.85 *(978-1-68048-114-3(2)*, Britannica Educational Publishing) Rosen Publishing Group, Inc., The.

Scheff, Matt. Aaron Rodgers, 1 vol. 2016. (ENG., Illus.). 32p. (J). *(978-1-62403-827-3(1)*, SportsZone) ABDO Publishing Co.

—Andrew Luck, 1 vol. 2016. (ENG., Illus.). 32p. (J). *(978-1-62403-825-9(5))* ABDO Publishing Co.

—Eli Manning: Football Superstar, 1 vol. 2014. (Superstar Athletes Ser.). (ENG.). 24p. (gr. 1-2). pap. 7.29 *(978-1-4765-9430-9(9))*; lib. bdg. 25.32 *(978-1-4765-8601-4(2))* Capstone Press of Coughlan Cos.

—J.J. Watt, 1 vol. 2016. (ENG., Illus.). 32p. (J). *(978-1-62403-828-0(X)*, 1391414, SportsZone) ABDO Publishing Co.

—Peyton Manning, 1 vol. 2016. (ENG., Illus.). 32p. (J). *(978-1-62403-826-6(3)*, 1391410, SportsZone) ABDO Publishing Co.

—Russell Wilson, 1 vol. 2016. (ENG., Illus.). 32p. (J). *(978-1-62403-829-7(8)*, SportsZone) ABDO Publishing Co.

—Tom Brady: Football Superstar, 1 vol. 2012. (Superstar Athletes Ser.). (ENG.). 24p. (gr. 1-2). pap. 7.29 *(978-1-4296-8006-6(7))*; lib. bdg. 25.32 *(978-1-4296-7685-4(X))* Capstone Press of Coughlan Cos.

—Tom Brady: Football Superstar. 2012. (Superstar Athletes Ser.). (ENG.). 24p. (gr. 1-2). pap. 41.70 *(978-1-4296-8496-5(8))* Capstone Press of Coughlan Cos.

Schoenfeld, Steve. Jake Plummer: The Comeback Cardinal. 2003. (SuperStar Ser.: Vol. 4). 96p. (gr. 4-7). 4.95 *(978-1-58261-165-5(3))* Sports Publishing, LLC.

Scholastic, Inc. Staff & Kelley, K. C. Football Superstars 2014. 2014. (ENG.). 32p. (J). (gr. 1-3). pap. 5.99 *(978-0-545-72219-3(5)*, Scholastic Paperbacks) Scholastic, Inc.

Schuh, Mari. Aaron Rodgers. 2013. (Football Stars up Close Ser.). 24p. (J). (gr. k-5). lib. bdg. 23.93 *(978-1-61772-714-6(8))* Bearport Publishing Co., Inc.

—Russell Wilson. 2016. (Famous Athletes Ser.). (ENG., Illus.). 24p. (gr. k-1). lib. bdg. 26.65 *(978-1-4914-8510-1(8)*, Pebble Plus) Capstone Press of Coughlan Cos.

Shalin, Mike. Drew Bledsoe: Patriot Rifle. 2003. (SuperStar Ser.: Vol. 6). 96p. (gr. 4-7). 4.95 *(978-1-58261-168-6(8))* Sports Publishing, LLC.

Side-By-Side Sports, 1 vol. 2014. (Side-By-Side Sports Ser.). (ENG.). 48p. (gr. 4-6). 111.96 *(978-1-4765-6168-4(0))* Capstone Press of Coughlan Cos.

Smithwick, John. Meet Peyton Manning: Football's Top Quarterback. 2009. (Amazing Athletes/Atletas increíbles Ser.). 32p. (ENG & SPA.). (gr. 1-2). 42.50 *(978-1-61511-307-1(X)*, Editorial Buenas Letras); (gr. 4-5). 47.90 *(978-1-61511-293-7(6)*, PowerKids Pr.) Rosen Publishing Group, Inc., The.

—Meet Shaun Alexander: Football's Top Running Back. (All-Star Players Ser.). 32p. (gr. 4-5). 2009. 47.90 *(978-1-61511-294-4(4)*, PowerKids Pr.) 2007. (Illus.). (YA). lib. bdg. 25.25 *(978-1-4042-3635-6(X))* Rosen Publishing Group, Inc., The.

Steenkamer, Paul. Sports Great Donovan Mcnabb. 2003. (Sports Great Bks.). (Illus.). 64p. (J). lib. bdg. 23.94 *(978-0-7660-2114-3(9))* Enslow Pubs., Inc.

Sterngass, Jon. Brian Urlacher. 2011. (Football Superstars Ser.). (Illus.). 131p. (gr. 6-12). 30.00 *(978-1-60413-752-1(5))* Facts On File, Inc.

—Dan Marino. 2008. (Football Superstars Ser.). 144p. (YA). (gr. 7-12). 30.00 *(978-0-7910-9606-2(8))* Facts On File, Inc.

—Jerry Rice. 2008. (Football Superstars Ser.). (Illus.). 144p. (YA). (gr. 7-12). 30.00 *(978-0-7910-9607-9(6))* Facts On File, Inc.

Stewart, Mark. Eli Manning. 2009. (Today's Superstars Ser.). 48p. (J). (gr. 5-8). (ENG.). pap. 14.05 *(978-1-4339-2159-9(6))*; lib. bdg. 31.95 *(978-1-4339-1966-4(4))* Stevens, Gareth Publishing LLLP.

Stewart, Mark Alan. Tom Brady: Heart of the Huddle. 2003. (Football's New Wave Ser.: up). (Illus.). 48p. (gr. 4-18). lib. bdg. 22.90 *(978-0-7613-2907-7(2)*, Millbrook Pr.) Lerner Publishing Group.

Thornley, Stew. Super Sports Star Brett Favre. 2003. (Super Sports Star Ser.). (Illus.). 48p. (J). (gr. 1-4). lib. bdg. 25.27 *(978-0-7660-2048-1(7))* Enslow Pubs., Inc.

—Super Sports Star Daunte Culpepper. 2003. (Super Sports Star Ser.). (Illus.). 48p. (J). (gr. 1-4). lib. bdg. 25.27 *(978-0-7660-2051-1(7))* Enslow Pubs., Inc.

—Super Sports Star Eddie George. 2003. (Super Sports Star Ser.). (Illus.). 48p. (J). (gr. 1-4). lib. bdg. 25.27 *(978-0-7660-2050-4(9))* Enslow Pubs., Inc.

—Super Sports Star Randy Moss. 2003. (Super Sports Star Ser.). (Illus.). 48p. (J). (gr. 1-4). lib. bdg. 25.27 *(978-0-7660-2049-8(5))* Enslow Pubs., Inc.

Tieck, Sarah. Eli Manning: Football Star, 1 vol. 2008. (Big Buddy Biographies Ser.). (ENG.). 32p. (J). (gr. 2-5). 28.50 *(978-1-60453-124-4(X))* ABDO Publishing Co.

—Eli Manning CD & Book. 2010. (Big Buddy Biographies CD+Book Ser.). 32p. (gr. 2-5). audio compact disk 57.00 *(978-1-61613-309-2(0)*, Big Buddy Bks.) ABDO Publishing Co.

—Eli Manning Site CD & Book. 2010. (Big Buddy Biographies Site CD+Book Ser.). 32p. (gr. 2-5). cd-rom 85.57 *(978-1-61613-281-1(7)*, Big Buddy Bks.) ABDO Publishing Co.

—Peyton Manning: Famous Quarterback, 1 vol. 2010. (Big Buddy Bks.). (ENG.). 32p. (J). (gr. 2-5). 28.50 *(978-1-61613-976-6(5))* ABDO Publishing Co.

—Russell Wilson: Super Bowl Champion, 1 vol. 2014. (Big Buddy Biographies Set 12 Ser.). (ENG.). 32p. (gr. 2-5). 28.50 *(978-1-62403-574-6(4))* ABDO Publishing Co.

—Tom Brady: Famous Quarterback, 1 vol. 2008. (Big Buddy Biographies Ser.). (ENG.). 32p. (J). (gr. 2-5). 28.50 *(978-1-60453-118-3(5))* ABDO Publishing Co.

Tihe Bookazines Staff. Sports Illustrated: Brett Favre: The Tribute. 2008. (YA). pap. 14.95 *(978-1-60320-549-8(7))* Time Inc. Bks.

Tillman, Charles. The Middle School Rules of Charles Tillman. 2015. (Middle School Rules Ser.). (ENG., Illus.). 176p. (J). (gr. 4-8). 14.99 *(978-1-4245-5101-9(3))* BroadStreet Publishing.

Torres, John. Tim Tebow. 2012. (J). lib. bdg. 25.70 *(978-1-61228-317-3(9))* Mitchell Lane Pubs., Inc.

Torsiello, David P. Read about Drew Brees. 2011. (I Like Sports Stars! Ser.). (Illus.). 24p. (J). (gr. k-18). pap. 7.95 *(978-1-59845-299-0(1)*, Enslow Elementary) Enslow Pubs., Inc.

—Read about Eli Manning. 2011. (I Like Sports Stars! Ser.). (Illus.). 24p. (J). (gr. k-18). pap. 7.95 *(978-1-59845-298-3(3)*, Enslow Elementary); (gr. 1-4). lib. bdg. 22.60 *(978-0-7660-3832-5(7))* Enslow Pubs., Inc.

Towle, Mike. Walter Payton: Football's Sweetest Superstar. 2005. (Great American Sports Legends Ser.). (ENG., Illus.). 225p. (gr. 3-7). per. 12.95 *(978-1-58182-476-6(9)*, 1249190) Turner Publishing Co.

Tracy, Kathleen. Day by Day with Eli Manning. 2011. (Day by Day with... Ser.). (Illus.). 32p. (J). (gr. -1-2). lib. bdg. 25.70 *(978-1-58415-985-8(5))* Mitchell Lane Pubs., Inc.

—Troy Polamalu. 2011. (Robbie Reader Ser.). (Illus.). 32p. (J). (gr. 2-5). lib. bdg. 25.70 *(978-1-61228-059-2(5))* Mitchell Lane Pubs., Inc.

—What It's Like to Be Mark Sanchez. de la Vega, Eida, tr. from ENG. 2011. (What It's Like to Be... = Que Se Sienta Al Ser... Ser.). (ENG & SPA., Illus.). 32p. (J). (gr. -1-2). lib. bdg. 25.70 *(978-1-58415-994-0(4))* Mitchell Lane Pubs., Inc.

Trotter, Jim. Junior Seau: Overcoming the Odds. 2003. (SuperStar Ser.: Vol. 7). 96p. (gr. 4-7). 4.95 *(978-1-58261-169-3(6))* Sports Publishing, LLC.

Wargin, Kathy-jo. Win One for the Gipper: America's Football Hero. Langton, Bruce, illus. 2004. (ENG.). 40p. (J). (gr. k-6). 16.95 *(978-1-58536-221-9(2))* Sleeping Bear Pr.

Weber, Terri. Ricky Williams. 2004. (J). pap. *(978-1-932724-33-2(8))*; lib. bdg. *(978-1-932724-32-5(X))* Panda Publishing, L.L.C. (Bios for Kids).

Wheeler, Jill C. Michael Vick. 2006. (Awesome Athletes Ser.). (Illus.). 32p. (J). (gr. 3-7). lib. bdg. 22.78 *(978-1-59928-308-1(5))* ABDO Publishing Co.

Whiting, Jim. Liverpool FC: Soccer Champions. 2016. (Soccer Champions Ser.). (ENG.). 48p. (J). (gr. 5-9). pap. 12.00 *(978-1-62832-193-7(8)*, Creative Paperbacks) Creative Co., The.

—Troy Polamalu. 2012. (Superstars of Pro Football Ser.). 64p. (J). 22.95 *(978-1-4222-2725-1(1))* Mason Crest.

Williams, Zella. Mark Sanchez: Quarterback on the Rise. 2010. (Hispanic Headliners Ser.). (ENG.). 24p. (J). pap. 8.25 *(978-1-4488-1484-6(7)*, PowerKids Pr.) Rosen Publishing Group, Inc., The.

—Mark Sanchez: Quarterback on the Rise - Mariscal de Campo en Ascenso. 2010. (Hispanic Headliners / Hispanos en Las Noticias Ser.). (ENG & SPA.). 24p. (J). (gr. 2-5). 22.60 *(978-1-4488-1171-7(6))* Rosen Publishing Group, Inc., The.

—Tony Romo: Star Quarterback. 2010. (Hispanic Headliners Ser.). (ENG.). 24p. (J). pap. 8.25 *(978-1-4488-1476-3(6))*; lib. bdg. 22.60 *(978-1-4488-1456-5(1))* Rosen Publishing Group, Inc., The. (PowerKids Pr.).

—Tony Romo: Star Quarterback - Tony Romo - Mariscal de Campo Estrella. 2010. (Hispanic Headliners / Hispanos en Las Noticias Ser.). (ENG & SPA.). 24p. (J). (gr. 2-5). lib. bdg. 22.60 *(978-1-4488-0712-3(3))* Rosen Publishing Group, Inc., The.

Willis, Chris. Dutch Clark: The Life of an NFL Legend & the Birth of the Detroit Lions. 2012. (ENG., Illus.). 422p. 72.00 *(978-0-8108-8520-2(4))* Scarecrow Pr., Inc.

Wilner, Barry. Buffalo Bills. 2015. (Insider's Guide to Pro Football Ser.). (ENG.). 32p. (J). (gr. k-3). 28.50 *(978-1-63143-987-2(1)*, 208822) Child's World, Inc., The.

—Eli Manning: A Football Star Who Cares. 2013. (Sports Stars Who Care Ser.). 48p. (J). 25.27 *(978-0-7660-4300-8(2))*; (gr. 3-4). pap. 8.95 *(978-1-4644-0545-7(X)*, Enslow Elementary) Enslow Pubs., Inc.

—Football's Top 10 Quarterbacks. 2010. (Top 10 Sports Stars Ser.). (Illus.). 48p. (J). (gr. 5-9). 25.27 *(978-0-7660-3469-3(0))* Enslow Pubs., Inc.

—Football's Top 10 Running Backs. 2010. (Top 10 Sports Stars Ser.). (Illus.). 48p. (J). (gr. 5-9). 25.27 *(978-0-7660-3468-6(2))* Enslow Pubs., Inc.

—Peyton Manning: A Football Star Who Cares. 2011. (Sports Stars Who Care Ser.). (Illus.). 48p. (J). (gr. 3-18). pap. 8.95 *(978-1-59845-232-7(0)*, Enslow Elementary); (gr. 2-5). lib. bdg. 25.27 *(978-0-7660-3774-8(6))* Enslow Pubs., Inc.

—Sports Great Peyton Manning. 2003. (Sports Great Bks.). (Illus.). 64p. (J). (gr. 4-10). lib. bdg. 23.94 *(978-0-7660-2033-7(9))* Enslow Pubs., Inc.

—Tom Brady: A Football Star Who Cares. 2011. (Sports Stars Who Care Ser.). (Illus.). 48p. (J). (gr. 3-18). pap. 8.95 *(978-1-59845-233-4(9)*, Enslow Elementary); (gr. 2-5). lib. bdg. 25.27 *(978-0-7660-3773-1(8))* Enslow Pubs., Inc.

Wilson, J. H. Bright Sunset. 2006. (ENG., Illus.). 144p. (J). per. 7.99 *(978-1-84550-114-3(4)*, b61e23be-8f6b-4f53-b2ba-20d49c6ad50e) Christian Focus Pubns. GBR. Dist: Bookmasters Distribution.

Woog, Adam. Joe Montana. 2008. (Football Superstars Ser.). (Illus.). 120p. (YA). (gr. 7-12). 30.00 *(978-0-7910-9568-3(1))* Facts On File, Inc.

—LaDainian Tomlinson. 2011. (Football Superstars Ser.). (Illus.). 124p. (gr. 6-12). 30.00 *(978-1-60413-757-6(6))* Facts On File, Inc.

—Reggie Bush. 2011. (Football Superstars Ser.). (Illus.). 126p. (gr. 6-12). 30.00 *(978-1-60413-756-9(8)*, Chelsea Hse.) Facts On File, Inc.

—Walter Payton. 2008. (Football Superstars Ser.). 136p. (YA). (gr. 7-12). 30.00 *(978-0-7910-9567-6(3))* Facts On File, Inc.

Worthington, Joe. The Mannings: Football's Famous Family. 2005. (High Five Reading - Blue Ser.). (ENG., Illus.). 48p. (gr. 3-4). per. 9.00 *(978-0-7368-5741-3(9)*, High Five Reading (RBL)) Capstone Press of Coughlan Cos.

Yomtov, Nel. Colin Kaepernick. 2014. (Football Stars up Close Ser.). 24p. (J). (gr. 1-6). lib. bdg. 23.93 *(978-1-62724-085-7(3))* Bearport Publishing Co., Inc.

—Robert Griffin III. 2014. (Football Stars up Close Ser.). 24p. (J). (gr. 1-6). lib. bdg. 23.93 *(978-1-62724-083-3(7))* Bearport Publishing Co., Inc.

Zuehlke, Jeffrey. Ben Roethlisberger. 2009. pap. 6.95 *(978-0-7613-5418-5(2)*, Lerner Pubns.) 2008. pap. 40.95 *(978-0-8225-9284-6(3))* 2007. (Illus.). 32p. (J). (gr. -1-3). per. 6.95 *(978-0-8225-7665-5(1)*, First Avenue Editions) Lerner Publishing Group.

—Donovan Mcnabb. 2006. (Amazing Athletes Ser.). (J). lib. bdg. 26.65 *(978-0-8225-5957-3(9)*, Lerner Pubns.) Lerner Publishing Group.

FOOTBALL—FICTION

Adler, David A. Don't Throw It to Mo! Ricks, Sam, illus. 2015. (Mo Jackson Ser.: bk.1). (ENG.). 32p. (J). (gr. 1-2). 14.99 *(978-0-670-01631-0(4)*, Penguin Young Readers) Penguin Young Readers Group.

—Don't Throw It to Mo! 2016. (Penguin Young Readers Level 2 Ser.). lib. bdg. 13.55 *(978-0-606-38852-8(4))* Turtleback Bks.

Allard, Harry & Marshall, James. Miss Nelson Has a Field Day. 2015. 32p. pap. 7.00 *(978-1-61003-506-4(2))* Center for the Collaborative Classroom.

Allard, Harry G., Jr. Miss Nelson Has a Field Day, 1 vol. Marshall, James, illus. 2012. (ENG.). 32p. (J). (gr. -1-3). audio compact disk 10.99 *(978-0-547-75376-8(4))* Houghton Mifflin Harcourt Publishing Co.

Anonymous. The Book of David. 2014. (ENG., Illus.). 288p. (YA). (gr. 9). pap. 9.99 *(978-1-4424-8985-1(5)*, Simon Pulse) Simon Pulse.

Arnold, Tedd. Hooray for Fly Guy! 2008. (Fly Guy Ser.: 6). (ENG.). 32p. (J). (gr. -1-3). 6.99 *(978-0-545-00724-5(0))* Scholastic, Inc.

Aryal, Aimee. Go, Pack, Go! De Angel, Miguel, illus. 2007. 24p. (J). (gr. -1-3). 14.95 *(978-1-932888-94-2(2))* Mascot Bks., Inc.

—Here We Go, Steelers! 2007. (YA). 14.95 *(978-1-932888-78-2(0))* Mascot Bks., Inc.

—How 'Bout Them Cowboys! De Angel, Miguel, illus. 2007. 24p. (J). 17.95 *(978-1-932888-90-4(X))* Mascot Bks., Inc.

—How 'Bout Them Cowboys! Coloring Book. 2007. (YA). pap. 4.95 *(978-1-932888-77-5(2))* Mascot Bks., Inc.

—Let's Go, Chiefs! De Angel, Miguel, illus. 2007. 24p. (J). lib. bdg. 14.95 *(978-1-932888-93-5(4))* Mascot Bks., Inc.

—Let's Go, Colts! 2007. (YA). 14.95 *(978-1-932888-86-7(1))* Mascot Bks., Inc.

—Lets Go Illini! Shrestha, Anuj, illus. 2004. 24p. (J). lib. bdg. 19.95 *(978-1-932888-21-8(7))* Mascot Bks., Inc.

—Let's Go, Panthers! De Angel, Miguel, illus. 2007. 24p. (J). (gr. -1-3). 14.95 *(978-1-932888-97-3(7))* Mascot Bks., Inc.

—Let's Go, Seahawks! De Angel, Miguel, illus. 2007. 24p. (J). lib. bdg. 14.95 *(978-1-932888-95-9(0))* Mascot Bks., Inc.

—Let's Go, Vikings! De Angel, Miguel, illus. 2007. 24p. (J). 14.95 *(978-1-932888-99-7(3))* Mascot Bks., Inc.

Attanas, John. Eddie & the Jets. 2005. 142p. (J). (gr. 4-7). lib. bdg. 15.95 *(978-1-58196-026-6(3)*, Darby Creek) Lerner Publishing Group.

Bacskai, Andrew. Fighting the Legend, 1 vol. unabr. ed. 2011. (District 13 Ser.). (ENG.). 48p. (YA). (gr. 9-12). pap. 7.95 *(978-1-61651-278-1(4))* Saddleback Educational Publishing, Inc.

Banks, Anna. Joyride. 2015. (ENG.). 288p. (YA). (gr. 7). 17.99 *(978-1-250-03961-3(4)*, 9781250039613) Feiwel & Friends.

Barber, Ronde & Barber, Tiki. Go Long! 2011. (Barber Game Time Bks.). (ENG.). 160p. (J). (gr. 3-7). pap. 7.99 *(978-1-4169-8573-0(5)*, Simon & Schuster/Paula Wiseman Bks.) Simon & Schuster/Paula Wiseman Bks.

Barber, Tiki & Barber, Ronde. End Zone. (Barber Game Time Bks.). (ENG., Illus.). (J). (gr. 3-7). 2014. 192p. pap. 7.99 *(978-1-4169-9098-7(4))* 2012. 176p. 15.99 *(978-1-4169-9097-0(6))* Simon & Schuster/Paula Wiseman Bks. (Simon & Schuster/Paula Wiseman Bks.).

—Goal Line. (Barber Game Time Bks.). (ENG., Illus.). 176p. (J). (gr. 3-7). 2013. pap. 6.99 *(978-1-4169-9096-3(8))* 2011. 15.99 *(978-1-4169-9095-6(X))* Simon & Schuster/Paula Wiseman Bks. (Simon & Schuster/Paula Wiseman Bks.).

—Kickoff! 2007. (Barber Game Time Bks.). (ENG.). 160p. (J). (gr. 3-7). 15.99 *(978-1-4169-3618-3(1)*, Simon & Schuster/Paula Wiseman Bks.) Simon & Schuster/Paula Wiseman Bks.

—Red Zone. (Barber Game Time Bks.). (ENG., 176p. (J). (gr. 3-7). 2013. Illus.). pap. 7.99 *(978-1-4169-6861-0(X))* 2010. 15.99 *(978-1-4169-6860-3(1))* Simon & Schuster/Paula Wiseman Bks. (Simon & Schuster/Paula Wiseman Bks.).

—Wild Card. (Barber Game Time Bks.). (ENG.). 160p. (J). (gr. 3-7). 2012. pap. 7.99 *(978-1-4169-6859-7(8))* 2009. 15.99 *(978-1-4169-6858-0(X))* Simon & Schuster/Paula Wiseman Bks. (Simon & Schuster/Paula Wiseman Bks.).

Barbour, Ralph Henry. Behind the Line: A Story of College Life & Football. 2006. (Illus.). pap. *(978-1-4065-0775-1(X))* Dodo Pr.

—The Half-Back. 2005. 27.95 *(978-1-4218-1494-0(3))*; 220p. pap. 12.95 *(978-1-4218-1594-7(X))* 1st World Publishing, Inc. (1st World Library - Literary Society).

—The Half-Back. 2006. (Illus.). pap. *(978-1-4065-0776-8(8))* Dodo Pr.

—The Half-Back. 2007. 132p. per. *(978-1-4068-3665-3(6))* Echo Library.

—Left Tackle Thayer. 2006. (Illus.). pap. *(978-1-4065-0777-5(6))* Dodo Pr.

—Right Guard Grant. Crump, Leslie, illus. 2011. 304p. 48.95 *(978-1-258-10515-0(2))* Literary Licensing, LLC.

Barrow, Shelley. My Life: The Story of a NFL Child. 2007. (J). 16.99 *(978-0-9792647-0-2(7))* Mikenzi's Kardz & Bks. Llc.

Bee, Clair. Fourth down Showdown: A Chip Hilton Sports Story. 2011. 222p. (gr. 3-8). 44.95 *(978-1-258-07163-9(0))* Literary Licensing, LLC.

—Freshman Quarterback: Chip Hilton Sports Story No. 9. 2011. 222p. (gr. 8-12). 44.95 *(978-1-258-07328-2(5))* Literary Licensing, LLC.

—Ten Seconds to Play: A Chip Hilton Sports Story. 2011. 222p. (gr. 8-12). 44.95 *(978-1-258-09715-8(X))* Literary Licensing, LLC.

—Triple Threat Trouble: A Chip Hilton Sports Story. 2011. 192p. (gr. 4-7). 42.95 *(978-1-258-10118-3(1))* Literary Licensing, LLC.

Bee, Clair Francis. A Pass & a Prayer: A Chip Hilton Sports Story. 2011. 224p. 44.95 *(978-1-258-06272-9(0))* Literary Licensing, LLC.

Behrens, Andy. The Fast & the Furriest. 2011. (ENG.). 256p. (J). (gr. 3-7). 7.99 *(978-0-375-85900-7(4)*, Yearling) Random Hse. Children's Bks.

Benson, Linda Sue. Hey Latrell, 1 vol. Johnson, Bruce, illus. 2009. 48p. pap. 16.95 *(978-1-60813-961-3(1))* America Star Bks.

Berenstain, Mike. The Berenstain Bears Play Football! Berenstain, Mike, illus. 2017. (I Can Read Level 1 Ser.). (Illus.). 32p. (J). (gr. -1-3). pap. 3.99 ***(978-0-06-235033-6(1))*** HarperCollins Pubs.

—The Berenstain Bears Play Football! 2017. (Berenstain Bears — I Can Read Ser.). lib. bdg. 13.55 ***(978-0-606-40068-8(0))*** Turtleback Bks.

Berrill, Jack. Under the Friday Night Lights! A Gil Thorp Football Collection. 2004. (Illus.). 328p. per. 32.95 *(978-0-930099-14-5(1))* Take Five Pubs.

Berrios, Frank. Football with Dad. Biggs, Brian, illus. 2015. (Little Golden Book Ser.). (ENG.). 24p. (J). (-k). 4.99 *(978-0-385-37925-0(0)*, Golden Bks.) Random Hse. Children's Bks.

Bildner, Phil. The Greatest Game Ever Played. Pullen, Zachary, illus. 2015. (ENG.). 40p. (J). (gr. k-3). 8.99 *(978-0-14-751451-6(7)*, Puffin Books) Penguin Young Readers Group.

—Turkey Bowl. Payne, C. F., illus. 2008. (ENG.). 32p. (J). (gr. k-3). 15.99 *(978-0-689-87896-1(6)*, Simon & Schuster Bks. For Young Readers) Simon & Schuster Bks. For Young Readers.

Bogart, Mike. The Henderson Twins in Muckleball! 2006. 107p. pap. 16.95 *(978-1-4241-3050-4(6))* PublishAmerica, Inc.

Born to be a Tiger. 2004. (J). per. 18.50 net. *(978-0-615-12596-1(4))* Little Band Man Co., LLC, The.

Bowen, Carl. Quarterback Rush, 1 vol. Garcia, Eduardo, illus. 2014. (Sports Illustrated Kids Graphic Novels Ser.). (ENG.). 72p. (gr. 2-5). 26.65 *(978-1-4342-6489-3(0))* Stone Arch Bks.

Bowen, Fred. Quarterback Season, 1 vol. 2011. (ENG.). 144p. (J). (gr. 2-7). pap. 5.95 *(978-1-56145-594-2(6)*, Peachtree Junior) Peachtree Pubs.

—Touchdown Trouble, 1 vol. 2009. (Fred Bowen Sports Story Ser.). (ENG.). 128p. (J). (gr. 2-7). pap. 5.95 *(978-1-56145-497-6(4))* Peachtree Pubs.

Bradley, John Ed. Call Me by My Name. (ENG.). (YA). (gr. 7). 2015. 288p. pap. 11.99 *(978-1-4424-9794-8(7))* 2014. (Illus.). 272p. 17.99 *(978-1-4424-9793-1(9)*, Atheneum Bks. for Young Readers) Simon & Schuster Children's Publishing.

Bradman, Tony. Game Over! 2003. 169p. pap. *(978-0-552-54762-8(X)*, Corgi) Transworld Publishers Ltd.

Brooks, Walter R. Freddy Plays Football. Wiese, Kurt, illus. 2013. (ENG.). 288p. (gr. 4-13). pap. 10.99 *(978-1-4683-0667-5(7)*, 460667) Overlook Pr., The.

Brouwer, Sigmund. Cobra Strike, 1 vol. 2007. (Orca Sports Ser.). (ENG.). 176p. (YA). (gr. 6-10). per. 9.95 *(978-1-55143-725-5(2))* Orca Bk. Pubs. USA.

Brown, Herman. The Option. 2014. (Red Zone Ser.: 3). (ENG.). 104p. (YA). (gr. 6-12). pap. 7.95 *(978-1-4677-4473-7(5)*, Darby Creek); lib. bdg. 27.93 *(978-1-4677-2128-8(X))* Lerner Publishing Group.

Buchholz, Chris. Beckett 81. 2010. 147p. pap. 10.00 *(978-0-557-27451-2(6))* Lulu Pr., Inc.

Carlson, Nancy. Louanne Pig in Making the Team. 2005. (Louanne Pig Ser.). (Illus.). 32p. (J). (gr. k-2). lib. bdg. 15.95 *(978-1-57505-914-3(2))* Lerner Publishing Group.

Cassidy, Anne & Durant, Alan. Doing the Double. 2007. (Sharp Shades Ser.). (ENG., Illus.). 64p. (J). (gr. 6-8). pap. 8.99 *(978-0-237-53447-9(9))* Evans Brothers, Ltd. GBR. Dist: Independent Pubs. Group.

Christopher, Matt. Catch That Pass! 2005. (Sports Classics III Ser.). 110p. (J). lib. bdg. 15.00 *(978-1-59054-748-9(9))* Fitzgerald Bks.

—Catch That Pass! l.t. ed. 2007. (New Matt Christopher Sports Library). 128p. (J). (gr. 4-6). lib. bdg. 26.60 *(978-1-59953-105-2(4))* Norwood Hse. Pr.

—The Dog That Called the Signals. Ogden, Bill, illus. 2010. (Matt Christopher Sports Readers Ser.). 48p. (J). (gr. 1-3). lib. bdg. 23.93 *(978-1-59953-349-0(9))* Norwood Hse. Pr.

—The Dog That Stole Football Plays. Vasconcellos, Daniel et al, illus. 2013. (Passport to Reading Level 3 Ser.). (ENG.). 32p. (J). (gr. 1-4). pap. 4.99 *(978-0-316-21849-8(9))* Little, Brown Bks. for Young Readers.

—The Dog That Stole the Football Plays. Ogden, Bill, illus. 2010. (Matt Christopher Sports Readers Ser.). 48p. (J). (gr. 1-3). lib. bdg. 23.93 *(978-1-59953-350-6(2))* Norwood Hse. Pr.

—Football Double Threat. 2008. (ENG.). 128p. (J). (gr. 3-7). pap. 5.99 *(978-0-316-01632-2(2))* Little, Brown Bks. for Young Readers.

—The Great Quarterback Switch. 2008. (New Matt Christopher Sports Library). 144p. (J). (gr. 4-6). lib. bdg. 26.60 *(978-1-59953-216-5(6))* Norwood Hse. Pr.

—Halfback Attack. Meyer, Karen, illus. 2005. (Sports Classics II Ser.). 104p. (J). lib. bdg. 15.00 *(978-1-59054-752-6(7))* Fitzgerald Bks.

—Long-Arm Quarterback. 2007. (New Matt Christopher Sports Library). 113p. (J). (gr. 4-6). lib. bdg. 26.60 *(978-1-59953-114-4(3))* Norwood Hse. Pr.

—Long Arm Quarterback. 2005. (Sports Classics II Ser.). 117p. (J). lib. bdg. 15.00 *(978-1-59054-761-8(6))* Fitzgerald Bks.

—QB Blitz. 2011. (ENG.). 144p. (J). (gr. 3-7). pap. 5.99 *(978-0-316-17682-8(6))* Little, Brown Bks. for Young Readers.

—The Team That Couldn't Lose. 2010. (Matt Christopher Sports Library). 128p. (J). (gr. 4-6). lib. bdg. 26.60 *(978-1-59953-358-2(8))* Norwood Hse. Pr.

—Tough to Tackle. 2010. (Matt Christopher Sports Library). 128p. (J). (gr. 4-6). lib. bdg. 26.60 *(978-1-59953-359-9(6))* Norwood Hse. Pr.

Ciencin, Scott & Fuentes, Benny. End Zone Thunder, 1 vol. Sandoval, Gerardo, illus. 2010. (Sports Illustrated Kids Graphic Novels Ser.). (ENG.). 56p. (gr. 2-3). 26.65 *(978-1-4342-2010-3(9))*; pap. 7.19 *(978-1-4342-2784-3(7))* Stone Arch Bks.

Cohen, Joshua C. Leverage. 2012. (ENG.). 432p. (YA). (gr. 9). pap. 8.99 *(978-0-14-242086-7(7)*, Speak) Penguin Young Readers Group.

Cole, Bob. Charging Forward: Heart, Team & Eight Seconds, the Boys that Refuse to Lose, 1 vol. 2009. 149p. pap. 24.95 *(978-1-61546-775-4(0))* America Star Bks.

Coleman, K. Showdown. 2017. (Gridiron Ser.). (ENG.). (YA). (gr. 6-12). 112p. pap. 7.99 ***(978-1-5124-5354-6(4))***; lib. bdg. 26.65 ***(978-1-5124-3978-6(9))*** Lerner Publishing Group. (Darby Creek).

—Signing Day. 2017. (Gridiron Ser.). (ENG.). (YA). (gr. 6-12). 120p. pap. 7.99 ***(978-1-5124-5355-3(2))***; lib. bdg. 26.65 ***(978-1-5124-3983-0(5))*** Lerner Publishing Group. (Darby Creek).

Coleman, K. R. The Late Hit. 2017. (Gridiron Ser.). (ENG.). 128p. (YA). (gr. 6-12). 26.65 ***(978-1-5124-3982-3(7))***; pap. 7.99 ***(978-1-5124-5352-2(8))*** Lerner Publishing Group. (Darby Creek).

Collar, Bill. It;s More Than A Game! Vervoort, Sarah, illus. 2007. (J). per. 6.95 *(978-1-933556-81-9(1))* Publishers' Graphics, L.L.C.

Counts, Monika, illus. Alabama Countdown to Touchdown. 2010. (Countdown to Touchdown Ser.). 20p. (J). 14.95 *(978-1-61524-080-7(2)*, Intervisual/Piggy Toes) Bendon, Inc.

—Florida Countdown to Touchdown. 2010. (Countdown to Touchdown Ser.). 20p. 14.95 *(978-1-61524-082-1(9)*, Intervisual/Piggy Toes) Bendon, Inc.

—LSU Countdown to Touchdown. 2010. (Countdown to Touchdown Ser.). 20p. 14.95 *(978-1-61524-081-4(0)*, Intervisual/Piggy Toes) Bendon, Inc.

Coy, John. Crackback. 2007. 201p. (gr. 7-12). 17.00 *(978-0-7569-8274-4(X))* Perfection Learning Corp.

Daniel, Claire. A Winning Attitude. Winborn, Marsha, illus. 2007. 14p. pap. 4.75 *(978-0-15-377381-5(2))* Harcourt Schl. Pubs.

Davie, Jan. Apollo Cafe. 2005. 76p. pap. *(978-1-84401-565-8(3))* Athena Pr.

De Angel, Miguel, illus. Let's Go, Patriots! 2007. 24p. (J). (gr. -1-3). 14.95 *(978-1-932888-98-0(5))* Mascot Bks., Inc.

Deuker, Carl. Gutless. (ENG.). 336p. (YA). (gr. 7). 2017. pap. 9.99 ***(978-1-328-74206-3(7))*** 2016. 17.99 *(978-0-544-64961-3(3))* Houghton Mifflin Harcourt Publishing Co. (HMH Books For Young Readers).

Deuker, Carl. Gym Candy. 2008. (ENG.). 320p. (YA). (gr. 7). pap. 9.99 *(978-0-547-07631-7(2))* Houghton Mifflin Harcourt Publishing Co.

—Gym Candy. 2008. 313p. 19.00 *(978-1-60686-376-3(2))* Perfection Learning Corp.

Dickson, Darnell G. Small Town, Big Dreams: A Dane Jordan Sports Novel. 2008. pap. 14.99 *(978-1-59955-229-3(9))* Cedar Fort, Inc./CFI Distribution.

Dixon, Franklin W. Kickoff to Danger. 2005. (Hardy Boys I Ser.: No. 170). 149p. (J). lib. bdg. 15.00 *(978-1-59054-843-1(4))* Fitzgerald Bks.

Dooley, Vince. How 'Bout Them Dawgs! De Angel, Miguel, illus. 2006. 24p. (J). lib. bdg. 17.95 *(978-1-932888-46-1(2))* Mascot Bks., Inc.

Double or Nothing. 2014. (It Takes Two Ser.: 3). (ENG., Illus.). 160p. (J). (gr. 3-7). pap. 6.99 *(978-1-4814-1652-8(9)*, Simon Spotlight) Simon Spotlight.

Double Reverse, 1 vol. 2014. (Sports Stories Ser.). (ENG.). 128p. (J). (gr. 2-6). pap. 5.95 *(978-1-56145-807-3(4))* Peachtree Pubs.

Doyle, Bill. The Big Foot in the End Zone. Lee, Jared, illus. 2012. (Scream Team Ser.). (ENG.). 96p. (J). (gr. 2-5). pap. 4.99 *(978-0-545-47977-6(0)*, Scholastic Paperbacks) Scholastic, Inc.

Draper, Sharon M. November Blues. 2009. (Jericho Trilogy Ser.). (ENG.). 400p. (YA). (gr. 7). mass mkt. 8.99 *(978-1-4169-0699-5(1)*, Simon Pulse) Simon Pulse.

Dungy, Tony & Dungy, Lauren. A Team Stays Together! Newton, Vanessa Brantley, illus. 2011. (Tony & Lauren Dungy Ready-To-Reads Ser.). (ENG.). 32p. (J). (gr. k-2). pap. 3.99 *(978-1-4424-3539-1(9)*, Simon Spotlight) Simon Spotlight.

Durant, Alan. Spider's Big Match. Hopman, Philip, illus. 2007. (Collins Big Cat Ser.). (ENG.). 32p. (J). (gr. 2-4). pap. 8.99 *(978-0-00-723081-5(8))* HarperCollins Pubs. Ltd. GBR. Dist: Independent Pubs. Group.

Dyan, Penelope. I Like Football — for Boys Only(r). Dyan, Penelope, illus. 2010. (Illus.). 34p. pap. 11.95 *(978-1-935630-27-2(X))* Bellissima Publishing, LLC.

Dye, Pat. War Eagle! De Angel, Miguel, illus. 2006. 24p. (J). lib. bdg. 17.95 *(978-1-932888-47-8(0))* Mascot Bks., Inc.

Elkeles, Simone. Better Than Perfect. 2014. (Wild Cards Ser.). (ENG.). 352p. (YA). (gr. 9). pap. 9.99 *(978-0-8027-3725-0(0)*, 9780802737250, Bloomsbury USA Childrens) Bloomsbury Publishing USA.

—Wild Cards. 2013. 352p. (YA). pap. *(978-0-8027-3738-0(2))* Walker & Co.

Emery, R. G. T-Quarterback. 2011. 206p. 44.95 *(978-1-258-10163-3(7))* Literary Licensing, LLC.

Eulo, Elena Yates. The Great Receiver. 2008. (ENG.). 192p. (J). (gr. 7-18). 16.95 *(978-0-8234-1888-6(X))* Holiday Hse., Inc.

Faul, Pamela. Tc's Big Game. 2010. 24p. pap. 14.95 *(978-1-60911-266-0(0)*, Strategic Bk. Publishing) Strategic Book Publishing & Rights Agency (SBPRA).

Feinstein, John. Cover-Up: Mystery at the Super Bowl. 2008. (Sports Beat Ser.). (ENG.). 320p. (J). (gr. 5). 7.99 *(978-0-440-42205-1(1)*, Yearling) Random Hse. Children's Bks.

—The Walk On. 2015. (Triple Threat Ser.). (ENG.). 384p. (J). (gr. 5). pap. 7.99 *(978-0-385-75349-4(7)*, Yearling) Random Hse. Children's Bks.

—The Walk On. 2015. (Triple Threat Ser.: 1). lib. bdg. 18.40 *(978-0-606-37704-1(2))* Turtleback Bks.

Franckowiak, Jon. When I Grow up I Want to be a Nittany Lion. 2008. 32p. pap. 9.95 *(978-0-9715415-0-4(7))* Franckowiak, Jon.

Fuentes, Benny & Hoena, Blake A. Sack Attack!, 1 vol. Sandoval, Gerardo, illus. 2011. (Sports Illustrated Kids Graphic Novels Ser.). (ENG.). 56p. (gr. 2-3). pap. 7.19 *(978-1-4342-3404-9(5))*; lib. bdg. 26.65 *(978-1-4342-2243-5(8))* Stone Arch Bks.

Ganzer, Diane. Patrick the Wayward Setter: A Christmas Miracle. 2005. 60p. pap. 16.95 *(978-1-4137-8351-3(1))* PublishAmerica, Inc.

Geddes, Diana. Es Temporada de Americano (6 Pack) Palmer, Kate Salley, illus. 2007.Tr. of It's Football Time. (SPA.). 12p. (gr. k-1). pap. *(978-1-57874-330-8(3)*, Kaeden Bks.) Kaeden Corp.

—Es Temporada de Futbol Americano. Palmer, Kate Salley, illus. 2007.Tr. of It's Football Time. (SPA.). 12p. (gr. k-1). pap. 8.95 *(978-1-57874-329-2(X)*, Kaeden Bks.) Kaeden Corp.

Girvan, Gregor. A Trial for Iris. 2013. 32p. pap. 3.95 *(978-1-78035-666-2(8)*, Fastprint Publishing) Upfront Publishing Ltd. GBR. Dist: Printondemand-worldwide.com.

Glines, Abbi. After the Game: A Field Party Novel. 2017. (YA). ***(978-1-5344-0168-6(7)***, Simon Pulse) Simon Pulse.

—Under the Lights. 2016. (Field Party Ser.: 2). (ENG., Illus.). 336p. (YA). (gr. 9). 17.99 *(978-1-4814-3889-6(1)*, Simon Pulse) Simon Pulse.

—Until Friday Night. 2015. (Field Party Ser.: Bk. 1). (ENG.). 336p. (YA). pap. *(978-1-4711-2502-7(5)*, Simon Pulse) Simon Pulse.

Goodnight Football, 1 vol. 2014. (Sports Illustrated Kids Bedtime Bks.). (ENG., Illus.). 32p. (gr. -1-2). lib. bdg. 22.60 *(978-1-4795-5177-4(5))* Capstone Press of Coughlan Cos.

Grab, Daphne. Halftime. 2010. (J). *(978-0-385-90693-7(5))*; *(978-0-385-73783-8(1))* Random House Publishing Group. (Delacorte Pr).

Grambling, Lois G. Nicky Jones & the Roaring Rhinos. Geer, William J., illus. 2004. 32p. (J). 6.95 *(978-1-877810-14-5(2))* Rayve Productions, Inc.

Green, Tim. The Big Time. (Football Genius Ser.: 4). (ENG.). (J). (gr. 3-7). 2011. 304p. pap. 6.99 *(978-0-06-168621-4(2))* 2010. 288p. 16.99 *(978-0-06-168619-1(0))* HarperCollins Pubs.

—Deep Zone. 2011. (Football Genius Ser.: 5). (ENG.). 272p. (J). (gr. 3-7). 16.99 *(978-0-06-201244-9(4))* HarperCollins Pubs.

—Deep Zone. 2012. (Football Genius Ser.: 5). (J). lib. bdg. 17.20 *(978-0-606-26854-7(5)*, Turtleback) Turtleback Bks.

—First Team. 2015. (ENG.). 352p. (J). (gr. 3-7). pap. 6.99 *(978-0-06-220876-7(4))* HarperCollins Pubs.

—First Team. 2014. (ENG.). 336p. (J). (gr. 3-7). 16.99 *(978-0-06-220875-0(6))* HarperCollins Pubs.

—Football Champ. (Football Genius Ser.: 3). (ENG.). (J). (gr. 3-7). 2010. 304p. pap. 6.99 *(978-0-06-162691-3(0))* 2009. (Illus.). 288p. 16.99 *(978-0-06-162689-0(9))* HarperCollins Pubs.

—Football Genius. (Football Genius Ser.: 1). (ENG.). (J). (gr. 5-9). 2008. 272p. pap. 6.99 *(978-0-06-112273-6(4))* 2007. (Illus.). 256p. 16.99 *(978-0-06-112270-5(X))* HarperCollins Pubs.

—Football Genius. l.t. ed. 2008. (Thorndike Literacy Bridge Ser.). 291p. (YA). (gr. 8-12). 23.95 *(978-1-4104-0497-8(8))* Thorndike Pr.

—Football Hero. (Football Genius Ser.: 2). (ENG.). (J). (gr. 3-7). 2009. 320p. pap. 6.99 *(978-0-06-112276-7(9))* 2008. (Illus.). 304p. 16.99 *(978-0-06-112274-3(2))* HarperCollins Pubs.

—Football Hero. l.t. ed. 2008. (YA). 23.95 *(978-1-4104-1116-7(8))* Thorndike Pr.

—Kid Owner. (J). (gr. 3-7). 2016. 352p. pap. 6.99 *(978-0-06-229380-0(X))* 2015. (ENG.). 336p. 16.99 *(978-0-06-229379-4(6))* HarperCollins Pubs.

—Left Out. (J). (gr. 3-7). 2017. 368p. pap. 6.99 ***(978-0-06-229383-1(4))*** 2016. 352p. 16.99 *(978-0-06-229382-4(6))* HarperCollins Pubs.

—Perfect Season. (Football Genius Ser.: 6). (ENG.). (J). (gr. 3-7). 2014. 416p. pap. 6.99 *(978-0-06-220870-5(5))* 2013. 400p. 16.99 *(978-0-06-220869-9(1))* HarperCollins Pubs.

—Touchdown Kid. 2017. 320p. (J). (gr. 3-7). 16.99 ***(978-0-06-229385-5(0))*** HarperCollins Pubs.

Green, Tim. Unstoppable. (ENG.). (J). (gr. 4-7). 2013. 368p. pap. 6.99 *(978-0-06-208957-1(9))* 2012. 352p. 16.99 *(978-0-06-208956-4(0))* HarperCollins Pubs.

Greene, Janice. The Ritual, 1 vol. unabr. ed. 2010. (Q Reads Ser.). (ENG.). 32p. (YA). (gr. 9-12). pap. 6.95 *(978-1-61651-185-2(0))* Saddleback Educational Publishing, Inc.

Gresh, Dannah. Danika's Totally Terrible Toss. 2008. (Secret Keeper Girl Fiction Ser.). (ENG.). 112p. pap. 7.99 *(978-0-8024-8702-5(5))* Moody Pubs.

Gresh, Dannah & Mylin, Janet. Just Call Me Kate. 2008. (Secret Keeper Girl Fiction Ser.). (ENG.). 112p. pap. 7.99 *(978-0-8024-8703-2(3))* Moody Pubs.

Gresh, Dannah K. & Weibel, Suzy. T Is for AnTONIa. 2008. (Secret Keeper Girl Fiction Ser.). (ENG.). 96p. pap. 7.99 *(978-0-8024-8705-6(X))* Moody Pubs.

Grindele, Jenny. Josh, the Jock of High School. 2005. 48p. pap. 16.95 *(978-1-4137-6950-0(0))* America Star Bks.

Gutman, Dan. Coach Hyatt Is a Riot! Paillot, Jim, illus. 2008. (My Weird School Daze Ser.: 4). 112p. (J). (gr. 1-5). lib. bdg. 15.89 *(978-0-06-155408-7(1))*; 4th ed. (ENG.). pap. 4.99 *(978-0-06-155406-3(5))* HarperCollins Pubs.

—The Day Roy Riegels Ran the Wrong Way. Talbott, Kerry, illus. 2011. (ENG.). 40p. (J). (gr. -1-8). 16.99 *(978-1-59990-494-8(2)*, 9781599904948, Bloomsbury USA Childrens) Bloomsbury Publishing USA.

Hale, Bruce. This Gum for Hire. 2003. (Chet Gecko Ser.: 6). (ENG., Illus.). 144p. (J). (gr. 2-5). pap. 5.99 *(978-0-15-202497-0(2))* Houghton Mifflin Harcourt Publishing Co.

—This Gum for Hire. 2007. (Chet Gecko Mystery Ser.). (Illus.). 115p. (J). (gr. 4-7). pap. 6.60 *(978-1-4189-5216-7(8))* Houghton Mifflin Harcourt Supplemental Pubs.

Hamley, Dennis. Haunted United. Fenoughty, Charles, illus. 2004. 148p. per. *(978-1-904529-11-8(9)*, Back to Front) Solidus.

Hancock, H. Irving. The High School Captain of the Team. rev. ed. 2006. 212p. 27.95 (978-1-4218-1740-8(3)); pap. 12.95 (978-1-4218-1840-5(X)) 1st World Publishing, Inc. (1st World Library - Literary Society).

—The High School Captain of the Team. 2007. 176p. per. (978-1-4065-1987-7(1)) Dodo Pr.

—The High School Left End. rev. ed. 2006. 212p. 27.95 (978-1-4218-1742-2(X)); pap. 12.95 (978-1-4218-1842-9(6)) 1st World Publishing, Inc. (1st World Library - Literary Society).

—The High School Left End. 2007. 176p. per. (978-1-4065-1989-1(8)) Dodo Pr.

—The High School Left End, or Dick & Co. Grilling on the Football Gridiron. 2006. (ENG.). 156p. pap. 19.99 (978-1-4264-6385-3(5)); 174p. pap. 21.99 (978-1-4264-6459-1(2)) Creative Media Partners, LLC.

Hand, Cynthia. Unearthly. 2011. (Unearthly Ser.: 1). (ENG.). 464p. (YA). (gr. 8). pap. 9.99 (978-0-06-199617-7(3), HarperTeen) HarperCollins Pubs.

Hand, Jimmie. The Long Way Around. 2005. (Dream Ser.). 150p. (gr. 3-8). pap. 9.95 (978-0-9708992-7-9(0)) Scobre Pr. Corp.

Hanson, Ed. The Pass. 2003. (Barclay Family Adventure Ser.: Bk. 9). (Illus.). 64p. (J). (gr. k-6). per. 3.95 (978-1-56254-557-4(4), SP 5574) Saddleback Educational Publishing, Inc.

Harmon, Michael. Stick. 2015. (ENG.). 240p. (YA). (gr. 9). 17.99 (978-0-385-75436-1(1)); lib. bdg. 20.99 (978-0-385-75437-8(X)) Random Hse. Children's Bks. (Knopf Bks. for Young Readers).

Harris, Michael. Young Marques Becomes a Quiet Storm. 2011. 40p. pap. 22.50 (978-1-4634-4532-4(6)) AuthorHouse.

Hautman, Pete. Rash. 2007. (ENG., Illus.). 272p. (YA). (gr. 7-12). pap. 10.99 (978-0-689-86904-4(5), Simon & Schuster Bks. For Young Readers) Simon & Schuster Bks. For Young Readers.

Heidring, Thatcher. The Football Girl. 2017. (YA). **(978-0-375-99026-7(7)**, Delacorte Pr) Random House Publishing Group.

Heller, Alyson. Touchdown! Björkman, Steve, illus. 2010. (After-School Sports Club Ser.). (ENG.). 32p. (J). (gr. -1-1). pap. 3.99 (978-1-4169-9413-8(0), Simon Spotlight) Simon Spotlight.

Hellman, Charles. Adventures in SportsLand - the Football Bully (with accompanying CD) Tiritilli, Robert, illus. 2008. (Adventures in SportsLand: the Bully Ser.). 32p. (J). (gr. -1-3). 19.95 (978-0-935938-30-2(3)) Williams, Michael.

Hellman, Charles S. The Football Bully. Tiritilli, Robert A., illus. 2013. 34p. pap. 9.25 (978-0-935938-22-7(2)) LuckySports.

Hengel, Katherine. Before the Snap, 1 vol. unabr. ed. 2011. (District 13 Ser.). (ENG.). 48p. (YA). (gr. 9-12). 7.95 (978-1-61651-581-2(3)) Saddleback Educational Publishing, Inc.

Herbach, Geoff. Anything You Want. 2016. (ENG.). 320p. (YA). (gr. 7-12). pap. 9.99 (978-1-4022-9144-9(2), 9781402291449) Sourcebooks, Inc.

—Stupid Fast. 2011. (Felton Reinstein Trilogy Ser.: 1). (ENG.). 320p. (YA). (gr. 7-12). pap. 10.99 (978-1-4022-5630-1(2), 9781402256301) Sourcebooks, Inc.

Heyliger, William. Quarterback Hothead. Grubb, W. B., illus. 2011. 262p. 47.95 (978-1-258-09738-7(9)) Literary Licensing, LLC.

Hillert, Margaret. Touchdown! Dear Dragon. Schimmell, David, illus. 2009. (BeginningtoRead Ser.). 32p. (J). (gr. k-2). lib. bdg. 22.60 (978-1-59953-296-7(4)) Norwood Hse. Pr.

Hoblin, Paul. The Clutch. 2017. (Gridiron Ser.). (ENG.). 120p. (YA). (gr. 6-12). 26.65 **(978-1-5124-3980-9(0))** Lerner Publishing Group.

—False Start. 2017. (Gridiron Ser.). (ENG.). 128p. (YA). (gr. 6-12). 26.65 **(978-1-5124-3979-3(7))**; pap. 7.99 **(978-1-5124-5351-5(X))** Lerner Publishing Group. (Darby Creek).

Hoena, Blake A. & Gonzalez, Jorge. Kickoff Blitz. Ruiz, Alfonso, illus. 2010. (Sports Illustrated Kids Graphic Novels Ser.). 56p. pap. 0.50 (978-1-4342-3205-2(0)); (ENG.). (gr. 2-3). pap. 7.19 (978-1-4342-2292-3(6)); (ENG.). (gr. 2-3). 26.65 (978-1-4342-1909-1(7)) Stone Arch Bks.

Honeyman, Kay. Interference. 2016. (ENG.). 352p. (YA). (gr. 7). 17.99 (978-0-545-81232-0(1), Levine, Arthur A. Bks.) Scholastic, Inc.

Howling, Eric. Red Zone Rivals, 1 vol. 2014. (Lorimer Sports Stories Ser.). (ENG.). 136p. (J). (gr. 4-8). pap. 9.95 (978-1-4594-0714-5(8), 9781459407145) Lorimer, James & Co., Ltd., Pubs. CAN. Dist: Casemate Pubs. & Bk. Distributors, LLC.

Hughes, Mair Wynn & Davidson, Nadine. Colli Pêl. 2005. (WEL., Illus.). 15p. pap. (978-0-86243-454-0(8)) Y Lolfa.

Hupf, Zetta & Hupf, Mitchellx. Detective Buddy & the Case of the Missing Football, 1 vol. Hupf, Zetta, illus. 2009. (Illus.). 23p. pap. 19.95 (978-1-61582-312-3(3)) PublishAmerica, Inc.

Inagaki, Riichiro. Eyeshield 21, Vol. 8. Murata, Yusuke, illus. 2006. (Eyeshield 21 Ser.: 8). (ENG.). 208p. pap. 9.99 (978-1-4215-0637-1(8)) Viz Media.

—Eyeshield 21, Vol. 9. Murata, Yusuke, illus. 2006. (ENG.). 208p. (gr. 11). pap. 9.99 (978-1-4215-0638-8(6)) Viz Media.

Jacobs, Evan. Screaming Quietly, 1 vol. 2013. (Gravel Road Ser.). (ENG.). 212p. (YA). (gr. 9-12). pap. 9.95 (978-1-62250-003-1(2)) Saddleback Educational Publishing, Inc.

—Screaming Quietly. 2013. (Gravel Road Ser.). (YA). lib. bdg. 20.80 (978-0-606-32029-0(6), Turtleback) Turtleback Bks.

Jacobs, Evan. The Underdogs, 1 vol. 2016. (White Lightning Ser.). (ENG.). 97p. (J). (gr. 6-8). pap. 8.95 **(978-1-68021-144-3(7))** Saddleback Educational Publishing, Inc.

Jacobs, John Hornor & Priest, A. Breakthrough. 2014. (Red Zone Ser.: 2). (ENG.). 104p. (YA). (gr. 6-12). lib. bdg. 27.93 (978-1-4677-2131-8(X)) Lerner Publishing Group.

Jarman, Benjamin. Tony's Last Touchdown. 2012. (Champion Sports Story Ser.). 104p. (J). (gr. 3-18). pap. 10.95 (978-1-4644-0004-9(0)); 27.94 (978-0-7660-3885-1(8)) Enslow Pubs., Inc.

Jenkins, Donna. When I Grow up, I Want to Be a Football Player. 2010. 16p. pap. 10.49 (978-1-4490-6496-9(5)) AuthorHouse.

Jones, Patrick. Out of the Tunnel. 2014. (Red Zone Ser.: 1). (ENG.). 104p. (YA). (gr. 6-12). pap. 7.95 (978-1-4677-4471-3(9), Darby Creek); lib. bdg. 27.93 (978-1-4677-2126-4(3)) Lerner Publishing Group.

Jones, Patrick & Chartier, Brent. At All Costs. 2014. (Red Zone Ser.: 4). 104p. (YA). (gr. 6-12). (ENG.). pap. 7.95 (978-1-4677-4475-1(1)); lib. bdg. 27.93 (978-1-4677-2129-5(8)) Lerner Publishing Group. (Darby Creek).

—The Franchise. 2013. (Opportunity Ser.). (ENG.). 104p. (YA). (gr. 6-12). pap. 7.95 (978-1-4677-1496-9(8)); lib. bdg. 27.93 (978-1-4677-1375-7(9)) Lerner Publishing Group. (Darby Creek).

Jon's Football Team, Level 1. 2016. (Ladybird Readers Ser.). (ENG., Illus.). 48p. (J). (gr. 2-4). pap. 9.99 (978-0-241-25411-0(6)) Penguin Bks., Ltd. GBR. Dist: Independent Pubs. Group.

Jordan, Brian. I Told You I Can Play! 2008. (Illus.). 32p. 6.95 (978-1-60349-001-6(9), Marimba Bks.) Hudson Publishing Group, The.

Kearney, Tom John. Cougars Big Game. 2004. (Illus.). 11p. (J). bds. 7.95 (978-0-9745454-1-7(4)) Timberwood Pr.

Kelly, David A. The Football Fumble. Brundage, Scott, illus. 2016. (Most Valuable Players Ser.: 3). (ENG.). 128p. (J). (gr. 1-4). 4.99 (978-0-553-51325-7(7), Random Hse. Bks. for Young Readers) Random Hse. Children's Bks.

Kelly, Kelley R. Sundays with Daddy. Cook, Jeffrey, illus. 2010. 32p. pap. 13.99 (978-1-4490-6082-4(X)) AuthorHouse.

Kenneally, Miranda. Catching Jordan. 2011. (Hundred Oaks Ser.: Bk. 1). (ENG.). 288p. (YA). (gr. 7-12). pap. 9.99 (978-1-4022-6227-2(2)) Sourcebooks, Inc.

Keplinger, Kody. Shut Out. 2012. (ENG.). 288p. (YA). (gr. 10-17). pap. 10.99 (978-0-316-17555-5(2), Poppy) Little, Brown Bks. for Young Readers.

Klass, David & Klass, Perri. Second Impact. 2013. (ENG.). 288p. (YA). (gr. 7). 16.99 (978-0-374-37996-4(3), 9780374379964, Farrar, Straus & Giroux (BYR)) Farrar, Straus & Giroux.

—Second Impact. 2014. (ENG.). 304p. (YA). (gr. 7). pap. 10.99 (978-1-250-04436-5(7), 9781250044365) Square Fish.

Knudsen, Shannon. Rise Above. 2014. (Red Zone Ser.: 6). (ENG.). 104p. (YA). (gr. 6-12). pap. 7.95 (978-1-4677-4476-8(X), Darby Creek) Lerner Publishing Group.

Korman, Gordon. Jake, Reinvented (repackage) 2017. (ENG.). 192p. (J). (gr. 5-9). pap. 8.99 **(978-1-4847-9842-3(2))** Hyperion Bks. for Children.

—No More Dead Dogs. 2017. Orig. Title: Touchdown Stage Left. (J). lib. bdg. 17.20 **(978-0-606-40570-6(4))** Turtleback Bks.

—No More Dead Dogs (repackage) 2017. (ENG.). 240p. (J). (gr. 5-9). pap. 6.99 (978-1-4847-9844-7(9)) Hyperion Bks. for Children.

—Pop. 272p. (YA). (gr. 8). 2011. pap. 9.99 (978-0-06-174261-3(9)) 2009. 16.99 (978-0-06-174228-6(7)) HarperCollins Pubs.

Kremer, Kevin. The Year Our Teacher Won Super Bowl. Ely, Dave, illus. 2010. (ENG.). 178p. pap. 6.50 (978-0-9824611-1-2(9)) Snow In Sarasota Publishing.

Kuskowski, Alex. Down & Out, 1 vol. unabr. ed. 2011. (District 13 Ser.). (ENG.). 48p. (YA). (gr. 9-12). 7.95 (978-1-61651-582-9(1)) Saddleback Educational Publishing, Inc.

LeBoutillier, Nate. A Running Back Can't Always Rush, 1 vol. Santillan, Jorge H., illus. 2010. (Sports Illustrated Kids Victory School Superstars Ser.). (ENG.). 56p. (gr. 1-3). 26.65 (978-1-4342-2055-4(9)); pap. 5.95 (978-1-4342-2805-5(3)) Stone Arch Bks.

Lipsyte, Robert. Raiders Night. (YA). (gr. 9-12). 2007. (ENG.). 256p. pap. 9.99 (978-0-06-059948-5(0)) 2006. 232p. 15.99 (978-0-06-059946-1(4)) 2006. 232p. lib. bdg. 16.89 (978-0-06-059947-8(2)) HarperCollins Pubs. (HarperTeen).

Literature Connections English: Maniac Magee. 2004. (gr. 6-12). (978-0-395-77524-0(8), 2-80093) Holt McDougal.

Lord, Michelle. The Quick Quarterback, 1 vol. Harpster, Steve, illus. 2012. (My First Graphic Novel Ser.). (ENG.). 32p. (gr. k-2). pap. 6.25 (978-1-4342-3861-0(X), My First Graphic Novel) Stone Arch Bks.

Loughlin, Patrick. Football High - Fire Up, Vol. 2. 2016. (Football High Ser.: 2). (ENG.). 192p. (J). (gr. 3-7). pap. 12.99 (978-1-925324-52-5(4)) Random Hse. Australia AUS. Dist: Independent Pubs. Group.

—Football High 3. 2016. (Football High Ser.: 3). (ENG.). 192p. (J). (gr. 3-5). pap. 12.99 **(978-1-925324-54-9(0))** Random Hse. Australia AUS. Dist: Independent Pubs. Group.

—Football High 4. 2016. (Football High Ser.: 4). (ENG.). 192p. (J). (gr. 3-5). pap. 12.99 **(978-1-925324-56-3(7))** Random Hse. Australia AUS. Dist: Independent Pubs. Group.

Lupica, Mike. The Extra Yard. 2016. (Home Team Ser.). (ENG., Illus.). 304p. (J). (gr. 3-7). 17.99 (978-1-4814-1000-7(8), Simon & Schuster Bks. For Young Readers) Simon & Schuster Bks. For Young Readers.

—The Extra Yard. 2017. (Home Team Ser.). lib. bdg. 18.40 **(978-0-606-39757-5(4))** Turtleback Bks.

—Fantasy League. 2014. (ENG.). 304p. (J). (gr. 5). 17.99 (978-0-399-25607-3(5), Philomel Bks.) Penguin Publishing Group.

—Fantasy League. 2015. (ENG.). 320p. (J). (gr. 5). pap. 7.99 (978-0-14-751494-3(0), Puffin Books) Penguin Young Readers Group.

—Game Changers. (Game Changers Ser.: 1). (ENG.). 224p. (J). (gr. 3-7). 2013. pap. 6.99 (978-0-545-38179-6(7))Bk. 1. 2012. 16.99 (978-0-545-38182-6(7)) Scholastic, Inc. (Scholastic Pr.).

—Last Man Out. (ENG.). (J). (gr. 5). 2017. 272p. 8.99 **(978-0-14-751491-2(6)**, Puffin Books) 2016. 256p. 17.99 (978-0-399-17279-3(3), Philomel Bks.) Penguin Young Readers Group.

—Million-Dollar Throw. 2010. (ENG.). 272p. (J). (gr. 5-18). 7.99 (978-0-14-241558-0(8), Puffin Books) Penguin Young Readers Group.

—Million-Dollar Throw. 2010. (Million Dollar Sports Ser.). lib. bdg. 18.40 (978-0-606-25316-1(5), Turtleback) Turtleback Bks.

—Qb 1. 2013. (ENG.). 272p. (J). (gr. 5). 17.99 (978-0-399-25228-0(2), Philomel Bks.) Penguin Publishing Group.

—Qb 1. 2014. (ENG.). 288p. (J). (gr. 5). pap. 7.99 (978-0-14-751152-2(6), Puffin Books) Penguin Young Readers Group.

—Two-Minute Drill, 1 vol. 2012. (Comeback Kids Ser.). (ENG.). 192p. (J). (gr. 4-8). lib. bdg. 27.07 (978-1-59961-179-2(1)) Spotlight.

—The Underdogs. (ENG.). (J). (gr. 5-18). 2012. 304p. pap. 7.99 (978-0-14-242139-0(1), Puffin Books) 2011. 288p. 17.99 (978-0-399-25001-9(8), Philomel Bks.) Penguin Young Readers Group.

Lynch, Chris. Hit Count. (ENG.). 368p. (YA). (gr. 9-12). 2016. pap. 9.95 (978-1-61620-593-5(8)) 2015. 17.95 (978-1-61620-250-7(5)) Algonquin Bks. of Chapel Hill.

—Hit Count. 2016. lib. bdg. 20.80 (978-0-606-37956-4(8)) Turtleback Bks.

—Inexcusable. 2005. (ENG., Illus.). 176p. (YA). (gr. 7-18). 19.99 (978-0-689-84789-9(0), Atheneum Bks. for Young Readers) Simon & Schuster Children's Publishing.

—Inexcusable: 10th Anniversary Edition. 10th ed. 2015. (ENG., Illus.). 192p. (YA). (gr. 8). pap. 9.99 (978-1-4814-3202-3(8), Simon & Schuster Bks. For Young Readers) Simon & Schuster Bks. For Young Readers.

Maddox, Jake. En la línea de Ataque. Heck, Claudia M., tr. from ENG. Tiffany, Sean, illus. 2012. (Jake Maddox en Español Ser.). (SPA.). 72p. (gr. 2-3). 25.32 (978-1-4342-3813-9(X)) Stone Arch Bks.

—Gridiron Bully, 1 vol. Tiffany, Sean, illus. 2009. (Jake Maddox Sports Stories Ser.). (ENG.). 72p. (gr. 2-3). 25.32 (978-1-4342-1201-6(7)) Stone Arch Bks.

—Gridiron Showdown, 1 vol. Ray, Mike, illus. 2014. (Jake Maddox JV Ser.). (ENG.). 96p. (gr. 3-4). 25.99 (978-1-4342-9155-4(3)) Stone Arch Bks.

—Home-Field Football, 1 vol. Tiffany, Sean, illus. 2012. (Jake Maddox Sports Stories Ser.). (ENG.). 72p. (gr. 2-3). pap. 5.95 (978-1-4342-4206-8(4)); 25.32 (978-1-4342-4008-8(8)) Stone Arch Bks.

—Linebacker Block, 1 vol. Tiffany, Sean, illus. 2010. (Team Jake Maddox Sports Stories Ser.). (ENG.). 72p. (gr. 2-3). lib. bdg. 25.32 (978-1-4342-1635-9(7)); pap. 5.95 (978-1-4342-2779-9(0)) Stone Arch Bks.

—On the Line, 1 vol. Tiffany, Sean, illus. 2006. (Jake Maddox Sports Stories Ser.). (ENG.). 72p. (gr. 2-3). 25.32 (978-1-59889-062-4(X)); pap. 5.95 (978-1-59889-240-6(1)) Stone Arch Bks.

—Quarterback Comeback, 1 vol. Tiffany, Sean, illus. 2010. (Team Jake Maddox Sports Stories Ser.). (ENG.). 72p. (gr. 2-3). lib. bdg. 25.32 (978-1-4342-1634-2(9)); pap. 5.95 (978-1-4342-2778-2(2)) Stone Arch Bks.

—Quarterback Sneak, 1 vol. Tiffany, Sean, illus. 2008. (Jake Maddox Sports Stories Ser.). (ENG.). 72p. (gr. 2-3). lib. bdg. 25.32 (978-1-4342-0464-6(2)); per. 5.95 (978-1-4342-0514-8(2)) Stone Arch Bks.

—Running Back Dreams, 1 vol. Tiffany, Sean, illus. 2010. (Team Jake Maddox Sports Stories Ser.). (ENG.). 72p. (gr. 2-3). lib. bdg. 25.32 (978-1-4342-1637-3(3)); pap. 5.95 (978-1-4342-2781-2(2)) Stone Arch Bks.

—Speed Receiver, 1 vol. Tiffany, Sean, illus. 2010. (Team Jake Maddox Sports Stories Ser.). (ENG.). 72p. (gr. 2-3). lib. bdg. 25.32 (978-1-4342-1636-6(5)); pap. 5.95 (978-1-4342-2780-5(4)) Stone Arch Bks.

—Touchdown Triumph. Aburto, Jesus, illus. 2015. (Jake Maddox Sports Stories Ser.). (ENG.). 72p. (gr. 2-3). lib. bdg. 25.32 (978-1-4965-0492-0(5)) Stone Arch Bks.

—Wildcats Blitz, 1 vol. Tiffany, Sean, illus. 2010. (Team Jake Maddox Sports Stories Ser.). (ENG.). 208p. (gr. 3-6). pap. 7.95 (978-1-4342-2887-1(8)) Stone Arch Bks.

Manning, Peyton, et al. Family Huddle. Madsen, Jim, illus. 2009. (J). (978-0-545-21351-6(7), Scholastic Pr.) Scholastic, Inc.

Marsh, Carole. The Football Phantom. 2006. 64p. (gr. 2-4). 14.95 (978-0-635-06223-9(2)); pap. 3.99 (978-0-635-06217-8(8)) Gallopade International.

Masterson, Hoss. Wild Receiver. Alves, Josh, illus. 2017. (Animal All-Stars Ser.). (ENG.). 56p. (gr. 1-3). lib. bdg. 25.32 (978-1-4965-4307-3(6)) Stone Arch Bks.

Matchett, Gillian. The Adventures of Weston Super Cat with Activities. 2009. (Illus.). 92p. pap. 30.49 (978-1-4389-2241-6(8)) AuthorHouse.

McCarty, Peter. Fall Ball. McCarty, Peter, illus. 2013. (ENG., Illus.). 32p. (J). (gr. -1-3). 16.99 (978-0-8050-9253-0(6), 9780805092530, Holt, Henry & Co. Bks. For Young Readers) Holt, Henry & Co.

McEwan, Jamie. Rufus the Scrub Does Not Wear a Tutu. Margeson, John, illus. 2006. 64p. (J). (gr. 2-3). 14.95 (978-1-58196-060-0(3), Darby Creek) Lerner Publishing Group.

McKissack, Fredrick, Jr. Shooting Star. 2010. (ENG.). 288p. (YA). (gr. 7). pap. 9.99 (978-1-4169-9774-0(1), Atheneum Bks. for Young Readers) Simon & Schuster Children's Publishing.

McKissack, Fredrick L. Shooting Star. 2009. (ENG., Illus.). 288p. (YA). (gr. 7-18). 16.99 (978-1-4169-4745-5(0), Atheneum Bks. for Young Readers) Simon & Schuster Children's Publishing.

McKnight, Marty. Jim Nasium Is a Football Fumbler. Jones, Chris B., illus. 2015. (Jim Nasium Ser.). (ENG.). 88p. (gr. 2-3). lib. bdg. 25.32 (978-1-4965-0522-4(0)) Stone Arch Bks.

Meddaugh, Susan. Football Fumble. 2013. (Martha Speaks Ser.). (ENG., Illus.). 24p. (J). (gr. -1-3). pap. 3.99 (978-0-544-08902-0(2)) Houghton Mifflin Harcourt Publishing Co.

—Martha Speaks: Football Fumble (Reader) 2013. (Martha Speaks Ser.). (ENG., Illus.). 24p. (J). (gr. -1-3). 12.99 (978-0-544-08764-4(X)) Houghton Mifflin Harcourt Publishing Co.

Millett, Peter & Chambers, Mal. Goal! 2008. (Rigby Focus Forward: Level O Ser.). (Illus.). 24p. (J). (gr. 4-7). pap. (978-1-4190-3845-7(1), Rigby) Pearson Education Australia.

Mills, Emma. First & Then. 2015. (ENG.). 272p. (YA). (gr. 9-12). 17.99 (978-1-62779-235-6(X), 9781627792356, Holt, Henry & Co. Bks. For Young Readers) Holt, Henry & Co.

Mitchell, Carolyn. The Tale of the Pumpkin Seed Squad. 2006. (ENG.). 40p. per. 16.99 (978-1-4259-7004-8(4)) AuthorHouse.

Monninger, Joseph. Game Change. 2017. (ENG.). 240p. (YA). (gr. 9). 17.99 **(978-0-544-53122-2(1)**, HMH Books For Young Readers) Houghton Mifflin Harcourt Publishing Co.

Moore, Stephanie Perry. Forever Hot/Truly Fine. 2013. (Grovehill Giants Ser.). (YA). lib. bdg. 26.90 (978-0-606-31877-8(1), Turtleback) Turtleback Bks.

—Yell Out/Do You. 2012. (Lockwood Lions Ser.). (YA). lib. bdg. 26.90 (978-0-606-26493-8(0), Turtleback) Turtleback Bks.

Moore, Stephanie Perry & Moore, Derrick. Forever Hot/Truly Fine, 1 vol. 2013. (Grovehill Giants Ser.: Bk. 1). (ENG.). 318p. (YA). (gr. 9-12). pap. 14.95 (978-1-62250-683-5(9)) Saddleback Educational Publishing, Inc.

—Golden Heart - Deep Soul, 1 vol. 2013. (Grovehill Giants Ser.: Bk. 2). (ENG.). 320p. (YA). (gr. 9-12). pap. 14.95 (978-1-62250-684-2(7)) Saddleback Educational Publishing, Inc.

Moore, Steve. King of the Bench: Control Freak. Moore, Steve, illus. 2017. (King of the Bench Ser.: 2). (Illus.). 224p. (J). (gr. 3-7). 13.99 **(978-0-06-220332-8(0))** HarperCollins Pubs.

Morait, Tracey. Goalden Girl. 2007. 160p. pap. 13.95 (978-1-84799-758-6(9)) Lulu Pr., Inc.

Mortensen, Lori. The End Zone, 1 vol. Sullivan, Mary, illus. 2009. (My First Graphic Novel Ser.). (ENG.). 32p. (gr. k-2). pap. 6.25 (978-1-4342-1408-9(7), My First Graphic Novel) Stone Arch Bks.

Murdock, Catherine Gilbert. Dairy Queen. 2007. (ENG.). 304p. (YA). (gr. 7-12). pap. 9.99 (978-0-618-86335-8(4)) Houghton Mifflin Harcourt Publishing Co.

—The off Season. 2011. (ENG.). 304p. (YA). (gr. 7). pap. 8.99 (978-0-618-93493-5(6)) Houghton Mifflin Harcourt Publishing Co.

Neil Wallace, Sandra. Muckers. 2013. (ENG.). 288p. (YA). (gr. 7). 16.99 (978-0-375-86754-5(6), Knopf Bks. for Young Readers) Random Hse. Children's Bks.

Norris, Shana. Troy High. 2009. (ENG.). 272p. (YA). (gr. 7-11). 16.95 (978-0-8109-4647-7(5), Amulet Bks.) Abrams, Inc.

Opitz, Todd. The Football & the Fly. 2012. 24p. pap. 24.95 (978-1-4626-9847-9(6)) America Star Bks.

Paratore, Coleen Murtagh. Mack Mcginn's Big Win. 2014. (ENG., Illus.). 192p. (J). (gr. 5-9). pap. 9.99 (978-1-4814-4490-3(5), Simon & Schuster Bks. For Young Readers) Simon & Schuster Bks. For Young Readers.

Parker, Laurie. Mad for Maroon. 2005. (Illus.). (J). 17.95 (978-0-9772096-1-3(X)) Wild Hare Publishing.

Patterson, James & Tebbetts, Chris. Just My Rotten Luck. Park, Laura, illus. 2015. (Middle School Ser.: 7). (ENG.). 320p. (J). (gr. 3-7). 13.99 (978-0-316-28477-6(7), Jimmy Patterson) Little Brown & Co.

Payton, Belle. A Whole New Ball Game. 2014. (It Takes Two Ser.: 1). (ENG., Illus.). 160p. (J). (gr. 3-7). pap. 6.99 (978-1-4814-0641-3(8), Simon Spotlight) Simon Spotlight.

Pee-Wee Football. 2003. (J). per. (978-1-57657-940-4(9)) Paradise Pr., Inc.

Phillips, Lyda. Mr Touchdown. 2008. 184p. 23.95 (978-1-4401-0976-8(1)); pap. 13.95 (978-1-60528-029-5(1)) iUniverse, Inc. (iUniverse Star).

Powell, Randy. Three Clams & an Oyster. 2007. 216p. (gr. 7-12). 16.95 (978-0-7569-8184-6(0)) Perfection Learning Corp.

Price, Roxanne M. Troy & the Championship Trophy. 2007. 20p. per. 11.95 (978-1-4327-0613-5(6)) Outskirts Pr., Inc.

Priest, A. L. Breakthrough. 2014. (Red Zone Ser.: 2). (ENG.). 104p. (YA). (gr. 6-12). pap. 7.95 (978-1-4677-4472-0(7), Darby Creek) Lerner Publishing Group.

Ransome, James E. Gunner, Football Hero. Ransome, James E., illus. 2010. (ENG., Illus.). 32p. (J). (gr. -1-3). 16.95 (978-0-8234-2053-7(1)) Holiday Hse., Inc.

Regan, Peter. Shannon Harps. Myler, Terry, illus. 2003. (Shannon Harps Ser.: 01). (ENG.). 128p. (J). (gr. 3-18). pap. 10.95 (978-1-901737-41-7(1)) Anvil Bks., Ltd. IRL. Dist: Dufour Editions, Inc.

Regard, Jady. Born to be a Longhorn. 2007. 32p. 19.95 (978-0-9789475-2-1(5)) Slice of Lime Publishing.

Rennie, Cliff. Goal Behind the Curtain. 2011. (Freestyle Fiction 12+ Ser.). (ENG.). 176p. (J). mass mkt. 8.99 (978-1-871676-47-1(9), df3a7515-5c5f-4709-ab1d-e32b03bb9c87) Christian Focus Pubns. GBR. Dist: Bookmasters Distribution.

Revenge of the Bully. 2014. (How to Beat the Bully Ser.). (ENG., Illus.). 288p. (J). (gr. 3-7). 17.99 (978-1-4424-5677-8(9), Simon & Schuster/Paula Wiseman Bks.) Simon & Schuster/Paula Wiseman Bks.

Richards, Sonja. My Maize & Blue Day. Viall, Pauline, illus. 2008. 32p. (J). 19.95 (978-0-9794935-1-5(X)) Olde Towne Publishing.

Richmond, Peter. Always a Catch. 2014. (ENG.). 288p. (YA). (gr. 7). 17.99 (978-0-399-25055-2(7), Philomel Bks.) Penguin Young Readers Group.

Rigby, Ed & Dooley, Angela. Mouse of the Match. 2009. 41p. pap. 10.50 (978-1-4452-2692-7(8)) Lulu Pr., Inc.

Riley, Zach. Quarterback Crisis. Ricci, Andrés, illus. 2012. (Zach Riley Ser.). 80p. (J). (gr. 3-6). lib. bdg. 27.07 (978-1-61783-534-6(X)) Magic Wagon.

Rise Above. 2014. (Red Zone Ser.: 6). (ENG.). 104p. (YA). (gr. 6-12). lib. bdg. 27.93 (978-1-4677-2127-1(1)) Lerner Publishing Group.

Robins, Eleanor. Back-up Quarterback. 2004. (Carter High Chronicles (High-Interest Readers) Ser.). (Illus.). 48p. per. 3.95 (978-1-56254-675-5(9), SP6759) Saddleback Educational Publishing, Inc.

—Break All Rules, 1 vol. unabr. ed. 2011. (Choices Ser.). (ENG.). 48p. (YA). (gr. 9-12). 7.95 (978-1-61651-590-4(2)) Saddleback Educational Publishing, Inc.

—Lucky Falcon Mystery, 1 vol. unabr. ed. 2011. (Carter High Mysteries Ser.). (ENG.). 47p. (YA). (gr. 9-12). 7.95 (978-1-61651-565-2(1)) Saddleback Educational Publishing, Inc.

—The Missing Test Mystery, 1 vol. unabr. ed. 2011. (Carter High Mysteries Ser.). (ENG.). 47p. (YA). (gr. 9-12). 7.95 (978-1-61651-566-9(X)) Saddleback Educational Publishing, Inc.

—A Very Good Year, 1 vol. unabr. ed. 2011. (Carter High Senior Year Ser.). (ENG.). 49p. (YA). (gr. 9-12). pap. 7.95 (978-1-61651-332-0(2)) Saddleback Educational Publishing, Inc.

Rud, Jeff. First & Ten, 1 vol. 2007. (ENG.). 176p. (J). (gr. 3-7). per. 7.95 (978-1-55143-690-6(6)) Orca Bk. Pubs. USA.

—Paralyzed, 1 vol. 2008. (Orca Sports Ser.). (ENG.). 176p. (YA). (gr. 6-10). pap. 9.95 (978-1-55469-059-6(5)) Orca Bk. Pubs. USA.

Rylant, Cynthia. The High-Rise Private Eye: The\Case of the Troublesome Turtle. Karas, G. Brian, illus. 2003. (High-Rise Private Eyes Ser.: No. 4). (J). (gr. k-3). 25.95 incl. audio *(978-1-59112-202-9(3))* Live Oak Media.

Saddleback Educational Publishing Staff, ed. Score, 1 vol. unabr. ed. 2011. (Heights Ser.). (ENG.). 50p. (gr. 5-8). 7.95 *(978-1-61651-624-6(0))* Saddleback Educational Publishing, Inc.

S.C.A.M. 170p. (J). pap. *(978-1-4114-0441-0(6)*, SparkNotes) Barnes & Noble, Inc.

Schroeder, Lisa. The Bridge from Me to You. 2014. (ENG.). 336p. (J). (gr. 7). 17.99 *(978-0-545-64601-7(4))* Scholastic, Inc.

Shultz, Charles M. & Katschke, Judy. Kick the Football, Charlie Brown!, 1 vol. 2011. (Peanuts Ready-To-Reads Ser.). (ENG., Illus.). 32p. (gr. -1-2). lib. bdg. 24.21 *(978-1-59961-803-6(6))* Spotlight.

Skead, Robert. Elves Can't Tackle. 2004. (J). pap. 7.99 *(978-1-929478-64-4(X))* Cross Training Publishing.

Skidmore, Steve & Barlow, Steve. Football Fanatic. 2014. (Read On Ser.). (ENG., Illus.). 48p. (J). (gr. 5). 9.99 *(978-0-00-746474-6(6))* HarperCollins Pubs. Ltd. GBR. Dist: Independent Pubs. Group.

Smith, Andrew. Stand-off. Bosma, Sam, illus. 2016. (ENG.). 432p. (YA). (gr. 7). pap. 10.99 *(978-1-4814-1830-0(0)*, Simon & Schuster Bks. For Young Readers) Simon & Schuster Bks. For Young Readers.

Smith, Wade & Lamm, Jayme. Smitty Hits the Play Books. 2016. (ENG., Illus.). 24p. (J). 19.95 *(978-1-942945-33-8(7)*, 9781942945338) Bright Sky Pr.

Stabler, Ken. Roll Tide! De Angel, Miguel, illus. 2006. 24p. (J). lib. bdg. 17.95 *(978-1-932888-48-5(9))* Mascot Bks., Inc.

Stadler, John. Snail Saves the Day, 1 vol. 2006. (ENG., Illus.). 32p. (J). (gr. -1-3). reprint ed. pap. 5.95 *(978-1-59572-045-0(6))* Star Bright Bks., Inc.

Stahler, David, Jr. Doppelganger. (YA). 2008. (ENG.). 272p. (gr. 8). pap. 8.99 *(978-0-06-087234-2(9)*, HarperTeen) 2006. (Illus.). 272p. (gr. 7-12). 16.99 *(978-0-06-087232-8(2))* 2006. (Illus.). 258p. (gr. 7-12). lib. bdg. 17.89 *(978-0-06-087233-5(0))* HarperCollins Pubs.

Stine, R. L. Lose, Team, Lose! Park, Trip, illus. 2008. (Rotten School Ser.: 4). (ENG.). 128p. (J). (gr. 3-7). pap. 5.99 *(978-0-06-078810-0(0))* HarperCollins Pubs.

—Lose, Team, Lose!, 1 vol. Park, Trip, illus. 2011. (Rotten School Ser.: No. 4). (ENG.). 128p. (gr. 2-5). 24.21 *(978-1-59961-828-9(1))* Spotlight.

—Rotten School #12: Battle of the Dum Diddys. Park, Trip, illus. 4.99 *(978-0-06-078835-3(6))* HarperCollins Pubs.

Terrell, Brandon. Daydream Receiver. 2017. (Jake Maddox Graphic Novels Ser.). (ENG., Illus.). 72p. (gr. 2-5). lib. bdg. 26.65 *(978-1-4965-3702-7(5))* Stone Arch Bks.

—Dive for the Goal Line. 2014. (ENG.). 80p. (J). *(978-1-63235-046-6(7))* Pr. Room Editions LLC.

—Take Away. 2014. (Red Zone Ser.: 5). (ENG.). 104p. (YA). (gr. 6-12). pap. 7.95 *(978-1-4677-4474-4(3)*, Darby Creek); lib. bdg. 27.93 *(978-1-4677-2130-1(1))* Lerner Publishing Group.

Terrell, Brandon & Fuentes, Benny. Quarterback Scramble, 1 vol. Sandoval, Gerardo, illus. 2011. (Sports Illustrated Kids Graphic Novels Ser.). (ENG.). 56p. (gr. 2-3). pap. 7.19 *(978-1-4342-3070-6(8))*; lib. bdg. 26.65 *(978-1-4342-2220-6(9))* Stone Arch Bks.

Tewkesbury, Alexa. Danny's Daring Days, 1 vol. 2009. (Topz Secret Diaries). (ENG., Illus.). 128p. pap. *(978-1-85345-502-5(4))* Crusade for World Revival.

Thaler, Mike. The Big Game from the Black Lagoon. Lee, Jared D., illus. 2013. 63p. (J). pap. *(978-0-545-61639-3(5))* Scholastic, Inc.

Tharp, Tim. Knights of the Hill Country. 2008. 233p. 17.00 *(978-1-60686-365-7(7))* Perfection Learning Corp.

—Knights of the Hill Country. 2013. (ENG.). 240p. (YA). (gr. 7). pap. 8.99 *(978-0-449-81287-7(1)*, Ember) Random Hse. Children's Bks.

Thomas, Chericia. Buffy the Football Player. 2010. 20p. 12.49 *(978-1-4490-9708-0(1))* AuthorHouse.

Tuck, Justin. Home-Field Advantage. Rodriguez, Leonardo, illus. 2011. (ENG.). 40p. (J). (gr. -1-3). 16.99 *(978-1-4424-0369-7(1)*, Simon & Schuster Bks. For Young Readers) Simon & Schuster Bks. For Young Readers.

Tyson, Peter K. The Winning Touch: A story about football for teenage boys (and maybe a few Girls) 2011. 96p. pap. 19.95 *(978-1-4626-0422-7(6))* America Star Bks.

Unsworth, Anne. Danny Is Dyslexic. 2011. 68p. (gr. 4-6). pap. 12.10 *(978-1-4567-8417-1(X))* AuthorHouse.

Van Wright, Cornelius & Hu, Ying-Hwa, illus. I Told You I Can Play! 2006. (ENM.). 32p. (J). 16.95 *(978-1-933491-06-6(X))* Just Us Bks., Inc.

Volponi, Paul. Crossing Lines. 2011. (ENG.). 256p. (YA). (gr. 7). E-Book *(978-1-101-52904-1(0))*; 16.99 *(978-0-670-01214-5(9))* Penguin Young Readers Group. (Viking Books for Young Readers).

—Top Prospect. 2016. (ENG.). 280p. (gr. 4-9). (J). 17.99 *(978-1-4677-9433-6(3))*; 35.99 *(978-1-5124-0887-4(5))* Lerner Publishing Group. (Carolrhoda Bks.).

Votruba, Erik C. The Cowboy Mile. 2009. 231p. pap. 14.99 *(978-0-557-09002-0(4))* Lulu Pr., Inc.

Wallace, Rich. Emergency Quarterback. 5th ed. 2006. (Winning Season Ser.: No. 5). (ENG., Illus.). 128p. (J). (gr. 3-7). 5.99 *(978-0-14-240615-1(5)*, Puffin Books) Penguin Young Readers Group.

—The Roar of the Crowd. 2005. (Winning Season Ser.). (ENG.). 128p. (J). (gr. 3-7). pap. 5.99 *(978-0-14-240443-0(8)*, Puffin Books) Penguin Young Readers Group.

—Roar of the Crowd. 2004. 101p. (J). lib. bdg. 15.38 *(978-1-4242-2165-3(X))* Fitzgerald Bks.

—War & Watermelon. 2012. (ENG.). 192p. (J). (gr. 5-18). pap. 6.99 *(978-0-14-242138-3(3)*, Puffin Books) Penguin Young Readers Group.

Walter, Dan. Hello, Willie! 2007. (J). 14.95 *(978-1-932888-52-2(7))* Mascot Bks., Inc.

Walters, Eric. Juice, 1 vol. 2005. (Orca Soundings Ser.). (ENG.). 128p. (YA). (gr. 8-12). per. 9.95 *(978-1-55143-351-6(6))* Orca Bk. Pubs. USA.

Wertheim, L. Jon & Moskowitz, Tobias J. The Rookie Bookie. (ENG., Illus.). 272p. (J). (gr. 3-7). 2015. pap. 7.00 *(978-0-316-24979-9(3))* 2014. 17.00 *(978-0-316-24981-2(5))* Little, Brown Bks. for Young Readers.

West, Joseph, Jr. Watching the Hokies with Daddy. 2005. (Illus.). 23p. (J). 18.95 *(978-0-9770680-0-5(5))* Titan Publishing.

West, Shelia. Porky Porcupine Tackles Football. Written by Shelia West; Illustrated by D, illus. 2011. 20p. pap. 24.95 *(978-1-4560-5528-8(3))* America Star Bks.

Weyn, Suzanne. Full Impact. 2013. (Surviving Southside Ser.). (ENG.). 104p. (YA). (gr. 6-12). pap. 7.95 *(978-1-4677-0705-3(8))*; lib. bdg. 27.93 *(978-1-4677-0311-6(7))* Lerner Publishing Group.

—Recruited. (Surviving Southside Ser.). (ENG.). 104p. (YA). (gr. 6-12). 2015. 34.65 *(978-1-4677-6010-2(2)*, Lerner Digital) 2011. pap. 7.95 *(978-0-7613-6167-1(7))* 2011. lib. bdg. 27.93 *(978-0-7613-6153-4(7))* Lerner Publishing Group.

Wheeler, Lisa. Dino-Football. Gott, Barry, illus. 2012. (Carolrhoda Picture Bks.). (ENG.). 32p. (J). (gr. k-3). lib. bdg. 16.95 *(978-0-7613-6394-1(7))* Lerner Publishing Group.

Whitaker, Nathan. Snap Decision, 1 vol. 2015. (Game Face Ser.). (ENG.). 272p. (J). pap. 8.99 *(978-0-310-73703-2(6))* Zonderkidz.

White, Tim. A Single Heart. 2006. 193p. pap. 24.95 *(978-1-4137-9418-2(1))* PublishAmerica, Inc.

Wojciechowska, Maia. Dreams of the Super Bowl. Karsky, A. K., illus. (Dreams of...Ser.). 80p. (J). 14.50 *(978-1-883740-20-7(7))* Pebble Beach Pr., Ltd.

Wright, Gail R. The Adventures of Alfred in the Greatest Fruit of All: Conflicts & Resolutions. 2011. 112p. (gr. 1-2). 28.95 *(978-1-4497-1586-1(9))*; pap. 11.95 *(978-1-4497-1585-4(0))* Author Solutions, Inc. (WestBow Pr.).

Ylvisaker, Anne. Button Down. (ENG.). 192p. (J). (gr. 3-7). 2013. pap. 6.99 *(978-0-7636-6463-3(4))* 2012. (Illus.). 15.99 *(978-0-7636-5396-5(9))* Candlewick Pr.

FOOTBALL—HISTORY

Adamson, Thomas K. The Houston Texans Story. 2016. (NFL Teams Ser.). (ENG., Illus.). 32p. (J). (gr. 3-7). lib. bdg. 26.95 *(978-1-62617-367-5(2)*, Torque Bks.) Bellwether Media.

—The New England Patriots Story. 2016. (NFL Teams Ser.). (ENG., Illus.). 32p. (J). (gr. 3-7). lib. bdg. 26.95 *(978-1-62617-373-6(7)*, Torque Bks.) Bellwether Media.

—The New York Jets Story. 2016. (NFL Teams Ser.). (ENG., Illus.). 32p. (J). (gr. 3-7). lib. bdg. 26.95 *(978-1-62617-376-7(1)*, Torque Bks.) Bellwether Media.

—The Tennessee Titans Story. 2016. (NFL Teams Ser.). (ENG., Illus.). 32p. (J). (gr. 3-7). lib. bdg. 26.95 *(978-1-62617-385-9(0)*, Torque Bks.) Bellwether Media.

America's Most Winning Teams: Sets 1 - 2. 2013. (America's Most Winning Teams Ser.). 48p. (J). (gr. 5-8). 351.00 *(978-1-4777-0613-8(5))*; pap. 846.00 *(978-1-4777-2684-6(5))*; pap. 141.00 *(978-1-4777-2683-9(7))* Rosen Publishing Group, Inc., The.

Aretha, David. Top 10 Craziest Plays in Football. 2016. (Sports Greats Ser.). (Illus.). 48p. (J). pap. 11.70 *(978-0-7660-8304-2(7))* Enslow Pubs., Inc.

—Top 10 Games in Football. 2016. (Sports Greats Ser.). (Illus.). 48p. (J). pap. 11.70 *(978-0-7660-8312-7(8))* Enslow Pubs., Inc.

Bailey, Diane. Texas Football. 2013. (America's Most Winning Teams Ser.). 48p. (J). (gr. 5-8). 29.25 *(978-1-4488-9398-0(4))*; pap. 70.50 *(978-1-4488-9445-1(X))*; pap. 11.75 *(978-1-4488-9442-0(5))* Rosen Publishing Group, Inc., The.

Barber, Phil. Football & Player Safety. 2017. (Illus.). 64p. (J). *(978-1-4222-3576-8(9))* Mason Crest.

Bell, Lonnie. The History of the New England Patriots. 2004. (NFL Today Ser.). (Illus.). 32p. (YA). (gr. 5-9). 18.95 *(978-1-58341-304-3(9))* Creative Co., The.

—The History of the New Orleans Saints. 2004. (NFL Today Ser.). (Illus.). 32p. (YA). (gr. 5-9). 18.95 *(978-1-58341-305-0(7))* Creative Co., The.

—The History of the San Francisco 49ers. 2004. (NFL Today Ser.). (Illus.). 32p. (YA). (gr. 5-9). 18.95 *(978-1-58341-313-5(8))* Creative Co., The.

Borth, Teddy. Football: Great Moments, Records, & Facts, 1 vol. 2014. (Great Sports Ser.). (ENG., Illus.). 24p. (J). (gr. 2-4). lib. bdg. 28.50 *(978-1-62970-689-4(2))* ABDO Publishing Co.

Brar, Aneel. Super Bowl. (J). 2012. *(978-1-61913-061-6(0))* 2012. pap. *(978-1-61913-623-6(6))* 2007. (Illus.). 32p. (gr. 4-6). lib. bdg. 26.00 *(978-1-59036-689-9(1))* 2007. (Illus.). 32p. (gr. 4-7). per. 9.95 *(978-1-59036-690-5(5))* Weigl Pubs., Inc.

Bryant, Howard. Legends: The Best Players, Games, & Teams in Football. 2016. (ENG., Illus.). 320p. (J). (gr. 3-7). 8.99 *(978-0-14-751256-7(5)*, Puffin Books) Penguin Young Readers Group.

Bryant, Howard & Mack, Jeff. Legends: The Best Players, Games, & Teams in Football. 2015. (ENG., Illus.). 336p. (J). (gr. 3-7). bds. 17.99 *(978-0-399-16904-5(0)*, Philomel Bks.) Penguin Young Readers Group.

Caffrey, Scott. The Story of the Dallas Cowboys. 2011. (NFL Today Ser.). (ENG.). 48p. (J). (gr. 5-17). pap. 9.99 *(978-0-89812-534-4(0)*, Creative Paperbacks) Creative Co., The.

Coleman, Miriam. Plan It: Conducting Short-Term & Long-Term Research. 2012. (Core Skills Ser.). (ENG., Illus.). 32p. (J). (gr. 3-6). pap. 10.00 *(978-1-4488-7523-8(4))*; lib. bdg. 25.25 *(978-1-4488-7450-7(5))* Rosen Publishing Group, Inc., The. (PowerKids Pr.).

Cox, Gene. Go Big Red! A History of Leon High School Football 1916-2001. 2003. (Illus.). 400p. (YA). (gr. 7-12). 46.50 *(978-0-9669672-1-0(6))* Cox, Gene.

Day, Chuck. Jacksonville Football History. 2004. (YA). lib. bdg. 29.95 *(978-0-9760906-0-1(0))* Spectrum Films Inc.

Diemer, Lauren. Rose Bowl. 2013. (J). *(978-1-62127-367-7(9))*; pap. *(978-1-62127-372-1(5))* Weigl Pubs., Inc.

Dittmer, Lori. The Story of the San Francisco 49ers. 2011. (NFL Today Ser.). (ENG.). 48p. (J). (gr. 5-17). pap. 9.99 *(978-0-89812-538-2(3)*, Creative Paperbacks) Creative Co., The.

Doeden, Matt. The College Football Championship: The Fight for the Top Spot. 2015. (ENG., Illus.). 64p. (gr. 5-12). (J). 33.27 *(978-1-4677-1897-4(1))*; 33.32 *(978-1-4677-8852-6(X))* Lerner Publishing Group. (Millbrook Pr.).

—Outrageous Football Rivalries. 2015. (Sports Rivalries Ser.). (ENG.). 32p. (gr. 3-4). lib. bdg. 27.99 *(978-1-4914-2026-3(X))* Capstone Press of Coughlan Cos.

Doeden, Matt. The Super Bowl: Chasing Football Immortality. 2017. (Spectacular Sports Ser.). (ENG., Illus.). 64p. (J). (gr. 5-12). 33.32 ***(978-1-5124-2754-7(3)***, Millbrook Pr.) Lerner Publishing Group.

Flynn, Jim. Tampa Bay Buccaneers, 1 vol. 2010. (Inside the NFL Ser.). (ENG.). 48p. (YA). (gr. 3-6). lib. bdg. 32.79 *(978-1-61714-030-3(9))* ABDO Publishing Co.

Frager, Ray. LSU Tigers, 1 vol. 2012. (Inside College Football Ser.). (ENG.). 48p. (J). (gr. 3-6). 32.79 *(978-1-61783-497-4(1))* ABDO Publishing Co.

Frederick, Sara. The History of the Cincinnati Bengals. 2004. (NFL Today Ser.). (Illus.). 32p. (YA). (gr. 5-9). 18.95 *(978-1-58341-292-3(1))* Creative Co., The.

Frederick, Shane. Football Stats & the Stories Behind Them: What Every Fan Needs to Know. 2016. (Sports Stats & Stories Ser.). (ENG., Illus.). 48p. (gr. 4-6). lib. bdg. 31.99 *(978-1-4914-8214-8(1))* Capstone Press of Coughlan Cos.

Frisch, Aaron. Baltimore Ravens. 2011. (Super Bowl Champions Ser.). (J). (gr. 1-3). 24.25 *(978-1-60818-014-1(X))* Creative Co., The.

—The History of the Chicago Bears. 2004. (NFL Today Ser.). (Illus.). 32p. (YA). (gr. 5-9). 18.95 *(978-1-58341-291-6(3))* Creative Co., The.

—The History of the Detroit Lions. 2004. (NFL Today Ser.). (Illus.). 32p. (YA). (gr. 5-9). 18.95 *(978-1-58341-296-1(4))* Creative Co., The.

—The History of the Minnesota Vikings. 2004. (NFL Today Ser.). (Illus.). 32p. (YA). (gr. 5-9). 18.95 *(978-1-58341-303-6(0))* Creative Co., The.

—The History of the Oakland Raiders. 2003. (NFL Today Ser.). (Illus.). 32p. (YA). (gr. 5-9). 18.95 *(978-1-58341-308-1(1))* Creative Co., The.

—The History of the Tennessee Titans. 2004. (NFL Today Ser.). (Illus.). 32p. (YA). (gr. 5-9). 18.95 *(978-1-58341-316-6(2))* Creative Co., The.

—Indianapolis Colts. 2014. (Illus.). 24p. (J). *(978-1-60818-377-7(7)*, Creative Education) Creative Co., The.

—Kansas City Chiefs. 2014. (Illus.). 24p. (J). *(978-1-60818-378-4(5)*, Creative Education) Creative Co., The.

—New England Patriots. 2014. (Illus.). 24p. (J). *(978-1-60818-380-7(7)*, Creative Education) Creative Co., The.

—New Orleans Saints. 2011. (Super Bowl Champions Ser.). (J). (gr. 1-3). 24.25 *(978-1-60818-103-2(0))* Creative Co., The.

—New York Jets. 2014. (Illus.). 24p. (J). *(978-1-60818-383-8(1)*, Creative Education) Creative Co., The.

—Oakland Raiders. 2014. (Illus.). 24p. (J). *(978-1-60818-384-5(X)*, Creative Education) Creative Co., The.

—Pittsburgh Steelers. 2011. (Super Bowl Champions Ser.). (J). (gr. 1-3). 24.25 *(978-1-60818-026-4(3))* Creative Co., The.

—Pittsburgh Steelers. 2014. (Illus.). 24p. (J). *(978-1-60818-385-2(8)*, Creative Education) Creative Co., The.

—San Francisco 49ers. 2011. (Super Bowl Champions Ser.). (J). (gr. 1-3). 24.25 *(978-1-60818-028-8(X))* Creative Co., The.

Gilbert, Sara. The History of the Arizona Cardinals. 2004. (NFL Today Ser.). (Illus.). 32p. (YA). (gr. 5-9). 18.95 *(978-1-58341-286-2(7))* Creative Co., The.

—The History of the Cleveland Browns. 2004. (NFL Today Ser.). (Illus.). 32p. (YA). (gr. 5-9). 18.95 *(978-1-58341-293-0(X))* Creative Co., The.

—The History of the Seattle Seahawks. 2004. (NFL Today Ser.). (Illus.). 32p. (YA). (gr. 5-9). 18.95 *(978-1-58341-314-2(6))* Creative Co., The.

—The Story of the Cincinnati Bengals. 2009. (NFL Today Ser.). 48p. (YA). (gr. 5-9). 22.95 *(978-1-58341-751-5(6))* Creative Co., The.

Gitlin, Martin. Florida Gators, 1 vol. 2012. (Inside College Football Ser.). (ENG., Illus.). 48p. (J). (gr. 3-6). 32.79 *(978-1-61783-496-7(3))* ABDO Publishing Co.

—Ohio State Buckeyes, 1 vol. 2012. (Inside College Football Ser.). (ENG., Illus.). 48p. (J). (gr. 3-6). 32.79 *(978-1-61783-501-8(3))* ABDO Publishing Co.

Goodman, Michael E. The History of the Atlanta Falcons. 2004. (NFL Today Ser.). (Illus.). 32p. (YA). (gr. 5-9). 18.95 *(978-1-58341-287-9(5))* Creative Co., The.

—The History of the Carolina Panthers. 2004. (NFL Today Ser.). (Illus.). 32p. (YA). (gr. 5-9). 18.95 *(978-1-58341-290-9(5))* Creative Co., The.

—The History of the New York Giants. 2004. (NFL Today Ser.). (Illus.). 32p. (YA). (gr. 5-9). 18.95 *(978-1-58341-306-7(5))* Creative Co., The.

—The History of the New York Jets. 2004. (NFL Today Ser.). (Illus.). 32p. (YA). (gr. 5-9). 18.95 *(978-1-58341-307-4(3))* Creative Co., The.

—The History of the Tampa Bay Buccaneers. 2004. (NFL Today Ser.). (Illus.). 32p. (YA). (gr. 5-9). 18.95 *(978-1-58341-315-9(4))* Creative Co., The.

—The History of the Washington Redskins. 2004. (NFL Today Ser.). (Illus.). 32p. (YA). (gr. 5-9). 18.95 *(978-1-58341-317-3(0))* Creative Co., The.

Grabowski, John F. The Minnesota Vikings. 2003. (Great Sports Teams in History Ser.). (ENG., Illus.). 112p. (J). 30.85 *(978-1-56006-943-0(0)*, Lucent Bks.) Cengage Gale.

Hawkes, Brian. The History of the Dallas Cowboys. 2004. (NFL Today Ser.). (Illus.). 32p. (YA). (gr. 5-9). 18.95 *(978-1-58341-294-7(8))* Creative Co., The.

—The History of the Indianapolis Colts. 2004. (NFL Today Ser.). (Illus.). 32p. (YA). (gr. 5-9). 18.95 *(978-1-58341-299-2(9))* Creative Co., The.

—The History of the Jacksonville Jaguars. 2004. (NFL Today Ser.). (Illus.). 32p. (YA). (gr. 5-9). 18.95 *(978-1-58341-300-5(6))* Creative Co., The.

—The History of the Kansas City Chiefs. 2004. (NFL Today Ser.). (Illus.). 32p. (YA). (gr. 5-9). 18.95 *(978-1-58341-301-2(4))* Creative Co., The.

Heos, Bridget. Alabama Football. 2013. (America's Most Winning Teams Ser.). 48p. (J). (gr. 5-8). 29.25 *(978-1-4488-9402-4(6))*; pap. 11.75 *(978-1-4488-9424-6(7))*; pap. 70.50 *(978-1-4488-9425-3(5))* Rosen Publishing Group, Inc., The.

Hetrick, Hans. The Super Bowl: All about Pro Football's Biggest Event. 2012. (Winner Takes All Ser.). (ENG.). 32p. (gr. 3-4). pap. 41.70 *(978-1-4296-9443-8(2))*; lib. bdg. 27.99 *(978-1-4296-6573-5(4))* Capstone Press of Coughlan Cos.

Holder, Larry & Howell, Brian. New Orleans Saints, 1 vol. 2010. (Inside the NFL Ser.). (ENG.). 48p. (YA). (gr. 3-6). lib. bdg. 32.79 *(978-1-61714-020-4(1))* ABDO Publishing Co.

Holmes, Parker. Alabama vs. Auburn. 2013. (J). *(978-1-4777-1168-2(6))*; pap. *(978-1-4777-1167-5(8))*; lib. bdg. *(978-1-4777-1160-6(0))* Rosen Publishing Group, Inc., The. (PowerKids Pr.).

—Texas vs. Oklahoma. 2013. (J). *(978-1-4777-1162-0(7))*; pap. *(978-1-4777-1161-3(9))*; lib. bdg. *(978-1-4777-1157-6(0))* Rosen Publishing Group, Inc., The. (PowerKids Pr.).

Howell, Brian. Auburn Tigers, 1 vol. 2012. (Inside College Football Ser.). (ENG., Illus.). 48p. (J). (gr. 3-6). 32.79 *(978-1-61783-495-0(5))* ABDO Publishing Co.

—Notre Dame Fighting Irish, 1 vol. 2012. (Inside College Football Ser.). (ENG., Illus.). 48p. (J). (gr. 3-6). 32.79 *(978-1-61783-500-1(5))* ABDO Publishing Co.

Jasner, Andy. Baltimore Ravens, 1 vol. 2010. (Inside the NFL Ser.). (ENG.). 48p. (YA). (gr. 3-6). lib. bdg. 32.79 *(978-1-61714-003-7(1))* ABDO Publishing Co.

Jones, Rob Lloyd. Story of Football. 2007. 64p. 8.99 *(978-0-7945-1553-9(3)*, Usborne) EDC Publishing.

Kirkpatrick, Rob. Doug Flutie: International Football Star. 2003. (Reading Power Ser.). (Illus.). 24p. (J). (gr. 1). lib. bdg. 17.25 *(978-0-8239-5537-4(0)*, PowerKids Pr.) Rosen Publishing Group, Inc., The.

Kovacs, Vic. Touchdown! The History of Football. 2016. (ENG., Illus.). 32p. (J). *(978-0-7787-2297-7(X))* Crabtree Publishing Co.

Lester, Brian. San Francisco 49ers, 1 vol. 2010. (Inside the NFL Ser.). (ENG.). 48p. (YA). (gr. 3-6). lib. bdg. 32.79 *(978-1-61714-027-3(9))* ABDO Publishing Co.

Mabry-Gordon, Sherri. Top 10 Wide Receivers in Football. 2016. (Sports Greats Ser.). 48p. (J). pap. 11.70 *(978-0-7660-8320-2(9))* Enslow Pubs., Inc.

Mack, Larry. The Carolina Panthers Story. 2016. (NFL Teams Ser.). (ENG., Illus.). 32p. (J). (gr. 3-7). lib. bdg. 26.95 *(978-1-62617-359-0(1)*, Torque Bks.) Bellwether Media.

Monnig, Alex. Arkansas Razorbacks, 1 vol. 2013. (Inside College Football Set 2 Ser.). (ENG.). 48p. (J). (gr. 3-6). lib. bdg. 32.79 *(978-1-61783-651-0(6)*, SportsZone) ABDO Publishing Co.

—Nebraska Cornhuskers, 1 vol. 2012. (Inside College Football Ser.). (ENG., Illus.). 48p. (J). (gr. 3-6). 32.79 *(978-1-61783-499-8(8))* ABDO Publishing Co.

—Oklahoma Sooners, 1 vol. 2012. (Inside College Football Ser.). (ENG., Illus.). 48p. (J). (gr. 3-6). 32.79 *(978-1-61783-502-5(1))* ABDO Publishing Co.

Monteverde, Matthew. Giants vs. Cowboys. 2014. (J). 49.50 *(978-1-4777-2783-6(3))*; pap. 8.25 *(978-1-4777-2782-9(5))*; 24p. (gr. 2-5). lib. bdg. 22.60 *(978-1-4777-2781-2(7))* Rosen Publishing Group, Inc., The. (PowerKids Pr.).

—Michigan vs. Ohio State. 2013. (J). *(978-1-4777-1166-8(X))*; pap. *(978-1-4777-1165-1(1))*; lib. bdg. *(978-1-4777-1159-0(7))* Rosen Publishing Group, Inc., The. (PowerKids Pr.).

Morey, Allan. The Denver Broncos Story. 2016. (NFL Teams Ser.). (ENG., Illus.). 32p. (J). (gr. 3-7). lib. bdg. 26.95 *(978-1-62617-364-4(8)*, Torque Bks.) Bellwether Media.

—The Kansas City Chiefs Story. 2016. (NFL Teams Ser.). (ENG., Illus.). 32p. (J). (gr. 3-7). lib. bdg. 26.95 *(978-1-62617-370-5(2)*, Torque Bks.) Bellwether Media.

—The San Diego Chargers Story. 2016. (NFL Teams Ser.). (ENG., Illus.). 32p. (J). (gr. 3-7). lib. bdg. 26.95 *(978-1-62617-380-4(X)*, Torque Bks.) Bellwether Media.

Myers, Dan. Story of the Cotton Bowl, 1 vol. 2016. (ENG., Illus.). 48p. (J). ***(978-1-62403-887-7(5)**, SportsZone)* ABDO Publishing Co.

Nichols, John. The History of the Baltimore Ravens. 2004. (NFL Today Ser.). (Illus.). 32p. (YA). (gr. 5-9). 18.95 *(978-1-58341-288-6(3))* Creative Co., The.

Omoth, Tyler. The Story of the Denver Broncos. 2011. (NFL Today Ser.). (ENG.). 48p. (J). (gr. 5-17). pap. 9.99 *(978-0-89812-535-1(9)*, Creative Paperbacks) Creative Co., The.

Publications International Ltd. Staff. Yesterday & Today Football Universary of Florida. 2009. 144p. 9.95 *(978-1-4127-6111-6(5))* Publications International, Ltd.

—Yesterday & Today Football Universary of Gerogia. 2009. 144p. 15.95 *(978-1-4127-1657-4(8))* Publications International, Ltd.

—Yesterday & Todayfootball Universary of Arkansas. 2009. 144p. 24.95 *(978-1-4127-7516-8(7))* Publications International, Ltd.

Publishers, Chelsea House, creator. Football Superstars Set, 12-Volumes. 2008. (Football Superstars Ser.). (gr. 6-12). 360.00 *(978-0-7910-9886-8(9)*, Chelsea Hse.) Facts On File, Inc.

Rappoport, Ken. Michigan Wolverines, 1 vol. 2012. (Inside College Football Ser.). (ENG., Illus.). 48p. (J). (gr. 3-6). 32.79 *(978-1-61783-498-1(X))* ABDO Publishing Co.

Robinson, Tom. Pittsburgh Steelers, 1 vol. 2010. (Inside the NFL Ser.). (ENG.). 48p. (YA). (gr. 3-6). lib. bdg. 32.79 *(978-1-61714-025-9(2))* ABDO Publishing Co.

—Tennessee Titans, 1 vol. 2010. (Inside the NFL Ser.). (ENG.). 48p. (YA). (gr. 3-6). lib. bdg. 32.79 *(978-1-61714-031-0(7))* ABDO Publishing Co.

Roselius, J. Chris. Texas Longhorns, 1 vol. 2012. (Inside College Football Ser.). (ENG., Illus.). 48p. (J). (gr. 3-6). 32.79 *(978-1-61783-504-9(8))* ABDO Publishing Co.

Rosen Central, creator. Inside College Football. 2007. (J). 159.00 *(978-1-4042-1102-5(0)*, Rosen Reference) Rosen Publishing Group, Inc., The.

Schmalzbauer, Adam. The History of the Denver Broncos. 2004. (NFL Today Ser.). (Illus.). 32p. (YA). (gr. 5-9). 18.95 *(978-1-58341-295-4(6))* Creative Co., The.

—The History of the Miami Dolphins. 2004. (NFL Today Ser.). (Illus.). 32p. (YA). (gr. 5-9). 18.95 *(978-1-58341-302-9(2))* Creative Co., The.

E
F
G

—The History of the Philadelphia Eagles. 2004. (NFL Today Ser.). (Illus.). 32p. (YA). (gr. 5-9). 18.95 (978-1-58341-309-8(X)) Creative Co., The.

—The History of the Pittsburgh Steelers. 2004. (NFL Today Ser.). (Illus.). 32p. (YA). (gr. 5-9). 18.95 (978-1-58341-310-4(3)) Creative Co., The.

—The History of the San Diego Chargers. 2004. (NFL Today Ser.). (Illus.). 32p. (YA). (gr. 5-9). 18.95 (978-1-58341-312-8(X)) Creative Co., The.

Seidel, Jeff. Alabama Crimson Tide, 1 vol. 2012. (Inside College Football Ser.). (ENG., Illus.). 48p. (J). (gr. 3-6). 32.79 (978-1-61783-494-3(7)) ABDO Publishing Co.

Stewart, Mark. The Georgia Bulldogs. 2010. (Team Spirit Ser.). 48p. (J). (gr. 3-6). lib. bdg. 26.60 (978-1-59953-334-6(0)) Norwood Hse. Pr.

—The Michigan Wolverines. 2009. (Team Spirit College Ser.). 48p. (J). (gr. 3-6). lib. bdg. 26.60 (978-1-59953-278-3(6)) Norwood Hse. Pr.

—The Ohio State Buckeyes. (Team Spirit College Ser.). 48p. (J). 2009. (gr. 3-6). lib. bdg. 26.60 (978-1-59953-277-6(8)) 2008. pap. 10.95 (978-1-59953-307-0(3)) Norwood Hse. Pr.

Suen, Anastasia. La historia del fútbol americano (the Story of Football) 2009. (Historia de los deportes (Sports History) Ser.). (SPA.). 24p. (gr. 2-2). 42.50 (978-1-61513-312-3(7), Editorial Buenas Letras) Rosen Publishing Group, Inc., The.

Watson, Stephanie. Brain Injuries in Football, 1 vol. 2014. (Essential Issues Set 4 Ser.). (ENG., Illus.). 112p. (J). (gr. 6-12). lib. bdg. 35.64 (978-1-62403-417-6(9), Essential Library) ABDO Publishing Co.

Whiting, Jim. Real Madrid: Soccer Champions. 2016. (Soccer Champions Ser.). (ENG.). 48p. (J). (gr. 5-9). pap. 12.00 (978-1-62832-196-8(2), Creative Paperbacks) Creative Co., The.

—The Story of the Pittsburgh Steelers. 2013. (J). 35.65 (978-1-60818-316-6(5), Creative Education) Creative Co., The.

Wilner, Barry. Story of the Fiesta Bowl, 1 vol. 2016. (ENG., Illus.). 48p. (J). **(978-1-62403-888-4(3)**, SportsZone) ABDO Publishing Co.

—Super Bowl, 1 vol. 2013. (Sports' Great Championships Ser.). (ENG.). 64p. (J). (gr. 4-6). lib. bdg. 32.79 (978-1-61783-673-2(7), SportsZone) ABDO Publishing Co.

—Tennessee Volunteers, 1 vol. 2012. (Inside College Football Ser.). (ENG.). 48p. (J). (gr. 3-6). 32.79 (978-1-61783-503-2(X)) ABDO Publishing Co.

Yomtov, Nel. Being Your Best at Football. 2016. (True Book(tm), a — Sports & Entertainment Ser.). (ENG., Illus.). 48p. (J). lib. bdg. 31.00 (978-0-531-23264-4(6), Children's Pr.) Scholastic Library Publishing.

Zappa, Marcia. Chicago Bears, 1 vol. 2014. (NFL's Greatest Teams Ser.). (ENG.). 32p. (gr. 7-11). lib. bdg. 28.50 (978-1-62403-359-9(8), Big Buddy Bks.) ABDO Publishing Co.

—Dallas Cowboys, 1 vol. 2014. (NFL's Greatest Teams Ser.). (ENG.). 32p. (gr. 7-11). lib. bdg. 28.50 (978-1-62403-360-5(1), Big Buddy Bks.) ABDO Publishing Co.

—Green Bay Packers, 1 vol. 2014. (NFL's Greatest Teams Ser.). (ENG.). 32p. (gr. 7-11). lib. bdg. 28.50 (978-1-62403-361-2(X), Big Buddy Bks.) ABDO Publishing Co.

FOOTBALL TEAMS

ABDO Publishing Company Staff. NFL's Greatest Teams. 2014. (NFL's Greatest Teams Ser.: 8). (ENG.). 32p. (gr. 7-11). lib. bdg. 228.00 (978-1-62403-358-2(X), Big Buddy Bks.) ABDO Publishing Co.

Adamson, Thomas K. The Arizona Cardinals Story. 2016. (NFL Teams Ser.). (ENG., Illus.). 32p. (J). (gr. 3-7). lib. bdg. 26.95 (978-1-62617-355-2(9), Torque Bks.) Bellwether Media.

—The Buffalo Bills Story. 2016. (NFL Teams Ser.). (ENG., Illus.). 32p. (J). (gr. 3-7). lib. bdg. 26.95 (978-1-62617-358-3(3), Torque Bks.) Bellwether Media.

—The Jacksonville Jaguars Story. 2016. (NFL Teams Ser.). (ENG., Illus.). 32p. (J). (gr. 3-7). lib. bdg. 26.95 (978-1-62617-369-9(9), Torque Bks.) Bellwether Media.

—The San Francisco 49ers Story. 2016. (NFL Teams Ser.). (ENG., Illus.). 32p. (J). (gr. 3-7). lib. bdg. 26.95 (978-1-62617-381-1(8), Torque Bks.) Bellwether Media.

Aretha, David. Steel Tough: The Pittsburgh Steelers. 2007. (Sensational Sports Teams Ser.). (Illus.). 128p. (J). (gr. 3-7). lib. bdg. 34.60 (978-1-59845-047-7(6), MyReportLinks.com Bks.) Enslow Pubs., Inc.

—Top 10 Football Teams. 2010. (Sports Greats Ser.). (Illus.). 48p. (J). 27.93 (978-0-7660-8310-3(1)) Enslow Pubs., Inc.

—Top 10 Teams in Football. 2016. (Sports Greats Ser.). (Illus.). 48p. (J). pap. 11.70 (978-0-7660-8308-0(X)) Enslow Pubs., Inc.

Artell, Mike. Drew Brees: Football Superstar, 1 vol. 2011. (Superstar Athletes Ser.). (ENG.). 24p. (gr. 1-2). pap. 7.29 (978-1-4296-7305-1(2)); pap. 41.70 (978-1-4296-7306-8(0)); lib. bdg. 25.32 (978-1-4296-6565-0(3)) Capstone Press of Coughlan Cos.

Ashby, Neal, et al. Goodnight Tiger Stadium. 2012. (J). 14.95 (978-1-62086-032-8(5)) Mascot Bks., Inc.

Barber, Genise. The Tryouts. 2010. 32p. pap. 12.77 (978-1-4520-7630-0(8)) AuthorHouse.

Barnes, Luke. The Saints. 2015. (ENG.). 96p. pap. 17.95 (978-1-78319-155-0(4)) Oberon Bks., Ltd. GBR. Dist: Consortium Bk. Sales & Distribution.

Bell, Lonnie. The History of the New Orleans Saints. 2004. (NFL Today Ser.). (Illus.). 32p. (YA). (gr. 5-9). 18.95 (978-1-58341-305-0(7)) Creative Co., The.

—The History of the San Francisco 49ers. 2004. (NFL Today Ser.). (Illus.). 32p. (YA). (gr. 5-9). 18.95 (978-1-58341-313-5(8)) Creative Co., The.

Bryant, Howard & Mack, Jeff. Legends: The Best Players, Games, & Teams in Football. 2015. (ENG., Illus.). 336p. (J). (gr. 3-7). bds. 17.99 (978-0-399-16904-5(0), Philomel Bks.) Penguin Young Readers Group.

Burgess, Zack. Meet the Arizona Cardinals. 2016. (Big Picture Sports Ser.). (ENG., Illus.). 24p. (J). (gr. k-3). lib. bdg. 22.60 (978-1-59953-728-3(1)) Norwood Hse. Pr.

—Meet the Atlanta Falcons. 2016. (Big Picture Sports Ser.). (ENG., Illus.). 24p. (J). (gr. k-3). lib. bdg. 22.60 (978-1-59953-735-1(4)) Norwood Hse. Pr.

—Meet the Baltimore Ravens. 2016. (Big Picture Sports Ser.). (ENG., Illus.). 24p. (J). (gr. k-3). lib. bdg. 22.60 (978-1-59953-745-0(1)) Norwood Hse. Pr.

—Meet the Buffalo Bills. 2016. (Big Picture Sports Ser.). (ENG., Illus.). 24p. (J). (gr. k-3). lib. bdg. 22.60 (978-1-59953-725-2(7)) Norwood Hse. Pr.

—Meet the Houston Texans. 2016. (Big Picture Sports Ser.). (ENG., Illus.). 24p. (J). (gr. k-3). lib. bdg. 22.60 (978-1-59953-750-4(8)) Norwood Hse. Pr.

—Meet the Jacksonville Jaguars. 2016. (Big Picture Sports Ser.). (ENG., Illus.). 24p. (J). (gr. k-3). lib. bdg. 22.60 (978-1-59953-737-5(0)) Norwood Hse. Pr.

—Meet the Los Angeles Rams. 2016. (Big Picture Sports Ser.). (ENG., Illus.). 24p. (J). (gr. k-3). lib. bdg. 22.60 (978-1-59953-744-3(3)) Norwood Hse. Pr.

—Meet the New Orleans Saints. 2016. (Big Picture Sports Ser.). (ENG., Illus.). 24p. (J). (gr. k-3). lib. bdg. 22.60 (978-1-59953-747-4(8)) Norwood Hse. Pr.

—Meet the Philadelphia Eagles. 2016. (Big Picture Sports Ser.). (ENG., Illus.). 24p. (J). (gr. k-3). lib. bdg. 22.60 (978-1-59953-734-4(6)) Norwood Hse. Pr.

—Meet the Pittsburgh Steelers. 2016. (Big Picture Sports Ser.). (ENG., Illus.). 24p. (J). (gr. k-3). lib. bdg. 22.60 (978-1-59953-749-8(4)) Norwood Hse. Pr.

—Meet the San Francisco 49ers. 2016. (Big Picture Sports Ser.). (ENG., Illus.). 24p. (J). (gr. k-3). lib. bdg. 22.60 (978-1-59953-722-1(2)) Norwood Hse. Pr.

—Meet the Tampa Bay Buccaneers. 2016. (Big Picture Sports Ser.). (ENG., Illus.). 24p. (J). (gr. k-3). lib. bdg. 22.60 (978-1-59953-727-6(3)) Norwood Hse. Pr.

—Meet the Tennessee Titans. 2016. (Big Picture Sports Ser.). (ENG., Illus.). 24p. (J). (gr. k-3). lib. bdg. 22.60 (978-1-59953-751-1(6)) Norwood Hse. Pr.

Byers, Ann. Ohio State Football. 2013. (America's Most Winning Teams Ser.). 48p. (J). (gr. 5-8). 29.25 (978-1-4488-9401-7(8)); pap. 70.50 (978-1-4488-9439-0(5)); pap. 11.75 (978-1-4488-9438-3(7)) Rosen Publishing Group, Inc., The.

Caffrey, Scott. The Story of the Buffalo Bills. 2009. (NFL Today Ser.). 48p. (YA). (gr. 5-9). 22.95 (978-1-58341-748-5(6)) Creative Co., The.

—The Story of the Oakland Raiders. 2009. (NFL Today Ser.). (Illus.). 48p. (YA). (gr. 5-9). 22.95 (978-1-58341-765-2(6)) Creative Co., The.

Carr, Aaron. San Francisco 49ers. (Illus.). 32p. (J). 2015. pap. (978-1-4896-0887-1(7)) 2014. (ENG., (gr. 4-7). lib. bdg. 28.55 (978-1-4896-0886-4(9), AV2 by Weigl) Weigl Pubs., Inc.

Castle, George. Chicago Bears, 1 vol. 2010. (Inside the NFL Ser.). (ENG.). 48p. (YA). (gr. 3-6). lib. bdg. 32.79 (978-1-61714-006-8(6)) ABDO Publishing Co.

Coleman, Miriam. Plan It: Conducting Short-Term & Long-Term Research. 2012. (Core Skills Ser.). (ENG., Illus.). 32p. (J). (gr. 3-6). pap. 10.00 (978-1-4488-7523-8(4)); lib. bdg. 25.25 (978-1-4488-7450-7(5)) Rosen Publishing Group, Inc., The. (PowerKids Pr.).

Dittmer, Lori. The Story of the San Francisco 49ers. 2009. (NFL Today Ser.). (Illus.). 48p. (YA). (gr. 5-9). 22.95 (978-1-58341-770-6(2)) Creative Co., The.

—The Story of the St. Louis Rams. 2009. (NFL Today Ser.). (Illus.). 48p. (YA). (gr. 5-9). 22.95 (978-1-58341-768-3(0)) Creative Co., The.

—The Story of the Tennessee Titans. 2009. (NFL Today Ser.). 48p. (YA). (gr. 5-9). 22.95 (978-1-58341-773-7(7)) Creative Co., The.

Doeden, Matt. Luke Kuechly. 2017. (Sports All-Stars Ser.). (ENG.). 32p. (J). (gr. 2-5). 12.99 **(978-1-5124-3789-8(1)**, Lerner Pubns.); 39.99 **(978-1-5124-2829-2(9)**, Lerner Pubns.); 39.99 **(978-1-5124-3788-1(3)**, Lerner Pubns.); (Illus.). 26.65 (978-1-5124-2584-0(2)) Lerner Publishing Group.

Epstein, Brad. Philadelphia Eagles 101. 2010. (Illus.). 24p. (J). bds. (978-1-60730-123-3(7), 101 Bk.) Michaelson Entertainment.

Epstein, Brad M. Arizona Cardinals 101: My First Team-Board-Book. 2013. (Illus.). 24p. (J). bds. (978-1-60730-100-4(8), 101 Bk.) Michaelson Entertainment.

—Chicago Bears 101. 2010. (Illus.). 28p. (J). bds. (978-1-60730-105-9(9), 101 Bk.) Michaelson Entertainment.

—New Orleans Saints 101. 2010. (Illus.). 24p. (J). bds. (978-1-60730-119-6(9), 101 Bk.) Michaelson Entertainment.

—Pittsburgh Steelers 101. 2010. (ENG., Illus.). 24p. (J). bds. (978-1-60730-124-0(5), 101 Bk.) Michaelson Entertainment.

—San Francisco 49ers 101. 2010. (ENG., Illus.). 24p. (J). bds. (978-1-60730-127-1(X), 101 Bk.) Michaelson Entertainment.

—St Louis Rams 101. 2010. (ENG., Illus.). 24p. (J). bds. (978-1-60730-125-7(3), 101 Bk.) Michaelson Entertainment.

epstein, brad M. & lee-Epstein, michael. Pittsburgh Steelers Doodle Playbook: For Kids & Fans. 2012. (ENG., Illus.). 200p. (J). pap. (978-1-60730-324-4(8)) Michaelson Entertainment.

Frederick, Shane. The Best of Everything Football Book, 1 vol. 2010. (All-Time Best of Sports Ser.). (ENG.). 64p. (gr. 3-4). lib. bdg. 34.65 (978-1-4296-5466-1(X)) Capstone Press of Coughlan Cos.

—The Ultimate Guide to Pro Football Teams. 2010. (Ultimate Pro Team Guides (Sports Illustrated for Kids) Ser.). (ENG.). 72p. (gr. 3-4). pap. 53.70 (978-1-4296-5735-8(9)) Capstone Press of Coughlan Cos.

Frisch, Aaron. Baltimore Ravens. 2014. 24p. pap. 27.10 (978-1-60818-372-2(6), Creative Education) Creative Co., The.

—The History of the Tennessee Titans. 2004. (NFL Today Ser.). (Illus.). 32p. (YA). (gr. 5-9). 18.95 (978-1-58341-316-6(2)) Creative Co., The.

—New Orleans Saints. 2014. (Illus.). 24p. (J). (978-1-60818-381-4(5), Creative Education) Creative Co., The.

—San Francisco 49ers. 2014. (Illus.). 24p. (J). (978-1-60818-387-6(4), Creative Education) Creative Co., The.

—The Story of the Baltimore Ravens. 2009. (NFL Today Ser.). 48p. (YA). (gr. 5-9). 22.95 (978-1-58341-747-8(8)) Creative Co., The.

—Tampa Bay Buccaneers. 2014. (Illus.). 24p. (J). (978-1-60818-388-3(2), Creative Education) Creative Co., The.

Frisch, Nate. NFL Today: Atlanta Falcons. 2013. (NFL Today Ser.). (ENG.). 48p. (J). (gr. 4-7). pap. 12.00 (978-0-89812-846-8(3), Creative Paperbacks) Creative Co., The.

—NFL Today: Carolina Panthers. 2013. (NFL Today Ser.). (ENG., Illus.). 48p. (J). (gr. 4-7). pap. 12.00 (978-0-89812-849-9(8), Creative Paperbacks) Creative Co., The.

—NFL Today: Houston Texans. 2013. (NFL Today Ser.). (ENG.). 48p. (J). (gr. 4-7). pap. 12.00 (978-0-89812-857-4(9), Creative Paperbacks) Creative Co., The.

—NFL Today: Jacksonville Jaguars. 2013. (NFL Today Ser.). (ENG.). 48p. (J). (gr. 4-7). pap. 12.00 (978-0-89812-859-8(5), Creative Paperbacks) Creative Co., The.

—NFL Today: Philadelphia Eagles. 2013. (NFL Today Ser.). (ENG., Illus.). 48p. (J). (gr. 4-7). pap. 12.00 (978-0-89812-868-0(4), Creative Paperbacks) Creative Co., The.

—NFL Today: St. Louis Rams. 2013. (NFL Today Ser.). (ENG.). 48p. (J). (gr. 4-7). pap. 12.00 (978-0-89812-870-3(6), Creative Paperbacks) Creative Co., The.

—NFL Today: Tampa Bay Buccaneers. 2013. (NFL Today Ser.). (ENG., Illus.). 48p. (J). (gr. 4-7). pap. 12.00 (978-0-89812-874-1(9), Creative Paperbacks) Creative Co., The.

—The Story of the Atlanta Falcons. 2013. (J). 35.65 (978-1-60818-293-0(2), Creative Education) Creative Co., The.

—The Story of the Carolina Panthers. 2013. (Illus.). 48p. (J). 35.65 (978-1-60818-296-1(7), Creative Education) Creative Co., The.

—The Story of the Houston Texans. 2013. (J). 35.65 (978-1-60818-304-3(1), Creative Education) Creative Co., The.

—The Story of the Jacksonville Jaguars. 2013. (J). 35.65 (978-1-60818-306-7(8), Creative Education) Creative Co., The.

—The Story of the Philadelphia Eagles. 2013. (Illus.). 48p. (J). 35.65 (978-1-60818-315-9(7), Creative Education) Creative Co., The.

—The Story of the St. Louis Rams. 2013. (J). 35.65 (978-1-60818-317-3(3), Creative Education) Creative Co., The.

—The Story of the Tampa Bay Buccaneers. 2013. (Illus.). 48p. (J). 35.65 (978-1-60818-321-0(1), Creative Education) Creative Co., The.

Gigliotti, Jim. Eli Manning. 2016. (Football Heroes Making a Difference Ser.). (ENG.). 24p. (J). (gr. 1-6). 16.96 (978-1-943553-40-2(8)) Bearport Publishing Co., Inc.

Gilbert, Sara. The History of the Arizona Cardinals. 2004. (NFL Today Ser.). (Illus.). 32p. (YA). (gr. 5-9). 18.95 (978-1-58341-286-2(7)) Creative Co., The.

—NFL Today: Baltimore Ravens. 2013. (NFL Today Ser.). (ENG.). 48p. (J). (gr. 4-7). pap. 12.00 (978-0-89812-847-5(1), Creative Paperbacks) Creative Co., The.

—NFL Today: Buffalo Bills. 2013. (NFL Today Ser.). (ENG.). 48p. (J). (gr. 4-7). pap. 12.00 (978-0-89812-848-2(X), Creative Paperbacks) Creative Co., The.

—NFL Today: Tennessee Titans. 2013. (NFL Today Ser.). (ENG.). 48p. (J). (gr. 4-7). pap. 12.00 (978-0-89812-875-8(7), Creative Paperbacks) Creative Co., The.

—The Story of the Arizona Cardinals. 2009. (NFL Today Ser.). (Illus.). 48p. (YA). (gr. 5-9). 22.95 (978-1-58341-745-4(1)) Creative Co., The.

—The Story of the Baltimore Ravens. 2013. (J). 35.65 (978-1-60818-294-7(0), Creative Education) Creative Co., The.

—The Story of the New Orleans Saints. 2009. (NFL Today Ser.). 48p. (YA). (gr. 5-9). 22.95 (978-1-58341-764-5(8)) Creative Co., The.

—The Story of the Tampa Bay Buccaneers. 2009. (NFL Today Ser.). 48p. (YA). (gr. 5-9). 22.95 (978-1-58341-772-0(9)) Creative Co., The.

—The Story of the Tennessee Titans. 2013. (J). 35.65 (978-1-60818-322-7(X), Creative Education) Creative Co., The.

Gillespie, Katie. Arizona Cardinals. 2016. (J). **(978-1-4896-5478-6(X))** Weigl Pubs., Inc.

Gitlin, Martin. Drew Brees: Super Bowl Champ, 1 vol. 2011. (Playmakers Ser.). (ENG., Illus.). 32p. (YA). (gr. 3-6). 27.07 (978-1-61714-743-2(5)) ABDO Publishing Co.

—Michigan Football. 2013. (America's Most Winning Teams Ser.). 48p. (J). (gr. 5-8). 29.25 (978-1-4488-9397-3(6)); pap. 70.50 (978-1-4488-9426-0(3)); pap. 11.75 (978-1-4488-9423-9(9)) Rosen Publishing Group, Inc., The.

—Ole Miss Rebels, 1 vol. 2013. (Inside College Football Set 2 Ser.). (ENG.). 48p. (J). (gr. 3-6). lib. bdg. 32.79 (978-1-61783-655-8(9), SportsZone) ABDO Publishing Co.

—Wisconsin Badgers, 1 vol. 2013. (Inside College Football Set 2 Ser.). (ENG.). 48p. (J). (gr. 3-6). lib. bdg. 32.79 (978-1-61783-658-9(3), SportsZone) ABDO Publishing Co.

Glave, Tom. Houston Texans. 2015. (Insider's Guide to Pro Football Ser.). (ENG.). 32p. (J). (gr. k-3). 28.50 (978-1-63143-995-7(2), 208830) Child's World, Inc., The.

—Jacksonville Jaguars. 2015. (Insider's Guide to Pro Football Ser.). (ENG.). 32p. (J). (gr. k-3). 28.50 (978-1-63143-997-1(9), 208832) Child's World, Inc., The.

—Pittsburgh Steelers. 2015. (Insider's Guide to Pro Football Ser.). (ENG.). 32p. (J). (gr. k-3). 28.50 (978-1-63143-994-0(4), 208829) Child's World, Inc., The.

—Tennessee Titans. 2015. (Insider's Guide to Pro Football Ser.). (ENG.). 32p. (J). (gr. k-3). 28.50 (978-1-63143-998-8(7), 208833) Child's World, Inc., The.

Goodman, Michael E. The History of the Atlanta Falcons. 2004. (NFL Today Ser.). (Illus.). 32p. (YA). (gr. 5-9). 18.95 (978-1-58341-287-9(5)) Creative Co., The.

—The History of the Carolina Panthers. 2004. (NFL Today Ser.). (Illus.). 32p. (YA). (gr. 5-9). 18.95 (978-1-58341-290-9(5)) Creative Co., The.

—The History of the Tampa Bay Buccaneers. 2004. (NFL Today Ser.). (Illus.). 32p. (YA). (gr. 5-9). 18.95 (978-1-58341-315-9(4)) Creative Co., The.

—The Story of the Atlanta Falcons. 2009. (NFL Today Ser.). 48p. (YA). (gr. 5-9). 22.95 (978-1-58341-746-1(X)) Creative Co., The.

—The Story of the Carolina Panthers. 2009. (NFL Today Ser.). 48p. (YA). (gr. 5-9). 22.95 (978-1-58341-749-2(4)) Creative Co., The.

Grayson, Robert. Plaxico Burress. 2009. (Superstars of Pro Football Ser.). (Illus.). 64p. (YA). (gr. 7-12). lib. bdg. 22.95 (978-1-4222-0552-5(5)) Mason Crest.

Harmon, Daniel E. Notre Dame Football. 2013. (America's Most Winning Teams Ser.). 48p. (J). (gr. 5-8). 29.25 (978-1-4488-9399-7(2)); pap. 11.75 (978-1-4488-9436-9(0)); pap. 70.50 (978-1-4488-9437-6(9)) Rosen Publishing Group, Inc., The.

Hawkes, Brian. The History of the Indianapolis Colts. 2004. (NFL Today Ser.). (Illus.). 32p. (YA). (gr. 5-9). 18.95 (978-1-58341-299-2(9)) Creative Co., The.

—The History of the Jacksonville Jaguars. 2004. (NFL Today Ser.). (Illus.). 32p. (YA). (gr. 5-9). 18.95 (978-1-58341-300-5(6)) Creative Co., The.

Heath, Steve & Gitlin, Martin. Arizona Cardinals, 1 vol. 2010. (Inside the NFL Ser.). (ENG.). 48p. (YA). (gr. 3-6). lib. bdg. 32.79 (978-1-61714-001-3(5)) ABDO Publishing Co.

Holmes, Parker. The Alabama Crimson Tide. 2012. (Champions of College Football Ser.). (ENG., Illus.). 24p. (J). (gr. 2-5). pap. 10.60 (978-1-4488-9200-6(7)); lib. bdg. 23.95 (978-1-4488-9192-4(2)) Rosen Publishing Group, Inc., The. (PowerKids Pr.).

—The Auburn Tigers. 2012. (Champions of College Football Ser.). (ENG., Illus.). 24p. (J). (gr. 2-5). pap. 10.60 (978-1-4488-9197-9(3)); lib. bdg. 23.95 (978-1-4488-9193-1(0)) Rosen Publishing Group, Inc., The. (PowerKids Pr.).

Howell, Brian. Miami Hurricanes, 1 vol. 2013. (Inside College Football Set 2 Ser.). (ENG.). 48p. (J). (gr. 3-6). lib. bdg. 32.79 (978-1-61783-654-1(0), SportsZone) ABDO Publishing Co.

Jasner, Andy. Baltimore Ravens, 1 vol. 2010. (Inside the NFL Ser.). (ENG.). 48p. (YA). (gr. 3-6). lib. bdg. 32.79 (978-1-61714-003-7(1)) ABDO Publishing Co.

—Buffalo Bills, 1 vol. 2010. (Inside the NFL Ser.). (ENG.). 48p. (YA). (gr. 3-6). lib. bdg. 32.79 (978-1-61714-004-4(X)) ABDO Publishing Co.

Joura, Brian. Carolina Panthers, 1 vol. 2010. (Inside the NFL Ser.). (ENG.). 48p. (YA). (gr. 3-6). lib. bdg. 32.79 (978-1-61714-005-1(8)) ABDO Publishing Co.

Kelley, K. C. Football: Dynamic Duos. 2014. (ENG.). 32p. (J). (gr. 2-5). pap. 3.99 (978-0-545-72218-6(7), Scholastic Paperbacks) Scholastic, Inc.

—Quarterback Superstars 2015. 2015. (ENG., Illus.). 32p. (J). (gr. 2-5). pap. 3.99 (978-0-545-82635-8(7), Scholastic Paperbacks) Scholastic, Inc.

Kimmich, Ian. Antonio Gates. 2009. (Superstars of Pro Football Ser.). (Illus.). 64p. (YA). (gr. 7-12). lib. bdg. 22.95 (978-1-4222-0553-2(3)) Mason Crest.

Krumenauer, Heidi. Brett Favre. 2008. (Blue Banner Biography Ser.). (Illus.). 32p. (YA). (gr. 4-7). lib. bdg. 25.70 (978-1-58415-670-3(8)) Mitchell Lane Pubs., Inc.

Leboutillier, Nate. San Francisco 49ers. 2005. (Super Bowl Champions Ser.). (Illus.). 24p. (J). (gr. 1-4). lib. bdg. 16.95 (978-1-58341-391-3(X), Creative Education) Creative Co., The.

—St. Louis Rams. 2005. (Super Bowl Champions Ser.). (Illus.). 24p. (J). (gr. 5-9). lib. bdg. 16.95 (978-1-58341-390-6(1)) Creative Co., The.

Lee, Tony. Clemson Tigers, 1 vol. 2013. (Inside College Football Set 2 Ser.). (ENG., Illus.). 48p. (J). (gr. 3-6). lib. bdg. 32.79 (978-1-61783-652-7(4), SportsZone) ABDO Publishing Co.

Mack, Larry. The New Orleans Saints Story. 2016. (NFL Teams Ser.). (ENG., Illus.). 32p. (J). (gr. 3-7). lib. bdg. 26.95 (978-1-62617-374-3(5), Torque Bks.) Bellwether Media.

—The Philadelphia Eagles Story. 2016. (NFL Teams Ser.). (ENG., Illus.). 32p. (J). (gr. 3-7). lib. bdg. 26.95 (978-1-62617-378-1(8), Torque Bks.) Bellwether Media.

—The Tampa Bay Buccaneers Story. 2016. (NFL Teams Ser.). (ENG., Illus.). 32p. (J). (gr. 3-7). lib. bdg. 26.95 (978-1-62617-384-2(2), Torque Bks.) Bellwether Media.

MacRae, Sloan. The New Orleans Saints. 2011. (America's Greatest Teams Ser.). (Illus.). 24p. (J). pap. 8.25 (978-1-4488-2745-9(0)); lib. bdg. 22.60 (978-1-4488-2578-3(4)) Rosen Publishing Group, Inc., The. (PowerKids Pr.).

—The Pittsburgh Steelers. (Illus.). 24p. (J). 2010. pap. 8.25 (978-1-4358-3396-8(1)) 2009. lib. bdg. 22.60 (978-1-4042-8131-8(2)) Rosen Publishing Group, Inc., The. (PowerKids Pr.).

—The San Francisco 49ers. 2011. (America's Greatest Teams Ser.). (Illus.). 24p. (J). pap. 8.25 (978-1-4488-3170-8(9)); lib. bdg. 22.60 (978-1-4488-3166-1(0)) Rosen Publishing Group, Inc., The. (PowerKids Pr.).

—The Washington Redskins. 2011. (America's Greatest Teams Ser.). (Illus.). 24p. (J). pap. 8.25 (978-1-4488-3176-0(8)); lib. bdg. 22.60 (978-1-4488-3169-2(5)) Rosen Publishing Group, Inc., The. (PowerKids Pr.).

McMahon, Dave. Atlanta Falcons, 1 vol. 2010. (Inside the NFL Ser.). (ENG.). 48p. (YA). (gr. 3-6). lib. bdg. 32.79 (978-1-61714-002-0(3)) ABDO Publishing Co.

Monnig, Alex. Arkansas Razorbacks, 1 vol. 2013. (Inside College Football Set 2 Ser.). (ENG.). 48p. (J). (gr. 3-6). lib. bdg. 32.79 (978-1-61783-651-0(6), SportsZone) ABDO Publishing Co.

—Florida State Seminoles, 1 vol. 2013. (Inside College Football Set 2 Ser.). (ENG.). 48p. (J). (gr. 3-6). lib. bdg. 32.79 (978-1-61783-653-4(2), SportsZone) ABDO Publishing Co.

—New Orleans Saints. 2015. (Insider's Guide to Pro Football Ser.). (ENG.). 32p. (J). (gr. k-3). 28.50 (978-1-63407-013-3(5), 208848) Child's World, Inc., The.

—San Francisco 49ers. 2015. (Insider's Guide to Pro Football Ser.). (ENG.). 32p. (J). (gr. k-3). 28.50 (978-1-63407-016-4(X), 208851) Child's World, Inc., The.

—St. Louis Rams. 2015. (Insider's Guide to Pro Football Ser.). (ENG.). 32p. (J). (gr. k-3). 28.50 (978-1-63407-018-8(6), 208853) Child's World, Inc., The.

—Tampa Bay Buccaneers. 2015. (Insider's Guide to Pro Football Ser.). (ENG.). 32p. (J). (gr. k-3). 28.50 (978-1-63407-014-0(3), 208849) Child's World, Inc., The.

Monteverde, Matthew. Notre Dame vs. USC. 2013. (J). *(978-1-4777-1164-4(3))*; pap. *(978-1-4777-1163-7(5))*; lib. bdg. *(978-1-4777-1158-3(9))* Rosen Publishing Group, Inc., The. (PowerKids Pr.).

Mooney, Carla. Nebraska Football. 2013. (America's Most Winning Teams Ser.). 48p. (J). (gr. 5-8). 29.25 *(978-1-4488-9400-0(X))*; pap. 70.50 *(978-1-4488-9434-5(4))*; pap. 11.75 *(978-1-4488-9433-8(6))* Rosen Publishing Group, Inc., The.

Morey, Allan. The Baltimore Ravens Story. 2016. (NFL Teams Ser.). (ENG., Illus.). 32p. (J). (gr. 3-7). lib. bdg. 26.95 *(978-1-62617-357-6(5)*, Torque Bks.) Bellwether Media.

—The Los Angeles Rams. 2016. (NFL Teams Ser.). (ENG., Illus.). 32p. (J). (gr. 3-7). lib. bdg. 26.95 *(978-1-62617-383-5(4)*, Torque Bks.) Bellwether Media.

—The Pittsburgh Steelers Story. 2016. (NFL Teams Ser.). (ENG., Illus.). 32p. (J). (gr. 3-7). lib. bdg. 26.95 *(978-1-62617-379-8(6)*, Torque Bks.) Bellwether Media.

Nichols, John. The History of the Baltimore Ravens. 2004. (NFL Today Ser.). (Illus.). 32p. (YA). (gr. 5-9). 18.95 *(978-1-58341-288-6(3))* Creative Co., The.

—The Story of the Pittsburgh Steelers. 2009. (NFL Today Ser.). 48p. (YA). (gr. 5-9). 22.95 *(978-1-58341-767-6(2))* Creative Co., The.

Norman, J. T. Houston Texans. 2017. (Illus.). 32p. (J). ***(978-1-68079-894-4(4)***, SportsZone) ABDO Publishing Co.

Omoth, Tyler. The Story of the Indianapolis Colts. 2009. (NFL Today Ser.). 48p. (YA). (gr. 5-9). 22.95 *(978-1-58341-758-4(3))* Creative Co., The.

—The Story of the Philadelphia Eagles. 2009. (NFL Today Ser.). 48p. (YA). (gr. 5-9). 22.95 *(978-1-58341-766-9(4))* Creative Co., The.

Patrick, James. Football Madness: The Road to Super Bowl XXXVII. 2003. (Illus.). 24p. (J). *(978-0-439-48650-7(5))* Scholastic, Inc.

Peters, Rob, illus. Kansas City Chiefs ABCs And 1-2-3s. 2015. (ENG.). 26p. (J). bds. 18.95 *(978-0-9961944-0-2(1))* Ascend Bks., LLC.

Portman, Michael. Drew Brees. 2010. (Today's Superstars Ser.). (Illus.). 48p. (gr. 5-8). 31.95 *(978-1-4339-3992-1(4))*; pap. 14.05 *(978-1-4339-3993-8(2))* Stevens, Gareth Publishing LLLP.

Pueschner, Gordon. The Story of the Houston Texans. 2009. (NFL Today Ser.). 48p. (YA). (gr. 5-9). 22.95 *(978-1-58341-757-7(5))* Creative Co., The.

—The Story of the Jacksonville Jaguars. 2009. (NFL Today Ser.). (Illus.). 48p. (YA). (gr. 5-9). 22.95 *(978-1-58341-759-1(1))* Creative Co., The.

Pulditor, Seth H. DeSean Jackson. 2009. (Superstars of Pro Football Ser.). 64p. (YA). (gr. 5-18). pap. 9.95 *(978-1-4222-1983-6(6))* Mason Crest.

Rappoport, Ken. Texas a & M Aggies, 1 vol. 2013. (Inside College Football Set 2 Ser.). (ENG.). 48p. (J). (gr. 3-6). lib. bdg. 32.79 *(978-1-61783-657-2(5)*, SportsZone) ABDO Publishing Co.

Read Together Books Inc Staff & Shoule, Michael. My Daddy Loves Boston College Football. 2010. (ENG.). 20p. (J). bds. 11.95 *(978-0-9822615-0-7(0)*, 9780982261507) Read Together Bks.

Robson, David W. Brian Westbrook. 2009. (Superstars of Pro Football Ser.). (Illus.). 64p. (YA). (gr. 7-12). lib. bdg. 22.95 *(978-1-4222-0547-1(9))* Mason Crest.

Roselius, J. Chris. Houston Texans, 1 vol. 2010. (Inside the NFL Ser.). (ENG.). 48p. (YA). (gr. 3-6). lib. bdg. 32.79 *(978-1-61714-013-6(9))* ABDO Publishing Co.

Ross, Dalton. The Top Teams Ever: Football, Baseball, Basketball & Hockey Winners. 2005. (Sports Illustrated for Kids Books Ser.). (Illus.). 176p. (YA). (gr. 7-12). lib. bdg. 33.25 *(978-0-8239-3693-9(7))* Rosen Publishing Group, Inc., The.

Sandler, Michael. Drew Brees & the New Orleans Saints. 2010. (Super Bowl Superstars Ser.). 24p. (YA). (gr. k-3). lib. bdg. 22.61 *(978-1-936088-27-0(4))* Bearport Publishing Co., Inc.

—Joe Montana & the San Fransisco 49ers. 2008. (Super Bowl Superstars Ser.). (Illus.). 24p. (J). (gr. k-3). lib. bdg. 22.61 *(978-1-59716-738-3(X))* Bearport Publishing Co., Inc.

—Pro Football's Dream Teams. 2010. (Football-O-Rama Ser.). 24p. (YA). (gr. 3-6). lib. bdg. 22.61 *(978-1-936088-24-9(X))* Bearport Publishing Co., Inc.

Savage, Jeff. Drew Brees. 2010. pap. 39.62 *(978-0-7613-6967-7(8))* Lerner Publishing Group.

Schmalzbauer, Adam. The History of the Philadelphia Eagles. 2004. (NFL Today Ser.). (Illus.). 32p. (YA). (gr. 5-9). 18.95 *(978-1-58341-309-8(X))* Creative Co., The.

—The History of the Pittsburgh Steelers. 2004. (NFL Today Ser.). (Illus.). 32p. (YA). (gr. 5-9). 18.95 *(978-1-58341-310-4(3))* Creative Co., The.

Stewart, Mark. The Arizona Cardinals. rev. ed. 2012. (Team Spirit Ser.). (ENG.). 48p. (J). (gr. 3-6). lib. bdg. 29.27 *(978-1-59953-512-8(2))* Norwood Hse. Pr.

—The Atlanta Falcons. rev. ed. 2012. (Team Spirit Ser.). (ENG.). 48p. (J). (gr. 3-6). lib. bdg. 29.27 *(978-1-59953-513-5(0))* Norwood Hse. Pr.

—The Auburn Tigers. 2011. (Team Spirit College Ser.). 48p. (J). (gr. 3-6). 26.60 *(978-1-59953-461-9(4))* Norwood Hse. Pr.

—The Baltimore Ravens. rev. ed. 2012. (Team Spirit Ser.). (ENG.). 48p. (J). (gr. 3-6). lib. bdg. 29.27 *(978-1-59953-514-2(9))* Norwood Hse. Pr.

—The Carolina Panthers. rev. ed. 2012. (Team Spirit Ser.). (ENG.). 48p. (J). (gr. 3-6). lib. bdg. 29.27 *(978-1-59953-516-6(5))* Norwood Hse. Pr.

—The Chicago Bears. rev. ed. 2012. (Team Spirit Ser.). (ENG.). 48p. (J). (gr. 3-6). lib. bdg. 29.27 *(978-1-59953-517-3(3))* Norwood Hse. Pr.

—The Cincinnati Bengals. rev. ed. 2012. (Team Spirit Ser.). (ENG.). 48p. (J). (gr. 3-6). lib. bdg. 29.27 *(978-1-59953-518-0(1))* Norwood Hse. Pr.

—The Dallas Cowboys. rev. ed. 2012. (Team Spirit Ser.). (ENG., Illus.). 48p. (J). (gr. 3-6). lib. bdg. 29.27 *(978-1-59953-520-3(3))* Norwood Hse. Pr.

—The Detroit Lions. rev. ed. 2012. (Team Spirit Ser.). (ENG.). 48p. (J). (gr. 3-6). lib. bdg. 29.27 *(978-1-59953-522-7(X))* Norwood Hse. Pr.

—The Florida Gators. 2010. (Team Spirit Ser.). 48p. (J). (gr. 3-6). 26.60 *(978-1-59953-333-9(2))* Norwood Hse. Pr.

—The Houston Texans. rev. ed. 2012. (Team Spirit Ser.). (ENG.). 48p. (J). (gr. 3-6). lib. bdg. 29.27 *(978-1-59953-524-1(6))* Norwood Hse. Pr.

—The Jacksonville Jaguars. rev. ed. 2012. (Team Spirit Ser.). (ENG.). 48p. (J). (gr. 3-6). lib. bdg. 29.27 *(978-1-59953-526-5(2))* Norwood Hse. Pr.

—The Kansas City Chiefs. rev. ed. 2012. (Team Spirit Ser.). (ENG.). 48p. (J). (gr. 3-6). lib. bdg. 29.27 *(978-1-59953-527-2(0))* Norwood Hse. Pr.

—The Minnesota Vikings. rev. ed. 2012. (Team Spirit Ser.). (ENG.). 48p. (J). (gr. 3-6). lib. bdg. 29.27 *(978-1-59953-529-6(7))* Norwood Hse. Pr.

—The Notre Dame Fighting Irish. 2010. (Team Spirit Ser.). (ENG.). 48p. (J). (gr. 3-6). lib. bdg. 26.60 *(978-1-59953-279-0(4))* Norwood Hse. Pr.

—The Philadelphia Eagles. rev. ed. 2012. (Team Spirit Ser.). (ENG.). 48p. (J). (gr. 3-6). lib. bdg. 29.27 *(978-1-59953-535-7(1))* Norwood Hse. Pr.

—The San Diego Chargers. rev. ed. 2012. (Team Spirit Ser.). (ENG.). 48p. (J). (gr. 3-6). lib. bdg. 29.27 *(978-1-59953-537-1(8))* Norwood Hse. Pr.

—The San Francisco 49ers. rev. ed. 2012. (Team Spirit Ser.). (ENG.). 48p. (J). (gr. 3-6). lib. bdg. 29.27 *(978-1-59953-538-8(6))* Norwood Hse. Pr.

—The Seattle Seahawks. rev. ed. 2012. (Team Spirit Ser.). (ENG.). 48p. (J). (gr. 3-6). lib. bdg. 29.27 *(978-1-59953-539-5(4))* Norwood Hse. Pr.

—The St. Louis Rams. rev. ed. 2012. (Team Spirit Ser.). (ENG.). 48p. (J). (gr. 3-6). lib. bdg. 29.27 *(978-1-59953-540-1(8))* Norwood Hse. Pr.

—The Tampa Bay Buccaneers. rev. ed. 2012. (Team Spirit Ser.). (ENG.). 48p. (J). (gr. 3-6). lib. bdg. 29.27 *(978-1-59953-541-8(6))* Norwood Hse. Pr.

—The Tennessee Titans. rev. ed. 2012. (Team Spirit Ser.). (ENG.). 48p. (J). (gr. 3-6). lib. bdg. 29.27 *(978-1-59953-542-5(4))* Norwood Hse. Pr.

—The Washington Redskins. rev. ed. 2012. (Team Spirit Ser.). (ENG.). 48p. (J). (gr. 3-6). lib. bdg. 29.27 *(978-1-59953-543-2(2))* Norwood Hse. Pr.

The Story of the Buffalo Bills. 2013. (J). 35.65 *(978-1-60818-295-4(9)*, Creative Education) Creative Co., The.

Temple, Ramey. Tampa Bay Buccaneers. 2014. (Inside the NFL Ser.). (ENG., Illus.). 32p. (J). (gr. 4-7). lib. bdg. 28.55 *(978-1-4896-0898-7(2)*, AV2 by Weigl) Weigl Pubs., Inc.

Torsiello, David P. Read about Drew Brees. 2011. (I Like Sports Stars! Ser.). (Illus.). 24p. (J). (gr. k-18). pap. 7.95 *(978-1-59845-299-0(1)*, Enslow Elementary); (gr. 1-4). lib. bdg. 22.60 *(978-0-7660-3831-8(9))* Enslow Pubs., Inc.

Tustison, Matt. Jacksonville Jaguars, 1 vol. 2010. (Inside the NFL Ser.). (ENG.). 48p. (YA). (gr. 3-6). lib. bdg. 32.79 *(978-1-61714-015-0(5))* ABDO Publishing Co.

Weaver, Jack. Uga Hunkers down in Athens Town. Ingram, Glenda Brown, illus. 2004. (J). *(978-0-9773370-0-2(6))* Weaver, Jack R. Company.

Whiting, Jim. NFL Today: Arizona Cardinals. 2013. (NFL Today Ser.). (ENG.). 48p. (J). (gr. 4-7). pap. 12.00 *(978-0-89812-845-1(5)*, Creative Paperbacks) Creative Co., The.

—NFL Today: New Orleans Saints. 2013. (NFL Today Ser.). (ENG., Illus.). 48p. (J). (gr. 4-7). pap. 12.00 *(978-0-89812-864-2(1)*, Creative Paperbacks) Creative Co., The.

—NFL Today: Pittsburgh Steelers. 2013. (NFL Today Ser.). (ENG.). 48p. (J). (gr. 4-7). pap. 12.00 *(978-0-89812-869-7(2)*, Creative Paperbacks) Creative Co., The.

—NFL Today: San Francisco 49ers. 2013. (NFL Today Ser.). (ENG.). 48p. (J). (gr. 4-7). pap. 12.00 *(978-0-89812-872-7(2)*, Creative Paperbacks) Creative Co., The.

—The Story of the Arizona Cardinals. 2013. (J). 35.65 *(978-1-60818-292-3(4)*, Creative Education) Creative Co., The.

—The Story of the San Francisco 49ers. 2013. (J). 35.65 *(978-1-60818-319-7(X)*, Creative Education) Creative Co., The.

Williams, Doug. Oregon Ducks, 1 vol. 2013. (Inside College Football Set 2 Ser.). (ENG., Illus.). 48p. (J). (gr. 3-6). lib. bdg. 32.79 *(978-1-61783-656-5(7)*, SportsZone) ABDO Publishing Co.

Wilner, Barry. Philadelphia Eagles. 2015. (Insider's Guide to Pro Football Ser.). (ENG.). 32p. (J). (gr. k-3). 28.50 *(978-1-63407-005-8(4)*, 208840) Child's World, Inc., The.

—USC Trojans, 1 vol. 2012. (Inside College Football Ser.). (ENG., Illus.). 48p. (J). (gr. 3-6). 32.79 *(978-1-61783-505-6(6))* ABDO Publishing Co.

Wyner, Zach. Seattle Seahawks. 2014. 32p. pap. *(978-1-4896-0890-1(7))* Weigl Pubs., Inc.

Wyner, Zach. Arizona Cardinals. 2014. (Inside the NFL Ser.). (ENG., Illus.). 32p. (J). (gr. 4-7). lib. bdg. 28.55 *(978-1-4896-0782-9(X)*, AV2 by Weigl) Weigl Pubs., Inc.

—Atlanta Falcons. (Illus.). 32p. 2015. pap. *(978-1-4896-0787-4(0))* 2014. (ENG., (J). (gr. 4-7). lib. bdg. 28.55 *(978-1-4896-0786-7(2)*, AV2 by Weigl) Weigl Pubs., Inc.

—Baltimore Ravens. (Illus.). 32p. (J). 2015. pap. *(978-1-4896-0791-1(9))* 2014. (ENG., (gr. 4-7). lib. bdg. 28.55 *(978-1-4896-0790-4(0)*, AV2 by Weigl) Weigl Pubs., Inc.

—Buffalo Bills. 2015. (Illus.). 32p. (J). *(978-1-4896-0794-2(3))* Weigl Pubs., Inc.

—Carolina Panthers. 2015. (Illus.). 32p. (J). *(978-1-4896-0798-0(6))* Weigl Pubs., Inc.

—Cleveland Browns. 2015. (Illus.). 32p. pap. *(978-1-4896-0811-6(7))* Weigl Pubs., Inc.

—Houston Texans. (Illus.). 32p. (J). 2015. pap. *(978-1-4896-0831-4(1))* 2014. (ENG., (gr. 4-7). lib. bdg. 28.55 *(978-1-4896-0830-7(3)*, AV2 by Weigl) Weigl Pubs., Inc.

—Jacksonville Jaguars. (Illus.). 32p. 2015. pap. *(978-1-4896-0839-0(7))* 2014. (ENG., (J). (gr. 4-7). lib. bdg. 28.55 *(978-1-4896-0838-3(9)*, AV2 by Weigl) Weigl Pubs., Inc.

—New Orleans Saints. (Illus.). 32p. (J). 2015. pap. *(978-1-4896-0859-8(1))* 2014. (ENG., (gr. 4-7). lib. bdg. 28.55 *(978-1-4896-0858-1(3)*, AV2 by Weigl) Weigl Pubs., Inc.

—Philadelphia Eagles. (Illus.). 32p. 2015. pap. *(978-1-4896-0875-8(3))* 2014. (ENG., (J). (gr. 4-7). lib. bdg. 28.55 *(978-1-4896-0874-1(5)*, AV2 by Weigl) Weigl Pubs., Inc.

—Pittsburgh Steelers. 2014. (Inside the NFL Ser.). (ENG., Illus.). 32p. (J). (gr. 4-7). lib. bdg. 28.55 *(978-1-4896-0878-9(8)*, AV2 by Weigl) Weigl Pubs., Inc.

—St. Louis Rams. (Illus.). 32p. 2015. pap. *(978-1-4896-0895-6(8))* 2014. (ENG., (J). (gr. 4-7). lib. bdg. 28.55 *(978-1-4896-0894-9(X)*, AV2 by Weigl) Weigl Pubs., Inc.

—Tennessee Titans. 2014. (Inside the NFL Ser.). (ENG., Illus.). 32p. (J). (gr. 4-7). lib. bdg. 28.55 *(978-1-4896-0902-1(4)*, AV2 by Weigl) Weigl Pubs., Inc.

—TennesseeTitans. 2015. (Illus.). 32p. (J). pap. *(978-1-4896-0903-8(2))* Weigl Pubs., Inc.

Zappa, Marcia. New Orleans Saints, 1 vol. 2014. (NFL's Greatest Teams Set 2 Ser.). (ENG.). 32p. (gr. 2-5). 28.50 *(978-1-62403-588-3(4))* ABDO Publishing Co.

—Pittsburgh Steelers, 1 vol. 2014. (NFL's Greatest Teams Ser.). (ENG.). 32p. (gr. 7-11). 28.50 *(978-1-62403-365-0(2))* ABDO Publishing Co.

—San Francisco 49ers, 1 vol. 2014. (NFL's Greatest Teams Ser.). (ENG.). 32p. (gr. 7-11). 28.50 *(978-1-62403-366-7(0))* ABDO Publishing Co.

FORCE AND ENERGY

see also Dynamics; Mechanics; Motion

Angliss, Sarah, et al. Hands-On Science: Forces & Motion. 2013. (Hands-On Science Ser.). (ENG., Illus.). 32p. (J). (gr. 2-5). pap. 7.99 *(978-0-7534-6972-9(3)*, 9780753469729, Kingfisher) Roaring Brook Pr.

Armentrout, David & Armentrout, Patricia. Biofuels. 2008. (ENG., Illus.). 48p. (gr. 4-8). pap. 10.95 *(978-1-60694-906-1(3))* Rourke Educational Media.

Bailey, Gerry & Law, Felicia. Energy & Movement. 2015. (Stone Age Science Ser.). (ENG., Illus.). 32p. (J). (gr. 3-7). lib. bdg. *(978-0-7787-1888-8(3))* Crabtree Publishing Co.

Ballard, Carol. Exploring Forces & Movement. 2008. (How Does Science Work? Ser.). (Illus.). 32p. (J). (gr. 3-7). lib. bdg. 26.50 *(978-1-4042-4277-7(5))* Rosen Publishing Group, Inc., The.

Barchers, Suzanne I. Conservation of Energy. 2015. (Science Readers: Content & Literacy Ser.). (Illus.). 32p. (gr. 5-5). pap. 8.99 *(978-1-4807-4723-4(8))* Teacher Created Materials, Inc.

—Energy, 1 vol. rev. ed. 2014. (Science Readers: Content & Literacy Ser.). (ENG.). 32p. (gr. 2-2). pap. 8.99 *(978-1-4807-4605-3(3))* Teacher Created Materials, Inc.

—Friction, 1 vol. rev. ed. 2014. (Science Readers: Content & Literacy Ser.). (ENG.). 32p. (gr. 2-2). pap. 8.99 *(978-1-4807-4606-0(1))* Teacher Created Materials, Inc.

Benchmark Education Company, LLC Staff, compiled by. Forces & Energy: Theme Set. 2006. (J). 136.00 *(978-1-4108-7061-2(8))* Benchmark Education Co.

—Forces & Motion. 2006. spiral bd. 330.00 *(978-1-4108-7014-8(6))* 2006. (J). 178.00 *(978-1-4108-7030-8(8))* 2005. (J). spiral bd. 265.00 *(978-1-4108-5760-6(3))* Benchmark Education Co.

—Forces & Motion: Theme Set. 2006. (J). 183.00 *(978-1-4108-7146-6(0))* Benchmark Education Co.

—Science Theme: Forces & Motion. 2005. spiral bd. 115.00 *(978-1-4108-5312-7(8))* Benchmark Education Co.

Bethea, Nikole Brooks. Power Plays: The Next 100 Years of Energy. Pota, Giovanni et al, illus. 2016. (Our World: the Next 100 Years Ser.). (ENG.). 32p. (gr. 3-4). lib. bdg. 30.65 *(978-1-4914-8267-4(2)*, Graphic Library) Capstone Press of Coughlan Cos.

Bishop, Amanda. Energy Conservation. 2008. (Saving Our World Ser.). 32p. (gr. 4-18). lib. bdg. 28.50 *(978-0-7614-3224-1(8)*, Benchmark Bks.) Marshall Cavendish Corp.

Biskup, Agnieszka. Aliens & Energy, 1 vol. Aón, Carlos, illus. 2011. (Monster Science Ser.). (ENG.). 32p. (gr. 3-4). pap. 8.10 *(978-1-4296-7325-9(7))*; pap. 47.70 *(978-1-4296-7326-6(5))*; lib. bdg. 30.65 *(978-1-4296-6580-3(7))* Capstone Press of Coughlan Cos. (Graphic Library).

—The Gripping Truth about Forces & Motion. Lum, Bernice, illus. 2012. (LOL Physical Science Ser.). (ENG.). 32p. (gr. 3-4). pap. 47.70 *(978-1-4296-9299-1(5)*, Fact Finders); pap. 8.10 *(978-1-4296-9298-4(7))*; lib. bdg. 27.32 *(978-1-4296-8601-3(4))* Capstone Press of Coughlan Cos.

—The Powerful World of Energy with Max Axiom, Super Scientist, 1 vol. 2009. (Graphic Science Ser.). (ENG.). 32p. (gr. 3-4). pap. 8.10 *(978-1-4296-3450-2(2)*, Graphic Library) Capstone Press of Coughlan Cos.

—Super Cool Forces & Motion Activities with Max Axiom. Baez, Marcelo, illus. 2015. (Max Axiom Science & Engineering Activities Ser.). (ENG.). 32p. (gr. 3-4). lib. bdg. 30.65 *(978-1-4914-2079-9(0)*, Graphic Library) Capstone Press of Coughlan Cos.

Bitterman, Quinn. Push & Pull: Understanding Force & Motion. 2013. (Rosen Readers Ser.). (ENG.). 24p. (J). (gr. 2-3). pap. 8.25 *(978-1-4777-2354-8(4))*; pap. 49.50 *(978-1-4777-2355-5(2))* Rosen Publishing Group, Inc., The. (Rosen Classroom).

Blaisdell, Molly. Our Sun. 2008. (Discovering & Exploring Science Ser.). (Illus.). 16p. (J). (gr. -1-3). 12.95 *(978-0-7569-8257-7(X))* Perfection Learning Corp.

Bodach, Vijaya Khisty. Energy. 2008. (Discovering & Exploring Science Ser.). (Illus.). 16p. (J). (gr. -1-3). lib. bdg. 12.95 *(978-0-7569-8415-1(7))* Perfection Learning Corp.

Bonnet, Robert L. & Keen, Dan. Home Run! Science Projects with Baseball & Softball. 2009. (Score! Sports Science Projects Ser.). (Illus.). 104p. (J). (gr. 5-9). lib. bdg. 33.27 *(978-0-7660-3365-8(1))* Enslow Pubs., Inc.

Boothroyd, Jennifer. Give It A Push! Give it A Pull! 2010. pap. 45.32 *(978-0-7613-6931-8(7))* Lerner Publishing Group.

—Give It a Push! Give It a Pull! A Look at Forces. 2010. (Lightning Bolt Books (tm) — Exploring Physical Science Ser.). (ENG., Illus.). 32p. (gr. k-2). lib. bdg. 26.60 *(978-0-7613-5431-4(X))* Lerner Publishing Group.

—Many Ways to Move. 2010. pap. 45.32 *(978-0-7613-6932-5(5))* Lerner Publishing Group.

—Many Ways to Move: A Look at Motion. 2010. (Lightning Bolt Books (tm) — Exploring Physical Science Ser.). (ENG.). 32p. (gr. k-2). pap. 7.95 *(978-0-7613-6060-5(3))*; (Illus.). lib. bdg. 26.60 *(978-0-7613-5434-5(4))* Lerner Publishing Group.

Bradley, Kimberly Brubaker. Forces Make Things Move. Meisel, Paul, illus. 2005. (Let's-Read-And-Find-Out Science 2 Ser.). (ENG.). 40p. (J). (gr. k-4). pap. 5.99 *(978-0-06-445214-4(X))* HarperCollins Pubs.

Bryant-Mole, Karen. Forces. 2016. (Science All Around Me Ser.). (ENG.). 24p. (gr. 1-3). pap. 7.49 *(978-1-4846-3651-0(1)*, NA-h) Heinemann-Raintree.

Bug, Amy L. Forces & Motion. 2008. (Physics in Action Ser.). 134p. (YA). (gr. 9-12). 35.00 *(978-0-7910-8931-6(2))* Facts On File, Inc.

Burton, Margie, et al. What Pushes? What Pulls? 2011. (Early Connections Ser.). (J). *(978-1-61672-548-6(6))* Benchmark Education Co.

—What Pushes? What Pulls? & ¿Qué empuja? ¿Qué Jala? 6 English, 6 Spanish Adaptations. 2011. (J). spiral bd. 75.00 net. *(978-1-4108-5641-8(0))* Benchmark Education Co.

Carlson Berne, Emma. Speeding! Mechanical Energy. 2013. (Energy Everywhere Ser.). (ENG., Illus.). 24p. (J). (gr. 3-6). 22.60 *(978-1-4488-9651-6(7))*; pap. 8.25 *(978-1-4488-9760-5(2))* Rosen Publishing Group, Inc., The. (PowerKids Pr.).

Cavell-Clarke, Steffi. Pushes & Pulls. 2017. (First Science Ser.). 24p. (J). (gr. 1-1). pap. 8.25 ***(978-1-5345-2080-6(5))***; lib. bdg. 24.60 ***(978-1-5345-2082-0(1))*** Greenhaven Publishing LLC. (KidHaven Publishing).

Challoner, Jack & Green, Dan. DK Eyewitness Books: Energy. 2016. (DK Eyewitness Bks.). (ENG., Illus.). 72p. (J). (gr. 3-7). pap. 9.99 *(978-1-4654-5104-0(8)*, DK Children) Dorling Kindersley Publishing, Inc.

—Energy. 2016. (DK Eyewitness Bks.). (ENG., Illus.). 72p. (J). (gr. 3-7). lib. bdg. 19.99 *(978-1-4654-5105-7(6)*, DK Children) Dorling Kindersley Publishing, Inc.

Cherry Lake Publishing Staff, compiled by. Power Up! 2009. (21st Century Skills Library: Power Up! Ser.). 32p. lib. bdg. 199.50 *(978-1-60279-107-7(4)*, 200050) Cherry Lake Publishing.

Chiang, Mona. Isaac Newton & His Laws of Motion: Text Pairs. 2008. (Bridges/Navigators Ser.). (J). (gr. 6). 94.00 *(978-1-4108-8442-8(2))* Benchmark Education Co.

Claybourne, Anna. Forces & Motion. 2016. (Mind Webs Ser.). (ENG., Illus.). 32p. (J). (gr. 4-6). pap. 11.99 *(978-0-7502-8983-2(X)*, Wayland) Hachette Children's Group GBR. Dist: Hachette Bk. Group.

—Forms of Energy. 2016. (Sci-Hi: Physical Science Ser.). (ENG.). 48p. (gr. 4-4). pap. 8.99 *(978-1-4109-8532-3(6)*, Sci-Hi) Heinemann-Raintree.

—Pushes & Pulls. 2012. (Illus.). 24p. (gr. k-4). pap. 7.95 *(978-1-926853-59-8(8))* Saunders Bk. Co. CAN. Dist: RiverStream Publishing.

Clemens, Nora & Greenberger, Robert. Discovering the Nature of Energy. 2011. (Scientist's Guide to Physics Ser.). (YA). (gr. 7-12). lib. bdg. 34.60 *(978-1-4488-4702-0(8))* Rosen Publishing Group, Inc., The.

Close, Edward. Force & Motion, 1 vol., 1. 2014. (Discovery Education: How It Works). (ENG.). 32p. (gr. 3-6). 26.25 *(978-1-4777-6317-9(1)*, PowerKids Pr.) Rosen Publishing Group, Inc., The.

Coan, Sharon. Empujar y Jalar (Pushes & Pulls) 2016. (TIME for KIDS(r) Nonfiction Readers Ser.). (SPA.). 12p. (J). (gr. k-k). 4.99 *(978-1-4938-2961-3(0))* Teacher Created Materials, Inc.

—Pushes & Pulls, 1 vol. 2015. (TIME for KIDS(r) Nonfiction Readers Ser.). (ENG., Illus.). 12p. (gr. k-k). 4.99 *(978-1-4938-2052-8(4))* Teacher Created Materials, Inc.

Colson, Mary. The Science of Forces. 2016. (Flowchart Smart Ser.). (ENG.). 48p. (J). (gr. 4-5). pap. 14.05 *(978-1-4824-4135-2(7))* Stevens, Gareth Publishing LLLP.

Cook, Trevor. Experiments with Forces. 2009. (Science Lab Ser.). (J). (ENG., Illus.). 32p. (gr. 4-6). pap. 10.00 *(978-1-4358-3217-6(5))*; lib. bdg. 26.50 *(978-1-4358-2804-9(6))* Rosen Publishing Group, Inc., The. (PowerKids Pr.).

Crawford, Leslie & Holm, Amy E. Environmental Action. 26p. (YA). (gr. 6-12). pap. 8.50 *(978-0-201-49549-2(X))* Globe Fearon Educational Publishing.

David, Sarah B. Reducing Your Carbon Footprint at Home. 2009. (Your Carbon Footprint Ser.). 48p. (gr. 5-5). 53.00 *(978-1-60854-910-8(0)*, Rosen Reference) Rosen Publishing Group, Inc., The.

Davis, Fredrick. Forms of Energy. 2009. (Amazing Science Ser.). 24p. (gr. 3-3). 42.50 *(978-1-61511-327-9(4)*, PowerKids Pr.) Rosen Publishing Group, Inc., The.

Dawson, Emily C. Push & Pull. 2010. (Everyday Science Ser.). 24p. (J). (gr. k-3). 25.65 *(978-1-60753-021-3(X))* Amicus Publishing.

de Pinna, Simon. Transfer of Energy. 2007. (Gareth Stevens Vital Science: Physical Science Ser.). (Illus.). 48p. (gr. 5-12). pap. 14.05 *(978-0-8368-8100-4(1))*; lib. bdg. 27.00 *(978-0-8368-8091-5(9))* Stevens, Gareth Publishing LLLP. (Gareth Stevens Secondary Library).

Dicker, Katie. Forces & Motion. 2010. (Sherlock Bones Looks at Physical Science Ser.). (ENG.). 32p. (YA). (gr. 3-6). lib. bdg. 25.25 *(978-1-61533-211-3(1))* Windmill Bks.

Doudna, Kelly. Super Simple Things to Do with Pressure: Fun & Easy Science for Kids, 1 vol. 2011. (Super Simple Science Ser.). (ENG., Illus.). 24p. (J). (gr. k-3). lib. bdg. 25.65 *(978-1-61714-675-6(7))* ABDO Publishing Co.

Duke, Shirley. Forces & Motion at Work. 2011. (ENG., Illus.). 48p. (gr. 4-6). pap. 10.95 *(978-1-61741-990-4(7))* Rourke Educational Media.

Dunne, Abbie. Forces. 2016. (Physical Science Ser.). (ENG., Illus.). 24p. (gr. k-1). lib. bdg. 26.65 *(978-1-5157-0936-7(1)*, Pebble Plus) Capstone Press of Coughlan Cos.

Encyclopaedia Britannica, Inc. Staff, compiled by. Britannica Illustrated Science Library: Energy & Movement. 2009. 29.95 *(978-1-59339-855-2(7))* Encyclopaedia Britannica, Inc.

Encyclopedia Britannica Staff, creator. Energy & Movement. 2011. (Britannica Illustrated Science Library Ser.). 104p. (J). 37.44 *(978-1-61535-467-2(0))* Encyclopaedia Britannica, Inc.

Energy. 2011. (Introduction to Physics Ser.). (ENG.). 80p. (YA). (gr. 7-12). 63.40 *(978-1-61530-776-0(1))* Rosen Publishing Group, Inc., The.

Energy - English Take Home Book. 2007. (Journeys Ser.). (J). pap. 20.00 *(978-1-4042-9535-3(6)*, Rosen Classroom) Rosen Publishing Group, Inc., The.

EFG

Enz, Tammy. Harness It: Invent New Ways to Harness Energy & Nature, 1 vol. 2012. (Invent It Ser.). (ENG.). 32p. (gr. 3-4). pap. 8.10 *(978-1-4296-7982-4(4))*; pap. 47.70 *(978-1-4296-8456-9(9))* Capstone Press of Coughlan Cos. (Fact Finders).

Evans Ogden, Lesley J. Forces & Motion. 2011. (J). (gr. 4-6). pap. 12.95 *(978-1-61690-733-4(9)*, AV2 by Weigl); (Illus.). 24p. (gr. 3-6). 27.13 *(978-1-61690-729-7(0))* Weigl Pubs., Inc.

—Studying Forces & Motion. 2016. (Illus.). 24p. (J). *(978-1-5105-1124-8(5))* SmartBook Media, Inc.

Everyday Forces: Individual Title Six-Packs. (Discovery World Ser.). 24p. (gr. 1-2). 33.00 *(978-0-7635-8480-1(0))* Rigby Education.

Fiedler, Julie. Learning about Force & Motion with Graphic Organizers. 2007. (Graphic Organizers in Science Ser.: Vol. 3). (ENG., Illus.). 24p. (J). (gr. 3-7). lib. bdg. 22.60 *(978-1-4042-3410-9(1))* Rosen Publishing Group, Inc., The.

Flounders, Anne. Power for the Planet. 2014. (Our Green Earth Ser.). (Illus.). 32p. (gr. 2-4). pap. 8.95 *(978-1-939656-33-9(8))* Red Chair Pr.

Foland, Andrew Dean. Energy. 2007. (Physics in Action Ser.). (Illus.). 127p. (YA). (gr. 9-12). lib. bdg. 35.00 *(978-0-7910-8930-9(4))* Facts On File, Inc.

Frost, Adriana. Making Things Move: Force & Motion. 2013. (InfoMax Readers Ser.). (ENG.). 24p. (J). (gr. 2-3). pap. 49.50 *(978-1-4777-2336-4(6))*; (Illus.). pap. 8.25 *(978-1-4777-2335-7(8))* Rosen Publishing Group, Inc., The. (Rosen Classroom).

Gardner, Robert. Bicycle Science Fair Projects. 2015. (Prize-Winning Science Fair Projects Ser.). (ENG.). 128p. (J). (gr. 7-7). lib. bdg. 37.27 *(978-0-7660-7016-5(6))* Enslow Pubs., Inc.

—Bicycle Science Projects: Physics on Wheels. 2004. (Science Fair Success Ser.). (Illus.). 112p. (J). lib. bdg. 27.94 *(978-0-7660-1630-9(7))* Enslow Pubs., Inc.

—Energy Experiments Using Ice Cubes, Springs, Magnets, & More: One Hour or Less Science Experiments. 2012. (Last-Minute Science Projects Ser.). (Illus.). 48p. (J). (gr. 5-18). 25.27 *(978-0-7660-3959-9(5))* Enslow Pubs., Inc.

—Forces & Motion Science Fair Projects, Revised & Expanded Using the Scientific Method. LaBaff, Tom & LaBaff, Stephanie, illus. 2010. (Physics Science Projects Using the Scientific Method Ser.). 160p. (J). (gr. 5-18). 35.94 *(978-0-7660-3415-0(1))* Enslow Pubs., Inc.

—The Physics of Sports Science Projects. 2013. (Exploring Hands-On Science Projects Ser.). 128p. (J). (gr. 5-12). pap. 10.95 *(978-1-4644-0222-7(1))*; lib. bdg. 27.94 *(978-0-7660-4146-2(8))* Enslow Pubs., Inc.

—Sizzling Science Projects with Heat & Energy. LaBaff, Tom, illus. 2006. (Fantastic Physical Science Experiments Ser.). 48p. (J). (gr. 3-4). lib. bdg. 25.27 *(978-0-7660-2586-8(1)*, Enslow Elementary) Enslow Pubs., Inc.

Gardner, Robert & Goodstein, Madeline P. Ace Your Forces & Motion Science Project: Great Science Fair Ideas. 2009. (Ace Your Physics Science Project Ser.). (Illus.). 128p. (J). (gr. 5-18). lib. bdg. 33.27 *(978-0-7660-3222-4(1))* Enslow Pubs., Inc.

Goodstein, Madeline P. Goal! Science Projects with Soccer. 2009. (Score! Sports Science Projects Ser.). (Illus.). 104p. (J). (gr. 5-9). lib. bdg. 33.27 *(978-0-7660-3106-7(3))* Enslow Pubs., Inc.

Graham, Ian. Forces & Motion: Investigating a Car Crash, 1 vol. Stayte, James, illus. 2013. (Anatomy of an Investigation Ser.). (ENG.). 56p. (gr. 7-8). pap. 9.95 *(978-1-4329-7608-8(7))* Heinemann-Raintree.

—The Science of a Bicycle: The Science of Forces. 2009. (Science of... Ser.). 32p. (YA). (gr. 3-6). lib. bdg. 26.00 *(978-1-4339-0040-2(8))* Stevens, Gareth Publishing LLLP.

Graham, Stella. Forces & Motion at the Playground. 2009. (Real Life Readers Ser.). 16p. (gr. 2-3). pap. 7.05 *(978-1-4358-0057-1(5)*, Rosen Classroom) Rosen Publishing Group, Inc., The.

Gray, Leon. Forces & Motion. 2013. (Physical Science Ser.). 48p. (J). (gr. 4-6). pap. 84.30 *(978-1-4339-9506-4(9))*; pap. 14.05 *(978-1-4339-9505-7(0))*; (ENG., Illus.). lib. bdg. 31.95 *(978-1-4339-9504-0(2))* Stevens, Gareth Publishing LLLP.

Green, Jen. Saving Energy. 2005. (Improving Our Environment Ser.). (Illus.). 32p. (gr. 3-6). lib. bdg. 26.00 *(978-0-8368-4430-6(0)*, Gareth Stevens Learning Library) Stevens, Gareth Publishing LLLP.

Greenberger, Robert. How Do We Know the Nature of Energy. (Great Scientific Questions & the Scientists Who Answered Them Ser.). 112p. (gr. 7-12). 2009. 63.90 *(978-1-61513-201-0(5))* 2005. (Illus.). (J). lib. bdg. 34.60 *(978-1-4042-0076-0(2))* Rosen Publishing Group, Inc., The.

Gregory, Helen. Pushes & Pulls, 1 vol. (Wonder Readers Next Steps: Science Ser.). (ENG.). (gr. -1-1). 2013. 20p. lib. bdg. 22.65 *(978-1-4765-0039-3(8))* 2011. 16p. pap. 35.94 *(978-1-4296-8139-1(X))* 2011. 32p. pap. 5.99 *(978-1-4296-7813-1(5))* Capstone Press of Coughlan Cos. (Wonder Readers).

Haber-Schaim, Uri, et al. Force, Motion, & Energy Assessment Package. 2003. pap. *(978-1-882057-15-3(5)*, SCI-777-3393) Science Curriculum, Inc.

Hammond, Richard. Can You Feel the Force? 2015. (Big Questions Ser.). (ENG., Illus.). 96p. (J). (gr. 3-7). pap. 9.99 *(978-1-4654-3904-8(8)*, DK Children) Dorling Kindersley Publishing, Inc.

Hawbacker, Emily. Energy Lab for Kids: 40 Exciting Experiments to Explore, Create, Harness, & Unleash Energy. 2017. (Lab Ser.). (ENG., Illus.). 144p. (J). (gr. 5-9). pap. 22.99 *(978-1-63159-250-8(5)*, Quarry Bks.) Quarto Publishing Group USA.

Hawkins, Jay. Push & Pull: The Science of Forces. 2013. (Big Bang Science Experiments Ser.). (ENG., Illus.). 32p. (gr. 3-6). 26.50 *(978-1-4777-0324-3(1))*; pap. 11.75 *(978-1-4777-0368-7(3))* Windmill Bks.

Heitkamp, Kristina Lyn. What Is Mechanical Energy? 2017. (Let's Find Out! Forms of Energy Ser.). 32p. (gr. 6-8). pap. 12.90 ***(978-1-68048-709-1(4)***, Britannica Educational Publishing) Rosen Publishing Group, Inc., The.

Herweck, Don. All about Energy, 1 vol. 2007. (Science Readers Ser.) (SPA & ENG.). 32p. (J). (gr. 4-4). pap. 8.99 *(978-0-7439-0571-8(7))* Shell Educational Publishing.

Hesse, Leah. How Do Dams Work? 2013. (Rosen Readers Ser.). (ENG.). 24p. (J). (gr. 3-4). pap. 8.25 *(978-1-4777-2554-2(7))*; pap. 49.50 *(978-1-4777-2555-9(5))* Rosen Publishing Group, Inc., The. (Rosen Classroom).

Hewitt, Sally. Amazing Forces & Movement. 2007. (Amazing Science Ser.). (ENG.). 32p. (J). pap. *(978-0-7787-3625-7(3))* Crabtree Publishing Co.

—Energy. (Illus.). 32p. (YA). (gr. 1-18). lib. bdg. 27.10 *(978-1-931983-93-8(3))* Chrysalis Education.

—Forces & Motion. (Illus.). 32p. (YA). (gr. 2-18). lib. bdg. 27.10 *(978-1-932333-32-9(0))* Chrysalis Education.

Hicks, Terry Allan. The Pros & Cons of Biofuel. 2014. (Economics of Energy Ser.). 80p. (YA). (gr. 7-10). lib. bdg. 35.64 *(978-1-62712-933-6(2))* Cavendish Square Publishing.

Higgins, Nadia. Marvelous Motion, 1 vol. Ricci, Andres Martinez, illus. 2008. (Science Rocks Ser.). (ENG.). 32p. (gr. -1-4). 28.50 *(978-1-60270-278-3(0)*, 1287326, Looking Glass Library- Nonfiction) Magic Wagon.

—Marvelous Motion CD+Book. Martinez Ricci, Andres, illus. 2010. (Science Rocks! Set 2 CD+Book Ser.). 32p. lib. bdg. 54.14 incl. cd-rom *(978-1-60270-993-5(9))* ABDO Publishing Co.

—Marvelous Motion Site CD+Book. Martinez Ricci, Andres, illus. 2010. (Science Rocks! Set 2 Site CD+Book Ser.). 32p. lib. bdg. 84.14 incl. cd-rom *(978-1-61641-010-0(8))* ABDO Publishing Co.

Hirsch, Rebecca. Science Lab: Motion & Forces. 2011. (Explorer Library: Language Arts Explorer Ser.). (ENG.). 32p. (gr. 4-8). 28.50 *(978-1-61080-205-5(5)*, 201186); pap. 14.21 *(978-1-61080-294-9(2)*, 201216) Cherry Lake Publishing.

Hock, Peggy. Clean Energy. 2008. (ENG.). 24p. (J). pap. 6.95 *(978-0-531-20433-7(2)*, Children's Pr.) Scholastic Library Publishing.

—Helping Out. 2008. (ENG., Illus.). 24p. (J). pap. 6.95 *(978-0-531-20431-3(6)*, Children's Pr.) Scholastic Library Publishing.

—Saving Energy. 2008. (ENG., Illus.). 24p. (J). pap. 6.95 *(978-0-531-20435-1(9)*, Children's Pr.) Scholastic Library Publishing.

Hoffmann, Sara. Going from Here to There. 2012. (First Step Nonfiction - Balance & Motion Ser.). (ENG., Illus.). 8p. (gr. -1-1). pap. 4.95 *(978-1-4677-0516-5(0)*, Lerner Pubns.) Lerner Publishing Group.

Holt, Rinehart and Winston Staff. Holt Science & Technology Chapter 9: Physical Science: Energy & Energy Resources. 5th ed. 2004. (Illus.). pap. 12.86 *(978-0-03-030396-8(6))* Holt McDougal.

Housel, Debra J. Forces, 1 vol. rev. ed. 2014. (Science Readers: Content & Literacy Ser.). (ENG.). 32p. (gr. 2-2). pap. 8.99 *(978-1-4807-4604-6(5))* Teacher Created Materials, Inc.

—Motion, 1 vol. rev. ed. 2014. (Science Readers: Content & Literacy Ser.). (ENG.). 32p. (gr. 2-2). pap. 8.99 *(978-1-4807-4607-7(X))* Teacher Created Materials, Inc.

Hughes, Mónica. Pushing & Pulling. 2005. (Big Cat Ser.). (gr. k-2). pap. 6.50 *(978-0-60457-025-0(3))* Pacific Learning, Inc.

Hyde, Natalie. Changing Direction. 2014. (ENG., Illus.). 24p. (J). *(978-0-7787-0528-4(5))* Crabtree Publishing Co.

—Pushing & Pulling. 2014. (ENG., Illus.). 24p. (J). *(978-0-7787-0529-1(3))* Crabtree Publishing Co.

Issues, Evidence & You - Energy Mega Module Complete Materials Package. 2003. (Illus.). (YA). tchr. ed., stu. ed., per. *(978-1-887725-62-0(8))* Lab-Aids, Inc.

Ives, Rob. Fun Experiments with Forces & Motion: Hovercrafts, Rockets, & More. Sassin, Eva, illus. 2017. (Amazing Science Experiments Ser.). (ENG.). (J). (gr. 3-6). lib. bdg. 26.65 ***(978-1-5124-3217-6(2))*** Lerner Publishing Group.

Jackson, Tom. Power & Energy. 2012. (FAYFT: Invention & Technology Ser.). 64p. (gr. 4-10). lib. bdg. 39.95 *(978-1-936333-39-4(2))* Brown Bear Bks.

Jennings, Terry. Forces. 2009. (Science Alive Ser.). (Illus.). 32p. (J). pap. *(978-1-897563-54-0(X))* Saunders Bk. Co.

Jennings, Terry J. Forces. 2009. (J). 28.50 *(978-1-59920-269-3(7))* Black Rabbit Bks.

Jerome, Kate Boehm. Forces That Move. 2007. (Language, Literacy, & Vocabulary - Reading Expeditions Ser.). (ENG., Illus.). 36p. (J). pap. 18.95 *(978-0-7922-5437-9(6))* CENGAGE Learning.

Johanson, Paula. What Is Energy? 2014. (Let's Find Out! Ser.). 32p. (J). (gr. 3-6). 23.45 *(978-1-62275-492-2(1))* Rosen Publishing Group, Inc., The.

Juettner, Bonnie. Motion. 2004. (KidHaven Science Library). (ENG., Illus.). 48p. (J). (gr. 4-7). 27.50 *(978-0-7377-1536-1(7)*, Greenhaven Pr., Inc.) Cengage Gale.

Karam, P. Andrew & Stein, Ben P. Matter & Energy. 2011. (Science Foundations Ser.). (Illus.). 128p. (gr. 6-12). 35.00 *(978-1-60413-345-5(7)*, Chelsea Hse.) Facts On File, Inc.

Kenney, Karen Latchana. The Science of Race Cars: Studying Forces & Motion, 1 vol. 2016. (Science in Action Ser.). (ENG., Illus.). 32p. (J). (gr. 3-6). 27.07 *(978-1-62403-963-8(4))* ABDO Publishing Co.

—The Science of Roller Coasters: Understanding Energy, 1 vol. 2016. (Science in Action Ser.). (ENG., Illus.). 32p. (J). (gr. 3-6). 27.07 *(978-1-62403-964-5(2))* ABDO Publishing Co.

Kessler, Colleen. A Project Guide to Forces & Motion. 2011. (Physical Science Projects for Kids Ser.). (Illus.). 48p. (J). (gr. 3-6). lib. bdg. 29.95 *(978-1-58415-965-0(0)*, 1327815) Mitchell Lane Pubs., Inc.

Lancaster, Juliana. PBIS- Building Big Things. 2005. pap., stu. ed. 8.00 *(978-1-58591-565-1(3))* It's About Time, Herff Jones Education Div.

Lilly, Melinda. Energy. Thompson, Scott M., photos by. 2005. (Rourke Discovery Library). (Illus.). 24p. (J). (gr. 1-4). lib. bdg. 22.79 *(978-1-59515-401-9(9)*, 1244272) Rourke Educational Media.

Lindeen, Mary. Speed. 2017. (BeginningtoRead Ser.). (ENG.). 32p. (J). (-2). 22.60 ***(978-1-59953-880-8(6))***; pap. 11.94 ***(978-1-68404-099-5(X))*** Norwood Hse. Pr.

Llewellyn, Claire. And Everyone Shouted, Pull! A First Look at Forces & Motion. Abel, Simone, illus. 2004. (First Look: Science Ser.). (ENG.). 32p. (gr. -1-2). 26.65 *(978-1-4048-0656-6(3))* Picture Window Bks.

—Forces & Movement. 2010. (Start-Up Connections Ser.). (ENG., Illus.). 24p. (J). (gr. 2-4). pap. 14.99 *(978-0-237-54172-9(6))* Evans Brothers, Ltd. GBR. Dist: Independent Pubs. Group.

Macken, JoAnn Early. Toys. 2010. (Everyday Science Ser.). 24p. (J). (gr. k-3). 25.65 *(978-1-60753-017-6(1))* Amicus Publishing.

Madgwick, Wendy. First Science Library: On the Move. 2014. (ENG., Illus.). 32p. (J). (gr. k-2). 8.99 *(978-1-86147-356-1(7)*, Armadillo) Anness Publishing GBR. Dist: National Bk. Network.

Maloof, Torrey. Transferring Energy. 2015. (Science Readers: Content & Literacy Ser.). (ENG., Illus.). 32p. (gr. 4-4). pap. 8.99 *(978-1-4807-4683-1(5))* Teacher Created Materials, Inc.

Manolis, Kay. Energy. 2007. (First Science Ser.). (ENG., Illus.). 24p. (J). (gr. 2-5). lib. bdg. 25.95 *(978-1-60014-096-9(3))* Bellwether Media.

—Energy. (Blastoff! Readers Ser.). 24p. (J). 2011. (Illus.). (gr. 2). pap. 5.95 *(978-0-531-28453-7(0))* 2007. (ENG.). (gr. k-2). 20.00 *(978-0-531-14724-5(X))* Scholastic Library Publishing. (Children's Pr.).

—Motion. 2011. (Blastoff! Readers Ser.). 24p. (J). pap. 5.95 *(978-0-531-28458-2(1)*, Children's Pr.) Scholastic Library Publishing.

Margulies, Philip. The Department of Energy. 2006. (This Is Your Government Ser.). (ENG., Illus.). 64p. (gr. 4-8). per. 12.95 *(978-1-4042-0661-8(2))* Rosen Publishing Group, Inc., The.

Marsico, Katie. Key Discoveries in Physical Science. 2015. (Science Discovery Timelines Ser.). (ENG., Illus.). 48p. (J). (gr. 6-8). pap. 8.99 *(978-1-4677-6160-4(5))*; lib. bdg. 30.65 *(978-1-4677-5785-0(3))* Lerner Publishing Group. (Lerner Pubns.).

Mason, Adrienne. Move It! Motion, Forces & You. Dávila, Claudia, illus. 2005. (Primary Physical Science Ser.). (ENG.). 32p. (J). (gr. -1-2). pap. 7.95 *(978-1-55337-759-7(1))* Kids Can Pr., Ltd. CAN. Dist: Hachette Bk. Group.

Masters, Nancy Robinson. How Did That Get to My House? Natural Gas. 2009. (Community Connections: How Did That Get to My House? Ser.). (ENG.). 24p. (gr. 2-5). lib. bdg. 25.64 *(978-1-60279-479-5(0)*, 200248) Cherry Lake Publishing.

Matter & Energy Lesson Plans & Blackline Masters (National Version) 2009. (Journeys Ser.). 20.00 *(978-1-4042-9489-9(9)*, Rosen Classroom) Rosen Publishing Group, Inc., The.

Matter & Energy Word-picture match cards, Memory game cards, Labeled picture Cards. 2008. (Journeys Ser.). 46.60 *(978-1-4042-9490-5(2)*, Rosen Classroom) Rosen Publishing Group, Inc., The.

McLeish, Ewan. Challenges to Our Energy Supply. 2009. (Can the Earth Survive? Ser.). 48p. (ENG.). (YA). pap. 11.75 *(978-1-4358-5490-1(X)*, Rosen Reference); (Illus.). (J). (gr. 5-9). lib. bdg. 29.25 *(978-1-4358-5357-7(1))* Rosen Publishing Group, Inc., The.

McNeil, Niki, et al. HOCPP 1091 Forces. 2006. spiral bd. 19.50 *(978-1-60308-091-0(0))* In the Hands of a Child.

McNeilly, Linden. What's Your Potential? The Energy of Motion. 2016. (Let's Explore Science Ser.). (ENG., Illus.). 48p. (gr. 5-8). 35.64 *(978-1-68191-394-0(1))* Rourke Educational Media.

Monroe, Tilda. What Do You Know about Forces & Motion? 2010. (20 Questions: Physical Science Ser.). (ENG.). 24p. (J). pap. 8.25 *(978-1-4488-1254-7(2)*, PowerKids Pr.); (gr. 2-5). lib. bdg. 22.60 *(978-1-4488-0673-7(9))* Rosen Publishing Group, Inc., The.

Moore, David. Expl on Your Own on the Farm. 2009. (Explore on Your Own Ser.). (ENG.). 12p. (C). pap. 7.95 *(978-0-7362-5551-6(6))* National Geographic School Publishing, Inc.

Morgan, Elizabeth. What Is Energy? 2013. (Rosen Readers Ser.). (ENG.). 24p. (J). (gr. 3-4). pap. 8.25 *(978-1-4777-2597-9(0))*; pap. 49.50 *(978-1-4777-2598-6(9))* Rosen Publishing Group, Inc., The. (Rosen Classroom).

Morris, Neil. Biomass Power. 2006. (Energy Sources Ser.). (Illus.). 32p. (YA). (gr. 4-7). lib. bdg. 28.50 *(978-1-58340-816-2(9))* Black Rabbit Bks.

—Biomass Power: Now & in the Future. 2010. (J). 34.25 *(978-1-59920-337-9(5))* Black Rabbit Bks.

Motion & Force: Integrated Physics & Chemistry / Algebra I Instructional Unit. 2003. (Region IV ESC Resources for Mathematics & Science Ser.). stu. ed., per. *(978-1-932524-69-7(X))* Region IV Education Service Ctr.

Motion & Forces. 2011. (Science Made Simple Ser.). (ENG.). 64p. (YA). pap. 12.95 *(978-1-4488-2240-9(8))* Rosen Publishing Group, Inc., The.

Muldoon, Kathleen M. Forces & Motion in the Real World. 2013. (Science in the Real World EBook Ser.). (ENG.). 48p. (J). pap. 15.64 *(978-1-61783-790-6(3)*, Core Library); (gr. 3-6). lib. bdg. 32.79 *(978-1-61783-740-1(7))* ABDO Publishing Co.

Mullins, Matt. Energy. 2011. (True Book(tm), a — Physical Science Ser.). (ENG., Illus.). 48p. (J). (gr. 3-5). 31.00 *(978-0-531-26320-4(7))*; pap. 6.95 *(978-0-531-26582-6(X))* Scholastic Library Publishing. (Children's Pr.).

Murphy, Brian. Movement. 2004. (Experiment with Ser.). (SPA., Illus.). 32p. (J). (gr. 2-5). 9.95 *(978-1-58728-248-5(8)*, Two-Can Publishing) T&N Children's Publishing.

Murphy, John, ed. Physics: Understanding the Properties of Matter & Energy. 2014. (Study of Science Ser.). (Illus.). 160p. (J). (gr. 7-12). 35.25 *(978-1-62275-418-2(2))* Rosen Publishing Group, Inc., The.

Murray, Julie. Hot & Cold, 1 vol. 2006. (First Science Ser.). (ENG., Illus.). 24p. (J). (gr. k-4). 25.65 *(978-1-59679-825-0(4)*, Buddy Bks.) ABDO Publishing Co.

Natural Resources Defense Council Staff, et al. Simple Steps Toward a Healthier Earth. Carpenter, Tad, illus. 2010. (ENG.). 80p. (J). (gr. 3-17). pap., act. bk. ed. 12.99 *(978-0-8118-7141-9(X))* Chronicle Bks. LLC.

Nelson, Robin. Cómo Se Mueven Las Cosas. Translations.com Staff, tr. from ENG. 2007. (Mi Primer Paso Al Mundo Real - Fuerzas y Movimiento (First Step Nonfiction - Forces & Motion) Ser.). (SPA., Illus.). 24p. (gr. k-2). lib. bdg. 23.93 *(978-0-8225-7811-6(5)*, Ediciones Lerner) Lerner Publishing Group.

—Como Se Mueven Las Cosas; Way Things Move. 2008. pap. 34.95 *(978-0-8225-9894-7(9))* Lerner Publishing Group.

—Empujar y Jalar. Translations.com Staff, tr. from ENG. 2007. (Mi Primer Paso Al Mundo Real - Fuerzas y Movimiento (First Step Nonfiction - Forces & Motion) Ser.). (SPA., Illus.). 24p. (gr. k-2). lib. bdg. 23.93 *(978-0-8225-7810-9(7)*, Ediciones Lerner) Lerner Publishing Group.

—Empujar Y Jalar; Push & Pull. 2008. pap. 34.95 *(978-0-8225-9895-4(7))* Lerner Publishing Group.

—Fuerzas Y Movimiento; Forces & Motion: Classroom Set. 2008. pap. 28.95 *(978-1-58013-615-0(X))* Lerner Publishing Group.

—Fuerzas Y Movimiento (Forces & Motion) Complete Set. 2008. pap. 173.95 *(978-1-58013-616-7(8))* Lerner Publishing Group.

—Push & Pull. 2004. (First Step Nonfiction - Forces & Motion Ser.). (ENG., Illus.). 24p. (gr. k-2). lib. bdg. 23.93 *(978-0-8225-5134-8(9))* Lerner Publishing Group.

—Ways Things Move. (Forces & Motion Ser.). (Illus.). (J). 2005. 22p. pap. 5.95 *(978-0-8225-5300-7(7))* 2004. 24p. lib. bdg. 18.60 *(978-0-8225-5136-2(5))* Lerner Publishing Group.

Newell, Ella. Energy. 2013. (Physical Science Ser.). 48p. (J). (gr. 4-6). pap. 14.05 *(978-1-4339-9509-5(3))*; pap. 84.30 *(978-1-4339-9510-1(7))*; (ENG., Illus.). lib. bdg. 31.95 *(978-1-4339-9508-8(5))* Stevens, Gareth Publishing LLLP.

Newman, Patricia. Biofuels. 2013. (Explorer Library: Language Arts Explorer Ser.). (ENG.). 32p. (gr. 4-8). 28.50 *(978-1-61080-893-4(2)*, 202551); pap. 14.21 *(978-1-61080-918-4(1)*, 202553) Cherry Lake Publishing.

Newton, Joan. Gravity in Action: Roller Coasters! 2009. (Real Life Readers Ser.). 24p. (gr. 3-4). pap. 8.25 *(978-1-4358-0008-3(7)*, Rosen Classroom); (J). (gr. 2-5). lib. bdg. 22.60 *(978-1-4358-2976-3(X)*, PowerKids Pr.) Rosen Publishing Group, Inc., The.

Orme, Helen. Energy for the Future. 2008. (Earth in Danger Ser.). (Illus.). 32p. (YA). (gr. 3-6). lib. bdg. 25.27 *(978-1-59716-727-7(4)*, 1284324) Bearport Publishing Co., Inc.

Orr, Tamra. Motion & Forces. 2011. (Science Made Simple Ser.). (Illus.). 64p. (YA). (gr. 5-8). lib. bdg. 31.95 *(978-1-4488-1232-5(1))* Rosen Publishing Group, Inc., The.

Oxlade, Chris. Energy Technology. 2010. (New Technology Ser.). (ENG., Illus.). 48p. (J). 23.99 *(978-0-237-53430-1(4))* Evans Brothers, Ltd. GBR. Dist: Independent Pubs. Group.

—Forces & Motion: An Investigation. 2008. (Science Investigations Ser.). (Illus.). 32p. (YA). (gr. 4-7). lib. bdg. 26.50 *(978-1-4042-4283-8(X))* Rosen Publishing Group, Inc., The.

—Simple Experiments with Levers. 2013. (Science Experiments with Simple Machines Ser.). 32p. (J). (gr. k-3). 26.50 *(978-1-61533-756-9(3))*; pap. 11.75 *(978-1-61533-829-0(2))*; pap. 70.50 *(978-1-61533-830-6(6))* Windmill Bks.

—Simple Experiments with Pulleys. 2013. (Science Experiments with Simple Machines Ser.). 32p. (J). (gr. k-3). 26.50 *(978-1-61533-751-4(2))*; pap. 11.75 *(978-1-61533-819-1(5))*; pap. 70.50 *(978-1-61533-820-7(9))* Windmill Bks.

—Simple Experiments with Wedges. 2013. (Science Experiments with Simple Machines Ser.). 32p. (J). (gr. k-3). 26.50 *(978-1-61533-755-2(5))*; pap. 11.75 *(978-1-61533-827-6(6))*; pap. 70.50 *(978-1-61533-828-3(4))* Windmill Bks.

Oxlade, Chris & Jennings, Terry. Energy. 2009. (Science Alive Ser.). (Illus.). 32p. (J). pap. *(978-1-897563-53-3(1))* Saunders Bk. Co.

Oxlade, Chris & Jennings, Terry J. Energy. 2009. (J). 28.50 *(978-1-59920-273-0(5))* Black Rabbit Bks.

Pamplona, Alberto Hernández. A Visual Guide to Energy & Movement. 2017. (Visual Exploration of Science Ser.). 96p. (J). (gr. 12-13). 37.10 ***(978-1-5081-7582-7(9)***, Rosen Young Adult) Rosen Publishing Group, Inc., The.

Paris, Stephanie. Drag! Friction & Resistance, 1 vol. 2nd rev. ed. 2013. (Nonfiction Readers Ser.). (ENG.). 64p. (J). (gr. 5-5). pap. 10.99 *(978-1-4333-4940-9(X))* Teacher Created Materials, Inc.

—¡Fsst! Fricción y Resistencia. 2016. (TIME for Kids en Español - Level 5 Ser.). (SPA.). 64p. (gr. 5-5). lib. bdg. 31.99 *(978-1-5157-2930-3(3))* Time for Kids Inc AUS. Dist: Capstone Pub.

—Pop! Air & Water Pressure, 1 vol. 2nd rev. ed. 2013. (Nonfiction Readers Ser.). (ENG.). 64p. (J). (gr. 5-5). pap. 10.99 *(978-1-4333-4939-3(6))* Teacher Created Materials, Inc.

—¡Pop! Presión Del Aire y Del Agua. 2016. (TIME for Kids en Español - Level 5 Ser.). (SPA.). 64p. (gr. 5-5). lib. bdg. 31.99 *(978-1-5157-2931-0(1))* Time for Kids Inc AUS. Dist: Capstone Pub.

—Vroom! Speed & Acceleration, 1 vol. 2nd rev. ed. 2013. (Nonfiction Readers Ser.). (ENG.). 64p. (J). (gr. 5-5). pap. 10.99 *(978-1-4333-4938-6(8))* Teacher Created Materials, Inc.

Parker, Russ. Energy Supplies in Crisis. 2009. (Planet in Crisis Ser.). 32p. (YA). (gr. 5-8). lib. bdg. 25.25 *(978-1-4358-5251-8(6)*, Rosen Reference) Rosen Publishing Group, Inc., The.

Petersen, Kristen. Understanding Kinetic Energy. 2015. (J). lib. bdg. *(978-1-62713-435-4(2))*; (ENG.). 48p. (gr. 7-7). 31.36 *(978-1-5026-0144-5(3))* Cavendish Square Publishing.

Peterson, Megan Cooley. Scooby-Doo! a Science of Energy Mystery: The High-Voltage Ghost. 2016. (Scooby-Doo Solves It with S. T. E. M. Ser.). (ENG., Illus.). 32p. (gr. 3-4). 27.99 *(978-1-5157-2591-6(X))* Capstone Press of Coughlan Cos.

—Scooby-Doo! a Science of Forces & Motion Mystery: The Rogue Robot. 2016. (Scooby-Doo Solves It with S. T. E. M. Ser.). (ENG., Illus.). 32p. (gr. 3-4). 27.99 *(978-1-5157-2590-9(1))* Capstone Press of Coughlan Cos.

Phelan, Glen. Forces & Motion in Sports: Set Of 6. 2011. (Navigators Ser.). (J). pap. 50.00 net. *(978-1-4108-5088-1(9))* Benchmark Education Co.

—Forces & Motion on Earth: Set Of 6. 2011. (Navigators Ser.). (J). pap. 50.00 net. *(978-1-4108-5087-4(0))* Benchmark Education Co.

—Introduction to Energy. 2007. (Nonfiction Reading & Writing Workshops Ser.). (ENG., Illus.). 32p. (J). pap. 17.95 *(978-0-7922-4580-3(6))* CENGAGE Learning.

—Newton's Laws. 2007. (Reading Expeditions Ser.). (ENG., Illus.). 32p. (J). pap. 17.95 *(978-0-7922-4584-1(9))* CENGAGE Learning.

Plummer, Todd. I've Discovered Energy! 2008. (Eureka! Ser.). 32p. (gr. 4-18). lib. bdg. 28.50 *(978-0-7614-3202-9(7),* Benchmark Bks.) Marshall Cavendish Corp.
—I've Discovered Force! 2008. (Eureka! Ser.). 32p. (gr. 4-18). lib. bdg. 28.50 *(978-0-7614-3204-3(3),* Benchmark Bks.) Marshall Cavendish Corp.
Polinsky, Paige V. Super Simple Experiments with Forces: Fun & Innovative Science Projects. 2016. (ENG., Illus.). 32p. (J). *(978-1-68078-169-4(3))* ABDO Publishing Co.
Rand, Casey. Forces & Motion. 2016. (Sci-Hi: Physical Science Ser.). (ENG.). 48p. (gr. 4-4). pap. 8.99 *(978-1-4109-8633-7(0),* Sci-Hi) Heinemann-Raintree.
Richards, Julie. Biofuels. 2009. (J). 19.95 *(978-0-7614-4432-9(7))* Marshall Cavendish GBR. Dist: Marshall Cavendish Corp.
Riley, Peter. Forces & Magnets. 2016. (Moving up with Science Ser.). 00032p. (J). (gr. 3-4). pap. 10.00 *(978-1-4994-3141-4(4),* PowerKids Pr.) Rosen Publishing Group, Inc., The.
Rowell, Rebecca. Forces & Motion Through Infographics. Dean, Venitia, illus. 2013. (Super Science Infographics Ser.). (ENG.). 32p. (gr. 3-5). (J). lib. bdg. 26.60 *(978-1-4677-1291-0(4),* Lerner Pubns.); pap. 8.95 *(978-1-4677-1591-1(3))* Lerner Publishing Group.
Royston, Angela. All about Forces. 2016. (All about Science Ser.). (ENG., Illus.). 32p. (gr. 1-3). lib. bdg. 27.32 *(978-1-4846-2689-4(3),* Heinemann First Library) Heinemann-Raintree.
—Forces: Pushes & Pulls. 2012. (Science Corner Ser.). (Illus.). 24p. (J). (gr. 1-4). lib. bdg. 22.60 *(978-1-4488-5292-5(7))* Rosen Publishing Group, Inc., The.
—Forces & Motion, 1 vol. 2013. (Essential Physical Science Ser.). (ENG.). 48p. (gr. 4-6). 33.32 *(978-1-4329-8145-7(5),* Heinemann InfoSearch) Heinemann-Raintree.
—Looking at Forces & Motion: How Do Things Move? 2008. (Looking at Science: How Things Change Ser.). (Illus.). 32p. (J). (gr. 3-7). lib. bdg. 23.94 *(978-0-7660-3089-3(X),* Enslow Elementary) Enslow Pubs., Inc.
—Race That Bike! Forces in Vehicles. 2015. (Feel the Force Ser.). (ENG., Illus.). 48p. (gr. 3-6). 33.32 *(978-1-4846-2599-6(4))* Heinemann-Raintree.
—Win That Sprint! Forces in Sport. 2015. (Feel the Force Ser.). (ENG., Illus.). 48p. (gr. 3-6). 33.32 *(978-1-4846-2597-2(8))* Heinemann-Raintree.
Roza, Greg. Reducing Your Carbon Footprint on Vacation. 2009. (Your Carbon Footprint Ser.). 48p. (gr. 5-5). 53.00 *(978-1-60854-913-9(5),* Rosen Reference) Rosen Publishing Group, Inc., The.
Ruschmann, Paul. Energy Policy. 2009. (Point/Counterpoint Ser.). 144p. (C). (gr. 9-18). 35.00 *(978-1-60413-333-2(3),* Chelsea Hse.) Facts On File, Inc.
The Science of Energy. 2016. (Illus.). 48p. (J). *(978-1-4222-3513-3(0))* Mason Crest.
Silverman, Buffy. Energy All Around. 2012. (ENG.). 24p. (gr. 3-4). pap. 8.95 *(978-1-61810-228-7(1))* Rourke Educational Media.
—Pull It, Push It. 2012. (ENG.). 24p. (gr. 3-4). pap. 8.95 *(978-1-61810-229-4(X))* Rourke Educational Media.
—Stop & Go, Fast & Slow. 2011. (ENG., Illus.). 24p. (gr. k-1). pap. 8.95 *(978-1-61741-929-4(X))* Rourke Educational Media.
Silverstein, Alvin, et al. Forces & Motion. 2008. (Science Concepts, Second Ser.). (ENG., Illus.). 112p. (gr. 6-8). lib. bdg. 31.93 *(978-0-8225-7514-6(0))* Lerner Publishing Group.
Slade, Suzanne. Zap! Wile E. Coyote Experiments with Energy, 1 vol. Ricci, Andrés Martinez, illus. 2014. (Wile E. Coyote, Physical Science Genius Ser.). (ENG.). 32p. (gr. 3-4). 30.65 *(978-1-4765-4223-2(6));* pap. 8.95 *(978-1-4765-5214-9(2))* Capstone Press of Coughlan Cos.
Smith, A. Energy, Forces & Motion. 2004. (Internet-Linked Library of Science). 64p. (J). pap. 9.95 *(978-0-7945-0084-9(6),* Usborne); lib. bdg. 17.95 *(978-1-58086-374-2(4))* EDC Publishing.
Sohn, Emily. Experiments in Forces & Motion with Toys & Everyday Stuff. 2015. (Fun Science Ser.). (ENG., Illus.). 24p. (gr. 1-2). lib. bdg. 25.32 *(978-1-4914-5032-1(0))* Capstone Press of Coughlan Cos.
Sohn, Emily & Fellows, Fred. Levers & Pulleys: Lift Anything! 2011. (IScience Readers Ser.). 48p. (J). (gr. 5-6). lib. bdg. 23.94 *(978-1-59953-426-8(6))* Norwood Hse. Pr.
Sohn, Emily & Tsang, Nina. Matter & Energy: Finding the Power. 2011. (IScience Readers Ser.). 32p. (J). (gr. 3-4). lib. bdg. 22.60 *(978-1-59953-416-9(9))* Norwood Hse. Pr.
Solway, Andrew. Energy & Matter. 2010. (CC: 21st Century Science Ser.). 112p. (gr. 6-12). 42.80 *(978-1-933834-72-6(2))* Brown Bear Bks.
—Exploring Forces & Motion. 2007. (Exploring Physical Science Ser.). (Illus.). 48p. (YA). (gr. 5-9). lib. bdg. 26.50 *(978-1-4042-3747-6(X))* Rosen Publishing Group, Inc., The.
Spilsbury, Louise & Spilsbury, Richard. Fly to Mars! Forces in Space. 2015. (Feel the Force Ser.). (ENG., Illus.). 48p. (gr. 3-6). 33.32 *(978-1-4846-2600-9(1))* Heinemann-Raintree.
Spilsbury, Louise, et al. Feel the Force. 2015. (Feel the Force Ser.). (ENG.). 48p. (gr. 3-6). 133.28 *(978-1-4846-2601-6(X),* Heinemann InfoSearch) Heinemann-Raintree.
Spilsbury, Richard & Spilsbury, Louise. Biomass Power. 2012. (Let's Discuss Energy Resources Ser.). (Illus.). 32p. (YA). (gr. 4-7). lib. bdg. 26.50 *(978-1-4488-5260-4(9))* Rosen Publishing Group, Inc., The.
—Ride That Rollercoaster! Forces at an Amusement Park. 2015. (Feel the Force Ser.). (ENG., Illus.). 48p. (gr. 3-6). 33.32 *(978-1-4846-2598-9(6))* Heinemann-Raintree.
—What Are Forces & Motion? Exploring Science with Hands-on Activities. 2008. (In Touch with Basic Science Ser.). (Illus.). 32p. (J). (gr. 3-4). lib. bdg. 23.94 *(978-0-7660-3095-4(4),* Enslow Elementary) Enslow Pubs., Inc.
—What Is Energy? Exploring Science with Hands-on Activities. 2008. (In Touch with Basic Science Ser.). (Illus.). 32p. (J). (gr. 3-4). lib. bdg. 23.94 *(978-0-7660-3099-2(7),* Enslow Elementary) Enslow Pubs., Inc.
Spiro, Ruth & Chan, Irene. Baby Loves Thermodynamics! 2017. (ENG., Illus.). 20p. (J). (— 1). bds. 8.99 ***(978-1-58089-768-6(1))*** Charlesbridge Publishing, Inc.
Stille, Darlene R. Energy: Heat, Light, & Fuel. Boyd, Sheree, illus. 2004. (Amazing Science Ser.). (ENG.). 24p. (gr. k-4). 26.65 *(978-1-4048-0249-0(5))* Picture Window Bks.
—Motion: Push & Pull, Fast & Slow. Boyd, Sheree, tr. Boyd, Sheree, illus. 2004. (Amazing Science Ser.). (ENG.). 24p. (gr. k-4). 26.65 *(978-1-4048-0250-6(9))* Picture Window Bks.
—El Movimiento: Tira y Empuja, Rápido y Despacio. Robledo, Sol, tr. from ENG. Boyd, Sheree, illus. 2007. (Ciencia Asombrosa Ser.). (SPA.). 24p. (gr. k-4). lib. bdg. 26.65 *(978-1-4048-3222-0(X))* Picture Window Bks.
Stille, Darlene R. & Picture Window Books Staff. La Energia: Calor, Luz y Combustible. Robledo, Sol, tr. from ENG. Boyd, Sheree, illus. 2007. (Ciencia Asombrosa Ser.). (SPA.). 24p. (gr. k-4). 26.65 *(978-1-4048-3213-8(0))* Picture Window Bks.
Stoyles, Pennie & Pentland, Peter. Earth & Space. 2011. (Energy in Action Ser.). (Illus.). 32p. (J). (gr. 4). 28.50 *(978-1-60870-566-5(8))* Marshall Cavendish Corp.
—Everyday Technology. 2011. (Energy in Action Ser.). 32p. (gr. 4). 28.50 *(978-1-60870-567-2(6))* Marshall Cavendish Corp.
Sundance/Newbridge LLC Staff. Energy. 2007. (Early Science Ser.). (gr. k-3). 18.95 *(978-1-4007-6549-2(8));* pap. 6.10 *(978-1-4007-6545-4(5))* Sundance/Newbridge Educational Publishing.
—Push & Pull. 2007. (Early Science Ser.). (gr. k-3). 18.95 *(978-1-4007-6134-0(4));* pap. 6.10 *(978-1-4007-6130-2(1))* Sundance/Newbridge Educational Publishing.
Swanson, Jennifer. The Attractive Truth about Magnetism. Lum, Bernice, illus. 2012. (LOL Physical Science Ser.). (ENG.). 32p. (gr. 3-4). pap. 47.70 *(978-1-4296-9297-7(9),* Fact Finders) Capstone Press of Coughlan Cos.
—Explore Force & Motion! With 25 Great Projects. Stone, Bryan, illus. 2016. (Explore Your World Ser.). (ENG.). 96p. (gr. 1-5). 19.95 *(978-1-61930-351-5(5))* Open City Bks.
Thomas, Elizabeth. Conserving Energy. 2011. (Go Green! Ser.). (ENG., Illus.). 32p. (J). (gr. 1-4). lib. bdg. 28.50 *(978-1-60973-172-4(7),* 201151) Child's World, Inc., The.
Thomas, Isabel. Experiments with Forces. 2015. (Read & Experiment Ser.). (ENG., Illus.). 32p. (gr. 2-4). 30.65 *(978-1-4109-7921-6(0))* Heinemann-Raintree.
Troupe, Thomas Kingsley. Are Bowling Balls Bullies? Learning about Forces & Motion with the Garbage Gang. Toye, Derek, illus. 2015. (Garbage Gang's Super Science Questions Ser.). (ENG.). 24p. (gr. k-2). lib. bdg. 26.65 *(978-1-4795-7057-7(5))* Picture Window Bks.
Uttley, Colin. Experiments with Force & Motion. 2010. (Cool Science Ser.). (Illus.). 32p. (J). (gr. 5-6). pap. 10.50 *(978-1-4339-3460-5(4));* lib. bdg. 28.00 *(978-1-4339-3459-9(0),* 1309302) Stevens, Gareth Publishing LLLP. (Gareth Stevens Learning Library).
VanCleave, Janice. Janice VanCleave's Energy for Every Kid: Easy Activities That Make Learning Science Fun. 2005. (Science for Every Kid Ser.: 15). (ENG., Illus.). 236p. (gr. 3-7). pap. 14.95 *(978-0-471-33099-8(X),* Wiley) Wiley, John & Sons, Inc.
—Step-by-Step Science Experiments in Energy. 2012. (Janice VanCleave's First-Place Science Fair Projects Ser.). (ENG., Illus.). 80p. (J). (gr. 5-8). 33.25 *(978-1-4488-6979-4(X));* pap. 14.15 *(978-1-4488-8471-1(3))* Rosen Publishing Group, Inc., The. (Rosen Reference).
VanVoorst, Jenny Fretland. Boomerangs. 2016. (Early Physics Fun). 24p. (J). (gr. 2-5). lib. bdg. 25.65 *(978-1-62031-315-2(4),* Pogo) Jump! Inc.
—Hula Hoops. 2016. (Early Physics Fun). 24p. (J). (gr. 2-5). lib. bdg. 25.65 *(978-1-62031-316-9(2),* Pogo) Jump! Inc.
—Slides. 2016. 24p. (J). (gr. 2-5). lib. bdg. 25.65 *(978-1-62031-318-3(9),* Pogo) Jump! Inc.
—Trampolines. 2016. (Early Physics Fun). 24p. (J). (gr. 2-5). lib. bdg. 25.65 *(978-1-62031-319-0(7),* Pogo) Jump! Inc.
Viegas, Jennifer. Kinetic & Potential Energy: Understanding Changes Within Physical Systems. (Library of Physics Ser.). 48p. (gr. 7-7). 2009. 53.00 *(978-1-60853-802-7(8))* 2004. (Illus.). (J). lib. bdg. 29.25 *(978-1-4042-0333-4(8))* Rosen Publishing Group, Inc., The.
Vogel, Julia. Discover Energy. Yamada, Jane, illus. 2014. (Science Around Us Ser.). (ENG.). 24p. (J). (gr. -1-2). 25.64 *(978-1-62687-303-2(8),* 207144) Child's World, Inc., The.
Wadsworth, Pamela. Defnyddio Egni. 2005. (WEL., Illus.). 24p. pap. *(978-1-85596-243-9(8))* Dref Wen.
—Golwg Gyntaf Ar Egni. 2005. (WEL., Illus.). 24p. pap. *(978-1-85596-257-6(8))* Dref Wen.
—Grymoedd a Symud. 2005. (WEL., Illus.). 24p. pap. *(978-1-85596-227-9(6))* Dref Wen.
—Rhagor Am Ddefnyddio Egni. 2005. (WEL., Illus.). 24p. pap. *(978-1-85596-244-6(6))* Dref Wen.
—Rhagor Am Rymoedd a Symud. 2005. (WEL., Illus.). 24p. pap. *(978-1-85596-228-6(4))* Dref Wen.
Walker, Niki. Biomass: Fueling Change. 2006. (Energy Revolution Ser.). (ENG., Illus.). 32p. (J). (gr. 4-7). lib. bdg. *(978-0-7787-2914-3(1),* 1259460) Crabtree Publishing Co.
Walker, Sally M. Libros de Energia para Madrugadores; Early Bird Energy: Classroom Set. 2008. pap. 52.95 *(978-0-8225-9052-1(2))* Lerner Publishing Group.
Walker, Sally M. & Feldmann, Roseann. Put Pulleys to the Test. 2011. (Searchlight Books (tm) — How Do Simple Machines Work? Ser.). (ENG., Illus.). 40p. (gr. 3-5). lib. bdg. 27.93 *(978-0-7613-5322-5(4))* Lerner Publishing Group.
Watt's UP? The Energy Around Us. 2007. (Illus.). 30p. (J). pap. 6.00 *(978-0-9815308-3-3(4))* Amazement Square.
Weakland, Mark. Do-4U the Robot Experiences Forces & Motion. Moran, Mike, illus. 2012. (In the Science Lab Ser.). (ENG.). 24p. (gr. 2-3). pap. 9.95 *(978-1-4048-7239-4(6))* Picture Window Bks.
—Do-4U the Robot Experiences Forces & Motion. Moran, Michael & Moran, Mike, illus. 2012. (In the Science Lab Ser.). (ENG.). 24p. (gr. 2-3). lib. bdg. 26.65 *(978-1-4048-7145-8(4))* Picture Window Bks.
—Thud! Wile E. Coyote Experiments with Forces & Motion, 1 vol. Cornia, Christian, illus. 2014. (Wile E. Coyote, Physical Science Genius Ser.). (ENG.). 32p. (gr. 3-4). 30.65 *(978-1-4765-4221-8(X))* Capstone Press of Coughlan Cos.
—Whoosh! Wile E. Coyote Experiments with Flight & Gravity. Brown, Alan, illus. 2017. (Wile E. Coyote, Physical Science Genius Ser.). (ENG.). 32p. (gr. 3-5). lib. bdg. 30.65 *(978-1-5157-3732-2(2))* Capstone Press of Coughlan Cos.
—Zombies & Forces & Motion, 1 vol. Gervasio, illus. 2011. (Monster Science Ser.). (ENG.). 32p. (gr. 3-4). lib. bdg. 30.65 *(978-1-4296-6577-3(7),* Graphic Library) Capstone Press of Coughlan Cos.
Weir, Jane. Investigating Forces & Motion, 1 vol. 2007. (Science Readers Ser.). (ENG.). 32p. (J). (gr. 4-4). pap. 8.99 *(978-0-7439-0573-2(3))* Shell Educational Publishing.
West, Herbert. Forms of Energy. 2009. (Real Life Readers Ser.). 24p. (gr. 3-4). pap. 8.25 *(978-1-4358-0123-3(7),* Rosen Classroom); (Illus.). (J). (gr. 2-5). lib. bdg. 22.60 *(978-1-4358-2975-6(1),* PowerKids Pr.) Rosen Publishing Group, Inc., The.
Wheeler, Jill C. Eye on Energy, 1 vol., Set. Incl. Alternative Cars. 27.07 *(978-1-59928-803-1(6));* Everyday Conservation. 27.07 *(978-1-59928-804-8(4));* Fossil Fuels. 27.07 *(978-1-59928-805-5(2));* Nature Power. 27.07 *(978-1-59928-806-2(0));* Nuclear Power. 27.07 *(978-1-59928-807-9(9));* Renewable Fuels. 27.07 *(978-1-59928-808-6(7));* (Illus.). (gr. k-6). (Eye on Energy Ser.: 6). (ENG.). 32p. 2008. 162.42 *(978-1-59928-802-4(8),* Checkerboard Library) ABDO Publishing Co.
Wheeler-Toppen, Jodi. Science Experiments That Explode & Implode: Fun Projects for Curious Kids, 1 vol. 2010. (Kitchen Science Ser.). (ENG.). 32p. (gr. 3-4). lib. bdg. 27.99 *(978-1-4296-5427-2(9),* Edge Bks.) Capstone Press of Coughlan Cos.
Whitehouse, Patty. Energia Por Dondequiera / Energy Everywhere. 2006. (Construction Forces Discovery Library). (Illus.). 24p. (J). (gr. k-2). lib. bdg. 22.79 *(978-1-60044-274-2(9))* Rourke Educational Media.
—Pushes & Pulls. 2006. (Construction Forces Discovery Library). (Illus.). 24p. (J). (gr. k-2). lib. bdg. 22.79 *(978-1-60044-193-6(9))* Rourke Educational Media.
Whiting, Jim. Energy. 2012. (Mysteries of the Universe Ser.). (Illus.). 48p. (J). (gr. 5-12). 23.95 *(978-1-60818-187-2(1),* Creative Education) Creative Co., The.
—Mysteries of the Universe: Energy. 2013. (Mysteries of the Universe Ser.). (ENG., Illus.). 48p. (J). (gr. 4-7). pap. 12.00 *(978-0-89812-912-0(5),* Creative Paperbacks) Creative Co., The.
—The Science of Hitting a Home Run: Forces & Motion in Action. 2010. (Action Science Ser.). (ENG.). 32p. (gr. 3-4). pap. 47.70 *(978-1-4296-5076-2(1),* Fact Finders) Capstone Press of Coughlan Cos.
Wilson, Anthony. Science Museum Book of Amazing Facts: Energy. (Illus.). 119p. pap. *(978-0-340-71477-5(8))* Hodder & Stoughton.
Winterberg, Jenna. Balanced & Unbalanced Forces, 1 vol. 2015. (Science Readers: Content & Literacy Ser.). (ENG., Illus.). 32p. (gr. 3-3). pap. 8.99 *(978-1-4807-4646-6(0))* Teacher Created Materials, Inc.
World Book, Inc Staff, contrib. by. Encyclopedia of Matter & Energy. 2013. (Illus.). 245p. (J). *(978-0-7166-7521-1(8))* World Bk., Inc.
—Learning about Energy, Forces, & Motion. 2011. (J). *(978-0-7166-0233-0(4))* World Bk., Inc.
Young, June. Energy Is Everywhere. 2006. (Rookie Read-About Science Ser.). (ENG., Illus.). 32p. (J). (gr. 1-2). pap. 4.95 *(978-0-516-28003-5(1),* Children's Pr.) Scholastic Library Publishing.
Zuchora-Walske, Christine. Science Lab: The Transfer of Energy. 2011. (Explorer Library: Language Arts Explorer Ser.). (ENG.). 32p. (gr. 4-8). pap. 14.21 *(978-1-61080-298-7(5),* 201220); lib. bdg. 28.50 *(978-1-61080-209-3(8),* 201194) Cherry Lake Publishing.

FORD, GERALD R., 1913-2006

Francis, Sandra. Gerald R. Ford. 2008. (Presidents of the U. S. A. Ser.). (ENG., Illus.). 48p. (J). (gr. 3-6). 32.79 *(978-1-60253-066-9(1),* 200705) Child's World, Inc., The.
Gunderson, Megan M. Gerald Ford, 1 vol. 2009. (United States Presidents Ser.). (ENG., Illus.). 40p. (YA). (gr. 3-6). 27.07 *(978-1-60453-451-1(6))* ABDO Publishing Co.
Mara, Wil. Gerald Ford. 2009. (Presidents & Their Times 3 Ser.). 96p. (gr. 6). 34.21 *(978-0-7614-3629-4(4))* Marshall Cavendish GBR. Dist: Marshall Cavendish Corp.
Margaret, Amy. Gerald R. Ford Library & Museum. (Presidential Libraries Ser.). 24p. 2009. (gr. 3-3). 42.50 *(978-1-60851-485-4(4))* 2004. (Illus.). (J). lib. bdg. 22.60 *(978-0-8239-6270-9(9))* Rosen Publishing Group, Inc., The. (PowerKids Pr.).
O'Shei, Tim. Gerald R. Ford: A MyReportLinks.com Book. 2003. (Presidents Ser.). (Illus.). 48p. (J). (gr. 5-10). lib. bdg. 25.26 *(978-0-7660-5050-1(5),* MyReportLinks.com Bks.) Enslow Pubs., Inc.
Plaut, Michael. How to Draw the Life & Times of Gerald R. Ford. 2009. (Kid's Guide to Drawing the Presidents of the United States of America Ser.). 32p. (gr. 4-4). 50.50 *(978-1-61511-141-1(7),* PowerKids Pr.) Rosen Publishing Group, Inc., The.
Plaut, Michael F. How to Draw the Life & Times of Gerald R. Ford. 2005. (Kid's Guide to Drawing the Presidents of the United States of America Ser.). (Illus.). 32p. (YA). (gr. 2-5). lib. bdg. 26.50 *(978-1-4042-3014-9(9))* Rosen Publishing Group, Inc., The.
Venezia, Mike. Gerald R. Ford: Thirty-Eighth President, 1974-1977. Venezia, Mike, illus. (Getting to Know the U. S. Presidents Ser.). (ENG., Illus.). 32p. (J). (gr. 3-4). 2008. pap. 7.95 *(978-0-516-25597-2(5))* 2007. 28.00 *(978-0-516-22642-2(8))* Scholastic Library Publishing. (Children's Pr.).
Waxman, Laura Hamilton. Gerald R. Ford. 2009. pap. 52.95 *(978-0-7613-4954-9(5))* 2008. (ENG.). 48p. (gr. 3-6). 27.93 *(978-0-8225-7985-4(5),* Lerner Pubns.) Lerner Publishing Group.
Winget, Mary Mueller. Gerald R. Ford. 2007. (Presidential Leaders Ser.). (Illus.). 112p. (J). (gr. 3-7). lib. bdg. 29.27 *(978-0-8225-1509-8(1),* Twenty-First Century Bks.) Lerner Publishing Group.

FORD, HENRY, 1863-1947

Armstrong, Linda. Henry Ford. 2009. pap. 13.25 *(978-1-60559-062-2(2))* Hameray Publishing Group, Inc.
Arrathoon, Leigh A. Men Who Changed the World Vol. I: The Henry Ford Story. Davio, John, ed. Hajdyla, Ken, illus. 56p. (J). (gr. 5-6). pap. 5.95 *(978-0-9648564-5-5(X))* Archus Pr., LLC.
Brown, Jonatha A. Henry Ford. 2005. (Gente que hay que conocer (People We Should Know- Spanish) Ser.). 24p. (gr. 1-4). (SPA.). lib. bdg. 22.00 *(978-0-8368-4582-2(X));* (Illus.). pap. 8.15 *(978-0-8368-4473-3(4));* (Illus.). lib. bdg. 22.00 *(978-0-8368-4466-5(1))* Stevens, Gareth Publishing LLLP. (Weekly Reader Leveled Readers).
Burgan, Michael. Who Was Henry Ford? Hammond, Ted, illus. 2014. 105p. (J). lib. bdg. *(978-1-4844-3671-4(7),* Grosset & Dunlap) Penguin Publishing Group.
—Who Was Henry Ford? Hammond, Ted & Harrison, Nancy, illus. 2014. (Who Was? Ser.). (ENG.). 112p. (J). (gr. 3-7). 5.99 *(978-0-448-47957-6(5),* Grosset & Dunlap) Penguin Young Readers Group.
—Who Was Henry Ford? 2014. (Who Was... ? Ser.). (Illus.). 105p. (J). lib. bdg. 16.00 *(978-0-606-36169-9(3))* Turtleback Bks.
Davis, Lynn. Henry Ford, 1 vol. 2016. (ENG., Illus.). 24p. (J). *(978-1-62403-724-5(0))* ABDO Publishing Co.
Ford, Carin T. Henry Ford: The Car Man. 2003. (Famous Inventors Ser.). (Illus.). 32p. (J). (gr. 1-4). lib. bdg. 22.60 *(978-0-7660-2179-2(3))* Enslow Pubs., Inc.
Green, Sara. Ford. 2016. (Brands We Know Ser.). (ENG., Illus.). 24p. (J). (gr. 3-8). 25.95 *(978-1-62617-408-5(3),* Pilot Bks.) Bellwether Media.
Greene, Lila. Henry Ford's Fantastic Factory: Identify & Explain Patterns in Arithmetic. 2014. (Rosen Common Core Math Readers Ser.). (ENG., Illus.). 24p. (J). (gr. 3-4). pap. 8.25 *(978-1-4777-4941-8(1),* Rosen Classroom) Rosen Publishing Group, Inc., The.
Gregory, Josh. Henry Ford: Father of the Auto Industry. 2013. (True Book(tm), a — Great American Business Ser.). (ENG.). 48p. (J). 31.00 *(978-0-531-24777-8(5));* pap. 6.95 *(978-0-531-28463-6(8))* Scholastic Library Publishing.
James, Emily. Henry Ford. 2017. (Great Scientists & Inventors Ser.). (ENG.). 24p. (gr. k-1). lib. bdg. 26.65 *(978-1-5157-3880-0(9),* Pebble Plus) Capstone Press of Coughlan Cos.
Kent, Zachary. The Story of Henry Ford & the Automobile: Cornerstones of Freedom. 2004. (Illus.). 31p. (J). (gr. k-4). reprint ed. 17.00 *(978-0-7567-7648-0(1))* DIANE Publishing Co.
Kulling, Monica. Eat My Dust! Henry Ford's First Race. Walz, Richard, illus. 2004. (Step into Reading Ser.). 48p. (J). (gr. 1-3). 11.65 *(978-0-7569-3231-2(9))* Perfection Learning Corp.
—Eat My Dust! Henry Ford's First Race. Walz, Richard, illus. 2004. (Step into Reading Ser.). (ENG.). 48p. (J). (gr. k-3). pap. 3.99 *(978-0-375-81510-2(4),* Random Hse. Bks. for Young Readers) Random Hse. Children's Bks.
Kuskowski, Alex & Craig, Diane. Super Simple Automobile Projects: Inspiring & Educational Science Activities, 1 vol. 2016. (ENG., Illus.). 32p. (J). 18.95 *(978-1-62403-729-0(1))* ABDO Publishing Co.
Mara, Wil. Henry Ford: Automotive Innovator. 2017. (Rookie Biographies Ser.). (ENG.). 32p. (J). lib. bdg. 25.00 ***(978-0-531-23225-5(5),*** Children's Pr.) Scholastic Library Publishing.
Marsh, Carole. Henry Ford. 2004. 12p. (gr. k-4). 2.95 *(978-0-635-02365-0(2))* Gallopade International.
McDowell, Pamela. Henry Ford. 2014. (Illus.). 24p. (J). *(978-1-62127-306-6(7))* Weigl Pubs., Inc.
Mitchell, Don. Driven: A Photobiography of Henry Ford. 2010. (Photobiographies Ser.). (ENG., Illus.). 64p. (J). (gr. 5-18). 27.90 *(978-1-4263-0156-8(1));* 18.95 *(978-1-4263-0155-1(3))* National Geographic Society. (National Geographic Children's Bks.).
Nagelhout, Ryan. Henry Ford in His Own Words. 2014. (Eyewitness to History Ser.). 32p. (J). (gr. 4-6). pap. 63.00 *(978-1-4824-1218-5(7))* Stevens, Gareth Publishing LLLP.
O'Hearn, Michael. Henry Ford & the Model T, 1 vol. Miller, Phil et al, illus. 2006. (Inventions & Discovery Ser.). (ENG.). 32p. (gr. 3-4). 30.65 *(978-0-7368-6480-0(6),* Graphic Library) Capstone Press of Coughlan Cos.
Parker, Lewis K. Henry Ford & the Automobile Industry. (American Tycoons Ser.). 24p. 2009. (gr. 3-3). 42.50 *(978-1-61511-390-3(8))* 2003. (Illus.). (J). lib. bdg. 22.60 *(978-0-8239-6451-2(5))* Rosen Publishing Group, Inc., The. (PowerKids Pr.).
Rausch, Monica L. Henry Ford & the Model T Car. 2007. (Inventors & Their Discoveries Ser.). (Illus.). 24p. (gr. 1-4). lib. bdg. 22.00 *(978-0-8368-7500-3(1),* Weekly Reader Leveled Readers) Stevens, Gareth Publishing LLLP.
—Henry Ford y el Automovil Modelo T. 2007. (Inventores y sus descubrimientos (Inventors & Their Discoveries) Ser.). (ENG & SPA., Illus.). 24p. (gr. 1-4). pap. 8.15 *(978-0-8368-8000-7(5));* lib. bdg. 22.00 *(978-0-8368-7995-7(3))* Stevens, Gareth Publishing LLLP. (Weekly Reader Leveled Readers).
Reis, Ronald A. Henry Ford for Kids: His Life & Ideas, with 21 Activities. 2016. (For Kids Ser.). (ENG., Illus.). 144p. (J). (gr. 4). pap. 16.95 *(978-1-61373-090-4(X))* Chicago Review Pr., Inc.
Roberts, Steven. Henry Ford. 2013. (Jr. Graphic American Inventors Ser.). (ENG., Illus.). 24p. (J). (gr. 3-6). pap. 10.60 *(978-1-4777-0143-0(5));* lib. bdg. 25.25 *(978-1-4777-0079-2(X))* Rosen Publishing Group, Inc., The. (PowerKids Pr.).
Roop, Peter & Roop, Connie. Let's Drive, Henry Ford! 2004. (Before I Made History Ser.). (Illus.). 59p. (J). pap. *(978-0-439-67624-3(X))* Scholastic, Inc.
Royston, Angela. Henry Ford & the Assembly Line, 01 vols., 1. 2016. (Inventions That Changed the World Ser.). (ENG.). 32p. (J). pap. 10.00 *(978-1-5081-4627-8(6),* PowerKids Pr.) Rosen Publishing Group, Inc., The.
Roza, Greg. Henry Ford: Pioneer of Modern Industry. 2009. (Real Life Readers Ser.). 24p. (gr. 3-4). pap. 8.25 *(978-1-4358-0137-0(7),* Rosen Classroom) Rosen Publishing Group, Inc., The.
Slade, Suzanne. The Inventor's Secret: What Thomas Edison Told Henry Ford. Reinhardt, Jennifer Black, illus. 2015. (ENG.). 48p. (J). (gr. 1-4). lib. bdg. 16.95 *(978-1-58089-667-2(7))* Charlesbridge Publishing, Inc.
Tallinda, Theodore. Math at Henry Ford's Factory: Identify & Explain Patterns in Arithmetic, 1 vol. 2015. (InfoMax Common Core Math Readers Ser.). (ENG.). 24p. (J). pap. 8.25 *(978-1-4777-4684-4(6),* Rosen Classroom) Rosen Publishing Group, Inc., The.
Venezia, Mike. Henry Ford: Big Wheel in the Auto Industry. Venezia, Mike, illus. 2009. (Getting to Know the World's Greatest Inventors & Scientists Ser.). (ENG., Illus.). 32p. (J). (gr. 3-4). pap. 6.95 *(978-0-531-21335-3(8),* Children's Pr.); (gr. 2-5). 28.00 *(978-0-531-23726-7(5))* Scholastic Library Publishing.

York, M. J. Henry Ford: Manufacturing Mogul, 1 vol. 2010. (Essential Lives Set 5 Ser.). (ENG.). 112p. (J). (gr. 6-12). lib. bdg. 35.64 *(978-1-61613-514-0(X))* ABDO Publishing Co.

Young, Jeff C. Henry Ford: Genius Behind the Affordable Car. 2007. (Inventors Who Changed the World Ser.). (Illus.). 128p. (J). (gr. 4-7). lib. bdg. 34.60 *(978-1-59845-053-8(0)*, MyReportLinks.com Bks.) Enslow Pubs., Inc.

Zuehlke, Jeffrey. Henry Ford. 2007. (History Maker Bios Ser.). (Illus.). 48p. (J). (gr. 3-7). lib. bdg. 26.60 *(978-0-8225-6583-3(8)*, Lerner Pubns.) Lerner Publishing Group.

FORD, WHITEY, 1928-

Nolan, Arthea. Whitey Ford. (Baseball Hall of Famers Ser.). 112p. (gr. 5-8). 2009. 63.90 *(978-1-61511-518-1(8))* 2004. (Illus.). lib. bdg. 34.60 *(978-0-8239-3784-4(4))* Rosen Publishing Group, Inc., The. (Rosen Reference).

FORD AUTOMOBILE

Bradley, Michael. Ford Truck. 2008. (Cars Ser.). 32p. (gr. 3-18). lib. bdg. 28.50 *(978-0-7614-2979-1(4)*, Benchmark Bks.) Marshall Cavendish Corp.

Green, Sara. Ford. 2016. (Brands We Know Ser.). (ENG., Illus.). 24p. (J). (gr. 3-8). 25.95 *(978-1-62617-408-5(3)*, Pilot Bks.) Bellwether Media.

Kent, Zachary. The Story of Henry Ford & the Automobile: Cornerstones of Freedom. 2004. (Illus.). 31p. (J). (gr. k-4). reprint ed. 17.00 *(978-0-7567-7648-0(1))* DIANE Publishing Co.

Maurer, Tracy Nelson. Ford Thunderbird. 2007. (Full Throttle 2 (High Interest) Ser.). (Illus.). 32p. (J). (gr. 3-7). lib. bdg. 28.50 *(978-1-60044-572-9(1))* Rourke Educational Media.

Publications International Ltd. Staff. Yesterday & Today Ford. 2009. (Illus.). 160p. *(978-1-60553-338-4(6)*, 1605533386) Publications International, Ltd.

Rausch, Monica L. Henry Ford & the Model T Car. 2007. (Inventors & Their Discoveries Ser.). (Illus.). 24p. (gr. 1-4). lib. bdg. 22.00 *(978-0-8368-7500-3(1)*, Weekly Reader Leveled Readers) Stevens, Gareth Publishing LLLP.

—Henry Ford y el Automovil Modelo T. 2007. (Inventores y sus descubrimientos (Inventors & Their Discoveries) Ser.). (ENG & SPA., Illus.). 24p. (gr. 1-4). pap. 8.15 *(978-0-8368-8000-7(5))*; lib. bdg. 22.00 *(978-0-8368-7995-7(3))* Stevens, Gareth Publishing LLLP. (Weekly Reader Leveled Readers).

FORD MOTOR COMPANY

Green, Sara. Ford. 2016. (Brands We Know Ser.). (ENG., Illus.). 24p. (J). (gr. 3-8). 25.95 *(978-1-62617-408-5(3)*, Pilot Bks.) Bellwether Media.

Kent, Zachary. The Story of Henry Ford & the Automobile: Cornerstones of Freedom. 2004. (Illus.). 31p. (J). (gr. k-4). reprint ed. 17.00 *(978-0-7567-7648-0(1))* DIANE Publishing Co.

Musolf, Nell. The Story of Ford. (Built for Success Ser.). (Illus.). 2011. (ENG.). 48p. (J). (gr. 4-7). pap. 12.00 *(978-1-897563-02-1(7)*, Creative Paperbacks) 2008. 46p. (YA). (gr. 5-9). 22.95 *(978-1-58341-604-4(8))* Creative Co., The.

O'Hearn, Michael. Henry Ford & the Model T, 1 vol. Miller, Phil et al, illus. 2006. (Inventions & Discovery Ser.). (ENG.). 32p. (gr. 3-4). 30.65 *(978-0-7368-6480-0(6)*, Graphic Library) Capstone Press of Coughlan Cos.

Parker, Lewis K. Henry Ford & the Automobile Industry. (American Tycoons Ser.). 24p. 2009. (gr. 3-3). 42.50 *(978-1-61511-390-3(8))* 2003. (Illus.). (J). lib. bdg. 22.60 *(978-0-8239-6451-2(5))* Rosen Publishing Group, Inc., The. (PowerKids Pr.).

Roza, Greg. Henry Ford: Pioneer of Modern Industry. 2009. (Real Life Readers Ser.). 24p. (gr. 3-4). pap. 8.25 *(978-1-4358-0137-0(7)*, Rosen Classroom) Rosen Publishing Group, Inc., The.

FORECASTING, WEATHER

see Weather Forecasting

FOREIGN AID PROGRAM

see Economic Assistance

FOREIGN ECONOMIC RELATIONS

see International Economic Relations

FOREIGN MISSIONS

see Missions

FOREIGN POPULATION

see Immigrants; Minorities

FOREIGN RELATIONS

see International Relations

see names of countries with subdivision Foreign Relations

FOREIGNERS

see Immigrants

FORENSIC SCIENCES

Ballard, Carol. At the Crime Scene! Collecting Clues & Evidence. 2009. (Solve That Crime! Ser.). (Illus.). 48p. (J). (gr. 5-9). lib. bdg. 25.27 *(978-0-7660-3373-3(2))* Enslow Pubs., Inc.

—Crime under the Microscope! In the Forensics Lab. 2009. (Solve That Crime! Ser.). (Illus.). 48p. (J). (gr. 5-9). lib. bdg. 25.27 *(978-0-7660-3374-0(0))* Enslow Pubs., Inc.

Bauchner, Elizabeth. Computer Investigation. Noziglia, Carla Miller & Siegel, Jay A., eds. 2013. (Solving Crimes with Science: Forensics Ser.: 12). (Illus.). 112p. (J). (gr. 7-18). 22.95 *(978-1-4222-2862-3(2))* Mason Crest.

—Document Analysis. Noziglia, Carla Miller & Siegel, Jay A., eds. 2013. (Solving Crimes with Science: Forensics Ser.: 12). (Illus.). 112p. (J). (gr. 7-18). 22.95 *(978-1-4222-2865-4(7))* Mason Crest.

Bedell, J. M. So, You Want to Work with the Ancient & Recent Dead? Unearthing Careers from Paleontology to Forensic Science. 2015. (Be What You Want Ser.). (ENG., Illus.). 256p. (J). (gr. 3-7). pap. 11.99 *(978-1-58270-545-3(3))* Aladdin/Beyond Words.

Beres, D. B. Sticky Evidence: Burglar Caught on Tape. 2011. (J). pap. *(978-0-545-32803-6(9))* Scholastic, Inc.

Bodden, Valerie. Identification. 2016. (J). *(978-1-60818-681-5(4)*, Creative Education) Creative Co., The.

—Lab Analysis. 2016. (J). *(978-1-60818-682-2(2)*, Creative Education) Creative Co., The.

—Medical Examination. 2016. (J). *(978-1-60818-683-9(0)*, Creative Education) Creative Co., The.

—Mind of a Criminal. 2016. (J). *(978-1-60818-684-6(9)*, Creative Education) Creative Co., The.

—Odysseys in Crime Scene Science: Digital Forensics. 2017. (Odysseys in Crime Scene Science Ser.). (ENG.). 80p. (J). (gr. 7-11). pap. 14.99 ***(978-1-62832-469-3(4)***, Creative Paperbacks) Creative Co., The.

—Odysseys in Crime Scene Science: Identification. 2017. (Odysseys in Crime Scene Science Ser.). (ENG.). 80p. (J). (gr. 7-11). pap. 14.99 ***(978-1-62832-470-9(8)***, Creative Paperbacks) Creative Co., The.

—Odysseys in Crime Scene Science: Lab Analysis. 2017. (Odysseys in Crime Scene Science Ser.). (ENG.). 80p. (J). (gr. 7-11). pap. 14.99 ***(978-1-62832-471-6(6)***, Creative Paperbacks) Creative Co., The.

—Odysseys in Crime Scene Science: Medical Examination. 2017. (Odysseys in Crime Scene Science Ser.). (ENG.). 80p. (J). (gr. 7-11). pap. 14.99 ***(978-1-62832-472-3(4)***, Creative Paperbacks) Creative Co., The.

—Odysseys in Crime Scene Science: Mind of a Criminal. 2017. (Odysseys in Crime Scene Science Ser.). (ENG.). 80p. (J). (gr. 7-11). pap. 14.99 ***(978-1-62832-473-0(2)***, Creative Paperbacks) Creative Co., The.

Careers in Focus: Forensics. 2010. (Careers in Focus Ser.). (Illus.). 208p. (gr. 6-12). 32.95 *(978-0-8160-8020-5(8)*, Ferguson Publishing Co.) Facts On File, Inc.

Carmichael, L. E. Discover Forensic Science. 2016. (Searchlight Books (tm) — What's Cool about Science? Ser.). (ENG., Illus.). 40p. (J). (gr. 3-5). 30.65 *(978-1-5124-0805-8(0))* Lerner Publishing Group.

—Forensic Science: In Pursuit of Justice, 1 vol. 2014. (History of Science Ser.). (ENG.). 112p. (J). (gr. 6-12). lib. bdg. 35.64 *(978-1-62403-561-6(2)*, Essential Library) ABDO Publishing Co.

Crime Science. 2013. (Crime Science Ser.). 48p. (J). (gr. 4-8). 191.70 *(978-1-4339-9680-1(4))*; pap. 505.80 *(978-1-4339-9801-0(7))*; pap. 84.30 *(978-1-4339-9800-3(9))* Stevens, Gareth Publishing LLLP.

Crime Solvers. 2017. (Crime Solvers Ser.). 48p. (gr. 6-6). pap. 84.30 ***(978-1-5382-0611-9(0))*** Stevens, Gareth Publishing LLLP.

Ebner, Aviva. Forensic Science Experiments. 2011. (Experiments for Future Scientists Ser.). (Illus.). 172p. (gr. 5-8). 35.00 *(978-1-60413-850-4(5))* Facts On File, Inc.

Eldridge, Stephen. Investigating Trace Evidence. 2017. (J). ***(978-0-7660-9187-0(2))*** Enslow Pubs., Inc.

Eldridge, Stephen. Trace Evidence: Dead People Do Tell Tales. 2011. (True Forensic Crime Stories Ser.). (Illus.). 104p. (J). (gr. 5-18). pap. 10.95 *(978-1-59845-366-9(1))*; (gr. 7-12). lib. bdg. 33.27 *(978-0-7660-3664-2(2))* Enslow Pubs., Inc.

Engdahl, Sylvia. Forensic Technology. Gale Editors, ed. 2010. (Current Controversies Ser.). (ENG.). 240p. 40.95 *(978-0-7377-4911-3(3))*; pap. 28.45 *(978-0-7377-4912-0(1))* Cengage Gale. (Greenhaven Pr., Inc.).

Esherick, Joan. Criminal Psychology & Personality Profiling. Noziglia, Carla Miller & Siegel, Jay A., eds. 2013. (Solving Crimes with Science: Forensics Ser.: 12). (Illus.). 112p. (J). (gr. 7-18). 22.95 *(978-1-4222-2863-0(0))* Mason Crest.

Faulk, Michelle. Gun Crimes: Dead People Do Tell Tales. 2011. (True Forensic Crime Stories Ser.). (Illus.). 104p. (J). (gr. 5-18). pap. 10.95 *(978-1-59845-365-2(3))*; (gr. 7-12). lib. bdg. 33.27 *(978-0-7660-3763-2(0))* Enslow Pubs., Inc.

Ford, Jean. Explosives & Arson Investigation. Noziglia, Carla Miller & Siegel, Jay A., eds. 2013. (Solving Crimes with Science: Forensics Ser.: 12). (Illus.). 112p. (J). (gr. 7-18). 22.95 *(978-1-4222-2867-8(3))* Mason Crest.

—Forensics in American Culture. 2013. (J). *(978-1-4222-2861-6(4))* Mason Crest.

—Forensics in American Culture. Noziglia, Carla Miller & Siegel, Jay A., eds. 2013. (Solving Crimes with Science: Forensics Ser.: 12). (Illus.). 112p. (J). (gr. 7-18). 22.95 *(978-1-4222-2870-8(3))* Mason Crest.

Forensic Archaeology. 2011. (Crime Scene Investigations Ser.). 128p. lib. bdg. 33.45 *(978-1-4205-0548-1(3)*, Lucent Bks.) Cengage Gale.

Gardner, Robert. Forensic Science Experiments in Your Own Crime Lab. 2015. (Design, Build, Experiment Ser.). (ENG.). 128p. (J). (gr. 7-7). lib. bdg. 37.27 *(978-0-7660-6955-8(9))* Enslow Pubs., Inc.

—Who Can Solve the Crime? Science Projects Using Detective Skills. 2010. (Who Dunnit? Forensic Science Experiments Ser.). (Illus.). 48p. (J). (gr. 2-5). 25.27 *(978-0-7660-3247-7(7))* Enslow Pubs., Inc.

—Who Forged This Document? Crime-Solving Science Projects. 2010. (Who Dunnit? Forensic Science Experiments Ser.). (Illus.). 48p. (J). (gr. 2-5). 25.27 *(978-0-7660-3246-0(9))* Enslow Pubs., Inc.

—Whose Bones Are These? Crime-Solving Science Projects. 2010. (Who Dunnit? Forensic Science Experiments Ser.). (Illus.). 48p. (J). (gr. 2-5). 25.27 *(978-0-7660-3248-4(5))* Enslow Pubs., Inc.

—Whose Fingerprints Are These? Crime-Solving Science Projects. 2010. (Who Dunnit? Forensic Science Experiments Ser.). (Illus.). 48p. (J). (gr. 2-5). 25.27 *(978-0-7660-3245-3(0))* Enslow Pubs., Inc.

Gardner, Robert & Conklin, Joshua. Experiments for Future Forensic Scientists. 2016. (Experiments for Future STEM Professionals Ser.). 128p. (J). lib. bdg. 37.27 *(978-0-7660-8202-1(4))* Enslow Pubs., Inc.

Glenn, John. Civil Engineers. 2015. (Illus.). 48p. (J). *(978-1-4222-3416-7(9))* Mason Crest.

Graham, Ian. Forensic Technology. 2011. (New Technology Ser.). 48p. (YA). (gr. 7-12). lib. bdg. 34.25 *(978-1-59920-532-8(7))* Black Rabbit Bks.

Gray, Susan H. Forensic Psychologist. 2015. (21st Century Skills Library: Cool STEAM Careers Ser.). (ENG., Illus.). 32p. (J). (gr. 4-7). 29.93 *(978-1-63362-559-4(1)*, 206420) Cherry Lake Publishing.

Hamilton, Sue L. Crime Scene Investigation, 6 vols., Set. Incl. DNA Analysis: Forensic Fluids & Follicles. 27.07 *(978-1-59928-987-8(3))*; Fingerprint Analysis: Hints from Prints. 27.07 *(978-1-59928-988-5(1))*; Forensic Artist: Solving the Case with a Face. 27.07 *(978-1-59928-989-2(X))*; Forensic Ballistics: Styles of Projectiles. 27.07 *(978-1-59928-990-8(3))*; Forensic Entomology: Bugs & Bodies. 27.07 *(978-1-59928-991-5(1))*; 32p. (gr. 4-8). (Crime Scene Investigation Ser.). 2008. 162.42 *(978-1-59928-986-1(5)*, Abdo & Daughters) ABDO Publishing Co.

—DNA Analysis: Forensic Fluids & Follicles, 1 vol. 2008. (Crime Scene Investigation Ser.). (ENG.). 32p. (gr. 4-8). 27.07 *(978-1-59928-987-8(3)*, Abdo & Daughters) ABDO Publishing Co.

Heos, Bridget. Blood, Bullets, & Bones: The Story of Forensic Science from Sherlock Holmes to DNA. 2016. (Illus.). 272p. (YA). (gr. 9). 18.99 *(978-0-06-238762-2(6))* HarperCollins Pubs.

Herweck, Diana. En Escena: La Vida de un CSI. 2017. (TIME for Kids en Español - Level 4 Ser.). (SPA., Illus.). 48p. (gr. 4-4). lib. bdg. 31.99 *(978-1-5157-5130-4(9))* Time for Kids Inc AUS. Dist: Capstone Pub.

—On the Scene: A CSI's Life, 1 vol. 2nd rev. ed. 2013. (Nonfiction Readers Ser.). (ENG., Illus.). 48p. (J). (gr. 4-4). pap. 29.96 *(978-1-4807-1101-3(2))* Shell Educational Publishing.

Hunter, William. DNA Analysis. Noziglia, Carla Miller & Siegel, Jay A., eds. 2013. (Solving Crimes with Science: Forensics Ser.: 12). (Illus.). 112p. (J). (gr. 7-18). 22.95 *(978-1-4222-2864-7(9))* Mason Crest.

—DNA Analysis. 2007. (Forensics Ser.). (Illus.). 112p. (YA). (gr. 7-18). lib. bdg. 22.95 *(978-1-4222-0026-1(4))* Mason Crest.

—Mark & Trace Analysis. Siegel, Jay A., ed. 2013. (Solving Crimes with Science: Forensics Ser.: 12). (Illus.). 112p. (J). (gr. 7-18). 22.95 *(978-1-4222-2871-5(1))* Mason Crest.

—Solving Crimes with Physics. Noziglia, Carla Miller & Siegel, Jay A., eds. 2013. (Solving Crimes with Science: Forensics Ser.: 12). (Illus.). 112p. (J). (gr. 7-18). 22.95 *(978-1-4222-2873-9(8))* Mason Crest.

Innes, Brian. Forensic Science, Vol. 20. Gomez, Manny, ed. 2016. (Crime & Detection Ser.). (Illus.). 96p. (J). (gr. 7). 24.95 *(978-1-4222-3477-8(0))* Mason Crest.

Kawa, Katie. Forensic Detectives, 01 vols., 1. 2016. (Out of the Lab: Extreme Jobs in Science Ser.). (ENG., Illus.). 32p. (J). pap. 10.00 *(978-1-5081-4521-9(0)*, PowerKids Pr.) Rosen Publishing Group, Inc., The.

Kling, Andrew A. Surveillance. 2007. (Crime Scene Investigations Ser.). (ENG., Illus.). 128p. (gr. 7-12). lib. bdg. 40.40 *(978-1-59018-991-7(4))* Cengage Gale.

Lane, Brian, et al. Eyewitness Books - Crime & Detection. Crawford, Andy, photos by. 2005. (DK Eyewitness Bks.). (ENG., Illus.). 72p. (J). (gr. 3-7). 16.99 *(978-0-7566-1386-0(8)*, DK Children) Dorling Kindersley Publishing, Inc.

Latta, Sara L. Bones: Dead People Do Tell Tales. 2011. (True Forensic Crime Stories Ser.). (Illus.). 104p. (J). (gr. 5-18). pap. 10.95 *(978-1-59845-363-8(7))*; (gr. 7-12). lib. bdg. 33.27 *(978-0-7660-3669-7(3))* Enslow Pubs., Inc.

—DNA & Blood: Dead People Do Tell Tales. 2011. (True Forensic Crime Stories Ser.). (Illus.). 104p. (J). (gr. 7-12). lib. bdg. 33.27 *(978-0-7660-3667-3(7))* Enslow Pubs., Inc.

—DNA & Blood: Dead People DO Tell Tales. 2011. (True Forensic Crime Stories Ser.). (Illus.). 104p. (J). (gr. 5-18). pap. 10.95 *(978-1-59845-362-1(9))* Enslow Pubs., Inc.

Libal, Angela. Fingerprints, Bite Marks, Ear Prints. Noziglia, Carla Miller & Siegel, Jay A., eds. 2013. (Solving Crimes with Science: Forensics Ser.: 12). (Illus.). 112p. (J). (gr. 7-18). 22.95 *(978-1-4222-2868-5(1))* Mason Crest.

—Forensic Anthropology. Noziglia, Carla Miller & Siegel, Jay A., eds. 2013. (Solving Crimes with Science: Forensics Ser.: 12). (Illus.). 112p. (J). (gr. 7-18). 22.95 *(978-1-4222-2869-2(X))* Mason Crest.

Litmanovich, Ellina & Latta, Sara L. Investigating Bones. 2017. (J). ***(978-0-7660-9182-5(1))*** Enslow Pubs., Inc.

MacLeod, Elizabeth. Bones Never Lie: How Forensics Helps Solve History's Mysteries. 3rd ed. 2013. (ENG., Illus.). 160p. (J). (gr. 5-7). 24.95 *(978-1-55451-483-0(5)*, 9781554514830); pap. 14.95 *(978-1-55451-482-3(7)*, 9781554514823) Annick Pr., Ltd. CAN. Dist: Publishers Group West (PGW).

Marzilli, Alan. DNA Evidence. 2004. (Point/Counterpoint Ser.). (Illus.). 112p. (C). (gr. 9-13). 35.00 *(978-0-7910-8092-4(7)*, Chelsea Hse.) Facts On File, Inc.

Meyer, Terry Teague. Careers in Computer Forensics. 2013. (Careers in Computer Technology Ser.). (ENG., Illus.). 80p. (YA). (gr. 9-12). lib. bdg. 33.25 *(978-1-4488-9593-9(6)*, Rosen Classroom) Rosen Publishing Group, Inc., The.

Mooney, Carla. Forensics: Uncover the Science & Technology of Crime Scene Investigation. Carbaugh, Samuel, illus. 2013. (Inquire & Investigate Ser.). (ENG.). 128p. (YA). (gr. 6-10). 21.95 *(978-1-61930-188-7(1))*; pap. 16.95 *(978-1-61930-184-9(9))* Open City Bks.

Murray, Elizabeth A. Forensic Identification: Putting a Name & Face on Death. 2012. (Exceptional Science Titles for Upper Grades Ser.). (ENG., Illus.). 72p. (J). (gr. 6-12). lib. bdg. 30.60 *(978-0-7613-6696-6(2))* Lerner Publishing Group.

Orr, Tamra B. Crime Scene Investigator. 2015. (21st Century Skills Library: Cool STEAM Careers Ser.). (ENG., Illus.). 32p. (J). (gr. 4-7). 29.93 *(978-1-63362-556-3(7)*, 206408) Cherry Lake Publishing.

—Forensic Science Investigator. 2015. (21st Century Skills Library: Cool STEAM Careers Ser.). (ENG., Illus.). 32p. (J). (gr. 4-7). 29.93 *(978-1-63362-560-0(5)*, 206424) Cherry Lake Publishing.

—Investigating a Crime Scene. 2014. (Explorer Library: Follow the Clues Ser.). (ENG.). 32p. (J). (gr. 4-8). 28.50 *(978-1-62431-777-4(4)*, 203304) Cherry Lake Publishing.

Parker, Janice. Crime. 2009. (Science Q & A Ser.). (Illus.). 48p. (YA). (gr. 5-8). pap. 10.95 *(978-1-60596-069-2(1))*; lib. bdg. 29.05 *(978-1-60596-068-5(3))* Weigl Pubs., Inc.

—Crime Q & A. 2014. (Science Discovery Ser.). (ENG., Illus.). 48p. (J). (gr. 5-8). pap. 13.95 *(978-1-4896-0685-3(8)*, AV2 by Weigl) Weigl Pubs., Inc.

Parks, Peggy J. DNA Evidence & Investigation. 2010. (Compact Research Ser.). 96p. (YA). (gr. 7-12). lib. bdg. 25.95 *(978-1-60152-102-6(2))* ReferencePoint Pr., Inc.

Peppas, Lynn. Forensics: The Scene of the Crime. 2014. (ENG., Illus.). 48p. (J). *(978-0-7787-1363-0(6))* Crabtree Publishing Co.

Perritano, John. Forensics, Vol. 10. 2016. (Stem in Current Events Ser.). (Illus.). 64p. (J). (gr. 7). 23.95 *(978-1-4222-3592-8(0))* Mason Crest.

—Science Beats Crime. 2010. (Cool Science Ser.). 48p. (J). (gr. 3-6). 28.50 *(978-1-60870-078-3(X))* Marshall Cavendish Corp.

Prokos, Anna. Guilty by a Hair! Real-Life DNA Matches! 2007. (24/7: Science Behind the Scenes Ser.). (ENG., Illus.). 64p. (J). (gr. 9-12). 29.00 *(978-0-531-11821-4(5)*, Watts, Franklin) Scholastic Library Publishing.

Rainis, Kenneth G. Blood & DNA Evidence: Crime-Solving Science Experiments. 2006. (Forensic Science Projects Ser.). (Illus.). 104p. (J). (gr. 3-7). lib. bdg. 33.27 *(978-0-7660-1958-4(6))* Enslow Pubs., Inc.

Rauf, Don & Williams, Judith. Forensic Science Specialists: Making Sense of Crime Scene Evidence. 2015. (Extreme Science Careers Ser.). (ENG., Illus.). 128p. (J). (gr. 7-7). lib. bdg. 37.27 *(978-0-7660-6962-6(1)*, 1392186) Enslow Pubs., Inc.

Royston, Angela. Science vs. Crime. 2013. (Science Fights Back Ser.). (Illus.). 48p. (J). (gr. 4-6). 31.95 *(978-1-4339-8683-3(3))*; pap. 14.05 *(978-1-4339-8684-0(1))* Stevens, Gareth Publishing LLLP. (Gareth Stevens Learning Library).

—Science vs. Natural Disasters. 2013. (Science Fights Back Ser.). (Illus.). 48p. (J). (gr. 4-6). 31.95 *(978-1-4339-8691-8(4))*; pap. 14.05 *(978-1-4339-8692-5(2))* Stevens, Gareth Publishing LLLP. (Gareth Stevens Learning Library).

Siegel, Jay. Forensic Science at Work. 2011. (Contemporary Issues Ser.). (Illus.). 166 ndash; 308p. (YA). (gr. 9-12). 37.95 *(978-1-4488-1864-8(8))* Rosen Publishing Group, Inc., The.

Spilsbury, Richard. Bones Speak! Solving Crimes from the Past. 2009. (Solve That Crime! Ser.). (Illus.). 48p. (J). (gr. 5-9). lib. bdg. 25.27 *(978-0-7660-3377-1(5))* Enslow Pubs., Inc.

Stefoff, Rebecca. Crime Labs. 2010. (Forensic Science Investigated 2 Ser.). (Illus.). 80p. (J). (gr. 5). lib. bdg. 34.21 *(978-0-7614-4140-3(9))* Marshall Cavendish Corp.

—Forensics & Modern Disasters. 2010. (Forensic Science Investigated 2 Ser.). (Illus.). 80p. (J). (gr. 5). lib. bdg. 34.21 *(978-0-7614-4144-1(1))* Marshall Cavendish Corp.

Stiefel, Chana. Fingerprints: Dead People Do Tell Tales. 2011. (True Forensic Crime Stories Ser.). (Illus.). 104p. (J). (gr. 5-18). pap. 10.95 *(978-1-59845-364-5(5))*; (gr. 7-12). lib. bdg. 33.27 *(978-0-7660-3689-5(8))* Enslow Pubs., Inc.

Sutherland, Adam. Police Forensics. 2012. (On the Radar: Defend & Protect Ser.). (ENG., Illus.). 32p. (gr. 4-8). lib. bdg. 26.60 *(978-0-7613-7774-0(3)*, Lerner Pubns.) Lerner Publishing Group.

Sutinis, Beth. Crime Scene Techs!, Vol. 10. 2015. (Scientists in Action Ser.). 48p. (J). (gr. 5). lib. bdg. 20.95 *(978-1-4222-3423-5(1))* Mason Crest.

T R Thomas & Thomas, T. R. DNA Evidence, 1 vol. unabr. ed. 2010. (True Crime Ser.). (ENG.). 64p. (YA). (gr. 9-12). pap. 8.95 *(978-1-59905-438-4(8))* Saddleback Educational Publishing, Inc.

—Forensics: True Crime, 1 vol. unabr. ed. 2010. (True Crime Ser.). (ENG.). 64p. (YA). (gr. 9-12). pap. 8.95 *(978-1-59905-439-1(6))* Saddleback Educational Publishing, Inc.

Townsend, John. Famous Forensic Cases. 2011. (Amazing Crime Scene Science Ser.). 32p. (YA). (gr. 4-7). 19.95 *(978-1-60753-169-2(0))* Amicus Publishing.

Walker, Maryalice. Entomology & Palynology. Noziglia, Carla Miller & Siegel, Jay A., eds. 2013. (Solving Crimes with Science: Forensics Ser.: 12). (Illus.). 112p. (J). (gr. 7-18). 22.95 *(978-1-4222-2866-1(5))* Mason Crest.

—Pathology. Noziglia, Carla Miller & Siegel, Jay A., eds. 2013. (Solving Crimes with Science: Forensics Ser.: 12). (Illus.). 112p. (J). (gr. 7-18). 22.95 *(978-1-4222-2872-2(X))* Mason Crest.

Wood, Alix. Hunting the Cyber Trail: Be a Computer Forensic Scientist. 2017. (Crime Solvers Ser.). 48p. (gr. 6-6). pap. 84.30 ***(978-1-5382-0619-5(6))*** Stevens, Gareth Publishing LLLP.

Woog, Adam. Careers in Forensic Science. 2012. (J). 34.21 *(978-1-60870-958-8(2))* Marshall Cavendish Corp.

Wright, John D. & Singer, Jane. DNA & Body Evidence, 4 bks., Set. Incl. Hair & Fibers. (ENG., Illus.). 96p. (C). (gr. 6-18). 2008. lib. bdg. 158.00 *(978-0-7656-8116-4(1)*, Y182555); (ENG., Illus.). 96p. 2007. Set lib. bdg. 158.00 *(978-0-7656-8113-3(7)*, Y182327) Routledge.

Zullo, Allan. Crime Scene Investigators. 2008. 149p. (J). pap. *(978-0-439-93406-0(0))* Scholastic, Inc.

FOREST ANIMALS

Alaina, Maria. Rainforest. 2011. (Wonder Readers Early Level Ser.). (ENG & ABK.). (gr. -1-1). 32p. pap. 5.99 *(978-1-4296-8057-8(1))*; 16p. pap. 35.94 *(978-1-4296-8171-1(3))* Capstone Press of Coughlan Cos. (Wonder Readers).

Allgor, Marie. Endangered Forest Animals. 2012. (Save Earth's Animals! Ser.). (ENG., Illus.). 24p. (J). (gr. k-5). pap. 8.25 *(978-1-4488-7497-2(1))*; lib. bdg. 22.60 *(978-1-4488-7424-8(6))* Rosen Publishing Group, Inc., The. (PowerKids Pr.).

—Endangered Rain Forest Animals. 2012. (Save Earth's Animals! Ser.). (ENG., Illus.). 24p. (J). (gr. k-5). pap. 8.25 *(978-1-4488-7495-8(5))*; lib. bdg. 22.60 *(978-1-4488-7422-4(X))* Rosen Publishing Group, Inc., The. (PowerKids Pr.).

Amstutz, Lisa J. Rain Forest Animal Adaptations. 2011. (Amazing Animal Adaptations Ser.). (ENG.). 32p. (gr. 1-2). pap. 47.70 *(978-1-4296-7037-1(1)*, Aplus Bks.) Capstone Press of Coughlan Cos.

—What Eats What in a Forest Food Chain, 1 vol. McLaughlin, Zack, illus. 2012. (Food Chains Ser.). (ENG.). 24p. (gr. 2-3). 25.99 *(978-1-4048-7388-9(0))*; pap. 8.95 *(978-1-4048-7692-7(8))* Picture Window Bks.

—What Eats What in a Rain Forest Food Chain, 1 vol. Wertheim, Anne, illus. 2012. (Food Chains Ser.). (ENG.). 24p. (gr. 2-3). 25.99 *(978-1-4048-7387-2(2))*; pap. 8.95 *(978-1-4048-7694-1(4))* Picture Window Bks.

Anderson, Sheila. What Can Live in a Forest? 2010. (First Step Nonfiction - Animal Adaptations Ser.). (ENG.). 24p. (gr. k-2). pap. 6.95 *(978-0-7613-5675-2(4))*; (Illus.). (J). lib. bdg. 23.93 *(978-0-7613-4571-8(X))* Lerner Publishing Group.

—What Can Live in A Forest? 2010. pap. 33.92 *(978-0-7613-6908-0(2))* Lerner Publishing Group.

Andrews, Alexa. In the Forest. Keimig, Candice, illus. 2013. (Penguin Young Readers, Level 1 Ser.). (ENG.). 32p. (J). (gr. k-1). pap. 3.99 *(978-0-448-46719-1(4),* Penguin Young Readers) Penguin Young Readers Group.

Arnold, Caroline. A Day & Night in the Forest. Arnold, Caroline, illus. 2015. (Caroline Arnold's Habitats Ser.). (ENG., Illus.). 24p. (gr. 2-3). lib. bdg. 27.99 *(978-1-4795-6075-2(8))* Picture Window Bks.

—A Day & Night in the Rain Forest. Arnold, Caroline, illus. 2015. (Caroline Arnold's Habitats Ser.). (ENG., Illus.). 24p. (gr. 2-3). lib. bdg. 27.99 *(978-1-4795-6074-5(X))* Picture Window Bks.

AZ Books. Forest Animals. 2012. (Touch & Feel Ser.). (ENG.). 10p. (J). (— 1). bds. 12.95 *(978-1-61889-222-5(3))* AZ Bks. LLC.

AZ Books, creator. Who Lives in the Forest? 2012. (Funny Animals Ser.). (ENG., Illus.). 10p. (J). (gr. -1-k). bds. 8.95 *(978-1-61889-003-0(4))* AZ Bks. LLC.

AZ Books Staff. In the Forest. Ulasevich, Olga & Goncharik, Irina, eds. 2012. (Animal Sounds Ser.). (ENG.). 14p. (J). (gr. -1-k). bds. 7.95 *(978-1-61889-126-6(X))* AZ Bks. LLC.

Barlowe, Dot. Forest Animals. 2011. (Dover Nature Coloring Book Ser.). (ENG.). 32p. (J). (gr. 1-5). pap. 5.99 *(978-0-486-47894-4(7))* Dover Pubns., Inc.

Benjamin, Tina. Let's Walk in the Woods. 2015. (Let's Go Outdoors! Ser.). (ENG.). 24p. (J). (gr. k-k). lib. bdg. 22.60 *(978-1-4824-2635-9(8));* (Illus.). pap. 8.15 *(978-1-4824-2633-5(1))* Stevens, Gareth Publishing LLLP.

Berkes, Marianne. Over in the Jungle: A Rainforest Rhyme. Canyon, Jeanette, illus. 2007. 32p. (J). (gr. -1-2). 16.95 *(978-1-58469-091-7(7))* Dawn Pubns.

—Over in the Jungle: A Rainforest Rhyme, 1 vol. Canyon, Jeanette, illus. 2007. (Sharing Nature with Children Book Ser.). (ENG.). 32p. (J). (gr. -1-3). 8.95 *(978-1-58469-092-4(5))* Dawn Pubns.

Boothroyd, Jennifer. Let's Visit the Deciduous Forest. 2016. (Lightning Bolt Books (tm) — Biome Explorers Ser.). (ENG., Illus.). 32p. (J). (gr. 1-3). 26.65 *(978-1-5124-1189-8(2))* Lerner Publishing Group.

Bradley, Timothy. Terror en Los Trópicos. 2016. (TIME for Kids en Español - Level 5 Ser.). (SPA.). 64p. (gr. 5-5). lib. bdg. 31.99 *(978-1-5157-2939-6(7))* Time for Kids Inc AUS. Dist: Capstone Pub.

Bredeson, Carmen. Baby Animals of the Tropical Rain Forest. (Nature's Baby Animals Ser.). (Illus.). 24p. (J). 2012. (gr. k-18). pap. 7.95 *(978-1-59845-408-6(0),* Enslow Elementary) 2008. (gr. 1-3). lib. bdg. 22.60 *(978-0-7660-3004-6(0))* Enslow Pubs., Inc.

—Baby Animals of the Woodland Forest. (Nature's Baby Animals Ser.). (Illus.). 24p. (J). 2012. (gr. k-18). pap. 7.95 *(978-1-59845-409-3(9),* Enslow Elementary) 2008. (gr. 1-3). lib. bdg. 22.60 *(978-0-7660-3005-3(9))* Enslow Pubs., Inc.

Brocoli, Steffie & Bidet, Catherine. Through the Forest. 2016. (ENG., Illus.). 30p. (J). (gr. k-2). 19.95 *(978-0-500-65076-9(4),* 565076) Thames & Hudson.

Callery, Sean. Life Cycles: Forest. 2013. (Lifecycles Ser.). (ENG., Illus.). 32p. (J). (gr. 2-5). 6.99 *(978-0-7534-7065-7(9),* 9780753470657, Kingfisher) Roaring Brook Pr.

Carlson-Voiles, Polly. Someone Walks By. 2008. 32p. (J). (gr. 1-2). 18.95 *(978-0-9801045-5-4(6))* Raven Productions, Inc.

—Someone Walks By: The Wonders of Winter Wildlife. 2008. 32p. (J). (gr. 1-2). pap. 9.95 *(978-0-9801045-6-1(4))* Raven Productions, Inc.

Claus, Matteson. Animals & Deforestation. 2013. (Animal 911: Environmental Threats Ser.). (Illus.). 48p. (J). (gr. 3-5). pap. 14.05 *(978-1-4339-9707-5(X),* 1358474); pap. 84.30 *(978-1-4339-9708-2(8),* 1358474); (ENG., lib. bdg. 31.95 *(978-1-4339-9706-8(1),* 1358474) Stevens, Gareth Publishing LLLP.

Creatures of the Forest Habitat. 2016. (Creatures of the Forest Habitat Ser.). 00024p. (J). (gr. 3-3). 141.60 *(978-1-4994-2639-7(9),* PowerKids Pr.) Rosen Publishing Group, Inc., The.

Dayton, Connor. Forest Animals. 2009. (American Habitats Ser.). (gr. 2-5). (ENG., Illus.). 24p. (J). pap. 8.25 *(978-1-4358-3193-3(4),* PowerKids Pr.); 24p. 42.50 *(978-1-61511-351-4(7),* PowerKids Pr.); (YA). lib. bdg. 22.60 *(978-1-4358-2764-6(3))* Rosen Publishing Group, Inc., The.

de Lambilly-Bresson, Elisabeth. Animals in the Forest. 2007. (Animal Show & Tell Ser.). (Illus.). 16p. (gr. -1-3). lib. bdg. 19.00 *(978-0-8368-8205-6(9),* Gareth Stevens Learning Library) Stevens, Gareth Publishing LLLP.

deMarin, Layne. Amazon Adventure, 1 vol. 2011. (Wonder Readers: Science Ser.). (ENG.). (gr. -1-2). 20p. lib. bdg. 22.65 *(978-1-4296-8634-1(0));* 16p. pap. 35.94 *(978-1-4296-8069-1(5));* 32p. pap. 5.99 *(978-1-4296-7907-7(7))* Capstone Press of Coughlan Cos. (Wonder Readers).

Diaz, Joanne Ruelos. Animals in the Rain Forest, 1 vol. Mendez, Simon, illus. 2014. (Animals All Day! Ser.). (ENG.). 32p. (gr. k-2). 27.27 *(978-1-4795-5698-4(X))* Picture Window Bks.

Dils, Tracey E. Down in the Jungle 1,2,3: A Rainforest Counting Book. 2015. (1, 2, 3... Count with Me Ser.). (ENG., Illus.). 24p. (J). (gr. k-2). 19.95 *(978-1-60753-715-1(X))* Amicus Publishing.

Duke, Kate. In the Rainforest. Duke, Kate, illus. 2014. (Let's-Read-And-Find-Out Science 2 Ser.). (ENG., Illus.). 40p. (J). (gr. -1-3). 17.99 *(978-0-06-028259-2(2));* pap. 5.99 *(978-0-06-445197-0(6))* HarperCollins Pubs.

Feely, Jenny. The Forest. 2004. (Illus.). 12p. (J). pap. *(978-0-7608-7866-8(8))* Sundance/Newbridge Educational Publishing.

Fennell, Clare, illus. Forest Homes. 2017. (Push & Pull Ser.). (ENG.). 8p. (J). (gr. -1 — 1). bds. 5.99 *(978-0-7641-6891-8(6))* Barron's Educational Series, Inc.

Fleisher, Paul. Forest Food Webs in Action. 2013. (Searchlight Books What Is a Food Web Ser.). (ENG., Illus.). 40p. (gr. 3-5). lib. bdg. 27.93 *(978-1-4677-1254-5(X),* Lerner Pubns.) Lerner Publishing Group.

A Forest Ecosystem. 2012. (Nature Trail Ser.). (ENG., Illus.). 32p. (J). (gr. k-5). 23.95 *(978-1-4488-6641-0(3),* PowerKids Pr.) Rosen Publishing Group, Inc., The.

Franklin, Carolyn, illus. Rain Forest Animals. 2013. (World of Wonder Ser.). 32p. (gr. 1-3). 31.35 ***(978-1-904642-67-1(5))*** Book Hse. GBR. Dist: Black Rabbit Bks.

Franklin, Carolyn & Stewart, David. Rain Forest Animals. Franklin, Carolyn, illus. 2008. (World of Wonder Ser.). (ENG., Illus.). 32p. (J). (gr. 1-4). 29.00 *(978-0-531-20452-8(9),* Children's Pr.) Scholastic Library Publishing.

Fredericks, Anthony D. A Is for Anaconda: A Rainforest Alphabet. Regan, Laura, illus. 2009. (Science Ser.). (ENG.). 40p. (J). (gr. 1-5). 17.95 *(978-1-58536-317-9(0))* Sleeping Bear Pr.

—Around One Log: Chipmunks, Spiders, & Creepy Insiders, 1 vol. DiRubbio, Jennifer, illus. 2011. 32p. (J). (gr. -1-5). (ENG.). 16.95 *(978-1-58469-137-2(9));* pap. 8.95 *(978-1-58469-138-9(7))* Dawn Pubns.

Fredericks, Anthony D. Tall Tall Tree, 1 vol. Wallace, Chad, illus. 2017. (ENG.). 32p. (J). (gr. -1-3). 16.95 ***(978-1-58469-601-8(X));*** pap. 8.95 ***(978-1-58469-602-5(8))*** Dawn Pubns.

Gaarder-Juntti, Oona. What Lives in the Forest?, 1 vol. 2008. (Animal Habitats Ser.). (ENG., Illus.). 24p. (J). (gr. k-3). 25.65 *(978-1-60453-174-9(6))* ABDO Publishing Co.

Ganeri, Anita. Lifesize: Rainforest: See Rainforest Creatures at Their Actual Size. Jackson-Carter, Stuart, illus. 2014. (Lifesize Ser.). (ENG.). 32p. (J). (gr. k-5). 16.99 *(978-0-7534-7190-6(6),* 9780753471906, Kingfisher) Roaring Brook Pr.

Golding, Elizabeth. Moonlight Animals. Lodge, Ali, illus. 2011. (ENG.). 12p. (J). (gr. -1-3). 12.95 *(978-0-7624-4316-1(2))* Running Pr. Bk. Pubs.

Gordon, Sharon. Animales de la Selva Tropical. Victory Productions, Inc. Staff, tr. from ENG. 2008. (Animales Salvajes Ser.). (SPA.). 24p. (gr. k-1). lib. bdg. 15.95 *(978-0-7614-3428-3(3),* Benchmark Bks.) Marshall Cavendish Corp.

Gregoire, Maryellen. Animals in the Forest, 1 vol. 2012. (Wonder Readers Emergent Level Ser.). (ENG.). (gr. -1-1). 32p. pap. 5.99 *(978-1-4296-9193-2(X));* 16p. pap. 35.94 *(978-1-4296-9203-8(0))* Capstone Press of Coughlan Cos. (Wonder Readers).

Groves, Julia, illus. Animal Babies in the Forest! 2016. (Animal Babies Ser.: 4). (ENG.). 14p. (J). bds. *(978-1-84643-878-3(0))* Child's Play International Ltd.

Hess, Paul. Rainforest Animals. Hess, Paul, illus. 2009. (Animal Verse Ser.). (ENG., Illus.). 24p. (J). (gr. -1-k). pap. *(978-1-84089-560-5(8))* Zero to Ten, Ltd.

Hodge, Deborah. Forest Animals. Stephens, Pat, illus. 2009. (Who Lives Here? Ser.). (ENG.). 24p. (J). (gr. -1-2). 5.95 *(978-1-55453-071-7(7));* 14.95 *(978-1-55453-070-0(9))* Kids Can Pr., Ltd. CAN. Dist: Hachette Bk. Group.

—Rain Forest Animals. Stephens, Pat, illus. 2008. (Who Lives Here? Ser.). (ENG.). 24p. (J). (gr. -1-2). 14.95 *(978-1-55453-041-0(5));* pap. 5.95 *(978-1-55453-042-7(3))* Kids Can Pr., Ltd. CAN. Dist: Hachette Bk. Group.

Holland, Trish. Who Lives in Trees? 2010. (Illus.). 24p. (J). *(978-1-60617-131-8(3))* Teaching Strategies, LLC.

Honovich, Nancy. The Field Guide to Rainforest Animals: Explore the Amazon Jungle. 2015. (Field Guides). (ENG., Illus.). 32p. (J). (gr. 2). pap. 15.95 *(978-1-62686-005-6(X),* Silver Dolphin Bks.) Readerlink Distribution Services, LLC.

Jackson, Tom. Parrots & Rainforest Birds: Macaws, Hummingbirds, Flamingos, Toucans & Other Exotic Species, All Shown in More Than 180 Pictures: 2014. (ENG., Illus.). 64p. (J). (gr. -1-3). 12.99 *(978-1-86147-329-5(X),* Armadillo) Anness Publishing GBR. Dist: National Bk. Network.

Jewitt, Kathryn & Dogi, Fiametta. 3D Theater: Rainforest. 2011. (3D Theater Ser.). (ENG., Illus.). 20p. (J). (gr. -1-3). 19.99 *(978-0-7534-6467-0(5),* 9780753464670, Kingfisher) Roaring Brook Pr.

Johnson, Robin. Rain Forests Inside Out. 2014. (ENG.). 32p. (J). *(978-0-7787-0637-3(0))* Crabtree Publishing Co.

Kalman, Bobbie. Baby Animals in Forest Habitats. 2011. (Habitats of Baby Animals Ser.). (ENG.). 24p. (J). (gr. k-3). *(978-0-7787-7726-7(X));* pap. *(978-0-7787-7739-7(1))* Crabtree Publishing Co.

—Baby Animals in Northern Forests. 2013. (ENG., Illus.). 24p. (J). pap. *(978-0-7787-1031-8(9))* Crabtree Publishing Co.

—Baby Animals in Rainforest Habitats. 2011. (ENG.). 24p. (J). pap. *(978-0-7787-7745-8(6))* Crabtree Publishing Co.

Katirgis, Jane. Baby Forest Animals. 2010. (All about Baby Animals Ser.). (Illus.). 24p. (J). pap. 7.95 *(978-1-59845-161-0(8));* lib. bdg. 22.60 *(978-0-7660-3798-4(3))* Enslow Pubs., Inc. (Enslow Elementary).

Kenan, Tessa. Es un Camaleón! 2017. (Bumba Books (tm) en Español — Animales de la Selva Tropical (Rain Forest Animals) Ser.). (SPA., Illus.). 24p. (J). (gr. -1-1). 25.32 ***(978-1-5124-4127-7(9))*** Lerner Publishing Group.

—Es un Chimpancé! 2017. (Bumba Books (tm) en Español — Animales de la Selva Tropical (Rain Forest Animals) Ser.). (SPA., Illus.). 24p. (J). (gr. -1-1). pap. 6.99 ***(978-1-5124-5409-3(5))*** Lerner Publishing Group.

—Es un Jaguar! 2017. (Bumba Books (tm) en Español — Animales de la Selva Tropical (Rain Forest Animals) Ser.). (SPA., Illus.). 24p. (J). (gr. -1-1). pap. 6.99 ***(978-1-5124-5410-9(9))*** Lerner Publishing Group.

—Es un Murciélago Vampiro! 2017. (Bumba Books (tm) en Español — Animales de la Selva Tropical (Rain Forest Animals) Ser.). (SPA.). 24p. (J). (gr. -1-1). 25.32 ***(978-1-5124-4129-1(5))*** Lerner Publishing Group.

—Es una Boa Constrictora! 2017. (Bumba Books (tm) en Español — Animales de la Selva Tropical (Rain Forest Animals) Ser.). (SPA., Illus.). 24p. (J). (gr. -1-1). pap. 6.99 ***(978-1-5124-5407-9(9))*** Lerner Publishing Group.

—Es una Rana Arbórea de Ojos Rojos! 2017. (Bumba Books (tm) en Español — Animales de la Selva Tropical (Rain Forest Animals) Ser.). (SPA.). 24p. (J). (gr. -1-1). 25.32 ***(978-1-5124-4128-4(7))*** Lerner Publishing Group.

—It's a Boa Constrictor! 2017. (Bumba Books (tm) — Rain Forest Animals Ser.). (ENG.). 24p. (J). (gr. -1-1). 25.32 *(978-1-5124-2567-3(2));* 12.99 ***(978-1-5124-3747-8(6),*** Lerner Pubns.); 38.65 ***(978-1-5124-3746-1(8),*** Lerner Pubns.); 38.65 ***(978-1-5124-2757-8(8),*** Lerner Pubns.) Lerner Publishing Group.

—It's a Chameleon! 2017. (Bumba Books (tm) — Rain Forest Animals Ser.). (ENG.). 24p. (J). (gr. -1-1). 12.99 ***(978-1-5124-3750-8(6),*** Lerner Pubns.); 38.65 ***(978-1-5124-3749-2(2),*** Lerner Pubns.); 38.65 ***(978-1-5124-2758-5(6),*** Lerner Pubns.); (Illus.). 25.32 *(978-1-5124-2568-0(0))* Lerner Publishing Group.

—It's a Chimpanzee! 2017. (Bumba Books (tm) — Rain Forest Animals Ser.). (ENG.). 24p. (J). (gr. -1-1). 12.99 ***(978-1-5124-3753-9(0),*** Lerner Pubns.); 38.65 ***(978-1-5124-2759-2(4),*** Lerner Pubns.); 38.65 ***(978-1-5124-3752-2(2),*** Lerner Pubns.); (Illus.). 25.32 *(978-1-5124-2572-7(9))* Lerner Publishing Group.

—It's a Jaguar! 2017. (Bumba Books (tm) — Rain Forest Animals Ser.). (ENG.). 24p. (J). (gr. -1-1). 12.99 ***(978-1-5124-3756-0(5),*** Lerner Pubns.); 38.65 ***(978-1-5124-3755-3(7),*** Lerner Pubns.); 38.65 ***(978-1-5124-2760-8(8),*** Lerner Pubns.); (Illus.). 25.32 *(978-1-5124-2571-0(0))* Lerner Publishing Group.

—It's a Red-Eyed Tree Frog! 2017. (Bumba Books (tm) — Rain Forest Animals Ser.). (ENG.). 24p. (J). (gr. -1-1). 12.99 ***(978-1-5124-3759-1(X),*** Lerner Pubns.); 38.65 ***(978-1-5124-2761-5(6),*** Lerner Pubns.); 38.65 ***(978-1-5124-3758-4(1),*** Lerner Pubns.); (Illus.). 25.32 *(978-1-5124-2569-7(9))* Lerner Publishing Group.

—It's a Vampire Bat! 2017. (Bumba Books (tm) — Rain Forest Animals Ser.). (ENG.). 24p. (J). (gr. -1-1). 12.99 ***(978-1-5124-3762-1(X),*** Lerner Pubns.); 38.65 ***(978-1-5124-3761-4(1),*** Lerner Pubns.); 38.65 ***(978-1-5124-2762-2(4),*** Lerner Pubns.); (Illus.). 25.32 *(978-1-5124-2570-3(2))* Lerner Publishing Group.

Kingfisher Editors. Baby Animals in the Forest. 2011. (Baby Animals Ser.). (ENG., Illus.). 14p. (J). (gr. -1-k). bds. 5.99 *(978-0-7534-6566-0(3),* 9780753465660, Kingfisher) Roaring Brook Pr.

Kopp, Megan. What Do You Find in a Rainforest Tree? 2016. (ENG., Illus.). 24p. (J). *(978-0-7787-2261-8(9))* Crabtree Publishing Co.

Kratter, Paul. The Living Rain Forest: An Animal Alphabet. Kratter, Paul, illus. rev. ed. 2010. (ENG., Illus.). 32p. (J). (gr. 1-4). pap. 7.95 *(978-1-58089-393-0(7))* Charlesbridge Publishing, Inc.

Kuskowski, Alex. A Herd of Deer: Animal Groups in the Forest, 1 vol. 2012. (Animal Groups Ser.). (ENG.). 24p. (J). (gr. k-3). lib. bdg. 24.21 *(978-1-61783-539-1(0),* SandCastle) ABDO Publishing Co.

—Super Simple Forest Critter Crafts: Fun & Easy Animal Crafts. 2016. (ENG., Illus.). 32p. (J). *(978-1-68078-162-5(6))* ABDO Publishing Co.

Levy, Janey. Life in a Rain Forest Ecosystem. 2009. (Science Scope Ser.). 32p. (gr. 5-5). 47.90 *(978-1-60853-054-0(X),* PowerKids Pr.) Rosen Publishing Group, Inc., The.

Lewin, Ted. Can You See Me? Lewin, Ted, illus. 2014. (I Like to Read(r) Ser.). (ENG., Illus.). 24p. (J). (gr. -1-3). 14.95 *(978-0-8234-2940-0(7))* Holiday Hse., Inc.

Lewin, Ted & Lewin, Ted. Can You See Me? 2015. (I Like to Read(r) Ser.). (ENG.). 24p. (J). (gr. -1-3). 6.99 *(978-0-8234-3299-8(8))* Holiday Hse., Inc.

Lewis, J. Patrick. My Home in the Rainforest. 2017. (Rookie Poetry(tm) — Animal Homes Ser.). (ENG., Illus.). 24p. (J). lib. bdg. 25.00 *(978-0-531-22873-9(8),* Children's Pr.) Scholastic Library Publishing.

Lindeen, Mary. Forest Doubles. 2011. (Wonder Readers Fluent Level Ser.). (ENG.). (gr. -1-2). 16p. pap. 35.94 *(978-1-4296-8089-9(X));* 32p. pap. 5.99 *(978-1-4296-7922-0(0))* Capstone Press of Coughlan Cos. (Wonder Readers).

—In the Woods. 2015. (BeginningtoRead Ser.). (ENG.). 32p. (J). (gr. k-2). pap. 11.94 *(978-1-60357-757-1(2));* (Illus.). lib. bdg. 22.60 *(978-1-59953-697-2(8))* Norwood Hse. Pr.

Llewellyn, Claire. Forests, 1 vol. 2012. (Habitat Survival Ser.). (ENG.). 32p. (gr. 2-4). pap. 8.29 *(978-1-4109-4604-1(5));* lib. bdg. 30.65 *(978-1-4109-4595-2(2))* Heinemann-Raintree. (Raintree Perspectives).

Lynette, Rachel. Who Lives in a Wet, Wild Rain Forest? 2010. (Exploring Habitats Ser.). (ENG.). 24p. (J). pap. 8.25 *(978-1-4488-1283-7(6));* lib. bdg. 22.60 *(978-1-4488-0678-2(X))* Rosen Publishing Group, Inc., The. (PowerKids Pr.).

Marianne, Berkes. Over in the Jungle: A Rainforest Rhyme. Jeanette, Canyon, illus. 2008. 26p. (J). (gr. -1). bds. 7.95 *(978-1-58469-108-2(5))* Dawn Pubns.

Markle, Sandra. Finding Olinguito. 2017. (ENG., Illus.). 40p. (J). (gr. 3-6). 30.65 *(978-1-5124-1015-0(2),* Millbrook Pr.) Lerner Publishing Group.

Markle, Sandra. The Search for Olinguito: Discovering a New Species. 2017. (Nonfiction — Grades 4-8 Ser.). (ENG.). 40p. (J). (gr. 3-6). 16.99 ***(978-1-5124-3875-8(8));*** 46.65 ***(978-1-5124-3876-5(6));*** (Illus.). 46.65 ***(978-1-5124-2842-1(6))*** Lerner Publishing Group. (Millbrook Pr.).

Mattern, Joanne. Que Comen los Animales del Bosque?/What Forest Animals Eat. 2006. (Nature's Food Chains/ Las cadenas alimentarias en la naturaleza Ser.). (SPA., Illus.). 24p. (gr. k-3). lib. bdg. 22.00 *(978-0-8368-7372-6(6),* Weekly Reader Leveled Readers) Stevens, Gareth Publishing LLLP.

—What Forest Animals Eat. 2006. (Nature's Food Chains Ser.). (Illus.). 24p. (gr. k-3). pap. 8.15 *(978-0-8368-6878-4(1));* lib. bdg. 22.00 *(978-0-8368-6871-5(4))* Stevens, Gareth Publishing LLLP. (Weekly Reader Leveled Readers).

—What Forest Animals Eat/¿Qué Comen los Animales del Bosque? 2006. (Nature's Food Chains/ Las cadenas alimentarias en la naturaleza Ser.). (ENG & SPA., Illus.). 24p. (gr. k-3). pap. 8.15 *(978-0-8368-7379-5(3),* Weekly Reader Leveled Readers) Stevens, Gareth Publishing LLLP.

McGehee, Claudia. A Woodland Counting Book. 2006. (Bur Oak Book Ser.). (Illus.). 32p. (J). (gr. 3-7). 17.95 *(978-0-87745-989-7(4))* Univ. of Iowa Pr.

McKissack, Fredrick L. & McKissack, Lisa Beringer. Counting in the Rain Forest. 2008. (Counting in the Biomes Ser.). (Illus.). 32p. (J). (gr. 1-3). lib. bdg. 23.94 *(978-0-7660-2992-7(1),* Enslow Elementary) Enslow Pubs., Inc.

—Counting in the Temperate Forest. 2008. (Counting in the Biomes Ser.). (Illus.). 32p. (J). (gr. 1-3). lib. bdg. 23.94 *(978-0-7660-2990-3(5),* Enslow Elementary) Enslow Pubs., Inc.

Miller, Debbie S. Are Trees Alive? Schuett, Stacey, illus. 2003. (ENG.). 32p. (J). (gr. -1-3). 17.99 *(978-0-8027-8801-6(7),* 9780802788016, Bloomsbury USA Childrens) Bloomsbury Publishing USA.

Morgan, Sally. Under a Leaf in Forests & Jungles. 2006. (Hidden Habitats Ser.). (J). *(978-1-59389-284-5(5))* Chrysalis Education.

Murray, Aaron R. Counting in the Forest 1-2-3. 2012. (All about Counting in the Biomes Ser.). (Illus.). 24p. (J). (gr. -1-1). 22.60 *(978-0-7660-4053-3(4))* Enslow Pubs., Inc.

National Geographic Kids Staff & Evans, Shira. In the Forest. 2016. (Readers Ser.). (ENG., Illus.). 48p. (J). (-k). pap. 4.99 *(978-1-4263-2621-9(1),* National Geographic Children's Bks.) National Geographic Society.

Neuman, Susan B. Swing, Sloth! Explore the Rain Forest. 2014. (Readers Ser.). (ENG., Illus.). 24p. (J). (-k). pap. 3.99 *(978-1-4263-1506-0(6),* National Geographic Children's Bks.) National Geographic Society.

Newland, Sonya. Woodland & Forest Animals. 2011. (Saving Wildlife Ser.). 32p. (gr. 4-7). 31.35 *(978-1-59920-662-2(5))* Black Rabbit Bks.

Ottina, Laura. In the Forest. Ranchetti, Sebastiano, illus. 2009. (Learn with Animals Ser.). (ENG.). 24p. (J). (gr. -1-2). pap. 8.15 *(978-1-4339-2089-9(1));* lib. bdg. 22.00 *(978-1-4339-1912-1(5))* Stevens, Gareth Publishing LLLP. (Weekly Reader Leveled Readers).

Patent, Dorothy Hinshaw. Flashy Fantastic Rain Forest Frogs. Jubb, Kendahl Jan, illus. 2015. 32p. pap. 8.00 *(978-1-61003-544-6(5))* Center for the Collaborative Classroom.

Peluso, Beth A. The Charcoal Forest: How Fire Helps Animals & Plants. Peluso, Beth A., illus. 2007. (Illus.). 56p. (J). (gr. -1-3). pap. 12.00 *(978-0-87842-532-7(2))* Mountain Pr. Publishing Co., Inc.

Pettiford, Rebecca. Rain Forest Food Chains. 2016. (Who Eats What?). 24p. (J). (gr. 2-5). lib. bdg. 25.65 *(978-1-62031-304-6(9),* Pogo) Jump! Inc.

Phillips, Dee. Find It in a Rain Forest. 2006. (Can You Find It? Ser.). (Illus.). 24p. (gr. k-3). lib. bdg. 23.00 *(978-0-8368-6299-7(6),* Gareth Stevens Learning Library) Stevens, Gareth Publishing LLLP.

Radley, Gail. Forests & Jungles. Sherlock, Jean, illus. (Vanishing from Ser.). 32p. 2005. (gr. 6-12). lib. bdg. 22.60 *(978-1-57505-405-6(1))* 2003. (J). (gr. 3-5). 6.95 *(978-1-57505-567-1(8))* Lerner Publishing Group.

Rake, Matthew. Creatures of the Rain Forest. Mendez, Simon, illus. 2015. (Real-Life Monsters Ser.). (ENG.). 32p. (J). (gr. 3-6). lib. bdg. 26.65 *(978-1-4677-6363-9(2))* Lerner Publishing Group.

Rissman, Rebecca. Counting in the Forest, 1 vol. 2012. (I Can Count! Ser.). (ENG.). 24p. (J). (gr. -1-k). pap. 9.95 *(978-1-4329-6698-0(7));* lib. bdg. 25.32 *(978-1-4329-6693-5(6))* Heinemann-Raintree.

Rivera, Sheila. Forest. 2005. (Illus.). 24p. (J). pap. 5.95 *(978-0-8225-5371-7(6));* (ENG., lib. bdg. 23.93 *(978-0-8225-2596-7(8),* Lerner Pubns.) Lerner Publishing Group.

Rustad, Martha E. H. Animal Camouflage in the Forest [Scholastic]. 2010. (Hidden in Nature Ser.). pap. 0.52 *(978-1-4296-5047-2(8),* Pebble Plus) Capstone Press of Coughlan Cos.

Salas, Laura Purdie. Temperate Deciduous Forests: Lands of Falling Leaves, 1 vol. Yesh, Jeff, illus. 2007. (Amazing Science: Ecosystems Ser.). (ENG.). 24p. (J). (gr. k-3). lib. bdg. 25.99 *(978-1-4048-3099-8(5),* Nonfiction Picture Bks.) Picture Window Bks.

Scholastic, Inc. Staff, contrib. by. Bedtime for Rainforest Babies. 2016. (Rookie Toddler(tm) Ser.). (ENG.). 12p. (J). bds. 6.95 *(978-0-531-22697-1(2),* Children's Pr.) Scholastic Library Publishing.

Scott, Janine. Rain Forest Life, 1 vol. 2011. (Habitats Around the World Ser.). (ENG.). 24p. (gr. k-1). pap. 7.29 *(978-1-4296-7152-1(1));* pap. 41.70 *(978-1-4296-7156-9(4))* Capstone Press of Coughlan Cos. (Pebble Plus).

Senisi, Ellen B. All in a Rainforest Day. Marent, Thomas, photos by. (Illus.). (J). 2016. (ENG.). (gr. -1-3). pap. 7.95 ***(978-0-9912337-1-7(9))*** 2016. (gr. -1-3). 45.99 ***(978-0-9912337-2-4(7))*** 2014. (ENG., 32p. 17.95 *(978-0-9912337-0-0(0))* EdTechLens.

Serafini, Frank. Looking Closely Through the Forest, 0 vols. Serafini, Frank, illus. 2014. (Looking Closely Ser.). (ENG., Illus.). 40p. (J). (gr. -1-2). pap. 7.95 *(978-1-77138-118-5(3))* Kids Can Pr., Ltd. CAN. Dist: Hachette Bk. Group.

Sharp, Zoe, et al. In the Tree. 2007. (Windows on Literacy Ser.). (ENG., Illus.). 12p. (J). pap. 10.95 *(978-0-7922-8461-1(5))* CENGAGE Learning.

Silverman, Buffy. Let's Visit the Rain Forest. 2016. (Lightning Bolt Books (tm) — Biome Explorers Ser.). (ENG.). 32p. (J). (gr. 1-3). 26.65 *(978-1-5124-1195-9(7))* Lerner Publishing Group.

Sovak, Jan. Lost in the Amazon: Hidden Pictures. 2011. (Dover Children's Activity Bks.). (ENG., Illus.). 48p. (J). (gr. 3-6). pap. 4.99 *(978-0-486-48230-9(8))* Dover Pubns., Inc.

Spilsbury, Louise & Spilsbury, Richard. A Nature Walk in the Woods, 1 vol. 2014. (Nature Walks Ser.). (ENG., Illus.). 24p. (gr. k-2). 23.32 *(978-1-4846-0403-8(2),* Heinemann Read & Learn) Heinemann-Raintree.

Summers, Portia & Grady, Colin. The Deciduous Forest Biome. 2016. (Zoom in on Biomes Ser.). (Illus.). 24p. (J). (gr. 2-2). pap. 9.35 *(978-0-7660-7748-5(9))* Enslow Pubs., Inc.

Underwood, Deborah. Hiding in Forests, 1 vol. 2010. (Creature Camouflage Ser.). (ENG.). 32p. (gr. 1-3). 27.32 *(978-1-4329-4022-5(8),* Heinemann First Library) Heinemann-Raintree.

—Hiding in Rain Forests, 1 vol. 2010. (Creature Camouflage Ser.). (ENG.). 32p. (gr. 1-3). pap. 8.29 *(978-1-4329-4035-5(X),* Heinemann First Library) Heinemann-Raintree.

Wallace, Marianne D. America's Forests: Guide to Plants & Animals. 2009. (America's Ecosystems Ser.). (ENG.). 48p. (J). (gr. 1-5). pap. 11.95 *(978-1-55591-595-7(7))* Fulcrum Publishing.

Waxman, Laura Hamilton. Life in a Forest. 2016. (Biomes Alive! Ser.). (ENG., Illus.). 24p. (J). (gr. k-3). lib. bdg. 25.95 *(978-1-62617-317-0(6),* Blastoff! Readers) Bellwether Media.

World Book, Inc Staff, contrib. by. Seasonal Forests. 2012. (J). *(978-0-7166-0444-0(2))* World Bk., Inc.

—Tropical Regions & Rain Forests. 2012. (J). *(978-0-7166-0449-5(3));* (Illus.). 48p. *(978-0-7166-0441-9(8))* World Bk., Inc.

E
F
G

Zondervan Staff. Rainforest Friends, 1 vol. 2011. (I Can Read! / Made by God Ser.). (ENG.). 32p. (J). pap. 3.99 *(978-0-310-72182-6(2))* Zonderkidz.

Zorzi, Gina & Sánchez, Lucía M. Bosques: This Is a Forest. 2011. (2G Ecosistemas Ser.). (SPA.). 28p. (J). (gr. k-2). pap. 6.99 *(978-1-61541-426-0(6))* American Reading Co.

Zorzi, Gina & Sanchez, Lucia M. Bosques (This Is a Forest) 2011. (poder de 100 - Ecosistemas Ser.). 28p. pap. 45.32 *(978-1-61541-427-7(4))* American Reading Co.

FOREST CONSERVATION

see Forests and Forestry

FOREST ECOLOGY

see also Rain Forest Ecology

Allgor, Marie. Endangered Forest Animals. 2012. (Save Earth's Animals! Ser.). (ENG., Illus.). 24p. (J). (gr. k-5). pap. 8.25 *(978-1-4488-7497-2(1))*; lib. bdg. 22.60 *(978-1-4488-7424-8(6))* Rosen Publishing Group, Inc., The. (PowerKids Pr.).

Amstutz, Lisa J. What Eats What in a Forest Food Chain, 1 vol. McLaughlin, Zack, illus. 2012. (Food Chains Ser.). (ENG.). 24p. (gr. 2-3). 25.99 *(978-1-4048-7388-9(0))*; pap. 8.95 *(978-1-4048-7692-7(8))* Picture Window Bks.

—What Eats What in a Rain Forest Food Chain, 1 vol. Wertheim, Anne, illus. 2012. (Food Chains Ser.). (ENG.). 24p. (gr. 2-3). 25.99 *(978-1-4048-7387-2(2))*; pap. 8.95 *(978-1-4048-7694-1(4))* Picture Window Bks.

Aspen-Baxter, Linda. Rainforests. 2011. (J). (gr. 5-8). pap. 13.95 *(978-1-61690-646-7(4)*, AV2 by Weigl); (Illus.). 32p. (gr. 2-5). 28.55 *(978-1-61690-640-5(5))* Weigl Pubs., Inc.

Benoit, Peter. Temperate Forests. 2011. (True Bk Ser.). (Illus.). 48p. (J). (ENG.). pap. 6.95 *(978-0-531-28101-7(9))*; (gr. 3-5). 29.00 *(978-0-531-20552-5(5))* Scholastic Library Publishing. (Children's Pr.).

Blomgren, Jennifer. Where Would I Be in an Evergreen Tree? Gabriel, Andrea, illus. 2011. (ENG.). 32p. (J). (gr. -1-2). pap. 10.99 *(978-1-57061-753-9(8)*, Little Bigfoot) Sasquatch Bks.

Boothroyd, Jennifer. Let's Visit the Deciduous Forest. 2016. (Lightning Bolt Books (tm) — Biome Explorers Ser.). (ENG., Illus.). 32p. (J). (gr. 1-3). 26.65 *(978-1-5124-1189-8(2))* Lerner Publishing Group.

Bow, James. Forests Inside Out. 2015. (ENG.). 32p. (J). *(978-0-7787-1495-8(0))* Crabtree Publishing Co.

Brenner, Barbara. One Small Place in a Tree. Leonard, Tom, illus. 2004. (ENG.). 32p. (J). (gr. k-3). 17.99 *(978-0-688-17180-3(X))* HarperCollins Pubs.

Callery, Sean. Life Cycles: Forest. 2013. (Lifecycles Ser.). (ENG., Illus.). 32p. (J). (gr. 2-5). 6.99 *(978-0-7534-7065-7(9)*, 9780753470657, Kingfisher) Roaring Brook Pr.

Carlisi, Alison & Foxx, Teralene S. The Forest & the Fire. 2005. (Illus.). (J). 15.00 *(978-0-941232-31-9(X))* Bathtub Row Pr.

Cefrey, Holly. The Coniferous Forest. 2009. (Biomes Ser.). 24p. (gr. 2-3). 42.50 *(978-1-61511-593-8(5)*, PowerKids Pr.) Rosen Publishing Group, Inc., The.

—Coniferous Forests. 2003. (Biomes Ser.). (Illus.). 24p. (J). lib. bdg. 22.60 *(978-0-8239-6455-0(8)*, PowerKids Pr.) Rosen Publishing Group, Inc., The.

—The Deciduous Forest. (Biomes Ser.). 24p. 2009. (gr. 2-3). 42.50 *(978-1-61511-594-5(3))* 2003. (Illus.). (J). lib. bdg. 22.60 *(978-0-8239-6454-3(X))* Rosen Publishing Group, Inc., The. (PowerKids Pr.).

Cleavitt, Natalie. Seeking the Wolf Tree. Leggitt, Marjorie, illus. 2015. (Long Term Ecological Research Ser.). (ENG.). 32p. (J). (gr. 3-7). 15.95 *(978-1-63076-145-5(1))* Taylor Trade Publishing.

Cole, Melissa S. Forest. 2003. (Wild America Habitats Ser.). (Illus.). 24p. (J). 21.20 *(978-1-56711-802-5(X)*, Blackbirch Pr., Inc.) Cengage Gale.

Dorling Kindersley Publishing Staff & Lock, Deborah. Forest. 2003. (ENG., Illus.). 48p. (J). (gr. 6-6). 10.99 *(978-0-7894-9759-8(X)*, DK Children) Dorling Kindersley Publishing, Inc.

Eshbach, Charles. Twig's Guide to My Old Growth Forest. 2012. (ENG.). pap. *(978-1-4675-2565-7(0))* Independent Pub.

Fleisher, Paul. Early Bird Food Webs. 2008. pap. 52.95 *(978-0-8225-9054-5(9))*; pap. 316.95 *(978-0-8225-9196-2(0))* Lerner Publishing Group.

—Forest Food Webs. 2008. pap. 52.95 *(978-0-8225-9349-2(1))* 2007. (Illus.). 48p. (J). (gr. 2-5). lib. bdg. 26.60 *(978-0-8225-6729-5(6)*, Lerner Pubns.) Lerner Publishing Group.

—Forest Food Webs in Action. 2013. (Searchlight Books What Is a Food Web Ser.). (ENG., Illus.). 40p. (gr. 3-5). pap. 8.95 *(978-1-4677-1553-9(0))*; lib. bdg. 27.93 *(978-1-4677-1254-5(X)*, Lerner Pubns.) Lerner Publishing Group.

Flounders, Anne. Healthy Trees, Healthy Planet. 2014. (Our Green Earth Ser.). (Illus.). 32p. (gr. 2-4). pap. 8.95 *(978-1-939656-32-2(X))* Red Chair Pr.

Food and Agriculture Organization of the United Nations Staff & Youth and United Nations Global Alliance Staff. The Youth Guide to Forests. 2014. (ENG.). 236p. pap. 54.00 *(978-92-5-108435-9(1))* Food & Agriculture Organization of the United Nations ITA. Dist: Rowman & Littlefield Publishers, Inc.

A Forest Ecosystem. 2012. (Nature Trail Ser.). (ENG., Illus.). 32p. (J). (gr. k-5). 23.95 *(978-1-4488-6641-0(3)*, PowerKids Pr.) Rosen Publishing Group, Inc., The.

Forest Habitats. 2013. (Discovery Education: Habitats Ser.). 32p. (J). (gr. 3-6). pap. 60.00 *(978-1-4777-1488-1(X)*, PowerKids Pr.) Rosen Publishing Group, Inc., The.

Franchino, Vicky. South American Cloud Forest. 2016. (Community Connections: Getting to Know Our Planet Ser.). (ENG., Illus.). 24p. (J). (gr. 2-5). 27.07 *(978-1-63470-519-6(X)*, 207807) Cherry Lake Publishing.

Gaarder-Juntti, Oona. What Lives in the Forest?, 1 vol. 2008. (Animal Habitats Ser.). (ENG., Illus.). 24p. (J). (gr. k-3). 25.65 *(978-1-60453-174-9(6))* ABDO Publishing Co.

Gagne, Tammy. Forest Ecosystems. 2018. (ENG.). 32p. (gr. 3-6). ***(978-1-63235-455-6(1)***, 12-Story Library) Pr. Room Editions LLC.

Gardeski, Christina Mia. All about Forests. 2017. (Habitats Ser.). (ENG.). 24p. (gr. k-1). lib. bdg. 21.99 ***(978-1-5157-7638-3(7)***, Pebble Bks.) Capstone Press of Coughlan Cos.

Gardner, Robert. Temperate Forest Expements: 8 Science Experiments in One Hour or Less. 2014. (Last Minute Science Projects with Biomes Ser.). 48p. (J). (gr. 5-12). 25.27 *(978-0-7660-5922-1(7))* Enslow Pubs., Inc.

—Temperate Forest Experiments: 8 Science Experiments in One Hour or Less. 2014. (Last Minute Science Projects with Biomes Ser.). (Illus.). 48p. (YA). (gr. 5-12). pap. 8.95 *(978-0-7660-5923-8(5)*, Enslow Elementary) Enslow Pubs., Inc.

Group/McGraw-Hill, Wright. La Vida en la Selva Tropical, 6 vols., Vol. 2. (First Explorers. Primeros Exploradores Nonfiction Sets Ser.). (SPA.). (gr. 1-2). 29.95 *(978-0-7699-1487-9(X))* Shortland Pubns. (U. S. A.) Inc.

Guiberson, Brenda Z. Life in the Boreal Forest. Spirin, Gennady, illus. 2009. (ENG.). 40p. (J). (gr. k-4). 18.99 *(978-0-8050-7718-6(9)*, 9780805077186, Holt, Henry & Co. Bks. For Young Readers) Holt, Henry & Co.

Heos, Bridget. Do You Really Want to Visit a Temperate Forest? Fabbri, Daniele, illus. 2014. (Do You Really Want to Visit... ? Ser.). (ENG.). 24p. (J). (gr. 1-4). lib. bdg. 27.10 *(978-1-60753-451-8(7))* Amicus Publishing.

Hurtig, Jennifer. Deciduous Forests. (J). 2011. (gr. 5-8). pap. 13.95 *(978-1-61690-647-4(2)*, AV2 by Weigl) 2011. (Illus.). 32p. (gr. 2-5). 28.55 *(978-1-61690-641-2(3))* 2006. 9.95 *(978-1-59036-441-3(4))* Weigl Pubs., Inc.

Hyde, Natalie. Amazon Rainforest Research Journal. 2017. (Illus.). 32p. (J). ***(978-0-7787-3467-3(6))***; pap. ***(978-0-7787-3492-5(7))*** Crabtree Publishing Co.

Johansson, Philip. The Taiga: Discover This Forested Biome. 2015. (Discover the World's Biomes Ser.). 48p. (J). (gr. 3-4). pap. 8.95 *(978-0-7660-6411-9(5)*, Enslow Elementary) Enslow Pubs., Inc.

—The Temperate Forest: Discover This Wooded Biome. 2015. (Discover the World's Biomes Ser.). 48p. (J). (gr. 3-4). pap. 8.95 *(978-0-7660-6416-4(6))*; lib. bdg. 25.27 *(978-0-7660-6415-7(8))* Enslow Pubs., Inc. (Enslow Elementary).

Kalman, Bobbie. Baby Animals in Forest Habitats. 2011. (Habitats of Baby Animals Ser.). (ENG.). 24p. (J). (gr. k-3). *(978-0-7787-7726-7(X))*; pap. *(978-0-7787-7739-7(1))* Crabtree Publishing Co.

—Baby Animals in Northern Forests. 2013. (ENG., Illus.). 24p. (J). pap. *(978-0-7787-1031-8(9))* Crabtree Publishing Co.

—Cadenas Alimentarias del Bosque. 2006. (Cadenas Alimentarias Ser.). (SPA., Illus.). 32p. (J). (gr. 3-7). lib. bdg. *(978-0-7787-8529-3(7))* Crabtree Publishing Co.

—Forest Food Chains. 2004. (Food Chains Ser.). (ENG., Illus.). 32p. (J). pap. *(978-0-7787-1989-2(8))*; lib. bdg. *(978-0-7787-1943-4(X))* Crabtree Publishing Co.

—A Forest Habitat. 2006. (Introducing Habitats Ser.). (ENG., Illus.). 32p. (J). (gr. 3-7). pap. *(978-0-7787-2979-2(6))*; lib. bdg. *(978-0-7787-2951-8(6))* Crabtree Publishing Co.

—Un Habitat de Bosque. 2007. (Introduction a Los Habitats Ser.). (SPA., Illus.). 32p. (J). (gr. 3-7). lib. bdg. *(978-0-7787-8327-5(8))* Crabtree Publishing Co.

—Un Hábitat de Bosque. rev. ed. 2007. (Introduccion a Los Habitats/Introducing Habitats Ser.). (SPA., Illus.). 32p. (J). (gr. k-3). pap. *(978-0-7787-8351-0(0))* Crabtree Publishing Co.

Kalman, Bobbie & Smithyman, Kathryn. La Foret. 2004. (Petit Monde Vivant Ser.). (FRE., Illus.). 32p. (J). pap. 10.95 *(978-2-89579-012-9(4))* Bayard Canada Livres CAN. Dist: Crabtree Publishing Co.

Kawa, Katie. Forest Food Chains, 1 vol. 2015. (ENG., Illus.). 24p. (J). lib. bdg. 23.60 *(978-1-4777-5997-4(2)*, PowerKids Pr.) Rosen Publishing Group, Inc., The.

King, Zelda. Examining Forest Habitats. 2009. (Graphic Organizers: Habitats Ser.). 24p. (gr. 2-4). (Illus.). (J). pap. 8.25 *(978-1-4358-3122-3(5))*; 42.50 *(978-1-61513-094-8(2))*; (J). lib. bdg. 22.60 *(978-1-4358-2718-9(X))* Rosen Publishing Group, Inc., The. (PowerKids Pr.).

Knowles, Laura. Once upon a Jungle. Boast, James, illus. 2017. (ENG.). 32p. (J). (gr. k-3). 18.95 ***(978-1-77085-971-5(3)***, 9781770859715) Firefly Bks., Ltd.

Laber-Warren, Emily. A Walk in the Woods: Into the Field Guide. 2013. (ENG.). 112p. (J). (gr. k). pap. 9.99 *(978-1-935703-26-6(9))* Downtown Bookworks.

LaPlante, Walter. There's a Forest in My Backyard! 2016. (Backyard Biomes Ser.). 00024p. (J). pap. 8.15 *(978-1-4824-5559-5(5))* Stevens, Gareth Publishing LLLP.

Llewellyn, Claire. Forests, 1 vol. 2012. (Habitat Survival Ser.). (ENG.). 32p. (gr. 2-4). pap. 8.29 *(978-1-4109-4604-1(5))*; lib. bdg. 30.65 *(978-1-4109-4595-2(2))* Heinemann-Raintree. (Raintree Perspectives).

Lynette, Rachel. Who Lives in a Wet, Wild Rain Forest? 2010. (Exploring Habitats Ser.). (ENG.). 24p. (J). pap. 8.25 *(978-1-4488-1283-7(6))*; lib. bdg. 22.60 *(978-1-4488-0678-2(X))* Rosen Publishing Group, Inc., The. (PowerKids Pr.).

MacMillan, Dianne M. Life in a Deciduous Forest. 2003. (Ecosystems in Action Ser.). (ENG., Illus.). 72p. (gr. 5-9). 26.60 *(978-0-8225-4684-9(1))* Lerner Publishing Group.

McFadzean, Lesley. Forest Habitats. 2013. (Discovery Education: Habitats Ser.). 32p. (J). (gr. 3-6). 25.25 *(978-1-4777-1326-6(3))*; pap. 10.00 *(978-1-4777-1487-4(1))* Rosen Publishing Group, Inc., The. (PowerKids Pr.).

McKissack, Fredrick L. & McKissack, Lisa Beringer. Counting in the Temperate Forest. 2008. (Counting in the Biomes Ser.). (Illus.). 32p. (J). (gr. 1-3). lib. bdg. 23.94 *(978-0-7660-2990-3(5)*, Enslow Elementary) Enslow Pubs., Inc.

McNeil, Niki, et al. Forest Habitats. 2007. (In the Hands of a Child: Custom Designed Project Pack Ser.). (Illus.). 96p. spiral bd. 22.50 *(978-1-60308-099-6(6))* In the Hands of a Child.

Miller, Debbie S. Are Trees Alive? Schuett, Stacey, illus. 2003. (ENG.). 32p. (J). (gr. -1-3). 17.99 *(978-0-8027-8801-6(7)*, 9780802788016, Bloomsbury USA Childrens) Bloomsbury Publishing USA.

Miller-Schroeder, Patricia. Boreal Forests. (J). 2011. (gr. 5-8). pap. 13.95 *(978-1-61690-648-1(0)*, AV2 by Weigl) 2011. (Illus.). 32p. (gr. 2-5). 28.55 *(978-1-61690-642-9(1))* 2005. (Illus.). 32p. (gr. 3-7). per. 9.95 *(978-1-59036-351-5(5))* Weigl Pubs., Inc.

Moore, Peter D. & Garratt, Richard. Tropical Forests. 2007. (Ecosystems Ser.). (Illus.). 272p. (C). (gr. 9). 70.00 *(978-0-8160-5934-8(9))* Facts On File, Inc.

Morgan, Sally. Under a Leaf in Forests & Jungles. 2006. (Hidden Habitats Ser.). (J). *(978-1-59389-284-5(5))* Chrysalis Education.

Murray, Aaron R. Counting in the Forest 1-2-3. 2012. (All about Counting in the Biomes Ser.). (Illus.). 24p. (J). (gr. -1-1). 22.60 *(978-0-7660-4053-3(4))* Enslow Pubs., Inc.

Nagle, Jeanne. Coniferous Forests: An Evergreen World. 2009. (Biomes of the World Ser.). 48p. (gr. 5-8). 53.00 *(978-1-61511-596-9(X)*, Rosen Reference) Rosen Publishing Group, Inc., The.

—Deciduous Forests: Seasons of Survival. 2009. (Biomes of the World Ser.). 48p. (gr. 5-8). (ENG., Illus.). (J). pap. 11.75 *(978-1-4358-5427-7(6))*; 53.00 *(978-1-61511-599-0(4)*, Rosen Reference); (YA). lib. bdg. 29.25 *(978-1-4358-5001-9(7))* Rosen Publishing Group, Inc., The.

Nagle, Jeanne M. Coniferous Forests: An Evergreen World. 2009. (Biomes of the World Ser.). 48p. (gr. 5-8). (ENG., Illus.). (J). pap. 11.75 *(978-1-4358-5426-0(8))*; (YA). lib. bdg. 29.25 *(978-1-4358-5000-2(9))* Rosen Publishing Group, Inc., The.

National Geographic Kids Staff & Evans, Shira. In the Forest. 2016. (Readers Ser.). (ENG., Illus.). 48p. (J). (-k). pap. 4.99 *(978-1-4263-2621-9(1)*, National Geographic Children's Bks.) National Geographic Society.

Newland, Sonya. Woodland & Forest Animals. 2011. (Saving Wildlife Ser.). 32p. (gr. 4-7). 31.35 *(978-1-59920-662-2(5))* Black Rabbit Bks.

Owen, Ruth. Welcome to the Forest. 2016. (Nature's Neighborhoods: All about Ecosystems Ser.). (ENG.). 32p. (J). (gr. -1-3). lib. bdg. 19.95 *(978-1-910549-64-3(9))* Bearport Publishing Co., Inc.

Peluso, Beth A. The Charcoal Forest: How Fire Helps Animals & Plants. Peluso, Beth A., illus. 2007. (Illus.). 56p. (J). (gr. -1-3). pap. 12.00 *(978-0-87842-532-7(2))* Mountain Pr. Publishing Co., Inc.

Pfeffer, Wendy. A Log's Life. Brickman, Robin, illus. 2007. (ENG.). 32p. (J). (gr. -1-3). 6.99 *(978-1-4169-3483-7(9)*, Aladdin) Simon & Schuster Children's Publishing.

Pyers, Greg. Biodiversity of Temperate Forests. 2011. (Biodiversity 2 Ser.). (Illus.). 32p. (J). (gr. 4). 28.50 *(978-1-60870-532-0(3))* Marshall Cavendish GBR. Dist: Marshall Cavendish Corp.

—Biodiversity of Woodlands. 2010. (Biodiversity Ser.). 32p. (gr. 4-18). 28.50 *(978-1-60870-074-5(7))* Marshall Cavendish Corp.

Quinlan, Susan E. The Case of the Monkeys That Fell from the Trees: And Other Mysteries in Tropical Nature. 2010. (ENG.). 172p. (J). (gr. 4-6). pap. 10.95 *(978-1-59078-775-5(7))* Boyds Mills Pr.

Raven, Catherine. Forestry. 2006. (Green World Ser.). (Illus.). 125p. (gr. 6-12). lib. bdg. 37.50 *(978-0-7910-8752-7(2))* Facts On File, Inc.

Rice, Bill. Survival! Jungle, 1 vol. 2nd rev. ed. 2013. (Nonfiction Readers Ser.). (ENG., Illus.). 48p. (J). (gr. 4-4). pap. 29.96 *(978-1-4807-1096-2(2))* Shell Educational Publishing.

Rivera, Sheila. Forest. 2005. (Illus.). 24p. (J). pap. 5.95 *(978-0-8225-5371-7(6))* Lerner Publishing Group.

Russo, Monica. Treecology: 30 Activities & Observations for Exploring the World of Trees & Forests. Byron, Kevin, photos by. 2016. (Young Naturalists Ser.). (ENG., Illus.). 144p. (J). (gr. 2). pap. 15.99 *(978-1-61373-396-7(8))* Chicago Review Pr., Inc.

Saunders, Gary L. My Life with Trees: A Sylvan Journey. 2015. (ENG.). 256p. pap. *(978-1-55447-151-5(6))* Gaspereau Pr.

Schaefer, Lola M. & Schaefer, Adam. Acorn. Preston-Gannon, Frann, illus. 2016. (ENG.). 36p. (J). (gr. -1-k). 16.99 *(978-1-4521-1242-8(8))* Chronicle Bks. LLC.

Scraper, Katherine. What Is in a Forest? 2006. (Early Explorers Ser.). (J). pap. *(978-1-4108-6022-4(1))* Benchmark Education Co.

Sharp, Zoe, et al. In the Tree. 2007. (Windows on Literacy Ser.). (ENG., Illus.). 12p. (J). pap. 10.95 *(978-0-7922-8461-1(5))* CENGAGE Learning.

Silverman, Buffy. Let's Visit the Evergreen Forest. 2016. (Lightning Bolt Books (tm) — Biome Explorers Ser.). (ENG., Illus.). 32p. (J). (gr. 1-3). 26.65 *(978-1-5124-1191-1(4))* Lerner Publishing Group.

—Let's Visit the Rain Forest. 2016. (Lightning Bolt Books (tm) — Biome Explorers Ser.). (ENG.). 32p. (J). (gr. 1-3). 26.65 *(978-1-5124-1195-9(7))* Lerner Publishing Group.

Slade, Suzanne. What If There Were No Gray Wolves? A Book about the Temperate Forest Ecosystem, 1 vol. Schwartz, Carol, illus. 2010. (Food Chain Reactions Ser.). (ENG.). 24p. (gr. 2-4). pap. 9.95 *(978-1-4048-6395-8(8))* Picture Window Bks.

Spilsbury, Louise & Spilsbury, Richard. A Nature Walk in the Woods, 1 vol. 2014. (Nature Walks Ser.). (ENG., Illus.). 24p. (gr. k-2). 23.32 *(978-1-4846-0403-8(2)*, Heinemann Read & Learn) Heinemann-Raintree.

Staub, Frank J., photos by. America's Forests & Woodlands. 2006. (Illus.). 48p. (J). pap. *(978-1-59034-806-2(0))* Mondo Publishing.

Stille, Darlene R. Protecting Land. 2011. (Go Green! Ser.). (ENG., Illus.). 32p. (J). (gr. 1-4). lib. bdg. 28.50 *(978-1-60973-175-5(1)*, 201154) Child's World, Inc., The.

Stone, Lynn M. Forests. 2003. (Rourke Discovery Library). (Illus.). 24p. (J). 20.64 *(978-1-58952-684-6(8))* Rourke Educational Media.

Summers, Portia & Grady, Colin. The Deciduous Forest Biome. 2016. (Zoom in on Biomes Ser.). (Illus.). 24p. (J). (gr. 2-2). pap. 9.35 *(978-0-7660-7748-5(9))* Enslow Pubs., Inc.

Taylor, Trace & Sanchez, Lucia M. En el bosque (in the Woods) 2011. (Lugares adonde voy Ser.). (SPA.). 16p. pap. 39.62 *(978-1-61541-457-4(6))* American Reading Co.

Taylor, Trace, et al. En el Bosque. 2011. (2Y Lugares Adonde Voy Ser.).Tr. of In the Woods. (SPA.). 12p. (J). (gr. k-2). pap. 6.99 *(978-1-61541-456-7(8))* American Reading Co.

Tocci, Salvatore. Life in the Temperate Forests. 2005. (Watts Library). (ENG., Illus.). 64p. (J). (gr. 5-7). lib. bdg. 25.50 *(978-0-531-12363-8(4)*, Watts, Franklin) Scholastic Library Publishing.

Vasillu, Michelle. The Future of Forests. 2007. (Action Numeracy Middle Primary Ser.). 32p. pap. 9.95 *(978-0-86431-678-3(X))* ACER Pr. AUS. Dist: ISBS Publisher Services.

Vogel, Julia. Deciduous Forest Food Chains, 1 vol. Adams, Hazel, illus. 2010. (Fascinating Food Chains Ser.). (ENG.). 32p. 28.50 *(978-1-60270-792-4(8)*, Looking Glass Library-Nonfiction) Magic Wagon.

Wallace, Marianne D. America's Forests: Guide to Plants & Animals. 2009. (America's Ecosystems Ser.). (ENG.). 48p. (J). (gr. 1-5). pap. 11.95 *(978-1-55591-595-7(7))* Fulcrum Publishing.

Warhol, Tom. Forest. 2006. (Earth's Biomes Ser.). (Illus.). 80p. (J). lib. bdg. 32.79 *(978-0-7614-2189-4(0)*, Benchmark Bks.) Marshall Cavendish Corp.

Waxman, Laura Hamilton. Life in a Forest. 2016. (Biomes Alive! Ser.). (ENG., Illus.). 24p. (J). (gr. k-3). lib. bdg. 25.95 *(978-1-62617-317-0(6)*, Blastoff! Readers) Bellwether Media.

Welch, Martha Mckeen. Close Looks in a Spring Woods. 2011. (J). *(978-0-396-07998-9(9))* Dodd, Mead & Co., U. S.

Wojahn, Rebecca Hogue & Donald. A Rain Forest Food Chain: A Who-Eats-What Adventures in South America. 2009. pap. 58.95 *(978-0-7613-4660-9(0))* Lerner Publishing Group.

—A Savanna Food Chain: A Who-Eats-What Adventure in Africa. 2009. pap. 58.95 *(978-0-7613-4661-6(9))* Lerner Publishing Group.

—A Tundra Food Chain: A Who-Eats-What in the Arctic. 2009. pap. 58.95 *(978-0-7613-4663-0(5))* Lerner Publishing Group.

Wojahn, Rebecca Hogue & Wojahn, Donald. A Cloud Forest Food Chain: A Who-Eats-What Adventure in Africa. 2009. (Follow That Food Chain Ser.). (ENG.). 64p. (gr. 3-5). 30.60 *(978-0-8225-7612-9(0))* Lerner Publishing Group.

—An Estuary Food Chain: A Who-Eats-What Adventure in North America. 2009. (Follow That Food Chain Ser.). (ENG., Illus.). 64p. (J). (gr. 3-5). 30.60 *(978-0-8225-7616-7(3))* Lerner Publishing Group.

—A Temperate Forest Food Chain: A Who-Eats-What Adventure in North America. 2009. (Follow That Food Chain Ser.). (ENG.). 64p. (gr. 3-5). pap. 9.95 *(978-0-7613-4191-8(9))* Lerner Publishing Group.

Woodward, John. Temperate Forests, 1 vol. 2nd ed. 2010. (Biomes Atlases Ser.). (ENG., Illus.). 64p. (gr. 6-9). 34.65 *(978-1-4329-4180-2(1))* Heinemann-Raintree.

World Book, Inc Staff, contrib. by. Forests & Wetlands. 2008. (J). *(978-0-7166-1401-2(4))* World Bk., Inc.

—Tropical Regions & Rain Forests. 2012. (Illus.). 48p. (J). *(978-0-7166-0441-9(8))* World Bk., Inc.

Zorzi, Gina & Sánchez, Lucía M. Bosques: This Is a Forest. 2011. (2G Ecosistemas Ser.). (SPA.). 28p. (J). (gr. k-2). pap. 6.99 *(978-1-61541-426-0(6))* American Reading Co.

Zorzi, Gina & Sanchez, Lucia M. Bosques (This Is a Forest) 2011. (poder de 100 - Ecosistemas Ser.). 28p. pap. 45.32 *(978-1-61541-427-7(4))* American Reading Co.

FOREST FIRES

Apel, Melanie Ann. The Yellowstone Park Fire of 1988. 2004. (Tragic Fires Throughout History Ser.). (Illus.). 48p. (gr. 5-8). lib. bdg. 29.25 *(978-0-8239-4490-3(5)*, Rosen Reference) Rosen Publishing Group, Inc., The.

—The Yellowstone Park Fire Of 1988. 2009. (Tragic Fires Throughout History Ser.). 48p. (gr. 5-8). 53.00 *(978-1-60854-585-8(7)*, Rosen Reference) Rosen Publishing Group, Inc., The.

Ball, Jacqueline A. Wildfire! The 1871 Peshtigo Firestorm. 2005. (X-Treme Disasters That Changed America Ser.). 32p. (J). lib. bdg. 25.27 *(978-1-59716-011-7(3))* Bearport Publishing Co., Inc.

Baltzer, Rochelle. Wildfires, 1 vol. 2011. (Natural Disasters Ser.). (ENG., Illus.). 32p. (J). (gr. 2-5). 28.50 *(978-1-61783-036-5(4))* ABDO Publishing Co.

Barber, Nicola, et al. Inside Fires & Floods. 2006. (Inside Nature's Disasters Ser.). (Illus.). 36p. (gr. 3-7). lib. bdg. 26.00 *(978-0-8368-7248-4(7)*, Gareth Stevens Learning Library) Stevens, Gareth Publishing LLLP.

Bell, Samantha S. Detecting Wildfires. 2017. (Detecting Disasters (paperback) Ser.). (ENG., Illus.). 32p. (J). (gr. 4-7). pap. 9.95 ***(978-1-63517-063-4(X)***, Focus Readers) North Star Editions.

Bond, Rebecca. Out of the Woods: A True Story of an Unforgettable Event. 2015. (ENG., Illus.). 40p. (J). (gr. k-4). 17.99 *(978-0-374-38077-9(5)*, 9780374380779, Farrar, Straus & Giroux (BYR)) Farrar, Straus & Giroux.

Brezina, Corona. Disappearing Forests: Deforestation, Desertification, & Drought. 2009. (Extreme Environmental Threats Ser.). 64p. (gr. 6-6). 58.50 *(978-1-61512-426-8(8))* Rosen Publishing Group, Inc., The.

Carlisi, Alison & Foxx, Teralene S. The Forest & the Fire. 2005. (Illus.). (J). 15.00 *(978-0-941232-31-9(X))* Bathtub Row Pr.

Costain, Meredith. Devouring Flames: The Story of Forest Fires. 2006. (Science Chapters Ser.). (ENG., Illus.). 48p. (J). (gr. 1-4). lib. bdg. 17.90 *(978-0-7922-5944-2(0)*, National Geographic Children's Bks.) National Geographic Society.

Cunningham, Kevin. Wildfires. 2009. (Extreme Threats Ser.). 112p. (YA). lib. bdg. 28.95 *(978-1-59935-120-9(X))* Reynolds, Morgan Inc.

Garbe, Suzanne. The Worst Wildfires of All Time, 1 vol. 2012. (Epic Disasters Ser.). (ENG., Illus.). 32p. (gr. 3-4). lib. bdg. 27.99 *(978-1-4296-8418-7(6))* Capstone Press of Coughlan Cos.

Jakubiak, David J. What Can We Do about Deforestation? 2012. (Illus.). 24p. (J). 49.50 *(978-1-4488-5120-1(3)*, PowerKids Pr.); pap. 8.25 *(978-1-4488-5119-5(X)*, PowerKids Pr.); (gr. 2-5). lib. bdg. 22.60 *(978-1-4488-4986-4(1))* Rosen Publishing Group, Inc., The.

Jones, Emma. Smokejumpers, 01 vols., 1. 2016. (Careers for Heroes Ser.). (ENG.). 24p. (J). 23.60 *(978-1-4994-1853-8(1)*, PowerKids Pr.) Rosen Publishing Group, Inc., The.

Katirgis, Jane & Droham, Michele Ingber. Fearsome Forest Fires. 2015. (Earth's Natural Disasters Ser.). (ENG., Illus.). 32p. (J). (gr. 3-4). 25.27 *(978-0-7660-6811-7(0))* Enslow Pubs., Inc.

Katirgis, Jane & Ingber Drohan, Michele. Fearsome Forest Fires. 2015. (Earth's Natural Disasters Ser.). (ENG.). 32p. (J). (gr. 3-4). pap. 10.52 *(978-0-7660-6809-4(9))* Enslow Pubs., Inc.

Knickelbine, Scott. The Great Peshtigo Fire: Stories & Science from America's Deadliest Fire. 2012. (ENG., Illus.). 88p. (J). pap. 15.95 *(978-0-87020-499-9(8))* Wisconsin Historical Society.

Menon, Sujatha. Fire & Floods. 2009. (Wild Nature Ser.). 48p. (gr. 4-5). 53.00 *(978-1-60854-793-7(0)*, PowerKids Pr.) Rosen Publishing Group, Inc., The.

Merrick, Patrick. Forest Fires. 2015. (Forces of Nature Ser.). (ENG.). 24p. (J). (gr. 2-5). 27.07 *(978-1-63143-766-3(6)*, 208606) Child's World, Inc., The.

Minden, Cecilia. Wildfires! 2010. (21st Century Basic Skills Library: Natural Disasters Ser.). (ENG.). 24p. (gr. k-3). lib. bdg. 22.79 *(978-1-60279-865-6(6),* 200596) Cherry Lake Publishing.

Orr, Tamra B. Wildfires. 2012. (21st Century Skills Library: Real World Math Ser.). (ENG., Illus.). 32p. (J). (gr. 4-8). pap. 14.21 *(978-1-61080-412-7(0),* 201344); lib. bdg. 28.50 *(978-1-61080-329-8(9),* 201310) Cherry Lake Publishing.

Peppas, Lynn. Wildfire Alert! 2004. (Disaster Alert! Ser.). (ENG., Illus.). 32p. (J). pap. *(978-0-7787-1606-8(6));* lib. bdg. *(978-0-7787-1574-0(4))* Crabtree Publishing Co.

Piehl, Janet. Forest Fires. 2008. pap. 40.95 *(978-0-8225-9442-0(0));* (ENG., Illus.). 32p. lib. bdg. 22.60 *(978-0-8225-7907-6(3),* Lerner Pubns.) Lerner Publishing Group.

Rice, William B. Fires, 1 vol. 2009. (Science Readers: a Closer Look Ser.). (ENG.). 32p. (J). (gr. 2-2). pap. 8.99 *(978-1-4333-0314-2(0))* Teacher Created Materials, Inc.

Rowell, Rebecca. Wildfires. 2013. (J). pap. 15.64 *(978-1-62403-008-6(4),* Core Library); (ENG., Illus.). 48p. (gr. 3-6). lib. bdg. 32.79 *(978-1-61783-943-6(4))* ABDO Publishing Co.

Thiessen, Mark. Extreme Wildfire: Smoke Jumpers, High-Tech Gear, Survival Tactics, & the Extraordinary Science of Fire. 2016. (ENG., Illus.). 112p. (J). (gr. 3-7). pap. 12.99 *(978-1-4263-2530-4(4),* National Geographic Children's Bks.) National Geographic Society.

Thomas, William David. Forest Firefighter. 2008. (Cool Careers: Adventure Careers Ser.). (Illus.). 32p. (gr. 5-8). pap. 10.50 *(978-0-8368-8889-8(8));* lib. bdg. 26.00 *(978-0-8368-8882-9(0))* Stevens, Gareth Publishing LLLP.

White, Katherine. The 2000-2002 Forest Fires in the Western United States. (Tragic Fires Throughout History Ser.). 48p. (gr. 5-8). 2009. 53.00 *(978-1-60854-580-3(6))* 2004. (Illus.). (J). lib. bdg. 29.25 *(978-0-8239-4488-0(3))* Rosen Publishing Group, Inc., The. (Rosen Reference).

World Book, Inc Staff, contrib. by. Wildfires. (J). 2007. *(978-0-7166-9816-6(1))* 2nd ed. 2009. (Illus.). 47p. *(978-0-7166-9832-6(3))* World Bk., Inc.

FOREST FIRES—FICTION

Acton, Vanessa. Backfire. 2017. (Day of Disaster Ser.). (ENG.). 112p. (gr. 6-12). (J). 26.65 *(978-1-5124-2775-2(6));* (YA). 12.99 ***(978-1-5124-3504-7(X),*** Darby Creek); (YA). 39.99 ***(978-1-5124-3503-0(1),*** Darby Creek); (YA). 39.99 ***(978-1-5124-2782-0(9),*** Darby Creek) Lerner Publishing Group.

Daher, Anita. Flight from Big Tangle, 1 vol. 2003. (Orca Young Readers Ser.). (ENG., Illus.). 144p. (J). (gr. 3-6). pap. 7.95 *(978-1-55143-234-2(X))* Orca Bk. Pubs. USA.

Ellis, Edward Sylvester. Through Forest & Fire. 2005. pap. 14.95 *(978-1-59224-221-4(9))* Wildside Pr., LLC.

Ellsworth, Mark R. Capped for Courage. 2008. 20p. pap. 24.95 *(978-1-60474-095-0(7))* America Star Bks.

Garretson, Dee. Wildfire Run. 2011. (ENG.). 288p. (J). (gr. 3-7). pap. 6.99 *(978-0-06-195350-7(4))* HarperCollins Pubs.

Gleitzman, Morris. Now. 2013. (Once Ser.: 3). (ENG.). 192p. (YA). (gr. 7). pap. 9.99 *(978-1-250-03417-5(5),* 9781250034175) Square Fish.

Hanson, Ed. Forest Fire. 2003. (Barclay Family Adventure Ser.: Bk. 4). (Illus.). 64p. (J). (gr. k-6). per. 3.95 *(978-1-56254-553-6(1),* SP 5531) Saddleback Educational Publishing, Inc.

Holden, Pam. Jungle Fire. Hatam, Samer, illus. 2015. (ENG.). 16p. (-1). pap. *(978-1-77654-132-4(4),* Red Rocket Readers) Flying Start Bks.

Ingold, Jeanette. The Big Burn: Teddy Roosevelt & the Fire That Saved America. 2003. (Illus.). 301p. (YA). (gr. 8-12). 14.60 *(978-0-7569-4283-0(7))* Perfection Learning Corp.

Ingold, Jeanette & Egan, Timothy. The Big Burn: Teddy Roosevelt & the Fire That Saved America. 2003. (ENG., Illus.). 320p. (YA). (gr. 7-12). pap. 6.95 *(978-0-15-204924-9(X))* Houghton Mifflin Harcourt Publishing Co.

Irwin, Bindi & Black, Jess. Bushfire! 2011. (Bindi's Wildlife Adventures Ser.: 3). (ENG.). 112p. (gr. 3-6). pap. 4.99 *(978-1-4022-5520-5(9),* Sourcebooks Jabberwocky) Sourcebooks, Inc.

Lewis, Carolyn & DeVince, James. Hairy Beary Book Three: The Blue Ribbon Hero, 3 bks., Vol. 3. DeVince, James, ed. Porcheron, Tammy, illus. 2003. (Hairy Beary Ser.: 3). 46p. (J). pap. 9.95 *(978-0-9712641-2-0(0))* J M D's Business Services.

Livingston, Mary A. & Shufelberger, Amanda. Buddy & the Magic Chicken Tree, 2 bks. Livingston, Tim, illus. 2014th ed. 2014. (ENG.). 34p. (J). 19.99 *(978-0-9635757-3-9(2))* Red Tail Publishing.

Livingston, Timothy J. & Livingston, Mary A. FireStorm in the Forest: When a Forest Burns. Livingston, Timothy J., illus. 2006. (Illus.). 32p. (J). 19.99 *(978-0-9635757-1-5(6))* Red Tail Publishing.

London, Jonathan. Little Lost Tiger, 0 vols. Spirin, Ilya, illus. 2012. (ENG.). 32p. (J). (gr. k-3). 17.99 *(978-0-7614-6130-2(2),* 9780761461302, Amazon Children's Publishing) Amazon Publishing.

Longenecker, Jeff & Longenecker, Brenda. The Adventures of Critterville: The Beginning of Critterville. 2011. 44p. 16.59 *(978-1-4520-7458-0(5))* AuthorHouse.

McNeal, Laura. Dark Water. 2011. (ENG.). 324p. (YA). (gr. 7). pap. 9.99 *(978-0-375-84330-3(2),* Ember) Random Hse. Children's Bks.

Nesbit, Troy. Forest Fire Mystery. 2014. (Wilderness Mystery Ser.). (ENG., Illus.). 284p. (J). (gr. 3-7). pap. 12.95 *(978-1-58979-869-4(4))* Taylor Trade Publishing.

Roddy, Lee. Escape down the Raging Rapids. 2008. (D. J. Dillon Adventure Ser.: No. 10). (J). 7.99 *(978-0-88062-274-5(1))* Mott Media.

Rodenberg, Charlotte Vivian. Bronto, Friend of Ceratops. Rodenberg, Charlotte Vivian, illus. 2013. (ENG., Illus.). 32p. (J). 14.99 *(978-0-9844422-9-4(4))* Craigmore Creations.

Schaaf, Ron. BearClaw: Finding Courage Within. 2007. (J). *(978-0-9787555-1-5(0))* Hickory Tales Publishing.

Shafer, Patty. Annie the Texas Ranch Dog - Injured Hero. Retzlaff, Shay, illus. 2012. 96p. (J). pap. 9.95 *(978-1-61899-008-2(X),* Tadpole Pr. 4 Kids) Smooth Sailing Pr., LLC.

Smith, Debra. Hattie Marshall & the Dangerous Fire, 1 vol. 2007. (Hattie Marshall Ser.). (ENG.). 128p. (J). (gr. 3-6). per. 7.95 *(978-1-58980-492-0(9))* Pelican Publishing Co., Inc.

FOREST PLANTS

Alaina, Maria. Rainforest. 2011. (Wonder Readers Early Level Ser.). (ENG.). (gr. -1-1). 16p. pap. 35.94 *(978-1-4296-8171-1(3));* 32p. pap. 5.99 *(978-1-4296-8057-8(1))* Capstone Press of Coughlan Cos. (Wonder Readers).

Boothroyd, Jennifer. Let's Visit the Deciduous Forest. 2016. (Lightning Bolt Books (tm) — Biome Explorers Ser.). (ENG., Illus.). 32p. (J). (gr. 1-3). 26.65 *(978-1-5124-1189-8(2))* Lerner Publishing Group.

Dils, Tracey E. Down in the Jungle 1,2,3: A Rainforest Counting Book. 2015. (1, 2, 3... Count with Me Ser.). (ENG., Illus.). 24p. (J). (gr. k-2). 19.95 *(978-1-60753-715-1(X))* Amicus Publishing.

Duke, Kate. In the Rainforest. Duke, Kate, illus. 2014. (Let's-Read-And-Find-Out Science 2 Ser.). (ENG., Illus.). 40p. (J). (gr. -1-3). 17.99 *(978-0-06-028259-2(2));* pap. 5.99 *(978-0-06-445197-0(6))* HarperCollins Pubs.

Fleisher, Paul. Forest Food Webs in Action. 2013. (Searchlight Books What Is a Food Web Ser.). (ENG., Illus.). 40p. (gr. 3-5). lib. bdg. 27.93 *(978-1-4677-1254-5(X),* Lerner Pubns.) Lerner Publishing Group.

Levy, Janey. Life in a Rain Forest Ecosystem. 2009. (Science Scope Ser.). 32p. (gr. 5-5). 47.90 *(978-1-60853-054-0(X),* PowerKids Pr.) Rosen Publishing Group, Inc., The.

Lindeen, Mary. In the Woods. 2015. (BeginningtoRead Ser.). (ENG.). 32p. (J). (gr. k-2). pap. 11.94 *(978-1-60357-757-1(2));* (Illus.). lib. bdg. 22.60 *(978-1-59953-697-2(8))* Norwood Hse. Pr.

McGehee, Claudia. A Woodland Counting Book. 2006. (Bur Oak Book Ser.). (Illus.). 32p. (J). (gr. 3-7). 17.95 *(978-0-87745-989-7(4))* Univ. of Iowa Pr.

Numminen, Mark. Rain Forest Plants. 2009. (Real Life Readers Ser.). 8p. (gr. k-2). pap. 5.15 *(978-1-4042-7950-6(4),* Rosen Classroom) Rosen Publishing Group, Inc., The.

Peluso, Beth A. The Charcoal Forest: How Fire Helps Animals & Plants. Peluso, Beth A., illus. 2007. (Illus.). 56p. (J). (gr. -1-3). pap. 12.00 *(978-0-87842-532-7(2))* Mountain Pr. Publishing Co., Inc.

Rivera, Sheila. Forest. 2005. (Illus.). 24p. (J). pap. 5.95 *(978-0-8225-5371-7(6));* (ENG., lib. bdg. 23.93 *(978-0-8225-2596-7(6),* Lerner Pubns.) Lerner Publishing Group.

Salas, Laura Purdie. Temperate Deciduous Forests: Lands of Falling Leaves, 1 vol. Yesh, Jeff, illus. 2007. (Amazing Science: Ecosystems Ser.). (ENG.). 24p. (J). (gr. k-3). lib. bdg. 25.99 *(978-1-4048-3099-8(5),* Nonfiction Picture Bks.) Picture Window Bks.

Senisi, Ellen B. All in a Rainforest Day. Marent, Thomas, photos by. (Illus.). (J). 2016. (ENG.). (gr. -1-3). pap. 7.95 *(978-0-9912337-1-7(9))* 2016. (gr. -1-3). 45.99 ***(978-0-9912337-2-4(7))*** 2014. (ENG., 32p. 17.95 *(978-0-9912337-0-0(0))* EdTechLens.

Serafini, Frank. Looking Closely Through the Forest, 0 vols. Serafini, Frank, illus. 2014. (Looking Closely Ser.). (ENG., Illus.). 40p. (J). (gr. -1-2). pap. 7.95 *(978-1-77138-118-5(3))* Kids Can Pr., Ltd. CAN. Dist: Hachette Bk. Group.

Sovak, Jan. Lost in the Amazon: Hidden Pictures. 2011. (Dover Children's Activity Bks.). (ENG., Illus.). 48p. (J). (gr. 3-6). pap. 4.99 *(978-0-486-48230-9(8))* Dover Pubns., Inc.

Wallace, Marianne D. America's Forests: Guide to Plants & Animals. 2009. (America's Ecosystems Ser.). (ENG.). 48p. (J). (gr. 1-5). pap. 11.95 *(978-1-55591-595-7(7))* Fulcrum Publishing.

Waxman, Laura Hamilton. Life in a Forest. 2016. (Biomes Alive! Ser.). (ENG., Illus.). 24p. (J). (gr. k-3). lib. bdg. 25.95 *(978-1-62617-317-0(6),* Blastoff! Readers) Bellwether Media.

Zorzi, Gina & Sánchez, Lucía M. Bosques: This Is a Forest. 2011. (2G Ecosistemas Ser.). (SPA.). 28p. (J). (gr. k-2). pap. 6.99 *(978-1-61541-426-0(6))* American Reading Co.

Zorzi, Gina & Sanchez, Lucia M. Bosques (This Is a Forest) 2011. (poder de 100 - Ecosistemas Ser.). 28p. pap. 45.32 *(978-1-61541-427-7(4))* American Reading Co.

FORESTRY

see Forests and Forestry

FORESTS AND FORESTRY

see also Forest Plants; Lumber and Lumbering; Rain Forests; Tree Planting; Trees; Wood

Andrews, Alexa. In the Forest. Keimig, Candice, illus. 2013. (Penguin Young Readers, Level 1 Ser.). (ENG.). 32p. (J). (gr. k-1). pap. 3.99 *(978-0-448-46719-1(4),* Penguin Young Readers) Penguin Young Readers Group.

Armentrout, David & Armentrout, Patricia. Fires. 2006. (Earth's Power Ser.). (Illus.). 32p. (YA). (gr. 2-5). lib. bdg. 28.50 *(978-1-60044-231-5(5))* Rourke Educational Media.

AZ Books. Forest Life. 2013. (Matching Pictures Ser.). (ENG.). 20p. (J). (gr. -1-k). spiral bd. 5.95 *(978-1-61889-308-6(4))* AZ Bks. LLC.

AZ Books Staff. Living Book of the Forest. Vasilkova, Elena, ed. 2012. (Our Amazing World Ser.). (ENG.). 12p. (J). (gr. 1-3). bds. 19.95 *(978-1-61889-022-1(0))* AZ Bks. LLC.

—Making the Forest. Sisoj, Natalja, ed. 2012. (Modeling Clay Bks.). (ENG.). 12p. (J). (gr. -1-2). bds. 10.95 *(978-1-61889-199-0(5))* AZ Bks. LLC.

—Sounds of the Forest. Sheljagovich, Yana, ed. 2012. (Sounds Around Us Ser.). (ENG.). 16p. (J). (gr. 1-3). bds. 17.95 *(978-1-61889-028-3(X))* AZ Bks. LLC.

—Visiting the Forest. Zuk, Valentina, ed. 2012. (Lively Pictures Ser.). (ENG.). 10p. (J). (gr. -1-k). bds. 9.95 *(978-1-61889-178-5(2))* AZ Bks. LLC.

Bailey, Diane. Saving the Rainforests: Inside the World's Most Diverse Habitat. 2017. (Protecting the Earth's Animals Ser.). (ENG.). (J). (gr. 5-8). 23.95 ***(978-1-4222-3880-6(6))*** Mason Crest.

Baker, Chris. A Year in Barrowswold Forest: Band 15/Emerald. 2017. (ENG.). 48p. (J). pap. 8.99 ***(978-0-00-820886-8(7))*** HarperCollins Pubs. Ltd. GBR. Dist: Independent Pubs. Group.

Barrett, Susan. Day & Night in Forest. Barrett, Peter, illus. 2009. 38p. (J). (gr. 2-5). 14.99 *(978-0-8437-0943-8(X))* Hammond World Atlas Corp.

Beilenson, Suzanne. Rain Forest Scratch & Sketch: An Art Activity Book for Adventurous Artists & Explorers of All Ages. 2007. (Illus.). 64p. (YA). 12.99 *(978-1-59359-862-4(9))* Peter Pauper Pr. Inc.

Benchmark Education Company. Forests (Teacher Guide) 2005. *(978-1-4108-4664-8(4))* Benchmark Education Co.

Bishop, Nic. The Cloud Forest. Bishop, Nic, photos by. 2005. (Collins Big Cat Ser.). (ENG., Illus.). 1p. (J). (gr. 2-3). pap. 7.99 *(978-0-00-718641-9(X))* HarperCollins Pubs. Ltd. GBR. Dist: Independent Pubs. Group.

Bjornlund, Lydia D. Deforestation. 2009. (Compact Research Ser.). (YA). (gr. 7-12). 25.95 *(978-1-60152-075-3(1))* ReferencePoint Pr., Inc.

Blyton, Enid. Tower in Ho-Ho Wood: And Other Stories. 2013. (ENG., Illus.). 192p. (J). 9.95 *(978-1-84135-463-7(5))* Award Pubns. Ltd. GBR. Dist: Parkwest Pubns., Inc.

Bow, James. Forests Inside Out. 2015. (ENG.). 32p. (J). *(978-0-7787-1495-8(0))* Crabtree Publishing Co.

Brannon, Barbara. Discover Forests. 2005. (J). pap. *(978-1-4108-5138-3(9))* Benchmark Education Co.

Brett, Anna. Magical Forest: Color & Create Your Own Beautiful 3D Scenes. 2017. (3D Colorscapes Ser.). (ENG.). 48p. (J). (gr. 3-7). bds. 10.99 *(978-0-7641-6883-3(5))* Barron's Educational Series, Inc.

Brezina, Corona. Disappearing Forests: Deforestation, Desertification, & Drought. 2009. (Extreme Environmental Threats Ser.). (ENG., Illus.). 64p. (J). (gr. 7-12). pap. 12.95 *(978-1-4358-5374-4(1),* 1291449); (YA). (gr. 5-9). lib. bdg. 31.95 *(978-1-4358-5018-7(1))* Rosen Publishing Group, Inc., The.

Burzynski, Roberta. Why Would Anyone Cut a Tree Down? Forest Service (U.S.), Northeastern Area State and Private Forestry, ed. Watts, Juliette, illus. 2013. (ENG.). 40p. pap. 10.00 *(978-0-16-091626-7(7),* Forest Service) United States Government Printing Office.

Butterfield, Moira. Protecting Temperate Forests. 2005. (Protecting Habitats Ser.). (Illus.). 32p. (J). (gr. 4-7). lib. bdg. 26.00 *(978-0-8368-4995-0(7),* Gareth Stevens Learning Library) Stevens, Gareth Publishing LLLP.

Callery, Sean. Life Cycles: Forest. 2013. (Lifecycles Ser.). (ENG., Illus.). 32p. (J). (gr. 2-5). 6.99 *(978-0-7534-7065-7(9),* 9780753470657, Kingfisher) Roaring Brook Pr.

Carlisi, Alison & Foxx, Teralene S. The Forest & the Fire. 2005. (Illus.). (J). 15.00 *(978-0-941232-31-9(X))* Bathtub Row Pr.

Casper, Julie Kerr. Forests: More Than Just Trees. 2007. (Natural Resources Ser.). (Illus.). 194p. (YA). (gr. 7-12). lib. bdg. 39.50 *(978-0-8160-6355-0(9))* Facts On File, Inc.

Cefrey, Holly. The Deciduous Forest. 2009. (Biomes Ser.). 24p. (gr. 2-3). 42.50 *(978-1-61511-594-5(3),* PowerKids Pr.) Rosen Publishing Group, Inc., The.

Chinery, Michael & Michael, Chinery. Los Bosques.Tr. of Forests. (SPA.). 40p. (J). (gr. 3-5). 12.76 *(978-84-241-2057-3(4))* Everest Editora ESP. Dist: Lectorum Pubns., Inc.

Cole, Melissa S. Forest. 2003. (Wild America Habitats Ser.). (Illus.). 24p. (J). 21.20 *(978-1-56711-802-5(X),* Blackbirch Pr., Inc.) Cengage Gale.

Cooper, Jenny, illus. Forest Life to Color. 2013. (Nature Coloring Bks). 32p. (J). pap. 5.99 *(978-0-7945-3305-2(1),* Usborne) EDC Publishing.

Cowan, Mary Morton. Timberrr! A History of Logging in New England. 2003. (Women at War Ser.). (Illus.). 128p. (gr. 5-18). lib. bdg. 25.90 *(978-0-7613-1866-8(6),* Twenty-First Century Bks.) Lerner Publishing Group.

Daly, Ruth. Forestry. 2017. ***(978-1-5105-1935-0(1))*** SmartBook Media, Inc.

Dennard, Deborah. Koala Country: A Story of an Australian Eucalyptus Forest. McKinnon, James, illus. 2005. (Wild Habitats Ser.: Vol. 17). (ENG.). 36p. (J). (gr. 1-4). 15.95 *(978-1-56899-887-9(2),* B7018) Soundprints.

Dorling Kindersley Publishing Staff. Forest Life & Woodland Creatures. 2017. (ENG., Illus.). 32p. (J). (-k). 8.99 *(978-1-4654-5659-5(7),* DK Children) Dorling Kindersley Publishing, Inc.

—Woodland & Forests. 2017. (ENG., Illus.). 64p. (J). (gr. 1-3). 9.99 *(978-1-4654-5754-7(2),* DK Children) Dorling Kindersley Publishing, Inc.

Dorling Kindersley Publishing Staff & Hickey, Cathriona. DK Findout! Forest. 2017. (DK Find Out! Ser.). (ENG., Illus.). 64p. (J). (gr. 1-4). pap. 10.99 ***(978-1-4654-6232-9(5),*** DK Children) Dorling Kindersley Publishing, Inc.

First Discovery Staff & Mettler, René. Jungle. Mettler, René, illus. 2006. (ENG., Illus.). 36p. (J). (gr. k-3). pap. 11.99 *(978-1-85103-183-2(9))* Moonlight Publishing, Ltd. GBR. Dist: Independent Pubs. Group.

Flatt, Lizann. Life in a Forestry Community. 2009. (Learn about Rural Life Ser.). (ENG., Illus.). 32p. (J). (gr. 3-6). pap. *(978-0-7787-5086-4(8));* lib. bdg. *(978-0-7787-5073-4(6))* Crabtree Publishing Co.

Food and Agriculture Organization of the United Nations Staff. The Forests Challenge Badge. 2014. (ENG., Illus.). 152p. pap. 20.00 *(978-92-5-107973-7(0))* Food & Agriculture Organization of the United Nations ITA. Dist: Rowman & Littlefield Publishers, Inc.

Food and Agriculture Organization of the United Nations Staff & Youth and United Nations Global Alliance Staff. The Youth Guide to Forests. 2014. (ENG.). 236p. pap. 54.00 *(978-92-5-108435-9(1))* Food & Agriculture Organization of the United Nations ITA. Dist: Rowman & Littlefield Publishers, Inc.

Forest. 2003. (J). per. *(978-1-57657-887-2(9))* Paradise Pr., Inc.

Franchino, Vicky. Canadian Taiga. 2016. (Community Connections: Getting to Know Our Planet Ser.). (ENG., Illus.). 24p. (J). (gr. 2-5). 27.07 *(978-1-63470-515-8(7),* 207791) Cherry Lake Publishing.

Franklin, Yvonne. Las Selvas, 1 vol. rev. ed. 2010. (Science Readers: a Closer Look Ser.). (SPA., Illus.). 32p. (J). (gr. 2-3). pap. 8.99 *(978-1-4333-2143-6(2))* Shell Educational Publishing.

Fuhr, Ute & Sautai, Raoul. Woods & Forests. 2013. (ENG., Illus.). 36p. (J). (gr. -1-k). 12.99 *(978-1-85103-421-5(8))* Moonlight Publishing, Ltd. GBR. Dist: Independent Pubs. Group.

Gardeski, Christina Mia. All about Forests. 2017. (Habitats Ser.). (ENG.). 24p. (gr. k-1). lib. bdg. 21.99 ***(978-1-5157-7638-3(7),*** Pebble Bks.) Capstone Press of Coughlan Cos.

Gardner, Jane P. Timber & Forest Products, Vol. 12. 2015. (North American Natural Resources Ser.). (Illus.). 64p. (J). (gr. 7). 23.95 *(978-1-4222-3389-4(8))* Mason Crest.

Gardner, Robert. Taiga Experiments: 12 Science Experiments in One Hour or Less. 2014. (Last Minute Science Projects with Biomes Ser.). (Illus.). 48p. (J). (gr. 5-12). lib. bdg. 25.27 *(978-0-7660-5932-0(4))* Enslow Pubs., Inc.

Gazlay, Suzy. Managing Green Spaces: Careers in Wilderness & Wildlife Management. 2009. (Green-Collar Careers Ser.). (ENG., Illus.). 64p. (J). (gr. 5-8). pap. *(978-0-7787-4866-3(9));* lib. bdg. *(978-0-7787-4855-7(3))* Crabtree Publishing Co.

Gilkerson, Patricia. My Adventure in an Enchanted Forest. 2006. 44p. (J). 8.99 *(978-1-59092-277-4(8))* Blue Forge Pr.

Greeley, August. Fading Forests: The Destruction of Our Rainforests. 2003. (Man-Made Disasters Ser.). (Illus.). 24p. (J). lib. bdg. 22.60 *(978-0-8239-6486-4(8),* PowerKids Pr.) Rosen Publishing Group, Inc., The.

Green, Emily K. Forests. 2006. (Learning about the Earth Ser.). (ENG., Illus.). 24p. (J). (gr. k-3). lib. bdg. 25.95 *(978-1-60014-036-5(X))* Bellwether Media.

—Forests. 2011. (Blastoff! Readers Ser.). 24p. (J). pap. 5.95 *(978-0-531-26028-9(3),* Children's Pr.) Scholastic Library Publishing.

Greene, Carol. I Love Our Forests. 2012. (I Love Our Earth Ser.). (Illus.). 24p. (J). (gr. 3-4). 22.60 *(978-0-7660-4039-7(9),* Enslow Elementary) Enslow Pubs., Inc.

Hamilton, John. Wildfires, 1 vol. 2006. (Nature's Fury Ser.). (ENG., Illus.). 32p. (gr. 3-8). 27.07 *(978-1-59679-330-9(9),* Abdo & Daughters) ABDO Publishing Co.

Heos, Bridget. Do You Really Want to Visit a Temperate Forest? Fabbri, Daniele, illus. 2014. (Do You Really Want to Visit... ? Ser.). (ENG.). 24p. (J). (gr. 1-4). lib. bdg. 27.10 *(978-1-60753-451-8(7))* Amicus Publishing.

Howard, Fran. Forests, 1 vol. 2006. (Habitats Ser.). (ENG., Illus.). 32p. (gr. -1-3). 27.07 *(978-1-59679-777-2(0),* Buddy Bks.) ABDO Publishing Co.

Johansson, Philip. The Temperate Forest: A Web of Life. 2004. (World of Biomes Ser.). (Illus.). 48p. (J). lib. bdg. 25.27 *(978-0-7660-2198-3(X))* Enslow Pubs., Inc.

Johnson, Rebecca L. A Walk in the Deciduous Forest. Saroff, Phyllis V., illus. Braasch, Gary, photos by. 2005. (Biomes of North America Ser.). 48p. (gr. 3-6). lib. bdg. 23.93 *(978-1-57505-155-0(9))* Lerner Publishing Group.

Kalman, Bobbie. Where on Earth Are Forests? 2014. (ENG., Illus.). 32p. (J). *(978-0-7787-0500-0(5))* Crabtree Publishing Co.

Kalman, Bobbie & Smithyman, Kathryn. La Foret. 2004. (Petit Monde Vivant Ser.). (FRE., Illus.). 32p. (J). pap. 10.95 *(978-2-89579-012-9(4))* Bayard Canada Livres CAN. Dist: Crabtree Publishing Co.

King, Zelda. Examining Forest Habitats. 2009. (Graphic Organizers: Habitats Ser.). 24p. (gr. 2-4). (Illus.). (J). pap. 8.25 *(978-1-4358-3122-3(5));* 42.50 *(978-1-61513-094-8(2));* (J). lib. bdg. 22.60 *(978-1-4358-2718-9(X))* Rosen Publishing Group, Inc., The. (PowerKids Pr.).

Levete, Sarah. Jungle Crash! 2011. (ENG.). 24p. (J). pap. *(978-0-7787-7871-4(1));* (gr. 3-6). *(978-0-7787-7849-3(5))* Crabtree Publishing Co.

Levine, Mathea. I'm Lucy: A Day in the Life of a Young Bonobo. Brickner, Marian, illus. 2008. 32p. (gr. -1-3). 19.95 *(978-0-615-18110-3(4))* Blue Bark Pr.

Linde, Barbara M. Deforestation & Desertification: Set Of 6. 2011. (Navigators Ser.). (J). pap. 50.00 net. *(978-1-4108-5090-4(0))* Benchmark Education Co.

Llewellyn, Claire. Forests, 1 vol. 2012. (Habitat Survival Ser.). (ENG.). 32p. (gr. 2-4). pap. 8.29 *(978-1-4109-4604-1(5));* lib. bdg. 30.65 *(978-1-4109-4595-2(2))* Heinemann-Raintree. (Raintree Perspectives).

Lonely Planet Publications Staff, et al. Let's Explore... Jungle, 1 vol. 2016. (Lonely Planet Kids Ser.). (ENG.). 48p. (J). pap. 9.99 *(978-1-76034-038-4(3),* 5144) Lonely Planet Pubns.

Lya, Maria. The Wise Parrot & a Plan to Save the Forest: A Plan to Save the Forest. 2011. (Illus.). 28p. (gr. -1). pap. 20.16 *(978-1-4567-8106-4(5))* AuthorHouse.

Lynette, Rachel. Julia Butterfly Hill: Saving the Ancient Redwoods. 2007. (Young Heros Ser.). (ENG., Illus.). 48p. (J). (gr. 4-7). lib. bdg. 30.50 *(978-0-7377-3628-1(3),* Kidhaven) Cengage Gale.

MacMillan, Dianne M. Life in a Deciduous Forest. 2003. (Ecosystems in Action Ser.). (ENG., Illus.). 72p. (gr. 5-9). 26.60 *(978-0-8225-4684-9(1))* Lerner Publishing Group.

Marshall, Pam. From Tree to Paper. 2013. (Start to Finish, Second Series: Everyday Products Ser.). (ENG., Illus.). 24p. (gr. k-3). pap. 6.95 *(978-1-4677-0797-8(X))* Lerner Publishing Group.

McKissack, Fredrick L. & McKissack, Lisa Beringer. Counting in the Temperate Forest. 2008. (Counting in the Biomes Ser.). (Illus.). 32p. (J). (gr. 1-3). lib. bdg. 23.94 *(978-0-7660-2990-3(5),* Enslow Elementary) Enslow Pubs., Inc.

Minden, Cecilia. Forests. 2010. (21st Century Basic Skills Library: the World Around Us Ser.). (ENG.). 24p. (gr. k-3). lib. bdg. 22.79 *(978-1-60279-862-5(1),* 200590) Cherry Lake Publishing.

Moore, Peter D. & Garratt, Richard. Tropical Forests. 2007. (Ecosystems Ser.). (Illus.). 272p. (C). (gr. 9). 70.00 *(978-0-8160-5934-8(9))* Facts On File, Inc.

Nagle, Jeanne. Deciduous Forests: Seasons of Survival. 2009. (Biomes of the World Ser.). 48p. (gr. 5-8). 53.00 *(978-1-61511-599-0(4),* Rosen Reference) Rosen Publishing Group, Inc., The.

National Geographic Kids Staff & Evans, Shira. In the Forest. 2016. (Readers Ser.). (ENG., Illus.). 48p. (J). (-k). pap. 4.99 *(978-1-4263-2621-9(1),* National Geographic Children's Bks.) National Geographic Society.

National Geographic Kids Staff & Neuman, Susan B. Hop, Bunny! 2014. (Readers Ser.). (ENG., Illus.). 24p. (J). (-k). pap. 3.99 *(978-1-4263-1739-2(5),* National Geographic Children's Bks.) National Geographic Society.

Newland, Sonya. Woodland & Forest Animals. 2011. (Saving Wildlife Ser.). 32p. (gr. 4-7). 31.35 *(978-1-59920-662-2(5))* Black Rabbit Bks.

E
F
G

Owen, Ruth. Jungle Survival Guide. 2010. (ENG., Illus.). 32p. (J). pap. *(978-0-7787-7555-3(0))*; lib. bdg. *(978-0-7787-7533-1(X))* Crabtree Publishing Co.

Palazeti, Toulla. A Seed Was Planted. 2009. (ENG.). 32p. (J). (gr. -1-3). 16.95 *(978-1-934960-09-7(8)*, Raven Tree Pr.,Csi) Continental Sales, Inc.

—A Seed Was Planted/Sembré una Semilla. Barcita, Pamela, illus. 2009. (ENG & SPA.). 32p. (J). (gr. -1-3). 16.95 *(978-1-932748-89-5(X))*; pap. 7.95 *(978-1-932748-88-8(1))* Continental Sales, Inc. (Raven Tree Pr.,Csi).

Parsons, Michelle Hyde. Forests. 2005. (J). pap. *(978-1-4108-4616-7(4))* Benchmark Education Co.

La Proteccion del Basque. (Colección Biblioteca Juvenil de Ecología). (SPA., Illus.). (YA). (gr. 5-8). pap. *(978-958-04-2407-9(1)*, 80424079) Norma S.A. COL. Dist: Lectorum Pubns., Inc.

Randall, Jory. My Day in the Forest. 2009. (Kid's Life! Ser.). 24p. (J). (ENG.). pap. 8.25 *(978-1-4358-2475-1(X))*; (Illus.). lib. bdg. 22.60 *(978-1-4042-8078-6(2))* Rosen Publishing Group, Inc., The. (PowerKids Pr.).

Raven, Catherine. Forestry. 2006. (Green World Ser.). (Illus.). 125p. (gr. 6-12). lib. bdg. 37.50 *(978-0-7910-8752-7(2))* Facts On File, Inc.

Rettore. Forest. 2017. (Baby Sees Cloth Bks.). (ENG.). 6p. (J). (gr. -1 — 1). 10.99 *(978-1-4380-7758-1(0))* Barron's Educational Series, Inc.

Rice, Howard. Step into the Forest, 1 vol. 2nd rev. ed. 2013. (Nonfiction Readers Ser.). (ENG., Illus.). 28p. (J). (gr. 2-2). pap. 23.96 *(978-1-4807-1049-8(0))* Shell Educational Publishing.

—Step into the Forest, 1 vol. 2nd rev. ed. 2011. (Nonfiction Readers Ser.). (ENG.). 28p. (J). (gr. 2-2). pap. 6.99 *(978-1-4333-3628-7(6))* Teacher Created Materials, Inc.

Rice, William & Franklin, Yvonne. Forests, 1 vol. 2009. (Science Readers: a Closer Look Ser.). (ENG.). 32p. (J). (gr. 3-3). pap. 8.99 *(978-1-4333-0317-3(5))* Teacher Created Materials, Inc.

Santos, Penelope. All about Forests. 2015. (Rosen REAL Readers: STEM & STEAM Collection). (ENG.). 8p. pap. 5.46 *(978-1-4994-9642-0(7)*, Rosen Classroom) Rosen Publishing Group, Inc., The.

Selvas. (Coleccion Planeta Vivo).Tr. of Forests. (SPA.). (J). (gr. 5-8). 12.00 *(978-84-342-1976-2(X))* Parramon Ediciones S.A. ESP. Dist: Distribuidora Norma, Inc.

Spilsbury, Richard. Deforestation. 2011. (Development or Destruction? Ser.). (ENG., Illus.). 48p. (YA). (gr. 5-8). pap. 11.75 *(978-1-4488-6996-1(X))*; lib. bdg. 29.25 *(978-1-4488-6989-3(7))* Rosen Publishing Group, Inc., The. (Rosen Reference).

—Deforestation Crisis. 2009. (Can the Earth Survive? Ser.). (Illus.). 48p. (J). (gr. 5-9). lib. bdg. 29.25 *(978-1-4358-5353-9(9))* Rosen Publishing Group, Inc., The.

Staub, Frank J., photos by. America's Forests & Woodlands. 2006. (Illus.). 48p. (J). pap. *(978-1-59034-806-2(0))* Mondo Publishing.

Stenstrup, Allen. Forests. 2009. (Diminishing Resources Ser.). 112p. (J). lib. bdg. 28.95 *(978-1-59935-116-2(1))* Reynolds, Morgan Inc.

Stone, Lynn M. Forests. 2003. (Rourke Discovery Library). (Illus.). 24p. (J). 20.64 *(978-1-58952-684-6(8))* Rourke Educational Media.

Summers, Portia & Grady, Colin. The Coniferous Forest Biome. 2016. (Zoom in on Biomes Ser.). 24p. (J). (gr. 2-2). pap. 9.35 *(978-0-7660-7743-0(8))* Enslow Pubs., Inc.

—The Deciduous Forest Biome. 2016. (Zoom in on Biomes Ser.). (Illus.). 24p. (J). (gr. 2-2). pap. 9.35 *(978-0-7660-7748-5(9))* Enslow Pubs., Inc.

Taylor, Barbara. Temperate Forest Habitats. 2006. (Exploring Habitats Ser.). (Illus.). 36p. (J). (gr. 3-7). lib. bdg. 26.00 *(978-0-8368-7257-6(6)*, Gareth Stevens Learning Library) Stevens, Gareth Publishing LLLP.

Taylor, Trace & Sanchez, Lucia M. En el bosque (in the Woods) 2011. (Lugares adonde voy Ser.). (SPA.). 16p. pap. 39.62 *(978-1-61541-457-4(6))* American Reading Co.

Taylor, Trace & Zorzi, Gina. This Is a Forest. 2011. (Power 100 - Ecosystems Ser.). 28p. pap. 45.32 *(978-1-61541-269-3(7))* American Reading Co.

Taylor, Trace, et al. En el Bosque. 2011. (2Y Lugares Adonde Voy Ser.).Tr. of In the Woods. (SPA.). 12p. (J). (gr. k-2). pap. 6.99 *(978-1-61541-456-7(8))* American Reading Co.

Toupin, Laurie Peach. The Taiga: Life in the Boreal Forest. 2005. (Watts Library). (ENG., Illus.). 64p. (J). (gr. 5-7). lib. bdg. 25.50 *(978-0-531-12387-4(1)*, Watts, Franklin) Scholastic Library Publishing.

Tribuzi, Luke. What's the Difference Between Forests & Prairies? 2013. (Rosen Readers Ser.). (ENG.). 24p. (J). (gr. 3-4). pap. 49.50 *(978-1-4777-2450-7(8))*; pap. 8.25 *(978-1-4777-2449-1(4))* Rosen Publishing Group, Inc., The. (Rosen Classroom).

Turning Trees into Paper. 2014. (Step-By-Step Transformations Ser.). 24p. (J). (gr. k-2). lib. bdg. 24.21 *(978-1-62713-007-3(1))* Cavendish Square Publishing.

Vasillu, Michelle. The Future of Forests. 2007. (Action Numeracy Middle Primary Ser.). 32p. pap. 9.95 *(978-0-86431-678-3(X))* ACER Pr. AUS. Dist: ISBS Publisher Services.

Veitch, Catherine. The Natural World. 2013. (Natural World Ser.). (ENG.). 24p. (gr. -1-1). pap. 23.96 *(978-1-4109-5410-7(2)*, NA-r) Heinemann-Raintree.

Wallace, Marianne D. America's Forests: Guide to Plants & Animals. 2009. (America's Ecosystems Ser.). (ENG.). 48p. (J). (gr. 1-5). pap. 11.95 *(978-1-55591-595-7(7))* Fulcrum Publishing.

Warhol, Tom. Forest. 2006. (Earth's Biomes Ser.). (Illus.). 80p. (J). lib. bdg. 32.79 *(978-0-7614-2189-4(0)*, Benchmark Bks.) Marshall Cavendish Corp.

Waxman, Laura Hamilton. Life in a Forest. 2016. (Biomes Alive! Ser.). (ENG., Illus.). 24p. (J). (gr. k-3). lib. bdg. 25.95 *(978-1-62617-317-0(6)*, Blastoff! Readers) Bellwether Media.

Weinhold, Angela. El Bosque. 2007. (Junior (Silver Dolphin) Ser.). (Illus.). 16p. (J). (gr. -1). *(978-970-718-493-0(0)*, Silver Dolphin en Español) Advanced Marketing, S. de R. L. de C. V.

Wickman, Allen, ed. Forest Management Digest. 9th ed. 2004. 460p. (YA). reprint ed. pap. 45.00 *(978-0-913163-36-8(8)*, KAP22004) Hobar Pubns.

Wilkes, Angela. Wild Places: Combined Volume. 2009. (Explainers Ser.). 96p. (J). pap. 12.99 *(978-0-7945-2499-9(0)*, Usborne) EDC Publishing.

World Book, Inc Staff, contrib. by. Forests & Wetlands. 2008. (J). *(978-0-7166-1401-2(4))* World Bk., Inc.

Zak, Monica. Salven Mi Selva. Runnerstrom, Bengt-Arne, illus. (SPA.). 29p. (J). (gr. 3-18). pap. 12.95 *(978-968-6048-23-0(5))* volcano pr.

FORESTS AND FORESTRY—FICTION

Addy, Sharon. In Grandpa's Woods. Akins, Tamlyn, illus. 2004. (J). *(978-1-931599-42-9(4)*, Trails Bks.) Bower Hse.

The Adventures of Chip Green the Forestry Kid l.t. ed. 2005. (Illus.). 34p. (J). per. *(978-0-9729753-8-4(1))* Really Big Coloring Bks., Inc.

Aldrick, Shirley H. F. Tobias & the Pale, Pale Leprechaun. 2009. 52p. pap. 19.50 *(978-1-60693-959-8(9)*, Strategic Bk. Publishing) Strategic Book Publishing & Rights Agency (SBPRA).

Amore, Sandra. The Princess Who Lived on the 174th Floor. 2011. 58p. pap. 18.68 *(978-1-4653-5854-7(4))* Xlibris Corp.

Anderson, P. The Secret World of Fairies. 2010. 116p. pap. 39.99 *(978-0-557-44401-4(2))* Lulu Pr., Inc.

Andrews, Jackie. Goldilocks & the Three Bears. Taylor, Lawrie, illus. 2012. (ENG.). 32p. (J). pap. 6.50 *(978-1-84135-191-9(1))* Award Pubns. Ltd. GBR. Dist: Parkwest Pubns., Inc.

Archambault, Marc. Hal the Unwashed Dragon. 2009. 28p. pap. 18.98 *(978-0-557-09894-1(7))* Lulu Pr., Inc.

—Hal the Unwashed Dragon (perfect Bound) 2009. 32p. pap. 18.97 *(978-0-557-12009-3(8))* Lulu Pr., Inc.

Arias, Carlos Ballesteros. The Magic Forest. 2006. (J). pap. 8.00 *(978-0-8059-7022-7(3))* Dorrance Publishing Co., Inc.

Arnauld, D. S. Zertelo & the Road of Fire: Book Two. Scott, Sara, ed. 2007. 210p. (J). per. 9.95 *(978-0-9801408-1-1(1))* Heroes & Leaders.

Avalos, Francisco. Amazon Tale. 2013. 124p. 29.99 *(978-1-4797-6689-5(5))*; pap. 19.99 *(978-1-4797-6688-8(7))* Xlibris Corp.

AZ Books, creator. Magic Forest. 2012. (Baby Book Ser.). (ENG., Illus.). 10p. (J). (gr. -1 — 1). bds. 4.95 *(978-1-61889-287-4(8))* AZ Bks. LLC.

AZ Books Staff. My Forest. Yaroshevich, Angelica, ed. 2012. (Open the Book-I Am Alive Ser.). (ENG.). 8p. (J). (— 1). bds. 5.95 *(978-1-61889-042-9(5))* AZ Bks. LLC.

Baggett, Shirley Reed. Adventures of Bandit: A Little Racoon Goes into the Forbidden Forest. 2011. 16p. (gr. 1-2). pap. 9.99 *(978-1-4567-6575-0(2))* AuthorHouse.

Baglio, Ben M. Colt on Christmas Eve. Baum, Ann & Lasher, Mary Ann, illus. 2005. 142p. (J). pap. *(978-0-439-77522-9(1))* Scholastic, Inc.

Ballman, Swanee. The Chocolate Kingdom Caper. Brunson, Stephanie, illus. 2003. 32p. (J). per. 6.95 *(978-1-59094-025-9(3)*, 1590940253) Jawbone Publishing Corp.

Barbieri, Sandra Birriel. Cristal & the Secret of the Enchanted Forest: Cristal y el Secreto Del Bosque Encantado. 2013. 64p. pap. 23.99 *(978-1-4525-6512-5(0))* Balboa Pr.

Barnard, Bobbie. The Fairies of the Big Forest. 2013. 16p. pap. 24.95 *(978-1-63004-359-9(1))* America Star Bks.

Barnes, Kenneth Edward. Invasion of the Dregs. 2011. 164p. (gr. 10-12). pap. 13.50 *(978-1-4634-0745-2(9))*; (gr. 4-6). 22.23 *(978-1-4634-0726-1(2))* AuthorHouse.

Barron, T. A. Tree Girl. 2013. (ENG.). 144p. (J). (gr. 3-7). pap. 7.99 *(978-0-14-242708-8(X)*, Puffin Books) Penguin Young Readers Group.

Barroux. Where's the Elephant? Barroux, illus. 2016. (ENG., Illus.). 32p. (J). (gr. -1-2). 14.99 *(978-0-7636-8110-4(5))* Candlewick Pr.

Baum, Roger S. The Oz Odyssey. Seitzinger, Victoria, illus. 2006. 176p. (J). 19.95 *(978-1-57072-299-8(4))* Overmountain Pr.

Baumbach, Rudolph. Summer Legends. 2004. reprint ed. pap. 21.95 *(978-1-4191-4993-1(8))*; pap. 1.99 *(978-1-4192-4993-8(2))* Kessinger Publishing, LLC.

Baumgartner, John Robert. Ron's Ghost: The Secret of the Stone Stairs. 2012. 296p. 27.95 *(978-1-4626-6310-1(9))* America Star Bks.

Bentley, Dawn & Studio Mouse Staff. Triceratops. Carr, Karen, illus. 2008. (ENG.). 24p. (J). (gr. 3-7). 4.99 *(978-1-59069-622-4(0))* Studio Mouse LLC.

—Tyrannosaurus Rex. Carr, Karen, illus. 2008. (ENG.). 24p. (J). (gr. 3-7). 4.99 *(978-1-59069-621-7(2))* Studio Mouse LLC.

Berenstain, Stan & Berenstain, Jan. The Berenstain Bears Happy Halloween! 2013. (First Time Books(R) Ser.). (ENG., Illus.). 96p. (J). (gr. -1-2). 9.99 *(978-0-385-37191-9(8)*, Random Hse. Bks. for Young Readers) Random Hse. Children's Bks.

Bertagnolli, Daniel. Whooo Turned Out the Lights? Bertagnolli, Daniel, illus. 2009. (Illus.). 20p. pap. 9.14 *(978-1-4269-0590-2(4))* Trafford Publishing.

Bhandari, D. Growing Wings: Parrot's Day Out. 2010. 28p. 17.99 *(978-1-4520-1102-8(8))* AuthorHouse.

Bickford-Smith, Coralie. The Fox & the Star. 2015. (ENG., Illus.). 64p. (J). 20.00 *(978-0-14-310867-2(0)*, Penguin Books) Penguin Publishing Group.

Birkenstock, Michelle M. Harry the Caterpillar. 2010. 20p. pap. 10.95 *(978-1-60911-250-9(4)*, Eloquent Bks.) Strategic Book Publishing & Rights Agency (SBPRA).

Bissonette, Aimee M. North Woods Girl. McGehee, Claudia, illus. 2015. (ENG.). 32p. (J). 16.95 *(978-0-87351-966-3(3))* Minnesota Historical Society Pr.

Blackwood, Sage. Jinx. (Jinx Ser.: 3). 400p. (J). (gr. 3-7). 2016. pap. 7.99 *(978-0-06-212997-0(X))* 2015. (ENG.). 16.99 *(978-0-06-212996-3(1))* 2014. (ENG.). 16.99 *(978-0-06-212993-2(7))* HarperCollins Pubs. (Tegen, Katherine Bks).

Bobulski, Chelsea. The Wood. 2017. (ENG.). 320p. (YA). 17.99 *(978-1-250-09426-1(7)*, 9781250094261) Feiwel & Friends.

Bramlett, Timothy A. Thomas in the Land of the Blips. 2012. 26p. pap. 19.99 *(978-1-4772-9576-2(3))* AuthorHouse.

Braunns, Melissa. Big Bear Cares. 2009. 24p. pap. 11.50 *(978-1-60860-636-8(8)*, Strategic Bk. Publishing) Strategic Book Publishing & Rights Agency (SBPRA).

Briggs, Mark T. Jermaine Peterman & the Encounter in the Forest. 2012. 44p. pap. 16.95 *(978-1-4626-8431-1(9))* America Star Bks.

Brocklehurst, Ruth & Doherty, Gillian. Illustrated Grimm's Fairy Tales. 2011. (Illustrated Stories Ser.). 303p. (J). ring bd. 19.99 *(978-0-7945-2409-8(5)*, Usborne) EDC Publishing.

Brooks, John. The Sundarbans Tiger. 2006. 115p. (J). pap. 13.58 *(978-0-9661789-4-4(7))* Canis Lupus Productions.

Brooks, Walter R. & Slayton-Mitchell, Joyce. Knuckleboom Loaders Load Logs: A Trip to the Sawmill. Wiese, Kurt & Boms, Steven, illus. 2003. (ENG.). 40p. (gr. 4-13). 16.95 *(978-1-58567-368-1(4)*, 856368) Overlook Pr., The.

Brown, Audrey E. Angels of Freedom. 2012. (ENG.). 135p. pap. 9.95 *(978-1-4327-8337-2(8))* Outskirts Pr., Inc.

Brown, Carron, ed. The Three Little Pigs & Little Red Riding Hood: Two Tales & Their Histories. 2009. (World of Fairy Tales Ser.). (Illus.). 32p. (J). (gr. -1-2). pap. 10.55 *(978-1-60754-641-2(8))*; lib. bdg. 22.60 *(978-1-60754-640-5(X))* Windmill Bks.

Burgess, Thornton W. The Adventures of Happy Jack. 2004. (Dover Children's Thrift Classics Ser.). (ENG., Illus.). 128p. (J). (gr. 3-8). pap. 4.00 *(978-0-486-43321-9(8))* Dover Pubns., Inc.

—Whitefoot the Wood Mouse. Cady, Harrison, illus. 2006. (Dover Children's Thrift Classics Ser.). (ENG.). 112p. (J). (gr. 3-8). per. 4.00 *(978-0-486-44944-9(0))* Dover Pubns., Inc.

—Whitefoot the Woodmouse. 2007. 120p. per. 10.95 *(978-1-60312-258-0(3))*; 22.95 *(978-1-60312-756-1(9))* Aegypan.

—Whitefoot the Woodmouse. 2011. 118p. 23.95 *(978-1-4638-9567-9(4))* Rodgers, Alan Bks.

Burks, James. Bird & Squirrel on Fire. 2017. (Bird & Squirrel Ser.). (ENG.). 192p. (J). (gr. 2-5). 18.99 *(978-0-545-80429-5(9)*, Graphix) Scholastic, Inc.

The Busy Forest. (J). 26.20 *(978-0-8136-8414-7(5))*; 26.20 *(978-0-8136-8413-0(7))*; (gr. -1-3). 59.50 *(978-0-8136-7948-8(6))* Modern Curriculum Pr.

Calcutt, David. Robin Hood. Baker-Smith, Grahame, illus. 2012. (ENG.). 176p. (J). (gr. 4-6). pap. 12.99 *(978-1-84686-799-6(1))* Barefoot Bks., Inc.

Campbell, Lori. The Adventures of Tinkerbelle & Peanut. 2012. 36p. pap. 21.99 *(978-1-4771-4835-8(3))* Xlibris Corp.

Carter, Alden R. Walkaway. 2008. (ENG.). 192p. (YA). (gr. 7-18). 16.95 *(978-0-8234-2106-0(6))* Holiday Hse., Inc.

Carver, David. Leafy Leafs Where Is Lester?, 1 vol. Carver, Erin, illus. 34p. 2010. 24.95 *(978-1-4512-1069-9(8))* 2009. pap. 19.95 *(978-1-4489-2203-1(8))* PublishAmerica, Inc.

Cerimele, Ron. Winup. 2012. 28p. pap. 21.99 *(978-1-4771-1144-4(1))* Xlibris Corp.

Chambers, Melinda. We Are Whoooo We Are. Spiker, Sue Ann, illus. 2006. 32p. (J). 16.95 *(978-0-929915-46-3(1))* Headline Bks., Inc.

Chandler Goldstein. Georgette: A Little Frog Discovers the Value in Revealing Her True Self! 2012. 20p. pap. 15.99 *(978-1-4772-0835-9(6))* AuthorHouse.

Chandler, Jeff. The New Kitten: A Story about a Foster Puppy, 1 vol. 2009. 48p. pap. 24.95 *(978-1-61546-176-9(0))* America Star Bks.

Chapman, Charlotte. The Adventures of Little Payton. 2008. 24p. pap. 14.49 *(978-1-4343-9598-6(7))* AuthorHouse.

Cheverton, Mark. Terrors of the Forest. 2017. (Mystery of Entity303 Ser.: 1). lib. bdg. 20.85 ***(978-0-606-40312-2(4))*** Turtleback Bks.

Chin, Jason. Redwoods. Chin, Jason, illus. 2009. (ENG., Illus.). 40p. (J). (gr. -1-3). 18.99 *(978-1-59643-430-1(9)*, 9781596434301) Roaring Brook Pr.

Cohen, Jerianne. Max A. Million's Birthday Party. 2008. 193p. pap. 24.95 *(978-1-60672-844-4(X))* America Star Bks.

Coleman, K. R. Truth or Dare. 2017. (Midnight Ser.). (ENG.). 104p. (YA). (gr. 6-12). lib. bdg. 26.65 *(978-1-5124-2768-4(3))*; 12.99 ***(978-1-5124-3495-8(7))***; 39.99 ***(978-1-5124-2788-2(8))***; 39.99 ***(978-1-5124-3494-1(9))*** Lerner Publishing Group. (Darby Creek).

Collier, Kevin Scott. Tales from Kensington Forest. l.t. ed. 2006. (Illus.). 26p. (J). E-Book 5.00 incl. cd-rom *(978-1-933090-26-9(X))* Guardian Angel Publishing, Inc.

Collins, Christine. The Knight Meets Ole Dragon. 2009. 100p. pap. 28.95 *(978-1-4327-4128-0(4))* Outskirts Pr., Inc.

Connelly, Peg. If the Forest Is Silent, Beware! 2007. 108p. pap. 19.95 *(978-1-60441-548-3(7))* America Star Bks.

Corwin, Katherine A. R. Greg the Bearded Dragon & Thomas the Sea Turtle: A Tale of Adventure, Discovery, & Friendship. 2012. 28p. pap. 19.99 *(978-1-4685-7958-1(4))* AuthorHouse.

Cote, Denis. La Foret aux Cent Perils. Poulin, Stephane, tr. 2003. (Roman Jeunesse Ser.). (FRE., Illus.). 96p. (J). (gr. 4-7). pap. *(978-2-89021-647-1(0))* Diffusion du livre Mirabel (DLM).

Côté, Denis. La Forêt aux Mille et un Périls, Tome 2. Poulin, Stephane, illus. 2004. (Roman Jeunesse Ser.). (FRE.). 96p. (J). (gr. 4-7). pap. *(978-2-89021-696-9(9))* Diffusion du livre Mirabel (DLM).

Cox, Dorothy Ayling. Children's Stories. 2013. 108p. pap. 11.95 *(978-1-4787-0220-7(6))* Outskirts Pr., Inc.

Cvetkovic, Judith Lynn. Mandy's Lost Adventure. 2008. 48p. per. 24.95 *(978-1-4241-9709-5(0))* PublishAmerica, Inc.

Dal Santo, Sandy. My Fantasy Forest. 2009. 36p. pap. 15.65 *(978-1-4389-6035-7(2))* AuthorHouse.

Daniels, Cheri & Nicewander, Carol. Shadow Tail Meets the Gang. 2008. 24p. pap. 11.49 *(978-1-4389-3259-0(6))* AuthorHouse.

Darling, Pollyanna. Heartwood. Chalmers, Kirsty, illus. 2013. 66p. (J). pap. *(978-0-9871164-4-4(4))* Imaginaria.

de Brunhoff, Laurent. Babar et ses Amis en Foret. (Babar Ser.). (FRE., Illus.). 48p. (J). (gr. -1-3). 19.95 *(978-0-7859-8811-3(4))* French & European Pubns., Inc.

De Sena, Joseph. Little Sammy Sunshine & the Frightful Forest. 2008. 64p. pap. 27.95 *(978-1-4327-3119-9(X))* Outskirts Pr., Inc.

Dek, Maria. A Walk in the Forest. 2017. (ENG.). 48p. (J). (gr. -1-1). 17.95 *(978-1-61689-569-3(1))* Princeton Architectural Pr.

Derrick, Patricia & Sibbett, Joyce. Montgomery the Moose Can Shake His Caboose. Martinez, J-P Loppo, illus. 2007. 32p. (J). (gr. -1). 18.95 incl. audio compact disk *(978-1-933818-18-4(2))* Animalations.

Devlin, Ivy. Low Red Moon. 2010. (ENG., Illus.). 256p. (YA). (gr. 7-18). 16.99 *(978-1-59990-510-5(8)*, 9781599905105, Bloomsbury USA Childrens) Bloomsbury Publishing USA.

D'Ghent, Laurie. Dryer Sheet Fairy. 2013. 20p. pap. 24.95 *(978-1-63000-960-1(1))* America Star Bks.

Dietrich, Sean, illus. Hansel & Gretel: The Graphic Novel, 1 vol. 2008. (Graphic Spin Ser.). (ENG.). 40p. (gr. 1-3). 25.32 *(978-1-4342-0767-8(6)*, Graphic Revolve) Stone Arch Bks.

Dimplechin, Lord Reginald. Does a Wuzz. 2012. 38p. 24.95 *(978-1-4626-6151-0(3))* America Star Bks.

Divenuto, John. Scruffy Hawk & Freddy Ferret. 2011. 32p. pap. 13.00 *(978-1-60976-702-0(0)*, Eloquent Bks.) Strategic Book Publishing & Rights Agency (SBPRA).

Dixon, Bob. Rooty the Tree Troll. 2009. 28p. pap. 13.99 *(978-1-4389-9129-0(0))* AuthorHouse.

Du Chaillu, Paul. The World of the Great Forest: How Animals, Birds, Reptiles & Insects Talk, Think, Work & Live. Knight, C. R., illus. 2004. reprint ed. pap. 31.95 *(978-1-4179-0914-8(5))* Kessinger Publishing, LLC.

Ducote, Billie Seaon. The Adventures of Artie Eco Part One: The Problem with Greed, 2 vols, Vol. 1. Ducote, Billie Seaon, illus. 2007. (ENG., Illus.). 26p. (J). 18.95 *(978-0-9787597-5-9(3))* PureLight Pubns.

—The Adventures of Artie Eco Part Two: The Problem with Greed Artie Eco Goes to Dirtyville, 2 vols., Vol. 2. Ducote, Billie Seaon, illus. 2007. (Illus.). 26p. (J). act. bk. ed. 18.95 *(978-0-9787597-1-1(0))* PureLight Pubns.

Dufresne, Michele. Adventure in the Purple Forest. 2003. (Spaceboy Set 1 Ser.). (ENG., Illus.). (J). pap. 7.33 *(978-1-932570-06-9(3))* Pioneer Valley Bks.

Dugan, Karen. Ms. April & Ms. Mae: A Fable. 2009. (ENG., Illus.). 40p. (J). (gr. 3-6). 17.95 *(978-0-940719-07-1(X))* Gryphon Pr., The.

Duvoisin, Roger, illus. Happy Hunter. 2016. (ENG.). 40p. (J). (gr. -1-3). 16.95 *(978-1-59270-205-3(8))* Enchanted Lion Bks., LLC.

Ebeltoft, Christine. Koo & Jay in the Rainforest. 2004. 34p. pap. 24.95 *(978-1-4137-3698-4(X))* PublishAmerica, Inc.

Edwards, Carol. Jacy Meets Betsy: Jacy's Search for Jesus Book 2. Frey, Daniel, illus. 2006. 32p. (J). 15.95 *(978-0-9755314-1-9(7))* Majestic Publishing, LLC.

Ely, Kosa. The Peaceable Forest: India's Tale of Kindness to Animals. Johansson, Anna, illus. 2012. (ENG.). 32p. (gr. k). 16.99 *(978-1-60887-115-5(0))* Mandala Publishing.

Engle, Margarita. Forest World. 2017. (ENG., Illus.). 208p. (J). (gr. 5). 16.99 ***(978-1-4814-9057-3(5)***, Atheneum Bks. for Young Readers) Simon & Schuster Children's Publishing.

Epps, Lawrence. Stomping on Toad Stools. 2011. 40p. pap. 24.95 *(978-1-4560-3702-4(1))* America Star Bks.

Esbaum, Jill. I Am Cow, Hear Me Moo! Gordon, Gus, illus. 2014. (ENG.). 32p. (J). (gr. -1-k). 16.99 *(978-0-8037-3524-8(3)*, Dial Bks) Penguin Young Readers Group.

Fabrizio, Anthony. The Last Forest, 1 vol. 2009. 64p. pap. 19.95 *(978-1-61546-861-4(7))* America Star Bks.

Fei, Kanara. Kalani's Wish. 2009. 44p. pap. 16.99 *(978-1-4389-8118-5(X))* AuthorHouse.

Fernandez, Martina. Jellybean: Jellybean Finds a Home. 2012. 28p. pap. 19.99 *(978-1-4772-7237-4(2))* AuthorHouse.

Ferry, Ann. Gusty the Cloud & Streakie the Snail. Swope, Brenda, illus. 2011. 28p. pap. 24.95 *(978-1-4560-0928-1(1))* America Star Bks.

Finnigan, Mary C. Our Family Trees. 2011. 28p. pap. 15.00 *(978-1-4634-1354-5(8))* AuthorHouse.

Fisscher, Tiny. RUBY & the LION. 2008. (ENG.). 48p. (J). (gr. 1-7). 11.95 *(978-1-60136-014-4(2))* Audio Holdings, LLC.

The Forest of the Frendibles. 2006. (J). mass mkt. *(978-0-9791982-0-5(8))* Pine Cone Pr.

Francis-Harris, Annabel. The Other Side of the Forest. 2006. pap. 19.95 *(978-1-59526-458-9(2))* Aeon Publishing Inc.

Fulcomer, Betty. My Friend Kate Is a Forest Ranger, 1 vol. 2010. 34p. 24.95 *(978-1-4489-4764-5(2))* America Star Bks.

Furgang, Kathy. The Great Green Forest: Set Of 6. 2010. (Early Connections Ser.). (J). pap. 37.00 net. *(978-1-4108-1373-2(8))* Benchmark Education Co.

Gaichies, Sarah. Mirabelle the Lost Kitten. 2010. (Illus.). 76p. pap. 24.99 *(978-1-4490-5593-6(1))* AuthorHouse.

Gallego Garcia, Laura. Retorno a la Isla Blanca. 2004. 143p. pap. 14.00 *(978-84-931888-6-3(7))* Editorial Brief ESP. Dist: Independent Pubs. Group.

Galvin, Laura Gates & Studiomouse Staff. The Hungry T-Rex. Carr, Karen, illus. 2011. (Read, Play & Go Ser.). (ENG.). 20p. (gr. -1-k). 9.99 *(978-1-60727-288-5(1))* Studio Mouse LLC.

Gault, Linda Fulford. The Chosen Tree. 2011. 28p. pap. 12.95 *(978-1-4567-1561-8(5))* AuthorHouse.

Gi Gi. The Adventures of Trueword the Bear. 2012. 28p. pap. 24.95 *(978-1-4626-8042-9(9))* America Star Bks.

Giachetti, Julia & Benchmark Education Co. Staff. A Tail for a Tail - Cherokee Trickster Tales. 2014. (Text Connections Ser.). (J). (gr. 5). *(978-1-4900-1375-6(X))* Benchmark Education Co.

Gifford, Dorinda. Harriet the Ferret, 1 vol. Luevano, Raul, illus. 2009. 20p. pap. 24.95 *(978-1-59129-405-4(3))* America Star Bks.

Gilbert, Harry. Year of Sharing, Level 1. Oxford University Press Staff & Bassett, Jennifer, eds. 3rd ed. 2008. (ENG., Illus.). 64p. 10.00 *(978-0-19-479077-2(0))* Oxford Univ. Pr., Inc.

Gile, John. El Primer Bosque. Kohen-Klieman, Clarita, tr. 2006.Tr. of First Forest. (SPA., Illus.). 40p. per. 9.95 *(978-0-910941-15-0(7))* JGC/United Publishing Corps.

Gillingham, Sara. In My Forest. Siminovich, Lorena, illus. 2010. (ENG.). 12p. (J). (gr. -1 — 1). bds. 8.99 *(978-0-8118-7566-0(0))* Chronicle Bks. LLC.

Gogonya, Carol. The Adventure of Red Robin in the African Forest. 2012. 24p. pap. 28.03 *(978-1-4691-7922-3(9))* Xlibris Corp.

Golden Books Staff. Oh, the Things Spring Brings! Ruiz, Aristides, illus. 2013. (Color Plus Stencil Ser.). (ENG.). 64p. (J). (-k). pap. 5.99 *(978-0-307-98123-3(1)*, Golden Bks.) Random Hse. Children's Bks.

Goldilocks & the Three Bears. 2004. (My First Fairy Tales Ser.). (Illus.). 24p. (J). pap. 3.99 *(978-1-85854-686-5(9))* Brimax Books Ltd. GBR. Dist: Byeway Bks.

Goldilocks & the Three Bears. (Ladybird Bks.). (ARA., Illus.). 52p. (J). 12.95 incl. audio *(978-0-86685-254-8(9)*, LDL109C) International Bk. Ctr., Inc.

Gonzalez, Bruno. Savior of the Rain Forest: An Adventure of Zalvator the Black Panther. 2010. 40p. pap. 19.99 *(978-1-4269-3185-7(9))* Trafford Publishing.
Grahame, Kenneth. The Wind in the Willows. Ingpen, Robert R., illus. 2012. (Sterling Illustrated Classics Ser.). (ENG.). 224p. (J). (gr. 2-8). 19.95 *(978-1-4027-8283-1(7))* Sterling Publishing Co., Inc.
Grandma Bette. The Excellent Adventures of Max & Madison: Bedtime Stories for Youngsters. 2013. 32p. pap. 16.95 *(978-1-4525-7264-2(X))*; 36p. pap. 16.95 *(978-1-4525-7270-3(4))*; 32p. pap. 16.95 *(978-1-4525-7268-0(2))*; 32p. pap. 16.95 *(978-1-4525-7266-6(6))* Author Solutions, Inc. (Balboa Pr.).
Greathouse, Rebecca. Katie & Riley's Magical Adventures: Journey to the Amazon. 2006. 48p. pap. 16.95 *(978-1-4241-5341-1(7))* America Star Bks.
Green, John. Terdellaline: A Free-Sprited, Energeti. 2005. 48p. pap. 16.95 *(978-1-4137-9528-8(5))* PublishAmerica, Inc.
Grimm, Jacob & Grimm, Wilhelm K. Little Red Riding Hood: Caperucita Roja. Surges, James, tr. Estrada, Pau, illus. 2006. 22p. (J). (gr. k-4). reprint ed. 15.00 *(978-0-7567-9994-6(5))* DIANE Publishing Co.
Grindley, Sally. Keep Out! Bears About! 2015. (ENG., Illus.). 32p. (J). (gr. -1-k). pap. 12.99 *(978-1-4449-1416-0(2))* Hodder & Stoughton GBR. Dist: Hachette Bk. Group.
Guerra, Elisa Puricelli. The Forest of Talking Trees. Zeni, Marco, tr. from ITA. Bernstein, Gabriel León, illus. 2015. (Minerva Mint Ser.). (ENG.). 160p. (gr. 2-4). lib. bdg. 25.32 *(978-1-4342-9673-3(3))* Stone Arch Bks.
Gummelt, Donna & Melchiorre, Dondino. Michelina the Magical Musical Good Witch of the Forest. Wall, Randy Hugh, ed. Varela, Juan D., tr. Varela, Juan D., illus. 2006. (SPA.). 34p. (J). 14.95 *(978-0-9764798-6-4(9))* Story Store Collection Publishing.
Gwyer, Gillian K. Podnockery Forest - Owl & the Trickster. 2013. 40p. *(978-1-4602-3974-2(1))* FriesenPress.
H. P. Lawrence. The Adventures of Wilfred & Henri: The Staff of Knowledge. 2009. 88p. pap. 10.49 *(978-1-4389-6374-7(2))* AuthorHouse.
Hahn, Rebecca. A Creature of Moonlight. 2014. (ENG.). 224p. (YA). (gr. 7-12). 17.99 *(978-0-544-10935-3(X)*, HMH Books For Young Readers) Houghton Mifflin Harcourt Publishing Co.
Haig, Matt. Samuel Blink & the Forbidden Forest. 2008. (ENG.). 352p. (J). (gr. 3-7). 7.99 *(978-0-14-241191-9(4)*, Puffin Books) Penguin Young Readers Group.
—Shadow Forest. 2009. pap. 1.00 *(978-1-4074-4391-1(7))* Recorded Bks., Inc.
Hall, Kirsten. The Gold Leaf. Forsythe, Matthew, illus. 2017. (ENG.). 48p. (J). (gr. -1-3). 18.95 *(978-1-59270-214-5(7))* Enchanted Lion Bks., LLC.
Hamilton, Elizabeth L. Charley Chimp's Jungle Fairness. l.t. ed. 2005. (Character Critters Ser.: No. 10). (Illus.). 32p. (J). per. 5.95 *(978-0-9754629-7-3(0)*, Character-in-Action) Quiet Impact, Inc.
Harary, Keith. The Owls of the Enchanted Forest. Gonina, Luba, illus. 2008. 52p. (J). pap. 15.88 *(978-0-9799196-8-8(1))* Owl Pals.
—The Owls of the Enchanted Forest - 2007 Special Collector's Edition. Gonina, Luba, illus. 2007. 50p. (J). 50.00 incl. DVD *(978-0-9799196-3-3(0))* Owl Pals.
Harden, Mark E. The Bug in the Big White Forest. 2009. 32p. pap. 12.99 *(978-1-4389-6477-5(3))* AuthorHouse.
Haseley, Dennis. My Father Doesn't Know about the Woods & Me. 2013. (ENG., Illus.). 32p. (J). (gr. -1-3). 16.99 *(978-1-4814-0159-3(9)*, Atheneum Bks. for Young Readers) Simon & Schuster Children's Publishing.
Haugen, Timothy A. The Castle of Gloom, 1 vol. 2009. (ENG.). 175p. pap. 24.95 *(978-1-61546-106-6(X))* America Star Bks.
Hawthorne, Rachel. Shadow of the Moon. 2010. (Dark Guardian Ser.: 4). (ENG.). 256p. (YA). (gr. 9-18). pap. 8.99 *(978-0-06-196290-5(2)*, HarperTeen) HarperCollins Pubs.
Hayes, J. B. Freddy the Frog's First Christmas. 2012. 44p. pap. 21.99 *(978-1-4772-2870-8(5))* AuthorHouse.
Heinrich, Julie. Bob White & Whippoorwill. 2008. 32p. 14.50 *(978-1-4357-1074-0(6))* Lulu Pr., Inc.
Heinz, Brian. The Great North Woods. Rothman, Michael, illus. 2016. (ENG.). 32p. (J). (gr. 1-3). 18.99 *(978-1-56846-275-2(1)*, Creative Editions) Creative Co., The.
Helget, Nicole. The End of the Wild. 2017. (ENG., Illus.). 272p. (J). (gr. 3-7). 16.99 *(978-0-316-24511-1(9))* Little, Brown Bks. for Young Readers.
Higesanbon. Mo Mo Mo Mo Monster: Mon Monster. 2011. 56p. pap. 34.95 *(978-1-4327-4149-5(7))* Outskirts Pr., Inc.
Holland, Francis. KoKo's New Home. 2008. 32p. pap. 24.95 *(978-1-60474-706-5(4))* America Star Bks.
Holmes, Sara. The Wolf Hour. 2017. (J). pap. ***(978-0-545-10798-3(9)***, Levine, Arthur A. Bks.) Scholastic, Inc.
Hood, Karen Jean Matsko. Opening Day. Whispering Pine Press International, ed. Artistic Design Service Staff, illus. l.t. ed. 2014. (Bernadette's Bakery Ser.). 224p. pap. 22.95 *(978-1-930948-27-3(1))* Whispering Pine Pr. International, Inc.
Hooper, Leta. The Dream That Saved Grizzly Forest. 2010. 16p. pap. 9.00 *(978-1-4490-5087-0(5))* AuthorHouse.
Hopgood, Sally. In the Forest: A Pull-The-Tab Book. Hinton, Stephanie, illus. 2014. (J). *(978-1-4351-5689-0(7))* Barnes & Noble, Inc.
Hovaguimian, Vroni. Deep in the Woods. 2011. 32p. pap. 13.00 *(978-0-557-70332-6(8))* Lulu Pr., Inc.
Howard-Parlnam, Pam. If You Go into the Forest. Meier, Kerry L., illus. l.t. ed. 2005. (HRL Board Book Ser.). (J). (gr. -1-k). pap. 10.95 *(978-1-57332-324-6(1)*, HighReach Learning, Incorporated) Carson-Dellosa Publishing, LLC.
Hughes, Carol. The Princess & the Unicorn. 2010. (ENG.). 288p. (J). (gr. 3-7). 7.99 *(978-0-375-85563-4(7)*, Bluefire) Random Hse. Children's Bks.
Hulst, W. G. van de & Hulst, Willem G. van de, illus. Annie & the Goat. 2014. (J). *(978-1-928136-06-4(0))* Inheritance Pubns.
—The Woods Beyond the Wall. 2017. (J). *(978-1-928136-08-8(7))* Inheritance Pubns.
Huneck, Stephen. Sally in the Forest. 2014. (Sally Board Bks.). (ENG., Illus.). 20p. (J). (gr. -1 — 1). bds. 7.95 *(978-1-4197-1226-5(8)*, Abrams Appleseed) Abrams, Inc.
Hunter, Erin. Battles of the Clans. 2010. (Warriors Field Guide Ser.). 208p. (J). (gr. 3-7). (ENG.). 16.99 *(978-0-06-170230-3(7))*; lib. bdg. 17.89 *(978-0-06-170231-0(5))* HarperCollins Pubs.
—Bluestar's Prophecy. McLoughlin, Wayne, illus. 2010. (Warriors Super Edition Ser.: 2). (ENG.). 560p. (J). (gr. 3-7). pap. 7.99 *(978-0-06-158250-9(6))* HarperCollins Pubs.
—The Forgotten Warrior. Richardson, Owen & Douglas, Allen, illus. 2012. (Warriors: Omen of the Stars Ser.: 5). (ENG.). 384p. (J). (gr. 3-7). pap. 6.99 *(978-0-06-155526-8(6))* HarperCollins Pubs.
—The Heart of a Warrior. Barry, James L., illus. 2010. (Warriors Manga Ser.: 3). (ENG.). 112p. (J). (gr. 3-7). pap. 6.99 *(978-0-06-168867-6(3))* HarperCollins Pubs.
—A Hidden Enemy. (Survivors Ser.: 2). (J). (gr. 3-7). 2014. (ENG.). 304p. pap. 7.99 *(978-0-06-210262-1(1))* 2013. 288p. lib. bdg. 17.89 *(978-0-06-210261-4(3))* 2013. (ENG.). 288p. 16.99 *(978-0-06-210260-7(5))* HarperCollins Pubs.
—A Hidden Enemy. 2014. (Survivors Ser.: 2). (J). lib. bdg. 18.40 *(978-0-606-35056-3(X)*, Turtleback) Turtleback Bks.
—Skyclan's Destiny. McLoughlin, Wayne, illus. 2010. (Warriors Super Edition Ser.: 3). (ENG.). 528p. (J). (gr. 3-7). 17.99 *(978-0-06-169994-8(2))* HarperCollins Pubs.
—Warriors, 6, Set. 2007. (Warriors Ser.: Bks. 1-6). 2112p. (J). (gr. 3-7). pap. 36.99 *(978-0-06-147793-5(1))* HarperCollins Pubs.
Hunter, Erin & Jolley, Dan. Escape from the Forest. Hudson, Don, illus. 2008. (Warriors Manga Ser.: 2). (ENG.). 112p. (J). (gr. 3-7). pap. 7.99 *(978-0-06-154793-5(X))* HarperCollins Pubs.
Hunter, Tammy. Tede's Search for his Mom. 2004. 27p. pap. 24.95 *(978-1-4137-2854-5(5))* PublishAmerica, Inc.
Ichikawa, Satomi. En Busca de Tesoros. (SPA., Illus.). 40p. (J). (gr. k-2). *(978-84-95150-33-2(6)*, COR0428) Corimbo, Editorial S.L. ESP. Dist: Lectorum Pubns., Inc.
Interiano, Jeffrey. Critters of Forest City. 2006. pap. 10.00 *(978-1-4257-1721-6(7))* Xlibris Corp.
Iwamura, Kazuo. Bedtime in the Forest. 2010. (ENG., Illus.). 32p. (J). (gr. -1-3). 16.95 *(978-0-7358-2310-5(3))* North-South Bks., Inc.
Jacques, Brian. The Bellmaker. Curless, Allan, illus. 2004. (Redwall Ser.). (ENG.). 352p. (J). (gr. 5-18). reprint ed. pap. 8.99 *(978-0-14-240030-2(0)*, Firebird) Penguin Young Readers Group.
Janesh, Ron. Ariela Aparecida E O Vale Da Neblina Da Cachoeir. Gonçalves da Silva, Fabio, illus. 2012. 56p. pap. 20.50 *(978-1-60976-925-3(2)*, Strategic Bk. Publishing) Strategic Book Publishing & Rights Agency (SBPRA).
Janvier Gibeau, Claire. Discoveries. 2009. 24p. pap. 12.99 *(978-1-4490-3790-1(9))* AuthorHouse.
Jeanfield. Twinkle, a Christmas Story. 2009. 36p. pap. 13.95 *(978-1-60693-745-7(6)*, Eloquent Bks.) Strategic Book Publishing & Rights Agency (SBPRA).
Jensen, Derrick. Mischief in the Forest: A Yarn Yarn. McMillan, Stephanie, illus. 2010. (Flashpoint Press Ser.). (ENG.). 40p. (J). (gr. -1-k). pap. 14.95 *(978-1-60486-081-8(2))* PM Pr.
Johnson, Amy. Tales of the Forest. 2011. (Illus.). 64p. pap. 13.95 *(978-1-4670-1976-7(3))* AuthorHouse.
Jones, Cloteal Mae. The Five Little Ducks Went to the Forest. 2012. 24p. (-18). pap. 15.99 *(978-1-4797-0274-9(9))* Xlibris Corp.
—The Five Little Ducks Went to the Forest: The Work Book. 2012. 44p. (-18). pap. 21.99 *(978-1-4797-1000-3(8))* Xlibris Corp.
Joseph, A. Valentine. The Forest Is Our Home. 2012. 88p. pap. 9.95 *(978-1-4759-4400-6(4))* iUniverse, Inc.
Kamon. Hooty & the Magic Power. Krit, Joey, illus. 2011. 36p. pap. 14.39 *(978-1-4634-1042-1(5))* AuthorHouse.
Keister, Douglas. El Regalo de Fernando. Keister, Douglas, photos by. 2004.Tr. of Fernando's Gift. (SPA., Illus.). 32p. (J). (gr. 3-3). reprint ed. 16.95 *(978-0-87156-414-6(9))* Sierra Club Bks. for Children.
Kent, Neville. The Secrets of the Forest - the Time Zone. 2013. 88p. pap. *(978-1-78299-795-5(4))* FeedARead.com.
Kerwin, Betsy. The Adventures of Floret the Woodland Fairy: The Adventures Begin. 2008. 44p. pap. 18.49 *(978-1-4343-9426-2(3))* AuthorHouse.
Kiernan, Tim. Liams Luck & Finnegans Fortune. 2009. (ENG.). 144p. pap. 10.95 *(978-1-933918-48-4(6)*, Ferne Pr.) Nelson Publishing & Marketing.
Kilgore, Lee. The Riddle of the Rustled Reindeer: A Christmas Mystery. 2009. 50p. pap. 16.95 *(978-1-61546-863-8(3))* America Star Bks.
Kirkwood, Edith Brown. Animal Children: The Friends of the Forest & the Plain. Ross, M. T., illus. 2007. 100p. per. *(978-1-4065-2907-4(9))* Dodo Pr.
Kleczka, John A. Flick the Butterfly: Flick & Mom Go to Grandma's. 2008. 48p. per. 24.95 *(978-1-60441-290-1(9))* America Star Bks.
Kline, Trish & Donev, Mary. A Scary Day in the Forest: KA Reader 5. 2007. (Illus.). 32p. (J). per. 20.00 *(978-0-9717234-8-1(6))* Ghost Hunter Productions.
Knapman, Timothy. Time Now to Dream. Oxenbury, Helen, illus. 2017. (ENG.). 32p. (J). (gr. -1-2). 16.99 *(978-0-7636-9078-6(3))* Candlewick Pr.
Kramer, Alan & Kramer, Candice. Brer Rabbit Hears a Big Noise in the Woods: An African /American Folktale. 2006. (J). pap. *(978-1-4108-7163-3(0))* Benchmark Education Co.
Kratzert, Barbara & Probst, Sharon Patrice. Bobby Bubblebug in the Bubblegum Tree Forest. 2009. 24p. pap. 11.49 *(978-1-4389-4480-7(2))* AuthorHouse.
Kreidler, Shannon. The Adventures of Sally the Squirrel: Interactive... Educational & Earn Gold Stars. 2013. 28p. pap. 15.99 *(978-1-4797-7674-0(2))* Xlibris Corp.
Lagerlöf, Selma. The Further Adventures of Nils. Howard, Velma Swanston, tr. 2003. 284p. pap. 14.95 *(978-1-59224-320-4(7))*; 32.95 *(978-1-59224-541-3(2))* Wildside Pr., LLC.
LaMarche, Jim. Pond. LaMarche, Jim, illus. 2016. (ENG., Illus.). 40p. (J). (gr. -1-3). 17.99 *(978-1-4814-4735-5(1)*, Simon & Schuster/Paula Wiseman Bks.) Simon & Schuster/Paula Wiseman Bks.
Lancett, Peter. Dark Words. 2007. (Dark Man Ser.). (ENG.). 36p. pap. *(978-1-84167-602-9(0))* Ransom Publishing Ltd.
Lasky, Kathryn. Sugaring Time. 2003. (Illus.). 21.25 *(978-0-8446-7248-9(3))* Smith, Peter Pub., Inc.
Lee, R. Denzil. Found in the Forest. 2012. 24p. pap. 11.50 *(978-1-60976-741-9(1)*, Strategic Bk. Publishing) Strategic Book Publishing & Rights Agency (SBPRA).
Leigh-Crawford, Lynda. Hovis the Hedgehog: Bonfire Night. 2009. (Illus.). 16p. pap. 9.49 *(978-1-4490-3675-1(9))* AuthorHouse.
LeMonde', Stephanie. The Misty Forest. 2007. (Illus.). 154p. (J). (gr. -1-3). 14.95 *(978-1-934138-13-7(4))* Bouncing Ball Bks., Inc.
Leone, Jason, illus. the Enchantress of Caratunk. Manna, Elizabeth, photos by. 2003. 30p. (J). (gr. 1-5). pap. 9.95 *(978-0-9729807-0-8(9))* Murray, David M.
Lewis, Anne. Dragonchild. 2003. (Bwgan-Wood Ser.: 3). (ENG., Illus.). 208p. (J). (gr. 3-6). pap. 7.95 *(978-1-870206-55-6(X))* Honno Welsh Women's Pr. GBR. Dist: Independent Pubs. Group.
Lewis, Cindy (Didas). The Sugar Spigot. 2011. 34p. pap. 16.95 *(978-1-4560-7012-0(6))* America Star Bks.
Lewis, Regina N. The Smallest Forest. Moore, P. M., illus. 2013. 60p. pap. 12.95 *(978-1-935083-12-2(0))* CyPress Pubns.
Livingston, Mary A. & Shufelberger, Amanda. Buddy & the Magic Chicken Tree, 2 bks. Livingston, Tim, illus. 2014th ed. 2014. (ENG.). 34p. (J). 19.99 *(978-0-9635757-3-9(2))* Red Tail Publishing.
Llama, Gram. The Bunny Fuzz Mystery. 2007. 32p. per. 24.95 *(978-1-4241-8371-5(5))* America Star Bks.
Lois, Lowry. Messenger. 2006. (ENG.). 176p. (J). (gr. 3-7). mass mkt. 7.99 *(978-0-440-23912-3(5)*, Laurel Leaf) Random Hse. Children's Bks.
London, Olivia. Welcome to the Everfree Forest! 2014. (My Little Pony 8X8 Picture Bks.). (J). lib. bdg. 13.55 *(978-0-606-35940-5(0))* Turtleback Bks.
Long, Ruth Frances. The Treachery of Beautiful Things. 2013. (ENG.). 384p. (YA). (gr. 7). pap. 9.99 *(978-0-14-242606-7(7)*, Speak) Penguin Young Readers Group.
Lootens, Ann. The Birthday Surprise. Faas, Linde, illus. 2013. (Wild Woods Ser.). (ENG.). 32p. (J). (gr. -1-k). 15.95 *(978-1-60537-147-4(5))* Cobblestone Publishing Co.
Lopatina, Irina. Tales from the Frog Forest. Lopatin, Dmitry, tr. Shapiro, Alla, illus. 2012. (ENG.). 48p. (J). 18.00 *(978-1-61153-022-3(9))* Light Messages Publishing.
Lopez, Maria Lorena. The Bird's Party, Birds in the Tropical Dry Forest. 2009. 28p. pap. 13.00 *(978-1-60860-156-1(0)*, Eloquent Bks.) Strategic Book Publishing & Rights Agency (SBPRA).
Lopez, Minia. Friends in the Forest. Jimenez, Resu, illus. 2006. (J). 8.00 *(978-0-9773531-4-9(1))* Charming Pubns.
Lunsford, Susie. The Magical Wishing Well Forest Series. 2006. pap. 25.32 *(978-1-4134-9491-4(9))* Xlibris Corp.
Lyon, George Ella. What Forest Knows. 2014. (ENG., Illus.). 40p. (J). (gr. -1-3). 17.99 *(978-1-4424-6775-0(4)*, Atheneum Bks. for Young Readers) Simon & Schuster Children's Publishing.
MacCarthy, Patricia. Moon Forest. 2013. (ENG., Illus.). 32p. (J). (gr. -1-1). 17.99 *(978-1-84780-283-5(4)*, Frances Lincoln) Quarto Publishing Group UK GBR. Dist: Hachette Bk. Group.
MacHale, D. J. Black Water. 2004. (Pendragon Ser.: 5). (ENG.). 448p. (J). (gr. 5-9). pap. 10.99 *(978-0-689-86911-2(8)*, Aladdin) Simon & Schuster Children's Publishing.
Mackey, Heather. Dreamwood. 2014. (ENG.). 352p. (J). (gr. 5). 16.99 *(978-0-399-25067-5(0)*, G.P. Putnam's Sons Books for Young Readers) Penguin Young Readers Group.
Marie, E. The Porcupine Connection: The Story of a Young Girl's Journey from Tragedy to Healing, with the Help of Her Forest Friends. 2004. 48p. pap. 16.95 *(978-1-4137-3480-5(4))* America Star Bks.
Markowitz, Krista. Mrs Tipperwillow's Afterlife Adventures. 2008. 316p. 28.95 *(978-0-595-49079-0(4))*; pap. 18.95 *(978-0-595-44671-1(X))* iUniverse, Inc.
Markowitz, Susan Meredith. The Great Green Forest & el gran bosque Verde: 6 English, 6 Spanish Adaptations. 2011. (ENG & SPA.). (J). 75.00 net. *(978-1-4108-5653-1(4))* Benchmark Education Co.
Martin, JoElle. Moonlight in the Forest. 2009. (ENG.). 280p. (YA). pap. 14.99 *(978-1-59092-563-8(7))* Blue Forge Pr.
Martin, Michelle Nicole. Princess & Missy's Magical Adventures: The Crystal Heart. 2010. 55p. pap. 10.95 *(978-1-4327-4954-5(4))* Outskirts Pr., Inc.
Massie, Rosemary. Rhymen the Rabbit: Meeting the Forest Ranger, 2011. 28p. pap. 13.95 *(978-1-4634-2572-2(4))* AuthorHouse.
—Rhymen the Rabbit: Save the Forest. 2011. 28p. pap. 13.95 *(978-1-4634-1597-6(4))* AuthorHouse.
Mazzola, Lori E. The Forbidden Forest: Tales of the Tree People, 1 vol. 2009. 151p. pap. 24.95 *(978-1-4489-2656-5(4))* America Star Bks.
McCarty, Bryan. Devyn's Gold. 2008. pap. 17.00 *(978-0-8059-8640-2(5))* Dorrance Publishing Co., Inc.
McCorkle, Barbara. Brutis' New Friend. Taylor, David A., illus. 2007. 30p. (J). 13.99 *(978-1-59879-439-7(6))* Lifevest Publishing, Inc.
McDonald, Dawn M. Kiki Koala Wanders Away. 2008. 28p. per. 24.95 *(978-1-4241-9924-2(7))* America Star Bks.
McDowell, Andrew. Beyond the Forest. 2007. 286p. pap. 16.95 *(978-0-7414-4238-3(8))* Infinity Publishing.
McIntyre, Sheila Adam. The Cave in the Forest. 2012. pap. 9.95 *(978-0-7414-7480-3(8))* Infinity Publishing.
McKenzie, Tiffany M. The Adventures of Alan & the Man-Eating Rabbits. 2013. 24p. pap. 24.95 *(978-1-63000-143-8(0))* America Star Bks.
McQuestion, Karen. Celia & the Fairies, 0 vols. unabr. ed. 2010. (ENG.). 142p. (gr. 4-6). pap. 7.95 *(978-1-935597-28-5(0)*, 9781935597285, Two Lions) Amazon Publishing.
Merritt, Kory. The Dreadful Fate of Jonathan York. 2015. (ENG.). 128p. (J). pap. 9.99 *(978-1-4494-7100-2(5))* Andrews McMeel Publishing.
Mestas. Nolan & the Magic Bridge. 2009. 28p. pap. 13.99 *(978-1-4490-0812-3(7))* AuthorHouse.
Mitton, Tony. Forest Adventure. Parker, Ant, illus. 2015. (Amazing Animals Ser.). (ENG.). 24p. (J). (gr. -1-1). pap. 4.99 *(978-0-7534-7229-3(5)*, 9780753472293, Kingfisher) Roaring Brook Pr.
Miyakoshi, Akiko. The Tea Party in the Woods. Miyakoshi, Akiko, illus. 2015. (ENG., Illus.). 32p. (J). (gr. -1-2). 16.95 *(978-1-77138-107-9(8))* Kids Can Pr., Ltd. CAN. Dist: Hachette Bk. Group.
Mohler, Marie. Little Bird's Earth Nest. 2008. 32p. 18.95 *(978-1-4357-1711-4(2))* Lulu Pr., Inc.
Monaghan, Joseph. The Boy Who Loved Trees. 2013. (Illus.). 24p. pap. 19.82 *(978-1-4817-8225-8(8))* AuthorHouse.
Mooney, Carla. The Forest Surprise, 1 vol. Harpster, Steve, illus. 2011. (My First Graphic Novel Ser.). (ENG.). 32p. (gr. k-2). pap. 6.25 *(978-1-4342-3064-5(3))*; lib. bdg. 24.65 *(978-1-4342-2520-7(8))* Stone Arch Bks. (My First Graphic Novel).
Moreau, Laurent. Masks in the Forest: A Story Told with Masks. 2016. (ENG., Illus.). 40p. (J). (gr. -1-3). 19.95 *(978-3-89955-763-3(8))* Die Gestalten Verlag DEU. Dist: Penguin Random Hse. LLC.
Moss, Patricia Crocker. Dillie & the Baby Deer. 2011. (J). 44p. 27.99 *(978-1-4568-4999-3(9))*; 48p. pap. 17.49 *(978-1-4568-4998-6(0))* Xlibris Corp.
Musick, David. Jeremy Daniels with the Bambles: The Adventure in the Mountains. 2003. 172p. pap. 12.95 *(978-0-595-27944-9(9))* iUniverse, Inc.
Nichills, Dee. Visit the Rainforest. 2013. 42p. pap. 9.99 *(978-1-60820-857-9(5))* MLR Pr., LLC.
The Night Crossing: Individual Title, 6 packs. (Bookweb Ser.). 32p. (gr. 4-18). 34.00 *(978-0-7635-3729-6(2))* Rigby Education.
Noe, Katherine Schlick. Something to Hold. 2011. (ENG., Illus.). 256p. (J). (gr. 5-7). 17.99 *(978-0-547-55813-4(9))* Houghton Mifflin Harcourt Publishing Co.
Nooks, Nanny. Nina in the Forest of Faces. 2011. 46p. pap. 16.00 *(978-1-61204-606-8(1)*, Strategic Bk. Publishing) Strategic Book Publishing & Rights Agency (SBPRA).
Nuttall, Lesley. Ollie the Ogre. 2012. (Illus.). 16p. pap. 18.30 *(978-1-4678-8908-7(3))* AuthorHouse.
O'Garden, Irene. Forest, What Would You Like? Schories, Pat, illus. 2013. (ENG.). 32p. (J). (gr. -1-3). 16.95 *(978-0-8234-2322-4(0))* Holiday Hse., Inc.
Ohizep, Zoiea. Rainbow's Ring. 2011. 24p. pap. 15.99 *(978-1-4567-5574-4(9))* AuthorHouse.
Olena Rudge. The Adventures of Sophie & Katia in the Enchanted Forest. 2013. 220p. pap. *(978-3-85438-685-8(0))* united p.c. Verlag.
Paderewski, Elliot. The Forest near My House. 2016. (Rosen REAL Readers: STEM & STEAM Collection). 8p. (gr. 1-k). pap. 5.46 *(978-1-5081-2613-3(5)*, Rosen Classroom) Rosen Publishing Group, Inc., The.
Page, Terry. The Fathers of the Friendly Forest. Page, Terry, illus. (Illus.). 24p. (J). (gr. 2-6). pap. 4.00 *(978-1-887864-69-5(5))*; lib. bdg. 7.00 *(978-1-887864-38-1(5))* Boo Bks., Inc.
Parrish, Terry. Wiffenpoof. 2012. 28p. pap. 24.95 *(978-1-4626-7942-3(0))* America Star Bks.
Perkins, Lynne Rae. Nuts to You. Perkins, Lynne Rae, illus. 2014. (ENG., Illus.). 272p. (J). (gr. 3-7). 16.99 *(978-0-06-009275-7(0)*, Greenwillow Bks.) HarperCollins Pubs.
Perkins, T. J. The Secret in Phantom Forest: A Kim & Kelly Mystery. 2004. (Illus.). 130p. (YA). 10.99 *(978-0-9777538-1-9(6))* GumShoe Press.
Perry, Dakota. Brim's Journey. 2008. 36p. pap. 24.95 *(978-1-60703-938-9(9))* America Star Bks.
Perry, Holly Lynn. Spinner's Mystic Travels: Lost in the Black Forest. 2003. pap. 9.00 *(978-0-8059-6291-8(3))* Dorrance Publishing Co., Inc.
Pevear, Ted F. & Pevear, Linda W. Finding Little Feathers a Hub-A-Son. 2012. 24p. 24.95 *(978-1-4626-5874-9(1))* America Star Bks.
Pferdehirt, Julia. Wisconsin Forest Tales. 2004. (Illus.). vii, 152p. (J). *(978-1-931599-47-4(5)*, Trails Bks.) Bower Hse.
Pfitsch, Patricia Curtis. Riding the Flume. 2004. (Aladdin Historical Fiction Ser.). 232p. (gr. 5-9). 15.00 *(978-0-7569-2938-1(5))* Perfection Learning Corp.
Pike, Christopher, pseud. The Cold People. 2015. (Spooksville Ser.: 5). (ENG., Illus.). 128p. (J). (gr. 3-7). pap. 6.99 *(978-1-4814-1061-8(X)*, Aladdin) Simon & Schuster Children's Publishing.
Pintozzi, Nick. Bentley & the Cactus Rustlers. Pintozzi, Nick & Pintozzi, Connie, illus. 2006. per. 11.00 *(978-0-9749465-4-2(0))* BentDaiSha, LLC.
Polanco, Amparo. The Magical Forest. 2016. (ENG., Illus.). (J). 16.95 ***(978-1-5069-0268-5(5))***; pap. 12.95 ***(978-1-5069-0269-2(3))*** First Edition Design eBook Publishing.
Pranali. The Secret Storybook. 2013. 64p. pap. 23.95 *(978-1-4828-0147-7(7))* Partridge Pub.
Preston, Helen M. Gra Gra's Stories. 2012. 72p. pap. 28.99 *(978-1-4772-9783-4(9))* AuthorHouse.
Ramsey, Byra L. Little Stick. 2009. 28p. pap. 13.99 *(978-1-4490-3371-2(7))* AuthorHouse.
Ransome, Arthur. Old Peter's Russian Tales. 2005. 35.00 *(978-1-55742-465-5(9))*; pap. 15.95 *(978-1-55742-456-3(X))* Wildside Pr., LLC.
Rauscher, C D. The Fairies of the Clouds. 2008. 68p. pap. 25.49 *(978-1-4343-5153-1(X))* AuthorHouse.
Rawlings, Marjorie Kinnan. The Secret River. Dillon, Leo & Dillon, Diane, illus. 2011. (ENG.). 56p. (J). (gr. -1-3). 19.99 *(978-1-4169-1179-1(0)*, Atheneum Bks. for Young Readers) Simon & Schuster Children's Publishing.
Reed, T. K. Quasar & the Eye of the Serpent. 2009. 136p. 21.95 *(978-1-4401-2753-0(0))*; pap. 11.95 *(978-1-4401-2751-9(4))* iUniverse, Inc.
Reid, James. This Is My Story by Frederick G. Frog, 1 vol. rev. ed. 2013. (Fiction Readers Ser.). (ENG., Illus.). 20p. (J). (gr. 1-1). pap. 15.96 *(978-1-4807-1140-2(3))*; pap. 4.99 *(978-1-4333-5484-7(5))* Shell Educational Publishing.
Reid, Roger. Longleaf. 2007. 133p. (J). (gr. 3-7). 19.95 *(978-1-58838-194-1(3)*, Junebug Bks.) NewSouth, Inc.
RH Disney Staff. Bambi. unabr. ed. (Read-Along Ser.). (J). 7.99 incl. audio *(978-1-55723-008-9(0))* Walt Disney Records.
Richardson, Tracy. Indian Summer. 2010. (ENG.). 198p. (YA). (gr. 7). pap. 11.95 *(978-1-935462-25-5(3))* Luminis Bks., Inc.
Richter, Jeff, photos by. White Deer: Ghost of the Forest. 2007. (Illus.). 96p. pap. 19.95 *(978-0-9741883-1-7(X))* Nature's Pr.

EFG

Rothman, Lorne. Southcrop Forest. 2008. 184p. pap. 13.95 *(978-0-595-49588-7(5))* iUniverse, Inc.

Rouncville, Bibi. Gimbels & Gooseberries. 2010. 52p. pap. 9.50 *(978-0-557-21585-0(4))* Lulu Pr., Inc.

S., Lisa Hamilton Ed. The Tale of the Talking Trees: The Tale of the Talking Trees a Story of Suspense & Surprise. 2012. 32p. pap. 21.99 *(978-1-4691-7846-2(X))* Xlibris Corp.

Saccheri, Josephine. The Secret to Easter Eggs. Saccheri, Briana, illus. 2008. 28p. pap. 24.95 *(978-1-60474-210-7(0))* America Star Bks.

Salten, Felix. A Forest World. Greenburger, Sanford Jerome & Milton, Paul R., trs. 2013. (Bambi's Classic Animal Tales Ser.). (ENG., Illus.). 288p. (J). (gr. 3-7). pap. 6.99 *(978-1-4424-8637-9(6)*, Aladdin) Simon & Schuster Children's Publishing.

—A Forest World. Greenburger, Sanford Jerome & Milton, Paul R., trs. 2013. (Bambi's Classic Animal Tales Ser.). (ENG., Illus.). 288p. (J). (gr. 3-7). 16.99 *(978-1-4424-8638-6(4)*, Simon & Schuster/Paula Wiseman Bks.) Simon & Schuster/Paula Wiseman Bks.

Sansone, V. K. Katie Bear: Fun Days at School. WillowRaven, Aidana, illus. 2007. 84p. pap. 16.95 *(978-0-9798154-7-8(9))* Living Waters Publishing Co.

Schmidt, Werner. The Forests of Adventure. 2005. 137p. pap. 12.50 *(978-1-4116-4721-3(1))* Lulu Pr., Inc.

Schofield Sr., Derrick. A Frog's Tale. 2012. 20p. pap. 13.77 *(978-1-4669-2009-5(2))* Trafford Publishing.

Sealls, Arthur. The Three Little Heroes: Book One of Kirk, Chelsea, & Samantha's Adventures. 2007. 84p. per. 8.95 *(978-0-595-44083-2(5))* iUniverse, Inc.

Seidman, Amy. The Adventures of Bebop Bunny. 2009. (Illus.). 20p. pap. 14.95 *(978-0-9824530-1-8(9)*, Epigraph Bks.) Monkfish Bk. Publishing Co.

Sempebwa, Christina. Tales of Zindan. 2012. 154p. pap. *(978-1-908895-48-6(9))* FeedARead.com.

Senior, Patricia. Mischief on Mumpit Mountain. 2009. 36p. pap. 14.75 *(978-1-60693-661-0(1)*, Eloquent Bks.) Strategic Book Publishing & Rights Agency (SBPRA).

Serino, Robert. The Adventures of Pea-Shooter: Into the Forbidden Forest. Lally, Cory, illus. 2012. 32p. pap. 24.95 *(978-1-4626-8019-1(4))* America Star Bks.

Sherwood-Sitts, Herm. The Fox & Farmer Beeching. 2011. 28p. pap. 24.95 *(978-1-4626-0914-7(7))* America Star Bks.

Simone, Kriss. Fairy Forest. 2007. 86p. pap. 7.78 *(978-1-84799-156-0(4))* Lulu Pr., Inc.

Smith-Rogers & Smith, Brady A. The Culinary Capers of Canon & Lily: Canon Grows a Garden. 2009. 20p. pap. 11.49 *(978-1-4490-1305-9(8))* AuthorHouse.

Smith, Timothy R. The Owls Don't Give a Hoot. 2007. (Buck Wilder's Adventure Ser.: 4). (Illus.). 80p. (J). (gr. -1-3). per. 5.95 *(978-1-934133-11-8(6)*, Mackinac Island Press, Inc.) Charlesbridge Publishing, Inc.

Sontag, Mary G. Bruno's Adventures. 2009. 128p. pap. 38.49 *(978-1-4490-1769-9(X))* AuthorHouse.

Spetzler, Carl. Goldilocks Meets Desidero. Meyers, Mark, illus. 2011. 36p. pap. 16.86 *(978-1-4634-2684-2(4))* AuthorHouse.

Srinivasan, Divya. Little Owl's 1-2-3. Srinivasan, Divya, illus. 2015. (ENG., Illus.). 18p. (J). (— 1). 5.99 *(978-0-451-47454-4(6)*, Viking Books for Young Readers) Penguin Young Readers Group.

—Little Owl's Day. Srinivasan, Divya, illus. 2014. (ENG., Illus.). 32p. (J). (gr. -1-k). 16.99 *(978-0-670-01650-1(0)*, Viking Books for Young Readers) Penguin Young Readers Group.

—Little Owl's Night. (ENG., 32p. (J). 2013. Illus.). (— 1). bds. 6.99 *(978-0-670-01579-5(2))* 2011. (gr. -1-k). 16.99 *(978-0-670-01295-4(5))* Penguin Young Readers Group. (Viking Books for Young Readers).

Stephens, Sarah Hines & Hines-Stephens, Sarah. Rumble in the Rainforest, 1 vol. Schoening, Dan, illus. (Wonder Woman Ser.). (ENG.). 56p. (gr. 2-3). 2014. pap. 4.95 *(978-1-4342-2765-2(0))* 2010. 26.65 *(978-1-4342-1992-3(5))* Stone Arch Bks. (DC Super Heroes).

Stewart, A. W. Rooktime. 2010. 284p. pap. 15.49 *(978-1-4520-1460-9(4))* AuthorHouse.

Stewart, Paul & Riddell, Chris. Beyond the Deepwoods. 2008. (Edge Chronicles Ser.: Bk. 1). (ENG.). 288p. (J). (gr. 3-7). 8.99 *(978-0-440-42087-3(3)*, Bluefire) Random Hse. Children's Bks.

Stolberg, Tina. Little Shrew Caboose. O'Neill, Philomena, illus. 2009. (ENG.). 32p. (J). (gr. k-2). 16.95 *(978-0-9792035-7-2(0))* Pleasant St. Pr.

Stone Arch Books (Firm: Afton, Minn.) Staff. Hansel & Gretel: The Graphic Novel, 1 vol. Dietrich, Sean, illus. 2008. (Graphic Spin Ser.). (ENG.). 40p. (gr. 1-3). pap. 5.95 *(978-1-4342-0863-7(X)*, Graphic Revolve) Stone Arch Bks.

Stone, Laura. Tulia Turtle Finds Her Talents. 2010. 33p. pap. 16.95 *(978-0-557-32227-4(3))* Lulu Pr., Inc.

Stratton-Porter, Gene. Freckles. (J). reprint ed. lib. bdg. 24.95 *(978-0-89190-949-1(4)*, Rivercity Pr.) Amereon Ltd.

Stubben, Michael. Clark vs. the Rainforest. 2012. 110p. pap. 9.99 *(978-1-105-54615-0(2))* Lulu Pr., Inc.

Suits, Barbara Bradford. The Hidden Treasure. 2013. 48p. pap. 7.95 *(978-1-61286-199-9(7))* Avid Readers Publishing Group.

Summers, Gillian. The Secret of the Dread Forest: The Faire Folk Trilogy. 2009. (Faire Folk Saga Ser.: 3). (ENG.). 288p. (YA). pap. 9.95 *(978-0-7387-1411-0(9)*, Flux) North Star Editions.

Sunday, Bonnie. Sparkles, Dragons, & Dragonfly Land. 2012. 32p. pap. 19.99 *(978-1-4772-2914-9(0))* AuthorHouse.

Swarabi, Fatma Abdulla & El Amin, Khalid Hamid. Marim & Her Grandmother. 2010. 28p. pap. 13.99 *(978-1-4490-8156-0(8))* AuthorHouse.

Tara, Stephanie Lisa. Eliza's Forever Trees. Walton, Alex, illus. 2012. 290p. (J). pap. 9.99 net. *(978-1-61254-067-2(8))* Brown Books Publishing Group.

Tardif, Elizabeth. A Bunny Named Apple. Buehrle, Jacquelyn, illus. 2011. 28p. pap. 24.95 *(978-1-4560-0946-5(X))* America Star Bks.

Tatsuyama, Sayuri. Happy Happy Clover, Vol. 1. Tatsuyama, Sayuri, illus. 2009. (ENG., Illus.). 200p. (J). pap. 7.99 *(978-1-4215-2656-0(5))* Viz Media.

Taylor, Dereen. The Lost Treasure of the Jungle Temple: Peek Inside the 3D Windows! Hutchinson, Tim, illus. 2013. (ENG.). 12p. (J). (gr. 1-8). 16.99 *(978-1-84322-822-6(X)*, Armadillo) Anness Publishing GBR. Dist: National Bk. Network.

Theiss, Lewis E. The Young Wireless Operator -As a Fire. 2006. pap. *(978-1-4068-1180-3(7))* Echo Library.

Thomas, Dagny. Courageous Hearts. 2007. 190p. pap. 11.98 *(978-0-615-17087-9(0))* Thomastar Publishing.

Thorpe, Roslyn C. Rayray's Amazing Dream: An Adventurous Week. 2012. 24p. pap. 15.99 *(978-1-4771-5366-6(7))* Xlibris Corp.

Thrasher, Amanda M. Mischief in the Mushroom Patch. 2010. 174p. pap. 10.50 *(978-1-60911-165-6(6)*, Strategic Bk. Publishing) Strategic Book Publishing & Rights Agency (SBPRA).

Tibo, Gilles & Vaillancourt, François. El Senor Patapum. (Barril Sin Fondo Ser.). (SPA.). (J). (gr. 3-5). pap. *(978-968-6465-58-7(8))* Casa de Estudios de Literatura y Talleres Artisticos Amaquemecan A.C. MEX. Dist: Lectorum Pubns., Inc.

Toma, Al. Rainbow on the Tree of Life. 2005. (J). pap. 15.00 *(978-0-8059-6607-7(2))* Dorrance Publishing Co., Inc.

Tomlin, S. E. Children of Baimbough Forest. 2012. (ENG.). 79p. pap. 9.95 *(978-1-4327-9857-4(X))*; pap. 17.95 *(978-1-4787-1735-5(1))* Outskirts Pr., Inc.

Tonderum, Angela. Kaycee Kangaroo Lost in Alphabet Forest: Adventures of Kaycee Kangaroo. Carlson, Christine, illus. 2008. 41p. pap. 24.95 *(978-1-60672-601-3(3))* America Star Bks.

Troyer, Gloria Irene. Beatrice & the Snow People. 2013. 114p. pap. 14.95 *(978-1-62646-481-0(2))* Booklocker.com, Inc.

Tumbrello, Shannon. Freedom Forest. 2007. 17.00 *(978-0-8059-8880-2(7))* Dorrance Publishing Co., Inc.

Turner, Tracie & Dyson, Kyree. The Adventures of Kyree the Chocolate Moose. 2013. 20p. pap. 24.95 *(978-1-62709-178-7(5))* America Star Bks.

Twin Sister Produtions & Shepherd, Jodie. Sesame Street Big Red Riding Hood. 2010. (J). (gr. k-2). 14.99 *(978-1-59922-635-4(9))* Twin Sisters IP, LLC.

Twin Sister Produtions Staff & Shepherd, Jodie. Sesame Street Big Red Riding Hood. 2010. (J). (gr. k-2). 14.99 *(978-1-59922-526-5(3))* Twin Sisters IP, LLC.

Tyler, Brenda. The Tomtes of Hilltop Wood, 1 vol. 2010. (ENG., Illus.). 32p. (J). (gr. -1-3). 17.95 *(978-0-86315-772-1(6))* Floris Bks. GBR. Dist: SteinerBooks, Inc.

Tyler, William H. Who Let the Mongoose Loose? 2011. 48p. pap. 18.41 *(978-1-4269-5694-2(0))* Trafford Publishing.

Tyrrell, Melissa. Hansel & Gretel. McMullen, Nigel, illus. 2005. (Fairytale Friends Ser.). 12p. (J). bds. 5.95 *(978-1-58117-152-5(8)*, Intervisual/Piggy Toes) Bendon, Inc.

Wainscott, Bud. The Candy Well. 2012. 52p. pap. 11.95 *(978-1-4772-5349-6(1))* AuthorHouse.

—The Wounded Hawk. 2012. 48p. pap. 11.95 *(978-1-4772-5354-0(8))* AuthorHouse.

Walker, Mary. The Flower Tree. 2010. (Illus.). 50p. pap. 12.95 *(978-1-4327-3588-3(8))* Outskirts Pr., Inc.

Ward, C. L. Portia the Porcupine Visits the Doctor. 2010. 36p. pap. 16.95 *(978-1-4490-9230-6(6))* AuthorHouse.

Welsh, Kenneth Wilbur. The Oak Brothers. 2011. 16p. 12.00 *(978-1-4520-6079-8(7))* AuthorHouse.

West, Carly Anne. The Bargaining. 2015. (ENG., Illus.). 416p. (YA). (gr. 9). 17.99 *(978-1-4424-4182-8(8)*, Simon Pulse) Simon Pulse.

West, Kathryn E. Garden of Roses. 2007. 328p. 29.95 *(978-0-595-70333-3(X))*; per. 19.95 *(978-0-595-45295-8(7))* iUniverse, Inc.

Weston Woods Staff, creator. Hansel & Gretel. 2011. 38.75 *(978-0-439-80425-7(6))* Weston Woods Studios, Inc.

—Red Riding Hood. 2011. 18.95 *(978-0-439-72882-9(7))*; 38.75 *(978-0-439-72883-6(5))*; 29.95 *(978-0-439-73518-6(1))* Weston Woods Studios, Inc.

White, Kittie. The Magic Butterfly: And Other Tales. 2008. (ENG.). 52p. pap. 11.99 *(978-1-4196-9096-9(5))* CreateSpace Independent Publishing Platform.

Whybrow, Ian. Little Wolf, Forest Detective. Ross, Tony, illus. 2005. 112p. (J). (gr. 3-6). pap. 6.95 *(978-1-57505-829-0(4))* Lerner Publishing Group.

Wilhelm, Hans. Hello, Sun! Wilhelm, Hans, illus. 2005. (Illus.). 32p. (gr. k-2). 15.25 *(978-1-57505-348-6(9))* Lerner Publishing Group.

Williams, Annik. Mr. Mole's Day Off: With Goodnight Little Birdie. 2010. 20p. 15.78 *(978-1-4520-3756-1(6))* AuthorHouse.

Williams, T. D. Happy Village. 2010. 24p. 13.99 *(978-1-4269-3492-6(0))* Trafford Publishing.

Williams, Teresa Ann. Friends of Wildwood, 1 vol. 2009. 48p. pap. 16.95 *(978-1-4489-9419-9(5))* America Star Bks.

Wilson, Karma. Bear's New Friend. Chapman, Jane, illus. 2006. (Bear Bks.). (ENG.). 40p. (J). (gr. -1-3). 17.99 *(978-0-689-85984-7(8)*, McElderry, Margaret K. Bks.) McElderry, Margaret K. Bks.

Wilson, Melissa Anne. Nalyn & the Indigo Pearl. 2008. (Illus.). 24p. (J). pap. 8.00 *(978-0-8059-7409-6(1))* Dorrance Publishing Co., Inc.

Winfield, Arthur M. The Rover Boys in the Jungle. 2004. reprint ed. pap. 21.95 *(978-1-4191-8118-4(1))*; pap. 1.99 *(978-1-4192-8118-1(6))* Kessinger Publishing, LLC.

Wolf, Gita & Anastasio, Andrea. Alone in the Forest. Shyam, Bhajju, illus. 2013. (ENG.). 40p. (J). (gr. -1). 16.95 *(978-81-923171-5-1(3))* Tara Books Agency IND. Dist: Publishers Group West (PGW).

Wolfe, Carolyn. The Unhappy Little Dragon: Lessons Begin. Mathis, Leslie, illus. 2009. 38p. pap. 12.99 *(978-1-935105-42-8(6))* Avid Readers Publishing Group.

Wood, Barbie. The Adventure of Mookin Munchkin. Klick, Gloria, illus. 2013. 32p. pap. 24.95 *(978-1-63004-041-3(X))* America Star Bks.

Woszczylo, Noushka. Escape. 2012. 36p. pap. 21.99 *(978-1-4771-5035-1(8))* Xlibris Corp.

Yorke, Peter & Batley, Alan. Tales from Fidgety Forest. 2011. (Illus.). 80p. (gr. 1-2). pap. 12.52 *(978-1-4567-7961-0(3))* AuthorHouse.

Yusuf. Butterfly & Bumble Bee: Adventure in Yellow Stone National Park. 2010. 16p. 8.49 *(978-1-4520-4022-6(2))* AuthorHouse.

Zabel, Alanna. The Seven Doors. 2006. 59p. pap. 18.50 *(978-1-4116-4369-7(0))* Lulu Pr., Inc.

Zahorak, Sarah. Candyland Forest. 2009. 24p. pap. 12.50 *(978-1-4343-9905-2(2))* AuthorHouse.

Zalonis, C. B. Strangers in the Forest. 2006. (J). pap. 8.00 *(978-0-8059-6820-0(2))* Dorrance Publishing Co., Inc.

FORGERY OF WORKS OF ART

see Art—Forgeries

FORMER SOVIET REPUBLICS

Here are entered works discussing collectively the independent countries that emerged from the dissolution of the former Soviet Union in 1991.

Minahan, James. The Former Soviet Union's Diverse Peoples: A Reference Sourcebook, 1 vol. Barkan, Elliott Robert, ed. 2004. (Ethnic Diversity Within Nations Ser.). (Illus.). 389p. (C). 75.00 *(978-1-57607-823-5(X)*, SVDPLEC) ABC-CLIO, LLC.

FORMOSA

see Taiwan

FORREST, NATHAN BEDFORD, 1821-1877

Seabrook, Lochlainn. The Quotable Nathan Bedford Forrest: Selections from the Writings & Speeches of the Confederacy's Most Brilliant Cavalryman. 2012. (Illus.). 130p. pap. 12.95 *(978-0-9838185-5-7(X))* Sea Raven Pr.

—Saddle, Sword, & Gun: A Biography of Nathan Bedford Forrest for Teens. 2013. 116p. pap. 9.95 *(978-0-9858632-6-5(9))* Sea Raven Pr.

FORT, CHARLES, 1874-1932

Walker, Kathryn. Mysteries of the Cosmic Joker. 2009. (Unsolved! Ser.). (ENG., Illus.). 32p. (J). (gr. 3-5). pap. *(978-0-7787-4161-9(3))*; (gr. 4-6). *(978-0-7787-4148-0(6))* Crabtree Publishing Co.

FORTEN, JAMES, 1766-1842

Figley, Marty Rhodes. Prisoner for Liberty. Orback, Craig, illus. 2008. (On My Own History Ser.). (ENG.). 48p. (gr. 2-4). lib. bdg. 25.26 *(978-0-8225-7280-0(X)*, Millbrook Pr.) Lerner Publishing Group.

Figley, Mary Rhodes. Prisoner for Liberty. 2009. pap. 40.95 *(978-0-7613-4796-5(8))* Lerner Publishing Group.

FORTIFICATION

see also Military Engineering

also names of countries with the subdivision Defenses, e.g. United States—Defenses, etc.

Copeland, Peter F. Historic North American Forts. 2012. (Dover History Coloring Book Ser.). (ENG.). 48p. (gr. 3-8). pap. 4.99 *(978-0-486-41036-4(6))* Dover Pubns., Inc.

Davis, Susan Burdick. Old Forts & Real Folks. 2006. pap. 31.95 *(978-1-4286-5582-9(4))* Kessinger Publishing, LLC.

Gravett, Christopher. Castle. 2008. (DK Eyewitness Bks.). (ENG.). 72p. (J). (gr. 3-7). 16.99 *(978-0-7566-3769-9(4)*, DK Children) Dorling Kindersley Publishing, Inc.

Hamilton, John. Castles & Dungeons, 1 vol. 2006. (Fantasy & Folklore Ser.). (ENG., Illus.). 32p. (gr. 5-8). 27.07 *(978-1-59679-335-4(X)*, Abdo & Daughters) ABDO Publishing Co.

Hicks, Peter. How Castles Were Built. 2008. (Age of Castles Ser.). (Illus.). 48p. (J). (gr. 3-7). lib. bdg. 29.25 *(978-1-4042-4293-7(7)*, PowerKids Pr.) Rosen Publishing Group, Inc., The.

Hoggard, Brian. Crusader Castles: Christian Fortresses in the Middle East. (Library of the Middle Ages Ser.). 64p. (gr. 5-8). 2009. 58.50 *(978-1-60853-897-3(4)*, Rosen Reference) 2004. (Illus.). (YA). lib. bdg. 31.95 *(978-0-8239-4212-1(0))* Rosen Publishing Group, Inc., The.

Kerrigan, Juliet. Life & Death in a Hill Fort. 2015. (Collins Big Cat Ser.). (ENG., Illus.). 32p. (J). (gr. 3-3). pap. 8.95 *(978-0-00-812773-2(5))* HarperCollins Pubs. Ltd. GBR. Dist: Independent Pubs. Group.

Macaulay, David. Castle: Revised & in Full Color. 2013. (ENG., Illus.). 80p. (J). (gr. 5-7). 19.99 *(978-0-544-10226-2(6))* Houghton Mifflin Harcourt Publishing Co.

Macaulay, David & Keenan, Sheila. Castle: How It Works. 2015. (ENG., Illus.). 32p. (J). (gr. 1-4). 17.99 *(978-1-62672-208-8(0)*, 9781626722088, Macaulay, David Studio) Roaring Brook Pr.

Macdonald, Fiona. Warfare in the Middle Ages. 2015. (Warriors Ser.). (Illus.). 48p. (gr. 4-7). 37.10 *(978-1-62588-356-8(0))* Black Rabbit Bks.

—You Wouldn't Want to Be in a Medieval Dungeon! Prisoners You'd Rather Not Meet. Antram, David, illus. 2013. (You Wouldn't Want to... Ser.). (ENG.). (J). 40p. pap. 9.95 *(978-0-531-24504-0(7))*; 32p. 29.00 *(978-0-531-25948-1(X))* Scholastic Library Publishing. (Watts, Franklin).

—You Wouldn't Want to Be in a Medieval Dungeon! Prisoners You'd Rather Not Meet. 2013. (You Wouldn't Want To... Ser.). lib. bdg. 20.80 *(978-0-606-31629-3(9)*, Turtleback) Turtleback Bks.

Malam, John. Hill Forts: Discover Stone, Bronze & Iron Age Britain. 2017. (Prehistoric Adventures Ser.). (ENG., Illus.). 32p. (J). (gr. 2-4). 17.99 *(978-0-7502-9593-2(7)*, Wayland) Hachette Children's Group GBR. Dist: Hachette Bk. Group.

Maynard, Charles W. Castillo de San Marcos. 2009. (Famous Forts Throughout American History Ser.). 24p. (gr. 3-4). 42.50 *(978-1-61512-514-2(0)*, PowerKids Pr.) Rosen Publishing Group, Inc., The.

Patrick, Bethanne Kelly. Forts of the West. 2004. (History of the Old West Ser.). (Illus.). 64p. (YA). (gr. 5-18). lib. bdg. 19.95 *(978-1-59084-071-9(2))* Mason Crest.

Snyder, Sally. Hold the Fort. Snyder, Sally, illus. 2003. (Illus.). 45p. (J). 20.00 *(978-1-882203-99-4(2))* Orange Frazer Pr.

Stewart, David. You Wouldn't Want to Be in a Medieval Dungeon! Antram, David, illus. rev. ed. 2013. (You Wouldn't Want to... Ser.). (ENG.). 32p. (J). 29.00 *(978-0-531-25949-8(8)*, Watts, Franklin) Scholastic Library Publishing.

Stiles, David. Forts for Kids. 2011. (ENG., Illus.). 96p. pap. 16.95 *(978-0-7627-6453-2(8)*, Lyons Pr.) Globe Pequot Pr., The.

Truran, Stacy. Troy's Tree Fort: Measure Lengths in Standard Units. 2014. (Rosen Common Core Math Readers Ser.). (ENG.). 24p. (J). (gr. 2-3). pap. 8.25 *(978-1-4777-4784-1(2)*, Rosen Classroom) Rosen Publishing Group, Inc., The.

FORTS

see Fortification

FORTUNE

see Probabilities; Success

FORTUNE-TELLING

see also Astrology; Cards; Clairvoyance; Dreams

Filipak, Christine & Vargo, Joseph, illus. Madame Endora's Fortune Cards. 2003. mass mkt. 17.99 *(978-0-9675756-3-6(X))* Monolith Graphics.

Green, Carl R. & Sanford, William R. The Mysterious Secrets of Dreams. Kelley, Gerald, illus. 2011. (Investigating the Unknown Ser.). 48p. (J). (gr. 5-9). lib. bdg. 25.27 *(978-0-7660-3821-9(1))* Enslow Pubs., Inc.

—The Mystery of Fortune-Telling. Kelley, Gerald, illus. 2011. (Investigating the Unknown Ser.). 48p. (J). (gr. 5-18). pap. 8.95 *(978-1-59845-304-1(1))*; lib. bdg. 25.27 *(978-0-7660-3819-6(X))* Enslow Pubs., Inc.

Heiman, Diane & Suneby, Elizabeth. Origami Fortune Tellers. Archer, Christine, illus. 2011. (Dover Origami Papercraft Ser.). (ENG.). 32p. (J). (gr. 2-7). pap. 7.99 *(978-0-486-47826-5(2))* Dover Pubns., Inc.

Kanto, Erik & Kanto, Ilona. Your Face Tells All: Learn the Wisdom of the Chinese Art of Face Reading. 2004. (Illus.). 176p. pap. 16.95 *(978-1-929956-13-5(4))* Kanto Productions, LLC.

Krohn, Katherine. Fortune-Telling. 2008. (Mysterious Encounters Ser.). (ENG., Illus.). 48p. (J). (gr. 4-8). lib. bdg. 29.00 *(978-0-7377-4085-1(X)*, LML02109-242880, Kidhaven) Cengage Gale.

Moss, Marissa. Amelia Tells All. Moss, Marissa, illus. 2007. (Amelia Ser.). (ENG., Illus.). 64p. (J). (gr. 2-5). 9.99 *(978-1-4169-0918-7(4)*, Simon & Schuster/Paula Wiseman Bks.) Simon & Schuster/Paula Wiseman Bks.

Storm, Rayne. Elemental Tarot for Kids, 1 vol. 2012. (ENG., Illus.). 96p. (J). pap. 34.99 *(978-0-7643-4130-4(8)*, 9780764341304) Schiffer Publishing, Ltd.

FORTUNES

see Income

FOSSIL MAMMALS

see Mammals, Fossil

FOSSIL PLANTS

see Plants, Fossil

FOSSILS

see also Extinct Animals; Mammals, Fossil; Plants, Fossil; Reptiles, Fossil

ABDO Publishing Company Staff. Prehistoric Animals Set 2. 2003. (Prehistoric Animals Set 2 Ser.). (gr. k-4). 153.90 *(978-1-57765-972-3(4)*, Buddy Bks.) ABDO Publishing Co.

Agenbroad, Larry D. & Nelson, Lisa W. Mammoths: Ice-Age Giants. 2003. (Illus.). 120p. (J). (gr. 7-12). pap. 7.95 *(978-0-8225-0470-2(7))* Lerner Publishing Group.

Aliki. Digging up Dinosaurs. 33p. (J). (gr. 1-3). pap. 4.95 *(978-0-8072-1339-1(X)*, Listening Library) Random Hse. Audio Publishing Group.

—Fossils Tell of Long Ago. Aliki, illus. 2016. (Let's-Read-And-Find-Out Science 2 Ser.). (Illus.). 32p. (J). (gr. -1-3). pap. 6.99 *(978-0-06-238207-8(1))* HarperCollins Pubs.

Alonso, Juan Carlos & Paul, Gregory S. The Early Cretaceous: Notes, Drawings, & Observations from Prehistory. 2015. (Ancient Earth Journal Ser.). (ENG., Illus.). 112p. (J). (gr. 3-7). 19.95 *(978-1-63322-033-1(8)*, 1394805, Walter Foster Jr) Quarto Publishing Group USA.

American Museum of Natural History & Lach, Will. I Am NOT a Dinosaur! Lambert, Jonny, illus. 2016. (ENG.). 40p. (J). (gr. -1-2). 14.95 *(978-1-4549-1491-4(2))* Sterling Publishing Co., Inc.

Amiot, Romain. Dinosaurs. Méhée, Loic, illus. 2017. (ENG.). 32p. (J). 12.99 ***(978-1-4413-2474-0(7)***, 993b8c32-b56d-4ab5-a26e-28e02dfd336c) Peter Pauper Pr. Inc.

Anderson, Michael. Investigating Minerals, Rocks, & Fossils. 2011. (Illus.). 88p. (J). lib. bdg. 31.70 *(978-1-61530-500-1(9))* Rosen Publishing Group, Inc., The.

Arato, Rona. Fossils: Clues to Ancient Life. 2004. (Rocks, Minerals, & Resources Ser.). (ENG., Illus.). 32p. (J). pap. *(978-0-7787-1451-4(9))* Crabtree Publishing Co.

Arnold, Caroline. Living Fossils: Clues to the Past. Plant, Andrew, illus. 2016. (ENG.). 32p. (J). (gr. 2-5). lib. bdg. 16.95 *(978-1-58089-691-7(X))* Charlesbridge Publishing, Inc.

Bacchin, Matteo, illus. A Jurassic Mystery: Archaeopteryx. 2008. (Dinosaurs: Ser.). (ENG.). 64p. (J). (gr. 3-7). 15.95 *(978-0-7892-0979-5(9)*, Abbeville Kids) Abbeville Pr., Inc.

Bacchin, Matteo & Signore, Marco. The Journey: Plateosaurus. Shore, Marguerite, tr. from ITA. 2008. (Dinosaurs: Ser.). (ENG., Illus.). 61p. (J). (gr. 4-12). 18.95 *(978-0-7892-1015-9(0)*, Abbeville Kids) Abbeville Pr., Inc.

—A Jurassic Mystery: Archaeopteryx. Shore, Marguerite, tr. from ITA. 2008. (Dinosaurs: Ser.). (ENG., Illus.). 61p. (J). (gr. 4-6). 18.95 *(978-0-7892-1016-6(9)*, Abbeville Kids) Abbeville Pr., Inc.

Bailey, Jacqui. Monster Bones: The Story of a Dinosaur Fossil, 1 vol. Lilly, Matthew, illus. 2004. (Science Works). (ENG.). 32p. (gr. 3-6). 27.99 *(978-1-4048-0565-1(6))* Picture Window Bks.

Bard, Mariel. Amphibian Fossils. 2016. (Fossil Files Ser.). 00032p. (J). (gr. 5-5). pap. 10.00 *(978-1-4994-2720-2(4)*, PowerKids Pr.) Rosen Publishing Group, Inc., The.

Bardoe, Cheryl. Mammoths & Mastodons: Titans of the Ice Age. 2010. (ENG., Illus.). 48p. (J). (gr. 3-7). 19.95 *(978-0-8109-8413-4(X)*, Abrams Bks. for Young Readers) Abrams, Inc.

Barker, Charles Ferguson. Under New England: The Story of New England's Rocks & Fossils. Barker, Charles Ferguson, illus. 2008. (ENG., Illus.). 72p. (J). (gr. 2-7). 12.95 *(978-1-58465-696-8(4))* Univ. Pr. of New England.

—Under Ohio: The Story of Ohio's Rocks & Fossils. Barker, Charles Ferguson, illus. 2007. (Illus.). 56p. (J). (gr. 3-7). 26.95 *(978-0-8214-1755-3(X))* Ohio Univ. Pr.

Barner, Bob. Dinosaur Bones. Barner, Bob, illus. unabr. ed. 2006. (Illus.). (J). (gr. -1-2). 29.95 *(978-0-439-90580-0(X))* Weston Woods Studios, Inc.

Bedell, J. M. So, You Want to Work with the Ancient & Recent Dead? Unearthing Careers from Paleontology to Forensic Science. 2015. (Be What You Want Ser.). (ENG., Illus.). 256p. (J). (gr. 3-7). pap. 11.99 *(978-1-58270-545-3(3))* Aladdin/Beyond Words.

Bedry, Christa. Fish. 2004. (Prehistoric Life Ser.). (J). pap. 9.95 *(978-1-59036-172-6(5))*; (Illus.). 32p. lib. bdg. 26.00 *(978-1-59036-112-2(1))* Weigl Pubs., Inc.

—Insects. 2004. (Prehistoric Life Ser.). (Illus.). 32p. (J). (gr. -1-3). per. 9.95 *(978-1-59036-173-3(3))*; lib. bdg. 26.00 *(978-1-59036-113-9(X))* Weigl Pubs., Inc.

Benanti, Carol. Real Fossils. Frank, Michael, ed. Dickens, Earl, illus. (Real Collections). 32p. (Orig.). (J). (gr. 3-8). pap. 6.95 (978-1-880592-06-9(1)) Pace Products, Inc.

Benchmark Education Company. Plant & Animal Fossils (Teacher Guide) 2005. (978-1-4108-4669-3(5)) Benchmark Education Co.

Benduhn, Tea. Oil, Gas, & Coal. 2008. (Energy for Today Ser.). 24p. (gr. 2-6). (J). lib. bdg. 22.00 (978-0-8368-9261-1(5)); (SPA & ENG.). pap. 8.15 (978-0-8368-9360-1(3)) Stevens, Gareth Publishing LLLP. (Weekly Reader Leveled Readers).

—Petróleo, Gas y Carbón. 2008. (Energía para el presente (Energy for Today) Ser.). (SPA & ENG.). 24p. (gr. 2-6). pap. 8.15 (978-0-8368-9366-3(2), Weekly Reader Leveled Readers) Stevens, Gareth Publishing LLLP.

Bennett, Leonie. Dinosaur Fossils. 2007. (I Love Reading Ser.). (Illus.). 24p. (J). (gr. -1-2). lib. bdg. 19.96 (978-1-59716-555-6(7)) Bearport Publishing Co., Inc.

—Dinosaur Hunting. 2007. (I Love Reading Ser.). (Illus.). 24p. (J). (gr. -1-2). lib. bdg. 19.96 (978-1-59716-554-9(9)) Bearport Publishing Co., Inc.

Birch, Robin. Relatives of Dinosaurs. 2nd rev. ed. 2008. (Dinosaur World Ser.). 32p. (J). (gr. 2-4). 23.00 (978-1-60413-408-7(9)) Facts On File, Inc.

Blaisdell, Molly. Fossils. 2008. (Discovering & Exploring Science Ser.). (Illus.). 16p. (J). (gr. -1-3). lib. bdg. 12.95 (978-0-7569-8411-3(4)) Perfection Learning Corp.

Boelts, Maribeth. Fossils Give Us Clues. 2016. (Spring Forward Ser.). (J). (gr. 2). (978-1-4900-2249-9(X)) Benchmark Education Co.

Bonner, Hannah. When Dinos Dawned, Mammals Got Munched, & Pterosaurs Took Flight: A Cartoon Prehistory of Life in the Triassic. 2012. (ENG., Illus.). 48p. (J). (gr. 3-7). lib. bdg. 25.90 (978-1-4263-0863-5(9), National Geographic Children's Bks.) National Geographic Society.

—When Fish Got Feet, Sharks Got Teeth, & Bugs Began to Swarm: A Cartoon Prehistory of Life Long Before Dinosaurs. 2009. (ENG., Illus.). 48p. (J). (gr. 5). pap. 7.95 (978-1-4263-0546-7(X), National Geographic Children's Bks.) National Geographic Society.

—When Fish Got Feet, Sharks Got Teeth, & Bugs Began to Swarm: A Cartoon Prehistory of Life Long Before Dinosaurs. Bonner, Hannah, illus. 2007. (ENG., Illus.). 48p. (J). (gr. 5-18). lib. bdg. 25.90 (978-1-4263-0079-0(4)); 16.95 (978-1-4263-0078-3(6)) National Geographic Society. (National Geographic Children's Bks.).

—When Fish Got Feet, When Bugs Were Big, & When Dinos Dawned: A Cartoon Prehistory of Life on Earth. 2015. (ENG., Illus.). 128p. (J). (gr. 3-7). pap. 12.99 (978-1-4263-2104-7(X), National Geographic Children's Bks.) National Geographic Society.

Bonner, Hannah & National Geographic Kids Staff. When Dinos Dawned, Mammals Got Munched, & Pterosaurs Took Flight: A Cartoon PreHistory of Life in the Triassic. 2012. (ENG., Illus.). 48p. (J). (gr. 3-7). 17.95 (978-1-4263-0862-8(0), National Geographic Children's Bks.) National Geographic Society.

Bowman, Chris. Fossils. 2014. (Earth Science Rocks! Ser.). (ENG., Illus.). 24p. (J). (gr. k-3). lib. bdg. 25.95 (978-1-60014-979-5(0), Blastoff! Readers) Bellwether Media.

Bramwell, Martyn. Rocks & Fossils. Bramwell, Martyn, ed. Jackson, Ian & Suttie, Alan, illus. rev. ed. 2007. (Hobby Guides). 31p. (J). pap. 6.99 (978-0-7945-1526-3(6), Usborne) EDC Publishing.

Brannon, Barbara. Discover Fossils. 2005. (J). pap. (978-1-4108-5121-5(4)) Benchmark Education Co.

Brown, Cynthia Light & Brown, Grace. Explore Fossils! With 25 Great Projects. Stone, Bryan, illus. 2016. (Explore Your World Ser.). (ENG.). 96p. (J). (gr. 1-5). 19.95 (978-1-61930-331-7(0), 1401070) Octavio Publishing.

Bureau Of Land Management, et al. Junior Explorer Geology & Fossils Activity Book. 2012. 26p. pap. (978-1-78266-060-6(7)) Military Studies Pr.

Burton, Virginia Lee. Life Story. 2009. (ENG., Illus.). 80p. (J). (gr. 2-5). pap. 8.99 (978-0-547-20359-1(4)) Houghton Mifflin Harcourt Publishing Co.

Butz, Steve. The Bone Race: A Quest for Dinosaur Fossils. 2007. (ENG.). 248p. (YA). (gr. 7). pap. (978-1-933255-30-9(7)) DNA Pr.

Carpenter, Elizabeth. DinoMazes: The Colossal Fossil Book - 31 Poster-Size Prehistoric Fossil Nazes. 2011. (ENG., Illus.). 41p. (J). (gr. 3-12). pap. 11.95 (978-0-7611-6575-0(4), 16575) Workman Publishing Co., Inc.

Chandler, Fiona, et al. The Usborne Internet-Linked Prehistoric World. Firenze, Inklink, illus. 2005. 96p. (J). pap. (978-0-439-78504-4(9)) Scholastic, Inc.

Channing, Margot. Incredible Creatures. 2015. (Inside Eye Ser.). (Illus.). 32p. (gr. 3-6). 31.35 (978-1-906370-80-0(X)) Book Hse. GBR. Dist: Black Rabbit Bks.

Chapman, Todd & Judge, Lita. D Is for Dinosaur: A Prehistoric Alphabet. Judge, Lita, illus. 2007. (Science Alphabet Ser.). (ENG., Illus.). 48p. (J). (gr. 1-4). 19.99 (978-1-58536-242-4(5), 202065) Sleeping Bear Pr.

Clarke, Ginjer L. Maxed Out! Gigantic Creatures from the Past. Mueller, Pete, illus. 2010. (Penguin Young Readers, Level 3 Ser.). (ENG.). 48p. (J). (gr. 1-3). mass mkt. 3.99 (978-0-448-44827-5(0), Penguin Young Readers) Penguin Young Readers Group.

Clemson, Wendy & Clemson, David. Digging for Dinosaurs. 2007. (Math Adventures Ser.). (Illus.). 32p. (gr. 1-4). pap. 10.50 (978-0-8368-8137-0(0)); lib. bdg. 26.00 (978-0-8368-7838-7(8)) Stevens, Gareth Publishing LLLP. (Gareth Stevens Learning Library).

Colson, Rob. Dinosaur Bones: And What They Tell Us. 2016. (ENG., Illus.). 96p. (J). (gr. 5-12). 19.95 (978-1-77085-717-9(6), 9781770857179); pap. 12.95 (978-1-77085-694-3(3), 9781770856943) Firefly Bks., Ltd.

Connors, Kathleen. Human Fossils. 2012. (Fossilized! Ser.). (Illus.). 24p. (J). (gr. 2-5). pap. 8.15 (978-1-4339-6414-5(7)); lib. bdg. 22.60 (978-1-4339-6412-1(0)) Stevens, Gareth Publishing LLLP.

Croy, Anita. Exploring the Past. 2010. (Invisible Worlds Ser.). 48p. (gr. 4). 28.50 (978-0-7614-4194-6(8)) Marshall Cavendish GBR. Dist: Marshall Cavendish Corp.

Cunningham, Laura. The Bay Area Through Time. 2015. (Illus.). (J). (978-1-59714-301-1(4)) Heyday.

Dayton, Connor. Fossils. (Rocks & Minerals Ser.). 24p. (gr. 2-3). 2009. 42.50 (978-1-60852-499-0(X), PowerKids Pr.) 2007. (Illus.). (YA). lib. bdg. 22.60 (978-1-4042-3689-9(9)) Rosen Publishing Group, Inc., The.

Dickmann, Nancy. Burning Out: Energy from Fossil Fuels. 2016. (ENG., Illus.). 32p. (J). (978-0-7787-2372-1(0)) Crabtree Publishing Co.

Dinosaurios y animales prehistoricos/Dinosaurs & Prehistoric Animals [Becker's]. 2010. (Dinosaurios y animales prehistoricos/Dinosaurs & Prehistoric Animals Ser.). 89.80 (978-1-4296-5776-1(6)) Capstone Digital.

Dinosaurios y animales prehistoricos/Dinosaurs & Prehistoric Animals [Becker's]. 2010. (Dinosaurios y animales prehistoricos/Dinosaurs & Prehistoric Animals Ser.). 24p. pap. 27.80 (978-1-4296-5775-4(8), Pebble Plus Bilingue/Bilingual) Capstone Press of Coughlan Cos.

Dinosaurs & Prehistoric Animals [Becker's]. 2010. (Dinosaurs & Prehistoric Animals Ser.). 24p. pap. 27.80 (978-1-4296-5774-7(X), Pebble Plus) Capstone Press of Coughlan Cos.

Dinosaurs Dominate: Jurassic Life. 2013. (Awesome Ancient Animals Ser.). (Illus.). 32p. (J). (gr. 2-6). (978-1-84898-628-2(9), TickTock Books) Octopus Publishing Group.

Dippold-Brady, Melissa. Florida Fossils for Kids. 2009. pap. (978-1-61584-678-8(6)) Independent Pub.

DiSiena, Laura Lyn & Eliot, Hannah. Dinosaurs Live On! And Other Fun Facts. Spurgeon, Aaron, illus. 2015. (Did You Know? Ser.). (ENG.). 32p. (J). (gr. -1-3). pap. 6.99 (978-1-4814-2424-0(6), Little Simon) Little Simon.

Donald, Rhonda Lucas. Dino Tracks, 1 vol. Morrison, Cathy, illus. 2013. (ENG.). 32p. (J). (gr. 1-4). pap. 9.95 (978-1-60718-631-1(4)) Arbordale Publishing.

—Dino Treasures, 1 vol. Morrison, Cathy, illus. 2015. (ENG.). 32p. (J). (gr. 1-4). 17.95 (978-1-62855-450-2(9)) Arbordale Publishing.

Dorling Kindersley Publishing Staff. Dinosaurs. 2013. (Visual Encyclopedia Ser.). (ENG.). 304p. (J). (gr. 2-5). pap. 19.99 (978-1-4654-1233-1(6), DK Children) Dorling Kindersley Publishing, Inc.

—DK Eyewitness Books: Fossil. 2017. (DK Eyewitness Bks.). (ENG.). 72p. (J). (gr. 3-7). pap. 9.99 **(978-1-4654-6247-3(3)**, DK Children) Dorling Kindersley Publishing, Inc.

—Fossil. 2017. (DK Eyewitness Bks.). (ENG.). 72p. (J). (gr. 3-7). lib. bdg. 19.99 **(978-1-4654-6255-8(4)**, DK Children) Dorling Kindersley Publishing, Inc.

Dowell, Lori. Be a Paleontologist. 2014. (Be a Scientist! Ser.). 32p. (J). (gr. 3-6). pap. 10.50 (978-1-4824-1209-3(8)) Stevens, Gareth Publishing LLLP.

Dunn, Mary. My Adventure on a Dinosaur Dig. 2006. 44p. (J). 8.99 (978-1-59092-281-1(6)) Blue Forge Pr.

EDC Publishing, creator. Rocks & Fossils Kid Kit. 2009. (Usborne Kid Kits Ser.). (Illus.). (J). (gr. 5). pap. 15.99 (978-1-60130-025-6(5)) EDC Publishing.

Edelstein, June. Fossils. 2011. (Early Connections Ser.). (J). (978-1-61672-634-8(2)) Benchmark Education Co.

Eid, Alain. 1000 Photos of Minerals & Fossils. Viard, Michel, illus. 2003. (One Thousand Photos Ser.). 128p. (YA). (gr. 5-18). pap. 24.95 (978-0-7641-5218-4(1)) Barron's Educational Series, Inc.

Facchini, Fiorenzo. A Day with Homo Sapiens: Life 15,000 Years Ago. 2003. (Early Humans Ser.). (Illus.). 48p. (gr. 6-18). lib. bdg. 23.90 (978-0-7613-2768-4(1), Twenty-First Century Bks.) Lerner Publishing Group.

Faulkner, Rebecca. Fossils. 2016. (Geology Rocks! Ser.). (ENG.). 48p. (gr. 3-3). pap. 9.49 (978-1-4109-8634-4(9), Raintree Freestyle Express) Heinemann-Raintree.

Fossil Files. 2016. (Fossil Files Ser.). 00032p. (J). (gr. 5-5). 157.50 (978-1-4994-2642-7(9), PowerKids Pr.) Rosen Publishing Group, Inc., The.

Francis, Suzanne. Ancient Animals. 2006. (Illus.). 32p. (J). pap. (978-0-439-83876-4(2)) Scholastic, Inc.

—Prehistoric Hunters. 2006. (Illus.). 32p. (J). (978-0-439-83863-4(0)) Scholastic, Inc.

Franklin, Carolyn. Prehistoric Animals. Francis, John, illus. 2013. (World of Wonder Ser.). (ENG.). 32p. (gr. 1-3). lib. bdg. 31.35 (978-1-904642-65-7(9)) Book Hse. GBR. Dist: Black Rabbit Bks.

—Scary Dinosaurs. 2010. (Top 10 Worst Ser.). (Illus.). 32p. (J). (gr. 3-6). (ENG.). pap. 10.50 (978-1-4339-4074-3(4)); lib. bdg. 26.60 (978-1-4339-4073-6(6)) Stevens, Gareth Publishing LLLP. (Gareth Stevens Learning Library).

Furgang, Kathy. Finding Fossils & en busca de Fósiles: 6 English, 6 Spanish Adaptations. 2011. (ENG & SPA.). (J). 75.00 net. (978-1-4108-5654-8(2)) Benchmark Education Co.

Gilbert, Sara. Dire Wolves. 2017. (Illus.). 24p. (J). (978-1-60818-765-2(9), Creative Education) Creative Co., The.

—Ice Age Mega Beasts: Dire Wolves. 2017. (Ice Age Mega Beasts Ser.). (ENG., Illus.). 24p. (J). (gr. 1-3). pap. 8.99 **(978-1-62832-373-3(6)**, Creative Paperbacks) Creative Co., The.

—Ice Age Mega Beasts: Giant Short-Faced Bears. 2017. (Ice Age Mega Beasts Ser.). (ENG., Illus.). 24p. (J). (gr. 1-3). pap. 8.99 **(978-1-62832-374-0(4)**, Creative Paperbacks) Creative Co., The.

—Ice Age Mega Beasts: Mammoths. 2017. (Ice Age Mega Beasts Ser.). (ENG., Illus.). 24p. (J). (gr. 1-3). pap. 8.99 **(978-1-62832-375-7(2)**, Creative Paperbacks) Creative Co., The.

—Ice Age Mega Beasts: Stag-Moose. 2017. (Ice Age Mega Beasts Ser.). (ENG., Illus.). 24p. (J). (gr. 1-3). pap. 8.99 **(978-1-62832-378-8(7)**, Creative Paperbacks) Creative Co., The.

Gish, Melissa & Shaw, Nancy J. Fossils. (Illus.). 32p. pap. 8.95 (978-0-89812-319-7(4)) Creative Co., The.

Goecke, Michael P. American Mastodon, 1 vol. 2003. (Prehistoric Animals Set II Ser.). (ENG., Illus.). 24p. (gr. k-4). 25.65 (978-1-57765-973-0(2), Buddy Bks.) ABDO Publishing Co.

—Dire Wolf, 1 vol. 2003. (Prehistoric Animals Ser.). (ENG.). 24p. (gr. k-4). 25.65 (978-1-57765-966-2(X), Buddy Bks.) ABDO Publishing Co.

—Giant Ape, 1 vol. 2003. (Prehistoric Animals Ser.). (ENG.). 24p. (gr. k-4). 25.65 (978-1-57765-967-9(8), Buddy Bks.) ABDO Publishing Co.

—Giant Armadillo, 1 vol. 2003. (Prehistoric Animals Set II Ser.). (ENG.). 24p. (gr. k-4). 25.65 (978-1-57765-974-7(0), Buddy Bks.) ABDO Publishing Co.

—Giant Ground Sloth, 1 vol. 2003. (Prehistoric Animals Ser.). (ENG.). 24p. (gr. k-4). 25.65 (978-1-57765-968-6(6), Buddy Bks.) ABDO Publishing Co.

—Giant Rhino, 1 vol. 2003. (Prehistoric Animals Ser.). (ENG.). 24p. (gr. k-4). 25.65 (978-1-57765-969-3(4), Buddy Bks.) ABDO Publishing Co.

—Irish Elk, 1 vol. 2003. (Prehistoric Animals Set II Ser.). (ENG.). 24p. (gr. k-4). 25.65 (978-1-57765-975-4(9), Buddy Bks.) ABDO Publishing Co.

—Prehistoric Animals Set 1. 2003. (Prehistoric Animals Set 1 Ser.). (gr. k-4). 153.90 (978-1-57765-965-5(1), Buddy Bks.) ABDO Publishing Co.

—Scimitar Cat, 1 vol. 2003. (Prehistoric Animals Set II Ser.). (ENG.). 24p. (gr. k-4). 25.65 (978-1-57765-977-8(5), Buddy Bks.) ABDO Publishing Co.

—Short-Faced Bear, 1 vol. 2003. (Prehistoric Animals Set II Ser.). (ENG.). 24p. (gr. k-4). 25.65 (978-1-57765-976-1(7), Buddy Bks.) ABDO Publishing Co.

—Woolly Rhinoceros, 1 vol. 2003. (Prehistoric Animals Set II Ser.). (ENG.). 24p. (gr. k-4). 25.65 (978-1-57765-978-5(3), Buddy Bks.) ABDO Publishing Co.

Goldish, Meish. The Fossil Feud: Marsh & Cope's Bone Wars. 2006. (Fossil Hunters Ser.). (Illus.). 32p. (YA). (gr. 2-5). lib. bdg. 25.27 (978-1-59716-256-2(6)) Bearport Publishing Co., Inc.

Goldsmith, Mike. Digging for Dinosaurs. Daubney, Kate, illus. 2015. (I Explore Ser.). (ENG.). 12p. (J). (gr. -1-k). bds. 6.95 (978-1-4549-1501-0(3)) Sterling Publishing Co., Inc.

Goodman, Polly. Understanding Fossil Fuels. 2010. (World of Energy Ser.). (ENG.). 48p. (J). (gr. 6-8). lib. bdg. 31.95 (978-1-4339-4118-4(X), Gareth Stevens Learning Library) Stevens, Gareth Publishing LLLP.

Grambo, Rebecca L. Digging Canadian Dinosaurs, 1 vol. Bonder, Dianna, illus. 2004. (ENG.). 64p. (J). (gr. 2-6). pap. (978-1-55285-395-5(0)) Whitecap Bks., Ltd.

Gray, Susan H. Dinosaur Dig! 2007. (Scholastic News Nonfiction Readers Ser.). (ENG., Illus.). 24p. (J). (gr. 1-2). 22.00 (978-0-531-17482-1(4)) Scholastic Library Publishing.

—Dinosaur Eggs. 2007. (Scholastic News Nonfiction Readers Ser.). (ENG., Illus.). 24p. (J). (gr. 1-2). 22.00 (978-0-531-17483-8(2)) Scholastic Library Publishing.

—Dinosaur Tracks. 2007. (Scholastic News Nonfiction Readers Ser.). (ENG., Illus.). 24p. (J). (gr. 1-2). 22.00 (978-0-531-17485-2(9)) Scholastic Library Publishing.

—Paleontology: The Study of Prehistoric Life. 2012. (True Book Ser.). (ENG.). 48p. (J). pap. 6.95 (978-0-531-28274-8(0)); lib. bdg. 29.00 (978-0-531-24680-1(9)) Scholastic Library Publishing. (Children's Pr.).

Gregory, Josh. If You Were a Kid Discovering Dinosaurs. 2017. (If You Were a Kid Ser.). (ENG.). 32p. (J). pap. 7.95 **(978-0-531-23948-3(9))**; lib. bdg. 26.00 **(978-0-531-23747-2(8))** Scholastic Library Publishing. (Children's Pr.).

Greve, Tom. Fossils, Uncovering the Past. 2011. (ENG., Illus.). 48p. (gr. 4-6). pap. 10.95 (978-1-61741-984-3(2)) Rourke Educational Media.

Group/McGraw-Hill, Wright. Fossils Reveal Clues about Ancient Life, 6 vols. (Book2WebTM Ser.). (gr. 4-8). 36.50 (978-0-322-04431-9(6)) Wright Group/McGraw-Hill.

Halls, Kelly Milner. Dinosaur Mummies: Beyond Bare-Bone Fossils. 2007. (J). pap. 8.95 (978-1-58196-034-1(4), Darby Creek) Lerner Publishing Group.

—Dinosaur Mummies: Beyond Bare-Bone Fossils. Spears, Rick, illus. 2003. (Junior Library Guild Selection Ser.). 48p. (J). (gr. 4-18). 17.95 (978-1-58196-000-6(X), Darby Creek) Lerner Publishing Group.

Hansen, Grace. Fosiles. 2016. (¡Súper Geología! Ser.). (SPA.). 24p. (J). (gr. 1-6). pap. 7.95 (978-1-4966-0678-5(7)) Capstone Classroom.

—Fossils, 1 vol. 2016. (ENG., Illus.). 24p. (978-1-62970-905-5(0), 1391183) ABDO Publishing Co.

Hantula, Richard. Rocks & Fossils. 2007. (Gareth Stevens Vital Science: Earth Science Ser.). (Illus.). 48p. (gr. 5-12). pap. 14.05 (978-0-8368-7876-9(0), Gareth Stevens Secondary Library) Stevens, Gareth Publishing LLLP.

Harris, Nicolas. Dinosaurs Through Time. Dennis, Peter, illus. 2009. (Fast Forward Ser.). 32p. (YA). (gr. 2-5). lib. bdg. 25.25 (978-1-4358-2802-5(X)) Rosen Publishing Group, Inc., The.

Havercroft, Elizabeth. A Year in the World of Dinosaurs. 2008. (Time Goes By Ser.). (ENG.). (gr. k-2). pap. 39.62 (978-0-7613-4714-9(3)); (Illus.). 24p. lib. bdg. 22.60 (978-1-58013-548-1(X)) Lerner Publishing Group.

Haynes, Danielle. Mammal Fossils. 2016. (Fossil Files Ser.). 00032p. (J). (gr. 5-5). 26.25 (978-1-4994-2859-9(6)); pap. 10.00 (978-1-4994-2743-1(3)) Rosen Publishing Group, Inc., The. (PowerKids Pr.).

Heal, Edith. How the World Began. Nelson, Don, illus. 2012. 112p. 39.95 (978-1-258-23527-7(7)); pap. 24.95 (978-1-258-24549-8(3)) Literary Licensing, LLC.

Heitkamp, Kristina Lyn. Digging for Poop Fossils. 2017. (J). pap. **(978-0-7660-9097-2(3))** Enslow Pubs., Inc.

Heitkamp, Kristina Lyn. The Rift Valley & the Archaeological Evidence of the First Humans. 2016. (First Humans & Early Civilizations Ser.). 64p. (J). (gr. 6-6). pap. 12.95 (978-1-4994-6318-7(9)) Rosen Publishing Group, Inc., The.

Hirsch, Rebecca E. De-Extinction: The Science of Bringing Lost Species Back to Life. 2017. (Nonfiction — Young Adult Ser.). (ENG.). 120p. (gr. 8-12). (YA). 19.99 **(978-1-5124-3902-1(9)**, Twenty-First Century Bks.); (YA). 53.32 **(978-1-5124-2848-3(5)**, Twenty-First Century Bks.); (YA). 53.32 **(978-1-5124-3903-8(7)**, Twenty-First Century Bks.); (Illus.). (J). lib. bdg. 35.99 (978-1-4677-9490-9(2)) Lerner Publishing Group.

Hodge, Judith. Riches from Earth & Las riquezas de la Tierra: 6 English, 6 Spanish Adaptations. 2011. (ENG & SPA.). (J). 97.00 net. (978-1-4108-5716-3(6)) Benchmark Education Co.

Hoffman, Steven M. Fossils: History in the Rocks. 2011. (Rock It! Ser.). (Illus.). 24p. (J). pap. 8.25 (978-1-4488-2702-2(7)); lib. bdg. 22.60 (978-1-4488-2558-5(X)) Rosen Publishing Group, Inc., The. (PowerKids Pr.).

Holmes, Thom. Dinosaur Scientist: Careers Digging up the Past. 2009. (Wild Science Careers Ser.). (Illus.). 128p. (J). (gr. 5-18). lib. bdg. 33.27 (978-0-7660-3053-4(9)) Enslow Pubs., Inc.

—Paleontologists: Searching for Dinosaur Bones. 2015. (Extreme Science Careers Ser.). (ENG., Illus.). 128p. (J). (gr. 7-7). 37.27 (978-0-7660-6964-0(8)) Enslow Pubs., Inc.

—The Prehistoric Earth Set, 10-Volumes. 2008. (Prehistoric Earth Ser.). (C). (gr. 9-18). 350.00 (978-0-8160-7841-7(6), Chelsea Hse.) Facts On File, Inc.

Holmes, Thom & Holmes, Laurie. Baby Dinosaurs: Eggs, Nests, & Recent Discoveries. Skrepnick, Michael William, illus. 2003. (Dinosaur Library). 104p. (J). (gr. 6-12). lib. bdg. 26.60 (978-0-7660-2074-0(6)) Enslow Pubs., Inc.

—Great Dinosaur Expeditions & Discoveries: Adventures with the Fossil Hunters. Skrepnick, Michael William, illus. 2003. (Dinosaur Library). 112p. (J). lib. bdg. 26.60 (978-0-7660-2078-8(9)) Enslow Pubs., Inc.

—Prehistoric Flying Reptiles: The Pterosaurs. Skrepnick, Michael William, illus. 2003. (Dinosaur Library). 104p. (J). (gr. 6-12). lib. bdg. 26.60 (978-0-7660-2072-6(X)) Enslow Pubs., Inc.

Holtz, Thomas R., Jr. Digging for Brachiosaurus: A Discovery Timeline. 2015. (Dinosaur Discovery Timelines Ser.). (ENG.). 32p. (gr. 4-5). lib. bdg. 27.99 (978-1-4914-2123-9(1)) Capstone Press of Coughlan Cos.

—Digging for Stegosaurus: A Discovery Timeline. 2015. (Dinosaur Discovery Timelines Ser.). (ENG., Illus.). 32p. (gr. 4-5). pap. 7.95 (978-1-4914-2365-3(X)) Capstone Press of Coughlan Cos.

—Digging for Triceratops: A Discovery Timeline. 2015. (Dinosaur Discovery Timelines Ser.). (ENG., Illus.). 32p. (gr. 4-5). pap. 7.95 (978-1-4914-2367-7(6)) Capstone Press of Coughlan Cos.

—Digging for Tyrannosaurus Rex: A Discovery Timeline. 2015. (Dinosaur Discovery Timelines Ser.). (ENG.). 32p. (gr. 4-5). lib. bdg. 27.99 (978-1-4914-2125-3(8)) Capstone Press of Coughlan Cos.

Honders, Christine. Reptile Fossils. 2016. (Fossil Files Ser.). 00032p. (J). (gr. 5-5). pap. 10.00 (978-1-4994-2741-7(7), PowerKids Pr.) Rosen Publishing Group, Inc., The.

Horn, Geoffrey M., et al. Coal, Oil, & Natural Gas. 2010. (Energy Today Ser.). 48p. (J). (gr. 3-6). 30.00 (978-1-60413-785-9(1)) Facts On File, Inc.

Horner, Jack. Digging up Dinosaurs. Rath, Robert & Wilson, Phil, illus. 2007. 49p. (J). (gr. 3-7). pap. 14.95 (978-1-56037-396-4(2)) Farcountry Pr.

Houran, Lori Haskins. Dig Those Dinosaurs. Marquez, Francisca, illus. 2013. (ENG.). 24p. (J). (gr. -1-2). 15.99 (978-0-8075-1579-2(5)) Whitman, Albert & Co.

Huge Hunters Roam the Earth: Ancient Mammals. 2013. (Awesome Ancient Animals Ser.). 32p. (gr. 2-6). (978-1-84898-624-4(6), TickTock Books) Octopus Publishing Group.

Hutmacher, Kimberly. Fossils & Rocks. 2012. (ENG.). 24p. (gr. 4-5). pap. 8.95 (978-1-61810-236-2(2)) Rourke Educational Media.

Hyde, Natalie. Animal Fossils. 2013. (ENG.). 32p. (J). (978-0-7787-1261-9(3)); (Illus.). pap. (978-0-7787-1265-7(6)) Crabtree Publishing Co.

—Human Fossils. 2013. (ENG., Illus.). 32p. (J). (978-0-7787-1263-3(X)); pap. (978-0-7787-1267-1(2)) Crabtree Publishing Co.

—What Are Fossils? 2012. (ENG., Illus.). 32p. (J). pap. (978-0-7787-7219-4(5)); (gr. 3-6). lib. bdg. (978-0-7787-7214-9(4)) Crabtree Publishing Co.

Interior Dept. (U.S.) & Land Management Bureau (U.S.), eds. Junior Explorer Geology & Fossils Activity Book. 2012. (ENG., Illus.). 25p. 7.00 (978-0-16-091363-1(2), Interior Dept.) United States Government Printing Office.

Jackson, Tom. The Magnificent Book of Dinosaurs & Other Prehsitoric Creatures. Farkas, Rudolf, illus. 2017. (ENG.). 80p. (J). (gr. 2). 18.99 (978-1-62686-743-7(7), Silver Dolphin Bks.) Readerlink Distribution Services, LLC.

Jobes, Cecily. Fossils. 2016. (Spotlight on Earth Science Ser.). 00024p. (J). (gr. 4-6). pap. 10.00 (978-1-4994-2513-0(9), PowerKids Pr.) Rosen Publishing Group, Inc., The.

Johnson, Anne Janette & Raham, Gary. Fossils. 2009. (Restless Earth Ser.). (Illus.). 112p. (YA). (gr. 5-9). 35.00 (978-0-7910-9703-8(X)) Facts On File, Inc.

Johnson, Jinny. Flying Reptiles. 2015. (Discovering Dinosaurs Ser.). (ENG., Illus.). 24p. (J). pap. 8.95 (978-1-77092-162-7(1)) RiverStream Publishing.

—Mighty Killers. 2015. (Discovering Dinosaurs Ser.). (ENG., Illus.). 24p. (J). pap. 8.95 (978-1-77092-163-4(X)) RiverStream Publishing.

—Peaceful Plant Eaters. 2014. (Discovering Dinosaurs Ser.). (Illus.). 24p. (gr. 3-6). 28.50 (978-1-62588-016-1(2)) Black Rabbit Bks.

—Peaceful Plant-Eaters. 2015. (Discovering Dinosaurs Ser.). (ENG., Illus.). 24p. (J). pap. 8.95 (978-1-77092-164-1(8)) RiverStream Publishing.

—Speedy Dinosaurs. 2014. (Discovering Dinosaurs Ser.). (Illus.). 24p. (gr. 3-6). 28.50 (978-1-62588-017-8(0)) Black Rabbit Bks.

—Speedy Hunters. 2015. (Discovering Dinosaurs Ser.). (ENG., Illus.). 24p. (J). pap. 8.95 (978-1-77092-165-8(6)) RiverStream Publishing.

Johnson, Rebecca L., et al. Paul Sereno: Digging for Dinosaurs. 2007. (Reading Expeditions Ser.). (ENG., Illus.). 32p. (J). pap. 17.95 (978-0-7922-8887-9(4)) CENGAGE Learning.

Johnston, Ginny & Cutchins, Judy. Ice Age Giants of the South. 2015. (Southern Fossil Discoveries Ser.). (ENG., Illus.). 48p. (J). pap. 14.95 (978-1-56164-793-4(4)) Pineapple Pr., Inc.

Kim, F. S. Dig Deep! Looking for Dinosaurs. 2006. (Illus.). 32p. (J). pap. (978-0-439-83877-1(0)) Scholastic, Inc.

Kralick, Evelyn. Famous Fossils: Measure Lengths in Standard Units. 2014. (Math Masters: Measurement & Data Ser.). 24p. (J). (gr. 2-3). 23.60 (978-1-4777-6437-4(2)); (ENG.). pap. 8.25 (978-1-4777-4792-6(3)) Rosen Publishing Group, Inc., The. (Rosen Classroom).

Kulavis, Allyson. Fossil-Icious. 2012. (Science with Stuff Ser.: 3). (ENG.). 48p. (J). (gr. 1). 11.99 (978-1-935703-51-8(X)) Downtown Bookworks.

Kurtz, Jane. Mister Bones: Dinosaur Hunter. Haverfield, Mary, illus. 2004. (Ready-To-Reads Ser.). (ENG.). 32p. (J). (gr.

-1-1). pap. 3.99 *(978-0-689-85960-1(0)*, Simon Spotlight) Simon Spotlight.

Lappi, Megan. Birds. 2004. (Prehistoric Life Ser.). (Illus.). 32p. (J). (gr. -1-3). per. 9.95 *(978-1-59036-170-2(9))*; lib. bdg. 24.45 *(978-1-59036-111-5(3))* Weigl Pubs., Inc.

—Fossils. 2016. (Illus.). 24p. (J). *(978-1-5105-1150-7(4))* SmartBook Media, Inc.

—Fossils. (Focus on Earth Science Ser.). (gr. 3-7). 2015. (ENG.). (J). lib. bdg. 27.13 *(978-1-4896-4081-9(9)*, AV2 by Weigl) 2010. (Illus.). 24p. (J). pap. 11.95 *(978-1-60596-974-9(5))* 2010. (Illus.). 24p. (YA). lib. bdg. 25.70 *(978-1-60596-973-2(7))* 2006. (Illus.). 24p. (J). lib. bdg. 24.45 *(978-1-59036-213-6(6))* Weigl Pubs., Inc.

Lee, Sally. Allosaurus. 2015. (Little Paleontologist Ser.). (ENG.). 32p. (gr. 1-3). lib. bdg. 27.99 *(978-1-4914-2127-7(4))* Capstone Press of Coughlan Cos.

—Apatosaurus. 2015. (Little Paleontologist Ser.). (ENG.). 32p. (gr. 1-3). lib. bdg. 27.99 *(978-1-4914-2128-4(2))* Capstone Press of Coughlan Cos.

—Iguanodon. 2015. (Little Paleontologist Ser.). (ENG.). 32p. (gr. 1-3). lib. bdg. 27.99 *(978-1-4914-2129-1(0))* Capstone Press of Coughlan Cos.

—Little Paleontologist. 2015. (Little Paleontologist Ser.). (ENG.). 32p. (gr. 1-3). lib. bdg. 111.96 *(978-1-4914-2617-3(9))* Capstone Press of Coughlan Cos.

—Megalosaurus. 2015. (Little Paleontologist Ser.). (ENG.). 32p. (gr. 1-3). lib. bdg. 27.99 *(978-1-4914-2130-7(4))* Capstone Press of Coughlan Cos.

Lessem, Don. Carnivoros Gigantes. Bindon, John, illus. 2005.Tr. of Giant Meat-Eating Dinosaurs. (SPA.). 32p. (J). (gr. 2-4). pap. 6.95 *(978-0-8225-2963-7(7))* Lerner Publishing Group.

—Carnivoros Gigantes. Translations.com Staff, tr. from ENG. Bindon, John, illus. 2005. (Conoce A Los Dinosaurios (Meet the Dinosaurs) Ser.).Tr. of Giant Meat-Eating Dinosaurs. (SPA.). 32p. (gr. 2-4). lib. bdg. 23.93 *(978-0-8225-2962-0(9))* Lerner Publishing Group.

—Giant Plant-Eating Dinosaurs. Bindon, John, illus. 2004. (Meet the Dinosaurs Ser.). 32p. (J). (gr. 3-7). lib. bdg. 23.93 *(978-0-8225-1371-1(4))* Lerner Publishing Group.

—Sea Giants of Dinosaur Time. Bindon, John, illus. 2005. 32p. (J). (gr. 2-5). pap. 6.95 *(978-0-8225-2623-0(9))*; (gr. 3-7). lib. bdg. 23.93 *(978-0-8225-1425-1(7))* Lerner Publishing Group.

Lewis, Brenda Ralph. Prehistoric Creatures in the Sea & Sky. 2006. (Nature's Monsters Ser.). (Illus.). 32p. (gr. 2-6). lib. bdg. 26.00 *(978-0-8368-6845-6(5)*, Gareth Stevens Learning Library) Stevens, Gareth Publishing LLLP.

Linde, Barbara M. Insect Fossils. 2016. (Fossil Files Ser.). 00032p. (J). (gr. 5-5). 26.25 *(978-1-4994-2860-5(X))*; pap. 10.00 *(978-1-4994-2744-8(1))* Rosen Publishing Group, Inc., The. (PowerKids Pr.).

Lindsay, William. Prehistoric Life. 2012. (DK Eyewitness Bks.). (ENG.). 72p. (J). (gr. 3-7). 19.99 *(978-0-7566-9078-6(1))*; 16.99 *(978-0-7566-9077-9(3))* Dorling Kindersley Publishing, Inc. (DK Children).

Macken, JoAnn Early. The Dinosaur Museum. 2010. (My Community Ser.). 24p. (J). 25.65 *(978-1-60753-023-7(6))* Amicus Publishing.

Malam, John. Prehistoric Scary Creatures. 2008. (Scary Creatures Ser.). (ENG.). 32p. (J). 27.00 *(978-0-531-21747-4(7))*; (gr. 2-4). pap. 8.95 *(978-0-531-21901-0(1))* Scholastic Library Publishing. (Watts, Franklin).

Markle, Sandra. Outside & Inside Dinosaurs. 2003. (ENG., Illus.). 40p. (J). (gr. k-4). 9.99 *(978-0-689-85778-2(0)*, Aladdin) Simon & Schuster Children's Publishing.

Matthews, Rupert. Prehistoric Life. 2010. (Unpredictable Nature Ser.). (Illus.). 48p. (J). (gr. 3-18). lib. bdg. 19.95 *(978-1-4222-2003-0(6))* Mason Crest.

McConnell, William. Rocks & Fossils. (Reading Room Collection 1 Ser.). 16p. (gr. 2-3). 2009. 37.50 *(978-1-60851-950-7(3)*, PowerKids Pr.) 2006. (Illus.). (J). lib. bdg. 17.25 *(978-1-4042-3344-7(X))* Rosen Publishing Group, Inc., The.

McGowan, Chris. Dinosaur Discovery: Everything You Need to Be a Paleontologist. Schmidt, Erica Lyn, illus. 2011. (ENG.). 48p. (J). (gr. 2-6). 18.99 *(978-1-4169-4764-6(7)*, Simon & Schuster Bks. For Young Readers) Simon & Schuster Bks. For Young Readers.

Mead, Brian. Monsters of the Ice Age Coloring Book. 2003. 32p. (J). (gr. -1-3). pap. 3.99 *(978-0-9717509-2-0(0))* Mead, Brian Publishing.

Meehan, Sara. Bird Fossils. 2016. (Fossil Files Ser.). 00032p. (J). (gr. 5-5). 26.25 *(978-1-4994-2861-2(8))*; pap. 10.00 *(978-1-4994-2745-5(X))* Rosen Publishing Group, Inc., The. (PowerKids Pr.).

Mehing, Carl. Before the Dinosaurs. 2009. (Discovering Dinosaurs Ser.). (Illus.). 48p. (YA). (gr. 2-6). pap. 12.85 *(978-1-60754-780-8(5))*; (gr. 4-7). 29.25 *(978-1-60754-772-3(4))* Windmill Bks.

—Giant Meat-Eating Dinosaurs. 2009. (Discovering Dinosaurs Ser.). (Illus.). 48p. (YA). (gr. 2-6). pap. 12.85 *(978-1-60754-785-3(6))*; (gr. 4-7). 29.25 *(978-1-60754-777-8(5))* Windmill Bks.

—Prehistoric Creatures of the Sea & Skies. 2009. (Discovering Dinosaurs Ser.). (Illus.). 48p. (YA). (gr. 2-6). pap. 12.85 *(978-1-60754-781-5(3))*; (gr. 4-7). 29.25 *(978-1-60754-773-0(2))* Windmill Bks.

—Small & Deadly Dinosaurs. 2009. (Discovering Dinosaurs Ser.). (Illus.). 48p. (YA). (gr. 2-6). pap. 12.85 *(978-1-60754-784-6(8))*; (gr. 4-7). 29.25 *(978-1-60754-776-1(7))* Windmill Bks.

Mehling, Carl. Giant Plant-Eating Dinosaurs. 2009. (Discovering Dinosaurs Ser.). (Illus.). 48p. (YA). (gr. 4-7). 29.25 *(978-1-60754-778-5(3))* Windmill Bks.

Mehling, Carl, ed. Giant Plant-Eating Dinosaurs. Mehling, Carl, . 2010. (Discovering Dinosaurs Ser.). (Illus.). 48p. (YA). (gr. 2-6). pap. 12.85 *(978-1-60754-786-0(4))* Windmill Bks.

Meredith, Susan Markowitz. Finding Fossils: Set Of 6. 2010. (Early Connections Ser.). (J). pap. 37.00 net. *(978-1-4108-1086-1(0))* Benchmark Education Co.

Michaels, Eric. Fossils, 6 vols. 2004. (Phonics Readers Books 37-72 Ser.). (ENG.). 8p. (gr. k-1). pap. 35.70 *(978-0-7368-4081-1(8)*, Phonics Readers) Capstone Press of Coughlan Cos.

Miller, Connie Colwell. I'll Be a Paleontologist. Baroncelli, Silvia, illus. 2016. (When I Grow Up Ser.). (ENG.). 24p. (J). (gr. k-3). 20.95 *(978-1-60753-763-2(X))* Amicus Publishing.

Miller, Debbie S. A Woolly Mammoth Journey. 2010. (ENG., Illus.). 32p. (J). 15.95 *(978-1-60223-099-6(4))* Univ. of Alaska Pr.

—A Woolly Mammoth Journey. Van Zyle, Jon, illus. 2010. (ENG.). 32p. (J). pap. 9.95 *(978-1-60223-098-9(6))* Univ. of Alaska Pr.

Mooney, Carla. Fossils. 2016. (Geology Rocks! Ser.). (ENG.). 24p. (J). (gr. 3-6). 28.50 *(978-1-5038-0800-3(9)*, 210636) Child's World, Inc., The.

Moore Niver, Heather. Marine Fossils. 2016. (Fossil Files Ser.). 00032p. (J). (gr. 5-5). pap. 10.00 *(978-1-4994-2742-4(5)*, PowerKids Pr.) Rosen Publishing Group, Inc., The.

Morgan, Ben & Palmer, Douglas. Rock & Fossil Hunter. 2015. (ENG., Illus.). 72p. (J). (gr. 3-7). pap. 9.99 *(978-1-4654-3015-1(6)*, DK Children) Dorling Kindersley Publishing, Inc.

Morris, Neil. Everyday Life in Prehistory. 2005. (Uncovering History Ser.). (Illus.). 46p. (J). (gr. 6-9). lib. bdg. 29.95 *(978-1-58340-709-7(X))* Black Rabbit Bks.

Morris, Ting & Morris, Neil. Dinosaurs. Levy, Ruth & Cowne, Joanne, illus. 2006. (Sticky Fingers Ser.). 32p. (J). lib. bdg. 28.50 *(978-1-59771-029-9(6))* Sea-To-Sea Pubns.

National Geographic Editors & Esbaum, Jill. Angry Birds Playground - Dinosaurs. Tempesta, Franco, illus. 2013. (ENG.). 128p. (J). (gr. -1-3). lib. bdg. 21.90 *(978-1-4263-1325-7(X)*, National Geographic Children's Bks.) National Geographic Society.

National Geographic Kids Staff & Esbaum, Jill. Dinosaurs: A Prehistoric Adventure! Tempesta, Franco, illus. 2013. (ENG.). 128p. (J). (gr. -1-3). 14.95 *(978-1-4263-1324-0(1)*, National Geographic Children's Bks.) National Geographic Society.

Nelson, Lisa W. & Agenbroad, Larry D. Mammoths: Ice-Age Giants. Jansen, Paula, illus. Jansen, Paula, photos by. 2005. (Discovery! Ser.). 120p. (gr. 5-12). lib. bdg. 27.93 *(978-0-8225-2862-3(2))* Lerner Publishing Group.

Nelson, Maria. The Rock Cycle. 2013. (That Rocks! Ser.). (Illus.). 24p. (J). (gr. 2-5). pap. 8.15 *(978-1-4339-8326-9(5))*; lib. bdg. 22.60 *(978-1-4339-8325-2(7))* Stevens, Gareth Publishing LLLP.

Olien, Rebecca. How Do We Know about Dinosaurs? A Fossil Mystery, 1 vol. McDee, Katie, illus. 2011. (First Graphics: Science Mysteries Ser.). (ENG.). 24p. (gr. 1-2). pap. 6.29 *(978-1-4296-7173-6(4))*; pap. 35.70 *(978-1-4296-7177-4(7))* Capstone Press of Coughlan Cos.

Ollhoff, Jim. Fossil Fuels, 1 vol. 2010. (Future Energy Ser.). (ENG.). 32p. (YA). (gr. 4-7). 27.07 *(978-1-60453-935-6(6))* ABDO Publishing Co.

Orr, Tamra B. Unearthing Fossils. 2014. (Explorer Library: Follow the Clues Ser.). (ENG., Illus.). 32p. (J). (gr. 4-8). 28.50 *(978-1-62431-781-1(2)*, 203320) Cherry Lake Publishing.

Owen, Ruth. Paleontologists & Archaeologists. 2013. (Out of the Lab: Extreme Jobs in Science Ser.). 32p. (J). (gr. 3-6). 25.25 *(978-1-4777-1290-0(9))*; pap. 60.00 *(978-1-4777-1387-7(5))*; pap. 10.00 *(978-1-4777-1380-8(8))* Rosen Publishing Group, Inc., The. (PowerKids Pr.).

Padma, T. V. The Albertosaurus Mystery: Philip Currie's Hunt in the Badlands. 2006. (Fossil Hunters Ser.). (Illus.). 32p. (J). (gr. 2-5). lib. bdg. 25.27 *(978-1-59716-254-8(X))* Bearport Publishing Co., Inc.

Paiva, Johannah Gilman, ed. The Awesome Book of Prehistoric Animals. Various, illus. 2013. (World of Wonder (Library) Ser.). (ENG.). 32p. (J). (gr. 3-7). 7.99 *(978-1-77093-780-2(3))* Flowerpot Pr.

Palmer, Douglas. Firefly Encyclopedia of Dinosaurs & Prehistoric Animals. 2014. (ENG., Illus.). 256p. (J). (gr. 4-7). pap. 19.95 *(978-1-77085-460-4(6)*, 9781770854604) Firefly Bks., Ltd.

Parker, Gary & Parker, Mary. The Fossil Book. 2006. (Wonders of Creation Ser.). 36p. (J). (gr. 4-7). pap. 3.99 *(978-1-60092-007-3(1))* Master Bks.

Parker, Gary E. & Parker, Mary. The Fossil Book. 2005. (Wonders of Creation Ser.). (Illus.). 80p. (J). (gr. 5-8). 5.99 *(978-0-89051-438-2(0)*, 303-212) Master Bks.

Parker, Steve. Creatures of the Sky. 2011. (ENG., Illus.). 32p. (J). pap. 10.95 *(978-1-77092-011-8(0))* Saunders Bk. Co. CAN. Dist: RiverStream Publishing.

—Fossils. 2010. (Unpredictable Nature Ser.). (Illus.). 48p. (J). (gr. 3-18). lib. bdg. 19.95 *(978-1-4222-2000-9(1))* Mason Crest.

—Ice Age Giants. 2011. (ENG., Illus.). 32p. (J). pap. 10.95 *(978-1-77092-012-5(9))* Saunders Bk. Co. CAN. Dist: RiverStream Publishing.

—Land Roamers. 2011. (ENG., Illus.). 32p. (J). pap. 10.95 *(978-1-77092-013-2(7))* Saunders Bk. Co. CAN. Dist: RiverStream Publishing.

—Sea Monsters. 2011. (ENG., Illus.). 32p. (J). pap. 10.95 *(978-1-77092-014-9(5))* Saunders Bk. Co. CAN. Dist: RiverStream Publishing.

Patterson, Haley. Fossils Around the World: Measure Lengths in Standard Units, 1 vol. 2015. (InfoMax Common Core Math Readers Ser.). (ENG.). 24p. (J). pap. 8.25 *(978-1-4777-4777-3(X)*, Rosen Classroom) Rosen Publishing Group, Inc., The.

Paul, Gregory. The Early Cretaceous Volume 1: Notes, Drawings, & Observations from Prehistory. Alonso, Juan, illus. 2017. (Ancient Earth Journal Ser.). (ENG.). (J). (gr. 3-8). lib. bdg. 31.99 ***(978-1-942875-30-7(4)***, Walter Foster Jr) Quarto Publishing Group USA.

—The Early Cretaceous Volume 2: Notes, Drawings, & Observations from Prehistory. Alonso, Juan, illus. 2017. (Ancient Earth Journal Ser.). (ENG.). (J). (gr. 3-8). lib. bdg. 31.99 ***(978-1-942875-31-4(2)***, Walter Foster Jr) Quarto Publishing Group USA.

—The Early Jurassic Vol. 1: Notes, Drawings, & Observations from Prehistory. Alonso, Juan, illus. 2017. (Ancient Earth Journal Ser.). (ENG.). (J). (gr. 3-8). lib. bdg. 31.99 ***(978-1-942875-32-1(0)***, Walter Foster Jr) Quarto Publishing Group USA.

—The Early Jurassic Vol. 2: Notes, Drawings, & Observations from Prehistory. Alonso, Juan, illus. 2017. (Ancient Earth Journal Ser.). (ENG.). (J). (gr. 3-8). lib. bdg. 31.99 ***(978-1-942875-33-8(9)***, Walter Foster Jr) Quarto Publishing Group USA.

Pearcey, Alice, ed. Dinosaur Jigsaw Atlas. Bird, Glen, illus. 2004. 20p. (J). 14.95 *(978-0-7945-0913-2(4)*, Usborne) EDC Publishing.

Pellant, Chris. Fossils of the World. 2004. (World Book's Science & Nature Guides Ser.). (Illus.). 80p. (J). *(978-0-7166-4212-1(3))* World Bk., Inc.

Pellant, Chris & Pellant, Helen. Fossils. 2008. (Rock Stars Ser.). (Illus.). 24p. (YA). (gr. 1-4). lib. bdg. 23.00 *(978-0-8368-9223-9(2))* Stevens, Gareth Publishing LLLP.

Petersen, Christine. Fantastic Fossils, 1 vol. 2010. (Rock on!: a Look at Geology Ser.). (ENG.). 32p. (YA). (gr. 3-6). 27.07 *(978-1-60453-742-0(6))* ABDO Publishing Co.

Peterson, Judy Monroe. Fossil Finders: Paleontologists. 2009. (Extreme Scientists Ser.). 24p. (gr. 2-3). 42.50 *(978-1-61512-452-7(7)*, PowerKids Pr.); (Illus.). (YA). lib. bdg. 22.60 *(978-1-4042-4524-2(3))* Rosen Publishing Group, Inc., The.

Phelan, Glen, et al. Uncovering Earth's History. 2006. (Avenues Ser.). (ENG., Illus.). 32p. (YA). pap. 17.95 *(978-0-7922-8878-7(5))* CENGAGE Learning.

Prehistoric Animals. (First Facts about Ser.). 24p. (J). (gr. 3-7). pap. *(978-1-882210-19-0(0))* Action Publishing, Inc.

Rake, Matthew. The Dawn of Planet Earth. Minister, Peter, illus. 2015. (Prehistoric Field Guides). (ENG.). 32p. (J). (gr. 3-6). 26.65 *(978-1-4677-6348-6(9)*, Lerner Pubns.) Lerner Publishing Group.

—The Last Days of the Dinosaurs. Minister, Peter, illus. 2015. (Prehistoric Field Guides). (ENG.). 32p. (J). (gr. 3-6). lib. bdg. 26.65 *(978-1-4677-6350-9(0))* Lerner Publishing Group.

—Prehistoric Ancestors of Modern Animals. Mendez, Simon, illus. 2017. (If Extinct Beasts Came to Life Ser.). (ENG.). 32p. (J). (gr. 3-6). 7.99 *(978-1-5124-1159-1(0))*; 7.99 ***(978-1-5124-3609-9(7))***; 39.99 ***(978-1-5124-0906-2(5))***; 39.99 ***(978-1-5124-3608-2(9))*** Lerner Publishing Group.

Rake, Matthew. Prehistoric Giants. Mendez, Simon, illus. 2017. (If Extinct Beasts Came to Life Ser.). (ENG.). 32p. (J). (gr. 3-6). 26.65 *(978-1-5124-0635-1(X))*; 7.99 ***(978-1-5124-3612-9(7))***; 39.99 ***(978-1-5124-0912-3(X))***; 39.99 ***(978-1-5124-3611-2(9))*** Lerner Publishing Group.

Reed, M. K. Dinosaurs: Fossils & Feathers. Flood, Joe, illus. 2016. 117p. (J). ***(978-1-4844-7999-5(8)***, First Second Bks.) Roaring Brook Pr.

Reed, M. K. Science Comics: Dinosaurs. Flood, Joe, illus. 2016. (Science Comics Ser.). (ENG.). 128p. (J). pap. 12.99 *(978-1-62672-143-2(2)*, 9781626721432, First Second Bks.) Roaring Brook Pr.

Reid, Struan & McConnell, William. Rocks & Fossils. 2006. (Rosen Real Readers Big Bookstm Ser.). (ENG.). 16p. (gr. 2-3). 37.95 *(978-1-4042-6221-8(0))* Rosen Publishing Group, Inc., The.

Reptiles Rule: Triassic Life. 2013. (Awesome Ancient Animals Ser.). 32p. (gr. 2-6). *(978-1-84898-629-9(7)*, TickTock Books) Octopus Publishing Group.

Rhonda Lucas Donald, Rhonda Lucas. Dino Tracks, 1 vol. Morrison, Cathy, illus. 2013. (ENG.). 32p. (J). (gr. 1-4). 17.95 *(978-1-60718-619-9(5))* Arbordale Publishing.

Richards, Julie. Fossil Fuels. 2009. (J). *(978-0-7614-4434-3(3))* Marshall Cavendish.

Richardson, Hazel. Dinosaurs & Prehistoric Life. 2003. (Smithsonian Handbooks Ser.). (ENG., Illus.). 224p. pap. 22.00 *(978-0-7894-9361-3(6)*, DK) Dorling Kindersley Publishing, Inc.

Ripley, Esther. The Big Dinosaur Dig. 2003. (DK Readers Ser.). (Illus.). 48p. (J). (gr. -1-3). 11.65 *(978-0-7569-3355-5(2))* Perfection Learning Corp.

—Big Dinosaur Dig, Level 3. 2009. (DK Readers Ser.). (ENG.). 48p. (J). (gr. 2-4). 3.99 *(978-0-7566-5595-2(1)*, DK Children) Dorling Kindersley Publishing, Inc.

Robb, Jackie & Stringle, Berny. The Story of Plankton. Duncan, Karen & Stringle, Sam, illus. 2004. (Bang on the Door Ser.). 32p. (YA). pap. *(978-1-85602-336-8(2)*, Pavilion Children's Books) Pavilion Bks.

The Rock Cycle. 2013. (That Rocks! Ser.). 24p. (J). (gr. 2-5). pap. 48.90 *(978-1-4339-8327-6(3))* Stevens, Gareth Publishing LLLP.

Rockwood, Leigh. Hadrosaurus. 2012. (Illus.). 24p. (J). 49.50 *(978-1-4488-5097-6(5))*; pap. 8.25 *(978-1-4488-5096-9(7))*; lib. bdg. 22.60 *(978-1-4488-4973-4(X))* Rosen Publishing Group, Inc., The. (PowerKids Pr.).

—Iguanodon. 2012. (Illus.). 24p. (J). 49.50 *(978-1-4488-5099-0(1))*; pap. 8.25 *(978-1-4488-5098-3(3))*; lib. bdg. 22.60 *(978-1-4488-4974-1(8))* Rosen Publishing Group, Inc., The. (PowerKids Pr.).

Romero, Libby. Plant & Animal Fossils. 2005. (J). pap. *(978-1-4108-4621-1(0))* Benchmark Education Co.

Rooney, Anne & Collins UK Staff. Creatures from the Past. 2016. (ENG.). 56p. (J). (gr. 5-6). pap. 9.95 *(978-0-00-816402-7(9))* HarperCollins Pubs. Ltd. GBR. Dist: Independent Pubs. Group.

Rupert, Matthews. Visual Factfinder Dinosaurs & Prehistoric Life. 2008. 512p. pap. *(978-1-84810-078-7(7))* Miles Kelly Publishing, Ltd.

—Visual Factfinder Rocks & Fossils. 2008. 512p. pap. *(978-1-84810-080-0(9))* Miles Kelly Publishing, Ltd.

—What about Dinosaurs. 2008. 400p. pap. *(978-1-84810-067-1(1))* Miles Kelly Publishing, Ltd.

Ruzicka, Oldrich. Prehistoric Atlas: A Voyage of Discovery for Young Paleontologists. Tumas, Tomás, illus. 2017. (ENG.). 30p. (J). (gr. 3-5). 16.95 *(978-1-4549-2252-0(4))* Sterling Publishing Co., Inc.

Saber Tooths Are the Big Cats: Ice Age. 2013. (Awesome Ancient Animals Ser.). 32p. (gr. 2-6). *(978-1-84898-627-5(0)*, TickTock Books) Octopus Publishing Group.

Sampson, Scott D. You Can Be a Paleontologist! Discovering Dinosaurs with Dr. Scott. 2017. (ENG., Illus.). 32p. (J). (gr. -1-3). 16.99 *(978-1-4263-2728-5(5)*, National Geographic Children's Bks.) National Geographic Society.

Scheele, William E. Ancient Elephants. 2011. 66p. 36.95 *(978-1-258-01254-0(5))* Literary Licensing, LLC.

Schomp, Virginia. Stegosaurus: And Other Plate-Backed Plant-Eaters. 2003. (Prehistoric World Ser.). (Illus.). 32p. (gr. 4-18). lib. bdg. 20.95 *(978-0-7614-1544-2(0)*, Benchmark Bks.) Marshall Cavendish Corp.

Schroeter, Chloe. Why Why Why... Were Mammoths Wooly? 2010. (Why Why Why Ser.). 32p. (J). (gr. 1-3). lib. bdg. 18.95 *(978-1-4222-1589-0(X))* Mason Crest.

Sea Creatures Crawl on Land: Early Life. 2013. (Awesome Ancient Animals Ser.). (Illus.). 32p. (J). (gr. k-3). *(978-1-84898-626-8(2)*, TickTock Books) Octopus Publishing Group.

Sereno, Paul C. & Lunis, Natalie. Supercroc: Paul Sereno's Dinosaur Eater. 2016. (Fossil Hunters Ser.). (ENG.). 32p. (J). (gr. 2-7). pap. 8.95 *(978-1-944998-74-5(8))* Bearport Publishing Co., Inc.

Sherman, Jill. Fossil Fuels. 2017. (J). pap. ***(978-0-7660-9151-1(1))*** Enslow Pubs., Inc.

Shofner, Melissa Raé. Gareth's Guide to Unearthing a Dinosaur. 2017. (Gareth Guides to an Extraordinary Life Ser.). 32p. (J). (gr. 4-5). lib. bdg. 26.60 ***(978-1-5382-0360-6(X))*** Stevens, Gareth Publishing LLLP.

Shore, Marguerite, tr. from ITA. The Journey: Plateosaurus. Bacchin, Matteo, illus. 2008. (Dinosaurs: Ser.: Vol. 1). (ENG.). 63p. (J). (gr. 3-6). 15.95 *(978-0-7892-0978-8(0)*, Abbeville Kids) Abbeville Pr., Inc.

Sian Revision Fossil Formations. 2004. (Science in A Nutshell Ser.). (J). *(978-1-59242-032-2(X))* Delta Education, LLC.

Slade, Suzanne. What Do You Know about Fossils? (20 Questions: Science Ser.). 24p. (gr. 2-3). 2009. 42.50 *(978-1-60854-963-4(1)*, PowerKids Pr.) 2008. (Illus.). (YA). lib. bdg. 22.60 *(978-1-4042-4197-8(3))* Rosen Publishing Group, Inc., The.

Sohn, Emily & Kentor Schmauss, Judy. Structures of Life: What Is this Fossil? 2011. (IScience Readers Ser.). 32p. (J). (gr. 3-4). lib. bdg. 22.60 *(978-1-59953-420-6(7))* Norwood Hse. Pr.

Sovak, Jan. Invisible Prehistoric Animals Magic Picture Book. 2004. (Dover Little Activity Bks.). (ENG., Illus.). 32p. (J). (gr. -1-2). pap. 1.50 *(978-0-486-43719-4(1))* Dover Pubns., Inc.

Spilsbury, Louise. Fósiles. 2011. (Las Rocas Ser.). (SPA.). 32p. (gr. 3-5). pap. 8.29 *(978-1-4329-5658-5(2))*; lib. bdg. 33.32 *(978-1-4329-5650-9(7))* Heinemann-Raintree. (Heinemann InfoSearch).

Spilsbury, Louise & Spilsbury, Richard. Fossils, 1 vol. 2011. (Let's Rock Ser.). (ENG.). 32p. (gr. 3-6). pap. 8.29 *(978-1-4329-4690-6(0))*; lib. bdg. 33.32 *(978-1-4329-4682-1(X))* Heinemann-Raintree. (Heinemann InfoSearch).

Squire, Ann O. Fossils. 2012. (ENG.). 48p. (J). 29.00 *(978-0-531-26142-2(5))*; pap. 6.95 *(978-0-531-26250-4(2))* Scholastic Library Publishing.

Stamper, Judith Bauer & Willows, Vicky. Fossils. 2010. (Illus.). 32p. (J). *(978-0-545-28546-9(1))* Scholastic, Inc.

Staunton, Joseph. Dinosaurs in the Sea. 2010. (Discover the Dinosaurs Ser.). 32p. (J). (gr. 2-5). 28.50 *(978-1-60753-107-4(0))* Amicus Publishing.

—Meat-Eating Dinosaurs. 2010. (Discover the Dinosaurs Ser.). 32p. (J). (gr. 2-5). 28.50 *(978-1-60753-109-8(7))* Amicus Publishing.

—Plant-Eating Dinosaurs. 2010. (Discover the Dinosaurs Ser.). 32p. (J). (gr. 2-5). 28.50 *(978-1-60753-110-4(0))* Amicus Publishing.

Staunton, Joseph & Flinthart, Dirk. Meat Eating Dinosaurs. Rey, Luis, illus. 2011. (Inside Crime Ser.). 48p. (YA). (gr. 5-9). 34.25 *(978-1-59920-395-9(2))* Black Rabbit Bks.

Stewart, Melissa. Dino-Mite Jokes about Prehistoric Life: Laugh & Learn about Science. Kelley, Gerald, illus. 2012. (Super Silly Science Jokes Ser.). 48p. (J). (gr. 3-4). 25.27 *(978-0-7660-3968-1(4)*, Enslow Elementary) Enslow Pubs., Inc.

—How Does a Bone Become a Fossil? 2016. (How Does It Happen Ser.). (ENG.). 32p. (gr. 3-5). pap. 8.29 *(978-1-4109-8529-3(6)*, Raintree Perspectives) Heinemann-Raintree.

Storad, Conrad J. Fossil Fuels. 2008. pap. 52.95 *(978-0-8225-9111-5(1))* 2007. (ENG., Illus.). 48p. (gr. 2-5). lib. bdg. 26.60 *(978-0-8225-6736-3(9)*, Lerner Pubns.) Lerner Publishing Group.

Surget, Alain & Hirsinger, Julien. Half & Half-People of the Caves. Avril, Francois & Duffour, Jean-Pierre, illus. 2008. 48p. (J). 9.95 *(978-1-60115-205-3(1))*; pap. 4.99 *(978-1-60115-206-0(X))* Treasure Bay, Inc.

Switek, Brian. Prehistoric Predators. Csotonyi, Julius, illus. 2015. (ENG.). 104p. (J). 19.95 *(978-1-60433-552-1(1)*, Applesauce Pr.) Cider Mill Pr. Bk. Pubs., LLC.

T-Rex Is King: Cretaceous Life. 2013. (Awesome Ancient Animals Ser.). (Illus.). 32p. (J). (gr. 2-4). *(978-1-84898-625-1(4)*, TickTock Books) Octopus Publishing Group.

Taplin, Sam. First Encyclopedia of Dinosaurs & Prehistoric Life: Internet-Linked. Hancock, David, illus. 2004. (Usborne First Encyclopedia Library). 64p. (J). (gr. 2-18). lib. bdg. 17.95 *(978-1-58086-657-6(3)*, Usborne) EDC Publishing.

—First Encyclopedia of Dinosaurs II. rev. ed. 2011. (First Encyclopedias Ser.). 64p. (J). pap. 9.99 *(978-0-7945-3047-1(8)*, Usborne) EDC Publishing.

Thimmesh, Catherine. Scaly Spotted Feathered Frilled: How Do We Know What Dinosaurs Really Looked Like? 2013. (ENG., Illus.). 64p. (J). (gr. 5-7). 17.99 *(978-0-547-99134-4(7))* Houghton Mifflin Harcourt Publishing Co.

Thomson, Sarah L. Ancient Animals: Terror Birds. Plant, Andrew, illus. 2013. (ENG.). 32p. (J). (gr. 1-4). pap. 5.95 *(978-1-58089-399-2(6))* Charlesbridge Publishing, Inc.

Throp, Claire. Fantasy Science Field Trips, 1 vol. 2014. (Fantasy Science Field Trips Ser.). (ENG.). 32p. (gr. 1-3). lib. bdg. 119.96 *(978-1-4109-6201-0(6)*, Read Me!) Heinemann-Raintree.

—A Weekend with Dinosaurs: Fantasy Science Field Trips, 1 vol. 2014. (Fantasy Science Field Trips Ser.). (ENG., Illus.). 32p. (gr. 1-3). pap. 8.95 *(978-1-4109-6203-4(2))*; lib. bdg. 29.99 *(978-1-4109-6198-3(2))* Heinemann-Raintree. (Read Me!).

tictock Media, Ltd. The Ultimate Guide to Dinosaurs. 2009. (ENG.). 128p. (J). (gr. 4-7). pap. 12.95 *(978-1-84696-988-1(3)*, TickTock Books) Octopus Publishing Group GBR. Dist: Independent Pubs. Group.

Upgrade kit dsm-3 Dinos&fossils. (J). 2004. *(978-1-59242-528-0(3))* 2003. *(978-1-59242-411-5(2))* Delta Education, LLC.

VanVoorst, Jenny Fretland. Fossils, 1 vol. 2014. (Rocks & Minerals Ser.). (ENG.). 48p. (gr. 8-12). lib. bdg. 32.79 *(978-1-62403-385-8(7))* ABDO Publishing Co.

Venezia, Mike. Mary Leakey - Archaeologist Who Really Dug Her Work. Venezia, Mike, illus. 2009. (Getting to Know the World's Greatest Inventors & Scientists Ser.). (ENG., Illus.). 32p. (J). (gr. 2-5). 28.00 *(978-0-531-23727-4(3))* Scholastic Library Publishing.

Walker, Sally M. Figuring Out Fossils. 2013. (Searchlight Books (tm) — Do You Dig Earth Science? Ser.). (ENG.). 40p. (gr. 3-5). lib. bdg. 27.93 *(978-1-4677-0019-1(3)*, Lerner Pubns.); (Illus.). pap. 8.95 *(978-1-4677-0791-6(0))* Lerner Publishing Group.

—Fossils. 2006. (Early Bird Earth Science Ser.). (ENG., Illus.). 48p. (gr. 2-5). lib. bdg. 26.60 *(978-0-8225-5945-0(5)*, Lerner Pubns.) Lerner Publishing Group.

—The Search for Antarctic Dinosaurs. 2009. pap. 40.95 *(978-0-7613-4822-1(0))* Lerner Publishing Group.

—The Search for Antarctic Dinosaurs. Bindon, John, illus. 2007. (On My Own Science Ser.). (ENG.). 48p. (gr. 2-4). lib. bdg. 25.26 *(978-0-8225-6749-3(0)*, Millbrook Pr.) Lerner Publishing Group.

—Supercroc Found. Hood, Philip, illus. 2005. (On My Own Science Ser.). 48p. (J). (gr. 3-7). lib. bdg. 25.26 *(978-1-57505-760-6(3))* Lerner Publishing Group.

—SuperCroc Found. Hood, Philip, illus. 2006. (On My Own Science Ser.). 48p. (J). (gr. 3-7). per. 6.95 *(978-1-57505-852-8(9)*, First Avenue Editions) Lerner Publishing Group.

Washington, Curtis. The Story of Sue. 2005. (Illus.). 12p. (J). pap. *(978-0-328-14253-8(0)*, Scott Foresman) Addison-Wesley Educational Pubs., Inc.

Waters, Kate. Curious about Fossils. 2016. (Smithsonian Ser.). (ENG., Illus.). 32p. (J). (gr. 1-3). pap. 3.99 *(978-0-448-49019-9(6)*, Grosset & Dunlap) Penguin Young Readers Group.

Wenzel, Gregory. The Feathered Dinosaurs of China. Wenzel, Gregory, illus. 2004. (ENG., Illus.). 32p. (J). (gr. 1-4). pap. 7.95 *(978-1-57091-562-8(8))* Charlesbridge Publishing, Inc.

West, David. Ankylosaurus & Other Armored & Plated Herbivores. 2010. (Dinosaurs Ser.). (Illus.). 32p. (J). (gr. 3-6). (ENG.). pap. 10.50 *(978-1-4339-4231-0(3))*; lib. bdg. 26.60 *(978-1-4339-4230-3(5))* Stevens, Gareth Publishing LLLP. (Gareth Stevens Learning Library).

—Brachiosaurus & Other Long-Necked Herbivores. 2010. (Dinosaurs Ser.). (Illus.). 32p. (J). (gr. 3-6). (ENG.). pap. 10.50 *(978-1-4339-4222-8(4))*; lib. bdg. 26.60 *(978-1-4339-4221-1(6))* Stevens, Gareth Publishing LLLP. (Gareth Stevens Learning Library).

—Cetiosaurus & Other Dinosaurs & Reptiles from the Middle Jurassic. 2012. (Dinosaurs! Ser.). (ENG., Illus.). 32p. (J). (gr. 3-6). 26.60 *(978-1-4339-6707-8(3))*; pap. 10.50 *(978-1-4339-6709-2(X))* Stevens, Gareth Publishing LLLP. (Gareth Stevens Learning Library).

—Coelophysis & Other Dinosaurs & Reptiles from the Upper Triassic. West, David, illus. 2012. (Dinosaurs! Ser.). (ENG., Illus.). 32p. (J). (gr. 3-6). pap. 10.50 *(978-1-4339-6713-9(8))*; lib. bdg. 26.60 *(978-1-4339-6711-5(1))* Stevens, Gareth Publishing LLLP. (Gareth Stevens Learning Library).

—Dinosaurs of the Lower Cretaceous: 25 Dinosaurs from 144 — 127 Million Years Ago. 2016. (Firefly Dinosaur Ser.). (ENG., Illus.). 32p. (J). (gr. 3-6). pap. 6.95 *(978-1-77085-831-2(8)*, 9781770858312) Firefly Bks., Ltd.

—Dinosaurs of the Middle Cretaceous: 25 Dinosaurs from 126 — 89 Million Years Ago. 2016. (Firefly Dinosaur Ser.). (ENG., Illus.). 32p. (J). (gr. 3-6). pap. 6.95 *(978-1-77085-833-6(4)*, 9781770858336) Firefly Bks., Ltd.

—Dinosaurs of the Middle Jurassic: 25 Dinosaurs from 175 — 165 Million Years Ago. 2016. (Firefly Dinosaur Ser.). (ENG., Illus.). 32p. (J). (gr. 3-6). pap. 6.95 *(978-1-77085-835-0(0)*, 9781770858350) Firefly Bks., Ltd.

—Dinosaurs of the Upper Cretaceous: 25 Dinosaurs from 89 — 65 Million Years Ago. 2016. (Firefly Dinosaur Ser.). (ENG., Illus.). 32p. (J). (gr. 3-6). pap. 6.95 *(978-1-77085-837-4(7)*, 9781770858374) Firefly Bks., Ltd.

—Dinosaurs of the Upper Jurassic: 25 Dinosaurs from 164 — 145 Million Years Ago. 2016. (Firefly Dinosaur Ser.). (ENG., Illus.). 32p. (J). (gr. 3-6). pap. 6.95 *(978-1-77085-839-8(3)*, 9781770858398) Firefly Bks., Ltd.

—Dinosaurs of the Upper Triassic & the Lower Jurassic: 25 Dinosaurs from 227 — 175 Million Years Ago. 2016. (Firefly Dinosaur Ser.). (ENG., Illus.). 32p. (J). (gr. 3-6). pap. 6.95 *(978-1-77085-841-1(5)*, 9781770858411) Firefly Bks., Ltd.

—Lesothosaurus & Other Dinosaurs & Reptiles from the Lower Jurassic. West, David, illus. 2012. (Dinosaurs! Ser.). (ENG., Illus.). 32p. (J). (gr. 3-6). pap. 10.50 *(978-1-4339-6717-7(0))*; lib. bdg. 26.60 *(978-1-4339-6715-3(4))* Stevens, Gareth Publishing LLLP. (Gareth Stevens Learning Library).

—Parasaurolophus & Other Duck-Billed & Beaked Herbivores. 2010. (Dinosaurs Ser.). (Illus.). 32p. (J). (gr. 3-6). (ENG.). pap. 10.50 *(978-1-4339-4228-0(3))*; lib. bdg. 26.60 *(978-1-4339-4227-3(5))* Stevens, Gareth Publishing LLLP. (Gareth Stevens Learning Library).

—Prehistoric Flying Reptiles, 01 vols., 1. 2016. (Prehistoric Animals Ser.). (ENG., Illus.). 24p. (J). pap. 8.25 *(978-1-5081-9037-0(2)*, Windmill Bks.) Rosen Publishing Group, Inc., The.

—The Rise of Humans. 2014. (Prehistoric! Ser.). (Illus.). 32p. (J). (gr. 2-5). 31.35 *(978-1-62588-087-1(1))* Black Rabbit Bks.

—Triceratops & Other Horned Herbivores. 2010. (Dinosaurs Ser.). (Illus.). 32p. (J). (gr. 3-6). pap. 10.50 *(978-1-4339-4234-1(8))*; lib. bdg. 26.60 *(978-1-4339-4233-4(X))* Stevens, Gareth Publishing LLLP. (Gareth Stevens Learning Library).

—Tyrannosaurus Rex & Other Giant Carnivores. 2010. (Dinosaurs Ser.). (Illus.). 32p. (J). (gr. 3-6). (ENG.). pap. 10.50 *(978-1-4339-4237-2(2))*; lib. bdg. 26.60 *(978-1-4339-4236-5(4))* Stevens, Gareth Publishing LLLP. (Gareth Stevens Learning Library).

—Velociraptor & Other Raptors & Small Carnivores. 2010. (Dinosaurs Ser.). (Illus.). 32p. (J). (gr. 3-6). pap. 10.50 *(978-1-4339-4225-9(9))*; lib. bdg. 26.60 *(978-1-4339-4224-2(0))* Stevens, Gareth Publishing LLLP. (Gareth Stevens Learning Library).

Wheeler, Jill C. Fossil Fuels, 1 vol. 2008. (Eye on Energy Ser.). (ENG., Illus.). 32p. (gr. k-6). 27.07 *(978-1-59928-805-5(2)*, Checkerboard Library) ABDO Publishing Co.

Whitfield, Philip. Scholastic's Children's Guide to Dinosaurs. (Illus.). 96p. (J). pap. 21.95 *(978-0-590-24329-2(2))* Scholastic, Inc.

Williams, Judith. Descubriendo Dinosaurios con un Cazador de Fsiles. Skrepnick, Michael W., illus. 2008. (I Like Science! Bilingual Ser.).Tr. of Discovering Dinosaurs with a Fossil Hunter. (SPA & ENG.). 24p. (J). (gr. 3-7). lib. bdg. 22.60 *(978-0-7660-2978-1(6)*, Enslow Elementary) Enslow Pubs., Inc.

—Discovering Dinosaurs with a Fossil Hunter. Skrepnick, Michael William, illus. 2004. (I Like Science! Ser.). 24p. (J). lib. bdg. 22.60 *(978-0-7660-2267-6(6))* Enslow Pubs., Inc.

—The Discovery & Mystery of a Dinosaur Named Jane. 2007. (Prime (Elementary) Ser.). (Illus.). 48p. (J). (gr. 4-7). lib. bdg. 25.27 *(978-0-7660-2730-5(9))*; per. 8.95 *(978-0-7660-2709-1(0))* Enslow Pubs., Inc.

Wittmann, Kelly. The Bone Wars: The Race to Dig up Dinosaurs. 2017. (Great Race: Fight to the Finish Ser.). 48p. (gr. 4-5). pap. 84.30 ***(978-1-5382-0803-8(2))*** Stevens, Gareth Publishing LLLP.

Wood, Robert Muir. Discovering Prehistory. 2012. (ENG., Illus.). 48p. (J). 15.00 *(978-1-899762-87-3(6))* Award Pubns. Ltd. GBR. Dist: Parkwest Pubns., Inc.

World Book, Inc Staff, contrib. by. Birdlike Dinosaurs: Small Theropods & Prehistoric Birds. 2012. (J). *(978-0-7166-0368-9(3))* World Bk., Inc.

World Book, Inc. Staff, contrib. by. Extinct! 2014. (J). *(978-0-7166-5628-9(0))* World Bk., Inc.

World Book, Inc Staff, contrib. by. Fierce Dinosaurs: The Large Theropods. 2012. (J). *(978-0-7166-0369-6(1))* World Bk., Inc.

—Resources & Cumulative Index. 2005. (World Book's Science & Nature Guides Ser.). 80p. (J). *(978-0-7166-4216-9(6))* World Bk., Inc.

Zabludoff, Marc. Dire Wolf. Bollinger, Peter, illus. 2009. (Prehistoric Beasts Ser.). 32p. (gr. 2-8). 29.93 *(978-0-7614-3998-1(6))* Marshall Cavendish Corp.

—Doedicurus. Bollinger, Peter, illus. 2010. (Prehistoric Beasts 2 Ser.). 32p. (J). (gr. 2). 29.93 *(978-1-60870-033-2(X))* Marshall Cavendish Corp.

—Gastornis. Bollinger, Peter, illus. 2009. (Prehistoric Beasts Ser.). 32p. (gr. 2-8). 29.93 *(978-0-7614-4000-0(3))* Marshall Cavendish Corp.

—Giant Ground Sloth. Bollinger, Peter, illus. 2009. (Prehistoric Beasts Ser.). 32p. (gr. 2-8). 29.93 *(978-0-7614-3997-4(8))* Marshall Cavendish Corp.

—Hyracotherium. Bollinger, Peter, illus. 2010. (Prehistoric Beasts 2 Ser.). 32p. (J). (gr. 2). 29.93 *(978-1-60870-034-9(8))* Marshall Cavendish GBR. Dist: Marshall Cavendish Corp.

—Mastodon. Bollinger, Peter, illus. 2010. (Prehistoric Beasts 2 Ser.). 32p. (gr. 2). 29.93 *(978-1-60870-036-3(4))* Marshall Cavendish Corp.

—Saber-Toothed Cat. Bollinger, Peter, illus. 2010. (Prehistoric Beasts 2 Ser.). 32p. (gr. 2). 29.93 *(978-1-60870-037-0(2))* Marshall Cavendish GBR. Dist: Marshall Cavendish Corp.

Zeiger, Jennifer. Mammoth & Mastodon. 2015. (21st Century Junior Library: Dinosaurs & Prehistoric Creatures Ser.). (ENG., Illus.). 24p. (J). (gr. 2-5). lib. bdg. 27.07 *(978-1-63362-383-5(1)*, 206952) Cherry Lake Publishing.

FOSTER HOME CARE

see also Adoption

Berry, Joy. I Love Daycare. Regan, Dana, illus. 2010. (Teach Me About Ser.). (ENG.). 20p. (J). (gr. k — 1). bds. 5.99 *(978-1-60577-016-1(7))* Berry, Joy Enterprises.

Bradex, Melissa A. Little Gregory. Crane, Eddie, illus. 2009. 32p. pap. 14.99 *(978-1-4490-3549-5(3))* AuthorHouse.

Braley and Thompson, Inc. Staff. Treatment Team Foster Care. (Illus.). 100p. (J). 4th ed. pap. 6.00 *(978-1-883239-00-8(1))* 5th ed. pap. 6.00 *(978-1-883239-01-5(X))* Braley & Thompson, Inc.

Do You Have What It Takes. 2007. (YA). per. 35.00 *(978-0-9661256-9-6(X))* Youth Communication - New York Center.

Fraser, Theresa. Billy Had to Move. Walton, Alex, illus. 2009. (J). pap. 14.95 *(978-1-932690-87-3(5))* Loving Healing Pr., Inc.

—Billy Had to Move: A Foster Care Story. Walton, Alex, illus. 2011. 32p. (gr. 3-7). 32.95 *(978-1-61599-118-1(2))* Loving Healing Pr., Inc.

Hardaway, Francine. Foster Mom: A Journey of Self-Discovery. 2004. 152p. (YA). pap. 14.95 *(978-0-595-31431-7(7))* iUniverse, Inc.

Levy, Janice. Finding the Right Spot: When Kids Can't Live with Their Parents. Martin, Whitney, illus. 2004. 48p. (J). 14.95 *(978-1-59147-073-1(0))*; pap. 9.95 *(978-1-59147-074-8(9))* American Psychological Assn. (Magination Pr.).

Libal, Joyce. A House Between Homes: Youth in the Foster Care System. 2003. (Youth with Special Needs Ser.). (Illus.). 127p. (YA). pap. 14.95 *(978-1-4222-0419-1(7))* Mason Crest.

Meese, Ruth Lyn. Family Matters: Adoption & Foster Care in Children's Literature, 1 vol. 2009. 147p. (C). pap. 35.00 *(978-1-59158-782-8(4)*, TIP8782, Libraries Unlimited) ABC-CLIO, LLC.

Nelson, Julie. Kids Are Important: A Book for Young Children in Foster Care. 2003. (Illus.). (J). *(978-0-9743826-1-6(2))* Lifetrack Resources.

—Kids Need to Be Safe: A Book for Children in Foster Care. Gallagher, Mary, illus. 2005. (Kids Are Important Ser.). (ENG.). 32p. (J). (gr. -1-5). pap. 9.99 *(978-1-57542-192-6(5))* Free Spirit Publishing, Inc.

Poole, H. W. Foster Families, Vol. 12. 2016. (Families Today Ser.). (Illus.). 48p. (J). (gr. 5). 20.95 *(978-1-4222-3615-4(3))* Mason Crest.

Rhodes-Courter, Ashley. Three Little Words: A Memoir. 2009. (ENG.). 336p. (YA). (gr. 9). pap. 12.99 *(978-1-4169-4807-0(4)*, Atheneum Bks. for Young Readers) Simon & Schuster Children's Publishing.

Rissman, Rebecca. Foster Parents, 1 vol. 2011. (Families Ser.). (ENG., Illus.). 24p. (gr. -1-1). 22.65 *(978-1-4329-4657-9(9))*; pap. 6.29 *(978-1-4329-4665-4(X))* Heinemann-Raintree. (Acorn).

Stewart, Sheila. A House Between Homes: Kids in the Foster Care System. 2009. (Kids Have Troubles Too Ser.). 48p. (YA). (gr. 5-18). pap. 7.95 *(978-1-4222-1905-8(4))* Mason Crest.

Stewart, Sheila & Flath, Camden. A House Between Homes: Kids in the Foster Care System. 2010. (Kids Have Troubles Too Ser.). 48p. (YA). (gr. 5-18). lib. bdg. 19.95 *(978-1-4222-1692-7(6))* Mason Crest.

FOSTER HOME CARE—FICTION

Alper, Joanne. Billy Says... Six Therapeutic Storybooks to Help Children on Their Journey Through Fostering or Adoption. 2015. (ENG., Illus.). 120p. (J). pap. 64.95 *(978-1-84905-667-0(6)*, 8049) Kingsley, Jessica Pubs. GBR. Dist: Macmillan Distribution Ltd.

Anderson, Jessica Lee. Calli. 2011. (ENG.). 198p. (J). (gr. 6). 16.95 *(978-1-57131-702-5(3))*; pap. 8.00 *(978-1-57131-699-8(X))* Milkweed Editions.

Archway Care Sons and Daughters Group & Archway Care Sons And Daughters Group. How Does Jorge Feel ? 2011. 12p. pap. 7.70 *(978-1-4467-1645-8(7))* Lulu Pr., Inc.

At Aunt Hattie's House. 2005. (YA). 12.00 net. *(978-0-9763793-1-7(7))* Mitchell, Karan.

Ayarbe, Heidi. Compromised. (ENG.). (YA). (gr. 8). 2011. 480p. pap. 8.99 *(978-0-06-172851-8(9))* 2010. 464p. 16.99 *(978-0-06-172849-5(7))* HarperCollins Pubs. (HarperTeen).

Bare, Bart. Girl. 2010. 188p. (YA). pap. 11.95 *(978-0-9825396-4-4(9))* Canterbury Hse. Publishing, Ltd.

Bennett, Cindy C. Geek Girl. 2011. 280p. (J). pap. 15.99 *(978-1-59955-925-4(0))* Bonneville B.V. NLD. Dist: Cedar Fort, Inc./CFI Distribution.

Bernard, Romily. Find Me. 2014. (Find Me Ser.: 1). (ENG.). 336p. (YA). (gr. 8). pap. 9.99 *(978-0-06-222904-5(4)*, HarperTeen) HarperCollins Pubs.

—Remember Me. 2014. (Find Me Ser.: 2). (ENG.). 368p. (YA). (gr. 8). 17.99 *(978-0-06-222906-9(0)*, HarperTeen) HarperCollins Pubs.

Bishop, Michele. Mummy's Happy Tears. Sharp, Craig, illus. 2013. 18p. pap. *(978-1-78148-186-8(5))* Grosvenor Hse. Publishing Ltd.

Booth, Coe. Bronxwood. 2013. (ENG.). 336p. (J). (gr. 9). pap. 10.99 *(978-0-439-92535-8(5)*, PUSH) Scholastic, Inc.

—Kinda Like Brothers. 2015. (ENG.). 256p. (J). (gr. 3-7). pap. 6.99 *(978-0-545-22497-0(7)*, Scholastic Paperbacks) Scholastic, Inc.

Briggs, Elizabeth. Future Shock. 2016. (YA). (Future Shock Ser.: 1). (ENG.). 288p. (gr. 8-12). pap. 9.99 *(978-0-8075-2680-4(0))*; *(978-0-8075-2683-5(5))*; (Future Shock Ser.: 1). (ENG.). 272p. (gr. 8-12). 16.99 *(978-0-8075-2682-8(7))* Whitman, Albert & Co.

Brody, Jessica. Unremembered. 2013. (Unremembered Trilogy Ser.: 1). (ENG.). 320p. (YA). (gr. 7). 17.99 *(978-0-374-37991-9(2)*, 9780374379919, Farrar, Straus & Giroux (BYR)) Farrar, Straus & Giroux.

—Unremembered. 2014. (Unremembered Trilogy Ser.: 1). (ENG.). 352p. (YA). (gr. 7). pap. 9.99 *(978-1-250-04002-2(7)*, 9781250040022) Square Fish.

Bunting, Eve. Train to Somewhere. Himler, Ronald, illus. 2004. 32p. (gr. -1-3). 18.00 *(978-0-7569-4260-1(8))* Perfection Learning Corp.

Canady, Mary Monica. Why Is My Name Sam? Papeo, Maria Eugenia & Saumell, Marina, illus. 2008. 24p. pap. 24.95 *(978-1-60474-028-8(0))* America Star Bks.

Castleman, Virginia. Sara Lost & Found. 2016. (ENG., Illus.). 320p. (J). (gr. 3-7). 16.99 *(978-1-4814-3871-1(9)*, Aladdin) Simon & Schuster Children's Publishing.

Champion, Dionne N., et al. The Spirit of the Baobab Tree. Champion, Dionne N. & Champion, Daryl, illus. 2008. 37p. (J). 31.99 *(978-1-4363-7842-0(7))* Xlibris Corp.

Cooney, Caroline B. They Never Came Back. 2011. (ENG., Illus.). 208p. (YA). (gr. 7). pap. 7.99 *(978-0-385-73809-5(9)*, Ember) Random Hse. Children's Bks.

Crowder, Melanie. Three Pennies. 2017. (ENG., Illus.). 192p. (J). (gr. 3-7). 16.99 ***(978-1-4814-7187-9(2)***, Atheneum Bks. for Young Readers) Simon & Schuster Children's Publishing.

Davis, Tanita S. Peas & Carrots. 2016. (ENG.). 288p. (YA). (gr. 7). 17.99 *(978-0-553-51281-6(1))*; lib. bdg. 20.99 *(978-0-553-51282-3(X))* Random Hse. Children's Bks. (Knopf Bks. for Young Readers).

De la Peña, Matt. Ball Don't Lie. 2007. (ENG.). 288p. (YA). (gr. 9-12). pap. 9.99 *(978-0-385-73425-7(5)*, Ember) Random Hse. Children's Bks.

DeGarmo, John & DeGarmo, Kelly. A Different Home: A New Foster Child's Story. Trammell, Norma Jeanne, illus. 2014. (ENG.). 48p. (J). 14.95 *(978-1-84905-987-9(X)*, 2757) Kingsley, Jessica Pubs. GBR. Dist: Macmillan Distribution Ltd.

Dowell, Frances O'Roark. Where I'd Like to Be. 2004. (Aladdin Fiction Ser.). 232p. (gr. 5-9). 17.00 *(978-0-7569-4357-8(4))* Perfection Learning Corp.

—Where I'd Like to Be. (ENG., (J). (gr. 5-9). 2003. Illus.). 240p. 17.99 *(978-0-689-84420-1(4))* 2004. 256p. reprint ed. pap. 7.99 *(978-0-689-87067-5(1))* Simon & Schuster Children's Publishing. (Atheneum Bks. for Young Readers).

—Where I'd Like to Be. l.t. ed. 2003. 162p. (J). 22.95 *(978-0-7862-5741-6(5))* Thorndike Pr.

Encyclopaedia Britannica, Inc. Staff, compiled by. My Little Foster Sister. 2008. 49.95 *(978-1-59339-666-4(X))* Encyclopaedia Britannica, Inc.

Engle, Margarita. Mountain Dog. Ivanov, Aleksey & Ivanov, Olga, illus. 2013. (ENG.). 224p. (J). (gr. 3-7). 17.99 *(978-0-8050-9516-6(0)*, 9780805095166, Holt, Henry & Co. Bks. For Young Readers) Holt, Henry & Co.

—Mountain Dog. Ivanov, Aleksey & Ivanov, Olga, illus. 2014. (ENG.). 240p. (J). (gr. 3-7). pap. 7.99 *(978-1-250-04424-2(3)*, 9781250044242) Square Fish.

Ferguson, Alane & Skurzynski, Gloria. Running Scared. 2008. (Mysteries in Our National Park Ser.). (ENG., Illus.). 160p. (J). (gr. 3-7). mass mkt. 4.99 *(978-1-4263-0182-7(0)*, National Geographic Children's Bks.) National Geographic Society.

Fleischman, Paul. Breakout. 2003. (ENG.). 160p. (J). 15.95 *(978-0-8126-2696-4(6))* Cricket Bks.

—Breakout. 2005. (ENG.). 144p. (YA). (gr. 7). reprint ed. pap. 6.99 *(978-0-689-87189-4(9)*, Simon Pulse) Simon Pulse.

Fogelin, Adrian. Anna Casey's Place in the World. 2003. (ENG.). 224p. (J). (gr. 3-7). pap. 7.95 *(978-1-56145-295-8(5)*, Q32694) Peachtree Pubs.

—The Sorta Sisters, 1 vol. 2007. (ENG., Illus.). 224p. (J). (gr. 3-7). 15.95 *(978-1-56145-424-2(9))* Peachtree Pubs.

—Sorta Sisters, 1 vol. Fogelin, Adrian, illus. 2011. (ENG., Illus.). 288p. pap. 7.95 *(978-1-56145-592-8(X)*, Peachtree Junior) Peachtree Pubs.

Gagnon, Michelle. Don't Let Go. 2014. (Don't Turn Around Ser.: 3). (ENG.). 352p. (YA). (gr. 8). 17.99 *(978-0-06-210296-6(6))* HarperCollins Pubs.

—Don't Turn Around. 2013. (Don't Turn Around Ser.: 1). (ENG.). 336p. (YA). (gr. 8). pap. 9.99 *(978-0-06-210291-1(5))* HarperCollins Pubs.

Giff, Patricia Reilly. Pictures of Hollis Woods. 2014. (ENG.). 176p. (J). (gr. 3-7). 11.24 *(978-1-63245-318-1(5))* Lectorum Pubns., Inc.

—Pictures of Hollis Woods. 2004. (ENG.). 176p. (J). (gr. 3-7). 7.99 *(978-0-440-41578-7(0)*, Yearling) Random Hse. Children's Bks.

Gilman, Jan Levinson. Murphy's Three Homes: A Story for Children in Foster Care. O'Malley, Kathy, illus. 2008. 32p. (J). (gr. -1-2). 14.95 *(978-1-4338-0384-0(4))*; pap. 9.95 *(978-1-4338-0385-7(2))* American Psychological Assn. (Magination Pr.).

Gonzales, Rebecca. Beauty & the Basketcase. 2007. 103p. pap. 14.94 *(978-1-4303-2379-2(5))* Lulu Pr., Inc.

Gray, Dianne & Gray, Dianne E. Holding up the Earth. 2006. (ENG.). 210p. (J). (gr. 5-7). pap. 12.95 *(978-0-618-73747-5(2))* Houghton Mifflin Harcourt Publishing Co.

Grimes, Nikki. The Road to Paris. 2008. 153p. (gr. 3-7). 17.00 *(978-0-7569-8932-3(9))* Perfection Learning Corp.

—Road to Paris. 2008. (ENG.). 160p. (J). (gr. 3-7). 6.99 *(978-0-14-241082-0(9)*, Puffin Books) Penguin Young Readers Group.

Hahn, Mary Downing. Where I Belong. 2014. (ENG.). 240p. (J). (gr. 5-7). 16.99 *(978-0-544-23020-0(5))* Houghton Mifflin Harcourt Publishing Co.

Hansen, Joyce. One True Friend. Giblin, James Cross, ed. 2005. (ENG.). 160p. (J). (gr. 5-7). pap. 11.95 *(978-0-618-60991-8(1))* Houghton Mifflin Harcourt Publishing Co.

Heneghan, James & Charles, Norma M. Bank Job, 1 vol. 2009. (ENG.). 176p. (J). (gr. 4-8). pap. 14.95 *(978-1-55143-855-9(0))* Orca Bk. Pubs. USA.

Henson, Heather. Dream of Night. 2010. (ENG.). 224p. (J). (gr. 3-7). 15.99 *(978-1-4169-4899-5(6)*, Atheneum Bks. for Young Readers) Simon & Schuster Children's Publishing.

Hernandez, Jo Ann Yolanda. The Throwaway Piece. 2006. 246p. (J). (gr. 6). per. 9.95 *(978-1-55885-353-9(7)*, Piñata Books) Arte Publico Pr.

Higgins, Heather. The Foal That Doesn't Have a Family. 2007. 24p. 13.95 *(978-1-4303-2336-5(1))* Lulu Pr., Inc.

Hill, Janet Muirhead. Kendall's Storm. Leonhard, Herb, illus. 2011. (J). pap. 12.00 *(978-0-9820893-0-9(9))* Raven Publishing Inc. of Montana.

—Kyleah's Tree. Leonhard, Herb, illus. 2011. (J). pap. 12.00 *(978-0-9827377-9-8(3))* Raven Publishing Inc. of Montana.

Horowitz, Anthony. Raven's Gate. 2006. (Gatekeepers Ser.: 1). (ENG.). 272p. (J). (gr. 3-7). pap. 8.99 *(978-0-439-68009-7(3)*, Scholastic Paperbacks) Scholastic, Inc.

—Raven's Gate. 2005. 288p. pap. *(978-1-84428-619-5(3))* Walker Bks., Ltd.

Horvath, Polly. Everything on a Waffle. 2008. (Illus.). 154p. (gr. 5-9). 18.00 *(978-0-7569-8776-3(8))* Perfection Learning Corp.

—Everything on a Waffle. 2008. (ENG., Illus.). 176p. (J). (gr. 5-9). pap. 7.99 *(978-0-312-38004-5(6)*, 9780312380045) Square Fish.

—One Year in Coal Harbor. 2014. (ENG.). 224p. (J). (gr. 4-7). 7.99 *(978-0-385-38653-1(2)*, Yearling) Random Hse. Children's Bks.

Hubler, Marsha. Blue Ribbon Champ, 1 vol. rev. ed. 2010. (Keystone Stables Ser.). (ENG.). 112p. (J). pap. 7.99 *(978-0-310-71797-3(3))* Zonderkidz.

—A Horse to Love, 1 vol. ed. 2009. (Keystone Stables Ser.). (ENG.). 144p. (J). pap. 4.99 *(978-0-310-71792-8(2))* Zonderkidz.

—Leading the Way, 1 vol. 2010. (Keystone Stables Ser.). (ENG.). 128p. (J). pap. 7.99 *(978-0-310-71796-6(5))* Zonderkidz.

—The Long Ride Home, 1 vol. 2010. (Keystone Stables Ser.). (ENG.). 144p. (J). pap. 7.99 *(978-0-310-71692-1(6))* Zonderkidz.

—On the Victory Trail, 1 vol. rev. ed. 2009. (Keystone Stables Ser.). (ENG.). 144p. (J). pap. 7.99 *(978-0-310-71793-5(0))* Zonderkidz.

—Southern Belle's Special Gift, 1 vol. 2009. (Keystone Stables Ser.). (ENG.). 128p. (J). pap. 7.99 *(978-0-310-71794-2(9))* Zonderkidz.

—Whispering Hope, 1 vol., Bk. 7. 2010. (Keystone Stables Ser.). (ENG.). 144p. (J). pap. 7.99 *(978-0-310-71691-4(8))* Zonderkidz.

Hugger, M. A. Danny Malloy & His Mississippi River Samurai. 2008. 132p. 21.95 *(978-0-595-49382-1(3))*; pap. 11.95 *(978-0-595-48462-1(X))* iUniverse, Inc.

Hunt, Lynda Mullaly. One for the Murphys. (ENG.). (J). (gr. 5). 2013. 256p. pap. 7.99 *(978-0-14-242652-4(0)*, Puffin Books) 2012. 288p. 16.99 *(978-0-399-25615-8(6)*, Nancy Paulsen Books) Penguin Young Readers Group.

Huser, Glen. Skinnybones & the Wrinkle Queen, 1 vol. 2008. (ENG.). 192p. (J). (gr. 6-10). pap. 8.95 *(978-0-88899-733-3(7))* Groundwood Bks. CAN. Dist: Publishers Group West (PGW).

Israelievitch, Gabrielle. Where's Home? 2011. (Illus.). 64p. (J). pap. 15.95 *(978-0-937404-72-0(1))* Triad Publishing Co.

Ius, Dawn. Overdrive. 2016. (ENG., Illus.). 352p. (YA). (gr. 9). 17.99 *(978-1-4814-3944-2(8)*, Simon Pulse) Simon Pulse.

Jansen, Karen. The Coming of an Astronaut. 2009. 68p. pap. 9.99 *(978-1-60911-076-5(5)*, Eloquent Bks.) Strategic Book Publishing & Rights Agency (SBPRA).

Jean, Emiko. We'll Never Be Apart. 2015. (ENG.). 288p. (YA). (gr. 9). 17.99 *(978-0-544-48200-5(X)*, HMH Books For Young Readers) Houghton Mifflin Harcourt Publishing Co.

Johnston, Julie. Adam & Eve & Pinch-Me. 2003. (ENG.). 232p. (J). (gr. 5). pap. 9.95 *(978-0-88776-648-0(X)*, Tundra Bks.) Tundra Bks. CAN. Dist: Penguin Random Hse. LLC.

Jones Med, Marquita J. Marvette Made Fun of Me. 2012. (ENG.). 34p. (J). pap. 23.95 *(978-1-4327-8551-2(6))* Outskirts Pr., Inc.

EFG

Jones, Patrick. Outburst. 2014. (Alternative Ser.). (ENG.). 104p. (YA). (gr. 6-12). lib. bdg. 27.93 *(978-1-4677-3901-6(4))* Lerner Publishing Group.
—Outburst. 2014. (Alternative Ser.). (ENG.). 104p. (YA). (gr. 6-12). pap. 7.95 *(978-1-4677-4484-3(0),* Darby Creek) Lerner Publishing Group.
—Taking Sides. 2015. (Locked Out Ser.). (ENG.). 104p. (J). (gr. 6-12). lib. bdg. 27.99 *(978-1-4677-5800-0(0))* Lerner Publishing Group.
Katherine, Paterson. The Great Gilly Hopkins. 2014. (Trophy Bk Ser.). (ENG.). 192p. (J). (gr. 7-12). 10.24 *(978-1-63245-107-1(7))* Lectorum Pubns., Inc.
Kehret, Peg. Runaway Twin. 2011. (ENG.). 208p. (J). (gr. 5-18). 6.99 *(978-0-14-241849-9(8),* Puffin Books) Penguin Young Readers Group.
Kennedy, Marlane. Disaster Strikes #3: Blizzard Night. 2014. (Disaster Strikes Ser.: 3). (ENG.). 128p. (J). (gr. 2-5). pap. 4.99 *(978-0-545-53048-4(2),* Scholastic Paperbacks) Scholastic, Inc.
Kirby, Susan E. A No-Fuss Christmas. 2010. (J). *(978-1-60682-059-9(1))* BJU Pr.
Koertge, Ronald. Strays. (ENG.). 176p. (YA). (gr. 9). 2010. Illus.). pap. 7.99 *(978-0-7636-4377-5(7))* 2007. 16.99 *(978-0-7636-2705-8(4))* Candlewick Pr.
Larcombe, Jennifer Rees. Stone of Evil. 173p. pap. *(978-0-340-58754-6(7))* Hodder & Stoughton.
Laughlin, Florence. The Little Leftover Witch. 2013. (ENG.). 96p. (J). (gr. 3-7). 15.99 *(978-1-4424-8677-5(5));* pap. 5.99 *(978-1-4424-8672-0(4))* Simon & Schuster Bks. For Young Readers. (Simon & Schuster Bks. For Young Readers).
Lewis, Richard. The Demon Queen. 2012. (ENG.). 240p. (YA). (gr. 7). pap. 11.99 *(978-1-4169-3590-2(8),* Simon & Schuster Bks. For Young Readers) Simon & Schuster Bks. For Young Readers.
Loftin, Nikki. Nightingale's Nest. (ENG.). (J). (gr. 3-7). 2015. 272p. pap. 8.99 *(978-1-59514-623-6(7))* 2014. 256p. 16.99 *(978-1-59514-546-8(X))* Penguin Young Readers Group. (Razorbill).
Lois, Lowry. Gossamer. 2006. (ENG.). 144p. (J). (gr. 5-7). 17.99 *(978-0-618-68550-9(2))* Houghton Mifflin Harcourt Publishing Co.
—Gossamer. 2008. (ENG.). 176p. (J). (gr. 3-7). 6.99 *(978-0-385-73416-5(6),* Yearling) Random Hse. Children's Bks.
Lord, Cynthia. Touch Blue. 2012. (ENG.). 192p. (J). (gr. 3-7). pap. 6.99 *(978-0-545-03532-3(5),* Scholastic Pr.) Scholastic, Inc.
Lowell, Pamela. Returnable Girl. 0 vols. 2009. (ENG.). 240p. (J). (gr. 8-12). pap. 9.99 *(978-0-7614-5592-9(2),* 9780761455929, Amazon Children's Publishing) Amazon Publishing.
—Returnable Girl. 2006. 229p. (YA). (gr. 8-12). 16.99 *(978-0-7614-5317-8(2))* Marshall Cavendish Corp.
Lupica, Mike. Fast Break. 2015. (ENG.). 272p. (J). (gr. 5-8). 17.99 *(978-0-399-25606-6(7),* Philomel Bks.) Penguin Publishing Group.
—Fast Break. 2016. (ENG.). 288p. (J). (gr. 5). pap. 8.99 *(978-1-101-99783-3(4),* Puffin Books) Penguin Young Readers Group.
—Fast Break. 2016. (ENG.). 288p. (J). (gr. 5). 19.65 *(978-0-606-39313-3(7))* Turtleback Bks.
Magnin, Joyce. Cake: Love, Chickens, & a Taste of Peculiar. 1 vol. Ivanov, Alexsey & Ivanov, Olga, illus. 2013. (ENG.). 224p. (J). 14.99 *(978-0-310-73333-1(2))* Zonderkidz.
McClintock, Norah. Dead & Gone. 2014. (Mike & Riel Mysteries Ser.: No. 3). 224p. (YA). (gr. 6-12). lib. bdg. 27.93 *(978-1-4677-2607-8(9));* (ENG.). pap. 8.95 *(978-1-4677-2615-3(X))* Lerner Publishing Group. (Darby Creek).
—Dead Silence. 2014. (Mike & Riel Mysteries Ser.: No. 5). 240p. (YA). (gr. 6-12). lib. bdg. 27.93 *(978-1-4677-2609-2(5));* (ENG.). pap. 8.95 *(978-1-4677-2619-1(2))* Lerner Publishing Group. (Darby Creek).
—Seeing & Believing. 2014. (Mike & Riel Mysteries Ser.: No. 4). 240p. (YA). (gr. 6-12). lib. bdg. 27.93 *(978-1-4677-2608-5(7),* Darby Creek) Lerner Publishing Group.
—Truth & Lies. 2014. (Mike & Riel Mysteries Ser.: No. 2). 216p. (YA). (gr. 6-12). lib. bdg. 27.93 *(978-1-4677-2606-1(0),* Darby Creek) Lerner Publishing Group.
Mitchell, Christine. Family Day: Celebrating Ethan's Adoption Anniversary. 2009. 32p. pap. 13.95 *(978-1-4389-5542-1(1))* AuthorHouse.
Montgomery, L. M. Anne of Green Gables. Devereux, Cecily, ed. 2004. (Broadview Editions Ser.). (ENG., Illus.). 400p. pap. *(978-1-55111-362-3(7))* Broadview Pr.
Muldoon, Kathleen M. The Runaway Skeleton. Hilliker, Phillip, illus. 2008. (Vortex Bks.). (ENG.). 112p. (gr. 2-3). 26.65 *(978-1-4342-0800-2(1),* Vortex Bks.) Stone Arch Bks.
Mussi, Sarah. The Door of No Return. (ENG.). 400p. (YA). (gr. 7). 2009. pap. 10.99 *(978-1-4169-6825-2(3))* 2008. 17.99 *(978-1-4169-1550-8(8))* McElderry, Margaret K. Bks. (McElderry, Margaret K. Bks.).
Myers, Kate Kae. The Vanishing Game. (ENG.). (YA). (gr. 7). 2014. 384p. pap. 9.99 *(978-1-61963-127-4(X),* 9781619631274) 2012. 368p. 17.99 *(978-1-59990-694-2(5),* 9781599906942) Bloomsbury Publishing USA. (Bloomsbury USA Childrens).
Nation, Kaleb. The Specter Key. 2010. (ENG.). 352p. (J). (gr. 4-7). pap. 7.99 *(978-1-4022-4059-1(7),* Sourcebooks Jabberwocky) Sourcebooks, Inc.
Paterson, Katherine. La Gran Gilly Hopkins.Tr. of Great Gilly Hopkins. (SPA.). 160p. (J). (gr. 1-6). 8.95 *(978-84-204-3222-9(9))* Santillana USA Publishing Co., Inc.
—The Great Gilly Hopkins. 2004. (Trophy Bk.). (ENG.). 192p. (J). (gr. 5-18). reprint ed. pap. 6.99 *(978-0-06-440201-9(0))* HarperCollins Pubs.
Patterson, James & Papademetriou, Lisa. Homeroom Diaries. Keino, illus. 2014. (ENG.). 272p. (YA). (gr. 7-17). 18.00 *(978-0-316-20762-1(4),* Jimmy Patterson) Little Brown & Co.
Powers, Elizabeth. Where Are You Taking Me? 2008. 28p. pap. 24.95 *(978-1-60563-033-5(0))* America Star Bks.
Robe, Adam D. Meeting My Cas. Robe, Kim A., ed. Gavet, Nathalie, illus. 2009. 16p. pap. 11.99 *(978-0-9817403-5-5(9))* Robe Communications, Inc.
—Moving to Another Foster Home. Robe, Kim A., ed. Gavet, Nathalie, illus. 2009. 16p. pap. 11.99 *(978-0-9817403-4-8(0))* Robe Communications, Inc.
—Robbie's Trail Through Foster Care. Robe, Kim A., ed. Gavet, Nathalie, illus. 2010. 40p. pap. 23.99 *(978-1-935831-00-6(3))* Robe Communications, Inc.
—Robbie's Trail Through Foster Care — Activity Book. Robe, Kim A., ed. Gavet, Nathalie, illus. 2010. 36p. pap. 16.99 *(978-1-935831-01-3(1))* Robe Communications, Inc.
—Robbie's Trail Through Foster Care — Adult Guide. Robe, Kim A., ed. Gavet, Nathalie, illus. 2010. 28p. pap. 16.99 *(978-1-935831-02-0(X))* Robe Communications, Inc.
—Wanting to Belong. Robe, Kim A., ed. Gavet, Nathalie, illus. 2009. 16p. pap. 11.99 *(978-0-9817403-6-2(7))* Robe Communications, Inc.
Rutkoski, Marie. The Shadow Society. 2013. (ENG.). 448p. (YA). (gr. 7-12). pap. 9.99 *(978-1-250-03424-3(8))* Square Fish.
Salisbury, Linda G. The Mysterious Jamestown Suitcase: A Bailey Fish Adventure. Grotke, Christopher A., illus. 2006. (Bailey Fish Adventures Ser.). 191p. (J). (gr. 3-7). per. 8.95 *(978-1-881539-43-8(1))* Tabby Hse. Bks.
Scaletta, Kurtis. Mudville. 2010. (ENG.). 272p. (J). (gr. 3-7). 8.99 *(978-0-375-84472-0(4),* Yearling) Random Hse. Children's Bks.
Scelsa, Kate. Fans of the Impossible Life. 2015. (ENG.). 368p. (YA). (gr. 9). 17.99 *(978-0-06-233175-5(2))* HarperCollins Pubs.
Schmidt, Gary D. Orbiting Jupiter. 2015. (ENG.). 192p. (J). (gr. 7). 17.99 *(978-0-544-46222-9(X),* Clarion Bks.) Houghton Mifflin Harcourt Publishing Co.
—Orbiting Jupiter. 2017. (ENG.). (YA). (gr. 7). lib. bdg. 20.85 ***(978-0-606-39818-3(X))*** Turtleback Bks.
Schraff, Anne. The Forever Boy. 1 vol. 2016. (Red Rhino Ser.). (ENG.). 62p. (J). (gr. 3-6). pap. 7.95 *(978-1-62250-957-7(9))* Saddleback Educational Publishing, Inc.
Schuster, Judith A. No Place to Call Home: Book Two-the Eddie Brewster Adventures. 2008. 196p. pap. 24.95 *(978-1-60563-559-0(6))* PublishAmerica, Inc.
Shafer, Audrey. The Mailbox. 2008. (ENG.). 192p. (J). (gr. 3-7). 6.99 *(978-0-440-42134-4(9),* Yearling) Random Hse. Children's Bks.
Shaw, Susan. The Boy from the Basement. 2006. (ENG.). 208p. (YA). (gr. 7-18). 6.99 *(978-0-14-240546-8(9),* Speak) Penguin Young Readers Group.
Sherrard, Valerie. Searching for Yesterday: A Shelby Belgarden Mystery. 2008. (ENG.). 224p. (YA). (gr. 6-10). pap. 12.99 *(978-1-55002-788-4(3),* Boardwalk Bks.) Dundurn CAN. Dist: Ingram Publisher Services.
Skurzynski, Gloria & Ferguson, Alane. Cliff-Hanger: A Mystery in Mesa Verde National Park. 2007. (Mysteries in Our National Park Ser.). (ENG., Illus.). 160p. (J). (gr. 3-7). per. 4.99 *(978-1-4263-0092-9(1),* National Geographic Children's Bks.) National Geographic Society.
—Out of the Deep. 2008. (Mysteries in Our National Park Ser.). (ENG., Illus.). 160p. (J). (gr. 3-7). pap. 4.99 *(978-1-4263-0251-0(7),* National Geographic Children's Bks.) National Geographic Society.
—Over the Edge. 2008. (Mysteries in Our National Park Ser.). (ENG., Illus.). 160p. (J). (gr. 3-7). per. 4.99 *(978-1-4263-0177-3(4),* National Geographic Children's Bks.) National Geographic Society.
—Valley of Death: A Mystery in Death Valley National Park. 2008. (Mysteries in Our National Park Ser.). (ENG., Illus.). 160p. (J). (gr. 3-7). per. 4.99 *(978-1-4263-0178-0(2),* National Geographic Children's Bks.) National Geographic Society.
Sobel, M., et al. Poison Plate. 1 vol. Cunningham, Kelley, illus. 2006. (Vortex Bks.). (ENG.). 112p. (gr. 2-3). per. 7.19 *(978-1-59889-280-2(0),* Vortex Bks.) Stone Arch Bks.
Sourcebooks. Twisted. 2016. (ENG.). 320p. (YA). (gr. 8-12). pap. 10.99 *(978-1-4926-3179-8(5),* 9781492631798) Sourcebooks, Inc.
Stephenson, Lynda. Dancing with Elvis. 2006. (ENG.). 331p. (YA). (gr. 7). per. 8.00 *(978-0-8028-5300-4(5),* Eerdmans Bks For Young Readers) Eerdmans, William B. Publishing Co.
Sullivan, Therese M. & Bitner, Pamela. A Gift from Valentine. 2007. 24p. (J). per. 12.95 *(978-1-58939-981-5(1))* Virtualbookworm.com Publishing, Inc.
Thill, Mary Kay. Wablenica: The Tale of a Lakotah Orphan. 2004. 240p. (J). per. *(978-0-9743908-0-2(1),* 1232791) Balance Bks., Inc.
Ulch, Virginia. Love, Bandit - a Tail of Foster Care. 2007. 36p. per. 18.95 *(978-1-59858-353-3(0))* Dog Ear Publishing, LLC.
Ure, Jean. Babycakes. 2006. 164p. per. *(978-1-904529-27-9(5),* Back to Front) Solidus.
—Here Comes Ellen. 2006. 164p. per. *(978-1-904529-26-2(7),* Back to Front) Solidus.
—Meet the Radish. 2006. 164p. per. *(978-1-904529-25-5(9),* Back to Front) Solidus.
—My Sister Sam. 2006. 164p. per. *(978-1-904529-24-8(0),* Back to Front) Solidus.
Watson, Stephanie Elaine. Elvis & Olive: Super Detectives. 2010. (ENG.). 288p. (J). (gr. 3-7). 15.99 *(978-0-545-15148-1(1),* Scholastic Pr.) Scholastic, Inc.
Wierenga, Emily Theresa. Save My Children: The Story of a Father's Love. 2008. *(978-1-897213-35-3(2))* BayRidge Bks.
Wilson, Jacqueline. The Story of Tracy Beaker. Sharratt, Nick, illus. 2004. (ENG.). 133p. 16.00 *(978-0-7569-3205-3(X))* Perfection Learning Corp.
Wolfson, Jill. What I Call Life. 2008. (ENG.). 288p. (J). (gr. 5-9). pap. 19.99 *(978-0-312-37752-6(5),* 9780312377526) Square Fish.
Woodson, Jacqueline. Peace, Locomotion. (ENG.). (J). 2010. 176p. (gr. 5-18). 8.99 *(978-0-14-241512-2(X),* Puffin Books) 2009. 144p. (gr. 4-7). 15.99 *(978-0-399-24655-5(X),* G.P. Putnam's Sons Books for Young Readers) Penguin Young Readers Group.
Yelchin, Eugene. Arcady's Goal. Yelchin, Eugene, illus. 2014. (ENG., Illus.). 240p. (J). (gr. 4-7). 15.99 *(978-0-8050-9844-0(5),* 9780805098440, Holt, Henry & Co. Bks. For Young Readers) Holt, Henry & Co.
—Arcady's Goal. Yelchin, Eugene, illus. 2015. (ENG., Illus.). 256p. (J). (gr. 4-7). pap. 7.99 *(978-1-250-06814-9(2),* 9781250068149) Square Fish.

FOURTH DIMENSION

see also Space And Time

Eikum, John. The 4th Dimension & Beyond: Imagining Worlds with 0, 1, 2, 3, 4 Dimensions & More. 2007. 120p. (J). per. 16.95 *(978-1-59298-172-4(0))* Beaver's Pond Pr., Inc.
Kallen, Stuart A. Time Travel. 2009. (Mysterious Encounters Ser.). 48p. (J). 29.00 *(978-0-7377-4573-3(8),* Kidhaven) Cengage Gale.

FOURTH OF JULY

Aloian, Molly. Independence Day. 2009. (Celebrations in My World Ser.). (ENG., Illus.). 32p. (J). (gr. k-2). pap. *(978-0-7787-4772-7(7));* (gr. 1-3). *(978-0-7787-4754-3(9))* Crabtree Publishing Co.
Appleby, Alex. Feliz Cuatro de Julio! / Happy Fourth of July!, Vol. 1. 2014. (¡Felices Fiestas! / Happy Holidays! Ser.). (SPA & BYN., Illus.). 24p. (J). (gr. k-k). 22.60 *(978-1-4339-9962-8(5))* Stevens, Gareth Publishing LLLP.
—Happy Fourth of July!, Vol. 1. 2014. (Happy Holidays! Ser.). (Illus.). 24p. (J). (gr. k-k). (ENG.). 22.60 *(978-1-4824-0207-0(6));* pap. 8.15 *(978-1-4824-0209-4(2))* Stevens, Gareth Publishing LLLP.
Dayton, Connor. Independence Day. 2012. (American Holidays Ser.). (ENG.). 24p. (J). (gr. k-3). pap. 8.25 *(978-1-4488-6238-2(8));* lib. bdg. 22.60 *(978-1-4488-6140-8(3))* Rosen Publishing Group, Inc., The. (PowerKids Pr.).
—Independence Day: Día de la Independencia. Alamán, Eduardo, tr. from ENG. 2012. (American Holidays / Celebraciones en los Estados Unidos Ser.). (SPA & ENG., Illus.). 24p. (J). (gr. k-3). lib. bdg. 22.60 *(978-1-4488-6706-6(1),* PowerKids Pr.) Rosen Publishing Group, Inc., The.
Dean, Sheri. Fourth of July. 2010. (Our Country's Holidays Ser.). (ENG.). 24p. (J). (gr. k-3). pap. 8.15 *(978-1-4339-3915-0(0));* lib. bdg. 22.60 *(978-1-4339-3914-3(2))* Stevens, Gareth Publishing LLLP.
—Fourth of July (Cuatro de Julio) 2006. (Our Country's Holidays/ Las fiestas de nuestra nacion Ser.). (ENG & SPA., Illus.). 24p. (J). (gr. k-3). pap. 8.15 *(978-0-8368-6526-4(X));* lib. bdg. 22.00 *(978-0-8368-6519-6(7))* Stevens, Gareth Publishing LLLP. (Weekly Reader Leveled Readers).
DeRubertis, Barbara. Let's Celebrate Independence Day. 2016. (Holidays & Heroes Ser.). (ENG., Illus.). 32p. (J). (gr. 1-4). pap. 7.95 *(978-1-57565-747-9(3))* Kane Press, Inc.
Felix, Rebecca. We Celebrate Independence Day in Summer. 2014. (21st Century Basic Skills Library: Let's Look at Summer Ser.). (ENG., Illus.). 24p. (J). (gr. k-3). 22.79 *(978-1-63137-599-6(7),* 205179); pap. 12.79 *(978-1-63137-644-3(6),* 205180) Cherry Lake Publishing.
Foran, Jill. Independence Day. 2015. (Illus.). 24p. (J). *(978-1-5105-0110-2(X));* pap. *(978-1-5105-0260-4(2))* SmartBook Media, Inc.
—Independence Day. 2004. (American Holidays Ser.). (Illus.). 24p. (J). lib. bdg. 24.45 *(978-1-59036-109-2(1));* (gr. 1-3). per. 8.95 *(978-1-59036-165-8(2))* Weigl Pubs., Inc.
—Independence Day with Code. 2012. (American Celebrations Ser.). (ENG., Illus.). 24p. (J). (gr. 3-5). pap. 12.95 *(978-1-61913-867-4(0));* lib. bdg. 27.13 *(978-1-61913-864-3(6))* Weigl Pubs., Inc. (AV2 by Weigl).
Gillespie, Katie. Independence Day. 2015. (Let's Celebrate American Holidays Ser.). (ENG.). (J). lib. bdg. 27.13 *(978-1-4896-3625-6(0),* AV2 by Weigl) Weigl Pubs., Inc.
Goeller, Dorothy. The 4th of July. 2010. (All about Holidays Ser.). (Illus.). 24p. (J). 22.60 *(978-0-7660-3806-6(8));* pap. 7.95 *(978-1-59845-175-7(8))* Enslow Pubs., Inc. (Enslow Elementary).
Grack, Rachel. Independence Day. 2017. (Celebrating Holidays! Ser.). (ENG.). 24p. (J). (gr. k-3). lib. bdg. 25.95 ***(978-1-62617-622-5(1),*** Blastoff! Readers) Bellwether Media.
Harcourt School Publishers Staff. Timefor Kids, 5 Pack., Bk. 12. 3rd ed. 2003. (Horizontes (Social Studies) Ser.). (SPA.). (gr. 1-18). pap. 24.00 *(978-0-15-333731-4(1))* Harcourt Schl. Pubs.
Hayes, Amy. Celebrate Independence Day. 2015. (Our Holidays Ser.). (ENG., Illus.). 24p. (J). (gr. 1-1). pap. 8.22 *(978-1-5026-0232-9(6))* Cavendish Square Publishing.
Kaplan, Leslie C. Independence Day. (Library of Holidays Ser.). 24p. 2009. (gr. 2-3). 42.50 *(978-1-60853-713-6(7))* 2004. (Illus.). (J). lib. bdg. 22.60 *(978-0-8239-6663-9(1))* Rosen Publishing Group, Inc., The. (PowerKids Pr.).
Landau, Elaine. What Is the 4th of July? 2011. (I Like Holidays! Ser.). (Illus.). 24p. (J). (gr. k-18). pap. 7.95 *(978-1-59845-292-1(4),* Enslow Elementary); (gr. 1-4). lib. bdg. 22.60 *(978-0-7660-3703-8(7))* Enslow Pubs., Inc.
McGee, Randel. Paper Crafts for the 4th of July. 2011. (Paper Craft Fun for Holidays Ser.). (Illus.). 48p. (J). (gr. 2-5). lib. bdg. 25.27 *(978-0-7660-3727-4(4));* (gr. 3-18). pap. 8.95 *(978-1-59845-332-4(7),* Enslow Elementary) Enslow Pubs., Inc.
Mercer, Abbie. Happy 4th of July. 2009. (Holiday Fun Ser.). 24p. (gr. 2-3). 42.50 *(978-1-61513-374-1(7),* PowerKids Pr.) Rosen Publishing Group, Inc., The.
Merrick, Patrick. Fourth of July Fireworks. 2015. (Our Holiday Symbols Ser.). (ENG.). 24p. (J). (gr. 1-4). 25.64 *(978-1-63143-744-1(5),* 208553) Child's World, Inc., The.
Murray, Julie. Independence Day. 1 vol. 2005. (Buddy Book Ser.). (ENG., Illus.). 24p. (gr. k-4). 25.65 *(978-1-59197-588-5(3),* Buddy Bks.) ABDO Publishing Co.
Nelid, Piper. Independence Day. 01 vols., 1. 2016. (Rosen REAL Readers: Social Studies Nonfiction / Fiction: Family, Community, & the World Ser.). (ENG.). 12p. (J). pap. 6.33 *(978-1-5081-1752-0(7),* Rosen Classroom) Rosen Publishing Group, Inc., The.
Owen, Ruth. Independence Day Origami. 2012. (Holiday Origami Ser.). (ENG., Illus.). 32p. (J). (gr. 3-6). 26.50 *(978-1-4488-7863-5(2));* pap. 11.75 *(978-1-4488-7922-9(1))* Rosen Publishing Group, Inc., The. (PowerKids Pr.).
Ponto, Joanna. Independence Day. 2016. (Story of Our Holidays Ser.). (ENG.). 32p. (J). (gr. 3-3). 25.27 *(978-0-7660-7459-0(5))* Enslow Pubs., Inc.
Trueit, Trudi Strain & Strain-Trueit, Trudi. Independence Day. rev. ed. 2006. (Rookie Read-About Holidays Ser.). (ENG., Illus.). 32p. (J). (gr. 1-2). pap. 5.95 *(978-0-531-11838-2(X),* Children's Pr.) Scholastic Library Publishing.
Williams, Colleen Madonna Flood. My Adventure on the Fourth of July. 2009. (ENG.). 44p. (J). 8.99 *(978-1-59092-560-7(2))* Blue Forge Pr.
Wood, Ira. The Fourth of July. (Real Readers - Upper Emergent Ser.). (ENG., Illus.). 12p. (gr. 1-2). 2008. pap. 5.90 *(978-0-8239-8199-1(1))* 2006. 33.50 *(978-1-4042-6217-1(2))* Rosen Publishing Group, Inc., The.
Zocchi, Judy. On Independence Day. Wallis, Rebecca, illus. 2005. (Holiday Happenings Ser.). 32p. (J). pap. 10.95 *(978-1-59646-208-3(6));* lib. bdg. 21.65 *(978-1-891997-43-3(2))* Dingles & Co.
—On Independence Day/el día de la Independencia. Wallis, Rebecca, illus. 2005. (Holiday Happenings Ser.).Tr. of día de la Independencia. (ENG & SPA.). 32p. (J). pap. 10.95 *(978-1-59646-210-6(8));* lib. bdg. 21.65 *(978-1-891997-44-0(0))* Dingles & Co.

FOURTH OF JULY—FICTION

Anastasio, Dina & Jenkins, Amanda. Jake Digs a Hole, Luke & the Bug Man. 2011. (Readers' & Writers' Genre Workshop Ser.). (YA). pap. *(978-1-4509-3022-2(0))* Benchmark Education Co.
Berenstain, Mike & Berenstain, Stan. The Berenstain Bears God Bless Our Country. 1 vol. 2015. (Berenstain Bears/Living Lights Ser.). (ENG.). 24p. (J). pap. 4.99 *(978-0-310-73485-7(1))* Zonderkidz.
Clark, Katie. Grandma Drove the Garbage Truck. Huntington, Amy, illus. 2006. (ENG.). 32p. (J). (gr. -1-17). 15.95 *(978-0-89272-698-1(9))* Down East Bks.
Flor Ada, Alma. Celebrate Fourth of July with Champ, the Scamp. Mazali, Gustavo, illus. 2006. (Cuentos para Celebrar / Stories to Celebrate Ser.). 30p. (gr. k-6). per. 11.95 *(978-1-59820-131-4(X))* Santillana USA Publishing Co., Inc.
Freeman, Don. Corduroy's Fourth of July. McCue, Lisa, illus. 2007. (Corduroy Ser.). (ENG.). 16p. (J). (gr. -1 — 1). bds. 5.99 *(978-0-670-06159-4(X),* Viking Books for Young Readers) Penguin Young Readers Group.
Grosgebauer, Clare Ham. Snickerdoodle's Star-Spangled Fourth of July! Rissing, Karen, illus. 4th ed. 2005. 36p. (J). (gr. -1-3). 12.99 *(978-0-9741888-6-7(7))* Small Wonders Enterprises.
Henry, Henther French. Life, Liberty & the Pursuit of Jellybeans: A Fourth of July Story. Henry, Henther French, illus. 2004. (Claire's Holiday Adventures Ser.). (ENG., Illus.). 32p. (J). (gr. k-4). 15.95 *(978-0-9706341-6-0(1))* Cubbie Blue Publishing.
—Life, Liberty & the Pursuit of Jellybeans: An Independence Day Story. Henry, Henther French, illus. 2004. (Claire's Holiday Adventures Ser.). (ENG., Illus.). 32p. (J). (gr. k-4). 16.95 *(978-0-9706341-5-3(3))* Cubbie Blue Publishing.
Hillert, Margaret. Let's Go, Dear Dragon. Pullan, Jack, illus. 2016. (BeginningtoRead Ser.). (ENG.). 32p. (J). (-2). lib. bdg. 22.60 *(978-1-59953-774-0(5))* Norwood Hse. Pr.
Hillert, Margaret. Vamos, Querido Dragón. Pullan, Jack, illus. 2017. (BeginningtoRead Ser.).Tr. of Let's Go, Dear Dragon. (ENG & SPA.). 32p. (J). (-2). 22.60 ***(978-1-59953-837-2(7))*** Norwood Hse. Pr.
Hodges, Meredith. Jasper: A Fabulous Fourth. Shields, Bonnie, illus. 2006. 83p. (J). *(978-1-928624-24-0(3))* Lucky 3 Ranch, Inc.
Kane, Bob. Month of Waters & Independence Day. Nguyen, Dustin, illus. 2015. (Batman: Li'l Gotham Ser.). (ENG.). 32p. (gr. 2-3). lib. bdg. 22.60 *(978-1-4342-9666-5(0))* Stone Arch Bks.
Manushkin, Fran. Red, White, & Blue & Katie Woo!. 1 vol. Lyon, Tammie, illus. 2010. (Katie Woo Ser.). (ENG.). 32p. (gr. k-2). lib. bdg. 21.32 *(978-1-4048-5985-2(3));* pap. 5.95 *(978-1-4048-6364-4(8))* Picture Window Bks.
McDonald, Kirsten. The Sparkly Night. 2016. (Carlos & Carmen Set 3 Ser.). (ENG., Illus.). (J). (gr. -1-3). lib. bdg. 27.07 ***(978-1-62402-185-5(9))*** ABDO Publishing Co.
McGrath, Barbara Barbieri. The M & M's(r) Brand All-American Parade Book. Tagel, Peggy, illus. 2004. 12p. (J). (gr. -1-k). bds. 6.95 *(978-1-57091-430-0(3))* Charlesbridge Publishing, Inc.
Montgomery, Lewis B. The Case of the July 4th Jinx. Wummer, Amy, illus. 2010. (Milo & Jazz Mysteries Ser.). 96p. (J). (gr. 2-6). (ENG.). pap. 6.95 *(978-1-57565-308-2(7));* lib. bdg. 22.60 *(978-1-57565-315-0(X))* Kane Press, Inc.
—The Case of the July 4th Jinx. 5th rev. ed. 2010. pap. 39.62 *(978-0-7613-6520-4(6))* Kane Press, Inc.
Morse, William A. and & Morse, William A. And Dana Jo. Kurkle Kids: Spirit of America. 2009. 44p. pap. 16.99 *(978-1-4490-1009-6(1))* AuthorHouse.
Peschke, Marci. Singing Queen. 1 vol. Mourning, Tuesday, illus. 2012. (Kylie Jean Ser.). (ENG.). 112p. (gr. 2-3). pap. 5.95 *(978-1-4048-7211-0(6));* lib. bdg. 22.65 *(978-1-4048-6800-7(3))* Picture Window Bks. (Kylie Jean).
Renero, Joaquin. The Enchanted Scrapbook: Welcome to the Wilburton Society. 2011. 320p. 29.95 *(978-1-4502-6140-1(X));* pap. 19.95 *(978-1-4502-6138-8(8))* iUniverse, Inc.
Rose, Lisa. Shmulik Paints the Town. Echeverri, Catalina, illus. 2016. (ENG.). 32p. (J). (gr. -1-3). 17.99 *(978-1-4677-5239-8(8),* Kar-Ben Publishing) Lerner Publishing Group.
Roy, Ron. July Jitters. Gurney, John Steven, illus. 2012. (Calendar Mysteries Ser.: 7). (ENG.). 80p. (J). (gr. 1-4). 4.99 *(978-0-375-86882-5(8),* Random Hse. Bks. for Young Readers) Random Hse. Children's Bks.
—July Jitters. 2012. (Calendar Mysteries Ser.: 7). lib. bdg. 14.75 *(978-0-606-26402-0(7),* Turtleback) Turtleback Bks.
—The Talking T. Rex. Gurney, John Steven, illus. 2003. (to Z Mysteries Ser.: 20). (ENG.). 96p. (J). (gr. 1-4). pap. 4.99 *(978-0-375-81369-6(1),* Random Hse. Bks. for Young Readers) Random Hse. Children's Bks.
Schories, Pat, illus. Biscuit's Fourth of July. 2005. (J). *(978-1-4156-0311-6(1),* HarperFestival) HarperCollins Pubs.
Shea, Therese. Flags & Fireworks. 2006. (Neighborhood Readers Ser.). (ENG.). 8p. (gr. -1-3). pap. 5.15 *(978-1-4042-5726-9(8),* Rosen Classroom) Rosen Publishing Group, Inc., The.
Stein, Garth. Enzo & the Fourth of July Races. Alley, R. W., illus. 2017. 40p. (J). (gr. -1-3). 17.99 *(978-0-06-238059-3(1))* HarperCollins Pubs.
Wing, Natasha & dePaola, Tomie. The Night Before the Fourth of July. Wummer, Amy, illus. 2015. (Night Before Ser.). (ENG.). 32p. (J). (gr. -1-k). bds. 4.99 *(978-0-448-48712-0(8),* Grosset & Dunlap) Penguin Young Readers Group.
Wong, Janet S. Apple Pie Fourth of July. Chodos-Irvine, Margaret, illus. 2006. (ENG.). 40p. (J). (gr. -1-3). pap. 7.99 *(978-0-15-205708-4(0))* Houghton Mifflin Harcourt Publishing Co.

Zschock, Martha Day. Hello, Rhode Island! 2011. (Hello! Ser.). (ENG., Illus.). 16p. (J). (gr. -1-k). bds. 9.95 (978-1-933212-62-3(4), Commonwealth Editions) Applewood Bks.

FOXES

Barnard, Edward S. Foxes. 2009. (Amazing Animals Ser.). (ENG.). 48p. (J). (gr. 2-6). pap. 10.50 (978-1-4339-2121-6(9), Gareth Stevens Learning Library); (YA). (gr. 3-6). lib. bdg. 28.00 (978-0-8368-9117-1(1)) Stevens, Gareth Publishing LLLP.

—Foxes. 2007. (J). (978-1-59939-120-5(1), Reader's Digest Young Families, Inc.) Studio Fun International.

Berger, Melvin & Berger, Gilda. Foxes. 2010. (Illus.). 16p. (J). (978-0-545-24435-0(8)) Scholastic, Inc.

Borgert-Spaniol, Megan. Baby Foxes. 2015. (Super Cute! Ser.). (ENG., Illus.). 24p. (J). (gr. k-3). lib. bdg. 25.95 (978-1-62617-215-9(3), Blastoff! Readers) Bellwether Media.

—Red Foxes. 2015. (North American Animals Ser.). (ENG., Illus.). 24p. (J). (gr. k-3). lib. bdg. 25.95 (978-1-62617-193-0(9), Blastoff! Readers) Bellwether Media.

Budayr, Valarie. The Fox Diaries: The Year the Foxes Came to Our Garden. 2011. (ENG., Illus.). 80p. (J). 14.95 (978-1-936426-18-8(8)) Audrey Pr.

Carr, Aaron. Foxes. 2014. (J). (978-1-4896-2942-5(4)) Weigl Pubs., Inc.

Donovan, Sandy. A Fox in Its Den. 2003. (Where Do Animals Live? Ser.). (J). pap. (978-1-58417-191-1(X)) Lake Street Pubs.

Doudna, Kelly. It's a Baby Red Fox!, 1 vol. 2008. (Baby Mammals Ser.). (ENG., Illus.). 24p. (J). (gr. k-3). lib. bdg. 24.21 (978-1-60453-031-5(6)) ABDO Publishing Co.

Emily Rose Townsend. Arctic Foxes [Scholastic]. 2009. (Polar Animals Ser.). 24p. (gr. k-1). pap. 0.34 (978-1-4296-4227-9(0), Pebble Bks.) Capstone Press of Coughlan Cos.

Franchino, Vicky. Arctic Foxes. 2013. (ENG.). 48p. (J). 28.00 (978-0-531-23354-2(5)); pap. 6.95 (978-0-531-25152-2(7)) Scholastic Library Publishing.

Ganeri, Anita. Fennec Fox, 1 vol. 2011. (Day in the Life: Desert Animals Ser.). (ENG., Illus.). 24p. (gr. k-2). pap. 6.79 (978-1-4329-4780-4(X), Heinemann Read & Learn) Heinemann-Raintree.

Gardner, Jane P. Fennec Foxes. 2013. (Wild Canine Pups Ser.). 24p. (J). (gr. -1-3). lib. bdg. 21.32 (978-1-61772-925-6(6)) Bearport Publishing Co., Inc.

—Gray Foxes. 2013. (Wild Canine Pups Ser.). 24p. (J). (gr. -1-3). lib. bdg. 21.32 (978-1-61772-931-7(0)) Bearport Publishing Co., Inc.

George, Jean Craighead. Summer Moon. 2003. (J). (gr. 3-7). 20.75 (978-0-8446-7243-4(2)) Smith, Peter Pub., Inc.

Gish, Melissa. Foxes. (Living Wild Ser.). (Illus.). (J). 2017. (ENG.). 48p. (gr. 4-7). pap. 12.00 (978-1-62832-300-9(0), Creative Paperbacks) 2016. 46p. (978-1-60818-704-1(7), Creative Education) Creative Co., The.

Green, Emily. Foxes. 2010. (Backyard Wildlife Ser.). (ENG., Illus.). 24p. (J). (gr. k-3). lib. bdg. 25.95 (978-1-60014-441-7(1), Blastoff! Readers) Bellwether Media.

Green, Jen. Red Fox. 2008. (Illus.). 52p. (J). (978-0-7172-6282-3(0)) Grolier, Ltd.

Holland, Mary. Ferdinand Fox's First Summer, 1 vol. 2013. (ENG., Illus.). 32p. (J). (gr. 1-4). 17.95 (978-1-60718-614-4(4)) Arbordale Publishing.

—El Primer Verano Del Zorro Fernando, 1 vol. 2013. (SPA., Illus.). 32p. (J). (gr. 1-4). 17.95 (978-1-60718-710-3(8)) Arbordale Publishing.

Johnson, J. Angelique. Red Foxes, 1 vol. (Nocturnal Animals Ser.). (ENG., 24p. (gr. k-1). 2011. Illus.). pap. 7.29 (978-1-4296-6195-9(X)) 2011. pap. 41.70 (978-1-4296-6364-9(2)) 2010. lib. bdg. 26.65 (978-1-4296-5285-8(3)) Capstone Press of Coughlan Cos. (Pebble Plus).

Johnson, Jinny. Fox. Rosewarne, Graham, illus. 2010. (J). 28.50 (978-1-59920-354-6(5)) Black Rabbit Bks.

Kalman, Bobbie. Baby Foxes. 2010. (ENG., Illus.). 24p. (J). (978-0-7787-3960-9(0)); pap. (978-0-7787-3979-1(1)) Crabtree Publishing Co.

—Fox Family Adventures. 2016. (ENG., Illus.). 32p. (J). (978-0-7787-2232-8(5)) Crabtree Publishing Co.

Lake, G. G. Red Foxes. 2016. (Woodland Wildlife Ser.). (ENG., Illus.). 24p. (gr. k-1). lib. bdg. 26.65 (978-1-5157-0815-5(2), Pebble Plus) Capstone Press of Coughlan Cos.

Leach, Michael. Fox. 2009. (Animal Neighbors Ser.). 32p. (gr. k-5). pap. 10.60 (978-1-4042-4569-3(3), Rosen Classroom); (Illus.). (J). lib. bdg. 25.25 (978-1-4358-4992-1(2), PowerKids Pr.) Rosen Publishing Group, Inc., The.

Lee, David. Foxes. 2016. (Creatures of the Forest Habitat Ser.). 00024p. (J). (gr. 3-3). pap. 8.25 (978-1-4994-2712-7(3), PowerKids Pr.) Rosen Publishing Group, Inc., The.

Levine, Michelle. Red Foxes. 2004. (Pull Ahead Bks.). (Illus.). 32p. (J). 22.60 (978-0-8225-3774-8(5), Carolrhoda Bks.); (ENG., pap. 7.95 (978-0-8225-9887-9(6)) Lerner Publishing Group.

Markle, Sandra. Foxes. 2009. (Animal Predators Ser.). (ENG.). 40p. (gr. 3-6). 26.60 (978-1-58013-536-8(6)) Lerner Publishing Group.

Marsico, Katie. Arctic Fox, 1 vol. 2011. (Day in the Life: Polar Animals Ser.). (ENG.). 24p. (gr. k-2). pap. 6.79 (978-1-4329-5336-2(2)); 23.32 (978-1-4329-5329-4(X)) Heinemann-Raintree. (Heinemann Read & Learn).

Mason, Cherie. Wild Fox: A True Story. Stammen, JoEllen McAllister, illus. 2013. (ENG.). 56p. 14.99 (978-1-60893-212-2(5)) Down East Bks.

Moore Niver, Heather. Foxes after Dark. 2016. (Animals of the Night Ser.). (ENG.). 32p. (J). (gr. 3-3). pap. 10.52 (978-0-7660-7212-1(6)) Enslow Pubs., Inc.

Murray, Julie. Arctic Foxes, 1 vol. 2013. (Arctic Animals Ser.). (ENG.). 32p. (J). (gr. 2-5). lib. bdg. 28.50 (978-1-61783-797-5(0), Big Buddy Bks.) ABDO Publishing Co.

Niver, Heather Moore. Foxes after Dark. 2016. (Animals of the Night Ser.). (ENG., Illus.). 32p. (J). (gr. 3-3). 25.27 (978-0-7660-7214-5(2)) Enslow Pubs., Inc.

Nobleman, Marc Tyler. Foxes. 2006. (Animals Animals Ser.). (Illus.). 48p. (gr. 3-7). lib. bdg. 29.93 (978-0-7614-2237-2(4), Benchmark Bks.) Marshall Cavendish Corp.

Orr, Nicole. Backyard Jungle Safari Foxes. 2015. (ENG., Illus.). 32p. (J). 26.50 (978-1-62469-098-3(X)) Purple Toad Publishing, Inc.

Owen, Ruth. Arctic Fox Pups. 2011. (Wild Baby Animals Ser.). 24p. (J). (gr. k-3). lib. bdg. 19.96 (978-1-61772-156-4(5)); lib. bdg., E-Book 39.93 (978-1-61772-238-7(3)) Bearport Publishing Co., Inc.

—Arctic Foxes. 2013. (Polar Animals: Life in the Freezer Ser.). (ENG., Illus.). 32p. (gr. k-5). 25.25 (978-1-4777-0222-2(9)); pap. 10.00 (978-1-4777-0231-4(8)) Windmill Bks.

Person, Stephen. Arctic Fox: Very Cool! (Uncommon Animals Ser.). 32p. (gr. 2-7). 2016. (ENG.). (J). pap. 8.95 (978-1-944998-59-2(4)) 2008. (Illus.). (YA). lib. bdg. 25.27 (978-1-59716-730-7(4), 1284372) Bearport Publishing Co., Inc.

Petrie, Kristin. Fennec Foxes, 1 vol. 2010. (Nocturnal Animals Ser.). (ENG.). 24p. (YA). (gr. 3-6). 25.65 (978-1-60453-736-9(1)) ABDO Publishing Co.

Phillips, Dee. Arctic Fox. 2015. (Arctic Animals: Life Outside the Igloo Ser.). (ENG.). 24p. (J). (gr. -1-3). lib. bdg. 23.93 (978-1-62724-530-2(8)) Bearport Publishing Co., Inc.

—Fox's Den. 2012. (Hole Truth! Underground Animal Life Ser.). 24p. (J). (gr. -1-3). lib. bdg. 23.93 (978-1-61772-409-1(2)) Bearport Publishing Co., Inc.

Pope, Kristen. Fennec Foxes. 2015. (Endangered Animals Ser.). (ENG.). 24p. (J). (gr. 1-4). 27.07 (978-1-63143-968-1(5), 208803) Child's World, Inc., The.

Pringle, Laurence. The Secret Life of the Red Fox. Garchinsky, Kate, illus. 2017. (ENG.). 32p. (J). (gr. k-4). 16.95 (978-1-62979-260-6(8)) Boyds Mills Pr.

Raabe, Emily. Flying Foxes. 2009. (Library of Bats Ser.). 24p. (gr. 3-3). 42.50 (978-1-60853-562-0(2), PowerKids Pr.) Rosen Publishing Group, Inc., The.

Read, Tracy C. Exploring the World of Foxes. 2010. (Exploring the World Of Ser.). (ENG., Illus.). 24p. (J). (gr. 2-5). 16.95 (978-1-55407-625-3(0), 9781554076253); pap. 6.95 (978-1-55407-616-1(1), 9781554076161) Firefly Bks., Ltd.

Rigby Education Staff. The Fox: Jumbled Tumble. (gr. k-2). 21.00 (978-0-7635-2422-7(0)) Rigby Education.

Rissman, Rebecca. Red Foxes: Nocturnal Predators, 1 vol. 2014. (Night Safari Ser.). (ENG., Illus.). 24p. (gr. k-2). 23.32 (978-1-4846-0312-3(5), Heinemann Read & Learn) Heinemann-Raintree.

Rudolph, Jessica. MIS Orejas Son Enormes y Peludas (Fennec Fox) 2016. (Pistas de Animales 2 Ser.). (SPA.). 24p. (J). (gr. -1-3). 17.95 (978-1-944102-75-3(2)) Bearport Publishing Co., Inc.

—My Ears Are Huge & Fuzzy. 2016. (Zoo Clues 2 Ser.). (ENG.). 24p. (J). (gr. -1-3). lib. bdg. 17.95 (978-1-944102-57-9(4)) Bearport Publishing Co., Inc.

Rustad, Martha E. Foxes & Their Dens [Scholastic]. 2010. (Animal Homes Ser.). 24p. pap. 0.49 (978-1-4296-5795-2(2), Pebble Plus) Capstone Press of Coughlan Cos.

Rustad, Martha E. H. Foxes. 2013. (ENG., Illus.). 24p. (J). lib. bdg. 25.65 (978-1-62031-069-4(4)) Jump! Inc.

Sebastian, Emily. Foxes. 2012. (Illus.). 24p. (J). 49.50 (978-1-4488-5057-0(6), PowerKids Pr.); pap. 8.25 (978-1-4488-5056-3(8), PowerKids Pr.); lib. bdg. 22.60 (978-1-4488-4953-6(5)) Rosen Publishing Group, Inc., The.

Siemens, Jared. Fennec Fox. 2016. (J). **(978-1-4896-5375-8(9))** Weigl Pubs., Inc.

Sisk, Maeve T. Arctic Foxes. 2010. (Animals That Live in the Tundra Ser.). (ENG.). 24p. (J). (gr. -1-3). 22.60 (978-1-4339-3887-0(1)); pap. 8.15 (978-1-4339-3888-7(X)) Stevens, Gareth Publishing LLLP.

Smith van Frankenhuyzen, Robbyn. Saving Samantha: A True Story. van Frankenhuyzen, Gijsbert, illus. 2004. (Hazel Ridge Farm Stories Ser.). (ENG.). 32p. (J). 17.95 (978-1-58536-220-2(4)) Sleeping Bear Pr.

Strother, Ruth. Red Foxes. 2013. (Wild Canine Pups Ser.). 24p. (J). (gr. -1-3). lib. bdg. 21.32 (978-1-61772-927-0(2)) Bearport Publishing Co., Inc.

Stuhr, Carri. Arctic Foxes. 2009. (Early Bird Nature Bks.). (ENG.). 48p. (gr. 2-5). 26.60 (978-0-8225-9432-1(3), Lerner Pubns.) Lerner Publishing Group.

Terp, Gail. Red Foxes. 2017. (Wild Animal Kingdom Ser.). (ENG., Illus.). 32p. (J). (gr. 3-7). 31.35 **(978-1-68072-057-0(0)**, Bolt); **(978-0-7166-9443-4(3))** Black Rabbit Bks.

Thomas, Isabel. Fox: City Safari, 1 vol. 2014. (City Safari Ser.). (ENG., Illus.). 24p. (gr. 1-1). lib. bdg. 23.32 (978-1-4329-8808-1(5), Heinemann Read & Learn) Heinemann-Raintree.

Ventana, Jose. Foxes & Kits. 2017. (Animal Family Ser.). 24p. (gr. k-k). pap. 8.15 **(978-1-4824-6381-1(4))** Stevens, Gareth Publishing LLLP.

Windsor, Jo. Foxes: Early Level Satellite Individual Title Six-Packs. (Sails Literacy Ser.). 16p. (gr. 1-2). 27.00 (978-0-7578-2941-3(4)) Rigby Education.

Yasuda, Anita. Foxes. 2011. (J). (gr. 2-4). pap. 12.95 (978-1-61690-626-9(X), AV2 by Weigl); (Illus.). 24p. 27.13 (978-1-61690-620-7(0)) Weigl Pubs., Inc.

Zubek, Adeline. Foxes in the Dark. 2012. (Creatures of the Night Ser.). (Illus.). 24p. (J). (gr. 1-3). pap. 8.15 (978-1-4339-6370-4(1)); lib. bdg. 22.60 (978-1-4339-6368-1(X)) Stevens, Gareth Publishing LLLP.

FOXES—FICTION

Aesop. The Fox & the Crane. 2012. (J). 29.99 (978-1-61913-109-5(9)) Weigl Pubs., Inc.

—The Rooster & the Fox: A Tale about Being Clever. 2006. (Famous Fables Ser.). (Illus.). (J). (978-1-59939-038-3(8), Reader's Digest Young Families, Inc.) Studio Fun International.

Akin, Sean, illus. Henny Penny. 2010. (J). (978-1-60617-133-2(X)) Teaching Strategies, LLC.

Alborough, Jez. Six Little Chicks. 2013. (ENG.). 32p. (J). (gr. -1-1). pap. 6.99 (978-1-4380-0181-4(9)) Barron's Educational Series, Inc.

Allen, Jan. Now I Know the Story of Samson. l.t. ed. 2006. (Illus.). 40p. (J). (978-0-9765514-1-6(1)) Light Bugs Publishing.

Aman, Kimiko. The Fox Wish. Sakai, Komako, illus. 2017. (ENG.). 32p. (J). 16.99 (978-1-4521-5188-5(1)) Chronicle Bks. LLC.

Appelt, Kathi & Mcghee, Alison. Maybe a Fox. 2016. (ENG., Illus.). 272p. (J). (gr. 5-9). 17.99 (978-1-4424-8242-5(7), Atheneum/Caitlyn Dlouhy Books) Simon & Schuster Children's Publishing.

Augustyn, Heather. Chi-Town Coyote. 2005. 215p. pap. 12.59 (978-1-4116-3365-0(2)) Lulu Pr., Inc.

Award, Anna, et al. The Fox & the Stork & the Man, His Son & the Donkey. 2014. (ENG.). 24p. (J). pap. 6.95 (978-1-84135-955-7(6)) Award Pubns. Ltd. GBR. Dist: Parkwest Pubns., Inc.

Aylesworth, Jim. The Gingerbread Man. McClintock, Barbara, illus. 2010. (ENG.). 32p. (J). (gr. k — 1). bds. 6.99 (978-0-545-23514-3(6), Cartwheel Bks.) Scholastic, Inc.

Baia, Edward. The Flying Fox & the Cockatoo. Mape, Michael, illus. 2013. 22p. pap. (978-9980-86-507-6(5)) University of Papua New Guinea Press.

Bailey, Arthur Scott. Sleepy-Time Tales: The Tale of Tommy Fox. 2006. pap. (978-1-4065-0453-8(X)) Dodo Pr.

—The Tale of Tommy Fox. 2004. reprint ed. pap. 1.99 (978-1-4192-8481-6(9)); pap. 15.95 (978-1-4191-8481-9(4)) Kessinger Publishing, LLC.

Bailey, Linda. Toads on Toast. Jack, Colin, illus. 2012. (ENG.). 32p. (J). (gr. -1-2). 16.95 (978-1-55453-662-7(6)) Kids Can Pr., Ltd. CAN. Dist: Hachette Bk. Group.

Baker, Harriet Lila. Boyduck Goose: His Life & Times, Bk. II. 2005. (J). pap. 9.00 (978-0-8059-6694-7(3)) Dorrance Publishing Co., Inc.

Baker, Liza. I Love You Because You're You. McPhail, David, illus. (ENG.). (J). (gr. -1-k). 2008. 24p. bds. 8.99 (978-0-545-02931-5(7), Cartwheel Bks.) 2006. 9.99 (978-0-439-89558-3(8)) Scholastic, Inc.

Baltz, Kimberly. Frieda Tails: Freida Goes to Town & Freida, Jack, & the Box. 2012. 28p. 24.99 (978-1-4575-1294-0(7)); pap. 13.95 (978-1-4575-1291-9(2)) Dog Ear Publishing, LLC.

Barkaw, Henniette. Don't Cry Sly: Big Book English Only. Johnson, Richard, illus. 2004. (J). (978-1-85269-999-4(X)) Mantra Lingua.

Barkow, Henriette. Buri & the Maroow. Finlay, Lizzie, illus. 2004. (ENG & FRE.). 24p. (J). pap. (978-1-85269-583-5(8)) Mantra Lingua.

Beha, Eileen. Tango: The Tale of an Island Dog. 2010. (ENG.). 256p. (YA). (gr. 3-6). pap. 7.99 (978-1-59990-485-6(3), 9781599904856, Bloomsbury USA Childrens) Bloomsbury Publishing USA.

Bergren, Lisa T. God Found Us You. Bryant, Laura J., illus. 2009. (J). lib. bdg. 3.99 (978-0-06-113177-6(6)) HarperCollins Pubs.

—God Found Us You. Bryant, Laura J., illus. 2009. (HarperBlessings Ser.). (ENG.). 40p. (J). (gr. -1-2). 10.99 (978-0-06-113176-9(8)) HarperCollins Pubs.

Bickford-Smith, Coralie. The Fox & the Star. 2015. (ENG., Illus.). 64p. (J). 20.00 (978-0-14-310867-2(0), Penguin Books) Penguin Publishing Group.

Bishop, Poppy. Bear's House of Books. Edgson, Alison, illus. 2017. (ENG.). 32p. (J). (gr. -1-2). 16.99 **(978-1-68010-038-9(6))** Tiger Tales.

Blackaby, Susan. Brownie Groundhog & the February Fox. Segovia, Carmen, illus. 2011. (ENG.). 32p. (J). (gr. -1-2). 14.95 (978-1-4027-4336-8(X)) Sterling Publishing Co., Inc.

—Brownie Groundhog & the Wintry Surprise. Segovia, Carmen, illus. 2013. (ENG.). 32p. (J). (gr. -1). 14.95 (978-1-4027-9836-8(9)) Sterling Publishing Co., Inc.

Blevins, Wiley. Stella... Almost: Self-Confidence. Nez, John Abbott, illus. 2015. (ENG.). 24p. (J). (gr. k-2). lib. bdg. 19.99 (978-1-63440-006-0(2), 1392169) Red Chair Pr.

Bloom, Suzanne. Alone Together. Bloom, Suzanne, illus. 2014. (Goose & Bear Stories Ser.). (ENG., Illus.). 32p. (J). (gr. -1-k). 16.95 (978-1-62091-736-7(X)) Boyds Mills Pr.

—Oh! What a Surprise! 2012. (Goose & Bear Stories Ser.). (ENG.). 32p. (J). (gr. -1-k). 16.95 (978-1-59078-892-9(3)) Boyds Mills Pr.

—What about Bear? (Goose & Bear Stories Ser.). (ENG., Illus.). 32p. (J). (gr. -1-1). 2012. pap. 7.95 (978-1-59078-913-1(X)) 2010. 16.95 (978-1-59078-528-7(2)) Boyds Mills Pr.

Bloom, Suzanne, illus. Bear Can Dance! 2015. (Goose & Bear Stories Ser.). (ENG.). 40p. (J). (-k). 16.95 (978-1-62979-442-6(2)) Boyds Mills Pr.

Bonnet, Rosalinde. Daddy Honk Honk! Bonnet, Rosalinde, illus. 2017. (ENG., Illus.). 32p. (J). (-k). 16.99 (978-0-399-18676-9(X), Dial Bks) Penguin Young Readers Group.

Book Buddy: Fox with Story Book. Orig. Title: Child's Play. (Illus.). 10p. (J). (gr. -1-3). reprint ed. (978-1-881469-46-9(8)) Safari, Ltd.

Boujon, Claude. Bon Appetit Monsieur Renard. pap. 14.95 (978-2-211-04878-1(1)) Archimede Editions FRA. Dist: Distribooks, Inc.

Bowler, Tim. Buried Thunder. 2011. (ENG.). 224p. (J). 16.95 (978-0-8234-2397-2(2)) Holiday Hse., Inc.

Bradman, Tom. King Fox Purple Band. Bernstein, Galia, illus. 2016. (Cambridge Reading Adventures Ser.). (ENG.). 24p. pap. 7.19 (978-1-107-56215-8(5)) Cambridge Univ. Pr.

Britt, Fanny. Jane, the Fox & Me, 1 vol. Ouriou, Susan & Morelli, Christelle, trs. from FRE. Arsenault, Isabelle, illus. 2013. (ENG.). 104p. (J). (gr. 5). 19.95 (978-1-55498-360-5(6)) Groundwood Bks. CAN. Dist: Publishers Group West (PGW).

Bryson, Theresa. The Hungry Fox: Set Of 6. 2010. (Early Connections Ser.). (J). 33.00 net. (978-1-59000-721-1(2)) Benchmark Education Co.

Burgess, Thornton W. The Adventures of Reddy Fox. 2005. 26.95 (978-1-4218-0995-3(8)); 84p. pap. 10.95 (978-1-59540-695-8(6)) 1st World Publishing, Inc. (1st World Library - Literary Society).

—The Adventures of Reddy Fox. 2007. 108p. (gr. 4-7). per. 9.95 (978-1-60312-155-2(2)); 22.95 (978-1-60312-838-4(7)) Aegypan.

—The Adventures of Reddy Fox. (J). 18.95 (978-0-8488-0380-3(9)) Amereon Ltd.

—The Adventures of Reddy Fox. 2007. (ENG.). 60p. per. (978-1-4065-5338-3(7)) Dodo Pr.

—The Adventures of Reddy Fox. 2004. reprint ed. pap. 1.99 (978-1-4192-5161-0(9)); pap. 15.95 (978-1-4191-5161-3(4)) Kessinger Publishing, LLC.

—The Adventures of Reddy Fox. Frost, Maddie, illus. 2017. (Thornton Burgess Library). (ENG.). 128p. (J). (gr. -1-2). pap. 9.95 **(978-1-63322-368-4(X)**, Seagrass) Quarto Publishing Group USA.

—The Adventures of Reddy Fox. 2011. 108p. 23.95 (978-1-4638-9571-6(2)) Rodgers, Alan Bks.

—The Adventures of Reddy Fox & Prickly Porky. 2007. 118p. pap. 18.99 (978-1-4346-4026-0(4)); (ENG.). 136p. pap. 19.99 (978-1-4346-4073-4(6)) Creative Media Partners, LLC.

—Old Granny Fox. 124p. 2008. per. 10.95 (978-1-60312-415-7(2)) 2007. 23.95 (978-1-60312-593-2(0)) Aegypan.

—Old Granny Fox. (J). 18.95 (978-0-8488-0392-6(2)) Amereon Ltd.

—Old Granny Fox. 2010. (Dover Children's Thrift Classics Ser.). (ENG., Illus.). 96p. (J). (gr. 3-8). pap. 3.00 (978-0-486-41659-5(3)) Dover Pubns., Inc.

—Old Granny Fox. 2011. 122p. 24.95 (978-1-4638-9559-4(3)) Rodgers, Alan Bks.

—Old Mother West Wind. 2008. 112p. per. 9.95 (978-1-60312-453-9(5)); 22.95 (978-1-60312-551-2(5)) Aegypan.

Camcam, Princesse, creator. Fox's Garden. 2014. (Stories Without Words Ser.). (ENG., Illus.). 32p. (J). (gr. -1-3). 14.95 (978-1-59270-167-4(1)) Enchanted Lion Bks., LLC.

Cartwright, Stan & Dixon, Edna. Strong Fox: How Fox Came to Help a Village Grow Stronger. 2010. 28p. pap. 12.49 (978-1-4490-4376-6(3)) AuthorHouse.

Choi, JeongIm. Who's Coming Tonight? Gang, MinJeong, illus. rev. ed. 2014. (MySELF Bookshelf Ser.). (ENG.). 32p. (J). (gr. k-2). lib. bdg. 25.27 (978-1-59953-653-8(6)) Norwood Hse. Pr.

Chrustowski, Rick. My Little Fox. Chrustowski, Rick, illus. 2017. (ENG., Illus.). 40p. (J). (gr. -1-k). 17.99 **(978-1-4814-6961-6(4)**, Beach Lane Bks.) Beach Lane Bks.

Constantine, Clélia. The Planet of Music. Smith, Owen & Collins Smith, Anne, trs. ÉLyum Studio, illus. 2012. (Little Prince Ser.: 3). (ENG.). 56p. (J). (gr. 4-8). pap. 7.95 (978-0-8225-9424-6(2), Graphic Universe™) Lerner Publishing Group.

Cook, Sherry & Johnson, Terri. X. E. Ecology, 26. Kuhn, Jesse, illus. l.t. ed. 2006. (Quirkles — Exploring Phonics through Science Ser.: 24). 32p. (J). 7.99 (978-1-933815-23-7(X), Quirkles, The) Creative 3, LLC.

Crenshaw, Glenda. Friends of the Enchanted Forest: How they Save Christmas. 2011. 28p. pap. 15.47 (978-1-4520-0512-6(5)) AuthorHouse.

Dahl, Michael. Playdate for Panda. Vidal, Oriol, illus. 2016. (Hello Genius Ser.). (ENG.). 20p. (gr. 1-2). bds. 7.99 (978-1-4795-8741-4(9)) Picture Window Bks.

Dahl, Roald. Fantastic Mr. Fox. 2009. 8.32 (978-0-7848-2303-3(0), Everbind) Marco Bk. Co.

—Fantastic Mr. Fox. Blake, Quentin, illus. 2007. 17.00 (978-0-7569-8286-7(3)) Penguin Publishing Group.

—Fantastic Mr. Fox. 2012. (ENG.). 96p. (J). (gr. 3-7). mass mkt. 14.99 (978-0-14-242343-1(2), Puffin Books) Penguin Young Readers Group.

—Fantastic Mr. Fox. Blake, Quentin, illus. 2007. (ENG.). 112p. (J). (gr. 3-7). 7.99 (978-0-14-241034-9(9), Puffin Books) Penguin Young Readers Group.

—Fantastic Mr. Fox. 2007. 18.40 (978-1-4177-8615-2(9), Turtleback) Turtleback Bks.

—El Superzorro. Elena, Horacio, illus. 2003.Tr. of Fantastic Mr Fox. (SPA.). 96p. (J). (gr. 5-8). pap. 9.95 (978-968-19-0719-8(1)) Santillana USA Publishing Co., Inc.

Dalton, Kippy. The Fox & the Crane. 2016. (Spring Forward Ser.). (J). (gr. 1). (978-1-4900-9392-5(3)) Benchmark Education Co.

Davey, Owen, illus. Foxly's Feast. 2014. (ENG.). 32p. (J). (-k). 14.95 (978-1-62914-608-9(0), Sky Pony Pr.) Skyhorse Publishing Co., Inc.

Defosse, Rosana Curiel. Santiago & the Fox of Hatsune. Barradas, Leticia, illus. (SPA.). 32p. (J). (gr. 3-5). pap. 7.95 (978-970-29-0134-1(0)) Santillana USA Publishing Co., Inc.

Denis, Kasey. Henry the Hippo. 2012. 24p. pap. 17.99 (978-1-4772-6558-1(9)) AuthorHouse.

deRubertis, Barbara. Frances Frog's Forever Friend. Alley, R. W., illus. 2010. (Animal Antics A to Z Ser.). 32p. (J). (gr. -1-3). (ENG.). pap. 7.95 (978-1-57565-310-5(9)); lib. bdg. 22.60 (978-1-57565-317-4(6)) Kane Press, Inc.

deRubertis, Barbara & DeRubertis, Barbara. Frances Frog's Forever Friend. Alley, R. W., illus. 2012. (Animal Antics A to Z Ser.). 32p. (J). (gr. 2 — 1). cd-rom 7.95 (978-1-57565-399-0(0)) Kane Press, Inc.

DiDomenico, Allison. You Can Do It, Fiona! 2010. 28p. pap. 12.95 (978-1-4490-9913-8(0)) AuthorHouse.

Dodd, Emma. Foxy. Dodd, Emma, illus. 2012. (ENG., Illus.). 40p. (J). (gr. -1-2). 14.99 (978-0-06-201419-1(6)) HarperCollins Pubs.

—Foxy in Love. Dodd, Emma, illus. 2013. (ENG., Illus.). 40p. (J). (gr. -1-3). 17.99 (978-0-06-201422-1(6)) HarperCollins Pubs.

—Foxy in Love. 2013. (Illus.). (J). lib. bdg. (978-0-06-201423-8(4)) HarperCollins Pubs.

Donald, David R. Tikoloshe & the Three Fox Cubs. 2012. (Illus.). 56p. pap. 13.66 (978-1-4772-3496-9(9)) AuthorHouse.

Donaldson, Julia. The Quick Brown Fox Cub. 2006. (Red Bananas Ser.). (ENG., Illus.). 48p. (J). (gr. -1-3). lib. bdg. (978-0-7787-1080-6(7)) Crabtree Publishing Co.

Don't Cry Sly. 2004. (J). E-Book incl. cd-rom (978-1-84444-457-1(0)) Mantra Lingua.

Dubos, Delphine. The Planet of Wind. Burrell, Carol klio, tr. Élyum Studio Staff, illus. 2012. (Little Prince Ser.: 1). (ENG.). 56p. (J). (gr. 4-8). pap. 7.95 (978-0-8225-9422-2(6), Graphic Universe™) Lerner Publishing Group.

Eggleton, Jill. The Robber Fox: 3-in-1 Package. (Sails Literacy Ser.). 24p. (gr. 1-18). 57.00 (978-0-7578-8621-8(3)) Rigby Education.

Ekholm, Jan. The Little Red Rascal. 2011. 88p. pap. 30.28 (978-1-4567-9501-6(5)) AuthorHouse.

Emmett, Jonathan. Foxes in the Snow, 11. Harry, Rebecca, illus. 3rd ed. 2012. (ENG.). 32p. (J). (gr. -1-k). pap. 9.99 (978-0-230-71229-4(0)) Pan Macmillan GBR. Dist: Independent Pubs. Group.

Ernst, Lisa Campbell. The Gingerbread Girl. Ernst, Lisa Campbell, illus. 2009. (Illus.). 32p. (J). (gr. -1-k). pap. 6.99 (978-0-14-241448-4(4), Puffin) Penguin Publishing Group.

—The Gingerbread Girl. Ernst, Lisa Campbell, illus. 2006. (ENG., Illus.). 32p. (J). (gr. -1-k). 16.99 *(978-0-525-47667-2(9))*, Dutton Books for Young Readers) Penguin Young Readers Group.

EsterSonia. Sissi My Story - My life with my loving Owners. 2010. 78p. pap. 33.50 *(978-1-4452-1215-9(3))* Lulu Pr., Inc.

Evans, Sarah. The Moose, the Flea, the Fly. 2007. 16p. pap. 24.95 *(978-1-4241-8533-7(5))* America Star Bks.

Faulkner, Georgene. The Gingerbread Boy: Fairy Tales from the World Over. Winter, Milo & Becker, Charlotte, illus. 2011. 98p. 38.95 *(978-1-258-09946-6(2))* Literary Licensing, LLC.

Fenske, Jonathan. A Pig, a Fox, & Stinky Socks. 2017. (Penguin Young Readers Level 2 Ser.). lib. bdg. 13.55 ***(978-0-606-39771-1(X))*** Turtleback Bks.

Fenske, Jonathan & Bader, Bonnie. A Pig, a Fox, & a Box. Fenske, Jonathan, illus. 2015. (Penguin Young Readers, Level 2 Ser.). (ENG., Illus.). 32p. (J). (gr. 1-2). 3.99 *(978-0-448-48510-2(9))*, Penguin Young Readers) Penguin Young Readers Group.

Fenwick, Margaret. Lonnie the Lost Lamb. 2010. 32p. pap. 13.00 *(978-1-60911-038-3(2))*, Eloquent Bks.) Strategic Book Publishing & Rights Agency (SBPRA).

Filipek, Nina. The Gingerbread Man. O'Toole, Jeanette, illus. 2009. (Fairy Tale Firsts Ser.). 12p. (J). (gr. -1-k). bds. 11.40 *(978-1-60754-694-8(9))* Windmill Bks.

Fitzgerald-Rodriguez, Mary. 20 Foxes. 2008. 30p. pap. 24.95 *(978-1-60672-282-4(4))* America Star Bks.

The Fix It Fox. (Little Book Practice Reader Ser.). (J). *(978-0-8136-0690-3(X))* Modern Curriculum Pr.

Football, Virginia. How the Fox Saved the People. Wedzin, James, illus. 2009. (Fox Ser.). (ENG & DGR.). 56p. (gr. k-6). 26.95 *(978-1-894778-75-6(8))* Theytus Bks., Ltd. CAN. Dist: Univ. of Toronto Pr.

Football, Virginia & Mantla, Rosa. How the Fox Got His Crossed Legs. Siemens, Mary, tr. Wedzin, James, illus. 2009. (Fox Ser.). (ENG & DGR.). 32p. (gr. 2-3). 20.95 *(978-1-894778-74-9(X))* Theytus Bks., Ltd. CAN. Dist: Univ. of Toronto Pr.

Ford, Carole S. Freddie the Fox & Peter the Cheetah. Edwin, Kimberly, illus. 30p. (J). (gr. -1). pap. 4.95 *(978-1-891533-03-7(7))* Calvin Partnership, LLC.

Foster, Sheilagh. Mr Coyote Visits the Robson Valley. 2011. 26p. pap. 11.97 *(978-1-61204-439-2(5))*, Strategic Bk. Publishing) Strategic Book Publishing & Rights Agency (SBPRA).

The Fox & the Grapes: 6 Small Books. (gr. k-2). 23.00 *(978-0-7635-8504-4(1))* Rigby Education.

Fox & the Hound. (Read-Along Ser.). (J). 7.99 incl. audio *(978-1-55723-019-5(6))* Walt Disney Records.

Fox, Culpeo S., illus. The Fox & the Crow. 2014. (ENG.). 28p. (J). (gr. -1). 17.95 *(978-81-8190-303-7(X))* Karadi Tales Co. Pvt. Ltd. IND. Dist: Consortium Bk. Sales & Distribution.

Fox, L. B. The Adventures of Marky, Slash & Levy. 2006. (ENG.). 184p. per. 24.95 *(978-1-4241-4992-6(4))* PublishAmerica, Inc.

Fox's Socks. (Acorn Wood Lift-the-Flap Bks.). (Illus.). (YA). bds. 3.50 net. *(978-1-56021-379-6(5))* W.J. Fantasy, Inc.

Gagné, Michel. The Saga of Rex. 2010. (ENG., Illus.). 200p. (J). (gr. 4-7). pap. 17.99 *(978-1-60706-322-3(0))*, 9781607063223) Image Comics.

Galdone, Paul. The Gingerbread Boy, 1 vol. Galdone, Paul, illus. 2008. (Paul Galdone Classics Ser.). (ENG., Illus.). 40p. (J). (gr. -1-3). audio compact disk 10.99 *(978-0-618-89498-7(5))* Houghton Mifflin Harcourt Publishing Co.

—The Gingerbread Boy Big Book. 2006. (Paul Galdone Classics Ser.). (ENG., Illus.). 40p. (J). (gr. -1-3). 26.99 *(978-0-618-83686-4(1))* Houghton Mifflin Harcourt Publishing Co.

Galera Staff. Cuervo y la Raposa (Raven & the Fox) (SPA.). 24p. (J). 9.95 *(978-84-246-1601-4(4))* La Galera, S.A. Editorial ESP. Dist: AIMS International Bks., Inc.

El Gallo, la Zorra, y el Perro. (Coleccion Fabulas y Cuentos Populares). (SPA.). (J). (gr. 2-4). *(978-84-246-1559-8(X))*, GL0414) La Galera, S.A. Editorial ESP. Dist: Lectorum Pubns., Inc.

Gardiner, John Reynolds. Stone Fox. Sewall, Marcia, illus. 25th anniv. ed. 2005. (ENG.). 96p. (J). (gr. 2-6). 16.99 *(978-0-690-03983-2(2))* HarperCollins Pubs.

—Stone Fox. Sewall, Marcia & Hargreaves, Greg, illus. 30th anniv. ed. 2010. (Trophy Bk.). (ENG.). 96p. (J). (gr. 2-6). pap. 6.99 *(978-0-06-440132-6(4))* HarperCollins Pubs.

—Stone Fox. 48p. (J). pap. 4.50 *(978-0-8072-1267-7(9))*, Listening Library) Random Hse. Audio Publishing Group.

Gardiner, John Reynolds & Gardiner, J. Stone Fox. 2010. (J). (gr. 3-6). 17.20 *(978-0-8085-6651-9(2))*, Turtleback) Turtleback Bks.

Garis, Howard Roger. Buddy & Brighteyes Pigg. 2004. reprint ed. pap. 15.95 *(978-1-4191-1107-5(8))*; pap. 1.99 *(978-1-4192-1107-2(2))* Kessinger Publishing, LLC.

Garson, Sarah. Daydream Dan. 2008. (ENG., Illus.). 32p. (J). (gr. -1-k). 19.95 *(978-1-84270-721-0(3))* Andersen Pr. GBR. Dist: Independent Pubs. Group.

Gliori, Debi. No Matter What. (ENG., Illus.). 24p. (J). (gr. -1 — 1). 2012. bds. 12.99 *(978-0-547-71905-4(1))* 2008. bds. 6.99 *(978-0-15-206343-6(9))* Houghton Mifflin Harcourt Publishing Co.

Graegin, Stephanie. Little Fox in the Forest. 2017. (ENG., Illus.). 40p. (J). (gr. -1-3). 17.99 *(978-0-553-53789-5(X))*, Schwartz & Wade Bks.) Random Hse. Children's Bks.

Hagen, Oddmund. Campo Abierto (Open Field) Santos, Nuria G., tr. from NOR. Dezakin, Akin, illus. 2003. (Rosa y Manzana Ser.). (SPA.). 32p. 16.95 *(978-84-89804-42-5(7))* Lóguez Ediciones ESP. Dist: Baker & Taylor Bks.

Hamilton, Martha & Weiss, Mitch. How Fox Became Red. O'Malley, Kathy, illus. 2005. (ENG.). 12p. (J). 5.75 *(978-1-57274-717-3(X))*, 2749, Bks. for Young Learners) Owen, Richard C. Pubs., Inc.

—Two Fables of Aesop. MacDonald, Bruce, illus. 2005. (ENG.). 16p. (J). 5.75 *(978-1-57274-718-0(8))*, 2788, Bks. for Young Learners) Owen, Richard C. Pubs., Inc.

Hansen, Alli. Huevos Rancheros. 2008. 32p. pap. 24.95 *(978-1-60672-993-9(4))* PublishAmerica, Inc.

Harmon, Alison L. The Adventures of Feeda Fox; Everybody's Different. 2010. 24p. 14.99 *(978-0-557-05931-7(3))* Lulu Pr., Inc.

Hartwell, Joe. Hunted Down. 2005. 204p. pap. 14.95 *(978-1-4208-1841-3(4))* AuthorHouse.

Hartzell, Andy. Fox Bunny Funny. 2007. (ENG., Illus.). 104p. pap. 10.00 *(978-1-891830-97-6(X))*, 9781891830976) Top Shelf Productions.

Harvey, Damian. Mr. Fox's Socks. Rescek, Sanja, illus. 2004. (ENG.). 16p. (J). lib. bdg. 23.65 *(978-1-59646-678-4(2))* Dingles & Co.

HB Staff. Good-bye, Fox. 97th ed. 2003. (First-Place Reading Ser.). (gr. 1-18). pap. 16.50 *(978-0-15-308139-2(2))* Harcourt Schl. Pubs.

Head, Mat. Warduff & the Corn Cob Caper. Head, Mat, illus. 2011. (Andersen Press Picture Books Ser.). (Illus.). 16.95 *(978-0-7613-8095-5(7))* Andersen Pr. GBR. Dist: Lerner Publishing Group.

Heinz, Brian J. Red Fox at McCloskey's Farm. Sheban, Chris, illus. 2006. 32p. (J). (gr. -1-3). 17.95 *(978-1-56846-195-3(X))*, Creative Editions) Creative Co., The.

Henry, Marguerite. Cinnabar, the One O'Clock Fox. Dennis, Wesley, illus. (ENG.). 144p. (J). (gr. 3-7). 2015. 19.99 *(978-1-4814-0401-3(6))* 2014. pap. 6.99 *(978-1-4814-0400-6(8))* Simon & Schuster Children's Publishing. (Aladdin).

Hilkene, Ruth Miller & Gugle, Marie. Willie Fox's Diary. 2011. 128p. 40.95 *(978-1-258-09801-8(6))* Literary Licensing, LLC.

Hindley, Judy. Do Like a Duck Does! Bates, Ivan, illus. 2007. (ENG.). 40p. (J). (gr. -1-2). 4.99 *(978-0-7636-3284-7(8))* Candlewick Pr.

—Do Like a Duck Does! Bates, Ivan, illus. 2007. (gr. -1-k). 15.00 *(978-0-7569-8127-3(1))* Perfection Learning Corp.

—Do Like A Duck Does! 2007. 14.75 *(978-1-4177-8331-1(1))*, Turtleback) Turtleback Bks.

Hogrogian, Nonny. One Fine Day. Hogrogian, Nonny, illus. 2nd ed. 2005. (Stories to Go! Ser.). (ENG., Illus.). 32p. (J). 4.99 *(978-1-4169-0312-3(7))*, Simon & Schuster/Paula Wiseman Bks.) Simon & Schuster/Paula Wiseman Bks.

Holden, Pam. Dinner with Fox. Hatam, Samer, illus. 2015. (ENG.). 16p. (-1). pap. *(978-1-77654-129-4(4))*, Red Rocket Readers) Flying Start Bks.

Holland, Trish. I'm Not Sleepy. Kennedy, Anne, illus. 2017. (Little Golden Book Ser.). (ENG.). 24p. (J). (-k). 4.99 *(978-0-399-55058-4(5))*, Golden Bks.) Random Hse. Children's Bks.

Hollenbeck, Kathleen M. Red Fox at Hickory Lane. Smith, Wendy, illus. 2005. (Smithsonian's Backyard Ser.). (ENG.). 32p. (J). (gr. -1-2). 8.95 *(978-1-59249-117-9(0))*, SC5025); 9.95 *(978-1-59249-120-9(0))*, PB5075); 19.95 *(978-1-59249-116-2(2))*, BC5025); 4.95 *(978-1-59249-114-8(6))*, B5075) Soundprints.

—Red Fox at Hickory Lane. Smith, Wendy, tr. Smith, Wendy, illus. 2005. (Smithsonian's Backyard Ser.). (ENG.). 32p. (J). (gr. -1-2). 15.95 *(978-1-59249-113-1(8))*, B5025); pap. 6.95 *(978-1-59249-115-5(4))*, S5025) Soundprints.

Horvath, Polly. Mr. & Mrs. Bunny: Detectives Extraordinaire! Blackall, Sophie, illus. 2012. (ENG.). 256p. (J). (gr. 3-7). 16.99 *(978-0-375-86755-2(4))*, Schwartz & Wade Bks.) Random Hse. Children's Bks.

Houser, Martin. The Secret of Squirrel Meadow. 2006. (Adventures of Little Fox Ser.). (Illus.). 171p. (J). 16.95 *(978-0-9752703-4-9(6))*; per. 7.95 *(978-0-9752703-5-6(4))* Marhouse, Inc.

Houser, Martin L. The Adventures of Little Fox, Book Four, Escape. 2010. (Adventures of Little Fox Ser.). (J). 16.95 *(978-0-9752703-8-7(9))*; pap. 7.95 *(978-0-9752703-9-4(7))* Marhouse, Inc.

—The Adventures of Little Fox Book One, Generations: Teacher's Guide & Student Reproducibles. 2007. (Illus.). 99p. tchr. ed., per. 11.95 *(978-0-9752703-2-5(X))* Marhouse, Inc.

—The Adventures of Little Fox, Book Three, Unfamiliar Territory. 2009. (Adventures of Little Fox Ser.). (J). 16.95 *(978-0-9752703-6-3(2))*; pap. 7.95 *(978-0-9752703-7-0(0))* Marhouse, Inc.

—The Adventures of Little Fox, Generations, Bk. 1. 2006. (Illus.). 208p. (J). pap. 7.95 *(978-0-9752703-1-8(1))*; (Adventures of Little Fox Ser.: Bk. 1). 16.95 *(978-0-9752703-0-1(3))* Marhouse, Inc.

How the Chick Tricked the Fox. (Little Book Practice Reader Ser.). (J). *(978-0-8136-0821-1(X))* Modern Curriculum Pr.

Hughes, Devon. Escape from Lion's Head. 2017. (Unnaturals Ser.: 2). 384p. (J). (gr. 3-7). 16.99 *(978-0-06-225757-4(9))*, Tegen, Katherine Bks) HarperCollins Pubs.

Hutchins, Pat. Rosie's Walk. 2009. 9.00 *(978-0-7848-2915-8(2))*, Everbind) Marco Bk. Co.

ImageBooks Staff & Chronicle Books Staff. Little Fox: Finger Puppet Book. Put, Klaartje van der, illus. 2015. (ENG.). 12p. (J). (gr. -1 — 1). bds. 6.99 *(978-1-4521-4230-2(0))* Chronicle Bks. LLC.

Inglis, Karen. Ferdinand Fox's Big Sleep Colouring Book. Kundalic, Damir, illus. 2013. 32p. pap. *(978-0-9569323-4-1(7))* Well Said Pr.

Iserles, Inbali. The Elders. 2016. (Foxcraft Ser.: 2). (ENG.). 304p. (J). (gr. 3-7). 16.99 *(978-0-545-69084-3(6))*, Scholastic Pr.) Scholastic, Inc.

—The Elders (Foxcraft, Book 2) 2017. (Foxcraft Ser.: 2). (ENG.). 304p. (J). (gr. 3-7). pap. 6.99 ***(978-0-545-69085-0(4))***, Scholastic Paperbacks) Scholastic, Inc.

Iserles, Inbali. The Taken. 2015. (Foxcraft Ser.). (ENG., Illus.). 272p. (J). (gr. 3-7). 16.99 *(978-0-545-69081-2(1))*, Scholastic Pr.) Scholastic, Inc.

Iserles, Inbali, illus. The Taken. 2015. 252p. (J). pap. ***(978-0-545-91869-5(3)***, Scholastic Pr.) Scholastic, Inc.

Jacobs, Joseph. Most Delectable History of Reynard the F. 2006. (Illus.). pap. 28.95 *(978-1-4286-1364-3(6))* Kessinger Publishing, LLC.

Jacques, Brian. Eulalia! 2010. (Redwall Ser.). (ENG.). 400p. (J). (gr. 5-18). 8.99 *(978-0-14-241495-8(6))*, Firebird) Penguin Young Readers Group.

Janssen, Ian. The Perils of Pierre Book 1, Gold Fever. 2013. 26p. pap. 12.99 *(978-1-61160-594-5(6))* Whiskey Creek Restorations.

—The Perils of Pierre Book 2, Hunger Rules. 2013. 26p. pap. 13.95 *(978-1-61160-823-6(6))* Whiskey Creek Restorations.

Jayne, Mitch. Forest in the Wind. 2009. 146p. pap. 15.00 *(978-1-882467-48-8(5))* Wildstone Media.

Jones, Elisabeth & Jones, Lis. A Walk in the Wild Woods. Coplestone, Jim, illus. 2010. (ENG.). 32p. (J). (gr. -1-1). 16.95 *(978-1-84507-956-7(6))*, Frances Lincoln) Quarto Publishing Group UK GBR. Dist: Hachette Bk. Group.

Jones, Helen. Poco - a Chiropractic Story. 2013. 40p. pap. 15.99 *(978-1-4525-8144-6(4))*, Balboa Pr.) Author Solutions, Inc.

Jones, Wendy Lou. Quest for Golden Downs. 2013. 246p. pap. 10.95 *(978-0-9777110-2-4(1))* Royal Knight Inc.

Josephine Breglia. The Adventures of Poke Sa' Baar. 2012. 28p. pap. 24.95 *(978-1-4626-8820-3(9))* America Star Bks.

Kaltovich, Edith Rusconi. The Adventures of Juan, the Fox: Argentine Tales & Fables. 2010. 64p. pap. 26.49 *(978-1-4490-8778-4(7))* AuthorHouse.

Kasza, Keiko. My Lucky Day. Kasza, Keiko, illus. (ENG., Illus.). 32p. (J). (gr. -1-3). 2005. pap. 5.99 *(978-0-14-240456-0(X))*, Puffin Books) 2003. 16.99 *(978-0-399-23874-1(3))*, G.P. Putnam's Sons Books for Young Readers) Penguin Young Readers Group.

—My Lucky Day. Kasza, Keiko, illus. 2005. (Illus.). (gr. -1-3). lib. bdg. 16.00 *(978-0-7569-5492-5(4))* Perfection Learning Corp.

—My Lucky Day. 2006. (J). (gr. k-3). 29.95 incl. audio compact disk *(978-0-8045-4136-7(1))*, SACD4136); incl. audio *(978-0-8045-6937-8(1))*, SAC6937) Spoken Arts, Inc.

Kelly, Thomas E. The Fox & the Young Rooster. Ward, Kelly, illus. 2011. 44p. pap. 24.95 *(978-1-4626-0343-5(2))* America Star Bks.

Kimura, Yuichi. On the Seesaw Bridge. Hata, Kowshiro, illus. 2011. (ENG.). 36p. (J). (gr. -1-3). 14.95 *(978-1-935654-18-6(7))*, Vertical) Vertical, Inc.

Kinross, Robin. No! Go Away! 2013. 40p. pap. 16.95 *(978-1-4525-0979-2(4))* Balboa Pr.

Knoch, Frank. The Big Rescue: The Greenwood Forest Series, 1 vol. Meierhofer, Brian, illus. 2010. 32p. pap. 24.95 *(978-1-4489-6158-0(0))* PublishAmerica, Inc.

Korba, Joanna. The Fox & the Cheese Queen. 2006. (J). pap. *(978-1-4108-7174-9(6))* Benchmark Education Co.

Korschunow, Irina. El Zorrito Abandonado. (Torre de Papel Ser.).Tr. of Abandoned Fox. (SPA., Illus.). (J). (gr. 2). 7.95 *(978-958-04-1380-6(0))* Norma S.A. COL. Dist: Distribuidora Norma, Inc.

Kvasnosky, Laura McGee. The Big Picture. Kvasnosky, Laura McGee, illus. 2010. (Zelda & Ivy Ser.). (ENG., Illus.). 48p. (J). (gr. k-4). 14.99 *(978-0-7636-4180-1(4))* Candlewick Pr.

—The Runaways. Kvasnosky, Laura McGee, illus. 2006. (Zelda & Ivy Ser.). (ENG., Illus.). 48p. (J). (gr. k-4). 14.99 *(978-0-7636-2689-1(9))* Candlewick Pr.

—The Runaways. 2007. (Zelda & Ivy Ser.). (Illus.). 42p. (J). (gr. -1-3). 12.65 *(978-0-7569-8140-2(9))* Perfection Learning Corp.

—Zelda & Ivy - Keeping Secrets. Kvasnosky, Laura McGee, illus. 2013. (Candlewick Sparks Ser.). (ENG., Illus.). 48p. (J). (gr. k-4). pap. 3.99 *(978-0-7636-6636-1(X))* Candlewick Pr.

—Zelda & Ivy - The Big Picture. Kvasnosky, Laura McGee, illus. 2013. (Candlewick Sparks Ser.). (ENG., Illus.). 48p. (J). (gr. k-4). pap. 3.99 *(978-0-7636-6637-8(8))* Candlewick Pr.

—Zelda & Ivy - The Runaways. Kvasnosky, Laura McGee, illus. 2013. (Candlewick Sparks Ser.). (ENG., Illus.). 48p. (J). (gr. k-4). pap. 3.99 *(978-0-7636-6635-4(1))* Candlewick Pr.

—Zelda & Ivy & the Boy Next Door. Kvasnosky, Laura McGee, illus. (Candlewick Sparks Ser.). (ENG., Illus.). 40p. (J). (gr. k-4). 2014. pap. 3.99 *(978-0-7636-7182-2(7))* 2008. 15.99 *(978-0-7636-4004-0(2))* Candlewick Pr.

—Zelda & Ivy One Christmas. Kvasnosky, Laura McGee, illus. 2013. (Candlewick Sparks Ser.). (ENG., Illus.). 40p. (J). (gr. k-4). pap. 3.99 *(978-0-7636-6865-5(6))* Candlewick Pr.

La Coccinella. Little Star. 2014. (Look & See! Ser.). (ENG., Illus.). 24p. (J). (gr. -1 — 1). bds. 6.95 *(978-1-4549-0599-8(9))* Sterling Publishing Co., Inc.

Lane, Jessica E. Fletcher: The Quickest Chicken Catcher. 2009. 52p. pap. 31.99 *(978-1-4415-3461-3(X))* Xlibris Corp.

Lee, Maxine. Big Whoop! 2014. (ENG., Illus.). 32p. (J). (gr. 1-4). 16.95 *(978-1-57687-683-1(7))*, powerHouse Bks.) powerHouse Cultural Entertainment, Inc.

Leedy, Loreen. Crazy Like a Fox. Leedy, Loreen, illus. 2009. (ENG., Illus.). 32p. (J). (gr. -1-3). 7.99 *(978-0-8234-2248-7(8))* Holiday Hse., Inc.

LeTourneau, Marie, illus. Argyle Fox. 2017. (ENG.). 32p. (J). (gr. -1-2). 17.99 *(978-1-939100-09-2(7))* Tanglewood Pr.

Liwska, Renata. Red Wagon. Liwska, Renata, illus. 2013. (ENG., Illus.). 32p. (J). (gr. -1 — 1). 6.99 *(978-0-399-16239-8(9))*, Philomel Bks.) Penguin Young Readers Group.

Lowry, Amy & Aesop. Fox Tails: Four Fables from Aesop. 2012. (ENG., Illus.). 32p. (J). 17.95 *(978-0-8234-2400-9(6))* Holiday Hse., Inc.

Luciani, Brigitte. The Carnival. Tharlet, Eve, illus. 2014. (ENG.). 32p. (J). pap. 6.95 *(978-1-4677-4204-7(X))*; lib. bdg. 25.26 *(978-1-4677-4203-0(1))*, Graphic Universe™) Lerner Publishing Group.

—A Hubbub. Gauvin, Edward, tr. from FRE. Tharlet, Eve, illus. 2010. (Mr. Badger & Mrs. Fox Ser.: 2). (ENG.). 32p. (J). (gr. k-3). pap. 6.95 *(978-0-7613-5632-5(0))*, Graphic Universe™);Bk. 2. 25.26 *(978-0-7613-5626-4(6))* Lerner Publishing Group.

—The Meeting. Burrell, Carol, tr. from FRE. Tharlet, Eve, illus. 2010. (Mr. Badger & Mrs. Fox Ser.: 1). (ENG.). 32p. (J). (gr. k-3). lib. bdg. 25.26 *(978-0-7613-5625-7(8))* Lerner Publishing Group.

—The Meeting. Burrell, Carol, tr. from FRE. Tharlet, Eve, illus. 2010. 1. (ENG.). 32p. (C). (gr. k-3). pap. 10.95 *(978-0-7613-5631-8(2))* National Geographic School Publishing, Inc.

—Peace & Quiet. Burrell, Carol, tr. Tharlet, Eve, illus. 2012. (Mr. Badger & Mrs. Fox Ser.: 4). (ENG.). 32p. (J). (gr. k-3). pap. 6.95 *(978-0-8225-9163-4(4))*; lib. bdg. 25.26 *(978-0-7613-8520-2(7))* Lerner Publishing Group. (Graphic Universe™).

—What a Team! Gauvin, Edward, tr. from FRE. Tharlet, Eve, illus. 2011. (Mr. Badger & Mrs. Fox Ser.: 3). (ENG.). 32p. (J). (gr. k-3). 25.26 *(978-0-7613-5627-1(4))*; pap. 6.95 *(978-0-7613-5633-2(9))*, Graphic Universe™) Lerner Publishing Group.

Magnet, Julien. The Planet of the Firebird. Klio Burrell, Carol, tr. ÉLyum Studio, illus. 2012. (Little Prince Ser.: 2). (ENG.). 56p. (J). (gr. 4-8). pap. 7.95 *(978-0-8225-9423-9(4))*, Graphic Universe™) Lerner Publishing Group.

Magruder, Nilah. How to Find a Fox. 2016. (ENG., Illus.). 40p. (J). 16.99 *(978-1-250-08656-3(6))*, 9781250086563) Feiwel & Friends.

Malone, Geoffrey. Torn Ear. (Illus.). 157p. pap. *(978-0-340-68295-1(7))* Hodder & Stoughton.

Marshall, Edward & Marshall, James. Fox & His Friends. (Fox Ser.). 56p. (J). (gr. k-2). pap. 3.99 *(978-0-8072-1350-6(0))*, Listening Library) Random Hse. Audio Publishing Group.

—Fox at School. (Fox Ser.). 48p. (J). (gr. k-2). pap. 3.99 *(978-0-8072-1349-0(7))*, Listening Library) Random Hse. Audio Publishing Group.

—Fox in Love. (Fox Ser.). 48p. (J). (gr. k-2). pap. 3.99 *(978-0-8072-1352-0(7))*, Listening Library) Random Hse. Audio Publishing Group.

—Fox on Wheels. (Fox Ser.). 48p. (J). (gr. k-2). pap. 3.99 *(978-0-8072-1353-7(5))*, Listening Library) Random Hse. Audio Publishing Group.

Martinez, Rocio, illus. The Fox & the Crow. 2007. (First Reading Level 1 Ser.). 32p. (J). (gr. -1-3). 8.99 *(978-0-7945-1813-4(3))*, Usborne) EDC Publishing.

Marwood, Diane. The Fox & the Crow. 2012. (ENG., Illus.). 24p. (J). *(978-0-7787-7892-9(4))*; pap. *(978-0-7787-7904-9(1))* Crabtree Publishing Co.

Matalonis, Anne. The Fox Behind the Chatterbox. McGhee, Chelsea, illus. 2008. 32p. pap. 17.95 *(978-1-59858-783-8(8))* Dog Ear Publishing, LLC.

Matteren, Joanne. The Old Lion & the Fox. 2005. (J). pap. *(978-1-4108-4206-0(1))* Benchmark Education Co.

Mcauliffe, Timothy & McAuliffe, John Jobin. Snappy the Fox & Other Sleep Time Stories. 2008. 64p. pap. 18.95 *(978-1-4327-1934-0(3))* Outskirts Pr., Inc.

McBratney, Sam. I'll Always Be Your Friend. 2004. (Illus.). (J). (gr. k-3). spiral bd. *(978-0-616-14587-6(X))*; spiral bd. *(978-0-616-14588-3(8))* Canadian National Institute for the Blind/Institut National Canadien pour les Aveugles.

—I'll Always Be Your Friend. Lewis, Kim, illus. 2004. (ENG.). 32p. (J). (gr. -1-3). pap. 6.99 *(978-0-06-055548-1(3))*, Harper Trophy) HarperCollins Pubs.

McCanna, Tim. Water Song. Smythe, Richard, illus. 2017. (ENG.). 32p. (J). (gr. -1-3). 17.99 *(978-1-4814-6881-7(2))*, Simon & Schuster/Paula Wiseman Bks.) Simon & Schuster/Paula Wiseman Bks.

McDermott, Gerald. The Fox & the Stork. 2003. (Green Light Readers Level 2 Ser.). (ENG., Illus.). 24p. (J). (gr. -1-3). pap. 3.95 *(978-0-15-204837-2(5))* Houghton Mifflin Harcourt Publishing Co.

Meadows, Daisy. Nora the Arctic Fox Fairy. 2015. (Baby Animal Rescue Fairies Ser.: 7). (ENG.). 80p. (J). (gr. 2-5). pap. 4.99 *(978-0-545-70856-2(7))*, Scholastic Paperbacks) Scholastic, Inc.

—Nora the Arctic Fox Fairy. 2015. (Rainbow Magic — Baby Animal Rescue Fairies Ser.: 7). lib. bdg. 14.75 *(978-0-606-37055-4(2))* Turtleback Bks.

—Ruby Fuzzybrush's Star Dance. 2016. (Magic Animal Friends Ser.: 7). (ENG., Illus.). 112p. (J). (gr. 2-5). pap. 4.99 *(978-0-545-90745-3(4))*, Scholastic Paperbacks) Scholastic, Inc.

Mellgren, Jöns. Elsa & the Night. 2014. (ENG., Illus.). 32p. (J). (gr. -1-3). 19.95 *(978-3-89955-716-9(6))* Die Gestalten Verlag DEU. Dist: Penguin Random Hse. LLC.

Mercer, M. J. O'No It's Henry. 2010. 24p. 12.99 *(978-1-4520-2125-6(2))* AuthorHouse.

Mesce, Bill. Big Hug. 2016. (ENG.). 32p. pap. 12.00 *(978-1-62288-136-9(2))* Austin, Stephen F. State Univ. Pr.

Metzger, Steve. The Amazing Turkey Rescue. Paillot, Jim, illus. 2007. (J). ***(978-0-545-01420-5(4))*** Scholastic, Inc.

Meyer, Ronald. Freddy Fox. 2005. (ENG., Illus.). 32p. (J). 19.95 *(978-0-9754701-0-7(8))* Natures Beauty Publishing.

Migy. And Away We Go! Migy, illus. 2014. (ENG., Illus.). 40p. (J). (gr. -1-1). 17.99 *(978-0-8050-9901-0(8))*, 9780805099010, Holt, Henry & Co. Bks. For Young Readers) Holt, Henry & Co.

Miller, Dorothy North. How Mr Foxy Fox Was Outfoxed. 2009. 32p. pap. 14.95 *(978-0-9825086-1-9(1))* Fiction Publishing, Inc.

Miller, Janet. Fox Tail Farms. 2011. 172p. pap. 19.95 *(978-1-257-85817-0(3))* Lulu Pr., Inc.

Mini Cuentos: Atletas se Entrenan, Zorro y la Cigüena.Tr. of Mini Fairy Tales: Fox & the Swan. (SPA.). (J). (gr. k-4). 4.98 *(978-970-607-621-2(2))* Larousse, Ediciones, S. A. de C. V. MEX. Dist: Continental Bk. Co., Inc.

Mitcham Davis, Zipporah. The Fox & Emily's Long Migration. 2008. 28p. pap. 13.99 *(978-1-4389-0326-2(X))* AuthorHouse.

Moore, Stephen. Skin & Bone. mass mkt. 8.99 *(978-0-340-70455-4(1))* Hodder & Stoughton GBR. Dist: Trafalgar Square Publishing.

Moran, Alex. Six Silly Foxes. Baker, Keith, illus. 2003. (Green Light Readers Level 1 Ser.). (ENG.). 24p. (J). (gr. -1-3). pap. 3.95 *(978-0-15-204863-1(4))* Houghton Mifflin Harcourt Publishing Co.

—Six Silly Foxes. Baker, Keith, illus. 2003. (Green Light Readers — Level 1 Ser.). (gr. -1-3). lib. bdg. 13.50 *(978-0-613-64595-9(2))*, Turtleback) Turtleback Bks.

Moroney, Tracey, illus. Little Fox's Surprise. 2015. (J). ***(978-0-545-84956-2(X))*** Scholastic, Inc.

Morpurgo, Michael. Little Foxes. 2nd ed. 2009. (ENG., Illus.). 208p. (J). (gr. 2-4). pap. 11.99 *(978-1-4052-3339-2(7))* Egmont Bks., Ltd. GBR. Dist: Independent Pubs. Group.

Myers, Tim. Basho & the Fox, 1 vol. Han, Oki S., illus. 2005. (ENG.). 32p. (J). pap. 5.95 *(978-0-7614-5190-7(0))* Marshall Cavendish Corp.

Myers, Tim J. Basho & the River Stones, 0 vols. Han, Oki, illus. 2013. (ENG.). 34p. (J). (gr. 1-4). pap. 9.99 *(978-1-4778-1682-0(8))*, 9781477816820, Amazon Children's Publishing) Amazon Publishing.

—The Outfoxed Fox: Based on a Japanese Kyogen, 0 vols. 2013. (ENG.). 32p. (J). (gr. k-3). pap. 9.99 *(978-1-4778-1681-3(X))*, 9781477816813, Amazon Children's Publishing) Amazon Publishing.

Nagle, Barbara. Duck & Spider, 1 vol. 2009. 37p. pap. 24.95 *(978-1-60749-980-0(0))* America Star Bks.

Neal, Michael. Rex's Secret: A Courageous CrittersTM Book. 2004. 56p. (J). pap. 8.95 *(978-0-595-30773-9(6))* iUniverse, Inc.

Niland, Kilmeny. The Gingerbread Man. 2006. (Illus.). 16p. *(978-1-921049-49-1(9))* Little Hare Bks. AUS. Dist: HarperCollins Pubs. Australia.

Nolan, Tina. The Injured Fox Kit. Chernyshova, Anna, illus. 2017. (Animal Rescue Center Ser.). (ENG.). 112p. (J). (gr. 1-3). pap. 4.99 ***(978-1-58925-499-2(6))*** Tiger Tales.

Nolte, Nancy. The Gingerbread Man. Scarry, Richard, illus. 2004. (Big Little Golden Book Ser.). (ENG.). 32p. (J). (gr. -1-2). 8.99 *(978-0-375-82589-7(4),* Golden Bks.) Random Hse. Children's Bks.

Oates, Joyce Carol. Where Is Little Reynard? Graham, Mark, illus. 2003. 32p. (J). 16.89 *(978-0-06-029583-7(X))* HarperCollins Pubs.

Ohi, Ruth. Fox & Squirrel. Ohi, Ruth, illus. 2013. (ENG., Illus.). 32p. (gr. -1-2). *(978-1-4431-1914-6(8))* Scholastic Canada, Ltd.

Once upon a Time Spanish Version-the Gingerbread Man. 2005. (J). *(978-1-57022-556-7(7))* ECS Learning Systems, Inc.

O'Toole-Freel, Judy. Zigzag the Rocking Roadrunner. Freel, Mirle, illus. 2012. 40p. 24.95 *(978-1-4626-9970-4(7))* America Star Bks.

Ozgur, Lynne Emily. Darryl & the Mountain. Abay, Ismail, illus. 2009. (ENG.). 32p. (J). (gr. 2-4). 9.95 *(978-1-59784-138-2(2))* Tughra Bks.

Page, Sam. Clearwell Copse: Farlie Fox Has an Invisible Friend. 2012. 32p. pap. 14.51 *(978-1-4669-2026-2(2))* Trafford Publishing.

Papish, Ram. The Little Fox: An Alaska Adventure. Papish, Ram & Papish, Ram, illus. 2008. (ENG., Illus.). 38p. (gr. 3-7). 15.95 *(978-1-889963-87-7(9))* Univ. of Alaska Pr.

Parker, Amy. Night Night, Daddy, 1 vol. 2016. (Night Night Ser.). (ENG., Illus.). 20p. (J). bds. 9.99 *(978-0-7180-4230-1(1))* Nelson, Thomas Inc.

Parker, Vic, ed. The Fox & the Stork & Other Fables. 2014. (Aesop's Fables Ser.). 40p. (J). (gr. 2-5). pap. 84.95 *(978-1-4824-1255-0(1))* Stevens, Gareth Publishing LLLP.

Pascoe, Bruce. Fog a Dox. l.t. ed. 2013. 108p. pap. *(978-1-4596-7080-8(9))* ReadHowYouWant.com, Ltd.

Paul, Dwain. The Fox the Hare the Wolf & the Sheep. 2011. 28p. 16.10 *(978-1-4269-5573-0(1))* Trafford Publishing.

Pauli, Lorenz. Fox in the Library. Schaerer, Kathrin, illus. 2013. (ENG.). 32p. (J). (gr. -1-3). 17.95 *(978-0-7358-4150-5(0))* North-South Bks., Inc.

—The Fox in the Library. Schärer, Kathrin, illus. 2015. (ENG.). 32p. (J). pap. 7.95 *(978-0-7358-4213-7(2))* North-South Bks., Inc.

Pavlick, Leon E. & PAVLICK, A. N. N. M. Foxes on the Ridge. Calvert, Lissa, illus. 2012. 48p. pap. *(978-1-77097-852-2(6))* FriesenPress.

PC Treasures Staff, prod. The Gingerbread Man. 2007. (J). *(978-1-60072-015-4(3))* PC Treasures, Inc.

Pennypacker, Sara. Pax. Klassen, Jon, illus. 2016. (ENG.). (J). (gr. 3-3). 16.99 ***(978-0-06-245703-5(9))*** Blackstone Audio, Inc.

—Pax. Klassen, Jon, illus. 2016. 288p. (J). (gr. 3-7). 16.99 *(978-0-06-237701-2(9))* HarperCollins Pubs.

—Pax. 2017. (SPA.). lib. bdg. 29.35 ***(978-0-606-40010-7(9))*** Turtleback Bks.

—PAX: UNA HISTORIA DE PAZ Y AMISTAD. 2017. (SPA.). 304p. (gr. -1-2). pap. 16.95 ***(978-84-15594-95-6(X),*** Nube De Tinta) Penguin Random House Grupo Editorial ESP. Dist: Two Rivers Distribution.

Percy, Graham. The Fox & the Stork. 2009. (Aesop's Fables Ser.). (ENG., Illus.). 32p. (J). (gr. k-3). 28.50 *(978-1-60253-200-7(1),* 200036) Child's World, Inc., The.

Pertile, Paula, illus. The Gingerbread Man. 2010. (J). *(978-1-60617-141-7(0))* Teaching Strategies, LLC.

Petras, Emery G. The Foxes Three. 2009. 24p. pap. 12.50 *(978-1-4490-2826-8(8))* AuthorHouse.

Pierce, Christa. Did You Know That I Love You? Pierce, Christa, illus. 2014. (ENG., Illus.). 32p. (J). (gr. -1-3). 17.99 *(978-0-06-229744-0(9))* HarperCollins Pubs.

Pink, A. J. The Fox at Christmas. 2009. (Illus.). 52p. pap. *(978-1-84748-586-1(3))* Athena Pr.

Porter, Matthew. Fox on the Loose! Porter, Matthew, illus. 2014. (ENG., Illus.). 20p. (J). (— 1). bds. 9.99 *(978-1-57061-928-1(X),* Little Bigfoot) Sasquatch Bks.

Priddy, Roger. Follow Me. 2016. (Finger Mazes Ser.). (ENG.). 16p. (J). bds. 9.99 *(978-0-312-52058-8(1),* 9780312520588, Priddy Bks.) St. Martin's Pr.

Randy. Charlie the Fox & Mr Cricket. 2009. 28p. pap. 15.99 *(978-1-4415-4254-0(X))* Xlibris Corp.

Rawlinson, Julia. Fletcher & the Falling Leaves. Beeke, Tiphanie, illus. 2008. (ENG.). 32p. (J). (gr. -1-2). pap. 7.99 *(978-0-06-157397-2(3),* Greenwillow Bks.) HarperCollins Pubs.

—Fletcher & the Falling Leaves. 2011. (J). (gr. -1-2). 29.95 *(978-0-545-19699-4(X));* 18.95 *(978-0-545-19705-2(8))* Weston Woods Studios, Inc.

—Fletcher & the Snowflake Christmas. Beeke, Tiphanie, illus. 2010. (ENG.). 32p. (J). (gr. -1-2). 16.99 *(978-0-06-199033-5(7),* Greenwillow Bks.) HarperCollins Pubs.

—Fletcher & the Springtime Blossoms. Beeke, Tiphanie, illus. 2009. (ENG.). 32p. (J). (gr. -1-2). 17.99 *(978-0-06-168855-3(X),* Greenwillow Bks.) HarperCollins Pubs.

—Fletcher & the Springtime Blossoms. 2011. (J). (gr. -1-2). 29.95 *(978-0-545-32738-1(5))* Weston Woods Studios, Inc.

Rawlinson, Julia & Rawlinson. Fletcher & the Falling Leaves. Beeke, Tiphanie, illus. 2006. (ENG.). 32p. (J). (gr. -1-2). 16.99 *(978-0-06-113401-2(5),* Greenwillow Bks.) HarperCollins Pubs.

Ray, Christie Jones & Ray, Christie Jones. Fox Family of Franklin. 2012. (Illus.). 16p. pap. 10.00 *(978-0-9853223-3-5(0))* Rose Water Cottage Pr.

Raye, Marianna & Raye, Daniel. Olis & the Big Outside. 2011. (Illus.). 32p. pap. 14.09 *(978-1-4567-7157-7(4))* AuthorHouse.

Reilly, Carmel & Culic, Ned. Ben Fox Saves the Day. 2008. (Rigby Focus Forward: Level D Ser.). (Illus.). 24p. (J). (gr. 4-7). pap. *(978-1-4190-3665-1(3),* Rigby) Pearson Education Australia.

Remolina, Tere. Un Cambio de Piel. Martinez, Enrique, illus. (Barril Sin Fondo Ser.). (SPA.). (J). (gr. 3-5). pap. *(978-968-6465-20-4(0))* Casa de Estudios de Literatura y Talleres Artisticos Amaquemecan A.C. MEX. Dist: Lectorum Pubns., Inc.

Renner, Benjamin. The Big Bad Fox. 2017. (ENG., Illus.). 192p. (J). pap. 15.99 *(978-1-62672-331-3(1),* 9781626723313, First Second Bks.) Roaring Brook Pr.

Rice, Dona Herwick. The Fox & the Crow, 1 vol. 2008. (Building Fluency Through Reader's Theater Ser.). (ENG.). 24p. (J). (gr. 1-3). pap. 6.99 *(978-1-4333-0295-4(0))* Teacher Created Materials, Inc.

Roberts, Charles G. D. Red Fox. 2008. (Fiction Treasures Ser.). (ENG., Illus.). 270p. (YA). pap. 16.95 *(978-0-88780-737-4(2),* 9780887807374) Formac Publishing Co., Ltd. CAN. Dist: Casemate Pubs. & Bk. Distributors, LLC.

Robinson, Peewee. Spot. 2012. 40p. pap. *(978-1-77097-358-9(3))* FriesenPress.

Rodriguez, Béatrice. The Chicken Thief. 2010. (Stories Without Words Ser.).Tr. of Voleur de Poule. (ENG., Illus.). 32p. (J). (gr. -1-2). 14.95 *(978-1-59270-092-9(6))* Enchanted Lion Bks., LLC.

Rodriguez, Béatrice, illus. Fox & Hen Together. 2011. (Stories Without Words Ser.). (ENG.). 32p. (J). (gr. -1-3). 14.95 *(978-1-59270-109-4(4))* Enchanted Lion Bks., LLC.

Roldan, Gustavo. Cuentos del Zorro. (Cuentamerica Ser.). (SPA.). 64p. (J). (gr. 4-6). *(978-950-07-1557-7(0),* SA30061) Editorial Sudamericana S.A. ARG. Dist: Lectorum Pubns., Inc.

Ross, Dev. We Both Read-Fox's Best Trick Ever: Level 1. Reinhart, Larry, illus. 2006. (We Both Read Ser.). 44p. (J). (gr. -1-3). 7.99 *(978-1-891327-69-8(0))* Treasure Bay, Inc.

Rumaner, Marc. Tundra Finds Her Howler. 2008. 28p. pap. 12.49 *(978-1-4389-4461-6(6))* AuthorHouse.

Russell, Karen Elizabeth. All the Little Foxes. 2015. (ENG., Illus.). 60p. (J). pap. *(978-1-61984-920-4(8))* Price World Publishing.

Salzano, Tammi J. One Windy Day. Wood, Hannah, illus. 2012. (ENG.). 24p. (J). bds. *(978-1-58925-875-4(4))* Tiger Tales.

Sanders, Cecilia. Wanted Dead or Alive. 2010. 36p. pap. 16.99 *(978-1-4520-7023-0(7))* AuthorHouse.

Sargent, Dave & Sargent, David M. Buzz Buzzard: Obey the Rules, 19 vols., Vol. 5. Lenoir, Jane, illus. 2003. (Feather Tales Ser.: 5). 42p. (J). pap. 10.95 *(978-1-56763-728-1(0));* 2nd ed. lib. bdg. 20.95 *(978-1-56763-727-4(2))* Ozark Publishing.

Sargent, Dave & Sargent, Pat. Redi Fox: Friendship, 15 vols., Vol. 3. Huff, Jeane, illus. 2nd rev. ed. 2003. (Animal Pride Ser.: 3). 42p. (J). pap. 10.95 *(978-1-56763-764-9(7));* lib. bdg. 20.95 *(978-1-56763-763-2(9))* Ozark Publishing.

—Young Redi: Friendship!, Vol. 3. Woodward, Elaine, illus. 2003. (Young Animal Pride Ser.: 3). 24p. (J). pap. 10.95 *(978-1-56763-868-4(6));* lib. bdg. 20.95 *(978-1-56763-867-7(8))* Ozark Publishing.

Sawyer, J. Scott. The Broccoli Bush. Bozeman, Gary, illus. 2012. 36p. pap. 24.95 *(978-1-4626-2501-7(0))* America Star Bks.

Scarry, Richard. Richard Scarry's Mr. Fixit's Whacky Toolbox: Lift-The Flap Book. 2015. (ENG., Illus.). 10p. (J). (gr. -1 — 1). bds. 7.99 *(978-0-7641-6811-6(8))* Barron's Educational Series, Inc.

Schorr, Titus. Tricky Fox, 01 vols., 1. 2016. (Rosen REAL Readers: STEM & STEAM Collection). (ENG.). 12p. (J). pap. 6.33 *(978-1-5081-1530-4(3),* Rosen Classroom) Rosen Publishing Group, Inc., The.

Schweizer, Chris. Tricky Fox Tales. Paroline, Shelli & Paroline, Michelle, illus. 2011. (Tricky Journeys Ser.: 3). (ENG.). (J). (gr. 2-4). pap. 39.62 *(978-0-7613-8627-8(0))* Lerner Publishing Group.

—Tricky Fox Tales. Paroline, Shelli, illus. 2011. (Tricky Journeys Ser.: 3). (ENG.). 64p. (J). (gr. 2-4). pap. 6.95 *(978-0-7613-7861-7(8))* Lerner Publishing Group.

—Tricky Fox Tales, No. 3. Paroline, Shelli & Paroline, Michelle, illus. 2011. (Tricky Journeys Ser.: 3). (ENG.). 64p. (J). (gr. 2-4). lib. bdg. 27.93 *(978-0-7613-6605-8(9))* Lerner Publishing Group.

Scraper, Katherine. Fox in the Forest. 2006. (Early Explorers Ser.). (J). pap. *(978-1-4108-6023-1(X))* Benchmark Education Co.

Sedrak, Asham. The Santa Claus Fox. 2011. 28p. pap. 13.59 *(978-1-4670-2484-6(8))* AuthorHouse.

Seton, Ernest Thompson. The Biography of a Silver Fox. 2005. pap. 24.95 *(978-1-885529-39-8(2))* Stevens Publishing.

Seuss, Dr. Fox in Socks. (Big Bright & Early Board Book Ser.). (ENG., Illus.). (J). 2015. 24p. (— 1). bds. 6.99 *(978-0-553-51336-3(2))* 2005. 64p. (gr. -1-2). 9.95 *(978-0-375-83494-3(X))* Random Hse. Children's Bks. (Random Hse. Bks. for Young Readers).

—Fox in Socks: Dr. Seuss's Book of Tongue Tanglers. 2011. (Bright & Early Board Books Ser.). (ENG., Illus.). 24p. (J). (gr. k-1). bds. 4.99 *(978-0-307-93180-1(3),* Random Hse. Bks. for Young Readers) Random Hse. Children's Bks.

—Fox in Socks & Socks in Box. 2015. (ENG., Illus.). 24p. (J). (— 1). 11.99 *(978-0-553-52424-6(0),* Random Hse. Bks. for Young Readers) Random Hse. Children's Bks.

—Fox in Socks, Bricks & Blocks. Gerardi, Jan, illus. 2011. (Dr. Seuss Nursery Collection). (ENG.). 14p. (J). (gr. -1 — 1). 7.99 *(978-0-375-87209-9(4),* Random Hse. Bks. for Young Readers) Random Hse. Children's Bks.

Shah, Idries. The Man & the Fox. Mallam, Sally, illus. 2006. 32p. (J). (gr. -1). 18.00 *(978-1-883536-43-5(X));* pap. 7.99 *(978-1-883536-60-2(X))* I S H K. (Hoopoe Bks.).

Shapiro, Esmé. Ooka. 2016. (ENG., Illus.). 40p. (J). (gr. -1-2). 16.99 *(978-1-101-91844-9(6),* Tundra Bks.) Tundra Bks. CAN. Dist: Penguin Random House. LLC.

Sherwood-Sitts, Herm. The Fox & Farmer Beeching. 2011. 28p. pap. 24.95 *(978-1-4626-0914-7(7))* America Star Bks.

Slater, Teddy. Tim Feels Scared. Rescek, Sanja, illus. 2011. (J). *(978-0-545-35179-9(0))* Scholastic, Inc.

Sly Fox & Red Hen, Level 2. 2016. (Ladybird Readers Ser.). (ENG.). 48p. (J). (gr. 2-4). pap. 9.99 *(978-0-241-25443-1(4))* Penguin Bks., Ltd. GBR. Dist: Independent Pubs. Group.

Sly Fox & the Little Red Hen. 2005. (J). bds. 3.99 *(978-1-933200-11-8(1))* Family Bks. at Home.

Small, David. Eulalie & the Hopping Head. Small, David, illus. 2003. (Illus.). pap. 35.95 incl. audio compact disk *(978-1-59112-520-4(0))* Live Oak Media.

Smith, Alex T. Foxy & Egg: Starring Vivien Vixen As Foxy Dubois - Introducing Edward l'Ouef As Egg. Smith, Alex T., illus. 2011. (Illus.). 32p. (J). (gr. -1-3). 17.95 *(978-0-8234-2330-9(1))* Holiday Hse., Inc.

Smith, Ivy. Roxie & the Deer. 2011. (Illus.). 32p. (J). 19.95 *(978-0-9635757-7-7(5));* (ENG., pap. 11.99 *(978-0-9635757-8-4(3))* Red Tail Publishing.

Smith, Lesley & Award Publications Staff. Brer Rabbit & Brer Fox. 2014. (ENG., Illus.). 24p. (J). pap. 6.95 *(978-1-84135-962-5(9))* Award Pubns. Ltd. GBR. Dist: Parkwest Pubns., Inc.

Smith, Sindy. Ervin & Alma's Little Mouse House. 2013. 38p. 24.95 *(978-1-63004-209-7(9));* 40p. pap. 24.95 *(978-1-62709-189-3(0))* America Star Bks.

Snell, Roy J. Little White Fox & His Arctic Friends. 2008. 108p. 22.95 *(978-1-60664-935-0(3));* 104p. pap. 9.95 *(978-1-60664-055-5(0))* Aegypan.

Sommer, Carl. The Donkey, Fox, & the Lion. Noé, Ignacio, illus. 2016. (ENG.). 32p. (J). (gr. k-4). lib. bdg. 16.95 *(978-1-57537-926-5(0),* Another Sommer-Time Story) Advance Publishing, Inc.

—The Sly Fox & the Chicks. James, Kennon, illus. 2014. (J). pap. *(978-1-57537-966-1(X))* Advance Publishing, Inc.

—The Sly Fox & the Chicks. 2003. (Another Sommer-Time Story Ser.). (Illus.). 48p. (J). (gr. 1-4). 16.95 incl. audio *(978-1-57537-553-3(2))* Advance Publishing, Inc.

—The Sly Fox & the Chicks. James, Kennon, illus. 2003. (Another Sommer-Time Story Ser.). (ENG.). 48p. (J). 16.95 incl. audio compact disk *(978-1-57537-504-5(4))* Advance Publishing, Inc.

—The Sly Fox & the Chicks Read-along. 2003. (Another Sommer-Time Story Ser.). (Illus.). 48p. (J). lib. bdg. 23.95 incl. audio *(978-1-57537-754-4(3))* Advance Publishing, Inc.

—The Sly Fox & the Chicks Read-along. James, Kennon, illus. 2003. (Another Sommer-Time Story Ser.). (ENG.). 48p. (J). lib. bdg. 23.95 incl. audio compact disk *(978-1-57537-704-9(7))* Advance Publishing, Inc.

—The Sly Fox & the Chicks(El Zorro Astuto y los Pollitos) James, Kennon, illus. 2009. (Another Sommer-Time Story Bilingual Ser.). (SPA & ENG.). 48p. (J). lib. bdg. 16.95 *(978-1-57537-166-5(9))* Advance Publishing, Inc.

Soo, Kean, illus. The Great Desert Rally. 2015. (March Grand Prix Ser.). (ENG.). 48p. (gr. 1-3). lib. bdg. 33.32 *(978-1-4342-9641-2(5))* Capstone Young Readers of Coughlan Cos.

—The Race at Harewood. 2015. (March Grand Prix Ser.). (ENG.). 48p. (gr. 1-3). lib. bdg. 33.32 *(978-1-4342-9639-9(3))* Capstone Young Readers of Coughlan Cos.

Souhami, Jessica, illus. King Pom & the Fox. 2009. (ENG.). 36p. (J). (gr. -1-2). pap. 7.95 *(978-1-84507-365-7(7),* Frances Lincoln) Quarto Publishing Group UK GBR. Dist: Hachette Bk. Group.

Squamish Nation Education Department. Hussa. 2011. 24p. (gr. -1). pap. 10.96 *(978-1-4251-7645-7(3))* Trafford Publishing.

Starfall Education. Mox's Shop. Starfall Education, ed. 2004. (ENG., Illus.). 8p. (J). pap. *(978-1-59577-004-2(6))* Starfall Education.

Steig, William. Doctor de Soto. 2003. (Picture Books Collection). (SPA.). 32p. (J). (gr. k-3). 16.95 *(978-84-372-6616-9(5))* Altea, Ediciones, S.A. - Grupo Santillana ESP. Dist: Santillana USA Publishing Co., Inc.

—Doctor de Soto. 2004. (J). (gr. k-3). spiral bd. *(978-0-616-01784-5(7));* spiral bd. *(978-0-616-01785-2(5))* Canadian National Institute for the Blind/Institut National Canadien pour les Aveugles.

—Roland the Minstrel Pig. 2016. (ENG., Illus.). 32p. (J). (gr. -1-3). 18.99 *(978-0-374-30088-3(7),* 9780374300883, Farrar, Straus & Giroux (BYR)) Farrar, Straus & Giroux.

Stilton, Geronimo. Secret Agent. 2008. (Geronimo Stilton Ser.: 34). (ENG., Illus.). 128p. (J). (gr. 2-5). pap. 7.99 *(978-0-545-02134-0(0),* Scholastic Paperbacks) Scholastic, Inc.

Stone, Forrest. The Fox & Grapes at Belleville Elementary. 2006. (J). pap. *(978-1-4108-7172-5(X))* Benchmark Education Co.

Stowell, Louie. Brer Rabbit down the Well. Muszynski, Eva, illus. 2010. (First Reading Level 2 Ser.). 32p. (J). 6.99 *(978-0-7945-2674-0(8),* Usborne) EDC Publishing.

Szabo, Erika. Our Summer Guests. 2008. 32p. pap. 24.95 *(978-1-60441-946-7(6))* America Star Bks.

Tabor, Corey R. Fox & the Jumping Contest. Tabor, Corey R., illus. 2016. (Illus.). 32p. (J). (gr. -1-3). 17.99 *(978-0-06-239874-1(1))* HarperCollins Pubs.

Tatsuyama, Sayuri. Happy Happy Clover, Vol. 1. Tatsuyama, Sayuri, illus. 2009. (ENG., Illus.). 200p. (J). pap. 7.99 *(978-1-4215-2656-0(5))* Viz Media.

—Happy Happy Clover, Vol. 4. Tatsuyama, Sayuri, illus. 2010. (ENG., Illus.). 192p. (J). pap. 7.99 *(978-1-4215-2735-2(9))* Viz Media.

TerKeurst, Lysa. It Will Be Okay: Trusting God Through Fear & Change, 1 vol. 2014. (ENG., Illus.). 32p. (J). 14.99 *(978-1-4003-2419-4(X))* Nelson, Thomas Inc.

Tessa on Her Own: Evaluation Guide. 2006. (J). *(978-1-55942-422-6(2))* Witcher Productions.

Thompson, Jolene & Thompson, Justin K. Faraway Fox. Thompson, Jolene & Thompson, Justin K., illus. 2016. (ENG., Illus.). 32p. (J). (gr. -1-3). 17.99 *(978-0-544-70711-5(7),* HMH Books For Young Readers) Houghton Mifflin Harcourt Publishing Co.

Thompson, Margaret. Fox Winter. Akin, Galan, tr. 2005. (Illus.). 60p. (J). (gr. 3-5). 8.95 *(978-0-9730831-5-6(8))* Hodgepog Bks. CAN. Dist: Coteau Bks.

Tompert, Ann. Grandfather Tang's Story. Parker, Robert A., illus. 2015. (ENG.). 32p. (J). (gr. -1-2). 16.99 *(978-0-517-57487-4(X),* Knopf Bks. for Young Readers) Random Hse. Children's Bks.

Tompert, Ann & Lister, Ralph. Little Fox Goes to the End of the World, 0 vols. Bryant, Laura J., illus. 2010. (ENG.). 32p. (J). (gr. -1-2). 16.99 *(978-0-7614-5703-9(8),* 9780761457039, Amazon Children's Publishing) Amazon Publishing.

Top That! Playtime Shapes (large Version) Parry, Jo, illus. 2007. 10p. (J). (gr. -1). *(978-1-84666-555-4(8),* Tide Mill Pr.) Top That! Publishing PLC.

Turnbull, Victoria. Pandora. 2017. (ENG., Illus.). 32p. (J). (gr. -1-3). 16.99 *(978-0-544-94733-7(9),* Clarion Bks.) Houghton Mifflin Harcourt Trade & Reference Pubs.

Twohy, Mike. Outfoxed. Twohy, Mike, illus. 2013. (ENG., Illus.). 40p. (J). (gr. -1-3). 16.99 *(978-1-4424-7392-8(4),* Simon & Schuster Bks. For Young Readers) Simon & Schuster Bks. For Young Readers.

Vue, Jeng Tong & Vue, See. Baby Chick & the Fox. 2009. 44p. pap. 9.95 *(978-1-936107-27-8(9))* Salem Author Services.

Ward, Helen, illus. & retold by. The Rooster & the Fox. Ward, Helen, retold by. 2003. 40p. (J). (gr. k-3). 16.95 *(978-0-7613-1846-0(1),* First Avenue Editions) Lerner Publishing Group.

Ward, Helen & Ward, Helen. The Rooster & the Fox. 2003. (Single Titles Ser.: Vol. 3). 40p. (gr. k-4). lib. bdg. 24.90 *(978-0-7613-2920-6(X),* Millbrook Pr.) Lerner Publishing Group.

Wendling, Peter. Matthew Leads the Animal Parade, 1 vol. 2010. 30p. 24.95 *(978-1-4512-1836-7(2))* PublishAmerica, Inc.

Weston, Avalon. All the Sky. 2013. 138p. pap. *(978-1-78407-151-6(X))* FeedARead.com.

Weston, Carrie. If a Chicken Stayed for Supper. Fatus, Sophie, illus. 2007. (ENG.). 32p. (J). (gr. -1-3). 16.95 *(978-0-8234-2067-4(1))* Holiday Hse., Inc.

Weston Woods Staff, creator. Fletcher & the Falling Leaves. 2011. 38.75 *(978-0-545-19710-6(4))* Weston Woods Studios, Inc.

—Fletcher & the Snowflake Christmas. 2011. 29.95 *(978-0-545-42619-0(7))* Weston Woods Studios, Inc.

—One Fine Day. 2011. 29.95 *(978-0-545-23362-0(3));* 18.95 *(978-0-545-23363-7(1));* 38.75 *(978-0-545-23364-4(X))* Weston Woods Studios, Inc.

White, Mark. The Fox & the Grapes: A Retelling of Aesop's Fable, 1 vol. Pérez, Sara Rojo, illus. (My First Classic Story Ser.). (ENG.). 24p. (gr. k-3). 2013. pap. 7.10 *(978-1-4795-1856-2(5),* My First Classic Story) 2008. per. 3.95 *(978-1-4048-0467-8(6),* Easy Readers) Picture Window Bks.

—La Zorra y Las Uvas. Abello, Patricia, tr. Pérez, Sara Rojo, illus. 2008. (Read-It! Readers en Español: Cuentos Folclóricos Ser.). (SPA.). 24p. (gr. k-3). per. 3.95 *(978-1-4048-2141-5(4),* Easy Readers) Picture Window Bks.

White, Mark & Aesop Enterprise Inc. Staff. The Fox & the Grapes: A Retelling of Aesop's Fable, 1 vol. Pérez, Sara Rojo, illus. 2011. (My First Classic Story Ser.). (ENG.). 24p. (gr. k-3). lib. bdg. 22.65 *(978-1-4048-6508-2(X),* My First Classic Story) Picture Window Bks.

Whybrow, Ian. Little Wolf's Diary of Daring Deeds. Ross, Tony, illus. (Middle Grade Fiction Ser.). 132p. (gr. 3-6). 2005. 14.95 *(978-1-57505-411-7(6))* 2003. (J). pap. 6.95 *(978-0-87614-536-4(5),* Carolrhoda Bks.) Lerner Publishing Group.

Wild, Margaret. Fox. Brooks, Ron, illus. 2006. (ENG.). 32p. (J). (gr. 1). pap. 7.99 *(978-1-933605-15-9(4))* Kane Miller.

Wiley, Melissa. Fox & Crow Are Not Friends. Braun, Sebastien, illus. 2012. (Step into Reading Ser.). (ENG.). 48p. (J). (gr. k-3). pap. 3.99 *(978-0-375-86982-2(4),* Random Hse. Bks. for Young Readers) Random Hse. Children's Bks.

—Fox & Crow Are Not Friends. 2012. (Step into Reading Level 3 Ser.). lib. bdg. 13.55 *(978-0-606-26806-6(5),* Turtleback) Turtleback Bks.

Willems, Mo. That Is Not a Good Idea! Willems, Mo, illus. 2013. (ENG., Illus.). 48p. (J). (gr. k-3). 17.99 *(978-0-06-220309-0(6))* HarperCollins Pubs.

Wilson, Barbara. Mrs. Piglin Visits Sick Mr. Fox. Caracino, Leah, illus. 2012. (ENG.). 16p. (gr. k-3). pap. 9.00 *(978-1-56778-541-8(7))* Wilson Language Training.

Ylvis & Løchstøer, Christian. What Does the Fox Say? Nyhus, Svein, illus. 2013. (ENG.). 32p. (J). (gr. -1-3). 17.99 *(978-1-4814-2223-9(5),* Simon & Schuster Bks. For Young Readers) Simon & Schuster Bks. For Young Readers.

Zubeyr Mohamed. The Fox & the Hyen. 2013. 32p. pap. 17.25 *(978-1-4669-7232-2(7))* Trafford Publishing.

Zuckerman, Linda. A Taste for Rabbit. 2007. (J). *(978-0-439-86978-2(1),* Levine, Arthur A. Bks.) Scholastic, Inc.

FOXES—SONGS AND MUSIC

Spier, Peter. The Fox Went Out on a Chilly Night: An Old Song. 2014. (ENG., Illus.). 48p. (J). (gr. -1-2). 17.99 *(978-0-385-37616-7(2));* lib. bdg. 20.99 *(978-0-375-97207-2(2))* Random Hse. Children's Bks. (Doubleday Bks. for Young Readers).

Spier, Peter, illus. The Fox Went Out on a Chilly Night: An Old Song. unabr. ed. 2006. (J). (gr. -1-3). pap. 16.95 incl. audio *(978-1-59112-440-5(9));*Set. pap. 39.95 incl. audio compact disk *(978-1-59112-443-6(3));*Set. pap. 37.95 incl. audio *(978-1-59112-442-9(5))* Live Oak Media.

FOWL, ARTEMIS (FICTITIOUS CHARACTER)—FICTION

Colfer, Eoin. The Arctic Incident. 2009. (Artemis Fowl Ser.). (ENG.). 304p. (J). (gr. 5-9). pap. 8.99 *(978-1-4231-2454-2(5))* Hyperion Pr.

—The Arctic Incident. 2003. (Artemis Fowl Ser.: 2). 277p. (J). (gr. 5-7). lib. bdg. 19.65 *(978-0-613-62927-0(2),* Turtleback) Turtleback Bks.

—Artemis Fowl, 3 vols., Set. 2010. (Artemis Fowl Ser.). (ENG.). 944p. (J). (gr. 5-17). pap. 19.99 *(978-1-4231-3681-1(0))* Disney Pr.

—Artemis Fowl. (Artemis Fowl Ser.: Bk. 1). (FRE.). pap. 34.95 *(978-2-07-054681-7(0))* Gallimard, Editions FRA. Dist: Distribooks, Inc.

—Artemis Fowl. rev. ed. 2009. (Artemis Fowl Ser.). (ENG.). 304p. (J). (gr. 5-9). pap. 8.99 *(978-1-4231-2452-8(9))* Hyperion Pr.

—Artemis Fowl. (Artemis Fowl Ser.: Bk. 1). pap. 34.95 *(978-88-04-49788-2(2))* Mondadori ITA. Dist: Distribooks, Inc.

—Artemis Fowl. (Artemis Fowl Ser.: 1). (YA). 2007. 1.25 *(978-1-4193-6020-6(5))* 2006. 52.75 *(978-1-4193-6023-7(X))* 2006. 54.75 *(978-1-4193-6021-3(3))* 2006. 54.75 *(978-1-4193-6026-8(4))* 2006. 132.75 *(978-1-4193-6022-0(1))* 2005. 56.75 *(978-1-4193-6024-4(8))* Recorded Bks., Inc.

—Artemis Fowl. 2009. (Artemis Fowl Ser.: 1). (J). (gr. 5-8). lib. bdg. 19.65 *(978-0-613-60637-0(X),* Turtleback) Turtleback Bks.

—Artemis Fowl. Feldmann, Claudia, tr. (Artemis Fowl Ser.: Bk. 1). (GER.). pap. 24.95 *(978-3-548-60320-9(3))* Ullstein-Taschenbuch-Verlag DEU. Dist: Distribooks, Inc.

E
F
G

—Artemis Fowl & the Atlantis Complex. 2012. (ENG.). 384p. (J). (gr. 5-9). pap. 8.99 *(978-1-4231-2972-1(5))* Hyperion Pr.
—The Atlantis Complex. 2010. (Artemis Fowl Ser.: 7). (ENG.). 368p. (J). (gr. 5-9). 17.99 *(978-1-4231-2819-9(2))* Hyperion Pr.
—The Atlantis Complex. 2012. (Artemis Fowl Ser.: 7). (J). lib. bdg. 19.65 *(978-0-606-23614-0(7),* Turtleback) Turtleback Bks.
—The Eternity Code. rev. ed. 2009. (Artemis Fowl Ser.). (ENG.). 336p. (J). (gr. 5-9). pap. 8.99 *(978-1-4231-2453-5(7))* Hyperion Pr.
—The Last Guardian. 2012. (Artemis Fowl Ser.). (ENG.). 336p. (J). (gr. 5-9). 18.99 *(978-1-4231-6161-5(0))* Hyperion Pr.
—The Last Guardian. 2014. (Artemis Fowl Ser.: 8). (J). lib. bdg. 19.65 *(978-0-606-32288-1(4),* Turtleback) Turtleback Bks.
—EL MUNDO SUBTERRÁNEO (ARTEMIS FOWL 1) (Artemis Fowl Ser.: Bk. 1). (SPA.). 288p. pap. *(978-84-8441-115-4(X),* MO31567) Grijalbo Mondadori, S.A.-Montena.
—The Opal Deception. 2006. (Artemis Fowl Ser.: Bk. 4). 17.10 *(978-0-7569-6828-1(3))* Disney Pr.
—The Opal Deception. rev. ed. 2009. (Artemis Fowl Ser.). (ENG.). 368p. (J). (gr. 5-9). pap. 8.99 *(978-1-4231-2455-9(3))* Hyperion Pr.
—The Opal Deception. (Artemis Fowl Ser.: 4). (J). 2007. 1.25 *(978-1-4193-6041-1(8))* 2006. 72.75 *(978-1-4193-6045-9(0))* 2006. 69.75 *(978-1-4193-6047-3(7))* Recorded Bks., Inc.
—The Time Paradox. 2009. (Artemis Fowl Ser.). (ENG.). 448p. (J). (gr. 5-9). pap. 8.99 *(978-1-4231-0837-5(X))* Hyperion Pr.
—The Time Paradox. 2009. (Artemis Fowl Ser.: 6). (J). lib. bdg. 19.65 *(978-0-606-10579-8(4),* Turtleback) Turtleback Bks.
Colfer, Eoin & Donkin, Andrew. Artemis Fowl. Rigano, Giovanni & Lamanna, Paolo, illus. 2007. (Artemis Fowl Ser.). (ENG.). 112p. (J). (gr. 5-9). 18.99 *(978-0-7868-4881-2(2));* pap. 12.99 *(978-0-7868-4882-9(0))* Hyperion Pr.
—The Eternity Code. Rigano, Giovanni & Lamanna, Paolo, illus. 2013. (Artemis Fowl Ser.: 3). (ENG.). 112p. (J). (gr. 5-9). 19.99 *(978-1-4231-4527-1(5))* Hyperion Pr.

FOYT, A. J., 1935-

Wilker, Josh & Prentzas, G. S., texts. A. J. Foyt. rev. ed. 2007. (Race Car Legends Ser.). (Illus.). 72p. (YA). (gr. 5-9). lib. bdg. 25.00 *(978-0-7910-8759-6(X))* Facts On File, Inc.

FRACTIONS

Adamson, Thomas K. and Heather. Half You Heard of Fractions? 2012. (Fun with Numbers Ser.). (ENG.). 32p. (gr. 1-2). pap. 47.70 *(978-1-4296-8306-7(6),* Aplus Bks.) Capstone Press of Coughlan Cos.
Adler, David A. Fractions, Decimals, & Percents. Miller, Edward, illus. (ENG.). 32p. (J). 2011. pap. 7.99 *(978-0-8234-2354-5(9))* 2010. (gr. 1-5). 17.95 *(978-0-8234-2199-2(6))* Holiday Hse., Inc.
—Fractions, Decimals, & Percents. Miller, Edward, illus. 2010. (J). *(978-0-545-25162-4(1))* Scholastic, Inc.
—Working with Fractions. Miller, Edward, illus. 2009. (ENG.). 32p. (J). (gr. 1-5). pap. 7.99 *(978-0-8234-2207-4(0))* Holiday Hse., Inc.
Aihara, Masaaki & Sarris, Eno, eds. Grade 4 Decimals & Fractions: Kumon Math Workbooks. 2008. (J). per. 7.95 *(978-1-933241-58-6(6))* Kumon Publishing North America, Inc.
—Grade 5 Decimals & Fractions: Kumon Math Workbooks. 2008. (J). per. 7.95 *(978-1-933241-59-3(4))* Kumon Publishing North America, Inc.
—Grade 6 Fractions: Kumon Math Workbooks. 2008. (J). per. 7.95 *(978-1-933241-60-9(8))* Kumon Publishing North America, Inc.
Alaina, Maria. Fractions, 1 vol. (Wonder Readers Next Steps: Math Ser.). (ENG.). (gr. -1-1). 2013. 20p. 22.65 *(978-1-4765-2368-2(1))* 2011. 16p. pap. 35.94 *(978-1-4296-8090-5(3))* 2011. 32p. pap. 5.99 *(978-1-4296-7804-9(6))* Capstone Press of Coughlan Cos. (Wonder Readers).
Arias, Lisa. Dandy Decimals: Add, Subtract, Multiply, & Divide. 2014. (ENG.). 32p. (gr. 3-6). 32.79 *(978-1-62717-718-4(3))* Rourke Educational Media.
—Dazzling Decimals: Decimals & Fractions. 2014. (ENG.). 32p. (gr. 3-6). 32.79 *(978-1-62717-714-6(0))* Rourke Educational Media.
—Dynamic Denominators: Compare, Add, & Subtract. 2014. (ENG., Illus.). 32p. (gr. 3-6). 32.79 *(978-1-62717-716-0(7))* Rourke Educational Media.
—Fraction Action: Fractions Are Numbers Too. 2014. (ENG.). 32p. (gr. 3-6). 32.79 *(978-1-62717-709-2(4))* Rourke Educational Media.
—Funky Fractions: Multiply & Divide. 2014. (ENG.). 32p. (gr. 3-6). 32.79 *(978-1-62717-717-7(5))* Rourke Educational Media.
Atwood, Megan. Cuddly Kittens: Discovering Fractions, 1 vol. Holm, Sharon, illus. 2012. (Count the Critters Ser.). (ENG.). 24p. (J). (gr. k-3). 27.07 *(978-1-61641-853-3(2))* Magic Wagon.
Bennet, Janice. Flag Fractions! Develop Understanding of Fractions & Numbers. 2014. (Rosen Common Core Math Readers Ser.). (ENG.). 24p. (J). (gr. 3-4). pap. 8.25 *(978-1-4777-4924-1(1),* PowerKids Pr.) Rosen Publishing Group, Inc., The.
Burton, Margie, et al. Parts Make up a Whole. 2011. (Early Connections Ser.). (J). *(978-1-61672-533-4(8))* Benchmark Education Co.
—Parts of a Whole. 2011. (Early Connections Ser.). (J). *(978-1-61672-267-8(3))* Benchmark Education Co.
Bussell, Linda. Pizza Parts: Fractions! 2008. (Math in Our World - Level 3 Ser.). 24p. (gr. 2-5). (J). lib. bdg. 22.00 *(978-0-8368-9289-5(5));* pap. 8.15 *(978-0-8368-9388-5(3))* Stevens, Gareth Publishing LLLP. (Weekly Reader Leveled Readers).
—Pizza Por Partes: Fracciones! 2008. (Las matemáticas en nuestro mundo - Nivel 3 (Math in Our World - Level 3) Ser.). (SPA.). 24p. (gr. 2-5). pap. 8.15 *(978-0-8368-9396-0(4),* Weekly Reader Leveled Readers) Stevens, Gareth Publishing LLLP.
—Pizza por Partes: ¡FRACCIONES! 2008. (Matemáticas en Nuestro Mundo - Nivel 3 (Math in Our World - Level 3) Ser.). (SPA.). 24p. (J). (gr. 2-5). lib. bdg. 22.00 *(978-0-8368-9297-0(6),* Weekly Reader Leveled Readers) Stevens, Gareth Publishing LLLP.
Caron, Lucille & St. Jacques, Philip M. Fraction & Decimal Smarts! 2011. (Math Smarts! Ser.). (Illus.). 64p. (J). (gr. 5-18). pap. 8.95 *(978-1-59845-321-8(1))* Enslow Pubs., Inc.
—Percent & Ratio Smarts! 2011. (Math Smarts! Ser.). (Illus.). 64p. (J). (gr. 5-18). pap. 8.95 *(978-1-59845-317-1(3))* Enslow Pubs., Inc.
Caron, Lucille, et al. Fraction & Decimal Smarts! 2011. (Math Smarts! Ser.). (Illus.). 64p. (J). (gr. 5-18). lib. bdg. 29.27 *(978-0-7660-3936-0(6))* Enslow Pubs., Inc.
—Percent & Ratio Smarts! 2011. (Math Smarts! Ser.). (Illus.). 64p. (J). (gr. 5-18). lib. bdg. 29.27 *(978-0-7660-3940-7(4))* Enslow Pubs., Inc.
Carson-Dellosa Publishing Staff. Fractions. 2006. (ENG., Illus.). 54p. (gr. 3-5). 2.99 *(978-0-7696-7733-0(9),* Brighter Child) Carson-Dellosa Publishing, LLC.
Cefrey, Holly. Let's Take a Hike! Converting Fractions to Decimals. 2009. (PowerMath Ser.). (ENG., Illus.). 24p. (J). (gr. 3-4). pap. 8.25 *(978-0-8239-8928-7(3),* PowerKids Pr.) Rosen Publishing Group, Inc., The.
Cleary, Brian P. A Fraction's Goal: Parts of a Whole. Gable, Brian, illus. 2011. (Math Is CATegorical (r) Ser.). (ENG.). 32p. (J). (gr. k-3). lib. bdg. 16.95 *(978-0-8225-7881-9(6),* Millbrook Pr.) Lerner Publishing Group.
—A Fraction's Goal - Parts of a Whole. Gable, Brian, illus. 2013. (Math Is CATegorical (r) Ser.). (ENG.). 32p. (gr. k-3). pap. 6.95 *(978-1-4677-1380-1(5),* Millbrook Pr.) Lerner Publishing Group.
Clement, Christine. My Family Reunion: Learning to Recognize Fractions as Part of a Group. 2009. (Math for the REAL World Ser.). 16p. (gr. 2-3). pap. 7.05 *(978-0-8239-8923-2(2),* Rosen Classroom) Rosen Publishing Group, Inc., The.
Cocca, Lisa Colozza. Pie Graphs. 2013. (J). *(978-1-61080-990-0(4));* (ENG.). 24p. (gr. 1-4). 28.50 *(978-1-61080-915-3(7),* 202639); (ENG.). 24p. (gr. 1-4). pap. 12.79 *(978-1-61080-940-5(8),* 202641) Cherry Lake Publishing.
Collins Easy Learning, Collins Easy. Fractions & Decimals Bumper Book Ages 7-9. 2017. (Collins Easy Learning KS2 Ser.). (ENG.). 64p. (J). (gr. 2-4). pap. 9.99 ***(978-0-00-821243-8(0))*** HarperCollins Pubs. Ltd. GBR. Dist: Independent Pubs. Group.
Collins Easy Learning Staff & Blackwood, Mel. Fractions & Decimals, Ages 7-9. 2015. (Collins Easy Learning Ser.). (ENG.). 32p. (J). (gr. 2-4). pap. 6.95 *(978-0-00-813445-7(6))* HarperCollins Pubs. Ltd. GBR. Dist: Independent Pubs. Group.
Collins, Kathleen. Music Math: Exploring Different Interpretations of Fractions. (Powermath Ser.). 32p. 2009. (ENG., Illus.). (J). (gr. 4-5). pap. 10.00 *(978-0-8239-8877-8(5))* 2009. (gr. 4-5). 47.90 *(978-1-60851-398-7(X))* 2004. (Illus.). (J). lib. bdg. 25.25 *(978-0-8239-8984-3(4))* Rosen Publishing Group, Inc., The. (PowerKids Pr.).
Colson, Rob. Fraction Frenzy: Fractions & Decimals. 2017. (Math Everywhere Ser.). (ENG.). 32p. (J). pap. 8.95 ***(978-0-531-23317-7(0))***; lib. bdg. 27.00 ***(978-0-531-22881-4(9))*** Scholastic Library Publishing. (Children's Pr.).
Cominskey, Michael J. The Number System & Common & Decimal Fractions, 1 vol. 2015. (ENG.). 64p. (J). 31.70 *(978-1-62275-524-0(3),* Britannica Educational Publishing) Rosen Publishing Group, Inc., The.
Dobson, Christina. The Pizza Counting. Holmes, Matthew, illus. 2003. (ENG.). 32p. (J). (gr. 1-4). pap. 7.95 *(978-0-88106-339-4(8))* Charlesbridge Publishing, Inc.
Dodds, Dayle Ann. Full House: An Invitation to Fractions. Carter, Abby, illus. 2012. (ENG.). 32p. (J). (gr. 1-4). pap. 24.99 *(978-0-7636-6090-1(6))* Candlewick Pr.
Dorling Kindersley Publishing Staff. 10 Minutes a Day: Fractions, Fourth Grade: Fractions, Fourth Grade. 2014. (ENG.). 80p. (J). (gr. 3-7). pap. 9.99 *(978-1-4654-2824-0(0),* DK Children) Dorling Kindersley Publishing, Inc.
Dowdy, Penny. Fractions. 2008. (My Path to Math Ser.). (ENG., Illus.). 24p. (J). (gr. k-3). pap. *(978-0-7787-4356-9(X));* lib. bdg. *(978-0-7787-4338-5(1))* Crabtree Publishing Co.
Einhorn, Edward. Fractions in Disguise: A Math Adventure. Clark, David, illus. 2014. (ENG.). 32p. (J). (gr. 2-5). pap. 7.95 *(978-1-57091-774-5(4));* lib. bdg. 16.95 *(978-1-57091-773-8(6))* Charlesbridge Publishing, Inc.
Encyclopaedia Britannica Publishers, Inc. Staff. Math in Context: Fraction Times. 6th ed. 2005. (Math in Context Ser.). pap. 10.60 *(978-0-03-039619-9(0))* Harcourt Schl. Pubs.
Feldman, Jean R. & Karapetkova, Holly. Fraction Pizza (Tune, He's Got the Whole World in His Hands) 2010. (ENG., Illus.). 12p. (gr. -1-k). 9.95 *(978-1-61590-222-4(8))* Rourke Educational Media.
Fischer, James. Game Math. 2013. (Math 24/7 Ser.: 10). 48p. (J). (gr. 5-18). 19.95 *(978-1-4222-2907-1(6))* Mason Crest.
Flash Kids Editors, ed. Fraction Activities: Grade 3 (Flash Skills) 2010. (Flash Skills Ser.). (ENG.). 64p. (J). pap. 3.95 *(978-1-4114-3467-7(6),* Spark Publishing Group) Sterling Publishing Co., Inc.
Fosnot, Catherine Twomey. Field Trips & Fund-Raisers: Introducing Fractions. 2008. (ENG.). 64p. (gr. 4-5). pap. 31.25 *(978-0-325-01023-6(4),* E01023, Firsthand) Heinemann.
Fract Burger Foam New in Center. 2004. (J). *(978-1-59242-142-8(3))* Delta Education, LLC.
Fraction Basics (Gr. 2-3) 2003. (J). *(978-1-58232-089-2(6))* ECS Learning Systems, Inc.
Fraction Basics Spanish Version. 2007. (J). per. *(978-1-58232-158-5(2))* ECS Learning Systems, Inc.
Fraction Burger Magnetic. 2004. (J). *(978-1-59242-145-9(8))* Delta Education, LLC.
Fractions Cards Staff. LP-Fractions: Level 2 Math. 2004. (ENG.). (J). 9.99 *(978-1-59204-020-9(9))* Learning Wrap-Ups, Inc.
Fractions with Fish. 2013. (Animal Math Ser.). 24p. (J). (gr. 1-3). pap. 48.90 *(978-1-4339-9310-7(4))* Stevens, Gareth Publishing LLLP.
Frenetti, Jackson. Flags of the World: Develop Understanding of Fractions & Numbers, 1 vol. 2015. (InfoMax Common Core Math Readers Ser.). (ENG.). 24p. (J). pap. 8.25 *(978-1-4777-4615-8(3),* Rosen Classroom) Rosen Publishing Group, Inc., The.
Furgang, Kathy. Pizza Parts. 2011. (Early Connections Ser.). (J). *(978-1-61672-669-0(5))* Benchmark Education Co.
George, Gale. We're in the Band: Develop Understanding of Fractions & Numbers. 2014. (Rosen Common Core Math Readers Ser.). (ENG., Illus.). 24p. (J). (gr. 3-4). pap. 8.25 *(978-1-4777-4927-2(6),* Rosen Classroom) Rosen Publishing Group, Inc., The.
George, Lynn. Civil War Recipes: Adding & Subtracting Simple Fractions. (PowerMath Ser.). (ENG., 24p. (gr. 3-4). 2009. Illus.). (J). pap. 8.25 *(978-0-8239-8896-9(1),* PowerKids Pr.) 2004. 43.95 *(978-0-8239-7643-0(2))* Rosen Publishing Group, Inc., The.
Gifford, Scott. Piece = Part = Portion. Thaler, Shmuel, photos by. 2008. (SPA & ENG., Illus.). 32p. (J). (gr. 1-4). pap. 7.99 *(978-1-58246-261-5(5),* Tricycle Pr.) Random Hse. Children's Bks.
Gorstko, Aleksandr. Daddy! Mom! at Last I Know Fractions! 2011. 124p. pap. *(978-1-84903-016-8(2))* Schiel & Denver Publishing Ltd.
Harcourt School Publishers Staff. Math Program Development, Grades 3-6: Fraction Concepts Binder Package. 3rd ed. 2003. ring bd. 360.00 *(978-0-15-340578-5(3))* Harcourt Schl. Pubs.
Hunt, Darleen L. Baby's Fraction Lunch. Komarck, Michael, illus. 2003. (Sherman's Math Corner Ser.). (J). (gr. -1-3). *(978-1-929591-07-7(1))* Reading Rock, Inc.
Jones, Kadeem. Healthy Fractions: Develop Understanding of Fractions & Numbers. 2014. (Rosen Common Core Math Readers Ser.). (ENG., Illus.). 24p. (J). (gr. 3-4). pap. 8.25 *(978-1-4777-4920-3(9),* Rosen Classroom) Rosen Publishing Group, Inc., The.
Kiernan, Denise. Fractions & Decimals: Familiar & Flexible Games with Dozens of Variations That Help Struggling Learners Practice & Really Master Basic Fraction & Decimal Facts. 2007. (Math Games to Master Basic Skills Ser.). (ENG., Illus.). 48p. pap. 10.99 *(978-0-439-51772-0(9),* Teaching Resources) Scholastic, Inc.
Kompelien, Tracy. I Know Fractions by Their Actions!, 1 vol. 2007. (Math Made Fun Ser.). (ENG., Illus.). 24p. (J). (gr. k-3). lib. bdg. 24.21 *(978-1-59928-529-0(0),* SandCastle) ABDO Publishing Co.
Krech, Bob & Novelli, Joan. Fractions & Decimals: Engaging Story Problems for Students to Read, Fill-In, Solve, & Sharpen Their Math Skills. 2009. (50 Fill-in Math Word Problems Ser.). (ENG.). 64p. (gr. 4-6). pap. 11.99 *(978-0-545-07486-5(X),* Teaching Resources) Scholastic, Inc.
Kumon Publishing, ed. Focus on Reducing & Calculating Fractions. 2012. (Illus.). 64p. (J). pap. 5.95 *(978-4-7743-0022-1(5))* Kumon Publishing North America, Inc.
Levy, Janey. Recipes for a Medieval Feast: Medieval Feast: Working Flexibly with Fractions. 2009. (PowerMath: Advanced Proficiency Plus Ser.). 32p. (gr. 5-5). 47.90 *(978-1-60851-364-2(5),* PowerKids Pr.) Rosen Publishing Group, Inc., The.
—Recipes for a Medieval Feast: Working Flexibly with Fractions. (Math for the Real World Ser.). (Illus.). 32p. 2009. (ENG.). (gr. 6-7). pap. 10.00 *(978-1-4042-6061-0(7))* 2006. (YA). (gr. 5-9). lib. bdg. 25.25 *(978-1-4042-3354-6(7))* Rosen Publishing Group, Inc., The.
Linde, Barbara. Managing Your Money: Understanding Math Operations Involving Decimals & Integers. 2009. (PowerMath: Advanced Proficiency Plus Ser.). 32p. (gr. 5-5). 47.90 *(978-1-60851-361-1(0),* PowerKids Pr.) Rosen Publishing Group, Inc., The.
Linde, Barbara M. Managing Your Money: Understanding Math Operations Involving Decimals & Integers. (Math for the Real World Ser.). (Illus.). 32p. 2009. (ENG.). (gr. 6-7). pap. 10.00 *(978-1-4042-6091-7(9))* 2006. (YA). (gr. 5-9). lib. bdg. 25.25 *(978-1-4042-3369-0(5))* Rosen Publishing Group, Inc., The.
Loughran, Donna. Tending the Tide Pool: The Parts Make a Whole. 2013. (IMath Ser.). (Illus.). 24p. (J). (gr. k-2). pap. 11.94 *(978-1-60357-494-5(8));* lib. bdg. 21.27 *(978-1-59953-555-5(6))* Norwood Hse. Pr.
Loughran, Donna & Brunner-Jass, Renata. The Garden Club: Operations with Fractions. 2013. (IMath Ser.). (Illus.). 48p. (J). (gr. 5-6). pap. 11.94 *(978-1-60357-509-6(X));* lib. bdg. 23.94 *(978-1-59953-570-8(X))* Norwood Hse. Pr.
Meredith, Susan. Half or Whole? 2010. (ENG., Illus.). 24p. (gr. k-2). pap. 8.95 *(978-1-61590-532-4(4))* Rourke Educational Media.
Midthun, Joseph. Fractions. Hiti, Samuel, illus. 2013. (Building Blocks of Mathematics Ser.). 32p. (J). pap. 169.00 *(978-0-7166-1435-7(9))* World Bk., Inc.
Miller, Reagan & Berry, Minta. Comparing Fractions. Crabtree Publishing Staff, ed. 2011. (My Path to Math Ser.: No. 34). (ENG., Illus.). 24p. (J). pap. *(978-0-7787-5264-6(X),* 1325389) Crabtree Publishing Co.
—Comparing Fractions. 2011. (ENG., Illus.). 24p. (J). lib. bdg. *(978-0-7787-5275-2(5),* 1325389) Crabtree Publishing Co.
Moore, Sharon. Food Fractions: Learning How Fractional Parts Equal a Whole. 2009. (Math for the REAL World Ser.). 16p. (gr. 2-3). pap. 7.05 *(978-0-8239-8852-5(X),* Rosen Classroom) Rosen Publishing Group, Inc., The.
Morado, Leah. What's on My Plate? Develop Understanding of Fractions & Numbers, 1 vol. 2015. (InfoMax Common Core Math Readers Ser.). (ENG.). 24p. (J). pap. 8.25 *(978-1-4777-4609-7(9),* Rosen Classroom) Rosen Publishing Group, Inc., The.
Muschla, Erin. Fractions & Decimals. 2012. (Practice Makes Perfect Ser.). (ENG., Illus.). 176p. pap. 18.00 *(978-0-07-177286-0(3),* 0071772863) McGraw-Hill Education.
Nagda, Ann Whitehead & Bickel, Cindy. Polar Bear Math: Learning about Fractions from Klondike & Snow. 2007. (ENG., Illus.). 32p. (J). (gr. -1-3). per. 8.99 *(978-0-312-37749-6(5),* 9780312377496) Square Fish.
Onish, Liane. Solve-the-Riddle Math Practice - Fractions & Decimals: 50+ Reproducible Activity Sheets That Help Students Master Fraction & Decimal Skills. 2012. (ENG.). 64p. (gr. 3-3). pap. 11.99 *(978-0-545-40033-6(3),* Teaching Resources) Scholastic, Inc.
Pallotta, Jerry. Pizza Fractions. Bolster, Rob, illus. 2007. 32p. (J). pap. *(978-0-545-00687-3(2))* Scholastic, Inc.
Perritano, John. Seeing Halves: Symmetry in Our World. 2013. (IMath Ser.). 32p. (J). (gr. 3-4). lib. bdg. 22.60 *(978-1-59953-564-7(5))* Norwood Hse. Pr.
Pistoia, Sara. Fractions. 2013. (Simply Math Ser.). (ENG.). 24p. (J). (gr. -1-2). 27.07 *(978-1-62323-529-1(4),* 206335) Child's World, Inc., The.
—Fractions. 2016. (J). *(978-1-4896-5104-4(7))* Weigl Pubs., Inc.
Quinlivan, Ada. Blake the Baker: Develop Understanding of Fractions & Numbers. 2014. (Rosen Common Core Math Readers Ser.). (ENG.). 24p. (J). (gr. 3-4). pap. 8.25 *(978-1-4777-4930-2(6),* PowerKids Pr.) Rosen Publishing Group, Inc., The.
Rasmussen, Steven & Key Curriculum Press Staff. Fraction Concepts, Bk. 1. 2012. (Key To... workbooks Ser.: Bk. 1). (ENG.). 40p. (gr. 6-8). spiral bd., wbk. ed. 5.64 *(978-0-913684-91-7(0),* 0913684910) McGraw-Hill Education.
—Mixed Numbers, Bk. 4. 2012. (Key To... workbooks Ser.: Bk. 4). (ENG.). 40p. (gr. 6-8). spiral bd., wbk. ed. 5.64 *(978-0-913684-94-8(5),* 0913684945) McGraw-Hill Education.
—Multiplying & Dividing, Bk. 2. 2012. (Key To... workbooks Ser.: Bk. 2). (ENG.). 40p. (gr. 6-8). spiral bd., wbk. ed. 5.64 *(978-0-913684-92-4(9),* 0913684929) McGraw-Hill Education.
Robinson, C. L. MATH1on1 Fractions & Decimals. 2006. (YA). per. 9.99 *(978-0-9786767-1-1(8))* Robinson, Consuelo.
—MATH1on1 Multiply & Divide Fractions. 2006. (YA). per. 9.99 *(978-0-9786767-3-5(4))* Robinson, Consuelo.
Roy, Jennifer Rozines & Roy, Gregory. Holiday Fractions. 2005. (Math All Around Ser.). (Illus.). 32p. (gr. 2-7). lib. bdg. 29.93 *(978-0-7614-2001-9(0),* Benchmark Bks.) Marshall Cavendish Corp.
Roza, Greg. Olympic Math: Working with Percentages & Decimals. 2009. (PowerMath: Advanced Proficiency Plus Ser.). 32p. (gr. 5-5). 47.90 *(978-1-60851-363-5(7),* PowerKids Pr.) Rosen Publishing Group, Inc., The.
—Olympic Math: Working with Percents & Decimals. (Math for the Real World Ser.). (Illus.). 32p. 2009. (ENG.). (gr. 6-7). pap. 10.00 *(978-1-4042-6057-3(9))* 2006. (J). lib. bdg. 23.95 *(978-1-4042-3352-2(0))* Rosen Publishing Group, Inc., The.
Scholastic, Inc. Staff, contrib. by. Fractions. 2010. (Scholastic Success with Ser.). (ENG.). 48p. (gr. 4-4). pap. 5.99 *(978-0-545-20088-2(1),* Teaching Resources) Scholastic, Inc.
—Fractions & Decimals. 2010. (Scholastic Success with Ser.). (ENG.). 48p. (gr. 5-5). pap. 5.99 *(978-0-545-20089-9(X),* Teaching Resources) Scholastic, Inc.
School Zone Interactive Staff. Time, Money & Fractions. rev. ed. 2004. (ENG.). 64p. (J). (gr. k-2). 15.99 *(978-1-58947-832-9(0))* School Zone Publishing Co.
School Zone Staff, ed. Time, Money & Fractions. 2003. (ENG.). (J). (gr. 1-2). cd-rom 19.99 *(978-1-58947-930-2(0))* School Zone Publishing Co.
Shaskan, Trisha Speed. If You Were a Fraction, 1 vol. Carabelli, Francesca, illus. 2008. (Math Fun Ser.). (ENG.). 24p. (gr. 2-4). pap. 7.95 *(978-1-4048-4791-0(X))* Picture Window Bks.
Sisk, Maeve T. Fractions with Fish. 2013. (Animal Math Ser.). 24p. (J). (gr. 1-3). 22.60 *(978-1-4339-9308-4(2));* pap. 8.15 *(978-1-4339-9309-1(0))* Stevens, Gareth Publishing LLLP.
Smart, Margaret & Tuel, Patricia. Focus on Fractions, 3 bks., Set. Incl. Bk. 1. 1986. 7.95 *(978-0-918932-14-3(9),* A-1394); Bk. 2. 1989. 7.95 *(978-0-918932-15-0(7),* A-1395); Bk. 3. 1987. 7.95 *(978-0-918932-16-7(5),* A-1396); (Illus.). 48p. (J). (gr. 5-9). Set pap. 23.85 *(978-0-918932-69-3(6))* Activity Resources Co., Inc.
Solodar, Marisol. Bailey's Band: Develop Understanding of Fractions & Numbers, 1 vol. 2015. (InfoMax Common Core Math Readers Ser.). (ENG.). 24p. (J). pap. 8.25 *(978-1-4777-4618-9(8),* Rosen Classroom) Rosen Publishing Group, Inc., The.
Stckvagn. AC Ems Fractions. 2004. pap. *(978-0-7398-9856-7(6))* Harcourt Schl. Pubs.
Steck-Vaughn Staff. At-Home Workbooks: Fractions. 2004. (Illus.). pap., wbk. ed. *(978-0-7398-8530-7(8))* Steck-Vaughn.
—Early Math: Fractions I, 10 Pack. 2005. pap. 29.95 *(978-1-4190-0354-7(2))* Steck-Vaughn.
—Early Math: Fractions II, 10 Pack. 2005. pap. 29.95 *(978-1-4190-0364-6(X))* Steck-Vaughn.
—Focus on Math Level C 10-pack: Fractions. 2005. pap. 29.95 *(978-1-4190-0291-5(0))* Harcourt Schl. Pubs.
—Focus on Math Level D: Fractions. 2005. pap. 2.99 *(978-1-4190-0273-1(2));* pap. 2.99 *(978-1-4190-0267-0(8))* Harcourt Schl. Pubs.
—Focus on Math Level D 10-pack: Fractions. 2005. pap. 29.95 *(978-1-4190-0297-7(X))* Harcourt Schl. Pubs.
—Focus on Math Level E: Fractions. 2005. pap. 2.99 *(978-1-4190-0280-9(5))* Harcourt Schl. Pubs.
—Focus on Math Level E 10-pack: Fractions. 2005. pap. 29.95 *(978-1-4190-0304-2(6))* Harcourt Schl. Pubs.
—Focus on Math Level F: Fractions. 2005. pap. 2.99 *(978-1-4190-0285-4(6))* Harcourt Schl. Pubs.
—Focus on Math Level F 10-pack: Fractions. 2005. pap. 29.95 *(978-1-4190-0309-7(7))* Harcourt Schl. Pubs.
—Math Remediation 10-Pack: Fractions. 2005. pap. 54.95 *(978-1-4190-0389-9(5))* Harcourt Schl. Pubs.
—Top Line Math: Fractions. 2005. pap. 5.49 *(978-1-4190-0368-4(2))* Harcourt Schl. Pubs.
Sterling, Kristin. Fractions. 2008. pap. 22.95 *(978-0-8225-9360-7(2));* (ENG.). 8p. (gr. -1-1). pap. 4.95 *(978-0-8225-8847-4(1))* Lerner Publishing Group.
Stern, Margaret, creator. The Fraction Set. 2010. (J). 50.00 *(978-0-9845392-6-0(3))* Stern Math, LLC.
Townsend, Donna. Apple Fractions. 2005. (Rookie Read-About Math Ser.). (ENG., Illus.). 32p. (J). (gr. 1-2). pap. 5.95 *(978-0-516-24670-3(4),* Children's Pr.) Scholastic Library Publishing.
Vaughan, Susan. Making Muffins: Learning the Fractions 1/2, 1/3 & 1/4. 2009. (Math for the REAL World Ser.). 12p. (gr. 1-2). pap. 5.90 *(978-0-8239-8891-4(0),* Rosen Classroom) Rosen Publishing Group, Inc., The.

Wingard-Nelson, Rebecca. Decimals & Fractions. 2008. (Math Busters Ser.). (Illus.). 64p. (J). (gr. 4-7). lib. bdg. 29.27 *(978-0-7660-2877-7(1))* Enslow Pubs., Inc.

—Decimals & Fractions: It's Easy. 2014. (Easy Genius Math Ser.). 64p. (J). pap. 8.95 *(978-1-4644-0447-4(X))*; (gr. 4-18). 29.27 *(978-0-7660-4252-0(9))* Enslow Pubs., Inc.

—Fraction & Decimal Word Problems: No Problem! 2010. (Math Busters Word Problems Ser.). (Illus.). 64p. (J). 29.27 *(978-0-7660-3371-9(6))* Enslow Pubs., Inc.

—Fractions & Decimals. 2012. (Ace Your Math Test Ser.). (Illus.). 104p. (J). (gr. 5-18). 33.27 *(978-0-7660-3780-9(0))* Enslow Pubs., Inc.

—Fractions & Decimals: Ace Your Math Test. 2012. (Ace Your Math Test Ser.). (Illus.). 104p. (J). (gr. 5-18). pap. 10.95 *(978-1-4644-0007-0(5))* Enslow Pubs., Inc.

—Fun Food Word Problems Starring Fractions: Math Word Problems Solved. 2009. (Math Word Problems Solved Ser.). (Illus.). 48p. (J). (gr. 2-5). lib. bdg. 25.27 *(978-0-7660-2919-4(0))* Enslow Pubs., Inc.

—Percents & Ratios: Ace Your Math Test. 2012. (Ace Your Math Test Ser.). (Illus.). 104p. (J). (gr. 5-18). pap. 10.95 *(978-1-4644-0008-7(3))* Enslow Pubs., Inc.

—Ready for Fractions & Decimals. LaBaff, Tom, illus. 2014. (Ready for Math Ser.). 48p. (J). pap. 8.95 *(978-1-4644-0437-5(2)*, Enslow Elementary); (gr. 3-18). 25.27 *(978-0-7660-4247-6(2))* Enslow Pubs., Inc.

—Sports Word Problems Starring Decimals & Percents. 2009. (Math Word Problems Solved Ser.). (Illus.). 48p. (J). (gr. 2-5). lib. bdg. 25.27 *(978-0-7660-2920-0(4))* Enslow Pubs., Inc.

Wingard-Nelson, Rebecca & Williams, Zella. Word Problems Using Decimals & Percentages. 2016. (Mastering Math Word Problems Ser.). 48p. (J). pap. 11.70 *(978-0-7660-8256-4(3))* Enslow Pubs., Inc.

—Word Problems Using Fractions. 2016. (Mastering Math Word Problems Ser.). 48p. (J). pap. 11.70 *(978-0-7660-8260-1(1))* Enslow Pubs., Inc.

World Book, Inc Staff, contrib. by. Fractions. 2012. (J). *(978-0-7166-1434-0(0))*; pap. *(978-0-7166-1475-3(8))* World Bk., Inc.

Zuravicky, Orli. The Stock Market: Understanding & Applying Ratios, Decimals, Fractions, & Percentages. (PowerMath Ser.). 32p. 2009. (ENG., Illus.). (gr. 5-6). pap. 10.00 *(978-1-4042-5121-2(9))* 2009. (gr. 4-5). 47.90 *(978-1-60851-426-7(9)*, PowerKids Pr.) 2005. (Illus.). (J). (gr. 3-6). lib. bdg. 25.25 *(978-1-4042-2929-7(9)*, PowerKids Pr.) Rosen Publishing Group, Inc., The.

FRACTURES

Ballard, Carol. What Happens to Broken Bones? Bones, 1 vol. 2011. (Inside My Body Ser.). (ENG.). 32p. (gr. 3-5). 30.65 *(978-1-4109-4011-7(X))*; pap. 8.95 *(978-1-4109-4022-3(5))* Heinemann-Raintree. (NA-r).

Earhart, Kristin. The Magic School Bus Fixes a Bone. Bracken, Carolyn, illus. 2010. 32p. (J). pap. *(978-0-545-23950-9(8)*, Cartwheel Bks.) Scholastic, Inc.

Landau, Elaine. Broken Bones. 2008. (Head-to-Toe Health Ser.). 32p. (gr. 2-7). lib. bdg. 28.50 *(978-0-7614-2847-3(X)*, Benchmark Bks.) Marshall Cavendish Corp.

FRACTURES—FICTION

Barkley, Callie. Marion Takes a Break. Riti, Marsha, illus. 2013. (Critter Club Ser.: 4). (ENG.). 128p. (J). (gr. k-2). 16.99 *(978-1-4424-6773-6(8))*; pap. 5.99 *(978-1-4424-6772-9(X))* Little Simon. (Little Simon).

—Marion Takes a Break. 2013. (Critter Club Ser.: 4). lib. bdg. 16.00 *(978-0-606-32045-0(8)*, Turtleback) Turtleback Bks.

Hillert, Margaret. Dear Dragon Goes to the Hospital. Schimmell, David, illus. rev. ed. 2014. (BeginningtoRead Ser.). (ENG.). 32p. (J). (gr. k-2). lib. bdg. 22.60 *(978-1-59953-581-4(5))* Norwood Hse. Pr.

Sheinmel, Courtney. Broken Birthday. Bell, Jennifer A., illus. 2017. (Stella Batts Ser.). (ENG.). 160p. (J). (gr. 2-3). 9.99 *(978-1-58536-921-8(7)*, 204228) Sleeping Bear Pr.

Weston Woods Staff, creator. Ready, Freddy! #3: Homework Hassles. 2011. 20.95 *(978-0-545-05007-4(3))* Weston Woods Studios, Inc.

FRAMING OF PICTURES

see Picture Frames and Framing

FRANCE

Alcraft, Rob & Herweck, Diana. A Visit to France. 2016. (TIME for Kids en Español - Level 5 Ser.). (SPA., Illus.). 64p. (gr. 5-5). lib. bdg. 31.99 *(978-1-5157-2951-8(6))* Time for Kids Inc AUS. Dist: Capstone Pub.

Bankston, John. The Evolution of Government & Politics in France. 2014. 48p. (gr. 4-8). 29.95 *(978-1-61228-583-2(X))* Mitchell Lane Pubs., Inc.

Boutan, Mila. Renoir & Me. 2010. (ENG., Illus.). 48p. (J). (gr. 3-7). pap. 17.95 *(978-1-4081-2384-3(3)*, 9781408123843, A&C Black) Bloomsbury Publishing Plc GBR. Dist: Macmillan.

Bryant, Jen. Six Dots: A Story of Young Louis Braille. Kulikov, Boris, illus. 2016. (ENG.). 40p. (J). (gr. -1-3). 17.99 *(978-0-449-81337-9(1)*, Knopf Bks. for Young Readers) Random Hse. Children's Bks.

Burnham, Brad. Cave of Lascaux: The Cave of Prehistoric Wall Paintings. (Famous Caves of the World Ser.). 24p. 2009. (gr. 3-4). 42.50 *(978-1-61512-495-4(0))* 2003. (Illus.). (J). (gr. k-4). lib. bdg. 22.60 *(978-0-8239-6257-0(1))* Rosen Publishing Group, Inc., The. (PowerKids Pr.).

Byers, Helen. Colors of France. Byers, Helen, illus. 2005. (Colors of the World Ser.). (Illus.). 24p. (gr. 3-6). 5.95 *(978-1-57505-565-7(1))* Lerner Publishing Group.

Candlewick Press, Candlewick. France. Krauss, Trisha, illus. 2015. (Panorama Pops Ser.). (ENG.). 30p. (J). (gr. k-4). 8.99 *(978-0-7636-7836-4(8))* Candlewick Pr.

Cook, Diane. Paul Gauguin: 18th Century French Painter. 2013. (People of Importance Ser.: 21). (Illus.). 32p. (J). (gr. 4-18). 19.95 *(978-1-4222-2854-8(1))* Mason Crest.

Crean, Susan. Discover France. 2012. (Discover Countries Ser.). (Illus.). 32p. (YA). (gr. 4-7). lib. bdg. 26.50 *(978-1-4488-5267-3(6))* Rosen Publishing Group, Inc., The.

Discovering Major Cities of France. 2007. (YA). 13.95 *(978-1-931463-22-5(0))* Aaron Levy Pubns., LLC.

Donaldson-Forbes, Jeff. Jacques Cartier. 2009. (Primary Source Library of Famous Explorers Ser.). 24p. (gr. 4-4). 42.50 *(978-1-60854-126-3(6)*, PowerKids Pr.) Rosen Publishing Group, Inc., The.

—Jacques Marquette & Louis Jolliet. 2009. (Primary Source Library of Famous Explorers Ser.). 24p. (gr. 4-4). 42.50 *(978-1-60854-127-0(4)*, PowerKids Pr.) Rosen Publishing Group, Inc., The.

Donaldson, Madeline. Louis Braille. 2008. pap. 52.95 *(978-0-8225-9393-5(9))* Lerner Publishing Group.

Edison, Erin. Marie Curie, 1 vol. 2014. (Great Women in History Ser.). (ENG.). 24p. (gr. k-1). lib. bdg. 21.99 *(978-1-4765-4216-4(3)*, Pebble Bks.) Capstone Press of Coughlan Cos.

Feinstein, Stephen. Louis Pasteur: The Father of Microbiology. 2008. (Inventors Who Changed the World Ser.). (Illus.). 128p. (J). (gr. 6-18). lib. bdg. 34.60 *(978-1-59845-078-1(6)*, MyReportLinks.com Bks.) Enslow Pubs., Inc.

Fiscus, James. The Suez Crisis. 2009. (War & Conflict in the Middle East Ser.). 64p. (gr. 5-5). 58.50 *(978-1-60854-741-8(8))* Rosen Publishing Group, Inc., The.

Fiscus, James W. The Suez Crisis. 2004. (War & Conflict in the Middle East Ser.). (Illus.). 64p. (gr. 7-12). lib. bdg. 31.95 *(978-0-8239-4550-4(2))* Rosen Publishing Group, Inc., The.

Glavich, Mary Kathleen. Saint Therese of Lisieux: The Way of Love. Esquinaldo, Virginia, tr. Esquinaldo, Virginia, illus. 2003. (Encounter the Saints Ser.). 132p. (J). pap. 5.95 *(978-0-8198-7074-2(9)*, 332-370) Pauline Bks. & Media.

Gofen, Ethel. France. 2013. (Cultures of the World 4 Ser.). 144p. (J). (gr. 6-9). pap. 23.51 *(978-1-62712-158-3(7))* Cavendish Square Publishing.

Gordon, Susan. Montesquieu: The French Philosopher Who Shaped Modern Government. 2009. (Philosophers of the Enlightenment Ser.). 112p. (gr. 5-8). 66.50 *(978-1-60851-166-2(9)*, Rosen Reference) Rosen Publishing Group, Inc., The.

Hardyman, Robyn. Celebrate: France. 2009. (Celebrate Country Ser.). 32p. (gr. 4-6). 28.00 *(978-1-60413-263-2(9)*, Chelsea Clubhouse) Facts On File, Inc.

Henderson, Harry. The Curie Family. 2012. (Trailblazers in Science & Technology Ser.). 136p. (gr. 6-12). 35.00 *(978-1-60413-675-3(8)*, Chelsea Hse.) Facts On File, Inc.

Hesse, Joseph M. Les Régions de France. 2nd ed. 2004. (Geography Capsules Ser.). (FRE.). 144p. (YA). (gr. 7-12). 88.00 *(978-1-885888-32-7(5))* Global Awareness Publishing Co.

Jett, Stephen C. & Roberts, Lisa. France. 2003. (Modern World Nations Ser.). (Illus.). 150p. (gr. 6-12). 35.00 *(978-0-7910-7607-1(5)*, Chelsea Hse.) Facts On File, Inc.

Klepeis, Alicia. France. 2016. (Exploring World Cultures Ser.). 32p. (J). pap. 10.58 *(978-1-5026-2142-9(8))* Cavendish Square Publishing.

Larkin, Tanya. Jacques Marquette & Louis Jolliet: Explorers of the Mississippi. 2009. (Library of Explorers & Exploration Ser.). 112p. (gr. 5-8). 66.50 *(978-1-60853-608-5(4)*, Rosen Reference) Rosen Publishing Group, Inc., The.

Marsh, Carole. France: The Ooh-lala Country Everyone Loves! 2009. (It's Your World Ser.). 48p. (J). (gr. 2-9). pap. 7.99 *(978-0-635-06810-1(9))* Gallopade International.

McCully, Emily Arnold. The Secret Cave: Discovering Lascaux. McCully, Emily Arnold, illus. 2010. (ENG., Illus.). 40p. (J). (gr. 1-4). 18.99 *(978-0-374-36694-0(2)*, 9780374366940, Farrar, Straus & Giroux (BYR)) Farrar, Straus & Giroux.

Medina, Nico & Tomie, dePaola. Who Was Jacques Cousteau? Putra, Dede & Harrison, Nancy, illus. 2015. (Who Was? Ser.). (ENG.). 112p. (J). (gr. 3-7). 5.99 *(978-0-448-48234-7(7)*, Grosset & Dunlap) Penguin Young Readers Group.

Pickwell, Linda. France. 2004. (QEB Travel Through Ser.). (Illus.). 32p. (J). lib. bdg. 18.95 *(978-1-59566-062-6(3))* QEB Publishing Inc.

Popper, Garry. Paul in France. Johnson, Andi, illus. 2004. 36p. (gr. -1-7). 4.00 *(978-1-84161-056-6(9))* Ravette Publishing, Ltd. GBR. Dist: Parkwest Pubns., Inc.

Poussin, Nichol. Still Spins the Spider of Rennes-le-Chateau. I.t. ed. 2004.Tr. of L' arraignee tisse sa toile a Rennes-le-Chateaua. (Illus.). 347p. pap. *(978-0-9541527-1-0(9)*, http//www.keysofantiquity.com) DEK Publishing.

Powell, Jillian. Descubramos Francia. 2007. (Descubramos paises del mundo (Looking at Countries) Ser.). (ENG & SPA.). 32p. (gr. 1-5). pap. 10.50 *(978-0-8368-7960-5(0))*; (Illus.). lib. bdg. 26.00 *(978-0-8368-7953-7(8))* Stevens, Gareth Publishing LLLP. (Gareth Stevens Learning Library).

—Looking at France. 2007. (Looking at Countries Ser.). (Illus.). 32p. (gr. 1-5). pap. 10.50 *(978-0-8368-7675-8(X))*; lib. bdg. 26.00 *(978-0-8368-7668-0(7))* Stevens, Gareth Publishing LLLP. (Gareth Stevens Learning Library).

Raabe, Emily. A Primary Source Guide to France. 2009. (Countries of the World). 24p. (gr. 2-3). 42.50 *(978-1-61512-031-4(9)*, PowerKids Pr.) Rosen Publishing Group, Inc., The.

—A Prmiary Source Guide to France. 2005. (Countries of the World). (Illus.). 24p. (J). (gr. k-5). lib. bdg. 22.60 *(978-1-4042-2752-1(0)*, PowerKids Pr.) Rosen Publishing Group, Inc., The.

Savery, Annabel. France. 2011. (ENG., Illus.). 32p. (J). pap. 10.95 *(978-1-77092-023-1(4))* Saunders Bk. Co. CAN. Dist: RiverStream Publishing.

Smith, Linda Wasmer. Louis Pasteur: Genius Disease Fighter. 2015. (Genius Scientists & Their Genius Ideas Ser.). 96p. (J). (gr. 5-12). pap. 10.95 *(978-0-7660-6576-5(6))* Enslow Pubs., Inc.

Sommers, Michael A. France: A Primary Source Cultural Guide. (Primary Sources of World Cultures Ser.). 128p. 2009. (gr. 4-5). 79.90 *(978-1-60851-920-0(1))* 2005. (Illus.). (J). (gr. 5-8). lib. bdg. 37.25 *(978-1-4042-2909-9(4))* Rosen Publishing Group, Inc., The.

Spengler, Kremena T. France: A Question & Answer Book, 1 vol. 2004. (Questions & Answers: Countries Ser.). (ENG.). 32p. (gr. 3-4). 26.65 *(978-0-7368-2689-1(0)*, Fact Finders) Capstone Press of Coughlan Cos.

Streissguth, Tom. France. 2009. pap. 52.95 *(978-0-7613-4727-9(5))* Lerner Publishing Group.

Tecco, Betsy Dru. How to Draw France's Sights & Symbols. 2009. (Kid's Guide to Drawing the Countries of the World Ser.). 48p. (gr. 4-4). 53.00 *(978-1-61511-110-7(7)*, PowerKids Pr.) Rosen Publishing Group, Inc., The.

Throp, Claire. Marie Curie. 2015. (Against the Odds Biographies Ser.). (ENG., Illus.). 48p. (gr. 3-6). 33.32 *(978-1-4846-2467-8(X))* Heinemann-Raintree.

Tidmarsh, Celia. Focus on France. 2006. (World in Focus Ser.). (Illus.). 64p. (gr. 5-12). pap. 14.05 *(978-0-8368-6236-2(8))*; lib. bdg. 34.00 *(978-0-8368-6217-1(1))* Stevens, Gareth Publishing LLLP. (Gareth Stevens Secondary Library).

Tieck, Sarah. France, 1 vol. 2013. (Explore the Countries Ser.). (ENG.). 40p. (J). (gr. 2-5). lib. bdg. 29.93 *(978-1-61783-810-1(1)*, Big Buddy Bks.) ABDO Publishing Co.

Walker, Ida. France, 1 vol. 2011. (Countries of the World Set 1 Ser.). (ENG., Illus.). 144p. (J). (gr. 6-12). lib. bdg. 37.07 *(978-1-61783-109-6(3))* ABDO Publishing Co.

Yaccarino, Dan. The Fantastic Undersea Life of Jacques Cousteau. 2012. (ENG.). 40p. (J). (gr. 1-4). pap. 7.99 *(978-0-375-84470-6(8)*, Dragonfly Bks.) Random Hse. Children's Bks.

Yount, Lisa. Antoine Lavoisier: Genius of Modern Chemistry. 2015. (Genius Scientists & Their Genius Ideas Ser.). 96p. (J). (gr. 5-12). pap. 10.95 *(978-0-7660-6521-5(9))* Enslow Pubs., Inc.

FRANCE—ARMEE

Gilbert, Adrian D. Voices of the Foreign Legion: The History of the World's Most Famous Fighting Corps. 2010. (ENG.). 288p. 24.95 *(978-1-61608-032-7(9)*, 608032) Skyhorse Publishing Co., Inc.

FRANCE—FICTION

Adler, Irene. The Cathedral of Fear. McGuinness, Nanette, tr. from ITA. Bruno, Iacopo, illus. 2015. (Sherlock, Lupin, & Me Ser.). (ENG.). 256p. (gr. 4-8). lib. bdg. 26.65 *(978-1-4965-0490-6(9))* Stone Arch Bks.

—The Dark Lady, 1 vol. Bruno, Iacopo, illus. 2014. (Sherlock, Lupin, & Me Ser.). (ENG.). 240p. (gr. 4-8). 12.95 *(978-1-62370-040-9(X))* Capstone Young Readers of Coughlan Cos.

Alender, Katie. Marie Antoinette, Serial Killer. (ENG.). 304p. (J). (gr. 7). 2014. pap. 9.99 *(978-0-545-46810-7(8)*, Scholastic Paperbacks) 2013. 18.99 *(978-0-545-46809-1(4))* Scholastic, Inc.

Alter, Anna. Sprout Street Neighbors: Bon Voyage. 2017. (Sprout Street Neighbors Ser.: 3). (ENG., Illus.). 96p. (J). (gr. 1-4). pap. 6.99 ***(978-1-5247-0053-9(3)***, Yearling) Random Hse. Children's Bks.

Angeletti, Roberta. The Cave Painter of Lascaux. 2004. (Illus.). 32p. (J). 16.95 *(978-1-56290-323-7(3))* Crystal Productions.

Anholt, Laurence. The Magical Garden of Claude Monet. 2003. (ENG., Illus.). 32p. (J). 16.99 *(978-0-7641-5574-1(1))* Barron's Educational Series, Inc.

—Matisse: the King of Color. 2007. (Anholt's Artists Books for Children Ser.). (ENG., Illus.). 32p. (J). (gr. 1-3). 16.99 *(978-0-7641-6047-9(8))* Barron's Educational Series, Inc.

—Van Gogh & the Sunflowers. 2007. (Anholt's Artists Books for Children Ser.). (ENG., Illus.). 32p. (J). (gr. -1-3). *(978-0-7641-3854-6(5))* Barron's Educational Series, Inc.

Avalon-Pai, Phyllis. Children's Stories from Around the World. Arrott, Nancy, illus. 2008. 70p. pap. 9.95 *(978-0-9788283-8-7(0))* Acacia Publishing, Inc.

Baccellia, Kim. Goddesses Can Wait. 2015. (YA). *(978-1-61271-297-0(5))* Zumaya Pubns. LLC.

Banks, Kate. The Cat Who Walked Across France. Hallensleben, Georg, illus. 2004. (ENG.). 40p. (J). (gr. -1-2). 18.99 *(978-0-374-39968-9(9)*, 9780374399689, Farrar, Straus & Giroux (BYR)) Farrar, Straus & Giroux.

Bea's Own Good: Evaluation Guide. 2006. (J). *(978-1-55942-401-1(X))* Witcher Productions.

Beka. Why Are We Here Again? Poupard et al, illus. 2007. (Rugger Boys Ser.: 1). (ENG.). 48p. (J). (gr. 4-7). per. 9.99 *(978-1-905460-33-5(3))* CineBook GBR. Dist: National Bk. Network.

Bell, Anthea, tr. from FRE. Nicholas in Trouble. Sempé, Jean-Jacques, illus. 2008. (ENG.). 128p. (gr. 1-4). 19.95 *(978-0-7148-4813-6(1))* Phaidon Pr., Inc.

Bemelmans, Ludwig. Madeline: Edicion en Espanol. Anasal, Arshes, ed. 2005. (SPA., Illus.). 44p. (J). (gr. k-4). reprint ed. 16.00 *(978-0-7567-8842-1(0))* DIANE Publishing Co.

—Madeline 75th Anniversary Edition. 2014. (Madeline Ser.). (ENG.). 56p. (J). (gr. -1-2). 25.00 *(978-0-670-78540-7(7)*, Viking Books for Young Readers) Penguin Young Readers Group.

—Madeline's Rescue. 2004. (J). (gr. -1-2). spiral bd. *(978-0-616-11864-1(3))* Canadian National Institute for the Blind/Institut National Canadien pour les Aveugles.

Benni, Stefano & Curtis, Howard. The Story of Cyrano de Bergerac. Tranco, Miguel, illus. 2017. (Save the Story Ser.). (ENG.). 104p. (J). (gr. 3-7). 19.95 *(978-1-78269-021-4(2)*, Pushkin Children's Bks.) Steerforth Pr.

Blain, Christophe. Los Hielos, Vol. 2. 2005. (Isaac el Pirata Ser.). (SPA., Illus.). 48p. (YA). (gr. 8-17). 19.95 *(978-1-59497-114-3(5))* Public Square Bks.

Brannen, Sarah S. Madame Martine. Brannen, Sarah S., illus. 2014. (ENG., Illus.). 32p. (J). (gr. -1-3). 16.99 *(978-0-8075-4905-6(3))* Whitman, Albert & Co.

Brett, Jan. Beauty & the Beast. Brett, Jan, illus. 2011. (ENG., Illus.). 32p. (J). (gr. k-3). 17.99 *(978-0-399-25731-5(4)*, G.P. Putnam's Sons Books for Young Readers) Penguin Young Readers Group.

Brown, Carron, ed. Beauty & the Beast & Jack & the Beanstalk: Two Tales & Their Histories. 2009. (World of Fairy Tales Ser.). (Illus.). 32p. (J). (gr. -1-2). pap. 10.55 *(978-1-60754-650-4(7))*; lib. bdg. 22.60 *(978-1-60754-649-8(3))* Windmill Bks.

Burn, Michael. Childhood at Oriol. 2005. (ENG., Illus.). 360p. pap. 16.95 *(978-1-885586-32-2(9))* Turtle Point Pr.

Burnett, Frances Hodgson. Esmeralda, Mère Giraud's Little Daughter, Little Saint Elizabeth & Other Stories: A Collection of Short Stories by Frances Hodgson Burnett. 2012. 378p. *(978-1-78139-164-8(5))* Benediction Classics.

Cach, Lisa. Wake unto Me. 2011. (ENG.). 320p. (YA). (gr. 7-18). 8.99 *(978-0-14-241436-1(0)*, Speak) Penguin Young Readers Group.

Cadic, Olivier & Gheysens, Francois. Queen Margot - The Age of Innocence. Derenne, Juliette & Barroux, Sophie, illus. 2007. (Queen Margot Ser.: 1). (ENG.). 48p. (J). (gr. 4-7). per. 13.95 *(978-1-905460-10-6(4))* CineBook GBR. Dist: National Bk. Network.

Casanova, Mary. Curse of a Winter Moon. 2014. (ENG.). 144p. pap. 9.95 *(978-0-8166-9207-1(6))* Univ. of Minnesota Pr.

Clark Mancuso, Jackie. Hudson in Provence: A Paris-Chien Adventure. Clark Mancuso, Jackie, illus. I.t. ed. 2015. (Paris-Chien Adventure Ser.). (ENG., Illus.). 32p. (J). (gr. k-2). 17.95 *(978-0-9886058-4-8(8))* La Librairie Parisienne.

Craig, Joe. Jimmy Coates: Killer. 2007. 261p. (J). (gr. 5-9). 15.99 *(978-0-06-077266-6(2))* HarperCollins Pubs.

Crane, Walter. Beauty & the Beast, & Other Tales. (Illus.). [47] p.:p. *(978-0-87099-303-9(8))* Bow Historical Bks.

Curtin, Judi. Bonjour Alice. Fox, Woody, illus. 2015. (ENG.). 256p. (J). pap. 12.00 *(978-1-84717-689-9(5))* O'Brien Pr., Ltd., The IRL. Dist: Dufour Editions, Inc.

Cyr, Joe. Shadi, the Shadow Who Wanted to Be Free. Owen, Ramon, illus. 2010. 40p. pap. 14.95 *(978-1-936343-08-9(8))* Peppertree Pr., The.

de Las Casas, Dianne. Cinderellaphant, 1 vol. Jolet, Stefan, illus. 2014. (ENG.). 32p. (J). (gr. k-3). 16.99 *(978-1-4556-1900-9(0))* Pelican Publishing Co., Inc.

Defoe, Daniel & Perry, John Jasiel. Atalantis Major. 2011. 54p. 15.95 *(978-1-4638-9670-6(0))* Rodgers, Alan Bks.

Dennard, Susan. A Darkness Strange & Lovely. 2017. (Something Strange & Deadly Trilogy Ser.: 2). 432p. (YA). (gr. 9). pap. 9.99 *(978-0-06-265816-6(6)*, HarperTeen) HarperCollins Pubs.

Disney Book Group Staff & Green, Rico. Cinderella Kindness & Courage, Level 2. 2015. (World of Reading Ser.). (ENG.). 32p. (J). (gr. 1-3). pap. 3.99 *(978-1-4847-1112-5(2))* Disney Pr.

Druon, Maurice. The King Without a Kingdom (the Accursed Kings, Book 7) 2016. (Accursed Kings Ser.: 7). (ENG.). 368p. 14.99 *(978-0-00-814486-9(9))* HarperCollins Pubs.

Dumas, Alexandre. The Three Musketeers. Helquist, Brett, illus. 2011. (ENG.). 384p. (J). (gr. 5). pap. 6.99 *(978-0-06-206013-6(9))* HarperCollins Pubs.

—Los Tres Mosqueteros.Tr. of Trois Mousquetaires. (SPA.). (J). 2.49 *(978-968-890-125-0(3))* Edivision Compania Editorial, S.A. de C.V. MEX. Dist: Continental Bk. Co., Inc.

Dunn, Joeming W. & Dunn, Ben. D-Day. Dunn, Joeming W. & Dunn, Ben, illus. 2016. (Graphic Warfare Ser.). (ENG., Illus.). 32p. (J). (gr. 3-8). 28.50 *(978-1-61641-979-0(2))* Magic Wagon.

Egea, Marcelo. Sobe, the Cat That Thinks He's a Dog. 2012. 24p. pap. 15.99 *(978-1-4691-5925-6(2))* Xlibris Corp.

Ellis, Deborah. No Safe Place. 2013. 224p. pap. *(978-1-4596-6447-0(7))* ReadHowYouWant.com, Ltd.

Evans, Cambria. Bone Soup. 2008. (ENG., Illus.). 32p. (J). (gr. 2-5). 16.99 *(978-0-618-80908-0(2))* Houghton Mifflin Harcourt Publishing Co.

Fabian, Ingrid. The Black Arabian Foal. 2011. (Illus.). 53p. pap. 15.95 *(978-1-84624-530-5(3))* Book Guild, Ltd. GBR. Dist: Trans-Atlantic Pubns., Inc.

Fitzhugh, Percy K. Tom Slade with the Boys over There. 2005. (Illus.). pap. 24.95 *(978-1-885529-89-3(9))* Stevens Publishing.

Friedman, Aimee. Two Summers. 2016. (ENG.). 368p. (J). (gr. 7). 17.99 *(978-0-545-51807-9(5))* Scholastic, Inc.

Gay, Homel D. On the Road Again! More Travels with My Family. Gay, Marie-Louise, illus. 2008. (ENG.). 120p. (J). (gr. 1-5). 15.95 *(978-0-88899-846-0(5))* Groundwood Bks. CAN. Dist: Publishers Group West (PGW).

Gill, Heidi. 2 Kurious Kids: France. Carter, Kris, illus. 2012. 38p. (J). 14.95 *(978-1-936319-90-9(X))* Mascot Bks., Inc.

Gilley, Jane. Christmas on Troglodyte Hill - Book Three of the Troglodyte Trilogy. 2008. 16p. pap. *(978-1-906210-71-7(3))* Grosvenor Hse. Publishing Ltd.

—Roodery's Birthday - Book One of the Troglodyte Trilogy. 2008. 16p. pap. *(978-1-906210-72-4(1))* Grosvenor Hse. Publishing Ltd.

—Thibault Goes Missing - Book Two of the Troglodyte Trilogy. 2008. 16p. pap. *(978-1-906210-73-1(X))* Grosvenor Hse. Publishing Ltd.

Goscinny, René. Nicholas on Vacation. Bell, Anthea, tr. Sempé, Jean-Jacques, illus. 2013. (ENG.). 136p. (J). (gr. 1-4). pap. 9.95 *(978-0-7148-6224-8(X))* Phaidon Pr., Inc.

Guillain, Charlotte. Pandarella, 1 vol. Beacon, Dawn, illus. 2013. (Animal Fairy Tales Ser.). (ENG.). 24p. (gr. -1-2). pap. 6.49 *(978-1-4109-5031-4(X))*; lib. bdg. 23.99 *(978-1-4109-5025-3(5))* Heinemann-Raintree. (NA-r).

Guillain, Charlotte & Perrault, Charles. Pandarella. Beacon, Dawn, illus. 2013. (Animal Fairy Tales Ser.). (ENG.). 24p. (gr. -1-2). 26.00 *(978-1-4109-5043-7(3)*, NA-r) Heinemann-Raintree.

Hapka, Cathy, pseud. Pardon My French. 2005. (S. A. S. S. Ser.). (ENG., Illus.). 224p. (YA). (gr. 7-7). 7.99 *(978-0-14-240459-1(4)*, Speak) Penguin Young Readers Group.

Hayes, Clair W. The Boy Allies at Verdun. 2005. 28.95 *(978-1-4218-0324-1(0))*; 264p. pap. 13.95 *(978-1-4218-0424-8(7))* 1st World Publishing, Inc. (1st World Library - Literary Society).

—The Boy Allies at Verdun or Saving France from the Enemy. 2007. 124p. (gr. -1-7). per. *(978-1-4068-1712-6(0))* Echo Library.

—The Boy Allies in the Trenches: Midst Shot & Shell along the Aisne. 2007. (ENG.). 180p. pap. 19.99 *(978-1-4346-2323-2(8))*; 192p. pap. 21.99 *(978-1-4346-2381-2(5))* Creative Media Partners, LLC.

Hayes, Clair Wallace. The Boy Allies at Verdun: Saving France from the Enemy. 2007. (ENG.). 174p. pap. 19.99 *(978-1-4264-7694-5(9))*; 190p. pap. 21.99 *(978-1-4264-7752-2(X))* Creative Media Partners, LLC.

Henty, George Alfred. In the Reign of Terror: The Adventures of a Westminster Boy. 2004. reprint ed. pap. 26.95 *(978-1-4191-2606-2(7))*; pap. 1.99 *(978-1-4192-2606-9(1))* Kessinger Publishing, LLC.

Hergé. The Castafiore Emerald. (Illus.). 62p. (J). 19.95 *(978-0-8288-5016-2(X))* French & European Pubns., Inc.

Higgins, Nadia. Beauty & the Beast. Petelinsek, Kathleen, illus. 2013. (Fairy Tale Collection). (ENG.). 24p. (J). (gr. k-3). 28.50 *(978-1-62323-607-6(X)*, 206374) Child's World, Inc., The.

Hirota, Denise. Little Zippy Duffelbag Goes to France. 2012. 24p. pap. 12.45 *(978-1-4624-0443-8(X)*, Inspiring Voices) Author Solutions, Inc.

Hobbie, Holly. Top of the World. 2008. (Toot & Puddle Ser.: 6). (ENG.). 32p. (gr. -1-3). pap. 7.99 *(978-0-316-03384-8(7))* Little, Brown Bks. for Young Readers.

Horowitz, Anthony. Eagle Strike. (Alex Rider Ser.). (ENG.). (J). (gr. 5-18). 2006. 368p. 8.99 *(978-0-14-240613-7(9)*, Puffin

Books) 2004. (Illus.). 272p. 17.99 *(978-0-399-23979-3(0),* Philomel Bks.) Penguin Young Readers Group.

Jablonski, Carla. Defiance, Bk. 2. Purvis, Leland, illus. 2011. (Resistance Ser.: 2). (ENG.). 128p. (YA). (gr. 7-12). pap. 18.99 *(978-1-59643-292-5(6),* 9781596432925, First Second Bks.) Roaring Brook Pr.

—Resistance, Bk. 1. Purvis, Leland, illus. 2010. (Resistance Ser.: 1). (ENG.). 128p. (YA). (gr. 7-12). pap. 17.99 *(978-1-59643-291-8(8),* 9781596432918, First Second Bks.) Roaring Brook Pr.

Jacob, Le Bibliophile & Hunt, J. Timothy. Madame de Sévigné & Her Children at the Court of Versailles. 2011. 102p. pap. 12.00 *(978-0-578-06275-4(5))* Adhemar Pr. USA.

Jinks, Catherine. Pagan in Exile. 2005. (Pagan Chronicles Ser.: 2). (ENG., Illus.). 336p. (YA). (gr. 7-18). reprint ed. pap. 6.99 *(978-0-7636-2691-4(0))* Candlewick Pr.

Joffo, Joseph. A Bag of Marbles: The Graphic Novel. 2013. 128p. pap. 29.27 *(978-1-4677-1651-2(0))* Lerner Publishing Group.

—A Bag of Marbles: The Graphic Novel. Gauvin, Edward, tr. Bailly, Vincent, illus. 2013. (ENG.). 128p. (gr. 7-12). pap. 9.95 *(978-1-4677-1516-4(6));* lib. bdg. 29.27 *(978-1-4677-0700-8(7))* Lerner Publishing Group. (Graphic Universe™).

Johnson, D. B. Magritte's Marvelous Hat. Johnson, D. B., illus. 2012. (ENG., Illus.). 32p. (J). (gr. -1-3). 17.99 *(978-0-547-55864-6(3))* Houghton Mifflin Harcourt Publishing Co.

Johnston, Annie Fellows. The Giant Scissors. 2007. 188p. (gr. -1-7). 32.95 *(978-1-4344-9582-2(5));* per. 16.95 *(978-1-4344-9581-5(7))* Wildside Pr., LLC.

Jones, Wendy Lou. Bastian - Defender of Golden Downs. 2013. 234p. pap. 10.95 *(978-0-9777110-3-1(X))* Royal Knight Inc.

Kickliy. Musnet: The Mouse of Monet. 2016. (Musnet Ser.: 1). (ENG., Illus.). 56p. (J). (gr. 2). 19.95 *(978-1-941250-09-9(2),* odod bks.) Uncivilized Bks.

Kidd, Rob. Day of the Shadow. 4th ed. 2009. (Pirates of the Caribbean Ser.: No. 5). 256p. (YA). (gr. 5-18). pap. 6.99 *(978-1-4231-1041-5(2))* Disney Pr.

Kimmel, Eric A. Cactus Soup, 0 vols. Huling, Phil, illus. 2011. (ENG.). 34p. (J). (gr. -1-3). pap. 9.99 *(978-0-7614-5832-6(8),* 9780761458326, Amazon Children's Publishing) Amazon Publishing.

Kurlansky, Mark. The Girl Who Swam to Euskadi: Euskadiraino Igerian Joan Zen Neska. Kurlansky, Mark, illus. 2005. (ENG & BAQ., Illus.). 32p. (J). (gr. -1-3). 18.95 *(978-1-877802-54-6(9))* Ctr. for Basque Studies.

Lagonegro, Melissa. A Dream for a Princess (Disney Princess) Saichann, Alberto & Estudio, Pulsar, illus. 2016. (Step into Reading Ser.). (ENG.). 24p. (J). (gr. -1-1). pap. 4.99 *(978-0-7364-3668-7(5),* RH/Disney) Random Hse. Children's Bks.

Lambe, Mona. Yintin Tales. 2013. (Illus.). 60p. pap. *(978-0-9576015-0-5(6))* Moyin Bks.

Laski, Deirdre. Hidden in the Next Step. 2008. 224p. 25.95 *(978-0-595-50565-4(1));* pap. 15.95 *(978-0-595-50807-5(3))* iUniverse, Inc.

Lee, Mackenzi. This Monstrous Thing. 2015. (ENG.). 384p. (YA). (gr. 8). 17.99 *(978-0-06-238277-1(2))* HarperCollins Pubs.

Lee, Margaret. The Adventures of Sebastian the Helpful Seagull. 2012. (Illus.). 72p. pap. 41.99 *(978-1-4771-0672-3(3))* Xlibris Corp.

Lee, Tony. Messenger: the Legend of Joan of Arc. Hart, Sam, illus. 2015. (ENG.). 112p. (J). (gr. 5). 21.99 *(978-0-7636-7613-1(6))* Candlewick Pr.

LeTourneau, Marie & Baty, Danielle Reed. The Mice of Bistrot des Sept Frères. 2008. (ENG & FRE.). 32p. (J). (gr. -1-3). pap. 7.95 *(978-1-933718-18-7(8))* Tanglewood Pr.

Littlewood, Kathryn. A Dash of Magic: A Bliss Novel. McGuire, Erin, illus. 2013. (Bliss Bakery Trilogy Ser.: 2). (ENG.). 368p. (J). (gr. 3-7). 16.99 *(978-0-06-208429-3(1),* Tegen, Katherine Bks) HarperCollins Pubs.

MacDonald, Maryann. Odette's Secrets. 2013. (ENG., Illus.). 240p. (YA). (gr. 5-8). 16.99 *(978-1-59990-750-5(X),* 9781599907505, Bloomsbury USA Childrens) Bloomsbury Publishing USA.

Maddox, Joseph & Maddox, Diana. See You in Hell. 2004. 215p. (YA). pap. 14.95 *(978-0-7414-1872-2(X))* Infinity Publishing.

McDonough, Yona Zeldis. The Bicycle Spy. 2016. (ENG.). 208p. (J). (gr. 3-7). 16.99 *(978-0-545-85095-7(9),* Scholastic Pr.) Scholastic, Inc.

Meade, L. T. The Children's Pilgrimage. 2007. (ENG.). 254p. pap. 21.99 *(978-1-4346-4863-1(X));* 280p. pap. 23.99 *(978-1-4346-4864-8(8))* Creative Media Partners, LLC.

Merveille, David. Hello Mr. Hulot. 2013. (ENG., Illus.). 32p. (J). (gr. -1-3). 17.95 *(978-0-7358-4135-2(7))* North-South Bks., Inc.

Metaxas, Eric. Puss in Boots, 1 vol. Le-Tan, Pierre, illus. 2007. (Rabbit Ears: A Classic Tale Ser.). (ENG.). 36p. (gr. -1-3). 25.65 *(978-1-59961-311-6(5))* Spotlight.

Meyer, Susan Lynn. Black Radishes. 2011. (ENG.). 240p. (J). (gr. 3-7). 6.99 *(978-0-375-85822-2(9),* Yearling) Random Hse. Children's Bks.

Molesworth & Molesworth, Mary Louisa S. Grandmother Dear. 2008. 128p. pap. 10.95 *(978-1-60664-225-2(1))* Aegypan.

Morpurgo, Michael. Meeting Cezanne. Place, Francois, illus. 2013. (ENG.). 80p. (J). (gr. 2-5). 15.99 *(978-0-7636-4896-1(5))* Candlewick Pr.

Mosher, Richard. Zazoo. 2004. (ENG.). 272p. (YA). (gr. 7-18). reprint ed. pap. 15.95 *(978-0-618-43904-1(8))* Houghton Mifflin Harcourt Publishing Co.

Mullarkey, Lisa & Mullarkey, John. Mary Molds a Monster, 1 vol. Bernard, Courtney, illus. 2015. (ENG.). 128p. (J). *(978-1-62402-088-9(7))* Magic Wagon.

—Monet Changes Mediums, 1 vol. Bernard, Courtney, illus. 2015. (ENG.). 128p. (J). *(978-1-62402-089-6(5))* Magic Wagon.

Neale, J. B. In the Shadow of the Guillotine. 2008. 180p. pap. 13.95 *(978-1-4092-0391-9(3))* Lulu Pr., Inc.

Nesbø, Jo. Bubble in the Bathtub. Chace, Tara, tr. from NOR. Lowery, Mike, illus. 2011. (Doctor Proctor's Fart Powder Ser.). (ENG.). 432p. (J). (gr. 3-7). 17.99 *(978-1-4169-7974-6(3),* Aladdin) Simon & Schuster Children's Publishing.

Newsome, Richard. The Mask of Destiny. Duddle, Jonny, illus. 2013. 384p. (J). (gr. 3-7). pap. 6.99 *(978-0-06-194495-6(5),* Waldon Pond Pr.) HarperCollins Pubs.

Norris, Zack. Tunnel of Bones. 2012. (Double Detectives Ser.). (ENG.). 144p. (J). (gr. 3-7). pap. 4.95 *(978-1-4027-9147-5(X))* Sterling Publishing Co., Inc.

Olena Rudge. The Adventures of Sophie & Katia in the Enchanted Forest. 2013. 220p. pap. *(978-3-85438-685-8(0))* united p.c. Verlag.

O'Porter, Dawn. Paper Airplanes. 2015. (ENG.). 288p. (YA). (gr. 9-17). pap. 8.95 *(978-1-4197-1655-3(7),* Amulet Bks.) Abrams, Inc.

Outram, Evelyn. Sav & Josh O Lucky's Christmas Adventure & Magic Street. 2010. 56p. pap. 17.95 *(978-1-60911-876-1(6),* Eloquent Bks.) Strategic Book Publishing & Rights Agency (SBPRA).

Peacock, Shane. Last Message, 1 vol. 2012. (Seven (the Series) Ser.). (ENG., Illus.). 256p. (J). (gr. 5-10). pap. 9.95 *(978-1-55469-935-3(5))* Orca Bk. Pubs. USA.

Perrault, Charles. Cenicienta. Porras, Javier Fernando, illus. 2003. (Coleccion Letras Pegadas Ser.). (SPA.). 70p. (J). (gr. -1-7). pap. *(978-958-30-0547-3(9))* Panamericana Editorial.

—Puss in Boots. Adams, Frank & Lawrence, C. H., illus. 2009. (ENG.). 16p. (J). (gr. -1-3). pap. 9.95 *(978-1-59583-361-7(7),* 9781595833617) Laughing Elephant.

—Puss in Boots. Arthur, Malcolm, tr. Marcellino, Fred, illus. 2011. (ENG.). 32p. (J). (gr. -1-3). pap. 8.99 *(978-0-312-65945-5(8),* 9780312659455) Square Fish.

Peterfreund, Diana. Ascendant. (ENG.). (YA). (gr. 9). 2012. 416p. pap. 8.99 *(978-0-06-149005-7(9))* 2010. 400p. 17.99 *(978-0-06-149002-6(4))* HarperCollins Pubs. (HarperTeen).

Plum, Amy. Until I Die. 2013. (Die for Me Ser.: 2). (ENG.). 384p. (YA). (gr. 9). pap. 9.99 *(978-0-06-200405-5(0),* HarperTeen) HarperCollins Pubs.

Rabley, Stephen. Marcel & the Mona Lisa. 2nd ed. 2009. (ENG., Illus.). 20p. pap. 11.99 *(978-1-4058-6955-3(0))* Pearson Education.

Resau, Laura. The Ruby Notebook. 2012. (ENG.). 384p. (YA). (gr. 7). pap. 9.99 *(978-0-375-84525-3(9),* Ember) Random Hse. Children's Bks.

Ruellan, Susan. The Lost Treasure of Finistere. 2008. (ENG & FRE., Illus.). 83p. (J). (gr. 4-7). pap. 9.95 *(978-1-933916-24-8(9))* Nelson Publishing & Marketing.

Schweizer, Chris. The Crogan Adventures. 2015. (ENG., Illus.). 224p. (J). pap. 17.99 *(978-1-62010-243-5(9),* 9781620102435) Oni Pr., Inc.

Scimone, Diana. Adventures with Pawpaw: France. Wiedemer, Leah, illus. 2003. (Adventures with PawPaw Ser.). 32p. (J). 8.85 *(978-0-9729507-1-8(0))* Peapod Publishing, Inc.

Shakespeare, William. Henry V: The Graphic Novel. 2010. (Classic Graphic Novel Collection). (ENG.). 160p. (gr. 7-12). 39.40 *(978-1-4205-0371-5(5))* Cengage Gale.

Sherman, M. Zachary. A Time for War, 1 vol. Casas, Fritz, illus. 2011. (Bloodlines Ser.). (ENG.). 88p. (gr. 4-8). pap. 6.95 *(978-1-4342-3097-3(X));* 26.65 *(978-1-4342-2558-0(5))* Stone Arch Bks.

Smith, Annie Laura. Will Paris Burn? Casteel, Kay, illus. 2004. (ENG.). (YA). mass mkt. 6.99 *(978-0-9753367-4-8(6))* Onstage Publishing, LLC.

Spillebeen, Geert. Kipling's Choice. Edelstein, Terese, tr. 2007. (ENG.). 160p. (YA). (gr. 7-9). pap. 12.95 *(978-0-618-80035-3(2))* Houghton Mifflin Harcourt Publishing Co.

Still, Cynthia W. Gypsy Travels the World. 2012. 48p. pap. 21.99 *(978-1-4685-5839-5(0))* AuthorHouse.

Stokholm, Susan Mary. Between a Shadow & the Moon. 2010. 252p. pap. 14.49 *(978-1-4520-1752-5(2))* AuthorHouse.

Stone Arch Books Staff. Beauty & the Beast: The Graphic Novel, 1 vol. Feldman, Luke, illus. 2008. (Graphic Spin Ser.). (ENG.). 40p. (gr. 1-3). pap. 5.95 *(978-1-4342-0861-3(3),* Graphic Revolve) Stone Arch Bks.

Thomson, Sarah L. Cinderella, 0 vols. Ceccoli, Nicoletta, illus. 2012. (ENG.). 32p. (J). (gr. k-3). 17.99 *(978-0-7614-6170-8(1),* 9780761461708, Amazon Children's Publishing) Amazon Publishing.

Turetsky, Bianca. The Time-Traveling Fashionista at the Palace of Marie Antoinette. 2013. (Time-Traveling Fashionista Ser.: 2). (ENG., Illus.). 272p. (J). (gr. 3-7). pap. 9.00 *(978-0-316-10535-4(X),* Poppy) Little, Brown Bks. for Young Readers.

Vaugelade, Anaïs. The War. Vaugelade, Anaïs, illus. 2007. (Carolrhoda Picture Bks.). (ENG., Illus.). 32p. (J). (gr. k-4). per. 6.95 *(978-1-57505-918-1(5),* First Avenue Editions) Lerner Publishing Group.

Weston Woods Staff, creator. Stone Soup. 2011. 38.75 *(978-0-439-84572-4(6));* 29.95 *(978-0-439-74595-6(0))* Weston Woods Studios, Inc.

Whelan, Gloria. The Boy Who Wanted to Cook. Adams, Steve, illus. 2011. (Tales of the World Ser.). (ENG.). 40p. (gr. k-5). lib. bdg. 16.95 *(978-1-58536-534-0(3))* Sleeping Bear Pr.

Whitney, Daisy. Starry Nights. 2014. (ENG.). 304p. (YA). (gr. 7). pap. 9.99 *(978-1-61963-436-7(8),* 9781619634367, Bloomsbury USA Childrens) Bloomsbury Publishing USA.

Willett, Edward. Twist of the Blade, 1 vol. 2014. (Shards of Excalibur Ser.: 2). (ENG.). 232p. (YA). (gr. 7-10). pap. 14.95 *(978-1-55050-599-3(8))* Coteau Bks. CAN. Dist: Orca Bk. Pubs. USA.

Wyre, Yvonne. The Further Adventures of Cuthbert the Coal Lorry & all His Friends. 2007. (Illus.). 204p. pap. *(978-1-84401-801-7(6))* Athena Pr.

Yolen, Jane. Stone Angel. Green, Katie May, illus. 2015. (ENG.). 40p. (J). (gr. k-3). 16.99 *(978-0-399-16741-6(2),* Philomel Bks.) Penguin Young Readers Group.

Yorinks, Arthur. Harry & Lulu. braille ed. 2004. (Illus.). (J). (gr. k-3). spiral bd. *(978-0-616-07249-3(0));* spiral bd. *(978-0-616-07250-9(3))* Canadian National Institute for the Blind/Institut National Canadien pour les Aveugles.

—Harry & Lulu. Matje, Martin, illus. 32p. (J). pap. 4.99 *(978-0-7868-1221-9(4))* Hyperion Paperbacks for Children.

Zeller, Michelle. Maya's Magic Carpet. 2006. (J). per. 11.95 *(978-1-889743-48-6(8))* Robbie Dean Pr.

Zlamik, Natalie. Madeleine's Light: A Story of Camille Claudel. Dunn, Robert, illus. 2012. (ENG.). 32p. (J). (gr. k-2). 17.95 *(978-1-59078-855-4(9))* Boyds Mills Pr.

FRANCE—HISTORY

Amis, Nancy. The Orphans of Normandy: A True Story of World War II Told Through Drawings by Children. 2016. (ENG., Illus.). 48p. (J). (gr. 3-7). pap. 13.99 *(978-1-4814-9470-0(8),* Atheneum Bks. for Young Readers) Simon & Schuster Children's Publishing.

Bedford, Kathryn. The (True?) Story of Eustace the Monk. 2012. (Illus.). 36p. pap. *(978-1-908381-10-1(8))* Sacristy Pr.

Bhote, Themina. Charlemagne: Life & Times of an Early Medieval Emperor. 2004. (Leaders of the Middle Ages Ser.). (Illus.). 112p. (YA). (gr. 5-9). lib. bdg. 34.60 *(978-1-4042-0161-3(0))* Rosen Publishing Group, Inc., The.

—Charlemagne: The Life & Times of an Early Medieval Emperor. 2009. (Leaders of the Middle Ages Ser.). 112p. (gr. 5-8). 66.50 *(978-1-61513-896-8(X),* Rosen Reference) Rosen Publishing Group, Inc., The.

Bird, Julia & Lynch, Annabelle. France. 2014. (My Country Ser.). 24p. (gr. k-3). lib. bdg. 28.50 *(978-1-59920-905-0(5))* Black Rabbit Bks.

Bliven, Bruce. Invasion: The Story of D-Day. 2017. (Young Voyageur Ser.). (ENG.). 176p. (YA). (gr. 4-8). pap. 12.99 ***(978-0-7603-5436-0(7),*** Voyageur Pr.) Quarto Publishing Group USA.

Boutet de Monvel, Maurice. The Story of Joan of Arc. 2010. (Dover Children's Classics Ser.). (ENG., Illus.). 64p. (J). (gr. 4-7). pap. 14.99 *(978-0-486-47026-9(1))* Dover Pubns., Inc.

Brooks, Susie. Let's Visit France. 2009. (Around the World Ser.). (Illus.). 32p. (J). (ENG.). pap. 10.00 *(978-1-4358-8606-3(2));* (gr. 2-5). lib. bdg. 25.25 *(978-1-4358-3026-4(1))* Rosen Publishing Group, Inc., The. (PowerKids Pr.).

Burgan, Michael. Turning Point: The Story of the d-Day Landings. 2017. (Tangled History Ser.). (ENG., Illus.). 112p. (gr. 3-4). lib. bdg. 31.99 *(978-1-5157-3607-3(5))* Capstone Press of Coughlan Cos.

Caravantes, Peggy. The Many Faces of Josephine Baker: Dancer, Singer, Activist, Spy. 2015. (Women of Action Ser.). (ENG., Illus.). 208p. (YA). (gr. 7). 19.95 *(978-1-61373-034-8(9))* Chicago Review Pr., Inc.

Colson, Mary. France, 1 vol. 2011. (Countries Around the World Ser.). (ENG.). 48p. (gr. 3-6). pap. 9.95 *(978-1-4329-5228-0(5));* 33.32 *(978-1-4329-5203-7(X))* Heinemann-Raintree. (NA-h).

Conboy, Fiona & NgCheong-Lum, Roseline. France. 2010. (Welcome to My Country Ser.). 48p. (gr. 3-5). 28.50 *(978-1-60870-153-7(0))* Marshall Cavendish Corp.

Cunningham, Mark E. & Zwier, Lawrence. The Aftermath of the French Defeat in Vietnam. 2009. (Aftermath of History Ser.). (ENG.). 160p. (gr. 9-12). 38.60 *(978-0-8225-9093-4(X))* Lerner Publishing Group.

De la Bédoyère, Camilla. France. 2010. (Countries in Our World Ser.). 32p. (gr. 4-7). lib. bdg. 31.35 *(978-1-59920-437-6(1))* Black Rabbit Bks.

Demi. Joan of Arc, 0 vols. 2011. (ENG.). 56p. (J). (gr. 3-7). 19.99 *(978-0-7614-5953-8(7),* 9780761459538, Amazon Children's Publishing) Amazon Publishing.

Forest, Jim. Silent As a Stone: Mother Maria of Paris & the Trash Can Rescue. Pancheshnaya, Dasha, illus. 2007. (ENG.). 32p. (J). 18.00 *(978-0-88141-314-4(3))* St. Vladimir's Seminary Pr.

France. 2013. (Britannica Guide to Countries of the European Union Ser.). 376p. (YA). (gr. 9-12). 106.00 *(978-1-61530-982-5(9))* Rosen Publishing Group, Inc., The.

Freedman, Jeri. Strategic Inventions of the Napoleonic Wars. 2016. (Tech in the Trenches Ser.). 112p. (J). 42.79 *(978-1-5026-2351-5(X))* Cavendish Square Publishing.

Ganeri, Anita. France: A Benjamin Blog & His Inquisitive Dog Guide, 1 vol. Isik, Semur, illus. 2014. (Country Guides, with Benjamin Blog & His Inquisitive Dog Ser.). (ENG.). 32p. (gr. 1-3). pap. 7.99 *(978-1-4109-6676-6(3),* Read Me!) Heinemann-Raintree.

Goldsworthy, Kaite. France. 2014. (J). *(978-1-4896-1010-2(3))* Weigl Pubs., Inc.

Greenblatt, Miriam. Napoleon Bonaparte & Imperial France. 2005. (Rulers & Their Times Ser.). (Illus.). 96p. (J). (gr. 3-7). lib. bdg. *(978-0-7614-1837-5(7),* Benchmark Bks.) Marshall Cavendish Corp.

Hardyman, Robyn. Pierre & Marie Curie. 2014. (Dynamic Duos of Science Ser.). 48p. (YA). (gr. 5-8). pap. 84.30 *(978-1-4824-1287-1(X))* Stevens, Gareth Publishing LLLP.

Havemeyer, Janie. Catherine de' Medici: "The Black Queen" Malone, Peter, illus. 2011. (Thinking Girl's Treasury of Dastardly Dames Ser.). (ENG.). 32p. (J). (gr. 3-8). 18.95 *(978-0-9834256-3-2(9))* Goosebottom Bks. LLC.

Hilliam, David. Joan of Arc: Heroine of France. 2004. (Leaders of the Middle Ages Ser.). (Illus.). 112p. (J). lib. bdg. 34.60 *(978-1-4042-0164-4(5))* Rosen Publishing Group, Inc., The.

Hilliam, Paul. William the Conqueror: First Norman King of England. (Leaders of the Middle Ages Ser.). 112p. 2009. (gr. 5-8). 66.50 *(978-1-61513-903-3(6),* Rosen Reference) 2004. (Illus.). (J). lib. bdg. 34.60 *(978-1-4042-0166-8(1))* Rosen Publishing Group, Inc., The.

Hockinson, Liz. Marie Antoinette "Madame Deficit" Malone, Peter, illus. 2011. (Thinking Girl's Treasury of Dastardly Dames Ser.). (ENG.). 32p. (J). (gr. 3-8). 18.95 *(978-0-9834256-4-9(7))* Goosebottom Bks. LLC.

Hoffman, Megan Mills. Napoleon Bonaparte. 2017. (J). ***(978-1-5026-2782-7(5))*** Cavendish Square Publishing.

Horton, Casey. The French: From New France to Louisiana. 2006. (Illus.). 32p. (J). (gr. 4-8). reprint ed. 19.00 *(978-0-7567-9910-6(4))* DIANE Publishing Co.

Hubbard, Margaret Ann. Saint Louis & the Last Crusade. Barton, Harry, illus. 2013. (ENG.). 157p. pap. 9.95 *(978-1-58617-647-1(1))* Ignatius Pr.

Jeffrey, Gary. War in the Air. 2013. (ENG., Illus.). 48p. (J). *(978-0-7787-0914-5(0));* pap. *(978-0-7787-0924-4(8))* Crabtree Publishing Co.

Juettner Fernandes, Bonnie. The Large Hadron Collider. 2014. (Great Idea Ser.). (ENG., Illus.). 48p. (J). (gr. 4-6). lib. bdg. 26.60 *(978-1-59953-600-2(5))* Norwood Hse. Pr.

Kacer, Kathy. Hiding Edith: A True Story, 1 vol. 2006. (Holocaust Remembrance Ser.). (ENG., Illus.). 120p. (J). (gr. 4-8). pap. 14.95 *(978-1-897187-06-7(8))* Second Story Pr. CAN. Dist: Orca Bk. Pubs. USA.

Kalman, Bobbie. Spotlight on France. 2013. (ENG.). 32p. (J). *(978-0-7787-0865-0(9));* (Illus.). pap. *(978-0-7787-0869-8(1))* Crabtree Publishing Co.

Kemper, Bitsy. France. 2015. (One World, Many Countries Ser.). (ENG.). 32p. (J). (gr. 1-4). 28.50 *(978-1-63407-043-0(7),* 208873) Child's World, Inc., The.

Kenison, Misti, illus. France - The Tiny Traveler: A Book of Colors. 2015. (ENG.). 24p. (J). (— 1). bds. 5.95 *(978-1-62914-609-6(9),* Sky Pony Pr.) Skyhorse Publishing Co., Inc.

Knowles, Johanna. Jacques Cousteau. 2011. (Conservation Heroes Ser.). (Illus.). 120p. (YA). (gr. 6-12). 35.00 *(978-1-60413-947-1(1),* Chelsea Hse.) Facts On File, Inc.

Lace, William W. Joan of Arc & the Hundred Years' War in World History. 2003. (In World History Ser.). (Illus.). 128p. (J). (gr. 5-12). lib. bdg. 27.94 *(978-0-7660-1938-6(1))* Enslow Pubs., Inc.

Le Normand, Bruno. The Palace of Versailles. Heinrich, Christian, illus. 2012. (ENG.). 30p. (J). (gr. 2-6). pap. 11.99 *(978-1-85103-373-7(4))* Moonlight Publishing, Ltd. GBR. Dist: Independent Pubs. Group.

Leavitt, Amie Jane. My Home Is My Castle Versailles: Versailles. 2015. (ENG., Illus.). 48p. (J). 29.95 *(978-1-62469-140-9(4))* Purple Toad Publishing, Inc.

Lin, Yoming S. The Curies & Radioactivity. 2012. (Eureka! Ser.). (Illus.). 24p. (YA). (gr. 3-6). lib. bdg. 22.60 *(978-1-4488-5033-4(9))* Rosen Publishing Group, Inc., The.

Lynch, Annabelle. Living in France. 2017. (Living In Ser.). (ENG., Illus.). 24p. (J). (gr. 1-3). 16.99 *(978-1-4451-4838-0(2),* Franklin Watts) Hachette Children's Group GBR. Dist: Hachette Bk. Group.

Marsico, Katie. The Oldest & the Newest. 2015. (True Book(tm) — Extreme Places Ser.). (ENG., Illus.). 48p. (J). pap. 6.95 *(978-0-531-21785-6(X),* Children's Pr.) Scholastic Library Publishing.

Mason, Anthony. Versailles. 2005. (Places in History Ser.). (Illus.). 48p. (gr. 5-12). lib. bdg. 31.00 *(978-0-8368-5815-0(8),* World Almanac Library) Stevens, Gareth Publishing LLLP.

McGowen, Tom & Mcgowen, Tom. D-Day. 2008. (Cornerstones of Freedom Ser.). (ENG.). 48p. (J). (gr. 4-6). pap. 5.95 *(978-0-531-20831-1(1),* Children's Pr.) Scholastic Library Publishing.

McMenemy, Sarah. Paris: A 3D Keepsake Cityscape. McMenemy, Sarah, illus. 2012. (Panorama Pops Ser.). (ENG., Illus.). 20p. (J). (gr. k-12). 8.99 *(978-0-7636-5894-6(4))* Candlewick Pr.

Miller, Terry. D-Day at Omaha Beach: Turning the Tide of World War II. 2011. (J). *(978-0-545-32945-3(0))* Scholastic, Inc.

O'Brien, Cynthia. Explore with Sieur de la Salle. 2014. (ENG., Illus.). 32p. (J). *(978-0-7787-1430-9(6))* Crabtree Publishing Co.

Otfinoski, Steven & Gofen, Ethel. France. 3rd ed. 2013. 144p. (J). (gr. 6-9). 47.07 *(978-1-60870-867-3(5))* Cavendish Square Publishing.

Parker, Lewis K. French Colonies in the Americas. 2003. (European Colonies in the Americas Ser.). (Illus.). 24p. (J). lib. bdg. 22.60 *(978-0-8239-6473-4(6),* PowerKids Pr.) Rosen Publishing Group, Inc., The.

Parkes, Elle. Let's Explore France. 2017. (Bumba Books (tm) — Let's Explore Countries Ser.). (ENG.). 24p. (J). (gr. -1-1). 25.32 ***(978-1-5124-3366-1(7))*** Lerner Publishing Group.

Plain, Nancy. Eleanor of Aquitaine & the High Middle Ages. 2005. (Rulers & Their Times Ser.). (Illus.). 80p. (gr. 6-7). lib. bdg. 23.95 *(978-0-7614-1834-4(2),* Benchmark Bks.) Marshall Cavendish Corp.

Polette, Nancy. The Spy with the Wooden Leg: The Story of Virginia Hall. 2012. (ENG.). 160p. (J). pap. 12.95 *(978-1-934617-16-8(4));* 16.95 *(978-1-934617-15-1(6))* Elva Resa Publishing, LLC. (Alma Little).

Polisar, Patti. Inside France's DGSE: General Directorate for External Security. 2005. (Inside the World's Most Famous Intelligence Agencies Ser.). (Illus.). 64p. (YA). (gr. 7-12). lib. bdg. 31.95 *(978-0-8239-3814-8(X))* Rosen Publishing Group, Inc., The.

—Inside France's DGSE: The General Directorate for External Security. 2005. (Illus.). 63p. (gr. 4-8). reprint ed. 20.00 *(978-0-7567-8670-0(3))* DIANE Publishing Co.

—Inside France's DGSE: The General Directorate for External Security. 2009. (Inside the World's Most Famous Intelligence Agencies Ser.). 64p. (gr. 5-5). 58.50 *(978-1-61513-569-1(3))* Rosen Publishing Group, Inc., The.

Pollack, Pamela D. & Belviso, Meg. Who Was Joan of Arc? Thomson, Andrew & Harrison, Nancy, illus. 2016. (Who Was? Ser.). (ENG.). 112p. (J). (gr. 3-7). pap. 5.99 *(978-0-448-48304-7(1),* Grosset & Dunlap) Penguin Young Readers Group.

—Who Was Joan of Arc? 2016. (Who Was... ? Ser.). lib. bdg. 16.00 *(978-0-606-38395-0(6))* Turtleback Bks.

Rau, Dana Meachen & dePaola, Tomie. Who Was Marie Antoinette? O'brien, John, illus. 2015. (Who Was? Ser.). (ENG.). 112p. (J). (gr. 3-7). 5.99 *(978-0-448-48310-8(6),* Grosset & Dunlap) Penguin Young Readers Group.

Ray, Michael, ed. France. 2013. (Britannica Guide to Countries of the European Union Ser.). 376p. (YA). (gr. 9-12). 53.00 *(978-1-61530-964-1(0))* Rosen Publishing Group, Inc., The.

Rechner, Amy. France. 2017. (Country Profiles Ser.). (ENG., Illus.). 32p. (J). (gr. 3-8). lib. bdg. 26.95 ***(978-1-62617-680-5(9),*** Blastoff! Discovery) Bellwether Media.

Rice, Earle. The Life & Times of Clovis. 2009. (Biography from Ancient Civilizations Ser.). 48p. (J). (gr. 4-8). 29.95 *(978-1-58415-742-7(9))* Mitchell Lane Pubs., Inc.

Ross, Nancy Wilson. Joan of Arc. 2003. vii, 182p. pap. 29.00 *(978-0-7581-5017-2(2))* Textbook Pubs.

Rossi, Renzo. Paris. 2003. (Great Cities Through the Ages Ser.). (Illus.). 44p. (J). 18.95 *(978-1-59270-004-2(7))* Enchanted Lion Bks., LLC.

Rubin, Susan Goldman. Hot Pink: The Life & Fashions of Elsa Schiaparelli. 2015. (ENG., Illus.). 56p. (J). (gr. 5-9). 21.95 *(978-1-4197-1642-3(5),* Abrams Bks. for Young Readers) Abrams, Inc.

Ruelle, Karen Gray. The Grand Mosque of Paris: A Story of How Muslims Rescued Jews During the Holocaust. DeSaix, Deborah Durland, illus. 2010. (ENG.). 40p. (J). (gr. 3-18). pap. 8.95 *(978-0-8234-2304-0(2))* Holiday Hse., Inc.

—Hidden on the Mountain: Stories of Children Sheltered from the Nazis in le Chambon. DeSaix, Deborah Durland, illus. 2007. (ENG.). 272p. (J). (gr. 5-18). 24.95 *(978-0-8234-1928-9(2))* Holiday Hse., Inc.

Sanna, Jeanine & Indovino, Shaina C. France. Bruton, John, ed. 2012. (Major European Union Nations Ser.). 64p. (J). (gr. 7). 22.95 *(978-1-4222-2242-3(X))* Mason Crest.
Sanna, Jeanine & Indovino, Shaina Carmel. France. 2012. (J). pap. *(978-1-4222-2273-7(X))* Mason Crest.
Sapet, Kerrily. Eleanor of Aquitaine: Medieval Queen. 2006. (European Queens Ser.). (Illus.). 192p. (J). (gr. 6-12). lib. bdg. 26.95 *(978-1-931798-90-7(7))* Reynolds, Morgan Inc.
Schlesinger, Arthur M., Jr., intro. Ancient World Leaders. (Illus.). (gr. 6-12). lib. bdg. *(978-0-7910-8056-6(0)*, Chelsea Hse.) Facts On File, Inc.
Schmermund, Elizabeth & McGowan, Tom. Maximilien Robespierre & the French Revolution. 2016. (People & Events That Changed the World Ser.). (ENG., Illus.). 128p. (J). (gr. 7-8). lib. bdg. 37.27 *(978-0-7660-7294-7(0))* Enslow Pubs., Inc.
Sidinger, Jim. Eternal Companions: Faces of the Pere Lachaise, Paris. 2003. (Illus.). 48p. pap. 24.95 *(978-0-9729414-0-2(1)*, SIDJAM-0305) Catslip Arts, LLC.
Sonnebom, Liz. France. 2013. (Enchantment of the World™, Second Ser.). (ENG.). 144p. (J). 40.00 *(978-0-531-25600-8(6)*, Children's Pr.) Scholastic Library Publishing.
Spence, David. The Impressionists: Monet, Cezanne, Renoir, Degas. 2010. (ENG.). 128p. (J). (gr. 4-7). pap. 12.95 *(978-1-84696-217-2(X)*, TickTock Books) Octopus Publishing Group GBR. Dist: Independent Pubs. Group.
Spielman, Gloria. Marcel Marceau: Master of Mime. Gauthier, Manon, illus. 2011. (Kar-Ben Biographies Ser.). (ENG.). 32p. (J). (gr. 3-5). lib. bdg. 17.95 *(978-0-7613-3961-8(2)*, Kar-Ben Publishing) Lerner Publishing Group.
State, Paul. France. 2010. (Brief History Ser.). (Illus.). 416p. (C). (gr. 9). pap. 19.95 *(978-0-8160-8328-2(2))* Facts On File, Inc.
Streissguth, Thomas. France. 2008. (Country Explorers Ser.). (J). (gr. 2-5). 27.93 *(978-0-8225-9412-3(9))* Lerner Publishing Group.
Tagliaferro, Linda. Palace of Versailles: France's Royal Jewel. 2005. (Castles, Palaces, & Tombs Ser.). 32p. (J). lib. bdg. 25.27 *(978-1-59716-003-2(2))* Bearport Publishing Co., Inc.
Thiel, Kristin. Joan of Arc. 2017. (J). ***(978-1-5026-2791-9(4))*** Cavendish Square Publishing.
Thompson, Paul B. Joan of Arc: Warrior Saint of France. 2007. (Rulers of the Middle Ages Ser.). (Illus.). 160p. (YA). (gr. 6-12). lib. bdg. 35.94 *(978-0-7660-2716-9(3))* Enslow Pubs., Inc.
Thomson, Ruth. France. 2011. (Countries Ser.). (Illus.). 24p. (J). (gr. k-3). lib. bdg. 22.60 *(978-1-4488-3275-0(6))* Rosen Publishing Group, Inc., The.
Tieck, Sarah. Daft Punk: Electronic Music Duo, 1 vol. 2014. (Big Buddy Biographies Set 12 Ser.). (ENG.). 32p. (J). (gr. 2-5). 28.50 *(978-1-62403-567-8(1))* ABDO Publishing Co.
Webb, Sarah Powers. Marie Antoinette: Fashionable Queen or Greedy Royal? 2015. (Perspectives on History Ser.). (ENG.). 32p. (gr. 3-4). pap. 7.95 *(978-1-4914-2216-8(5))* Capstone Press of Coughlan Cos.
Whiting, Jim. The Life & Times of Charlemagne. 2005. (Biography from Ancient Civilizations Ser.). (Illus.). 48p. (J). (gr. 4-8). lib. bdg. 29.95 *(978-1-58415-346-7(6))* Mitchell Lane Pubs., Inc.
—The Life & Times of Joan of Arc. 2005. (Biography from Ancient Civilizations Ser.). (Illus.). 48p. (J). (gr. 4-8). lib. bdg. 29.95 *(978-1-58415-345-0(8))* Mitchell Lane Pubs., Inc.
Wilbur, Helen & L Wilbur, Helen. E Is for Eiffel Tower: A France Alphabet. 2016. (Av2 Fiction Readalong 2017 Ser.). (ENG.). (J). (gr. k-6). 34.28 ***(978-1-4896-5209-6(4)***, AV2 by Weigl) Weigl Pubs., Inc.
Wilbur, Helen L. E Is for Eiffel Tower: A France Alphabet. Nascimbene, Yan, illus. 2010. (Discover the World Ser.). (ENG.). 40p. (J). (gr. 1-3). 17.95 *(978-1-58536-505-0(X)*, 202199) Sleeping Bear Pr.
Wilkinson, Philip. Joan of Arc: The Teenager Who Saved Her Nation. (National Geographic World History Biographies Ser.). (ENG., Illus.). 64p. (J). (gr. 3-7). 2009. pap. 7.99 *(978-1-4263-0415-6(3))* 2007. 17.95 *(978-1-4263-0116-2(2))* 2007. lib. bdg. 27.90 *(978-1-4263-0117-9(0))* National Geographic Society. (National Geographic Children's Bks.).
Wolny, Philip. Joan of Arc: French Soldier & Saint. 2017. (Women Who Changed History Ser.). 48p. (gr. 10-12). pap. 14.05 ***(978-1-68048-645-2(4)***, Britannica Educational Publishing) Rosen Publishing Group, Inc., The.
Wood, Alix. Edgar Degas, 1 vol. 2015. (ENG., Illus.). 32p. (J). lib. bdg. 26.25 *(978-1-4777-5409-2(1)*, Windmill Bks.) Rosen Publishing Group, Inc., The.
—Paul Gauguin, 1 vol. 2015. (ENG., Illus.). 32p. (J). lib. bdg. 26.25 *(978-1-4777-5405-4(9)*, Windmill Bks.) Rosen Publishing Group, Inc., The.
Zaloga, Steven J. The Most Daring Raid of World War II: D-Day — Pointe-Du-Hoc. 2011. (Most Daring Raids in History Ser.). (Illus.). 64p. (YA). (gr. 7-12). lib. bdg. 31.95 *(978-1-4488-1867-9(2))* Rosen Publishing Group, Inc., The.

FRANCE—HISTORY—BIOGRAPHY

Abrams, Dennis. Coco Chanel. 2011. (Famous Fashion Designers Ser.). (Illus.). 128p. (gr. 6-12). 35.00 *(978-1-60413-925-9(0)*, Chelsea Hse.) Facts On File, Inc.
Alkayat, Zena. Coco Chanel. Cosford, Nina, illus. 2016. (ENG.). 128p. (J). 16.95 *(978-1-4521-5024-6(9))* Chronicle Bks. LLC.
Allport, Alan. Jacques Chirac. 2007. (Modern World Leaders Ser.). (Illus.). 111p. (YA). (gr. 7-12). lib. bdg. 30.00 *(978-0-7910-9265-1(8))* Facts On File, Inc.
Brezina, Corona. Jacques Cartier. 2016. (Spotlight on Explorers & Colonization Ser.). 00048p. (J). (gr. 6-6). pap. 11.75 *(978-1-5081-7206-2(4))* Rosen Publishing Group, Inc., The.
Collins, Kathleen. El Marques de Lafayette: Heroe Frances de la Guerra de Independencia. 2004. (Grandes personajes en la historia de los Estados Unidos Ser.). (SPA.). 32p. (gr. 3-6). pap. 10.00 *(978-0-8239-4233-6(3)*, Rosen Classroom) Rosen Publishing Group, Inc., The.
Donohue, Moira Rose. Jacques Cartier. 2013. (Illus.). 24p. (J). *(978-1-938813-03-0(0))* State Standards Publishing, LLC.
Fryer, Mary Beacock. Champlain: Peacemaker & Explorer. 2011. (ENG., Illus.). 152p. (YA). (gr. 6). pap. 19.99 *(978-1-55488-940-2(5))* Dundurn CAN. Dist: Ingram Publisher Services.
Gagne, Tammy. Charlemagne. 2017. (Junior Biography From Ancient Civilization Ser.). (gr. 4-6). 29.95 *(978-1-68020-020-1(8))* Mitchell Lane Pubs., Inc.
Goldberg, Jan. Napoleon Bonaparte. 2004. (ZB Reads Trio Books). 87p. (gr. 5-7). pap. 5.00 *(978-0-7367-1799-1(4))* Zaner-Bloser, Inc.
Heuston, Kimberley. Napoleon I: Emperor & Conqueror. 2010. (Wicked History Ser.). (ENG.). 128p. (J). (gr. 6-12). pap. 5.95 *(978-0-531-22823-4(1)*, Watts, Franklin) Scholastic Library Publishing.
Hilliam, David. Eleanor of Aquitaine: The Richest Queen in Medieval Europe. (Leaders of the Middle Ages Ser.). 112p. 2009. (gr. 5-8). 66.50 *(978-1-61513-897-5(8)*, Rosen Reference) 2004. (Illus.). (J). lib. bdg. 34.60 *(978-1-4042-0162-0(9))* Rosen Publishing Group, Inc., The.
Hoffman, Megan Mills. Napoleon Bonaparte. 2017. (J). ***(978-1-5026-2782-7(5))*** Cavendish Square Publishing.
Kallen, Stuart A. Claude Monet. 2008. (Eye on Art Ser.). (ENG., Illus.). 112p. (YA). (gr. 7-10). lib. bdg. 34.80 *(978-1-4205-0074-5(0)*, LML02109-242078, Lucent Bks.) Cengage Gale.
Koestler-Grack, Rachel A. Eleanor of Aquitaine: Heroine of the Middle Ages. 2005. (Makers of the Middle Ages & Renaissance Ser.). (Illus.). 168p. (gr. 5-8). lib. bdg. 32.95 *(978-0-7910-8633-9(X)*, Chelsea Hse.) Facts On File, Inc.
—Marie Curie: Scientist. 2009. (Women of Achievement Ser.). (Illus.). 136p. (gr. 6-12). 35.00 *(978-1-60413-086-7(5)*, Chelsea Hse.) Facts On File, Inc.
Kudlinski, Kathleen. Joan of Arc. 2008. (DK Biography Ser.). (ENG., Illus.). 128p. (J). (gr. 5-12). pap. 6.99 *(978-0-7566-3526-8(8)*, DK Children) Dorling Kindersley Publishing, Inc.
Ladybird Books Staff & Peach, L. Du Garde. The a Ladybird Adventure from History Book Story of Nelson. 2016. (Adventure from History Ser.). (ENG., Illus.). 56p. (J). (gr. 3-7). 9.99 *(978-0-7232-9799-4(1))* Penguin Bks., Ltd. GBR. Dist: Independent Pubs. Group.
Landau, Elaine. Napoleon Bonaparte. 2006. (Illus.). 112p. (J). 27.93 *(978-0-8225-3420-4(7)*, Twenty-First Century Bks.) Lerner Publishing Group.
Lowery, Lawrence F. Up, Up in a Balloon. 2013. (I Wonder Why Ser.). (ENG., Illus.). 36p. (J). (gr. k-3). pap. 11.95 *(978-1-938946-14-1(6))* National Science Teachers Assn.
Macdonald, Fiona. You Wouldn't Want to Be Joan of Arc! A Mission You Might Want to Miss. Antram, David, illus. 2010. (You Wouldn't Want to Ser.). (ENG.). 32p. (J). 29.00 *(978-0-531-20473-3(1))*; (gr. 3-18). pap. 9.95 *(978-0-531-22828-9(2))* Scholastic Library Publishing.
Maraval-Hutin, Sophie. Bernadette: The Girl from Lourdes. 2010. 36p. 14.99 *(978-1-58617-510-8(6))* Ignatius Pr.
Morse, Letitia M. Yellow Roses on Her Feet. 2008. (J). pap. *(978-0-9815075-0-7(6))* Bienna Bks.
Pelleschi, Andrea. Samuel de Champlain. 2013. (Jr. Graphic Famous Explorers Ser.). (ENG., Illus.). 24p. (J). (gr. 3-6). pap. 10.60 *(978-1-4777-0133-1(8))*; lib. bdg. 25.25 *(978-1-4777-0074-7(9))* Rosen Publishing Group, Inc., The. (PowerKids Pr.).
Peppas, Lynn. Why Sieur de La Salle Matters to Texas. 2014. (Illus.). 32p. (J). lib. bdg. 26.25 *(978-1-4777-0917-7(7))* Rosen Publishing Group, Inc., The.
Rau, Dana Meachen. Who Was Marie Antoinette? O'brien, John, illus. 2015. 106p. (J). *(978-1-4806-9210-7(7)*, Grosset & Dunlap) Penguin Publishing Group.
—Who Was Marie Antoinette? 2015. (Who Was... ? Ser.). lib. bdg. 16.00 *(978-0-606-37554-2(6))* Turtleback Bks.
Rice, Earle. The Life & Times of Eleanor of Aquitaine. 2009. (Biography of Ancient Civilizations Ser.). 48p. (J). (gr. 4-8). 29.95 *(978-1-58415-743-4(7))* Mitchell Lane Pubs., Inc.
Roberts, Russell. The Life & Times of Nostradamus. 2007. (Biography from Ancient Civilizations Ser.). (Illus.). 48p. (J). (gr. 4-8). lib. bdg. 29.95 *(978-1-58415-544-7(2))* Mitchell Lane Pubs., Inc.
Smith, Linda Wasmer. Louis Pasteur: Genius Disease Fighter. 2015. (Genius Scientists & Their Genius Ideas Ser.). 96p. (J). (gr. 5-12). 27.94 *(978-0-7660-6575-8(8))* Enslow Pubs., Inc.
Steinberg, D. J. King Louie's Shoes. Neubecker, Robert, illus. 2017. (ENG.). 48p. (J). (gr. -1-3). 17.99 ***(978-1-4814-2657-2(5)***, Beach Lane Bks.) Beach Lane Bks.
Trouvé, Marianne Lorraine. Saint Catherine Labouré: And Our Lady of the Miraculous Medal. 2011. (ENG.). (J). pap. 7.95 *(978-0-8198-7224-1(5))* Pauline Bks. & Media.
Van Gorp, Lynn. Antoine Lavoisier: Founder of Modern Chemistry, 1 vol. 2007. (Science Readers Ser.). (SPA & ENG.). 32p. (J). (gr. 3-3). pap. 8.99 *(978-0-7439-0582-4(2))* Shell Educational Publishing.
Wilkinson, Philip. Joan of Arc: The Teenager Who Saved Her Nation. 2007. (National Geographic World History Biographies Ser.). (ENG., Illus.). 64p. (J). (gr. 3-7). 17.95 *(978-1-4263-0116-2(2))*; lib. bdg. 27.90 *(978-1-4263-0117-9(0))* National Geographic Society. (National Geographic Children's Bks.).
Yount, Lisa. Antoine Lavoisier: Genius of Modern Chemistry. 2015. (Genius Scientists & Their Genius Ideas Ser.). 96p. (J). (gr. 5-12). 27.94 *(978-0-7660-6520-8(0))* Enslow Pubs., Inc.

FRANCE—HISTORY—FICTION

Andrews, Julie & Hamilton, Emma Walton. Dragon. 2004. (Julie Andrews Collection). 192p. (J). (gr. 4-18). 16.99 *(978-0-06-057119-1(5))*; lib. bdg. 17.89 *(978-0-06-057120-7(9))* HarperCollins Pubs. (Julie Andrews Collection).
Anton, Maggie. Secret Scholar. 2008. (ENG.). 160p. (gr. 4-7). pap. 14.00 *(978-0-8276-0869-6(1))* Jewish Pubn. Society.
Barker, Michelle. A Year of Borrowed Men. Benoit, Renne, illus. 2016. (ENG.). 40p. (J). (gr. 1-4). 18.95 *(978-1-927485-83-5(5))* Pajama Pr. CAN. Dist: Ingram Publisher Services.
Blake, Lily. Reign: The Prophecy. 2014. (ENG.). 240p. (YA). (gr. 7-17). pap. 14.00 *(978-0-316-33459-4(6)*, Poppy) Little, Brown Bks. for Young Readers.
Bond, Douglas. Hammer of the Huguenots. 2015. (Illus.). 226p. (J). pap. 12.99 *(978-1-59638-763-8(7))* P & R Publishing.
Cadic, Oliver, et al. Queen Margot - The Bloody Wedding. 2007. (Queen Margot Ser.: 2). (ENG., Illus.). 48p. (J). (gr. -1-12). pap. 13.95 *(978-1-905460-19-9(8))* CineBook GBR. Dist: National Bk. Network.
Chandler, Pauline. Warrior Girl: A Novel of Joan of Arc. 2006. 354p. (J). (gr. 5-9). 17.89 *(978-0-06-084103-4(6))* HarperCollins Pubs.
Dumas, Alexandre. The Count of Monte Cristo, 1 vol. Fisher, Scott, illus. 2011. (Calico Illustrated Classics Ser.). (ENG.). 112p. (YA). (gr. 3-6). 27.07 *(978-1-60270-744-3(8))* Magic Wagon.
—The Man in the Iron Mask. Howell, Troy, illus. 2008. (Classic Starts(tm) Ser.). (ENG.). 160p. (J). (gr. 2-4). 6.95 *(978-1-4027-4579-9(6))* Sterling Publishing Co., Inc.
—The Man in the Iron Mask. 2003. (Saddleback Classics Ser.). (Illus.). 48p. (J). per. 17.95 *(978-1-56254-528-4(0)*, SP5280); 79p. (YA). (gr. 8-12). per. 6.95 *(978-1-56254-527-7(2)*, SP5272) Saddleback Educational Publishing, Inc.
—The Three Musketeers, 1 vol. Lacey, Mike, illus. 2011. (Calico Illustrated Classics Ser.). (ENG.). 112p. (YA). (gr. 3-6). 27.07 *(978-1-60270-751-1(0))* Magic Wagon.
—The Three Musketeers. Hochman, Eleanor, tr. from FRE. 2006. (ENG., Illus.). 672p. (gr. 12-18). 7.95 *(978-0-451-53003-5(9)*, Signet) Penguin Publishing Group.
—The Three Musketeers. Laurel Associates Inc. Staff & Saddleback Educational Publishing Staff, eds. 2008. (Illustrated Classics Ser.). (ENG., Illus.). 16p. (YA). (gr. 9-12). pupil's gde. ed. 7.95 incl. cd-rom *(978-1-59905-313-4(6))* Saddleback Educational Publishing, Inc.
—The Three Musketeers. 2007. (Illustrated Classics Ser.). (Illus.). 40p. (gr. 3-6). lib. bdg. 26.00 *(978-0-8368-7664-2(4)*, Gareth Stevens Learning Library) Stevens, Gareth Publishing LLLP.
—The Three Musketeers. Dunn, Robert, illus. 2013. 46p. (J). *(978-1-4351-4812-3(6))* Barnes & Noble, Inc.
—The Three Musketeers. Akib, Jamel, illus. 2007. (Classic Starts(tm) Ser.). (ENG.). 160p. (J). (gr. 2-4). 6.95 *(978-1-4027-3695-7(9))* Sterling Publishing Co., Inc.
—The Three Musketeers. 2004. reprint ed. pap. 1.99 *(978-1-4192-8527-1(0))* Kessinger Publishing, LLC.
—The Three Musketeers, 1 vol. 2010. (Illustrated Classics Ser.). (ENG., Illus.). 64p. (YA). (gr. 9-12). pap. 9.95 *(978-1-56254-942-8(1))* Saddleback Educational Publishing, Inc.
Dumas, Alexandre & Thomas, Roy. The Three Musketeers, 1 vol. Petrus, Hugo et al, illus. 2009. (Man in the Iron Mask Ser.: Vol. 1). (ENG.). 24p. (gr. 7-18). 24.21 *(978-1-59961-594-3(0))* Spotlight.
Everett-Green, Evelyn. A Heroine of France. 2006. (ENG.). 188p. pap. 19.99 *(978-1-4264-7060-8(6))* 2007. 206p. pap. 22.99 *(978-1-4264-7136-0(X))* Creative Media Partners, LLC.
Farenhorst, Christine. Wings Like a Dove: The Courage of Queen Jeanne D'Albret. 2006. (Chosen Daughters Ser.). 207p. (YA). (gr. 7). per. 11.99 *(978-0-87552-642-3(X))* P & R Publishing.
Farrant, Natasha. What We Did for Love: Resistance, Heartbreak, Betrayal. 2014. (Illus.). 208p. (YA). (gr. 6-12). pap. 10.95 *(978-1-62324-029-5(8))* Enslow Pubs., Inc.
Flegg, Aubrey M. The Rainbow Bridge. 2nd rev. ed. 2006. (Louise Trilogy Ser.: 02). (ENG.). 272p. (J). pap. 12.95 *(978-0-86278-917-6(6))* O'Brien Pr., Ltd., The IRL. Dist: Dufour Editions, Inc.
Gibbs, Stuart. The Last Musketeer. 2012. (Last Musketeer Ser.: 1). (ENG.). 272p. (J). (gr. 3-7). pap. 6.99 *(978-0-06-204839-4(2))* HarperCollins Pubs.
Giff, Patricia Reilly. Genevieve's War. Stadtlander, Becca, illus. 2017. (ENG.). 240p. (J). (gr. 3-7). 16.95 *(978-0-8234-3800-6(7))* Holiday Hse., Inc.
Goscinny, René. Asterix & Cleopatra. Uderzo, Albert, illus. 2004. (ENG.). 48p. 17.99 *(978-0-7528-6606-2(0)*, Orion) Orion Publishing Group, Ltd. GBR. Dist: Hachette Bk. Group.
—Asterix & the Banquet. Uderzo, Albert, illus. 2004. (ENG.). 48p. 17.99 *(978-0-7528-6608-6(7)*, Orion) Orion Publishing Group, Ltd. GBR. Dist: Hachette Bk. Group.
—Asterix & the Cauldron. Uderzo, Albert, illus. 2004. (ENG.). 48p. 17.99 *(978-0-7528-6628-4(1)*, Orion) Orion Publishing Group, Ltd. GBR. Dist: Hachette Bk. Group.
—Asterix & the Golden Sickle. Uderzo, Albert, illus. 2004. (ENG., Illus.). 48p. 17.99 *(978-0-7528-6612-3(5)*, Orion) Orion Publishing Group, Ltd. GBR. Dist: Hachette Bk. Group.
—Asterix & the Normans. (Illus.). (J). pap. 9.95 *(978-0-02-497290-3(8))* International Language Centre.
—Asterix aux Jeux Olympiques. (FRE.). (J). pap. 21.95 *(978-2-01-210144-9(5))* Hachette Groupe Livre FRA. Dist: Distribooks, Inc.
—Asterix et Cleopatre. (FRE.). (J). pap. 21.95 *(978-2-01-210138-8(0))*; (Illus.). 21.95 *(978-2-01-210111-1(9))* Hachette Groupe Livre FRA. Dist: Distribooks, Inc.
—Asterix in Britain. Uderzo, Albert, illus. 2004. (ENG.). 48p. 17.99 *(978-0-7528-6618-5(4)*, Orion) Orion Publishing Group, Ltd. GBR. Dist: Hachette Bk. Group.
—Asterix in Switzerland. Uderzo, Albert, illus. 2004. (ENG.). 48p. 17.99 *(978-0-7528-6634-5(6)*, Orion) Orion Publishing Group, Ltd. GBR. Dist: Hachette Bk. Group.
—The Gaul. Uderzo, Albert, illus. 2004. (ENG.). 48p. 17.99 *(978-0-7528-6604-8(4)*, Orion) Orion Publishing Group, Ltd. GBR. Dist: Hachette Bk. Group.
Goscinny, René & Uderzo, Albert. Asterix & Caesar's Gift. 2004. (ENG., Illus.). 48p. 17.99 *(978-0-7528-6645-1(1)*, Orion) Orion Publishing Group, Ltd. GBR. Dist: Hachette Bk. Group.
—Asterix & Cleopatra. Uderzo, Albert, illus. 2004. (ENG., Illus.). 48p. pap. 12.99 *(978-0-7528-6607-9(9)*, Orion) Orion Publishing Group, Ltd. GBR. Dist: Hachette Bk. Group.
—Asterix & the Big Fight. 2004. (ENG., Illus.). 48p. 17.99 *(978-0-7528-6616-1(8)*, Orion) Orion Publishing Group, Ltd. GBR. Dist: Hachette Bk. Group.
—Asterix & the Big Fight. Uderzo, Albert, illus. 2004. (ENG., Illus.). 48p. pap. 12.99 *(978-0-7528-6617-8(6)*, Orion) Orion Publishing Group, Ltd. GBR. Dist: Hachette Bk. Group.
—Asterix & the Great Crossing. 2004. (ENG., Illus.). 48p. 17.99 *(978-0-7528-6647-5(8)*, Orion) Orion Publishing Group, Ltd. GBR. Dist: Hachette Bk. Group.
—Asterix & the Laurel Wreath. Uderzo, Albert, illus. 2004. (ENG., Illus.). 48p. 17.99 *(978-0-7528-6636-9(2)*, Orion) Orion Publishing Group, Ltd. GBR. Dist: Hachette Bk. Group.
—Asterix & the Normans. Uderzo, Albert, illus. 2004. (ENG., Illus.). 48p. 17.99 *(978-0-7528-6622-2(2)*, Orion) Orion Publishing Group, Ltd. GBR. Dist: Hachette Bk. Group.
—Asterix & the Soothsayer. Uderzo, Albert, illus. 2004. (ENG., Illus.). 48p. 17.99 *(978-0-7528-6641-3(9)*, Orion) Orion Publishing Group, Ltd. GBR. Dist: Hachette Bk. Group.
—Asterix at the Olympic Games. Uderzo, Albert, illus. 2004. (ENG., Illus.). 48p. 17.99 *(978-0-7528-6626-0(5)*, Orion) Orion Publishing Group, Ltd. GBR. Dist: Hachette Bk. Group.
—Asterix in Britain. Uderzo, Albert, illus. 2004. (ENG., Illus.). 48p. pap. 12.99 *(978-0-7528-6619-2(2)*, Orion) Orion Publishing Group, Ltd. GBR. Dist: Hachette Bk. Group.
—Asterix the Gladiator. Uderzo, Albert, illus. 2004. (ENG., Illus.). 48p. 17.99 *(978-0-7528-6610-9(9)*, Orion) Orion Publishing Group, Ltd. GBR. Dist: Hachette Bk. Group.
Goscinny, René & Uderzo, M. Asterix el Galo. (SPA., Illus.). (J). (gr. 7-10). 24.95 *(978-0-8288-4933-3(1))* French & European Pubns., Inc.
—Streit um Asterix. (GER., Illus.). (J). 24.95 *(978-0-8288-4906-7(4))* French & European Pubns., Inc.
Gosling, Sharon. The Ruby Airship. 2015. (Diamond Thief Ser.). (ENG.). 496p. (gr. 9-12). 16.95 *(978-1-63079-004-2(4))* Switch Pr.
Hartnett, Sonya. The Silver Donkey. Spudvilas, Anne, illus. 2004. viii, 193p. (J). *(978-0-670-04240-1(4)*, Viking Adult) Penguin Publishing Group.
Hendry, Frances. Quest for a Queen: The Lark. 2006. (Illus.). 251p. pap. *(978-1-905665-04-4(0))* Pollinger In Print.
Henty, George Alfred. No Surrender! A Tale of the Rising in la Vendee. l.t. ed. 2007. 330p. pap. 24.99 *(978-1-4346-3575-4(9))* Creative Media Partners, LLC.
Hofmeyr, Dianne. Zeraffa Giraffa. Ray, Jane, illus. 2015. (ENG.). 40p. (J). pap. 9.99 *(978-1-84780-661-1(9)*, Frances Lincoln Children's Bks.) Quarto Publishing Group UK GBR. Dist: Littlehampton Bk Services, Ltd.
Holmes, Mary Tavener & Harris, John. A Giraffe Goes to Paris, 0 vols. Cannell, Jon, illus. 2010. (ENG.). 32p. (J). (gr. 1-4). 17.99 *(978-0-7614-5595-0(7)*, 9780761455950, Amazon Children's Publishing) Amazon Publishing.
Hugo, Victor. The Hunchback of Notre Dame. 2008. (Bring the Classics to Life Ser.). (Illus.). 72p. (gr. 2-12). pap., act. bk. ed. 10.95 *(978-1-55576-324-4(3)*, EDCTR-208B) EDCON Publishing Group.
—The Hunchback of Notre Dame: Illustrated Edition, 1 vol. 2012. (Calico Illustrated Classics Ser.: No. 4). (ENG., Illus.). 112p. (J). (gr. 3-6). 27.07 *(978-1-61641-614-0(9))* Magic Wagon.
—The Hunchback of Notre Dame: With a Discussion of Compassion. Butterfield, Ned, tr. Butterfield, Ned, illus. 2003. (Values in Action Illustrated Classics Ser.). (J). *(978-1-59203-049-1(1))* Learning Challenge, Inc.
The Hunchback of Notre Dame. (Read-Along Ser.). (J). 7.99 incl. audio *(978-1-55723-992-1(4))* Walt Disney Records.
Jinks, Catherine. Babylonne. 2008. (ENG., Illus.). 400p. (YA). (gr. 7). 18.99 *(978-0-7636-3650-0(9))* Candlewick Pr.
Kesterson, Casie. The Goldfish in the Chandelier. Hovland, Gary, illus. 2012. (ENG.). 32p. 17.95 *(978-1-60606-094-0(5)*, J. Paul Getty Museum) Getty Pubns.
Klimo, Kate. Stubby. Jessell, Tim, illus. 2015. (Dog Diaries: 7). (ENG.). 160p. (J). (gr. 2-5). lib. bdg. 12.99 *(978-0-385-39244-0(3)*, Random Hse. Bks. for Young Readers) Random Hse. Children's Bks.
Ladybird, Ladybird & Dumas, Alexandre. The Three Musketeers. Hayden, Sean, illus. 2016. (Ladybird Classics Ser.). (ENG.). 72p. (J). (gr. 3-7). 8.99 *(978-1-4093-1355-7(7))* Penguin Bks., Ltd. GBR. Dist: Independent Pubs. Group.
LaFevers, Robin. Grave Mercy. (His Fair Assassin Ser.: 1). (ENG., Illus.). (YA). (gr. 9). 2013. 576p. pap. 9.99 *(978-0-544-02249-2(1))* 2012. 560p. 17.99 *(978-0-547-62834-9(X))* Houghton Mifflin Harcourt Publishing Co.
—Grave Mercy, 10 vols. 2012. (His Fair Assassin Trilogy: Bk. 1). (YA). 132.75 *(978-1-4640-2388-0(3))*; 130.75 *(978-1-4640-2390-3(5))*; 130.75 *(978-1-4640-2387-3(5))*; 287.75 *(978-1-4640-2386-6(7))* Recorded Bks., Inc.
—Mortal Heart. 2014. (His Fair Assassin Ser.: 3). (ENG.). 464p. (YA). (gr. 9). 17.99 *(978-0-547-62840-0(4)*, HMH Books For Young Readers) Houghton Mifflin Harcourt Publishing Co.
Levene, Rebecca, ed. Three Musketeers. Tavares, Victore, illus. 2009. (Young Reading 3 Ser.). 64p. (J). (gr. 2). 6.99 *(978-0-7945-1946-9(6)*, Usborne) EDC Publishing.
Malot, Hector & Crewe-Jones, Florence. Nobody's Boy: Companion Story to Nobody's Girl. Gooch, Thelma & Gruelle, Johnny, illus. 2006. 237p. (J). pap. *(978-1-894666-75-6(5))* Inheritance Pubns.
—Nobody's Girl: Companion Story to Nobody's Boy. Gooch, Thelma, illus. 2006. 220p. (J). pap. *(978-1-894666-76-3(3))* Inheritance Pubns.
McCaughrean, Geraldine. The Death-Defying Pepper Roux. 2010. 336p. (J). (gr. 5-18). 16.99 *(978-0-06-183665-7(6))* HarperCollins Pubs.
Milton, Nancy. The Giraffe That Walked to Paris. Roth, Roger, illus. 2013. (ENG.). 32p. (J). (gr. -1-3). 18.95 *(978-1-930900-67-7(8))* Purple Hse. Pr.
Osborne, Mary Pope, et al. La Noche de los Nuevos Magos. Murdocca, Sal, illus. 2016. (SPA.). (J). (gr. 2-4). pap. 5.99 ***(978-1-63245-645-8(1))*** Lectorum Pubns., Inc.
Richmond, Caroline Tung. Darkest Hour. 2016. (ENG.). 320p. (J). (gr. 7). 17.99 *(978-0-545-80127-0(3)*, Scholastic Pr.) Scholastic, Inc.
Spradlin, Michael P. Trail of Fate, 2 vols., Bk. 2. 2010. (Youngest Templar Ser.: 2). (ENG.). 256p. (J). (gr. 5-7). 7.99 *(978-0-14-241707-2(6)*, Puffin Books) Penguin Young Readers Group.
Strang, Herbert. With Marlborough to Malplaquet. 2006. pap. *(978-1-4068-3126-9(3))* Echo Library.
Tucker, Charlotte Maria. Driven into Exile: A Story of the Huguenots. 2003. (Huguenot Inheritance Ser.: Vol. 5). (Illus.). 141p. (J). *(978-0-921100-66-9(3))* Inheritance Pubns.
Venable, Alan. The Man in the Iron Mask. 2007. (Classic Adventures Ser.). pap. 9.95 *(978-1-4105-0860-7(9))* Johnston, Don Inc.
Vogel, Eva. Facing the Music. 2003. 284p. 19.95 *(978-1-880582-94-7(5))* Judaica Pr., Inc., The.

EFG

Weil, Sylvie. Elvina's Mirror. 2009. (ENG.). 150p. (gr. 5-18). pap. 14.00 *(978-0-8276-0885-6(3))* Jewish Pubn. Society.

—My Guardian Angel. Rosner, Gillian, tr. from FRE. 2014. (ENG., Illus.). 208p. (J). pap. 14.95 *(978-0-8276-1211-2(7))* Jewish Pubn. Society.

Zafón, Carlos Ruiz. The Watcher in the Shadows. 2014. (ENG.). 288p. (YA). (gr. 7-17). pap. 10.99 *(978-0-316-04475-2(X))* Little, Brown Bks. for Young Readers.

FRANCE—HISTORY—TO 1328—FICTION

Berry, Julie. The Passion of Dolssa. 2016. (ENG.). 496p. (YA). (gr. 7). 18.99 *(978-0-451-46992-2(5),* Viking Books for Young Readers) Penguin Young Readers Group.

Gidwitz, Adam. The Inquisitor's Tale: Or, the Three Magical Children & Their Holy Dog. Aly, Hatem, illus. 2016. (ENG.). 384p. (J). (gr. 5). 17.99 *(978-0-525-42616-5(7),* Dutton Books for Young Readers) Penguin Young Readers Group.

FRANCE—HISTORY—HOUSE OF VALOIS, 1328-1589

see also Hundred Years' War, 1339-1453

Joan of Arc. 2010. (Women of Achievement Ser.). (Illus.). 128p. (gr. 6-12). 35.00 *(978-1-60413-710-1(X),* Chelsea Hse.) Facts On File, Inc.

FRANCE—HISTORY—HOUSE OF VALOIS, 1328-1589—FICTION

Avi. The End of Time. 2011. (ENG.). 240p. (J). (gr. 5). pap. 6.99 *(978-0-06-174083-1(7))* HarperCollins Pubs.

LaFevers, Robin. Dark Triumph. (His Fair Assassin Ser.: 2). (ENG.). 400p. (YA). (gr. 9). 2014. pap. 9.99 *(978-0-544-22720-0(4),* HMH Books For Young Readers) 2013. 17.99 *(978-0-547-62838-7(2))* Houghton Mifflin Harcourt Publishing Co.

—Dark Triumph, 10 vols. 2013. (His Fair Assassin Ser.: 2). (YA). *(978-1-4640-2397-2(2))* Recorded Bks., Inc.

FRANCE—HISTORY—BOURBONS, 1589-1789—FICTION

Dumas, Alexandre. The Three Musketeers. Tayal, Amit, illus. 2011. (Campfire Graphic Novels Ser.). (ENG.). 104p. (YA). (gr. 3-7). pap. 12.99 *(978-93-80028-57-6(1),* Campfire) Steerforth Pr.

FRANCE—HISTORY—REVOLUTION, 1789-1799

Adcock, Michael. Cambridge Checkpoints VCE History - French Revolution 2014-16. 2013. (Cambridge Checkpoints Ser.). (ENG.). pap., stu. ed. *(978-1-107-67445-5(X))* Cambridge Univ. Pr.

—Cambridge Checkpoints VCE History - French Revolution 2014-16 & Quiz Me More. 2013. (Cambridge Checkpoints Ser.). (ENG.). pap., stu. ed. *(978-1-107-65836-3(5))* Cambridge Univ. Pr.

Davenport, John C. The French Revolution & the Rise of Napoleon. 2011. (Milestones in Modern World History Ser.). (Illus.). 127p. (C). (gr. 9). 35.00 *(978-1-60413-919-8(6),* Chelsea Hse.) Facts On File, Inc.

Daynes, Katie. Marie Antoinette. Mistry, Nilesh, illus. 2005. 64p. (J). 8.95 *(978-0-7945-1049-7(3),* Usborne) EDC Publishing.

Freedman, Jeri. Strategic Inventions of the French Revolution. 2016. (Tech in the Trenches Ser.). 112p. (J). lib. bdg. 42.79 *(978-1-5026-2347-8(1))* Cavendish Square Publishing.

French Revolution: Dba. 2003. spiral bd. 16.95 *(978-1-56004-110-8(2))* Social Studies Schl. Service.

Green, Robert. Cause & Effect the French Revolution: The French Revolution. 2015. (ENG., Illus.). 80p. (J). lib. bdg. *(978-1-60152-796-7(9))* ReferencePoint Pr., Inc.

Gregory, Josh. The French Revolution. 2013. (ENG.). 64p. (J). 30.00 *(978-0-531-28203-8(1));* pap. 8.95 *(978-0-531-27668-6(6))* Scholastic Library Publishing.

Haywood, Karen Diane. The French Revolution: The Power of the People. 2017. (World History Ser.). 104p. (YA). (gr. 7-7). lib. bdg. 39.90 ***(978-1-5345-6051-2(3),*** Lucent Pr.) Greenhaven Publishing LLC.

Klar, Jeremy. The French Revolution, Napoleon, & the Republic: Liberte, égalité, Fraternité. 2015. (Age of Revolution Ser.). (ENG., Illus.). 128p. (J). (gr. 9-10). 35.25 *(978-1-68048-023-8(5),* Britannica Educational Publishing) Rosen Publishing Group, Inc., The.

Klar, Jeremy, ed. The French Revolution, Napoleon, & the Republic: Liberté, Égalité, Fraternité. 2015. (Age of Revolution Ser.). (ENG.). 128p. (YA). (gr. 9-10). 70.50 *(978-1-68048-024-5(3),* Britannica Educational Publishing) Rosen Publishing Group, Inc., The.

McNeil, Niki, et al. HOCPP 1060 the French Revolution. 2006. spiral bd. 20.00 *(978-1-60308-060-6(0))* In the Hands of a Child.

Nardo, Don. The French Revolution. 2008. (World History Ser.). (ENG., Illus.). 104p. (YA). (gr. 7-10). 34.95 *(978-1-4205-0098-1(8),* Lucent Bks.) Cengage Gale.

Peal, Robert. KS3 History the French Revolution. 2017. (Knowing History Ser.). (ENG.). 16p. (J). (gr. 6-9). 3.99 *(978-0-00-819540-3(4))* HarperCollins Pubs. Ltd. GBR. Dist: Independent Pubs. Group.

Pipe, Jim. Be an Aristocrat in the French Revolution! A Horrible Time in Paris You'd Rather Avoid. Antram, David, illus. 2007. (You Wouldn't Want to...: History of the World Ser.). (ENG.). 32p. (J). (gr. 2-5). 29.00 *(978-0-531-18745-6(4),* Watts, Franklin) Scholastic Library Publishing.

Riggs, Kate. The French Revolution. 2009. (Days of Change Ser.). (Illus.). 48p. (YA). (gr. 4-7). 22.95 *(978-1-58341-734-8(6))* Creative Co., The.

—The French Revolution: Days of Change. 2015. (Illus.). 80p. (J). *(978-1-60818-526-9(5),* Creative Education) Creative Co., The.

—The French Revolution: Odysseys in History. 2016. (Odysseys in History Ser.). (ENG., Illus.). 80p. (J). (gr. 7-10). pap. 14.99 *(978-1-62832-127-2(X),* Creative Paperbacks) Creative Co., The.

Schwartz, Heather. The French Revolution: Terror & Triumph, 1 vol. 2012. (Primary Source Readers Ser.). (ENG.). 32p. (J). (gr. 5-5). pap. 8.99 *(978-1-4333-5011-5(4))* Teacher Created Materials, Inc.

Sebag-Montefiore, Mary, ed. Tale of Two Cities: Internet-Referenced. Ablett, Barry, illus. 2009. (Young Reading 3 Ser.). 64p. (J). 6.99 *(978-0-7945-2319-0(6),* Usborne) EDC Publishing.

FRANCE—HISTORY—REVOLUTION, 1789-1799—FICTION

Bradley, Kimberly Brubaker. The Lacemaker & the Princess. 2009. (ENG.). 208p. (J). (gr. 3-7). pap. 7.99 *(978-1-4169-8583-9(2),* McElderry, Margaret K. Bks.) McElderry, Margaret K. Bks.

Coatsworth, Elizabeth Jane. The Fair American. Sewell, Helen, illus. 2005. (Sally (Bethlehem Books) Ser.). 137p. (J). pap. 11.95 *(978-1-883937-85-0(X))* Bethlehem Bks.

Dickens, Charles. A Tale of Two Cities: A Classic Retelling. 2006. (Classic Retelling Ser.). (Illus.). 240p. (YA). (gr. 8-12). *(978-0-618-03150-4(2),* 2-00144) Holt McDougal.

Dickens, Charles & Hawksley, L. Dickens. A Tale of Two Cities. 2004. (Paperback Classics Ser.). 144p. (J). pap. 4.95 *(978-0-7945-0390-1(X));* lib. bdg. 12.95 *(978-1-58086-515-9(1))* EDC Publishing.

Duble, Kathleen Benner. Madame Tussaud's Apprentice: An Untold Story of Love in the French Revolution. 2014. (ENG.). 224p. (YA). 17.99 *(978-1-4405-8116-8(9),* Simon Pulse) Simon Pulse.

Elliott, Patricia. The Pale Assassin. 320p. (YA). 2010. (ENG.). (gr. 6-18). pap. 8.95 *(978-0-8234-2312-5(3))* 2009. (gr. 7-18). 17.95 *(978-0-8234-2250-0(X))* Holiday Hse., Inc.

Gardner, Sally. The Red Necklace. 2009. (ENG.). 400p. (YA). (gr. 7-18). 8.99 *(978-0-14-241488-0(3),* Speak) Penguin Young Readers Group.

—The Red Necklace: A Story of the French Revolution. l.t. ed. 2008. 583p. 23.95 *(978-1-4104-1016-0(1))* Thorndike Pr.

—The Silver Blade. 2010. (ENG.). 384p. (YA). (gr. 7-18). 8.99 *(978-0-14-241731-7(9),* Speak) Penguin Young Readers Group.

Higgins, Joanna. Waiting for the Queen: A Novel of Early America. 2013. (ENG.). 256p. (J). (gr. 4-10). 16.95 *(978-1-57131-700-1(7))* Milkweed Editions.

MacColl, Michaela. Secrets in the Snow: A Novel of Intrigue & Romance. 2016. (ENG., Illus.). 288p. (YA). (gr. 7-12). 16.99 *(978-1-4521-3358-4(1))* Chronicle Bks. LLC.

Meyer, Carolyn. The Bad Queen: Rules & Instructions for Marie-Antoinette. 2011. (Young Royals Ser.). (ENG.). 432p. (YA). (gr. 7). pap. 9.99 *(978-0-547-48249-1(3))* Houghton Mifflin Harcourt Publishing Co.

Orczy, Emmuska. The Gallant Pimpernel - Unabridged - Lord Tony's Wife, the Way of the Scarlet Pimpernel, Sir Percy Leads the Band, the Triumph of the Scarlet Pimpernel. 2012. 804p. *(978-1-78139-227-0(7))* Benediction Classics.

—I Will Repay. 2008. 168p. pap. 13.95 *(978-1-60664-230-6(8))* Rodgers, Alan Bks.

—The League of the Scarlet Pimpernel. 2008. 200p. 27.95 *(978-1-60664-797-4(0))* Aegypan.

—The Scarlet Pimpernel. 2016. (J). pap. *(978-1-5124-2624-3(5))* Lerner Publishing Group.

Rees, Celia. Sovay. 2010. (ENG.). 432p. (YA). (gr. 7). pap. 9.99 *(978-1-59990-483-2(7),* 9781599904832, Bloomsbury USA Childrens) Bloomsbury Publishing USA.

—Sovay. 2009. 1.00 *(978-1-4074-4516-8(2))* Recorded Bks., Inc.

Stevens, Dan. The Magic of the Brass Ring. 2009. 84p. pap. 19.95 *(978-1-4489-7759-8(2))* America Star Bks.

A Tale of Two Cities. abr. ed. (ARA., Illus.). 48p. (J). 12.00 *(978-0-86685-627-0(7))* International Bk. Ctr., Inc.

Williams, Maiya. The Golden Hour. 2006. (ENG.). 288p. (J). (gr. 5-10). per. 5.95 *(978-0-8109-9216-0(7))* Abrams, Inc.

FRANCE—HISTORY—1799-1914—FICTION

Meyer, L. A. My Bonny Light Horseman: Being an Account of the Further Adventures of Jacky Faber, in Love & War. 2010. (Bloody Jack Adventures Ser.: 6). (ENG., Illus.). 448p. (YA). (gr. 7). pap. 9.99 *(978-0-547-32794-5(3))* Houghton Mifflin Harcourt Publishing Co.

FRANCE—HISTORY—CONSULATE AND FIRST EMPIRE, 1799-1815—FICTION

Bill, Alfred Hoyt & Darlington, Franklin. Highroads of Peril: Being the Adventures of Franklin Darlington. 2012. 342p. 51.95 *(978-1-258-23792-9(X));* pap. 36.95 *(978-1-258-24525-2(6))* Literary Licensing, LLC.

Meyer, L. A. My Bonny Light Horseman: Being an Account of the Further Adventures of Jacky Faber, in Love & War. 2008. (Bloody Jack Adventures Ser.: 6). (ENG., Illus.). 448p. (YA). (gr. 7-18). 17.00 *(978-0-15-206187-6(8))* Houghton Mifflin Harcourt Publishing Co.

FRANCE—HISTORY—GERMAN OCCUPATION, 1940-1945

Draper, Allison Stark. Pastor Andre Trocme: Spiritual Leader of the French Village, Le Chambon. 2005. (Holocaust Biographies Ser.). (Illus.). 112p. (YA). (gr. 7-12). lib. bdg. 34.60 *(978-0-8239-3378-5(4))* Rosen Publishing Group, Inc., The.

—Pastor André Trocmé: Spiritual Leader of the French Village le Chambon. 2009. (Holocaust Biographies Ser.). 112p. (gr. 7-12). 63.90 *(978-1-61513-390-1(9))* Rosen Publishing Group, Inc., The.

FRANCE—HISTORY—GERMAN OCCUPATION, 1940-1945—FICTION

Barry, Rick. Gunner's Run: A World War II Novel. 2007. 215p. (YA). (gr. 8-12). per. 8.99 *(978-1-59166-761-2(5))* BJU Pr.

Bradley, Kimberly Brubaker. For Freedom: The Story of a French Spy. 2005. 181p. 16.00 *(978-0-7569-5091-0(0))* Perfection Learning Corp.

—For Freedom: The Story of a French Spy. 2005. (ENG.). 192p. (YA). (gr. 7-9). mass mkt. 5.99 *(978-0-440-41831-3(3),* Laurel Leaf) Random Hse. Children's Bks.

Burnford, Sheila. Bel Ria: Dog of War. 2006. (New York Review Children's Collection). (ENG.). 256p. (J). (gr. 4-7). 17.95 *(978-1-59017-211-7(6),* NYR Children's Collection) New York Review of Bks., Inc., The.

Calkhoven, Laurie. Michael at the Invasion of France 1943, 3 vols. 2012. (Boys of Wartime Ser.: 3). (ENG.). 240p. (J). (gr. 4-7). 16.99 *(978-0-8037-3724-2(6),* Dial Bks) Penguin Young Readers Group.

Dauvillier, Loïc & Salsedo, Greg. Hidden. Lizano, Marc, illus. 2014. (ENG.). 80p. (J). (gr. 1-5). 16.99 *(978-1-59643-873-6(8),* 9781596438736, First Second Bks.) Roaring Brook Pr.

Elliott, L. M. Under a War-Torn Sky. 2003. (J). (gr. 7-12). lib. bdg. 17.20 *(978-0-613-69092-8(3),* Turtleback) Turtleback Bks.

Graber, Janet. Resistance. 2005. 144p. (YA). 15.95 *(978-0-7614-5214-0(1))* Marshall Cavendish Corp.

Jablonski, Carla. Victory: Resistance Book 3. Purvis, Leland, illus. 2012. (Resistance Ser.: 3). (ENG.). 128p. (YA). (gr. 7-3). pap. 17.99 *(978-1-59643-293-2(4),* 9781596432932, First Second Bks.) Roaring Brook Pr.

McAllister, Cameron. The Tin Snail. Usher, Sam, illus. 2016. (ENG.). 288p. (J). (gr. 4-7). 16.99 *(978-0-553-53638-6(9),* Delacorte Bks. for Young Readers) Random Hse. Children's Bks.

Polacco, Patricia. The Butterfly. 2009. (ENG.). 48p. (J). (gr. 1-4). pap. 7.99 *(978-0-14-241306-7(2),* Puffin Books) Penguin Young Readers Group.

Wein, Elizabeth. Code Name Verity. (ENG.). (YA). (gr. 9-17). 2013. 368p. pap. 9.99 *(978-1-4231-5288-0(3))* 2012. 352p. 16.99 *(978-1-4231-5219-4(0))* Hyperion Pr.

—Code Name Verity. 2013. (YA). lib. bdg. 20.85 *(978-0-606-31760-3(0),* Turtleback) Turtleback Bks.

Yolen, Jane. Stone Angel. Green, Katie May, illus. 2015. (ENG.). 40p. (J). (gr. k-3). 16.99 *(978-0-399-16741-6(2),* Philomel Bks.) Penguin Young Readers Group.

FRANCE—SOCIAL LIFE AND CUSTOMS

Coster, Patience. My Life in France. 2015. (J). pap. *(978-1-62713-332-6(1))* Cavendish Square Publishing.

Dubowski, Mark. Discovery in the Cave. Barnard, Bryn, illus. 2010. (Step into Reading Ser.). (ENG.). 48p. (J). (gr. 2-4). pap. 3.99 *(978-0-375-85893-2(8),* Random Hse. Bks. for Young Readers) Random Hse. Children's Bks.

Elgin, Kathy. France. 2008. (Costume Around the World Ser.). (Illus.). 32p. (gr. 4-6). 28.00 *(978-0-7910-9766-3(8),* Chelsea Clubhouse) Facts On File, Inc.

—France. 2010. (World of Food Ser.). 32p. (YA). (gr. 4-7). lib. bdg. 24.95 *(978-1-934545-10-2(4))* Oliver Pr., Inc.

Garratt, Richard. France, Vol. 12. 2015. (Major Nations in a Global World: Tradition, Culture, & Daily Life Ser.). (Illus.). 64p. (J). (gr. 7). 23.95 *(978-1-4222-3343-6(X))* Mason Crest.

Klepeis, Alicia. France. 2016. (Exploring World Cultures Ser.). 32p. (J). lib. bdg. 28.50 *(978-1-5026-2144-3(4))* Cavendish Square Publishing.

Manning, Jack. Christmas in France, 1 vol. 2013. (Christmas Around the World Ser.). (ENG.). 24p. (gr. 1-2). 25.32 *(978-1-4765-3102-1(1),* First Facts) Capstone Press of Coughlan Cos.

McKay, Susan. France. 2010. (Festivals of the World Ser.). 32p. (gr. 3). 28.50 *(978-1-60870-099-8(2))* Marshall Cavendish Corp.

Mitchell, Alycen. France. 2004. (Cultures & Costumes Ser.). (Illus.). 64p. (YA). (gr. 7-18). lib. bdg. 19.95 *(978-1-59084-442-7(4),* 1247999) Mason Crest.

Parks, Peggy J. Foods of France. 2005. (Taste of Culture Ser.). (ENG., Illus.). 64p. (gr. 3-6). lib. bdg. 35.20 *(978-0-7377-3032-6(3))* Cengage Gale.

Peppas, Lynn. Cultural Traditions in France. 2014. (ENG., Illus.). 32p. (J). *(978-0-7787-0302-0(9))* Crabtree Publishing Co.

Roholt, Christine VeLure. Foods of France. 2014. (Cook with Me Ser.). (ENG., Illus.). 24p. (J). (gr. 3-7). lib. bdg. 25.95 *(978-1-62617-117-6(3),* Express Bks.) Bellwether Media.

Scarry, Huck. Life on a Farm: A Sketchbook. (J). 16.95 *(978-0-945912-32-3(3))* Pippin Pr.

Sexton, Colleen & Grack, Rachel. France. 2010. (Exploring Countries Ser.). (ENG., Illus.). 32p. (J). (gr. 3-7). lib. bdg. 26.95 *(978-1-60014-480-6(2),* Blastoff! Readers) Bellwether Media.

Streissguth, Thomas. France. 2008. (Country Explorers Ser.). (J). (gr. 2-5). 27.93 *(978-0-8225-9412-3(9))* Lerner Publishing Group.

Teacher Created Resources Staff. France: Come on a Journey of Discovery. 2008. (Qeb Travel Through Ser.). (ENG., Illus.). 32p. (gr. 4-7). pap. 7.99 *(978-1-4206-8282-3(2))* Teacher Created Resources, Inc.

FRANCIS, OF ASSISI, SAINT, 1182-1226

Billington, Rachel. The Life of Saint Francis. (Illus.). 48p. pap. 11.99 *(978-0-340-71427-0(1))* Hodder & Stoughton GBR. Dist: Trafalgar Square Publishing.

De Roma, Giuseppino. Francis of Assisi. (Illus.). 31p. 7.95 *(978-1-875570-64-5(0))* St Pauls Pubns. AUS. Dist: St Pauls/Alba Hse. Pubs.

Demi. Saint Francis of Assisi. 2012. (ENG., Illus.). 56p. (J). (gr. -1-3). 19.95 *(978-1-937786-04-5(8))* World Wisdom, Inc.

Gray, Tricia. The Wondrous Adventures of St. Francis of Assisi. rev. ed. 2003. (Illus.). 164p. (J). pap. 14.95 *(978-0-86716-480-0(8))* Franciscan Media.

Matas, Toni. Saint Francis of Assisi, Messenger of Peace. Picanyol, illus. 2013. 64p. (J). 8.95 *(978-0-8198-7297-5(0))* Pauline Bks. & Media.

Streit, Jakob. Brother Francis: The Life of Francis of Assisi. Kuettel, Nina, tr. from GER. 2013. (ENG., Illus.). 56p. (J). pap. 10.00 *(978-1-936367-40-5(8))* Waldorf Publications.

Visconti, Guido. Clare & Francis. Landmann, Bimba, illus. 2004. 40p. 20.00 *(978-0-8028-5269-4(6))* Eerdmans, William B. Publishing Co.

FRANCIS, OF ASSISI, SAINT, 1182-1226—FICTION

Campbell, Jeffrey. St. Francis & the Christmas Miracle of Greccio. Bianco, Francesca, illus. 2014. (ENG.). 28p. (J). 14.95 *(978-0-9796766-3-5(0),* Tau Publishing) Vesuvius Pr. Inc.

Hendey, Lisa M. The Whisper in the Ruins. Bower, Jenn, illus. 2016. (Chime Travelers Ser.: 3). (ENG.). 128p. (gr. 2-5). pap. 6.99 *(978-1-63253-036-3(8),* Servant Bks.) Franciscan Media.

Joslin, Mary. Saint Francis: The Good Man of Assisi. Wisenfeld, Alison, illus. 2015. (ENG.). 32p. (J). (gr. k-4). 9.99 *(978-0-7459-6492-8(3))* Lion Hudson PLC GBR. Dist: Independent Pubs. Group.

Langton, Jane P. Saint Francis & the Wolf. Plume, Ilse, illus. 2007. (ENG.). 32p. (J). (gr. -1-3). 16.95 *(978-1-56792-320-9(8))* Godine, David R. Pub.

Mora, Pat. The Song of Francis & the Animals. Frampton, David, illus. 2005. 32p. (J). (gr. -1-2). 16.00 *(978-0-8028-5253-3(X))* Eerdmans, William B. Publishing Co.

Nobisso, Josephine. Francis Woke up Early. Hyde, Maureen, illus. 2011. (ENG.). 32p. (J). (gr. k-2). 17.95 *(978-0-940112-20-9(5));* pap. 9.95 *(978-0-940112-22-3(1))* Gingerbread Hse.

O'Dell, Scott. The Road to Damietta. 2004. (ENG.). 320p. (YA). (gr. 7). pap. 17.99 *(978-0-618-49493-4(6))* Houghton Mifflin Harcourt Publishing Co.

Strasser, Myrna A. Saint Francis & the Nativity, 1 vol. Bianchi, Fausto, illus. 2010. (ENG.). 40p. (J). (gr. -1-2). 16.99 *(978-0-310-70890-2(7))* Zonderkidz.

Welborn, Amy. Adventures in Assisi: on the Path with St. Francis: On the Path with St. Francis. Engelhart, Ann Kissane, illus. 2014. (ENG.). 32p. (J). (gr. k-3). 15.99 *(978-1-61636-650-6(8))* Franciscan Media.

FRANCISCANS

Anderson, Zachary. Discovering Mission La Purísima Concepción. 2014. (California Missions Ser.). (Illus.). 48p. (J). (gr. 4-6). lib. bdg. 31.36 *(978-1-62713-094-3(2))* Cavendish Square Publishing.

—Discovering Mission Nuestra Señora de la Soledad. 2014. (California Missions Ser.). 48p. (J). (gr. 4-6). 31.36 *(978-1-62713-079-0(9))* Cavendish Square Publishing.

—Discovering Mission San Antonio de Padua. 2014. (California Missions Ser.). (Illus.). 48p. (J). (gr. 4-6). lib. bdg. 31.36 *(978-1-62713-082-0(9))* Cavendish Square Publishing.

Buckley, Jeannette. Discovering Mission San Juan Capistrano. 2016. (California Missions Ser.). (ENG.). 48p. (J). (gr. 4-4). pap. 12.95 *(978-1-5026-1217-5(8))* Cavendish Square Publishing.

—Discovering Mission San Luis Obispo de Tolosa. 2014. (California Missions Ser.). (Illus.). 48p. (J). (gr. 4-6). lib. bdg. 31.36 *(978-1-62713-091-2(8))* Cavendish Square Publishing.

—Discovering Mission San Luis Rey de Francia. (California Missions Ser.). 48p. (J). (gr. 4-4). 2016. (ENG.). pap. 12.95 *(978-1-5026-1226-7(7))* 2014. 31.36 *(978-1-62713-112-4(4))* Cavendish Square Publishing.

Cantillo, Oscar. Discovering Mission San Fernando Rey de España. (California Missions Ser.). 48p. (J). (gr. 4-4). 2016. (ENG.). pap. 12.95 *(978-1-5026-1224-3(0))* 2014. lib. bdg. 31.36 *(978-1-62713-106-3(X))* Cavendish Square Publishing.

—Discovering Mission San Francisco de Asís. 2014. (J). lib. bdg. *(978-1-62713-061-5(6))* Musa Publishing.

—Discovering Mission San Francisco Solano. 2016. (California Missions Ser.). (ENG.). 48p. (J). (gr. 4-4). pap. 12.95 *(978-1-5026-1207-6(0))* Cavendish Square Publishing.

Ching, Jacqueline. Mission San Rafael Arcangel. 2003. (Missions of California Ser.). 64p. (J). 26.50 *(978-0-8239-5886-3(8),* PowerKids Pr.) Rosen Publishing Group, Inc., The.

—Mission Santa Ines. 2009. (Missions of California Ser.). 64p. (gr. 4-4). 58.50 *(978-1-60854-042-6(1),* PowerKids Pr.) Rosen Publishing Group, Inc., The.

Ching, Jacqueline & Connelly, Jack. Discovering Mission San Rafael Arcángel. 2014. (California Missions Ser.). (Illus.). 48p. (J). (gr. 4-6). lib. bdg. 31.36 *(978-1-62713-058-5(6))* Cavendish Square Publishing.

Connelly, Jack. Discovering Mission Santa Bárbara. 2014. (California Missions Ser.). 48p. (J). (gr. 4-6). lib. bdg. 31.36 *(978-1-62713-100-1(0))* Cavendish Square Publishing.

Dickmann, Nancy. Earth's Landforms. 2016. (Earth Figured Out Ser.). (ENG., Illus.). 32p. (J). (gr. 4-4). pap. 10.58 *(978-1-5026-0866-6(9),* 1399805) Cavendish Square Publishing.

Ditchfield, Christin. Spanish Missions. 2006. (True Bks.). (Illus.). 48p. (J). (gr. 3-7). pap. 6.95 *(978-0-516-21746-8(1),* Children's Pr.) Scholastic Library Publishing.

Draper, Allison Stark. Mission San Francisco de Solano. 2003. (Missions of Californiatm Ser.). (Illus.). 64p. (J). (gr. 4-18). 26.50 *(978-0-8239-5884-9(1))* Rosen Publishing Group, Inc., The.

Edgar, Kathleen J. & Edgar, Susan E. Mission San Carlos Borromeo Del Rio Carmelo. 2003. (Missions of Californiatm Ser.). (Illus.). 64p. (YA). (gr. 4-7). 26.50 *(978-0-8239-5890-0(6))* Rosen Publishing Group, Inc., The.

—Mission San Francisco de Asis. 2003. (Missions of Californiatm Ser.). (Illus.). 64p. (J). (gr. 4-18). 26.50 *(978-0-8239-5887-0(6))* Rosen Publishing Group, Inc., The.

Edgar, Kathleen J., et al. Discovering Mission San Juan Capistrano. 2014. (California Missions Ser.). (Illus.). 48p. (J). (gr. 4-6). lib. bdg. 31.36 *(978-1-62713-085-1(3))* Cavendish Square Publishing.

—Discovering Mission San Miguel Arcángel. 2014. (California Missions Ser.). 48p. (J). (gr. 4-6). lib. bdg. 31.36 *(978-1-62713-088-2(8))* Cavendish Square Publishing.

Gasnick, Roy M. & Grycan, Julien. Serra: American Founding Father. 2010. (ENG., Illus.). 35p. pap. 2.95 *(978-0-86716-942-3(7))* Franciscan Media.

Gendell, Megan. Spanish Missions of California. 2010. (True Book(tm), a — Spanish Missions Ser.). (Illus.). 48p. (J). (gr. 2-5). 31.00 *(978-0-531-20577-8(0))* Scholastic Library Publishing.

—The Spanish Missions of California. 2010. (True Book Ser.). (ENG.). 48p. (J). (gr. 3-5). pap. 6.95 *(978-0-531-21240-0(8),* Children's Pr.) Scholastic Library Publishing.

—The Spanish Missions of Texas. 2010. (True Book(tm), a — Spanish Missions Ser.). (ENG.). 48p. (J). (gr. 2-5). 31.00 *(978-0-531-20580-8(0));* (Illus.). pap. 6.95 *(978-0-531-21243-1(2))* Scholastic Library Publishing.

Hamilton, Sam. Discovering Mission San Buenaventura. 2014. (California Missions Ser.). 48p. (J). (gr. 4-6). lib. bdg. 31.36 *(978-1-62713-103-2(5))* Cavendish Square Publishing.

—Discovering Mission San Diego de Alcalá. 2014. (California Missions Ser.). 48p. (J). (gr. 4-6). lib. bdg. 31.36 *(978-1-62713-109-4(4))* Cavendish Square Publishing.

Hamilton, Sam C. Discovering Mission San Buenaventura. 2016. (California Missions Ser.). (ENG.). 48p. (J). (gr. 4-4). pap. 12.95 *(978-1-5026-1223-6(2))* Cavendish Square Publishing.

Hardwick, Michael R. La Purisima Concepcion: The Enduring History of a California Mission. 2015. (Brief History Ser.). (ENG., Illus.). 144p. pap. 19.99 *(978-1-62619-984-2(1),* History Pr., The) Arcadia Publishing.

Herrera, Matthew D. History Guide to Old Mission San Luis Obispo de Tolosa. 2003. (Illus.). 77p. 9.95 *(978-0-9723720-1-5(6))* Tixlini Scriptorium, Inc.

Levy, Janey & Donnell, Kerri. The Missions of Texas. 2010. (Spotlight on Texas Ser.). (Illus.). 32p. (J). (gr. 3-4). (ENG.).

pap. 11.75 *(978-1-61532-456-9(9))*; 25.25 *(978-1-61532-465-1(8))* Rosen Publishing Group, Inc., The.

Lyon, Robin. The Spanish Missions of Arizona. 2010. (True Book(tm), a — Spanish Missions Ser.). 48p. (J). (gr. 2-5). 31.00 *(978-0-531-20576-1(2))*; (ENG.). pap. 6.95 *(978-0-531-21239-4(4))* Scholastic Library Publishing.

—Spanish Missions of New Mexico. 2010. (True Book(tm), a — Spanish Missions Ser.). (ENG.). 48p. (J). (gr. 2-5). 31.00 *(978-0-531-20579-2(7))* Scholastic Library Publishing.

—The Spanish Missions of New Mexico. 2010. (True Book Ser.). (ENG.). 48p. (J). pap. 6.95 *(978-0-531-21242-4(4)*, Children's Pr.) Scholastic Library Publishing.

Margaret, Amy. Mission San Buenaventura. 2003. (Missions of Californiatm Ser.). (Illus.). 64p. (J). (gr. 4-18). 26.50 *(978-0-8239-5888-7(4))* Rosen Publishing Group, Inc., The.

—Mission Santa Barbara. (Missions of California Ser.). 64p. (gr. 4-4). 2009. 58.50 *(978-1-60854-037-2(5)*, PowerKids Pr.) 2003. (Illus.). (J). 26.50 *(978-0-8239-5880-1(9))* Rosen Publishing Group, Inc., The.

—Mission Santa Clara de Asis. 2003. (Missions of Californiatm Ser.). (Illus.). 64p. (J). (gr. 4-18). 26.50 *(978-0-8239-5883-2(3))* Rosen Publishing Group, Inc., The.

McGinty, Alice B. Mission San Gabriel Arcangel. 2003. (Missions of Californiatm Ser.). (Illus.). 64p. (J). (gr. 4-18). 26.50 *(978-0-8239-5892-4(2))* Rosen Publishing Group, Inc., The.

McGinty, Alice B. & Stevens, Madeline. Discovering Mission San Gabriel Arcángel. 2014. (California Missions Ser.). 48p. (J). (gr. 4-6). lib. bdg. 31.36 *(978-1-62713-115-5(9))* Cavendish Square Publishing.

Nuñes, Sofia. Discovering Mission Santa Clara de Asís. 2016. (California Missions Ser.). (ENG.). 48p. (J). (gr. 4-4). pap. 12.95 *(978-1-5026-1211-3(9))* Cavendish Square Publishing.

—Discovering Mission Santa Cruz. 2016. (California Missions Ser.). (ENG.). 48p. (J). (gr. 4-4). pap. 12.95 *(978-1-5026-1212-0(7))* Cavendish Square Publishing.

—Discovering Mission Santa Inés. 2014. (California Missions Ser.). (Illus.). 48p. (J). (gr. 4-6). lib. bdg. 31.36 *(978-1-62713-097-4(7))* Cavendish Square Publishing.

—Discovering Mission Santa Inés. 2016. (California Missions Ser.). (ENG.). 48p. (J). (gr. 4-4). pap. 12.95 *(978-1-5026-1221-2(6))* Cavendish Square Publishing.

Ostrow, Kim. Mission Nuestra Senora de la Soledad. 2003. (Missions of Californiatm Ser.). (Illus.). 64p. (J). (gr. 4-18). 26.50 *(978-0-8239-5882-5(5))* Rosen Publishing Group, Inc., The.

—Mission Santa Cruz. 2009. (Missions of California Ser.). 64p. (gr. 4-4). 58.50 *(978-1-60854-041-9(3)*, PowerKids Pr.) Rosen Publishing Group, Inc., The.

Ostrow, Kim & Nuñes, Sofia. Discovering Mission Santa Cruz. 2014. (California Missions Ser.). (Illus.). 48p. (J). (gr. 4-6). lib. bdg. 31.36 *(978-1-62713-070-7(5))* Cavendish Square Publishing.

Perritano, John. Spanish Missions. 2010. (True Book(tm), a — Spanish Missions Ser.). (Illus.). 48p. (J). (gr. 2-5). 31.00 *(978-0-531-20575-4(4))*; pap. 6.95 *(978-0-531-21238-7(6))* Scholastic Library Publishing.

Serafin, Kim. Mission San Antonio de Padua. 2003. (Missions of Californiatm Ser.). (Illus.). 64p. (J). (gr. 4-18). 26.50 *(978-0-8239-5891-7(4))* Rosen Publishing Group, Inc., The.

Stevens, Madeline. Discovering Mission San Juan Bautista. 2014. (California Missions Ser.). (Illus.). 48p. (J). (gr. 4-6). lib. bdg. 31.36 *(978-1-62713-073-8(X))* Cavendish Square Publishing.

Suben, Eric. The Spanish Missions of Florida. 2010. (True Book(tm), a — Spanish Missions Ser.). 48p. (J). (gr. 2-5). 31.00 *(978-0-531-20578-5(9))*; (gr. 3-5). pap. 6.95 *(978-0-531-21241-7(6))* Scholastic Library Publishing.

Williams, Jack S. Padres of the California Mission Frontier. 2009. (People of the California Missions Ser.). 64p. (gr. 4-4). 58.50 *(978-1-60851-158-7(8)*, PowerKids Pr.) Rosen Publishing Group, Inc., The.

Williams, Jack S. & Davis, Thomas L. Padres of the California Mission Frontier. 2004. (People of the California Missions Ser.). (Illus.). 64p. (J). lib. bdg. 26.50 *(978-0-8239-6283-9(0)*, PowerKids Pr.) Rosen Publishing Group, Inc., The.

FRANK, ANNE, 1929-1945

Abramson, Ann. Who Was Anne Frank? Harrison, Nancy, illus. 2007. (Who Was? Ser.). (ENG.). 112p. (J). (gr. 3-7). pap. 5.99 *(978-0-448-44482-6(8)*, Grosset & Dunlap) Penguin Young Readers Group.

—Who Was Anne Frank? Harrison, Nancy, illus. 2007. (Who Was... ? Ser.). 103p. (gr. 2-6). 15.00 *(978-0-7569-8166-2(2))* Perfection Learning Corp.

—Who Was Anne Frank? Harrison, Nancy, illus. 2007. (Who Was... ? Ser.). 103p. (J). (gr. 4-7). 16.00 *(978-1-4177-6854-7(1)*, Turtleback) Turtleback Bks.

Ashby, Ruth. Anne Frank: Young Diarist. 2005. 186p. (J). lib. bdg. 18.46 *(978-1-4242-2208-7(7))* Fitzgerald Bks.

—Anne Frank: Young Diarist. 2005. (Childhood of World Figures Ser.). (ENG.). 192p. (J). (gr. 3-7). pap. 7.99 *(978-0-689-87468-0(5)*, Aladdin) Simon & Schuster Children's Publishing.

Boas, Jacob. We Are Witnesses: Five Diaries of Teenagers Who Died in the Holocaust. 2009. (ENG.). 208p. (YA). (gr. 6-10). pap. 9.99 *(978-0-312-53567-4(8)*, 9780312535674) Square Fish.

Brown, Jonatha A. Anne Frank. 2004. (People to Know Ser.). (Illus.). 24p. (gr. 1-4). lib. bdg. 22.00 *(978-0-8368-4309-5(6)*, Weekly Reader Leveled Readers) Stevens, Gareth Publishing LLLP.

—Anne Frank. Acosta, Tatiana & Gutierrez, Guillermo, trs. 2004. (Gente Que Hay Que Conocer Ser.). (SPA., Illus.). 24p. (gr. 1-4). lib. bdg. 22.00 *(978-0-8368-4351-4(7)*, Weekly Reader Leveled Readers) Stevens, Gareth Publishing LLLP.

Brown, Jonatha A. & Goff, Elizabeth Hudson. Ana Frank. McHargue, D. et al, illus. 2007. (Biografías Gráficas (Graphic Biographies) Ser.). (SPA.). 32p. (gr. 5-8). lib. bdg. 27.00 *(978-0-8368-7880-6(9))* Stevens, Gareth Publishing LLLP.

—Anne Frank. Floor, Guus & Timmons, Jonathan, illus. 2006. (Graphic Biographies (World Almanac Library (Firm))). 32p. (gr. 5-8). lib. bdg. 27.00 *(978-0-8368-6196-9(5))* Stevens, Gareth Publishing LLLP.

Carney, Elizabeth & Zapruder, Alexandra. National Geographic Readers: Anne Frank. 2013. (Readers Bios Ser.). (ENG., Illus.). 48p. (J). (gr. 1-4). pap. 3.99 *(978-1-4263-1352-3(7))*; lib. bdg. 13.90 *(978-1-4263-1353-0(5))* National Geographic Society. (National Geographic Children's Bks.).

Colbert, David. Anne Frank. 2008. (10 Days Ser.). (ENG., Illus.). 160p. (J). (gr. 3-8). pap. 7.99 *(978-1-4169-6445-2(2)*, Aladdin) Simon & Schuster Children's Publishing.

Dunn, Joe. Anne Frank, 1 vol. 2007. (Bio-Graphics Ser.). (ENG., Illus.). 32p. (gr. 3-6). 28.50 *(978-1-60270-065-9(6)*, Graphic Planet- Nonfiction) ABDO Publishing Co.

Frank, Ana. The Diary of a Anne Frank. adapted ed. pap., tchr. ed. 4.95 *(978-0-8359-0138-3(6))* Globe Fearon Educational Publishing.

Gil, Carmen & Gali, Merce. Ana Frank. 2010. (Me Llamo... Ser.). (SPA., Illus.). 63p. (J). pap. *(978-84-342-3339-3(8))* Parramon Ediciones S.A.

Goff, Elizabeth Hudson & Brown, Jonatha A. Anne Frank. 2006. (Graphic Biographies (World Almanac Library (Firm))). (Illus.). 32p. (gr. 5-8). pap. 10.50 *(978-0-8368-6248-5(1))* Stevens, Gareth Publishing LLLP.

Heims, Neil. Reading the Diary of Anne Frank. 2005. (Engaged Reader Ser.). (Illus.). 104p. (gr. 5-8). lib. bdg. 25.00 *(978-0-7910-8829-6(4)*, Chelsea Hse.) Facts On File, Inc.

Hermann, Spring. Anne Frank: Hope in the Shadows of the Holocaust. 2005. (Holocaust Heroes & Nazi Criminals Ser.). (Illus.). 160p. (YA). (gr. 6-12). lib. bdg. 29.27 *(978-0-7660-2531-8(4))* Enslow Pubs., Inc.

Hollingsworth, Tamara. Anne Frank: A Light in the Dark, 1 vol. 2nd rev. ed. 2013. (Nonfiction Readers Ser.). (ENG., Illus.). 48p. (J). (gr. 4-4). pap. 29.96 *(978-1-4807-1117-4(9))* Shell Educational Publishing.

—Anne Frank: A Light in the Dark, 1 vol. 2nd rev. ed. 2012. (TIME for KIDS(r) Nonfiction Readers Ser.). (ENG.). 48p. (J). (gr. 4-4). pap. 9.99 *(978-1-4333-4865-5(9))* Teacher Created Materials, Inc.

—Anne Frank: Una Luz en la Oscuridad. 2017. (TIME for Kids en Español - Level 4 Ser.). (SPA & ENG., Illus.). 48p. (gr. 4-4). lib. bdg. 31.99 *(978-1-5157-5146-5(5))* Time for Kids Inc AUS. Dist: Capstone Pub.

Hudson Goff, Elizabeth & Brown, Jonatha A. Ana Frank. 2007. (Biografías Graficas (Graphic Biographies) Ser.). (SPA.). 32p. (gr. 5-8). pap. 10.50 *(978-0-8368-7887-5(6))* Stevens, Gareth Publishing LLLP.

Killcoyne, Hope Lourie. Anne Frank: Heroic Diarist of the Holocaust, 01 vols., 1. 2016. (Britannica Beginner Bios Ser.). (ENG., Illus.). 32p. (J). pap. 12.90 *(978-1-5081-0061-4(6)*, Britannica Educational Publishing) Rosen Publishing Group, Inc., The.

Kramer, Ann. Anne Frank: The Young Writer Who Told the World Her Story. (National Geographic World History Biographies Ser.). (ENG., Illus.). 64p. (J). (gr. 3-7). 2009. 7.99 *(978-1-4263-0414-9(5))* 2007. 17.95 *(978-1-4263-0004-2(2))* 2007. lib. bdg. 27.90 *(978-1-4263-0005-9(0))* National Geographic Society. (National Geographic Children's Bks.).

Lee, Carol Ann. Anne Frank & the Children of the Holocaust. 2008. (ENG., Illus.). 256p. (J). (gr. 5-18). 7.99 *(978-0-14-241069-1(1)*, Puffin Books) Penguin Young Readers Group.

Mara, Wil. Anne Frank: A Life in Hiding. 2016. (Rookie Biographies(tm) Ser.). (ENG., Illus.). 32p. (J). lib. bdg. 25.00 *(978-0-531-21683-5(7)*, Children's Pr.) Scholastic Library Publishing.

Mccann, Michelle Roehm & Welden, Amelie. Girls Who Rocked the World: From Anne Frank to Natalie Portman. 2012. lib. bdg. 22.10 *(978-0-606-26898-1(7)*, Turtleback) Turtleback Bks.

McDowell, Pamela. Anne Frank. 2014. (J). *(978-1-4896-2456-7(2))* Weigl Pubs., Inc.

Miklowitz, Gloria. Anne Frank. 2009. pap. 13.25 *(978-1-60559-053-0(3))* Hameray Publishing Group, Inc.

Poole, Josephine. Ana Frank. Barrett, Angela, illus. 2005. (SPA.). 32p. (J). (gr. 3-4). 17.99 *(978-1-930332-87-4(4))* Lectorum Pubns., Inc.

Van Maarsen, Jacqueline. A Friend Called Anne: One Girl's Story of War, Peace, & a Unique Friendship with Anne Frank. 2007. (Illus.). 163p. (J). (gr. 5-9). 14.65 *(978-0-7569-8146-4(8))* Perfection Learning Corp.

Van Maarsen, Jacqueline & Lee, Carol Ann. A Friend Called Anne. 2007. (ENG., Illus.). 176p. (J). (gr. 3-7). 6.99 *(978-0-14-240719-6(4)*, Puffin Books) Penguin Young Readers Group.

Waxman, Laura Hamilton. Anne Frank. 2009. (History Maker Biographies Ser.). (ENG.). 48p. (gr. 3-6). 27.93 *(978-0-7613-4221-2(4)*, Lerner Pubns.) Lerner Publishing Group.

Whiting, Jim. Anne Frank. 2007. (What's So Great About... ? Ser.). (Illus.). 32p. (YA). (gr. 2-4). lib. bdg. 25.70 *(978-1-58415-581-2(7))* Mitchell Lane Pubs., Inc.

FRANKENSTEIN (FICTITIOUS CHARACTER)—FICTION

Bradman, Tony. The Frankenstein Teacher. Kavanagh, Peter, illus. 2014. (Colour First Reader Ser.). (ENG.). 80p. (J). (gr. k-2). pap. 9.99 *(978-0-552-56899-9(6))* Transworld Publishers Ltd. GBR. Dist: Independent Pubs. Group.

Cheshire, Simon. The Frankenstein Inheritance. 2012. 204p. pap. *(978-0-9565049-7-5(3))* Cheshire, Simon.

Oppel, Kenneth. Such Wicked Intent. (ENG., 320p. (YA). (gr. 7). 2012. Illus.). 16.99 *(978-1-4424-0318-5(7))*Bk. 2. 2013. pap. 9.99 *(978-1-4424-0319-2(5))* Simon & Schuster Bks. For Young Readers. (Simon & Schuster Bks. For Young Readers).

Rex, Adam. Frankenstein Takes the Cake. 2012. (ENG., Illus.). 48p. (J). (gr. 1-4). pap. 7.99 *(978-0-547-85062-7(X))* Houghton Mifflin Harcourt Publishing Co.

Shelley, Mary. Frankenstein. Barr, Ken, illus. 2005. (Reader's Workshop Ser.). (ENG.). 80p. (C). pap. 17.95 *(978-0-7362-2793-3(8))* CENGAGE Learning.

—Frankenstein. Irving, Frazer, illus. 2005. 176p. (gr. 3-7). 21.00 *(978-0-7569-5809-1(1))* Perfection Learning Corp.

—Frankenstein. 2010. (ENG., Illus.). 28p. 29.95 *(978-0-7893-2085-8(1))* Universe Publishing.

—Frankenstein. Williams, Anthony, illus. 2014. (ENG.). 32p. pap. 8.95 *(978-1-78404-356-8(7))* Arcturus Publishing GBR. Dist: Bookmasters Distribution.

—Frankenstein. abr. ed. 2010. (Dover Classic Stories Coloring Book Ser.). (ENG.). 48p. (J). (gr. 3-8). pap. 4.99 *(978-0-486-47415-1(1))* Dover Pubns., Inc.

—Frankenstein: The Graphic Novel. 2010. (Classic Graphic Novel Collection). (ENG., Illus.). 144p. (YA). (gr. 7-12). 34.80 *(978-1-4205-0374-6(X))* Cengage Gale.

—Gris Grimly's Frankenstein. Grimly, Gris, illus. 2013. (ENG.). 208p. (YA). (gr. 8). 24.99 *(978-0-06-186297-7(5))* HarperCollins Pubs.

—Gris Grimly's Frankenstein. Grimly, Gris, illus. 2015. (ENG.). 208p. (YA). (gr. 8). pap. 16.99 *(978-0-06-186298-4(3))* HarperCollins Pubs.

Shelley, Mary & Shelley, Mary. Frankenstein. Jones, Barry, illus. 2004. (Paperback Classics Ser.). 144p. (J). pap. 4.95 *(978-0-7945-0090-0(0)*, Usborne) EDC Publishing.

—Frankenstein. (J). 9.95 *(978-1-56156-309-8(9))* Kidsbooks, LLC.

Sonnebom, Scott. The Frankenstein Journals: Guts or Bust. Banks, Timothy, illus. 2015. (Frankenstein Journals). (ENG.). 160p. (gr. 2-3). 9.95 *(978-1-4965-0223-0(X))* Stone Arch Bks.

—No Guts, No Gloria. Banks, Timothy, illus. 2015. (Frankenstein Journals). (ENG.). 80p. (gr. 2-3). 22.65 *(978-1-4965-0221-6(3))* Stone Arch Bks.

—A Pain in the Butt. Banks, Timothy, illus. 2015. (Frankenstein Journals). (ENG.). 80p. (gr. 2-3). 22.65 *(978-1-4965-0222-3(1))* Stone Arch Bks.

Weyn, Suzanne. Dr. Frankenstein's Daughters. 2013. (ENG.). 256p. (J). (gr. 7). 17.99 *(978-0-545-42533-9(6)*, Scholastic Pr.) Scholastic, Inc.

FRANKLIN (FICTITIOUS CHARACTER: BOURGEOIS)—FICTION

Bourgeois, Paulette. Benjamin et Sa Petite Soeur. 2004.Tr. of Franklin's Baby Sister. (FRE., Illus.). (J). (gr. k-3). spiral bd. *(978-0-616-14597-5(7))* Canadian National Institute for the Blind/Institut National Canadien pour les Aveugles.

—Finders Keepers for Franklin. Clark, Brenda, illus. 2013. (Franklin Ser.). (ENG.). 32p. (J). (gr. -1-3). pap. 5.95 *(978-1-77138-003-4(9))* Kids Can Pr., Ltd. CAN. Dist: Hachette Bk. Group.

—Franklin & Harriet. Clark, Brenda, illus. 2nd ed. 2011. (Franklin Ser.). (ENG.). 32p. (J). (gr. -1-3). pap. 5.95 *(978-1-55453-727-3(4))* Kids Can Pr., Ltd. CAN. Dist: Hachette Bk. Group.

—Franklin & the Thunderstorm. Clark, Brenda, illus. 2nd ed. 2011. (Franklin Ser.). (ENG.). 32p. (J). (gr. -1-3). pap. 5.95 *(978-1-55453-729-7(0))* Kids Can Pr., Ltd. CAN. Dist: Hachette Bk. Group.

—Franklin & the Tooth Fairy. Clark, Brenda, illus. 2nd ed. 2011. (Franklin Ser.). (ENG.). 32p. (J). (gr. -1-3). pap. 5.95 *(978-1-55453-734-1(7))* Kids Can Pr., Ltd. CAN. Dist: Hachette Bk. Group.

—Franklin Es un Mandon. Varela, Alejandra López, tr. Clark, Brenda, illus.Tr. of Franklin Is Bossy. (SPA.). 10.95 *(978-1-930332-16-4(5)*, LC6564) Lectorum Pubns., Inc.

—Franklin Fibs. Clark, Brenda, illus. 2nd ed. 2011. (Franklin Ser.). (ENG.). 32p. (J). (gr. -1-3). pap. 5.95 *(978-1-55453-774-7(6))* Kids Can Pr., Ltd. CAN. Dist: Hachette Bk. Group.

—Franklin Goes to School. Clark, Brenda, illus. 2013. (Franklin Ser.). (ENG.). 32p. (J). (gr. -1-3). pap. 5.95 *(978-1-77138-010-2(1))* Kids Can Pr., Ltd. CAN. Dist: Hachette Bk. Group.

—Franklin Goes to the Hospital. 2004. (Illus.). (J). (gr. -1-2). spiral bd. *(978-0-616-03024-0(X))*; spiral bd. *(978-0-616-04547-3(6))* Canadian National Institute for the Blind/Institut National Canadien pour les Aveugles.

—Franklin Has a Sleepover. Clark, Brenda, illus. 2nd ed. 2011. (Franklin Ser.). (ENG.). 32p. (J). (gr. -1-3). pap. 5.95 *(978-1-55453-736-5(3))* Kids Can Pr., Ltd. CAN. Dist: Hachette Bk. Group.

—Franklin in the Dark. 2004. (Illus.). (J). (gr. -1-2). spiral bd. *(978-0-616-01575-9(5))*; spiral bd. *(978-0-616-01574-2(7))* Canadian National Institute for the Blind/Institut National Canadien pour les Aveugles.

—Franklin in the Dark. Clark, Brenda, illus. 2013. (Franklin Ser.). (ENG.). 32p. (J). (gr. -1-3). pap. 5.95 *(978-1-77138-007-2(1))* Kids Can Pr., Ltd. CAN. Dist: Hachette Bk. Group.

—Franklin in the Dark: 25th Anniversary Edition. Clark, Brenda, illus. 2nd ed. 2011. (Franklin Ser.). (ENG.). 48p. (J). (gr. -1-3). 18.95 *(978-1-55453-616-0(2))* Kids Can Pr., Ltd. CAN. Dist: Hachette Bk. Group.

—Franklin Is Bossy. Clark, Brenda, illus. 2nd ed. 2011. (Franklin Ser.). (ENG.). 32p. (J). (gr. -1-3). 5.95 *(978-1-55453-785-3(1))* Kids Can Pr., Ltd. CAN. Dist: Hachette Bk. Group.

—Franklin Is Lost. Clark, Brenda, illus. 2nd ed. 2011. (Franklin Ser.). (ENG.). 32p. (J). (gr. -1-3). pap. 5.95 *(978-1-55453-735-8(5))* Kids Can Pr., Ltd. CAN. Dist: Hachette Bk. Group.

—Franklin Is Messy. Clark, Brenda, illus. 2013. (Franklin Ser.). (ENG.). 32p. (J). (gr. -1-3). pap. 5.95 *(978-1-77138-000-3(4))* Kids Can Pr., Ltd. CAN. Dist: Hachette Bk. Group.

—Franklin Rides a Bike. Clark, Brenda, illus. 2nd ed. 2011. (Franklin Ser.). (ENG.). 32p. (J). (gr. -1-3). pap. 5.95 *(978-1-55453-731-0(2))* Kids Can Pr., Ltd. CAN. Dist: Hachette Bk. Group.

—Franklin Says I Love You. 2004. (Illus.). (J). (gr. k-3). spiral bd. *(978-0-616-14561-6(6))*; spiral bd. *(978-0-616-14562-3(4))* Canadian National Institute for the Blind/Institut National Canadien pour les Aveugles.

—Franklin Says I Love You. Clark, Brenda, illus. 2nd ed. 2011. (Franklin Ser.). (ENG.). 32p. (J). (gr. -1-3). pap. 5.95 *(978-1-55453-728-0(2))* Kids Can Pr., Ltd. CAN. Dist: Hachette Bk. Group.

—Franklin Wants a Badge. Clark, Brenda, illus. 2003. (Franklin TV Storybook Ser.). (ENG.). 32p. (J). (gr. -1-3). 4.95 *(978-1-55337-468-8(1))*; 10.95 *(978-1-55337-467-1(3))* Kids Can Pr., Ltd. CAN. Dist: Hachette Bk. Group.

—Franklin Wants a Pet. Clark, Brenda, illus. 2013. (Franklin Ser.). (ENG.). 32p. (J). (gr. -1-3). pap. 5.95 *(978-1-77138-004-1(7))* Kids Can Pr., Ltd. CAN. Dist: Hachette Bk. Group.

—Franklin y el Dia de Accion de Gracias. Varela, Alejandra López, tr. Clark, Brenda, illus.Tr. of Franklin's Thanksgiving. (SPA.). (J). (gr. k-2). 10.95 *(978-1-930332-07-2(6)*, LC30184) Lectorum Pubns., Inc.

—Franklin's Baby Sister. 2004. (Illus.). (J). (gr. k-3). spiral bd. *(978-0-616-07218-9(X))* Canadian National Institute for the Blind/Institut National Canadien pour les Aveugles.

—Franklin's Baby Sister. Clark, Brenda, illus. (Franklin Ser.). (ENG.). 32p. (J). (gr. -1-3). *(978-1-55074-858-1(0))* Kids Can Pr., Ltd.

—Franklin's Baby Sister. Clark, Brenda, illus. 2013. (Franklin Ser.). (ENG.). 32p. (J). (gr. -1-3). pap. 5.95 *(978-1-77138-002-7(0))* Kids Can Pr., Ltd. CAN. Dist: Hachette Bk. Group.

—Franklin's Bad Day. Clark, Brenda, illus. 2nd ed. 2011. (Franklin Ser.). (ENG.). 32p. (J). (gr. -1-3). pap. 5.95 *(978-1-55453-732-7(0))* Kids Can Pr., Ltd. CAN. Dist: Hachette Bk. Group.

—Franklin's Blanket. Clark, Brenda, illus. 2nd ed. 2011. (Franklin Ser.). (ENG.). 32p. (J). (gr. -1-3). pap. 5.95 *(978-1-55453-733-4(9))* Kids Can Pr., Ltd. CAN. Dist: Hachette Bk. Group.

—Franklin's Christmas: A Sticker Activity Book. Clark, Brenda, illus. 2003. (ENG.). 16p. (J). 6.95 *(978-1-55337-561-6(0))*; 6.95 *(978-1-55337-506-7(8))* Kids Can Pr., Ltd. CAN. Dist: Hachette Bk. Group.

—Franklin's Christmas Gift. Clark, Brenda, illus. 2013. (Franklin Ser.). (ENG.). 32p. (J). (gr. -1-3). pap. 5.95 *(978-1-77138-001-0(2))* Kids Can Pr., Ltd. CAN. Dist: Hachette Bk. Group.

—Franklin's Class Trip. Clark, Brenda, illus. 2012. (Franklin Ser.). (ENG.). 32p. (J). (gr. -1-3). pap. 5.95 *(978-1-55453-936-9(6))* Kids Can Pr., Ltd. CAN. Dist: Hachette Bk. Group.

—Franklin's Family Treasury. Clark, Brenda, illus. 2003. (Franklin Ser.). (ENG.). 128p. (J). (gr. -1-3). 15.95 *(978-1-55337-479-4(7))* Kids Can Pr., Ltd. CAN. Dist: Hachette Bk. Group.

—Franklin's Halloween. Clark, Brenda, illus. 2nd ed. 2011. (Franklin Ser.). (ENG.). 32p. (J). (gr. -1-3). pap. 5.95 *(978-1-55453-786-0(X))* Kids Can Pr., Ltd. CAN. Dist: Hachette Bk. Group.

—Franklin's New Friend. Clark, Brenda, illus. (Franklin Ser.). (ENG.). 32p. (J). (gr. -1-3). *(978-1-55074-363-0(5))* Kids Can Pr., Ltd.

—Franklin's New Friend. 2004. (Illus.). (J). (gr. k-3). spiral bd. *(978-0-616-01590-2(9))*; spiral bd. *(978-0-616-01591-9(7))* Canadian National Institute for the Blind/Institut National Canadien pour les Aveugles.

—Franklin's New Friend. Clark, Brenda, illus. 2nd ed. 2011. (Franklin Ser.). (ENG.). 32p. (J). (gr. -1-3). pap. 5.95 *(978-1-55453-773-0(8))* Kids Can Pr., Ltd. CAN. Dist: Hachette Bk. Group.

—Franklin's School Play. Clark, Brenda, illus. 2012. (Franklin Ser.). (ENG.). 32p. (J). (gr. -1-3). pap. 5.95 *(978-1-55453-935-2(8))* Kids Can Pr., Ltd. CAN. Dist: Hachette Bk. Group.

—Franklin's Secret Club. 2004. (Illus.). (J). (gr. k-3). spiral bd. *(978-0-616-01594-0(1))*; spiral bd. *(978-0-616-01593-3(3))* Canadian National Institute for the Blind/Institut National Canadien pour les Aveugles.

—Franklin's Secret Club. Clark, Brenda, illus. 2012. (Franklin Ser.). (ENG.). 32p. (J). (gr. -1-3). pap. 5.95 *(978-1-55453-934-5(X))* Kids Can Pr., Ltd. CAN. Dist: Hachette Bk. Group.

—Fun with Franklin: A Learning to Read Book. Clark, Brenda, illus. (Franklin Ser.). (J). (gr. -1-3). *(978-1-55074-646-4(4))* Kids Can Pr., Ltd.

—Hurry up, Franklin. Clark, Brenda, illus. 2012. (Franklin Ser.). (ENG.). 32p. (J). (gr. -1-3). pap. 5.95 *(978-1-55453-819-5(X))* Kids Can Pr., Ltd. CAN. Dist: Hachette Bk. Group.

—Neighborhood. 2004. (Illus.). (J). (gr. k-3). spiral bd. *(978-0-616-01588-9(7))*; spiral bd. *(978-0-616-01589-6(5))* Canadian National Institute for the Blind/Institut National Canadien pour les Aveugles.

—Un Nouvel Ami pour Benjamin. 2004.Tr. of Franklin's New Friend. (FRE., Illus.). (J). (gr. -1-2). spiral bd. *(978-0-616-01828-6(2))* Canadian National Institute for the Blind/Institut National Canadien pour les Aveugles.

Bourgeois, Paulette & Clark, Brenda. Franklin & the Computer. 2003. (Franklin TV Storybook Ser.). (ENG., Illus.). 32p. (J). (gr. -1-3). 4.95 *(978-1-55337-363-6(4))* Kids Can Pr., Ltd. CAN. Dist: Hachette Bk. Group.

—Franklin & the Cookies. 2005. (Kids Can Read Ser.). (ENG., Illus.). 32p. (J). (gr. 1-2). 14.95 *(978-1-55337-716-0(8))* Kids Can Pr., Ltd. CAN. Dist: Hachette Bk. Group.

—Franklin & the Gecko Games. 2013. (Franklin & Friends Ser.). (ENG., Illus.). 24p. (J). (gr. -1-2). pap. 5.95 *(978-1-55453-966-6(8))* Kids Can Pr., Ltd. CAN. Dist: Hachette Bk. Group.

—Franklin & the Little Sisters. 2013. (Franklin & Friends Ser.). (ENG., Illus.). 24p. (J). (gr. -1-2). 5.95 *(978-1-894786-92-8(0))* Kids Can Pr., Ltd. CAN. Dist: Hachette Bk. Group.

—Franklin & the New Teacher. 2004. (Franklin TV Storybook Ser.). (ENG., Illus.). 32p. (J). (gr. -1-3). 4.95 *(978-1-55337-500-5(9))* Kids Can Pr., Ltd. CAN. Dist: Hachette Bk. Group.

—Franklin Celebrates. 2005. (Franklin TV Storybook Ser.). (ENG., Illus.). 32p. (J). (gr. -1-3). 10.95 *(978-1-55337-501-2(7))* Kids Can Pr., Ltd. CAN. Dist: Hachette Bk. Group.

—Franklin in the Stars. 2013. (Franklin & Friends Ser.). (ENG., Illus.). 24p. (J). (gr. -1-2). 5.95 *(978-1-55453-965-9(X))* Kids Can Pr., Ltd. CAN. Dist: Hachette Bk. Group.

—Franklin Stays Up. Sinker, Alice, illus. 2003. (Kids Can Read Ser.). (ENG.). 32p. (J). (gr. 1-2). 3.95 *(978-1-55337-372-8(3))*; 14.95 *(978-1-55337-371-1(5))* Kids Can Pr., Ltd. CAN. Dist: Hachette Bk. Group.

—Franklin the Detective. 2004. (Kids Can Read Ser.). (ENG., Illus.). 32p. (J). (gr. 1-2). 14.95 *(978-1-55337-497-8(5))* Kids Can Pr., Ltd. CAN. Dist: Hachette Bk. Group.

—Franklin's Pumpkin. Southern, Shelley, illus. 2004. (Kids Can Read Ser.). (ENG.). 32p. (J). (gr. 1-2). 3.95 *(978-1-55337-496-1(7))*; 14.95 *(978-1-55337-495-4(9))* Kids Can Pr., Ltd. CAN. Dist: Hachette Bk. Group.

—Franklin's Spaceship. 2013. (Franklin & Friends Ser.). (ENG., Illus.). 24p. (J). (gr. -1-2). pap. 5.95 *(978-1-55453-967-3(6))* Kids Can Pr., Ltd. CAN. Dist: Hachette Bk. Group.

E
F
G

—Franklin's Surprise. 2003. (Kids Can Read Ser.). (ENG., Illus.). 32p. (J). (gr. 1-2). 3.95 *(978-1-55337-466-4(5))*; 14.95 *(978-1-55337-465-7(7))* Kids Can Pr., Ltd. CAN. Dist: Hachette Bk. Group.

—Franklin's Ups & Downs. 2013. (Franklin & Friends Ser.). (ENG., Illus.). 24p. (J). (gr. -1-2). 5.95 *(978-1-55453-838-6(6))* Kids Can Pr., Ltd. CAN. Dist: Hachette Bk. Group.

Bourgeois, Paulette, et al. Franklin's Big Book of Stories: A Collection of 6 First Readers. 2013. (Kids Can Read Ser.). (ENG., Illus.). 184p. (J). (gr. 1-2). 12.95 *(978-1-77138-028-7(4))* Kids Can Pr., Ltd. CAN. Dist: Hachette Bk. Group.

Endrulat, Harry, et al. The Adventures of Franklin & Friends: A Collection of 8 Stories. 2013. (Franklin & Friends Ser.). (ENG., Illus.). 192p. (J). (gr. -1-2). 13.95 *(978-1-77138-027-0(6))* Kids Can Pr., Ltd. CAN. Dist: Hachette Bk. Group.

—Franklin & the Best Friend Problem. 2013. (Franklin & Friends Ser.). (ENG., Illus.). 24p. (J). (gr. -1-2). pap. 5.95 *(978-1-894786-91-1(2))* Kids Can Pr., Ltd. CAN. Dist: Hachette Bk. Group.

—Franklin Feels at Home. 2013. (Franklin & Friends Ser.). (ENG., Illus.). 24p. (J). (gr. -1-2). pap. 5.95 *(978-1-894786-93-5(9))* Kids Can Pr., Ltd. CAN. Dist: Hachette Bk. Group.

—Franklin's Christmas Spirit. 2013. (Franklin & Friends Ser.). (ENG., Illus.). 24p. (J). (gr. -1-2). pap. 5.95 *(978-1-894786-90-4(4))* Kids Can Pr., Ltd. CAN. Dist: Hachette Bk. Group.

Jennings, Sharon. Franklin & the Cookies. Gagnon, Celeste et al, illus. 2005. 32p. (J). lib. bdg. 15.38 *(978-1-4242-1167-8(0))* Fitzgerald Bks.

—Franklin & the Scooter. Gagnon, Celeste et al, illus. 2004. 32p. (J). lib. bdg. 15.38 *(978-1-4242-1169-2(7))* Fitzgerald Bks.

—Franklin Stays Up. Jeffrey, Sean et al, illus. 2003. 32p. (J). pap. *(978-0-439-41815-7(1))* Scholastic, Inc.

—Franklin the Detective. Gagnon, Celeste et al, illus. 2004. 32p. (J). lib. bdg. 15.38 *(978-1-4242-1171-5(9))* Fitzgerald Bks.

—Franklin's Pond Phantom. McIntyre, Sasha et al, illus. 2005. 32p. (J). lib. bdg. 15.38 *(978-1-4242-1181-4(6))* Fitzgerald Bks.

Jennings, Sharon, et al, adapted by. Franklin & the Computer. 2003. (Franklin TV Storybook Ser.). (ENG., Illus.). 32p. (J). (gr. -1-3). 10.95 *(978-1-55337-362-9(6))* Kids Can Pr., Ltd. CAN. Dist: Hachette Bk. Group.

—Franklin's Picnic. 2006. (Kids Can Read Ser.). (ENG., Illus.). 32p. (J). (gr. 1-2). 14.95 *(978-1-55337-714-6(1))* Kids Can Pr., Ltd. CAN. Dist: Hachette Bk. Group.

Jennings, Sharon & Bourgeois, Paulette. A Classic Franklin Story: Franklin's Thanksgiving. Clark, Brenda, illus. 2013. (Franklin Ser.). (ENG.). 32p. (J). (gr. -1-3). pap. 5.95 *(978-1-77138-005-8(5))* Kids Can Pr., Ltd. CAN. Dist: Hachette Bk. Group.

—Franklin Goes to the Hospital. Clark, Brenda, illus. 2nd ed. 2011. (Franklin Ser.). (ENG.). 32p. (J). (gr. -1-3). 5.95 *(978-1-55453-725-9(8))* Kids Can Pr., Ltd. CAN. Dist: Hachette Bk. Group.

—Franklin's Valentines. Clark, Brenda, illus. 2013. (Franklin Ser.). (ENG.). 32p. (J). (gr. -1-3). pap. 5.95 *(978-1-77138-006-5(3))* Kids Can Pr., Ltd. CAN. Dist: Hachette Bk. Group.

Jennings, Sharon, et al. Franklin's Library Book. Gagnon, Céleste, illus. 2005. 32p. (J). *(978-0-439-82297-8(1))* Scholastic, Inc.

Kids Can Press Staff. Franklin & the Big Small Case. 2012. (Franklin & Friends Ser.). (ENG., Illus.). 24p. (J). (gr. -1-2). pap. 5.95 *(978-1-55453-968-0(4))* Kids Can Pr., Ltd. CAN. Dist: Hachette Bk. Group.

—Franklin & the Wonder. 2012. (Franklin & Friends Ser.). (ENG., Illus.). 24p. (J). (gr. -1-2). 5.95 *(978-1-55453-836-2(X))* Kids Can Pr., Ltd. CAN. Dist: Hachette Bk. Group.

—Franklin, the Little Bubble. 2012. (Franklin & Friends Ser.). (ENG., Illus.). 24p. (J). (gr. -1-2). 5.95 *(978-1-55453-837-9(8))* Kids Can Pr., Ltd. CAN. Dist: Hachette Bk. Group.

—Franklin's Partner. 2012. (Franklin & Friends Ser.). (ENG., Illus.). 24p. (J). (gr. -1-2). 5.95 *(978-1-55453-835-5(1))* Kids Can Pr., Ltd. CAN. Dist: Hachette Bk. Group.

Kids Can Press Staff, ed. Franklin & the Stopwatch. 2007. (Kids Can Read Ser.). (ENG., Illus.). 32p. (J). (gr. 1-2). 14.95 *(978-1-55337-890-7(3))* Kids Can Pr., Ltd. CAN. Dist: Hachette Bk. Group.

Kidscan Staff. Franklin's Day with Dad. 2014. (Franklin & Friends Ser.). (ENG., Illus.). 24p. (J). (gr. -1-2). pap. 5.95 *(978-1-77138-115-4(9))* Kids Can Pr., Ltd. CAN. Dist: Hachette Bk. Group.

—Franklin's Rocket Team. 2014. (Franklin & Friends Ser.). (ENG., Illus.). 24p. (J). (gr. -1-2). pap. 5.95 *(978-1-77138-116-1(7))* Kids Can Pr., Ltd. CAN. Dist: Hachette Bk. Group.

McIntyre, Sasha & Ghione, Yvette. Franklin's Easter: A Sticker Activity Book. 2004. (ENG., Illus.). 16p. (J). 6.95 *(978-1-55337-521-0(1))* Kids Can Pr., Ltd. CAN. Dist: Hachette Bk. Group.

Smith, Caitlin Drake, et al. Franklin & the Case of the New Friend. 2014. (Franklin & Friends Ser.). (ENG., Illus.). 24p. (J). (gr. -1-2). pap. 5.95 *(978-1-77138-122-2(1))* Kids Can Pr., Ltd. CAN. Dist: Hachette Bk. Group.

—Franklin & the Radio. 2014. (Franklin & Friends Ser.). (ENG., Illus.). 24p. (J). (gr. -1-2). pap. 5.95 *(978-1-77138-123-9(X))* Kids Can Pr., Ltd. CAN. Dist: Hachette Bk. Group.

FRANKLIN, BENJAMIN, 1706-1790

Adams, Colleen. Benjamin Franklin: American Inventor. 2009. (Reading Room Collection 2 Ser.). 24p. (gr. 3-4). 42.50 *(978-1-60851-959-0(7)*, PowerKids Pr.) Rosen Publishing Group, Inc., The.

Adler, David A. A Picture Book of Benjamin Franklin. Wallner, John & Wallner, Alexandra, illus. 2008. (Picture Book Biography Ser.). (J). (gr. k-3). 28.95 incl. audio compact disk *(978-1-4301-0340-0(X))* Live Oak Media.

—A Picture Book of Benjamin Franklin. 2008. (J). (gr. k-3). pap. 39.95 incl. audio compact disk *(978-1-4301-0341-7(8))* Live Oak Media.

—A Picture Book of Benjamin Franklin, 4 bks., Set. Wallner, John & Wallner, Alexandra, illus. 2008. (Picture Book Biography Ser.). (J). (gr. k-3). pap. 37.95 incl. audio *(978-1-4301-0338-7(8))* Live Oak Media.

Ashby, Ruth. The Amazing Mr. Franklin: Or the Boy Who Read Everything, 1 vol. Montgomery, Michael, illus. 2004. (ENG.). 144p. (J). (gr. 2-5). 12.95 *(978-1-56145-306-1(4))* Peachtree Pubs.

Baldwin, James. Four Great Americans. 2006. pap. *(978-1-4065-0509-2(9))* Dodo Pr.

Barretta, Gene. Now & Ben: The Modern Inventions of Benjamin Franklin. 2007. (J). (gr. 2-5). 29.95 incl. audio compact disk *(978-0-8045-4175-6(2))*; 27.95 incl. audio *(978-0-8045-6952-1(5))* Spoken Arts, Inc.

—Now & Ben: The Modern Inventions of Benjamin Franklin. Barretta, Gene, illus. 2008. (ENG., Illus.). 40p. (J). (gr. k-4). pap. 8.99 *(978-0-312-53569-8(4)*, 9780312535698) Square Fish.

Benge, Janet & Benge, Geoff. Heroes of History - Benjamin Franklin: Live Wire. 2005. (Heroes of History Ser.). (ENG., Illus.). 208p. (YA). (gr. 5). pap. 9.99 *(978-1-932096-14-9(0))* Emerald Bks.

Benjamin Franklin. 2007. (Illus.). 41p. (J). per. 6.95 *(978-0-9795887-2-3(3))* EZ Comics.

Bennett, Doraine & Scott, Clark C. Benjamin Franklin. 2012. (Illus.). 24p. (J). *(978-1-935884-38-5(7))*; pap. *(978-1-935884-47-7(6))* State Standards Publishing, LLC.

Bloom, Harold & Hayes, Kevin J., eds. Benjamin Franklin. 2008. (Bloom's Classic Critical Views Ser.). 264p. (YA). (gr. 9-12). 45.00 *(978-1-60413-135-2(7))* Facts On File, Inc.

Boekhoff, P. M. & Kallen, Stuart A. Benjamin Franklin. 2006. (Illus.). 48p. (J). (gr. 4-8). 17.00 *(978-1-4223-5322-6(2))* DIANE Publishing Co.

Byrd, Robert. Electric Ben: The Amazing Life & Times of Benjamin Franklin. 2012. (ENG.). 40p. (J). (gr. k-3). 17.99 *(978-0-8037-3749-5(1)*, Dial Bks) Penguin Young Readers Group.

Colbert, David. Benjamin Franklin. 2008. (10 Days Ser.). (ENG.). 160p. (J). (gr. 3-8). pap. 8.99 *(978-1-4169-6446-9(0)*, Simon & Schuster/Paula Wiseman Bks.) Simon & Schuster/Paula Wiseman Bks.

Collard, Sneed B., III. Benjamin Franklin: The Man Who Could Do Just about Anything. 2006. (American Heroes Ser.). (Illus.). 48p. (gr. 3-7). lib. bdg. 29.93 *(978-0-7614-2161-0(0)*, Benchmark Bks.) Marshall Cavendish Corp.

Conklin, Wendy. Benjamin Franklin, 1 vol. 2004. (Primary Source Readers Ser.). (ENG.). 24p. (J). (gr. 4-4). pap. 8.99 *(978-0-7439-8755-4(1))* Shell Educational Publishing.

—Benjamin Franklin (America's Early Years) 2016. (Primary Source Readers Ser.). (Illus.). 32p. (gr. 4-5). pap. 8.99 *(978-1-4938-3884-4(9))* Teacher Created Materials, Inc.

Cousins, Margaret. Ben Franklin of Old Philadelphia. 2004. (Landmark Bks.: No. 10). (ENG., Illus.). 160p. (J). (gr. 3-7). reprint ed. 5.99 *(978-0-394-84928-7(0)*, Random Hse. Bks. for Young Readers) Random Hse. Children's Bks.

Crawford, Laura. Benjamin Franklin from A to Z, 1 vol. Hierstein, Judith, illus. 2013. (ENG.). 32p. (J). (gr. k-3). 16.99 *(978-1-4556-1713-5(X))* Pelican Publishing Co., Inc.

Eberle, Irmengarde. Benjamin Franklin, Man of Science: A First Biography. Gillette, Henry S., illus. 2011. 156p. 41.95 *(978-1-258-08044-0(3))* Literary Licensing, LLC.

Espinosa, Rod. Benjamin Franklin, 1 vol. Espinosa, Rod, illus. 2007. (Bio-Graphics Ser.). (ENG., Illus.). 32p. (gr. 3-6). 28.50 *(978-1-60270-066-6(4)*, Graphic Planet- Nonfiction) ABDO Publishing Co.

Feinstein, Stephen. Read about Benjamin Franklin. 2006. (I Like Biographies! Ser.). (Illus.). 24p. (J). (gr. 1-3). lib. bdg. 22.60 *(978-0-7660-2596-7(9)*, Enslow Elementary) Enslow Pubs., Inc.

Fingeroth, Danny. Democracy's Signature: Benjamin Franklin & the Declaration of Independence. 2009. (Great Moments in American History Ser.). 32p. (gr. 3-3). 47.90 *(978-1-61513-141-9(8))* Rosen Publishing Group, Inc., The.

Fleming, Candace. Ben Franklin's Almanac: Being a True Account of the Good Gentleman's Life. 2003. (ENG., Illus.). 128p. (J). (gr. 5-9). 21.99 *(978-0-689-83549-0(3)*, Atheneum Bks. for Young Readers) Simon & Schuster Children's Publishing.

Fleming, Thomas. Ben Franklin: Inventing America. (Great Leaders & Events Ser.). (ENG.). 208p. (J). (gr. 4-8). 2017. lib. bdg. 35.99 ***(978-1-942875-23-9(1))*** 2016. (Illus.). pap. 12.99 *(978-0-7603-5228-1(3))* Quarto Publishing Group USA. (Voyageur Pr.).

Ford, Carin T. Benjamin Franklin: Inventor & Patriot. 2003. (Meeting Famous People Ser.). (Illus.). 32p. (J). (gr. 1-4). lib. bdg. 22.60 *(978-0-7660-1859-4(8))* Enslow Pubs., Inc.

Foster, Leila Merrell. Benjamin Franklin: Statesman & Inventor. 2015. (Legendary American Biographies Ser.). 96p. (J). (gr. 6-12). 27.94 *(978-0-7660-6445-4(X))*; pap. 10.95 *(978-0-7660-6446-1(8))* Enslow Pubs., Inc.

Fradin, Dennis Brindell. Who Was Ben Franklin? O'brien, John, illus. 2003. (Who Was... ? Ser.). 105p. (gr. 4-7). 15.00 *(978-0-7569-1589-6(9))* Perfection Learning Corp.

Franklin, Benjamin. Benjamin Franklin's Wise Words. Harper, Fred, illus. 2017. (ENG.). 128p. (J). (gr. 3-7). 16.99 *(978-1-4263-2699-8(8))*; lib. bdg. 26.90 *(978-1-4263-2700-1(5))* National Geographic Society. (National Geographic Children's Bks.).

Freedman, Russell. Becoming Ben Franklin: How a Candle-Maker's Son Helped Light the Flame of Liberty. 2013. (ENG.). 96p. (J). (gr. 5). 24.95 *(978-0-8234-2374-3(3))* Holiday Hse., Inc.

Friedman, Estelle. Ben Franklin. Caraway, James, illus. 2011. 44p. 35.95 *(978-1-258-07275-9(0))* Literary Licensing, LLC.

Furgang, Kathy. The Declaration of Independence & Benjamin Franklin of Pennsylvania. 2009. (Framers of the Declaration of Independence Ser.). 24p. (gr. 3-3). 42.50 *(978-1-61512-629-3(5)*, PowerKids Pr.) Rosen Publishing Group, Inc., The.

Gaustad, Edwin S. Benjamin Franklin: Inventing America. 2006. 143p. (J). (gr. 4-8). reprint ed. 22.00 *(978-1-4223-5227-4(7))* DIANE Publishing Co.

Giblin, James Cross. The Amazing Life of Benjamin Franklin. Dooling, Michael, illus. 2006. 48p. (gr. -1-3). 18.00 *(978-0-7569-6551-8(9))* Perfection Learning Corp.

—The Amazing Life of Benjamin Franklin. Dooling, Michael, illus. 2006. (ENG.). 48p. (J). (gr. 3-7). per. 7.99 *(978-0-439-81065-4(5)*, Scholastic Paperbacks) Scholastic, Inc.

Gilman, Sarah. Ben Franklin. 2016. (Explore Colonial America Ser.). (Illus.). 48p. (J). (gr. 5-4). 27.93 *(978-0-7660-7873-4(6))* Enslow Pubs., Inc.

Glass, Maya. Benjamin Franklin: Early American Genius. (Primary Sources of Famous People in American History Ser.). 32p. 2009. (gr. 2-3). 47.90 *(978-1-60851-654-4(7))* 2004. (ENG., Illus.). (gr. 4-8). pap. 10.00 *(978-0-8239-4175-9(2))* Rosen Publishing Group, Inc., The.

—Benjamin Franklin: Early American Genius / Político e inventor Estadounidense. 2009. (Famous People in American History/Grandes personajes en la historia de los Estados Unidos Ser.). (ENG & SPA.). 32p. (gr. 2-3). 47.90 *(978-1-61512-538-8(8)*, Editorial Buenas Letras) Rosen Publishing Group, Inc., The.

—Benjamin Franklin: Politico e inventor Estadounidense. 2004. (Grandes personajes en la historia de los Estados Unidos Ser.). (SPA.). 32p. (gr. 5-8). pap. 10.00 *(978-0-8239-4221-3(X)*, Rosen Classroom) Rosen Publishing Group, Inc., The.

—Benjamin Franklin: Político e inventor estadounidense (Benjamin Franklin: Early American Genius) 2009. (Grandes personajes en la historia de los Estados Unidos (Famous People in American History) Ser.). (SPA.). 32p. (gr. 2-3). 47.90 *(978-1-61512-790-0(9)*, Editorial Buenas Letras) Rosen Publishing Group, Inc., The.

Gosman, Gillian. Benjamin Franklin. 2011. (Life Stories Ser.). (Illus.). 24p. (J). pap. 8.25 *(978-1-4488-2759-6(0))*; (gr. 1-4). lib. bdg. 22.60 *(978-1-4488-2585-1(7))* Rosen Publishing Group, Inc., The. (PowerKids Pr.).

—Benjamín Franklin. 2011. (Life Stories / Biografías Ser.). (ENG & SPA., Illus.). 24p. (J). (gr. 1-4). lib. bdg. 22.60 *(978-1-4488-3219-4(5))* Rosen Publishing Group, Inc., The.

Gould, Jane H. Benjamin Franklin. 2012. (Jr. Graphic Founding Fathers Ser.). (ENG., Illus.). 24p. (J). (gr. 3-6). pap. 10.60 *(978-1-4488-7990-8(6))*; lib. bdg. 25.25 *(978-1-4488-7896-3(9))* Rosen Publishing Group, Inc., The. (PowerKids Pr.).

Greene, Victor. The Life of Benjamin Franklin. 2012. (InfoMax Readers Ser.). (ENG., Illus.). 24p. (J). (gr. 1-2). pap. 8.25 *(978-1-4488-8992-1(8)*, Rosen Classroom) Rosen Publishing Group, Inc., The.

Haldy, Emma E. Benjamin Franklin. Bane, Jeff, illus. 2016. (My Early Library: My Itty-Bitty Bio Ser.). (ENG.). 24p. (J). (gr. k-1). 28.50 *(978-1-63470-478-6(9)*, 207643) Cherry Lake Publishing.

Harness, Cheryl. The Remarkable Benjamin Franklin. 2008. (ENG., Illus.). 48p. (J). (gr. 2-5). 7.95 *(978-1-4263-0297-8(5)*, National Geographic Children's Bks.) National Geographic Society.

—The Remarkable Benjamin Franklin. Harness, Cheryl, illus. 2005. (National Geographic Ser.). (ENG., Illus.). 48p. (J). (gr. 2-5). 17.95 *(978-0-7922-7882-5(8)*, National Geographic Children's Bks.) National Geographic Society.

—The Remarkable Benjamin Franklin. 2005. (ENG., Illus.). 48p. (J). (gr. 2-5). 27.90 *(978-0-7922-7884-9(4)*, National Geographic Children's Bks.) National Geographic Society.

Hesleden, Michael. Benjamin Franklin: American Diplomat. 2015. (Spotlight on American History Ser.). (ENG., Illus.). 24p. (J). (gr. 4-6). pap. 10.00 *(978-1-4994-1782-1(9)*, PowerKids Pr.) Rosen Publishing Group, Inc., The.

Hirschfeld, Leila & Hirschfeld, Tom. You Decide, Ben Franklin! Weber, Lisa K., illus. 2016. (J). pap. *(978-0-553-50952-6(7)*, Salamander Bks.) Pavilion Bks.

Jango-Cohen, Judith. Ben Franklin's Big Shock. Lepp, Kevin, illus. 2006. (On My Own Science Ser.). 48p. (J). (gr. k-3). per. 5.95 *(978-0-8225-6450-8(5)*, First Avenue Editions); lib. bdg. 25.26 *(978-1-57505-873-3(1)*, Millbrook Pr.) Lerner Publishing Group.

Kelly, Jack. Benjamin Franklin. Tafalla, Ortiz, illus. 2005. (Heroes of America Ser.). 239p. (gr. 3-8). 27.07 *(978-1-59679-257-9(4)*, Abdo & Daughters) ABDO Publishing Co.

Kenison, Misti. Cheer up, Ben Franklin! 2017. (ENG.). 28p. (J). bds. 9.99 ***(978-1-4926-5247-2(4)***, Sourcebooks Jabberwocky) Sourcebooks, Inc.

Krensky, Stephen & Dorling Kindersley Publishing Staff. Benjamin Franklin. 2007. (DK Biography Ser.). (ENG., Illus.). 128p. (J). (gr. 5-12). pap. 6.99 *(978-0-7566-3528-2(4)*, DK Children) Dorling Kindersley Publishing, Inc.

Krull, Kathleen. Benjamin Franklin. Kulikov, Boris, illus. 2014. (Giants of Science Ser.). (ENG.). 128p. (J). (gr. 3-7). pap. 7.99 *(978-0-14-751178-2(X)*, Puffin Books) Penguin Young Readers Group.

Lace, William W. Benjamin Franklin. 2010. (Leaders of the Colonial Era Ser.). (Illus.). 120p. (gr. 5-8). 35.00 *(978-1-60413-737-8(1)*, Chelsea Hse.) Facts On File, Inc.

Landau, Elaine. Meet Ben Franklin with Elaine Landau. 2006. (Explore Colonial America with Elaine Landau Ser.). (Illus.). 48p. (J). (gr. 3-4). lib. bdg. 25.27 *(978-0-7660-2555-4(1)*, Enslow Elementary) Enslow Pubs., Inc.

Lantos, James, ed. & compiled by. Benjamin Franklin. Lantos, James, compiled by. 2010. (Applewood's Pictorial America Ser.). (ENG., Illus.). 56p. pap. 9.95 *(978-1-60889-016-3(3))* Applewood Bks.

Leavitt, Amie Jane. Who Really Discovered Electricity? (Race for History Ser.). (ENG.). 32p. (gr. 3-4). 2011. pap. 47.70 *(978-1-4296-6416-5(9))* 2010. lib. bdg. 27.32 *(978-1-4296-3345-1(X))* Capstone Press of Coughlan Cos. (Fact Finders).

Mara, Wil. Benjamin Franklin. (Rookie Biographies(r) Ser.). (Illus.). (J). 2014. (ENG.). 32p. pap. 5.95 *(978-0-531-21201-1(7))* 2014. (ENG., 32p. lib. bdg. 25.00 *(978-0-531-20558-7(4))* 2003. (ENG., 32p. (gr. 1-2). pap. 4.95 *(978-0-516-27341-9(8)*, Children's Pr.) 2007. 31p. (gr. 1-2). pap. 4.95 *(978-0-531-12591-5(2)*, Children's Pr.) Scholastic Library Publishing.

Marcovitz, Hal. Benjamin Franklin: Scientist, Inventor, Printer, & Statesman. 2006. (Leaders of the American Revolution Ser.). (Illus.). 100p. (gr. 5-8). lib. bdg. 30.00 *(978-0-7910-9219-4(4)*, Chelsea Hse.) Facts On File, Inc.

McCurdy, Michael. So Said Ben. 2007. (ENG., Illus.). 32p. (J). (gr. 1-3). 17.95 *(978-1-56846-147-2(X)*, Creative Editions) Creative Co., The.

McDowell, Pamela. Benjamin Franklin. 2013. *(978-1-62127-307-3(5))*; pap. *(978-1-62127-313-4(X))* Weigl Pubs., Inc.

McLeese, Don. Benjamin Franklin. 2005. (Heroes of the American Revolution Ser.). (Illus.). 32p. (gr. 2-5). 19.95 *(978-1-59515-216-9(4))* Rourke Educational Media.

McNeil, Niki, et al. HOCPP 1058 Benjamin Franklin. 2006. spiral bd. 18.50 *(978-1-60308-058-3(9))* In the Hands of a Child.

Miller, Brandon Marie. Benjamin Franklin, American Genius: His Life & Ideas with 21 Activities. 2009. (For Kids Ser.). (ENG., Illus.). 144p. (J). (gr. 4-7). pap. 16.95 *(978-1-55652-757-9(8))* Chicago Review Pr., Inc.

Miller, Chuck. Benjamin Franklin. 2003. (America's Founders Ser.). (J). pap. *(978-1-58417-084-6(0))*; lib. bdg. *(978-1-58417-021-1(2))* Lake Street Pubs.

Mills, Nathan & Coleridge, Margaret. Who Was Benjamin Franklin? 2012. (Rosen Readers Ser.). (ENG., Illus.). 24p. (J). (gr. 1-2). pap. 8.25 *(978-1-4488-8773-6(9)*, Rosen Classroom) Rosen Publishing Group, Inc., The.

Morlock, Theresa. 20 Fun Facts about Benjamin Franklin. 2017. (Fun Fact File: Founding Fathers Ser.). 32p. (gr. 2-3). pap. 63.00 ***(978-1-5382-0271-5(9))*** Stevens, Gareth Publishing LLLP.

Nelson, Maria. The Life of Ben Franklin. 2012. (Famous Lives Ser.). (ENG.). 24p. (J). (gr. k-3). lib. bdg. 22.60 *(978-1-4339-6345-2(0))*; (gr. 1-4). pap. 8.15 *(978-1-4339-6347-6(7))* Stevens, Gareth Publishing LLLP.

—The Life of Ben Franklin / la Vida de BenjamíN Franklin. 2012. (Famous Lives / Vidas extraordinarias Ser.). (ENG & SPA., Illus.). 24p. (J). (gr. k-3). 22.60 *(978-1-4339-6653-8(0))* Stevens, Gareth Publishing LLLP.

Nettleton, Pamela Hill. Benjamin Franklin: Writer, Inventor, Statesman, 1 vol. Yesh, Jeff, illus. 2003. (Biographies Ser.). (ENG.). 24p. (gr. k-3). per. 8.95 *(978-1-4048-0459-3(5))* Picture Window Bks.

Owens, L. L. Benjamin Franklin, 1 vol. 2007. (Essential Lives Set 1 Ser.). (ENG., Illus.). 112p. (J). (gr. 6-12). lib. bdg. 35.64 *(978-1-59928-840-6(0))* ABDO Publishing Co.

Pingry, Patricia A. Discover Benjamin Franklin: Printer, Scientist, Statesman. Britt, Stephanie, illus. 2005. (Discovery Readers Ser.). (ENG.). 32p. (J). (gr. 1-2). pap. 4.35 *(978-0-8249-5509-0(9)*, Ideal Pubns.) Worthy Publishing.

Proudfit, Benjamin. Benjamin Franklin. 2015. (What You Didn't Know about History Ser.). (ENG., Illus.). 24p. (J). (gr. 2-3). pap. 8.15 *(978-1-4824-1926-9(2))* Stevens, Gareth Publishing LLLP.

Randolph, Ryan P. Benjamin Franklin: Inventor, Writer & Patriot. 2005. (Library of American Lives & Times). (Illus.). 112p. (YA). (gr. 4-8). lib. bdg. 34.60 *(978-0-8239-5751-4(9))* Rosen Publishing Group, Inc., The.

—Benjamin Franklin: Inventor, Writer, & Patriot. 2009. (Library of American Lives & Times Ser.). 112p. (gr. 5-5). 69.20 *(978-1-60853-472-2(3))* Rosen Publishing Group, Inc., The.

Rausch, Monica. Benjamín Franklin. 2007. (Grandes personajes (Spanish- Great Americans) Ser.). 24p. (gr. 1-4). (ENG & SPA.). pap. 8.15 *(978-0-8368-7988-9(0))*; (Illus.). pap. 8.15 *(978-0-8368-7689-5(X))*; (Illus.). lib. bdg. 22.00 *(978-0-8368-7682-6(2))* Stevens, Gareth Publishing LLLP. (Weekly Reader Leveled Readers).

Rausch, Monica L. Benjamin Franklin. 2007. (Grandes personajes (Great Americans) Ser.). (ENG & SPA., Illus.). 24p. (gr. 1-4). lib. bdg. 22.00 *(978-0-8368-7981-0(3)*, Weekly Reader Leveled Readers) Stevens, Gareth Publishing LLLP.

Riley, Gail Blasser. Benjamin Franklin & Electricity. 2004. (Cornerstones of Freedom Ser.). (ENG., Illus.). 48p. (YA). (gr. 4-7). 26.00 *(978-0-516-24240-8(7))* Scholastic Library Publishing.

Riley, John B. Benjamin Franklin: A Photo Biography. l.t. ed. 2004. (First Biographies Ser.). (Illus.). 24p. (YA). (gr. 5-18). 16.95 *(978-1-883846-64-0(1)*, First Biographies) Reynolds, Morgan Inc.

Rockliff, Mara. Mesmerized: How Ben Franklin Solved a Mystery That Baffled All of France. Bruno, Iacopo, illus. (ENG.). 48p. (J). (gr. 1-4). 2017. 7.99 ***(978-0-7636-9515-6(7))*** 2015. 17.99 *(978-0-7636-6351-3(4))* Candlewick Pr.

Roop, Peter & Roop, Connie. Go Fly a Kite, Ben Franklin! 2003. (Illus.). 60p. (J). *(978-0-439-55442-8(X))* Scholastic, Inc.

Rosenstock, Barb. Ben Franklin's Big Splash: The Mostly True Story of His First Invention. Schindler, S. D., illus. 2014. (ENG.). 32p. (J). (gr. 3). 16.95 *(978-1-62091-446-5(8)*, Calkins Creek) Boyds Mills Pr.

Rushby, Pamela. Ben Franklin: Printer, Author, Inventor, Politician. 2007. (History Chapters Ser.). (ENG., Illus.). 48p. (J). (gr. 1-4). lib. bdg. 17.90 *(978-1-4263-0191-9(X)*, National Geographic Children's Bks.) National Geographic Society.

Saddleback Educational Publishing Staff, ed. Benjamin Franklin, 1 vol. unabr. ed. 2008. (Graphic Biographies Ser.). (ENG., Illus.). 25p. (YA). (gr. 9-12). pap. 7.95 *(978-1-59905-217-5(2))* Saddleback Educational Publishing, Inc.

Salzmann, Mary Elizabeth. Benjamin Franklin, 1 vol. 2016. (ENG., Illus.). 24p. (J). *(978-1-68078-157-1(X))* ABDO Publishing Co.

Satterfield, Kathryn Hoffman. Benjamin Franklin A Man of Many Talents. 2005. 44p. (J). lib. bdg. 15.00 *(978-1-4242-0846-3(7))* Fitzgerald Bks.

Schroeder, Alan. Ben Franklin: His Wit & Wisdom from A to Z. O'brien, John, illus. 2011. (ENG.). 32p. (J). (gr. 1-5). 16.95 *(978-0-8234-1950-0(9))* Holiday Hse., Inc.

—Ben Franklin: His Wit & Wisdom from A-Z. O'brien, John, illus. 2012. (ENG.). 32p. (J). pap. 7.95 *(978-0-8234-2435-1(9))* Holiday Hse., Inc.

Streissguth, Thomas & Streissguth, Tom. Benjamin Franklin. 2005. (Biography Ser.). (Illus.). 112p. (gr. 6-12). 27.93 *(978-0-8225-4997-0(2))* Lerner Publishing Group.

Streissguth, Tom. Benjamin Franklin. 2005. (Bios for Challenged Readers Ser.). (Illus.). 112p. (J). (gr. 6-12). lib. bdg. 27.93 *(978-0-8225-2210-2(1))* Lerner Publishing Group.

Thayer, William Makepeace. From Boyhood to Manhood: Life of Benjamin Franklin. 2006. pap. *(978-1-4068-0906-0(3))* Echo Library.

Time for Kids Editors. Benjamin Franklin - A Man of Many Talents. 2005. (Time for Kids Ser.). (ENG., Illus.). 48p. (J).

(gr. 2-4). pap. 3.99 *(978-0-06-057609-7(X))* HarperCollins Pubs.

Uglow, Loyd. Benjamin Franklin: You Know What to Say. Budwine, Greg, illus. 2003. (J). lib. bdg. 23.95 incl. audio *(978-1-57537-791-9(8))* Advance Publishing, Inc.

Van Vleet, Carmella. Amazing Ben Franklin Inventions. 2007. (Build It Yourself Ser.). (ENG., Illus.). 128p. (J). (gr. 3-7). 19.95 *(978-0-9792268-8-5(0))* Octavio Publishing.

—Amazing Ben Franklin Inventions: You Can Build Yourself. 2007. (Build It Yourself Ser.). (ENG., Illus.). 128p. (J). (gr. 3-7). per. 15.95 *(978-0-9771294-7-8(0))* Octavio Publishing.

Venezia, Mike. Benjamin Franklin: Electrified the World with New Ideas. Venezia, Mike, illus. 2009. (Getting to Know the World's Greatest Inventors & Scientists Ser.). (ENG., Illus.). 32p. (J). (gr. 2-5). 28.00 *(978-0-531-23701-4(X))* Scholastic Library Publishing.

Warrick, Karen Clemens. Benjamin Franklin: Creating a Nation. 2004. (America's Founding Fathers Ser.). (Illus.). 128p. (J). lib. bdg. 27.94 *(978-0-7660-2195-2(5))* Enslow Pubs., Inc.

Whiting, Jim. Benjamin Franklin. 2006. (Profiles in American History Ser.). (Illus.). 48p. (J). (gr. 3-7). lib. bdg. 29.95 *(978-1-58415-435-8(7))* Mitchell Lane Pubs., Inc.

FRANKLIN, BENJAMIN, 1706-1790—FICTION

Anderson, Jessica. Brownies with Benjamin Franklin. 2016. (Time Hop Sweets Shop Ser.). (ENG.). 32p. (gr. k-3). 25.65 *(978-1-68191-375-9(5))* Rourke Educational Media.

Avery, Ben G. Turtle Trouble, 1 vol. Gaudiamo, Adi Darda, illus. 2007. (Z Graphic Novels / TimeFlyz Ser.). (ENG.). 160p. (J). (gr. 3-7). pap. 6.99 *(978-0-310-71362-3(5))* Zondervan.

d'Lacey, Chris. Franklin's Bear. Taylor, Thomas, illus. 2005. (Red Go Bananas Ser.). (ENG.). 48p. (J). (gr. 2-3). lib. bdg. *(978-0-7787-2674-6(6))* Crabtree Publishing Co.

Fleming, Candace, et al. The Hatmaker's Sign: A Story Benjamin Franklin. Parker, Robert Andrew, illus. 2003. (Avenues Ser.). (ENG.). 40p. (C). (gr. k-4). pap. 10.95 *(978-0-531-07174-8(X))* National Geographic School Publishing, Inc.

Gutman, Dan. Back in Time with Benjamin Franklin. 2005. (ENG.). 192p. (J). (gr. 3-7). pap. 7.99 *(978-0-689-87884-8(2)*, Simon & Schuster Bks. For Young Readers) Simon & Schuster Bks. For Young Readers.

Hedstrom-Page, Deborah. From Settlement to City with Benjamin Franklin. Martinez, Sergio, illus. 2007. (My American Journey Ser.). 84p. (J). (gr. 3-9). 9.99 *(978-0-8054-3267-1(1))* B&H Publishing Group.

Hi-stories Presents Bengalmin Franklin. 2005. (J). per. *(978-0-9763233-1-0(1))* Little Germ That Could...Creations, Inc., The.

Hume, Stephen Eaton. Ben Franklin's War. 2006. (ENG.). 120p. (J). (gr. 4-8). pap. 10.99 *(978-1-55002-638-2(0))* Dundurn CAN. Dist: Ingram Publisher Services.

Kramer, Candice. De visita con Benjamin Franklin & Ben Franklin's Visit A When Machine Play. 2005. spiral bd. 76.00 *(978-1-4108-5787-3(5))* Benchmark Education Co.

Mansbach, Adam & Zweibel, Alan. Benjamin Franklin: Huge Pain in My... 2015. (Benjamin Franklin Ser.). (ENG., Illus.). 208p. (J). (gr. 5-9). 12.99 *(978-1-4847-1304-4(4))* Hyperion Bks. for Children.

—Benjamin Franklin: Huge Pain in My... 2017. (Benjamin Franklin Ser.). (ENG.). 224p. (J). (gr. 5-9). pap. 7.99 *(978-1-4847-2537-5(9))* Hyperion Bks. for Children.

McElligott, Matthew & Tuxbury, Larry David. Benjamin Franklinstein Lives! McElligott, Matthew, illus. 2010. (Benjamin Franklinstein Ser.: 1). (ENG., Illus.). 128p. (J). (gr. 3-7). 12.99 *(978-0-399-25229-7(0)*, G.P. Putnam's Sons Books for Young Readers) Penguin Young Readers Group.

—Benjamin Franklinstein Meets the Fright Brothers. McElligott, Matthew, illus. 2011. (Benjamin Franklinstein Ser.). (ENG., Illus.). 176p. (J). (gr. 3-7). E-Book *(978-1-101-53556-1(3)*, Puffin Books) Penguin Young Readers Group.

Potter, David. The Left Behinds: the IPhone That Saved George Washington. 2016. (Left Behinds Ser.). (ENG.). 368p. (J). (gr. 3-7). 7.99 *(978-0-385-39059-0(9)*, Yearling) Random Hse. Children's Bks.

Renfroe, Vicki. Franklin. 2008. 63p. pap. 19.95 *(978-1-60563-391-6(7))* America Star Bks.

Thomson, Sarah L. The Eureka Key. 2016. (Secrets of the Seven Ser.). (ENG.). 240p. (J). 16.99 *(978-1-61963-731-3(6)*, 9781619637313, Bloomsbury USA Childrens) Bloomsbury Publishing USA.

Woodruff, Elvira. George Washington's Spy. (Time Travel Adventures Ser.). (ENG.). 240p. (J). (gr. 3-7). 2012. pap. 6.99 *(978-0-545-10488-3(2)*, Scholastic Paperbacks) 2010. 16.99 *(978-0-545-10487-6(4)*, Scholastic Pr.) Scholastic, Inc.

—George Washington's Spy. 2012. lib. bdg. 17.20 *(978-0-606-26216-3(4)*, Turtleback) Turtleback Bks.

FRANKLIN, JOHN, 1786-1847

O'Brien, Cynthia. Explore with John Franklin. 2015. (Travel with the Great Explorers Ser.). (ENG., Illus.). 32p. (J). (gr. 3-6). *(978-0-7787-1703-4(8))* Crabtree Publishing Co.

FRANKLIN D. ROOSEVELT LIBRARY

Margaret, Amy. Franklin D. Roosevelt Library & Museum. (Presidential Libraries Ser.). 24p. 2009. (gr. 3-3). 42.50 *(978-1-60851-483-0(8))* 2004. (Illus.). (J). lib. bdg. 22.60 *(978-0-8239-6268-6(7))* Rosen Publishing Group, Inc., The. (PowerKids Pr.).

FRANZ FERDINAND, ARCHDUKE OF AUSTRIA, 1863-1914—ASSASSINATION

Bodden, Valerie. The Assassination of Archduke Ferdinand. 2009. (Days of Change Ser.). 48p. (YA). (gr. 4-7). 22.95 *(978-1-58341-731-7(1))* Creative Co., The.

FRAUD

see also Impostors and Imposture

Bauchner, Elizabeth. Document Analysis. Noziglia, Carla Miller & Siegel, Jay A., eds. 2013. (Solving Crimes with Science: Forensics Ser.: 12). (Illus.). 112p. (J). (gr. 7-18). 22.95 *(978-1-4222-2865-4(7))* Mason Crest.

Benson, Michael. Cons & Frauds. 2008. (Criminal Investigations Ser.). (Illus.). 112p. (C). (gr. 9-12). 35.00 *(978-0-7910-9404-4(9)*, Chelsea Hse.) Facts On File, Inc.

Berry, Joy Wilt. A Book about Cheating. 2005. (Illus.). (J). *(978-0-7172-8583-9(9))* Scholastic, Inc.

Mason, Paul. Frauds & Counterfeits. 2010. (Solve It with Science Ser.). (YA). (gr. 5-9). 34.25 *(978-1-59920-329-4(4))* Black Rabbit Bks.

Swanson, Diane. Nibbling on Einstein's Brain: The Good, the Bad & the Bogus in Science. Blake, Francis, illus. 2nd rev. ed. 2009. (ENG.). 160p. (J). (gr. 1-12). 24.95 *(978-1-55451-187-7(9)*, 9781554511877); pap. 12.95 *(978-1-55451-186-0(0)*, 9781554511860) Annick Pr., Ltd. CAN. Dist: Publishers Group West (PGW).

Wolny, Philip. Understanding Financial Frauds & Scams. 2012. (Real World Economics Ser.). (ENG., Illus.). 80p. (J). (gr. 7-12). 33.25 *(978-1-4488-6784-4(3))* Rosen Publishing Group, Inc., The.

Yes Magazine Editors. Hoaxed! Fakes & Mistakes in the World of Science. Woo, Howie, illus. 2009. (ENG.). 48p. (J). (gr. 3-7). 16.95 *(978-1-55453-206-3(X))* Kids Can Pr., Ltd. CAN. Dist: Hachette Bk. Group.

—Hoaxed! Fakes & Mistakes in the World of Science. Yes Magazine Editors, ed. Woo, Howie, illus. 2009. (ENG.). 48p. (J). (gr. 3-7). pap. 8.95 *(978-1-55453-207-0(8))* Kids Can Pr., Ltd. CAN. Dist: Hachette Bk. Group.

FRAUD—FICTION

Alger, Horatio. Hector's Inheritance: Or, The Boys of Smith Institute. 2006. pap. *(978-1-4065-0708-9(3))* Dodo Pr.

—Hector's Inheritance: Or: the Boys of Smith Institute. 2007. (ENG.). 186p. pap. 19.99 *(978-1-4346-5065-8(0))*; 192p. pap. 21.99 *(978-1-4346-5066-5(9))* Creative Media Partners, LLC.

Alger Jr. Horatio Staff. Hector's Inheritance. rev. ed. 2006. 276p. 28.95 *(978-1-4218-1758-3(6))*; pap. 13.95 *(978-1-4218-1858-0(2))* 1st World Publishing, Inc. (1st World Library - Literary Society).

Curtis, Christopher Paul. Bucking the Sarge. 2006. (Readers Circle Ser.). (ENG.). 288p. (YA). (gr. 7-7). reprint ed. mass mkt. 6.99 *(978-0-440-41331-8(1)*, Laurel Leaf) Random Hse. Children's Bks.

Thomas, Paul R., reader. The Reeve's Tale. 2006. pap. 10.00 *(978-0-8425-2667-8(6))* Brigham Young Univ.

West, Tracey. The Clothing Capers. Harrington, Rich, illus. 2007. 96p. (J). pap. *(978-0-439-91452-9(3))* Scholastic, Inc.

FREAKS

see Monsters

FREDDY THE DETECTIVE (FICTITIOUS CHARACTER)—FICTION

Brooks, Walter R. Freddy & the Ignormus, 4 vols. 2003. (Freddy the Pig Ser.). (J). 57.75 *(978-0-7887-2996-6(9)*, 40878) Recorded Bks., Inc.

—Freddy & the Men from Mars. Wiese, Kurt, illus. 2011. (ENG.). 256p. 10.99 *(978-1-59020-695-9(9)*, 902695) Overlook Pr., The.

—Freddy & the Popinjay. Wiese, Kurt, illus. 2011. (ENG.). 256p. (gr. 2-18). 10.99 *(978-1-59020-468-9(9))* Overlook Pr., The.

FREE SPEECH

see Freedom of Speech

FREE VERSE

Early Macken, JoAnn. Read, Write, & Recite Free Verse Poetry. 2014. (ENG., Illus.). 32p. (J). *(978-0-7787-0408-9(4))* Crabtree Publishing Co.

FREEBOOTERS

see Pirates

FREEDOM

see Liberty

FREEDOM MARCHES (CIVIL RIGHTS)

see Civil Rights Demonstrations

FREEDOM OF ASSEMBLY

see Assembly, Right of

FREEDOM OF RELIGION

see also Church and State

Cahill, Bryon. Freedom to Worship. 2013. (Four Freedoms Ser.). (ENG., Illus.). 32p. (J). (gr. 3-6). pap. 8.95 *(978-1-937529-84-0(3))*; lib. bdg. 19.95 net. *(978-1-937529-92-5(4))* Red Chair Pr.

Cavell-Clarke, Steffi. Celebrating Different Beliefs. 2017. (Illus.). 24p. (J). **(978-0-7787-3261-7(4))** Crabtree Publishing Co.

Connolly, Sean. Religious Freedom. 2005. (Campaigns for Change Ser.). (Illus.). 48p. (J). (gr. 6-9). lib. bdg. 29.95 *(978-1-58340-514-7(3)*, 1247337) Black Rabbit Bks.

Conway, John Richard. A Look at the First Amendment: Freedom of Speech & Religion. 2008. (Constitution of the United States Ser.). (Illus.). 128p. (J). (gr. 5-9). lib. bdg. 34.60 *(978-1-59845-069-9(7))* Enslow Pubs., Inc.

Currie, Stephen. Religious Oppression. 2003. (Great Escapes Ser.). (ENG., Illus.). 112p. (J). 30.85 *(978-1-59018-280-2(4)*, Lucent Bks.) Cengage Gale.

Head, Tom. Freedom of Religion. 2005. (American Rights Ser.). (Illus.). 144p. (gr. 5-8). 35.00 *(978-0-8160-5664-4(1))* Facts On File, Inc.

Hirst, Mike. Freedom of Belief. 2005. (What Do We Mean by Human Rights? Ser.). (Illus.). 46p. (YA). (gr. 5-9). lib. bdg. 29.95 *(978-1-932889-66-6(3))* Sea-To-Sea Pubns.

Holt, David H. Religious, Cultural, & Minority Rights, Vol. 8. Lansford, Tom, ed. 2016. (Foundations of Democracy Ser.). (Illus.). 64p. (J). (gr. 7). 23.95 *(978-1-4222-3632-1(3))* Mason Crest.

Hoover, Stephanie. Freedom of Religion. 2016. (Our Basic Freedoms Ser.). 00048p. (J). pap. 14.05 **(978-1-4824-6106-0(4))** Stevens, Gareth Publishing LLLP.

Jones, Molly. First Amendment: Freedom of Speech, the Press, & Religion. 2011. (Amendments to the United States Constitution: the Bill of Rights Ser.). (ENG., Illus.). 64p. (YA). pap. 12.95 *(978-1-4488-2302-4(1)*, Rosen Reference) Rosen Publishing Group, Inc., The.

—The First Amendment: Freedom of Speech, the Press, & Religion. 2011. (Amendments to the United States Constitution: the Bill of Rights Ser.). (Illus.). 64p. (YA). (gr. 5-9). lib. bdg. 31.95 *(978-1-4488-1252-3(6))* Rosen Publishing Group, Inc., The.

LaClair, Teresa. The Northern Colonies: Freedom to Worship (1600-1770) 2012. (J). pap. *(978-1-4222-2411-3(2))* Mason Crest.

—The Northern Colonies: Freedom to Worship (1600-1770) Rakove, Jack N., ed. 2012. (How America Became America Ser.). 48p. (J). (gr. 3-4). 19.95 *(978-1-4222-2397-0(3))* Mason Crest.

MacDonald, Joan Vos. Religion & Free Speech Today: A Pro/con Debate. 2008. (Issues in Focus Today Ser.). (Illus.). 112p. (J). (gr. k-6). lib. bdg. 33.27 *(978-0-7660-2915-6(8))* Enslow Pubs., Inc.

Micklos, John, Jr. The First Amendment: Freedom of Speech & Religion. 2017. (Cause & Effect: the Bill of Rights Ser.). (ENG.). 32p. (gr. 3-4). lib. bdg. 27.32 ***(978-1-5157-7164-7(4)***, Fact Finders) Capstone Press of Coughlan Cos.

Nichols, Joan K. A Matter of Conscience: The Trial of Anne Hutchinson. Krovatin, Dan, illus. 2009. (Steck-Vaughn Stories of America Ser.). (ENG.). 112p. (gr. 3-8). pap. 14.20 *(978-0-8114-8073-4(9))* Houghton Mifflin Harcourt Publishing Co.

Porterfield, Jason. The Separation of Church & State: Interpreting the Constitution. 2014. (Understanding the United States Constitution Ser.). (Illus.). 112p. (YA). (gr. 7-12). 35.60 *(978-1-4777-7508-0(0))* Rosen Publishing Group, Inc., The.

Rokutani, John. Freedom of Speech, the Press, & Religion: The First Amendment. 2017. (Bill of Rights Ser.). 48p. (J). (gr. 5-6). 27.93 **(978-0-7660-8549-7(X))** Enslow Pubs., Inc.

Smith, Rich. First Amendment: The Right of Expression, 1 vol. 2007. (Bill of Rights Ser.). (ENG.). 32p. (gr. 3-7). 27.07 *(978-1-59928-914-4(8)*, Abdo & Daughters) ABDO Publishing Co.

Ullmann, Carol & Zott, Lynn M. Religious Liberty. 2014. (Opposing Viewpoints Ser.). (ENG., Illus.). 224p. (gr. 7-12). pap. 33.80 *(978-0-7377-6665-3(4))*; lib. bdg. 48.80 *(978-0-7377-6664-6(6))* Cengage Gale. (Greenhaven Pr., Inc.).

FREEDOM OF SPEECH

see also Assembly, Right of

Allport, Alan, et al. Freedom of Speech. 2nd rev. ed. 2011. (Point/Counterpoint Ser.). (Illus.). 108p. (C). (gr. 9). 35.00 *(978-1-60413-759-0(2)*, Chelsea Hse.) Facts On File, Inc.

Axelrod-Contrada, Joan. Reno V. ACLU Internet Censorship. 2006. (Supreme Court Milestones Ser.). (Illus.). 128p. (gr. 7-7). lib. bdg. 42.79 *(978-0-7614-2144-3(0)*, Benchmark Bks.) Marshall Cavendish Corp.

Barbour, William. Censorship. 2010. (Opposing Viewpoints Ser.). (Illus.). 240p. (J). pap. 29.45 *(978-0-7377-4762-1(5)*, Greenhaven Pr., Inc.) Cengage Gale.

Cahill, Bryon. Freedom of Speech & Expression. 2013. (Four Freedoms Ser.). (ENG., Illus.). 32p. (J). (gr. 3-6). pap. 8.95 *(978-1-937529-83-3(5))*; lib. bdg. 19.95 net. *(978-1-937529-91-8(6))* Red Chair Pr.

Ditchfield, Christin. Freedom of Speech. 2004. (True Bks.). (ENG., Illus.). 48p. (J). (gr. 3-5). pap. 6.95 *(978-0-516-27909-1(2)*, Children's Pr.) Scholastic Library Publishing.

Edwards, Nicola. Voice. 2004. (Children's Rights Ser.). (J). lib. bdg. 27.10 *(978-1-58340-423-2(6))* Black Rabbit Bks.

Egendorf, Laura K. Free Speech. 2007. (Compact Research Ser.). (Illus.). 103p. (YA). (gr. 7-12). lib. bdg. 25.95 *(978-1-60152-018-0(2))* ReferencePoint Pr., Inc.

Engdahl, Sylvia. Blogs. 2008. (Current Controversies Ser.). (ENG., Illus.). 224p. (gr. 10-12). lib. bdg. 46.40 *(978-0-7377-3954-1(1))*; pap. 32.00 *(978-0-7377-3955-8(X))* Cengage Gale. (Greenhaven Pr., Inc.).

Freedom of Speech DBA. 2003. spiral bd. 16.95 *(978-1-56004-150-4(1))* Social Studies Schl. Service.

Friedman, Ian C. Freedom of Speech & the Press. 2005. (American Rights Ser.). (Illus.). 144p. (gr. 5-8). 35.00 *(978-0-8160-5662-0(5))* Facts On File, Inc.

Furgang, Adam. Edward Snowden. 2017. (J). **(978-0-7660-9208-2(9))** Enslow Pubs., Inc.

Ganchy, Sally & Isler, Claudia. Understanding Your Right to Free Speech. 2011. (Personal Freedom & Civic Duty Ser.). (Illus.). 152p. (YA). (gr. 7-12). lib. bdg. 35.95 *(978-1-4488-4667-2(6))* Rosen Publishing Group, Inc., The.

Gitlin, Marty. When Is Free Speech Hate Speech? 2017. (J). **(978-1-5345-0077-8(4))** Greenhaven Publishing LLC.

Gold, Susan Dudley. Clear & Present Danger: Schenck V. United States. 2014. (J). lib. bdg. *(978-1-62712-387-7(3))* Cavendish Square Publishing.

—Clear & Present Danger: Schenck V. United States. 2013. (J). 42.79 *(978-1-60870-909-0(4))* Marshall Cavendish Corp.

—Protecting Hate Speech: R.A.V. V. St. Paul. 2014. lib. bdg. *(978-1-62712-393-8(8))* Cavendish Square Publishing.

—Saluting the Flag: West Virginia State Board of Education V. Barnette. 2014. lib. bdg. *(978-1-62712-396-9(2))* Cavendish Square Publishing.

—Saluting the Flag: West Virginia State Board of Education V. Barnette. 2012. (J). 42.79 *(978-1-60870-911-3(6))* Marshall Cavendish Corp.

—Tinker V. des Moines: Free Speech for Students. 2006. (Supreme Court Milestones Ser.). (Illus.). 128p. (gr. 7-7). lib. bdg. 42.79 *(978-0-7614-2142-9(4)*, Benchmark Bks.) Marshall Cavendish Corp.

Icenoggle, Jodi. Schenck V. United States & the Freedom of Speech Debate: Debating Supreme Court Decisions. 2005. (Debating Supreme Court Decisions Ser.). (Illus.). 128p. (J). (gr. 7-13). lib. bdg. 27.94 *(978-0-7660-2392-5(3))* Enslow Pubs., Inc.

Lerner, Alicia Cafferty & Lerner, Adrienne Wilmoth. Freedom of Expression. 2009. (Global Viewpoints Ser.). (ENG., Illus.). 224p. (YA). (gr. 10-12). 27.95 *(978-0-7377-4155-1(4)*, LML02109-243056, Greenhaven Pr., Inc.); (gr. 9-12). lib. bdg. 40.45 *(978-0-7377-4154-4(6)*, LML02109-243050) Cengage Gale.

Lusted, Marcia Amidon & Thain, Gerald J. Tinker v. Des Moines: The Right to Protest in Schools, 1 vol. 2012. (Landmark Supreme Court Cases Ser.). (ENG., Illus.). 160p. (J). (gr. 6-12). 37.07 *(978-1-61783-477-6(7))* ABDO Publishing Co.

Mason, Jennifer. Freedom of Speech. 2016. (Our Basic Freedoms Ser.). 00048p. (J). pap. 14.05 **(978-1-4824-6108-4(0))** Stevens, Gareth Publishing LLLP.

Micklos, John, Jr. The First Amendment: Freedom of Speech & Religion. 2017. (Cause & Effect: the Bill of Rights Ser.). (ENG.). 32p. (gr. 3-4). lib. bdg. 27.32 ***(978-1-5157-7164-7(4)***, Fact Finders) Capstone Press of Coughlan Cos.

Pauly, Robert J. Speech, Media, & Protest, Vol. 8. Lansford, Tom, ed. 2016. (Foundations of Democracy Ser.). 64p. (J). (gr. 7). 23.95 *(978-1-4222-3633-8(1))* Mason Crest.

Rokutani, John. Freedom of Speech, the Press, & Religion: The First Amendment. 2017. (Bill of Rights Ser.). 48p. (J). (gr. 5-6). 27.93 **(978-0-7660-8549-7(X))** Enslow Pubs., Inc.

Smith, Rich. First Amendment: The Right of Expression, 1 vol. 2007. (Bill of Rights Ser.). (ENG.). 32p. (gr. 3-7). 27.07 *(978-1-59928-914-4(8)*, Abdo & Daughters) ABDO Publishing Co.

Steele, Philip. Freedom of Speech. 2005. (What Do We Mean by Human Rights? Ser.). (Illus.). 46p. (YA). (gr. 5-9). lib. bdg. 29.95 *(978-1-932889-67-3(1))* Sea-To-Sea Pubns.

Steffens, Bradley. Free Speech. 2007. (Ripped from the Headlines Ser.). (YA). (gr. 7-12). 23.95 *(978-1-60217-015-5(0))* Erickson Pr.

FREEDOM OF THE PRESS

Engdahl, Sylvia. Free Press. 2011. (Teen Rights & Freedoms Ser.). (ENG., Illus.). 176p. (gr. 10-12). 42.00 *(978-0-7377-5827-6(9))* Cengage Gale.

Freedom of the Press DBA. 2003. spiral bd. 16.95 *(978-1-56004-149-8(8))* Social Studies Schl. Service.

Friedman, Ian C. Freedom of Speech & the Press. 2005. (American Rights Ser.). (Illus.). 144p. (gr. 5-8). 35.00 *(978-0-8160-5662-0(5))* Facts On File, Inc.

Gold, Susan Dudley. Parody of Public Figures: Hustler Magazine Inc. V. Falwell. 2013. (J). 42.79 *(978-1-60870-906-9(X))* Marshall Cavendish Corp.

Hagler, Gina. Understanding Freedom of the Press. 2013. (Personal Freedom & Civic Duty Ser.). (ENG., Illus.). 112p. (YA). (gr. 7-12). lib. bdg. 34.60 *(978-1-4488-9465-9(4)*, Rosen Classroom) Rosen Publishing Group, Inc., The.

Hall, Homer L. High School Journalism Teacher's Workbook & Guide. 2009. (High School Journalism Ser.). 136p. 53.00 *(978-1-61513-266-9(X))* Rosen Publishing Group, Inc., The.

Herda, D. J. Fighting Censorship: New York Times V. United States. 2016. (US Supreme Court Landmark Cases Ser.). (Illus.). 128p. (J). 37.27 *(978-0-7660-8432-2(9))* Enslow Pubs., Inc.

—New York Times V. United States: National Security & Censorship. rev. ed. 2010. (Landmark Supreme Court Cases, Gold Edition Ser.). (Illus.). 112p. (J). (gr. 6-18). 33.27 *(978-0-7660-3429-7(1))* Enslow Pubs., Inc.

Hoover, Stephanie. Freedom of the Press. 2016. (Our Basic Freedoms Ser.). 00048p. (J). pap. 14.05 **(978-1-4824-6110-7(2))** Stevens, Gareth Publishing LLLP.

Rokutani, John. Freedom of Speech, the Press, & Religion: The First Amendment. 2017. (Bill of Rights Ser.). 48p. (J). (gr. 5-6). 27.93 **(978-0-7660-8549-7(X))** Enslow Pubs., Inc.

Smith, Rich. First Amendment: The Right of Expression, 1 vol. 2007. (Bill of Rights Ser.). (ENG.). 32p. (gr. 3-7). 27.07 *(978-1-59928-914-4(8)*, Abdo & Daughters) ABDO Publishing Co.

FREEDOM OF WORSHIP

see Freedom of Religion

FREEMAN, ELIZABETH, 1744?-1829

Woelfle, Gretchen. Mumbet's Declaration of Independence. Delinois, Alix, illus. 2014. (ENG.). 32p. (J). (gr. 1-4). 17.95 *(978-0-7613-6589-1(3)*, Carolrhoda Bks.) Lerner Publishing Group.

FREEMASONS

Vang, Richard. My Dad Is a Freemason. Vang, Richard, illus. 2006. (Masonic Family Ser.). (ENG., Illus.). 31p. per. 16.95 *(978-0-9789066-0-3(8))* Square Circle Pr. LLC.

FREEZING

see Ice; Refrigeration and Refrigerating Machinery

FREIGHT AND FREIGHTAGE

see also Aeronautics, Commercial

Clapper, Nikki Bruno. Freight Trains. 2015. (All Aboard! Ser.). (ENG., Illus.). 24p. (gr. k-1). lib. bdg. 26.65 *(978-1-4914-6038-2(5)*, Pebble Plus) Capstone Press of Coughlan Cos.

DeRouin, Edward M. North Shore Line - Interurban Freight. 2005. (Midwestern Rail Ser.: #2). (Illus.). 96p. per. 34.95 *(978-0-9728743-1-1(3))* Pixels Publishing.

Gilbert, Sara. Built for Success: the Story of FedEx. 2013. (Built for Success Ser.). (ENG.). 48p. (J). (gr. 4-7). pap. 12.00 *(978-0-89812-762-1(9)*, Creative Paperbacks) Creative Co., The.

—The Story of FedEx. 2012. (Built for Success Ser.). (Illus.). 48p. (J). (gr. 5-12). 23.95 *(978-1-60818-177-3(4)*, Creative Education) Creative Co., The.

Richardson, Adele D. Freight Trains in Action, 1 vol. 2011. (Transportation Zone Ser.). (ENG.). 24p. (gr. 1-2). lib. bdg. 25.32 *(978-1-4296-6828-6(8)*, First Facts) Capstone Press of Coughlan Cos.

Schauer, Donald D. Careers in Trucking. 2009. (Career Resource Library). 192p. (gr. 7-12). 63.90 *(978-1-60853-407-4(3))* Rosen Publishing Group, Inc., The.

Syrewicz, Connor. Truck Driver. 2013. (Earning $50,000 - $100,000 with a High School Diploma or Less Ser.: 14). 64p. (J). (gr. 7-18). 22.95 *(978-1-4222-2900-2(9))* Mason Crest.

FREMONT, JESSIE BENTON, 1824-1902

Higgins, Marguerite & Berg, Rea. Jessie Benton Fremont: California Pioneer. 2008. (Illus.). 183p. *(978-1-893103-33-7(1))* Beautiful Feet Bks.

FREMONT, JOHN CHARLES, 1813-1890

Marsh, Carole. John C. Fremont. 2004. 12p. (gr. k-4). 2.95 *(978-0-635-02380-3(6))* Gallopade International.

Maynard, Charles W. John Charles Fremont: The Pathfinder. 2003. (Famous Explorers of the American West Ser.). (Illus.). 24p. (J). lib. bdg. 22.60 *(978-0-8239-6289-1(X)*, PowerKids Pr.) Rosen Publishing Group, Inc., The.

Petrie, Kristin. John C. Fremont, 1 vol. 2004. (Explorers Set 1 Ser.). (ENG., Illus.). 32p. (gr. k-6). 27.07 *(978-1-59197-602-8(2)*, Checkerboard Library) ABDO Publishing Co.

Sanford, William R. & Green, Carl R. John C. Frémont: Courageous Pathfinder of the Wild West. 2012. (Courageous Heroes of the American West Ser.). (Illus.). 48p. (J). pap. 8.95 *(978-1-4644-0091-9(1))*; (gr. 5-18). 22.60 *(978-0-7660-4008-3(9))* Enslow Pubs., Inc.

Souza, D. M. John C. Fremont. 2004. (Watts Library). (ENG., Illus.). 64p. (J). (gr. 5-7). pap. 8.95 *(978-0-531-16652-9(X)*, Watts, Franklin) Scholastic Library Publishing.

FRENCH—AMERICA

Deiters, Erika & Deiters, Jim. The French Community in America. 2003. (J). *(978-1-58417-031-0(X))*; pap. *(978-1-58417-094-5(8))* Lake Street Pubs.

Parker, Lewis K. French Colonies in the Americas. 2009. (European Colonies in the Americas Ser.). 24p. (gr. 2-2).

42.50 (978-1-61512-318-6(0), PowerKids Pr.) Rosen Publishing Group, Inc., The.

FRENCH—UNITED STATES—FICTION

Magee, Helen. What's French for Help, George? l.t. ed. 2007. pap. (978-1-905665-68-6(7)) Pollinger In Print.

FRENCH AND INDIAN WAR, 1755-1763

see United States—History—French and Indian War, 1755-1763

FRENCH-CANADIANS

Pelletier, Fran. Little Pine to King Spruce: A Franco-American Childhood, 1 vol. 2003. (ENG., Illus.). 192p. pap. 15.00 (978-0-88448-254-3(5), 884254) Tilbury Hse. Pubs.

FRENCH-CANADIANS—FICTION

Beckhorn, Susan Williams. Moose Power! Muskeg Saves the Day. Huntington, Amy, illus. 2010. (ENG.). 40p. (J). (gr. -1-3). 16.95 (978-0-89272-762-9(4)) Down East Bks.

Brandeis, Madeline. Little Anne of Canad. 2011. 176p. 42.95 (978-1-258-09048-7(1)) Literary Licensing, LLC.

Donovan, Lois. Winds of l'Acadie. 2006. (ENG., Illus.). 216p. (YA). (gr. 8-12). per. (978-1-55380-047-7(8)) Ronsdale Pr.

Finger, Mary E. Charlotte Bakeman Has Her Say. Batti, Kimberly Rose, illus. 2007. 96p. (J). 16.00 (978-0-9746911-2-1(7)) Little Pear Pr.

Shaw, Tucker. Anxious Hearts. 2010. (ENG.). 272p. (YA). (gr. 7-11). 16.95 (978-0-8109-8718-0(X), Amulet Bks.) Abrams, Inc.

FRENCH LANGUAGE

Amery, H. First Thousand Words. rev. ed. 2004. (First Learning Ser.). (FRE.). 64p. (J). 12.99 (978-0-7945-0283-6(0)) EDC Publishing.

Amery, Heather & Cartwright, Stephen. First French Word Book. 2004. (Farmyard Tales First Words Ser.). (ENG & FRE., Illus.). 48p. (J). 10.95 (978-0-7945-0295-9(4), Usborne) EDC Publishing.

Ayotte-Irwin, Tracy & Jordan, Sara. Bilingual Songs - English-French, 2 vols., Vol. 2. 2003. (Bilingual Song English-French Ser.: 2). (FRE., Illus.). 48p. (J). 17.95 (978-1-894262-80-4(8), 1894262808) Jordan, Sara Publishing.

Blake, Quentin. Ten Frogs: A Book about Counting in English & French. Blake, Quentin, illus. 2008. (FRE & ENG., Illus.). 32p. (J). (gr. -1-k). 14.95 (978-1-84365-104-8(1)) Pavilion Bks. GBR. Dist: Independent Pubs. Group.

Bourdais, Danièle & Finnie, Sue. Panorama Francophone 17 Jun 2015, 5 bks., Pack. Talon, Geneviève & Ollerenshaw, Jenny, eds. 2015. (IB Diploma Ser.). (ENG.). 200p. pap. 61.88 (978-1-107-57269-0(X)) Cambridge Univ. Pr.

Bruzzone, Catherine. French for Children. 2003. (FRE & ENG., Illus.). 80p. (J). (gr. 1-6). 29.95 (978-0-8442-9179-6(X)) McGraw-Hill Trade.

Carole Marsh. False Paw! French for Kids. 2004. (Little Linguist Ser.). 32p. (gr. 2-6). pap. 5.95 (978-0-635-02430-5(6)) Gallopade International.

Collins Publishers Staff & Collins KS3 Staff. Key Stage 3 French. 2014. (ENG & FRE.). 216p. (YA). (gr. 6-9). pap. 16.95 (978-0-00-756285-5(3)) HarperCollins Pubs. Ltd. GBR. Dist: Independent Pubs. Group.

—KS3 French. 2014. (ENG & FRE.). 144p. (YA). (gr. 6-9). pap. 12.95 (978-0-00-756284-8(5)) HarperCollins Pubs. Ltd. GBR. Dist: Independent Pubs. Group.

Daynes, Katie & Irving, N. Easy French. 2004. (Easy Languages Ser.). (FRE., Illus.). 128p. (J). (gr. 6-18). lib. bdg. 20.95 (978-1-58086-429-9(5)) EDC Publishing.

Demado. Se Allez, Viens! En Route!, Level 1B. 6th ed. 2006. (Holt Allez, Viens! Ser.). (FRE & ENG.). 304p. (gr. 7-7). 70.75 (978-0-03-036972-8(X)) Houghton Mifflin Harcourt Publishing Co.

Discovering French Blanc, Euro Edition. 2003. (YA). (-12). stu. ed. (978-0-618-03505-2(2)) Holt McDougal.

Discovering French Rouge, Euro Edition. 2003. (YA). (-12). stu. ed. (978-0-618-03506-9(0)); (FRE.). act. bk. ed. (978-0-618-04710-9(7)) Holt McDougal.

Dopffer, Guillaume. 1000 First Words in French. Lacome, Susie, illus. 2013. (ENG & FRE.). 96p. (J). (gr. k-4). 12.99 (978-1-84322-957-5(9)) Anness Publishing GBR. Dist: National Bk. Network.

Dopffer, Guillaume & Nicola, Baxter. My First 200 Words in French: Learning Is Fun with Teddy the Bear! Lacome, Susie, illus. 2016. (ENG & FRE.). 24p. (J). (gr. -1-12). pap. 7.99 (978-1-86147-760-6(0), Armadillo) Anness Publishing GBR. Dist: National Bk. Network.

Dunn, Opal. Un Deux Trois: First French Rhymes. Aggs, Patrice, illus. 2006. (FRE & ENG.). 24p. (J). (gr. k-3). pap. 9.99 (978-1-84507-623-8(0), Frances Lincoln Children's Bks.) Quarto Publishing Group UK GBR. Dist: Hachette Bk. Group.

Fatus, Sophie & Couëlle, Jennifer. My Big Barefoot Book of French & English Words. 2016. (FRE & ENG.). (J). pap. (978-1-78285-303-9(0)) Barefoot Bks., Inc.

Fedoruk, Dennis, prod. Bilingual Baby - Flashcard Set - French. 2013. (FRE.). (J). 7.99 (978-1-892703-74-3(2)) Small Fry Beginnings.

Fulcher, Roz. Color & Learn Easy French Phrases for Kids. 2015. (Dover Little Activity Bks.). (ENG.). 64p. (J). (gr. k-3). pap. 1.99 (978-0-486-80361-6(9)) Dover Pubns., Inc.

Hazan, Maurice, creator. Le Chemin: Practicing Everyday Vocabulary for French. (FRE.). (J). 124.95 (978-1-932770-60-5(7), FC5) Symtalk, Inc.

—The Conversation Game for French. (FRE.). (YA). 124.95 (978-1-932770-63-6(1), FG8) Symtalk, Inc.

—Dis moi qui c Est: French Dialogues Level 2. (FRE.). (J). 134.95 (978-1-932770-61-2(5), FG6) Symtalk, Inc.

—Escrivons: Introduction to Writing in French. (FRE.). (J). 199.95 (978-1-932770-66-7(6), FG11) Symtalk, Inc.

—French Conjugating Cards. (FRE.). 149.95 (978-1-932770-87-2(9), FCC) Symtalk, Inc.

—The French Question Game. (FRE.). (YA). 134.95 (978-1-932770-64-3(X), FG9) Symtalk, Inc.

—Objects, Colors & Numbers Bingo for French. (FRE.). (J). 124.95 (978-1-932770-57-5(7), FG2) Symtalk, Inc.

—Phrases et Photos: Long sentence Bingo. (FRE.). (YA). 199.95 (978-1-932770-62-9(3), FG7) Symtalk, Inc.

—Resto Presto French. (FRE.). (J). 169.95 (978-1-932770-58-2(5), FC3) Symtalk, Inc.

—Savoir, devoir, vouloir, Pouvoir: Symtalk Verb + Verb Infinitive Game for French. (FRE.). (YA). 134.95 (978-1-932770-65-0(8), FG10) Symtalk, Inc.

—Les Verbes: Symtalk Verb Bingo. (FRE.). (J). 124.95 (978-1-932770-56-8(9), FG1) Symtalk, Inc.

Hazan, Maurice, illus. French, Bk. 1. 2004. (FRE.). (J). 140.00 (978-1-932770-30-8(5), FC-FB1) Symtalk, Inc.

Hazan, Maurice, illus. & creator. French. Hazan, Maurice, creator. 2004. (FRE.). Bk. 2. (J). 175.00 (978-1-932770-32-2(1), FC-FB2)Bk. 3. 199.00 (978-1-932770-34-6(8), FC-FB3) Symtalk, Inc.

Hendry, Linda & Farris, Katherine. Mon Plus Bel Album de Mots Illustres. (FRE., Illus.). (J). pap. 11.99 (978-0-590-73945-0(X)) Scholastic, Inc.

Holt, Rinehart and Winston Staff. En Avant/En Route. 4th annot. ed. 2003. (J). tchr. ed. 70.00 (978-0-03-070184-9(8)) Holt McDougal.

HOP, LLC. Hooked on French. 2006. 99.99 (978-1-933863-87-0(0)) HOP, LLC.

Kalz, Jill. My First French Phrases, 1 vol. Translations.com Staff, tr. Fabbri, Daniele, illus. 2012. (Speak Another Language! Ser.). (FRE & ENG.). 32p. (gr. 1-3). pap. 8.95 (978-1-4048-7244-8(2)); lib. bdg. 26.65 (978-1-4048-7153-3(5)) Picture Window Bks.

Leigh, Susannah. L' Ile Fantastique: Fantastic Island. Gemmell, Kathy & Irving, Nicole, eds. Haw, Brenda, illus. (FRE.). 25p. (J). (gr. 2-3). reprint ed. 17.00 (978-0-7881-9300-2(7)) DIANE Publishing Co.

Leroy-Bennett, Veronique. Les Animaux: First French. 2016. (ENG & FRE., Illus.). 64p. 12.99 (978-1-86147-632-6(9), Armadillo) Anness Publishing GBR. Dist: National Bk. Network.

—Chez Moi: An Introduction to Commonly Used French Words & Phrases Around the Home, with 500 Lively Photographs. 2016. (ENG & FRE., Illus.). 64p. (J). (gr. -1-12). 12.99 (978-1-86147-696-8(5), Armadillo) Anness Publishing GBR. Dist: National Bk. Network.

—First French: Chez Moi. 2014. (FRE & ENG., Illus.). 64p. (J). (gr. 4-7). pap. 7.99 (978-1-84476-524-9(5)) Anness Publishing GBR. Dist: National Bk. Network.

Levesque, Suzanne, tr. from ENG. Le Secret de Sindbad. 2003. (FRE & SPA., Illus.). 32p. (J). (gr. 1-4). 17.95 (978-0-88776-623-7(4)) Tundra Bks. CAN. Dist: Penguin Random Hse. LLC.

Levine, Julia Pimsleur. Little Pim: Numbers. 2012. (ENG.). 10p. (J). (gr. -1-k). bds. 8.95 (978-1-4197-0175-7(4)) Abrams, Inc.

Litchfield, Jo. The Usborne Book of Everyday Words in French. 2006. (Everyday Words Ser.). (Illus.). 48p. (J). (gr. -1-3). per. 9.99 (978-0-7945-0882-1(0), Usborne) EDC Publishing.

Litchfield, Jo, des. Usborne Everyday Words French Flashcards. rev. ed. 2005. (J). (gr. -1-3). 8.95 (978-0-7945-0885-2(5), Usborne) EDC Publishing.

McCoy, Heather. French Crossword Puzzles for Practice & Fun. 2012. (Dover Language Guides French Ser.). (FRE & ENG.). 120p. pap. 8.95 (978-0-486-48585-0(4)) Dover Pubns., Inc.

McGraw-Hill Staff. Bon Voyage, Level 1. 2005. (Glencoe French Ser.). (ENG.). (gr. 9-12). pap., stu. ed. 139.36 (978-0-07-868657-3(1), 0078686571) McGraw-Hill Education.

Milet Publishing Staff. Animals. 2011. (My First Bilingual Book Ser.). (FRE & ENG., Illus.). 24p. (J). (gr. k — 1). bds. 8.99 (978-1-84059-612-0(0)) Milet Publishing.

—Fruit (English-French) 2011. (My First Bilingual Book Ser.). (FRE & ENG., Illus.). 24p. (J). (gr. k — 1). bds. 7.99 (978-1-84059-628-1(7)) Milet Publishing.

—Home (English-French) 2011. (My First Bilingual Book Ser.). (FRE & ENG., Illus.). 24p. (J). (gr. k — 1). bds. 8.99 (978-1-84059-644-1(9)) Milet Publishing.

—Milet Interactive for Kids - French for English Speakers. 2012. (Milet Interactive for Kids Ser.). (FRE & ENG., Illus.). 1p. (J). (gr. k-2). cd-rom 24.95 (978-1-84059-677-9(5)) Milet Publishing.

—My Bilingual Book-Hearing (English-French) 2014. (My Bilingual Book Ser.). (ENG & FRE., Illus.). 28p. (J). (gr. -1-k). 9.95 (978-1-84059-776-9(3)) Milet Publishing.

—My Bilingual Book-Sight (English-French) 2014. (My Bilingual Book Ser.). (ENG & FRE., Illus.). 28p. (J). (gr. -1-k). 9.95 (978-1-84059-792-9(5)) Milet Publishing.

—My First Bilingual Book - Vegetables. 2011. (My First Bilingual Book Ser.). (FRE & ENG., Illus.). 24p. (J). (gr. k — 1). bds. 8.99 (978-1-84059-660-1(0)) Milet Publishing.

—Smell (English-French) 2014. (My Bilingual Book Ser.). (ENG & FRE., Illus.). 28p. (J). (gr. -1-k). 9.95 (978-1-84059-808-7(5)) Milet Publishing.

—Taste - My Bilingual Book. 2014. (My Bilingual Book Ser.). (ENG & FRE., Illus.). 28p. (J). (gr. -1-k). 9.95 (978-1-84059-824-7(7)) Milet Publishing.

—Taste / Das Schmecken. 2014. (My Bilingual Book Ser.). (ENG & GER., Illus.). 28p. (J). (gr. -1-k). 9.95 (978-1-84059-825-4(5)) Milet Publishing.

—Touch - My Bilingual Book. 2014. (My Bilingual Book Ser.). (ENG & FRE., Illus.). 28p. (J). (gr. -1-k). 9.95 (978-1-84059-840-7(9)) Milet Publishing.

Ninos Aprenden Ingles Corp. Children Learning French. 2004. (Illus.). 119p. (J). pap. 19.95 (978-1-934665-08-4(8)) Ninos Aprenden Ingles Corp.

Nunn, Daniel. Colors in French: Les Couleurs, 1 vol. 2012. (World Languages - Colors Ser.). (ENG, FRE & MUL.). 24p. (gr. 1-3). pap. 6.29 (978-1-4329-6658-4(8)); lib. bdg. 22.65 (978-1-4329-6651-5(0)) Heinemann-Raintree. (Acorn).

—Families in French: Les Familles. 2013. (World Languages - Families Ser.). (ENG, MUL & FRE., Illus.). 24p. (gr. 1-3). pap. 6.29 (978-1-4329-7179-3(4), Acorn) Heinemann-Raintree.

—Families in French - Les Familles. 2013. (World Languages - Families Ser.). (ENG, MUL & FRE., Illus.). 24p. (gr. 1-3). lib. bdg. 22.65 (978-1-4329-7172-4(7), Acorn) Heinemann-Raintree.

—Numbers in French: Les Chiffres - 1 2 3. 2012. (World Languages - Numbers Ser.). (ENG & MUL.). 24p. (gr. 1-3). pap. 6.29 (978-1-4329-6679-9(0), Acorn) Heinemann-Raintree.

—Numbers in French - Les Chiffres: Un, Deux, Trois... 2012. (World Languages - Numbers Ser.). (ENG & MUL.). 24p. (gr. 1-3). lib. bdg. 22.65 (978-1-4329-6672-0(3), Acorn) Heinemann-Raintree.

Paradis, Anne. Caillou, My First French Word Book: Learn a New Language with Caillou! Brignaud, Pierre & Sévigny, Éric, illus. 2016. (ENG & FRE.). 32p. (J). (gr. -1-k). 9.99 (978-2-89718-305-9(5)) Caillouet, Gerry.

Paré, Roger. L' Alphabet. 2003. (Gout de Savoir Ser.). (FRE., Illus.). 24p. (J). (gr. -1-18). pap. (978-2-89021-224-4(6)) Diffusion du livre Mirabel (DLM).

Stanley, Mandy. My First French Book: A Bilingual Introduction to Words, Numbers, Shapes, & Colors. 2007. (ENG & FRE., Illus.). 48p. (J). (gr. -1-k). 7.99 (978-0-7534-5998-0(1), 9780753459980, Kingfisher) Roaring Brook Pr.

Thibaut, Francois. Unassigned. 2004. (FRE.). (J). 0.01 (978-0-9755659-7-1(4)) Language Workshop for Children, The.

Valette, Jean-Paul & Valette, Rebecca M. Discovering French: Nouveau! 1B, Bleu, Deuxieme Partie. l.t. ed. 2004. (YA). (gr. 6-8). 56.52 (978-0-395-88143-9(9)) Holt McDougal.

—Discovering French Blanc, Euro Edition. 2006. (FRE., Illus.). 342p. (-12). per., act. bk. ed. (978-0-618-04709-3(3)) Holt McDougal.

—Discovering French Bleu, Euro Edition. 2006. (Illus.). 397p. (gr. 9-12). stu. ed. (978-0-618-03504-5(4)) Holt McDougal.

Walz, Joel & Piriou, Jean Pierre. Rapports: An Introduction to French Language & Francophone Culture. 5th ed. 2003. (ENG & FRE.). 540p. (YA). pap. 128.36 incl. cd-rom (978-0-618-26705-7(0), 313971) CENGAGE Learning.

Welling, Peter J. Michael le Souffle & the April Fool, 1 vol. Welling, Peter J., illus. 2003. (ENG., Illus.). 32p. (J). (gr. k-3). 16.99 (978-1-58980-105-9(9)) Pelican Publishing Co., Inc.

Woods, Caroline. Quick Revision KS3 French. 2007. pap. 9.95 (978-0-340-94311-3(4), Hodder Education) Hodder Education Group GBR. Dist: Trans-Atlantic Pubns., Inc.

FRENCH LANGUAGE—CONVERSATION AND PHRASE BOOKS

Batot, Yvonne & Gose, Senora. Flip Flop French: Ages 3-5: Level 1. 2007. (Illus.). 84p. (J). spiral bd. 25.00 (978-1-60402-967-3(6)) Flip n Flop Learning, LLC.

Crosbie, Duncan. Find Out about France: Learn French Words & Phrases & about Life in France. Hutchinson, Tim, illus. 2006. (Find Out about Bks.). (ENG.). 64p. (J). (gr. 3-18). 13.99 (978-0-7641-5953-4(4)) Barron's Educational Series, Inc.

Cullis, Megan. Essential French Phrases Internet-Referenced. 2010. (Essential French Phrases Ser.). 64p. (J). pap. 9.99 (978-0-7945-2650-4(0), Usborne) EDC Publishing.

Delaney, Sally & Richards, Wendy. How Do You Say That in French? 1000 Words & Phrases for Kids. Galloway, Ruth, illus. 2014. (FRE & ENG.). 64p. (J). (gr. 2-6). 12.99 (978-1-84322-915-5(3), Armadillo) Anness Publishing GBR. Dist: National Bk. Network.

Mahoney, Judy. Teach Me Everyday French Vol 1, Vol 1. Girouard, Patrick, illus. 2008. (FRE & ENG.). 32p. (J). (gr. -1). 19.95 (978-1-59972-101-9(5)) Teach Me Tapes, Inc.

Pirz, Therese S. Kids Stuff French: Easy French Phrases for You & Your Kids. 2010. (Bilingual Kids Ser.). (FRE & ENG., Illus.). 186p. (J). pap. 22.95 (978-0-9606140-5-9(2)) Chou Chou Pr.

Poulin, Stephane. As-Tu Vu Josephine? 2003. (FRE & SPA., Illus.). 24p. (J). (gr. k-3). pap. 6.95 (978-0-88776-645-9(5)) Tundra Bks. CAN. Dist: Penguin Random Hse. LLC.

Rivera, Donald S. LinguaFun! French. 2004. (Travel Ser.). (ENG & FRE.). 54p. 12.95 (978-1-56015-603-1(1)) Penton Overseas, Inc.

Sandviks HOP, Inc. Staff. Hooked on French: Premium Edition. abr. ed. 2007. 64.99 (978-1-60143-380-0(8)) HOP, LLC.

Tulip, Jenny, illus. My First French Word Book. 2004. (ENG & FRE.). 48p. (J). 5.99 (978-1-85854-237-9(5)) Brimax Books Ltd. GBR. Dist: Byeway Bks.

Watson, Carol & Moyle, Philippa. Let's Learn French. Foster, Teresa, illus. 2003. (Let's Learn Ser.). (ENG.). 32p. pap. 9.95 (978-0-7818-1014-2(0)) Hippocrene Bks., Inc.

Wightwick, Jane. Way Cool French Phrasebook. 2005. (ENG & FRE., Illus.). 96p. 12.95 (978-0-07-144839-0(X), 007144839X) McGraw-Hill Cos., The.

FRENCH LANGUAGE—DICTIONARIES

Award, Anna. English/French. Burton, Terry, illus. 2012. (FRE & ENG.). 96p. (J). 11.50 (978-1-84135-798-0(7)) Award Pubns. Ltd. GBR. Dist: Parkwest Pubns., Inc.

Bruzzone, Catherine & Millar, Louise. My French Sticker Dictionary: Everyday Words & Popular Themes in Colorful Sticker Scenes. Comfort, Louise, illus. 2013. (Sticker Dictionaries Ser.). (ENG.). 24p. (J). (gr. -1-1). pap. 6.99 (978-1-4380-0253-8(X)) Barron's Educational Series, Inc.

Bruzzone, Catherine, et al. French-English Picture Dictionary. Comfort, Louise & Dix, Steph, illus. 2011. (First Bilingual Picture Dictionaries Ser.). (FRE & ENG.). 48p. (J). (gr. -1-3). pap. 7.99 (978-0-7641-4660-2(2)) Barron's Educational Series, Inc.

Collins Dictionaries Staff. Collins Very First French Dictionary. 2nd rev. ed. 2014. (Collins Primary Dictionaries Ser.). (FRE & ENG., Illus.). 80p. (J). (gr. 1-4). pap. 9.95 (978-0-00-758354-6(0)) HarperCollins Pubs. Ltd. GBR. Dist: Independent Pubs. Group.

Davies, H. French Dictionary for Beginners Internet-Referenced. 2010. (Beginners Dictionaries Ser.). 128p. (J). pap. 12.99 (978-0-7945-2633-7(0), Usborne) EDC Publishing.

Davies, H. & Holmes, F. French Dictionary for Beginners. 2004. (Beginner's Dictionaries Ser.). (FRE & ENG.). 128p. (J). pap. 12.99 (978-0-7945-0287-4(3)) EDC Publishing.

Davies, Helen. French Dictionary for Beginners. Irving, Nicole, ed. Shackell, John, illus. 2006. (Beginner's Dictionaries Ser.). (FRE.). 128p. (J). (gr. 4). lib. bdg. 20.95 (978-1-58086-475-6(9)) EDC Publishing.

Harrap & Chambers Editors. French Student's Dictionary. (ENG & FRE., Illus.). 800p. (978-0-245-60676-2(9)) Harrap, Larousse Pubs.

Larousse Staff. Mon premier Larousse du Monde. (FRE.). pap. 39.95 (978-2-03-553015-8(6)) Librairie Larousse FRA. Dist: Distribooks, Inc.

Milet Publishing Staff. Bilingual Visual Dictionary. 2011. (Milet Multimedia Ser.). (FRE & ENG., Illus.). 1p. (J). (gr. k-2). cd-rom 19.95 (978-1-84059-584-0(1)) Milet Publishing.

Schmitt, Conrad J., et al. Glencoe French 1B Bon Voyage! 2nd ed. 2004. (Glencoe French Ser.). (FRE & ENG., Illus.). 120p. (gr. 6-8). stu. ed., spiral bd., wbk. ed. 22.32 (978-0-07-865629-3(X), 007865629X) McGraw-Hill Education.

FRENCH LANGUAGE—DICTIONARIES—ENGLISH

Amery, Heather. First Hundred Words in French II. 2015. (First Hundred Words Ser.). (ENG.). 32p. (J). pap. 6.99 (978-0-7945-3515-5(1), Usborne) EDC Publishing.

Brooks, Felicity. My First French Word Book. 2015. (My First Word Bks.). (ENG.). 20p. (J). 9.99 (978-0-7945-3492-9(9), Usborne) EDC Publishing.

—Very First Dictionary in French - Internet Referenced. 2008. (Very First Dictionaries Ser.). 80p. (J). 11.99 (978-0-7945-2047-2(2), Usborne) EDC Publishing.

Collins. Collins French School Dictionary. 3rd rev. ed. 2011. (FRE & ENG.). 640p. (J). pap. 9.95 (978-0-00-736785-6(6)) HarperCollins Pubs. Ltd. GBR. Dist: Independent Pubs. Group.

Collins Dictionaries. Collins French School Dictionary. 4th rev. ed. 2015. (FRE & ENG.). 640p. (YA). (gr. 6-11). pap. 9.99 (978-0-00-756931-1(9)); (Illus.). (gr. 5-11). pap. 10.99 (978-0-00-756935-9(1)) HarperCollins Pubs. Ltd. GBR. Dist: Independent Pubs. Group.

—Collins Primary French Dictionary. 2014. (FRE & ENG., Illus.). 640p. (J). (gr. 2-6). 14.99 (978-0-00-757874-0(1)) HarperCollins Pubs. Ltd. GBR. Dist: Independent Pubs. Group.

Kenny, Chantal Lacourcière. The Kids Can Press French & English Phrase Book. Hendry, Linda, illus. 2004. (ENG.). 40p. (J). 7.95 (978-1-55337-650-7(1)) Kids Can Pr., Ltd. CAN. Dist: Hachette Bk. Group.

Turhan, Sedat. New Bilingual Visual Dictionary (English-French) 2nd ed. 2017. (New Bilingual Visual Dictionary Ser.). (FRE & ENG., Illus.). 144p. (J). (gr. k-2). 19.95 (978-1-78508-885-8(8)) Milet Publishing.

York, M. J. Learn French Words. Petelinsek, Kathleen, illus. 2014. (Foreign Language Basics Ser.). (ENG.). 24p. (J). (gr. 2-5). 27.07 (978-1-62687-374-2(7), 207121) Child's World, Inc., The.

FRENCH LANGUAGE—GRAMMAR

Delaney, Sally & Richards, Wendy. How Do You Say That in French? 1000 Words & Phrases for Kids. Galloway, Ruth, illus. 2014. (FRE & ENG.). 64p. (J). (gr. 2-6). 12.99 (978-1-84322-915-5(3), Armadillo) Anness Publishing GBR. Dist: National Bk. Network.

Fawbush, Karla Winther, et al. C'est a Toi! French Grammar & Vocabulary Exercises, Level 1. rev. ed. (FRE.). (YA). (gr. 9-12). pap. 15.95 (978-0-8219-1980-4(6), 40674) EMC/Paradigm Publishing.

Foundations of French Grammar-Negatives, Question Words, Articles. 2004. (YA). 9.95 (978-1-931463-21-8(2)) Aaron Levy Pubns., LLC.

Foundations of French Grammar-Object Pronouns & Prepositions. 2004. (YA). 9.95 (978-1-931463-20-1(4)) Aaron Levy Pubns., LLC.

Hazan, Maurice, illus. & creator. Les Animaux et les verbes flash card Set. Hazan, Maurice, creator. 2003. (FRE.). (J). 95.00 (978-1-932770-38-4(0), FC-FWLB1) Symtalk, Inc.

—Chiffres, couleurs, verbes et phrases flash card Set. Hazan, Maurice, creator. 2003. (FRE.). (J). 115.00 (978-1-932770-39-1(9), FC-FWLB2) Symtalk, Inc.

McNab, Rosi. French Club, Bk. 1. 2009. (FRE & ENG., Illus.). 48p. (J). (gr. 2-4). pap. 15.99 (978-0-00-728756-7(9)) HarperCollins Pubs. Ltd. GBR. Dist: Independent Pubs. Group.

Milet Publishing Staff. La Musique. 2012. (My First Bilingual Book Ser.).Tr. of Music. (FRE & ENG., Illus.). 24p. (J). (gr. k — 1). bds. 7.99 (978-1-84059-720-2(8)) Milet Publishing.

—Opposites. 2012. (My First Bilingual Book Ser.). (FRE & ENG., Illus.). 24p. (J). (gr. k — 1). bds. 7.99 (978-1-84059-736-3(4)) Milet Publishing.

—Sports - My First Bilingual Book. 2012. (My First Bilingual Book Ser.). (FRE & ENG., Illus.). 24p. (J). (gr. k — 1). bds. 7.99 (978-1-84059-752-3(6)) Milet Publishing.

Pattis, Anne-Francoise. Let's Learn French Coloring Book. 2003. (ENG & FRE., Illus.). 64p. pap. 8.00 (978-0-07-142141-6(6), 0071421416) McGraw-Hill Education.

Travis, Joelle & Figueras, Ligaya, eds. Les Animaux et les Verbes. Hazan, Maurice, illus. 2003. (FRE.). (J). per. 20.00 (978-1-932770-18-6(6), FWLB1) Symtalk, Inc.

—Chiffres, Couleurs, Verbes et Phrases. Hazan, Maurice, illus. 2003. (FRE.). 114p. (J). per. 20.00 (978-1-932770-19-3(4), FWLB2) Symtalk, Inc.

FRENCH LANGUAGE—READERS

Berwick, Gwen, et al. Voila! For the National Framework. 2005. (ENG., Illus.). 160p. (YA). pap., stu. ed. 29.50 (978-0-7487-9094-4(2)) Nelson Thornes Ltd. GBR. Dist: Trans-Atlantic Pubns., Inc.

Blackstone, Stella. La Famille Active de l'Ours. 2012.Tr. of Bear's Busy Family. (FRE & ENG.). (J). pap. 6.99 (978-1-84686-772-9(X)) Barefoot Bks., Inc.

—L'Ours au Travail. 2012.Tr. of Bear at Work. (FRE & ENG.). (J). 6.99 (978-1-84686-770-5(3)) Barefoot Bks., Inc.

Bruzzone, Catherine. First French with Superchat: Learn French the Super-Fun Way Through Games, Activities & Songs. Beaton, Clare, illus. 2007. (Teach Yourself Ser.). (ENG.). 32p. (gr. 8-12). 13.95 (978-0-07-148101-4(X), 007148101X) McGraw-Hill Cos., The.

Burke, David. Beauty & the Beast: Level 3: Learn French Through Fairy Tales. Sandoval, Migs, illus. 2006. (Learn French Through Fairy Tales Ser.). (ENG & FRE.). 29p. (J). (gr. -1-3). pap. 14.95 incl. audio compact disk (978-1-891888-87-8(0)) Slangman Publishing.

Burnett, Frances Hodgson. La Petit Princesse.Tr. of Little Princess. (J). pap. 12.95 (978-2-07-056710-2(9)) Gallimard, Editions FRA. Dist: Distribooks, Inc.

Chatel, Kim. Clip-Clop, Tippity-Tap French Vocabulary on the Farm. Bullock, Kathleen, illus. 2011. 24p. pap. 10.95 (978-1-61633-136-8(4)) Guardian Angel Publishing, Inc.

Crossley, David, illus. ABC. 2004. (Baby's First Learning Ser.). 12p. (J). bds. 4.99 (978-1-85854-890-6(X)) Brimax Books Ltd. GBR. Dist: Byeway Bks.

Dahl, Roald. James et la Grosse Peche.Tr. of James & the Giant Peach. (FRE.). (J). pap. 17.95 (978-2-07-051374-1(2)) Gallimard, Editions FRA. Dist: Distribooks, Inc.

Deluc, Yves & Ruck. Prisunic. (FRE.). 48p. (YA). (gr. 9-12). pap. 5.99 *(978-0-88436-905-9(6)*, 40287) EMC/Paradigm Publishing.
Demado. En Route: Enhanced Online Edition. 4th ed. 2003. cd-rom 54.80 *(978-0-03-031976-1(5))* Holt McDougal.
Fralin, Alfred G. & Szeps-Fralin, Christiane. Le Francais Vivant 1. (YA). (gr. 6-8). pap. 9.95 *(978-0-8219-0517-3(1)*, 40662); pap. 118.00 incl. audio *(978-0-8219-0560-9(0)*, 40046) EMC/Paradigm Publishing.
—Le Francais Vivant 2. (J). stu. ed. 45.95 *(978-0-8219-0604-0(6)*, 40455); (YA). pap., wbk. ed. 10.50 *(978-0-8219-0606-4(2)*, 40663) EMC/Paradigm Publishing.
Fralin, Alfred G., et al. Le Francais Vivant 3. (YA). (gr. 9-12). stu. ed. 46.95 *(978-0-8219-0892-1(8)*, 40456); pap., wbk. ed. 10.95 *(978-0-8219-0893-8(6)*, 40664) EMC/Paradigm Publishing.
Holt, Rinehart and Winston Staff. En Route: Online Edition. 4th ed. 2003. 43.86 *(978-0-03-031817-7(3))* Holt McDougal.
Levine, Julia Pimsleur. Little Pim - Feelings. 2011. (ENG, FRE & SPA., Illus.). 10p. (J). (gr. -1 — 1). bds. 8.95 *(978-1-4197-0018-7(9)*, Abrams Bks. for Young Readers) Abrams, Inc.
Lomba, Ana. Boucle d'or et les Trois Ours. Wenzel, Dominique, tr. Cornejo, Santiago, illus. 2006.Tr. of Goldilocks & the Three Bears. (FRE & ENG.). 48p. (gr. -1-3). 17.00 *(978-0-07-146173-3(6)*, 0071461736) McGraw-Hill Cos., The.
—Le Petit Chaperon Rouge. Wenzel, Dominique, tr. Cornejo, Santiago, illus. 2006.Tr. of Little Red Riding Hood/The Fun Way to Learn 50 New French Words! (ENG & FRE.). 48p. (gr. -1-3). 17.00 incl. audio compact disk *(978-0-07-146167-2(1)*, 0071461671) McGraw-Hill Cos., The.
Look & Learn ABC Book. (Illus.). 18p. (J). bds. *(978-1-86515-520-3(9))* Hinkler Bks. Pty, Ltd.
Milet Publishing Staff. My First Bilingual Book - Colours. 2010. (My First Bilingual Book Ser.). (FRE & ENG., Illus.). 24p. (J). (gr. k — 1). bds. 8.99 *(978-1-84059-535-2(3))* Milet Publishing.
—Numbers - My First Bilingual Book. 2010. (My First Bilingual Book Ser.). (FRE & ENG., Illus.). 24p. (J). (gr. k — 1). bds. 7.99 *(978-1-84059-541-3(8))* Milet Publishing.
La Petite Sirene: Family, The Weather, Gardens, Underwater Life. (FRE & ENG., Illus.). 24p. (J). (gr. -1-5). pap., stu. ed. 5.95 *(978-88-8148-361-7(0))* EMC/Paradigm Publishing.
Sandoval, Migs, illus. Goldilocks & the 3 Bears: Level 2: Learn French Through Fairy Tales. 2006. (Learn French Through Fairy Tales Ser.). (ENG & FRE.). 29p. (J). (gr. -1-3). pap. 14.95 incl. audio compact disk *(978-1-891888-81-6(1))* Slangman Publishing.
Szeps-Fralin, Christiane. Drole de Mission. (FRE.). (YA). (gr. 9-12). stu. ed. 6.95 *(978-0-8219-0024-6(2)*, 40292); pap., wbk. ed. 5.95 *(978-0-8219-0025-3(0)*, 40654); pap., tchr.'s training gde. ed. 5.95 *(978-0-8219-0026-0(9)*, 40816) EMC/Paradigm Publishing.
—Poursuite Inattendue. (FRE.). (gr. 9-12). (J). stu. ed. 6.95 *(978-0-8219-0021-5(8)*, 40291); (YA). pap., wbk. ed. 5.95 *(978-0-8219-0022-2(6)*, 40653); (YA). pap., tchr.'s training gde. ed. 5.95 *(978-0-8219-0023-9(4)*, 40815) EMC/Paradigm Publishing.
wintranslation.com, tr. Carry Me (French/English), 1 vol. 2010. (ENG & FRE., Illus.). 20p. (J). 6.95 *(978-1-59572-216-4(5))* Star Bright Bks., Inc.
Zola, Émile. Trois Nouvelles, Level C. (FRE.). (YA). (gr. 7-12). 9.99 *(978-0-88436-744-4(4)*, 40311) EMC/Paradigm Publishing.

FRENCH LANGUAGE—STUDY AND TEACHING

AA Publishing. French. 2013. (AA Kids Phrasebooks Ser.). (FRE & ENG., Illus.). 128p. (J). (gr. 2-7). pap. 10.99 *(978-0-7495-7417-8(8))* Automobile Assn. GBR. Dist: Independent Pubs. Group.
Amery, H. First 100 Words in French. 2004. (First Hundred Words Ser.). (FRE., Illus.). 34p. (J). lib. bdg. 14.99 *(978-1-58086-394-0(9))* EDC Publishing.
Amery, Heather. First 100 Words in French. 2004. (First Hundred Words Ser.). (FRE & ENG.). 34p. (J). pap. 6.99 *(978-0-7945-0013-9(7)*, Usborne) EDC Publishing.
Bruzzone, Catherine & Martinneau, Susan. Hide & Speak French. Comfort, Louise, illus. 2003. (Hide & Speak Ser.). (FRE & ENG.). 32p. (J). pap. 8.99 *(978-0-7641-2588-1(5))* Barron's Educational Series, Inc.
Croteau, Marie-Danielle. La Petite Reine au Nez Rouge. St. Aubin, Bruno, illus. 2004. (Premier Roman Ser.). (FRE.). 64p. (J). (gr. 1-4). pap. *(978-2-89021-706-5(X))* Diffusion du livre Mirabel (DLM).
Dorling Kindersley Publishing Staff. 10 Minutes a Day: French, Beginner. 2016. (ENG.). 80p. (J). (gr. 3-7). pap. 9.99 *(978-1-4654-4409-7(2)*, DK Children) Dorling Kindersley Publishing, Inc.
Gilbert-Dumas, Mylène. Mystique. 2004. (Mon Roman Ser.). (FRE.). 256p. (J). (gr. 2). pap. *(978-2-89021-652-5(7))* Diffusion du livre Mirabel (DLM).
Gingras, Charlotte. La Boite a Bonheur. Jorisch, Stéphane, illus. 2004. (Mon Roman Ser.). (FRE.). 64p. (J). (gr. 2). pap. *(978-2-89021-668-6(3))* Diffusion du livre Mirabel (DLM).
Gintrac, Brigitte. Let's Play with Lou. 2010. 24p. pap. 15.95 *(978-1-4389-5243-7(0))* AuthorHouse.
Hanson, Tracie, des. New World Baby - French. 2007. (ENG, FRE, SPA & GER., Illus.). 28p. (J). 14.00 *(978-0-9799185-1-3(0))* Hanson, Tracie.
Lemieux, Jean. Le Fil de la Vie. Casson, Sophie, illus. 2004. (Premier Roman Ser.). (FRE.). 64p. (J). (gr. 1-4). pap. *(978-2-89021-644-0(6))* Diffusion du livre Mirabel (DLM).
Marie-France, Marcie. Bilingual Beginners Kit: English-French, 2 vols. 2010. (FRE., Illus.). 48p. (J). 17.95 *(978-1-55386-120-1(5)*, 1553861205) Jordan, Sara Publishing.
—Bilingual Kids Beginners - English-French: Ready-to-Use Reproducible Worksheets & Exercises. Content-Based Units Making Language Acquisition Easy Fun. 2010. (FRE.). 64p. (J). 15.95 *(978-1-55386-122-5(1)*, 1553861221) Jordan, Sara Publishing.
My First 100 Words in French/English. 2003. (First Words & Pictures Book Ser.).Tr. of My First 100 Words. (FRE.). 32p. (J). 11.95 *(978-0-7525-7768-5(9))* Parragon, Inc.
Wightwick, Jane. Way Cool French Phrasebook. 2005. (ENG & FRE., Illus.). 96p. 12.95 *(978-0-07-144839-0(X)*, 007144839X) McGraw-Hill Cos., The.

FRENCH LITERATURE—HISTORY AND CRITICISM

Bloom, Harold, ed. & tr. Emile Zola. Bloom, Harold, tr. 2003. (Bloom's Modern Critical Views Ser.). 150p. (C). (gr. 9). 45.00 *(978-0-7910-7663-7(6)*, Chelsea Hse.) Facts On File, Inc.
Saddleback Educational Publishing Staff, ed. Around the World in 80 Days. 2011. (Timeless Classics Ser.). (ENG.). 48p. (YA). (gr. 9-12). pupil's gde. ed. 19.95 incl. cd-rom *(978-1-61651-127-2(3))* Saddleback Educational Publishing, Inc.
—The Count of Monte Cristo. 2011. (Timeless Classics Ser.). (ENG.). 48p. (YA). (gr. 9-12). pupil's gde. ed. 19.95 incl. cd-rom *(978-1-61651-131-9(1))* Saddleback Educational Publishing, Inc.
—Hunchback of Notre Dame. 2011. (Timeless Classics Ser.). (ENG.). 48p. (YA). (gr. 9-12). pupil's gde. ed. 19.95 incl. cd-rom *(978-1-61651-138-8(9))* Saddleback Educational Publishing, Inc.
—Man in the Iron Mask. 2011. (Timeless Classics Ser.). (ENG.). 48p. (YA). (gr. 9-12). pupil's gde. ed. 19.95 incl. cd-rom *(978-1-61651-143-2(5))* Saddleback Educational Publishing, Inc.
—The Three Musketeers. 2011. (Timeless Classics Ser.). (ENG.). 48p. (YA). (gr. 9-12). pupil's gde. ed. 19.95 incl. cd-rom *(978-1-61651-153-1(2))* Saddleback Educational Publishing, Inc.
—20,000 Leagues under the Sea. 2011. (Timeless Classics Ser.). (ENG.). 48p. (YA). (gr. 9-12). pupil's gde. ed. 19.95 incl. cd-rom *(978-1-61651-156-2(7))* Saddleback Educational Publishing, Inc.

FRENCH REVOLUTION

see France—History—Revolution, 1789-1799

FRESHWATER ANIMALS

see also Aquariums; Marine Animals
also names of individual fresh-water animal, e.g. Beavers, etc.

Anderson, Sheila. What Can Live in a Lake? 2010. (First Step Nonfiction - Animal Adaptations Ser.). (ENG.). 24p. (gr. k-2). pap. 6.95 *(978-0-7613-5677-6(0))* Lerner Publishing Group.
Buckley, Arabella B. By Pond & River. 2008. (Illus.). 60p. pap. 9.95 *(978-1-59915-272-1(X))* Yesterday's Classics.
Callery, Sean. Life Cycles - River. 2013. (Lifecycles Ser.). (ENG., Illus.). 32p. (J). (gr. 2-5). 6.99 *(978-0-7534-7066-4(7)*, 9780753470664, Kingfisher) Roaring Brook Pr.
Clarke, Nadine. Get Bushwise: on Safari Desert, River, Bushveld: A Young Explorer's Guide. 2013. 192p. pap. 23.00 *(978-1-4317-0206-0(4))* Penguin Random House Grupo Editorial ESP. Dist: Casemate Pubs. & Bk. Distributors, LLC.
Goldish, Meish. Amazing Water Frogs. 2010. (Amphibiana Ser.). (Illus.). 24p. (YA). (gr. k-3). lib. bdg. 22.61 *(978-1-936087-34-1(0))* Bearport Publishing Co., Inc.
Hammersmith, Craig. Life in the Pond. 2011. (Habitats Around the World Ser.). (ENG.). 24p. (gr. k-1). pap. 41.70 *(978-1-4296-7153-8(X)*, Pebble Plus) Capstone Press of Coughlan Cos.
Heinz, Brian. Butternut Hollow Pond. Marstall, Bob, illus. 2006. (ENG.). 32p. (J). (gr. 2-6). pap. 6.95 *(978-0-8225-5993-1(5)*, First Avenue Editions) Lerner Publishing Group.
Kalman, Bobbie. Baby Animals in Rivers. 2013. (ENG., Illus.). 24p. (J). *(978-0-7787-1019-6(X))*; pap. *(978-0-7787-1033-2(5))* Crabtree Publishing Co.
Kopp, Megan. What Do You Find in a Pond? 2016. (ENG., Illus.). 24p. (J). *(978-0-7787-2259-5(7))* Crabtree Publishing Co.
Ridley, Kimberly. Secret Pool. Raye, Rebekah, illus. 2013. (Tilbury House Nature Book Ser.: 0). (ENG.). 32p. (gr. 1-7). 16.95 *(978-0-88448-339-7(8)*, 884339) Tilbury Hse. Pubs.
Sullivan, Laura. Saltwater & Freshwater Creatures Explained. 2016. (Distinctions in Nature Ser.). 32p. (J). pap. 10.58 *(978-1-5026-2185-6(1))* Cavendish Square Publishing.
West, David. Freshwater Animals. 2016. (Safari Sam's Wild Animals Ser.). 24p. (gr. k-3). 28.50 *(978-1-62588-071-0(5)*, Smart Apple Media) Black Rabbit Bks.
—Pond Life. (Nora the Naturalist's Animals Ser.). 24p. (gr. k-3). 2014. pap. 8.95 *(978-1-62588-053-6(7))* 2013. (Illus.). 28.50 *(978-1-62588-001-7(4))* Black Rabbit Bks.
World Book, Inc. Staff, contrib. by. Freshwater Life of the United States & Canada. 2004. (World Book's Science & Nature Guides Ser.). (Illus.). 80p. (J). *(978-0-7166-4213-8(1))* World Bk., Inc.
Worth, Bonnie. Would You Rather Be a Pollywog? All about Pond Life. Ruiz, Aristides & Mathieu, Joseph, illus. 2010. (Cat in the Hat's Learning Library). (ENG.). 48p. (J). (gr. -1-3). 9.99 *(978-0-375-82883-6(4)*, Random Hse. Bks. for Young Readers) Random Hse. Children's Bks.

FRESHWATER BIOLOGY

see also Aquariums; Freshwater Animals; Freshwater Plants; Marine Biology

Aspen-Baxter, Linda. Fresh Waters. 2006. (Biomes Ser.). (J). (Illus.). 32p. (gr. 3-7). lib. bdg. 26.00 *(978-1-59036-442-0(2))*; 9.95 *(978-1-59036-443-7(0))* Weigl Pubs., Inc.
Bussell, Linda. Measuring at the Pond. 2008. (Math in Our World - Level 3 Ser.). 24p. (gr. 2-5). (J). lib. bdg. 22.00 *(978-0-8368-9291-8(7))*; pap. 8.15 *(978-0-8368-9390-8(5))* Stevens, Gareth Publishing LLLP. (Weekly Reader Leveled Readers).
—Vamos a Medir en el Estanque. 2008. (Matemáticas en Nuestro Mundo - Nivel 3 (Math in Our World - Level 3) Ser.). (SPA.). 24p. (gr. 2-5). (J). lib. bdg. 22.00 *(978-0-8368-9299-4(2))*; pap. 8.15 *(978-0-8368-9398-4(0))* Stevens, Gareth Publishing LLLP. (Weekly Reader Leveled Readers).
Coss, Lauren. Life in Ponds. 2014. (Life in Water Biomes Ser.). (ENG.). 24p. (J). (gr. 2-5). 28.50 *(978-1-62687-298-1(8)*, 207139) Child's World, Inc., The.
DeStrulle, Arlene & Johnson, Tora. Guide to Freshwater Animals Without Backbones. Sayre, Tamara, illus. Date not set. (Orig.). (J). (gr. 4-6). pap. 10.95 *(978-0-9616712-6-6(2))* Catskill Ctr. for Conservation & Development, Inc.
Fleisher, Paul. Lake & Pond Food Webs. 2008. pap. 52.95 *(978-0-8225-9352-2(1))* 2007. (ENG., Illus.). 48p. (gr. 2-5). lib. bdg. 26.60 *(978-0-8225-6731-8(8)*, Lerner Pubns.) Lerner Publishing Group.
Gagne, Tammy. Freshwater Ecosystems. 2018. (ENG.). 32p. (gr. 3-6). ***(978-1-63235-456-3(X)***, 12-Story Library) Pr. Room Editions LLC.
Gray, Leon. Rivers & Lakes. 2015. (Amazing Biomes Ser.). (Illus.). 32p. (gr. 3-6). 31.35 *(978-1-78121-244-8(9)*, 1389646) Brown Bear Bks.
Grove, Craig J. Frog Water. 2013. 24p. *(978-1-4602-2634-6(8))*; pap. *(978-1-4602-2635-3(6))* FriesenPress.
Harkins, Susan Sales & Harkins, William H. Design Your Own Pond & Water Garden. 2008. (Gardening for Kids Ser.). (Illus.). 48p. (YA). (gr. 1-4). lib. bdg. 29.95 *(978-1-58415-635-2(X))* Mitchell Lane Pubs., Inc.
Heinz, Brian. Butternut Hollow Pond. Marstall, Bob, illus. 2006. (ENG.). 32p. (J). (gr. 2-6). pap. 6.95 *(978-0-8225-5993-1(5)*, First Avenue Editions) Lerner Publishing Group.
Hibbert, Adam. Life in a Pond. 2010. (Nature in Focus Ser.). (Illus.). 32p. (gr. 2-5). (J). pap. 10.50 *(978-1-4339-3412-4(4)*, Gareth Stevens Learning Library); (YA). lib. bdg. 26.00 *(978-1-4339-3411-7(6))* Stevens, Gareth Publishing LLLP.
Holmes, Porter. Plants in My Pond. 2017. (Plants in My World Ser.). 24p. (gr. 4-6). pap. 8.25 ***(978-1-5383-2124-9(6)***, PowerKids Pr.) Rosen Publishing Group, Inc., The.
Holt, Rinehart and Winston Staff. Holt Science & Technology Chapter 11: Earth Science: The Flow of Fresh Water. 5th ed. 2004. (Illus.). pap. 12.86 *(978-0-03-030316-6(8))* Holt McDougal.
Ivancic, Linda. Invasive Freshwater Species. 2016. (Invasive Species Ser.). (Illus.). 48p. (J). (gr. 4-4). 31.36 *(978-1-5026-1850-4(8))* Cavendish Square Publishing.
King, Zelda. Examining Pond Habitats. 2009. (Graphic Organizers: Habitats Ser.). (Illus.). 24p. (J). (gr. 2-4). pap. 8.25 *(978-1-4358-3121-6(7))*; 24p. (gr. 2-3). 42.50 *(978-1-61513-100-6(0))*; (J). lib. bdg. 22.60 *(978-1-4358-2717-2(1))* Rosen Publishing Group, Inc., The. (PowerKids Pr.).
Kochanoff, Peggy. Be a Pond Detective, 1 vol. 2016. (ENG., Illus.). 40p. (J). (gr. -1-4). pap. 14.95 *(978-1-77108-394-2(8))* Nimbus Publishing, Ltd. CAN. Dist: Orca Bk. Pubs. USA.
Kopp, Megan. Lakes & Ponds Inside Out. 2015. (ENG., Illus.). 32p. (J). *(978-0-7787-1499-6(3))* Crabtree Publishing Co.
—What Do You Find in a Pond? 2016. (ENG., Illus.). 24p. (J). *(978-0-7787-2259-5(7))* Crabtree Publishing Co.
Lindeen, Carol K. & Lindeen, Carol K. Life in a Pond. 2016. (Living in a Biome Ser.). (ENG.). 24p. (gr. k-1). pap. 7.29 *(978-1-5157-3463-5(3)*, Pebble Plus) Capstone Press of Coughlan Cos.
Lindeen, Mary. At the Pond. 2015. (BeginningtoRead Ser.). (ENG.). 32p. (J). (gr. k-2). pap. 11.94 *(978-1-60357-755-7(6))*; (Illus.). lib. bdg. 22.60 *(978-1-59953-695-8(1))* Norwood Hse. Pr.
Miller, Mirella S. Life in Freshwater Lakes. 2014. (Life in Water Biomes Ser.). (ENG.). 24p. (J). (gr. 2-5). 28.50 *(978-1-62687-295-0(3)*, 207136) Child's World, Inc., The.
Mooney, Carla. Explore Rivers & Ponds! With 25 Great Projects. Stone, Bryan, illus. 2012. (Explore Your World Ser.). (ENG.). 96p. (J). (gr. k-4). pap. 12.95 *(978-1-936749-80-5(7))* Open City Bks.
Owen, Ruth. Welcome to the Pond. 2016. (Nature's Neighborhoods: All about Ecosystems Ser.). (ENG.). 32p. (J). (gr. -1-3). lib. bdg. 19.95 *(978-1-910549-66-7(5))* Bearport Publishing Co., Inc.
Ridley, Kimberly. Secret Pool. Raye, Rebekah, illus. 2013. (Tilbury House Nature Book Ser.: 0). (ENG.). 32p. (gr. 1-7). 16.95 *(978-0-88448-339-7(8)*, 884339) Tilbury Hse. Pubs.
—The Secret Pool, 1 vol. Raye, Rebekah, illus. 2016. (Tilbury House Nature Book Ser.: 0). (ENG.). 36p. (gr. 1-7). pap. 8.95 *(978-0-88448-494-3(7)*, 884494) Tilbury Hse. Pubs.
Ross, Michael Elsohn. Pond Watching with Ann Morgan. Smith, Wendy, illus. 2005. (Naturalist's Apprentice Biographies Ser.). 48p. (gr. 3-6). lib. bdg. 19.93 *(978-1-57505-385-1(3))* Lerner Publishing Group.
Schomp, Virginia. 24 Hours in a Pond. 2013. (Day in an Ecosystem Ser.). 48p. (J). (gr. 4-8). pap. 12.93 *(978-1-62712-067-8(X))* Cavendish Square Publishing.
Sexton, Colleen. Ponds. 2011. (Blastoff! Readers Ser.). 24p. (J). pap. 5.95 *(978-0-531-26033-3(X)*, Children's Pr.) Scholastic Library Publishing.
Spilsbury, Louise. Pond. Hanna, Gary, illus. 2013. (Look Inside Ser.). (ENG.). 32p. (gr. 1-3). 27.32 *(978-1-4329-7196-0(4))*; pap. 8.29 *(978-1-4329-7203-5(0))* Heinemann-Raintree. (Heinemann First Library).
Sundance/Newbridge LLC Staff. Life in a Pond. 2007. (Early Science Ser.). (gr. k-3). 18.95 *(978-1-4007-6377-1(0))*; pap. 6.10 *(978-1-4007-6373-3(8))* Sundance/Newbridge Educational Publishing.
Taylor, Barbara. Inland Water Habitats. 2006. (Exploring Habitats Ser.). (Illus.). 36p. (gr. 3-7). lib. bdg. 26.00 *(978-0-8368-7254-5(1)*, Gareth Stevens Learning Library) Stevens, Gareth Publishing LLLP.
Toupin, Laurie. Freshwater Habitats: Life in Freshwater Ecosystems. 2005. (Watts Library). (ENG., Illus.). 64p. (J). (gr. 5-7). pap. 8.95 *(978-0-531-16675-8(9)*, Watts, Franklin) Scholastic Library Publishing.
West, David. Pond Life. (Nora the Naturalist's Animals Ser.). 24p. (gr. k-3). 2014. pap. 8.95 *(978-1-62588-053-6(7))* 2013. (Illus.). 28.50 *(978-1-62588-001-7(4))* Black Rabbit Bks.

FRESHWATER PLANTS

see also Aquariums; Marine Plants

Buckley, Arabella B. By Pond & River. 2008. (Illus.). 60p. pap. 9.95 *(978-1-59915-272-1(X))* Yesterday's Classics.
Callery, Sean. Life Cycles - River. 2013. (Lifecycles Ser.). (ENG., Illus.). 32p. (J). (gr. 2-5). 6.99 *(978-0-7534-7066-4(7)*, 9780753470664, Kingfisher) Roaring Brook Pr.
Wilkins, John-Paul. What Can Live in the River?, 1 vol. 2014. (What Can Live There? Ser.). (ENG., Illus.). 24p. (gr. -1-1). 22.65 *(978-1-4846-0575-2(6)*, Heinemann Read & Learn) Heinemann-Raintree.

FREUD, SIGMUND, 1856-1939

Bankston, John. Sigmund Freud: Exploring the Mysteries of the Mind. 2006. (Great Minds of Science Ser.). (Illus.). 128p. (J). (gr. 4-10). lib. bdg. 33.27 *(978-0-7660-2336-9(2))* Enslow Pubs., Inc.
Gillam, Scott. Sigmund Freud: Famous Neurologist, 1 vol. 2011. (Essential Lives Set 7 Ser.). (ENG., Illus.). 112p. (J). (gr. 6-12). lib. bdg. 35.64 *(978-1-61783-004-4(6))* ABDO Publishing Co.
Krull, Kathleen. Sigmund Freud. 2009. (Giants of Science Ser.). (ENG.). 144p. (J). (gr. 3-7). pap. 7.99 *(978-0-14-241266-4(X)*, Puffin Books) Penguin Young Readers Group.

FRICTION

Barchers, Suzanne I. Friction, 1 vol. rev. ed. 2014. (Science Readers: Content & Literacy Ser.). (ENG.). 32p. (gr. 2-2). pap. 8.99 *(978-1-4807-4606-0(1))* Teacher Created Materials, Inc.
Boothroyd, Jennifer. Give It A Push! Give It A Pull! 2010. pap. 45.32 *(978-0-7613-6931-8(7))* Lerner Publishing Group.
—Give It a Push! Give It a Pull! A Look at Forces. 2010. (Lightning Bolt Books (tm) — Exploring Physical Science Ser.). (ENG., Illus.). 32p. (gr. k-2). lib. bdg. 26.60 *(978-0-7613-5431-4(X))* Lerner Publishing Group.
—Why Do Moving Objects Slow Down? 2010. pap. 45.32 *(978-0-7613-6935-6(X))* Lerner Publishing Group.
—Why Do Moving Objects Slow Down? A Look at Friction. 2010. (Lightning Bolt Books (tm) — Exploring Physical Science Ser.). (ENG.). 32p. (gr. k-2). pap. 7.95 *(978-0-7613-6057-5(3))*; lib. bdg. 26.60 *(978-0-7613-5432-1(8))* Lerner Publishing Group.
Figorito, Marcus. Friction & Gravity: Snowboarding Science. 2009. (Real Life Readers Ser.). (ENG., Illus.). 32p. (J). (gr. 5-6). pap. 10.00 *(978-1-4358-0185-1(7))*; 32p. (gr. 5-5). 47.90 *(978-1-60853-053-3(1))*; (J). (gr. 4-6). lib. bdg. 25.25 *(978-1-4358-2995-4(6))* Rosen Publishing Group, Inc., The. (PowerKids Pr.).
Guillain, Charlotte. Brillante U Opaco, 1 vol. 2010. (Las Propiedades de Los Materiales Ser.). (SPA.). 24p. (gr. -1-1). pap. 6.29 *(978-1-4329-4249-6(2)*, Bellota) Heinemann-Raintree.
Hawkins, Jay. Push & Pull: The Science of Forces. 2013. (Big Bang Science Experiments Ser.). (ENG., Illus.). 32p. (gr. 3-6). 26.50 *(978-1-4777-0324-3(1))*; pap. 11.75 *(978-1-4777-0368-7(3))* Windmill Bks.
Howse, Jennifer. Inclined Planes. 2009. (Science Matters Ser.). (Illus.). 24p. (J). (gr. 3-5). pap. 8.95 *(978-1-60596-036-4(5))*; lib. bdg. 24.45 *(978-1-60596-035-7(7))* Weigl Pubs., Inc.
Idzikowski, Lisa. What Is Friction? 2014. (Let's Find Out! Ser.). 32p. (J). (gr. 3-6). 23.45 *(978-1-62275-502-8(2))* Rosen Publishing Group, Inc., The.
Jerome, Kate Boehm. Forces That Move. 2007. (Language, Literacy, & Vocabulary - Reading Expeditions Ser.). (ENG., Illus.). 36p. (J). pap. 18.95 *(978-0-7922-5437-9(6))* CENGAGE Learning.
Macken, JoAnn Early. Toys. 2010. (Everyday Science Ser.). 24p. (J). (gr. k-3). 25.65 *(978-1-60753-017-6(1))* Amicus Publishing.
Manolis, Kay. Motion. 2011. (Blastoff! Readers Ser.). 24p. (J). pap. 5.95 *(978-0-531-28458-2(1)*, Children's Pr.) Scholastic Library Publishing.
Mara, Wil. From Sharks to... Swimsuits. 2012. (21st Century Skills Innovation Library: Innovations from Nature Ser.). (ENG.). 32p. (gr. 4-8). 28.50 *(978-1-61080-499-8(6)*, 202109); pap. 14.21 *(978-1-61080-673-2(5)*, 202283) Cherry Lake Publishing.
Mullins, Matt. Friction: Phosphorus Matches Were Invented in 1831. 2011. (True Book(tm), a — Physical Science Ser.). (ENG., Illus.). 48p. (J). lib. bdg. 31.00 *(978-0-531-26321-1(5))*; pap. 6.95 *(978-0-531-26583-3(8))* Scholastic Library Publishing. (Children's Pr.).
Oxlade, Chris. Simple Experiments with Wheels & Axles. 2013. (Science Experiments with Simple Machines Ser.). 32p. (J). (gr. k-3). 26.50 *(978-1-61533-754-5(7))*; pap. 11.75 *(978-1-61533-825-2(X))*; pap. 70.50 *(978-1-61533-826-9(8))* Windmill Bks.
Paris, Stephanie. Drag! Friction & Resistance, 1 vol. 2nd rev. ed. 2013. (Nonfiction Readers Ser.). (ENG.). 64p. (J). (gr. 5-5). pap. 10.99 *(978-1-4333-4940-9(X))* Teacher Created Materials, Inc.
—¡Fsst! Fricción y Resistencia. 2016. (TIME for Kids en Español - Level 5 Ser.). (SPA.). 64p. (gr. 5-5). lib. bdg. 31.99 *(978-1-5157-2930-3(3))* Time for Kids Inc AUS. Dist: Capstone Pub.
Rising, Heather. Is It Smooth or Rough? 2012. (ENG., Illus.). 24p. (J). *(978-0-7787-2051-5(9))*; pap. *(978-0-7787-2058-4(6))* Crabtree Publishing Co.
Schwartz, Heather E. The Science of a Race Car: Reactions in Action. 2010. (Action Science Ser.). (ENG.). 32p. (gr. 3-4). pap. 47.70 *(978-1-4296-5074-8(5)*, Fact Finders) Capstone Press of Coughlan Cos.
Trumbauer, Lisa. What Is Friction? 2004. (Rookie Read-About Science Ser.). (ENG.). (J). 32p. (gr. 1-2). pap. 4.95 *(978-0-516-25843-0(5)*, Children's Pr.); (Illus.). 31p. 20.50 *(978-0-516-23447-2(1)*, Watts, Franklin) Scholastic Library Publishing.
VanVoorst, Jenny Fretland. Hula Hoops. 2016. (Early Physics Fun). 24p. (J). (gr. 2-5). lib. bdg. 25.65 *(978-1-62031-316-9(2)*, Pogo) Jump! Inc.
—Slides. 2016. 24p. (J). (gr. 2-5). lib. bdg. 25.65 *(978-1-62031-318-3(9)*, Pogo) Jump! Inc.
Walker, Sally M. & Feldmann, Roseann. Put Pulleys to the Test. 2011. (Searchlight Books (tm) — How Do Simple Machines Work? Ser.). (ENG., Illus.). 40p. (gr. 3-5). lib. bdg. 27.93 *(978-0-7613-5322-5(4))* Lerner Publishing Group.

FRIENDS, SOCIETY OF

see Society of Friends

FRIENDSHIP

see also Love

Akwudike, Joshua. Mom, Mitchell Refuses to Play with Me. 2012. 38p. pap. 16.95 *(978-1-4626-9547-8(7))* America Star Bks.
All about Us Interactive Packages: Making Friends. (Pebble Soup Explorations Ser.). (gr. -1-18). 52.00 *(978-0-7578-5228-2(9))* Rigby Education.
Amistad: Juego Entero. (SPA.). 150.00 *(978-1-55883-109-4(6)*, 602605) C R C World Literature Ministries/Libros Desafio.
Amistad: Manual para Lideres. (SPA.). tchr. ed. 25.00 *(978-1-55883-108-7(8)*, 602604) C R C World Literature Ministries/Libros Desafio.
Amistad: Recursos para Adultos. (SPA.). 11.75 *(978-1-55883-107-0(X)*, 602603) C R C World Literature Ministries/Libros Desafio.

Amistad: Recursos para Jovenes. (SPA.). (YA). (gr. 5-18). stu. ed. 11.75 (978-1-55883-106-3(1), 602602) C R C World Literature Ministries/Libros Desafio.

Amoroso, Cynthia. Friendliness. 2013. (Values to Live By Ser.). (ENG.). 24p. (J). (gr. -1-2). 25.64 (978-1-62323-518-5(9), 206289) Child's World, Inc., The.

Amos, Janine & Spenceley, Annabel. Let's Make Friends. 2009. (Best Behavior Ser.). (Illus.). 32p. (J). (gr. -1-2). 22.60 (978-1-60754-500-2(4)); pap. 10.55 (978-1-60754-499-9(7)) Windmill Bks.

Andrus, Aubre. Five-Minute True Stories: Animal BFFs. 2016. (ENG., Illus.). 160p. (J). (gr. -1-3). 12.99 (978-0-545-91419-2(1), Scholastic Nonfiction) Scholastic, Inc.

Anza, Ana Luisa. Amigos del Otro Lado. Gomez, Eddie Martinez, illus. rev. ed. 2004. (Castillo de la Lectura Naranja Ser.). (SPA & ENG.). 136p. (J). pap. 7.95 (978-970-20-0130-0(7)) Castillo, Ediciones, S. A. de C. V. MEX. Dist: Macmillan.

Austen, Mary. I Learn from My Friends. 2016. (Things I Learn Ser.). (Illus.). 24p. (J). (gr. 1-1). pap. 8.25 (978-1-4994-2345-7(4), PowerKids Pr.) Rosen Publishing Group, Inc., The.

Bailey, Debbie. Mis Amigos. Huszar, Susan, photos by. 2003. (Hablemos Ser.).Tr. of My Friends. (SPA., Illus.). 16p. (J). (gr. -1 — 1). bds. 5.95 (978-1-55037-827-6(9), 9781550378276) Annick Pr., Ltd. CAN. Dist: Publishers Group West (PGW).

—My Friends. Huszar, Susan, photos by. 6th ed. 2003. (Talk-About-Bks.: 17). (ENG., Illus.). 16p. (J). (gr. -1 — 1). bds. 6.95 (978-1-55037-817-7(1), 9781550378177) Annick Pr., Ltd. CAN. Dist: Publishers Group West (PGW).

Bailey, Diane. Girls: Being Best Friends. 2012. (Relationships 101 Ser.). (ENG., Illus.). 48p. (J). (gr. 5-8). 27.95 (978-1-4488-6831-5(9)); pap. 11.75 (978-1-4488-6834-6(3)) Rosen Publishing Group, Inc., The.

Basen, Ryan. Got Your Back: Dealing with Friends & Enemies, 1 vol. 2010. (Essential Health: a Guy's Guide Ser.). (ENG.). 112p. (J). (gr. 6-12). lib. bdg. 35.64 (978-1-61613-540-9(9)) ABDO Publishing Co.

Basic Friendship Curriculum: Year 2. stu. ed. 13.25 (978-1-56212-732-9(2), 300210); instr.'s gde. ed. 22.25 (978-1-56212-730-5(6), 300200) Faith Alive Christian Resources.

Basic Friendship Curriculum: Year 3. (YA). (gr. 5-18). stu. ed. 13.25 (978-1-56212-737-4(3), 300320) Faith Alive Christian Resources.

Be a Friend. 2006. 16p. (J). pap. 1.99 (978-0-7847-1451-5(7), 22130) Standard Publishing.

Becnel, Barbara, ed. Gangs & Friends: Stanley Tookie Williams Street Peace Series, 8 bks., Vol. 1, Bk. 5. 2008. 24p. (J). 6.95 (978-0-9753584-5-0(6)) Damamli Publishing Co.

Bell, Cece. El Deafo. Lasky, David, illus. 2014. (ENG.). 248p. (J). (gr. 3-7). 21.95 (978-1-4197-1020-9(6)); pap. 10.95 (978-1-4197-1217-3(9)) Abrams, Inc. (Amulet Bks.).

—El Deafo. 2014. (J). lib. bdg. 22.05 (978-0-606-36148-4(0)) Turtleback Bks.

Benchmark Education Company, LLC Staff, compiled by. Families & Friends: Theme Set. 2006. (J). 274.00 (978-1-4108-7069-8(3)) Benchmark Education Co.

Bender, Alexandra Sabina. Alana's Advice... When There's a Clique, You've Got to Think Quick. 2007. (Illus.). 152p. (J). (gr. 4-10). per. 14.95 (978-1-84590-075-5(8)) Crown Hse. Publishing.

Berman, Jax, compiled by. Friends: the Family We Choose (Mini Book) 2015. (ENG., Illus.). 80p. 5.95 (978-1-4413-1831-2(3), 9781441318312) Peter Pauper Pr. Inc.

Berry, Joy. I Love My Friends. Regan, Dana, illus. 2010. (Teach Me About Ser.). (ENG.). 20p. (J). (gr. k — 1). bds. 5.99 (978-1-60577-017-8(5)) Berry, Joy Enterprises.

Birchall, Mark. Copy Cat. 2010. (Child's Play Library). (ENG., Illus.). 32p. (J). (gr. 1-2). (978-1-84643-367-2(3)) Child's Play International Ltd.

Brown, Laurie Krasny. How to Be a Friend. Brown, Marc, illus. 2014. 32p. pap. 7.00 (978-1-61003-381-7(7)) Center for the Collaborative Classroom.

Bullard, Lisa. This Is My Country. Marts, Doreen & Mulryan, Doreen, illus. 2016. (Cloverleaf Books (tm) — Where I Live Ser.). (ENG.). 24p. (J). (gr. k-2). lib. bdg. 25.32 (978-1-4677-9524-1(0), Millbrook Pr.) Lerner Publishing Group.

Burks, Catherine. Different Friends, 5 bks., Set. Lee, Rudolph, illus. Incl. Vol. 1. Hi! Let's Meet Billy. pap. 6.95 (978-1-892750-00-6(7)); Vol. 2. Hi! Let's Meet Pete. pap. 6.95 (978-1-892750-01-3(5)); Vol. 3. Hi! Let's Meet Sam. pap. 6.95 (978-1-892750-02-0(3)); Vol. 4. Hi! Let's Meet Bertha. pap. 6.95 (978-1-892750-03-7(1)); Vol. 5. Hi! Let's Meet Doris. pap. 6.95 (978-1-892750-05-1(8)); (J). (gr. 1-5). 1998. (Illus.). 34.75 (978-1-892750-04-4(X)) Different Friends.

Burns, Jan. Friendship: A How-to Guide. 2011. (Life—a How-To Guide Ser.). (Illus.). 128p. (J). (gr. 6-18). pap. 10.95 (978-1-59845-315-7(7)) Enslow Pubs., Inc.

Burstein, John. Will You Be My Friend? Buddy-Building Strategies. 2009. (Slim Goodbody's Life Skills 101 Ser.). (ENG., Illus.). 32p. (J). (gr. 3-6). lib. bdg. (978-0-7787-4793-2(X)) Crabtree Publishing Co.

—Will You Be My Friend? Buddy Building Strategies. 2009. (Slim Goodbody's Life Skills 101 Ser.). (ENG., Illus.). 32p. (J). (gr. 3-6). pap. (978-0-7787-4809-0(X)) Crabtree Publishing Co.

Burton, Margie, et al. Alone & Together. 2011. (Early Connections Ser.). (J). (978-1-61672-514-3(1)) Benchmark Education Co.

—Alone & Together & Sola y Acompañada: 6 English, 6 Spanish Adaptations. 2011. (J). spiral bd. 75.00 net. (978-1-4108-5629-6(1)) Benchmark Education Co.

Burton, Natasha. 101 Quizzes for BFFs: Crazy Fun Tests to See Who Knows Who Best! 2014. (ENG.). 168p. pap. 10.99 (978-1-4405-8420-6(6)) Adams Media Corp.

Cain, Marie Mowery. Best Friends. 2013. (Big Books, Blue Ser.). (ENG & SPA., Illus.). 16p. pap. 33.00 (978-1-59246-018-2(6)) Big Books, by George!

Canetti, Yanitzia. Friends to the End: Together Is Better. 2010. 24p. (J). 5.99 (978-1-59835-145-3(1), BrickHouse Education) Cambridge BrickHouse, Inc.

—Siempre contigo mi Amigo: La alegria de estar Juntos. 2010. (SPA.). (J). pap. 5.99 (978-1-59835-143-9(5), BrickHouse Education) Cambridge BrickHouse, Inc.

Carlson, Melody & Rue, Nancy N. Dear Nancy: Answers to Letters from Girls Like You, 1 vol. 2008. (Faithgirlz Ser.). (ENG.). 160p. (J). pap. 7.99 (978-0-310-71496-5(6)) Zonderkidz.

Carrell, Elizabeth. A Cat Named Romeo. 2011. 28p. pap. 12.03 (978-1-4670-2559-1(3)) AuthorHouse.

Castle, Jennifer & Spring, Bill. Famous Friends: Best Buds, Rocky Relationships, & Awesomely Odd Couples from Past to Present. 2017. (ENG.). 112p. (J). (gr. 3-7). pap. 8.99 (978-0-545-94253-9(5), Scholastic Paperbacks) Scholastic, Inc.

Cavell-Clarke, Steffi. Making Friends. 2017. 24p. (J). **(978-0-7787-3720-9(9))** Crabtree Publishing Co.

Chatlos, Timothy J. Because Daddy's Coming Home Today. Knight, Michael T., illus. 2012. 24p. (J). pap. 12.99 (978-1-59755-300-1(X), Advantage Childrens) Advantage Bks.

Chen, D. M. & Sun, Michelle. Tie a Wish with Bracelets: Easy & Fun Chinese Knotting. 2012. (ENG., Illus.). 71p. (J). (gr. 4). pap. 10.95 (978-1-937489-01-4(9)) StoryRobin Co.

Coats, Lucy. Bear's Best Friend. Dyer, Sarah, illus. 2014. (ENG.). 32p. (J). (gr. -1-k). 21.00 (978-1-4088-2725-3(5), 9781408827253, Bloomsbury USA Childrens) Bloomsbury Publishing USA.

Coe, Julie L. The Friendship Puzzle: Helping Kids Learn about Accepting & Including Kids with Autism. Brassel, Sondra, illus. 2009. 24p. (J). (gr. k-2). 14.95 (978-0-9789182-4-8(X)) Larstan Publishing, Inc.

Conlon, Mara. Butterflies & Friends: An Art Activity Book for Adventurous Artists of All Ages. Zschock, Martha, illus. 2009. (Scratch & Sketch Ser.). 64p. (J). (gr. 1). spiral bd., act. bk. ed. 12.99 (978-1-59359-841-9(6)) Peter Pauper Pr. Inc.

Cosson, M. J. The Smart Kid's Guide to Friendships. Rooney, Ronnie, illus. 2014. (Smart Kid's Guide to Everyday Life Ser.). (ENG.). 32p. (J). (gr. 2-5). 28.50 (978-1-62687-342-1(9), 207182) Child's World, Inc., The.

Crimi-Trent, Ellen & Priddy, Roger. Super Sticker Book. 2014. (Schoolies Ser.). (ENG.). 130p. (J). (gr. -1-1). pap. 12.99 (978-0-312-51724-3(6), 9780312517243, Priddy Bks.) St. Martin's Pr.

Crist, James J. The Survival Guide for Making & Being Friends. 2014. (ENG., Illus.). 128p. (J). (gr. 4-7). pap. 13.99 (978-1-57542-472-9(X)) Free Spirit Publishing, Inc.

—What to Do When You're Cranky & Blue. 2013. (ENG., Illus.). 128p. (J). (gr. 4-8). pap. 10.99 (978-1-57542-430-9(4)) Free Spirit Publishing, Inc.

Criswell, Patti Kelley. A Smart Girl's Guide to Friendship Troubles: Dealing with Fights, Being Left Out & the Whole Popularity Thing. Martini, Angela, illus. 2003. (ENG.). 88p. pap. 9.95 (978-1-58485-711-2(0)) American Girl Publishing, Inc.

Currie, Lisa. Me, You, Us: A Book to Fill Out Together. 2014. (ENG., Illus.). 186p. (gr. k-12). pap. 15.00 (978-0-399-16794-2(3), TarcherPerigee) Penguin Publishing Group.

Davi. Chichonazo! 2004.Tr. of Bump on the Head! (SPA.). (J). pap. 7.99 (978-84-236-6323-1(X)) Edebé ESP. Dist: Lectorum Pubns., Inc.

Dellasega, Cheryl & Sourcebooks, Inc Staff. The Girl's Friendship Journal. 2005. (ENG.). 128p. (J). (gr. 4-7). pap. 16.00 (978-1-932783-59-9(8)) Sourcebooks, Inc.

Dietrich, Julie. David & His Friend, Jonathan. Ramsey, Marcy, illus. 2005. (Arch Bks.). (ENG.). 16p. (J). 1.99 (978-0-7586-0723-2(7)) Concordia Publishing Hse.

Doe, Jayne, et al. Jon & Jayne's Guide to Making Friends & Getting the Guy (Or Girl) 2008. (Jon & Jayne Doe Ser.). (ENG., Illus.). 128p. (gr. 7-11). pap. 9.95 (978-0-7573-0659-4(4)) Health Communications, Inc.

Dorling Kindersley Publishing Staff. The Adventure Guide. 2015. (ENG., Illus.). 96p. (J). (gr. k-4). lib. bdg. 16.99 (978-1-4654-3623-8(5), DK Children) Dorling Kindersley Publishing, Inc.

Duck Egg Blue & Autumn Publishing. Press-Out & Make Dolly Dressing — Fashionable Friends. 2013. (Dover Paper Dolls Ser.). (ENG.). 16p. (J). (gr. k-5). 6.99 (978-0-486-49130-1(7)) Dover Pubns., Inc.

Dzuver, Leo, et al. How to Get a Girlfriend. 2014. (Illus.). 31p. (J). pap. (978-0-545-80577-3(5)) Scholastic, Inc.

Engelbreit, Mary. The Blessings of Friendship Treasury, 1 vol. 2014. (ENG., Illus.). 40p. (J). 15.99 (978-0-310-74509-9(8)) Zonderkidz.

Espeland, Pamela & Verdick, Elizabeth. Making Choices & Making Friends: The Social Competencies Assets. 2006. (Adding Assets Series for Kids Ser.). (ENG., Illus.). 80p. (J). (gr. 3-7). pap. 7.99 (978-1-57542-201-5(8)) Free Spirit Publishing, Inc.

Feldman, Jean R. & Karapetkova, Holly. Good Bye, Friends (Tune, Buffalo Gal) Lap Book. 2010. (ENG., Illus.). 12p. (gr. -1-k). 9.95 (978-1-61590-220-0(1)) Rourke Educational Media.

Fontes, Justine. Rude Ralph: A Rookie Reader. Jordan, Charles, illus. 2011. (Rookie Ready to Learn - My Family & Friends Ser.). 40p. (J). (gr. -1-k). lib. bdg. 23.00 (978-0-531-26529-1(3), Children's Pr.) Scholastic Library Publishing.

Foster, Dylan. My Friend Sammy. 2011. 28p. (gr. 1-2). pap. 14.95 (978-1-4634-1063-6(8)) AuthorHouse.

Freedman, Russell. Abraham Lincoln & Frederick Douglass: The Story Behind an American Friendship. 2012. (ENG., Illus.). 128p. (J). (gr. 5-7). 18.99 (978-0-547-38562-4(5)) Houghton Mifflin Harcourt Publishing Co.

Friendship & Hair Braiding. 2003. 32p. 12.98 (978-1-4054-1639-9(4)) Parragon, Inc.

Friendship Bracelets. 2004. (Whizz Kits Ser.). (Illus.). 48p. (J). (978-1-84229-938-8(7)) Top That! Publishing PLC.

Fry, Erin. The Power of Friendship. 2005. (Illus.). 16p. (J). pap. (978-0-7367-2920-8(8)) Zaner-Bloser, Inc.

Gamblin, Rose Tooley. The Birthday Party. 2007. (J). (978-0-8127-0464-8(9)) Autumn Hse. Publishing Co.

George, Liz. Conflict Resolution: When Friends Fight. 2015. (Rookie Talk about It(tm) Ser.). (ENG.). 32p. (J). pap. 5.95 (978-0-531-21381-0(1), Children's Pr.) Scholastic Library Publishing.

Gibbons, Jolian A. A Giggly Gaggle of Friends. 2012. 32p. pap. 19.99 (978-1-4772-8147-5(9)) AuthorHouse.

Giovanni, Nikki. Lincoln & Douglass: An American Friendship. Collier, Bryan, illus. 2008. (ENG.). 40p. (J). (gr. 2-6). 16.95 (978-0-8050-8264-7(6), 9780805082647, Holt, Henry & Co. Bks. For Young Readers) Holt, Henry & Co.

—Lincoln & Douglass: An American Friendship. Collier, Bryan, illus. 2013. (ENG.). 40p. (J). (gr. 2-6). 8.99 (978-1-250-01869-4(2), 9781250018694) Square Fish.

Goldsack, Gaby. The Ultimate Sleepover Pack. Reeves, Sue, illus. 24p. (J). 79.60 (978-0-7641-7662-3(5)) Barron's Educational Series, Inc.

Golosi, Rosanne. Best Friends Forever! Martini, Angela, illus. 2005. 64p. (J). (978-0-439-80072-3(2)) Scholastic, Inc.

The Good, the Bad, & Everything Else: Individual Title Six-Packs. (Action Packs Ser.). 104p. (gr. 3-5). 44.00 (978-0-7635-2994-9(X)) Rigby Education.

Gregory, Cam. Where Can I Find A Good Friend? 2014. (Little Books of Answers: Level d Ser.). (Illus.). 16p. (gr. k-2). pap. 7.95 (978-1-927136-33-1(4)) Three Crows Media NZL. Dist: RiverStream Publishing.

Gresh, Dannah. My Secret Keeper Girl(r) Diary. 2014. (ENG.). 160p. (J). 9.99 (978-0-7369-6000-7(7)) Harvest Hse. Pubs.

Greve, Meg. Friends. 2012. (ENG.). 24p. (gr. k-2). pap. 8.95 (978-1-61810-262-1(1)) Rourke Educational Media.

Hale, Shannon. Real Friends. Pham, LeUyen, illus. 2017. (ENG.). 224p. (J). 21.99 (978-1-62672-416-7(4), 9781626724167, First Second Bks.) Roaring Brook Pr.

Hale, Shannon & Pham, LeUyen. Real Friends. 2017. (J). lib. bdg. 24.50 **(978-0-606-39954-8(2))** Turtleback Bks.

Hamilton, Lily & Myers, Barbara. Lily Goes to School. Sellaro, Brendan, illus. 2012. (ENG.). 32p. (J). 17.95 (978-0-938467-59-5(X)) Headline Bks., Inc.

Hammond, Charmaine. Toby, the Pet Therapy Dog, & His Hospital Friends. Prevac, Rose Anne, illus. 2011. (ENG.). 36p. (J). pap. 12.99 (978-0-9836045-0-1(9), Kendahl Hse. Pr.) Youngs, Bettie Bks.

—Toby, the Pet Therapy Dog, Says Be a Buddy, Not a Bully. 2013. (ENG., Illus.). 34p. (J). pap. 12.99 (978-0-9836045-4-9(1)) Youngs, Bettie Bks.

—Toby, the Pet Therapy Dog, Says Be a Buddy Not a Bully. Prevec, Rose Anne, illus. 2013. (ENG.). (J). pap. 12.95 (978-0-9836045-5-6(X), Kendahl Hse. Pr.) Youngs, Bettie Bks.

Hardyman, Robyn. Relationships. 2010. (Being Healthy, Feeling Great Ser.). (ENG.). 32p. (J). pap. 10.60 (978-1-61532-380-7(5), PowerKids Pr.); (gr. 3-6). lib. bdg. 26.50 (978-1-61532-371-5(6)) Rosen Publishing Group, Inc., The.

Hatkoff, Craig, et al. Owen & Mzee: The Language of Friendship. Greste, Peter, photos by. 2007. (Owen & Mzee Ser.). (ENG., Illus.). 40p. (J). (gr. -1-3). 18.99 (978-0-439-89959-8(1), Scholastic Pr.) Scholastic, Inc.

—Owen & Mzee: The True Story of a Remarkable Friendship. Greste, Peter, illus. 2006. (Owen & Mzee Ser.). (ENG.). 40p. (J). (gr. -1-3). 17.99 (978-0-439-82973-1(9), Scholastic Pr.) Scholastic, Inc.

Head, Honor. Family & Friends. 2013. (Let's Read & Talk about Ser.). (Illus.). 32p. (J). (gr. 2-5). 28.50 (978-1-59771-397-9(X)) Sea-To-Sea Pubns.

Holland, Jennifer S. Unlikely Friendships for Kids: The Dog & the Piglet - And Four Other Stories of Animal Friendships. 2012. (Unlikely Friendships for Kids Ser.). (ENG., Illus.). 48p. (J). (gr. 2-12). 7.95 (978-0-7611-7012-9(X), 17012) Workman Publishing Co., Inc.

—Unlikely Friendships for Kids: The Monkey & the Dove - And 4 Other Stories of Animal Friendships. 2012. (Unlikely Friendships for Kids Ser.). (ENG., Illus.). 48p. (J). (gr. 2-12). 7.95 (978-0-7611-7011-2(1), 17011) Workman Publishing Co., Inc.

—Unlikely Friendships for Kids: the Leopard & the Cow: And Four Other Stories of Animal Friendships. 2012. (Unlikely Friendships for Kids Ser.). (ENG., Illus.). 48p. (J). (gr. 2-12). 7.95 (978-0-7611-7013-6(8), 17013) Workman Publishing Co., Inc.

Hopkins, Amy. Girlfriends Make the Best Friends. 2005. 96p. pap. 9.95 (978-1-84601-011-8(X)) M Q Pubns.

How Can I Help? Friends Helping Friends. 2016. (How Can I Help? Friends Helping Friends Ser.). 00064p. (J). (gr. 6-6). 206.70 (978-1-5081-7352-6(4), Rosen Young Adult) Rosen Publishing Group, Inc., The.

Hunt, Rameck, et al. We Beat the Street: How a Friendship Pact Led to Success. 2006. (ENG., Illus.). 208p. (J). (gr. 5-18). 7.99 (978-0-14-240627-4(9), Puffin Books) Penguin Young Readers Group.

I Love You Because You're. 2004. (J). pap. 6.99 (978-0-439-57711-3(X)) Scholastic, Inc.

Innes, Shona & Agocs, Irisz. Friendship Is Like a Seesaw. 2014. (Big Hug Ser.). (ENG.). 32p. (J). (gr. -1-2). 10.99 (978-0-7641-6748-5(0)) Barron's Educational Series, Inc.

Johnson, Kevin. Stick: Glue Yourself to Godly Friends, 1 vol. 2007. (Deeper Ser.). (ENG.). 112p. (gr. 13). pap. 7.99 (978-0-310-27490-2(7)) Zondervan.

Johnson, Nerissa & Parra, Angelo. Teen Reflections, Then & Now. 2011. (Readers' & Writers' Genre Workshop Ser.). (YA). pap. (978-1-4509-3025-3(5)) Benchmark Education Co.

Johnston, Kurt, et al. My Friends, 1 vol. 2007. (Middle School Survival Ser.). (ENG., Illus.). 192p. (YA). (gr. 3-7). pap. 9.99 (978-0-310-27881-8(3)) Zondervan.

Jones, Grace. My Friends. 2017. (Illus.). 24p. (J). **(978-0-7787-3247-1(9))** Crabtree Publishing Co.

Jones, Jen. Are You a Good Friend?, 1 vol. 2011. (Friendship Quizzes Ser.). (ENG.). 32p. (gr. 3-4). lib. bdg. 27.99 (978-1-4296-6541-4(6), Snap Bks.) Capstone Press of Coughlan Cos.

Jones, Jen & Wittrock, Jeni. Friendship Quizzes. 2011. (Friendship Quizzes Ser.). (ENG.). 32p. (gr. 3-4). lib. bdg. 111.96 (978-1-4296-6543-8(2), Snap Bks.) Capstone Press of Coughlan Cos.

Jones, Kip. The Power of Bystanders: Willie Bohanon & Friends Learn to Handle Bullying Like a Boss. Isely, Chad, illus. 2015. (ENG.). 32p. (J). pap. 10.95 (978-1-934490-79-2(2)) Boys Town Pr.

Jones, Lynda. Mrs. Lincoln's Dressmaker: The Unlikely Friendship of Elizabeth Keckley & Mary Todd Lincoln. 2009. (ENG., Illus.). 80p. (J). (gr. 5). lib. bdg. 27.90 (978-1-4263-0378-4(5)); 18.95 (978-1-4263-0377-7(7)) National Geographic Society. (National Geographic Children's Bks.).

Kalman, Bobbie. These Are My Friends. 2010. (My World Ser.). (ENG., Illus.). 16p. (J). (gr. k-2). (978-0-7787-9439-4(3)); pap. (978-0-7787-9483-7(0)) Crabtree Publishing Co.

Keating-Velasco, Joanna L. A Is for Autism, F Is for Friend: A Kid's Book on Making Friends with a Child Who Has Autism. 2007. (Illus.). 54p. per. 12.95 (978-1-931282-43-7(9)) Autism Asperger Publishing Co.

Kerley, Barbara. With a Friend by Your Side. 2015. (ENG., Illus.). 48p. (J). (gr. -1-3). 17.99 (978-1-4263-1905-1(3), National Geographic Children's Bks.) National Geographic Society.

Kirchmeier, Jenn-Ann, illus. The Tails of Brinkley the Berner: The Beginning. 2008. 32p. (J). 16.95 (978-0-9793288-0-0(2)) Brinkley Bks., Inc.

Klutz Editors & Dzwonik, Cristian. Amigas para Siempre. Esteve, Laura, tr. 2005. (SPA., Illus.). 33p. (J). spiral bd. 18.95 (978-987-1078-29-5(3)) Klutz Latino MEX. Dist: Independent Pubs. Group.

Kranz, Rachel. Opening Night. 2011. (Navigators Ser.). (J). pap. (978-1-61672-960-8(0)) Benchmark Education Co.

Ladin - Bramet, Lisa. I Was Told That Angels Don't Need Friends. 2011. 120p. pap. 35.98 (978-1-4269-4891-6(3)) Trafford Publishing.

Langrish, Bob. Horses & Friends Poster Book. 2004. (ENG., Illus.). 64p. (J). (gr. 3-8). pap. 10.95 (978-1-58017-580-7(5), 67580) Storey Publishing, LLC.

Lluch, Isabel B. & Lluch, Emily. B. F. F. Best Friends Forever: Have Fun, Share, & Laugh While Getting to Know Your Best Friends! 2010. (ENG.). 112p. (J). (gr. 6-7). pap. 9.95 (978-1-934386-89-7(8)) WS Publishing.

Loewen, Nancy & Skelley, Paula. Besties, Sleepovers, & Drama Queens: Questions & Answers about Friends. Mora, Julissa, illus. 2015. (Girl Talk Ser.). (ENG.). 32p. (gr. 3-4). lib. bdg. 27.99 (978-1-4914-1859-8(1), Snap Bks.) Capstone Press of Coughlan Cos.

Loria, Laura. Etiquette among Friends. 2016. (Etiquette Rules! Ser.). 00048p. (J). (gr. 6-6). pap. 11.75 (978-1-4994-6488-7(6)) Rosen Publishing Group, Inc., The.

Lowery, Zoe & Bezdecheck, Bethany. Women in Relationships. 2017. (Women in the World Ser.). 112p. (gr. 12-11). 37.10 **(978-1-5081-7443-1(1)**, Rosen Young Adult) Rosen Publishing Group, Inc., The.

Luster, Hope. Friends till the End. 2010. 36p. 16.99 (978-1-4520-5054-6(6)) AuthorHouse.

Lutz, W. Bryant. Hercules the Mighty Steed Meets Ginger the Sparrow: A Diversity Book- Allows Everyone to Feel Special & Good about Each Other. 2010. 20p. 12.99 (978-1-4520-1807-2(3)) AuthorHouse.

MacKenzie, Carine. David the Fugitive: True Friendship. 2009. (Bible Alive Ser.). (ENG., Illus.). 24p. (J). 3.99 (978-1-84550-487-8(9), cf0ac043-f2de-40dc-874b-d61d7396ad4f) Christian Focus Pubns. GBR. Dist: Bookmasters Distribution.

March, Hunter. TBH - A True Story Collab. 2017. (ENG.). 256p. (J). (gr. 7). pap. 14.99 **(978-1-338-05399-9(X)**, Scholastic Nonfiction) Scholastic, Inc.

Mattern, Joanne. Do You Help Others? 2007. (Are You a Good Friend? Ser.). (Illus.). 24p. (gr. k-3). lib. bdg. 22.00 (978-0-8368-8273-5(3), Weekly Reader Leveled Readers) Stevens, Gareth Publishing LLLP.

—Do You Listen? 2007. (Are You a Good Friend? Ser.). 24p. (gr. k-3). pap. 8.15 (978-0-8368-8279-7(2)); (Illus.). lib. bdg. 22.00 (978-0-8368-8274-2(1)) Stevens, Gareth Publishing LLLP. (Weekly Reader Leveled Readers).

—Do You Listen?/Escuchas? 2007. (Are You a Good Friend?/Buenos Amigos Ser.). (ENG & SPA., Illus.). 24p. (gr. k-3). lib. bdg. 22.00 (978-0-8368-8284-1(9), Weekly Reader Leveled Readers) Stevens, Gareth Publishing LLLP.

—Do You Share? 2007. (Are You a Good Friend? Ser.). (Illus.). 24p. (gr. k-3). lib. bdg. 22.00 (978-0-8368-8275-9(X), Weekly Reader Leveled Readers) Stevens, Gareth Publishing LLLP.

—Do You Share?/Compartes? 2007. (Are You a Good Friend?/Buenos Amigos Ser.). (ENG & SPA., Illus.). 24p. (gr. k-3). lib. bdg. 22.00 (978-0-8368-8285-8(7), Weekly Reader Leveled Readers) Stevens, Gareth Publishing LLLP.

—Do You Take Turns? 2007. (Are You a Good Friend? Ser.). (Illus.). 24p. (gr. k-3). lib. bdg. 22.00 (978-0-8368-8276-6(8), Weekly Reader Leveled Readers) Stevens, Gareth Publishing LLLP.

—Do You Take Turns?/¿Te Turnas con Otros? 2007. (Are You a Good Friend?/Buenos Amigos Ser.). (SPA.). 24p. (gr. k-3). pap. 8.15 (978-0-8368-8291-9(1), Weekly Reader Leveled Readers) Stevens, Gareth Publishing LLLP.

—Do You Take Turns?/Te Turnas con Otros? 2007. (Are You a Good Friend?/Buenos Amigos Ser.). (ENG & SPA., Illus.). 24p. (gr. k-3). lib. bdg. 22.00 (978-0-8368-8286-5(5), Weekly Reader Leveled Readers) Stevens, Gareth Publishing LLLP.

Mattern, Joanne & National Geographic Learning Staff. Do You Share? 2010. (Rise & Shine Ser.). (ENG., Illus.). 24p. (C). (gr. k-3). pap. 13.95 (978-0-8368-8280-3(6)) National Geographic School Publishing, Inc.

—Do You Take Turns? 2010. (Rise & Shine Ser.). (ENG., Illus.). 24p. (C). (gr. k-3). pap. 13.95 (978-0-8368-8281-0(4)) National Geographic School Publishing, Inc.

Mayer, Cassie. Hacer Amigos. 2007. (Civismo Ser.). (SPA., Illus.). 24p. (gr. -1-1). pap. 6.29 (978-1-4329-0411-1(6), Bellota) Heinemann-Raintree.

Mefford, David. How to Make A Friend in Three Days or Less. 2004. (YA). (978-0-9762143-0-4(X)) Mefford, David.

Meyer, Jared. Making Friends: The Art of Social Networking in Life & Online. 2011. (Communicating with Confidence Ser.). (ENG.). 80p. (YA). (gr. 7-12). pap. 14.15 (978-1-4488-5633-6(7)); lib. bdg. 33.25 (978-1-4488-5522-3(5)) Rosen Publishing Group, Inc., The.

Mi Amigo. 2003. 63.50 (978-0-8136-8139-9(1)) Modern Curriculum Pr.

Michelson, Richard. As Good As Anybody. Colón, Raúl, illus. 2013. (ENG.). 40p. (J). (gr. 1-4). 7.99 (978-0-385-75387-6(X), Dragonfly Bks.) Random Hse. Children's Bks.

Mikayla. Our Friend Mikayla. Resh, Kimberly, ed. 2007. (Illus.). 48p. (J). (gr. k-3). 14.95 (978-1-4243-0734-0(1)) Independent Publisher Services.

Miles, Lisa & Chown, Xanna Eve. How to Survive Mean Girls. 2013. (Girl Talk Ser.). 48p. (J). (gr. 5-8). pap. 70.50 (978-1-4777-0722-7(0), Rosen Reference); (ENG., Illus.). pap. 11.75 (978-1-4777-0721-0(2), Rosen Classroom); (ENG., Illus.). lib. bdg. 29.25 (978-1-4777-0707-4(7), Rosen Reference) Rosen Publishing Group, Inc., The.

Miller, Amanda. Let's Be Friends. 2009. (Scholastic News Nonfiction Readers Ser.). (ENG.). 24p. (J). (gr. 1-2). pap. 6.95 (978-0-531-21444-2(3), Children's Pr.); lib. bdg. 22.00 (978-0-531-21344-5(7)) Scholastic Library Publishing.

Miller, Sophia. Aussie's Adventures. Heath, illus. 2nd rev. ed. 2016. (ENG.). (J). (gr. -1-4). 9.99 (978-1-945033-07-0(X), Atlas Publishing) Atlas Publishing LLC.

Mills, Nathan & Kurkowiak, Anne. Tyler's New Friend. 2012. (Rosen Readers Ser.). (ENG., Illus.). 16p. (J). (gr. k-1). pap. 7.00 (978-1-4488-8731-6(3), Rosen Classroom) Rosen Publishing Group, Inc., The.

Modern Staff. Best Friends: Short e; Consonants f, y; Blends fr, fl, Level A. 2003. ("Plaid" Phonics & Stories Libraries). (gr. 1-2). 38.50 (978-0-8136-9142-8(7)) Modern Curriculum Pr.

Moehn, Heather. Everything You Need to Know about Cliques. (Need to Know Library). 64p. 2009. (gr. 5-5). 58.50 (978-1-60854-058-7(8)) 2005. (Illus.). (J). (gr. 7-12). 31.95 (978-0-8239-3326-6(1)) Rosen Publishing Group, Inc., The.

Molesworth. The Rectory Children. 2007. (ENG.). 130p. pap. 18.99 (978-1-4264-5149-2(0)); 146p. pap. 19.99 (978-1-4264-5450-9(3)) Creative Media Partners, LLC.

—The Rectory Children. 2006. 92p. pap. (978-1-84702-690-3(7)) Echo Library.

—The Rectory Children. 2006. pap. 12.95 (978-1-55742-913-1(8)) Wildside Pr., LLC.

Nelson, Maria. I Am a Good Friend. 2013. (Kids of Character Ser.). 24p. (J). (gr. 1-3). 22.60 (978-1-4339-9017-5(2)); pap. 48.90 (978-1-4339-9019-9(9)); (ENG., Illus.). pap. 8.15 (978-1-4339-9018-2(0)) Stevens, Gareth Publishing LLLP.

Nelson, Robin. Am I a Good Friend? A Book about Trustworthiness. 2014. (Show Your Character Ser.). (ENG., Illus.). 32p. (gr. 1-3). pap. 8.95 (978-1-4677-2386-2(X)); lib. bdg. 26.60 (978-1-4677-1361-0(9), Lerner Pubns.) Lerner Publishing Group.

Nunn, Daniel. I Can Be a Friend. 2014. (Me & My Friends Ser.). (ENG.). 24p. (gr. -1-1). pap. 5.99 (978-1-4846-0245-4(5), Acorn) Heinemann-Raintree.

—Me & My Friends, 1 vol. 2014. (Me & My Friends Ser.). (ENG.). 24p. (gr. -1-1). pap. 23.96 (978-1-4846-0249-2(8), Acorn) Heinemann-Raintree.

Orr, Tamra B. Friendliness. 2016. (21st Century Basic Skills Library: Feelings Ser.). (ENG., Illus.). 24p. (J). (gr. k-3). 24.21 (978-1-63471-043-5(6), 208252) Cherry Lake Publishing.

Owens, L. L. Make Friends, 1 vol. Davidson, Chris, illus. 2010. (Let's Be Social Ser.). (ENG.). 32p. 28.50 (978-1-60270-802-0(9), Looking Glass Library- Nonfiction) Magic Wagon.

Painter, Carol. Friends Helping Friends: A Handbook for Helpers. 2nd ed. 2003. (ENG., Illus.). 224p. (J). pap. 10.95 (978-1-930572-21-8(2)) Educational Media Corp.

—Leading a Friends Helping Friends Peer Program. 2nd ed. 2003. (ENG.). 120p. (J). spiral bd. 9.95 (978-1-930572-22-5(0)) Educational Media Corp.

Parnell, Declan. My Friend Lives in Canada, 01 vols., 1. 2016. (Rosen REAL Readers: Social Studies Nonfiction / Fiction: Family, Community, & the World Ser.). (ENG.). 8p. (J). pap. 5.46 (978-1-5081-1653-0(9), Rosen Classroom) Rosen Publishing Group, Inc., The.

Patrick, Denise Lewis. A Lesson for Martin Luther King, Jr. Pate, Rodney S., illus. 2003. (Ready-To-read COFA Ser.). (ENG.). 32p. (J). (gr. k-2). pap. 3.99 (978-0-689-85397-5(1), Simon Spotlight) Simon Spotlight.

Pearson, Darrell, et al. Can I Really Relate? 2004. (Custom Curriculum Ser.). (Illus.). 256p. pap., per. 19.99 (978-0-7814-4088-2(2), 0781440882) Cook, David C.

Peckham, Lori. Guide's Greatest Friendship Stories. 2016. 158p. (J). pap. (978-0-8163-6144-1(4)) Pacific Pr. Publishing Assn.

Petz, Moritz. The Day Everything Went Wrong. Jackowski, Amélie, illus. 2015. (ENG.). 32p. (J). 17.95 (978-0-7358-4209-0(4)) North-South Bks., Inc.

Phidal Publishing Staff, ed. Girls World: My Best Friends. (Illus.). 64p. (J). pap. (978-2-7643-0145-6(6)) Phidal Publishing, Inc./Editions Phidal, Inc.

Phillips, Karen & Klutz Editors. Friendship Pixies: Charmed Little Dolls to Make & Share. 2011. (ENG.). 40p. (J). (gr. 3-3). 16.99 (978-1-59174-917-2(4)) Klutz.

Piper, Noël. Do You Want a Friend? Schoonmaker, Gail, illus. 2009. 32p. (J). (gr. -1-2). 12.99 (978-1-4335-0621-5(1)) Crossway.

Plattner, Josh. Manners with Friends, 1 vol. 2016. (ENG., Illus.). 24p. (J). (978-1-62403-719-1(4)) ABDO Publishing Co.

Pope, Ellen Dittman. Friends with a Difference. Dixon, Carol, illus. 2009. (J). (978-0-929915-92-0(5)) Headline Bks., Inc.

Powell, Jillian. My New Friend. 2012. (New Beginnings Ser.). (ENG., Illus.). 24p. (J). (gr. k-3). 21.25 (978-1-4488-6633-5(2), PowerKids Pr.) Rosen Publishing Group, Inc., The.

Priddy, Roger. We Are Best Friends (Small Format) 2015. (ENG.). 20p. (J). bds. 7.99 (978-0-312-52030-4(1), 9780312520304, Priddy Bks.) St. Martin's Pr.

Quienes Son Tus Amigos? 2003. 63.50 (978-0-8136-8049-1(2)); suppl. ed. 8.95 (978-0-8136-8046-0(8)) Modern Curriculum Pr.

Rameck, Hunt, et al. We Beat the Street: How a Friendship Pact Led to Success. 2014. (ENG.). 208p. (J). 12.24 (978-1-63245-093-7(3)) Lectorum Pubns., Inc.

Ray, Nan. Friends, Friends, Friends. 2004. (J). per. 24.95 (978-0-9760280-1-7(8)) You're On!, Inc.

Reader, Jenny. Girl 2 Girl: The Swap Book You Share with Your Friends. Martin, Caroline & Davies, Nic, illus. 2003. 96p. (J). pap. (978-0-439-56743-5(2)) Scholastic, Inc.

Rice, Ashley. Friends Rule: A Very Special Book of Friendship Especially for Girls. 2003. (Illus.). 64p. (J). pap. (978-0-88396-772-0(3), Blue Mountain Pr.) Blue Mountain Arts Inc.

Richards, Laurae. Coming Home. 2013. 28p. pap. 16.95 (978-1-4624-0769-9(2), Inspiring Voices) Author Solutions, Inc.

Rigby Education Staff. Friends Together. (Illus.). 8p. (J). bds. 3.95 (978-0-7635-6435-3(4), 764354C99) Rigby Education.

Rotner, Shelley & Kelly, Sheila M. All Kinds of Friends. Rotner, Shelley, photos by. 2017. (ENG., Illus.). (J). (gr. k-2). 32p. pap. 7.99 **(978-1-5124-8632-2(9))**; lib. bdg. 26.65 **(978-1-5124-3105-6(2))** Lerner Publishing Group. (Millbrook Pr.).

Rowe, Brooke. What Kind of Friend Are You? (Illus.). 32p. (J). 2016. pap. 14.21 (978-1-63470-066-5(X)) 2015. (978-1-63470-039-9(2)) Cherry Lake Publishing.

Rustad, Martha. Michael Makes Friends at School. Becker, Paula, illus. 2017. (Cloverleaf Books (tm) — off to School Ser.). (ENG.). (J). (gr. k-2). pap. 7.99 **(978-1-5124-5577-9(6))**; lib. bdg. 25.32 **(978-1-5124-3937-3(1))** Lerner Publishing Group. (Millbrook Pr.).

Santos, D. Friends: Learning the FR Sound. 2009. (PowerPhonics Ser.). 24p. (gr. 1-1). 39.90 (978-1-60851-442-7(0), PowerKids Pr.) Rosen Publishing Group, Inc., The.

Saunders, Catherine. Character Encyclopedia. 2014. (ENG.). 176p. (J). (gr. k-4). 18.99 (978-1-4654-2135-7(1), DK Children) Dorling Kindersley Publishing, Inc.

—LEGO Friends Character Encyclopedia. 2014. (ENG.). 176p. (J). (gr. k-4). 18.99 (978-1-4654-1894-4(6), DK Children) Dorling Kindersley Publishing, Inc.

Senker, Cath. Relationships, 1 vol. 2012. (Teen Issues Ser.). (ENG.). 56p. (gr. 6-10). pap. 9.99 (978-1-4329-6541-9(7)); lib. bdg. 34.65 (978-1-4329-6536-5(0)) Heinemann-Raintree.

Sévigny, Eric, illus. My Imaginary Friend. 2003. (Clubhouse Ser.). (ENG.). 24p. (J). (gr. -1-1). pap. 3.95 (978-2-89450-478-9(0)) Ellipsis Pr.

Shanks, Cindy. Alfonso Grows up on the Sheep Trail. 2010. 40p. pap. 18.99 (978-1-4520-7980-6(3)) AuthorHouse.

Shapiro, Lawrence E. & Holmes, Julia. Let's Be Friends: A Workbook to Help Kids Learn Social Skills & Make Great Friends. 2008. (Instant Help Ser.). (ENG., Illus.). 144p. (J). (gr. k-5). pap. 16.95 (978-1-57224-610-2(3), Instant Help Books) New Harbinger Pubns.

Sheehan, Jennifer E. Miss Bumples Lands on Earth. 2003. (Illus.). 31p. (J). (978-0-9700952-6-8(0)) Bumples.

Snow, Todd. You Are Friendly. Strong, Melodee, illus. 2007. (You Are Important Ser.). (ENG.). 24p. (J). (gr. -1-k). bds. 7.99 (978-1-934277-09-6(6)) Marn Green Publishing, Inc.

—You Are Friendly (PB) Strong, Melodee, illus. 2008. (ENG.). 24p. (J). pap. 8.99 (978-1-934277-18-8(5)) Marn Green Publishing, Inc.

Solomon, Iris L. & Solomon, Ron. Friendz Pakz: Friends. 2003. (YA). (gr. 3-18). 4.99 (978-1-930680-04-3(X), SSP-08FR) Swingset Pr., LLC.

Soto, Gary. Cebollas Enterradas. 2003. (la Orilla del Viento Ser.). (SPA.). 150p. (J). pap. 8.50 (978-968-16-6669-9(0)) Fondo de Cultura Economica USA.

Sperry, Amanda. Let's Be Friends. Krone, Mike, illus. 2004. (Elements of Reading: Phonics Ser.). 8p. pap. 40.00 (978-0-7398-9008-0(5)) Houghton Mifflin Harcourt Supplemental Pubs.

Spilsbury, Louise. Family & Friends. 2012. (Healthy & Happy Ser.). (Illus.). 32p. (J). (gr. 1-4). lib. bdg. 26.50 (978-1-4488-5275-8(7)) Rosen Publishing Group, Inc., The.

Sportelli-Rehak, Angela. Moving Again Mom! Hinlicky, Gregg, illus. (J). 2004. (Uncle Sam's Kids Ser.: Bk. 2). 40p. (gr. -1-7). pap. 7.95 (978-0-9714515-0-6(8)) 2003. (gr. k-7). pap. (978-0-9714515-3-7(2)) Abidenme Bks.

—Uncle Sam's Kids: Moving Again Mom. Hinlicky, Gregg, illus. 2004. (Uncle Sam's Kids Ser.: Bk. 2). 40p. (gr. k-6). 16.95 (978-0-9714515-2-0(4)) Abidenme Bks.

Tavolacci, Joyce. Teen Wise Guide to Relationships. 2012. (USA TODAY Teen Wise Guides: Time, Money, & Relationships Ser.). (ENG., Illus.). 64p. (gr. 8-12). lib. bdg. 31.93 (978-0-7613-7018-5(8)) Lerner Publishing Group.

Terrell, Cheryl. The Beginning of a Good Friendship. 2012. 16p. pap. 15.99 (978-1-4772-5655-8(5)) AuthorHouse.

Thebo, Patricia J. Uncle Looker & the Hurricane. 2003. (Illus.). 50p. (J). (gr. k-9). 16.50 (978-0-9725706-0-2(8)) Seaforth Publishing.

Thornborough, Kathy. Family & Friends. Petelinsek, Kathleen, illus. 2014. (Talking Hands Ser.). (ENG.). 24p. (J). (gr. k-3). 25.64 (978-1-62687-317-9(8), 207157) Child's World, Inc., The.

Tourville, Amanda Doering. Manners at a Friend's House, 1 vol. Lensch, Chris, illus. 2009. (Way to Be!: Manners Ser.). (ENG.). 24p. (gr. -1-2). lib. bdg. 26.65 (978-1-4048-5305-8(7)) Picture Window Bks.

Townes-Richards, Carolyn. Nothing Like Christine: Living Through Literature with Aunt Curly's Collection. 2009. 90p. pap. 13.50 (978-1-4251-1129-8(7)) Trafford Publishing.

Treasuree Cash. Tyler Learns to Do Tricks! 2013. 36p. pap. 16.95 (978-1-4908-1491-9(4), WestBow Pr.) Author Solutions, Inc.

True Friends. 2004. (Fun Kits Ser.). (Illus.). 48p. (J). (978-1-84229-862-6(3)) Top That! Publishing PLC.

Vander Pluym, Andrea. Mission: Sisterhood. Waters, Susy Pilgrim, illus. 2010. 80p. (YA). (978-0-88441-753-8(0)) Girl Scouts of the USA.

Verderosa, Laura. With My Friends. 2010. (Sight Word Readers Ser.). (J). 3.49 (978-1-60719-610-5(7)) Newmark Learning LLC.

Webber, Diane. Your Space: Dealing with Friends & Peers. 2008. (Scholastic Choices Ser.). (ENG., Illus.). 112p. (YA). (gr. 8-12). pap. 8.95 (978-0-531-14774-0(6), Watts, Franklin) Scholastic Library Publishing.

Whelon, Chuck. What to Doodle? Best Friends Forever! 2011. (Dover Doodle Bks.). (ENG., Illus.). 64p. (J). (gr. 2-5). pap. 5.99 (978-0-486-48527-0(7)) Dover Pubns., Inc.

Who Can Be a Friend? (J). 26.20 (978-0-8136-8401-7(3)); 26.20 (978-0-8136-8402-4(1)) Modern Curriculum Pr.

Widenhouse, Kathy. The Christian Girl's Guide to Friendship. 2004. (Illus.). 192p. (J). pap. 9.99 (978-1-58411-043-9(0), Legacy Pr.) Rainbow Pubs. & Legacy Pr.

Wigand, Molly. How to Be a Friend: A Book about Friendship... Just for Me! Fitzgerald, Anne, illus. 2012. 32p. (J). pap. 7.95 (978-0-87029-503-4(9)) Abbey Pr.

Will, Heidi. The Ghillie Girls: Irish Dance Pals. Will, Heidi, illus. 2008. (Illus.). 24p. (J). pap. 9.99 (978-0-9821065-0-1(5)) Cinealta Pr.

Williams, Dave. Windgalore Farm. 2005. (Illus.). 182p. pap. 21.95 (978-0-937921-56-2(4)) Acorn Publishing.

FRIENDSHIP—FICTION

A Caribbean Experience Con Amor. There's a Coqui in My Shoe! 2007. (Illus.). 66p. (J). 21.99 (978-0-9797641-0-3(6)) Chi Chi Rodriguez Bks.

Aaron, Taylor. Pumpkin Goblin Makes Friends. 2008. 36p. (J). 16.95 (978-1-934572-00-9(4)) Emerald Bk. Co.

Abbott, Hailey. Forbidden Boy. 2008. (ENG.). 256p. (YA). (gr. 9-18). pap. 8.99 (978-0-06-125382-9(0), HarperTeen) HarperCollins Pubs.

—Getting Lost with Boys. 2006. (ENG.). 240p. (YA). (gr. 9). pap. 8.99 (978-0-06-082432-7(8), HarperTeen) HarperCollins Pubs.

—The Other Boy. 2008. (ENG.). 272p. (YA). (gr. 9-18). pap. 8.99 (978-0-06-125383-6(9), HarperTeen) HarperCollins Pubs.

—The Perfect Boy. 2007. (ENG.). 272p. (YA). (gr. 9-18). pap. 8.99 (978-0-06-082434-1(4), HarperTeen) HarperCollins Pubs.

—The Secrets of Boys. 2006. (ENG.). 272p. (YA). (gr. 9). pap. 8.99 (978-0-06-082433-4(6), HarperTeen) HarperCollins Pubs.

Abbott, Monica. L T Makes New Friends. 2010. 24p. pap. 13.50 (978-1-4520-6128-3(9)) AuthorHouse.

Abbott Orloff, Chrissy. Lady Humming Fly's Lesson on Staying Safe. 2009. 80p. pap. 28.99 (978-1-4389-9938-8(0)) AuthorHouse.

Abbott, Tony. The Race to Doobesh. 2005. (Secrets of Droon Ser.: No. 24). (Illus.). 127p. (J). lib. bdg. 15.38 (978-1-4242-0311-6(2)) Fitzgerald Bks.

Abdo, Kenny. Comic Relief, 1 vol. Doucet, Bob, illus. 2013. (Haven't Got a Clue! Ser.). (ENG.). 80p. (J). (gr. 3-6). lib. bdg. 27.07 (978-1-61641-951-6(2), Calico Chapter Bks) Magic Wagon.

Abdo Publishing. Abby & the Book Bunch, 1 vol. 2013. (Abby & the Book Bunch Ser.: 6). (ENG.). 80p. (J). (gr. 2-5). lib. bdg. 162.42 (978-1-61641-911-0(3), Calico Chapter Bks) Magic Wagon.

—My Little Pony: Friendship Is Magic. 2015. (My Little Pony: Friendship Is Magic Ser.: Vol. 8). (ENG.). 24p. (J). (gr. 2-5). 193.68 (978-1-61479-375-5(1)) ABDO Publishing Co.

ABDO Publishing Company Staff. Monster Hunters, 1 vol. 2014. (Monster Hunters Ser.: 4). (ENG.). 80p. (J). (gr. 8-12). lib. bdg. 108.28 (978-1-62402-043-8(7), Calico Chapter Bks) Magic Wagon.

Abdullah, Shaila & Abdullah, Aanyah. My Friend Suhana: A Story of Friendship & Cerebral Palsy. 2014. 30p. pap. 14.95 (978-1-61599-211-9(1)) Loving Healing Pr., Inc.

Abela, Deborah. Hollywood. O'Connor, George, illus. 2007. (Spy Force Ser.: 4). (ENG.). 240p. (J). (gr. 3-7). pap. 10.99 (978-1-4169-3969-6(5), Aladdin) Simon & Schuster Children's Publishing.

Ablondi, Richard. The Ball, the Bat, & the Unforgiving BRAT. 2013. 46p. pap. 13.99 (978-1-62509-956-3(8)) Salem Author Services.

Abrams, Amir. Caught Up. 2014. (ENG., Illus.). 336p. (YA). (gr. 13). pap. 9.95 (978-0-7582-9478-4(6), K-Teen) Kensington Publishing Corp.

Abramson, Jill & O'Connor, Jane. Holiday Helper. Melmon, Deborah, illus. 2014. (Penguin Young Readers, Level 2 Ser.). (ENG.). 32p. (J). (gr. 1-3). pap. 3.99 (978-0-448-45677-5(X), Penguin Young Readers) Penguin Young Readers Group.

Acampora, Paul. I Kill the Mockingbird. 2014. (ENG.). 176p. (J). (gr. 5-9). 16.99 (978-1-59643-742-5(1), 9781596437425) Roaring Brook Pr.

—I Kill the Mockingbird. 2015. (ENG.). 192p. (J). (gr. 5-9). pap. 7.99 (978-1-250-06808-8(8), 9781250068088) Square Fish.

—Rachel Spinelli Punched Me in the Face. 2013. (ENG.). 192p. (J). (gr. 3-7). pap. 8.99 (978-1-250-01669-0(X), 9781250016690) Square Fish.

Acevedo, Jenny. Ginger's Grand Adventure. 2012. 36p. pap. 24.95 (978-1-4626-2472-0(3)) America Star Bks.

Ackelsberg, Amy. Berry Bitty Bakers. MJ Illustrations Staff, illus. 2011. (Strawberry Shortcake Ser.). (ENG.). 24p. (J). (gr. -1-k). pap. 4.99 (978-0-448-45695-9(8), Grosset & Dunlap) Penguin Young Readers Group.

—Happy New Year! 2014. (Strawberry Shortcake Ser.). (ENG., Illus.). 24p. (J). (gr. -1-k). 4.99 (978-0-448-48248-4(7), Grosset & Dunlap) Penguin Young Readers Group.

—Puppy Love! Artful Doodlers Limited Staff, illus. 2014. (Strawberry Shortcake Ser.). (ENG.). 24p. (J). (gr. -1-k). 4.99 (978-0-448-48150-0(2), Grosset & Dunlap) Penguin Young Readers Group.

—The Sweetest Friends. 2013. (Lalaloopsy Ser.). (ENG., Illus.). 24p. (J). (gr. -1-3). 4.99 (978-0-545-53366-9(X)) Scholastic, Inc.

—Valentine's Day Mix-Up. MJ Illustrations Staff, illus. 2011. (Strawberry Shortcake Ser.). (ENG.). 24p. (J). (gr. -1-k). mass mkt. 4.99 (978-0-448-45696-6(6), Grosset & Dunlap) Penguin Young Readers Group.

Ackerman, Helen. Casper's Paper Caper. 2013. 36p. pap. 18.41 (978-1-4669-7448-7(6)) Trafford Publishing.

Ackerman, Tova. Group Soup. Gorbachev, Valeri, illus. (Orig.). pap. 6.95 (978-0-9720183-0-2(1)) Puppetry in Practice.

Acton, Vanessa. Aftershock. 2017. (Day of Disaster Ser.). (ENG.). 112p. (gr. 6-12). (J). 26.65 (978-1-5124-2777-6(2)); (YA). 12.99 **(978-1-5124-3502-3(3)**, Darby Creek); (YA). 39.99 **(978-1-5124-2785-1(3)**, Darby Creek); (YA). 39.99 **(978-1-5124-3500-9(7)**, Darby Creek) Lerner Publishing Group.

Adair Scott, Paul. Benito Botón e Isabel Hilo. Adair, Pam, tr. 2004. Orig. Title: Blue Button & Red Thread. (SPA., Illus.). 25p. (J). pap. 5.95 (978-0-9740419-2-6(0)) words4u.

Adam D. Levine. Knights: Reign of Hellfire. 2010. (ENG.). 184p. 23.95 (978-1-4401-7614-2(0)); pap. 13.95 (978-1-4401-7618-0(3)) iUniverse, Inc.

Adamchuk, Rachelle G. Disappearance: The First Part of Trickery & Honest Deception. 2006. 169p. pap. 16.99 (978-1-4120-8991-3(3)) Trafford Publishing.

Adams, Alane. The Red Sun. 2015. (Legends of Orkney Ser.). (ENG., Illus.). 346p. (YA). pap. 17.00 (978-1-940716-24-4(1)) SparkPr. (a Bks.parks Imprint).

Adams, Ann. Moppet the Hero. 2012. (Illus.). 54p. pap. 6.00 (978-1-78035-372-2(3), Fastprint Publishing) Upfront Publishing Ltd. GBR. Dist: Printondemand-worldwide.com.

Adams, Jackie. Without a Blink. 2008. 40p. (J). 10.99 (978-0-9800327-0-3(9)) Speranza's Pr.

Adams, Jean Ekman. Clarence & the Purple Horse Bounce into Town. Adams, Jean Ekman, illus. 2003. (Illus.). 32p. (J). (gr. -1-3). 15.95 (978-0-87358-826-3(6), Rising Moon Bks. for Young Readers) Northland Publishing.

Adams, Jeanette. Within the Circle, one. 2003. (Camelot Rabbitry Ser.: Two). 108p. (YA). per. 9.95 (978-0-9672375-2-7(1)) Camelot Tales.

Adams, Jeff. Philemon: Real Friendships in an Unreal World. Date not set. (J). 14.95 (978-0-9643021-9-8(5)) Reality Living Publishing, Inc.

Adams, Katharine. Blackthorn. 2011. 222p. 44.95 (978-1-258-06889-9(3)) Literary Licensing, LLC.

Adams, Keith. The Tales of Henry Tuffin - Henry Goes to School. Hewitt, Geoff, ed. Mawson, Alan, illus. 2013. 20p. pap. (978-1-78222-103-6(4)) Paragon Publishing, Rothersthorpe.

—The Tales of Henry Tuffin - Henry's Christmas. Geoff Hewitt, ed. Mawson, Alan, illus. 2013. 32p. pap. (978-1-78222-172-2(7)) Paragon Publishing, Rothersthorpe.

—The Tales of Henry Tuffin - Henry's Sore Foot & a New Arrival. Hewitt, Geoff, ed. Mawson, illus. 2013. 20p. pap. (978-1-78222-105-0(0)) Paragon Publishing, Rothersthorpe.

—The Tales of Henry Tuffin - the Day the Light Went Out. Hewitt, Geoff, ed. Mawson, Alan, illus. 2013. 20p. pap. (978-1-78222-104-3(2)) Paragon Publishing, Rothersthorpe.

Adams, Kylie. Beautiful Disaster. 2006. (Fast Girls, Hot Boys Ser.: 3). (ENG.). 240p. (gr. 8-12). pap. 16.95 (978-1-4165-2042-9(2), MTV Bks.) MTV Books.

—Bling Addiction: Fast Girls, Hot Boys Series. 2006. (Fast Girls, Hot Boys Ser.: 2). (ENG.). 240p. (gr. 10-13). pap. 15.99 (978-1-4165-2041-2(4), MTV Bks.) MTV Books.

Adams, Lacole Sessions. Maggie & Her Tree. 2011. 28p. (gr. -1). pap. 15.29 (978-1-4567-2416-0(9)) AuthorHouse.

Adams, Mark. Bucky's Best Friend, Vol. 1. Dolan, Amy, illus. 2006. 15p. (J). pap. 5.00 (978-0-9670245-4-7(4)) Enthusi Adams, Inc.

Adams, Michael. The Last Shot. 2017. (Last Trilogy Ser.: 2). (ENG.). 416p. (YA). (gr. 9). pap. 12.99 **(978-1-76029-342-0(3))** Allen & Unwin AUS. Dist: Independent Pubs. Group.

Adams, Michael. The Little King & the Honeybee. 2005. (J). per. 9.95 (978-1-58597-327-9(0)) Leathers Publishing.

Adams, Peggy J. Arnie Aardvark & Friends. 2012. (ENG.). (J). pap. 7.95 (978-1-4675-5225-7(9)) Independent Pub.

Adams, Sarah. Gary & Ray. 2012. (Illus.). 36p. (J). pap. (978-1-84780-260-6(5), Frances Lincoln) Quarto Publishing Group UK.

Adams, Sherred Willcox. Five Little Friends. 2006. pap. (978-1-4065-0483-5(1)) Dodo Pr.

—Five Little Friends. 2006. pap. 15.95 (978-1-4304-4149-6(6)) 2004. reprint ed. pap. 1.99 (978-1-4192-1988-7(X)) Kessinger Publishing, LLC.

Adams, Tonya. Sam the Walrus: A Grumpy Day to Play. Johnson, Amber W., illus. 2008. 28p. pap. 24.95 (978-1-60672-861-1(X)) America Star Bks.

Adams, Wayne. Laci the Ladybug. Kern, Shelly, illus. 2012. 16p. pap. 24.95 (978-1-4626-7615-6(4)) America Star Bks.

Addie's Bad Day. 2003. 22.95 (978-0-673-75904-7(0)) Celebration Pr.

Adkins, Kurt. The Summer of Mucus Mcbain. 2013. 188p. (gr. 4-6). pap. 13.99 (978-1-4582-1138-5(X), Abbott Pr.) Author Solutions, Inc.

Adkins, Ryan. Dream Catcher. 2013. 28p. pap. 16.99 (978-1-4808-0326-8(X)) Archway Publishing.

Adler, Cs. The Magic of the Glits: A Tale of Loss, Love, & Lasting Friendship. 2007. 112p. per. 7.95 (978-1-58348-838-6(3), iUniverse Star) iUniverse, Inc.

Adler, David A. Danny's Doodles: the Dog Biscuit Breakfast. 2015. (Danny's Doodles Ser.: 3). (ENG.). 144p. (J). (gr. 2-5). 14.99 (978-1-4926-1668-9(0), Sourcebooks Jabberwocky) Sourcebooks, Inc.

—Danny's Doodles: The Dog Biscuit Breakfast. 2015. (Danny's Doodles Ser.: 3). (ENG., Illus.). 144p. (J). (gr. 2-5). pap. 4.99 (978-1-4926-1665-8(6), Sourcebooks Jabberwocky) Sourcebooks, Inc.

—Danny's Doodles: The Donut Dilemma. 2014. (Danny's Doodles Ser.: 2). (ENG., Illus.). 144p. (J). (gr. 2-5). pap. 4.99 (978-1-4022-8728-2(3), 9781402287282, Sourcebooks Jabberwocky) Sourcebooks, Inc.

—Danny's Doodles: The Jelly Bean Experiment. 2013. (Danny's Doodles Ser.: 1). (ENG.). 112p. (J). (gr. 2-5). pap. 5.99 (978-1-4022-8721-3(6), 9781402287213, Sourcebooks Jabberwocky) Sourcebooks, Inc.

—Danny's Doodles: the Squirting Donuts. 2014. (Danny's Doodles Ser.: 2). (ENG.). 144p. (J). (gr. 2-5). 14.99 (978-1-4926-1401-2(7), Sourcebooks Jabberwocky) Sourcebooks, Inc.

—Don't Talk to Me about the War. 2009. (ENG.). 224p. (J). (gr. 3-7). 7.99 (978-0-14-241372-2(0), Puffin Books) Penguin Young Readers Group.

—The Many Troubles of Andy Russell. Hillenbrand, Will, illus. 2005. (Andy Russell Ser.: 1). (ENG.). 144p. (J). (gr. 1-4). pap. 6.99 (978-0-15-205440-3(5)) Houghton Mifflin Harcourt Publishing Co.

—The Many Troubles of Andy Russell. 2008. (J). (gr. 2-4). pap. 24.95 incl. audio (978-1-4301-0479-7(1)) Live Oak Media.

Adoff, Jaime. Names Will Never Hurt Me. 2005. (ENG.). 192p. (YA). (gr. 7-7). 5.99 (978-0-14-240457-7(8), Speak) Penguin Young Readers Group.

The Adventures of the Original Pumpkin Patch Pals. l.t. ed. 2005. (Illus.). 32p. (J). 15.00 (978-0-9770960-1-5(7)) 3 Pals Media, LLC.

Afanasyev, Alexander. The Tale of Tsarevich Ivan, the Firebird, & the Grey Wolf. Bilibin, Ivan, illus. 2013. 28p. pap. (978-1-909115-50-7(9)) Planet, The.

Aguayo, Sal. The Tiny Detective. 2008. 48p. pap. 16.95 (978-1-60703-859-7(5)) America Star Bks.

—The Tiny Telepaths: A Continuing Saga, 1 vol. 2010. 62p. pap. 19.95 (978-1-4489-5212-0(3)) America Star Bks.

Ahmad, M. I. Aldebaram. 2009. 95p. pap. 13.00 (978-0-557-08323-7(0)) Lulu Pr., Inc.

Ahrens, Albrecht. Simply Out in the Woods: An Inspirational Children's Story. 2013. 232p. pap. (978-1-4602-0688-1(6)) FriesenPress.

Aiken, Joan. Bridle the Wind. 2007. (ENG., Illus.). 352p. (J). (gr. 5-7). pap. 21.95 *(978-0-15-206058-9(8))* Houghton Mifflin Harcourt Publishing Co.

Ailes, Mark Cusco. The Tree of No Boundaries: Book One. 2009. 196p. 24.95 *(978-0-595-63594-8(6))*; pap. 14.95 *(978-0-595-52834-9(1))* iUniverse, Inc.

Aimard, Gustave. The Indian Scout: a Story of the Aster City. 2006. (ENG.). 464p. per. 37.95 *(978-1-4286-1776-6(0))* Kessinger Publishing, LLC.

Ain, Beth. Starring Jules (As Herself) 2014. (Starring Jules Ser.: 1). (ENG., Illus.). 160p. (J). (gr. 2-5). pap. 5.99 *(978-0-545-44353-1(9)*, Scholastic Paperbacks) Scholastic, Inc.

—Starring Jules (As Herself) 2014. (Starring Jules Ser.: 1). lib. bdg. 16.00 *(978-0-606-35365-6(8))* Turtleback Bks.

—Starring Jules (in Drama-Rama) Higgins, Anne Keenan, illus. 2013. (Starring Jules Ser.: 2). (ENG.). 176p. (J). (gr. 2-5). 14.99 *(978-0-545-44354-8(7)*, Scholastic Pr.) Scholastic, Inc.

Ainsworth, Kimberly. Little Monkey. Berg, Michelle, illus. 2008. (Little Green Bks.). (ENG.). 8p. (J). (gr. -1 — 1). 9.99 *(978-1-4169-6175-8(5)*, Little Simon) Little Simon.

—Little Panda. Berg, Michelle, illus. 2008. (Little Green Bks.). (ENG.). 8p. (J). (gr. -1 — 1). 9.99 *(978-1-4169-6173-4(9)*, Little Simon) Little Simon.

Airgood, Ellen. Prairie Evers. (ENG.). 224p. (J). (gr. 3-7). 2014. pap. 7.99 *(978-0-14-242668-5(7)*, Puffin Books) 2012. 15.99 *(978-0-399-25691-2(1)*, Nancy Paulsen Books) Penguin Young Readers Group.

Aitchison, Jim & Sparks, Marilyn. Tin Pot Puppy. 2013. (Illus.). 76p. pap. 7.50 *(978-1-78035-579-5(3)*, Fastprint Publishing) Upfront Publishing Ltd. GBR. Dist: Printondemand-worldwide.com.

Aitken, Amber. Perfect Match, Vol. 4. 2011. (Cupid Company Ser.). (ENG.). 240p. (J). (gr. 4-6). pap. 9.99 *(978-0-00-736263-9(3))* HarperCollins Pubs. Ltd. GBR. Dist: Independent Pubs. Group.

Akchurin, Sergo. Blackie & the Magic Stone. 2011. 16p. 12.99 *(978-1-4269-6337-7(8))* Trafford Publishing.

Aker, Don. The First Stone. 2004. (ENG.). 304p. (J). mass mkt. 6.99 *(978-0-00-639286-6(5)*, Harper Trophy) HarperCollins Pubs.

Akers, Darla G. The Man, the Moon, & the Star. 2008. 24p. per. 24.95 *(978-1-60474-030-1(2))* PublishAmerica, Inc.

Akey, Maureen. The Adventures of Molly the Monarch Butterfly & Friends¬Series: Molly. 2009. 28p. pap. 14.99 *(978-1-4389-4229-2(X))* AuthorHouse.

Akin, Sean, illus. Henny Penny. 2010. (J). *(978-1-60617-133-2(X))* Teaching Strategies, LLC.

Akins, Joni. Dean the Bean. 2007. 24p. per. 24.95 *(978-1-4241-5015-1(9))* America Star Bks.

Akubue, Chira. Azuka. 2012. (Illus.). 16p. pap. 18.30 *(978-1-4670-0796-2(X))* AuthorHouse.

Al-Emadi, Hesham. The Savior's Threshold: The Chronicles of Dourren. 2010. 192p. pap. 13.95 *(978-1-4502-1846-7(6))* iUniverse, Inc.

—The Savior's Threshold: The Chronicles of Dourren. 2010. 192p. 23.95 *(978-1-4502-1848-1(2))* iUniverse, Inc.

Albert, Lisa. Mercy Lily. 2011. (ENG.). 240p. (YA). pap. 9.95 *(978-0-7387-2699-1(0)*, Flux) North Star Editions.

Albertalli, Becky. Simon vs. the Homo Sapiens Agenda. (YA). (gr. 9). 2016. 336p. pap. 10.99 *(978-0-06-234868-5(X))* 2015. (ENG.). 320p. 17.99 *(978-0-06-234867-8(1))* HarperCollins Pubs.

—The Upside of Unrequited. 2017. 352p. (YA). (gr. 9). 17.99 *(978-0-06-234870-8(1))* HarperCollins Pubs.

Alberto, Daisy. Pete for President! Sims, Blanche, illus. 2004. (Social Studies Connects). 32p. (J). (gr. 1-3). pap. 5.95 *(978-1-57565-142-2(4))* Kane Press, Inc.

Alborozo, Gabriel. The Mouse & the Moon. Alborozo, Gabriel, illus. 2016. (ENG., Illus.). 32p. (J). 16.99 *(978-1-62779-224-0(4)*, 9781627792240, Holt, Henry & Co. Bks. For Young Readers) Holt, Henry & Co.

Albuquerque, Blossom. Dashing Duke & His Dodgy Adventures. Flinn, Hannah, illus. 2011. 36p. pap. 13.95 *(978-1-60911-743-6(3)*, Strategic Bk. Publishing) Strategic Book Publishing & Rights Agency (SBPRA).

Alcott, Jessica. Even When You Lie to Me. 2015. (ENG.). 352p. (YA). (gr. 9). 17.99 *(978-0-385-39116-0(1)*, Crown Books For Young Readers) Random Hse. Children's Bks.

Alcott, Louisa May. Jack & Jill. 2005. 29.95 *(978-1-4218-1069-0(7))*; 320p. pap. 14.95 *(978-1-4218-1169-7(3))* 1st World Publishing, Inc. (1st World Library - Literary Society).

—Jack & Jill. Date not set. 352p. (YA). 25.95 *(978-0-8488-2671-0(X))* Amereon Ltd.

—Jack & Jill. 2012. (ENG., Illus.). 368p. (J). (gr. 3-9). pap. 17.95 *(978-1-4290-9310-1(2))* Applewood Bks.

—Jack & Jill. 2007. (ENG.). 252p. pap. 21.99 *(978-1-4346-2587-8(7))*; 276p. pap. 23.99 *(978-1-4346-2665-3(2))* Creative Media Partners, LLC.

—Jack & Jill. 2005. pap. *(978-1-4065-0100-1(X))* Dodo Pr.

—Jack & Jill. l.t. ed. 2005. 496p. pap. *(978-1-84637-054-0(X))* Echo Library.

—Jack & Jill. 2013. (Works of Louisa May Alcott). 425p. reprint ed. lthr. 79.00 *(978-0-7812-1638-8(9))* Reprint Services Corp.

—Under the Lilacs. 2005. 28.95 *(978-1-4218-1487-2(0))*; 280p. pap. 13.95 *(978-1-4218-1587-9(7))* 1st World Publishing, Inc. (1st World Library - Literary Society).

—Under the Lilacs. 2012. (ENG., Illus.). 328p. (gr. 3-9). pap. 17.95 *(978-1-4290-9311-8(0))* Applewood Bks.

—Under the Lilacs. 2007. 228p. pap. 20.99 *(978-1-4346-3618-8(6))*; 248p. pap. 22.99 *(978-1-4346-3635-5(6))* Creative Media Partners, LLC.

—Under the Lilacs. 2005. pap. *(978-1-4065-0105-6(0))* Dodo Pr.

—Under the Lilacs. 2013. (Works of Louisa May Alcott). 302p. reprint ed. lthr. 79.00 *(978-0-7812-1637-1(0))* Reprint Services Corp.

—Under the Lilacs. 2011. 226p. 26.95 *(978-1-4638-9588-4(7))* Rodgers, Alan Bks.

—Under the Lilacs. 2007. 296p. per. 13.45 *(978-1-59462-879-5(3)*, Book Jungle) Standard Pubns., Inc.

—Under the Lilacs. 2007. 316p. (gr. 4-7). 32.95 *(978-1-4344-8357-7(6))*; per. 19.95 *(978-1-4344-8356-0(8))* Wildside Pr., LLC.

Alderson, Sarah. Losing Lila. 2013. (ENG.). 352p. (J). pap. 10.00 *(978-0-85707-197-2(1)*, Simon & Schuster Children's) Simon & Schuster, Ltd. GBR. Dist: Simon & Schuster, Inc.

Aldrich, Sandra D. Trouble in the Park. 2012. 28p. 19.95 *(978-1-4626-8818-0(7))* America Star Bks.

—Willie's Lesson. 2012. 28p. 19.95 *(978-1-4626-9663-5(5))* America Star Bks.

Aldrick, Shirley H. F. Tobias & the Pale, Pale Leprechaun. 2009. 52p. pap. 19.50 *(978-1-60693-959-8(9)*, Strategic Bk. Publishing) Strategic Book Publishing & Rights Agency (SBPRA).

Aldridge, Janet. Meadow Brook Girls Afloat. l.t. ed. 2006. (ENG.). 156p. pap. 21.99 *(978-1-4264-0859-5(5))* Creative Media Partners, LLC.

—Meadow Brook Girls Afloat: Or the Stormy Cruise of the Red Rover. 2006. 160p. pap. 19.99 *(978-1-4264-0878-6(1))* Creative Media Partners, LLC.

—The Meadow-Brook Girls under Canvas (Ill. 2006. pap. *(978-1-4065-0695-2(8))* Dodo Pr.

Alegria, Malin. Estrella's Quinceañera. (ENG.). (YA). (gr. 7-18). 2007. 288p. pap. 10.99 *(978-0-689-87810-7(9))* 2006. (Illus.). 272p. 15.99 *(978-0-689-87809-1(5))* Simon & Schuster Bks. For Young Readers. (Simon & Schuster Bks. For Young Readers).

—Pueblo Fronterizo No. 2: Guerra de Quinceañeras. 2013. (Pueblo Fronterizo Ser.: 2). (SPA.). 208p. (J). (gr. 7). pap. 5.99 *(978-0-545-56565-3(0)*, Scholastic en Espanol) Scholastic, Inc.

Aleixandre, Marilar & Aleixandre, Marilar. La Branda Sin Futuro. 2003. (SPA.). 156p. *(978-84-348-7193-9(9)*, SM30543) SM Ediciones ESP. Dist: Lectorum Pubns., Inc.

Alemagna, Beatrice. Bugs in a Blanket. 2009. (ENG.). 42p. (gr. -1-4). 12.95 *(978-0-7148-4970-6(7))* Phaidon Pr., Inc.

—Bugs in the Garden. 2011. (ENG.). 40p. (gr. -1-2). 12.95 *(978-0-7148-6238-5(X))* Phaidon Pr., Inc.

Alemagna, Béatrice. What Is a Child? 2016. (ENG., Illus.). 36p. (J). (gr. -1-3). 19.95 *(978-1-84976-412-4(3))* Tate Publishing, Ltd. GBR. Dist: Abrams, Inc.

Alex, Smith. Home. Alex, Smith, illus. 2010. (ENG., Illus.). 32p. (J). (gr. -1-2). 15.95 *(978-1-58925-088-8(5))* Tiger Tales.

Alexander. Phonic Comics: Princess School - Level 1. 2011. (ENG., Illus.). 24p. (J). (gr. 1-17). pap. 3.99 *(978-1-60169-110-1(6))* Innovative Kids.

Alexander, Brooke. Little Mia's Big Heart. 2013. 72p. pap. *(978-1-4602-1670-5(9))* FriesenPress.

Alexander, Heather. Be a Star! Le Feyer, Diane, illus. 2015. (Amazing Stardust Friends Ser.: 2). (ENG.). 96p. (J). (gr. 1-3). pap. 4.99 *(978-0-545-75754-6(1))* Scholastic, Inc.

—Step into the Spotlight! Le Feyer, Diane, illus. 2015. (Amazing Stardust Friends Ser.: 1). (ENG.). 96p. (J). (gr. 1-3). pap. 4.99 *(978-0-545-75752-2(5))* Scholastic, Inc.

—Wallace & Grace & the Lost Puppy. Zarrin, Laura, illus. 2017. (Wallace & Grace Ser.). (ENG.). 80p. (J). 9.99 ***(978-1-68119-012-9(5)***, 9781681190129, Bloomsbury USA Childrens) Bloomsbury Publishing USA.

Alexander, Heather. Wallace & Grace Take the Case. Zarrin, Laura, illus. 2017. (Wallace & Grace Ser.). (ENG.). 80p. (J). 9.99 *(978-1-61963-988-1(2)*, 9781619639881, Bloomsbury USA Childrens) Bloomsbury Publishing USA.

Alexander, Jill S. The Sweetheart of Prosper County. 2010. (ENG.). 240p. (YA). (gr. 7-12). pap. 18.99 *(978-0-312-54857-5(5)*, 9780312548575) Square Fish.

Alexander, John. The Adventures of Thunder & Avalanche: Up & Away. Alexander, John, illus. 2013. (Illus.). 48p. 15.99 *(978-0-9887625-1-0(X))* Mountain Thunder Publishing.

Alexander, Louise. My Little Pony: Happy Haunting. 2016. (ENG.). 24p. (J). (gr. -1-3). 8.99 *(978-0-316-36150-7(X))* Little, Brown Bks. for Young Readers.

Alexandria, Shalayne. Nyville High No. 1: Welcome to Nyville. 2007. 124p. (YA). per. 10.00 *(978-0-9786180-1-8(7))* 5 Muses Publishing.

Alfaro, Manuel. Super Griego the Great & the Secret Mission to the Moon. Harrington, David, illus. 2009. 40p. pap. 15.95 *(978-1-60844-028-3(1))* Dog Ear Publishing, LLC.

Alger, Horatio. Bound to Rise: Or: up the Ladder. 2007. (ENG.). 172p. per. 19.99 *(978-1-4346-5059-7(6))*; 188p. per. 21.99 *(978-1-4346-5060-3(X))* Creative Media Partners, LLC.

—Do & Dare: Or, A Brave Boy's Fight for Fortune. 2006. 182p. pap. 19.99 *(978-1-4264-0680-9(3))*; 170p. pap. 21.99 *(978-1-4264-0861-8(7))* Creative Media Partners, LLC.

—Do & Dare: Or, A Brave Boy's Fight for Fortune. 2006. pap. *(978-1-4065-0701-0(6))* Dodo Pr.

—Fame & Fortune: Or: the Progress of Richard Hunter. 2007. (ENG.). 160p. per. 19.99 *(978-1-4346-5061-0(8))*; 176p. per. 21.99 *(978-1-4346-5062-7(6))* Creative Media Partners, LLC.

—Making His Way. 2005. 28.95 *(978-1-4218-1456-8(0))*; 260p. pap. 13.95 *(978-1-4218-1556-5(7))* 1st World Publishing, Inc. (1st World Library - Literary Society).

Aliaga, Roberto. Dorothy: A Different Kind of Friend. 2013. (ENG., Illus.). 28p. (J). (gr. -1-k). 16.95 *(978-84-15619-81-9(2))* Eastern National.

Alimonti, Frederick & Tedesco, Ann. Tommy & the T-Tops: Helping Children Overcome Prejudice. Hazard, John, illus. 2009. (Let's Talk Ser.). (ENG.). 48p. (J). (gr. -1-4). pap. 8.95 *(978-0-88282-305-8(1))* New Horizon Pr. Pubs., Inc.

All Aboard! Softi's Adventures. 2003. (J). mass mkt. *(978-1-932233-36-0(9))* Aurora Libris Corp.

Allem, Jolyia. The Maiden & the Prince: A Tale of Devotion. 2009. 16p. pap. 8.75 *(978-1-4490-2350-8(9))* AuthorHouse.

Allen, Bryony. Otoli. 2011. 144p. (YA). pap. *(978-1-907728-12-9(0))* Pneuma Springs Publishing.

Allen, C. William. The African Interior Mission. Lee, Xiongpao, illus. 2006. 232p. (J). pap. 20.00 *(978-0-9653308-5-5(0))* Africana Homestead Legacy Pubs., Inc.

Allen, Cassandra R. Morty the Alien: The Beginnings... 2009. 16p. pap. 12.50 *(978-1-4389-7283-1(0))* AuthorHouse.

Allen, Crystal. The Magnificent Mya Tibbs: the Wall of Fame Game. Kaban, Eda, illus. 2017. 272p. (J). (gr. 3-7). 16.99 *(978-0-06-234236-2(3))* HarperCollins Pubs.

—Spirit Week Showdown. Kaban, Eda, illus. (Magnificent Mya Tibbs Ser.: 1). (J). (gr. 3-7). 2017. 256p. pap. 6.99 *(978-0-06-234234-8(7))* 2016. 240p. 16.99 *(978-0-06-234233-1(9))* HarperCollins Pubs.

Allen, Elaine Ann. Olly's Treasure, 1 vol. Nash, Kelli, illus. 2011. (ENG.). 40p. (J). 16.99 *(978-0-7643-3772-7(6)*, 9780764337727, Schiffer Publishing Ltd) Schiffer Publishing, Ltd.

Allen, Elise & Stanford, Halle. Autumn's Secret Gift. Pooler, Paige, illus. 2014. (Enchanted Sisters Ser.). (ENG.). 128p. (J). (gr. 2-4). pap. 5.99 *(978-1-61963-254-7(3)*, 9781619632547, Bloomsbury USA Childrens) Bloomsbury Publishing USA.

—Summer's Friendship Games. Pooler, Paige, illus. 2015. (Enchanted Sisters Ser.). (ENG.). 128p. (J). (gr. 2-4). 15.99 *(978-1-61963-271-4(3)*, 9781619632714, Bloomsbury USA Childrens) Bloomsbury Publishing USA.

—Winter's Flurry Adventure. Pooler, Paige, illus. 2014. (Enchanted Sisters Ser.). (ENG.). 128p. (YA). (gr. 2-4). pap. 5.99 *(978-1-61963-267-7(5)*, 9781619632677, Bloomsbury USA Childrens) Bloomsbury Publishing USA.

—Winter's Flurry Adventure. Pooler, Paige, illus. 2014. (Enchanted Sisters Ser.: 2). (YA). lib. bdg. 16.00 *(978-0-606-36217-7(7))* Turtleback Bks.

Allen, J. J. Hello Kitty's Fun Friend Day! 2003. (Illus.). 32p. (J). pap. *(978-0-439-44917-5(0))* Scholastic, Inc.

Allen, Jean. Esmerelda Finds a Friend. 2012. 24p. 24.95 *(978-1-4626-5127-6(5))* America Star Bks.

Allen, M. Misty, Mattie, or Kim. 2012. 44p. pap. 16.95 *(978-1-4626-9414-3(4))* America Star Bks.

Allen, Pamela. Mr. Archimedes' Bath. Allen, Pamela, illus. 2004. (Illus.). 81p. (J). (gr. -1-1). pap. 11.00 *(978-0-207-17285-4(4))* HarperCollins Pubs.

Allen, Rachael. The Revenge Playbook. 2015. (ENG.). 368p. (YA). (gr. 8). pap. 9.99 *(978-0-06-228136-4(4)*, HarperTeen) HarperCollins Pubs.

—17 First Kisses. 2014. (ENG.). 352p. (YA). (gr. 8). pap. 9.99 *(978-0-06-228134-0(8)*, HarperTeen) HarperCollins Pubs.

Allen-Wilson, Regina. Bobo & the Pooch. 2013. 26p. pap. 12.00 *(978-1-4575-2084-6(2))* Dog Ear Publishing, LLC.

Allison, John. Bad Machinery Vol. 3: The Case of the Simple Soul. 2014. (ENG., Illus.). 136p. (YA). pap. 19.99 *(978-1-62010-193-3(9)*, 9781620101933) Oni Pr., Inc.

Allison, T. A. Noah's Harbour. 2013. 116p. pap. *(978-1-78299-579-1(X))* FeedARead.com.

Almeida, Jose-Gabriel. Lodiville: Adventure Land. 2008. 52p. pap. 16.95 *(978-1-60563-989-5(3))* America Star Bks.

Almond, David. A Song for Ella Grey. 2015. (ENG.). 272p. (YA). (gr. 7). 16.99 *(978-0-553-53359-0(2)*, Delacorte Pr.) Random Hse. Children's Bks.

The (Almost) Perfect Guide to Imperfect Boys. 2014. (Mix Ser.). (ENG., Illus.). 304p. (J). (gr. 4-8). pap. 7.99 *(978-1-4814-0563-8(2)*, Aladdin) Simon & Schuster Children's Publishing.

Alonso, Fernando & Fernando, Alonso. La Historia de un Hombrecillo de Papel. (Leer Es Vivir Serie Teatro). (SPA.). 96p. (J). (gr. 3-5). 6.36 *(978-84-241-7711-9(8))* Everest Editora ESP. Dist: Lectorum Pubns., Inc.

Alpert, Sandra F. Horrible Howard: The Bully & Coward. Date not set. (Bully Busting Ser.: Bk. 1). (Illus.). (Orig.). (J). (gr. k-5). pap. *(978-1-884931-02-4(2))* Global Commitment Publishing.

Alpine, Rachele. Operation Pucker Up. 2015. (Mix Ser.). (ENG., Illus.). 256p. (J). (gr. 4-8). 17.99 *(978-1-4814-3236-8(2)*, Aladdin) Simon & Schuster Children's Publishing.

Alsaid, Adi. Let's Get Lost. 2015. (ENG.). 384p. (YA). pap. 9.99 *(978-0-373-21149-4(X)*, Harlequin Teen) Harlequin Enterprises, Ltd. CAN. Dist: HarperCollins Pubs.

Alsenas, Linas. The Princess of 8th Street. 2012. (ENG., Illus.). 32p. (J). (gr. k-2). 16.95 *(978-0-8109-8972-6(7)*, Abrams Bks. for Young Readers) Abrams, Inc.

Alsop - Jinks, A. G. Kylie & the Butterfly. 2011. 16p. pap. 8.32 *(978-1-4634-0859-6(5))* AuthorHouse.

Alston, Colin. The Invisible Boy. 2009. 32p. pap. 13.75 *(978-1-60860-598-9(1)*, Eloquent Bks.) Strategic Book Publishing & Rights Agency (SBPRA).

Altebrando, Tara. The Battle of Darcy Lane. 2014. (ENG.). 208p. (J). (gr. -1-2). 14.95 *(978-0-7624-4948-4(9)*, Running Pr. Kids) Running Pr. Bk. Pubs.

Altein, Chani. The Gift of Friendship. 2006. 144p. (J). (gr. 3-7). 14.95 *(978-1-932443-47-9(9)*, GOFH) Judaica Pr., Inc., The.

—Hashem Is Truly Everywhere. Rosenfeld, D. L. & Leverton, Yossi, eds. Lumer, Marc, illus. 2011. 28p. (J). 12.95 *(978-1-929628-57-5(9))* Hachai Publishing.

Alter, Anna. Sprout Street Neighbors - A New Arrival. 2016. (Sprout Street Neighbors Ser.). (ENG., Illus.). 128p. (J). (gr. 1-4). 12.99 *(978-0-385-75562-7(7)*, Knopf Bks. for Young Readers) Random Hse. Children's Bks.

Alter, Anna. Sprout Street Neighbors: a New Arrival. 2017. (Sprout Street Neighbors Ser.: 2). (ENG.). 128p. (J). (gr. 1-4). pap. 6.99 ***(978-0-385-75564-1(3)***, Yearling) Random Hse. Children's Bks.

Alvarez, Julia. Devolver Al Remitente. 2010.Tr. of Return to Sender. (SPA & ENG.). 368p. (J). (gr. 3-7). 7.99 *(978-0-375-85124-7(0)*, Yearling) Random Hse. Children's Bks.

—Return to Sender. 2010. (ENG.). 352p. (J). (gr. 3-7). 6.99 *(978-0-375-85123-0(2)*, Yearling) Random Hse. Children's Bks.

Alvord, Larry. Down by Ol' Chooster's Pond. 2011. 56p. pap. 21.99 *(978-1-4628-7652-5(8))* Xlibris Corp.

Amani, Alexander. The Guardians. 2010. 148p. 24.95 *(978-1-4490-8572-8(5))*; pap. 16.99 *(978-1-4490-8571-1(7))* AuthorHouse.

Amarone, Morgan. Madison's Journey. Ruocco, Paul, illus. 2011. 30p. (J). pap. 16.99 *(978-0-9841934-5-5(6))* Bryson Taylor Publishing.

Amateau, Gigi. Dante of the Maury River. 2015. (Horses of the Maury River Ser.). (ENG.). 320p. (J). (gr. 3-7). 15.99 *(978-0-7636-7004-7(9))* Candlewick Pr.

Amato, Anne McCoy. Moving Shelly: A Novel. 2010. 148p. (gr. 4-6). 22.95 *(978-1-4502-2586-1(1))*; pap. 12.95 *(978-1-4502-2584-7(5))* iUniverse, Inc.

Amato, Mary. Get Happy. (ENG.). 244p. (gr. 7-12). 2016. pap. 9.99 *(978-1-5124-2627-4(X)*, Carolrhoda Bks.) 2014. (J). 16.99 *(978-0-7613-6984-1(3)*, Carolrhoda Lab™) Lerner Publishing Group.

Ambrose, Adrianne. What I Learned from Being a Cheerleader. 2010. 202p. pap. 12.95 *(978-1-935661-94-8(9)*, Bell Bridge Bks.) BelleBks., Inc.

Ambrose, Sophie. The Lonely Giant. Ambrose, Sophie, illus. 2016. (ENG., Illus.). 32p. (J). (gr. -1-3). 16.99 *(978-0-7636-8225-5(X))* Candlewick Pr.

Ameen, Judith. Harold & the Magic Books. 2005. 40p. pap. 8.95 *(978-1-933265-42-1(6))* Wasteland Pr.

Amelia Asks Have You Seen L. B. 2007. (J). 3.99 *(978-0-9726075-5-1(2))* EPI Bks.

Amelio, Paul. Jack & Zach: The Talk of the Town. 2013. 78p. pap. 10.97 *(978-1-62857-120-2(9)*, Strategic Bk. Publishing) Strategic Book Publishing & Rights Agency (SBPRA).

Amerikaner, Susan. Game On! 2012. (Step into Reading Level 2 Ser.). lib. bdg. 13.55 *(978-0-606-26799-1(9)*, Turtleback) Turtleback Bks.

Ammirato, Lidia. Why Does the Dog Chase the Cat & the Cat Chase the Mouse? 2012. 24p. pap. 15.99 *(978-1-4771-0651-8(0))* Xlibris Corp.

Amore, Dani, et al. Samurai Summer, 0 vols. Carlsson, Per, tr. 2013. (ENG.). 256p. (YA). (gr. 7-12). 17.99 *(978-1-4778-1654-7(2)*, 9781477816547, Amazon Children's Publishing) Amazon Publishing.

Amundson, Sandi. Zach & Dougie Dragonfly's Adventure. 2011. 55p. pap. 23.95 *(978-1-4327-3536-4(5))* Outskirts Pr., Inc.

Amy Brooks. Randy & Her Friends. 2007. 126p. pap. 18.99 *(978-1-4346-3978-3(9))*; (ENG.). 140p. pap. 19.99 *(978-1-4346-3979-0(7))* Creative Media Partners, LLC.

Ana, Moh. Kookaburra Tales: Shy Not, My Friend. 2013. 16p. pap. 17.03 *(978-1-4669-3193-0(0))* Trafford Publishing.

Anastasiu, Heather & Brown, Anne Greenwood. Girl Last Seen. 2016. (ENG.). 272p. (YA). (gr. 8-12). pap. 9.99 *(978-0-8075-8141-4(0))* Whitman, Albert & Co.

and Ellen Brenneman, John W. Lane. A Friend Indeed. 2009. 36p. pap. 16.90 *(978-0-557-11601-0(5))* Lulu Pr., Inc.

Andersen, Hans Christian. La Reina de las Nieves.Tr. of Snow Queen. (SPA., Illus.). 48p. (J). (gr. 3-5). *(978-84-241-5526-1(2)*, EV1028) Everest Editora ESP. Dist: Lectorum Pubns., Inc.

—La Reina de las Nieves. Bravo-Villasante, Carmen, tr. Catagan, Tino, illus.Tr. of Snow Queen. (SPA.). (J). (gr. 2-4). 6.50 *(978-84-355-0695-3(9))* Minon, S.A. ESP. Dist: Lectorum Pubns., Inc.

Anderson, Carolyn. No Counting Sheep, 1 vol. 2010. 34p. 24.95 *(978-1-4489-9078-8(5))* PublishAmerica, Inc.

—Water Queen & the Sea of Kings. 2013. 28p. pap. 24.95 *(978-1-63000-446-0(4))* America Star Bks.

Anderson, Cathysue. Through Grandmother's Window. 2013. 32p. pap. 13.99 *(978-1-4624-0579-4(7)*, Inspiring Voices) Author Solutions, Inc.

Anderson, Clay. Mary Margaret Hammersmith & the Lady of the Roundtable, 1 vol. 2009. 134p. pap. 24.95 *(978-1-4489-1892-8(8))* America Star Bks.

Anderson, Derek. Blue Burt & Wiggles. Anderson, Derek, illus. 2014.Tr. of Signed in American Sign Language. (ENG., Illus.). 32p. (J). (gr. -1-3). 16.99 *(978-1-4814-1933-8(1)*, Simon & Schuster Bks. For Young Readers) Simon & Schuster Bks. For Young Readers.

—Romeo & Lou Blast Off. Anderson, Derek, illus. 2014. (ENG., Illus.). 32p. (J). (gr. -1-3). 16.99 *(978-1-4814-1932-1(3)*, Simon & Schuster Bks. For Young Readers) Simon & Schuster Bks. For Young Readers.

Anderson, Dwayne. Partially Human. 2006. (YA). per. 12.00 *(978-0-9788612-0-9(5))* Capri Publishing.

Anderson, Jeff. Zack Delacruz 2 (working Title) 2016. (Zack Delacruz Ser.). (ENG., Illus.). 192p. (J). (gr. 5-8). 12.95 *(978-1-4549-2067-0(X))* Sterling Publishing Co., Inc.

Anderson, Jennifer. Spider. 2013. 174p. pap. 10.99 *(978-1-62237-146-4(1))* Turquoise Morning Pr.

Anderson, Jessica Lee. Trudy. 2005. (Milkweed Prize for Children's Literature Ser.). (ENG.). 192p. (J). (gr. 3-8). per. 6.95 *(978-1-57131-659-2(0))* Milkweed Editions.

Anderson, Jodi Lynn. Love & Peaches. 2009. (Peaches Ser.: 3). (ENG.). 256p. (YA). (gr. 8). pap. 8.99 *(978-0-06-073313-1(6)*, HarperTeen) HarperCollins Pubs.

—Midnight at the Electric. 2017. 272p. (YA). (gr. 9). 17.99 *(978-0-06-239354-8(5)*, HarperTeen) HarperCollins Pubs.

—The Secrets of Peaches. 2012. (Peaches Ser.: 2). (ENG.). 368p. (YA). (gr. 9-12). pap. 8.99 *(978-0-06-073310-0(1)*, HarperTeen) HarperCollins Pubs.

Anderson, John David. Ms. Bixby's Last Day. 2016. 320p. (J). (gr. 3-7). 16.99 *(978-0-06-233817-4(X)*, Waldon Pond Pr.) HarperCollins Pubs.

—Posted. 2017. 384p. (J). (gr. 3-7). 16.99 *(978-0-06-233820-4(X)*, Waldon Pond Pr.) HarperCollins Pubs.

Anderson, Laurie Halse. Forge. l.t. ed. 2017. (Seeds of America Ser.). (ENG.). 418p. 22.99 ***(978-1-4104-9918-9(9))*** Cengage Gale.

Anderson, Lena & Sandin, Joan. Hedgehog, Pig, & the Sweet Little Friend. Sandin, Joan, tr. from SWE. 2007. (Illus.). 32p. (J). (gr. -1-1). 16.00 *(978-91-29-66742-4(9))* R & S Bks. SWE. Dist: Macmillan.

Anderson, Lily. The Only Thing Worse Than Me Is You. 2016. (ENG.). 352p. (YA). 18.99 *(978-1-250-07909-1(8)*, 9781250079091, St. Martin's Griffin) St. Martin's Pr.

Anderson, M. T. Jasper Dash & the Flame-Pits of Delaware. Cyrus, Kurt, illus. (Pals in Peril Tale Ser.). (ENG.). (J). (gr. 5-9). 2010. 448p. pap. 6.99 *(978-1-4424-0838-8(3))* 2009. 432p. 16.99 *(978-1-4169-8639-3(1))* Beach Lane Bks. (Beach Lane Bks.).

—Thirsty. 2008. (ENG., Illus.). 256p. (YA). (gr. 7). pap. 8.99 *(978-0-7636-3895-5(1))* Candlewick Pr.

—Whales on Stilts! Cyrus, Kurt, illus. 2010. (Pals in Peril Tale Ser.). (ENG.). (J). (gr. 5-9). 208p. 17.99 *(978-1-4424-0695-7(X))*; 224p. pap. 7.99 *(978-1-4424-0701-5(8))* Beach Lane Bks. (Beach Lane Bks.).

—Whales on Stilts! Cyrus, Kurt, illus. 2006. (M. T. Anderson's Thrilling Tales Ser.). 188p. (gr. 5-9). 15.95 *(978-0-7569-7213-4(2))* Perfection Learning Corp.

Anderson, Max Elliot. Newspaper Caper. (Tweener Press Adventure Ser.). 2004. 135p. (J). (gr. 4-7). per. 9.95 *(978-0-9729256-4-8(3))* 2003. 136p. 16.95 *(978-0-9729256-5-5(1))* Baker Trittin Pr. (Tweener Pr.).

Anderson, Rachael. Los Mejores Amigos. McNicholas, Shelagh, illus. 2003. (SPA.). 120p. (J). (gr. 3-5). 9.95 *(978-84-204-4377-5(8))* Ediciones Alfaguara ESP. Dist: Santillana USA Publishing Co., Inc.

Anderson, Shel. Spoofaloof's Adventures: Rainy Day Fun. Anderson, Shauna, illus. 2008. 52p. pap. 22.50 *(978-1-4389-1689-7(2))* AuthorHouse.

Anderson, Steven. Leap & Twirl. DeAnguelo Hout, Sarah, illus. 2012. 34p. (J). pap. 10.99 *(978-0-692-01667-1(8))* BalletMet Dance Centre.

Anderson, T. L. Fifth Street: The Birthday Wish. 2011. 28p. 12.99 *(978-1-4520-9847-0(6))* AuthorHouse.

Anderson, Trey. Jesse & Midnight. 2007. 56p. per. 16.95 *(978-1-60474-062-2(0))* America Star Bks.

Andracki, Zenon. Dear Ashley: A Middle Grade Novel. 2006. (ENG.). 84p. per. 19.95 *(978-1-4241-6168-3(1))* America Star Bks.

Andrade, Brigitte. The Adventures of Bibi & Friends: Summer Season in Miami Beach, 17 vols. 7th ed. 2004. Orig. Title: The Adventures of Bibi 7 Friends. (Illus.). 64p. per. 7.95 *(978-0-9754329-0-7(7))* BB International Productions, Inc.

Andrefski, Jodie. The Society. 2016. (ENG.). 304p. (YA). pap. 9.99 *(978-1-63375-318-1(2)*, 9781633753181) Entangled Publishing, LLC.

Andrew, Joe. The Three Lady Fish: A Friend in Need. Andrew, Joe, illus. 2007. (Illus.). (J). (gr. -1-3). pap. 9.95 *(978-0-9787995-6-4(9))* High-Pitched Hum Inc.

Andrews, Andy. Henry Hodges Needs a Friend, 1 vol. 2015. (ENG., Illus.). 32p. (J). 14.99 *(978-0-529-11576-8(X))* Nelson, Thomas Inc.

Andrews, Cynthia. Molly Goes to Preschool. 2012. 16p. pap. 15.99 *(978-1-4772-7894-9(X))* AuthorHouse.

Andrews, D. M. The Serpent in the Glass. 2012. 234p. pap. *(978-1-78176-773-3(4))* FeedARead.com.

Andrews, Jesse. The Haters. (ENG.). 336p. (YA). (gr. 8-17). 2017. pap. 9.95 *(978-1-4197-2370-4(7))* 2016. 18.95 *(978-1-4197-2078-9(3))* Abrams, Inc. (Amulet Bks.).

—The Haters. 2017. (YA). lib. bdg. 20.80 ***(978-0-606-39688-2(8))*** Turtleback Bks.

Andrews, Jesse. Me & Earl & the Dying Girl. (ENG.). 304p. (YA). (gr. 9-17). 2012. 17.95 *(978-1-4197-0176-4(2)*, Amulet Bks.) 2015. 17.95 *(978-1-4197-2027-7(9))* 2015. 17.95 *(978-1-4197-2013-0(9)*, Amulet Bks.) 2015. pap. 9.95 *(978-1-4197-1960-8(2)*, Amulet Bks.) Abrams, Inc.

—Me & Earl & the Dying Girl. 2015. (CHI.). 320p. (YA). (gr. 9-17). pap. *(978-986-344-282-0(8))* Rye Field Publishing, Co.

—Me & Earl & the Dying Girl. 2015. lib. bdg. 20.80 *(978-0-606-37113-1(3))* Turtleback Bks.

Andrews, Julie & Hamilton, Emma Walton. A Spooky, Sparkly Halloween. 2016. (Very Fairy Princess Ser.). (J). lib. bdg. 16.00 *(978-0-606-38317-2(4))* Turtleback Bks.

—Valentines from the Heart. 2015. (Very Fairy Princess Ser.). (J). lib. bdg. 16.00 *(978-0-606-37466-8(3))* Turtleback Bks.

Andrews, Sandy. Best Friends - the Depression Years. 2012. 218p. pap. 12.95 *(978-1-937912-87-1(6))* Cordon Pubns.

Angelin. Date not set. *(978-0-517-80137-6(X))* Random Hse. Value Publishing.

Angelina, Laura. A Little Girl's Wish. 2013. 32p. pap. 19.99 *(978-1-4772-9896-1(7))* AuthorHouse.

Angleberger, Tom. Poop Fountain! (Qwikpick Papers). (ENG., Illus.). (J). (gr. 3-7). 2015. 160p. pap. 6.95 *(978-1-4197-1636-2(0))* 2014. 144p. 12.95 *(978-1-4197-0425-3(7))* Abrams, Inc. (Amulet Bks.).

—The Rat with the Human Face. 2015. (Qwikpick Papers). (ENG., Illus.). 160p. (J). (gr. 3-7). 12.95 *(978-1-4197-1489-4(9)*, Amulet Bks.) Abrams, Inc.

—The Rat with the Human Face: The Qwikpick Papers. 2016. (Qwikpick Papers). (ENG., Illus.). 176p. (J). (gr. 3-7). pap. 6.95 *(978-1-4197-1940-0(8)*, Amulet Bks.) Abrams, Inc.

—The Secret of the Fortune Wookiee. 3rd ed. 2012. 160p. pap. *(978-1-4197-0517-5(2))* Abrams, Inc.

Anglen, Becca. Nightmare in the Woods. McKeown, Christian, illus. 2007. 36p. (J). pap. 9.00 *(978-0-8059-7655-7(8))* Dorrance Publishing Co., Inc.

Angus, Sam. Captain. Roberto, Anna, ed. 2016. (ENG.). 240p. (J). 16.99 *(978-1-250-06137-9(7)*, 9781250061379) Feiwel & Friends.

Anhalt, Ariela. Freefall. 2011. (ENG.). 252p. (YA). (gr. 9). pap. 14.99 *(978-0-547-55216-3(5))* Houghton Mifflin Harcourt Publishing Co.

Anholt, Laurence. Van Gogh & the Sunflowers. 2007. (Anholt's Artists Books for Children Ser.). (ENG., Illus.). 32p. (J). (gr. -1-3). *(978-0-7641-3854-6(5))* Barron's Educational Series, Inc.

Animal Friends Squeaky. 2005. (J). bds. *(978-1-4194-0094-0(0))* Paradise Pr., Inc.

Animal Friends Squeaky - Cat. 2005. (J). bds. *(978-1-4194-0092-6(4))* Paradise Pr., Inc.

Anjelais, M. Breaking Butterflies. 2014. (ENG.). 272p. (J). (gr. 9). 17.99 *(978-0-545-66766-1(6)*, Chicken Hse., The) Scholastic, Inc.

Ann, Cameron. The Stories Julian Tells. 2014. (Stepping Stone Book Ser.). (ENG.). 80p. (J). 9.24 *(978-1-63245-217-7(0))* Lectorum Pubns., Inc.

Ann, Dee. Burden of Silence. 2013. 136p. pap. *(978-1-4602-2099-3(4))* FriesenPress.

Anna, Holly. Sparkle Fairies & the Imaginaries. Santos, Genevieve, illus. 2017. (Daisy Dreamer Ser.: 3). (ENG.). 128p. (J). (gr. k-4). pap. 5.99 ***(978-1-4814-9185-3(7)***, Little Simon) Little Simon.

Anne, Paula. Sultry Smith. 2009. 80p. pap. 9.99 *(978-1-60860-970-3(7)*, Eloquent Bks.) Strategic Book Publishing & Rights Agency (SBPRA).

The Ant & the Grasshopper: Individual Title Six-Packs. (Story Steps Ser.). (gr. k-2). 32.00 *(978-0-7635-9846-4(1))* Rigby Education.

The Ant & the Grasshopper: Small Book. (Pebble Soup Explorations Ser.). 16p. (gr. -1-18). 5.00 *(978-0-7635-7049-1(4))* Rigby Education.

Ant, Exupery. L apprends a compter avec Le. pap. 10.95 *(978-2-07-054270-3(X))* Gallimard, Editions FRA. Dist: Distribooks, Inc.

—Piccolo Principe el Suio. pap. 13.95 *(978-88-451-2266-8(2))* Fabbri Editori - RCS Libri ITA. Dist: Distribooks, Inc.

Anthony, David & David, Charles. Knightscares #5: (Knightscares) 2004. (Illus.). 200p. (J). per. 5.99 *(978-0-9728461-4-1(X)*, 1236107) Sigil Publishing.

Anthony, Wes. Binger & Stumpy the B D Dawg Series - Book. 2010. 534p. 35.95 *(978-1-60911-088-8(9)*, Eloquent Bks.) Strategic Book Publishing & Rights Agency (SBPRA).

Anton, Amy Way. Ina the Octopus & Her Shipwreck Adventure. Way, MaryFaye, illus. 2008. 28p. pap. 13.99 *(978-1-4389-2177-8(2))* AuthorHouse.

Anton, Jackie. Backyard Horse Tales Sox: 2nd Edition. 2012. 124p. pap. 11.99 *(978-1-4575-0949-0(0))* Dog Ear Publishing, LLC.

Anyanwu, Francis Eze. The Awesome Dog: How the Dog Became Man's Best Friend. 2011. 73p. pap. 14.95 *(978-1-4327-5666-6(4))* Outskirts Pr., Inc.

Apostolina, M. Hazing Meri Sugarman. 2005. (ENG.). 272p. (YA). pap. 8.99 *(978-1-4169-0610-0(X)*, Simon Pulse) Simon Pulse.

Appelt, Kathi. Bubba & Beau, Best Friends. Howard, Arthur, illus. 2006. (Bubba & Beau Ser.). (ENG.). 32p. (J). (gr. -1-3). pap. 6.99 *(978-0-15-205580-6(0))* Houghton Mifflin Harcourt Publishing Co.

Applegate, Anne. The Last Academy. 2013. (ENG.). 320p. (J). (gr. 7). 17.99 *(978-0-545-50204-7(7))* Scholastic, Inc.

Applegate, K. A., pseud. Animorphs #7: the Stranger. 2012. (Animorphs Ser.: 7). (ENG.). 176p. (J). (gr. 3-7). pap. 6.99 *(978-0-545-42414-1(3)*, Scholastic Paperbacks) Scholastic, Inc.

Applegate, Katherine. Beach Blondes. 2008. (Summer Ser.: 1). (ENG.). 736p. (YA). (gr. 9). pap. 9.99 *(978-1-4169-6133-8(X)*, Simon Pulse) Simon Pulse.

—Crenshaw. 2015. (ENG.). 256p. (J). (gr. 5-9). 16.99 *(978-1-250-04323-8(9)*, 9781250043238) Feiwel & Friends.

—Crenshaw. 2017. (ENG.). 272p. (J). pap. 7.99 ***(978-1-250-09166-6(7)***, 9781250091666) Square Fish.

—Crenshaw. 2017. (J). lib. bdg. 18.40 ***(978-0-606-40539-3(9))*** Turtleback Bks.

—Crenshaw. 2016. (SPA.). 192p. (J). (gr. 5-8). pap. 13.99 *(978-987-747-067-3(5))* V&R Editoras.

—Never Glue Your Friends to Chairs. Biggs, Brian, illus. 2016. (Roscoe Riley Rules Ser.: 1). 128p. (J). (gr. 1-5). pap. 4.99 *(978-0-06-239248-0(4))* HarperCollins Pubs.

—Roscoe Riley Rules: Never Glue Your Friends to Chairs, Never Swipe a Bully's Bear, Don't Swap Your Sweater for a Dog, & Never Swim in Applesauce. Biggs, Brian, illus. 2016. (Roscoe Riley Rules Ser.). 448p. (J). (gr. 1-5). 14.99 *(978-0-06-256427-6(7))* HarperCollins Pubs.

—Tan Lines: Sand, Surf, & Secrets; Rays, Romance, & Rivalry; Beaches, Boys, & Betrayal. 2008. (Summer Ser.: 2). (ENG.). 544p. (YA). (gr. 9). pap. 9.99 *(978-1-4169-6134-5(8)*, Simon Pulse) Simon Pulse.

Applegate, Katherine. Wishtree. 2017. (ENG., Illus.). 224p. (J). 16.99 ***(978-1-250-04322-1(0)***, 9781250043221) Feiwel & Friends.

Arbogast, Christian Hunt. Heaven's Dentist. 2011. 15.00 *(978-1-936319-58-9(6))* Mascot Bks., Inc.

Arce, Andrea. Under the Influence. 2013. 170p. pap. 13.95 *(978-1-4633-6688-9(4))* Palibrio.

Archambault, John. Cat in the Tree. Cooper, Stephanie, illus. 2007. (J). *(978-1-58669-230-8(5))* Childcraft Education Corp.

Archbold, David M. The Amazing Adventures of Chumley, Robin, Snickers & Mac. 2011. 48p. (gr. 4-6). pap. 19.26 *(978-1-4634-1518-1(4))* AuthorHouse.

Arden, Lynne. Guess What Happened to Me, Auntie Kate! Marino, Natalie, illus. 2008. 52p. pap. 18.95 *(978-1-59858-733-3(1))* Dog Ear Publishing, LLC.

Arena, Jacqueline. Basketball Showdown. Foye, Lloyd, illus. 2005. (Girlz Rock! Ser.). (J). pap. *(978-1-59336-704-6(X))* Mondo Publishing.

—Horsing Around. Maddock, Monika, illus. 2005. (Girlz Rock! Ser.). (J). pap. *(978-1-59336-703-9(1))* Mondo Publishing.

Armistead, John. The Return of Gabriel. Gregory, Fran, illus. 2004. 218p. (gr. 3-8). 17.45 *(978-0-7569-3460-6(5))* Perfection Learning Corp.

Armistead, John & Gregory, Fran. The $66 Summer: A Novel of the Segregated South. 2nd ed. 2006. (Milkweed Prize for Children's Literature Ser.). (ENG., Illus.). 240p. (J). (gr. 3-8). reprint ed. per. 8.00 *(978-1-57131-663-9(9))* Milkweed Editions.

Armo, Nancy. A Friend for Mole, 1 vol. Armo, Nancy, illus. 2016. (ENG., Illus.). 32p. (J). (gr. -1-k). 16.95 *(978-1-56145-865-3(1))* Peachtree Pubs.

Armstrong, Cindy. Boudreaux & His Buddies. 2006. 98p. pap. 16.95 *(978-1-4241-3906-4(6))* PublishAmerica, Inc.

Armstrong, Rachel. Fair Folk in Knob's End. 2013. 274p. pap. 14.99 *(978-1-60820-851-7(6))* MLR Pr., LLC.

Arno, Ronni. Dear Poppy. 2016. (Mix Ser.). (ENG., Illus.). 256p. (J). (gr. 4-8). pap. 7.99 *(978-1-4814-3759-2(3)*, Aladdin) Simon & Schuster Children's Publishing.

Arnold, Beth. Elijah Makes New Friends. Arnold, Beth, illus. 2012. (Illus.). 30p. pap. 9.99 *(978-0-9860272-3-9(5))* Get Happy Tips, LLC.

Arnold, Caroline. Wiggle & Waggle. Peterson, Mary, illus. 2009. (ENG.). 48p. (J). (gr. k-3). pap. 5.95 *(978-1-58089-307-7(4))* Charlesbridge Publishing, Inc.

Arnold, David. Kids of Appetite. (ENG.). (YA). (gr. 9). 2017. 368p. pap. 10.99 ***(978-0-14-751366-3(9)***, Speak) 2016. 352p. 18.99 *(978-0-451-47078-2(8)*, Viking Books for Young Readers) Penguin Young Readers Group.

—Kids of Appetite. 2017. lib. bdg. 22.10 ***(978-0-606-40491-4(0))*** Turtleback Bks.

Arnold, Elana K. The Question of Miracles. 2016. (ENG.). 256p. (J). (gr. 5-7). pap. 6.99 *(978-0-544-66852-2(9)*, HMH Books For Young Readers) Houghton Mifflin Harcourt Publishing Co.

Arnold, Lobel. Frog & Toad Are Friends. 2014. (I Can Read Book 2 Ser.). (ENG.). 64p. (J). (gr. 7-12). 8.24 *(978-1-63245-259-7(6))* Lectorum Pubns., Inc.

—Frog & Toad Together. 2014. (I Can Read Book 2 Ser.). (ENG.). 64p. (J). (gr. 3-7). 8.24 *(978-1-63245-246-7(4))* Lectorum Pubns., Inc.

Arnold, Louise. Golden & Grey: An Unremarkable Boy & a Rather Remarkable Ghost. 2006. (ENG., Illus.). 272p. (J). (gr. 3-7). reprint ed. pap. 6.99 *(978-0-689-87585-4(1)*, McElderry, Margaret K. Bks.) McElderry, Margaret K. Bks.

—Golden & Grey: The Nightmares That Ghosts Have. 2007. (ENG.). 304p. (J). (gr. 3-7). pap. 5.99 *(978-0-689-87587-8(8)*, McElderry, Margaret K. Bks.) McElderry, Margaret K. Bks.

Arnold, Shari. Mystique. 2012. (YA). *(978-1-4521-0363-1(1))* Chronicle Bks. LLC.

Arnold, Tedd. Fly Guy & the Frankenfly. 2013. (Fly Guy Ser.: 13). (ENG., Illus.). 32p. (J). (gr. -1-3). 6.99 *(978-0-545-49328-4(5)*, Cartwheel Bks.) Scholastic, Inc.

—Fly Guy & the Frankenfly. 2013. (Fly Guy Ser.: 13). lib. bdg. 17.20 *(978-0-606-32440-3(2)*, Turtleback) Turtleback Bks.

—Fly Guy's Amazing Tricks. 2014. (Illus.). (J). (Fly Guy Ser.: 14). (ENG.). 32p. (gr. -1-3). 6.99 *(978-0-545-49329-1(3)*, Cartwheel Bks.); 30p. *(978-0-545-76926-6(4))* Scholastic, Inc.

—Fly Guy's Amazing Tricks. 2014. (Fly Guy Ser.: 14). lib. bdg. 17.20 *(978-0-606-36267-2(3))* Turtleback Bks.

—Fly Guy's Ninja Christmas. Arnold, Tedd, illus. 2016. (Fly Guy Ser.: 16). (ENG., Illus.). 32p. (J). (gr. -1-3). 6.99 *(978-0-545-66277-2(X))* Scholastic, Inc.

Aronskind, Ofer. Escape from Sunday School. 2009. 152p. pap. 12.95 *(978-1-4401-3217-9(8))* iUniverse, Inc.

—That Same Summer. 2008. 156p. pap. 12.95 *(978-0-595-50605-7(4))* iUniverse, Inc.

Aros, Angela. Aunt Emma's Secret Recipe, 1 vol. 2009. 15p. pap. 19.95 *(978-1-60813-862-3(3))* PublishAmerica, Inc.

Arpaci, Halis. Eric & Derrick. 2011. (ENG.). 160p. (J). (gr. 3-7). 11.95 *(978-1-59784-232-7(X))* Tughra Bks.

Arps, Melissa & Lagonegro, Melissa. Friends Forever. Random House Disney Staff, illus. 2009. (Step into Reading Ser.). (ENG.). 32p. (J). (gr. k-3). pap. 3.99 *(978-0-7364-2597-1(7)*, RH/Disney) Random Hse. Children's Bks.

Arthur Hamilton & His Dog. 2004. reprint ed. pap. 1.99 *(978-1-4192-0774-7(1))*; pap. 15.95 *(978-1-4191-0774-0(7))* Kessinger Publishing, LLC.

Arthur, Peggy Ann. Come & Look in Grandma's Garden. 2012. 26p. 24.95 *(978-1-4560-3988-2(1))* America Star Bks.

Aryal, Aimee. Hello Albert! F. Pflueger, Maura McArdle, illus. 2004. 24p. (J). 19.95 *(978-1-932888-12-6(8))* Mascot Bks., Inc.

—Hello Aubie! Moore, Danny, illus. 2004. 22p. (J). 19.95 *(978-0-9743442-8-7(1))* Mascot Bks., Inc.

—Hello Baldwin! Goh, Tai Hwa, illus. 2004. 24p. (J). 19.95 *(978-1-932888-13-3(6))* Mascot Bks., Inc.

—Hello Bully! Moore, Danny, illus. 2004. 24p. (J). 19.95 *(978-0-9743442-6-3(5))* Mascot Bks., Inc.

—Hello CavMan! Perez, Gerry, illus. 2004. 24p. (J). 19.95 *(978-0-9743442-3-2(0))* Mascot Bks., Inc.

—Hello Goldy! Sable, Katherine, illus. 2004. 24p. (J). 19.95 *(978-0-9743442-4-9(9))* Mascot Bks., Inc.

—Hello Otto! Shrestha, Anuj, illus. 2004. 22p. (J). 19.95 *(978-0-9743442-2-5(2))* Mascot Bks., Inc.

Asani, Samantha. Everyone Is Special: A Lesson in Teamwork. 2012. 28p. pap. 19.99 *(978-1-4685-5320-8(8))* AuthorHouse.

Asch, Frank. The Earth & I. 2010. (Rise & Shine Ser.). (ENG., Illus.). 32p. (C). (gr. -1-3). pap. 11.95 *(978-0-15-206395-5(1))* National Geographic School Publishing, Inc.

—Here Comes the Cat! Vagin, Vladimir, illus. 25th ed. 2011. (ENG & RUS.). 32p. (J). (gr. -1-3). 12.95 *(978-1-936365-41-8(3))* McSweeney's Publishing.

—Moonbear's Bargain. Asch, Frank, illus. 2014. (Moonbear Ser.). (ENG., Illus.). 32p. (J). (gr. -1-3). 17.99 *(978-1-4424-9436-7(0)*, Aladdin) Simon & Schuster Children's Publishing.

—Moonbear's Pet. Asch, Frank, illus. 2014. (Moonbear Ser.). (ENG., Illus.). 32p. (J). (gr. -1-3). 17.99 *(978-1-4424-9430-5(1)*, Simon & Schuster/Paula Wiseman Bks.) Simon & Schuster/Paula Wiseman Bks.

—Moonbear's Shadow. Asch, Frank, illus. 2014. (Moonbear Ser.). (ENG., Illus.). 32p. (J). (gr. -1-3). 7.99 *(978-1-4424-9426-8(3)*, Aladdin) Simon & Schuster Children's Publishing.

Aschermann, Kurt. Bj & the Amazing Doctor Directions. 2008. 172p. pap. 11.99 *(978-1-4343-7708-1(3))* AuthorHouse.

Ashby, Lenore. The Magic of the Bear. 2003. (Illus.). 162p. (YA). per. 7.95 *(978-0-9728535-0-7(2)*, 853502) Grandma Chubby's Bks.

Ashby, Norman. Magic Fireplace. 2003. (Illus.). 50p. pap. *(978-1-84401-066-0(X))* Athena Pr.

Ashdown, Rebecca. Bob & Flo. 2015. (ENG., Illus.). 32p. (J). (gr. -1-3). 16.99 *(978-0-544-44430-0(2)*, HMH Books For Young Readers) Houghton Mifflin Harcourt Publishing Co.

—Bob & Flo & the Missing Bucket (Board Book) 2017. (ENG., Illus.). 26p. (J). (— 1). bds. 7.99 *(978-0-544-86711-6(4)*, HMH Books For Young Readers) Houghton Mifflin Harcourt Publishing Co.

Asher, Diana Harmon. Sidetracked. 2017. (ENG.). 240p. (J). (gr. 3-7). 16.99 ***(978-1-4197-2601-9(3)***, Amulet Bks.) Abrams, Inc.

Asher, Jay & Mackler, Carolyn. The Future of Us. 2012. (ENG., Illus.). 384p. (YA). (gr. 7). pap. 10.99 *(978-1-59514-516-1(8)*, Razorbill) Penguin Young Readers Group.

—The Future of Us. 2012. lib. bdg. 20.85 *(978-0-606-26498-3(1)*, Turtleback) Turtleback Bks.

Ashes to Ashes. 2014. (ENG., Illus.). 400p. (YA). (gr. 9). 18.99 *(978-1-4424-4081-4(3)*, Simon & Schuster Bks. For Young Readers) Simon & Schuster Bks. For Young Readers.

Ashley, Brook, et al. The Lonely Doll Makes New Friends. 2006. (ENG., Illus.). 44p. per. 17.99 *(978-1-4257-0410-0(7))* Xlibris Corp.

Ashley, Elana. Splunkunio Splunkey Detective & Peacemaker Detective y Pacificador: Case One: The Missing Friendship Bracelet Caso Primero: El Brazalete de la Amistad Desaparecido. Nikolov, Stefan V., tr. Ashley, Elana, photos by. 2005. (SPA & ENG., Illus.). 32p. (J). (gr. k-3). 17.95 *(978-0-9744812-1-0(1))* Dream Image Pr., LLC.

Ashley, Sharon. I Wish I Could See. 2013. 24p. pap. 24.95 *(978-1-4626-9700-7(3))* America Star Bks.

Ashton, Kenneth. Gale's Gold Ring: The Legend of Lincoln's Lost Gold. Ashton-Briggs, Shelley, illus. 2012. (ENG.). 198p. pap. 14.95 *(978-1-4327-8224-5(X))* Outskirts Pr., Inc.

Asquith, Ros. Letters from an Alien Schoolboy. 2013. (ENG., Illus.). 192p. (J). (gr. 1-5). 12.95 *(978-1-62087-536-0(5)*, 620536, Sky Pony Pr.) Skyhorse Publishing Co., Inc.

—Trixie Ace Ghost Buster. 2008. (Trixie Ser.). (ENG., Illus.). 176p. (J). (gr. 3-6). pap. 7.99 *(978-0-00-725909-0(3))* HarperCollins Pubs. Ltd. GBR. Dist: Independent Pubs. Group.

Atchison, David C. The Adventures of Black Bart: Dry Bones. 2008. 84p. pap. 7.94 *(978-0-615-20238-9(1))* Black Bart Bks.

Atkinson, Cale. To the Sea. Atkinson, Cale, illus. 2015. (ENG., Illus.). 48p. (J). (gr. -1-k). 16.99 *(978-1-4847-0813-2(X))* Disney Publishing Worldwide.

Atwater, Jillene. Small & Sassy. DeBroeck, Sarah, illus. 2011. 36p. pap. 24.95 *(978-1-4489-8374-2(6))* America Star Bks.

Atwater-Rhodes, Amelia. Bloodwitch. 2015. lib. bdg. 20.85 *(978-0-606-37648-8(8))* Turtleback Bks.

Atwood, Megan. The Bridge of Death. 2012. (Paranormalists Ser.: 4). (ENG.). 104p. (YA). (gr. 6-12). pap. 7.95 *(978-0-8225-9090-3(5)*, Darby Creek); lib. bdg. 27.93 *(978-0-7613-8335-2(2))* Lerner Publishing Group.

—Dear Molly, Dear Olive. Fleming, Lucy, illus. 2016. (Dear Molly, Dear Olive Ser.). (ENG.). 96p. (gr. 1-3). 87.96 *(978-1-4795-8701-8(X))* Picture Window Bks.

—The Haunting of Apartment 101. 2012. (Paranormalists Ser.: 1). (ENG.). 112p. (YA). (gr. 6-12). pap. 7.95 *(978-0-8225-9077-4(8)*, Darby Creek) Lerner Publishing Group.

—Ice Cream Summer. Andrewson, Natalie, illus. 2017. (Orchard Novel Ser.: 1). (ENG.). 272p. (J). (gr. 2-6). 12.99 ***(978-1-4814-9047-4(8)***, Aladdin) Simon & Schuster Children's Publishing.

—The Mayhem on Mohawk Avenue. 2012. (Paranormalists Ser.: 3). (ENG.). 104p. (YA). (gr. 6-12). pap. 7.95 *(978-0-8225-9088-0(3)*, Darby Creek); lib. bdg. 27.93 *(978-0-7613-8334-5(4))* Lerner Publishing Group.

—Molly Discovers Magic (Then Wants to un-Discover It) Fleming, Lucy, illus. 2016. (Dear Molly, Dear Olive Ser.). (ENG.). 96p. (gr. 1-3). lib. bdg. 21.99 *(978-1-4795-8694-3(3))* Picture Window Bks.

—Molly Discovers Magic (Then Wants to Un-Discover It) Fleming, Lucy, illus. 2017. (Dear Molly, Dear Olive Ser.). (ENG.). 96p. (gr. 1-3). pap. 5.95 *(978-1-62370-616-6(5))* Picture Window Bks.

—Molly Meets Trouble (Whose Real Name Is Jenna) Fleming, Lucy, illus. 2016. (Dear Molly, Dear Olive Ser.). (ENG.). 96p. (gr. 1-3). lib. bdg. 21.99 *(978-1-4795-8696-7(X))* Picture Window Bks.

—Olive Finds Treasure (of the Most Precious Kind) Fleming, Lucy, illus. (Dear Molly, Dear Olive Ser.). (ENG.). 96p. (gr. 1-3). 2017. pap. 5.95 *(978-1-62370-615-9(7))* 2016. lib. bdg. 21.99 *(978-1-4795-8693-6(5))* Picture Window Bks.

—Olive Spins a Tale (and It's a Doozy!) Fleming, Lucy, illus. 2016. (Dear Molly, Dear Olive Ser.). (ENG.). 96p. (gr. 1-3). lib. bdg. 21.99 *(978-1-4795-8695-0(1))* Picture Window Bks.

—The Terror of Black Eagle Tavern. 2012. (Paranormalists Ser.: 2). (ENG.). 104p. (YA). (gr. 6-12). pap. 7.95 *(978-0-8225-9078-1(6)*, Darby Creek); lib. bdg. 27.93 *(978-0-7613-8333-8(6))* Lerner Publishing Group.

Auborn, Jodi. Secrets of the North Country: The Hobo's Story. 2012. 210p. pap. 24.95 *(978-1-4626-7898-3(X))* America Star Bks.

Aubuchon, Hope L. Tiger, Ruler of the Universe. 2009. 48p. pap. 24.95 *(978-1-60749-896-4(0))* America Star Bks.

Auch, Mary Jane. A Dog on His Own. 2009. (ENG., Illus.). 160p. (J). (gr. 3-7). pap. 7.95 *(978-0-8234-2243-2(7))* Holiday Hse., Inc.

Audibert, Tara. Matthew Loses His Laugh. 2009. 32p. pap. 16.00 *(978-0-557-09385-4(6))* Lulu Pr., Inc.

Aulbach, Kathy. Meet the Flowers. 2009. 31p. 15.95 *(978-0-615-21179-4(8))* Flower Sprouts.

Auntie Annie. Knute: Dreams of Africa. 2013. 32p. pap. 17.25 *(978-1-4669-7519-4(9))* Trafford Publishing.

—Knute: In the Magical Meadow. 2013. 32p. pap. 17.25 *(978-1-4669-9778-3(8))* Trafford Publishing.

—Knute: Meets Mike in the Magical Meadow. 2013. 28p. pap. 16.09 *(978-1-4669-9780-6(X))* Trafford Publishing.

Aureliani, Franco. Dino-Mike & the Museum Mayhem. Aureliani, Franco, illus. 2015. (Dino-Mike! Ser.). (ENG., Illus.). 128p. (gr. 1-3). lib. bdg. 25.32 *(978-1-4342-9628-3(8)*, Dino-Mike!) Stone Arch Bks.

Aureliani, Franco, illus. Dino-Mike & the Museum Mayhem. 2015. (J). lib. bdg. *(978-1-4062-9391-3(1))* Stone Arch Bks.

Austin, Jamie Lea-Elizabeth. Reverie. 2012. 312p. 29.95 *(978-1-4626-6734-5(1))* PublishAmerica, Inc.

Austin, Jeanne J. Unlikely Friends. 2009. 24p. pap. 14.99 *(978-1-4343-2348-4(X))* AuthorHouse.

Austin, Rikey. Chunky & the Bone: Alice's Bear Shop. 2012. 28p. pap. *(978-1-78092-152-5(7))* MX Publishing, Ltd.

Authement, Louise. Diaries of the Fifth Grade Miseries. 2013. 68p. pap. 10.95 *(978-1-4327-9996-0(7))* Outskirts Pr., Inc.

Auty, Rob. A Hare's Tale 2 - the Golden Hare. Wood, Chaz, illus. 2013. 102p. pap. *(978-1-908098-90-0(2))* 2QT, Ltd. (Publishing).

Avasthi, Swati. Chasing Shadows. Phillips, Craig, illus. (ENG.). (YA). (gr. 9). 2015. 336p. pap. 10.99 *(978-0-375-86343-1(5)*, Ember) 2013. 320p. 17.99 *(978-0-375-86342-4(7)*, Knopf Bks. for Young Readers) 2013. 320p. lib. bdg. 20.99 *(978-0-375-96341-4(3)*, Knopf Bks. for Young Readers) Random Hse. Children's Bks.

Averiss, Corrinne. A Dot in the Snow. Woodcock, Fiona, illus. 2016. (ENG.). 32p. (J). (gr. -1-2). 14.95 *(978-1-4549-2101-1(3))* Sterling Publishing Co., Inc.

Avery, Lara. The Memory Book. 2016. (ENG.). 368p. (YA). (gr. 10-17). 17.99 *(978-0-316-28374-8(6)*, Poppy) Little, Brown Bks. for Young Readers.

—The Memory Book. 2017. (YA). lib. bdg. 20.85 ***(978-0-606-39907-4(0))*** Turtleback Bks.

Avery, Tom. My Brother's Shadow. 2014. (ENG.). 176p. (J). (gr. 4-7). 16.99 *(978-0-385-38487-2(4)*, Schwartz & Wade Bks.) Random Hse. Children's Bks.

Avi. Old Wolf. Floca, Brian, illus. 2015. (ENG.). 160p. (J). (gr. 3-7). 16.99 *(978-1-4424-9921-8(4))* Simon & Schuster Children's Publishing.

—Poppy & Ereth. Floca, Brian, illus. 2011. (Poppy Stories Ser.). (ENG.). 224p. (J). (gr. 3-7). pap. 6.99 *(978-0-06-111971-2(7))* HarperCollins Pubs.

—Romeo & Juliet Together (and Alive!) at Last. 2012. (ENG.). 128p. (J). (gr. 5-9). pap. 6.99 *(978-0-545-43097-5(6)*, Scholastic Paperbacks) Scholastic, Inc.

Award Staff & Award, Anna. Desert Adventure. 2015. (ENG., Illus.). 32p. (J). pap. 9.99 *(978-1-78270-018-0(8))* Award Pubns. Ltd. GBR. Dist: Parkwest Pubns., Inc.

—The Journey Begins. 2015. (ENG., Illus.). 32p. (J). pap. 9.99 *(978-1-78270-017-3(X))* Award Pubns. Ltd. GBR. Dist: Parkwest Pubns., Inc.

—Meerkat Mayhem. 2015. (ENG., Illus.). 32p. (J). pap. 9.99 *(978-1-78270-050-0(1))* Award Pubns. Ltd. GBR. Dist: Parkwest Pubns., Inc.

—The Search for the Rainbow Gem. 2015. (ENG., Illus.). 32p. (J). pap. 9.99 *(978-1-78270-051-7(X))* Award Pubns. Ltd. GBR. Dist: Parkwest Pubns., Inc.

Awdry, W. Brave Little Engines (Thomas & Friends) Durk, Jim, illus. 2014. (Deluxe Paint Box Book Ser.). (ENG.). 128p. (J). (gr. -1-2). pap. 7.99 *(978-0-385-38510-7(2)*, Golden Bks.) Random Hse. Children's Bks.

—Bust My Buffers! (Thomas & Friends) 2014. (Color Plus 1,000 Stickers Ser.). (ENG.). 64p. (J). (gr. -1-2). pap. 9.99 *(978-0-385-38537-4(4)*, Golden Bks.) Random Hse. Children's Bks.

—Busy, Busy Thomas. Stubbs, Tommy, illus. 2013. (Nifty Lift-And-Look Ser.). (ENG.). 12p. (J). (— 1). bds. 5.99 *(978-0-449-81642-4(7)*, Random Hse. Bks. for Young Readers) Random Hse. Children's Bks.

—The Lost Ship. Courtney, Richard, illus. 2015. (Step into Reading Ser.). (ENG.). 32p. (J). (gr. -1-1). lib. bdg. 12.99 *(978-0-553-52172-6(1)*, Random Hse. Bks. for Young Readers) Random Hse. Children's Bks.

—Not So Fast, Bash & Dash! 2013. (Thomas & Friends Step into Reading Ser.). lib. bdg. 13.55 *(978-0-606-32228-7(0)*, Turtleback) Turtleback Bks.

—Percy's Promise (Thomas & Friends) Dalby, C. Reginald, illus. 2017. (ENG.). 24p. (J). (— 1). bds. 6.99 *(978-0-399-55774-3(1)*, Random Hse. Bks. for Young Readers) Random Hse. Children's Bks.

—Story Time Collection. Courtney, Richard & Stubbs, Tommy, illus. 2014. (ENG.). 320p. (J). (gr. -1-2). 15.99 *(978-0-553-49678-9(6)*, Random Hse. Bks. for Young Readers) Random Hse. Children's Bks.

—Tale of the Brave. 2014. (Little Golden Book Ser.). (ENG., Illus.). 24p. (J). (-k). 4.99 *(978-0-385-37916-8(1)*, Golden Bks.) Random Hse. Children's Bks.

—Tale of the Brave (Thomas & Friends) Stubbs, Tommy, illus. 2014. (Big Golden Book Ser.). (ENG.). 48p. (J). (gr. -1-2). 9.99 *(978-0-385-37915-1(3)*, Golden Bks.) Random Hse. Children's Bks.

—Thomas & the Monster (Thomas & Friends) 2014. (Color Plus Chunky Crayons Ser.). (ENG.). 48p. (J). (gr. -1-2). pap. 3.99 *(978-0-385-38511-4(0)*, Golden Bks.) Random Hse. Children's Bks.

—Thomas' Big Book of Beginner Books. Random House Staff, illus. 2013. (Beginner Books Ser.). (ENG.). 224p. (J). (gr. -1-1). 16.99 *(978-0-449-81643-1(5)*, Random Hse. Bks. for Young Readers) Random Hse. Children's Bks.

Awdry, W. & Berrios, Frank. Thomas & Friends Puzzle Book. Random House Staff, illus. 2010. (Puzzle Book Ser.). (ENG.). 10p. (J). (gr. -1-2). 8.99 *(978-0-375-86168-0(8)*, Random Hse. Bks. for Young Readers) Random Hse. Children's Bks.

Awdry, Wilbert V. Full Steam Ahead! Golden Books, illus. 2012. (Color Plus Tattoos Ser.). (ENG.). 48p. (J). (gr. -1-2). pap. 3.99 *(978-0-307-93120-7(X)*, Golden Bks.) Random Hse. Children's Bks.

—Good Night, Thomas (Thomas & Friends) Random House Staff, illus. 2012. (Glow-In-the-Dark Board Book Ser.). (ENG.). 12p. (J). (gr. k-k). bds. 6.99 *(978-0-307-97697-0(1)*, Random Hse. Bks. for Young Readers) Random Hse. Children's Bks.

—King of the Railway. Golden Books Staff, illus. 2013. (Little Golden Book Ser.). (ENG.). 24p. (J). (gr. -1-1). 4.99 *(978-0-449-81537-3(4)*, Golden Bks.) Random Hse. Children's Bks.

—The Lost Crown of Sodor. Random House Staff, illus. 2013. (Pictureback Ser.). (ENG.). 24p. (J). (gr. -1-2). 3.99 *(978-0-449-81533-5(1)*, Random Hse. Bks. for Young Readers) Random Hse. Children's Bks.

—Rolling on the Rails. Golden Books Staff, illus. 2011. (Thomas & Friends Ser.). (ENG.). 12p. (J). (gr. k — 1). bds. 8.99 *(978-0-375-87304-1(X)*, Golden Bks.) Random Hse. Children's Bks.

—The Secret of the Mine. Durk, Jim, illus. 2013. (Glow-In-the-Dark Sticker Book Ser.). (ENG.). 48p. (J). (gr. -1-2). pap. 3.99 *(978-0-449-81711-7(3)*, Golden Bks.) Random Hse. Children's Bks.

—Thomas' Christmas Star. Durk, Jim, illus. 2013. (Color Plus Card Stock Ser.). (ENG.). 48p. (J). (gr. -1-2). pap. 3.99 *(978-0-449-81880-0(2)*, Golden Bks.) Random Hse. Children's Bks.

—Thomas' Valentine Party. Durk, Jim, illus. 2011. (Full-Color Activity Book with Stickers Ser.). (ENG.). 32p. (J). (gr. -1-2). pap. 3.99 *(978-0-375-86815-3(1)*, Golden Bks.) Random Hse. Children's Bks.

—Up, up & Away! Golden Books Staff & Durk, Jim, illus. 2013. (Color Plus Chunky Crayons Ser.). (ENG.). 48p. (J). (gr. -1-1). pap. 3.99 *(978-0-307-98199-8(1)*, Golden Bks.) Random Hse. Children's Bks.

Awdry, Wilbert V. & Awdry, W. Calling All Engines! Courtney, Richard, illus. 2005. (Pictureback(R) Ser.). (ENG.). 24p. (J). (gr. -1-2). pap. 3.99 *(978-0-375-83119-5(3)*, Random Hse. Bks. for Young Readers) Random Hse. Children's Bks.

Awdry, Wilbert V. & Random House Disney Staff. Thomas' Mixed-Up Day - Thomas Puts the Brakes On. Random House Disney Staff, illus. 2010. (Pictureback(R) Ser.). (ENG., Illus.). 32p. (J). (gr. -1-2). pap. 4.99 *(978-0-375-85919-9(5)*, Random Hse. Bks. for Young Readers) Random Hse. Children's Bks.

Awdry, Wilbert V. & Wrecks, Billy. Thomas Looks up (Thomas & Friends) Random House Staff, illus. 2012. (ENG.). 16p. (J). (gr. k-k). 7.99 *(978-0-307-93092-7(0)*, Random Hse. Bks. for Young Readers) Random Hse. Children's Bks.

Awdry, Wilbert Were. The Missing Christmas Tree. Stubbs, Tommy, illus. 2013. (Glitter Board Book Ser.). (ENG.). 12p. (J). (— 1). bds. 6.99 *(978-0-449-81713-1(X)*, Golden Bks.) Random Hse. Children's Bks.

Axmacher, Denise. Mrs. FireFly. 2008. 32p. 16.50 *(978-1-4357-0864-8(4))* Lulu Pr., Inc.

Ayarbe, Heidi. Freeze Frame. 2010. (ENG.). 400p. (YA). (gr. 8). pap. 8.99 *(978-0-06-135175-4(X)*, HarperTeen) HarperCollins Pubs.

Ayers, Michelle. Michael. 2011. 134p. pap. 9.99 *(978-0-557-78630-5(4))* Lulu Pr., Inc.

AZ Books. Hedgehog & His Friends. 2013. (Amusing Stories Ser.). (ENG.). 10p. (J). (-k). bds. 7.95 *(978-1-61889-305-5(X))* AZ Bks. LLC.

AZ Books, creator. Kitten Searches for a Friend. 2012. (Plush Baby Ser.). (ENG., Illus.). 10p. (J). (gr. -1 — 1). bds. 11.95 *(978-1-61889-219-5(3))* AZ Bks. LLC.

Babcock, Nona Burroughs. Little Wolf's Adventure: A Medicine Dream & Warrior Ghosts. 2008. 212p. 24.95 *(978-0-595-49087-5(5))*; pap. 14.95 *(978-0-595-46072-4(0))* iUniverse, Inc.

Baby Lauren & Theodore, Paperback. 2007. (J). pap. 9.95 *(978-0-9779643-0-7(2))* Healing Tree Arts.

Baccalario, P. D. Suitcase of Stars, 1 vol. Bruno, Iacopo, illus. 2014. (Enchanted Emporium Ser.). (ENG.). 240p. (gr. 4-8). pap. 9.25 *(978-1-4342-6519-7(6))* Stone Arch Bks.

—Suitcase of Stars, 1 vol. Pernigotti, Chiara, tr. from ITA. Bruno, Iacopo, illus. 2014. (Enchanted Emporium Ser.). (ENG.). 240p. (gr. 4-8). 26.65 *(978-1-4342-6516-6(1))* Stone Arch Bks.

Baccalario, Pierdomenico. Star of Stone. Janeczko, Leah D., tr. 2011. (Century Ser.). (ENG.). 320p. (J). (gr. 3-7). 7.99 *(978-0-375-85796-6(6)*, Yearling) Random Hse. Children's Bks.

—Suitcase of Stars, 1 vol. Bruno, Iacopo, illus. 2014. (Enchanted Emporium Ser.). (ENG.). 240p. (gr. 4-8). 12.95 *(978-1-62370-039-3(6))* Capstone Young Readers of Coughlan Cos.

Baccalario, Pierdomenico, et al. The Story of Snowflake & Inkdrop. 2015. (ENG., Illus.). 56p. (J). (gr. -1-3). 22.95 *(978-1-59270-186-5(8))* Enchanted Lion Bks., LLC.

Baccellia, Kim. Goddesses Can Wait. 2015. (YA). *(978-1-61271-297-0(5))* Zumaya Pubns. LLC.

Backer, Marni. Food Allergy Friends. 2012. (ENG.). pap. 14.99 *(978-1-4675-4513-6(9))* Independent Pub.

Bacon, C. G. Mean Mandy. 2009. 103p. pap. 11.00 *(978-0-557-05740-5(X))* Lulu Pr., Inc.

Bacon, Lee. The Dominion Key. 2014. (Joshua Dread Ser.: 3). (ENG.). 256p. (J). (gr. 4-7). 16.99 *(978-0-385-74382-2(3))*; lib. bdg. 19.99 *(978-0-375-99130-1(1))* Random Hse. Children's Bks. (Delacorte Bks. for Young Readers).

—The Nameless Hero. 2014. (Joshua Dread Ser.: 2). (ENG., Illus.). 304p. (J). (gr. 4-7). 7.99 *(978-0-307-92997-6(3)*, Yearling) Random Hse. Children's Bks.

Baczynski, Jolanta & Baczynski, Olga. Freddie & Jet. 2013. 36p. pap. *(978-0-9918166-4-4(1))* Flower Pr.

Badger, Hilary. State of Grace. 2015. (ENG.). 304p. 17.95 *(978-1-63079-015-8(X))* Switch Pr.

Bagley, Jessixa. Before I Leave. 2016. (ENG., Illus.). 40p. (J). 17.99 *(978-1-62672-040-4(1)*, 9781626720404) Roaring Brook Pr.

Baglio, Ben M. & Daniels, Lucy. Labrador on the Lawn. Gregory, Jenny, illus. 2005. (Animal Ark Hauntings Ser.: No. 38). (ENG.). 144p. (J). (gr. 2-5). 3.99 *(978-0-439-68488-0(9))* Scholastic, Inc.

Bahk, Jane. Juna's Jar. Hoshino, Felicia, illus. 2015. (ENG.). 32p. (J). 17.95 *(978-1-60060-853-7(1)*, 9781600000000) Lee & Low Bks., Inc.

Baiker, Karen. Barnyard Friends. (Felt Read-and-Play Ser.). (Illus.). 14p. (J). 17.95 *(978-1-59354-052-4(3))* Handprint Bks.

Bail, Mina Mauerstein. Max & Voltaire Getting to Know You. Choquette, Gabriel, illus. 2015. 66p. (J). pap. 16.95 *(978-1-59095-151-4(4))* TotalRecall Pubns.

Bailey, Charles. Slick Glickman, Unlikely Hero. 2008. 164p. 22.95 *(978-0-595-49014-1(X))*; pap. 12.95 *(978-0-595-48014-2(4))* iUniverse, Inc.

Bailey, Kevin. Anthony Meets the Playground Bully. 2009. 20p. pap. 13.50 *(978-1-60860-072-4(6)*, Eloquent Bks.) Strategic Book Publishing & Rights Agency (SBPRA).

Bailey, Margaret A. Dragonworld & the Room of Strange Hangings. 2009. 172p. pap. 11.99 *(978-1-4389-8252-6(6))* AuthorHouse.

Bailey, Mary. Vhan Zeely & the Time Prevaricators. 2009. 192p. 25.50 *(978-1-60693-477-7(5)*, Eloquent Bks.) Strategic Book Publishing & Rights Agency (SBPRA).

Bailey, S. D. All While Holding My Ladybug Lunch Pail. 2008. 24p. pap. 11.49 *(978-1-4389-0617-1(X))* AuthorHouse.

Bailey, William. Shalamar Book I. 2010. 37p. pap. 17.59 *(978-0-557-55781-3(X))* Lulu Pr., Inc.

Bailie, Helen. The Azura Stones. 2007. 212p. (YA). per. 18.00 *(978-1-58982-374-7(5)*, Bedside Bks.) American Bk. Publishing Group.

Bain, Michelle. The Adventures of Thumbs up Johnnie Johnnie's Missing Boot! Johnnie's Missing Boot! Lizana, Lorenzo, illus. 2007. (J). 14.95 *(978-0-9761421-8-8(X))* Pixie Stuff LLC.

Baisden, Crystal. Carlie's New Friend. 2012. 24p. pap. 24.95 *(978-1-4626-8405-2(X))* America Star Bks.

Baker, Andrea. Worlds Apart: Leah. 2013. 284p. pap. 14.99 *(978-0-9892854-3-8(X))* Taylor Street Publishing LLC.

Baker, Barbara. Digby & Kate & the Beautiful Day. Winborn, Marsha, illus. 2004. (Puffin Easy-to-Read Ser.). 48p. (J). (gr. 1-4). 11.65 *(978-0-7569-2959-6(8))* Perfection Learning Corp.

Baker, Brianna & Hastie, F. Bowman. Little White Lies. 2017. (ENG.). 272p. (YA). (gr. 9). pap. 10.99 *(978-1-61695-707-0(7)*, Soho Teen) Soho Pr., Inc.

Baker, Ed. The Story of Kitten Cuckoo. Baker, Ed, illus. 2007. (ENG., Illus.). 32p. (J). (gr. -1-17). 15.95 *(978-1-933572-04-8(3))* Centro Bks., LLC.

Baker, Jennifer. Sworn to Silence. 2014. (ENG., Illus.). 192p. (YA). (gr. 7). pap. 13.99 *(978-1-4814-2877-4(2)*, Simon Pulse) Simon Pulse.

Baker, Kage. The Hotel under the Sand. Law, Stephanie Pui-Mun, illus. 2009. (ENG.). 179p. (J). (gr. 2-7). pap. *(978-1-892391-89-6(9))* Temmen, Edition, Horst Temmen.

Baker, Lavayne L. The Return of the Black Dinosaur. 2009. 28p. pap. 12.49 *(978-1-4490-1723-1(1))* AuthorHouse.

Baker, Mary. Christmas Annie. 2009. 70p. pap. 7.96 *(978-0-557-17289-4(6))* Lulu Pr., Inc.

Baker, Matthew. If You Find This. 2015. (ENG.). 368p. (J). (gr. 3-7). 17.00 *(978-0-316-24008-6(7))* Little, Brown Bks. for Young Readers.

Baker, Michelle M. The Geese of Belle Isle: Volume I. 2011. 28p. pap. 24.95 *(978-1-4626-3715-7(9))* America Star Bks.

Baker, Roe. What's Wrong with Gretel Goann. 2010. 24p. pap. 11.50 *(978-1-60976-050-2(6)*, Eloquent Bks.) Strategic Book Publishing & Rights Agency (SBPRA).

Bakewell, Lori. Savannah Adventure: Pirate's Treasure. 2007. 173p. (J). pap. 12.95 *(978-0-9799473-9-1(1))* Tailwind Press.

Balaam, Steven & Balaam, Lisa. Abbey the Cavi: And Friends. 2007. (Illus.). 102p. (J). per. 9.95 *(978-0-9785585-0-5(2))* Balaam Books LLC.

Balazy, Elizabeth M. Prince to the Rescue. 2008. 48p. pap. 24.95 *(978-1-60474-812-3(5))* America Star Bks.

Balboni, Mary. The Birds of Winslow. 2010. 20p. 10.49 *(978-1-4490-2712-4(1))* AuthorHouse.

Baldwin, Faith. Judy: A Story of Divine Corners. Beebe, Robb, illus. 2011. 264p. 47.95 *(978-1-258-08877-4(0))* Literary Licensing, LLC.

Balfour, Melissa. The Magic Footprints. Julian, Russell, illus. 2005. (Green Bananas Ser.). (ENG.). 48p. (J). lib. bdg. *(978-0-7787-1023-3(8))* Crabtree Publishing Co.

Balfour, Melissa, et al. Yr Olion Traed Hud. 2005. (WEL., Illus.). 48p. pap. *(978-1-85596-677-2(8))* Dref Wen.

Balgassi, Haemi. Tae's Sonata. 2005. (Reader's Workshop Ser.). (ENG.). 164p. (C). pap. 19.95 *(978-0-7362-2801-5(2))* National Geographic School Publishing, Inc.

Balkovec, Lisa. Setting It Straight. 2006. (YA). per. 13.95 *(978-1-932172-24-9(6))* McKenna Publishing Group.

Ball, Georgia & Mebberson, Amy. Strawberry Shortcake, Vol. 1. 2013. (ENG., Illus.). 104p. (J). (gr. 4-8). pap. 14.99 *(978-1-937676-61-2(7)*, 9781937676612) Ape Entertainment.

Ball, Nate. Alien in My Pocket: Radio Active. Pamintuan, Macky, illus. 2014. (Alien in My Pocket Ser.: 3). (ENG.). 144p. (J). (gr. 1-5). 15.99 *(978-0-06-231493-2(9))* HarperCollins Pubs.

—Alien in My Pocket - Blast Off! Pamintuan, Macky, illus. 2014. (Alien in My Pocket Ser.: 1). (ENG.). 160p. (J). (gr. 1-5). pap. 4.99 *(978-0-06-221623-6(6))* HarperCollins Pubs.

—Alien in My Pocket - The Science Unfair. Pamintuan, Macky, illus. 2014. (Alien in My Pocket Ser.: 2). (ENG.). 144p. (J). (gr. 1-5). pap. 4.99 *(978-0-06-221625-0(2))* HarperCollins Pubs.

—Alien in My Pocket #5: Ohm vs. Amp. Pamintuan, Macky, illus. 2015. (Alien in My Pocket Ser.: 5). (ENG.). 144p. (J). (gr. 1-5). 15.99 *(978-0-06-231489-5(0))* HarperCollins Pubs.

—Alien in My Pocket #6: Forces of Nature. Pamintuan, Macky, illus. 2015. (Alien in My Pocket Ser.: 6). (ENG.). 144p. (J). (gr. 1-5). pap. 4.99 *(978-0-06-221633-5(3))* HarperCollins Pubs.

—Alien in My Pocket: on Impact! Pamintuan, Macky, illus. 2014. (Alien in My Pocket Ser.: 4). (ENG.). 128p. (J). (gr. 1-5). pap. 4.99 *(978-0-06-221629-8(5))* HarperCollins Pubs.

—Radio Active. 2014. (Alien in My Pocket Ser.: 3). (J). lib. bdg. 14.75 *(978-0-606-35349-6(6))* Turtleback Bks.

—The Science Unfair. Pamintuan, Macky, illus. 2014. (Alien in My Pocket Ser.: 2). (ENG.). 144p. (J). (gr. 1-5). 15.99 *(978-0-06-231494-9(7))* HarperCollins Pubs.

—The Science Unfair. 2014. (Alien in My Pocket Ser.: 2). (J). lib. bdg. 14.75 *(978-0-606-35182-9(5))* Turtleback Bks.

—Telescope Troubles. Pamintuan, Macky, illus. 2016. (Alien in My Pocket Ser.: 7). 144p. (J). (gr. 1-5). pap. 4.99 *(978-0-06-237088-4(X))* HarperCollins Pubs.

Ballantyne, R. M. Blown to Bits; or, the Lonely Man of Rak. 2006. pap. *(978-1-4065-0515-3(3))* Dodo Pr.

Ballard, Kim. Light at Summer's End. 2007. 116p. per. 15.95 *(978-1-60290-047-9(7))* OakTara Publishing Group LLC.

Ballesteros, Jason. Sideways. 2010. 145p. pap. 14.72 *(978-0-557-28699-7(9))* Lulu Pr., Inc.

Balmer, Fred. Festus & His New Job. Newcomb, Kristene, illus. 2004. 26p. (J). per. 7.00 *(978-0-9760790-1-9(1))* Folsom Fallies Pr.

—Festus & the Hole in the Fence Gang. Newcomb, Kristene, illus. 2005. 33p. (J). per. 7.00 *(978-0-9760790-3-3(8))* Folsom Fallies Pr.

—Festus & the Missing Bag of Feed. Newcomb, Kristene, illus. 2004. 26p. (J). per. 7.00 *(978-0-9760790-0-2(3))* Folsom Fallies Pr.

—Festus & the Stranger. Miller, Callie, ed. Newcomb, Kristene, illus. 2007. 30p. (J). per. 7.00 *(978-0-9760790-4-0(6))* Folsom Fallies Pr.

Balouch, Kristen. The Little Little Girl with the Big Big Voice. Balouch, Kristen, illus. 2011. (ENG., Illus.). 32p. (J). (gr. -1-k). 12.99 *(978-1-4424-0808-1(1)*, Little Simon) Little Simon.

Baltazar, Armand. Diego & the Rangers of the Vastlantic. Baltazar, Armand, illus. 2017. (Timeless Ser.: 1). (Illus.). 624p. (J). (gr. 3-7). 19.99 *(978-0-06-240236-3(6)*, Tegen, Katherine Bks) HarperCollins Pubs.

Bamboo Zoo Set: Meet Lester Panda & his Friends. 2006. (J). 17.95 *(978-0-9774493-1-6(9))* Bamboo Zoo, LLC.

Bancks, Tristan. Noob, Crimebuster. Gorissen, Dean, illus. 2015. (Legends in Their Own Lunchbox Ser.). (ENG.). 48p. (gr. 1-2). pap. 7.99 *(978-1-4966-0241-1(2)*, Legends in Their Own Lunchbox) Capstone Classroom.

—Noob, the Boy Who Could Fly. Gorissen, Dean, illus. 2015. (Legends in Their Own Lunchbox Ser.). (ENG.). 56p. (gr. 2-3). pap. 7.99 *(978-1-4966-0259-6(5)*, Legends in Their Own Lunchbox) Capstone Classroom.

Bandy, Sheena. Magdlynn in Flames. 2008. 164p. pap. 19.95 *(978-1-4116-7780-7(3))* Lulu Pr., Inc.

Banks, Anna. Of Poseidon, 1 vol. 2012. 59.95 *(978-0-7927-9019-8(7)*, Sound Library) AudioGO.

Banks, Jane Whelen. Liam Knows What to Do When Kids Act Snitty: Coping When Friends Are Tactless. 2008. (ENG., Illus.). 32p. 12.95 *(978-1-84310-902-0(6)*, 7167) Kingsley, Jessica Pubs. GBR. Dist: Macmillan Distribution Ltd.

Banks, Jane Whelen & Whelen-Banks, Jane. Liam Says "Sorry" Repairing an Encounter Gone Sour. 2008. (ENG., Illus.). 32p. 12.95 *(978-1-84310-903-7(4)*, 5373) Kingsley, Jessica Pubs. GBR. Dist: Macmillan Distribution Ltd.

Banks, Kate & Sheldrake, Rupert. Boy's Best Friend. 2015. (ENG.). 224p. (J). (gr. 3-7). 15.99 *(978-0-374-38008-3(2)*, 9780374380083, Farrar, Straus & Giroux (BYR)) Farrar, Straus & Giroux.

Banks, Rosie. Cloud Island. 2014. (Secret Kingdom Ser.: 3). lib. bdg. 14.75 *(978-0-606-35807-1(2))* Turtleback Bks.

—Mermaid Reef. 2014. (Secret Kingdom Ser.: 4). lib. bdg. 14.75 *(978-0-606-35842-2(0))* Turtleback Bks.

—Secret Kingdom #3: Cloud Island. 2014. (Secret Kingdom Ser.: 3). (ENG.). 128p. (J). (gr. 2-5). pap. 4.99 *(978-0-545-53555-7(7)*, Scholastic Paperbacks) Scholastic, Inc.

—Secret Kingdom #4: Mermaid Reef. 2014. (Secret Kingdom Ser.: 4). (ENG.). 128p. (J). (gr. 2-5). pap. 4.99 *(978-0-545-53556-4(5)*, Scholastic Paperbacks) Scholastic, Inc.

Banks, Sara Harrell. The Everlasting Now, 1 vol. 2010. (ENG.). 168p. (J). (gr. 3-7). 15.95 *(978-1-56145-525-6(3)*, Peachtree Junior) Peachtree Pubs.

Bannister, Bram. Rupert, the Alien & the Bank Robbery. 2007. 56p. per. 8.95 *(978-0-595-44839-5(9))* iUniverse, Inc.

Bansch, Helga. Petra. 2010. (SPA., Illus.). 48p. (J). 15.95 *(978-84-9871-003-8(0))* OQO, Editora ESP. Dist: Baker & Taylor Bks.

Bapiraju Gandham. The Wizard of Ants. 2010. 88p. pap. 33.48 *(978-1-4269-1940-4(9))* Trafford Publishing.

Barad-Cutler, Alexis. Walking with Dinosaurs: Friends Stick Together. 2013. (I Can Read Level 2 Ser.). (ENG., Illus.). 32p. (J). (gr. -1-3). 16.99 *(978-0-06-223286-1(X))*; pap. 3.99 *(978-0-06-223285-4(1))* HarperCollins Pubs.

Barandela, Jeremy. United We Stand. 2007. 376p. per. 20.95 *(978-1-4327-1495-6(3))* Outskirts Pr., Inc.

Barbari, Nader. Eddy the Elephant. 2010. 32p. pap. 13.99 *(978-1-4490-9430-0(9))* AuthorHouse.

Barber, Antonia. Dancing Shoes Friends & Rivals. (Illus.). 96p. (J). 5.95 *(978-0-14-038684-4(X))* Penguin Publishing Group.

Barbieri, Sandra Birriel. Cristal & the Secret of the Enchanted Forest: Cristal y el Secreto Del Bosque Encantado. 2013. 64p. pap. 23.99 *(978-1-4525-6512-5(0))* Balboa Pr.

Barbo, Maria S. The Rescue Mission. 2016. (Pokemon Reader Ser.: 1). lib. bdg. 13.55 ***(978-0-606-39736-0(1))*** Turtleback Bks.

Barbour, Ralph Henry. The Half-Back. 2006. (Illus.). pap. *(978-1-4065-0776-8(8))* Dodo Pr.

Barchers, Suzanne I. Kip Gets Sick, 1 vol. 2011. (Targeted Phonics Ser.). (ENG., Illus.). 16p. (J). (gr. k-2). pap. 5.99 *(978-1-4333-2422-2(9))* Teacher Created Materials, Inc.

Barden, Laura. The Fail Free Zone. Ebertsch, Ted, illus. 2010. 100p. pap. 10.49 *(978-1-4520-0857-8(4))* AuthorHouse.

Barden, Stephanie. Cinderella Smith. Goode, Diane, illus. (Cinderella Smith Ser.: 1). (ENG.). (J). 2011. 160p. (gr. 3-7). 16.99 *(978-0-06-196423-7(9))* Vol. 3. 2013. 144p. (gr. 1-5). 16.99 *(978-0-06-200443-7(3))* HarperCollins Pubs.

—The More the Merrier. Goode, Diane, illus. (Cinderella Smith Ser.: 2). (ENG.). (J). (gr. 3-7). 2013. 160p. pap. 5.99 *(978-0-06-200442-0(5))* 2012. 144p. 15.99 *(978-0-06-200440-6(9))* HarperCollins Pubs.

Bardhan-Quallen, Sudipta. The Adventures of Caveboy. Wight, Eric, illus. 2017. (Caveboy Ser.). (ENG.). 80p. (J). 9.99 *(978-1-61963-986-7(6)*, 9781619639867, Bloomsbury USA Childrens) Bloomsbury Publishing USA.

—Chasing Magic. Random House Disney Staff & Gurihiru Staff, illus. 2016. (Stepping Stone Book Ser.). (ENG.). 128p. (J). (gr. 1-4). 9.99 *(978-0-7364-3290-0(6)*, RH/Disney) Random Hse. Children's Bks.

—Purrmaids #1: the Scaredy Cat. 2017. (Purrmaids Ser.: 1). (ENG.). 96p. (J). (gr. 1-4). lib. bdg. 12.99 ***(978-1-5247-0162-8(9))***; (Illus.). 4.99 ***(978-1-5247-0161-1(0))*** Random Hse. Children's Bks. (Random Hse. Bks. for Young Readers).

—Purrmaids #2: the Catfish Club. 2017. (Purrmaids Ser.: 2). (ENG.). 96p. (J). (gr. 1-4). lib. bdg. 12.99 ***(978-1-5247-0165-9(3))***; (Illus.). 4.99 ***(978-1-5247-0164-2(5))*** Random Hse. Children's Bks. (Random Hse. Bks. for Young Readers).

Bargellini, Demetrio, et al. The Secret of the Sphinx. Cooper-McGuinness, Nanette, tr. 2009. (Geronimo Stilton Graphic Novels Ser.). (ENG., Illus.). 56p. (J). (gr. 2-6). 9.99 *(978-1-59707-159-8(5)*, 9781597071598) Papercutz.

Bargiel, Nina G. & Amsterdam, Shane. Fintastic Friends Forever. 2016. (Illus.). 32p. (J). ***(978-1-5182-1661-9(7))*** Little Brown & Co.

Barkley, Callie. All about Ellie. Riti, Marsha, illus. 2013. (Critter Club Ser.: 2). (ENG.). 128p. (J). (gr. k-2). 15.99 *(978-1-4424-5789-8(9))*; pap. 5.99 *(978-1-4424-5788-1(0))* Little Simon. (Little Simon).

—All about Ellie. 2013. (Critter Club Ser.: 2). lib. bdg. 16.00 *(978-0-606-27024-3(8)*, Turtleback) Turtleback Bks.

—The Critter Club: Amy & the Missing Puppy; All about Ellie; Liz Learns a Lesson. Riti, Marsha, illus. 2014. (Critter Club Ser.). (ENG.). 368p. (J). (gr. k-4). pap. 8.99 *(978-1-4814-2770-8(9)*, Little Simon) Little Simon.

—Ellie & the Good-Luck Pig. Riti, Marsha, illus. 2015. (Critter Club Ser.: 10). (ENG.). 128p. (J). (gr. k-4). pap. 5.99 *(978-1-4814-2402-8(5)*, Little Simon) Little Simon.

—Ellie's Lovely Idea. Riti, Marsha, illus. 2013. (Critter Club Ser.: 6). (ENG.). 128p. (J). (gr. k-4). 16.99 *(978-1-4424-8219-7(2))*; pap. 5.99 *(978-1-4424-8218-0(4))* Little Simon. (Little Simon).

—Ellie's Lovely Idea. 2013. (Critter Club Ser.: 6). (J). lib. bdg. 16.00 *(978-0-606-32321-5(X)*, Turtleback) Turtleback Bks.

—Liz & the Sand Castle Contest. Riti, Marsha, illus. 2015. (Critter Club Ser.: 11). (ENG.). 128p. (J). (gr. k-4). pap. 5.99 *(978-1-4814-2405-9(X)*, Little Simon) Little Simon.

—Liz at Marigold Lake. Riti, Marsha, illus. 2014. (Critter Club Ser.: 7). (ENG.). 128p. (J). (gr. k-4). pap. 5.99 *(978-1-4424-9525-8(1)*, Little Simon) Little Simon.

—Liz at Marigold Lake. 2014. (Critter Club Ser.: 7). lib. bdg. 16.00 *(978-0-606-35445-5(X))* Turtleback Bks.

—Liz Learns a Lesson. Riti, Marsha, illus. 2013. (Critter Club Ser.: 3). (ENG.). 128p. (J). (gr. -1-2). 16.99 *(978-1-4424-6770-5(3))*; pap. 5.99 *(978-1-4424-6768-2(1))* Little Simon. (Little Simon).

—Liz Learns a Lesson. 2013. (Critter Club Ser.: 3). lib. bdg. 16.00 *(978-0-606-32032-0(6)*, Turtleback) Turtleback Bks.

—Marion Takes a Break. Riti, Marsha, illus. 2013. (Critter Club Ser.: 4). (ENG.). 128p. (J). (gr. k-2). 16.99 *(978-1-4424-6773-6(8))*; pap. 5.99 *(978-1-4424-6772-9(X))* Little Simon. (Little Simon).

—Marion Takes a Break. 2013. (Critter Club Ser.: 4). lib. bdg. 16.00 *(978-0-606-32045-0(8)*, Turtleback) Turtleback Bks.

Barkley, Roger C. Johnny Grasshopper. 2006. 52p. pap. 16.95 *(978-1-4241-0221-1(9))* PublishAmerica, Inc.

Barlau, Martin. Lenny Was a Leaf: Learning about Life. 2013. 38p. pap. 16.95 *(978-1-4908-1150-5(8)*, WestBow Pr.) Author Solutions, Inc.

Barlone, M. J. A Mouse & Rabbits Tale. 2010. (Illus.). 40p. pap. 16.99 *(978-1-4490-7771-6(4))* AuthorHouse.

Barnaby, Hannah. Garcia & Colette Go Exploring. Joyner, Andrew, illus. 2017. (ENG.). 32p. (J). (-k). 16.99 *(978-0-399-17675-3(6),* G.P. Putnam's Sons Books for Young Readers) Penguin Young Readers Group.

Barnard, Lucy, illus. Squirrel's Busy Day. 2014. 24p. (J). **(978-1-4351-5602-9(1))** Barnes & Noble, Inc.

Barnes, David-Matthew. Mesmerized. 2010. (ENG.). 264p. (J). (gr. 7). pap. 13.95 *(978-1-60282-191-0(7))* Bold Strokes Bks.

—Swimming to Chicago. 2011. (ENG.). 264p. (J). (gr. 7). pap. 13.95 *(978-1-60282-572-7(6))* Bold Strokes Bks.

Barnes, Derrick D. We Could Be Brothers. 2010. (J). *(978-0-545-13574-0(5),* Scholastic Pr.) Scholastic, Inc.

Barnes, Jennifer Lynn. Fate. 2009. (ENG.). 368p. (YA). (gr. 7-18). pap. 8.99 *(978-0-385-73537-7(5),* Delacorte Bks. for Young Readers) Random Hse. Children's Bks.

—Tattoo. 2007. (ENG.). 272p. (YA). (gr. 7-12). pap. 7.99 *(978-0-385-73347-2(X),* Delacorte Bks. for Young Readers) Random Hse. Children's Bks.

Barnes, John. Tales of the Madman Underground. 2011. (ENG.). 544p. (YA). (gr. 9-18). 9.99 *(978-0-14-241702-7(5),* Speak) Penguin Young Readers Group.

Barnett, Mac. Leo: A Ghost Story. Robinson, Christian, illus. 2015. (ENG.). 52p. (J). (gr. -1-k). 16.99 *(978-1-4521-3156-6(2))* Chronicle Bks. LLC.

—Triangle. Klassen, Jon, illus. 2017. (ENG.). 48p. (J). (gr. k-4). 15.99 *(978-0-7636-9603-0(X))* Candlewick Pr.

Barnett, Mac & John, Jory. The Terrible Two. Cornell, Kevin, illus. (Terrible Two Ser.). (ENG.). (J). (gr. 3-7). 2016. 224p. 13.95 *(978-1-4197-1680-5(8),* Amulet Bks.) 2016. pap. 7.95 *(978-1-4197-1925-7(4))* 2015. 224p. 13.95 *(978-1-4197-1491-7(0),* Amulet Bks.) Abrams, Inc.

—The Terrible Two. 2017. (Terrible Two Ser.: 1). lib. bdg. 18.40 **(978-0-606-40723-6(5))**; lib. bdg. 18.40 **(978-0-606-40724-3(3))** Turtleback Bks.

Barnhill, Kelly. The Girl Who Drank the Moon. 2016. (ENG.). 400p. (J). (gr. 5-9). 17.95 *(978-1-61620-567-6(9))* Algonquin Bks. of Chapel Hill.

—The Mostly True Story of Jack. 2012. (ENG.). 352p. (J). (gr. 3-7). pap. 8.99 *(978-0-316-05672-4(3))* Little, Brown Bks. for Young Readers.

—The Witch's Boy. 2014. (ENG.). 384p. (J). (gr. 4). 17.95 *(978-1-61620-351-1(X),* 73351) Algonquin Bks. of Chapel Hill.

Barnholdt, Lauren. Devon Delaney Should Totally Know Better. 2009. (Mix Ser.). (ENG.). 288p. (J). (gr. 4-8). pap. 6.99 *(978-1-4169-8019-3(9),* Aladdin) Simon & Schuster Children's Publishing.

—Fake Me a Match. 2011. (Mix Ser.). (ENG.). 288p. (J). (gr. 4-9). 15.99 *(978-1-4424-2258-2(0),* Simon & Schuster/Paula Wiseman Bks.) Simon & Schuster/Paula Wiseman Bks.

—Four Truths & a Lie. 2008. (Mix Ser.). (ENG.). 272p. (J). (gr. 4-8). pap. 5.99 *(978-1-4169-3504-9(5),* Aladdin) Simon & Schuster Children's Publishing.

—From This Moment. 2015. (Moment of Truth Ser.: 3). (ENG.). 272p. (YA). (gr. 8). pap. 9.99 *(978-0-06-232143-5(9),* HarperTeen) HarperCollins Pubs.

—Heat of the Moment. 2015. (Moment of Truth Ser.: 1). (ENG.). 304p. (YA). (gr. 8). pap. 9.99 *(978-0-06-232139-8(0),* HarperTeen) HarperCollins Pubs.

—One Moment in Time. 2015. (Moment of Truth Ser.: 2). (ENG.). 304p. (YA). (gr. 8). pap. 9.99 *(978-0-06-232141-1(2),* HarperTeen) HarperCollins Pubs.

—Rules for Secret Keeping. 2010. (Mix Ser.). (ENG.). 288p. (J). (gr. 4-9). 15.99 *(978-1-4169-8020-9(2),* Aladdin) Simon & Schuster Children's Publishing.

—The Secret Identity of Devon Delaney. 2007. (Mix Ser.). (ENG.). 272p. (J). (gr. 4-8). pap. 5.99 *(978-1-4169-3503-2(7),* Aladdin) Simon & Schuster Children's Publishing.

Barnickle, Angela. Miles Gardner & the Secret of Blissville: A Blissville Mystery Series. 2011. 128p. (gr. 4-6). 23.89 *(978-1-4634-1675-1(X))*; pap. 12.01 *(978-1-4634-1676-8(8))* AuthorHouse.

Baroff, Raina. The Chanukah Puppet Show. 2008. 20p. per. 24.95 *(978-1-4241-8612-9(9))* America Star Bks.

Baron, Charlie & Gamson, Alyse. Peanut Butter & Jelly. 2013. 12p. pap. 10.97 *(978-1-62212-388-9(3),* Strategic Bk. Publishing) Strategic Book Publishing & Rights Agency (SBPRA).

Barr, Marilynn G. Miss Pitty Pat & Friends. 2012. 38p. pap. 12.95 *(978-1-937257-13-2(4))* Little Acorn Assocs., Inc.

Barradell, Isabel. Even More Tales from the Toyshop. 2008. 380p. pap. 29.95 *(978-1-60474-508-5(8))* America Star Bks.

Barrett, Jennifer. Lethal Delivery, Postage Prepaid. (Thumbprint Mysteries Ser.). 32.86 *(978-0-8092-0425-0(8))* McGraw-Hill/Contemporary.

Barrett, Michellene. Englisha & David's Adventurous Vacation. 2009. 86p. (gr. 3-3). pap. 9.95 *(978-1-4401-2319-1(5))* iUniverse, Inc.

Barrett, Susanna. Isabella Goes to the City. 2011. 20p. pap. 11.99 *(978-1-4634-0203-7(1))* AuthorHouse.

Barrie, J. M. Peter Pan: An Illustrated Classic for Kids & Young Readers (Excellent for Bedtime & Young Readers) eMusic, Tom, ed. Friday, Arthur, illus. 2013. 38p. pap. 6.99 *(978-1-62321-067-0(4))* Tommye-music Corp. DBA Tom eMusic.

—Tommy & Grizel. (J). reprint ed. lib. bdg. 98.00 *(978-0-7426-2515-0(X))* Classic Bks.

Barrow, Rebecca. You Don't Know Me but I Know You. 2017. 336p. (YA). (gr. 9). 17.99 **(978-0-06-249419-1(8),** HarperTeen) HarperCollins Pubs.

Barrows, Annie. Ivy + Bean. Blackall, Sophie, illus. (Ivy & Bean Ser.: IVYB). (ENG.). 120p. (J). (gr. 1-5). 2007. pap. 5.99 *(978-0-8118-4909-8(0))*Bk. 1. 2006. 14.99 *(978-0-8118-4903-6(1))* Chronicle Bks. LLC.

—Ivy + Bean. Blackall, Sophie, illus. 2007. (Ivy & Bean Ser.: Bk. 1). 120p. (gr. 1-5). 16.00 *(978-0-7569-8142-6(5))* Perfection Learning Corp.

—Ivy + Bean. Blackall, Sophie, illus. 2007. (Ivy & Bean Ser.: 1). (J). lib. bdg. 16.00 *(978-1-4177-7972-7(1),* Turtleback) Turtleback Bks.

—Ivy + Bean: No News Is Good News. Blackall, Sophie, illus. 2012. (Ivy & Bean Ser.). (ENG.). 144p. (J). (gr. 1-5). pap. 5.99 *(978-1-4521-0781-3(5))* Chronicle Bks. LLC.

—Ivy + Bean - Make the Rules. Blackall, Sophie, illus. 2012. (Ivy & Bean Ser.). (ENG.). 127p. (J). (gr. 1-5). 14.99 *(978-1-4521-0295-5(3))* Chronicle Bks. LLC.

—Ivy + Bean - What's the Big Idea? Blackall, Sophie, illus. 2011. (ENG.). 132p. (J). (gr. 1-5). pap. 5.99 *(978-1-4521-0236-8(8))* Chronicle Bks. LLC.

—Ivy + Bean & the Ghost That Had to Go. Blackall, Sophie, illus. (Ivy & Bean Ser.: IVYB). (ENG.). 136p. (J). (gr. 1-5). 2007. pap. 5.99 *(978-0-8118-4911-1(2))*Bk. 2. 2006. 14.99 *(978-0-8118-4910-4(4))* Chronicle Bks. LLC.

—Ivy + Bean Boxed Set: Books 7-9. Blackall, Sophie, illus. 2013. (Ivy & Bean Ser.). (ENG.). 428p. (J). (gr. 1-5). 19.99 *(978-1-4521-1732-4(2))* Chronicle Bks. LLC.

—Ivy + Bean Break the Fossil Record. Blackall, Sophie, illus. 2007. (Ivy & Bean Ser.: IVYB). (ENG.). (J). (gr. 1-5). 124p. pap. 5.99 *(978-0-8118-6250-9(X))*; 132p. 14.99 *(978-0-8118-5683-6(6))* Chronicle Bks. LLC.

—Ivy + Bean Doomed to Dance. Blackall, Sophie, illus. (ENG.). 136p. (J). (gr. 1-5). 2010. pap. 5.99 *(978-0-8118-7666-7(7))* 2009. (Ivy & Bean Ser.: IVYB). 14.99 *(978-0-8118-6266-0(6))* Chronicle Bks. LLC.

—Ivy + Bean Make the Rules, Bk. 9. Blackall, Sophie, illus. 2013. (Ivy & Bean Ser.: 9). (ENG.). 144p. (J). (gr. 1-5). pap. 5.99 *(978-1-4521-1148-3(0))* Chronicle Bks. LLC.

—Ivy + Bean Make the Rules. 2013. (Ivy & Bean Ser.: 9). (J). lib. bdg. 16.00 *(978-0-606-32296-6(5),* Turtleback) Turtleback Bks.

—Ivy + Bean No News Is Good News. Blackall, Sophie, illus. 2011. (Ivy & Bean Ser.: IVYB). (ENG.). 128p. (J). (gr. 1-5). 14.99 *(978-0-8118-6693-4(9))* Chronicle Bks. LLC.

—Ivy + Bean Take Care of the Babysitter. Blackall, Sophie, illus. 2008. (Ivy & Bean Ser.: IVYB). (ENG.). 144p. (J). (gr. 1-5). 14.99 *(978-0-8118-5685-0(2))* Chronicle Bks. LLC.

—Ivy + Bean Take the Case. Blackall, Sophie, illus. (ENG.). (J). (gr. 1-4). 2014. 136p. pap. 5.99 *(978-1-4521-2871-9(5))* 2013. 128p. 14.99 *(978-1-4521-0699-1(1))* Chronicle Bks. LLC.

—Ivy & Bean & the Ghost That Had to Go. Blackall, Sophie, illus. 2007. (Ivy & Bean Ser.: 2). (J). lib. bdg. 16.00 *(978-1-4177-9273-3(6),* Turtleback) Turtleback Bks.

—Ivy & Bean Take the Case. 2014. (Ivy & Bean Ser.: 10). (J). lib. bdg. 16.00 *(978-0-606-36537-6(0))* Turtleback Bks.

—No News Is Good News. Blackall, Sophie, illus. 2012. (Ivy & Bean Ser.: 8). (J). lib. bdg. 16.00 *(978-0-606-26950-6(9),* Turtleback) Turtleback Bks.

Barrows, Annie & Blackall, Sophie. Ivy + Bean, Set. 2010. (ENG., Illus.). 392p. (J). (gr. 1-5). 19.99 *(978-0-8118-7665-0(9))* Chronicle Bks. LLC.

—Ivy + Bean, 1 vol. 2011. (Ivy & Bean Ser.). (ENG., Illus.). 128p. (J). (gr. 1-4). 24.21 *(978-1-59961-928-6(8))* Spotlight.

—Ivy + Bean & the Ghost That Had to Go, 1 vol. 2011. (Ivy & Bean Ser.). (ENG., Illus.). 136p. (J). (gr. 1-4). 24.21 *(978-1-59961-929-3(6))* Spotlight.

—Ivy + Bean Break the Fossil Record, 1 vol. 2011. (Ivy & Bean Ser.). (ENG., Illus.). 128p. (J). (gr. 1-4). 24.21 *(978-1-59961-930-9(X))* Spotlight.

—Ivy + Bean Doomed to Dance, 1 vol. 2011. (Ivy & Bean Ser.). (ENG., Illus.). 136p. (J). (gr. 1-4). 24.21 *(978-1-59961-933-0(4))* Spotlight.

Barry, Cotter. The Adventures of Morgan Morgan the Rhymester. 2010. 16p. 12.99 *(978-1-4520-0116-6(2))* AuthorHouse.

Barry, Dave & Pearson, Ridley. Peter & the Starcatchers. Call, Greg, illus. rev. ed. 2006. (Peter & the Starcatchers Ser.). (ENG.). 480p. (J). (gr. 5-9). reprint ed. pap. 9.99 *(978-0-7868-4907-9(X),* Disney Editions) Disney Pr.

Barry, Debra R. Debbie's Eyes. Tessier, Beth Marie, photos by. 2011. (Illus.). 32p. pap. 24.95 *(978-1-4560-5272-0(1))* America Star Bks.

Barry, Nick. Escape of the Terra-Cotta Soldiers: An Ethan Sparks Adventure. 2008. 180p. 23.95 *(978-0-595-49365-4(3))*; pap. 13.95 *(978-0-595-45413-6(5))* iUniverse, Inc.

Barshaw, Ruth McNally. The Ellie McDoodle Diaries: Ellie for President. Barshaw, Ruth McNally, illus. 2014. (Ellie Mcdoodle Ser.). (ENG., Illus.). 176p. (J). (gr. 3-6). 12.99 *(978-1-61963-061-1(3),* 9781619630611, Bloomsbury USA Childrens) Bloomsbury Publishing USA.

—The Show Must Go On. Barshaw, Ruth McNally, illus. 2013. (Ellie Mcdoodle Diaries). (ENG., Illus.). 176p. (YA). (gr. 3-6). 12.99 *(978-1-61963-059-8(1),* 9781619630598, Bloomsbury USA Childrens) Bloomsbury Publishing USA.

Barson, Kelly. Charlotte Cuts It Out. 2016. (ENG.). 368p. (YA). (gr. 7). 17.99 *(978-0-451-46893-2(7),* Viking Books for Young Readers) Penguin Young Readers Group.

Bart, Kathleen. Town Teddy & Country Bear Tour the USA. Bart, Kathleen, illus. 2008. (Illus.). 32p. (J). (gr. -1-3). pap. 16.95 *(978-1-932485-50-9(3))* Reverie Publishing Co.

Bartels, Korin. A Secret in My Shoes. l.t. ed. 2005. (Illus.). 20p. (J). per. 10.00 *(978-1-59879-031-3(5))* Lifevest Publishing, Inc.

Barth, Kathleen E. The Amazing Adventures of Quigley D Pigley & His Friends. 2009. 16p. pap. 8.49 *(978-1-4389-8322-6(0))* AuthorHouse.

—The Amazing Adventures of Quigley D Pigley & His Friends: How to Become an Astronaut. 2009. 16p. pap. 8.49 *(978-1-4389-8606-7(8))* AuthorHouse.

Bartha, Alysa. Petal's Wish. 2010. 32p. 14.99 *(978-1-4490-7417-3(0))* AuthorHouse.

Bartolome, Teresita Africano. We Lost Our House, 1 vol. 2010. 24p. 24.95 *(978-1-4489-7338-5(4))* PublishAmerica, Inc.

Barton, Chris. Muddymania! Cummings, Troy, illus. 2017. 32p. (J). (gr. -1-3). 17.99 *(978-0-06-234479-3(X))* HarperCollins Pubs.

Barton, Tamra Clum. The Adventures of Lucky the Leaf. 2007. 32p. per. 18.65 *(978-1-4257-3026-0(4))* Xlibris Corp.

Barwin, Steven. Rock Dogs, 1 vol. 2009. (Lorimer Sports Stories Ser.). (ENG.). 104p. (J). (gr. 4-8). 16.95 *(978-1-55277-028-3(1),* 9781552770283); 8.95 *(978-1-55277-027-6(3),* 9781552770276) Lorimer, James & Co., Ltd., Pubs. CAN. Dist: Casemate Pubs. & Bk. Distributors, LLC.

Basha, Irena Canaj. The Birthday Party, It Was Saturday... 2013. 16p. pap. 24.95 *(978-1-62709-182-4(3))* America Star Bks.

Basham, Tom. Sailing Home. Calvert, Lissa, illus. 2012. 168p. *(978-1-77097-370-1(2))* FriesenPress.

Basham, Tom & Calvert, Lissa. Sailing Home. 2012. 168p. pap. *(978-1-77097-371-8(0))* FriesenPress.

Bashe, Kayla. Kitty Cadawell & the Shadowslayers of Fyrn. 2008. 290p. pap. 16.50 *(978-0-557-01916-8(8))* Lulu Pr., Inc.

Bashline, Trent. How Jake & Daisy Stopped Bullying at Dogwood Elementary. 2011. 32p. pap. 12.79 *(978-1-4634-2895-2(2))* AuthorHouse.

Baskin, Nora Raleigh. Ruby on the Outside. 2015. (ENG., Illus.). 176p. (J). (gr. 3-7). 18.99 *(978-1-4424-8503-7(5),* Simon & Schuster Bks. For Young Readers) Simon & Schuster Bks. For Young Readers.

—The Summer Before Boys. (ENG.). 208p. (J). (gr. 4-7). 2012. pap. 6.99 *(978-1-4169-8674-4(X))* 2011. 16.99 *(978-1-4169-8673-7(1))* Simon & Schuster Bks. For Young Readers. (Simon & Schuster Bks. For Young Readers).

Bass, Guy. The Ghost of Grotteskew, 1 vol. Williamson, Pete, illus. 2014. (Stitch Head Ser.). (ENG.). 208p. (gr. 3-4). 10.95 *(978-1-62370-030-0(2))* Capstone Young Readers of Coughlan Cos.

—The Pirate's Eye, 1 vol. Williamson, Pete, illus. 2013. (Stitch Head Ser.). (ENG.). 208p. (gr. 3-4). 10.95 *(978-1-62370-008-9(6))* Capstone Young Readers of Coughlan Cos.

—The Spider's Lair. Williamson, Pete, illus. 2015. (Stitch Head Ser.). (ENG.). 208p. (gr. 3-4). 10.95 *(978-1-62370-192-5(9))* Capstone Young Readers of Coughlan Cos.

—Stitch Head, 1 vol. Williamson, Pete, illus. 2013. (Stitch Head Ser.). (ENG.). 192p. (gr. 3-4). 10.95 *(978-1-62370-007-2(8))* Capstone Young Readers of Coughlan Cos.

Bass, Patrik Henry. The Zero Degree Zombie Zone. Craft, Jerry, illus. 2014. (ENG.). 144p. (J). (gr. 3-7). 16.99 *(978-0-545-13210-7(X),* Scholastic Pr.) Scholastic, Inc.

Bass, Ruth. Sarah's Daughter. 2007. 389p. (YA). (gr. 8-12). per. 14.95 *(978-0-9774053-4-3(6))* North River Pr. Publishing Corp., The.

Bastet - Evaluation Guide: Evaluation Guide. 2006. (J). *(978-1-55942-400-4(1))* Witcher Productions.

Batchelor, Rhonda. She Loves You. 2008. (ENG.). 136p. (YA). (gr. 7-8). pap. 11.99 *(978-1-55002-789-1(1),* Sandcastle Bks.) Dundurn CAN. Dist: Ingram Publisher Services.

Bateman, Marinna. The Toogles' Big Move, 1 vol. 2009. 24p. pap. 24.95 *(978-1-61546-537-8(5))* America Star Bks.

Bateman, Teresa. Leprechaun under the Bed. Meisel, Paul, illus. 2012. (ENG.). 32p. (J). 17.95 *(978-0-8234-2221-0(6))* Holiday Hse., Inc.

Bates, Angie. Hey Baby! 2010. (Sleepover Club Ser.). (ENG., Illus.). 144p. (J). (gr. 2-6). pap. 6.99 *(978-0-00-727704-9(0))* HarperCollins Pubs. Ltd. GBR. Dist: Independent Pubs. Group.

Bateson, Catherine. Being Bee. (ENG.). 136p. (J). 2008. (gr. 3-7). pap. 7.95 *(978-0-8234-2208-1(9))* 2007. (Illus.). (gr. 4-7). 16.95 *(978-0-8234-2104-6(X))* Holiday Hse., Inc.

Battiste, Alyse. Super Sally's Fantastic Fun Day. 2007. (Illus.). 68p. (J). pap. 15.97 *(978-0-9798217-1-4(1))* Candalyse Publishing.

Batton, Doris. Snicker & Snore, 1 vol. Griffin, Cheri, illus. 2010. 40p. pap. 24.95 *(978-1-4489-6113-9(0))* PublishAmerica, Inc.

Bauer, A. C. E. Gil Marsh. 2013. (ENG.). 192p. (YA). (gr. 7). pap. 7.99 *(978-0-375-87374-4(0),* Ember) Random Hse. Children's Bks.

Bauer, A. C. E. & Shakespeare, William. Come Fall. 2011. (ENG.). 240p. (J). (gr. 3-7). pap. 6.99 *(978-0-375-85826-0(1),* Yearling) Random Hse. Children's Bks.

Bauer, Joan. Sticks. 2005. (ENG., Illus.). 192p. (YA). (gr. 7-5). pap. 7.99 *(978-0-14-240428-7(4),* Speak) Penguin Young Readers Group.

Bauer, Marion Dane. The Double-Digit Club. 2004. (ENG.). 126p. (J). (gr. 4-6). tchr. ed. 16.95 *(978-0-8234-1805-3(7))* Holiday Hse., Inc.

—Killing Miss Kitty & Other Sins. 2008. (ENG.). 176p. (YA). (gr. 7). pap. 12.95 *(978-0-547-07614-0(2))* Houghton Mifflin Harcourt Publishing Co.

—On My Honor. 2012. lib. bdg. 18.40 *(978-0-606-24717-7(3),* Turtleback) Turtleback Bks.

Bauer, Michael Gerard. The Running Man. 2008. 304p. (YA). (gr. 9-18). lib. bdg. 17.89 *(978-0-06-145509-4(1),* HarperTeen) HarperCollins Pubs.

—The Running Man. 2004. 280p. (YA). pap. *(978-1-86291-575-6(X),* Omnibus Bks.) Scholastic Australia.

Baum, L. Frank. Ozma of Oz. 2007. 108p. (gr. 4-7). per. 9.95 *(978-1-60312-150-7(1))* Aegypan.

Baum, L. Frank & Bancroft, Laura. Twinkle & Chubbins. 2011. 106p. 22.95 *(978-1-4638-9604-1(2))* Rodgers, Alan Bks.

Baum, Robert. Portal Masters: A New Beginning. 2004. 282p. (YA). 27.95 *(978-0-595-66942-4(5))* iUniverse, Inc.

Baumgartner, John Robert. Like Losing Your Left Hand. 2011. 244p. pap. 24.95 *(978-1-4560-4043-7(X))* America Star Bks.

Be Kind, Be Friendly, Be Thankful: The Adventures of Brisky Bear & Trooper Dog. 2007. Orig. Title: Friends for Always. (J). pap. 7.95 incl. audio compact disk *(978-0-9795127-0-4(0))* Glory Be Collectibles.

Beacon Street Girls Staff. Meet the Beacon Street Girls. 2004. (Illus.). 36p. (J). pap. 3.99 *(978-0-9746587-5-9(8),* Beacon Street Girls) B*tween Productions, Inc.

Beale, Madeline. Sarah's BFF (Best Friend Forever) Goh, Douglas, illus. 2017. (ENG.). 24p. 10.00 *(978-981-4751-87-2(1))* Marshall Cavendish International (Asia) Private Ltd. SGP. Dist: National Bk. Network.

Beam, Cris. I Am J. 2012. (ENG.). 352p. (YA). (gr. 10-17). pap. 10.99 *(978-0-316-05360-0(0))* Little, Brown Bks. for Young Readers.

Beamish, Diane. Brucie Learns a Lesson. 2006. 25p. (J). 10.25 *(978-1-4116-6631-3(3))* Lulu Pr., Inc.

—Gentle Jack. 2006. 25p. (J). 10.25 *(978-1-4116-5553-9(2))* Lulu Pr., Inc.

Bear, F. T. Connor Finn: The Secret of Snow. 2013. 258p. pap. *(978-0-646-91485-5(5))* F. T. Bear.

Beard, Darleen Bailey. The Flimflam Man. Christelow, Eileen, illus. 2003. (ENG.). 96p. (J). (gr. 2-5). per. 10.99 *(978-0-374-42345-2(8),* 9780374423452, Farrar, Straus & Giroux (BYR)) Farrar, Straus & Giroux.

Beasley, Cassie. Circus Mirandus. 2016. (SPA.). 25.99 *(978-84-246-5686-7(5))* La Galera, S.A. Editorial ESP. Dist: Lectorum Pubns., Inc.

—Circus Mirandus. (ENG., Illus.). 304p. (J). (gr. 4-7). 2016. pap. 8.99 *(978-0-14-751554-4(8),* Puffin Books) 2015. 17.99 *(978-0-525-42843-5(7),* Dial Bks) Penguin Young Readers Group.

—Circus Mirandus. 2016. (ENG.). 304p. (J). (gr. 3-7). 19.65 *(978-0-606-39311-9(0))* Turtleback Bks.

Beasley, Cassie. Tumble & Blue. 2017. (ENG.). 400p. (J). (gr. 3-7). 17.99 **(978-0-525-42844-2(5),** Dial Bks) Penguin Young Readers Group.

Beatty, Cherie B. Meet Lewis the Duck. 2009. 24p. pap. 12.99 *(978-1-4389-5116-4(7))* AuthorHouse.

Beatty, Robert. Serafina & the Black Cloak. (Serafina Ser.). (ENG.). (J). (gr. 3-7). 2016. 320p. pap. 7.99 *(978-1-4847-1187-3(4))* 2015. 304p. 16.99 *(978-1-4847-0901-6(2))* Hyperion Bks. for Children.

—Serafina & the Black Cloak. 2016. (J). lib. bdg. 18.40 *(978-0-606-38336-3(0))* Turtleback Bks.

Beatty, Robert. Serafina & the Splintered Heart. 2017. (Serafina Ser.: bk.3). (ENG.). 368p. (J). (gr. 3-7). 16.99 **(978-1-4847-7504-2(X))** Hyperion Bks. for Children.

Beaudry, Len. Luther the Looney Bird: In Luther's First Walk. 2010. 12p. 8.49 *(978-1-4520-0358-0(0))* AuthorHouse.

Beaufrand, M. J. The Rise & Fall of the Gallivanters. 2015. (ENG., Illus.). 288p. (YA). (gr. 9-17). 16.95 *(978-1-4197-1495-5(3),* Amulet Bks.) Abrams, Inc.

Because of Winn Dixie. 2011. 9.14 *(978-0-7848-3659-0(0),* Everbind) Marco Bk. Co.

Beck, A. E. Master-E: Travel into Mystical Dragon Dimensions: Collision of Fantasy, Science Fiction & Physics. 2010. 212p. pap. 49.49 *(978-1-4490-3612-6(0))* AuthorHouse.

Beck, Andrea. Elliot's Fire Truck, 1 vol. Beck, Andrea, illus. 2010. (ENG., Illus.). 32p. (J). (gr. -1-3). 19.95 *(978-1-55469-143-2(5))* Orca Bk. Pubs. USA.

Beck, Bev. Benny at the Bop. 2011. 28p. pap. 24.95 *(978-1-4560-6151-7(8))* America Star Bks.

Beck, Ernie. Skinni Mini & Friends in the Valley of Hope. Beck, Blaze, illus. 2012. 74p. pap. 13.99 *(978-0-9858398-5-7(6))* Mindstir Media.

Becker and Mayer! Books Staff. Hello Kitty Super-Sweet Stencils. Sanrio Company, Ltd. Staff, illus. 2013. (ENG.). 24p. (J). (gr. k-2). spiral bd. 14.95 *(978-1-4197-0631-8(4),* Abrams Bks. for Young Readers) Abrams, Inc.

Becker, Bonny. A Bedtime for Bear. Denton, Kady MacDonald, illus. 2010. (J). (Bear & Mouse Ser.: 3). (ENG.). 48p. (gr. -1-2). 16.99 *(978-0-7636-4101-6(4))*; *(978-0-7636-5364-4(0))* Candlewick Pr.

—A Birthday for Bear. Denton, Kady MacDonald, illus. (Candlewick Sparks Ser.). (ENG.). (J). 2013. 56p. (gr. k-4). pap. 3.99 *(978-0-7636-6861-7(3))* 2012. 48p. (gr. -1-2). 16.99 *(978-0-7636-5823-6(5))* Candlewick Pr.

—The Sniffles for Bear. Denton, Kady MacDonald, illus. 2011. (Bear & Mouse Ser.). (ENG.). 32p. (J). (gr. -1-2). 16.99 *(978-0-7636-4756-8(X))* Candlewick Pr.

—A Visitor for Bear. Denton, Kady MacDonald, illus. (Bear & Mouse Ser.). (ENG.). 56p. (J). 2012. (gr. k-k). pap. 6.99 *(978-0-7636-4611-0(3))* 2008. (gr. -1-2). 16.99 *(978-0-7636-2807-9(7))* Candlewick Pr.

—A Visitor for Bear. Denton, Kady MacDonald, illus. 2012. lib. bdg. 17.20 *(978-0-606-26930-8(4),* Turtleback) Turtleback Bks.

Becker, Brooke. The Adventures of Sammy Snowflake, Vol. 1. Gentry, Kyle, illus. 2007. (ENG.). 64p. (gr. 4-7). 19.95 *(978-0-9795260-0-8(0))* Courtyard Publishing, LLC.

Becker Holstein, Barbara. Secrets: Diary of a Gutsy Teen. 2015. (ENG.). 144p. (J). (gr. 2-7). 12.95 *(978-1-62914-626-3(9),* Sky Pony Pr.) Skyhorse Publishing Co., Inc.

Becker, Suzy. Bud & Scooter. Date not set. 48p. (J). (gr. k-3). pap. 3.99 *(978-0-06-444286-2(1))* HarperCollins Pubs.

—Bud & Scooter. Becker, Suzy, illus. Date not set. (Illus.). 48p. (J). (gr. k-3). 16.89 *(978-0-06-028971-3(6))*; 15.99 *(978-0-06-028970-6(8))* HarperCollins Pubs.

—Kate the Great Except When She's Not. Becker, Suzy, illus. 2014. (Kate the Great Ser.: 1). (ENG., Illus.). 272p. (J). (gr. 3-7). 12.99 *(978-0-385-38742-2(3),* Crown Books For Young Readers) Random Hse. Children's Bks.

—Kate the Great, Except When She's Not. Becker, Suzy, illus. 2014. (Kate the Great Ser.). (ENG., Illus.). 272p. (J). (gr. 3-7). lib. bdg. 15.99 *(978-0-385-38743-9(1),* Crown Books For Young Readers) Random Hse. Children's Bks.

—Kate the Great: Winner Takes All. Becker, Suzy, illus. 2016. (Kate the Great Ser.). (ENG., Illus.). 256p. (J). (gr. 3-7). 12.99 *(978-0-385-38880-1(2),* Crown Books For Young Readers) Random Hse. Children's Bks.

Beckerman, Menucha. Friends on the Farm. 2004. (My Smiling World Ser.: No. 1). (Illus.). 32p. (J). 11.95 *(978-1-931681-53-7(8))* Israel Bookshop Pubns.

—My Middos World: Michael & the Secret of Making Friends, 9. 2003. (My Middos World Ser.: Vol. 9). (Illus.). 24p. (J). (gr. k-5). 11.95 *(978-1-931681-15-5(5))* Israel Bookshop Pubns.

Beckley, N. K. The Three-Some: Book 2. 2012. 66p. 24.99 *(978-1-4771-2938-8(3))* Xlibris Corp.

Bedford, David. Ahora Me Toca a Mi! Field, Elaine, illus. (SPA.). 32p. (J). *(978-84-8418-051-7(4))* Corimbo, Editorial S.L. ESP. Dist: Lectorum Pubns., Inc.

—The Copy Crocs. Bolam, Emily, tr. Bolam, Emily, illus. 2004. (ENG.). 32p. (J). (gr. k-3). 15.95 *(978-1-56145-304-7(8))* Peachtree Pubs.

Bedford, David & James, Ann. The Way I Love You Box Set. 2007. 24p. *(978-1-921049-95-8(2))* Little Hare Bks. AUS. Dist: HarperCollins Pubs. Australia.

Bedford, David A. Angela. 2009. 190p. 25.50 *(978-1-60860-755-6(0),* Eloquent Bks.) Strategic Book Publishing & Rights Agency (SBPRA).

Bednar, Martin. Sandy's Vision. 2006. (J). lib. bdg. 19.95 *(978-1-933732-15-2(6))* Big Ransom Studio.

Bee, Nanny. William. 2012. 52p. (-18). pap. 16.95 *(978-1-4626-9765-6(8))* America Star Bks.

Bee, Stevie J. Cross Your Heart. 2009. 216p. 25.50 *(978-1-60860-133-2(1),* Eloquent Bks.) Strategic Book Publishing & Rights Agency (SBPRA).

Beech, Sandy. Worst Class Trip Ever. Holder, Jimmy, illus. 2005. (Castaways Ser.: 1). (ENG.). 176p. (J). (gr. 3-7). pap. 9.99 *(978-0-689-87596-0(7),* Aladdin) Simon & Schuster Children's Publishing.

E
F
G

Beer, Henry, photos by. Girl Defective. 2015. (ENG., Illus.). 320p. (YA). (gr. 9). pap. 10.99 *(978-1-4424-9761-0(0))* Simon & Schuster Children's Publishing.

Beggs, Melissa. Pompety-Pooh: Purplest Penguin in Zonkety Zoo. Laible, Steve William, ed. Almanstotter, Susanne, illus. 2013. 52p. pap. 12.95 *(978-0-9844784-9-1(3)*, Empire Holdings) Kodel Group, LLC, The.

Behems, Kathryn J. The Gateway. 2016. (Atlas of Cursed Places Ser.). (ENG.). 104p. (YA). (gr. 6-12). lib. bdg. 26.65 *(978-1-5124-1325-0(9)*, Darby Creek) Lerner Publishing Group.

Behl, Colin. Noüm. 2007. 108p. per. 16.95 *(978-1-4241-4518-8(X))* PublishAmerica, Inc.

Behling, Steve. Daring Dino Rescue! (Rusty Rivets) Lovett, Nate, illus. 2017. (Big Golden Book Ser.). (ENG.). 48p. (J). (gr. -1-2). 9.99 ***(978-1-5247-1678-3(2)***, Golden Bks.) Random Hse. Children's Bks.

Behrens, Rebecca. When Audrey Met Alice. 2014. (ENG.). 304p. (J). (gr. 4-7). 16.99 *(978-1-4022-8642-1(2)*, 9781402286421, Sourcebooks Jabberwocky) Sourcebooks, Inc.

Beighey, Carole La Flamme. The Waddodles of Hollow Lake: Ruffed Grouse Courtship Ceremony. 2010. (ENG.). 284p. pap. 15.49 *(978-1-4490-3255-5(9))* AuthorHouse.

Beil, Michael D. The Red Blazer Girls. 2010. (Red Blazer Girls Ser.). (ENG.). 320p. (J). (gr. 3-7). 7.99 *(978-0-375-84303-7(5)*, Yearling) Random Hse. Children's Bks.

—The Red Blazer Girls: the Vanishing Violin. 2011. (Red Blazer Girls Ser.). (ENG.). 336p. (J). (gr. 3-7). 8.99 *(978-0-375-85454-5(1)*, Yearling) Random Hse. Children's Bks.

Beinstein, Phoebe. ¡A nadar, Boots! (Swim, Boots, Swim!) Roper, Robert, illus. 2009. (Dora la Exploradora Ser.). (SPA.). 24p. (J). pap. 3.99 *(978-1-4169-7939-5(5)*, Libros Para Ninos) Libros Para Ninos.

—Swim, Boots, Swim! Roper, Robert, illus. 2009. (Dora the Explorer Ser.: 29). (ENG.). 24p. (J). (gr. -1-2). pap. 3.99 *(978-1-4169-7195-5(5)*, Simon Spotlight/Nickelodeon) Simon Spotlight/Nickelodeon.

Bekis, Joanne. Bubble & Butterfly. 2009. 20p. pap. 10.50 *(978-1-60693-696-2(4)*, Strategic Bk. Publishing) Strategic Book Publishing & Rights Agency (SBPRA).

Bell, Cece. Chuck & Woodchuck. Bell, Cece, illus. 2016. (ENG., Illus.). 32p. (J). (gr. -1-3). 15.99 *(978-0-7636-7524-0(5))* Candlewick Pr.

—Rabbit & Robot. 2014. (Candlewick Sparks Ser.). lib. bdg. 13.55 *(978-0-606-35169-0(8))* Turtleback Bks.

—Rabbit & Robot: The Sleepover. Bell, Cece, illus. 2012. (ENG., Illus.). 56p. (J). (gr. k-4). 14.99 *(978-0-7636-5475-7(2))* Candlewick Pr.

—Rabbit & Robot - The Sleepover. Bell, Cece, illus. 2014. (Candlewick Sparks Ser.). (ENG., Illus.). 56p. (J). (gr. k-4). pap. 3.99 *(978-0-7636-6875-4(3))* Candlewick Pr.

—Rabbit & Robot & Ribbit. Bell, Cece, illus. 2016. (ENG., Illus.). 48p. (J). (gr. k-4). 14.99 *(978-0-7636-7935-4(6))* Candlewick Pr.

Bell, Eric. Alan Cole Is Not a Coward. 2017. 272p. (J). (gr. 3-7). 16.99 ***(978-0-06-256702-4(0)***, Tegen, Katherine Bks) HarperCollins Pubs.

Bell, G. F. Angel Wings & S'Mores. 2008. 152p. 29.99 *(978-1-4257-7491-2(1))*; pap. 19.99 *(978-1-4257-7489-9(X))* Xlibris Corp.

Bell, Krista & Smith, Craig. If the Shoe Fits. 2008. (Illus.). (Orig.). (J). 60p. (gr. -1-3). 14.95 *(978-1-58089-338-1(4))*; (ENG., 64p. (gr. 4-7). pap. 5.95 *(978-1-58089-339-8(2))* Charlesbridge Publishing, Inc.

Bell, Lucy J. Rufus Loses His Cape. Garton, Michael, illus. 2017. (J). 12.99 ***(978-1-5064-1788-2(4)***, Sparkhouse Family) Augsburg Fortress, Pubs.

—Uri & the Busy Day. Garton, Michael, illus. 2017. (J). 12.99 ***(978-1-5064-1787-5(6)***, Sparkhouse Family) Augsburg Fortress, Pubs.

Bell, Patricia A. Timothy Caterpillar Gets New Shoes. 2012. 24p. 24.95 *(978-1-62709-669-0(8))*; 20p. pap. 24.95 *(978-1-4626-9147-0(1))* America Star Bks.

Bell, Phillip. Kurt the Dog & His Friend Lisa the Cat. 2012. 20p. pap. 24.95 *(978-1-4626-8140-2(9))* America Star Bks.

Bell, Rebecca. Capitano Ricco. Bell, Rebecca, illus. 2005. (Illus.). 36p. (J). 9.95 *(978-1-934138-06-9(1))* Bouncing Ball Bks., Inc.

Bell, Sophie. Lilac Attack! 2014. (Ultra Violets Ser.: 3). (ENG., Illus.). 304p. (J). (gr. 3-7). 12.99 *(978-1-59514-648-9(2)*, Razorbill) Penguin Young Readers Group.

—Power to the Purple! Battle, Christina, illus. 2013. (Ultra Violets Ser.: 2). (ENG.). 336p. (J). (gr. 3-7). 12.99 *(978-1-59514-647-2(4)*, Razorbill) Penguin Young Readers Group.

Bell, Taryn. In the Spotlight. 2010. (ENG.). 256p. pap. 8.99 *(978-0-545-21444-5(0))* Scholastic, Inc.

Bellingham, Brenda. Lilly Makes a Friend, 1 vol. MacDonald, Clarke, illus. 2004. (Formac First Novels Ser.: 29). (ENG.). 64p. (J). (gr. 1-5). 4.95 *(978-0-88780-624-7(4)*, 9780887806247); 14.95 *(978-0-88780-625-4(2)*, 9780887806254) Formac Publishing Co., Ltd. CAN. Dist: Casemate Pubs. & Bk. Distributors, LLC.

—Lilly Traps the Bullies. MacDonald, Clarke, illus. 2011. (Formac First Novels Ser.). (ENG.). 64p. (J). (gr. 2-3). 14.95 *(978-0-88780-961-3(8)*, 9780887809613); pap. 5.95 *(978-0-88780-959-0(6)*, 9780887809590) Formac Publishing Co., Ltd. CAN. Dist: Casemate Pubs. & Bk. Distributors, LLC.

—Lilly's Special Gift. MacDonald, Clarke, illus. 2005. (Formac First Novels Ser.: 32). (ENG.). 64p. (gr. 2-5). 14.95 *(978-0-88780-665-0(1)*, 9780887806650) Formac Publishing Co., Ltd. CAN. Dist: Casemate Pubs. & Bk. Distributors, LLC.

—Lilly's Special Gift, 1 vol. MacDonald, Clarke & Kaulbach, Kathy, illus. 2005. (Formac First Novels Ser.: 32). (ENG.). 64p. (gr. 2-5). 4.95 *(978-0-88780-664-3(3)*, 9780887806643) Formac Publishing Co., Ltd. CAN. Dist: Casemate Pubs. & Bk. Distributors, LLC.

Bellis, Jill. The Return of the Magnificent Six: A Christmas Adventure. Farmer, Zoe, illus. 2008. (The Magnificent Six: Vol. 2). 62p. pap. 14.00 *(978-1-58690-073-1(0))* Players Pr., Inc.

Bellisario, Gina. An Extra-Ordinary Girl. Von Innerebner, Jessika, illus. 2016. (Ellie Ultra Ser.). (ENG.). 128p. (gr. 2-3). lib. bdg. 25.99 *(978-1-4965-3139-1(6))* Stone Arch Bks.

—Queen of the Spelling Bee. Von Innerebner, Jessika, illus. 2016. (Ellie Ultra Ser.). (ENG.). 128p. (gr. 2-3). lib. bdg. 25.99 *(978-1-4965-3141-4(8))* Stone Arch Bks.

—Team Earth Takeover. Von Innerebner, Jessika, illus. 2016. (Ellie Ultra Ser.). (ENG.). 128p. (gr. 2-3). lib. bdg. 25.99 *(978-1-4965-3143-8(4))* Stone Arch Bks.

Benchmark Education Co., LLC. My Friends Big Book. 2014. (Shared Reading Foundations Ser.). (J). (gr. -1). *(978-1-4509-9423-1(7))* Benchmark Education Co.

—Where Is Moggie? Big Book. 2014. (Shared Reading Foundations Ser.). (J). (gr. -1). *(978-1-4509-9429-3(6))* Benchmark Education Co.

Bender, Randy L. Bunko's Journey. LaGrange, Tiffany, illus. 2008. 44p. pap. 13.95 *(978-0-9818683-2-5(0))* Peppertree Pr., The.

Benedictus, David. Return to the Hundred Acre Wood. Burgess, Mark, illus. 2009. (Winnie-The-Pooh Ser.). (ENG.). 216p. (J). (gr. 3-7). 19.99 *(978-0-525-42160-3(2)*, Dutton Books for Young Readers) Penguin Young Readers Group.

Benedis-Grab, Daphne. Clementine for Christmas. 2015. (ENG.). 256p. (J). (gr. 3-7). 16.99 *(978-0-545-83951-8(3)*, Scholastic Pr.) Scholastic, Inc.

Benitez, Diana. The Butterfly Keeper. 2011. 102p. pap. 19.95 *(978-1-4626-2616-8(5))* America Star Bks.

Benjamin, Ali. The Thing about Jellyfish. (ENG.). 352p. (J). (gr. 5-17). 2017. pap. 8.99 *(978-0-316-38084-3(9))* 2015. 17.99 *(978-0-316-38086-7(5))* Little, Brown Bks. for Young Readers.

—The Thing about Jellyfish. 2017. (J). lib. bdg. 19.65 ***(978-0-606-40218-7(7))*** Turtleback Bks.

Benn, Iris H. Penelope's New Friends: Early Childhood Life Lesson. 2013. 32p. 29.95 *(978-1-4787-1210-7(4))* Outskirts Pr., Inc.

Bennese, Ray & Bennese, Kristian. Till the Train Runs Out of Track. 2007. 76p. per. 19.95 *(978-1-4241-7567-3(4))* America Star Bks.

Bennett, Bonnie. Howard the Worm. 2011. 28p. pap. 16.95 *(978-1-4626-0004-5(2))* America Star Bks.

—Meet Cinnamon Bear. 2009. 48p. pap. 16.95 *(978-1-60749-496-6(5))* America Star Bks.

Bennett, Cindy C. Geek Girl. 2011. 280p. (J). pap. 15.99 *(978-1-59955-925-4(0))* Bonneville B.V. NLD. Dist: Cedar Fort, Inc./CFI Distribution.

Bennett, Eric. Noodles & Albie. Bannish, Liz, illus. 2014. (ENG.). (J). 17.95 *(978-1-937650-40-7(5))* Small Batch Bks.

Bennett, Holly. The Bonemender, 1 vol. 2005. (Bonemender Ser.: 1). (ENG., Illus.). 208p. (YA). (gr. 8-12). per. 9.95 *(978-1-55143-336-3(2))* Orca Bk. Pubs. USA.

—Redwing, 1 vol. 2012. (ENG.). 208p. (YA). (gr. 8-12). pap. 12.95 *(978-1-4598-0038-0(9))* Orca Bk. Pubs. USA.

Bennett, Kelly. No a Norman: La Historia de un Pececito Dorado. Jones, Noah Z., illus. 2016. (ENG & SPA.). 32p. (J). 6.99 *(978-0-7636-8906-3(8))* Candlewick Pr.

—Not Norman: A Goldfish Story. Jones, Noah Z., illus. 2008. (ENG.). 32p. (J). (gr. -1-3). pap. 6.99 *(978-0-7636-2763-8(1))* Candlewick Pr.

Bennett, Marilyn J. The Poinsettia Adventure. 2010. 60p. pap. 21.99 *(978-1-4490-7108-0(2))* AuthorHouse.

Bennett, Shirley. Missy - a Tail-Wagging Good Life. 2012. 32p. pap. 19.99 *(978-1-4685-9476-8(1))* AuthorHouse.

Bennett, Sophia. Sequins, Secrets, & Silver Linings. 2011. (ENG.). 304p. (J). (gr. 7-11). 16.99 *(978-0-545-24241-7(X)*, Chicken Hse., The) Scholastic, Inc.

Benson, Cindy. Chloe & Hairy Go to School. 2012. 32p. pap. 12.99 *(978-0-9855202-9-8(9))* Kids At Heart Publishing, LLC.

Benson, Donald. Tommy Turtle Turns Blue. 2007. 28p. (J). pap. 12.78 *(978-1-4251-2087-0(3))* Trafford Publishing.

Benson, Donna. Dog Gone Drama, the Cupcakes Club #2. 2008. 130p. (J). pap. 7.95 *(978-0-9799159-1-8(0))* Pink Lemonade, LLC.

Benson, Glenda. The Adventures of Pepe & Gracie: Trouble in the Park. 2012. 20p. pap. 13.77 *(978-1-4669-0840-6(8))* Trafford Publishing.

Benson, Jeffrey. The Adventures of Avortit & Rooney. 2005. pap. *(978-1-84401-490-3(8))* Athena Pr.

Benson, Ken. Leela's Great Life. 2012. 28p. pap. 15.99 *(978-1-4771-2713-1(5))* Xlibris Corp.

Benson, Linda Sue. It's Okay, Leon, 1 vol. 2009. 74p. pap. 19.95 *(978-1-4489-2173-7(2))* America Star Bks.

Bentley, Dawn. Velociraptor. Carr, Karen, illus. 2005. (Smithsonian's Prehistoric Pals Ser.). (ENG.). 36p. (J). (gr. -1-2). 9.95 *(978-1-59249-168-1(5)*, PS2453) Soundprints.

Bentley, Sue. Chocolate Wishes #1. Swan, Angela, illus. 2013. (Magic Bunny Ser.: 1). (ENG.). 128p. (J). (gr. 1-3). pap. 5.99 *(978-0-448-46727-6(5)*, Grosset & Dunlap) Penguin Young Readers Group.

—Classroom Chaos, 2 vols. Swan, Angela & Farley, Andrew, illus. 2008. (Magic Kitten Ser.: 2). (ENG.). 128p. (J). (gr. 1-3). pap. 5.99 *(978-0-448-44999-9(4)*, Grosset & Dunlap) Penguin Young Readers Group.

—Dancing Days #5. Swan, Angela & Farley, Andrew, illus. 2014. (Magic Bunny Ser.: 5). (ENG.). 128p. (J). (gr. 1-3). 4.99 *(978-0-448-46793-1(3)*, Grosset & Dunlap) Penguin Young Readers Group.

—Firelight Friends. 2014. (Magic Kitten Ser.: 10). lib. bdg. 14.75 *(978-0-606-34136-3(6)*, Turtleback) Turtleback Bks.

—Friendship Forever #10. Swan, Angela, illus. 2013. (Magic Puppy Ser.: 10). (ENG.). 128p. (J). (gr. 1-3). 5.99 *(978-0-448-46733-7(X)*, Grosset & Dunlap) Penguin Young Readers Group.

—The Perfect Secret. 2014. (Magic Puppy Ser.: 14). lib. bdg. 14.75 *(978-0-606-35686-2(X))* Turtleback Bks.

—The Perfect Secret #14. Swan, Angela & Farley, Andrew, illus. 2014. (Magic Puppy Ser.: 14). (ENG.). 128p. (J). (gr. 1-3). 5.99 *(978-0-448-46799-3(2)*, Grosset & Dunlap) Penguin Young Readers Group.

—Seaside Mystery. 2013. (Magic Kitten Ser.: 9). lib. bdg. 16.00 *(978-0-606-32121-1(7)*, Turtleback) Turtleback Bks.

—A Shimmering Splash #11. Swan, Angela & Farley, Andrew, illus. 2014. (Magic Kitten Ser.: 11). (ENG.). 128p. (J). (gr. 1-3). 4.99 *(978-0-448-46789-4(5)*, Grosset & Dunlap) Penguin Young Readers Group.

—A Splash of Magic. 2013. (Magic Bunny Ser.: 3). lib. bdg. 14.75 *(978-0-606-31677-4(9)*, Turtleback) Turtleback Bks.

—A Splash of Magic #3. Swan, Angela, illus. 2013. (Magic Bunny Ser.: 3). (ENG.). 128p. (J). (gr. 1-3). pap. 5.99 *(978-0-448-46729-0(1)*, Grosset & Dunlap) Penguin Young Readers Group.

—Vacation Dreams. 2013. (Magic Bunny Ser.: 2). lib. bdg. 16.00 *(978-0-606-31676-7(0)*, Turtleback) Turtleback Bks.

—Vacation Dreams #2. Swan, Angela, illus. 2013. (Magic Bunny Ser.: 2). (ENG.). 128p. (J). (gr. 1-3). pap. 5.99 *(978-0-448-46728-3(3)*, Grosset & Dunlap) Penguin Young Readers Group.

Bentley, Tadgh. Samson: The Piranha Who Went to Dinner. Bentley, Tadgh, illus. 2017. (Illus.). 40p. (J). (gr. -1-3). 17.99 *(978-0-06-233537-1(5))* HarperCollins Pubs.

Benton, Jim. The Fran with Four Brains. Benton, Jim, illus. 2007. (Franny K. Stein, Mad Scientist Ser.: 6). (ENG., Illus.). 112p. (J). (gr. 2-5). pap. 5.99 *(978-1-4169-0232-4(5)*, Simon & Schuster Bks. For Young Readers) Simon & Schuster Bks. For Young Readers.

—Frantastic Voyage. Benton, Jim, illus. 2006. (Franny K. Stein, Mad Scientist Ser.: 5). (ENG., Illus.). 112p. (J). (gr. 2-5). 15.99 *(978-1-4169-0229-4(5)*, Simon & Schuster Bks. For Young Readers) Simon & Schuster Bks. For Young Readers.

—The Invisible Fran. Benton, Jim, illus. 2004. (Franny K. Stein, Mad Scientist Ser.: 3). (ENG., Illus.). 112p. (J). (gr. 2-5). 17.99 *(978-0-689-86293-9(8)*, Simon & Schuster Bks. For Young Readers) Simon & Schuster Bks. For Young Readers.

—Let's Do a Thing! 2017. (Victor Shmud, Total Expert Ser.: 1). (ENG.). 128p. (J). (gr. 2-5). pap. 5.99 ***(978-0-545-93229-5(7))***; lib. bdg. 16.99 ***(978-0-545-93233-2(5))*** Scholastic, Inc. (Scholastic Paperbacks).

—Let's Pretend This Never Happened. Benton, Jim, illus. 2004. (Dear Dumb Diary Ser.: 1). (ENG., Illus.). 128p. (J). (gr. 4-7). pap. 6.99 *(978-0-439-62904-1(7)*, Scholastic Paperbacks) Scholastic, Inc.

—Me (Just Like You, Only Better) Benton, Jim, illus. 2011. (Dear Dumb Diary Ser.: 12). (ENG., Illus.). 160p. (J). (gr. 3-7). pap. 6.99 *(978-0-545-11616-9(3)*, Scholastic Paperbacks) Scholastic, Inc.

—Nobody's Perfect. I'm As Close As It Gets. Benton, Jim, illus. 2013. (Dear Dumb Diary Year Two Ser.: 3). (ENG., Illus.). 144p. (J). (gr. 3-7). pap. 5.99 *(978-0-545-37764-5(1)*, Scholastic Paperbacks) Scholastic, Inc.

—Nobody's Perfect. I'm As Close As It Gets. 2013. (Dear Dumb Diary: Year Two Ser.: 3). lib. bdg. 16.00 *(978-0-606-31535-7(7)*, Turtleback) Turtleback Bks.

—Okay, So Maybe I Do Have Superpowers. Benton, Jim, illus. 2011. (Dear Dumb Diary Ser.: 11). (ENG., Illus.). 160p. (J). (gr. 3-7). pap. 6.99 *(978-0-545-11615-2(5)*, Scholastic Paperbacks) Scholastic, Inc.

—That's What Friends Aren't For. Benton, Jim, illus. 2010. (Dear Dumb Diary Ser.: 9). (ENG., Illus.). 144p. (J). (gr. 3-7). 6.99 *(978-0-545-11612-1(0)*, Scholastic Paperbacks) Scholastic, Inc.

—You Can Bet on That. Benton, Jim, illus. 2014. (Dear Dumb Diary Year Two Ser.: 5). (ENG., Illus.). 160p. (J). (gr. 3-7). pap. 5.99 *(978-0-545-64257-6(4)*, Scholastic Paperbacks) Scholastic, Inc.

Bentz, Lindsay. Really Good Friends. 2007. (ENG.). 182p. pap. 12.95 *(978-1-59526-720-7(4)*, Llumina Pr.) Aeon Publishing Inc.

Benway, Robin. Emmy & Oliver. (YA). (gr. 8). 2017. 368p. pap. 9.99 ***(978-0-06-233060-4(8))*** 2015. (ENG.). 352p. 17.99 *(978-0-06-233059-8(4))* HarperCollins Pubs. (HarperTeen).

Benwell, Sarah. The Last Leaves Falling. 2015. (ENG., Illus.). 368p. (YA). (gr. 9). 17.99 *(978-1-4814-3065-4(3))* Simon & Schuster Children's Publishing.

Benz, Derek & Lewis, J. S. The Relic Hunters: Even Heroes Have to Go to School. 2012. (Grey Griffins: the Clockwork Chronicles Ser.: 2). (ENG.). 384p. (J). (gr. 3-7). pap. 7.99 *(978-0-316-04520-9(9))* Little, Brown Bks. for Young Readers.

Beranek, Malinda. Rocky, the Country Squirrel. 2008. 12p. pap. 24.95 *(978-1-60563-018-2(7))* America Star Bks.

Berarie, Denis. The Little Soul & His Friend. 2012. (Illus.). 32p. pap. 21.35 *(978-1-4772-2634-6(6))* AuthorHouse.

Berdes, George R. The Girl Without a Name. 2011. 36p. pap. 16.95 *(978-1-4560-4922-5(4))* America Star Bks.

Berend, Janet Eoff. Vertical. 2012. (ENG.). 160p. (J). (gr. 5-10). pap. 12.95 *(978-1-891369-98-8(9))* Breakaway Bks.

Berenda, M. J. Helping with Pocket Change. 2011. 24p. pap. 12.95 *(978-1-4567-5836-3(5))* AuthorHouse.

Berenstain, Jan & Berenstain, Mike. The Berenstain Bears Friendship Blessings Collection, 1 vol. 2017. (Berenstain Bears/Living Lights Ser.). (ENG.). 160p. (J). 10.99 *(978-0-310-75338-4(4))* Zonderkidz.

Berenstain, Jan, et al. The Berenstain Bears Lose a Friend. Berenstain, Jan et al, illus. 2007. (Berenstain Bears Ser.). (ENG.). 32p. (J). (gr. -1-2). pap. 3.99 *(978-0-06-057389-8(9)*, HarperFestival) HarperCollins Pubs.

Berenstain, Mike, et al. The Berenstain Bears & the Golden Rule, 1 vol. 2008. (Berenstain Bears/Living Lights Ser.). (ENG., Illus.). 32p. (J). (gr. -1-2). pap. 3.99 *(978-0-310-71247-3(5))* Zonderkidz.

—Faithful Friends, 1 vol. Berenstain, Stan, illus. 2009. (Berenstain Bears/Living Lights Ser.). (ENG.). 32p. (J). (gr. -1-2). pap. 3.99 *(978-0-310-71253-4(X))* Zonderkidz.

Berenstain, Stan, et al. Berenstain Bears Love Their Neighbors, 1 vol. Berenstain, Stan, illus. 2009. (Berenstain Bears/Living Lights Ser.). (ENG., Illus.). 32p. (J). (gr. -1-2). pap. 3.99 *(978-0-310-71249-7(1))* Zonderkidz.

Berg, Brook. What Marion Taught Willis. Alberg, Nathan, illus. 2005. (J). 16.95 *(978-1-932146-31-8(8)*, 1242215) Highsmith Inc.

Berg, Dorlisa H. Fat Freddy Gets Fit. 2012. 158p. pap. 19.99 *(978-1-4797-6309-2(8))* Xlibris Corp.

Berger, Carin. Forever Friends. Berger, Carin, illus. 2010. (ENG., Illus.). 40p. (J). (gr. -1-1). 16.99 *(978-0-06-191528-4(9)*, Greenwillow Bks.) HarperCollins Pubs.

Berger, Samantha & Brockenbrough, Martha. Back to School with Bigfoot. Pressler, Dave, illus. 2017. (ENG.). 40p. (J). (gr. -1-3). 16.99 *(978-0-545-85973-8(5))* Scholastic, Inc.

Berggren, Joyce D. The Hustle & Bustle of Poor Mrs. Tustle. Muellner, Nancy, illus. 2010. 32p. pap. 12.95 *(978-0-9819860-5-0(6))* Amber Skye Publishing LLC.

Berk, Josh. Say It Ain't So. (Lenny & the Mikes Ser.). (ENG.). 288p. (J). (gr. 3-7). 2015. pap. 7.99 *(978-0-307-93007-1(6)*, Yearling) 2014. 16.99 *(978-0-375-87009-5(1)*, Knopf Bks. for Young Readers) Random Hse. Children's Bks.

—Strike Three, You're Dead. 2014. (Lenny & the Mikes Ser.). (ENG.). 272p. (J). (gr. 3-7). 6.99 *(978-0-307-93006-4(8)*, Yearling) Random Hse. Children's Bks.

Berk, Sheryl. Dance Divas - Showstopper. 2015. (Dance Divas Ser.). (ENG.). 144p. (YA). (gr. 3-6). 15.99 *(978-1-61963-575-3(5)*, 9781619635753, Bloomsbury USA Childrens) Bloomsbury Publishing USA.

—Showstopper. 2015. (Dance Divas Ser.). (ENG.). 144p. (YA). (gr. 3-6). pap. 5.99 *(978-1-61963-576-0(3)*, 9781619635760, Bloomsbury USA Childrens) Bloomsbury Publishing USA.

Berk, Sheryl & Berk, Carrie. Baby Cakes. 2014. (Cupcake Club Ser.: 5). (ENG.). 160p. (J). (gr. 3-6). pap. 6.99 *(978-1-4022-8330-7(X)*, Sourcebooks Jabberwocky) Sourcebooks, Inc.

—Bakers on Board. 2016. (Cupcake Club Ser.: 9). (ENG.). 128p. (J). (gr. 3-7). pap. 7.99 *(978-1-4926-2085-3(8)*, 9781492620853, Sourcebooks Jabberwocky) Sourcebooks, Inc.

—The Cupcake Club: Truth, Love & Cupcakes. 2012. (Cupcake Club Ser.: 1). (ENG.). 208p. (J). (gr. 3-7). pap. 6.99 *(978-1-4022-6449-8(6)*, Sourcebooks Jabberwocky) Sourcebooks, Inc.

—Cupcake Club Box Set: Books 1-3. 2013. (Cupcake Club Ser.: 0). (ENG.). (J). (gr. 3-6). 19.99 *(978-1-4022-9139-5(6)*, Sourcebooks Jabberwocky) Sourcebooks, Inc.

—Icing on the Cake. 2013. (Cupcake Club Ser.: 4). (ENG.). 160p. (J). (gr. 3-6). pap. 6.99 *(978-1-4022-8327-7(X)*, Sourcebooks Jabberwocky) Sourcebooks, Inc.

—Royal Icing: The Cupcake Club. 2014. (Cupcake Club Ser.: 6). (ENG.). 144p. (J). (gr. 3-7). pap. 6.99 *(978-1-4022-8333-8(4)*, Sourcebooks Jabberwocky) Sourcebooks, Inc.

—Sugar & Spice: The Cupcake Club. 2015. (Cupcake Club Ser.: 7). (ENG.). 160p. (J). (gr. 3-7). pap. 6.99 *(978-1-4022-8336-9(9)*, Sourcebooks Jabberwocky) Sourcebooks, Inc.

—Sweet Victory. 2015. (Cupcake Club Ser.: 8). (ENG.). 128p. (J). (gr. 3-7). pap. 6.99 *(978-1-4926-2082-2(3)*, Sourcebooks Jabberwocky) Sourcebooks, Inc.

Berkove, Lawrence I. How Butterflies Got Colored Wings. Barshishat, Malka Michaela, illus. 2017. (J). pap. ***(978-1-5011-4872-9(9))*** Meadowbrook Pr.

Bernal, Estela. Can You See Me Now? 2014. (ENG.). (YA). pap. 10.95 *(978-1-55885-783-4(4)*, Piñata Books) Arte Publico Pr.

Berne, Emma Carlson. Never Let You Go. 2012. (ENG.). 256p. (YA). (gr. 9). pap. 9.99 *(978-1-4424-4017-3(1)*, Simon Pulse) Simon Pulse.

Berrios, Frank. Bad Weather! (DC Super Friends) Beavers, Ethen, illus. 2014. (Little Golden Book Ser.). (ENG.). 24p. (J). (-k). 4.99 *(978-0-385-38440-7(8)*, Golden Bks.) Random Hse. Children's Bks.

—Lightning Loves Racing! (Disney/Pixar Cars) Random House Disney Staff, illus. 2013. (Pictureback(R) Ser.). (ENG.). 16p. (J). (gr. -1-2). 4.99 *(978-0-7364-3138-5(1)*, RH/Disney) Random Hse. Children's Bks.

—Plane Pals. 2014. (Step into Reading Level 1 Ser.). lib. bdg. 13.55 *(978-0-606-35202-4(3))* Turtleback Bks.

—Radiator Springs 500. RH Disney Staff, illus. deluxe ed. 2015. (Pictureback(R) Ser.). (ENG.). 24p. (J). (gr. -1-2). 4.99 *(978-0-7364-3281-8(7)*, RH/Disney) Random Hse. Children's Bks.

Berrow, G. M. Fluttershy & the Fine Furry Friends Fair. 2015. (My Little Pony Chapter Bks.). (J). lib. bdg. 16.00 *(978-0-606-35942-9(7))* Turtleback Bks.

—Friendship Is Magic. 2016. (ENG., Illus.). 144p. (J). (gr. 3-7). pap. 5.99 *(978-0-316-26631-4(0))* Little, Brown Bks. for Young Readers.

—My Little Pony: Equestria Girls: Through the Mirror. 2013. (Equestria Girls Ser.: 1). (ENG.). 240p. (J). (gr. 3-7). 9.99 *(978-0-316-24762-7(6))* Little, Brown Bks. for Young Readers.

—My Little Pony: Rarity & the Curious Case of Charity. 2014. (ENG.). 176p. (J). (gr. 3-7). pap. 5.99 *(978-0-316-24808-2(8))* Little, Brown Bks. for Young Readers.

—Pinkie Pie & the Rockin' Ponypalooza Party! 2013. (My Little Pony Chapter Bks.). (J). lib. bdg. 16.00 *(978-0-606-35299-4(6))* Turtleback Bks.

Berry, Carolyn. Buster Tells It All: Stories from Pony Creek Ranch. Cash, Eric, illus. 2011. 24p. (J). 16.95 *(978-1-61254-011-5(2))* Brown Books Publishing Group.

Berry, Eileen M. Haiku on Your Shoes. Regan, Dana, illus. 2005. 56p. (J). (gr. -1-3). per. 7.49 *(978-1-59166-374-4(1))* BJU Pr.

Berry, Jacqueline. Teeny Tiny Topper, the Grasshopper. 2007. 20p. per. 24.95 *(978-1-4241-8338-8(3))* America Star Bks.

Berry, Nessa. Protectors of Little Africa. 2005. 108p. per. 9.99 *(978-1-58832-132-9(0))* Unlimited Publishing LLC.

Berry, Nina. Othermoon. 2013. (ENG.). 320p. (YA). (gr. 9). pap. 9.95 *(978-0-7582-7693-3(1)*, K-Teen) Kensington Publishing Corp.

—Othersphere. 2013. (Otherkin Ser.). (ENG.). 320p. (YA). (gr. 9). pap. 9.95 *(978-0-7582-9238-4(4)*, K-Teen) Kensington Publishing Corp.

Berry, R. A. I Can Do It by Myself. 2010. 16p. 12.99 *(978-1-4520-2418-9(9))* AuthorHouse.

Bertier, Anne, creator. Wednesday. 2014. (ENG., Illus.). 48p. (J). (gr. -1-2). 17.95 *(978-1-59270-152-0(3))* Enchanted Lion Bks., LLC.

Bertrand, Diane Gonzales. Cecilia & Miguel Are Best Friends. Ventura, Gabriela Baeza, tr. Muraida, Thelma, illus. 2014.Tr. of Cecilia y Miguel Son Mejores Amigos. (SPA & ENG.). 32p. (J). 17.95 *(978-1-55885-794-0(X))* Arte Publico Pr.

—El Momento de Trino. Sanmiguel, Rosario, tr. from ENG. 2006. (SPA.). 181p. (J). (gr. 3-7). per. 9.95 *(978-1-55885-473-4(8)*, Piñata Books) Arte Publico Pr.

—My Pal Victor. Sweetland, Robert, illus. 2010.Tr. of Mi Amigo, Victor. (ENG.). 32p. (J). (gr. 4-7). 16.95

(978-1-934960-84-4(5), Raven Tree Pr.,Csi) Continental Sales, Inc.
—My Pal, Victor/Mi Amigo, Victor. de La Vega, Eida, tr. 2008. (ENG., Illus.). 32p. (J). (gr. -1-3). per. 7.95 (978-1-932748-72-7(5), Raven Tree Pr.,Csi) Continental Sales, Inc.
Best, Cari. My Three Best Friends & Me, Zulay. Brantley-Newton, Vanessa, illus. 2015. (ENG.). 40p. (J). (gr. -1-3). 17.99 (978-0-374-38819-5(9), 9780374388195, Farrar, Straus & Giroux (BYR)) Farrar, Straus & Giroux.
Best-Everette, Shabarbara. Will You Be My Friend? 2010. 32p. pap. 17.25 (978-1-4269-4186-3(2)) Trafford Publishing.
Best Friends My Fabulous Life. 2007. (Best Friends Club Ser.). 48p. (978-1-4054-9448-9(4)) Parragon, Inc.
Bethel, Ellie. Michael Recycle Meets Litterbug Doug. Colombo, Alexandra, illus. 2009. (Michael Recycle Ser.). (ENG.). 24p. (J). (gr. 2-5). 15.99 (978-1-60010-392-6(8), 9781600103926) Idea & Design Works, LLC.
Bette, Grandma. The Excellent Adventures of Max & Madison: Bedtime stories for Youngsters. 2012. 116p. pap. 42.95 (978-1-4525-0432-2(6)) Balboa Pr.
Bettenberg, Barbie. Edgar, the Near-Sighted Eagle. Clement, Marilyn, illus. 2008. 27p. (J). (978-0-9822534-0-3(0)) Cricket XPress of Minnesota.
Bettinger, John & Kina. Koa Becomes a Friend. 2012. 32p. (-18). pap. 13.95 (978-1-4497-6153-0(4), WestBow Pr.) Author Solutions, Inc.
Betts, A. J. Zac & Mia. 2016. (ENG.). 304p. (YA). (gr. 9). pap. 8.99 (978-0-544-66878-2(2), HMH Books For Young Readers) Houghton Mifflin Harcourt Publishing Co.
Beus, Bryan. Westly: A Spider's Tale. Beus, Bryan, illus. 2015. (Illus.). 171p. (J). 15.99 (978-1-62972-068-5(2), Shadow Mountain) Deseret Bk. Co.
Bevan, Sharon L. Bella Blue Fairy Finds a New Friend. 2009. (Illus.). 48p. pap. (978-1-84748-632-5(0)) Athena Pr.
Bevans, Donna. Sally & Sadie. 2011. 24p. (gr. -1). pap. 11.32 (978-1-4634-0211-2(2)) AuthorHouse.
—Scooter & His Friends. 2012. 40p. pap. 16.99 (978-1-4772-1288-2(4)) AuthorHouse.
Beylon, Cathy. I Love Ballet/Me Encanta el Ballet: Bilingual Coloring Book. Gongora, Oscar, tr. 2011. (Dover Children's Bilingual Coloring Book Ser.). (ENG & SPA., Illus.). 32p. (J). (gr. k-5). pap. 3.99 (978-0-486-47815-9(7)) Dover Pubns., Inc.
Bhoola, Prisha. Hashay Says Goodbye & Hello. 2013. 24p. pap. 22.68 (978-1-4669-9209-2(3)) Trafford Publishing.
Bial, Raymond. Shadow Island: A Tale of Lake Superior. 2006. 172p. (J). (gr. 3-7). 18.95 (978-1-883953-37-9(5)); per. 12.95 (978-1-883953-36-2(7)) Great Lakes Literary, LLC. (Blue Horse Books).
Bickford-Smith, Coralie. The Fox & the Star. 2015. (ENG., Illus.). 64p. (J). 20.00 (978-0-14-310867-2(0), Penguin Books) Penguin Publishing Group.
Bicknell, Anita. I Don't Wanna Be Here! 2011. 40p. 18.46 (978-1-4520-5222-9(0)) AuthorHouse.
Bickta, Brenda L. Tad's Life in the Lily Pond. 2008. 74p. pap. 19.95 (978-1-60672-647-1(1)) America Star Bks.
Biddle, Wharton. The Story of Timmy Sprite. 2012. 60p. pap. 24.99 (978-1-4772-8066-9(9)) AuthorHouse.
Bidoli, Katie. Karate Adventures of Kisho, Hana, & Nobu: Karate Is for Everyone! 2006. (Illus.). 16p. (J). 10.00 (978-1-60243-029-7(2)) Keen's Martial Arts Academy.
Bidwell, Dafne. Danger Unlimited: Action, Mystery & Adventure. 2007. 244p. pap. 15.50 (978-1-921064-89-0(7)) Fremantle Pr. AUS. Dist: Independent Pubs. Group.
Bidzilya, Kristin. Two Girls Dreams Come True. 2007. 64p. per. 9.95 (978-1-934246-87-0(5)) Peppertree Pr., The.
Biedrzycki, David. Groundhog's Runaway Shadow. Biedrzycki, David, illus. 2016. (ENG., Illus.). 32p. (J). (gr. -1-3). 16.95 (978-1-58089-734-1(7)) Charlesbridge Publishing, Inc.
Big Idea Entertainment, LLC. Where's God When I'm S-Scared? Jones, Cory, illus. 2016. (VeggieTales Ser.). (ENG.). 32p. (J). (gr. -1-3). pap. 3.99 (978-1-4336-4353-8(7), B&H Kids) B&H Publishing Group.
The Big Race: Individual Title Six-Packs. (gr. k-1). 23.00 (978-0-7635-9061-1(4)) Rigby Education.
Biggs, Pauline. A Wild Ride. Mayne, Michael, illus. 2004. 20p. (J). per. 12.95 (978-0-9760129-0-0(1)) The Publishing Place LLC.
Bigham, Madge A. Little Folks' Land. Ripperton, Lisa M., ed. 2009. 452p. pap. 15.95 (978-1-59915-375-9(0)) Yesterday's Classics.
Bildner, Phil. Tournament of Champions. Probert, Tim, illus. 2017. (Rip & Red Ser.: 3). (ENG.). 256p. (J). 16.99 (978-0-374-30507-9(2), 9780374305079, Farrar, Straus & Giroux (BYR)) Farrar, Straus & Giroux.
—A Whole New Ballgame. Probert, Tim, illus. 2015. (Rip & Red Ser.: 1). (ENG.). 256p. (J). (gr. 3-7). 16.99 (978-0-374-30130-9(1), 9780374301309, Farrar, Straus & Giroux (BYR)) Farrar, Straus & Giroux.
—A Whole New Ballgame. 2016. (Rip & Red Ser.: 1). (J). lib. bdg. 17.20 (978-0-606-38553-4(3)) Turtleback Bks.
Billet, Marion. Littleland. Billet, Marion, illus. 2013. (ENG., Illus.). 32p. (J). (gr. k-k). 14.99 (978-0-7636-6550-0(9), Nosy Crow) Candlewick Pr.
Billings, David. Louie the Buoy. 2010. 36p. pap. 16.99 (978-1-4520-3010-4(3)) AuthorHouse.
Billingsley, ReShonda Tate. Boy Trouble. 2014. (Rumor Central Ser.). (ENG., Illus.). 208p. (YA). (gr. 13). pap. 9.95 (978-0-7582-8959-9(6), K-Teen) Kensington Publishing Corp.
—Fair-Weather Friends. 2008. (Good Girlz Ser.: 5). (ENG.). 224p. pap. 15.99 (978-1-4165-5876-7(4), Gallery Bks.) Gallery Bks.
—Friends 'Til the End. 2009. (Good Girlz Ser.: 6). (ENG., Illus.). 208p. pap. 11.00 (978-1-4165-5877-4(2), Gallery Bks.) Gallery Bks.
—With Friends Like These. 2007. (Good Girlz Ser.: 3). (ENG., Illus.). 256p. (gr. 8-12). pap. 16.99 (978-1-4165-2562-2(9), Gallery Bks.) Gallery Bks.
—You Don't Know Me Like That. 2013. (Rumor Central Ser.). (ENG., Illus.). 224p. (YA). (gr. 9). pap. 9.95 (978-0-7582-8953-7(7), K-Teen/Dafina) Kensington Publishing Corp.
Bingham, Kelly. Circle, Square, Moose. Zelinsky, Paul O., illus. 2014. (ENG.). 48p. (J). (gr. -1-3). 17.99 (978-0-06-229003-8(7), Greenwillow Bks.) HarperCollins Pubs.
Bird Song: The Little Stories of Manoosh & Baloosh. 2003. (J). mass mkt. (978-1-932233-02-5(4)) Aurora Libris Corp.
Birdsall, Jeanne. The Penderwicks: A Summer Tale of Four Sisters, Two Rabbits, & a Very Interesting Boy. (Penderwicks Ser.). (ENG.). (J). (gr. 3-7). 2007. 288p. 7.99 (978-0-440-42047-7(4), Yearling) 2005. 272p. 16.99 (978-0-375-83143-0(6), Knopf Bks. for Young Readers) Random Hse. Children's Bks.
—The Penderwicks: A Summer Tale of Four Sisters, Two Rabbits & a Very Interesting Boy. 2007. (Penderwicks (Hardback) Ser.). 262p. (gr. 3-7). 18.00 (978-0-7569-7798-6(3)) Perfection Learning Corp.
—The Penderwicks: A Summer Tale of Four Sisters, Two Rabbits, & a Very Interesting Boy. 2007. (Penderwicks Ser.: 1). (Illus.). 262p. (gr. 4-7). lib. bdg. 18.40 (978-1-4177-7275-9(1)) Turtleback Bks.
—The Penderwicks: A Summer Tale of Four Sisters, Two Rabbits & a Very Interesting Boy. 2009. 8.80 (978-0-7848-2826-7(1), Everbind) Marco Bk. Co.
—The Penderwicks: A Summer Tale of Four Sisters, Two Rabbits & a Very Interesting Boy. l.t. ed. 2006. (Penderwick Ser.). 304p. (J). (gr. 3-7). 23.95 (978-0-7862-8897-7(3)) Thorndike Pr.
Birdsong, Michelle. Sneasy the Greasy Babysits Abigail. 2009. 20p. pap. 7.32 (978-1-4120-7205-2(0)) Trafford Publishing.
Birkenstock, Michelle M. Harry the Caterpillar. 2010. 20p. pap. 10.95 (978-1-60911-250-9(4), Eloquent Bks.) Strategic Book Publishing & Rights Agency (SBPRA).
Birle, Pete. Locals Only. 2013. (Av2 Audio Chapter Bks.). (ENG.). 121p. (J). 27.13 (978-1-62127-985-3(5), AV2 by Weigl) Weigl Pubs., Inc.
Birney, Betty G. Friendship According to Humphrey. (Humphrey Ser.: 2). (ENG.). (J). (gr. 3-7). 2006. 176p. 5.99 (978-0-14-240633-5(3), Puffin Books) 2005. 160p. 15.99 (978-0-399-24264-9(3), G.P. Putnam's Sons Books for Young Readers) Penguin Young Readers Group.
—Friendship According to Humphrey. 2007. (Humphrey Ser.). 150p. (gr. 4-7). 16.00 (978-0-7569-8277-5(4)) Perfection Learning Corp.
—School Days According to Humphrey. (Humphrey Ser.: 7). (ENG.). (J). (gr. 3-7). 2012. 176p. pap. 5.99 (978-0-14-242106-2(5), Puffin Books) 2011. 160p. 15.99 (978-0-399-25413-0(7), G.P. Putnam's Sons Books for Young Readers) Penguin Young Readers Group.
—School Days According to Humphrey. 2012. (According to Humphrey Ser.: 7). lib. bdg. 16.00 (978-0-606-26085-5(4), Turtleback) Turtleback Bks.
Biro, Val. For Forever! (Illus.). 26p. (J). (978-0-340-71448-5(4)) Hodder & Stoughton.
Birtles, Andrew. Chinese Whispers. 2013. (Illus.). 52p. pap. (978-1-908878-09-0(6)) Cornovia Pr., The.
Bise, Jr. J. David & Bise, Jr. In Search of a Name a Seahorse Story. 2011. 44p. pap. 15.50 (978-1-60976-288-9(6), Strategic Bk. Publishing) Strategic Book Publishing & Rights Agency (SBPRA).
Bishop, Beverly. My Friend with Autism: Enhanced Edition with FREE CD of Coloring Pages! Bishop, Craig, illus. 2011. (ENG.). 41p. (J). pap. 14.95 (978-1-935274-18-6(X)) Future Horizons, Inc.
Bishop, Jenn. 14 Hollow Road. 2017. (ENG.). 288p. (J). (gr. 3-7). 16.99 **(978-1-101-93875-1(7))**; lib. bdg. 19.99 **(978-1-101-93876-8(5))** Random Hse. Children's Bks. (Knopf Bks. for Young Readers).
Bishop, Jennie. The Garden Wall: A Story of Love Based on I Corinthians 13. Stoddard, Jeff, illus. 2006. (ENG.). 32p. (J). (gr. 2-7). 12.99 (978-1-59317-168-1(4)) Warner Pr., Inc.
Bistricean, Karen. The Adventures of Fergus & Lady: Home Sweet Home. Bistricean, Claudius, illus. 2006. (J). (978-0-9786975-1-8(0)) Fergus & Lady Publishing.
—The Adventures of Fergus & Lady: The Beginning. Bistricean, Claudius, illus. 2006. (J). (978-0-9786975-0-1(2)) Fergus & Lady Publishing.
Bitner, Pamela. A Brother-Sister Team. Poppen, Alex, illus. 2008. 16p. pap. 24.95 (978-1-60474-583-2(5)) America Star Bks.
Bjorkman, Lauren. Miss Fortune Cookie. 2012. (ENG.). 288p. (YA). (gr. 9-13). 16.99 (978-0-8050-8951-6(9), Holt, Henry & Co. Bks. For Young Readers) Holt, Henry & Co.
Blabey, Aaron. Pearl Barley & Charlie Parsley. 2008. (ENG., Illus.). 32p. (J). (gr. -1-3). 16.95 (978-1-59078-596-6(7), Front Street) Boyds Mills Pr.
—Pig the Pug. 2016. (ENG., Illus.). 32p. (J). (gr. -1-k). 14.99 (978-1-338-11245-0(7), Scholastic Pr.) Scholastic, Inc.
Blace, Maria. Lunie Balloonies. Swope, Brenda, illus. 2011. 24p. pap. 24.95 (978-1-4560-0947-2(8)) America Star Bks.
Black, Allyson. Fashion Face-off. Johnson, Shane L., illus. 2011. (Scarlett & Crimson Ser.). (ENG.). 112p. (J). (gr. 3-7). pap. 6.99 (978-1-4169-5937-3(8), Simon Spotlight) Simon Spotlight.
Black, Cary & Schott, Gretchen Victoria. French Quarter Tori & the Red Owl. Travis, Caroline, illus. 2012. 38p. pap. 12.95 (978-0-9754279-8-9(9)); pap. 14.95 (978-0-9754279-7-2(0)) Red Owl Pubns.
Black, Holly. Doll Bones. Wheeler, Eliza, illus. 2013. (ENG.). 256p. (J). (gr. 5-9). 18.99 (978-1-4169-6398-1(7), McElderry, Margaret K. Bks.) McElderry, Margaret K. Bks.
—Doll Bones. 2015. lib. bdg. 18.40 (978-0-606-36308-2(4)) Turtleback Bks.
Black, Holly & Clare, Cassandra. The Bronze Key. 2016. (Magisterium Ser.: 3). (ENG., Illus.). 256p. (J). (gr. 3-7). 17.99 (978-0-545-52231-1(5), Scholastic Pr.) Scholastic, Inc.
—The Copper Gauntlet. (Magisterium Ser.: 2). (ENG.). 272p. (J). 2016. (gr. 4-7). pap. 7.99 (978-0-545-52229-8(3)) 2015. (gr. 3-7). 17.99 (978-0-545-52228-1(5), Scholastic Pr.) Scholastic, Inc.
Black, Pam, illus. Candee Bar. 42p. (J). 2007. spiral bd. (978-0-9800791-2-8(8)) 2nd rev. ed. 2008. spiral bd. 18.95 (978-0-9800791-3-5(6)) Moore Publishing.
Blackaby, Susan. Brownie Groundhog & the Wintry Surprise. Segovia, Carmen, illus. 2013. (ENG.). 32p. (J). (gr. -1). 14.95 (978-1-4027-9836-8(9)) Sterling Publishing Co., Inc.
Blackaby, Tom & Osborne, Rick. Sammy Experiences Jesus. Kung, Isabella, illus. 2014. (Experiencing God at Home Ser.). (ENG.). 32p. (J). (gr. -1-3). 14.99 (978-1-4336-7981-0(7), B&H Kids) B&H Publishing Group.
Blackburn, Sheila M. Stewie Scraps & the Super Sleigh. 2008. 72p. pap. (978-1-903853-89-4(3)) Brilliant Pubns.
Blackdog, J. M. Loni Talltree: The world's greatest tree Climber. 2012. 24p. pap. 14.99 (978-1-4685-5319-2(4)) AuthorHouse.
Blackford, Cheryl. Lizzie & the Lost Baby. 2016. (ENG.). 192p. (J). (gr. 5-7). 16.99 (978-0-544-57099-3(5), HMH Books For Young Readers) Houghton Mifflin Harcourt Publishing Co.
Blackhurst, Rebecca. Count Grumpula & the Wood Witch. Errington, Rachael, illus. 2013. 18p. (978-0-473-24899-4(9)) Cobble Creep Productions.
Blackman, Jizelle. Buddy & Fred: The Adventurous Chronicles. 2012. 28p. pap. 19.99 (978-1-4772-1276-9(0)) AuthorHouse.
Blackmon, Rodney Allan. A Kitten Named Buddy: Buddy Makes a Friend. 2013. 24p. pap. 24.95 (978-1-62709-676-8(0)) America Star Bks.
—A Kitten Named Buddy: Buddy Stays Clean. 2013. 20p. pap. 24.95 (978-1-62709-675-1(2)) America Star Bks.
—A Kitten Named Buddy, Buddy's Circus. 2013. 20p. pap. 24.95 (978-1-62709-674-4(4)) America Star Bks.
Blackshaw, Win. David's Dinosaur. 2009. 104p. pap. 17.55 (978-1-4092-3704-4(4)) Lulu Pr., Inc.
Blackstone, Stella. Cleo & Caspar. Mockford, Caroline, illus. 2013. (ENG.). 24p. (J). 6.99 (978-1-78285-053-3(8)) Barefoot Bks., Inc.
—Cleo the Cat. Mockford, Caroline, illus. 2013. (ENG.). 24p. (J). (gr. -1-k). pap. 6.99 (978-1-78285-051-9(1)) Barefoot Bks., Inc.
Blackwell, Nancy. Andy the Ant in Precious Cargo. Ettinger, Charles, illus. 2011. 40p. pap. 14.99 (978-1-937129-03-3(9)) Faithful Life Pubs.
Blade, Adam. Deep Dive #3: Manak the Manta Ray. 2013. (Deep Dive Ser.: 3). (ENG.). 128p. (J). (gr. 2-5). pap. 4.99 (978-0-545-42769-2(X), Scholastic Paperbacks) Scholastic, Inc.
Blaha-Black, Caroline. Anika & the Magic Top. 2008. 60p. pap. 11.95 (978-1-4357-1194-5(7)) Lulu Pr., Inc.
Blaisdell, Patty. The Haunted Shed, 1 vol. 2009. 32p. pap. 24.95 (978-1-60836-674-3(X)) America Star Bks.
Blake, Ashley Herring. How to Make a Wish. 2017. (ENG.). 336p. (YA). (gr. 9). 17.99 (978-0-544-81519-3(X), HMH Books For Young Readers) Houghton Mifflin Harcourt Publishing Co.
Blake, Robert J. Painter & Ugly. Blake, Robert J., illus. 2011. (ENG., Illus.). 48p. (J). (gr. k-3). 16.99 (978-0-399-24323-3(2), Philomel Bks.) Penguin Young Readers Group.
Blake, Stephanie J. My Rotten Friend. Epelbaum, Mariano, illus. 2015. (ENG.). 32p. (J). (gr. -1-3). 16.99 (978-0-8075-5327-5(1)) Whitman, Albert & Co.
Blakemore, Megan Frazer. The Daybreak Bond. 2017. (ENG.). 336p. (J). 16.99 **(978-1-68119-479-0(1)**, 9781681194790, Bloomsbury USA Childrens) Bloomsbury Publishing USA.
—The Firefly Code. (ENG.). (J). 2017. 368p. pap. 7.99 **(978-1-68119-527-8(5)**, 9781681195278) 2016. 352p. 16.99 (978-1-61963-636-1(0), 9781619636361) Bloomsbury Publishing USA. (Bloomsbury USA Childrens).
—The Firefly Code. 2017. (J). lib. bdg. 18.40 **(978-0-606-40543-0(7))** Turtleback Bks.
Blakemore, Megan Frazer. The Friendship Riddle. (ENG.). 2016. 384p. (J). pap. 7.99 (978-1-68119-019-8(2), 9781681190198) 2015. 368p. (YA). (gr. 3-6). 16.99 (978-1-61963-630-9(1), 9781619636309) Bloomsbury Publishing USA. (Bloomsbury USA Childrens).
Blakeney, Crystal Denise. Paradise & Cove Counts Feathered Friends. 2012. 16p. pap. 15.99 (978-1-4772-5962-7(7)) AuthorHouse.
Blakeslee, S. E. Once upon a Blue Moon: The Chronicles of the Blue Moon. Blakeslee, S. E., illus. 2007. (ENG., Illus.). 32p. (J). 17.95 (978-0-9789031-0-7(2)) Blaumond Pr.
Blance, Ellen & Cook, Tony. Monster Looks for Friend. Date not set. (Illus.). 16p. pap. 129.15 (978-0-582-18591-3(2)) Addison-Wesley Longman, Ltd. GBR. Dist: Trans-Atlantic Pubns., Inc.
Bland, Nick. The Very Cranky Bear. Bland, Nick, illus. 2014. (ENG., Illus.). 32p. (J). (gr. -1-k). 16.99 (978-0-545-61269-2(1), Orchard Bks.) Scholastic, Inc.
Blankenship, Julianna. Sally Lumpkin's Party: A story of 6 true Friends. Dionne, Deanna, illus. 2008. 32p. pap. 15.56 (978-1-4343-6860-7(2)) AuthorHouse.
Blatchford, David. The Story of Mr Tomkins. 2012. (Illus.). 50p. pap. (978-1-908773-29-6(4)) Iponymous Publishing, Ltd.
Blaylock, Kathy. Adventures of Buddy Fairy & Friends. 2007. 48p. 16.95 (978-1-4137-9195-2(6)) America Star Bks.
Bledsoe Jr, Reuben Booo. Bullybuster. 2013. (ENG.). 98p. (J). pap. 14.95 (978-1-4787-1215-2(5)) Outskirts Pr., Inc.
Blevins-Counts, Charlotte. A Pot Full of Te. 2009. 24p. pap. 12.95 (978-1-59858-962-7(8)) Dog Ear Publishing, LLC.
Blevins, Wiley. Bear's Bad Day: Bullies Can Change. Clegg, Dave, illus. 2015. (ENG.). 24p. (J). (gr. k-2). lib. bdg. 19.99 (978-1-63440-012-1(7)) Red Chair Pr.
—A New Friend. 2013. (Penguin Young Readers, Level 1 Ser.). (ENG.). 32p. (J). (gr. k-1). 14.99 (978-0-448-46572-2(8)); pap. 3.99 (978-0-448-46180-9(3)) Penguin Young Readers Group. (Penguin Young Readers).
—A New Friend. 2013. (Penguin Young Readers Level 1 Ser.). lib. bdg. 13.55 (978-0-606-31705-4(8), Turtleback) Turtleback Bks.
—The on-Again, off-Again Friend: Standing up for Friends. Alley, R. W., illus. 2015. (ENG.). 24p. (J). (gr. k-2). lib. bdg. 19.99 (978-1-63440-015-2(1)) Red Chair Pr.
Blevins, Wiley & Bader, Bonnie. Max Finds an Egg. Clanton, Ben, illus. 2015. (Penguin Young Readers, Level 1 Ser.). (ENG.). 32p. (J). (gr. k-1). 3.99 (978-0-448-47993-4(1), Penguin Young Readers) Penguin Young Readers Group.
Block, Betty Mitchell. The Magic Pork Chop Bone. 2013. (ENG.). 76p. (YA). pap. 8.95 (978-1-4787-1482-8(4)) Outskirts Pr., Inc.
Block, F. L. My Miserable Life. Hemingway, Edward, illus. 2016. (ENG.). 192p. (J). 13.99 (978-0-8050-9628-6(0), 9780805096286, Holt, Henry & Co. Bks. For Young Readers) Holt, Henry & Co.
Block, Francesca Lia. The Island of Excess Love. 2014. (ENG.). 224p. (YA). (gr. 9). 16.99 (978-0-8050-9631-6(0), 9780805096316, Holt, Henry & Co. Bks. For Young Readers) Holt, Henry & Co.
—Weetzie Bat. 2004. (Weetzie Bat Ser.: 1). (ENG.). 128p. (YA). (gr. 9). pap. 8.99 (978-0-06-073625-5(9), HarperTeen) HarperCollins Pubs.
Blocker, Adam P. Joshua & the Spider. Taylor, Josh, illus. 2013. (ENG.). 72p. 17.99 (978-1-939418-08-1(9)) Writer of the Round Table Pr.
Bloom, C. P. The Monkey & the Bee. Raymundo, Peter, illus. 2015. (Monkey Goes Bananas Ser.). (ENG.). 40p. (J). (gr. -1-2). 14.95 (978-1-4197-0886-2(4), Abrams Bks. for Young Readers) Abrams, Inc.
Bloom, Janice Stitziel. Wonderfully Made under My Bed. Woodcock, Marcy, illus. 2007. 36p. (J). per. 15.99 (978-1-934643-00-6(9)) Villager Bk. Publishing.
Bloom, Suzanne. Alone Together. Bloom, Suzanne, illus. 2014. (Goose & Bear Stories Ser.). (ENG., Illus.). 32p. (J). (gr. -1-k). 16.95 (978-1-62091-736-7(X)) Boyds Mills Pr.
—A Splendid Friend, Indeed. Bloom, Suzanne, illus. 2009. (Goose & Bear Stories Ser.). (ENG., Illus.). 32p. (J). (gr. -1-k). pap. 7.95 (978-1-59078-488-4(X)) Boyds Mills Pr.
—A Splendid Friend, Indeed. 2005. (Goose & Bear Stories Ser.). (ENG., Illus.). 32p. (J). (gr. -1-k). 16.95 (978-1-59078-286-6(0)) Boyds Mills Pr.
—Treasure. (Goose & Bear Stories Ser.). (ENG.). 32p. (J). (gr. -1-1). 2012. pap. 7.95 (978-1-59078-920-9(2)) 2007. (Illus.). 15.95 (978-1-59078-457-0(X)) Boyds Mills Pr.
—What about Bear? (Goose & Bear Stories Ser.). (ENG., Illus.). 32p. (J). (gr. -1-1). 2012. pap. 7.95 (978-1-59078-913-1(X)) 2010. 16.95 (978-1-59078-528-7(2)) Boyds Mills Pr.
Bloom, Suzanne, illus. Bear Can Dance! 2015. (Goose & Bear Stories Ser.). (ENG.). 40p. (J). (-k). 16.95 (978-1-62979-442-6(2)) Boyds Mills Pr.
—A Splendid Friend, Indeed. 2015. (Goose & Bear Stories Ser.). (ENG.). 32p. (J). (— 1). bds. 7.99 (978-1-62979-408-2(2)) Boyds Mills Pr.
Bloomberg, Georgina & Hapka, Catherine. Rein It In. 2013. (a Circuit Ser.). (ENG.). 240p. (YA). (gr. 7). pap. 9.99 (978-1-61963-102-1(4), 9781619631021, Bloomsbury USA Childrens) Bloomsbury Publishing USA.
Bloomfield, Glynis. Jake's Secret. 2011. 194p. pap. 13.95 (978-1-60976-615-3(6), Strategic Bk. Publishing) Strategic Book Publishing & Rights Agency (SBPRA).
Bloomsbury USA. Lift-The-Flap Friends: Pirates. 2017. (ENG.). 14p. (J). bds. 9.99 (978-1-68119-241-3(1), 9781681192413, Bloomsbury Activity Bks.) Bloomsbury Publishing USA.
Bloser, Cheryl. Little Mouse & the Muddy Feet. 2012. 28p. pap. 9.99 (978-0-9836771-1-6(5)) Mindstir Media.
Bloss, Josie. Faking Faith. 2011. (ENG.). 240p. (YA). pap. 9.95 (978-0-7387-2757-8(1), Flux) North Star Editions.
Blount, Patty. TMI. 2013. (ENG.). 336p. (YA). (gr. 7-12). pap. 9.99 (978-1-4022-7340-7(1), 9781402273407) Sourcebooks, Inc.
Blue, Parker. Catch Me. 2015. (ENG., Illus.). 222p. (J). pap. 14.95 (978-1-61194-623-9(9)) BelleBks., Inc.
Blue, Sebastien. Liquid Diamond. 2013. 176p. pap. (978-1-4602-3346-7(8)) FriesenPress.
Bluecloud. A Space in Time. 2012. 24p. pap. 17.99 (978-1-4685-6407-5(2)) AuthorHouse.
Blume, Judy. BFF: Just as Long as We're Together/Here's to You, Rachel Robinson. 2007. (ENG., Illus.). 512p. (J). (gr. 3-7). 18.99 (978-0-385-73407-3(7), Delacorte Bks. for Young Readers) Random Hse. Children's Bks.
—Blubber. 153p. (J). (gr. 4-6). pap. 3.99 (978-0-8072-1404-6(3), Listening Library) Random Hse. Audio Publishing Group.
—Here's to You, Rachel Robinson. 2010. (ENG.). 208p. (J). (gr. 5). pap. 8.99 (978-0-385-73987-0(7), Delacorte Bks. for Young Readers) Random Hse. Children's Bks.
—Iggie's House. 2014. (ENG., Illus.). (J). (gr. 3-7). 160p. 17.99 (978-1-4814-1410-4(0)); 176p. pap. 7.99 (978-1-4814-1104-2(7)) Simon & Schuster Children's Publishing. (Atheneum Bks. for Young Readers).
—Just As Long As We're Together. 2010. (ENG.). 288p. (YA). (gr. 7). pap. 8.99 (978-0-385-73988-7(5), Delacorte Bks. for Young Readers) Random Hse. Children's Bks.
—Otherwise Known as Sheila the Great. 2007. (ENG.). 176p. (J). (gr. 3-7). 7.99 (978-0-14-240879-7(4), Puffin Books) Penguin Young Readers Group.
—Otherwise Known as Sheila the Great. 2007. 154p. (gr. 4-7). 16.00 (978-0-7569-7915-7(3)) Perfection Learning Corp.
—Otherwise Known as Sheila the Great. 2007. (Fudge Bks.: 2). 138p. (gr. 4-7). lib. bdg. 18.40 (978-1-4177-8370-0(2), Turtleback) Turtleback Bks.
—Superfudge. (Fudge Ser.).Tr. of Superfudge. 166p. (J). (gr. 2-4). pap. 4.99 (978-0-8072-1457-2(4), Listening Library) Random Hse. Audio Publishing Group.
Blume, Lesley M. M. Cornelia & the Audacious Escapades of the Somerset Sisters. (ENG.). 272p. (J). (gr. 3-7). 2008. 7.99 (978-0-440-42110-8(1), Yearling) 2006. 15.95 (978-0-375-83523-0(7), Knopf Bks. for Young Readers) Random Hse. Children's Bks.
Blumenstock, Jacqueline & Pool, David. Making New Friends. 2nd ed. 2005. (Illus.). 32p. (J). per. 5.95 (978-0-9764647-0-9(5)) Big Brown Box, Inc., The.
—Making New Friends. Madden, Colleen, illus. 2nd ed. 2005. 32p. (J). lib. bdg. 14.95 (978-0-9764647-1-6(3)) Big Brown Box, Inc., The.
Blumstein, Amy Beth. Jamie & Tallulah. 2009. 16p. pap. 12.00 (978-1-4389-3997-1(3)) AuthorHouse.
Bocanegra, Deborah. Winky Sue's Peppermint Birthday. Buehrle, Jacquelyn, illus. 2012. 26p. 24.95 (978-1-4560-7282-7(X)) America Star Bks.
Bock, Danuta. The Flying Turtle: A Test of Friendship & Understanding. 2007. 56p. per. 12.95 (978-1-4327-0918-1(6)) Outskirts Pr., Inc.
Bodenstein, Dan. Steven the Vegan. Ronald, Robrahn, illus. 2012. 38p. (J). pap. 12.99 (978-0-9843228-9-3(2)) Totem Tales Publishing.
Bodi, Sari. The Ghost in Allie's Pool. 2007. 192p. (J). (gr. 5-18). pap. 8.95 (978-0-9768126-6-1(5)) Brown Barn Bks.
Boelts, Maribeth. A Bike Like Sergio's. Jones, Noah Z., illus. 2016. (ENG.). 40p. (J). (gr. k-3). 15.99 (978-0-7636-6649-1(1)) Candlewick Pr.
Bogaerts, Jorge. El Día Que Hizo Mucho Viento. (SPA.). 112p. (J). (978-84-207-3535-1(3)) Grupo Anaya, S.A.

E
F
G

Bogan, Paulette. Virgil & Owen. 2015. (ENG., Illus.). 32p. (J). (gr. k-3). 16.99 (978-1-61963-372-8(8), 9781619633728, Bloomsbury USA Childrens) Bloomsbury Publishing USA.

—Virgil & Owen Stick Together. Bogan, Paulette, illus. 2016. (ENG., Illus.). 32p. (J). 16.99 (978-1-61963-373-5(6), 9781619633735, Bloomsbury USA Childrens) Bloomsbury Publishing USA.

Bogart, Jo Ellen. The Big Tree Gang, 1 vol. Griffiths, Dean, illus. 2005. (Orca Echoes Ser.). (ENG.). 64p. (J). (gr. 2-3). per. 6.95 (978-1-55143-345-5(1)) Orca Bk. Pubs. USA.

Bogart, Mike. Ice Warriors, 1 vol. 2010. 72p. pap. 19.95 (978-1-4489-3885-8(6)) America Star Bks.

Boiger, Alexandra. Max & Marla. Boiger, Alexandra, illus. 2015. (ENG., Illus.). 32p. (J). (-k). 17.99 (978-0-399-17504-6(0), G.P. Putnam's Sons Books for Young Readers) Penguin Young Readers Group.

Bojunga, Lygia. Los Amigos. (SPA.). (J). 8.95 (978-958-04-6262-0(3)) Norma S.A. COL. Dist: Distribuidora Norma, Inc.

Boland, Gerry. Marco: Master of Disguise. McGuinness, Áine, illus. 2012. (ENG.). 64p. (J). 12.95 (978-1-84717-273-0(3)) O'Brien Pr., Ltd., The IRL. Dist: Dufour Editions, Inc.

Boldt, Claudia. You're a Rude Pig, Bertie. 2013. (ENG., Illus.). 34p. (J). (gr. -1-3). 17.95 (978-0-7358-4152-9(7)) North-South Bks., Inc.

Bollinger/Papp, illus. King Kong: Meet Kong & Ann. 2005. 32p. (J). lib. bdg. 13.85 (978-1-4242-0615-5(4)) Fitzgerald Bks.

Bomgaars, Sharon. The Best Clubhouse Ever. 2009. 232p. pap. 14.49 (978-1-4259-9306-1(0)) AuthorHouse.

Bonaste, Sophie. The Sacrifices We Make [Library Edition]. 2014. 190p. pap. 14.99 (978-1-62798-187-3(X), Harmony Ink Pr.) Dreamspinner Pr.

Bond, Gwenda. Double Down. 2016. (Lois Lane Ser.). (ENG.). 384p. (gr. 9-12). 16.95 (978-1-63079-038-7(9)) Switch Pr.

Bond, Rebecca. Pig & Goose & the First Day of Spring. Bond, Rebecca, illus. 2017. (ENG., Illus.). 48p. (J). (gr. k-3). lib. bdg. 12.99 (978-1-58089-594-1(8)) Charlesbridge Publishing, Inc.

Bondanella Filutze, Ann M. On Gramma's Rocker: Animal Tales & Other Short Stories. 2013. 84p. pap. 27.95 (978-1-4624-0498-8(7), Inspiring Voices) Author Solutions, Inc.

Bongiovanni-Sharp, Debbie. Mom, but I Don't Want To. 2011. 42p. pap. 16.95 (978-1-4560-3992-9(X)) America Star Bks.

Bonin, Liane. Idol Talk: Fame Unlimited. 2007. 288p. (YA). (gr. 6-18). pap. 9.99 (978-0-451-22143-8(5), N A L Trade) Penguin Publishing Group.

—Pretty on the Outside: Fame Unlimited. 2007. 288p. (YA). pap. 9.99 (978-0-451-22122-3(2), N A L Trade) Penguin Publishing Group.

Bonnell, Kris. Can We Be Friends? 2007. (J). pap. 5.95 (978-1-933727-59-2(4)) Reading Reading Bks., LLC.

—The Happy Moon. 2006. (J). pap. 5.95 (978-1-933727-30-1(6)) Reading Reading Bks., LLC.

—The Little Boat. 2006. (J). pap. 5.95 (978-1-933727-34-9(9)) Reading Reading Bks., LLC.

—Mmm, Apples. 2006. (J). pap. 3.95 (978-1-933727-22-6(5)) Reading Reading Bks., LLC.

Bonnice, Lindsey. Libby & Pearl: The Best of Friends. Bonnice, Lindsey, illus. 2016. (Illus.). 32p. (J). (gr. -1-3). 14.99 (978-0-06-245927-5(9)) HarperCollins Pubs.

Bonwill, Ann. I Am Not a Copycat! Rickerty, Simon, illus. 2013. (ENG.). 32p. (J). (gr. -1-1). 15.99 (978-1-4424-8053-7(X)) Simon & Schuster Children's Publishing.

—I Don't Want to Be a Pea! Rickerty, Simon, illus. 2012. (ENG.). 32p. (J). (gr. -1-1). 14.99 (978-1-4424-3614-5(X), Atheneum Bks. for Young Readers) Simon & Schuster Children's Publishing.

Boonstra, Juan S. El Evangelio en Nuestro Mundo. 2004. (SPA.). 348p. 11.99 (978-0-85151-808-4(7)) Banner of Truth, The.

Booraem, Ellen. The Unnameables. 2011. (ENG., Illus.). 336p. (J). (gr. 5-7). pap. 18.99 (978-0-547-55213-2(0)) Houghton Mifflin Harcourt Publishing Co.

Booton, F. F. The Adventures of Elk. 2011. (Illus.). 180p. pap. 17.09 (978-1-4567-7517-9(0)) AuthorHouse.

Bootsma, Verner. Talking to the Moon. LaGrange, Tiffany, illus. 2007. 32p. per. 12.95 (978-1-934246-70-2(0)) Peppertree Pr., The.

Border, Terry. Peanut Butter & Cupcake. Border, Terry, illus. 2014. (ENG., Illus.). 32p. (J). (gr. -1-2). 17.99 (978-0-399-16773-7(0), Philomel Bks.) Penguin Publishing Group.

Border, Terry & Mack, Jeff. Happy Birthday, Cupcake! Border, Terry, illus. 2015. (ENG., Illus.). 32p. (J). (gr. k-3). bds. 17.99 (978-0-399-17160-4(6), Philomel Bks.) Penguin Young Readers Group.

Bordiglioni, Stephen & Bordiglioni, Stefano. Desert Adventure. Bertolucci, Federico, illus. 2009. (Dinodino's Dinosaur Adventures Ser.). 56p. (J). (gr. k-4). 27.95 (978-1-60754-714-3(7)); pap. 12.85 (978-1-60754-721-1(X)) Windmill Bks.

Boricchio, Frances. The Adventure of Rodney & Diane. 2012. 26p. pap. 17.99 (978-1-4685-6445-7(5)) AuthorHouse.

Bornemann, Elsa. Cuadernos de un Delfín. 2003. (SPA., Illus.). 125p. (J). (gr. 5-8). pap. 11.95 (978-950-511-724-6(8)) Santillana USA Publishing Co., Inc.

Bornstein, Ruth. Little Gorilla Book & CD. 2014. (ENG., Illus.). 32p. (J). (— 1). audio compact disk 10.99 (978-0-544-22794-1(8), HMH Books For Young Readers) Houghton Mifflin Harcourt Publishing Co.

Borraga, Charles R. The Old Parson's House. 2008. 24p. pap. 11.49 (978-1-4389-0698-0(6)) AuthorHouse.

Bossley, Michele Martin. Kicker, 1 vol. 2007. (Orca Sports Ser.). (ENG.). 160p. (YA). (gr. 6-10). per. 9.95 (978-1-55143-706-4(6)) Orca Bk. Pubs. USA.

Bost, Richard. Taekwon Tales. 2012. 120p. pap. 9.99 (978-0-9848626-1-0(7)) ImBost Inc.

Bostick, B. k. Huber Hill & the Golden Staff of Cibola. 2013. (J). pap. 14.99 (978-1-4621-1098-8(3), Horizon Pubs.) Cedar Fort, Inc./CFI Distribution.

Botelho, R. J. G. A. R. T. H. (Genetically Altered Radically Transformed Human) Book III: Downeast Maine: A New Beginning. 2006. 90p. pap. 16.95 (978-1-4241-2305-6(4)) PublishAmerica, Inc.

Botha, Si. Goosala Goop. 2009. 48p. pap. 16.50 (978-1-60860-124-0(2), Strategic Bk. Publishing) Strategic Book Publishing & Rights Agency (SBPRA).

Botterill, Ron E. Big, Green & Mean, Ogie, the Misunderstood Monster. 2009. 28p. pap. 13.00 (978-1-60860-712-9(7), Eloquent Bks.) Strategic Book Publishing & Rights Agency (SBPRA).

Bottner, Barbara. Raymond & Nelda, 1 vol. Hayashi, Nancy, illus. 2007. (ENG.). 32p. (J). (gr. k-3). 15.95 (978-1-56145-394-8(3)) Peachtree Pubs.

—Rosa's Room, 1 vol. Spiegel, Beth, illus. 2014. (ENG.). 32p. (J). (gr. -1-3). pap. 7.95 (978-1-56145-776-2(0)) Peachtree Pubs.

—Rosa's Room, 1 vol. Spiegel, Beth, tr. Spiegel, Beth, illus. 2004. (ENG.). 32p. (J). (gr. k-3). 15.95 (978-1-56145-302-3(1)) Peachtree Pubs.

Bottner, Barbara & Kruglik, Gerald. Wallace's Lists. Landstrom, Olof, tr. Landstrom, Olof, illus. 2004. (ENG.). 40p. (J). (gr. -1-2). 16.99 (978-0-06-000224-4(7), Tegen, Katherine Bks) HarperCollins Pubs.

—Wallace's Lists. Landstrom, Olof, illus. 2011. (J). (gr. 1-3). 29.95 (978-0-545-04275-8(5)) Weston Woods Studios, Inc.

Bouchard, John L. A Taste of Soda. 2006. 92p. pap. 16.95 (978-1-4241-2482-4(4)) PublishAmerica, Inc.

Boulden, James. Buddy Gets Angry Video Kit. 2003. (J). pap. 39.95 incl. VHS (978-1-892421-86-9(0), 739) Boulden Publishing.

Bourgeois, Paulette. Franklin & the Computer. Clark, Brenda, illus. 2003. (Franklin Ser.: Bk. 16). 32p. (J). pap. 4.50 (978-0-439-43121-7(2)) Scholastic, Inc.

—Franklin's New Friend. Clark, Brenda, illus. (Franklin Ser.). (ENG.). 32p. (J). (gr. -1-3). (978-1-55074-363-0(5)) Kids Can Pr., Ltd.

—Franklin's New Friend. 2004. (Illus.). (J). (gr. k-3). spiral bd. (978-0-616-01590-2(9)); spiral bd. (978-0-616-01591-9(7)) Canadian National Institute for the Blind/Institut National Canadien pour les Aveugles.

Bourgeois, Paulette & Clark, Brenda. Franklin Forgives. 2004. (Franklin TV Storybook Ser.). (ENG., Illus.). 32p. (J). (gr. -1-3). 4.95 (978-1-55337-488-6(6)) Kids Can Pr., Ltd. CAN. Dist: Hachette Bk. Group.

—Franklin's Nickname. Southern, Shelley, tr. Southern, Shelley, illus. 2004. (Franklin TV Storybook Ser.). (ENG.). 32p. (J). (gr. -1-3). 4.95 (978-1-55337-490-9(8)); 10.95 (978-1-55337-489-3(4)) Kids Can Pr., Ltd. CAN. Dist: Hachette Bk. Group.

Bourne, Tracey. Not Just a Dream! 2009. (Illus.). 52p. pap. 11.49 (978-1-4389-4819-5(0)) AuthorHouse.

Bowater, Alan. A Pig Called Pete Meets a Cat Called Kitty. Pascoe, Pete, illus. 2009. (Pig Called Pete Ser.). 32p. (J). (gr. -1-2). 22.60 (978-1-60754-561-3(6)); pap. 10.55 (978-1-60754-562-0(4)) Windmill Bks.

—A Pig Called Pete Meets a Cow Called Carlotta. Pascoe, Pete, illus. 2009. (Pig Called Pete Ser.). 32p. (J). (gr. -1-2). 22.60 (978-1-60754-567-5(5)); pap. 10.55 (978-1-60754-568-2(3)) Windmill Bks.

—A Pig Called Pete Meets a Dog Called Doug. Pascoe, Pete, illus. 2009. (Pig Called Pete Ser.). 32p. (J). (gr. -1-2). 22.60 (978-1-60754-564-4(0)); pap. 10.55 (978-1-60754-565-1(9)) Windmill Bks.

—A Pig Called Pete Meets a Sheep Called Sean. Pascoe, Pete, illus. 2009. (Pig Called Pete Ser.). 32p. (J). (gr. -1-2). 22.60 (978-1-60754-570-5(5)); pap. 10.55 (978-1-60754-571-2(3)) Windmill Bks.

Bowe, Julie. Big & Little Questions (According to Wren Jo Byrd) 2017. (ENG.). 240p. (J). (gr. 2-4). 16.99 (978-0-8037-3693-1(2), Kathy Dawson Books) Penguin Young Readers Group.

—Curve Ball. 2017. (Victoria Torres, Unfortunately Average Ser.). (ENG.). 160p. (gr. 4-4). pap. 5.95 (978-1-4965-3820-8(X)); lib. bdg. 26.65 (978-1-4965-3818-5(8)) Stone Arch Bks.

—Face the Music. 2015. (Victoria Torres, Unfortunately Average Ser.). (ENG.). 160p. (gr. 4-4). pap. 5.95 (978-1-4965-0538-5(7)) Stone Arch Bks.

—My Best Frenemy. 2011. (Friends for Keeps Ser.). (ENG.). 256p. (J). (gr. 3-7). 6.99 (978-0-14-241880-2(3), Puffin Books) Penguin Young Readers Group.

—My Extra Best Friend. 2013. (Friends for Keeps Ser.: 5). (ENG.). 240p. (J). (gr. 3-7). pap. 6.99 (978-0-14-242603-6(2), Puffin Books) Penguin Young Readers Group.

—My Forever Friends. 2012. (Friends for Keeps Ser.). (ENG.). 240p. (J). (gr. 3-7). pap. 6.99 (978-0-14-242104-8(9), Puffin Books) Penguin Young Readers Group.

—My Last Best Friend. 2008. (Friends for Keeps Ser.). (ENG., Illus.). 160p. (J). (gr. 2-5). pap. 5.99 (978-0-15-206197-5(5)) Houghton Mifflin Harcourt Publishing Co.

—My New Best Friend. 2010. (Friends for Keeps Ser.). (ENG.). 192p. (J). (gr. 2-5). pap. 6.99 (978-0-547-32869-0(9)) Houghton Mifflin Harcourt Publishing Co.

—Vicka for President! 2016. (Victoria Torres, Unfortunately Average Ser.). (ENG., Illus.). 160p. (gr. 4-4). lib. bdg. 26.65 (978-1-4965-3800-0(5)) Stone Arch Bks.

—Victoria Torres, Unfortunately Average. 2015. (Victoria Torres, Unfortunately Average Ser.). (ENG.). 160p. (gr. 4-4). 106.60 (978-1-4965-2028-9(9)) Stone Arch Bks.

—Victoria Torres, Unfortunately Average: Fall 2016, 2 vols. 2016. (Victoria Torres, Unfortunately Average Ser.). (ENG.). 160p. (gr. 4-4). pap. 11.90 (978-1-4965-3832-1(3)) Stone Arch Bks.

Bowen, Fred. Dugout Rivals, 1 vol. 2010. (Fred Bowen Sports Stories Ser.). (ENG.). 128p. (J). (gr. 2-7). pap. 6.95 (978-1-56145-515-7(6)) Peachtree Pubs.

—The Final Cut, 1 vol. 2009. (All-Star Sports Story Ser.). (ENG., Illus.). 112p. (J). pap. 6.95 (978-1-56145-510-2(5)) Peachtree Pubs.

Bowers, Tim. A New Home. 2003. (Green Light Readers Level 1 Ser.). (ENG., Illus.). 24p. (J). (gr. -1-3). pap. 3.95 (978-0-15-204848-8(0)) Houghton Mifflin Harcourt Publishing Co.

Bowles, B. R. Pauley the Pancake Boy. 2012. 24p. 24.95 (978-1-4626-6026-1(6)) America Star Bks.

Bowlin, Serina. Wandering Sam. Thrasher, Brian, illus. 2011. 20p. pap. 9.97 (978-1-61204-280-0(5), Eloquent Bks.) Strategic Book Publishing & Rights Agency (SBPRA).

Bowman, Crystal. Little David & His Best Friend. Hartung, Susan Kathleen & Endersly, Frank, illus. 2010. (I Can Read! / Little David Ser.). (ENG.). 32p. (J). pap. 3.99 (978-0-310-71710-2(8)) Zonderkidz.

Bowser, Ken. Bobbi's Big Brake. Bowser, Ken, illus. 2016. (Funny Bone Readers: Truck Pals on the Job Ser.). (ENG., Illus.). 24p. (gr. k-2). lib. bdg. 19.99 (978-1-63440-062-6(3)) Red Chair Pr.

—Bobbi's Big Brake: Self-Confidence. Bowser, Ken, illus. 2016. (Funny Bone Readers: Truck Pals on the Job Ser.). (ENG., Illus.). 24p. (gr. k-2). 30.65 (978-1-63440-064-0(X)) Red Chair Pr.

—Gus & the Mighty Mess. Bowser, Ken, illus. 2016. (Funny Bone Readers: Truck Pals on the Job Ser.). (ENG., Illus.). 24p. (gr. k-2). lib. bdg. 19.99 (978-1-63440-065-7(8), 1401366) Red Chair Pr.

—Gus & the Mighty Mess: Helping Others. Bowser, Ken, illus. 2016. (Funny Bone Readers: Truck Pals on the Job Ser.). (ENG., Illus.). 24p. (gr. k-2). 30.65 (978-1-63440-067-1(4)) Red Chair Pr.

—Hal & Al. Bowser, Ken, illus. 2016. (Funny Bone Readers: Truck Pals on the Job Ser.). (ENG., Illus.). 24p. (gr. k-2). lib. bdg. 19.99 (978-1-63440-068-8(2)) Red Chair Pr.

—Hal & Al: Self-Esteem. Bowser, Ken, illus. 2016. (Funny Bone Readers: Truck Pals on the Job Ser.). (ENG., Illus.). 24p. (gr. k-2). 30.65 (978-1-63440-070-1(4)) Red Chair Pr.

—Hitch Takes Off. Bowser, Ken, illus. 2016. (Funny Bone Readers: Truck Pals on the Job Ser.). (ENG., Illus.). 24p. (gr. k-2). lib. bdg. 19.99 (978-1-63440-071-8(2), 1401368) Red Chair Pr.

—Hitch Takes Off: Perseverance. Bowser, Ken, illus. 2016. (Funny Bone Readers: Truck Pals on the Job Ser.). (ENG., Illus.). 24p. (gr. k-2). 30.65 (978-1-63440-073-2(9)) Red Chair Pr.

—Lawni Takes the Field. Bowser, Ken, illus. 2016. (Funny Bone Readers: Truck Pals on the Job Ser.). (ENG., Illus.). 24p. (gr. k-2). lib. bdg. 19.99 (978-1-63440-074-9(7), 1401369) Red Chair Pr.

—Lawni Takes the Field: Teamwork. Bowser, Ken, illus. 2016. (Funny Bone Readers: Truck Pals on the Job Ser.). (ENG., Illus.). 24p. (gr. k-2). 30.65 (978-1-63440-076-3(3)) Red Chair Pr.

—One Wrong Turn. Bowser, Ken, illus. 2016. (Funny Bone Readers: Truck Pals on the Job Ser.). (ENG., Illus.). 24p. (gr. k-2). lib. bdg. 19.99 (978-1-63440-077-0(1), 1401370) Red Chair Pr.

—One Wrong Turn: Helping Those in Need. Bowser, Ken, illus. 2016. (Funny Bone Readers: Truck Pals on the Job Ser.). (ENG., Illus.). 24p. (gr. k-2). 30.65 (978-1-63440-079-4(8)) Red Chair Pr.

Bowser, Kimberly M. The Circus Dogs. 2012. 20p. pap. 24.95 (978-1-4626-6524-2(1)) America Star Bks.

The Box. 2012. (ENG.). 30p. (J). (gr. -1-k). 16.95 (978-1-60537-134-4(3)) Cobblestone Publishing Co.

The Boy I Love. 2014. (ENG., Illus.). 288p. (YA). (gr. 7). 17.99 (978-1-4424-8056-8(4), Atheneum Bks. for Young Readers) Simon & Schuster Children's Publishing.

Boyack, Merrilee. The Mismatched Nativity. Tenney, Shawna J. C., illus. 2016. (J). 18.99 (978-1-62972-239-9(1)) Deseret Bk. Co.

Boyce, Frank Cottrell. The Astounding Broccoli Boy. 2017. 400p. (J). (gr. 3-7). pap. 6.99 (978-0-06-240019-2(3), Waldon Pond Pr.) HarperCollins Pubs.

Boyd, Benjamin. The Adventures of Kid Humpty Dumpty. 2009. 60p. pap. 19.50 (978-1-60693-265-0(9), Eloquent Bks.) Strategic Book Publishing & Rights Agency (SBPRA).

Boyd, David. Pearl Harbor. Ng, Drew, illus. 2007. 48p. (J). lib. bdg. 23.08 (978-1-4242-1640-6(0)) Fitzgerald Bks.

Boyd, Kate & Brixton, Iris. The Quercus Quest. 2006. 159p. pap. 12.72 (978-1-4116-8843-8(0)) Lulu Pr., Inc.

Boyden, Linda. Boy & Poi Poi Puppy. Boyden, Linda, illus. 2013. (ENG., Illus.). 50p. (J). (gr. -1-2). 17.95 (978-1-940834-00-9(7)) Rising Phoenix Pr.

Boylan, Jennifer Finney. Falcon Quinn & the Black Mirror. Dorman, Brandon, illus. (Falcon Quinn Ser.: 1). (ENG.). (J). (gr. 5-9). 2011. 512p. pap. 7.99 (978-0-06-172834-1(9)) 2010. 496p. 16.99 (978-0-06-172832-7(2)) HarperCollins Pubs. (Tegen, Katherine Bks).

—Falcon Quinn & the Crimson Vapor. 2011. (Falcon Quinn Ser.: 2). (ENG.). 384p. (J). (gr. 5-9). 16.99 (978-0-06-172835-8(7), Tegen, Katherine Bks) HarperCollins Pubs.

Boyle, Amanda N. The Dream. 2007. 59p. per. 8.95 (978-1-59824-506-6(6)) E-BookTime LLC.

Boyle, Bob. Rosie & Rex: A Nose for Fun! Boyle, Bob, illus. 2014. (ENG., Illus.). 40p. (J). (gr. -1-3). 15.99 (978-0-06-221131-6(5)) HarperCollins Pubs.

Boyle, Karen Cother. Butterhead's Dream. 2010. 152p. pap. 15.49 (978-0-557-53742-6(8)) Lulu Pr., Inc.

Boyne, John. The Boy in the Striped Pajamas. (ENG.). (YA). (gr. 7). 2006. 224p. 17.99 (978-0-385-75106-3(0)) 2008. 240p. pap. 9.99 (978-0-385-75189-6(3)) Fickling, David Bks. GBR. Dist: Penguin Random Hse. LLC.

—The Boy in the Striped Pajamas. 2011. 10.54 (978-0-7848-3514-2(4), Everbind) Marco Bk. Co.

—The Boy in the Striped Pajamas. 2008. 215p. (gr. 7-12). 20.00 (978-0-7569-8943-9(4)) Perfection Learning Corp.

—The Boy in the Striped Pajamas. 2007. (ENG.). 224p. (YA). (gr. 7-18). pap. 9.99 (978-0-385-75153-7(2), Ember) Random Hse. Children's Bks.

—The Boy in the Striped Pajamas. rev. l.t. ed. 2007. (Thorndike Literacy Bridge Ser.). 247p. (YA). (gr. 7-12). 23.95 (978-0-7862-9425-1(6)) Thorndike Pr.

—The Boy in the Striped Pajamas. 2007. 215p. (YA). (gr. 7-12). 20.85 (978-1-4178-1823-5(9), Turtleback) Turtleback Bks.

—The Boy in the Striped Pajamas (Deluxe Illustrated Edition) Jeffers, Oliver, illus. 2016. (ENG.). 352p. (YA). (gr. 7). 18.99 (978-0-399-55931-0(0), Knopf Bks. for Young Readers) Random Hse. Children's Bks.

Boynton, Sandra. Your Personal Penguin. 2006. (ENG., Illus.). 24p. (J). (gr. k — 1). bds. 6.95 (978-0-7611-4372-7(6), 14372) Workman Publishing Co., Inc.

Bracken, Beth. The Little Bully, 1 vol. Bell, Jennifer A., illus. 2012. (Little Boost Ser.). (ENG.). 32p. (gr. k-3). lib. bdg. 23.99 (978-1-4048-6795-6(3), Little Boost) Picture Window Bks.

Bracken, Beth & Fraser, Kay. At the Edge of the Woods, 1 vol. Sawyer, Odessa, illus. 2013. (Faerieground Ser.). (ENG.). 96p. (gr. 1-3). lib. bdg. 23.99 (978-1-4342-4489-5(X)) Stone Arch Bks.

—Believe, 1 vol. Sawyer, Odessa, illus. 2014. (Faerieground Ser.). (ENG.). 288p. (gr. 4-8). 12.95 (978-1-62370-113-0(9)) Capstone Young Readers of Coughlan Cos.

—Bloodfate, 1 vol. Sawyer, Odessa, illus. 2012. (Faerieground Ser.). (ENG.). 96p. (gr. 1-3). lib. bdg. 23.99 (978-1-4342-3305-9(7), Faerieground) Stone Arch Bks.

—Faerieground. Sawyer, Odessa, illus. 2013. (Faerieground Ser.). (ENG.). 96p. (gr. 1-3). 191.92 (978-1-4342-6049-9(6)); 95.96 (978-1-4342-6050-5(X)) Stone Arch Bks. (Faerieground).

—Fate of the Willow Queen. Sawyer, Odessa, illus. 2013. (Faerieground Ser.). (ENG.). 96p. (gr. 1-3). 23.99 (978-1-4342-4492-5(X), Faerieground) Stone Arch Bks.

—The Hidden Things, 1 vol. Sawyer, Odessa, illus. 2014. (Faerieground Ser.). (ENG.). 96p. (gr. 1-3). 23.99 (978-1-4342-9185-1(5), Faerieground) Stone Arch Bks.

—A Murder of Crows, 1 vol. Sawyer, Odessa, illus. 2013. (Faerieground Ser.). (ENG.). 96p. (gr. 1-3). lib. bdg. 23.99 (978-1-4342-4491-8(1)) Stone Arch Bks.

—The Seventh Kingdom, 1 vol. Sawyer, Odessa, illus. 2014. (Faerieground Ser.). (ENG.). 96p. (gr. 1-3). 23.99 (978-1-4342-9186-8(3), Faerieground) Stone Arch Bks.

—The Shadows, 1 vol. Sawyer, Odessa, illus. 2012. (Faerieground Ser.). (ENG.). 96p. (gr. 1-3). lib. bdg. 23.99 (978-1-4342-3306-6(5), Faerieground) Stone Arch Bks.

—Two Mothers. Sawyer, Odessa, illus. 2013. (Faerieground Ser.). (ENG.). 96p. (gr. 1-3). 23.99 (978-1-4342-4490-1(3), Faerieground) Stone Arch Bks.

—The Willow Queen's Gate, 1 vol. Sawyer, Odessa, illus. 2012. (Faerieground Ser.). (ENG.). 96p. (gr. 1-3). lib. bdg. 23.99 (978-1-4342-3304-2(9), Faerieground) Stone Arch Bks.

—Wish, 1 vol. Sawyer, Odessa, illus. 2013. (Faerieground Ser.). (ENG.). 304p. (gr. 4-8). 12.95 (978-1-62370-003-4(5)) Stone Arch Bks.

—A Wish in the Woods, 1 vol. Sawyer, Odessa, illus. 2012. (Faerieground Ser.). (ENG.). 96p. (gr. 1-3). lib. bdg. 23.99 (978-1-4342-3303-5(0), Faerieground) Stone Arch Bks.

Brackett, Michael. The Adventures of Bunny & Hare. 2010. 138p. pap. 11.00 (978-1-60911-296-7(2), Eloquent Bks.) Strategic Book Publishing & Rights Agency (SBPRA).

Bradbury, Jennifer. Shift. (ENG., Illus.). (YA). (gr. 7). 2012. 272p. pap. 10.99 (978-1-4424-0852-4(9)) 2008. 256p. 17.99 (978-1-4169-4732-5(9)) Simon & Schuster Children's Publishing. (Atheneum Bks. for Young Readers).

Bradby, Marie. Some Friend. 2007. (ENG.). 240p. (J). (gr. 3-7). pap. 7.99 (978-1-4169-3452-3(9), Atheneum Bks. for Young Readers) Simon & Schuster Children's Publishing.

Braddock, Paige. Jane's World, Vol. 4. 2006. (ENG., Illus.). 160p. pap. 15.00 (978-0-9766707-3-5(9), 9780976670735) Girl Twirl Comics.

Bradford James Nolan. The Mouse Who Lived in Fenway Park. Jim Connelly, illus. 2009. 36p. pap. 19.99 (978-1-4389-4491-3(8)) AuthorHouse.

Bradley, John Ed. Call Me by My Name. (ENG.). (YA). (gr. 7). 2015. 288p. pap. 11.99 (978-1-4424-9794-8(7)) 2014. (Illus.). 272p. 17.99 (978-1-4424-9793-1(9), Atheneum Bks. for Young Readers) Simon & Schuster Children's Publishing.

Bradley, Kimberly Brubaker. The Lacemaker & the Princess. 2009. (ENG.). 208p. (J). (gr. 3-7). pap. 7.99 (978-1-4169-8583-9(2), McElderry, Margaret K. Bks.) McElderry, Margaret K. Bks.

Bradley, Natasha R. & Bradley, Jasmine N. Jessika's Diaries:Life's Not Fair. 2008. 132p. pap. 14.95 (978-0-615-21079-7(1)) On The Ball Publishing.

Bradley, Sharon. Walking Away from Texas. 2004. 112p. (YA). pap. 10.95 (978-0-595-32672-3(2)) iUniverse, Inc.

Brady, Carolyn. The Adventures of Pelican Mcfeet: The Big Lumpy Green Monster. Phillips, Deborah, illus. 2008. 32p. pap. 16.95 (978-1-4389-3539-3(0)) AuthorHouse.

Brager, Allison. Off-Colored Rainbows. 2005. 64p. pap. 16.95 (978-1-4241-0267-9(7)) PublishAmerica, Inc.

Brahney, Jenny. Spotty, 1 vol. 2010. 30p. pap. 24.95 (978-1-4489-8497-8(1)) PublishAmerica, Inc.

Brallier, Max. The Last Kids on Earth. Holgate, Douglas, illus. (J). 2017. pap. **(978-0-425-28872-6(2))** 2016. (Last Kids on Earth Ser.: Vol. 2). (ENG.). 304p. (gr. 3-7). 13.99 (978-0-670-01662-4(4)) 2015. (Last Kids on Earth Ser.: 1). (ENG.). 240p. (gr. 3-7). 13.99 (978-0-670-01661-7(6)) Penguin Young Readers Group. (Viking Books for Young Readers).

Bramsen, Carin. Hey, Duck! 2013. (ENG., Illus.). 40p. (J). (gr. -1-2). 17.99 (978-0-375-86990-7(5), Random Hse. Bks. for Young Readers) Random Hse. Children's Bks.

—Just a Duck? 2015. (ENG., Illus.). 40p. (J). (gr. -1-2). 17.99 (978-0-385-38415-5(7), Random Hse. Bks. for Young Readers) Random Hse. Children's Bks.

Bramwell, Wendie & Normand, Bridgid. Rhymitis. Kim, Julie J., tr. Kim, Julie J., illus. 2003. 32p. (J). pap. (978-0-9741388-8-6(6)) Committee for Children.

Bramwell, Wendie, et al. The Friendship Alphabet. Ziegler, Michael, illus. Ziegler, Michael, photos by. 2003. 32p. (J). pap. (978-0-9741388-3-1(5)) Committee for Children.

Brand, Jack. Freddy Tangles - Champ or Chicken? Jellett, Tom, illus. 2017. (Freddy Tangles Ser.: 2). (ENG.). 128p. (J). (gr. 2-5). 7.99 **(978-1-76011-035-2(3))** Allen & Unwin AUS. Dist: Independent Pubs. Group.

Brand, Jack. Freddy Tangles - Legend or Loser? Jellett, Tom, illus. 2017. (Freddy Tangles Ser.: 1). (ENG.). 128p. (J). (gr. 2-5). 7.99 (978-1-76011-034-5(5)) Allen & Unwin AUS. Dist: Independent Pubs. Group.

Brandeis, Madeline. The Little Dutch Tulip Girl. 2011. 194p. 42.95 (978-1-258-09813-1(X)) Literary Licensing, LLC.

Brandes, Wendy L. Claire's Cursed Camping Trip. Lorenzet, Eleonora, illus. 2016. (Summer Camp Ser.). (ENG.). 96p. (gr. 4-6). lib. bdg. 24.65 (978-1-4965-2600-7(7)) Stone Arch Bks.

—Emily's Pranking Problem. Lorenzet, Eleonora, illus. 2016. (Summer Camp Ser.). (ENG.). 96p. (gr. 4-6). lib. bdg. 24.65 (978-1-4965-2599-4(X)) Stone Arch Bks.

—MJ's Camp Crisis. Lorenzet, Eleonora, illus. 2016. (Summer Camp Ser.). (ENG.). 96p. (gr. 4-6). lib. bdg. 24.65 (978-1-4965-2598-7(1)) Stone Arch Bks.

—Nina's Not Boy Crazy! (She Just Likes Boys) Lorenzet, Eleonora, illus. 2016. (Summer Camp Ser.). (ENG.). 96p. (gr. 4-6). lib. bdg. 24.65 (978-1-4965-2601-4(5)) Stone Arch Bks.

—Summer Camp, 4 vols. Lorenzet, Eleonora, illus. 2016. (Summer Camp Ser.). (ENG.). 96p. (gr. 4-6). 98.60 *(978-1-4965-2749-3(6))* Stone Arch Bks.
Brandon, Barbara. Homer the H Shaped Tree. 2005. (J). 8.00 *(978-0-9776480-5-4(2),* MSP) Main St Publishing, Inc.
Branford, Anna. Violet Mackerel's Possible Friend. Allen, Elanna, illus. 2014. (Violet Mackerel Ser.). (ENG.). 128p. (J). (gr. 1-5). 15.99 *(978-1-4424-9455-8(7),* Atheneum Bks. for Young Readers) Simon & Schuster Children's Publishing.
—Violet Mackerel's Remarkable Recovery. Allen, Elanna, illus. 2013. (Violet Mackerel Ser.). (ENG.). 128p. (J). (gr. 1-5). 15.99 *(978-1-4424-3588-9(7));* pap. 5.99 *(978-1-4424-3589-6(5))* Simon & Schuster Children's Publishing. (Atheneum Bks. for Young Readers).
Brashares, Ann. Forever in Blue: The Fourth Summer of the Sisterhood. 2008. (Sisterhood of the Traveling Pants Ser.: Bk. 4). (ENG.). 416p. (YA). (gr. 7-12). pap. 9.99 *(978-0-385-73401-1(8),* Ember) Random Hse. Children's Bks.
—Girls in Pants. 2006. (Sisterhood of the Traveling Pants Ser.: Bk. 3). (ENG.). 384p. (YA). (gr. 7-12). reprint ed. per. 9.99 *(978-0-553-37593-0(8),* Ember) Random Hse. Children's Bks.
—The Sisterhood of the Traveling Pants. 2003. (Sisterhood of the Traveling Pants Ser.: Bk. 1). (ENG.). 336p. (YA). (gr. 7-18). pap. 9.99 *(978-0-385-73058-7(6),* Ember) Random Hse. Children's Bks.
—The Sisterhood of the Traveling Pants Set: The Sisterhood of the Traveling Pants - The Second Summer of the Sisterhood - Girls in Pants, 3 vols. 2006. (Sisterhood of the Traveling Pants Ser.: Vols. 1-3). (ENG.). (YA). pap., pap., pap. 26.85 *(978-0-385-73424-0(7),* Ember) Random Hse. Children's Bks.
Brashear Hopper, Celia. The Merry Adventures of Blade & Friends. 2007. (YA). lib. bdg. 26.95 *(978-0-9795460-1-3(X))* Creative Bk. Pubs.
Bratley, Colleen m. The Easter Spirit Eggs. 2012. (ENG.). (J). pap. 15.50 *(978-1-4675-2523-7(5))* Independent Pub.
Braun, Sebastien. Whoosh & Chug! Braun, Sebastien, illus. 2014. (Illus.). 32p. (J). (gr. -1-3). 16.99 *(978-0-06-207754-7(6))* HarperCollins Pubs.
Bray, Pamela. The Day Lonyaie's Life Changed. 2008. 32p. pap. 24.95 *(978-1-60474-859-8(1))* America Star Bks.
—Elephant & Ant. 2012. 36p. 24.95 *(978-1-4626-5986-9(1))* America Star Bks.
Braymer, Donna. The Adventures of Rowdy Raccoon. 2006. (J). audio compact disk 5.99 *(978-0-9766823-8-7(9))* Sable Creek Pr. LLC.
Breathed, Berkeley. The Bill the Cat Story: A Bloom County Epic. Breathed, Berkeley, illus. 2016. (ENG., Illus.). 40p. (J). (gr. -1-3). 18.99 *(978-0-399-54662-4(6),* Philomel Bks.) Penguin Young Readers Group.
—Pete & Pickles. Breathed, Berkeley, illus. 2008. (ENG., Illus.). 48p. (J). (gr. -1-k). 17.99 *(978-0-399-25082-8(4),* Philomel Bks.) Penguin Young Readers Group.
Breckenridge, Trula & Breckenridge, Scott. Squiggly the Roach. Breckenridge, Trula & Breckenridge, Scott, illus. 2004. (Illus.). (J). per. *(978-0-9749480-6-5(3),* MSPpress) Mama Specific Productions.
Bredeson, Michelle. Legends. 2012. 220p. pap. *(978-1-61706-158-5(1))* Roxby Media Ltd.
Bremner-Lewis, P. L. My Friend, the Unicorn. 2009. 28p. pap. 12.95 *(978-1-4389-8966-2(0))* AuthorHouse.
Brenda, Jones. No, I Don't Want to Play Today: An African Tale about Bullying. 2010. 40p. pap. 14.95 *(978-1-60911-387-2(X),* Eloquent Bks.) Strategic Book Publishing & Rights Agency (SBPRA).
Brenda Seabrooke. Jerry on the Line. 2010. 132p. pap. 10.95 *(978-1-4401-8766-7(5))* iUniverse, Inc.
Brenda Slack, Slack & Brenda Slack. Everybody. 2010. 28p. pap. 13.85 *(978-1-4269-0264-2(6))* Trafford Publishing.
Brennan, Sarah Rees. In Other Lands. Nowak, Carolyn, illus. 2017. (ENG.). 432p. 19.95 *(978-1-61873-120-3(3),* Big Mouth Hse.) Small Beer Pr.
Brent, Alexander Michael. Play Date with T-Rex: The Adventures of Jake & Sammy Wiggles. 2010. 52p. pap. 19.50 *(978-1-4520-7531-0(X))* AuthorHouse.
Breshears, Alyce Park. Friends - a Collection of Stories. 2013. 88p. pap. 10.95 *(978-1-60414-682-0(6))* Fideli Publishing, Inc.
Breslin, Jayne. The Princess Jelly Tutu Adventures. 2011. (Illus.). 28p. (gr. -1). pap. 14.09 *(978-1-4567-7611-4(8))* AuthorHouse.
Brett, Jan. Gingerbread Friends. Brett, Jan, illus. 2008. (ENG., Illus.). 32p. (J). (gr. -1-k). 17.99 *(978-0-399-25161-0(8),* G.P. Putnam's Sons Books for Young Readers) Penguin Young Readers Group.
Brewer, Dottie A. Saul the Pelican. Naenix, Robin, illus. 2004. 30p. (J). 4.95 *(978-0-9707945-9-8(2))* Billion $ Baby Pubns.
Brewin, Barbara. Sidney Snail's Wonderful World of Adventure. 2009. (Illus.). 32p. pap. 14.49 *(978-1-4389-4100-4(5))* AuthorHouse.
Brewis, Megan. Henry & Boo. Brewis, Megan, illus. 2017. (Child's Play Library). (ENG., Illus.). 32p. (J). ***(978-1-84643-999-5(X));*** pap. ***(978-1-84643-998-8(1))*** Child's Play International Ltd.
Brezenoff, Steve. The Case of the Counterfeit Painting. Weber, Lisa K., illus. 2016. (Museum Mysteries Ser.). (ENG.). 128p. (gr. 2-3). pap. 6.95 *(978-1-4965-2522-2(1));* lib. bdg. 26.65 *(978-1-4965-2518-5(3))* Stone Arch Bks. (Museum Mysteries).
—The Case of the Soldier's Ghost. Weber, Lisa K., illus. 2016. (Museum Mysteries Ser.). (ENG.). 128p. (gr. 2-3). lib. bdg. 26.65 *(978-1-4965-2519-2(1),* Museum Mysteries) Stone Arch Bks.
—I Dare You! Hilliker, Phillip, illus. 2008. (Vortex Bks.). (ENG.). 112p. (gr. 2-3). 26.65 *(978-1-4342-0798-2(6),* Vortex Bks.) Stone Arch Bks.
—Lost Island, 1 vol. Pinelli, Amerigo, illus. 2013. (Ravens Pass Ser.). (ENG.). 96p. (gr. 2-3). pap. 6.15 *(978-1-4342-6214-1(6))* Stone Arch Bks.
—Lost Island. 2013. (Ravens Pass Ser.). (ENG.). 96p. (gr. 2-3). pap. 35.70 *(978-1-4342-6290-5(1))* Stone Arch Bks.
—Lost Island, 1 vol. Pinelli, Amerigo, illus. 2013. (Ravens Pass Ser.). (ENG.). 96p. (gr. 2-3). lib. bdg. 25.32 *(978-1-4342-4614-1(0))* Stone Arch Bks.
—Overboard, 1 vol. Murphy, Scott, illus. 2012. (Return to Titanic Ser.). (ENG.). 112p. (gr. 2-3). pap. 6.95 *(978-1-4342-3912-9(8));* lib. bdg. 25.32 *(978-1-4342-3302-8(2))* Stone Arch Bks. (Return to Titanic).
—Stowaways, 1 vol. Murphy, Scott, illus. 2012. (Return to Titanic Ser.). (ENG.). 112p. (gr. 2-3). pap. 6.95 *(978-1-4342-3910-5(1));* lib. bdg. 25.32 *(978-1-4342-3300-4(6))* Stone Arch Bks. (Return to Titanic).
—Time Voyage, 1 vol. Murphy, Scott, illus. 2012. (Return to Titanic Ser.). (ENG.). 112p. (gr. 2-3). pap. 6.95 *(978-1-4342-3909-9(8));* lib. bdg. 25.32 *(978-1-4342-3299-1(9))* Stone Arch Bks. (Return to Titanic).
—An Unsinkable Ship, 1 vol. Murphy, Scott, illus. 2012. (Return to Titanic Ser.). (ENG.). 112p. (gr. 2-3). pap. 6.95 *(978-1-4342-3911-2(X));* lib. bdg. 25.32 *(978-1-4342-3301-1(4))* Stone Arch Bks. (Return to Titanic).
Brezenoff, Steven. Case of the Counterfeit Painting. Weber, Lisa K., illus. 2017. 118p. (J). pap. *(978-1-4965-2530-7(2))* Stone Arch Bks.
—The Case of the Haunted History Museum. Weber, Lisa K., illus. 2015. (Museum Mysteries Ser.). (ENG.). 128p. (gr. 2-3). lib. bdg. 26.65 *(978-1-4342-9687-0(3))* Stone Arch Bks.
—The Case of the Missing Mom. Weber, Lisa K., illus. 2016. (Museum Mysteries Ser.). (ENG.). 128p. (gr. 2-3). 26.65 *(978-1-4965-2517-8(5))* Stone Arch Bks.
—The Case of the Missing Museum Archives. Weber, Lisa K., illus. 2015. (Museum Mysteries Ser.). (ENG.). 128p. (gr. 2-3). lib. bdg. 26.65 *(978-1-4342-9688-7(1))* Stone Arch Bks.
—The Case of the Portrait Vandal. Weber, Lisa K., illus. 2015. (Museum Mysteries Ser.). (ENG.). 128p. (gr. 2-3). lib. bdg. 26.65 *(978-1-4342-9685-6(7))* Stone Arch Bks.
—The Case of the Stolen Sculpture. Weber, Lisa K., illus. 2015. (Museum Mysteries Ser.). (ENG.). 128p. (gr. 2-3). lib. bdg. 26.65 *(978-1-4342-9686-3(5))* Stone Arch Bks.
—The Case of the Stolen Space Suit. Weber, Lisa K., illus. 2016. (Museum Mysteries Ser.). (ENG.). 128p. (gr. 2-3). 26.65 *(978-1-4965-2516-1(7))* Stone Arch Bks.
Brian, Kate. A Private Collection, 4 vols., Set; Vols. 1-4. 2007. (Private Ser.: Nos. 1-4). (ENG.). 1032p. (YA). (gr. 9). pap. 34.99 *(978-1-4169-5818-5(5),* Simon & Schuster Bks. For Young Readers) Simon & Schuster Bks. For Young Readers.
Brian, Kate, pseud. Fake Boyfriend. 2009. (ENG.). 288p. (YA). (gr. 9). pap. 8.99 *(978-1-4169-1368-9(8),* Simon & Schuster Bks. For Young Readers) Simon & Schuster Bks. For Young Readers.
—Inner Circle. 2007. (Private Ser.: No. 5). (ENG.). 224p. (YA). (gr. 9-12). pap. 9.99 *(978-1-4169-5041-7(9),* Simon & Schuster Bks. For Young Readers) Simon & Schuster Bks. For Young Readers.
—Invitation Only. 2006. (Private Ser.: No. 2). (ENG.). 272p. (YA). (gr. 9-18). pap. 9.99 *(978-1-4169-1874-5(4),* Simon & Schuster Bks. For Young Readers) Simon & Schuster Bks. For Young Readers.
—Legacy. 2008. (Private Ser.: No. 6). (ENG.). 256p. (YA). (gr. 9). pap. 9.99 *(978-1-4169-5042-4(7),* Simon & Schuster Bks. For Young Readers) Simon & Schuster Bks. For Young Readers.
—Lucky T. 2007. (ENG.). 304p. (YA). (gr. 9-12). pap. 9.99 *(978-1-4169-3545-2(2),* Simon & Schuster Bks. For Young Readers) Simon & Schuster Bks. For Young Readers.
—Paradise Lost. 2009. (Private Ser.: 9). (ENG.). 256p. (YA). (gr. 9-18). pap. 9.99 *(978-1-4169-5884-0(3),* Simon & Schuster Bks. For Young Readers) Simon & Schuster Bks. For Young Readers.
—Private. 2006. (Private Ser.: No. 1). (ENG.). 240p. (YA). (gr. 9-12). pap. 10.99 *(978-1-4169-1873-8(6),* Simon & Schuster Bks. For Young Readers) Simon & Schuster Bks. For Young Readers.
—Revelation. 2008. (Private Ser.: No. 8). (ENG.). 288p. (YA). (gr. 9-18). pap. 11.99 *(978-1-4169-5883-3(5),* Simon & Schuster Bks. For Young Readers) Simon & Schuster Bks. For Young Readers.
—Suspicion. 2009. (Private Ser.: No. 10). (ENG.). 224p. (YA). (gr. 9-18). pap. 9.99 *(978-1-4169-5885-7(1),* Simon & Schuster Bks. For Young Readers) Simon & Schuster Bks. For Young Readers.
—Untouchable. 2009. (Private Ser.: No. 3). (ENG.). 256p. (YA). pap. 9.99 *(978-1-4169-9948-5(5),* Simon & Schuster Bks. For Young Readers) Simon & Schuster Bks. For Young Readers.
—The V Club. 2004. (ENG., Illus.). 288p. (YA). (gr. 9). 14.95 *(978-0-689-86764-4(6),* Simon & Schuster Bks. For Young Readers) Simon & Schuster Bks. For Young Readers.
Bridges, Eunice. A Day Like Mine. Goodwin, Adrienne Annette, illus. 2011. 32p. pap. 24.95 *(978-1-4560-5766-4(9))* America Star Bks.
Bridwell, Norman. Clifford's Pals. unabr. ed. 2008. (Clifford, the Big Red Dog Ser.). (ENG.). (J). (gr. -1-3). 18.95 *(978-0-545-05249-8(1))* Scholastic, Inc.
Briggs-Greenberg, Ruthie. Felicity the Dragon. 2015. (ENG., Illus.). 32p. (J). (gr. -1-2). 15.95 *(978-1-63076-062-5(5))* Taylor Trade Publishing.
Bright, J. E. Best Friends - Continental Drift. 2012. (I Can Read Level 2 Ser.). (ENG.). 32p. (J). (gr. k-3). pap. 3.99 *(978-0-06-210483-0(7))* HarperCollins Pubs.
Bright, Paul. Fidgety Fish & Friends. Galloway, Ruth, illus. 2008. (Tiger Tales Ser.). 24p. (J). (gr. -1-2). pap. 6.95 *(978-1-58925-409-1(0))* Tiger Tales.
—There's a Bison Bouncing on the Bed! Chatterton, Chris, illus. 2016. (ENG.). 32p. (J). (gr. -1-2). 16.99 *(978-1-68010-006-8(8))* Tiger Tales.
Bright, Rachel. The Lion Inside. Field, Jim, illus. 2016. (ENG.). 32p. (J): (gr. -1-k). 16.99 *(978-0-545-87350-5(9),* Scholastic Pr.) Scholastic, Inc.
—Love Monster & the Perfect Present. 2014. (ENG., Illus.). 32p. (J). (gr. -1-k). 17.99 *(978-0-374-34648-5(8),* 9780374346485, Farrar, Straus & Giroux (BYR)) Farrar, Straus & Giroux.
—Side by Side. Gliori, Debi, illus. 2015. (ENG.). 32p. (J). (gr. -1-k). 17.99 *(978-0-545-81326-6(3),* Scholastic Pr.) Scholastic, Inc.
—Walter & the No-Need-To-Worry Suit (the Wonderful World of Walter & Winnie) 2015. (Wonderful World of Walter & Winnie Ser.). (ENG.). 32p. (J). 17.99 *(978-0-00-758594-6(2),* HarperCollins Children's Bks.) HarperCollins Pubs. Ltd. GBR. Dist: HarperCollins Pubs.
Brightman, Michelle. If I Were. 2012. 24p. pap. 15.99 *(978-1-4771-3385-9(2))* Xlibris Corp.
Brightwood, Laura, illus. Red Hat / Blue Hat. Brightwood, Laura, . 2006. (J). *(978-0-9779290-5-4(1))* 3-C Institute for Social Development.
Brignull, Irena. The Hawkweed Prophecy. 2017. (Hawkweed Ser.: 1). (ENG.). 384p. (gr. 7-17). pap. 10.99 ***(978-1-60286-313-2(X),*** Weinstein Bks.) Perseus Bks. Group.
Brill, Calista. Tugboat Bill & the River Rescue. Carpenter, Tad, illus. 2017. 40p. (J). (gr. -1-3). 17.99 *(978-0-06-236618-4(1))* HarperCollins Pubs.
Brimner, Larry Dane. The Cool Coats. Tripp, Christine, illus. 2003. (Rookie Choices Ser.). 31p. (J). (gr. 1-2). 13.60 *(978-0-7569-3259-6(9))* Perfection Learning Corp.
Brink Hull, Amanda. Maslyn: A Different Kind of Name for a Delightful Little Girl. 2009. (Illus.). 36p. pap. 16.99 *(978-1-4389-9338-6(2))* AuthorHouse.
Brinkley, Inez. Rainbows & Promises. 2006. 43p. (J). 15.98 *(978-1-4116-9579-5(8))* Lulu Pr., Inc.
Britland, Jan. The Adventures of Rodger Dodger Dog. Swaim, Michael, illus. 2009. 40p. pap. 15.95 *(978-1-936051-23-6(0))* Peppertree Pr., The.
Britt, Chris. Blabbering Bethann, 1 vol. 2014. (ENG., Illus.). 32p. (J). (gr. k-3). 16.99 *(978-1-4556-2004-3(1))* Pelican Publishing Co., Inc.
Brittenham, Skip. Between Worlds. 2016. (ENG., Illus.). 256p. (YA). (gr. 7). 18.99 *(978-0-399-17689-0(6),* G.P. Putnam's Sons Books for Young Readers) Penguin Young Readers Group.
Britto, Romero. Where Is Friendship Bear? Britto, Romero, illus. 2010. (ENG., Illus.). 16p. (J). (gr. -1-k). 12.99 *(978-1-4169-9623-1(0),* Little Simon) Little Simon.
Brix, Liz. Josephine Prairie Dog. 2009. 28p. pap. 12.70 *(978-1-4389-4448-7(9))* AuthorHouse.
Broach, Elise. James to the Rescue. Murphy, Kelly, illus. 2015. (Masterpiece Adventures Ser.: 2). (ENG.). 112p. (J). (gr. 1-4). 15.99 *(978-1-62779-316-2(X),* 9781627793162, Holt, Henry & Co. Bks. For Young Readers) Holt, Henry & Co.
—The Miniature World of Marvin & James. Murphy, Kelly, illus. 2014. (Masterpiece Adventures Ser.: 1). (ENG.). 112p. (J). (gr. 1-4). 15.99 *(978-0-8050-9190-8(4),* 9780805091908, Holt, Henry & Co. Bks. For Young Readers) Holt, Henry & Co.
—Trouble at School for Marvin & James. Murphy, Kelly, illus. 2017. (Masterpiece Adventures Ser.: 3). (ENG.). 112p. (J). 15.99 *(978-1-62779-318-6(6),* 9781627793186, Holt, Henry & Co. Bks. For Young Readers) Holt, Henry & Co.
—The Wolf Keepers. Ratterree, Alice, illus. 2016. (ENG.). 352p. (J). 16.99 *(978-0-8050-9899-0(2),* 9780805098990, Holt, Henry & Co. Bks. For Young Readers) Holt, Henry & Co.
Brockmann, Suzanne & Brockmann, Melanie. Wild Sky: A Night Sky Novel. 2015. (Night Sky Ser.: 2). (ENG.). 448p. (YA). (gr. 8-12). 16.99 *(978-1-4926-0484-6(4));* pap. 9.99 *(978-1-4926-2314-4(8))* Sourcebooks, Inc.
Broderick, Lonia. Muffy, Fluffy, & Dexter In. 2013. 20p. pap. 9.99 *(978-1-62697-848-5(4))* Salem Author Services.
Broderick, Lonia R. Muffy, Fluffy, & Dexter In. Broderick, Al R., illus. 2013. 20p. 20.99 *(978-1-62839-255-5(X))* Salem Author Services.
Brodsky, Irene. The Adventures of Silly Kitty, Princess Jasmine & First Puppy. 2010. (Illus.). 44p. (J). pap. 23.95 *(978-1-4327-5552-2(8))* Outskirts Pr., Inc.
Brodsky, Kathy. A CatFish Tale. Bennett, Cameron, illus. 2012. (ENG.). (J). 19.99 *(978-0-9828529-3-4(2))* Helpingwords.
—My Bent Tree. Bennett, Cameron, illus. 2008. (ENG.). 44p. (J). 19.95 *(978-0-615-16066-5(2))* Helpingwords.
Brody, Jessica. Addie Bell's Shortcut to Growing Up. 2017. (ENG.). 368p. (J). (gr. 5). 16.99 *(978-0-399-55510-7(2),* Delacorte Bks. for Young Readers) Random Hse. Children's Bks.
—Boys of Summer. 2016. (ENG., Illus.). 352p. (YA). (gr. 9). 17.99 *(978-1-4814-6349-2(7),* Simon Pulse) Simon Pulse.
—A Week of Mondays. 2016. (ENG.). 464p. (YA). 17.99 *(978-0-374-38270-4(0),* 9780374382704, Farrar, Straus & Giroux (BYR)) Farrar, Straus & Giroux.
Brokamp, Elizabeth. Circle of Three: Enough Friendship to Go Around? Stringfield, Joni, illus. 2008. 44p. (J). (gr. 3-7). 14.95 *(978-1-4338-0321-5(6));* pap. 9.95 *(978-1-4338-0322-2(4))* American Psychological Assn. (Magination Pr.).
Bronte, Jules & Oapos, Jem, illus. The Castle Adventure. 2013. 171p. pap. *(978-1-908804-08-2(4))* Bingham Mayne & Smith, Ltd.
Brooke, Lauren. The New Class. 2005. (Chestnut Hill Ser.: No. 1). 212p. (J). (gr. 4-7). lib. bdg. 12.65 *(978-0-7569-6479-5(2))* Perfection Learning Corp.
Brooke, Samantha. Best Friends Forever. 2011. (Strawberry Shortcake Ser.). (ENG.). 24p. (J). (gr. -1-k). pap. 4.99 *(978-0-448-45721-5(0),* Grosset & Dunlap) Penguin Young Readers Group.
—Makeover Madness. Thomas, Laura, illus. 2011. (Strawberry Shortcake Ser.). (ENG.). 24p. (J). (gr. -1-k). pap. 4.99 *(978-0-448-45720-8(2),* Grosset & Dunlap) Penguin Young Readers Group.
—Princess Parade. movie tie-in ed. 2013. (Lalaloopsy Ser.). (ENG., Illus.). 24p. (J). (gr. -1-3). 3.99 *(978-0-545-58126-4(5))* Scholastic, Inc.
Brookover, Brian D. Neddy & Little Roy Go to Town. 2013. 40p. pap. 20.99 *(978-1-4817-1185-2(7))* AuthorHouse.
Brooks, Bruce. The Moves Make the Man. 2003. (ENG.). 256p. (YA). (gr. 8-18). pap. 8.99 *(978-0-06-447022-3(9),* HarperTeen) HarperCollins Pubs.
—The Moves Make the Man. 3rd ed. (J). pap. 3.95 *(978-0-13-800079-0(4))* Prentice Hall (Schl. Div.).
Brooks, Chelsey. Yokeville Yokinton. 2008. 42p. pap. 24.95 *(978-1-60703-823-8(4))* America Star Bks.
Brooks, Donna. The Golden Spindle. 2010. 112p. pap. 30.00 *(978-1-60860-852-2(2),* Eloquent Bks.) Strategic Book Publishing & Rights Agency (SBPRA).
Brooks, Erik. Later, Gator! 2016. (ENG., Illus.). 40p. (J). (gr. -1). 14.95 *(978-1-4549-1816-5(0))* Sterling Publishing Co., Inc.
Brooks, Kevin. Martyn Pig. 2003. 230p. (J). (gr. 5-9). 15.65 *(978-0-7569-7217-2(5))* Perfection Learning Corp.
Brooks, Martha. Being with Henry, 1 vol. (ENG.). 174p. pap. 8.95 *(978-0-88899-502-5(4))* Groundwood Bks. CAN. Dist: Publishers Group West (PGW).
Brooks, Robert. Sonrieta. Urban, Helle, illus. 2008. 40p. (YA). 17.95 *(978-0-9792294-0-4(5))* Mystic Jaguar Publishing.
Brooks-Scrivanich, Olivia. Fiscal Pear & Shimmer in the Call of River Whale. 2008. (ENG.). 92p. pap. 14.99 *(978-1-4196-9589-6(4))* CreateSpace Independent Publishing Platform.
Brophy, Ann. Novus 3 & Me: Six Short Stories about Friendship. 2010. 44p. pap. 18.49 *(978-1-4490-7132-5(5))* AuthorHouse.
Brosgol, Vera. Anya's Ghost. Brosgol, Vera, illus. 2011. (ENG., Illus.). 224p. (YA). (gr. 7-12). pap. 17.99 *(978-1-59643-552-0(6),* 9781596435520, First Second Bks.) Roaring Brook Pr.
Brouillet, Chrystine. Mon Amie Clémentine. 2003. (Premier Roman Ser.). (FRE.). 64p. (J). (gr. 2-5). pap. *(978-2-89021-313-5(7))* Diffusion du livre Mirabel (DLM).
Brouwer, Sigmund. Justine Mckeen, Pooper Scooper, 1 vol. Whamond, Dave, illus. 2012. (Orca Echoes Ser.). (ENG.). 64p. (J). (gr. 2-3). pap. 6.95 *(978-1-55469-931-5(2))* Orca Bk. Pubs. USA.
Brown, Alison. Eddie & Dog, 1 vol. 2014. (ENG.). 32p. (J). pap. *(978-1-62370-115-4(5))* Capstone Young Readers of Coughlan Cos.
Brown, Anne Greenwood & Anastasiu, Heather. Girl Last Seen. 2016. (ENG.). 272p. (YA). (gr. 8-12). 16.99 *(978-0-8075-8140-7(2))* Whitman, Albert & Co.
Brown, Brooklyn. Kifaru Tries Something New. 2012. 32p. (-18). pap. 16.95 *(978-1-4575-1470-8(2))* Dog Ear Publishing, LLC.
Brown, Daniel. Chipper Learns a Lesson. 2013. 28p. pap. 5.99 *(978-0-9897549-4-1(4))* Story and Logic Media Group.
Brown, Derrick. Valentine the Porcupine Dances Funny. Lewis, Jenn, illus. 2011. (ENG.). 44p. 20.00 *(978-1-935904-18-2(3))* Write Bloody Publishing.
Brown, Donna. Crippled Like Me. 2009. 36p. pap. 14.75 *(978-1-60693-986-4(6),* Eloquent Bks.) Strategic Book Publishing & Rights Agency (SBPRA).
Brown, Gladys M. Home Away from Home. 2005. 36p. pap. 6.95 *(978-1-4116-3026-0(2))* Lulu Pr., Inc.
Brown, Gregory R. K. My Best Friend Jason. 2011. 28p. pap. 15.99 *(978-1-4568-9507-5(9))* Xlibris Corp.
Brown, Hazel. Prince Henry St. Clair Earl of Orkney. Bramadat, Dawn, ed. Brown, Hazel, illus. 2013. (Illus.). 106p. pap. 25.95 *(978-1-935786-57-1(1))* St. Clair Pubns.
Brown, J. A. Busy Bee. Knight, Paula, illus. 2003. (Funny Faces Ser.). 10p. (J). bds. 3.95 *(978-1-58925-715-3(4))* Tiger Tales.
Brown, Jason Robert & Elish, Dan. 13. 2008. (Illus.). 208p. (J). lib. bdg. 16.89 *(978-0-06-078750-9(3),* Geringer, Laura Book) HarperCollins Pubs.
Brown, Jeff. Flat Stanley's Worldwide Adventures #10: Showdown at the Alamo. Pamintuan, Macky, illus. 2013. (Flat Stanley's Worldwide Adventures Ser.: 10). (ENG.). 112p. (J). (gr. 1-5). 15.99 *(978-0-06-218988-2(3))* HarperCollins Pubs.
—Showdown at the Alamo. Pamintuan, Macky, illus. 2013. (Flat Stanley's Worldwide Adventures Ser.: 10). (ENG.). 112p. (J). (gr. 1-5). pap. 4.99 *(978-0-06-218987-5(5))* HarperCollins Pubs.
—Showdown at the Alamo. 2013. (Flat Stanley's Worldwide Adventures Ser.: 10). (J). lib. bdg. 14.75 *(978-0-606-35046-4(2),* Turtleback) Turtleback Bks.
Brown, Jennifer. Life on Mars. 2014. (ENG.). 240p. (YA). (gr. 3-6). 16.99 *(978-1-61963-252-3(7),* 9781619632523, Bloomsbury USA Childrens) Bloomsbury Publishing USA.
—Pennybaker School Is Headed for Disaster. Kissi, Marta, illus. 2017. (ENG.). 320p. (J). 16.99 *(978-1-68119-174-4(1),* 9781681191744, Bloomsbury USA Childrens) Bloomsbury Publishing USA.
Brown, Kathryn. Freddy the Brave. 2010. 43p. pap. 12.50 *(978-1-4461-2959-3(4))* Lulu Pr., Inc.
Brown, Kathy. Wesley's World. Parsloe, Alismarie, illus. 2011. 36p. pap. 24.95 *(978-1-4489-8461-9(0))* America Star Bks.
Brown Lcsw, Jennifer. Star Realizes She Is Not Alone. 2013. 28p. pap. 19.99 *(978-1-4772-7043-1(4))* AuthorHouse.
Brown, Linnet. Secrets Can Be Told. 2013. 74p. pap. 10.99 *(978-1-62697-265-0(6))* Salem Author Services.
Brown, Marc. Arthur Jumps into Fall. 2006. (ENG., Illus.). 24p. (J). (gr. -1-1). pap. 3.99 *(978-0-316-05775-2(4))* Little, Brown Bks. for Young Readers.
—Arthur's Homework. 2004. (ENG., Illus.). 24p. (J). (gr. -1-1). pap. 3.99 *(978-0-316-73387-8(3))* Little, Brown Bks. for Young Readers.
—Arthur's Mystery Babysitter. Brown, Marc, illus. 2004. (ENG., Illus.). 24p. (J). (gr. -1-1). pap. 3.99 *(978-0-316-73394-6(6),* Tingley, Megan Bks.) Little, Brown Bks. for Young Readers.
—Francine, Believe It or Not! unabr. ed. 2004. (Arthur Chapter Bks.: Bk. 14). 58p. (J). (gr. 2-4). pap. 17.00 incl. audio *(978-0-8072-0345-3(9),* Listening Library) Random Hse. Audio Publishing Group.
Brown, Merry. The Second Fall. 2013. 290p. pap. 11.99 *(978-0-9899934-0-1(X))* YA Bks.
Brown, Monica. Lola Levine & the Ballet Scheme. 2016. (Lola Levine Ser.: 3). (ENG., Illus.). 112p. (J). (gr. 1-5). 14.99 *(978-0-316-25844-9(X))* Little, Brown Bks. for Young Readers.
Brown, Palmer. Hickory. Brown, Palmer, illus. 2013. (ENG., Illus.). 56p. (J). (gr. -1-2). 16.95 *(978-1-59017-627-6(8),* NYR Children's Collection) New York Review of Bks., Inc., The.
Brown, Peter. The Wild Robot. 2016. (ENG., Illus.). 288p. (J). (gr. 3-7). 16.99 *(978-0-316-38199-4(3))* Little, Brown Bks. for Young Readers.
—You Will Be My Friend! 2011. (Starring Lucille Beatrice Bear Ser.). (ENG., Illus.). 40p. (J). (gr. -1-3). 18.00 *(978-0-316-07030-0(0))* Little, Brown Bks. for Young Readers.
Brown, Ruth E. The Goontoff Kingdom Chronicles: The Bogus King. 2011. 46p. pap. 16.95 *(978-1-4560-8346-5(5))* America Star Bks.
Brown, Sam. Sometimes I Forget You're a Robot. 2013. (ENG., Illus.). 32p. (J). (gr. -1-k). 16.99 *(978-0-8037-3825-6(0),* Dial Bks) Penguin Young Readers Group.
Brown, Sheila M. A Dog Named Ben & His Two Best Friends. 2011. 16p. (gr. 1-2). 9.95 *(978-1-4567-2478-8(9))* AuthorHouse.

E
F
G

Brown, Tena L. Tena, Joshua & Friends, 22 vols., Set. Brown, Tena L., illus. Incl. Always, Forever & Five Days Are 5 Big Words. (gr. -1-4). spiral bd. 5.00 (978-1-890925-13-0(6)); Be Careful What You Do: Your Friends Are Always Watching You. (gr. -1-4). spiral bd. 5.00 (978-1-890925-07-9(1)); Clean Your Room. (gr. -1-4). spiral bd. 5.00 (978-1-890925-19-2(5)); Eat Your Veggies. (gr. -1-4). spiral bd. 5.00 (978-1-890925-20-8(9)); Family Comes 1st Is What We Say: Family Comes 1st Each & Everyday. (gr. -1-4). spiral bd. 5.00 (978-1-890925-04-8(7)); Follow Your Dreams to the Stars. (gr. -1-4). spiral bd. 5.00 (978-1-890925-14-7(4)); I Am Me. (gr. -1-4). spiral bd. 5.00 (978-1-890925-15-4(2)); It Is Okay to Be #1. (gr. -1-4). spiral bd. 5.00 (978-1-890925-18-5(7)); It Is Okay to Like You & Everything That You Do: No One Is a Misfit. (gr. -1-4). spiral bd. 5.00 (978-1-890925-11-6(X)); Just Say No & Turn & Walk Away. (gr. -1-4). spiral bd. 5.00 (978-1-890925-17-8(9)); Learn Reading, Writing & Arithmetic: You Cannot Get over If You Think That You Are Slick. (gr. -1-4). spiral bd. 5.00 (978-1-890925-12-3(8)); My 1-2-3's Say Be Kind to You & Me. (gr. -1-4). spiral bd. 5.00 (978-1-890925-08-6(X)); My A-B-Cs Say Be Kind to You & Me. (gr. -1-4). spiral bd. 5.00 (978-1-890925-09-3(8)); No One Is Perfect: Just Be the Best That You Can Be. (gr. -1-4). spiral bd. 5.00 (978-1-890925-06-2(3)); Take Care of Your Body. (gr. -1-4). spiral bd. 5.00 (978-1-890925-10-9(1)); Tena & Joshua Friends 'til the End. (gr. -1-4). spiral bd. 5.00 (978-1-890925-02-4(0)); Tena Gets Help from Her Friend Joshua. (gr. -1-4). per. 5.00 (978-1-890925-01-7(2)); Traffic Light Name Game. spiral bd. 5.00 (978-1-890925-21-5(7)); Trust, Honor & Loyalty - That Is What Friends Are Made Of. (gr. -1-4). spiral bd. 5.00 (978-1-890925-03-1(9)); Use Your Brain for Your Present, Future & Past. (gr. -1-4). spiral bd. 5.00 (978-1-890925-16-1(0)); We Are Growing up Too Fast. (gr. -1-4). spiral bd. 5.00 (978-1-890925-05-5(5)); When Will I Be 1 Year Old. (gr. -1-4). spiral bd. 5.00 (978-1-890925-22-2(5)); 24p. (J). 1997. (Illus.). 125.00 (978-1-890925-00-0(4)) Stori Tyme Huggggs, Inc.

Brownlee, Browne. Bad Breath. 2007. 108p. 19.95 (978-1-4241-5487-6(1)) America Star Bks.

Brownlow, Brooke. The Magic of Old Oak Hill. 2005. 48p. pap. 16.95 (978-1-4241-0223-5(5)) PublishAmerica, Inc.

Bruce, Sheila. Todos Ganan! Billin-Frye, Paige, illus. 2006. (Math Matters en Espanol Ser.). (SPA.). 32p. (J). (gr. -1-3). pap. 5.95 (978-1-57565-162-0(9)) Kane Press, Inc.

Bruckner, Tai. Lemon Path Encounter, 1 vol. Bruckner, Wes, illus. 2009. 15p. pap. 24.95 (978-1-60836-407-7(0)) America Star Bks.

Bruder, Eryka Naomi. Lilyen's Worn-Out Brown Boots. 2011. 28p. pap. (978-1-4269-7308-6(X)) Trafford Publishing (UK) Ltd.

Bruel, Robert O. Bob & Otto. Bruel, Nick, illus. 2007. (ENG.). 32p. (J). (gr. -1-3). 17.99 (978-1-59643-203-1(9), 9781596432031) Roaring Brook Pr.

Bruins, David. The Legend of Ninja Cowboy Bear. Leung, Hilary, illus. 2009. (Ninja Cowboy Bear Ser.). (ENG.). 32p. (J). (gr. -1-2). 16.95 (978-1-55453-486-9(0)) Kids Can Pr., Ltd. CAN. Dist: Hachette Bk. Group.

Brummett, Charlotte K. Doozy, the Lonely Firefly. 2006. (Illus.). 24p. (J). (gr. -1-3). per. 16.00 (978-1-58961-464-2(X)) PageFree Publishing, Inc.

Brummit, Ariyana. A Soldier's Way Home. 2013. 124p. pap. 11.97 (978-0-9801060-7-7(9)) Heard Word Publishing, LLC.

Brun-Cosme, Nadine. Big Wolf & Little Wolf, Such a Beautiful Orange! Tallec, Olivier & Sorman, Joy, illus. 2011. (ENG.). 32p. (J). (gr. -1-3). 16.95 (978-1-59270-106-3(X)) Enchanted Lion Bks., LLC.

Bruna, Dick. Miffy's Happy New Year! 2004. (Illus.). 24p. (J). pap. 3.99 (978-1-59226-233-5(3)) Big Tent Entertainment, Inc.

Bruno, Yvonne. Lisa Finds a New Friend. 2011. 24p. 12.79 (978-1-4567-1780-3(4)) AuthorHouse.

Bruton, Catherine & Shearwater, Cate. Rising Star. 2015. (Somersaults & Dreams Ser.: 2). (ENG.). 288p. (J). (gr. 4-6). pap. 11.99 (978-1-4052-6879-0(4)) Egmont Bks., Ltd. GBR. Dist: Independent Pubs. Group.

Bryan, Barbara. Starfish, Seashells, Coral & Gems. 2010. 47p. (J). pap. 27.95 (978-1-4327-6265-0(6)); pap. 21.95 (978-1-4327-6009-0(2)) Outskirts Pr., Inc.

Bryan, Jennifer. El Dragón Diferente. Hosler, Danamarie, illus. 2nd ed. 2015.Tr. of Different Dragon. (SPA.). 36p. (Orig.). (J). pap. 12.95 (978-0-9674468-9-9(9)) Two Lives Publishing.

Bryan, Jennifer Liu. Hilda, A Very Loyal Goat. 2009. 40p. (J). 15.95 (978-0-9816265-1-2(3)) Next Chapter Pr.

Bryant, Ann. Dancing Forever. 2006. (Ballerina Dreams Ser.). (Illus.). 105p. (J). (gr. 5). lib. bdg. 12.99 (978-1-58086-920-1(3), Usborne) EDC Publishing.

—Dragons vs Dinos. 2014. (ENG., Illus.). 32p. (J). (978-0-7787-1328-9(8)) Crabtree Publishing Co.

Bryant, Annie. Bad News/Good News. 2004. (Beacon Street Girls Ser.: No. 2). 236p. (J). 7.99 (978-0-9746587-0-4(7), Beacon Street Girls) B*tween Productions, Inc.

—Bad News/Good News. 2008. (Beacon Street Girls Ser.: 2). (ENG., Illus.). 256p. (J). (gr. 4-8). pap. 7.99 (978-1-4169-6425-4(8), Aladdin) Simon & Schuster Children's Publishing.

—Charlotte in Paris. 2008. (Beacon Street Girls Ser.: No. 1). (ENG.). 224p. (J). (gr. 5-8). pap. 8.99 (978-1-4169-6428-5(2), Aladdin) Simon & Schuster Children's Publishing.

—Crush Alert. 2008. (Beacon Street Girls Ser.: 14). (ENG.). 288p. (J). (gr. 4-8). pap. 8.99 (978-1-4169-6437-7(1), Aladdin) Simon & Schuster Children's Publishing.

—Fashion Frenzy. 2006. (Beacon Street Girls Ser.: No. 9). (Illus.). 203p. (J). (gr. 4-8). per. 7.99 (978-1-933566-02-3(7), Beacon Street Girls) B*tween Productions, Inc.

—Freaked Out. 2009. (Beacon Street Girls Ser.: 7). (ENG.). 272p. (J). (gr. 4-8). pap. 8.99 (978-1-4169-6433-9(9), Aladdin) Simon & Schuster Children's Publishing.

—Freestyle with Avery. 2009. (Beacon Street Girls Ser.). (ENG.). 240p. (J). (gr. 4-8). pap. 8.99 (978-1-4169-6435-3(5), Aladdin) Simon & Schuster Children's Publishing.

—Ghost Town. 2007. (Beacon Street Girls Ser.: No. 11). (Illus.). 217p. (J). (gr. 4-7). per. 7.10 (978-1-933566-09-2(4)) B*tween Productions, Inc.

—Ghost Town. 2009. (Beacon Street Girls Ser.: 11). (ENG.). 240p. (J). (gr. 4-8). pap. 7.99 (978-1-4169-6441-4(X), Aladdin) Simon & Schuster Children's Publishing.

—The Great Scavenger Hunt. 2009. (Beacon Street Girls Ser.: 15). (ENG.). 304p. (J). (gr. 4-8). pap. 8.99 (978-1-4169-6442-1(8), Aladdin) Simon & Schuster Children's Publishing.

—Green Algae & Bubble Gum Wars. 2008. (Beacon Street Girls Ser.: 13). (ENG.). 256p. (J). (gr. 4-8). pap. 7.99 (978-1-4169-6429-2(0), Aladdin) Simon & Schuster Children's Publishing.

—Isabel's Texas Two-Step. 2008. (Beacon Street Girls Ser.: No. 5). (ENG.). 256p. (J). (gr. 4-8). pap. 7.99 (978-1-4169-6423-0(1), Aladdin) Simon & Schuster Children's Publishing.

—Just Kidding. 2007. (Beacon Street Girls Ser.: No. 10). (Illus.). 247p. (J). (gr. 3-8). per. 7.99 (978-1-933566-07-8(8)) B*tween Productions, Inc.

—Just Kidding. 2009. (Beacon Street Girls Ser.: 10). (ENG.). 256p. (J). (gr. 4-8). pap. 7.99 (978-1-4169-6440-7(1), Aladdin) Simon & Schuster Children's Publishing.

—Lake Rescue. 2008. (Beacon Street Girls Ser.: 6). (ENG.). 256p. (J). (gr. 4-8). pap. 7.99 (978-1-4169-6431-5(2), Aladdin) Simon & Schuster Children's Publishing.

—Letters from the Heart. 2008. (Beacon Street Girls Ser.: 3). (ENG., Illus.). 256p. (J). (gr. 4-8). pap. 6.99 (978-1-4169-6426-1(6), Aladdin) Simon & Schuster Children's Publishing.

—Lucky Charm. 2006. (Beacon Street Girls Ser.: No. 8). (Illus.). 233p. (J). (gr. 4-8). per. 7.99 (978-0-9758511-9-7(5)) B*tween Productions, Inc.

—Lucky Charm. 2009. (Beacon Street Girls Ser.: 8). (ENG.). 272p. (J). (gr. 4-8). pap. 9.99 (978-1-4169-6434-6(7), Aladdin) Simon & Schuster Children's Publishing.

—Maeve on the Red Carpet. 2007. (Beacon Street Girls Special Adventure Ser.: No. 3). 221p. (J). (gr. 4-7). per. 7.10 (978-1-933566-08-5(6)) B*tween Productions, Inc.

—Maeve on the Red Carpet. 2009. (Beacon Street Girls Ser.: No. 3). (ENG.). 240p. (J). (gr. 4-8). pap. 6.99 (978-1-4169-6432-2(0), Aladdin) Simon & Schuster Children's Publishing.

—Out of Bounds. 2008. (Beacon Street Girls Ser.: 4). (ENG., Illus.). 288p. (J). (gr. 4-8). pap. 8.99 (978-1-4169-6427-8(4), Aladdin) Simon & Schuster Children's Publishing.

—Ready! Set! Hawaii! 2009. (Beacon Street Girls Ser.: No. 7). (ENG.). 304p. (J). (gr. 4-8). pap. 8.99 (978-1-4169-6436-0(3), Aladdin) Simon & Schuster Children's Publishing.

—Sweet Thirteen. 2009. (Beacon Street Girls Ser.: 16). (ENG.). 304p. (J). (gr. 4-8). pap. 7.99 (978-1-4169-6438-4(X), Aladdin) Simon & Schuster Children's Publishing.

—Time's Up. 2008. (Beacon Street Girls Ser.: 12). (ENG.). 208p. (J). (gr. 4-8). pap. 7.99 (978-1-4169-6422-3(3), Aladdin) Simon & Schuster Children's Publishing.

—Worst Enemies/Best Friends. 2004. (Beacon Street Girls Ser.: No. 1). 232p. (J). 7.99 (978-0-9746587-6-6(6), Beacon Street Girls) B*tween Productions, Inc.

—Worst Enemies/Best Friends. 2008. (Beacon Street Girls Ser.: 1). (ENG.). 240p. (J). (gr. 4-8). pap. 8.99 (978-1-4169-6424-7(X), Aladdin) Simon & Schuster Children's Publishing.

Bryant, Bonnie. Horse Play. 2007. (Saddle Club(R) Ser.: No. 7). (ENG.). 144p. (J). (gr. 3-7). 5.99 (978-0-553-15754-3(X), Yearling) Random Hse. Children's Bks.

Bryant, Jim. An Apple for Rose. 2009. 28p. pap. 12.49 (978-1-4389-4879-9(4)) AuthorHouse.

Bryant, Phoebe. What Is That in the Air? A play date with Sayde. 2009. (Illus.). 28p. pap. 12.99 (978-1-4490-2209-9(X)) AuthorHouse.

Bryce, Celia. Anthem for Jackson Dawes. 2013. (ENG.). 240p. (YA). (gr. 7-12). 16.99 (978-1-59990-975-2(8), 9781599909752, Bloomsbury USA Childrens) Bloomsbury Publishing USA.

Bryce, Conor. Wesco P. Mcsnaffle & the Great Brave Quest. 2008. 127p. pap. 22.50 (978-1-4092-1273-7(4)) Lulu Pr., Inc.

Bryson, Brenda. The Adventures of Roo & Winston. 2007. 78p. pap. 12.95 (978-1-4357-0145-8(3)) Lulu Pr., Inc.

Buchanan, Andrea J. Gift. 2012. (ENG.). 326p. (YA). (gr. 7-12). pap. 9.99 (978-1-4532-2023-8(2), Open Road Media E-riginal) Open Road Integrated Media, Inc.

Buchanan, Darlene. Smiley's World. 2009. 64p. pap. 11.49 (978-1-4490-2675-2(3)) AuthorHouse.

Buchanan, Paul & Buchanan, P. The Last Place I Want to Be, 1 vol. 2009. 176p. (J). pap. 7.99 (978-0-8254-2408-3(9)) Kregel Pubns.

Buchwald, Emilie. Floramel & Esteban. Robinson, Charles, illus. 2009. (ENG.). 80p. (J). (gr. 1-6). 16.95 (978-1-57131-688-2(4)) Milkweed Editions.

Buckeridge, Anthony. Jennings' Little Hut. l.t. ed. 2005. (Dales Ser.). (Illus.). 272p. (J). 23.99 (978-1-84262-370-1(2)) Magna Large Print Bks. GBR. Dist: Ulverscroft Large Print Bks., Ltd.

Buckingham-Smith, Celestia. College Life in Paradise: Hawaiian Style, 1 vol. 2010. 260p. pap. 27.95 (978-1-4489-6689-9(2)) America Star Bks.

Buckmaster, Heath L. The Venus Diary. 2008. 136p. pap. 13.50 (978-0-615-20678-3(6));Bk. 2. 132p. (YA). lib. bdg. 19.95 (978-0-9771802-6-4(3)) Transaltar Publishing.

Buddenberg, Laura J. & Montgomery, Alesia K. Friend Me: 10 Awesome Steps to Fun & Friendship. 2012. (ENG., Illus.). 130p. (J). pap. 9.95 (978-1-934490-38-9(5)) Boys Town Pr.

Budhos, Marina. Tell Us We're Home. (ENG.). (YA). (gr. 7). 2011. 320p. pap. 9.99 (978-1-4424-2128-8(2)) 2010. 304p. 17.99 (978-1-4169-0352-9(6)) Simon & Schuster Children's Publishing. (Atheneum Bks. for Young Readers).

Budic, Hannah Purdy. Ebenezer Flea & the Right Thing to Do, 1 vol. Rosendahl, Melissa M., illus. 2008. (ENG.). 30p. 24.95 (978-1-60441-750-0(1)) America Star Bks.

Bulbring, Edyth. Cornelia Button & the Globe of Gamagion. 2009. (ENG.). 208p. (J). (gr. 4-7). pap. 18.00 (978-1-77009-501-4(2)) Jacana Media ZAF. Dist: Independent Pubs. Group.

—100 Days of April-May. 2013. (April-May Ser.). (ENG.). 224p. (J). (gr. 4-7). pap. 9.99 (978-1-4714-0051-3(4)) Bonnier Publishing GBR. Dist: Independent Pubs. Group.

Bulion, Leslie. The Trouble with Rules, 1 vol. (ENG.). 160p. (J). 2011. pap. 6.95 (978-1-56145-576-8(8)) 2008. (gr. 2-6). 14.95 (978-1-56145-440-2(0)) Peachtree Pubs.

Bullock, Miranda. Mama Where Are You? 2008. 36p. pap. 16.99 (978-1-4389-2962-0(5)) AuthorHouse.

Bumble's Sweet Surprise. 2003. (Daisy Board Books Ser.). 10p. (J). bds. 9.95 (978-0-7525-8297-9(6)) Parragon, Inc.

Bunting, Eve. Frog & Friends. 2012. (I AM a READER! Frog & Friends Ser.: 4). (ENG., Illus.). 48p. (J). (gr. 1-3). pap. 3.99 (978-1-58536-806-8(7)) Sleeping Bear Pr.

—Frog & Friends. Masse, Josée, illus. 2011. (I Am A Reader! Ser.). (ENG.). 40p. (gr. k-3). pap. 3.99 (978-1-58536-689-7(7)); lib. bdg. 9.95 (978-1-58536-548-7(3)) Sleeping Bear Pr.

—Frog & Friends: Frog's Flying Adventure. 2012. (I AM a READER! Frog & Friends Ser.: 4). (ENG., Illus.). 48p. (J). (gr. 1-3). 9.95 (978-1-58536-805-1(9)) Sleeping Bear Pr.

—Frog & Friends: Outdoor Surprises. Masse, Josée, illus. 2013. (I AM a READER!: Frog & Friends Ser.). (ENG.). 48p. (J). (gr. 1-2). 9.95 (978-1-58536-807-5(5), 202361); pap. 3.99 (978-1-58536-808-2(3), 202370) Sleeping Bear Pr.

—Frog & Friends: The Best Summer Ever. 2012. (I Am A Reader!, Frog & Friends Ser.). (ENG., Illus.). 48p. (J). (gr. k-3). pap. 3.99 (978-1-58536-691-0(9)); lib. bdg. 9.95 (978-1-58536-550-0(5)) Sleeping Bear Pr.

—Frog & Friends Celebrate Thanksgiving, Christmas, & New Year's Eve. Masse, Josée, illus. 2015. (I AM a READER!: Frog & Friends Ser.). (ENG.). 40p. (J). (gr. 1-2). 9.99 (978-1-58536-897-6(0), 203949) Sleeping Bear Pr.

—Frog's Lucky Day. Masse, Josée, illus. 2014. (I Am a Reader!: Frog & Friends Ser.). (ENG.). 40p. (J). (gr. 1-2). 9.99 (978-1-58536-892-1(X), 203014) Sleeping Bear Pr.

—I Love You, Too! Sweet, Melissa, illus. 2015. (ENG.). 24p. (J). (— 1). bds. 7.99 (978-0-545-81390-7(5), Cartwheel Bks.) Scholastic, Inc.

—My Robot. Fehlau, Dagmar, illus. 2006. (Green Light Readers Level 2 Ser.). (ENG.). 24p. (J). (gr. -1-3). pap. 3.95 (978-0-15-205617-9(3)) Houghton Mifflin Harcourt Publishing Co.

—My Robot. Fehlau, Dagmar, illus. 2006. (Green Light Readers Level 2 Ser.). (gr. k-2). lib. bdg. 13.95 (978-0-7569-7211-0(6)) Perfection Learning Corp.

—Snowboarding on Monster Mountain. Ritz, Karen, illus. 2003. (ENG.). 64p. (J). 15.95 (978-0-8126-2704-6(0)) Cricket Bks.

Burach, Ross. Pine & Boof: the Lucky Leaf. Burach, Ross, illus. 2017. (Illus.). 40p. (J). (gr. -1-3). 17.99 **(978-0-06-241850-0(5))** HarperCollins Pubs.

Burchett, Loni R. Bear & Katie in a Day with Friends, Vol. 3. l.t. ed. 2005. (Illus.). 68p. (J). per. 11.95 (978-0-9742815-2-0(2), bk003) Black Lab Publishing LLC.

Burgess, Melvin. El Fantasma tras la Pared. (SPA.). (J). 8.95 (978-958-04-6483-9(9)) Norma S.A. COL. Dist: Distribuidora Norma, Inc.

Burgess, Thornton W. The Adventures of Prickly Porky. 2007. 140p. (gr. 4-7). per. 11.95 (978-1-60312-048-7(3)); 24.95 (978-1-60312-953-4(7)) Aegypan.

—The Adventures of Prickly Porky. 2011. 138p. 25.95 (978-1-4638-9572-3(0)) Rodgers, Alan Bks.

—Billy Mink. Cady, Harrison, illus. 2012. (Dover Children's Thrift Classics Ser.). (ENG.). 128p. (J). (gr. k-3). pap. 4.00 (978-0-486-48107-4(7)) Dover Pubns., Inc.

—Mother West Wind 'How' Stories. 2008. 108p. (gr. -1-3). 22.95 (978-1-60664-893-3(4)); pap. 9.95 (978-1-60664-012-8(7)) Aegypan.

Burggraaf, Deborah. Crow No More. Lumsden, Matt, illus. 2011. 28p. (J). pap. 10.95 (978-0-9845161-8-6(2)) Protective Hands Communications.

Burke, Christina. Melvin et le Grand Match de Hockey. Minguet, Anne, tr. Franfou, illus. 2013. 52p. (978-0-9918561-3-8(9)); pap. (978-0-9918561-2-1(0)) Stars Aligned Publishing.

Burke, Ruth. Gowandale Adventure: And other stories for Boys. 2007. (Illus.). 96p. 9.00 (978-1-84625-070-5(6)) DayOne Pubns. GBR. Dist: Send The Light Distribution LLC.

Burket, Shelia. Silver & Gold: Sissy Stringbean Meets Morris Norris. 2012. 28p. 24.95 (978-1-4626-3591-7(1)) America Star Bks.

Burkhart, Jessica. Behind the Bit. 2009. (Canterwood Crest Ser.: 3). (ENG.). 272p. (J). (gr. 4-8). pap. 7.99 (978-1-4169-5842-0(8), Aladdin) Simon & Schuster Children's Publishing.

—Best Enemies. 2009. (Canterwood Crest Ser.: 5). (ENG.). 272p. (J). (gr. 4-8). pap. 7.99 (978-1-4169-9037-6(2), Aladdin) Simon & Schuster Children's Publishing.

—Canterwood Crest Stable of Stories: Take the Reins; Chasing Blue; Behind the Bit; Triple Fault. 2014. (Canterwood Crest Ser.). (ENG., Illus.). 1088p. (J). (gr. 4-8). pap. 31.99 (978-1-4814-1474-6(7), Aladdin) Simon & Schuster Children's Publishing.

—Chasing Blue. 2009. (Canterwood Crest Ser.: 2). (ENG.). 272p. (J). (gr. 4-8). pap. 7.99 (978-1-4169-5841-3(X), Aladdin) Simon & Schuster Children's Publishing.

—Comeback. 2012. (Canterwood Crest Ser.: 15). (ENG.). 208p. (J). (gr. 5-8). pap. 7.99 (978-1-4424-1952-0(0), Aladdin) Simon & Schuster Children's Publishing.

—Home for Christmas. 2013. (Canterwood Crest Ser.). lib. bdg. 18.40 (978-0-606-32322-2(8), Turtleback) Turtleback Bks.

—Home for Christmas: Super Special. 2013. (Canterwood Crest Ser.). (ENG., Illus.). 240p. (J). (gr. 4-8). pap. 7.99 (978-1-4424-3661-9(1), Aladdin) Simon & Schuster Children's Publishing.

—Initiation. 2012. (Canterwood Crest Ser.: 13). (ENG.). 320p. (J). (gr. 4-8). pap. 7.99 (978-1-4424-1948-3(2), Aladdin) Simon & Schuster Children's Publishing.

—Little White Lies. 2009. (Canterwood Crest Ser.: 6). (ENG.). 240p. (J). (gr. 4-8). pap. 7.99 (978-1-4169-9038-3(0), Aladdin) Simon & Schuster Children's Publishing.

—Masquerade. 2012. (Canterwood Crest Ser.: 16). (ENG.). 256p. (J). (gr. 4-7). pap. 7.99 (978-1-4424-3655-8(7), Aladdin) Simon & Schuster Children's Publishing.

—Scandals, Rumors, Lies. 2010. (Canterwood Crest Ser.: 11). lib. bdg. 18.40 (978-0-606-15241-9(5), Turtleback) Turtleback Bks.

—Take the Reins. 2009. (Canterwood Crest Ser.: 1). (ENG.). 256p. (J). (gr. 4-8). pap. 7.99 (978-1-4169-5840-6(1), Aladdin) Simon & Schuster Children's Publishing.

—Triple Fault. 2009. (Canterwood Crest Ser.: 4). (ENG.). 288p. (J). (gr. 4-8). pap. 7.99 (978-1-4169-5843-7(6), Aladdin) Simon & Schuster Children's Publishing.

—Unfriendly Competition. 2011. (Canterwood Crest Ser.: 12). (ENG.). 192p. (J). (gr. 4-8). pap. 7.99 (978-1-4424-0386-4(1), Aladdin) Simon & Schuster Children's Publishing.

Burkhart, Kiersi & Keyser, Amber J. At Top Speed. 2017. (Quartz Creek Ranch Ser.). (ENG.). 240p. (J). (gr. 4-8). 27.99 (978-1-4677-9255-4(1)) Lerner Publishing Group.

—One Brave Summer. 2017. (Quartz Creek Ranch Ser.). (ENG.). 224p. (J). (gr. 4-8). 27.99 (978-1-4677-9254-7(3)) Lerner Publishing Group.

Burkhart, Lorene. Raccoon Tales: Hip, Flip, Skip & Boo & Their Friend Stu. 2007. (Illus.). (J). 8.95 (978-0-9790975-1-5(7)) Burkhart Bks.

Burks, Megan. Sally the Circle. 2012. 28p. pap. 21.99 (978-1-4771-3343-9(7)) Xlibris Corp.

Burnette, Leon P. Peeka-Boo Fables: Land of the Golems. 2012. 24p. pap. 15.99 (978-1-4797-4616-3(9)) Xlibris Corp.

Burnham, Molly B. Almost an Outlaw. Spencer, Trevor, illus. 2017. (Teddy Mars Ser.: 3). 288p. (J). (gr. 3-7). 16.99 (978-0-06-227816-6(9), Tegen, Katherine Bks) HarperCollins Pubs.

—Teddy Mars: Almost a World Record Breaker. Spencer, Trevor, illus. (Teddy Mars Ser.: 2). (J). (gr. 3-7). 2016. 288p. 16.99 (978-0-06-227813-5(4), Tegen, Katherine Bks) 2016. 240p. pap. 6.99 (978-0-06-227811-1(8), Tegen, Katherine Bks) 2015. (ENG.). 224p. 16.99 (978-0-06-227810-4(X)) HarperCollins Pubs.

Burningham, John. Picnic. Burningham, John, illus. 2014. (ENG., Illus.). 32p. (J). (-k). 16.99 (978-0-7636-6945-4(8)) Candlewick Pr.

Burns, Catherine Lloyd. The Good, the Bad & the Beagle. 2014. (ENG.). 336p. (J). (gr. 5-7). 16.99 (978-0-374-30039-5(9), 9780374300395, Farrar, Straus & Giroux (BYR)) Farrar, Straus & Giroux.

Burns, Laura J. Bewitched in Oz, 1 vol. Peters, Liam, illus. 2014. (Bewitched in Oz Ser.). (ENG.). 256p. (gr. 4-8). 12.95 (978-1-62370-129-1(5)); lib. bdg. 30.65 (978-1-4342-9207-0(X)) Stone Arch Bks.

Burroughs, Scott, illus. Hopping Mad. 2010. (Hardy Boys: the Secret Files Ser.: 4). (ENG.). 96p. (J). (gr. 1-4). pap. 5.99 (978-1-4169-9395-7(9), Aladdin) Simon & Schuster Children's Publishing.

—A Monster of a Mystery. 2011. (Hardy Boys: the Secret Files Ser.: 5). (ENG.). 96p. (J). (gr. 1-4). pap. 4.99 (978-1-4169-9166-3(2), Aladdin) Simon & Schuster Children's Publishing.

—Mystery Map. 2010. (Hardy Boys: the Secret Files Ser.: 3). (ENG.). 96p. (J). (gr. 1-4). pap. 5.99 (978-1-4169-9165-6(4), Aladdin) Simon & Schuster Children's Publishing.

Burrows, Jennifer S. Most Beautiful. 2012. (ENG.). 50p. (J). (gr. 4-7). pap. 9.99 (978-0-89824-376-5(9)) Royal Fireworks Publishing Co.

Burton, Martin Nelson. Dear Mr. Leprechaun: Letters from My First Friendship. Hansen, Clint, illus. Tanner, Dean, photos by. 2003. (ENG.). 32p. (J). 17.00 (978-0-9666490-0-0(1)) London Town Pr.

Burton, Rebecca. Leaving Jetty Road. 2004. 272p. (978-0-207-20015-1(7)) HarperCollins Pubs. Australia.

Burton, Virginia Lee. La Casita.Tr. of Little House. (SPA., Illus.). (J). (gr. 1-2). pap. 9.95 (978-970-629-050-2(8), SI6411) Sistemas Tecnicos de Edicion, S.A. de C.V. MEX. Dist: AIMS International Bks., Inc.

Burwick, Josh. Dad, I Wish I Was Your Age. Monroe, Dan, illus. 2012. 40p. (J). pap. 14.99 (978-0-9852146-3-0(5)) AM Ink Publishing.

Busch, Darcy J. Lily & the Hidden Secrets, 1 vol. 2009. 164p. pap. 24.95 (978-1-60836-498-5(4)) America Star Bks.

Busch, Jean. Colleen & the Willow Fairy. 2008. 48p. pap. 16.95 (978-1-60672-212-1(3)) America Star Bks.

Bush, Emilie P. Steamduck Learns to Fly! Petty, William Kevin, illus. 2012. 36p. pap. 11.95 (978-0-9849028-1-1(3)) Coal City Stories.

Bush, Leanne. A Very Special Christmas with Grandm. 2008. 18p. pap. 24.95 (978-1-4241-9777-4(5)) America Star Bks.

Bush, Martha Faircloth. Helping Hurting Children: a Journey of Healing: Children's Workbook. 2013. 174p. pap. 19.95 (978-1-4497-8527-7(1), WestBow Pr.) Author Solutions, Inc.

Bushman, Janet. A Shiny Red Apple. 2010. 16p. 8.95 (978-1-4389-7861-1(8)) AuthorHouse.

Bushnell, Candace. The Carrie Diaries. (Carrie Diaries: 1). (ENG.). (YA). (gr. 9). 2011. 416p. pap. 9.99 (978-0-06-172892-1(6)) 2010. 400p. 18.99 (978-0-06-172891-4(8)) 2012. 416p. pap. 10.99 (978-0-06-223684-5(9)) HarperCollins Pubs.

—Summer & the City. (Carrie Diaries: 2). (ENG.). 416p. (YA). (gr. 9). 2012. pap. 9.99 (978-0-06-172900-3(0)) 2013. pap. 10.99 (978-0-06-223686-9(5)) HarperCollins Pubs.

Bussereth, Bianca. Sky Rod. 2010. 80p. pap. 6.95 (978-1-60594-391-6(6), Llumina Pr.) Aeon Publishing Inc.

Bustard, Anne. Anywhere but Paradise. 2015. (ENG.). 288p. (gr. 5). 16.99 (978-1-60684-585-1(3)); (J). 16.99 (978-1-5124-0110-3(2)) Lerner Publishing Group. (Carolrhoda Bks.).

Butcher, Derek. Max the ed up Dog: Max & Matts Adventures. 2009. 56p. pap. 10.49 (978-1-4389-6551-2(6)) AuthorHouse.

Butineau, W. Turning Thirteen. 2005. 165p. pap. 24.95 (978-1-4137-5817-7(7)) America Star Bks.

Butler, Berwyn. Dinky the Doorknob: The Adventures of Sir Dinkum Wilhelm, the Third Earl of Surridge. 2005. (J). per. 11.95 (978-1-933732-02-2(4)) Big Ransom Studio.

Butler, Berwyn & McClean, Shorty. Dinky the Doorknob. 2006. (J). lib. bdg. 21.95 (978-1-933732-04-6(0)) Big Ransom Studio.

Butler, Berwyn G. Amazing Moonshine Mcpool. 2012. 72p. pap. 41.99 (978-1-4691-5185-4(5)) Xlibris Corp.

Butler, Darren J. The Secret of Crybaby Hollow. 2004. (YA). mass mkt. 6.99 (978-0-9753367-5-5(4)) Onstage Publishing, LLC.

Butler, Dori Hillestad. The Haunted Library #1. Damant, Aurore, illus. 2014. (Haunted Library: 1). (ENG.). 128p. (J).

(gr. 1-3). 5.99 (978-0-448-46242-4(7), Grosset & Dunlap) Penguin Young Readers Group.
—Trading Places with Tank Talbott. 2003. (ENG.). 144p. (J). (gr. 3-7). 15.99 (978-0-8075-1708-6(9)) Whitman, Albert & Co.
Butler, M. Christina. One Noisy Night. Macnaughton, Tina, illus. 2016. (ENG.). 32p. (J). (gr. -1-2). 16.99 (978-1-68010-034-1(3)) Tiger Tales.
—Snow Friends. Macnaughton, Tina, illus. 2016. (ENG.). 16p. (J). (— 1). bds. 9.99 (978-1-5107-1116-7(3), Sky Pony Pr.) Skyhorse Publishing Co., Inc.
Butler, Shirley. The First-Class Adventure of Flat Freddie. 2008. 60p. pap. 19.95 (978-1-60672-882-6(2)) America Star Bks.
Butterworth, Nick. Albert the Bear to the Rescue. 2008. (J). 16.99 (978-0-06-147046-2(5)) HarperCollins Pubs.
Buxbaum, Julie. What to Say Next. 2017. (ENG.). 304p. (YA). (gr. 7). 18.99 (978-0-553-53568-6(4), Delacorte Pr.) Random Hse. Children's Bks.
Buyea, Robert W. Saving Mr. Terupt. 2015. (ENG.). 384p. (J). (gr. 4-7). lib. bdg. 19.99 (978-0-375-99120-2(4), Delacorte Bks. for Young Readers) Random Hse. Children's Bks.
Buzo, Laura. Love & Other Perishable Items. (ENG.). 256p. (YA). (gr. 9). 2013. pap. 8.99 (978-0-307-92974-7(4), Ember) 2012. 17.99 (978-0-375-87000-2(8), Knopf Bks. for Young Readers) Random Hse. Children's Bks.
Byars, Betsy. The Blossoms Meet the Vulture Lady. 2008. (Blossom Family Book Ser.: 2). (ENG., Illus.). 134p. (J). (gr. 4-7). 6.95 (978-0-8234-2144-2(9)) Holiday Hse., Inc.
—The Cybil War. l.t. ed. 2003. (LRS Large Print Heritage Ser.). 122p. (J). lib. bdg. 27.95 (978-1-58118-111-1(6)) LRS.
—King of Murder. 2007. (Herculeah Jones Mystery Ser.). (ENG.). 144p. (J). (gr. 3-7). 5.99 (978-0-14-240759-2(3), Puffin Books) Penguin Young Readers Group.
—The Pinballs. 137p. (J). (gr. 4-6). pap. 4.95 (978-0-8072-1383-4(7)); pap. 4.95 (978-0-8072-1356-8(X)) Random Hse. Audio Publishing Group. (Listening Library).
Byars, Betsy & Byars. The Pinballs. 2004. (Apple Paperback Ser.). (ENG.). 144p. (J). (gr. 3-7). pap. 6.99 (978-0-06-440198-2(7)) HarperCollins Pubs.
Byng, Georgia. Molly Moon y el Increible Libro. 2003. (SPA.). 349p. (J). 18.99 (978-84-348-9076-3(3)) SM Ediciones ESP. Dist: Lectorum Pubns., Inc.
—Molly Moon's Incredible Book of Hypnotism. 2003. 135.92 (978-0-06-057217-4(5)) 2003. (Molly Moon Ser.: 1). (Illus.). 384p. (J). (gr. 3-7). 17.99 (978-0-06-051406-8(X)) 2004. (Molly Moon Ser.: 1). (ENG., Illus.). 384p. (J). (gr. 3-7). reprint ed. pap. 7.99 (978-0-06-051409-9(4)) HarperCollins Pubs.
—Molly Moon's Incredible Book of Hypnotism. 2004. (Molly Moon Ser.). 371p. (gr. 3-7). 18.00 (978-0-7569-3484-2(2)) Perfection Learning Corp.
Byrd, Betty. They Call Me Pharaoh. 2008. 20p. pap. 24.95 (978-1-60563-008-3(X)) America Star Bks.
Byrd, Debbie. Ayla by the Sea. 2010. 28p. pap. 13.99 (978-1-4520-6454-3(7)) AuthorHouse.
Byrd, Jeff, illus. A Tale of Two Tails, el Perro con Dos Colas: A children's story in English & Spanish. 2004.Tr. of Perro con Dos Colas. (SPA.). (J). (gr. -1-3). per. 14.95 (978-0-9746024-0-0(X)) One Arm Publishing.
Byrd, Lee Merrill. Treasure on Gold Street/El Tesoro de la Calle D'Oro: A Neighborhood Story in Spanish & English. Castro L., Antonio, illus. 2003. (ENG & SPA.). 40p. (J). (gr. 4-6). 16.95 (978-0-938317-75-3(X)) Cinco Puntos Pr.
—El Ttesoro en la Calle Oro: A Neighborhood Story in English & Spanish. Franco, Sharon, tr. Castro L., Antonio, illus. 2007.Tr. of Treasure on Gold Street. (SPA & ENG.). 40p. (J). (gr. 4-6). pap. 8.95 (978-1-933693-11-8(8)) Cinco Puntos Pr.
Byrd, Michael. The Adventures of Banter & Jafar: Spoiled Rotten, 1 vol. Bai, Jenny, illus. 2009. 36p. pap. 24.95 (978-1-60836-131-1(4)) America Star Bks.
Byrne, Bob. Robots Don't Cry. 2006. (Flyers Ser.: 15). (ENG., Illus.). 64p. (J). pap. 9.95 (978-1-84717-005-7(6)) O'Brien Pr., Ltd., The IRL. Dist: Dufour Editions, Inc.
Byrne, Marlene. Follow the Leader. Graber, Jesse, illus. 2009. (ENG.). 39p. (J). 14.99 (978-0-9777135-1-6(2)) Celtic Marketing Inc.
Byrne, Marlene F. Treasure Hunt. Graber, Jesse, illus. 2009. 36p. (J). 14.99 (978-0-9777135-0-9(4)) Celtic Marketing Inc.
Byrne, Richard. Spotty Lottie & Me. Byrne, Richard, illus. 2015. (ENG., Illus.). 32p. (J). 22.99 (978-1-78344-117-4(8)) Andersen Pr. GBR. Dist: Independent Pubs. Group.
Byun, You. Dream Friends. Byun, You, illus. 2013. (ENG., Illus.). 32p. (J). (gr. -1-k). 16.99 (978-0-399-25739-1(X), Nancy Paulsen Books) Penguin Young Readers Group.
C. Larene Hall. Martha's Freedom Train. 2009. 100p. pap. 10.49 (978-1-4389-7977-9(0)) AuthorHouse.
Cabot, Meg. Moving Day. 2009. (Allie Finkle's Rules for Girls Ser.: Bk. 1). (ENG.). 256p. (J). (gr. 3-7). 6.99 (978-0-545-04041-9(8), Scholastic Paperbacks) Scholastic, Inc.
—Moving Day. 2009. (Allie Finkle's Rules for Girls Ser.: 1). lib. bdg. 17.20 (978-0-606-06818-5(X), Turtleback) Turtleback Bks.
—The New Girl. 2008. (Allie Finkle's Rules for Girls Ser.: 2). (ENG.). 240p. (J). (gr. 3-7). 15.99 (978-0-545-04049-5(3), Scholastic Pr.) Scholastic, Inc.
—Stage Fright. 2010. (Allie Finkle's Rules for Girls Ser.: 4). (ENG.). 240p. (J). (gr. 3-7). 6.99 (978-0-545-04046-4(9)) Scholastic, Inc.
Cabrini, Joe. Chicco's Nicedream Van - Daniel's Winning Goal. Cabrini, Joe, illus. 2007. (Illus.). 32p. per. (978-0-7552-0300-0(3)) Authors OnLine, Ltd.
Cadell, Ava. NeuroLoveology: The Power to Mindful Love & Sex. 2014. (ENG.). 310p. pap. 14.99 (978-1-4976-6112-7(9)) Open Road Integrated Media, Inc.
Cafaro, Phyllis. Captain Mcfinn & Friends Meet Coral Rose. 2012. (ENG.). 24p. (J). 19.99 (978-0-9799283-5-2(4), 9780979928352) Cold River Pubns.
Cafaro, Phyllis C. Captain Mcfinn & Friends Encounter the Bully Bunker. 2012. (ENG., Illus.). 24p. (J). 17.99 (978-0-9859482-2-1(1), 9780985948221); pap. 9.99 (978-0-9859482-3-8(X), 9780985948238) Cold River Pubns.
Cagan, Kayla. Piper Perish. 2017. (ENG., Illus.). 416p. (YA). 17.99 (978-1-4521-5583-8(6)) Chronicle Bks. LLC.
Cahill, Bear. We're Brothers & Sisters. Collier, Kevin Scott, illus. 2008. 20p. pap. 9.95 (978-1-933090-70-2(7)) Guardian Angel Publishing, Inc.
Caird, Frankie Telfer. The Secret of Ellis Meadow. 2013. 160p. pap. 12.95 (978-1-60911-616-3(X), Strategic Bk. Publishing) Strategic Book Publishing & Rights Agency (SBPRA).
Calame, Don. Call the Shots. 2013. (ENG.). 464p. (YA). (gr. 9). pap. 7.99 (978-0-7636-6454-1(5)) Candlewick Pr.
—Swim the Fly. 2009. (ENG., Illus.). 352p. (YA). (gr. 9). 16.99 (978-0-7636-4157-3(X)) Candlewick Pr.
Calder, C. J. Busy Truck, 1 vol. Rooney, Ronnie & Peterson, Shauna, illus. 2012. (Truck Buddies Ser.). (ENG.). 16p. (gr. -1-k). bds. 7.95 (978-1-4342-4388-1(5)) Stone Arch Bks.
Caldwell, Daisy L. Sarah the Oh So Silly, but Shy Stegosaurus, 1 vol. 2009. 24p. pap. 24.95 (978-1-61546-319-0(4)) America Star Bks.
Caletti, Deb. The Last Forever. 2014. (ENG., Illus.). 336p. (YA). (gr. 7-7). 17.99 (978-1-4424-5000-4(2), Simon Pulse) Simon Pulse.
Callaghan, Cindy. Sydney Mackenzie Knocks 'Em Dead. 2017. (ENG., Illus.). 256p. (J). (gr. 4-8). 17.99 (978-1-4814-6569-4(4), Simon & Schuster/Paula Wiseman Bks.) Simon & Schuster/Paula Wiseman Bks.
Callahan, Susan. Always Right. 2012. 20p. pap. 15.99 (978-1-4772-0424-5(5)) AuthorHouse.
—A New Way. 2012. 20p. pap. 17.99 (978-1-4772-4507-1(3)) AuthorHouse.
Callen, Sharon. Boris & Bea, 1 vol. 2013. (Fiction Readers Ser.). (ENG., Illus.). 24p. (J). (gr. 2-2). pap. 6.99 (978-1-4333-5530-1(2)) Shell Educational Publishing.
—Max, 1 vol. rev. ed. 2013. (Fiction Readers Ser.). (ENG., Illus.). 12p. (J). (gr. 1-1). 4.99 (978-1-4333-5452-6(7)); pap. 12.96 (978-1-4807-1131-0(4)) Shell Educational Publishing.
—Soo Yun's Book, 1 vol. 2013. (Fiction Readers Ser.). (ENG., Illus.). 28p. (J). (gr. 2-2). pap. 6.99 (978-1-4333-5573-8(6)) Shell Educational Publishing.
—What Can You See?, 1 vol. rev. ed. 2013. (Fiction Readers Ser.). (ENG., Illus.). 20p. (J). (gr. 1-1). pap. 4.99 (978-1-4333-5490-8(X)); pap. 15.96 (978-1-4807-1146-4(2)) Shell Educational Publishing.
Calloway, Nathaniel. The Missing Tape Recorder: An Original Child's Tale. 2013. 12p. pap. 12.68 (978-1-4669-6423-5(5)) Trafford Publishing.
Calmenson, Stephanie. May I Pet Your Dog? The How-to Guide for Kids Meeting Dogs (and Dogs Meeting Kids) Ormerod, Jan, illus. 2007. (ENG.). 32p. (J). (gr. -1-3). 13.99 (978-0-618-51034-4(6), Clarion Bks.) Houghton Mifflin Harcourt Trade & Reference Pubs.
Calmenson, Stephanie & Cole, Joanna. Hot Diggity Dogs. Ross, Heather, illus. 2015. (Ready, Set, Dogs! Ser.: 2). (ENG.). 112p. (J). (gr. 1-4). 14.99 (978-0-8050-9649-1(3), 9780805096491, Holt, Henry & Co. Bks. For Young Readers) Holt, Henry & Co.
—No Dogs Allowed. Ross, Heather, illus. 2014. (Ready, Set, Dogs! Ser.: 1). (ENG.). 144p. (J). (gr. 1-4). pap. 5.99 (978-1-250-04414-3(6), 9781250044143) Square Fish.
—Teacher's Pets. Ross, Heather, illus. 2015. (Ready, Set, Dogs! Ser.: 2). (ENG.). 144p. (J). (gr. 1-4). pap. 5.99 (978-1-250-05705-1(1), 9781250057051) Square Fish.
Calonita, Jen. Battle of the Bands. 2016. (VIP Ser.: 2). (ENG., Illus.). 320p. (J). (gr. 3-7). 16.99 (978-0-316-25977-4(2)) Little, Brown Bks. for Young Readers.
Calucag, Angela. Little Freddy S Journey. 2012. 32p. pap. 17.99 (978-1-62419-840-3(6)) Salem Author Services.
Camacho, Norma I. Mikey/Jackster. 2011. 48p. (gr. 4-6). pap. 9.89 (978-1-4669-0155-1(1)) Trafford Publishing.
Cameron, Harriet. Nomad's Joyous Christmas. 2012. (Illus.). 24p. 12.00 (978-1-4251-2391-8(0)) Trafford Publishing.
Cameron, Sam. The Missing Juliet: a Fisher Key Adventure. 2013. (ENG.). 264p. (gr. 7). pap. 11.95 (978-1-60282-959-6(4)) Bold Strokes Bks.
Cameron, Sharon. The Forgetting. (ENG.). 416p. (gr. 7-7). 2017. (J). pap. 9.99 **(978-1-338-16071-0(0))** 2016. (YA). 18.99 (978-0-545-94521-9(6)) Scholastic, Inc. (Scholastic Pr.).
Cameron, Thomas "Tom". Freddy's Adventure on the Safari River. 2012. 36p. pap. 24.95 (978-1-4626-7436-7(4)) America Star Bks.
Campbell, Angella. Engel und Turkish. 2012. 32p. pap. 19.99 (978-1-4772-2556-1(0)) AuthorHouse.
Campbell, H. David. The Adventurous Jill: And Her Friend Jack. 2012. 112p. pap. 13.95 (978-1-4772-7241-1(0)) AuthorHouse.
—Merribell: A Comforting Story. 2011. 218p. (gr. 2-2). 23.95 (978-1-4620-4477-1(8)); pap. 13.95 (978-1-4620-4476-4(X)) iUniverse, Inc.
Campbell, Julie. The Secret of the Mansion: Trixie Belden. 2004. 236p. (J). (gr. 3-7). pap. 29.00 incl. audio (978-1-4000-9000-6(8), Listening Library) Random Hse. Audio Publishing Group.
Campbell, Mari. Maggiemoosetracks: Making Friends. Katsumoto, Sayaka, tr. Jennings, Randy, illus. 2013. 108p. pap. 21.99 (978-0-9895205-6-0(0)) MaggieMooseTracks.
—Maggiemoosetracks: Making Friends. Jennings, Randy, illus. 2013. 84p. pap. 21.00 (978-0-9895205-0-8(1)) MaggieMooseTracks.
—Maggiemoosetracks: Wolf Pack. Jennings, Randy, illus. 2013. 106p. pap. 21.00 (978-0-9895205-5-3(2)) MaggieMooseTracks.
Campbell, S. E. Tasting Silver. 2013. 178p. pap. 10.99 (978-1-62237-220-1(4)) Turquoise Morning Pr.
Campbell, Todd M. Puppy Dog's New Friend. 2012. 24p. 24.95 (978-1-4626-6127-5(0)) America Star Bks.
Campbell, Yma Orne. Manners & Morals in Minutes for Children. 2010. 44p. pap. 16.99 (978-1-4520-8251-6(0)) AuthorHouse.
Camper, Cathy. Low Riders in Space. Raúl, III, illus. 2014. (ENG & SPA.). 112p. (J). (gr. 3-7). pap. 9.99 (978-1-4521-2869-6(3));Bk. 1. 22.99 (978-1-4521-2155-0(9)) Chronicle Bks. LLC.
Campisi, Stephanie. The Ugly Dumpling. Kober, Shahar, illus. 2016. (ENG.). 32p. (J). (-3). 15.95 (978-1-938063-67-1(8), Mighty Media Kids) Mighty Media Pr.
Camus, William. Azules Contra Grises. (Barco de Vapor). (SPA.). 200p. (YA). (gr. 5-8). 7.95 (978-84-348-1455-4(2)) SM Ediciones ESP. Dist: AIMS International Bks., Inc.
Canavan, Charles Patrick. Rocky's Road to Sunshine. 2013. (ENG., Illus.). 30p. (J). pap. 19.95 (978-1-4787-1251-0(1)) Outskirts Pr., Inc.
Candlewick Press Staff. Peppa Pig & the Lost Christmas List. Ladybird Books Staff, illus. 2012. (Peppa Pig Ser.). (ENG.). 32p. (J). (gr. k-k). 12.99 (978-0-7636-6276-9(3), Candlewick Entertainment) Candlewick Pr.
A Candy Fairies Sugar-Tastic Collection, Bks. 5-8. 2014. (Candy Fairies Ser.). (ENG., Illus.). 512p. (J). (gr. 3-5). pap. 23.99 (978-1-4814-1659-7(6), Aladdin) Simon & Schuster Children's Publishing.
Cantor, Jillian. Searching for Sky. 2014. (ENG.). 288p. (YA). (gr. 7-12). 17.99 (978-1-61963-351-3(5), 9781619633513, Bloomsbury USA Childrens) Bloomsbury Publishing USA.
Capetta, Amy Rose. Entangled. (ENG.). (YA). (gr. 9). 2014. 352p. pap. 9.99 (978-0-544-33624-7(0), HMH Books For Young Readers) 2013. 336p. 17.99 (978-0-544-08744-6(5)) Houghton Mifflin Harcourt Publishing Co.
Caplan, Frank A. The Donkey Who Lost His Tail. 2010. (Illus.). 20p. 12.49 (978-1-4520-2778-4(1)) AuthorHouse.
Capone, Deb & compiled by. Tooth Fairy Tales Learning & Activity Guide. Capone, Deb, compiled by. 2007. (Illus.). 20p. (J). 9.95 (978-0-9728666-8-2(X)) As Simple As That Publishing.
Caprin, K. F. The Adventures of the Little Savages. 2009. (ENG.). 167p. pap. 16.95 (978-1-4092-3379-4(0)) Lulu Pr., Inc.
Capucilli, Alyssa Satin. Biscuit & the Little Pup. Schories, Pat, illus. 2007. (Biscuit: My First I Can Read! Ser.). 29p. (J). (gr. -1-3). lib. bdg. 13.55 (978-1-4178-1002-4(5), Turtleback) Turtleback Bks.
—Biscuit Visits the Doctor. Berlin, Rose Mary & Schories, Pat, illus. 2008. (Biscuit Ser.). (ENG.). 24p. (J). (gr. -1-1). pap. 3.99 (978-0-06-112843-1(0), HarperFestival) HarperCollins Pubs.
—Biscuit's Big Friend. Schories, Pat, illus. 2003. (My First I Can Read Ser.). 32p. (J). (gr. -1 — 1). (ENG.). pap. 3.99 (978-0-06-444288-6(8)); (ENG.). 16.99 (978-0-06-029167-9(2)); lib. bdg. 17.89 (978-0-06-029168-6(0)) HarperCollins Pubs.
—Katy Duck Ready-To-Read Value Pack: Starring Katy Duck; Katy Duck Makes a Friend; Katy Duck Meets the Babysitter; Katy Duck & the Tip-Tip Tap Shoes; Katy Duck, Flower Girl; Katy Duck Goes to Work. Cole, Henry, illus. 2014. (Katy Duck Ser.). (ENG.). 144p. (J). (gr. -1-1). pap. 15.96 (978-1-4814-2600-8(1), Simon Spotlight) Simon Spotlight.
—Where Is Love, Biscuit? A Pet & Play Book. Berlin, Rose Mary & Schories, Pat, illus. 2009. (Biscuit Ser.). (ENG.). 12p. (J). (gr. -1 — 1). bds. 7.99 (978-0-06-162521-3(3), HarperFestival) HarperCollins Pubs.
Cardarelli, Mario. Bunny, an Orphan's Story. 2008. 44p. pap. 18.99 (978-1-4389-1597-5(7)) AuthorHouse.
—Kid Jack Adventures: Prevent Bullying. 2011. 48p. pap. 15.49 (978-1-4567-2296-8(4)) AuthorHouse.
Cardona, Nancy. Beethoven. Swope, Brenda, illus. 2011. 28p. pap. 24.95 (978-1-4560-0961-8(3)) America Star Bks.
Cardoza, Kristina. Pinky Bunny's First Day of Kindergarten. 2011. 16p. pap. 8.75 (978-1-4634-8753-9(3)) AuthorHouse.
Carelli, Anne O'Brien. Amina's New Friends. 2009. 32p. 6.95 (978-1-60349-026-9(4), Marimba Bks.) Hudson Publishing Group, The.
Carey, Catherine Elaine. The Colorful & Playful Animal Friends, 1 vol. 2009. 73p. pap. 16.95 (978-1-60749-480-5(9)) PublishAmerica, Inc.
Carey-Costa, Denise. Lucky. Sjostrom, Nicole & Iseminger, Jonathan, illus. 2011. 34p. pap. 12.99 (978-1-61170-035-0(3)) Robertson Publishing.
Caring, Angela. Becoming Bryn. 2013. (ENG.). 297p. (YA). (gr. 7). pap. 11.95 (978-1-935089-66-7(8)) Acacia Publishing, Inc.
Carkhuff Jr., Sam. The Ranch Race. Crow, Katie, illus. 2012. 36p. 16.99 (978-1-939054-03-6(6)); pap. 11.99 (978-1-939054-02-9(8)) Rowe Publishing and Design.
Carle, Eric. Amigos. Carle, Eric, illus. 2016. (SPA., Illus.). 22p. (J). (— 1). bds. 7.99 (978-0-399-54506-1(9), Philomel Bks.) Penguin Young Readers Group.
—Friends. Carle, Eric, illus. 2013. (ENG., Illus.). 32p. (J). (gr. -1-k). 17.99 (978-0-399-16533-7(9), Philomel Bks.) Penguin Publishing Group.
—Friends. Carle, Eric, illus. 2015. (ENG., Illus.). 24p. (J). (gr. -1-k). bds. 7.99 (978-0-399-17206-9(8), Philomel Bks.) Penguin Young Readers Group.
—A House for Hermit Crab. Carle, Eric, illus. 2005. (ENG., Illus.). 32p. (J). (gr. -1-3). 4.99 (978-1-4169-0309-3(7), Simon & Schuster/Paula Wiseman Bks.) Simon & Schuster/Paula Wiseman Bks.
—Rooster Is off to See the World. 2013. (Eric Carle Ready-To-Read Ser.). lib. bdg. 13.55 (978-0-606-32063-4(6), Turtleback) Turtleback Bks.
Carlin, Mike. The Flintsones & the Jetsons. 2017. (ENG., Illus.). 144p. (gr. 3-7). pap. 12.99 (978-1-4012-7240-1(1)) DC Comics.
Carlson, Melody. Bitsy's Harvest Party. Reagan, Susan Joy, illus. 2005. 32p. (J). (gr. -1-4). 12.99 (978-0-8054-2684-7(1)) B&H Publishing Group.
—Bright Purple: Color Me Confused. 2006. (Truecolors Ser.: 10). (ENG.). 224p. (YA). (gr. 4-7). per. 14.99 (978-1-57683-950-8(8), Th1nk Bks.) NavPress Publishing Group.
—Dark Blue: Color Me Lonely. 2004. (Truecolors Ser.: 1). (ENG.). 208p. (YA). pap. 14.99 (978-1-57683-529-6(4), Th1nk Bks.) NavPress Publishing Group.
—Girl Power, 1 vol. 2016. (Faithgirlz / Girls of Harbor View Ser.). (ENG.). 272p. (J). pap. 9.99 (978-0-310-75361-2(9)) Zonderkidz.
—Glamour, 1 vol. 2014. (On the Runway Ser.). (ENG.). 224p. (YA). pap. 9.99 (978-0-310-74887-8(9)) Zondervan.
—Raising Faith, 1 vol. 2016. (Faithgirlz / Girls of Harbor View Ser.). (ENG.). 272p. (J). pap. 9.99 (978-0-310-75375-9(9)) Zonderkidz.
—Secret Admirer, 1 vol. 2016. (Faithgirlz / Girls of Harbor View Ser.). (ENG.). 272p. (J). pap. 9.99 (978-0-310-75371-1(6)) Zonderkidz.
—Take Charge, 1 vol. 2016. (Faithgirlz / Girls of Harbor View Ser.). (ENG.). 272p. (J). (gr. 3-7). pap. 9.99 (978-0-310-75373-5(2)) Zonderkidz.
Carlson, Nancy. Harriet & Walt. Carlson, Nancy, illus. unabr. ed. (Illus.). (J). (gr. k-3). 24.95 incl. audio (978-0-941078-59-7(0)); pap. 15.95 incl. audio (978-0-941078-57-3(4)); pap., tchr. ed. 31.95 incl. audio (978-0-941078-58-0(2)) Live Oak Media.
—Louanne Pig in Witch Lady. 2006. (Illus.). 32p. (J). (gr. -1-3). lib. bdg. 15.95 (978-0-8225-6196-5(4), Carolrhoda Bks.) Lerner Publishing Group.
—Louanne Pig in Witch Lady. Carlson, Nancy, illus. rev. ed. 2006. (ENG., Illus.). 32p. (J). (gr. k-2). per. 9.95 (978-0-8225-6197-2(2), First Avenue Editions) Lerner Publishing Group.
—My Best Friend Moved Away. Carlson, Nancy, illus. 2012. (Nancy Carlson Picture Bks). (Illus.). 32p. (J). (gr. k-2). 56.72 (978-0-7613-9309-2(9)); (ENG., 9.95 (978-0-7613-8954-5(7)) Lerner Publishing Group. (Carolrhoda Bks.).
—Snowden. Carlson, Nancy, illus. 2012. (Nancy Carlson Picture Bks). (Illus.). 32p. (J). (gr. k-2). (ENG.). 9.95 (978-0-7613-8952-1(0)); 56.72 (978-0-7613-9307-8(2)) Lerner Publishing Group. (Carolrhoda Bks.).
Carlson, Ron. The Speed of Light. 2003. (Illus.). 288p. (J). (ENG.). 15.99 (978-0-380-97837-3(7)); 16.89 (978-0-06-029825-8(1)) HarperCollins Pubs. (HarperTeen).
Carman, Debby. Kittywimpuss Got Game. Carman, Debby, illus. 2007. (Illus.). 28p. (J). (gr. -1-1). 14.99 (978-0-9777340-4-7(8)) Faux Paw Media Group.
—Purrlonia's Lullaby. Carman, Debby, illus. 2008. (Illus.). 28p. (J). (gr. -1-1). 14.99 (978-0-9777340-1-6(3)) Faux Paw Media Group.
Carman, Patrick. Floozombies! Sheesley, Brian, illus. 2016. (Fizzopolis Ser.: 2). 176p. (J). (gr. 3-7). 12.99 (978-0-06-239392-0(8), Tegen, Katherine Bks) HarperCollins Pubs.
—The House of Power. 2008. (Atherton Ser.: 1). (ENG., Illus.). 384p. (J). (gr. 3-7). pap. 9.99 (978-0-316-16671-3(5)) Little, Brown Bks. for Young Readers.
—Rivers of Fire. 2009. (Atherton Ser.: 2). (ENG., Illus.). 336p. (J). (gr. 3-7). pap. 9.99 (978-0-316-16673-7(1)) Little Brown & Co.
Carmody, Isobelle. The Farseekers. 2003. (Obernewtyn Chronicles: Bk. 2). (Illus.). 316p. (J). 13.65 (978-0-7569-4608-1(5)) Perfection Learning Corp.
—The Red Queen. 7th ed. 2016. (Obernewtyn Chronicles Ser.: 7). (ENG.). 1120p. (YA). (gr. 7). 29.99 (978-0-670-07640-6(6)) Penguin Books Australia AUS. Dist: Independent Pubs. Group.
—The Red Queen. 2011. (Obernewtyn Chronicles: Bk. 7). 544p. (YA). (gr. 7-18). mass mkt. 7.99 (978-0-375-85774-4(5), Random Hse. Bks. for Young Readers) Random Hse. Children's Bks.
Carnes, Daphane. Grace. 2009. 48p. (J). pap. 12.95 (978-1-4327-3380-3(X)) Outskirts Pr., Inc.
Carnesi, Mônica. Sleepover with Beatrice & Bear. Carnesi, Mônica, illus. 2014. (ENG., Illus.). 32p. (J). (gr. -1-k). 15.99 (978-0-399-25667-7(9), Nancy Paulsen Books) Penguin Young Readers Group.
Carney, Karin. Prince Braden's Animal Kingdom. 2011. 40p. pap. 18.95 (978-1-4357-9406-1(0)) Lulu Pr., Inc.
Carney, Larry, adapted by. Silly Friends. 2010. (ENG., Illus.). 24p. (J). pap. 6.95 (978-1-60072-158-8(3)) PC Treasures, Inc.
Carney, Riley. The Final Alliance: Book Five of the Reign of the Elements. 2012. (Reign of the Elements Ser.: Bk. 5). (Illus.). 312p. (J). 20.95 (978-0-9841307-9-5(9)) BookLight Pr.
Carol, Darlene. A Puppy Called Runt: The Adventure Begins. 2008. 224p. pap. 12.95 (978-1-935105-00-8(0)) Avid Readers Publishing Group.
Carothers, Nina. Gold Old Gets a Little Help from His Friends. Nilsen, Richard J., ed. Padovano, Chris, illus. 2013. 32p. pap. 12.97 (978-1-937376-29-1(X)) All Star Pr.
Carpenter, Angie. Digewi Deer: The Tale of a Blind Deer. Bemer Coble, Lynn, ed. 2013. 82p. (J). pap. 8.99 (978-0-9846724-3-1(5)) Paws and Claws Publishing, LLC.
Carpenter Czerw, Nancy. Friends on the Farm. Berlin, Rose Mary & Bauer, Dana, illus. 2006. (Itty & Bitty Ser.). (ENG.). 32p. (J). (gr. -1-3). 15.95 (978-0-9755618-3-6(9)) McWitty Pr., Inc.
Carpenter, Joyce M. An Unexpected Friend. 2010. 24p. 11.49 (978-1-4520-0758-8(6)) AuthorHouse.
Carr, David. Trebb the Troll. 2005. 86p. (YA). pap. 8.36 (978-1-4116-3865-5(4)) Lulu Pr., Inc.
Carr, Debra. The Curry Comb Caper. Carr, Stephen, illus. 2006. 48p. per. 8.95 (978-1-933912-59-2(6)) Westview Publishing Co., Inc.
—The Feed Trough Thriller. Carr, Stephen, illus. 2007. 56p. per. 8.95 (978-1-933912-66-0(9)) Westview Publishing Co., Inc.
Carr, Elias. Hal y el Nuevo Compañero. Garton, Michael, illus. 2016. (SPA.). (J). **(978-1-5064-2098-1(2))** Augsburg Fortress, Pubs.
Carrier, Therese & Carrier, Stephen. Josiah's School Fun Day. Hatfield, Tommy, illus. 2007. 29p. (J). 16.95 (978-0-9797648-0-6(7)) Carrier, Therese.
Carroll, Claudia. Old Dumpling & the Rainy Day. 2008. 55p. pap. 9.95 (978-0-557-01565-8(0)) Lulu Pr., Inc.
Carroll, Harlisha. Miracle Mouse & Jesus - Book: (Short Stories 1) 2012. 36p. pap. 24.95 (978-1-4626-6615-7(9)) America Star Bks.
Carroll, Jody. Mitsy Morgan: Six Monkeys Past Midnight. 2010. 44p. pap. 18.75 (978-1-4520-0796-0(9)) AuthorHouse.
Carroll, Katie L. Elixir Bound. 2013. 158p. pap. (978-1-77127-465-4(4)) MuseItUp Publishing.
Carroll, Michael Shane. Bye-Bye Brewster. Carroll, Katie, illus. 2012. 20p. pap. 5.00 (978-1-937260-14-9(3)) Sleepytown Pr.
Carruthers, Deborah. Olivia's Birthday. Zvonarova, Jenny Desneige, illus. 2011. 20p. (gr. 1-2). 14.99 (978-1-4269-4967-8(7)) Trafford Publishing.
Cars & Disney Book Group Staff. Cars. 2010. (Read-Along Storybook & CD Ser.). (ENG.). 32p. (J). (gr. -1 — 1). pap. 6.99 (978-1-4231-3332-2(3)) Disney Pr.
Carson, Jana. We Both Read-The New Tribe. Treatner, Meryl, illus. 2013. 44p. (J). pap. 4.99 (978-1-60115-264-0(7)) Treasure Bay, Inc.
Carson, Jeanelle. Lexi Lou Meets Jadie Bear. 2010. 36p. pap. 15.49 (978-1-4520-9449-6(7)) AuthorHouse.
Carson, John E. & Carson, Marlene R. The Wire Forest of Peru. 2007. (Ramblin' Rose Ser.). 205p. (YA). (gr. 8-12). per. 8.99 (978-0-9776043-9-5(X)) Aspirations Media, Inc.

Carson, Penny & Hess, Amy. Simon's Day of Rain. 2008. 17p. 10.94 (978-1-4357-2168-5(3)) Lulu Pr., Inc.

Carta, Karla K. Fairy Jane. 2005. 25p. 13.28 (978-1-4116-2296-8(0)) Lulu Pr., Inc.

Carter, Caela. My Best Friend, Maybe. 2014. (ENG.). 352p. (YA). (gr. 9). 17.99 (978-1-59990-970-7(7), 9781599909707, Bloomsbury USA Childrens) Bloomsbury Publishing USA.

—Tumbling. 2016. (ENG.). 432p. (YA). (gr. 7). 17.99 (978-0-451-47300-4(0), Viking Books for Young Readers) Penguin Young Readers Group.

Carter, Cathy. You Are My Very Best Friend: The Adventures of Mike & Gabe (in English & Spanish) 2012. 26p. 24.95 (978-1-4626-7072-7(5)) America Star Bks.

Carter, Darlene. Little Spit-N-Gasser Finds New Friends. 2009. 16p. pap. 8.90 (978-1-4389-5168-3(X)) AuthorHouse.

Carter, Jimmy. The Little Baby Snoogle- Fleejer. Carter, Amy, illus. 2014. (ENG.). 24p. (J). 19.95 (978-1-55728-671-0(X)) Univ. of Arkansas Pr.

Carter, Lara. Crusher Field Opening Day. 2009. 28p. pap. 12.49 (978-1-4389-3389-4(4)) AuthorHouse.

Carter, Nikki. Step to This. 2009. (ENG., Illus.). 240p. (YA). (gr. 9). 9.95 (978-0-7582-3439-1(2), K-Teen/Dafina) Kensington Publishing Corp.

Carter, Olivia. Through My Eyes, Book One: Jake. 2013. (ENG.). 235p. (YA). (gr. 7). pap. 10.95 (978-1-935089-63-6(3)) Acacia Publishing, Inc.

Carter, Scott William. The Last Great Getaway of the Water Balloon Boys. 2010. (ENG.). 208p. (YA). (gr. 7-18). 16.99 (978-1-4169-7156-6(4), Simon & Schuster Bks. For Young Readers) Simon & Schuster Bks. For Young Readers.

Cartwheel: A Sequel to Double Eagle. 2013. (ENG.). 252p. (YA). 17.00 (978-0-9844460-3-2(6)) Bucking Horse Bks.

Caruso, Paul. The Lonely Nail. 2010. (Illus.). 26p. (J). pap. 17.95 (978-1-4327-5646-8(X)) Outskirts Pr., Inc.

Carver, David. Leafy Leafs Where Is Lester?, 1 vol. Carver, Erin, illus. 2010. 34p. 24.95 (978-1-4512-1069-9(8)) PublishAmerica, Inc.

—Lester Returns Home with His New Friend La'doo, 1 vol. Carver, Erin, illus. 2010. 28p. 24.95 (978-1-4489-6340-9(0)) PublishAmerica, Inc.

Casad, Patricia E. Bubbykins: (Life on the Farm) 2008. 46p. pap. 24.95 (978-1-4241-9140-6(8)) America Star Bks.

Casanova, Mary. Danger at Snow Hill. Rayyan, Omar, illus. 2006. (Dog Watch Ser.: 3). (ENG.). 128p. (J). (gr. 3-7). pap. 4.99 (978-0-689-86812-2(X), Simon & Schuster/Paula Wiseman Bks.) Simon & Schuster/Paula Wiseman Bks.

—Dog-Napped! Rayyan, Omar, illus. 2006. (Dog Watch Ser.: 2). (ENG.). 144p. (J). (gr. 3-7). pap. 8.99 (978-0-689-86811-5(1), Simon & Schuster/Paula Wiseman Bks.) Simon & Schuster/Paula Wiseman Bks.

—Wolf Shadows. 2nd ed. 2009. (J). (978-0-9793444-1-1(7)) Quercus Press.

Cascioli, Lucia. Shifters. 2011. 126p. 25.99 (978-1-257-86200-9(6)); pap. 9.99 (978-1-257-86197-2(2)) Lulu Pr., Inc.

Cascone, Annette & Cascone, Gina. Little Magic Shop of Horrors. 2013. (Deadtime Stories Ser.: 5). (ENG.). 192p. (J). (gr. 3-7). pap. 6.99 (978-0-7653-3069-7(5), 9780765330697, Starscape) Doherty, Tom Assocs., LLC.

Cascone, Gina & Cascone, Annette. Little Magic Shop of Horrors. 2012. (Deadtime Stories Ser.: 5). (ENG.). 192p. (J). (gr. 3-7). 14.99 (978-0-7653-3075-8(X), 9780765330758, Starscape) Doherty, Tom Assocs., LLC.

Caselo-Atassi, Rosemarie. Camel's Tales: The Journey to Bethlehem. 2013. 86p. pap. 15.99 (978-1-4797-7565-1(7)) Xlibris Corp.

Cass, Isabella. Don't Stop Believing, Bk. 4. 2011. (Superstar High Ser.: 3). (ENG.). 496p. (J). (gr. 4-7). pap. 8.99 (978-0-552-56092-4(8)) Transworld Publishers Ltd. GBR. Dist: Independent Pubs. Group.

Cassidy, Cathy. Indigo Blue. 2006. (ENG.). 240p. (J). (gr. 5-18). 7.99 (978-0-14-240703-5(8), Puffin Books) Penguin Young Readers Group.

Cassity, Brittney. Fiddlebug. 2008. 52p. pap. 22.49 (978-1-4389-2537-0(9)) AuthorHouse.

Castellucci, Cecil. Odd Duck. Varon, Sara, illus. 2013. (ENG.). 96p. (J). (gr. 1-5). 15.99 (978-1-59643-557-5(7), 9781596435575, First Second Bks.) Roaring Brook Pr.

—The Queen of Cool. 2007. (ENG., Illus.). 176p. (YA). (gr. 9-18). pap. 7.99 (978-0-7636-3413-1(1)) Candlewick Pr.

—The Year of the Beasts. Powell, Nate, illus. 2012. (ENG.). 192p. (YA). (gr. 7-12). 16.99 (978-1-59643-686-2(7), 9781596436862) Roaring Brook Pr.

—The Year of the Beasts. Powell, Nate, illus. 2014. (ENG.). 208p. (YA). (gr. 7-12). pap. 9.99 (978-1-250-05076-2(6), 9781250050762) Square Fish.

Castle, M. E. Cloneward Bound. 2013. (Clone Chronicles Ser.: No. 2). (ENG.). 272p. (J). (gr. 3-7). pap. 6.99 (978-1-60684-473-1(3), Darby Creek) Lerner Publishing Group.

Castor, Harriet. Hit the Beach! 2010. (Sleepover Club Ser.). (ENG.). 128p. (J). (gr. 2-6). pap. 6.99 (978-0-00-727256-3(1), HarperCollins Children's Bks.) HarperCollins Pubs. Ltd. GBR. Dist: HarperCollins Pubs.

Castro, Shirley. The Pelican Family Series — Telly's Story. Castro, Christopher, illus. 2008. 36p. (J). 15.00 (978-0-9790307-1-0(4)) Castro, Shirley.

Castrovilla, Selene. The Girl Next Door. 2010. 240p. (YA). (gr. 9-12). 16.95 (978-1-934813-15-7(X)) Westside Bks.

Catalanotto, Peter. Monkey & Robot. Catalanotto, Peter, illus. (ENG., Illus.). 64p. (J). (gr. 1-4). 2014. pap. 5.99 (978-1-4424-2979-6(8), Atheneum Bks. for Young Readers) 2013. 12.99 (978-1-4424-2978-9(X), Atheneum/Richard Jackson Bks.) Simon & Schuster Children's Publishing.

—More of Monkey & Robot. Catalanotto, Peter, illus. 2014. (ENG., Illus.). 64p. (J). (gr. 1-4). 15.99 (978-1-4424-5251-0(X), Atheneum/Richard Jackson Bks.) Simon & Schuster Children's Publishing.

Caton, Peter. Josh: Hero. 2012. 114p. pap. (978-1-908128-40-9(2)) Spiderwize.

Cattanach, Ann. Malpas the Dragon. Renouf, Michael, illus. 2007. (ENG.). 28p. (J). (gr. 3-7). per. 15.95 (978-1-84310-572-5(1), 1774) Kingsley, Jessica Pubs. GBR. Dist: Macmillan Distribution Ltd.

Caudle, P. L. The Tale of Strawberry Snow, 1 vol. Simmonds, Frank H., illus. 2012. (ENG.). 48p. (J). 16.99 (978-0-7643-4076-5(X), 9780764340765) Schiffer Publishing, Ltd.

Cavanaugh, Nancy. Just Like Me. 2016. (ENG.). 256p. (J). (gr. 3-7). 16.99 (978-1-4926-0427-3(5), 9781492604273, Sourcebooks Jabberwocky) Sourcebooks, Inc.

Cavanna, Betty. A Touch of Magic. Gretzer, John, illus. 2011. 188p. 42.95 (978-1-258-07218-6(1)) Literary Licensing, LLC.

Cavender, Barbara. B Is for Ben. 2009. 84p. (J). pap. 12.95 (978-1-4327-3513-5(6)) Outskirts Pr., Inc.

Cazet, Denys. Snail & Slug. Cazet, Denys, illus. 2016. (ENG., Illus.). 32p. (J). (gr. -1-3). 17.99 (978-1-4814-4506-1(5), Atheneum/Richard Jackson Bks.) Simon & Schuster Children's Publishing.

Cecelia And Andrew Davis. A Budgie Tale: Rascal Meets Emmit. 2009. 12p. pap. 8.49 (978-1-4389-3304-7(5)) AuthorHouse.

Cecil, Carrie Gerlach & cecil, charli. Charli & Wilbur a Dancing Dog's Dream. 2012. 24p. pap. 7.99 (978-0-615-62081-7(7)) Anachel Communications.

Cecil, Kimberly. The Adventures of Hebear, 1 vol. 2010. 24p. pap. 24.95 (978-1-60749-915-2(0)) PublishAmerica, Inc.

Cecil, Lauren. Lalaloopsy: Halloween Surprise. Fruchter, Jason, illus. 2012. (Lalaloopsy Ser.). (ENG.). 24p. (J). (gr. -1-3). pap. 3.99 (978-0-545-43388-4(6)) Scholastic, Inc.

—Lalaloopsy: Lala-Oopsies: Meet the Lala-Oopsies. 2013. (ENG.). 24p. (J). (gr. -1-3). pap. 3.99 (978-0-545-57224-8(X)) Scholastic, Inc.

Celestin, Marie. The Unaccepted Child. 2003. (Illus.). 16p. (J). pap. 5.99 (978-1-890035-35-8(1), 119) New Century Pr.

Cerebellum Corporation, prod. Willow Pond Storybook. 2011. cd-rom 39.95 (978-1-61867-207-0(X)) Cerebellum Corp.

Cerimele, Ron. Hee, Haw, & a Donkey Named Sam. 2007. (ENG.). 20p. per. 24.95 (978-1-4241-9013-3(4)) America Star Bks.

Cerullo, Claudio V. Isabella's Rainy Day with Her Friends. 2011. 16p. pap. 24.95 (978-1-4626-2463-8(4)) America Star Bks.

Cervantes, Angela. Allie, First at Last. 2016. (ENG.). 208p. (J). (gr. 3-7). 16.99 (978-0-545-81223-8(2), Scholastic Pr.) Scholastic, Inc.

Cesmat, Sheryl. Poppy. 2013. 44p. pap. 20.72 (978-1-4669-8643-5(3)) Trafford Publishing.

Chabert, Jack. The Locker Ate Lucy! Ricks, Sam, illus. 2014. (Eerie Elementary — Branches Ser.: bk.2). (ENG.). 96p. (J). (gr. 1-3). 15.99 (978-0-545-62396-4(0)); pap. 4.99 (978-0-545-62395-7(2)) Scholastic, Inc.

—The Locker Ate Lucy! 2014. (Eerie Elementary — Branches Ser.: bk.2). (ENG.). (J). lib. bdg. 14.75 (978-0-606-36052-4(2)) Turtleback Bks.

—Recess Is a Jungle! Ricks, Sam, illus. 2016. (Eerie Elementary — Branches Ser.: bk.3). (ENG.). 96p. (J). (gr. 1-3). 15.99 (978-0-545-87353-6(3)) Scholastic, Inc.

—Sam Battles the Machine! Ricks, Sam, illus. 2017. (Eerie Elementary — Branches Ser.: bk.6). (ENG.). 96p. (J). (gr. 1-3). pap. 4.99 **(978-0-545-87378-9(9))** Scholastic, Inc.

—Sam Battles the Machine! 2017. (Eerie Elementary — Branches Ser.: bk.6). (ENG.). (J). lib. bdg. 14.75 **(978-0-606-40191-3(1))** Turtleback Bks.

—School Freezes Over! Ricks, Sam, illus. 2016. (Eerie Elementary — Branches Ser.: bk.5). (ENG.). 96p. (J). (gr. 1-3). pap. 4.99 (978-0-545-87373-4(8)) Scholastic, Inc.

—The School Is Alive! Ricks, Sam, illus. 2014. (Eerie Elementary — Branches Ser.: bk.1). (ENG.). 96p. (J). (gr. 1-3). 15.99 (978-0-545-62393-3(6)); pap. 4.99 (978-0-545-62392-6(8)) Scholastic, Inc.

—The School Is Alive! 2014. (Eerie Elementary — Branches Ser.: bk.1). (ENG.). (J). lib. bdg. 14.75 (978-0-606-35822-4(6)) Turtleback Bks.

—The Science Fair Is Freaky! Ricks, Sam, illus. 2016. (Eerie Elementary — Branches Ser.: bk.4). (ENG.). 96p. (J). (gr. 1-3). pap. 4.99 (978-0-545-87368-0(1)) Scholastic, Inc.

—The Science Fair Is Freaky! 2016. (Eerie Elementary — Branches Ser.: bk.4). (ENG.). (J). lib. bdg. 14.75 (978-0-606-38806-1(0)) Turtleback Bks.

Chace, Rebecca. June Sparrow & the Million-Dollar Penny. Schwartz, Kacey, illus. 2017. 352p. (J). (gr. 3-7). 16.99 (978-0-06-246498-9(1)) HarperCollins Pubs.

Chaconas, Dori. The Babysitters. McCue, Lisa, illus. 2014. (Cork & Fuzz Ser.: 6). (ENG.). 32p. (J). (gr. 1-3). pap. 3.99 (978-0-448-48050-3(6), Penguin Young Readers) Penguin Young Readers Group.

—Best Friends No. 1. McCue, Lisa, illus. 2010. (Cork & Fuzz Ser.: 1). (ENG.). 32p. (J). (gr. 1-3). mass mkt. 3.99 (978-0-14-241593-1(6), Penguin Young Readers) Penguin Young Readers Group.

—The Collectors, 4 vols. McCue, Lisa, illus. 2010. (Cork & Fuzz Ser.: 4). (ENG.). 32p. (J). (gr. 1-3). mass mkt. 3.99 (978-0-14-241714-0(9), Penguin Young Readers) Penguin Young Readers Group.

—Cork & Fuzz. McCue, Lisa, illus. 2005. (Cork & Fuzz Ser.: 1). (ENG.). 32p. (J). (gr. 1-3). 13.99 (978-0-670-03602-8(1), Viking Books for Young Readers) Penguin Young Readers Group.

—Cork & Fuzz - The Collectors. McCue, Lisa, illus. 2008. (Cork & Fuzz Ser.: 4). (ENG.). 32p. (J). (gr. k-3). 13.99 (978-0-670-06286-7(3), Viking Books for Young Readers) Penguin Young Readers Group.

—Finders Keepers, 5 vols. McCue, Lisa, illus. 2011. (Cork & Fuzz Ser.: 5). (ENG.). 32p. (J). (gr. 1-3). mass mkt. 3.99 (978-0-14-241869-7(2), Penguin Young Readers) Penguin Young Readers Group.

—Good Sports. McCue, Lisa, illus. 2010. (Cork & Fuzz Ser.: 3). (ENG.). 32p. (J). (gr. 1-3). mass mkt. 3.99 (978-0-14-241713-3(0), Penguin Young Readers) Penguin Young Readers Group.

—Looking for Easter. Moore, Margie, illus. 2012. (J). 34.28 (978-1-61913-120-0(X)) Weigl Pubs., Inc.

—Merry Merry Holly Holly. McCue, Lisa, illus. 2015. (Cork & Fuzz Ser.: 11). (ENG.). 32p. (J). (gr. -1-k). 16.99 (978-0-451-47501-5(1), Viking Books for Young Readers) Penguin Young Readers Group.

—Short & Tall No. 2, 2 vols. McCue, Lisa, illus. 2010. (Cork & Fuzz Ser.: 2). (ENG.). 32p. (J). (gr. 1-3). mass mkt. 3.99 (978-0-14-241594-8(4), Penguin Young Readers) Penguin Young Readers Group.

—Spring Cleaning. 2016. (Penguin Young Readers Level 3 Ser.). lib. bdg. 13.55 (978-0-606-38427-8(8)) Turtleback Bks.

—Swimming Lesson, 7 vols. McCue, Lisa, illus. 2011. (Cork & Fuzz Ser.: 7). (ENG.). 32p. (J). (gr. 1-3). 13.99 (978-0-670-01281-7(5), Viking Books for Young Readers) Penguin Young Readers Group.

—The Swimming Lesson. McCue, Lisa, illus. 2014. (Cork & Fuzz Ser.: 7). (ENG.). 32p. (J). (gr. 1-3). pap. 3.99 (978-0-448-48051-0(4), Penguin Young Readers) Penguin Young Readers Group.

Chaconas, Dori & Bader, Bonnie. Spring Cleaning. McCue, Lisa, illus. 2015. (Cork & Fuzz Ser.: 10). (ENG.). 32p. (J). (gr. 1-3). 14.99 (978-0-670-01686-0(1), Penguin Young Readers) Penguin Young Readers Group.

—Wait a Minute. McCue, Lisa, illus. 2015. (Cork & Fuzz Ser.: 9). (ENG.). 32p. (J). (gr. 1-3). 3.99 (978-0-14-750856-0(8), Penguin Young Readers) Penguin Young Readers Group.

Chadwick, Jennie. The Peach Tree Kids: Jaws of Dragon. 2010. 52p. pap. 9.99 (978-1-60911-991-1(6), Eloquent Bks.) Strategic Book Publishing & Rights Agency (SBPRA).

Chaffey, Tim & Westbrook, Joe. The Truth Chronicles: The Ark. 2013. 146p. pap. (978-1-936835-15-7(0)) Roxby Media Ltd.

Chainani, Soman. The Last Ever After. Bruno, Iacopo, illus. 2015. 655p. (J). (978-0-06-241756-5(8)) Harper & Row Ltd.

—The Last Ever After. 2015. (School for Good & Evil Ser.: 3). (ENG., Illus.). 672p. (J). (gr. 3-7). 17.99 (978-0-06-210495-3(0)) HarperCollins Pubs.

—The School for Good & Evil. (School for Good & Evil Ser.). (J). (gr. 3). 2016. 1760p. pap. 23.97 (978-0-06-245624-3(5)) 2015. (ENG.). 1334p. 53.97 (978-0-06-243497-5(7)) HarperCollins Pubs.

—The School for Good & Evil. Bruno, Iacopo, illus. (ENG.). (J). (gr. 3-7). 2014. (School for Good & Evil Ser.: 1). 544p. pap. 7.99 (978-0-06-210490-8(X)) 2013. (School for Good & Evil Trilogy: No. 1). 400p. 17.99 (978-0-06-210489-2(6)) HarperCollins Pubs.

—The School for Good & Evil. Bruno, Iacopo, illus. 2014. (School for Good & Evil Ser.: 1). 496p. (J). lib. bdg. 17.20 (978-0-606-36513-0(3)) Turtleback Bks.

—The School for Good & Evil #4: Quests for Glory. 2017. (School for Good & Evil Ser.: 4). 576p. (J). (gr. 3-7). 17.99 **(978-0-06-265847-0(6))** HarperCollins Pubs.

Chainani, Soman. A World Without Princes. 2014. (School for Good & Evil Trilogy: No. 2). 448p. (J). pap. (978-0-06-233135-9(3)) Harper & Row Ltd.

—A World Without Princes. Bruno, Iacopo, illus. 2014. (School for Good & Evil Trilogy: No. 2). (ENG.). 400p. (J). (978-0-06-234072-6(7)) Harper & Row Ltd.

—A World Without Princes. Bruno, Iacopo, illus. 2015. (School for Good & Evil Ser.: 2). (ENG.). 512p. (J). (gr. 3-7). pap. 7.99 (978-0-06-210493-9(4)) HarperCollins Pubs.

—A World Without Princes. 2014. (School for Good & Evil Trilogy: No. 2). (ENG., Illus.). 448p. (J). (gr. 3-7). 17.99 (978-0-06-210492-2(6)) HarperCollins Pubs.

—A World Without Princes. 2015. (School for Good & Evil Ser.: 2). (J). lib. bdg. 17.20 (978-0-606-36514-7(1)) Turtleback Bks.

Chalmers, Jason. Camp Sacrowee. 2011. 84p. pap. 19.95 (978-1-4241-7494-2(5)) America Star Bks.

—Fall Nightmares. 2011. 166p. pap. 24.95 (978-1-4560-8988-7(9)) America Star Bks.

Chambers, Aidan. The Toll Bridge. 2009. (ENG.). 288p. (YA). (gr. 9-17). pap. 9.95 (978-0-8109-8358-8(3), Amulet Bks.) Abrams, Inc.

Chambers, Cindy. Beamer Learns the Signs of a Stroke & How to Help. 2013. 28p. pap. 14.95 (978-1-4575-1725-9(6)) Dog Ear Publishing, LLC.

Chan, Marty. Barnabas Bigfoot: a Hairy Tangle. 2012. (ENG.). 104p. (gr. 4-6). 9.95 (978-1-927068-05-2(3)) Thistledown Pr., Ltd. CAN. Dist: Univ. of Toronto Pr.

Chan, Ruth. Georgie's Best Bad Day. 2017. (Georgie & Friends Ser.). (ENG., Illus.). 40p. (J). 17.99 (978-1-62672-270-5(6), 9781626722705) Roaring Brook Pr.

—Where's the Party? 2016. (Georgie & Friends Ser.). (ENG., Illus.). 40p. (J). 17.99 (978-1-62672-269-9(2), 9781626722699) Roaring Brook Pr.

Chance, C. The Trepets Book Three Rabbit Race Day. Champion, Vanessa, illus. 2007. 112p. per. (978-0-9551289-2-9(7), Bumble Bks.) Dragonfly Bks. & Arts.

Chand, Emlyn. Larry the Lonely: A Bird Brain Book. Giffin, Noelle, illus. l.t. ed. 2013. 9. (ENG.). 62p. (gr. k-3). pap. 10.95 (978-1-62253-128-8(0)) Evolved Publishing.

Chandler, Tony. The Journey. 2013. 242p. pap. (978-1-77115-091-0(2)) Double Dragon ebooks.

Chang, Margaret. Celia's Robot. 2009. (ENG.). 208p. (J). (gr. 3-7). 16.95 (978-0-8234-2181-7(3)) Holiday Hse., Inc.

Chapman, Allan W. Mr Wugidgem & the Dark Journey. 2012. 40p. pap. 7.99 (978-0-9796780-3-5(X)) AC Writings.

Chapman, Brenda. Trail of Secrets. 2009. (Jennifer Bannon Mystery Ser.: 4). (ENG.). 144p. (YA). (gr. 7-18). pap. 9.95 (978-1-894917-76-6(6), Napoleon & Co.) Dundurn CAN. Dist: Ingram Publisher Services.

Chapman, Bunny. Shanu the Watcher. 2013. 138p. pap. 9.99 (978-0-9855008-4-9(0)) Champlain Avenue Bks., Inc.

Chapman, Carlene. Jackson Goes to the Beach. 2010. 24p. pap. 11.95 (978-1-4490-9768-4(5)) AuthorHouse.

Chapman, Erica M. Teach Me to Forget. 2016. (ENG.). 288p. (YA). 17.99 (978-1-4405-9457-1(0), Simon Pulse) Simon Pulse.

Chapman, Jared. Pirate, Viking & Scientist. 2014. (ENG., Illus.). 40p. (J). (gr. -1-3). 17.00 (978-0-316-25389-5(8)) Little, Brown Bks. for Young Readers.

Chapman, Karean. The Adventures of Northern the Moose & a Dragon Named Zeus. Ciesinka, Izabela, illus. 2010. 38p. pap. 12.95 (978-1-935268-44-4(9)) Halo Publishing International.

Chapman, Lara. Flawless. 2011. (ENG.). 272p. (YA). (gr. 7-12). 16.99 (978-1-59990-631-7(7), 9781599906317); pap. 9.99 (978-1-59990-596-9(5), 9781599905969) Bloomsbury Publishing USA. (Bloomsbury USA Childrens).

Chapman, Linda & Cole, Steve. The Last Phoenix. 2010. (ENG.). 288p. (J). (gr. 3-7). 16.99 (978-0-06-125222-8(0)) HarperCollins Pubs.

Chapmon, Rachelle. Mari. 2009. 148p. pap. 11.99 (978-1-4389-6310-5(6)) AuthorHouse.

Chappell, Crissa-Jean. Snow Birds. 2017. (ENG.). 272p. (YA). 17.99 (978-1-5072-0069-8(2), Simon Pulse) Simon Pulse.

Charisse, April. Say Hello to Me: A Story about a Little Girl on the Autism Spectrum. 2012. 16p. pap. 15.99 (978-1-4685-9475-1(3)) AuthorHouse.

Charles, Norma M. Sophie's Friend in Need. 2004. (ENG.). 136p. (J). (gr. 6). pap. 6.95 (978-0-88878-449-0(X)) Dundurn CAN. Dist: Ingram Publisher Services.

Charles, Rie. No More Dragons. 2010. (ENG., Illus.). 112p. (J). (gr. 5-7). pap. 9.95 (978-1-926607-12-2(0), Napoleon & Co.) Dundurn CAN. Dist: Ingram Publisher Services.

Charles, Valerie. The Dancing Light. 2013. 118p. pap. (978-1-84944-167-4(7)) UKUnpublished.

Charlton-Trujillo, E. E. Fat Angie. 2013. (ENG.). 272p. (YA). (gr. 9). 16.99 (978-0-7636-6119-9(8)) Candlewick Pr.

Chase, Dakota. Mad about the Hatter. (ENG., Illus.). (YA). 2016. 24.99 **(978-1-63533-045-8(9))** 2015. 190p. pap. 14.99 (978-1-63476-148-2(0)) Dreamspinner Pr. (Harmony Ink Pr.).

Chase, Diana. Daisy Street. Bradley, Vanessa, illus. 2005. 128p. (Orig.). (J). pap. 13.50 (978-1-920731-11-3(3)) Fremantle Pr. AUS. Dist: Independent Pubs. Group.

Chase, Kit. Charlie's Boat. Chase, Kit, illus. 2017. (ENG., Illus.). 32p. (J). (-k). 16.99 (978-0-399-25702-5(0), G.P. Putnam's Sons Books for Young Readers) Penguin Young Readers Group.

—Lulu's Party. Chase, Kit, illus. 2015. (ENG., Illus.). 32p. (J). (gr. -1-k). 16.99 (978-0-399-25701-8(2), G.P. Putnam's Sons Books for Young Readers) Penguin Young Readers Group.

—Oliver's Tree. Chase, Kit, illus. 2014. (ENG., Illus.). 32p. (J). (gr. -1-k). 16.99 (978-0-399-25700-1(4), G.P. Putnam's Sons Books for Young Readers) Penguin Young Readers Group.

Chase, L. P. Elliot Stone & the Mystery of the Summer Vacation Sea Monster. DiRocco, Carl, illus. 2011. (ENG.). 165p. (J). pap. 8.99 (978-0-9792918-7-6(9)) Blue Marlin Pubns.

Chasing Gold. 2014. (Marguerite Henry's Ponies of Chincoteague Ser.: 3). (ENG., Illus.). 192p. (J). (gr. 3-7). pap. 6.99 (978-1-4814-0342-9(7), Aladdin) Simon & Schuster Children's Publishing.

Chast, Roz. Marco Goes to School. Chast, Roz, illus. 2012. (ENG., Illus.). 32p. (J). (gr. -1-3). 16.99 (978-1-4169-8475-7(5), Atheneum Bks. for Young Readers) Simon & Schuster Children's Publishing.

Chastain, Emma. Confessions of a High School Disaster. 2017. (Chloe Snow's Diary Ser.). (ENG., Illus.). 352p. (YA). (gr. 7). 17.99 (978-1-4814-8875-4(9), Simon Pulse) Simon Pulse.

Chaud, Benjamin. Farewell Floppy. 2015. (ENG., Illus.). 40p. (J). (gr. -1-k). 17.99 (978-1-4521-3734-6(X)) Chronicle Bks. LLC.

Chbosky, Stephen. The Perks of Being a Wallflower. 2014. (ENG.). 224p. (gr. 7-12). 18.25 (978-1-63245-042-5(9)) Lectorum Pubns., Inc.

—The Perks of Being a Wallflower. 2012. (ENG.). 224p. 21.00 (978-1-4516-9620-2(5)); pap. 14.99 (978-1-4516-9619-6(1)) MTV Books. (MTV Bks.).

—The Perks of Being a Wallflower. 2009. 13.77 (978-0-7848-1530-4(5), Everbind) Marco Bk. Co.

—The Perks of Being a Wallflower. 2008. (ENG.). 24.30 (978-1-60686-308-4(8), Covercraft) Perfection Learning Corp.

—The Perks of Being a Wallflower. 2007. 1.25 (978-1-4281-3271-9(6)) Recorded Bks., Inc.

Cheaney, J. B. My Friend the Enemy. 2007. 266p. (gr. 4-7). 16.50 (978-0-7569-7946-1(3)) Perfection Learning Corp.

Chef Jeff. Do Cows Eat Cake? 2008. 28p. pap. 13.99 (978-1-4389-0494-8(0)) AuthorHouse.

Chen, E. C. Bad Alphabet. 2013. 62p. 15.99 (978-0-9891510-0-9(X)) Zebra Ginkgo.

Chen, Wei Dong. Monkey King: Enemies & a New Friend. Peng, Chao, illus. 2012. (Monkey King Ser.: 4). (ENG.). 176p. (gr. 5-8). lib. bdg. 29.27 (978-89-94208-72-5(0)) JR Comics KOR. Dist: Lerner Publishing Group.

Cheng, Andrea. The Lace Dowry. 2005. (ENG.). 115p. (J). (gr. 6-9). 16.95 (978-1-932425-20-8(9), Lemniscaat) Boyds Mills Pr.

—Where Do You Stay? 2011. (ENG.). 136p. (J). (gr. 5-7). 17.95 (978-1-59078-707-6(2)) Boyds Mills Pr.

—The Year of the Baby. Barton, Patrice, illus. 2014. (Anna Wang Novel Ser.: 2). (ENG.). 176p. (J). (gr. 1-4). pap. 5.99 (978-0-544-22525-1(2), HMH Books For Young Readers) Houghton Mifflin Harcourt Publishing Co.

—The Year of the Book. Halpin, Abigail, illus. (Anna Wang Novel Ser.: 1). (ENG.). 160p. (J). (gr. 1-4). 2013. pap. 5.99 (978-0-544-02263-8(7)) 2012. 16.99 (978-0-547-68463-5(0)) Houghton Mifflin Harcourt Publishing Co.

—The Year of the Garden. Barton, Patrice, illus. 2017. (Anna Wang Novel Ser.: 5). (ENG.). 128p. (J). (gr. 1-4). 15.99 (978-0-544-66444-9(2), HMH Books For Young Readers) Houghton Mifflin Harcourt Publishing Co.

—The Year of the Three Sisters. Barton, Patrice, illus. (Anna Wang Novel Ser.: 4). (ENG.). 160p. (J). (gr. 1-4). 2016. pap. 5.99 (978-0-544-66849-2(9)) 2015. 16.99 (978-0-544-34427-3(8)) Houghton Mifflin Harcourt Publishing Co. (HMH Books For Young Readers).

Chenous, Brad. Stories from Farmer Ready's. 2011. 52p. (gr. 4-6). pap. 9.99 (978-1-4634-0001-9(2)) AuthorHouse.

Cherry, Alison. Willows vs. Wolverines. 2017. (Mix Ser.). (ENG., Illus.). 352p. (J). (gr. 4-8). 17.99 (978-1-4814-6354-6(3), Simon & Schuster/Paula Wiseman Bks.) Simon & Schuster/Paula Wiseman Bks.

Cherry Kathleen. Everyday Hero, 1 vol. 2016. (ENG.). 168p. (J). (gr. 4-7). pap. 9.95 (978-1-4598-0982-6(3)) Orca Bk. Pubs. USA.

Chester, Laura. Marvel the Marvelous. Lippincott, Gary A., illus. 2008. (ENG.). 176p. (J). 18.95 (978-1-59543-841-6(6)) Willow Creek Pr., Inc.

Chetdav, Rain S. Acidrain. 2003. 108p. (YA). pap. 9.95 (978-0-595-26560-2(X), Writers Club Pr.) iUniverse, Inc.

Cheverton, Mark. Saving Crafter. 2015. (ENG.). 304p. (J). (gr. 3). pap. 9.99 (978-1-5107-0014-7(5), Sky Pony Pr.) Skyhorse Publishing Co., Inc.

Chew, Ruth. A Matter-Of-Fact Magic Book: Witch in the House. 2016. (Matter-Of-Fact Magic Book Ser.). (ENG., Illus.). 144p. (J). (gr. 2-5). 5.99 (978-0-449-81586-1(2), Random Hse. Bks. for Young Readers) Random Hse. Children's Bks.

—Witch's Broom. 2015. (Matter-Of-Fact Magic Book Ser.). (ENG., Illus.). 144p. (J). (gr. 2-5). pap. 5.99

(978-0-449-81578-6(1), Random Hse. Bks. for Young Readers) Random Hse. Children's Bks.
Chiarello, Robin Taylor. The Blue Lobster's Holiday! Bohart, Lisa, illus. 2012. 40p. pap. 16.95 *(978-1-61493-053-2(8))* Peppertree Pr., The.
Chiarini, Chynna. Hippy Potto's Travel Adventure. 2010. 48p. pap. 11.99 *(978-1-4520-3447-8(8))* AuthorHouse.
Chic, Suzy & Touvay, Monique. Watching. 2007. (ENG.). 48p. (J). (gr. k-2). 12.00 *(978-1-905341-07-8(5))* WingedChariot Pr. GBR. Dist: Independent Pubs. Group.
Chichester Clark, Emma. Bears Don't Read! Chichester Clark, Emma, illus. 2016. (Illus.). 32p. (J). 12.99 *(978-1-61067-366-2(2))* Kane Miller.
—Beside the Sea. Chichester Clark, Emma, illus. 2007. (Melrose & Croc Ser.). (ENG., Illus.). 32p. (J). (gr. -1-2). pap. 8.95 *(978-0-00-718244-2(9),* HarperCollins Children's Bks.) HarperCollins Pubs. Ltd. GBR. Dist: HarperCollins Pubs.
—Find a Smile, Vol. 1. 2009. (Melrose & Croc Ser.). (ENG., Illus.). 32p. (J). (gr. -1-2). pap. 8.95 *(978-0-00-718241-1(4))* HarperCollins Pubs. Ltd. GBR. Dist: Independent Pubs. Group.
—Go to Town. Chichester Clark, Emma, illus. 2007. (Melrose & Croc Ser.). (ENG., Illus.). 32p. (J). (gr. -1-2). pap. 8.95 *(978-0-00-718243-5(0),* HarperCollins Children's Bks.) HarperCollins Pubs. Ltd. GBR. Dist: HarperCollins Pubs.
—We Are Not Fond of Rat! Chichester Clark, Emma, illus. 2006. (Collins Big Cat Phonics Ser.). (ENG., Illus.). 16p. (J). (gr. -1-1). pap. 5.99 *(978-0-00-723590-2(9))* HarperCollins Pubs. Ltd. GBR. Dist: Independent Pubs. Group.
Chichester Clark, Emma, tr. & illus. Will & Squill. Chichester Clark, Emma, illus. 2006. 32p. (J). (gr. -1-k). 15.95 *(978-1-57505-936-5(3),* Carolrhoda Bks.) Lerner Publishing Group.
Chick, Bryan. Riddles & Danger. 2011. (Secret Zoo Ser.: 3). (ENG.). 288p. (J). (gr. 3-7). 16.99 *(978-0-06-198927-8(4),* Greenwillow Bks.) HarperCollins Pubs.
—The Secret Zoo: Traps & Specters. 2012. (Secret Zoo Ser.: 4). (ENG.). 320p. (J). (gr. 3-7). 16.99 *(978-0-06-219222-6(1),* Greenwillow Bks.) HarperCollins Pubs.
—The Secret Zoo: Raids & Rescues. (Secret Zoo Ser.: 5). (ENG.). 272p. (J). (gr. 3-7). 2014. pap. 6.99 *(978-0-06-219229-5(9))* 2013. 16.99 *(978-0-06-219228-8(0))* HarperCollins Pubs. (Greenwillow Bks.).
—Secrets & Shadows. 2011. (Secret Zoo Ser.: 2). (ENG.). 272p. (J). (gr. 3-7). pap. 6.99 *(978-0-06-198926-1(6));* 16.99 *(978-0-06-198925-4(8))* HarperCollins Pubs. (Greenwillow Bks.).
—Traps & Specters. 2013. (Secret Zoo Ser.: 4). (ENG.). 320p. (J). (gr. 3-7). pap. 6.99 *(978-0-06-219223-3(X),* Greenwillow Bks.) HarperCollins Pubs.
Chiew, Suzanne. Friends to the Rescue. Pedler, Caroline, illus. 2016. (ENG.). 32p. (J). (gr. -1-2). 16.99 *(978-1-68010-007-5(6))* Tiger Tales.
Chiew, Suzanne. That's What Friends Are For. Pedler, Caroline, illus. 2017. (ENG.). 32p. (J). (gr. -1-2). 16.99 ***(978-1-68010-040-2(8))*** Tiger Tales.
Child, Lauren. Clarice Bean Spells Trouble. Child, Lauren, illus. 2006. (Clarice Bean Ser.). (Illus.). 189p. (J). (gr. 3-6). 13.65 *(978-0-7569-7919-5(6))* Perfection Learning Corp.
—I Am Really, Really Concentrating. 2008. (Charlie & Lola Ser.). (ENG.). 24p. (J). (gr. -1-k). mass mkt. 3.99 *(978-0-448-44905-0(6),* Grosset & Dunlap) Penguin Young Readers Group.
—I Can Do Anything That's Everything All on My Own. 2008. (Charlie & Lola Ser.). (ENG., Illus.). 24p. (J). (gr. -1-k). mass mkt. 3.99 *(978-0-448-44792-6(4),* Grosset & Dunlap) Penguin Young Readers Group.
—My Best, Best Friend. 2011. (Charlie & Lola Ser.). (ENG.). 32p. (J). (gr. -1-k). 16.99 *(978-0-8037-3586-6(3),* Dial Bks) Penguin Young Readers Group.
—Slightly Invisible. Child, Lauren, illus. 2016. (Charlie & Lola Ser.). (ENG., Illus.). 40p. (J). (gr. -1-3). 19.65 *(978-0-606-39107-8(X))* Turtleback Bks.
—Spells Trouble. Child, Lauren, illus. 2006. (Clarice Bean Ser.). (ENG., Illus.). 192p. (J). (gr. 3-7). pap. 6.99 *(978-0-7636-2903-8(0))* Candlewick Pr.
—You Can Be My Friend. 2007. (Charlie & Lola Ser.). (ENG., Illus.). 24p. (J). (gr. -1-k). mass mkt. 3.99 *(978-0-448-44840-4(8),* Grosset & Dunlap) Penguin Young Readers Group.
Childress, H. Lee. The Cane. 2007. pap. 9.00 *(978-0-8059-8453-8(4))* Dorrance Publishing Co., Inc.
Childs, Barbara. Sammy & the Cow Bird. 2009. 48p. pap. 21.99 *(978-1-4389-8025-6(6))* AuthorHouse.
Chipponeri, Kelli. The Big Win. Aikins, Dave, illus. 2008. (SpongeBob SquarePants Ser.: 13). (ENG.). 32p. (J). (gr. k-2). pap. 3.99 *(978-1-4169-4938-1(0),* Simon Spotlight/Nickelodeon) Simon Spotlight/Nickelodeon.
Chisolm, Melinda. Remembering to Breathe. Cross, Jo Ellen, illus. 2009. 31p. pap. 24.95 *(978-1-60703-914-3(1))* America Star Bks.
Chmakova, Svetlana. Brave. 2017. (J). lib. bdg. 22.10 ***(978-0-606-40456-3(2))*** Turtleback Bks.
Choffel, Theodora L. A Coat for Ebony. 2007. (ENG.). 32p. pap. 16.00 *(978-1-4196-7719-9(5))* CreateSpace Independent Publishing Platform.
Choi, SeoYun. Let's Be Friends. Furukawa, Masumi, illus. rev. ed. 2014. (MySELF Bookshelf Ser.). (ENG.). 32p. (J). (gr. k-2). pap. 11.94 *(978-1-60357-658-1(4));* lib. bdg. 25.27 *(978-1-59953-649-1(8))* Norwood Hse. Pr.
Choldenko, Gennifer. Chasing Secrets. 2015. (ENG.). 288p. (J). (gr. 4-7). lib. bdg. 19.99 *(978-0-375-99063-2(1),* Lamb, Wendy Bks.) Random Hse. Children's Bks.
—Chasing Secrets. 2016. lib. bdg. 18.40 *(978-0-606-38879-5(6))* Turtleback Bks.
Choo, Missy. What Color Is Monday. 2010. 32p. pap. 17.25 *(978-1-4269-3070-6(4))* Trafford Publishing.
Chotjewitz, David. Daniel Half Human. Orgel, Doris, tr. from GER. 2006. (ENG., Illus.). 336p. (YA). (gr. 7). reprint ed. mass mkt. 8.99 *(978-0-689-85748-5(9),* Simon Pulse) Simon Pulse.
Chotjewitz, David & Orgel, Doris. Daniel, Half Human: And the Good Nazi. 2004. 298p. (J). *(978-3-551-58045-0(6))* Carlsen Verlag DEU. Dist: Distribooks, Inc.
Choyce, Lesley. Hell's Hotel, 1 vol. rev. ed. 2008. (Lorimer SideStreets Ser.). (ENG.). 224p. (YA). (gr. 9-12). 9.95 *(978-1-55277-022-1(2),* 9781552770221) Lorimer, James & Co., Ltd., Pubs. CAN. Dist: Casemate Pubs. & Bk. Distributors, LLC.
—Last Chance, 1 vol. 2009. (Lorimer SideStreets Ser.). (ENG.). 152p. (YA). (gr. 9-12). 9.95 *(978-1-55277-444-1(9),* 9781552774441) Lorimer, James & Co., Ltd., Pubs. CAN. Dist: Casemate Pubs. & Bk. Distributors, LLC.
—Reckless, 1 vol. 2010. (Orca Currents Ser.). (ENG.). (gr. 5-9). 128p. (J). pap. 9.95 *(978-1-55469-223-1(7));* 112p. (YA). lib. bdg. 16.95 *(978-1-55469-224-8(5))* Orca Bk. Pubs. USA.
—Scam. 2016. (Orca Soundings Ser.). lib. bdg. 20.80 *(978-0-606-38703-3(X))* Turtleback Bks.
Christenson, Deanna. Best Friends! 2011. 44p. pap. 21.99 *(978-1-4568-6560-3(9))* Xlibris Corp.
Christian, Diana. The Lucky Seven. 2005. 71p. pap. 19.95 *(978-1-4137-5471-1(6))* America Star Bks.
Christian Mauricio Constante. What a Catch! 2009. 24p. pap. 11.49 *(978-1-4389-6423-2(4))* AuthorHouse.
Christiansen, Candace. The Mitten Tree. Greenstein, Elaine, illus. 2009. (ENG.). 32p. (J). (gr. -1-1). pap. 10.95 *(978-1-55591-733-3(X))* Fulcrum Publishing.
Christianson, Leslie Rose. Malinda Matters: And Priscilla the Praying Mantis. 2010. 36p. pap. 15.49 *(978-1-4490-6914-8(2))* AuthorHouse.
Christopher, Kathleen. Janie's First Day of School. 2012. 32p. pap. 24.95 *(978-1-62709-914-1(X))* America Star Bks.
Christopher, Matt. Baseball World Series. (Little League Ser.: 5). (ENG., 208p. (J). (gr. 3-7). 2015. Illus.). pap. 7.00 *(978-0-316-21295-3(4))* 2014. 16.00 *(978-0-316-22046-0(9))* Little, Brown Bks. for Young Readers.
—Day of the Dragon, No. 2. 2004. (ENG., Illus.). 64p. (J). (gr. 1-4). pap. 13.99 *(978-0-316-73753-1(4))* Little, Brown Bks. for Young Readers.
—The Extreme Team: Skateboard Moves. Leonard, David, illus. 2013. (Passport to Reading Level 3 Ser.: 1). (ENG.). 32p. (J). (gr. 1-4). 3.99 *(978-0-316-25230-0(1))* Little, Brown Bks. for Young Readers.
—Football Double Threat. 2008. (ENG.). 128p. (J). (gr. 3-7). pap. 5.99 *(978-0-316-01632-2(2))* Little, Brown Bks. for Young Readers.
—Hook Shot Hero: A Nothin' but Net Sequel. 2011. (ENG.). 144p. (J). (gr. 3-7). pap., pap. 5.99 *(978-0-316-10296-4(2))* Little, Brown Bks. for Young Readers.
—Into the Danger Zone. Koelsch, Michael, illus. 6th ed. 2004. (ENG.). 64p. (J). (gr. 1-4). pap. 13.99 *(978-0-316-76267-0(9),* Tingley, Megan Bks.) Little, Brown Bks. for Young Readers.
—Little Lefty. 2009. (J). pap. 7.95 *(978-1-933523-38-5(7))* Bella Rosa Bks.
—On Thin Ice. Koelsch, Michael, illus. 4th ed. 2004. (ENG.). 64p. (J). (gr. 1-4). pap. 13.99 *(978-0-316-73739-5(9))* Little, Brown Bks. for Young Readers.
—One Smooth Move. Koelsch, Michael, illus. 2004. (ENG.). 64p. (J). (gr. 1-4). pap. 13.99 *(978-0-316-73749-4(6))* Little, Brown Bks. for Young Readers.
—Roller Hockey Rumble. Koelsch, Michael, tr. Koelsch, Michael, illus. 3rd ed. 2004. (ENG.). 64p. (J). (gr. 1-4). pap. 13.99 *(978-0-316-73755-5(0))* Little, Brown Bks. for Young Readers.
—Slam Dunk. 2004. (ENG., Illus.). 128p. (J). (gr. 3-7). pap. 5.99 *(978-0-316-60762-9(2))* Little, Brown Bks. for Young Readers.
—Slide, Danny, Slide. 2010. (ENG.). 138p. (YA). pap. 9.95 *(978-1-933523-39-2(5))* Bella Rosa Bks.
—Stranger in Right Field. Dodson, Bert, illus. 2009. (New Peach Street Mudders Sports Library). 64p. (J). (gr. 2-4). lib. bdg. 23.93 *(978-1-59953-322-3(7))* Norwood Hse. Pr.
Christy, Jana, illus. The Never Girls Collecton #3 (Disney: the Never Girls), 4 vols. 2016. (ENG.). 512p. (J). (gr. 1-4). 23.96 *(978-0-7364-3521-5(2),* RH/Disney) Random Hse. Children's Bks.
Chung, Helena. Jennifer, the Special One. 2004. (J). pap. 8.00 *(978-0-8059-6395-3(2))* Dorrance Publishing Co., Inc.
Church, Caroline Jayne. Ruff! And the Wonderfully Amazing Busy Day. Church, Caroline Jayne, illus. 2013. (ENG., Illus.). 32p. (J). (gr. k-3). 17.99 *(978-0-06-201498-6(6))* HarperCollins Pubs.
Churchman, Jennifer & Churchman, John. Brave Little Finn. 2016. (Sweet Pea & Friends Ser.). (ENG., Illus.). 40p. (J). (gr. -1-3). 17.99 *(978-0-316-27359-6(7))* Little, Brown Bks. for Young Readers.
Chuslo-Shur, Lauren, ed. The Golden Friendship. 2012. (ENG.). (J). pap. *(978-1-4675-4581-5(3))* Independent Pub.
Ciminera, Siobhan. Farm Animal Friends. Collection/Jupiterimages Unlimited, illus. 2009. (ENG.). 48p. (J). (gr. -1-2). 12.99 *(978-1-4169-6786-6(9),* Simon Scribbles) Simon Scribbles.
Ciminera, Siobhan, adapted by. Get the Sillies Out! 2009. (Yo Gabba Gabba! Ser.). (ENG.). 16p. (J). (gr. -1-1). pap. 5.99 *(978-1-4169-7099-6(1),* Simon Spotlight) Simon Spotlight.
Ciminera, Siobhan & Rao, Lisa. Hello, Friends! Yoe! Studio Staff, illus. 2009. (Yo Gabba Gabba! Ser.). (ENG.). 64p. (J). 4.99 *(978-1-4169-7460-4(1),* Simon Scribbles) Simon Scribbles.
Ciocca, Gina. Last Year's Mistake. 2015. (ENG., Illus.). 320p. (YA). (gr. 9). 17.99 *(978-1-4814-3223-8(0),* Simon Pulse) Simon Pulse.
Cioffi, Erin. The Lost Carrot. 2012. 16p. pap. 15.99 *(978-1-4772-2078-8(X))* AuthorHouse.
Ciraolo, Simona, illus. Hug Me. 2014. (ENG.). 32p. (J). (gr. -1-2). 17.95 *(978-1-909263-49-9(4))* Flying Eye Bks. GBR. Dist: Consortium Bk. Sales & Distribution.
Cirrone, Dorian. The First Last Day. (ENG., Illus.). 240p. (J). (gr. 3-7). 2017. pap. 7.99 ***(978-1-4814-5814-6(0))*** 2016. 17.99 *(978-1-4814-5813-9(2))* Simon & Schuster Children's Publishing. (Aladdin).
Citra, Becky. After the Fire, 1 vol. 2010. (ENG.). 192p. (J). (gr. 4-7). pap. 10.95 *(978-1-55469-246-0(6))* Orca Bk. Pubs. USA.
Clairmont, Patsy. 5 Cheesy Stories: About Friendship, Bravery, Bullying, & More, 1 vol. Oeltjenbruns, Joni, illus. 2007. (Tails from the Pantry Ser.). (ENG.). 144p. (gr. -1-2). 15.99 *(978-1-4003-1042-5(3))* Nelson, Thomas Inc.
Clamp Staff. Cardcaptor Sakura, Vol. 6. rev. ed. 2005. (Illus.). 192p. pap. 9.99 *(978-1-59182-883-9(X),* Tokyopop Kids) TOKYOPOP, Inc.
Clanton, Ben. Narwhal: Unicorn of the Sea! 2016. (Narwhal & Jelly Book Ser.). (ENG., Illus.). 64p. (J). (gr. 1-4). pap. 7.99 *(978-1-101-91871-5(3),* Tundra Bks.) Tundra Bks. CAN. Dist: Penguin Random Hse. LLC.
—Rex Wrecks It! Clanton, Ben, illus. 2014. (ENG., Illus.). 40p. (J). (gr. -1-2). 15.99 *(978-0-7636-6501-2(0))* Candlewick Pr.
Clapp. Eloy the Elk & His Desert Friends. Clapp, ed. Drotar, illus. 2009. (J). pap. 9.95 *(978-0-9825181-0-6(2))* Arizona Elk Society.
Clar, David Austin, illus. Follow the Leader. 2003. (Rainbow Fish & Friends Ser.). (ENG.). 24p. (J). (gr. -1-2). 3.99 *(978-1-59014-106-9(7))* North-South Bks., Inc.
Clark, Catherine. Eleven Things I Promised. 2016. 304p. (YA). (gr. 8). pap. 9.99 *(978-0-06-226453-4(2),* HarperTeen) HarperCollins Pubs.
—Picture Perfect. 2008. (ENG.). 352p. (YA). (gr. 9-18). pap. 5.99 *(978-0-06-137497-5(0),* HarperTeen) HarperCollins Pubs.
Clark, Jay. The Edumacation of Jay Baker. 2012. (ENG.). 288p. (YA). (gr. 9-12). pap. 9.99 *(978-1-250-01675-1(4))* Square Fish.
Clark, Joan. Ann Drew Jackson. Clark, Nathan, illus. 2007. 122p. per. 17.95 *(978-1-931282-45-1(5))* Autism Asperger Publishing Co.
—Jackson Whole Wyoming. 2005. 16.00 *(978-1-931282-72-7(2),* 9945) Autism Asperger Publishing Co.
Clark, Johnny C. Poor Poor Ollie. 2012. 20p. pap. 24.95 *(978-1-62709-099-5(1))* America Star Bks.
Clark, Kristin Elizabeth. Jess, Chunk, & the Road Trip to Infinity. 2016. (ENG.). 272p. (YA). 17.99 *(978-0-374-38006-9(6),* 9780374380069, Farrar, Straus & Giroux (BYR)) Farrar, Straus & Giroux.
Clark, Leslie Ann. Peepsqueak Wants a Friend! Clark, Leslie Ann, illus. 2013. (ENG., Illus.). 32p. (J). (gr. -1-3). 15.99 *(978-0-06-207804-9(6))* HarperCollins Pubs.
Clark, Maxine. Build-A-Bear Workshop Furry Friends Hall of Fame: The Official Collector's Guide. 2005. (Illus.). 159p. (J). (gr. 4-7). *(978-1-59258-142-9(0))* Hylas Publishing.
Clark, Melissa. Bear Witness: A Novel. 2015. (ENG.). 118p. pap. 13.00 *(978-1-940716-75-6(6))* SparkPr. (a Bks.parks Imprint).
Clark, Ruth. Airport Mouse Works the Nightshift. 2008. (ENG.). 32p. (J). 15.95 *(978-0-9792963-3-8(1))* Hollywood Operating System.
Clark, Ruth E. Airport Mouse. Jones, Phil, illus. 2008. (ENG.). 32p. (J). (gr. -1-3). 15.95 *(978-0-9792963-2-1(3))* Hibiscus Publishing.
—Airport Mouse Activity Fun Book 1. Jones, Phil, illus. 2010. 16p. (J). pap. 5.99 *(978-0-9792963-6-9(6))* Huntington Ludlow Media Group.
—Airport Mouse Becomes a VIP/VIM World Traveler. Jones, Phil, illus. 2009. 32p. (J). 15.95 *(978-0-9792963-5-2(8))* Kimball, Jane A.
—Airport Mouse Explores on Opening Day Activity Fun Book 3. Jones, Phil, illus. 2010. 16p. (J). pap. 5.99 *(978-0-9792963-8-3(2))* Kimball, Jane A.
Clark Sherryl Staff. Bone Song. 2008. (Cutting Edge Ser.). (ENG.). 200p. pap. *(978-1-84167-751-4(5))* Ransom Publishing Ltd.
Clarke, Cat. Undone. 2014. (ENG.). 384p. (YA). (gr. 8-12). 16.99 *(978-1-4022-9224-8(4),* 9781402292248) Sourcebooks, Inc.
Clarke, David. Snake Bite: A Novel. 2009. 188p. 23.95 *(978-0-595-71833-7(7));* pap. 13.95 *(978-0-595-48406-5(9))* iUniverse, Inc.
Clarke, Graham. Fluffy Rabbit & Friends. 2016. (ENG.). 117p. (J). (gr. 1-2). 10.95 *(978-1-78554-339-5(3),* 80259502-e5fd-4c6b-93c4-99cb4e1f5c2c) Austin, Stan AUS. Dist: Bookmasters Distribution.
Clarke, Jane. G. E. M. Parsons, Garry, illus. 2008. (ENG.). 32p. (J). (gr. -1-k). pap. 9.95 *(978-0-09-948012-9(3),* Red Fox) Random House Children's Books GBR. Dist: Independent Pubs. Group.
Clarke, Jane & Fuge, Charles. Gilbert the Great. 2016. (ENG., Illus.). 32p. (J). (gr. -1-2). 6.95 *(978-1-4549-1912-4(4))* Sterling Publishing Co., Inc.
Clarke, Lizzy. The Spirit of the Jaguar. 2013. 92p. (gr. -1). 21.38 *(978-1-4907-0602-3(X))* Trafford Publishing.
Clasky, Leonard. Kate's Camp Friends: Putting Data in Order. 2017. (Computer Science for the Real World Ser.). 16p. (gr. 7-8). pap. 7.95 ***(978-1-5383-5196-3(X),*** Rosen Classroom) Rosen Publishing Group, Inc., The.
Classic Goosebumps & Stine, R. L. Say Cheese & Die! 2009. (Classic Goosebumps Ser.: 8). (ENG.). 160p. (J). (gr. 3-7). 6.99 *(978-0-545-03525-5(2),* Scholastic Paperbacks) Scholastic, Inc.
Claudine Sherels Johnson. Nire Goes to the Color Books Bookstore: Featuring God Is Awesome & Pink Carnation. 2009. 84p. pap. 10.49 *(978-1-4389-5952-8(4))* AuthorHouse.
Clausman, Rachel. Phineas the Talker. 2011. 28p. pap. 12.99 *(978-1-4634-1088-9(3))* AuthorHouse.
Clay, Dorian. Freddie Loses His Game. 2012. 64p. pap. 5.95 *(978-1-938056-04-8(3))* ARIVA Publishing.
—Freddie Loses His Game. Clay, Dorian, illus. 2012. (Illus.). 64p. pap. 12.99 *(978-1-938056-03-1(5))* ARIVA Publishing.
Clayton, Dallas. Lily the Unicorn. Clayton, Dallas, illus. 2014. (ENG., Illus.). 48p. (J). (gr. -1-3). 17.99 *(978-0-06-211668-0(1))* HarperCollins Pubs.
Cleary, Beverly. Mitch & Amy. Tiegreen, Alan & Dockray, Tracy, illus. 2008. (Cleary Reissue Ser.). (ENG.). 288p. (J). (gr. 3-7). pap. 6.99 *(978-0-380-70925-0(2))* HarperCollins Pubs.
—Ramona la Chinche. Palacios, Argentina, tr. Darling, Louis, illus. 2006. (Ramona Quimby Spanish Ser.: 2).Tr. of Ramona the Pest. (SPA.). 181p. (J). (gr. 4-7). lib. bdg. 16.00 *(978-0-613-00464-0(7),* Turtleback) Turtleback Bks.
Cleary, Christopher. Writing on the Wall. 2007. 198p. (YA). per. 9.99 *(978-0-9795753-5-8(4))* Immortality Pr.
Clement-Moore, Rosemary. Hell Week. 2009. (Maggie Quinn: Girl vs Evil Ser.). (ENG.). 336p. (YA). (gr. 9). pap. 9.99 *(978-0-385-73415-8(8),* Delacorte Bks. for Young Readers) Random Hse. Children's Bks.
Clements, Andrew. Extra Credit. Elliott, Mark, illus. 2009. (ENG.). 192p. (J). (gr. 3-7). 16.99 *(978-1-4169-4929-9(1),* Atheneum Bks. for Young Readers) Simon & Schuster Children's Publishing.
—Jake Drake, Know-It-All. Frazee, Marla & Pedersen, Janet, illus. 2007. (Jake Drake Ser.: Bk. 2). 88p. (gr. 2-5). 15.00 *(978-0-7569-8212-6(X))* Perfection Learning Corp.
—Jake Drake, Know-It-All. Pedersen, Janet & Frazee, Marla, illus. 2007. (Jake Drake Ser.: Bk. 2). (ENG.). 112p. (J). (gr. 2-5). pap. 5.99 *(978-1-4169-3931-3(8),* Atheneum Bks. for Young Readers) Simon & Schuster Children's Publishing.
—The Last Holiday Concert. Selznick, Brian, illus. 2004. (ENG.). 176p. (J). (gr. 3-7). 17.99 *(978-0-689-84516-1(2),* Atheneum Bks. for Young Readers) Simon & Schuster Children's Publishing.
—Lost & Found. Elliott, Mark, illus. 2008. (ENG.). 176p. (J). (gr. 3-7). 16.99 *(978-1-4169-0985-9(0),* Atheneum Bks. for Young Readers) Simon & Schuster Children's Publishing.
—The Map Trap. Andreasen, Dan, illus. 2016. (ENG.). 160p. (J). (gr. 3-7). pap. 7.99 *(978-1-4169-9728-3(8))* Simon & Schuster Children's Publishing.
—The Map Trap. LaMarche, Jim & Andreasen, Dan, illus. 2014. (ENG.). 144p. (J). (gr. 3-7). 17.99 *(978-1-4169-9727-6(X),* Atheneum Bks. for Young Readers) Simon & Schuster Children's Publishing.
—The Map Trap. 2016. lib. bdg. 18.40 *(978-0-606-38977-8(6))* Turtleback Bks.
—The Report Card. (ENG., Illus.). (J). (gr. 3-7). 2004. 176p. 18.99 *(978-0-689-84515-4(4))* 2006. 192p. reprint ed. pap. 7.99 *(978-0-689-84524-6(3))* Simon & Schuster Children's Publishing. (Atheneum Bks. for Young Readers).
—Room One: A Mystery or Two. Blair, Chris & Elliott, Mark, illus. 2006. (ENG.). 176p. (J). (gr. 3-7). 17.99 *(978-0-689-86686-9(0),* Atheneum Bks. for Young Readers) Simon & Schuster Children's Publishing.
—We the Children. Stower, Adam, illus. 2010. (Benjamin Pratt & the Keepers of the School Ser.: 1). (ENG.). 160p. (J). (gr. 2-5). 14.99 *(978-1-4169-3886-6(9),* Atheneum Bks. for Young Readers) Simon & Schuster Children's Publishing.
Clendenin, Arlene M. & Clendenin, Bernard S. The Adventures of the Yellow Beak Bird & the Flying Cats: Yellow Beak Bird & the Flying Cats. 2013. 48p. pap. 11.99 *(978-0-9897662-1-0(7))* Clendenin Fine Art Concepts.
Cline, H. R. Baxter's Backyard Adventures. 2009. 32p. pap. 13.99 *(978-1-4389-5939-9(7))* AuthorHouse.
Clocktowerhill Research & Publishing Group. Loyd & Boyd & the Slug Monster of Webster County. 2011. (ENG., Illus.). 104p. (J). 12.99 *(978-0-9832130-0-0(3),* Lucas Violet) Clocktower Hill Research & Publishing Group, LLC.
Clough, Lisa. Petal & Poppy. Briant, Ed, illus. 2014. (Green Light Readers Level 2 Ser.). (ENG.). 32p. (J). (gr. -1-3). pap. 3.99 *(978-0-544-11380-0(2),* HMH Books For Young Readers) Houghton Mifflin Harcourt Publishing Co.
—Petal & Poppy & the Penguin. Briant, Ed, illus. 2014. (Green Light Readers Level 2 Ser.). (ENG.). 32p. (J). (gr. -1-3). 12.99 *(978-0-544-13770-7(1));* pap. 3.99 *(978-0-544-13330-3(7))* Houghton Mifflin Harcourt Publishing Co. (HMH Books For Young Readers).
Clulow, Helen. The Frog Prince of Barker's Bay. 2003. 162p. pap. *(978-0-7022-3335-7(8))* Univ. of Queensland Pr.
Coatsworth, Elizabeth Jane. The Fair American. Sewell, Helen, illus. 2005. (Sally (Bethlehem Books) Ser.). 137p. (J). pap. 11.95 *(978-1-883937-85-0(X))* Bethlehem Bks.
Cobb, Amy. First Chair, 1 vol. Cattish, Anna, illus. 2015. (ENG.). 112p. (J). *(978-1-62402-074-2(7))* Magic Wagon.
—Mr. Byrd Flies the Nest. 2016. (Band Geeks Set 2 Ser.). (ENG.). (J). (gr. 3-6). lib. bdg. 27.07 ***(978-1-62402-173-2(5))*** ABDO Publishing Co.
—Nothing but Treble. 2016. (Band Geeks Set 2 Ser.). (ENG.). (J). (gr. 3-6). lib. bdg. 27.07 ***(978-1-62402-174-9(3))*** ABDO Publishing Co.
Cobb, Shawna. Little Sticker. 2012. 32p. pap. 24.95 *(978-1-62709-940-0(9))* America Star Bks.
Cochran, Randy. Critter Golf: The Adventures at Owl's Nest. 2013. (ENG.). 84p. (YA). pap. 8.95 *(978-1-4787-1263-3(5))* Outskirts Pr., Inc.
—Critter Golf Ii: Chaos at Owl's Nest. 2013. 148p. pap. 10.95 *(978-1-4787-0302-0(4))* Outskirts Pr., Inc.
—Critter Golf Iii: The Storm. 2013. 140p. pap. 10.95 *(978-1-4787-1610-5(X))* Outskirts Pr., Inc.
Cochrane, Mick. The Girl Who Threw Butterflies. 2010. (ENG.). 192p. (J). (gr. 3-7). 6.99 *(978-0-375-84610-6(7),* Yearling) Random Hse. Children's Bks.
Cockburn, Gerrie L. Why Turtles Have Shells. Cockburn, Ian, ed. Cockburn, Gerrie L., illus. (Friendship Ser.). (Illus.). 31p. (Orig.). (J). (gr. k-4). pap. 5.95 *(978-1-887461-00-9(0))* Cockburn Publishing.
Cocks, Nancy. Fergie Tries to Fly. Marton, Jirina, illus. 2003. 16p. pap. *(978-2-89507-275-1(2))* Novalis Publishing.
—Where, Oh Where, Is Fergie? Marton, Jirina, illus. 2003. 16p. pap. *(978-2-89507-273-7(6))* Novalis Publishing.
—You Can Count on Fergie. Marton, Jirina, illus. 2003. 16p. pap. *(978-2-89507-272-0(8))* Novalis Publishing.
Cocks, Nancy & Marton, Jirina. Nobody Loves Fergie. 2003. (Illus.). 16p. pap. *(978-2-89507-274-4(4))* Novalis Publishing.
Coe, Mary E. Willy: the Best Christmas Gift Ever. 2008. 127p. 25.95 *(978-0-557-02890-0(6));* pap. 10.95 *(978-1-4357-1627-8(2))* Lulu Pr., Inc.
—Willy: the Best Christmas Gift Ever a Children's Book. 2009. 95p. pap. 9.95 *(978-0-557-09420-2(8))* Lulu Pr., Inc.
—Willy: the Best Christmas Gift Ever A Children's Book. 2009. 55p. pap. 9.95 *(978-0-557-08687-0(6))* Lulu Pr., Inc.
Coffey, Ethel. How Meg Changed Her Mind. Schweitzer-Johnson, Betty, illus. 2014. (ENG.). 32p. pap. 11.95 *(978-1-4525-8377-8(3),* Balboa Pr.) Author Solutions, Inc.
Coffey, Stephen. Rosemary Herbb & the Zodiac Ghosts. 2009. 148p. pap. 14.50 *(978-1-4092-9751-2(9))* Lulu Pr., Inc.
Coh, Smiljana. Princesses on the Run. 2013. (ENG., Illus.). 40p. (J). (gr. -1-17). 15.95 *(978-0-7624-4612-4(9),* Running Pr. Kids) Running Pr. Bk. Pubs.
Cohagan, Carolyn. The Lost Children. 2011. (ENG.). 320p. (J). (gr. 3-7). pap. 7.99 *(978-1-4169-8617-1(0),* Aladdin) Simon & Schuster Children's Publishing.
—The Lost Children. 2010. (ENG.). 320p. (J). (gr. 3-7). 16.99 *(978-1-4169-8616-4(2),* Simon & Schuster/Paula Wiseman Bks.) Simon & Schuster/Paula Wiseman Bks.
Cohen, Barbara S. Forever Friends. Hall, Dorothy Louise, illus. 2015. (ENG.). 100p. (J). reprint ed. pap. 9.95 *(978-1-931290-54-8(7))* Tallfellow Pr.

E
F
G

Cohen, Jerianne. Max A. Million's Birthday Party. 2008. 193p. pap. 24.95 (978-1-60672-844-4(X)) America Star Bks.
Cohen, Leah. Sophie. 2010. 24p. 11.49 (978-1-4520-1854-6(5)) AuthorHouse.
Cohen, Marina. The Inn Between. Watts, Sarah, illus. 2016. (ENG.). 208p. (J). 16.99 (978-1-62672-202-6(1), 9781626722026) Roaring Brook Pr.
Cohen, Miriam. Two Little Mittens, 1 vol. Cohen, Miriam, illus. 2006. (ENG., Illus.). 32p. (J). (gr. -1). pap. 6.95 (978-1-59572-044-3(8)) Star Bright Bks., Inc.
—Will I Have a Friend?, 1 vol. Himler, Ronald, illus. 2008. (ENG.). 32p. (J). (gr. k-3). 15.95 (978-1-59572-069-6(3)) Star Bright Bks., Inc.
Cohen, Morris L. & Cohen, Miriam. Best Friends. 2007. (ENG.). 32p. (J). (gr. -1-3). 10.99 (978-1-4169-6501-5(7), Simon & Schuster/Paula Wiseman Bks.) Simon & Schuster/Paula Wiseman Bks.
Cohen, Pamela June. Ashie: Lost in the Hurricane. Lang, Allison, illus. 2008. 40p. pap. 24.95 (978-1-60474-961-8(X)) America Star Bks.
Cohen, Paula Marantz. Beatrice Bunson's Guide to Romeo & Juliet. 2016. (ENG.). 200p. (J). (gr. 4-9). pap. 11.95 (978-1-58988-105-1(2)) Dry, Paul Bks., Inc.
Cohn, Diana. Namaste! Cordova, Amy, illus. 2012. (ENG.). 32p. (J). pap. 9.95 (978-1-62148-005-1(4)) SteinerBooks, Inc.
Coia, Kristina. Lymeria. 2007. 120p. (YA). 20.95 (978-0-595-69347-4(4)); per. 10.95 (978-0-595-45268-2(X)) iUniverse, Inc.
Colasanti, Susane. City Love. 2015. (City Love Ser.: 1). (ENG.). 336p. (YA). (gr. 9). 17.99 (978-0-06-230768-2(1), Tegen, Katherine Bks) HarperCollins Pubs.
—Something Like Fate. 2011. (ENG., Illus.). 304p. (YA). (gr. 7-18). 9.99 (978-0-14-241882-6(X), Speak) Penguin Young Readers Group.
Colbert, Cory. Sammy the Sea Otter Makes New Friends: Adventures of Sammy the Sea Otter. 2011. 18p. pap. 11.95 (978-1-4327-7648-0(7)) Outskirts Pr., Inc.
Cole, Anjennetta. Cory's Classroom Rules. 2012. 28p. pap. 15.99 (978-1-4685-3652-2(4)) AuthorHouse.
Cole, Barbara H. Wash Day, 1 vol. Himler, Ronald, illus. 2004. (ENG.). 32p. (J). 15.95 (978-1-932065-36-7(9), 7187849112) Star Bright Bks., Inc.
Cole, Brock. Celine. 2003. (ENG.). 224p. (YA). (gr. 7-12). pap. 16.99 (978-0-374-41082-7(8), 9780374410827, Farrar, Straus & Giroux (BYR)) Farrar, Straus & Giroux.
—The Goats. 2003. 20.75 (978-0-8446-7238-0(6)) Smith, Peter Pub., Inc.
—The Goats. Cole, Brock, illus. 2010. (ENG., Illus.). 192p. (YA). (gr. 7-10). pap. 9.99 (978-0-312-61191-0(9), 9780312611910) Square Fish.
Cole, Bud. The Mystery of Little Bear. 2012. pap. 12.95 (978-0-7414-8106-1(5)) Infinity Publishing.
Cole, Frank. The Adventures of Hashbrown Winters. 2009. (J). pap. 7.99 (978-1-59955-303-0(1)) Cedar Fort, Inc./CFI Distribution.
Cole, Frank. The World's Greatest Adventure Machine. 2017. (J). **(978-0-399-55284-7(7))** Penguin Publishing Group.
Cole, Frank L. The World's Greatest Adventure Machine. 2017. (ENG.). 320p. (J). (gr. 4-7). 16.99 **(978-0-399-55282-3(0)**, Delacorte Bks. for Young Readers) Random Hse. Children's Bks.
Cole, Henry. Brambleheart. Cole, Henry, illus. 2016. (Brambleheart Ser.: 1). (Illus.). 272p. (J). (gr. 3-7). 16.99 (978-0-06-224546-5(5)) HarperCollins Pubs.
—Brambleheart: A Story about Finding Treasure & the Unexpected Magic of Friendship. Cole, Henry, illus. 2017. (Brambleheart Ser.: 1). (Illus.). 288p. (J). (gr. 3-7). pap. 6.99 (978-0-06-224544-1(9), Tegen, Katherine Bks) HarperCollins Pubs.
Cole, Kathryn. Sign up Here: A Story about Friendship, 1 vol. Leng, Qin, illus. 2016. (I'm a Great Little Kid Ser.). (ENG.). 24p. (J). (gr. 1-3). 15.95 (978-1-927583-90-6(X)) Second Story Pr. CAN. Dist: Orca Bk. Pubs. USA.
Cole, Kenneth. Friends & Neighbors: We Love to Learn. Ruebartsch, John, photos by. 2005. (Illus.). (J). pap. 9.95 (978-0-9770816-1-5(3)) SHARP Literacy, Inc.
—Friends & Neighbors: We Love to Learn. Ruebartsch, John, photos by. 2005. (Illus.). (J). 16.95 (978-0-9770816-0-8(5)) SHARP Literacy, Inc.
Cole-McCrea, Candace. The Seeing-Eye Dog: A Story of Brotherly Love. 2012. 28p. pap. 13.95 (978-1-4624-0050-8(7), Inspiring Voices) Author Solutions, Inc.
Cole, Penelope Ann. Magical Matthew. Collier, Kevin Scott, illus. 2012. 24p. pap. 10.95 (978-1-61633-326-3(X)) Guardian Angel Publishing, Inc.
Cole, Penelope Anne. Magical Matthew. Collier, Kevin Scott, illus. 2012. 24p. 19.95 (978-1-61633-325-6(1)) Guardian Angel Publishing, Inc.
—Magico Mateo. Collier, Kevin, illus. 2013. 24p. pap. 10.95 (978-1-61633-421-5(5)) Guardian Angel Publishing, Inc.
Cole, Stacey. Fluffy's Very Special Christmas. 2010. (Illus.). 32p. (J). pap. 26.95 (978-1-4327-4569-1(7)) Outskirts Pr., Inc.
Coleman, K. Showdown. 2017. (Gridiron Ser.). (ENG.). (YA). (gr. 6-12). 112p. pap. 7.99 **(978-1-5124-5354-6(4))**; lib. bdg. 26.65 **(978-1-5124-3978-6(9))** Lerner Publishing Group. (Darby Creek).
—Signing Day. 2017. (Gridiron Ser.). (ENG.). (YA). (gr. 6-12). 120p. pap. 7.99 **(978-1-5124-5355-3(2))**; lib. bdg. 26.65 **(978-1-5124-3983-0(5))** Lerner Publishing Group. (Darby Creek).
Coleman, K. R. The Late Hit. 2017. (Gridiron Ser.). (ENG.). 128p. (YA). (gr. 6-12). 26.65 **(978-1-5124-3982-3(7))**; pap. 7.99 **(978-1-5124-5352-2(8))** Lerner Publishing Group. (Darby Creek).
Coleman, Ryan. Folli: Children's Book of Characters. 2004. 20p. (J). pap. 24.95 (978-1-4137-4098-1(7)) PublishAmerica, Inc.
Coley, Patrick. The Chronicles of Maxwell & His Runaways. 2012. 134p. 29.99 (978-1-4797-0759-1(7)); pap. 19.99 (978-1-4797-0758-4(9)) Xlibris Corp.
Colfer, Chris. Stranger Than Fanfiction. 2017. (ENG.). (J). 304p. (gr. 10-17). 18.99 (978-0-316-38344-8(9)); 432p. (gr. 9-17). 20.99 (978-0-316-39678-3(8)) Little, Brown Bks. for Young Readers.
Colfer, Eoin. Benny & Babe. 2003. 240p. (YA). pap. 7.95 (978-0-86278-603-8(7)) O'Brien Pr., Ltd., The IRL. Dist: Independent Pubs. Group.
—Imaginary Fred. Jeffers, Oliver, illus. 2015. (ENG.). 48p. (J). (gr. -1-3). 18.99 (978-0-06-237955-9(0)) HarperCollins Pubs.
—The Supernaturalist. 2012. (Supernaturalist Ser.). (ENG.). 272p. (J). (gr. 5-9). pap. 7.99 (978-1-4231-4679-7(4)) Hyperion Pr.
Collard, Sneed B., III. Dog 4491. 2013. (Illus.). 256p. (J). 13.99 (978-0-9844460-4-9(4)) Bucking Horse Bks.
Collard, Sneed B., 3rd. Dog 4491. 2013. (ENG., Illus.). 256p. (J). pap. 8.00 (978-0-9844460-5-6(2)) Mountain Pr. Publishing Co., Inc.
Collett, Debra. The Reluctant Butterfly. 2013. (Illus.). 32p. pap. 13.95 (978-1-4908-1245-8(8), WestBow Pr.) Author Solutions, Inc.
Collier, James Lincoln. Me & Billy, 0 vols. unabr. ed. 2013. (ENG.). 194p. (J). (gr. 5-7). pap. 9.99 (978-1-4778-1706-3(9), 9781477817063, Amazon Children's Publishing) Amazon Publishing.
Collier, Kristen. Joy the Jellyfish. 2007. (Illus.). 24p. (J). per. (978-0-9797574-7-1(9)); (978-0-9797574-6-4(0)) Dragonfly Publishing, Inc.
Collier, Kristen & Collier, Kevin. Natalie's Ark. 2009. 84p. pap. 8.95 (978-1-61633-007-1(4)) Guardian Angel Publishing, Inc.
Collier, Kristi. Jericho Walls. 2007. (ENG.). 224p. (YA). (gr. 4-9). pap. 10.99 (978-0-8050-8184-8(4), 9780805081848, Holt, Henry & Co. Bks. For Young Readers) Holt, Henry & Co.
Collier, Talina L. Jacob & the Orange. 2012. 20p. pap. 24.95 (978-1-4626-8046-7(1)) America Star Bks.
—Jacob & the Turtle Race. 2012. 28p. pap. 24.95 (978-1-4626-8045-0(3)) America Star Bks.
Collins, Amanda. Bff!!! or Not??? 2007. 168p. per. 20.99 (978-1-4257-3370-4(0)) Xlibris Corp.
Collins, Amanda E. Bff!!! or Not??? 2007. 168p. 30.99 (978-1-4257-3371-1(9)) Xlibris Corp.
Collins, Ellen M. My Book: Fun Favorite Stories. 2010. 68p. pap. 26.99 (978-1-4490-5236-2(3)) AuthorHouse.
Collins, Lynette. The Round Door: The Willow Tree. 2017. (Round Door Ser.: Bk. 2). (ENG., Illus.). (J). pap. 28.22 **(978-1-5245-6171-0(1))** Xlibris Corp.
Collins, P. J. Sarah. Sam & Nate. Jin, Katherine, illus. 2005. 60p. (J). lib. bdg. 20.00 (978-1-4242-1261-3(8)) Fitzgerald Bks.
—Sam & Nate, 1 vol. Jin, Katherine, illus. 2005. (Orca Echoes Ser.). (ENG.). 64p. (J). (gr. 2-3). per. 6.95 (978-1-55143-334-9(6)) Orca Bk. Pubs. USA.
Collins, Paul. Lucy in a Jam. Bocquée, Christian, illus. 2015. (Legends in Their Own Lunchbox Ser.). (ENG.). 48p. (gr. 1-2). pap. 7.99 (978-1-4966-0248-0(X), Legends in Their Own Lunchbox) Capstone Classroom.
—Lucy, Kung-Fu Queen. Bocquée, Christian, illus. 2015. (Legends in Their Own Lunchbox Ser.). (ENG.). 48p. (gr. 1-2). pap. 7.99 (978-1-4966-0242-8(0), Legends in Their Own Lunchbox) Capstone Classroom.
Collins, Rachel. Fiddle Faddle Frog & Piddle Paddle Polliwog. 2010. 32p. pap. 16.95 (978-0-557-53411-1(9)) Lulu Pr., Inc.
Collins, Rudy. Vanessa Owens & the Bond of Sisterhood. 2011. 106p. pap. 19.95 (978-1-4560-7873-7(9)) America Star Bks.
Collins, Stephan. The Chronicles of Timothy Tabbis. 2009. 45p. pap. 8.55 (978-0-557-09266-6(3)) Lulu Pr., Inc.
Combs, Sarah. Breakfast Served Anytime. (ENG.). 272p. (gr. 7). 2016. (YA). pap. 7.99 (978-0-7636-8752-6(9)) 2014. (J). 16.99 (978-0-7636-6791-7(9)) Candlewick Pr.
Comyns, Barbara. Juniper Tree. 2011. (ENG.). 197p. pap. 14.95 (978-1-907429-19-4(0), Capuchin Classics) Stacey Publishing GBR. Dist: Casemate Pubs. & Bk. Distributors, LLC.
Concordia International School Shanghai. Stories from Room 113: International Adventures. 2008. 304p. pap. 18.95 (978-0-595-53090-8(7)) iUniverse, Inc.
Condenzio, Mary. The Mouse & the Star. Long, Paulette Rich, illus. 2008. 13p. pap. 24.95 (978-1-60441-449-3(9)) America Star Bks.
Condie, Ally. Reunion. 2008. 288p. (YA). pap. 15.95 (978-1-59038-989-8(1)) Deseret Bk. Co.
—Summerlost. (ENG.). 272p. (J). (gr. 5). 2017. 8.99 (978-0-399-18721-6(9), Puffin Books) 2016. 17.99 (978-0-399-18719-3(7), Dutton Books for Young Readers) Penguin Young Readers Group.
—Summerlost. 2017. lib. bdg. 19.65 **(978-0-606-40105-0(9))** Turtleback Bks.
Condie, Ally. Yearbook. 2006. 208p. (YA). pap. 14.95 (978-1-59038-690-3(6)) Deseret Bk. Co.
Condon, Bill. Riley & the Treasure. Hopgood, Andrew, illus. 2015. (Legends in Their Own Lunchbox Ser.). (ENG.). 56p. (gr. 2-3). pap. 7.99 (978-1-4966-0258-9(7), Legends in Their Own Lunchbox) Capstone Classroom.
—Riley Clowns Around. Hopgood, Andrew, illus. 2015. (Legends in Their Own Lunchbox Ser.). (ENG.). 48p. (gr. 1-2). pap. 7.99 (978-1-4966-0240-4(4), Legends in Their Own Lunchbox) Capstone Classroom.
—Riley Versus the Giant Banana. Hopgood, Andrew, illus. 2015. (Legends in Their Own Lunchbox Ser.). (ENG.). 48p. (gr. 1-2). pap. 7.99 (978-1-4966-0246-6(3), Legends in Their Own Lunchbox) Capstone Classroom.
Conklin, Wendy. Dos Amigos Planos Viajan por el Mundo, 1 vol. rev. ed. 2007. (Building Fluency Through Reader's Theater Ser.).Tr. of Two Flat Friends Travel the World. (SPA.). 24p. (J). (gr. 3-4). pap. 6.99 (978-1-4333-0022-6(2)) Teacher Created Materials, Inc.
Conkling, Keri. Glove of Their Own. Lambiase, Lauren, illus. 2008. 32p. 15.95 (978-0-9760469-5-0(4)) Franklin Mason Pr.
Conley, Cindy Taylor. For Little Louie Someday. 2013. 44p. pap. 24.95 (978-1-63000-044-8(2)) America Star Bks.
Conley, Deane W. Angelino & Friends. 2007. (J). lib. bdg. 19.95 (978-1-933732-25-1(3)) Big Ransom Studio.
Connell, Karen. The Adventures of Katie & Sam: A Day to Fly, 1 vol. 2009. 16p. pap. 24.95 (978-1-60813-702-2(3)) America Star Bks.
—Slow Down: The Adventures of Katie & Sam, 1 vol. 2010. 16p. 24.95 (978-1-4512-2073-5(1)) PublishAmerica, Inc.
Connelly, Neil. Into the Hurricane. 2017. (ENG.). 240p. (J). (gr. 9). 17.99 **(978-0-545-85381-1(8)**, Levine, Arthur A. Bks.) Scholastic, Inc.
Connelly, Peg. A Madman Hunts for Bigfoot. 2008. 110p. pap. 19.95 (978-1-60672-322-7(7)) America Star Bks.
Conner, Guy. Elizabeth & Parr. 2013. 90p. 24.00 (978-0-578-12011-9(9)) GRC Bks.
Connolly, Timothy. Joy's Journey Home. Sullivan, Mary, illus. 2012. (ENG.). 92p. (J). 17.95 (978-0-9859986-2-2(8)); pap. 8.95 (978-0-9859986-1-5(X)) Nectar Pubns.
Connor, D. E. L. Spirit Warriors: The Concealing. 2013. 186p. pap. 13.95 (978-1-62015-180-8(4), Booktrope Editions) Booktrope.
Connor, James. Surfing Summer. 2011. 138p. 22.99 (978-1-4568-8368-3(2)); pap. 15.99 (978-1-4568-8367-6(4)) Xlibris Corp.
—Surfing Summers. 2011. 138p. 22.99 (978-1-4568-9545-7(1)); pap. 15.99 (978-1-4568-9544-0(3)) Xlibris Corp.
Connor, Leslie. Waiting for Normal. (ENG.). (J). (gr. 5). 2010. 320p. pap. 6.99 (978-0-06-089090-2(8)) 2008. 304p. 16.99 (978-0-06-089088-9(6)) HarperCollins Pubs. (Tegen, Katherine Bks).
Connor, Lexi. The Runaway Spell. 2011. (B Magical Ser.: 3). (ENG.). 144p. (J). (gr. 3-7). pap. 5.99 (978-0-545-26552-2(5), Scholastic Paperbacks) Scholastic, Inc.
Conrad, Lauren. Infamous. 2013. (Fame Game Ser.: 3). (ENG.). 288p. (YA). (gr. 9). 18.99 (978-0-06-207984-8(0)) HarperCollins Pubs.
—L. A. Candy. (L. A. Candy Ser.: 1). (ENG.). (YA). (gr. 9-18). 2010. 352p. pap. 9.99 (978-0-06-176759-3(X)) 2009. 336p. 17.99 (978-0-06-176758-6(1)) HarperCollins Pubs.
Conroe, Lindy. Rockafella Jones & the Hidden Treasure. Riette, Susanne, illus. 2011. 108p. (J). pap. 10.95 (978-1-935199-00-7(5)) Blue Mustang Pr.
Conte, Alexander. Snow Storm. 2003. (J). per. 14.95 (978-1-932303-56-8(1), Llumina Pr.) Aeon Publishing Inc.
Converse, P. J. Subway Girl. 2011. (ENG.). 224p. (YA). (gr. 9-18). 16.99 (978-0-06-157514-3(3), HarperTeen) HarperCollins Pubs.
Cook, Beatrice. A Journey with the Spider & Snake to Arizona. Campis, Adrian, Jr., illus. 2007. (J). 14.95 (978-0-9795867-0-5(4)) Travel America Bks.
Cook, Diana. Wink Fish: Nate's Missed Adventure. 2011. 72p. pap. 41.99 (978-1-4628-8607-4(8)) Xlibris Corp.
Cook, Eileen. Fourth Grade Fairy. 2011. (Fourth Grade Fairy Ser.: 1). (ENG.). 176p. (J). (gr. 3-7). pap. 7.99 (978-1-4169-9811-2(X), Aladdin) Simon & Schuster Children's Publishing.
—Remember. 2015. (ENG., Illus.). 320p. (YA). (gr. 9). 17.99 (978-1-4814-1696-2(0), Simon Pulse) Simon Pulse.
—Used to Be: The Education of Hailey Kendrick & Getting Revenge on Lauren Wood. 2012. (ENG., Illus.). 608p. (YA). (gr. 9). pap. 11.99 (978-1-4424-7514-4(5), Simon Pulse) Simon Pulse.
—What Would Emma Do? 2008. (ENG.). 320p. (YA). (gr. 9-10). pap. 8.99 (978-1-4169-7432-1(6), Simon Pulse) Simon Pulse.
—Wishes for Beginners. 2011. (Fourth Grade Fairy Ser.: 2). (ENG.). 160p. (J). (gr. 3-7). pap. 6.99 (978-1-4169-9812-9(8), Aladdin) Simon & Schuster Children's Publishing.
—Year of Mistaken Discoveries. 2014. (ENG., Illus.). 272p. (YA). (gr. 9). 17.99 (978-1-4424-4022-7(8), Simon Pulse) Simon Pulse.
Cook, Jacqueline. On to Nationals. 2008. 296p. per. 12.95 (978-1-4327-1681-3(6)) Outskirts Pr., Inc.
Cook, Jeremy. Illusion of Time, 1 vol. 2010. 118p. pap. 19.95 (978-1-4489-6235-8(8)) America Star Bks.
—The Illusion Stick. 2008. 115p. pap. 19.95 (978-1-60474-705-8(6)) America Star Bks.
Cook, Julia. Making Friends Is an Art! Barnes, Bridget A., illus. 2012. (ENG.). 32p. (J). pap. 10.95 (978-1-934490-30-3(X)) Boys Town Pr.
Cook, Katie. My Little Pony: Friendship Is Magic Part 1: Friendship Is Magic Part 1. Price, Andy, illus. 2013. (My Little Pony Ser.). (ENG.). 52p. (J). (gr. 2-5). pap. 6.99 (978-1-61377-628-5(4), 9781613776285) Idea & Design Works, LLC.
—My Little Pony: Friendship Is Magic Volume 3: Friendship Is Magic Volume 3. Price, Andy, illus. 2014. (My Little Pony Ser.). (ENG.). 104p. pap. 17.99 (978-1-61377-854-8(6), 9781613778548) Idea & Design Works, LLC.
Cook, Melissa. Anna & the Garden Fairy: Anna's Little Black Bear. 2009. (ENG., Illus.). 20p. (J). 14.95 (978-1-57197-501-0(2), Ivy House Publishing Group) Pentland Pr., Inc.
Cook, Sherry & Johnson, Martin. Underwater Utley, 26. Kuhn, Jesse, illus. l.t. ed. 2006. (Quirkles — Exploring Phonics through Science Ser.: 21). 32p. (J). 7.99 (978-1-933815-20-6(5), Quirkles, The) Creative 3, LLC.
Cook, Sherry & Johnson, Terri. Gilbert Gas, 26 vols. Kuhn, Jesse, illus. l.t. ed. 2006. (Quirkles — Exploring Phonics through Science Ser.: 7). 32p. (J). 7.99 (978-1-933815-06-0(X), Quirkles, The) Creative 3, LLC.
—Hallie Heat, 26 vols. Kuhn, Jesse, illus. l.t. ed. 2006. (Quirkles — Exploring Phonics through Science Ser.: 8). 32p. (J). 7.99 (978-1-933815-07-7(8), Quirkles, The) Creative 3, LLC.
—Jazzy Jet, 26 vols. Kuhn, Jesse, illus. l.t. ed. 2006. (Quirkles — Exploring Phonics through Science Ser.: 10). 32p. (J). 7.99 (978-1-933815-09-1(4), Quirkles, The) Creative 3, LLC.
—Kitchen Chemistry Kal, 26 vols. Kuhn, Jesse, illus. l.t. ed. 2006. (Quirkles — Exploring Phonics through Science Ser.: 11). 32p. (J). 7.99 (978-1-933815-10-7(8), Quirkles, The) Creative 3, LLC.
—Mary Motion, 26 vols. Kuhn, Jesse, illus. l.t. ed. 2006. (Quirkles — Exploring Phonics through Science Ser.: 13). 32p. (J). 7.99 (978-1-933815-12-1(4), Quirkles, The) Creative 3, LLC.
—Nosey Nina, 26 vols. Kuhn, Jesse, illus. l.t. ed. 2006. (Quirkles — Exploring Phonics through Science Ser.: 14). 32p. (J). 7.99 (978-1-933815-13-8(2), Quirkles, The) Creative 3, LLC.
—Ollie Oxygen, 26 vols. Kuhn, Jesse, illus. l.t. ed. 2006. (Quirkles — Exploring Phonics through Science Ser.: 15). 32p. (J). 7.99 (978-1-933815-14-5(0), Quirkles, The) Creative 3, LLC.
—Pressure Pete, 26 vols. Kuhn, Jesse, illus. l.t. ed. 2006. (Quirkles — Exploring Phonics through Science Ser.: 16). 32p. (J). 7.99 (978-1-933815-15-2(9), Quirkles, The) Creative 3, LLC.
—Ronnie Rock, 26. Kuhn, Jesse, illus. l.t. ed. 2006. (Quirkles — Exploring Phonics through Science Ser.: 18). 32p. (J). 7.99 (978-1-933815-17-6(5), Quirkles, The) Creative 3, LLC.
—Susie Sound, 26. Kuhn, Jesse, illus. l.t. ed. 2006. 32p. (J). 7.99 (978-1-933815-18-3(3), Quirkles, The) Creative 3, LLC.
—Timothy Tornado, 26. Kuhn, Jesse, illus. l.t. ed. 2006. (Quirkles — Exploring Phonics through Science Ser.: 20). 32p. 7.99 (978-1-933815-19-0(1), Quirkles, The) Creative 3, LLC.
—Vinnie Volcano, 26. Kuhn, Jesse, illus. l.t. ed. 2006. (Quirkles — Exploring Phonics through Science Ser.: 22). 32p. (J). 7.99 (978-1-933815-21-3(3), Quirkles, The) Creative 3, LLC.
—Watery William, 26. Kuhn, Jesse, illus. l.t. ed. 2006. (Quirkles — Exploring Phonics through Science Ser.: 23). 32p. (J). 7.99 (978-1-933815-22-0(1), Quirkles, The) Creative 3, LLC.
—X. E. Ecology, 26. Kuhn, Jesse, illus. l.t. ed. 2006. (Quirkles — Exploring Phonics through Science Ser.: 24). 32p. (J). 7.99 (978-1-933815-23-7(X), Quirkles, The) Creative 3, LLC.
—Zany Science Zeke, 26. Kuhn, Jesse, illus. l.t. ed. 2006. (Quirkles — Exploring Phonics through Science Ser.: 26). 32p. (J). 7.99 (978-1-933815-25-1(6), Quirkles, The) Creative 3, LLC.
Cooke, Eunice Perneel. The Awesome Lost & Found Society. 2012. 56p. pap. (978-1-4602-0087-2(X)) FriesenPress.
Cooke, Tobias. The Secret of the Lost Soul: A Ben Street Mystery. 2011. 272p. pap. (978-1-907499-80-7(6)) Pen Pr. Pubs., Ltd.
Cooley Peterson, Megan. Scooby-Doo Solves It with S. T. E. M. Brizuela, Dario & Cornia, Christian, illus. 2016. (Scooby-Doo Solves It with S. T. E. M. Ser.). (ENG.). 32p. (gr. 3-4). 111.96 (978-1-5157-2663-0(0)) Capstone Press of Coughlan Cos.
Coombes, Patrick. The Witch's Assistant. 2013. 34p. pap. (978-1-909593-74-9(5)) Legend Pr.
Coon, Kathyann. We Are Different. 2013. 16p. pap. 24.95 (978-1-63004-413-8(X)) America Star Bks.
Cooner, Donna. Worthy. 2017. (ENG.). 288p. (J). (gr. 7). 17.99 (978-0-545-90393-6(9)) Scholastic, Inc.
Cooney, Caroline B. Hit the Road. rev. l.t. ed. 2007. (Thorndike Literacy Bridge Ser.). 259p. (YA). (gr. 7-12). 23.95 (978-0-7862-9429-9(9)) Thorndike Pr.
—The Voice on the Radio. 2012. (ENG.). 208p. (YA). (gr. 7). pap. 9.99 (978-0-385-74240-5(1), Ember) Random Hse. Children's Bks.
—The Voice on the Radio. 2012. (Janie Bks.: 3). lib. bdg. 20.85 (978-0-606-26369-6(1), Turtleback) Turtleback Bks.
Cooney, Doug. I Know Who Likes You. Bernardin, James, illus. 2005. (ENG.). 224p. (J). (gr. 3-7). pap. 10.99 (978-1-4169-0261-4(9), Simon & Schuster Bks. For Young Readers) Simon & Schuster Bks. For Young Readers.
Coons, Susan Anderson. Lighthouse Mouse Meets Simon the Cat. Sanne, Don, illus. 2012. 52p. pap. 10.03 (978-1-4669-1223-6(5)) Trafford Publishing.
Cooper, Abby. Bubbles. 2017. (ENG.). 272p. (J). 16.99 (978-0-374-30290-0(1), 9780374302900, Farrar, Straus & Giroux (BYR)) Farrar, Straus & Giroux.
—Sticks & Stones. 2016. (ENG.). 288p. (J). 16.99 (978-0-374-30287-0(1), 9780374302870, Farrar, Straus & Giroux (BYR)) Farrar, Straus & Giroux.
—Sticks & Stones. 2017. (J). lib. bdg. 18.40 **(978-0-606-39950-0(X))** Turtleback Bks.
Cooper, E. E. Avenged. 2016. (Vanished Ser.: 2). 352p. (YA). (gr. 9). 17.99 (978-0-06-229392-3(3), Tegen, Katherine Bks) HarperCollins Pubs.
—Vanished. 2015. (Vanished Ser.: 1). (ENG.). 320p. (YA). (gr. 9). 17.99 (978-0-06-229390-9(7), Tegen, Katherine Bks) HarperCollins Pubs.
Cooper, Elisha. Big Cat, Little Cat. 2017. (ENG., Illus.). 40p. (J). 16.99 (978-1-62672-371-9(0), 9781626723719) Roaring Brook Pr.
Cooper, Gael. Kermeena Kermudgeon Meets Gordon. 2010. 36p. 15.49 (978-1-4490-6735-9(2)) AuthorHouse.
Cooper, Helen S. Pumpkin Soup. Cooper, Helen S., illus. 2005. (ENG., Illus.). 32p. (J). (gr. -1-3). per. 7.99 (978-0-374-46031-0(0), 9780374460310) Square Fish.
Cooper, Ilene. The Worst Noel: A Novel. 2006. 143p. (J). (gr. 4-8). reprint ed. pap. 4.00 (978-1-4223-5411-7(3)) DIANE Publishing Co.
Cooper, John. In the Groove Vol. 2: Heroes Start As Kids! l.t. ed. 2003. (Dewey Does Ser.: 2). (Illus.). 95p. (J). (gr. -1-3). pap. 5.95 (978-0-9711474-7-8(7)) A B C-123 Publishing.
Cooper, Mimi. Me Versus Bedtime. 2006. 17p. 9.99 (978-1-4116-8255-9(6)) Lulu Pr., Inc.
Cooper, Robert. The Light Behind Their Eyes: The Story of Jack & Bunny Rabbit. 2005. 92p. pap. 33.75 (978-1-4184-0722-3(4)) AuthorHouse.
Coover, Colleen & Tobin, Paul. Adventure Time: The Flip Side. 2014. lib. bdg. 33.05 (978-0-606-36120-0(0)) Turtleback Bks.
Coppock, Phil & Bower's 2008-2009 4th Grade Class. Rubber Tuesday. 2010. 70p. pap. 12.95 (978-1-4327-5751-9(2)) Outskirts Pr., Inc.
Corbett Sampson, Natalie. Game Plan. 2013. 362p. pap. (978-1-927746-09-7(4)) Fierce ink Pr. Co-Op, Ltd.
Corderoy, Tracey. Flower in the Snow. Allsopp, Sophie, illus. 2012. (ENG.). 32p. (J). (-3). 16.99 (978-1-4022-7740-5(7), 1350490, Sourcebooks Jabberwocky) Sourcebooks, Inc.
—Just Right for Two. Beardshaw, Rosalind, illus. 2014. (ENG.). 32p. (J). (gr. -1-2). 15.99 (978-0-7636-7344-4(7), Nosy Crow) Candlewick Pr.
cordone-warner, debra. Starzzee & A Day of Play. 2010. 40p. pap. 18.99 (978-0-557-54780-7(6)) Lulu Pr., Inc.
Coren, Alan. Klondike Arthur. 2004. (Illus.). 64p. (978-0-903895-93-4(5), Robson Bks. Ltd.) Pavilion Bks.
Corgliano, K. L. Millie & Me, 1 vol. 2009. 29p. pap. 24.95 (978-1-60813-935-4(2)) America Star Bks.
Corianne, Strupp. Friends for Keeps. 2013. 124p. (J). pap. 12.99 (978-0-9882940-8-0(7)) Bryson Taylor Publishing.
Cornfield, Lynda Ellis. Rocks for Clean Oceans. 2009. 28p. pap. 13.99 (978-1-4389-8417-9(0)) AuthorHouse.
Coronado, Mark & Jackson, Dominic. Swamp Life. 2012. 16p. pap. 15.99 (978-1-4772-1042-0(3)) AuthorHouse.

Corp, Carey & Langdon, Lorie. Doon, 1 vol. 2014. (Doon Novel Ser.). (ENG.). 416p. (YA). pap. 12.99 *(978-0-310-74239-5(0))* Blink.

Corrigan, Eireann. Accomplice. 2010. (ENG.). 304p. (J). (gr. 7-7). 17.99 *(978-0-545-05236-8(X)*, Scholastic Pr.) Scholastic, Inc.

Corsetto, Danielle. Adventure Time: Pixel Princesses. 2013. lib. bdg. 23.30 *(978-0-606-35464-6(6))* Turtleback Bks.

Corthron, Kara Lee. The Truth of Right Now. 2017. (ENG., Illus.). 288p. (YA). (gr. 9). 17.99 *(978-1-4814-5947-1(3)*, Simon Pulse) Simon Pulse.

Corwin, Katherine A. R. Greg the Bearded Dragon & Thomas the Sea Turtle: A Tale of Adventure, Discovery, & Friendship. 2012. 28p. pap. 19.99 *(978-1-4685-7958-1(4))* AuthorHouse.

Cosgrove, Stephen. Bee Double Bopp: Respecting Others. Arroyo, Fian, illus. 2004. (J). *(978-1-58804-350-4(9))* P C I Education.

—Big Bubba Bigg, Jr: Dealing with Bullies. Arroyo, Fian, illus. 2004. (J). *(978-1-58804-352-8(5))* P C I Education.

—Gnome from Nome. James, Robin, illus. 2012. (Paws IV Ser.). (ENG.). 32p. (J). (gr. -1-2). pap. 10.99 *(978-1-57061-777-5(5)*, Little Bigfoot) Sasquatch Bks.

—Pickles & the P-Flock Bullies. James, Robin, illus. 2014. (ENG.). 32p. (J). (gr. k-3). 16.99 *(978-1-57061-887-1(9)*, Little Bigfoot) Sasquatch Bks.

Cosper, Andy. The Adventures of Drew Kreeger: Book 1. 2008. 56p. pap. 14.95 *(978-1-4327-3320-9(6))* Outskirts Pr., Inc.

Cossanteli, Veronica. The Extincts. Muradov, Roman, illus. 2016. (ENG.). 240p. (J). 16.99 *(978-1-62779-403-9(4)*, 9781627794039, Holt, Henry & Co. Bks. For Young Readers) Holt, Henry & Co.

Costa, Maria S. How to Find a Friend. 2017. (ENG., Illus.). 32p. (J). (gr. -1-3). 16.99 *(978-0-544-92678-3(1))* Houghton Mifflin Harcourt Publishing Co.

Costales, Amy. Lupe Vargas & Her Super Best Friend/Lupe Vargas y Su Super Mejor Amiga. 2006. (ENG, SPA & MUL., Illus.). 32p. (J). (gr. -1-3). 15.95 *(978-0-87358-888-1(6))* Cooper Square Publishing Llc.

Costamagna, Beatrice, illus. Polar Bear Munch! 2016. (Crunchy Board Bks.). (ENG.). 12p. (J). (gr. -1 — 1). bds. 6.99 *(978-1-4998-0345-7(1))* Little Bee Books Inc.

Côté, Geneviève. Me & You. Côté, Geneviève, illus. 2009. (Piggy & Bunny Ser.). (ENG., Illus.). 32p. (J). (gr. -1-k). 16.95 *(978-1-55453-446-3(1))* Kids Can Pr., Ltd. CAN. Dist: Hachette Bk. Group.

Côté, Geneviève. Mr. King's Castle. Côté, Geneviève, illus. 2013. (Mr. King Ser.). (ENG., Illus.). 32p. (J). (gr. -1-2). 16.95 *(978-1-55453-972-7(2))* Kids Can Pr., Ltd. CAN. Dist: Hachette Bk. Group.

—Without You. Côté, Geneviève, illus. 2011. (Piggy & Bunny Ser.). (ENG., Illus.). 32p. (J). (gr. -1-k). 16.95 *(978-1-55453-620-7(0))* Kids Can Pr., Ltd. CAN. Dist: Hachette Bk. Group.

Cote, Nancy. Leonard's Beard. 2016. (ENG., Illus.). 32p. (J). (gr. -1-k). 16.99 *(978-1-5107-0796-2(4)*, Sky Pony Pr.) Skyhorse Publishing Co., Inc.

—Watch the Cookie! Cote, Nancy, illus. 2014. (ENG., Illus.). 32p. (J). (gr. -1-k). 16.95 *(978-1-62914-630-0(7)*, Sky Pony Pr.) Skyhorse Publishing Co., Inc.

Cote, Nancy, illus. Watch the Birdie! 2016. (ENG.). 32p. (J). (gr. -1-k). 16.99 *(978-1-63450-202-3(7)*, Sky Pony Pr.) Skyhorse Publishing Co., Inc.

Cotler, Steve. Cheesie Mack Is Not a Genius or Anything. McCauley, Adam, illus. (Cheesie Mack Ser.). (ENG.). 240p. (J). (gr. 3-7). 2012. 6.99 *(978-0-375-86394-3(X)*, Yearling) 2011. 15.99 *(978-0-375-86437-7(7)*, Random Hse. Bks. for Young Readers) Random Hse. Children's Bks.

—Cheesie Mack Is Not Exactly Famous. Holgate, Douglas, illus. 2014. (Cheesie Mack Ser.). (ENG.). 256p. (J). (gr. 3-7). 15.99 *(978-0-385-36984-8(0)*, Random Hse. Bks. for Young Readers) Random Hse. Children's Bks.

—Cheesie Mack Is Running Like Crazy! Holgate, Douglas, illus. (Cheesie Mack Ser.). (ENG.). (J). (gr. 3-7). 2014. 256p. pap. 6.99 *(978-0-307-97716-8(1)*, Yearling) 2013. 240p. 15.99 *(978-0-307-97713-7(7)*, Random Hse. Bks. for Young Readers) Random Hse. Children's Bks.

—Cheesie Mack Is Sort of Freaked Out. Holgate, Douglas, illus. 2014. (Cheesie Mack Ser.). (ENG.). 256p. (J). (gr. 3-7). 15.99 *(978-0-385-36988-6(3)*, Random Hse. Bks. for Young Readers) Random Hse. Children's Bks.

Cotton, Connie. Crashing. 2009. 52p. pap. 16.95 *(978-1-61546-198-1(1))* America Star Bks.

Cotton, Katie. Dear Bunny. Gomez, Blanca, illus. 2015. (ENG.). 24p. (J). (gr. -1-1). 16.99 *(978-1-84780-685-7(6)*, Frances Lincoln) Quarto Publishing Group UK GBR. Dist: Littlehampton Bk Services, Ltd.

Cottringer, Anne. Hot Dog. Walker, Katherine, illus. 2005. (ENG.). 24p. (J). lib. bdg. 23.65 *(978-1-59646-738-5(X))* Dingles & Co.

—Mary Is Scary. Gale, Cathy, illus. 2007. (Bloomsbury Paperbacks Ser.). (ENG.). 32p. (J). (gr. k-2). pap. 9.99 *(978-0-7475-7927-4(X))* Bloomsbury Publishing Plc GBR. Dist: Independent Pubs. Group.

—Singing It. 2007. (ENG.). 224p. (YA). (gr. 7). pap. 11.95 *(978-1-84270-678-7(0))* Andersen Pr. GBR. Dist: Independent Pubs. Group.

Cottswold, Wooley. Rose & the Bald-Headed Elephant. 2009. (Illus.). 28p. (J). 16.95 *(978-0-9779064-0-6(X))* Archie Publishing.

Cotugno, Katie. Fireworks. 2017. 336p. (YA). (gr. 8). 17.99 *(978-0-06-241827-2(0))* HarperCollins Pubs.

Couch, Caroline. Ally Gator & Her Search for a Rainbow, 1 vol. 2009. 19p. pap. 24.95 *(978-1-60836-182-3(9))* America Star Bks.

Coughlin, Denise & Pappas, Maria. Petal Pals. 2008. 32p. 14.95 *(978-0-9705100-7-5(1))* NK Pubns.

Couric, Katie. The Brand New Kid. 2004. (Illus.). (J). (gr. -1-3). spiral bd. *(978-0-616-07225-7(2))*; spiral bd. *(978-0-616-07226-4(0))* Canadian National Institute for the Blind/Institut National Canadien pour les Aveugles.

Cousins, C. J. Bailey & Friends Have a Party. 2012. 16p. pap. 15.99 *(978-1-4772-7346-3(8))* AuthorHouse.

Cousins, Lucy. I'm the Best. Cousins, Lucy, illus. 2013. (ENG., Illus.). 32p. (J). (-k). 6.99 *(978-0-7636-6348-3(4))* Candlewick Pr.

—Maisy Goes on Vacation. Cousins, Lucy, illus. 2012. (Maisy Ser.). (ENG., Illus.). 32p. (J). (gr. -1-2). pap. 6.99 *(978-0-7636-6039-0(6))* Candlewick Pr.

—Maisy Goes to Preschool: A Maisy First Experiences Book. Cousins, Lucy, illus. 2009. (Maisy Ser.). (ENG., Illus.). 32p. (J). (gr. -1-k). 12.99 *(978-0-7636-4254-9(1))* Candlewick Pr.

—Maisy Plays Soccer. Cousins, Lucy, illus. 2014. (Maisy Ser.). (ENG., Illus.). 32p. (J). (gr. -1-2). pap. 6.99 *(978-0-7636-7238-6(6))* Candlewick Pr.

—Maisy Plays Soccer. 2014. (Maisy First Experiences Ser.). lib. bdg. 17.20 *(978-0-606-35155-3(8))* Turtleback Bks.

—Maisy Te Quiere. 2004.Tr. of Maisy Loves You. (SPA., Illus.). 12p. (J). bds. 9.99 *(978-84-8488-077-6(X))* Serres, Ediciones, S. L. ESP. Dist: Lectorum Pubns., Inc.

—Maisy's Animals (Los Animales de Maisy) Cousins, Lucy, illus. 2009. (Maisy Ser.). (SPA & ENG., Illus.). 16p. (J). (gr. -1-2). bds. 5.99 *(978-0-7636-4517-5(6))* Candlewick Pr.

—Maisy's Band. Cousins, Lucy, illus. 2012. (Maisy Ser.). (ENG., Illus.). 16p. (J). (gr. -1-2). 17.99 *(978-0-7636-6044-4(2))* Candlewick Pr.

—Maisy's Bus. Cousins, Lucy, illus. 2017. (Maisy Ser.). (ENG., Illus.). 18p. (J). (— 1). bds. 5.99 *(978-0-7636-9406-7(1))* Candlewick Pr.

—Maisy's Christmas Tree. Cousins, Lucy, illus. 2014. (Maisy Ser.). (ENG., Illus.). 16p. (J). (-k). bds. 6.99 *(978-0-7636-7457-1(5))* Candlewick Pr.

—Maisy's Fairground: A Maisy Pop-Up-and-Play Book. 2013. (Maisy Ser.). (ENG., Illus.). 16p. (J). (gr. k-k). 17.99 *(978-0-7636-6491-6(X))* Candlewick Pr.

—Maisy's First Colors: A Maisy Concept Book. Cousins, Lucy, illus. 2013. (Maisy Ser.). (ENG., Illus.). 14p. (J). (-k). bds. 6.99 *(978-0-7636-6804-4(4))* Candlewick Pr.

—Los Mejores Amigos de Maisy. 2004.Tr. of Maisy's Best Friends. (SPA., Illus.). 10p. (J). bds. 11.99 *(978-84-8488-123-0(7))* Serres, Ediciones, S. L. ESP. Dist: Lectorum Pubns., Inc.

Coven, Wanda. Heidi Heckelbeck & the Big Mix-Up. Burris, Priscilla, illus. 2016. (Heidi Heckelbeck Ser.: 18). (ENG.). 128p. (J). (gr. k-4). pap. 5.99 *(978-1-4814-7169-5(4)*, Little Simon) Little Simon.

—The Heidi Heckelbeck Collection: A Bewitching Four-Book Boxed Set: Heidi Heckelbeck Has a Secret; Heidi Heckelbeck Casts a Spell; Heidi Heckelbeck & the Cookie Contest; Heidi Heckelbeck in Disguise. Burris, Priscilla, illus. 2013. (Heidi Heckelbeck Ser.). (ENG.). 512p. (J). (gr. k-4). pap. 23.99 *(978-1-4424-8976-9(6)*, Little Simon) Little Simon.

—Heidi Heckelbeck Goes to Camp! Burris, Priscilla, illus. 2013. (Heidi Heckelbeck Ser.: 8). (ENG.). 128p. (J). (gr. k-2). 15.99 *(978-1-4424-6481-0(X))*; pap. 5.99 *(978-1-4424-6480-3(1))* Little Simon. (Little Simon).

—Heidi Heckelbeck Goes to Camp! 2013. (Heidi Heckelbeck Ser.: 8). lib. bdg. 16.00 *(978-0-606-32031-3(8)*, Turtleback) Turtleback Bks.

—Heidi Heckelbeck Is Not a Thief! Burris, Priscilla, illus. 2015. (Heidi Heckelbeck Ser.: 13). (ENG.). 128p. (J). (gr. k-4). pap. 5.99 *(978-1-4814-2324-3(X)*, Little Simon) Little Simon.

Coverly, Dave. Night of the Living Shadows. 2016. (Speed Bump & Slingshot Misadventure Ser.). (ENG., Illus.). 128p. (J). 13.99 *(978-0-8050-8887-8(3)*, 9780805088878, Holt, Henry & Co. Bks. For Young Readers) Holt, Henry & Co.

—Night of the Living Worms: A Speed Bump & Slingshot Misadventure. Coverly, Dave, illus. 2015. (Speed Bump & Slingshot Misadventure Ser.). (ENG., Illus.). 128p. (J). (gr. 2-5). 13.99 *(978-0-8050-8886-1(5)*, 9780805088861, Holt, Henry & Co. Bks. For Young Readers) Holt, Henry & Co.

Covey, Sean. Goob & His Grandpa. Curtis, Stacy, illus. 2013. (7 Habits of Happy Kids Ser.: 7). (ENG.). 32p. (J). (gr. -1-1). 7.99 *(978-1-4424-7653-0(2)*, Simon & Schuster Bks. For Young Readers) Simon & Schuster Bks. For Young Readers.

Coville, Bruce. Always October. 2012. (ENG.). 384p. (J). (gr. 3-7). 16.99 *(978-0-06-089095-7(9))* HarperCollins Pubs.

—Goblins in the Castle. Coville, Katherine, illus. 2015. (ENG.). 208p. (J). (gr. 3-7). 17.99 *(978-1-4814-3900-8(6)*, Aladdin) Simon & Schuster Children's Publishing.

—Goblins on the Prowl. 2015. (ENG., Illus.). 272p. (J). (gr. 3-7). 17.99 *(978-1-4169-1440-2(4)*, Aladdin) Simon & Schuster Children's Publishing.

—Jeremy Thatcher, Dragon Hatcher: A Magic Shop Book. Lippincott, Gary A., illus. 20th ed. 2007. (Magic Shop Book Ser.: 2). (ENG.). 176p. (J). (gr. 5-7). pap. 7.99 *(978-0-15-206252-1(1))* Houghton Mifflin Harcourt Publishing Co.

—The Skull of Truth: A Magic Shop Book. Lippincott, Gary A., illus. 2007. (Magic Shop Book Ser.: 4). (ENG.). 208p. (J). (gr. 5-7). pap. 7.99 *(978-0-15-206084-8(7))* Houghton Mifflin Harcourt Publishing Co.

Covington, Nichole. Melinda the Miserable: Eeriness in the Attic. 2011. 116p. pap. 19.95 *(978-1-4560-7250-6(1))* America Star Bks.

Cowan, Brad V. Skinner's Banks, 1 vol. 2013. (Seven Stair Crew Ser.). (ENG., Illus.). 160p. (J). (gr. 4-7). 19.95 *(978-1-4594-0521-9(8)*, 9781459405219); pap. 12.95 *(978-1-4594-0522-6(6)*, 9781459405226) Lorimer, James & Co., Ltd., Pubs. CAN. Dist: Casemate Pubs. & Bk. Distributors, LLC.

Cowan, Catherine. My Life with the Wave. 2004. (Illus.). (J). (gr. k-3). spiral bd. *(978-0-616-01621-3(2))* Canadian National Institute for the Blind/Institut National Canadien pour les Aveugles.

—My Life with the Wave. Buehner, Mark, illus. 2004. (ENG.). 32p. (J). (gr. -1-3). reprint ed. pap. 7.99 *(978-0-06-056200-7(5))* HarperCollins Pubs.

Cowley, Joy. Friends: Snake & Lizard. Bishop, Gavin, illus. 2011. (Gecko Press Titles Ser.). (ENG.). 144p. 16.95 *(978-1-877579-01-1(7))* Gecko Pr. NZL. Dist: Lerner Publishing Group.

Cox, Rhonda. Best Friends. Cox, Rhonda, photos by. 2003. (ENG., Illus.). 16p. (J). pap. 15.00 *(978-1-57274-699-2(8)*, BB2126, Bks. for Young Learners) Owen, Richard C. Pubs., Inc.

Coy, John. Eyes on the Goal, Bk. 2. 2012. (4 For 4 Ser.: 2). (ENG.). 192p. (J). (gr. 3-7). pap. 7.99 *(978-0-312-65922-6(9)*, 9780312659226) Square Fish.

—Take Your Best Shot. 2012. (4 For 4 Ser.: 4). (ENG.). 192p. (J). (gr. 3-7). 16.99 *(978-0-312-37332-0(5)*, 9780312373320) Feiwel & Friends.

—Top of the Order. 2010. (4 For 4 Ser.: 1). (ENG.). 208p. (J). (gr. 3-7). pap. 8.99 *(978-0-312-61111-8(0)*, 9780312611118) Square Fish.

Coyle, Carmela Lavigna. Do Princesses Have Best Friends Forever? Gordon, Mike & Gordon, Carl, illus. 2010. (J). *(978-1-58979-543-3(1))* Taylor Trade Publishing.

—Do Princesses Have Best Friends Forever? Gordon, Carl & Gordon, Mike, illus. 2010. (ENG.). 32p. (J). (gr. -1-3). 15.95 *(978-1-58979-542-6(3))* Taylor Trade Publishing.

Cozzo, Karole. The Truth about Happily Ever After. 2017. (ENG.). 320p. (YA). 17.99 *(978-1-250-12797-6(1)*, 9781250127976) Feiwel & Friends.

Crabtree, Julie. Discovering Pig Magic. 2008. (ENG.). 144p. (J). (gr. 2-8). 16.95 *(978-1-57131-683-7(3))*; pap. 6.95 *(978-1-57131-684-4(1))* Milkweed Editions.

Craft, Elizabeth. Love Bytes. 2013. (@cafe Ser.: 1). (ENG., Illus.). 224p. (YA). (gr. 7). pap. 15.99 *(978-1-4814-2110-2(7)*, Simon Pulse) Simon Pulse.

—Make Mine to Go. 2013. (@cafe Ser.: 3). (ENG., Illus.). 192p. (YA). (gr. 7). pap. 13.99 *(978-1-4814-2112-6(3)*, Simon Pulse) Simon Pulse.

Craig, Bobby & Manifold, Delwyn. The Learning Adventures of Spot. 2011. 28p. pap. 24.95 *(978-1-4560-3110-7(4))* America Star Bks.

Crane, Cheri J. Moment of Truth: A Novel. 2005. 238p. (YA). *(978-1-59156-727-1(0))* Covenant Communications.

Crane, Noelle L. The Clever Pug. Crane, Noelle L., illus. 2013. (Illus.). 66p. pap. 9.99 *(978-0-9846119-8-0(3))* Pluriverse Publishing.

Crane, Phyllis F. Anything but the Most Boring Place on Earth. 2011. 174p. pap. 24.95 *(978-1-4560-6802-8(4))* America Star Bks.

Crangle, Claudine, illus. Priscilla the Pack Rat: Making Room for Friendship. 2017. 32p. (J). 15.95 *(978-1-4338-2335-0(7)*, Magination Pr.) American Psychological Assn.

Cranse, Pratima. All the Major Constellations. 2015. (ENG.). 336p. (YA). (gr. 9). 17.99 *(978-0-670-01645-7(4)*, Viking Books for Young Readers) Penguin Young Readers Group.

Crashland. 2014. (Twinmaker Ser.: 2). (ENG.). 480p. (YA). (gr. 8). 17.99 *(978-0-06-220324-3(X))* HarperCollins Pubs.

Crawford, Deborah & Crawford, Ryan. Pity's Porch. Ballard, Merry, illus. 2012. 24p. pap. 11.50 *(978-1-60976-796-9(9)*, Strategic Bk. Publishing) Strategic Book Publishing & Rights Agency (SBPRA).

Crawford-Haynes, Debra. Bedtime with Julian. 2010. 32p. 16.99 *(978-1-4520-6943-2(3))* AuthorHouse.

Crawford, Ruth. Squirrel Boy & Brad: The Storm. 2010. 24p. pap. 12.99 *(978-1-4490-1611-1(1))* AuthorHouse.

—Squirrel Boy & Brad Become Friends. 2009. 24p. pap. 12.99 *(978-1-4490-1533-6(6))* AuthorHouse.

Crawford, Susan. The Sea Sprites. 2011. 12p. 12.68 *(978-1-4269-5009-4(8))* Trafford Publishing.

Crawford, Tammy. Gaby & Her Big Surprise. 2009. 36p. pap. 15.49 *(978-1-4389-3323-8(1))* AuthorHouse.

Creech, Sharon. The Boy on the Porch. 2013. 160p. (J). (gr. 3-7). (ENG.). 16.99 *(978-0-06-189235-6(1))*; lib. bdg. 17.89 *(978-0-06-189237-0(8))* HarperCollins Pubs.

—Granny Torrelli Makes Soup. Raschka, Chris, illus. 2004. (Joanna Cotler Bks.). 141p. (gr. 3-7). 17.00 *(978-0-7569-4604-3(2))* Perfection Learning Corp.

—Heartbeat. 2012. (ENG.). 208p. (J). (gr. 3-7). pap. 6.99 *(978-0-06-054024-1(9))* HarperCollins Pubs.

—Walk Two Moons. (Walk Two Moons Ser.: 1). (J). (gr. 3-7). 2011. 288p. pap. 7.99 *(978-0-06-440517-1(6))* 2003. 304p. pap. 7.99 *(978-0-06-056013-3(4)*, HarperTeen) HarperCollins Pubs.

—Walk Two Moons. 280p. (J). (gr. 4-6). pap. 4.95 *(978-0-8072-1509-8(0)*, Listening Library) Random Hse. Audio Publishing Group.

—Walk Two Moons. (J). 2011. (gr. 5-8). lib. bdg. 18.40 *(978-0-613-00204-2(0))* 2003. (gr. 7-12). 18.40 *(978-0-613-81971-8(3))* Turtleback Bks. (Turtleback).

Creech, Sharon. Walk Two Moons: a Harper Classic. 2017. (Harper Classic Ser.). 288p. (J). (gr. 3-7). 16.99 ***(978-0-06-265877-8(8))*** HarperCollins Pubs.

Creek, Silent. All the Ice of Afric. 2009. 160p. 22.95 *(978-1-4401-2118-0(4))* iUniverse, Inc.

Crenshaw, Glenda. Friends of the Enchanted Forest: How they Save Christmas. 2011. 28p. pap. 15.47 *(978-1-4520-0512-6(5))* AuthorHouse.

Crew, Gary. The Watertower. 2014. (ENG.). 32p. (J). (gr. 2-9). pap. 8.95 *(978-1-56656-331-4(3)*, Crocodile Bks.) Interlink Publishing Group, Inc.

Crews, G. S. Ellen G Goes to the Haunted Planetarium. Designs, Marion, photos by. 2009. (Illus.). 50p. pap. 20.00 *(978-0-9795236-4-9(8))* Crews Pubns., LLC.

Crider, Mike. Gonzo & the Almost Invisible Man. 2012. (ENG.). 140p. (J). (gr. 3-7). pap. 8.99 *(978-1-4424-8128-2(5)*, Simon & Schuster/Paula Wiseman Bks.) Simon & Schuster/Paula Wiseman Bks.

Crimi, Carolyn. Boris & Bella. Grimly, Gris, illus. 2006. (ENG.). 32p. (J). (gr. -1-3). reprint ed. pap. 7.99 *(978-0-15-205900-2(8))* Houghton Mifflin Harcourt Publishing Co.

The Critter Club Collection: A Purrfect Four-Book Boxed Set: Amy & the Missing Puppy; All about Ellie; Liz Learns a Lesson; Marion Takes a Break. 2014. (Critter Club Ser.). (ENG., Illus.). 512p. (J). (gr. k-4). pap. 23.99 *(978-1-4814-0664-2(7)*, Little Simon) Little Simon.

Crocker, Nancy. Billie Standish Was Here. 2007. (ENG.). 288p. (YA). (gr. 9-12). 16.99 *(978-1-4169-2423-4(X)*, Simon & Schuster Bks. For Young Readers) Simon & Schuster Bks. For Young Readers.

Crompton, Paul. Remarkable for Short. 2005. 113p. pap. 19.95 *(978-1-4241-0287-7(1))* PublishAmerica, Inc.

Cromwell, Ellen S. Wiggle-Dee-Dee: A Story about Friendship. 2011. 28p. pap. 15.99 *(978-1-4628-9458-1(5))* Xlibris Corp.

Cronin, Doreen. Boom Snot Twitty. Liwska, Renata, illus. 2014. (ENG.). 32p. (J). (gr. -1-k). 16.99 *(978-0-670-78575-9(X)*, Viking Books for Young Readers) Penguin Young Readers Group.

—Boom Snot Twitty This Way That Way. Liwska, Renata, illus. 2015. (ENG.). 32p. (J). (-k). 16.99 *(978-0-670-78577-3(6)*, Viking Books for Young Readers) Penguin Young Readers Group.

—Smick! Medina, Juana, illus. 2015. (ENG.). 34p. (J). (gr. -1-k). 16.99 *(978-0-670-78578-0(4)*, Viking Books for Young Readers) Penguin Young Readers Group.

Cronin, Susan L. Gidget Goes Away. 2006. 54p. pap. 16.95 *(978-1-4137-9878-4(0))* PublishAmerica, Inc.

Cross, Kady. Vigilante. 2017. (ENG.). 288p. 18.99 *(978-0-373-21177-7(5)*, Harlequin Teen) Harlequin Enterprises, Ltd. CAN. Dist: HarperCollins Pubs.

Cross, Mimi. Before Goodbye, 0 vols. 2016. (ENG.). 389p. (YA). (gr. 8-12). pap. 9.99 *(978-1-5039-4972-0(9)*, 9781503949720, Skyscape) Amazon Publishing.

Cross, P. W. The Idea Miners: The Lost Lake Dig. 2009. 288p. (J). pap. 7.99 *(978-0-9662800-8-1(3))* Appalachian Hse.

Crossman, David. The Legend of Burial Island: A Bean & Ab Mystery. 2009. (ENG.). 201p. (J). (gr. 3-7). pap. 11.95 *(978-0-89272-797-1(7))* Down East Bks.

Croteau-Fleury, Marie-Danielle. Des Citrouilles pour Cendrillon. 2003. (Premier Roman Ser.). (FRE., Illus.). 64p. (J). (gr. 2-5). pap. *(978-2-89021-359-3(5))* Diffusion du livre Mirabel (DLM).

Crouse, Donna J. The Ruby Ring: The Whispering Cove Kids Club. 2005. 114p. pap. 12.99 *(978-0-9765339-0-0(1))* Crouse, Donna J.

Crow, A. D. Daisy & Her Shiny Heart. 2012. 20p. pap. 24.95 *(978-1-4626-8039-9(9))* America Star Bks.

Crow, Kristyn. Hello, Hippo! Goodbye, Bird! Bernatene, Poly, illus. 2016. (ENG.). 32p. (J). (gr. -1-2). 15.99 *(978-0-553-50990-8(X)*, Knopf Bks. for Young Readers) Random Hse. Children's Bks.

—Zombelina: School Days. Idle, Molly, illus. (ENG.). (J). 2017. 40p. 16.99 *(978-1-61963-641-5(7)*, 9781619636415) 2013. 32p. (gr. -1-3). 16.99 *(978-0-8027-2803-6(0)*, 9780802728036) Bloomsbury Publishing USA. (Bloomsbury USA Childrens).

—Zombelina Dances the Nutcracker. Idle, Molly, illus. 2015. (ENG.). 40p. (J). (gr. -1-3). 16.99 *(978-1-61963-640-8(9)*, 9781619636408, Bloomsbury USA Childrens) Bloomsbury Publishing USA.

Crow, Matthew. The Brilliant Light of Amber Sunrise. 2015. (ENG., Illus.). 304p. (YA). (gr. 9). 17.99 *(978-1-4814-1873-7(4)*, Simon Pulse) Simon Pulse.

Crow, Melinda Melton. Camiones Amigos/Truck Buddies, 1 vol. Heck, Claudia M., tr. from ENG. Rooney, Ronnie, illus. 2012. (Camiones Amigos/Truck Buddies Ser.). (ENG, SPA & MUL.). 32p. (gr. -1-1). pap. 5.05 *(978-1-4342-3913-6(6))*; lib. bdg. 22.65 *(978-1-4342-3774-3(5))* Stone Arch Bks. (Bilingual Stone Arch Readers).

—Llos en la Nieve. Heck, Claudia M., tr. from ENG. Rooney, Ronnie, illus. 2012. (Camiones Amigos/Truck Buddies Ser.).Tr. of Snow Trouble. (MUL, SPA & ENG.). 32p. (gr. -1-1). pap. 5.05 *(978-1-4342-3914-3(4)*, Bilingual Stone Arch Readers) Stone Arch Bks.

—Little Lizard's New Friend, 1 vol. Rowland, Andrew, illus. 2011. (Little Lizards Ser.). (ENG.). 32p. (gr. -1-1). pap. 6.25 *(978-1-4342-3048-5(1))* Stone Arch Bks.

Crow, Nosy. Pip & Posy: the Bedtime Frog. Scheffler, Axel, illus. 2014. (Pip & Posy Ser.). (ENG.). 32p. (J). (-k). 12.99 *(978-0-7636-7068-9(5)*, Nosy Crow) Candlewick Pr.

—Pip & Posy: the Scary Monster. Scheffler, Axel, illus. 2014. (Pip & Posy Ser.). (ENG.). 24p. (J). (-k). bds. 6.99 *(978-0-7636-7231-7(9)*, Nosy Crow) Candlewick Pr.

Crowell, Marcia. The Adventures of Little Blackie & Friends. 2009. 36p. pap. 15.99 *(978-1-4389-0386-6(3))* AuthorHouse.

Crowley, Cath. A Little Wanting Song. 2011. (ENG.). 288p. (YA). (gr. 9). pap. 8.99 *(978-0-375-85449-1(5)*, Ember) Random Hse. Children's Bks.

Cruea, Kim. Summer Falls Junior Rangers: The First Adventures. 2008. 73p. pap. 19.95 *(978-1-60474-552-8(5))* America Star Bks.

Crummel, Susan Stevens. City Dog, Country Dog, 0 vols. Donohue, Dorothy, illus. 2010. (ENG.). 42p. (J). (gr. k-4). pap. 9.99 *(978-0-7614-5538-7(8)*, 9780761455387, Amazon Children's Publishing) Amazon Publishing.

Crummel, Susan Stevens & Donohue, Dorothy. City Dog & Country Dog. Donohue, Dorothy, illus. unabr. ed. 2006. (Illus.). (J). (gr. k-3). 27.95 incl. audio *(978-0-8045-6942-2(8)*, SAC6942) Spoken Arts, Inc.

Crummel, Susan Stevens & Stevens, Janet. Shoe Town. 2003. (Green Light Readers Level 2 Ser.). (ENG., Illus.). 32p. (J). (gr. -1-3). pap. 3.95 *(978-0-15-204842-6(1))* Houghton Mifflin Harcourt Publishing Co.

Crutcher, Chris. Staying Fat for Sarah Byrnes. 2003. (YA). lib. bdg. 20.85 *(978-0-613-61464-1(X)*, Turtleback) Turtleback Bks.

Cruz Garcia, Juanita. Yocumal & Juno. 2009. 16p. pap. 8.99 *(978-1-4490-2631-8(1))* AuthorHouse.

Cruzan, Patricia. The Wonder in the Woods. Brewer, Kathaleen, illus. 2013. 250p. pap. 15.00 *(978-0-9653543-7-0(7))* Clear Creek Pubs.

Crystow, Charisse. Dainty Dee & Lanky Lee. 2012. (ENG.). 26p. (J). pap. 14.95 *(978-1-59713-120-9(2))* Goose River Pr.

Cuasay, Alison Taimanglo. Tasi & Matina: The Story of the First Clown Fish. 2010. 28p. pap. 12.99 *(978-1-4520-6672-1(8))* AuthorHouse.

Cuevas, Michelle. Confessions of an Imaginary Friend: A Memoir by Jacques Papier. 2015. (ENG., Illus.). 176p. (J). (gr. 4-7). 16.99 *(978-0-525-42755-1(4)*, Dial Bks) Penguin Young Readers Group.

—Confessions of an Imaginary Friend: A Memoir of Jacques Papier. 2017. lib. bdg. 18.40 ***(978-0-606-39786-5(8))*** Turtleback Bks.

Cuevas, Michelle. The Uncorker of Ocean Bottles. Stead, Erin E., illus. 2016. (ENG.). 34p. (J). (gr. -1-3). 17.99 *(978-0-8037-3868-3(4)*, Dial Bks) Penguin Young Readers Group.

Culbertson, Kim. Catch a Falling Star. 2014. (ENG.). 304p. (J). (gr. 7). 17.99 *(978-0-545-62704-7(4)*, Scholastic Pr.) Scholastic, Inc.

Culbertson, Kim. The Wonder of Us. 2017. (ENG.). 336p. (J). (gr. 7). 17.99 ***(978-0-545-73151-5(8))*** Scholastic, Inc.

Cullagh, Yolanda. Sabina the Beach Fly. 2007. (ENG.). 28p. pap. 10.99 *(978-1-4196-7950-6(3))* CreateSpace Independent Publishing Platform.

E
F
G

Cumbie, Patricia. Where People Like Us Live. 2008. 224p. (YA). (gr. 7-18). lib. bdg. 17.89 (978-0-06-137598-9(5), Geringer, Laura Book) HarperCollins Pubs.
Cumming, Hannah. The Red Boat. Cumming, Hannah, illus. 2012. (Child's Play Library). (ENG., Illus.). 32p. (J). (978-1-84643-493-8(9)) Child's Play International Ltd.
Cummings, Lindsay. The Pillars of Ponderay. 2015. (Balance Keepers Ser.: 2). (ENG.). 384p. (J). (gr. 3-7). 16.99 (978-0-06-227521-9(6), Tegen, Katherine Bks) HarperCollins Pubs.
Cummings, Priscilla. Red Kayak. 2006. (ENG.). 224p. (J). (gr. 5-18). 7.99 (978-0-14-240573-4(6), Puffin Books) Penguin Young Readers Group.
Cummings, Troy. Attack of the Shadow Smashers. 2013. (Notebook of Doom Ser.: 3). (ENG.). 96p. (J). (gr. 1-3). pap. 4.99 (978-0-545-55297-4(4)) Scholastic, Inc.
—Attack of the Shadow Smashers. 2013. (Notebook of Doom Ser.: 3). lib. bdg. 14.75 (978-0-606-32369-7(4), Turtleback) Turtleback Bks.
—Charge of the Lightning Bugs. Cummings, Troy, illus. 2015. (Notebook of Doom Ser.: 8). (ENG., Illus.). 96p. (J). (gr. 1-3). 15.99 (978-0-545-79554-8(0)); pap. 4.99 (978-0-545-79555-5(9)) Scholastic, Inc.
—Chomp of the Meat-Eating Vegetables. 2014. (Notebook of Doom Ser.: 4). (ENG.). 96p. (J). (gr. 1-3). 15.99 (978-0-545-55300-1(8)); (Illus.). pap. 4.99 (978-0-545-55299-8(0)) Scholastic, Inc.
—Chomp of the Meat-Eating Vegetables. 2014. (Notebook of Doom Ser.: 4). lib. bdg. 14.75 (978-0-606-35362-5(3)) Turtleback Bks.
—Flurry of the Snombies. 2015. (Notebook of Doom Ser.: 7). (ENG., Illus.). 96p. (J). (gr. 1-3). 15.99 (978-0-545-79551-7(6)); pap. 4.99 (978-0-545-79550-0(8)) Scholastic, Inc.
—Rumble of the Coaster Ghost. Cummings, Troy, illus. 2016. (Notebook of Doom Ser.: 9). (ENG., Illus.). 96p. (J). (gr. 1-3). pap. 4.99 (978-0-545-86497-8(6)) Scholastic, Inc.
—Snap of the Super-Goop - A Branches Book. Cummings, Troy, illus. 2016. (Notebook of Doom Ser.: 1). (ENG., Illus.). 96p. (J). (gr. 1-3). pap. 4.99 (978-0-545-86499-2(2)) Scholastic, Inc.
—Sneeze of the Octo-Schnozz: a Branches Book (the Notebook of Doom #11) 2016. (Notebook of Doom Ser.: 11). (ENG.). 96p. (J). (gr. 1-3). pap. 4.99 (978-1-338-03448-6(0)) Scholastic, Inc.
—Whack of the P-Rex. 2014. (Notebook of Doom Ser.: 5). (ENG.). 96p. (J). (gr. 1-3). pap. 4.99 (978-0-545-69895-5(2)) Scholastic, Inc.
Cumyn, Alan. Dear Sylvia, 1 vol. 2009. (ENG.). 184p. (J). pap. 8.95 (978-0-88899-848-4(1)) Groundwood Bks. CAN. Dist: Publishers Group West (PGW).
Cuniffe, April. Willy the Weeping Willow. 2008. 36p. pap. 24.95 (978-1-60441-613-8(0)) America Star Bks.
Cunningham, Mary. Cynthias Attic Magicians Castle. 2009. 158p. pap. 10.99 (978-1-59080-656-2(5)) Echelon Press Publishing.
—The Missing Locket. 2005. (Cynthia's Attic Ser.). 152p. (J). (gr. 5). per. 9.99 (978-1-59080-441-4(4)) Echelon Press Publishing.
Curato, Mike. Little Elliot, Big City. Curato, Mike, illus. 2014. (Little Elliot Ser.). (ENG., Illus.). 40p. (J). (gr. -1-3). 16.99 (978-0-8050-9825-9(9), 9780805098259, Holt, Henry & Co. Bks. For Young Readers) Holt, Henry & Co.
—Little Elliot, Big Family. Curato, Mike, illus. 2015. (Little Elliot Ser.). (ENG., Illus.). 40p. (J). (gr. -1-3). 17.99 (978-0-8050-9826-6(7), 9780805098266, Holt, Henry & Co. Bks. For Young Readers) Holt, Henry & Co.
—Little Elliot, Big Fun. Curato, Mike, illus. 2016. (Little Elliot Ser.). (ENG., Illus.). 40p. (J). 17.99 (978-0-8050-9827-3(5), 9780805098273, Holt, Henry & Co. Bks. For Young Readers) Holt, Henry & Co.
Cureton-Heifner, Donna Lynn. The Adventures of Itsy & Willy Wabbit: In Search of Lillian the Ladybug. 2012. 16p. pap. 24.95 (978-1-4626-8547-9(1)) America Star Bks.
Currey, Anna. The Christmas Unicorn. 2013. (Illus.). (J). (978-1-4351-5017-1(1)) Barnes & Noble, Inc.
Currinder, Michael. Running Full Tilt. 2017. (ENG.). 336p. (YA). (gr. 7). lib. bdg. 17.99 **(978-1-58089-802-7(5)**, Charlesbridge Teen) Charlesbridge Publishing, Inc.
Curry, Cicero. The Tickle Man. Ledbetter, John'el, illus. 2013. 44p. pap. 24.95 (978-1-63000-015-8(9)) America Star Bks.
Curry, Judi. The Moose & the Elk. 2010. 32p. 14.49 (978-1-4520-8980-5(9)) AuthorHouse.
Curry, Kenneth. Star & Peanut. 2007. (Illus.). 22p. (J). 10.95 (978-0-9798364-9-7(2)) Curry Brothers Publishing Group.
Curtin, Ann. Dreamcatcher. 2015. 201p. (YA). (978-1-61271-246-8(0)) Zumaya Pubns. LLC.
Curtin, Judi. Alice Again. Fox, Woody, illus. 2006. (ENG.). 240p. (J). pap. 12.95 (978-0-86278-956-5(7)) O'Brien Pr., Ltd., The IRL. Dist: Dufour Editions, Inc.
—Alice & Megan Forever. Fox, Woody, illus. 2nd rev. ed. 2015. (ENG.). 288p. (J). pap. 12.00 (978-1-84717-690-5(9)) O'Brien Pr., Ltd., The IRL. Dist: Dufour Editions, Inc.
—Alice in the Middle. Fox, Woody, illus. 2nd rev. ed. 2015. (ENG.). 256p. (J). 13.00 (978-1-84717-673-8(9)) O'Brien Pr., Ltd., The IRL. Dist: Dufour Editions, Inc.
—Alice Next Door. Fox, Woody, illus. 2005. (ENG.). 208p. (J). pap. 12.95 (978-0-86278-898-8(6)) O'Brien Pr., Ltd., The IRL. Dist: Dufour Editions, Inc.
—Alice to the Rescue. Fox, Woody, illus. 2015. (ENG.). 272p. (J). pap. 12.00 (978-1-84717-691-2(7)) O'Brien Pr., Ltd., The IRL. Dist: Dufour Editions, Inc.
—Bonjour Alice. Fox, Woody, illus. 2015. (ENG.). 256p. (J). pap. 12.00 (978-1-84717-689-9(5)) O'Brien Pr., Ltd., The IRL. Dist: Dufour Editions, Inc.
—Don't Ask Alice. Fox, Woody, illus. (ENG.). 256p. (J). 2007. pap. 12.95 (978-1-84717-023-1(4)) 2nd rev. ed. 2015. 13.00 (978-1-84717-672-1(0)) O'Brien Pr., Ltd., The IRL. Dist: Dufour Editions, Inc.
—Eva & the Hidden Diary. Fox, Woody, illus. 2013. (ENG.). 240p. (J). pap. 13.95 (978-1-84717-588-5(0)) O'Brien Pr., Ltd., The IRL. Dist: Dufour Editions, Inc.
—Eva's Holiday. 2012. (Eva Ser.). (ENG.). 272p. (J). pap. 12.95 (978-1-84717-280-8(6)) O'Brien Pr., Ltd., The IRL. Dist: Dufour Editions, Inc.
Curtin, Judi & Meaney, Roisin. See If I Care. 2007. (Journals). (ENG.). 192p. (J). pap. 12.95 (978-1-84717-021-7(8)) O'Brien Pr., Ltd., The IRL. Dist: Dufour Editions, Inc.
Curtis, Alice Turner. A Yankee Girl at Fort Sumter. 2005. 180p. pap. 11.95 (978-1-4218-0401-9(8), 1st World Library - Literary Society) 1st World Publishing, Inc.
Curtis, Christopher Paul. The Madman of Piney Woods. 2016. (ENG.). 363p. (J). (gr. 3-7). lib. bdg. 18.40 (978-0-606-38061-4(2)) Turtleback Bks.
Curtis, D. D. Catching Rodeo Fever. 2011. 32p. pap. 16.95 (978-1-4560-7328-2(1)) America Star Bks.
Curtis, Joan Scott. The Number Fairy. 2012. (ENG.). (J). pap. 18.00 (978-1-4675-5219-6(4)) Independent Pub.
Curtis, Kelli. Amber & the Fallen Bridge. 2009. 32p. pap. 13.00 (978-1-60860-631-3(7), Strategic Bk. Publishing) Strategic Book Publishing & Rights Agency (SBPRA).
Curtis, Marci Lyn. The One Thing. 2015. (ENG., Illus.). 336p. (YA). (gr. 7-12). 17.99 (978-1-4847-0902-3(0)) Hyperion Bks. for Children.
—The One Thing. 2017. (YA). lib. bdg. 20.85 (978-0-606-39172-6(X)) Turtleback Bks.
Curtis, Morgan. Second-hand Alligata: A Cajun Tale. 2010. 20p. 13.99 (978-1-4520-1673-3(9)) AuthorHouse.
Curtis, Shelly. Shellbear's Adventures. 2012. 56p. pap. (978-1-4602-0601-0(0)) FriesenPress.
Curtis, Vanessa & Quarto Generic Staff. The Taming of Lilah May. 2012. (ENG.). 192p. (J). (gr. 7-9). pap. 8.99 (978-1-84780-149-4(8), Frances Lincoln) Quarto Publishing Group UK GBR. Dist: Hachette Bk. Group.
Cusack, Dale. Grace & the Drawl. 2008. (Illus.). 169p. pap. 11.95 (978-1-4357-0926-3(8)) Lulu Pr., Inc.
Cutler, Betty Jackson. The Flight of SaraJane. 2008. 29p. pap. 24.95 (978-1-60672-025-7(2)) America Star Bks.
Cutler-Broyles, Teresa. One Eyed Jack. 2013. 190p. pap. (978-1-908910-51-6(8)) Crooked Cat Publishing.
Cutler, Jane. Family Dinner. 2011. 116p. pap. 9.95 (978-1-4502-5374-1(1)) iUniverse, Inc.
—The Song of the Molimo: A Pygmy at the St. Louis World's Fair. 2008. 192p. (gr. 4-7). pap. 13.95 (978-0-595-52895-0(3)) iUniverse, Inc.
—Susan Marcus Bends the Rules. 2014. (ENG.). 112p. (J). (gr. 3-7). pap. 16.95 (978-0-8234-3047-5(2)) Holiday Hse., Inc.
Cutler, Stephen. Rally Caps. 2007. 88p. per. 19.95 (978-1-4241-7381-5(7)) America Star Bks.
Cuyler, Margery. Best Friends. Walker, David L., illus. 2017. (Step into Reading Ser.). (ENG.). 32p. (J). (gr. -1-1). pap. 4.99 (978-0-399-55369-1(X), Random Hse. Bks. for Young Readers) Random Hse. Children's Bks.
—Bullies Never Win. Howard, Arthur, illus. 2009. (ENG.). 32p. (J). (gr. k-3). 17.99 (978-0-689-86187-1(7), Simon & Schuster Bks. For Young Readers) Simon & Schuster Bks. For Young Readers.
—I Repeat, Don't Cheat! Howard, Arthur, illus. 2010. (ENG.). 32p. (J). (gr. k-3). 15.99 (978-1-4169-7167-2(X), Simon & Schuster Bks. For Young Readers) Simon & Schuster Bks. For Young Readers.
Cyr, Joe. Magical Trees & Crayons: Great Stories. 2006. (Illus.). pap. 9.95 (978-0-9778525-6-7(3)) Peppertree Pr., The.
Cyrus, Kurt. Invisible Lizard. Atkins, Andy, illus. 2017. (ENG.). 32p. (J). (gr. k-2). 16.99 **(978-1-58536-378-0(2)**, 204320) Sleeping Bear Pr.
D C Thomson Staff, ed. People's Friend Annual 2004. 2004. (Illus.). 176p. 9.95 (978-0-85116-832-6(9)) Thomson, D.C. & Co., Ltd. GBR. Dist: APG Sales & Distribution Services.
Dadey, Debbie. Battle of the Best Friends. Avakyan, Tatevik, illus. 2012. (Mermaid Tales Ser.: 2). (ENG.). 112p. (J). (gr. 1-4). 15.99 (978-1-4424-4979-4(9)); pap. 5.99 (978-1-4424-2982-6(8)) Simon & Schuster Children's Publishing. (Aladdin).
—The Crook & the Crown. Avakyan, Tatevik, illus. 2015. (Mermaid Tales Ser.: 13). (ENG.). 128p. (J). (gr. 1-4). pap. 5.99 (978-1-4814-4075-2(6), Aladdin) Simon & Schuster Children's Publishing.
—Danger in the Deep Blue Sea. Avakyan, Tatevik, illus. 2013. (Mermaid Tales Ser.: 4). (ENG.). 112p. (J). (gr. 1-4). 15.99 (978-1-4424-5319-7(2)); pap. 5.99 (978-1-4424-2986-4(0)) Simon & Schuster Children's Publishing. (Aladdin).
—Mermaid Tales 4-Books-In-1! Trouble at Trident Academy; Battles of the Best Friends; a Whale of a Tale; Danger in the Deep Blue Sea. Avakyan, Tatevik, illus. 2016. (Mermaid Tales Ser.). (ENG.). 416p. (J). (gr. 1-4). 14.99 (978-1-4814-7592-1(4), Aladdin) Simon & Schuster Children's Publishing.
—The Polar Bear Express. Avakyan, Tatevik, illus. 2015. (Mermaid Tales Ser.: 11). (ENG.). 128p. (J). (gr. 1-4). pap. 5.99 (978-1-4814-0260-6(9), Aladdin) Simon & Schuster Children's Publishing.
—Treasure in Trident City. Avakyan, Tatevik, illus. 2014. (Mermaid Tales Ser.: 8). (ENG.). 128p. (J). (gr. 1-4). pap. 5.99 (978-1-4424-8266-1(4), Aladdin) Simon & Schuster Children's Publishing.
—Trouble at Trident Academy. Avakyan, Tatevik, illus. 2012. (Mermaid Tales Ser.: 1). (ENG.). 112p. (J). (gr. 1-4). 15.99 (978-1-4424-4978-7(0)); pap. 5.99 (978-1-4424-2980-2(1)) Simon & Schuster Children's Publishing. (Aladdin).
—Twist & Shout. Avakyan, Tatevik, illus. 2016. (Mermaid Tales Ser.: 14). (ENG.). 112p. (J). (gr. 1-4). pap. 5.99 (978-1-4814-4078-3(0), Aladdin) Simon & Schuster Children's Publishing.
Dadey, Debby & Dadey, Debbie. Battle of the Best Friends, 1 vol., Bk. 2. 2015. (Mermaid Tales Ser.). (ENG.). 104p. (J). (gr. 2-4). 24.21 (978-1-61479-323-6(9), Spotlight) ABDO Publishing Co.
—Danger in the Deep Blue Sea, 1 vol., Bk. 4. 2015. (Mermaid Tales Ser.). (ENG.). 104p. (J). (gr. 2-4). 24.21 (978-1-61479-325-0(5), Spotlight) ABDO Publishing Co.
—Treasure in Trident City, 1 vol., Bk. 8. 2015. (Mermaid Tales Ser.). (ENG.). 120p. (J). (gr. 2-4). 24.21 (978-1-61479-329-8(8), Spotlight) ABDO Publishing Co.
—Trouble at Trident Academy, 1 vol., Bk. 1. 2015. (Mermaid Tales Ser.). (ENG.). 104p. (J). (gr. 2-4). 24.21 (978-1-61479-322-9(0), Spotlight) ABDO Publishing Co.
—Whale of a Tale, 1 vol., Bk. 3. 2015. (Mermaid Tales Ser.). (ENG.). 120p. (J). (gr. 2-4). 24.21 (978-1-61479-324-3(7), Spotlight) ABDO Publishing Co.
Daggett, Wade. Coco's New Friend. 2004. 35p. pap. 24.95 (978-1-4137-2001-3(3)) PublishAmerica, Inc.
Dagostino, Argus. Belcher Bomb. 2008. 53p. pap. 16.95 (978-1-60441-596-4(7)) America Star Bks.
Dahl, Elisabeth. Genie Wishes. 2013. (ENG., Illus.). 288p. (J). (gr. 3-7). 17.95 (978-1-4197-0526-7(1), Amulet Bks.) Abrams, Inc.
Dahl, Michael. Cold Feet, 1 vol. Ornia-Blanco, Miguel, illus. 2010. (Monster Street Ser.). (ENG.). 32p. (gr. 1-3). lib. bdg. 23.99 (978-1-4048-6070-4(3), Monster Street) Picture Window Bks.
—Dark Tower Rising, 1 vol. Kovar, Ben, illus. 2012. (Troll Hunters Ser.). (ENG.). 112p. (gr. 2-3). lib. bdg. 25.32 (978-1-4342-3308-0(1), Troll Hunters) Stone Arch Bks.
—Dragon Theft Auto, 1 vol. Rong, Yap Kun, illus. 2010. (Dragonblood Ser.). (ENG.). 40p. (gr. 1-3). pap. 6.25 (978-1-4342-2310-4(8), Zone Bks.) Stone Arch Bks.
—Dragon Theft Auto, 1 vol. Evans, Mark & Kun Rong, Yap, illus. 2009. (Dragonblood Ser.). (ENG.). 40p. (gr. 1-3). 23.99 (978-1-4342-1264-1(5), Zone Bks.) Stone Arch Bks.
—The Dragon with the Girl Tattoo, 1 vol. Aime, Luigi, illus. 2012. (Dragonborn Ser.). (ENG.). 72p. (gr. 1-3). pap. 7.10 (978-1-4342-4257-0(9)); lib. bdg. 23.99 (978-1-4342-4041-5(X)) Stone Arch Bks.
—Fallen Star, 1 vol. Kovar, Ben, illus. 2012. (Troll Hunters Ser.). (ENG.). 112p. (gr. 2-3). lib. bdg. 25.32 (978-1-4342-3310-3(3), Troll Hunters) Stone Arch Bks.
—The Lava Crown, 1 vol. Kovar, Ben, illus. 2012. (Troll Hunters Ser.). (ENG.). 112p. (gr. 2-3). lib. bdg. 25.32 (978-1-4342-3309-7(X), Troll Hunters) Stone Arch Bks.
—Skyfall, 1 vol. Kovar, Ben, illus. 2012. (Troll Hunters Ser.). (ENG.). 112p. (gr. 2-3). lib. bdg. 25.32 (978-1-4342-3307-3(3), Troll Hunters) Stone Arch Bks.
—Troll Hunters, 1 vol. Kovar, Ben, illus. 2012. (Troll Hunters Ser.). (ENG.). 320p. (gr. 4-4). 12.95 (978-1-4342-4590-8(X)) Stone Arch Bks.
—Two Heads Are Better Than One, 1 vol. Ornia-Blanco, Miguel, illus. 2010. (Monster Street Ser.). (ENG.). 32p. (gr. 1-2). lib. bdg. 23.99 (978-1-4048-6067-4(3), Monster Street) Picture Window Bks.
Dahl, Michael & Aime, Luigi. Duel of Dragons, 1 vol. 2012. (Dragonborn Ser.). (ENG., Illus.). 72p. (gr. 1-3). pap. 7.10 (978-1-4342-4254-9(4)); lib. bdg. 23.99 (978-1-4342-4039-2(8)) Stone Arch Bks.
Daigle, Damien. The Fish That Went Roar. Daigle, Casie, illus. 2011. 28p. pap. 24.95 (978-1-4560-5080-1(X)) America Star Bks.
Dailey, Reid. Ross the Reader & the Adventure of the Pirate's Treasure. Edgerley, Ross, illus. 2009. 44p. pap. 16.95 (978-1-59858-900-9(8)) Dog Ear Publishing, LLC.
Dairman, Tara. All Four Stars. 2014. (All Four Stars Ser.: Bk. 1). (ENG.). 288p. (J). (gr. 3-7). 16.99 (978-0-399-16252-7(6), G.P. Putnam's Sons Books for Young Readers) Penguin Young Readers Group.
—The Stars of Summer. 2015. (All Four Stars Ser.: Bk. 2). (ENG.). 336p. (J). (gr. 3-7). 16.99 (978-0-399-17069-0(3), G.P. Putnam's Sons Books for Young Readers) Penguin Young Readers Group.
Dal Santo, Sandy. I Live on a Colorful Street. 2009. 32p. pap. 13.49 (978-1-4389-3978-0(7)) AuthorHouse.
Daley, Michael J. Pinch & Dash & the Terrible Couch. Yezerski, Thomas F., illus. 2013. (ENG.). 48p. (J). (gr. k-3). 12.95 (978-1-58089-379-4(1)); pap. 5.95 (978-1-58089-380-0(5)) Charlesbridge Publishing, Inc.
—Pinch & Dash Make Soup. Yezerski, Thomas F., illus. 2012. (ENG.). 48p. (J). (gr. k-3). 12.95 (978-1-58089-346-6(5)); pap. 5.95 (978-1-58089-347-3(3)) Charlesbridge Publishing, Inc.
Daley-Prado, M. J. Buzz. 2008. 36p. pap. 17.95 (978-1-4357-1352-9(4)) Lulu Pr., Inc.
Dallas, Sandra. The Quilt Walk. (ENG.). 216p. (J). 2013. (gr. 4-7). pap. 9.95 (978-1-58536-799-3(0), 202373) 2012. 18.95 (978-1-58536-800-6(8)) Sleeping Bear Pr.
D'Allessandro, Alan. Growing Out of Fear. 2005. 62p. pap. 16.95 (978-1-4137-8547-0(6)) PublishAmerica, Inc.
Dalton, Andrew & Boatfield, Jonny. The New Empire of Malplaquet. 2009. (ENG., Illus.). 192p. (gr. 4-7). 35.00 (978-0-7188-3096-0(2)); pap. 17.50 (978-0-7188-3093-9(8)) Lutherworth Pr., The GBR. Dist: Casemate Academic.
Dalton, Annie. Lilac Peabody, No. 3. Griff, illus. 2009. (ENG.). 96p. (J). pap. 5.99 (978-0-00-713773-2(7), HarperCollins Children's Bks.) HarperCollins Pubs. Ltd. GBR. Dist: HarperCollins Pubs.
Dalton, Susan. The Magic Glasses. 2012. 36p. pap. 19.95 (978-1-4685-2586-1(7)) AuthorHouse.
Daly, Kathleen. Howdy Doody's Animal Friends. Seiden, Art, illus. 2011. 26p. 35.95 (978-1-258-02771-1(2)) Literary Licensing, LLC.
Damaged. 2014. (ENG., Illus.). 384p. (YA). (gr. 8). 17.99 (978-1-4424-5699-0(X), Simon Pulse) Simon Pulse.
Damerau, Diane Deci. The Petoskey Stones, 1 vol. 2009. 135p. pap. 24.95 (978-1-60749-903-9(7)) America Star Bks.
Damian, Gabriela Georgeta. The Chocolate Tree. 2010. 50p. pap. 19.88 (978-0-557-14739-7(5)) Lulu Pr., Inc.
Damman, Matthew. The Small Sports Take the Field! Eisenbraun, Patty, illus. 2nd ed. 2013. (ENG.). 32p. (J). 15.99 (978-0-9856967-0-2(2)) MAP Creative LLC.
Dammier, Patti. Got Carrots? Rescued Horse: The Winter Vacation. 2012. 142p. 21.95 (978-1-4759-2842-6(4)); pap. 11.95 (978-1-4759-2840-2(8)) iUniverse, Inc.
Dana, Barbara. Spencer & His Friends. 2014. (ENG., Illus.). 128p. (J). (gr. 3-7). pap. 13.99 (978-1-4814-3754-7(2), Atheneum Bks. for Young Readers) Simon & Schuster Children's Publishing.
Dandan-Albano, Corazon & Romulo, Liana. Filipino Friends. 2006. (ENG., Illus.). 32p. (J). (gr. 1-3). 15.95 (978-0-8048-3822-1(4)) Tuttle Publishing.
D'Andra, Anastasia. In the Shadows: Book 2 Rosegrove Series. 2012. 186p. pap. 24.95 (978-1-4626-5920-3(9)) America Star Bks.
Daneshvari, Gitty. Ghoulfriends Just Want to Have Fun. 2013. (ENG., Illus.). 272p. (J). (gr. 3-7). 12.99 (978-0-316-22253-2(4)) Little, Brown Bks. for Young Readers.
—Ghoulfriends 'Til the End. 2014. (Monster High Ghoulfriends Ser.: 4). (ENG., Illus.). 256p. (J). (gr. 3-7). 13.99 (978-0-316-22251-8(8)) Little, Brown Bks. for Young Readers.
—The Ghouls Rule Boxed Set, Set. 2013. (ENG., Illus.). 816p. (J). (gr. 3-7). 39.00 (978-0-316-32361-1(6)) Little, Brown Bks. for Young Readers.
—Who's That Ghoulfriend? 2013. Bk. 3. (ENG., Illus.). 272p. (J). (gr. 3-7). 13.00 (978-0-316-22254-9(2)) Little, Brown Bks. for Young Readers.
Daniell, G. Dusty & Albert's Beaver Tales. 2009. 50p. pap. 24.00 (978-0-557-08541-5(1)) Lulu Pr., Inc.
Daniels, Lucy. Oscar's Best Friends. 2005. 57p. (978-0-439-68199-5(5)) Scholastic, Inc.
Danna, Minnie. Miss Poppy & Red Jeans: Adventure to Willie Willie's Garden. Danna Sr., Gerald, illus. 2012. 66p. pap. 12.95 (978-0-9852608-0-4(7)) Flower Publishing.
Danziger, Paula. Amber Brown Goes Fourth. Ross, Tony, illus. 2007. (Amber Brown Ser.: No. 3). 101p. (gr. 2-5). 15.00 (978-0-7569-8197-6(2)) Perfection Learning Corp.
—Amber Brown Goes Fourth. (Amber Brown Ser.: No. 3). 112p. (J). (gr. 3-6). pap. 3.99 (978-0-8072-1291-2(1), Listening Library) Random Hse. Audio Publishing Group.
—Amber Brown Goes Fourth. Ross, Tony, illus. 2007. (Amber Brown Ser.: 3). (ENG.). 128p. (J). (gr. 2-5). 5.99 (978-0-14-240901-5(4), Puffin Books) Penguin Young Readers Group.
—Amber Brown Is Not a Crayon. Ross, Tony, illus. 2006. (Amber Brown Ser.: 1). (ENG.). 96p. (J). (gr. 2-5). 5.99 (978-0-14-240619-9(8), Puffin Books) Penguin Young Readers Group.
—Amber Brown Is Not a Crayon. (Amber Brown Ser.: No. 1). 80p. (J). (gr. 3-6). pap. 3.50 (978-0-8072-1289-9(X), Listening Library) Random Hse. Audio Publishing Group.
—Es Dia de Feria, Ambar Dorado. Ross, Tony, illus. 2007. (de Ambar / a Is for Amber Easy-To-Read Ser.).Tr. of It's a Fair Day, Amber Brown. (SPA.). 48p. (gr. k-3). pap. 8.95 (978-1-59820-596-1(X)) Santillana USA Publishing Co., Inc.
—Forever Amber Brown. 2008. (Amber Brown Ser.: 5). (ENG.). 128p. (J). (gr. 2-5). 5.99 (978-0-14-241201-5(5), Puffin Books) Penguin Young Readers Group.
—It's a Fair Day, Amber Brown. Ross, Tony, illus. 2003. pap. 31.95 incl. audio compact disk (978-1-59112-564-8(2)); pap. 31.95 incl. audio compact disk (978-1-59112-564-8(2)); (J). (gr. -1-2). audio compact disk 28.95 (978-1-59112-565-5(0)); (J). (gr. -1-2). audio compact disk 28.95 (978-1-59112-565-5(0)) Live Oak Media.
—It's a Fair Day, Amber Brown. Ross, Tony, illus. 2003. (Is for Amber Ser.). (ENG.). 48p. (J). (gr. 1-3). pap. 3.99 (978-0-698-11982-6(7), Penguin Young Readers) Penguin Young Readers Group.
—It's a Fair Day, Amber Brown. 2003. (Young Amber Brown Easy-To-Read Ser.: 4). (gr. k-3). lib. bdg. 13.55 (978-0-613-61635-5(9), Turtleback) Turtleback Bks.
—It's Justin Time, Amber Brown. Ross, Tony, illus. (Amber Brown Ser.). 9.95 (978-1-59112-294-4(5)) Live Oak Media.
—Justo a Tiempo, Ambar Dorado. Ross, Tony, illus. 2007. (Amber Brown Ser.). (SPA.). 48p. (gr. k-3). per. 8.95 (978-1-59820-595-4(1), Alfaguara) Santillana USA Publishing Co., Inc.
—Remember Me to Harold Square. (Remember Me to Harold Square Ser.: No. 1). 139p. (YA). (gr. 6-18). pap. 3.99 (978-0-8072-1472-5(8), Listening Library) Random Hse. Audio Publishing Group.
—¿Seguiremos Siendo Amigos? 97th ed. 2003.Tr. of Amber Brown is Not a Crayon. (SPA., Illus.). 106p. (gr. 3-5). 24.60 (978-84-204-4857-2(5), SAN8575) Harcourt Schl. Pubs.
Danziger, Paula & Martin, Ann M. P. S. Longer Letter Later. (Tara Starr & Elizabeth Ser.). 240p. (J). (gr. 3-5). pap. 4.99 (978-0-8072-1537-1(6), Listening Library) Random Hse. Audio Publishing Group.
—Snail Mail No More. unabr. ed. 2004. (Tara Starr & Elizabeth Ser.). 307p. (J). (gr. 3-7). pap. 36.00 incl. audio (978-0-8072-8413-1(0), Listening Library) Random Hse. Audio Publishing Group.
Darcy, Kate. Winnie Windmill: The Village Fete. 2012. (Illus.). 52p. pap. 24.40 (978-1-4678-8382-5(4)) AuthorHouse.
Darden, Hunter. Pete's Angel. Vaca, Sally, illus. 2008. 44p. pap. 12.00 (978-1-60693-264-3(0), Strategic Bk. Publishing) Strategic Book Publishing & Rights Agency (SBPRA).
Darke, J. A. Fade to Black. Evans, Neil, illus. 2016. (Spine Shivers Ser.). (ENG.). 128p. (gr. 3-4). lib. bdg. 26.65 (978-1-4965-3070-7(5)) Stone Arch Bks.
Darling, Angela. Lindsay Likes Nick Crush: Does He Like Her Too? 2013. (Crush Ser.: 3). (ENG., Illus.). 144p. (J). (gr. 3-7). 15.99 (978-1-4424-8045-2(9), Simon Spotlight) Simon Spotlight.
—Lindsay's Surprise Crush. 2013. (Crush Ser.: 3). (ENG., Illus.). 144p. (J). (gr. 3-7). pap. 5.99 (978-1-4424-8042-1(4), Simon Spotlight) Simon Spotlight.
Darnton, Kate. Chloe in India. 2016. (ENG.). 224p. (J). (gr. 4-7). 16.99 (978-0-553-53504-4(8), Delacorte Bks. for Young Readers) Random Hse. Children's Bks.
Dashner, James. A Mutiny in Time. 2012. (Infinity Ring Ser.: Bk. 1). (ENG.). 192p. (J). (gr. 3-7). 12.99 (978-0-545-38696-8(9)); 16.99 (978-0-545-48321-6(2)) Scholastic, Inc.
—A Mutiny in Time. 2015. (Infinity Ring Ser.: 1). lib. bdg. 17.20 (978-0-606-37765-2(4)) Turtleback Bks.
Dauer, Marty. Harvey's Woods: the Royal Adventures. LaRiccia, Mike, illus. 2007. 52p. per. 16.95 (978-1-4241-7924-4(6)) America Star Bks.
Daughtrey, Patricia & Benson, Gary. Shanaya & Friends: Litter Bugs Turn Eco H. E. R. O. S. Balkovek, Jim, illus. 2011. 40p. pap. 14.95 (978-1-60911-475-6(2), Eloquent Bks.) Strategic Book Publishing & Rights Agency (SBPRA).
Davenport, Eddie. Bunnyburg: The Newcomers. 2013. (ENG.). 30p. (J). pap. 14.95 (978-1-4787-2062-1(X)) Outskirts Pr., Inc.
David, Lawrence. The Terror of the Pink Dodo Balloons. Gott, Barry, illus. 2003. (Horace Splattly Ser.). 153p. (J). (gr. 4-7). 12.65 (978-0-7569-2816-2(8)) Perfection Learning Corp.
Davidson, Thomas A. Penny Found in Willowbrooke. 2009. 40p. pap. 14.75 (978-1-60693-774-7(X), Strategic Bk. Publishing) Strategic Book Publishing & Rights Agency (SBPRA).
Davie, Jan. Stairway to the Stars. 2005. 76p. pap. (978-1-84401-569-6(6)) Athena Pr.

Davies, Jacqueline. Nothing but Trouble. 2016. (Nothing but Trouble Ser.: 1). 320p. (J). (gr. 3-7). 16.99 *(978-0-06-236988-8(1)*, Tegen, Katherine Bks) HarperCollins Pubs.

Davies, Jocelyn. The Odds of Lightning. 2016. (ENG., Illus.). 384p. (YA). (gr. 9). 17.99 *(978-1-4814-4053-0(5)*, Simon Pulse) Simon Pulse.

Davies, Katie. The Great Rabbit Rescue. Shaw, Hannah, illus. 2011. (Great Critter Capers Ser.). (ENG.). 224p. (J). (gr. 3-7). 12.99 *(978-1-4424-2064-9(2)*, Beach Lane Bks.) Beach Lane Bks.

Davies, Linda. Longbow Girl. 2016. (ENG.). 336p. (J). (gr. 7). 17.99 *(978-0-545-85345-3(1)*, Chicken Hse., The) Scholastic, Inc.

Davies, Nicola. King of the Sky. Carlin, Laura, illus. 2017. (ENG.). 48p. (J). (gr. -1-3). 17.99 *(978-0-7636-9568-2(8))* Candlewick Pr.

Davies, Rob. Henhouse High Jinx: Mr. Stevens & Friends. 2013. 176p. 21.99 *(978-1-4669-9492-8(4))*; pap. 11.99 *(978-1-4669-9491-1(6))* Trafford Publishing.

Davies, Stephen. Sophie & the Albino Camel. 2009. 1.00 *(978-1-4074-4344-7(5))* Recorded Bks., Inc.

Davis, Alexus. Juke Joint. 2010. 169p. pap. 9.76 *(978-0-557-23687-9(8))* Lulu Pr., Inc.

Davis, Anne. Bud & Gabby. Davis, Anne, illus. 2006. (Illus.). 32p. (J). (gr. -1-2). lib. bdg. 16.89 *(978-0-06-075351-1(X))* HarperCollins Pubs.

—No Dogs Allowed!, No. 1. Davis, Anne, illus. 2011. (ENG., Illus.). 32p. (J). (gr. -1-3). 16.99 *(978-0-06-075353-5(6))* HarperCollins Pubs.

Davis, Beneta. My Covers. 2008. 24p. pap. 24.95 *(978-1-60441-584-1(3))* America Star Bks.

Davis, Bertha M. Jay's Friend Kitty Brew. Bowman, Todd A., illus. 2013. 28p. pap. 14.99 *(978-0-9886360-5-7(0))* Kids At Heart Publishing, LLC.

Davis, Danielle. Zinnia & the Bees. Horton, Laura K., illus. 2017. (Middle-Grade Novels Ser.). (ENG.). 240p. (gr. 4-7). lib. bdg. 26.65 ***(978-1-4965-4661-6(X))*** Stone Arch Bks.

Davis, Jacky. Ladybug Girl & the Best Ever Playdate. Soman, David, illus. 2015. (Ladybug Girl Ser.). (ENG.). 40p. (J). (gr. -1-k). 17.99 *(978-0-8037-4030-3(1)*, Dial Bks) Penguin Young Readers Group.

Davis, Jacky & Soman, David. Ladybug Girl & Bumblebee Boy. Soman, David, illus. 2009. (Ladybug Girl Ser.). (ENG., Illus.). 40p. (J). (gr. -1-k). 17.99 *(978-0-8037-3339-8(9)*, Dial Bks) Penguin Young Readers Group.

—Ladybug Girl Makes Friends. Soman, David, illus. 2012. (Ladybug Girl Ser.). (ENG., Illus.). 12p. (J). (gr. -1 — 1). bds. 5.99 *(978-0-448-45764-2(4)*, Grosset & Dunlap) Penguin Young Readers Group.

—Who Can Play? Soman, David, illus. 2013. (Ladybug Girl Ser.). (ENG., Illus.). 32p. (J). (gr. k-1). pap. 3.99 *(978-0-448-46501-2(9)*, Penguin Young Readers) Penguin Young Readers Group.

Davis, Katie. The Curse of Addy Mcmahon. 2008. (ENG., Illus.). 288p. (J). (gr. 5-9). 16.99 *(978-0-06-128711-4(3)*, Greenwillow Bks.) HarperCollins Pubs.

—The Curse of Addy McMahon. 2008. (Illus.). 288p. (J). (gr. 5-9). lib. bdg. 17.89 *(978-0-06-128712-1(1)*, Greenwillow Bks.) HarperCollins Pubs.

Davis, Lynda S. & Weisel, Kaitlyn E. Christopher James Mcabee & the Wonderful Tree. Trone, Melody Karns, illus. 2013. 54p. pap. 6.99 *(978-0-9889907-0-8(9))* Sruvis Publishing.

Davis, Mandy. Superstar. 2017. 336p. (J). (gr. 3-7). 16.99 *(978-0-06-237777-7(9))* HarperCollins Pubs.

Davis, Melissa. Remy's First Day of School. Kalpart, illus. 2013. 20p. pap. 10.95 *(978-1-62212-480-0(4)*, Strategic Bk. Publishing) Strategic Book Publishing & Rights Agency (SBPRA).

Davis, Mike. Land of the Lost Mammoths: A Science Adventure. 2003. (Illus.). 174p. (J). 15.95 *(978-0-9747078-8-5(5))* Perceval Pr.

Davis, Milton J. Amber & the Hidden City. 2013. 220p. pap. 16.95 *(978-0-9800842-7-6(X))* MVmedia.

Davis, Rhonda L. Faces of Darkness: The Daredevil Friends. 2008. 284p. pap. 14.95 *(978-1-934925-75-1(6)*, Eloquent Bks.) Strategic Book Publishing & Rights Agency (SBPRA).

DAVIS, Tamika. If i knew back then what i know Now. 2010. 119p. pap. 15.00 *(978-0-557-37544-8(4))* Lulu Pr., Inc.

—Now i Know. 2010. 152p. pap. 17.00 *(978-0-557-58446-8(9))* Lulu Pr., Inc.

Davis, Toby K. The Ever Part of Always: Keely Tucker's First Adventure. 2012. 208p. (gr. 4-6). 24.95 *(978-1-4697-4592-3(5))*; pap. 14.95 *(978-1-4697-4591-6(7))* iUniverse, Inc.

Davis, Trevor. The Adventures of Charley Mcchoochoo: Danny & the Whistling Engine. Davis, Natalie, ed. Anderson, Lochlin, illus. 2012. 34p. pap. 9.99 *(978-0-9853650-5-9(6))* Mindstir Media.

Dawe, Ted. Into the River. 2016. (ENG.). 304p. (J). (gr. 7). 17.99 *(978-1-943818-19-8(3))* Polis Bks.

Dawson, Dorothy M. Email on a Special Journey. 2008. 32p. per. 24.95 *(978-1-4241-9338-7(9))* America Star Bks.

Dawson, JoAnn. Willie to the Rescue. 2006. 264p. 15.95 *(978-0-9746561-0-6(0))*; pap. 8.95 *(978-0-9746561-2-0(7))* FT Richards Publishing.

Dawson, Piper. The Adventures of Fenway & Becc. 2012. 76p. pap. 8.95 *(978-1-4502-8646-6(1))* iUniverse, Inc.

Dawson, Stephanie Mara. The best recess Ever. 2nd ed. 2004. (Illus.). 28p. (J). per. 15.95 *(978-0-9748990-0-8(3))* Bk. Nook Productions.

Day, Karen. A Million Miles from Boston. 2012. (ENG.). 224p. (J). (gr. 3-7). pap. 6.99 *(978-0-375-85974-8(8)*, Yearling) Random Hse. Children's Bks.

—No Cream Puffs. 2010. (ENG.). 224p. (J). (gr. 3-7). 6.99 *(978-0-375-83776-0(0)*, Yearling) Random Hse. Children's Bks.

Day, Ralph M. Peter Porcupine One Quill. 2010. 40p. 19.95 *(978-1-4269-3747-7(4))* Trafford Publishing.

DC Super Friends, 1 vol. 2014. (DC Super Friends Ser.). (ENG.). 32p. (gr. 1-2). 271.20 *(978-1-4342-9525-5(7))* Stone Arch Bks.

de Bree, Alexander. Casting Dragon, 1 vol. 2010. 94p. pap. 19.95 *(978-1-4512-8691-5(0))* America Star Bks.

de Brunhoff, Laurent. Babar's Little Girl. rev. ed. 2012. (ENG., Illus.). 40p. (J). (gr. k-2). 16.95 *(978-1-4197-0340-9(4)*, Abrams Bks. for Young Readers) Abrams, Inc.

De Campi, Alex. Kat & Mouse, Vol. 3. 2017. (ENG., Illus.). 96p. pap. 5.99 *(978-1-59816-550-0(X)*, 9781598165500) TOKYOPOP, Inc.

—Kat & Mouse Vol. 1: Teacher Torture, 1 vol. Manfredi, Federica, illus. 2009. (Tokyopop Ser.). (ENG.). 96p. (gr. 2-6). 25.65 *(978-1-59961-564-6(9))* Spotlight.

—Kat & Mouse Vol. 2: Tripped, 1 vol. Manfredi, Federica, illus. 2009. (Tokyopop Ser.). (ENG.). 96p. (gr. 2-6). 25.65 *(978-1-59961-565-3(7))* Spotlight.

De Fombelle, Timothée. A Prince Without a Kingdom. 2015. (ENG., Illus.). 464p. (YA). (gr. 7). 17.99 *(978-0-7636-7950-7(X))* Candlewick Pr.

—Vango: Between Sky & Earth. 2014. (ENG., Illus.). 432p. (YA). (gr. 5). 17.99 *(978-0-7636-7196-9(7))* Candlewick Pr.

de Fombelle, Timothée. Vango: Between Sky & Earth. Ardizzone, Sarah, tr. 2016. (ENG.). 432p. (YA). (gr. 7). pap. 9.99 *(978-0-7636-8781-6(2))* Candlewick Pr.

De Fonté, Desiree. Zach: A Story of Obedience. 2012. 36p. pap. 24.95 *(978-1-4626-5114-6(3))* America Star Bks.

De Fonte', Desiree. Gaining the Heart of a Man: A Story of Hope & Forgiveness. 2011. 28p. pap. 24.95 *(978-1-4626-0274-2(6))* America Star Bks.

De Goldi, Kate. The 10 PM Question. 2012. (ENG., Illus.). 256p. (YA). (gr. 7). pap. 6.99 *(978-0-7636-5848-9(0))* Candlewick Pr.

de Gramont, Nina. The Boy I Love. 2015. (ENG., Illus.). 288p. (YA). (gr. 7). pap. 10.99 *(978-1-4424-8057-5(2)*, Atheneum Bks. for Young Readers) Simon & Schuster Children's Publishing.

—Every Little Thing in the World. (ENG., Illus.). 288p. (YA). (gr. 9). 2011. pap. 8.99 *(978-1-4169-8015-5(6))* 2010. 16.99 *(978-1-4169-8013-1(X))* Simon & Schuster Children's Publishing. (Atheneum Bks. for Young Readers).

De Jong, Riet M. W. I. Little Freebie & All His Friends. 2011. 124p. pap. 42.75 *(978-1-4269-5243-2(0))* Trafford Publishing.

De la Cruz, Melissa. The Ashleys. 2008. (Ashleys Ser.: Bk. 1). (ENG.). 272p. (J). (gr. 4-8). pap. 9.99 *(978-1-4169-3406-6(5)*, Simon & Schuster Bks. For Young Readers) Simon & Schuster Bks. For Young Readers.

—The Au Pairs. 2005. (Au Pairs Ser.: Bk. 1). (ENG.). 320p. (YA). reprint ed. pap. 9.99 *(978-0-689-87319-5(0)*, Simon & Schuster Bks. For Young Readers) Simon & Schuster Bks. For Young Readers.

—Beach Lane. 2013. (Beach Lane Ser.: 1). (ENG., Illus.). 320p. (YA). (gr. 9). pap. 9.99 *(978-1-4424-7409-3(2)*, Simon & Schuster Bks. For Young Readers) Simon & Schuster Bks. For Young Readers.

—Birthday Vicious. 2008. (Ashleys Ser.: Bk. 3). (ENG.). 256p. (J). (gr. 4-8). pap. 9.99 *(978-1-4169-3408-0(1)*, Simon & Schuster Bks. For Young Readers) Simon & Schuster Bks. For Young Readers.

—Crazy Hot. (Beach Lane Ser.: 4). (ENG., (YA). (gr. 9). 2013. Illus.). 288p. pap. 9.99 *(978-1-4424-7412-3(2))* 2008. 320p. pap. 9.99 *(978-1-4169-4808-7(2))* Simon & Schuster Bks. For Young Readers. (Simon & Schuster Bks. For Young Readers).

—Skinny-Dipping. (Beach Lane Ser.: 2). (ENG., (YA). (gr. 9). 2013. Illus.). 320p. pap. 9.99 *(978-1-4424-7410-9(6))* 2006. 304p. reprint ed. pap. 8.99 *(978-1-4169-0383-3(6))* Simon & Schuster Bks. For Young Readers. (Simon & Schuster Bks. For Young Readers).

—Sun-Kissed. (Beach Lane Ser.: 3). (ENG., (YA). (gr. 9). 2013. Illus.). 336p. pap. 9.99 *(978-1-4424-7411-6(4))* 2007. 320p. pap. 8.99 *(978-1-4169-1747-2(0))* Simon & Schuster Bks. For Young Readers. (Simon & Schuster Bks. For Young Readers).

De la Peña, Matt. Curse of the Ancients. 2015. (Infinity Ring Ser.: 4). (ENG.). 192p. (J). (gr. 3-7). pap. 6.99 *(978-0-545-90119-2(7))* Scholastic, Inc.

—Curse of the Ancients. 2015. (Infinity Ring Ser.: 4). lib. bdg. 17.20 *(978-0-606-37789-8(1))* Turtleback Bks.

—We Were Here. 2010. (ENG.). 368p. (YA). (gr. 9). pap. 9.99 *(978-0-385-73670-1(3)*, Ember) Random Hse. Children's Bks.

de Lint, Charles. Dingo. 2008. (ENG.). 224p. (YA). (gr. 7-18). 11.99 *(978-0-14-240816-2(6)*, Firebird) Penguin Young Readers Group.

De Los Heros, Luis & Wilson, Elizabeth. Chifa Chi's Little Adventure in New York City. 2011. 44p. pap. 21.99 *(978-0-557-91842-3(1))* Lulu Pr., Inc.

—Chifa Chi's Little Adventure in Washington Dc. 2010. 40p. pap. 21.99 *(978-0-557-23085-3(3))* Lulu Pr., Inc.

de los Santos, Marisa & Teague, David. Connect the Stars. 2015. (ENG.). 352p. (J). (gr. 3-7). 16.99 *(978-0-06-227465-6(1))* HarperCollins Pubs.

De Saint-Exupéry, Antoine. The Little Prince. l.t. ed. 2005.Tr. of Petit Prince. (ENG.). 168p. pap. 10.95 *(978-0-7862-7539-7(1))* Thorndike Pr.

De Saulnier, Gia Volterra. Journey to Jazzland. Zieroth, Emily, illus. 2013. 44p. 14.99 *(978-0-9851492-8-4(0))* Flying Turtle Publishing.

De Sena, Joseph. Little Sammy Sunshine & the Frightful Forest. 2008. 64p. pap. 27.95 *(978-1-4327-3119-9(X))* Outskirts Pr., Inc.

De Stefano, Lauren. A Curious Tale of the In-Between. 2016. (J). lib. bdg. 18.40 *(978-0-606-39553-3(9))* Turtleback Bks.

De Witt, Peter. Toaster Pond. 2006. (ENG.). 248p. (YA). (gr. 7-12). per. 16.95 *(978-1-933255-21-7(8))* DNA Pr.

Dean, James. Cavecat Pete. Dean, James, illus. 2015. (Pete the Cat Ser.). (ENG., Illus.). 24p. (J). (gr. -1-3). pap. 4.99 *(978-0-06-219863-1(7)*, HarperFestival) HarperCollins Pubs.

—Pete the Cat - Robo-Pete. Dean, James, illus. 2015. (Pete the Cat Ser.). (ENG., Illus.). 24p. (J). (gr. -1-3). pap. 4.99 *(978-0-06-230427-8(5)*, HarperFestival) HarperCollins Pubs.

—Pete's Big Lunch. 2013. (Pete the Cat I Can Read Ser.). (J). lib. bdg. 13.55 *(978-0-606-27146-2(5)*, Turtleback) Turtleback Bks.

Dean, James & Dean, Kimberly. Pete the Cat & the Missing Cupcakes. Dean, James, illus. 2016. (Pete the Cat Ser.). (Illus.). 40p. (J). (gr. -1-3). 17.99 *(978-0-06-230434-6(8))*; lib. bdg. 18.89 *(978-0-06-230435-3(6))* HarperCollins Pubs.

—Pete the Cat & the New Guy. Dean, James, illus. 2014. (Pete the Cat Ser.). (ENG., Illus.). 40p. (J). (gr. -1-3). 17.99 *(978-0-06-227560-8(7))*; lib. bdg. 18.89 *(978-0-06-227561-5(5))* HarperCollins Pubs.

Dean Van Scoyoc, Andrea. Graveyard katie & her Pals. 2008. 52p. pap. 20.00 *(978-0-557-01337-1(2))* Lulu Pr., Inc.

Dearing, Ruth. Tommy & the Hiccups. 2013. 44p. pap. 10.00 *(978-0-9843487-9-4(4))* Painting the Pages Publishing.

Deas, Mike, illus. Dalen & Gole: Scandal in Port Angus, 1 vol. 2011. (ENG.). 128p. (J). (gr. 3-6). pap. 9.95 *(978-1-55469-800-4(6))* Orca Bk. Pubs. USA.

Deb, Capone. Dumplings are Delicious Learning & Activity Guide. Stan, Jaskiel, illus. 2007. 20p. (J). 9.95 *(978-0-9728666-9-9(8))* As Simple As That Publishing.

Deborah, Wiles. Freedom Summer. 2014. (ENG.). 32p. (J). (gr. k-3). 12.24 *(978-1-63245-316-7(9))* Lectorum Pubns., Inc.

Debose, Alison. Lenny & Di in the Frog & the Fly. 2011. 28p. pap. 24.95 *(978-1-4626-0394-7(7))* PublishAmerica, Inc.

Debruzzi, Jeremy. A Minnesota Fish Tail. 2012. 48p. 24.99 *(978-1-4628-8580-0(2))*; pap. 15.99 *(978-1-4628-8579-4(9))* Xlibris Corp.

Decary, Marie. Le Combats des Chocolats. Brignaud, Pierre, illus. 2003. (Roman Jeunesse Ser.). (FRE.). 96p. (J). (gr. 4-7). pap. *(978-2-89021-611-2(X))* Diffusion du livre Mirabel (DLM).

Decker-Ahmed, Stasia. The Weirder the Better. 2011. (ENG.). 175p. (J). (gr. 4-6). pap. 8.99 *(978-0-930773-97-7(7))* Black Heron Pr.

Decker, Wendy. The Bedazzling Bowl. 2006. pap. 13.99 *(978-1-60034-468-8(2))* Salem Author Services.

Decter, Ed. Expedition to Pine Hollow. Yuen, Sammy, Jr. & Yuen Jr., Sammy, illus. 2007. (Outriders Ser.: 3). (ENG.). 240p. (J). (gr. 3-7). pap. 11.99 *(978-1-4169-1307-8(6)*, Simon & Schuster/Paula Wiseman Bks.) Simon & Schuster/Paula Wiseman Bks.

Dee, Barbara. This Is Me from Now On. 2010. (Mix Ser.). (ENG.). 272p. (J). (gr. 4-8). pap. 7.99 *(978-1-4169-9414-5(9)*, Aladdin) Simon & Schuster Children's Publishing.

Dee, Barbara. Truth or Dare. (ENG.). (J). (gr. 4-8). 2017. 272p. pap. 7.99 ***(978-1-4814-5969-3(4))*** 2016. (Illus.). 256p. 16.99 *(978-1-4814-5968-6(6))* Simon & Schuster Children's Publishing. (Aladdin).

Deem, James M. 3 NBs of Julian Drew. 2004. (ENG.). 208p. (YA). (gr. 7-18). pap. 13.95 *(978-0-618-43907-2(2))* Houghton Mifflin Harcourt Publishing Co.

DeFelice, Cynthia. Fort. 2015. (ENG.). 208p. (J). (gr. 3-7). 16.99 *(978-0-374-32427-8(1)*, 9780374324278, Farrar, Straus & Giroux (BYR)) Farrar, Straus & Giroux.

—Fort. 2016. (ENG.). 224p. (J). pap. 6.99 *(978-1-250-07973-2(X)*, 9781250079732) Square Fish.

—Fort. 2016. (J). lib. bdg. 17.20 *(978-0-606-38552-7(5))* Turtleback Bks.

DeFelice, Cynthia C. Signal. 2011. (ENG.). 176p. (J). (gr. 5-8). pap. 8.99 *(978-0-312-61776-9(3)*, 9780312617769) Square Fish.

Defreitas, Henrietta. Henratty Mortimer: We Were Only Strawberry Picking. 2011. (Illus.). 176p. (gr. -1). pap. 15.66 *(978-1-4567-8911-4(2))* AuthorHouse.

Degarmo, Serena. Penny Sue the Pure Hearted. De Marco, Arielle, illus. 2013. 30p. pap. 7.99 *(978-1-936341-55-9(7))* DeWard Publishing Co., Ltd.

Degen, Bruce. Nate Likes to Skate. Degen, Bruce, illus. 2016. (I Like to Read(r) Ser.). (ENG., Illus.). 24p. (J). (gr. -1-3). 6.99 *(978-0-8234-3543-2(1))*; 14.95 *(978-0-8234-3456-5(7))* Holiday Hse., Inc.

deGennaro, Sue. The Pros & Cons of Being a Frog. deGennaro, Sue, illus. 2016. (ENG., Illus.). 40p. (J). (gr. -1-3). 17.99 *(978-1-4814-7130-5(9)*, Simon & Schuster/Paula Wiseman Bks.) Simon & Schuster/Paula Wiseman Bks.

deGroat, Diane. Happy Birthday to You, You Belong in a Zoo. deGroat, Diane, illus. 2007. (Gilbert & Friends Ser.). (ENG., Illus.). 32p. (J). (gr. -1-3). pap. 6.99 *(978-0-06-001029-4(0))* HarperCollins Pubs.

—Happy Birthday to You, You Belong in a Zoo. deGroat, Diane, illus. 2007. (Gilbert & Friends Ser.). (Illus.). (gr. -1-3). 17.00 *(978-0-7569-8108-2(5))* Perfection Learning Corp.

—No More Pencils, No More Books, No More Teacher's Dirty Looks! deGroat, Diane, illus. (Gilbert Ser.). (Illus.). 32p. (J). (gr. -1-3). 2009. (ENG.). pap. 6.99 *(978-0-06-079116-2(0))* 2006. 15.99 *(978-0-06-079114-8(4))* 2006. lib. bdg. 18.89 *(978-0-06-079115-5(2))* HarperCollins Pubs.

DeHart, Leslie Marie. Paloma: The Lilly Fairy, 1 vol. 2010. 50p. pap. 16.95 *(978-1-4489-6818-3(6))* America Star Bks.

Dehghanpisheh, Corine. Buddy's Dream. Dehghanpisheh, Corine, illus. 2013. (Illus.). 34p. pap. 12.95 *(978-0-9851930-4-1(2))* Dehghanpisheh, Corine.

—Can We Play Again? Dehghanpisheh, Corine, illus. 2012. (Illus.). 32p. pap. 12.95 *(978-0-9851930-1-0(8))* Dehghanpisheh, Corine.

Dehm, Debbie. Animal Stories of the Desert. 2009. (Illus.). 41p. (J). pap. 20.95 *(978-1-4327-3461-9(X))* Outskirts Pr., Inc.

Del Rio, Adam. Teo in Palo Verde/Teo en Palo Verde. Ill, Noel, illus. 2008. (ENG & SPA.). 32p. (J). (gr. k-3). pap. 8.95 *(978-1-60448-001-6(7))* Lectura Bks.

Del Rizzo, Suzanne. My Beautiful Birds. Del Rizzo, Suzane, illus. 2017. (ENG.). 32p. (J). (gr. 1-3). 17.95 *(978-1-77278-010-9(3))* Pajama Pr. CAN. Dist: Ingram Publisher Services.

Delacre, Lulu. Alicia Afterimage. 2008. (ENG.). 144p. (YA). (gr. 7-18). 19.95 *(978-1-60060-242-9(8))* Lee & Low Bks., Inc.

Delacre, Lulu & Swanson, Katharine. Jay & Ben. Delacre, Lulu, illus. 2013. (ENG., Illus.). 18p. (J). bds. 20.00 *(978-1-60060-460-7(9))* Lee & Low Bks., Inc.

DeLaCroix, Alice. The Best Horse Ever. Himler, Ronald, illus. 2010. (ENG.). 80p. (J). (gr. 1-5). 15.95 *(978-0-8234-2254-8(2))* Holiday Hse., Inc.

Delafontaine, Ariane. Prince des Montagnes. 2012. 190p. pap. 38.59 *(978-1-291-11264-1(2))* Lulu Pr., Inc.

Delaronde, Deborah L. Duck's Bay. Dawson, Sheldon, illus. 2004. 48p. (J). pap. *(978-1-894717-24-3(4)*, Spotlight Poets) Pemmican Pubns., Inc.

Delashmit, Margaret V. Thief! 2012. 148p. (gr. 4-6). pap. 12.99 *(978-1-4624-0348-6(4)*, Inspiring Voices) Author Solutions, Inc.

Delessert, Etienne. Fuzzy, Furry Hat. Delessert, Etienne, illus. 2016. (ENG., Illus.). 32p. (J). (gr. 1-3). 18.99 *(978-1-56846-296-7(4)*, Creative Editions) Creative Co., The.

Delgado, Linda D. Hijab-Ez Friends. 2006. (YA). per. *(978-0-9767861-6-0(8))* Muslim Writers Publishing.

Delibero, Bob. Petrucchio. 2012. 234p. 24.95 *(978-1-4626-6155-8(6))* America Star Bks.

Delios, Louis & Sharma, Vicky. Tomorrow Will Be a New Day. 2011. 20p. pap. *(978-1-4269-7318-5(7))* Trafford Publishing (UK) Ltd.

Deliso, Chris & Dorling Kindersley Publishing Staff. Playtime with Sophie. 2014. (ENG., Illus.). 14p. (J). (gr. -1 — 1). bds. 5.99 *(978-1-4654-2042-8(8)*, DK Children) Dorling Kindersley Publishing, Inc.

Dell, Bella. Rosie the Robin. 2013. 24p. pap. 24.95 *(978-1-63000-892-5(3))* America Star Bks.

Dell, Pamela. Blood in the Water: A Story of Friendship During the Mexican War. 2003. (Scrapbooks of America Ser.). (ENG., Illus.). 48p. (J). (gr. 3-6). 32.79 *(978-1-59187-042-5(9)*, 200805) Child's World, Inc., The.

Dellaira, Ava. Love Letters to the Dead. 2015. (YA). lib. bdg. 20.85 *(978-0-606-37590-0(2))* Turtleback Bks.

Deluna, Alicia C. Tippy Gets a Friend. 2012. 20p. pap. 17.99 *(978-1-4685-5513-4(8))* AuthorHouse.

Demas, Corinne. Everything I Was. (Carolrhoda YA Ser.). (ENG.). 216p. (YA). (gr. 6-10). 2012. pap. 9.95 *(978-0-7613-9011-4(1))* 2011. 17.95 *(978-0-7613-7303-2(9))* Lerner Publishing Group. (Carolrhoda Lab™).

—Here Comes Trouble! Jones, Noah, illus. 2013. (J). *(978-0-545-55449-7(7)*, Scholastic Pr.) Scholastic, Inc.

Dembo, Jaiden. Finding Strider. 2010. 52p. pap. 15.54 *(978-0-557-39981-9(5))* Lulu Pr., Inc.

Demcak, Andrew. Ghost Songs. 2016. (ENG., Illus.). (J). 24.99 ***(978-1-63533-019-9(X))*** 2014. 210p. pap. 14.99 *(978-1-62798-795-0(9))* Dreamspinner Pr. (Harmony Ink Pr.).

—A Little Bit Langston. 2016. (ENG., Illus.). (YA). (gr. 9-12). 24.99 ***(978-1-63477-928-9(2)***, Harmony Ink Pr.) Dreamspinner Pr.

Demers, Dominique. Today, Maybe, 1 vol. Grimard, Gabrielle, illus. 2011. (ENG.). 32p. (J). (gr. -1-3). 19.95 *(978-1-55469-400-6(0))* Orca Bk. Pubs. USA.

Demetrios, Heather. I'll Meet You There. 2015. (ENG.). 400p. (YA). (gr. 9). 17.99 *(978-0-8050-9795-5(3)*, 9780805097955, Holt, Henry & Co. Bks. For Young Readers) Holt, Henry & Co.

DeMico, Judy. The Bus Trip, 1 vol. Johnson, Catherine LeAnn, illus. 2010. 26p. pap. 24.95 *(978-1-4489-2767-8(6))* PublishAmerica, Inc.

Demonia, Lori. Leah's Voice. 2013. 28p. 16.95 *(978-1-61244-240-2(4))* Halo Publishing International.

DeMonte, Joe. Lucy & the Magic Factory. 2008. 79p. pap. 19.95 *(978-1-60813-119-8(X))* America Star Bks.

Dempsey, Sheena. Bruno & Titch. Dempsey, Sheena, illus. 2014. (ENG., Illus.). 32p. (J). (gr. -1-2). 16.99 *(978-0-7636-7316-1(1))* Candlewick Pr.

Dempsey, Tami. We Are a Champion! 2010. 36p. pap. 15.49 *(978-1-4490-8102-7(9))* AuthorHouse.

Denis, Kasey. Henry the Hippo. 2012. 24p. pap. 17.99 *(978-1-4772-6558-1(9))* AuthorHouse.

Denman, K. L. Mirror Image, 1 vol. 2007. (Orca Currents Ser.). (ENG.). 128p. (J). (gr. 5-9). per. 9.95 *(978-1-55143-665-4(5))* Orca Bk. Pubs. USA.

Denofsky, Howard. Sillyishis, Beanie & the Hobblebobs. 2012. 32p. 24.95 *(978-1-4626-6211-1(0))* America Star Bks.

Dent, Jenny. The Story of Hoppy's Friend Pickle. (Illus.). 28p. (J). (gr. k-3). 2.25 *(978-0-85487-074-5(1))* White Eagle Publishing Trust GBR. Dist: DeVorss & Co.

Denton, P. J. Keeping Secrets. Denos, Julia, illus. 4th ed. 2008. (Sleepover Squad Ser.: 4). (ENG.). 96p. (J). (gr. 1-4). pap. 4.99 *(978-1-4169-2801-0(4)*, Aladdin) Simon & Schuster Children's Publishing.

DeNucci, Sharon. Ava Goes to Africa. DeNucci, Corinne, illus. 2010. 32p. pap. 16.99 *(978-1-4520-4091-2(5))* AuthorHouse.

Denucci, Sharon. Grammie & the Gecko. DeNucci, Corinne, illus. 2008. 40p. pap. 16.99 *(978-1-4389-1790-0(2))* AuthorHouse.

dePaola, Tomie. Andy & Sandy & the First Snow. dePaola, Tomie, illus. 2016. (Andy & Sandy Book Ser.). (ENG., Illus.). 32p. (J). (gr. -1-3). 8.99 *(978-1-4814-4159-9(0)*, Simon & Schuster Bks. For Young Readers) Simon & Schuster Bks. For Young Readers.

—Andy & Sandy's Anything Adventure. 2016. (Andy & Sandy Book Ser.). (ENG., Illus.). 32p. (J). (gr. -1-3). 8.99 *(978-1-4814-4157-5(4)*, Simon & Schuster Bks. For Young Readers) Simon & Schuster Bks. For Young Readers.

—Four Friends at Christmas. dePaola, Tomie, illus. 2009. (ENG., Illus.). 32p. (J). (gr. -1-1). 12.99 *(978-1-4169-9175-5(1)*, Aladdin) Simon & Schuster Children's Publishing.

—Four Friends in Autumn. dePaola, Tomie, illus. 2004. (ENG., Illus.). 32p. (J). (gr. -1-3). 17.99 *(978-0-689-85980-9(5)*, Simon & Schuster Bks. For Young Readers) Simon & Schuster Bks. For Young Readers.

—Four Friends in Summer. dePaola, Tomie, illus. 2003. (ENG., Illus.). 32p. (J). (gr. -1-3). reprint ed. 17.99 *(978-0-689-85693-8(8)*, Simon & Schuster Bks. For Young Readers) Simon & Schuster Bks. For Young Readers.

dePaola, Tomie, illus. When Andy Met Sandy. 2016. (Andy & Sandy Book Ser.). (ENG.). 32p. (J). (gr. -1-3). 8.99 *(978-1-4814-4155-1(8)*, Simon & Schuster Bks. For Young Readers) Simon & Schuster Bks. For Young Readers.

dePaola, Tomie & Lewis, Jim. Andy & Sandy & the Big Talent Show. dePaola, Tomie, illus. 2017. (Andy & Sandy Book Ser.). (ENG., Illus.). 32p. (J). (gr. -1-3). 8.99 ***(978-1-4814-7947-9(4)***, Simon & Schuster Bks. For Young Readers) Simon & Schuster Bks. For Young Readers.

Depken, Kristen L. Castle Caper. Cartobaleno, illus. 2015. (Pictureback(R) Ser.). (ENG.). 24p. (J). (gr. -1-2). 5.99 *(978-0-553-52313-3(9)*, Random Hse. Bks. for Young Readers) Random Hse. Children's Bks.

—Let's Go to the Circus! (Pocoyo) 2014. (Little Golden Book Ser.). (ENG., Illus.). 24p. (J). (-k). 3.99 *(978-0-385-37512-2(3)*, Golden Bks.) Random Hse. Children's Bks.

—Merry Christmas, Woody (Disney/Pixar Toy Story) RH Disney Staff, illus. 2013. (Pictureback Ser.). (ENG.). 16p. (J). (gr. -1-2). 3.99 *(978-0-7364-3070-8(9)*, RH/Disney) Random Hse. Children's Bks.

—Wally's Best Friends. Random House, illus. 2015. (Friendship Box Ser.). (ENG.). 48p. (J). (-k). bds. 10.99 *(978-0-553-52311-9(2)*, Random Hse. Bks. for Young Readers) Random Hse. Children's Bks.

—We Love to Dance! 2015. (Dora the Explorer Step into Reading Ser.). lib. bdg. 14.75 *(978-0-606-36396-9(3))* Turtleback Bks.

—We Love to Dance! (Dora & Friends) Aikins, David, illus. 2015. (Step into Reading Ser.). (ENG.). 24p. (J). (gr. -1-1). 4.99 *(978-0-553-50857-4(1)*, Random Hse. Bks. for Young Readers) Random Hse. Children's Bks.

Depperschmidt, Dustin & Andrea. The Adventures of Dax: The Golden Hammer. 2012. 28p. pap. 13.95 *(978-1-4497-7601-5(9)*, WestBow Pr.) Author Solutions, Inc.

DePrisco, Dorothea. Meet Gator: A Picture Clues Touch & Feel Book. Croft, James Lee, illus. 2005. (Learn to Read Ser.). 10p. (J). (gr. -1-18). 10.95 *(978-1-58117-123-5(4)*, Intervisual/Piggy Toes) Bendon, Inc.

Derbez, Eugenio. Lonjito Moco y Sus Amigos.Tr. of Lonjito Moco & His Friends. (SPA.). 4.98 *(978-968-890-497-8(X))* Edivision Compania Editorial, S.A. de C.V. MEX. Dist: Continental Bk. Co., Inc.

Deriso, Christine Hurley. The Right-Under Club: Second Stage. 2010. (J). *(978-0-385-73621-3(5))*; lib. bdg. *(978-0-385-90593-0(9))* Random House Publishing Group. (Delacorte Pr).

—Talia Talk. 2009. 184p. (J). pap. *(978-0-375-84496-6(1)*, Delacorte Pr) Random House Publishing Group.

DeRosier, Cher. The Plight of the Jelly Bean. Contreras, Gilbert, illus. 2005. (J). *(978-1-891685-50-7(3))* Dearborn Publishing.

Derting, Kimberly. Body Finder. 2011. (Body Finder Ser.: 1). (ENG.). 352p. (YA). (gr. 9). pap. 9.99 *(978-0-06-177983-1(0))* HarperCollins Pubs.

—Desires of the Dead. 2012. (Body Finder Ser.: 2). (ENG.). 384p. (YA). (gr. 9). pap. 8.99 *(978-0-06-177986-2(5))* HarperCollins Pubs.

—The Taking. 2014. (Taking Ser.: 1). (ENG.). 368p. (YA). (gr. 9). 17.99 *(978-0-06-229360-2(5)*, HarperTeen) HarperCollins Pubs.

deRubertis, Barbara. Corky Cub's Crazy Caps. Alley, R. W., illus. 2010. (Animal Antics A to Z Ser.). 32p. (J). lib. bdg. 22.60 *(978-1-57565-306-8(0))*; (ENG.). (gr. -1-3). pap. 7.95 *(978-1-57565-302-0(8))* Kane Press, Inc.

Derubertis, Barbara. Frances Frog's Forever Friend. 2010. pap. 45.32 *(978-0-7613-6508-2(7))* Kane Press, Inc.

deRubertis, Barbara. Frances Frog's Forever Friend. Alley, R. W., illus. 2010. (Animal Antics A to Z Ser.). 32p. (J). (gr. -1-3). (ENG.). pap. 7.95 *(978-1-57565-310-5(9))*; lib. bdg. 22.60 *(978-1-57565-317-4(6))* Kane Press, Inc.

deRubertis, Barbara & DeRubertis, Barbara. Corky Cub's Crazy Caps. Alley, R. W., illus. 2012. (Animal Antics A to Z Ser.). 32p. (J). (gr. 2 — 1). cd-rom 7.95 *(978-1-57565-396-9(6))* Kane Press, Inc.

—Frances Frog's Forever Friend. Alley, R. W., illus. 2012. (Animal Antics A to Z Ser.). 32p. (J). (gr. 2 — 1). cd-rom 7.95 *(978-1-57565-399-0(0))* Kane Press, Inc.

Desbordes, Astrid. Edmond, the Moonlit Party. Boutavant, Marc, illus. 2015. (ENG.). 32p. (J). (gr. -1-3). 17.95 *(978-1-59270-174-2(4))* Enchanted Lion Bks., LLC.

Desbordes, Astrid. The Thing. Boutavant, Marc, illus. 2017. (ENG.). 32p. (J). (gr. -1-3). 17.95 ***(978-1-59270-217-6(1))*** Enchanted Lion Bks., LLC.

Desbordes, Astrid & Martin, Pauline. Daydreams of a Solitary Hamster. 2010. (ENG., Illus.). 56p. (J). (gr. 1-2). 17.95 *(978-1-59270-093-6(4))* Enchanted Lion Bks., LLC.

Desclouds, Rick. My Year with the ESL Boys. 2009. 280p. pap. 22.92 *(978-1-4269-0621-3(8))* Trafford Publishing.

Deshmukh, Manisha. Chinu's Day Out. 2008. 24p. pap. 11.49 *(978-1-4389-0601-0(3))* AuthorHouse.

Desir, C. & Perry, Jolene. Love Blind. 2016. (ENG., Illus.). 320p. (YA). (gr. 9). 17.99 *(978-1-4814-1693-1(6)*, Simon Pulse) Simon Pulse.

Desmet, Sara. Scared Silly. Desmet, Sara, illus. 2006. (Illus.). 32p. (J). (gr. -1-3). 15.95 *(978-1-60108-009-7(3))* Red Cygnet Pr.

Dessen, Sarah. Saint Anything. (ENG.). (YA). (gr. 7). 2016. 448p. pap. 10.99 *(978-0-14-751603-9(X)*, Speak) 2015. 432p. 19.99 *(978-0-451-47470-4(8)*, Viking Books for Young Readers) Penguin Young Readers Group.

—Saint Anything. 2016. lib. bdg. 22.10 *(978-0-606-38833-7(8))* Turtleback Bks.

—Someone Like You. 2011. 10.36 *(978-0-7848-3539-5(X)*, Everbind) Marco Bk. Co.

—Someone Like You. 2004. (ENG.). 304p. (YA). (gr. 7-7). 10.99 *(978-0-14-240177-4(3)*, Speak) Penguin Young Readers Group.

—Someone Like You. 2004. 281p. (YA). (gr. 7). 16.65 *(978-0-7569-4967-9(X))* Perfection Learning Corp.

—Someone Like You. 2004. 281p. (gr. 7). lib. bdg. 22.10 *(978-1-4176-2674-8(7)*, Turtleback) Turtleback Bks.

Dessers, Rik. Rosie & Roger. Schuurmans, Hilde, illus. 2015. (ENG.). 100p. (J). pap. 16.95 *(978-1-931290-09-8(1))* Tallfellow Pr.

DeStefano, Lauren. A Curious Tale of the In-Between. 2015. (ENG.). 240p. (YA). (gr. 3-6). 16.99 *(978-1-61963-600-2(X)*, 9781619636002, Bloomsbury USA Childrens) Bloomsbury Publishing USA.

—The Peculiar Night of the Blue Heart. (ENG.). 2017. 224p. pap. 7.99 *(978-1-61963-645-3(X)*, 9781619636453) 2016. 208p. (J). 16.99 *(978-1-61963-643-9(3)*, 9781619636439) Bloomsbury Publishing USA. (Bloomsbury USA Childrens).

Destiny, A. & Hapka, Catherine. Virtually in Love. 2015. (Flirt Ser.). (ENG., Illus.). 240p. (YA). (gr. 7). pap. 9.99 *(978-1-4814-2118-8(2)*, Simon Pulse) Simon Pulse.

Destiny, A. & Helms, Rhonda. Never Too Late. 2015. (Flirt Ser.). (ENG., Illus.). 224p. (YA). (gr. 7). pap. 9.99 *(978-1-4814-5188-8(X)*, Simon Pulse) Simon Pulse.

Dettman, Eric. Any Day Friends. 2012. 28p. pap. 19.99 *(978-1-4685-4297-4(4))* AuthorHouse.

Detweiler, Katelyn & Wells, Rosemary. Immaculate. 2015. (ENG.). 464p. (YA). (gr. 9). bds. 17.99 *(978-0-451-46962-5(3)*, Viking Books for Young Readers) Penguin Young Readers Group.

Deubreau, Sharon. Heather & Avery & the Magic Kite. Pileggi, Steve, illus. l.t. ed. 2006. 23p. (J). per. 11.99 *(978-1-59879-143-3(5))* Lifevest Publishing, Inc.

Deuker, Carl. Gutless. (ENG.). 336p. (YA). (gr. 7). 2017. pap. 9.99 ***(978-1-328-74206-3(7))*** 2016. 17.99 *(978-0-544-61964-3(3))* Houghton Mifflin Harcourt Publishing Co. (HMH Books For Young Readers).

—Heart of a Champion. 2007. (ENG.). 208p. (YA). (gr. 7-17). per. 9.99 *(978-0-316-06726-3(1))* Little, Brown Bks. for Young Readers.

—Night Hoops. 2009. (ENG.). 224p. (YA). (gr. 7). pap. 8.99 *(978-0-547-24891-2(1))* Houghton Mifflin Harcourt Publishing Co.

—Night Hoops. 2009. 250p. (gr. 7-12). lib. bdg. 19.65 *(978-0-613-61919-6(6)*, Turtleback) Turtleback Bks.

Deutsch, Neil. Rose & the Pelican. 2013. 32p. pap. 19.99 *(978-1-4817-0947-7(X))* AuthorHouse.

Deutsch, Stacia. The Friendship Code. Fernandez, Andrea, illus. 2017. (Girls Who Code Ser.: 1). (ENG.). 144p. (J). (gr. 3-7). 12.99 ***(978-0-399-54251-0(5)***, Penguin Workshop) Penguin Young Readers Group.

Deutsch, Stacia. Quest for the Keys. 2015. (LEGO Elves Chapter Book Ser.: 1). lib. bdg. 16.00 *(978-0-606-37769-0(7))* Turtleback Bks.

Devargas, Casey Anthony. The Kindergarten Treasure. 2012. 44p. pap. 7.00 *(978-0-9859042-0-3(8))* CD Publishing.

deVet, L. J. Teddy's Christmas Wish. Zabarylo-Duma, Ewa, illus. 2013. 46p. (J). pap. *(978-0-9873686-5-2(6))* Print-Rite Publishers.

DeVillers, Julia. Liberty Porter, First Daughter. Pooler, Paige, illus. (Liberty Porter, First Daughter Ser.: 1). (ENG.). (J). (gr. 3-7). 2010. 192p. pap. 6.99 *(978-1-4169-9127-4(1))* 2009. 176p. 15.99 *(978-1-4169-9126-7(3))* Simon & Schuster/Paula Wiseman Bks. (Simon & Schuster/Paula Wiseman Bks.).

Devine, Ginger. Hooray for the Circus: A Story of Sam the Lamb. 2008. 36p. pap. 16.99 *(978-1-4389-1826-6(7))* AuthorHouse.

Devore, Laurie. How to Break a Boy. 2017. (ENG.). 352p. (YA). 17.99 *(978-1-250-08286-2(2)*, 9781250082862) Imprint IND. Dist: Macmillan.

Dewolfe, Jeannee'. The Adventures of Billy Chicken Toes & the Wolf: Add Your Own Art Children's Books. 2012. 56p. pap. 11.97 *(978-1-61204-921-2(4)*, Strategic Bk. Publishing) Strategic Book Publishing & Rights Agency (SBPRA).

Dexter & His Mystery Friend. 2004. (J). per. 15.99 *(978-0-9753533-5-6(7))* Golden Eagle Publishing Hse., Inc.

Dey, Lorraine. The Rainforest Party / Fiesta en el bosque Tropical. 2012. (ENG.). 32p. 16.95 *(978-1-936299-28-7(3)*, Raven Tree Pr.,Csi) Continental Sales, Inc.

Dharma Publishing Staff. Golden Foot: A Story about Unselfish Love. 3rd ed. 2013. (ENG.). 36p. (gr. -1-7). pap. 8.95 *(978-0-89800-517-2(5))* Dharma Publishing.

—The Value of Friends: A Story about Helping Friends in Need. 2nd ed. 2015. (ENG.). 36p. (gr. -1-7). pap. 8.95 *(978-0-89800-493-9(4))* Dharma Publishing.

Diamond, Jill. Lou Lou & Pea & the Mural Mystery. Vamos, Lesley, illus. 2016. (ENG.). 272p. (J). 16.99 *(978-0-374-30295-5(2)*, 9780374302955, Farrar, Straus & Giroux (BYR)) Farrar, Straus & Giroux.

Diaz, Cynthia. Sunny & Cubby's Real Life: ... Venturing Through Darkness. 2012. 24p. pap. 14.93 *(978-1-4669-4316-2(5))* Trafford Publishing.

DiCamillo, Kate. Because of Winn-Dixie. aut. ed. 2010. (Because of Winn-Dixie Ser.). (ENG., Illus.). 192p. (J). (gr. 4-7). 50.00 *(978-0-7636-5185-5(0))*; 15.99 *(978-0-7636-5007-0(2))* Candlewick Pr.

—Raymie Nightingale. 2016. (ENG.). 272p. (J). (gr. 5-7). 16.99 *(978-0-7636-8117-3(2))* Candlewick Pr.

—Raymie Nightingale. 2016. (J). lib. bdg. 29.40 *(978-0-606-37935-9(5))* Turtleback Bks.

—The Tiger Rising. (ENG.). (J). (gr. 5). 2015. 144p. pap. 6.99 *(978-0-7636-8087-9(7))* 2011. (Illus.). 128p. 15.99 *(978-0-7636-5270-8(9))* Candlewick Pr.

—The Tiger Rising. Sheban, Chris, illus. 2006. 144p. (J). (gr. 5). pap. 5.99 *(978-0-7636-2916-8(2))* Candlewick Pr.

—The Tiger Rising. aut. ed. 2011. (ENG., Illus.). 128p. (J). (gr. 5). 50.00 *(978-0-7636-5383-5(7))* Candlewick Pr.

—The Tiger Rising. unabr. ed. 2004. (Middle Grade Cassette Librariestm Ser.). 128p. (J). (gr. 5-9). pap. 29.00 incl. audio *(978-0-8072-0998-1(8)*, S YA 285 SP, Listening Library) Random Hse. Audio Publishing Group.

DiCamillo, Kate & Moghee, Alison. Best Friends Forever. Fucile, Tony, illus. (Bink & Gollie Ser.). (ENG.). (J). (gr. 1-4). 2014. 88p. pap. 6.99 *(978-0-7636-7092-4(8))* 2013. 96p. 15.99 *(978-0-7636-3497-1(2))* Candlewick Pr.

—Best Friends Forever. 2014. (Bink & Gollie Ser.: 3). lib. bdg. 17.20 *(978-0-606-35172-0(8))* Turtleback Bks.

—Bink & Gollie. Fucile, Tony, illus. (Bink & Gollie Ser.). (ENG.). (J). (gr. 1-4). 2012. 88p. pap. 6.99 *(978-0-7636-5954-7(1))* 2010. 96p. 15.99 *(978-0-7636-3266-3(X))* Candlewick Pr.

—Bink & Gollie. 2012. (Bink & Gollie Ser.: 1). lib. bdg. 17.20 *(978-0-606-23813-7(1)*, Turtleback) Turtleback Bks.

—Bink & Gollie - The Completely Marvelous Collection. Fucile, Tony, illus. 2014. (Bink & Gollie Ser.). (ENG.). (J). (gr. 1-4). pap. 19.99 *(978-0-7636-7536-3(9))* Candlewick Pr.

—Two for One. Fucile, Tony, illus. (Bink & Gollie Ser.). (ENG.). 96p. (J). (gr. 1-4). 2013. pap. 6.99 *(978-0-7636-6445-9(6))* 2012. 15.99 *(978-0-7636-3361-5(5))* Candlewick Pr.

—Two for One. 2013. (Bink & Gollie Ser.: 2). lib. bdg. 17.20 *(978-0-606-31607-1(8)*, Turtleback) Turtleback Bks.

DiCicco, Sue, illus. Totally Monster: Best Friends. 2013. (Totally Monsters Ser.). (ENG.). 14p. (J). 12.95 *(978-1-60710-643-2(4)*, Silver Dolphin Bks.) Readerlink Distribution Services, LLC.

Dickens, Frank. Fly Away Peter. 2017. (ENG., Illus.). 32p. (J). (gr. k-2). pap. 9.99 ***(978-1-84365-321-9(4)***, Pavilion) Pavilion Bks. GBR. Dist: Independent Pubs. Group.

Dickman, Jacqueline Rosett. Rebecca & Mom: Friends Forever, 1 vol. 2010. 116p. pap. 19.95 *(978-1-4489-4088-2(5))* America Star Bks.

Dickson, Irene. Blocks. Dickson, Irene, illus. 2016. (ENG., Illus.). 32p. (J). (-k). 14.99 *(978-0-7636-8656-7(5)*, Nosy Crow) Candlewick Pr.

Dickson, Robert. Sam Ferret Mysteries. 2010. 88p. pap. 14.95 *(978-1-4259-2741-7(6))* AuthorHouse.

DiDomenico, Allison. You Can Do It, Fiona! 2010. 28p. pap. 12.95 *(978-1-4490-9913-8(0))* AuthorHouse.

Diego, Marene. Hyper Spin, 1 vol. 2010. 190p. pap. 24.95 *(978-1-4489-2490-5(1))* America Star Bks.

Diesen, Deborah. The Pout-Pout Fish. Hanna, Dan, illus. (Pout-Pout Fish Adventure Ser.: 1). (ENG.). (J). (gr. -1 — 1). 2013. 36p. bds. 7.99 *(978-0-374-36097-9(9)*, 9780374360979) 2008. 32p. 16.99 *(978-0-374-36096-2(0)*, 9780374360962) Farrar, Straus & Giroux. (Farrar, Straus & Giroux (BYR)).

Dietl, Erhard. Andres y Su Nuevo Amigo. (Torre de Papel Ser.). (SPA.). (J). 7.95 *(978-958-04-4111-3(1))* Norma S.A. COL. Dist: Distribuidora Norma, Inc.

Dietrich, Cale. The Love Interest. 2017. (ENG.). 384p. (YA). 17.99 *(978-1-250-10713-8(X)*, 9781250107138) Feiwel & Friends.

DiGuardo, Maggie & Leventis, Kelly. Celly. 2012. (J). 14.95 *(978-1-937406-17-2(2))* Mascot Bks., Inc.

Dillard, Sarah. First Day at Zoo School. Dillard, Sarah, illus. 2014. (ENG., Illus.). 40p. (J). (gr. k-2). 14.99 *(978-1-58536-890-7(3)*, 203670) Sleeping Bear Pr.

—Mouse Scouts: Make a Difference. 2016. (Mouse Scouts Ser.). (ENG., Illus.). 144p. (J). (gr. 2-5). 12.99 *(978-0-385-75603-7(8)*, Knopf Bks. for Young Readers) Random Hse. Children's Bks.

Dilley, Ray. Brian's Lighthouse. 2013. 40p. pap. 19.99 *(978-1-4772-6663-2(1))* AuthorHouse.

Dillingham, Mike. Rivers Book Two: Through the Eyes of a Blind Sled Dog. 2003. (YA). pap. 13.95 *(978-1-59433-004-9(2))* Publication Consultants.

Dillon, Elena. Crushing. 2013. 368p. (YA). pap. 13.99 *(978-0-9886353-4-0(8))* Dillon, Elena.

Dilloway, Margaret. Momotaro Xander & the Lost Island of Monsters. Yung, Choong, illus. 2016. (Momotaro Ser.). (ENG.). 310p. (J). (gr. 3-7). 16.99 *(978-1-4847-2487-3(9))* Disney Publishing Worldwide.

—Momotaro Xander & the Lost Island of Monsters. Yoon, Choong, illus. 2017. (Momotaro Ser.). (ENG.). 336p. (J). (gr. 3-7). pap. 6.99 *(978-1-4847-4681-3(3))* Hyperion Bks. for Children.

—Xander & the Lost Island of Monsters. 2017. (J). lib. bdg. 17.20 *(978-0-606-39503-8(2))* Turtleback Bks.

Dinardo, Jeff. Bunny & Bird Are Best Friends: Making New Friends. Ho, Jannie, illus. 2014. (Funny Bone Readers: Being a Friend Ser.). 24p. (gr. -1-1). pap. 4.99 *(978-1-939656-02-5(8))* Red Chair Pr.

—Klink & Klank: Accepting Differences. Paillot, Jim, illus. 2014. (Funny Bone Readers: Being a Friend Ser.). 24p. (gr. -1-1). pap. 4.99 *(978-1-939656-04-9(4))* Red Chair Pr.

Ding, Yuhui Andrew. Warrior Soul. 2009. 28p. pap. 15.99 *(978-1-4415-6734-5(8))* Xlibris Corp.

Dinnison, Kris. You & Me & Him. (ENG.). 288p. (YA). (gr. 9). 2016. pap. 8.99 *(978-0-544-67175-1(9))* 2015. 17.99 *(978-0-544-30112-2(9))* Houghton Mifflin Harcourt Publishing Co. (HMH Books For Young Readers).

Dinosaur Friends. 2014. (Dinosaur Friends Ser.). 32p. (J). (gr. k-3). 105.00 *(978-1-4777-9112-7(4))* Windmill Bks.

Dionne, Erin. Models Don't Eat Chocolate Cookies. 2009. (ENG.). 256p. (J). (gr. 3-7). pap. 6.99 *(978-0-8037-3296-4(1)*, Dial Bks) Penguin Young Readers Group.

Dipucchio, Kelly. Dress-Up Mess-Up. Ross, Heather, illus. 2013. (Crafty Chloe Ser.). (ENG.). 40p. (J). (gr. -1-3). 16.99 *(978-1-4424-2124-0(X))* Simon & Schuster Children's Publishing.

—Everyone Loves Cupcake. Wight, Eric, illus. 2016. (ENG.). 40p. (J). 17.99 *(978-0-374-30293-1(6)*, 9780374302931, Farrar, Straus & Giroux (BYR)) Farrar, Straus & Giroux.

Diroma, Joseph. Pinuccio. Jones, Bob, illus. 2009. 24p. pap. 14.99 *(978-1-60844-036-8(2))* Dog Ear Publishing, LLC.

Dirst, Tracy. The Adventures of Pixie & Pete: They Meet. 2011. 16p. 9.50 *(978-1-4567-1077-4(X))* AuthorHouse.

Disney. Disney Miles from Tomorrowland: Galactic Explorers! 2016. (ENG.). 24p. (J). (gr. -1-1). 14.99 *(978-0-7944-3790-9(7)*, Reader's Digest Children's Bks.) Studio Fun International.

—Disney Pixar Finding Dory: I Love My Friends. 2016. (ENG.). 10p. (J). (gr. -1-k). bds. 7.99 *(978-0-7944-3882-1(2)*, Reader's Digest Children's Bks.) Studio Fun International.

Disney & Fox, Jennifer. Meet Nyx the Scout Fairy. 2015. (Passport to Reading Level 1 Ser.). (ENG., Illus.). 32p. (J). (gr. -1-1). pap. 3.99 *(978-0-316-28352-6(5))* Little, Brown Bks. for Young Readers.

Disney Book Group. Elena of Avalor My Best Friend's Birthday. Disney Storybook Art Team, illus. 2017. (ENG.). 24p. (J). (gr. 1-3). pap. 4.99 *(978-1-4847-7495-3(7))* Disney Pr.

—Girl Meets World Friend Power. No New Art Needed, illus. 2016. (Girl Meets World Junior Novel Ser.). (ENG.). 128p. (J). (gr. 3-7). pap. 5.99 *(978-1-4847-6715-3(2))* Disney Pr.

—Miles from Tomorrowland Mighty Merc. Disney Storybook Art Team, illus. 2015. (ENG.). 24p. (J). (gr. -1-k). pap. 3.99 *(978-1-4847-1552-9(7))* Disney Pr.

—Minnie Pop Star Minnie. Disney Storybook Art Team, illus. 2015. (ENG.). 24p. (J). (gr. -1-k). pap. 4.99 *(978-1-4231-8403-4(3))* Disney Pr.

—Standard Characters - Mickey Reader Bind Up. Disney Storybook Art Team, illus. 2016. (World of Reading Ser.). (ENG.). 96p. (J). (gr. -1-k). pap. 7.99 *(978-1-4847-9034-2(0))* Disney Pr.

—World of Reading: Sofia the First Adventure Stories: Five Favorites. Disney Storybook Art Team, illus. 2016. (Wonderful World of Reading Ser.). (ENG.). 160p. (J). (gr. -1-k). pap. 7.99 *(978-1-4847-7502-8(3))* Disney Pr.

Disney Book Group & Hurley, Kalikolehua. The Mighty Maui Makes a Friend. Disney Storybook Art Team & Isvandi, Mehrdad, illus. 2017. (ENG.). 32p. (J). (gr. 1-3). 16.99 *(978-1-4847-8292-7(5))* Disney Pr.

Disney Book Group, et al. Clover Time. 2016. (Sofia the First World of Reading Ser.). (Illus.). 32p. (J). lib. bdg. 13.55 *(978-0-606-37534-4(1))* Turtleback Bks.

Disney Book Group Staff. Disney 5-Minute Fairy Tales. Disney Storybook Artists Staff, illus. 2013. (5-Minute Stories Ser.). (ENG.). 192p. (J). (gr. -1 — 1). 12.99 *(978-1-4231-6766-2(X))* Disney Pr.

—Disney Junior 5-Minute Sofia the First & Friends Stories. Disney Storybook Art Team, illus. 2015. (5-Minute Stories Ser.). (ENG.). 192p. (J). (gr. -1-k). 12.99 *(978-1-4847-1327-3(3))* Disney Pr.

—Doc Mcstuffins Training Army Al. Disney Storybook Art Team, illus. 2014. (ENG.). 24p. (J). (gr. -1-k). pap. 3.99 *(978-1-4847-1419-5(9))* Disney Pr.

—Girl Meets World Follow Your Heart. 2015. (Girl Meets World Junior Novel Ser.). (ENG., Illus.). 128p. (J). (gr. 3-7). pap. 5.99 *(978-1-4847-2812-3(2))* Disney Pr.

—Haunted Clubhouse. 2010. (ENG., Illus.). 12p. (J). (gr. -1-k). bds. 6.99 *(978-1-4231-2832-8(X))* Disney Pr.

—The Inside Scoop. Peake, Marilyn, ed. movie tie-in ed. 2009. (ENG.). 32p. (J). (gr. 1-4). pap. 3.99 *(978-1-4231-1819-0(7))* Disney Pr.

—Thumper Finds a Friend. Disney Storybook Artists Staff & Disney Storybook Art Team, illus. 2010. (ENG.). 32p. (J). (gr. -1-k). pap. 3.99 *(978-1-4231-2313-2(1))* Disney Pr.

Disney Book Group Staff & LaRose, Melinda. Jake & the Never Land Pirates - Winter Never Land. Disney Storybook Art Team, illus. 2014. (ENG.). 12p. (J). (gr. -1-k). bds. 7.99 *(978-1-4231-9424-8(1))* Disney Pr.

Disney Book Group Staff & Ryals, Lexi. Crush Crazy. 2013. (Jessie Junior Novel Ser.). (ENG.). 128p. (J). (gr. 3-7). pap. 5.99 *(978-1-4231-8374-7(6))* Disney Pr.

Disney Book Group Staff, et al. It's a Small World. Chou, Joey, illus. 2011. (Disney Parks Presents Ser.). (ENG.). 32p. (J). (gr. -1 — 1). 16.99 *(978-1-4231-4689-6(1))* Disney Pr.

Disney Editors. Belle's Friendship Invention / Tiana's Friendship Fix-Up. 2016. (Disney Princess 8x8 Ser.). lib. bdg. 16.00 ***(978-0-606-39853-4(8))*** Turtleback Bks.

—Cinderella Takes the Stage. 2017. (Disney Princess Beginnings Ser.). lib. bdg. 17.20 ***(978-0-606-39857-2(0))*** Turtleback Bks.

—Olaf Loves... Everything! 2016. (Frozen 8X8 Ser.). lib. bdg. 14.75 ***(978-0-606-39858-9(9))*** Turtleback Bks.

Disney Enterprises Inc. Staff, creator. Disney Caritas Felices: Simba. 2007. (Illus.). 8p. (J). (gr. -1). *(978-970-718-392-6(6)*, Silver Dolphin en Español) Advanced Marketing, S. de R. L. de C. V.

Disney Junior Staff & Higginson, Sheila Sweeny. Disney Doc McStuffins Carryalong Play Book. Hall, Susan, illus. 2014. (CarryAlong Book Ser.). (ENG.). 14p. (J). (gr. -1-k). bds. 14.99 *(978-0-7944-3178-5(X))* Reader's Digest Assn., Inc., The.

Disney Minnie, Disney. Disney Minnie - My Colorful Closet. 2014. (ENG.). 10p. (J). (gr. -1-1). 12.99 *(978-0-7944-3141-9(0))* Reader's Digest Assn., Inc., The.

Disney Press Editors. Ewoks Join the Fight. 2015. (Star Wars: World of Reading Ser.). (J). lib. bdg. 13.55 *(978-0-606-36912-1(0))* Turtleback Bks.

Disney Press Staff, ed. Mickey's New Friend. 2011. (Illus.). 32p. (J). *(978-1-4231-4585-1(2))* Disney Pr.

Disney Press Staff & Disney Book Group Staff. Furry Friends! Disney Storybook Artists Staff, illus. 2011. (Touch-And-feel Book Ser.). (ENG.). 16p. (J). (gr. -1-k). bds. 7.99 *(978-1-4231-4183-9(0))* Disney Pr.

Disney, Princesses, ed. Snow White, My Best Friends Audio Tales: Disney. 2009. 32p. 8.99 *(978-1-59069-772-6(3))* Studio Mouse LLC.

Disney Staff. Beauty & the Beast. 2004. (J). (gr. -1-2). spiral bd. *(978-0-616-01631-2(X))* Canadian National Institute for the Blind/Institut National Canadien pour les Aveugles.

Disney Storybook Art Team, illus. Legend of the Neverbeast. 2015. (Read-Along Storybook & CD Ser.). (ENG.). 32p. (J). (gr. 1-3). pap. 6.99 *(978-1-4847-1075-3(4))* Disney Pr.

Disney Storybook Artists Staff, ed. Disney/Pixar Cars Drawing Book & Kit. 2008. 32p. pap. 10.95 *(978-1-60058-102-1(1))* Quarto Publishing Group USA.

Disney Storybook Artists Staff, et al, illus. Disney's the Lion King. 2007. (Play-A-Sound Ser.). 16p. (J). (gr. -1-3). 16.98 *(978-1-4127-8776-5(9))* Publications International, Ltd.

DiTerlizzi, Tony. Ted. 2004. (J). (gr. k-3). spiral bd. *(978-0-616-07230-1(9))* Canadian National Institute for the Blind/Institut National Canadien pour les Aveugles.

—Ted. DiTerlizzi, Tony, illus. 2004. (ENG., Illus.). 40p. (J). (gr. -1-3). reprint ed. 7.99 *(978-0-689-86374-5(8)*, Simon & Schuster Bks. For Young Readers) Simon & Schuster Bks. For Young Readers.

DiTerlizzi, Tony & DiTerlizzi, Angela. Big Fun! DiTerlizzi, Tony, illus. 2009. (Adventure of Meno Ser.: 1). (ENG., Illus.). 48p. (J). (gr. -1-k). 9.99 *(978-1-4169-7148-1(3)*, Simon & Schuster Bks. For Young Readers) Simon & Schuster Bks. For Young Readers.

—Wet Friend! DiTerlizzi, Tony, illus. 2009. (Adventure of Meno Ser.: 2). (ENG., Illus.). 48p. (J). (gr. -1-k). 9.99 *(978-1-4169-7149-8(1)*, Simon & Schuster Bks. For Young Readers) Simon & Schuster Bks. For Young Readers.

Dittman, Jeffery. Jungle Heroes. 2013. 36p. pap. 15.95 *(978-1-4327-9935-9(5))* Outskirts Pr., Inc.

Divine, L. The Fight. 2008. (Drama High Ser.: Vol. 1). 202p. (gr. 8-12). 19.95 *(978-0-7569-8830-2(6))* Perfection Learning Corp.

—Frenemies. 2008. (ENG., Illus.). 304p. (YA). (gr. 9-12). 15.00 *(978-0-7582-2532-0(6)*, K-Teen/Dafina) Kensington Publishing Corp.

—Hustlin' 2009. (ENG., Illus.). 256p. (YA). (gr. 9). pap. 15.00 *(978-0-7582-3105-5(9)*, K-Teen/Dafina) Kensington Publishing Corp.

Dix, Catherine R. Rosetta Stones. 2009. (ENG.). 213p. pap. 14.95 *(978-0-9798452-2-2(X))* Central Ave. Pr.

Dixon, Amy. Sophie's Animal Parade. Wish, Katia, illus. 2015. (ENG.). 32p. (J). (gr. -1-k). 16.99 *(978-1-63220-403-5(7)*, Sky Pony Pr.) Skyhorse Publishing Co., Inc.

Dixon, Bob. Rooty the Tree Troll. 2009. 28p. pap. 13.99 *(978-1-4389-9129-0(0))* AuthorHouse.

Dixon, Dallas L. Shelby's Collection Day. Williams, Nancy E., ed. Forrest, Grace Metzger, illus. 2013. 24p. (J). pap. 12.98 *(978-1-938526-54-1(6))* Laurus Bks.

Dixon, Danielle. Project: Purest. 2012. 370p. pap. 19.99 *(978-1-4691-8247-6(5))* Xlibris Corp.

Dixon, Franklin W. The Race Is On. 2015. (Hardy Boys: Secret Files Ser.: 19). lib. bdg. 16.00 *(978-0-606-37840-6(5))* Turtleback Bks.

Dixon, Ken. Cobweb Jack & the Sacred Khunjar. 2009. 210p. pap. 28.50 *(978-1-4092-8919-7(2))* Lulu Pr., Inc.

Dixon, Kirstie. Pickles Helps a Friend. 2012. 16p. pap. 15.99 *(978-1-4772-6445-4(0))* AuthorHouse.

d'Lacey, Chris. A Dark Inheritance. 2014. (UFiles Ser.). (ENG.). 304p. (J). (gr. 3-7). 16.99 *(978-0-545-60876-3(7)*, Scholastic Pr.) Scholastic, Inc.

—The Fire Eternal. 2010. (Last Dragon Chronicles Ser.: 4). (ENG.). 512p. (J). (gr. 3-7). 8.99 *(978-0-545-05164-4(9)*, Orchard Bks.) Scholastic, Inc.

—UFiles #1: a Dark Inheritance. 2014. (UFiles Ser.: 1). (ENG.). 304p. (J). (gr. 3-7). pap. 7.99 (978-0-545-60878-7(3), Scholastic Paperbacks) Scholastic, Inc.

—The Wearle. 2016. (Erth Dragons Ser.: 1). (ENG.). 320p. (J). (gr. 3-7). 16.99 (978-0-545-90018-8(2), Scholastic Pr.) Scholastic, Inc.

Dobrina, Elena. The Beaver Kid's Adventures. 2007. (Illus.). 120p. (J). pap. 88.00 (978-0-8059-7451-5(2)) Dorrance Publishing Co., Inc.

Docherty, Thomas. Big Scary Monster. Docherty, Thomas, illus. 2010. (ENG., Illus.). 40p. (J). (gr. -1-2). 15.99 (978-0-7636-4787-2(X), Templar) Candlewick Pr.

—Little Boat. Docherty, Thomas, illus. 2009. (ENG., Illus.). 40p. (J). (gr. -1-2). 15.99 (978-0-7636-4428-4(5), Templar) Candlewick Pr.

Dockray, Tracy. My Life Story. Dockray, Tracy, illus. 2003. (Illus.). 40p. (J). lib. bdg. 15.95 (978-1-58717-218-2(6), SeaStar Bks.) Chronicle Bks. LLC.

Doe, Cheyenne. Kitty Kats. 2012. 264p. 27.95 (978-1-4626-7201-1(9)) America Star Bks.

Doerrfeld, Cori. Truth in Sight. Doerrfeld, Cori & Page, Tyler, illus. 2016. (Cici: a Fairy's Tale Ser.: 2). (ENG.). 48p. (J). (gr. 2-5). lib. bdg. 26.65 (978-1-4677-6153-6(2), Graphic Universe™) Lerner Publishing Group.

Doherty, Patrick. Cold Waves, Cold Blood. Warner, Christopher, ed. Struntz, D. J., photos by. 2015. (Illus.). 146p. (YA). (gr. 9-12). pap. 11.95 (978-0-9963756-3-4(5)) All About Kids Publishing.

Dokey, Cameron. Boys Camp: Zack's Story. Orback, Craig, illus. 2015. (ENG.). 128p. (J). (gr. 1-5). pap. 9.95 (978-1-62914-805-2(9), Sky Pony Pr.) Skyhorse Publishing Co., Inc.

—Zack's Story, Bk. 1. Orback, Craig, illus. 2013. (ENG.). 128p. (J). (gr. 2-5). 14.95 (978-1-62087-528-5(4), 620528, Sky Pony Pr.) Skyhorse Publishing Co., Inc.

Doktorski, Jennifer Salvato. How My Summer Went up in Flames. 2013. (ENG.). 320p. (YA). (gr. 9). 17.99 (978-1-4424-5940-3(9)); pap. 10.99 (978-1-4424-5939-7(5)) Simon Pulse. (Simon Pulse).

Doll, Nancy L. Buddee the Bugger & Me: Told by Mac, 1 vol. 2009. 48p. pap. 24.95 (978-1-60749-979-4(7)) America Star Bks.

Dolphin Halloween & Elsie's Scrapbook. l.t. ed. 2004. (Illus.). 32p. (J). mass mkt. 4.99 (978-0-9760868-0-2(8)) Pluegl Bks.

Dominguez, Angela. How Do You Say? / ¿Cómo Se Dice? Dominguez, Angela, illus. 2016. (SPA & ENG., Illus.). 32p. (J). 17.99 (978-1-62779-496-1(4), 9781627794961, Holt, Henry & Co. Bks. For Young Readers) Holt, Henry & Co.

Domínguez, José A. Mamerto: A Children's Story. 2006. (J). mass mkt. 12.50 (978-1-59835-022-7(6)) Cambridge BrickHouse, Inc.

Dompierre, Judith. Little Bear's & Friend's Summer Trip. 32p. 2012. 29.95 (978-1-4626-9272-9(9)) 2011. pap. 24.95 (978-1-4512-6624-5(3)) America Star Bks.

Dompierre, Judith E. Little Bear's & Friend's Summer Trip. 2012. 32p. pap. 24.95 (978-1-4626-9325-2(3)) America Star Bks.

Donaldson, Julia. Night Monkey, Day Monkey. Richards, Lucy, illus. 2016. (ENG.). 26p. (J). (gr. -1-k). bds. 10.99 (978-1-4052-8334-2(3)) Egmont Bks., Ltd. GBR. Dist: Independent Pubs. Group.

—The Spiffiest Giant in Town. Scheffler, Axel, illus. 2005. (ENG.). 32p. (J). (gr. -1-2). reprint ed. pap. 6.99 (978-0-14-240275-7(3), Puffin Books) Penguin Young Readers Group.

—What the Jackdaw Saw: Book & CD Pack, 2 vols. Sharratt, Nick, illus. 2015. (ENG.). 32p. (J). (gr. -1-k). 14.99 (978-1-5098-0622-5(9)) Pan Macmillan GBR. Dist: Independent Pubs. Group.

Donaldson, Julia & Richards, Lucy. Night Monkey, Day Monkey. 2012. (ENG., Illus.). 32p. (J). (gr. -1-k). pap. 10.99 (978-0-7497-4893-7(1)) Egmont Bks., Ltd. GBR. Dist: Independent Pubs. Group.

Donegan, Noel & Donegan, Luz. The Hot-Headed Bassoon. 2013. (Magical Mozart & His Musical Ser.). (ENG.). 32p. (J). pap. 8.95 (978-1-84730-392-9(7)) Veritas Pubns. IRL. Dist: Dufour Editions, Inc.

—The Sad Little Violin. 2013. (Magical Mozart & His Musical Ser.). (ENG.). 32p. (J). pap. 8.95 (978-1-84730-393-6(5)) Veritas Pubns. IRL. Dist: Dufour Editions, Inc.

Donnell, Annie Hamilton. Four Girls & A Compact. 2005. 26.95 (978-1-4218-0906-9(0), 1st World Library - Literary Society) 1st World Publishing, Inc.

Donnelly, Liza. The End of the Rainbow. Donnelly, Liza, illus. 2015. (I Like to Read(r) Ser.). (ENG., Illus.). 24p. (J). (gr. -1-3). 6.99 (978-0-8234-3396-4(X)); 14.95 (978-0-8234-3291-2(2)) Holiday Hse., Inc.

Donofrio, Beverly. Where's Mommy? McClintock, Barbara, illus. 2014. (Mary & the Mouse Ser.). (ENG.). 32p. (J). (gr. -1-2). 17.99 (978-0-375-84423-2(6), Schwartz & Wade Bks.) Random Hse. Children's Bks.

Donovan, Dan. A Christmas Tail! 2008. 28p. pap. 14.50 (978-1-4389-1220-2(X)) AuthorHouse.

Donovan, Jane. Just Perfect! 2008. 16p. pap. 12.95 (978-1-4389-0936-3(5)) AuthorHouse.

Donovan, Kevin. Billy & His Friends Witness a Miracle. 2003. (Illus.). 32p. 10.95 (978-0-9641338-2-2(2)) Billy the Bear & His Friends, Inc.

Donzelli, Janine. I Am Like You, & You Are Like Me. 2012. 24p. pap. 17.99 (978-1-4685-4128-1(5)) AuthorHouse.

Dooley, Sarah. Wilfred & Harold's Dinner Party Disaster . 2004. 35p. pap. 17.95 (978-1-4137-1585-9(0)) PublishAmerica, Inc.

Dopson, Jennifer. Life Goes On. 2008. 202p. pap. 12.96 (978-0-557-01741-6(6)) Lulu Pr., Inc.

Doren, Greg Van. Obleo. 2010. 24p. pap. 11.49 (978-1-4490-8811-8(2)) AuthorHouse.

Dorion, Betty F. & Dorion, Betty. Whose Side Are You On?, 1 vol. 2005. (ENG., Illus.). 216p. (J). (gr. 6-18). pap. 7.95 (978-1-55050-179-7(8)) Coteau Bks. CAN. Dist: Fitzhenry & Whiteside, Ltd.

Dorling Kindersley Publishing Staff. The Adventures of Brer Rabbit & Friends. Copeland, Eric, illus. 2006. (ENG.). 64p. (J). (gr. 5-12). per. 6.99 (978-0-7566-1813-1(4), DK Children) Dorling Kindersley Publishing, Inc.

—Disney Pixar Character Encyclopedia. 2012. (ENG.). 208p. (J). (gr. 2-5). 16.99 (978-0-7566-9885-0(5), DK Children) Dorling Kindersley Publishing, Inc.

—Lego Friends: The Adventure Guide. 2015. (ENG., Illus.). 96p. (J). (gr. k-4). 16.99 (978-1-4654-3549-1(2), DK Children) Dorling Kindersley Publishing, Inc.

—Sophie la Girafe: Sophie's Big Noisy Day Book! 2015. (ENG., Illus.). 12p. (J). (— 1). bds. 14.99 (978-1-4654-3803-4(3), DK Children) Dorling Kindersley Publishing, Inc.

—Sophie Pop-Up Peekaboo! 2014. (ENG., Illus.). 12p. (J). (gr. -1 — 1). bds. 9.99 (978-1-4654-2041-1(X), DK Children) Dorling Kindersley Publishing, Inc.

—Summer Adventures. 2013. (DK Reader Level 3 Ser.). lib. bdg. 13.55 (978-0-606-31476-3(8), Turtleback) Turtleback Bks.

Dorling Kindersley Publishing Staff & Beecroft, Simon. R2-D2 & Friends, Level 2. 2008. (DK Readers Ser.). (ENG.). 32p. (J). (gr. 1-3). pap. 3.99 (978-0-7566-4516-8(6), DK Children) Dorling Kindersley Publishing, Inc.

Dorling Kindersley Publishing Staff & Saunders, Catherine. Let's Explore! 2015. (DK Adventures Ser.). (ENG.). 128p. (J). (gr. 3-7). pap. 5.99 (978-1-4654-3533-0(6), DK Children) Dorling Kindersley Publishing, Inc.

Doman, Dave. Tree Talkers: A Christmas Story, 1 vol. Swope, Brenda, illus. 2009. 32p. pap. 24.95 (978-1-61546-180-6(9)) America Star Bks.

Dorothy Disanto-Morrell. Dorotea & Friends Visit the Hospital. 2010. 20p. pap. 7.31 (978-1-4269-2557-3(3)) Trafford Publishing.

Dorpinghaus, Penny. Fear Balls & Button Wads. 2006. 52p. pap. 16.95 (978-1-4241-2281-3(3)) PublishAmerica, Inc.

Dorsey, Angela. Autumn in Snake Canyon. 2012. 122p. pap. (978-1-927100-23-4(2)) Enchanted Pony Bks.

—The Time Thief. 2011. (ENG.). 144p. (YA). (gr. 6). pap. 9.99 (978-1-926607-27-6(9), Napoleon & Co.) Dundurn CAN. Dist: Ingram Publisher Services.

—Winter of Sinking Waters. 2012. 130p. pap. (978-1-927100-25-7(9)) Enchanted Pony Bks.

Dossantos, Laurie Staples. The Adventures of Stormy. 2009. 34p. pap. 10.50 (978-1-60693-365-7(5), Eloquent Bks.) Strategic Book Publishing & Rights Agency (SBPRA).

Dotlich, Rebecca Kai. Bella & Bean. Leijten, Aileen, illus. 2009. (ENG.). 40p. (J). (gr. -1-3). 17.99 (978-0-689-85616-7(4), Atheneum Bks. for Young Readers) Simon & Schuster Children's Publishing.

Doty, Kathryn Adams. Wild Orphan. 2006. (ENG.). 144p. (gr. 3-7). per. 14.95 (978-1-889020-20-4(6)) Edinborough Pr.

Doty, Linda. Hydrangea Hill: A New Home for Amy Manchester. 2008. 182p. pap. 24.95 (978-1-60610-840-6(9)) America Star Bks.

Doty, M. Surviving High School. 2012. (Surviving High School Ser.: 1). (ENG.). 224p. (YA). (gr. 7-17). pap. 10.00 (978-0-316-22015-6(9), Poppy) Little, Brown Bks. for Young Readers.

Doucette, Christina. Gordon's Treasure! A Sparkle Cove Adventure. 2011. 44p. (gr. 1-2). pap. 19.99 (978-1-4634-0487-1(5)) AuthorHouse.

Dougherty, Brandi. The Friendship Experiment. 2009. 147p. (J). pap. (978-0-545-07929-7(2)) Scholastic, Inc.

—The Littlest Pilgrim. Richards, Kirsten, illus. 2008. (ENG.). 32p. (J). (gr. -1-k). pap. 3.99 (978-0-545-05372-3(2), Cartwheel Bks.) Scholastic, Inc.

—The Valentine's Day Disaster. 2008. 204p. (J). pap. (978-0-545-03168-4(0)) Scholastic, Inc.

Douglas, Helen. After Eden. 2013. (ENG.). 288p. (YA). (gr. 7). 17.99 (978-1-61963-130-4(X), 9781619631304, Bloomsbury USA Childrens) Bloomsbury Publishing USA.

Douglas, Ryke Leigh. Molly the Trolley & Bud. 2008. 24p. pap. 11.95 (978-1-4327-2207-4(7)) Outskirts Pr., Inc.

—Sam's Surprise. 2008. 28p. per. 12.95 (978-1-4327-0850-4(3)) Outskirts Pr., Inc.

Douglass, E. The Squirrel Friends Adventures: The Monster & the Great Storm. 2013. 100p. 19.95 (978-1-4759-6640-4(7)); pap. 9.95 (978-1-4759-6638-1(5)) iUniverse, Inc.

Douglass Thom, Kara. Soccer Girl Cassie's Story: Teamwork Is the Goal. Seatter, Pamela, illus. 2014. (Go! Go! Sports Girls Ser.). (ENG.). 32p. (J). (gr. k-2). pap. 4.99 (978-1-940731-00-1(3)) Dream Big Toy Co.

Douthwaite, Wendy. The Orange Pony. 2003. (ENG., Illus.). 96p. (J). (gr. 2-7). mass mkt. 6.99 (978-0-330-33631-4(2), Pan) Pan Macmillan GBR. Dist: Trafalgar Square Publishing.

Doutrive, Kaleb D. The Funny Chaps. 2012. 24p. pap. 11.00 (978-0-9851574-1-8(0)) Bran Nue Productions.

Dowding, Philippa. The Gargoyle at the Gates. 2012. (Lost Gargoyle Ser.: 3). (ENG.). 192p. (J). pap. 10.99 (978-1-4597-0394-0(4), 9781459703940) Dundurn CAN. Dist: Ingram Publisher Services.

Dowell, Frances O'Roark. Phineas L. MacGuire & His Highly Scientific Notebooks ... All of Them! Phineas L. MacGuire ... Erupts!; Phineas L. MacGuire ... Gets Slimed!; Phineas L. MacGuire ... Blasts off!;Phineas L. MacGuire ... Gets Cooking! McDaniels, Preston, illus. 2016. (From the Highly Scientific Notebooks of Phineas L. MacGuire Ser.). (ENG.). 848p. (J). (gr. 3-7). pap. 27.99 (978-1-4814-9965-1(3), Atheneum/Caitlyn Dlouhy Books) Simon & Schuster Children's Publishing.

Dowell, Frances O'Roark. Blasts Off! McDaniels, Preston, illus. 2011. (From the Highly Scientific Notebooks of Phineas L. MacGuire Ser.). (ENG.). 224p. (J). (gr. 3-7). pap. 7.99 (978-1-4424-2204-9(1), Atheneum Bks. for Young Readers) Simon & Schuster Children's Publishing.

—Chicken Boy. Krause, George, photos by. 2007. (ENG., Illus.). 224p. (J). (gr. 5-9). pap. 6.99 (978-1-4169-3482-0(0), Atheneum Bks. for Young Readers) Simon & Schuster Children's Publishing.

—Chicken Boy. 2005. (ENG.). 208p. (J). (gr. 5-9). 17.99 (978-0-689-85816-1(7), Atheneum Bks. for Young Readers) Simon & Schuster Children's Publishing.

—Erupts! McDaniels, Preston, illus. 2006. (From the Highly Scientific Notebooks of Phineas L. MacGuire Ser.). (ENG.). 176p. (J). (gr. 3-7). 16.99 (978-1-4169-0195-2(7), Atheneum Bks. for Young Readers) Simon & Schuster Children's Publishing.

—The Kind of Friends We Used to Be. (Secret Language of Girl Trilogy Ser.). (ENG., Illus.). (J). (gr. 3-7). 2010. 256p. pap. 7.99 (978-1-4169-9779-5(2)) 2009. 240p. 16.99 (978-1-4169-5031-8(1)) Simon & Schuster Children's Publishing. (Atheneum Bks. for Young Readers).

—Phineas L. MacGuire ... Gets Cooking! McDaniels, Preston, illus. 2015. (From the Highly Scientific Notebooks of Phineas L. MacGuire Ser.). (ENG.). 224p. (J). (gr. 3-7). pap. 6.99 (978-1-4814-0100-5(9)) Simon & Schuster Children's Publishing.

—Phineas L. Macguire... Blasts Off! McDaniels, Preston, illus. 2008. (From the Highly Scientific Notebooks of Phineas L. MacGuire Ser.). (ENG.). 208p. (J). (gr. 3-7). 16.99 (978-1-4169-2689-4(5), Atheneum Bks. for Young Readers) Simon & Schuster Children's Publishing.

—Phineas L. Macguire... Erupts! McDaniels, Preston, illus. 2007. (From the Highly Scientific Notebooks of Phineas L. MacGuire Ser.). (ENG.). 176p. (J). (gr. 3-7). pap. 6.99 (978-1-4169-4734-9(5), Atheneum Bks. for Young Readers) Simon & Schuster Children's Publishing.

—Phineas L. MacGuire... Gets Slimed! McDaniels, Preston, illus. (From the Highly Scientific Notebooks of Phineas L. MacGuire Ser.). (ENG.). (J). (gr. 3-7). 2010. 224p. pap. 6.99 (978-1-4169-9775-7(X)) 2007. 208p. 16.99 (978-1-4169-0196-9(5)) Simon & Schuster Children's Publishing. (Atheneum Bks. for Young Readers).

—Phineas L. MacGuire... Gets Slimed! McDaniels, Preston, illus. l.t. ed. 2008. (From the Highly Scientific Notebooks of Phineas L. MacGuire Ser.). 159p. (J). (gr. 3-7). 22.95 (978-1-4104-0440-4(4)) Thorndike Pr.

—The Second Life of Abigail Walker. (ENG., Illus.). (J). (gr. 3-7). 2013. 272p. pap. 5.99 (978-1-4424-0594-3(5)) 2012. 240p. 16.99 (978-1-4424-0593-6(7)) Simon & Schuster Children's Publishing. (Atheneum Bks. for Young Readers).

—The Secret Language of Girls. 2005. 247p. (gr. 3-7). 17.00 (978-0-7569-5463-5(0)) Perfection Learning Corp.

—The Secret Language of Girls. (Secret Language of Girl Trilogy Ser.). (ENG., Illus.). 256p. (J). (gr. 3-7). 2005. pap. 7.99 (978-1-4169-0717-6(3)) 2004. 19.99 (978-0-689-84421-8(2)) Simon & Schuster Children's Publishing. (Atheneum Bks. for Young Readers).

—The Secret Language of Girls Trilogy: The Secret Language of Girls; the Kind of Friends We Used to Be; the Sound of Your Voice, Only Really Far Away. 2015. (Secret Language of Girl Trilogy Ser.). (ENG., Illus.). 768p. (J). (gr. 5-9). pap. 22.99 (978-1-4814-3831-5(X), Atheneum Bks. for Young Readers) Simon & Schuster Children's Publishing.

—The Sound of Your Voice, Only Really Far Away. 2013. (Secret Language of Girl Trilogy Ser.). (ENG., Illus.). 240p. (J). (gr. 5-9). 16.99 (978-1-4424-3289-5(6)) Simon & Schuster Children's Publishing.

Dower, Laura. Return of Mega Mantis. Schlafman, Dave, illus. 2009. (Monster Squad Ser.: 2). (ENG.). 144p. (J). (gr. 2-4). pap. 5.99 (978-0-448-44913-5(7), Grosset & Dunlap) Penguin Young Readers Group.

Dowley, Ruth. Hard Rock. 2006. (ENG.). 160p. (J). (gr. 4-7). pap. 9.99 (978-1-84270-467-7(2)) Andersen Pr. GBR. Dist: Independent Pubs. Group.

Dowling, Iris Gray. A Change of Hats. Bouthyette, Valerie, illus. 2012. 28p. pap. 14.99 (978-1-937129-36-1(5)) Faithful Life Pubs.

—A Pony for My Birthday. Bouthyette, Valerie, illus. 2012. 36p. pap. 10.99 (978-1-937129-50-7(0)) Faithful Life Pubs.

Dowling, Joni. Friends Forever. 2007. (J). per. 8.99 net. (978-1-60402-244-5(2)) Independent Pub.

Downer, Denise. Soul Mates. Frampton, Otis, illus. 2013. (Tombstone Twins Ser.). (ENG.). 48p. (gr. 1-3). lib. bdg. 23.99 (978-1-4342-2248-0(9)) Stone Arch Bks.

—Tombstone Twins: Soul Mates, 1 vol. Frampton, Otis, illus. 2013. (Tombstone Twins Ser.). (ENG.). 48p. (gr. 1-3). pap. 5.95 (978-1-4342-3873-3(3)) Stone Arch Bks.

—Tombstone Twins Package: Soul Mates. Frampton, Otis, illus. 2013. (ENG.). 41p. (J). (gr. 2-4). pap. 35.70 (978-1-4342-3955-6(1)) Stone Arch Bks.

Downes, Alice. Lucy & the Magic Loom: A Rainbow Loomer's Adventure Story. 2015. (ENG.). 112p. (gr. k-5). pap. 7.99 (978-1-63450-137-8(3), Sky Pony Pr.) Skyhorse Publishing Co., Inc.

Downest, Madeline. Lucy & the Magic Loom: the Daring Rescue: A Rainbow Loomer's Adventure Story. 2016. (ENG.). 112p. (J). (gr. k-5). pap. 7.99 (978-1-63450-215-3(9), Sky Pony Pr.) Skyhorse Publishing Co., Inc.

Downey, Joni J. Will You Be My Friend? — We Really Are No Different. Brudos, Susan E., illus. 2004. (J). pap. (978-0-932991-34-8(3)) Place In The Woods, The.

Downham, Jenny. Before I Die. 2009. (ENG.). 336p. (YA). (gr. 9). pap. 9.99 (978-0-385-75183-4(4), Ember) Random Hse. Children's Bks.

Downing, Erin. Best Friends (until Someone Better Comes Along) 2014. (Mix Ser.). (ENG., Illus.). 240p. (J). (gr. 4-8). pap. 6.99 (978-1-4424-8519-8(1), Aladdin) Simon & Schuster Children's Publishing.

Downing, Erin. Moon Shadow. 2017. (ENG., Illus.). 256p. (J). (gr. 3-7). 17.99 **(978-1-4814-7521-1(5)**, Aladdin) Simon & Schuster Children's Publishing.

Downing, Sue. Look, Look! Baby Animal Friends. 2016. (ENG., Illus.). 10p. (J). bds. 7.99 (978-1-61963-832-7(0), 9781619638327, Bloomsbury USA Childrens) Bloomsbury Publishing USA.

Doyle, Brian. You Can Pick Me up at Peggy's Cove, 1 vol. 2nd ed. 2006. (ENG.). 104p. (J). (gr. 4-8). pap. 6.95 (978-0-88899-709-8(4)) Groundwood Bks. CAN. Dist: Publishers Group West (PGW).

Doyle, Malachy. Long Gray Norris. 2006. (Yellow Bananas Ser.). (ENG., Illus.). 48p. (J). (gr. -1-3). lib. bdg. (978-0-7787-0956-5(6)) Crabtree Publishing Co.

—Rory's Lost His Voice. Semple, David, illus. 2005. (ENG.). 24p. (J). lib. bdg. 23.65 (978-1-59646-714-9(2)) Dingles & Co.

Doyle, V. L. & Rohm, Robert. Four Friends Find Fun. Zulewski, Timothy, illus. 2005. 32p. (J). 18.95 (978-0-9651672-4-6(0)) Eklektika Pr., Inc.

Dragonblood, A. The Whispering V: Children of the Others Collection. 2010. 84p. pap. 10.49 (978-1-4520-3250-4(5)) AuthorHouse.

Drake, Christina M. Milo the Monkey. 2013. 88p. (978-1-4602-2323-9(3)) FriesenPress.

Drakeford, Lisa. The Baby. 2016. (ENG.). 256p. (J). (gr. 9). 17.99 (978-0-545-94027-6(3)) Scholastic, Inc.

Draper, Adrian. Chili Peppers in Oatmeal. 2012. 30p. 24.95 (978-1-4626-5553-3(X)) America Star Bks.

Draper, Penny. Ice Storm!, 1 vol. 2011. (Disaster Strikes! Ser.: 6). (ENG.). 192p. (J). (gr. 4-8). pap. 8.95 (978-1-55050-451-4(7)) Coteau Bks. CAN. Dist: Orca Bk. Pubs. USA.

Draper, Rohan. Sunny & Mayo. 2012. 146p. 46.72 (978-1-4771-0446-0(1)); pap. 28.03 (978-1-4771-0445-3(3)) Xlibris Corp.

Draper, Sharon M. Copper Sun. 2006. (ENG.). 320p. (YA). (gr. 8-18). 19.99 (978-0-689-82181-3(6), Atheneum Bks. for Young Readers) Simon & Schuster Children's Publishing.

—Double Dutch. 2004. 183p. (gr. 6-9). 17.00 (978-0-7569-2934-3(2)) Perfection Learning Corp.

—Double Dutch. 2004. (ENG.). 192p. (J). (gr. 5-9). pap. 7.99 (978-0-689-84231-3(7), Atheneum Bks. for Young Readers) Simon & Schuster Children's Publishing.

Dreher, Gidge. Gus, Scruffy, Clara & Friends. 2007. 80p. per. 9.95 (978-1-933912-24-0(3)) Westview Publishing Co., Inc.

Dreisbach, Kristin Wolf. Winston the Duck & His Big Orange Bill. Dreisbach, Kristin Wolf & Foreman, Austin Lee, illus. 2013. 20p. pap. 13.97 (978-1-62212-897-6(4), Strategic Bk. Publishing) Strategic Book Publishing & Rights Agency (SBPRA).

Dreistadt, Jessica R. Ashley & Tiana. 2009. 96p. pap. 10.00 (978-0-578-02239-0(7)) Dreistadt, Jessica R.

Drescher, Henrik. Love the Beastie: A Spin-and-Play Book. 2011. (ENG., Illus.). 11p. (J). (gr. -1-3). 12.95 (978-0-7611-6109-7(0), 16109) Workman Publishing Co., Inc.

Drew And Hilary McSherry. Terrance the Trapezoid. 2013. 40p. pap. 16.99 (978-1-4808-0131-8(3)) Archway Publishing.

Driscoll, Amanda. Duncan the Story Dragon. 2015. (ENG., Illus.). 40p. (J). (gr. -1-2). 16.99 (978-0-385-75507-8(4), Knopf Bks. for Young Readers) Random Hse. Children's Bks.

Driscoll, Laura & Disney Book Group Staff. Thumper Finds an Egg. Tyminski, Lori et al, illus. 2009. (ENG.). 24p. (J). (gr. -1-k). pap. 3.99 (978-1-4231-1717-9(4)) Disney Pr.

Driving Mom Crazy 6 Packs: Individual Title. (gr. -1-2). 27.00 (978-0-7635-9446-6(6)) Rigby Education.

Drummond, Ree. Charlie's New Friend. 2014. (I Can Read! Level 1 Ser.). (J). lib. bdg. 13.55 (978-0-606-35041-9(1), Turtleback) Turtleback Bks.

Dube, Tory. A Trixi, a Shmoop & a Monster. Vasilevsky, Marina, illus. 2013. 32p. 19.99 (978-0-9886193-1-9(8)) Dube, Tory.

Dube, Tory Lee. A Trixi, a Shmoop & a Monster. 2013. 32p. pap. 9.99 (978-0-9886193-0-2(X)) Dube, Tory.

Dubisch, Mike, illus. The Haunted Cabin Mystery. 2009. (Boxcar Children Graphic Novels Ser.: 9). (ENG.). 32p. (J). (gr. 1-5). pap. 6.99 (978-0-8075-3180-8(4)) Whitman, Albert & Co.

—Tree House Mystery. 2009. (Boxcar Children Graphic Novels Ser.: 8). (ENG.). 32p. (J). (gr. 1-5). pap. 6.99 (978-0-8075-8088-2(0)) Whitman, Albert & Co.

Dubison, Valentine. Willington Woods. 2008. 52p. pap. 7.95 (978-1-4327-2153-4(4)) Outskirts Pr., Inc.

Dubois, Ricardo. Ghost Squirrel. 2007. 99p. pap. 12.49 (978-0-615-15411-4(5)) Dubois, Ricardo S.

Dubos, Delphine. The Planet of Wind. Burrell, Carol klio, tr. Elyum Studio Staff, illus. 2012. (Little Prince Ser.: 1). (ENG.). 56p. (J). (gr. 4-8). pap. 7.95 (978-0-8225-9422-2(6), Graphic Universe™) Lerner Publishing Group.

Dubosarsky, Ursula. The Golden Day. 2013. (ENG.). 160p. (YA). (gr. 7). 15.99 (978-0-7636-6399-5(9)) Candlewick Pr.

Dubuc, Marianne, creator. The Lion & the Bird. 2014. (ENG., Illus.). 64p. (J). (gr. -1). 17.95 (978-1-59270-151-3(5)) Enchanted Lion Bks., LLC.

Duchesne, Christiane. Edmond et Amandine. 2004. (FRE., Illus.). (J). (gr. -1-3). spiral bd. (978-0-616-11143-7(6)) Canadian National Institute for the Blind/Institut National Canadien pour les Aveugles.

Duddle, Jonny. The Pirates Next Door. 2012. (ENG., Illus.). 44p. (J). (gr. -1-2). 15.99 (978-0-7636-5842-7(1), Templar) Candlewick Pr.

Dudley, Blanche R. Siggy's Parade: Helping Kids with Disabilities Find Their Strengths. 2014. (ENG., Illus.). 48p. (J). (gr. -1-2). 9.95 (978-0-88282-469-7(4)) New Horizon Pr. Pubs., Inc.

Due, Kirsten L. Bearen Bear & the Bunbury Tales. Berends, Jenny, illus. 2013. 194p. pap. (978-0-9884916-3-2(X)) Roxby Media Ltd.

Duey, Kathleen. Arthur. Epstein, Eugene, illus. Gould, Robert, photos by. 2004. (Time Soldiers Ser.: Bk. 4). (ENG.). 48p. (J). (gr. k-2). 15.95 (978-1-929945-05-4(1)) Big Guy Bks., Inc.

—Time Soldiers - Patch. Epstein, Eugene, illus. Gould, Robert, photos by. 2003. (Time Soldiers Ser.: Vol. 3). (ENG.). 48p. (J). (gr. k-2). pap. 8.95 (978-1-929945-28-3(0)); 15.95 (978-1-929945-02-3(7)) Big Guy Bks., Inc.

Duey, Kathleen & Bale, Karen A. Flood: Mississippi 1927. 2015. (Survivors Ser.). (ENG., Illus.). 176p. (J). (gr. 3-7). pap. 6.99 (978-1-4814-1642-9(1), Aladdin) Simon & Schuster Children's Publishing.

Duff, Hilary. Devoted. 2011. (Elixir Ser.). (ENG.). 368p. (YA). (gr. 9). 17.99 (978-1-4424-0855-5(3), Simon & Schuster Bks. For Young Readers) Simon & Schuster Bks. For Young Readers.

Duff, Jc. Tornado Watch. 2012. 32p. pap. 21.99 (978-1-4771-1866-5(7)) Xlibris Corp.

Duffy, Cr. The Return of the Dark Star. 2012. 188p. (gr. 4-6). 30.95 (978-1-4525-4168-6(X)); pap. 13.99 (978-1-4525-4167-9(1)) Balboa Pr.

DuJardin, Rosamond. One of the Crowd. 2003. (YA). pap. 12.95 (978-1-930009-73-8(9), 800-691-7779) Image Cascade Publishing.

—The Real Thing. 2003. (YA). pap. 12.95 (978-1-930009-71-4(2), 800-691-7779) Image Cascade Publishing.

Dukes, Janet Walton. Harold & Tyler: Bravery. Dukes, Jazalyn D., ed. 2013. (ENG.). 32p. (J). pap. 9.95 (978-1-4787-0231-3(1)) Outskirts Pr., Inc.

Dukes, LeRoy. The Chill Street Gang. 2005. (Illus.). 40p. (J). 6.99 (978-0-9664506-1-3(2)) Dukes World, Inc.

Dukes, Martin. Worm Winds of Zanzibar. 2013. 420p. pap. (978-0-9575679-0-0(1)) Dukes, Martin.

E
F
G

Dunagan, Ted M. Secret of the Satilfa. 2010. (ENG.). 208p. (J). (gr. 3-18). 21.95 *(978-1-58838-249-8(4),* NewSouth Bks.) NewSouth, Inc.
Dunbar, Helene. What Remains. 2015. (ENG.). 264p. (YA). pap. 9.99 *(978-0-7387-4430-8(1),* Flux) North Star Editions.
Dunbar, Polly. Hello, Tilly. Dunbar, Polly, illus. 2008. (Tilly & Friends Ser.). (ENG., Illus.). 32p. (J). (gr. -1-2). 12.99 *(978-0-7636-4109-2(X))* Candlewick Pr.
—Pretty Pru: A Tilly & Friends Book. Dunbar, Polly, illus. 2009. (Tilly & Friends Ser.). (ENG., Illus.). 32p. (J). (gr. -1-2). 12.99 *(978-0-7636-4272-3(X))* Candlewick Pr.
Duncan, Daniel. South. 2017. (ENG., Illus.). 40p. (J). (gr. k-2). 17.95 *(978-1-4197-2299-8(9),* Abrams Bks. for Young Readers) Abrams, Inc.
Duncan, Jodi. Happy Flowers. 2009. 24p. pap. 14.50 *(978-1-60693-519-4(4),* Eloquent Bks.) Strategic Book Publishing & Rights Agency (SBPRA).
Duncan, Tisha Admire. Myrtle the Blue Eyed Turtle: A My Dirty Cat Mutt Adventure. 2012. 28p. pap. 14.95 *(978-1-4497-5727-4(8),* WestBow Pr.) Author Solutions, Inc.
Dungy, Tony & Dungy, Lauren. You Can Be a Friend. Mazellan, Ron, illus. 2011. (ENG.). 32p. (J). (gr. -1-2). 16.99 *(978-1-4169-9771-9(7),* Little Simon Inspirations) Little Simon Inspirations.
Dunham, Wendy. My Name Is River. 2015. (ENG.). 144p. (J). (gr. 2-7). pap. 7.99 *(978-0-7369-6461-6(4))* Harvest Hse. Pubs.
Dunker, Kristina. Summer Storm, 0 vols. Dembo, Margot Battauer, tr. from GER. unabr. ed. 2011. (ENG.). 146p. (YA). (gr. 7-9). pap. 9.95 *(978-1-61109-030-7(X),* 9781611090307) Amazon Publishing.
Dunlap, Sonya. Responza the Bull Learns the Ropes of Friendship. Snider, Sharon, illus. 2009. 32p. pap. 17.95 *(978-0-9815245-8-0(3))* Accelerator Bks.
Dunmore, Helen. The Deep. 2009. (Ingo Ser.: 3). 336p. (YA). (gr. 5-18). 16.99 *(978-0-06-081858-6(1))* HarperCollins Pubs.
Dunn, Gaby & Raskin, Allison. I Hate Everyone but You. 2017. (ENG.). 352p. (YA). 18.99 ***(978-1-250-12932-1(X),*** 9781250129321, Wednesday Bks.) St. Martin's Pr.
Dunn, Mark. The Age Altertron, Bk. 1. 2009. (ENG.). 175p. (gr. 4). *(978-1-59692-345-4(8))* MacAdam/Cage Publishing, Inc.
Dunrea, Olivier. Gansi y Gerti/Gossie & Gertie Bilingual Board Book. 2013. (Gossie & Friends Ser.). (SPA & ENG., Illus.). 32p. (J). (gr. -1-3). bds., bds. 4.99 *(978-0-544-07773-7(3))* Houghton Mifflin Harcourt Publishing Co.
—Gossie & Friends Big Book of Adventures. 2017. (Gossie & Friends Ser.). (ENG., Illus.). 288p. (J). (gr. -1-3). 15.99 *(978-0-544-77980-8(0),* HMH Books For Young Readers) Houghton Mifflin Harcourt Publishing Co.
—Gossie & Friends Sticker Fun. 2012. (Gossie & Friends Ser.). (ENG., Illus.). 24p. (J). (gr. -1-3). pap. 4.99 *(978-0-547-64300-7(4))* Houghton Mifflin Harcourt Publishing Co.
—Gossie & Gertie. Dunrea, Olivier, illus. 2007. (Gossie & Friends Ser.). (ENG., Illus.). 16p. (J). (gr. -1 — 1). bds. 6.99 *(978-0-618-74793-1(1))* Houghton Mifflin Harcourt Publishing Co.
—Gossie & Gertie. 2014. (Gossie & Friends — Green Light Readers Ser.). lib. bdg. 13.55 *(978-0-606-33981-0(7),* Turtleback) Turtleback Bks.
—Gossie & Gertie. 2006. (Illus.). 32p. pap. *(978-1-4063-0119-9(1))* Walker Bks., Ltd.
—Gossie & Gertie Padded Board Book. 2015. (Gossie & Friends Ser.). (ENG., Illus.). 32p. (J). (— 1). bds. 8.99 *(978-0-544-50644-2(8),* HMH Books For Young Readers) Houghton Mifflin Harcourt Publishing Co.
—Gossie & Gertie (Reader) 2014. (Gossie & Friends Ser.). (ENG., Illus.). 32p. (J). (gr. -1-3). pap. 3.99 *(978-0-544-10535-5(4))* Houghton Mifflin Harcourt Publishing Co.
—Jasper & Joop. 2013. (Gossie & Friends Ser.). (ENG., Illus.). 32p. (J). (— 1). 9.99 *(978-0-547-86762-5(X))* Houghton Mifflin Harcourt Publishing Co.
—Jasper & Joop (Reader) 2015. (Gossie & Friends Ser.). (ENG., Illus.). 32p. (J). (gr. -1-3). pap. 3.99 *(978-0-544-50381-6(3),* HMH Books For Young Readers) Houghton Mifflin Harcourt Publishing Co.
—Ollie's Valentine. 2015. (Gossie & Friends Ser.). (ENG., Illus.). 14p. (J). (— 1). bds. 6.99 *(978-0-544-50269-7(8),* HMH Books For Young Readers) Houghton Mifflin Harcourt Publishing Co.
—Say Good Night. 2017. (Gossie & Friends Ser.). (ENG., Illus.). 18p. (J). (— 1). bds. 8.99 *(978-0-544-91503-9(8),* HMH Books For Young Readers) Houghton Mifflin Harcourt Publishing Co.
Dupont, Matthew. As I Look in Your Eyes. Gutierez, Francisco & Renteria, Justin, illus. 2003. 20p. (YA). pap. 5.99 *(978-0-9728134-0-2(3))* A & E Children's Pr.
DuPrau, Jeanne. The City of Ember. 2008. (Book of Ember Ser.). (J). 44.99 *(978-0-7393-7097-1(9))* Findaway World, LLC.
Duquin, Judy. Rusty. 2011. 160p. (gr. -1). 23.00 *(978-1-4634-2559-3(7));* pap. 13.00 *(978-1-4634-2560-9(0))* AuthorHouse.
Duran, Magdalena. Jewel of Friendship. 2nd ed. 2009. (Jataka Tales Ser.). (ENG., Illus.). 32p. (J). (gr. -1-3). pap. 8.95 *(978-0-89800-426-1(4))* Dharma Publishing.
Durfee, Jody Wind. Hadley-Hadley Benson. 2013. (ENG.). 144p. (J). pap. 11.99 *(978-1-62108-151-7(6))* Covenant Communications, Inc.
Dussling, Jennifer. Gotcha! Nez, John, illus. 2003. (Science Solves It! Ser.). 32p. (J). pap. 5.95 *(978-1-57565-124-8(6))* Kane Press, Inc.
Dutka, Pamela. Madame Cecil's Swamp. 2005. 48p. pap. 16.95 *(978-1-4137-9701-5(6))* PublishAmerica, Inc.
Dwyer, Joe & Levison, Doug. Daniel - the Miracle Beagle: A Story for Young Readers. 2012. 34p. pap. 14.95 *(978-1-4575-1381-7(1))* Dog Ear Publishing, LLC.
Dwyer, Kevin & Dwyer, Shawnae. The Blue Baboon. Harman, Micah, illus. 2007. 40p. per. 13.95 *(978-1-59800-247-8(3))* Outskirts Pr., Inc.
Dyan, Penelope. Hush! 2011. 34p. pap. 11.95 *(978-1-935630-53-1(9))* Bellissima Publishing, LLC.
—Mikey & Me & the Fly — -the Continuing Story of a Girl & Her Dog. Dyan, Penelope, illus. 2010. (Illus.). 50p. pap. 14.95 *(978-1-935118-94-7(3))* Bellissima Publishing, LLC.
—Mikey & Me & the Spider — -the Continuing Story of a Girl & Her Dog. Dyan, Penelope, illus. 2010. (Illus.). 50p. pap. 14.95 *(978-1-935118-95-4(1))* Bellissima Publishing, LLC.
Dyas, Amy. The Robins of St Lawrence Church. 2009. 128p. pap. 29.96 *(978-0-9786567-8-2(4))* Parson Place Pr., LLC.
Dyckman, Ame. Boy & Bot. Yaccarino, Dan, illus. (ENG.). (J). (-k). 2016. 24p. bds. 7.99 *(978-1-101-93688-7(6))* 2012. 32p. E-Book *(978-0-375-98724-3(X))* 2012. 32p. 16.99 *(978-0-375-86756-9(2))* Random Hse. Children's Bks. (Knopf Bks. for Young Readers).
—Girl + Bot. Yaccarino, Dan, illus. 2017. (J). ***(978-1-5247-0072-0(X))*** Knopf, Alfred A. Inc.
Dyckman, Ame. Horrible Bear! OHora, Zachariah, illus. 2016. (ENG.). 40p. (J). (gr. -1-3). 17.99 *(978-0-316-28283-3(9))* Little Brown & Co.
Dye, Troy & Kelesides, Tom. Goblin Chronicles 01A. 2008. (YA). 3.50 *(978-0-9801314-0-6(5))* Ape Entertainment.
—Goblin Chronicles #1B. 2008. (YA). 3.50 *(978-0-9801314-1-3(3))* Ape Entertainment.
—Goblin Chronicles #2A. 2008. (Illus.). 32p. (J). 3.50 *(978-0-9801314-2-0(1))* Ape Entertainment.
—Goblin Chronicles #2B. 2008. (Illus.). 32p. (J). 3.50 *(978-0-9801314-3-7(X))* Ape Entertainment.
Dyer, K. C. A Walk Through a Window. 2009. (ENG.). 240p. (J). (gr. 5-7). pap. 12.50 *(978-0-385-66637-4(3),* Doubleday Canada) Penguin Random House Canada Young Readers CAN. Dist: Penguin Random Hse. LLC.
Dzidrums, Christine. Princess Dessabelle Makes a Friend. Muths, Tohn, illus. 2011. 32p. (J). pap. 9.99 *(978-0-9826435-6-3(X));* 17.99 *(978-0-9826435-7-0(8))* Creative Media Publishing.
E. S. Townsend. The Secrets of Marsh House. 2013. 208p. pap. *(978-1-907011-44-3(7))* Esteemworld Pubns.
E.A. Budd. Stella Saves the Game. Lucas, Diane, illus. 2012. 24p. pap. 12.95 *(978-1-61244-059-0(2))* Halo Publishing International.
Eaddy, Susan. Poppy's Best Paper. Bonnet, Rosalinde, illus. 2015. (ENG.). 40p. (J). (gr. k-3). lib. bdg. 15.95 *(978-1-58089-614-6(6))* Charlesbridge Publishing, Inc.
—Poppy's Best Paper (1 Hardcover/1 CD) Bonnet, Rosalinde, illus. 2016. (ENG.). (J). (gr. 1-4). audio compact disk 29.95 *(978-1-4301-2187-9(4))* Live Oak Media.
Eakins, Bonny Mae. Wonder Island. Eakins, Bonny Mae & Hoffbauer, Wyng, illus. 2nd ed. 2013. 80p. pap. 14.95 *(978-1-893660-26-7(5))* Ravenhawk Bks.
Eareckson Tada, Joni. You've Got a Friend. Meyer, Jeff, illus. 2004. 31p. (gr. -1-3). 14.99 *(978-1-58134-060-0(5))* Crossway.
Earhart, Kristin. Roscoe & the Pony Parade. Gurney, John Steven, illus. 2008. (Little Apple Ser.). 88p. (J). *(978-0-545-08094-1(0))* Scholastic, Inc.
Earl, David G. Koala Koala, I'm Not a Bear, I'm a Koala. Gentry, T. Kyle, illus. 2009. 32p. pap. 12.95 *(978-1-936051-22-9(2))* Peppertree Pr., The.
Earle, Phil. The Bubble Wrap Boy. (ENG.). 288p. (J). (gr. 5). 2016. 7.99 *(978-0-553-51318-9(4),* Yearling) 2015. (Illus.). 19.99 *(978-0-553-51316-5(8),* Delacorte Bks. for Young Readers) 2015. (Illus.). 16.99 *(978-0-553-51315-8(X),* Delacorte Bks. for Young Readers) Random Hse. Children's Bks.
—The Bubble Wrap Boy. 2016. (ENG.). 288p. (J). (gr. 5). 18.40 *(978-0-606-39343-0(9))* Turtleback Bks.
Earnhardt, Heather L. The Wandering Goose: A Modern Fable of How Love Goes. Clements, Frida, illus. 2013. (ENG.). 64p. 15.95 *(978-1-57061-881-9(X))* Sasquatch Bks.
Easer, Katherine. Vicious Little Darlings. 2012. (ENG.). 320p. (YA). (gr. 9-12). pap. 9.99 *(978-1-59990-854-0(9),* 9781599908540, Bloomsbury USA Childrens) Bloomsbury Publishing USA.
Eason, Alethea. Hungry. 2007. 197p. (J). (gr. 5-18). lib. bdg. 16.89 *(978-0-06-082555-3(3),* Eos) HarperCollins Pubs.
East, Bob. Tommy Cat & the Haunted Well, 1 vol. 2009. 42p. pap. 24.95 *(978-1-60703-754-5(8))* America Star Bks.
East, Jacqueline, illus. The Town Mouse & the Country Mouse. 2007. (Picture Book Classics Ser.). 24p. (J). (gr. -1-3). 9.99 *(978-0-7945-1877-6(X),* Usborne) EDC Publishing.
Eastman, P. D. Big Dog ... Little Dog: A Bedtime Story. 2006. (Bright & Early Board Books(TM) Ser.). (ENG., Illus.). 24p. (J). (— 1). bds. 4.99 *(978-0-375-87539-7(5),* Random Hse. Bks. for Young Readers) Random Hse. Children's Bks.
Eastman, P. D. & Eastman, Tony. Big Dog... Little Dog. Eastman, P. D. & Eastman, Tony, illus. 2003. (Beginner Books(R) Ser.). (ENG., Illus.). 48p. (J). (gr. -1-2). 9.99 *(978-0-375-82297-1(6),* Random Hse. Bks. for Young Readers) Random Hse. Children's Bks.
Eastman, Peter. Fred & Ted's Road Trip. 2011. (Beginner Books(R) Ser.). (ENG., Illus.). 48p. (J). (gr. -1-2). 9.99 *(978-0-375-86764-4(3),* Random Hse. Bks. for Young Readers) Random Hse. Children's Bks.
Easton, Marilyn. New Girl in Town. 2013. (ENG., Illus.). 64p. (J). (gr. 2-5). pap. 4.99 *(978-0-545-54762-8(8))* Math Solutions.
—New Girl in Town. 2013. (LEGO Friends Chapter Bks.: 1). lib. bdg. 14.75 *(978-0-606-31548-7(9),* Turtleback) Turtleback Bks.
Eaves, Victor Caleb. Vee's the Chapters of Expudict: Book One. 2008. 128p. pap. 12.00 *(978-1-4389-3385-6(1))* AuthorHouse.
Ebeltoft, Christine. Koo & Jay in the Rainforest. 2004. 34p. pap. 24.95 *(978-1-4137-3698-4(X))* PublishAmerica, Inc.
Eboch, M. M. Monster Island. 2015. (ENG.). 96p. (gr. 3-6). 31.36 *(978-1-63430-394-1(6))* Rourke Educational Media.
Echerique, Alfredo Bryce & Duenas, Ana Maria. Goig. Roederer, Charlotte, illus. (Literary Encounters Ser.). (SPA.). (J). (gr. 3-5). pap. *(978-968-494-065-9(3),* CI7706) Centro de Informacion y Desarrollo de la Comunicacion y la Literatura MEX. Dist: Lectorum Pubns., Inc.
Echols, Jennifer. The One That I Want. 2012. (ENG.). 288p. (YA). (gr. 7). pap. 9.99 *(978-1-4424-5236-7(6),* Simon Pulse) Simon Pulse.
Ecton, Emily. Project Jackalope. 2012. (ENG., Illus.). 256p. (J). (gr. 3-7). 15.99 *(978-1-4521-0155-2(8))* Chronicle Bks. LLC.
Edelman, Lana. School Friends. 2012. (Penguin Young Readers Level 2 Ser.). lib. bdg. 13.55 *(978-0-606-26023-7(4),* Turtleback) Turtleback Bks.
Edgemon, Darcie. Seamore, the Very Forgetful Porpoise. Seibold, J. Otto, illus. 2008. 48p. (J). (gr. -1-3). lib. bdg. 17.89 *(978-0-06-085076-0(0))* HarperCollins Pubs.
Edgerton, Martha. Civility Matters: Anna Moves to the Big City. 2011. 38p. pap. 16.95 *(978-1-4626-4211-3(X))* America Star Bks.
Edgeworth, Maria. The Bracelets or Amiability & Industry Rewarded. 2004. reprint ed. pap. 1.99 *(978-1-4192-5513-7(4));* pap. 15.95 *(978-1-4191-5513-0(X))* Kessinger Publishing, LLC.
Edgin, Brenda. Little Winston & his Big Adventures in Natchez: Down in the Bayou. 2011. 16p. 12.95 *(978-1-4567-4421-2(6))* AuthorHouse.
Edman Lamote, Lisa. Booklet Goes to the Doctor. Wilson, Alisha, illus. 2006. (Bookmann Family Presents Ser.). 32p. (J). (gr. k-3). 15.99 *(978-1-933673-02-8(8),* BookMann Pr.) Mann Publishing Group.
Edmonds, Lin. Jaden & the Terrible Terrible Toad. 2011. 36p. pap. 15.14 *(978-1-4634-1112-1(X))* AuthorHouse.
—Patric the Pony & the Flash of Lightning. 2009. 34p. pap. 13.99 *(978-1-4389-6302-0(5))* AuthorHouse.
—Patric the Pony & the Race for Freedom. 2011. 32p. pap. 15.50 *(978-1-4670-3662-7(5))* AuthorHouse.
—Patric the Pony Finds a Friend. Connors, Mary, illus. 2009. 32p. pap. 12.99 *(978-1-4389-5167-6(1))* AuthorHouse.
Edwards, Amelia. Playground Friends, 1 vol. rev. ed. 2013. (Fiction Readers Ser.). (ENG., Illus.). 12p. (J). (gr. 1-1). 4.99 *(978-1-4333-5449-6(7));* pap. 12.96 *(978-1-4807-1128-0(4))* Shell Educational Publishing.
Edwards, Helen L. Clara's Imagination. Doggett, Al, illus. 2005. 19.95 *(978-0-9765414-0-0(8))* Bad Publishing.
Edwards, Jean Pearce. Little Jean's War. 2008. (Illus.). 208p. pap. 14.49 *(978-1-4343-9133-9(7))* AuthorHouse.
Edwards, Judith. At the Top of the Mountain: The Adventures of Will Ryan & the Civilian Conservation Corps, 1936-38, Book III. 2013. (ENG., Illus.). 144p. (J). (gr. 3-7). pap. 12.95 *(978-1-884592-63-8(5))* Images from the Past, Inc.
Edwards, Karl Newsom. I Got a New Friend. 2017. (ENG., Illus.). 32p. (J). (gr. -1-3). 16.99 *(978-0-399-55700-2(8),* Knopf Bks. for Young Readers) Random Hse. Children's Bks.
Edwards, Linda M. Emma & Topsy's Story: The Art of Loving & Letting Go. Maher, Bob, illus. 2010. 20p. pap. 10.95 *(978-1-60911-808-2(1),* Eloquent Bks.) Strategic Book Publishing & Rights Agency (SBPRA).
Edwards, M. J. Dontayan. 2008. 62p. pap. 19.95 *(978-1-60610-026-4(2))* America Star Bks.
Edwards, Mamie. Magical Mix-Ups: Friends & Fashion. Hodgkinson, Leigh, illus. 2012. (Magical Mix-Ups Ser.). (ENG.). 96p. (J). (gr. 2-5). pap. 6.99 *(978-0-7636-6166-3(X),* Nosy Crow) Candlewick Pr.
—Magical Mix-Ups: Spells & Surprises. Hodgkinson, Leigh, illus. 2014. (Magical Mix-Ups Ser.). (ENG.). (J). (gr. 2-5). pap. 6.99 *(978-0-7636-6610-1(6),* Nosy Crow) Candlewick Pr.
Edwards, Meinir Wyn. Rhys & Meinir. Wade, Gini, illus. 2007. (ENG.). 24p. (J). pap. 4.95 *(978-1-84771-020-8(4))* Y Lolfa GBR. Dist: Dufour Editions, Inc.
Edwards, Michelle. Pa Lia's First Day. 2005. (Jackson Friends Ser.: 1). (ENG., Illus.). 64p. (J). (gr. -1-3). pap. 5.99 *(978-0-15-205748-0(X))* Houghton Mifflin Harcourt Publishing Co.
—Pa Lia's First Day. 2005. (Jackson Friends Bks.). (Illus.). 55p. (gr. 1-4). 15.95 *(978-0-7569-5773-5(7))* Perfection Learning Corp.
Edwards, Pamela Duncan. Gigi & Lulu's Gigantic Fight. Cole, Henry, tr. Cole, Henry, illus. 2004. 40p. (J). (gr. -1-2). lib. bdg. 15.89 *(978-0-06-050753-4(5))* HarperCollins Pubs.
—Teddy Bear Hide-and-Seek. Birkett, Georgie, illus. 2008. (ENG.). 20p. (J). (gr. 2-5). 14.95 *(978-0-230-01442-8(9),* Macmillan) Pan Macmillan GBR. Dist: Trans-Atlantic Pubns., Inc.
Egan, Catherine. Bone, Fog, Ash & Star, 1 vol. 2014. (Last Days of Tian Di Ser.: 3). (ENG.). 320p. (J). (gr. 6-10). pap. 12.95 *(978-1-55050-593-1(9))* Coteau Bks. CAN. Dist: Orca Bk. Pubs. USA.
Egan, Kate, adapted by. World's Apart. 2005. (W. I. T. C. H. Ser.: Bk. 14). 134p. (J). lib. bdg. 16.92 *(978-1-4242-0788-6(6))* Fitzgerald Bks.
Egart, Patricia. Alley Learns Something New. 2012. (ENG., Illus.). 32p. pap. 8.95 *(978-0-9831839-3-8(7))* Amber Skye Publishing LLC.
Eggleston, Edward. Mr. Blake's Walking Stick. 2013. (Collected Works of Edward Eggleston). 425p. reprint ed. lthr. 79.00 *(978-0-7812-1170-3(0))* Reprint Services Corp.
Egielski, Richard. Slim & Jim. Date not set. 32p. (J). (gr. -1-2). pap. 5.99 *(978-0-06-443564-2(4))* HarperCollins Pubs.
Eglington, Tara. How to Keep a Boy from Kissing You. 2016. (ENG.). 320p. (YA). 18.99 *(978-1-250-04953-7(9),* 9781250049537) St. Martin's Pr.
Ehlert, Lois. Heart to Heart. Ehlert, Lois, illus. 2017. (ENG., Illus.). 72p. (J). (gr. -1-3). 9.99 *(978-1-4814-8087-1(1),* Beach Lane Bks.) Beach Lane Bks.
—Nuts to You! 2004. (ENG., Illus.). 40p. (J). (gr. -1-3). reprint ed. pap. 7.99 *(978-0-15-205064-1(7))* Houghton Mifflin Harcourt Publishing Co.
Ehlin, Gina. Emma & Friends: Emma's Airport Adventure. Ayzenberg, Nina, illus. l.t. ed. 2005. 32p. (J). per. 10.99 *(978-1-59879-014-6(5))* Lifevest Publishing, Inc.
—Emma & Friends; Emma Rescues Cali. Ayzenberg, Nina, illus. l.t. ed. 2006. 24p. (J). per. 10.99 *(978-1-59879-112-9(5))* Lifevest Publishing, Inc.
—Emma's Airport Adventure. Ayesenberg, Nina, illus. l.t. ed. 2005. (Emma & Friends Ser.). 34p. (J). 15.99 *(978-1-59879-015-3(3))* Lifevest Publishing, Inc.
Ehrenberg, Pamela. Ethan, Suspended. 2009. (ENG.). 272p. (J). (gr. 6-9). pap. 8.50 *(978-0-8028-5317-2(X))* 2007. 266p. (YA). (gr. 7-18). 16.00 *(978-0-8028-5324-0(2),* Eerdmans Bks For Young Readers) Eerdmans, William B. Publishing Co.
Ehrenhaft, Daniel. 10 Things to Do Before I Die. 2006. (ENG.). 224p. (YA). (gr. 7). per. 7.95 *(978-0-385-73406-6(9),* Delacorte Bks. for Young Readers) Random Hse. Children's Bks.
Eichler, Darlene. Where's the Kitty. Wyles, Betty, illus. 2013. 52p. pap. 18.95 *(978-0-9893063-1-7(3))* ProsePress.
Eichler, Ken. Swift Eagle's Vision Quest, 1 vol. 2009. 95p. pap. 19.95 *(978-1-60703-649-4(5))* America Star Bks.
Eickhoff, Kim, et al. Bamboo Zoo: Meet Lester Panda & his Friends! 2005. (Bamboo Zoo Ser.: Bk. 1). (Illus.). (J). per. 9.95 *(978-0-9774493-0-9(0))* Bamboo Zoo, LLC.
Eisan, Daniel. The Lonely Peach. 2011. (Illus.). 48p. pap. 15.99 *(978-1-4628-5634-3(9))* Xlibris Corp.
Eisele, Barbara. Miss Thistle & Friends. 2009. 48p. pap. 12.99 *(978-1-4490-2007-1(0))* AuthorHouse.
Eitner-England, Lita. Bullmina the Courageous Bulldog to the Rescue. 2010. 588p. 33.99 *(978-1-4490-8225-3(4));* pap. 15.00 *(978-1-4490-8224-6(6))* AuthorHouse.
Eke, Vincent. The Turtle's Shell. 2013. (Illus.). 46p. pap. *(978-1-909688-00-1(2))* Lionpen Publishing.
Elaine Vanier. Crystal Lights: Awaken the Power. 2009. 116p. pap. 10.95 *(978-1-4401-8357-7(0))* iUniverse, Inc.
Eland, Lindsay. Five Times Revenge. 2016. 384p. (J). (gr. 3-7). 16.99 *(978-0-06-239730-0(3),* Greenwillow Bks.) HarperCollins Pubs.
—A Summer of Sundays. 2013. (ENG.). 336p. (J). (gr. 3-7). 16.99 *(978-1-60684-030-6(4),* Carolrhoda Bks.) Lerner Publishing Group.
Elder, Elizabeth. When I'm with You. Mansmann, Leslie, illus. 2003. (ENG.). 32p. (J). 15.95 *(978-0-9671662-8-5(4))* Islandport Pr., Inc.
Eldridge, Jim. The Final Showdown: Match Six. 2016. (Wrestling Trolls Ser.: 6). (ENG., Illus.). 176p. (J). (gr. k-3). pap. 9.99 *(978-1-4714-0269-2(X))* Bonnier Publishing GBR. Dist: Independent Pubs. Group.
Elga Learns to Juggle. 2006. (J). 6.99 *(978-0-9770918-0-5(5))* Forelle Graphics.
Eliopulos, Nick & Random House Staff. DC Super Friends: Flying High. Wallace, Loston et al, illus. 2008. (Step into Reading Ser.). (ENG.). 32p. (J). (gr. -1-1). pap. 3.99 *(978-0-375-85208-4(5),* Random Hse. Bks. for Young Readers) Random Hse. Children's Bks.
Eliotte, Lisa J. The Adventures of Derby Doodle. 2009. 640p. pap. 25.99 *(978-1-4389-3058-9(5))* AuthorHouse.
Elk, Ronit. A Surprise at Dancing Fields. 2009. 76p. pap. 10.49 *(978-1-4490-2064-4(X))* AuthorHouse.
Elkeles, Simone. Leaving Paradise. 2007. (Leaving Paradise Novel Ser.: 1). (ENG.). 312p. (YA). (gr. 3-7). per. 11.99 *(978-0-7387-1018-1(0),* 1265837, Flux) North Star Editions.
Elkhouly, Mona Henri. Take Me along Series: How It All Started. 2011. 28p. pap. 18.95 *(978-1-4634-7432-4(6))* AuthorHouse.
Elkins, J. Theron. You Are the Pea, & I Am the Carrot. Lemaître, Pascal, illus. 2013. (ENG.). 32p. (J). (gr. k-2). 16.95 *(978-1-4197-0850-3(3),* Abrams Bks. for Young Readers) Abrams, Inc.
Elkins, Stephen. Ebony & Ivory: Discovering 10 Keys to Racial Harmony. Reisch, Jessie, illus. 2003. 32p. (J). (gr. k-18). 14.99 incl. audio compact disk *(978-0-8054-2674-8(4))* B&H Publishing Group.
Ellen, Connie. Marvel Mansion Gang. 2012. 114p. 22.19 *(978-1-4269-6666-8(0));* pap. 12.19 *(978-1-4269-5968-4(0))* Trafford Publishing.
Elliott, Ann. GypsyBridge Friends: The Vine. 2003. 40p. pap. 12.95 *(978-0-9721825-0-8(0))* Open Vision Entertainment Corp.
Elliott, David. This Orq. (He Cave Boy.) Nichols, Lori, illus. 2014. (ENG.). 40p. (J). (gr. -1-2). 15.95 *(978-1-62091-521-9(9))* Boyds Mills Pr.
—The Two Tims. Alborozo, Gabriel, illus. 2016. (ENG.). 32p. (J). (gr. -1-1). 15.99 *(978-0-7636-7264-5(5))* Candlewick Pr.
Elliott, Emilia. Patricia. 2007. 64p. per. *(978-1-4065-2466-6(2))* Dodo Pr.
Elliott, Kate, pseud. Court of Fives. 2015. (Court of Fives Ser.: Bk. 1). (ENG., Illus.). 448p. (YA). (gr. 7-17). 18.00 *(978-0-316-36419-5(3))* Little Brown & Co.
—Court of Fives. 2016. (Court of Fives Ser.: 1). (ENG., Illus.). 464p. (YA). (gr. 7-17). pap. 10.99 *(978-0-316-36430-0(4))* Little, Brown Bks. for Young Readers.
Elliott, Laura Malone. Hunter's Best Friend at School. Munsinger, Lynn, illus. 2005. (gr. -1-2). 17.00 *(978-0-7569-5786-5(9))* Perfection Learning Corp.
—Hunter's Best Friend at School. Munsinger, Lynn, illus. 2005. (ENG.). 32p. (J). (gr. -1-2). reprint ed. pap. 6.99 *(978-0-06-075319-1(6),* Tegen, Katherine Bks) HarperCollins Pubs.
Elliott, Marc. The House at the End of the Tracks. 2007. 48p. per. 16.95 *(978-1-4241-6876-7(7))* America Star Bks.
Elliott, Rebecca. Baxter Is Missing. 2017. (Owl Diaries — Branches Ser.: 6). lib. bdg. 14.75 ***(978-0-606-40189-0(X))*** Turtleback Bks.
—Eva & the New Owl. 2016. (Owl Diaries: 4). (ENG., Illus.). 80p. (J). (gr. k-2). pap. 4.99 *(978-0-545-82559-7(8))* Scholastic, Inc.
—Eva's Treetop Festival. Bk. 1. Elliott, Rebecca, illus. 2015. (Owl Diaries: 1). (ENG., Illus.). 80p. (J). (gr. k-2). pap. 4.99 *(978-0-545-68362-3(9))* Scholastic, Inc.
—My Stinky New School. Elliott, Rebecca, illus. 2015. (ENG., Illus.). 32p. (J). (gr. -1-1). 16.99 *(978-0-7459-6949-7(6))* Lion Hudson PLC GBR. Dist: Independent Pubs. Group.
—Warm Hearts Day: A Branches Book. Elliott, Rebecca, illus. 2016. (Owl Diaries: 5). (ENG., Illus.). 80p. (J). (gr. k-2). pap. 4.99 *(978-1-338-04280-1(7))* Scholastic, Inc.
Ellis, Ann Dee. This Is What I Did. 2009. (ENG.). 176p. (J). (gr. 7-17). pap. 7.99 *(978-0-316-01362-8(5))* Little, Brown Bks. for Young Readers.
Ellis, Deborah. The Breadwinner. 2015. (Breadwinner Ser.: 1). lib. bdg. 20.80 *(978-0-606-37232-9(6))* Turtleback Bks.
Ellis, Elina. The Big Adventure. 2015. (ENG., Illus.). 32p. (J). (gr. -1-3). 16.99 *(978-1-4998-0109-5(2))* Little Bee Books Inc.
Ellis, Sarah. Ben Says Goodbye. LaFave, Kim, illus. 2016. (ENG.). 32p. (J). (gr. -1-1). 16.95 *(978-1-927485-79-8(7))* Pajama Pr. CAN. Dist: Ingram Publisher Services.
Ellis, Sue. Gorgeous Gwendolen Goose & Other Stories. 2015. (ENG.). 49p. (J). (gr. 3-4). mass mkt. 13.95 *(978-1-78455-571-9(1),* 32f7fc86-9367-414f-b0a7-4ad5f341c9cb) Austin, Stan AUS. Dist: Bookmasters Distribution.
Ellison, Joy D. Carol & Connie. 2008. 28p. per. 24.95 *(978-1-4241-9276-2(5))* America Star Bks.
Elmendorf, Dana. South of Sunshine. 2016. (ENG.). 256p. (YA). (gr. 8-12). 16.99 *(978-0-8075-7568-0(2))* Whitman, Albert & Co.

Else, Barbara. The Queen & the Nobody Boy. Broad, Sam, illus. 2013. (Tales of Fontania Ser.). (ENG.). 328p. (J). (gr. 4-7). *(978-1-877579-49-3(1))* Gecko Pr.

Ely, Lesley & Dunbar, Polly. Measuring Angels. Dunbar, Polly, illus. 2008. (ENG., Illus.). 32p. (J). (gr. -1-3). 16.95 *(978-1-84507-639-9(7)*, Frances Lincoln) Quarto Publishing Group UK GBR. Dist: Hachette Bk. Group.

Elys Dayton, Arwen. Disruptor. 2017. (Seeker Ser.). (ENG.). 384p. (YA). (gr. 9). 18.99 *(978-0-385-74411-9(0)*, Delacorte Pr.) Random Hse. Children's Bks.

Emanuel, Lora. The Puppy Tree, 1 vol. Swope, Brenda, illus. 2009. 30p. pap. 24.95 *(978-1-60749-614-4(3))* America Star Bks.

Emberley, Rebecca. Spare Parts. Emberley, Ed, illus. 2015. (ENG.). 32p. (J). (gr. -1-2). 17.99 *(978-1-59643-723-4(5)*, 9781596437234) Roaring Brook Pr.

Emde, Nicole. Alabaster the Albino Alligator. 2008. 40p. per. 24.95 *(978-1-4241-9778-1(3))* America Star Bks.

Emerson, Alice B. Ruth Fielding on Cliff Island: Or the Old Hunter's Treasure Box. 2007. (ENG.). 136p. pap. 18.99 *(978-1-4346-2493-2(5))*; 148p. pap. 19.99 *(978-1-4346-2535-9(4))* Creative Media Partners, LLC.

Emerson, Kevin. The Dark Shore. 2014. (Atlanteans Ser.: 2). (ENG.). 496p. (YA). (gr. 8). pap. 9.99 *(978-0-06-206283-3(2)*, Tegen, Katherine Bks) HarperCollins Pubs.

—Last Day on Mars. 2017. (Chronicle of the Dark Star Ser.: 1). 336p. (J). (gr. 3-7). 16.99 *(978-0-06-230671-5(5)*, Walden Pond Pr.) HarperCollins Pubs.

Emert, Sarah. Chanier & Friends: Backyard Camping. 2013. (ENG.). 30p. (J). pap. 7.99 *(978-1-936815-81-4(8))* Yawn's Bks. & More, Inc.

Emery, Anne. Dinny Gordon, Freshman. 2004. (J). per. 9.95 *(978-1-930009-97-4(6))* Image Cascade Publishing.

—Dinny Gordon Sophomore. 2004. (J). per. 9.95 *(978-1-930009-98-1(4))* Image Cascade Publishing.

Emin, Rebecca. When Dreams Come True. 2012. 164p. pap. *(978-1-4710-9204-6(6))* Lulu.com.

Emma Treehouse Ltd. My Friends. Davis, Caroline, illus. 2007. (Easy Flaps Ser.). 10p. (J). (gr. -1). bds. 6.95 *(978-1-58925-823-5(1))* Tiger Tales.

Emmett, Jonathan & Reed, Nathan. What Friends Do Best. (ENG., Illus.). (J). (gr. k-2). 2005. 26p. 15.99 *(978-0-00-714120-3(3)*, Collins) 2004. 32p. pap. 9.99 *(978-0-00-714121-0(1))* HarperCollins Pubs. Ltd. GBR. Dist: Independent Pubs. Group.

Emond, Stephen. Bright Lights, Dark Nights. 2015. (ENG., Illus.). 384p. (YA). (gr. 7). 17.99 *(978-1-62672-206-4(4))* Roaring Brook Pr.

—Winter Town. 2012. (ENG., Illus.). 352p. (YA). (gr. 7-17). pap. 10.99 *(978-0-316-13331-9(0))* Little, Brown Bks. for Young Readers.

Enderle, Dotti. Book 13: Yo Ho No!, 1 vol. 2014. (Ghost Detectors Set 3 Ser.). (ENG., Illus.). 80p. (J). (gr. 2-5). lib. bdg. 27.07 *(978-1-62402-001-8(1)*, Calico Chapter Bks) Magic Wagon.

—Book 15: Rock & Roll!, 1 vol. 2014. (Ghost Detectors Set 3 Ser.). (ENG., Illus.). 80p. (J). (gr. 2-5). lib. bdg. 27.07 *(978-1-62402-003-2(8)*, Calico Chapter Bks) Magic Wagon.

Enge-Grandbois, Kathryn L. Suzy Q. 2008. 48p. pap. 16.95 *(978-1-4241-7650-2(6))* America Star Bks.

Engholm, Evelyn. Ted & Danny's Secret. 2007. 96p. per. 9.95 *(978-1-4327-0183-3(5))* Outskirts Pr., Inc.

Engle, Dawn A. Ella's Golden Heart Goes to Camp. 2011. 40p. pap. 14.95 *(978-1-60911-392-6(6)*, Eloquent Bks.) Strategic Book Publishing & Rights Agency (SBPRA).

English, Karen. Birthday Blues. Freeman, Laura, illus. 2010. (ENG.). 96p. (J). (gr. 1-4). pap. 5.99 *(978-0-547-24893-6(8))* Houghton Mifflin Harcourt Publishing Co.

—Dog Days. Freeman, Laura, illus. 2014. (Carver Chronicles Ser.). (ENG.). 128p. (J). (gr. 1-4). pap. 5.99 *(978-0-544-33912-5(6)*, HMH Books For Young Readers) Houghton Mifflin Harcourt Publishing Co.

—Francie. 2007. (ENG.). 208p. (J). (gr. 4-8). per. 8.99 *(978-0-312-37383-2(X)*, 9780312373832) Square Fish.

—The Newsy News Newsletter. Freeman, Laura, illus. 2011. (ENG.). 96p. (J). (gr. 1-4). pap. 5.99 *(978-0-547-40626-8(6))* Houghton Mifflin Harcourt Publishing Co.

—Nikki & Deja. Freeman, Laura, illus. 2009. (ENG.). 80p. (J). (gr. -1-3). pap. 5.99 *(978-0-547-13362-1(6))* Houghton Mifflin Harcourt Publishing Co.

—Nikki & Deja: Substitute Trouble. Freeman, Laura, illus. 2014. (ENG.). 112p. (J). (gr. 1-4). pap. 5.99 *(978-0-544-22388-2(8)*, HMH Books For Young Readers) Houghton Mifflin Harcourt Publishing Co.

—Wedding Drama. Freeman, Laura, illus. 2013. (ENG.). 112p. (J). (gr. 1-4). pap. 5.99 *(978-0-544-00324-8(1))* Houghton Mifflin Harcourt Publishing Co.

Enright, Elizabeth. Thimble Summer. unabr. ed. 2004. 136p. (J). (gr. 3-7). pap. 36.00 incl. audio *(978-0-8072-0671-3(7)*, Listening Library) Random Hse. Audio Publishing Group.

Eone, illus. Around the World with Peppa. 2017. (Scholastic Reader, Level 1 Ser.). (ENG.). 32p. (J). (gr. -1-k). 3.99 ***(978-1-338-13980-8(0))*** Scholastic, Inc.

Epstein, Adam Jay & Jacobson, Andrew. The Familiars. Chiu, Bobby, illus. 2010. (Familiars Ser.: 1). (ENG.). 368p. (J). (gr. 3-7). 16.99 *(978-0-06-196108-3(6))* HarperCollins Pubs.

Erickson, Mary Ellen. Who Jinxed the CG Ranch? 2009. 196p. 24.95 *(978-1-4401-4218-5(1))*; pap. 14.95 *(978-1-4401-4216-1(5))* iUniverse, Inc.

Ericson, Nora. Dill & Bizzy: An Odd Duck & a Strange Bird. Ericson, Lisa, illus. 2016. 40p. (J). (gr. -1-3). 17.99 *(978-0-06-230452-0(6))* HarperCollins Pubs.

—Dill & Bizzy: Opposite Day. Ericson, Lisa, illus. 2017. 40p. (J). (gr. -1-3). 17.99 *(978-0-06-230453-7(4))* HarperCollins Pubs.

Erlbruch, Wolf. Duck, Death & the Tulip. Erlbruch, Wolf, illus. 2011. (ENG., Illus.). 38p. (J). 17.95 *(978-1-877579-02-8(5))* Gecko Pr. NZL. Dist: Lerner Publishing Group.

Erlbruch, Wolf & Chidgey, Catherine. Duck, Death & the Tulip. Erlbruch, Wolf, illus. 2016. (ENG., Illus.). 38p. (gr. 4-12). 16.99 *(978-1-877467-14-1(6))* Gecko Pr. NZL. Dist: Lerner Publishing Group.

Ernst, Cindy Kathleen. Sunny the Sunflower. 2012. 32p. pap. *(978-1-4602-0276-0(7))* FriesenPress.

Ernst, Kathleen. The Runaway Friend. Tibbles, Jean-Paul, illus. 2008. (ENG.). 192p. (gr. 3-7). pap. 6.95 *(978-1-59369-298-8(6))* American Girl Publishing, Inc.

Erskine, Kathryn. The Badger Knight. 2014. (Illus.). (J). 325p. *(978-0-545-66293-2(1))*; (ENG.). 352p. (gr. 3-7). 17.99 *(978-0-545-46442-0(0))* Scholastic, Inc. (Scholastic Pr.).

Erwin, Kay. A Sheepdog's Christmas. 2008. 56p. pap. 10.99 *(978-1-60647-698-7(X))* Salem Author Services.

Esbaum, Jill. Elwood Bigfoot: Wanted: Birdie Friends! Wragg, Nate, illus. 2015. (ENG.). 32p. (J). (gr. -1-2). 14.95 *(978-1-4549-0879-1(3)*, 1394145) Sterling Publishing Co., Inc.

—Teeny Tiny Toady. Yamaguchi, Keika, illus. 2016. (ENG.). 40p. (J). (gr. -1-2). 14.95 *(978-1-4549-1454-9(8))* Sterling Publishing Co., Inc.

Escher, Jill. The Boneyville Dogs - Scuba Dogs. 2011. 24p. 12.79 *(978-1-4567-1908-1(4))* AuthorHouse.

Eshed, Tina. The Adventures of Bunzy: The Beginning. 2009. 60p. pap. 24.49 *(978-1-4389-2673-5(1))* AuthorHouse.

Eskye, Tony. The Adventures of Fojo the Frog. 2009. (Illus.). 224p. pap. 14.49 *(978-1-4389-9530-4(X))* AuthorHouse.

Espinoza, Vicki. Donnie Dollar. 2008. 38p. pap. 16.78 *(978-0-557-01616-7(9))* Lulu Pr., Inc.

Estes, Eleanor. The Alley. Ardizzone, Edward, illus. 2003. (ENG.). 288p. (J). (gr. 2-5). pap. 18.95 *(978-0-15-204918-8(5))* Houghton Mifflin Harcourt Publishing Co.

—The Alley. Ardizzone, Edward, illus. 2004. (Odyssey/Harcourt Young Classic Ser.). 283p. 15.95 *(978-0-7569-3475-0(3))* Perfection Learning Corp.

—The Hundred Dresses. Slobodkin, Louis, illus. anniv. ed. 2004. (ENG.). 96p. (J). (gr. 1-4). 16.99 *(978-0-15-205170-9(8))*; pap. 7.99 *(978-0-15-205260-7(7))* Houghton Mifflin Harcourt Publishing Co.

—The Tunnel of Hugsy Goode. Ardizzone, Edward, illus. 2003. (ENG.). 256p. (J). (gr. 2-5). pap. 14.95 *(978-0-15-204916-4(9))* Houghton Mifflin Harcourt Publishing Co.

Estes-Hill, Katrina. My Imagination. Kwong, Alvina, illus. 2007. 32p. (J). (gr. -1-2). 15.95 *(978-0-9745715-6-0(3))* KRBY Creations, LLC.

Etemo-Harris, Jacqueline. Be'Be: A Very Special Friendship. Cagle, Eddie, illus. 2009. 28p. pap. 14.99 *(978-1-4389-8846-7(X))* AuthorHouse.

Etting, Tali. Max's Amazing Adventure. 2011. (Illus.). 32p. 14.09 *(978-1-4567-7251-2(1))* AuthorHouse.

Eubank, Patricia Reeder. The Leprechaun's Big Pot of Gold. Eubank, Patricia Reeder, illus. 2012. (Illus.). 20p. (J). bds. 6.99 *(978-0-8249-1877-4(0)*, Ideal Pubns.) Worthy Publishing.

Eulberg, Elizabeth. Better off Friends. 2014. (ENG.). 288p. (J). (gr. 7). 17.99 *(978-0-545-55145-8(5))* Scholastic, Inc.

—The Great Shelby Holmes. 2017. (ENG., Illus.). 272p. (J). pap. 7.99 ***(978-1-68119-053-2(2)***, 9781681190532, Bloomsbury USA Childrens) Bloomsbury Publishing USA.

—The Great Shelby Holmes: Girl Detective. 2016. (ENG., Illus.). 256p. (J). 16.99 *(978-1-68119-051-8(6)*, 9781681190518, Bloomsbury USA Childrens) Bloomsbury Publishing USA.

—Just Another Girl. 2017. (ENG.). 256p. (J). (gr. 7). 17.99 *(978-0-545-95628-4(5))* Scholastic, Inc.

—Take a Bow. 2013. (ENG.). 288p. (J). (gr. 7). pap. 9.99 *(978-0-545-33476-1(4)*, Scholastic Paperbacks) 2012. (ENG.). 288p. (J). (gr. 7). 17.99 *(978-0-545-33474-7(8))* 2012. 280p. (YA). pap. *(978-0-545-43982-4(5))* Scholastic, Inc.

Evans, Cathy. Halo & the Rainbows. 2013. 36p. pap. 16.95 *(978-1-4624-0704-0(8)*, Inspiring Voices) Author Solutions, Inc.

Evans, Courtney. Percy the Penguin, 1 vol. 2010. 26p. pap. 24.95 *(978-1-4489-4881-9(9))* PublishAmerica, Inc.

Evans, Len. Yr Enillwyr. 2005. (WEL.). 64p. pap. *(978-1-85596-218-7(7))* Dref Wen.

Evans, Mari. Dear Corinne, Tell Somebody! Love, Annie: A Book about Secrets. 2004. (J). pap. 6.95 *(978-0-940975-90-3(4))*; (Illus.). 64p. (gr. 3-7). 12.95 *(978-0-940975-81-1(5))* Just Us Bks., Inc. (Sankofa Bks.).

Evans, Pamela. Tina Queen of the Dragons. 2006. 101p. pap. 16.95 *(978-1-4241-3356-7(4))* PublishAmerica, Inc.

Evans, Rhonda Boone. Johnny Lumpkin Wants a Friend. Evans, Chadrick Michael, illus. 2007. 32p. per. 24.95 *(978-1-4241-8614-3(5))* America Star Bks.

—Thanksgiving with the Lumpkins. 2009. 40p. pap. 16.50 *(978-1-60860-783-9(6)*, Eloquent Bks.) Strategic Book Publishing & Rights Agency (SBPRA).

Evans, Richard. Battle of the Ampere. (Michael Vey Ser.: 3). (ENG., Illus.). 320p. (YA). (gr. 7). 2014. pap. 11.99 *(978-1-4424-7512-0(9))* 2013. 17.99 *(978-1-4424-7511-3(0))* Simon Pulse/Mercury Ink. (Simon Pulse/Mercury Ink).

—An Electrifying Michael Vey Set. 2013. (Michael Vey Ser.). (ENG., Illus.). 1008p. (YA). (gr. 7). 53.99 *(978-1-4424-9550-0(2)*, Simon Pulse/Mercury Ink) Simon Pulse/Mercury Ink.

—Hunt for Jade Dragon. 2015. (Michael Vey Ser.: 4). (ENG., Illus.). 336p. (YA). (gr. 7). pap. 11.99 *(978-1-4814-2439-4(4))* Simon & Schuster, Inc.

—Michael Vey 5. 2015. (Michael Vey Ser.: 5). (ENG., Illus.). 288p. (YA). (gr. 7). 18.99 *(978-1-4814-4410-1(7)*, Simon Pulse/Mercury Ink) Simon Pulse/Mercury Ink.

—Michael Vey Books One & Two: The Prisoner of Cell 25; Rise of the Elgen. 2014. (Michael Vey Ser.). (ENG., Illus.). 720p. (YA). (gr. 7). pap. 13.99 *(978-1-4814-2034-1(8)*, Simon Pulse/Mercury Ink) Simon Pulse/Mercury Ink.

—The Prisoner of Cell 25. (Michael Vey Ser.: 1). (ENG., Illus.). (YA). (gr. 7). 2012. 352p. pap. 11.99 *(978-1-4424-6812-2(2))* 2011. 336p. 19.99 *(978-1-4516-5650-3(5))* Simon Pulse/Mercury Ink. (Simon Pulse/Mercury Ink).

—Rise of the Elgen. (Michael Vey Ser.: 2). (ENG., Illus.). 352p. (YA). (gr. 7). 2013. pap. 11.99 *(978-1-4424-7510-6(2))* 2012. 17.99 *(978-1-4424-5414-9(8))* Simon Pulse/Mercury Ink. (Simon Pulse/Mercury Ink).

Evans, Zoe. Revenge of the Titan. Barrager, Brigette, illus. 2012. (Cheer! Ser.: 5). (ENG.). 224p. (J). (gr. 3-7). pap. 6.99 *(978-1-4424-4634-2(X)*, Simon Spotlight) Simon Spotlight.

Eve, Laure. The Graces. 2016. (ENG.). 352p. (YA). (gr. 8-17). 18.95 *(978-1-4197-2123-6(2)*, Amulet Bks.) Abrams, Inc.

Eveleigh, Victoria. Katy's Pony Challenge. 2016. (Katy's Exmoor Ponies Ser.). (ENG., Illus.). 144p. (J). (gr. 2-4). 7.99 *(978-1-4440-1451-8(X)*, Orion Children's Bks.) Hachette Children's Group GBR. Dist: Hachette Bk. Group.

Everett, Anita. Abc Adventures Continued: D e F G. 2012. 44p. pap. 21.99 *(978-1-4691-7797-7(8))* Xlibris Corp.

Everett, George W. G. W. Frog & the Circus Lion. 2010. 32p. 16.95 *(978-1-4497-0443-8(3)*, WestBow Pr.) Author Solutions, Inc.

Everett, Reese. Monster in the Mangroves. 2015. (ENG.). 48p. (gr. k-3). 27.07 *(978-1-63430-377-4(6))* Rourke Educational Media.

Everitt, Sandra. My Imaginary Friends. 2017. (ENG.). 68p. pap. 15.95 ***(978-1-78612-232-2(4)***, b3019e73-8027-4430-874f-a6c2033377a5) Austin, Stan AUS. Dist: Bookmasters Distribution.

Evert, Lori. The Brave Little Puppy. Breiehagen, Per, illus. 2016. (ENG.). 28p. (J). (-k). bds. 8.99 *(978-0-399-54945-8(5)*, Random Hse. Bks. for Young Readers) Random Hse. Children's Bks.

Every Day but Sunday, 6 Packs. (gr. -1-2). 23.00 *(978-0-7635-9004-8(5))* Rigby Education.

Ewert, Marcus. 10,000 Dresses. Ray, Rex, illus. 2008. (ENG.). 32p. (J). (gr. k-4). 14.95 *(978-1-58322-850-0(0)*, Triangle Square) Seven Stories Pr.

Ewing, John. The Adventures of Rennie & Bodger, 1 vol. 2010. 42p. 24.95 *(978-1-4489-5654-8(4))* PublishAmerica, Inc.

Ewing, Lynne. The Lure. 2014. (ENG.). 288p. (YA). (gr. 9). 17.99 *(978-0-06-220688-6(5))* HarperCollins Pubs.

Extraordinary Warren Saves the Day. 2014. (Pix Ser.). (ENG., Illus.). 64p. (J). (gr. 1-4). 12.99 *(978-1-4814-0352-8(4)*, Aladdin) Simon & Schuster Children's Publishing.

Eyre, Lindsay. The Mean Girl Meltdown. 2015. (Sylvie Scruggs Ser.: 2). (ENG., Illus.). 160p. (J). (gr. 2-5). pap. 5.99 *(978-0-545-62030-7(9)*, Levine, Arthur A. Bks.) Scholastic, Inc.

Fabbella, Teresa. Forever Friends. Giaquinta, Maria, illus. 2010. 26p. pap. 9.95 *(978-1-60911-366-7(7)*, Eloquent Bks.) Strategic Book Publishing & Rights Agency (SBPRA).

Faber, Polly. Mango & Bambang: The Not-a-Pig. Vulliamy, Clara, illus. 2016. (ENG.). 144p. (J). (gr. 1-4). 14.99 *(978-0-7636-8226-2(8))* Candlewick Pr.

Facey, La-Toya S. Brielle-Elaine Tries to Fit In! 2011. 24p. pap. 14.99 *(978-1-4634-2353-7(5))* AuthorHouse.

Fagan, Cary. Danny, Who Fell in a Hole, 1 vol. Pavlovic, Milan, illus. 2013. (ENG.). 96p. (J). 14.95 *(978-1-55498-311-7(8))* Groundwood Bks. CAN. Dist: Publishers Group West (PGW).

—Danny, Who Fell in a Hole. 2013. 84p. pap. *(978-1-4596-6456-2(6))* ReadHowYouWant.com, Ltd.

—Ella May & the Wishing Stone. Cote, Genevieve, illus. 2011. (ENG.). 32p. (J). (gr. -1-1). 17.95 *(978-1-77049-225-7(9)*, Tundra Bks.) Tundra Bks. CAN. Dist: Penguin Random Hse. LLC.

Fahy, Davene & Mueller, Dagmar H. Anthony Best: A Picture Book about Asperger's. Inouye, Carol, illus. 2013. (ENG.). 32p. (J). (gr. -1-3). 16.95 *(978-1-61608-961-0(X)*, 608961, Sky Pony Pr.) Skyhorse Publishing Co., Inc.

Fairchild Hawks, Lyn. How Wendy Redbird Dancing Survived the Dark Ages of Nought. 2013. (ENG.). 286p. (C). pap. 16.99 *(978-0-9888837-2-7(4))* Hawks, Lyn.

Fairfield, J. S. Cunning Foe: Faulkil. 2009. 88p. pap. 19.95 *(978-1-61546-603-0(7))* America Star Bks.

Fairlie, Emily. The Lost Treasure of Tuckernuck. Caparo, Antonio Javier, illus. 2012. (Tuckernuck Mysteries Ser.). (ENG.). 304p. (J). (gr. 3-7). 16.99 *(978-0-06-211890-5(0)*, Tegen, Katherine Bks) HarperCollins Pubs.

Falcone, David A. The Adventures of Miss Aiden in Dinoland. 2011. 28p. pap. 15.99 *(978-1-4568-4015-0(0))* Xlibris Corp.

Falconer, Ian, et al. Olivia & Her Great Adventures. Osterhold, Jared & Johnson, Shane L., illus. 2012. (J). *(978-1-4351-4316-6(7)*, Simon Spotlight) Simon Spotlight.

Falk, Elizabeth Sullivan. Lettie's North Star. Wolf, Elizabeth, illus. 2006. (J). *(978-1-59336-694-0(9))* Mondo Publishing.

Falki, Pamela Marie. The Perfect Christmas Tree: Petrie & Toby's Holiday Adventure. 2009. 24p. pap. 11.49 *(978-1-4343-9983-0(4))* AuthorHouse.

Falkner, Brian. Maddy West & the Tongue Taker, 1 vol. Bixley, Donovan, illus. 2014. (ENG.). 256p. (gr. 4-8). 12.95 *(978-1-62370-084-3(1))* Capstone Young Readers of Coughlan Cos.

Falkner, John Meade. Moonfleet. l.t. ed. 2004. (Large Print Ser.). 370p. 26.00 *(978-1-58287-658-0(4))* North Bks.

Falkoff, Michelle. Playlist for the Dead. 2015. (ENG.). 288p. (YA). (gr. 8). 17.99 *(978-0-06-231050-7(X)*, HarperTeen) HarperCollins Pubs.

Falligant, Erin. A Surprise Find. Studios, Arcana, illus. 2011. (ENG.). 120p. (J). pap. 8.95 *(978-1-59369-908-6(5))* American Girl Publishing, Inc.

Fallin, Rachel. Little Blessings. 2012. 24p. pap. 17.99 *(978-1-4685-6209-5(6))* AuthorHouse.

Fallows, Ralph. Ralphie's after-School Adventure. 2012. 32p. pap. 14.51 *(978-1-4669-2227-3(3))* Trafford Publishing.

Falwell, Cathryn. Los Dibujos de David. de La Vega, Eida, tr. from ENG. Falwell, Cathryn, illus. 2005. (SPA., Illus.). 32p. (J). (gr. -1-5). pap. 9.95 *(978-1-58430-258-2(5))* Lee & Low Bks., Inc.

Falwell, Cathryn & National Geographic Learning Staff. David's Drawings. 2010. (Rise & Shine Ser.). (ENG., Illus.). 32p. (C). (gr. -1-2). pap. 14.95 *(978-1-58430-261-2(5))* National Geographic School Publishing, Inc.

Fanny, Nanny. The New Girl in Town: A Children's Book. Fanny, Nanny, illus. 2013. (Illus.). 32p. pap. 12.99 *(978-1-62516-179-6(4)*, Strategic Bk. Publishing) Strategic Book Publishing & Rights Agency (SBPRA).

farahay, m. l. The BUTTERFLY, the BEE & the SPIDER, Sc3. 2009. 32p. pap. 14.94 *(978-0-557-15287-2(9))* Lulu Pr., Inc.

Farber, E. S. Fish Finelli (Book 2) Operation Fireball. Beene, Jason, illus. 2015. (Fish Finelli Ser.). (ENG.). 184p. (J). (gr. 3-7). pap. 6.99 *(978-1-4521-2875-7(8))* Chronicle Bks. LLC.

—Fish Finelli (Book 3) Warrick, Jessica, illus. 2016. (Fish Finelli Ser.). (ENG.). 176p. (J). (gr. 3-7). 15.99 *(978-1-4521-3815-2(X))* Chronicle Bks. LLC.

—Operation Fireball. Beene, Jason, illus. 2014. (Fish Finelli Ser.). (ENG.). 172p. (J). (gr. 3-7). 15.99 *(978-1-4521-1083-7(2))* Chronicle Bks. LLC.

Farber, Erica. Kooky Campout. Scarry, Huck, illus. 2015. (Richard Scarry's Great Big Schoolhouse Ser.). (ENG.). 24p. (J). (gr. 1-2). 12.95 *(978-1-4027-9914-3(4))* Sterling Publishing Co., Inc.

Faria, N. K. The Little Smart Rabbit & the Greedy Wolf: Finding Carrots. 2009. (Illus.). 24p. pap. 11.49 *(978-1-4490-1004-1(0))* AuthorHouse.

Faris, Stephanie. 25 Roses. 2015. (Mix Ser.). (ENG., Illus.). 224p. (J). (gr. 4-8). pap. 7.99 *(978-1-4814-2420-2(3)*, Aladdin) Simon & Schuster Children's Publishing.

—30 Days of No Gossip. 2014. (ENG., Illus.). 208p. (J). (gr. 4-8). 17.99 *(978-1-4424-8282-1(6)*, Aladdin) Simon & Schuster Children's Publishing.

Farizan, Sara. If You Could Be Mine. (ENG.). (YA). (gr. 9-12). 2014. 272p. pap. 9.95 *(978-1-61620-455-6(9)*, 73455) 2013. 256p. 16.95 *(978-1-61620-251-4(3)*, 73251) Algonquin Bks. of Chapel Hill.

—Tell Me Again How a Crush Should Feel. 2014. (ENG.). 304p. (YA). (gr. 9-12). 16.95 *(978-1-61620-284-2(X)*, 73284) Algonquin Bks. of Chapel Hill.

Farley, Jan. Fleur & Cedarick: Book Two in Fleur Series. 2011. 58p. pap. 16.95 *(978-1-4560-7837-9(2))* America Star Bks.

Farley, Robin. Mia & the Big Sister Ballet. 2012. (Mia I Can Read Bks.). (J). lib. bdg. 13.55 *(978-0-606-26282-8(2)*, Turtleback) Turtleback Bks.

—Mia & the Daisy Dance. Ivanov, Olga & Ivanov, Aleksey, illus. 2012. (My First I Can Read Ser.). (ENG.). 32p. (J). (gr. -1-3). 16.99 *(978-0-06-173306-2(7))*; pap. 3.99 *(978-0-06-173305-5(9))* HarperCollins Pubs.

—Mia & the Dance for Two. Ivanov, Olga & Ivanov, Aleksey, illus. 2011. (My First I Can Read Ser.). (ENG.). 32p. (J). (gr. -1-3). 16.99 *(978-0-06-173304-8(0))*; pap. 3.99 *(978-0-06-173303-1(2))* HarperCollins Pubs.

—Mia & the Girl with a Twirl. Ivanov, Olga & Ivanov, Aleksey, illus. 2013. (My First I Can Read Ser.). (ENG.). 32p. (J). (gr. -1-3). 16.99 *(978-0-06-208689-1(8))*; pap. 3.99 *(978-0-06-208688-4(X))* HarperCollins Pubs.

—Mia & the Tiny Toe Shoes. 2012. (Mia I Can Read Bks.). (J). lib. bdg. 13.55 *(978-0-606-26863-9(4)*, Turtleback) Turtleback Bks.

Farnell, Chris. Mark II. 2006. (ENG., Illus.). 144p. (gr. 8-10). per. 14.95 *(978-0-9547913-9-1(8)*, Tindal Street Pr.) Profile Bks. Ltd. GBR. Dist: Independent Pubs. Group.

Farnol, Jeffery. Money Moon. 2006. pap. 13.95 *(978-1-4218-3066-7(3))* 1st World Publishing, Inc.

Farnsworth-Simpson, Patricia Ann. Flick the Karate Pig. 2008. 163p. pap. 16.50 *(978-1-4357-2843-1(2))* Lulu Pr., Inc.

Farrell, Connie. Sam's Harvest Party, 1 vol. Ellingsworth, Colleen, illus. 2009. 29p. pap. 24.95 *(978-1-60813-937-8(9))* America Star Bks.

Farrell, Darren. Doug-Dennis & the Flyaway Fib. 2010. (ENG.). 40p. (J). (gr. k-3). 16.99 *(978-0-8037-3437-1(9)*, Dial Bks) Penguin Young Readers Group.

Farrell, Lynne. Bennie's Forever Gift. 2012. 40p. pap. 15.95 *(978-1-4497-6133-2(X)*, WestBow Pr.) Author Solutions, Inc.

Farrell-Whelan, Max. Something Fishy Aboard the Red Herring: Can You Catch the Killer? 2013. 130p. pap. 11.95 *(978-1-61204-239-8(2)*, Strategic Bk. Publishing) Strategic Book Publishing & Rights Agency (SBPRA).

Farrelly, Linda. Elliot's Amazing Adventures Number 1. Farrelly, Linda & Hopkins, Simon, illus. 2013. 52p. pap. *(978-0-9560331-5-4(6))* Children' Story Pubs.

Farrey, Brian. The Secret of Dreadwillow Carse. 2016. (ENG.). 256p. (J). (gr. 3-7). 16.95 *(978-1-61620-505-8(9))* Algonquin Bks. of Chapel Hill.

—With or Without You. 2011. (ENG., Illus.). 368p. (YA). (gr. 11-18). pap. 8.99 *(978-1-4424-0699-5(2)*, Simon Pulse) Simon Pulse.

Farrow, G. e. & Farrow, G. E. The Wallypug in London. 2011. 106p. pap. 9.95 *(978-1-60664-480-5(7))* Rodgers, Alan Bks.

Farruggia, M. E. Lost Memories. 2013. 352p. pap. 21.99 *(978-1-4582-1247-4(5)*, Abbott Pr.) Author Solutions, Inc.

Fass, Amanda L. Farm Friends. Swope, Brenda, illus. 2011. 28p. pap. 24.95 *(978-1-4560-0894-9(3))* America Star Bks.

Fatio, Louise. The Happy Lion. Duvoisin, Roger, illus. (ENG.). 40p. (J). (gr. -1-2). 2015. 6.99 *(978-0-553-50850-5(4))* 2010. pap. 7.99 *(978-0-553-11364-8(X))* Random Hse. Children's Bks. (Dragonfly Bks.).

Faul, Nicole. The Great Animal Race & Trap the Angry Elephant Finds a Friend. 2009. (Illus.). 44p. pap. 18.49 *(978-1-4389-3320-7(7))* AuthorHouse.

Faust, Lauren. The Magic Begins, Vol. 1. 2013. (My Little Pony Ser.). (ENG., Illus.). 112p. (J). (gr. 2-5). pap. 7.99 *(978-1-61377-754-1(X)*, 9781613777541) Idea & Design Works, LLC.

Fay, Nicole. Andy & Armadillio Are Astronauts. 2008. 20p. pap. 10.49 *(978-1-4389-1057-4(6))* AuthorHouse.

Faye Morningstar. Little Dream Athe: The Sand Prince. 2012. 20p. pap. 17.99 *(978-1-4772-9540-3(2))* AuthorHouse.

Feagins, Sistah L. E. T. M. E. TELL'YA Bernadine. Hakim & Terrance Shadow Mystery ! 2009. 68p. pap. 15.72 *(978-0-557-09041-9(5))* Lulu Pr., Inc.

The Fearful Fairy. 2007. (ENG., Illus.). 39p. (J). 16.95 *(978-0-9793823-0-7(0))* StonesThrow Publishing, LLC.

Fechner, Maggie. Growing Up Gracie. 2010. 240p. pap. 15.99 *(978-1-59955-453-2(4))* Cedar Fort, Inc./CFI Distribution.

Fedderesen, Jill. The Very Best Friend There Ever Could Be. Sabanski, Helen, illus. 2004. 8p. pap. 5.73 *(978-1-4116-0898-6(4))* Lulu Pr., Inc.

Feder, Jane. Spooky Friends. Downing, Julie, illus. 2013. (ENG.). 40p. (J). (gr. k-2). 16.99 *(978-0-545-47815-1(4)*, Scholastic Pr.) Scholastic, Inc.

—Spooky Friends, Level 2. Downing, Julie, illus. 2013. (Scholastic Reader Level 2 Ser.). (ENG.). 40p. (J). (gr. 1-2). pap. 3.99 *(978-0-545-47816-8(2)*, Scholastic Pr.) Scholastic, Inc.

Feder, Joel A. Kokomo Superhero. 2011. 32p. pap. 14.99 *(978-1-4634-4748-9(5))* AuthorHouse.

—Kokomo's Halloween Adventure. 2012. 32p. pap. 15.99 *(978-1-4685-7331-2(4))* AuthorHouse.

Federle, Tim. Better Nate Than Ever. 2014. lib. bdg. 18.40 *(978-0-606-35430-1(1))* Turtleback Bks.

—Five, Six, Seven, Nate! (ENG., Illus.). (J). (gr. 5-9). 2015. 320p. pap. 7.99 *(978-1-4424-4695-3(1))* 2014. 304p. 16.99 *(978-1-4424-4693-9(5))* Simon & Schuster Bks. For Young Readers. (Simon & Schuster Bks. For Young Readers).

Fee, J. M. The Amazing Adventures of Phineas Screwdriver. 2012. 64p. pap. 20.95 *(978-1-4497-7236-9(6)*, WestBow Pr.) Author Solutions, Inc.

EFG

Feld, Ellen F. Annie: The Mysterious Morgan Horse. Mellin, Jeanne, illus. 2007. 206p. (J). per. 9.95 (978-0-9709002-9-6(5)) Willow Bend Publishing.

Feldman, Jody. The Gollywhopper Games: Friend or Foe. Jamieson, Victoria, illus. 2016. (Gollywhopper Games Ser.: 3). 432p. (J). (gr. 3-7). pap. 6.99 (978-0-06-221129-3(3), Greenwillow Bks.) HarperCollins Pubs.

Feldman, Karen. Glorious Wings. 2011. 36p. pap. 24.95 (978-1-4560-8352-6(X)) America Star Bks.

Feldman, Thea. Fun Around the Town. 2006. 3p. 5.99 (978-1-932915-34-1(6)) Sandvik Publishing.

—Thomas & Friends: Best Day Ever! 2015. (ENG.). 12p. (J). (gr. -1-k). 15.99 (978-0-7944-3512-7(2), Reader's Digest Children's Bks.) Studio Fun International.

Fenn, G. Manville. Brownsmith's Boy. 2008. 260p. pap. 15.95 (978-1-60664-154-5(9)) Aegypan.

—The Rajah of Dah. 2011. 194p. 26.95 (978-1-4638-9697-3(2)) Rodgers, Alan Bks.

Fenske, Jonathan. Woodward & Mctwee. Fenske, Jonathan, illus. 2014. (Penguin Young Readers, Level 2 Ser.). (ENG., Illus.). 32p. (J). (gr. 1-2). pap. 3.99 (978-0-448-47991-0(5), Penguin Young Readers) Penguin Young Readers Group.

Fenske, Jonathan & Bader, Bonnie. A Pig, a Fox, & a Box. Fenske, Jonathan, illus. 2015. (Penguin Young Readers, Level 2 Ser.). (ENG., Illus.). 32p. (J). (gr. 1-2). 3.99 (978-0-448-48510-2(9), Penguin Young Readers) Penguin Young Readers Group.

Fenwick, Margaret. Lonnie the Lost Lamb. 2010. 32p. pap. 13.00 (978-1-60911-038-3(2), Eloquent Bks.) Strategic Book Publishing & Rights Agency (SBPRA).

Fergus, Maureen. Buddy & Earl. 1 vol. Sookocheff, Carey, illus. 2015. (Buddy & Earl Ser.: 1). (ENG.). 32p. (J). (gr. -1-2). 16.95 (978-1-55498-712-2(1)) Groundwood Bks. CAN. Dist: Publishers Group West (PGW).

Ferguson, Dwayne. Mess at Loch Ness. 2004. (Kid Caramel). 72p. (J). pap. 4.50 (978-0-940975-74-3(2), Sankofa Bks.) Just Us Bks., Inc.

Ferguson, Gloria. Fair Money. 2012. 62p. 19.95 (978-1-4626-3037-0(5)) America Star Bks.

Ferguson, Jamianne. Lost in Past Remembrence. 2010. 265p. pap. 17.25 (978-0-557-52788-5(0)) Lulu Pr., Inc.

Ferguson, Sarah & Duchess of York Staff. Little Red's Autumn Adventure. Williams, Sam, illus. 2009. (ENG.). 40p. (J). (gr. -1-1). 16.99 (978-0-689-84341-9(0), Simon & Schuster/Paula Wiseman Bks.) Simon & Schuster/Paula Wiseman Bks.

—Little Red's Christmas Story. Williams, Sam, illus. 2011. (ENG.). 40p. (J). (gr. -1-2). pap. 19.99 (978-1-4424-3076-1(1), Simon & Schuster/Paula Wiseman Bks.) Simon & Schuster/Paula Wiseman Bks.

Fern, Fanny. Little Ferns for Fanny's Little Friends by the Author of Fern Leaves. 2006. 320p. per. 23.99 (978-1-4255-3132-4(6)) Michigan Publishing.

Ferrari, Michael. Born to Fly. 2011. (ENG.). 224p. (J). (gr. 3-7). 6.99 (978-0-375-84607-6(7), Yearling) Random Hse. Children's Bks.

Ferreira, Ann Devine & Bailey. Hi I'm Bailey & I'm Getting A New Special Family. 2011. 32p. 17.95 (978-1-4269-5303-3(8)) Trafford Publishing.

Ferrell, Deen. Cryptic Spaces: Book One. 2013. 396p. pap. 16.95 (978-1-60047-864-2(6)) Wasteland Pr.

Ferris, Jean. Of Sound Mind. 2004. (ENG.). 224p. (YA). (gr. 7). reprint ed. pap. 10.99 (978-0-374-45584-2(8), 9780374455842, Farrar, Straus & Giroux (BYR)) Farrar, Straus & Giroux.

Ferry, Ann. Cozy the Pine Tree & Swaylee the Elm in Featherwood Forest. 1 vol. 2010. 24p. 24.95 (978-1-4512-1742-1(0)) PublishAmerica, Inc.

Ferry, Beth. Stick & Stone. Lichtenheld, Tom, illus. 2015. (ENG.). 48p. (J). (gr. -1-3). 16.99 (978-0-544-03256-9(X), HMH Books For Young Readers) Houghton Mifflin Harcourt Publishing Co.

Fessahaye, Miss Mehret. Layla the Animals' Friend. 2012. (Illus.). 40p. pap. 22.81 (978-1-4772-5086-0(7)) AuthorHouse.

Few, Valerie. Filbert & Friends. 2008. 56p. pap. (978-1-84748-346-1(1)) Athena Pr.

Fiani, M. A Cat Named Monkey. 2008. 24p. pap. 14.99 (978-1-4389-1966-9(2)) AuthorHouse.

Fickey, Brenda. Beckoning Shadows. 1 vol. 2009. (ENG.). 179p. pap. 24.95 (978-1-61546-330-5(5)) America Star Bks.

—Echoing Silence. 2008. 123p. pap. 19.95 (978-1-60563-816-4(1)) America Star Bks.

Ficklin, Jonene H. The Garden Gate. 2005. (YA). 14.95 (978-0-9761188-2-4(3)) Victor's Crown Publishing.

Fiedler, Lisa. The Green-Eyed Monster. 2012. 168p. (J). (978-0-545-48424-4(3)) Scholastic, Inc.

Fiedler, Lisa & Wallach, Anya. Showstopper! 2015. (Stagestruck Ser.). (ENG.). 280p. (J). (gr. 4-6). 11.99 (978-1-58536-925-6(X), 203948) Sleeping Bear Pr.

Fields, Jan. Facing a Frenemy. 1 vol. 2014. (Meri's Mirror Ser.). (ENG., Illus.). 80p. (J). (gr. 2-5). lib. bdg. 27.07 (978-1-62402-008-7(9), Calico Chapter Bks) Magic Wagon.

—Meri Mercer Doesn't Lie, Mostly. 1 vol. 2014. (Meri's Mirror Ser.). (ENG., Illus.). 80p. (J). (gr. 2-5). lib. bdg. 27.07 (978-1-62402-009-4(7), Calico Chapter Bks) Magic Wagon.

—Terrible Twin Mania. 1 vol. 2014. (Meri's Mirror Ser.). (ENG.). 80p. (J). (gr. 2-5). lib. bdg. 27.07 (978-1-62402-011-7(9), Calico Chapter Bks) Magic Wagon.

Fiesta Girls: A Paper Doll Cut-Out Book. 2006. (J). pap. 8.95 (978-0-9787319-0-8(5)) Kolluri, Alina M.

Figiel, Lisa. Swimming Is Fun! 2010. 24p. pap. 11.49 (978-1-4490-5520-2(6)) AuthorHouse.

Figurska, A. B. The Island of Harklitt. 1 vol. 2010. 108p. pap. 19.95 (978-1-4489-4176-6(8)) PublishAmerica, Inc.

Filali, Lisa. Faith Team 1: Taking Briar Falls. 2007. 84p. per. 19.95 (978-1-4137-8030-7(X)) America Star Bks.

Filaretos, William. The Potion of Time: A Story of Demetrios. 2006. per. 12.95 (978-0-9724520-0-7(1)) Filaretos, William.

Filbin, Sandra A. The Enchanted World: A Tooth Fairy's Tale. 2010. 158p. pap. 14.50 (978-1-60860-379-4(2), Strategic Bk. Publishing) Strategic Book Publishing & Rights Agency (SBPRA).

Filoche, Eric. Hey ! We're Talking about Ourselves ! 2013. 68p. pap. (978-2-9538737-4-0(0)) Koshkindom.

Finally, Lil Rose. Slowpoke the Turtle & Company. Drape, Kaitlin, illus. 2005. (J). pap. 8.00 (978-0-8059-6778-4(8)) Dorrance Publishing Co., Inc.

Finch, Donna. Amanda the Panda. 1 vol. Bolund, Inna, illus. 2009. (ENG.). 27p. pap. 24.95 (978-1-61546-797-6(1)) America Star Bks.

Findlay, Chris. Ae Sma Voice. 2008. 152p. pap. (978-1-84923-144-2(3)) YouWriteOn.

Fine, Anne. Jamie & Angus Together. Dale, Penny, illus. 2007. (ENG.). 112p. (J). (gr. -1-1). 15.99 (978-0-7636-3374-5(7)) Candlewick Pr.

Finley, Leah. The One & Only Mr C. 2009. 82p. pap. 8.95 (978-1-935118-75-6(7)) Bellissima Publishing, LLC.

Finn, Perdita. Equestria Girls: Friendship Games. 2015. (Equestria Girls Ser.: 5). (ENG., Illus.). 208p. (J). (gr. 3-7). 9.99 (978-0-316-41080-9(2)) Little, Brown Bks. for Young Readers.

—The Mane Event. 2014. (Equestria Girls Ser.: 3). (ENG.). 240p. (J). (gr. 3-7). 9.99 (978-0-316-24777-1(4)) Little, Brown Bks. for Young Readers.

—Monster High: Electrified: the Deluxe Junior Novel. 2017. (ENG.). 144p. (J). (gr. 3-7). 9.99 **(978-0-316-54826-7(X))** Little, Brown Bks. for Young Readers.

—Monster High: Electrified: the Junior Novel. 2017. (ENG.). 144p. (J). (gr. 3-7). pap. 6.99 **(978-0-316-54836-6(7))** Little, Brown Bks. for Young Readers.

Finn, Perdita. Rainbow Rocks. 2014. (Equestria Girls Ser.: 2). (ENG.). 192p. (J). (gr. 3-7). 9.99 (978-0-316-28486-8(6)) Little, Brown Bks. for Young Readers.

Fiore, Kelly, et al. Just Like the Movies. (If Only... Ser.). (ENG.). (YA). (gr. 7-12). 2016. 304p. pap. 9.99 (978-1-61963-356-8(6), 9781619633568) 2014. 288p. 17.99 (978-1-61963-354-4(X), 9781619633544) Bloomsbury Publishing USA. (Bloomsbury USA Childrens).

Fiori, Natalie. Lobsters in Seacliff. 2009. 52p. pap. 20.99 (978-1-4490-1811-5(4)) AuthorHouse.

Firestone, Carrie. The Unlikelies. 2017. (ENG.). 336p. (YA). (gr. 9-17). 17.99 **(978-0-316-38286-1(8))** Little, Brown Bks. for Young Readers.

Firth, Norma. Tasha a Fraidy Cat. 2012. 28p. pap. 15.99 (978-1-4685-6079-4(4)) AuthorHouse.

Fischer, David. Heir to Oswyn. 2011. 66p. pap. 19.95 (978-1-4626-2581-9(9)) America Star Bks.

Fisher, Annabelle. Pixie Piper & the Matter of the Batter. 2017. (Pixie Piper Ser.: 2). 336p. (J). (gr. 3-7). 16.99 (978-0-06-239380-7(4), Greenwillow Bks.) HarperCollins Pubs.

—The Secret Destiny of Pixie Piper. Andrewson, Natalie, illus. 2016. (Pixie Piper Ser.: 1). 320p. (J). (gr. 3-7). 16.99 (978-0-06-239377-7(4), Greenwillow Bks.) HarperCollins Pubs.

Fisher, Meaghan. Giuseppe's Famous Pizza Pies. Barrett, Diana, illus. 2013. 24p. pap. 8.99 (978-1-938768-20-0(5)) Gypsy Pubns.

FitzGerald, Dawn. Getting in the Game. 2007. (ENG.). 144p. (J). (gr. 4-8). pap. 16.99 (978-0-312-37753-3(3), 9780312377533) Square Fish.

Fitzgerald, Laura Marx. Under the Egg. (ENG.). 256p. (J). (gr. 3-7). 2015. 7.99 (978-0-14-242765-1(9), Puffin Books) 2014. 16.99 (978-0-8037-4001-3(8), Dial Bks) Penguin Young Readers Group.

Fitzgerald, Mary. Samson's Best Friend. 2012. (ENG.). 32p. (J). 22.95 (978-1-4327-9039-4(0)) Outskirts Pr., Inc.

Fitzgerald, Sarah Moore. The Apple Tart of Hope. 2016. (ENG.). 208p. (J). (gr. 5). 16.95 (978-0-8234-3561-6(X)) Holiday Hse., Inc.

Fitzhugh, Louise. Harriet the Spy. 50th anniv. ed. 2014. (ENG.). 336p. (J). (gr. 3-7). 17.99 (978-0-385-37610-5(3), Delacorte Bks. for Young Readers) Random Hse. Children's Bks.

Fitzpatrick, Becca. The Complete Hush, Hush Saga: Hush, Hush; Crescendo; Silence; Finale. 2012. (Hush, Hush Saga Ser.: Bks. 1-4). (ENG.). 1744p. (YA). (gr. 9). 74.99 (978-1-4424-7372-0(X), Simon & Schuster Bks. For Young Readers) Simon & Schuster Bks. For Young Readers.

—Hush, Hush. (SPA.). 368p. 2010. (Hush, Hush Saga: Bk. 1). (YA). pap. 20.95 (978-84-666-4417-4(2)) pap. 13.95 (978-84-9872-932-0(7)) Ediciones B ESP. Dist: Spanish Pubs., LLC.

—Hush, Hush. 3 vols. Ruiz, Derek, ed. 2012. (Hush, Hush Saga: Bk. 1). (Illus.). 120p. (YA). 19.95 (978-0-9836131-1-4(7)) Sea Lion Bks.

—Hush, Hush. (Hush, Hush Saga Ser.: Bk. 1). (ENG.). (YA). (gr. 9-18). 2010. 432p. pap. 11.99 (978-1-4169-8942-4(0)) 2009. 400p. 21.99 (978-1-4169-8941-7(2)) Simon & Schuster Bks. For Young Readers. (Simon & Schuster Bks. For Young Readers).

Fitzpatrick, Huntley. The Boy Most Likely To. 2015. (ENG.). 432p. (YA). (gr. 9). 17.99 (978-0-8037-4142-3(1), Dial Bks) Penguin Young Readers Group.

Fitzpatrick, Marie-Louise. Owl Bat Bat Owl. Fitzpatrick, Marie-Louise, illus. 2017. (ENG., Illus.). 32p. (J). (gr. -1-2). 15.99 (978-0-7636-9161-5(5)) Candlewick Pr.

Fitzsimmons, Christy. Krissy & the Indians. 1 vol. Steckler, Megan, illus. 2009. 28p. pap. 24.95 (978-1-61546-206-3(6)) America Star Bks.

Flake, Sharon. Unstoppable Octobia May. 2014. (ENG.). 288p. (J). (gr. 3-7). 16.99 (978-0-545-60960-9(7), Scholastic Pr.) Scholastic, Inc.

Flake, Sharon G. Pinned. (ENG.). 240p. (J). 2014. (gr. 9). pap. 9.99 (978-0-545-05733-2(7)) 2012. (gr. 8-9). 17.99 (978-0-545-05718-9(3)) Scholastic, Inc. (Scholastic Pr.).

Flanagan, John. The Ghostfaces. 2016. (Brotherband Chronicles Ser.: 6). (ENG.). 400p. (J). (gr. 5). 18.99 (978-0-399-16357-9(3), Philomel Bks.) Penguin Young Readers Group.

—The Hunters. (Brotherband Chronicles Ser.: 3). (ENG.). (J). (gr. 5). 2014. 448p. pap. 8.99 (978-0-14-242664-7(4), Puffin Books) 2012. 416p. 18.99 (978-0-399-25621-9(0), Philomel Bks.) Penguin Young Readers Group.

—The Hunters. 2014. (Brotherband Chronicles Ser.: 3). lib. bdg. 19.65 (978-0-606-35708-1(4)) Turtleback Bks.

—The Invaders. (Brotherband Chronicles Ser.: 2). (ENG.). (J). (gr. 5). 2013. 448p. pap. 8.99 (978-0-14-242663-0(6), Puffin Books) 2012. 432p. 18.99 (978-0-399-25620-2(2), Philomel Bks.) Penguin Young Readers Group.

—The Invaders. 2013. (Brotherband Chronicles Ser.: 2). lib. bdg. 19.65 (978-0-606-26637-6(2), Turtleback) Turtleback Bks.

—The Outcasts. 2011. (Brotherband Chronicles: Bk. 1). (ENG.). (J). (gr. 3-7). 54.99 (978-1-61657-043-9(1)) Findaway World, LLC.

—The Outcasts. (Brotherband Chronicles Ser.: 1). (ENG.). (J). (gr. 5). 2012. 464p. pap. 8.99 (978-0-14-242194-9(4), Puffin Books) 2011. 448p. 18.99 (978-0-399-25619-6(9), Philomel Bks.) Penguin Young Readers Group.

—The Outcasts. 2012. (Brotherband Chronicles Ser.: 1). lib. bdg. 19.65 (978-0-606-26636-9(4), Turtleback) Turtleback Bks.

—Slaves of Socorro. 2014. (Brotherband Chronicles Ser.: Bk. 4). (ENG., Illus.). 480p. (J). 18.99 (978-0-399-16355-5(7), Philomel Bks.) Penguin Publishing Group.

—Slaves of Socorro. 2015. (Brotherband Chronicles Ser.: 4). (ENG.). 496p. (J). (gr. 5). pap. 8.99 (978-0-14-242726-2(8), Puffin Books) Penguin Young Readers Group.

—Slaves of Socorro. 2015. (Brotherband Chronicles Ser.: 4). lib. bdg. 19.65 (978-0-606-36771-4(3)) Turtleback Bks.

Flanagan, Liz. Eden Summer. 2017. (ENG.). 288p. (J). (gr. 7). 18.99 **(978-1-338-12120-9(0))** Scholastic, Inc.

Fleming, Bryn. Cassie & Jasper: Cattle Drive Danger. 2016. (Range Riders Ser.). (ENG.). 147p. (J). pap. 10.99 (978-1-941821-95-4(2), West Winds Pr.) Graphic Arts Ctr. Publishing Co.

—Cassie & Jasper: Kidnapped Cattle. 2016. (Range Riders Ser.). (ENG.). 147p. (J). 24.99 (978-1-943328-66-6(8), West Winds Pr.) Graphic Arts Ctr. Publishing Co.

—Cassie & Jasper to the Rescue. 2014. (Range Riders Ser.). (ENG.). 128p. (YA). (gr. 3-7). 23.99 (978-1-941821-04-6(9)); pap. 9.99 (978-0-88240-992-4(1)) Graphic Arts Ctr. Publishing Co. (West Winds Pr.).

Fleming, Meg. Ready, Set, Build! Jarvis, illus. 2017. (ENG.). 32p. (J). (gr. -1-3). 16.99 (978-1-4998-0175-0(0)) Little Bee Books Inc.

Fleming, Sean & Ewald, Jenny, eds. To Catch a Mall Thief. 2004. 85p. (YA). pap. 9.95 (978-0-7414-2196-8(8)) Infinity Publishing.

Flemmer, Chip. Out of Texas. 1 vol. 2010. 183p. pap. 24.95 (978-1-4489-2918-4(0)) America Star Bks.

Flood, C. J. Infinite Sky. (ENG., Illus.). 256p. (YA). (gr. 7). 2015. pap. 10.99 (978-1-4814-0659-8(0)) 2014. 17.99 (978-1-4814-0658-1(2), Atheneum Bks. for Young Readers) Simon & Schuster Children's Publishing.

Flood, Pansie Hart. Secret Holes. Marshall, Felicia, illus. 2004. 128p. (J). (gr. 3-6). 15.95 (978-0-87614-923-2(9), Carolrhoda Bks.) Lerner Publishing Group.

—Tiger's Trouble with Donut Head. Wummer, Amy, illus. 2005. 71p. (J). lib. bdg. 19.93 (978-1-57505-814-6(6), Carolrhoda Bks.) Lerner Publishing Group.

Floppy's Friends. 2004. (J). (ENG & TUR.). (978-1-84444-664-3(6)); (ENG & VIE.). (978-1-84444-666-7(2)); (ENG & PAN.). (978-1-84444-658-2(1)); (ENG & TAM.). (978-1-84444-663-6(8)); (ENG & SPA.). (978-1-84444-662-9(X)); (ENG & SOM.). (978-1-84444-661-2(1)); (ENG & POR.). (978-1-84444-660-5(3)); (ALB & ENG.). (978-1-84444-647-6(6)); (ARA & ENG.). (978-1-84444-648-3(4)); (CHI & ENG.). (978-1-84444-651-3(4)); (CRO & ENG.). (978-1-84444-652-0(2)); (ENG & PER.). (978-1-84444-653-7(0)); (ENG & FRE.). (978-1-84444-654-4(9)); (ENG & GUJ.). (978-1-84444-655-1(7)); (ENG & HIN.). (978-1-84444-656-8(5)); (ENG & LAO.). (978-1-84444-657-5(3)) Mantra Lingua.

Florence, Debbi Michiko. Jasmine Toguchi, Mochi Queen. Vukovic, Elizabet, illus. 2017. (Jasmine Toguchi Ser.: 1). (ENG.). 128p. (J). pap. 5.99 **(978-0-374-30834-6(9)**, 9780374308346, Farrar, Straus & Giroux (BYR)) Farrar, Straus & Giroux.

—Jasmine Toguchi, Super Sleuth. Vukovic, Elizabet, illus. 2017. (J). pap. **(978-0-374-30414-0(9))**; (Jasmine Toguchi Ser.: 2). (ENG.). 128p. pap. 5.99 **(978-0-374-30835-3(7)**, 9780374308353, Farrar, Straus & Giroux (BYR)) Farrar, Straus & Giroux.

Florence, Nancy L. Harold the Goat. 2004. (ENG.). 30p. 24.95 (978-1-4137-3941-1(5)) PublishAmerica, Inc.

Flores, Eileen. To All a Good Knight. 2008. 92p. pap. 12.50 (978-1-4389-2267-6(1)) AuthorHouse.

Flower, Amanda. Andi under Pressure. 1 vol. 2014. (Andi Boggs Novel Ser.). (ENG.). 176p. (J). 10.99 (978-0-310-73702-5(8)) Zonderkidz.

—Andi under Pressure: An Andi Boggs Novel. 2014. 176p. (J). pap. (978-0-310-74022-3(3)) Zondervan.

The Flower Child. 2013. (Illus.). 28p. 17.99 (978-0-9891510-1-6(8)) Zebra Ginkgo.

Flower, Graham Jessie. Grace Harlowe's Junior Year at High School: Or Fast Friends in the Sororities. 2007. (ENG.). 162p. pap. 19.99 (978-1-4346-1306-6(2)); 178p. pap. 21.99 (978-1-4346-1358-5(5)) Creative Media Partners, LLC.

Flowers, Natasha. Sammy the Snail. 2006. 10.00 (978-0-8059-9158-1(1)) Dorrance Publishing Co., Inc.

Flynn, Dave. Nick & the Old Man of the Mountain. 2010. 40p. pap. 18.49 (978-1-4389-9356-0(0)) AuthorHouse.

Fogelin, Adrian. The Sorta Sisters. 1 vol. 2007. (ENG., Illus.). 224p. (J). (gr. 3-7). 15.95 (978-1-56145-424-2(9)) Peachtree Pubs.

—Sorta Sisters. 1 vol. Fogelin, Adrian, illus. 2011. (ENG., Illus.). 288p. pap. 7.95 (978-1-56145-592-8(X), Peachtree Junior) Peachtree Pubs.

Fogg, K. L. Diamondback Cave: A Novel. 2008. 377p. (J). (978-1-59811-512-3(X)) Covenant Communications.

—Serpent Tide. 2006. 16.95 (978-1-59156-861-2(7)) Covenant Communications, Inc.

—Widow's Revenge: A Novel. 2007. 355p. (J). (978-1-59811-319-8(4)) Covenant Communications.

Fogle, Llynda & González, Althea. A Friendship Place. 2005. (ENG & SPA., Illus.). (J). (978-0-9760282-6-0(3)) RAPC - Sparkle & Shine Project.

Fogleman, Laurie. Jimmy, What Are You Eating?! 2011. 64p. (gr. -1). pap. 9.99 (978-1-4634-1206-7(1)) AuthorHouse.

Foley, Alyssa Christine. A Secret at Half Past Noon: A Christmas Story. 2008. 28p. pap. 13.99 (978-1-4389-2013-9(X)) AuthorHouse.

Foley, Greg. Willoughby & the Lion. Foley, Greg, illus. 2009. (ENG., Illus.). 40p. (J). (gr. -1-2). 17.99 (978-0-06-154750-8(6)) HarperCollins Pubs.

Foley, Jessie Ann. Neighborhood Girls. 2017. 368p. (YA). (gr. 9). 17.99 **(978-0-06-257185-4(0)**, HarperTeen) HarperCollins Pubs.

Foley, Monica. The Four of Us. 2008. pap. 9.00 (978-0-8059-8628-0(6)) Dorrance Publishing Co., Inc.

Folgueira, Rodrigo. Ribbit! Bernatene, Poly, illus. (ENG.). (J). 2016. 34p. (-k). bds. 8.99 (978-0-553-53721-5(0)) 2013. 32p. (gr. -1-k). 15.99 (978-0-307-98146-2(0)) Random Hse. Children's Bks. (Knopf Bks. for Young Readers).

Follett, Ross C. Beebear 2. Sievers, Lee, illus. 2013. (ENG.). 52p. (J). (gr. -1-3). 15.95 (978-0-9881748-0-1(4), OddInt Media) Greenwood Hill Pr.

Foltyn, Sue. Mayzeemioletu. 2009. 12p. pap. 9.95 (978-1-4490-2244-0(8)) AuthorHouse.

Fonte, Mary Roessler & Hoppe, Jessica. Big Green Gorilla. Verhoosky, Michele, illus. 2013. 34p. 17.99 (978-1-937260-92-7(5)) Sleepytown Pr.

Fontenot, Mary Alice. Clovis Crawfish & Silvie Sulphur. 1 vol. Buckner, Julie Dupre, illus. 2004. (Clovis Crawfish Ser.). (ENG & FRE.). 32p. (J). (gr. k-3). 16.99 (978-1-56554-864-0(7)) Pelican Publishing Co., Inc.

Fontes, Justine. Showdown in Crittertown. 2014. (Cheddar's Tales Ser.). (ENG.). 176p. (J). (gr. 2-4). pap. 5.99 (978-1-4380-0360-3(9)) Barron's Educational Series, Inc.

—Toy Trouble. Hefferan, Rob, illus. 2003. 24p. (J). pap. (978-1-59034-447-7(2)); 14.95 (978-1-59034-446-0(4)) Mondo Publishing.

Fontinalis. The Far Shore. 2011. 76p. pap. 6.99 (978-1-61667-309-3(5)) Raider Publishing International.

Foon, Dennis. Skud. 1 vol. 2004. (ENG.). 176p. (YA). pap. 9.95 (978-0-88899-549-0(0)) Groundwood Bks. CAN. Dist: Publishers Group West (PGW).

Ford, Bernette. Ballet Kitty: Christmas Recital. Williams, Sam, illus. 2012. (ENG.). 32p. (J). (gr. -1-1). 16.95 (978-1-907152-12-2(1)) Boxer Bks., Ltd. GBR. Dist: Sterling Publishing Co., Inc.

Ford, Bernette G. Princess Puppy. Williams, Sam, illus. 2013. (J). (978-0-545-53967-8(6), Cartwheel Bks.) Scholastic, Inc.

Foreman, Jack. Say Hello. Foreman, Michael, illus. 2012. (ENG.). 40p. (J). (gr. -1-2). pap. 6.99 (978-0-7636-6087-1(6)) Candlewick Pr.

Foreman, Jack & Foreman, Michael. Say Hello. 2015. 40p. pap. 7.00 (978-1-61003-409-8(0)) Center for the Collaborative Classroom.

Foreman, Michael. Friends. Foreman, Michael, illus. 2012. (Andersen Press Picture Bks). (ENG., Illus.). 32p. (J). (gr. -1-3). 16.95 (978-1-4677-0317-8(6)) Lerner Publishing Group.

—The Seeds of Friendship. Foreman, Michael, illus. 2015. (ENG., Illus.). 32p. (J). (gr. -1-3). 16.99 (978-0-7636-7834-0(1)) Candlewick Pr.

—Tufty. Foreman, Michael, illus. 2016. (ENG., Illus.). 32p. (gr. -1-3). (J). 17.99 (978-1-5124-0425-8(X)); 35.99 (978-1-5124-0448-7(9)) Lerner Publishing Group.

Forester, Victoria. The Boy Who Knew Everything. 2015. (ENG.). 416p. (J). (gr. 4-7). 16.99 (978-0-312-62600-6(2), 9780312626006) Feiwel & Friends.

Forler, Nan. Bird Child. Thisdale, Francois, illus. 2009. (ENG.). 32p. (J). (gr. k-3). 19.95 (978-0-88776-894-1(6), Tundra Bks.) Tundra Bks. CAN. Dist: Penguin Random Hse. LLC.

Forman, Gayle. I Was Here. l.t. ed. 2015. (ENG.). 420p. 24.99 (978-1-4104-8255-6(3)) Cengage Gale.

—I Was Here. 2015. (ENG.). 288p. (J). (gr. 9). 18.99 (978-0-451-47147-5(4), Viking Books for Young Readers) Penguin Publishing Group.

—I Was Here. 2016. (ENG.). 304p. (YA). (gr. 9). pap. 10.99 (978-0-14-751403-5(7), Speak) Penguin Young Readers Group.

—I Was Here. 2016. lib. bdg. 22.10 (978-0-606-38404-9(9)) Turtleback Bks.

—Sisters in Sanity. (YA). 2016. (ENG.). 304p. (gr. 8). pap. 9.99 (978-0-06-088749-0(4)) 2007. 290p. (gr. 7-12). lib. bdg. 17.89 (978-0-06-088748-3(6)) 2007. (ENG.). 304p. (gr. 7-18). 16.99 (978-0-06-088747-6(8)) HarperCollins Pubs. (HarperTeen).

Forney, Lane. The Super Power Teens. 2009. 140p. pap. 11.95 (978-0-557-00129-3(3)) Lulu Pr., Inc.

Forrester, Izola L. Kit of Greenacre Farm. 2007. (ENG.). 158p. pap. 19.99 (978-1-4264-8431-5(3)); 174p. pap. 21.99 (978-1-4264-8489-6(5)) Creative Media Partners, LLC.

Forsythe, Amanda J. The Contabulous Adventures of M.E. 2012. 28p. pap. 24.95 (978-1-4626-6531-0(4)) America Star Bks.

Fortner, Tama. God Is Always Good: Comfort for Kids Facing Grief, Fear, or Change. 1 vol. Vasylenko, Veronica, illus. 2014. (ENG.). 32p. (J). 12.99 (978-0-7180-1145-1(7)) Nelson, Thomas Inc.

Fortunato, Mike. Later Gator, in a While Crocodile. 2013. (ENG.). 40p. (J). pap. 14.95 (978-1-4787-1285-5(6)) Outskirts Pr., Inc.

Fortune, Emil. Root. 2014. (ENG.). 288p. (J). (gr. 6). pap. 10.99 (978-0-552-56635-3(7)) Transworld Publishers Ltd. GBR. Dist: Independent Pubs. Group.

Fosse, Mika. Garage People. 2008. 84p. pap. 9.95 (978-1-60693-500-2(3), Eloquent Bks.) Strategic Book Publishing & Rights Agency (SBPRA).

Foster, Claudie. Princess Vanilla of the Amazon Jungle. 2011. 48p. pap. 24.95 (978-1-60749-297-9(0)) America Star Bks.

Foster, Darlene. Amanda in England. 2012. (Amanda Travels Ser.: 3). (ENG.). 118p. (J). (gr. 3-8). pap. 9.95 (978-1-926760-77-3(8)) Central Avenue Publishing CAN. Dist: Independent Pubs. Group.

Foster, Stewart. Bubble. 2017. (ENG., Illus.). 352p. (J). (gr. 3-5). 16.99 **(978-1-4814-8742-9(6)**, Simon & Schuster Bks. For Young Readers) Simon & Schuster Bks. For Young Readers.

Foster, Thelma Louise Elisher. A Brand New House. 2011. 24p. pap. 15.99 (978-1-4568-4803-3(8)) Xlibris Corp.

Foster, Thomas. Travel Buddies: Robby & Sammy Visit China. 2006. (J). pap. 12.00 (978-1-890306-93-9(2)) Warwick Hse. Publishing.

Foster, Travis & Long, Ethan. Give Me Back My Book! 2017. (ENG., Illus.). 56p. (J). (gr. k-3). 16.99 **(978-1-4521-6040-5(6))** Chronicle Bks. LLC.

Foutz, Andrea. Friendships & Smiles. 2008. 18p. pap. 24.95 (978-1-60610-175-9(7)) America Star Bks.

Fowle, Patz. Remember When... 2008. (ENG.). 50p. pap. 10.99 (978-1-4196-7089-3(1)) CreateSpace Independent Publishing Platform.

Fox, Jennifer. Teen Titans Go! - Boys Versus Girls. 2015. (Passport to Reading Level 2 Ser.). (ENG., Illus.). 32p. (J). (gr. -1-3). pap. 4.99 (978-0-316-37727-0(9)) Little, Brown Bks. for Young Readers.

Fox, L. B. The Adventures of Marky, Slash & Levy. 2006. (ENG.). 184p. per. 24.95 (978-1-4241-4992-6(4)) PublishAmerica, Inc.

Fox, Nita. Captain Benjamin Dale. Wallace, Andrea, illus. 2008. 32p. (J). (gr. -1-3). pap. 5.99 (978-0-9816107-0-2(6)) Fox's Den Publishing.

Fox, Paula. A Likely Place. 2010. (ENG.). 80p. (J). (gr. 3-7). pap. 6.99 (978-1-4424-1677-2(7), Simon & Schuster/Paula Wiseman Bks.) Simon & Schuster/Paula Wiseman Bks.

Fox, R. J. Stuart & His Incredibly Obnoxious Magical Book: Soccer, 1 vol. 2009. 86p. pap. 19.95 (978-1-4489-9833-3(6)) America Star Bks.

Foxx, Darla J. Alexis Mcdougal starring in... Secrets Are Confidential Business!!! A sequel to Alexis Mcdougal starring in... the Day I Met My New Special Friend. 2006. (Illus.). 72p. (J). 9.95 (978-0-9768879-1-1(6), ISBN0976887916) Universal Messengers Pubns.

—Alexis Mcdougal starring in the Day I Met My New Special Friend. 2005. (Illus.). 79p. (J). per. 7.95 (978-0-9768879-0-4(8), AM-001) Universal Messengers Pubns.

Fraillon, Zana. The Bone Sparrow. 2016. (ENG.). 240p. (J). (gr. 4-7). 16.99 (978-1-4847-8151-7(1)) Hyperion Bks. for Children.

France, Richard. Joshua Stories: Book 1 - New School, New Friends. 2011. (Illus.). 104p. (gr. 4-6). pap. 14.09 (978-1-4567-7732-6(7)) AuthorHouse.

Francesca, Sieglinde De. A Donsy of Gnomes. 2009. pap. (978-1-61623-243-6(9)) Independent Pub.

Franciosa, John F. Little Johnny Lion. 2009. 24p. pap. 11.99 (978-1-4389-8810-8(9)) AuthorHouse.

Francis, Anwen. Siani Shetland. 2008. (ENG.). 84p. (J). pap. 9.95 (978-1-905762-62-0(3)) Parthian Bks. GBR. Dist: Independent Pubs. Group.

Francis, Jamaine. The Adventures of Pb & Brown Bear: Lost & Found. 2009. 28p. pap. 12.88 (978-1-4490-1817-7(3)) AuthorHouse.

Francis, JennaKay. Michael's Safari. Howarth, Craig, illus. 2013. 12p. pap. 8.95 (978-1-61633-411-6(8)) Guardian Angel Publishing, Inc.

Franck, Herman. Winnie & Thunderose: An Illustrated Story about Friendship. 2011. 128p. pap. 12.60 (978-1-4269-5647-8(9)) Trafford Publishing.

Francoeur, Christine Marie. The Adventures of Jimmy Su: The South Pole. 2008. 16p. pap. 9.95 (978-1-59858-720-3(X)) Dog Ear Publishing, LLC.

Francois, Saragine. The White Gorilla & the Three Chimpanzees a Day from the Zoo. 2011. 28p. pap. 14.99 (978-1-4520-3190-3(8)) AuthorHouse.

Francoise. Fanchette & Jeannot: A Little Story with Pictures. 2011. 26p. 35.95 (978-1-258-07322-0(6)) Literary Licensing, LLC.

Francour, Kathleen, illus. Friends Forever. 2003. (Puzzles Ser.). (J). bds. 10.95 (978-1-74047-342-2(6)) Book Co. Publishing Pty, Ltd., The AUS. Dist: Penton Overseas, Inc.

Frank, Lucy. Lucky Stars. 2014. (ENG.). 304p. (J). (gr. 5-9). pap. 14.99 (978-1-4814-2901-6(9), Atheneum Bks. for Young Readers) Simon & Schuster Children's Publishing.

Frank, Steven B. Armstrong & Charlie. 2017. (ENG.). 304p. (J). (gr. 5-7). 16.99 (978-0-544-82608-3(6), HMH Books For Young Readers) Houghton Mifflin Harcourt Publishing Co.

Frankel, Erin. Dare!, Bk. 2. Heaphy, Paula, illus. 2013. (Weird! Ser.). (ENG.). 48p. (J). (gr. k-4). pap. 9.99 (978-1-57542-439-2(8)) Free Spirit Publishing, Inc.

Franklin, Cathy. The Magical Ballet Shoes: A Pinta & Polly Story, 1 vol. Watkins, Tammy, illus. 2009. 25p. pap. 24.95 (978-1-4489-2007-5(8)) America Star Bks.

Franklin, Deborah. Annette's Christmas Gift. 2008. (Illus.). 24p. (YA). 7.00 (978-0-8059-7482-9(2)) Dorrance Publishing Co., Inc.

Franklin, Emily. Last Night at the Circle Cinema. 2015. (ENG.). 200p. (YA). (gr. 8-12). 18.99 (978-1-4677-7489-5(8)) Lerner Publishing Group.

Franklin, Miriam Spitzer. Extraordinary. 2015. (ENG.). 256p. (J). (gr. 2-7). 14.99 (978-1-63220-402-8(9), Sky Pony Pr.) Skyhorse Publishing Co., Inc.

Franklin, Teii L. Ameelia's Adventures: Ameelia's First Play. 2010. 32p. pap. 16.49 (978-1-4520-3613-7(6)) AuthorHouse.

Franz, Kevin. The Princess Sisters & the Underwater City. Stigler, Marilyn, illus. 2004. 112p. (J). per. 7.99 (978-0-9747774-1-2(2)) Starbell Bks.

Frashier, Giva. Bogey the Golf Bug. 2013. 36p. pap. 15.99 (978-1-4808-0126-4(7)) Archway Publishing.

Frati, Dorothy. Friendly Bubbles. 2012. 24p. pap. 17.99 (978-1-4772-6447-8(7)) AuthorHouse.

Frazee, Marla. A Couple of Boys Have the Best Week Ever. 2008. (ENG., Illus.). 40p. (J). (gr. 1-4). 17.99 (978-0-15-206020-6(0)) Houghton Mifflin Harcourt Publishing Co.

Frazin, Julian. A Little Dab of Paint. Schirmer, Susan, illus. 2012. 32p. (J). 22.95 (978-0-9838846-5-1(X)) Berwick Court Publishing.

Frederick, Heather Vogel. The Black Paw. 2013. (Spy Mice Ser.: 1). (ENG., Illus.). 224p. (J). (gr. 3-6). pap. 7.99 (978-1-4424-6701-9(0), Simon & Schuster Bks. For Young Readers) Simon & Schuster Bks. For Young Readers.

—Dear Pen Pal. (Mother-Daughter Book Club Ser.). (ENG.). (J). (gr. 4-7). 2010. 432p. pap. 7.99 (978-1-4424-0848-7(0)) 2009. 416p. 16.99 (978-1-4169-7430-7(X)) Simon & Schuster Bks. For Young Readers. (Simon & Schuster Bks. For Young Readers).

—Much Ado about Anne. 2008. (Mother-Daughter Book Club Ser.). (ENG., Illus.). 336p. (J). (gr. 4-7). 15.99 (978-0-689-85566-5(4), Simon & Schuster Bks. For Young Readers) Simon & Schuster Bks. For Young Readers.

Fredericks, Mariah. Crunch Time. 2007. (ENG.). 336p. (YA). (gr. 7-12). pap. 15.99 (978-1-4169-3973-3(3), Atheneum Bks. for Young Readers) Simon & Schuster Children's Publishing.

—Life. Watkins, Liselotte, illus. 2009. (In the Cards Ser.: No. 3). (ENG.). 272p. (J). pap. 5.99 (978-0-689-87659-2(9), Simon & Schuster/Paula Wiseman Bks.) Simon & Schuster/Paula Wiseman Bks.

Fredo, Sophia E. The Girls of Oak Court: Death at Whitford Pond. 2012. 172p. (gr. 10-12). pap. 13.95 (978-1-4759-4057-2(2)) iUniverse, Inc.

Freed, Christina. Sophie's Cross. 2007. 48p. per. 16.95 (978-1-4241-7677-9(8)) America Star Bks.

Freedman, Claire. Little Bear's Special Friend. Kolanovic, Dubravka, illus. 2007. (J). (978-0-545-06757-7(X)) Scholastic, Inc.

—The Monster of the Woods! Julian, Russell, illus. 2013. (ENG.). 32p. (J). pap. (978-0-545-51571-9(8), Cartwheel Bks.) Scholastic, Inc.

Freedman, Deborah. Shy. 2016. (ENG., Illus.). 40p. (J). (-k). 17.99 (978-0-451-47496-4(1), Viking Books for Young Readers) Penguin Young Readers Group.

—The Story of Fish & Snail. 3rd ed. 2013. (ENG., Illus.). 40p. (J). (gr. -1-k). 16.99 (978-0-670-78489-9(3), Viking Books for Young Readers) Penguin Young Readers Group.

Freeman, Don. Corduroy. 2011. (Corduroy Ser.). (ENG.). 28p. (J). (gr. -1 — 1). bds. 11.99 (978-0-670-01311-1(0), Viking Books for Young Readers) Penguin Young Readers Group.

—Gregory's Shadow. Freeman, Don, illus. 2003. (Readalongs for Beginning Readers Ser.). (Illus.). (J). 25.95 incl. audio (978-1-59112-238-8(4)); pap. 37.95 incl. audio (978-1-59112-239-5(2)) Live Oak Media.

Freeman, Gayle. Football Friends. 2008. 16p. pap. 8.49 (978-1-4343-5611-6(6)) AuthorHouse.

Freeman, Martha. Campfire Cookies. 2016. (Secret Cookie Club Ser.). (ENG., Illus.). 288p. (J). (gr. 3-7). 16.99 (978-1-4814-4821-5(8), Simon & Schuster/Paula Wiseman Bks.) Simon & Schuster/Paula Wiseman Bks.

—P. S. Send More Cookies. 2017. (Secret Cookie Club Ser.). (ENG., Illus.). 336p. (J). (gr. 3-7). 16.99 **(978-1-4814-4824-6(2)**, Simon & Schuster/Paula Wiseman Bks.) Simon & Schuster/Paula Wiseman Bks.

—The Secret Cookie Club. 2015. (Secret Cookie Club Ser.). (ENG., Illus.). 304p. (J). (gr. 3-7). 16.99 (978-1-4814-1046-5(6), Simon & Schuster Bks. For Young Readers) Simon & Schuster Bks. For Young Readers.

—The Spy Wore Shades. Date not set. 160p. (YA). (gr. 3-18). pap. 4.99 (978-0-06-440957-5(0)) HarperCollins Pubs.

—1,000 Reasons Never to Kiss a Boy. 2007. (ENG.). 240p. (YA). (gr. 7-18). 16.95 (978-0-8234-2044-5(2)) Holiday Hse., Inc.

Freeman, Shannon. High School High, 1 vol. 2013. (Port City High Ser.). (ENG.). 199p. (YA). (gr. 9-12). pap. 9.95 (978-1-62250-037-6(7)) Saddleback Educational Publishing, Inc.

—High School High. 2013. (Port City High Ser.: 1). (YA). lib. bdg. 20.80 (978-0-606-31773-3(2), Turtleback) Turtleback Bks.

—Listed. 2014. (Port City High Ser.: 6). (YA). lib. bdg. 20.80 (978-0-606-36618-2(0)) Turtleback Bks.

—Taken, 1 vol. 2013. (Port City High Ser.). (ENG.). 199p. (YA). (gr. 9-12). pap. 9.95 (978-1-62250-038-3(5)) Saddleback Educational Publishing, Inc.

—Traumatized. 2014. (Port City High Ser.: 7). (YA). lib. bdg. 20.80 (978-0-606-36619-9(9)) Turtleback Bks.

Freeman, Tor. Olive & the Big Secret. Freeman, Tor, illus. 2012. (ENG., Illus.). 32p. (J). (gr. -1-3). 15.99 (978-0-7636-6149-6(X), Templar) Candlewick Pr.

—Olive & the Embarrassing Gift. Freeman, Tor, illus. 2014. (ENG., Illus.). 32p. (J). (gr. -1-3). 15.99 (978-0-7636-7406-9(0), Templar) Candlewick Pr.

Frelinghuysen Eighth Grade Storytellers Staff. Flash Before My Eyes. 2008. 52p. pap. 8.95 (978-0-595-52714-4(0)) iUniverse, Inc.

French, Joyce. The Popcorn Tree. Hansen, Paisley, illus. 2012. 22p. 15.95 (978-1-60414-639-4(7)) Fideli Publishing, Inc.

French, Renee. Barry's Best Buddy. French, Renee, illus. 2013. (ENG., Illus.). 32p. (J). (gr. -1-3). 12.95 (978-1-935179-21-4(7)) TOON Books / RAW Junior, LLC.

—The Soap Lady. French, Renee, illus. 2005. (Illus.). 111p. (J). (gr. 4-8). reprint ed. 20.00 (978-0-7567-9419-4(6)) DIANE Publishing Co.

French, S. Terrell. Operation Redwood. 2011. (ENG.). 368p. (J). (gr. 3-7). pap. 9.95 (978-0-8109-9720-2(7), Amulet Bks.) Abrams, Inc.

French, Vivian. Princess Charlotte & the Enchanted Rose. Gibb, Sarah, illus. 2007. (Tiara Club Ser.: No. 7). 80p. (J). (gr. 1-4). pap. 3.99 (978-0-06-112441-9(9), Tegen, Katherine Bks) HarperCollins Pubs.

French, Vivian & Terry, Michael. Ellie & Elvis. 2007. (Bloomsbury Paperbacks Ser.). (ENG., Illus.). 32p. (J). (gr. k-2). 9.99 (978-0-7475-8403-2(6)) Bloomsbury Publishing Plc GBR. Dist: Independent Pubs. Group.

Frick, Lisa. "Evie" the Little Jack Russell with Brown Around Her Eyes. 2009. 64p. pap. 31.99 (978-1-4415-2911-4(X)) Xlibris Corp.

Fridman, Sashi. The Doll Maker's Gift. Schiffman, Jessica, illus. 2011. 36p. 14.95 (978-0-8266-0040-0(9)) Kehot Pubn. Society.

Friedman, Becky. Daniel's New Friend. 2015. (Daniel Tiger's Neighborhood 8X8 Ser.). lib. bdg. 13.55 (978-0-606-37143-8(5)) Turtleback Bks.

—Welcome to the Neighborhood! Style Guide Staff & Garwood, Gord, illus. 2014. (Daniel Tiger's Neighborhood Ser.). (ENG.). 24p. (J). (gr. -1-1). pap. 3.99 (978-1-4424-9741-2(6), Simon Spotlight) Simon Spotlight.

—Welcome to the Neighborhood! 2014. (Daniel Tiger's Neighborhood 8X8 Ser.). lib. bdg. 13.55 (978-0-606-35458-5(1)) Turtleback Bks.

Friedman, J. S. Casablanca. Beatrice, Chris, illus. 2013. (Maurice's Valises: Moral Tails in an Immoral World Ser.: Vol. 3). (ENG.). 45p. (J). (gr. k-4). pap. (978-94-91613-09-8(X)) Mouse Prints Pr.

Friedman, Laurie. Campfire Mallory. 2009. pap. 34.95 (978-0-7613-4787-3(9)) Lerner Publishing Group.

—Campfire Mallory. Kalis, Jennifer, illus. (Mallory Ser.: 9). (ENG.). 176p. (J). (gr. 2-5). 2009. pap. 5.95 (978-1-58013-841-3(1), First Avenue Editions) 2008. lib. bdg. 15.95 (978-0-8225-7657-0(0), Carolrhoda Bks.) Lerner Publishing Group.

—Change Is in the Air, Mallory. Kalis, Jennifer, illus. 2015. (Mallory Ser.: 24). (ENG.). 160p. (J). (gr. 2-5). 15.99 (978-1-4677-8822-9(8), Darby Creek) Lerner Publishing Group.

—Happy New Year, Mallory! Kalis, Jennifer, illus. (Mallory Ser.: 12). (ENG.). 176p. (J). (gr. 2-5). 2010. pap. 5.95 (978-0-7613-3947-2(7)) 2009. 15.95 (978-0-8225-8883-2(8)) Lerner Publishing Group. (Carolrhoda Bks.).

—Happy New Year, Mallory! 12th rev. ed. 2010. pap. 33.92 (978-0-7613-6996-7(1)) Lerner Publishing Group.

—Heart to Heart with Mallory. 2008. pap. 34.95 (978-0-8225-9439-0(0)) Lerner Publishing Group.

—Heart to Heart with Mallory. Pollak, Barbara, illus. (Mallory Ser.: 6). (ENG.). 160p. (J). (gr. 2-5). 2007. per. 5.95 (978-0-8225-7133-9(1), First Avenue Editions) 2006. lib. bdg. 15.95 (978-1-57505-932-7(0), Twenty-First Century Bks.) Lerner Publishing Group.

—High Five, Mallory! Kalis, Jennifer, illus. (Mallory Ser.: Vol. 26). (ENG.). 160p. (J). 2017. (gr. 2-5). pap. 5.95 **(978-1-5124-5867-1(8))** 2016. (gr. 3-3). E-Book 11.99 (978-1-5124-0898-0(0), 9781512408980) Lerner Publishing Group. (Darby Creek).

—High Five, Mallory! Kalis, Jennifer, illus. 2016. (Mallory Ser.: 26). (ENG.). 160p. (gr. 2-5). 15.95 (978-1-4677-5030-1(1)) Lerner Publishing Group.

—Mallory & Mary Ann Take New York. Kalis, Jennifer, illus. (Mallory Ser.: 19). (ENG.). 160p. (J). (gr. 2-5). 2014. pap. 5.95 (978-1-4677-0935-4(2), Darby Creek) 2013. 15.95 (978-0-7613-6074-2(3)) Lerner Publishing Group.

—Mallory in the Spotlight. Kalis, Jennifer, illus. (Mallory Ser.). 2011. pap. 33.92 (978-0-7613-8359-8(X), Darby Creek) 2011. (ENG.). 160p. (J). (gr. 2-5). pap. 5.95 (978-0-7613-3948-9(5), Darby Creek) 2010. (ENG.). 160p. (J). (gr. 2-5). 15.95 (978-0-8225-8884-9(6), Carolrhoda Bks.) Lerner Publishing Group.

—Mallory Mcdonald, Baby Expert. Kalis, Jennifer, illus. 2015. (Mallory Ser.: Vol. 22). (ENG.). 152p. (J). (gr. 2-5). pap. 5.95 (978-1-4677-0938-5(7), Darby Creek) Lerner Publishing Group.

—Mallory on Board. 2008. pap. 34.95 (978-0-8225-9440-6(4)) Lerner Publishing Group.

—Mallory on Board. Pollak, Barbara, illus. (Mallory Ser.: 7). (ENG.). 176p. (J). (gr. 2-5). 2008. per. 5.95 (978-0-8225-9023-1(9), First Avenue Editions) 2007. 15.95 (978-0-8225-6194-1(8), Carolrhoda Bks.) Lerner Publishing Group.

—Mallory on the Move. Schmitz, Tamara, illus. 2005. (Mallory Ser.: 1). (ENG.). 160p. (J). (gr. 2-5). per. 5.95 (978-1-57505-831-3(6)) Lerner Publishing Group.

—Mallory on the Move. Schmitz, Tamara, tr. Schmitz, Tamara, illus. 2004. (Mallory Ser.: 1). (ENG.). 160p. (J). (gr. 2-5). 15.95 (978-1-57505-538-1(4)) Lerner Publishing Group.

—Mallory Se Muda. Schmitz, Tamara, illus. 2007. (Mallory en español (Mallory in Spanish) Ser.). (SPA.). 160p. (J). (gr. 4-7). per. 5.95 (978-0-8225-7493-4(4), Ediciones Lerner) Lerner Publishing Group.

—Not What I Expected. Shaloshvili, Natasha, illus. 2015. (Mostly Miserable Life of April Sinclair Ser.: 5). (ENG.). 176p. (J). (gr. 5-9). 17.99 (978-1-4677-8829-8(5), Darby Creek) Lerner Publishing Group.

—Red, White, & True Blue Mallory. Kalis, Jennifer, illus. (Mallory Ser.: 11). (ENG.). 184p. (J). (gr. 2-5). 2010. pap. 5.95 (978-0-7613-3946-5(9)) 2009. 15.95 (978-0-8225-8882-5(X)) Lerner Publishing Group. (Carolrhoda Bks.).

—Step Fourth, Mallory! Kalis, Jennifer, illus. (Mallory Ser.: 10). (ENG.). 176p. (J). (gr. 2-5). 2009. pap. 5.95 (978-1-58013-842-0(X), First Avenue Editions) 2008. 15.95 (978-0-8225-8881-8(1), Carolrhoda Bks.) Lerner Publishing Group.

—Three's Company, Mallory! Kalis, Jennifer, illus. 2014. (Mallory Ser.: 21). (ENG.). 160p. (J). (gr. 2-5). 15.95 (978-1-4677-0921-7(2), Darby Creek) Lerner Publishing Group.

—Too Good to Be True. 2014. (Mostly Miserable Life of April Sinclair Ser.: 2). (ENG., Illus.). 168p. (J). (gr. 5-9). 17.95 (978-1-4677-0926-2(3), Darby Creek) Lerner Publishing Group.

—Too Much Drama. Shaloshvili, Natasha, illus. 2016. (Mostly Miserable Life of April Sinclair Ser.: 6). (ENG.). 184p. (gr. 5-9). (J). 17.95 (978-1-4677-8589-1(X)); 35.99 (978-1-4677-9570-8(4)) Lerner Publishing Group. (Darby Creek).

Friedman, Laurie B. Change Is in the Air, Mallory. Kalis, Jennifer, illus. 2015. (ENG.). 160p. (J). (gr. 2-5). 15.95 (978-1-4677-0924-8(7)) Lerner Publishing Group.

—Game Time, Mallory! Kalis, Jennifer, illus. 2015. (J). 15.99 (978-1-4677-6188-8(5)) Lerner Publishing Group.

—Love or Something Like It. 2015. (J). 5.99 (978-1-4677-7790-2(0)); (Mostly Miserable Life of April Sinclair Ser.: 4). (ENG.). 184p. (gr. 5-9). 17.95 (978-1-4677-0928-6(X)) Lerner Publishing Group.

—Mallory McDonald, Baby Expert. Kalis, Jennifer, illus. 2014. (Mallory Ser.: 22). (ENG.). 152p. (J). (gr. 2-5). 15.95 (978-1-4677-0922-4(0)) Lerner Publishing Group.

—Not What I Expected. Shaloshvili, Natasha, illus. 2015. (ENG.). 176p. (J). (gr. 5-9). 17.95 (978-1-4677-8588-4(1)) Lerner Publishing Group.

—Truth & Kisses. 2014. (Mostly Miserable Life of April Sinclair Ser.: 3). (ENG.). 168p. (J). (gr. 5-9). 17.95 (978-1-4677-0927-9(1)) Lerner Publishing Group.

Friedman, Michelle. Close Your Eyes. 2013. (Illus.). 32p. 25.95 (978-1-4582-1217-7(3), Abbott Pr.) Author Solutions, Inc.

Friedrich, Joachim. The Disappearing Bio Teacher. Date not set. (Illus.). 144p. (J). (gr. 3-7). 14.99 (978-0-7868-0700-0(8)) Hyperion Pr.

Friel, Maeve. Charlie's Story, 1 vol. 2004. (ENG.). 112p. (YA). (gr. 7-9). pap. 6.95 (978-1-56145-315-3(3)) Peachtree Pubs.

Friend, Alison. Freddy & Frito & the Clubhouse Rules. Friend, Alison, illus. 2015. (ENG., Illus.). 40p. (J). (gr. -1-3). 17.99 (978-0-06-228580-5(7)) HarperCollins Pubs.

Friend, Larry. Icy the Iceberg. Makis, Sidney, illus. 2008. 28p. pap. 13.95 (978-1-4327-3777-1(5)) Outskirts Pr., Inc.

Friend, Natasha. My Life in Black & White. 2012. (ENG.). 304p. (YA). (gr. 7-18). pap. 8.99 (978-0-670-78494-3(X), Viking Books for Young Readers) Penguin Young Readers Group.

—Perfect. 2004. (ENG.). 232p. (J). pap. 7.95 (978-1-57131-651-6(5)) Milkweed Editions.

A Friend with No Name. 2006. (ENG., Illus.). 28p. per. 11.95 (978-1-59800-476-2(X)) Outskirts Pr., Inc.

Friends. 2008. (YA). pap. 15.00 (978-0-9797521-1-7(6)) Ta-La-Vue Pub.

Friends & Heroes Activity & Coloring Book. 2008. (Friends & Heroes Ser.). (J). pap. (978-1-4143-2157-8(0), Tyndale Entertainment) Tyndale Hse. Pubs.

Friends Forever: Adventures. 2003. per. 12.95 net. (978-1-891929-96-0(8)) Four Seasons Pubs.

Friesen, Gayle. For Now. 2007. (ENG.). 248p. (J). (gr. 5-9). 7.95 (978-1-55453-133-2(0)) Kids Can Pr., Ltd. CAN. Dist: Hachette Bk. Group.

—The Isabel Factor. 2005. (ENG., Illus.). 256p. (J). (gr. 7-9). 7.95 (978-1-55337-738-2(9)) Kids Can Pr., Ltd. CAN. Dist: Hachette Bk. Group.

Fripp, Deborah & Fripp, Michael. Naya & Nathan. Fripp, Jean, ed. Barber, Carol, illus. 2003. (Dolphin Watch Ser.). 32p. (J). (gr. k-4). pap. 5.99 (978-0-9701008-4-9(1)) Bicast, Inc.

Frith, Nicholas John. Hector & Hummingbird. Frith, Nicholas John, illus. 2016. (ENG., Illus.). 32p. (J). (gr. -1-3). 17.99 (978-0-545-85701-7(5)) Scholastic, Inc.

—Hello, Mr. Dodo! 2017. (ENG.). 32p. (J). (gr. -1-3). 17.99 (978-1-338-08939-4(0)) Scholastic, Inc.

Froeb, Lori. A Sister's Love: Storybook & Necklace. 2016. (ENG.). 32p. (J). (gr. -1-k). 14.99 (978-0-7944-3574-5(2), Reader's Digest Children's Bks.) Studio Fun International.

From zero to Hero. 2007. (J). bds. 14.95 (978-0-9793882-1-7(X)) Over The Rainbow Bks. Publishing.

Frost, Helen. Crossing Stones. 2009. (ENG., Illus.). 192p. (YA). (gr. 7-18). 18.99 (978-0-374-31653-2(8), 9780374316532, Farrar, Straus & Giroux (BYR)) Farrar, Straus & Giroux.

—Salt: A Story of Friendship in a Time of War. 2013. (ENG.). 160p. (J). (gr. 5-9). 17.99 (978-0-374-36387-1(0), 9780374363871, Farrar, Straus & Giroux (BYR)) Farrar, Straus & Giroux.

Frosting & Friendship. 2014. (ENG., Illus.). 240p. (J). (gr. 3-7). pap. 6.99 (978-1-4424-7397-3(5), Aladdin) Simon & Schuster Children's Publishing.

Fruchter, Jason, illus. Daniel Feels Left Out. 2015. (Daniel Tiger's Neighborhood Ser.). (ENG.). 32p. (J). (gr. -1-k). 16.99 (978-1-4814-3836-0(0), Simon Spotlight) Simon Spotlight.

—Daniel Gets Scared. 2015. (Daniel Tiger's Neighborhood Ser.). (ENG.). 32p. (J). (gr. -1-k). pap. 3.99 (978-1-4814-5257-1(6), Simon Spotlight) Simon Spotlight.

—Daniel's New Friend. 2015. (Daniel Tiger's Neighborhood Ser.). (ENG.). 24p. (J). (gr. -1-2). pap. 3.99 (978-1-4814-3543-7(4), Simon Spotlight) Simon Spotlight.

—Friends Help Each Other. 2014. (Daniel Tiger's Neighborhood Ser.). (ENG.). 32p. (J). (gr. -1-k). pap. 3.99 (978-1-4814-0366-5(4), Simon Spotlight) Simon Spotlight.

—Happy Love Day, Daniel Tiger! 2015. (Daniel Tiger's Neighborhood Ser.). (ENG.). 14p. (J). (gr. -1-2). bds. 6.99 (978-1-4814-4855-0(2), Simon Spotlight) Simon Spotlight.

Fry, Erin. Secrets of the Book, 0 vols. 2014. (ENG.). 304p. (YA). (gr. 7-9). 14.99 (978-1-4778-4716-9(2), 9781477847169, Two Lions) Amazon Publishing.

Fryer, Samantha. A Sorcerer's Tale. 2008. 116p. pap. 14.95 (978-1-84799-366-3(4)) Lulu Pr., Inc.

Fuchs, Menucha. Chatzkel, Mendel & Me: An adventure Story. Daykin, Rachmiel, tr. from HEB. Hechtkopf, H., illus. 2005. Orig. Title: Mah Shekarah Ba'Ayarah. 192p. (J). 15.95 (978-1-932443-39-4(8), CHMH) Judaica Pr., Inc., The.

—The Flying Invitation. 2004. (Menucha V'Simcha Ser.). (Illus.). 20p. (J). 6.95 (978-1-932443-07-3(X), FLIH) Judaica Pr., Inc., The.

—The Most Beautiful Picture in the World. 2004. (Menucha V'Simcha Ser.). (Illus.). 20p. (J). 6.95 (978-1-932443-09-7(6)) Judaica Pr., Inc., The.

Fuchs, Michael. Keniff & Kieff. 2013. 28p. pap. 13.95 (978-1-4908-0002-8(6), WestBow Pr.) Author Solutions, Inc.

Fuchs-Rice, Dwayne. Shades of Ember. 2008. 456p. pap. 24.95 (978-0-595-53315-2(9)) iUniverse, Inc.

—Troika. 2007. 248p. per. 16.95 (978-0-595-45834-9(3)) iUniverse, Inc.

Fucile, Tony. Let's Do Nothing! Fucile, Tony, illus. 2012. (ENG., Illus.). 40p. (J). (gr. -1-3). pap. 6.99 (978-0-7636-5269-2(5)) Candlewick Pr.

Fujikawa, Brian. The Adventures of Bibole, Ri: The CURSE of the WEREMOUSE. 2012. 52p. pap. 18.41 (978-1-4669-3547-1(2)) Trafford Publishing.

Fulcomer, Betty. My Friend Kate Is a Forest Ranger, 1 vol. 2010. 34p. 24.95 (978-1-4489-4764-5(2)) America Star Bks.

Fuller, Dawn. Looper: Bullying. 2012. 32p. pap. 14.51 (978-1-4669-1989-1(2)) Trafford Publishing.

Fulton-Vengco, Aletha. Felicidad & Her Pen Pal Kamar. 2009. 33p. 13.90 (978-0-578-02728-9(3)) Vengco, Aletha Fulton.

Funk, Josh. Dear Dragon: A Pen Pal Tale. Montalvo, Rodolfo, illus. 2016. (ENG.). 40p. (J). (gr. -1-3). 16.99 (978-0-451-47230-4(6), Viking Books for Young Readers) Penguin Young Readers Group.

—Lady Pancake & Sir French Toast. Kearney, Brendan, illus. 2015. (Lady Pancake & Sir French Toast Ser.). (ENG.). 40p. (J). (gr. k). 14.95 (978-1-4549-1404-4(1), 1394148) Sterling Publishing Co., Inc.

Funk, Michele Housholder. The Adventures of Pete & Max: And the Lost Sock. 2011. (Illus.). 36p. pap. 16.86 (978-1-4567-3724-5(4)) AuthorHouse.

Funke, Cornelia. Ghost Knight. 2013.Tr. of Geisterritter. (ENG., Illus.). 352p. (J). (gr. 3-7). pap. 7.99 (978-0-316-05616-8(2)) Little, Brown Bks. for Young Readers.

Furman, Necah Stewart & Huff, Bailey. Lucy Swan's Circle. Clay, Joshua, illus. 2005. (Friends of Fairlane Woods Ser.). (ENG.). 40p. (J). (gr. -1-3). per. 16.99 (978-1-4134-8666-7(5)) Xlibris Corp.

Fusek Peters, Andrew. The Ant & the Big Bad Bully Goat. Wadham, Anna, illus. 2010. (Traditional Tales with a Twist Ser.). (ENG.). 32p. (J). (gr. -1-2). audio compact disk (978-1-84643-348-1(7)) Child's Play International Ltd.

Fuson, Robin Densmore. Rosita Valdez: And the Giant Sea Turtle. 2012. 108p. 28.99 (978-1-4497-6487-6(8)); pap. 11.99 (978-1-4497-6486-9(X)) Author Solutions, Inc. (WestBow Pr.).

Gaber, Susan, illus. The Little Red Hen: An Old Fable. 2015. (ENG.). 32p. (J). (gr. -1-3). pap. 8.95 (978-1-939160-97-3(9)) August Hse. Pubs., Inc.

Gabriel, Elizabeth P. & Gabriel, Pamela P. Ziccah Blows Her Horn. 2008. 24p. pap. 12.99 (978-1-4389-2447-2(X)) AuthorHouse.

Gág, Wanda. Snippy & Snappy. 2003. (Fesler-Lampert Minnesota Heritage Ser.). (Illus.). 48p. (gr. k-3). 14.95 (978-0-8166-4245-8(1)) Univ. of Minnesota Pr.

Gagnon, Mary. Are Those Your Shoes? 2008. 120p. pap. 11.95 (978-1-4357-2942-1(0)) Lulu Pr., Inc.

Gail, Cornelia. Juvey. 2015. 153p. (YA). per. 14.95 (978-0-9674454-4-1(2)) Girls In Da Game Publishing.

Gaines, Isabel & Milne, A. A. Pooh's Leaf Pile. Rigol, Francesc, illus. 2012. (J). (978-1-4351-4190-2(3)) Disney Pr.

Galante, Cecilia. Stealing Our Way Home. 2017. (ENG.). 304p. (J). (gr. 3-7). 17.99 **(978-1-338-04296-2(3)**, Scholastic Pr.) Scholastic, Inc.

Galante, Cecilia. Willowood. 2011. (ENG.). 288p. (J). (gr. 4-8). pap. 6.99 (978-1-4169-8303-3(1), Aladdin) Simon & Schuster Children's Publishing.

—Willowood. 2010. (ENG.). 272p. (J). (gr. 4-8). 16.99 (978-1-4169-8022-3(9), Simon & Schuster/Paula Wiseman Bks.) Simon & Schuster/Paula Wiseman Bks.

Galardi Mlis, Judith A. Judi Galardi's Thrae Back Atcha! 2011. 128p. (gr. -1). pap. 16.49 (978-1-4567-2388-0(X)) AuthorHouse.

Galbraith, Julie. Stable Ground: The Riding Series #1. 2013. 136p. pap. (978-1-927794-05-0(6)) Lechner Syndications.

Galbraith, Kathryn O. Two Bunny Buddies. Cepeda, Joe, illus. 2014. (ENG.). 32p. (J). (gr. -1-3). 16.99 (978-0-544-17652-2(9), HMH Books For Young Readers) Houghton Mifflin Harcourt Publishing Co.

Galdone, Paul. The Little Red Hen, 1 vol. 2006. (Paul Galdone Classics Ser.). (ENG., Illus.). 48p. (J). (gr. -1-3). audio compact disk 10.99 (978-0-618-75250-8(1)) Houghton Mifflin Harcourt Publishing Co.

Gale, Emily. Girl Out Loud. 2012. (YA). (978-0-545-30439-9(3)); (ENG.). 288p. (J). (gr. 7-7). 17.99 (978-0-545-30438-2(5)) Scholastic, Inc. (Chicken Hse., The).

Galer, Jeffrey & Galer, Christa. The Big Red Barn. Galer, Jeffrey, illus. 2003. (Illus.). 40p. (J). 11.49 (978-0-9706491-0-2(X)) Purple Crayon Studios.

Galing, Ed. Tony. Stead, Erin E., illus. 2017. (ENG.). 32p. (J). 16.99 (978-1-62672-308-5(7), 9781626723085) Roaring Brook Pr.

Gallagher, Brian. Stormclouds: New Friends. Old Differences. 2014. (ENG.). 224p. (J). 13.95 (978-1-84717-579-3(1)) O'Brien Pr., Ltd., The IRL. Dist: Dufour Editions, Inc.

Gallagher, Diana G. Advice about Friends: Claudia Cristina Cortez Uncomplicates Your Life. Garvey, Brann, illus. 2010. (Claudia Cristina Cortez Ser.). (ENG.). 80p. (gr. 2-3). pap. 6.10 (978-1-4342-2251-0(9), Claudia Cristina Cortez) Stone Arch Bks.

—The Doggone Dog, 1 vol. Juarez, Adriana & Puglisi, Adriana, illus. 2013. (Pet Friends Forever Ser.). (ENG.). 88p. (gr. 1-3). pap. 5.95 (978-1-4795-1865-4(4)); lib. bdg. 25.32 (978-1-4048-7502-9(6)) Picture Window Bks.

—The Great Kitten Challenge, 1 vol. Juarez, Adriana & Puglisi, Adriana, illus. 2013. (Pet Friends Forever Ser.). (ENG.). 88p. (gr. 1-3). pap. 5.95 (978-1-4795-1864-7(6)); lib. bdg. 25.32 (978-1-4048-7501-2(8)) Picture Window Bks.

—Haunted Love, 1 vol. (Claudia & Monica: Freshman Girls Ser.). (ENG.). 144p. (gr. 3-6). 2013. 9.95 (978-1-4342-6286-8(3)) 2012. lib. bdg. 26.65 (978-1-4342-3277-9(8)) Stone Arch Bks. (Claudia & Monica: Freshman Girls).

—Homecoming, 1 vol. 2012. (Claudia & Monica: Freshman Girls Ser.). (ENG.). 144p. (gr. 3-6). lib. bdg. 26.65 (978-1-4342-3276-2(X), Claudia & Monica: Freshman Girls) Stone Arch Bks.

—Mice Capades, 1 vol. Juarez, Adriana & Puglisi, Adriana, illus. 2013. (Pet Friends Forever Ser.). (ENG.). 88p. (gr. 1-3). pap. 5.95 (978-1-4795-1863-0(8)); lib. bdg. 25.32 (978-1-4048-7500-5(X)) Picture Window Bks.

—Monica & the Sweetest Song, 1 vol. 2011. (Monica Ser.). (ENG.). 88p. (gr. 2-3). lib. bdg. 26.65 (978-1-4342-2556-6(9)) Stone Arch Bks.

—New Firsts, 1 vol. 2012. (Claudia & Monica: Freshman Girls Ser.). (ENG.). 144p. (gr. 3-6). lib. bdg. 26.65 (978-1-4342-3275-5(1), Claudia & Monica: Freshman Girls) Stone Arch Bks.

—A No-Sneeze Pet, 1 vol. Juarez, Adriana & Puglisi, Adriana, illus. 2013. (Pet Friends Forever Ser.). (ENG.). 88p. (gr. 1-3). pap. 5.95 (978-1-4795-1862-3(X)); lib. bdg. 25.32 (978-1-4048-7499-2(2)) Picture Window Bks.

—Pet Friends Forever, 1 vol. (Pet Friends Forever Ser.). (ENG.). 88p. (gr. 1-3). 2014. 151.92 (978-1-4795-4433-2(7)) 2013. 101.28 (978-1-4795-2066-4(7)) 2013. pap. 23.80 (978-1-4795-1866-1(2)) Picture Window Bks.

—Tested, 1 vol. 2012. (Claudia & Monica: Freshman Girls Ser.). (ENG.). 144p. (gr. 3-6). lib. bdg. 26.65 (978-1-4342-3278-6(6), Claudia & Monica: Freshman Girls) Stone Arch Bks.

—Whatever! The Complicated Life of Claudia Cristina Cortez, 1 vol. Garvey, Brann, illus. 2007. (Claudia Cristina Cortez Ser.). (ENG.). 88p. (gr. 2-3). pap. 6.10 (978-1-59889-880-4(9)); lib. bdg. 26.65 (978-1-59889-839-2(6)) Stone Arch Bks. (Claudia Cristina Cortez).

Gallagher, Mary. The Legend of Lisnashee. 2006. (ENG., Illus.). 100p. (J). pap. 10.95 (978-1-903464-71-7(4)) Collins Pr., The IRL. Dist: Dufour Editions, Inc.

Gallagher, Mary Collins. Ginny Morris & Dads New Girlfriend. Martin, Whitney, illus. 2006. (Ginny Morris Ser.). 63p. (J). (gr. 3-7). 14.95 (978-1-59147-386-2(1)); per. 9.95 (978-1-59147-387-9(X)) American Psychological Assn. (Magination Pr.).

Gallant, Mark D. Christmas at Wildwood Farm. 2010. 140p. 22.49 (978-1-4520-2808-8(7)); pap. 11.99 (978-1-4520-2807-1(9)) AuthorHouse.

Gallego García, Laura. Retorno a la Isla Blanca. 2004. 143p. pap. 14.00 (978-84-931888-6-3(7)) Editorial Brief ESP. Dist: Independent Pubs. Group.

Gallego García, Laura & Peden, Margaret Sayers. The Valley of the Wolves. 2006. 247p. (J). pap. (978-0-439-58554-5(6), Levine, Arthur A. Bks.) Scholastic, Inc.

Gallemore, M. H. Annie & the Mermaid. 2005. 9.00 (978-0-8059-9787-3(3)) Dorrance Publishing Co., Inc.

Gallivan, Susan. The Return of Mr Jeffries. 2009. 88p. pap. 10.49 (978-1-4389-4183-7(8)) AuthorHouse.

Gallo, Tina, adapted by. Kung Fu Road Trip. 2014. (Kung Fu Panda TV Ser.). (ENG., Illus.). 32p. (J). (gr. k-2). 16.99 (978-1-4814-0489-1(X), Simon Spotlight) Simon Spotlight.

Galloway, Ruth. Clumsy Crab. Galloway, Ruth, illus. 2005. (Illus.). 32p. (J). (gr. -1-2). 15.95 (978-1-58925-050-5(8)) Tiger Tales.

Galveston, Louise. In Todd We Trust. 2015. (ENG., Illus.). 256p. (J). (gr. 3-7). 16.99 (978-1-59514-679-3(2), Razorbill) Penguin Young Readers Group.

Galvin, Laura. Pooh & Friends Colors & Shapes. 2008. (ENG.). 24p. (J). (gr. -1). 4.99 (978-1-59069-736-8(7)) Studio Mouse LLC.

Galvin, Laura Gates. Baby Lamb Finds a Friend. 2007. (ENG., Illus.). 16p. (gr. -1-k). 6.95 (978-1-59249-746-1(2)) Soundprints.

—Baby Pig Time to Play. 2008. (ENG., Illus.). 16p. (J). (gr. -1-k). 6.95 (978-1-59249-787-4(X)) Soundprints.

—Handy Manny: 1,2,3 Amigos. Parisi, Anthony, ed. 2011. (Learning Library). (ENG., Illus.). 24p. (gr. -1-k). 8.99 (978-1-60727-268-7(7)) Studio Mouse LLC.

—Handy Manny Counting on Friends. 2008. (ENG.). 32p. (J). (gr. -1-3). 4.99 (978-1-59069-735-1(9)) Studio Mouse LLC.

—Mickey Mouse Clubhouse Teamwork: Let's Do It Together. 2008. (ENG.). 40p. (J). (gr. -1). 12.99 (978-1-59069-738-2(3)) Studio Mouse LLC.

—Princess Counting Fun. Parisi, Anthony, ed. 2011. (Learning Library). (ENG., Illus.). 24p. (gr. -1). 8.99 (978-1-60727-265-6(2)) Studio Mouse LLC.

Galvin, Laura Gates & Studio Mouse Staff. Best Friends. rev. ed. 2006. (ENG., Illus.). 20p. (J). (gr. -1-3). 14.99 (978-1-59069-477-0(5)) Studio Mouse LLC.

GAMAGO. GAMAGO Yeti & Friends Place Mats. 2013. (ENG.). 96p. (J). (gr. -1-4). 12.99 (978-1-4521-1159-9(6)) Chronicle Bks. LLC.

—GAMAGO Yeti & Friends Puzzle. 2013. (ENG., Illus.). 16p. (J). (gr. -1 — 1). 14.99 (978-1-4521-1160-5(X)) Chronicle Bks. LLC.

Gambini, Josephine. Poetino Piccolino Saves the Day. Stafford, Jordan, illus. 2011. (ENG.). (J). pap. 19.95 (978-0-9829496-3-4(4)) Giusti-Gambini, J.M. Publishing, LLC.

Game On. 13th ed. 2009. (ENG.). 128p. (J). pap. 4.99 (978-1-4231-0972-3(4)) Disney Pr.

Gammon, Bob. Orange Polar Bears Don't Cry. 2008. 36p. pap. 18.50 (978-1-60693-393-0(0), Eloquent Bks.) Strategic Book Publishing & Rights Agency (SBPRA).

Gandy, Deborah A. A Squeaky Little Mouse Named Rainbow. 2011. 44p. pap. 21.99 (978-1-4568-7546-6(9)) Xlibris Corp.

Gannon, Nicholas. The Doldrums. 368p. (J). (gr. 3-7). 2017. pap. 7.99 **(978-0-06-232095-7(5))** 2015. (ENG., Illus.). 17.99 (978-0-06-232094-0(7)) HarperCollins Pubs. (Greenwillow Bks.).

Gansworth, Eric L. If I Ever Get Out of Here. (ENG.). 368p. (J). (gr. 7). 2015. pap. 10.99 (978-0-545-41731-0(7)) 2013. 17.99 (978-0-545-41730-3(9)) Scholastic, Inc. (Levine, Arthur A. Bks.).

Gant, Gene. The Battle for Jericho [Library Edition]. 2013. 240p. pap. 14.99 (978-1-62380-917-1(7), Harmony Ink Pr.) Dreamspinner Pr.

—The Thunder in His Head [Library Edition]. 2012. 200p. (-18). pap. 14.99 (978-1-62380-903-4(7), Harmony Ink Pr.) Dreamspinner Pr.

Gantos, Jack. The Follower. 2015. (ENG.). 224p. (YA). (gr. 7-10). 17.99 (978-0-374-37995-7(5), 9780374379957, Farrar, Straus & Giroux (BYR)) Farrar, Straus & Giroux.

—From Norvelt to Nowhere. 2015. (J). lib. bdg. 18.40 (978-0-606-37280-0(6)) Turtleback Bks.

Ganz, Yaffa. Raise a Rabbit, Grow a Goose. Klineman, Harvey, illus. 2008. 30p. 14.99 (978-1-59826-235-3(1)) Feldheim Pubs.

Ganzer, Diane & St. Croix, Sammy. Adventures of a Kitten Named Raspberry & Other Tales. 2009. 176p. pap. 9.95 (978-1-935105-30-5(2)) Avid Readers Publishing Group.

Garant, Andre J. Jake's Tree House. 2010. 128p. pap. 10.99 (978-1-4490-8369-4(2)) AuthorHouse.

García, Cristina. Dreams of Significant Girls. 2011. (ENG.). 256p. (YA). (gr. 9-18). 16.99 (978-1-4169-7920-3(4), Simon & Schuster Bks. For Young Readers) Simon & Schuster Bks. For Young Readers.

Garcia, Cristina. Dreams of Significant Girls. 2012. (ENG.). 256p. (J). (gr. 9). pap. 8.99 (978-1-4169-7930-2(1), Simon & Schuster Bks. For Young Readers) Simon & Schuster Bks. For Young Readers.

Garcia, Kami & Stohl, Margaret. Beautiful Redemption. 2013. (Beautiful Creatures Ser.: 4). (YA). lib. bdg. 24.50 (978-0-606-32282-9(5), Turtleback) Turtleback Bks.

Garcia, Katherine. Jojo & the Tule Tree. 2013. 20p. pap. 9.95 (978-1-935752-39-4(1)) Bryce Cullen Publishing.

García, Nasario. Grandpa Lolo's Navajo Saddle Blanket: La Tilma de Abuelito Lolo. Moeller, Richard, illus. Moeller, Richard, photos by. 2012. (J). (978-0-8263-5078-7(X)); 61p. pap. (978-0-8263-5080-0(1)); (SPA.). 72p. pap. (978-0-8263-5079-4(8)) Univ. of New Mexico Pr.

Garcia, Norma Lee. A Day with Smiles. 2012. 28p. pap. 24.95 (978-1-4626-8823-4(3)) America Star Bks.

Gard, Don. The Adventures of Beezer. Giancanelli, Candace, illus. 2006. 100p. per. 12.95 (978-1-59858-157-7(0)) Dog Ear Publishing, LLC.

Gardam, Jane. The Hollow Land. 2015. (ENG.). 160p. (gr. 12). pap. 15.00 (978-1-60945-246-9(1)) Europa Editions, Inc.

Gardener, Amanda & Sealey, Nanlie. Freddy the White Flamingo. 2013. 28p. pap. 12.99 (978-1-60820-900-2(8)) MLR Pr., LLC.

Gardner, Alecia. Peachy Penelope. 2010. 44p. pap. 19.99 (978-1-4490-0419-4(9)) AuthorHouse.

Gardner, Graham. The Santa Beacon. LeBlanc, Nancy, illus. 2012. 40p. (J). 19.95 (978-0-9859358-0-1(4), Belle Isle Bks.) Brandylane Pubs., Inc.

Gardner, Sally. Maggot Moon. Crouch, Julian, illus. (ENG.). 288p. (YA). (gr. 7). 2014. pap. 8.99 (978-0-7636-7169-3(X)) 2013. 16.99 (978-0-7636-6553-1(3)) Candlewick Pr.

Gardner, Whitney. You're Welcome, Universe. 2017. (ENG., Illus.). 304p. (YA). (gr. 7). 17.99 (978-0-399-55141-3(7), Knopf Bks. for Young Readers) Random Hse. Children's Bks.

Garfield, Leon. The Complete Bostock & Harris. 2014. (ENG.). 336p. (J). (gr. 3-7). 17.95 (978-1-59017-783-9(5), NYR Children's Collection) New York Review of Bks., Inc., The.

Garis, Howard R. The Curlytops & Their Playmates. 2009. 120p. 22.95 (978-1-60664-610-6(9)); pap. 10.95 (978-1-60664-342-6(8)) Rodgers, Alan Bks.

—Uncle Wiggily & Old Mother Hubbard. 2008. 116p. 22.95 (978-1-60664-970-1(1)) Aegypan.

Garis, Howard Roger. Uncle Wiggily's Travels. 2005. 26.95 (978-1-4218-1469-8(2)); 164p. pap. 11.95 (978-1-4218-1569-5(9)) 1st World Publishing, Inc. (1st World Library - Literary Society).

Garland, Michael. Big & Little: A Story of Two Friends. 2017. (ENG., Illus.). 32p. (J). (gr. -1-k). 14.99 (978-0-545-87097-9(6)) Scholastic, Inc.

Garland, Sarah, illus. Eddie's Toolbox: And How to Make & Mend Things. 2011. (ENG.). 40p. (J). (gr. -1-2). (978-1-84780-053-4(X)) Rough Guides, Ltd.

Garlick, Nicholas. Storm Horse. 2017. (J). pap. **(978-0-545-90415-5(3))** Scholastic, Inc.

Garralon, Claire. Black Cat & White Cat. 2016. (ENG.). 30p. (J). bds. 7.99 (978-1-4926-3781-3(5), 9781492637813, Sourcebooks Jabberwocky) Sourcebooks, Inc.

Garratt, Irene Joyce. Andrew's Activities: Two in One Stories. 2009. (Illus.). 20p. pap. 10.49 (978-1-4389-4235-3(4)) AuthorHouse.

Garrett, Christine. Dream Bunny's Tales - Saving the Land of Dreams. 2009. (Illus.). 48p. pap. 13.95 (978-1-60860-451-7(9), Eloquent Bks.) Strategic Book Publishing & Rights Agency (SBPRA).

Garrett, Kelly. The Last to Die. 2017. (ENG.). (YA). pap. 10.95 (978-1-929345-30-4(5)) Poisoned Pen Pr.

Garton, Carol. Isabella Barella. 2013. (ENG.). 300p. (YA). 32.95 (978-1-4787-1339-5(9)); pap. 17.95 (978-1-4787-1490-3(5)) Outskirts Pr., Inc.

Garton, Sam. I Am Otter. Garton, Sam, illus. 2014. (ENG., Illus.). 32p. (J). (gr. -1-3). 16.99 (978-0-06-224775-9(1)) HarperCollins Pubs.

—Otter Goes to School. Garton, Sam, illus. 2016. (Illus.). 32p. (J). (gr. -1-3). 17.99 (978-0-06-235225-5(3)) HarperCollins Pubs.

—Otter: Hello, Sea Friends! Garton, Sam, illus. 2016. (My First I Can Read Ser.). (Illus.). 32p. (J). (gr. -1-3). pap. 3.99 (978-0-06-236660-3(2)) HarperCollins Pubs.

—Otter in Space. Garton, Sam, illus. 2015. (ENG., Illus.). 32p. (J). (gr. -1-3). 16.99 (978-0-06-224776-6(X)) HarperCollins Pubs.

—Otter Loves Halloween! Garton, Sam, illus. 2015. (ENG., Illus.). 32p. (J). (gr. -1-3). 9.99 (978-0-06-236666-5(1), Balzer & Bray) HarperCollins Pubs.

—Otter: Oh No, Bath Time! Garton, Sam, illus. 2016. (My First I Can Read Ser.). (Illus.). 32p. (J). (gr. -1-3). pap. 3.99 (978-0-06-236657-3(2)) HarperCollins Pubs.

—Otter: the Best Job Ever! Garton, Sam, illus. 2016. (My First I Can Read Ser.). (Illus.). 32p. (J). (gr. -1-3). pap. 3.99 (978-0-06-236654-2(8)) HarperCollins Pubs.

Gasior, Julie. Samy the Star. 2008. 46p. 27.95 (978-0-615-18884-3(2)) Gasior, Julie.

Gassman, Julie A. Skating Is Hard When You're Homesick, 1 vol. Santillan, Jorge H., illus. 2011. (Sports Illustrated Kids Victory School Superstars Ser.). (ENG.). 56p. (gr. 1-3). pap. 5.95 (978-1-4342-3398-1(7)); lib. bdg. 26.65 (978-1-4342-2237-4(3)) Stone Arch Bks.

Gaston, Sharon D. Clean Your Own House & Misery Loves Company. 2009. 40p. pap. 18.50 (978-1-4389-7831-4(6)) AuthorHouse.

—Who's Laughing Now? & Don't Burn Your Bridge. 2009. 48p. pap. 19.50 (978-1-4389-7832-1(4)) AuthorHouse.

Gaudet, M. K. Marley to the Rescue! 2008. (Marley: I Can Read! Ser.). (Illus.). 32p. (J). (gr. -1-3). lib. bdg. 13.55 (978-1-4178-2918-7(4), Turtleback) Turtleback Bks.

Gaughen, A. C. Scarlet. 2013. (Scarlet Ser.: 1). (ENG.). 304p. (YA). (gr. 7-12). pap. 9.99 (978-0-8027-3424-2(3), 9780802734242, Bloomsbury USA Childrens) Bloomsbury Publishing USA.

Gausselin, Richard J. How the Grandmas & Grandpas Saved Christmas. 2012. 24p. pap. 17.99 (978-1-4772-4771-6(8)) AuthorHouse.

Gavagan, Cinda J. The Old Haunted House. 2011. 56p. pap. 16.95 (978-1-4560-8301-4(5)) PublishAmerica, Inc.

Gaven, Jim. Friends Find Fun for Food: All about Alliterations. 2013. 28p. pap. 24.95 (978-1-63000-140-7(6)) America Star Bks.

Gavin, Ciara. Bear Is Not Tired. 2016. (ENG., Illus.). 32p. (J). (gr. -1-2). 16.99 (978-0-385-75476-7(0), Knopf Bks. for Young Readers) Random Hse. Children's Bks.

Gay, Francis. The Friendship Book. 2005. (Illus.). 180p. 9.95 (978-1-84535-050-5(2)) Thomson, D.C. & Co., Ltd. GBR. Dist: APG Sales & Distribution Services.

—Friendship Book 2004. D C Thomson Staff, ed. 2004. (Illus.). 108p. 9.95 (978-0-85116-834-0(5)) Thomson, D.C. & Co., Ltd. GBR. Dist: APG Sales & Distribution Services.

Geiger, Eileen. The Adventures of Christina Crankypants. 2010. (ENG.). 80p. pap. 16.95 (978-1-4452-3771-8(7)) Lulu Pr., Inc.

Geiger, Kay. Treasure. 2010. 36p. pap. 19.95 (978-1-4457-6383-5(4)) Lulu Pr., Inc.

Gellman, Ellie B. Tamar's Sukkah. Kahn, Katherine Janus, illus. rev. ed. 2015. (ENG.). 32p. (J). (gr. -1-2). pap. 7.99 (978-1-4677-5637-2(7)); lib. bdg. 17.99 (978-1-4677-5636-5(9)) Lerner Publishing Group. (Kar-Ben Publishing).

—Tamar's Sukkah (Revised Edition) Kahn, Katherine Janus, illus. 2015. (ENG.). 32p. (J). (gr. -1-2). 6.99 (978-1-4677-8845-8(7), Kar-Ben Publishing) Lerner Publishing Group.

Gemeinhart, Dan. The Honest Truth. 2015. (ENG.). 240p. (J). (gr. 3-7). 16.99 (978-0-545-66573-5(6), Scholastic Pr.) Scholastic, Inc.

—The Honest Truth. 2015. (ENG.). 240p. (J). (gr. 3-7). lib. bdg. 17.20 (978-0-606-38060-7(4)) Turtleback Bks.

Gemmell, N. J. Coco Banjo Has Been Unfriended. 2016. (Coco Banjo Ser.: 2). (ENG.). 192p. (J). (gr. 1-3). pap. 9.99 (978-0-85798-735-8(6)) Random Hse. Australia AUS. Dist: Independent Pubs. Group.

Gendreau, Paula. The Adventures of Lilly Lou: The First Day at Camp Who Who. 2009. 16p. pap. 8.49 (978-1-4389-5950-4(8)) AuthorHouse.

Genhart, Michael. Cake & I Scream! ... Being Bossy Isn't Sweet. Mack, Steve, illus. 2017. (J). **(978-1-4338-2759-4(X)**, Magination Pr.) American Psychological Assn.

—Mac & Geeeez! ...being Real Is What It's All About. Mack, Steve, illus. 2017. (J). **(978-1-4338-2723-5(9)**, Magination Pr.) American Psychological Assn.

—Peanut Butter & Jellyous: ...sometimes Friendships Get Sticky. Mack, Steve, illus. 2017. (J). **(978-1-4338-2337-4(3)**, Magination Pr.) American Psychological Assn.

George & His Best Friend. 2003. (Illus.). 32p. (J). 6.99 (978-0-9744520-0-5(9)) Glitter Creek, Inc.

George, Jean Craighead. Ratas de Rio, S. A.Tr. of River Rats, Inc.. (SPA.). (YA). (gr. 5-8). pap. (978-84-345-8620-8(7)) Salvat Editores, S.A. ESP. Dist: Lectorum Pubns., Inc.

George, Jessica Day. Dragon Flight. 2009. (Dragon Slippers Ser.). (ENG.). 288p. (YA). (gr. 5-8). pap. 8.99 (978-1-59990-359-0(8), 9781599903590, Bloomsbury USA Childrens) Bloomsbury Publishing USA.

George, Kallie. The Melancholic Mermaid. Halpin, Abigail, illus. 2011. (ENG.). 64p. (J). (gr. k-4). 16.95 (978-1-897476-53-6(1)) Simply Read Bks. CAN. Dist: Ingram Publisher Services.

George, Madeleine. Looks. 2009. (ENG.). 256p. (YA). (gr. 7-18). 7.99 (978-0-14-241419-4(0), Speak) Penguin Young Readers Group.

George, McKelle. Speak Easy, Speak Love. 2017. 432p. (YA). (gr. 8). 17.99 **(978-0-06-256092-6(1)**, Greenwillow Bks.) HarperCollins Pubs.

Georgieva, Zoia. Herman the Earth Worm: Illustrated by Emma C. Van Dyke. 2008. pap. 18.00 (978-0-8059-8630-3(8)) Dorrance Publishing Co., Inc.

Gephart, Donna. How to Survive Middle School. 2011. (ENG.). 256p. (J). (gr. 3-7). 6.99 (978-0-375-85411-8(8), Yearling) Random Hse. Children's Bks.

—Lily & Dunkin. 2016. (ENG.). 352p. (J). (gr. 5). 16.99 (978-0-553-53674-4(5), Delacorte Bks. for Young Readers) Random Hse. Children's Bks.

Geraldi, Michele J. Pennies at Piper Park. 2009. 24p. pap. 12.99 (978-1-4389-2829-6(7)) AuthorHouse.

Gerard, Timothy. The City Brigade & Remember the Music. 2012. 112p. (gr. -1). 23.99 (978-1-4685-2420-8(8)); pap. 14.95 (978-1-4685-2421-5(6)) AuthorHouse.

Geras, Adèle. Pictures of the Night. 2005. (ENG.). 192p. (YA). (gr. 7-12). pap. 11.95 (978-0-15-205543-1(6)) Houghton Mifflin Harcourt Publishing Co.

Gerlach, Carolyn. Robert Lee. 2012. 24p. 24.95 (978-1-4626-6031-5(2)) America Star Bks.

German, Lana. Jake the Sadder Ladder. Miller, Mark, illus. 2012. 20p. (-18). pap. 24.95 (978-1-4626-9574-4(4)) America Star Bks.

Germano, Yveta. Bring Me Back. 2013. 298p. 27.99 (978-1-938516-75-7(3)); 318p. pap. 13.99 (978-1-938516-17-7(6)) Midnight Hologram, LLC.

Gerovasiliou, Oreanthy. Yuri the Lion: Three Stories. 2010. (Illus.). 48p. pap. 13.00 (978-1-60888-069-0(9)) Nimble Bks. LLC.

Gerowin, Sean. Catte au Lait & the Big Hurricane. 2005. 36p. (J). 8.99 (978-1-4116-5157-9(X)) Lulu Pr., Inc.

Gerrity, Arlene. The Tale of Chicken Noodle & Rabbit Stew Number Two. 2010. 24p. 10.99 (978-1-4251-6258-0(4)) Trafford Publishing.

Gerry's 4. The World of Round. 2012. 24p. pap. 12.56 (978-1-4669-6882-0(6)) Trafford Publishing.

Gershel, Yolande. Alice. 2007. 32p. (J). pap. 15.00 (978-0-8059-7613-7(2)) Dorrance Publishing Co., Inc.

Gerstein, Mordicai. You Can't Have Too Many Friends! Gerstein, Mordicai, illus. 2014. (ENG., Illus.). 32p. (J). (gr. -1-2). 16.95 (978-0-8234-2393-4(X)) Holiday Hse., Inc.

Gervay, Susanne. Always Jack. Wilcox, Cathy, illus. 2013. 148p. (J). (978-1-61067-226-9(7)) Kane Miller.

—Being Jack. Wilcox, Cathy, illus. 2015. 167p. (J). (978-1-61067-455-3(3)) Kane Miller.

Gervay, Susanne & Wilcox, Cathy. Always Jack. 2014. (ENG.). 160p. (J). pap. 5.99 (978-1-61067-130-9(9)) Kane Miller.

Geshell, Carmen. Waltah Melon: Local-Kine Hero. Pagay, Jeff, illus. 2004. 24p. (J). 10.95 (978-1-57306-205-3(7)) Bess Pr., Inc.

Gesvalli, Domanick. Jason's Journeys: Swim to Me. 2011. 28p. (gr. -1). pap. 16.09 (978-1-4269-7015-3(3)) Trafford Publishing.

Getsinger, Mary. A Dream Come True. 2009. 20p. pap. 9.50 (978-1-4251-8885-6(0)) Trafford Publishing.

Geyer, Clyde. The Awesome Adventures of Chuckie Chopper & Friends. 2012. 52p. pap. 15.95 (978-1-4575-0741-0(2)) Dog Ear Publishing, LLC.

Ghigna, Charles. Adeline Porcupine. East, Jacqueline, illus. 2015. (Tiny Tales Ser.). (ENG.). 64p. (gr. -1-2). lib. bdg. 23.99 (978-1-4795-6530-6(X)) Tiny Tales.

—Lucy Goose. East, Jacqueline, illus. 2015. (Tiny Tales Ser.). (ENG.). 64p. (gr. -1-2). lib. bdg. 23.99 (978-1-4795-6529-0(6)) Tiny Tales.

Gi Gi. The Adventures of Trueword the Bear. 2012. 28p. pap. 24.95 (978-1-4626-8042-9(9)) America Star Bks.

Gianferrari, Maria. The School Show. Heder, Thyra, illus. 2015. (Penny & Jelly Ser.). (ENG.). 32p. (J). (gr. -1-3). 16.99 (978-0-544-23014-9(0), HMH Books For Young Readers) Houghton Mifflin Harcourt Publishing Co.

Gibbons, Gail. The Quilting Bee. Gibbons, Gail, illus. 2004. (ENG., Illus.). 32p. (J). (gr. k-5). 17.99 (978-0-688-16397-6(1)) HarperCollins Pubs.

Gibbs, Gretchen. The Book of Maggie Bradstreet. 2012. (Bradstreet Chronicles). (ENG.). 183p. (YA). pap. 9.99 (978-0-9852948-0-9(9)) Glenmere Pr.

Gibbs, Lynne. Time to Share: A Story of Sharing. Mitchell, Melanie, illus. 2009. (Let's Grow Together Ser.). 32p. (J). (gr. -1-2). lib. bdg. 22.60 *(978-1-60754-757-0(0))* Windmill Bks.

Gibbs, May. The Complete Adventures of Snugglepot & Cuddlepie. 2007. (Illus.). 272p. *(978-0-7322-8428-2(7))* HarperCollins Pubs. Australia.

Gibbs, Stuart. Spy School Secret Service. 2017. (J). pap. ***(978-1-4814-7783-3(8)***, Simon & Schuster Bks. For Young Readers) Simon & Schuster Bks. For Young Readers.

Gibbs, Stuart. Spy Ski School. 2016. (Spy School Ser.). (ENG., Illus.). 368p. (J). (gr. 3-7). 16.99 *(978-1-4814-4562-7(6)*, Simon & Schuster Bks. For Young Readers) Simon & Schuster Bks. For Young Readers.

Gibson, Barbara Leonard, illus. The Dragonfly Door. rev. ed. 2007. (ENG.). 40p. (J). (gr. k-5). 17.95 *(978-1-934066-12-6(5))* Feather Rock Bks., Inc.

Gibson, Douglas. Tales of a Fifth-Grade Knight. Tuya, Jez, illus. 2015. (Middle-Grade Novels Ser.). (ENG.). 160p. (gr. 4-7). lib. bdg. 26.65 *(978-1-4965-0488-3(7))* Stone Arch Bks.

Gibson, Steve. Sparky the Firehouse Dog, 1 vol. Weishampel, Winifred Ann, illus. 2009. 20p. pap. 24.95 *(978-1-60836-254-7(X))* America Star Bks.

Gibson, Sylvia Scott. Ricky the Skating Worm & Friends, 1 vol. Gibson, Gregory V., illus. 2009. 21p. pap. 24.95 *(978-1-60836-473-2(9))* America Star Bks.

Gibson, Sylvia Scott & Gibson, James E. Latawnya the Naughty Horse Two, 1 vol. Gibson, Gregory V., illus. 2010. 22p. 24.95 *(978-1-4489-7859-5(9))* PublishAmerica, Inc.

Giddens, Martha Anne. The Unluckiest Kid in the Universe. 2006. 56p. pap. 9.95 *(978-1-4120-7935-8(7))* Trafford Publishing.

Gideon, John. The Little Soup Spoon. 2010. 32p. pap. 12.99 *(978-1-4520-3001-2(4))* AuthorHouse.

Giff, Patricia Reilly. All the Way Home. 2003. (ENG., Illus.). 176p. (J). (gr. 3-7). pap. 7.99 *(978-0-440-41182-6(3)*, Yearling) Random Hse. Children's Bks.

—B-E-S-T Friends. 73p. (J). (gr. 1-2). pap. 3.99 *(978-0-8072-1277-6(6)*, Listening Library) Random Hse. Audio Publishing Group.

—Jubilee. (ENG.). 160p. (J). (gr. 3-7). 2017. 6.99 ***(978-0-385-74489-8(7)***, Yearling) 2016. 16.99 *(978-0-385-74486-7(2)*, Lamb, Wendy Bks.) Random Hse. Children's Bks.

—Maggie's Door. 2005. (ENG.). 176p. (J). (gr. 3-7). 6.99 *(978-0-440-41581-7(0)*, Yearling) Random Hse. Children's Bks.

—Winter Sky. 2014. (ENG.). 160p. (J). (gr. 3-7). 15.99 *(978-0-375-83892-7(9)*, Lamb, Wendy Bks.) Random Hse. Children's Bks.

Gilani-Williams, Fawzia. Yaffa & Fatima: Shalom, Salaam. Fedele, Chiara, illus. 2017. (ENG.). 24p. (gr. -1-3). 17.99 *(978-1-4677-8938-7(0)*, Kar-Ben Publishing) Lerner Publishing Group.

Gilbert, George. George, Candy, & the Raccoon. Perez-Torres, Juliana, illus. 2008. 40p. pap. 16.99 *(978-1-4389-2848-7(3))* AuthorHouse.

Gilbert, Heather. Skyler the Pirate, 1 vol. 2009. 25p. pap. 24.95 *(978-1-60813-820-3(8))* America Star Bks.

Gilbert, Julie. Fire & Ice: A Mermaid's Journey. Fagan, Kirbi, illus. 2017. (Dark Waters Ser.). (ENG.). 160p. (gr. 2-4). lib. bdg. 26.65 *(978-1-4965-4168-0(5))* Stone Arch Bks.

—Neptune's Trident: A Mermaid's Journey. Fagan, Kirbi, illus. 2017. (Dark Waters Ser.). (ENG.). 160p. (gr. 2-4). lib. bdg. 26.65 *(978-1-4965-4169-7(3))* Stone Arch Bks.

—The Sighting: A Mermaid's Journey. Fagan, Kirbi, illus. 2017. (Dark Waters Ser.). (ENG.). 160p. (gr. 2-4). lib. bdg. 26.65 *(978-1-4965-4170-3(7))* Stone Arch Bks.

Gildea, Kathy. The Adventures of Baylee Beagle — Annabelle Beagle. Larson, Amanda, illus. 2005. 28p. (J). 7.95 *(978-0-9767096-1-9(9))* Maxim Pr.

—The Adventures of Baylee Beagle — Greenville. 2005. (Illus.). 20p. (J). 7.95 *(978-0-9767096-0-2(0))* Maxim Pr.

—The Adventures of Baylee Beagle — Hurricane Hound. Larson, Amanda, illus. 2005. 28p. (J). 7.95 *(978-0-9767096-2-6(7))* Maxim Pr.

Giles, Doris. Foursome. 2009. 24p. pap. 13.49 *(978-1-4389-1203-5(X))* AuthorHouse.

Giles, Lisa. The Adventures of Sunny the Bunny: The Easter Egg Hunt. 2010. 20p. 10.49 *(978-1-4520-1842-3(1))* AuthorHouse.

Gilks, Tina M. My Dog Mo. 2011. 32p. pap. 17.25 *(978-1-4269-4931-9(6))* Trafford Publishing.

Gill, J. Duddy. The Secret of Ferrell Savage. Chaghatzbanian, Sonia, illus. (ENG.). 176p. (J). (gr. 3-7). 2015. pap. 7.99 *(978-1-4424-6018-8(0))* 2014. 15.99 *(978-1-4424-6017-1(2))* Simon & Schuster Children's Publishing. (Atheneum Bks. for Young Readers).

Gill, Janie S. Just Like You. Lambson, Elizabeth, illus. Date not set. 5.95 *(978-0-89868-430-8(7))* ARO Publishing Co.

Gilleland, Linda. I Love You, Baby Deer. Irish, Leigh Ann, illus. 2012. 56p. 19.99 *(978-1-61254-025-2(2))* Brown Books Publishing Group.

Gillen-Connell, Linda. Laura the Loser. 2006. 66p. pap. 16.95 *(978-1-4241-0820-6(9))* PublishAmerica, Inc.

Gilley, Jane. Christmas on Troglodyte Hill - Book Three of the Troglodyte Trilogy. 2008. 16p. pap. *(978-1-906210-71-7(3))* Grosvenor Hse. Publishing Ltd.

—The Phantom Pum. 2008. 20p. pap. *(978-1-906210-74-8(8))* Grosvenor Hse. Publishing Ltd.

Gilley, Mel. Sam & the Sad Dinosaur. 2011. 28p. pap. 13.59 *(978-1-4567-6751-8(8))* AuthorHouse.

Gillingham, Sara. Busy Baby Friends. 2015. (ENG., Illus.). 10p. (J). (gr. -1 — 1). bds. 9.99 *(978-1-4521-4188-6(6))* Chronicle Bks. LLC.

—How to Grow a Friend. 2015. (ENG., Illus.). 40p. (J). (gr. -1-2). lib. bdg. 19.99 *(978-0-375-97325-3(7)*, Random Hse. Bks. for Young Readers) Random Hse. Children's Bks.

—In My Pond. Siminovich, Lorena, illus. 2009. (ENG.). 12p. (J). (gr. -1 — 1). bds. 8.99 *(978-0-8118-6556-2(8))* Chronicle Bks. LLC.

—Trucks. 2015. (ENG., Illus.). 10p. (J). (gr. -1 — 1). bds. 9.99 *(978-1-4521-4187-9(8))* Chronicle Bks. LLC.

Gilman, Grace. Dixie & the Big Bully. McConnell, Sarah, illus. 2013. (I Can Read Level 1 Ser.). (ENG.). 32p. (J). (gr. -1-3). 16.99 *(978-0-06-208637-2(5))* HarperCollins Pubs.

—Dixie & the Big Bully. 2013. (Dixie: I Can Read Ser.). (J). lib. bdg. 13.55 *(978-0-606-27136-3(8)*, Turtleback) Turtleback Bks.

—Dixie & the Good Deeds. McConnell, Sarah, illus. 2013. (I Can Read Level 1 Ser.). (ENG.). 32p. (J). (gr. -1-3). 16.99 *(978-0-06-208657-0(X))*; pap. 3.99 *(978-0-06-208643-3(X))* HarperCollins Pubs.

Gilmore, Grace. The New Kid. Brown, Petra, illus. 2016. (Tales from Maple Ridge Ser.: 6). (ENG.). 128p. (J). (gr. k-4). pap. 5.99 *(978-1-4814-4746-1(7)*, Little Simon) Little Simon.

Gilmore, Rachna. Roses for Gita. Priestley, Alice, illus. 2004. 24p. (J). *(978-1-85269-367-1(3))*; *(978-1-85269-369-5(X))* Mantra Lingua.

Ginesin, Lucia. Prince Jack, the Little Artist. Ginesin, Zack, illus. 2009. 28p. pap. 11.99 *(978-1-59858-983-2(0))* Dog Ear Publishing, LLC.

Gingold, Janet. Danger, Long Division. 2006. 188p. per. 14.99 *(978-1-59092-122-7(4))* Blue Forge Pr.

Gingras, Charlotte. Pieces of Me. Ouriou, Susan, tr. from FRE. 2009. (ENG.). 144p. (J). (gr. 7-9). 8.95 *(978-1-55453-432-6(1))* Kids Can Pr., Ltd. CAN. Dist: Hachette Bk. Group.

Ginkel, Anne. I've Got an Elephant, 1 vol. Bynum, Janie, illus. 2013. (ENG.). 32p. (J). (gr. -1-3). 7.95 *(978-1-56145-685-7(3))* Peachtree Pubs.

Gino, Alex. George. 2015. (ENG.). 208p. (J). (gr. 3-7). 16.99 *(978-0-545-81254-2(2)*, Scholastic Pr.) Scholastic, Inc.

Giordano, Anthony. Another Boring Summer... Again! 2009. 154p. (YA). pap. 11.25 *(978-1-60695-077-7(0))* Callanish Pr.

Gipson, Mary Willene. The Tattered Feather. 2012. 28p. pap. 13.95 *(978-1-4525-5036-7(0))* Balboa Pr.

Girard, Franck. Toby Goes Bananas. Bloch, Serge, illus. 2017. (ENG.). 96p. (J). (gr. 2-5). 19.99 ***(978-0-545-85284-5(6))***; pap. 9.99 ***(978-0-545-85283-8(8))*** Scholastic, Inc. (Graphix).

Girard, M-E. Girl Mans Up. 2016. 384p. (YA). (gr. 9). 17.99 *(978-0-06-240417-6(2)*, HarperTeen) HarperCollins Pubs.

Gist, Richard. Ayshus on the Inside. 2013. 104p. *(978-1-4602-1899-0(X))*; pap. *(978-1-4602-1900-3(7))* FriesenPress.

Gitau, Terri. Annie & Kindness the Frog. 2012. 16p. pap. 15.99 *(978-1-4634-4021-3(9))* AuthorHouse.

Glass, Sue. Helping Hop. 2nd ed. 2004. Orig. Title: What's Wrong with Hop? (J). spiral bd. 10.99 *(978-0-9763593-0-2(8))* Closer Looks Bks.

Glasthal, Jacqueline B. Liberty on 23rd Street. Reingold, Alan, illus. 2006. (Adventures in America Ser.). (gr. 4). 14.95 net. *(978-1-893110-45-8(1))* Silver Moon Pr.

Gleadhill, Christa J. Here Comes Lucky! 2011. 16p. pap. 9.99 *(978-1-257-03275-4(5))* Lulu Pr., Inc.

Gleeson, Libby. Half a World Away. Blackwood, Freya, illus. 2007. (J). pap. *(978-0-439-88978-0(2)*, Levine, Arthur A. Bks.) Scholastic, Inc.

Gleim, Jc. Leprechaun Kate. 2012. 56p. pap. 24.95 *(978-1-4626-7608-8(1))* America Star Bks.

Glendenning, Debra Morgan. Little Lost Baxter. 2009. 28p. pap. 24.95 *(978-1-60749-256-6(3))* America Star Bks.

Glennon, Michelle. My Big Green Teacher: Don't Rock the Boat: Saving Our Oceans. Glennon, Michelle, illus. 2008. (Illus.). 32p. (J). 19.95 *(978-0-9796625-2-2(4))* GDG Publishing.

—My Big Green Teacher: Seven Generations from Now. Glennon, Michelle, illus. 2008. (Illus.). (J). 19.95 *(978-0-9797952-1-3(4))* GDG Publishing.

—My Big Green Teacher: Take a Deep Breath: Saving Our Rainforests. Glennon, Michelle, illus. 2008. (ENG., Illus.). 32p. (J). 19.95 *(978-0-9797952-0-6(6))* GDG Publishing.

Glickman, Susan. Bernadette & the Lunch Bunch, 1 vol. Allard, Melanie, illus. 2009. (Lunch Bunch Ser.). (ENG.). 123p. (J). (gr. 1-4). pap. 6.95 *(978-1-897187-51-7(3))* Second Story Pr. CAN. Dist: Orca Bk. Pubs. USA.

—Bernadette in the Doghouse, 1 vol. 2011. (Lunch Bunch Ser.). (ENG., Illus.). 122p. (J). (gr. 2-4). pap. 8.95 *(978-1-897187-92-0(0))* Second Story Pr. CAN. Dist: Orca Bk. Pubs. USA.

Glines, Abbi. The Sea Breeze Collection: Breathe; Because of Low; While It Lasts; Just for Now. 2013. (Sea Breeze Ser.). (ENG., Illus.). 1312p. (YA). (gr. 11-11). pap. 39.99 *(978-1-4424-9608-8(8)*, Simon Pulse) Simon Pulse.

—Under the Lights. 2016. (Field Party Ser.: 2). (ENG., Illus.). 336p. (YA). (gr. 9). 17.99 *(978-1-4814-3889-6(1)*, Simon Pulse) Simon Pulse.

Glitterpony, Jessica Noelle. The Warkak & Snoozle. 2013. 42p. pap. 9.87 *(978-1-939896-16-2(9))* Levity Pr.

Glover, Clair. Fairy Penguin - the Penguin Who Loves to Play. 2013. 26p. pap. *(978-1-78222-119-7(0))* Paragon Publishing, Rothersthorpe.

Glover, Dennis W. The Talking Flower. 2010. 32p. pap. 12.99 *(978-1-4490-5599-8(0))* AuthorHouse.

Glover, Sandra. Dangerously Close. 2008. (ENG.). 176p. (YA). (gr. 7). pap. 9.99 *(978-1-84270-679-4(9))* Andersen Pr. GBR. Dist: Independent Pubs. Group.

Gnoske, Alexandra. Loui Saves the Earth. 2010. 16p. 9.49 *(978-1-4520-0034-3(4))* AuthorHouse.

Godbersen, Anna. Beautiful Days. 2012. (Bright Young Things Ser.: 2). (ENG.). 368p. (YA). (gr. 9). pap. 9.99 *(978-0-06-196269-1(4))* HarperCollins Pubs.

Goddard, Michael. The Adventure of Mike & Matt. 2010. 27p. 14.05 *(978-0-557-33766-8(6))* Lulu Pr., Inc.

Goertzen, Angelina. Tinsel the Christmas Tree. 2009. 32p. pap. 12.49 *(978-1-4389-8569-5(X))* AuthorHouse.

Goerzen, Christy. The Big Apple Effect, 1 vol. 2014. (Orca Currents Ser.). (ENG.). 136p. (J). (gr. 5-9). pap. 9.95 *(978-1-4598-0738-9(3))* Orca Bk. Pubs. USA.

—Farmed Out, 1 vol. 2011. (Orca Currents Ser.). (ENG.). 128p. (J). (gr. 5-9). pap. 9.95 *(978-1-55469-910-0(X))*; lib. bdg. 16.95 *(978-1-55469-911-7(8))* Orca Bk. Pubs. USA.

Goethals, Angela. The Sisterhood of the Traveling Pants. 2004. (Sisterhood of the Traveling Pants Ser.: Bk. 1). 320p. (YA). (gr. 7-18). pap. 40.00 incl. audio *(978-0-8072-2286-7(0)*, Listening Library) Random Hse. Audio Publishing Group.

Going, K. L. The Liberation of Gabriel King. 2007. (ENG.). 160p. (J). (gr. 3-7). 6.99 *(978-0-14-240766-0(6)*, Puffin Books) Penguin Young Readers Group.

—The Liberation of Gabriel King. 2007. 151p. (gr. 3-7). 17.00 *(978-0-7569-7762-7(2))* Perfection Learning Corp.

Goins, Debra Lynn. One Day I Tried to Catch the Sun. 2011. 24p. (gr. 1-2). pap. 11.32 *(978-1-4634-1872-4(8))* AuthorHouse.

Gold, Gina. Disney Minnie Mouse Hugs for Friends: A Hugs Book. 2014. (Hugs Book Ser.: 1). (ENG.). 10p. (J). (gr. -1-k). 10.99 *(978-0-7944-3004-7(X))* Reader's Digest Assn., Inc., The.

Gold, Maya & Fitzhugh, Louise. Harriet the Spy, Double Agent. 2007. (Harriet the Spy Adventures Ser.). (ENG.). 160p. (J). (gr. 3-7). 6.99 *(978-0-440-41691-3(4)*, Yearling) Random Hse. Children's Bks.

Gold, Rachel. Just Girls. 2014. (ENG.). 254p. (J). pap. 16.95 *(978-1-59493-419-3(3))* Bella Bks., Inc.

Goldberg, Whoopi & Underwood, Deborah. Plum Fantastic Bk. 1. Cato, Nancy & Roos, Maryn, illus. 2008. (ENG.). 160p. (J). (gr. 1-17). pap. 4.99 *(978-0-7868-5260-4(7)*, Jump at the Sun) Hyperion Bks. for Children.

Goldblatt, Mark. Finding the Worm. 2015. (ENG.). 352p. (J). (gr. 4-7). 16.99 *(978-0-385-39108-5(0)*, Random Hse. Bks. for Young Readers) Random Hse. Children's Bks.

—Finding the Worm (Twerp Sequel) 2016. (ENG.). 368p. (J). (gr. 4-7). 7.99 *(978-0-385-39111-5(0)*, Yearling) Random Hse. Children's Bks.

—Twerp. 2013. (ENG.). 288p. (J). (gr. 4-7). 16.99 *(978-0-375-97142-6(4)*, Random Hse. Bks. for Young Readers) Random Hse. Children's Bks.

Golden Books. ABC Animals (Dora the Explorer) McGee, Warner, illus. 2013. (Color Plus Card Stock Ser.). (ENG.). 48p. (J). (gr. -1-2). pap. 3.99 *(978-0-307-98218-6(1)*, Golden Bks.) Random Hse. Children's Bks.

—From Army Ants to Zebrafish: Animals That Hop, Fly & Swish! (Dr. Seuss/Cat in the Hat) Ruiz, Aristides, illus. 2013. (Deluxe Stickerific Ser.). (ENG.). 64p. (J). (gr. -1-2). pap. 5.99 *(978-0-449-81432-1(7)*, Golden Bks.) Random Hse. Children's Bks.

—I See Seeds! Ruiz, Aristides, illus. 2013. (Color Plus Chunky Crayons Ser.). (ENG.). 48p. (J). (gr. -1-2). pap. 3.99 *(978-0-307-98209-4(2)*, Golden Bks.) Random Hse. Children's Bks.

—Marshall to the Rescue! (Paw Patrol) Golden Books & Jackson, Mike, illus. 2016. (Big Golden Book Ser.). (ENG.). 32p. (J). (gr. -1-2). 9.99 *(978-1-101-93847-8(1)*, Golden Bks.) Random Hse. Children's Bks.

—One Spooky Night (Dora & Friends) Aikins, David, illus. 2015. (Hologramatic Sticker Book Ser.). (ENG.). 64p. (J). (gr. -1-2). pap. 4.99 *(978-0-553-52118-4(7)*, Golden Bks.) Random Hse. Children's Bks.

—The Pups Save Friendship Day! (PAW Patrol) Jackson, Mike, illus. 2016. (Big Golden Book Ser.). (ENG.). 32p. (J). (gr. -1-2). 9.99 *(978-1-5247-1388-1(0)*, Golden Bks.) Random Hse. Children's Bks.

—Snow Wonder! (Frosty the Snowman) Golden Books, illus. 2013. (Deluxe Paint Box Book Ser.). (ENG., Illus.). 128p. (J). (gr. -1-2). pap. 7.99 *(978-0-385-37179-7(9)*, Golden Bks.) Random Hse. Children's Bks.

—Thomas & Friends: Nine Favorite Tales (Thomas & Friends) A Little Golden Book Collection. 2014. (Little Golden Book Treasury Ser.). (ENG., Illus.). 224p. (J). (-k). 12.99 *(978-0-385-37644-0(8)*, Golden Bks.) Random Hse. Children's Bks.

Golden Books. Thomas & Friends Summer 2017 Movie Big Golden Book (Thomas & Friends) Stubbs, Tommy, illus. 2017. (Big Golden Book Ser.). (ENG.). 32p. (J). (gr. -1-2). 9.99 ***(978-1-5247-1662-2(6)***, Golden Bks.) Random Hse. Children's Bks.

Golden Books & Random House Disney Staff, illus. Nine Classic Tales. 2014. (Little Golden Book Treasury Ser.). (ENG.). 224p. (J). (-k). 12.99 *(978-0-7364-3260-3(4)*, Golden/Disney) Random Hse. Children's Bks.

Golden Books Staff. Puppy Hugs & Kisses! Golden Books Staff & Lovett, Nate, illus. 2016. (Hologramatic Sticker Book Ser.). (ENG.). 64p. (J). (gr. -1-2). pap. 4.99 *(978-0-399-55878-8(0)*, Golden Bks.) Random Hse. Children's Bks.

—Welcome to Wally's World! VanTuyle, David, illus. 2015. (Pictureback(R) Ser.). (ENG.). 16p. (J). (gr. -1-2). 3.99 *(978-0-385-38764-4(4)*, Golden Bks.) Random Hse. Children's Bks.

Golden Books Staff, illus. Favorites: Thomas Breaks a Promise - Thomas & the Big, Big Bridge/May the Best Engine Win! 2009. (Little Golden Book Favorites Ser.). (ENG.). 80p. (J). (gr. -1-2). 7.99 *(978-0-375-85554-2(8)*, Golden Bks.) Random Hse. Children's Bks.

Goldfinger, Jennifer P. Hello, My Name Is Tiger. Goldfinger, Jennifer P., illus. 2016. (Illus.). 40p. (J). (gr. -1-3). 17.99 *(978-0-06-239951-9(9))* HarperCollins Pubs.

Golding, Julia. The Chimera's Curse, 0 vols. 2010. (Companions Quartet Ser.: 4). (ENG.). 320p. (J). (gr. 4-7). pap. 9.99 *(978-0-7614-5726-8(7)*, 9780761457268, Amazon Children's Publishing) Amazon Publishing.

—Mines of the Minotaur, 0 vols., Bk. 3. unabr. ed. 2010. (Companions Quartet Ser.: 3). (ENG.). 288p. (gr. 5-9). pap. 9.99 *(978-0-7614-5796-1(8)*, 9780761457961, Amazon Children's Publishing) Amazon Publishing.

Goldsmith, Howard. Thomas Jefferson & the Ghostriders. Rose, Drew, illus. 2008. (Ready-To-read COFA Ser.). (ENG.). 32p. (J). (gr. k-2). pap. 3.99 *(978-1-4169-2692-4(5))*; lib. bdg. 13.89 *(978-1-4169-2749-5(2))* Simon Spotlight. (Simon Spotlight).

Goldstein, Mona Pastroff. Friends Forever: The Good Fight. 2009. (Illus.). 207p. pap. 15.00 *(978-1-58432-546-8(1))* Educa Vision Inc.

Gomes, Barbara K. Esau at the Big House. 2006. 76p. pap. 19.95 *(978-1-4241-2288-2(0))* America Star Bks.

Gómez Cerda, Alfredo. Barro de Medellín/ Mud of Medellin. Lopez, Xan, illus. 2010. (SPA.). 146p. (YA). (gr. 5-8). *(978-84-263-6849-2(2))* Vives, Luis Editorial (Edelvives).

Gomez, Sally. Too Many Freckles! Mitchell, Hazel, illus. 2008. (ENG.). 32p. pap. *(978-1-934363-32-4(4))* Zoe Life Publishing.

Gomi, Taro. My Friends. 2005. (ENG., Illus.). 34p. (J). (gr. -1 — 1). bds. 6.99 *(978-0-8118-4786-5(1))* Chronicle Bks. LLC.

Gonzales, Rebecca. Beauty & the Basketcase. 2007. 103p. pap. 14.94 *(978-1-4303-2379-2(5))* Lulu Pr., Inc.

Gonzalez, Christina Diaz. A Thunderous Whisper. 2013. (ENG., Illus.). 320p. (J). (gr. 5). pap. 7.99 *(978-0-375-87371-3(6)*, Yearling) Random Hse. Children's Bks.

Gonzalo, Angela. The Pig, Bear, & the Pear: The Pear Meets the Pig & Bear. 2013. 44p. pap. 17.45 *(978-1-4624-0576-3(2)*, Inspiring Voices) Author Solutions, Inc.

Gonzßlez Valdts, Alberto Domingo. Sueños de Obama/Obama's Dreams. 2008. (SPA.). 164p. pap. 15.00 *(978-1-4389-3773-1(3))* AuthorHouse.

Good, Dinah. Stay Away from Mean Jean! 2012. 48p. pap. 19.56 *(978-1-4685-2862-6(9))* AuthorHouse.

Goode, Laura. Sister Mischief. 2011. (ENG., Illus.). 384p. (YA). (gr. 9-18). 16.99 *(978-0-7636-4640-0(7))* Candlewick Pr.

Goodhart, Pippa. One Windy Day. Cassidy, Amber, illus. 2016. (Reading Ladder Ser.). (ENG.). 48p. (J). (gr. k-2). 7.99 *(978-1-4052-8233-8(9))* Egmont Bks., Ltd. GBR. Dist: Independent Pubs. Group.

Goodman, Hannah R. Fear of Falling. 2009. 168p. pap. 12.95 *(978-1-4401-5645-8(X))* iUniverse, Inc.

Goodman-Schneps, Oriana. The Seventh Chime. 2009. 52p. pap. 15.99 *(978-1-4415-2748-6(6))* Xlibris Corp.

Goodnight, Macy. The Toad & the Dragonfly. 2008. 24p. pap. 24.95 *(978-1-60474-785-0(4))* America Star Bks.

Goodrich, C. C. Barnabee: Meets New Friends. 2009. (Illus.). 24p. pap. 12.99 *(978-1-4389-8390-5(5))* AuthorHouse.

Goodrich, Carter. We Forgot Brock! Goodrich, Carter, illus. 2015. (ENG., Illus.). 48p. (J). (gr. -1-3). 17.99 *(978-1-4424-8090-2(4)*, Simon & Schuster Bks. For Young Readers) Simon & Schuster Bks. For Young Readers.

Goodspeed, Jjdy. Perky Turkey's 4th of July Adventure. 2008. (Illus.). 24p. (J). per. *(978-0-9801376-1-3(6))* Dragonfly Publishing, Inc.

Goodspeed, Judy. Perky Turkey Finds a Friend. (Illus.). 24p. (J). 2007. per. 11.99 *(978-0-9797574-2-6(8))* 2006. lib. bdg. 24.95 *(978-0-9778651-2-3(6))* Dragonfly Publishing, Inc.

—Perky Turkey Finds a Friend. Taylor, Chet, illus. l.t. ed. 2006. 24p. (J). pap. 14.99 *(978-0-9765786-6-2(2))* Dragonfly Publishing, Inc.

—Perky Turkey's 4th of July Adventure. 2008. (Illus.). 24p. (J). lib. bdg. *(978-0-9801376-0-6(8))* Dragonfly Publishing, Inc.

Goody, C. A. Charlie & the Rodent Queen Laaker, Terry, illus. l.t. ed. 2003. (Charlie's Great Adventures: No. 3). 88p. per. 5.95 *(978-0-9702546-2-7(8)*, 623-876-1518) GoodyGoody Bks.

Gopinath, Karin Ursula. Friends in the Garden. Sutanto, Tommy, illus. 2008. 34p. (J). per. 19.95 *(978-0-9800637-0-7(1))* Lotus Art Works Inc.

Gorbachev, Valeri. Me Too! Gorbachev, Valeri, illus. 2014. (I Like to Read(r) Ser.). (ENG., Illus.). 24p. (J). (gr. -1-3). 6.99 *(978-0-8234-3179-3(7))* Holiday Hse., Inc.

—Not Me! Gorbachev, Valeri, illus. 2016. (ENG., Illus.). 24p. (J). 14.95 *(978-0-8234-3546-3(6))*; pap. 6.99 *(978-0-8234-3547-0(4))* Holiday Hse., Inc.

Gordon, Amy. The Gorillas of Gill Park. 2003. (ENG., Illus.). 256p. (J). (gr. 4-6). tchr. ed. 16.95 *(978-0-8234-1751-3(4))* Holiday Hse., Inc.

—Return to Gill Park. 2006. (ENG., Illus.). 240p. (J). (gr. 4-7). 16.95 *(978-0-8234-1998-2(3))* Holiday Hse., Inc.

Gordon, David. Smitten. Gordon, David, illus. 2007. (ENG., Illus.). 40p. (J). (gr. -1-3). 17.99 *(978-1-4169-2440-1(X)*, Atheneum Bks. for Young Readers) Simon & Schuster Children's Publishing.

Gordon, Gus. Herman & Rosie. Gordon, Gus, illus. 2013. (ENG., Illus.). 32p. (J). (gr. 2-5). 17.99 *(978-1-59643-856-9(8)*, 9781596438569) Roaring Brook Pr.

Gordon, Sylvia. Further Adventures of the Potty Wizard & His Cat, Muddles. 2009. (Illus.). 60p. pap. 10.49 *(978-1-4389-6819-3(1))* AuthorHouse.

Gorey, Edward. The Osbick Bird. 2012. 32p. (J). 12.95 *(978-0-7649-6335-3(X))* Pomegranate Communications, Inc.

Gorey, Edward & Chess, Victoria. Fletcher & Zenobia. Chess, Victoria, illus. 2016. (ENG., Illus.). 72p. (J). (gr. k-2). 14.95 *(978-1-59017-963-5(3)*, NYR Children's Collection) New York Review of Bks., Inc., The.

Gorges, Julie A. Just Call Me Goody-Two-Shoes. 2006. 146p. (YA). per. 9.95 *(978-0-9763274-1-7(4))* I.Form Ink, Publishing.

Gormally, Eleanor. St Paul: The Man with the Letters. 2010. (ENG., Illus.). 32p. (J). pap. 16.95 *(978-1-84730-177-2(0))* Veritas Pubns. IRL. Dist: Dufour Editions, Inc.

Gorman, DI. Pudgy Wudgy: Pudgy Wudgy Meets a Friend. 2008. 32p. pap. 12.99 *(978-1-4389-2151-8(9))* AuthorHouse.

Gorman, Patrick. Alicia & Policia, 1 vol. Gorman, Kyrsten, illus. 2010. 24p. 24.95 *(978-1-4489-6425-3(3))* PublishAmerica, Inc.

Gorrell, Nancy. Anna Banana. 2006. (ENG., Illus.). 96p. (J). (gr. -1-2). per. 6.99 *(978-1-84550-182-2(9)*, 5a21ceaa-6b5b-4fb6-b215-15915b289e40) Christian Focus Pubns. GBR. Dist: Bookmasters Distribution.

Goscinny, René. Nicholas & the Gang. Bell, Anthea, tr. from FRE. Sempé, Jean-Jacques, illus. 2011. (ENG.). 120p. (gr. 4-7). pap. 9.95 *(978-0-7148-6226-2(6))* Phaidon Pr., Inc.

—Where's Asterix? Uderzo, Albert, illus. 2012. (ENG.). 32p. (J). (gr. 4-6). pap. 9.99 *(978-1-4440-0554-7(5)*, Orion) Orion Publishing Group, Ltd. GBR. Dist: Hachette Bk. Group.

Goscinny, René, et al. Nicholas Again. Bell, Anthea, tr. from FRE. 2006. (ENG., Illus.). 120p. 19.95 *(978-0-7148-4491-6(8))* Phaidon Pr., Inc.

Goslee, S. J. Whatever. 2016. (ENG.). 272p. (YA). 17.99 *(978-1-62672-399-3(0)*, 9781626723993) Roaring Brook Pr.

Gosselin, Jake & Gosselin, Laura. The Pinkaboos: Bitterly & the Giant Problem. 2016. (Pinkaboos Ser.: 1). (ENG.). 96p. (J). pap. 7.99 *(978-1-4494-7831-5(X))* Andrews McMeel Publishing.

Gosule, Bette & Longmire, Lynda. Sneakers Hangs Out. Dewitt, Kenny, illus. 2012. 26p. (J). 14.95 *(978-1-60131-129-0(X)*, Castlebridge Bks.) Big Tent Bks.

Gottesfeld, Jeff. Blackout, 1 vol. 2016. (Red Rhino Ser.). (ENG.). 63p. (J). (gr. 3-6). pap. 7.95 *(978-1-62250-956-0(0))* Saddleback Educational Publishing, Inc.

—The Code. 2014. (Red Rhino Ser.). (J). lib. bdg. 18.40 *(978-0-606-36199-6(5))* Turtleback Bks.

—Too Many Dogs, 1 vol. 2015. (Red Rhino Ser.). (ENG.). 68p. (J). (gr. 4-6). pap. 7.95 *(978-1-62250-951-5(X))* Saddleback Educational Publishing, Inc.

E
F
G

Gough, Simon. I Can'T Fly & I Can'T Swim. 2011. (Illus.). 24p. pap. 11.44 *(978-1-4567-8063-0(8))* AuthorHouse.
Gould, M. & Gould, R. About Gossip: What Would Jesus Do, 1 vol. Hurst, Debbie, illus. 2009. 28p. pap. 24.95 *(978-1-60749-680-9(1))* America Star Bks.
Gould, M&R. What Would Jesus Do? Purity of Intention. 2008. 35p. pap. 24.95 *(978-1-60672-675-4(7))* America Star Bks.
Gould, Terry. The Adventures of Sir Sniffsalot & His Friends. Proulx, Denis, illus. 2007. 48p. (gr. -1-3). pap. 15.99 *(978-0-9789057-3-6(3))* Huntington Ludlow Media Group.
—The Adventures of Sir Sniffsalot & His Friends. 2009. (Illus.). 48p. pap. 15.99 *(978-0-615-26181-2(7))* Write Away.
Goulis, Julie. Something Shiny, Something Round. Ferguson, John, illus. 2005. 32p. (J). (gr. 3-7). 14.99 *(978-0-9754621-1-9(3))* Bubblegum Bks.
Gow, Kailin. Loving Summer. 2012. 250p. (-18). pap. 9.99 *(978-1-59748-044-4(4),* The Edge) Sparklesoup LLC.
Gownley, Jimmy. Amelia in Fireflies & Time, 1 vol. 2013. (Amelia Rules! Set 2 Ser.). (ENG.). 36p. (J). (gr. 3-6). 24.21 *(978-1-61479-069-3(8))* Spotlight.
—Amelia in Heroes & Villains, 1 vol. 2013. (Amelia Rules! Set 2 Ser.). (ENG.). 36p. (J). (gr. 3-6). 24.21 *(978-1-61479-070-9(1))* Spotlight.
—Amelia in into Graceland, 1 vol. 2013. (Amelia Rules! Set 2 Ser.). (ENG.). 36p. (J). (gr. 3-6). 24.21 *(978-1-61479-071-6(X))* Spotlight.
—Amelia in Joy & Wonder, 1 vol. 2013. (Amelia Rules! Set 2 Ser.). (ENG.). 36p. (J). (gr. 3-6). 24.21 *(978-1-61479-072-3(8))* Spotlight.
—Her Permanent Record. Gownley, Jimmy, illus. 2012. (Amelia Rules! Ser.). (ENG., Illus.). 160p. (J). (gr. 2-7). 19.99 *(978-1-4169-8615-7(4));* pap. 11.99 *(978-1-4169-8614-0(6))* Simon & Schuster Children's Publishing. (Atheneum Bks. for Young Readers).
—Her Permanent Record. 2012. (Amelia Rules! Ser.: 8). lib. bdg. 23.30 *(978-0-606-26885-1(5),* Turtleback) Turtleback Bks.
—The Meaning of Life ... & Other Stuff. Gownley, Jimmy, illus. 2011. (Amelia Rules! Ser.). (ENG., Illus.). 160p. (J). (gr. 2-7). 19.99 *(978-1-4169-8613-3(8));* pap. 11.99 *(978-1-4169-8612-6(X))* Simon & Schuster Children's Publishing. (Atheneum Bks. for Young Readers).
—When the Past Is a Present. Gownley, Jimmy, illus. 2011. (Amelia Rules! Ser.). (ENG., Illus.). 176p. (J). (gr. 2-7). 19.99 *(978-1-4424-4541-3(6),* Atheneum Bks. for Young Readers) Simon & Schuster Children's Publishing.
—The Whole World's Crazy. Gownley, Jimmy, illus. 2009. (Amelia Rules! Ser.). (ENG., Illus.). 176p. (J). (gr. 2-7). pap. 12.99 *(978-1-4169-8604-1(9),* Atheneum Bks. for Young Readers) Simon & Schuster Children's Publishing.
Grabenstein, Chris. Riley Mack & the Other Known Troublemakers. 2012. (Riley Mack Ser.: 1). (ENG.). 272p. (J). (gr. 3-7). 16.99 *(978-0-06-202620-0(8))* HarperCollins Pubs.
—Riley Mack Stirs up More Trouble. 2013. (Riley Mack Ser.: 2). (ENG.). 336p. (J). (gr. 3-7). 16.99 *(978-0-06-202622-4(4))* HarperCollins Pubs.
Grace, N. B. Lights, Camera, Action! 14th ed. 2009. (ENG.). 128p. (J). pap. 4.99 *(978-1-4231-1609-7(7))* Disney Pr.
Graff, Keir. The Matchstick Castle. 2017. (ENG.). 288p. (J). (gr. 3-7). 16.99 *(978-1-101-99622-5(6),* G.P. Putnam's Sons Books for Young Readers) Penguin Young Readers Group.
Graff, Lisa. The Great Treehouse War. 2017. (ENG.). 288p. (J). (gr. 3-7). 16.99 *(978-0-399-17500-8(8),* Philomel Bks.) Penguin Young Readers Group.
—Lost in the Sun. 2015. (ENG.). 304p. (J). (gr. 5). 16.99 *(978-0-399-16406-4(5),* Philomel Bks.) Penguin Young Readers Group.
—Lost in the Sun. 2016. lib. bdg. 19.65 *(978-0-606-38835-1(4))* Turtleback Bks.
—Sophie Simon Solves Them All. Beene, Jason, illus. 2010. (ENG.). 112p. (J). (gr. 3-5). 14.99 *(978-0-374-37125-8(3),* 9780374371258, Farrar, Straus & Giroux (BYR)) Farrar, Straus & Giroux.
—Sophie Simon Solves Them All. Beene, Jason, illus. 2012. (ENG.). 112p. (J). (gr. 3-5). pap. 6.99 *(978-1-250-02898-3(1),* 9781250028983) Square Fish.
—The Thing about Georgie. 2008. (ENG.). 224p. (J). (gr. 3-7). pap. 6.99 *(978-0-06-087591-6(7))* HarperCollins Pubs.
Graftinvine, D. J. Hobbledehoy: Salvation. 2012. (ENG.). 73p. pap. 12.95 *(978-1-4787-1600-6(2))* Outskirts Pr., Inc.
Graham, Deborah. The Magic Comes Back: A Max & Sam Adventure. 2012. 66p. (gr. 2-4). pap. 8.95 *(978-1-4759-4758-8(5))* iUniverse, Inc.
Graham, Frank. The Adventures of Lil' Bull. 2009. 40p. pap. 16.50 *(978-1-60693-582-8(8),* Eloquent Bks.) Strategic Book Publishing & Rights Agency (SBPRA).
Graham, H. P. & De Bats, M. On the Heels of the Hunted. 2013. 346p. pap. *(978-1-78148-067-0(2))* Grosvenor Hse. Publishing Ltd.
Graham, Hilary Weisman. Reunited. (ENG., 336p. (YA). (gr. 7). 2013. Illus.). pap. 9.99 *(978-1-4424-0687-2(9))* 2012. 16.99 *(978-1-4424-3984-9(X))* Simon & Schuster Bks. For Young Readers. (Simon & Schuster Bks. For Young Readers).
Graham, J. Lee. In the Nick of Time. 2008. 108p. pap. 10.95 *(978-0-595-52621-5(7))* iUniverse, Inc.
Graham, Janice C. The Little Country Girl & Frisky the Squirrel. Allen, S. Joan & Graham, Jerry L., illus. 2008. 32p. pap. 24.95 *(978-1-60610-312-8(1))* America Star Bks.
Graham, Oakley. 3 Go to London. 2016. (Learning Journeys Ser.). (ENG.). 24p. (J). (gr. -1-k). 14.99 *(978-1-78445-312-1(9))* Top That! Publishing PLC GBR. Dist: Independent Pubs. Group.
Graham, Sabrina Depina. Breanna. 2008. 24p. pap. 21.99 *(978-1-4363-0900-4(X))* Xlibris Corp.
Grahame, Kenneth. The Gates of Dawn. Johnson, Joe, tr. Plessix, Michel, illus. 2003. (Wind in the Willows Ser.: Vol. 3). (ENG.). 32p. (gr. 4-7). pap. 15.95 *(978-1-56163-245-9(7))* NBM Publishing Co.
—Mr. Toad, Vol. 2. Johnson, Joe, tr. from FRE. 2003. (Wind in the Willows Ser.: Vol. 2). (ENG., Illus.). 32p. (gr. 4-7). 15.95 *(978-1-56163-218-3(X))* NBM Publishing Co.
—The Reluctant Dragon (Illustrated Edition) 2015. (ENG., Illus.). 42p. pap. *(978-1-5154-0330-2(0),* Illustrated Bks.) Jorge Pinto Bks.
—El Viento en los Sauces.Tr. of Wind in the Willows. (SPA.). 192p. (J). l. 9.50 *(978-84-372-1882-3(9))*ll. 9.50 *(978-84-372-1883-0(7))* Santillana USA Publishing Co., Inc.
—The Wind in the Willows. Bransom, Paul, illus. 2013. 176p. pap. 35.00 *(978-1-927558-25-6(5))* Birch Tree Publishing.
—The Wind in the Willows. Roberts, David, illus. 2013. (ENG.). 256p. (J). (gr. 5). 24.99 *(978-0-7636-6526-5(6))* Candlewick Pr.
—The Wind in the Willows. Moore, Inga, illus. 2009. 184p. pap. 12.99 *(978-0-7606-4211-5(7))* Candlewick Pr.
—The Wind in the Willows. Daily, Don, illus. 2014. (ENG.). 64p. (J). (gr. -1). 18.95 *(978-1-60433-478-4(9),* Applesauce Pr.) Cider Mill Pr. Bk. Pubs., LLC.
—The Wind in the Willows. Benson, Patrick, illus. 2009. (ENG.). 304p. pap. 11.99 *(978-0-00-647926-0(X))* HarperCollins Pubs.
—The Wind in the Willows. 2013. 258p. pap. 12.99 *(978-1-60796-643-2(3))* Meirovich, Igal.
—The Wind in the Willows. Taso, Alex, illus. 2006. (ENG.). 240p. (J). (gr. 5-18). 5.95 *(978-0-451-53014-1(4),* Signet) Penguin Publishing Group.
—The Wind in the Willows. 2005. (ENG.). 240p. (gr. 2-5). 14.00 *(978-0-14-303909-9(1),* Penguin Classics) Penguin Publishing Group.
—The Wind in the Willows. 2013. (Easy Reader Classics Ser.). (ENG., Illus.). 192p. (J). (gr. 1-3). pap. 9.95 *(978-1-4549-0590-5(5))* Sterling Publishing Co., Inc.
—The Wind in the Willows. Ingpen, Robert R., illus. 2012. (Sterling Illustrated Classics Ser.). (ENG.). 224p. (J). (gr. 2-8). 19.95 *(978-1-4027-8283-1(7))* Sterling Publishing Co., Inc.
—The Wind in the Willows. Hanft, Joshua, ed. (Great Illustrated Classics Ser.: Vol. 39). (Illus.). 240p. (J). (gr. 3-6). 9.95 *(978-0-86611-990-0(6))* Waldman Publishing Corp.
—The Wind in the Willows. Moore, Inga, illus. 2009. (Candlewick Illustrated Classics Ser.). (ENG.). 184p. (J). (gr. 5-12). pap. 14.99 *(978-0-7636-4211-2(8))* Candlewick Pr.
—The Wind in the Willows. Shepard, Ernest H., illus. 2007. 259p. (J). (gr. 5-6). reprint ed. lib. bdg. 22.95 *(978-0-88411-877-0(0))* Amereon Ltd.
—The Wind in the Willows. Kliros, Thea, illus. abr. ed. 2011. (Dover Children's Thrift Classics Ser.). (ENG.). 96p. (J). (gr. 3-8). pap. 4.00 *(978-0-486-28600-6(2))* Dover Pubns., Inc.
Grahame, Kenneth & Todd, Justin. The Wind in the Willows. 2013. (Calla Editions Ser.). (ENG., Illus.). 208p. (J). (gr. 3). 30.00 *(978-1-60660-044-3(3))* Dover Pubns., Inc.
Gram, Golden. Gail the Snail: Snailing Around. 2007. 20p. per. 11.95 *(978-1-59858-435-6(9))* Dog Ear Publishing, LLC.
Grambling, Lois G. & Grambling. Shoo! Scat!, 1 vol. Newman, Barbara Johansen, illus. 2004. (ENG.). 32p. (J). 16.95 *(978-0-7614-5167-9(6))* Marshall Cavendish Corp.
Grandmother Littlewolf. Littlestar, 1 vol. Macpherson, Carol, illus. 2010. (ENG.). 19p. pap. 24.95 *(978-1-4489-8619-4(2))* America Star Bks.
Granger, Trudi. Always There Bear. Llewhellin, Gareth, illus. 2015. (ENG.). 32p. (J). (-k). 16.99 *(978-1-63220-434-9(7),* Sky Pony Pr.) Skyhorse Publishing Co., Inc.
Granhold, Adriana. Mattie Knowsmath & the Great Shape Hunt. 2012. 32p. pap. 24.95 *(978-1-4626-7202-8(7))* America Star Bks.
G'rani, Elizebeth. Learning with Kailey & Anthony: Kailey Meets Anthony, 1 vol. 2010. 16p. pap. 24.95 *(978-1-4489-9510-3(8))* PublishAmerica, Inc.
Granny J. Pinky Makes a New Friend: Pinky Frink's Adventures. 2012. 36p. pap. 17.99 *(978-1-105-82663-4(5))* Lulu Pr., Inc.
—Pinky Visits Outer Space: Pinky Frink's Adventures. 2012. 38p. pap. 17.99 *(978-1-300-06064-2(6))* Lulu Pr., Inc.
Grant, Jacob. Cat Knit. 2016. (ENG., Illus.). 40p. (J). 16.99 *(978-1-250-05150-9(9),* 9781250051509) Feiwel & Friends.
Grant, Joan. Cat & Fish. Curtis, Neil, illus. 2005. (ENG.). 32p. (J). (gr. k-3). 16.95 *(978-1-894965-14-9(0))* Simply Read Bks. CAN. Dist: Ingram Publisher Services.
Grant, Karima. Sofie & the City. Montecalvo, Janet, illus. 2006. (ENG.). 32p. (J). (gr. 1-3). 15.95 *(978-1-59078-273-6(9))* Boyds Mills Pr.
Grant, Katy. Acting Out. 2008. (Summer Camp Secrets Ser.). (ENG.). 240p. (J). (gr. 3-7). pap. 7.99 *(978-1-4169-3577-3(0),* Aladdin) Simon & Schuster Children's Publishing.
—Friends Forever. 2008. (Summer Camp Secrets Ser.). (ENG.). 240p. (J). (gr. 3-7). pap. 7.99 *(978-1-4169-3578-0(9),* Aladdin) Simon & Schuster Children's Publishing.
—Pranked. 2008. (Summer Camp Secrets Ser.). (ENG.). 240p. (J). (gr. 3-7). pap. 7.99 *(978-1-4169-3576-6(2),* Aladdin) Simon & Schuster Children's Publishing.
—Rumors. 2010. (Summer Camp Secrets Ser.). (ENG.). 256p. (J). (gr. 3-7). pap. 6.99 *(978-1-4169-9163-2(8),* Aladdin) Simon & Schuster Children's Publishing.
—Tug-of-War. 2010. (Summer Camp Secrets Ser.). (ENG.). 256p. (J). (gr. 3-7). pap. 7.99 *(978-1-4169-9161-8(1),* Aladdin) Simon & Schuster Children's Publishing.
Grant, Myrna. Ivan & the Daring Escape. 2006. (Flamingo Fiction 9-13s Ser.). (ENG., Illus.). 144p. (J). (gr. 4-7). per. 6.99 *(978-1-84550-132-7(2),* 24be2b87-de69-4377-8a1b-bc7b2ad8cd87) Christian Focus Pubns. GBR. Dist: Bookmasters Distribution.
—Ivan & the Informer. 2013. (Flamingo Fiction 9-13s Ser.). (ENG., Illus.). 128p. (J). (gr. 1-8). per. 6.99 *(978-1-84550-134-1(9),* a4873bb8-0b7a-4393-a40a-6315d03042d2) Christian Focus Pubns. GBR. Dist: Bookmasters Distribution.
Grant, Neil. Rhino Chasers. 2003. (ENG., Illus.). 240p. (J). (gr. 11). pap. 13.95 *(978-1-86508-695-8(9))* Allen & Unwin AUS. Dist: Independent Pubs. Group.
Grant, Tess. Flying in the Dark. 2013. 186p. pap. 10.99 *(978-1-62237-167-9(4))* Turquoise Morning Pr.
Grant, Vicki. Triggered, 1 vol. 2013. (Orca Soundings Ser.). (ENG.). 128p. (YA). (gr. 8-12). pap. 9.95 *(978-1-4598-0526-2(7));* lib. bdg. 16.95 *(978-1-4598-0529-3(1))* Orca Bk. Pubs. USA.
Graphman, Wm. Matthew. Chel & Riley Adventures: The K9 Kidnapping Adventure. 2011. 80p. (gr. 4-6). pap. 9.99 *(978-1-4567-9574-0(0))* AuthorHouse.
Graves, Kassie. Brave Little Sailboat. Graves, Kassie, illus. 2003. (Illus.). 20p. (J). 14.95 *(978-0-9728019-0-4(1))* Bright Eyes Pr.
Graves, Susan Elaine. Rescued & Making New Friends. 2011. 50p. pap. 24.95 *(978-1-4560-6776-2(1))* America Star Bks.
Gravett, Emily. Bear & Hare Go Fishing. Gravett, Emily, illus. 2015. (Bear & Hare Ser.). (ENG., Illus.). 32p. (J). (gr. -1-3). 15.99 *(978-1-4814-2289-5(8),* Simon & Schuster Bks. For Young Readers) Simon & Schuster Bks. For Young Readers.
—Bear & Hare Snow! Gravett, Emily, illus. 2015. (Bear & Hare Ser.). (ENG., Illus.). 32p. (J). (gr. -1-3). 16.99 *(978-1-4814-4514-6(6),* Simon & Schuster Bks. For Young Readers) Simon & Schuster Bks. For Young Readers.
—Blue Chameleon. Gravett, Emily, illus. 2011. (ENG., Illus.). 32p. (J). (gr. -1-1). 16.99 *(978-1-4424-1958-2(X),* Simon & Schuster Bks. For Young Readers) Simon & Schuster Bks. For Young Readers.
—Where's Bear? Gravett, Emily, illus. 2016. (Bear & Hare Ser.). (ENG., Illus.). 32p. (J). (gr. -1-3). 16.99 *(978-1-4814-5615-9(6),* Simon & Schuster Bks. For Young Readers) Simon & Schuster Bks. For Young Readers.
Gravley, Debbie Bybee. Golden Lace & the Magical Mossy Woods. 2005. 25.00 *(978-0-9771793-0-5(3))* Gravley, Debbie Bybee.
Gray, Bianca. Back to School: Adventures of Alex & Joey. 2013. 20p. pap. 17.99 *(978-1-4817-0425-0(7))* AuthorHouse.
Gray, Clio. Peder & the Skincatcher. 2013. 188p. (J). pap. *(978-1-78299-157-1(3))* FeedARead.com.
Gray, Jacky. Rory. 2010. 199p. pap. 16.95 *(978-1-4461-5021-4(6))* Lulu Pr., Inc.
Gray, Keith. Ostrich Boys. 2011. (ENG.). 304p. (YA). (gr. 7). pap. 9.99 *(978-0-375-85844-4(X),* Random Hse. Bks. for Young Readers) Random Hse. Children's Bks.
Gray, Laurie. Summer Sanctuary. 2010. (ENG.). 193p. (YA). (gr. 7). pap. 11.95 *(978-1-935462-34-7(2))* Luminis Bks., Inc.
Gray, Libba Moore. Is There Room on the Feather Bed? 2004. (Illus.). (J). (gr. -1-2). spiral bd. *(978-0-616-03037-0(1));* spiral bd. *(978-0-616-04555-8(7))* Canadian National Institute for the Blind/Institut National Canadien pour les Aveugles.
Gray, Rev. Maxine A. Children's Lessons on Morality: Don't Use Your Friends. 2013. 24p. pap. 14.99 *(978-1-4669-8831-6(2))* Trafford Publishing.
Gray, Rick & Gray, Coral. Evangel Meets Orsen Whale. Headley, Aaron, illus. 2007. (ENG.). 32p. (J). (gr. -1-3). 14.95 *(978-0-9790210-1-5(4))* Evening Star Enterprise, Inc.
Gray, Stephen J. For the Love of a Cloud Maker. 2013. 28p. pap. 13.55 *(978-1-4669-8004-4(1))* Trafford Publishing.
Greathouse, Cindy. Robin the Abused Child. 2011. 28p. pap. 24.95 *(978-1-60749-065-4(X))* America Star Bks.
Greathouse, Rebecca. Katie & Riley's Magical Adventures: Journey to the Amazon. 2006. 48p. pap. 16.95 *(978-1-4241-5341-1(7))* America Star Bks.
Greeley, David. Seven Friends, 1 vol. Marquis, KariAnn, illus. 2010. 38p. 24.95 *(978-1-4489-4101-8(6))* PublishAmerica, Inc.
Green, Amy. Escape from Riddler's Pass, Vol. 2. 2011. (ENG., Illus.). 176p. (J). pap. 7.99 *(978-1-59317-433-0(0))* Warner Pr., Inc.
Green, D. L. Kaitlyn & the Competition. 2016. (Babysitter Chronicles Ser.). (ENG.). 160p. (gr. 4-7). pap. 6.95 *(978-1-4914-8861-4(1))* Stone Arch Bks.
—Zeke Meeks, 1 vol. Alves, Josh, illus. 2014. (Zeke Meeks Ser.). (ENG.). 128p. (gr. 2-2). 45.30 *(978-1-4795-2045-9(4),* Zeke Meeks) Picture Window Bks.
—Zeke Meeks vs the Big Blah-Rific Birthday, 1 vol. Alves, Josh, illus. 2013. (Zeke Meeks Ser.). (ENG.). 128p. (gr. 2-2). 8.95 *(978-1-4048-8105-1(0));* lib. bdg. 22.65 *(978-1-4048-7637-8(5))* Picture Window Bks. (Zeke Meeks).
—Zeke Meeks vs the Gruesome Girls, 1 vol. Alves, Josh, illus. 2012. (Zeke Meeks Ser.). (ENG.). 128p. (gr. 2-2). pap. 5.95 *(978-1-4048-7221-9(3));* lib. bdg. 22.65 *(978-1-4048-6805-2(4))* Picture Window Bks. (Zeke Meeks).
—Zeke Meeks vs the Putrid Puppet Pals, 1 vol. Alves, Josh, illus. 2012. (Zeke Meeks Ser.). (ENG.). 128p. (gr. 2-2). pap. 5.95 *(978-1-4048-7223-3(X));* lib. bdg. 22.65 *(978-1-4048-6803-8(8))* Picture Window Bks. (Zeke Meeks).
—Zeke Meeks vs the Stinkin' Science Fair, 1 vol. Alves, Josh, illus. 2012. (Zeke Meeks Ser.). (ENG.). 128p. (gr. 2-2). pap. 5.95 *(978-1-4048-7222-6(1));* lib. bdg. 22.65 *(978-1-4048-6802-1(X))* Picture Window Bks. (Zeke Meeks).
Green, John. Turtles All the Way Down. 2017. lib. bdg. 33.05 ***(978-0-606-40748-9(0))*** Turtleback Bks.
Green, John Patrick. Hippopotamister. 2016. (ENG., Illus.). 96p. (J). 17.99 *(978-1-62672-200-2(5),* 9781626722002, First Second Bks.) Roaring Brook Pr.
Green, Judith. A Family Secret. Hammah, Aisha, illus. 2013. 32p. pap. *(978-0-9810759-7-6(5))* WTL International.
Green, Kevin M. Livy Bug & Ally Gator in Best Friends. 2008. 16p. per. 24.95 *(978-1-4241-9385-1(0))* America Star Bks.
Green, Kim. Rinny Rhino Wants Pink Pearls & a Polka Dotted Penguin. 2013. 46p. pap. 14.99 *(978-1-61863-530-3(1))* Bookstand Publishing.
Green, Margaret. It Takes Teamwork! 2016. (Dinotrux 8X8 Ser.). (J). lib. bdg. 14.75 *(978-0-606-38319-6(0))* Turtleback Bks.
—Meet Garby! 2016. (Dinotrux Passport Reading Level 1 Ser.). (J). lib. bdg. 13.55 *(978-0-606-39189-4(4))* Turtleback Bks.
Green, Margaret. Monster High: Fierce Friends. 2017. (Passport to Reading Level 2 Ser.). (ENG., Illus.). 32p. (J). (gr. -1-3). pap. 3.99 ***(978-0-316-54838-0(3))*** Little, Brown Bks. for Young Readers.
Green, Poppy. A New Friend. Bell, Jennifer A., illus. 2015. (Adventures of Sophie Mouse Ser.: 1). (ENG.). 128p. (J). (gr. k-4). pap. 5.99 *(978-1-4814-2832-3(2),* Little Simon) Little Simon.
—A Surprise Visitor. Bell, Jennifer A., illus. 2016. (Adventures of Sophie Mouse Ser.: 8). (ENG.). 128p. (J). (gr. k-4). pap. 5.99 *(978-1-4814-6698-1(4),* Little Simon) Little Simon.
Green, Terry. Moonstone. 2010. 188p. pap. 14.49 *(978-1-4520-4634-1(4))* AuthorHouse.
Green, Tim. Force Out. 2013. (ENG.). 288p. (J). (gr. 3-7). 16.99 *(978-0-06-208959-5(5))* HarperCollins Pubs.
—Perfect Season. 2014. (Football Genius Ser.: 6). (ENG.). 416p. (J). (gr. 3-7). pap. 6.99 *(978-0-06-220870-5(5))* HarperCollins Pubs.
—Rivals: A Baseball Great Novel. (Baseball Great Ser.: 2). (ENG.). (J). (gr. 3-7). 2011. 288p. pap. 6.99 *(978-0-06-162694-4(5))* 2010. 272p. 16.99 *(978-0-06-162692-0(9))* HarperCollins Pubs.
Green, Vyridian E. Ruby Red Finds a New Home. 2015. (ENG.). 44p. (J). (gr. 2-3). mass mkt. 13.95 *(978-1-78455-723-2(4),* c74571f1-0c9e-4fc5-ac85-cb7c36470ecb) Austin, Stan AUS. Dist: Bookmasters Distribution.
Greene, Bette. I've Already Forgotten Your Name, Philip Hall! Jenkins, Leonard, illus. 2004. 176p. (J). (gr. 5-18). 15.99 *(978-0-06-051835-6(9))* HarperCollins Pubs.
Greene, Joshua M. Krishna & the Mystery of the Stolen Calves. Amendola, Dominique, illus. 2013. (ENG.). 24p. (gr. -1). 14.99 *(978-1-60887-173-5(8))* Mandala Publishing.
Greene, Kristy. How Penguins Lost Their Flight. 2012. 20p. pap. 24.95 *(978-1-4626-7697-2(9))* America Star Bks.
Greene, Richard. Lawrence the Locomotive. 2004. 49p. pap. 16.95 *(978-1-4137-5704-0(9))* America Star Bks.
Greene, Stephanie. Moose's Big Idea, 0 vols. Mathieu, Joe, illus. 2010. (Moose & Hildy Ser.: 0). (ENG.). 64p. (J). (gr. 1-4). pap. 6.99 *(978-0-7614-5698-8(8),* 9780761456988, Amazon Children's Publishing) Amazon Publishing.
—Owen Foote, Super Spy. Weston, Martha, illus. 2005. (ENG.). 96p. (J). (gr. 1-4). pap. 8.95 *(978-0-618-55159-0(X))* Houghton Mifflin Harcourt Publishing Co.
—Pig Pickin', 0 vols. Mathieu, Joe, illus. 2013. (Moose & Hildy Ser.). (ENG.). 68p. (J). (gr. -1-3). pap. 9.99 *(978-1-4778-1684-4(4),* 9781477816844, Amazon Children's Publishing) Amazon Publishing.
—Princess Posey & the First Grade Ballet. Sisson, Stéphanie Roth, illus. 2014. (Princess Posey, First Grader Ser.: 9). (ENG.). 96p. (J). (gr. k-3). pap. 5.99 *(978-0-14-751292-5(1),* Puffin Books) Penguin Young Readers Group.
—Princess Posey & the Monster Stew, 4 vols. Sisson, Stéphanie Roth, illus. 2012. (Princess Posey, First Grader Ser.: 4). (ENG.). 96p. (J). (gr. k-3). pap. 5.99 *(978-0-14-242105-5(7),* Puffin Books) Penguin Young Readers Group.
—Princess Posey & the New First Grader. Sisson, Stéphanie Roth, illus. 2013. (Princess Posey, First Grader Ser.: 6). (ENG.). 96p. (J). pap. 4.99 *(978-0-14-242763-7(2),* Puffin Books) Penguin Young Readers Group.
—Princess Posey & the Perfect Present, Bk. 2. Sisson, Stéphanie Roth, illus. 2011. (Princess Posey, First Grader Ser.: 2). (ENG.). 96p. (J). (gr. k-3). 5.99 *(978-0-14-241828-4(5),* Puffin Books); 12.99 *(978-0-399-25462-8(5),* G.P. Putnam's Sons Books for Young Readers) Penguin Young Readers Group.
—Queen Sophie Hartley. 2011. (ENG.). 144p. (J). (gr. 2-5). pap. 5.99 *(978-0-547-55021-3(9))* Houghton Mifflin Harcourt Publishing Co.
—The Show-Off, 0 vols. Mathieu, Joe, illus. (Moose & Hildy Ser.). (ENG.). 64p. (J). (gr. 1-4). 2013. pap. 9.99 *(978-1-4778-1686-8(0),* 9781477816868) 2007. lib. bdg. 14.99 *(978-0-7614-5374-1(1),* 9780761453741) Amazon Publishing. (Amazon Children's Publishing).
Greene, Thomas. Whacked Out Wrestling: Memorial - A tale of Headlocks, Hurricanranas, & High School. 2007. 228p. pap. 14.95 *(978-1-60145-175-0(X))* Booklocker.com, Inc.
Greenham, Caz. The Adventures of Eric Seagull. Homfray, Nick, illus. 2013. 40p. pap. *(978-1-78132-093-8(4))* SilverWood Bks.
Greenhill, Ms Jane. Jolly Olde Teenage Alien. 2013. 258p. pap. *(978-0-9918766-2-4(8))* Greenhill, Jane.
Greenwald, Lisa. Dog Beach Unleashed. 2015. (Seagate Summers Ser.). (ENG., Illus.). 240p. (YA). (gr. 5-9). 15.95 *(978-1-4197-1481-8(3),* Amulet Bks.) Abrams, Inc.
—Epic Kale: And Other Cleanses for a Broken Heart. 2017. (YA). pap. ***(978-0-399-55641-8(9))*** Random Hse., Inc.
—Kale, My Ex, & Other Things to Toss in a Blender. 2017. (ENG.). 272p. (YA). (gr. 7). 17.99 ***(978-0-399-55638-8(9),*** Random Hse. Bks. for Young Readers) Random Hse. Children's Bks.
—Sweet Treats & Secret Crushes. (ENG.). (YA). (gr. 3-7). 2011. 320p. pap. 7.95 *(978-1-4197-0029-3(4))* 2010. 304p. 16.95 *(978-0-8109-8990-0(5))* Abrams, Inc. (Amulet Bks.).
—Welcome to Dog Beach. 2014. (Seagate Summers Ser.). (ENG.). 272p. (YA). (gr. 3-7). 15.95 *(978-1-4197-1018-6(4),* Amulet Bks.) Abrams, Inc.
Greenwald, Lisa. 11 Before 12. 2017. 416p. (J). (gr. 3-7). 16.99 ***(978-0-06-241174-7(8),*** Tegen, Katherine Bks) HarperCollins Pubs.
Greenwald, Tommy. It's a Doggy Dog World. Stower, Adam, illus. 2016. (Crimebiters Ser.: 2). (ENG.). 240p. (J). (gr. 3-7). 12.99 *(978-0-545-78397-2(6),* Scholastic Pr.) Scholastic, Inc.
—Pete Milano's Guide to Being a Movie Star. Roher, Rebecca, illus. 2016. (ENG.). 256p. (J). 13.99 *(978-1-62672-167-8(X),* 9781626721678) Roaring Brook Pr.
—The Real Us. Burniac, Lauren, ed. Coovert, J. P., illus. 2017. (ENG.). 256p. (J). 16.99 *(978-1-62672-171-5(8),* 9781626721715) Roaring Brook Pr.
Greenwood, Anna. The Children at St Bartholomew's Hospital. 2008. 172p. pap. 13.95 *(978-1-4401-0558-6(8))* iUniverse, Inc.
Greenwood, Dwayne. The Tales of Wally the Whale & Sammy the Salmon. 2006. 17.00 *(978-0-8059-9074-4(7))* Dorrance Publishing Co., Inc.
Greer, Hannah. The Lighthouse Summer Greer, Tica, illus. 2009. 156p. pap. 24.95 *(978-1-60813-493-9(8))* America Star Bks.
Gregar, Steve. Buzz the Fly. 2004. 14p. pap. 9.98 *(978-1-4116-1147-4(0))* Lulu Pr., Inc.
Gregorowski, Christopher. Fly, Eagle, Fly: An African Tale. Daly, Niki, illus. 2008. (ENG.). 36p. (J). (gr. -1-3). 12.99 *(978-1-4169-7599-1(3),* Aladdin) Simon & Schuster Children's Publishing.
Gregory, Kristiana. Bronte's Book Club. 2008. (ENG., Illus.). 160p. (J). (gr. 3-7). pap. 7.95 *(978-0-8234-2209-8(7));* 16.95 *(978-0-8234-2136-7(8))* Holiday Hse., Inc.
Greiner, Gail. Patchwork Helps a Friend. Schmidt, Jacqueline, illus. 2013. (ENG.). 40p. (J). (gr. -1-2). 17.95 *(978-1-57687-642-8(X),* powerHouse Bks.) powerHouse Cultural Entertainment, Inc.
Gresh, Dannah. Danika's Totally Terrible Toss. 2008. (Secret Keeper Girl Fiction Ser.). (ENG.). 112p. pap. 7.99 *(978-0-8024-8702-5(5))* Moody Pubs.

Gresh, Dannah & Mylin, Janet. Just Call Me Kate. 2008. (Secret Keeper Girl Fiction Ser.). (ENG.). 112p. pap. 7.99 *(978-0-8024-8703-2(3))* Moody Pubs.
Gresh, Dannah K. & Weibel, Suzy. T Is for AnTONIa. 2008. (Secret Keeper Girl Fiction Ser.). (ENG.). 96p. pap. 7.99 *(978-0-8024-8705-6(X))* Moody Pubs.
Griebel, Roberta L. Joyful Noise! 2007. (ENG.). 56p. per. 16.95 *(978-1-4241-6037-2(5))* America Star Bks.
Griffin, Adele. The Julian Game. 2011. (ENG.). 208p. (YA). (gr. 7-18). 7.99 *(978-0-14-241973-1(7)*, Speak) Penguin Young Readers Group.
—The Knaveheart's Curse. 2009. (Vampire Island Ser.). (ENG.). 160p. (J). (gr. 3-7). 6.99 *(978-0-14-241407-1(7)*, Puffin Books) Penguin Young Readers Group.
Griffin, Adele & Sheinmel, Courtney. Agnes & Clarabelle. Palacios, Sara, illus. 2017. (Agnes & Clarabelle Ser.). (ENG.). 80p. (J). 9.99 *(978-1-61963-137-3(7)*, 9781619631373, Bloomsbury USA Childrens) Bloomsbury Publishing USA.
—Agnes & Clarabelle Celebrate! Palacios, Sara, illus. 2017. (Agnes & Clarabelle Ser.). (ENG.). 80p. (J). 9.99 *(978-1-61963-217-2(9)*, 9781619632172, Bloomsbury USA Childrens) Bloomsbury Publishing USA.
Griffin, Claire J. Nowhere to Run. 2013. 118p. 18.95 *(978-1-60898-144-1(4))*; pap. 9.95 *(978-1-60898-145-8(2))* namelos llc.
Griffin, N. The Whole Stupid Way We Are. (ENG., Illus.). 368p. (YA). (gr. 9). 2014. pap. 9.99 *(978-1-4424-3156-0(3))* 2013. 16.99 *(978-1-4424-3155-3(5))* Simon & Schuster Children's Publishing. (Atheneum Bks. for Young Readers).
Griffin, Paul. When Friendship Followed Me Home. 2016. (ENG.). 256p. (J). (gr. 5-9). 16.99 *(978-0-8037-3816-4(1)*, Dial Bks) Penguin Young Readers Group.
Griffin, Wiley Chase. Chase the Shark: Flies Like a Bird. 2010. 28p. pap. 12.50 *(978-1-4520-5173-4(9))* AuthorHouse.
Griffith, Christina. Jubilee & Ashanti Find Insects. 2011. 28p. (gr. 2-4). pap. 13.54 *(978-1-4269-7068-9(4))* Trafford Publishing.
—Why Jubilee & Ashanti go to the Doctor? 2011. 28p. pap. 13.54 *(978-1-4269-7069-6(2))* Trafford Publishing.
Griffiths, Andy. Ed & Ted & Ted's Dog Fred. Denton, Terry, illus. 2014. (My Readers Ser.). (ENG.). 32p. (J). (gr. -1-1). 15.99 *(978-1-250-04447-1(2)*, 9781250044471) Square Fish.
—Ed & Ted & Ted's Dog Fred. 2014. (My Readers: Level 2 Ser.). (J). lib. bdg. 13.55 *(978-0-606-35525-4(1))* Turtleback Bks.
Griffo, Michael. Starfall. 2014. (Darkborn Legacy Ser.). (ENG.). 384p. (YA). (gr. 13). pap. 20.00 *(978-0-7582-8076-3(9)*, K-Teen) Kensington Publishing Corp.
Griggs, Rosemarie. The Adventures of Donkey Tom Volume 2: Crystal Forest. 2012. 40p. pap. 32.70 *(978-1-4797-0553-5(5))* Xlibris Corp.
Griggs, Terry. Nieve. L'Hirondelle, Cheryl, illus. 2010. (ENG.). 264p. (J). (gr. 4-10). pap. 14.95 *(978-1-897231-87-6(3))* Biblioasis CAN. Dist: Consortium Bk. Sales & Distribution.
Grime, L. L. Do You Love Me? 2008. 48p. pap. 22.95 *(978-1-4357-1364-2(8))* Lulu Pr., Inc.
Grimes, Nikki. Danitra Brown, Class Clown. Lewis, E. B., illus. 2005. 32p. (J). lib. bdg. 17.89 *(978-0-688-17291-6(1))*; (ENG.). (gr. 3). 16.99 *(978-0-688-17290-9(3)*, Amistad) HarperCollins Pubs.
—Make Way for Dyamonde Daniel. Christie, R. Gregory, illus. (Dyamonde Daniel Book Ser.: 1). (ENG.). (J). (gr. 2-4). 2010. 112p. pap. 5.99 *(978-0-14-241555-9(3)*, Puffin Books) 2009. 96p. 10.99 *(978-0-399-25175-7(8)*, G.P. Putnam's Sons Books for Young Readers) Penguin Young Readers Group.
—Planet Middle School. 2011. (ENG.). 160p. (YA). 15.99 *(978-1-59990-284-5(2)*, 9781599902845, Bloomsbury USA Childrens) Bloomsbury Publishing USA.
—Rich. Christie, R. Gregory, illus. 2009. (Dyamonde Daniel Book Ser.: 2). (ENG.). 112p. (J). (gr. 2-4). 12.99 *(978-0-399-25176-4(6)*, G.P. Putnam's Sons Books for Young Readers) Penguin Young Readers Group.
Grimm, Jacob & Grimm, Wilhelm K. Hansel & Gretel/Hansel y Gretel. 2004. (Illus.). (J). *(978-1-933530-14-7(6))* Bingo Bks., Inc.
Grimm, Kristi. Mommy, Tell Me a Story about a Car, 2nd Edition. Grimm, Dave, illus. 2nd ed. 2013. 32p. pap. 13.99 *(978-0-9855699-9-0(9))* Richer Life, LLC.
—Mommy, Tell Me a Story about a Fish. 2013. (Illus.). 34p. pap. 13.99 *(978-0-9899001-3-3(4))* Richer Life, LLC.
—Mommy, Tell Me a Story about a Plane, 2nd Edition. Grimm, Dave, illus. 2nd ed. 2013. 36p. pap. 13.99 *(978-0-9855699-8-3(0))* Richer Life, LLC.
Grindley, Sally. Bravo, Max! Ross, Tony, illus. 2007. (ENG.). 160p. (J). (gr. 1-4). pap. 8.99 *(978-1-4169-3645-9(9)*, Simon & Schuster/Paula Wiseman Bks.) Simon & Schuster/Paula Wiseman Bks.
Grindley, Sally & Lucas, D J. Dear Max. Ross, Tony, illus. 2007. (ENG.). 144p. (J). (gr. 1-4). pap. 7.99 *(978-1-4169-3443-1(X)*, Simon & Schuster/Paula Wiseman Bks.) Simon & Schuster/Paula Wiseman Bks.
Grinnell, Suzanne. Where Is Beau? Peter, Joshua, illus. 2008. 24p. pap. 12.99 *(978-1-59858-612-1(2))* Dog Ear Publishing, LLC.
Griswold, Melissa. Friends, Like You. Fisher, Cynthia, illus. 2007. (J). 24.95 *(978-0-9797287-2-3(X))*; 32p. 15.00 *(978-0-9797287-3-0(8))* Mainstream Ctr., Schl. for the Deaf, The.
—Friends, Like You: Children's Activity Book. Fisher, Cynthia, illus. 2007. 16p. (J). *(978-0-9797287-4-7(6))* Mainstream Ctr., Schl. for the Deaf, The.
—Friends, Like You: Educator's Guide. 2007. 12p. *(978-0-9797287-5-4(4))* Mainstream Ctr., Schl. for the Deaf, The.
Griver, Jeanette A. CURIO a Shetland Sheepdog & her Pals: All ages Will enjoy the Tales of Friendship. 2007. (J). per. 8.50 *(978-0-929948-06-5(8))* Compsych Systems, Inc., Pubns. Div.
Groethe, Kd. The Boy Who Would Walk on Air. 2012. 118p. (gr. -1). 23.99 *(978-1-4772-9164-1(4))*; pap. 14.95 *(978-1-4772-9165-8(2))* AuthorHouse.
Grosgebauer, Clare Ham. Snickerdoodle's Star-Spangled Fourth of July! Rissing, Karen, illus. 4th ed. 2005. 36p. (J). (gr. -1-3). 12.99 *(978-0-9741888-6-7(7))* Small Wonders Enterprises.
Gross, S. D. Blue Frog. Lt. ed. 2006. (Illus.). 24p. (J). per. 11.99 *(978-1-59879-207-2(5))* Lifevest Publishing, Inc.
—Freddie. 2007. (Illus.). 22p. (J). per. 12.99 *(978-1-59879-342-0(X))* Lifevest Publishing, Inc.
—Freddie, Fireman Mike. 2007. (Illus.). 24p. (J). (gr. -1-3). per. 12.99 *(978-1-59879-343-7(8))* Lifevest Publishing, Inc.
Grosset & Dunlap. Berry Merry Holiday Treasury. 2014. (Strawberry Shortcake Ser.). (ENG.). 160p. (J). (gr. -1-k). 9.99 *(978-0-448-48360-3(2)*, Grosset & Dunlap) Penguin Young Readers Group.
Grossinger, Tania. Jackie & Me: A Very Special Friendship. Esperanza, Charles George, illus. 2013. (ENG.). 32p. (J). (gr. -1-3). 16.95 *(978-1-62087-683-1(3)*, 620683, Sky Pony Pr.) Skyhorse Publishing Co., Inc.
Grosso, Salvatore. The Butterfly & the Dinosaur: A true story of fiction Inspired by a Beautiful Butterfly. 2010. 32p. pap. 16.99 *(978-1-4490-6603-1(8))* AuthorHouse.
Grout, Claire. Emil & Ordi: Friends for All Time. 2012. 24p. pap. 15.99 *(978-1-4691-6279-9(2))* Xlibris Corp.
Grove, Malachai. The Return of Malachai. 2011. 24p. pap. 14.99 *(978-1-4567-6257-5(5))* AuthorHouse.
Groves, Odessa M. Playful Teeth: Login. 2008. (Illus.). 68p. pap. 21.95 *(978-0-9820002-1-2(9))* G Publishing LLC.
Grovet, Heather. Blondie's Big Ride. 2008. (Illus.). 95p. (J). pap. 5.97 *(978-0-8163-2225-1(2))* Pacific Pr. Publishing Assn.
—Super Star Problems. 2008. (J). pap. 5.97 *(978-0-8163-2255-8(4))* Pacific Pr. Publishing Assn.
Grovet, Heather Marie. Marvelous Mark & His No-Good Dog. 2003. (Review Kids Ser.). 128p. (J). pap. 7.99 *(978-0-8280-1734-3(4)*, 132-670) Review & Herald Publishing Assn.
Gruber, Daveda. More Tales of a Tiny Dog. 2009. 71p. pap. 32.50 *(978-1-4092-6657-0(5))* Lulu Pr., Inc.
Grund, Carol A. Anna Mei, Cartoon Girl. 2010. 140p. (J). (gr. 4-7). pap. 8.95 *(978-0-8198-0788-5(2))* Pauline Bks. & Media.
—Anna Mei, Escape Artist. 2011. 168p. (J). (gr. 4-7). pap. 8.95 *(978-0-8198-0794-6(X))* Pauline Bks. & Media.
Guardo, Attilio. A Special Time in Clear Creek. 2004. 184p. pap. 24.95 *(978-1-4137-2872-9(3))* America Star Bks.
Guatemala, Anne. The Story of Señor Pico. Frazao, Catia, illus. 2007.Tr. of Historia del Señor Pico. (ENG & SPA.). 32p. (J). pap. 17.00 *(978-0-8059-7818-6(6))* Dorrance Publishing Co., Inc.
Gudeon, Adam. Ping Wants to Play. Gudeon, Adam, illus. 2014. (I Like to Read(r) Ser.). (ENG., Illus.). 24p. (J). (gr. -1-3). 14.95 *(978-0-8234-2854-0(0))* Holiday Hse., Inc.
Gudeon, Adam & Gudeon, Adam. Ping Wants to Play. 2015. (I Like to Read(r) Ser.). (ENG.). 24p. (J). (gr. -1-3). 6.99 *(978-0-8234-3313-1(7))* Holiday Hse., Inc.
Guerra, Elisa Puricelli. The City of Lizards. Zeni, Marco, tr. from ITA. Bernstein, Gabriel León, illus. 2015. (Minerva Mint Ser.). (ENG.). 160p. (gr. 2-4). lib. bdg. 25.32 *(978-1-4342-9671-9(7))* Stone Arch Bks.
—The Forest of Talking Trees. Zeni, Marco, tr. from ITA. Bernstein, Gabriel León, illus. 2015. (Minerva Mint Ser.). (ENG.). 160p. (gr. 2-4). lib. bdg. 25.32 *(978-1-4342-9673-3(3))* Stone Arch Bks.
—The Legend of Black Bart, 1 vol. Pernigotti, Chiara, tr. from ITA. Bernstein, Gabo León, illus. 2014. (Minerva Mint Ser.). (ENG.). 160p. (gr. 2-4). pap. 7.99 *(978-1-4342-6515-9(3))* Capstone Young Readers of Coughlan Cos.
—The Legend of Black Bart, 1 vol. Pernigotti, Chiara, tr. from ITA. Bernstein, Gabo León, illus. 2014. (Minerva Mint Ser.). (ENG.). 160p. (gr. 2-4). 25.32 *(978-1-4342-6512-8(9))* Stone Arch Bks.
—Merlin's Island, 1 vol. Pernigotti, Chiara, tr. from ITA. Bernstein, Gabriel León, illus. 2014. (Minerva Mint Ser.). (ENG.). 160p. (gr. 2-4). pap. 7.99 *(978-1-4342-6514-2(5))* Capstone Young Readers of Coughlan Cos.
—Merlin's Island, 1 vol. Pernigotti, Chiara, tr. from ITA. Bernstein, Gabo León, illus. 2014. (Minerva Mint Ser.). (ENG.). 160p. (gr. 2-4). 25.32 *(978-1-4342-6511-1(0))* Stone Arch Bks.
—Minerva Mint, 1 vol. 2014. (Minerva Mint Ser.). (ENG.). 160p. (gr. 2-4). 75.96 *(978-1-4342-8932-2(X))* Stone Arch Bks.
—The Night of the Blue Turtles. Zeni, Marco, tr. from ITA. Bernstein, Gabriel León, illus. 2015. (Minerva Mint Ser.). (ENG.). 160p. (gr. 2-4). lib. bdg. 25.32 *(978-1-4342-9672-6(5))* Stone Arch Bks.
—The Order of the Owls, 1 vol. Bernstein, Gabo León, illus. 2014. (Minerva Mint Ser.). (ENG.). 160p. (gr. 2-4). 9.95 *(978-1-62370-038-6(8))* Capstone Young Readers of Coughlan Cos.
Guerra, S. F. Billy the Kid Is Not Crazy, 0 vols. 2013. (ENG.). 224p. (J). (gr. 4-6). 16.99 *(978-1-4778-1732-2(8)*, 9781477817322, Amazon Children's Publishing) Amazon Publishing.
Guerra, Stephanie. Torn, 0 vols. 2012. (ENG.). 272p. (YA). (gr. 10-12). 17.99 *(978-0-7614-6272-9(4)*, 9780761462729, Amazon Children's Publishing) Amazon Publishing.
Guerrera, Jeannette D. The Dumb-Dumb Angel. 2012. 20p. pap. 17.99 *(978-1-4685-5426-7(3))* AuthorHouse.
Guerrero, Rhonda. It's Me, Penny! The Hot Air Balloon Adventure. Leech, Jacob, illus. 2011. 28p. pap. 24.95 *(978-1-4489-7070-4(9))* America Star Bks.
Guertin, Chantel. The Rule of Thirds. 2013. (Pippa Greene Novel Ser.). (ENG., Illus.). 220p. (J). (gr. 7-11). pap. *(978-1-77041-159-3(3))* Me to We.
Guest, Elissa Haden. Iris & Walter. Davenier, Christine, illus. alt. ed. 2012. (Green Light Readers Level 3 Ser.). (ENG.). 44p. (J). (gr. 1-4). pap. 3.99 *(978-0-547-74555-8(9))* Houghton Mifflin Harcourt Publishing Co.
—Iris & Walter. 2012. (Iris & Walter — Green Light Reader Ser.). lib. bdg. 13.55 *(978-0-606-24229-5(5)*, Turtleback) Turtleback Bks.
—Iris & Walter & Baby Rose. Davenier, Christine, illus. 2012. (Green Light Readers Level 3 Ser.). (ENG.). 44p. (J). (gr. 1-4). pap. 3.99 *(978-0-547-85064-1(6))* Houghton Mifflin Harcourt Publishing Co.
—Iris & Walter & Cousin Howie. Davenier, Christine, illus. alt. ed. 2012. (Green Light Readers Level 3 Ser.). (ENG.). 44p. (J). (gr. 1-4). pap. 3.99 *(978-0-547-85068-9(9))* Houghton Mifflin Harcourt Publishing Co.
—Iris & Walter & the Field Trip. Davenier, Christine, illus. 2013. (Green Light Readers Level 3 Ser.). (ENG.). 44p. (J). (gr. 1-4). pap. 3.99 *(978-0-544-10665-9(2))* Houghton Mifflin Harcourt Publishing Co.
—Iris & Walter & the Field Trip. Davenier, Christine, illus. 2007. (Iris & Walter Ser.). 44p. (J). (gr. 1-4). 13.60 *(978-0-7569-8041-2(0))* Perfection Learning Corp.
—Iris & Walter & the Field Trip. 2013. (Iris & Walter — Green Light Reader Ser.). lib. bdg. 13.55 *(978-0-606-33987-2(6)*, Turtleback) Turtleback Bks.
—Iris & Walter Book & CD. Davenier, Christine, illus. 2015. (Green Light Readers Level 3 Ser.). (ENG.). 44p. (J). (gr. -1-3). audio compact disk 6.99 *(978-0-544-45604-4(1)*, HMH Books For Young Readers) Houghton Mifflin Harcourt Publishing Co.
—Iris & Walter: Substitute Teacher. Davenier, Christine, illus. 2014. (Green Light Readers Level 3 Ser.). (ENG.). 44p. (J). (gr. 1-4). pap. 3.99 *(978-0-544-22788-0(3)*, HMH Books For Young Readers) Houghton Mifflin Harcourt Publishing Co.
—Iris & Walter: the School Play. Davenier, Christine, illus. 2015. (Green Light Readers Level 3 Ser.). (ENG.). 44p. (J). (gr. 1-4). pap. 3.99 *(978-0-544-45602-0(5)*, HMH Books For Young Readers) Houghton Mifflin Harcourt Publishing Co.
—Iris & Walter: True Friends. Davenier, Christine, illus. 2015. (Green Light Readers Level 3 Ser.). (ENG.). 44p. (J). (gr. 1-4). pap. 3.99 *(978-0-544-45603-7(3)*, HMH Books For Young Readers) Houghton Mifflin Harcourt Publishing Co.
Guest, Jacqueline. Ghost Messages, 1 vol. 2011. (ENG.). 192p. (J). (gr. 4-8). pap. 8.95 *(978-1-55050-458-3(4))* Coteau Bks. CAN. Dist: Orca Bk. Pubs. USA.
Guettier, Nancy. I Wish. 2015. (ENG.). 32p. (J). pap. 9.95 *(978-1-63047-512-3(2))* Morgan James Publishing.
Guibert, Emmanuel. A Beautiful Cow. 2014. (Ariol Ser.: 4). (J). lib. bdg. 24.50 *(978-0-606-35103-4(5)*, Turtleback) Turtleback Bks.
—Bizbilla Hits the Bullseye. 2014. (Ariol Ser.: 5). (J). lib. bdg. 24.50 *(978-0-606-35534-6(0))* Turtleback Bks.
—Happy as a Pig... 2013. (Ariol Graphic Novels Ser.). (ENG., Illus.). 124p. (J). (gr. 1-5). pap. 12.99 *(978-1-59707-487-2(X)*, 9781597074872) Papercutz.
—Happy as a Pig... 2013. (Ariol Ser.: 3). (J). lib. bdg. 24.50 *(978-0-606-32310-9(4)*, Turtleback) Turtleback Bks.
Guiza, Vic, illus. Bat in the Bunk: Summer Camp Stories Seires. 2015. (ENG.). 32p. (J). (gr. 1-18). 19.99 *(978-0-9863743-0-2(X))* Summer Camp Stories LLC.
Gulley Sr, Wayne A. Michelangelo Tangelo - a Bully No More. Gulley, Robin, ed. Gulley SR, Wayne A., illus. 2012. 40p. pap. 13.99 *(978-0-9843505-5-1(1))* Gulley, Wayne.
Gunby, Stephanie. The Clever Clouds. 2010. 56p. pap. 24.20 *(978-1-4269-3902-0(7))* Trafford Publishing.
Gunderson, Jessica. I Just Have to Ride the Halfpipe! Santillan, Jorge H., illus. 2011. (Sports Illustrated Kids Victory School Superstars Ser.). (ENG.). 56p. (gr. 1-3). pap. 5.95 *(978-1-4342-3397-4(9))*; lib. bdg. 26.65 *(978-1-4342-2236-7(5))* Stone Arch Bks.
—Olivia Bitter, Spooked-Out Sitter! 2016. (Babysitter Chronicles Ser.). (ENG.). 160p. (gr. 4-7). pap. 6.95 *(978-1-4914-8862-1(X))* Stone Arch Bks.
Gunderson, Jessica A. How to Keep a Secret for Detectives. 2008. 206p. pap. 15.50 *(978-0-557-01369-2(0))* Lulu Pr., Inc.
Gunn, Robin Jones. Christy Miller Collection, Vol. 2. 2006. (Christy Miller Collection: Bks. 4-6). (ENG.). 496p. (J). (gr. 7-12). 16.99 *(978-1-59052-585-2(X)*, Multnomah Bks.) Crown Publishing Group.
—Christy Miller Collection Vol. 3, Vol. 3. 2006. (Christy Miller Collection: Bks. 7-9). (ENG.). 480p. (J). (gr. 7-12). 16.99 *(978-1-59052-586-9(8)*, Multnomah) Doubleday Religious Publishing Group, The.
—Christy Miller Collection, Vol 1, Vol. 1. 2005. (Christy Miller Collection: Bks. 1-3). (ENG., Illus.). 496p. (J). (gr. 7-12). 16.99 *(978-1-59052-584-5(1)*, Multnomah) Doubleday Religious Publishing Group, The.
—Christy Miller Collection, Vol 4, Vol. 4. 2006. (Christy Miller Collection: Bks. 10-12). (ENG.). 496p. (J). (gr. 7-12). 16.99 *(978-1-59052-587-6(6)*, Multnomah) Doubleday Religious Publishing Group, The.
Gunnery, Sylvia. Personal Best, 1 vol. 2005. (Lorimer Sports Stories Ser.). (ENG.). 112p. (J). (gr. 4-8). 16.95 *(978-1-55028-897-1(0)*, 9781550288971) Lorimer, James & Co., Ltd., Pubs. CAN. Dist: Casemate Pubs. & Bk. Distributors, LLC.
Gupta, Jennifer. Silly Turtle! That's Not on the Menu! 2008. 28p. pap. 13.99 *(978-1-4343-9183-4(3))* AuthorHouse.
Gurden, Gloria. The Adventures of Wersel Driftwood. 2011. 58p. (gr. 2-4). pap. 10.16 *(978-1-4269-9254-4(8))* Trafford Publishing.
Gurevich, Margaret. All or Nothing. Hagel, Brooke, illus. 2016. (Chloe by Design Ser.). (ENG.). 96p. (gr. 5-8). lib. bdg. 25.32 *(978-1-4965-3263-3(5))* Stone Arch Bks.
—Back to Basics. Hagel, Brooke, illus. 2016. (Chloe by Design Ser.). (ENG.). 96p. (gr. 5-8). lib. bdg. 25.32 *(978-1-4965-3261-9(9))* Stone Arch Bks.
—Chloe by Design: Measuring Up. Hagel, Brooke, illus. 2016. (Chloe by Design Ser.). (ENG.). 384p. (gr. 4-8). 14.95 *(978-1-62370-727-9(7))* Capstone Young Readers of Coughlan Cos.
—Fashion Week Finale. Hagel, Brooke, illus. 2015. (Chloe by Design Ser.). (ENG.). 96p. (gr. 5-8). 25.32 *(978-1-4965-0507-1(7))* Stone Arch Bks.
—The Final Cut. Hagel, Brooke, illus. 2016. (Chloe by Design Ser.). (ENG.). 96p. (gr. 5-8). lib. bdg. 25.32 *(978-1-4965-3264-0(3))* Stone Arch Bks.
—The First Cut, 1 vol. Hagel, Brooke, illus. 2014. (Chloe by Design Ser.). (ENG.). 96p. (gr. 5-8). 25.32 *(978-1-4342-9178-3(2))* Stone Arch Bks.
—Runway Rundown. Hagel, Brooke, illus. 2015. (Chloe by Design Ser.). (ENG.). 96p. (gr. 5-8). 25.32 *(978-1-4965-0506-4(9))* Stone Arch Bks.
—Unraveling, 1 vol. Hagel, Brooke, illus. 2014. (Chloe by Design Ser.). (ENG.). 96p. (gr. 5-8). 25.32 *(978-1-4342-9179-0(0))* Stone Arch Bks.
Gurtler, Janet. Cora's Decision. Wood, Katie, illus. 2015. (Mermaid Kingdom Ser.). (ENG.). 96p. (gr. 3-5). 23.99 *(978-1-4342-9695-5(4))* Stone Arch Bks.
—Deep-Water Drama. Wood, Katie, illus. 2016. (Mermaid Kingdom Ser.). (ENG.). 288p. (gr. 3-5). 12.95 *(978-1-62370-632-6(7))* Capstone Young Readers of Coughlan Cos.
—Rachel's Secret. Wood, Katie, illus. 2015. (Mermaid Kingdom Ser.). (ENG.). 96p. (gr. 3-5). 23.99 *(978-1-4342-9694-8(6))* Stone Arch Bks.
—Rachel's Worry. Wood, Katie, illus. 2016. (Mermaid Kingdom Ser.). (ENG.). 96p. (gr. 3-5). 23.99 *(978-1-4965-2607-6(4))* Stone Arch Bks.
—Secrets Beneath the Sea. Wood, Katie, illus. 2015. (Mermaid Kingdom Ser.). (ENG.). 288p. (gr. 3-5). 12.95 *(978-1-62370-187-1(2))* Capstone Young Readers of Coughlan Cos.
—Shyanna's Wish. Wood, Katie, illus. 2015. (Mermaid Kingdom Ser.). (ENG.). 96p. (gr. 3-5). 23.99 *(978-1-4342-9696-2(2))* Stone Arch Bks.
Gutenberg, S. R. Abby Longbotham & the Quilt. 2008. 28p. pap. 24.95 *(978-1-4241-9428-5(8))* America Star Bks.
Gutknecht, Allison. A Cast Is the Perfect Accessory: And Other Lessons I've Learned. Lewis, Stevie, illus. 2014. (ENG.). 160p. (J). (gr. 2-5). 16.99 *(978-1-4424-8396-5(2))*; pap. 5.99 *(978-1-4424-8395-8(4))* Simon & Schuster Children's Publishing. (Aladdin).
Gutman, Dan. The Homework Machine. 2007. (ENG.). 176p. (J). (gr. 3-7). pap. 6.99 *(978-0-689-87679-0(3)*, Simon & Schuster Bks. For Young Readers) Simon & Schuster Bks. For Young Readers.
—The Million Dollar Putt. 2007. 69p. (J). (gr. 3-7). 13.65 *(978-0-7569-8281-2(2))* Perfection Learning Corp.
—The Million Dollar Strike. 2004. 176p. (J). lib. bdg. 18.46 *(978-1-4242-2107-3(2))* Fitzgerald Bks.
—Mr. Hynde Is Out of His Mind! Paillot, Jim, illus. 2005. (My Weird School Ser.: 6). (ENG.). 112p. (J). (gr. 1-5). pap. 4.99 *(978-0-06-074520-2(7))* HarperCollins Pubs.
—Ms. Todd Is Odd! Paillot, Jim, illus. 2006. (My Weird School Ser.: 12). (ENG.). 112p. (J). (gr. 1-5). pap. 4.99 *(978-0-06-082231-6(7))* HarperCollins Pubs.
—The My Weird School Collection, Bks. 1-4. Paillot, Jim, illus. 2010. (My Weird School Ser.). (J). (gr. 1-5). pap. 16.99 *(978-0-06-189489-3(3))* HarperCollins Pubs.
Gutsche, Brigitte. The Intruder. 2006. (Holt's Friends Ser.). (J). pap. 9.99 *(978-0-88092-519-8(1))* Royal Fireworks Publishing Co.
Guy, Rosa. The Friends. 2006. (Reader's Workshop Ser.). (ENG.). 224p. (C). pap. 19.95 *(978-0-7362-3152-7(8))* CENGAGE Learning.
Guzzardi, Mary. The Magical Ice Skates. 2011. 50p. pap. 24.95 *(978-1-4560-3246-3(1))* PublishAmerica, Inc.
Gwaltney, Doris. Homefront. 2009. (ENG.). 320p. (J). (gr. 5-9). pap. 6.99 *(978-1-4169-9572-2(2)*, Simon & Schuster Bks. For Young Readers) Simon & Schuster Bks. For Young Readers.
Haas, Abigail. Dangerous Girls. (ENG., Illus.). 400p. (YA). (gr. 9). 2014. pap. 10.99 *(978-1-4424-8660-7(0))* 2013. 16.99 *(978-1-4424-8659-1(7))* Simon Pulse. (Simon Pulse).
Haas, Irene. Bess & Bella. Haas, Irene, illus. 2006. (ENG., Illus.). 32p. (J). (gr. -1-2). 17.99 *(978-1-4169-0013-9(6)*, McElderry, Margaret K. Bks.) McElderry, Margaret K. Bks.
Haas, Jessie. Bramble & Maggie: Give & Take. Friend, Alison, illus. 2013. (ENG.). 56p. (J). (gr. k-3). 14.99 *(978-0-7636-5021-6(8))* Candlewick Pr.
—Bramble & Maggie Give & Take. Friend, Alison, illus. 2015. (Candlewick Sparks Ser.). (ENG.). 56p. (J). (gr. k-4). pap. 3.99 *(978-0-7636-7787-9(6))* Candlewick Pr.
—Saige. Davis, Sarah, illus. 2012. (American Girl Today Ser.: Bk. 1). lib. bdg. 17.15 *(978-0-606-31568-5(3)*, Turtleback) Turtleback Bks.
—Saige Paints the Sky. Davis, Sarah, illus. 2012. (American Girl Today Ser.: Bk. 2). lib. bdg. 17.15 *(978-0-606-31569-2(1)*, Turtleback) Turtleback Bks.
Haase Wittler, Penny S. Emma, the Big Red Cow. 2011. 16p. pap. 9.99 *(978-1-4520-1959-8(2))* AuthorHouse.
Haber, Melissa Glenn. Dear Anjali. 2010. (ENG.). 288p. (J). (gr. 4-8). 16.99 *(978-1-4169-9599-9(4)*, Simon & Schuster/Paula Wiseman Bks.) Simon & Schuster/Paula Wiseman Bks.
—Your Best Friend, Meredith. 2011. (ENG.). 288p. (J). (gr. 4-8). pap. 6.99 *(978-1-4169-9600-2(1)*, Aladdin) Simon & Schuster Children's Publishing.
Haddix, Margaret Peterson. Because of Anya. 2004. (ENG.). 128p. (J). (gr. 3-7). reprint ed. pap. 6.99 *(978-0-689-86993-8(2)*, Simon & Schuster Bks. For Young Readers) Simon & Schuster Bks. For Young Readers.
—Dexter the Tough. Elliott, Mark, illus. 2008. (ENG.). 144p. (J). (gr. 2-5). pap. 6.99 *(978-1-4169-1170-8(7))* 2007. 141p. pap. 7.99 *(978-0-15-377020-3(1))* 2007. (ENG.). 144p. (J). (gr. 2-5). 17.99 *(978-1-4169-1159-3(6))* Simon & Schuster Bks. For Young Readers. (Simon & Schuster Bks. For Young Readers).
—Don't You Dare Read This, Mrs. Dunphrey. 2004. (ENG.). 128p. (YA). (gr. 7). mass mkt. 6.99 *(978-0-689-87102-3(3)*, Simon Pulse) Simon Pulse.
—Palace of Mirrors. 2010. (Palace Chronicles Ser.: 2). (ENG.). 320p. (J). (gr. 5-9). pap. 7.99 *(978-1-4424-0667-4(4)*, Simon & Schuster Bks. For Young Readers) Simon & Schuster Bks. For Young Readers.
Haden, Robbie. Run Girl Run. 2013. 116p. 28.95 *(978-1-4525-6779-2(4))*; pap. 11.99 *(978-1-4525-6777-8(8))* Author Solutions, Inc. (Balboa Pr.).
Hafner, Marylin. The Adventures of Molly & Emmett. (J). 7.95 *(978-0-8126-0052-0(5))* Open Court Publishing Co.
Hagemann, Bernhard. Charlie Gallina Ciega. (Torre de Papel Ser.). (SPA., Illus.). (J). 7.95 *(978-958-04-5032-0(3))* Norma S.A. COL. Dist: Distribuidora Norma, Inc.
Hahn, Mary Downing. Closed for the Season. 2010. (ENG.). 192p. (J). (gr. 5-7). pap. 6.99 *(978-0-547-39853-2(0))* Houghton Mifflin Harcourt Publishing Co.
—The Old Willis Place. 2007. (ENG.). 208p. (J). (gr. 5-7). pap. 7.99 *(978-0-618-89741-4(0))* Houghton Mifflin Harcourt Publishing Co.
—One for Sorrow: A Ghost Story. 2017. (ENG.). 304p. (J). (gr. 5-7). 16.99 *(978-0-544-81809-5(1))* Houghton Mifflin Harcourt Publishing Co.
—Where I Belong. 2014. (ENG.). 240p. (J). (gr. 5-7). 16.99 *(978-0-544-23020-0(5))* Houghton Mifflin Harcourt Publishing Co.
Haislip, Phyllis Hall. Anybody's Hero: The Battle of Old Men & Young Boys. 2004. (Illus.). 220p. (J). pap. 8.95 *(978-1-57249-343-8(7)*, White Mane Kids) White Mane Publishing Co., Inc.

Halahmy, Miriam. Behind Closed Doors. 2017. (ENG.). 208p. (J). (gr. 9). 16.95 (978-0-8234-3641-5(1)) Holiday Hse., Inc.

Halbrook, Kristin. Every Last Promise. 2015. (ENG.). 288p. (YA). (gr. 8). pap. 9.99 (978-0-06-212128-6(X), HarperTeen) HarperCollins Pubs.

Halcomb, Suzanne. The Mcfee Family Harvest. 2012. 40p. pap. 19.75 (978-1-4269-9647-4(0)) Trafford Publishing.

Hale, Bruce. Afraid of the Dark. Francis, Guy, illus. 2015. (Clark the Shark Ser.). (ENG.). 32p. (J). (gr. -1-3). 17.99 (978-0-06-237450-9(8)) HarperCollins Pubs.

—Clark the Shark. 2016. (Clark the Shark: I Can Read Level 1 Ser.). (J). lib. bdg. 13.55 (978-0-606-38774-3(9)) Turtleback Bks.

—Clark the Shark Takes Heart. Francis, Guy, illus. 2014. (Clark the Shark Ser.). (ENG.). 32p. (J). (gr. -1-3). 17.99 (978-0-06-219227-1(2)) HarperCollins Pubs.

—Curse of the Were-Hyena: A Monstertown Mystery. Hale, Bruce, illus. 2016. (Monstertown Mysteries Ser.). (ENG., Illus.). 220p. (J). (gr. 3-7). 14.99 (978-1-4847-1325-9(7)) Disney Pr.

—Mutant Mantis Lunch Ladies! 2017. (Monstertown Mysteries Ser.). (ENG.). 208p. (J). (gr. 3-7). 14.99 (978-1-4847-1324-2(9)) Disney Pr.

Hale, Kathleen. No One Else Can Have You. 2014. (Kippy Bushman Ser.). (ENG.). 384p. (YA). (gr. 9). 17.99 (978-0-06-221119-4(6)) HarperCollins Pubs.

Hale, Marian. The Truth about Sparrows. 2007. (ENG.). 288p. (YA). (gr. 7-12). per. 9.99 (978-0-312-37133-3(0), 9780312371333) Square Fish.

Hale, Mary. Karly & Sheila's Walk. 2012. (ENG.). 23p. (J). pap. 11.95 (978-1-4327-8647-2(4)) Outskirts Pr., Inc.

Hale, R. A. Best Friends. 2005. (J). 6.00 (978-0-9708959-5-0(X), Accent Pubns.) Ajoyin Publishing, Inc.

Hale, Rachael. Baby's Best Friend. 2011. (ENG.). 20p. (J). (gr. -1 — 1). bds. 6.99 (978-0-316-12962-6(3)) Little, Brown Bks. for Young Readers.

—Furry Friends. rev. ed. 2007. (Paw Pals Ser.). (ENG., Illus.). 20p. (J). (gr. -1 — 1). bds. 6.99 (978-0-316-11319-9(0)) Little, Brown Bks. for Young Readers.

Hale, Shannon. Real Friends. Pham, LeUyen, illus. 2017. (ENG.). 224p. (J). pap. 12.99 (978-1-62672-785-4(6), 9781626727854, First Second Bks.) Roaring Brook Pr.

—The Storybook of Legends. 2013. (Ever after High Ser.). (ENG., Illus.). 320p. (J). (gr. 3-7). 14.99 (978-0-316-40122-7(6)) Little, Brown Bks. for Young Readers.

—The Storybook of Legends. 2017. (Ever after High Ser.: 1). (J). lib. bdg. 18.40 **(978-0-606-40630-7(1))** Turtleback Bks.

Hale, Shannon. The Unfairest of Them All. 2014. (Ever after High Ser.). (ENG.). 336p. (J). (gr. 3-7). 14.99 (978-0-316-28201-7(4)) Little, Brown Bks. for Young Readers.

Hale, Shannon & Hale, Dean. The Princess in Black & the Mysterious Playdate. Pham, LeUyen, illus. 2017. (Princess in Black Ser.: 5). (ENG.). 96p. (J). (gr. k-3). 14.99 **(978-0-7636-8826-4(6))** Candlewick Pr.

Halevy, Hanita H. Dragonlions & the Spacemen. Heler, Shraga, illus. 2012. (ENG.). 140p. (J). pap. 13.00 (978-965-550-085-1(3)) Contento De Semrik ISR. Dist: Bookmasters Distribution.

Haley, Annie. Rumpus & Bumpus: If we could do Anything... ... 2008. 32p. pap. 13.95 (978-1-59858-803-3(6)) Dog Ear Publishing, LLC.

Haley, Barbara. Boot Camp. 2006. (Flamingo Fiction 9-13s Ser.). (ENG., Illus.). 128p. (J). (gr. 4-7). per. 6.99 (978-1-84550-128-0(4), b92d6d0e-c252-4095-839b-1c07c368f656) Christian Focus Pubns. GBR. Dist: Bookmasters Distribution.

Hall, Bureda Ann Greathouse. Stories of My Little Blue Monkey. 2007. (Illus.). 32p. (J). pap. 15.00 (978-0-8059-7397-6(4)) Dorrance Publishing Co., Inc.

Hall, Caroline V. Rhett & Abby: Abby's New Home. 2011. 40p. pap. 15.95 (978-1-4497-1887-9(6), WestBow Pr.) Author Solutions, Inc.

Hall, Hannah. God Bless My Friends, 1 vol. Whitlow, Steve, illus. 2016. (God Bless Book Ser.). (ENG.). 20p. (J). bds. 9.99 (978-0-7180-8953-5(7)) Nelson, Thomas Inc.

Hall, J. Darroll. The Lollipop Club. 2011. (ENG.). 290p. pap. 4.99 (978-0-615-56231-5(0)) Fantasy Island Bk. Publishing.

Hall, John. Is He or Isn't He? 2006. (ENG.). 304p. (YA). (gr. 9). pap. 8.99 (978-0-06-078747-9(3), HarperTeen) HarperCollins Pubs.

Hall, Kirsten. Double Trouble: All about Colors. Luedecke, Bev, illus. 2003. (Beastieville Ser.). 32p. (J). (gr. -1-1). 19.50 (978-0-516-22892-1(7), Children's Pr.) Scholastic Library Publishing.

—Help! All about Telling Time. Luedecke, Bev, illus. 2003. (Concept Bks.). 32p. (J). 19.50 (978-0-516-22890-7(0), Children's Pr.) Scholastic Library Publishing.

—Little Lies: All about Math. Luedecke, Bev, illus. 2003. (Beastieville Ser.). 32p. (J). 19.50 (978-0-516-22896-9(X), Children's Pr.) Scholastic Library Publishing.

Hall, Mike. Chirpi. 2012. 24p. pap. 15.99 (978-1-4691-4955-4(9)) Xlibris Corp.

Hall, Natalie Susan. Andy Anole's Adventure, 1 vol. 2009. 26p. pap. 24.95 (978-1-60813-350-5(8)) America Star Bks.

Hall, Noelle Chason & Joanne Beeker Clurman. Sweetpea County's Secret Quilt. Caprara, Collette, illus. 2011. 28p. pap. 24.95 (978-1-4626-2248-1(8)) America Star Bks.

Hall, Patricia. Old Friends, New Friends. Winfield, Alison, illus. 2005. (Ready-to-Read Ser.). 32p. (J). lib. bdg. 15.00 (978-1-59054-930-8(9)) Fitzgerald Bks.

Hall, Sharon J. Ridgeway Middle School: Choosing to Embrace Diversity 360 Degrees. 2007. 316p. per. 18.95 (978-0-595-45109-8(8)) iUniverse, Inc.

Hall, Stan And Carol. Carl Barconey & Friends. 2011. 24p. pap. 14.95 (978-1-4520-9647-6(3)) AuthorHouse.

Hall, Susan T., illus. Presentamos a Diego! 2005. (Dora the Explorer Ser.). Orig. Title: Meet Diego! (SPA.). 24p. (J). pap. 3.99 (978-0-689-87749-0(8), Libros Para Ninos) Libros Para Ninos.

Hall, Tessa Emily. Purple Moon. 2013. 328p. pap. 13.95 (978-1-938499-87-6(5)) Lighthouse Publishing of the Carolinas.

Hall, William. Just Like Me: My Diggety Dog - Paws4Learning. 2013. 32p. pap. (978-1-4602-1368-1(8)) FriesenPress.

Hallagin, Janet. The Way of Courage. 2006. 30.99 (978-1-4257-1249-5(5)); pap. 20.99 (978-1-4257-1248-8(7)) Xlibris Corp.

Haller, Reese. Making Friends, 2. Galsterer, Lynne, illus. 2nd ed. 2006. (Fred the Mouse Ser.). 112p. (J). per. 4.97 (978-0-9772321-0-9(7)) Personal Power Pr.

Hallinan, P. K. Forever Friends! 2003. (ENG., Illus.). 28p. (J). (gr. -1-k). bds. 7.95 (978-0-8249-5454-3(8), Ideal Pubns.) Worthy Publishing.

—Let's Be Friends. 2008. (ENG., Illus.). 26p. (J). (gr. -1-k). bds. 7.95 (978-0-8249-6587-7(6), Ideal Pubns.) Worthy Publishing.

—My Brother & I. 2008. (ENG., Illus.). 24p. (J). (gr. -1-k). bds. 7.95 (978-0-8249-5455-0(6), Ideal Pubns.) Worthy Publishing.

—A Rainbow of Friends. 2005. (ENG., Illus.). 32p. (J). (gr. -1-3). 4.35 (978-0-8249-5519-9(6), Ideal Pubns.) Worthy Publishing.

Hallstrand, John & Sarah & Hawley, Karen. Zoey Helps the Mystery Dog Find a Home. 2011. 24p. pap. 11.99 (978-1-4634-1094-0(8)) AuthorHouse.

Halpern, Julie. The F - It List. 2013. (ENG.). 256p. (YA). (gr. 8). 17.99 (978-1-250-02565-4(6), 9781250025654) Feiwel & Friends.

—Into the Wild Nerd Yonder. 2011. (ENG.). 272p. (YA). (gr. 8-13). pap. 16.99 (978-0-312-65307-1(7), 9780312653071) Square Fish.

Halsey, Jacqueline. Peggy's Letters, 1 vol. 2005. (Orca Young Readers Ser.). (ENG., Illus.). 132p. (J). (gr. 3-6). per. 5.95 (978-1-55143-363-9(X)) Orca Bk. Pubs. USA.

Halter, Loretta. Lacy's Journey: The Life of a Decorator Crab. 2010. (ENG.). 64p. (J). 19.95 (978-0-9822942-1-5(2)) Nature's Hopes & Heroes.

Haltigan, Susanne. Seymour the Sea Turtle Saves His Sea Friends. 2011. 28p. pap. 11.95 (978-1-4567-6549-1(3)) AuthorHouse.

Halverson, Barbara. Farm Friends Forever: Everyone Needs Friends. 2013. (ENG.). 27p. (J). pap. 13.95 (978-1-4787-1380-7(1)) Outskirts Pr., Inc.

Hambrick, Sharon. Tommy's Race. Manning, Maurie J., illus. 2004. (Fig Street Kids Ser.). 95p. (J). (gr. 1-2). 7.49 (978-1-59166-286-0(9)) BJU Pr.

—Tommy's Rocket. Manning, Maurie J., illus. 2003. (Fig Street Kids Ser.). 83p. (J). (gr. 1-2). 7.49 (978-1-59166-186-3(2)) BJU Pr.

Hamilton, Patricia D. Peaches the Private Eye Poodle: Finding Dipsey Doodle. 2008. 32p. pap. 13.50 (978-1-60693-276-6(4), Eloquent Bks.) Strategic Book Publishing & Rights Agency (SBPRA).

—Peaches the Private Eye Poodle: Finding Foster a Home. 2010. 36p. (gr. -1-3). pap. 13.50 (978-1-60911-108-3(7), Eloquent Bks.) Strategic Book Publishing & Rights Agency (SBPRA).

—Peaches the Private Eye Poodle: Where Is Loosey Goosey? 2009. 32p. pap. 13.50 (978-1-60860-063-2(7), Eloquent Bks.) Strategic Book Publishing & Rights Agency (SBPRA).

Hamilton, Virginia. The Planet of Junior Brown. 2006. 210p. (gr. 3-7). 17.00 (978-0-7569-6783-3(X)) Perfection Learning Corp.

—The Planet of Junior Brown. 2006. (ENG., Illus.). 224p. (J). (gr. 3-7). pap. 7.99 (978-1-4169-1410-5(2), Simon & Schuster/Paula Wiseman Bks.) Simon & Schuster/Paula Wiseman Bks.

Hammond, Barbara, illus. The Duffy Chronicles. Hammond, Barbara, . 2007. 60p. pap. 11.99 (978-0-9800675-4-5(5)) Mirror Publishing.

Hammond, James F. Ski Challenge. 2008. 100p. pap. 16.95 (978-1-60703-493-3(X)) PublishAmerica, Inc.

Hampton, Brooke. Enchanted Cedar: The Journey Home. 2013. 38p. pap. 16.99 (978-1-4525-6896-6(0)) Balboa Pr.

Han, Jenny. The Complete Summer I Turned Pretty Trilogy: The Summer I Turned Pretty; It's Not Summer Without You; We'll Always Have Summer. 2013. (Summer I Turned Pretty Ser.). (ENG., Illus.). 928p. (YA). (gr. 7). pap. 32.99 (978-1-4424-9832-7(3), Simon & Schuster Bks. For Young Readers) Simon & Schuster Bks. For Young Readers.

—It's Not Summer Without You. 6 vols. 2010. (Summer I Turned Pretty Ser.: 2). (YA). 90.75 (978-1-4498-2018-3(2)); 73.75 (978-1-4498-2016-9(6)); 1.25 (978-1-4498-2022-0(0)); 230.75 (978-1-4498-2015-2(8)); 88.75 (978-1-4498-2020-6(4)) Recorded Bks., Inc.

—It's Not Summer Without You. (Summer I Turned Pretty Ser.). (ENG.). (YA). (gr. 7). 2011. 320p. pap. 10.99 (978-1-4169-9556-2(0)) 2010. 288p. 18.99 (978-1-4169-9555-5(2)) Simon & Schuster Bks. For Young Readers. (Simon & Schuster Bks. For Young Readers).

—P.S. I Still Love You. 2015. (ENG., Illus.). 352p. (YA). (gr. 7). 17.99 (978-1-4424-2673-3(X)); (To All the Boys I've Loved Before Ser.: 2). E-Book (978-1-4424-2675-7(6)) Simon & Schuster Bks. For Young Readers. (Simon & Schuster Bks. For Young Readers).

—P.S. I Still Love You. 2017. (To All the Boys I've Loved Before Ser.: 2). (ENG.). 352p. (YA). (gr. 7). pap. 10.99 (978-1-4424-2674-0(8)) Simon & Schuster Children's Publishing.

—Shug. (ENG.). 256p. 2007. (J). (gr. 4-8). pap. 7.99 (978-1-4169-0943-9(5), Simon & Schuster/Paula Wiseman Bks.) 2006. (Illus.). (YA). (gr. 7-7). 16.99 (978-1-4169-0942-2(7), Simon & Schuster Bks. For Young Readers) Simon & Schuster Bks. For Young Readers.

—The Summer I Turned Pretty. (Summer I Turned Pretty Ser.). (ENG.). (YA). (gr. 7). 2010. 304p. pap. 10.99 (978-1-4169-6829-0(6)) 2009. 288p. 19.99 (978-1-4169-6823-8(7)) Simon & Schuster Bks. For Young Readers. (Simon & Schuster Bks. For Young Readers).

—The Summer I Turned Pretty. 2010. lib. bdg. 22.10 (978-0-606-14529-9(X), Turtleback) Turtleback Bks.

Han, Jenny & Vivian, Siobhan. Burn for Burn. (ENG.). (YA). (gr. 9). 2013. Illus.). 400p. pap. 10.99 (978-1-4424-4076-0(7)) 2012. 368p. 17.99 (978-1-4424-4075-3(9)) Simon & Schuster Bks. For Young Readers. (Simon & Schuster Bks. For Young Readers).

—Fire with Fire. 2013. (ENG., Illus.). 528p. (YA). (gr. 9). 17.99 (978-1-4424-4078-4(3), Simon & Schuster Bks. For Young Readers) Simon & Schuster Bks. For Young Readers.

Hancock, H. Irving. The High School Captain of the Team. 2006. (ENG.). 156p. pap. 19.99 (978-1-4264-6386-0(3)); 172p. pap. 21.99 (978-1-4264-6460-7(6)) Creative Media Partners, LLC.

—The High School Left End, or Dick & Co. Grilling on the Football Gridiron. 2006. (ENG.). 156p. pap. 19.99 (978-1-4264-6385-3(5)); 174p. pap. 21.99 (978-1-4264-6459-1(2)) Creative Media Partners, LLC.

Hancock, Susan G. The Wind & Little Cloud. Simmons, Robert, illus. 2006. (J). (ENG.). 40p. spiral bd. 17.95 (978-0-9741743-3-4(5)); 48p. (gr. -1-3). per. 10.95 (978-0-9741743-0-3(0)) Perlycross Pubs.

Hand, Cynthia, et al. My Lady Jane. 512p. (YA). (gr. 8). 2017. pap. 9.99 (978-0-06-239176-6(3)) 2016. 17.99 (978-0-06-239174-2(7)) HarperCollins Pubs. (HarperTeen).

Hand, Reuben W. The Thirst for Life, 1 vol. 2010. 52p. pap. 16.95 (978-1-4489-4897-0(5)) America Star Bks.

Haneberg, Janet. Mighty Mitt. 2006. 36p. (J). pap. 14.99 (978-1-4116-4168-6(X)) Lulu Pr., Inc.

Hanlon, Abby. Dory & the Real True Friend. 2016. (Dory Ser.: 2). lib. bdg. 18.40 (978-0-606-38846-7(X)) Turtleback Bks.

—The Real True Friend. 2015. (Dory Fantasmagory Ser.: 2). (ENG., Illus.). 160p. (J). (gr. 1-3). 14.99 (978-0-525-42866-4(6), Dial Bks) Penguin Young Readers Group.

Hannan, Peter. The Greatest Snowman in the World! Hannan, Peter, illus. 2010. (ENG., Illus.). 32p. (J). (gr. -1-3). 16.99 (978-0-06-128480-9(7)) HarperCollins Pubs.

Hannigan, Katherine. True (... Sort Of) (ENG.). (J). (gr. 3-7). 2012. 384p. pap. 6.99 (978-0-06-196875-4(7)) 2011. (Illus.). 368p. 16.99 (978-0-06-196873-0(0)) HarperCollins Pubs. (Greenwillow Bks.).

Hanny, Diane. Wispy Willy. Baskey, Kim, illus. 2011. 24p. pap. 12.00 (978-1-4520-9975-0(8)) AuthorHouse.

Hano, Patricia. Tyler Meets the Moon. 2010. 28p. pap. 11.99 (978-1-60911-189-2(3), Eloquent Bks.) Strategic Book Publishing & Rights Agency (SBPRA).

Hansen, Dustin. Microsaurs: Adventure Awaits. Hansen, Dustin, illus. 2017. (Microsaurs Ser.: 1). (ENG., Illus.). 224p. (J). 13.99 (978-1-250-09021-8(0), 9781250090218) Feiwel & Friends.

—Microsaurs: Tiny-Raptor Pack Attack. Hansen, Dustin, illus. 2017. (Microsaurs Ser.: 2). (ENG., Illus.). 240p. (J). 13.99 (978-1-250-09025-6(3), 9781250090256) Feiwel & Friends.

Hansen, Joyce. The Gift-Giver. 2005. (ENG.). 132p. (J). (gr. 5-7). pap. 7.99 (978-0-618-61123-2(1)) Houghton Mifflin Harcourt Publishing Co.

—The Gift-Giver. 2011. 8.97 (978-0-7848-3614-9(0), Everbind) Marco Bk. Co.

—One True Friend. Giblin, James Cross, ed. 2005. (ENG.). 160p. (J). (gr. 5-7). pap. 11.95 (978-0-618-60991-8(1)) Houghton Mifflin Harcourt Publishing Co.

—Yellow Bird & Me. 2005. (ENG.). 160p. (J). (gr. 5-7). pap. 6.95 (978-0-618-61116-4(9)) Houghton Mifflin Harcourt Publishing Co.

—Yellow Bird & Me. 2005. (163rd Street Ser.). 155p. (gr. 5-9). 16.95 (978-0-7569-6228-9(5)) Perfection Learning Corp.

Hansen, Kate. Spike the Sewer Cat. Illustrations byVoigt, Karen S., illus. 2008. 27p. pap. 24.95 (978-1-60474-094-3(9)) America Star Bks.

Hanson, Anders. Lone Shark, 1 vol. Haberstroh, Anne, illus. 2007. (Critter Chronicles Ser.). (ENG.). 24p. (J). (gr. k-3). lib. bdg. 24.21 (978-1-59928-452-1(9), SandCastle) ABDO Publishing Co.

Hanson, Shelley. K9 Crew Beginnings. 2004. 160p. (J). per. 9.99 (978-0-9752887-0-2(9)) Tail Wagging Productions.

Hao, K. T. Best Friends. Kung, Annie, tr. Ferri, Giuliano, illus. 2008. (ENG.). 32p. (J). (gr. -1). 15.95 (978-1-933327-38-9(3)); lib. bdg. 16.50 (978-1-933327-39-6(1)) Purple Bear Bks., Inc.

Hapka, Catherine, pseud. Back in the Saddle. 2016. (Marguerite Henry's Ponies of Chincoteague Ser.: 7). (ENG., Illus.). 192p. (J). (gr. 3-7). pap. 6.99 (978-1-4814-5993-8(7), Aladdin) Simon & Schuster Children's Publishing.

—Blue Ribbon Summer. 2014. (Marguerite Henry's Ponies of Chincoteague Ser.: 2). (ENG., Illus.). 208p. (J). (gr. 3-7). pap. 6.99 (978-1-4814-0339-9(7), Aladdin) Simon & Schuster Children's Publishing.

—Dolphin Dreams. 2017. (ENG.). 224p. (J). (gr. 3-7). pap. 6.99 **(978-1-338-13642-5(9))** Scholastic, Inc.

—The Enchanted Science Fair. 2014. (Sofia the First Ser.). (J). lib. bdg. 14.75 (978-0-606-35911-5(7)) Turtleback Bks.

—Forever Free. 5th ed. 2009. (ENG.). 288p. pap. 7.99 (978-1-4231-1668-4(2)) Disney Pr.

—Friends 4 Ever? 2008. (High School Musical Stories from East High Ser.). 124p. (J). (gr. 3-7). 12.65 (978-0-7569-8820-3(9)) Perfection Learning Corp.

—A Winning Gift. 2015. (Marguerite Henry's Ponies of Chincoteague Ser.: 5). (ENG., Illus.). 192p. (J). (gr. 3-7). pap. 6.99 (978-1-4814-3968-8(5), Aladdin) Simon & Schuster Children's Publishing.

—A Winning Gift. 2015. (Ponies of Chincoteague Ser.: 5). lib. bdg. 17.20 (978-0-606-37135-3(4)) Turtleback Bks.

Hapka, Catherine, pseud & Bloomberg, Georgina. The A Circuit. 2011. (a Circuit Ser.). (ENG.). 288p. (YA). (gr. 7-12). 16.99 (978-1-59990-641-6(4), 9781599906416); pap. 9.99 (978-1-59990-634-8(1), 9781599906348) Bloomsbury Publishing USA. (Bloomsbury USA Childrens).

—My Favorite Mistake: An a Circuit Novel. 2012. (a Circuit Ser.). (ENG.). 256p. (YA). pap. 9.99 (978-1-59990-642-3(2), 9781599906423, Bloomsbury USA Childrens) Bloomsbury Publishing USA.

—Off Course. 2012. (a Circuit Ser.). (ENG.). 256p. (YA). (gr. 7-12). pap. 9.99 (978-1-59990-909-7(X), 9781599909097, Bloomsbury USA Childrens) Bloomsbury Publishing USA.

Hapka, Cathy, pseud. Disney Sofia the First - Sofia's Magical World: The First Hidden Stories. 2015. (Hidden Stories Ser.: 2). (ENG.). 10p. (J). (gr. -1-1). 15.99 (978-0-7944-3201-0(8), Reader's Digest Children's Bks.) Studio Fun International.

—Heart of a Dolphin. 2016. (Illus.). 186p. (J). pap. **(978-1-338-03282-6(8))** Scholastic, Inc.

—LEGO Friends: Mystery in the Whispering Woods (Chapter Book #3) 2013. (LEGO Friends Ser.). (ENG.). 64p. (J). (gr. 2-5). pap. 4.99 (978-0-545-56669-8(X)) Scholastic, Inc.

—Lights, Camera, Girl Power! 2013. (ENG.). 64p. (J). (gr. 2-5). pap. 4.99 (978-0-545-51654-9(4)) Math Solutions.

—Lights, Camera, Girl Power! 2013. (LEGO Friends Chapter Bks.: 2). lib. bdg. 14.75 (978-0-606-31550-0(0), Turtleback) Turtleback Bks.

—Mystery in the Whispering Woods. 2013. (LEGO Friends Chapter Bks.: 3). lib. bdg. 14.75 (978-0-606-32394-9(5), Turtleback) Turtleback Bks.

Hapka, Cathy, pseud, et al. Pooh's Halloween Pumpkin. Disney Storybook Artists Staff, illus. 2013. (ENG.). 10p. (J). (gr. -1-k). bds. 5.99 (978-1-4231-6767-9(8)) Disney Pr.

Happel-Holtz, Ruby H. Kool Kat Charlie of Cocoa Beach. 2011. 72p. pap. (978-1-4269-9484-5(2)) Trafford Publishing (UK) Ltd.

Happel, Kathleen. The Smartest Kid I Ever Met. Behles, Liza, illus. 2005. 57p. (J). per. 12.50 (978-0-9763993-3-9(4), Ithaca Pr.) Authors & Artists Publishers of New York, Inc.

Happel, Roberta L. Lynd. 2009. 16p. pap. 8.99 (978-1-4389-4088-5(2)) AuthorHouse.

Harcrow, Melissa. Where're Your Manners, William? 2008. 26p. pap. 24.95 (978-1-60563-470-8(0)) America Star Bks.

Hardwell, Gary D. A Boo Bears' Story: Stormy Night. 2007. (Illus.). 36p. per. 10.00 (978-0-9792016-9-1(1)) Professional Publishing Hse. LLC.

Hardy, Zoey. Brockway High. 2006. 318p. per. 12.95 (978-0-9765423-1-5(5)) Eudon Publishing.

A Hare, a Hound & Shy Mousey Brown. 2013. (J). (978-1-4351-4729-4(4)) Barnes & Noble, Inc.

Harewood, Sean C. It's Only the First Day. 2008. 48p. pap. 19.49 (978-1-4343-7367-0(3)) AuthorHouse.

Hargrave, Kiran Millwood. The Cartographer's Daughter. 2016. (ENG.). 224p. (J). (gr. 5). 16.99 (978-0-553-53528-0(5), Knopf Bks. for Young Readers) Random Hse. Children's Bks.

Hargreaves, Adam. Little Miss Hug. Hargreaves, Adam, illus. 2014. (Mr. Men & Little Miss Ser.). (ENG., Illus.). 32p. (J). (gr. -1-2). 4.99 (978-0-8431-8059-6(5), Price Stern Sloan) Penguin Young Readers Group.

Hargreaves, Roger. Mr. Men 40th Anniversary Box Set. 2011. (Mr. Men & Little Miss Ser.). (ENG.). 32p. (J). (gr. -1-2). 26.00 (978-0-8431-9835-5(4), Price Stern Sloan) Penguin Young Readers Group.

Harimann, Sierra. Puppies on Parade. 2014. (Illus.). 30p. (J). pap. (978-0-545-59211-6(9)) Scholastic, Inc.

Harimann, Sierra, et al. Adventures of Strawberry Shortcake! Beighley, Marci et al, illus. 2016. 126p. (J). **(978-1-101-95018-0(8))** Penguin Random Hse. LLC.

Harkrader, Lisa. Ruby Makes It Even! Odd/Even Numbers. Wummer, Amy, illus. 2015. (Math Matters(r) Ser.). (ENG.). 32p. (gr. k-2). 11.99 (978-1-57565-806-3(2)) Kane Press, Inc.

Harlan. My Best Friend. 2011. 28p. pap. 9.95 (978-1-4327-7164-5(7)) Outskirts Pr., Inc.

Harley, Bill. The Amazing Flight of Darius Frobisher, 1 vol. 2009. (ENG.). 160p. (J). pap. 7.95 (978-1-56145-494-5(X)) Peachtree Pubs.

Harlow, Joan Hiatt. Blown Away! (ENG.). 272p. (J). (gr. 4-7). 2008. pap. 7.99 (978-1-4169-0782-4(3)) 2007. 16.99 (978-1-4169-0781-7(5)) McElderry, Margaret K. Bks. (McElderry, Margaret K. Bks.).

—Shadows on the Sea. (ENG., Illus.). (J). (gr. 3-7). 2005. 272p. pap. 7.99 (978-0-689-84927-5(3)) 2003. 256p. 17.99 (978-0-689-84926-8(5)) McElderry, Margaret K. Bks. (McElderry, Margaret K. Bks.).

Harmening, Gail. How Did Clancey Get His Color?, 1 vol. 2009. 45p. pap. 24.95 (978-1-60836-440-4(2)) America Star Bks.

Harner, Ron. Move It Milton! Surrey, Michael, illus. 2009. 36p. pap. 11.95 (978-1-59858-738-8(2)) Dog Ear Publishing, LLC.

Harney, D. G. Meet Mr. Ugly, 1 vol. 2010. 133p. pap. 24.95 (978-1-4489-5191-8(7)) America Star Bks.

Harold & I. 2007. (ENG., Illus.). 291p. (J). (gr. 3-8). per. 13.99 (978-0-7684-2432-4(1)) Send The Light Distribution LLC.

Harpan, Gaile. The Ballad of Omar the Cat. Reddy, Sneha, illus. 2008. 28p. pap. 12.95 (978-0-9820479-1-0(6)) Peppertree Pr., The.

Harper, Ben. Super Friends: Going Bananas. Random House Staff, illus. 2009. (Step into Reading Ser.). (ENG.). 32p. (J). (gr. -1-1). pap. 3.99 (978-0-375-85613-6(7), Random Hse. Bks. for Young Readers) Random Hse. Children's Bks.

Harper, Benjamin & Scieszka, Jon. All Around Trucktown. Shannon, David et al, illus. 2008. (Jon Scieszka's Trucktown Ser.). (ENG.). 32p. (J). (gr. -1-1). 3.99 (978-1-4169-4194-1(0), Simon Scribbles) Simon Scribbles.

Harper, Charise Mericle. Alien Encounter. Harper, Charise Mericle, illus. 2014. (Sasquatch & Aliens Ser.: 1). (ENG., Illus.). 208p. (J). (gr. 2-5). 12.99 (978-0-8050-9621-7(3), 9780805096217, Holt, Henry & Co. Bks. For Young Readers) Holt, Henry & Co.

—The Ball. 2013. (Bean Dog & Nugget Ser.). lib. bdg. 14.75 (978-0-606-31944-7(1), Turtleback) Turtleback Bks.

—The Cookie. 2013. (Bean Dog & Nugget Ser.). lib. bdg. 14.75 (978-0-606-31945-4(X), Turtleback) Turtleback Bks.

—Cupcake. Harper, Charise Mericle, illus. 2010. (ENG., Illus.). 32p. (J). (gr. -1-1). 14.99 (978-1-4231-1897-8(9)) Hyperion Pr.

—Just Grace. 2008. (Just Grace Ser.: 1). (ENG., Illus.). 144p. (J). (gr. 1-4). pap. 5.99 (978-0-547-01440-1(6)) Houghton Mifflin Harcourt Publishing Co.

—Just Grace & the Super Sleepover. 2014. (Just Grace Ser.: 11). (ENG., Illus.). 208p. (J). (gr. 1-4). 15.99 (978-0-544-04584-2(X)) Houghton Mifflin Harcourt Publishing Co.

—Just Grace Gets Crafty. 2014. (Just Grace Ser.: 12). (ENG., Illus.). 192p. (J). (gr. 1-4). 15.99 (978-0-544-08023-2(8), HMH Books For Young Readers) Houghton Mifflin Harcourt Publishing Co.

—Just Grace Goes Green. 2009. (Just Grace Ser.: 4). (ENG., Illus.). 192p. (J). (gr. 1-4). pap. 5.99 (978-0-547-24821-9(0)) Houghton Mifflin Harcourt Publishing Co.

—Lights, Camera, Cook! Blard-Quintard, Aurélie, illus. 2017. (Next Best Junior Chef Ser.: 1). (ENG.). 192p. (J). (gr. 2-5). 12.99 **(978-0-544-91260-1(8)**, HMH Books For Young Readers) Houghton Mifflin Harcourt Publishing Co.

—Mae & June & the Wonder Wheel. Spires, Ashley, illus. 2017. (ENG.). 128p. (J). (gr. 1-4). 15.99 (978-0-544-63063-5(7), HMH Books For Young Readers) Houghton Mifflin Harcourt Publishing Co.

—Still Just Grace. (Just Grace Ser.: 2). (ENG., Illus.). 160p. (J). 2009. (gr. 1-4). pap. 5.99 (978-0-618-93482-9(0)) 2007. (gr. 2-5). 15.99 (978-0-618-64643-2(4)) Houghton Mifflin Harcourt Publishing Co.

—Super Sasquatch Showdown. Harper, Charise Mericle, illus. 2015. (Sasquatch & Aliens Ser.: 2). (ENG., Illus.). 176p. (J). (gr. 2-5). 13.99 (978-0-8050-9622-4(1), 9780805096224, Holt, Henry & Co. Bks. For Young Readers) Holt, Henry & Co.

Harper, Jo. Whistling Willie. 2005. 32p. (J). (978-0-7868-2095-5(0)) Hyperion Pr.

Harper, Ken. Mystery in Mansfield. 2008. 60p. pap. 19.95 (978-1-60441-055-6(8)) America Star Bks.

Harrington, Jane. Four Things My Geeky-Jock-of-a-Best-Friend Must Do in Europe. 2006. (ENG.). 160p. (J). (gr. 6-9). 15.95 (978-1-58196-041-9(7), Darby Creek) Lerner Publishing Group.

Harrington, K. A. Forget Me. 2014. (ENG.). 288p. (YA). (gr. 7). 17.99 (978-0-399-16529-0(0), G.P. Putnam's Sons Books for Young Readers) Penguin Young Readers Group.

Harrington, Linda. Holly's Backyard Adventures, 1 vol. 2010. 20p. pap. 24.95 (978-1-4512-9277-0(5)) PublishAmerica, Inc.

Harris, Brenda. Ride Like the Wind. 2011. (Illus.). 40p. (J). pap. 12.95 (978-1-936076-93-2(4)) Innovo Publishing, LLC.

Harris, Christine. Four Tails: An Anthology of Four Tales for Children. 2011. (Illus.). 92p. (gr. -1). pap. 12.10 (978-1-4520-7643-0(X)) AuthorHouse.

Harris, Donna. Dust Bunnies Do Love Donuts. 2009. 40p. pap. 16.99 (978-1-4490-0628-0(0)) AuthorHouse.

—Lucie & the Garden Fairies. 2008. (Illus.). 40p. pap. 18.49 (978-1-4389-1312-4(5)) AuthorHouse.

Harris, Harris. Union Cross: New Seasons. 2013. 234p. (J). pap. 9.00 (978-1-60039-202-3(4)) Lamp Post Inc.

Harris, Lewis. A Taste for Red. 2010. (ENG.). 180p. (J). (gr. 5-7). pap. 12.95 (978-0-547-39851-8(4)) Houghton Mifflin Harcourt Publishing Co.

Harris, Nikki. Adventures in Friendship for Benji Butterfly & Tom Turkey. 2013. 24p. pap. 24.95 (978-1-63004-741-2(4)) America Star Bks.

Harris, Patricia. Rowdy Racket in the Jungle. 2017. (Jungle Fun Ser.). 24p. (gr. 4-6). pap. 8.25 **(978-1-5383-2128-7(9)**, PowerKids Pr.) Rosen Publishing Group, Inc., The.

—Teddy Finds Some Friends. 2017. (Teddy's Colorful World Ser.). 24p. (gr. 4-6). pap. 8.25 **(978-1-5383-2155-3(6)**, PowerKids Pr.) Rosen Publishing Group, Inc., The.

Harris, Philip. Trever & the Phoenix. 2009. 40p. pap. 16.99 (978-1-4389-9537-3(7)) AuthorHouse.

Harris, Robie H. Turtle & Me. Freeman, Tor, illus. 2015. (ENG.). 40p. (J). (gr. -1-3). 16.99 (978-1-4998-0046-3(0)) Little Bee Books Inc.

Harris, Sally M. Color Me Happy. Paplinksie, Cecilia, illus. 2009. 24p. pap. 10.95 (978-1-935137-75-7(1)) Guardian Angel Publishing, Inc.

Harris, Shelly J. A Snowman's Love, 1 vol. 2009. 19p. pap. 24.95 (978-1-60836-708-5(8)) America Star Bks.

Harris, Teresa E. American Girl: Girl of the Year: 2017, Novel 1. 2016. (American Girl Contempory Middle Grade Ser.: 1). lib. bdg. 20.85 **(978-0-606-39986-9(0))** Turtleback Bks.

—Girl of the Year - 2017 Novel 2. 2017. (American Girl Contempory Middle Grade Ser.: 2). lib. bdg. 20.85 **(978-0-606-39987-6(9))** Turtleback Bks.

Harris, Trudy. Tally Cat Keeps Track. Harris, Andrew, illus. 2010. (Math Is Fun! Ser.). (ENG.). 32p. (gr. k-2). lib. bdg. 22.60 (978-0-7613-4451-3(9), Millbrook Pr.) Lerner Publishing Group.

Harris, Wendell. Elton's Shoes. 2012. 100p. (gr. -1). pap. 13.95 (978-1-4520-8143-4(3)) AuthorHouse.

Harrison, Dorothy. A Better Tomorrow? 2003. 128p. pap. 13.95 (978-0-595-28429-0(9), Backinprint.com) iUniverse, Inc.

Harrison, Emma. The Best Girl. 2007. (ENG.). 288p. (YA). (gr. 9-18). pap. 5.99 (978-0-06-122824-7(9), HarperTeen) HarperCollins Pubs.

—Finding What's Real. 2017. (ENG., Illus.). 304p. (YA). (gr. 9). 17.99 (978-1-4814-4215-2(5), Simon Pulse) Simon Pulse.

Harrison, Hannah E. My Friend Maggie. 2016. (ENG., Illus.). 40p. (J). (gr. -1-3). 17.99 (978-0-525-42916-6(6), Dial Bks) Penguin Young Readers Group.

Harrison, John. Fergal Onions. 2005. (Illus.). 32p. pap. (978-0-7022-3481-1(8)) Univ. of Queensland Pr.

Harrison, Lisi. Best Friends for Never. 2004. (Clique Ser.: 2). (ENG.). 208p. (YA). (gr. 7-17). pap. 9.99 (978-0-316-70131-0(9), Poppy) Little, Brown Bks. for Young Readers.

—Best Friends for Never. 2008. (Clique Novels Ser.). 197p. 20.00 (978-1-60686-290-2(1)) Perfection Learning Corp.

—Bratfest at Tiffany's, No. 9. 2008. (Clique Ser.: 9). (ENG., Illus.). 256p. (YA). (gr. 7-17). per. 9.99 (978-0-316-00680-4(7), Poppy) Little, Brown Bks. for Young Readers.

—Charmed & Dangerous: The Clique Prequel. 2012. (Clique Ser.). (ENG.). 208p. (YA). (gr. 7-17). pap. 8.99 (978-0-316-05536-9(0), Poppy) Little, Brown Bks. for Young Readers.

—The Clique. 2004. (Clique Ser.: 1). (ENG.). 224p. (YA). (gr. 7-17). pap. 9.99 (978-0-316-70129-7(7), Poppy) Little, Brown Bks. for Young Readers.

—It's Not Easy Being Mean. 2008. (Clique Ser.). 193p. 20.00 (978-1-60686-330-5(4)) Perfection Learning Corp.

—Sealed with a Diss. 2008. (Clique Novels Ser.). 248p. 20.00 (978-1-60686-345-9(2)) Perfection Learning Corp.

—A Tale of Two Pretties. 2011. (Clique Ser.: 14). (ENG.). 224p. (YA). (gr. 7-17). pap. 9.99 (978-0-316-08442-0(5), Poppy) Little, Brown Bks. for Young Readers.

—These Boots Are Made for Stalking. 12th ed. 2010. (Clique Ser.: 12). (ENG.). 256p. (YA). (gr. 7-17). pap. 9.99 (978-0-316-00683-5(1), Poppy) Little, Brown Bks. for Young Readers.

Harrison, Patrick Gb. Who says Kist Can't Fight Global Warming. 2009. pap. 16.97 (978-1-61584-921-5(1)) Independent Pub.

Harrison, Paula. The Ice Diamond. 2014. (Rescue Princesses Ser.: 1). (ENG.). 128p. (J). (gr. 2-5). pap. 4.99 (978-0-545-66164-5(1), Scholastic Paperbacks) Scholastic, Inc.

Harrison, Zac. Crash Landing, 1 vol. 2013. (Hyperspace High Ser.). (ENG.). 288p. (gr. 4-8). 27.32 (978-1-4342-6306-3(1)) Stone Arch Bks.

—Galactic Battle, 1 vol. 2014. (Hyperspace High Ser.). (ENG., Illus.). 288p. (gr. 4-8). 27.32 (978-1-4342-6569-2(2)) Stone Arch Bks.

—Hyperspace High, 1 vol. (Hyperspace High Ser.). (ENG.). 288p. (gr. 4-8). 2014. 54.64 (978-1-4342-8935-3(4)) 2013. 109.28 (978-1-4342-6314-8(2)) 2013. pap. 35.80 (978-1-4342-9039-7(5)) Stone Arch Bks.

—Robot Warriors, 1 vol. 2013. (Hyperspace High Ser.). (ENG.). 288p. (gr. 4-8). pap. 8.95 (978-1-4342-6312-4(6)); 27.32 (978-1-4342-6308-7(8)) Stone Arch Bks.

—Space Plague, 1 vol. 2014. (Hyperspace High Ser.). (ENG., Illus.). 288p. (gr. 4-8). 27.32 (978-1-4342-6568-5(4)) Stone Arch Bks.

—Warlord's Revenge, 1 vol. 2013. (Hyperspace High Ser.). (ENG.). 288p. (gr. 4-8). pap. 8.95 (978-1-4342-6313-1(4)); 27.32 (978-1-4342-6309-4(6)) Stone Arch Bks.

Harrod-Eagles, Cynthia. A Church Anniversary. 2011. 44p. pap. 18.46 (978-1-4567-6493-7(4)) AuthorHouse.

Harrold, A. F. The Imaginary. Gravett, Emily, illus. 2015. (ENG.). 240p. (YA). (gr. 3-6). 16.99 (978-0-8027-3811-0(7), 9780802738110, Bloomsbury USA Childrens) Bloomsbury Publishing USA.

—The Song from Somewhere Else. Pinfold, Levi, illus. 2017. (ENG.). 240p. (J). 16.99 (978-1-68119-401-1(5), 9781681194011, Bloomsbury USA Childrens) Bloomsbury Publishing USA.

Harrop, Isobel. The Isobel Journal, 1 vol. 2014. (ENG.). 208p. (gr. 10-12). 16.95 (978-1-63079-003-5(6)) Switch Pr.

Harry, Rebecca. Snow Bunny's Christmas Gift. 2015. (ENG., Illus.). 32p. (J). (gr. -1-3). 17.99 (978-1-4998-0164-4(5)) Little Bee Books Inc.

—Snow Bunny's Christmas Wish. Harry, Rebecca, illus. 2013. (ENG., Illus.). 32p. (J). (gr. -1-3). 16.99 (978-0-545-54103-9(4), Orchard Bks.) Scholastic, Inc.

Hart, Caryl & Lord, Leonie. The Wolf Who Wouldn't Go to School. 2015. (ENG.). 32p. (J). (gr. -1-k). pap. 8.99 (978-1-4380-0620-8(9)) Barron's Educational Series, Inc.

Hart, J. Tristan. The Adventures of Friendly & Barnackel: Book 1 Friendly & Barnackel. 2010. 36p. pap. 15.49 (978-1-4490-9721-9(9)) AuthorHouse.

—The Adventures of Friendly & Barnackel: Book 2. 2011. 36p. pap. 15.14 (978-1-4567-6284-1(2)) AuthorHouse.

Hart, Jeff. Undead with Benefits. 2014. (Eat, Brains, Love Ser.: 2). (ENG.). 416p. (YA). (gr. 8). pap. 9.99 (978-0-06-220036-5(4), HarperTeen) HarperCollins Pubs.

Hart, Julie Anne. Miss Molly Mare. 2011. 16p. 8.50 (978-1-4520-5172-7(0)) AuthorHouse.

Hart, Kate. After the Fall. 2017. (ENG.). 336p. (YA). 17.99 (978-0-374-30269-6(3), 9780374302696, Farrar, Straus & Giroux (BYR)) Farrar, Straus & Giroux.

Hart-Plaugher, Teresa. Little Bird & the Wind. Swope, Brenda, illus. 2011. 28p. pap. 24.95 (978-1-4512-9102-5(7)) America Star Bks.

Hart, Teresa. The Ant & the Alligator. 2007. 84p. per. 19.95 (978-1-4241-7182-8(2)) America Star Bks.

—The Ant & the Lost Spider, 1 vol. 2009. 76p. pap. 19.95 (978-1-60749-296-2(2)) America Star Bks.

Hartinger, Brent. Project Sweet Life. 2009. (J). lib. bdg. 17.89 (978-0-06-082412-9(3)); (ENG.). 288p. (YA). (gr. 8-18). 16.99 (978-0-06-082411-2(5)) HarperCollins Pubs. (HarperTeen).

—Three Truths & a Lie. 2016. (ENG., Illus.). 272p. (YA). (gr. 9). 17.99 (978-1-4814-4960-1(5), Simon Pulse) Simon Pulse.

Hartley, Susan. Jake's Sleepover. 2011. (Early Connections Ser.). (J). (978-1-61672-583-9(4)) Benchmark Education Co.

Hartry, Nancy. Watching Jimmy. 2009. (ENG.). 160p. (YA). (gr. 4-7). 16.95 (978-0-88776-871-2(7), Tundra Bks.) Tundra Bks. CAN. Dist: Penguin Random Hse. LLC.

Hartt-Sussman, Heather. Noni Says No. Côté, Geneviève, illus. 2011. (ENG.). 24p. (J). (gr. -1-2). 17.95 (978-1-77049-233-2(X), Tundra Bks.) Tundra Bks. CAN. Dist: Penguin Random Hse. LLC.

Harvey, Damian. Snail's Legs. Paul, Korky, illus. 2015. (ENG.). 32p. (J). (gr. -1-2). pap. 8.99 (978-1-84780-712-0(7), Frances Lincoln) Quarto Publishing Group UK GBR. Dist: Hachette Bk. Group.

Harvey-Fitzhenry, Alyxandra. Broken, 1 vol. 2010. (ENG., Illus.). 176p. (YA). (gr. 7-12). pap. 12.95 (978-1-896580-41-8(6)) Tradewind Bks. CAN. Dist: Orca Bk. Pubs. USA.

Harvey, Irene J. William the Fairground Car. 2008. 116p. pap. 30.95 (978-1-60693-210-0(1), Eloquent Bks.) Strategic Book Publishing & Rights Agency (SBPRA).

Harvey, Jacqueline. Alice-Miranda Holds the Key. Yinfoo, Anne, illus. 2017. (Alice-Miranda Ser.: 15). (ENG.). 384p. (J). (gr. 3-7). 9.99 **(978-0-14-378070-0(0))** Random Hse. Australia AUS. Dist: Independent Pubs. Group.

—Alice-Miranda on Vacation. 2013. (ENG.). 288p. (J). (gr. 2-5). 7.99 (978-0-385-73996-2(6), Yearling) Random Hse. Children's Bks.

—Clementine Rose & the Special Promise. 2016. (Clementine Rose Ser.: 11). (ENG.). 160p. (J). (gr. 1-3). pap. 8.99 (978-0-85798-786-0(0)) Random Hse. Australia AUS. Dist: Independent Pubs. Group.

Harvey, John. My New Skates. 2006. (Neighborhood Readers Ser.). (ENG.). 16p. (gr. 1-3). pap. 6.50 (978-1-4042-7172-2(4), Rosen Classroom) Rosen Publishing Group, Inc., The.

Harvey, Keith. Tiberius & the Friendly Dragon. Kirk, Heather, illus. 2010. (Tiberius Tales Ser.). 24p. (J). (gr. -1-2). pap. 8.15 (978-1-60754-834-8(8)); lib. bdg. 22.60 (978-1-60754-830-0(5)) Windmill Bks.

Harvey, Keith & Kirk, Heather. Tiberius & the Friendly Dragon. 2014. (ENG., Illus.). 24p. pap. 8.95 (978-1-84135-917-5(3)) Award Pubns. Ltd. GBR. Dist: Parkwest Pubns., Inc.

Harvey, Pam & Panckridge, Michael. Ghost of a Chance. 2007. 208p. (978-0-207-20063-2(7)) HarperCollins Pubs. Australia.

—Into the Fire. 2008. 192p. (J). (978-0-207-20061-8(0)) HarperCollins Pubs. Australia.

Harvey, Sarah N. The Lit Report, 1 vol. 2008. (ENG.). 208p. (YA). (gr. 7-12). pap. 12.95 (978-1-55143-905-1(0)) Orca Bk. Pubs. USA.

Harvie, Ronald Anthony. The Adventures of Peter Potato & Friends. 2005. (Illus.). 71p. (J). per. 15.95 (978-0-9771939-0-5(X), 0002) New World Publishing.

Hasak-Lowy, Todd. 33 Minutes. Barton, Bethany, illus. (ENG.). 224p. (J). (gr. 3-7). 2014. pap. 7.99 (978-1-4424-4501-7(7)) 2013. 16.99 (978-1-4424-4500-0(9)) Simon & Schuster Children's Publishing. (Aladdin).

Hasan, Jamal I. A Journey to Remember. 2007. 64p. per. 8.95 (978-0-595-43375-9(8)) iUniverse, Inc.

Hasbro. Around Equestria! 2016. (ENG.). 160p. (J). (gr. -1-3). 11.99 (978-0-316-39529-8(3)) Little, Brown Bks. for Young Readers.

—Friendship Through the Ages, Set. 2015. (ENG., Illus.). 960p. (J). (gr. 3-7). 40.00 (978-0-316-30778-9(5)) Little, Brown Bks. for Young Readers.

—My Little Pony: Chapter Book Bind-Up. 2016. (ENG., Illus.). 416p. (J). (gr. 3-7). pap. 12.99 (978-0-316-27259-9(0)) Little, Brown Bks. for Young Readers.

—My Little Pony: Ponyville Reading Adventures. 2015. (Passport to Reading Level 2 Ser.). (ENG., Illus.). 192p. (J). (gr. -1-3). 9.99 (978-0-316-33740-3(4)) Little, Brown Bks. for Young Readers.

Hasbro Industries Incorporated Staff & Snider, Brandon T. Wonderbolts Academy Handbook. 2016. (ENG.). 192p. (J). (gr. 3-7). 17.99 (978-0-316-39499-4(8)) Little, Brown Bks. for Young Readers.

Hasbro My Little Pony, Hasbro My. My Little Pony New Episode 2014. 2014. (Panorama Sticker Storybook Ser.: 12). (ENG.). 24p. (J). (gr. -1-2). pap. 7.99 (978-0-7944-3117-4(8)) Reader's Digest Assn., Inc., The.

—My Little Pony Pony Friends Are Forever/La Amistad de los Ponis Es Para Siempre: An English/Spanish Lift-the-Flap Book. 2014. (Lift-The-Flap Ser.: 30). (ENG.). 10p. (J). (gr. -1-1). bds. 9.99 (978-0-7944-3144-0(5)) Reader's Digest Assn., Inc., The.

Hasiuk, Brenda. Your Constant Star, 1 vol. 2014. (ENG.). 248p. (YA). (gr. 8-12). pap. 12.95 (978-1-4598-0368-8(X)) Orca Bk. Pubs. USA.

Hasting, Lori A. Green with N. V. 2012. (ENG.). pap. 14.95 (978-1-4675-4195-4(8)) Independent Pub.

Hatch, Justina. Charlie the Caterpillar, 1 vol. 2010. 44p. pap. 24.95 (978-1-4489-9256-0(7)) PublishAmerica, Inc.

Hatch, Thomas. Larry the Moose. 2009. 32p. pap. 15.99 (978-1-4389-8533-6(9)) AuthorHouse.

Hathaway, Jill. Impostor. 2013. (Slide Ser.: 2). (ENG.). 272p. (YA). (gr. 9). 17.99 (978-0-06-207798-1(8)) HarperCollins Pubs.

—Slide. (Slide Ser.: 1). (ENG.). (YA). (gr. 9). 2013. 272p. pap. 9.99 (978-0-06-207796-7(1)) 2012. 256p. 17.99 (978-0-06-207790-5(2)) HarperCollins Pubs.

Hatke, Ben. Zita the Spacegirl. Hatke, Ben, illus. 2011. (Zita the Spacegirl Ser.: 1). (ENG., Illus.). 192p. (J). (gr. 3-7). 19.99 (978-1-59643-695-4(6), 9781596436954); pap. 12.99 (978-1-59643-446-2(5), 9781596434462) Roaring Brook Pr. (First Second Bks.).

—Zita the Spacegirl. 2011. (Zita the Spacegirl Ser.: 1). (J). lib. bdg. 24.50 (978-0-606-21623-4(5), Turtleback) Turtleback Bks.

Hattemer, Kate. The Vigilante Poets of Selwyn Academy. 2014. (ENG.). 336p. (YA). (gr. 7). 16.99 (978-0-385-75378-4(0), Knopf Bks. for Young Readers) Random Hse. Children's Bks.

Hatton, Laura. The Fairy's Garden. 2012. 64p. pap. 26.52 (978-1-4669-3961-5(3)) Trafford Publishing.

Hauf, Kyle. Annabelle Discovers the Missing Lunch Money. PA Illustrator, illus. 2011. 36p. pap. 24.95 (978-1-4560-3656-0(4)) America Star Bks.

Haugen, Timothy A. The Castle of Gloom, 1 vol. 2009. (ENG.). 175p. pap. 24.95 (978-1-61546-106-6(X)) America Star Bks.

Hauser, Michele. The Crystal Palace Ii: Rebellion in Fairyland. 2009. (Illus.). 130p. pap. 9.95 (978-1-4327-1153-5(9)) Outskirts Pr., Inc.

Hautman, Pete. Invisible. Hautman, Pete, illus. 2006. (ENG., Illus.). 160p. (YA). (gr. 7-12). reprint ed. pap. 9.99 (978-0-689-86903-7(7), Simon & Schuster Bks. For Young Readers) Simon & Schuster Bks. For Young Readers.

—What Boys Really Want. 2012. (ENG.). 304p. (J). (gr. 7). 17.99 (978-0-545-11315-1(6), Scholastic Pr.) Scholastic, Inc.

Havill, Juanita. Jamaica Tag-Along, 1 vol. O'Brien, Anne Sibley, illus. 2011. (ENG.). 32p. (J). (gr. -1-3). audio compact disk 10.99 (978-0-547-48105-0(5)) Houghton Mifflin Harcourt Publishing Co.

Hawes, Adrienne Hill. Moving Danielle. 2008. 22p. pap. 24.95 (978-1-4241-4977-3(0)) America Star Bks.

Hawkins, Colin & Hawkins, Jacqui. Foxy & Friends Go Racing. (Illus.). 32p. (J). 8.95 (978-0-00-664565-8(8), HarperSport) HarperCollins Pubs. Ltd. GBR. Dist: Trafalgar Square Publishing.

Hawkins, Nicole. Blue. 2013. 20p. pap. 24.95 (978-1-4137-3232-0(1)) America Star Bks.

Hawkins, Rachel. Hex Hall, Bk. 1. 2010. (ENG.). 336p. (J). (gr. 7-17). 16.99 (978-1-4231-2130-5(9)) Hyperion Pr.

—Journey's End. 2016. (ENG.). 304p. (J). (gr. 3-7). 16.99 (978-0-399-16960-1(1), G.P. Putnam's Sons Books for Young Readers) Penguin Young Readers Group.

Hawkins, Wendy. Binky Goes to School. 2009. 20p. pap. 13.99 (978-1-4389-6990-9(2)) AuthorHouse.

Hawley, Bobby. Matt & the Wonder of Wishes, 1 vol. 2009. 165p. pap. 24.95 (978-1-60836-743-6(6)) America Star Bks.

Hawley, Jim. Homer & Friends. 2012. 50p. pap. (978-1-77097-709-9(0)) FriesenPress.

Hawthorne, Rachel. The Boyfriend League. 2007. (ENG.). 336p. (YA). (gr. 9-12). pap. 8.99 (978-0-06-113837-9(1), HarperTeen) HarperCollins Pubs.

—The Boyfriend Project. 2015. (ENG.). 352p. (YA). (gr. 9). pap. 9.99 (978-0-06-233073-4(X), HarperTeen) HarperCollins Pubs.

—Suite Dreams. 2008. (ENG.). 288p. (YA). (gr. 9-18). pap. 5.99 (978-0-06-168806-5(1), HarperTeen) HarperCollins Pubs.

—Thrill Ride. 2006. (ENG.). 320p. (YA). (gr. 9). pap. 5.99 (978-0-06-083954-3(6), HarperTeen) HarperCollins Pubs.

Haxhia, Miranda. The Dolls Nose. Kohler, Ursula, illus. 2007. 32p. (J). (POL & ENG.). pap. 16.95 (978-1-60195-097-0(7)); (ARA & ENG.). pap. 16.95 (978-1-60195-087-1(X)) International Step by Step Assn.

Haxhia, Miranda. The Doll's Nose. Kohrer, Ursula, illus. 2014. (ARA.). (J). **(978-0-9856237-4-6(8))** East West Discovery Pr.

Hay, Sam. Night of the Howling Hound, No. 3. Cooper, Simon, illus. 2014. (Undead Pets Ser.: 3). (ENG.). 112p. (J). (gr. 1-3). 5.99 (978-0-448-47797-8(1), Grosset & Dunlap) Penguin Young Readers Group.

—Night of the Howling Hound. 2014. (Undead Pets Ser.: 3). lib. bdg. 16.00 (978-0-606-36219-1(3)) Turtleback Bks.

Hayatian, MaryAnn. Cookie, a cat's Tale. 2010. 32p. pap. 20.00 (978-0-557-70819-2(2)) Lulu Pr., Inc.

Haydel, Catherine. Uno the Cat & Hurricane Katrina. 2006. 18.00 (978-0-8059-7341-9(9)) Dorrance Publishing Co., Inc.

Haydon, David J. The Spuds - the Circus Comes to Town. 2012. 20p. pap. (978-1-78222-051-0(8)) Paragon Publishing, Rothersthorpe.

—The Spuds - the Fancy Dress Party. Ferns, Kevin, illus. 2011. 20p. pap. (978-1-908341-08-2(4)) Paragon Publishing, Rothersthorpe.

Haydu, Corey Ann. Life by Committee. 2014. (ENG.). 304p. (YA). (gr. 9). 17.99 (978-0-06-229405-0(9), Tegen, Katherine Bks) HarperCollins Pubs.

—Making Pretty. 2015. (ENG.). 368p. (YA). (gr. 9). 17.99 (978-0-06-229408-1(3), Tegen, Katherine Bks) HarperCollins Pubs.

Hayes, Daniel. Flyers. 2013. (ENG.). 208p. (YA). (gr. 7). pap. 10.99 (978-1-4424-8881-6(6), Simon & Schuster Bks. For Young Readers) Simon & Schuster Bks. For Young Readers.

Hayes, Denis. Silly Animal Stories for Kids. 2014. 80p. pap. 36.26 (978-1-4828-9436-3(X)) Partridge Pub.

Hayes, Felix. Doctor Monkey. Broadway, Hannah, illus. 2013. (Monkey & Robot Ser.). (ENG.). 32p. (J). (gr. -1-k). pap. 10.99 (978-1-4088-0654-8(1), 9781408806548, Bloomsbury USA Childrens) Bloomsbury Publishing USA.

Hayes, Geoffrey. Benny & Penny in the Big No-No! Hayes, Geoffrey, illus. 2014. (Benny & Penny Ser.). (ENG., Illus.). 32p. (J). (gr. -1-3). pap. 6.99 (978-1-935179-35-1(7)) TOON Books / RAW Junior, LLC.

Hayes, J. B. Freddy the Frog's First Christmas. 2012. 44p. pap. 21.99 (978-1-4772-2870-8(5)) AuthorHouse.

Hayes, James. Tuggy the Little Tug Boat. 2012. 24p. pap. 17.99 (978-1-4772-9075-0(3)) AuthorHouse.

Hayes, K. M. My Little Brony: An Unofficial Novel about Finding the Magic of Friendship. 2015. (ENG.). 272p. (J). (gr. 6). pap. 8.99 (978-1-63450-676-2(6)) Skyhorse Publishing Co., Inc.

Hayes, Karel. The Christmas Visitors. 2013. (ENG., Illus.). 32p. (J). (gr. -1-3). 16.95 (978-1-60893-248-1(6)) Down East Bks.

Hayes, Sonia. Eye Candy. 2008. (YA). per. 9.95 (978-0-9777573-2-9(3)) NUA Multimedia.

—Urban Goddess. 2007. 224p. (YA). per. 9.95 (978-0-9777573-1-2(5)) NUA Multimedia.

Hayes, Terri. The Day the Blue Puff Trees Bloomed. 2011. 36p. pap. 24.95 (978-1-4560-6096-1(1)) America Star Bks.

Haynes, Marilee. Pictures of Me. 2016. 149p. (J). pap. (978-0-8198-6019-4(0)) Pauline Bks. & Media.

Hays, Anna. Portia's Exclusive & Confidential Rules on True Friendship. 2009. (Mix Ser.). (ENG.). 224p. (J). (gr. 4-8). pap. 5.99 (978-1-4169-7806-0(2), Aladdin) Simon & Schuster Children's Publishing.

Hays, Tommy. What I Came to Tell You. 2014. (ENG., Illus.). 304p. (J). (gr. 5). pap. 8.99 (978-1-60684-545-5(4), Carolrhoda Bks.) Lerner Publishing Group.

Haywood, Carolyn. Betsy & the Boys. 2004. (ENG., Illus.). 160p. (J). (gr. 1-4). pap. 10.95 (978-0-15-205102-0(3)) Houghton Mifflin Harcourt Publishing Co.

—Here's a Penny. 2005. (ENG., Illus.). 160p. (J). (gr. 1-4). pap. 6.99 (978-0-15-205225-6(9)) Houghton Mifflin Harcourt Publishing Co.

—Primrose Day. 2005. (ENG., Illus.). 176p. (J). (gr. 1-4). pap. 10.95 (978-0-15-205229-4(1)) Houghton Mifflin Harcourt Publishing Co.

Haywood, Ebony. There Was Once a Potato. 2009. 42p. (J). pap. 21.95 (978-1-4327-3871-6(2)) Outskirts Pr., Inc.

Hazell, Carolyn. Pav the Plumber Saves the Day. 2011. 84p. (gr. 4-6). pap. 11.76 (978-1-4567-8148-4(0)) AuthorHouse.

Hazuka, Tom. Last Chance for First. 2008. 296p. (YA). (gr. 9-18). pap. 8.95 (978-0-9798824-0-1(0)) Brown Barn Bks.

HB Staff. My Wild Woolly. 97th ed. 2003. (First-Place Reading Ser.). (gr. 1-18). pap. 16.50 (978-0-15-308163-7(5)) Harcourt Schl. Pubs.

Healey, Vittoria. Rebecca & Her Bushland Friends. 2016. (ENG.). 105p. (J). pap. 10.95 (978-1-78455-783-6(8), 427c9885-3abf-4fdc-a0c3-5d8c8beffa44) Austin, Stan AUS. Dist: Bookmasters Distribution.

Heasley, Gwendolyn. Don't Call Me Baby. 2014. (ENG.). 304p. (YA). (gr. 8). pap. 9.99 (978-0-06-220852-1(7), HarperTeen) HarperCollins Pubs.

Heath, Clyde. Kids Have Ups & Downs Too! 2012. 62p. pap. 17.99 (978-0-9853650-1-1(3)) Mindstir Media.

Heather, Cherry. Surviving High School: The Journey of an Angst Filled Teen, 1 vol. 2010. 74p. pap. 19.95 (978-1-4489-4145-2(8)) PublishAmerica, Inc.

Heathfield, Lisa. Paper Butterflies. 2017. (ENG.). 272p. (YA). (gr. 7-12). 18.99 **(978-1-5124-8241-6(2)**, Carolrhoda Bks.) Lerner Publishing Group.

Hecker, Vera, illus. A Home for Rainbow. 2007. 32p. (J). (978-0-9799729-0-4(6)) Banta, Sandra.

Heeney, Bronwyn. A Dragon Called Wilbur: How a Fire-Breathing Dragon Made Friends. Fekete, Lucy, illus. 2012. 40p. pap. 16.97 (978-1-61204-803-1(X), Strategic Bk. Publishing) Strategic Book Publishing & Rights Agency (SBPRA).

Heer, Dusty Rhoades. The Forest That Rains Frogs. 2012. (ENG.). 58p. pap. 19.95 (978-1-4327-9303-6(9)) Outskirts Pr., Inc.

Heffernan, John. Hotaka: Through My Eyes - Natural Disaster Zones. White, Lyn, ed. 2017. (Through My Eyes Ser.). (ENG.). 224p. (J). (gr. 6-9). pap. 12.99 **(978-1-76011-376-6(X))** Allen & Unwin AUS. Dist: Independent Pubs. Group.

Hegarty, Patricia. Bear's Truck Is Stuck! 2015. (Amazing Changing Pictures! Ser.). (ENG.). 14p. (J). (gr. -1-3). 12.99 (978-1-68010-001-3(7)) Tiger Tales.

Hegedus, Bethany. Between Us Baxters. 2009. 306p. (YA). (gr. 7-9). 17.95 (978-1-934813-02-7(8)) 2011. 9.14 (978-1-934813-18-8(4)) Westside Bks.

Heible, Bev. A Collection of Short Tails. 2012. 60p. 17.95 (978-1-62709-686-7(8)); pap. 17.95 (978-1-62709-343-9(5)) America Star Bks.

Heidbreder, Robert. Crocodiles Play! Mate, Rae, illus. 2009. (ENG.). 32p. (J). (gr. -1-3). 16.95 (978-1-894965-86-6(8)) Simply Read Bks. CAN. Dist: Ingram Publisher Services.

Heide, Florence Parry. Princess Hyacinth (the Surprising Tale of a Girl Who Floated) Smith, Lane, illus. 2016. (ENG.). 48p.

(J). (gr. -1-3). 7.99 (978-0-553-53804-5(7), Dragonfly Bks.) Random Hse. Children's Bks.
—That's What Friends Are For. Meade, Holly, illus. 2007. 40p. pap. 6.99 (978-0-7636-3283-0(X)) Candlewick Pr.
Heide, Florence Parry & Clief, Sylvia Van. That's What Friends Are For. Meade, Holly, illus. 2007. 30p. (gr. -1-3). 17.00 (978-0-7569-8126-6(3)) Perfection Learning Corp.
Heiman, Herb. Running on Dreams. 2007. 293p. (YA). (gr. 8-14). per. 22.95 (978-1-931282-28-4(5)) Autism Asperger Publishing Co.
Heimbuch, Carol. Shadow Stallion. 2011. 170p. pap. 11.50 (978-1-59330-693-9(8)) Aventine Pr.
Heimbuch, Carol Jo. Condor Caper. Martin, Fred, illus. 2008. 128p. pap. 11.50 (978-1-59330-560-4(5)) Aventine Pr.
Heine, Helme. Trois Amis.Tr. of Three Friends. (FRE.). (J). pap. 12.95 (978-2-07-050533-3(2)) Gallimard, Editions FRA. Dist: Distribooks, Inc.
Heldring, Thatcher. The Football Girl. 2017. (YA). (978-0-375-99026-7(7), Delacorte Pr) Random House Publishing Group.
Heldring, Thatcher. Toby Wheeler: Eighth Grade Benchwarmer. 2008. (ENG.). 224p. (J). (gr. 3-7). 6.99 (978-0-440-42183-2(7), Yearling) Random Hse. Children's Bks.
Helfenbein, DeWayne. The Treasure Hunt. 2006. pap. 9.99 (978-1-60034-562-3(X)) Salem Author Services.
Helgeson, Kat & Moskowitz, Hannah. Gena/Finn. 2016. (ENG., Illus.). (YA). (gr. 7-12). 17.99 (978-1-4521-3839-8(7)) Chronicle Bks. LLC.
Helidoniotis, Kathy. Horse Mad Heroes. 2007. 272p. (J). (978-0-7322-8423-7(6)) HarperCollins Pubs. Australia.
Heling, Kathryn & Hembrook, Deborah. I Wish I Had Freckles Like Abby. Adamson, Bonnie, illus. 2010. (I Wish Ser.). (ENG.). 32p. (J). (gr. 4-7). pap. 7.95 (978-1-934960-47-9(0), Raven Tree Pr.,Csi) Continental Sales, Inc.
—I Wish I Had Freckles Like Abby/Quisiera Tener Pecas Como Abby. Adamson, Bonnie, illus. 2007. (SPA & ENG.). 32p. (J). (gr. -1-3). pap. 7.95 (978-0-9770906-6-2(3), Raven Tree Pr.,Csi) Continental Sales, Inc.
—I Wish I Had Glasses Like Rosa. Adamson, Bonnie, illus. 2010. (I Wish Ser.). (ENG.). 32p. (J). (gr. 4-7). pap. 7.95 (978-1-934960-49-3(7), Raven Tree Pr.,Csi) Continental Sales, Inc.
Heling, Kathryn, et al. I Wish I Had Freckles Like Abby/Quisiera Tener Pecas Como Abby. de La Vega, Eida, tr. Adamson, Bonnie, illus. 2007. (I Wish Ser.). (SPA & ENG.). 32p. (J). (gr. -1-3). 16.95 (978-0-9724973-8-1(2), 626999, Raven Tree Pr.,Csi) Continental Sales, Inc.
The Hell House Experience. 2008. (ENG.). 70p. 14.99 (978-0-9817520-8-2(X)) Torch Legacy Pubns.
Heller, Alyson. Soccer Day. Björkman, Steve, illus. 2009. (After-School Sports Club Ser.). (ENG.). 32p. (J). (gr. -1-1). pap. 3.99 (978-1-4169-9410-7(6), Simon Spotlight) Simon Spotlight.
Heller, Sarah. Tinker Bell My Music MP3 Player: Storybook & Personal Music Player. 2008. (RD Innovative Book & Player Format Ser.). (ENG.). 36p. (YA). bds. 24.99 (978-0-7944-1673-7(X)) Reader's Digest Assn., Inc., The.
Helmetag Murdock, Kita. Future Flash. 2014. (ENG.). 208p. (J). (gr. 2-7). 12.95 (978-1-62873-622-3(7), Sky Pony Pr.) Skyhorse Publishing Co., Inc.
Helou, Sandra & Chown, Xanna Eve. Grover on the Case: Follow the Reader Level 1. 2008. (Sesame Street Ser.). (ENG.). 24p. (J). 24.99 (978-1-4169-5852-9(5), Simon Scribbles) Simon Scribbles.
Helsel, Sandra. Pokey & the Rooster. Snyder, Joe, illus. 2009. 28p. pap. 9.95 (978-0-9818488-1-5(8)) Ajoyin Publishing, Inc.
Hemery, Kathleen Maresh. Sunflower Promise. Bordelois, Augusto, illus. 2005. (J). (978-1-56123-188-1(6)) Centering Corp.
Hemingway, Edith M. Road to Tater Hill. 2011. (ENG.). 224p. (J). (gr. 3-7). 7.99 (978-0-375-84544-4(5), Yearling) Random Hse. Children's Bks.
Hemingway, Edward. Bad Apple: A Tale of Friendship. Hemingway, Edward, illus. 2012. (ENG., Illus.). 32p. (J). (gr. -1-k). 16.99 (978-0-399-25191-7(X), G.P. Putnam's Sons Books for Young Readers) Penguin Young Readers Group.
—Bad Apple's Perfect Day. Hemingway, Edward, illus. 2014. (ENG., Illus.). 32p. (J). (gr. -1-k). 16.99 (978-0-399-16036-3(1), G.P. Putnam's Sons Books for Young Readers) Penguin Young Readers Group.
Hemmerle, Jamie. The Lost & Found Summer. 2010. (Illus.). 312p. pap. 15.95 (978-1-4327-6268-1(0)) Outskirts Pr., Inc.
Henderson, Lauren. Kiss Me Kill Me. 2009. (ENG.). 272p. (YA). (gr. 9). pap. 8.99 (978-0-385-73488-2(3), Delacorte Pr.) Random Hse. Children's Bks.
Henderson, Maryel. Squirt Saves the Day: A Stinkbug's Story. Henderson, Maryel, illus. 2017. (ENG., Illus.). 42p. (J). pap. 8.95 (978-1-68350-043-8(1)) Morgan James Publishing.
Henderson, Milagros. Lulu the Bouncing Kangaroo. 2012. 36p. (-18). pap. 20.99 (978-1-4772-8899-3(6)) AuthorHouse.
Henderson, Virginia. Zippy the Dreamer. 2010. 20p. 13.77 (978-1-4269-3448-3(3)) Trafford Publishing.
Hendricks, Brenda K. What's the Buzz, Bumbly Bee? Hendricks, Brenda K., illus. 2013. (Illus.). 30p. pap. 9.99 (978-0-9826582-3-9(0)) Two Small Fish Pubns.
Hendricks, Linda K. The Rainbow Egg. 2012. 26p. pap. 12.95 (978-1-4497-7539-1(X), WestBow Pr.) Author Solutions, Inc.
Hendrix, Jennifer & Schmitt, Laura. Oscar. 2012. 50p. pap. 20.95 (978-1-4525-4938-5(9)) Balboa Pr.
Hengel, Katherine. Taking Control, 1 vol. unabr. ed. 2011. (District 13 Ser.). (ENG.). 48p. (YA). (gr. 9-12). pap. 7.95 (978-1-61651-276-7(8)) Saddleback Educational Publishing, Inc.
Henkes, Kevin. Bird Lake Moon. (ENG.). 192p. (J). (gr. 3-7). 2010. pap. 5.99 (978-0-06-147079-0(1)) 2008. 17.99 (978-0-06-147076-9(7)) HarperCollins Pubs. (Greenwillow Bks.).
—Chester's Way. (Illus.). 25.95 incl. audio (978-1-59112-968-4(0)); 28.95 incl. audio compact disk (978-1-59112-972-1(9)); pap. 33.95 incl. audio (978-1-59112-969-1(9)); pap. 35.95 incl. audio compact disk (978-1-59112-973-8(7)) Live Oak Media.
—Egg. Henkes, Kevin, illus. 2017. (Illus.). 40p. (J). (gr. -1-3). 17.99 (978-0-06-240872-3(0), Greenwillow Bks.) HarperCollins Pubs.
—Words of Stone. 2005. (ENG.). 160p. (J). (gr. 3-7). reprint ed. pap. 6.99 (978-0-06-078230-6(7), Greenwillow Bks.) HarperCollins Pubs.
Hennessy, Mary-Christine. My Hidden Friend. 2011. 24p. pap. 12.79 (978-1-4567-6137-0(4)) AuthorHouse.
Henry, April. Blood Will Tell. 2015. (Point Last Seen Ser.: 2). (ENG.). 272p. (YA). (gr. 7). 17.99 (978-0-8050-9853-2(4), 9780805098532, Holt, Henry & Co. Bks. For Young Readers) Holt, Henry & Co.
—The Body in the Woods. 2014. (Point Last Seen Ser.: 1). (ENG.). 272p. (YA). (gr. 7). 17.99 (978-0-8050-9852-5(6), 9780805098525, Holt, Henry & Co. Bks. For Young Readers) Holt, Henry & Co.
Henry, Jed. Cheer up, Mouse! Henry, Jed, illus. 2013. (ENG., Illus.). 32p. (J). (gr. -1-3). 12.99 (978-0-547-68107-8(0)) Houghton Mifflin Harcourt Publishing Co.
—Good Night, Mouse! Henry, Jed, illus. 2013. (ENG., Illus.). 32p. (J). (gr. -1-3). 16.99 (978-0-547-98156-7(2)) Houghton Mifflin Harcourt Publishing Co.
Henry, Kristina. The Rat Tank, 1 vol. Ambler, Laura & Brown, Amanda, illus. 2011. (ENG.). 40p. (J). 16.99 (978-0-7643-3842-7(0), 9780764338427, Schiffer Publishing Ltd) Schiffer Publishing, Ltd.
Henry, Regene. The Barefoot Boys of Fayette. Stich, Carolyn R., illus. 2005. 180p. (J). (gr. 4-7). pap. 9.95 (978-0-9749412-3-3(9)) EDCO Publishing, Inc.
Hensdill, Norma Mae. Friends Are Forever. 2009. 36p. pap. 17.99 (978-1-4389-5053-2(5)) AuthorHouse.
Henshon, Suzanna E. Spiders on the Ceiling. 2006. (J). (978-0-88092-614-0(7)) Royal Fireworks Publishing Co.
Hensler, K. Why Worry? The Adventures of Bay/Bob/A/Loo/Bop Everything in Moderation. 2008. 48p. pap. 24.95 (978-1-60610-813-0(1)) America Star Bks.
Hepler, Heather. Frosted Kisses. 2015. (ENG.). 272p. (J). (gr. 7). 17.99 (978-0-545-79055-0(7)) Scholastic, Inc.
Hepler, Linda McGhee. How to Survive Seventh Grade (If You're Lucky) 2008. 146p. pap. 24.95 (978-1-60563-610-8(X)) America Star Bks.
Heppermann, Christine & Koertge, Ron. Jess's Story. Marcero, Deborah, illus. 2016. (Backyard Witch Ser.: 2). 192p. (J). (gr. 3-7). 16.99 (978-0-06-233841-9(2), Greenwillow Bks.) HarperCollins Pubs.
Heppermann, Christine & Koertge, Ronald. Sadie's Story. Marcero, Deborah, illus. 2015. (Backyard Witch Ser.: 1). (ENG.). 176p. (J). (gr. 3-7). 16.99 (978-0-06-233838-9(2), Greenwillow Bks.) HarperCollins Pubs.
Herbauts, Anne. Monday. 2006. (ENG., Illus.). 36p. (J). (gr. -1-3). 16.95 (978-1-59270-057-8(8)) Enchanted Lion Bks., LLC.
Herbert, Frances. Fran's Van & the Magic Box. Herbert, Frances, illus. 2013. (Illus.). 24p. pap. (978-1-78222-085-5(2)) Paragon Publishing, Rothersthorpe.
Herman, Gail. Peppa Pig & Her Best Friend. 2007. (My First I Can Read Bks.). 32p. (J). pap. 3.99 (978-0-06-117305-9(3), Harper Trophy) HarperCollins Pubs.
Herman, R. A. Pal & Sal's New Friend. 2005. (978-0-439-68119-3(7)) Scholastic, Inc.
Hermes, Patricia. Emma Dilemma & the Camping Nanny, 0 vols. Carter, Abby, illus. 2009. (Emma Dilemma Ser.: 4). (ENG.). 144p. (J). (gr. 3-6). 15.99 (978-0-7614-5534-9(5), 9780761455349, Amazon Children's Publishing) Amazon Publishing.
—Emma Dilemma, the Nanny, & the Best Horse Ever, 0 vols. Carter, Abby, illus. 2013. (Emma Dilemma Ser.: 6). (ENG.). 144p. (J). (gr. 3-6). pap. 9.99 (978-1-4778-1633-2(X), 9781477816332, Amazon Children's Publishing) Amazon Publishing.
Hernandez, Christopher. Scaredycrow. 2013. lib. bdg. 14.75 (978-0-606-31953-9(0), Turtleback) Turtleback Bks.
Hernandez, David. No More Us for You. 2009. (YA). 281p. lib. bdg. 17.89 (978-0-06-117334-9(7)); (ENG.). 288p. (gr. 9-18). 16.99 (978-0-06-117333-2(9)) HarperCollins Pubs. (HarperTeen).
Hernandez, Mary L. Como el Viento Paso a Ser Tormenta. Maval Publishing Inc. Staff, illus.Tr. of How the Tornado Got It's Wind. (SPA.). (J). (gr. -1-3). pap. 7.50 (978-1-59134-015-7(2)) Maval Publishing, Inc.
Herndon, Lee G. The Land of Always & Forever: The Trilogy, 1 vol. 2009. 77p. pap. 19.95 (978-1-60836-898-3(X)) America Star Bks.
Herr, Brandy. The Adventures of Freddie Spaghetti & Meat Ball. 2012. 24p. pap. 24.95 (978-1-4626-7834-1(3)) America Star Bks.
Herren, Greg. Sorceress. 2010. (ENG.). 434p. (J). (gr. 6). pap. 18.95 (978-0-9845318-1-3(5)) Tiny Stachel Pr.
Herrick, Amy. The Time Fetch. 2014. (ENG.). 336p. (J). (gr. 4-7). pap. 6.95 (978-1-61620-453-2(2), 73453) Algonquin Bks. of Chapel Hill.
Herrick, Steven. Do-Wrong Ron. Magerl, Caroline, illus. 2005. (ENG.). 132p. (J). (gr. 1-5). pap. 11.99 (978-1-86508-661-3(4)) Allen & Unwin AUS. Dist: Independent Pubs. Group.
Herring, Bruce D. The Wizard of Wonderland, 1 vol. 2010. 192p. pap. 24.95 (978-1-4489-5844-3(X)) America Star Bks.
Herrndorf, Wolfgang. Why We Took the Car. Mohr, Tim, tr. from GER. 2014. (ENG.). 256p. (J). (gr. 9). 17.99 (978-0-545-48180-9(5), Levine, Arthur A. Bks.) Scholastic, Inc.
—You, Me, & a Russian Jeep. 2013. (YA). pap. (978-0-545-48181-6(3), Levine, Arthur A. Bks.) Scholastic, Inc.
Herrold. City & Village Planning & Zon. 2013. (Fesler-Lampert Minnesota Heritage Ser.). (ENG.). 136p. pap. 9.95 (978-0-8166-9031-2(6)) Univ. of Minnesota Pr.
Hershey, Mary. My Big Sister Is So Bossy She Says You Can't Read This Book. 2006. (ENG., Illus.). 176p. (J). (gr. 3-7). per. 6.99 (978-0-553-48797-8(3), Yearling) Random Hse. Children's Bks.
Hertz, Kellen. American Girl. 2017. (American Girl Contempory Middle Grade Ser.: 1). lib. bdg. 20.85 (978-0-606-39988-3(7)) Turtleback Bks.
—Tenney in the Key of Friendship. 2017. (American Girl Contempory Middle Grade Ser.: 2). lib. bdg. 20.85 (978-0-606-39989-0(5)) Turtleback Bks.
Herzog, Pearl. The Amazing Fishing Rod. Bodel, Itai, photos by. 2013. (Illus.). 34p. (J). (978-1-4226-1436-5(0)) Mesorah Pubns., Ltd.
Hesse, Karen. Phoenix Rising. 2009. (ENG.). 208p. (J). (gr. 6-11). pap. 9.99 (978-0-312-53562-9(7), 9780312535629) Square Fish.
—Safekeeping. 2012. (ENG., Illus.). 304p. (YA). (gr. 7-12). 17.99 (978-1-250-01134-3(5), 9781250011343) Feiwel & Friends.
Hest, Amy. Mr. George Baker. Muth, Jon J., illus. 2007. (Reading Rainbow Bks.). (ENG.). 32p. (J). (gr. k-3). 6.99 (978-0-7636-3308-0(9)) Candlewick Pr.
—Mr. George Baker. 2007. lib. bdg. 17.20 (978-1-4177-9067-8(9), Turtleback) Turtleback Bks.
Heuvel, Eric & Miller, Lorraine T. A Family Secret. Miller, Lorraine T., tr. from DUT. Heuvel, Eric, illus. 2009. (ENG., Illus.). 64p. (J). (gr. 5-9). pap. 11.99 (978-0-374-42265-3(6), 9780374422653) Square Fish.
Hewett, Katherine. Smile Doodle Bug! 2009. 26p. 21.80 (978-0-578-03065-4(9)) Hewett, Katherine J.E.
Hewitt, Megan. Eagle Rises. 2013. 118p. (J). pap. 12.99 (978-1-300-55242-0(5)) Lulu Pr., Inc.
Hichens, Joanne. Stained. 2008. (Cutting Edge Ser.). (ENG.). 200p. pap. (978-1-84167-715-6(9)) Ransom Publishing Ltd.
Hickey, Caroline. Isabelle's Boyfriend. 2009. (ENG.). 192p. (J). (gr. 6-9). pap. 18.99 (978-0-312-60273-4(1), 9780312602734) Square Fish.
Hickey, Laura L. What's in the Woods. 2012. 84p. pap. 19.95 (978-1-4626-9025-1(4)) America Star Bks.
Hickey, Tony. Where's Jacko? Myler, Terry, illus. 2006. (ENG.). 64p. (J). pap. 10.95 (978-1-901737-47-9(0)) Anvil Bks., Ltd. IRL. Dist: Dufour Editions, Inc.
Hickner, Hayden. A Bear & the Bees. 2010. 36p. 15.49 (978-1-4520-5087-4(2)) AuthorHouse.
Hicks, Aniya & Hicks, Michelle. Fun Back in Ruskin Town. 2012. 24p. pap. 24.95 (978-1-4626-8245-4(6)) America Star Bks.
Hicks, Clifford B. Alvin Fernald, Foreign Trader. Schluenderfritz, Theodore, illus. 2007. (Alvin Fernald Mysteries Ser.). 181p. (J). (gr. 4). per. 11.95 (978-1-883937-74-4(4)) Bethlehem Bks.
Hicks, Esther & Hicks, Jerry. Solomon's Fine Featherless Friends. 2nd ed. 2007. (ENG., Illus.). 256p. pap. 15.99 (978-1-4019-1159-1(5)) Hay Hse., Inc.
Hicks, Esther, et al. Sara Learns the Secret about the Law of Attraction. Garrett, Caroline S., illus. 2nd ed. 2007. (ENG.). 192p. per. 14.99 (978-1-4019-1158-4(7)) Hay Hse., Inc.
Hicks, Faith Erin. The Nameless City. 2016. (Nameless City Ser.: 1). (ENG., Illus.). 240p. (J). pap. 14.99 (978-1-62672-156-2(4), 9781626721562, First Second Bks.) Roaring Brook Pr.
Hicks, Kelli. Field Trip Fiasco. 2015. (ENG.). 48p. (gr. k-3). 27.07 (978-1-63430-371-2(7)) Rourke Educational Media.
Hicks, Robert Z. Tommie Turtle's Secret. Rolseth, Ruthie, illus. 2007. (ENG.). 40p. (J). 16.95 (978-0-9792031-0-7(4)) R.Z. Enterprises of Florida.
Hidier, Tanuja Desai. Born Confused. 2014. (ENG.). 512p. (J). (gr. 9). pap. 10.99 (978-0-545-66451-6(9), PUSH) Scholastic, Inc.
Higginbotham, Mary. Only Feature. 2012. 56p. pap. 16.95 (978-1-4626-7953-9(6)) America Star Bks.
Higgins, Chris. The Secrets Club: Alice in the Spotlight. 2015. (Secrets Club Ser.: 1). (ENG.). 208p. (J). (gr. 2-4). pap. 9.99 (978-0-14-133522-3(X)) Penguin Bks., Ltd. GBR. Dist: Independent Pubs. Group.
—The Secrets Club: No Match for Dani. 3rd ed. 2016. (Secrets Club Ser.: 3). (ENG.). 176p. (J). (gr. 2-4). pap. 9.99 (978-0-14-133524-7(6)) Penguin Bks., Ltd. GBR. Dist: Independent Pubs. Group.
—The Truth about Tash. 2nd ed. 2015. (Secrets Club Ser.: 2). (ENG.). 192p. (J). (gr. 2-4). 9.99 (978-0-14-133523-0(8)) Penguin Bks., Ltd. GBR. Dist: Independent Pubs. Group.
Higgins, Jim. The Enchanted Nursery: Heather & Hamish, Fun in Florida, Reggie Rabbit at the Seaside, Percy Penguin's Friends. 2009. (Illus.). 36p. pap. 15.49 (978-1-4389-9904-3(6)) AuthorHouse.
Higgins, Joanna. Waiting for the Queen: A Novel of Early America. 2013. (ENG.). 256p. (J). (gr. 4-10). 16.95 (978-1-57131-700-1(7)) Milkweed Editions.
Higgins, Ryan. Wilfred. Higgins, Ryan, illus. 2013. (ENG., Illus.). 40p. (J). (gr. -1-k). 16.99 (978-0-8037-3732-7(7), Dial Bks) Penguin Young Readers Group.
Higginson, Hadley. Keeker & the Pony Camp Catastrophe, Bk. 5. Perrett, Lisa, illus. 2007. (Keeker & the Sneaky Pony Ser.: KEEK). (ENG.). 56p. (J). (gr. k-3). per. 4.99 (978-0-8118-5597-6(X)) Chronicle Bks. LLC.
Higginson, Sheila Sweeny & Disney Book Group Staff. Bubble Trouble. Disney Storybook Artists Staff & Disney Storybook Art Team, illus. 2013. (ENG.). 24p. (J). (gr. -1-k). pap. 4.99 (978-1-4231-6454-8(7)) Disney Pr.
Higginson, Sheryl. Dilbert's Pets, 1 vol. 2010. 94p. pap. 19.95 (978-1-4489-5757-6(5)) America Star Bks.
Higgs, Carolyn. One Village Boy Loses His Friends. 2011. 20p. pap. 24.95 (978-1-4489-4290-9(X)) America Star Bks.
Higman, Anita. The Living Darkness: Texas Caves. 2nd ed. 2003. (Illus.). xiii, 93p. (J). (978-1-57168-763-8(1), Eakin Pr.) Eakin Pr.
Hiiasen, Carl. Hoot. 2014. 17.00 (978-1-63419-707-6(0)) Perfection Learning Corp.
Hildahl, Melita K. Life Is an Adventure with Ernie. 2008. 156p. per. 15.99 (978-1-60477-139-8(9)) Salem Author Services.
Hileman, Linda L. Dawn's Secret. 2006. (J). per. 9.95 (978-1-59571-117-5(1)) Word Association Pubs.
Hill, C. J. Slayers: Friends & Traitors. 2013. (Slayers Ser.: 2). (ENG.). 400p. (YA). (gr. 7). 16.99 (978-1-250-02461-9(7), 9781250024619) Feiwel & Friends.
Hill, Chris. Lucky. 2016. (ENG.). 208p. (J). (gr. 2-5). 16.99 (978-0-545-83977-8(7), Chicken Hse., The) Scholastic, Inc.
Hill, Clarissa. God Deserves Your Best. Hill, Stephanie, illus. 2005. (ENG.). 20p. (J). pap. 11.00 (978-0-9785539-0-6(X)) Hill, Stephanie & Clarissa.
Hill, Ryan. J P Trouble. 2012. 32p. pap. 12.95 (978-1-886057-15-9(X)) Warren Publishing, Inc.
Hill, Sarah. Posie Pixie & the Copper Kettle. O'Gorman, Sarah, ed. Mauchline, Sarah, illus. 2013. 52p. pap. (978-1-909302-20-4(1)) Abela Publishing.
Hill, Susan. Ruby Bakes a Cake. Moore, Margie, illus. 2004. (My First I Can Read Bks.). 32p. (J). (gr. k-3). lib. bdg. 16.89 (978-0-06-008976-4(8)) HarperCollins Pubs.
—Ruby Bakes a Cake, 1 vol. Moore, Margie, illus. 2010. (I Can Read! / Ruby Raccoon Ser.). (ENG.). 32p. (J). pap. 3.99 (978-0-310-72022-5(2)) Zonderkidz.
—Ruby's Perfect Day. Moore, Margie, illus. 2006. (I Can Read Bks.). 32p. (J). (gr. -1-3). 15.99 (978-0-06-008962-5(2)) HarperCollins Pubs.
—Ruby's Perfect Day, 1 vol. Moore, Margie, illus. 2010. (I Can Read! / Ruby Raccoon Ser.). (ENG.). 32p. (J). pap. 3.99 (978-0-310-72024-9(9)) Zonderkidz.
Hillenbrand, Jane. What a Treasure! Hillenbrand, Will, illus. 2006. (ENG.). 24p. (J). (gr. -1-3). 16.95 (978-0-8234-1896-1(0)) Holiday Hse., Inc.
—What a Treasure! Hillenbrand, Will, illus. 2017. (ENG.). 24p. (J). (gr. -1-1). bds. 7.99 (978-0-8234-3763-4(9)) Holiday Hse., Inc.
Hillert, Margaret. Una Amiga para Querido Dragón. Pullan, Jack, illus. 2017. (BeginningtoRead Ser.).Tr. of Friend for Dear Dragon. (ENG & SPA.). 32p. (J). (-2). 22.60 (978-1-59953-828-0(8)) Norwood Hse. Pr.
—Four Good Friends. Collier-Morales, Roberta, illus. 2016. (BeginningtoRead Ser.). (ENG.). 32p. (J). (gr. -1-2). pap. 11.94 (978-1-60357-906-3(0)) Norwood Hse. Pr.
—A Friend for Dear Dragon. Pullan, Jack, illus. 2016. (BeginningtoRead Ser.). (ENG.). 32p. (J). (-2). lib. bdg. 22.60 (978-1-59953-765-8(6)); (gr. 1-2). pap. 11.94 (978-1-60357-878-3(1)) Norwood Hse. Pr.
Hillhouse, Joanne C. With Grace: By Joanne C. Hillhouse. Ward, Cherise, illus. 2017. (J). pap. (978-1-934370-62-9(2)) Editorial Campana.
Hilliard, Regina Foster. Tim & Tom: Frog Friends. 2011. (Illus.). 19p. (J). pap. 14.95 (978-1-4327-5917-9(5)) Outskirts Pr., Inc.
Hillner, Brenda. The Invisible Girl. 2012. 86p. 19.10 (978-1-4669-5398-7(5)); pap. 9.10 (978-1-4669-5396-3(9)) Trafford Publishing.
Hills, Frederic F. & Hills, Tad. Rocket's 100th Day of School. 2014. (Rocket Ser.). (ENG.). 32p. (J). (gr. 1-4). pap. 3.99 (978-0-385-39097-2(1), Random Hse. Bks. for Young Readers) Random Hse. Children's Bks.
Hills, Tad. Duck & Goose Go to the Beach. 2014. (Duck & Goose Ser.). (ENG., Illus.). 40p. (J). (gr. -1-2). 17.99 (978-0-385-37235-0(3), Schwartz & Wade Bks.) Random Hse. Children's Bks.
—Duck, Duck, Goose. Hills, Tad, illus. 2007. (Duck & Goose Ser.). (ENG., Illus.). 40p. (J). (gr. -1-2). 17.99 (978-0-375-84068-5(0), Schwartz & Wade Bks.) Random Hse. Children's Bks.
Hillyer, Lexa. Proof of Forever. 352p. (YA). (gr. 8). 2016. pap. 9.99 (978-0-06-233038-3(1)) 2015. (ENG.). 17.99 (978-0-06-233037-6(3)) HarperCollins Pubs. (HarperTeen).
Hillyer, Rhonda. Butterfly Magic. Wood, Steve, illus. 2013. 84p. pap. 12.00 (978-1-62212-306-3(9), Strategic Bk. Publishing) Strategic Book Publishing & Rights Agency (SBPRA).
Hilton, Marilyn. Found Things. (ENG.). 240p. (J). (gr. 4-7). 2015. pap. 7.99 (978-1-4424-6088-1(1)) 2014. 16.99 (978-1-4424-6087-4(3)) Simon & Schuster Children's Publishing.
Himmelman, John. Katie & the Puppy Next Door. Himmelman, John, illus. 2013. (ENG., Illus.). 32p. (J). (gr. -1-1). 16.99 (978-0-8050-9484-8(9), 9780805094848, Holt, Henry & Co. Bks. For Young Readers) Holt, Henry & Co.
—Katie Loves the Kittens. Himmelman, John, illus. 2008. (ENG., Illus.). 32p. (J). (gr. -1-3). 18.99 (978-0-8050-8682-9(X), 9780805086829, Holt, Henry & Co. Bks. For Young Readers) Holt, Henry & Co.
Hines, Anna Grossnickle. Pieces: A Year in Poems & Quilts. Hines, Anna Grossnickle, illus. 2003. (ENG., Illus.). 32p. (J). (gr. k-5). pap. 6.99 (978-0-06-055960-1(8), Greenwillow Bks.) HarperCollins Pubs.
Hinkel, Patricia. Frog in My Bucket. 2012. 16p. pap. 15.99 (978-1-4772-4815-7(3)) AuthorHouse.
Hinson, Beverly. Breezy & Friends: Life Lessons Learned in the Rain Forest. 2016. (ENG., Illus.). 30p. (J). pap. 12.95 (978-1-934898-56-7(2)) McClanahan Publishing Hse., Inc.
Hinton, Maureen. William's Troublesome Tongue. 2010. 36p. pap. 13.95 (978-1-60911-396-4(9), Eloquent Bks.) Strategic Book Publishing & Rights Agency (SBPRA).
Hiranandani, Veera. Lunch Will Never Be the Same! Dreidemy, Joëlle, illus. 2014. (Phoebe G. Green Ser.: 1). (ENG.). 96p. (J). (gr. 1-3). pap. 4.99 (978-0-448-46695-8(3), Grosset & Dunlap) Penguin Young Readers Group.
Hirota, Denise. Little Zippy Duffelbag Goes to France. 2012. 24p. pap. 12.45 (978-1-4624-0443-8(X), Inspiring Voices) Author Solutions, Inc.
Hirsch, Andy. Varmints. 2016. (ENG., Illus.). 224p. (J). pap. 16.99 (978-1-62672-279-8(X), 9781626722798, First Second Bks.) Roaring Brook Pr.
Hirsch, Jeff. Magisterium. 2012. (ENG.). 320p. (J). (gr. 7). 17.99 (978-0-545-29018-0(X), Scholastic Pr.) Scholastic, Inc.
Hirst, Daisy. Hilda & the Runaway Baby. Hirst, Daisy, illus. 2017. (ENG., Illus.). 32p. (J). (-k). 16.99 (978-0-7636-9490-6(8)) Candlewick Pr.
Hissey, Jane. Old Bear. 2013. (ENG., Illus.). 36p. (J). (gr. -1-1). 17.95 (978-1-77049-481-7(2), Tundra Bks.) Tundra Bks. CAN. Dist: Penguin Random Hse. LLC.
Hitchcock, Bonnie-Sue. The Smell of Other People's Houses. 2016. (ENG., Illus.). 240p. (YA). (gr. 7). 17.99 (978-0-553-49778-6(2), Lamb, Wendy Bks.) Random Hse. Children's Bks.
Hitchcock, Shannon. Ruby Lee & Me. 2016. (ENG., Illus.). 272p. (J). (gr. 3-7). 16.99 (978-0-545-78230-2(9), Scholastic Pr.) Scholastic, Inc.
Hoban, Russell. A Bargain for Frances. Hoban, Lillian, illus. l.t. ed. 2003. (I Can Read Level 2 Ser.). (ENG.). 64p. (J). (gr. k-3). pap. 3.99 (978-0-06-444001-1(X)) HarperCollins Pubs.
—Best Friends for Frances. Hoban, Lillian, illus. (J). 2016. (ENG.). 32p. (gr. -1-3). pap. 5.99 (978-0-06-239244-2(1), HarperFestival) 2009. 48p. (gr. -1-3). 16.99 (978-0-06-083801-0(9)) 2009. (ENG.). 48p. (gr. k-3). pap. 3.99 (978-0-06-083803-4(5)) HarperCollins Pubs.
Hobbie, Holly. Let It Snow. 2016. (J). lib. bdg. 17.20 (978-0-606-39186-3(X)) Turtleback Bks.
—Toot & Puddle. 2010. (Toot & Puddle Ser.: 1). (ENG., Illus.). 32p. (J). (gr. -1-3). pap. 7.99 (978-0-316-08080-4(2)) Little, Brown Bks. for Young Readers.
—Toot & Puddle. Hobbie, Holly, illus. 2007. (Toot & Puddle Ser.: 1). (ENG., Illus.). 32p. (J). (gr. -1-3). 17.99

(978-0-316-16702-4(9)) Little, Brown Bks. for Young Readers.
—Toot & Puddle: Let It Snow. 2016. (Toot & Puddle Ser.: 11). (ENG.). 32p. (J). (gr. -1-3). 6.99 *(978-0-316-35224-6(1))* Little, Brown Bks. for Young Readers.
—Top of the World. 2008. (Toot & Puddle Ser.: 6). (ENG.). 32p. (gr. -1-3). pap. 7.99 *(978-0-316-03384-8(7))* Little, Brown Bks. for Young Readers.
—You Are My Sunshine. 2010. (Toot & Puddle Ser.: 3). (ENG., Illus.). 32p. (J). (gr. -1-3). pap. 7.99 *(978-0-316-16703-1(7))* Little, Brown Bks. for Young Readers.
Hobbs, Constance. Bugsy's Special Event. 2008. 64p. pap. 10.50 *(978-0-9556783-7-0(4))* Hobbs, Constance GBR. Dist: Lulu Pr., Inc.
Hobbs, Will. Crossing the Wire. (ENG.). 224p. (J). (gr. 5-9). 2007. pap. 7.99 *(978-0-06-074140-2(6))* 2006. (Illus.). 16.99 *(978-0-06-074138-9(4))* HarperCollins Pubs.
—Crossing the Wire. 2007. (Illus.). 216p. (gr. 5-9). 17.00 *(978-0-7569-8053-5(4))* Perfection Learning Corp.
Hoberman, Mary Ann. And to Think That We Thought That We'd Never Be Friends. Hawkes, Kevin, illus. 2003. (ENG.). 40p. (J). (gr. -1-2). pap. 7.99 *(978-0-440-41776-7(7),* Dragonfly Bks.) Random Hse. Children's Bks.
—Strawberry Hill. 2010. (ENG., Illus.). 240p. (J). (gr. 3-7). pap. 7.99 *(978-0-316-04135-5(1))* Little, Brown Bks. for Young Readers.
Hodge, Deborah. Bear's Winter Party. 1 vol. Cinar, Lisa, illus. 2016. (ENG.). 32p. (J). (gr. -1-2). 16.95 *(978-1-55498-853-2(5))* Groundwood Bks. CAN. Dist: Publishers Group West (PGW).
Hodges, Ronald. Buff Bears. 2011. 68p. (gr. -1). pap. 11.99 *(978-1-4567-9437-8(X))* AuthorHouse.
Hodgkinson, Jo. A Big Day for Migs. Hodgkinson, Jo, illus. 2014. (ENG., Illus.). 32p. (J). (gr. -1-3). 16.95 *(978-1-4677-5014-1(X))* Lerner Publishing Group.
Hoena, Blake. Brains vs. Brawn. Regan, Dana, illus. 2014. (Jess & Jaylen Ser.). (ENG.). 48p. (J). (gr. 1-4). 27.07 *(978-1-63143-436-5(5),* 208260) Child's World, Inc., The.
—Coming Clean. Regan, Dana, illus. 2014. (Jess & Jaylen Ser.). (ENG.). 48p. (J). (gr. 1-4). 27.07 *(978-1-63143-437-2(3),* 208261) Child's World, Inc., The.
—Daring, 1 vol. Cano, Fernando, illus. 2014. (Tony Hawk: Live2Skate Ser.). (ENG.). 72p. (gr. 4-5). lib. bdg. 25.32 *(978-1-4342-9139-4(1))* Stone Arch Bks.
—Halloween Scream. Regan, Dana, illus. 2014. (Jess & Jaylen Ser.). (ENG.). 48p. (J). (gr. 1-4). 27.07 *(978-1-63143-438-9(1),* 208262) Child's World, Inc., The.
—Monster Heroes, 4 vols. Bardin, Dave, illus. 2016. (Monster Heroes Ser.). (ENG.). 32p. (gr. 1-2). 85.28 *(978-1-4965-3770-6(X))* Stone Arch Bks.
—Museum Mystery. Regan, Dana, illus. 2014. (Jess & Jaylen Ser.). (ENG.). 48p. (J). (gr. 1-4). 27.07 *(978-1-63143-439-6(X),* 208263) Child's World, Inc., The.
—Video Game Zombie. Regan, Dana, illus. 2014. (Jess & Jaylen Ser.). (ENG.). 48p. (J). (gr. 1-4). 27.07 *(978-1-63143-443-3(8),* 208267) Child's World, Inc., The.
—Witch's Brew. Bardin, Dave, illus. 2016. (Monster Heroes Ser.). (ENG.). 32p. (gr. 1-2). lib. bdg. 21.32 *(978-1-4965-3756-0(4))* Stone Arch Bks.
Hoena, Blake & Hoena, Blake A. The Ghost Trap. Bardin, Dave, illus. 2016. (Monster Heroes Ser.). (ENG.). 32p. (gr. 1-2). lib. bdg. 21.32 *(978-1-4965-3757-7(2))* Stone Arch Bks.
—Vampires & Veggies. Bardin, Dave, illus. 2016. (Monster Heroes Ser.). (ENG.). 32p. (gr. 1-2). lib. bdg. 21.32 *(978-1-4965-3755-3(6))* Stone Arch Bks.
—Zombies & Meatballs. Bardin, Dave, illus. 2016. (Monster Heroes Ser.). (ENG.). 32p. (gr. 1-2). lib. bdg. 21.32 *(978-1-4965-3754-6(8))* Stone Arch Bks.
Hoena, Blake A. Raw. Cano, Fernando, illus. 2013. (Tony Hawk: Live2Skate Ser.). (ENG.). 72p. (gr. 3-4). pap. 35.70 *(978-1-4342-6268-4(5),* Tony Hawk's 900 Revolution) Stone Arch Bks.
—Raw, 1 vol. Cano, Fernando, illus. 2013. (Tony Hawk: Live2Skate Ser.). (ENG.). 72p. (gr. 4-5). pap. 5.95 *(978-1-4342-6188-5(3));* lib. bdg. 25.32 *(978-1-4342-4086-6(X))* Stone Arch Bks.
Hoena, Blake A. & Terrell, Brandon. Tony Hawk's 900 Revolution. 2013. (Tony Hawk's 900 Revolution Ser.). (ENG.). 128p. (gr. 3-4). 106.60 *(978-1-4342-4109-2(2),* Tony Hawk's 900 Revolution) Stone Arch Bks.
Hoena, Blake A. & Tortosa, Wilson. Amplified, Vol. 5. Ito, Leonardo, illus. 2012. (Tony Hawk's 900 Revolution Ser.). (ENG.). 128p. (gr. 3-4). pap. 7.19 *(978-1-4342-3887-0(3));* lib. bdg. 26.65 *(978-1-4342-3311-0(1))* Stone Arch Bks. (Tony Hawk's 900 Revolution).
Hoes, Holly. When Aliens Took over the World. 2012. 44p. pap. 21.99 *(978-1-4797-4870-9(6))* Xlibris Corp.
Hoff, Syd. Danny & the Dinosaur. 2017. (Danny & the Dinosaur — I Can Read Ser.). lib. bdg. 13.55 ***(978-0-606-40063-3(X))*** Turtleback Bks.
—Danny & the Dinosaur & the Big Storm. Hoff, Syd, illus. 2017. (Illus.). 24p. (J). (gr. -1-3). pap. 4.99 *(978-0-06-241045-0(8),* HarperFestival) HarperCollins Pubs.
—Danny & the Dinosaur: School Days. Hoff, Syd, illus. 2017. (I Can Read Level 1 Ser.). (Illus.). 32p. (J). (gr. -1-3). pap. 3.99 *(978-0-06-228161-6(5))* HarperCollins Pubs.
Hoffman, Alice. Indigo. 2003. (ENG.). 96p. (J). (gr. 3-7). pap. 6.99 *(978-0-439-25636-0(4),* Scholastic Paperbacks) Scholastic, Inc.
Hoffman, Cj. The Dragons & the Simmies: A Friendly Story. 2008. 20p. pap. 10.49 *(978-1-4389-1452-7(0))* AuthorHouse.
Hoffman, Judy. The Art of Flying: A Novel. Graegin, Stephanie, illus. 2014. (ENG.). 320p. (J). (gr. 3-7). pap. 7.99 *(978-1-4231-5907-0(1))* Hyperion Bks. for Children.
Hoffman, Mary. Bravo, Grace! 2011. (ENG.). 112p. (J). (gr. 3-7). 5.99 *(978-0-14-241850-5(1),* Puffin Books) Penguin Young Readers Group.
—Encore, Grace! 2011. (ENG.). 112p. (J). (gr. 3-7). 5.99 *(978-0-14-241854-3(4),* Puffin Books) Penguin Young Readers Group.
Hoffman, Robert M. The Adventures of Mia & Squeaky: Tails of Imagination. 2011. 32p. pap. 14.99 *(978-1-257-37254-6(8))* Lulu Pr., Inc.
Hoffmann, Burton R. Millicent the Magnificent. du Houx, Emily C., illus. 2004. 64p. pap. 12.00 *(978-1-882190-68-3(8))* Polar Bear & Co.
Hofmann, Ginnie. One Teddy Bear Is Enough! 2003. (Illus.). 32p. (Orig.). (J). pap. *(978-1-932485-02-8(3))* Reverie Publishing Co.
Hofmann-Maniyar, Ariane. That's NOT How You Do It! Hofmann-Maniyar, Ariane, illus. 2017. (Child's Play Library). (ENG., Illus.). 32p. (J). *(978-1-84643-929-2(9))* Child's Play International Ltd.
Hofmeister, Alan, et al. Ann & Nan. (Reading for All Learners Ser.). (Illus.). (J). pap. *(978-1-56861-085-6(8))* Swift Learning Resources.
—Mit & the Weed. (Reading for All Learners Ser.). (Illus.). (J). pap. *(978-1-56861-113-6(7))* Swift Learning Resources.
—Nell & Ed. (Reading for All Learners Ser.). (Illus.). (J). pap. *(978-1-56861-097-9(1))* Swift Learning Resources.
—The Pond. (Reading for All Learners Ser.). (Illus.). (J). pap. *(978-1-56861-131-0(5))* Swift Learning Resources.
Hogan, Anne Harmon. The Three Amigos. 2011. 26p. pap. 14.95 *(978-1-61434-276-2(8))* Booklocker.com, Inc.
Hoke, Jeehyun. Boy & the Little Violet Flower. 2012. (ENG.). (J). pap. 10.99 *(978-1-4675-2921-1(4))* Independent Pub.
Hol, Coby. Punch & His Friends. (Illus.). 24p. (J). 14.95 *(978-0-86315-206-1(6),* 1823) Floris Bks. GBR. Dist: Gryphon Hse., Inc.
Holder, Ramona V. Paco & Lexus Are Good Friends: Paco y Lexus son Buen Amigos. 2009. 24p. pap. 12.99 *(978-1-4389-5778-4(5))* AuthorHouse.
Holding, James Malcolm, 3rd. et al. The Mullet Masters. 2007. pap. 8.00 *(978-0-8059-7147-7(5))* Dorrance Publishing Co., Inc.
The Hole in the Hill: Individual Title Six-Packs. (Action Packs Ser.). 104p. (gr. 3-5). 44.00 *(978-0-7635-2993-2(1))* Rigby Education.
Hole, Stian. Garmann's Secret. Hole, Stian, illus. 2011. (ENG., Illus.). 56p. (J). 17.00 *(978-0-8028-5400-1(1),* Eerdmans Bks For Young Readers) Eerdmans, William B. Publishing Co.
Hole, Stian & Bartlett, Don. Garmann's Street. 2010. (ENG.). 44p. (J). (gr. 1-5). 17.00 *(978-0-8028-5357-8(9),* Eerdmans Bks For Young Readers) Eerdmans, William B. Publishing Co.
Holland, Dwayne K. Princess Laura & the Magic Waterfall. 2010. 42p. pap. 15.50 *(978-1-60860-744-0(5),* Strategic Bk. Publishing) Strategic Book Publishing & Rights Agency (SBPRA).
Holliday, D. L. Adventures of Tommy. 2013. (ENG.). 34p. (J). pap. 14.95 *(978-1-4787-0953-4(7))* Outskirts Pr., Inc.
Holliday, Patricia. You & me makes Two. 2008. 32p. pap. 17.35 *(978-1-4357-5321-1(6))* Lulu Pr., Inc.
Holliday, Susan. Dream Cave. l.t. ed. 2007. 216p. per. *(978-1-905665-23-5(7))* Pollinger In Print.
Hollis, Nicole Phillips. My Neighborhood Super Kids. 2012. 44p. pap. 21.99 *(978-1-4685-6169-2(3))* AuthorHouse.
Holm, Jennifer L. & Holm, Matthew. Pod vs. Pod. 2016. (Squish Ser.: 8). lib. bdg. 17.20 *(978-0-606-38880-1(X))* Turtleback Bks.
—Queen of the World! 2005. (Babymouse Ser.: 1). (ENG., Illus.). 96p. (J). (gr. 2-5). pap. 6.99 *(978-0-375-83229-1(7));* lib. bdg. 12.99 *(978-0-375-93229-8(1))* Random Hse. Children's Bks. (Random Hse. Bks. for Young Readers).
—Squish #8: Pod vs. Pod. Holm, Jennifer L. & Holm, Matthew, illus. 2016. (Squish Ser.). (ENG., Illus.). 96p. (J). (gr. 2-5). pap. 6.99 *(978-0-307-98308-4(0));* lib. bdg. 12.99 *(978-0-307-98309-1(9))* Random Hse. Children's Bks. (Random Hse. Bks. for Young Readers).
Holman, Donna Buckman. Little Angel Friends. 2013. 24p. pap. 10.95 *(978-1-4525-8494-2(X),* Balboa Pr.) Author Solutions, Inc.
Holmes, Anna. Tickety Toc: Pirate Time. 2014. (ENG.). 24p. (J). (gr. -1-k). pap. 3.99 *(978-0-545-61475-7(9))* Scholastic, Inc.
Holmes, Harold H. The Tale of the Purple Chicken & Orange Frog. 2010. 26p. pap. 12.00 *(978-1-60911-653-8(4),* Eloquent Bks.) Strategic Book Publishing & Rights Agency (SBPRA).
Holmes, Janet A. Me & You. Rossell, Judith, illus. 2009. (ENG.). 32p. (J). (gr. -1-3). 14.95 *(978-0-7358-2250-4(6))* North-South Bks., Inc.
Holmes, Quentin. Real Street Kidz: Chasing Action. 2010. 88p. pap. 10.99 *(978-1-60844-521-9(6))* Dog Ear Publishing, LLC.
Holmes, Stephanie. Grady Goes to Puppy School. 2011. 20p. (gr. 1-2). pap. 11.99 *(978-1-4634-1000-1(X))* AuthorHouse.
Holmqvist, Carin. African Tales. 2010. 64p. pap. 28.70 *(978-0-557-18184-1(4))* Lulu Pr., Inc.
Holsather, Kent /Wilson. Sara's Moon. 2007. (Illus.). 176p. (YA). per. 12.95 *(978-0-9729101-3-2(1))* Lonejack Mountain Pr.
Holt, K. A. Rhyme Schemer. 2014. (ENG., Illus.). 176p. (J). (gr. 5-9). 15.99 *(978-1-4521-2700-2(X))* Chronicle Bks. LLC.
Holt, Kimberly Willis. My Louisiana Sky. 208p. (YA). (gr. 5-18). 4.99 *(978-0-8072-8291-5(X),* Listening Library) Random Hse. Audio Publishing Group.
—My Louisiana Sky. 2011. (ENG.). 224p. (J). (gr. 4-7). pap. 7.99 *(978-0-312-66095-6(2),* 9780312660956) Square Fish.
—Piper Reed, Forever Friend. Davenier, Christine, illus. 2013. (Piper Reed Ser.: 6). (ENG.). 176p. (J). (gr. 3-6). pap. 6.99 *(978-1-250-02725-2(X),* 9781250027252) Square Fish.
—When Zachary Beaver Came to Town. unabr. ed. 2004. 227p. (J). (gr. 5-9). pap. 36.00 incl. audio *(978-0-8072-8394-3(0),* Listening Library) Random Hse. Audio Publishing Group.
—When Zachary Beaver Came to Town. 2011. (ENG.). 256p. (J). (gr. 5-9). pap. 7.99 *(978-0-312-63212-0(6),* 9780312632120) Square Fish.
Holt, Tami. Friends Forever. 2013. 108p. pap. 10.99 *(978-1-937129-78-1(0))* Faithful Life Pubs.
Holub, Joan. Don't Get Lost, Odysseus! Patricelli, Leslie, illus. 2016. (Mini Myths Ser.). (ENG.). 24p. (J). (gr. -1 — 1). bds. 6.95 *(978-1-4197-1897-7(5),* Abrams Appleseed) Abrams, Inc.
—Good Job, Athena! Patricelli, Leslie, illus. 2016. (Mini Myths Ser.). (ENG.). 24p. (J). (gr. -1 — 1). bds. 6.95 *(978-1-4197-1898-4(3),* Abrams Appleseed) Abrams, Inc.
Holub, Joan & Williams, Suzanne. Apollo & the Battle of the Birds. 2014. (Heroes in Training Ser.: 6). lib. bdg. 16.00 *(978-0-606-35442-4(5))* Turtleback Bks.
—Cassandra the Lucky. 2013. (Goddess Girls Ser.: 12). (ENG., Illus.). 256p. (J). (gr. 3-7). 16.99 *(978-1-4424-8818-2(2));* pap. 7.99 *(978-1-4424-8817-5(4))* Simon & Schuster Children's Publishing. (Aladdin).
—Cassandra the Lucky. 2013. (Goddess Girls Ser.: 12). lib. bdg. 18.40 *(978-0-606-32329-1(5),* Turtleback) Turtleback Bks.
—Cinderella Stays Late. 2014. (Grimmtastic Girls Ser.: 1). (ENG.). 192p. (J). (gr. 3-7). pap. 5.99 *(978-0-545-51983-0(7))* Scholastic, Inc.
—Cinderella Stays Late. 2014. (Grimmtastic Girls Ser.: 1). lib. bdg. 16.00 *(978-0-606-35395-3(X))* Turtleback Bks.
—Goddess Girls the Glittering Collection: Athena the Wise - Aphrodite the Diva - Artemis the Loyal - Medusa the Mean. 2013. (Goddess Girls Ser.). (ENG., Illus.). 1088p. (J). (gr. 3-7). pap. 23.99 *(978-1-4424-9925-6(7),* Aladdin) Simon & Schuster Children's Publishing.
—Goldilocks Breaks In. 2015. (Grimmtastic Girls Ser.: 6). lib. bdg. 16.00 *(978-0-606-37075-2(7))* Turtleback Bks.
—Medusa the Mean. (Goddess Girls Ser.: 8). (ENG., 256p. (J). (gr. 3-7). 2013. Illus.). 16.99 *(978-1-4424-8595-2(7))* 2012. pap. 7.99 *(978-1-4424-3379-3(5))* Simon & Schuster Children's Publishing. (Aladdin).
—Medusa the Mean. 2012. (Goddess Girls Ser.: 8). lib. bdg. 18.40 *(978-0-606-26348-1(9),* Turtleback) Turtleback Bks.
—Poseidon & the Sea of Fury. Phillips, Craig, illus. 2012. (Heroes in Training Ser.: 2). (ENG.). 128p. (J). (gr. 1-4). 16.99 *(978-1-4424-5798-0(8));* pap. 5.99 *(978-1-4424-5265-7(X))* Simon & Schuster Children's Publishing. (Aladdin).
—Red Riding Hood Gets Lost. 2014. (Grimmtastic Girls Ser.: 2). (ENG.). 192p. (J). (gr. 3-7). pap. 5.99 *(978-0-545-51984-7(5))* Scholastic, Inc.
—Sleeping Beauty Dreams Big. 2015. (Grimmtastic Girls Ser.: 5). (ENG.). 192p. (J). (gr. 3-7). pap. 5.99 *(978-0-545-78393-4(3),* Scholastic Paperbacks) Scholastic, Inc.
—Snow White Lucks Out. 2014. (Grimmtastic Girls Ser.: 3). lib. bdg. 16.00 *(978-0-606-35852-1(8))* Turtleback Bks.
Holub, Joan, et al. Aphrodite the Diva. 2011. (Goddess Girls Ser.: 6). (ENG.). 288p. (J). (gr. 3-7). pap. 7.99 *(978-1-4424-2100-4(2),* Aladdin) Simon & Schuster Children's Publishing.
Holy Peace: The Story of Iz & Pal. 2003. 91p. (YA). per. 5.99 *(978-0-9704361-3-9(0))* L W S Bks.
Homan, Michael. Grendel Gander the Sinister Goose. Duggins, Peat, illus. 2012. 48p. pap. 14.95 *(978-1-60808-049-6(8),* WriteLife Publishing) Boutique of Quality Books Publishing Co., Inc.
Homer, Elizabeth. Peter Wolfe & the Scepter of Myleah. 2008. 212p. pap. 13.95 *(978-1-60693-197-4(0),* Eloquent Bks.) Strategic Book Publishing & Rights Agency (SBPRA).
Homzie, Hillary. The Hot List. 2011. (Mix Ser.). (ENG.). 256p. (J). (gr. 4-8). pap. 6.99 *(978-1-4424-0657-5(7),* Aladdin) Simon & Schuster Children's Publishing.
—Things Are Gonna Get Ugly. 2009. (Mix Ser.). (ENG.). 272p. (J). (gr. 4-8). pap. 5.99 *(978-1-4169-7563-2(2),* Aladdin) Simon & Schuster Children's Publishing.
Hone, Sallie. Phoenix. 2011. (Illus.). 48p. 20.36 *(978-1-4567-0074-4(X))* AuthorHouse.
Honey, Elizabeth. The Ballad of Cauldron Bay. 2005. (ENG., Illus.). 312p. (YA). (gr. 7-17). pap. 12.95 *(978-1-74114-255-6(5))* Allen & Unwin AUS. Dist: Independent Pubs. Group.
Hong, Catherine Thao. The Adventures of Miss Turtle. Pipe, Jasper, illus. 2012. 24p. (J). pap. *(978-0-9873790-0-9(3))* Icky Grass Books.
Hong, J. Gabriela Gil. Chaos & Mother Earth / Caos y Madre Tierr. 2012. 44p. pap. 17.44 *(978-1-4669-6969-8(5))* Trafford Publishing.
Honsinger, Lea. Mike's New Friends. 2005. 35p. (J). pap. 5.92 *(978-1-4116-3070-3(X))* Lulu Pr., Inc.
Hoogstad, Alice. BOLDER & BOAT. 2008. (ENG.). 32p. (J). (gr. 1-7). 13.95 *(978-1-60136-015-1(0))* Audio Holdings, LLC.
Hooke, R. Schuyler. Thomas' Night Before Christmas. Courtney, Richard, illus. 2013. (Little Golden Book Ser.). (ENG.). 24p. (J). (gr. -1-k). 4.99 *(978-0-449-81663-9(X),* Golden Bks.) Random Hse. Children's Bks.
Hooks, Gwendolyn. Three's a Crowd. Walker, Sylvia, illus. 2004. 32p. (J). lib. bdg. 15.00 *(978-1-4242-0240-9(X))* Fitzgerald Bks.
Hooper, Jaci. Gary: #Exodus 20. 2013. 32p. pap. 16.95 *(978-1-4908-1120-8(6),* WestBow Pr.) Author Solutions, Inc.
Hoover, P. J. The Navel of the World. 2013. (ENG.). 304p. (J). (gr. 6-9). pap. 8.95 *(978-1-933767-20-8(0))* CBAY Bks.
Hoover, T. A. The Last Eagle. Kaths, Kathy, illus. 2004. 38p. (J). 16.00 *(978-0-9702216-3-6(0))* Sport Story Publishing.
Hopgood, Tim. Ping & Pong Are Best Friends (Mostly) 2013. (Illus.). (J). *(978-1-4351-4730-0(8))* Barnes & Noble, Inc.
Hopkins, Cathy. Friend Me: Mates, Dates, & Inflatable Bras; Mates, Dates, & Cosmic Kisses; Mates, Dates, & Designer Divas. 2009. (Mates, Dates Ser.). (ENG.). 528p. (YA). (gr. 7). pap. 8.99 *(978-1-4169-7836-7(4),* Simon Pulse) Simon Pulse.
—Mates, Dates, & Great Escapes. 2011. (Mates, Dates Ser.). (ENG.). 224p. (YA). (gr. 7). pap. 10.99 *(978-1-4424-3080-8(X),* Simon Pulse) Simon Pulse.
—Mates, Dates, & Inflatable Bras. 2011. (Mates, Dates Ser.). (ENG.). 176p. (YA). (gr. 7). pap. 9.99 *(978-1-4424-3113-3(X),* Simon Pulse) Simon Pulse.
—Mates, Dates, & Sleepover Secrets. 2010. (Mates, Dates Ser.). (ENG.). 208p. (YA). (gr. 7). pap. 10.99 *(978-1-4424-1421-1(9),* Simon Pulse) Simon Pulse.
—The Princess of Pop. 2012. (Truth or Dare Ser.). (ENG.). 224p. (YA). (gr. 7). pap. 10.99 *(978-1-4424-6057-7(1),* Simon Pulse) Simon Pulse.
Hopkins, Jackie Mims. Prairie Chicken Little, 1 vol. Cole, Henry, illus. 2015. (ENG.). 32p. (J). (gr. 1-3). pap. 7.95 *(978-1-56145-834-9(1))* Peachtree Pubs.
Hopkins, Lee Bennett. Full Moon & Star. Hall, Marcellus, illus. 2011. (ENG.). 32p. (J). (gr. -1-k). 16.95 *(978-1-4197-0013-2(8),* Abrams Bks. for Young Readers) Abrams, Inc.
—Mother Goose & Her Animal Friends. Fehlau, Dagmar et al, illus. 2005. (Lee Bennett Hopkins Mother Goose Ser.). (YA). (gr. -1-1). 76.50 *(978-0-8215-0470-3(3))* Sadlier, William H. Inc.
Hopkinson, Deborah. Abe Lincoln Crosses a Creek: A Tall, Thin Tale (Introducing His Forgotten Frontier Friend) Hendrix, John, illus. (ENG.). 40p. (J). (gr. -1-3). 2016. 7.99 *(978-1-5247-0158-1(0),* Dragonfly Bks.) 2008. 17.99 *(978-0-375-83768-5(X),* Schwartz & Wade Bks.) Random Hse. Children's Bks.
Hopper, Celia. The Merry Adventures of Blade & Friends. 2006. (J). lib. bdg. 26.95 *(978-0-9779662-8-8(3))* Creative Bk. Pubs.
Hoppey, Tim. Jungle Scout: A Vietnam War Story, 1 vol. Espinoza, Ramon, illus. 2008. (Historical Fiction Ser.). (ENG.). 56p. (gr. 2-3). pap. 6.25 *(978-1-4342-0846-0(X),* Graphic Flash) Stone Arch Bks.
Horácek, Petr. Puffin Peter. Horácek, Petr, illus. 2013. (ENG., Illus.). 40p. (J). (gr. -1-2). 16.99 *(978-0-7636-6572-2(X))* Candlewick Pr.
Horan, Pamela. Newman the Gnome. 2012. 66p. pap. 17.95 *(978-1-4626-9461-7(6))* America Star Bks.
Horatio Alger Jr. Cast upon the Breakers. l.t. ed. 2007. 226p. pap. 22.99 *(978-1-4264-8224-3(8))* Creative Media Partners, LLC.
Hordos, Sandra. Marissa Plans a Princess Tea Party. Allen, Joshua, illus. 2010. 28p. pap. 12.49 *(978-1-4520-2557-5(6))* AuthorHouse.
Horowitz, Dave. Little Big Horse. 2014. (Scholastic Reader Level 1 Ser.). lib. bdg. 13.55 *(978-0-606-35375-5(5))* Turtleback Bks.
Horowitz, Jeanine. Latch Key Kid. 2006. 75p. (YA). lib. bdg. 12.99 *(978-1-934190-10-4(1))* Ocean Front Bk. Publishing, Inc.
Horowitz, Lena. Dancing with Molly. 2016. (ENG.). 272p. (YA). (gr. 9). pap. 10.99 *(978-1-4814-1551-4(4),* Simon Pulse) Simon Pulse.
Horowitz, Ruth. Are We Still Friends? Gomez, Blanca, illus. 2017. (ENG.). 40p. (J). (gr. -1-3). 16.99 *(978-0-545-64521-8(2),* Scholastic Pr.) Scholastic, Inc.
Horsfall, S. J. Jodie & Lilly... & the Fake Mansion. 2009. 58p. pap. 7.50 *(978-0-557-12474-9(3))* Lulu Pr., Inc.
—Jodie & Lilly & the Joy of Christmas. 2010. 19p. 12.95 *(978-1-4452-4148-7(X))* Lulu Pr., Inc.
Horton, Jim. The Foot Log Incident. 2008. 30p. pap. 24.95 *(978-1-60610-706-5(2))* America Star Bks.
Hostetter, Joyce Moyer. Blue. (Bakers Mountain Stories Ser.). (ENG.). 200p. (J). 2010. (gr. 6-9). pap. 7.95 *(978-1-59078-835-6(4))* 2006. (gr. 5). 16.95 *(978-1-59078-389-4(1))* Boyds Mills Pr. (Calkins Creek).
Hotchkins, Dewayne. Pen Pals. 2016. (Rosen REAL Readers: Social Studies Nonfiction / Fiction: Family, Community, & the World Ser.). 12p. (gr. 1-k). pap. 6.33 *(978-1-5081-2547-1(3),* Rosen Classroom) Rosen Publishing Group, Inc., The.
Hotte, Sylvain. Power Forward. Roberts, Casey, tr. 2012. (Break Away Ser.). (ENG., Illus.). 180p. (YA). (gr. 8). pap. 16.95 *(978-1-926824-42-0(3))* Baraka Bks. CAN. Dist: Independent Pubs. Group.
Houdek, Andi. J P S Halloween Parade. Collier, Kevin, illus. 2012. 20p. pap. 9.95 *(978-1-61633-263-1(8))* Guardian Angel Publishing, Inc.
Hourihan, Kelly. 4 to 16 Characters. 2013. 376p. pap. 11.50 *(978-0-9897411-0-1(9))* Lemon Sherbet Pr.
House, B. J. What's Wrong with Pauly? Cash, Paul, illus. 2013. 36p. 11.99 *(978-0-9835843-6-0(2),* Lonely Swan Bks.) Cosmic Gargoyle Creative Solutions.
House, Megan. The Big Black Bear. 2008. 32p. per. 24.95 *(978-1-4241-9315-8(X))* America Star Bks.
House, Silas. Eli the Good. (ENG., Illus.). 304p. (YA). (gr. 7). 2011. pap. 8.99 *(978-0-7636-5288-3(1))* 2009. 16.99 *(978-0-7636-4341-6(6))* Candlewick Pr.
House, Silas & Vaswani, Neela. Same Sun Here. Schenker, Hilary, illus. (ENG.). (J). 2013. 304p. (gr. 4-7). pap. 7.99 *(978-0-7636-6451-0(0))* 2012. 288p. (gr. 5). 15.99 *(978-0-7636-5684-3(4))* Candlewick Pr.
Houser, Marlin L. The Adventures of Little Fox, Book Four, Escape. 2010. (Adventures of Little Fox Ser.). (J). 16.95 *(978-0-9752703-8-7(9));* pap. 7.95 *(978-0-9752703-9-4(7))* Marhouse, Inc.
—The Adventures of Little Fox, Book Three, Unfamiliar Territory. 2009. (Adventures of Little Fox Ser.). (J). 16.95 *(978-0-9752703-6-3(2));* pap. 7.95 *(978-0-9752703-7-0(0))* Marhouse, Inc.
Houston, Anna. Daisy's Bug. 2009. 32p. pap. 14.49 *(978-1-4389-6696-0(2))* AuthorHouse.
Houtman, Jacqueline. The Reinvention of Edison Thomas. (ENG.). 192p. (J). (gr. 3-7). 2012. pap. 8.95 *(978-1-59078-951-3(2))* 2010. 17.95 *(978-1-59078-708-3(0),* Front Street) Boyds Mills Pr.
Hovanec, Deb. Lots & Lots of Friends! 2012. 28p. pap. 15.99 *(978-1-4797-6208-8(3))* Xlibris Corp.
How, Barbara. My Friend: Beth. 2010. 52p. pap. 14.99 *(978-1-4269-4707-0(0))* Trafford Publishing.
Howard, Arthur. When I Was Five. 2014. 40p. pap. 7.00 *(978-1-61003-185-1(7))* Center for the Collaborative Classroom.
Howard, J. J. That Time I Joined the Circus. 2013. (ENG.). 272p. (J). (gr. 7). 17.99 *(978-0-545-43381-5(9))* Scholastic, Inc.
Howard, Kate. Double Trouble. 2016. (LEGO NEXO Knights Ser.). (ENG.). 80p. (J). (gr. 2-5). pap. 4.99 *(978-1-338-03803-3(6))* Scholastic, Inc.
Howard, Kate, illus. On Our Way to First Grade. 2015. 32p. (J). *(978-0-545-82340-1(4))* Scholastic, Inc.
Howard, Reginald. The Big, Big Wall. Aruego, Jose & Dewey, Ariane, illus. 2003. (Green Light Readers Level 1 Ser.). (ENG.). 24p. (J). (gr. -1-3). pap. 3.95 *(978-0-15-204853-2(7))* Houghton Mifflin Harcourt Publishing Co.
—The Big, Big Wall. Dewey, Ariane & Aruego, Jose, illus. 2003. (Green Light Readers — Level 1 Ser.). (J). (gr. -1-3). 13.50 *(978-0-613-66350-2(0),* Turtleback) Turtleback Bks.
—The Big, Big Wall/No Puedo Bajar. Flor Ada, Alma & Campoy, F. Isabel, trs. Dewey, Ariane & Aruego, Jose, illus. 2009. (Green Light Readers Level 1 Ser.). (SPA & ENG.). 28p. (J). (gr. -1-3). pap. 3.99 *(978-0-547-25548-4(9))* Houghton Mifflin Harcourt Publishing Co.
Howard, Victoria. The Adventures of Max: Max & His Friends Save the World. 2013. 68p. pap. 28.99 *(978-1-4817-0732-9(9))* AuthorHouse.
—The Adventures of Max & Molly: A Love Story about a Dog & a Horse. 2012. 52p. pap. 24.99 *(978-1-4772-4866-9(8))* AuthorHouse.

E
F
G

Howe, James. Also Known As Elvis. (Misfits Ser.). (ENG., Illus.). (J). (gr. 5-9). 2015. 304p. pap. 7.99 (978-1-4424-4511-6(4)) 2014. 288p. 16.99 (978-1-4424-4510-9(6), Atheneum Bks. for Young Readers) Simon & Schuster Children's Publishing.

—The Complete Misfits Collection: The Misfits; Totally Joe; Addie on the Inside; Also Known As Elvis. 2015. (Misfits Ser.). (ENG., Illus.). 1072p. (J). (gr. 5-9). pap. 27.99 (978-1-4814-2898-9(5), Atheneum Bks. for Young Readers) Simon & Schuster Children's Publishing.

—Horace & Morris, but Mostly Dolores. Waldrod, Amy, illus. 2003. pap. 39.95 incl. audio compact disk (978-1-59112-538-9(3)); 25.95 incl. audio (978-1-59112-242-5(2)); pap. 37.95 incl. audio (978-1-59112-243-2(0)) Live Oak Media.

—Horace & Morris but Mostly Dolores. Walrod, Amy, illus. 2003. 30p. (J). (gr. -1-3). 15.65 (978-0-7569-2936-7(9)) Perfection Learning Corp.

—Horace & Morris Join the Chorus (but What about Dolores?) Walrod, Amy, illus. 2005. (ENG.). 32p. (J). (gr. -1-3). 7.99 (978-1-4169-0616-2(9), Atheneum Bks. for Young Readers) Simon & Schuster Children's Publishing.

—Hot Fudge. Mack, Jeff, illus. 2006. (Bunnicula & Friends Ser.). 42p. (gr. k-4). 14.00 (978-0-7569-7224-0(8)) Perfection Learning Corp.

—Houndsley & Catina. Gay, Marie-Louise, illus. (ENG.). 40p. (J). (gr. k-4). 2013. (Candlewick Sparks Ser.). pap. 3.99 (978-0-7636-6638-5(6)) 2006. (Houndsley & Catina Ser.: 1). 15.99 (978-0-7636-2404-0(7)) Candlewick Pr.

—Houndsley & Catina. Gay, Marie-Louise, illus. 2007. 36p. (J). (gr. k-2). lib. bdg. 12.65 (978-0-7569-8141-9(7)) Perfection Learning Corp.

—Houndsley & Catina. 2013. (Candlewick Sparks Ser.). lib. bdg. 13.55 (978-0-606-31608-8(6), Turtleback) Turtleback Bks.

—Houndsley & Catina & the Birthday Surprise. Gay, Marie-Louise, illus. (ENG.). 48p. (J). (gr. k-4). 2013. (Candlewick Sparks Ser.). pap. 3.99 (978-0-7636-6639-2(4)) 2006. (Houndsley & Catina Ser.: 2). 15.99 (978-0-7636-2405-7(5)) Candlewick Pr.

—Houndsley & Catina & the Quiet Time. Gay, Marie-Louise, illus. (ENG.). 48p. (J). (gr. k-4). 2013. (Candlewick Sparks Ser.). pap. 3.99 (978-0-7636-6863-1(X)) 2008. (Houndsley & Catina Ser.: 3). 15.99 (978-0-7636-3384-4(4)) Candlewick Pr.

—Houndsley & Catina Plink & Plunk. Gay, Marie-Louise, illus. 2013. (Candlewick Sparks Ser.). (ENG.). 48p. (J). (gr. k-4). pap. 3.99 (978-0-7636-6640-8(8)) Candlewick Pr.

—The Misfits. 2003. (Misfits Ser.). (ENG.). 304p. (J). (gr. 5-9). mass mkt. 7.99 (978-0-689-83956-6(1), Atheneum Bks. for Young Readers) Simon & Schuster Children's Publishing.

—Plink & Plunk. Gay, Marie-Louise, illus. 2009. (Houndsley & Catina Ser.). (ENG.). 48p. (J). (gr. k-4). 15.99 (978-0-7636-3385-1(2)) Candlewick Pr.

—Totally Joe. (Misfits Ser.). (J). 2007. 224p. (gr. 4-8). pap. 7.99 (978-0-689-83958-0(8)) 2005. (Illus.). 208p. (gr. 5-9). 17.99 (978-0-689-83957-3(X)) Simon & Schuster Children's Publishing. (Atheneum Bks. for Young Readers).

Howe, Katherine. Conversion. (ENG.). 432p. (YA). (gr. 7). 2015. pap. 10.99 (978-0-14-751155-3(0), Speak) 2014. 18.99 (978-0-399-16777-5(3), G.P. Putnam's Sons Books for Young Readers) Penguin Young Readers Group.

Howe, Norma. Angel in Vegas: The Chronicles of Noah Sark. 2009. (ENG., Illus.). 256p. (YA). (gr. 7-18). 16.99 (978-0-7636-3985-3(0)) Candlewick Pr.

Howell, Jessica. Lilly Lu & the Pink Tutu. 2007. 29p. pap. 24.95 (978-1-4241-8398-2(7)) America Star Bks.

Howell, Julie. The Pepper Tree, How the Seeds Were Planted! LaGrange, Tiffany, illus. 2007. 28p. per. 12.95 (978-1-934246-51-1(4)) Peppertree Pr., The.

Howell, Julie Ann. The Pepper Tree, How the Seeds Were Planted! LaGrange, Tiffany, illus. 2008. 28p. pap. 12.95 (978-0-9820479-0-3(8)) Peppertree Pr., The.

—The Pepper Tree, How the Seeds Were Planted. LaGrange, Tiffany, illus. 2012. 28p. 24.95 (978-1-61493-059-4(7)) Peppertree Pr., The.

Howell, Ruth. Fairy Friends. Bachmann, B. L., illus. 2013. 28p. 12.95 (978-0-9899275-2-9(0)) Ravenwood Publishing.

Howell, Trisha Adelena. The Adventures of Melon & Turnip. Lopez, Paul, illus. 2004. 32p. 15.95 (978-1-931210-04-1(7)) Howell Canyon Pr.

—Talia & the Great Sapphire of Knowledge. Hohn, David, illus. 2005. 128p. (J). pap. 11.95 (978-1-931210-11-9(X)) Howell Canyon Pr.

Howitt, Mary Botham. Strive & Thrive a Tale by Mary Howitt. 2006. 180p. per. 18.99 (978-1-4255-1426-6(X)) Michigan Publishing.

Howland, Leila. Nantucket Blue. 2014. (Nantucket Blue Ser.). (ENG.). 320p. (YA). (gr. 9-17). pap. 8.99 (978-1-4231-6139-4(4)) Hyperion Bks. for Children.

Hoyle, K. B. The Bone Whistle. 2016. (ENG., Illus.). (J). 32.99 **(978-1-61213-401-7(7))** Writer's Coffee Shop, The.

—The Oracle. 2016. (ENG., Illus.). (J). 29.99 **(978-1-61213-397-3(5))** Writer's Coffee Shop, The.

—The White Thread. 2016. (ENG., Illus.). (J). 29.99 **(978-1-61213-398-0(3))** Writer's Coffee Shop, The.

Hoyt, Charlene. Where the Leprechauns Hide. Fischer, Sandi, illus. 2007. (ENG.). 40p. per. 12.99 (978-0-9792258-9-5(2)) Bezalel Bks.

Hrdlitschka, Shelley. Kat's Fall. 2005. 168p. 18.95 (978-0-7569-6315-6(X)) Perfection Learning Corp.

Huang, Yu-Hsuan. Fairy Friends. 2017. (ENG., Illus.). 10p. (J). (gr. -1-k). bds. 7.99 **(978-1-5098-3578-2(4))** Pan Macmillan GBR. Dist: Independent Pubs. Group.

Hubbard, Jenny. Paper Covers Rock. 2012. (ENG.). 192p. (YA). (gr. 9). pap. 7.99 (978-0-385-74056-2(5), Ember) Random Hse. Children's Bks.

Hubbard, Mandy. You Wish. 2010. (ENG.). 304p. (YA). (gr. 7-18). pap. 8.99 (978-1-59514-292-4(4), Razorbill) Penguin Young Readers Group.

Huber, Mike. The Amazing Erik. Cowman, Joseph, illus. 2014. (ENG.). 32p. (gr. -1). 15.95 (978-1-60554-209-6(1)) Redleaf Pr.

—Bree Finds a Friend. Cowman, Joseph, illus. 2014. (ENG.). 32p. (gr. -1). 15.95 (978-1-60554-211-9(3)) Redleaf Pr.

—Evette's Invitation. Cowman, Joseph, illus. 2014. (ENG.). 32p. (gr. -1). 15.95 (978-1-60554-212-6(1)) Redleaf Pr.

—Rita & the Firefighters. Cowman, Joseph, illus. 2014. (ENG.). 32p. (gr. -1-k). 15.95 (978-1-60554-208-9(3)) Redleaf Pr.

Hubler, Marsha. On the Victory Trail, 1 vol. rev. ed. 2009. (Keystone Stables Ser.). (ENG.). 144p. (J). pap. 7.99 (978-0-310-71793-5(0)) Zonderkidz.

Huckerby, Mark & Ostler, Nick. Defender of the Realm. 2017. (ENG.). 320p. (J). (gr. 3-7). 17.99 (978-0-545-93666-8(7), Scholastic Pr.) Scholastic, Inc.

Hudgins, Larry. My Dog Spike, 1 vol. 2009. 55p. pap. 16.95 (978-1-60836-421-3(6)) America Star Bks.

Hudson, Katy. Too Many Carrots. 2016. (ENG., Illus.). 32p. (gr. -1-1). 14.95 (978-1-62370-638-8(6)) Capstone Young Readers of Coughlan Cos.

Hudson, Wade. Friends I Love to Meet. 2009. 24p. 3.99 (978-1-60349-012-2(4), Marimba Bks.) Hudson Publishing Group, The.

—Places I Love to Go. 2008. (Illus.). 24p. (J). (gr. -1-3). 3.99 (978-1-60349-008-5(6), Marimba Bks.) Hudson Publishing Group, The.

—Puddin', Jeffrey & Leah. 2008. (Illus.). 16p. (gr. -1). 6.95 (978-1-60349-006-1(X), Marimba Bks.) Hudson Publishing Group, The.

—Puddin' Jeffrey & Leah. 2009. 16p. 6.95 (978-1-60349-018-4(3), Marimba Bks.) Hudson Publishing Group, The.

—Puddin' Jeffrey & Leah: Happy Birthday Puddin'! Happy Birthday Puddin'! 2009. 16p. 6.95 (978-1-60349-019-1(1), Marimba Bks.) Hudson Publishing Group, The.

Hudspeth, Jodi. Unconditional Love. 2009. 80p. pap. 28.99 (978-1-4343-6383-1(X)) AuthorHouse.

Hudspith, Will. Stairgate - Gordon's Adventures on Everest. 2013. 64p. pap. (978-1-4602-1219-6(3)) FriesenPress.

Hughes, Emily C. My Little Pony: Ponies Love Pets! 2014. (Passport to Reading Level 1 Ser.). (ENG., Illus.). 32p. (J). (gr. -1-3). pap. 3.99 (978-0-316-36885-8(7)) Little, Brown Bks. for Young Readers.

—Ponies Love Pets! 2014. (Passport to Reading Level 1 Ser.). (J). lib. bdg. 13.55 (978-0-606-35298-7(8)) Turtleback Bks.

Hughes, Jack. Dachy's Deaf. 2014. (Dinosaur Friends Ser.). (Illus.). 32p. (J). (gr. k-3). lib. bdg. 26.25 (978-1-4777-9222-3(8)) Windmill Bks.

—Emmy's Eczema. 2014. (Dinosaur Friends Ser.). (Illus.). 32p. (J). (gr. k-3). lib. bdg. 26.25 (978-1-4777-9234-6(1)) Windmill Bks.

—Rex's Specs. 2014. (Dinosaur Friends Ser.). (Illus.). 32p. (J). (gr. k-3). lib. bdg. 26.25 (978-1-4777-9226-1(0)) Windmill Bks.

—Steggie's Stutter. 2014. (Dinosaur Friends Ser.). (Illus.). 32p. (J). (gr. k-3). lib. bdg. 26.25 (978-1-4777-9230-8(9)) Windmill Bks.

Hughes, Jenny. A Horse by Any Other Name. 2014. (ENG.). 224p. (J). (gr. 3-7). pap. 9.95 (978-1-62124-009-9(6)) Breakaway Bks.

—Horse in the Portrait. 2014. (ENG.). 128p. (J). (gr. 3-7). pap. 9.95 (978-1-62124-013-6(4)) Breakaway Bks.

Hughes, Mair Wynn & Ward, Jonathan. Ffrindiau Pennaf. 2005. (WEL., Illus.). 13p. pap. (978-0-86243-456-4(4)) Y Lolfa.

Hughes, Melissa. Myles & Otis: A Story of Friendship. 2009. (Illus.). 30p. (J). pap. 14.95 (978-1-4327-5182-1(4)) Outskirts Pr., Inc.

Hughes, Monica. The Game. 2010. (ENG.). 208p. (YA). (gr. 7). pap. 9.99 (978-1-4424-0939-2(8), Simon Pulse) Simon Pulse.

Hughes, Shirley. Alfie & His Very Best Friend. 2016. (Alfie Ser.). (ENG., Illus.). 32p. (J). (gr. -1-k). 19.99 **(978-1-78230-061-8(9))** Random Hse. GBR. Dist: Independent Pubs. Group.

Hughes, Shirley. Digby o'Day in the Fast Lane. Vulliamy, Clara, illus. 2014. (ENG.). 128p. (J). (gr. k-3). 12.99 (978-0-7636-7369-7(2)) Candlewick Pr.

Hughes, Susan. Earth to Audrey. Poulin, Stéphane, illus. 2007. (ENG.). 32p. (J). (gr. k-3). 6.95 (978-1-55453-165-3(9)) Kids Can Pr., Ltd. CAN. Dist: Hachette Bk. Group.

—Murphy. 2016. (Puppy Pals Ser.: 3). (ENG.). 128p. (J). (gr. 2-5). pap. 5.99 (978-1-4926-3400-3(X), 9781492634003, Sourcebooks Jabberwocky) Sourcebooks, Inc.

—Riley. 2016. (Puppy Pals Ser.: 2). (ENG.). 128p. (J). (gr. 2-5). pap. 5.99 (978-1-4926-3397-6(6), 9781492633976, Sourcebooks Jabberwocky) Sourcebooks, Inc.

Hughes, Suz. The Night the Stars Went Out. 2016. (Fiction Picture Bks.). (ENG.). 32p. (gr. 1-2). lib. bdg. 23.32 (978-1-5158-0214-3(0), Fiction Picture Bks.) Picture Window Bks.

Huizenga, Nathaniel. Justice in Winter: Justice the Dog Series. 2009. 28p. pap. 13.99 (978-1-4389-7361-6(6)) AuthorHouse.

Hull, Bunny. The Friendship Seed. Fleming, Kye, illus. 2007. (Young Masters Ser.). 28p. (J). (gr. -1-2). per. 13.95 incl. audio compact disk (978-0-9721478-6-6(1), Dream A World) BrassHeart Music.

Hulst, W. G. van de & Hulst, Willem G. van de, illus. Herbie, the Runaway Duck. 2014. (J). (978-1-928136-19-4(2)) Inheritance Pubns.

—The Secret Hiding Place. 2014. (J). (978-1-928136-16-3(8)) Inheritance Pubns.

Humann, Amanda. Out of Sync. 2013. (Counterattack Ser.). (ENG.). 104p. (YA). (gr. 6-12). pap. 7.95 (978-1-4677-0719-0(8)); lib. bdg. 27.93 (978-1-4677-0304-8(4)) Lerner Publishing Group.

Humphrey, Anna. Mission (un)Popular. 2013. (ENG.). 416p. (J). (gr. 5-9). pap. 6.99 (978-1-4231-2321-7(2)) Hyperion Pr.

—Rhymes with Cupid. 2010. (ENG.). 240p. (YA). (gr. 8). pap. 7.99 (978-0-06-193501-5(8), HarperTeen) HarperCollins Pubs.

Hundal, Nancy. Kaleidoscopes & Butterfly Dreams. 2009. (ENG.). 112p. (YA). (gr. 5-9). pap. 12.95 (978-0-88982-256-6(5)) Oolichan Bks. CAN. Dist: Univ. of Toronto Pr.

Hunt, Debbie Colleen. The Dinosaur Who Loved to Bake & Eat Cakes. Hunt, Craig J. S., illus. 2012. 32p. 24.95 (978-1-4626-3213-8(0)) America Star Bks.

—Wollie the Wheelbarrow. Burket, Shelia, illus. 24p. 2012. 24.95 (978-1-4626-9969-8(3)) 2011. pap. 24.95 (978-1-4626-2980-0(6)) America Star Bks.

Hunt for Jade Dragon. 2014. (Michael Vey Ser.: No. 4). (ENG., Illus.). 336p. (YA). (gr. 7). 19.99 (978-1-4814-2438-7(6), Simon Pulse/Mercury Ink) Simon Pulse/Mercury Ink.

Hunt, Julie. KidGlovz. Newman, Dale, illus. 2017. (ENG.). 288p. (J). (gr. 3-7). 19.99 **(978-1-74237-852-7(8))** Allen & Unwin AUS. Dist: Independent Pubs. Group.

Hunter, Alex. Game Over. Rew, Jen, illus. 2012. 126p. pap. (978-1-78176-771-9(8)) FeedARead.com.

—Game over - Book Three. 2013. 268p. (J). pap. (978-1-78299-394-0(0)) FeedARead.com.

Hunter, Erin. Forest of Wolves. 2015. (Seekers: Return to the Wild Ser.: 4). (ENG.). 304p. (J). (gr. 3-7). pap. 6.99 (978-0-06-199645-0(9)) HarperCollins Pubs.

—The Heart of a Warrior. Barry, James L., illus. 2010. (Warriors Manga Ser.: 3). (ENG.). 112p. (J). (gr. 3-7). pap. 6.99 (978-0-06-168867-6(3)) HarperCollins Pubs.

Hunter, Jana. Trick or Treat. 2010. (Sleepover Club Ser.). (ENG., Illus.). 112p. (J). (gr. 2-6). pap. 6.99 (978-0-00-727254-9(5), HarperCollins Children's Bks.) HarperCollins Pubs. Ltd. GBR. Dist: HarperCollins Pubs.

Hunter, K. N. Hollow: N2 the Hollow World. 2008. 62p. pap. 16.95 (978-1-4241-0220-4(0)) PublishAmerica, Inc.

Huntley, Amy. The Everafter. 2010. (ENG.). 272p. (YA). (gr. 8). pap. 9.99 (978-0-06-177681-6(5)) HarperCollins Pubs.

Hurd, Pamela. Switch Witch: An Old Fashioned Witch Learns a New Trick. 2011. 20p. pap. 11.99 (978-1-4634-4587-4(3)) AuthorHouse.

Hurley, Tonya. Ghostgirl. 2010. (Ghostgirl Ser.: 1). (ENG.). 336p. (YA). (gr. 7-17). pap. 9.99 (978-0-316-03635-1(8)) Little, Brown Bks. for Young Readers.

—Ghostgirl. Frieyro, Alicia, tr. Impey, Allison & Phillips, Craig, illus. 2009. (SPA.). 1200p. (YA). (gr. 8-12). pap. 19.99 (978-607-11-0185-3(9), Alfaguara Juvenil) Santillana USA Publishing Co., Inc.

—Homecoming. 2010. (Ghostgirl Ser.: 2). (ENG.). 304p. (YA). (gr. 7-17). pap. 10.00 (978-0-316-08943-2(5)) Little, Brown Bks. for Young Readers.

—Lovesick. 2011. (Ghostgirl Ser.: 3). (ENG.). 320p. (YA). (gr. 7-17). pap. 9.99 (978-0-316-13316-6(7)) Little, Brown Bks. for Young Readers.

Hurrell, Dianne. Tom Burrows & Friends: Short Stories, Rhymes & Poems. 2010. (ENG., Illus.). 50p. pap. (978-1-84748-782-7(3)) Athena Pr.

Hurst, Elva. The Pony Cart Adventure. 2014. (Farm Life Ser.). 64p. pap. 6.99 (978-0-7369-6089-2(9)) Harvest Hse. Pubs.

—The Pony Cart Adventure: A True Story. 2014. (Farm Life Ser.). (ENG., Illus.). 64p. (J). pap. 6.99 (978-0-7369-6088-5(0)) Harvest Hse. Pubs.

Hurtado, Patricia. The Magical Feline & the White Haven. 2009. 142p. pap. 10.95 (978-1-60594-325-1(8), Llumina Pr.) Aeon Publishing Inc.

Hurwin, Davida Wills. A Time for Dancing. 2009. (ENG.). 272p. (YA). (gr. 7-17). pap. 10.00 (978-0-316-03634-4(X)) Little Brown & Co.

Hurwitz, Michele Weber. The Summer I Saved the World ... in 65 Days. 2015. (ENG.). 272p. (J). (gr. 5). pap. 9.99 (978-0-385-37109-4(8), Ember) Random Hse. Children's Bks.

Husby, Greg. The Zoebirds. 2008. 40p. pap. 21.99 (978-1-4363-4941-3(9)) Xlibris Corp.

Huston, Deirdre. Jake, Zee-Bee & the Crystal Quest. 2010. 52p. pap. 31.50 (978-1-4452-2404-6(6)) Lulu Pr., Inc.

Hutchens, Calvin. The Adventures of Otis Possum. 2007. 52p. per. 16.95 (978-1-4241-7065-4(6)) America Star Bks.

Hutchins, Hazel. Robyn's Party-in-the-Park. Cathcart, Yvonne, illus. 2005. (Formac First Novels Ser.: 31). (ENG.). 64p. (J). (gr. 2-5). 14.95 (978-0-88780-663-6(5), 9780887806636) Formac Publishing Co., Ltd. CAN. Dist: Casemate Pubs. & Bk. Distributors, LLC.

—Robyn's Party in the Park, 1 vol. Cathcart, Yvonne, illus. 2005. (Formac First Novels Ser.: 31). (ENG.). 64p. (J). (gr. 2-5). 4.95 (978-0-88780-662-9(7), 9780887806629) Formac Publishing Co., Ltd. CAN. Dist: Casemate Pubs. & Bk. Distributors, LLC.

Hutchinson, Shaun David. Deathday Letter. 2010. (ENG.). 256p. (YA). (gr. 9-18). pap. 9.99 (978-1-4169-9608-8(7), Simon Pulse) Simon Pulse.

Huthmaker, Dixie. Trapped in Half Position. 2005. pap. 10.95 (978-1-59330-317-4(3)) Aventine Pr.

Hutton, Gaila. Frank the Colorful Frog. Knox, Anna Mae, illus. 2011. 28p. pap. 24.95 (978-1-4560-5607-0(7)) America Star Bks.

Huxley, Sheila M. One Lovely Summer: The Stories of One Little Butterfly & His Friends. 2009. (Illus.). 48p. pap. 19.49 (978-1-4389-2987-3(0)) AuthorHouse.

Hyde, Heidi Smith. Shanghai Sukkah. Tsong, Jing Jing, illus. 2015. (ENG.). 32p. (J). (gr. k-4). 17.99 (978-1-4677-3474-5(8)); pap. 7.99 (978-1-4677-3475-2(6)) Lerner Publishing Group. (Kar-Ben Publishing).

Hyde, Lara. Mosquito Bites. 2009. 132p. 21.95 (978-0-595-51697-1(1)); pap. 11.95 (978-0-595-52079-4(0)) iUniverse, Inc.

Hyman, Fracaswell. Mango Delight. Morrison, Frank, illus. 2017. (ENG.). 224p. (J). (gr. 4-8). 14.95 **(978-1-4549-2332-9(6))** Sterling Publishing Co., Inc.

I Want a Friend. 2017. (ENG., Illus.). 32p. (J). (gr. -1-k). 16.99 **(978-0-7459-7707-2(3))** Lion Hudson PLC GBR. Dist: Independent Pubs. Group.

Iacovone, Lauren Marie. Here Lies Thomas Crawford, 1 vol. 2010. 252p. pap. 27.95 (978-1-61582-690-2(4)) America Star Bks.

Ian Pugh. Wolfstorm: The First Danny Piper Adventure. 2010. 388p. pap. 22.95 (978-1-4269-0238-3(7)) Trafford Publishing.

Ianieri, Tom. Polar Pals. 2011. 28p. pap. 15.99 (978-1-4628-5403-5(6)) Xlibris Corp.

Ibarra, Maria Teresa Ornelas. Penny & Me. 2006. (J). 4.95 (978-0-9774306-6-6(9)) Acacia Publishing, Inc.

Ibarrola, Begonia. Chusco the Stray Dog. Herranz, Yésica, ed. Souto, Jose, illus. 2013. (ENG.). 40p. (J). (gr. k-2). 13.95 (978-84-95923-99-8(8)) Primera Persona ESP. Dist: Independent Pubs. Group.

Ibbotson, Eva. Not Just a Witch. Hawkes, Kevin, illus. 2004. (ENG.). 192p. (J). (gr. 3-7). pap. 5.99 (978-0-14-240232-0(X), Puffin Books) Penguin Young Readers Group.

Ibbott, Penny. Scarcode. 2013. 358p. pap. (978-1-78299-864-8(0)) FeedARead.com.

Ichikawa, Satomi. En Busca de Tesoros. (SPA., Illus.). 40p. (J). (gr. k-2). (978-84-95150-33-2(6), COR0428) Corimbo, Editorial S.L. ESP. Dist: Lectorum Pubns., Inc.

If I Play the Tubalatrumlute, Will You Still Be My Friend? 2008. (J). 16.99 (978-1-60336-482-9(X)) Mainstream Connections Publishing.

Ignatow, Amy. The Awesomely Awful Melodies. 2014. (Popularity Papers). (ENG., Illus.). 208p. (J). (gr. 3-7). pap. 8.95 (978-1-4197-1308-8(6), Amulet Bks.) Abrams, Inc.

—The Popularity Papers. 2011. (Popularity Papers). (ENG., Illus.). 208p. (J). (gr. 3-7). pap. 8.95 (978-0-8109-9723-3(1), Amulet Bks.) Abrams, Inc.

—The Popularity Papers: Research for the Social Improvement & General Betterment of Lydia Goldblatt & Julie Graham-Chang. 2010. (Popularity Papers). (ENG., Illus.). 208p. (J). (gr. 3-7). 16.95 (978-0-8109-8421-9(0), Amulet Bks.) Abrams, Inc.

—The Popularity Papers: The Less-Than-Hidden Secrets & Final Revelations of Lydia Goldblatt & Julie Graham-Chang. 2014. (Popularity Papers). (ENG., Illus.). 208p. (J). (gr. 3-7). 15.95 (978-1-4197-1270-8(5), Amulet Bks.) Abrams, Inc.

—The Awesomely Awful Melodies of Lydia Goldblatt & Julie Graham-Chang. 2013. (Popularity Papers). (ENG., Illus.). 208p. (J). (gr. 3-7). 16.95 (978-1-4197-0536-6(9), Amulet Bks.) Abrams, Inc.

—Words of (Questionable) Wisdom. 2013. (Popularity Papers). (ENG., Illus.). 208p. (J). (gr. 3-7). pap. 8.95 (978-1-4197-0535-9(0), Amulet Bks.) Abrams, Inc.

—Words of (Questionable) Wisdom from Lydia Goldblatt & Julie Graham-Chang, Bk. 3. 2011. (Popularity Papers). (ENG., Illus.). 208p. (J). (gr. 3-7). 16.95 (978-1-4197-0063-7(4), Amulet Bks.) Abrams, Inc.

Ikeda, Daisaku. Over the Deep Blue Sea. McCraughrean, Geraldine, tr. from JPN. Wildsmith, Brian, illus. 2013. 6.95 (978-1-935523-59-8(7)) World Tribune Pr.

Ikegami, Aiko. Friends. Ikegami, Aiko, illus. 2016. (ENG., Illus.). 32p. (J). (gr. -1-3). 16.99 (978-0-8075-2550-0(2)) Whitman, Albert & Co.

Illek, Nuala. The Chinese Sausage Dog, the Panicky Porcupine & Mrs Shoo an Animal Tale of Friendship in Chin. 2009. 50p. pap. 9.99 (978-1-60860-781-5(X), Eloquent Bks.) Strategic Book Publishing & Rights Agency (SBPRA).

ImageBooks Staff. Little Shark: Finger Puppet Book. Put, Klaartje van der, illus. 2013. (Little Finger Puppet Board Bks.). (ENG.). 12p. (J). (gr. -1 — 1). bds. 6.99 (978-1-4521-1251-0(7)) Chronicle Bks. LLC.

Imaginism Studios Inc. Staff & Disney Storybook Art Team, illus. Vampirina Going Batty. 2017. (ENG.). 24p. (J). (gr. -1-k). pap. 5.99 **(978-1-368-00619-4(1))** Disney Pr.

Impey, Rose. Best Friends! 2008. (Sleepover Club Ser.). (ENG., Illus.). 128p. (J). (gr. 2-6). pap. 6.99 (978-0-00-726494-0(1), HarperCollins Children's Bks.) HarperCollins Pubs. Ltd. GBR. Dist: HarperCollins Pubs.

Inches, Alison. My Visit with Periwinkle. Levy, David B., illus. 2003. (Blue's Clues Ser.). (ENG.). 24p. (J). pap. 3.99 (978-0-689-85230-5(4), Simon Spotlight/Nickelodeon) Simon Spotlight/Nickelodeon.

Ing, Dean. It's up to Charlie Hardin. 2015. (Baen Ser.: 1). (ENG.). 256p. (YA). (gr. 5). 16.99 (978-1-4767-8030-6(7)) Baen Bks.

Ingram, Jacquelyn. Dakota's Doggie Tale. 2009. 32p. pap. 14.99 (978-1-4490-1327-1(9)) AuthorHouse.

Inkpen, Mick. Silly Big Bear. 2017. (Wibbly Pig Ser.). (ENG., Illus.). 32p. (J). (gr. -1-k). pap. 8.99 **(978-1-4449-3125-9(3))** Hachette Children's Group GBR. Dist: Hachette Bk. Group.

InSeon, Chae. Handy Mr. Hippo. YouDae, Kim, illus. rev. ed. 2014. (MySELF Bookshelf Ser.). (ENG.). 32p. (J). (gr. k-2). pap. 11.94 (978-1-60357-661-1(4)); lib. bdg. 25.27 (978-1-59953-652-1(8)) Norwood Hse. Pr.

Ioannides, Mara W. Cohen. A Shout in the Sunshine. 2007. (ENG.). 120p. (gr. 5). per. 14.95 (978-0-8276-0838-2(1)) Jewish Pubn. Society.

Iossa, Federica, illus. Peekaboo Teddy. 2016. (Peekaboo Bks.). (ENG.). 8p. (J). (gr. -1 — 1). bds. 7.99 (978-0-7641-6862-8(2)) Barron's Educational Series, Inc.

Ippolito, Heidi. Bobo's New Home. 2009. 24p. pap. 11.50 (978-1-60860-220-9(6), Strategic Bk. Publishing) Strategic Book Publishing & Rights Agency (SBPRA).

Ira Sleeps Over. 2005. (J). (978-1-59564-973-7(5)) Steps To Literacy, LLC.

The Iris House. 2006. (YA). per. 12.95 (978-0-9677047-7-7(4)) Marble Hse. Editions.

Iriyama, Satoshi. Good Night, Chirp. 2015. (Chirp the Chick Ser.). (ENG., Illus.). 36p. (J). (— 1). 8.99 (978-0-544-35994-9(1), HMH Books For Young Readers) Houghton Mifflin Harcourt Publishing Co.

Irvine, Jenny. My Friend, Mi Amigo. 2010. 32p. pap. 14.49 (978-1-4490-1619-7(7)) AuthorHouse.

Irwin, Esther. Jesse & His New Friends. Puett, Gayle, ed. Vroman, Dave, illus. 2006. (J). spiral bd. 10.00 (978-0-9778462-1-4(0)) Irwin, Esther L.

Irwin, Gayle. Sage Learns to Share, 1 vol. Araujo, Katie, illus. 2009. 45p. pap. 24.95 (978-1-60836-409-1(7)) America Star Bks.

Irwin, Inez Haynes. Maida's Little House. 2004. reprint ed. pap. 27.95 (978-1-4179-4236-7(3)) Kessinger Publishing, LLC.

Irwin, Judy. What's It to You? 2013. 106p. pap. (978-0-9877088-7-8(2)) Irwin, Judy.

Irwin, Kate. Alfie's Great Escape. Elsom, Clare, illus. 2016. (Reading Ladder Ser.). (ENG.). 48p. (J). (gr. k-2). 7.99 (978-1-4052-8217-8(7)) Egmont Bks., Ltd. GBR. Dist: Independent Pubs. Group.

Irwin, Ms. Judy. We're Done. 2012. 104p. pap. (978-0-9877088-4-7(8)) Irwin, Judy.

—What Did You Say? 2012. 78p. pap. (978-0-9877088-5-4(6)) Irwin, Judy.

Isaac, Lowell. Mr. Cat & the End of the World. 2013. 36p. pap. 20.99 (978-1-4817-0297-3(1)) AuthorHouse.

Isabel, Michelle. Murtle the Sea Turtle. Isabel, Michelle & Thomas, Franselica, illus. 2011. 24p. pap. 24.95 (978-1-4626-0114-1(6)) America Star Bks.

Isbell, Shaun. The Mouse & the Witch, 1 vol. 2009. 56p. pap. 16.95 (978-1-61546-892-8(7)) PublishAmerica, Inc.

Isern, Susanna. The Magic Ball of Wool. 2013. (ENG., Illus.). 32p. (J). (gr. -1-k). 16.95 *(978-84-15619-89-5(8))* Eastern National.

Islam, Hina. An Eid for Everyone. 2009. 16p. pap. 9.99 *(978-1-4389-4845-4(X))* AuthorHouse.

Israel, Julie. Juniper Lemon's Happiness Index. 2017. (ENG.). 352p. (YA). (gr. 7). 17.99 ***(978-0-7352-2817-7(5)***, Kathy Dawson Books) Penguin Young Readers Group.

Istvan & Schritter "Istvansch", Istvan. Federica Aburrida. 2004. (SPA.). 32p. (J). 6.50 *(978-84-348-7817-4(8))* SM Ediciones ESP. Dist: Lectorum Pubns., Inc.

Itani, Frances. Best Friend Trouble, 1 vol. Després, Geneviève, illus. 2014. (ENG.). 32p. (J). (gr. -1-3). 19.95 *(978-1-55469-891-2(X))* Orca Bk. Pubs. USA.

Ivan, Benson. The Snow That Just Wouldn't Stop. Scott, Rosseau, illus. 2008. 24p. (J). pap. 8.95 *(978-0-9774754-4-5(1))* Spiritbuilding.

Ivanoff, George & Quarmby, Toby. My Best Friend Thinks I'm a Genius. 2008. (Rigby Focus Forward Ser.). (ENG., Illus.). 24p. (gr. 3-8). pap. 11.20 *(978-1-4190-3849-5(4))* Houghton Mifflin Harcourt Publishing Co.

Iversen, Jeremy. 21. 2005. (ENG.). 272p. (YA). pap. 6.99 *(978-0-689-87623-3(8)*, Simon Pulse) Simon Pulse.

Ivey, Lisa. The Christmas Tree That Didn't Get Picked. 2007. 64p. per. 19.95 *(978-1-4241-8276-3(X))* America Star Bks.

Iwasa, Megumi. Yours Sincerely, Giraffe. Takabatake, Jun, illus. 2017. (Gecko Press Titles Ser.). (ENG.). 104p. (gr. k-3). 9.99 ***(978-1-77657-114-7(2))*** Gecko Pr. NZL. Dist: Lerner Publishing Group.

J, Granny. Pinky Gets a New Puppy: Pinky Frink's Adventures. 2012. 38p. pap. 17.99 *(978-1-105-86479-7(0))* Lulu Pr., Inc.

J. Katyn. Boo & the Halloween Grin. 2011. 36p. pap. *(978-1-4269-7197-6(4))* Trafford Publishing (UK) Ltd.

Jabaley, Jennifer. Crush Control. 2011. (ENG.). 336p. (YA). (gr. 7-18). 9.99 *(978-1-59514-424-9(2)*, Razorbill) Penguin Young Readers Group.

Jablonski, Carla. Defiance, Bk. 2. Purvis, Leland, illus. 2011. (Resistance Ser.: 2). (ENG.). 128p. (YA). (gr. 7-12). pap. 18.99 *(978-1-59643-292-5(6)*, 9781596432925, First Second Bks.) Roaring Brook Pr.

—Resistance, Bk. 1. Purvis, Leland, illus. 2010. (Resistance Ser.: 1). (ENG.). 128p. (YA). (gr. 7-12). pap. 17.99 *(978-1-59643-291-8(8)*, 9781596432918, First Second Bks.) Roaring Brook Pr.

Jablonski, Carrie. Spots New Friends. 2012. 20p. pap. 24.95 *(978-1-4626-8398-7(3))* America Star Bks.

Jack, Gordon. The Boomerang Effect. 2016. 352p. (YA). (gr. 9). 17.99 *(978-0-06-239939-7(X)*, HarperTeen) HarperCollins Pubs.

Jackson, Al, Jr. Adventures of Middle School: The Handbook. 2013. (ENG.). 60p. (YA). pap. 12.95 *(978-1-4787-0892-6(1))* Outskirts Pr., Inc.

Jackson, Armitra L. Eating Safe with Ace & Mace! 2007. 44p. per. 15.95 *(978-1-4327-1255-6(1))* Outskirts Pr., Inc.

Jackson, Barry E. Danny Diamondback. Jackson, Barry E., illus. 2008. (Illus.). 40p. (J). (gr. k-2). lib. bdg. 17.89 *(978-0-06-113185-1(7))* HarperCollins Pubs.

Jackson, Ciandress. Chloe the Jumbo Jet: First Class to Seoul! Let's Rock & Roll. 2013. 26p. pap. 9.99 *(978-1-61286-196-8(2))* Avid Readers Publishing Group.

—Chloe the Jumbo Jet the Best Cancelled Christmas Ever. 2013. 28p. pap. 9.99 *(978-1-61286-200-2(4))* Avid Readers Publishing Group.

Jackson, Colter & dePaola, Tomie. Elephants Make Fine Friends. 2015. (ENG., Illus.). 32p. (J). (gr. -1-k). bds. 3.99 *(978-0-448-48505-8(2)*, Grosset & Dunlap) Penguin Young Readers Group.

Jackson, Corrine. If I Lie. (ENG.). 288p. (YA). (gr. 9). 2013. pap. 12.99 *(978-1-4424-4000-5(7))* 2012. 16.99 *(978-1-4424-5413-2(X))* Simon Pulse. (Simon Pulse).

Jackson, Debra. Canines on Patrol: Special Lessons. 2009. (Illus.). 28p. pap. 12.49 *(978-1-4343-8806-3(9))* AuthorHouse.

Jackson, Dessi. The Saint & His Bees. Brandenburg, Claire, illus. 2013. 28p. pap. 9.99 *(978-1-62395-487-1(8))* Xist Publishing.

Jackson, Jasmine. Robert's Really Restless. 2011. 24p. pap. 15.99 *(978-1-4568-5343-3(0))* Xlibris Corp.

Jackson, Laura Gower. The Snowman & the Magic Eyeglasses. 2010. 24p. 11.99 *(978-1-4520-3544-4(X))* AuthorHouse.

Jackson, Maureen. You Count Too. 2012. 20p. pap. 17.99 *(978-1-4772-1241-7(8))* AuthorHouse.

Jackson, Ruth Montgomery. A Bit of Magic with Wee Willie & Double Trouble. 2011. 76p. pap. 27.50 *(978-1-4567-0050-8(2))* AuthorHouse.

Jackson, Spring. The Little Faucet That Never Stopped Dripping. 2012. 24p. pap. 17.99 *(978-1-4685-4266-0(4))* AuthorHouse.

Jacobs, Britany R. The Kraken's Rules to Making Friends. 2016. (ENG., Illus.). 40p. (J). (gr. -1-2). 18.95 *(978-1-57687-814-9(7)*, powerHouse Bks.) powerHouse Cultural Entertainment, Inc.

Jacobs Cfp, Sheila. Jake's Big Bang. 2012. 28p. pap. 11.99 *(978-1-4685-5736-7(X))* AuthorHouse.

Jacobs, Evan. Clan Castles, 1 vol. 2014. (Red Rhino Ser.). (ENG.). 68p. (J). (gr. 4-6). pap. 7.95 *(978-1-62250-921-8(8))* Saddleback Educational Publishing, Inc.

—Varsity 170, 1 vol., Bk. 10. 2015. (Gravel Road Ser.). (ENG.). (YA). (gr. 9-12). pap. 9.95 *(978-1-62250-889-1(0))* Saddleback Educational Publishing, Inc.

Jacobs, Jerry L. Koda. 2013. 80p. pap. 12.99 *(978-0-9855202-5-0(6))* Kids At Heart Publishing, LLC.

Jacobs, John Hornor & Priest, A. Breakthrough. 2014. (Red Zone Ser.: 2). (ENG.). 104p. (YA). (gr. 6-12). lib. bdg. 27.93 *(978-1-4677-2131-8(X))* Lerner Publishing Group.

Jacobson, Jennifer Richard. Andy Shane & the Barn Sale Mystery. Carter, Abby, illus. (Andy Shane Ser.: 5). (ENG.). 64p. (J). (gr. k-3). 2010. 4.99 *(978-0-7636-4827-5(2))* 2009. 14.99 *(978-0-7636-3599-2(5))* Candlewick Pr.

—Andy Shane Is Not in Love. Carter, Abby, illus. 2009. (Andy Shane Ser.: 4). (ENG.). 64p. (J). (gr. k-3). 4.99 *(978-0-7636-4403-1(X))* Candlewick Pr.

Jacques, Florence Page. There Once Was a Puffin. Halpern, Shari, illus. 2016. (ENG.). 32p. (J). 15.95 *(978-0-7358-4245-8(0))* North-South Bks., Inc.

Jacques, Taryn Elise. What's Wrong with the New Girl? Reilly, Meghan M., illus. 2004. 33p. pap. 24.95 *(978-1-4137-1999-4(6))* PublishAmerica, Inc.

Jafa, Manorama. The Parrot & the Mynah (English) 2013. (ENG.). 16p. pap. 4.95 *(978-93-5036-080-4(2))* Ratna Sagar Pvt. Ltd. IND. Dist: Midpoint Trade Bks., Inc.

Jaggi, Harleen. Mystery at the Book Store. 2007. (J). per. *(978-0-9790896-0-2(3))* Booksmart Pubns.

Jahn-Clough, Lisa. Felicity & Cordelia: A Tale of Two Bunnies. Jahn-Clough, Lisa, illus. 2011. (ENG., Illus.). 40p. (J). (gr. -1-3). 16.99 *(978-0-374-32300-4(3)*, 9780374323004, Farrar, Straus & Giroux (BYR)) Farrar, Straus & Giroux.

—My Friend & I. 2003. (ENG., Illus.). 32p. (J). (gr. -1-3). 6.99 *(978-0-618-39108-0(8))* Houghton Mifflin Harcourt Publishing Co.

Jahn-Clough, Lisa, et al. Petal & Poppy & the Mystery Valentine. Briant, Ed, illus. 2015. (Green Light Readers Level 2 Ser.). (ENG.). 32p. (J). (gr. 1-4). pap. 3.99 *(978-0-544-55549-5(X)*, HMH Books For Young Readers) Houghton Mifflin Harcourt Publishing Co.

Jaimet, Kate. Dunces Rock, 1 vol. 2014. (ENG.). 224p. (J). (gr. 4-7). pap. 9.95 *(978-1-4598-0585-9(2))* Orca Bk. Pubs. USA.

Jakobs, D. My Little Pony: Holly, Jolly Harmony. 2013. (Passport to Reading Level 2 Ser.). (ENG., Illus.). 32p. (J). (gr. -1-3). 4.99 *(978-0-316-22816-9(8))* Little, Brown Bks. for Young Readers.

Jakubowski, Michele. Beach Bummer. Waters, Erica-Jane, illus. 2014. (Perfectly Poppy Ser.). (ENG.). 32p. (gr. k-2). lib. bdg. 22.65 *(978-1-4795-2284-2(8))* Picture Window Bks.

—Best Friends Forever? Fekete, Hedi, illus. 2016. (Ashley Small & Ashlee Tall Ser.). (ENG.). 64p. (gr. 1-3). lib. bdg. 20.65 *(978-1-4795-9191-6(2))* Picture Window Bks.

—Big Dog Decisions, 1 vol. Montalto, Luisa, illus. 2014. (Sidney & Sydney Ser.). (ENG.). 128p. (gr. 1-3). 25.32 *(978-1-4795-5226-9(7))* Picture Window Bks.

—Brushes & Basketballs. Fekete, Hedi, illus. 2016. (Ashley Small & Ashlee Tall Ser.). (ENG.). 64p. (gr. 1-3). lib. bdg. 20.65 *(978-1-5158-0010-1(5))* Picture Window Bks.

—Dodgeball, Drama, & Other Dilemmas. Montalto, Luisa, illus. (Sidney & Sydney Ser.). (ENG.). 128p. (gr. 1-3). 2016. pap. 6.95 *(978-1-4795-6755-3(8))* 2013. 8.95 *(978-1-4795-2116-6(7))* 2013. lib. bdg. 25.32 *(978-1-4048-8061-0(5))* Picture Window Bks.

—The Grass Is Always Greener. (Ashley Small & Ashlee Tall Ser.). (ENG., Illus.). 64p. (gr. 1-3). 2017. pap. 4.95 *(978-1-5158-0016-3(4))* 2016. lib. bdg. 20.65 *(978-1-5158-0012-5(1))* Picture Window Bks.

—Mick's Buried Treasure. Pinelli, Amerigo, illus. 2016. (Sleuths of Somerville Ser.). (ENG.). 144p. (gr. 4-6). lib. bdg. 25.99 *(978-1-4965-3178-0(7))* Stone Arch Bks.

—Outside Surprise. Waters, Erica-Jane, illus. 2015. (Perfectly Poppy Ser.). (ENG.). 32p. (gr. k-2). 22.65 *(978-1-4795-5802-5(8))* Picture Window Bks.

—Poppy's Puppy. Waters, Erica-Jane, illus. 2015. (Perfectly Poppy Ser.). (ENG.). 32p. (gr. k-2). 22.65 *(978-1-4795-5799-8(4))* Picture Window Bks.

—The Professor's Discovery. Pinelli, Amerigo, illus. 2017. (Sleuths of Somerville Ser.). (ENG.). 144p. (gr. 4-6). pap. 6.95 *(978-1-4965-3181-0(7))* Stone Arch Bks.

—Secrets in Somerville. Pinelli, Amerigo, illus. 2016. (Sleuths of Somerville Ser.). (ENG.). 144p. (gr. 4-6). lib. bdg. 25.99 *(978-1-4965-3175-9(2))* Stone Arch Bks.

—Sidney & Sydney, 1 vol. (Sidney & Sydney Ser.). (ENG.). 128p. (gr. 1-3). 2014. 75.96 *(978-1-4795-5749-3(8))* 2013. 50.64 *(978-1-4795-1696-4(1))* Picture Window Bks.

—Sleepover. 2017. (Ashley Small & Ashlee Tall Ser.). (ENG., Illus.). 64p. (gr. 1-3). pap. 4.95 *(978-1-5158-0015-6(6))* Capstone Press of Coughlan Cos.

—Sleepover. 2016. (Ashley Small & Ashlee Tall Ser.). (ENG., Illus.). 64p. (gr. 1-3). lib. bdg. 20.65 *(978-1-5158-0011-8(3))* Picture Window Bks.

—Soccer Star. Waters, Erica-Jane, illus. 2015. (Perfectly Poppy Ser.). (ENG.). 32p. (gr. k-2). 22.65 *(978-1-4795-5800-1(1))* Picture Window Bks.

—Talent Trouble. Waters, Erica-Jane, illus. 2014. (Perfectly Poppy Ser.). (ENG.). 32p. (gr. k-2). lib. bdg. 22.65 *(978-1-4795-2281-1(3))* Picture Window Bks.

—Third Grade Mix-Up. Montalto, Luisa, illus. (Sidney & Sydney Ser.). (ENG.). 128p. (gr. 1-3). 2015. pap. 7.15 *(978-1-4795-6754-6(X))* 2013. 8.95 *(978-1-4048-8104-4(2))* 2013. lib. bdg. 25.32 *(978-1-4048-8001-6(1))* Picture Window Bks.

—Tour of Trouble. Pinelli, Amerigo, illus. 2016. (Sleuths of Somerville Ser.). (ENG.). 144p. (gr. 4-6). lib. bdg. 25.99 *(978-1-4965-3176-6(0))* Stone Arch Bks.

—Tour of Trouble. Pinelli, Amerigo, illus. 2017. (Sleuths of Somerville Ser.). (ENG.). 144p. (gr. 4-6). pap. 6.95 *(978-1-4965-3180-3(9))* Stone Arch Bks.

James, Andrea. Adventures at Ja-Mar Farms: Pup-Pup, Padluck & PIG Take a Walk in the Wet Woods, 1 vol. 2010. 48p. 24.95 *(978-1-4512-1005-7(1))* 2005. 47p. pap. 24.95 *(978-1-4137-3437-9(5))* PublishAmerica, Inc.

James, Ann. Bird & Bear. James, Ann, illus. 2015. (ENG., Illus.). 40p. (J). (gr. -1-2). 16.99 *(978-1-4998-0037-1(1))* Little Bee Books Inc.

James, Arthur. Jason & the Kodikats. 2013. 118p. pap. *(978-0-9918166-2-0(5))* Flower Pr.

James, Catherine. Bobby Cottontail's Gift. Collier, Kevin Scott, illus. 2008. 28p. pap. 10.95 *(978-1-935137-07-8(7))* 2006. 32p. (J). E-Book 9.95 incl. cd-rom *(978-1-933090-24-5(3))* Guardian Angel Publishing, Inc.

—The Sad Little House. Collier, Kevin Scott, illus. 2008. 24p. pap. 10.95 *(978-1-935137-06-1(9))* Guardian Angel Publishing, Inc.

James, Howe. The Misfits. 2014. (Misfits Ser.). (ENG.). 304p. (J). 11.24 *(978-1-63245-171-2(9))* Lectorum Pubns., Inc.

—Pinky & Rex & the Bully. 2014. (Pinky & Rex Ser.). (ENG.). 48p. (J). (gr. 1-3). 8.24 *(978-1-63245-347-1(9))* Lectorum Pubns., Inc.

James, Martin. William Is Going Green. 2008. 38p. 14.95 *(978-0-9799465-1-6(4))* Martin, James Jr.

James, Simon. Leon & Bob. James, Simon, illus. 2016. (ENG., Illus.). 32p. (J). (gr. -1-3). 7.99 *(978-0-7636-8175-3(X))* Candlewick Pr.

James, Suzi. Matilda Bear & Father Bear: I Love You Father Bear. 2012. (Illus.). 52p. pap. 23.95 *(978-1-4525-4822-7(6))* Balboa Pr.

James, Wayan. My Friend the Painter. 2016. (Rosen REAL Readers: STEM & STEAM Collection). 12p. (gr. 1-k). pap. 6.33 *(978-1-5081-2661-4(5)*, Rosen Classroom) Rosen Publishing Group, Inc., The.

Jamieson, Victoria. All's Faire in Middle School, 9 vols. 2017. (ENG.). (J). pap. 116.91 ***(978-0-525-48668-8(2))***; (Illus.). 248p. (gr. 4-7). 20.99 ***(978-0-525-42998-2(0))***; (Illus.). 248p. (gr. 4-7). pap. 12.99 ***(978-0-525-42999-9(9))*** Penguin Young Readers Group. (Dial Bks).

—All's Faire in Middle School. 2017. lib. bdg. 24.50 ***(978-0-606-40484-6(8))*** Turtleback Bks.

Jamieson, Victoria. Roller Girl. 2015. (ENG., Illus.). 240p. (J). (gr. 4-7). 20.99 *(978-0-525-42967-8(0))*; pap. 12.99 *(978-0-8037-4016-7(6))* Penguin Young Readers Group. (Dial Bks).

—Roller Girl. 2015. (J). lib. bdg. 24.50 *(978-0-606-37112-4(5))* Turtleback Bks.

Jamison, Lori. Running for Dave. (Illus.). 86p. *(978-1-897039-11-3(5))* High Interest Publishing (HIP).

Jan Baer. And the Mystery of the Silent Circus. 2005. (J). per. 10.00 *(978-1-930052-29-1(4))* Cherokee Bks.

Jane, Pamela. Noelle of the Nutcracker. Brett, Jan, illus. 2003. (ENG.). 64p. (J). (gr. 5-7). pap. 8.95 *(978-0-618-36922-5(8))* Houghton Mifflin Harcourt Publishing Co.

Jane, Rebecca. Hamster Heroes to the Rescue: The Mystery of the Shadow in the Yard & Retirement. 2012. 84p. 19.95 *(978-1-4626-6862-5(3))* America Star Bks.

Janeway, Paul. Dragon Eye Connection. 2011. 202p. pap. 14.95 *(978-1-60976-854-6(X)*, Strategic Bk. Publishing) Strategic Book Publishing & Rights Agency (SBPRA).

Janover, Caroline D. Zipper: The Kid with ADHD. 2007. 172p. per. 12.95 *(978-0-595-47615-2(5)*, Backinprint.com) iUniverse, Inc.

Janovitz, Marilyn. I Will Try. Janovitz, Marilyn, illus. (I Like to Read(r) Ser.). (ENG., Illus.). 24p. (J). 2013. pap. 6.99 *(978-0-8234-2756-7(0))* 2012. 14.95 *(978-0-8234-2399-6(9))* Holiday Hse., Inc.

Janski, Beverly. A Little Birdie Told Me. 2012. 48p. pap. 14.95 *(978-1-4497-5263-7(2)*, WestBow Pr.) Author Solutions, Inc.

Janssen, Ian. The Perils of Pierre Book 1, Gold Fever. 2013. 26p. pap. 12.99 *(978-1-61160-594-5(6))* Whiskey Creek Restorations.

Jarek, Janice. Emma & Her Angels. 2012. 24p. 24.95 *(978-1-4626-6255-5(2))* America Star Bks.

—Mya & the Mermaid. 2012. 28p. 24.95 *(978-1-4626-3277-0(7))* America Star Bks.

Jarman, Julia. Ants in Your Pants! Parker-Rees, Guy, illus. 2011. (ENG.). 32p. (J). (gr. -1-k). pap. 10.99 *(978-1-4083-0525-6(9))* Hodder & Stoughton GBR. Dist: Hachette Bk. Group.

—A Friend in Need! Pankhurst, Kate, illus. 2015. (Friends Ser.: 2). (ENG.). 96p. (J). (gr. 2-4). 11.99 *(978-1-84939-576-2(4))* Andersen Pr. GBR. Dist: Independent Pubs. Group.

—Friends Forever. Pankhurst, Kate, illus. 2015. (ENG.). 288p. (J). pap. 12.99 *(978-1-78344-234-8(4))* Andersen Pr. GBR. Dist: Independent Pubs. Group.

—Make Friends - Break Friends. Pankhurst, Kate, illus. 2015. (Friends Ser.: 1). (ENG.). 96p. (J). (gr. 2-4). pap. 6.99 *(978-1-84939-509-0(8))* Andersen Pr. GBR. Dist: Independent Pubs. Group.

—New Friend Old Friends. Pankhurst, Kate, illus. 2015. (Friends Ser.: 3). (ENG.). 112p. (J). (gr. 2-4). 6.99 *(978-1-78344-004-7(X))* Andersen Pr. GBR. Dist: Independent Pubs. Group.

Jarrell, Pamela R. Caillou's Family & Friends. Meier, Kerry L., illus. l.t. ed. 2005. (HRL Board Book Ser.). (J). (gr. k-18). pap. 10.95 *(978-1-57332-327-7(6)*, HighReach Learning, Incorporated) Carson-Dellosa Publishing, LLC.

Jarrett, Clare. Dancing Maddy. (Illus.). 26p. (J). pap. *(978-0-00-664670-9(0))* HarperCollins Canada, Ltd.

Jarvis. Fred Forgets. Jarvis, illus. 2016. (Illus.). 32p. (J). (gr. -1-3). 17.99 *(978-0-06-234916-3(3))* HarperCollins Pubs.

Jarvis, James & Waterman, Russell. Vortigern's Machine: And the Great Sage of Wisdom. Jarvis, James, illus. 2006. (Illus.). 48p. per. 24.00 *(978-3-89955-098-6(6))* Die Gestalten Verlag DEU. Dist: Prestel Publishing.

Jarvis, Mary Rowles. Dick Lionheart. 2007. (Illus.). 76p. per. *(978-1-4065-2709-4(2))* Dodo Pr.

Jasmine, Jean-Pierre. It's Raining Uber. 2013. 166p. (J). pap. 13.99 *(978-1-4808-0122-6(4))* Archway Publishing.

Jasnoch, Dorothy. Frankie the Bunny: Helping the Birds. Korzeniowski, Samson O., ed. Jasnoch, Dorothy, illus. 2013. (Illus.). 28p. 17.99 *(978-1-937752-20-0(8))* Owl About Bks. Pub., Inc.

—Frankie the Bunny: Newfound Friends. Korzeniowski, Samson O., ed. Jasnoch, Dorothy, illus. 2013. (Illus.). 28p. 17.99 *(978-1-937752-15-6(1))* Owl About Bks. Pub., Inc.

—Frankie the Bunny: Wheels of Fortune. Korzeniowski, Samson O., ed. Jasnoch, Dorothy, illus. 2013. (Illus.). 28p. 17.99 *(978-1-937752-17-0(8))* Owl About Bks. Pub., Inc.

—Frankie the Bunny: Woodland Warning. Korzeniowski, Samson, ed. Jasnoch, Dorothy, illus. 2012. (Illus.). 28p. pap. 12.99 *(978-1-937752-03-3(8))* Owl About Bks. Pub., Inc.

—Frankie the Bunny the Fall Scramble Begins. Korzeniowski, Samson, ed. Jasnoch, Dorothy, illus. 2012. (Illus.). 28p. pap. 12.99 *(978-1-937752-04-0(6))* Owl About Bks. Pub., Inc.

Jason. Jason & Edeia. pap. 6.95 *(978-0-394-74096-6(3))* Random Hse., Inc.

Javaherbin, Mina. Goal! Ford, A. G., illus. 2012. (ENG.). 40p. (J). (gr. 1-4). pap. 6.99 *(978-0-7636-5822-9(7))* Candlewick Pr.

Jax, T. L. Fraidy-Frieda's Light Show. Jax, T. L., illus. l.t. ed. 2004. (Illus.). 30p. (J). 9.95 *(978-0-9743890-2-8(1))* Flaxenfluff Pr., LLC.

Jayne, Hannah. The Dare. 2014. (ENG.). 288p. (YA). (gr. 7-12). pap. 9.99 *(978-1-4022-9457-0(3)*, 9781402294570) Sourcebooks, Inc.

Jazz. Gizmo & Scatz: A Tail of Friendship. 2012. (Illus.). 16p. pap. 17.55 *(978-1-4678-8267-5(4))* AuthorHouse.

Jean. Jean's Story. 2009. 40p. pap. 18.49 *(978-1-4389-4531-6(0))* AuthorHouse.

Jeanne Taylor Thomas Illustrator: Pr. Austin & Harlow's First Adventure. Hardy, Pris, illus. 2011. 28p. pap. 24.95 *(978-1-4560-8383-0(X))* America Star Bks.

Jeffers, Dawn. Vegetable Dreams/Huerto Sonado. de La Vega, Eida, tr. Schneider, Claude, illus. 2006. (SPA & ENG.). 32p. (J). (gr. -1-3). 16.95 *(978-0-9741992-9-0(X)*, 626999, Raven Tree Pr.,Csi) Continental Sales, Inc.

Jeffers, Oliver. Lost & Found. Jeffers, Oliver, illus. 2005. (ENG., Illus.). 32p. (J). (gr. -1-2). 17.99 *(978-0-399-24503-9(0)*, Philomel Bks.) Penguin Young Readers Group.

—Up & Down. Jeffers, Oliver, illus. 2010. (ENG., Illus.). 40p. (J). (gr. -1-2). 17.99 *(978-0-399-25545-8(1)*, Philomel Bks.) Penguin Young Readers Group.

Jeffers, Stewart. The Collapse of the Crew. 2005. 111p. pap. 19.95 *(978-1-4137-8714-6(2))* PublishAmerica, Inc.

Jeffers, Sunni. Eyes on the Prize. 2009. (Tales from Grace Chapel Inn Ser.). (ENG.). 328p. pap. 13.99 *(978-0-8249-4787-3(8)*, Ideal Pubns.) Worthy Publishing.

Jefferson, E. Louis. The Little Caterpillar-A Story of Kindness. 2012. 38p. pap. 17.00 *(978-1-105-76076-1(6))* Lulu Pr., Inc.

—The Little Caterpillar-A Story of Kindness-Companion Coloring Book. 2012. 52p. pap. 8.00 *(978-1-105-92194-0(8))* Lulu Pr., Inc.

—The Little Tadpole-A Story of Friendship: Companion Coloring Book. 2012. 48p. pap. 7.00 *(978-1-105-61123-0(X))* Lulu.com GBR. Dist: Lulu Pr., Inc.

—Terry-The Little Tadpole-Making New Friends. 2013. 90p. pap. 35.00 *(978-1-300-61843-0(4))* Lulu Pr., Inc.

Jefferson Elementary Art Club, illus. Domino. 2007. 32p. (J). 15.00 *(978-0-9767244-2-1(1))* SkyMacSyd Publishing.

Jeffery, John. Freddie & the Garden Circus. 2015. (ENG.). 47p. (J). (gr. 2-3). mass mkt. 14.95 *(978-1-78455-729-4(3)*, ffaea993-f2af-431a-bb31-29d73a42d220) Austin, Stan AUS. Dist: Bookmasters Distribution.

Jeffrey, Rosemary. Allio, Are you Free. 2010. 176p. pap. 12.00 *(978-0-557-75342-0(2))* Lulu Pr., Inc.

Jeffries, Alison. Sam & the Bag. Andreasen, Dan, illus. 2004. (Green Light Readers Level 1 Ser.). (gr. -1-1). 13.95 *(978-0-7569-4331-8(0))* Perfection Learning Corp.

Jeffs, Dixie. Molly's Promise. 2013. 28p. pap. 24.95 *(978-1-62709-116-9(5))* America Star Bks.

Jenkins, Emily. Skunkdog. Pratt, Pierre, illus. 2008. (ENG.). 32p. (J). (gr. -1-3). 16.95 *(978-0-374-37009-1(5)*, 9780374370091, Farrar, Straus & Giroux (BYR)) Farrar, Straus & Giroux.

—Tiger & Badger. Gay, Marie-Louise, illus. 2016. (ENG.). 32p. (J). (-k). 15.99 *(978-0-7636-6604-0(1))* Candlewick Pr.

—Toy Dance Party. Zelinsky, Paul O., illus. 2010. (Toys Go Out Ser.). (ENG.). 176p. (J). (gr. 1-4). 6.99 *(978-0-375-85525-2(4)*, Yearling) Random Hse. Children's Bks.

—Toy Dance Party: Being the Further Adventures of a Bossyboots Stingray, a Courageous Buffalo, & a Hopeful Round Someone Called Plastic. Zelinsky, Paul O., illus. 2008. (Toys Go Out Ser.). (ENG.). 176p. (J). (gr. 1-4). 16.99 *(978-0-375-83935-1(6)*, Schwartz & Wade Bks.) Random Hse. Children's Bks.

—Toys Come Home: Being the Early Experiences of an Intelligent Stingray, a Brave Buffalo, & a Brand-New Someone Called Plastic. Zelinsky, Paul O., illus. 2011. (Toys Go Out Ser.). (ENG.). 144p. (J). (gr. 1-4). 16.99 *(978-0-375-86200-7(5)*, Schwartz & Wade Bks.) Random Hse. Children's Bks.

—Toys Go Out: Being the Adventures of a Knowledgeable Stingray, a Toughy Little Buffalo, & Someone Called Plastic. Zelinsky, Paul O., illus. (Toys Go Out Ser.). (ENG.). (J). (gr. 1-4). 2008. 144p. 6.99 *(978-0-385-73661-9(4)*, Yearling) 2006. 128p. 16.95 *(978-0-375-83604-6(7)*, Schwartz & Wade Bks.) Random Hse. Children's Bks.

Jenkins, Gloria. Storm: The Peace Maker. 2006. (J). pap. 8.00 *(978-0-8059-7116-3(5))* Dorrance Publishing Co., Inc.

Jenkins, Jerry B. & LaHaye, Tim. Heat Wave: Surviving the Fourth Bowl Judgment. 2004. (Left Behind: the Kids Ser.: 37). (ENG.). 208p. (YA). mass mkt. 5.99 *(978-0-8423-8347-9(6))* Tyndale Hse. Pubs.

—The Perils of Love: Breaking Through the Darkness. 2004. (Left Behind: the Kids Ser.: 38). (ENG.). 208p. (YA). mass mkt. 5.99 *(978-0-8423-8348-6(4))* Tyndale Hse. Pubs.

Jennicrai, Susanna. Button & Bow: Friends Forever. 2013. 28p. pap. 16.09 *(978-1-4669-8779-1(0))* Trafford Publishing.

Jennie Lyon Wood. Bath Time Bears Have So Much Fun. Kristie Kryssing, illus. 2009. 24p. pap. 12.99 *(978-1-4389-4420-3(9))* AuthorHouse.

Jennings, Carol E. Marshall & Satchmo. 2008. 40p. pap. 21.32 *(978-1-4363-7117-9(1))* Xlibris Corp.

Jennings, Patrick. Bat & Rat. Cordell, Matthew, illus. 2012. (ENG.). 40p. (J). (gr. k-2). 16.95 *(978-1-4197-0160-3(6)*, Abrams Bks. for Young Readers) Abrams, Inc.

—Odd, Weird & Little. 2014. (ENG.). 160p. (J). (gr. 3-7). 15.99 *(978-1-60684-374-1(5)*, Carolrhoda Bks.) Lerner Publishing Group.

Jennings, Richard W. Scribble. 2004. (ENG.). 160p. (YA). (gr. 5-9). tchr. ed. 15.00 *(978-0-618-43367-4(8))* Houghton Mifflin Harcourt Publishing Co.

Jennings, Sharon. Batnapped. *(978-1-897039-30-4(1))* High Interest Publishing (HIP).

—Home Free, 1 vol. 2009. (Gutsy Girl Ser.). (ENG., Illus.). 160p. (J). (gr. 4-7). pap. 8.95 *(978-1-897187-55-5(6))* Second Story Pr. CAN. Dist: Orca Bk. Pubs. USA.

—Jingle Bats. Malloy, Kalle, illus. 72p. pap. *(978-1-897039-22-9(0))* High Interest Publishing (HIP).

Jennings, Terri & Gold, Paul Daniel. Cadbury's Big Move. 2007. 52p. per. 19.95 *(978-1-4327-0705-7(1))* Outskirts Pr., Inc.

Jensen, Peder Skytte. Anton & Rosita: All Roads Lead to Rome. 2011. (Illus.). 40p. (gr. 1-2). pap. 20.38 *(978-1-4567-8077-7(8))* AuthorHouse.

Jentsch, R. D. Froggy & Friends Go to the Creek, 1 vol. Jentsch, Joyce Harp, illus. 2009. 41p. pap. 24.95 *(978-1-60836-966-9(8))* America Star Bks.

Jesrani, Asha. Shirley the Poppy Fairy & the Little Girl Lucky. 2012. (Illus.). 28p. pap. 21.35 *(978-1-4772-1939-3(0))* AuthorHouse.

Jesse, Mary. Abbey & Friends M Is for Manners. Cherif, Jennifer, illus. 2003. 48p. (J). 15.95 *(978-0-9729958-0-1(3))* Hexagon Blue.

Jewell, Teresa. How Charlie Mouse Learned about Cystic Fibrosis. 2011. 48p. pap. 21.66 *(978-1-4567-2557-0(2))* AuthorHouse.

Jewl, Terry. The Pixies in Home Sweet Home. 2012. 24p. pap. 24.95 *(978-1-4626-5585-4(8))* America Star Bks.

EFG

Jiang, Ji-Li. Lotus & Feather. Downing, Julie, illus. 2016. (ENG.). 40p. (J). (gr. -1-k). 17.99 *(978-1-4231-2754-3(4))* Disney Pr.

Jiménez, Juan Ramón. Platero & I/Platero y Yo: A Dual-Language Book. Appelbaum, Stanley, ed. Appelbaum, Stanley, tr. from SPA. 2004. (Dover Dual Language Spanish Ser.). (ENG & SPA.). 192p. pap. 12.95 *(978-0-486-43565-7(2))* Dover Pubns., Inc.

—Platero y Yo. (SPA.). 192p. (J). 13.95 *(978-84-206-1851-7(9),* AZ1851); (Illus.). 159p. 15.95 *(978-84-206-3408-1(5))* Alianza Editorial, S. A. ESP. Dist: Continental Bk. Co., Inc., Distribooks, Inc.

—Platero y Yo. (SPA.). (J). pap. 9.95 *(978-968-432-357-5(3),* PM223) Editorial Porrua MEX. Dist: Continental Bk. Co., Inc.

—Platero y Yo. annot. ed. (SPA., Illus.). 232p. (J). 15.95 *(978-84-207-2636-6(2),* ANY010) Grupo Anaya, S.A. ESP. Dist: Continental Bk. Co., Inc.

—Platero y Yo (Platero & I) (SPA.). (J). pap. 9.95 *(978-968-416-022-4(4),* AOR01) Fernandez USA Publishing.

Jimmie the Crab: An Adventure in the Chesapeake Bay. 2013. (Illus.). 28p. pap. 13.97 *(978-1-62516-364-6(9),* Strategic Bk. Publishing) Strategic Book Publishing & Rights Agency (SBPRA).

Jitchotvisut, Donna M. Mittens for Christmas. 2009. 376p. 31.95 *(978-1-4401-0372-8(0));* pap. 21.95 *(978-1-4401-0370-4(4))* iUniverse, Inc.

Job, et al. Yakari & the Beavers. 2007. (Yakari Ser.: 3). (ENG., Illus.). 48p. (J). (gr. 4-7). per. 11.95 *(978-1-905460-09-0(0))* CineBook GBR. Dist: National Bk. Network.

Jofre, Paola. Lilliput Blasts Off! 2010. 36p. 17.50 *(978-1-4490-7450-0(2))* AuthorHouse.

Johannes, Shelley. Beatrice Zinker, Upside down Thinker. Johannes, Shelley, illus. 2017. (Beatrice Zinker, Upside down Thinker Ser.). (ENG., Illus.). 160p. (J). (gr. 2-5). 14.99 ***(978-1-4847-6738-2(1))*** Hyperion Bks. for Children.

Johansen, Hanna & Barrett, John S. The Duck & the Owl. Bhend, Käthi, illus. 2005. (ENG.). 72p. (J). 17.95 *(978-1-56792-285-1(6))* Godine, David R. Pub.

Johansson, J. R. Insomnia. 2013. (Night Walkers Ser.: 1). (ENG.). 360p. (YA). pap. 9.99 *(978-0-7387-3593-1(0),* Flux) North Star Editions.

John, Clement. Best Friends: A Bedtime Story. 2011. (Illus.). 40p. pap. 21.93 *(978-1-4520-7922-6(6))* AuthorHouse.

John, Jory. I Love You Already! Davies, Benji, illus. 2015. 32p. (J). (gr. -1-3). 17.99 *(978-0-06-237095-2(2))* HarperCollins Pubs.

Johns, Rebecca. Julie Forgets Annie. l.t. ed. 2003. (Illus.). 8p. (J). *(978-0-9740833-1-5(3))* Port Town Publishing.

Johnson, Angela. A Certain October. (ENG.). 176p. (YA). (gr. 9). 2013. pap. 9.99 *(978-0-689-87065-1(5))* 2012. 16.99 *(978-0-689-86505-3(8))* Simon & Schuster Bks. For Young Readers. (Simon & Schuster Bks. For Young Readers).

—Lottie Paris & the Best Place. Fischer, Scott M., illus. 2013. (ENG.). 32p. (J). (gr. k-4). 16.99 *(978-0-689-87378-2(6),* Simon & Schuster Bks. For Young Readers) Simon & Schuster Bks. For Young Readers.

Johnson, Bob. The Lost Mine of the Mechanical Spider. Johnson, Bob, illus. 2006. (Squatland Chronicles Ser.). (Illus.). 53p. (J). (gr. -1-3). per. 11.00 *(978-1-60002-185-5(9),* 3977) Mountain Valley Publishing, LLC.

Johnson, Cara. The Dream Travelers, Book Two: The Butterfly Voyage. 2007. 176p. (J). per. 9.99 *(978-0-9768870-1-0(0))* Whirling Dirvish Publishing.

—Looking Forward Back: The Dream Travelers Book Three. 2008. 162p. (J). per. 9.99 *(978-0-9768870-3-4(7))* Whirling Dirvish Publishing.

Johnson, Carl & Johnson, Gwen. Diggin' the Big'un. Johnson, Gwen, illus. 2007. (Illus.). 16p. (YA). 14.95 *(978-0-9795860-1-9(1))* Fish Tales Publishing.

—Dreamland Friends. Johnson, Gwen, illus. 2007.Tr. of Amigos del Tierra del Sue#324;os. (ENG & SPA., Illus.). 18p. (J). 5.95 *(978-0-9795860-7-1(0))* Fish Tales Publishing.

Johnson, Carole. Pennie the Piglet. 2007. 60p. per. 16.95 *(978-1-4241-7019-7(2))* America Star Bks.

Johnson-Choong, Shelly. A Light to Come Home By. 2nd unabr. ed. 2004. 212p. (C). reprint ed. pap. 12.95 *(978-1-932280-52-4(9),* 80529) Granite Publishing & Distribution.

Johnson, Dawn M. I Have a Chuck. Klein, Ellen Marie, illus. 2013. 28p. pap. 24.95 *(978-1-62709-628-7(0))* America Star Bks.

Johnson, Deanna. Blarron Creek Chronicles. 2009. 108p. 23.49 *(978-1-4389-5580-3(4))* AuthorHouse.

Johnson, Gillian. Thora. Johnson, Gillian, illus. 2003. (Illus.). 128p. *(978-0-207-19815-1(2))* HarperCollins Pubs. Australia.

Johnson, Grace. The Little Fish Who Was Afraid to Swim. 2008. 36p. pap. 15.49 *(978-1-4389-2262-1(0))* AuthorHouse.

Johnson, James A. The Terror & the Talking Stick: Sundown Stories II. 2011. 56p. pap. 8.95 *(978-1-4502-8156-0(7))* iUniverse, Inc.

Johnson, Janet. The Last Great Adventure of the PB & J Society. 2016. (ENG.). 256p. (gr. 4-8). 12.95 *(978-1-62370-636-4(X))* Capstone Young Readers of Coughlan Cos.

Johnson, Jesse Edward. Yearbook. 2017. (ENG.). 260p. (J). (gr. 6). pap. 11.95 *(978-1-58988-118-1(4))* Dry, Paul Bks., Inc.

Johnson, Jo. My Dad Makes Awesome Boats. 2017. (ENG.). 32p. (C). pap. 6.95 ***(978-0-86388-999-8(9),*** Y328881) Routledge.

Johnson, Joanne Gail. Donkey & the Racehorse. Ferris, Carole Anne, illus. 2011. (ENG.). 48p. pap. 12.00 *(978-0-230-02552-3(8),* Macmillan) Pan Macmillan GBR. Dist: Macmillan.

Johnson, Joshua C. The Raccoon in My Room. 2010. 20p. 10.49 *(978-1-4520-7273-9(6))* AuthorHouse.

Johnson, Judy K. What Is It Like to Be Blind? 2009. 34p. pap. 15.58 *(978-0-557-08477-7(6))* Lulu Pr., Inc.

Johnson, Lois Walfrid. The Invisible Friend, Vol. 3. 2004. (Viking Quest Ser.: 3). (ENG.). 224p. (J). (gr. 3). pap. 8.99 *(978-0-8024-3114-1(3))* Moody Pubs.

Johnson, Maureen. Devilish. 2013. (ENG.). 304p. (YA). (gr. 7). pap. 9.99 *(978-0-14-750855-3(X),* Speak) Penguin Young Readers Group.

Johnson, Melinda & Johnson, Mindy. Tinker Bell: An Evolution. 2013. (Disney Editions Deluxe (Film) Ser.). (ENG., Illus.). 192p. (YA). (gr. 13-17). 40.00 *(978-1-4231-7201-7(9),* Disney Editions) Disney Pr.

Johnson Mockler, Nicole. Alex Has Had Enough! Mockler, Sean, illus. 2011. 64p. pap. *(978-1-77067-334-2(2))* FriesenPress.

Johnson, Peter. The Life & Times of Benny Alvarez. 2014. (ENG.). 224p. (J). (gr. 3-7). 16.99 *(978-0-06-221596-3(5))* HarperCollins Pubs.

Johnson, Sandi. Lost Island. Johnson, Britt & Durant, Sybrina, eds. Sturgeon, Bobbi, illus. l.t. ed. 2014. 28p. (J). (gr. k-5). pap. 12.99 *(978-1-929063-69-7(5),* 168) Moons & Stars Publishing For Children.

Johnson, Varian. The Great Greene Heist. 2014. (ENG.). 240p. (J). (gr. 4-7). 16.99 *(978-0-545-52552-7(7),* Levine, Arthur A. Bks.) Scholastic, Inc.

—To Catch a Cheat. 2016. (ENG.). 256p. (J). (gr. 3-7). 16.99 *(978-0-545-72239-1(X),* Levine, Arthur A. Bks.) Scholastic, Inc.

Johnston, Annie Fell. The Story of Dago. 2006. (Illus.). pap. *(978-1-4065-1127-7(7))* Dodo Pr.

—Two Little Knights of Kentucky (Illustra. 2006. pap. *(978-1-4065-1133-8(1))* Dodo Pr.

Johnston-Brown, A. M. The Chronicles of Pleasant Grove. 2006. (J). pap. 12.95 *(978-0-9760718-5-3(1))* Retriever Pr.

Johnston, Carol Shaw. Lily & Sophie: Sisters & Best Friends. 2010. 65p. pap. 26.99 *(978-0-557-35894-6(9))* Lulu Pr., Inc.

Johnston, Cindy. Zip, Burp & Hula. 2006. (Illus.). 32p. (J). per. 10.95 *(978-0-9787930-5-0(6))* Virtual Word Publishing.

Johnston, E. K. Exit, Pursued by a Bear. 2016. (ENG.). 256p. (YA). (gr. 9). 17.99 *(978-1-101-99458-0(4),* Dutton Books for Young Readers) Penguin Young Readers Group.

Johnston, Jan. Ruby - the Naughty Little Black Kitten: Hello! My Name Is Ruby ... 2013. (Illus.). 24p. pap. 17.99 *(978-1-4817-8023-0(9))* AuthorHouse.

Johnston, Tamra L. Libby the Little Leprechaun: Exploring the Opposite Side of South Africa. 2012. 50p. pap. 21.99 *(978-1-4772-0782-6(1))* AuthorHouse.

Johnston, Tony. Bone by Bone by Bone. 2007. (ENG.). 192p. (YA). (gr. 7-12). 29.99 *(978-1-59643-113-3(X),* 9781596431133) Roaring Brook Pr.

—First Grade, Here I Come! Sweet, Melissa & Walker, David, illus. 2015. (ENG.). 32p. (J). (gr. k-2). 8.99 *(978-0-545-20143-8(8),* Cartwheel Bks.) Scholastic, Inc.

—Hanging Out. DiTerlizzi, Tony, illus. 2003. (Allen & Possum Ser.). 48p. (J). 11.65 *(978-0-7569-1544-5(9))* Perfection Learning Corp.

—A Small Thing ... but Big. Hooper, Hadley, illus. 2016. (ENG.). 40p. (J). 17.99 *(978-1-62672-256-9(0),* 9781626722569) Roaring Brook Pr.

Jonas. Three's a Crowd. 6th ed. 2010. 128p. pap. 4.99 *(978-1-4231-2282-1(8))* Disney Pr.

Jonell, Bob. Penny the Chinstrap Penguin, 1 vol. Prince, Brian, illus. 2010. 22p. 24.95 *(978-1-4489-5334-9(0))* PublishAmerica, Inc.

Jones, C. B. The Cats' Meow. Green, Chris, illus. 2017. (Bog Hollow Boys Ser.). (ENG.). 72p. (gr. 4-5). lib. bdg. 25.32 *(978-1-4965-4057-7(3))* Stone Arch Bks.

—Gone to the Buzzards. Green, Chris, illus. 2017. (Bog Hollow Boys Ser.). (ENG.). 72p. (gr. 4-5). lib. bdg. 25.32 *(978-1-4965-4058-4(1))* Stone Arch Bks.

—Kiss of the Snake. Green, Chris, illus. 2017. (Bog Hollow Boys Ser.). (ENG.). 72p. (gr. 4-5). lib. bdg. 25.32 *(978-1-4965-4056-0(5))* Stone Arch Bks.

—Sleeping with the Fishes. Green, Chris, illus. 2017. (Bog Hollow Boys Ser.). (ENG.). 72p. (gr. 4-5). lib. bdg. 25.32 *(978-1-4965-4055-3(7))* Stone Arch Bks.

Jones, Darynda. Death & the Girl He Loves. 2013. (Darklight Ser.: 3). (ENG.). 272p. (YA). (gr. 8-12). pap. 9.99 *(978-0-312-62522-1(7),* 9780312625221, St. Martin's Griffin) St. Martin's Pr.

Jones, Elwynn. Frank's Frantic Friday. 2010. 40p. pap. 16.95 *(978-1-60911-750-4(6),* Eloquent Bks.) Strategic Book Publishing & Rights Agency (SBPRA).

Jones, Harmony. Girl vs. Boy Band: The Right Track. 2016. (ENG.). 240p. (J). 16.99 *(978-1-61963-947-8(5),* 9781619639478, Bloomsbury USA Childrens) Bloomsbury Publishing USA.

—The High Note. 2017. (ENG.). 240p. (J). 16.99 *(978-1-61963-949-2(1),* 9781619639492, Bloomsbury USA Childrens) Bloomsbury Publishing USA.

Jones, James Lucas & Torres, J., eds. Yo Gabba Gabba: Comic Book Time. 2011. (Illus.). 128p. (J). 24.99 *(978-1-934964-49-1(2))* Oni Pr., Inc.

Jones, Jasmine, adapted by. Head over Heels. 2004. (Lizzie Mcguire Ser.). (Illus.). 152p. (J). 12.65 *(978-0-7569-2723-3(4))* Perfection Learning Corp.

—The Importance of Being Gordo. 2005. (Illus.). 138p. (J). *(978-1-4155-7362-4(X))* Disney Pr.

—Importance of Being Gordo. 2005. 138p. (J). lib. bdg. 16.92 *(978-1-4242-0688-9(X))* Fitzgerald Bks.

Jones, Jen. Ashley Goes Viral. Franco, Paula, illus. 2015. (Sleepover Girls Ser.). (ENG.). 128p. (gr. 3-5). pap. 6.95 *(978-1-62370-306-6(9))* Stone Arch Bks.

—Brooke's Big Decision, No. 8. Adams, Liz, illus. 2012. (Team Cheer Ser.). (ENG.). 112p. (gr. 4-4). 25.32 *(978-1-4342-4036-1(3))* Stone Arch Bks.

—Brooke's Big Decision: #8, 1 vol. 2013. (Team Cheer Ser.). (ENG.). 112p. (gr. 4-4). pap. 7.19 *(978-1-4342-4262-4(5),* Team Cheer) Stone Arch Bks.

—Brooke's Quest for Captain, No. 2. 2011. (Team Cheer Ser.). (ENG.). 112p. (gr. 4-4). lib. bdg. 25.32 *(978-1-4342-2995-3(5),* Team Cheer) Stone Arch Bks.

—Brooke's Quest for Captain: # 2, 1 vol. 2012. (Team Cheer Ser.). (ENG.). 112p. (gr. 4-4). pap. 7.19 *(978-1-4342-4250-1(1),* Team Cheer) Stone Arch Bks.

—The Competition for Gaby, No. 4. 2011. (Team Cheer Ser.). (ENG.). 112p. (gr. 4-4). lib. bdg. 25.32 *(978-1-4342-2997-7(1),* Team Cheer) Stone Arch Bks.

—The Competition for Gaby: # 4, 1 vol. 2012. (Team Cheer Ser.). (ENG.). 112p. (gr. 4-4). pap. 7.19 *(978-1-4342-4252-5(8),* Team Cheer) Stone Arch Bks.

—Delaney vs. the Bully. Franco, Paula, illus. 2015. (Sleepover Girls Ser.). (ENG.). 128p. (gr. 3-5). lib. bdg. 22.65 *(978-1-4965-0541-5(7))* Stone Arch Bks.

—Dog Days for Delaney. Franco, Paula, illus. 2014. (Sleepover Girls Ser.). (ENG.). 128p. (gr. 3-5). 22.65 *(978-1-4342-9756-3(X))* Stone Arch Bks.

—Faith & the Camp Snob, No. 1. 2011. (Team Cheer Ser.). (ENG.). 112p. (gr. 4-4). lib. bdg. 25.32 *(978-1-4342-2994-6(7),* Team Cheer) Stone Arch Bks.

—Faith & the Camp Snob: # 1, 1 vol. 2012. (Team Cheer Ser.). (ENG.). 112p. (gr. 4-4). pap. 7.19 *(978-1-4342-4249-5(8),* Team Cheer) Stone Arch Bks.

—Faith & the Dance Drama, No. 5. Adams, Liz, illus. 2012. (Team Cheer Ser.: No. 5). (ENG.). 112p. (gr. 4-4). lib. bdg. 25.32 *(978-1-4342-4033-0(9))* Stone Arch Bks.

—Faith & the Dance Drama: #5, 1 vol. 2013. (Team Cheer Ser.). (ENG.). 112p. (gr. 4-4). pap. 7.19 *(978-1-4342-4263-1(3),* Team Cheer) Stone Arch Bks.

—Lissa & the Fund-Raising Funk, No. 3. 2011. (Team Cheer Ser.). (ENG.). 112p. (gr. 4-4). lib. bdg. 25.32 *(978-1-4342-2996-0(3),* Team Cheer) Stone Arch Bks.

—Lissa & the Fund-Raising Funk: # 3, 1 vol. 2012. (Team Cheer Ser.). (ENG.). 112p. (gr. 4-4). pap. 7.19 *(978-1-4342-4251-8(X),* Team Cheer) Stone Arch Bks.

—Lissa on the Sidelines, No. 6. Adams, Liz, illus. 2012. (Team Cheer Ser.). (ENG.). 112p. (gr. 4-4). lib. bdg. 25.32 *(978-1-4342-4034-7(7))* Stone Arch Bks.

—Lissa on the Sidelines: #6, 1 vol. 2013. (Team Cheer Ser.). (ENG.). 112p. (gr. 4-4). pap. 7.19 *(978-1-4342-4264-8(1),* Team Cheer) Stone Arch Bks.

—Maren Loves Luke Lewis. Franco, Paula, illus. 2014. (Sleepover Girls Ser.). (ENG.). 128p. (gr. 3-5). lib. bdg. 22.65 *(978-1-4342-9755-6(1))* Stone Arch Bks.

—The New Ashley. Franco, Paula, illus. 2014. (Sleepover Girls Ser.). (ENG.). 128p. (gr. 3-5). lib. bdg. 22.65 *(978-1-4342-9758-7(6))* Stone Arch Bks.

—Save Our Squad, Gaby, No. 7. Adams, Liz, illus. 2012. (Team Cheer Ser.). (ENG.). 112p. (gr. 4-4). lib. bdg. 25.32 *(978-1-4342-4035-4(5))* Stone Arch Bks.

—Save Our Squad, Gaby: #7, 1 vol. 2013. (Team Cheer Ser.). (ENG.). 112p. (gr. 4-4). pap. 7.19 *(978-1-4342-4265-5(X),* Team Cheer) Stone Arch Bks.

—Team Cheer. 2013. (Team Cheer Ser.). (ENG.). 112p. (gr. 4-4). pap. 55.60 *(978-1-4342-6326-1(6),* Team Cheer) Stone Arch Bks.

—Willow's Spring Break Adventure. Franco, Paula, illus. 2015. (Sleepover Girls Ser.). (ENG.). 128p. (gr. 3-5). pap. 6.95 *(978-1-62370-305-9(0))* Stone Arch Bks.

—Willow's Boy-Crazy Birthday. Franco, Paula, illus. 2014. (Sleepover Girls Ser.). (ENG.). 128p. (gr. 3-5). lib. bdg. 22.65 *(978-1-4342-9757-0(8))* Stone Arch Bks.

Jones, Karen Lee. Giggle with Friends from Imagination Way. 2007. pap. 11.00 *(978-0-8059-8475-0(5))* Dorrance Publishing Co., Inc.

Jones, Kia. The Adventures of Shamya & Friends: The Thanksgiving Day Wish. 2009. 28p. pap. 12.49 *(978-1-4389-5127-0(2))* AuthorHouse.

Jones, Kim P. Maggie & the Halloween Bandit. 2007. 124p. per. 19.95 *(978-1-60441-158-4(9))* America Star Bks.

Jones, Kip. The Power of a Positive No: Willie Bohanon & Friends Learn the Power of Resisting Peer Pressure. Isely, Chad, illus. 2016. (Urban Character Education Ser.: Vol. 4). (ENG.). 32p. (J). pap. 10.95 *(978-1-944882-06-8(5))* Boys Town Pr.

—The Power of Self-D: Willie Bohanon & Friends Learn the Power of Self-Determination. Isely, Chad, illus. 2014. (ENG.). 32p. (J). pap. 10.95 *(978-1-934490-66-2(0))* Boys Town Pr.

Jones, Lara. Me Gustan Los Besos y Abrazos. (SPA.). 10p. 17.95 *(978-84-272-7866-0(7))* Molino, Editorial ESP. Dist: Distribooks, Inc.

Jones, Lori M. Riley's Heart MacHine. Hammond, Julie, illus. 2012. 16p. pap. 9.95 *(978-1-61633-312-6(X))* Guardian Angel Publishing, Inc.

Jones, Marcia Thornton & Dadey, Debbie. Guys & Ghouls. Francis, Guy, illus. 2006. (Ghostville Elementary Ser.: Bk. 13). 81p. *(978-0-439-79402-2(1))* Scholastic, Inc.

Jones, Mary Noble. Itsy Rabbit & Friends: Itsy's First Adventure. Jones, Mary Noble, illus. 2007. (Illus.). 28p. (J). per. 15.00 *(978-0-9796209-8-0(8))* Righter Publishing Co., Inc.

Jones, Milo. Snow Friends. Lewis, Stephen, illus. 2010. 16p. (J). pap. *(978-0-545-24823-5(X))* Scholastic, Inc.

Jones, Nancy. The Grandpaws. 2005. 57p. pap. 16.95 *(978-1-4137-4778-2(7))* America Star Bks.

Jones, Patrick. Friend or Foe. 2016. (Unbarred Ser.). (ENG.). 120p. (YA). (gr. 6-12). lib. bdg. 27.99 *(978-1-5124-0005-2(X),* Darby Creek) Lerner Publishing Group.

—Friend or Foe. 2016. (Unbarred Ser.). (ENG.). 120p. (YA). (gr. 6-12). pap. 7.99 *(978-1-5124-0095-3(5),* Darby Creek) Lerner Publishing Group.

—Friend or Foe. 2016. (Unbarred Ser.). (ENG.). 120p. (YA). (gr. 6-12). 42.65 *(978-1-5124-0096-0(3),* Darby Creek) Lerner Publishing Group.

Jones, Patrick & Chartier, Brent. At All Costs. 2014. (Red Zone Ser.: 4). 104p. (YA). (gr. 6-12). (ENG.). pap. 7.95 *(978-1-4677-4475-1(1));* lib. bdg. 27.93 *(978-1-4677-2129-5(8))* Lerner Publishing Group. (Darby Creek).

Jones, Rachel. The Adventures of AJ & Hunter: Lost in the Back Yard. sheltrown, karen, illus. 2011. (ENG.). 24p. pap. 6.99 *(978-1-4681-0130-0(7))* CreateSpace Independent Publishing Platform.

Jones, Rebecca C. Matthew & Tillie. Peck, Beth, illus. 2015. 32p. pap. 7.00 *(978-1-61003-532-3(1))* Center for the Collaborative Classroom.

Jones, Rene'. A New Friend for Dilly. Nielson, Ginger, illus. 2011. 32p. pap. 14.99 *(978-0-9826423-0-6(X))* 4RV Publishing, LLC.

Jones, Sandra O. A Voice on the Wind: I Know about the Apple... do You? 2012. 24p. pap. 17.99 *(978-1-4567-3553-1(5))* AuthorHouse.

Jones, Shelley V. & Sprick, Marilyn. Turtle in the Tuba: Read Well Level K Unit 8 Storybook. McDonnell, Kevin, illus. 2004. (Read Well Level K Ser.). 20p. *(978-1-57035-672-8(6))* Cambium Education, Inc.

Jones, Stella J. The Perfect Present. Pedler, Caroline, illus. 2016. (ENG.). 32p. (J). (gr. -1-2). pap. 16.99 *(978-1-68010-036-5(X))* Tiger Tales.

Jones, Yevad. The Sea Quill. 2010. 112p. pap. 14.95 *(978-1-4452-7066-1(8))* Lulu Pr., Inc.

Jonsberg, Barry. The Categorical Universe of Candice Phee. 2014. (ENG.). 242p. (J). (gr. 5-8). 16.99 *(978-1-4521-3351-5(4))* Chronicle Bks. LLC.

Joosse, Barbara M. Evermore Dragon. Cecil, Randy, illus. 2015. (ENG.). 32p. (J). (gr. -1-2). 15.99 *(978-0-7636-6882-2(6))* Candlewick Pr.

—Friends (Mostly) Milian, Tomaso, illus. 2010. (ENG.). 32p. (J). (gr. -1-3). 16.99 *(978-0-06-088221-1(2),* Greenwillow Bks.) HarperCollins Pubs.

—Lovabye Dragon. Cecil, Randy, illus. 2012. (ENG.). 32p. (J). (gr. -1-2). 15.99 *(978-0-7636-5408-5(6))* Candlewick Pr.

Jordan, Apple. Driving Buddies. Disney Storybook Artists Staff & Random House Disney Staff, illus. 2006. (Step into Reading Ser.). (ENG.). 32p. (J). (gr. k-3). pap. 3.99 *(978-0-7364-2339-7(7),* RH/Disney) Random Hse. Children's Bks.

Jordan, Rosa. The Last Wild Place, 1 vol. 2008. (ENG.). 256p. (J). (gr. 3-7). 15.95 *(978-1-56145-458-7(3),* Peachtree Junior) Peachtree Pubs.

—Wild Spirits. 2010. (ENG.). 272p. (J). (gr. 6). pap. 12.99 *(978-1-55488-729-3(1))* Dundurn CAN. Dist: Ingram Publisher Services.

Jorgensen, Norman & Harrison-Lever, Brian. The Call of the Osprey. 2004. (Illus.). 36p. (J). 22.50 *(978-1-920731-85-4(7))* Fremantle Pr. AUS. Dist: Independent Pubs. Group.

Joseph, Lila. The Boy Who Could Talk to Animals. 2008. 36p. pap. 18.95 *(978-1-4327-2873-1(3))* Outskirts Pr., Inc.

Journey to see the King. 2006. (J). *(978-0-9791168-0-3(5))* Lighthouse Bk. Publishing.

Joy, Linda. Little Wave & the Mystery of the Lost Whale. 2011. 28p. pap. 15.99 *(978-1-4628-9711-7(8))* Xlibris Corp.

Joy, N. The Secret Olivia Told Me. Devard, Nancy, illus. 2007. 32p. (J). (gr. -1-3). 16.95 *(978-1-933491-08-0(6))* Just Us Bks., Inc.

Joyce, William. Rolie Polie Olie. Joyce, William, illus. 2017. (World of William Joyce Ser.). (ENG., Illus.). 48p. (J). (gr. -1-2). 17.99 ***(978-1-4814-8957-7(7),*** Atheneum Bks. for Young Readers) Simon & Schuster Children's Publishing.

Joyner, Andrew. Boris for the Win. 2013. (Boris Ser.: 3). (ENG.). 80p. (J). (gr. k-2). pap. 4.99 *(978-0-545-48449-7(9))* Scholastic, Inc.

—Boris for the Win. 2013. (Boris Ser.: 3). lib. bdg. 14.75 *(978-0-606-31976-8(X),* Turtleback) Turtleback Bks.

—Boris Sees the Light. 2013. (Boris Ser.: 4). (ENG.). 80p. (J). (gr. k-2). pap. 4.99 *(978-0-545-48454-1(5))* Scholastic, Inc.

—Boris Sees the Light. 2013. (Boris Ser.: 4). lib. bdg. 14.75 *(978-0-606-32363-5(5),* Turtleback) Turtleback Bks.

Juby, Susan. The Fashion Committee. 2017. (ENG.). 320p. (YA). (gr. 7). 18.99 *(978-0-451-46878-9(3),* Viking Books for Young Readers) Penguin Young Readers Group.

Juckes, Deborah Sioux. Meesha, Guardian of Grand Mountain: Book One of the Guardian Series. McCleary, Twila, illus. 2005. (Guardian Ser.: Bk. 1). (YA). pap. 12.95 *(978-0-9767748-0-8(1))* Red Earth Publishing.

—Meesha, Guardian of Grand Mountain: Book One of the Guardian Series. McCleary, Twila, illus. 2005. (YA). 18.95 *(978-0-9767748-1-5(X))* Red Earth Publishing.

Judd, Merlynne. Circle of Friendship. 2010. 76p. pap. 24.99 *(978-1-4520-6783-4(X))* AuthorHouse.

Jude, Sarah. The May Queen Murders. 2016. (ENG.). 304p. (YA). (gr. 9). 17.99 *(978-0-544-64041-2(1),* HMH Books For Young Readers) Houghton Mifflin Harcourt Publishing Co.

Jude, Tracey. Mr. Topaz Takes a Walk. 2005. 43p. (J). spiral bd. 16.99 *(978-1-4116-5691-8(1))* Lulu Pr., Inc.

Judge, Chris. The Snow Beast. Judge, Chris, illus. 2015. (ENG., Illus.). 32p. (J). (gr. -1-3). 17.99 *(978-1-4677-9313-1(2))* Andersen Pr. GBR. Dist: Lerner Publishing Group.

Jukes, Mavis. The New Kid. (ENG.). 288p. (J). 2012. (gr. 4-7). 7.99 *(978-0-375-85367-8(7),* Yearling) 2011. (gr. 3-7). 14.99 *(978-0-375-85879-6(2),* Knopf Bks. for Young Readers) Random Hse. Children's Bks.

Jules, Jacqueline. Picnic at Camp Shalom. Melmon, Deborah, illus. 2011. (ENG.). 32p. (J). (gr. k-3). pap. 7.95 *(978-0-7613-6662-1(8),* Kar-Ben Publishing) Lerner Publishing Group.

Jules, Jacqueline & Hechtkopf, Jacqueline. Picnic at Camp Shalom. Melmon, Deborah, illus. 2011. (Kar-Ben Favorites Ser.). (ENG.). 32p. (J). (gr. k-3). 17.95 *(978-0-7613-6661-4(X),* Kar-Ben Publishing) Lerner Publishing Group.

Julie Marie. The Adventures of Fred the Five Pound Note. 2009. (Illus.). 52p. pap. 10.49 *(978-1-4389-4921-5(9))* AuthorHouse.

June-Bug. Sweetbread & Tattletale. 2012. 32p. 24.95 *(978-1-4626-6040-7(1))* America Star Bks.

Jung, Mike. Unidentified Suburban Object. 2016. (ENG.). 272p. (J). (gr. 3-7). 16.99 *(978-0-545-78226-5(0),* Levine, Arthur A. Bks.) Scholastic, Inc.

Jungle Limbo. l.t. ed. 2003. (Illus.). 31p. (J). spiral bd. 7.95 *(978-0-9741074-0-0(9))* Catterfly Pr.

Juscik, Andy. Tear Catchers. 2010. 36p. pap. 14.95 *(978-1-60911-488-6(4),* Eloquent Bks.) Strategic Book Publishing & Rights Agency (SBPRA).

Juslin, Lee. Nurse Frosty & the Wond'ear'ful Adventure. 2010. 32p. pap. 21.99 *(978-0-557-52512-6(8))* Lulu Pr., Inc.

Just for Boys. 2008. (Amazing Body Growing Up Ser.). 96p. *(978-1-4075-1570-0(5))* Parragon, Inc.

Justesen, Kim Williams. Kiss, Kiss, Bark! 2nd ed. 2012. (ENG.). 176p. (J). (gr. 4). pap. 8.95 *(978-1-933718-76-7(5))* Tanglewood Pr.

Justice, Tonya. Millie Mathison's Imagination: Cowboys, Indians, & no Red Cards. 2009. 24p. pap. 11.99 *(978-1-4389-9519-9(9))* AuthorHouse.

K. B. Kendricks. Travis Taylor & the Dragon Quest. 2010. 344p. 29.95 *(978-1-4502-0261-9(6));* pap. 19.95 *(978-1-4502-0259-6(4))* iUniverse, Inc.

Kadence, Sam. On the Right Track. 2016. (ENG., Illus.). (YA). (gr. 9-12). 24.99 ***(978-1-63533-057-1(2))*** 2013. 184p. pap. 14.99 *(978-1-62798-069-2(5))* Dreamspinner Pr. (Harmony Ink Pr.).

Kadilak, Kathy. Tommy Finds His Forever Home. 2009. 28p. pap. 12.49 *(978-1-4490-0177-3(7))* AuthorHouse.

Kadohata, Cynthia. Kira-Kira. (ENG., Illus.). (J). (gr. 5-9). 2004. 256p. 17.99 *(978-0-689-85639-6(3))* 2006. 272p. reprint ed. pap. 7.99 *(978-0-689-85640-2(7))* Simon & Schuster Children's Publishing. (Atheneum Bks. for Young Readers).

Kagiliery, Theodore. Angelo & Peter. 2012. 32p. pap. 19.99 *(978-1-4772-2893-7(4))* AuthorHouse.

Kain, P. G. Dramatic Pause. 2012. (Commercial Breaks Ser.: 3). (ENG.). 288p. (J). (gr. 4-9). pap. 6.99 *(978-1-4169-9788-7(1),* Aladdin) Simon & Schuster Children's Publishing.

—The Social Experiments of Dorie Dilts: Dumped by Popular Demand. 2007. (Mix Ser.). (ENG., Illus.). 272p. (J). (gr. 4-8). pap. 5.99 *(978-1-4169-3519-3(3),* Simon & Schuster/Paula Wiseman Bks.) Simon & Schuster/Paula Wiseman Bks.

—The Social Experiments of Dorie Dilts: The School for Cool. 2008. (Mix Ser.). (ENG.). 288p. (J). (gr. 4-8). pap. 13.99 *(978-1-4169-3520-9(7),* Simon & Schuster/Paula Wiseman Bks.) Simon & Schuster/Paula Wiseman Bks.

Kai's Cake. 2004. (Illus.). 23p. (J). pap. *(978-0-9749469-0-0(7))* Crunchpeep Media.

Kale, Ann Stephanian. Artie - The Ugly Frog. Kale, Ann Stephanian, illus. 2004. (Illus.). 20p. (J). pap. 10.00 *(978-0-9704131-6-1(5))* Abril BookStore & Publishing.

Kam, Jennifer Wolf. Devin Rhodes Is Dead. 2014. (YA). (ENG.). 240p. (gr. 7). 16.95 *(978-1-934133-59-0(0),* Mackinac Island Press, Inc.); 228p. *(978-1-60734-706-4(7))* Charlesbridge Publishing, Inc.

Kanakia, Rahul. Enter Title Here. 2017. (ENG.). 352p. (YA). (gr. 9-17). pap. 9.99 ***(978-1-4847-3406-3(8))*** Hyperion Bks. for Children.

Kane, P. B. & Kane, Paul. The Rainbow Man. 2013. 162p. pap. 9.99 *(978-0-9823322-3-8(8))* Rocket Ride Bks.

Kaneko, Amanda Bullard. Darza the Little Dragon. Hildebrandt, Lowell, illus. 2010. 28p. 13.99 *(978-1-4520-4198-8(9))* AuthorHouse.

Kanemaki, Tomoco, et al. Kingdom Hearts II. 2017. (Kingdom Hearts II: the Novel Ser.: 1). (ENG.). 272p. pap. 16.00 ***(978-0-316-47193-0(3),*** Yen Pr.) Orbit.

Kang, A. N. Papillon, Book 2 Papillon Goes to the Vet. Kang, A. N., illus. 2017. (Papillon Ser.). (ENG., Illus.). 40p. (J). (gr. -1-k). 16.99 ***(978-1-4847-2881-9(5))*** Hyperion Bks. for Children.

Kann, Victoria. Cherry Blossom. Kann, Victoria, illus. 2015. (I Can Read Level 1 Ser.). (ENG., Illus.). 32p. (J). (gr. -1-3). 16.99 *(978-0-06-224593-9(7));* pap. 3.99 *(978-0-06-224594-6(5))* HarperCollins Pubs.

—Pinkalicious: Pinkie Promise. Kann, Victoria, illus. 2011. (I Can Read Level 1 Ser.). (ENG., Illus.). 32p. (J). (gr. -1-3). pap. 3.99 *(978-0-06-192887-1(9))* HarperCollins Pubs.

—Pinkalicious: Fashion Fun. Kann, Victoria, illus. 2016. (I Can Read Level 1 Ser.). (Illus.). 32p. (J). (gr. -1-3). pap. 3.99 *(978-0-06-241076-4(8))* HarperCollins Pubs.

—Pinkalicious: Tutu-Rrific. Kann, Victoria, illus. 2017. (I Can Read Level 1 Ser.). (Illus.). 40p. (J). (gr. -1-3). 9.99 ***(978-0-06-257278-3(4))*** HarperCollins Pubs.

—Pinkie Promise. Kann, Victoria, illus. 2011. (I Can Read Level 1 Ser.). (ENG., Illus.). 32p. (J). (gr. -1-3). 16.99 *(978-0-06-192888-8(7))* HarperCollins Pubs.

—Tutu-Rrific! 2014. (Pinkalicious I Can Read Ser.). (J). lib. bdg. 13.55 *(978-0-606-35958-0(3))* Turtleback Bks.

—Tutu-Rrific! Pinkalicious. Kann, Victoria, illus. 2014. (I Can Read Level 1 Ser.). (ENG., Illus.). 32p. (J). (gr. -1-3). pap. 3.99 *(978-0-06-218795-6(3))* HarperCollins Pubs.

Kantner, Seth. Pup & Pokey. Hill, Beth, illus. 2014. 48p. pap. 14.95 *(978-1-60223-241-9(5))* Univ. of Alaska Pr.

Kantor, Melissa. Maybe One Day. 2014. (ENG.). 400p. (YA). (gr. 8). 17.99 *(978-0-06-227920-0(3),* HarperTeen) HarperCollins Pubs.

Karalius, Kimberly. Love Charms & Other Catastrophes. 2016. (Grimbaud Ser.). (ENG.). 384p. (YA). pap. 10.99 *(978-1-250-08404-0(0),* 9781250084040) Feiwel & Friends.

Karasyov, Carrie & Kargman, Jill. Jet Set. 2008. 256p. (J). (gr. 7-18). 16.99 *(978-0-06-143177-7(X))* HarperCollins Pubs.

Karen Bisset. Rahab's Story. 2010. 20p. 8.99 *(978-1-4251-8724-8(2))* Trafford Publishing.

Kares, P. S. The Prairie Orphans' Journey. 2008. 32p. per. 24.95 *(978-1-4241-8396-8(0))* America Star Bks.

Kargbo, Ms Mariatu. Three Themne Titi Girls. 2013. 24p. (J). pap. 24.95 *(978-1-63004-790-0(2))* America Star Bks.

Kargman, Jill & Karasyov, Carrie. Bittersweet Sixteen. 2006. (YA). (gr. 7-12). (ENG.). 240p. 15.99 *(978-0-06-077844-6(X));* 230p. lib. bdg. 16.89 *(978-0-06-077845-3(8))* HarperCollins Pubs.

Karim, Sheba. That Thing We Call a Heart. 2017. 288p. (YA). (gr. 8). 17.99 *(978-0-06-244570-4(7),* HarperTeen) HarperCollins Pubs.

Karol, Leslee. Sylvie the Littlest Guardian Angel: Cassie Makes a Friend. 2013. 48p. pap. 21.99 *(978-1-4817-0864-7(3))* AuthorHouse.

Karr, Kathleen. Worlds Apart, 0 vols. unabr. ed. 2013. (ENG.). 208p. (J). (gr. 5-7). pap. 9.99 *(978-1-4778-1710-0(7),* 9781477817100, Amazon Children's Publishing) Amazon Publishing.

Kasischke, Laura. Feathered. 2008. (ENG.). 272p. (YA). (gr. 9-18). 16.99 *(978-0-06-081317-8(2),* HarperTeen) HarperCollins Pubs.

Kasper, Kathy. Mary Jean Learns to Shine. 2008. 51p. pap. 16.95 *(978-1-60441-680-0(7))* America Star Bks.

Kasza, Keiko. Silly Goose's Big Story. Kasza, Keiko, illus. 2012. (ENG., Illus.). 32p. (J). (gr. -1-k). 16.99 *(978-0-399-25542-7(7),* G.P. Putnam's Sons Books for Young Readers) Penguin Young Readers Group.

Katcher, Brian. Almost Perfect. 2010. (ENG.). 368p. (YA). (gr. 9). pap. 9.99 *(978-0-385-73665-7(7),* Delacorte Bks. for Young Readers) Random Hse. Children's Bks.

—Playing with Matches. 2009. (ENG.). 304p. (YA). (gr. 9). mass mkt. 8.99 *(978-0-385-73545-2(6),* Laurel Leaf) Random Hse. Children's Bks.

Katie, Byron & Wilhelm, Hans. Tiger-Tiger, Is It True? Four Questions to Make You Smile Again. 2009. (ENG., Illus.). 32p. 14.95 *(978-1-4019-2560-4(X),* 1076) Hay Hse., Inc.

Kats, Jewel. Teddy Bear Princess: A Story about Sharing & Caring. Arts, Richa Kinra, illus. 2012. 24p. (-18). pap. 13.95 *(978-1-61599-163-1(8),* Marvelous Spirit Pr.) Loving Healing Pr., Inc.

Katschke, Judy, et al. Shore Thing. 2003. (ENG., Illus.). 112p. *(978-0-00-714464-8(4),* HarperCollins Children's Bks.) HarperCollins Pubs. Ltd.

Katy Duck & the Secret Valentine. 2014. (Katy Duck Ser.). (ENG., Illus.). 24p. (J). (gr. -1-1). pap. 3.99 *(978-1-4424-9809-9(9),* Simon Spotlight) Simon Spotlight.

Katz, Bebe Weinberg. A Best Friend for Claudia. 2008. 77p. pap. 19.95 *(978-1-60563-485-2(9))* America Star Bks.

Katz, Karin Jill. There's a Fly in My Soup. 2012. 16p. pap. 15.99 *(978-1-4772-6331-0(4))* AuthorHouse.

Kauffman, Tracy. Gwendolyn's Wish. 2012. (-18). 24p. 24.95 *(978-1-62709-555-6(1));* 20p. pap. 24.95 *(978-1-4626-7207-3(8))* America Star Bks.

Kay, Cassandra. A Week in the Life of Mertyle. 2009. 96p. pap. 10.49 *(978-1-4389-4049-6(1))* AuthorHouse.

Kay, L. M. Frederick's Birthday Surprise. 2009. 36p. pap. 24.95 *(978-1-60836-944-7(7))* America Star Bks.

Kay, Regina. I Just Want to Be Liked. Kinard, Brandi, illus. 2013. (J). 19.95 *(978-1-56411-592-8(5),* CB Publishing & Design) UBUS Communications Systems.

Kayaalp, Suzan. The Adventures of Lucky the Duck. 2010. 90p. pap. 9.95 *(978-1-60693-716-7(2),* Eloquent Bks.) Strategic Book Publishing & Rights Agency (SBPRA).

Kaye, Marilyn. Jill's Happy Un-Birthday: The after School Club. 2014. (ENG., Illus.). 80p. (J). (gr. 3-7). pap. 13.99 *(978-1-4814-2885-9(3),* Simon & Schuster/Paula Wiseman Bks.) Simon & Schuster/Paula Wiseman Bks.

Kaye, Shelley. Saving Private Woods. 2012. (Illus.). 76p. pap. 8.50 *(978-1-78035-510-8(6),* Fastprint Publishing) Upfront Publishing Ltd. GBR. Dist: Printondemand-worldwide.com.

Kear, Nicole C. The Fix-It Friends: Have No Fear! Dockray, Tracy, illus. 2017. (Fix-It Friends Ser.: 1). (ENG.). 144p. (J). pap. 5.99 *(978-1-250-08584-9(5),* 9781250085849) Imprint IND. Dist: Macmillan.

—The Fix-It Friends: Have No Fear! Dockray, Tracy, illus. 2017. (Fix-It Friends Ser.). (ENG.). 144p. (J). 16.99 *(978-1-250-11577-5(9),* 9781250115775) Imprint IND. Dist: Macmillan.

—The Fix-It Friends: Sticks & Stones. Dockray, Tracy, illus. 2017. (Fix-It Friends Ser.: 2). (ENG.). 144p. (J). pap. 5.99 *(978-1-250-08586-3(1),* 9781250085863) Imprint IND. Dist: Macmillan.

—The Fix-It Friends: the Show Must Go On. Dockray, Tracy, illus. 2017. (Fix-It Friends Ser.: 3). (ENG.). 160p. (J). pap. 5.99 ***(978-1-250-08668-6(X),*** 9781250086686) Imprint IND. Dist: Macmillan.

—The Fix-It Friends: Wish You Were Here. Dockray, Tracy, illus. 2017. (Fix-It Friends Ser.: 4). (ENG.). 160p. (J). pap. 5.99 ***(978-1-250-08670-9(1),*** 9781250086709) Imprint IND. Dist: Macmillan.

Keating, Jess. How to Outfox Your Friends When You Don't Have a Clue. 2015. (My Life Is a Zoo Ser.: 3). (ENG.). 304p. (J). (gr. 4-7). pap. 7.99 *(978-1-4926-1794-5(6),* 9781492617945, Sourcebooks Jabberwocky) Sourcebooks, Inc.

Keefer, Nick T. Pear-A-Dise. Bowser, Sean T., illus. 2013. 28p. pap. 12.95 *(978-0-9894814-6-5(8))* Warren Publishing, Inc.

Keeling, Evan. CrumbSnatchers. 2008. 60p. (J). per. 5.95 *(978-0-9796902-4-2(2))* Silent Devil Productions.

Keenan-Bolger, Andrew, et al. Jack & Louisa - Act 1. Webster, Kyle T., illus. 2015. (Jack & Louisa Ser.: 1). (ENG.). 240p. (J). (gr. 3-7). bds. 16.99 *(978-0-448-47839-5(0),* Grosset & Dunlap) Penguin Young Readers Group.

Keene, Carolyn. April Fool's Day. Pamintuan, Macky, illus. 2009. (Nancy Drew & the Clue Crew Ser.: 19). (ENG.). 96p. (J). (gr. 1-4). pap. 5.99 *(978-1-4169-7518-2(7),* Aladdin) Simon & Schuster Children's Publishing.

—Babysitting Bandit. Pamintuan, Macky, illus. 2009. (Nancy Drew & the Clue Crew Ser.: 23). (ENG.). 96p. (J). (gr. 1-4). pap. 5.99 *(978-1-4169-7813-8(5),* Aladdin) Simon & Schuster Children's Publishing.

—Candy Kingdom Chaos. Francis, Peter, illus. 2017. (Nancy Drew Clue Book Ser.: 7). (ENG.). 96p. (J). (gr. 1-4). pap. 5.99 *(978-1-4814-5826-9(4),* Simon & Schuster/Paula Wiseman Bks.) Simon & Schuster/Paula Wiseman Bks.

—Cape Mermaid Mystery. Pamintuan, Macky, illus. 2012. (Nancy Drew & the Clue Crew Ser.: 32). (ENG.). 96p. (J). (gr. 1-4). pap. 5.99 *(978-1-4424-4625-0(0),* Aladdin) Simon & Schuster Children's Publishing.

—Cat Burglar Caper. Pamintuan, Macky, illus. 2010. (Nancy Drew & the Clue Crew Ser.: 27). (ENG.). 96p. (J). (gr. 1-4). pap. 5.99 *(978-1-4169-9436-7(X),* Aladdin) Simon & Schuster Children's Publishing.

—Last Lemonade Standing. Francis, Peter, illus. 2015. (Nancy Drew Clue Book Ser.: 2). (ENG.). 96p. (J). (gr. 1-4). pap. 5.99 *(978-1-4814-3748-6(8),* Aladdin) Simon & Schuster Children's Publishing.

—Pets on Parade. Francis, Peter, illus. 2016. (Nancy Drew Clue Book Ser.: 6). (ENG.). 96p. (J). (gr. 1-4). pap. 5.99 *(978-1-4814-5823-8(X),* Aladdin) Simon & Schuster Children's Publishing.

—Thanksgiving Thief. Pamintuan, Macky, illus. 2008. (Nancy Drew & the Clue Crew Ser.: 16). (ENG.). 96p. (J). (gr. 1-4). pap. 5.99 *(978-1-4169-6777-4(X),* Aladdin) Simon & Schuster Children's Publishing.

Kehret, Peg. The Ghost's Grave. 2007. 224p. pap. 5.99 *(978-0-14-280819-1(9),* Puffin) Penguin Publishing Group.

—The Ghost's Grave. 2007. (ENG.). 224p. (J). (gr. 5-18). 6.99 *(978-0-14-240819-3(0),* Puffin Books) Penguin Young Readers Group.

Kehret, Peg & the Cat, Pete. The Stranger Next Door. 2008. (Pete the Cat Ser.). (ENG.). 176p. (J). (gr. 3-7). 5.99 *(978-0-14-241248-0(1),* Puffin Books) Penguin Young Readers Group.

—Trapped! 2008. (Pete the Cat Ser.). (ENG.). 192p. (J). (gr. 3-7). 5.99 *(978-0-14-241189-6(2),* Puffin Books) Penguin Young Readers Group.

Keil, Melissa. Life in Outer Space, 1 vol. (ENG.). 320p. (YA). (gr. 7-11). 2016. pap. 9.95 ***(978-1-56145-975-9(5))*** 2013. 16.95 *(978-1-56145-742-7(6))* Peachtree Pubs.

Keiser, Frances R. Annie the River Otter: The Adventures of Pelican Pete. Keiser, Hugh M., illus. I.t. ed. 2006. (ENG.). 34p. (J). 19.99 *(978-0-9668845-4-8(X))* Sagaponack Bks.

Keith, Patty J. I Wish I Was a Mallard but God Made Me a Pekin Instead. Keith, Patty J., photos by. 2013. (Illus.). 32p. pap. 12.95 *(978-0-9893303-0-5(3))* Patty's Blooming Words.

—Will You Be My Friend? Even If I Am Different from You. Keith, Patty J., photos by. 2013. (Illus.). 36p. pap. 12.95 *(978-0-615-78050-4(4))* Patty's Blooming Words.

Keithley, Laura Lee. Ellie's Big Day. Holliday, Holly, illus. 2008. 40p. pap. 24.95 *(978-1-60672-474-3(6))* America Star Bks.

Kellenbarger, Sandy Hurst. Magic Gnomes. 2012. 24p. (gr. 2-4). pap. 14.93 *(978-1-4669-6526-3(6))* Trafford Publishing.

Keller, Holly. Farfallina & Marcel. Keller, Holly, illus. 2005. (ENG., Illus.). 32p. (J). (gr. -1-4). reprint ed. pap. 6.99 *(978-0-06-443872-8(4),* Greenwillow Bks.) HarperCollins Pubs.

—Farfallina & Marcel. Keller, Holly, illus. 2005. (Illus.). (gr. -1-3). 17.00 *(978-0-7569-5785-8(0))* Perfection Learning Corp.

—Help! A Story of Friendship. Keller, Holly, illus. 2007. (ENG., Illus.). 40p. (J). (gr. -1-3). 16.99 *(978-0-06-123913-7(5),* Greenwillow Bks.) HarperCollins Pubs.

—Sophie's Window. Keller, Holly, illus. 2005. (Illus.). 32p. (J). 16.89 *(978-0-06-056283-0(8))* HarperCollins Pubs.

Keller, Laurie. Arnie the Doughnut. Keller, Laurie, illus. 2005. (Illus.). (J). (gr. k-4). 29.95 *(978-0-439-76641-8(9),* WHCD649) Weston Woods Studios, Inc.

Keller, William B. Olivia & the Mystery. 2011. 88p. pap. 14.95 *(978-1-4327-7636-7(3))* Outskirts Pr., Inc.

Kelley, Jane. The Book of Dares for Lost Friends. 2015. (ENG.). 304p. (J). (gr. 3-7). 16.99 *(978-1-250-05087-8(1),* 9781250050878) Feiwel & Friends.

—The Desperate Adventures of Zeno & Alya. 2013. (ENG.). 208p. (J). (gr. 3-7). 15.99 *(978-1-250-02348-3(3),* 9781250023483) Feiwel & Friends.

—Nature Girl. 2011. (ENG., Illus.). 256p. (J). (gr. 3-7). pap. 6.99 *(978-0-375-85635-8(8),* Yearling) Random Hse. Children's Bks.

Kelley Ludovici, Joanne Dzioba. Maggie Stone Becomes Morning Starr. 2013. 28p. pap. 16.09 *(978-1-4669-9291-7(3))* Trafford Publishing.

Kelley, Marty. The Best Friend Bandit. Kelley, Marty, illus. 2017. (Molly Mac Ser.). (ENG., Illus.). 56p. (gr. k-2). lib. bdg. 22.65 *(978-1-5158-0836-7(X))* Picture Window Bks.

Kelly, Cheryl. Adam the Adventurous Ant. 2011. 24p. pap. 15.99 *(978-1-4568-6366-1(5))* Xlibris Corp.

Kelly, David A. The Football Fumble. Brundage, Scott, illus. 2016. (Most Valuable Players Ser.: 3). (ENG.). 128p. (J). (gr. 1-4). 4.99 *(978-0-553-51325-7(7),* Random Hse. Bks. for Young Readers) Random Hse. Children's Bks.

—The Gold Medal Mess. Brundage, Scott, illus. 2016. (Most Valuable Players Ser.: 1). (ENG.). 128p. (J). (gr. 1-4). 4.99 *(978-0-553-51319-6(2),* Random Hse. Bks. for Young Readers) Random Hse. Children's Bks.

—The Soccer Surprise. Brundage, Scott, illus. 2016. (Most Valuable Players Ser.: 2). (ENG.). 128p. (J). (gr. 1-4). 4.99 *(978-0-553-51322-6(2),* Random Hse. Bks. for Young Readers) Random Hse. Children's Bks.

Kelly, Erin Entrada. Hello, Universe. Roxas, Isabel, illus. 2017. 320p. (J). (gr. 3-7). 16.99 *(978-0-06-241415-1(1),* Greenwillow Bks.) HarperCollins Pubs.

Kelly, Joan L. The Dna Connection: Tannenhauser's Theory. 2013. 198p. pap. 9.99 *(978-1-936453-25-2(8))* Bezalel Bks.

Kelly, Lynda. Magazine-Page Pony. 2013. 190p. pap. *(978-1-903053-37-9(4))* Kelly Pubns.

Kelly, Margo. Unlocked. 2016. (ENG.). 304p. (YA). 17.99 *(978-1-4405-9359-8(0),* Simon Pulse) Simon Pulse.

Kelly, Mij & Fuge, Charles. Friendly Day. 2013. (ENG., Illus.). 32p. (J). (gr. -1-1). pap. 8.99 *(978-1-4380-0345-0(5))* Barron's Educational Series, Inc.

Kelly, Theresa. Tony the Pony: Bugs Are Not Bad. Sampson, Jody, illus. 2005. (J). per. 7.95 *(978-1-59466-030-6(1))* Port Town Publishing.

Kelsey, Annie. Pippa Morgan's Diary. Larsen, Kate, illus. 2015. (Pippa Morgan's Diary Ser.: 1). (ENG.). 160p. (J). (gr. 3-7). 12.99 *(978-1-4926-2328-1(8),* 9781492623281, Sourcebooks Jabberwocky) Sourcebooks, Inc.

Kelsey-Livin, Barbara. The Monkey & the Frog. 2012. 30p. 24.95 *(978-1-4626-6161-9(0))* America Star Bks.

Kelton, G F. The Land of Cigam. 2007. 144p. per. 10.95 *(978-0-595-46947-5(7))* iUniverse, Inc.

Kemnitz, Dianna. King Eli Speaks to Jack. 2012. 38p. 24.95 *(978-1-4626-6727-7(9))* America Star Bks.

—Meet Jack & His New Friend. 2011. 36p. pap. 24.95 *(978-1-4560-8776-0(2))* America Star Bks.

—A New Hat for Jack. 2012. 38p. 24.95 *(978-1-4626-6816-8(X))* America Star Bks.

Kemp, Hill & Kemp, Siena. Lucky Penny. 2007. 88p. pap. 6.95 *(978-1-933090-87-0(1))* Guardian Angel Publishing, Inc.

Kemp, Kristin. The Boy in the Striped Pajamas: An Instructional Guide for Literature. 2015. (Great Works). (ENG., Illus.). 72p. (gr. 4-8). pap. 9.99 *(978-1-4807-8507-6(5))* Shell Educational Publishing.

—Of Mice & Men: An Instructional Guide for Literature. 2015. (Great Works). (ENG., Illus.). 72p. (gr. 9-12). pap. 9.99 *(978-1-4807-8508-3(3))* Shell Educational Publishing.

Kendall, Carolyn. Phibby & Ribby. 2013. 32p. pap. *(978-1-4602-0387-3(9))* FriesenPress.

Kendall, Gillian Murray. The Garden of Darkness. 2014. (ENG.). 336p. (YA). (gr. 6-12). pap. 9.99 *(978-1-78108-248-5(0),* Ravenstone) Rebellion GBR. Dist: Simon & Schuster, Inc.

Kendrick, Evelyn R. Molly & Bailey Make New Friends, 1 vol. 2010. 24p. pap. 24.95 *(978-1-4489-9169-3(2))* PublishAmerica, Inc.

Kenley, Holli. Another Way: A Novel. 2015. 155p. (YA). pap. *(978-1-61599-259-1(6))* Loving Healing Pr., Inc.

Kenneally, Miranda. Jesse's Girl. 2015. (Hundred Oaks Ser.: Bk. 6). (ENG.). 304p. (YA). (gr. 8-12). 16.99 *(978-1-4022-8482-3(9),* 9781402284823) Sourcebooks, Inc.

Kennedy. Dabbling Doezee. 2014. (ENG., Illus.). (J). 16.95 *(978-0-9915194-0-8(X))* Fabula.

Kennedy, J. Aday. Cobbledom's Curse. Foster, Jack, illus. 2012. 20p. pap. 9.95 *(978-1-61633-265-5(4))* Guardian Angel Publishing, Inc.

—Itcha Itcha Goo Goo Blues. Foster, Jack, illus. 2012. 20p. pap. 10.95 *(978-1-61633-294-5(8))* Guardian Angel Publishing, Inc.

Kennedy, Leo B. Devin & the Greedy Ferret. 2013. 86p. (gr. 4-6). pap. 9.99 *(978-1-4497-8429-4(1),* WestBow Pr.) Author Solutions, Inc.

Kennedy, Marlane. Disaster Strikes #1: Earthquake Shock. 2014. (Disaster Strikes Ser.: 1). (ENG.). 128p. (J). (gr. 2-5). pap. 4.99 *(978-0-545-53044-6(X),* Scholastic Paperbacks) Scholastic, Inc.

Kennedy, Triona. Benny Bunny. 2010. 28p. pap. 12.50 *(978-1-60860-559-0(0),* Eloquent Bks.) Strategic Book Publishing & Rights Agency (SBPRA).

Kenner, Crystal R. The King of All Tickle Bugs & Other Stories. 2011. (Illus.). 124p. (gr. -1). pap. 10.95 *(978-1-4502-9466-9(9))* iUniverse, Inc.

Kenney, Cindy. Project Precious Paws, Bk. 3. 2009. 86p. (J). 9.95 *(978-0-9817159-5-7(8));* pap. 5.99 *(978-0-9817159-4-0(X))* Precious Moments, Inc.

Kent, Renee Holmes. Adventures in Misty Falls, Vol. 8. 2004. (Adventures in Misty Falls Ser.: Vol. 8). (Illus.). 100p. (gr. 4-7). pap. 4.99 *(978-1-56309-456-9(8),* N017104) Woman's Missionary Union.

—Best Friends Forever?, Vol. 2. 2004. (Adventures in Misty Falls Ser.: Bk. 2). (Illus.). 100p. (gr. 4-7). pap. 4.99 *(978-1-56309-734-8(6),* N007117) New Hope Pubs.

—Girl Talk, Vol. 7. 2004. (Adventures in Misty Falls Ser.: Vol. 7). (Illus.). 100p. (J). (gr. 4-7). pap. 4.99 *(978-1-56309-455-2(X),* N017103) New Hope Pubs.

Keough, Kevin. Snoozy Dog: And Curly Cat Too! 2011. 24p. (gr. -1). pap. 12.98 *(978-1-4389-4794-5(1))* AuthorHouse.

Kephart, Beth. The Heart Is Not a Size. 2010. (ENG.). 256p. (YA). (gr. 8-18). 16.99 *(978-0-06-147048-6(1),* HarperTeen) HarperCollins Pubs.

Keplinger, Kody. Lying Out Loud: A Companion to the DUFF. 2015. (ENG.). 288p. (J). (gr. 9). 17.99 *(978-0-545-83109-3(1))* Scholastic, Inc.

—Lying Out Loud: a Companion to the DUFF. 2016. (ENG.). 304p. (J). (gr. 9). pap. 9.99 *(978-0-545-83110-9(5),* Scholastic Paperbacks) Scholastic, Inc.

—Run. (ENG.). 304p. (gr. 9). 2017. (J). pap. 10.99 ***(978-0-545-83114-7(8),*** Scholastic Paperbacks) 2016. (YA). 17.99 *(978-0-545-83113-0(X),* Scholastic Pr.) Scholastic, Inc.

Keplinger, Kody. The Swift Boys & Me. 2014. (ENG.). 272p. (J). (gr. 3-7). 16.99 *(978-0-545-56200-3(7),* Scholastic Pr.) Scholastic, Inc.

Kerbel, Deborah. Feathered. 2016. (ENG., Illus.). 146p. (J). (gr. 4-8). 15.95 *(978-1-77138-341-7(0))* Kids Can Pr., Ltd. CAN. Dist: Hachette Bk. Group.

Kerr, Esme. The Girl with the Glass Bird. 2015. (ENG.). 272p. (J). (gr. 3-7). 16.99 *(978-0-545-69984-6(3))* Scholastic, Inc.

—Mischief at Midnight. 2016. (ENG.). 272p. (J). (gr. 3-7). 16.99 *(978-0-545-90403-2(X),* Chicken Hse., The) Scholastic, Inc.

Kerr, M. E., pseud. The Son of Someone Famous. 2014. (ENG.). 200p. (J). (gr. 6). pap. 12.95 *(978-1-939601-29-2(0))* Ig Publishing, Inc.

—Your Eyes in Stars. 2006. (YA). (gr. 7-12). (ENG.). 240p. 16.99 *(978-0-06-075682-6(9));* 229p. lib. bdg. 17.89 *(978-0-06-075683-3(7))* HarperCollins Pubs.

Kerrin, Jessica Scott. Out of Orbit! Kelly, Joseph, illus. 2007. (Martin Bridge Ser.). (ENG.). 112p. (J). (gr. 2-5). 6.95 *(978-1-55453-149-3(7))* Kids Can Pr., Ltd. CAN. Dist: Hachette Bk. Group.

Kerz, Anna. The Gnome's Eye, 1 vol. 2010. (ENG.). 224p. (J). (gr. 4-7). pap. 9.95 *(978-1-55469-195-1(8))* Orca Bk. Pubs. USA.

Keselman, Gabriela. El Mejor Amigo. 2003. (SPA.). 48p. (J). 6.95 *(978-84-670-0302-4(2))* Espasa Calpe, S.A. ESP. Dist: Planeta Publishing Corp.

Kessler, Liz. The Castle in the Mist. Ledwidge, Natacha & Gibb, Sarah, illus. 2007. (Emily Windsnap Ser.: 3). (ENG.). 208p. (J). (gr. 3-7). 15.99 *(978-0-7636-3330-1(5))* Candlewick Pr.

—The Castle in the Mist. 2012. (Emily Windsnap Ser.: 3). lib. bdg. 16.00 *(978-0-606-25596-7(6),* Turtleback) Turtleback Bks.

—Emily Windsnap & the Castle in the Mist. Ledwidge, Natacha, illus. 2012. (Emily Windsnap Ser.: 3). (ENG.). 208p. (J). (gr. 3-7). pap. 5.99 *(978-0-7636-6017-8(5))* Candlewick Pr.

—Has Anyone Seen Jessica Jenkins? 2015. (ENG.). 288p. (J). (gr. 3-7). 15.99 *(978-0-7636-7060-3(X))* Candlewick Pr.

—North of Nowhere. 2015. (ENG.). 272p. (J). (gr. 4-7). pap. 7.99 *(978-0-7636-7672-8(1))* Candlewick Pr.

—Philippa Fisher & the Dream-Maker's Daughter. 2015. (Philippa Fisher Ser.: 2). (ENG.). 288p. (J). (gr. 3-7). pap. 6.99 *(978-0-7636-7460-1(5))* Candlewick Pr.

—Philippa Fisher & the Fairy Godsister. 2015. (Philippa Fisher Ser.: 1). (ENG.). 288p. (J). (gr. 3-7). pap. 6.99 *(978-0-7636-7462-5(1))* Candlewick Pr.

—Philippa Fisher & the Fairy's Promise. (Philippa Fisher Ser.: 3). (ENG.). (J). (gr. 3-7). 2015. 288p. pap. 6.99 *(978-0-7636-7461-8(3))* 2010. (Illus.). 274p. 15.99 *(978-0-7636-5031-5(5))* Candlewick Pr.

—Philippa Fisher's Fairy Godsister. 2008. (Philippa Fisher Ser.: 1). (ENG., Illus.). 256p. (J). (gr. 3-7). 15.99 *(978-0-7636-4070-5(0))* Candlewick Pr.

—A Year Without Autumn. (ENG.). 304p. (J). (gr. 4-7). 2012. pap. 7.99 *(978-0-7636-6060-4(4))* 2011. (Illus.). 15.99 *(978-0-7636-5595-2(3))* Candlewick Pr.

Kessler, MacKenzie. Murphy the Lonely Robot/Cecil the Lonely Pterodactyl. 2010. 52p. pap. 14.00 *(978-0-557-22226-1(5))* Lulu Pr., Inc.

Ketteman, Helen. Armadilly Chili. Terry, Will, illus. 2004. (ENG.). 32p. (J). (gr. k-3). pap. 7.99 *(978-0-8075-0458-1(0))* Whitman, Albert & Co.

Kettle, Shey. Surf Girls. Thomas, Meredith, illus. 2005. (Girlz Rock! Ser.). (J). pap. *(978-1-59336-708-4(2))* Mondo Publishing.

Kew, Trevor. Trading Goals, 1 vol. 2009. (Lorimer Sports Stories Ser.). (ENG.). 144p. (J). (gr. 4-8). 16.95 *(978-1-55277-425-0(2),* 9781552774250) Lorimer, James & Co., Ltd., Pubs. CAN. Dist: Casemate Pubs. & Bk. Distributors, LLC.

Keyes, Joseph W. The Sparrows of Saint Thomas. 2007. 92p. pap. 14.95 *(978-1-4303-1410-3(9))* Lulu Pr., Inc.

Keyser, Amber J. Pointe, Claw. 2017. (Fiction — Young Adult Ser.). (ENG.). 288p. (YA). (gr. 8-12). 9.99 ***(978-1-5124-3431-6(0));*** 38.65 ***(978-1-5124-0895-9(6));*** 38.65 ***(978-1-5124-3432-3(9))*** Lerner Publishing Group. (Carolrhoda Lab™).

—Pointe, Claw. Burrell, Carol klio, tr. 2017. (ENG.). 288p. (YA). (gr. 8-12). 18.99 *(978-1-4677-7591-5(6))* Lerner Publishing Group.

Keyser, Amber J. & Burkhart, Kiersi. At Top Speed. 2017. (Quartz Creek Ranch Ser.). (ENG.). 240p. (gr. 4-8). 35.99 ***(978-1-5124-2697-7(0),*** Darby Creek) Lerner Publishing Group.

—One Brave Summer. 2017. (Quartz Creek Ranch Ser.). (ENG.). 224p. (gr. 4-8). 35.99 ***(978-1-5124-0892-8(1),*** Darby Creek) Lerner Publishing Group.

Keyser, Francois. Tiger Loses His Stripes. 2013. (ENG.). 24p. pap. 20.00 *(978-1-4669-9203-0(4))* Trafford Publishing.

E
F
G

Keyworth, R. L. Gregory Giraffe's New Friends Adventure: Gregory Giraffe Is about to find some altogether different but new friends at his watering Hole. 2009. 20p. pap. 10.99 *(978-1-4389-3284-2(7))* AuthorHouse.

Kezar, Wanda. It's a Scamp's Life! Derby, Sarah, illus. 2013. 186p. pap. 14.99 *(978-1-62839-371-2(8))* Salem Author Services.

Khan, Hana. Taylor's Birthday Party. Kemble, Mai S., illus. 2008. (J). *(978-1-60108-048-6(4))* Red Cygnet Pr.

Kidwell, Leigh-Anne. The Year i Lost My Popularity! 2005. 115p. pap. 19.95 *(978-1-4137-8376-6(7))* PublishAmerica, Inc.

Kiefer, Janet Kennedy & Barrett, Jill. Can I Play with You? Freckles Book 2. 2013. 42p. pap. *(978-1-4602-0038-4(1))* FriesenPress.

Kiely, Brendan. The Gospel of Winter. (ENG., Illus.). (YA). (gr. 9). 2015. 320p. pap. 11.99 *(978-1-4424-8490-0(X))* 2014. 304p. 19.99 *(978-1-4424-8489-4(6))* McElderry, Margaret K. Bks. (McElderry, Margaret K. Bks.).

Kieslich, Anita Hilliker. Friends Forever: Adventures of Henderson. 2010. 32p. pap. 14.49 *(978-1-4490-7997-0(0))* AuthorHouse.

Kijinski, Paul. Camp Limestone. 2006. (Illus.). 104p. (YA). per. 7.99 *(978-1-59958-016-6(0))* Journey Stone Creations, LLC.

Killian, Beth. Everything She Wants. 2006. (310 Ser.). (ENG.). 240p. (gr. 8-12). pap. 15.99 *(978-1-4165-2168-6(2)*, MTV Bks.) MTV Books.

Kilpatrick, Irene. Let's Use Our Imaginations! Giles, Mike, illus. 2009. (Yo Gabba Gabba! Ser.). (ENG.). 24p. (J). (gr. -1-2). pap. 3.99 *(978-1-4169-7854-1(2)*, Simon Spotlight) Simon Spotlight.

Kim, Cecil. Friendship Quilt. Jeong, HaJin, illus. rev. ed. 2014. (MySELF Bookshelf Ser.). (ENG.). 32p. (J). (gr. k-2). pap. 11.94 *(978-1-60357-659-8(2))*; lib. bdg. 25.27 *(978-1-59953-650-7(1))* Norwood Hse. Pr.

Kim, JiYu. Zippy the Runner. Seon, JeongHyeon, illus. rev. ed. 2014. (MySELF Bookshelf Ser.). (ENG.). 32p. (J). (gr. k-2). pap. 11.94 *(978-1-60357-656-7(8))*; lib. bdg. 25.27 *(978-1-59953-647-7(1))* Norwood Hse. Pr.

Kim, YeShil. My Best Buddy. Tanco, Miguel, illus. 2014. (MySELF Bookshelf Ser.). (ENG.). 32p. (J). (gr. k-2). pap. 11.94 *(978-1-60357-693-2(2))*; lib. bdg. 25.27 *(978-1-59953-658-3(7))* Norwood Hse. Pr.

Kimmel, Elizabeth Cody. Leading Ladies. Mingus, Cathi, illus. 2012. (Forever Four Ser.: 2). (ENG.). 224p. (J). (gr. 3-7). pap. 6.99 *(978-0-448-45549-5(8)*, Grosset & Dunlap) Penguin Young Readers Group.

—Lily B. on the Brink of Cool. 2005. 245p. (J). (gr. 5-9). 14.65 *(978-0-7569-5653-0(6))* Perfection Learning Corp.

—My Penguin Osbert in Love. Lewis, H. B., illus. 2010. (ENG.). 48p. (J). (gr. -1-3). 7.99 *(978-0-7636-5001-8(3))* Candlewick Pr.

—Stories from New York, No. 3. Mingus, Cathi, illus. 2012. (Forever Four Ser.: 3). (ENG.). 208p. (J). (gr. 3-7). pap. 6.99 *(978-0-448-45550-1(1)*, Grosset & Dunlap) Penguin Young Readers Group.

—Suddenly Supernatural 4: Crossing Over. 2011. (Suddenly Supernatural Ser.: 4). (ENG.). 256p. (J). (gr. 3-7). pap. 5.99 *(978-0-316-13345-6(0))* Little, Brown Bks. for Young Readers.

—Suddenly Supernatural: Scaredy Kat. 2010. (Suddenly Supernatural Ser.: 2). (ENG.). 272p. (J). (gr. 3-7). pap. 5.99 *(978-0-316-08745-2(9))* Little, Brown Bks. for Young Readers.

—Suddenly Supernatural: School Spirit. 2010. (Suddenly Supernatural Ser.: 1). (ENG.). 336p. (J). (gr. 3-7). pap. 7.99 *(978-0-316-07821-4(2))* Little, Brown Bks. for Young Readers.

—#1 Forever Four. Mingus, Cathi, illus. 2012. (Forever Four Ser.: 1). (ENG.). 224p. (J). (gr. 3-7). pap. 6.99 *(978-0-448-45548-8(X)*, Grosset & Dunlap) Penguin Young Readers Group.

Kimmel, Elizabeth Cody & Buck, Lewis. My Penguin Osbert in Love, Set. Lewis, H. B., illus. 2008. (ENG.). 48p. (J). (gr. -1-3). 16.99 *(978-0-7636-3032-4(2))* Candlewick Pr.

Kimmel, Eric A. Medio Pollito: A Spanish Tale, 0 vols. Docampo, Valeria, illus. 2010. (ENG.). 32p. (J). (gr. k-3). 17.99 *(978-0-7614-5705-3(4)*, 9780761457053, Amazon Children's Publishing) Amazon Publishing.

Kimmelman, Leslie. Sam & Charlie (and Sam Too) at Camp! Owl, William, illus. 2015. (ENG.). 48p. (J). (gr. k-3). 13.99 *(978-0-8075-7217-7(9))* Whitman, Albert & Co.

Kimpton, Diana. Princess Ellie to the Rescue. Finlay, Lizzie, illus. 2006. (ENG.). 96p. (gr. 1-4). pap. 3.99 *(978-0-7868-4870-6(7))* Hyperion Pr.

Kimpton, Paul & Kimpton, Ann Kaczkowski. Summer of Firsts: WWII Is Ending, but the Music Adventures Are Just Beginning. 2013. (Adventures with Music Ser.: 3). (ENG., Illus.). 288p. (J). (gr. 4-7). pap. 8.95 *(978-1-57999-972-8(7))* G I A Pubns., Inc.

Kimura & North, Lucy. One Stormy Night. Abe, Hiroshi, illus. 2005. 48p. (J). (gr. 1-3). 16.00 *(978-4-7700-2970-6(5))* Kodansha International JPN. Dist: Cheng & Tsui Co.

—One Sunny Day, 2 vols., Vol. 2. Abe, Hiroshi, illus. 2005. 48p. (J). 16.00 *(978-4-7700-2971-3(3))* Kodansha International JPN. Dist: Cheng & Tsui Co.

Kinard, Kami. The Boy Prediction: Notes & Observations of Tabitha Reddy. 2014. (ENG., Illus.). 272p. (J). (gr. 3-7). 12.99 *(978-0-545-57586-7(9)*, Scholastic Pr.) Scholastic, Inc.

Kinch, Michael. The Fires of New Sun. 2012. (Blending Time Ser.: 2). (ENG.). 288p. (YA). pap. 9.95 *(978-0-7387-3076-9(9)*, Flux) North Star Editions.

—The Rebels of New SUN. 2013. (Blending Time Ser.: 3). (ENG.). 288p. (YA). pap. 9.99 *(978-0-7387-3151-3(X)*, Flux) North Star Editions.

Kinerk, Robert. Clorinda Takes Flight. Kellogg, Steven, illus. 2007. (ENG.). 40p. (J). (gr. -1-3). 17.99 *(978-0-689-86864-1(2)*, Simon & Schuster/Paula Wiseman Bks.) Simon & Schuster/Paula Wiseman Bks.

King, A. S. Glory O'Brien's History of the Future. 2014. (ENG.). 320p. (YA). (gr. 10-17). 18.00 *(978-0-316-22272-3(0))* Little, Brown Bks. for Young Readers.

—Please Ignore Vera Dietz. 2012. (ENG.). 336p. (YA). (gr. 9). pap. 9.99 *(978-0-375-86564-0(0)*, Ember) Random Hse. Children's Bks.

King, Aby. Lupo & the Lost Pirate of Kensington Palace Lupo & the Lost Pirate of Kensington Palace. 2016. (Lupo Ser.). (ENG., Illus.). 240p. (J). (gr. 4-17). pap. 7.99 *(978-1-4449-2157-1(6))* Hachette Children's Group GBR. Dist: Hachette Bk. Group.

King, Amy Sarig. Me & Marvin Gardens. 2017. (ENG.). 256p. (J). (gr. 3-7). 16.99 *(978-0-545-87074-0(7)*, Levine, Arthur A. Bks.) Scholastic, Inc.

King, Carrie. Joni-Pip. Boddy, James & Moon, Paul, illus. 2010. 476p. pap. *(978-0-9555246-9-1(5))* Bothy Bks., Corwall, A Div. of Grace & Patrick Pubs., Ltd.

King, Ms Marcy Cockerille. The Orples Learn to Read. 2012. 40p. pap. 10.95 *(978-0-9850752-2-4(8))* King, Marcy.

King, Philip. Bluey, the Little Drip. King, Janet, illus. 2011. 40p. pap. 14.95 *(978-1-60976-661-0(X)*, Eloquent Bks.) Strategic Book Publishing & Rights Agency (SBPRA).

King, Sharon. Oops Was Bullied? Hey, Why Did You Hurt Me That Way? LaRoe, Misty Bailey, illus. 2013. (ENG.). 32p. (J). pap. 16.95 *(978-1-4787-1364-7(X))* Outskirts Pr., Inc.

King-smith, Dick. Dinosaur Trouble. Bruel, Nick, illus. 2012. (ENG.). 128p. (J). (gr. 2-5). pap. 16.99 *(978-1-59643-935-1(1)*, 9781596439351) Roaring Brook Pr.

King, Stephen Michael. You: A Story of Love & Friendship. King, Stephen Michael, illus. 2011. (Illus.). 32p. (J). 14.99 *(978-0-06-206014-3(7)*, Greenwillow Bks.) HarperCollins Pubs.

King, Steve. The Stone Dragon. 2005. 80p. pap. 16.95 *(978-1-4137-9628-5(1))* PublishAmerica, Inc.

King, Trey. Friends & Foes. 2015. (LEGO DC Super Heroes 8X8 Ser.). (Illus.). (J). lib. bdg. 13.55 *(978-0-606-36361-7(0))* Turtleback Bks.

Kinney, Jeff. Carnet de Bord de Greg Heffley. Zimmerman, Natalie, tr. 2012. (Journal d'un Degonfle Ser.: Vol. 1). (FRE., Illus.). 223p. (J). (gr. 4-8). pap. *(978-2-02-101196-8(8))* Editions du Seuil.

—El Diario de Greg, un Renacuajo. Morán, Esteban, tr. 2008. (SPA.). 218p. (J). (gr. 3-6). 17.99 *(978-1-933032-52-8(9))* Lectorum Pubns., Inc.

—Diary of a Wimpy Kid. 2014. pap. *(978-1-4197-1499-3(6))* 2013. pap. *(978-1-4197-1176-3(8))* 2009. pap. *(978-0-8109-8888-0(7))* 2007. (Diary of a Wimpy Kid Ser.). (ENG., Illus.). 224p. (J). (gr. 2-8). 13.95 *(978-0-8109-9313-6(9))* 2007. pap. *(978-0-8109-8292-5(7))* 2007. pap. *(978-0-8109-8893-4(3))* 2007. (Diary of a Wimpy Kid Ser.: Bk. 1). 217p. pap. *(978-0-8109-9455-3(0))*Bks. 1-4. 2014. (ENG.). 896p. (J). (gr. 3-7). 56.00 *(978-1-4197-1669-0(7))* Abrams, Inc. (Amulet Bks.).

—Diary of a Wimpy Kid. (Diary of a Wimpy Kid Ser.). (CHI., Illus.). (J). 2009. (gr. 4-8). ***(978-986-84847-4-0(X))*** 2008. (gr. 3-7). ***(978-986-84847-0-2(7))*** DaskoviK, Izdatel'sko-torgovaja korporacija.

—Diary of a Wimpy Kid. 2013. (Diary of a Wimpy Kid Ser.: 16). (CHI.). (J). pap. 13.95 *(978-7-5405-7891-6(2))* Guangdong New Era Publishing Hse. CHN. Dist: Chinasprout, Inc.

—Diary of a Wimpy Kid. 2009. (Diary of a Wimpy Kid Ser.: Bk. 1). 1.00 *(978-1-4074-4434-5(4))* 2008. (Diary of a Wimpy Kid Ser.: 1). (J). 75.75 *(978-1-4361-3290-9(8))* 2008. (Diary of a Wimpy Kid Ser.: 1). (J). 44.75 *(978-1-4281-8196-0(2))* 2008. (Diary of a Wimpy Kid Ser.: 1). (J). 46.75 *(978-1-4281-8194-6(6))* 2008. (Diary of a Wimpy Kid Ser.: 1). (J). 173.75 *(978-1-4281-8195-3(4))* 2008. (Diary of a Wimpy Kid Ser.: 1). (J). 1.25 *(978-1-4281-8191-5(1))* 2008. (Diary of a Wimpy Kid Ser.: 1). (J). 46.75 *(978-1-4281-8198-4(9))* 2008. (Diary of a Wimpy Kid Ser.: 1). (J). 44.75 *(978-1-4281-8200-4(4))* Recorded Bks., Inc.

—Diary of a Wimpy Kid. 2007. (Diary of a Wimpy Kid Ser.: 1). (Illus.). 217p. (J). lib. bdg. 25.70 *(978-0-606-23662-1(7)*, Turtleback) Turtleback Bks.

—Hard Luck. 2013. (Diary of a Wimpy Kid Ser.: Bk. 8). (ENG., Illus.). 224p. (J). (gr. 3-7). 13.95 *(978-1-4197-1132-9(6)*, Amulet Bks.) Abrams, Inc.

—Hard Luck. 2013. (Diary of a Wimpy Kid Ser.: 8). (J). lib. bdg. 25.70 *(978-0-606-32062-7(8)*, Turtleback) Turtleback Bks.

—The Third Wheel. 2012. (Diary of a Wimpy Kid Ser.). (ENG., Illus.). 224p. (J). (gr. 3-7). 13.95 *(978-1-4197-0584-7(9)*, Amulet Bks.) Abrams, Inc.

—The Third Wheel. 2012. (Diary of a Wimpy Kid Ser.: 7). (Illus.). 217p. (YA). lib. bdg. 25.70 *(978-0-606-26514-0(7)*, Turtleback) Turtleback Bks.

—The Ugly Truth. 2010. (Diary of a Wimpy Kid Ser.). (ENG.). 224p. (J). (gr. 3-7). 13.95 *(978-0-8109-8491-2(1)*, Amulet Bks.) Abrams, Inc.

—The Ugly Truth. 2010. (Diary of a Wimpy Kid Ser.: Bk. 5). (JPN., Illus.). 221p. (J). (gr. 4-7). *(978-4-591-12117-7(8))* Poplar Publishing.

—The Ugly Truth, 2 vols. 2010. (Diary of a Wimpy Kid Ser.: 5). (J). 44.75 *(978-1-4498-4534-6(7))*; 46.75 *(978-1-4498-4532-2(0))*; 173.75 *(978-1-4498-4530-8(4))*; 44.75 *(978-1-4498-4531-5(2))*; 1.25 *(978-1-4498-4535-3(5))* Recorded Bks., Inc.

—The Ugly Truth. 2010. (Diary of a Wimpy Kid Ser.: 5). (J). lib. bdg. 25.70 *(978-0-606-23666-9(X)*, Turtleback) Turtleback Bks.

Kinsella, Sophie, pseud. Finding Audrey. (ENG.). 304p. (YA). (gr. 7). 2016. pap. 9.99 *(978-0-553-53653-9(2)*, Ember) 2015. 18.99 *(978-0-553-53651-5(6)*, Delacorte Pr.) Random Hse. Children's Bks.

—Finding Audrey. 2016. lib. bdg. 20.85 *(978-0-606-38874-0(5))* Turtleback Bks.

Kinton, P. D. Wishing for Wizards & Chips for Te. 2010. 28p. pap. *(978-1-907211-26-3(8))* Grosvenor Hse. Publishing Ltd.

Kirby, Matthew J. Cave of Wonders. 2013. (Infinity Ring Ser.: 5). (ENG.). 192p. (J). (gr. 3-7). 16.99 *(978-0-545-48460-2(X))* Scholastic, Inc.

—The Clockwork Three. (ENG.). 400p. (J). (gr. 3-7). 2011. 7.99 *(978-0-545-20338-8(4)*, Scholastic Paperbacks) 2010. 17.99 *(978-0-545-20337-1(6)*, Scholastic Pr.) Scholastic, Inc.

—Spell Robbers. 2014. (Quantum League Ser.: No. 1). (ENG.). 272p. (J). (gr. 3-7). 16.99 *(978-0-545-50226-9(8)*, Scholastic Pr.) Scholastic, Inc.

Kirby, Stan. Captain Awesome & the New Kid. O'Connor, George, illus. 2012. (Captain Awesome Ser.: 3). (ENG.). 128p. (J). (gr. k-4). 16.99 *(978-1-4424-4200-9(X))*; pap. 5.99 *(978-1-4424-4199-6(2))* Little Simon. (Little Simon).

—Captain Awesome & the New Kid. 2012. (Captain Awesome Ser.: 3). lib. bdg. 16.00 *(978-0-606-26324-5(1)*, Turtleback) Turtleback Bks.

—Captain Awesome vs. Nacho Cheese Man. O'Connor, George, illus. 2012. (Captain Awesome Ser.: 2). (ENG.). 128p. (J). (gr. -1-2). 16.99 *(978-1-4424-4091-3(0))*; (gr. k-4). pap. 5.99 *(978-1-4424-3563-6(1))* Little Simon. (Little Simon).

—Captain Awesome vs. Nacho Cheese Man. 2012. (Captain Awesome Ser.: 2). lib. bdg. 16.00 *(978-0-606-26323-8(3)*, Turtleback) Turtleback Bks.

Kirk, Daniel. Ten Thank-You Letters. Kirk, Daniel, illus. 2014. (ENG., Illus.). 32p. (J). (gr. k-3). 16.99 *(978-0-399-16937-3(7)*, Nancy Paulsen Books) Penguin Young Readers Group.

—Ten Things I Love about You. Kirk, Daniel, illus. 2012. (ENG., Illus.). 36p. (J). (gr. k-3). 16.99 *(978-0-399-25288-4(6)*, Nancy Paulsen Books) Penguin Young Readers Group.

—You Are Not My Friend, but I Miss You. 2014. (ENG., Illus.). 32p. (J). (gr. k-2). 16.95 *(978-1-4197-1236-4(5)*, Abrams Bks. for Young Readers) Abrams, Inc.

Kirk, Trish. I Think There's a Bear Out There. 2009. 36p. pap. 16.99 *(978-1-4389-6097-5(2))* AuthorHouse.

Kirkham, Tyler & Kirkham, Rian. My Best Friend's a Booger. O'Reilly, Sean Patrick, ed. 2012. (Illus.). 32p. pap. 6.95 *(978-1-926914-36-7(8))* Arcana Studio, Inc.

Kirkpatrick, Kevin. Francisco's Friends: The Pachyderm Predicamen. 2012. 40p. pap. 24.95 *(978-1-4626-8881-4(0))* America Star Bks.

Kirkpatrick, Teresa. Roscoe's Forest Adventures. 2008. 177p. pap. 24.95 *(978-1-60672-328-9(6))* America Star Bks.

Kirkwood, Neville A. Jungle Heroes. 2011. 138p. pap. 11.50 *(978-1-60976-267-4(3)*, Eloquent Bks.) Strategic Book Publishing & Rights Agency (SBPRA).

Kirouac Bn, Nicole. I Am Unique. 2013. 32p. pap. 13.99 *(978-1-4525-7594-0(0)*, Balboa Pr.) Author Solutions, Inc.

Kiss, Kay. Mr B T Bumblebee. 2007. 28p. per. 11.95 *(978-1-4327-1744-5(8))* Outskirts Pr., Inc.

Kita, Suzanne. Three Whales: Who Won the Heart of the World. Sundram, Steve, illus. 2010. (ENG.). 40p. (J). (gr. 3). *(978-1-59700-761-0(7))* Island Heritage Publishing.

Kittscher, Kristen. The Tiara on the Terrace. 2016. 400p. (J). (gr. 3-7). 16.99 *(978-0-06-222798-0(X))* HarperCollins Pubs.

—The Wig in the Window. (J). (gr. 3-7). 2016. 384p. pap. 6.99 *(978-0-06-211051-0(9))* 2013. (ENG.). 368p. 16.99 *(978-0-06-211050-3(0))* HarperCollins Pubs.

Klages, Ellen. The Green Glass Sea. 2008. (ENG.). 368p. (J). (gr. 3-7). 8.99 *(978-0-14-241149-0(3)*, Puffin Books) Penguin Young Readers Group.

—The Green Glass Sea. 2008. 321p. (gr. 4-7). 19.00 *(978-0-7569-8931-6(0))* Perfection Learning Corp.

Klass, David. Losers Take All. 2015. (ENG.). 320p. (YA). (gr. 7). 17.99 *(978-0-374-30136-1(0)*, 9780374301361, Farrar, Straus & Giroux (BYR)) Farrar, Straus & Giroux.

—Losers Take All. 2016. (YA). lib. bdg. 20.85 *(978-0-606-39480-2(X))* Turtleback Bks.

Klausner, Julie. Art Girls Are Easy. 2013. (ENG.). 240p. (YA). (gr. 10-17). pap. 18.99 *(978-0-316-24362-9(0)*, Poppy) Little, Brown Bks. for Young Readers.

Kleback, Amanda. Hoo Hoo's Song. Kleback, Amanda & Kleback, Brian, illus. 2009. 24p. pap. 12.00 *(978-1-4389-1322-3(2))* AuthorHouse.

Klein, Abby. The King of Show-and-Tell. McKinley, John, illus. 2004. (Ready, Freddy! Ser.: 2). (ENG.). 96p. (J). (gr. -1-3). 5.99 *(978-0-439-55598-2(1)*, Blue Sky Pr., The) Scholastic, Inc.

—Second Grade Rules! McKinley, John, illus. 2014. 85p. (J). pap. *(978-0-545-69031-7(5))* Scholastic, Inc.

Klein, Adria F. Max Celebra el Ano Nuevo Chino, 1 vol. Robledo, Sol, tr. from ENG. Gallagher-Cole, Mernie, illus. 2007. (Read-It! Readers en Español: la Vida de Max Ser.). (SPA.). 24p. (gr. -1-3). lib. bdg. 21.32 *(978-1-4048-3794-2(9)*, Easy Readers) Picture Window Bks.

—Max Come Al Aire Libre, 1 vol. Robledo, Sol, tr. from ENG. Gallagher-Cole, Mernie, illus. 2007. (Read-It! Readers en Español: la Vida de Max Ser.). (SPA.). 24p. (gr. -1-3). lib. bdg. 21.32 *(978-1-4048-3795-9(7)*, Easy Readers) Picture Window Bks.

—Max Goes to the Farm, 1 vol. Gallagher-Cole, Mernie, illus. 2007. (Read-It! Readers: the Life of Max Ser.). (ENG.). 24p. (gr. -1-2). lib. bdg. 21.32 *(978-1-4048-3678-5(0)*, Easy Readers) Picture Window Bks.

—Max Goes to the Playground, 1 vol. Gallagher-Cole, Mernie, illus. 2007. (Read-It! Readers: the Life of Max Ser.). (ENG.). 24p. (gr. -1-2). lib. bdg. 21.32 *(978-1-4048-3681-5(0)*, Easy Readers) Picture Window Bks.

—Max Goes to the Zoo, 1 vol. Gallagher-Cole, Mernie, illus. 2007. (Read-It! Readers: the Life of Max Ser.). (ENG.). 24p. (gr. -1-2). lib. bdg. 21.32 *(978-1-4048-3677-8(2))*; per. 3.95 *(978-1-4048-3683-9(7))* Picture Window Bks. (Easy Readers).

—Max Se Queda a Dormir, 1 vol. Robledo, Sol, tr. from ENG. Gallagher-Cole, Mernie, illus. 2007. (Read-It! Readers en Español: la Vida de Max Ser.). (SPA.). 24p. (gr. -1-3). lib. bdg. 21.32 *(978-1-4048-3797-3(3)*, Easy Readers) Picture Window Bks.

—Max y la Fiesta de Adopcion, 1 vol. Robledo, Sol, tr. from ENG. Gallagher-Cole, Mernie, illus. 2007. (Read-It! Readers en Español: la Vida de Max Ser.). (SPA.). 24p. (gr. -1-3). lib. bdg. 21.32 *(978-1-4048-3793-5(0)*, Easy Readers) Picture Window Bks.

—Max's Fun Day, 1 vol. Gallagher-Cole, Mernie, illus. 2007. (Read-It! Readers: the Life of Max Ser.). (ENG.). 24p. (gr. -1-2). lib. bdg. 21.32 *(978-1-4048-3150-6(9)*, 1265797, Easy Readers) Picture Window Bks.

Klein, Jen. Shuffle, Repeat. (ENG.). (YA). (gr. 7). 2017. 352p. pap. 9.99 ***(978-0-553-50985-4(3)***, Ember) 2016. 336p. 17.99 *(978-0-553-50982-3(9)*, Random Hse. Bks. for Young Readers) Random Hse. Children's Bks.

Klein, Lisa. Love Disguised. 2013. (ENG., Illus.). 320p. (YA). (gr. 7). 17.99 *(978-1-59990-968-4(5)*, 9781599909684, Bloomsbury USA Childrens) Bloomsbury Publishing USA.

Kleinberg, Naomi. Circle of Friends (Sesame Street) Brannon, Tom, illus. 2012. (ENG.). 12p. (J). (gr. k-k). bds. 5.99 *(978-0-307-93185-6(4)*, Random Hse. Bks. for Young Readers) Random Hse. Children's Bks.

—Elmo's Book of Friends (Sesame Street) 2016. (ENG., Illus.). 16p. (J). (-k). bds. 7.99 *(978-0-399-55211-3(1)*, Random Hse. Bks. for Young Readers) Random Hse. Children's Bks.

—Have Yourself a Furry Little Christmas. Womble, Louis, illus. 2007. (ENG.). 12p. (J). (gr. k — 1). bds. 4.99 *(978-0-375-84133-0(4)*, Random Hse. Bks. for Young Readers) Random Hse. Children's Bks.

—In Elmo's Easter Parade. Moroney, Christopher, illus. 2009. (ENG.). 12p. (J). (gr. k — 1). bds. 4.99 *(978-0-375-84480-5(5)*, Random Hse. Bks. for Young Readers) Random Hse. Children's Bks.

Kleman, Jamie. Uncovered. 2005. 39p. pap. 10.95 *(978-1-4116-6198-1(2))* Lulu Pr., Inc.

Kleven, Elisa, illus. The Horribly Hungry Gingerbread Boy: A San Francisco Story. 2016. 40p. (J). *(978-1-59714-352-3(9))* Heyday.

Klim, Christopher. Firecracker Jones Is on the Case. (Illus.). (J). 2006. 116p. lib. bdg. 19.95 *(978-1-933435-11-4(9))* 2005. 111p. per. 9.95 *(978-0-9726906-7-6(0))* Hopewell Pubns., LLC.

Kline, Lisa Williams. Write Before Your Eyes. 2010. (ENG.). 192p. (J). (gr. 3-7). 6.99 *(978-0-440-42251-8(5)*, Yearling) Random Hse. Children's Bks.

Kline, Suzy. Horrible Harry & the Battle of the Bugs. 2017. (Horrible Harry Ser.). (ENG.). 80p. (J). (gr. 2-5). 14.99 *(978-0-425-28820-7(X)*, Viking Books for Young Readers) Penguin Young Readers Group.

—Horrible Harry & the Dragon War. Remkiewicz, Frank, illus. 2003. (Horrible Harry Ser.). (ENG.). 64p. (J). (gr. 2-4). 4.99 *(978-0-14-250166-5(2)*, Puffin Books) Penguin Young Readers Group.

—Horrible Harry & the Dragon War. 2003. (Horrible Harry Ser.: 14). lib. bdg. 14.75 *(978-0-613-92539-6(4)*, Turtleback) Turtleback Bks.

—Horrible Harry & the Secret Treasure. Wummer, Amy, illus. (Horrible Harry Ser.). (ENG.). 80p. (J). (gr. 2-4). 2012. 4.99 *(978-0-14-242021-8(2)*, Puffin Books) 2011. 14.99 *(978-0-670-01181-0(9)*, Viking Books for Young Readers) Penguin Young Readers Group.

—Horrible Harry & the Top-Secret Hideout. Wummer, Amy, illus. 2016. (Horrible Harry Ser.: Vol. 33). (ENG.). 80p. (J). (gr. 1-3). 14.75 *(978-0-606-39323-2(4))* Turtleback Bks.

Kline, Trish. The Fang Gang: KA Reader 4. 2007. (Illus.). 32p. (J). per. 20.00 *(978-0-9717234-6-7(X))* Ghost Hunter Productions.

—Super Hero: KA Reader 1. 2007. (Illus.). 32p. (J). per. 20.00 *(978-0-9717234-2-9(7))* Ghost Hunter Productions.

Kline, Trish & Donev, Mary. Don't Frown, Clown! KA Reader 9. 2007. (Illus.). 32p. (J). per. 20.00 *(978-1-934307-02-1(5))* Ghost Hunter Productions.

—Where Can Lost Bee Be? KA Reader 6. 2007. (Illus.). 32p. (J). per. 20.00 *(978-0-9717234-9-8(4))* Ghost Hunter Productions.

Kluger, Steve. My Most Excellent Year: A Novel of Love, Mary Poppins, & Fenway Park. 2009. (ENG.). 416p. (YA). (gr. 7-18). 9.99 *(978-0-14-241343-2(7)*, Speak) Penguin Young Readers Group.

Kneisley, Amy. The Gentle Elephant. Tina, Dunnier, illus. 2013. 24p. pap. 8.99 *(978-1-938768-21-7(3))* Gypsy Pubns.

Knife, Ivan M. Uses the. Black Thursday. 2010. 108p. pap. 15.99 *(978-1-4500-6311-1(X))* Xlibris Corp.

Knight, Chris. The Statue. 2013. 52p. pap. *(978-1-78299-440-4(8))* FeedARead.com.

Knight, Diedre. Beanie's Backyard. 2012. 28p. pap. 12.95 *(978-1-62141-812-2(X))* Booklocker.com, Inc.

Knight, P. B. The Little Orange & Red Butterfly, 1 vol. 2009. 16p. pap. 19.95 *(978-1-60749-693-9(3))* PublishAmerica, Inc.

—The Secret Passage, 1 vol. 2009. 73p. pap. 14.95 *(978-1-61546-421-0(2))* PublishAmerica, Inc.

Knowles, Jo. Lessons from a Dead Girl. (ENG., Illus.). 224p. (YA). (gr. 9). 2009. pap. 7.99 *(978-0-7636-4485-7(4))* 2007. 16.99 *(978-0-7636-3279-3(1))* Candlewick Pr.

—See You at Harry's. 2013. (ENG.). 320p. (J). (gr. 5). pap. 7.99 *(978-0-7636-6455-8(3))* Candlewick Pr.

Knowles, Johanna. Pearl. 2011. (ENG.). 224p. (YA). (gr. 7-12). 16.99 *(978-0-8050-9207-3(2)*, 9780805092073, Holt, Henry & Co. Bks. For Young Readers) Holt, Henry & Co.

Knudson, Mike. Cool Campers. 2011. (Raymond & Graham Ser.). (ENG.). 160p. (J). (gr. 3-7). 6.99 *(978-0-14-241875-8(7)*, Puffin Books) Penguin Young Readers Group.

Knudson, Mike & Wilkinson, Steve. Bases Loaded. 2011. (Raymond & Graham Ser.). (ENG.). 160p. (J). (gr. 3-7). 6.99 *(978-0-14-241751-5(3)*, Puffin Books) Penguin Young Readers Group.

—Dancing Dudes. Curtis, Stacy, illus. 2010. (Raymond & Graham Ser.). (ENG.). 144p. (J). (gr. 3-7). 6.99 *(978-0-14-241508-5(1)*, Puffin Books) Penguin Young Readers Group.

—Raymond & Graham Rule the School. Curtis, Stacy, illus. 2009. (Raymond & Graham Ser.). (ENG.). 144p. (J). (gr. 3-7). 6.99 *(978-0-14-241426-2(3)*, Puffin Books) Penguin Young Readers Group.

Kobald, Irena. My Two Blankets. Blackwood, Freya, illus. 2015. (ENG.). 32p. (J). (gr. 1-4). 17.99 *(978-0-544-43228-4(2)*, HMH Books For Young Readers) Houghton Mifflin Harcourt Publishing Co.

Kobus, Joanne. Mr Frog's Bad Day. 2009. 40p. pap. 16.99 *(978-1-4389-7513-9(9))* AuthorHouse.

Kocek, Sara. Promise Me Something. 2015. (ENG.). 320p. (YA). (gr. 8-12). pap. 9.99 *(978-0-8075-6643-5(8))* Whitman, Albert & Co.

Kochalka, James. The Best Little Ghost in the World! 2008. (Johnny Boo Ser.: 1). (ENG., Illus.). 40p. (J). (gr. 2-5). 9.95 *(978-1-60309-013-1(4)*, 9781603090131) Top Shelf Productions.

Koenig, Faydra. Two Homes for Daniel. 2013. 30p. pap. 10.95 *(978-0-9891471-1-8(8))* Alpine River Pr.

Koertge, Ronald. Boy Girl Boy. 2007. (ENG., Illus.). 180p. (YA). (gr. 9-18). pap. 12.95 *(978-0-15-205865-4(6))* Houghton Mifflin Harcourt Publishing Co.

—Deadville. 2008. (ENG., Illus.). 224p. (YA). (gr. 9). 16.99 *(978-0-7636-3580-0(4))* Candlewick Pr.

Kohl, T. Michelle. The Magical Adventures of Bailey Boo the Cockatoo: When the Family's Away, the Parrots Will Play! 2012. 24p. pap. 24.95 *(978-1-4626-6215-9(3))* America Star Bks.

Kohlhepp, Michael. Within the Hearthstone: Book 1: the Trea. 2006. 127p. pap. 19.95 *(978-1-4241-3744-2(6))* PublishAmerica, Inc.

Kollar, J. P. Three Tomato Brand. 2005. 127p. per. 12.95 *(978-1-59879-076-4(5))* Lifevest Publishing, Inc.
Koller, Jackie French. Someday. 2010. 228p. pap. 14.95 *(978-1-4401-8675-2(8))* iUniverse, Inc.
Komorn, Julie, adapted by. Out of the Dark. 2004. (W. I. T. C. H. Ser.: Bk. 8). (Illus.). 128p. (J). lib. bdg. 16.92 *(978-1-4242-0789-3(4))* Fitzgerald Bks.
Komorn, Julie & Lenhard, Elizabeth, adapted by. The Light of Meridian. 2004. (W. I. T. C. H. Ser.: Bk. 7). (Illus.). 144p. (J). lib. bdg. 16.92 *(978-1-4242-0794-7(0))* Fitzgerald Bks.
Kompelien, Tracy. Lion Manes, 1 vol. Haberstroh, Anne, illus. 2006. (Animal Tales Ser.). (ENG.). 24p. (J). (gr. k-3). lib. bdg. 24.21 *(978-1-59679-949-3(8)*, SandCastle) ABDO Publishing Co.
—Lion Manes. Nobens, C. A., illus. 2006. (Fact & Fiction Ser.). 24p. (J). pap. 48.42 *(978-1-59679-950-9(1))* ABDO Publishing Co.
Konen, Leah. The After Girls. 2013. (ENG.). 304p. (YA). 17.95 *(978-1-4405-6108-5(7)*, Simon Pulse) Simon Pulse.
Konigsberg, Bill. The Porcupine of Truth. 2015. (ENG.). 336p. (J). (gr. 9). 17.99 *(978-0-545-64893-6(9))* Scholastic, Inc.
Konigsburg, E. L. The E. L. Konigsburg Newbery Collection: From the Mixed-Up Files of Mrs. Basil E. Frankweiler; Jennifer, Hecate, Macbeth, William Mckinley, & Me, Elizabeth; the View from Saturday. 2013. (ENG., Illus.). 472p. (J). (gr. 3-7). pap. 23.99 *(978-1-4424-9743-6(2)*, Atheneum Bks. for Young Readers) Simon & Schuster Children's Publishing.
—Jennifer, Hecate, Macbeth, William McKinley, & Me, Elizabeth. 117p. (J). (gr. 3-6). pap. 4.99 *(978-0-8072-1417-6(5)*, Listening Library) Random Hse. Audio Publishing Group.
—Jennifer, Hecate, Macbeth, William Mckinley, & Me, Elizabeth. 2007. (ENG., Illus.). 128p. (J). (gr. 3-7). pap. 7.99 *(978-1-4169-3396-0(4)*, Atheneum Bks. for Young Readers) Simon & Schuster Children's Publishing.
—Jennifer, Hecate, Macbeth, William McKinley, & Me, Elizabeth. 2011. 8.32 *(978-0-7848-3469-5(5)*, Everbind) Marco Bk. Co.
—The Mysterious Edge of the Heroic World. (ENG.). 256p. (J). 2009. (gr. 5-9). pap. 7.99 *(978-1-4169-5353-1(1))* 2007. (Illus.). (gr. 4-8). 16.99 *(978-1-4169-4972-5(0))* Simon & Schuster Children's Publishing. (Atheneum Bks. for Young Readers).
—Sabato di Gloria. pap. 15.95 *(978-88-04-47046-5(1))* Mondadori ITA. Dist: Distribooks, Inc.
—Silent to the Bone. unabr. ed. 2004. (Middle Grade Cassette Librariestm Ser.). 272p. (J). (gr. 5-9). pap. 38.00 incl. audio *(978-0-8072-8741-5(5)*, S YA 253 SP, Listening Library) Random Hse. Audio Publishing Group.
—Silent to the Bone. 2004. (ENG.). 272p. (YA). (gr. 7). mass mkt. 7.99 *(978-0-689-86715-6(8)*, Simon Pulse) Simon Pulse.
—The View from Saturday. 280p. (YA). (gr. 5-18). pap. 4.95 *(978-0-8072-1511-1(2)*, Listening Library) Random Hse. Audio Publishing Group.
Könnecke, Ole. Anton & the Battle. Chidgey, Catherine, tr. from GER. 2013.Tr. of Anton und der grosse Streit. (ENG., Illus.). 32p. (gr. -1-3). 17.95 *(978-1-877579-26-4(2))* Gecko Pr. NZL. Dist: Lerner Publishing Group.
Koppens, Judith. The Seesaw. van Lindenhuizen, Eline, illus. 2013. (Animal Square Ser.). (ENG.). 32p. (J). (gr. -1-k). 13.95 *(978-1-60537-152-8(1))* Cobblestone Publishing Co.
Korda, Lerryn. Into the Wild. Korda, Lerryn, illus. 2010. (Playtime with Little Nye Ser.). (ENG., Illus.). 26p. (J). (gr. -1 — 1). 8.99 *(978-0-7636-4812-1(4))* Candlewick Pr.
—It's Vacation Time. Korda, Lerryn, illus. 2010. (Playtime with Little Nye Ser.). (ENG., Illus.). 26p. (J). (— 1). 8.99 *(978-0-7636-4813-8(2))* Candlewick Pr.
—Millions of Snow. Korda, Lerryn, illus. 2010. (Playtime with Little Nye Ser.). (ENG., Illus.). 32p. (J). (— 1). 8.99 *(978-0-7636-4651-6(2))* Candlewick Pr.
Korell, Jennifer. A Day at the Beach with Shrimp & Friends. 2013. 20p. pap. 24.95 *(978-1-63000-677-8(7))* America Star Bks.
Korman, Gordon. Framed. (J). 2011. (ENG.). 240p. (gr. 3-7). pap. 6.99 *(978-0-545-19763-2(5)*, Scholastic Paperbacks) 2010. *(978-0-545-27081-6(2)*, Scholastic Pr.) 2010. (Swindle Ser.: 3). (ENG.). 240p. (gr. 4-7). 16.99 *(978-0-545-17849-5(5)*, Scholastic Pr.) Scholastic, Inc.
—Jackpot. 2014. (Swindle Ser.: 6). (ENG.). 208p. (J). (gr. 3-7). pap. 6.99 *(978-0-545-56147-1(7))*; 16.99 *(978-0-545-56146-4(9))* Scholastic, Inc. (Scholastic Pr.).
—Jackpot. 2014. (Swindle Ser.: 6). lib. bdg. 17.20 *(978-0-606-36032-6(8))* Turtleback Bks.
—Jingle (Swindle #8) 2016. (Swindle Ser.: 8). (ENG.). 208p. (J). (gr. 3-7). 16.99 *(978-0-545-86142-7(X)*, Scholastic Pr.) Scholastic, Inc.
—The Juvie Three. 2010. (ENG.). 256p. (YA). (gr. 7-17). pap. 8.99 *(978-1-4231-0162-8(6))* Hyperion Pr.
—The Juvie Three (repackage) 2017. (ENG.). 256p. (J). (gr. 5-9). pap. 8.99 ***(978-1-4847-9843-0(0))*** Hyperion Bks. for Children.
—Slacker. 2016. (ENG.). 240p. (J). (gr. 3-7). 16.99 *(978-0-545-82315-9(3)*, Scholastic Pr.) Scholastic, Inc.
—Unleashed. 2015. (Swindle Ser.: 7). (ENG.). 208p. (J). (gr. 3-7). 16.99 *(978-0-545-70935-4(0)*, Scholastic Pr.) Scholastic, Inc.
Korman, Susan. Birds of a Feather. 2011. (Rio Ser.). (ENG.). 24p. (J). (gr. -1-2). pap. 3.99 *(978-0-06-202267-7(9)*, HarperFestival) HarperCollins Pubs.
—Continental Drift. 2012. (Ice Age Ser.). (ENG.). 144p. (J). (gr. 3-7). pap. 5.99 *(978-0-06-210485-4(3)*, HarperFestival) HarperCollins Pubs.
Korth, Melanie. The Roadrunner: Finds a Friend. 2009. 20p. pap. 10.49 *(978-1-4389-7540-5(6))* AuthorHouse.
Koss, Amy Goldman. The Cheat. 2004. (ENG.). 176p. (YA). (gr. 7-7). 5.99 *(978-0-14-240128-6(5)*, Speak) Penguin Young Readers Group.
—Gossip Times Three. 2005. (ENG.). 176p. (J). (gr. 3-7). reprint ed. pap. 6.99 *(978-0-14-240295-5(8)*, Puffin Books) Penguin Young Readers Group.
—Gossip Times Three. 2005. 170p. (gr. 5-9). 16.00 *(978-0-7569-5648-6(X))* Perfection Learning Corp.
Kostecki-Shaw, Jenny Sue. Same, Same but Different. Kostecki-Shaw, Jenny Sue, illus. 2011. (ENG., Illus.). 40p. (J). (gr. -1-2). 17.99 *(978-0-8050-8946-2(2)*, 9780805089462, Holt, Henry & Co. Bks. For Young Readers) Holt, Henry & Co.
Kountz, Charity. Jason, Lizzy & the Snowman Village. Klock, Kimberly, illus. 2013. 132p. 24.99 *(978-0-9859601-1-7(6))* Texas Pride Publishing.
Kowalski, Bernard. Alexis & Ralph the Dragon, 1 vol. 2010. 32p. 24.95 *(978-1-4512-1008-8(6))* PublishAmerica, Inc.
Kowalski, William. The Way It Works, 1 vol. 2010. (Rapid Reads Ser.). (ENG.). 128p. pap. 9.95 *(978-1-55469-367-2(5)*, Raven Bks.) Literations.
Kowitt, Holly. The Principal's Bra Is Missing. Kowitt, Holly, illus. 2017. (ENG., Illus.). 224p. (J). 16.99 *(978-1-250-09132-1(2)*, 9781250091321) Feiwel & Friends.
Krackow, Eric T. Have an Abominably Good Day, 1 vol. 2010. (ENG., Illus.). 64p. (J). 16.99 *(978-0-7643-3496-2(4)*, 9780764334962) Schiffer Publishing, Ltd.
—The Lollipop Monster Meets Clem the Klutz, 1 vol. 2013. (ENG., Illus.). 64p. (J). 16.99 *(978-0-7643-4287-5(8)*, 9780764342875) Schiffer Publishing, Ltd.
Krackow, Eric T. & Krackow, Krackow. Bill the Snowman, 1 vol. 2009. (ENG., Illus.). 64p. (J). 16.99 *(978-0-7643-3219-7(8)*, 9780764332197) Schiffer Publishing, Ltd.
Kraegel, Kenneth. The Song of Delphine. Kraegel, Kenneth, illus. 2015. (ENG., Illus.). 40p. (J). (gr. k-3). 15.99 *(978-0-7636-7001-6(4))* Candlewick Pr.
Kraft, Andrea. Gracie Blue Knows a Secret, 1 vol. 2010. 24p. 24.95 *(978-1-4512-1035-4(3))* PublishAmerica, Inc.
—Gracie Blue Knows a Secret, 1 vol. Kraft, Joe, illus. 2009. 23p. pap. 19.95 *(978-1-61582-554-7(1))* PublishAmerica, Inc.
Kraft, Erik P. Lenny & Mel. Kraft, Erik P., illus. 2012. (Ready-for-Chapters Ser.). (ENG., Illus.). 64p. (J). (gr. 2-5). pap. 6.99 *(978-0-689-85891-8(4)*, Aladdin) Simon & Schuster Children's Publishing.
Krakower, Harold. The Adventures of Jacob & Mr Ludicus. 2010. 28p. pap. 12.49 *(978-1-4520-1187-5(7))* AuthorHouse.
Kramer, Jackie Azúa. The Green Umbrella. Sassouni, Maral, illus. 2017. (ENG.). 32p. (J). (gr. -1-3). 17.95 *(978-0-7358-4218-2(3))* North-South Bks., Inc.
Krantz, Hazel. In the Garden of the Caliph. 2012. 132p. (gr. 4-6). 23.14 *(978-1-4669-2888-6(3))*; (J). pap. 13.14 *(978-1-4669-2886-2(7))* Trafford Publishing.
Kraszewski. Surf Angel. 2009. 40p. *(978-0-9821989-0-2(6))* Kraszewski, Terry.
Kravetz, Stacy. The Fosters: Keep Your Frenemies Close. 2015. (ENG.). 224p. (YA). (gr. 7-12). pap. 9.99 *(978-1-4847-1620-5(5))* Hyperion Bks. for Children.
Krebs, Laurie. We All Went on Safari: A Counting Journey Through Tanzania. Cairns, Julia, illus. 2010. (J). 18.10 *(978-0-7569-9319-1(9))* Perfection Learning Corp.
Krech, Bob & Krecht, R.J. Love Puppies & Corner Kicks. 2011. (ENG.). 224p. (J). (gr. 5-18). 7.99 *(978-0-14-241783-6(1)*, Puffin Books) Penguin Young Readers Group.
Kredensor, Diane. Ollie & Moon: Aloha! 2013. (Step into Reading Ser.). (ENG., Illus.). 48p. (J). (gr. 1-4). 3.99 *(978-0-307-97950-6(4)*, Random Hse. Bks. for Young Readers) Random Hse. Children's Bks.
Kreder Sr., Edward G. & Kreder, Mary Ellen DeLuca. Sparkle's Journey. Vanden Berg, Myra, illus. 2013. 32p. pap. 5.99 *(978-0-9913232-0-3(3))* Kreder, Mary Ellen DeLuca.
Kreie, Chris, et al. Battle for Home Plate, 1 vol. Aburtov, Jesus Aburto, illus. 2010. (Sports Illustrated Kids Graphic Novels Ser.). (ENG.). 56p. (gr. 2-3). pap. 7.19 *(978-1-4342-2290-9(X))* Stone Arch Bks.
—Battle for Home Plate, 1 vol. Aburto, Jesus, illus. 2010. (Sports Illustrated Kids Graphic Novels Ser.). (ENG.). 56p. (gr. 2-3). 26.65 *(978-1-4342-1913-8(5))* Stone Arch Bks.
Krejewski, Sandra. The Little Hermit Crab. 2009. 21p. (J). 12.00 *(978-1-60695-004-3(5))* Callanish Pr.
Krensky, Stephen. Pins & Needles. Litten, Kristyna, illus. 2014. (Penguin Core Concepts Ser.). (ENG.). 32p. (J). (gr. -1-k). 3.99 *(978-0-448-46209-7(5)*, Grosset & Dunlap) Penguin Young Readers Group.
Krepela, Rebecca. Vernon, Drake & Chomp. 2013. 20p. pap. 24.95 *(978-1-62709-841-0(0))* America Star Bks.
Kretzmann, Jane. Eddie & Harry. Ditewig, Diann, illus. 2014. 48p. (J). *(978-0-9846739-3-3(8))* Cornerstone Pr. Chicago.
Kretzmer, Alissa. Brandy's Day at the Beach. 2013. 16p. pap. 12.97 *(978-1-61897-357-3(6)*, Strategic Bk. Publishing) Strategic Book Publishing & Rights Agency (SBPRA).
Kriescher, Jeanette "Netty". A Big Message from a Little Book: A Color-Blind World. 2008. 25p. pap. 24.95 *(978-1-60563-376-3(3))* America Star Bks.
Krisher, Trudy. Fallout. 2006. (ENG.). 272p. (J). (gr. 3-7). 17.95 *(978-0-8234-2035-3(3))* Holiday Hse., Inc.
Krishnaswami, Uma. The Grand Plan to Fix Everything. Halpin, Abigail, illus. (ENG.). (J). (gr. 3-7). 2013. 288p. pap. 8.99 *(978-1-4169-9590-6(0))* 2011. 272p. 16.99 *(978-1-4169-9589-0(7))* Simon & Schuster Children's Publishing. (Atheneum Bks. for Young Readers).
—The Problem with Being Slightly Heroic. Halpin, Abigail, illus. (ENG.). 288p. (J). (gr. 3-7). 2014. pap. 6.99 *(978-1-4424-2329-9(3)*, Atheneum Bks. for Young Readers) 2013. 16.99 *(978-1-4424-2328-2(5))* Simon & Schuster Children's Publishing.
Kristen, Judith. My Name Is Henley: My life & times as a rescued Dog. 2007. 150p. (J). per. 11.95 *(978-0-9800448-0-5(4))* Aquinas & Krone Publishing, LLC.
—Once upon a Time in Liverpool. Cash, Eric, illus. 2012. 40p. pap. 15.95 *(978-0-9849505-2-2(4))* Aquinas & Krone Publishing, LLC.
Kristie Smith-Armand M.Ed Ctvi. Adventures of Abby Diamond: Out of Sight. 2009. 300p. pap. 18.95 *(978-1-4401-7013-3(4))* iUniverse, Inc.
Kristie Smith-Armand M.Ed Tvi. Adventures of Abby Diamond: Abby Diamond in Teenage Wizard & Secrets in the Attic. 2009. 276p. pap. 17.95 *(978-1-4401-6626-6(9))* iUniverse, Inc.
Kristina Takes the Stage. 2008. (Illus.). 56p. (J). mass mkt. 10.95 *(978-0-9792361-3-6(4))* Inspire U., LLC.
Kriszt, Ann Marie. Bestis Friends. 2008. 276p. pap. 27.95 *(978-1-60703-154-3(X))* PublishAmerica, Inc.
Krivinskas, Carol Italiano. Barnyard Babies to the Rescue. 2008. 20p. pap. 13.95 *(978-1-4327-2183-1(6))* Outskirts Pr., Inc.
Krommenacker, Mark. Dave the Duck Gets Active, 1 vol. 2010. 20p. 24.95 *(978-1-4512-1231-0(3))* PublishAmerica, Inc.
Kropp, Paul. The Edge Is Burning. Doherty, Catherine, illus. 2008. 112p. (YA). (gr. 7-18). pap. *(978-1-897039-33-5(6))* High Interest Publishing (HIP).
Krosoczka, Jarrett J. Peanut Butter & Jellyfish. 2014. (ENG.). 40p. (J). (gr. -1-2). 16.99 *(978-0-375-87036-1(9)*, Knopf Bks. for Young Readers) Random Hse. Children's Bks.
Kroupa, Robert J. Just Like You. 2011. (J). *(978-0-9825503-4-2(0))* IGI Pr.
Krueger, Anton. Sunnyside Sal. 2010. 120p. pap. *(978-0-9584915-6-3(9))* Deep South Bks.
Krueger, Jim & Rogers, Bud. Child of Destiny, 1 vol. Padilla, Ariel, illus. 2008. (Z Graphic Novels / Tomo Ser.). (ENG.). 160p. (J). (gr. 4-7). pap. 6.99 *(978-0-310-71302-9(1))* Zondervan.
Krulik, Nancy. Don't Sneeze! 2017. (Kid from Planet Z Ser.: 2). lib. bdg. 16.00 ***(978-0-606-40108-1(3))*** Turtleback Bks.
—Eww! What's on My Shoe? Blecha, Aaron, illus. 2013. (George Brown, Class Clown Ser.: 11). (ENG.). 128p. (J). (gr. 2-4). 4.99 *(978-0-448-46114-4(5)*, Grosset & Dunlap) Penguin Young Readers Group.
—Eww! What's on My Shoe? 2013. (George Brown, Class Clown Ser.: 11). lib. bdg. 14.75 *(978-0-606-32126-6(8)*, Turtleback) Turtleback Bks.
—Friends for Never, 14 vols. John and Wendy Staff, illus. 2004. (Katie Kazoo, Switcheroo Ser.: 14). (ENG.). 80p. (J). (gr. 2-4). pap. 4.99 *(978-0-448-43606-7(X)*, Grosset & Dunlap) Penguin Young Readers Group.
—How Do You Pee in Space? 2014. (George Brown, Class Clown Ser.: 13). lib. bdg. 14.75 *(978-0-606-36163-7(4))* Turtleback Bks.
—I Heard a Rumor. Martini, Angela, illus. 2007. (How I Survived Middle School Ser.: No. 3). 105p. (J). *(978-0-439-90091-1(3))* Scholastic, Inc.
—Karate Katie, 18 vols. John and Wendy Staff, illus. 2006. (Katie Kazoo, Switcheroo Ser.: 18). (ENG.). 80p. (J). (gr. 2-4). pap. 4.99 *(978-0-448-43767-5(8)*, Grosset & Dunlap) Penguin Young Readers Group.
—The Twelve Burps of Christmas. Blecha, Aaron, illus. 2012. (George Brown, Class Clown Ser.: No. 1). (ENG.). 192p. (J). (gr. 2-4). pap. 5.99 *(978-0-448-45680-5(X)*, Grosset & Dunlap) Penguin Young Readers Group.
—The Twelve Burps of Christmas. 2012. (George Brown, Class Clown Ser.: No. 1). lib. bdg. 16.00 *(978-0-606-26652-9(6)*, Turtleback) Turtleback Bks.
—A Whirlwind Vacation. John and Wendy Staff, illus. 2005. (Katie Kazoo, Switcheroo Ser.: No. 2). (ENG.). 160p. (J). (gr. 2-4). mass mkt. 4.99 *(978-0-448-43748-4(1)*, Grosset & Dunlap) Penguin Young Readers Group.
Krulik, Nancy E. It's a Bird, It's a Plane, It's Toiletman! 2016. (George Brown, Class Clown Ser.: 17). lib. bdg. 14.75 *(978-0-606-38417-9(0))* Turtleback Bks.
—Pup Art. 2015. (Magic Bone Ser.: 9). lib. bdg. 14.75 *(978-0-606-37546-7(5))* Turtleback Bks.
Krum, Atticus. The Taming. Donaera, Patrizia, illus. 2014. (ENG.). 227p. (J). pap. 12.99 *(978-0-9885349-1-9(6))* Huntly Hse.
Krumm, Brian & Kortenkamp, Steve. Exploring Space & Beyond. 2015. (Exploring Space & Beyond Ser.). (ENG.). (gr. 3-4). 114.61 *(978-1-4914-6659-9(6)*, Connect) Stone Arch Bks.
Kruusval, Catarina. Franny's Friends. Sandin, Joan, tr. from SWE. 2008. (Illus.). 32p. (J). (gr. -1-1). 16.00 *(978-91-29-66836-0(0))* R & S Bks. SWE. Dist: Macmillan.
Kuefler, Joseph. Rulers of the Playground. Kuefler, Joseph, illus. 2017. (Illus.). 48p. (J). (gr. -1-3). 17.99 *(978-0-06-242432-7(7))* HarperCollins Pubs.
Kuenzler, Lou. The Dragon Dance. 2017. (Princess DisGrace Ser.). (ENG., Illus.). 272p. (J). (gr. 3-7). 15.99 *(978-0-553-53781-9(4)*, Random Hse. Bks. for Young Readers) Random Hse. Children's Bks.
Kugler, Tina. Snail & Worm Again. 2017. (ENG., Illus.). 32p. (J). (gr. 1-4). 16.99 *(978-0-544-79249-4(1)*, HMH Books For Young Readers) Houghton Mifflin Harcourt Publishing Co.
Kügler, Tina & Kügler, Carson, illus. Snail & Worm: Meet My Friend. 2016. (ENG.). 32p. (J). (gr. 1-4). 16.99 *(978-0-544-49412-1(1)*, HMH Books For Young Readers) Houghton Mifflin Harcourt Publishing Co.
Kuhlman, Evan. Hank's Big Day: The Story of a Bug. Groenink, Chuck, illus. 2016. (ENG.). 40p. (J). (gr. -1-2). 16.99 *(978-0-553-51150-5(5)*, Schwartz & Wade Bks.) Random Hse. Children's Bks.
Kuhn, Douglas Wolcik. The Summer of the Monarch Butterflies. 2012. 28p. pap. 24.95 *(978-1-4626-9302-3(4))* America Star Bks.
Kuipers, Jennifer L. Lynn's Magic Trunk: An Adventure in King Arthur's Court. 2007. 76p. per. 19.95 *(978-1-4241-9860-3(7))* America Star Bks.
Kuivila, Janet. The Gamma Girls of Chagrin Falls: Lillie, Rose & Irisa. 2004. 146p. pap. 12.95 *(978-0-9763441-0-0(6))* Cats Ink.
Kumiega, Michelle. The Bunnies Who Learn Not to Bully. 2011. 24p. pap. 24.95 *(978-1-4560-6742-7(7))* America Star Bks.
Kuperman, Joshua & Kuperman, Laura. The Little Lost Cricket. 2011. 20p. 11.59 *(978-1-4269-5486-3(7))* Trafford Publishing.
Kurtz, Jane. Planet Jupiter. 2017. 288p. (J). (gr. 3-7). 16.99 *(978-0-06-056486-5(5)*, Greenwillow Bks.) HarperCollins Pubs.
Kurtz, John. Claus Kids Stickers. 2011. (Dover Little Activity Books Stickers Ser.). (ENG.). 4p. (J). (gr. k-3). pap. 1.50 *(978-0-486-48294-1(4))* Dover Pubns., Inc.
Kurzweil, Allen. Leon & the Champion Chip. Bertholf, Bret, illus. 2005. 352p. (J). lib. bdg. 16.89 *(978-0-06-053934-4(8))* HarperCollins Pubs.
Kusaka, Hidenori. Pokemon Xy, Vol. 11. 2017. (Pokemon X Y Ser.: 11). lib. bdg. 14.75 ***(978-0-606-40299-6(3))*** Turtleback Bks.
Kuskowski, Alex. Line Up, 1 vol. unabr. ed. 2011. (District 13 Ser.). (ENG.). 48p. (YA). (gr. 9-12). pap. 7.95 *(978-1-61651-279-8(2))* Saddleback Educational Publishing, Inc.
Kvamstrom, Todd M. The King of Pete's Pond. 2011. 84p. pap. 28.68 *(978-1-4634-3523-3(1))* AuthorHouse.
Kvasnosky, Laura McGee. Really Truly Bingo. Kvasnosky, Laura McGee, illus. 2008. (ENG., Illus.). 32p. (J). (gr. k-k). 15.99 *(978-0-7636-3210-6(4))* Candlewick Pr.
Kwiat, Ernie, illus. Abby Caddaby up & Down. 2013. (J). *(978-0-7636-6741-2(2))* Candlewick Pr.
Kyi, Tanya Lloyd. Truth, 1 vol. 2003. (Orca Soundings Ser.). (ENG.). 128p. (YA). (gr. 8-12). pap. 9.95 *(978-1-55143-265-6(X))* Orca Bk. Pubs. USA.
La Coccinella. Here Comes Leo Lion. 2015. (Pull & Play Ser.). (ENG., Illus.). 12p. (J). (gr. -1-k). bds. 7.95 *(978-1-4549-1582-9(X))* Sterling Publishing Co., Inc.
La-Marr, Chiquita. Sally's Adventures. 2012. 12p. pap. 10.67 *(978-1-4669-4294-3(0))* Trafford Publishing.
Labatt, Mary. A Friend for Sam. Sarrazin, Marisol, illus. 2003. (Kids Can Read Ser.). (ENG.). 32p. (J). (gr. k-1). 14.95 *(978-1-55337-374-2(X))*; pap. 3.95 *(978-1-55337-375-9(8))* Kids Can Pr., Ltd. CAN. Dist: Hachette Bk. Group.
Labeda, Patricia R. Miko & the Mystery Friend. Labeda, Patricia R., illus. 2007. (Illus.). 73p. (J). (gr. 4-7). per. 10.99 *(978-1-59879-415-1(9)*, Lifevest) Lifevest Publishing, Inc.
LaCaille, Link. Smoken Careers: Roots, Rock, Rap & Reggae Book 2, 1 vol. 2010. 44p. pap. 24.95 *(978-1-4489-2136-2(8))* PublishAmerica, Inc.
Lacasse, Michael. George & His Special New Friends. 2005. 48p. pap. 16.95 *(978-1-4137-8285-1(X))* PublishAmerica, Inc.
Lackey, Mercedes & Edghill, Rosemary. Legacies, No. 1. 2010. (Shadow Grail Ser.: 1). (ENG.). 320p. (YA). (gr. 8-12). pap. 11.99 *(978-0-7653-1761-2(3)*, Tor Teen) Doherty, Tom Assocs., LLC.
LaCour, Nina. The Disenchantments. (ENG.). (YA). (gr. 9). 2013. 336p. pap. 10.99 *(978-0-14-242391-2(2)*, Speak) 2012. 320p. 16.99 *(978-0-525-42219-8(6)*, Dutton Books for Young Readers) Penguin Young Readers Group.
—Hold Still. 2010. (ENG.). 272p. (YA). (gr. 7-18). 10.99 *(978-0-14-241694-5(0)*, Speak) Penguin Young Readers Group.
—We Are Okay. 2017. (ENG.). 240p. (YA). (gr. 9). 17.99 *(978-0-525-42589-2(6)*, Dutton Books for Young Readers) Penguin Young Readers Group.
Ladig, Kim. Ellie's Lake House. 2010. 48p. pap. 19.49 *(978-1-4490-5641-4(5))* AuthorHouse.
Ladybird. Anansi Helps a Friend, Level 1. 2016. (Ladybird Readers Ser.). (ENG.). 16p. (J). (gr. 2-4). pap., act. bk. ed. 5.99 *(978-0-241-25420-2(5))* Penguin Bks., Ltd. GBR. Dist: Independent Pubs. Group.
LaFleur, John & Dubin, Shawn. Dreary & Naughty: Friday the 13th of February, 1 vol. 2013. (ENG., Illus.). 64p. (J). 14.99 *(978-0-7643-4495-4(1)*, 9780764344954) Schiffer Publishing, Ltd.
LaFleur, Suzanne. Beautiful Blue World. (ENG., Illus.). (J). (gr. 3-7). 2017. 240p. pap. 6.99 *(978-0-307-98032-8(4)*, Yearling) 2016. 224p. lib. bdg. 19.99 *(978-0-375-99089-2(5)*, Lamb, Wendy Bks.) Random Hse. Children's Bks.
—Eight Keys. 2012. (ENG.). 224p. (J). (gr. 4-7). 6.99 *(978-0-375-87213-6(2)*, Yearling) Random Hse. Children's Bks.
—Love, Aubrey. 2011. (ENG.). 272p. (J). (gr. 3-7). pap. 7.99 *(978-0-375-85159-9(3)*, Yearling) Random Hse. Children's Bks.
LaFleur, Suzanne. Threads of Blue. 2017. (ENG.). 224p. (J). (gr. 3-7). 16.99 ***(978-1-101-93999-4(0))***; lib. bdg. 19.99 ***(978-1-101-94000-6(X))*** Random Hse. Children's Bks. (Lamb, Wendy Bks.).
LaFleur, Suzanne M. Threads of Blue. 2017. (J). pap. ***(978-1-101-94002-0(6)***, Delacorte Pr) Random House Publishing Group.
Lagartos, M. L., et al. Entre Amigos. (SPA & ENG., Illus.). (J). (gr. 4). 88p. wbk. ed. *(978-84-7861-045-7(6))*;Level 2. 2nd ed. 108p. tchr. ed. *(978-84-7861-038-9(3))*;Level 3. 74p. tchr. ed. *(978-84-7861-047-1(2))*;Level 3. 192p. stu. ed. *(978-84-7861-044-0(8))* Coloquio, Editorial S.A.
—Entre Amigos. (SPA & ENG.). (J). (gr. 4). Level 1. stu. ed. 25.95 *(978-84-7143-427-2(X)*, SGS427X)Level 1. 64p. wbk. ed. 15.95 *(978-84-7143-428-9(8)*, SGS4288)Level 2. 4th ed. (Illus.). 160p. stu. ed. 25.95 *(978-84-7143-472-2(5)*, SGS725)Level 2. 4th ed. (Illus.). 68p. wbk. ed. 15.95 *(978-84-7143-477-7(6)*, SGS776) Sociedad General Espanola de Libreria ESP. Dist: Continental Bk. Co., Inc.
Lagercrantz, Rose. Life According to Dani. Eriksson, Eva, illus. 2016. (My Happy Life Ser.: 4). (ENG.). 108p. (gr. k-3). 16.99 *(978-1-77657-070-6(7))* Gecko Pr. NZL. Dist: Lerner Publishing Group.
—My Happy Life. Eriksson, Eva, illus. 2013. (ENG.). 136p. (J). (gr. k-3). 16.95 *(978-1-877579-35-6(1))* Gecko Pr. NZL. Dist: Lerner Publishing Group.
—When I Am Happiest. Eriksson, Eva, illus. 2015. (ENG.). 128p. (J). (gr. k-3). 16.99 *(978-1-927271-90-2(8))* Gecko Pr. NZL. Dist: Lerner Publishing Group.
Lagonegro, Melissa. Friends for a Princess. 2004. (Disney Princess Step into Reading Ser.). (gr. -1-2). lib. bdg. 13.55 *(978-0-613-73713-5(X)*, Turtleback) Turtleback Bks.
—Friends for a Princess (Disney Princess) Harchy, Atelier Philippe, illus. 2016. (Step into Reading Ser.). (ENG.). 24p. (J). (gr. -1-1). pap. 4.99 *(978-0-7364-3670-0(7)*, RH/Disney) Random Hse. Children's Bks.
Lagonegro, Melissa & RH Disney Staff. Just Keep Swimming. Harchy, Atelier Philippe, illus. 2005. (Step into Reading Ser.). (ENG.). 32p. (J). (gr. k-3). pap. 3.99 *(978-0-7364-2319-9(2)*, RH/Disney) Random Hse. Children's Bks.
Lai, Trevor. Piggy. 2016. (ENG., Illus.). 32p. (J). 16.99 *(978-1-68119-065-5(6)*, 9781681190655, Bloomsbury USA Childrens) Bloomsbury Publishing USA.
Lake, A. J. The Circle of Stone. 2008. (Darkest Age Ser.). (ENG.). 304p. (YA). (gr. 4-7). 16.95 *(978-1-59990-079-7(3)*, 9781599900797, Bloomsbury USA Childrens) Bloomsbury Publishing USA.
Lake, Autumn. The Terrible Day. 2011. 32p. pap. 24.95 *(978-1-4560-0949-6(4))* America Star Bks.
Lamar, Lloyd. The Pond. 2007. 92p. per. 9.99 *(978-1-60477-286-9(7))* Salem Author Services.
LaMarche, Una. You in Five Acts. 2016. (ENG.). 352p. (YA). (gr. 7). 17.99 *(978-1-101-99893-9(8)*, Razorbill) Penguin Young Readers Group.
Lamb, Anne. Beat Bugs. 2017. (Beat Bugs Ser.). 32p. (J). (gr. -1-3). 9.99 *(978-0-06-264076-5(3)*, HarperFestival) HarperCollins Pubs.
—Beat Bugs: Magical Mystery Tour. 2017. (Beat Bugs Ser.). 24p. (J). (gr. -1-3). pap. 3.99 *(978-0-06-264062-8(3)*, HarperFestival) HarperCollins Pubs.

E
F
G

—Beat Bugs: Meet the Beat Bugs. 2017. (I Can Read Level 1 Ser.). 32p. (J). (gr. -1-3). pap. 3.99 *(978-0-06-264066-6(6))* HarperCollins Pubs.
—Beat Bugs: Rain. 2017. (Beat Bugs Ser.). 16p. (J). (gr. -1 — 1). bds. 6.99 *(978-0-06-264073-4(9),* HarperFestival) HarperCollins Pubs.
Lamb, Braden. Adventure Time. Paroline, Shelli, illus. 2014. (Adventure Time Ser.: 3). (ENG.). 128p. (J). (gr. 4). 34.99 *(978-1-60886-347-1(6))* Boom! Studios.
Lamb li, James. Jimmy Jimmy el Cordero Salto Cumple Phil el Pato. 2012. 28p. pap. 17.99 *(978-1-4685-5036-8(5))* AuthorHouse.
Lamb, Lenny. Moving Blues: Greener Grass. 2011. 32p. pap. 24.95 *(978-1-4626-4398-1(1))* America Star Bks.
Lambert, Janet. Where the Heart Is: A Christy Drayton Story. 2003. (J). pap. 9.95 *(978-1-930009-83-7(6),* 800-691-7779) Image Cascade Publishing.
Lambert, Nancy & Lamb, Anne. Help! 2017. (Beat Bugs Ser.). 24p. (J). (gr. -1-3). pap. 3.99 *(978-0-06-264060-4(7),* HarperFestival) HarperCollins Pubs.
Laminack, Lester L. The Ultimate Read-Aloud Resource: Making Every Moment Intentional & Instructional with Best Friend Books. 2016. (ENG.). 128p. (J). (gr. k-8). pap. 34.99 *(978-1-338-10925-2(1),* Teaching Resources) Scholastic, Inc.
Lammers, Elizabeth A. & McKinney, Dan. The Tale of the Black Igloo: Another Adventure of Pepe & Pierre, 1 vol. Epstein, Gabriela, illus. 2010. 26p. pap. 24.95 *(978-1-60610-433-0(0))* PublishAmerica, Inc.
Lamont, Tracey. The Adventures of Speedy & Creedy: Mrs. Smith's Kitchen. 2008. (ENG.). 32p. 14.49 *(978-1-4389-3043-5(7))* AuthorHouse.
—The Adventures of Speedy & Creedy: The Surprise. 2009. 36p. pap. 16.50 *(978-1-4389-7541-2(4))* AuthorHouse.
Lampard, Frank. Frankie vs. the Cowboy's Crew. 2014. (Frankie's Magic Soccer Ball Ser.: 4). (ENG., Illus.). 112p. (J). (gr. 2-5). pap. 4.99 *(978-0-545-66618-3(X),* Scholastic Paperbacks) Scholastic, Inc.
Lampley, Titra. Jazzy Dolls & Swaggro's Get's Revenge on Bullies. 2012. 42p. 16.95 *(978-1-4626-6137-4(8))* America Star Bks.
Lamuth, Nancy. Lucky & Me. Thomas, Richard A., illus. 2012. 20p. pap. 24.95 *(978-1-4626-0665-8(2))* America Star Bks.
Landolf, Diane Wright. Hog & Dog. Harris, Jennifer Beck, illus. 2005. (Step into Reading Ser.: Vol. 1). (ENG.). 32p. (J). (gr. -1-1). per. 3.99 *(978-0-375-83165-2(7),* Random Hse. Bks. for Young Readers) Random Hse. Children's Bks.
Landon, Kristen. Life in the Pit. 2008. (ENG., Illus.). 248p. (YA). (gr. 5-13). pap. 8.95 *(978-1-933831-08-4(1))* Blooming Tree Pr.
Landry, Cristy. Snowboarding with Courage. 2016. 98p. (YA). (gr. 8-12). pap. 10.95 *(978-0-9963756-0-3(0))* All About Kids Publishing.
Lane, Bruce Courand. The Friendly Little Martian. 2011. 28p. pap. 15.99 *(978-1-4568-6638-9(9))* Xlibris Corp.
Lane, Ronald. Avina's Song: A Children's Story. 2007. (ENG.). 48p. per. 16.95 *(978-1-4241-6252-9(1))* America Star Bks.
Lang, Valerie E. Jet's Day: A Whisker Team Story. 2011. 32p. pap. 13.00 *(978-1-61204-178-0(7),* Strategic Bk. Publishing) Strategic Book Publishing & Rights Agency (SBPRA).
Langan, Paul & Schraff, Anne. Summer of Secrets. 2008. (Bluford High Ser.: 10). (ENG.). 160p. (J). (gr. 7-18). 5.99 *(978-0-439-90491-9(9),* Scholastic Paperbacks) Scholastic, Inc.
Lange, Erin Jade. Dead Ends. 2013. (ENG.). 336p. (YA). (gr. 9). 17.99 *(978-1-61963-080-2(X),* 9781619630802, Bloomsbury USA Childrens); 288p. pap. 17.99 *(978-1-61963-081-9(8))* Bloomsbury Publishing USA.
Langreuter, Jutta. So Happy Together! Dahle, Stephanie, illus. 2017. (ENG.). 32p. (J). (gr. -1-3). 17.95 *(978-0-7358-4279-3(5))* North-South Bks., Inc.
Langrish, Katherine. The Shadow Hunt. 2010. 322p. lib. bdg. *(978-0-06-111678-0(5))* HarperCollins Pubs.
Lao, Samantha. The Scared Panda. 2009. 20p. pap. 10.49 *(978-1-4389-9226-6(2))* AuthorHouse.
Lariviere, Sarah. The Bad Kid. 2016. (ENG., Illus.). 304p. (J). (gr. 3-7). 16.99 *(978-1-4814-3581-9(7),* Simon & Schuster Bks. For Young Readers) Simon & Schuster Bks. For Young Readers.
Lamer, Eric. The Adventure of Paperman - Journey into Night. Schmolze, Ian, illus. 2013. 194p. pap. 16.99 *(978-1-883651-68-8(9))* Winters Publishing.
Laroche, M. The Perplexing Problems of Pea & Friends. 2011. 36p. pap. 21.99 *(978-1-4568-2288-0(8))* Xlibris Corp.
Larry Sweitzer. The Ghost, the Eggheads, & Babe Ruth's Piano: A Novel. 2009. 180p. 23.95 *(978-1-4401-7103-1(3));* pap. 13.95 *(978-1-4401-7104-8(1))* iUniverse, Inc.
Larsen, Alison. Thomas the Turtle's Adventures. 2006. (Illus.). 23p. (J). per. 14.95 *(978-1-60002-096-4(8),* 3962) Mountain Valley Publishing, LLC.
Larsen, Angela Sage. Broken Record, Bk. 4. 2013. (Fifties Chix Ser.: 4). (ENG., Illus.). 200p. (YA). pap. 9.95 *(978-1-60746-446-4(2),* Premiere) FastPrncil, Inc.
—Till the End of Time. 2013. (Fifties Chix Ser.: 5). (ENG.). 200p. (YA). pap. 9.95 *(978-1-60746-468-6(3),* Premiere) FastPrncil, Inc.
Larsen, Elizabeth. Buster Hardings: Buster Makes New Friends. 2008. 104p. pap. 19.95 *(978-1-60563-951-2(6))* America Star Bks.
—A Party for Buster & Haylee! 2011. 34p. pap. 16.95 *(978-1-4560-6954-4(3))* America Star Bks.
Larue, Ravyn. Sophie Browne Isn't Dead. 2011. 40p. pap. 19.95 *(978-0-557-91717-4(4))* Lulu Pr., Inc.
Lasenby, Jack. Taur. (Travellers Ser.: No. 2). (Illus.). 160p. (YA). (gr. 8-18). pap. *(978-1-877135-18-7(6),* Longacre Pr.) Random Hse. New Zealand.
Lasky, Kathryn. Poodle & Hound. Vane, Mitch, illus. 2011. (ENG.). 48p. (J). (gr. k-3). pap. 6.95 *(978-1-58089-323-7(6))* Charlesbridge Publishing, Inc.
Lasota, Mary. Kitty Piper Angel Cat: I Almost Lost My Best Friend. 2009. 36p. pap. 16.99 *(978-1-4490-2012-5(7))* AuthorHouse.
—Kitty Piper, Angel Cat, Book 2: The Venusians Have Landed. 2010. 40p. pap. 18.46 *(978-1-4520-8823-5(3))* AuthorHouse.
Lasser, Jessica. Stormy the Cloud. 2012. 24p. pap. 17.99 *(978-1-4685-6214-9(2))* AuthorHouse.
Latham, Frank Brown. The Fighting Quaker: The Southern Campaigns of General Nathaniel Greene. Vosburg, L., illus. 2011. 194p. 42.95 *(978-1-258-00848-2(3))* Literary Licensing, LLC.
Latham, Irene. Don't Feed the Boy. Graegin, Stephanie, illus. 2012. (ENG.). 288p. (J). (gr. 3-7). 17.99 *(978-1-59643-755-5(3),* 9781596437555) Roaring Brook Pr.
—Don't Feed the Boy. Graegin, Stephanie, illus. 2014. (ENG.). 304p. (J). (gr. 3-7). pap. 9.99 *(978-1-250-04428-0(6),* 9781250044280) Square Fish.
Lathrop, Brandy. Jalen Goes to Mars. 2008. 22p. pap. 24.95 *(978-1-4241-9010-2(X))* America Star Bks.
Latimer, Miriam. Dear Panda. 2014. (ENG., Illus.). 32p. (J). (gr. -1-3). 17.95 *(978-1-77147-078-0(X),* Owlkids) Owlkids Bks. Inc. CAN. Dist: Publishers Group West (PGW).
Latter, Kym & Stroud, Cassie. The Trouble with Bear Hugs: A Story about Asthma. 2012. (Illus.). 32p. (J). pap. *(978-0-9873747-0-7(2))* Latter, Kym.
Laubenstein, Sharon. Something about Sally. 2013. 24p. pap. 10.95 *(978-1-4908-0723-2(3),* WestBow Pr.) Author Solutions, Inc.
Laudati, Joe. Faela: A Fairy's Tale. 2008. 190p. pap. 14.50 *(978-0-615-20324-9(8))* Laudati, Joe.
Laure, Estelle. This Raging Light. 2015. (ENG.). 288p. (YA). (gr. 9). 17.99 *(978-0-544-53429-2(8),* HMH Books For Young Readers) Houghton Mifflin Harcourt Publishing Co.
Laurens, Jennifer. Falling for Romeo. 2007. (YA). per. 12.95 *(978-1-933963-94-5(8))* Grove Creek Publishing, LLC.
Laurentine, Florianne Daphne. The Mystery Chronicles: The Unknown Masterpiece & the Case of the Practical Joker. 2012. 98p. pap. 7.99 *(978-1-61667-427-4(X))* Raider Publishing International.
Laurie Douglas, Inez. No One Heard His Cry. 2008. 185p. pap. 11.95 *(978-1-4327-2870-0(9))* Outskirts Pr., Inc.
Lavi, Yifat. Fish Also Fade: Illustrated by: Oren Somech. 2011. (Illus.). 32p. pap. 14.58 *(978-1-4520-9084-9(X))* AuthorHouse.
Lavohn, Jodi. Sam's Adventure. 2011. 54p. pap. 16.95 *(978-1-4560-7758-7(9))* America Star Bks.
Lavoie, Jennifer. Andy Squared. 2012. (ENG.). 264p. (J). (gr. 7). pap. 11.95 *(978-1-60282-743-1(5))* Bold Strokes Bks.
Lawrence, Eve Pollard. My Friend Eddie. 2012. 30p. pap. 19.99 *(978-1-4685-7632-0(1))* AuthorHouse.
Lawrence, Hilary R. The Adventures of Little Ted. 2009. (ENG., Illus.). 154p. pap. *(978-1-84748-587-8(1))* Athena Pr.
Laws, Jamie Lynn. Cameron & the Mysterious Shack. 2008. pap. 16.95 *(978-1-60563-434-0(4))* America Star Bks.
Lawson, Dorie McCullough. Tex: A Book for Little Dreamers. 2011. (ENG., Illus.). 44p. (J). (gr. -1-k). 15.95 *(978-1-57076-501-8(4))* Trafalgar Square Bks.
Lawson, Gwendolynn. Jane's Secret Angel. 2009. 20p. pap. 12.49 *(978-1-4389-4061-8(0))* AuthorHouse.
Lawson, Jessica. Sharing & Making Friends. 2010. 20p. pap. 10.00 *(978-1-60911-707-8(7),* Eloquent Bks.) Strategic Book Publishing & Rights Agency (SBPRA).
Lawson, Rob, illus. Duke Finds a Home. 2006. (Duke's Tails Ser.). 32p. (J). *(978-0-9779308-0-7(7))* Bush Brothers & Co.
Lawton, Diana. Paulie the Penguin Meets Sammy the Seal. 2012. 30p. 24.95 *(978-1-4626-6782-6(1))* America Star Bks.
Lay, Eddie. Mystery of the Hats. 2006. 61p. pap. 16.95 *(978-1-4241-2649-1(5))* PublishAmerica, Inc.
Lay, Kathryn. Book 1: Time & Space. 2016. (Time Twisters Ser.). (ENG.). (J). (gr. 2-6). lib. bdg. 27.07 ***(978-1-62402-177-0(8))*** ABDO Publishing Co.
—Book 2: Haunted Time. 2016. (Time Twisters Ser.). (ENG.). (J). (gr. 2-6). lib. bdg. 27.07 ***(978-1-62402-178-7(6))*** ABDO Publishing Co.
—Book 3: the Curse of Time. 2016. (Time Twisters Ser.). (ENG.). (J). (gr. 2-6). lib. bdg. 27.07 ***(978-1-62402-179-4(4))*** ABDO Publishing Co.
Lay, Kathryn. Crown Me! 2004. (ENG.). 208p. (J). (gr. 4-6). tchr. ed. 17.95 *(978-0-8234-1845-9(6))* Holiday Hse., Inc.
Lazewnik, Libby. Out of the Woods. Scheinberg, Shepsil, illus. 2011. 320p. (J). *(978-1-4226-1176-0(0))* Mesorah Pubns., Ltd.
Lazo, Jeanne Rae. If Looks Could Kill. 2005. 160p. (J). lib. bdg. 14.95 *(978-0-9713756-4-2(X))* Stargazer Publishing Co.
Log. The Pencil Monster! 2011. 28p. pap. 14.95 *(978-0-557-94993-9(9))* Lulu Pr., Inc.
Le Blanc, Lennie. The Minnesota Summer. 2011. 116p. (gr. 4-6). pap. 10.95 *(978-1-4620-3887-9(5))* iUniverse, Inc.
Le Guin, Ursula K. Tom Mouse. 2004. (Illus.). (J). (gr. k-3). spiral bd. *(978-0-616-14584-5(5))* Canadian National Institute for the Blind/Institut National Canadien pour les Aveugles.
—Very Far Away from Anywhere Else. 2004. (ENG.). 144p. (YA). (gr. 7-12). pap. 6.95 *(978-0-15-205208-9(9))* Houghton Mifflin Harcourt Publishing Co.
Leader, Jessica. Nice & Mean. 2010. (Mix Ser.). (ENG.). 272p. (J). (gr. 4-8). pap. 6.99 *(978-1-4169-9160-1(3),* Aladdin) Simon & Schuster Children's Publishing.
Leah. The Alligator Named Ally, 1 vol. 2009. 20p. pap. 24.95 *(978-1-60749-726-4(3))* America Star Bks.
Leah's Song Apple. 2003. (J). pap. 2.75 *(978-0-590-44567-2(7))* Scholastic, Inc.
Lean, Sarah. Hero. 2015. (ENG.). 208p. (J). (gr. 3-7). 16.99 *(978-0-06-212238-4(X))* HarperCollins Pubs.
Lears, Laurie. Stay Away from Rat Boy! Hansen, Red, illus. 2009. (ENG.). 32p. (J). (gr. 2-3). 16.99 *(978-0-8075-6789-0(2))* Whitman, Albert & Co.
Lease, Janice. Pellina the Pelican. 2008. 48p. pap. 19.95 *(978-0-9800762-1-9(8))* Cinnamon Ridge Publishing.
Leathers, Philippa. The Black Rabbit. Leathers, Philippa, illus. 2016. (ENG., Illus.). 40p. (J). (gr. -1-2). 6.99 *(978-0-7636-8879-0(7))* Candlewick Pr.
Leathers, Ruth. Purple Mountain. 2008. 36p. pap. 20.95 *(978-1-4327-2685-0(4))* Outskirts Pr., Inc.
Leavitt, Lindsey. The Chapel Wars. 2014. (ENG.). 304p. (YA). (gr. 7). 17.99 *(978-1-59990-788-8(7),* 9781599907888, Bloomsbury USA Childrens) Bloomsbury Publishing USA.
Leavitt, Lindsey & Mellom, Robin. The Pages Between Us. Dening, Abby, illus. 2016. (Pages Between Us Ser.: 1). 288p. (J). (gr. 3-7). 16.99 *(978-0-06-237771-5(X))* HarperCollins Pubs.
—The Pages Between Us: in the Spotlight. 2017. (Pages Between Us Ser.: 2). 336p. (J). (gr. 3-7). 16.99 *(978-0-06-237774-6(4))* HarperCollins Pubs.
Leavy, Patricia. Blue. 2015. (ENG., Illus.). 168p. pap. *(978-94-6300-353-7(3))* Sense Pubs.
Leberer, Sigrid. The Adventures of the Three Best Friends. 2004. (Charming Collection of Five Short Stories Ser.). (Illus.). 22p. (J). bds. 6.99 *(978-1-59384-056-3(X))* Parklane Publishing.
Leblanc, Louise. Leo's Poster Challenge, 1 vol. Prud'homme, Jules & Cummins, Sarah, trs. from FRE. Prud'homme, Jules & Jules, Prud'homme, illus. 2003. (Formac First Novels Ser.). (ENG.). 64p. (J). (gr. 2-5). 4.95 *(978-0-88780-608-7(2),* 9780887806087); 14.95 *(978-0-88780-609-4(0),* 9780887806094) Formac Publishing Co., Ltd. CAN. Dist: Casemate Pubs. & Bk. Distributors, LLC.
—Leo's Skiing Surprise. Prud'homme, Jules, illus. 2007. (Formac First Novels Ser.). (ENG.). 64p. (J). (gr. 2-5). 14.95 *(978-0-88780-738-1(0),* 9780887807381) Formac Publishing Co., Ltd. CAN. Dist: Casemate Pubs. & Bk. Distributors, LLC.
—Leo's Skiing Surprise, 1 vol. Cummins, Sarah, tr. from FRE. Prud'homme, Jules, illus. 2007. (Formac First Novels Ser.). (ENG.). 64p. (J). (gr. 2-5). 4.95 *(978-0-88780-736-7(4),* 9780887807367) Formac Publishing Co., Ltd. CAN. Dist: Casemate Pubs. & Bk. Distributors, LLC.
Ledbetter, Penny S. Mushroom's Day Away. Garrett, Caroline S., illus. 2005. 32p. (J). 9.95 *(978-1-933251-19-6(0))* Parkway Pubs., Inc.
Leder, Meg. The Museum of Heartbreak. 2017. (ENG., Illus.). 288p. (YA). (gr. 7). pap. 10.99 *(978-1-4814-3211-5(7),* Simon Pulse) Simon Pulse.
—The Museum of Heartbreak. Wachter, Jill, photos by. 2016. (ENG., Illus.). 288p. (YA). (gr. 9). 17.99 *(978-1-4814-3210-8(9),* Simon Pulse) Simon Pulse.
Lee Badtke, Danica. Day Care. 2013. 26p. pap. 9.99 *(978-1-937165-36-9(1))* Orange Hat Publishing.
Lee, Cecelia In. The Alphabets. 2010. 292p. 25.99 *(978-1-4520-3626-7(8));* pap. 15.59 *(978-1-4520-3625-0(X))* AuthorHouse.
Lee, Dakota. Flash of Freedom. 2009. 128p. pap. 11.95 *(978-0-595-52557-7(1))* iUniverse, Inc.
Lee, Darrien. Grown in Sixty Seconds. 2009. (ENG., Illus.). 288p. (YA). (gr. 9). 9.95 *(978-1-933967-72-1(2),* Urban Renaissance) Kensington Publishing Corp.
Lee, Janice. Ethan's First Day of School. 2013. 20p. pap. 24.95 *(978-1-62709-501-3(2))* America Star Bks.
Lee, Janice G. The Adventures of Chewy & Tonk. 2003. (Illus.). 40p. (J). per. *(978-1-55306-599-9(9),* Guardian Bks.) Essence Publishing.
Lee, Jeffrey Lyndon. Locked in the Box. 2013. 40p. pap. 24.95 *(978-1-4626-6218-0(8))* America Star Bks.
Lee, Jihyeon. Pool. 2015. (ENG., Illus.). 56p. (J). (gr. -1-k). 16.99 *(978-1-4521-4294-4(7))* Chronicle Bks. LLC.
Lee, Johnie. Courtney. 2012. 108p. pap. 11.99 *(978-1-61996-498-3(8))* Salem Author Services.
Lee, Jonathan. So I Could Fly Free. 2008. (ENG., Illus.). 32p. (J). *(978-1-85345-434-9(6))* Crusade for World Revival.
Lee, Kathy. The Runaway Train. 2011. 144p. pap. *(978-1-84427-505-2(1))* Scripture Union.
Lee, Laura. Snail Race at Penny's Place. 2009. 24p. pap. 11.99 *(978-1-4389-9958-6(5))* AuthorHouse.
Lee, Mark. My Best Friend Is a Goldfish. 2017. (ENG.). 24p. (J). *(978-1-5124-2601-4(6),* Carolrhoda Bks.) Lerner Publishing Group.
Lee, Maxine. Big Whoop! 2014. (ENG., Illus.). 32p. (J). (gr. 1-4). 16.95 *(978-1-57687-683-1(7),* powerHouse Bks.) powerHouse Cultural Entertainment, Inc.
Lee, Michelle. Play with Me! Lee, Michelle, illus. 2017. (ENG., Illus.). 32p. (J). (-k). 16.99 *(978-0-399-54601-3(4),* G.P. Putnam's Sons Books for Young Readers) Penguin Young Readers Group.
Lee, Nancy. Baby Chipmunks & Backyard Friends. 2005. (J). 9.95 *(978-0-9772078-2-4(X))* Journey Pubns., LLC.
—Hoover's Funny Little Kids. 2005. (J). spiral bd. 8.95 *(978-0-9748087-8-9(4))* Journey Pubns., LLC.
Lee, Patty. Three Dogs & a Horse Named Blue. Lee, Jack, illus. 2009. 80p. pap. 10.49 *(978-1-4389-9685-1(3))* AuthorHouse.
Lee, Thomas. The Battle at Otter Lake. 2007. 167p. pap. 24.95 *(978-1-60441-488-2(X))* America Star Bks.
Lee, Tiffany A. Meadow City Presents: A New Friend. 2006. 52p. pap. 16.95 *(978-1-4241-4374-0(8))* PublishAmerica, Inc.
Lee, Vanessa Rose. The Haunted House of Riddles. Gillen, Rosemarie, illus. 2011. 28p. pap. 7.99 *(978-1-61286-053-4(2))* Avid Readers Publishing Group.
Leese, Jennifer L. B. Two Spots Bakery. 2004. 41p. pap. 24.95 *(978-1-4137-3207-8(0))* PublishAmerica, Inc.
Leeson, Christine. Molly & the Storm. Hansen, Gaby, illus. 2003. 32p. (J). (gr. k-2). tchr. ed. 15.95 *(978-1-58925-027-7(3))* Tiger Tales.
Leeuwen, Joke Van & Leeuwen, Joke van. Eep! Leeuwen, Joke van, illus. 2012. (Gecko Press Titles Ser.). (ENG., Illus.). 152p. (J). (gr. 2-5). pap. 7.95 *(978-1-877579-07-3(6))* Gecko Pr. NZL. Dist: Lerner Publishing Group.
Leffler, Silke & Janisch, Heinz. "I Have a Little Problem" Said the Bear. 2012. (ENG., Illus.). 32p. (J). (gr. -1-3). pap. 8.95 *(978-0-7358-4094-2(6))* North-South Bks., Inc.
LeFlore, Lyah B. Can't Hold Me Down. Warfield, D. L., illus. 2010. (Come Up Ser.). (ENG.). 272p. (J). (gr. 9-18). pap. 8.99 *(978-1-4169-7964-7(6),* Simon Pulse) Simon Pulse.
Legrand, Claire. The Cavendish Home for Boys & Girls. Watts, Sarah, illus. (ENG.). (J). (gr. 5). 2013. 368p. pap. 7.99 *(978-1-4424-4292-4(1))* 2012. 352p. 16.99 *(978-1-4424-4291-7(3))* Simon & Schuster Bks. For Young Readers. (Simon & Schuster Bks. For Young Readers).
—Foxheart. Zollars, Jaime, illus. 2016. 480p. (J). (gr. 3-7). 16.99 *(978-0-06-242773-1(3),* Greenwillow Bks.) HarperCollins Pubs.
Lehmkuhl, Pat, illus. Starlight, Star Bright: (the Starlight Books, 3), 6 vols. 2003. (Starlight Bks.: Bk. 3). 192p. (J). (gr. 3-7). per. 12.00 *(978-0-9714161-2-3(5))* Raven Publishing Inc. of Montana.
Lehrhaupt, Adam. I Will Not Eat You. Magoon, Scott, illus. 2016. (ENG.). 40p. (J). (gr. -1-3). 17.99 *(978-1-4814-2933-7(7),* Simon & Schuster Bks. For Young Readers) Simon & Schuster Bks. For Young Readers.
Lehrman, Maggie. The Cost of All Things. 2015. (ENG.). 416p. (YA). (gr. 9). 17.99 *(978-0-06-232074-2(2))* HarperCollins Pubs.
Leibenkop, T. The Sovereign of the Northern Winds. 2009. 30p. pap. 13.50 *(978-1-60693-847-8(9),* Eloquent Bks.) Strategic Book Publishing & Rights Agency (SBPRA).
Leigh, Autumn. Far-Out Friends. 2006. (Neighborhood Readers Ser.). (ENG.). 8p. (gr. -1-3). pap. 5.15 *(978-1-4042-6750-3(6),* Rosen Classroom) Rosen Publishing Group, Inc., The.
Leigh, Brittany. A New Friend in Jungletown. 2011. 40p. pap. 24.95 *(978-1-4560-3699-7(8))* America Star Bks.
Leliveld, Alette Wells. Remember Me. 2013. 64p. pap. *(978-1-77097-686-3(8))* FriesenPress.
Lemay, Didi. A Winter Solstice Celebration. Campbell, Jacquie, illus. 2008. 56p. pap. 23.99 *(978-1-4389-0998-1(5))* AuthorHouse.
Lemieux, Jean. Toby & the Mysterious Creature. Cummins, Sarah, tr. from FRE. Casson, Sophie, illus. 2008. (Formac First Novels Ser.). (ENG.). 64p. (J). (gr. 2-5). 14.95 *(978-0-88780-761-9(5),* 9780887807619) Formac Publishing Co., Ltd. CAN. Dist: Casemate Pubs. & Bk. Distributors, LLC.
—Toby's Best Friend. Cummins, Sarah, tr. from FRE. Casson, Sophie, illus. 2003. (Formac First Novels Ser.). (ENG.). 64p. (J). (gr. 2-5). 14.95 *(978-0-88780-611-7(2),* 9780887806117); (gr. 1-5). 4.95 *(978-0-88780-610-0(4),* 9780887806100) Formac Publishing Co., Ltd. CAN. Dist: Casemate Pubs. & Bk. Distributors, LLC.
Lemieux, Jean & Casson, Sophie. Toby & the Mysterious Creature, 1 vol. Cummins, Sarah, tr. from FRE. Casson, Sophie, illus. 2008. (Formac First Novels Ser.). (ENG., Illus.). 64p. (J). (gr. 2-5). 5.95 *(978-0-88780-759-6(3),* 9780887807596) Formac Publishing Co., Ltd. CAN. Dist: Casemate Pubs. & Bk. Distributors, LLC.
Lemke, Amy J. Too Short for the Court, 1 vol. Harpster, Steve, illus. 2012. (My First Graphic Novel Ser.). (ENG.). 32p. (gr. k-2). pap. 6.25 *(978-1-4342-3862-7(8));* lib. bdg. 24.65 *(978-1-4342-3282-3(4))* Stone Arch Bks. (My First Graphic Novel).
Lemke, Donald B. Drop In, 1 vol., Vol. 1. Majado, Caio et al, illus. 2011. (Tony Hawk's 900 Revolution Ser.). (ENG.). 128p. (gr. 3-4). pap. 7.19 *(978-1-4342-3451-3(7));* lib. bdg. 26.65 *(978-1-4342-3214-4(X))* Stone Arch Bks. (Tony Hawk's 900 Revolution).
Lemke, Donald B. & Pattison, Ronda. Captured off Guard: The Attack on Pearl Harbor, 1 vol. St. Aubin, Claude, illus. 2008. (Historical Fiction Ser.). (ENG.). 56p. (gr. 2-3). pap. 6.25 *(978-1-4342-0493-6(6),* Graphic Flash) Stone Arch Bks.
Lemon, Keith. The Beaver & the Elephant. 2016. (Anholt Family Favourites Ser.). (ENG.). 96p. (J). (gr. -1-k). 12.99 *(978-1-4440-1300-9(9))* Orion Publishing Group, Ltd. GBR. Dist: Hachette Bk. Group.
Lengacher, Janice. My Imaginary Other. 2012. 28p. (-18). pap. 14.95 *(978-1-4772-8795-8(7))* AuthorHouse.
L'Engle, Madeleine. And Both Were Young. 2011. (ENG.). 272p. (YA). (gr. 7-12). pap. 17.99 *(978-0-312-60277-2(4),* 9780312602772) Square Fish.
—A Wrinkle in Time. 2007. (Wrinkle in Time Quintet Ser.: 1). (ENG.). (J). (gr. 5-8). 224p. per. 6.99 *(978-0-312-36755-8(4),* 9780312367558); 256p. per. 6.99 *(978-0-312-36754-1(6),* 9780312367541) Square Fish.
Lenhard, Elizabeth. A Bridge Between Worlds. 2004. (W. I. T. C. H. Ser.: Bk. 10). 158p. (J). lib. bdg. 16.92 *(978-1-4242-0796-1(7))* Fitzgerald Bks.
—Different Path. 2004. (W. I. T. C. H. Ser.: Bk. 13). 158p. (J). lib. bdg. 16.92 *(978-1-4242-0791-6(6))* Fitzgerald Bks.
—The Disappearance. 2004. (W. I. T. C. H. Ser.: Bk. 2). 158p. (J). lib. bdg. 16.92 *(978-1-4242-0799-2(1))* Fitzgerald Bks.
—Finding Meridian. 2004. (W. I. T. C. H. Ser.: Bk. 3). 158p. (J). lib. bdg. 16.92 *(978-1-4242-0801-2(7))* Fitzgerald Bks.
—Power of Five. 2004. 158p. (J). lib. bdg. 16.92 *(978-1-4242-0795-4(9))* Fitzgerald Bks.
Lenhard, Elizabeth, adapted by. The Disappearance. 2004. (W. I. T. C. H. Ser.). (Illus.). 144p. (J). 12.65 *(978-0-7569-4620-3(4))* Perfection Learning Corp.
—The Return of a Queen. 2004. (W. I. T. C. H. Ser.: Bk. 12). 152p. (J). lib. bdg. 16.92 *(978-1-4242-0797-8(5))* Fitzgerald Bks.
Lennon, Maria T. Confessions of a So-Called Middle Child. 2014. (ENG.). 304p. (J). (gr. 3-7). pap. 6.99 *(978-0-06-212691-7(1))* HarperCollins Pubs.
—Watch Out, Hollywood! More Confessions of a So-Called Middle Child. 2014. (ENG.). 224p. (J). (gr. 3-7). 16.99 *(978-0-06-212693-1(8))* HarperCollins Pubs.
Lennon, Stella, et al. Revealed, Bk. 2. 2011. (Amanda Project Ser.: 2). (ENG.). 240p. (YA). (gr. 8-18). pap. 8.99 *(978-0-06-174215-6(5),* HarperTeen) HarperCollins Pubs.
Leno, Katrina. The Lost & Found. 2016. 352p. (J). (gr. 8). 17.99 *(978-0-06-223120-8(0),* HarperTeen) HarperCollins Pubs.
Leonard, Elise. Monday Morning Blitz. 2007. (Al's World Ser.: 1). (ENG.). 144p. (J). (gr. 5-9). pap. 8.99 *(978-1-4169-3464-6(2),* Simon & Schuster/Paula Wiseman Bks.) Simon & Schuster/Paula Wiseman Bks.
Leonard, M. G. Beetle Boy. (ENG.). (J). (gr. 3-7). 2017. 304p. pap. 6.99 ***(978-0-545-85347-7(8))*** 2016. 288p. 16.99 *(978-0-545-85346-0(X))* Scholastic, Inc. (Chicken Hse., The).
Leonard, Marcia. Mejores Amigas. Handelman, Dorothy, photos by. 2005. (ENG & SPA., Illus.). 32p. (J). (gr. -1-1). pap. 4.99 *(978-0-8225-3291-0(3))* Lerner Publishing Group.
—Mejores Amigas: Nivel 1. Handelman, Dorothy, photos by. 2005. (Lecturas para Niños de Verdad (Real Kids Readers) Ser.).Tr. of Best Friends. (SPA., Illus.). 32p. (J). (gr. 1-1). per. 5.95 *(978-0-8225-3290-3(5),* Ediciones Lerner) Lerner Publishing Group.
Leonard, Mary T. Three Best Friends. Russell, Terry, illus. 2004. 96p. (J). per. 12.00 *(978-0-9740683-8-1(1))* Authors & Artists Publishers of New York, Inc.
Leone, Dee. Bizz & Buzz Make Honey Buns. Marite, illus. 2014. (Penguin Core Concepts Ser.). (ENG.). 32p. (J). (gr. -1-k). 3.99 *(978-0-448-47927-9(3),* Grosset & Dunlap) Penguin Young Readers Group.

Leoni, Nancy. Toby Goes to Camp, 1 vol. Leoni, Nancy, illus. 2009. (Illus.). 21p. pap. 24.95 *(978-1-61546-417-3(4))* America Star Bks.

Lepere, J. Mindseed. 2013. 120p. 28.99 *(978-1-4808-0016-8(3))*; pap. 11.99 *(978-1-4808-0014-4(7))* Archway Publishing.

Lepri, Nancy Carty. Tiny Angel. 2009. 104p. pap. 8.95 *(978-1-935137-94-8(8))* Guardian Angel Publishing, Inc.

Lerangis, Peter. The Colossus Rises, Bk. 1. Norstrand, Torstein & Reagan, Mike, illus. 2013. (Seven Wonders Ser.: 1). (ENG.). 384p. (J). (gr. 3-7). pap. 6.99 *(978-0-06-207041-8(X))* HarperCollins Pubs.

—The Colossus Rises, Bk. 1. Reagan, Mike & Norstrand, Torstein, illus. 2013. (Seven Wonders Ser.: 1). (ENG.). 368p. (J). (gr. 3-7). 17.99 *(978-0-06-207040-1(1))* HarperCollins Pubs.

—The Colossus Rises, No. 1. Lerangis, Peter, illus. 2012. (Seven Wonders Ser.). (ENG., Illus.). 112p. (J). (gr. 3-7). 2.99 *(978-0-06-223889-4(2))* HarperCollins Pubs.

—The Colossus Rises. 2013. (Seven Wonders Ser.: 1). (J). lib. bdg. 17.20 *(978-0-606-32166-2(7),* Turtleback) Turtleback Bks.

—The Curse of the King. Norstrand, Torstein, illus. 2015. (Seven Wonders Ser.: Bk. 4). (ENG.). 320p. (J). (gr. 3-7). 17.99 *(978-0-06-207049-4(5))* HarperCollins Pubs.

LernerClassroom Editors. Mallory Teaching Guide. 2009. pap. 7.95 *(978-0-8225-7448-4(9))* Lerner Publishing Group.

Les Becquets, Diane. The Stones of Mourning Creek, 0 vols. 2005. (ENG.). 320p. (YA). (gr. 7-9). reprint ed. pap. 9.99 *(978-0-7614-5238-6(9),* 9780761452386, Amazon Children's Publishing) Amazon Publishing.

Lescarbeau, Nicole. Ellie's Allies. 2006. 79p. pap. 16.95 *(978-1-4241-0446-8(7))* PublishAmerica, Inc.

Lesczynski, Jim. The Walton Street Tycoons. 2007. 269p. (YA). pap. 9.95 *(978-0-9791283-0-1(7))* East River Pr.

Leslie, Robyn. Rinny & the Trail of Clues. 2003. Orig. Title: Miss President & the Trail of Clues. (Illus.). 192p. (J). pap. 7.95 *(978-0-9727388-8-0(6))* Sugar Ducky Bks., Inc.

Lester, Alison. The Circus Horse. Harvey, Roland, illus. 2009. (ENG.). 64p. (J). (gr. k-3). pap. 4.99 *(978-0-8118-6656-9(4))* Chronicle Bks. LLC.

—Noni the Pony Goes to the Beach. Lester, Alison, illus. 2015. (ENG., Illus.). 32p. (J). (gr. -1-3). 17.99 *(978-1-4814-4625-9(8),* Beach Lane Bks.) Beach Lane Bks.

Lester, Alison & Harvey, Roland. The Silver Horse Switch. 2009. (ENG., Illus.). 64p. (J). (gr. k-3). pap. 4.99 *(978-0-8118-6554-8(1))* Chronicle Bks. LLC.

Leth, Kate. Adventure Time Vol. 4. 2014. lib. bdg. 24.50 *(978-0-606-36119-4(7))* Turtleback Bks.

Lette, Lauren Britt. Kiwi's First Day of School. 2008. 32p. pap. 24.95 *(978-1-60441-418-9(9))* America Star Bks.

Lettrick, Robert. The Murk. Disney Storybook Art Team, illus. 2015. (ENG.). 320p. (J). (gr. 5-9). 16.99 *(978-1-4231-8695-3(8))* Hyperion Bks. for Children.

Leveen, Tom. Manicpixiedreamgirl. 2014. (ENG.). 256p. (YA). (gr. 9). pap. 8.99 *(978-0-375-87021-7(0),* Ember) Random Hse. Children's Bks.

—Shackled: The Truth Doesn't Always Set You Free. 2015. (ENG., Illus.). 224p. (YA). (gr. 9). 17.99 *(978-1-4814-2249-9(9),* Simon Pulse) Simon Pulse.

—Sick. (ENG.). 288p. (YA). (gr. 9-17). 2014. pap. 8.95 *(978-1-4197-1228-9(4))* 2013. 18.95 *(978-1-4197-0805-3(8))* Abrams, Inc. (Amulet Bks.).

Levering-Duff, Judy. Barnaby Wetzel, Boy Wizard. 2003. 128p. (J). 1450.00 *(978-0-9725874-2-6(X))*; pap. 7.50 *(978-0-9725874-3-3(8))* Outskirts Pr., Inc.

Levering, Vicki. Postcards from the Pound. 2008. 48p. pap. 23.99 *(978-1-4363-1406-0(2))* Xlibris Corp.

LeVerrier, Renee. The Four Friends. 2011. (Illus.). 44p. (J). pap. 18.99 *(978-1-59092-762-5(1))* Blue Forge Pr.

Levin, Betty. Thorn. 2005. (ENG.). 176p. (J). (gr. 9-12). 16.95 *(978-1-932425-46-8(2),* Lemniscaat) Boyds Mills Pr.

Levin, Michael & Pannell, Jack. Lunch Money Can't Shoot. 2017. (ENG.). 146p. pap. 12.95 *(978-1-68350-110-7(1))* Morgan James Publishing.

Levine, Caroline Anne. Jay Grows an Alien. 2007. 73p. (J). (gr. 5-13). pap. 13.95 *(978-1-931282-29-1(3))* Autism Asperger Publishing Co.

Levine, Deborah A. & Riley, JillEllyn. The Icing on the Cake. 2015. (Saturday Cooking Club Ser.: 2). (ENG., Illus.). 304p. (J). (gr. 4-9). 17.99 *(978-1-4424-9942-3(7),* Aladdin) Simon & Schuster Children's Publishing.

—Kitchen Chaos. 2015. (Saturday Cooking Club Ser.: 1). (ENG., Illus.). 336p. (J). (gr. 4-9). pap. 7.99 *(978-1-4424-9940-9(0),* Aladdin) Simon & Schuster Children's Publishing.

—Kitchen Chaos. Espinosa, Leo, illus. 2015. (Saturday Cooking Club Ser.: 1). (ENG.). 336p. (J). (gr. 4-9). 17.99 *(978-1-4424-9939-3(7),* Aladdin) Simon & Schuster Children's Publishing.

Levine, Gail Carson. Ella Enchanted. 2011. 238p. (J). (gr. 3-7). 18.40 *(978-0-613-07691-3(5),* Turtleback) Turtleback Bks.

—The Wish. 2005. (ENG.). 256p. (J). (gr. 3-7). pap. 6.99 *(978-0-06-075911-7(9),* HarperTeen) HarperCollins Pubs.

—The Wish. 2004. 197p. (gr. 3-7). 16.00 *(978-0-7569-4272-4(1))* Perfection Learning Corp.

Levine, Gail Carson & Levine, Gail C. Ella Enchanted. movie tie-in ed. 2004. (ENG.). 288p. (J). (gr. 3-7). pap. 6.99 *(978-0-06-055886-4(5),* HarperTeen) HarperCollins Pubs.

Levine, Kristin. The Best Bad Luck I Ever Had. 2010. (ENG.). 272p. (J). (gr. 5-18). 7.99 *(978-0-14-241648-8(7),* Puffin Books) Penguin Young Readers Group.

—The Lions of Little Rock. (ENG.). (J). (gr. 5-9). 2013. 320p. pap. 7.99 *(978-0-14-242435-3(8),* Puffin Books) 2012. 304p. 16.99 *(978-0-399-25644-8(X),* G.P. Putnam's Sons Books for Young Readers) Penguin Young Readers Group.

—The Paper Cowboy. 2016. (ENG.). (J). lib. bdg. 19.65 *(978-0-606-38394-3(8))* Turtleback Bks.

Levinson, Nancy Smiler. Prairie Friends. Schuett, Stacey, illus. 2003. (I Can Read Bks.). 64p. (J). (gr. k-3). 15.99 *(978-0-06-028001-7(8))* HarperCollins Pubs.

Levinson, Robin K. Shoshana & the Native Rose. Kehl, Drusilla, illus. 2006. 103p. (J). (gr. 3-5). per. 12.00 *(978-0-9773673-2-0(0))* Gali Girls, Inc.

Levis, Caron. Ida, Always. Santoso, Charles, illus. 2016. (ENG.). 40p. (J). (gr. -1-3). 17.99 *(978-1-4814-2640-4(0))* Simon & Schuster Children's Publishing.

Levithan, David. Boy Meets Boy. 2005. (ENG.). 224p. (YA). (gr. 7-12). reprint ed. per. 9.99 *(978-0-375-83299-4(8),* Ember) Random Hse. Children's Bks.

—Every You, Every Me. Levithan, David & Farmer, Jonathan, photos by. 2012. (ENG., Illus.). 256p. (YA). (gr. 7). pap. 9.99 *(978-0-375-85451-4(7),* Ember) Random Hse. Children's Bks.

Levoy, Myron. Alan & Naomi. 2011. 14.12 *(978-0-7848-3566-1(7),* Everbind) Marco Bk. Co.

Levy, Janice. Diva Duck Goes to Hollywood, 1 vol. Madden, Colleen M., illus. 2012. (Diva Duck Ser.). (ENG.). 32p. (J). (gr. -1-4). 28.50 *(978-1-61641-887-8(7))* Magic Wagon.

—Diva Duck Travels the World, 1 vol. Madden, Colleen M., illus. 2012. (Diva Duck Ser.). (ENG.). 32p. (J). (gr. -1-4). 28.50 *(978-1-61641-888-5(5))* Magic Wagon.

Levy, Joanne. Crushing It. 2017. (Mix Ser.). (ENG., Illus.). 240p. (J). (gr. 4-8). pap. 7.99 *(978-1-4814-6473-4(6),* Aladdin) Simon & Schuster Children's Publishing.

Levy, Marianne. Katie Cox Goes Viral. 2017. (ENG.). 368p. (J). (gr. 5-9). pap. 7.99 *(978-1-4926-4250-3(9),* 9781492642503, Sourcebooks Jabberwocky) Sourcebooks, Inc.

Levy, Michael. The Inspiring Story of Little Goody Two Shoes. 2007. 139p. (YA). per. 12.95 *(978-0-9668069-9-1(9))* Point of Life, Inc.

Lewis. Tomboy Terror in Bunk 109. 2008. (ENG.). 128p. (YA). (gr. 7). pap. 7.95 *(978-1-4169-7539-7(X),* Simon Pulse) Simon Pulse.

Lewis, Anne Margaret. The Runaway Santa. Zenz, Aaron, illus. 2015. (ENG.). 40p. (J). (gr. -1-k). 15.99 *(978-1-63450-589-5(1),* Sky Pony Pr.) Skyhorse Publishing Co., Inc.

Lewis, Clarajane. The House on the Hill. 2012. (Illus.). 26p. pap. 12.00 *(978-1-78035-399-9(5),* Fastprint Publishing) Upfront Publishing Ltd. GBR. Dist: Printondemand-worldwide.com.

Lewis, Doreen. The Bubblegum Babes' Guide to Sixth Grade. 2005. (J). per. 9.95 *(978-0-9769193-0-8(3))* Helm Publishing.

Lewis, E. B. & Public Domain Staff. This Little Light of Mine. 2005. (ENG., Illus.). 32p. (J). (gr. -1-3). 17.99 *(978-0-689-83179-9(X),* Simon & Schuster Bks. For Young Readers) Simon & Schuster Bks. For Young Readers.

Lewis, Elfyn. Scruff & Friends. 2012. (Illus.). 12p. pap. 18.30 *(978-1-4772-1449-7(6))* AuthorHouse.

Lewis, Gill. Wild Wings. Onoda, Yuta, illus. (ENG.). 304p. (J). (gr. 3-7). 2012. pap. 7.99 *(978-1-4424-1446-4(4))* 2011. 18.99 *(978-1-4424-1445-7(6))* Simon & Schuster Children's Publishing. (Atheneum Bks. for Young Readers).

Lewis, J. Patrick. Good Ship Crocodile. Felix, Monique, illus. 2013. (ENG.). 32p. (J). (gr. 1-3). 18.99 *(978-1-56846-238-7(7),* Creative Editions) Creative Co., The.

—That's What Friends Are For. Denise, Christopher, illus. 2012. (I Am A Reader! Ser.). (ENG.). 40p. (J). (gr. k-3). pap. 3.99 *(978-1-58536-687-3(0))* Sleeping Bear Pr.

—Tugg & Teeny. Denise, Christopher, illus. 2011. (I am a Reader Ser.). (ENG.). 40p. (J). (gr. k-2). pap. 3.99 *(978-1-58536-685-9(4))*;Bk. 1. lib. bdg. 9.95 *(978-1-58536-514-2(9))* Sleeping Bear Pr.

—Tugg & Teeny: That's What Friends Are For. Denise, Christopher, illus. 2012. (I Am A Reader! Ser.). (ENG.). 40p. (gr. k-3). lib. bdg. 9.95 *(978-1-58536-516-6(5))* Sleeping Bear Pr.

—Tugg & Teeny - Jungle Suprises, Bk. 2. Denise, Christopher, illus. 2011. (I am a Reader Ser.). (ENG.). 40p. (J). (gr. k-2). lib. bdg. 9.95 *(978-1-58536-515-9(7))* Sleeping Bear Pr.

—Tugg & Tweeny - Jungle Surprises, Bk. 2. Denise, Christopher, illus. 2011. (I am a Reader Ser.). (ENG.). 40p. (J). (gr. k-2). pap. 3.99 *(978-1-58536-686-6(2))* Sleeping Bear Pr.

Lewis, Judith. Not Like Any Bird I've Ever Heard. 2011. 24p. pap. 24.95 *(978-1-4626-2730-1(7))* America Star Bks.

Lewis, Kevin. Kj's Adventures. 2011. 28p. pap. 15.99 *(978-1-4653-3573-9(0))* Xlibris Corp.

Lewis, Linda. We Love Only Older Boys. 2008. (ENG.). 160p. (Orig.). (YA). (gr. 7). pap. 8.95 *(978-1-4169-7535-9(7),* Simon Pulse) Simon Pulse.

Lewis, Lorinne. Junior & Callie's Awesome Adventure. 2012. 36p. pap. 16.95 *(978-1-62709-269-2(2))* America Star Bks.

Lewis, Melinda. Bulls-Eye Bob & the Backyard Buddies. 2008. 68p. pap. 15.99 *(978-1-4363-3109-8(9))* Xlibris Corp.

Lewis, Rob. Friends. (ENG., Illus.). 32p. (J). pap. 8.95 *(978-0-09-926612-9(1),* Arrow Bks., Ltd.) Random Hse. GBR. Dist: Trafalgar Square Publishing.

Lewman, David. Branch & the Cooking Catastrophe (DreamWorks Trolls Chapter Book #2) Random House, illus. 2017. (ENG.). 128p. (J). (gr. 1-4). 6.99 ***(978-1-5247-1708-7(8))***; lib. bdg. 12.99 ***(978-1-5247-1709-4(6))*** Random Hse. Children's Bks. (Random Hse. Bks. for Young Readers).

Lewman, David. A Tale of Two Genies (Shimmer & Shine) Aikins, David, illus. 2016. (Big Golden Book Ser.). (ENG.). 32p. (J). (gr. -1-2). 9.99 *(978-0-553-52200-6(0),* Golden Bks.) Random Hse. Children's Bks.

Licata, Rosemarie & Reizer, Edwina. The Hare & the Hound. 2007. 17p. 14.95 *(978-1-4357-0439-8(8))* Lulu Pr., Inc.

Licciardi, Paula. Wasting Calvin's Time. 2006. 9.00 *(978-0-8059-8138-4(1))* Dorrance Publishing Co., Inc.

Lichtman, Wendy. Secrets, Lies, & Algebra. 2008. (Do the Math Ser.: 1). (ENG., Illus.). 208p. (YA). (gr. 8-8). pap. 6.99 *(978-0-06-122957-2(1),* Greenwillow Bks.) HarperCollins Pubs.

—The Writing on the Wall. 2008. (Do the Math Ser.: 2). (ENG.). 224p. (YA). (gr. 8-9). 16.99 *(978-0-06-122958-9(X),* Greenwillow Bks.) HarperCollins Pubs.

Lickel, Lisa J. The Potawatomi Boy. Hendricks, Brenda K., illus. 2013. 34p. pap. 5.95 *(978-0-9856215-2-0(4))* Fox Ridge Pubns.

Liddiard, Merrilee. Fairy Friends: an Opposites Primer, 1 vol. 2016. (ENG., Illus.). 22p. (J). bds. 9.99 *(978-1-4236-4537-5(5))* Gibbs Smith, Publisher.

—Seasons, 1 vol. 2016. (ENG., Illus.). 22p. (J). bds. 9.99 *(978-1-4236-4540-5(5))* Gibbs Smith, Publisher.

Liebert, Emily. Those Secrets We Keep. 2015. (ENG.). 336p. (gr. 12). pap. 16.00 *(978-0-451-47187-1(3),* Berkley) Penguin Publishing Group.

Light, Kelly. Louise & Andie: The Art of Friendship. Light, Kelly, illus. 2016. (Illus.). 40p. (J). (gr. -1-3). 17.99 *(978-0-06-234440-3(4))* HarperCollins Pubs.

Light, Steve. The Christmas Giant. Light, Steve, illus. 2010. (ENG., Illus.). 32p. (J). (gr. -1-2). 15.99 *(978-0-7636-4692-9(X))* Candlewick Pr.

Light's Adventure's with Friends. 2005. (J). spiral bd. 7.00 *(978-0-9743223-2-2(6))* Jones, Augustine R.

Likins, Kim. Charlie's Special Friends. 2004. (Illus.). 32p. (J). lib. bdg. 19.95 *(978-0-9729987-1-0(3))* Island Friends LLC.

Liliom, Laura. You Are a Really Good Friend of Mine. Vagharshyan, Lilit, illus. 2007. 32p. (J). (ARA & ENG.). pap. 16.95 *(978-1-60195-310-0(0))*; (POL & ENG.). pap. 16.95 *(978-1-60195-107-6(8))* International Step by Step Assn.

Lilly, Sara. The Inseparables. 2015. (ENG.). 77p. (J). (gr. 3-4). mass mkt. 14.95 *(978-1-78455-920-5(2),* d4b15bff-7ea4-4131-af5d-e5ff708023ca) Austin, Stan AUS. Dist: Bookmasters Distribution.

Limb, Sue. Girl, 15, Charming but Insane. 2005. (Girl, 15 Ser.). (ENG.). 240p. (YA). (gr. 7-12). reprint ed. pap. 8.99 *(978-0-385-73215-4(5),* Delacorte Bks. for Young Readers) Random Hse. Children's Bks.

Lin, Chris. Mandy & Pandy Play Sports. Villalta, Ingrid, illus. 2008. 20p. (J). (gr. -1-3). bds. 9.99 *(978-0-9800156-7-6(7))* Mandy & Pandy Bks., LLC.

—Mandy & Pandy Visit China. Villalta, Ingrid, illus. 2008. 20p. (J). (gr. -1-3). bds. 9.99 *(978-0-9800156-6-9(9))* Mandy & Pandy Bks., LLC.

Lin, Grace. The Year of the Rat. 2009. (Pacy Lin Novel Ser.). (ENG.). 208p. (J). (gr. 3-7). pap. 7.00 *(978-0-316-03361-9(8))* Little, Brown Bks. for Young Readers.

Lincoln, James. The Rainbow Jars. Smith, Jacqui, illus. 2013. 28p. (J). pap. 14.95 *(978-1-60131-153-5(2),* Castlebridge Bks.) Big Tent Bks.

Lind, Kathleen. Best Friends. Lind, Kathleen & Simonis, Cheryl, illus. 2005. (J). 4.95 *(978-1-58597-305-7(X))* Leathers Publishing.

Lindbergh, Anne M. The Worry Week. Hawkes, Kevin, illus. 2003. (ENG.). 144p. reprint ed. pap. 12.95 *(978-1-56792-239-4(2))* Godine, David R. Pub.

Lindeman, Craig. The Big Black Dog & the Big Blue Se. Shoop, Johanna, illus. 2009. 40p. pap. 15.95 *(978-1-60844-047-4(8))* Dog Ear Publishing, LLC.

Linder, Karen A. Jack the Curly Black Dog: Goes to the Beach. 2010. 20p. 13.80 *(978-1-4520-3434-8(5))* AuthorHouse.

Linder, Kim And Joe. The Story of Nastyman. 2012. 36p. (-18). pap. 15.99 *(978-1-4525-6151-6(6))* Balboa Pr.

Lindo, Elvira. Manolito Four-Eyes: the 2nd Volume of the Great Encyclopedia of My Life: The 2nd Volume of the Great Encyclopedia of My Life, 0 vols. Urberuaga, Emilio, illus. unabr. ed. 2013. (Manolito Four-Eyes Ser.: 2). (ENG.). 162p. (J). (gr. 3-7). pap. 9.99 *(978-1-4778-1700-1(X),* 9781477817001, Amazon Children's Publishing) Amazon Publishing.

Lindquist, N. J. The Best of Friends. 2016. (Circle of Friends Ser.: Vol. 1). (ENG., Illus.). (YA). pap. ***(978-1-927692-03-5(2))*** That's Life! Communications.

Lindsay, Elizabeth. Dancing Magic. 2012. (Silverlake Fairy School Ser.). 100p. (J). pap. 4.99 *(978-0-7945-3067-9(2),* Usborne) EDC Publishing.

Lindsay, Sierra. Spindly the Spider. Lindsay, Sierra, illus. 2012. (Illus.). 20p. pap. 10.99 *(978-0-9836641-9-2(6))* Kids At Heart Publishing, LLC.

Lindsey, Audrey. Against the Dawn, 1 vol. 2010. 74p. pap. 19.95 *(978-1-60749-097-5(8))* America Star Bks.

Lindstrom, Eric. Not If I See You First. 2015. (ENG.). 320p. (YA). (gr. 10-17). 18.00 *(978-0-316-25985-9(3))* Little Brown & Co.

Lindstrom, Florence M. Meeting New Friends. 2nd ed. 2007. (Illus.). 185p. pap. 8.95 *(978-1-932971-00-2(9))* Christian Liberty Pr.

Lindwall, Erika. The Moose & the Goose. Lindwall, Erika, illus. 2013. (Illus.). 32p. pap. 11.95 *(978-1-940728-01-8(0),* Simple Faith Bks.) Sunrise Mountain Bks.

Lindy J. & Hubbard, Bobbie. The Story of Becky & Zippy. 2012. 32p. pap. 19.99 *(978-1-4772-6489-8(2))* AuthorHouse.

Lingenfelser, Lynda L. Lizah Lizard: Koco's Tale. 2008. 50p. pap. 22.98 *(978-0-615-14072-8(6))* Lingenfelser, Lynda L.

Linney, Graham F. The Seaside Adventure of Carrot, Pea, & Friends. 2011. 32p. pap. 13.00 *(978-1-61204-435-4(2),* Strategic Bk. Publishing) Strategic Book Publishing & Rights Agency (SBPRA).

Linseman, Daniel. Shroobear's First Swim: Book I of the Shroobear Short Stories. 2008. 36p. pap. 15.49 *(978-1-4343-8252-8(4))* AuthorHouse.

Linz, Kathryn. Jim Brandon's Adventures. 2006. (ENG.). 100p. per. 19.95 *(978-1-4241-3160-0(X))* America Star Bks.

Lionni, Leo. An Extraordinary Egg. 2014. (ENG., Illus.). 40p. (J). (gr. -1-2). 17.99 *(978-0-679-85840-9(7),* Knopf Bks. for Young Readers) Random Hse. Children's Bks.

—Little Blue & Little Yellow. (ENG.). (J). (gr. -1-2). 2011. 42p. bds. 7.99 *(978-0-375-87290-7(6))* 2009. 48p. 16.99 *(978-0-375-86013-3(4))* Random Hse. Children's Bks. (Knopf Bks. for Young Readers).

—Swimmy. 2017. (ENG.). 32p. (J). (gr. -1-2). 7.99 *(978-0-399-55550-3(1),* Dragonfly Bks.) Random Hse. Children's Bks.

Liphardt, Linda. Secret in the Old Barn. 2008. 116p. pap. 19.95 *(978-1-60703-615-9(0))* America Star Bks.

Lipp, Frederick J. Bread Song. Gaillard, Jason, tr. Gaillard, Jason, illus. 2004. (J). 15.95 *(978-1-59336-000-9(2))*; pap. *(978-1-59336-001-6(0))* Mondo Publishing.

Lisle, Janet Taylor. Afternoon of the Elves. 2017. (ENG., Illus.). 128p. (J). (gr. 3-7). 16.99 ***(978-1-4814-9908-8(4),*** Atheneum Bks. for Young Readers) Simon & Schuster Children's Publishing.

Lisle, Janet Taylor. Black Duck. 2007. (ENG.). 256p. (J). (gr. 5-18). 7.99 *(978-0-14-240902-2(2),* Puffin Books) Penguin Young Readers Group.

List, Gloria A. A Heart That Finds His Way: More on the Line. Sturcke, Otto, illus. 2005. 18p. (J). pap. 7.95 *(978-0-9709861-0-8(6))* Fingerprint Bks.

Litchfield, David. The Bear & the Piano. 2016. (ENG., Illus.). 40p. (J). (gr. -1-3). 16.99 *(978-0-544-67454-7(5))* Houghton Mifflin Harcourt Publishing Co.

Litten, Kristyna. Blue & Bertie. Litten, Kristyna, illus. 2016. (ENG., Illus.). 32p. (J). (gr. -1-3). 17.99 *(978-1-4814-6154-2(0),* Simon & Schuster Bks. For Young Readers) Simon & Schuster Bks. For Young Readers.

Little Bear, Shena. How the lone wolf got her Name. 2008. 80p. pap. 9.95 *(978-0-578-00171-5(3))* Stone Castle Publishing.

Little Blue Kite & Friends Activity Book. 2005. (YA). per. *(978-1-59872-122-5(4))* Instant Pub.

Little, Celeste. At the Park with Tommy & Scales. Motz, Mike, illus. 2012. 26p. (J). (-18). 12.95 *(978-1-60131-139-9(7),* Castlebridge Bks.) Big Tent Bks.

Little China's Not So Mean after All. 2012. 28p. 24.95 *(978-1-4137-7549-5(7))* America Star Bks.

Little Dolphin & Friends. (Flocked Soft-to-Touch Board Ser.). 5p. bds. *(978-1-4054-9503-5(0))* Parragon, Inc.

Little Dragon Makes Friends. 2008. (Little Dragon Storybooks Ser.). 32p. *(978-1-4075-1288-4(9))* Parragon, Inc.

Little Elephant & Friends. (Flocked Soft-to-Touch Board Ser.). 5p. bds. *(978-1-4054-9445-8(X))* Parragon, Inc.

Little Engine- Animal Friends. 2005. (J). *(978-1-4194-0023-0(1))* Paradise Pr., Inc.

Little Engine-AV Friends Forever. 2005. (J). *(978-1-4194-0010-0(X))* Paradise Pr., Inc.

Little Engine-Circus Friends. 2005. (J). *(978-1-4194-0005-6(3))* Paradise Pr., Inc.

Little Is Big. 2006. (Illus.). (J). *(978-1-882601-58-5(0))* See-More's Workshop.

Little, Judy. Yody & Bippy the Boo: Friends for Life. 2010. 28p. pap. 12.49 *(978-1-4389-7145-2(1))* AuthorHouse.

Little Monkey & Friends. (Flocked Soft-to-Touch Board Ser.). 5p. bds. *(978-1-4054-9504-2(9))* Parragon, Inc.

Little Penguin & Friends. (Flocked Soft-to-Touch Board Ser.). 5p. bds. *(978-1-4054-9446-5(8))* Parragon, Inc.

Littman, Sarah Darer. Backlash. 2015. (ENG.). 336p. (J). (gr. 7). 17.99 *(978-0-545-65126-4(3),* Scholastic Pr.) Scholastic, Inc.

—Fairest of Them All. 2017. (ENG., Illus.). 224p. (J). (gr. 3-7). pap. 7.99 ***(978-1-4814-5129-1(4),*** Aladdin) Simon & Schuster Children's Publishing.

—In Case You Missed It. (ENG.). 320p. (gr. 7). 2017. (J). pap. 9.99 ***(978-1-338-16065-9(6),*** Scholastic Paperbacks) 2016. (YA). 17.99 *(978-0-545-90437-7(4),* Scholastic Pr.) Scholastic, Inc.

Littman, Sarah Darer. Purge. 2010. (ENG.). 240p. (J). (gr. 7). 8.99 *(978-0-545-05237-5(8),* Scholastic Paperbacks) Scholastic, Inc.

Litzenberger, Mona. Humble the Bumblebee. 2013. 24p. pap. 9.99 *(978-0-9894748-0-1(1))* Mindstir Media.

Livingston, A. A. B. Bear & Lolly: Off to School. Chou, Joey, illus. 2014. (ENG.). 32p. (J). (gr. -1-3). 15.99 *(978-0-06-219788-7(6))* HarperCollins Pubs.

—B. Bear & Lolly: Catch That Cookie! Chou, Joey, illus. 2015. (ENG.). 32p. (J). (gr. -1-3). 15.99 *(978-0-06-219791-7(6))* HarperCollins Pubs.

Lloyd-Caldwell, Marian. Dancing Watermelon Babies & Mr Mouse's Good Deed. 2008. 44p. pap. 18.49 *(978-1-4343-9555-9(3))* AuthorHouse.

Lloyd, Natalie. A Snicker of Magic. (ENG.). 320p. (J). (gr. 3-7). 2015. pap. 6.99 *(978-0-545-55273-8(7))* 2014. 16.99 *(978-0-545-55270-7(2))* Scholastic, Inc. (Scholastic Pr.).

—A Snicker of Magic. 2015. lib. bdg. 17.20 *(978-0-606-37089-9(7))* Turtleback Bks.

Lloyd, Natalie, et al. A Snicker of Magic. 2014. (ENG.). mass mkt. *(978-0-545-68447-7(1))* Scholastic, Inc.

Lloyd, Sylvia. A Little Turtle's Tale. 2005. pap. *(978-1-932077-96-4(0))* Athena Pr.

Lluch, Isabel. The Fabulous Book of Me! The Ultimate Girls' Guide Journal & Keepsake That's All about You! 2009. (ENG.). 100p. (J). (gr. 6-7). spiral bd. 12.95 *(978-1-934386-57-6(X))* WS Publishing.

Lo, Catherine. How It Ends. (ENG.). 304p. (YA). (gr. 9). 2017. pap. 9.99 *(978-0-544-93720-8(1))* 2016. 17.99 *(978-0-544-54006-4(9))* Houghton Mifflin Harcourt Publishing Co. (HMH Books For Young Readers).

Lobdell, Chanel Mickayla. Tale of Phoebe & Leonardo. Cain, Mary, illus. 2012. 32p. pap. *(978-0-9859892-0-0(3))* Roxby Media Ltd.

Lobel, Arnold. Days with Frog & Toad. Lobel, Arnold, illus. 25th ed. 2004. (I Can Read Level 2 Ser.). (ENG., Illus.). 64p. (J). (gr. -1-3). 16.99 *(978-0-06-023963-3(8))* HarperCollins Pubs.

—Días con Sapo y Sepo.Tr. of (Days with Frog & Toad). (SPA.). 72p. (J). (gr. 1-6). 8.95 *(978-84-204-3743-9(3))* Santillana USA Publishing Co., Inc.

—Frog & Toad Are Friends. Lobel, Arnold, illus. 2017. (I Can Read Level 2 Ser.). (Illus.). 72p. (J). (gr. -1-3). 9.99 *(978-0-06-257273-8(3))* HarperCollins Pubs.

—Frog & Toad Storybook Treasury. Lobel, Arnold, illus. 2013. (I Can Read Level 2 Ser.). (ENG., Illus.). 256p. (J). (gr. -1-3). 11.99 *(978-0-06-229258-2(7))* HarperCollins Pubs.

—Sapo y Sepo Son Amigos. Lobel, Arnold, illus. 2003.Tr. of Frog & Toad Are Friends. (SPA., Illus.). 66p. (J). (gr. k-3). pap. 12.95 *(978-968-19-0714-3(0))* Aguilar, Altea, Taurus, Alfaguara, S.A. de C.V MEX. Dist: Santillana USA Publishing Co., Inc.

Lockaby, Angie. Tad the Turtle It's Okay to Be Different. 2012. 28p. pap. 19.99 *(978-1-4772-7295-4(X))* AuthorHouse.

Lockard, Donna Lee. Sasha the Tortoise's Summer Vacation. 2013. (ENG.). 36p. (J). pap. 19.95 *(978-1-4787-0938-1(3))* Outskirts Pr., Inc.

Lockhart, E. The Boy Book: A Study of Habits & Behaviors, Plus Techniques for Taming Them. 2008. (Ruby Oliver Quartet Ser.). (ENG.). 224p. (YA). (gr. 7). pap. 8.99 *(978-0-385-73209-3(0),* Delacorte Pr.) Random Hse. Children's Bks.

—The Boyfriend List: 15 Guys, 11 Shrink Appointments, 4 Ceramic Frogs & Me, Ruby Oliver. 2006. (Ruby Oliver Quartet Ser.). (ENG.). 256p. (YA). (gr. 7-12). reprint ed. pap. 9.99 *(978-0-385-73207-9(4),* Ember) Random Hse. Children's Bks.

—The Disreputable History of Frankie Landau-Banks. 2009. (ENG.). 352p. (J). (gr. 5-9). pap. 9.99 *(978-0-7868-3819-6(1))* Hyperion Pr.

—The Disreputable History of Frankie Landau-Banks. l.t. ed. 2009. (ENG.). 502p. (YA). 23.95 *(978-1-4104-1439-7(6))* Thorndike Pr.

—Dramarama. 2007. (ENG.). 320p. (YA). 24.80 *(978-1-4287-4612-1(9))* Hyperion Pr.

—Genuine Fraud. 2017. (YA). ***(978-1-5247-7067-9(1),*** Delacorte Pr) Random House Publishing Group.

E
F
G

—Genuine Fraud, 9 vols. 2017. (ENG.). (YA). 170.91 **(978-0-525-50205-0(X))**; 75.96 **(978-0-525-50207-4(6))**; 170.91 **(978-0-525-50206-7(8))**; 288p. (gr. 7). 18.99 **(978-0-385-74477-5(3))**; 288p. (gr. 7). lib. bdg. 21.99 **(978-0-375-99184-4(0))** Random Hse. Children's Bks. (Delacorte Pr.).

—The Treasure Map of Boys: Noel, Jackson, Finn, Hutch, Gideon - And Me, Ruby Oliver. 2010. (Ruby Oliver Quartet Ser.). (ENG.). 256p. (J). (gr. 7). pap. 8.99 *(978-0-385-73427-1(1)*, Delacorte Pr.) Random Hse. Children's Bks.

—We Were Liars. 2014. (Illus.). 227p. (YA). *(978-0-385-39009-5(2)*, Delacorte Pr) Random House Publishing Group.

—We Were Liars. (ENG., (YA). (gr. 7). 2014. Illus.). 240p. 17.99 *(978-0-385-74126-2(X))* 2017. 272p. 18.99 **(978-1-5247-6458-6(2))** Random Hse. Children's Bks. (Delacorte Pr.).

Lockhart, E., et al. How to Be Bad. 2008. 325p. (YA). (gr. 9-12). lib. bdg. 17.89 *(978-0-06-128423-6(8)*, HarperTeen) HarperCollins Pubs.

Lockhart, Kendra. Favorite Hat. 2010. (Illus.). 24p. (J). pap. 14.95 *(978-0-9843883-3-2(6)*, Green Lady Pr., The) RealityIsBooks.com, Inc.

Lodding, Linda Ravin. Wakey, Wakey, Elephant! Robertson, Michael, illus. 2017. (ENG.). 32p. (J). (gr. -1). 16.95 **(978-1-4549-1999-5(X))** Sterling Publishing Co., Inc.

Lodge, Jo. La Casa del Senor Coc/ The House of Mr Coc. 2007. 8p. bds. 36.95 *(978-84-263-6454-8(3))* Vives, Luis Editorial (Edelvives) ESP. Dist: Baker & Taylor Bks.

Loe, Steve. The Hot Hurry of Mercurial Fleeting. 2016. (YA). pap. 9.99 *(978-0-88092-303-3(2))* Royal Fireworks Publishing Co.

Loftin, Nikki. Wish Girl. 2015. (ENG.). 256p. (J). (gr. 3-7). 16.99 *(978-1-59514-686-1(5)*, Razorbill) Penguin Young Readers Group.

Loftus, Tracy. Lucky Pup & Miss Millie Go Home. 2012. 28p. pap. 19.99 *(978-1-4772-6922-0(3))* AuthorHouse.

Logan, Dottie Colegrove. Picnic on the Beach: Nana & Me Series, Book Three. 2010. 16p. 12.99 *(978-1-4490-3689-8(9))* AuthorHouse.

Logan, Kenneth. True Letters from a Fictional Life. 2016. 336p. (J). (gr. 8). 17.99 *(978-0-06-238025-8(7)*, HarperTeen) HarperCollins Pubs.

Logie, Mark. Storm Troopers Tz9. 2011. 108p. pap. *(978-0-7552-1333-7(5))* Authors OnLine, Ltd.

Lois, Lowry. Anastasia Asusordenes. 2003. (Anastasia Krupnik Ser.).Tr. of Anastasia at Your Order. (SPA.). 120p. (J). 9.95 *(978-84-239-7073-5(6))* Espasa Calpe, S.A. ESP. Dist: Planeta Publishing Corp.

—Anastasia at Your Service. (Anastasia Krupnik Ser.). 149p. (J). (gr. 4-6). pap. 3.99 *(978-0-8072-1409-1(4)*, Listening Library) Random Hse. Audio Publishing Group.

—Compte les Etoiles. pap. 16.95 *(978-2-211-03436-4(5))* Archimede Editions FRA. Dist: Distribooks, Inc.

—Number the Stars. (ENG.). 160p. (J). (gr. 5-7). 2011. pap. 7.99 *(978-0-547-57709-8(5))* 25th anniv. ed. 2014. 17.99 *(978-0-544-34000-8(0)*, HMH Books For Young Readers) Houghton Mifflin Harcourt Publishing Co.

—Number the Stars. 2004. 144p. (J). (gr. 5-9). pap. 29.00 incl. audio *(978-1-4000-8637-5(X)*, Listening Library) Random Hse. Audio Publishing Group.

—The Silent Boy. 2017. (ENG., Illus.). 240p. (J). (gr. 5-7). pap. 7.99 *(978-0-544-93522-8(5)*, HMH Books For Young Readers) Houghton Mifflin Harcourt Publishing Co.

Lokko, CNN. Adventures of Elizabeth Sam. 2012. 280p. pap. *(978-9964-70-151-2(9))* Afram Pubns. Ghana, Ltd.

Lombard, Jenny. Drita, My Homegirl. 2008. 135p. (J). (gr. 4-6). 13.65 *(978-0-7569-8919-4(1))* Perfection Learning Corp.

Lombardi, Kristine. It's a Surprise Playhouse Storybook. Mattel Inc. Staff, illus. 2010. (Storybook & Playset Ser.). (ENG.). 16p. (J). (gr. -1-2). bds. 15.99 *(978-0-7944-2005-5(2))* Reader's Digest Assn., Inc., The.

Lombardi, Kristine A. Mr. Biddles. Lombardi, Kristine A., illus. 2017. (Illus.). 40p. (J). (gr. -1-3). 17.99 **(978-0-06-244114-0(0))** HarperCollins Pubs.

Lonborg, Rosemary. Helpin' Bugs. Houghton, Diane R., illus. 2006. 32p. (J). (gr. -1-3). reprint ed. pap. 7.00 *(978-1-4223-5405-6(9))* DIANE Publishing Co.

London, Jonathan. Froggy Builds a Tree House. 2013. (Froggy Ser.). (ENG.). 32p. (J). (-k). pap. 6.99 *(978-0-14-242533-6(8)*, Puffin Books) Penguin Young Readers Group.

—Froggy Builds a Tree House. 2013. (Froggy Ser.). lib. bdg. 17.20 *(978-0-606-30518-1(1)*, Turtleback) Turtleback Bks.

London, Kelli. Uptown Dreams. 2011. (ENG., Illus.). 256p. (YA). (gr. 9). 9.95 *(978-0-7582-6128-1(4)*, K-Teen/Dafina) Kensington Publishing Corp.

London, Kiara. Kiss Cam. 2016. (ENG.). 272p. (YA). pap. 9.99 *(978-1-250-07096-8(1)*, 9781250070968) Feiwel & Friends.

London, Olivia. Meet the Ponies of Ponyville. 2013. (Passport to Reading Level 1 Ser.). (J). lib. bdg. 14.75 *(978-0-606-31732-0(5)*, Turtleback) Turtleback Bks.

—My Little Pony: Welcome to Equestria! 2013. (ENG., Illus.). 24p. (J). (gr. -1-3). 3.99 *(978-0-316-22814-5(1))* Little, Brown Bks. for Young Readers.

—Welcome to Rainbow Falls! 2014. (My Little Pony 8X8 Picture Bks.). (J). lib. bdg. 14.75 *(978-0-606-35297-0(X))* Turtleback Bks.

Long, Claire Nicole. Dreaming of Dolphins. 2012. (Illus.). 52p. (gr. 4-6). pap. 13.66 *(978-1-4772-3937-7(5))* AuthorHouse.

Long, Ethan. Lion & Tiger & Bear: Tag! You're It! 2016. (Lion & Tiger & Bear Ser.). (ENG., Illus.). 40p. (J). (gr. k-2). 14.95 *(978-1-4197-1896-0(7))* Abrams, Inc.

—Pig Has a Plan. 2013. (I Like to Read(r) Ser.). (ENG.). 24p. (J). (gr. -1-3). pap. 6.99 *(978-0-8234-2911-0(3))* Holiday Hse., Inc.

Long, Loren. Otis's Busy Day. Long, Loren, illus. 2014. (Otis Ser.). (ENG., Illus.). 32p. (J). (gr. k-1). pap. 3.99 *(978-0-448-48130-2(8)*, Penguin Young Readers) Penguin Young Readers Group.

The Long-Lost Friends, 6 vols., Vol. 3. (Woodland Mysteriestm Ser.). 133p. (gr. 3-7). 42.50 *(978-0-322-02377-2(7))* Wright Group/McGraw-Hill.

Long, Michelle. Mckayla, the Girl with the Special Hug, Makes A Friend. 2009. (Illus.). 30p. (J). pap. 13.95 *(978-1-4327-4730-5(4))* Outskirts Pr., Inc.

Long, Tyler. Wires, 1 vol. Fleming, Christopher, illus. 2009. 28p. pap. 24.95 *(978-1-60836-217-2(5))* America Star Bks.

Longmeyer, C. M. My Life As a Third Grade Zombie. Blanding, Dexter, illus. 2013. (My Life As a Third Grade... Ser.). (ENG.). (J). (gr. -1-3). pap. 7.99 *(978-0-635-11131-9(4))* Gallopade International.

Longo, Jennifer. Six Feet over It. 2014. (ENG.). 352p. (YA). (gr. 7). 17.99 *(978-0-449-81871-8(3)*, Random Hse. Bks. for Young Readers) Random Hse. Children's Bks.

Longo, Kaitlin. The Secret in Olivia's Garden. 2012. 36p. pap. 20.99 *(978-1-4685-5222-5(8))* AuthorHouse.

Longo, Sharon. My Friend Daniel Doesn't Talk. 2007. (ENG., Illus.). 28p. (C). pap. 13.95 *(978-0-86388-562-4(4)*, Y329914, Routledge) Taylor & Francis Group GBR. Dist: Taylor & Francis Group.

Look, Lenore. Alvin Ho: Allergic to Camping, Hiking, & Other Natural Disasters. Pham, LeUyen, illus. 2010. (Alvin Ho Ser.). (ENG.). 192p. (J). (gr. 1-4). 6.99 *(978-0-375-85750-8(8)*, Yearling) Random Hse. Children's Bks.

—Ruby Lu, Brave & True. 2004. (Illus.). 104p. (J). lib. bdg. 15.00 *(978-1-4242-0914-9(5))* Fitzgerald Bks.

—Ruby Lu, Brave & True. Wilsdorf, Anne, illus. 2006. (ENG.). 112p. (J). (gr. 1-5). pap. 6.99 *(978-1-4169-1389-4(0)*, Atheneum Bks. for Young Readers) Simon & Schuster Children's Publishing.

—Ruby Lu, Empress of Everything. Wilsdorf, Anne, illus. (ENG.). 176p. (J). (gr. 1-5). 2007. pap. 5.99 *(978-1-4169-5003-5(6))* 2006. 16.99 *(978-0-689-86460-5(4))* Simon & Schuster Children's Publishing. (Atheneum Bks. for Young Readers).

Looper, Grace W. Molasses Making Time. l.t. ed. 2004. 152p. (YA). pap. 8.95 *(978-0-9747685-5-7(3))* Bella Rosa Bks.

Loos, Jody C. Alex the Alien: Bubble Magic. 2013. 24p. pap. 14.95 *(978-1-4787-0322-8(9))* Outskirts Pr., Inc.

Lopez, Barbara J. Pepper's Wish. 2009. 32p. pap. 14.49 *(978-1-4389-4976-5(6))* AuthorHouse.

Lopez, Christopher P. The Absolute Truth about Lying. Racine, Victoria, illus. 2011. 36p. pap. 24.95 *(978-1-4626-3245-9(9))* America Star Bks.

López, Diana. Ask My Mood Ring How I Feel. 2013. (ENG.). 336p. (J). (gr. 3-7). 17.00 *(978-0-316-20996-0(1))* Little Brown & Co.

—Nothing up My Sleeve. 2016. (ENG.). 400p. (J). (gr. 3-7). 16.99 *(978-0-316-34087-8(1))* Little, Brown Bks. for Young Readers.

López Narváez, Concha. El Arbol de los Pajaros Sin Vuelo. (SPA.). 128p. (YA). (gr. 5-8). *(978-84-207-2905-3(1))* Grupo Anaya, S.A. ESP. Dist: Lectorum Pubns., Inc.

Lopez, Patricia. A Dog Named Pom Pom & Friends. Lopez, Patricia, illus. l.t. ed. 2011. (ENG., Illus.). 34p. pap. 15.99 *(978-1-4610-4886-2(9))* CreateSpace Independent Publishing Platform.

Lopez, Sixto. Snarloff Duwaki's Adventures. 2011. 24p. pap. 24.95 *(978-1-4626-2557-4(6))* America Star Bks.

Lorbiecki, Marybeth. Jackie's Bat. Pinkney, Brian, illus. 2006. (ENG.). 40p. (J). (gr. k-3). 17.99 *(978-0-689-84102-6(7)*, Simon & Schuster Bks. For Young Readers) Simon & Schuster Bks. For Young Readers.

Lord, Bruce & Richards, Elisabeth. Humpty Dumpty Was Pushed: And Other Cracked Tales. 2008. 196p. 24.95 *(978-0-595-71559-6(1))*; pap. 14.95 *(978-0-595-47691-6(0))* iUniverse, Inc.

Lord, Cynthia. Half a Chance. 2014. (ENG.). 224p. (J). (gr. 3-7). 16.99 *(978-0-545-03533-0(3)*, Scholastic Pr.) Scholastic, Inc.

—A Handful of Stars. (ENG.). 192p. (J). (gr. 3-7). 2017. pap. 6.99 **(978-0-545-70028-3(0))** 2015. 16.99 *(978-0-545-70027-6(2))* Scholastic, Inc. (Scholastic Pr.).

—Happy Birthday Hamster. Anderson, Derek, illus. 2011. (ENG.). 40p. (J). (gr. -1-k). 18.99 *(978-0-545-25522-6(8)*, Scholastic Pr.) Scholastic, Inc.

—Hot Rod Hamster & the Wacky Whatever Race! Anderson, Derek, illus. 2014. (ENG.). 32p. (J). (gr. -1-3). pap. 3.99 *(978-0-545-62678-1(1)*, Scholastic Pr.) Scholastic, Inc.

Lord, Emery. Open Road Summer. 2015. (ENG.). 368p. (YA). (gr. 7). pap. 9.99 *(978-0-8027-3801-1(X)*, 9780802738011, Bloomsbury USA Childrens) Bloomsbury Publishing USA.

—The Start of Me & You. (ENG.). (YA). 2016. 416p. pap. 9.99 *(978-1-61963-938-6(6)*, 9781619639386) 2015. 384p. (gr. 7). 17.99 *(978-1-61963-359-9(0)*, 9781619633599) Bloomsbury Publishing USA. (Bloomsbury USA Childrens).

Lordon, Claire. Lorenzo, the Pizza-Loving Lobster. 2016. (ENG., Illus.). 32p. (J). (gr. -1-3). 16.99 *(978-1-4998-0228-3(5))* Little Bee Books Inc.

Lore, Pittacus. I Am Number Four. (YA). (gr. 9). 2016. (Lorien Legacies: the Lost Files Ser.). 416p. pap. 9.99 *(978-0-06-238771-4(5))* 2011. (Lorien Legacies Ser.: 1). (ENG.). 496p. pap. 9.99 *(978-0-06-196957-7(5))* 2010. (Lorien Legacies Ser.: 1). (ENG.). 448p. 17.99 *(978-0-06-196955-3(9))* 2011. (Lorien Legacies Ser.: 1). (ENG.). 496p. pap. 9.99 *(978-0-06-211655-0(X))* 2011. (Lorien Legacies Ser.: 1). (ENG.). 480p. 17.99 *(978-0-06-202624-8(0))* HarperCollins Pubs.

—I Am Number Four. 2009. (Lorien Legacies Ser.: Bk. 1). 11.04 *(978-0-7848-3715-3(5)*, Everbind) Marco Bk. Co.

—I Am Number Four. 2011. (I Am Number Four Ser.: Vol. 1). (ENG.). 440p. (gr. 9-12). 20.00 *(978-1-61383-207-3(9))* Perfection Learning Corp.

—I Am Number Four. 2011. (Lorien Legacies Ser.: 1). (YA). lib. bdg. 20.85 *(978-0-606-23545-7(0)*, Turtleback) Turtleback Bks.

—I Am Number Four: The Lost Files: Rebel Allies. 2015. (Lorien Legacies: the Lost Files Ser.). (ENG.). 416p. (YA). (gr. 9). pap. 9.99 *(978-0-06-236404-3(9))* HarperCollins Pubs.

—I Am Number Four: The Lost Files: Secret Histories. 2013. (Lorien Legacies: the Lost Files Ser.). (ENG.). 416p. (YA). (gr. 9). pap. 9.99 *(978-0-06-222367-8(4))* HarperCollins Pubs.

—The Legacies. 2012. (Lorien Legacies: the Lost Files Ser.). (YA). lib. bdg. 20.85 *(978-0-606-26874-5(X)*, Turtleback) Turtleback Bks.

—The Power of Six. (Lorien Legacies Ser.: 2). (ENG.). (YA). (gr. 9). 2012. 448p. pap. 9.99 *(978-0-06-197457-1(9))* 2011. 416p. 17.99 *(978-0-06-197455-7(2))* HarperCollins Pubs.

—The Power of Six. 2012. (Lorien Legacies Ser.: 2). (YA). lib. bdg. 20.85 *(978-0-606-26289-7(X)*, Turtleback) Turtleback Bks.

—The Rise of Nine. (Lorien Legacies Ser.: 3). (ENG.). 416p. (YA). (gr. 9). 2013. pap. 9.99 *(978-0-06-197460-1(9))* 2012. 17.99 *(978-0-06-197458-8(7))* HarperCollins Pubs.

—The Rise of Nine. 2013. (Lorien Legacies Ser.: 3). (YA). lib. bdg. 20.85 *(978-0-606-31830-3(5)*, Turtleback) Turtleback Bks.

—Secret Histories. 2013. (Lorien Legacies: the Lost Files Ser.). (YA). lib. bdg. 20.85 *(978-0-606-31823-5(2)*, Turtleback) Turtleback Bks.

Lorenzo, Lucia Ann. Lucky, My Best Friend. 2012. 24p. pap. 17.99 *(978-1-4772-8087-4(1))* AuthorHouse.

Lorey, Dean. Monster Law. 2009. 304p. 10.99 *(978-0-06-134048-2(0))* HarperCollins Pubs.

Lorraine. The Adventures of Ruthy: Ruthy Gets Lost. 2012. 32p. pap. 19.99 *(978-1-4772-6000-5(5))* AuthorHouse.

Lorsch-Saltzman, Laurie. Josh & George. 2011. 32p. pap. 24.95 *(978-1-4560-6552-2(1))* America Star Bks.

Lorton, Barbara. Sidney Seagull Marks Lighthouses & Buoys of the Chesapeake. 2013. (Illus.). 28p. pap. 16.99 *(978-1-4582-1055-5(3)*, Abbott Pr.) Author Solutions, Inc.

Lotfy, Evelyn. Ms. Plant & Friends. 2011. 24p. (gr. -1). pap. 14.98 *(978-1-4567-5448-8(3))* AuthorHouse.

Loth, Sebastian. Remembering Crystal. 2010. (ENG., Illus.). 64p. (J). (gr. -1-3). 14.95 *(978-0-7358-2300-6(6))* North-South Bks., Inc.

Loughead, Deb. Caught in the Act, 1 vol. 2013. (Orca Currents Ser.). (ENG.). 128p. (J). (gr. 5-9). pap. 9.95 *(978-1-4598-0496-8(1))*; lib. bdg. 16.95 *(978-1-4598-0510-1(0))* Orca Bk. Pubs. USA.

—A Pocketful of Fur. Birke, Lisa, tr. 2005. (Illus.). 60p. (J). (gr. 2-4). 6.95 *(978-0-9730831-6-3(6))* Hodgepog Bks. CAN. Dist: Fitzhenry & Whiteside, Ltd.

—Sidetracked, 1 vol. 2012. (Orca Sports Ser.). (ENG.). 136p. (YA). (gr. 6-10). pap. 9.95 *(978-1-4598-0250-6(0))* Orca Bk. Pubs. USA.

Lougher, Jenny. Ted & the Combine Harvester. Lewis, Wayne, illus. 2007. 23p. pap. *(978-1-905553-27-3(7))* BookPublishingWorld.

Louis, Sachar. There's a Boy in the Girls' Bathroom. 2014. (ENG.). 208p. (J). (gr. 7-12). 11.24 *(978-1-63245-256-6(1))* Lectorum Pubns., Inc.

Love, Emily. The Beginning of Freedom. 2010. 81p. pap. 9.00 *(978-0-557-56598-6(7))* Lulu Pr., Inc.

Love, Jessica. In Real Life: A Novel. 2016. (ENG.). 240p. (YA). 18.99 *(978-1-250-06471-4(6)*, 9781250064714, St. Martin's Griffin) St. Martin's Pr.

Lovejoy, Sharon. Running Out of Night. 2014. (ENG., Illus.). 304p. (J). (gr. 4-7). lib. bdg. 19.99 *(978-0-375-99147-9(6)*, Delacorte Bks. for Young Readers) Random Hse. Children's Bks.

Lovelace, Eloise. Elvin's Friends. 2012. 20p. pap. 17.99 *(978-1-4685-7615-3(1))* AuthorHouse.

Lovelace, Maud Hart. Betsy-Tacy. Lenski, Lois, illus. 60th anniv. ed. 2007. (Betsy-Tacy Ser.: 1). (ENG.). 144p. (J). (gr. 2-5). pap. 5.99 *(978-0-06-440096-1(4))* HarperCollins Pubs.

—The Betsy-Tacy Treasury: The First Four Betsy-Tacy Books. 2011. (P. S. Ser.). (ENG.). 736p. pap. 15.99 *(978-0-06-209587-9(0)*, Harper Perennial) HarperCollins Pubs.

Lovelace, Maud Hart & Lovelace, M. Betsy-Tacy. 2007. (Betsy-Tacy Ser.). (J). (gr. 3-6). lib. bdg. 16.00 *(978-0-8335-1338-0(9)*, Turtleback) Turtleback Bks.

Lovell, Patty. Have Fun, Molly Lou Melon. Lovell, Patty & Catrow, David, illus. 2012. (ENG.). 32p. (J). (gr. k-3). 16.99 *(978-0-399-25406-2(4)*, G.P. Putnam's Sons Books for Young Readers) Penguin Young Readers Group.

Loveridge, Pamela. Buzzy Bee. 2012. 24p. pap. 28.03 *(978-1-4797-4802-0(1))* Xlibris Corp.

Low, Chen-Chen-Chen. Lizzie May & Oshin. 2009. 46p. pap. 29.99 *(978-1-4092-5740-0(1))* Lulu Pr., Inc.

—Lizzie May & the Shoelaces. 2009. 44p. pap. 29.99 *(978-1-4092-5739-4(8))* Lulu Pr., Inc.

Low, J. H. The Visitor from Far Far Away. Low, J. H., illus. 2016. (ENG., Illus.). 32p. 10.00 *(978-981-4721-71-4(9))* Marshall Cavendish International (Asia) Private Ltd. SGP. Dist: National Bk. Network.

Lowe, E. Van. Never Slow Dance with a Zombie. 2009. (ENG.). 256p. (J). (gr. 8-12). pap. 18.99 *(978-0-7653-2040-7(1)*, 9780765320407, Tor Teen) Doherty, Tom Assocs., LLC.

Lowell, Pamela. Returnable Girl, 0 vols. 2009. (ENG.). 240p. (J). (gr. 8-12). pap. 9.99 *(978-0-7614-5592-9(2)*, 9780761455929, Amazon Children's Publishing) Amazon Publishing.

—Returnable Girl. 2006. 229p. (YA). (gr. 8-12). 16.99 *(978-0-7614-5317-8(2))* Marshall Cavendish Corp.

Lowery, Marie Hayes. Beau & Friends. 2012. 20p. pap. 17.99 *(978-1-4817-0106-8(1))* AuthorHouse.

Lowery, Rae. Charlie & the Case of the Big Bully: The Adventures of Charlie #4, 1 vol. 2010. 108p. pap. 19.95 *(978-1-4489-5558-9(0))* America Star Bks.

Lowrey-Christian, Jane. Quackless Duck Finds His Pals. 2009. 36p. pap. 21.99 *(978-1-4415-1374-8(4))* Xlibris Corp.

Loye, Scott. Moon Ring. 2011. 160p. (gr. 10-12). 22.95 *(978-1-4502-9682-3(3))*; pap. 12.95 *(978-1-4502-9680-9(7))* iUniverse, Inc.

Lubar, David. Punished! (Darby Creek Exceptional Titles Ser.). (ENG.). 96p. (J). (gr. 2-5). 2007. per. 4.99 *(978-1-58196-063-1(8))* 2006. 15.95 *(978-1-58196-042-6(5))* Lerner Publishing Group. (Darby Creek).

—Sophomores & Other Oxymorons. 2015. (ENG.). 432p. (YA). (gr. 7). 17.99 *(978-0-525-42970-8(0)*, Dutton Books for Young Readers) Penguin Young Readers Group.

—Stranger Things. Loveridge, Matt, illus. 2013. (Looniverse Ser.: 1). (ENG.). 96p. (J). (gr. 1-3). pap. 4.99 *(978-0-545-49602-5(0))* Scholastic, Inc.

—Stranger Things. 2013. (Looniverse Ser.: 1). lib. bdg. 14.75 *(978-0-606-31962-1(4)*, Turtleback) Turtleback Bks.

Luberto, Bradley. Clide & Druce: A Repulsive Tale of Trolls & Tax Money. 2006. (ENG.). 48p. per. 16.95 *(978-1-4241-5012-0(4))* PublishAmerica, Inc.

Lubner, Susan. A Horse's Tale: A Colonial Williamsburg Adventure. Moore, Margie, illus. 2008. (ENG.). 32p. (J). (gr. -1-1). 17.95 *(978-0-8109-9490-4(9)*, Abrams Bks. for Young Readers) Abrams, Inc.

Lucado, Max & Schmidt, Troy. Flo, the Lyin' Fly. 2005. 32p. (J). pap. 3.99 *(978-1-4003-0664-0(7))* Nelson, Thomas Inc.

Lucy's New Friend. 2005. 16p. (J). bds. 4.99 *(978-1-59384-079-2(9))* Bk. Club of America.

Luder, Doreen. Dax the Last Dragon. 2012. 24p. pap. 24.95 *(978-1-62709-988-2(3))* America Star Bks.

Ludwig, Trudy. Better Than You. Gustavson, Adam, illus. 2011. (ENG.). 32p. (J). (gr. 1-4). 15.99 *(978-1-58246-380-3(8)*, Knopf Bks. for Young Readers) Random Hse. Children's Bks.

—The Invisible Boy. Barton, Patrice, illus. 2013. (ENG.). 40p. (J). (gr. 1-4). 16.99 *(978-1-58246-450-3(2)*, Knopf Bks. for Young Readers) Random Hse. Children's Bks.

Lukic, Dragan. Friend to Friend. Vuchic-Radovich, Sladjana, tr. 2005. (Illus.). 36p. (J). *(978-0-9714039-6-3(1))* Zora.

Lundquist, Jenny. Plastic Polly. 2013. (Mix Ser.). (ENG.). 256p. (J). (gr. 4-8). pap. 6.99 *(978-1-4424-5248-0(X)*, Aladdin) Simon & Schuster Children's Publishing.

Lundquist, Mary. Cat & Bunny. Lundquist, Mary, illus. 2015. (ENG., Illus.). 32p. (J). (gr. -1-3). 17.99 *(978-0-06-228780-9(X))* HarperCollins Pubs.

Lunievicz, Joe. Open Wounds. 2011. 352p. (YA). (gr. 9-18). 16.95 *(978-1-934813-51-5(6))* Westside Bks.

Luper, Eric. The Spy's Secret. 2016. (Key Hunters Ser.: 2). (ENG.). 128p. (J). (gr. 2-5). pap. 4.99 *(978-0-545-82206-0(8))* Scholastic, Inc.

Lupica, Mike. Game Changers. (Game Changers Ser.: 1). (ENG.). 224p. (J). (gr. 3-7). 2013. pap. 6.99 *(978-0-545-38179-6(7))*Bk. 1. 2012. 16.99 *(978-0-545-38182-6(7))* Scholastic, Inc. (Scholastic Pr.).

—Heavy Hitters. (Game Changers Ser.: 3). (ENG.). 240p. (J). (gr. 3-7). 2015. pap. 6.99 *(978-0-545-38181-9(9)*, Scholastic Paperbacks) 2014. 16.99 *(978-0-545-38184-0(3))* Scholastic, Inc.

—Million-Dollar Throw. 2010. (ENG.). 272p. (J). (gr. 5-18). 7.99 *(978-0-14-241558-0(8)*, Puffin Books) Penguin Young Readers Group.

—Million-Dollar Throw. 2010. (Million Dollar Sports Ser.). lib. bdg. 18.40 *(978-0-606-25316-1(5)*, Turtleback) Turtleback Bks.

—The Only Game. 2015. (Home Team Ser.). (ENG., Illus.). 320p. (J). (gr. 3-7). 16.99 *(978-1-4814-0995-7(6)*, Simon & Schuster Bks. For Young Readers) Simon & Schuster Bks. For Young Readers.

—The Only Game. 2016. (Home Team Ser.). lib. bdg. 18.40 *(978-0-606-38252-6(6))* Turtleback Bks.

—Play Makers. 2014. (Game Changers Ser.: 2). (ENG.). 224p. (J). (gr. 3-7). pap. 6.99 *(978-0-545-38180-2(0)*, Scholastic Pr.) Scholastic, Inc.

—Two-Minute Drill, 1 vol. 2012. (Comeback Kids Ser.). (ENG.). 192p. (J). (gr. 4-8). lib. bdg. 27.07 *(978-1-59961-179-2(1))* Spotlight.

Lurie, Susan. Will You Be My Friend? Head, Murray, illus. 2016. (ENG.). 32p. (J). 16.99 *(978-1-250-04643-7(2)*, 9781250046437) Feiwel & Friends.

Lush, Nella. Gracie & Belle Never Again! 2007. 20p. per. 24.95 *(978-1-4241-8373-9(1))* America Star Bks.

Lustig, Loretta, illus. The Little Red Hen: A Tale about Cooperation. 2006. (J). 6.99 *(978-1-59939-018-5(3))* Cornerstone Pr.

Luthardt, Kevin. When Edgar Met Cecil, 1 vol. Luthardt, Kevin, illus. 2013. (ENG., Illus.). 32p. (J). (gr. -1-3). 15.95 *(978-1-56145-706-9(X))* Peachtree Pubs.

Luttrel, Bill. Redheaded Robbie's Christmas Story. Melanson, Luc, illus. 2003. (ENG.). 32p. (J). (gr. k-6). 16.95 *(978-1-58536-136-6(4))* Sleeping Bear Pr.

Lutz II, William. Seeking Mason. 2009. 212p. pap. 14.00 *(978-0-557-03737-7(9))* Lulu Pr., Inc.

Lux, Josephine Kei & Doerflinger, Marion. Daydreaming Daisy Part of the Daydreamer's Club Series. 2009. 40p. pap. 17.50 *(978-1-60860-252-0(4)*, Eloquent Bks.) Strategic Book Publishing & Rights Agency (SBPRA).

Lyen, Taylor Samuel. Pembroke: The Adventures of Arthur Bacterium & Patty Virus. 2012. 180p. (-18). pap. 13.95 *(978-1-4759-5855-3(2))* iUniverse, Inc.

Lyga, Barry. Bang. 2017. (ENG.). 304p. (J). (gr. 7-17). 17.99 *(978-0-316-31550-0(8))* Little, Brown Bks. for Young Readers.

—The Secret Sea. 2016. (ENG.). 448p. (J). 16.99 *(978-1-250-07283-2(2)*, 9781250072832) Feiwel & Friends.

Lyle-Soffe, Shari. Trouble Finds Rooter & Snuffle. Collier, Kevin Scott, illus. 2008. 20p. pap. 9.95 *(978-1-933090-72-6(3))* Guardian Angel Publishing, Inc.

Lynch, Brendan Denis. The Document. 2012. 218p. pap. 8.99 *(978-0-9825243-2-9(3))* 1776 Pr.

Lynch, Chris. Alive & Kicking. 2015. 182p. (J). *(978-0-545-78940-0(0)*, Scholastic Pr.) Scholastic, Inc.

—Hothouse. 2010. (ENG.). 208p. (YA). (gr. 8-18). 16.99 *(978-0-06-167379-5(X)*, HarperTeen) HarperCollins Pubs.

—I Pledge Allegiance. 2011. (Vietnam Ser.: 1). (ENG.). 192p. (J). (gr. 3-7). 16.99 *(978-0-545-27029-8(4)*, Scholastic Pr.); 183p. (YA). *(978-0-545-38415-5(X))* Scholastic, Inc.

—I Pledge Allegiance. 2013. (Vietnam Ser.: 1). lib. bdg. 17.20 *(978-0-606-31961-4(1)*, Turtleback) Turtleback Bks.

—The Liberators. 2015. (World War II Ser.: 4). (ENG.). 192p. (J). (gr. 5-9). 18.99 *(978-0-545-52304-2(4)*, Scholastic Pr.) Scholastic, Inc.

—Sharpshooter. (J). 2013. (Vietnam Ser.: 2). (ENG.). 192p. (gr. 5-9). pap. 7.99 *(978-0-545-27027-4(8))* 2012. *(978-0-545-43650-2(8))* Scholastic, Inc. (Scholastic Pr.).

—Sharpshooter. 2013. (Vietnam Ser.: 2). lib. bdg. 18.40 *(978-0-606-31962-1(X)*, Turtleback) Turtleback Bks.

—Sins of the Fathers. 2006. 232p. (YA). (gr. 9-12). lib. bdg. 17.89 *(978-0-06-074038-2(8)*, HarperTeen) HarperCollins Pubs.

—Slot Machine. 2003. 23.00 *(978-0-8446-7249-6(1))* Smith, Peter Pub., Inc.

—Vietnam #1: I Pledge Allegiance. 2013. (Vietnam Ser.: 1). (ENG.). 192p. (J). (gr. 5-9). pap. 7.99 *(978-0-545-27030-4(8)*, Scholastic Paperbacks) Scholastic, Inc.

—Walking Wounded, Bk. 5. 2014. (Vietnam Ser.: 5). (ENG.). 208p. (J). (gr. 5-9). 17.99 *(978-0-545-64013-8(X)*, Scholastic Pr.) Scholastic, Inc.

—World War II Book 2: Dead in the Water. 2014. (World War II Ser.: 2). (ENG.). 192p. (J). (gr. 5-9). 18.99 *(978-0-545-52298-4(6)*, Scholastic Pr.) Scholastic, Inc.

Lynch, Diane M., ed. Friend 2 Friend: Twelve Short Stories. 2009. (J). (gr. 3-6). pap. 7.95 *(978-0-8198-2685-5(5))* Pauline Bks. & Media.

Lynch, Lauren Boehm. Working As a Team: Down to the End of the Road & Back. DeBroeck, Sarah, illus. 2011. 28p. pap. 24.95 *(978-1-4560-0986-1(9))* America Star Bks.

—The Yellow Butterfly. DeBroeck, Sarah, illus. 2011. 28p. pap. 24.95 *(978-1-4560-0982-3(6))* America Star Bks.

Lynch, Sharon Boylan. The Nimbles of Nimbus. 2011. 32p. pap. 14.50 *(978-1-4389-6223-8(1))* AuthorHouse.

Lynch, Stephen D. The Travels of Kui, the African Spurred Tortoise. Richard, Keisha Luana, illus. 2007. 36p. per. 24.95 *(978-1-4137-1802-7(7))* America Star Bks.

Lyon, Nathan W. & Ellis, Kevin L. Sam the Clam. 2010. 28p. pap. 14.95 *(978-1-4520-7784-0(3))* AuthorHouse.

Lyons, C. J. Broken. 2014. (ENG.). 320p. (YA). (gr. 7-12). pap. 9.99 *(978-1-4022-9230-9(9))* Sourcebooks, Inc.

Lyons, Stefanie. Dating Down. 2015. (ENG., Illus.). 312p. (YA). pap. 9.99 *(978-0-7387-4337-0(2)*, Flux) North Star Editions.

Lytton, Deborah. Ruby Starr. 2017. (Ruby Starr Ser.: 1). (ENG.). 272p. (J). (gr. 3-7). pap. 7.99 ***(978-1-4926-4577-1(X)***, Sourcebooks Jabberwocky) Sourcebooks, Inc.

M. Alvarado. We Are Different, but the Same. 2012. 16p. pap. 15.99 *(978-1-4685-4425-1(X))* AuthorHouse.

M. Eugenia Coeymans. The Universe of the Aurus. 2013. 60p. pap. 20.99 *(978-1-4808-0366-4(9))* Archway Publishing.

M. F Feierabend, J. Olivia Ponty & Friends to the Rescue. 2012. 32p. pap. 32.70 *(978-1-4771-1081-2(X))* Xlibris Corp.

Mabille, Christine. Potato-Kid & the Adventure: Treasures Within, 1 vol. 2009. 76p. pap. 19.95 *(978-1-61582-981-1(4))* America Star Bks.

MacDonald, Frances. The Screaming Tunnel. 2012. (ENG.). 140p. (YA). pap. 15.99 *(978-1-926780-23-8(X))* Key Publishing Hse., Inc., The CAN. Dist: Bookmasters Distribution.

MacDonald, George. Princess & the Goblin. 2006. 128p. per. 10.95 *(978-1-59818-653-6(1))* Aegypan.

MacDonald, Ross. Henry's Hand. 2013. (ENG., Illus.). 48p. (J). (gr. k-2). 17.95 *(978-1-4197-0527-4(X)*, Abrams Bks. for Young Readers) Abrams, Inc.

MacDowell, Diane. Adventures of Timkin: The Early Years. 2012. 28p. pap. 19.99 *(978-1-4772-7101-8(5))* AuthorHouse.

Macenski, Geraldine. Healthy, Happy Gigi! 2009. 28p. pap. 15.99 *(978-1-4415-3644-0(2))* Xlibris Corp.

MacGregor, Joanne. Rock Steady. 2013. (ENG.). 284p. pap. 15.00 *(978-1-86919-903-6(0))* Protea Boekhuis ZAF. Dist: Casemate Pubs. & Bk. Distributors, LLC.

MacGuire, Maxine. Maddie & the Naughty Elf: Santa Learns a Lesson, 1 vol. 2010. 36p. 24.95 *(978-1-4489-8250-9(2))* PublishAmerica, Inc.

Machado, Ana Maria. Camilon, Comilon. (Barco de Vapor). (SPA.). 64p. (J). (gr. 2-3). *(978-84-348-2703-5(4))* SM Ediciones.

Machen, Sherry Ann. Hannah & Friends. 2004. 75p. (J). per. *(978-1-55306-833-4(5)*, Epic Pr.) Essence Publishing.

Maciel, Amanda. Lucky Girl. 2017. 320p. (YA). (gr. 9). 17.99 *(978-0-06-230533-6(6))* HarperCollins Pubs.

Mack, Iris Marie. Mama Says, Money Doesn't Grow on Trees! 2004. (World of Dr. Mackamatix Mathematics Edutainment Book Ser.). (Illus.). 48p. (J). per. 18.99 *(978-1-4134-0891-1(5))* Xlibris Corp.

Mack, Jeff. Hippo & Rabbit. Mack, Jeff, illus. 2011. (Scholastic Reader Level 1 Ser.). (ENG., Illus.). 32p. (J). (gr. -1-2). pap. 3.99 *(978-0-545-27445-6(1)*, Cartwheel Bks.) Scholastic, Inc.

—Look! Mack, Jeff, illus. 2015. (ENG., Illus.). 32p. (J). (gr. -1-k). 16.99 *(978-0-399-16205-3(4)*, Philomel Bks.) Penguin Young Readers Group.

Mack, Kelvin. Bullies Need Friends Too. 2011. 20p. 13.99 *(978-1-4269-6182-3(0))* Trafford Publishing.

Mack, Winnie. After All, You're Callie Boone. 2013. (ENG.). 192p. (J). (gr. 4-7). pap. 14.99 *(978-1-250-02735-1(7)*, 9781250027351) Square Fish.

Mackall, Dandi Daley. Friendly Foal. 2004. (Winnie the Horse Gentler Ser.: 7). (ENG.). 224p. (J). mass mkt. 5.99 *(978-0-8423-8723-1(4)*, Tyndale Kids) Tyndale Hse. Pubs.

—Natalie: School's First Day of Me, 1 vol. Blakeslee, Lys, illus. 2009. (That's Nat! Ser.). (ENG.). 96p. (J). (gr. 1-4). pap. 4.99 *(978-0-310-71568-9(7))* Zonderkidz.

—Natalie & the Bestest Friend Race, 1 vol. Blakeslee, Lys, illus. 2009. (That's Nat! Ser.). (ENG.). 96p. (J). (gr. 1-4). pap. 4.99 *(978-0-310-71570-2(9))* Zonderkidz.

—A Perfect Pony, 1 vol. Wolf, Claudia, illus. 2011. (I Can Read! / a Horse Named Bob Ser.). (ENG.). 32p. (J). pap. 3.99 *(978-0-310-71783-6(3))* Zonderkidz.

Mackay, Gregory. Anders & the Volcano. 2017. (Anders Ser.: 2). (ENG.). 176p. (J). (gr. 1-6). pap. 9.99 ***(978-1-76029-003-0(3))*** Allen & Unwin AUS. Dist: Independent Pubs. Group.

Mackel, Kathy. MadCat. 2005. (Illus.). 192p. (J). 15.99 *(978-0-06-054869-8(X))* HarperCollins Pubs.

MacKenzie, Catherine. The Dark Blue Bike at No 17: Tammy & Jake Learn about Friendship & Bullying. 2003. (Tales from Canterbury Place Ser.). (ENG., Illus.). 160p. (J). mass mkt. 6.99 *(978-1-85792-732-0(X))* Christian Focus Pubns. GBR. Dist: Send The Light Distribution LLC.

MacKenzie, Jill. Spin the Sky. 2016. (ENG.). 352p. (YA). (gr. 6). 17.99 *(978-1-5107-0686-6(0)*, Sky Pony Pr.) Skyhorse Publishing Co., Inc.

MacKenzie, Ross. Zac & the Dream Stealers. (J). 2013. 297p. *(978-0-545-40107-4(0))* 2012. (ENG.). 304p. (gr. 3-7). 16.99 *(978-0-545-40106-7(2))* Scholastic, Inc. (Chicken Hse., The).

MacKie, Ian. The Adventures of Hamish the Sea Eagle. Mackie, Marie-Anne, illus. 2013. 24p. *(978-1-78148-614-6(X))* Grosvenor Hse. Publishing Ltd.

Mackintosh, David. Marshall Armstrong Is New to Our School. 2011. (ENG., Illus.). 32p. (J). (gr. k-2). 17.95 *(978-1-4197-0036-1(7)*, Abrams Bks. for Young Readers) Abrams, Inc.

—What's up Mumu? Mackintosh, David, illus. 2015. (ENG., Illus.). 32p. (J). 17.99 *(978-0-00-812469-4(8)*, HarperCollins Children's Bks.) HarperCollins Pubs. Ltd. GBR. Dist: HarperCollins Pubs.

Mackler, Carolyn. Best Friend Next Door. 2015. (ENG.). 224p. (J). (gr. 3-7). 16.99 *(978-0-545-70944-6(X)*, Scholastic Pr.) Scholastic, Inc.

—Infinite in Between. 2015. (ENG.). 480p. (YA). (gr. 8). 17.99 *(978-0-06-173107-5(2)*, HarperTeen) HarperCollins Pubs.

MacLachlan, Patricia. The Boxcar Children Beginning. Jessell, Tim, illus. (Boxcar Children Mysteries Ser.). (ENG.). 144p. (J). (gr. 1-5). 2013. 6.99 *(978-0-8075-6617-6(9))* 2012. 16.99 *(978-0-8075-6616-9(0))* Whitman, Albert & Co.

—Skylark. 2004. (Sarah, Plain & Tall Ser.: 2). (ENG.). 128p. (J). (gr. 1-5). pap. 5.99 *(978-0-06-440622-2(9))* HarperCollins Pubs.

MacLean, Sarah. The Season. 2009. 345p. (J). *(978-0-545-24214-1(2))* Scholastic, Inc.

Maclear, Kyo. The Wish Tree. Turnham, Chris, illus. 2016. (ENG.). 40p. (J). (gr. -1 — 1). 16.99 *(978-1-4521-5065-9(6))* Chronicle Bks. LLC.

MacLellan, Erin. Run from the Nun! 2003. (ENG.). 128p. (J). (gr. 4-6). tchr. ed. 16.95 *(978-0-8234-1796-4(4))* Holiday Hse., Inc.

Macmillan, Sue. Bouncy, Pouncy Puppy. Ward, Sarah, illus. 2014. (Cheery Chasers Ser.). (ENG.). 8p. (J). (gr. -1 — 1). bds. 4.99 *(978-0-7641-6698-3(0))* Barron's Educational Series, Inc.

—Hoppy Frog's Fly Spy. Ward, Sarah, illus. 2014. (Cheery Chasers Ser.). (ENG.). 8p. (J). (gr. -1 — 1). bds. 4.99 *(978-0-7641-6700-3(6))* Barron's Educational Series, Inc.

Madden, Gloria. Grandmothers Bedtime Stories. 2008. 68p. (gr. -1-7). pap. 10.49 *(978-1-4343-9201-5(5))* AuthorHouse.

—Grandmothers Bedtime Stories: Book 5. 2008. 144p. pap. 11.99 *(978-1-4343-9515-3(4))* AuthorHouse.

Maddock, Lisa. The Bridezilla Who Stole Christmas: A Teddy & Pip Story. 2009. 108p. pap. 9.95 *(978-1-60844-258-4(6))* Dog Ear Publishing, LLC.

Maddox, Jake. BMX Bravery. 2016. (Jake Maddox JV Ser.). (ENG.). 96p. (gr. 3-4). lib. bdg. 25.99 *(978-1-4965-2630-4(9))* Stone Arch Bks.

—Board Battle, 1 vol. Aburtov, Jesus Aburto, illus. 2013. (Jake Maddox Sports Stories Ser.). (ENG.). 72p. (gr. 2-3). pap. 5.95 *(978-1-4342-6208-0(1))* Stone Arch Bks.

—Board Battle. 2013. (Jake Maddox Sports Stories Ser.). (ENG.). 72p. (gr. 2-3). pap. 35.70 *(978-1-4342-6235-6(9))* Stone Arch Bks.

—Board Battle, 1 vol. Aburtov, Jesus Aburto, illus. 2013. (Jake Maddox Sports Stories Ser.). (ENG.). 72p. (gr. 2-3). lib. bdg. 25.32 *(978-1-4342-5975-2(7))* Stone Arch Bks.

—Cheer Captain, 1 vol. Pulsar Studios Staff, illus. 2011. (Jake Maddox Girl Sports Stories Ser.). (ENG.). 72p. (gr. 2-3). 25.32 *(978-1-4342-2551-1(8))* Stone Arch Bks.

—Cheer Choice, 1 vol. Wood, Katie, illus. 2014. (Jake Maddox Girl Sports Stories Ser.). (ENG.). 72p. (gr. 2-3). 25.32 *(978-1-4342-4143-6(2))* Stone Arch Bks.

—Cycling Champion, 1 vol. Garcia, Eduardo, illus. 2012. (Jake Maddox Sports Stories Ser.). (ENG.). 72p. (gr. 2-3). pap. 5.95 *(978-1-4342-3904-4(7))*; lib. bdg. 25.32 *(978-1-4342-3290-8(5))* Stone Arch Bks.

—Dance Team Dilemma, 1 vol. Wood, Katie, illus. 2013. (Jake Maddox Girl Sports Stories Ser.). (ENG.). 72p. (gr. 2-3). pap. 5.95 *(978-1-4342-4201-3(3))*; lib. bdg. 25.32 *(978-1-4342-4014-9(2))* Stone Arch Bks.

—Dance Team Drama. 2016. (Jake Maddox JV Girls Ser.). (ENG.). 96p. (gr. 3-4). pap. 5.95 *(978-1-4965-3678-5(9))*; lib. bdg. 25.99 *(978-1-4965-3674-7(6))* Stone Arch Bks.

—Dancing Solo, 1 vol. Wood, Katie, illus. 2014. (Jake Maddox Girl Sports Stories Ser.). (ENG.). 72p. (gr. 2-3). 25.32 *(978-1-4342-4142-9(4))* Stone Arch Bks.

—Diving off the Edge, 1 vol. Tiffany, Sean, illus. 2009. (Jake Maddox Sports Stories Ser.). (ENG.). 72p. (gr. 2-3). lib. bdg. 25.32 *(978-1-4342-1205-4(X))* Stone Arch Bks.

—Gold Medal Swim, 1 vol. Garcia, Eduardo, illus. 2012. (Jake Maddox Sports Stories Ser.). (ENG.). 72p. (gr. 2-3). pap. 5.95 *(978-1-4342-3902-0(0))*; lib. bdg. 25.32 *(978-1-4342-3288-5(3))* Stone Arch Bks.

—Gridiron Showdown, 1 vol. Ray, Mike, illus. 2014. (Jake Maddox JV Ser.). (ENG.). 96p. (gr. 3-4). 25.99 *(978-1-4342-9155-4(3))* Stone Arch Bks.

—Heavyweight Takedown. 2015. (Jake Maddox JV Ser.). (ENG.). 96p. (gr. 3-4). lib. bdg. 25.99 *(978-1-4342-9638-2(5))* Stone Arch Bks.

—Hoop Hustle. Aburto, Jesus, illus. 2015. (Jake Maddox Sports Stories Ser.). (ENG.). 72p. (gr. 2-3). lib. bdg. 25.32 *(978-1-4965-0494-4(1))* Stone Arch Bks.

—Kart Competition, 1 vol. Aburtov, Jesus Aburto, illus. 2013. (Jake Maddox Sports Stories Ser.). (ENG.). 72p. (gr. 2-3). pap. 5.95 *(978-1-4342-6209-7(X))* Stone Arch Bks.

—Kart Competition. 2013. (Jake Maddox Sports Stories Ser.). (ENG.). 72p. (gr. 2-3). pap. 35.70 *(978-1-4342-6236-3(7))* Stone Arch Bks.

—Kart Competition, 1 vol. Aburtov, Jesus, illus. 2013. (Jake Maddox Sports Stories Ser.). (ENG.). 72p. (gr. 2-3). lib. bdg. 25.32 *(978-1-4342-5976-9(5))* Stone Arch Bks.

—Point Guard Prank, 1 vol. Tiffany, Sean, illus. 2012. (Jake Maddox Sports Stories Ser.). (ENG.). 72p. (gr. 2-3). pap. 5.95 *(978-1-4342-4207-5(2))*; 25.32 *(978-1-4342-4009-5(6))* Stone Arch Bks.

—Second-Chance Soccer, 1 vol. Ray, Mike, illus. 2014. (Jake Maddox JV Ser.). (ENG.). 96p. (gr. 3-4). 25.99 *(978-1-4342-9154-7(5))* Stone Arch Bks.

—Skateboard Idol. 2016. (Jake Maddox JV Ser.). (ENG.). 96p. (gr. 3-4). lib. bdg. 25.99 *(978-1-4965-2631-1(7))* Stone Arch Bks.

—Skating Showdown, 1 vol. Wood, Katie, illus. 2013. (Jake Maddox Girl Sports Stories Ser.). (ENG.). 72p. (gr. 2-3). pap. 5.95 *(978-1-4342-4204-4(8))*; lib. bdg. 25.32 *(978-1-4342-4012-5(6))* Stone Arch Bks.

—Slap-Shot Slump. 2015. (Jake Maddox JV Ser.). (ENG.). 96p. (gr. 3-4). lib. bdg. 25.99 *(978-1-4342-9635-1(0))* Stone Arch Bks.

—Snowboard Struggle. 2016. (Jake Maddox JV Ser.). (ENG., Illus.). 96p. (gr. 3-4). lib. bdg. 25.99 *(978-1-4965-3980-9(X))* Stone Arch Bks.

—Soccer Switch. Aburtov, Jesus Aburto, illus. 2017. (Jake Maddox Graphic Novels Ser.). (ENG.). 72p. (gr. 2-5). lib. bdg. 26.65 *(978-1-4965-3699-0(1))* Stone Arch Bks.

—Softball Surprise, 1 vol. Wood, Katie, illus. 2014. (Jake Maddox Girl Sports Stories Ser.). (ENG.). 72p. (gr. 2-3). 25.32 *(978-1-4342-4141-2(6))* Stone Arch Bks.

—Squad Struggles. Wood, Katie, illus. 2017. (Jake Maddox Girl Sports Stories Ser.). (ENG.). 72p. (gr. 2-3). lib. bdg. 25.32 ***(978-1-4965-4971-6(6))*** Stone Arch Bks.

—Striker Assist, 1 vol. Tiffany, Sean, illus. 2012. (Jake Maddox Sports Stories Ser.). (ENG.). 72p. (gr. 2-3). pap. 5.95 *(978-1-4342-4208-2(0))* Stone Arch Bks.

—Swimming the Distance. 2015. (Jake Maddox JV Ser.). (ENG.). 96p. (gr. 3-4). lib. bdg. 25.99 *(978-1-4342-9637-5(7))* Stone Arch Bks.

—Victory Vault, 1 vol. Pulsar Studios Staff, illus. 2011. (Jake Maddox Girl Sports Stories Ser.). (ENG.). 72p. (gr. 2-3). 25.32 *(978-1-4342-2498-9(8))* Stone Arch Bks.

Maddox, Jake & Berne, Emma Carlson. Horseback Hurdles, 1 vol. Wood, Katie, illus. 2012. (Jake Maddox Girl Sports Stories Ser.). (ENG.). 72p. (gr. 2-3). pap. 5.95 *(978-1-4342-3905-1(5))*; lib. bdg. 25.32 *(978-1-4342-3294-6(8))* Stone Arch Bks.

—Running Scared, 1 vol. Wood, Katie, illus. 2013. (Jake Maddox Girl Sports Stories Ser.). (ENG.). 72p. (gr. 2-3). pap. 5.95 *(978-1-4342-4203-7(X))*; lib. bdg. 25.32 *(978-1-4342-4015-6(0))* Stone Arch Bks.

Maddox, Nicklas. The Big Tiny Spaceman, 1 vol. 2010. 36p. 24.95 *(978-1-4489-7870-0(X))* PublishAmerica, Inc.

Madigan, L. K. Flash Burnout. 2010. (ENG.). 336p. (YA). (gr. 9). pap. 7.99 *(978-0-547-40493-6(X))* Houghton Mifflin Harcourt Publishing Co.

—The Mermaid's Mirror. 2011. (ENG.). 320p. (YA). (gr. 7). pap. 8.99 *(978-0-547-57735-7(4))* Houghton Mifflin Harcourt Publishing Co.

Madonna, Lenae. Lost & Found. Conde, Manuel, illus. 2012. 38p. (J). 16.95 *(978-1-60131-115-3(X)*, Castlebridge Bks.) Big Tent Bks.

Madonna, pseud. Being Binah, No. 6. Fulvimari, Jeffrey, illus. 2008. (English Roses Ser.: 6). (ENG.). 128p. (J). (gr. 3-7). 9.99 *(978-0-14-241095-0(0)*, Puffin Books) Penguin Young Readers Group.

—Big-Sister Blues, No. 5. Fulvimari, Jeffrey, illus. 2008. (English Roses Ser.: 5). (ENG.). 128p. (J). (gr. 3-7). 10.99 *(978-0-14-241093-6(4)*, Puffin Books) Penguin Young Readers Group.

—Friends for Life! Fulvimari, Jeffrey, illus. 2007. (English Roses Ser.: 1). (ENG.). 96p. (J). (gr. 3-7). 10.99 *(978-0-14-241114-8(0)*, Puffin Books) Penguin Young Readers Group.

—Good-Bye, Grace?, No. 2. Fulvimari, Jeffrey, illus. 2007. (English Roses Ser.: 2). (ENG.). 144p. (J). (gr. 3-7). 10.99 *(978-0-14-240883-4(2)*, Puffin Books) Penguin Young Readers Group.

—The New Girl, Vol. 3. Fulvimari, Jeffrey, illus. 2007. (English Roses Ser.: 3). (ENG.). 144p. (J). (gr. 3-7). 9.99 *(978-0-14-240884-1(0)*, Puffin Books) Penguin Young Readers Group.

—A Rose by Any Other Name. Fulvimari, Jeffrey, illus. 2007. (English Roses Ser.: 4). (ENG.). 144p. (J). (gr. 3-7). 10.99 *(978-0-14-240885-8(9)*, Puffin Books) Penguin Young Readers Group.

Madonna, pseud & Fulvimari, Jeffrey. The Runway Rose. 2009. (English Roses Ser.: 9). (ENG., Illus.). 128p. (J). (gr. 3-7). 9.99 *(978-0-14-241126-1(4)*, Puffin Books) Penguin Young Readers Group.

Madrzak, Carole. In the Shadows of Bington Manor. 2006. (ENG.). 132p. per. 24.95 *(978-1-4241-5168-4(6))* America Star Bks.

—Moonlight Dare. 2004. 48p. pap. 16.95 *(978-1-4137-5144-4(X))* America Star Bks.

—Secrets Inside Bington Manor. 2005. 108p. pap. 19.95 *(978-1-4241-0720-9(2))* America Star Bks.

Mae, Darcie. Sammy & Robert Go Home for the Holidays. 2011. 44p. pap. 24.95 *(978-1-4560-5702-2(2))* America Star Bks.

Magaziner, Lauren. The Only Thing Worse Than Witches. 2014. (ENG.). 272p. (J). (gr. 3-7). 16.99 *(978-0-8037-3918-5(4)*, Dial Bks) Penguin Young Readers Group.

Magee, Helen. A Ghost Called Clarence. Lt. ed. 2007. pap. *(978-1-905665-66-2(0))* Pollinger In Print.

Magical Max Makes Friends. 2005. (Adventures of Magical Max, Scarlet Feather & Little Lilly Woo-Woo Ser.). (Illus.). 16p. (J). (gr. k-4). 14.95 *(978-0-9762408-0-8(7))* Lead Life Pr., LLC.

Magill, Sharon L. Chloe Madison & the Beach Heists. 2009. 60p. pap. 10.49 *(978-1-4389-4191-2(9))* AuthorHouse.

Magnason, Andri Snaer. The Story of the Blue Planet. D'Arcy, Julian Meldon, tr. Jonsdottir, Aslaug, illus. 2013. (ENG.). 136p. (J). (gr. 2-5). pap. 9.95 *(978-1-60980-506-7(2)*, Triangle Square) Seven Stories Pr.

Magnusson, Sally. Horace & the Christmas Mystery. Stone, Norman, illus. 2015. (ENG.). 48p. (J). (gr. k). 14.99 ***(978-1-84502-791-9(4))*** Black and White Publishing Ltd. GBR. Dist: Independent Pubs. Group.

Magoon, Kekla. Camo Girl. 2012. (ENG.). 224p. (J). (gr. 3-9). pap. 7.99 *(978-1-4169-7805-3(4)*, Aladdin) Simon & Schuster Children's Publishing.

—Camo Girl. 2011. (ENG., Illus.). 224p. (J). (gr. 3-9). 16.99 *(978-1-4169-7804-6(6)*, Simon & Schuster/Paula Wiseman Bks.) Simon & Schuster/Paula Wiseman Bks.

Mahon, Matthew. The Defenders of All Thats Fall. 2008. 56p. pap. 24.95 *(978-1-4327-3169-4(6))* Outskirts Pr., Inc.

Mahoney, Jan. Moose Tales. 2010. 12p. 9.99 *(978-1-4520-6950-0(6))* AuthorHouse.

Maiden, Cecil. The Molliwumps. Price, Christine, illus. 2004. 160p. 12.95 *(978-0-9714612-9-1(5))* Green Mansion Pr. LLC.

Maier, Gary B. Key Masters: The Tyrannosaur Rebellion. 2013. 124p. pap. 11.50 *(978-1-62516-403-2(3)*, Strategic Bk. Publishing) Strategic Book Publishing & Rights Agency (SBPRA).

Maithya, Susan M. Struffel Cares: Struffel's New Pet. 2012. 40p. pap. 20.99 *(978-1-4772-3323-8(7))* AuthorHouse.

Maizel, Rebecca. A Season for Fireflies. 2016. 256p. (YA). (gr. 9). 17.99 *(978-0-06-232764-2(X)*, HarperTeen) HarperCollins Pubs.

Majumdar, Debu. Viku & the Elephant: A Story from the Forests of India. Wolfe, Lynn, illus. 2011. (ENG.). 54p. (J). pap. 12.99 *(978-0-9832227-0-5(3))* Bo-Tree Hse.

Malatesta, Resa. Jewel & Chin Chin's Adventure. 2013. 20p. pap. 10.95 *(978-1-4525-7610-7(6)*, Balboa Pr.) Author Solutions, Inc.

Maldonado, Luis, illus. Friends Having Fun. Maldonado, Luis, . 2007. 48p. (J). 3.95 *(978-0-9790699-1-8(2))* Empty Harbor Productions, LLC.

Mallat, Kathy. Just Ducky. 2004. (Illus.). 24p. (J). (gr. -1-1). 16.85 *(978-0-8027-8825-2(4))* Walker & Co.

Malone, Cheryl Lawton. Dario & the Whale. Masseva, Bistra, illus. 2016. (ENG.). 32p. (J). (gr. -1-3). 16.99 *(978-0-8075-1463-4(2))* Whitman, Albert & Co.

Malone, Jen. The Sleepover. 2017. (Mix Ser.). (ENG., Illus.). 256p. (J). (gr. 4-8). pap. 7.99 ***(978-1-4814-5260-1(6)***, Aladdin) Simon & Schuster Children's Publishing.

Malone, Jen & Nall, Gail. You're Invited. 2015. (ENG., Illus.). 336p. (J). (gr. 4-8). 17.99 *(978-1-4814-3197-2(8)*, Aladdin) Simon & Schuster Children's Publishing.

—You're Invited Too. 2016. (Mix Ser.). (ENG., Illus.). 304p. (J). (gr. 4-8). pap. 7.99 *(978-1-4814-3199-6(4)*, Aladdin) Simon & Schuster Children's Publishing.

Malone, Lee Gjertsen. The Last Boy at St. Edith's. 2016. (Max Ser.). (ENG., Illus.). 272p. (J). (gr. 3-7). 16.99 *(978-1-4814-4435-4(2)*, Aladdin) Simon & Schuster Children's Publishing.

—The Last Boy at St. Edith's. 2017. lib. bdg. 18.40 ***(978-0-606-40157-9(1))*** Turtleback Bks.

Malone, Nola. A Home. 2013. (ENG.). 28p. (J). (gr. -1-3). 14.99 *(978-1-4814-2128-7(X)*, Simon & Schuster Bks. For Young Readers) Simon & Schuster Bks. For Young Readers.

Malone, Sydney. Shop the Vote (Shopkins) 2017. (Shopkins Ser.). (ENG.). 24p. (J). (gr. -1-3). pap. 4.99 ***(978-1-338-13556-5(2))*** Scholastic, Inc.

Man-Kong, Mary. Friends, Fashion, & Fun! (Barbie) Golden Books Staff & Das Group Staff, illus. 2012. (Jumbo Coloring Book Ser.). (ENG.). 224p. (J). (gr. -1-2). pap. 5.99 *(978-0-375-87358-4(9)*, Golden Bks.) Random Hse. Children's Bks.

—Fun & Furry Friends (Barbie) 2014. (Friendship Box Ser.). (ENG., Illus.). 48p. (J). (gr. -1-2). bds. 10.99 *(978-0-385-38470-4(X)*, Random Hse. Bks. for Young Readers) Random Hse. Children's Bks.

—My Fabulous Friends! Golden Books Staff, illus. 2009. (Pictureback(R) Ser.). (ENG.). 16p. (J). (gr. -1-2). pap. 3.99 *(978-0-375-85789-8(3)*, Random Hse. Bks. for Young Readers) Random Hse. Children's Bks.

Man-Kong, Mary & Random House. A Surprise for a Friend (Barbie) 2015. (Pictureback(R) Ser.). (ENG., Illus.). 16p. (J). (gr. -1-2). 4.99 *(978-0-553-50942-7(X)*, Random Hse. Bks. for Young Readers) Random Hse. Children's Bks.

Mancil, Arlene. The Garden Fairy. 2008. 32p. pap. 24.95 *(978-1-60441-735-7(8))* PublishAmerica, Inc.

Mancini, Aly. Layne at Home. 2012. 24p. pap. 21.99 *(978-1-4797-5397-0(1))* Xlibris Corp.

Mancuso, Rudy. How to Be Famous in Six Seconds. 2016. (YA). pap. ***(978-1-5011-2767-0(5)***, Keywords Press) Atria Bks.

Maness, Patricia. Adventures of Ben & Golden. 2007. 192p. per. 24.95 *(978-1-4241-7721-9(9))* America Star Bks.

Maness, Rowan. Bombshell. 2017. (ENG., Illus.). 320p. (YA). (gr. 9). 18.99 ***(978-1-4814-4164-3(7)***, Simon Pulse) Simon Pulse.

Manley, Brenda Randazzo. The Misfits of Millville. 2010. (ENG.). 220p. pap. 14.99 *(978-1-4392-6496-6(1))* CreateSpace Independent Publishing Platform.

Manley, Curtis. Shawn Loves Sharks. Subisak, Tracy, illus. 2017. (ENG.). 32p. (J). 17.99 *(978-1-62672-134-0(3)*, 9781626721340) Roaring Brook Pr.

Mann, Greyson. When Lava Strikes: Secrets of a Minecraft Survivor. Sandford, Grace, illus. 2017. (Secrets of an Overworld Survivor Ser.). (ENG.). 112p. (J). (gr. 1-4). 13.99 *(978-1-5107-1328-4(X)*, Sky Pony Pr.) Skyhorse Publishing Co., Inc.

Mann, Jennifer Ann. Sunny Sweet Is So Not Scary. 2015. (Sunny Sweet Ser.). (ENG.). 192p. (YA). (gr. 3-6). 15.99 *(978-1-61963-507-4(0)*, 9781619635074, Bloomsbury USA Childrens) Bloomsbury Publishing USA.

Mann, Jennifer K. Sam & Jump. Mann, Jennifer K., illus. 2016. (ENG., Illus.). 32p. (J). (gr. -1-2). 15.99 *(978-0-7636-7947-7(X))* Candlewick Pr.

Mannering, Rose. Boo's Beard. Straker, Bethany, illus. 2015. (ENG.). 32p. (J). (gr. -1-k). 16.99 *(978-1-63450-207-8(8)*, Sky Pony Pr.) Skyhorse Publishing Co., Inc.

Manners I. Care. 2005. (J). pap. 5.99 *(978-0-9771143-4-4(1))* Child Life Bks., LLC.

Manners, Tyler. Continental Change of Heart. 2006. 65p. pap. 16.95 *(978-1-4137-9483-0(1))* PublishAmerica, Inc.

Manning, Matthew K. & Majado, Caio. Lockdown, Vol. 8. Ito, Leonardo, illus. 2012. (Tony Hawk's 900 Revolution Ser.). (ENG.). 128p. (gr. 3-4). pap. 7.19 *(978-1-4342-3890-0(3))*; lib. bdg. 26.65 *(978-1-4342-3314-1(6))* Stone Arch Bks. (Tony Hawk's 900 Revolution).

Manning, Sara. Wally the Whale: A Tale about a Whale with Seizures. 2011. 40p. pap. 18.46 *(978-1-4634-4160-9(6))* AuthorHouse.

Manson, Beverlie, illus. The Mermaid's Secret Diaries. 2013. (ENG.). 96p. (J). (gr. -1-2). 9.95 *(978-1-907967-59-7(1))* Boxer Bks., Ltd. GBR. Dist: Sterling Publishing Co., Inc.

Mantell, Paul, text. Nothin' but Net. 2003. (Matt Christopher Sports Ser.). 136p. (J). (gr. 3-7). 12.65 *(978-0-7569-3021-9(9))* Perfection Learning Corp.

Mantell, Paul & Christopher, Matt. Mountain Bike Mania. Lt. ed. 2007. (New Matt Christopher Sports Library). 160p. (J). (gr. 4-6). lib. bdg. 26.60 *(978-1-59953-108-3(9))* Norwood Hse. Pr.

Manushkin, Fran. Best Club. Lyon, Tammie, illus. 2016. (Katie Woo Ser.). (ENG.). 32p. (gr. k-2). lib. bdg. 21.32 *(978-1-4795-9639-3(6))* Picture Window Bks.

—Best Season Ever, 1 vol. Lyon, Tammie, illus. 2010. (Katie Woo Ser.). (ENG.). 32p. (gr. k-2). lib. bdg. 21.32 *(978-1-4048-5730-8(3))* Picture Window Bks.

—Katie Goes Camping, 1 vol. Lyon, Tammie, illus. 2010. (Katie Woo Ser.). (ENG.). 32p. (gr. k-2). lib. bdg. 21.32 *(978-1-4048-5731-5(1))* Picture Window Bks.

—Katie Saves the Earth, 1 vol. Lyon, Tammie, illus. 2013. (Katie Woo Ser.). (ENG.). 32p. (gr. k-2). pap. 5.95 *(978-1-4048-8046-7(1))*; lib. bdg. 21.32 *(978-1-4048-7652-1(9))* Picture Window Bks.

—Katie Woo, Set. Lyon, Tammie, illus. Incl. Big Lie. 21.32 (978-1-4048-5497-0(5)); Boss of the World. 21.32 (978-1-4048-5493-2(2)); Goodbye to Goldie. 21.32 (978-1-4048-5495-6(9)); Happy Day. 21.32 (978-1-4048-5496-3(7)); No More Teasing. 21.32 (978-1-4048-5492-5(4)); Too Much Rain. 21.32 (978-1-4048-5494-9(0)); (gr. k-2). (Katie Woo Ser.). (ENG., Illus.). 32p. 2009. 127.92 (978-1-4048-5679-0(X)) Picture Window Bks.

—Katie Woo & Friends, 1 vol. Lyon, Tammie, illus. 2012. (Katie Woo Ser.). (ENG.). 96p. (gr. k-2). pap. 4.95 (978-1-4048-7909-6(9)) Picture Window Bks.

—Katie Woo Book Club Kit. Lyon, Tammie, illus. 2013. (Katie Woo Ser.). (ENG.). 576p. (gr. k-2). pap. 29.70 (978-1-4795-5120-0(1)) Picture Window Bks.

—Katie Woo Celebrates, 1 vol. Lyon, Tammie, illus. 2013. (Katie Woo Ser.). (ENG.). 96p. (gr. k-2). pap. 4.95 (978-1-4048-8100-6(X)) Picture Window Bks.

—Katie Woo, Super Scout. Lyon, Tammie, illus. 2015. (Katie Woo Ser.). (ENG.). 32p. (gr. k-2). 21.32 (978-1-4795-6178-0(9)) Picture Window Bks.

—Katie's Spooky Sleepover. Lyon, Tammie, illus. 2016. (Katie Woo Ser.). (ENG.). 32p. (gr. k-2). lib. bdg. 21.32 (978-1-4795-9640-9(X)) Picture Window Bks.

—Moo, Katie Woo!, 1 vol. Lyon, Tammie, illus. 2013. (Katie Woo Ser.). (ENG.). 32p. (gr. k-2). pap. 5.95 (978-1-4048-8047-4(X)) Picture Window Bks.

—Pedro, First-Grade Hero. Lyon, Tammie, illus. 2016. (Pedro Ser.). (ENG.). 96p. (gr. k-2). pap. 4.95 (978-1-5158-0112-2(8)) Pedro Pubns. GBR. Dist: Capstone Pub.

—Pedro for President. Lyon, Tammie, illus. 2016. (Pedro Ser.). (ENG.). 32p. (gr. k-2). lib. bdg. 21.32 (978-1-5158-0087-3(3)) Pedro Pubns. GBR. Dist: Capstone Pub.

—Pedro's Big Goal. Lyon, Tammie, illus. 2016. (Pedro Ser.). (ENG.). 32p. (gr. k-2). lib. bdg. 21.32 (978-1-5158-0086-6(5)) Pedro Pubns. GBR. Dist: Capstone Pub.

—Pedro's Mystery Club. Lyon, Tammie, illus. 2016. (Pedro Ser.). (ENG.). 32p. (gr. k-2). lib. bdg. 21.32 (978-1-5158-0084-2(9)) Pedro Pubns. GBR. Dist: Capstone Pub.

—Pirate Pedro. Lyon, Tammie, illus. 2017. (Pedro Ser.). (ENG.). 32p. (gr. k-2). lib. bdg. 21.32 (978-1-5158-0872-5(6)) Pedro Pubns. GBR. Dist: Capstone Pub.

—What Happens Next, Katie? Writing a Narrative with Katie Woo, 1 vol. Lyon, Tammie, illus. 2013. (Katie Woo: Star Writer Ser.). (ENG.). 32p. (gr. k-2). pap. 6.95 (978-1-4795-1924-8(3)); lib. bdg. 20.65 (978-1-4048-8129-7(8)) Picture Window Bks.

Manwiller, S. A. The Adventures of Jack & Max the Truliest Meaning of Christmas. Manwiller, S. A. & Overly, Kristen V., illus. 2013. (ACH & ENG.). 38p. 24.99 (978-0-9838427-7-4(9)) SevenHorns Publishing.

Manzel, Michael, illus. Moby's Tale. 2004. 248p. (YA). pap. 19.95 (978-0-9746345-0-0(6)) River of Life Publishing.

Manzer, Jenny. Save Me, Kurt Cobain. 2016. (ENG.). 272p. (YA). (gr. 7). 17.99 (978-0-553-52126-9(8), Delacorte Pr.) Random Hse. Children's Bks.

Manzo, Christopher. Oliver Brightside: You Don't Want That Penny. Adams, Lisa, illus. 2016. (ENG.). 36p. (J). 16.95 (978-0-9963756-4-1(3)) All About Kids Publishing.

Maple, Daphne. All Paws on Deck. Metayer, Annabelle, illus. 2016. (Roxbury Park Dog Club Ser.: 4). 224p. (J). (gr. 3-7). pap. 6.99 (978-0-06-232773-4(9)) HarperCollins Pubs.

—A Bone to Pick. Metayer, Annabelle, illus. 2017. (Roxbury Park Dog Club Ser.: 6). 208p. (J). (gr. 3-7). pap. 6.99 (978-0-06-237102-7(9)) HarperCollins Pubs.

Mara, Cate. The Great Kieranski & the Bardbuy. 2012. 114p. pap. (978-0-9873204-2-1(4)) Breedles Publishing.

Marciniak, Christine. Honestly, Ali! 2014. (YA). (978-1-61271-249-9(5)) Zumaya Pubns. LLC.

Marcionette, Jake. Just Jake: Dog Eat Dog. Villa, Victor Rivas, illus. 2015. (Just Jake Ser.: No. 2). (ENG.). 196p. (J). (gr. 3-7). 11.99 (978-0-448-46693-4(7), Grosset & Dunlap) Penguin Young Readers Group.

Marconi, Martina. Birthday Wishes, 1 vol. 2010. 20p. pap. 24.95 (978-1-4489-6067-5(3)) PublishAmerica, Inc.

Marcus, Kimberly. Exposed. 2012. (ENG.). 272p. (YA). (gr. 9). pap. 8.99 (978-0-375-86591-6(8), Ember) Random Hse. Children's Bks.

Marcus, Ms. Elena N. Devon: The Wild Adventures of Devon & Friends. 2012. (ENG., Illus.). 74p. (gr. 1-6). pap. 18.00 (978-0-615-57545-2(5)) Elena Marcus Negoita.

Margaret I. Pascuzzo. Anton Finds a Treasure. Bicking, Judith, illus. 2008. 16p. pap. 12.00 (978-1-4251-8683-8(1)) Trafford Publishing.

Margolin, Phillip & Rome, Ami Margolin. Vanishing Acts. 2011. (ENG.). 176p. (J). (gr. 3-7). 16.99 (978-0-06-188556-3(8)) HarperCollins Pubs.

Margolis, Leslie. Everybody Bugs Out. (Annabelle Unleashed Ser.). (ENG.). (YA). (gr. 3-12). 2012. 224p. pap. 6.99 (978-1-59990-828-1(X), 9781599908281) 2011. 208p. 15.99 (978-1-59990-526-6(4), 9781599905266) Bloomsbury Publishing USA. (Bloomsbury USA Childrens).

—If I Were You. 2015. (ENG.). 224p. (YA). (gr. 5-9). 15.99 (978-0-374-30068-5(2), 9780374300685, Farrar, Straus & Giroux (BYR)) Farrar, Straus & Giroux.

—Monkey Business. (Annabelle Unleashed Ser.). (ENG.). 224p. (YA). (gr. 3-6). 2015. pap. 7.99 (978-1-61963-799-3(5), 9781619637993) 2014. 16.99 (978-1-61963-393-3(0), 9781619633933) Bloomsbury Publishing USA. (Bloomsbury USA Childrens).

—One Tough Chick. 2013. (Annabelle Unleashed Ser.). (ENG.). 176p. (YA). (gr. 3-6). 15.99 (978-1-59990-961-5(8), 9781599909615, Bloomsbury USA Childrens) Bloomsbury Publishing USA.

Marie, Jill Jana. Elsa Magda Val My Imaginary Pal. 2008. 24p. pap. 12.95 (978-1-4389-3411-2(4)) AuthorHouse.

Marie, Lynne. Hedgehog Goes to Kindergarten. Kennedy, Anne, illus. 2011. (J). pap. (978-0-545-29874-2(1)) Scholastic, Inc.

Marie, Tamara. The Adventures of Madison. 2010. 32p. pap. 17.99 (978-1-60957-972-2(0)) Salem Author Services.

Marin, Dale Diane. Friends Forever: A Rachel Beth Tale, 1 vol. Borstel, Ian von, illus. 2009. 31p. pap. 24.95 (978-1-61546-149-3(3)) America Star Bks.

Marino, Nan. Hiding Out at the Pancake Palace. 2013. (ENG.). 256p. (J). (gr. 3-7). 16.99 (978-1-59643-753-1(7), 9781596437531) Roaring Brook Pr.

—Hiding Out at the Pancake Palace. 2014. (ENG.). 272p. (J). (gr. 3-7). pap. 7.99 (978-1-250-04000-8(0), 9781250040008) Square Fish.

—Neil Armstrong Is My Uncle & Other Lies Muscle Man McGinty Told Me. 2012. (ENG.). 176p. (J). (gr. 3-7). pap. 6.99 (978-0-312-66548-7(2), 9780312665487) Square Fish.

Marino, Peter. Dough Boy. 2005. (ENG.). 176p. (YA). (gr. 7-12). 17.95 (978-0-8234-1873-2(1)) Holiday Hse., Inc.

—Magic & Misery. 2009. (ENG.). 272p. (YA). (gr. 9-18). 17.95 (978-0-8234-2133-6(3)) Holiday Hse., Inc.

Marion, L. K. Summer Holiday with Funny Bunny. 2012. 32p. pap. 17.25 (978-1-4669-6475-4(8)) Trafford Publishing.

Mariotte, Jeff. Dark Vengeance Vol. 1: Summer, Fall. 2011. (ENG.). 512p. (YA). (gr. 9). pap. 9.99 (978-1-4424-2975-8(5), Simon Pulse) Simon Pulse.

Markell, Denis. Click Here to Start. 2016. (ENG.). 320p. (J). (gr. 5-7). 16.99 (978-1-101-93187-5(6), Delacorte Bks. for Young Readers) Random Hse. Children's Bks.

Markowitz, Krista. Mrs Tipperwillow's Afterlife Adventures. 2008. 316p. 28.95 (978-0-595-49079-0(4)); pap. 18.95 (978-0-595-44671-1(X)) iUniverse, Inc.

Marks, Nancy Freeman. Just As You Are: The Story of Leon & Sam. Buchheim, Su Jen, illus. 2003. 32p. (J). 15.00 (978-0-9722430-1-8(1)) Wave Publishing.

Marlee. Harry the Elephant & His New Found Friends. 2009. 16p. pap. 9.49 (978-1-4490-5305-5(X)) AuthorHouse.

Marlin, Peggy. Wackydoodle. 2009. 20p. pap. 12.49 (978-1-4389-7573-3(2)) AuthorHouse.

Marlow, Herb. A Long Way Home. l.t. ed. 2003. (Illus.). 14p. (J). 19.95 (978-1-893595-35-4(8)) Four Seasons Bks., Inc.

Marlow, Layn. You Make Me Smile. 2013. (ENG., Illus.). 32p. (J). (gr. -1-1). 16.95 (978-0-8234-2922-6(9)) Holiday Hse., Inc.

Marlow, Susan K. Andi Saddles Up, 1 vol. 2017. (Circle C Stepping Stones Ser.: 1). 112p. (J). pap. 7.99 **(978-0-8254-4430-2(6))** Kregel Pubns.

Marlowe, Sara. My New Best Friend. Salom, Ivette, illus. 2016. (ENG.). 32p. (J). 15.95 (978-1-61429-353-8(8)) Wisdom Pubns.

Marman, Richard. Mcalister's Spark. Marman, Richard, illus. 2013. (Illus.). 364p. pap. (978-1-909302-21-1(X)) Abela Publishing.

Marr, Melissa. Challenge. Xian Nu Studio Staff, illus. 2010. (Wicked Lovely: Desert Tales Ser.: 2). (ENG.). 176p. (YA). (gr. 8-18). pap. 9.99 (978-0-06-149349-2(X)) HarperCollins Pubs.

Marranzino, Sami. The Littlest Ladybug. Currey, Andrew K., illus. 2012. 32p. pap. 24.95 (978-1-4626-7781-8(9)) America Star Bks.

Marsden, Carolyn. The Gold-Threaded Dress. 2006. (ENG.). 80p. (J). (gr. 2-4). reprint ed. per. 6.99 (978-0-7636-2993-9(6)) Candlewick Pr.

—The Gold-Threaded Dress. 2006. 73p. (gr. 2-4). 17.00 (978-0-7569-6574-7(8)) Perfection Learning Corp.

—Moon Runner. 2007. (ENG., Illus.). 112p. (J). (gr. 3-7). per. 6.99 (978-0-7636-3304-2(6)) Candlewick Pr.

—Take Me with You. 2010. (ENG., Illus.). 176p. (J). (gr. 5-18). 14.99 (978-0-7636-3739-2(4)) Candlewick Pr.

Marsh, Carole. The Case of the Crybaby Cowboy. 2006. (3 Amigos Ser.). (Illus.). 54p. (J). (gr. 4-7). 14.95 (978-0-635-06199-7(6)) Gallopade International.

—The Case of the Hunchback Hairdresser. 2006. (Criss Cross Applesauce Ser.). (Illus.). 54p. (J). (gr. 4-7). 14.95 (978-0-635-06202-4(X)) Gallopade International.

—The Wild Water Mystery of Niagra Falls. 2009. (Real Kids, Real Places Ser.). (Illus.). 146p. (J). (gr. 4-7). pap. 7.99 (978-0-635-06825-5(7), Marsh, Carole Bks.) Gallopade International.

Marsh, Laura. Take a Leap! 2009. (Toot & Puddle Ser.). (ENG., Illus.). 24p. (J). (gr. -1-2). pap. 3.99 (978-1-4263-0416-3(1)); lib. bdg. 11.90 (978-1-4263-0417-0(X)) National Geographic Society. (National Geographic Children's Bks.).

—Toot's Tour of India. 2009. (Toot & Puddle Ser.). (ENG., Illus.). 24p. (J). (gr. -1-2). pap. 3.99 (978-1-4263-0418-7(8)); lib. bdg. 11.90 (978-1-4263-0419-4(6)) National Geographic Society. (National Geographic Children's Bks.).

Marsh, Naomi Fawn. Mr. Crabby Pants the Crab. 2008. 36p. pap. 24.95 (978-1-60474-092-9(2)) PublishAmerica, Inc.

Marshall, Gwendolyn. Saving Crystallia, 1 vol. 2010. 32p. pap. 24.95 (978-1-4489-5637-1(4)) PublishAmerica, Inc.

Marshall, James. The Complete Stories of Two Best Friends. collector's ed. 2008. (ENG., Illus.). 368p. (J). (gr. 2-5). 29.99 (978-0-618-89195-5(1)) Houghton Mifflin Harcourt Publishing Co.

—George & Martha No. 4: The Best of Friends Early Reader. 2011. (Green Light Readers Level 2 Ser.). (ENG., Illus.). 32p. (J). (gr. -1-3). pap. 4.99 (978-0-547-51988-3(5)) Houghton Mifflin Harcourt Publishing Co.

—George & Martha Early Reader. 2010. (Green Light Readers Level 2 Ser.). (ENG., Illus.). 24p. (J). (gr. -1-3). pap. 4.99 (978-0-547-40624-4(X)) Houghton Mifflin Harcourt Publishing Co.

—George & Martha Two Great Friends Early Reader. 2010. (Green Light Readers Level 2 Ser.). (ENG., Illus.). 32p. (J). (gr. -1-3). pap. 4.99 (978-0-547-40625-1(8)) Houghton Mifflin Harcourt Publishing Co.

—Rise & Shine No. 5. 2011. (George & Martha Ser.). (ENG., Illus.). 40p. (J). (gr. -1-3). pap. 4.99 (978-0-547-57687-9(0)) Houghton Mifflin Harcourt Publishing Co.

—Round & Round, No. 3. 2011. (Green Light Readers Level 2 Ser.). (ENG., Illus.). 32p. (J). (gr. -1-3). pap. 3.99 (978-0-547-51982-1(6)) Houghton Mifflin Harcourt Publishing Co.

Marshall, James & Marshall, James. George & Martha Book & CD, 1 vol. 2007. (Read along Book & CD Ser.). (ENG., Illus.). 48p. (J). (gr. -1-3). audio compact disk 10.99 (978-0-618-83951-3(8)) Houghton Mifflin Harcourt Publishing Co.

—Wings: A Tale of Two Chickens. 2003. (ENG., Illus.). 32p. (J). (gr. -1-3). 6.95 (978-0-618-31659-5(0)) Houghton Mifflin Harcourt Publishing Co.

Marshall, Wendy. The O'Clocks: Mr. O'Clock Goes to A Party. 2008. 40p. pap. 18.49 (978-1-4389-2403-8(8)) AuthorHouse.

Martell, Ray. Brox the Bungling Badger. 2012. (Illus.). 88p. pap. 15.50 (978-1-78035-345-6(6), Fastprint Publishing) Upfront Publishing Ltd. GBR. Dist: Printondemand-worldwide.com.

Martens, Kara. The Two Missing Kids. 2008. 80p. pap. 11.49 (978-1-4343-8696-0(1)) AuthorHouse.

Martin, Abigail M. Welcome to Applewood Place. 2008. 24p. pap. 24.95 (978-1-60441-167-6(8)) America Star Bks.

Martin, Ann M. Best Friends. 2008. (Illus.). 195p. (J). pap. (978-0-545-05062-3(6)) Scholastic, Inc.

—Coming Apart. 2010. (Main Street Ser.: 9). (ENG.). 208p. (J). (gr. 3-7). pap. 6.99 (978-0-545-06896-3(7), Scholastic Paperbacks) Scholastic, Inc.

—A Corner of the Universe. 2004. (ENG.). 208p. (J). (gr. 3-7). pap. 7.99 (978-0-439-38881-8(3), Scholastic Paperbacks) Scholastic, Inc.

—Mary Anne Saves the Day. Telgemeier, Raina, illus. rev. ed. 2015. (Baby-Sitters Club Graphix Ser.: 3). (ENG.). 160p. (J). (gr. 3-7). 24.99 (978-0-545-88617-8(1)); pap. 10.99 (978-0-545-88621-5(X)) Scholastic, Inc. (Graphix).

—Needle & Thread. 2007. (Main Street Ser.). (Illus.). 205p. (J). (gr. 4-7). 14.65 (978-0-7569-8328-4(2)) Perfection Learning Corp.

—Needle & Thread. Andreasen, Dan, illus. 2007. 205p. (J). pap. (978-0-545-03660-3(7)) Scholastic, Inc.

—The Summer Before. 2010. (Baby-Sitters Club Ser.). (ENG.). 224p. (J). (gr. 3-7). 16.99 (978-0-545-16093-3(6)) Scholastic, Inc.

—Ten Good & Bad Things about My Life (So Far) 2013. (ENG.). 288p. (J). (gr. 4-7). pap. 7.99 (978-1-250-03413-7(2), 9781250034137) Square Fish.

—The Truth about Stacey. 2015. (Baby-Sitters Club Graphix Ser.: 2). lib. bdg. 22.10 (978-0-606-37027-1(7)) Turtleback Bks.

Martin, Ann M. & Telgemeier, Raina. Baby-Sitters Club Graphix, Bks. 1-4, Set. Telgemeier, Raina, illus. 2016. (Baby-Sitters Club Graphix Ser.). (ENG., Illus.). 192p. (J). (gr. 3-7). pap. 43.96 (978-1-338-11898-8(6)) Scholastic, Inc.

Martin, Anne E. Flip Flops for Paige. 2007. (Illus.). 36p. (J). per. 14.99 (978-1-59879-243-0(1)) Lifevest Publishing, Inc.

Martin, Bill, Jr. Brown Bear & Friends. Carle, Eric, illus. unabr. ed. 2011. (Brown Bear & Friends Ser.). (ENG.). (J). (gr. -1-k). 39.99 (978-1-4272-1448-5(4), 9781427214485) Macmillan Audio.

Martin, Bill. Lift-the-Tab: Baby Bear, Baby Bear, What Do You See? Carle, Eric, illus. 2016. (Brown Bear & Friends Ser.). (ENG.). 28p. (J). bds. 6.99 (978-1-62779-724-5(6), 9781627797245, Holt, Henry & Co. Bks. For Young Readers) Holt, Henry & Co.

Martin, Brenda Darnley. Freddie, Hector & Tish: The Treasure-Hunt Fish. 2008. 36p. per. 24.95 (978-1-60441-109-6(0)) America Star Bks.

Martin, Brian. The Gold of Angel Island. McDonald, Kim, illus. 2007. 46p. (J). (978-0-9798059-0-5(2)) Lunchbox Stories Inc.

Martin, Cheryl. Susie Lumpybothams: New & Improved. 2009. 28p. pap. 12.49 (978-1-4389-7853-6(7)) AuthorHouse.

Martin, David. Peep & Ducky. Walker, David, illus. (ENG.). (J). (— 1). 2015. 24p. bds. 6.99 (978-0-7636-7243-0(2)) 2013. 32p. 14.99 (978-0-7636-5039-1(0)) Candlewick Pr.

—Peep & Ducky Rainy Day. Walker, David, illus. 2015. (ENG.). 32p. (J). (— 1). 14.99 (978-0-7636-6884-6(2)) Candlewick Pr.

Martin, Denise R. Alicia's Dance. 2009. 72p. pap. 12.99 (978-1-4389-4194-3(3)) AuthorHouse.

Martin, Emily. The Year We Fell Apart. 2016. (ENG.). 320p. (YA). (gr. 9). 17.99 (978-1-4814-3841-4(7), Simon Pulse) Simon Pulse.

Martin, Gina. Mother Moon: Magic Pool in the Sky. 2008. 28p. pap. 12.49 (978-1-4389-0138-1(0)) AuthorHouse.

Martin, Joan Watson. Inventing Chloe. 2008. 140p. 19.95 (978-1-934335-25-3(8)); pap. 9.95 (978-1-934335-24-6(X)) WordWright.biz, Inc. (One Night Bks.).

Martin, Laura. The Ark Plan. DesChamps, Eric, illus. 2017. (Edge of Extinction Ser.: 1). (ENG.). (J). (gr. 3-7). lib. bdg. 17.20 **(978-0-606-40046-6(X))** Turtleback Bks.

Martin, Maria G. The Christmas Crown. Stratman, Kay, illus. 2010. 20p. pap. 10.95 (978-1-60911-442-8(6), Eloquent Bks.) Strategic Book Publishing & Rights Agency (SBPRA).

Martin, Martha M. Chipper, the Heroic Chipmunk. Matzen, Deon C., illus. 2004. 32p. (J). (gr. -1-3). 16.95 (978-0-9758580-0-4(9)) M & B Publishing.

Martin, Michelle Nicole. Princess & Missy's Magical Adventures: The Crystal Heart. 2010. 55p. pap. 10.95 (978-1-4327-4954-5(4)) Outskirts Pr., Inc.

Martin, Rosemary. Rosie's Story. 2011. (ENG., Illus.). 32p. pap. (978-1-84876-699-0(8)) Troubador Publishing Ltd.

Martin, T. Michael. Mr. Fahrenheit. 2016. 320p. (YA). (gr. 9). 17.99 (978-0-06-220183-6(2)) HarperCollins Pubs.

Martin, W. D. Dragonfly Valley: When Best Plans Go Awry. 2012. (ENG.). 176p. (J). pap. 11.95 (978-1-4787-1832-1(3)) Outskirts Pr., Inc.

Martínez, Jessica. The Vow. (ENG., (YA). (gr. 9). 2014. Illus.). 448p. pap. 11.99 (978-1-4424-5865-9(8)) 2013. 432p. 17.99 (978-1-4424-5864-2(X)) Simon Pulse. (Simon Pulse).

Martino, Alfred C. Pinned: There Can Be Only One Winner... 2006. (ENG., Illus.). 320p. (YA). (gr. 7-12). reprint ed. pap. 8.99 (978-0-15-205631-5(9)) Houghton Mifflin Harcourt Publishing Co.

Martone, Ginny. Trapped in Dead Man's Cave. 2007. 61p. pap. 19.95 (978-1-60474-227-5(5)) America Star Bks.

Marvelous Marty. 2008. (J). (978-0-9778113-4-2(4)); pap. (978-0-9778113-5-9(2)) HeartFelt Stories LLC.

Maschari, Jennifer. Things That Surprise You. 2017. 288p. (J). (gr. 3-7). 16.99 **(978-0-06-243892-8(1))** HarperCollins Pubs.

Masino, Brian. Cabbage Patch Kids: We Are All Best Friends. Karl, Linda, illus. 2006. (J). pap. (978-0-439-76820-7(9)) Scholastic, Inc.

Mason, Dianne. Danny's Ghost. 2007. 156p. pap. 9.39 (978-1-4116-4937-8(0)) Lulu Pr., Inc.

Mason, Jane B. & Stephens, Sarah Hines. Snowfall Surprise. 2009. (Candy Apple Ser.: 21). (ENG.). 144p. (J). (gr. 3-7). 5.99 (978-0-545-10067-0(4), Scholastic Paperbacks) Scholastic, Inc.

Mass, Wendy. The Candymakers. (ENG.). (J). (gr. 3-7). 2011. 480p. pap. 9.99 (978-0-316-00259-2(3)) 2010. 464p. 16.99 (978-0-316-00258-5(5)) 2015. 480p. 12.99 (978-0-316-26499-0(7)) Little, Brown Bks. for Young Readers.

—The Candymakers. 2011. (J). lib. bdg. 20.85 (978-0-606-23448-1(9), Turtleback) Turtleback Bks.

—The Candymakers & the Great Chocolate Chase. (ENG.). (J). (gr. 3-7). 2017. 560p. pap. 8.99 **(978-0-316-08918-0(4))** 2016. 544p. 18.99 (978-0-316-08919-7(2)) Little, Brown Bks. for Young Readers.

—Every Soul a Star. 2009. (ENG.). 336p. (J). (gr. 3-7). pap. 8.99 (978-0-316-00257-8(7)) Little, Brown Bks. for Young Readers.

—Every Soul a Star. 2009. 322p. 17.00 (978-1-60686-523-1(4)) Perfection Learning Corp.

—Graceful. 2015. (ENG.). 256p. (J). (gr. 3-7). 16.99 (978-0-545-77313-3(X), Scholastic Pr.) Scholastic, Inc.

—The Last Present. (ENG.). 256p. (J). (gr. 3-7). 2015. pap. 6.99 (978-0-545-31017-8(2)) 2013. 16.99 (978-0-545-31016-1(4), Scholastic Pr.) Scholastic, Inc.

—A Mango-Shaped Space. 2005. (ENG.). 240p. (YA). (gr. 3-7). per. 8.99 (978-0-316-05825-4(4)) Little, Brown Bks. for Young Readers.

—11 Birthdays. (ENG.). 272p. (J). (gr. 3-7). 2010. pap. 6.99 (978-0-545-05240-5(8), Scholastic Paperbacks) 2009. 17.99 (978-0-545-05239-9(4), Scholastic Pr.) Scholastic, Inc.

—11 Birthdays. 2010. (Willow Falls Ser.: 1). lib. bdg. 17.20 (978-0-606-13990-8(7), Turtleback) Turtleback Bks.

Massaro, Michael. Tony Towne & the Amazing Brain. 2011. (ENG.). 248p. pap. 9.55 (978-1-4565-2044-1(X)) CreateSpace Independent Publishing Platform.

Massenot, Véronique. The Mermaid & the Parakeet: A Children's Book Inspired by Henri Matisse. Hié, Vanessa, illus. 2016. (ENG.). 32p. (J). (gr. -1-3). 14.95 (978-3-7913-7265-5(3)) Prestel Verlag GmbH & Co KG. DEU. Dist: Penguin Random Hse. LLC.

Massey, Carol. Not a Friend. 2005. 79p. pap. 9.95 (978-0-7414-2319-1(7)) Infinity Publishing.

Masters, M. The Case of the Chocolate Snatcher: Can You Solve the Mystery #2. 2013. (Can You Solve the Mystery? Ser.: 2). (ENG.). 112p. (J). (gr. 1-7). pap. 4.99 (978-1-4424-6900-6(5)) Meadowbrook Pr.

Masterson, Carla Jo. What's on the Other Side of the Rainbow? The Secret of the Golden Mirror. Fochtman, Omra Jo, illus. 2006. 40p. (J). 24.95 (978-1-59975-228-0(X)) Father & Son Publishing.

Mastro, M. L. Return to Baladah. 2011. 88p. (gr. 10-12). pap. 9.99 (978-1-4520-7377-4(5)) AuthorHouse.

Mata, Julie. Kate Walden Directs: Bride of Slug Man. 2015. (ENG., Illus.). 288p. (J). (gr. 3-7). 16.99 (978-1-4231-9460-6(8)) Disney Pr.

—Kate Walden Directs: Bride of Slug Man. 2016. (Kate Walden Directs Ser.). (ENG.). 288p. (J). (gr. 3-7). pap. 6.99 (978-1-4847-4746-9(1)) Hyperion Bks. for Children.

—Night of the Zombie Chickens. 2014. (Kate Walden Ser.). (ENG., Illus.). 288p. (J). (gr. 3-7). 16.99 (978-1-4231-9459-0(4)) Hyperion Bks. for Children.

Matagrano, Joseph F. Forever Brothers. 2007. 396p. 26.95 (978-1-4327-0963-1(1)); per. 16.95 (978-1-4327-1524-3(0)) Outskirts Pr., Inc.

Mateboer, Hans. Peter the Cruise Ship - to Alaska. 2007. (Illus.). 32p. (J). 16.95 (978-0-9759487-2-9(5)) Mateboer, Johannes Aart.

Mateos, Pilar. Historias de Ninguno. (Barco de Vapor). (SPA.). 120p. (J). (gr. 4-5). (978-84-348-0907-9(9)) SM Ediciones.

—Molinete. (Barco de Vapor). (SPA.). 88p. (J). (gr. 4-5). (978-84-348-1372-4(6)) SM Ediciones.

Mateos, Pilar & Lucini, Chata. Lucas y Lucas. (Barco de Vapor). (SPA.). 88p. (YA). (gr. 5-8). (978-84-348-1233-8(9)) SM Ediciones.

Matheis, Mickie. A Berry Lucky St. Patrick's Day. Thomas, Laura, illus. 2015. (Strawberry Shortcake Ser.). (ENG.). 24p. (J). (gr. -1-k). 4.99 (978-0-448-48420-4(X), Grosset & Dunlap) Penguin Young Readers Group.

—Gymnastics Fun. Thomas, Laura, illus. 2014. (Strawberry Shortcake Ser.). (ENG.). 24p. (J). (gr. -1-k). 4.99 (978-0-448-46750-4(X), Grosset & Dunlap) Penguin Young Readers Group.

—Happy Birthday, Strawberry Shortcake. Thomas, Laura, illus. 2015. (Strawberry Shortcake Ser.). (ENG.). 32p. (J). (gr. -1-k). 16.99 (978-0-448-48748-9(9), Grosset & Dunlap) Penguin Young Readers Group.

Matherly, Ashley Page. Wonderful White Wintery Day: The Marvelous Misadventure of Katy Bear, 1 vol. Fennewald, Joseph Grant, illus. 2009. 43p. pap. 24.95 (978-1-61546-323-7(2)) PublishAmerica, Inc.

Mathews, Temple. The Sword of Armaggeddon. 2010. ix, 291p. (978-1-935618-17-1(2)) BenBella Bks.

Mathieson, Karen. Duel or Duet: Book Two of the Rosemary Ridge Trilogy. 2013. 160p. (J). pap. 7.99 (978-1-940350-05-9(0)) Portable COO, The.

—Liza, Elizabeth: Book Three of the Rosemary Ridge Trilogy. 2013. 164p. (J). pap. 7.99 (978-1-940350-08-0(5)) Portable COO, The.

Mathieu, Jennifer. Afterward. 2016. (ENG.). 320p. (YA). 17.99 (978-1-62672-238-5(2), 9781626722385) Roaring Brook Pr.

—Afterward. 2017. (ENG.). 336p. (YA). pap. 9.99 **(978-1-250-12962-8(1)**, 9781250129628) Square Fish.

—Afterward. 2017. (YA). lib. bdg. 20.85 **(978-0-606-40590-4(9))** Turtleback Bks.

Matlin, Marlee. Deaf Child Crossing. 2004. (ENG., Illus.). 208p. (J). (gr. 3-7). pap. 7.99 (978-0-689-86696-8(8), Simon & Schuster Bks. For Young Readers) Simon & Schuster Bks. For Young Readers.

Matson, Morgan. Since You've Been Gone. 2015. (ENG., Illus.). 480p. (YA). (gr. 7). pap. 9.99 (978-1-4424-3501-8(1), Simon & Schuster Bks. For Young Readers) Simon & Schuster Bks. For Young Readers.

—The Unexpected Everything. 2016. (ENG.). (YA). (gr. 7). pap. 12.99 (978-1-4814-8207-3(6)) Simon & Schuster.

—The Unexpected Everything. (ENG., Illus.). (YA). (gr. 7). 2017. 560p. pap. 9.99 (978-1-4814-0455-6(5)) 2016. 528p. 17.99 (978-1-4814-0454-9(7)) Simon & Schuster Bks. For Young Readers. (Simon & Schuster Bks. For Young Readers).

Matsumoto, Reiko Odate. The Princess with the Magic Bowl: As retold from the Japanese folk tale By. 2008. 48p. pap. 22.49 (978-1-4389-1225-7(0)) AuthorHouse.

Mattel. Ever after High - Sleepover Spellebration Party Planner. 2014. (Ever after High Ser.). (ENG., Illus.). 48p. (J). (gr. 3-7). 9.99 *(978-0-316-28359-5(2))* Little, Brown Bks. for Young Readers.
Mattel & Castle, Elizabelle. Ever after High - Madeline Hatter's Guide to Riddlish! 2015. (ENG., Illus.). 160p. (J). (gr. 3-7). act. bk. ed. 9.99 *(978-0-316-33744-1(7))* Little, Brown Bks. for Young Readers.
Mattel Inc. Staff & Finn, Perdita. Ever after High. 2016. (ENG., Illus.). 32p. (J). (gr. -1-3). pap. 3.99 *(978-0-316-35677-0(8))* Little, Brown Bks. for Young Readers.
Matthews Culp, Dawn. What's up Willie? the Birthday Puppy! 2008. (Illus.). 24p. (J). 28.95 *(978-0-615-22222-6(6))* Sprouting Peanut Pubs.
Matthews, Regina Stone. Elizabeth Marie Hutchinson - When I Dream. 2008. 48p. pap. 16.95 *(978-1-60563-112-7(4))* America Star Bks.
Matthew's Web Unplugged. 2003. (J). per. *(978-0-9716567-7-2(0))* Book Web Publishing, Limited.
Mattsson, Jude. Angus Emu & Sara Mare. 2011. 20p. 11.99 *(978-1-4567-3153-3(X))* AuthorHouse.
Maturana, Andrea. Life Without Nico. Olea, Francisco Javier, illus. 2016. (ENG.). 40p. (J). (gr. -1-2). 16.95 *(978-1-77138-611-1(8))* Kids Can Pr., Ltd. CAN. Dist: Hachette Bk. Group.
Matute, Ana María. El Polizón del Ulises. (SPA.). 126p. (YA). (gr. 5-18). 10.36 *(978-84-264-3022-9(8))*, LM0588) Editorial Lumen ESP. Dist: Lectorum Pubns., Inc.
Maunder, Roger. Mundy Pond. 2006. (ENG.). 195p. per. *(978-1-897174-09-8(8))*, Tuckamore Bks.) Creative Bk. Publishing.
Mawhinney, Art & Johnson, Shane L., illus. OLIVIA Meets Olivia. 2011. (Olivia TV Tie-In Ser.). (ENG.). 24p. (J). (gr. -1-2). pap. 3.99 *(978-1-4424-4707-3(9))*, Simon Spotlight) Simon Spotlight.
Maxwell, Andre L. & Maxwell, Amanda L. The Great Chicken Caper. Carter, Jill, illus. 2012. 34p. (-18). 18.00 *(978-0-9881811-1-3(8))* Maxwell, Andre.
May, Eleanor. Who Needs It? Sims, Blanche, illus. 2009. (Social Studies Connects Ser.). 32p. (J). (gr. 1-3). pap. 5.95 *(978-1-57565-281-8(1))* Kane Press, Inc.
—Who Needs It? Sims, Blanche, illus. 2009. (Social Studies Connects (r) Ser.). (ENG.). (gr. 1-3). pap. 33.92 *(978-0-7613-4804-7(2))* Lerner Publishing Group.
May, Kyla. Coco: My Delicious Life. 2013. (Lotus Lane Ser.: 2). (ENG., Illus.). 96p. (J). (gr. 1-3). 15.99 *(978-0-545-49615-5(2))*; pap. 4.99 *(978-0-545-44514-6(0))* Scholastic, Inc.
—Coco: My Delicious Life. 2013. (Lotus Lane Ser.: 2). lib. bdg. 14.75 *(978-0-606-31978-2(6))*, Turtleback) Turtleback Bks.
—Kiki: My Stylish Life. 2013. (Lotus Lane Ser.: 1). (ENG.). 96p. (J). (gr. 1-3). pap. 4.99 *(978-0-545-44512-2(4))* Scholastic, Inc.
—Kiki: My Stylish Life. 2013. (Lotus Lane Ser.: 1). lib. bdg. 14.75 *(978-0-606-31977-5(8))*, Turtleback) Turtleback Bks.
—Kiki Bk. 1: My Stylish Life. 2013. (Lotus Lane Ser.: 1). (ENG.). 96p. (J). (gr. 1-3). lib. bdg. 15.99 *(978-0-545-49613-1(6))* Scholastic, Inc.
—Lulu: My Glamorous Life. 2013. (Lotus Lane Ser.: 3). (ENG.). 96p. (J). (gr. 1-3). 15.99 *(978-0-545-49618-6(7))*; pap. 4.99 *(978-0-545-44516-0(7))*; E-Book *(978-0-545-49682-7(9))* Scholastic, Inc.
—Mika: My New Life. 2013. (Lotus Lane Ser.: 4). (ENG.). 96p. (J). (gr. 1-3). pap. 4.99 *(978-0-545-44519-1(1))* Scholastic, Inc.
—Mika: My New Life. 2013. (Lotus Lane Ser.: 4). lib. bdg. 14.75 *(978-0-606-32365-9(1))*, Turtleback) Turtleback Bks.
—My Glamorous Life. 2013. (Lotus Lane Ser.: 3). lib. bdg. 14.75 *(978-0-606-32364-2(3))*, Turtleback) Turtleback Bks.
May, Maggie. Pilot, Swaydy & Friends. Larade, April, illus. 2011. 30p. pap. 24.95 *(978-1-4560-8499-8(2))* America Star Bks.
May, R. B. Charlie Finds a Friend. 2010. 32p. pap. 12.99 *(978-1-4490-6913-1(4))* AuthorHouse.
May, Stephan. Leo the Entrepreneurial Hippo. 2008. (Illus.). 56p. pap. 10.95 *(978-1-4401-0480-0(8))* iUniverse, Inc.
Maycock, Dianne. Lucky's Mountain, 1 vol. 2007. (Orca Young Readers Ser.). (ENG.). 112p. (J). (gr. 3-8). per. 6.95 *(978-1-55143-682-1(5))* Orca Bk. Pubs. USA.
Mayer, Kirsten. I Am Aquaman. 2013. (Justice League Classic: I Can Read! Ser.). (J). lib. bdg. 13.55 *(978-0-606-31794-8(5))*, Turtleback) Turtleback Bks.
Mayer, Marianna. One Frog Too Many. Mayer, Marianna, illus. 2003. (Boy, a Dog, & a Frog Ser.). (ENG., Illus.). 32p. (J). (gr. -1-k). 6.99 *(978-0-8037-2885-1(9))*, Dial Bks) Penguin Young Readers Group.
Mayer, Marvin. The Day X Ran Away. 2013. (ENG., Illus.). 38p. (gr. -1-3). pap. 12.00 *(978-1-936205-87-5(4))* Austin, Stephen F. State Univ. Pr.
Mayer, Mercer. The Best Teacher Ever No. 6. Mayer, Mercer, illus. 2008. (Little Critter Ser.). (ENG., Illus.). 24p. (J). (gr. -1-2). pap. 3.99 *(978-0-06-053960-3(7))*, HarperFestival) HarperCollins Pubs.
—Frog on His Own. Mayer, Mercer, illus. 2003. (Boy, a Dog, & a Frog Ser.). (ENG., Illus.). 32p. (J). (gr. -1-k). 6.99 *(978-0-8037-2883-7(2))*, Dial Bks) Penguin Young Readers Group.
—Just Me & My Buddies. 2017. (Pictureback(R) Ser.). (ENG., Illus.). 48p. (J). (gr. -1-2). 5.99 *(978-0-399-55376-9(2))*, Random Hse. Bks. for Young Readers) Random Hse. Children's Bks.
—Little Critters, 1 vol. 2014. (ENG., Illus.). 24p. (J). bds. 9.99 *(978-1-4003-2250-3(2))* Nelson, Thomas Inc.
Mayer, Mercer & Mayer, Marianna. A Boy, a Dog, a Frog & a Friend. Mayer, Mercer & Mayer, Marianna, illus. 2003. (Boy, a Dog, & a Frog Ser.). (ENG., Illus.). 32p. (J). (gr. -1-k). 6.99 *(978-0-8037-2882-0(4))*, Dial Bks) Penguin Young Readers Group.
Mayfield, Jamie. Destiny. 2016. (ENG., Illus.). (J). 29.99 ***(978-1-63533-000-7(9))*** 2013. 310p. pap. 17.99 *(978-1-62380-864-8(2))* Dreamspinner Pr. (Harmony Ink Pr.).
—Determination. 2016. (ENG., Illus.). (J). 29.99 ***(978-1-63533-001-4(7))***, Harmony Ink Pr.) 2013. 336p. pap. 17.99 *(978-1-62798-009-8(1))* Dreamspinner Pr.
Mayfield, Sue. I Can, You Can, Toucan! 2006. (Green Bananas Ser.). (ENG., Illus.). 48p. (J). (gr. -1-3). lib. bdg. *(978-0-7787-1032-5(7))* Crabtree Publishing Co.
Mayhew, James. Bubble & Squeak. Vulliamy, Clara, illus. 2013. (J). *(978-1-4351-4770-6(7))* Barnes & Noble, Inc.
Maynor, Megan. Ella & Penguin: a Perfect Match. Bonnet, Rosalinde, illus. 2017. 32p. (J). (gr. -1-3). 17.99 *(978-0-06-233089-5(6))* HarperCollins Pubs.
—Ella & Penguin Stick Together. Bonnet, Rosalinde, illus. 2016. 32p. (J). (gr. -1-3). 17.99 *(978-0-06-233088-8(8))* HarperCollins Pubs.
Mazer, Anne. Everything New under the Sun. 2003. (Amazing Days of Abby Hayes Ser.: Bk. 10). (Illus.). 105p. (J). (gr. 4-7). 12.65 *(978-0-7569-3931-1(3))* Perfection Learning Corp.
—Good Things Come in Small Packages. 2003. (Amazing Days of Abby Hayes Ser.: Bk. 12). (Illus.). 101p. (J). (gr. 4-7). 12.65 *(978-0-7569-3935-9(6))* Perfection Learning Corp.
—It's Music to My Ears. 2005. (Amazing Days of Abby Hayes Ser.). (Illus.). 110p. (J). (gr. 3-7). 12.65 *(978-0-7569-5910-4(1))* Perfection Learning Corp.
—Some Things Never Change. 2004. (Amazing Days of Abby Hayes Ser.: Bk. 13). (Illus.). 101p. (J). (gr. 4-7). 12.65 *(978-0-7569-5302-7(2))* Perfection Learning Corp.
Mazer, Norma Fox. Babyface. 2007. (ENG., Illus.). 176p. (YA). (gr. 7). pap. 11.95 *(978-0-15-206277-4(7))* Houghton Mifflin Harcourt Publishing Co.
—Crazy Fish. 2007. (ENG., Illus.). 160p. (J). (gr. 2-5). pap. 11.95 *(978-0-15-206373-3(0))* Houghton Mifflin Harcourt Publishing Co.
—Ten Ways to Make My Sister Disappear. 2007. (ENG.). 128p. (J). (gr. 4-7). 16.99 *(978-0-439-83983-9(1))*, Levine, Arthur A. Bks.) Scholastic, Inc.
Mazzafro, Howard. No Room for George. 2011. (Illus.). 24p. (gr. -1). pap. 14.93 *(978-1-4269-6782-5(9))* Trafford Publishing.
McAllister, Angela. A Mouse So Small. Pedler, Caroline, illus. 2015. (ENG.). 32p. (J). (gr. -1-3). 16.99 *(978-1-58925-194-6(6))* Tiger Tales.
—Winter's Child. Baker-Smith, Grahame, illus. 2015. (ENG.). 40p. (J). (gr. -1-2). 16.99 *(978-0-7636-7964-4(X))*, Templar) Candlewick Pr.
Mcallister, Herb West. Doo West to Toadstool. 2011. 44p. pap. 21.99 *(978-1-4628-5530-8(X))* Xlibris Corp.
McAlpine, Stacy. To Be with You, 1 vol. 2010. 72p. pap. 19.95 *(978-1-4489-5087-4(2))* America Star Bks.
Mcandrew, Maria. The Invasion of the Evil Chocolate Chips. 2013. 24p. pap. 24.95 *(978-1-63004-186-1(6))* America Star Bks.
McAneney, Caitie. Koko the Cat. 2017. (Pet Tales! Ser.). 24p. (J). (gr. 4-6). pap. 8.25 ***(978-1-5081-5675-8(1))***, PowerKids Pr.) Rosen Publishing Group, Inc., The.
McAnulty, Stacy. Goldie Blox & the Three Dares. 2017. (Goldie Blox Ser.). lib. bdg. 17.20 ***(978-0-606-40255-2(1))*** Turtleback Bks.
McArdle, Donald. Santa's Newest Friend. 2007. 25p. (J). 21.50 *(978-0-615-14212-8(5))* McArdle, Donald.
McArthur, Shallee. The Unhappening of Genesis Lee. 2014. (ENG.). 352p. (J). (gr. 6). 16.95 *(978-1-62914-647-8(1))*, Sky Pony Pr.) Skyhorse Publishing Co., Inc.
McBride, Eve. Dandelions Help. 160p. (J). pap. *(978-0-9698752-5-3(8))* Shoreline.
McBride, Kristina. One Moment. 2017. (ENG.). 272p. (YA). (gr. 8). pap. 9.99 *(978-1-5107-1455-7(3))*, Sky Pony Pr.) Skyhorse Publishing Co., Inc.
McBride, Peter & McBride, Judith. Bug & Budgie. 2013. 32p. *(978-1-4602-2343-7(8))* FriesenPress.
—Bug & Budgie Fly Away. 2013. 48p. *(978-1-4602-3312-2(3))* FriesenPress.
McCabe, Jane. The Remarkable Story of the Very First Flower: And How She Changed the World. 2010. 56p. pap. 24.99 *(978-1-4490-8361-8(7))* AuthorHouse.
McCafferty, Megan. The (Totally Not) Guaranteed Guide to Popularity, Prettiness & Perfection. 2014. (Jessica Darling's It List Ser.: 1). (ENG.). 240p. (J). (gr. 3-7). pap. 8.99 *(978-0-316-24498-5(8))*, Poppy) Little, Brown Bks. for Young Readers.
McCahan, Erin. Love & Other Foreign Words. 2014. (ENG.). 336p. (YA). (gr. 7). 17.99 *(978-0-8037-4051-8(4))*, Dial Bks) Penguin Young Readers Group.
McCann, Jesse L., et al. Here Comes Krypto, 1 vol. 2014. (Krypto the Superdog Ser.). (ENG., Illus.). 32p. (gr. 1-2). 22.60 *(978-1-4342-4785-8(6))* Stone Arch Bks.
Mccants, Bruce C. Legend of the White Cockroach. 2012. 120p. 20.95 *(978-1-4759-4791-5(7))*; pap. 10.95 *(978-1-4759-4792-2(5))* iUniverse, Inc.
McCarry, Sarah. All Our Pretty Songs. 2013. (Metamorphoses Trilogy Ser.: 1). (ENG.). 240p. (YA). (gr. 8-12). pap. 9.99 *(978-1-250-02708-5(X))*, 9781250027085, St. Martin's Griffin) St. Martin's Pr.
—Dirty Wings. 2014. (Metamorphoses Trilogy Ser.: 2). (ENG.). 288p. (YA). (gr. 8-12). 19.99 *(978-1-250-04938-4(5))*, 9781250049384, St. Martin's Griffin) St. Martin's Pr.
McCarthy, Cori. You Were Here. 2016. (ENG., Illus.). 400p. (YA). (gr. 8-12). 17.99 *(978-1-4926-1704-4(0))*, 9781492617044) Sourcebooks, Inc.
McCarthy, Peggy & Rivers, Julia. Not for the Meek. 2013. (ENG.). 130p. (J). pap. 10.95 *(978-1-4327-9157-5(5))* Outskirts Pr., Inc.
McCarthy, Sally J. & McCarthy, Arica G. Hope & Wishie. 2013. (Illus.). 42p. pap. 12.95 *(978-0-9898968-1-8(1))* McCarthy, Sally Studios.
McCarty, Bryan. Devyn's Gold. 2008. pap. 17.00 *(978-0-8059-8640-2(5))* Dorrance Publishing Co., Inc.
McCarty, Peter. The Monster Returns. McCarty, Peter, illus. 2012. (Jeremy & the Monster Ser.). (ENG., Illus.). 40p. (J). (gr. -1-1). 16.99 *(978-0-8050-9030-7(4))*, 9780805090307, Holt, Henry & Co. Bks. For Young Readers) Holt, Henry & Co.
McCaughan, Timothy. Crimson Soul. 2005. 200p. per. 12.95 *(978-1-58961-438-3(0))* PageFree Publishing, Inc.
McClear, Preston. Frannie & Pickles. Dollak, Nicholas, illus. 2003. 48p. (J). (gr. k-5). 16.95 *(978-1-929084-13-5(7))* Malibu Bks. for Children.
McCleery, Peter. Bob & Joss Get Lost! Vogel, Vin, illus. 2017. 32p. (J). (gr. -1-3). 17.99 *(978-0-06-241531-8(X))* HarperCollins Pubs.
McClellan, Mae. Just Friends. 2004. (J). pap. 8.00 *(978-0-8059-6468-4(1))* Dorrance Publishing Co., Inc.
McClintock, Norah. My Side, 1 vol. 2013. (Orca Soundings Ser.). (ENG.). 128p. (YA). (gr. 8-12). pap. 9.95 *(978-1-4598-0511-8(9))*; lib. bdg. 16.95 *(978-1-4598-0517-0(8))* Orca Bk. Pubs. USA.
—El Regreso, 1 vol. 2011. (Spanish Soundings Ser.).Tr. of Back. (SPA.). 112p. (YA). (gr. 8-12). pap. 9.95 *(978-1-55469-973-5(8))* Orca Bk. Pubs. USA.
—Seeing & Believing. 2014. (Mike & Riel Mysteries Ser.: No. 4). 240p. (YA). (gr. 6-12). lib. bdg. 27.93 *(978-1-4677-2608-5(7))*, Darby Creek) Lerner Publishing Group.
—Snitch, 1 vol. 2005. (Orca Soundings Ser.). (ENG.). 128p. (YA). (gr. 8-12). per. 9.95 *(978-1-55143-484-1(9))* Orca Bk. Pubs. USA.
McCloskey, John J. Warrior Ching. 2006. 179p. pap. 24.95 *(978-1-4241-2389-6(5))* PublishAmerica, Inc.
McCluskey, J. E. The Adventures of Peter the Pleasant Platypus & Friends: First Adventure, Tidy Time. 2004. 48p. pap. 24.95 *(978-1-4137-2546-9(5))* PublishAmerica, Inc.
—Platypus Tales. 2009. 120p. pap. 14.95 *(978-1-4357-2635-2(9))* Lulu Pr., Inc.
McClymer, Kelly. She's a Witch Girl. 2007. (ENG.). 272p. (YA). (gr. 7-12). pap. 12.99 *(978-1-4169-4902-2(X))*, Simon Pulse) Simon Pulse.
McCoid, Uldine. Little Girls Play Dress Up. 2011. 28p. (gr. -1). pap. 12.03 *(978-1-4567-6841-6(7))* AuthorHouse.
McConchie, Lyn. Autumn of the Wild Poney. 2012. (ENG.). 126p. (YA). pap. 12.00 *(978-1-936021-40-6(4))*, Banana Oil Bks.) Cyberwizard Productions.
—Winter of Waiting. 2015. (YA). (gr. 5-18). pap. 15.00 *(978-1-936021-55-0(2))*, Banana Oil Bks.) Cyberwizard Productions.
McCorkle, Barbara. Brutis' New Friend. Taylor, David A., illus. 2007. 30p. (J). 13.99 *(978-1-59879-439-7(6))* Lifevest Publishing, Inc.
McCorkle, Denise. On Angels Wings - Softball. 2008. 32p. pap. 17.95 *(978-1-4327-3102-1(5))* Outskirts Pr., Inc.
McCormick, Michelle. Priscilla Willa, Party Planner: Night at the Haunted Hotel. 2013. (ENG.). 108p. (YA). pap. 9.95 *(978-1-4787-0890-2(5))* Outskirts Pr., Inc.
McCormick, Patricia. Sold. 2008. (ENG.). 272p. (J). (gr. 7-17). pap. 8.99 *(978-0-7868-5172-0(4))* Hyperion Pr.
—Sold. 2011. 10.36 *(978-0-7848-3420-6(2))*, Everbind) Marco Bk. Co.
—Sold. 2008. 263p. (J). (gr. 7-12). 19.65 *(978-1-4178-1810-5(7))*, Turtleback) Turtleback Bks.
McCorvie, D. Lawrence. Timothy Hunt: The Great Candy Caper. 2007. 232p. 30.00 *(978-1-4251-3618-5(4))* Trafford Publishing.
McCowan, Patricia. Honeycomb, 1 vol. 2014. (Orca Limelights Ser.). (ENG.). 152p. (J). (gr. 6-9). pap. 9.95 *(978-1-4598-0579-8(8))* Orca Bk. Pubs. USA.
McCoy, Mary. Camp So-And-So. 2017. (ENG.). 424p. (YA). (gr. 8-12). 18.99 *(978-1-5124-1597-1(9))*; 9.99 ***(978-1-5124-3428-6(0))***, Carolrhoda Lab™); 38.65 ***(978-1-5124-3429-3(9))***, Carolrhoda Lab™); 38.65 ***(978-1-5124-2693-9(8))***, Carolrhoda Lab™) Lerner Publishing Group.
McCoy, Tanya. If My Best Friend was an Elephant, 1 vol. 2010. 20p. 24.95 *(978-1-4512-1063-7(9))* PublishAmerica, Inc.
McCranie, Stephen. Belly Flop! Book 3. McCranie, Stephen, illus. 3rd ed. 2012. (Mal & Chad Ser.: 3). (ENG., Illus.). 240p. (J). (gr. 3-7). pap. 9.99 *(978-0-399-25658-5(X))*, Philomel Bks.) Penguin Young Readers Group.
McCreely, Havelock. My Zombie Hamster. 2014. (ENG.). 200p. (J). (gr. 3-7). 15.99 *(978-1-60684-491-5(1))*, Carolrhoda Bks.) Lerner Publishing Group.
McCrimmon, Linda. Can You Please tie My Shoes? 2007. (J). 10.95 *(978-0-9796978-2-1(4))* G Publishing LLC.
McCue, Lisa. Quiet Bunny & Noisy Puppy. (ENG., Illus.). (J). 2013. 30p. (gr. -1 — 1). bds. 7.95 *(978-1-4549-0860-9(2))* 2011. 32p. 14.95 *(978-1-4027-8559-7(3))* Sterling Publishing Co., Inc.
McCully, Emily Arnold. Pete Likes Bunny. McCully, Emily Arnold, illus. 2016. (I Like to Read(r) Ser.). (ENG., Illus.). 24p. (J). (gr. -1-2). 6.99 *(978-0-8234-3687-3(X))* Holiday Hse., Inc.
—Pete Likes Bunny. 2016. (I Like to Read(r) Ser.). (ENG., Illus.). 24p. (J). (gr. -1-2). 14.95 *(978-0-8234-3653-8(5))* Holiday Hse., Inc.
McCune, Susan. The Best Friend, 01 vols., 1. 2016. (Rosen REAL Readers: Social Studies Nonfiction / Fiction: Family, Community, & the World Ser.). (ENG.). 8p. (J). pap. 5.46 *(978-1-5081-1845-9(0))*, Rosen Classroom) Rosen Publishing Group, Inc., The.
McCusker, Paul. Danger Lies Ahead! 2006. (Adventures in Odyssey Bks.: No. 2). (ENG.). 336p. (J). (gr. 8-12). per. 15.99 *(978-1-58997-329-9(1))* Tyndale Hse. Pubs.
—Point of No Return. 2006. (Adventures in Odyssey Bks.). (ENG.). 336p. (J). (gr. 3-7). per. 15.99 *(978-1-58997-332-9(1))* Tyndale Hse. Pubs.
—Strange Journey Back. 2006. (Adventures in Odyssey Bks.: No. 1). (ENG., Illus.). 304p. (J). (gr. 3-7). per. 15.99 *(978-1-58997-325-1(9))* Tyndale Hse. Pubs.
McDaniel, Carren. Fresh Air Friends: The Dangers of Secondhand Smoke. 2012. (ENG.). 33p. (J). pap. 14.95 *(978-1-4327-9818-5(9))* Outskirts Pr., Inc.
McDaniel, Lurlene. Breathless. 2010. (ENG.). 180p. (YA). (gr. 7). mass mkt. 7.99 *(978-0-440-24016-7(6))*, Delacorte Bks. for Young Readers) Random Hse. Children's Bks.
—Heart to Heart. 2012. (ENG.). 224p. (YA). (gr. 7). pap. 8.99 *(978-0-440-24017-4(4))*, Ember) Random Hse. Children's Bks.
—Holly's Story. 2007. (Angels in Pink Ser.). (ENG.). 224p. (YA). (gr. 7-11). mass mkt. 6.99 *(978-0-440-23867-6(6))*, Laurel Leaf) Random Hse. Children's Bks.
—Raina's Story. 2006. (Angels in Pink Ser.). (ENG.). 208p. (YA). (gr. 7-12). mass mkt. 6.99 *(978-0-440-23866-9(8))*, Laurel Leaf) Random Hse. Children's Bks.
—True Love. 2009. (ENG.). 672p. (YA). (gr. 7). pap. 10.99 *(978-0-375-86148-2(3))*, Ember) Random Hse. Children's Bks.
—The Year of Chasing Dreams. 2014. (ENG.). 336p. (YA). (gr. 7). 16.99 *(978-0-385-74173-6(1))*, Delacorte Pr.) Random Hse. Children's Bks.
—The Year of Luminous Love. (ENG.). 384p. (YA). (gr. 7). 2014. pap. 9.99 *(978-0-385-74172-9(3))*, Ember) 2013. 16.99 *(978-0-385-74171-2(5))*, Delacorte Bks. for Young Readers) Random Hse. Children's Bks.
McDaniels, Preston. A Perfect Snowman. McDaniels, Preston, illus. 2007. (ENG., Illus.). 40p. (J). (gr. -1-3). 18.99 *(978-1-4169-1026-8(3))*, Simon & Schuster Bks. For Young Readers) Simon & Schuster Bks. For Young Readers.
McDaniels, Preston, illus. Phineas L. MacGuire ... Gets Cooking! 2014. (From the Highly Scientific Notebooks of Phineas L. MacGuire Ser.). (ENG.). 208p. (J). (gr. 3-7). 16.99 *(978-1-4814-0099-2(1))*, Atheneum Bks. for Young Readers) Simon & Schuster Children's Publishing.
McDavid-Jones, Elizabeth. Mystery on Skull Island. 2009. (Mysteries Through Time Ser.). 192p. (YA). (gr. 4-8). 31.95 *(978-1-60754-286-5(2))*; pap. 15.25 *(978-1-60754-302-2(8))* Windmill Bks.
McDonagh, Christelle, et al. Mission Magic Bubble. 2009. (Illus.). 56p. pap. 23.99 *(978-1-4389-0640-9(4))* AuthorHouse.
McDonald, Abby. Getting over Garrett Delaney. 2012. (ENG., Illus.). 336p. (YA). (gr. 9). 16.99 *(978-0-7636-5507-5(4))* Candlewick Pr.
—Sophomore Switch. 2010. (ENG., Illus.). 304p. (YA). (gr. 9). pap. 8.99 *(978-0-7636-4774-2(8))* Candlewick Pr.
McDonald, Ellie. Danger after Dark. 4th ed. 2005. (Creative Girls Club Mystery Book Ser.). (Illus.). 118p. (J). pap. *(978-1-59635-127-1(6))*, Annie's) Annie's Publishing, LLC.
McDonald, Fiona. Ghost Doll & Jasper. 2012. (ENG., Illus.). 112p. (J). (gr. 2-7). 12.95 *(978-1-62087-174-4(2))*, 620174, Sky Pony Pr.) Skyhorse Publishing Co., Inc.
McDonald, Megan. Ant & Honey Bee: A Pair of Friends at Halloween. Karas, G. Brian, illus. 2013. (Candlewick Sparks Ser.). (ENG.). 48p. (J). (gr. k-4). pap. 3.99 *(978-0-7636-6864-8(8))* Candlewick Pr.
—Ant & Honey Bee: A Pair of Friends in Winter. Karas, G. Brian, illus. (Candlewick Sparks Ser.). (ENG.). 64p. (J). (gr. k-4). 2014. pap. 3.99 *(978-0-7636-6862-4(1))* 2013. 14.99 *(978-0-7636-5712-3(3))* Candlewick Pr.
—April Fools', Mr. Todd! Madrid, Erwin, illus. 2017. (Judy Moody Ser.). (ENG.). 64p. (J). (gr. -1-1). 12.99 *(978-0-7636-8200-2(4))* Candlewick Pr.
—April Fools', Mr. Todd! Madrid, Erwin, illus. 2017. (Judy Moody & Friends Ser.). (ENG.). (J). (gr. -1-1). lib. bdg. 14.75 ***(978-0-606-39835-0(X))*** Turtleback Bks.
—Around the World in 8 1/2 Days. 2007. (Judy Moody Ser.: 7). (SPA.). (J). 1.25 *(978-1-4281-3376-1(3))* Recorded Bks., Inc.
—Around the World in 8 1/2 Days. Reynolds, Peter H., illus. 2010. (Judy Moody Ser.: 7). (ENG.). 176p. (J). (gr. 1-4). 15.99 *(978-0-7636-4864-0(7))* Candlewick Pr.
—Around the World in 8 1/2 Days. 2010. (Judy Moody Ser.: 7). lib. bdg. 16.00 *(978-0-606-12349-5(0))*, Turtleback) Turtleback Bks.
—Around the World in 8 1/2 Days, Bk. 7. Reynolds, Peter H., illus. 2010. (Judy Moody Ser.: 7). (ENG.). 176p. (J). (gr. 1-4). pap. 5.99 *(978-0-7636-4863-3(9))* Candlewick Pr.
—Frank Pearl in the Awful Waffle Kerfuffle. Madrid, Erwin, illus. 2014. (Judy Moody Ser.: 4). (ENG.). 64p. (J). (gr. -1-1). 12.99 *(978-0-7636-5717-8(4))* Candlewick Pr.
—Jessica Finch in Pig Trouble. Madrid, Erwin, illus. 2014. (Judy Moody Ser.: 1). (ENG.). 64p. (J). (gr. -1-1). 12.99 *(978-0-7636-5718-5(2))*; pap. 4.99 *(978-0-7636-7027-6(8))* Candlewick Pr.
—Jessica Finch in Pig Trouble. 2014. (Judy Moody & Friends Ser.). (Illus.). 60p. (J). lib. bdg. 14.75 *(978-0-606-35162-1(0))* Turtleback Bks.
—Judy Moody & Friends: Mrs. Moody in the Birthday Jinx. Madrid, Erwin, illus. 2016. (Judy Moody Ser.). (ENG.). 64p. (J). (gr. -1-1). 12.99 *(978-0-7636-8198-2(9))* Candlewick Pr.
—Mood Martian. Reynolds, Peter H., illus. 2015. (Judy Moody Ser.). (ENG.). 208p. (J). (gr. 1-4). pap. 5.99 *(978-0-7636-8015-2(X))* Candlewick Pr.
—Rocky Zang in the Amazing Mr. Magic. 2014. (Judy Moody & Friends Ser.). lib. bdg. 14.75 *(978-0-606-35163-8(9))* Turtleback Bks.
McDonald, Meinir & Evans, Anthony. Bant I Batagonia. 2005. (WEL., Illus.). 16p. pap. *(978-1-85644-543-6(7))* CAA.
McDonnell, Margot. Torn to Pieces. 2010. (ENG.). 272p. (YA). (gr. 7). pap. 8.99 *(978-0-385-73557-5(X))*, Delacorte Bks. for Young Readers) Random Hse. Children's Bks.
McDonnell, Patrick. The Gift of Nothing. (ENG., Illus.). 56p. (gr. -1-3). 2005. (J). 15.99 *(978-0-316-11488-2(X))* 2009. 19.99 *(978-0-316-05441-6(0))* Little, Brown Bks. for Young Readers.
—The Little Gift of Nothing. 2016. (ENG., Illus.). 30p. (J). (gr. -1 — 1). bds. 7.99 *(978-0-316-39473-4(4))* Little, Brown Bks. for Young Readers.
—Thank You & Good Night. 2015. (ENG., Illus.). 40p. (J). (gr. -1-3). 15.99 *(978-0-316-33801-1(X))* Little Brown & Co.
McDuffie, Linda. The Underwater Adventures of Little Ki. 2008. 26p. per. 21.99 *(978-1-4257-8392-1(9))* Xlibris Corp.
McElroy, Roland. Jibicle & Cobie: Friends at Last. 2006. (J). pap. 9.95 *(978-0-9673917-1-7(7))* McElroy & Assocs.
Mcevoy, Ariane. Little Monkey Learns to Share. 2012. 28p. pap. 15.99 *(978-1-4691-5830-3(2))* Xlibris Corp.
McFarland, Myndie. Squigley the Squirrel. 2012. 46p. pap. 12.95 *(978-1-886057-11-1(7))* Warren Publishing, Inc.
McGann, Erika. The Broken Spell. 2014. (Demon Notebook Ser.: 2). (ENG.). 352p. (J). (gr. 4-8). pap. 6.99 *(978-1-4926-0296-5(5))*, Sourcebooks Jabberwocky) Sourcebooks, Inc.
—The Demon Notebook. 2014. (Demon Notebook Ser.: 1). (ENG.). 288p. (J). (gr. 3-6). pap. 6.99 *(978-1-4022-9538-6(3))*, 9781402295386, Sourcebooks Jabberwocky) Sourcebooks, Inc.
McGarry, Katie. Long Way Home. 2017. (Thunder Road Ser.: 3). (ENG.). 416p. 18.99 *(978-0-373-21217-0(8))*, Harlequin Teen) Harlequin Enterprises, Ltd. CAN. Dist: HarperCollins Pubs.
McGarvey, A. J. Loyalty Unbroken: A Mustang's Tale. 2011. (Illus.). 84p. pap. 12.52 *(978-1-4520-5162-8(3))* AuthorHouse.
McGee, Katharine. The Dazzling Heights. 2017. (Thousandth Floor Ser.: 2). 432p. (YA). (gr. 8). 18.99 ***(978-0-06-241862-3(9))*** HarperCollins Pubs.
—The Thousandth Floor. (Thousandth Floor Ser.: 1). (YA). (gr. 8). 2017. 496p. pap. 9.99 ***(978-0-06-241860-9(2))*** 2016. (ENG.). 448p. 18.99 *(978-0-06-241859-3(9))* HarperCollins Pubs.
Mcgee, Ken. Forever. 2013. 224p. pap. 15.49 *(978-1-62509-504-6(X))* Salem Author Services.

McGee, Mami. Bear Can't Sleep! Julian, Sean, illus. 2015. (ENG.). 32p. (J). (gr. -1-3). 16.99 (978-1-58925-189-2(X)) Tiger Tales.

Mcghee, Alison. Firefly Hollow. Denise, Christopher, illus. 2015. (ENG.). 304p. (J). (gr. 3-7). 16.99 (978-1-4424-2336-7(6), Atheneum Bks. for Young Readers) Simon & Schuster Children's Publishing.

—Making a Friend. Rosenthal, Marc, illus. 2011. (ENG.). 40p. (J). (gr. -1-3). 16.99 (978-1-4169-8998-1(6), Atheneum Bks. for Young Readers) Simon & Schuster Children's Publishing.

McGhee, Holly M. Matylda, Bright & Tender. 2017. (ENG.). 224p. (J). (gr. 3-7). 16.99 (978-0-7636-8951-3(3)) Candlewick Pr.

McGill, Justin. Friends Forever, Signed Jeremy E. 2007. 48p. per. 16.95 (978-1-4241-8794-2(X)) America Star Bks.

McGill, Nichole. Girl #3. 2009. (ENG.). 224p. (YA). (gr. 7-18). pap. (978-1-55470-143-8(0)) Me to We.

McGinnis, Chelsea. Mk Frogg & the Lily Pad Adventures, 1 vol. 2009. 48p. pap. 24.95 (978-1-60813-548-6(9)) America Star Bks.

McGinnis, Mindy. The Female of the Species. (YA). (gr. 9). 2017. 368p. pap. 9.99 **(978-0-06-232090-2(4))** 2016. 352p. 17.99 (978-0-06-232089-6(0)) HarperCollins Pubs. (Tegen, Katherine Bks).

McGlame, Jack. Majik: The Beginning. 2012. 132p. 21.95 (978-1-4759-3289-8(8)) iUniverse, Inc.

McGovem, Suzanne. Gator & Pete - More Alike Than It Seems. Bizjak, Donna, illus. 2007. (J). 13.99 (978-0-9792558-0-9(5)) Hatch Ideas, Inc.

McGowan, Anthony. The Bare Bum Gang & the Holy Grail. 2009. (ENG., Illus.). 160p. (J). (gr. 2-4). pap. 11.99 (978-1-86230-389-8(4), Red Fox) Random House Children's Books GBR. Dist: Independent Pubs. Group.

—The Bare Bum Gang Battles the Dogsnatchers. 2010. (ENG., Illus.). 144p. (J). (gr. 2-4). pap. 11.99 (978-1-86230-387-4(8), Red Fox) Random House Children's Books GBR. Dist: Independent Pubs. Group.

—The Fall. 2012. (Stoke Books Titles Ser.). (ENG.). 64p. (YA). (gr. 8-12). pap. 6.95 (978-1-78112-094-1(3)); lib. bdg. 22.60 (978-1-78112-095-8(1)) Lerner Publishing Group.

—The Knife That Killed Me. 2011. (ENG.). 224p. (YA). (gr. 9). pap. 8.99 (978-0-375-85516-0(5), Ember) Random Hse. Children's Bks.

McGrath, Maureen. Spunky's Special Friend. 2009. (Illus.). 24p. pap. 13.50 (978-1-60693-735-8(9), Eloquent Bks.) Strategic Book Publishing & Rights Agency (SBPRA).

McGrath, Maureen Julie. The Tale of the Cat with the Crooked Tail. 2013. 24p. pap. 13.50 (978-1-62516-859-7(4), Strategic Bk. Publishing) Strategic Book Publishing & Rights Agency (SBPRA).

McGraw, Mike. Doodle Land. 2010. 28p. pap. 13.99 (978-1-4520-1290-2(3)) AuthorHouse.

McGregor, Melissa Lee. Ainsley & Owen: An Unexpected Friendship. 2013. 40p. pap. (978-1-4602-0111-4(6)) FriesenPress.

McGriff, Shawna A. Princess Pink: Princess Pink Helps Zion, Melinda, & Jasmine Learn to Communicate about Their Parents' Divorces. 2010. 56p. pap. 24.00 (978-1-4520-3941-1(0)) AuthorHouse.

—Princess Pink: Sam Loses Her Mother, but She Gains Her Mother's Heart. 2010. 32p. pap. 15.50 (978-1-4520-3937-4(2)) AuthorHouse.

McGuigan, Mary Ann. Morning in a Different Place. 2009. (ENG.). 195p. (YA). (gr. 7-18). 17.95 (978-1-59078-551-5(7), Front Street) Boyds Mills Pr.

McGuinness, Elle J. & Caron, Romi. Baby Turtle's Tale. 2011. (ENG.). 12p. (J). 9.99 (978-1-4494-0354-6(9)) Andrews McMeel Publishing.

McHale, Remme. No Place for Niappy. 2010. 28p. pap. 12.85 (978-1-4490-6900-1(2)) AuthorHouse.

McInnes, Nicole. 100 Days. 2016. (ENG.). 400p. (YA). 17.99 (978-0-374-30284-9(7), 9780374302849, Farrar, Straus & Giroux (BYR)) Farrar, Straus & Giroux.

McIntosh, Helen B. Eric, Jose, & the Peace Rug. 2nd ed. 2005. (J). per. 14.99 (978-0-9763949-0-7(1)) Peace Rug Company, Inc., The.

McIntyre, Mel & Mcintyre, Mel. Flutter Bunnies Fossil of Fortune. Grady, Kit, illus. 2011. 20p. pap. 9.95 (978-1-61633-170-2(4)) Guardian Angel Publishing, Inc.

McKann, Anna. Chavos: The Kids of Distrito Federal. 2006. (Illus.). 261p. (J). per. (978-0-9554438-0-0(6)) Sharon Hse. Publishing, Ltd.

McKay, Amanda S. The New Night Sky. 2012. 28p. pap. 19.99 (978-1-4685-2517-5(4)) AuthorHouse.

McKay, Hilary. Caddy's World. (ENG.). (J). (gr. 5-9). 2013. 288p. pap. 6.99 (978-1-4424-4106-4(2)) 2012. 272p. 16.99 (978-1-4424-4105-7(4)) McElderry, Margaret K. Bks. (McElderry, Margaret K. Bks.).

—Indigo's Star. 2006. (ENG.). 272p. (J). (gr. 3-7). reprint ed. per. 7.99 (978-1-4169-1403-7(X), McElderry, Margaret K. Bks.) McElderry, Margaret K. Bks.

—Permanent Rose. 2006. (ENG.). 256p. (J). (gr. 3-7). reprint ed. per. 7.99 (978-1-4169-2804-1(9), McElderry, Margaret K. Bks.) McElderry, Margaret K. Bks.

—Wishing for Tomorrow: The Sequel to a Little Princess. Maland, Nick, illus. (ENG.). 288p. (J). (gr. 3-7). 2011. pap. 6.99 (978-1-4424-0170-9(2)) 2010. 16.99 (978-1-4424-0169-3(9)) McElderry, Margaret K. Bks. (McElderry, Margaret K. Bks.).

McKay, Sharon E. Thunder over Kandahar. Gerszak, Rafal, photos by. 2010. (ENG., Illus.). 264p. (YA). (gr. 7-12). 19.95 (978-1-55451-267-6(0), 9781554512676); 3rd ed. pap. 12.95 (978-1-55451-266-9(2), 9781554512669) Annick Pr., Ltd. CAN. Dist: Publishers Group West (PGW).

McKay, Sharon E. & Lafrance, Daniel. War Brothers: The Graphic Novel. Lafrance, Daniel, illus. 2013. (ENG., Illus.). 176p. (YA). (gr. 9-12). 2nd ed. 27.95 (978-1-55451-489-2(4), 9781554514892) 3rd ed. pap. 18.95 (978-1-55451-488-5(6), 9781554514885) Annick Pr., Ltd. CAN. Dist: Publishers Group West (PGW).

McKay, Sindy. We Read Phonics-the Garden Crew. Johnson, Meredith, illus. 2011. 32p. (J). 9.95 (978-1-60115-345-6(7)); pap. 4.99 (978-1-60115-346-3(5)) Treasure Bay, Inc.

McKayhan, Norma J. The Mighty King & the Small Creature. 2012. 24p. pap. 12.55 (978-1-4669-1463-6(7)) Trafford Publishing.

McKee, David. Elmer, Level 4.9. McKee, David, illus. 3rd ed. 2003. (Picture Books Collection). (SPA., Illus.). 32p. (J). (gr. k-3). 12.95 (978-84-372-2186-1(2)) Altea, Ediciones, S.A. - Grupo Santillana ESP. Dist: Santillana USA Publishing Co., Inc.

—Elmer. McKee, David, illus. (Historias Para Dormir Ser.). (SPA., Illus.). 32p. (J). (gr. k-3). pap. 9.95 (978-968-19-1029-7(X)) Santillana USA Publishing Co., Inc.

—Elmer's Friends. 2010. (Elmer Ser.).Tr. of Amigos de Elmer. (ENG & POL., Illus.). 16p. (J). (gr. k — 1). 8.95 (978-1-84059-533-8(7)) Milet Publishing.

—Elmer's Friends. Umicini, Roberta, tr. 2004. (Elmer Ser.).Tr. of Amigos de Elmer. (ENG & ITA., Illus.). 14p. (J). (gr. -1). bds. 8.95 (978-1-84059-402-7(0)) Milet Publishing.

—Elmer's Friends. Mo'Allim, Nur M., tr. 2004. (Elmer Ser.).Tr. of Amigos de Elmer. (ENG & SOM., Illus.). 14p. (J). (gr. -1). bds. 8.95 (978-1-84059-403-4(9)) Milet Publishing.

—Elmer's Friends. Al-Hamdi, Ahmed, tr. 2004. (Elmer Ser.).Tr. of Amigos de Elmer. (ARA & ENG., Illus.). 14p. (J). (gr. -1). bds. 8.95 (978-1-84059-401-0(2)) Milet Publishing.

—Elmer's New Friend. 2003. (ENG., Illus.). 11p. (J). 8.99 (978-1-84270-034-1(0)) Andersen Pr. GBR. Dist: Trafalgar Square Publishing.

McKendall, Kerry. My Imagination Book. 2009. 48p. pap. 17.49 (978-1-4389-1299-8(4)) AuthorHouse.

McKenna, K. J. Take Three Girls. 2005. 96p. pap. 10.00 (978-1-4116-6290-2(3)) Lulu Pr., Inc.

McKennon, Tony. You're Moving Where?! 2008. 40p. pap. 18.55 (978-1-4389-1397-1(4)) AuthorHouse.

McKenzie, C. Lee. Alligators Overhead. 2012. (ENG.). 216p. pap. 12.95 (978-1-4327-8473-7(0)) Outskirts Pr., Inc.

McKinley, Mary. Beau, Lee, the Bomb & Me. 2014. (Rusty Winters Ser.: 1). (ENG.). 256p. (YA). (gr. 13). pap. 9.95 (978-1-61773-255-3(9), K-Teen) Kensington Publishing Corp.

McKinley, Ryan. The Lost Crew. 2012. (ENG.). 144p. pap. 9.95 (978-1-4327-9658-7(5)); pap. 14.95 (978-1-4327-9659-4(3)) Outskirts Pr., Inc.

McKinney, Frank & Mason, Kate. Dead Fred, Flying Lunchboxes & the Good Luck Circle. 2009. (ENG.). 336p. (J). (gr. 4-8). 18.95 (978-0-7573-1382-0(5)) Health Communications, Inc.

McKissack, Patricia C. A Friendship for Today. 2008. 172p. (J). pap. (978-0-545-06563-4(1)) Scholastic, Inc.

—A Song for Harlem. 2008. (Scraps of Time Ser.). (ENG.). 128p. (J). (gr. 3-7). 6.99 (978-0-14-241238-1(4), Puffin Books) Penguin Young Readers Group.

McLachlan, Jenny. Love Bomb. 2016. (Ladybirds Ser.: 2). (ENG.). 208p. (YA). 16.99 (978-1-250-06149-2(0), 9781250061492) Feiwel & Friends.

McLaughlin, Lauren. Mitzi Tulane, Preschool Detective in the Secret Ingredient. Ohi, Debbie Ridpath, illus. 2017. (ENG.). (J). (-k). 32p. 17.99 **(978-0-449-81916-6(7))**; 40p. lib. bdg. 20.99 **(978-0-375-97177-8(7))** Random Hse. Children's Bks. (Random Hse. Bks. for Young Readers).

McLaughlin, Richard. The Skunk with the Stinky Attitude. Wilson, Mark, illus. 2013. 44p. (YA). pap. 13.75 (978-1-939625-49-6(1)) Inkwell Books LLC.

McLaurin, Corey F. Larry, Lisa & the Missing Kite, 1 vol. Dixon, Corey, illus. 2009. 20p. pap. 24.95 (978-1-61546-590-3(1)) America Star Bks.

McLean, Hope. Battle of the Brightest. 2013. 140p. (J). (978-0-545-48292-9(5)) Scholastic, Inc.

—Jewel Society #3: Keep Friends Close, Emeralds Closer. 2013. (Jewel Thieves Ser.: 3). (ENG.). 144p. (J). (gr. 3-7). pap. 5.99 (978-0-545-60764-3(7)) Scholastic, Inc.

—Jewel Society #4: Battle of the Brightest. 2013. (Jewel Society Ser.: 4). (ENG.). 144p. (J). (gr. 3-7). pap. 5.99 (978-0-545-60765-0(5), Scholastic Paperbacks) Scholastic, Inc.

McLean, Matthew. A Bewitching Summer, 1 vol. 2009. 100p. pap. 19.95 (978-1-60836-686-6(3)) America Star Bks.

McLeese, Peggy Anne. The Magic. 2011. 64p. pap. 31.99 (978-1-4568-9558-7(3)) Xlibris Corp.

McLemore, Anna-Marie. When the Moon Was Ours. 2016. (ENG.). 288p. (YA). 18.99 (978-1-250-05866-9(X), 9781250058669) St. Martin's Pr.

Mcleod-Stecy, Tracey. The Stone Guardian. 2011. 144p. (gr. 4-6). pap. 11.95 (978-1-4620-3954-8(5)) iUniverse, Inc.

McMahen, Chris. Klutzhood, 1 vol. 2007. (ENG.). 168p. (J). (gr. 4-7). per. 7.95 (978-1-55143-710-1(4)) Orca Bk. Pubs. USA.

McMahon, Michael. Patrick & Paloma, 1 vol. 2013. (Fiction Readers Ser.). (ENG., Illus.). 24p. (J). (gr. 2-2). pap. 6.99 (978-1-4333-5532-5(9)) Shell Educational Publishing.

McMahon, Michele. The Butterfly Promise. 2010. 24p. 12.99 (978-1-4520-1510-1(4)) AuthorHouse.

McMaster, Alex. Giant George & Little Leo. 2012. 24p. pap. 14.95 (978-1-4669-5080-1(3)) Trafford Publishing.

McMillen, Charlotte Palmer. The Little Sea Rock & His Friend Arena. 2005. (Illus.). 32p. (J). per. 14.95 (978-0-9771939-4-3(2), 003) New World Publishing.

Mcmillen, Michelle. Brothers in the Storm. 2011. 120p. pap. 14.95 (978-1-4670-2518-8(6)) AuthorHouse.

McMullan, Kate. Five Days till Summer. Alley, R. W., illus. 2014. (Pearl & Wagner Ser.: 5). (ENG.). 48p. (J). (gr. 1-3). pap. 3.99 (978-0-448-48137-1(5), Penguin Young Readers) Penguin Young Readers Group.

—Four Eyes. Alley, R. W., illus. 2013. (Pearl & Wagner Ser.: 4). (ENG.). 48p. (J). (gr. 1-3). pap. 3.99 (978-0-448-47781-7(5), Penguin Young Readers) Penguin Young Readers Group.

—Two Good Friends. Alley, R. W., illus. 2011. (Pearl & Wagner Ser.: 2). (ENG.). 48p. (J). (gr. 1-3). pap. 3.99 (978-0-448-45690-4(7), Penguin Young Readers) Penguin Young Readers Group.

McMurtrie, Kevin. Have You Seen My Duck? 2012. 20p. pap. 13.77 (978-1-4669-4847-1(7)) Trafford Publishing.

McNally, Amber. Henry & the World of the Missing Socks. 2008. 60p. pap. 16.95 (978-1-60563-288-9(0)) America Star Bks.

McNamara, Margaret. The Fairy Bell Sisters Vol. 5: Sylva & the Lost Treasure. Denos, Julia, illus. 2014. (Fairy Bell Sisters Ser.: 5). (ENG.). 144p. (J). (gr. 1-5). 15.99 (978-0-06-226721-4(3)) HarperCollins Pubs.

—Halloween Fun. Gordon, Mike, illus. 2008. (Robin Hill School Ser.). (ENG.). 32p. (J). (gr. -1-1). pap. 3.99 (978-1-4169-3496-7(0), Simon Spotlight) Simon Spotlight.

—Rosy & the Secret Friend. Denos, Julia, illus. 2013. (Fairy Bell Sisters Ser.: 2). (ENG.). 128p. (J). (gr. 1-5). 15.99 (978-0-06-222805-5(6)); pap. 4.99 (978-0-06-222804-8(8)) HarperCollins Pubs.

—Rosy & the Secret Friend. 2013. (Fairy Bell Sisters Ser.: 2). (J). lib. bdg. 14.75 (978-0-606-31797-9(X), Turtleback) Turtleback Bks.

—Snow Day. Gordon, Mike, illus. 2007. (Robin Hill School Ser.). (ENG.). 32p. (J). (gr. -1-1). pap. 3.99 (978-1-4169-3493-6(6), Simon Spotlight) Simon Spotlight.

—Sylva & the Lost Treasure. Denos, Julia, illus. 2014. (Fairy Bell Sisters Ser.: 5). (ENG.). 144p. (J). (gr. 1-5). pap. 4.99 (978-0-06-226720-7(5)) HarperCollins Pubs.

McNeal, Tom. Far Far Away. (ENG.). (YA). (gr. 7). 2014. 400p. pap. 9.99 (978-0-375-84329-7(9), Ember) 2013. 384p. 17.99 (978-0-375-84972-5(6), Knopf Bks. for Young Readers) Random Hse. Children's Bks.

McNeely, Marian Hurd. The Jumping-off Place. Siegel, William, illus. 2008. 321p. (J). 15.95 (978-0-9798940-4-6(2), South Dakota State Historical Society Pr.) South Dakota State Historical Society Pr.

McNicoll, Sylvia. Best Friends Through Eternity. 2015. (ENG., Illus.). 184p. (YA). (gr. 7). 17.99 (978-1-77049-710-8(2), Tundra Bks.) Tundra Bks. CAN. Dist: Penguin Random Hse. LLC.

McOmber, Rachel B., ed. McOmber Phonics Storybooks: Hello Again. rev. ed. (Illus.). (J). (978-0-944991-84-8(X)) Swift Learning Resources.

—McOmber Phonics Storybooks: Jud & Nell. rev. ed. (Illus.). (J). (978-0-944991-33-6(5)) Swift Learning Resources.

—McOmber Phonics Storybooks: The Gal Pals. rev. ed. (Illus.). (J). (978-0-944991-42-8(4)) Swift Learning Resources.

McPhail, David. Bella Loves Bunny. Brukoff, Barry, photos by. 2013. (David Mcphail's Love Ser.). (ENG., Illus.). 22p. (J). (gr. -1 — 1). bds. 8.95 (978-1-4197-0543-4(1), Abrams Appleseed) Abrams, Inc.

—Ben Loves Bear. 2013. (David Mcphail's Love Ser.). (ENG., Illus.). 22p. (J). (gr. -1-k). bds. 8.95 (978-1-4197-0386-7(2), Abrams Appleseed) Abrams, Inc.

—Big Pig & Little Pig. 2003. (Green Light Readers Level 1 Ser.). (ENG., Illus.). 24p. (J). (gr. -1-3). pap. 3.95 (978-0-15-204857-0(X)) Houghton Mifflin Harcourt Publishing Co.

—Big Pig & Little Pig. 2003. (Green Light Readers — Level 1 Ser.). (gr. k-3). lib. bdg. 13.50 (978-0-613-63254-6(0), Turtleback) Turtleback Bks.

—Big Pig & Little Pig(Cerdo y Cerdito) 2009. (SPA & ENG., Illus.). 32p. (J). (gr. -1-1). 12.99 Houghton Mifflin Harcourt Trade & Reference Pubs.

—Budgie & Boo. 2009. (ENG., Illus.). 32p. (J). (gr. -1-k). 15.95 (978-0-8109-8324-3(9), Abrams Bks. for Young Readers) Abrams, Inc.

—Cerdo y Cerdito. Flor Ada, Alma & Campoy, F. Isabel, trs. from ENG. 2009. (Green Light Readers Level 1 Ser.).Tr. of Big Pig & Little Pig. (SPA & ENG., Illus.). 32p. (J). (gr. -1-3). pap. 3.99 (978-0-15-206561-4(X)) Houghton Mifflin Harcourt Publishing Co.

—Jack & Rick. 2003. (Green Light Readers Level 1 Ser.). (ENG., Illus.). 24p. (J). (gr. -1-3). pap. 3.95 (978-0-15-204859-4(6)) Houghton Mifflin Harcourt Publishing Co.

—Jack & Rick. 2003. (Green Light Readers — Level 1 Ser.). (Illus.). 20p. (gr. -1-3). lib. bdg. 13.50 (978-0-613-63167-9(6), Turtleback) Turtleback Bks.

—Olivia Loves Owl. 2016. (ENG., Illus.). 20p. (J). (gr. -1 — 1). bds. 8.95 (978-1-4197-2127-4(5), Abrams Appleseed) Abrams, Inc.

—Pig Pig Meets the Lion. McPhail, David, illus. 2012. (Illus.). pap. 15.95 (978-1-60734-080-5(1)); (ENG., 32p. (J). (gr. -1-3). 15.95 (978-1-58089-358-9(9)) Charlesbridge Publishing, Inc.

—Rick Is Sick. 2004. (Green Light Readers Level 1 Ser.). (ENG., Illus.). 24p. (J). (gr. -1-3). pap. 3.95 (978-0-15-205092-4(2)) Houghton Mifflin Harcourt Publishing Co.

—Rick Is Sick. 2004. (Green Light Readers — Level 1 Ser.). 13.50 (978-0-613-97286-4(4), Turtleback) Turtleback Bks.

—The Teddy Bear. McPhail, David, illus. 2005. (ENG., Illus.). 32p. (J). (gr. -1-1). reprint ed. pap. 8.99 (978-0-8050-7882-4(7), 9780805078824) Square Fish.

—Waddles. 2011. (ENG., Illus.). 32p. (J). (gr. k-2). 16.95 (978-0-8109-8415-8(6), Abrams Bks. for Young Readers) Abrams, Inc.

McPhate, Paul J. The Puggle King. 2008. 52p. pap. 16.95 (978-1-60703-709-5(2)) America Star Bks.

McPherson, Dottie. Kizzi's Special Friends. 2003. (Illus.). (J). 14.95 (978-0-9724979-0-9(0), Advocate Hse.) A Cappela Publishing.

McPike, Elizabeth. Little Bitty Friends. Barton, Patrice, illus. 2016. (ENG.). 32p. (J). (— 1). 16.99 (978-0-399-17255-7(6), G.P. Putnam's Sons Books for Young Readers) Penguin Young Readers Group.

McQuinn, Anna. My Friend Jamal. Frey, Ben, illus. McQuinn, Anna, photos by. 2008. (ENG.). 32p. (J). (gr. -1-2). 17.95 (978-1-55451-123-5(2), 9781554511235); pap. 8.95 (978-1-55451-122-8(4), 9781554511228) Annick Pr., Ltd. CAN. Dist: Publishers Group West (PGW).

—My Friend Mei Jing. Frey, Ben, illus. Cheung, Irvin, photos by. 2009. (ENG.). 32p. (J). (gr. -1-1). 17.95 (978-1-55451-153-2(4), 9781554511532) Annick Pr., Ltd. CAN. Dist: Publishers Group West (PGW).

McRary, Janie. The Rock That Became a Friend. 2011. 24p. pap. 12.74 (978-1-4634-3018-4(3)) AuthorHouse.

McRitchie, Mike. Best Friends. 2009. 25p. 13.95 (978-0-578-03644-1(4)) McRitchie, Mike.

McSorley, Paul J. & Bearss, Patricia. The Adventures of Forealdo: Finding Millie. 2012. 34p. 24.95 (978-1-4626-6721-5(X)) America Star Bks.

McVeigh, Mark. Hello Kitty: Superterrific Sleepover! 2004. pap. (978-0-439-67634-2(7)) Scholastic, Inc.

McVoy, Terra Elan. Drive Me Crazy. (J). (gr. 3-7). 2016. 320p. pap. 6.99 (978-0-06-232244-9(3)) 2015. (ENG.). 288p. 16.99 (978-0-06-232243-2(5)) HarperCollins Pubs. (Tegen, Katherine Bks).

—In Deep. 2014. (ENG., Illus.). 304p. (YA). (gr. 9). 17.99 (978-1-4814-0136-4(X), Simon Pulse) Simon Pulse.

—Pure. (ENG.). (YA). 2010. 352p. (gr. 7). pap. 9.99 (978-1-4169-6748-4(6)) 2009. 336p. (gr. 9-18). 16.99 (978-1-4169-7872-5(0)) Simon Pulse. (Simon Pulse).

McWatt, Irene. Pongo-Peter: The Life & Thoughts of an Extraordinary Mongrel. 2007. 168p. per. (978-1-906210-00-7(4)) Grosvenor Hse. Publishing Ltd.

Meachen Rau, Dana. Sweet Pea: Escape in the Garden. Hannon, Holly, illus. 2006. (J). (978-1-58987-200-4(2)) Kindermusik International.

Mead, David. The Forgetful Little Leprechaun. Sharp, Chris, illus. 2011. 18p. (J). (gr. -1-1). bds. 10.99 (978-0-8249-1509-4(7), Ideal Pubns.) Worthy Publishing.

Mead, Richelle. Bloodlines. 2012. (Bloodlines Ser.: 1). (ENG.). 448p. (YA). (gr. 7-18). pap. 10.99 (978-1-59514-473-7(0), Razorbill) Penguin Young Readers Group.

—Spirit Bound. 2011. (Vampire Academy Ser.: 5). (ENG.). 512p. (YA). (gr. 7-18). 9.99 (978-1-59514-366-2(1), Razorbill) Penguin Young Readers Group.

Meade, L. T. A Modern Tomboy. 2011. 328p. 50.95 (978-1-258-06028-2(0)) Literary Licensing, LLC.

Meadows, Daisy. Ava the Sunset Fairy. 2011. (Illus.). 63p. (J). (978-0-545-38040-9(5)) Scholastic, Inc.

—Bella Tabbypaw I Trouble. 2015. (Magic Animal Friends Ser.: 4). lib. bdg. 14.75 (978-0-606-37048-6(X)) Turtleback Bks.

—Best Friends in Fairyland. 2010. (Scholastic Reader Level 2 Ser.). (ENG.). 32p. (J). (gr. 1-3). pap. 3.99 (978-0-545-22293-8(1), Cartwheel Bks.) Scholastic, Inc.

—Carly the School Fairy. 2015. (Rainbow Magic — Special Edition Ser.). lib. bdg. 17.20 (978-0-606-37774-4(3)) Turtleback Bks.

—Ellie Featherbill All Alone. 2015. (Magic Animal Friends Ser.: 3). lib. bdg. 14.75 (978-0-606-37047-9(1)) Turtleback Bks.

—Emily Prickleback's Clever Idea. 2016. (Magic Animal Friends Ser.: 6). (ENG.). 112p. (J). (gr. 2-5). pap. 4.99 (978-0-545-90743-9(8), Scholastic Paperbacks) Scholastic, Inc.

—Esther the Kindness Fairy (Friendship Fairies #1) 2017. (Friendship Fairies Ser.: 1). (ENG.). 80p. (J). (gr. 2-5). pap. 4.99 **(978-1-338-15767-3(1)**, Scholastic Paperbacks) Scholastic, Inc.

—Florence the Friendship Fairy. 2012. (Rainbow Magic Ser.). (ENG., Illus.). 176p. (J). (gr. 2-5). pap. 6.99 (978-0-545-45572-5(3), Scholastic Paperbacks) Scholastic, Inc.

—Florence the Friendship Fairy. 2012. (Rainbow Magic — Special Edition Ser.). lib. bdg. 17.20 (978-0-606-26754-0(9), Turtleback) Turtleback Bks.

—Grace Woollyhop's Musical Mystery. 2016. (Magic Animal Friends Ser.: 12). lib. bdg. 14.75 (978-0-606-38802-3(8)) Turtleback Bks.

—Grace Woollyhop's Musical Mystery (Magic Animal Friends #12) 2016. (Magic Animal Friends Ser.: 12). (ENG., Illus.). 112p. (J). (gr. 2-5). pap. 4.99 (978-0-545-94079-5(6), Scholastic Paperbacks) Scholastic, Inc.

—Lucy Longwhiskers Gets Lost. 2015. (Magic Animal Friends Ser.: 1). lib. bdg. 14.75 (978-0-606-37045-5(5)) Turtleback Bks.

—Lydia the Reading Fairy. 2016. (Rainbow Magic — the School Day Fairies Ser.: 3). lib. bdg. 14.75 (978-0-606-38791-0(9)) Turtleback Bks.

—Mary the Sharing Fairy. 2017. (Rainbow Magic — Friendship Fairies Ser.: 2). lib. bdg. 14.75 **(978-0-606-40176-0(8))** Turtleback Bks.

—Mimi the Laughter Fairy. 2017. (Rainbow Magic — Friendship Fairies Ser.: 3). lib. bdg. 14.75 **(978-0-606-40177-7(6))** Turtleback Bks.

—Mimi the Laughter Fairy (Friendship Fairies #3) 2017. (Friendship Fairies Ser.: 3). (ENG.). 80p. (J). (gr. 2-5). pap. 4.99 **(978-1-338-15769-7(8)**, Scholastic Paperbacks) Scholastic, Inc.

—Molly Twinkletail Runs Away. 2015. (Magic Animal Friends Ser.: 2). lib. bdg. 14.75 (978-0-606-37046-2(3)) Turtleback Bks.

—Olivia Nibblesqueak's Messy Mischief. 2016. (Magic Animal Friends Ser.: 9). (ENG., Illus.). 112p. (J). (gr. 2-5). pap. 4.99 (978-0-545-94076-4(1), Scholastic Paperbacks) Scholastic, Inc.

—Olivia Nibblesqueak's Messy Mischief. 2016. (Magic Animal Friends Ser.: 9). lib. bdg. 14.75 (978-0-606-38804-7(4)) Turtleback Bks.

Mealue, Monique. Johnny Goes Camping. 2011. 28p. pap. 15.99 (978-1-4634-2488-6(4)) AuthorHouse.

Mechling, Lauren & Moser, Laura. All Q, No A: More Tales of a 10th-Grade Social Climber. 2006. (ENG.). 288p. (YA). (gr. 7-12). pap. 15.95 (978-0-618-66378-1(9)) Houghton Mifflin Harcourt Publishing Co.

—Foreign Exposure: The Social Climber Abroad. 2007. (ENG.). 320p. (YA). (gr. 7-18). pap. 18.95 (978-0-618-66379-8(7)) Houghton Mifflin Harcourt Publishing Co.

Mechling, Lauren, et al. The Rise & Fall of a 10th Grade Social Climber. 2005. (ENG.). 304p. (YA). (gr. 7). pap. 16.99 (978-0-618-55519-2(6)) Houghton Mifflin Harcourt Publishing Co.

Meddaugh, Susan. Martha Speaks: Meet Martha (Picture Reader) 2010. (Martha Speaks Ser.). (ENG., Illus.). 24p. (J). (gr. -1-3). 12.99 (978-0-547-36904-4(2)) Houghton Mifflin Harcourt Publishing Co.

—Meet Martha. 2010. (Martha Speaks Ser.). (ENG., Illus.). 24p. (J). (gr. -1-3). pap. 3.99 (978-0-547-21079-7(5)) Houghton Mifflin Harcourt Publishing Co.

—Pool Party. 2011. (Martha Speaks Ser.). (ENG., Illus.). 24p. (J). (gr. -1-3). pap. 3.99 (978-0-547-43882-5(6)) Houghton Mifflin Harcourt Publishing Co.

—Purrfect Friends. 2012. (Martha Speaks Ser.). (ENG., Illus.). 24p. (J). (gr. -1-3). pap. 3.99 (978-0-547-68123-8(2)) Houghton Mifflin Harcourt Publishing Co.

—Summer Fun, 3 bks. in 1. 2013. (Martha Speaks Ser.). (ENG., Illus.). 72p. (J). (gr. -1-3). pap. 7.99 (978-0-547-97025-7(0)) Houghton Mifflin Harcourt Publishing Co.

Medearis, Angela Shelf. Best Friends Forever? Papp, Robert, illus. 2004. 124p. (J). (978-0-439-52330-1(3)) Scholastic, Inc.

Medina, Nico. Fat Hoochie Prom Queen. 2008. (ENG.). 320p. (YA). (gr. 9-18). pap. 8.99 (978-1-4169-3603-9(3), Simon Pulse) Simon Pulse.

—The Straight Road to Kylie. 2007. (ENG.). 320p. (YA). (gr. 9-12). pap. 9.99 *(978-1-4169-3600-8(9),* Simon Pulse) Simon Pulse.
Medina, Sylvia M. & B alloxk-Dixon, Saige J. Gorilla's Roar. Eagle, Joy, illus. 2012. 36p. pap. 11.49 *(978-0-9836602-5-5(5))* Green Kids Club, Inc.
Medina, Sylvia M. & Ballock-Dixon, Saige J. Desert Mirage. Eagle, Joy, illus. 2012. 32p. pap. 11.59 *(978-0-9836602-6-2(3))* Green Kids Club, Inc.
Medlen, Ellen. A Voice for Joey. 2010. 92p. pap. 12.99 *(978-1-4490-2144-3(1))* AuthorHouse.
Meeko's New Friend Little Play. (J). 6.98 *(978-0-7853-1336-6(2))* Publications International, Ltd.
Meeks, Jane. Finding Home. 2011. 24p. pap. 15.99 *(978-1-4653-6606-1(7))* Xlibris Corp.
Mehnert, Robert. Spelunkers. 2012. 108p. pap. 19.95 *(978-1-62709-036-0(3))* America Star Bks.
Mehrlich Iii, Ferdinand Paul. Splugworth Saves the Day, 1 vol. Mehrlich, Cynthia, illus. 2009. 43p. pap. 24.95 *(978-1-60836-765-8(7))* America Star Bks.
Meisel, Paul, illus. Good Night, Bat! Good Morning, Squirrel! 2016. (ENG.). 40p. (J). (gr. -1-3). 16.95 *(978-1-62979-495-2(3))* Boyds Mills Pr.
Meister, Cari. Beat Bugs. 2017. (I Can Read Level 1 Ser.). 32p. (J). (gr. -1-3). pap. 3.99 *(978-0-06-264069-7(0))* HarperCollins Pubs.
—Beat Bugs: Penny Lane. 2017. (I Can Read Level 1 Ser.). 32p. (J). (gr. -1-3). pap. 3.99 *(978-0-06-264071-0(2))* HarperCollins Pubs.
—The Grumpy Lobster, 1 vol. Harpster, Steve, illus. 2012. (Ocean Tales Ser.). (ENG.). 32p. (gr. 2-4). pap. 6.25 *(978-1-4342-4230-3(7));* lib. bdg. 22.65 *(978-1-4342-4025-5(8))* Stone Arch Bks.
—Moopy el Monstruo Subterráneo/Moopy the Underground Monster. Heck, Claudia M., tr. from ENG. Messner, Dennis, illus. 2012. (Los Amigos Monstruos/Monster Friends Ser.). (SPA & MUL.). 32p. (gr. 2-3). lib. bdg. 22.65 *(978-1-4342-3785-9(0),* Bilingual Stone Arch Readers) Stone Arch Bks.
—The Stranded Orca, 1 vol. Harpster, Steve, illus. 2012. (Ocean Tales Ser.). (ENG.). 32p. (gr. 2-4). pap. 6.25 *(978-1-4342-4232-7(3));* lib. bdg. 22.65 *(978-1-4342-4026-2(6))* Stone Arch Bks.
Meistle, Jarrod. Victor the Vampire. 2011. 28p. pap. 12.99 *(978-1-4628-4514-9(2))* Xlibris Corp.
Melchionno, Marion. Patty & the Little Ponies That Could: Hunt for the Collar of Sparkle. 2013. 28p. pap. 24.95 *(978-1-4626-9973-5(1))* America Star Bks.
—Patty & the Little Pony That Could. 2012. 44p. 24.95 *(978-1-4626-9475-4(6));* pap. 24.95 *(978-1-4626-7552-4(2))* America Star Bks.
Meldrum, Margaret. Peter Panda & His Friends. 2009. (Illus.). 24p. pap. 11.49 *(978-1-4343-7826-2(8))* AuthorHouse.
Melendez-Shafe, Yvette. The Adventures of Mudpie. 2009. 100p. pap. 28.99 *(978-1-4389-6616-8(4))* AuthorHouse.
_Meli, Ayani & D., Jessie. God Says I've Changed Your Dna: Walk As Children of the Light. Mallette, Dania, illus. 2013. 24p. pap. 12.00 *(978-0-9846315-7-5(7))* JWD Publishing.
Mello, Alondra. Alanora's Magic Tree: Alanora's Spirit Journey. 2007. 48p. per. 12.97 *(978-1-932344-77-6(2))* Thornton Publishing, Inc.
Mellom, Robin. The Classroom Trick Out My School! Gilpin, Stephen, illus. 2014. (Classroom Novel Ser.). (ENG.). 288p. (J). (gr. 3-7). 12.99 *(978-1-4231-5065-7(1))* Hyperion Bks. for Children.
Meloy, Colin. Wildwood Imperium: The Wildwood Chronicles, Book III. Ellis, Carson, illus. 2015. (Wildwood Chronicles Ser.: 3). (ENG.). 592p. (J). (gr. 3). pap. 9.99 *(978-0-06-202476-3(0))* HarperCollins Pubs.
Meloy, Maile. The Apprentices. Schoenherr, Ian, illus. 2014. (Apothecary Ser.: 2). (ENG.). 432p. (J). (gr. 5). pap. 8.99 *(978-0-14-242598-5(2),* Puffin Books) Penguin Young Readers Group.
Menard, Lucille. The Top of the Bottom: Inky to the Rescue, Volume 1. 2013. 38p. pap. 12.50 *(978-0-9887969-6-6(1))* Four Menards, The.
Menard, Lucille R. & Menard, Michele R. Inky the Talent Scout. 2013. 38p. pap. 12.75 *(978-0-9891734-2-1(9))* Four Menards, The.
Menard, Menard & Menard, Michele. Wood, You Be Real! 2013. 36p. pap. 11.95 *(978-0-9891734-0-7(2))* Four Menards, The.
Menard, Michele R. The Canopy House - Vol 2- Gus & Ester Meet the Neighbors. 2013. 34p. pap. 12.50 *(978-0-9891734-1-4(0))* Four Menards, The.
—Who Do I Think You Are? 2013. 26p. pap. 10.95 *(978-0-9887969-5-9(3))* Four Menards, The.
Menchin, Scott. What Are You Waiting For? Phelan, Matt, illus. 2017. (ENG.). 32p. (J). 16.99 *(978-1-62672-152-4(1),* 9781626721524) Roaring Brook Pr.
mendelsohn, martha. Bromley Girls. 2015. (ENG.). 192p. (YA). pap. 14.95 *(978-0-89672-922-3(2))* Texas Tech Univ. Pr.
Menge, Dawn. Queen Vernita Visits the Islands of Enchantment. 2011. (ENG.). 32p. (J). pap. 16.95 *(978-1-4327-7312-0(7))* Outskirts Pr., Inc.
—Queen Vernita's Visitors. Switzer, Bobbi, illus. 2008. 36p. pap. 19.95 *(978-1-59800-714-5(9))* Outskirts Pr., Inc.
Mercer, Rita C. Earl the Squatchem. 2007. 9.00 *(978-0-8059-8823-9(8))* Dorrance Publishing Co., Inc.
Merchant, Eryn. My Little Bumblebee. 2013. 28p. pap. 24.95 *(978-1-63000-675-4(0))* America Star Bks.
Meredith, Susan Markowitz. A New Friend: Set Of 6. 2011. (Early Connections Ser.). (J). 37.00 net. *(978-1-4108-1096-0(8))* Benchmark Education Co.
—Stump Hill. 2011. (Early Connections Ser.). (J). *(978-1-61672-670-6(9))* Benchmark Education Co.
Merialdo, Lee K. Kidnapped. 2006. 112p. pap. 10.95 *(978-0-7414-3407-4(5))* Infinity Publishing.
Meridith, Brenda C. She's Funny That Way. Meridith, Brenda C., ed. 2003. (C). 22.00 *(978-0-9723570-0-5(9))* Dahomey Publishing Co.
Merkel, Ruth Vitrano. Hannah's Girls: Elaine. 2008. (Hannah's Girls Ser.: 5). (Illus.). 176p. (J). pap. 9.99 *(978-0-8280-1955-2(X))* Review & Herald Publishing Assn.
—Hannah's Girls: Erin (Born 1988) 2009. (J). 9.99 *(978-0-8280-1956-9(8))* Review & Herald Publishing Assn.
Merrick, M.R. Endure. 2013. 382p. pap. *(978-0-9917862-4-4(6))* Merrick, M.R.
Merritt, Michael. Tack & Mame Book. 2012. 48p. pap. 20.00 *(978-1-105-80829-6(7))* Lulu Pr., Inc.
Mescall, Ron. The Adventures of Goo Goo Malou: A Parent's Guide for Teaching Values. 2009. 24p. pap. 10.96 *(978-1-4269-0836-1(9))* Trafford Publishing.
Mesrobian, Carrie. Cut Both Ways. (YA). (gr. 9). 2017. 368p. pap. 9.99 *(978-0-06-234989-7(9))* 2015. (ENG.). 352p. 17.99 *(978-0-06-234988-0(0))* HarperCollins Pubs.
Messenger, Shannon. Neverseen. (Keeper of the Lost Cities Ser.: 4). (ENG., Illus.). 688p. (J). (gr. 3-7). 2016. pap. 9.99 *(978-1-4814-3230-6(3))* 2015. 19.99 *(978-1-4814-3229-0(X))* Simon & Schuster Children's Publishing. (Aladdin).
Messimer, Wanda Fay. Tiny Teacup & Pot Belly Pig Go to Africa to Meet the 'Great Lion' 2013. 24p. pap. 24.95 *(978-1-4626-8736-7(9))* America Star Bks.
Messina, Leslie-Ann. The Adventures of Dolly the Dollar Bill: Dolly Meets Matilda. 2012. 32p. pap. 19.95 *(978-1-4772-9235-8(7))* AuthorHouse.
Messner, Kate. The Brilliant Fall of Gianna Z. (ENG.). 224p. 2017. (J). pap. 8.99 ***(978-1-68119-547-6(X),*** 9781681195476) 2010. (YA). (gr. 3-6). pap. 8.99 *(978-0-8027-2173-0(7),* 9780802721730) Bloomsbury Publishing USA. (Bloomsbury USA Childrens).
—The Brilliant Fall of Gianna Z. 2017. (J). lib. bdg. 19.65 ***(978-0-606-40595-9(X))*** Turtleback Bks.
—Fergus & Zeke. Ross, Heather, illus. 2017. (ENG.). 56p. (J). (gr. k-3). 14.99 *(978-0-7636-7846-3(5))* Candlewick Pr.
—Spitfire. 2007. (J). *(978-1-59531-018-7(5))* North Country Bks., Inc.
—Wake up Missing. 2014. (ENG.). 288p. (YA). (gr. 5-8). pap. 7.99 *(978-0-8027-3748-9(X),* 9780802737489, Bloomsbury USA Childrens) Bloomsbury Publishing USA.
Metz, Melinda. The Mars Mission Mayhem. McKenzie, Heath, illus. 2016. (S. M. A. R. T. S. Ser.). (ENG.). 128p. (gr. 3-6). pap. 9.95 *(978-1-4965-3018-9(7))* Stone Arch Bks.
—S. M. A. R. T. S. & the 3-D Danger. McKenzie, Heath, illus. 2015. (S. M. A. R. T. S. Ser.). (ENG.). 128p. (gr. 3-6). 22.65 *(978-1-4965-0465-4(8))* S.M.A.R.T.S. Learning System.
—S. M. A. R. T. S. & the Mars Mission Mayhem. McKenzie, Heath, illus. 2016. (S. M. A. R. T. S. Ser.). (ENG.). 128p. (gr. 3-6). lib. bdg. 22.65 *(978-1-4965-3016-5(0))* S.M.A.R.T.S. Learning System.
Metz, Teresa L. Friends for Phoebe. 2010. 43p. pap. 24.40 *(978-0-557-16884-2(8))* Lulu Pr., Inc.
Metzger, Steve. Big Shark's Valentine Surprise. Hohnstadt, Cedric, illus. 2007. (J). pap. *(978-0-439-92251-7(8))* Scholastic, Inc.
—The Biggest Leaf Pile. Dubin, Jill, illus. 2003. (J). *(978-0-439-55657-6(0))* Scholastic, Inc.
—Dancing Clock. Nez, John Abbott, illus. 2011. (ENG.). 32p. 12.95 *(978-1-58925-100-7(8));* (J). pap. 7.95 *(978-1-58925-429-9(5))* Tiger Tales.
—We're Going on a Leaf Hunt. Sakamoto, Miki, illus. 2008. (ENG.). 32p. (J). (gr. -1-3). pap. 6.99 *(978-0-439-87377-2(0),* Cartwheel Bks.) Scholastic, Inc.
Mewburn, Kyle. Hill & Hole Are Best Friends. Roberto, Anna, ed. Unka, Vasanti, illus. 2016. (ENG.). 40p. (J). 17.99 *(978-1-250-07637-3(4),* 9781250076373) Feiwel & Friends.
Meyer, Brad. A Matchless Age. 2006. 302p. pap. 29.95 *(978-1-4241-0523-6(4))* PublishAmerica, Inc.
Meyer, Bryce L. Dolphin & Manatee Friends End to End: Formerly Grant's Book of Manatees & Dolphins. 2009. 32p. pap. 16.99 *(978-1-4269-1678-6(7))* Trafford Publishing.
Meyer, Carolyn. Diary of a Waitress: The Not-So-Glamorous Life of a Harvey Girl. 2015. (ENG., Illus.). 288p. (J). (gr. 4). 17.95 *(978-1-62091-652-0(5),* Calkins Creek) Boyds Mills Pr.
Meyer, Linda. The Kid in My Closet. Roberts, Miranda, illus. 2008. (ENG.). 32p. (J). pap. 12.95 *(978-1-887542-94-4(9))* Book Pubs. Network.
Meyerhoff, Jenny. The Barftastic Life of Louie Burger. Week, Jason, illus. 2013. (Barftastic Life of Louie Burger Ser.: 1). (ENG.). 240p. (J). (gr. 3-6). 13.99 *(978-0-374-30518-5(8),* 9780374305185, Farrar, Straus & Giroux (BYR)) Farrar, Straus & Giroux.
—Class B. U. R. P. Week, Jason, illus. 2014. (Barftastic Life of Louie Burger Ser.: 2). (ENG.). 288p. (J). (gr. 3-6). 13.99 *(978-0-374-30521-5(8),* 9780374305215, Farrar, Straus & Giroux (BYR)) Farrar, Straus & Giroux.
—Green Thumbs-Up! Chatelain, Éva, illus. 2015. (Friendship Garden Ser.: 1). (ENG.). 176p. (J). (gr. 2-5). pap. 5.99 *(978-1-4814-3904-6(9),* Aladdin) Simon & Schuster Children's Publishing.
—Project Peep. Chatelain, Éva, illus. 2016. (Friendship Garden Ser.: 3). (ENG.). 144p. (J). (gr. 2-5). pap. 5.99 *(978-1-4814-3913-8(8),* Aladdin) Simon & Schuster Children's Publishing.
—Project Peep. 2016. (Friendship Garden Ser.: 3). lib. bdg. 16.00 *(978-0-606-38264-9(X))* Turtleback Bks.
—Pumpkin Spice. Chatelain, Éva, illus. 2015. (Friendship Garden Ser.: 2). (ENG.). 144p. (J). (gr. 2-5). pap. 5.99 *(978-1-4814-3909-1(X),* Aladdin) Simon & Schuster Children's Publishing.
—Pumpkin Spice. 2015. (Friendship Garden Ser.: 2). lib. bdg. 16.00 *(978-0-606-37833-8(2))* Turtleback Bks.
—Starry Skies & Fireflies. Chatelain, Éva, illus. 2016. (Friendship Garden Ser.: 4). (ENG.). 128p. (J). (gr. 2-5). pap. 5.99 *(978-1-4814-3917-6(0),* Aladdin) Simon & Schuster Children's Publishing.
—Sweet Peas & Honeybees. 2016. (Friendship Garden Ser.: 4). lib. bdg. 16.00 *(978-0-606-38978-5(4))* Turtleback Bks.
Meyers, Dolores. Herbie's New Home. 2011. 20p. pap. 24.95 *(978-1-60749-665-6(8))* America Star Bks.
M.H.Pruitt. The Adventures of Rexie the Bear. 2009. 16p. pap. 8.99 *(978-1-4490-4211-0(2))* AuthorHouse.
Mi Amigo Es un Flash-Flash. (Raton de Biblioteca Coleccion). (SPA.). (J). (gr. 3). pap. 7.95 *(978-84-88061-82-9(X))* Serres, Ediciones, S. L. ESP. Dist: Lectorum Pubns., Inc.
Mia's Recipe for Disaster. 2014. (Cupcake Diaries: 22). (ENG., Illus.). 160p. (J). (gr. 3-7). pap. 6.99 *(978-1-4814-1864-5(5),* Simon Spotlight) Simon Spotlight.
Micchelli, Lauren. I Love My Pet Elephant. 2015. (ENG., Illus.). 28p. (J). pap. 14.95 *(978-1-62287-880-2(9))* First Edition Design eBook Publishing.
Michael. Bedwin, 1 vol. David, Amanda, illus. 2009. (ENG.). 46p. 24.95 *(978-1-60813-258-4(7))* America Star Bks.
Michael-Angelo Goes to School. 2012. (Illus.). 34p. pap. 9.99 *(978-1-937107-10-9(8))* Morning Joy Media.
Michael Batdorf. Pair of Jacks: A Novel. 2009. 332p. 29.95 *(978-1-4401-4482-0(6));* pap. 19.95 *(978-1-4401-4479-0(6))* iUniverse, Inc.
Michaelides, M. Rainbow Angel. 2012. 120p. (gr. 4-6). 20.95 *(978-1-4759-6249-9(5));* pap. 10.95 *(978-1-4759-6248-2(7))* iUniverse, Inc.
Michaels, Anna. Best Friends. Karas, G. Brian, illus. 2004. 24p. (J). lib. bdg. 10.00 *(978-1-4242-0217-1(5))* Fitzgerald Bks.
—Best Friends. Karas, G. Brian, illus. 2004. (Green Light Readers Level 1 Ser.). (ENG.). 32p. (J). (gr. -1-3). pap. 3.95 *(978-0-15-205133-4(3))* Houghton Mifflin Harcourt Publishing Co.
Michaels, Kat. Willow's Bend. 2006. (Illus.). 24p. (J). (gr. -1-3). 15.95 *(978-0-9745052-6-8(9))* Tree Of Life Publishing.
Michalak, Jamie. Joe & Sparky Get New Wheels. Remkiewicz, Frank, illus. 2013. (Candlewick Sparks Ser.). (ENG.). 48p. (J). (gr. k-4). pap. 3.99 *(978-0-7636-6641-5(6))* Candlewick Pr.
—Joe & Sparky Go to School. Remkiewicz, Frank, illus. 2014. (Candlewick Sparks Ser.). (ENG.). 48p. (J). (gr. k-4). pap. 3.99 *(978-0-7636-7181-5(9))* Candlewick Pr.
—Joe & Sparky, Superstars! Remkiewicz, Frank, illus. (Candlewick Sparks Ser.). (ENG.). 48p. (J). (gr. k-4). 2013. pap. 3.99 *(978-0-7636-6642-2(4))* 2011. 15.99 *(978-0-7636-4578-6(8))* Candlewick Pr.
—Judy Moody & the Thrill Points Race. Candlewick Press Staff, illus. 2011. (Judy Moody Ser.). (ENG.). 48p. (J). (gr. k-3). pap. 3.99 *(978-0-7636-5552-5(X))* Candlewick Pr.
—Larry & Rita. Newton, Jill, illus. 2007. (Brand New Readers Ser.). (ENG.). 48p. (J). (gr. -1-3). 14.99 *(978-0-7636-2963-2(4))* Candlewick Pr.
Michels, Anna. 26 Kisses. 2016. (ENG.). (YA). (gr. 9). pap. 12.99 *(978-1-4814-8515-9(6))* Simon & Schuster.
Michelson, Richard. Across the Alley. Lewis, E. B., illus. 2006. (ENG.). 32p. (J). (gr. -1-3). 16.99 *(978-0-399-23970-0(7),* G.P. Putnam's Sons Books for Young Readers) Penguin Young Readers Group.
Michener, Tara. No Longer Besties: And Other Assorted Teenage Drama. 2011. 192p. (gr. 10-12). pap. 14.99 *(978-1-4634-0118-4(3))* AuthorHouse.
—100% Real: A Who I Am Book. 2009. 48p. pap. 17.99 *(978-1-4490-2027-9(5))* AuthorHouse.
Michiko Florence, Debbi. The Hunt for the Perfect Present. Roe, Monika, illus. 2016. (Dorothy & Toto Ser.). (ENG.). 40p. (gr. k-2). lib. bdg. 21.32 *(978-1-4795-8703-2(6))* Capstone Press of Coughlan Cos.
—Jasmine Toguchi, Super Sleuth. Vukovic, Elizabet, illus. 2017. (Jasmine Toguchi Ser.). (ENG.). 128p. (J). 15.99 *(978-0-374-30413-3(0),* 9780374304133, Farrar, Straus & Giroux (BYR)) Farrar, Straus & Giroux.
Micinilio, Leanne Plein. Tia's Troubles: The First in a series of Tia's Adventures. 2011. 40p. pap. 16.99 *(978-1-4490-4695-8(9))* AuthorHouse.
Mickles Sr., Robert T. S. Blood Kin, a Savannah Story. 2007. 108p. per. 9.95 *(978-0-595-45129-6(2))* iUniverse, Inc.
Middlemiss, David. The Great Hamstini. Middlemiss, Laura B., illus. 2010. 108p. *(978-1-907211-18-8(7))* Grosvenor Hse. Publishing Ltd.
Middleton, Dana. The Infinity Year of Avalon James. 2016. (ENG.). 224p. (J). 16.99 *(978-1-250-08569-6(1),* 9781250085696) Feiwel & Friends.
Middleton Gray, Family Np. Maddie Goes to the Nurse Practitioner. 2008. 32p. pap. 13.50 *(978-1-4389-0220-3(4))* AuthorHouse.
Middleton, Patricia T. Given Strength. 2013. 24p. pap. 14.95 *(978-1-4787-1028-8(4))* Outskirts Pr., Inc.
Middleton, Sydney Elise. Green Dog & Red Cat. 2011. 12p. 8.79 *(978-1-4567-2736-9(2))* AuthorHouse.
Midorikawa, Yuki. Natsume's Book of Friends. Midorikawa, Yuki, illus. 2010. (ENG., Illus.). Vol. 1. 208p. pap. 9.99 *(978-1-4215-3243-1(3))* Vol. 3. 200p. pap. 9.99 *(978-1-4215-3245-5(X))* Vol. 4. 200p. pap. 9.99 *(978-1-4215-3246-2(8))* Viz Media.
—Natsume's Book of Friends, Vol. 2. Midorikawa, Yuki, illus. 2010. (ENG., Illus.). 208p. pap. 9.99 *(978-1-4215-3244-8(1))* Viz Media.
Mifae. 2013. 200p. *(978-1-4602-2049-8(8))* FriesenPress.
Miglis, Jenny. And the Winner Is... Meurer, Caleb, illus. 2004. (SpongeBob SquarePants Ser.). (ENG.). 24p. (J). pap. 3.99 *(978-0-689-86327-1(6),* Simon Spotlight/Nickelodeon) Simon Spotlight/Nickelodeon.
Migy. And Away We Go! Migy, illus. 2014. (ENG., Illus.). 40p. (J). (gr. -1-1). 17.99 *(978-0-8050-9901-0(8),* 9780805099010, Holt, Henry & Co. Bks. For Young Readers) Holt, Henry & Co.
Mikkelsen, Jon. Storm Shelter. Lueth, Nathan, illus. 2008. (We Are Heroes Ser.). (ENG.). 40p. (gr. 2-3). lib. bdg. 23.99 *(978-1-4342-0787-6(0),* Keystone Bks.) Stone Arch Bks.
Milbourne, Anna. How High Is the Sky? Riglietti, Serena, illus. 2009. (Picture Bks.). 24p. (J). (gr. -1). 10.99 *(978-0-7945-2273-5(4),* Usborne) EDC Publishing.
Miles, Chris. Spurt. 2017. (ENG., Illus.). 272p. (J). (gr. 6-9). 16.99 *(978-1-4814-7972-1(5),* Simon & Schuster Bks. For Young Readers) Simon & Schuster Bks. For Young Readers.
Miles, Ellen. Lucky. 2010. (Puppy Place Ser.: 15). (ENG.). 96p. (J). (gr. 2-5). 4.99 *(978-0-545-08347-8(8),* Scholastic Paperbacks) Scholastic, Inc.
—Maggie & Max. 2008. (Puppy Place Ser.: 10). (ENG.). 96p. (J). (gr. 2-5). 4.99 *(978-0-545-03456-2(6),* Scholastic Paperbacks) Scholastic, Inc.
Miles, Lisa. Best Friends: Over 1000 Reusable Stickers! 2014. (Little Hands Creative Sticker Play Ser.). (ENG.). 64p. (J). (gr. -1-2). pap. 9.99 *(978-1-4380-0390-0(0))* Barron's Educational Series, Inc.
—Let's Be Friends! Follow the Reader Level 2. 2008. (Littlest Pet Shop Ser.). (ENG., Illus.). 24p. (J). (gr. -1-2). 24.99 *(978-1-4169-4994-7(1),* Simon Scribbles) Simon Scribbles.
Milford, Diana Viola. Fuzzum & Wuzzum, 1 vol. 2010. 34p. pap. 24.95 *(978-1-4489-9168-6(4))* PublishAmerica, Inc.
Milgrim, David. See Pip Point. Milgrim, David, illus. 2016. (Adventures of Otto Ser.). (ENG., Illus.). 32p. (J). (gr. -1-k). pap. 3.99 *(978-1-4814-6784-1(0),* Simon Spotlight) Simon Spotlight.
Mill, Lynda. Let's Meet Harry, Ted & Mike. 2013. 40p. pap. 19.57 *(978-1-4669-9321-1(9))* Trafford Publishing.
Millar, Martin. Lonely Werewolf Girl. 2008. (ENG.). 560p. per. *(978-0-9796636-6-6(0))* CSA Telltapes, Ltd.
Miller, Albert G. Fury & the White Mare. 2011. 186p. 42.95 *(978-1-258-07408-1(7))* Literary Licensing, LLC.
Miller, Amanda K. Lily's Grand Adventures. 2011. 36p. pap. 24.95 *(978-1-4626-2493-5(6))* America Star Bks.
Miller, Austin. Sam Is Special. 2011. (Early Connections Ser.). (J). *(978-1-61672-597-6(4))* Benchmark Education Co.
Miller, Bobbi. Miss Sally Ann & the Panther. Lloyd, Megan, illus. 2012. (ENG.). 32p. (J). 16.95 *(978-0-8234-1833-6(2))* Holiday Hse., Inc.
Miller, Chris & Miller, Allan. Hunter Brown & the Consuming Fire, 3 bks., Bk.2. 2009. (ENG., Illus.). 352p. (J). pap. 13.99 *(978-1-59317-357-9(1))* Warner Pr., Inc.
Miller, Christopher & Miller, Allan. Hunter Brown & the Secret of the Shadow, 3 bks., Bk.1. 2008. (ENG., Illus.). 384p. (J). (gr. 9-18). pap. 13.99 *(978-1-59317-328-9(8))* Warner Pr., Inc.
Miller, Ed, illus. Minions Paradise: Phil Saves the Day! 2016. (ENG.). 24p. (J). (gr. -1-3). pap. 5.99 *(978-0-316-39296-9(0))* Little, Brown Bks. for Young Readers.
Miller, H. James. Willy the Worm Gets Lost. 2011. 24p. pap. 15.99 *(978-1-4568-9801-4(9))* Xlibris Corp.
Miller, Holly & Schwartzkopf, Jere. A Horse Named Princess: Hola Princess Adios Thistle. 2009. 48p. pap. 17.49 *(978-1-4343-6976-5(5))* AuthorHouse.
Miller, Jennifer. Best Friends for Life. Choi Sung Hwan, Aragon Noel, illus. 2006. (Trollz Ser.). (ENG.). 120p. (J). pap. 4.99 *(978-0-439-80311-3(X))* Scholastic, Inc.
—Jennifer Miller's Run, Rasputin Run! Rasputin's Redemption (Book 3) 2007. (Illus.). 136p. per. 14.50 *(978-1-4251-1029-1(0))* Trafford Publishing.
—Run, Rasputin, Run! Trials & Friendships (Book 2) 2006. (ENG., Illus.). 172p. per. 14.85 *(978-1-4120-8494-9(6))* Trafford Publishing.
Miller, John. Winston & George. Cucco, Giuliano, illus. 2014. (ENG.). 56p. (J). (gr. k-3). 17.95 *(978-1-59270-145-2(0))* Enchanted Lion Bks., LLC.
Miller-Johnston, Renee. Courtney Logan Kennedy Presents Zoe. 2008. 76p. pap. 19.95 *(978-1-60703-558-9(8))* America Star Bks.
—Double Trouble for Courtney Logan Kennedy, 1 vol. 2009. 88p. pap. 19.95 *(978-1-60836-384-1(8))* America Star Bks.
Miller, Kymberly. My Mommy's Having a Baby. 2012. 36p. (-18). pap. 18.99 *(978-1-4772-8660-9(8))* AuthorHouse.
—There's a Secret at My House. 2012. 24p. pap. 16.99 *(978-1-4685-9618-2(7))* AuthorHouse.
Miller, Marie. The Great Complaint: Oh! What a Day! 2012. 20p. pap. 17.99 *(978-1-4772-2439-7(4))* AuthorHouse.
Miller, Mary Beth. Aimee. 2004. (ENG., Illus.). 288p. (YA). (gr. 7-18). 8.99 *(978-0-14-240025-8(4),* Speak) Penguin Young Readers Group.
—Aimee. 2005. 276p. (gr. 9-12). 17.00 *(978-0-7569-6303-3(6))* Perfection Learning Corp.
Miller, Mona. Hey, Buddy! Fruchter, Jason, illus. 2010. (Super Coloring Book Ser.). (ENG.). 96p. (J). (gr. -1-2). pap. 3.99 *(978-0-375-86155-0(6),* Golden Bks.) Random Hse. Children's Bks.
Miller, Mona. Poppy & Branch's Big Adventure. 2017. (Illus.). 32p. (J). ***(978-1-5182-3647-1(2))*** Random Hse., Inc.
Miller, Pat Zietlow. Sophie's Squash. Wilsdorf, Anne, illus. 2013. (ENG.). 40p. (J). (gr. -1-2). 16.99 *(978-0-307-97896-7(6),* Schwartz & Wade Bks.) Random Hse. Children's Bks.
—Sophie's Squash Go to School. Wilsdorf, Anne, illus. 2016. (ENG.). 40p. (J). (gr. -1-2). 17.99 *(978-0-553-50944-1(6),* Schwartz & Wade Bks.) Random Hse. Children's Bks.
Miller, Patricia. Tale of Polly Puffin. 2010. 30p. (J). pap. 14.95 *(978-1-4327-5231-6(6))* Outskirts Pr., Inc.
Miller, Paula K. Amy, Louise & Me. 2008. 24p. pap. 24.95 *(978-1-4241-9757-6(0))* America Star Bks.
Miller, Ray JR. & Miller, Ray. How Kris Became Claus. 2009. (Illus.). 20p. pap. 12.99 *(978-1-4389-7474-3(4))* AuthorHouse.
Miller, Sara. My Pod: Libro de Cuentos y Reproductor Personal de Musica. Peterson, Stacy & Maberry, Maranda, illus. 2007. (SPA.). 38p. (J). (gr. -1-3). *(978-970-718-495-4(7),* Silver Dolphin en Español) Advanced Marketing, S. de R. L. de C. V.
Miller, Sara F. A Gift for Pooh. 2012. (ENG.). 24p. (J). (gr. -1-1). pap. 4.99 *(978-1-4231-3592-0(X))* Disney Pr.
Miller, Tim. Moo Moo in a Tutu. Miller, Tim, illus. 2017. (Moo Moo & Mr. Quackers Book Ser.). (Illus.). 32p. (J). (gr. -1-3). 17.99 *(978-0-06-241440-3(2))* HarperCollins Pubs.
Miller, Tiwana Mutch. Praying Time. 2008. (YA). per. 10.00 *(978-0-9788937-8-1(6))* Amani Publishing, LLC.
Miller, Vern. Gypsy the Goat. Cotes Stanley, Marsha, illus. 2013. 36p. pap. 11.95 *(978-1-61153-082-7(2))* Light Messages Publishing.
Millman, Calanitte. The Adventures of the Gimmel Gang III: The Cave. 2005. (J). pap. 8.95 *(978-1-931681-84-1(8))* Israel Bookshop Pubns.
Millman, M. C. Always Something Else: The whimsical adventures of Elisheva Raskin. 2005. (Illus.). 160p. (J). 14.95 *(978-1-932443-23-3(1),* ASEH) Judaica Pr., Inc., The.
—Always Something Else 2. 2006. (Illus.). 160p. (J). 14.95 *(978-1-932443-43-1(6),* ASE2H) Judaica Pr., Inc., The.
Millner, Denene. Miss You, Mina. 2010. 163p. (J). pap. *(978-0-545-25106-8(0))* Scholastic, Inc.
Mills, Charles. Wings over Oshkosh. 2005. (Honors Club Story Ser.: Vol. 5). 127p. (J). 7.99 *(978-0-8163-2089-9(6))* Pacific Pr. Publishing Assn.
Mills, Claudia. Annika Riz, Math Whiz. Shepperson, Rob, illus. 2014. (Franklin School Friends Ser.: 2). 160p. (J). (gr. 2-5). 15.99 *(978-0-374-30335-8(5),* 9780374303358, Farrar, Straus & Giroux (BYR)) Farrar, Straus & Giroux.
—Being Teddy Roosevelt. Alley, R. W., illus. 2007. (ENG.). 96p. (J). (gr. 2-5). 16.99 *(978-0-374-30657-1(5),* 9780374306571, Farrar, Straus & Giroux (BYR)) Farrar, Straus & Giroux.
—Being Teddy Roosevelt. Alley, R. W., illus. 2012. (ENG.). 112p. (J). (gr. 2-5). pap. 8.99 *(978-0-312-64018-7(8),* 9780312640187) Square Fish.
—Cody Harmon, King of Pets. Shepperson, Rob, illus. 2016. (Franklin School Friends Ser.: 5). (ENG.). 144p. (J). 15.99

EFG

(978-0-374-30223-8(5), 9780374302238, Farrar, Straus & Giroux (BYR)) Farrar, Straus & Giroux.

—Izzy Barr, Running Star. Shepperson, Rob, illus. 2015. (Franklin School Friends Ser.: 3). (ENG.). 144p. (J). (gr. 2-5). 15.99 (978-0-374-33578-6(8), 9780374335786, Farrar, Straus & Giroux (BYR)) Farrar, Straus & Giroux.

—Mason Dixon: Fourth-Grade Disasters. Francis, Guy, illus. 2012. (Mason Dixon Ser.). (ENG.). 176p. (J). (gr. 4-7). 6.99 (978-0-375-87275-4(2), Yearling) Random Hse. Children's Bks.

—Pet Disasters. Francis, Guy, illus. 2012. (Mason Dixon Ser.). (ENG.). 176p. (J). (gr. 4-7). 6.99 (978-0-375-87274-7(4), Yearling) Random Hse. Children's Bks.

—The Trouble with Ants. Kath, Katie, illus. (Nora Notebooks Ser.: 1). (ENG.). 176p. (J). (gr. 2-5). 2016. 6.99 (978-0-385-39163-4(3), Yearling) 2015. lib. bdg. 17.99 (978-0-385-39162-7(5), Knopf Bks. for Young Readers) Random Hse. Children's Bks.

—The Trouble with Friends. Kath, Katie, illus. 2017. (Nora Notebooks Ser.). (ENG.). 192p. (J). (gr. 2-5). 12.99 (978-0-385-39169-6(2), Knopf Bks. for Young Readers) Random Hse. Children's Bks.

Mills, Emma. This Adventure Ends. 2016. (ENG.). 320p. (YA). 17.99 (978-1-62779-935-5(4), 9781627799355, Holt, Henry & Co. Bks. For Young Readers) Holt, Henry & Co.

Mills, Robert. Lump of Gump. 2012. 28p. pap. 24.95 (978-1-4626-7489-3(5)) America Star Bks.

Mills, Susan & Shara, Diana. Frankie & Her Little Pals - Save the Watermelons. 2007. 32p. (J). (978-0-9790690-3-1(3)) Lucky Red Pr., LLC.

Mills, Tessa L. The Adventures of Avery & Cali. 2007. 60p. per. 16.95 (978-1-4241-7982-4(3)) America Star Bks.

Mills, Wendy. Positively Beautiful. (ENG.). 368p. (YA). 2016. pap. 9.99 (978-1-68119-025-9(7), 9781681190259) 2015. (gr. 9). 17.99 (978-1-61963-341-4(8), 9781619633414) Bloomsbury Publishing USA. (Bloomsbury USA Childrens).

Milton, Nina. Tough Luck. 2013. 180p. pap. (978-1-909734-13-5(6)) ThornBerry Publishing UK.

Minarik, Else Holmelund. Los Amigos de Osito. Benavides, Rosa, tr. Sendak, Maurice, illus. 2nd ed. (Infantil Alfaguara Ser.: 32).Tr. of Little Bear's Friends. (SPA.). 64p. (J). 7.95 (978-84-204-3049-2(8)) Santillana USA Publishing Co., Inc.

Minchin, Adele. The Beat Goes On. 2007. (ENG.). 224p. (YA). (gr. 7). pap. 11.95 (978-1-4169-6755-2(9), Simon Pulse) Simon Pulse.

Mineuittie, Abike. Nandi & Masani. Jacques Huiswood, illus. 2011. 40p. pap. 24.95 (978-1-4560-2700-1(X)) America Star Bks.

Minter, J. The Insiders. 2004. (Insiders Ser.). (ENG.). 288p. (YA). (gr. 9-18). pap. 8.95 (978-1-58234-895-7(2), 9781582348957, Bloomsbury USA Childrens) Bloomsbury Publishing USA.

Minton, Ross. Baseball, from the Street to the Diamond, 1 vol. 2010. 94p. pap. 19.95 (978-1-4489-4918-2(1)) America Star Bks.

Minz-Kammer, Koda. Pinpot Tiger & the Lost Monkey. 2008. 54p. pap. 20.00 (978-0-557-01646-4(0)) Lulu Pr., Inc.

Miracle Mouse Cranky's Miracle. 2006. (J). lib. bdg. 19.95 (978-1-934017-00-5(0)) Hignites, Tom Miracle Studio.

Mire - Umm Mariam, Sahra. The Boy with One Ear. 2011. (Illus.). 44p. pap. 23.50 (978-1-4567-8336-5(X)) AuthorHouse.

Miro. The Watermelon Story. Brown, Nick, illus. 2003. 103p. (J). pap. (978-1-84426-258-8(8)) Upfront Publishing Ltd.

Misra, Michelle. Angel Wings: New Friends. 2013. (ENG., Illus.). 112p. (J). pap. 5.99 (978-0-85707-623-6(X)) Simon & Schuster, Ltd. GBR. Dist: Simon & Schuster, Inc.

—Birthday Surprise. Chaffey, Samantha, illus. 2016. (Angel Wings Ser.: 2). (ENG.). 128p. (J). (gr. 1-4). pap. 5.99 (978-1-4814-5800-9(0), Aladdin) Simon & Schuster Children's Publishing.

—New Friends. Chaffey, Samantha, illus. 2016. (Angel Wings Ser.: 1). (ENG.). 128p. (J). (gr. 1-4). pap. 5.99 (978-1-4814-5797-2(7), Aladdin) Simon & Schuster Children's Publishing.

Miss Karen. Precious Gets a Surprise. 2011. 12p. pap. 9.99 (978-1-4634-3160-0(0)) AuthorHouse.

Mitaro, S. Ciara. The Good Eggs. 2013. 104p. pap. 16.95 (978-1-4575-1837-9(6)) Dog Ear Publishing, LLC.

Mitchell, Carol. Another Day. Ward, Cherise, illus. 2013. 206p. pap. 8.99 (978-0-9899305-0-5(5)) CaribbeanReads.

mitchell, Ed. You never can tell what's least expected Most. 2008. 228p. pap. 16.95 (978-1-4092-2539-3(9)) Lulu Pr., Inc.

Mitchell, Lance B. The Penguin Adventures of Ping & Pong. 2008. 32p. pap. 24.95 (978-1-60474-124-7(4)) America Star Bks.

Mitchell, Laurence. Friends & Forgiving! Character Tales. 2009. 24p. pap. 12.00 (978-1-4389-5423-3(9)) AuthorHouse.

Mitchell, Racquel L. Penny Pincher Teaches: Tithing. 2011. 24p. pap. 16.99 (978-1-4670-2472-3(4)) AuthorHouse.

Mitchell, Stan R. Oskar & Myer at the Lake. 2013. 24p. pap. 24.95 (978-1-63000-414-9(6)) America Star Bks.

Mitchell, Taylor. Blue Bell. 2012. 28p. pap. 15.99 (978-1-4797-0292-3(7)) Xlibris Corp.

Mitchell, Trish. Noah Pals: Journey to the Apple Tree. 2011. 32p. pap. 16.99 (978-1-4567-9939-7(8)) AuthorHouse.

—Noah Pals: Noah & Friends Awesome Adventure. 2011. 56p. pap. 23.88 (978-1-4520-0459-4(5)) AuthorHouse.

Mith with an Itch. 2008. (Illus.). 34p. (J). 10.95 (978-0-9800259-0-3(7)) Dream Weaver Ministries, Inc.

Mittal, Anjali. The Convent Rules. 2009. (Illus.). 80p. pap. 10.49 (978-1-4389-8575-6(4)) AuthorHouse.

Mitter, Matt. Grouchy Hugs. Brannon, Tom, illus. 2012. (Hugs Book Ser.). (ENG.). 12p. (J). (gr. -1-k). bds. 10.99 (978-0-7944-2194-6(6)) Reader's Digest Assn., Inc., The.

Mitter, Matt & Peyo. I Smurf You! Peyo, illus. 2011. (Smurfs Classic Ser.). (ENG., Illus.). 14p. (J). (gr. -1-k). bds. 10.99 (978-1-4424-3606-0(9), Simon Spotlight) Simon Spotlight.

Mitton, Tony. Snowy Bear. Brown, Alison, illus. (ENG.). (J). 2016. 26p. bds. 7.99 (978-1-68119-084-6(2), 9781681190846) 2015. 32p. (gr. -1-1). 16.99 (978-1-61963-905-8(X), 9781619639058) Bloomsbury Publishing USA. (Bloomsbury USA Childrens).

Miyares, Daniel. That Neighbor Kid. Miyares, Daniel, illus. 2017. (ENG., Illus.). 32p. (J). (gr. -1-3). 17.99 (978-1-4814-4979-3(6), Simon & Schuster Bks. For Young Readers) Simon & Schuster Bks. For Young Readers.

Mizutani, Fuka. Love at Fourteen. 2015. (Love at Fourteen Ser.: 3). (ENG., Illus.). 192p. (J). (gr. 8-17). pap. 15.00 (978-0-316-29876-6(X), Yen Pr.) Orbit.

MJ Illustrations (Group) Staff, contrib. by. Marshall to the Rescue! 2016. (Illus.). (J). (978-1-4806-9669-3(2), Golden Bks.) Random Hse. Children's Bks.

Mjolhus, Joy. Squirrel Babies & Friends. 2008. 16p. pap. 24.95 (978-1-4241-8562-7(9)) America Star Bks.

Mlynowski, Sarah. Abby in Wonderland. 2017. (Whatever After Ser.). (ENG.). 256p. (J). (gr. 3-7). 16.99 (978-0-545-74664-9(7), Scholastic Pr.) Scholastic, Inc.

—Cold As Ice. 2015. (Whatever After Ser.: 6). (ENG.). 176p. (J). (gr. 3-7). pap. 5.99 (978-0-545-62736-8(2), Scholastic Pr.) Scholastic, Inc.

—Cold as Ice. 2014. (Whatever After Ser.: 6). (ENG.). 176p. (J). (gr. 3-7). 14.99 (978-0-545-62734-4(6), Scholastic Pr.) Scholastic, Inc.

Mlynowski, Sarah. I See London, I See France. 2017. 384p. (YA). (gr. 9). 17.99 (978-0-06-239707-2(9), HarperTeen) HarperCollins Pubs.

Moceanu, Dominique & Thompson, Alicia. Reaching High. 2012. (Go-For-Gold Gymnasts Ser.). (ENG.). 224p. (J). (gr. 5-9). pap. 5.99 (978-1-4231-3657-6(8)) Hyperion Pr.

Modern Publishing, creator. Wheels to the Rails! 2011. (Chuggington Ser.). (ENG., Illus.). (J). (gr. -1-3). 2.99 (978-0-7666-3981-2(9)) Modern Publishing.

Modica, Cathy & Van Eyck, Laura. Niik & Bling: The Friendship Begins. Modica, Cathy, photos by. l.t. ed. 2005. (Illus.). 40p. (J). 19.95 (978-0-9762466-0-2(0)) Wholesome Puppy Tales.

Moffett, Elzater. Tenan & Colleen: Who Is Harry? 2011. 36p. pap. 16.86 (978-1-4567-5378-8(9)) AuthorHouse.

Moffitt, Debra. Best Kept Secret. 2011. (Pink Locker Society Novels Ser.: 2). (ENG.). 128p. (J). (gr. 3-7). pap. 16.99 (978-0-312-64503-8(1), 9780312645038, St. Martin's Griffin) St. Martin's Pr.

Mohler, Marie. The Habit of Rabbits. 2008. 32p. 18.95 (978-1-4357-1992-7(1)) Lulu Pr., Inc.

Moiser, Liam. Moore Field School & the Mystery. 2013. 118p. pap. 10.95 (978-1-62516-787-3(3), Strategic Bk. Publishing) Strategic Book Publishing & Rights Agency (SBPRA).

Moisher, Phil. Long Before I Knew Better. 2011. 70p. pap. 19.95 (978-1-4560-4007-9(3)) America Star Bks.

Moldavsky, Goldy. No Good Deed. 2017. (ENG.). 352p. (J). (gr. 9). 17.99 (978-0-545-86751-1(7)) Scholastic, Inc.

Mollis Lindquist, Melody Rose. Oak Tree. 2009. 16p. pap. 10.99 (978-1-4490-0859-8(3)) AuthorHouse.

Molnar, Cheri Eplin. Dee Diddly Dragon Is Not a Wimp. Gutwein, Gwendolyn, illus. 2004. 32p. (J). per. 17.95 (978-0-9746330-3-9(8)) Anton Berkshire Publishing.

Monahan, Hillary. Bloody Mary, Book 2 Mary: Unleashed. 2015. (Bloody Mary Ser.). (ENG.). 256p. (YA). (gr. 7-12). 17.99 (978-1-4231-8539-0(0)) Hyperion Bks. for Children.

—Mary: The Summoning. 2014. (Bloody Mary Ser.). (ENG.). 256p. (YA). (gr. 7-12). 16.99 (978-1-4231-8519-2(6)) Hyperion Bks. for Children.

—Summoning. 2015. (Bloody Mary Ser.). (ENG.). 272p. (YA). (gr. 7-12). pap. 9.99 (978-1-4231-8693-9(1)) Hyperion Bks. for Children.

Moncure, Jane Belk. Little Too-Tall: A Book about Friendship. DeSantis, Susan, illus. 2013. (Magic Castle Readers Ser.). (ENG.). 32p. (J). (gr. -1-2). 25.64 (978-1-62323-568-0(5), 206303) Child's World, Inc., The.

—What Do You Do with a Grumpy Kangaroo? A Book about Feelings. Gallagher-Cole, Mernie, illus. 2013. (Magic Castle Readers Ser.). (ENG.). 32p. (J). (gr. -1-2). 25.64 (978-1-62323-589-5(8), 206324) Child's World, Inc., The.

A Monkey Ate My Homework. 2007. 32p. pap. 4.50 (978-0-8341-2287-1(1), 083-412-2871) Beacon Hill Pr. of Kansas City.

Monlongo, Jorge & Chabot, Jacob. Hello Kitty: Just Imagine. Monlongo, Jorge, illus. 2014. (ENG., Illus.). 64p. (J). pap. 7.99 (978-1-4215-7362-5(8)) Viz Media.

Monninger, Joseph. Finding Somewhere. 2012. (ENG.). 240p. (YA). (gr. 7). pap. 8.99 (978-0-375-89755-9(0), Ember) Random Hse. Children's Bks.

Monroe, Ayshia. Kiki: Doin' It, 1 vol. unabr. ed. 2012. (Juicy Central Ser.). (ENG.). 128p. (YA). (gr. 9-12). pap. 9.95 (978-1-61651-669-7(0)) Saddleback Educational Publishing, Inc.

—Mamyke - The Fake Date, 1 vol. unabr. ed. 2012. (Juicy Central Ser.). (ENG.). 130p. (YA). (gr. 9-12). pap. 9.95 (978-1-61651-667-3(4)) Saddleback Educational Publishing, Inc.

—Nishell; Tempted, 1 vol. unabr. ed. 2012. (Juicy Central Ser.). (ENG.). 127p. (YA). (gr. 9-12). pap. 9.95 (978-1-61651-670-3(4)) Saddleback Educational Publishing, Inc.

—Sherise: Stalked, 1 vol. unabr. ed. 2012. (Juicy Central Ser.). (ENG.). 127p. (YA). (gr. 9-12). pap. 9.95 (978-1-61651-668-0(2)) Saddleback Educational Publishing, Inc.

—Tia; Diva. unabr. ed. 2012. (Juicy Central Ser.). (ENG.). 126p. (YA). (gr. 9-12). pap. 9.95 (978-1-61651-671-0(2)) Saddleback Educational Publishing, Inc.

Monroe, Ella. Secrets & Lies: A Capital Girls Novel. 2012. (Capital Girls Ser.: 2). (ENG.). 320p. (YA). (gr. 8). pap. 21.99 (978-0-312-62305-0(4), St. Martin's Griffin) St. Martin's Pr.

—Truth or Dare. 2013. (Capital Girls Ser.: 3). (ENG.). 304p. (YA). (gr. 8). pap. 20.99 (978-0-312-62304-3(6), 9780312623043, St. Martin's Griffin) St. Martin's Pr.

Montgomery Gibson, Jane. My Christmas Friend. Montgomery Gibson, Jane, illus. 2005. (Illus.). (YA). bds. 8.99 (978-1-4183-0066-1(7)) Christ Inspired, Inc.

Montgomery, L. M. Anne of Green Gables. 400p. 2005. 33.95 (978-1-4218-0660-0(6), 1st World Library - Literary Society) 2004. per. 16.95 (978-1-59540-110-6(5)) 1st World Publishing, Inc.

—Anne of Green Gables. 2009. 292p. 27.99 (978-1-60512-375-2(7)); pap. 14.99 (978-1-60512-475-9(3)) Akasha Publishing, LLC. (Akasha Classics).

—Anne of Green Gables. 2008. 316p. 29.99 (978-0-554-23545-5(5)) 2008. 316p. 28.99 (978-0-554-32848-5(8)) 2007. (ENG.). 312p. pap. 24.99 (978-1-4264-4662-7(4)) Creative Media Partners, LLC.

—Anne of Green Gables. 2008. (Anne of Green Gables Ser.). (ENG.). 366p. (J). (gr. 4-7). pap. 9.95 (978-0-9782552-6-8(7)) Davenport Pr. CAN. Dist: Independent Pubs. Group.

—Anne of Green Gables. 2007. per. 6.99 (978-1-4209-2922-5(4)) Digireads.com Publishing.

—Anne of Green Gables. 2007. 284p. per. (978-1-4065-6399-3(4)) Dodo Pr.

—Anne of Green Gables. 2007. 572p. (978-1-84702-773-3(3)) 2006. pap. (978-1-4068-2170-3(5)) Echo Library.

—Anne of Green Gables. 2008. 316p. pap. 16.95 (978-1-60096-565-4(2)); pap. 16.95 (978-1-60096-101-4(0)) Editorium, The.

—Anne of Green Gables. 2009. 242p. pap. 8.58 (978-0-217-43952-7(7)) General Bks. LLC.

—Anne of Green Gables. 2005. (My First Classics Ser.). 112p. (J). (gr. k-3). pap., pap. 4.99 (978-0-06-079147-6(0), HarperFestival) HarperCollins Pubs.

—Anne of Green Gables. 2005. 21.99 (978-1-4142-5125-7(4)) IndyPublish.com.

—Anne of Green Gables. 2008. (ENG.). 376p. (gr. k-12). pap. 14.95 (978-0-7710-9368-5(3), New Can Library) McClelland & Stewart CAN. Dist: Penguin Random Hse. LLC.

—Anne of Green Gables, 1 vol. 2016. (ENG.). 352p. (J). (gr. 2-5). pap. 10.95 (978-1-55109-249-2(2)) Nimbus Publishing, Ltd. CAN. Dist: National Bk. Network.

—Anne of Green Gables. Rubio, Mary Henley & Waterston, Elizabeth, eds. 2007. (Norton Critical Editions Ser.: 0). (ENG., Illus.). 464p. (C). (gr. 9-12). per. 15.02 (978-0-393-92695-8(8), 92695) Norton, W. W. & Co., Inc.

—Anne of Green Gables. 2003. (ENG.). 320p. (gr. 5-7). 5.95 (978-0-451-52882-7(4), Signet) Penguin Publishing Group.

—Anne of Green Gables. 2008. (Puffin Classics Ser.). (ENG., Illus.). 464p. (J). (gr. 3-7). 5.99 (978-0-14-132159-2(8), Puffin Books) Penguin Young Readers Group.

—Anne of Green Gables. 2003. 320p. (J). (gr. 4-7). 12.60 (978-0-7569-1848-4(0)) Perfection Learning Corp.

—Anne of Green Gables. 2013. (Word Cloud Classics Ser.). (ENG.). 264p. pap. 14.99 (978-1-60710-728-6(7), Thunder Bay Pr.) Readerlink Distribution Services, LLC.

—Anne of Green Gables. 2009. 224p. pap. 15.45 (978-1-4385-1847-3(1), Book Jungle) Standard Pubns., Inc.

—Anne of Green Gables. McKowen, Scott, illus. 2004. (Sterling Unabridged Classics Ser.). (ENG.). 312p. (J). (gr. 5). 9.95 (978-1-4027-1451-1(3)) Sterling Publishing Co., Inc.

—Anne of Green Gables. Corvino, Lucy, illus. 2005. (Classic Starts(tm) Ser.). (ENG.). 160p. (J). (gr. 2-4). 6.95 (978-1-4027-1130-5(1)) Sterling Publishing Co., Inc.

—Anne of Green Gables. 2008. (Modern Library Classics Ser.). (ENG.). 320p. pap. 9.00 (978-0-8129-7903-9(6), Modern Library) Random House Publishing Group.

—Anne of Green Gables. rev. ed. 2007. 280p. pap. 21.99 (978-1-4264-4611-5(X)) Creative Media Partners, LLC.

—Anne of Green Gables. l.t. ed. 2006. pap. (978-1-4068-3174-0(3)) Echo Library.

—Anne of Green Gables. 2004. reprint ed. pap. 27.95 (978-1-4191-0717-7(8)); pap. 1.99 (978-1-4192-0717-4(2)) Kessinger Publishing, LLC.

—Anne of Green Gables. l.t. ed. 2009. (World Classics Ser.). 288p. pap. 21.95 (978-1-59688-123-5(2)) Large Print Bk. Co., The.

—The Anne of Green Gables Collection: Six Complete & Unabridged Novels in One Volume. 2013. 1140p. (978-1-78139-344-4(3)) Benediction Classics.

—Anne of the Island. 2008. (Anne of Green Gables Ser.). (ENG.). 272p. (J). (gr. 4-7). pap. 9.95 (978-0-9782552-8-2(3)) Davenport Pr. CAN. Dist: Independent Pubs. Group.

—Emily Climbs. 2009. (ENG.). 376p. pap. 16.95 (978-0-7710-9382-1(9), New Can Library) McClelland & Stewart CAN. Dist: Random Hse., Inc.

—Magic for Marigold. 2014. (ENG.). 336p. (YA). (gr. 5-12). pap. 8.99 (978-1-4022-8921-7(9)) Sourcebooks, Inc.

Montgomery, L. M & Castelao, Patricia. Anne of Green Gables, 1 vol. 2012. (Calico Illustrated Classics Ser.: No. 4). (ENG., Illus.). 112p. (J). (gr. 3-6). 27.07 (978-1-61641-612-6(2)) Magic Wagon.

Montgomery, Ross. Perijee & Me. 2016. (ENG.). 224p. (J). (gr. 3-7). 16.99 (978-0-399-55397-4(5), Lamb, Wendy Bks.) Random Hse. Children's Bks.

Moody, Gloria. Two Beautiful Butterflies. Doering, Kimber, illus. l.t. ed. 2005. 25p. (YA). per. 8.99 (978-1-59879-002-3(1)) Lifevest Publishing, Inc.

Moon, Nicola. Margarine & Marbles. 2005. (Red Go Bananas Ser.). (ENG., Illus.). 48p. (J). (gr. 2-3). lib. bdg. (978-0-7787-2676-0(2)) Crabtree Publishing Co.

Moon, Poppy, illus. Kicky's Friendship Card Game. 2011. (J). 17.95 (978-1-59850-097-4(X)) Youthlight, Inc.

Moonbeam: The Little Elephant. 2005. (Illus.). 32p. (J). 16.95 (978-0-9763596-0-9(X)) BOOKGEMSFORKIDS.

Moore, Debbie. Penelope, the Peculiar Purple Porpoise. 2011. 48p. pap. 24.95 (978-1-4560-6577-5(7)) America Star Bks.

Moore, Inga. A House in the Woods. 2011. (ENG., Illus.). 48p. (J). (gr. -1-2). 16.99 (978-0-7636-5277-7(6)) Candlewick Pr.

Moore, Julianne. Best Friends Forever. Pham, LeUyen, illus. (Freckleface Strawberry Ser.). (ENG.). 40p. (J). (gr. -1-3). 2011. 17.89 (978-1-59990-552-5(3), 9781599905525) 2011. 16.99 (978-1-59990-551-8(5), 9781599905518) 2007. 17.99 (978-1-59990-107-7(2), 9781599901077) Bloomsbury Publishing USA. (Bloomsbury USA Childrens).

—Best Friends Forever. 2015. (CHI.). 40p. (J). (gr. -1-8). pap. (978-7-5133-1778-8(X)) New Star Publishing Hse.

—Best Friends Forever. Pham, LeUyen, illus. (Step into Reading Ser.). (ENG.). 32p. (J). (gr. -1-1). 2017. 15.99 (978-0-375-97369-7(9), Random Hse. Bks. for Young Readers) 2016. 12.99 (978-0-385-39198-6(6), Doubleday Bks. for Young Readers) 2016. pap. 3.99 (978-0-385-39197-9(8), Random Hse. Bks. for Young Readers) Random Hse. Children's Bks.

—Freckleface Strawberry: Monster Time! Pham, LeUyen, illus. 2017. (Step into Reading Ser.). (ENG.). 32p. (J). (gr. -1-1). pap. 3.99 (978-0-385-39200-6(1), Random Hse. Bks. for Young Readers) Random Hse. Children's Bks.

—Freckleface Strawberry: Backpacks! Pham, LeUyen, illus. 2015. (Step into Reading Ser.). (ENG.). 32p. (J). (gr. -1-1). lib. bdg. 15.99 (978-0-375-97367-3(2), Random Hse. Bks. for Young Readers) Random Hse. Children's Bks.

—Freckleface Strawberry: Lunch, or What's That? Pham, LeUyen, illus. 2015. (Step into Reading Ser.). (ENG.). 32p. (J). (gr. -1-1). lib. bdg. 15.99 (978-0-375-97366-6(4), Random Hse. Bks. for Young Readers) Random Hse. Children's Bks.

Moore, Kelly, et al. Amber House. 2012. (Amber House Ser.: 1). (ENG.). 368p. (J). (gr. 9). 17.99 (978-0-545-43416-4(5), Levine, Arthur A. Bks.) Scholastic, Inc.

Moore, Lorraine. Lidoo Woodo's Goes to Daycare. 2012. 28p. pap. 21.99 (978-1-4691-6576-9(7)) Xlibris Corp.

Moore, Roland D. Bugging in the City. 2011. 80p. pap. 32.26 (978-1-4567-4130-3(6)) AuthorHouse.

Moore, S. D. The Adventures of Pj & Split Pea. Switzer, Bobbi, illus. 2008. 36p. per. 12.95 (978-1-4327-1288-4(8)) Outskirts Pr., Inc.

Moore, Stephanie Perry. Equally Yoked, Vol. 3. 2003. (Laurel Shadrach Ser.: 3). (ENG.). 192p. (YA). (gr. 8). pap. 7.99 (978-0-8024-4037-2(1)) Moody Pubs.

—True Friends. 2005. (Carmen Browne Ser.: 1). (ENG.). 128p. (YA). pap. 6.99 (978-0-8024-8172-6(8), Lift Every Voice) Moody Pubs.

Moore, Stephanie Perry & Moore, Stephanie. The Way We Roll. 2009. (ENG., Illus.). 224p. (YA). (gr. 9). 9.95 (978-0-7582-3443-8(0), K-Teen/Dafina) Kensington Publishing Corp.

Moore, Thomas. Zoe & the Back Yard Boys: The Magic Garden Haunted House Adventure. 2012. 24p. pap. 17.99 (978-1-4772-9086-6(9)) AuthorHouse.

Moore, Victor L. The Pentacle of Northumbria. 2013. 432p. pap. (978-1-78222-073-2(9)) Paragon Publishing, Rothersthorpe.

Moore, Wes & Goodman, Shawn. This Way Home. 2015. (ENG.). 256p. (YA). (gr. 9). 20.99 (978-0-375-99019-9(4), Delacorte Pr.) Random Hse. Children's Bks.

Moores, Susanna. It's Not Yours, It's Mine! Moores, Susanna, illus. 2013. (Child's Play Library). (ENG., Illus.). 32p. (J). (gr. -1-2). (978-1-84643-600-0(1)) Child's Play International Ltd.

Moracho, Cristina. Althea & Oliver. 2014. (ENG.). 384p. (YA). (gr. 9). 17.99 (978-0-670-78539-1(3), Viking Books for Young Readers) Penguin Young Readers Group.

—Althea & Oliver. 2016. lib. bdg. 22.10 (978-0-606-37577-1(5)) Turtleback Bks.

Morah, Chizoba. The Anderson Twins. 2007. 76p. per. 19.95 (978-1-60441-015-0(9)) America Star Bks.

Moraja, Melissa Perry. Madison & G. A. - a Tale of the Slimy Spitball. Moraja, Melissa Perry, illus. 2012. (Illus.). 94p. pap. (978-0-9834751-7-0(2)) Roxby Media Ltd.

Moran, Alex. Boots for Beth. Ernst, Lisa Campbell, illus. 2003. (Green Light Readers Level 2 Ser.). (ENG.). 24p. (J). (gr. -1-3). pap. 3.95 (978-0-15-204838-9(3)) Houghton Mifflin Harcourt Publishing Co.

—Sam & Jack: Three Stories. Bowers, Tim, illus. 2003. (Green Light Readers Level 1 Ser.). (ENG.). 24p. (J). (gr. -1-3). pap. 3.95 (978-0-15-204862-4(6)) Houghton Mifflin Harcourt Publishing Co.

Moran, Kelly. The Tiny Caterpillar & the Great Big Tree. 2009. 50p. pap. 19.50 (978-0-557-09498-1(4)) Lulu Pr., Inc.

Mörchen, Roland. Wir Gehen in Die Bibliothek - A Visit to the Library: Deutsch-Englische Ausgabe. Kiefer, Katja, illus. 2010. (ENG.). 40p. (J). (gr. 3-7). 19.99 (978-3-487-08843-3(6)) Olms, Georg Verlag AG DEU. Dist: Independent Pubs. Group.

Moreira, Carol. Membrane, 1 vol. 2013. (ENG.). 269p. pap. (978-1-927746-05-9(1)); 282p. pap. (978-1-927746-04-2(3)) Fierce ink Pr. Co-Op, Ltd.

Morelli, Yamile, tr. Me Robaron a Mi Mejor Amig. 2012. 138p. pap. 5.99 (978-0-9831557-3-7(9)) WordWorks Publishing.

Morello, Jill. Lily Goes to School. 2010. 28p. pap. 13.99 (978-1-4490-6218-7(0)) AuthorHouse.

Morey, Walt. Gentle Ben. Schoenherr, John, illus. 2006. (ENG.). 192p. (J). (gr. 3-7). 6.99 (978-0-14-240551-2(5), Puffin Books) Penguin Young Readers Group.

Morgan, Alex. Hat Trick. 2015. (Kicks Ser.). (ENG., Illus.). 128p. (J). (gr. 3-7). 16.99 (978-1-4814-5096-6(4), Simon & Schuster Bks. For Young Readers) Simon & Schuster Bks. For Young Readers.

—Sabotage Season. (Kicks Ser.). (ENG., Illus.). (J). (gr. 3-7). 2014. 192p. pap. 6.99 (978-1-4424-8576-1(0)) 2013. 176p. 15.99 (978-1-4424-8574-7(4)) Simon & Schuster Bks. For Young Readers. (Simon & Schuster Bks. For Young Readers).

—Settle the Score. 2016. (Kicks Ser.). (ENG., Illus.). 128p. (J). (gr. 3-7). 16.99 (978-1-4814-5104-8(9), Simon & Schuster Bks. For Young Readers) Simon & Schuster Bks. For Young Readers.

—Under Pressure. 2017. (J). pap. (978-1-4814-8151-9(7)); (ENG., Illus.). 128p. (gr. 3-7). 16.99 (978-1-4814-8150-2(9)) Simon & Schuster Bks. For Young Readers. (Simon & Schuster Bks. For Young Readers).

Morgan, Alex. Win or Lose. 2014. (Kicks Ser.). (ENG., Illus.). 160p. (J). (gr. 3-7). 15.99 (978-1-4424-8580-8(9), Simon & Schuster Bks. For Young Readers) Simon & Schuster Bks. For Young Readers.

Morgan, Anna & Turkienicz, Rachael. My (Worst) Best Sleepover Party, 1 vol. 2007. (ENG., Illus.). 128p. (J). (gr. 2-5). pap. 7.95 (978-1-897187-20-3(3)) Second Story Pr. CAN. Dist: Orca Bk. Pubs. USA.

Morgan, Gloria. Dream Me Home. 2012. 294p. pap. 13.50 (978-1-84426-661-6(3), Fastprint Publishing) Upfront Publishing Ltd. GBR. Dist: Printondemand-worldwide.com.

Morgan, Kristy. The Adventures of Rocky & Skeeter: Rocky Goes to Jail. 2011. 52p. pap. 8.95 (978-1-4620-2219-9(7)) iUniverse, Inc.

Morgan, Mary. Hear Me Squeak! 2009. 24p. pap. 11.84 (978-1-4389-4632-0(5)) AuthorHouse.

Morgan, Mary Sue. Swifty. 2008. 24p. pap. 24.95 (978-1-60441-579-7(7)) America Star Bks.

Morgan, Melissa J. Alex's Challenge. 2005. (Camp Confidential Ser.: 4). (ENG.). 160p. (J). (gr. 3-7). mass mkt. 4.99 (978-0-448-43876-4(3), Grosset & Dunlap) Penguin Young Readers Group.

—Best (Boy) Friend Forever. 2006. (Camp Confidential Ser.: 9). (ENG.). 160p. (J). (gr. 3-7). pap. 4.99 (978-0-448-44325-6(2), Grosset & Dunlap) Penguin Young Readers Group.

—Extra Credit. 2009. (Camp Confidential Ser.: 22). (ENG.). 160p. (J). (gr. 4-7). pap. 4.99 (978-0-448-45216-6(2), Grosset & Dunlap) Penguin Young Readers Group.

—A Fair to Remember. 2007. (Camp Confidential Ser.: 13). (ENG.). 160p. (J). (gr. 3-7). pap. 4.99 (978-0-448-44451-2(8), Grosset & Dunlap) Penguin Young Readers Group.

—Falling in Like. 2006. (Camp Confidential Ser.: 11). (ENG.). 160p. (J). (gr. 3-7). pap. 4.99 (978-0-448-44391-1(0), Grosset & Dunlap) Penguin Young Readers Group.

—Golden Girls. 2007. (Camp Confidential Ser.: 16). (ENG.). 160p. (J). (gr. 3-7). pap. 4.99 (978-0-448-44541-0(7), Grosset & Dunlap) Penguin Young Readers Group.

—Grace's Twist. 2005. (Camp Confidential Ser.: 3). (ENG.). 160p. (J). (gr. 3-7). mass mkt. 4.99 (978-0-448-43875-7(5), Grosset & Dunlap) Penguin Young Readers Group.

—Over & Out. 2006. (Camp Confidential Ser.: 10). (ENG.). 160p. (J). (gr. 3-7). pap. 4.99 (978-0-448-44326-3(0), Grosset & Dunlap) Penguin Young Readers Group.

—Politically Incorrect. 2010. (Camp Confidential Ser.: 23). (ENG.). 176p. (J). (gr. 3-7). pap. 4.99 (978-0-448-45267-8(7), Grosset & Dunlap) Penguin Young Readers Group.

—Reality Bites, 15 vols. 2007. (Camp Confidential Ser.: 15). (ENG.). 160p. (J). (gr. 3-7). pap. 4.99 (978-0-448-44539-7(5), Grosset & Dunlap) Penguin Young Readers Group.

—RSVP. 2005. (Camp Confidential Ser.: 6). (ENG., Illus.). 160p. (J). (gr. 3-7). pap. 4.99 (978-0-448-43962-4(X), Grosset & Dunlap) Penguin Young Readers Group.

—Suddenly Last Summer. 2008. (Camp Confidential Ser.: 20). (ENG.). 160p. (J). (gr. 3-7). pap. 4.99 (978-0-448-44881-7(5), Grosset & Dunlap) Penguin Young Readers Group.

—Topsy-Turvy. 2010. (Camp Confidential Ser.: 24). (ENG.). 160p. (J). (gr. 3-7). pap. 4.99 (978-0-448-45372-9(X), Grosset & Dunlap) Penguin Young Readers Group.

—Wish You Weren't Here. 2006. (Camp Confidential Ser.: 8). (ENG.). 160p. (J). (gr. 4-7). pap. 4.99 (978-0-448-44266-2(3), Grosset & Dunlap) Penguin Young Readers Group.

Morgan, Melissa J. & Morgan, Melissa. Super Special No. 21. 2009. (Camp Confidential Ser.: 21). (ENG.). 256p. (J). (gr. 4-7). pap. 5.99 (978-0-448-45187-9(5), Grosset & Dunlap) Penguin Young Readers Group.

Morgan, Michaela. Band of Friends. Price, Nick, illus. 2005. (ENG.). 24p. (J). lib. bdg. 23.65 (978-1-59646-734-7(7)) Dingles & Co.

—Shy Shark. Gomez, Elena, illus. 2005. (ENG.). 24p. (J). lib. bdg. 23.65 (978-1-59646-722-4(3)) Dingles & Co.

Morgan, Michelle. Colorsaurus. 2009. 32p. pap. 18.00 (978-0-557-06120-4(2)) Lulu Pr., Inc.

Morgan, Nicola. The Highwayman's Curse. 2009. (J). (978-0-7636-4066-8(2)) Candlewick Pr.

Morgan, Winter. Skeleton Battle: The Unofficial Minecrafters Academy Series, Book Two. 2016. (Unofficial Minecrafters Academy Ser.). (ENG.). 112p. (J). (gr. 1-7). pap. 7.99 (978-1-5107-0595-1(3), Sky Pony Pr.) Skyhorse Publishing Co., Inc.

Morgante, Roxanne & Callies, Pat. Justin & Travis: Games They Play, 1 vol. 2010. 62p. pap. 19.95 (978-1-4489-4458-3(9)) PublishAmerica, Inc.

Moricz-Goodwin, Jennifer. Keys. 2004. 131p. (YA). per. 9.95 (978-0-9716442-3-6(3)) Jackson Publishing.

Morin, James F. Rothshield Chasing Shadows. 2006. pap. 14.95 (978-1-59330-422-5(6)) Aventine Pr.

Morley, Elizabeth. Let Sleeping Hedgehogs Spy. 2013. (Illus.). 154p. pap. (978-1-78299-107-6(7)) FeedARead.com.

Morningstar, Jeremy. Penalty Kick. 2005. 56p. pap. 9.00 (978-1-4116-6572-9(4)) Lulu Pr., Inc.

Moroney, Tracey, illus. A Snowman for Little Bear. 2016. (J). **(978-0-545-84958-6(6))** Scholastic, Inc.

Morpurgo, Michael. The War of Jenkins' Ear. 2nd ed. 2017. (ENG.). 192p. (J). (gr. 5-7). pap. 9.99 **(978-1-4052-2672-1(2))** Egmont Bks., Ltd. GBR. Dist: Independent Pubs. Group.

Morrall, Heather. Echo Glass. 2006. 192p. (YA). (gr. 7-18). pap. (978-0-9554252-0-2(4)) Rubery Pr.

Morris, Jennifer E. Ice Cream Shop. 2014. (Scholastic Reader Level 1 Ser.). lib. bdg. 13.55 (978-0-606-35819-4(6)) Turtleback Bks.

—Scholastic Reader Level 1: the Sea Monster: A Steve & Wessley Reader. 2014. (Scholastic Reader Level 1 Ser.). (ENG., Illus.). 32p. (J). (gr. -1-2). pap. 3.99 (978-0-545-61482-5(1)) Scholastic, Inc.

Morris, Lolita. Mike & Me-Sh. 2012. 24p. pap. 14.93 (978-1-4669-6169-2(4)) Trafford Publishing.

Morris, Lynn. Belinda the Butterfly's Beautiful Colors. 2011. 48p. (gr. -1). pap. 19.26 (978-1-4567-3521-0(7)) AuthorHouse.

Morris, M. R. Midnight's Court. 2012. 60p. pap. 24.99 (978-1-4685-9548-2(2)) AuthorHouse.

Morris, Paula. The Eternal City. 2015. (ENG.). 304p. (J). (gr. 7). 17.99 (978-0-545-25133-4(8)) Scholastic, Inc.

Morris, Paula. The Eternal City. 2015. 291p. (YA). **(978-0-545-91986-9(X))** Scholastic, Inc.

Morris, Taylor. The BFF Breakup. 2011. (Mix Ser.). (ENG.). 288p. (J). (gr. 4-8). pap. 6.99 (978-1-4424-0758-9(1), Aladdin) Simon & Schuster Children's Publishing.

Morrison, Kevin. I Can Speak Bully. Kemble, Mai S., illus. 2009. 32p. (J). 14.95 (978-0-8091-6744-9(1), Ambassador Bks.) Paulist Pr.

Morrow, Dj. Charlie & Joe. 2013. 28p. pap. 24.95 (978-1-62709-833-5(X)) America Star Bks.

Morrow, John. Ostrich Egg Omelets. 2017. (ENG., Illus.). (J). 19.99 (978-0-9790832-1-1(4)) 405 Pubns.

Morse, William A. Bip & the Bulb. 2009. 64p. pap. 23.49 (978-1-4490-2498-7(X)) AuthorHouse.

Mortensen, Lori. First Day, No Way!, 1 vol. Simard, Remy, illus. (My First Graphic Novel Ser.). (ENG.). 32p. (gr. k-2). 2011. pap. 6.25 (978-1-4342-3102-4(X)) 2010. 24.65 (978-1-4342-2015-8(X)) Stone Arch Bks. (My First Graphic Novel).

Morty, Ducktor. Can Do & Friends to the Rescue! A Story about Getting along & Working Together. l.t. ed. 2005. Orig. Title: Can Do & the Mall. (Illus.). 34p. (J). pap. (978-0-9768384-2-5(7)) Can Do Duck Publishing.

Moser, Elise. Lily & Taylor, 1 vol. 2013. (ENG.). 224p. (J). (gr. 8). 16.95 (978-1-55498-334-6(7)) Groundwood Bks. CAN. Dist: Publishers Group West (PGW).

Moser, Lisa. Squirrel's Fun Day. Gorbachev, Valeri, illus. 2015. (Candlewick Sparks Ser.). (ENG.). 48p. (J). (gr. k-4). pap. 3.99 (978-0-7636-7789-3(2)) Candlewick Pr.

Moses, Jennifer Anne. Tales from My Closet. 2014. (J). 298p. pap. (978-0-545-66811-8(5)); (ENG.). 304p. (gr. 7-9). 17.99 (978-0-545-51608-2(0)) Scholastic, Inc. (Scholastic Pr.).

Mosesson, Connie. Lovey Dovey & the Makeover Mistake. 2008. 40p. pap. 16.50 (978-1-60693-275-9(6), Eloquent Bks.) Strategic Book Publishing & Rights Agency (SBPRA).

Moskowitz, Hannah. A History of Glitter & Blood. 2015. (ENG., Illus.). 280p. (YA). (gr. 9-17). 18.99 (978-1-4521-2942-6(8)) Chronicle Bks. LLC.

Moss, Alexandra, pseud. Ellie's Chance to Dance. 2005. (Royal Ballet School Diaries: 1). (ENG.). 144p. (J). (gr. 3-7). mass mkt. 5.99 (978-0-448-43535-0(7), Grosset & Dunlap) Penguin Young Readers Group.

—Grace's Show of Strength. 2005. (Royal Ballet School Diaries: 6). (ENG.). 144p. (J). (gr. 3-7). pap. 5.99 (978-0-448-43772-9(4), Grosset & Dunlap) Penguin Young Readers Group.

Moss, Marissa. The All-New Amelia. Moss, Marissa, illus. (ENG., Illus.). (J). 2013. 5.99 (978-1-4169-1289-7(4)) 2007. 40p. (gr. 2-5). 12.99 (978-1-4169-0908-8(7)) Simon & Schuster/Paula Wiseman Bks. (Simon & Schuster/Paula Wiseman Bks.).

—Amelia's 7th-Grade Notebook. Moss, Marissa, illus. 2007. (Amelia Ser.). (ENG., Illus.). 80p. (J). (gr. 5-8). 12.99 (978-1-4169-3661-9(0), Simon & Schuster/Paula Wiseman Bks.) Simon & Schuster/Paula Wiseman Bks.

—Amelia's BFF. Moss, Marissa, illus. 2011. (Amelia Ser.). (ENG., Illus.). 64p. (J). (gr. 5-8). 9.99 (978-1-4424-0376-5(4), Simon & Schuster/Paula Wiseman Bks.) Simon & Schuster/Paula Wiseman Bks.

—Amelia's Cross-My-Heart, Hope-to-Die Guide to the Real, True You! Moss, Marissa, illus. 2010. (Amelia Ser.). (ENG., Illus.). 64p. (J). (gr. 5-8). 9.99 (978-1-4169-8710-9(X), Simon & Schuster/Paula Wiseman Bks.) Simon & Schuster/Paula Wiseman Bks.

—Amelia's Itchy-Twitchy, Lovey-Dovey Summer at Camp Mosquito. Moss, Marissa, illus. 2008. (Amelia Ser.). (ENG., Illus.). 80p. (J). (gr. 5-8). 12.99 (978-1-4169-4722-6(1), Simon & Schuster/Paula Wiseman Bks.) Simon & Schuster/Paula Wiseman Bks.

—Amelia's Middle-School Graduation Yearbook. 2015. (ENG., Illus.). 80p. (J). (gr. 4-8). 12.95 (978-1-939547-09-5(1)) Creston Bks.

—Amelia's Middle School Survival Guide: Amelia's Most Unforgettable Embarrassing Moments, Amelia's Guide to Gossip. Moss, Marissa, illus. 2009. (Amelia Ser.). (ENG., Illus.). 160p. (J). (gr. 5-8). 14.99 (978-1-4169-7987-6(5), Simon & Schuster/Paula Wiseman Bks.) Simon & Schuster/Paula Wiseman Bks.

—Amelia's Science Fair Disaster. Moss, Marissa, illus. 2008. (Amelia Ser.). (ENG., Illus.). 80p. (J). (gr. 5-8). 12.99 (978-1-4169-6494-0(0), Simon & Schuster/Paula Wiseman Bks.) Simon & Schuster/Paula Wiseman Bks.

—Amelia's Summer Survival Guide: Amelia's Longest, Biggest, Most-Fights-Ever Family Reunion; Amelia's Itchy-Twitchy, Lovey-Dovey Summer at Camp Mosquito. Moss, Marissa, illus. 2011. (Amelia Ser.). (ENG., Illus.). 160p. (J). (gr. 5-8). 12.99 (978-1-4424-2331-2(5), Simon & Schuster/Paula Wiseman Bks.) Simon & Schuster/Paula Wiseman Bks.

—The Fake Friend! Moss, Marissa, illus. 2012. (Daphne's Diary of Daily Disasters Ser.). (ENG., Illus.). 96p. (J). (gr. 2-5). 9.99 (978-1-4424-4014-2(7)); pap. 5.99 (978-1-4424-4015-9(5)) Simon & Schuster/Paula Wiseman Bks. (Simon & Schuster/Paula Wiseman Bks.).

—Friendship Survival Guide: And Trying to Be the Best BFF Amelia. Moss, Marissa, illus. 2013. (Amelia Ser.). (ENG., Illus.). 144p. (J). (gr. 5-8). 12.99 (978-1-4424-8304-0(0), Simon & Schuster/Paula Wiseman Bks.) Simon & Schuster/Paula Wiseman Bks.

Moss, Patricia Crocker. Dillie & the Baby Deer. 2011. (J). 44p. 27.99 (978-1-4568-4999-3(9)); 48p. pap. 17.49 (978-1-4568-4998-6(0)) Xlibris Corp.

Moss, Peggy & Lyon, Lea. Say Something, 1 vol. 2008. (ENG., Illus.). 32p. (J). (gr. 1-7). pap. 7.95 (978-0-88448-310-6(X)) Tilbury Hse. Pubs.

Moss, Peggy & Weber, Penny. One of Us, 1 vol. 2010. (ENG., Illus.). 32p. (gr. 1-7). 16.95 (978-0-88448-322-9(3), 884322) Tilbury Hse. Pubs.

Moss, Peggy, et al. Our Friendship Rules, 1 vol. Geis, Alissa Imre, illus. 2007. (ENG.). 32p. (gr. 2-6). 16.95 (978-0-88448-291-8(X), 884291) Tilbury Hse. Pubs.

Mosso, Tyfanny. The Mud Puddle Gang. 2006. pap. 17.00 (978-0-8059-9067-6(4)) Dorrance Publishing Co., Inc.

Mostoller, Marcia. Emma's Dilemm. 2011. 42p. pap. 16.95 (978-1-4560-9859-9(4)) America Star Bks.

—Emma's Summer Camp Dilemm. 2011. 64p. pap. 19.95 (978-1-4626-2814-8(1)) America Star Bks.

Motomi, Kyousuke. Dengeki Daisy , Vol. 16. 2015. (ENG.). 192p. pap. 9.99 (978-1-4215-7771-5(2)) Viz Media.

Mould, Paul, ed. The Magnificent Six. 2007. (Illus.). 52p. pap. (978-1-58690-048-9(X)) Mould, Paul Publishing.

Moulder, Holly. Crystal City Lights. 2013. (ENG.). 190p. (J). pap. 8.99 (978-0-9885295-0-2(5)) Blue Marlin Pubns.

Moulton, Erin E. Tracing Stars. 2013. (ENG.). 256p. (J). (gr. 3-7). pap. 6.99 (978-0-14-242653-1(9), Puffin Books) Penguin Young Readers Group.

Moulton, Mark Kimball. A Snowgirl Named Just Sue. Good, Karen Hillard, illus. 2008. (ENG.). 36p. (J). (gr. -1-3). 14.95 (978-0-8249-5150-4(6), Ideal Pubns.) Worthy Publishing.

—A Snowman Named Just Bob. Hillard Good, Karen, illus. 2006. (ENG.). 16p. (J). (gr. k-3). 14.95 (978-0-8249-1707-4(3), Ideal Pubns.) Worthy Publishing.

—A Snowman Named Just Bob. Crouch, Karen Hillard, illus. 2003. (ENG.). 36p. (J). 14.95 (978-0-8249-5860-2(8), 53876801, Ideal Pubns.) Worthy Publishing.

—The Very Best Pumpkin. Good, Karen Hillard, illus. 2010. (ENG.). 32p. (J). (gr. -1-3). 12.99 (978-1-4169-8288-3(4), Simon & Schuster/Paula Wiseman Bks.) Simon & Schuster/Paula Wiseman Bks.

Moulton, Mark Kimball & Good, Karen Hillard. A Snowman Named Just Bob. Good, Karen Hillard, illus. 2009. (Illus.). 32p. (J). (gr. -1-3). 18.99 (978-0-8249-5596-0(X), Ideal Pubns.) Worthy Publishing.

Mounteer, J. B. I Think My Brother Is a Werewolf. 2012. 50p. pap. 8.22 (978-1-4669-4868-6(X)) Trafford Publishing.

Mounts, Samia. Frunk the Skunk. Matricardi, Luca, illus. 2008. (ENG.). 150p. (J). (gr. 4-6). pap. 9.95 (978-0-9798841-0-8(1)) 4N Publishing LLC.

Mouser, Mary. Chigger: A Prairie Dog Tale. 2007. 152p. per. 24.95 (978-1-4241-9791-0(0)) America Star Bks.

Mowry, Tia & Mowry, Tamera. Twintuition: Double Dare. 2017. (Twintuition Ser.: 3). 208p. (J). (gr. 3-7). 16.99 (978-0-06-237292-5(0)) HarperCollins Pubs.

Mr Fizzle, the Man Who Went Boo!, 6 Packs. (gr. k-1). 23.00 (978-0-7635-8858-8(X)) Rigby Education.

Mracek, Ann. Friendship Flies the Sun: The Ancient Egyptian Legend of Scarab Beetle. l.t. ed. 2005. (DAN., Illus.). 32p. (J). per. 15.99 (978-0-9766488-0-2(6)) Mracek, Ann.

Ms. T. A Chincoteague Pony Finds a Friend. 2009. 28p. pap. 12.49 (978-1-4389-7981-6(9)) AuthorHouse.

Mucha, Mark. Adventures with Edison & His Friends Vol. 1: "Crab in a Bucket" 2008. 58p. pap. 11.95 (978-1-934449-29-5(6)) Legacy Publishing Services, Inc.

Mueller, Stephen R. Hermie & Bernie, 1 vol. 2009. 124p. pap. 19.95 (978-1-4489-1813-3(8)) PublishAmerica, Inc.

Mukherjee, Aiswarya & S., Bijan, illus. My Family! ABCs with Keesha. 2011. (J). pap. 2.99 (978-0-9767273-9-2(0)) Dodi Pr.

Mulder, Michelle. Maggie & the Chocolate War, 1 vol. 2008. (Kids' Power Book Ser.). (ENG., Illus.). 94p. (J). (gr. 4-8). pap. 14.95 (978-1-897187-27-2(0)) Second Story Pr. CAN. Dist: Orca Bk. Pubs. USA.

—Not a Chance, 1 vol. 2013. (ENG.). 160p. (J). (gr. 4-7). pap. 9.95 (978-1-4598-0216-2(0)) Orca Bk. Pubs. USA.

Muldrow, Diane. Turning up the Heat, No. 2. Pollak, Barbara, illus. 2nd ed. 2007. (Dish Ser.: 2). (ENG.). 160p. (J). (gr. 4-7). pap. 4.99 (978-0-448-44527-4(1), Grosset & Dunlap) Penguin Young Readers Group.

Mulford, Carolyn. The Feedsack Dress. 2007. (YA). per. 7.95 (978-0-9713497-4-2(6)) Cave Hollow Pr.

Mull, Brandon. Arcade Catastrophe. 2012. (Candy Shop War Ser.: 2). (ENG.). 448p. (J). (gr. 5). 18.99 (978-1-60907-179-0(4), Shadow Mountain) Shadow Mountain Publishing.

—Arcade Catastrophe. 2014. (Candy Shop War Ser.: 2). lib. bdg. 18.40 (978-0-606-35795-1(5)) Turtleback Bks.

—The Candy Shop War. 2011. E-Book 6.64 (978-1-60641-649-5(9)) Deseret Bk. Co.

—The Candy Shop War. (Candy Shop War Ser.: Bk. 1). 2008. 368p. pap. 6.99 (978-1-59038-970-6(0)) 2007. (Illus.). 409p. (J). (gr. 3-7). 19.99 (978-1-59038-783-2(X)) Shadow Mountain Publishing. (Shadow Mountain).

—The Candy Shop War. 2014. (Candy Shop War Ser.: 1). lib. bdg. 18.40 (978-0-606-35794-4(7)) Turtleback Bks.

—Crystal Keepers. 2016. (Five Kingdoms Ser.: 3). lib. bdg. 18.40 (978-0-606-38253-3(4)) Turtleback Bks.

—Pingo & the Playground Bully. Dorman, Brandon, illus. 2012. (Pingo Ser.: 2). (ENG.). 32p. (J). (gr. k-3). 17.99 (978-1-60907-178-3(6), Shadow Mountain) Shadow Mountain Publishing.

—Rogue Knight. (Five Kingdoms Ser.: 2). (ENG., Illus.). (J). (gr. 3-7). 2015. 496p. pap. 8.99 (978-1-4424-9704-7(1)) 2014. 480p. 17.99 (978-1-4424-9703-0(3)) Simon & Schuster Children's Publishing. (Aladdin).

—Rogue Knight. 2015. (Five Kingdoms Ser.: 2). lib. bdg. 19.65 (978-0-606-38254-0(2)) Turtleback Bks.

Mull, David Kenneth. His Date for the Dance was His Science Project. 2012. 80p. pap. 9.99 (978-0-89824-371-0(8)) Royal Fireworks Publishing Co.

Mullarkey, Lisa. The Artsy Fartsy Auction: Book 8, 1 vol. Harris, Phyllis, illus. 2012. (Katharine the Almost Great Ser.). (ENG.). 80p. (J). (gr. 1-4). 27.07 (978-1-61641-829-8(X)) Magic Wagon.

—Battle of the Bunks, 1 vol. Franco, Paula, illus. 2016. (ENG.). 112p. (J). lib. bdg. (978-1-62402-162-6(X)) Magic Wagon.

—The Campfire Capers, 1 vol. 2014. (Storm Cliff Stables Ser.). (ENG., Illus.). 112p. (J). (gr. 7-11). 27.07 (978-1-62402-049-0(6)) Magic Wagon.

—Carly, 1 vol. Franco, Paula, illus. 2016. (Pony Girls Ser.). (ENG.). 112p. (J). (gr. 1-4). 27.07 (978-1-62402-127-5(1)) Magic Wagon.

—Daniela, 1 vol. Franco, Paula, illus. 2016. (Pony Girls Ser.). (ENG.). 112p. (J). (gr. 1-4). 27.07 (978-1-62402-128-2(X)) Magic Wagon.

—A Feast of Fun, 1 vol. Franco, Paula, illus. 2016. (ENG.). 112p. (J). lib. bdg. (978-1-62402-163-3(8)) Magic Wagon.

—A Filming Fiasco, 1 vol. Franco, Paula, illus. 2016. (ENG.). 112p. (J). lib. bdg. (978-1-62402-164-0(6)) Magic Wagon.

—Gold Medal Glitch, 1 vol. 2014. (Storm Cliff Stables Ser.). (ENG., Illus.). 112p. (J). (gr. 7-11). 27.07 (978-1-62402-050-6(X)) Magic Wagon.

—Horsenapped!, 1 vol. 2014. (Storm Cliff Stables Ser.). (ENG., Illus.). 112p. (J). (gr. 7-11). 27.07 (978-1-62402-051-3(8)) Magic Wagon.

—TJ Zaps a Nightmare: Stopping Blackmail Bullying #5, 1 vol. LaCoste, Gary, illus. 2012. (TJ Trapper, Bully Zapper Ser.). (ENG.). 80p. (J). (gr. 2-5). lib. bdg. 27.07 (978-1-61641-909-7(1), Calico Chapter Bks) Magic Wagon.

—TJ Zaps the Freeze Out: Stopping the Silent Treatment #3, 1 vol. LaCoste, Gary, illus. 2012. (TJ Trapper, Bully Zapper Ser.). (ENG.). 80p. (J). (gr. 2-5). lib. bdg. 27.07 (978-1-61641-907-3(5), Calico Chapter Bks) Magic Wagon.

—TJ Zaps the One-Upper: Stopping One-Upping & Cell Phone Bullying #2, 1 vol. LaCoste, Gary, illus. 2012. (TJ Trapper, Bully Zapper Ser.). (ENG.). 80p. (J). (gr. 2-5). lib. bdg. 27.07 (978-1-61641-906-6(7), Calico Chapter Bks) Magic Wagon.

—Trail Ride Troubles, 1 vol. 2014. (Storm Cliff Stables Ser.). (ENG.). 112p. (J). (gr. 7-11). lib. bdg. 27.07 (978-1-62402-052-0(6), Calico Chapter Bks) Magic Wagon.

—The Write Stuff: Book 7, 1 vol. Harris, Phyllis, illus. 2012. (Katharine the Almost Great Ser.). (ENG.). 80p. (J). (gr. 1-4). 27.07 (978-1-61641-828-1(1)) Magic Wagon.

Mullen, Susan & Kun, Michael. We Are Still Tornadoes. 2016. (ENG.). 304p. (YA). 18.99 (978-1-250-09840-5(8), 9781250098405, St. Martin's Griffin) St. Martin's Pr.

Muller, Lisa M. Master smokey & mr. Duck. 2006. 15p. (J). 9.99 (978-1-4276-0027-1(9)) Aardvark Global Publishing.

Mullins, Julie. School Play Stars. Maddock, Monika, illus. 2005. (Girlz Rock! Ser.). (J). pap. (978-1-59336-706-0(6)) Mondo Publishing.

—The Sleepover. Foye, Lloyd, illus. 2005. (Girlz Rock! Ser.). (J). pap. (978-1-59336-707-7(4)) Mondo Publishing.

Mulryan, Doreen. Lucky Ducky. 2016. (ENG., Illus.). 32p. (J). (gr. k-2). 14.95 (978-1-4197-1467-2(8), Abrams Bks. for Young Readers) Abrams, Inc.

Mulubah, Sr. Denise's Pet Dove. 2009. 36p. pap. 16.99 (978-1-4389-7536-8(8)) AuthorHouse.

Mun-Ensor, Michelle. Aloh. 2011. 32p. pap. 24.95 (978-1-4560-9848-3(9)) America Star Bks.

—The Angel's Garden. 2011. 48p. pap. 24.95 (978-1-4560-5596-7(8)) America Star Bks.

—The Ten Bridesmaids. 2011. 28p. pap. 24.95 (978-1-4560-9003-6(8)) America Star Bks.

Munoz, R. C. In Honor of the Oak Tree. 2012. 20p. pap. 24.95 (978-1-4626-6454-2(7)) America Star Bks.

Munsch, Audrey. The Tale of the Red Ribbon. 2012. 16p. pap. 11.97 (978-1-61897-026-8(7), Strategic Bk. Publishing) Strategic Book Publishing & Rights Agency (SBPRA).

Munsch, Robert. We Share Everything! 2004. (Illus.). (J). (gr. -1-2). spiral bd. (978-0-616-01749-4(9)); spiral bd. (978-0-616-01750-0(2)) Canadian National Institute for the Blind/Institut National Canadien pour les Aveugles.

Munsell, Jill. What a Day for a Parade. 2010. 48p. pap. 19.95 (978-1-4389-9080-4(4)) AuthorHouse.

Munté, Marta. KUKU AND MWEWE: A SWAHILI FOLKTALE. 2013. (ENG., Illus.). 30p. (J). (gr. -1-k). 16.95 (978-84-15619-97-0(9)) Eastern National.

Murakami, Yasanuri & Kimura, ken, illus. 999 Frogs & a Little Brother. 2015. (ENG.). 40p. (J). 17.95 (978-0-7358-4202-1(7)) North-South Bks., Inc.

Murcray, Rod. Tuttle Stories. McDaniel, Rick, illus. 2012. 40p. pap. 14.95 (978-1-61897-654-3(0), Strategic Bk. Publishing) Strategic Book Publishing & Rights Agency (SBPRA).

Murguia, Bethanie Deeney. I Feel Five! Murguia, Bethanie Deeney, illus. 2014. (ENG., Illus.). 32p. (J). (gr. -1-3). 14.99 (978-0-7636-6291-2(7)) Candlewick Pr.

—Princess! Fairy! Ballerina! 2016. (ENG., Illus.). 40p. (J). (gr. -1-k). 17.99 (978-0-545-73240-6(9)) Scholastic, Inc.

Murphy, Jill. All for One. 2004. (Illus.). (J). (gr. -1-2). spiral bd. (978-0-616-14591-3(8)); spiral bd. (978-0-616-14592-0(6)) Canadian National Institute for the Blind/Institut National Canadien pour les Aveugles.

—On the Way Home. Murphy, Jill, illus. 2nd rev. ed. 2007. (ENG., Illus.). 32p. (J). (gr. k-2). pap. 11.95 (978-0-230-01584-5(0)) Pan Macmillan GBR. Dist: Independent Pubs. Group.

Murphy, Jim. Revenge of the Green Banana. 2017. (ENG.). 224p. (J). (gr. 5-7). 16.99 (978-0-544-78677-6(7), Clarion Bks.) Houghton Mifflin Harcourt Trade & Reference Pubs.

Murphy, Julie. Dumplin. (YA). (gr. 8). 2017. 400p. pap. 9.99 (978-0-06-232719-2(4)) 2015. (ENG.). 384p. 17.99 (978-0-06-232718-5(6)) HarperCollins Pubs.

—Dumplin. 2017. (YA). lib. bdg. 20.85 **(978-0-606-39647-9(0))** Turtleback Bks.

Murphy, Julie. Side Effects May Vary. (ENG.). (YA). (gr. 9). 2015. 352p. pap. 9.99 (978-0-06-224537-3(6)) 2014. 336p. 17.99 (978-0-06-224535-9(X)) HarperCollins Pubs.

Murphy, Mary. Panda Foo & the New Friend. Murphy, Mary, illus. 2007. (ENG., Illus.). 32p. (J). (gr. k-k). 15.99 (978-0-7636-3405-6(0)) Candlewick Pr.

Murphy, Pat. The Wild Girls. 2008. (ENG.). 304p. (YA). (gr. 7-18). 8.99 (978-0-14-241245-9(7), Speak) Penguin Young Readers Group.

—The Wild Girls. unabr. ed. 2007. (YA). (gr. 6-9). audio compact disk 45.00 (978-0-7393-5988-4(6)) Random Hse. Audio Publishing Group.

Murphy, Patricia J. I Need You. Bryant, Laura J., illus. 2003. (Rookie Reader Español Ser.). (ENG.). (J). (gr. k-2). pap. 4.95 (978-0-516-26966-5(6), Children's Pr.) Scholastic Library Publishing.

Murphy, Stuart J. Emma Hace Amigos. 2011. (I See I Learn Ser.). (SPA & ENG., Illus.). 32p. (J). (-k). 14.95 (978-1-58089-482-1(8)); pap. 6.95 (978-1-58089-483-8(6)) Charlesbridge Publishing, Inc.

—Emma's Friendwich. 2010. (I See I Learn Ser.). (ENG., Illus.). 32p. (J). (gr. -1-k). 14.95 (978-1-58089-450-0(X)); pap. 6.95 (978-1-58089-451-7(8)) Charlesbridge Publishing, Inc.

—Freda Says Please. Jones, Tim, illus. 2013. (I See I Learn Ser.). (ENG.). 32p. (J). (-k). pap. 6.95 (978-1-58089-475-3(5)) Charlesbridge Publishing, Inc.

—Freda Says Please. Jones, Tim, illus. 2013. (I See I Learn Ser.). (ENG.). 32p. (J). (-k). lib. bdg. 14.95 (978-1-58089-474-6(7)) Charlesbridge Publishing, Inc.

—Happy, Healthy Ajay! 2012. (I See I Learn Ser.). (ENG., Illus.). 32p. (J). (-k). 14.95 (978-1-58089-470-8(4)); pap. 6.95 (978-1-58089-471-5(2)) Charlesbridge Publishing, Inc.

Murphy, Tracy. Everyday Adventures with Mickey & Seed. 2011. (Illus.). 68p. (gr. -1). pap. 25.80 (978-1-4567-7351-9(8)) AuthorHouse.

Murray, Fisher C & Murray, Colleen O. One & Only Bernadette P. McMull. 2009. (ENG.). 32p. pap. 10.95 (978-1-933916-52-1(4), Ferne Pr.) Nelson Publishing & Marketing.

Murray, Guillermo. Te Dije Que No Miraras. rev. ed. 2005. (Ediciones Castillo Castillo Del Terror Ser.). (SPA & ENG.). 100p. (J). (gr. -1-7). pap. 6.95 (978-970-20-0308-3(3)) Castillo, Ediciones, S. A. de C. V. MEX. Dist: Macmillan.

Murray, Karessa M. Campbell. High Class: {Friendship, Love, Sex, Relationships & Money}, 1 vol. 2010. 164p. pap. 24.95 (978-1-4489-8464-0(5)) America Star Bks.

Murray, Martine. Molly & Pim & the Millions of Stars. 2017. (ENG., Illus.). 192p. (J). (gr. 3-7). 16.99 (978-0-399-55040-9(2), Knopf Bks. for Young Readers) Random Hse. Children's Bks.

Murray, Rosalie. Bobby & Bun Bun's Afternoon Adventure. Swope, Brenda, illus. 2012. 32p. pap. 24.95 (978-1-4560-5090-0(7)) America Star Bks.

Murray, Victoria Christopher. Aaliyah. 2009. (Divas Ser.). (ENG.). 208p. pap. 14.99 (978-1-4165-6351-8(2), Gallery Bks.) Gallery Bks.

Murrell, Belinda. Lulu Bell's Best Friends Ever. 2017. (Lulu Bell Ser.). (ENG.). 384p. (J). (gr. 1-4). 16.99 **(978-0-14-378257-5(6))** Random Hse. Australia AUS. Dist: Independent Pubs. Group.

Murrell, Diane. Friends Learn about Tobin. Murrell, Diane, illus. 2007. (ENG., Illus.). 29p. (J). (gr. -1-3). 16.95 (978-1-932565-41-6(8)) Future Horizons, Inc.

My Amazing Pet Snail. 2013. (Illus.). (J). (978-1-4351-4755-3(3)) Barnes & Noble, Inc.

My Awesome School Planner. 2008. (Best Friends Club Ser.). 160p. (978-1-4075-3175-5(1)) Parragon, Inc.

My Best Friends. (Girls' World Ser.). 16p. (J). (978-2-7643-0141-8(3)) Phidal Publishing, Inc./Editions Phidal, Inc.

My Monster Friends, 6 Packs. (Literatura 2000 Ser.). (gr. 1-2). 28.00 (978-0-7635-0102-0(6)) Rigby Education.

My Two, Very, Special Friends, 1. 2006. (Illus.). 19p. (J). per. 4.00 (978-0-9788386-1-4(0)) Taylor, Y. H.

My Uncle Has Wheels. 2005. (J). 8.00 (978-0-9767077-1-4(3)) Carson, Tracy.

Mydin, Liza. The Three Village Boys of Al Haidar: The First Adventure. 2012. 20p. pap. 16.00 (978-1-4669-2792-6(5)) Trafford Publishing.

Myers, Byrona. Turn Here for Strawberry Roam. Jauss, Anne Marie, illus. 2011. 134p. 40.95 (978-1-258-08195-9(4)) Literary Licensing, LLC.

—Yo Ho for Strawberry Roam! Jauss, Anne Marie, illus. 2011. 154p. 41.95 (978-1-258-08204-8(7)) Literary Licensing, LLC.

Myers, Linda. Stoney the Pony's Most Inspiring Year: Teaching Children about Addiction Through Metaphor. 2012. 36p. pap. 16.99 (978-1-4624-0311-0(5), Inspiring Voices) Author Solutions, Inc.

Myers, Walter Dean. Autobiography of My Dead Brother. Myers, Christopher, illus. 2006. (ENG.). 224p. (YA). (gr. 9). pap. 9.99 (978-0-06-058293-7(6), Amistad) HarperCollins Pubs.

—Autobiography of My Dead Brother. 2006. 20.00 (978-0-7569-6388-0(5)) Perfection Learning Corp.

—Darius & Twig. 2013. 208p. (YA). (gr. 8). (ENG.). 17.99 (978-0-06-172823-5(3)); lib. bdg. 18.89 (978-0-06-172824-2(1)) HarperCollins Pubs. (Amistad).

—Lockdown. (YA). (gr. 8). 2011. (ENG.). 272p. pap. 9.99 (978-0-06-121482-0(5)) 2010. 256p. lib. bdg. 17.89 (978-0-06-121481-3(7)) 2010. (ENG.). 256p. 16.99 (978-0-06-121480-6(9)) HarperCollins Pubs. (Amistad).

Myracle, Lauren. Awesome Blossom. 2013. (Flower Power Ser.). (ENG.). 272p. (J). (gr. 4-8). 17.95 (978-1-4197-0405-5(2), Amulet Bks.) Abrams, Inc.

—Awesome Blossom: A Flower Power Book. 2013. (Flower Power Ser.). (ENG.). 272p. (J). (gr. 3-7). pap. 7.95 (978-1-4197-0791-9(4), Amulet Bks.) Abrams, Inc.

—Bff: A Girlfriend Book You Write Together. 2009. (ENG., Illus.). 256p. (YA). (gr. 7-11). 10.95 (978-0-8109-8431-8(8), Amulet Bks.) Abrams, Inc.

—Eleven. 2005. (Winnie Years Ser.). (ENG.). 224p. (J). (gr. 3-7). reprint ed. pap. 7.99 (978-0-14-240346-4(6), Puffin Books) Penguin Young Readers Group.

—The Fashion Disaster That Changed My Life. 2008. (ENG.). 160p. (J). (gr. 5-18). 6.99 (978-0-14-240717-2(8), Puffin Books) Penguin Young Readers Group.

—Friends of a Feather. Henry, Jed, illus. 2015. (Life of Ty Ser.: 3). (ENG.). 144p. (J). (gr. 1-4). 5.99 (978-0-14-242320-2(3), Puffin Books); 12.99 (978-0-525-42288-4(9), Dutton Books for Young Readers) Penguin Young Readers Group.

—Kissing Kate. 2007. (ENG.). 208p. (YA). (gr. 7-18). 7.99 (978-0-14-240869-8(7), Speak) Penguin Young Readers Group.

—Luv Ya Bunches, Bk. 1. 2009. (Flower Power Ser.). (ENG., Illus.). 352p. (J). (gr. 3-7). 16.95 (978-0-8109-4211-0(9), Amulet Bks.) Abrams, Inc.

—Luv Ya Bunches: A Flower Power Book. 2010. (Flower Power Ser.). (ENG.). 352p. (J). (gr. 3-7). pap. 8.95 (978-0-8109-8982-5(4), Amulet Bks.) Abrams, Inc.

—Oopsy Daisy. 2012. (Flower Power Ser.). (ENG.). 368p. (J). (gr. 3-7). pap. 8.95 (978-1-4197-0418-5(4), Amulet Bks.) Abrams, Inc.

—Ten. (Winnie Years Ser.). (ENG.). (J). (gr. 3-7). 2012. 240p. pap. 7.99 (978-0-14-242134-5(0), Puffin Books) 2011. 272p. 16.99 (978-0-525-42356-0(7), Dutton Books for Young Readers) Penguin Young Readers Group.

—Thirteen. 2009. (Winnie Years Ser.). (ENG.). 272p. (J). (gr. 3-7). 7.99 (978-0-14-241370-8(4), Puffin Books) Penguin Young Readers Group.

—Twelve. 2008. (Winnie Years Ser.). (ENG.). 224p. (J). (gr. 5-18). 7.99 (978-0-14-241091-2(8), Puffin Books) Penguin Young Readers Group.

—Violet in Bloom. 2010. (Flower Power Ser.). (ENG., Illus.). 384p. (J). (gr. 3-7). 16.95 (978-0-8109-8983-2(2), Amulet Bks.) Abrams, Inc.

—Yolo. 2014. (Internet Girls Ser.). (ENG., Illus.). 208p. (YA). (gr. 8-17). 16.95 (978-1-4197-0871-8(6), Amulet Bks.) Abrams, Inc.

Myracle, Lauren, et al. How to Be Bad. 2015. (ENG.). 352p. (YA). (gr. 9). pap. 9.99 (978-0-06-240568-5(3), HarperTeen) HarperCollins Pubs.

Nœ–ez, Marisa. CHOCOLATE. 2007. (ENG., Illus.). 36p. (J). 17.95 (978-84-96788-83-1(0)) OQO, Editora ESP. Dist: Baker & Taylor Bks.

Na, Il Sung. Bird, Balloon, Bear. 2017. (ENG.). 32p. (J). (-k). 17.99 (978-0-399-55155-0(7), Knopf Bks. for Young Readers) Random Hse. Children's Bks.

Naas, Katy Newton. Missing Max. 2017. (ENG.). 36p. (J). pap. 8.99 (978-1-68350-088-9(1)) Morgan James Publishing.

Nabors, V. L. Mad Craze Middle School; the Case of the Crumpled Balls. 2010. 215p. pap. 16.95 (978-0-557-44140-2(4)) Lulu Pr., Inc.

Nadin, Joanna. Wonderland. 2011. (ENG., Illus.). 224p. (YA). (gr. 9-18). 16.99 (978-0-7636-4846-6(9)) Candlewick Pr.

Nagle, Barbara. Duck & Spider, 1 vol. 2009. 37p. pap. 24.95 (978-1-60749-980-0(0)) America Star Bks.

Nahal, Denise Abda. Hello Birdie! Tale of a Classroom Pet Based on a True Story. 2012. 16p. pap. 10.67 (978-1-4669-6822-6(2)) Trafford Publishing.

Nahall Nikoo Fells. Drowning in the Mainstream: Confessions of a Sister. 2010. 284p. 27.95 (978-1-4502-0552-8(6)); pap. 17.95 (978-1-4502-0554-2(2)) iUniverse, Inc.

Nahorniak, Mike. Kalico Jack. 2016. (ENG., Illus.). (J). 16.95 **(978-1-5069-0333-0(9))**; pap. 14.95 **(978-1-5069-0290-6(1))** First Edition Design eBook Publishing.

Naidoo, Beverley. Burn My Heart. 2008. (ENG.). 224p. (J). (gr. 5-18). 16.99 (978-0-06-143297-2(0), Amistad) HarperCollins Pubs.

Naidoo, Vahini. Fall to Pieces, 0 vols. 2012. (ENG.). 324p. (YA). (gr. 8-12). 16.99 (978-0-7614-6217-0(1), 9780761462170, Amazon Children's Publishing) Amazon Publishing.

Nakakuma, Chie. Whazzup, Wolly Ayaka? 2007. 128p. per. 10.95 (978-0-595-44646-9(9)) iUniverse, Inc.

Nalbandian, Paisely Lineyeia. Treasure Seekers. 2011. 28p. pap. 15.99 (978-1-4415-1375-5(2)) Xlibris Corp.

Namm, Diane. My Best Friend. Gordon, Mike, illus. 2004. (My First Reader Ser.). (ENG.). 32p. (J). (gr. k-1). pap. 3.95 (978-0-516-25504-0(5), Children's Pr.) Scholastic Library Publishing.

—My Best Friend. Gordon, Mike, tr. Gordon, Mike, illus. 2004. (My First Reader Ser.). (ENG.). 31p. (J). 18.50 (978-0-516-24416-7(7), Children's Pr.) Scholastic Library Publishing.

Nanette. The Black Alligator. 2004. (Life on Granny's Farm Ser.). (J). 12.95 (978-0-9741269-3-7(4)) St. Bernard Publishing, LLC.

—Little Red. 2004. (Life on Granny's Farm Ser.). (J). 12.95 (978-0-9741269-1-3(8)) St. Bernard Publishing, LLC.

—Pancake the Purple Pony. 2004. (Life on Granny's Farm Ser.). (J). 12.95 (978-0-9741269-8-2(5)) St. Bernard Publishing, LLC.

Napolitano, Gretchen. Christopher Lee & Bozzie Bear's First Day of School. 2012. (ENG.). 56p. 27.95 (978-1-4327-9443-9(4)); pap. 20.95 (978-1-4327-8487-4(0)) Outskirts Pr., Inc.

Nara, Yoshitomo. The Lonesome Puppy. 2008. (ENG., Illus.). 40p. (J). (gr. -1-17). 17.99 (978-0-8118-5640-9(2)) Chronicle Bks. LLC.

Narsimhan, Mahtab. Mission Mumbai. 2016. (ENG.). 272p. (J). (gr. 4-7). 16.99 (978-0-545-74651-9(5), Scholastic Pr.) Scholastic, Inc.

Narvaez, Concha Lopez. La Colina de Edeta. (SPA.). 124p. (YA). (gr. 5-8). (978-84-239-9050-4(8), EC3401) Espasa Calpe, S.A. ESP. Dist: Lectorum Pubns., Inc.

Nash, Andy. Marcus & His Monkey: For Kids Blessed with Popularity. 2010. (J). (978-0-8127-0452-5(5)) Autumn Hse. Publishing Co.

—Tatum & Her Tiger: For Kids Blessed with Passion. 2007. (Illus.). (J). 9.99 (978-0-8127-0451-8(7)) Autumn Hse. Publishing Co.

Nash, Arizona. Red Rooster, Green Rooster. 2009. 48p. pap. 16.99 (978-1-935436-98-0(8)) Rodaian Pr.

Nash, David. A Pete & Charley Adventure: The Sheri. 2005. 131p. pap. 24.95 (978-1-4137-9449-6(1)) PublishAmerica, Inc.

Nash, Susan Smith. The Good Deeds Society: Family Plot. 2008. (Illus.). 220p. (YA). pap. 18.00 (978-0-9797573-2-7(0)) Texture Pr.

Nathan, Sarah. Blue-Ribbon Bunny. 2014. (Sofia the First World of Reading Ser.). (J). lib. bdg. 13.55 (978-0-606-35264-2(3)) Turtleback Bks.

Nation, Kay. Jamie Learns to Love. 2006. pap. 10.00 (978-1-4257-0534-3(0)) Xlibris Corp.

Navarro-Talavera, Carmen. The Ant Lucy & the Hurricane. 2009. 48p. pap. 17.49 (978-1-4389-7788-1(3)) AuthorHouse.

—La Hormiguita Lucy y el Huracán. 2009. 48p. pap. 17.49 (978-1-4389-7787-4(5)) AuthorHouse.

Nayer, Judy. Best Wishes for Eddie. Franson, Leanne, illus. 2012. (First Chapters: Set 2 Ser.: Vol. 8). (ENG.). 64p. (J). (gr. 2-3). pap. 9.50 (978-0-7652-0884-2(9)) Modern Curriculum Pr.

Naylor, Phyllis Reynolds. The Alice Collection/Alice in Elementary: Starting with Alice; Alice in Blunderland; Lovingly Alice. 2016. (Alice Ser.). (ENG., Illus.). 672p. (J). (gr. 2-7). pap. 17.99 (978-1-4814-7874-8(5), Atheneum Bks. for Young Readers) Simon & Schuster Children's Publishing.

—The Alice Collection/High School & Beyond: I Like Him, He Likes Her; It's Not Like I Planned It This Way; Please Don't Be True; You & Me & the Space in Between; Now I'll Tell You Everything. 2016. (Alice Ser.). (ENG., Illus.). 3648p. (YA). (gr. 7). pap. 61.99 (978-1-4814-7876-2(1), Atheneum/Caitlyn Dlouhy Books) Simon & Schuster Children's Publishing.

—The Alice Collection/the Middle School Years: The Agony of Alice; Alice in Rapture, Sort of; Reluctantly Alice; All but Alice; Alice in-Between; Alice the Brave; Alice in Lace; Outrageously Alice; Achingly Alice; Alice on the Outside; the Grooming of Alice. 2016. (Alice Ser.). (ENG., Illus.). 2368p. (J). (gr. 5-9). pap. 81.99 (978-1-4814-7875-5(3), Atheneum/Caitlyn Dlouhy Books) Simon & Schuster Children's Publishing.

—Alice in Blunderland. 2005. 200p. (J). (gr. 2-7). 13.65 (978-0-7569-5075-0(9)) Perfection Learning Corp.

—Alice in Blunderland. 2012. (Alice Ser.). (ENG., Illus.). 240p. (J). (gr. 2-7). pap. 5.99 (978-1-4424-4643-4(9), Atheneum Bks. for Young Readers) Simon & Schuster Children's Publishing.

—Alice on Board. 2012. (Alice Ser.: 24). (ENG., Illus.). 288p. (YA). (gr. 9). 16.99 (978-1-4424-4588-8(2), Atheneum Bks. for Young Readers) Simon & Schuster Children's Publishing.

—Almost Alice. 2008. (Alice Ser.: 20). (ENG.). 288p. (YA). (gr. 9-18). 16.99 (978-0-689-87096-5(5), Atheneum Bks. for Young Readers) Simon & Schuster Children's Publishing.

—Almost Alice. 2009. (Alice Ser.: 20). (ENG.). 288p. (YA). (gr. 9). mass mkt. 6.99 (978-0-689-87097-2(3), Simon Pulse) Simon Pulse.

—Cricket Man. 2008. (ENG.). 208p. (YA). (gr. 7-18). 16.99 (978-1-4169-4981-7(X), Atheneum Bks. for Young Readers) Simon & Schuster Children's Publishing.

—Faith, Hope, & Ivy June. 2011. (ENG.). 288p. (J). (gr. 3-7). 6.99 (978-0-375-84491-1(0), Yearling) Random Hse. Children's Bks.

—The Grooming of Alice. 2012. (Alice Ser.: 12). (ENG., Illus.). 240p. (J). (gr. 5-9). pap. 6.99 (978-1-4424-3496-7(1), Atheneum Bks. for Young Readers) Simon & Schuster Children's Publishing.

—I Like Him, He Likes Her: Alice Alone; Simply Alice; Patiently Alice. 2010. (Alice Ser.). (ENG.). 640p. (YA). (gr. 7). pap. 12.99 (978-1-4424-0978-1(9), Atheneum Bks. for Young Readers) Simon & Schuster Children's Publishing.

—Lovingly Alice. 2004. (Alice Bks.). 166p. (J). (gr. 4-6). 13.65 (978-0-7569-6604-1(3)) Perfection Learning Corp.

—Lovingly Alice. 2006. (Alice Ser.). (ENG., Illus.). 176p. (J). (gr. 4-7). pap. 5.99 (978-0-689-84400-3(X), Atheneum Bks. for Young Readers) Simon & Schuster Children's Publishing.

—Now I'll Tell You Everything. 2013. (Alice Ser.: 25). (ENG., Illus.). 528p. (YA). (gr. 9). 17.99 (978-1-4424-4590-1(4)) Simon & Schuster Children's Publishing.

—Please Don't Be True: Dangerously Alice; Almost Alice; Intensely Alice. 2011. (Alice Ser.). (ENG., Illus.). 768p. (YA). (gr. 9). pap. 12.99 (978-1-4424-1721-2(8), Atheneum Bks. for Young Readers) Simon & Schuster Children's Publishing.

—Saving Shiloh. unabr. ed. 2004. 137p. (J). (gr. 3-7). pap. 29.00 incl. audio (978-0-8072-0456-6(0), Listening Library) Random Hse. Audio Publishing Group.

—Starting with Alice. 2004. (Alice Bks.). 181p. (J). (gr. 4-7). 12.65 (978-0-7569-2940-4(7)) Perfection Learning Corp.

—Starting with Alice. 2012. (Alice Ser.). (ENG., Illus.). 224p. (J). (gr. 2-7). pap. 6.99 (978-1-4424-4642-7(0), Atheneum Bks. for Young Readers) Simon & Schuster Children's Publishing.

—You & Me & the Space in Between: Alice in Charge; Incredibly Alice; Alice on Board. 2013. (Alice Ser.). (ENG., Illus.). 880p. (YA). (gr. 9). pap. 10.99 (978-1-4424-8664-5(3), Atheneum Bks. for Young Readers) Simon & Schuster Children's Publishing.

Nazemian, Abdi. The Authentics. 2017. 288p. (YA). (gr. 8). 17.99 (978-0-06-248646-2(2)) HarperCollins Pubs.

Necochea, Kristi Landry. The First Day of Forever. 2007. (J). (978-0-9792361-0-5(X)) Inspire U., LLC.

Neeck, Alessa. Bella Bunhead. 2013. 34p. pap. 9.99 (978-0-9894402-0-2(6)) Bella & Bruno Bks.

Needham B.Ed, Louise. Flossie's Escape to Freedom. 2010. (Illus.). 44p. pap. 16.99 (978-1-4490-9385-3(X)) AuthorHouse.

Needham, T. L. Kitty Claus. 2012. (ENG.). 27p. (J). (-18). pap. 19.95 (978-1-4787-1788-1(2)) Outskirts Pr., Inc.

Neel, Julien. Down in the Dumps. Neel, Julien, illus. 2012. (Lou! Ser.: 3). (ENG., Illus.). 48p. (J). (gr. 6-9). pap. 8.95 (978-0-8225-9165-8(0), Graphic Universe™) Lerner Publishing Group.

Neel, Julien & Burrell, Carol klio. Down in the Dumps. Neel, Julien, illus. 2012. (Lou! Ser.: 3). (ENG., Illus.). 48p. (J). (gr. 6-9). lib. bdg. 27.93 (978-0-7613-8779-4(X), Graphic Universe™) Lerner Publishing Group.

Neely, Wilma F. Aaron & Abbey Go to School: Trevor Tutors His Friends. 2009. 28p. pap. 12.49 (978-1-4389-5420-2(4)) AuthorHouse.

Neer, P. J. Cats Can't Fly: Teaching Children to Value New Friendships. Gazsi, Benjamin, illus. 2012. (Let's Talk Ser.). (ENG.). 48p. (J). (gr. -1-2). pap. 9.95 (978-0-88282-381-2(7)) New Horizon Pr. Pubs., Inc.

Nefflen, Marjorie E. Bashful the Brown-Eyed Dog Gets a Home. 2013. 36p. pap. 24.95 (978-1-4626-9881-3(6)) America Star Bks.

Neil, Deanna. The Land of Curiosities (Book 2)) Lost in Yellowstone, 1872-1873. 2009. 320p. (J). pap. 12.95 (978-0-9798800-2-5(5)) EcoSeekers, The.

Neilson, G. E. F. Cosmic Aviators - Nathaniel's 1st Adventure. 2013. 332p. pap. (978-0-9576132-0-1(2)) Buzzword Pr.

Neimark, Jill & Weiner, Marcella Bakur. Toodles & Teeny: A Story about Friendship. 2012. (J). pap. 9.95 (978-1-4338-1199-9(5)); (Illus.). 14.95 (978-1-4338-1198-2(7)) American Psychological Assn. (Magination Pr.).

Nelid, Piper. The Pen Pal, 01 vols., 1. 2016. (Rosen REAL Readers: Social Studies Nonfiction / Fiction: Family, Community, & the World Ser.). (ENG.). 12p. (J). pap. 6.33 (978-1-5081-1910-4(4), Rosen Classroom) Rosen Publishing Group, Inc., The.

Nelligan, Patty. Peppy Up: Eat Your Best, Be Your Best! Ocello, Salvatore & Nelligan, Kevin, illus. 2013. 32p. pap. 12.95 (978-1-939418-41-8(0)) Writer of the Round Table Pr.

Nelson, Bruce M. The Magician's Hat. 2006. 127p. pap. 19.95 (978-1-4241-2301-8(1)) America Star Bks.

Nelson, James Gary. Smileytooth & the Plaque Attack. Bumstead, Debbie, illus. 2008. 20p. pap. 10.95 (978-1-935137-48-1(4)) Guardian Angel Publishing, Inc.

Nelson, Jim. Crosstown Crush. 2005. 82p. Vol. 1, Bk. 1. (YA). pap. 9.00 (978-1-4116-5266-8(5)) Vol. 1,Bk. 2. pap. 9.00 (978-1-4116-6654-2(2)) Lulu Pr., Inc.

Nelson, Linda. Friends of Choice. 2010. 152p. 34.99 (978-0-557-53239-1(6)); 267p. pap. 19.99 (978-0-557-49742-3(6)) Lulu Pr., Inc.

Nelson, Marilyn. Ostrich & Lark. Artists of the Kuru Art Project in Botswana, San, illus. 2012. (ENG.). 32p. (J). (gr. k-4). 16.95 (978-1-59078-702-1(1)) Boyds Mills Pr.

—Snook Alone. Ering, Timothy Basil, illus. (ENG.). 48p. (J). (gr. -1-3). 2012. pap. 7.99 (978-0-7636-6120-5(1)) 2010. 16.99 (978-0-7636-2667-9(8)) Candlewick Pr.

Nelson, Peter. Herbert's Wormhole: The Rise & Fall of el Solo Libre. Rao, Rohitash, illus. 2014. (Herbert's Wormhole Ser.: 2). (ENG.). 336p. (J). (gr. 3-7). pap. 6.99 (978-0-06-201219-7(3)) HarperCollins Pubs.

—The Rise & Fall of el Solo Libre. Rao, Rohitash, illus. 2012. (Herbert's Wormhole Ser.: 2). (ENG.). 320p. (J). (gr. 3-7). 12.99 (978-0-06-201218-0(5)) HarperCollins Pubs.

Nelson, Sheila K. The Backpack Bears' Adventure: Friendship. 2009. 24p. pap. 16.50 (978-1-4490-0554-2(3)) AuthorHouse.

Nelson, Suzanne. Cake Pop Crush. 2016. (ENG.). 256p. (J). (gr. 4-7). pap. 6.99 (978-0-545-85734-5(1), Scholastic Paperbacks) Scholastic, Inc.

—Donut Go Breaking My Heart: a Wish Novel. 2017. (Wish Ser.). (ENG.). 288p. (J). (gr. 4-7). pap. 6.99 **(978-1-338-13742-2(5)**, Scholastic Paperbacks) Scholastic, Inc.

Nelson, Suzanne. Macarons at Midnight. 2016. (ENG.). 256p. (J). (gr. 4-7). pap. 6.99 (978-0-545-88425-9(X), Scholastic Paperbacks) Scholastic, Inc.

Nelson, Tamieka Lewis -. Step Friend. 2012. 28p. pap. 21.99 (978-1-4691-7852-3(4)) Xlibris Corp.

Nelson, Wendy Watson. The Not Even Once Club: My Promise to Heavenly Father. Dorman, Brandon, illus. 2013. 18.99 (978-1-60907-337-4(1)) Deseret Bk. Co.

Neri, G. Tru & Nelle. (ENG., Illus.). (J). (gr. 3-5). 2017. 352p. pap. 7.99 **(978-1-328-74095-3(1))** 2016. 336p. 16.99 (978-0-544-69960-1(2)) Houghton Mifflin Harcourt Publishing Co. (HMH Books For Young Readers).

Neri, Greg. Surf Mules. 2104. (ENG.). 288p. (YA). pap. (978-1-4677-4238-2(4)) Lerner Publishing Group.

Nesbet, Anne. Cloud & Wallfish. 2016. (ENG.). 400p. (J). (gr. 5-9). 16.99 (978-0-7636-8803-5(7)) Candlewick Pr.

Nesbit, E. The Story of the Amulet. 2009. 176p. (gr. -1-7). pap. 4.95 (978-1-60459-694-6(5)) Wilder Pubns., Corp.

Nesbø, Jo. Doctor Proctor's Fart Powder. Chace, Tara F., tr. Lowery, Mike, illus. 2010. (Doctor Proctor's Fart Powder Ser.). (ENG.). 288p. (J). (gr. 3-7). pap. 7.99 (978-1-4169-7973-9(5), Aladdin) Simon & Schuster Children's Publishing.

—Doctor Proctor's Fart Powder. Chace, Tara, tr. from GER. Lowery, Mike, illus. 2009. (Doctor Proctor's Fart Powder Ser.). (ENG.). 272p. (J). (gr. 3-7). 17.99 (978-1-4169-7972-2(7), Aladdin) Simon & Schuster Children's Publishing.

—Doctor Proctor's Fart Powder. 2010. (Dr. Proctor's Fart Powder Ser.: 1). lib. bdg. 18.40 (978-0-606-15419-2(1), Turtleback) Turtleback Bks.

Nettrour, Nelani. Sun Griffins: Dragonlands, Book 4. 2007. (Illus.). 190p. (J). pap. 16.95 (978-1-932657-90-6(8)) Third Millennium Pubns.

Neufeld, John. Lisa, Bright & Dark: A Novel. 2007. 152p. per. 12.95 (978-0-595-45048-0(2), Backinprint.com) iUniverse, Inc.

Neuhofer, Sheri L. Courageous Warrior. Amory, Deanna & O'Hara, Cynthia, illus. 2010. 28p. pap. 10.95 (978-0-9787472-7-5(5)) Ajoyin Publishing, Inc.

Neumann, Jeanne L. Wendell the Weasel. 2008. 16p. per. 24.95 (978-1-4241-9922-8(0)) America Star Bks.

Neuschwander, Angel & Johnston, Becky. Gretchen Asks, How Do Cars Work? 2009. 24p. pap. 12.99 (978-1-4389-2886-9(6)) AuthorHouse.

The Nevergreen. 2003. (J). 15.99 (978-0-9744565-9-1(4)) Heart-to-Heart Pubns.

New Frontiers Group. There's Nobody Like You! The World of Howie & Friends. 2006. (Illus.). (J). 2.99 (978-1-58597-370-5(X)) Leathers Publishing.

New, William. Sam Swallow & the Riddleworld League, 1 vol. Yayo, illus. 2013. (ENG.). 144p. (J). (gr. 3-5). pap. 12.95 (978-1-896580-98-2(X)) Tradewind Bks. CAN. Dist: Orca Bk. Pubs. USA.

Newberry, Peggy. Margie & the Goat. 2010. 24p. pap. 15.99 (978-1-4500-7475-9(8)) Xlibris Corp.

Newman, Barbara Johansen. Glamorous Glasses. 2012. (ENG.). 40p. (J). (gr. k-3). 16.95 (978-1-59078-878-3(8)) Boyds Mills Pr.

Newman, Catherine. One Mixed-Up Night. 2017. (ENG.). 208p. (J). (gr. 3-7). 16.99 **(978-0-399-55388-2(6))**; lib. bdg. 19.99 **(978-0-399-55389-9(4))** Random Hse. Children's Bks. (Random Hse. Bks. for Young Readers).

Newman, Samantha. Sammy Skizzors & the Rainbow Knight. 2010. 32p. 14.99 (978-1-4520-9976-7(6)) AuthorHouse.

Newton, Robert. Saturday Morning, Mozart & Burnt Toast. 2004. 150p. (J). (978-0-7022-3436-1(2)) Univ. of Queensland Pr.

Neylon, Robbie. The Real Me. 2013. 24p. pap. 15.99 (978-1-4797-5718-3(7)) Xlibris Corp.

Nicholas, Soraya. Gymkhana Hijinks. 2017. (Starlight Stables Ser.: 2). (ENG.). 192p. (J). (gr. 2-4). 8.99 **(978-0-14-330863-8(7))** Random Hse. Australia AUS. Dist: Independent Pubs. Group.

Nichols, Lori. Maple. Nichols, Lori, illus. 2014. (ENG., Illus.). 32p. (J). (gr. -1-k). 16.99 (978-0-399-16085-1(X), Nancy Paulsen Books) Penguin Young Readers Group.

—Maple & Willow Together. Nichols, Lori, illus. 2014. (ENG., Illus.). 32p. (J). (gr. -1-k). 16.99 (978-0-399-16283-1(6), Nancy Paulsen Books) Penguin Young Readers Group.

Nicholson, Simon. The Demon Curse. 2015. (Young Houdini Ser.: 2). (ENG.). 240p. (J). (gr. 5-8). 15.99 (978-1-4926-0335-1(X), 9781492603351, Sourcebooks Jabberwocky) Sourcebooks, Inc.

—The Magician's Fire. (Young Houdini Ser.: 1). (ENG.). (J). 2015. 272p. (gr. 4-7). pap. 7.99 (978-1-4926-0949-0(8)) 2014. (Illus.). 240p. (gr. 5-8). 15.99 (978-1-4926-0332-0(5), 9781492603320, Sourcebooks Jabberwocky) Sourcebooks, Inc.

Nick, Barbara. Bella the Dragon. Steckler, Elaine, illus. 2013. 36p. pap. 11.75 (978-1-938078-05-7(5)) Catto Creations, LLC.

Nickel, Scott. Garfield & Friends. Flowerpot Press, ed. 2012. (Illus.). 10p. (J). (978-1-926988-83-2(3)) Flowerpot Children's Pr. Inc.

Nickelodeon Dora the Explorer Staff. Say Boo! 2013. (Guess Who! Book Ser.: 1). (ENG.). 10p. (J). (gr. -1-1). bds. 10.99 (978-0-7944-2857-0(6)) Reader's Digest Assn., Inc., The.

Nickelodeon Staff & Nickelodeon / LeapFrog. Go Diego Go! Underwater Mystery. 2008. (J). 13.99 (978-1-59319-925-8(2)) LeapFrog Enterprises, Inc.

Nicklas, James. Study Hall Story. 2008. 146p. pap. 8.84 (978-1-4357-5691-5(6)) Lulu Pr., Inc.

Nicolle, Ethan. Kill the Devil. 2008. (ENG., Illus.). 120p. (YA). pap. 10.95 (978-1-59362-099-8(3), 9781593620998) Slave Labor Bks.

Niddrie, June. Great Scott & Otis. 2010. 56p. pap. 23.30 (978-0-557-31863-6(7)) Lulu Pr., Inc.

—Sweetpea & His Friends. 2010. 36p. pap. 17.30 (978-0-557-31853-7(X)) Lulu Pr., Inc.

Nielsen, Amy. Victor & the Sun Orb. 2008. 144p. 21.95 (978-0-595-50307-0(1)); pap. 11.95 (978-0-595-51212-6(7)) iUniverse, Inc.

Nielsen, Jennifer A. The Scourge. 2016. (ENG.). 368p. (J). (gr. 4-7). 16.99 (978-0-545-68245-9(2), Scholastic Pr.) Scholastic, Inc.

Nielsen, Susin. Optimists Die First. 2017. (ENG.). 240p. (YA). (gr. 7). 17.99 (978-0-553-49690-1(5), Lamb, Wendy Bks.) Random Hse. Children's Bks.

—Word Nerd. (ENG.). (J). (gr. 4-7). 2010. 264p. pap. 12.95 (978-0-88776-990-0(X)) 2008. 256p. 18.95 (978-0-88776-875-0(X)) Tundra Bks. CAN. (Tundra Bks.). Dist: Penguin Random Hse. LLC.

Niemi, Renee. Riia's Dream Diary. 2012. 54p. pap. 16.95 (978-1-4626-9942-1(1)) America Star Bks.

Night, P. J. Best Friends Forever. 2012. (You're Invited to a Creepover Ser.: 6). (ENG.). 160p. (J). (gr. 3-7). pap. 6.99 (978-1-4424-4150-7(X), Simon Spotlight) Simon Spotlight.
—Best Friends Forever. 2012. (Creepover Ser.: 6). lib. bdg. 17.20 (978-0-606-26336-8(5), Turtleback) Turtleback Bks.
—Is She for Real? 2012. (You're Invited to a Creepover Ser.: 7). (ENG.). 160p. (J). (gr. 3-7). pap. 6.99 (978-1-4424-5056-1(8), Simon Spotlight) Simon Spotlight.
—Is She for Real? 2012. (Creepover Ser.: 7). lib. bdg. 17.20 (978-0-606-26340-5(3), Turtleback) Turtleback Bks.
—No Trick-or-Treating! Superscary Superspecial. 2012. (You're Invited to a Creepover Ser.: 9). (ENG.). 208p. (J). (gr. 3-7). pap. 6.99 (978-1-4424-5053-0(3), Simon Spotlight) Simon Spotlight.
—The Ride of Your Life. 2014. (You're Invited to a Creepover Ser.: 18). (ENG., Illus.). 160p. (J). (gr. 3-7). pap. 6.99 (978-1-4424-9729-0(7), Simon Spotlight) Simon Spotlight.
—The Ride of Your Life. 2014. (Creepover Ser.: 18). lib. bdg. 17.20 (978-0-606-35431-8(X)) Turtleback Bks.
—What a Doll! 2013. (You're Invited to a Creepover Ser.: 12). (ENG.). 160p. (J). (gr. 3-7). pap. 6.99 (978-1-4424-5985-4(9), Simon Spotlight) Simon Spotlight.
—You Can't Come in Here!, 1 vol. 2013. (You're Invited to a Creepover Ser.). (ENG.). 160p. (J). (gr. 3-6). lib. bdg. 24.21 (978-1-61479-066-2(3), Essential Library) ABDO Publishing Co.
—You Can't Come in Here! 2011. (You're Invited to a Creepover Ser.: 2). (ENG.). 160p. (J). (gr. 3-7). pap. 6.99 (978-1-4424-2095-3(2), Simon Spotlight) Simon Spotlight.
—Your Worst Nightmare. 2013. (You're Invited to a Creepover Ser.: 17). (ENG., Illus.). 160p. (J). (gr. 3-7). pap. 6.99 (978-1-4424-8235-7(4), Simon Spotlight) Simon Spotlight.
Nikolet, C. T. From Bullies to Friends. Howe, Cindy T., illus. 2008. 25p. pap. 24.95 (978-1-60610-121-6(8)) America Star Bks.
Nilsson, Bo Sigvard. Come on, Brian! A Young Boy's Struggle to Play in an All-Star Hockey Tournament. 2012. 56p. (gr. 4-6). pap. 8.95 (978-1-4502-9301-3(8)) iUniverse, Inc.
Nitz, Kristin Wolden. Defending Irene, 1 vol. 2004. (ENG.). 224p. (J). (gr. 3-7). 14.95 (978-1-56145-309-2(9)) Peachtree Pubs.
Niven, Jennifer. All the Bright Places. 2015. (ENG.). 400p. pap. (978-0-14-135703-4(7)) Penguin Bks., Ltd.
—All the Bright Places. (ENG.). (YA). (gr. 9). 2016. 416p. pap. 10.99 (978-0-385-75591-7(0), Ember) 2015. 400p. lib. bdg. 20.99 (978-0-385-75589-4(9), Knopf Bks. for Young Readers) 2015. 400p. 17.99 (978-0-385-75588-7(0), Knopf Bks. for Young Readers) Random Hse. Children's Bks.
—All the Bright Places. 2016. lib. bdg. 22.10 (978-0-606-38876-4(1)) Turtleback Bks.
Noël, Alyson. Art Geeks & Prom Queens. 2005. (ENG.). 240p. (YA). (gr. 7-12). pap. 9.99 (978-0-312-33636-3(5), 9780312336363, St. Martin's Griffin) St. Martin's Pr.
—Keeping Secrets. 2012. (ENG.). 448p. (YA). (gr. 8-12). pap. 9.99 (978-1-250-01862-5(5), 9781250018625, St. Martin's Griffin) St. Martin's Pr.
Nolan, Alan. Conor's Caveman: The Amazing Adventures of Ogg. 2016. (ENG., Illus.). 144p. (J). pap. 11.00 (978-1-84717-732-2(8)) O'Brien Pr., Ltd., The IRL. Dist: Dufour Editions, Inc.
Nolen, Jerdine. Block Party Surprise. Henninger, Michelle, illus. 2015. 41p. (J). (978-1-4806-8574-1(7)) Harcourt.
—Bradford Street Buddies: Block Party Surprise. Henninger, Michelle, illus. 2015. (Green Light Readers Level 3 Ser.). (ENG.). 48p. (J). (gr. 1-4). pap. 3.99 (978-0-544-35863-8(5), HMH Books For Young Readers) Houghton Mifflin Harcourt Publishing Co.
Nolen, Jerdine, et al. Bradford Street Buddies: Backyard Camp-Out. Henninger, Michelle, illus. 2015. (Green Light Readers Level 3 Ser.). (ENG.). 48p. (J). (gr. 1-4). pap. 3.99 (978-0-544-36844-6(4), HMH Books For Young Readers) Houghton Mifflin Harcourt Publishing Co.
—Bradford Street Buddies: Backyard Camp-Out. Henninger, Michelle, illus. 2015. (Green Light Readers Level 3 Ser.). (ENG.). 48p. (J). (gr. 1-4). 12.99 (978-0-544-36843-9(6), HMH Books For Young Readers) Houghton Mifflin Harcourt Publishing Co.
Nolt, Debbie. Love for Lyndon. 2011. (Illus.). 62p. (J). (gr. 3-6). 3.40 (978-0-7399-2430-3(3)) Rod & Staff Pubs., Inc.
Nona Theresa Perez - Bayanin. Nadia Mei's First Spring: A Season of Growth. 2012. 32p. pap. 21.99 (978-1-4771-1006-5(2)) Xlibris Corp.
Nooks, Nanny. Nina in the Forest of Faces. 2011. 46p. pap. 16.00 (978-1-61204-606-8(1), Strategic Bk. Publishing) Strategic Book Publishing & Rights Agency (SBPRA).
Nord, Kristin Magnuson. Moosh & Grizzle. 2011. 28p. (gr. 1-2). 13.95 (978-1-4269-6167-0(7)) Trafford Publishing.
Nordling, Lee. Belinda the Unbeatable. Roberts, Scott, illus. 2017. (Game for Adventure Ser.). (ENG.). 32p. (J). (gr. k-3). pap. 6.99 **(978-1-5124-5413-0(3))**; lib. bdg. 25.32 **(978-1-5124-1331-1(3))** Lerner Publishing Group. (Graphic Universe™).
Nordquist, Donna M. Petey the Pigasaurus. Fortune, Leslie, illus. 2011. 32p. pap. 24.95 (978-1-4560-6051-0(1)) America Star Bks.
Nordqvist, Sven. Findus Disappears! 2014. (Adventures of Pettson & Findus Ser.). (ENG., Illus.). 32p. (J). 17.95 (978-0-7358-4184-0(5)) North-South Bks., Inc.
Norman, Kim. She'll Be Coming up the Mountain. Woodruff, Liza, illus. 2016. (ENG.). 32p. (J). (gr. -1). 14.95 (978-1-4549-1610-9(9)) Sterling Publishing Co., Inc.
Norris, Christine. The Talisman of Zandria. 2013. 240p. pap. 14.99 (978-1-61271-220-8(7)) Zumaya Pubns. LLC.
Norris, Johanna. The Day Prince Snot Nose Made Friends. 2011. 36p. (gr. -1). pap. 11.32 (978-1-4567-3283-7(8)) AuthorHouse.
Norris, Shana. Troy High. 2009. (ENG.). 272p. (YA). (gr. 7-11). 16.95 (978-0-8109-4647-7(5), Amulet Bks.) Abrams, Inc.
Norriss, Andrew. Friends for Life. 2015. (ENG.). 240p. (J). (gr. 3-7). 17.99 (978-0-545-85186-2(6)) Scholastic, Inc.
North, Lynne. Gerties Gets It Right. 2008. 204p. pap. (978-1-84923-231-9(8)) YouWriteOn.
North, Phoebe. Starbreak. 2014. (Starglass Sequence Ser.). (ENG., Illus.). 432p. (YA). (gr. 7). 17.99 (978-1-4424-5956-4(5), Simon & Schuster Bks. For Young Readers) Simon & Schuster Bks. For Young Readers.
North, Ryan. Adventure Time, Vol. 2. Paroline, Shelli & Lamb, Braden, illus. 2013. (Adventure Time Ser.: 1). (ENG.). 128p. (J). (gr. 4). 34.99 (978-1-60886-321-1(2)) Boom! Studios.
—Adventure Time Vol. 2. Paroline, Shelli & Lamb, Braden, illus. 2013. (Adventure Time Ser.). (ENG.). 112p. (J). (gr. 4). pap. 14.99 (978-1-60886-323-5(9)) Boom! Studios.
—Adventure Time Vol. 3. Paroline, Shelli & Lamb, Braden, illus. 2013. (Adventure Time Ser.). (ENG.). 112p. (J). (gr. 4). pap. 14.99 (978-1-60886-317-4(4)) Boom! Studios.
North, Ryan & Lamb, Branden. Adventure Time, Vol. 1. Paroline, Shelli, illus. 2012. (Adventure Time Ser.). (ENG.). 128p. (J). (gr. 4). pap. 14.99 (978-1-60886-280-1(1)) Boom! Studios.
Northrop, Michael. Gentlemen. 2009. (ENG.). 256p. (J). (gr. 9-18). 17.99 (978-0-545-09749-9(5), Scholastic Pr.) Scholastic, Inc.
—Rotten. 2013. (ENG.). 256p. (J). (gr. 7). 17.99 (978-0-545-49587-5(3), Scholastic Pr.) Scholastic, Inc.
Norton, Dr J. Renae & Norton, J. Renae. A Maji & Mongo Book. 2011. 28p. pap. 19.95 (978-1-4634-3334-5(4)) AuthorHouse.
Norton Kreider, Barbara. Mr Squealy Makes a Friend. Dimbylow, Jube, illus. 2013. 24p. pap. (978-1-921883-52-1(9)) Pick-a-Woo Woo Pubs.
Norton, Tamra. Make Me a Home. 2008. 159p. (J). (gr. 3-7). pap. 12.99 (978-1-59955-113-5(6)) Cedar Fort, Inc./CFI Distribution.
Nosotros Interactive Packages: Los Amigos. (Pebble Soup Exploraciones Ser.). (gr. -1-18). 52.00 (978-0-7578-5252-7(1)) Rigby Education.
Nosy Crow Staff. Cuddly Cow: A Farm Friends Sound Book. Scheffler, Axel, illus. 2017. (Farm Friends Sound Book Ser.). (ENG.). 12p. (J). (— 1). bds. 9.99 (978-0-7636-9325-1(1), Nosy Crow) Candlewick Pr.
—Higgly Hen: A Farm Friends Sound Book. Scheffler, Axel, illus. 2017. (Farm Friends Sound Book Ser.). (ENG.). 12p. (J). (— 1). bds. 9.99 (978-0-7636-9324-4(3), Nosy Crow) Candlewick Pr.
—Violet Rose & the Surprise Party. Ho, Jannie, illus. 2016. (ENG.). (J). (gr. -1-3). 8.99 (978-0-7636-8917-9(3), Nosy Crow) Candlewick Pr.
Novis, Jovita. The Tiny Ballerina in the Garden. 2013. 40p. pap. 15.95 (978-1-4497-9104-9(2), WestBow Pr.) Author Solutions, Inc.
Now I'll Tell You Everything. 2014. (Alice Ser.: 25). (ENG., Illus.). 544p. (YA). (gr. 9). pap. 12.99 (978-1-4424-4591-8(2), Atheneum Bks. for Young Readers) Simon & Schuster Children's Publishing.
Nowinski, Hanna. Meg & Linus. 2017. (ENG.). 336p. (YA). 17.99 (978-1-250-09860-3(2), 9781250098603) Feiwel & Friends.
Nowlin, Laura. If He Had Been with Me. 2013. (ENG.). 336p. (YA). (gr. 7-12). pap. 9.99 (978-1-4022-7782-5(2), 9781402277825) Sourcebooks, Inc.
—This Song Is (Not) for You. 2016. (ENG.). 240p. (YA). (gr. 8-12). pap. 9.99 (978-1-4926-0290-3(6), 9781492602903) Sourcebooks, Inc.
Nuchols, Galand A. Dragon Hatchling. 2007. 144p. per. 11.95 (978-0-595-46346-6(0)) iUniverse, Inc.
Nuhfer, Heather. Friendship Is Magic. Mebberson, Amy, illus. 2013. (My Little Pony Ser.). (ENG.). 104p. pap. 17.99 (978-1-61377-760-2(4), 9781613777602) Idea & Design Works, LLC.
Numeroff, Laura Joffe. Happy Valentine's Day, Mouse! Bond, Felicia, illus. 2009. (If You Give... Ser.). (ENG.). 24p. (J). (gr. -1-3). bds. 6.99 (978-0-06-180432-8(0)) HarperCollins Pubs.
—Happy Valentine's Day, Mouse! Lap Edition. Bond, Felicia, illus. 2015. (If You Give... Ser.). (ENG.). 24p. (J). (gr. -1-3). bds. 12.99 (978-0-06-242740-3(7)) HarperCollins Pubs.
Numeroff, Laura Joffe & Evans, Nate. The Jellybeans & the Big Art Adventure. Munsinger, Lynn, illus. 2012. (ENG.). 32p. (J). (gr. -1-k). 17.95 (978-1-4197-0171-9(1), Abrams Bks. for Young Readers) Abrams, Inc.
—The Jellybeans & the Big Book Bonanza. Munsinger, Lynn, illus. 2010. (ENG.). 32p. (J). (gr. k-2). 17.95 (978-0-8109-8412-7(1), Abrams Bks. for Young Readers) Abrams, Inc.
—The Jellybeans Love to Dance. Munsinger, Lynn, illus. 2013. (ENG.). 24p. (J). (gr. -1 — 1). bds. 7.95 (978-1-4197-0622-6(5), Abrams Appleseed) Abrams, Inc.
—The Jellybeans Love to Read. Munsinger, Lynn, illus. 2014. (ENG.). 24p. (J). (gr. -1-k). bds. 7.95 (978-1-4197-1162-6(8), Abrams Appleseed) Abrams, Inc.
Numeroff, Laura Joffe, et al. The Jellybeans & the Big Camp Kickoff. 2011. (ENG., Illus.). 32p. (J). (gr. k-2). 17.95 (978-0-8109-9765-3(7), Abrams Bks. for Young Readers) Abrams, Inc.
Nunes, Lygia Bojunga. La Bolsa Amarilla. (SPA.). (YA). (gr. 5-8). pap. (978-958-04-4148-9(0), NR5368) Norma S.A. COL. Dist: Lectorum Pubns., Inc.
—La Cuerda Floja. (SPA.). 136p. (YA). (gr. 5-8). (978-84-204-3122-2(2), AF1749) Ediciones Alfaguara ESP. Dist: Lectorum Pubns., Inc.
Nunez, Ralph da Costa & Ellison, Jesse Andrews. Voyage to Shelter Cove. Simon, Madeline Gerstein, illus. 2005. (J). pap. 5.00 (978-0-9724425-3-4(7)) Homes for the Homeless Institute, Inc.
Nunnery, Donna. The Leaf That Was Afraid to Fall, 1 vol. Scardina, Tom, illus. 2010. 26p. 24.95 (978-1-4489-5927-3(6)) PublishAmerica, Inc.
Nuo, Johnny. Dinh Van Binh: Vietnamese Village Boy. 2006. (Illus.). 176p. per. 15.12 (978-1-4120-9966-0(8)) Trafford Publishing.
Nussbaum, Ben & Studio Mouse Editorial. Snow White: A New Beginning. 2008. (ENG., Illus.). 36p. (J). (gr. -1). 7.99 (978-1-59069-437-4(6)) Studio Mouse LLC.
Nuzum, K. A. The Leanin' Dog. (ENG.). 256p. (J). (gr. 3-7). 2010. pap. 6.99 (978-0-06-113936-9(X)) 2008. 15.99 (978-0-06-113934-5(3)) HarperCollins Pubs.
Nye, Barry. Hannah & the Magic Blanket - Land of the Dinosaurs. 2009. 40p. pap. 18.50 (978-0-557-03682-0(8)) Lulu Pr., Inc.
—Hannah & the Magic Blanket - Land of the Robots. 2009. 40p. pap. 18.50 (978-0-557-06602-5(6)) Lulu Pr., Inc.
Nyeu, Tao. Squid & Octopus: Friends for Always. 2012. (ENG., Illus.). 40p. (J). (gr. -1-k). 16.99 (978-0-8037-3565-1(0), Dial Bks) Penguin Young Readers Group.
Nyikos, Stacy. Shelby. Sisneros, Shawn, illus. 2006. 32p. (J). (gr. -1-3). 15.95 (978-0-9764199-1-4(2)) Stonehorse Publishing, LLC.
Nykko. Book Six: The Tower of Shadows. Bannister, illus. 2013. (Elsewhere Chronicles Ser.: 6). (ENG.). 48p. (J). (gr. 4-8). pap. 6.95 (978-1-4677-1517-1(4)) Lerner Publishing Group.
—The Elsewhere Chronicles. 2009. (Elsewhere Chronicles Ser.). (ENG.). (J). (gr. 4-8). pap. 39.62 (978-0-7613-5088-0(8));Pack, Set. pap. 237.69 (978-0-7613-5090-3(X)) Lerner Publishing Group.
O' Byrne, Lorraine. The Hippity Dippity Witch. Martin, Laura & Kennedy, Seamus, illus. 2012. 138p. pap. (978-1-78176-391-9(7)) FeedARead.com.
Oakes, Cory Putman. Dinosaur Boy Saves Mars. 2016. (Dinosaur Boy Ser.: 2). (ENG., Illus.). 224p. (J). (gr. 3-7). 12.99 (978-1-4926-0540-9(9), 9781492605409, Sourcebooks Jabberwocky) Sourcebooks, Inc.
—Dinosaur Boy Saves Mars. 2016. (Dinosaur Boy Ser.: 2). (ENG.). 224p. (J). (gr. 3-7). 18.40 (978-0-606-39306-5(4)) Turtleback Bks.
Oates, Joyce Carol. Two or Three Things I Forgot to Tell You. (ENG.). (YA). (gr. 9). 2013. 304p. pap. 9.99 (978-0-06-211048-0(9)) 2012. 288p. 17.99 (978-0-06-211047-3(0)) HarperCollins Pubs. (HarperTeen).
Oberlin, Linda. Eco in the Garden. Oberlin, Linda, illus. 2013. (Illus.). 26p. pap. 10.00 (978-0-9911382-0-3(1)) Little Worm Publishing.
Obiols, Anna. Stegosaurus: the Friendliest Dinosaur. Subi, illus. 2012. (Dinosaur Bks.). (ENG.). 36p. (J). (gr. -1-1). pap. 6.99 (978-1-4380-0107-4(X)) Barron's Educational Series, Inc.
Oblich, Kathleen. Jake & the Scarecrow. 2007. 48p. pap. 16.95 (978-1-4241-3101-3(4)) PublishAmerica, Inc.
O'Brien, Lara. Chesca & the Spirit of Grace. 2013. 316p. pap. 13.99 (978-0-9896752-0-8(3)) O'Brien, Lara Publishing.
O'Callahan, Jay. Herman & Marguerite: An Earth Story, 1 vol. O'Callahan, Laura, illus. 2003. (ENG.). 36p. (J). (gr. k-3). pap. 7.95 (978-1-56145-283-5(1)) Peachtree Pubs.
Ocean Friends Books Set 800936, 2 vols. 2005. (J). (978-1-59794-095-5(X)) Environments, Inc.
Oceanak, Karla. Dumbstruck. Spanjer, Kendra, illus. 2011. (Aldo Zelnick Comic Novel Ser.: 4). (ENG.). 160p. (J). (gr. 3-7). 12.95 (978-1-934649-16-9(3)) Bailiwick Pr.
—Ignoramus. Spanjer, Kendra, illus. 2013. (Aldo Zelnick Comic Novel Ser.: 9). (ENG.). 160p. (J). (gr. 3-7). 12.95 (978-1-934649-41-1(4)) Bailiwick Pr.
Ockler, Sarah. #scandal. 2014. (ENG., Illus.). 416p. (YA). (gr. 9). 17.99 (978-1-4814-0124-1(6), Simon Pulse) Simon Pulse.
—Twenty Boy Summer. 2010. (ENG.). 320p. (YA). (gr. 7-17). pap. 10.99 (978-0-316-05158-3(6)) Little, Brown Bks. for Young Readers.
O'Connell, Jenny. The Book of Luke. 2007. (ENG.). 304p. pap. 11.00 (978-1-4165-2040-5(6), MTV Bks.) MTV Books.
O'Connell, Rebecca. Penina Levine Is a Hard-boiled Egg. Lue Sue, Majella, illus. 2009. (ENG.). 192p. (J). (gr. 3-7). pap. 18.99 (978-0-312-55026-4(X), 9780312550264) Square Fish.
O'Connor, Barbara. The Small Adventure of Popeye & Elvis. 2011. (ENG.). 176p. (J). (gr. 3-7). pap. 7.99 (978-0-312-65932-5(6), 9780312659325) Square Fish.
O'Connor, Grandma. Rodney the Robot: Why Rodney Rebels. 2008. 52p. pap. 8.95 (978-0-595-51055-9(8)) iUniverse, Inc.
O'connor, Jane. Best Reading Buddies. 2016. (Fancy Nancy - I Can Read! Ser.). (J). lib. bdg. 13.55 (978-0-606-39273-0(4)) Turtleback Bks.
O'Connor, Jane. Fancy Nancy: Pajama Day. Drainville, Beth et al, illus. 2009. (I Can Read Level 1 Ser.). (ENG.). 32p. (J). (gr. -1-3). 16.99 (978-0-06-170371-3(0)) HarperCollins Pubs.
—Fancy Nancy & the Boy from Paris. Enik, Ted & Glasser, Robin Preiss, illus. 2008. (I Can Read Level 1 Ser.). (ENG.). 32p. (J). (gr. -1-3). 16.99 (978-0-06-123610-5(1)); pap. 3.99 (978-0-06-123609-9(8)) HarperCollins Pubs.
—Fancy Nancy & the Dazzling Jewels. Glasser, Robin Preiss, illus. 2017. (Fancy Nancy Ser.). 24p. (J). (gr. -1-3). pap. 4.99 **(978-0-06-237793-7(0)**, HarperFestival) HarperCollins Pubs.
—Fancy Nancy & the Mermaid Ballet. Glasser, Robin Preiss & Bracken, Carolyn, illus. 2012. (Fancy Nancy Ser.). (ENG.). 32p. (J). (gr. -1-2). 17.99 (978-0-06-170381-2(8)) HarperCollins Pubs.
—Fancy Nancy: Best Reading Buddies. Glasser, Robin Preiss, illus. 2016. (I Can Read Level 1 Ser.). 32p. (J). (gr. -1-3). pap. 3.99 (978-0-06-237783-8(3)) HarperCollins Pubs.
—Pajama Day. Drainville, Beth et al, illus. 2009. (I Can Read Level 1 Ser.). (ENG.). 32p. (J). (gr. -1-3). pap. 3.99 (978-0-06-170370-6(2)) HarperCollins Pubs.
—Sand Castles & Sand Palaces. Glasser, Robin Preiss, illus. 2014. (Fancy Nancy Ser.). (ENG.). 24p. (J). (gr. -1-3). pap. 4.99 (978-0-06-226954-6(2), HarperFestival) HarperCollins Pubs.
—The Secret of the Silver Key. Glasser, Robin Preiss, illus. 2014. (Fancy Nancy Ser.). (ENG.). 128p. (J). (gr. 1-5). 9.99 (978-0-06-208299-2(X)) HarperCollins Pubs.
—Splendid Speller. Glasser, Robin Preiss, illus. 2011. (I Can Read Level 1 Ser.). (ENG.). 32p. (J). (gr. -1-3). 16.99 (978-0-06-200176-4(0)); pap. 3.99 (978-0-06-200175-7(2)) HarperCollins Pubs.
—Yours till Niagara Falls, Abby. Apple, Margot, illus. 2008. (ENG.). 128p. (J). (gr. 3-7). 7.99 (978-0-14-241151-3(5), Puffin Books) Penguin Young Readers Group.
O'Coyne, James. Gravelle's Land of Horror. Whispering Pine Press International, Inc. Staff, ed. Baer, Brian, illus. 2007. (ENG.). 120p. (J). per. 9.95 (978-1-59649-604-0(5)) Whispering Pine Pr. International, Inc.
Oddo, Jennifer M. Asim the Awesome Possum: Asim Gets His Awesome. Lamb, T. S., illus. 2012. 36p. 16.95 (978-0-9855906-2-8(9)) Pie Plate Publishing Co.
An Ode to Hoptoad. 2004. (Illus.). 11p. (J). 10.00 (978-0-9749161-0-1(2)) Ray Greer, Mary Lou.
O'Dell, Kathleen. Agnes Parker... Girl in Progress. 2004. (ENG.). 176p. (J). (gr. 2-5). reprint ed. 6.99 (978-0-14-240228-3(1), Puffin Books) Penguin Young Readers Group.
—Agnes Parker... Happy Camper? 2006. (ENG., Illus.). 160p. (J). (gr. 3-7). reprint ed. 6.99 (978-0-14-240618-2(X), Puffin Books) Penguin Young Readers Group.
—The Aviary. 2012. (ENG.). 352p. (J). (gr. 3-7). 7.99 (978-0-375-85226-8(3), Yearling) Random Hse. Children's Bks.
Odems, Carlee. A Thin Line. 2008. 88p. pap. 9.95 (978-0-595-50829-7(4)) iUniverse, Inc.
Odle, Ingrid. The Case of the Missing Abacus. 2012. 16p. pap. 15.99 (978-1-4772-5612-1(1)) AuthorHouse.
O'Donnell, Liam. Ganked: Geeked Out Mysteries #1. 2013. 214p. pap. (978-0-9919281-3-2(X)) Feeding Change Media.
O'Donnell, Tom. Hamstersaurus Rex vs. Squirrel Kong. Miller, Tim, illus. 2017. (Hamstersaurus Rex Ser.: 2). 304p. (J). (gr. 3-7). 12.99 **(978-0-06-237756-2(6))** HarperCollins Pubs.
Odu, Nkemakolam. My Horrible Trip to New York. 2012. (Illus.). 74p. (gr. 4-6). pap. 13.66 (978-1-4685-8217-8(8)) AuthorHouse.
Ogunsuyi, Melissa. The Grumpy Caterpillar. 2010. 28p. pap. 14.99 (978-1-4520-4613-6(1)) AuthorHouse.
Oh, Jiwon. Mr. Monkey's Classroom. Oh, Jiwon, illus. 2005. (Illus.). 32p. (J). (gr. -1-2). lib. bdg. 15.89 (978-0-06-055722-5(2)) HarperCollins Pubs.
O'Hara, Susan. Christie Plays Softball. Barrett, Rebecca, illus. 2013. 48p. pap. 15.97 (978-1-62516-519-0(6), Strategic Bk. Publishing) Strategic Book Publishing & Rights Agency (SBPRA).
Ohi, Ruth. Fox & Squirrel. Ohi, Ruth, illus. 2013. (ENG., Illus.). 32p. (gr. -1-2). (978-1-4431-1914-6(8)) Scholastic Canada, Ltd.
Oja, L. G. Little Miss Izzy's Adventures - Miss Izzy & the Monsters. 2013. 24p. pap. (978-1-4602-1421-3(8)) FriesenPress.
Okaty, Nicole. Orange Blossom's Fruity Fun Book: A Juicy Orange Adventure. 2004. (Illus.). 39p. (978-0-439-70466-3(9)) Scholastic, Inc.
Okeke, Paulicap Okechukwu. Biribamba the Lonely Elephant. 2011. (Illus.). 28p. pap. 13.50 (978-1-4634-2992-8(4)) AuthorHouse.
O'Kelley, Jeff. Sharing Our Stories. 2006. (Early Explorers Ser.). (J). pap. (978-1-4108-6127-6(9)) Benchmark Education Co.
Okimoto, Jean Davies. Dear Ichiro. Keith, Doug, illus. 2006. 29p. (J). (gr. 4-8). reprint ed. 17.00 (978-1-4223-5803-0(8)) DIANE Publishing Co.
Okorafor-Mbachu, Nnedi. Zahrah the Windseeker. 2008. (ENG., Illus.). 320p. (J). (gr. 5-7). pap. 8.99 (978-0-547-02028-0(7)) Houghton Mifflin Harcourt Publishing Co.
Older, Daniel José. Shadowshaper. 2016. (ENG.). 297p. (YA). (gr. 9). 20.85 (978-0-606-39124-5(7)) Turtleback Bks.
Oldfield, Jenny. Sugar & Spice, Bk. 14. (Illus.). 120p. (J). pap. 7.99 (978-0-340-69986-7(8)) Hodder & Stoughton GBR. Dist: Trafalgar Square Publishing.
Oldman, James. Superhighway. Ingram, Chris, illus. 2012. 184p. pap. (978-1-78176-206-6(6)) FeedARead.com.
Olena Rudge. The Adventures of Sophie & Katia in the Enchanted Forest. 2013. 220p. pap. (978-3-85438-685-8(0)) united p.c. Verlag.
Olfet, Omid. In the Dark: Parts 3 And 4. 2009. 74p. pap. 8.95 (978-1-4401-5811-7(8)) iUniverse, Inc.
Olin, Rita & Olin, Spencer. Trouble in Soccertown: A Lazer Mcnulty Adventure. 2009. 108p. 20.95 (978-1-4401-5374-7(4)); pap. 10.95 (978-1-4401-5376-1(0)) iUniverse, Inc.
Olin, Sean. Reckless Hearts. 2015. (Wicked Games Ser.: 2). (ENG.). 336p. (YA). (gr. 9). 17.99 (978-0-06-219241-7(8), Tegen, Katherine Bks) HarperCollins Pubs.
Oliveira, Luis. The Children of Hope 3. 2009. 56p. pap. 15.49 (978-0-578-00420-4(8)) Desktop Prepress Services.
Oliver, Amanda Eaddy. Cheyenne the Cat. 2010. 28p. 13.99 (978-1-4520-6218-1(8)) AuthorHouse.
Oliver, Andrew. If Photos Could Talk. 2005. (Sam & Stephanie Mystery Ser.). 264p. (J). per. 12.95 (978-0-9661009-6-9(4)) Adams-Pomeroy Pr.
Oliver, Charles Folkes. Little Willy & the Party Animals. 2011. (Illus.). 20p. (gr. -1). pap. 14.99 (978-1-4567-5138-8(7)) AuthorHouse.
Oliver, Lauren. Before I Fall Movie Tie-In Edition. 2017. 496p. (YA). (gr. 9). pap. 10.99 (978-0-06-265632-2(5)) HarperCollins Pubs.
—Requiem. 2013. (Delirium Trilogy: Bk. 3). (ENG.). 400p. (J). (gr. 9). 18.99 (978-0-06-201453-5(6)) HarperCollins Pubs.
Oliver, Lauren & Chester, H. C. The Screaming Statue. 2017. (Curiosity House Ser.: 2). 384p. (J). (gr. 3-7). pap. 6.99 (978-0-06-227085-6(0)) HarperCollins Pubs.
Olizon-Chikiamco, Norma, et al. Pan de Sal Saves the Day: A Filipino Children's Story. Salvatus, Mark & Salvatus III, Mark Ramsel N., illus. 2009. (ENG.). 24p. (J). (gr. k-3). 12.95 (978-0-8048-4078-1(4)) Tuttle Publishing.
Olker, Constance. The Punctuation Pals Go Snow Skiing. Guzman, Minerva, illus. 2005. 22p. (J). (gr. -1-3). per. 18.95 (978-1-933449-14-2(4)) Nightengale Pr.
Ollie. 2006. (J). 6.99 (978-0-9778922-0-4(4)) Hudson, Jessie.
Olsen, J. J. The Mystic Kingdom: A Jenny Dewberry Series. 2008. 400p. pap. 17.99 (978-1-4389-2598-1(0)) AuthorHouse.
Olsen, Judith K. I Can Hardly Wait. 2006. 100p. (J). pap. 7.95 (978-1-59800-999-6(0)) Outskirts Pr., Inc.
Olsen, Mary-Kate & Olsen, Ashley. Best Friends Forever, 2 vols. 2003. (ENG., Illus.). 128p. (978-0-00-714457-0(1), HarperCollins Children's Bks.) HarperCollins Pubs. Ltd.
—Closer Than Ever. 2004. (ENG., Illus.). 112p. (978-0-00-715881-2(5), HarperCollins Children's Bks.) HarperCollins Pubs. Ltd.
—Heart to Heart. 2005. (ENG., Illus.). 112p. (978-0-00-715889-8(0)) HarperCollins Pubs. Australia.
—Making a Splash. 2005. (ENG., Illus.). 112p. (978-0-00-715886-7(6)) HarperCollins Pubs. Australia.
—MKA Two of a Kind 2003 Boxed Set. 2003. mass mkt. 19.96 (978-0-06-072353-8(X), Harper Entertainment) HarperCollins Pubs.
—Spring Breakup. 2004. (ENG.). 128p. (Orig.). (978-0-00-718095-0(0)) HarperCollins Pubs. Australia.
Olson, Cynthia J. Kiera's Cry, 1 vol. 2009. 151p. pap. 24.95 (978-1-60749-280-1(6)) America Star Bks.
Olson, Jennifer Gray. Ninja Bunny. 2015. (ENG., Illus.). 32p. (J). (gr. -1-2). 16.99 (978-0-385-75493-4(0), Knopf Bks. for Young Readers) Random Hse. Children's Bks.

Olson, Jennifer Lynn. Chef Charlie & the Great Escape, 1 vol. 2010. 18p. 24.95 (978-1-4489-5638-8(2)) PublishAmerica, Inc.
Olson, Kayla. The Sandcastle Empire. 2017. 464p. (YA). (gr. 9). 17.99 (978-0-06-248487-1(7), HarperTeen) HarperCollins Pubs.
Olswanger, Anna. Greenhorn. Nerlove, Miriam, illus. 2012. (ENG.). (J). E-Book 9.99 (978-1-60306-159-9(2)); 48p. 17.95 (978-1-58838-235-1(4)) NewSouth, Inc. (NewSouth Bks.).
Olszewski, Raymond VanCe. Chucky the Car: A Children's Story & Coloring Book. 2010. (Illus.). 20p. 12.95 (978-1-4490-6821-9(9)) AuthorHouse.
Oltchick, Peter. Clean Clara. Jasuna, Aija, illus. 2012. 34p. (J). (-18). 16.95 (978-1-60131-127-6(3), Castlebridge Bks.) Big Tent Bks.
O'Malley Cerra, Kerry. Just a Drop of Water. (ENG.). 320p. (J). (gr. 2-7). 2016. pap. 7.99 (978-1-5107-1234-8(8)) 2014. 14.95 (978-1-62914-613-3(7)) Skyhorse Publishing Co., Inc. (Sky Pony Pr.).
O'Mara, Robert J. Friends Are Special, 1 vol. 2009. 26p. pap. 24.95 (978-1-60749-087-6(0)) America Star Bks.
Omawumi Kola-Lawal, Constance. We Learn about Road Safety. 2013. 32p. pap. (978-1-909204-29-4(3)) BookPublishingWorld.
Omaya, Tam. Passion & Pain. 2010. 216p. pap. 14.49 (978-1-4520-1444-9(2)) AuthorHouse.
Once upon a Time Spanish Version-the Little Red Hen. 2005. (J). (978-1-57022-561-1(3)) ECS Learning Systems, Inc.
O'Neill, Gemma. Monty's Magnificent Mane. O'Neill, Gemma, illus. 2015. (ENG., Illus.). 40p. (J). (gr. -1-2). 15.99 (978-0-7636-7593-6(8), Templar) Candlewick Pr.
—Oh Dear, Geoffrey! O'Neill, Gemma, illus. 2014. (ENG., Illus.). 32p. (J). (gr. -1-2). 15.99 (978-0-7636-6659-0(9), Templar) Candlewick Pr.
O'Neill, Rachael. Do You Want a Hug, Honey Bunny? O'Neill, Rachael, illus. 2008. (Tiger Tales Ser.). (Illus.). 12p. (J). (gr. -1-k). 8.95 (978-1-58925-829-7(0)) Tiger Tales.
O'Neill, Tom. Old Friends. 2010. (ENG.). 436p. (J). (gr. 3-7). pap. 12.99 (978-1-84840-941-5(9)) Little Island IRL. Dist: Independent Pubs. Group.
Oneto, Maria Teresa. Liliana, la Iguan. 2012. 52p. pap. 25.00 (978-1-4389-8241-0(0)) AuthorHouse.
Onwusilikam, Ify Chinedum. The Drama Queen. 2009. 56p. pap. 10.00 (978-1-60860-126-4(9), Strategic Bk. Publishing) Strategic Book Publishing & Rights Agency (SBPRA).
Opio, Leoncio. The Adventures of Mr. Nimbus & the School House Bullies. 2012. 98p. pap. 19.95 (978-1-4626-9442-6(X)) America Star Bks.
Opitz, Todd. The Football & the Fly. 2012. 24p. pap. 24.95 (978-1-4626-9847-9(6)) America Star Bks.
O'Porter, Dawn. Goose. 2015. (ENG.). 256p. (YA). (gr. 9-17). 16.95 (978-1-4197-1645-4(X), Amulet Bks.) Abrams, Inc.
—Paper Airplanes. (ENG.). (YA). (gr. 9-17). 2015. 288p. pap. 8.95 (978-1-4197-1655-3(7)) 2014. 272p. 16.95 (978-1-4197-1184-8(9)) Abrams, Inc. (Amulet Bks.).
Oram, Hiawyn. Filbert, the Good Little Fiend. Liao, Jimmy, illus. 2013. (ENG.). 32p. (J). (gr. -1-2). 15.99 (978-0-7636-5870-0(7)) Candlewick Pr.
—My Friend Fred. Reeve, Rosie, illus. 2012. (ENG.). 32p. (J). (978-1-58925-105-2(9)) Tiger Tales.
—What's Naughty? Reynolds, Adrian, illus. 32p. (J). pap. 11.99 (978-0-340-75447-4(8)) Hodder & Stoughton GBR. Dist: Trafalgar Square Publishing.
O'Reilly, Jane. The Secret of Goldenrod. 2016. (ENG.). 328p. (J). (gr. 3-6). 17.99 (978-1-5124-0135-6(8), Carolrhoda Bks.) Lerner Publishing Group.
O'Reilly, Sean. The Abominable Snow Kid, 1 vol. 2012. (Mighty Mighty Monsters Ser.). (ENG.). 48p. (gr. 2-3). lib. bdg. 23.99 (978-1-4342-3892-4(X)) Stone Arch Bks.
—Abominable Snow Kid. 2013. (Mighty Mighty Monsters Ser.). (ENG., Illus.). 48p. (gr. 2-3). pap. 6.10 (978-1-4342-4227-3(7)) Stone Arch Bks.
—The Gremlin's Curse, 1 vol. 2012. (Mighty Mighty Monsters Ser.). (ENG.). 48p. (gr. 2-3). lib. bdg. 23.99 (978-1-4342-3894-8(6)) Stone Arch Bks.
—Gremlin's Curse. 2013. (Mighty Mighty Monsters Ser.). (ENG., Illus.). 48p. (gr. 2-3). pap. 6.10 (978-1-4342-4228-0(5)) Stone Arch Bks.
—Homesick Witch, 1 vol. (Mighty Mighty Monsters Ser.). (ENG., 48p. (gr. 2-3). 2013. Illus.). pap. 6.10 (978-1-4342-4225-9(0)) 2012. lib. bdg. 23.99 (978-1-4342-3893-1(8)) Stone Arch Bks.
—Monster Beach, 1 vol. 2011. (Mighty Mighty Monsters Ser.). (ENG.). 48p. (gr. 2-3). lib. bdg. 23.99 (978-1-4342-3217-5(4)) Stone Arch Bks.
—Monster Beach, 1 vol. Arcana Studio Staff, illus. 2012. (Mighty Mighty Monsters Ser.). (ENG.). 48p. (gr. 2-3). pap. 6.10 (978-1-4342-4608-0(6)) Stone Arch Bks.
Orgel, Doris. Devil in Vienna. 2004. (ENG.). 256p. (J). (gr. 3-7). 7.99 (978-0-14-240236-8(2), Speak) Penguin Young Readers Group.
Ori, Anthony. Snow Makes a Snowman. 2008. 24p. pap. 24.95 (978-1-60703-308-0(9)) America Star Bks.
Orietta, Susan. The Day Tyson Became a Hero. 2011. 24p. pap. 15.99 (978-1-4628-6823-0(1)) Xlibris Corp.
Orme, David & Banks, J. Gateway to Hell. 2004. (Shades Ser.). 62p. (J). pap. (978-0-237-52623-8(9)) Evans Brothers, Ltd.
Orme, Helen. Boys! Brett, Cathy, illus. 2007. (Siti's Sisters Ser.). (ENG.). 36p. (J). per. (978-1-84167-600-5(4)) Ransom Publishing Ltd.
—Leave Her Alone. 2008. (Siti's Sisters Ser.). (ENG., Illus.). 36p. pap. (978-1-84167-742-2(6)) Ransom Publishing Ltd.
—Moving. 2008. (Siti's Sisters Ser.). (ENG., Illus.). 36p. pap. (978-1-84167-689-0(6)) Ransom Publishing Ltd.
—Odd One Out. Brett, Cathy, illus. 2007. (Siti's Sisters Ser.). (ENG.). 36p. (J). per. (978-1-84167-597-8(0)) Ransom Publishing Ltd.
—Party Time. 2008. (ENG., Illus.). 36p. pap. (978-1-84167-819-1(8)) Ransom Publishing Ltd.
—Secrets. 2008. (Siti's Sisters Ser.). (ENG., Illus.). 36p. pap. (978-1-84167-743-9(4)) Ransom Publishing Ltd.
—She's My Friend Now. 2008. (Siti's Sisters Ser.). (ENG., Illus.). 36p. pap. (978-1-84167-740-8(X)) Ransom Publishing Ltd.
—Sleepover. 2008. (Siti's Sisters Ser.). (ENG., Illus.). 36p. pap. (978-1-84167-741-5(8)) Ransom Publishing Ltd.
—Stalker. Brett, Cathy, illus. 2007. (Siti's Sisters Ser.). (ENG.). 36p. (J). per. (978-1-84167-595-4(4)) Ransom Publishing Ltd.
—Taken for a Ride. Brett, Cathy, illus. 2007. (Siti's Sisters Ser.). (ENG.). 36p. (J). per. (978-1-84167-596-1(2)) Ransom Publishing Ltd.
—Trouble with Teachers. Brett, Cathy, illus. 2007. (Siti's Sisters Ser.). (ENG.). 36p. (J). per. (978-1-84167-599-2(7)) Ransom Publishing Ltd.
—Who Can I Tell? 2008. (Siti's Sisters Ser.). (ENG., Illus.). 36p. pap. (978-1-84167-744-6(2)) Ransom Publishing Ltd.
Ormondroyd, Edward. David & the Phoenix. 2009. 76p. (gr. 4-7). pap. 4.75 (978-1-60459-691-5(0)) Wilder Pubns., Corp.
—Time at the Top. Ericksen, Barbara, illus. 40th anniv. ed. 2003. 191p. (J). 17.95 (978-1-930900-19-6(8)) Purple Hse. Pr.
Ormsbee, K. E. The Doorway & the Deep. 2016. (ENG., Illus.). 480p. (J). (gr. 3-7). 16.99 (978-1-4521-3636-3(X)) Chronicle Bks. LLC.
—The Water & the Wild. Mora, Elsa, illus. 2015. (ENG.). 448p. (J). (gr. 3-7). 16.99 (978-1-4521-1386-9(6)) Chronicle Bks. LLC.
Ormsbee, Kathryn. Lucky Few. (ENG., Illus.). (YA). (gr. 9). 2017. 400p. pap. 10.99 (978-1-4814-5529-9(X)) 2016. 384p. 17.99 (978-1-4814-5528-2(1)) Simon & Schuster Bks. For Young Readers. (Simon & Schuster Bks. For Young Readers).
Oroma Alikor-Adele. Bugerfly Finds Friends. 2010. 28p. pap. 15.99 (978-1-4535-6167-6(6)) Xlibris Corp.
O'Rourke, Erica. Torn. 2011. (ENG.). 336p. (YA). (gr. 9). 9.95 (978-0-7582-6703-0(7), K-Teen) Kensington Publishing Corp.
O'Rourke, Ryan. Bella, Up, Up & Away. O'Rourke, Ryan, illus. 2016. (Illus.). 40p. (J). (gr. -1-3). 17.99 (978-0-06-221863-6(8)) HarperCollins Pubs.
Orpinas, Jean-Paul & Tilley, Scott, illus. Cars. 2006. (Little Golden Book Ser.). (ENG.). 24p. (J). (gr. -1-2). 4.99 (978-0-7364-2347-2(8), Golden/Disney) Random Hse. Children's Bks.
Orr, Tina. The Misfits & the Magical Pond. 2012. 56p. (gr. -1). pap. 12.87 (978-1-4685-3658-4(3)) AuthorHouse.
Orr, Wendy. Nim's Island. Millard, Kerry, illus. 2008. (ENG.). 128p. (J). (gr. 3-7). 6.99 (978-0-385-73606-0(1), Yearling) Random Hse. Children's Bks.
Orsi, Tea. Tinker Bell & the Legend of the NeverBeast. 2015. (Disney Fairies Graphic Novels Ser.: 17). (J). lib. bdg. 18.40 (978-0-606-37295-4(4)) Turtleback Bks.
Orsi, Tea & Panaro, Carlo. Tinker Bell & the Lost Treasure. Razzi, Manuela et al, illus. 2013. (Disney Fairies Ser.: 12). (ENG.). 64p. (J). (gr. 1-6). pap. 7.99 (978-1-59707-428-5(4), 9781597074285) Papercutz.
Ortiz, Gilberto Rendon. Tuiiiii el Murcielago. (Barril Sin Fondo Ser.). (SPA.). (J). (gr. 3-5). pap. (978-968-6465-22-8(7)) Casa de Estudios de Literatura y Talleres Artisticos Amaquemecan A.C. MEX. Dist: Lectorum Pubns., Inc.
O'Ryan, Ray. Galaxy Zack: Hello, Nebulon!; Journey to Juno; the Prehistoric Planet. Jack, Colin, illus. 2015. (Galaxy Zack Ser.). (ENG.). 384p. (J). (gr. k-4). pap. 8.99 (978-1-4814-5641-8(5), Little Simon) Little Simon.
—Hello, Nebulon! Jack, Colin, illus. 2013. (Galaxy Zack Ser.: 1). (ENG.). 128p. (J). (gr. k-2). 16.99 (978-1-4424-5387-6(7)); pap. 5.99 (978-1-4424-5386-9(9)) Little Simon. (Little Simon).
—Monsters in Space! Jack, Colin, illus. 2013. (Galaxy Zack Ser.: 4). (ENG.). 128p. (J). (gr. k-2). 16.99 (978-1-4424-6721-7(5)); pap. 5.99 (978-1-4424-6718-7(5)) Little Simon. (Little Simon).
—Monsters in Space! 2013. (Galaxy Zack Ser.: 4). lib. bdg. 16.00 (978-0-606-32460-1(7), Turtleback) Turtleback Bks.
—Operation Twin Trouble. Kraft, Jason, illus. 2015. (Galaxy Zack Ser.: 12). (ENG.). 128p. (J). (gr. k-4). pap. 5.99 (978-1-4814-4399-9(2), Little Simon) Little Simon.
—Ready, Set, Blast Off! 2017. (Galaxy Zack Ser.: 15). lib. bdg. 16.00 **(978-0-606-39737-7(X))** Turtleback Bks.
—Return to Earth! Kraft, Jason, illus. 2015. (Galaxy Zack Ser.: 10). (ENG.). 128p. (J). (gr. k-4). pap. 5.99 (978-1-4814-2181-2(6), Little Simon) Little Simon.
—Three's a Crowd! Jack, Colin, illus. 2013. (Galaxy Zack Ser.: 5). (ENG.). 128p. (J). (gr. k-4). 16.99 (978-1-4424-8222-7(2)); pap. 5.99 (978-1-4424-8221-0(4)) Little Simon. (Little Simon).
—Three's a Crowd! 2013. (Galaxy Zack Ser.: 5). lib. bdg. 16.00 (978-0-606-35187-4(6)) Turtleback Bks.
O'Ryan, Ray & Jack, Colin. Hello, Nebulon!, 1 vol. 2015. (ENG.). 128p. (978-1-61479-367-0(0)) ABDO Publishing Co.
Osborne, Amber & Osborne, Dwight. Puffy Buffy Jones Jones Osborne Dadoot Da Do. Osborne, Amber, illus. 2006. (Illus.). (J). pap. 11.99 (978-0-9786431-0-2(0)) AAO Publishing.
O'Shea, M.J. Cold Moon [Library Edition]. 2nd ed. 2014. 180p. pap. 14.99 (978-1-62798-460-7(7), Harmony Ink Pr.) Dreamspinner Pr.
Oshiro, Kimberley. The Saga of Simon the Skinny Pig: Simon Saves the Day. Yee, Jeanne, illus. 2012. 38p. pap. 12.50 (978-1-61170-089-3(2)) Robertson Publishing.
Osteen, Victoria. Unexpected Treasures. Palmisciano, Diane, illus. 2009. (ENG.). 32p. (J). (gr. -1-3). 17.99 (978-1-4169-5550-4(X), Little Simon Inspirations) Little Simon Inspirations.
Osterhold, Jared, illus. OLIVIA Goes Camping. 2011. (Olivia TV Tie-In Ser.). (ENG.). 24p. (J). (gr. -1-1). 15.99 (978-1-4424-2253-7(X)); pap. 3.99 (978-1-4424-2135-6(5)) Simon Spotlight. (Simon Spotlight).
Osterweil, Adam & Smith, Craig. The Baseball Card Kid. Smith, Craig, illus. 2009. (ENG., Illus.). 199p. (J). (gr. 3-7). 17.95 (978-1-59078-526-3(6), Front Street) Boyds Mills Pr.
Ostow, Micol. What Would My Cell Phone Do? 2011. (ENG.). 272p. (YA). (gr. 7-18). 7.99 (978-0-14-241469-9(7), Speak) Penguin Young Readers Group.
Ostrander, P. Martin. P Martin Ostrander's Dangerous Four Series: Book #1. 2007. 112p. 20.95 (978-0-595-68250-8(2)); per. 10.95 (978-0-595-43582-1(3)) iUniverse, Inc.
Ostrom, Bob, illus. Friends till the End! 2005. (Teenage Mutant Ninja Turtles Ser.: No. 3). 24p. (J). lib. bdg. 15.00 (978-1-59054-833-2(7)) Fitzgerald Bks.
Otoshi, Kathryn. Two. 2014. (ENG., Illus.). 40p. (J). (gr. -1). 18.95 (978-0-9723946-6-6(4)) KO Kids Bks.
Otten, Charlotte F. Home in a Wilderness Fort: Copper Harbor 1844. 2006. (Illus.). 232p. (J). (gr. 2-7). per. 14.95 (978-0-9766104-5-8(0)) Arbutus Pr.
Out of the Blue. 2014. (J). pap. (978-0-8163-5016-2(7)) Pacific Pr. Publishing Assn.
Overington, Marcus. Lost on Bodmin Moor. 2012. (Illus.). 50p. pap. (978-1-909039-36-0(5)) Legend Pr.
Owen, Sarah. The Adventures of Molly & Polly. 2009. 43p. pap. 26.95 (978-1-4452-5925-3(7)) Lulu Pr., Inc.
Owens, Donna. NIBBLES: Volume 2, Nibbles Adventures. 2008. 38p. pap. 14.95 (978-1-4357-4621-3(X)) Lulu Pr., Inc.
Owens, L. L. If You Want My Advice- Tolson, Scott, illus. 2004. 25p. (978-1-57021-030-3(6)) Comprehensive Health Education Foundation.
—Kendra's Big Decision. 2004. (Illus.). 26p. pap. (978-1-57021-031-0(4)) Comprehensive Health Education Foundation.
—The Longest Car Ride Ever. Tolson, Scott, illus. 2004. 28p. (978-1-57021-032-7(2)) Comprehensive Health Education Foundation.
—The New Girl. Tolson, Scott, illus. 2004. 27p. (978-1-57021-029-7(2)) Comprehensive Health Education Foundation.
P. Cats & Cows & Moos & Meows. 2011. 28p. (gr. -1). pap. 13.50 (978-1-4567-3464-0(4)) AuthorHouse.
P., Angie. Sneakers. 2012. 32p. pap. 19.99 (978-1-4772-4548-4(0)) AuthorHouse.
Pace, Betty. Donald's Dump Truck. 2007. 36p. per. 12.95 (978-1-4327-0029-4(4)) Outskirts Pr., Inc.
Paciullo, Ursula. Max's Tale: Max Makes New Friends. 2012. 20p. pap. 17.99 (978-1-4772-7861-1(3)) AuthorHouse.
Packard, Mary. Where Is Jake? Allen, Joy, illus. 2003. (My First Reader Ser.). (ENG.). 32p. (J). 18.50 (978-0-516-22957-7(5), Children's Pr.) Scholastic Library Publishing.
Packham, Simon. Trust Games. 2016. (ENG.). 224p. (YA). (gr. 7). pap. 11.99 (978-1-84812-384-7(1)) Bonnier Publishing GBR. Dist: Independent Pubs. Group.
Padian, Maria. Brett McCarthy: Work in Progress. 2009. (ENG.). 288p. (YA). (gr. 7). pap. 8.99 (978-0-440-24055-6(7), Knopf Bks. for Young Readers) Random Hse. Children's Bks.
—Jersey Tomatoes Are the Best. 2012. (ENG.). 352p. (YA). (gr. 7). pap. 9.99 (978-0-375-86563-3(2), Ember) Random Hse. Children's Bks.
Padula, Stacy A. Montgomery Lake High #2-When Darkness Tries to Hide. 2011. 146p. pap. 11.50 (978-1-60976-857-7(4), Eloquent Bks.) Strategic Book Publishing & Rights Agency (SBPRA).
Page, Julie & Adams, Sabrina. The Treasure of Trust: The Hidden Treasures of My Kingdom Pals McTeer, Rhonda, ed. Motz, Mike, illus. 2005. 72p. (J). (gr. 4-7). 14.95 (978-0-9748251-0-6(7), 825106) Zoe Life Publishing.
Page, Rhonda G. The Most Important Thing to Have. 2003. pap. 8.00 (978-0-8059-5438-8(4)) Dorrance Publishing Co., Inc.
Pagel, Stace. Fletcher the Fly. 2008. (Illus.). 32p. pap. 14.95 (978-1-4389-2196-9(9)) AuthorHouse.
Painter, Grace. The Harry Bear Story. Kacer, Stephen, illus. 2011. 28p. pap. 24.95 (978-1-4626-3327-2(7)) America Star Bks.
Pair, Karma A. Before the Sun Could Answer. 2009. 20p. pap. 15.00 (978-1-4389-6252-8(5)) AuthorHouse.
Pakalne, Violeta. A Motorcyclist Croaker Lee. 2010. 80p. pap. 29.49 (978-1-4520-9578-3(7)) AuthorHouse.
Pakkala, Christine. Jasmine & Maddie. 2014. (ENG.). 192p. (J). (gr. 4-7). 16.95 (978-1-62091-739-8(4)) Boyds Mills Pr.
—Last-But-Not-Least Lola & the Cupcake Queens. Hoppe, Paul, illus. 2015. (Last-But-Not-Least Lola Ser.). (ENG.). 168p. (J). (gr. 1-5). 16.95 (978-1-62091-596-7(0)) Boyds Mills Pr.
—Last-But-Not-Least Lola & the Wild Chicken. Hoppe, Paul, illus. (Last-But-Not-Least Lola Ser.). (ENG.). 216p. (J). 2015. (gr. 1-5). pap. 7.95 (978-1-62979-404-4(X)) 2014. (gr. 2-5). 15.95 (978-1-59078-983-4(0)) Boyds Mills Pr.
—Last-but-Not-Least Lola Going Green. Hoppe, Paul, illus. 2013. (Last-But-Not-Least Lola Ser.). (ENG.). 192p. (J). (gr. 2-5). 15.95 (978-1-59078-935-3(0)) Boyds Mills Pr.
—Last-But-Not-Least Lola Going Green. Hoppe, Paul, illus. 2014. (Last-But-Not-Least Lola Ser.). (ENG.). 192p. (J). (gr. 2-5). pap. 7.95 (978-1-62979-113-5(X)) Boyds Mills Pr.
Palacio, R. J. Auggie & Me: Three Wonder Stories. 2015. (ENG.). 320p. (J). (gr. 3-7). 16.99 (978-1-101-93485-2(9), Knopf Bks. for Young Readers) Random Hse. Children's Bks.
Palacios, Tomas. Avengers: Age of Ultron: Friends & Foes. 2015. (Passport to Reading Level 2 Ser.). (J). lib. bdg. 13.55 (978-0-606-37216-9(4)) Turtleback Bks.
Palatini, Margie. Stuff. Jones, Noah Z., illus. 2011. (ENG.). 32p. (J). (gr. -1-2). 16.99 (978-0-06-171921-9(8), Tegen, Katherine Bks) HarperCollins Pubs.
Paley, Sasha. Huge. 2008. (ENG.). 272p. (YA). (gr. 7-12). pap. 8.99 (978-1-4169-5795-9(2), Simon & Schuster Bks. For Young Readers) Simon & Schuster Bks. For Young Readers.
Paley, Sasha & Greenwald, Lisa. Huge. 2007. (ENG.). 272p. (YA). (gr. 9-12). 15.99 (978-1-4169-3517-9(7), Simon & Schuster Bks. For Young Readers) Simon & Schuster Bks. For Young Readers.
Pallasch, Tina. Ever Atom: One. 2011. 46p. pap. 16.50 (978-1-60976-374-9(2), Eloquent Bks.) Strategic Book Publishing & Rights Agency (SBPRA).
Palma, B. El Dorado: A Palo Alto Adventure. 2012. 136p. (gr. -1). 23.99 (978-1-4634-3110-5(4)); pap. 13.99 (978-1-4634-3111-2(2)) AuthorHouse.
Palmer, Iva-Marie. Gabby Garcia's Ultimate Playbook. 2017. (Gabby Garcia's Ultimate Playbook Ser.: 1). 304p. (J). (gr. 3-7). 12.99 (978-0-06-239180-3(1), Tegen, Katherine Bks) HarperCollins Pubs.
Palmer, Robin. Cindy Ella. 2008. (ENG.). 336p. (YA). (gr. 7-18). 9.99 (978-0-14-240392-1(X), Speak) Penguin Young Readers Group.
—For Better or for Worse, 5 vols. 2012. (Yours Truly, Lucy B. Parker Ser.: 5). (ENG.). 224p. (J). (gr. 5-18). pap. 6.99 (978-0-14-241504-7(9), Puffin Books) Penguin Young Readers Group.
—Once upon a Kiss. 2016. (ENG.). 304p. (YA). (gr. 7). pap. 9.99 (978-0-14-750988-8(2), Speak) Penguin Young Readers Group.
—Take My Advice!, 4 vols. 2012. (Yours Truly, Lucy B. Parker Ser.: 4). (ENG.). 224p. (J). (gr. 5-18). 6.99 (978-0-14-241503-0(0), Puffin Books) Penguin Young Readers Group.
—Vote for Me!, 3 vols. 2011. (Yours Truly, Lucy B. Parker Ser.: 3). (ENG.). 224p. (J). (gr. 5-18). 6.99 (978-0-14-241502-3(2), Puffin Books) Penguin Young Readers Group.
Palmieri, Kathryn & Palmieri, Patricia. GYPSY McPHEE: The New Kid in Town. 2011. (Illus.). 40p. (J). pap. 12.95 (978-1-58909-750-6(5)) Bookstand Publishing.
Pampalone, Donna. The Adventures of Koco Koala & Friends: Book One: Cuisin' with Cameron. 2007. 60p. per. 16.95 (978-1-4241-8095-0(3)) America Star Bks.
Panaitescu, Simona. The Unseen Paths of the Forest: 13 Tales about Love & Friendship. Moscal, Manuela, illus. 2012. (ENG.). 263p. pap. 14.95 (978-1-4327-7908-5(7)) Outskirts Pr., Inc.
Pandelis, Bloomin' Harmony Judy E. Bloomin' Harmony. 2010. 32p. pap. 18.00 (978-0-557-32902-1(7)) Lulu Pr., Inc.
Panik, Alison Saeger. Berry Best Friends Book: A Fun with Friends Adventure. 2005. 39p. lib. bdg. (978-0-439-70469-4(3)) Scholastic, Inc.
Pantages, Joanna. Fairytale Fitness: Holygrain. 2009. 24p. pap. 12.49 (978-1-4389-4494-4(2)) AuthorHouse.
Paourou, Maria. Bubblebea Wants to Be a Hero. 2009. (Illus.). 40p. pap. 16.99 (978-1-4343-7330-4(4)) AuthorHouse.
Papademetriou, Lisa. Confectionately Yours #3: Sugar & Spice. 2013. (Confectionately Yours Ser.). (ENG.). 224p. (J). (gr. 3-7). pap. 6.99 (978-0-545-22230-3(3), Scholastic Paperbacks) Scholastic, Inc.
—Confectionately Yours #4: Something New. 2013. (Confectionately Yours Ser.: 3). (ENG.). 192p. (J). (gr. 3-7). pap. 6.99 (978-0-545-22231-0(1), Scholastic Paperbacks) Scholastic, Inc.
—Save the Cupcake! 2012. (Confectionately Yours Ser.: 1). (J). (ENG.). 240p. (gr. 3-7). pap. 6.99 (978-0-545-22228-0(1), Scholastic Paperbacks); 231p. (978-0-545-46039-2(5)) Scholastic, Inc.
—Taking the Cake! 2012. (Confectionately Yours Ser.: Bk. 2). 223p. (J). (978-0-545-49391-8(9)) Scholastic, Inc.
—A Tale of Highly Unusual Magic. 2015. (ENG.). 320p. (J). (gr. 3-7). 16.99 (978-0-06-237121-8(5)) HarperCollins Pubs.
Paquette, Ammi-Joan & Mack, Jeff. Princess Juniper of the Hourglass. 2015. (Princess Juniper Ser.). (ENG., Illus.). 288p. (J). (gr. 3-7). bds. 16.99 (978-0-399-17151-2(7), Philomel Bks.) Penguin Young Readers Group.
Paradis, Linzy. Fanny's Walk. 2008. 28p. pap. 24.95 (978-1-60672-714-0(1)) America Star Bks.
Parasciuc, Natalia. Beaverlini & Rodney Are Having Fun! 2011. 28p. pap. 12.99 (978-0-557-84882-9(2)) Lulu Pr., Inc.
Paratore, Coleen Murtagh. Wish I Might. 2011. (ENG.). 176p. (J). (gr. 5-9). pap. 6.99 (978-0-545-09402-3(X), Scholastic Paperbacks) Scholastic, Inc.
Parent, Dan. Betty & Veronica: Best Friends Forever. 2012. (Archie & Friends All-Stars Ser.: 16). (ENG.). 128p. (J). (gr. 4-7). pap. 9.99 (978-1-879794-76-4(4), Archie Comics) Archie Comic Pubns., Inc.
Parent, David D. Drummers Forward! Marching with Angels: The Exciting Tale of a Drummer Boy Serving with the First Vermont Brigade & His Adventures During the Americ. 2013. 188p. pap. 13.50 (978-1-62516-582-4(X), Strategic Bk. Publishing) Strategic Book Publishing & Rights Agency (SBPRA).
Parenteau, Shirley. Bears on Chairs. Walker, David, illus. 2009. (ENG.). 32p. (J). (gr. -1-k). 15.99 (978-0-7636-3588-6(X)) Candlewick Pr.
Paris, Jacqueline. Decision. 2011. 28p. pap. 15.99 (978-1-4568-8437-6(9)) Xlibris Corp.
Paris, Tom. Tom & Pearl's Udder Stand. 2012. 44p. pap. 17.45 (978-1-4669-4829-7(9)) Trafford Publishing.
Parish, Alex. Peter & the Flying Sergeant. 2009. 30p. 21.50 (978-0-9561613-0-7(8)) Parish, Alex GBR. Dist: Lulu Pr., Inc.
Parish, Herman. Amelia Bedelia Chapter Book #6: Amelia Bedelia Cleans Up (POB) Avril, Lynne, illus. 2015. (Amelia Bedelia Ser.). (ENG.). 160p. (J). (gr. 1-5). 9.99 (978-0-06-233403-9(4), Greenwillow Bks.) HarperCollins Pubs.
—Amelia Bedelia Chapter Book #8: Amelia Bedelia Dances Off. Avril, Lynne, illus. 2015. (Amelia Bedelia Ser.). (ENG.). 160p. (J). (gr. 1-5). 15.99 (978-0-06-233409-1(3), Greenwillow Bks.) HarperCollins Pubs.
—Amelia Bedelia Cleans Up. Avril, Lynne, illus. 2015. (Amelia Bedelia Ser.). (ENG.). 160p. (J). (gr. 1-5). pap. 4.99 (978-0-06-233400-8(X), Greenwillow Bks.) HarperCollins Pubs.
—Amelia Bedelia Joins the Club. Avril, Lynne, illus. 2014. (I Can Read Level 1 Ser.). (ENG.). 32p. (J). (gr. -1-3). 16.99 (978-0-06-222131-5(0)); pap. 3.99 (978-0-06-222130-8(2)) HarperCollins Pubs. (Greenwillow Bks.).
—Amelia Bedelia Joins the Club. 2014. (Amelia Bedelia: I Can Read! Ser.). (J). lib. bdg. 13.55 (978-0-606-35051-8(9), Turtleback) Turtleback Bks.
—Amelia Bedelia Makes a Friend. Avril, Lynne, illus. 2011. (I Can Read Level 1 Ser.). (ENG.). 32p. (J). (gr. k-3). 16.99 (978-0-06-207516-1(0)); pap. 3.99 (978-0-06-207515-4(2)) HarperCollins Pubs. (Greenwillow Bks.).
—Amelia Bedelia Makes a Splash. Avril, Lynne, illus. 2017. (Amelia Bedelia Ser.). 160p. (J). (gr. 1-5). pap. 4.99 (978-0-06-265839-5(5), Greenwillow Bks.) HarperCollins Pubs.
—Amelia Bedelia on the Job. 2016. (Amelia Bedelia Chapter Book Ser.: 9). (J). lib. bdg. 14.75 (978-0-606-38160-4(0)) Turtleback Bks.
—Amelia Bedelia Sets Sail. Avril, Lynne, illus. 2015. (Amelia Bedelia Ser.). (ENG.). 160p. (J). (gr. 1-5). pap. 4.99 (978-0-06-233404-6(2), Greenwillow Bks.) HarperCollins Pubs.
—Amelia Bedelia Takes the Cake. Avril, Lynne, illus. 2016. (I Can Read Level 1 Ser.). 32p. (J). (gr. -1-3). pap. 3.99 (978-0-06-233430-5(1), Greenwillow Bks.) HarperCollins Pubs.
—Amelia Bedelia Tries Her Luck. 2013. (Amelia Bedelia: I Can Read! Ser.). (J). lib. bdg. 13.55 (978-0-606-32445-8(3), Turtleback) Turtleback Bks.

—Sets Sail. Avril, Lynne, illus. 2015. (Amelia Bedelia Ser.). (ENG.). 160p. (J). (gr. 1-5). 15.99 *(978-0-06-233405-3(0)*, Greenwillow Bks.) HarperCollins Pubs.

Parish, Peggy. Amelia Bedelia I Can Read, Set. Siebel, Fritz et al, illus. 2016. (I Can Read Level 2 Ser.). 320p. (J). (gr. -1-3). pap. 16.99 *(978-0-06-244356-4(9)*, Greenwillow Bks.) HarperCollins Pubs.

Parisi, Bettie. The Quiet. 2009. 36p. pap. 15.00 *(978-1-4269-1015-9(0))* Trafford Publishing.

Parisi, Mark. Do Not Open! Parisi, Mark, illus. 2017. (Marty Pants Ser.: 1). (Illus.). 256p. (J). (gr. 3-7). 12.99 *(978-0-06-242776-2(8))* HarperCollins Pubs.

Park, Barbara. Junie B. Jones Books in a Bus (Books 1-28), 28 vols. Brunkus, Denise, illus. 2015. (ENG.). (J). (gr. 1-4). 139.72 *(978-1-101-93859-1(5)*, Random Hse. Bks. for Young Readers) Random Hse. Children's Bks.

—Toothless Wonder. Brunkus, Denise, illus. 2003. (Junie B. Jones Ser.: Bk. 3). 80p. (gr. 1-4). 15.00 *(978-0-7569-1621-3(6))* Perfection Learning Corp.

Park, Linda Sue. Keeping Score. 2010. (ENG.). 224p. (J). (gr. 2-5). pap. 7.99 *(978-0-547-24897-4(0))* Houghton Mifflin Harcourt Publishing Co.

—Project Mulberry. 2017. (ENG.). 272p. (J). (gr. 5-7). pap. 6.99 *(978-0-544-93521-1(7)*, HMH Books For Young Readers) Houghton Mifflin Harcourt Publishing Co.

—Project Mulberry. 2007. 225p. (gr. 4-7). 17.00 *(978-0-7569-7921-8(8))* Perfection Learning Corp.

—Project Mulberry. 2007. (ENG.). 240p. (J). (gr. 3-7). 6.99 *(978-0-440-42163-4(2)*, Yearling) Random Hse. Children's Bks.

Park, Louise. Three's a Crowd. May, Kyla & Matthews, Melanie, illus. 2015. (Star Girl Ser.). (ENG.). 80p. (gr. 1-4). lib. bdg. 22.65 *(978-1-4795-8278-5(6))* Picture Window Bks.

Parker, A. J. The Table of Shadows. 2007. 273p. pap. 16.95 *(978-1-84753-762-1(6))* Lulu Pr., Inc.

Parker, Danny & Bodman, Charlotte. Molly & Mae: A Friendship Journey. Blackwood, Freya, illus. 2017. (ENG.). 32p. (J). (gr. -1-3). 16.99 ***(978-1-328-71543-2(4)***, HMH Books For Young Readers) Houghton Mifflin Harcourt Publishing Co.

Parker, David. I'm a Good Friend! Ong, Cristina, illus. 2004. (J). pap. *(978-0-439-62807-5(5))* Scholastic, Inc.

—My Best Friend Is Moving. Lucas, Margeaux, illus. 2007. (J). *(978-0-545-00389-6(X))* Scholastic, Inc.

Parker, Emma. Albert & the Dragon. 2010. (Illus.). 20p. pap. *(978-1-877561-50-4(9))* First Edition Ltd.

—Sebastian the Ant. 2010. (Illus.). pap. *(978-1-877561-14-6(2))* First Edition Ltd.

Parker, Gilles N. A Visit to the Farm: A Vet Makes New Friends. 2013. 24p. pap. 24.99 *(978-1-4669-3524-2(3))* Trafford Publishing.

Parker, Jake. Little Bot & Sparrow. Parker, Jake, illus. 2016. (ENG., Illus.). 40p. (J). 17.99 *(978-1-62672-367-2(2)*, 9781626723672) Roaring Brook Pr.

Parker, Jim. Howard the Flying Bloodhound. 2011. 28p. 13.59 *(978-1-4567-4106-8(3))* AuthorHouse.

Parker, Jo Ann. The Cow That Could, & Did! (with a Little Help from Her Friends) 2012. 32p. pap. 19.99 *(978-1-4772-2909-5(4))* AuthorHouse.

Parker, Lucy. Acorn Meadow has a Secret. 2010. (ENG., Illus.). 80p. pap. *(978-1-84748-600-4(2))* Athena Pr.

Parker, Richard. Voyage to Tasmani. Seward, Prudence, illus. 2011. 128p. 40.95 *(978-1-258-08572-8(0))* Literary Licensing, LLC.

Parker, Robert. Edenville Owls. 2008. 194p. (gr. 4-6). 18.00 *(978-0-7569-8920-0(5))* Perfection Learning Corp.

Parker, Robert B. Chasing the Bear. 2010. (ENG.). 176p. (YA). (gr. 7-18). 8.99 *(978-0-14-241573-3(1)*, Speak) Penguin Young Readers Group.

Parkhurst, Liz S. Under One Flag: A Year at Rohwer. Clifton, Tom, illus. 2006. (ENG.). 32p. (J). (gr. 3-7). 16.95 *(978-0-87483-759-9(6)*, 1241971) August Hse. Pubs., Inc.

Parkins, Rebecca Katherine. Lilly the Little Lava Mouse. 2009. 180p. pap. 43.49 *(978-1-4389-4330-5(X))* AuthorHouse.

Parkinson, Ethelyn. Good Old Archibald. Stevens, Mary, illus. 2014. 145p. (J). pap. 14.95 *(978-1-932350-42-5(X))* Bethlehem Bks.

Parkinson, Will. Pitch. 2016. (ENG., Illus.). (J). 24.99 ***(978-1-63533-061-8(0))*** 2013. 190p. pap. 14.99 *(978-1-62798-034-0(2))* Dreamspinner Pr. (Harmony Ink Pr.).

Parnell, Declan. Marco's New Friend, 01 vols., 1. 2016. (Rosen REAL Readers: STEM & STEAM Collection). (ENG.). 8p. (J). pap. 5.46 *(978-1-5081-1420-8(X)*, Rosen Classroom) Rosen Publishing Group, Inc., The.

Parnell, Robyn. The Mighty Quinn. DeYoe, Katie & DeYoe, Aaron, illus. 2013. (ENG.). 272p. (gr. 2-7). pap. 10.95 *(978-1-938063-10-7(4)*, Mighty Media Junior Readers) Mighty Media Pr.

Parpan, Justin, illus. Gwango's Lonesome Trail. 2006. 32p. (J). (gr. -1-3). 15.95 *(978-1-60108-004-2(2))* Red Cygnet Pr.

Parr, Todd. Doggy Kisses 123. 2013. (ENG., Illus.). 24p. (J). (gr. -1 — 1). bds. 7.99 *(978-0-316-20737-9(3))* Little, Brown Bks. for Young Readers.

—Otto Goes to the Beach. 2014. (Passport to Reading Level 1 Ser.). (ENG., Illus.). 32p. (J). (gr. -1-1). 3.99 *(978-0-316-24602-6(6))* Little, Brown Bks. for Young Readers.

—Otto Goes to the Beach. 2014. (Passport to Reading Level 1 Ser.). (J). lib. bdg. 13.55 *(978-0-606-35303-8(8))* Turtleback Bks.

Parragon Staff, ed. Cerdito. 2010. pap. 4.95 *(978-1-4054-4915-1(2))* Parragon, Inc.

Parrish, Edith. Sarah the Purple Goose Gets Lost. Odom, Kelly, illus. 2011. 34p. 23.95 *(978-1-60844-930-9(0))* Dog Ear Publishing, LLC.

Parrish, Edith E. Sara the Purple Goose & Susan the Black Swan. 2010. 24p. pap. 17.99 *(978-1-4490-8879-8(1))* AuthorHouse.

Parrish, Kat. Micah & the Magic Helment: The Helmet & the Dragon. Milam, C. J., illus. 2011. (ENG.). 32p. (J). (gr. k-7). pap. 8.95 *(978-0-938467-29-8(8)*, Headline Kids) Headline Bks., Inc.

Parry, Linda & Parry, Alan. Christmastime with Mr Bear. 2006. 12p. (J). bds. 11.99 *(978-0-7847-1469-0(X)*, 04389) Standard Publishing.

Parry, Rosanne. The Turn of the Tide. 2016. (ENG., Illus.). 304p. (J). (gr. 3-7). 16.99 *(978-0-375-86972-3(7)*, Random Hse. Bks. for Young Readers) Random Hse. Children's Bks.

Parsons, Caroline Renee. The Coffins in the Basement. 2008. 134p. pap. 24.95 *(978-1-60563-140-0(X))* America Star Bks.

Parvela, Timo. Bicycling to the Moon. Talvitie, Virpi, illus. 2016. (ENG.). 128p. (gr. k-5). 16.99 *(978-1-77657-031-7(6))*; 16.99 *(978-1-77657-091-1(X))*; 9.99 *(978-1-77657-078-2(2))*; 16.99 *(978-1-77657-080-5(4))* Gecko Pr. NZL. Dist: Lerner Publishing Group.

Pascal, Francine. Fearless 3: Rebel; Heat; Blood. 2014. (Fearless Ser.: 3). (ENG., Illus.). 656p. (YA). (gr. 9). pap. 10.99 *(978-1-4814-0270-5(6)*, Simon Pulse) Simon Pulse.

—Flechazo. Orig. Title: Elizabeth's First Kiss. (SPA.). 152p. (J). 6.95 *(978-84-272-4643-0(9))* Molino, Editorial ESP. Dist: AIMS International Bks., Inc.

—La Guerra Entre los Gemelos.Tr. of War Between the Twins. (SPA.). 136p. (J). 6.95 *(978-84-272-3598-4(4))* Molino, Editorial ESP. Dist: AIMS International Bks., Inc.

—Jessica's Secreto. Orig. Title: Jessica's Secret. (SPA.). 144p. (J). 6.95 *(978-84-272-4642-3(0))* Molino, Editorial ESP. Dist: AIMS International Bks., Inc.

Paschal Shija. The Proud Kid & the Stream. 2005. (Illus.). 14p. pap. *(978-9987-686-97-1(4))* Mkuki na Nyoka Pubs. TZA. Dist: Michigan State Univ. Pr.

Pascual, Dennis Mark. The Adventures of Dj the Butterfly & Friends Series Presents Dj's Birthday Party. 2012. 20p. pap. 10.15 *(978-1-105-35838-8(0))* Lulu Pr., Inc.

Pastel, JoAnne & Fitzsimmons, Kakie. Bur Bur & Friends 3 volume Set. VanDeWeghe, Lindsay & Bohnet, Christopher, illus. 2007. (J). lib. bdg. 39.95 *(978-0-9777121-5-1(X))* IGI Pr.

Pastis, Stephan. Mistakes Were Made. 2015. (Timmy Failure Ser.: 1). lib. bdg. 18.40 *(978-0-606-36864-3(7))* Turtleback Bks.

—Now Look What You've Done. Pastis, Stephan, illus. 2014. (Timmy Failure Ser.: No. 2). (ENG., Illus.). 288p. (J). (gr. 3-7). 14.99 *(978-0-7636-6051-2(5))* Candlewick Pr.

—Stephan's Web: A Pearls Before Swine Collection. 2016. (Pearls Before Swine Ser.: 26). (ENG.). 128p. pap. 14.99 *(978-1-4494-8202-2(3))* Andrews McMeel Publishing.

Patchett, Mary Elwyn. Ajax: Golden Dog of the Australian Bush. Tansley, Eric, illus. 2011. 172p. 42.95 *(978-1-258-01103-1(4))* Literary Licensing, LLC.

—The Great Barrier Reef. Monroe, Joan Kiddell, illus. 2011. 210p. 44.95 *(978-1-258-08492-9(9))* Literary Licensing, LLC.

Paterakis, Paul. Henry the Friendly Shark. 2013. 24p. pap. 24.95 *(978-1-62709-447-4(4))* America Star Bks.

Paterson, Katherine. Bridge to Terabithia. Diamond, Donna, illus. (ENG.). (J). (gr. 3-7). 2017. 192p. 16.99 *(978-0-690-01359-7(0))* 2008. 208p. pap. 6.99 *(978-0-06-073401-5(9)*, HarperTeen) 2006. 176p. pap. 6.99 *(978-0-06-122728-8(5)*, HarperFestival) 2006. 208p. pap. 6.99 *(978-0-06-125370-6(7)*, HarperFestival) HarperCollins Pubs.

—Bridge to Terabithia. Diamond, Donna, illus. l.t. ed. 2007. (Literacy Bridge Middle Reader Ser.). 187p. (J). (gr. 4-7). 23.95 *(978-0-7862-9620-0(8))* Thorndike Pr.

—Bridge to Terabithia. Diamond, Donna, illus. 2017. (Trophy Bk.). (ENG.). 192p. (J). (gr. 3-7). reprint ed. pap. 7.99 *(978-0-06-440184-5(7))* HarperCollins Pubs.

—Bridge to Terabithia: a Harper Classic. Diamond, Donna, illus. 2017. (Harper Classic Ser.). 192p. (J). (gr. 3-7). 16.99 ***(978-0-06-265874-6(3))*** HarperCollins Pubs.

Paterson, Katherine. La Gran Gilly Hopkins. 2003.Tr. of Great Gilly Hopkins. (SPA., Illus.). 152p. (YA). (gr. 5-8). pap. 12.95 *(978-958-24-0172-6(9))* Santillana COL. Dist: Santillana USA Publishing Co., Inc.

—La Gran Gilly Hopkins.Tr. of Great Gilly Hopkins. (SPA.). 152p. (J). (gr. 5-8). pap. 9.95 *(978-84-204-4789-6(7))* Santillana USA Publishing Co., Inc.

Paticoff, Melanie. Sophie's Tales: Overcoming Obstacles. Vales, Chrissie, illus. 2012. 42p. 25.95 *(978-0-9851575-6-2(9))* Sophie's Tales, LLC.

Patrick, Ella. Rapunzel Finds a Friend (Disney Princess) Thomas, Jeffrey, illus. 2016. (ENG.). 32p. (J). (gr. -1-2). 7.99 *(978-0-7364-3388-4(0)*, RH/Disney) Random Hse. Children's Bks.

Patron, Susan. Lucky Breaks. Phelan, Matt, illus. 2010. (ENG.). 208p. (J). (gr. 3-7). pap. 7.99 *(978-1-4169-9772-6(5)*, Atheneum Bks. for Young Readers) Simon & Schuster Children's Publishing.

Patterson, Christine. On the Wings of a Butterfly. 2004. 21p. (J). per. 10.68 *(978-1-4116-0669-2(8))* Lulu Pr., Inc.

Patterson, Ellie. Baby Bear & the Big, Wide World. Kolanovic, Dubravka, illus. 2013. (J). *(978-1-4351-4929-8(7))* Barnes & Noble, Inc.

Patterson, Horace. Ernie the Ermine. Parker, Jack, illus. 2007. 28p. per. 7.99 *(978-1-58942-374-9(7))* R.H. Boyd Publishing Corp.

Patterson, James. Angel. 2011. (Maximum Ride Ser.). (YA). 54.99 *(978-1-60941-970-7(7))* Findaway World, LLC.

—Angel. (Maximum Ride Ser.: 7). (ENG.). (gr. 5-17). 2012. 352p. pap. 10.00 *(978-0-316-03832-4(6))* 2011. 384p. pap. 22.99 *(978-0-316-12201-6(7))* Little Brown & Co. (Jimmy Patterson).

—Angel. 2012. (Maximum Ride Ser.: 7). lib. bdg. 20.85 *(978-0-606-23452-8(7)*, Turtleback) Turtleback Bks.

—Nevermore: The Final Maximum Ride Adventure. 2012. (Maximum Ride Ser.: 8). (ENG.). 384p. (YA). (gr. 5-17). 17.99 *(978-0-316-10184-4(2)*, Jimmy Patterson) Little Brown & Co.

Patterson, James & Grabenstein, Chris. Daniel X: Lights Out. 2015. (Daniel X Ser.: 6). (ENG.). 272p. (J). (gr. 3-7). 17.00 *(978-0-316-20745-4(4)*, Jimmy Patterson) Little Brown & Co.

—I Funny TV: A Middle School Story. Park, Laura, illus. 2015. (I Funny Ser.: 4). (ENG.). 336p. (J). (gr. 3-7). 13.99 *(978-0-316-30109-1(4)*, Jimmy Patterson) Little Brown & Co.

—Pottymouth & Stoopid. Gilpin, Stephen, illus. 2017. (ENG.). 336p. (J). (gr. 3-7). 13.99 *(978-0-316-34963-5(1))* Little Brown & Co.

—Word of Mouse. Sutphin, Joe, illus. 2016. (ENG.). 304p. (J). (gr. 3-7). 13.99 *(978-0-316-34956-7(9)*, Jimmy Patterson) Little Brown & Co.

Patterson, James & Papademetriou, Lisa. Homeroom Diaries. Keino, illus. 2014. (ENG.). 272p. (YA). (gr. 7-17). 18.00 *(978-0-316-20762-1(4)*, Jimmy Patterson) Little Brown & Co.

Patterson, James & Tebbetts, Chris. How I Survived Bullies, Broccoli, & Snake Hill. Park, Laura, illus. 2013. (Middle School Ser.: 4). (ENG.). 336p. (J). (gr. 3-7). 14.00 *(978-0-316-23175-6(4)*, Jimmy Patterson) Little Brown & Co.

—Just My Rotten Luck. Park, Laura, illus. 2015. (Middle School Ser.: 7). (ENG.). 320p. (J). (gr. 3-7). 13.99 *(978-0-316-28477-6(7)*, Jimmy Patterson) Little Brown & Co.

—Save Rafe! Park, Laura, illus. 2014. (Middle School Ser.: 6). (ENG.). 288p. (J). (gr. 3-7). 13.99 *(978-0-316-32212-6(1)*, Jimmy Patterson) Little Brown & Co.

Patterson, James & Tebbetts, Christopher. From Hero to Zero. Park, Laura, illus. 2017. (J). pap. ***(978-0-316-35756-2(1))*** Little Brown & Co.

Patterson, James & Tebbetts, Christopher. Save Rafe! Park, Laura, illus. 2014. 269p. (J). *(978-0-316-28629-9(X))* Little Brown & Co.

Patterson, Nancy Ruth. The Shiniest Rock of All. 2009. 84p. pap. 8.95 *(978-1-4401-1620-9(2))* iUniverse, Inc.

Patterson, Sandra Jean. Crabby Crab. 2006. bds. 12.95 *(978-1-59700-246-2(1))* Island Heritage Publishing.

Patterson, Shannon. The Princess & the Cheese. 2010. 43p. pap. 19.95 *(978-0-557-51615-5(3))* Lulu Pr., Inc.

Patton, Julia. Drat That Fat Cat! Patton, Julia, illus. 2016. (ENG., Illus.). 32p. (J). (gr. -1-3). 16.99 *(978-0-8075-1713-0(5))* Whitman, Albert & Co.

Pauba, Judy. A Tale of Two Dogs. 2006. (Illus.). 32p. (J). per. 5.95 *(978-0-9747994-1-4(6))* Julenda Enterprises.

Paul. Best Friends. 2012. 24p. pap. 17.99 *(978-1-4772-0755-0(4))* AuthorHouse.

Paul & Lady Jan. Mako in My Backyard. Beeson, Jan, illus. 2013. 34p. pap. 12.99 *(978-0-9890482-3-1(3))* Beeson, Jan.

—Wesley the Wobbly Bear. Beeson, Jan, illus. 2013. 38p. pap. 12.99 *(978-0-9890482-4-8(1))* Beeson, Jan.

Paul, Donita K. Two Renegade Realms, 1 vol. 2014. (Realm Walkers Ser.). (ENG.). 416p. (YA). pap. 13.99 *(978-0-310-73581-6(5))* Zondervan.

Paul Frank Industries Staff & Chronicle Books Staff. High Five with Julius! & Friends. 2010. (ENG., Illus.). 10p. (J). (gr. -1 — 1). bds. 8.99 *(978-0-8118-7147-1(9))* Chronicle Bks. LLC.

Paul J McSorley; Illustrated By Patricia. The Adventures of Forealdo. Bearss, Patricia, illus. 2011. 36p. pap. 24.95 *(978-1-4560-8429-5(1))* America Star Bks.

Paul, Marcy Beller. Underneath Everything. Davis, Bill, illus. 2015. (ENG.). 304p. (YA). (gr. 9). 17.99 *(978-0-06-232721-5(6))* HarperCollins Pubs.

Paul, Miranda. Blobfish Throws a Party. Caton, Maggie, illus. 2017. (ENG.). 32p. (J). (gr. -1-3). 16.99 ***(978-1-4998-0422-5(9))*** Little Bee Books Inc.

Paul, Ruth. Hedgehog's Magic Tricks. Paul, Ruth, illus. 2013. (ENG., Illus.). 32p. (J). (gr. -1-2). 12.99 *(978-0-7636-6385-8(9))* Candlewick Pr.

Pauline Roberts & Donnie Obina. Promises! Promises! Who Can I Trust. 2013. 28p. pap. 16.09 *(978-1-4669-7959-8(3))* Trafford Publishing.

Paulits, John. Philip & the Case of the Mistaken Identity & Philip & the Baby. 2007. (ENG.). 150p. (YA). pap. 10.95 *(978-1-59705-897-1(1))* Wings ePress, Inc.

—Philip Gets Even. 2007. (YA). pap. 10.95 *(978-1-59705-928-2(5))* Wings ePress, Inc.

Paulk, William. The Creatures of Vision City: Pokie's Party, Book One. 2009. 48p. pap. 10.99 *(978-1-4389-5659-6(2))* AuthorHouse.

Paulsen, Aimee. Mambo & the Runaway Gorill. 2011. (Illus.). 40p. pap. 21.99 *(978-1-4628-5878-1(3))* Xlibris Corp.

Paulsen, Gary. Brian's Hunt. 2012. (Hatchet Adventure Ser.). (ENG.). 144p. (YA). (gr. 5). pap. 9.99 *(978-0-307-92959-4(0)*, Ember) Random Hse. Children's Bks.

—Flat Broke: The Theory, Practice & Destructive Properties of Greed. (ENG.). 128p. (J). (gr. 3-7). 2012. pap. 6.99 *(978-0-375-86612-8(4)*, Yearling) 2011. 12.99 *(978-0-385-74002-9(6)*, Lamb, Wendy Bks.) Random Hse. Children's Bks.

—Foxman. l.t. ed. 2004. (YA). (gr. 6-12). 27.95 *(978-1-58118-112-8(4))* LRS.

—Masters of Disaster. 2011. (ENG.). 112p. (J). (gr. 3-7). 5.99 *(978-0-375-86610-4(8)*, Yearling) Random Hse. Children's Bks.

—Six Kids & a Stuffed Cat. 2016. (ENG., Illus.). 144p. (J). (gr. 3-7). 16.99 *(978-1-4814-5223-6(1)*, Simon & Schuster Bks. For Young Readers) Simon & Schuster Bks. For Young Readers.

Paulson, Michael William. The Baker Street Bunch & the Hidden Map Mystery. 2005. (Illus.). (J). per. *(978-0-9754241-4-8(9))* MiMar Publishing.

Paver, Michelle. Outcast. Taylor, Geoff, illus. 2009. (Chronicles of Ancient Darkness Ser.: 4). 352p. (J). (gr. 5). pap. 6.99 *(978-0-06-072836-6(1)*, Tegen, Katherine Bks) HarperCollins Pubs.

Pavese, Candace. Caught in the Net. Holroyd, Geraldine, illus. 2013. 84p. pap. 9.95 *(978-1-937449-19-3(X))* YAV.

Pavlicin, Karen. Perch, Mrs. Sackets, & Crow's Nest. 2007. (J). (ENG.). 160p. 16.95 *(978-1-934617-00-7(8))*; pap. *(978-1-934617-01-4(6))* Elva Resa Publishing, LLC. (Alma Little).

Pavlova, Elena. Adventures at Tall Oaks: New Friends. 2004. (Illus.). 80p. (J). 19.95 *(978-0-9755839-0-6(5))* Read 2 Children.

Payne, Gregory. Chase to the Brazen Head. 2010. (ENG.). 228p. (YA). (gr. 4-7). pap. 11.95 *(978-988-18094-6-9(0))* Haven Bks.

Payne, K. E. Me@You.com. 2012. (ENG.). 288p. (J). (gr. 7). pap. 13.95 *(978-1-60282-592-5(0))* Bold Strokes Bks.

Payne, Richard A. The Banjo & the Telescope. 2008. 44p. per. 24.95 *(978-1-4241-9776-7(7))* America Star Bks.

Payot Karpathakis, Emmanuelle. Pixie en Vacaciones. 2013. 40p. pap. *(978-1-909193-28-4(3))* Summertime Publishing.

—Pixie's Holidays. 2013. 40p. pap. *(978-1-909193-25-3(9))* Summertime Publishing.

Paytras, C. J. The Littlest Homeless Angel: Darby's Story. 2011. 28p. pap. 24.95 *(978-1-4560-6708-3(7))* America Star Bks.

Peabody, Beth Leone. Chocolate Pie Therapy. 2008. 40p. pap. 18.49 *(978-1-4343-9684-6(3))* AuthorHouse.

PeachMoon Publishing. The Adventures of Lucky the Lizard Las aventuras del lagarto Lucky. 2008. (ENG & SPA., Illus.). 100p. (J). pap. 19.95 *(978-0-9795831-4-8(4))* PeachMoon Publishing.

Peacock, Carol Antoinette. Red Thread Sisters. 2012. (ENG.). 240p. (J). (gr. 3-7). 15.99 *(978-0-670-01386-9(2)*, Viking Books for Young Readers) Penguin Young Readers Group.

Pearce, Bryony. Phoenix Rising. 2017. (ENG.). 336p. (J). (gr. 4). 15.99 *(978-1-5107-0734-4(4)*, Sky Pony Pr.) Skyhorse Publishing Co., Inc.

Pearce, Jackson. The Inside Job: (and Other Skills I Learned As a Superspy) 2016. (ENG.). 272p. (J). 16.99 *(978-1-61963-420-6(1)*, 9781619634206, Bloomsbury USA Childrens) Bloomsbury Publishing USA.

Pearce, Jonathan. The Far Side of the Moon: A California Story. 2nd ed. 2004. 150p. (J). pap. 15.95 *(978-1-59411-011-5(5))* Writers' Collective, The.

Pearce, Philippa. The Little Gentleman. Pohrt, Tom, illus. 2004. 208p. (J). (gr. 3-18). lib. bdg. 16.89 *(978-0-06-073161-8(3))* HarperCollins Pubs.

Pearce, Philippa & Pearl, Matthew. The Little Gentleman, 3 vols. unabr. ed. 2005. (J). 55.75 *(978-1-4193-3601-0(0)*, 42047) Recorded Bks., Inc.

Pearce, Richard & Story, Ken. Dorkman. 2006. (YA). mass mkt. 8.50 *(978-0-9753367-8-6(9))* Onstage Publishing, LLC.

Pearl, B. B. Poerava's Heaven. 2011. (Illus.). 88p. pap. 12.85 *(978-1-4567-8985-5(6))* AuthorHouse.

Pearl, Beverly. Poison Ivy. 2008. 98p. pap. 9.99 *(978-1-4357-1386-4(9))* Lulu Pr., Inc.

—Poison Ivy, the Pocket Book. 2008. 105p. pap. 14.95 *(978-1-4357-2328-3(7))* Lulu Pr., Inc.

Pearsall, Shelley. All Shook Up. 2009. (ENG.). 272p. (J). (gr. 3-7). 6.99 *(978-0-440-42139-9(X)*, Yearling) Random Hse. Children's Bks.

Pearson, Jean W. & Dutto, Lisa M. Gravity Rocks. 2012. (Illus.). 60p. pap. 35.99 *(978-1-4685-2813-8(0))* AuthorHouse.

Pearson, Kathleen. Polka Dot Loves Her Friends a Lot! 2012. 28p. pap. 17.99 *(978-1-4772-4402-9(6))* AuthorHouse.

—We Love You a Lot, Little Polka Dot. 2011. 28p. (gr. -1). pap. 12.49 *(978-1-4567-4449-6(6))* AuthorHouse.

Pearson, Kimberly Ann. Mystling Glen Book I: The Tale of A Prince. 2009. 207p. pap. 14.95 *(978-1-4327-4169-3(1))* Outskirts Pr., Inc.

Pearson, Lance. A Byte of Charity. 2003. 264p. pap. 14.95 *(978-1-878044-69-3(9))* Mayhaven Publishing, Inc.

Pearson, Mary E. The Miles Between. 2011. (ENG.). 288p. (YA). (gr. 9-12). pap. 15.99 *(978-0-312-65926-4(1))* Square Fish.

Peaty, Mary Alice. The Girl Who Lived on the Moon. 2008. 44p. pap. 26.95 *(978-0-557-02225-0(8))* Lulu Pr., Inc.

Peck, Dale. Sprout. 2009. (ENG.). 288p. (YA). (gr. 9-12). 16.99 *(978-1-59990-160-2(9)*, 9781599901602, Bloomsbury USA Childrens) Bloomsbury Publishing USA.

Peck, James E. Meet Mr. Chair Bear. 2008. 52p. pap. 16.95 *(978-1-4241-7959-6(9))* America Star Bks.

Peck, Lisa J. A Challenge for Brittany: CTR Club - Book One, 4 bks. 2005. (J). pap. 6.95 *(978-0-9749241-5-1(6))* Golden Wings Enterprises.

—Meagan's Secret: CTR Club - Book Three, 4 bks. 2005. (J). pap. 6.95 *(978-0-9749241-7-5(2))* Golden Wings Enterprises.

Peck, Richard. Remembering the Good Times. 181p. (YA). (gr. 7-18). pap. 4.50 *(978-0-8072-1380-3(2)*, Listening Library) Random Hse. Audio Publishing Group.

—Three Quarters Dead. 2011. (ENG.). 224p. (YA). (gr. 7-18). 7.99 *(978-0-14-241942-7(7)*, Speak) Penguin Young Readers Group.

Peckover, Lyn. Sparkling Gold Dust. 2010. 86p. pap. 6.99 *(978-1-61667-074-0(6))* Raider Publishing International.

Peek, Megan. Friendly Furries: The Annual Animal County Hop-a-Thon , the un-Surprise Birthday , the New Soccer Friend , the School Play , the Cook-off Contest. 2007. 76p. per. 19.95 *(978-1-4241-6193-5(2))* America Star Bks.

Peeler, Penny. The Adventures of Spike & Sally. 2011. 52p. pap. 15.99 *(978-1-4568-9981-3(3))* Xlibris Corp.

Pefferly, Lawrence. Larry Tyler & the Planet Buksdahud. 2007. 312p. pap. 16.95 *(978-0-9789969-2-5(5))*; 24.95 *(978-0-9789969-1-8(7))* Tradition Publishing.

Peirce, Lincoln. Big Nate: Revenge of the Cream Puffs. 2016. (Big Nate Ser.: 15). (ENG.). 184p. (J). (gr. 3-7). pap. 9.99 *(978-1-4494-6228-4(6))* Andrews McMeel Publishing.

—Big Nate & Friends. 2011. (Illus.). 224p. (J). (Big Nate Ser.: 3). (ENG.). pap. 9.99 *(978-1-4494-2043-7(5))*; *(978-0-545-46801-5(9))*; *(978-1-60744-837-2(8))* Andrews McMeel Publishing.

—Big Nate Blasts Off. Peirce, Lincoln, illus. 2016. (Big Nate Ser.: 8). (ENG., Illus.). 224p. (J). (gr. 3-7). 13.99 *(978-0-06-211111-1(6))* HarperCollins Pubs.

—Big Nate Doodlepalooza. Peirce, Lincoln, illus. 2016. (Big Nate Activity Book Ser.: 3). (Illus.). 224p. (J). (gr. 3-7). pap. 6.99 *(978-0-06-234952-1(X))* HarperCollins Pubs.

—Big Nate Lives It Up. Peirce, Lincoln, illus. 2015. (Big Nate Ser.: 7). (Illus.). 224p. (J). (gr. 3-7). lib. bdg. 13.89 *(978-0-06-211109-8(4))* HarperCollins Pubs.

—Here Goes Nothing. Peirce, Lincoln, illus. 2012. (Big Nate Comix Ser.: 2). (ENG., Illus.). 224p. (J). (gr. 3-7). pap. 9.99 *(978-0-06-208696-9(0))* HarperCollins Pubs.

—What Could Possibly Go Wrong? Peirce, Lincoln, illus. 2012. (Big Nate Comix Ser.: 1). (ENG., Illus.). 224p. (J). (gr. 3-7). pap. 9.99 *(978-0-06-208694-5(4))* HarperCollins Pubs.

—What's a Little Noogie Between Friends? 2017. (Big Nate Ser.: 16). (ENG.). 176p. (J). pap. 9.99 *(978-1-4494-6229-1(4))* Andrews McMeel Publishing.

Peirce, Lincoln, illus. Big Nate Flips Out. 2013. 216p. (J). *(978-0-06-224637-0(2))* Harper & Row Ltd.

Peirs, Adam. Hopper's Helpful Day. 2012. 24p. pap. 14.99 *(978-1-105-25383-6(X))* Lulu Pr., Inc.

Pelelo-Ray, Sam. Athenrei. 2006. 56p. pap. 16.95 *(978-1-4137-9946-0(9))* PublishAmerica, Inc.

Pelton, Lisa. Logos & Adoption: Remi's Journey. 2012. 40p. pap. 14.95 *(978-1-4497-5378-8(7)*, WestBow Pr.) Author Solutions, Inc.

Pendergrass, D. Louis, a Blue Dragon. 2009. 32p. pap. 15.00 *(978-1-4389-9036-1(7))* AuthorHouse.

Penguin Young Readers. I Am Lily. 2013. (Peter Rabbit Animation Ser.). (ENG.). 32p. (J). (gr. 1-3). 14.99 *(978-0-7232-8083-5(5))*; pap. 3.99 *(978-0-7232-8074-3(6))* Penguin Young Readers Group. (Penguin Young Readers).

Penguin Young Readers Group Staff. I Am Peter. 2014. (Peter Rabbit Animation Ser.). (ENG.). 32p. (J). (gr. 1-3). pap. 3.99

(978-0-14-135006-6(7), Penguin Young Readers) Penguin Young Readers Group.

Pennels, Geraldine. The School Shenanigans of Amy & Nontand. 2009. 152p. pap. 33.50 (978-1-60860-496-8(9), Strategic Bk. Publishing) Strategic Book Publishing & Rights Agency (SBPRA).

Pennels, Geraldine M. The School Shenanigans of Amy & Nontand: Volume Two Fifth Grade. 2010. 144p. pap. 11.50 (978-1-60911-848-8(0), Eloquent Bks.) Strategic Book Publishing & Rights Agency (SBPRA).

Pennypacker, Sara. Clementine. Frazee, Marla, illus. (ENG.). (J). 2008. 160p. (gr. 2-5). pap. 5.99 (978-0-7868-3883-7(3)) 2006. 144p. (gr. 1-3). 14.99 (978-0-7868-3882-0(5)) Hyperion Pr.

—Clementine, Friend of the Week. Frazee, Marla, illus. (Clementine Book Ser.). (ENG.). 176p. (J). 2011. (gr. 1-3). pap. 5.99 (978-1-4231-1560-1(0)) 2010. (gr. 2-5). 14.99 (978-1-4231-1355-3(1)) Hyperion Pr.

Peot, Margaret. Crow Made a Friend. 2015. (I Like to Read(r) Ser.). (ENG., Illus.). 24p. (J). (gr. -1-3). 14.95 (978-0-8234-3297-4(1)) Holiday Hse., Inc.

Pepper, Lily. Bananas. 2012. (Illus.). 20p. pap. 19.82 (978-1-4772-1964-5(1)) AuthorHouse.

Pepper, Louise. Got your Back... A Story of Friendship & Caring. 2011. 24p. (gr. -1). pap. 11.50 (978-1-4567-5527-0(7)) AuthorHouse.

Pepper, Sly. Dugan Peckles Through the Manhole. 2004. 190p. (gr. 4-6). pap. 5.99 (978-0-9747668-0-5(1)) MindMaze Publishing Co.

Percival, Tom. Bubble Trouble. 2015. (ENG., Illus.). 32p. (J). (gr. -1-1). 17.99 (978-1-61963-679-8(4), 9781619636798, Bloomsbury USA Childrens) Bloomsbury Publishing USA.

—Herman's Letter. 2014. (ENG., Illus.). 32p. (J). (gr. -1-1). 17.99 (978-1-61963-423-7(6), 9781619634237, Bloomsbury USA Childrens) Bloomsbury Publishing USA.

—Herman's Vacation. 2016. (ENG., Illus.). 32p. (J). 17.99 (978-1-61963-990-4(4), 9781619639904, Bloomsbury USA Childrens) Bloomsbury Publishing USA.

Perelman, Helen. A Candy Fairies Sweet Collection: Chocolate Dreams; Rainbow Swirl; Caramel Moon; Cool Mint. Waters, Erica-Jane, illus. 2013. (Candy Fairies Ser.). (ENG.). 512p. (J). (gr. 2-5). pap. 23.99 (978-1-4424-9390-2(9), Aladdin) Simon & Schuster Children's Publishing.

—Frozen Treats. Waters, Erica-Jane, illus. 2014. (Candy Fairies Ser.: 13). (ENG.). 128p. (J). (gr. 2-5). pap. 5.99 (978-1-4424-5303-6(6), Aladdin) Simon & Schuster Children's Publishing.

—A Minty Mess. Waters, Erica-Jane, illus. 2016. (Candy Fairies Ser.: 19). (ENG.). 128p. (J). (gr. 2-5). pap. 5.99 (978-1-4814-4680-8(0), Aladdin) Simon & Schuster Children's Publishing.

—Rainbow Swirl. Waters, Erica-Jane, illus. 2010. (Candy Fairies Ser.: 2). (ENG.). 128p. (J). (gr. 2-5). pap. 5.99 (978-1-4169-9455-8(6), Aladdin) Simon & Schuster Children's Publishing.

—Rainbow Swirl. Waters, Erica-Jane, illus. 2012. (Candy Fairies Ser.: 2). (ENG.). 128p. (J). (gr. 2-5). 15.99 (978-1-4424-5776-8(7), cwvc, Simon & Schuster/Paula Wiseman Bks.) Simon & Schuster/Paula Wiseman Bks.

—Sweet Secrets. Waters, Erica-Jane, illus. 2015. (Candy Fairies Ser.: 15). (ENG.). 128p. (J). (gr. 2-5). pap. 5.99 (978-1-4814-0610-9(8), Aladdin) Simon & Schuster Children's Publishing.

Perera, Hilda. Kike. 13th ed. 2005. (SPA., Illus.). 128p. (J). (gr. 4-5). 7.95 (978-84-348-1288-8(6), SM0858) SM Ediciones ESP. Dist: Iaconi, Mariuccia Bk. Imports, Lectorum Pubns., Inc.

Peretti, Kim. Oodle Van Boodle & the Great Cake Adventure. 2010. (ENG., Illus.). 32p. (J). pap. 15.95 (978-0-9824461-4-0(4)) SDP Publishing.

Pérez, Celia C. The First Rule of Punk. 2017. (ENG., Illus.). 336p. (J). (gr. 4-7). 16.99 **(978-0-425-29040-8(9)**, Viking Books for Young Readers) Penguin Young Readers Group.

Perez, Maureen T. Friendliness. Perez, Maureen T. & Cesena, Denise, illus. l.t. ed. 2003. 28p. (J). 10.00 (978-0-9740418-0-3(7)) Night Light Pubns., LLC.

—Friendliness - Companion Book. Perez, Maureen T. & Cesena, Denise, illus. l.t. ed. 2003. 12p. (J). 2.00 (978-0-9740418-1-0(5)) Night Light Pubns., LLC.

Perez, Whitney Joan. Friendship. 2010. 65p. pap. 9.99 (978-0-557-35700-0(4)) Lulu Pr., Inc.

Perkins, Lynne Rae. All Alone in the Universe. unabr. ed. 2004. 143p. (J). (gr. 3-5). pap. 29.00 incl. audio (978-0-8072-0443-6(9), Listening Library) Random Hse. Audio Publishing Group.

—The Cardboard Piano. Perkins, Lynne Rae, illus. 2008. (ENG., Illus.). 32p. (J). (gr. -1-2). 17.99 (978-0-06-154265-7(2), Greenwillow Bks.) HarperCollins Pubs.

—Nuts to You. Perkins, Lynne Rae, illus. 2014. (ENG., Illus.). 272p. (J). (gr. 3-7). 16.99 (978-0-06-009275-7(0), Greenwillow Bks.) HarperCollins Pubs.

Perkins, Lynne Rae & Perkins, Lynne R. All Alone in the Universe. 2007. (ENG., Illus.). 224p. (J). (gr. 5-18). reprint ed. pap. 6.99 (978-0-380-73302-6(1), Greenwillow Bks.) HarperCollins Pubs.

Perkins, TJ. Fantasies Are Murder: A Kim & Kelly Mystery. novel ed. 2005. (Illus.). 148p. (YA). 10.99 (978-0-9777538-0-2(8)) GumShoe Press.

Perl, Erica S. Totally Tardy Marty. Krosoczka, Jarrett J., illus. 2015. (ENG.). 32p. (J). (gr. -1-3). 16.95 (978-1-4197-1661-4(1), Abrams Bks. for Young Readers) Abrams, Inc.

Perl, Lila. Me & Fat Glenda. 2014. (Fat Glenda Ser.). (ENG.). 200p. (gr. 3). pap. 12.95 (978-1-939601-03-2(7)) Ig Publishing, Inc.

Pernikoff, Doug. So What If Im a Bully. 2009. 40p. 11.99 (978-0-9816923-3-3(8)) Cochran, Russ Co., The.

—So What If Im Adopted. 2009. 36p. 11.99 (978-0-9816923-2-6(X)) Cochran, Russ Co., The.

—So What If My Parents Got Divorced. 2009. 36p. 11.99 (978-0-9816923-1-9(1)) Cochran, Russ Co., The.

Perrin. Rafi's Song & the Stones of Erebrus. 2006. 10.18 (978-0-9738036-0-0(6)) Ankh Bks. CAN. Dist: Mountain Bk. Co.

Perry, Brad Lee. Clumsy Claudia & the Gentle Forest Friends, 1 vol. Perry, Diana Torri, illus. 2010. 56p. pap. 16.95 (978-1-4489-4633-4(6)) America Star Bks.

Perry, Chrissie. Project Best Friend. 2017. (Penelope Perfect Ser.: 1). lib. bdg. 16.00 **(978-0-606-40210-1(1))** Turtleback Bks.

Perry, Fred. Gold Digger - Platinum, Vol. 2. 2011. (ENG.). 132p. (YA). pap., pap. 14.99 (978-0-9831823-4-4(5), 9780983182344) Antarctic Pr., Inc.

Perry, Jolene. All the Forever Things. 2017. (ENG.). 272p. (YA). (gr. 8-12). 16.99 (978-0-8075-2532-6(4)); pap. 9.99 **(978-0-8075-2534-0(0))** Whitman, Albert & Co.

Perry, Laurie. Kaycee's New School, 1 vol. 2009. 48p. pap. 16.95 (978-1-61582-638-4(6)) America Star Bks.

Perry, Marie/Fritz. Cecil's New Year's Eve Tail. Perry, Marie/Fritz, illus. 2007. (Illus.). 32p. (J). lib. bdg. (978-0-9755675-2-4(7)) Buttonweed Pr., L.L.C.

Perry, Phyllis J. The Secrets of the Rock. Lipking, Ron, illus. 2004. (Fribble Mouse Library Mystery Ser.). 96p. (J). 16.95 (978-1-932146-22-6(9), 1237661) Highsmith Inc.

Perry, Phyllis Jean. The Alien, the Giant, & Rocketman. Francis, Guy, illus. 2006. (J). pap. (978-1-59336-723-7(7)) Mondo Publishing.

Perry, Salena Maria. Recipe for Chocolate Soup. 2011. 28p. 12.95 (978-1-4567-1640-0(9)) AuthorHouse.

Perry, Sarah Catherine. Clara's Test. 2006. (J). per. (978-1-55452-022-0(3)) Essence Publishing.

Persinger, Eric. Plaid the Platypus. l.t. ed. 2004. (Illus.). (J). 25p. per. 8.99 (978-1-932338-54-6(3)); 34p. lib. bdg. 12.95 (978-1-932338-57-7(8)) Lifevest Publishing, Inc.

Pescatore, Faith. A Bell for Justin. 2009. 56p. pap. 10.99 (978-1-4389-6821-6(3)) AuthorHouse.

Peschke, Marci. Gymnastics Queen. Mourning, Tuesday, illus. 2016. (Kylie Jean Ser.). (ENG.). 112p. (gr. 2-3). lib. bdg. 22.65 (978-1-5158-0052-1(0)) Picture Window Bks.

—Pirate Queen. Mourning, Tuesday, illus. (Kylie Jean Ser.). (ENG.). 112p. (gr. 2-3). 2015. pap. 5.95 (978-1-4795-8020-0(1)) 2013. 8.95 (978-1-4048-8103-7(4)) 2013. lib. bdg. 22.65 (978-1-4048-7581-4(6)) Picture Window Bks. (Kylie Jean).

—Soccer Queen. Mourning, Tuesday, illus. 2015. (Kylie Jean Ser.). (ENG.). 112p. (gr. 2-3). 22.65 (978-1-4795-5882-7(6), Kylie Jean) Picture Window Bks.

—Summer Camp Queen, 1 vol. Mourning, Tuesday, illus. 2013. (Kylie Jean Ser.). (ENG.). 112p. (gr. 2-3). lib. bdg. 22.65 (978-1-4048-7583-8(2), Kylie Jean) Picture Window Bks.

Peters, Andrew Fusek. The Ant & the Big Bad Bully Goat. Wadham, Anna, illus. 2007. (Traditional Tales with a Twist Ser.). (ENG.). 32p. (J). (gr. 2-2). pap. (978-1-84643-079-4(8)) Child's Play International Ltd.

Peters, Julie Anne. Define Normal. 2003. (ENG., Illus.). 196p. (J). (gr. 7-17). pap. 9.99 (978-0-316-73489-9(6)) Little, Brown Bks. for Young Readers.

—It's Our Prom (So Deal with It) 2013. (ENG.). 352p. (YA). (gr. 7-17). pap. 8.99 (978-0-316-13144-5(X)) Little, Brown Bks. for Young Readers.

Peters, Karen Lynn. If I Only Had a Horse. 2013. 36p. 16.99 (978-0-9894748-4-9(4)) Mindstir Media.

Peters, Lou. The Owl & the Turtle. 2010. 32p. pap. 15.95 (978-0-557-51727-5(3)) Lulu Pr., Inc.

Peters, Stephanie True. The Wind in the Willows. Cano, Fern, illus. 2016. (Graphic Revolve: Common Core Editions Ser.). (ENG.). 72p. (gr. 2-3). pap. 6.95 (978-1-4965-3564-1(2), Graphic Revolve) Stone Arch Bks.

—The Wind in the Willows. Cano, Fern, illus. 2016. (Graphic Revolve: Common Core Editions Ser.). (ENG.). 72p. (gr. 2-3). lib. bdg. 27.99 (978-1-4965-3562-7(6), Graphic Revolve) Stone Arch Bks.

Peters, Suzanne. Misee Mouse. 2011. 36p. pap. 15.49 (978-1-4269-5738-3(6)) Trafford Publishing.

Petersen, Jeffrey Lee. A Boy a Dog & a Creek. 2013. 102p. pap. (978-1-78299-794-8(6)) FeedARead.com.

Peterson, Brian. The Popcornmaker. 2007. 232p. 25.95 (978-0-595-70458-3(1)); per. 15.95 (978-0-595-46727-3(X)) iUniverse, Inc.

Peterson, Kathryn. Reilly's Leap of Faith, 1 vol. 2010. 48p. pap. 16.95 (978-1-4512-0154-3(0)) America Star Bks.

Peterson, Tina L. Oscar & the Amazing Gravity Repellent. Bonet, Xavier, illus. 2015. (Middle-Grade Novels Ser.). (ENG.). 224p. (gr. 4-7). lib. bdg. 26.65 (978-1-4965-0000-7(8)) Stone Arch Bks.

Peto, Judith E. & Talwar, Robert B. Jenny & Benny: Friends 2005. (Illus.). 28p. (J). (gr. -1-3). 16.95 (978-0-9767511-0-6(0)) Lasting Bks. Publishing Co.

Petracca, C. A. B. The Chronicles of Petr The. 2005. 208p. per. 14.95 (978-1-59858-012-9(4)) Dog Ear Publishing, LLC.

Petre, Wanda E. The Watch Chicken: The Legend of Russell the Rooster & His Friend Hortense. 2006. 36p. (J). pap. 9.93 (978-1-4116-9990-8(4)) Lulu Pr., Inc.

Petrillo, Genevieve & Lyon, Lea. Keep Your Ear on the Ball, 1 vol. Lyon, Lea07/, illus. 2009. (ENG.). 32p. (gr. 2-6). pap. 7.95 (978-0-88448-324-3(X), 884324) Tilbury Hse. Pubs.

Petrucha, Stefan & Kinney, Sarah. Tiger Counter. 2008. (Nancy Drew Graphic Novels: Girl Detective Ser.: 15). (ENG., Illus.). 96p. (J). (gr. 3-7). 12.95 (978-1-59707-119-2(6), 9781597071192) Papercutz.

Petrucha, Stefan, et al. The Fake Heir. Ross, Daniel Vaughn, illus. 2006. (J). (978-1-59707-060-7(2)) Papercutz.

Pett, Mark. The Girl & the Bicycle. Pett, Mark, illus. 2014. (ENG., Illus.). 40p. (J). 17.99 (978-1-4424-8319-4(9), Simon & Schuster Bks. For Young Readers) Simon & Schuster Bks. For Young Readers.

Petterson, Aline. El Papalote y el Nopal. Pacheco, Gabriel, illus. 2003. (SPA.). 34p. (J). (gr. 3-5). 15.95 (978-968-19-0750-1(7)) Santillana USA Publishing Co., Inc.

Petty, Dini. The Queen, the Bear & the Bumblebee. Cowles, Rose, illus. 32p. (J). 19.95 (978-1-55285-151-7(6)) Whitecap Bks., Ltd. CAN. Dist: Graphic Arts Ctr. Publishing Co.

Peymani, Christine. Super Starz Masquerade. 2007. (Illus.). 94p. (J). pap. (978-0-439-91952-4(5)) Scholastic, Inc.

Pfeffer, Susan Beth. Revenge of the Aztecs. 2004. 118p. (J). lib. bdg. 16.92 (978-1-4242-0763-3(0)) Fitzgerald Bks.

Pfister, Marcus. The Adventures of Rainbow Fish. 2014. (Rainbow Fish Ser.). (ENG., Illus.). 144p. (J). 19.95 (978-0-7358-4185-7(3)) North-South Bks., Inc.

—Happiness Is... 2014. (ENG., Illus.). 32p. (J). 17.95 (978-0-7358-4179-6(9)) North-South Bks., Inc.

Phanton, Richard G. Frankie. Baker, David, illus. 2012. 40p. 24.95 (978-1-4560-3509-9(6)) America Star Bks.

Phanton, Rick. Boston & the Bean. 2012. 112p. pap. 19.95 (978-1-4626-4809-2(6)) America Star Bks.

Pheather, Heather. Sweater Trouble. 2013. 28p. pap. 24.95 (978-1-63004-667-5(1)) America Star Bks.

Phelan, Matt. Bluffton: My Summers with Buster. Phelan, Matt, illus. 2017. (ENG., Illus.). 232p. (J). (gr. 4-7). pap. 12.99 (978-0-7636-8706-9(5)) Candlewick Pr.

—Bluffton: My Summers with Buster. Phelan, Matt, illus. 2017. (ENG., Illus.). (J). (gr. 4-7). lib. bdg. 24.50 **(978-0-606-39837-4(6))** Turtleback Bks.

Phelps, Dawn. A Monstrous Problem. 2009. 32p. pap. 18.50 (978-1-4389-0848-9(2)) AuthorHouse.

Phelps, Donna & Phelps, Cameron. Cameron & the Dinosaur Heroes. 2011. 128p. 21.23 (978-1-4567-2476-4(2)); pap. 10.68 (978-1-4389-6353-2(X)) AuthorHouse.

Phifer, Larry & Phifer. World on a String. 2013. (ENG.). 17.95 (978-0-9886984-0-6(4)) Storytime Works.

Philbin, Joanna. The Daughters Break the Rules. 2011. (Daughters Ser.: 2). (ENG.). 304p. (J). (gr. 7-17). pap., pap. 10.00 (978-0-316-04905-4(0), Poppy) Little, Brown Bks. for Young Readers.

Philbrick, Rodman. Freak the Mighty. 20th anniv. ed. 2013. (ENG.). 208p. (J). (gr. 3-7). 16.99 (978-0-545-56645-2(2), Blue Sky Pr., The) Scholastic, Inc.

Philippou, Stefanie. Sammy Learns to Say I Am Sorry. 2011. 28p. pap. 21.99 (978-1-4653-6352-7(1)) Xlibris Corp.

Philipson, Sandra J. Forever Home. Campbell, Jenny, illus. 2007. (ENG.). 89p. (J). (gr. 3-7). bds. 7.95 (978-1-59624-080-3(6)) Cleveland Clinic Pr.

Phillips, Dee. Friends?, 1 vol. 2014. (Right Now! Ser.). (ENG.). 48p. (YA). (gr. 9-12). pap. 8.95 (978-1-62250-882-2(3)) Saddleback Educational Publishing, Inc.

—Who Can I Be? 2010. (Look at Me! Ser.). (ENG.). 5p. (J). (gr. -1-k). bds. 6.95 (978-1-84696-200-4(5), TickTock Books) Octopus Publishing Group GBR. Dist: Independent Pubs. Group.

Phillips, Dee & Ticktock Media, Ltd. Staff. What Do Monkeys Do? 2009. (What Do Animals Do? Ser.). (ENG.). 5p. (J). (gr. k — 1). bds. 4.95 (978-1-84696-960-7(3), TickTock Books) Octopus Publishing Group GBR. Dist: Independent Pubs. Group.

Phillips, Dixie. Angel Eyes. Sponaugle, Kim, illus. 2008. 24p. pap. 10.95 (978-1-933090-74-0(X)) Guardian Angel Publishing, Inc.

Phillips, Gin. The Hidden Summer. 2014. (ENG.). 208p. (J). (gr. 5). pap. 7.99 (978-0-14-242568-8(0), Puffin Books) Penguin Young Readers Group.

—A Little Bit of Spectacular. 2015. (ENG.). 176p. (J). (gr. 5). 16.99 (978-0-8037-3837-9(4), Dial Bks) Penguin Young Readers Group.

Phillips, Liam & Plumm, Gabi. Mumble & Jumble & the Great Corpsicle Conundrum. 2009. 278p. pap. 24.50 (978-1-4092-5577-2(8)) Lulu Pr., Inc.

Phillips, Lorri. Ragamuffin Friends. 2010. 71p. pap. 14.00 (978-0-557-73860-1(1)) Lulu Pr., Inc.

Phillips, Matthew. Ingo Flamingo, 1 vol. 2009. 19p. pap. 24.95 (978-1-60836-340-7(6)) America Star Bks.

Phillips, Rebecca. These Things I've Done. 2017. 352p. (YA). (gr. 9). 17.99 **(978-0-06-257090-1(0)**, HarperTeen) HarperCollins Pubs.

Phillips, Ruby Ann. Dream Birthday, 1 vol. Isik, Semur, illus. 2014. (Krystal Ball Ser.). (ENG.). 112p. (gr. 2-3). 25.32 (978-1-4795-2178-4(7)) Picture Window Bks.

—Fortune Cookie Fiasco. Isik, Semur, illus. 2015. (Krystal Ball Ser.). (ENG.). 112p. (gr. 2-3). lib. bdg. 25.32 (978-1-4795-5874-2(5)) Picture Window Bks.

—The Great & Powerful, 1 vol. Isik, Semur, illus. 2014. (Krystal Ball Ser.). (ENG.). 112p. (gr. 2-3). 25.32 (978-1-4795-2179-1(5)) Picture Window Bks.

—Pet Psychic. Isik, Semur, illus. 2015. (Krystal Ball Ser.). (ENG.). 112p. (gr. 2-3). lib. bdg. 25.32 (978-1-4795-5875-9(3)) Picture Window Bks.

Phillips, Sparkle. How to Meet the Man (or Woman) of your Dreams: Or at least, how I met Mine. 2009. (ENG., Illus.). 88p. per. 9.99 (978-0-9779960-3-2(4), Books To Believe In) Thornton Publishing, Inc.

Philpot, Chelsey. Be Good Be Real Be Crazy. 2016. 272p. (YA). (gr. 8). 17.99 (978-0-06-229372-5(9), HarperTeen) HarperCollins Pubs.

—Even in Paradise. (YA). (gr. 8). 2016. 384p. pap. 9.99 (978-0-06-229370-1(2)) 2014. (ENG.). 368p. 17.99 (978-0-06-229369-5(9)) HarperCollins Pubs.

Phineas and Ferb. Phineas & Ferb Batter Up! 2010. pap. 5.99 (978-1-4231-2408-5(1)) Disney Pr.

Piantedosi, John J. The Cat That Purred. Maglio-Macullar, Andrea, illus. 2014. (ENG.). (J). pap. 11.95 (978-1-56548-540-2(8)) New City Press of the Focolare.

Pickell, Sammy. Doxie. Everett, J. H., illus. 2013. (ENG.). (J). 18.99 (978-0-9827972-3-5(0)) MMJ Foundation.

Pickering, Sean & Morrill, Scott. The Adventures of Danny & Spike: Underground. 2007. 92p. per. 9.95 (978-0-595-44365-9(6)) iUniverse, Inc.

Pierro, Rita. No Veggies for Me. Iukel, Onur, illus. 2011. 32p. pap. 24.95 (978-1-4626-4554-1(2)) America Star Bks.

Pierson, Jan. The Haunted Horse of Gold Hill. 2005. (Ghostowners Ser.: Vol. 4). (Illus.). 109p. (J). per. 9.95 (978-0-9721800-3-0(6)) WildWest Publishing.

Pig & Small, 1 vol. 2014. (ENG., Illus.). 32p. (J). (gr. -1-3). 15.95 (978-1-56145-797-7(3)) Peachtree Pubs.

Piggy Toes Press, creator. Giggles & More! with Abby & Friends. 2010. (Illus.). 95p. (J). pap. 7.95 (978-1-61524-233-7(3), Intervisual/Piggy Toes) Bendon, Inc.

—Let's Read Together with Elmo & Friends. 2010. (Sesame Street Ser.). (Illus.). 96p. (J). pap. 7.95 (978-1-61524-234-4(1), Intervisual/Piggy Toes) Bendon, Inc.

Pike, Christopher, pseud. Remember Me: Her Death Will Not Go Unpunished... 2010. (Remember Me Ser.: Vols. 1-3). (ENG., Illus.). 848p. (YA). (gr. 9). pap. 9.99 (978-1-4424-0596-7(1), Simon Pulse) Simon Pulse.

Pilcher, Steve. Pixar Animation Studio Artist Showcase over There. Pilcher, Steve, illus. 2014. (Pixar Animation Studios Artist Showcase Ser.). (ENG., Illus.). 40p. (J). (gr. -1-k). 17.99 (978-1-4231-4793-0(6)) Hyperion Bks. for Children.

Pilger, Seamus. Blast from the Past. Gilpin, Stephen, illus. 2017. (Fart Squad Ser.: 6). 128p. (J). (gr. 1-5). pap. 4.99 (978-0-06-229055-7(X)) HarperCollins Pubs.

Pilkey, Dav. A Friend for Dragon. 2008. (Dragon Tales Ser.). (Illus.). (gr. -1-3). 16.00 (978-0-7569-8299-7(5)) Perfection Learning Corp.

—Uranium Unicorns from Uranus., Bk. 7. 2015. (Ricky Ricotta Ser.: 7). (ENG., Illus.). 128p. (J). (gr. -1-3). pap. 5.99 (978-0-545-63015-3(0)) Scholastic, Inc.

Pilutti, Deb. Bear & Squirrel Are Friends ... Yes, Really! Pilutti, Deb, illus. 2015. (ENG., Illus.). 40p. (J). (gr. -1-3). 17.99 (978-1-4814-2913-9(2), Simon & Schuster Bks. For Young Readers) Simon & Schuster Bks. For Young Readers.

Pino, Montana. Tessie & Tillie. 10th ed. 2004. (YA). lib. bdg. (978-0-9754365-1-6(1)) Thomson, J P.

Pinson, Mignon L. My Two Best Friends Are Hamsters. 2010. 24p. 12.99 (978-1-4520-3309-9(9)) AuthorHouse.

Pintozzi, Nick. Bentley & the Great Fire. Pintozzi, Nick et al, illus. 2004. 16.95 (978-0-9749465-2-8(4)) BentDaiSha, LLC.

Piper, Molly. Rosey & Amanda. Piper, Molly, illus. Date not set. (Illus.). (J). (gr. k-6). pap. 7.95 (978-1-891360-01-5(9)) Little Deer Pr.

Piper, William Bowman. Giraffe of Montana, Volume 3. 2007. (Giraffe of Montana Ser.). (Illus.). 144p. (J). 19.95 (978-0-9763359-6-2(4)) Little Pemberley Pr.

Pires, Curt. The Fiction. 2016. lib. bdg. 26.95 (978-0-606-38936-5(9)) Turtleback Bks.

Pirnot, Karen Hutchins. Sam's Perfect Plan. Ross, Julie, illus. 2008. 32p. pap. 12.95 (978-0-9814894-8-3(6)) Peppertree Pr., The.

Pirzada, Nefes & Simeone, Angelique. Young Equestrian: Something in Common. 2012. 386p. (gr. 4-18). pap. 21.14 (978-1-4669-5242-3(3)) Trafford Publishing.

Pitcher, Chelsea. The Last Changeling. 2014. (ENG.). 360p. (YA). pap. 11.99 (978-0-7387-4084-3(5), Flux) North Star Editions.

—The S-Word. 2013. (ENG.). 320p. pap. 19.99 (978-1-4516-9516-8(0), Gallery Bks.) Gallery Bks.

Pitkethly, Maggie. Graeme Goes Home. Farmer, Suzanne, illus. 2008. 32p. pap. 12.00 (978-0-9791402-8-0(5)) Stewart, R. J. Bks.

Pitman, Sandra. 10 Busy Bumble Bees, 1 vol. Sizemore, Carmen, illus. 2009. 20p. pap. 24.95 (978-1-60749-683-0(6)) America Star Bks.

Pittam, Lore M. The Golden Mushrooms. 2008. 48p. pap. 24.95 (978-1-60703-727-9(0)) America Star Bks.

Pittar, Gill. Milly, Molly & Beefy (book W/dolls) 2006. 28p. pap. (978-1-86972-090-2(3)) Milly Molly Bks.

—Milly, Molly & Henry. 2004. 28p. (978-1-86972-030-8(X)) Milly Molly Bks.

—Milly, Molly & Henry (book W/dolls) 2006. 28p. pap. (978-1-86972-103-9(9)) Milly Molly Bks.

—Milly, Molly & Jimmy's Seeds (book W/dolls) 2006. 28p. pap. (978-1-86972-091-9(1)) Milly Molly Bks.

—Milly, Molly & Oink. 28p. 2006. pap. (978-1-86972-093-3(8)) 2004. (Illus.). (978-1-86972-002-5(4)) Milly Molly Bks.

—Milly, Molly & Special Friends. 2004. 28p. (978-1-86972-017-9(2)) Milly Molly Bks.

—Milly, Molly & Special Friends (book W/dolls) 2006. 28p. pap. (978-1-86972-104-6(7)) Milly Molly Bks.

—Milly, Molly & the Runaway Bean. Morrell, Cris, illus. 2005. 28p. (J). (gr. -1). pap. (978-1-86972-049-0(0)) Milly Molly Bks.

—Milly, Molly & the Stowaways. 2004. 28p. (978-1-86972-026-1(1)) Milly Molly Bks.

—Milly, Molly & the Tree Hut. 2004. 28p. (978-1-86972-028-5(8)) Milly Molly Bks.

—Milly, Molly & What Was That? 2004. 28p. (978-1-86972-031-5(8)) Milly Molly Bks.

Pittar, Gill & Gill, Pittar. Las Ciruelas de Isa Bela. Rioja, Alberto Jimenez, tr. Morrell, Cris, illus. 2003. (Milly Molly Ser.). (SPA.). 24p. (J). pap. (978-84-241-8687-6(7)) Everest Editora ESP. Dist: Lectorum Pubns., Inc.

Pixie, B. R. Just a Little Human. 2011. 98p. pap. 19.95 (978-1-4512-3551-7(8)) America Star Bks.

Pixton, Amy. Mary Had a Little Lamb. 2010. (Indestructibles Ser.). (ENG., Illus.). 12p. (J). (gr. k — 1). pap. 5.95 (978-0-7611-5860-8(X), 15860) Workman Publishing Co., Inc.

Plant, Marilyn. Trinka's Magic Bracelet. 2012. 40p. pap. (978-1-77067-956-6(1)) FriesenPress.

Plaza, José María. Ya Soy Mayor. 2003. (Disney Collection). (SPA.). 48p. (J). 6.95 (978-84-670-0303-1(0)) Espasa Calpe, S.A. ESP. Dist: Planeta Publishing Corp.

Pledger, Maurice, illus. Daisy Duckling's Adventure. 2014. (ENG.). 16p. (J). (gr. -1). bds. 10.95 (978-1-62686-015-5(7), Silver Dolphin Bks.) Readerlink Distribution Services, LLC.

Pliszka, Jodi. Bella & Gizmo's Adventures: Bella Gets A New Sweater. 2005. (Illus.). 24p. (J). per. 18.95 (978-1-933449-04-3(7)) Nightengale Pr.

—Bella & Gizmo's Adventures — Bella Gets A New Sweater. 2005. 32p. (J). per. 18.95 (978-1-933449-26-5(8)) Nightengale Pr.

Pliszka, Jodi A. Bella & Gizmo's Adventures: The Hairless Sphynx Cats. 2005. (Illus.). 30p. (J). per. 18.95 (978-1-933449-03-6(9)) Nightengale Pr.

Plourde, Lynn. Maxi's Secrets: (or What You Can Learn from a Dog) (ENG.). 272p. (J). (gr. 5). 2017. 8.99 **(978-0-399-54568-9(9)**, Puffin Books) 2016. 16.99 (978-0-399-54567-2(0), Nancy Paulsen Books) Penguin Young Readers Group.

Plourde, Lynn. You're Doing That in the Talent Show?! Cornelison, Sue, illus. 2016. (ENG.). 32p. (J). (gr. -1-k). 16.99 (978-1-4847-1491-1(1)) Disney Pr.

Pluth, Lisa Anderson. A Haunting in Little River. 2011. 94p. pap. 19.95 (978-1-4560-9700-4(8)) America Star Bks.

Poblocki, Dan. The Book of Bad Things. 2014. (ENG.). 256p. (J). (gr. 5-9). 16.99 (978-0-545-64553-9(0), Scholastic Pr.) Scholastic, Inc.

—The Haunting of Gabriel Ashe. (ENG.). 288p. (J). (gr. 5-9). 2015. pap. 7.99 (978-0-545-40271-2(9)) 2013. 16.99 (978-0-545-40270-5(0)) Scholastic, Inc. (Scholastic Pr.).

Pocha, Michael J. Thomas James & the Ringmaster. 2011. 180p. pap. 24.95 (978-1-4560-6904-9(7)) America Star Bks.

Pochocki, Ethel. A Penny for a Hundred. Owens, Mary Beth, illus. 2005. 31p. (J). (gr. 2-5). pap. 9.95 (978-1-883937-52-2(3)) Bethlehem Bks.

—A Penny for a Hundred. 2014. (ENG., Illus.). 32p. (J). (gr. -1-3). 15.95 *(978-1-60893-311-2(3))* Down East Bks.

Pochocki, Ethel & Mosher, Barry. The Mushroom Man, 1 vol. 2006. (ENG., Illus.). 32p. (gr. 2-6). reprint ed. 7.95 *(978-0-88448-278-9(2),* 884278) Tilbury Hse. Pubs.

Pohlemann, Terri. She Lives in the Stars. 2012. 24p. pap. 24.95 *(978-1-4626-6190-9(4))* America Star Bks.

Poindexter, Stephanie. Octavious & His Busy Tentacles. 2010. 21p. 13.50 *(978-0-557-30136-2(X))* Lulu Pr., Inc.

Polacco, Patricia. Bully. Polacco, Patricia, illus. 2012. (ENG., Illus.). 48p. (J). (gr. 2-5). 17.99 *(978-0-399-25704-9(7),* G.P. Putnam's Sons Books for Young Readers) Penguin Young Readers Group.

—Chicken Sunday. 2015. 32p. pap. 8.00 *(978-1-61003-527-9(5))* Center for the Collaborative Classroom.

—Emma Kate. Polacco, Patricia, illus. (ENG., Illus.). (J). (gr. -1-k). 2008. 32p. pap. 6.99 *(978-0-14-241196-4(5),* Puffin Books) 2005. 40p. 17.99 *(978-0-399-24452-0(2),* Philomel Bks.) Penguin Young Readers Group.

—Pink & Say. (Illus.). (J). (gr. 3-4). pap. 7.99 net. *(978-1-930332-54-6(8))* Lectorum Pubns., Inc.

Polanco, Amparo. The Magical Forest. 2016. (ENG., Illus.). (J). 16.95 ***(978-1-5069-0268-5(5))***; pap. 12.95 ***(978-1-5069-0269-2(3))*** First Edition Design eBook Publishing.

Poland, Pitch & Poland, Inglan. Lost & Found. Rose, Drew, illus. 2013. 30p. (J). *(978-0-9853430-0-2(1))* Little P Pr. Co.

Polden, Kelly Carper. Puppy Tales: The Adventures of Adam the Australian Sheppard. 2007. (ENG.). 72p. pap. 11.99 *(978-1-4196-7458-7(7))* CreateSpace Independent Publishing Platform.

Polglase, Pamela. Handy & Dandy. 2008. 182p. pap. 15.96 *(978-0-557-02578-7(8))*; 27.76 *(978-1-4357-4588-9(4))* Lulu Pr., Inc.

Polisner, Gae. The Memory of Things. 2016. (ENG.). 288p. (YA). 18.99 *(978-1-250-09552-7(2),* 9781250095527, St. Martin's Griffin) St. Martin's Pr.

—The Memory of Things. 2017. (YA). lib. bdg. 22.10 ***(978-0-606-40599-7(2))*** Turtleback Bks.

—The Memory of Things: A Novel. 2017. (ENG.). 288p. (YA). pap. 10.99 ***(978-1-250-14442-3(6),*** 9781250144423, Wednesday Bks.) St. Martin's Pr.

Polisner, Gae. The Summer of Letting Go. (ENG.). (YA). (gr. 7-10). 2015. 336p. pap. 9.95 *(978-1-61620-480-8(X))* 2014. 320p. 16.95 *(978-1-61620-256-9(4),* 73256) Algonquin Bks. of Chapel Hill.

Pollack, Jenny. Klepto. 2008. (ENG.). 288p. (YA). (gr. 7-18). 8.99 *(978-0-14-241072-1(1),* Speak) Penguin Young Readers Group.

Pollard, Tara. Season's Christmas Quest: The Dog's Story. 2012. 138p. (gr. 1-1). 21.95 *(978-1-4759-4008-4(4))*; pap. 11.95 *(978-1-4759-4009-1(2))* iUniverse, Inc.

Polo & Cuddles. (J). 14.64 *(978-0-8136-0618-7(7))* Modern Curriculum Pr.

Ponti, Claude. DeZert Isle. Holliday, Mary Martin, tr. from FRE. Ponti, Claude, illus. 2003. (ENG., Illus.). 64p. (J). 16.95 *(978-1-56792-237-0(6))* Godine, David R. Pub.

Ponti, James. Framed! (Framed! Ser.: 1). (ENG., Illus.). (J). (gr. 3-7). 2017. 320p. pap. 7.99 ***(978-1-4814-3631-1(7))*** 2016. 304p. 17.99 *(978-1-4814-3630-4(9))* Simon & Schuster Children's Publishing. (Aladdin).

Pool, Catherine. Catrina's Journey to Her Musical Friends, 1 vol. 2010. 18p. pap. 24.95 *(978-1-4489-7237-1(X))* PublishAmerica, Inc.

Poole, Catherine Cheyenne. Batboy's Crazy Day. Murphy, Fredrick, illus. 2008. 24p. pap. 8.95 *(978-1-935105-18-3(3))* Avid Readers Publishing Group.

Poole, Cheryl J. A. Farmer & Me! Making Silage. 2012. (Illus.). 24p. pap. 19.82 *(978-1-4772-2360-4(6))* AuthorHouse.

—Farmer & Me! Milking the Cows. 2012. (Illus.). 24p. (-18). pap. 19.82 *(978-1-4772-3947-6(2))* AuthorHouse.

Poon, Janice. Claire & the Water Wish. Poon, Janice, illus. 2009. (ENG., Illus.). 120p. (J). (gr. 2-5). 15.95 *(978-1-55453-381-7(3))* Kids Can Pr., Ltd. CAN. Dist: Hachette Bk. Group.

Popcorn, Socks, & Salvation. 2008. 32p. pap. 4.99 *(978-0-8341-2350-2(9),* 083-412-3509) Beacon Hill Pr. of Kansas City.

Pope, Mildred. But I Don't Wanna Take a Bath! A Mike & Tyke Series. 2011. 36p. (gr. -1). 15.95 *(978-1-4567-3939-3(5))* AuthorHouse.

Pope, Stephanie L. Fedo the Frog Flew the Coop. 2012. 16p. pap. 15.99 *(978-1-4772-1656-9(1))* AuthorHouse.

Port City High Sample Set: High School High/Taken/Deported/the Public Eye. 2013. (ENG.). (YA). (gr. 8-12). pap. 39.80 *(978-1-62250-697-2(9))* Saddleback Educational Publishing, Inc.

Porta, Bill K. Rusty the Rescue Horse. 2011. 24p. pap. 11.32 *(978-1-4520-4452-1(X))* AuthorHouse.

Porter, Amber Leann. To Be a Champion. 2008. 31p. pap. 24.95 *(978-1-60610-222-0(2))* PublishAmerica, Inc.

Porter, Rhonda. Brody Learns about Strangers, 1 vol. 2009. 29p. pap. 19.95 *(978-1-61546-699-3(1))* PublishAmerica, Inc.

—Brody Meets a Bully. 2008. 16p. pap. 24.95 *(978-1-60610-311-1(3))* America Star Bks.

Portis, Antoinette. Best Frints in the Whole Universe. 2016. (ENG., Illus.). 40p. (J). 16.99 *(978-1-62672-136-4(X),* 9781626721364) Roaring Brook Pr.

Posner, Richard. Sparrows Flight. 2014. (ENG.). 222p. (J). (gr. 7-10). pap. 14.95 *(978-1-59077-316-1(0))* Evans, M. & Co., Inc.

Posner-Sanchez, Andrea. Always a Princess (Disney Princess) Disney Storybook Artists Staff, illus. 2011. (Friendship Box Ser.). (ENG.). 48p. (J). (gr. k — 1). bds. 10.99 *(978-0-7364-2848-4(8),* RH/Disney) Random Hse. Children's Bks.

—Dino-Might Tales. Random House Disney Staff, illus. 2016. (Friendship Box Ser.). (ENG.). 48p. (J). (gr. -1 — 1). bds. 10.99 *(978-0-7364-3224-5(8),* RH/Disney) Random Hse. Children's Bks.

Posner, Tina. Rabbit Tricks. Corbett, Liza, illus. 2006. 8p. (J). pap. *(978-0-439-73513-1(0))* Scholastic, Inc.

Poth, Karen. Sheerluck Holmes & the Case of the Missing Friend, 1 vol. 2014. (I Can Read! / Big Idea Books / VeggieTales Ser.). (ENG.). 32p. (J). pap. 3.99 *(978-0-310-74171-8(8))* Zonderkidz.

Poth, Karen, et al. The Pirates Who Don't Do Anything & Me! 2004. (Big Idea Books / VeggieTales Ser.). (ENG., Illus.). 32p. (J). 7.99 *(978-0-310-70725-7(0))* Zonderkidz.

Potter, Noel Gyro. Dibble Can't Dribble, 1 vol. Cannon, Joseph, illus. 2008. (Adventures of Marshall & Art Ser.). (ENG.). 32p. (gr. -1-4). 28.50 net. *(978-1-60270-197-7(0),* Looking Glass Library) ABDO Publishing Co.

—A Very Sticky Situation, 1 vol. Cannon, Joseph, illus. 2008. (Adventures of Marshall & Art Ser.). (ENG.). 32p. (gr. -1-4). 28.50 *(978-1-60270-201-1(2),* Looking Glass Library) ABDO Publishing Co.

Pottorf, Patricia D. Hebee, the Quibber. 2012. 64p. pap. 19.50 *(978-1-61897-350-4(9),* Strategic Bk. Publishing) Strategic Book Publishing & Rights Agency (SBPRA).

Pova, Rosie. Ladybug & Caterpillar: The Way to Friendship. 2008. 16p. pap. 24.95 *(978-1-60474-950-2(4))* America Star Bks.

Povandra, Shirley. My Imaginary Friend. 2007. 44p. pap. 17.95 *(978-1-59526-669-9(0))* Aeon Publishing Inc.

Powell, Eleanor. The Little Cloud That Cried. 2012. 24p. pap. 12.99 *(978-1-4691-4256-2(2))* Xlibris Corp.

Powell, GinaMarie. Ayiana & the Hurricane Katrina Classmate. Bray, Pamela, illus. 2008. 28p. pap. 24.95 *(978-1-60441-965-8(2))* America Star Bks.

Powell, Laura. Witch Fire. 2013. (ENG.). 336p. (YA). (gr. 7). 17.99 *(978-1-61963-006-2(0),* 9781619630062, Bloomsbury USA Childrens) Bloomsbury Publishing USA.

Powell, Randy. Three Clams & an Oyster. 2007. 216p. (gr. 7-12). 16.95 *(978-0-7569-8184-6(0))* Perfection Learning Corp.

Powelson, Jannifer. Rachel & Sammy Learn about Trees. 2012. (Illus.). 40p. pap. 15.00 *(978-1-61204-988-5(5),* Strategic Bk. Publishing) Strategic Book Publishing & Rights Agency (SBPRA).

Power, Molly. Up & down with Lena Larocha. Carter, Barbara, illus. 2013. 169p. pap. 15.00 *(978-1-60571-176-8(4),* Shires Press) Northshire Pr.

Prahin, Andrew. Brimsby's Hats. Prahin, Andrew, illus. 2013. (ENG., Illus.). 40p. (J). (gr. -1-3). 15.99 *(978-1-4424-8147-3(1),* Simon & Schuster Bks. For Young Readers) Simon & Schuster Bks. For Young Readers.

Prasad, Sunayna. Alyssa's African Adventures. 2011. pap. 11.95 *(978-0-7414-6619-8(8))* Infinity Publishing.

Pratico, Ariel R. Do You Know Where Z Is? 2011. 36p. pap. 24.95 *(978-1-4626-2560-4(6))* America Star Bks.

Prats, Joan de Déu. Un Topo en un Mar de Hierba. Caruncho, Isabel, illus. (SPA.). 31p. *(978-84-236-5040-8(5))* Edebé ESP. Dist: Lectorum Pubns., Inc.

Pratt, Non. Remix. 2017. (ENG.). 320p. (YA). (gr. 9). pap. 10.99 *(978-1-4424-9776-4(9))* Simon & Schuster Children's Publishing.

—Trouble. 2014. (ENG., Illus.). 384p. (YA). (gr. 9). 17.99 *(978-1-4424-9772-6(6),* Simon & Schuster Bks. For Young Readers) Simon & Schuster Bks. For Young Readers.

—Trouble. 2015. (ENG., Illus.). 400p. (YA). (gr. 9). pap. 10.99 *(978-1-4424-9773-3(4))* Simon & Schuster, Inc.

Pratt, Sally. The Adventures of Bernie the Bee in Sally's Garden. 2013. 46p. pap. 21.99 *(978-1-4772-9759-9(6))* AuthorHouse.

Preble, Laura. The Queen Geek Social Club. 2006. (ENG.). 336p. (YA). (gr. 7-18). 15.00 *(978-0-425-21164-9(9),* Berkley) Penguin Publishing Group.

Preller, James. Along Came Spider. 2008. (ENG.). 144p. (J). (gr. 3-7). 15.99 *(978-0-545-03299-5(7),* Scholastic Paperbacks) Scholastic, Inc.

Press, Julian. Operation Yellow Dragon, No. 3. 2008. (Get a Clue Ser.: 3). (ENG.). 128p. (J). (gr. 2-5). 7.99 *(978-0-448-44875-6(0),* Grosset & Dunlap) Penguin Young Readers Group.

Preston-Gannon, Frann. How to Lose a Lemur. 2016. (ENG., Illus.). 30p. (J). (gr. -1 — 1). bds. 6.95 *(978-1-4549-2095-3(5))* Sterling Publishing Co., Inc.

Preston, Helen M. Gra Gra's Stories. 2012. 72p. pap. 28.99 *(978-1-4772-9783-4(9))* AuthorHouse.

Preston, L. M. Explorer X: Beta. 2012. (ENG.). 264p. (YA). pap. 11.99 *(978-0-9841989-5-5(4))* Phenomenal One Pr.

Preus, Margi. The Bamboo Sword. (ENG., Illus.). (YA). (gr. 5-9). 2016. 368p. pap. 8.95 *(978-1-4197-0824-4(1))* 2015. 352p. 16.95 *(978-1-4197-0807-7(4))* Abrams, Inc. (Amulet Bks.).

Price, Audrey. My best Friend: Best Friend. 2004. (J). pap. 15.95 *(978-0-9778937-0-6(7))* Priceless Ink Publishing Co., Inc.

Price, Cheryl. The Golden Aspen. 2009. 36p. pap. 15.95 *(978-1-4490-2855-8(1))* AuthorHouse.

Price, David. Sly the Fox & Advice from la Princessa Roja. 2008. (Illus.). 34p. (J). 14.95 *(978-0-9779701-2-4(4))* Wishingstone Publishing.

Price, Mary Elizabeth. Wallbaby Bumblebees. 2004. (Illus.). 40p. (J). per. 15.75 *(978-0-9715402-2-4(5),* 410-707-6686) Barnhardt & Ashe Publishing, Inc.

Priddy Book. In the Yard; Fuzzy Bee & Friends. (Illus.). (J). 17.90 *(978-0-312-49377-6(0),* Priddy Bks.) St. Martin's Pr.

Priddy, Roger. Best Friends: We Are Best Friends. 2015. (Best Friends Ser.). (ENG.). 20p. (J). (gr. -1-1). bds. 9.99 *(978-0-312-51922-3(2),* 9780312519223, Priddy Bks.) St. Martin's Pr.

—Fluffy Chick & Friends. 2015. (Touch & Feel Cloth Bks.). (ENG.). 6p. (J). (gr. -1 — 1). 12.99 *(978-0-312-51892-9(7),* 9780312518929, Priddy Bks.) St. Martin's Pr.

—Follow Me. 2016. (Finger Mazes Ser.). (ENG.). 16p. (J). bds. 9.99 *(978-0-312-52058-8(1),* 9780312520588, Priddy Bks.) St. Martin's Pr.

—Fuzzy Bee & Friends. 2015. (Touch & Feel Cloth Bks.). (ENG.). 6p. (J). (gr. -1 — 1). 12.99 *(978-0-312-51891-2(9),* 9780312518912, Priddy Bks.) St. Martin's Pr.

—Hello Friends. 2014. (Little Friends Ser.). (ENG.). 24p. (J). (gr. -1 — 1). bds. 5.99 *(978-0-312-51684-0(3),* 9780312516840, Priddy Bks.) St. Martin's Pr.

—Home Sweet Home. 2014. (Little Friends Ser.). (ENG.). 10p. (J). (gr. -1 — 1). bds. 6.99 *(978-0-312-51679-6(7),* 9780312516796, Priddy Bks.) St. Martin's Pr.

—Little Friends: Home for Christmas. 2016. (Little Friends Ser.). (ENG.). 12p. (J). bds. 8.99 *(978-0-312-52144-8(8),* 9780312521448, Priddy Bks.) St. Martin's Pr.

—Little Friends: Little Monkey. 2015. (Little Friends Ser.). (ENG., Illus.). 10p. (J). (gr. -1 — 1). bds. 8.99 *(978-0-312-51779-3(3),* 9780312517793, Priddy Bks.) St. Martin's Pr.

—Sticker Friends: Love Bug. 2016. (Sticker Friends Ser.). (ENG.). 24p. (J). pap. 4.99 *(978-0-312-52146-2(4),* 9780312521462, Priddy Bks.) St. Martin's Pr.

—Tea Party Set. 2014. (Hello Kitty Ser.). (ENG.). 8p. (J). (gr. -1-1). bds. 14.99 *(978-0-312-51766-3(1),* 9780312517663, Priddy Bks.) St. Martin's Pr.

—We Are Better Together (Small Format) 2016. (ENG.). 20p. (J). bds. 7.99 *(978-0-312-52031-1(X),* 9780312520311, Priddy Bks.) St. Martin's Pr.

—Wiggle & the Whale: A Book of Funny Friends. 2016. (Alphaprints Ser.). (ENG.). 32p. (J). 16.99 *(978-0-312-52136-3(7),* 9780312521363, Priddy Bks.) St. Martin's Pr.

Priddy, Roger & Crimi-Trent, Ellen. Making Friends. 2013. (Schoolies Ser.). (ENG., Illus.). 28p. (J). (gr. -1-1). 4.99 *(978-0-312-51610-9(X),* 9780312516109, Priddy Bks.) St. Martin's Pr.

Priebe, Val. I Don't Want to Live on the Tennis Court, 1 vol. Santillan, Jorge H., illus. 2012. (Sports Illustrated Kids Victory School Superstars Ser.). (ENG.). 56p. (gr. 1-3). pap. 5.95 *(978-1-4342-3868-9(7))*; lib. bdg. 26.65 *(978-1-4342-3761-3(3))* Stone Arch Bks.

Priest, A. L. Breakthrough. 2014. (Red Zone Ser.: 2). (ENG.). 104p. (YA). (gr. 6-12). pap. 7.95 *(978-1-4677-4472-0(7),* Darby Creek) Lerner Publishing Group.

Priest, Cherie. I Am Princess X. Ciesemier, Kali, illus. 2015. (ENG.). 256p. (YA). (gr. 7). 18.99 *(978-0-545-62085-7(6),* Levine, Arthur A. Bks.) Scholastic, Inc.

Prignano, Barbara. The Tiny Tomato & His Terrific Manners. Kalpart, illus. 2013. 32p. pap. 12.95 *(978-1-62857-080-9(6),* Strategic Bk. Publishing) Strategic Book Publishing & Rights Agency (SBPRA).

Primavera, Elise. Louise the Big Cheese. Goode, Diane, illus. 2011. (ENG.). 40p. (J). (gr. k-3). 6.99 *(978-1-4424-2066-3(9),* Simon & Schuster/Paula Wiseman Bks.) Simon & Schuster/Paula Wiseman Bks.

—Louise the Big Cheese: Divine Diva. Goode, Diane, illus. 2009. (ENG.). 40p. (J). (gr. k-3). 16.99 *(978-1-4169-7180-1(7),* Simon & Schuster/Paula Wiseman Bks.) Simon & Schuster/Paula Wiseman Bks.

—Louise the Big Cheese & the Ooh-la-La Charm School. Goode, Diane, illus. 2012. (ENG.). 40p. (J). (gr. k-3). 16.99 *(978-1-4424-0599-8(6),* Simon & Schuster/Paula Wiseman Bks.) Simon & Schuster/Paula Wiseman Bks.

Prince, Liz. Clarence. 2016. lib. bdg. 26.95 *(978-0-606-39003-3(0))* Turtleback Bks.

Printers, Caxton. Rufus & Friends. 2012. (ENG.). pap. *(978-1-4675-4752-9(2))*; pap. *(978-1-4675-4751-2(4))* Independent Pub.

Prinz, Yvonne. Still There, Clare. 2005. (ENG.). 4p. (J). pap., tchr. ed. *(978-1-55192-821-0(3))* Raincoast Bk. Distribution CAN. Dist: Publishers Group West (PGW).

Prior, Natalie. Lily Quench & the Dragon of Ashby, No. 1. Dawson, Janine, illus. 2004. (ENG.). 160p. (J). (gr. 3-7). 6.99 *(978-0-14-240020-3(3),* Puffin Books) Penguin Young Readers Group.

Pritchard, Jean. Bobcat Bootcamp in Orange City. Dakins, Todd, illus. 2007. (J). *(978-0-9652491-6-4(6))* Cook, Ken Co.

Pritchett, Andy. Stick! 2013. (ENG., Illus.). 32p. (J). (gr. -1-2). 15.99 *(978-0-7636-6616-3(5))* Candlewick Pr.

Procter, Diann. It Happened in the Goldfish Bowl. Procter, Bill, illus. 2007. 28p. pap. 24.95 *(978-1-4241-8357-9(X))* America Star Bks.

Proimos, James. Mac & Cheese. Proimos, James, illus. 2016. (ENG., Illus.). 40p. (J). 16.99 *(978-0-8050-9156-4(4),* 9780805091564, Holt, Henry & Co. Bks. For Young Readers) Holt, Henry & Co.

—Waddle! Waddle! Proimos, James, illus. 2015. (ENG., Illus.). 32p. (J). (gr. -1-3). 17.99 *(978-0-545-41846-1(1),* Scholastic Pr.) Scholastic, Inc.

Prokash, Marie. Madison's Adventure. 2012. 28p. pap. 17.99 *(978-1-4772-3334-4(2))* AuthorHouse.

The Promise. 2012. 218p. pap. *(978-1-78176-337-7(2))* FeedARead.com.

Promise, 1 vol. 2014. (Faerieground Ser.). (ENG., Illus.). 96p. (gr. 1-3). lib. bdg. 23.99 *(978-1-4342-9188-2(X))* Stone Arch Bks.

Prose, Francine. Touch. 2010. (ENG.). 272p. (YA). (gr. 9). pap. 8.99 *(978-0-06-137519-4(5),* HarperTeen) HarperCollins Pubs.

Prostko, Andrea. Strike One! 2010. 220p. pap. 13.95 *(978-1-60911-546-3(5),* Eloquent Bks.) Strategic Book Publishing & Rights Agency (SBPRA).

Prou, Suzanne. Les Amis de Monsieur Paul, Level C. (FRE.). (YA). (gr. 7-12). 9.99 *(978-0-8219-1218-8(6),* 40331) EMC/Paradigm Publishing.

Provenzano, Stella Marie. How Rusty Rooster Found His Do. 2008. 16p. per. 24.95 *(978-1-4241-9362-2(1))* America Star Bks.

Provost, Gary & Stockwell, Gail Provost. David & Max. rev. ed. 2006. (ENG.). 185p. (gr. 5). per. 14.95 *(978-0-8276-0837-5(3))* Jewish Pubn. Society.

Pruett, Nichole Lee. My Best Friend. Rowton, Caitlin, illus. 2013. (ENG.). 46p. (J). pap. 14.95 *(978-1-936578-15-3(8))* 5 Fold Media LLC.

Pruitt, Vasta Z. Buttons & Babs Run Life's Race: Heavenly Pals Series. 2011. 168p. (gr. 4-6). 22.99 *(978-1-4567-6792-1(5))*; pap. 13.99 *(978-1-4567-6793-8(3))* AuthorHouse.

Pryce, Denise. Alexander & the Ring of Destiny. 2009. 72p. pap. 24.99 *(978-1-4251-8887-0(7))* Trafford Publishing.

Pryke, Gary. The Adventures of Spike & Johnny: Somewhere Close to Forty. 2011. 120p. (gr. -1). pap. 13.88 *(978-1-4269-2705-8(3))* Trafford Publishing.

Pryor, Michael. Leo Da Vinci vs the Ice-Cream Domination League. Faber, Jules, illus. 2015. (Leo Da Vinci Ser.). (ENG.). 144p. (J). (gr. 4-7). 8.99 *(978-0-85798-837-9(9))* Random Hse. Australia AUS. Dist: Independent Pubs. Group.

Publications International Ltd. Staff. My 1St Look & Find Disney Pixar Friends & Heroes. 2007. 18p. (J). 9.98 *(978-1-4127-6848-1(9),* PIL Kids) Publications International, Ltd.

—Rio Large Play As Ound. 2011. 24p. (J). 17.98 *(978-1-4508-0735-7(6))* Phoenix International Publications, Inc.

—Steering Wheel Sound Thomas the Tank. 2007. 12p. (J). bds. 17.98 *(978-1-4127-6811-5(X))* Phoenix International Publications, Inc.

—Thomas & Friends: First Look & Find. 2010. 18p. 7.98 *(978-1-4508-1139-2(6))* Phoenix International Publications, Inc.

Publications International Ltd. Staff, creator. Disney Best Friends. 2007. (My First Look & Find Ser.). (Illus.). 12p. (gr. -1-k). 7.98 *(978-1-4127-8738-3(6))* Publications International, Ltd.

—Thomas & Friends Musical Pop-up Treasury. 2007. (Thomas & Friends Ser.). (Illus.). 24p. (gr. -1). 15.98 *(978-1-4127-9293-6(2))* Publications International, Ltd.

Publications International Ltd. Staff, ed. Barney: Let's Play Together. 2011. 10p. (J). bds. 8.98 *(978-1-4508-0859-0(X))* Publications International, Ltd.

—The Big Fix-It Day. 2010. 14p. (J). 19.98 *(978-1-60553-110-6(3),* PIL Kids) Publications International, Ltd.

—Cars: Fun with Friends. 2010. (J). bds. 5.98 *(978-1-60553-038-3(7))* Phoenix International Publications, Inc.

—Disney(r) Frozen: Giant Look & Find(tm) 2014. 24p. (J). *(978-1-4508-9769-3(X),* 145089769X) Publications International, Ltd.

—Disney(r) Frozen Little Look & Find(tm) 2014. 24p. (J). *(978-1-4508-9259-9(0),* 1450892590) Publications International, Ltd.

—Disney(r) Junior Little Look & Find(tm) Fun with Friends. 2014. 24p. (J). *(978-1-4508-9479-1(8),* 1450894798) Publications International, Ltd.

—Disney(r) Princess Palace Pets: Little Pop-Up Songbook. 2014. 10p. (J). bds. *(978-1-4508-8635-2(3),* 1450886353) Publications International, Ltd.

—Dora's Desert Friends Plush Sound Book. 2010. 6p. (J). bds. 12.98 *(978-1-4127-3095-2(3),* 7229600) Phoenix International Publications, Inc.

—Let's Have a Race, Surprises, Little Engines. 2010. 14p. (J). 12.98 *(978-1-4127-4716-5(3))* Phoenix International Publications, Inc.

—Lights & Music Treasury 10Led Spa Disney Classics. 2009. 160p. 15.98 *(978-1-4127-5454-5(2))* Phoenix International Publications, Inc.

—Look & Find: Snoopy. 2013. 24p. (J). (gr. 1-3). 7.99 *(978-1-4127-1722-9(1),* 6273d751-5dbd-41ad-a19f-1ef74baf570f) Phoenix International Publications, Inc.

—Mickey Mouse Clubhouse: Mickey & Friends (Look & Find) 2010. 24p. (J). 7.98 *(978-1-60553-747-4(0))* Publications International, Ltd.

—Mickey Mouse Clubhouse: Mickey's Surprise! 2013. 14p. (J). (gr. k-3). bds. 16.99 *(978-1-4508-2188-9(X),* 87b7723a-b11c-4ce1-8b21-522e3e8ff7e2) Phoenix International Publications, Inc.

—My First Story Reader Sesame Street, 3 vols. 2007. (Illus.). (J). 31.98 *(978-1-4127-8989-9(3))* Phoenix International Publications, Inc.

—My Friends Tigger & Pooh. 2008. (J). bds. 5.98 *(978-1-4127-8483-2(2))* Publications International, Ltd.

—Record a Story with Thomas & Friends: Good Night, Little Engine. 2011. (Illus.). 20p. (J). bds. 25.98 *(978-1-4508-1164-4(7))* Phoenix International Publications, Inc.

—Rock & Roll with Elmo. 2010. 24p. (J). bds. 19.98 *(978-1-4127-4475-1(X),* PIL Kids) Publications International, Ltd.

—Rockin' on the Railway. 2010. 24p. (J). 17.98 *(978-1-60553-339-1(4),* PIL Kids) Publications International, Ltd.

—Sesame Street: Find a Friend: A Busy Box Book. 2010. 14p. (J). bds. 16.98 *(978-1-60553-622-4(9))* Phoenix International Publications, Inc.

—Thomas & Friends: Ding! Dong! A Visit from Thomas. 2011. 12p. (J). bds. 9.98 *(978-1-60553-985-0(6))* Phoenix International Publications, Inc.

—Thomas & Friends: Sodor Snapshots. 2010. 14p. (J). bds. 19.98 *(978-1-4127-1918-6(6))* Publications International, Ltd.

—Thomas & Friends(tm) Super Look & Find(r) Activity Pad: Spot the Find 'ems, Find the Differences! Giant Play Scene! More Than 50 Stickers! 2014. 64p. (J). *(978-1-4508-8559-1(4),* 1450885594) Publications International, Ltd.

—Tinker Bell. 2009. 24p. (J). 7.98 *(978-1-4127-7144-3(7),* PIL Kids) Publications International, Ltd.

—Toy Story 3: New Friends. 2010. 12p. (J). bds. 10.98 *(978-1-4127-4584-0(5),* PIL Kids) Publications International, Ltd.

—Treasure Hunt. 2010. 12p. (J). bds. 9.98 *(978-1-4127-9885-3(X))* Phoenix International Publications, Inc.

—Up & down! Play-a-Sound Book & Huggable Kai-lan. 2010. (J). 14.98 *(978-1-4127-5591-7(3))* Publications International, Ltd.

—A Very Busy Day for Sodor: (Stereo Play-a-Sound) 2010. 24p. (J). 19.98 *(978-1-4508-0010-5(6))* Publications International, Ltd.

—Write-And-Erase Look & Find(r) Disney(r) Sofia the First: More Than 100 Find 'ems! Find & Circle 'em. Wipe Clean & Play Again! 2014. 28p. (J). bds. *(978-1-4508-9034-2(2),* 1450890342) Publications International, Ltd.

—9 Button Record Story Pooh Friends & Fun. 2011. 18p. 19.98 *(978-1-4508-1994-7(X))* Publications International, Ltd.

Publications International Ltd. Staff & Red Giraffe, Ltd Staff, eds. The Big Race - Stories Come to Life, 3Bks. 2011. (J). *(978-1-4508-0586-5(8))* Phoenix International Publications, Inc.

Pugh, Ian. Wolfstorm: The First Danny Piper Adventure. 2010. 388p. 32.95 *(978-1-4269-0239-0(5))* Trafford Publishing.

Pugliano-Martin, Carol. See You in Spring! 2006. (Early Explorers Ser.). (J). pap. *(978-1-4108-6105-4(8))* Benchmark Education Co.

Purtill, C. Leigh. FaceSpace Face-Off! 2010. 240p. pap. 5.95 *(978-1-60747-781-5(5),* Pickwick Pr.) Phoenix Bks., Inc.

EFG

Puzzi, Jessica. Rosy & Simon's Front Yard Adventure, 1 vol. 2010. 18p. pap. 24.95 *(978-1-4489-2601-5(7))* PublishAmerica, Inc.

Puzzuoli, Jon. Wishing to Whistle. 2009. 32p. pap. 17.50 *(978-0-557-10420-8(3))* Lulu Pr., Inc.

Pyatt, A. K. Old Woman's Garbage. Hill, Lynn, illus. 2003. *(978-0-9718431-3-4(9))* M.O.T.H.E.R. Publishing Co., Inc., The.

Pybus, Judith. The Ladder. 2009. 136p. pap. 10.99 *(978-1-4490-0298-5(6))* AuthorHouse.

Pyne, Jane. Tommy's Secret. 2009. 86p. pap. 10.49 *(978-1-4389-9102-3(9))* AuthorHouse.

Pyros, Andrea. My Year of Epic Rock: How to Survive 7th Grade: Make Some Noise. 2014. (ENG.). 208p. (J). (gr. 4-8). pap. 7.99 *(978-1-4022-9300-9(3))*, 9781402293009, Sourcebooks Jabberwocky) Sourcebooks, Inc.

Quackenbush, Robert. Piet Potter Returns: A Piet Potter Mystery. 2010. 52p. (J). (gr. k-4). pap. 8.95 *(978-1-4502-1352-3(9))* iUniverse, Inc.

—Piet Potter Strikes Again: A Piet Potter Mystery. 2010. 52p. (J). (gr. k-4). pap. 8.95 *(978-1-4502-1530-5(0))* iUniverse, Inc.

Quarto Generic Staff. My Bear Griz. McGinness, Suzanne, illus. 2011. (ENG.). 32p. (J). (gr. -1-1). 17.95 *(978-1-84780-113-5(7))*, Frances Lincoln) Quarto Publishing Group UK GBR. Dist: Hachette Bk. Group.

Quayle, Susan. Mouse & the Storm. Muldoon, Melissa, illus. 2017. (ENG.). 56p. 15.95 *(978-1-84819-344-4(0))*, 9047, Singing Dragon) Kingsley, Jessica Pubs. GBR. Dist: Macmillan Distribution Ltd.

Queen Rania of Jordan Al Abdullah Staff, et al. The Sandwich Swap. Tusa, Tricia, illus. 2010. (ENG.). 32p. (J). (gr. -1-2). 16.99 *(978-1-4231-2484-9(7))* Hyperion Pr.

Quick, Matthew. Boy21. 2013. (ENG.). 272p. (YA). (gr. 7-17). pap. 10.99 *(978-0-316-12796-7(5))* Little, Brown Bks. for Young Readers.

—Forgive Me, Leonard Peacock. 2014. (ENG.). 304p. (YA). (gr. 10-17). pap. 10.99 *(978-0-316-22135-1(X))* Little, Brown Bks. for Young Readers.

Quiller-Couch, Arthur Thomas. True Tilda. 2006. 224p. per. 15.95 *(978-1-59818-052-7(5))* Aegypan.

Quin-Harkin, Janet. Forever Friday. 2014. (Tgif Ser.: 4). (ENG., Illus.). 128p. (J). (gr. 3-7). pap. 13.99 *(978-1-4814-2882-8(9))*, Simon & Schuster/Paula Wiseman Bks.) Simon & Schuster/Paula Wiseman Bks.

—Four's a Crowd. 2014. (Tgif Ser.: 3). (ENG., Illus.). 128p. (J). (gr. 3-7). pap. 13.99 *(978-1-4814-2881-1(0))*, Simon & Schuster/Paula Wiseman Bks.) Simon & Schuster/Paula Wiseman Bks.

—Secret Valentine. 2014. (Tgif Ser.: 6). (ENG., Illus.). 128p. (J). (gr. 3-7). pap. 13.99 *(978-1-4814-2884-2(5))*, Simon & Schuster/Paula Wiseman Bks.) Simon & Schuster/Paula Wiseman Bks.

—Sleepover Madness. 2014. (Tgif Ser.: 1). (ENG., Illus.). 128p. (J). (gr. 3-7). pap. 13.99 *(978-1-4814-2879-8(9))*, Simon & Schuster/Paula Wiseman Bks.) Simon & Schuster/Paula Wiseman Bks.

—Toe Shoe Trouble. 2014. (Tgif Ser.: 5). (ENG., Illus.). 128p. (J). (gr. 3-7). pap. 13.99 *(978-1-4814-2883-5(7))*, Simon & Schuster/Paula Wiseman Bks.) Simon & Schuster/Paula Wiseman Bks.

Quince, Lia. Abby & Jules. 2009. *(978-1-933791-14-2(4))* Finial Publishing.

Quinn, Jordan. The Lost Stone. McPhillips, Robert, illus. 2014. (Kingdom of Wrenly Ser.: 1). (ENG.). 128p. (J). (gr. k-4). pap. 5.99 *(978-1-4424-9690-3(8))*, Little Simon) Little Simon.

—The Lost Stone. 2014. (Kingdom of Wrenly Ser.: 1). lib. bdg. 16.00 *(978-0-606-35443-1(3))* Turtleback Bks.

—The Scarlet Dragon. McPhillips, Robert, illus. 2014. (Kingdom of Wrenly Ser.: 2). (ENG.). 128p. (J). (gr. k-4). pap. 5.99 *(978-1-4424-9693-4(2))*, Little Simon) Little Simon.

—The Scarlet Dragon. 2014. (Kingdom of Wrenly Ser.: 2). lib. bdg. 16.00 *(978-0-606-35444-8(1))* Turtleback Bks.

—Sea Monster! McPhillips, Robert, illus. 2014. (Kingdom of Wrenly Ser.: 3). (ENG.). 128p. (J). (gr. k-4). pap. 5.99 *(978-1-4814-0072-5(X))*, Little Simon) Little Simon.

—The Secret World of Mermaids. McPhillips, Robert, illus. 2015. (Kingdom of Wrenly Ser.: 8). (ENG.). 128p. (J). (gr. k-4). pap. 5.99 *(978-1-4814-3122-4(6))*, Little Simon) Little Simon.

—The Witch's Curse. McPhillips, Robert, illus. 2014. (Kingdom of Wrenly Ser.: 4). (ENG.). 128p. (J). (gr. k-4). pap. 5.99 *(978-1-4814-0075-6(4))*, Little Simon) Little Simon.

Quinn, Paul Michael. The Love Flute. 2013. 24p. pap. 24.95 *(978-1-63000-705-8(6))* America Star Bks.

Quintero, Isabel. Ugly Cat & Pablo. Knight, Tom, illus. 2017. (ENG.). 112p. (J). (gr. 2-5). pap. 6.99 ***(978-0-545-94091-7(5))***, Scholastic Pr.) Scholastic, Inc.

Quintero, Sofia. Show & Prove. 2015. (ENG.). 352p. (YA). (gr. 7). 17.99 *(978-0-375-84707-3(3))*, Knopf Bks. for Young Readers) Random Hse. Children's Bks.

Rabb, Margo. Kissing in America. 2015. (ENG.). 400p. (YA). (gr. 9). 17.99 *(978-0-06-232237-1(0))* HarperCollins Pubs.

Rabbett, Martin. Forever Buster: What a Name! What a Dog, We Exclaim! Burns, Donna, illus. 2007. (J). 13.95 *(978-0-9794649-0-4(0))* Hula Moon Pr.

Rabin, Staton. Betsy & the Emperor. 2006. (ENG., Illus.). 304p. (YA). (gr. 7). reprint ed. mass mkt. 7.99 *(978-1-4169-1336-8(X))*, Simon Pulse) Simon Pulse.

Rabley, Stephen & Pearson Education Staff. Maisie & the Dolphin. 2nd ed. 2009. (ENG.). 20p. pap. 11.99 *(978-1-4058-6954-6(2))* Pearson Education.

Radwan, Hassan & Stratford, Stevan. Rashid & the Haupmann Diamond. 2010. (ENG., Illus.). 112p. (J). (gr. 2-6). pap. 6.50 *(978-0-86037-357-5(6))* Kube Publishing Ltd. GBR. Dist: Consortium Bk. Sales & Distribution.

Rae, Angela. All of Us. 2009. 81p. pap. 12.99 *(978-0-557-05491-6(5))* Lulu Pr., Inc.

Rae, Kristin. What You Always Wanted: An If Only Novel. 2016. (If Only... Ser.). (ENG.). 320p. (YA). pap. 9.99 *(978-1-61963-345-2(0))*, 9781619633452, Bloomsbury USA Childrens) Bloomsbury Publishing USA.

Raffle, Diana. Moondragon. 2006. 161p. pap. 24.95 *(978-1-4241-0626-4(5))* PublishAmerica, Inc.

Ragin, M. K. Mildred Row & Improper Bounds. 2006. 185p. pap. 24.95 *(978-1-4137-9724-4(5))* America Star Bks.

Ragland, Jean. Let's Do the Right Thing! 2011. 24p. pap. 12.79 *(978-1-4634-4419-8(2))* AuthorHouse.

Rain, Mandy. Spring Fling. 2011. (School Gyrls Ser.). (ENG.). 144p. (J). (gr. 3-7). pap. 5.99 *(978-1-4424-0882-1(0))*, Simon & Schuster/Paula Wiseman Bks.) Simon & Schuster/Paula Wiseman Bks.

Ralph, Brian. Reggie-12. 2013. (ENG., Illus.). 96p. (YA). 21.95 *(978-1-77046-132-1(9))*, 9781770461321) Drawn & Quarterly Pubns. CAN. Dist: Macmillan.

Rameaka, T. Where's Dorothy? 2005. 73p. pap. 16.95 *(978-1-4137-9117-4(4))* PublishAmerica, Inc.

Ramirez, Martha. The Fabulous Adventures of Fred the Frog. 2008. 48p. pap. 24.95 *(978-1-60474-799-7(4))* America Star Bks.

Ramirez, Terry. Growing up with Olivi: The Beguiling Blue-Haired Beauty of Boysenberry Lane. 2009. 96p. pap. 9.95 *(978-0-595-47668-8(6))* iUniverse, Inc.

Ramljak, Marijan. Are You My Friend? 2009. (Look for Me Bks.). (Illus.). (J). bds. 9.99 *(978-1-934650-67-7(6))* Just For Kids Pr., LLC.

Ramos, Marielly. The Fast Getting Married Ugly Changing Bear. 2012. 24p. pap. 17.99 *(978-1-4772-8581-7(4))* AuthorHouse.

Ramos, Odalys Q. Allow Me to Introduce Myself. Graham, Michael, illus. 2012. 24p. (-18). pap. 12.95 *(978-1-61493-121-8(6))* Peppertree Pr., The.

Ramrattan Smith, Sherry & Smith, Benjamin Eric. Brothers: Best Friends Growing Up. 2010. 28p. pap. 14.95 *(978-1-4490-6339-9(X))* AuthorHouse.

Ramsay, Kim Heaton. Will You Be My Friend? 2012. 16p. pap. 15.99 *(978-1-4772-9503-8(8))* AuthorHouse.

Ramsey, Charmaine J. Frollica & Frenzi: New York City Friends. Steinlage, Kelly, illus. 2009. 36p. pap. 15.49 *(978-1-4490-0487-3(3))* AuthorHouse.

Ramsey, Jo. Jet Black. 2012. 220p. pap. 12.99 *(978-1-60820-630-8(0))* MLR Pr., LLC.

—Opening Up. 2013. 266p. pap. 14.99 *(978-1-60820-887-6(7))* MLR Pr., LLC.

Ramsnips, Tunder. The Hardly Boys. 2010. 196p. pap. 15.95 *(978-0-557-38767-0(1))* Lulu Pr., Inc.

Rand, Edward A. The Knights of the White Shield: Up-the-Ladder Club Series Round One Play. 2007. 166p. pap. 19.99 *(978-1-4264-8273-1(6))*; (ENG.). 184p. pap. 21.99 *(978-1-4264-8310-3(4))* Creative Media Partners, LLC.

—The Knights of the White Shield; or, up-the-Ladder Club Series, Round One Play. 2007. 120p. per. *(978-1-4068-3739-1(3))* Echo Library.

Rand, Jonathan. Freddie Fernortner #7 Bk 7: Fearless First Grader: the Magical Wading Pool. 2007. pap. 4.99 *(978-1-893699-91-5(9))* AudioCraft Publishing, Inc.

Randall, Bob & McInerney, Kunyi June-Anne. Tracker Tjugingji. 2003. (ENG.). 36p. (J). pap. 22.95 incl. audio compact disk *(978-1-86465-030-3(3))* IAD Pr. AUS. Dist: Independent Pubs. Group.

Randall, Ronne. Snuggle up, Little Penguin! Church, Caroline Jayne, illus. 2003. (Little Friends Ser.). 14p. (J). 12.95 *(978-1-57145-919-0(7))*, Silver Dolphin Bks.) Readerlink Distribution Services, LLC.

Randle, Kristen D. The Only Alien on the Planet. 2009. (ENG.). 240p. (YA). (gr. 7-12). pap. 11.99 *(978-1-4022-2669-4(1))*, 9781402226694, Sourcebooks Jabberwocky) Sourcebooks, Inc.

—Slumming. 2003. (Illus.). 240p. (J). lib. bdg. 16.89 *(978-0-06-001023-2(1))*, HarperTeen) HarperCollins Pubs.

Randolph, Robert. Ben Goes to the Farmer's Market, 1 vol. 2009. 37p. pap. 24.95 *(978-1-4489-1934-5(7))* PublishAmerica, Inc.

Random House. Fabulous Friends! (Shimmer & Shine) Random House, illus. 2017. (Friendship Box Ser.). (ENG., Illus.). 48p. (J). (-k). bds. 10.99 *(978-0-399-55790-3(3))*, Random Hse. Bks. for Young Readers) Random Hse. Children's Bks.

—The Fearsome Footprints/Thomas the Brave (Thomas & Friends) Stubbs, Tommy, illus. 2014. (Pictureback(R) Ser.). (ENG.). 24p. (J). (gr. -1-2). 4.99 *(978-0-385-37392-0(9))*, Random Hse. Bks. for Young Readers) Random Hse. Children's Bks.

—GoldieBlox Chapter Book #2 (GoldieBlox) Random House et al, illus. 2017. (Stepping Stone Book(TM) Ser.). (ENG.). 128p. (J). (gr. 1-4). 6.99 *(978-0-399-55636-4(2))*, Random Hse. Bks. for Young Readers) Random Hse. Children's Bks.

—Happy Howl-O-ween! (Barbie) 2016. (Pictureback(R) Ser.). (ENG., Illus.). 16p. (J). (gr. -1-2). 4.99 *(978-1-101-93748-8(3))*, Random Hse. Bks. for Young Readers) Random Hse. Children's Bks.

—Hide-And-Go-Swim! (Bubble Guppies) MJ Illustrations, illus. 2014. (Nifty Lift-And-Look Ser.). (ENG.). 12p. (J). (— 1). bds. 5.99 *(978-0-385-38515-2(3))*, Random Hse. Bks. for Young Readers) Random Hse. Children's Bks.

—Meet Rusty Rivets! (Rusty Rivets) Cassity, Donald, illus. 2017. (Step into Reading Ser.). (ENG.). 24p. (J). (gr. -1-1). pap. 4.99 ***(978-1-5247-1686-8(3))***; lib. bdg. 12.99 ***(978-1-5247-1687-5(1))*** Random Hse. Children's Bks. (Random Hse. Bks. for Young Readers).

—Meet Shimmer & Shine! (Shimmer & Shine) Cardona, Jose Maria, illus. 2016. (Step into Reading Ser.). (ENG.). 24p. (J). (gr. -1-1). 4.99 *(978-0-553-52203-7(5))*, Random Hse. Bks. for Young Readers) Random Hse. Children's Bks.

—Meet the Pets. Random House, illus. 2016. (Step into Reading Ser.). (ENG., Illus.). 32p. (J). (gr. -1-2). 4.99 *(978-0-399-55483-4(1))*, Random Hse. Bks. for Young Readers) Random Hse. Children's Bks.

—Patrol Pals (Paw Patrol) Random House, illus. 2015. (Friendship Box Ser.). (ENG., Illus.). 48p. (J). (— 1). bds. 10.99 *(978-0-553-50796-6(6))*, Random Hse. Bks. for Young Readers) Random Hse. Children's Bks.

—Poppy Follows Her Nose! Random House, illus. 2017. (Scratch-And-Sniff Book Ser.). (ENG., Illus.). 24p. (J). (gr. -1-2). 9.99 ***(978-1-5247-6642-9(9))***, Random Hse. Bks. for Young Readers) Random Hse. Children's Bks.

—Thomas & Friends: the Adventure Begins (Thomas & Friends) 2015. (Pictureback(R) Ser.). (ENG., Illus.). 24p. (J). (gr. -1-2). 3.99 *(978-0-553-53553-2(6))*, Random Hse. Bks. for Young Readers) Random Hse. Children's Bks.

Random House. Thomas at the Steelworks/Friends to the Rescue. 2017. (Pictureback(R) Ser.). (ENG., Illus.). 24p. (J). (gr. -1-2). pap. 4.99 ***(978-1-5247-1655-4(3))***, Random Hse. Bks. for Young Readers) Random Hse. Children's Bks.

Random House & Man-Kong, Mary. Meet the Pets. Random House, illus. 2016. (Step into Reading Ser.). (ENG., Illus.). 32p. (J). (gr. -1-2). 12.99 *(978-0-399-55484-1(X))*, Random Hse. Bks. for Young Readers) Random Hse. Children's Bks.

Random House Disney Staff. Disney/Pixar Story Collection. Random House Disney Staff, illus. 2008. (Step into Reading Ser.). (ENG., Illus.). 160p. (J). (gr. k-3). pap. 7.99 *(978-0-7364-2554-4(3))*, RH/Disney) Random Hse. Children's Bks.

—Race Around the World. Random House Disney Staff, illus. 2011. (Step into Reading Ser.). (ENG., Illus.). 32p. (J). (gr. k-3). pap. 3.99 *(978-0-7364-2808-8(9))*, RH/Disney) Random Hse. Children's Bks.

—Rose & the Wish Thing. Mageri, Caroline, illus. 2016. (ENG.). 40p. (J). (gr. -1-2). 16.99 *(978-0-553-53617-1(6))*, Doubleday Bks. for Young Readers) Random Hse. Children's Bks.

—Super Spies. Random House Disney Staff, illus. 2011. (Step into Reading Ser.). (ENG., Illus.). 32p. (J). (gr. k-3). pap. 3.99 *(978-0-7364-2807-1(0))*, RH/Disney) Random Hse. Children's Bks.

Random House Staff. A Friend at the Zoo (Bubble Guppies) Random House Staff & Nunn, Paul, illus. 2013. (Pictureback(R) Ser.). (ENG.). 16p. (J). (gr. -1-2). pap. 3.99 *(978-0-449-81389-8(4))*, Random Hse. Bks. for Young Readers) Random Hse. Children's Bks.

—I Love Colors (Dora the Explorer) Random House Staff, illus. 2013. (ENG., Illus.). 24p. (J). (-k). bds. 4.99 *(978-0-449-81481-9(5))*, Random Hse. Bks. for Young Readers) Random Hse. Children's Bks.

—Railway Adventures. Random House Staff, illus. 2010. (Step into Reading Ser.). (ENG., Illus.). 160p. (J). (gr. -1-1). pap. 7.99 *(978-0-375-86653-1(1))*, Random Hse. Bks. for Young Readers) Random Hse. Children's Bks.

—Time for School! (Bubble Guppies) Random House Staff, illus. 2013. (Pictureback(R) Ser.). (ENG., Illus.). 16p. (J). (gr. -1-2). pap. 4.99 *(978-0-449-81447-5(5))*, Random Hse. Bks. for Young Readers) Random Hse. Children's Bks.

Random House Staff, illus. Hero Story Collection (DC Super Friends) 2012. (Step into Reading Ser.). (ENG.). 160p. (J). (gr. -1-1). pap. 7.99 *(978-0-375-87298-3(1))*, Random Hse. Bks. for Young Readers) Random Hse. Children's Bks.

Rankin, Heather & Rankin, Heather. All It Takes Is One Friend. 2012. 46p. pap. *(978-0-9876945-0-2(1))* Our Farm Bks.

Rankin, Laura. My Turn! Rankin, Laura, illus. 2016. (ENG., Illus.). 32p. (J). 16.99 *(978-1-59990-174-9(9))*, 9781599901749, Bloomsbury USA Childrens) Bloomsbury Publishing USA.

Rankine-Van Wassenhoven, Jacqueline. A Little Honey for Serge. 2009. 16p. pap. 9.00 *(978-1-4490-0810-9(0))* AuthorHouse.

Ranson, Erin. One Little Bear & Her Friends. Gévry, Claudine, illus. 2007. 10p. (J). (gr. -1-k). bds. *(978-1-84666-354-3(7))*, Tide Mill Pr.) Top That! Publishing PLC.

Rao, Lisa & Gallo, Tina. It's Nice to Be Nice! Giles, Mike, illus. 2009. (Yo Gabba Gabba! Ser.). (ENG.). 24p. (J). (gr. -1-2). pap. 3.99 *(978-1-4169-7866-4(6))*, Simon Spotlight) Simon Spotlight.

Rao, Sirish. The Old Animals' Forest Band. Bai, Durga, illus. 2008. 40p. (J). (gr. -1-2). (ENG.). *(978-81-86211-45-8(4))*; *(978-81-86211-41-0(1))* Tara Publishing.

Raphael, Akili & Lewis, Harriet. Malik & the Malaria-Carrying Mosquito. 2012. 32p. pap. 19.99 *(978-1-4772-8813-9(9))* AuthorHouse.

—Malik Says, Turn off the Water! 2012. 36p. pap. 20.99 *(978-1-4772-9541-0(0))* AuthorHouse.

Raschka, Chris. Yo! Yes? Raschka, Chris, illus. 2007. (Scholastic Bookshelf Ser.). (ENG., Illus.). 32p. (J). (gr. -1-1). pap. 6.99 *(978-0-439-92185-5(6))* Scholastic, Inc.

Rasheed, Winona. Stories from Grandma's Garden. 2008. 41p. pap. 15.94 *(978-1-4357-5075-3(6))* Lulu Pr., Inc.

Ratcliff, Charline. The Princess, the Toad & the Whale. 2012. (ENG.). 36p. (J). (-18). pap. 12.95 *(978-1-4787-1672-3(X))* Outskirts Pr., Inc.

Rath, Tom & Reckmeyer, Mary. How Full Is Your Bucket? For Kids. Manning, Maurie J., illus. 2009. (ENG.). 32p. (J). (gr. -1-4). 17.95 *(978-1-59562-027-9(3))* Gallup Pr.

Rathbome, St. George. Canoe Mates in Canada; or, Three Boys Afloat on the Saskatchewan. 2007. 100p. per. *(978-1-4068-3746-9(6))* Echo Library.

Rathmell, Donna & Rathmell, Doreen. Octavia & Her Purple Ink Cloud, 1 vol. McLennan, Connie, illus. 2006. (ENG.). 32p. (J). (gr. -1-2). 15.95 *(978-0-9764943-5-5(3))* Arbordale Publishing.

Ratnayake, Kumari/Keiko. Monsieur Bagel's War. Ratnayake, Kumari/Keiko, illus. 2007. (Illus.). 25p. (J). spiral bd. 15.00 net. *(978-0-9797015-1-1(1))* Augustana College Geology Dept. Pr.

Rattay, Deidra. My Best Friend the Gnome. 2011. 24p. (gr. 2-4). pap. 14.93 *(978-1-4269-7077-1(3))* Trafford Publishing.

Ratto, Linda Lee. Perfection. 2004. (YA). per. 16.95 *(978-0-9748508-3-2(7))* Power Pr.

Ratzlaff, Aaron J. Quills. 2011. (ENG.). 40p. (J). pap. 13.99 *(978-0-8361-9509-5(4))* Herald Pr.

Rau, Dana Meachen. Corn Aplenty. Iwai, Melissa, illus. 2009. (Step into Reading Ser.). (ENG.). 32p. (J). (gr. -1-1). 3.99 *(978-0-375-85575-7(0))*, Random Hse. Bks. for Young Readers) Random Hse. Children's Bks.

Raudenbush, Amy. Lucy More Needs Less. 2006. 48p. (J). pap. 13.99 *(978-1-4116-6120-2(6))* Lulu Pr., Inc.

Raughley, Sarah. Fate of Flames. 2016. (Effigies Ser.: 1). (ENG., Illus.). 368p. (YA). (gr. 9). 17.99 *(978-1-4814-6677-6(1))*, Simon Pulse) Simon Pulse.

Raun, Robert L. Tales of the Clam Club: Turtle Soup. 2012. (ENG.). pap. *(978-1-4675-1923-6(5))* Independent Pub.

Rautenberg, Karen Rita. Ballerina Detective & the Missing Jeweled Tiara. 2009. (ENG.). 198p. (J). (gr. 5-8). pap. *(978-1-933255-47-7(1))* DNA Pr.

Rawlinson, Julia. Fletcher & the Snowflake Christmas. Beeke, Tiphanie, illus. 2010. (ENG.). 32p. (J). (gr. -1-2). 16.99 *(978-0-06-199033-5(7))*, Greenwillow Bks.) HarperCollins Pubs.

Ray Charles Lockamy, Inez Eason. The Adventures of Tracks & Cookout. 2010. 40p. pap. *(978-1-4269-2159-9(4))* Trafford Publishing (UK) Ltd.

Ray, Keri. The Saving Journey. 2009. 48p. pap. 10.49 *(978-1-4389-5008-2(X))* AuthorHouse.

Rayburn, Tricia. The Melting of Maggie Bean. 2007. (ENG.). 256p. (J). (gr. 4-8). pap. 6.99 *(978-1-4169-3348-9(4))*, Aladdin) Simon & Schuster Children's Publishing.

Raye, Donna. Edison the Firefly & Ford the Fly. 2013. 28p. pap. 9.99 *(978-0-9894748-2-5(8))* Mindstir Media.

—Edison the Firefly & Sierra the Special Spider. 2013. 28p. pap. 9.99 *(978-0-9910324-9-5(7))* Mindstir Media.

—Faith a Leapin' The Sign (Multilingual Edition) 2012. 30p. pap. 9.99 *(978-0-9883162-5-6(0))* Mindstir Media.

R.D.Haire & Francis, Richard E. When Good Got Better: The Adventures of Fred the Friendly Shark. 2012. 24p. pap. 15.99 *(978-1-4797-3797-0(6))* Xlibris Corp.

Rea, Monique F. The Original Story of Toulouse the Moose & His Friends: Book & CD. 2007. (J). *(978-0-9788926-2-3(3))* Trails of Discovery.

Read, Laurie. Blacky Longlegs Meets Freddy the Fly. 2008. 20p. pap. 14.00 *(978-1-4389-1231-8(5))* AuthorHouse.

Read, Sara. The Teenagers Guide to Self-Destruction. 2008. 92p. pap. 12.99 *(978-1-4343-6962-8(5))* AuthorHouse.

Reader's Digest Editors, ed. The Red Ribbon: A Book about Friendship. Taylor, Thomas, illus. 2004. (ENG.). 14p. (J). 12.99 *(978-0-7944-0401-7(4))*, Reader's Digest Children's Bks.) Studio Fun International.

Reader's Digest Editors, et al. Elmo Loves Hugs! 2009. (Hugs Book Ser.). (ENG., Illus.). 14p. (J). (gr. -1-k). bds. 10.99 *(978-0-7944-1914-1(3))*, Reader's Digest Children's Bks.) Studio Fun International.

Reader's Digest Staff & Rhodes, Lilly. Guess Who, Minnie! Loter Inc. Staff, illus. 2013. (Guess Who Ser.: 1). (ENG.). 10p. (J). (gr. -1-k). 10.99 *(978-0-7944-2555-5(0))* Reader's Digest Assn., Inc., The.

Reading Is Awesome! A Best Friend for Foofa; Friends Are Fun!; Fun with Plex; Mystery in Gabba Land; Super Gabba Friends!; the Gabba Land Band. 2014. (Yo Gabba Gabba! Ser.). (ENG., Illus.). 144p. (J). (gr. -1-k). pap. 15.99 *(978-1-4814-2152-2(2))*, Simon Spotlight) Simon Spotlight.

RealBuzz Studios Staff. Out of the Soup. 2007. (Goofyfoot Gurl Ser.: No. 4). 96p. (YA). pap. 4.97 *(978-1-59789-576-7(8))* Barbour Publishing, Inc.

—Space Cadet vs Drama Queen Terror from the Tarantula Nebula: Life Camera Action Book 1. 2007. 128p. (YA). pap. 4.97 *(978-1-59789-577-4(6))*, Barbour Bks.) Barbour Publishing, Inc.

Reasoner, Charles. Number Munch! 2009. (Bite Bks.). (Illus.). (J). bds. 7.99 *(978-1-934650-14-1(5))* Just For Kids Pr., LLC.

Reaves, Janice. Ser Inteligente y Tener a Dios en Tu Corazón Es Buena Ond. 2010. 44p. pap. 16.99 *(978-1-4490-8002-0(2))* AuthorHouse.

Rebal, Tara. Sarah Sue Smith: A Crooked Wharf Adventure. 2010. 52p. pap. 22.49 *(978-1-4520-7165-7(9))* AuthorHouse.

Rebbie, Kevin. Mr. Stinkas & the Little Cheese Shop. 2011. pap. 23.95 *(978-0-7414-6439-2(X))* Infinity Publishing.

Rebello, Kevin. Julia & Mckinley's Day at the Beach. 2009. 32p. pap. 12.99 *(978-1-4389-7330-2(6))* AuthorHouse.

Recob, Amy. The BugaBees: Friends with Food Allergies. 2009. (Illus.). 32p. (J). *(978-1-59298-279-0(4))* Beaver's Pond Pr., Inc.

Recorvits, Helen & Recorvits, H. Yoon & the Jade Bracelet. Swiatkowska, Gabi, illus. 2008. (ENG.). 32p. (J). (gr. -1-3). 18.99 *(978-0-374-38689-4(7))*, 9780374386894, Farrar, Straus & Giroux (BYR)) Farrar, Straus & Giroux.

Rector, Lori. Adventures of A. 2013. (ENG.). 21p. (J). pap. 12.95 *(978-1-4787-1005-9(5))* Outskirts Pr., Inc.

Redbank, Tennant. The Great Mountain Adventure. RH Disney et al, illus. 2016. (Disney Chapters Ser.). (ENG.). 64p. (J). (gr. 1-4). 5.99 *(978-0-7364-3636-6(7))*, RH/Disney) Random Hse. Children's Bks.

Redepenning, George. The Adventures of Webster. 2008. pap. 9.00 *(978-0-8059-8629-7(4))* Dorrance Publishing Co., Inc.

Redfern, Holly. The Adventures of Remmington the Dog: An Unexpected Friend. Burton, Claudia, illus. 2007. 28p. (gr. -1-3). per. 14.95 *(978-1-59858-317-5(4))* Dog Ear Publishing, LLC.

Rednose, Skiddles. Tale of the Land of Umble. 2013. 126p. pap. 18.99 *(978-1-938487-14-9(1))* Big Country Publishing, LLC.

Reece, Eva. The Boinking Bubble MacHine. Davis, Shelley L. A., illus. 2013. 24p. pap. 12.99 *(978-0-9886360-2-6(6))* Kids At Heart Publishing, LLC.

Reed, Amy. Over You. 2013. (ENG., Illus.). 320p. (YA). (gr. 9). 16.99 *(978-1-4424-5696-9(5))*, Simon Pulse) Simon Pulse.

Reed, Janet. Brave Dave & the Dragons. Fraser, Kara-Anne, illus. 2009. 12p. (J). *(978-0-545-16142-8(8))* Scholastic, Inc.

Reed, Jennifer. That's Not Fair! Dufalla, Anita, illus. 2012. (ENG.). 24p. (gr. 1-2). pap. 8.95 *(978-1-61810-309-3(1))* Rourke Educational Media.

Reed, Lynn Rowe. Oliver, the Spaceship, & Me. 2009. (ENG., Illus.). 32p. (J). (gr. -1-3). 16.95 *(978-0-8234-2193-0(7))* Holiday Hse., Inc.

Reed, Tom. Pookus & Buckie: A Children's Book Based on a True Story. Carter, Sandy Lewis, illus. l.t. ed. 2005. 36p. (J). per. 11.95 *(978-0-9749725-4-1(1))*, 10000, Lonestar Abilene Publishing) LoneStar Abilene Publishing, LLC.

Reeder, Marilou. The Daring Prince Dashing. West, Karl, illus. 2015. (ENG.). 32p. (J). (gr. -1-k). 16.99 *(978-1-63450-161-3(6))*, Sky Pony Pr.) Skyhorse Publishing Co., Inc.

Reedy, Trent. Stealing Air. 2012. (ENG.). 288p. (J). (gr. 3-7). 16.99 *(978-0-545-38307-3(2))*, Levine, Arthur A. Bks.) Scholastic, Inc.

Reel FX Inc. Staff, et al, illus. A Tale of Two Friends. 2014. (Book of Life Ser.). (ENG.). 32p. (J). (gr. k-2). pap. 3.99 *(978-1-4814-2573-5(0))*, Simon Spotlight) Simon Spotlight.

Reese, Jenn. Horizon. 2014. (Above World Ser.). (ENG.). 400p. (J). (gr. 5). 16.99 *(978-0-7636-6417-6(0))* Candlewick Pr.

Reeve, Penny. Water or Goo? Apps, Fred, illus. 2008. (Tania Abbey Adventure Ser.). (ENG.). 96p. (J). pap. 6.99 *(978-1-84550-341-3(4))*, 748295d7-9d18-4862-90d7-b454340bafc1) Christian Focus Pubns. GBR. Dist: Bookmasters Distribution.

Reeves, Heather. My Big Brother, He's My Best Friend, 1 vol. 2010. 18p. 24.95 *(978-1-4489-4021-9(4))* PublishAmerica, Inc.

Reeves, Laura. The Best Friend Necklace. 2007. (Illus.). 160p. (J). mass mkt. 7.99 *(978-0-9797165-0-8(0))* True Friends Bk. Club, LLC.

Regan, Dian. Cyberpals According to Kaley. 2006. (Illus.). 128p. (J). (gr. 3-7). 15.95 *(978-1-58196-051-8(4),* Darby Creek) Lerner Publishing Group.

Regan, Lisa. No Hitting, Henry: Don't Hurt. 2017. (You Choose Ser.). (Illus.). 32p. (J). (gr. 2-2). lib. bdg. 25.27 ***(978-0-7660-8702-6(6))*** Enslow Pubs., Inc.

Regan, Peter. Riverside: The Movie. 2006. (ENG.). 128p. (J). pap. 11.95 *(978-1-901737-50-9(0))* Anvil Bks., Ltd. IRL. Dist: Dufour Editions, Inc.

Reid, James. Across the Sea, 1 vol. rev. ed. 2013. (Fiction Readers Ser.). (ENG., Illus.). 12p. (J). (gr. 1-1). pap. 12.96 *(978-1-4807-1130-3(6));* pap. 4.99 *(978-1-4333-5451-9(9))* Shell Educational Publishing.

Reid, Kimberly. Perfect Liars. 2016. (ENG.). 384p. (YA). (gr. 7-12). 19.95 *(978-1-62014-273-8(2),* Tu Bks.) Lee & Low Bks., Inc.

Reid, Lainey. Takari. 2008. 156p. pap. 24.95 *(978-1-60672-717-1(6))* America Star Bks.

Reid-Tulloch, Joseth. Manu's Special Day. 2012. 16p. pap. 14.99 *(978-1-4520-9150-1(1))* AuthorHouse.

Reilly, Hope. The Ghost Horse at Cove House: A Book about the Strength of Friendship. 2013. 32p. pap. 13.00 *(978-1-61204-666-2(5),* Strategic Bk. Publishing) Strategic Book Publishing & Rights Agency (SBPRA).

Reimer, Charlotte. Problems with Pies. 2006. 68p. (YA). pap. 13.50 *(978-1-4116-7646-6(7))* Lulu Pr., Inc.

Reimiller, Diane. Brayden & Ryan's Summer Vacation. Jastrzebski, Brandy, illus. 2012. 24p. pap. 24.95 *(978-1-4626-7792-4(4))* America Star Bks.

Reimiller, Diane L. A Duck Named Quackers, 1 vol. Jastrzebski, Brandy, illus. 2009. 12p. pap. 24.95 *(978-1-60836-771-9(1))* America Star Bks.

Reis, Jason & Hurley, Meagan. The Adventures of Burt: Burt & the Big Race. 2012. 28p. pap. 19.99 *(978-1-4634-4126-5(6))* AuthorHouse.

Reisfeld, Randi. All Access. rev. ed. 2007. (ENG.). 288p. (gr. 7-12). pap. 8.99 *(978-1-4231-0503-9(6))* Hyperion Pr.

Reisinger, John. The Duckworth Chronicles. 2005. pap. 11.95 *(978-1-59330-269-6(X))* Aventine Pr.

Reiss, Kathryn. The Tangled Web: A Julie Mystery. Tibbles, Jean-Paul, illus. 2009. (ENG.). 168p. (J). (gr. 4-18). 10.95 *(978-1-59369-475-3(X))* American Girl Publishing, Inc.

Reisz, Kristopher. Unleashed. 2008. (ENG.). 352p. (YA). (gr. 9). pap. 7.99 *(978-1-4169-4001-2(4),* Simon Pulse) Simon Pulse.

Reiter, Naomi. Sandy the Stingray. 2007. 24p. per. 24.95 *(978-1-4241-8619-8(6))* America Star Bks.

Remenar, Kristen. Groundhog's Dilemma. Faulkner, Matt, illus. 2015. (ENG.). 32p. (J). (gr. -1-2). lib. bdg. 16.95 *(978-1-58089-600-9(6))* Charlesbridge Publishing, Inc.

Rempt, Fiona. Snail's Birthday Wish. Smit, Noelle, illus. 2007. (ENG.). 32p. (J). (gr. -1-1). 14.95 *(978-1-905417-52-0(7))* Boxer Bks., Ltd. GBR. Dist: Sterling Publishing Co., Inc.

Rene, Rochelle. Bella & the Bad Mood Busters: The Bad Mood Blues. 2012. (ENG.). 22p. (J). 24.95 *(978-1-4327-7279-6(1))* Outskirts Pr., Inc.

Renek, Nava. Venice Is for Cats. 2013. (Illus.). pap. 20.00 *(978-0-923389-53-6(9))* Spuyten Duyvil Publishing.

Renero, Joaquin. The Enchanted Scrapbook: Welcome to the Wilburton Society. 2011. 320p. 29.95 *(978-1-4502-6140-1(X));* pap. 19.95 *(978-1-4502-6138-8(8))* iUniverse, Inc.

Renfrew, Regan. Orphans of the Heart: A Young Girl & a Paint Filly Heal Each Other's Broken Hearts. 2013. (ENG.). 163p. (YA). pap. 12.95 *(978-1-4787-1686-0(X))* Outskirts Pr., Inc.

Renna, G. M. Meticulous Nicholas Goes to Camp. 2009. 64p. pap. 10.49 *(978-1-4490-2784-1(9))* AuthorHouse.

Rennison, Louise. Knocked Out by My Nunga-Nungas. 2006. (Confessions of Georgia Nicolson Ser.: 3). (ENG.). 208p. (YA). (gr. 8-18). pap. 8.99 *(978-0-06-447362-0(7),* HarperTeen) HarperCollins Pubs.

—On the Bright Side, I'm Now the Girlfriend of a Sex God: Further Confessions of Georgia Nicolson. (Confessions of Georgia Nicolson Ser.: 2). (ENG.). 2006. 272p. (YA). (gr. 8). pap. 8.99 *(978-0-06-447226-5(4),* HarperTeen) 2003. 256p. (J). pap. 6.99 *(978-0-06-052185-1(6))* HarperCollins Pubs.

Renshaw, Douglas. Around Our Feeder with George the Groundhog & Friends. Lamb, Janie, illus. 2008. 48p. pap. 24.95 *(978-1-60610-657-0(0))* America Star Bks.

Rentas, Donna. Leticia Goes to School. 2008. 16p. pap. 24.95 *(978-1-4241-8966-3(7))* America Star Bks.

Resau, Laura. Estrella en el Bosque (Star in the Forest) 2016. (ENG & SPA.). 160p. (J). (gr. 2-5). 18.40 *(978-0-606-39132-0(0))* Turtleback Bks.

—The Lightning Queen. 2015. (ENG.). 336p. (J). (gr. 3-7). 16.99 *(978-0-545-80084-6(6),* Scholastic Pr.) Scholastic, Inc.

—Star in the Forest. 2012. (ENG.). 160p. (J). (gr. 2-5). 6.99 *(978-0-375-85410-1(X),* Yearling) Random Hse. Children's Bks.

Resnikoff, Irene & Valas, Claudia. OG in Jerusalem. 2003. (OG the Terrible Ser.: Vol. 3). (HEB & ENG., Illus.). 24p. (J). pap. 4.50 *(978-0-939144-43-3(3))* EKS Publishing Co.

Restrepo, Bettina. Moose & Magpie, 1 vol. Rogers, Sherry, illus. 2009. (ENG.). 32p. (J). (gr. -1-3). pap. 8.95 *(978-1-60718-042-5(1))* Arbordale Publishing.

Restrepo, Bettina & Rogers, Sherry. Moose & Magpie, 1 vol. 2009. (ENG., Illus.). 32p. (J). (gr. -1-3). 16.95 *(978-1-934359-97-6(1))* Arbordale Publishing.

Rettore. Elephant & Friends. 2014. (Friends Cloth Bks.). (ENG.). 8p. (J). (gr. -1 — 1). 9.99 *(978-1-4380-0527-0(X))* Barron's Educational Series, Inc.

—Giraffe & Friends. 2014. (Friends Cloth Bks.). (ENG.). 8p. (J). (gr. -1 — 1). 9.99 *(978-1-4380-0528-7(8))* Barron's Educational Series, Inc.

Return to the Crows, 1 vol. 2014. (Faeregound Ser.). (ENG., Illus.). 96p. (gr. 1-3). lib. bdg. 23.99 *(978-1-4342-9187-5(1))* Stone Arch Bks.

Reul, Robin. My Kind of Crazy. 2016. (ENG.). 336p. (YA). (gr. 8-12). pap. 10.99 *(978-1-4926-3176-7(0),* 9781492631767) Sourcebooks, Inc.

Revere, John J. The Little Brown Horse. Harvancik, Monica, illus. 2011. 34p. 17.95 *(978-1-4327-8146-0(4))* Outskirts Pr., Inc.

Rex, Adam. Nothing Rhymes with Orange. 2017. (ENG., Illus.). 48p. (J). (gr. k-3). 16.99 ***(978-1-4521-5443-5(0))*** Chronicle Bks. LLC.

Rey, H. A. Curious George at the Park. Meyer, Emily, ed. 2010. (Curious George Ser.). (ENG., Illus.). 10p. (J). (gr. -1 — 1). bds. 6.99 *(978-0-547-24300-9(6))* Houghton Mifflin Harcourt Publishing Co.

—Curious George Farm to Table (CGTV 8x8) 2016. (Curious George Ser.). (ENG., Illus.). 24p. (J). (gr. -1-3). 12.99 *(978-0-544-65220-0(7),* HMH Books For Young Readers) Houghton Mifflin Harcourt Publishing Co.

—Curious George Home Run (Jorge el Curioso el Jonrón) 2012. (Curious George Ser.). (ENG & SPA., Illus.). 24p. (J). (gr. -1-3). pap. 3.99 *(978-0-547-69114-5(9))* Houghton Mifflin Harcourt Publishing Co.

—Curious George Neighborhood Friends. 2010. (Curious George Ser.). (ENG., Illus.). 12p. (J). (gr. -1 — 1). bds. 6.99 *(978-0-547-23875-3(4))* Houghton Mifflin Harcourt Publishing Co.

—Feliz Navidad, Jorge el Curioso. Young, Mary O'Keefe, illus. 2012. (Curious George Ser.).Tr. of Merry Christmas, Curious George. (ENG & SPA.). 32p. (J). (gr. -1-3). 10.99 *(978-0-547-74503-9(6))* Houghton Mifflin Harcourt Publishing Co.

—Jorge el Curioso Va a una Fiesta de Disfraces/Curious George Goes to a Costume Party (Bilingual) 2012. (Curious George Ser.). (ENG & SPA., Illus.). 24p. (J). (gr. -1-3). pap. 3.99 *(978-0-547-86575-1(9))* Houghton Mifflin Harcourt Publishing Co.

—Up, Up, & Away. 2009. (Curious George Ser.). (ENG., Illus.). 24p. (J). (gr. -1-3). pap. 4.99 *(978-0-547-11966-3(6))* Houghton Mifflin Harcourt Publishing Co.

Rey, H. A. & Rey, Margret. Happy Hanukkah. 2012. (Curious George Ser.). (ENG., Illus.). 14p. (J). (gr. k — 1). bds. 7.99 *(978-0-547-75731-5(X))* Houghton Mifflin Harcourt Publishing Co.

—Jorge el Curioso Vuela Una Cometa. 2012. (Curious George Ser.). (ENG & SPA., Illus.). 80p. (J). (gr. -1-3). pap. 7.99 *(978-0-547-69162-6(9))* Houghton Mifflin Harcourt Publishing Co.

Reyes, M. G. Vindicated. 2017. (Emancipated Ser.: 3). 352p. (YA). (gr. 9). 17.99 *(978-0-06-228901-8(2),* Tegen, Katherine Bks) HarperCollins Pubs.

Reynolds, Aaron. Nerdy Birdy. Davies, Matt, illus. (Nerdy Birdy Ser.). (ENG.). 40p. (J). 2017. 17.99 *(978-1-62672-128-9(9),* 9781626721289) 2015. 16.99 *(978-1-62672-127-2(0),* 9781626721272) Roaring Brook Pr.

Reynolds, Alison. A New Friend for Marmalade. McKenzie, Heath, illus. 2014. (ENG.). 40p. (J). (gr. -1-1). 15.99 *(978-1-4814-2046-4(1),* Little Simon) Little Simon.

—A Year with Marmalade. McKenzie, Heath, illus. 2013. (ENG.). 40p. (J). (gr. -1-1). 15.99 *(978-1-4424-8105-3(6),* Little Simon) Little Simon.

Reynolds, Betty. Little Lies. 2012. 102p. pap. 7.99 *(978-0-9856724-0-9(4))* Personal.

Reynolds, Caroline. Bead Street-the Fable of Red Clover. 2009. 116p. pap. 22.50 *(978-1-60693-579-8(8),* Eloquent Bks.) Strategic Book Publishing & Rights Agency (SBPRA).

Reynolds, Cynthia Furlong. Across the Reach. 2007. 269p. (J). (gr. 3-7). 16.95 *(978-1-58726-518-1(4),* Mitten Pr.) Ann Arbor Editions LLC.

Reynolds, Eleanor Davenport. Why Aren't You My Friend? the Story of Bullying, Diversity, & Friendship. 2nd ed. 2013. 140p. pap. 11.95 *(978-0-9882209-5-9(4))* Wyatt Hse. Publishing.

Reynolds Jr., R. A. Simon's Big Move. Balek, Dayna Courtney, illus. 2008. 19p. pap. 24.95 *(978-1-60672-676-1(5))* America Star Bks.

Reynolds, Judy. A Blue Jay's Choice. 2010. 72p. pap. 10.49 *(978-1-4520-6455-0(5))* AuthorHouse.

Reynolds, Lori. My Name Is Mac. Cardwell, Brett, illus. 2016. (ENG.). (J). ***(978-1-925515-56-5(7));*** pap. ***(978-1-925515-45-9(1))*** Vivid Publishing.

Reynolds, Mignon C. Life as Bonkers. 2006. 137p. pap. 12.95 *(978-1-4116-7357-1(3))* Lulu Pr., Inc.

Reynolds, Peter H. I'm Here. Reynolds, Peter H., illus. 2011. (ENG., Illus.). 32p. (J). (gr. -1-3). 16.99 *(978-1-4169-9649-1(4),* Atheneum Bks. for Young Readers) Simon & Schuster Children's Publishing.

Reznik, Anastassia, ed. The Little Horse Gornok: Russian Fairy Tale. 2009. 40p. pap. 18.95 *(978-1-4343-9830-7(7))* AuthorHouse.

RH Disney. Belle's Friendship Invention/Tiana's Friendship Fix-Up (Disney Princess) RH Disney, illus. 2016. (Pictureback(R) Ser.). (ENG., Illus.). 48p. (J). (gr. -1-2). pap. 5.99 *(978-0-7364-3735-6(5),* RH/Disney) Random Hse. Children's Bks.

—A Fairy's Fire. RH Disney, illus. 2016. (Never Girls Ser.). (ENG., Illus.). 224p. (J). (gr. 1-4). lib. bdg. 17.99 *(978-0-7364-8175-5(3),* RH/Disney) Random Hse. Children's Bks.

— Fairy's Fire. RH Disney, illus. 2016. (Never Girls Ser.). (ENG., Illus.). 224p. (J). (gr. 1-4). 14.99 *(978-0-7364-3556-7(5),* RH/Disney) Random Hse. Children's Bks.

—Finding Dory Pictureback with Stickers (Disney/Pixar Finding Dory) RH Disney, illus. 2016. (Pictureback(R) Ser.). (ENG., Illus.). 24p. (J). (gr. -1-2). pap. 4.99 *(978-0-7364-3708-0(8),* RH/Disney) Random Hse. Children's Bks.

—Flounder Loves Ariel (Disney Princess) RH Disney, illus. 2016. (Padded Board Book Ser.). (ENG., Illus.). 26p. (J). (gr. -1-1). bds. 9.99 *(978-0-7364-3707-3(X),* RH/Disney) Random Hse. Children's Bks.

—Gus Loves Cinderella (Disney Princess) RH Disney, illus. 2016. (Padded Board Book Ser.). (ENG., Illus.). 26p. (J). (gr. -1-1). bds. 9.99 *(978-0-7364-3706-6(1),* RH/Disney) Random Hse. Children's Bks.

—Pete's Dragon (Disney: Pete's Dragon) RH Disney, illus. 2016. (Little Golden Book Ser.). (ENG., Illus.). 24p. (J). (-k). 4.99 *(978-0-7364-3522-2(0),* Golden/Disney) Random Hse. Children's Bks.

—Tutu Terrific! (Disney Palace Pets: Whisker Haven Tales) Wu, Vivien, illus. 2016. (Little Golden Book Ser.). (ENG.). 24p. (J). (-k). 4.99 *(978-0-7364-3504-8(2),* Golden/Disney) Random Hse. Children's Bks.

RH Disney & Posner-Sanchez, Andrea. Olaf Loves ... Everything! (Disney Frozen) RH Disney, illus. 2016. (Pictureback(R) Ser.). (ENG., Illus.). 16p. (J). (gr. -1-1). pap. 4.99 *(978-0-7364-3590-1(5),* RH/Disney) Random Hse. Children's Bks.

RH Disney Staff. Finding Nemo. Tilley, Scott & RH Disney Staff, illus. 2003. (Little Golden Book Ser.). (ENG.). 24p. (J). (gr. -1-2). lib. bdg. 4.99 *(978-0-7364-2139-3(4),* Golden/Disney) Random Hse. Children's Bks.

—Finding Nemo. novel ed. 2003. (Junior Novel Ser.). (ENG., Illus.). 128p. (J). (gr. 4-7). 4.99 *(978-0-7364-2130-0(0),* RH/Disney) Random Hse. Children's Bks.

—Monsters University Little Golden Book (Disney/Pixar Monsters University) RH Disney Staff, illus. 2013. (Little Golden Book Ser.). (ENG., Illus.). 24p. (J). (-k). 3.99 *(978-0-7364-3034-0(2),* Golden/Disney) Random Hse. Children's Bks.

—Scaring Lessons. RH Disney Staff, illus. 2013. (Step into Reading Ser.). (ENG., Illus.). 32p. (J). (gr. -1-1). 3.99 *(978-0-7364-3035-7(0),* RH/Disney) Random Hse. Children's Bks.

Rhiger, Tenna. The Story about How the Spotted Wobblepig Got Its Spots. 2012. 40p. pap. *(978-1-84903-152-3(5))* Schiel & Denver Publishing Ltd.

Rhodes, Carol. Gene the Pumpkin Man. 2008. 32p. pap. 16.95 *(978-1-4327-1416-1(3))* Outskirts Pr., Inc.

Rhodes, Danny W. I Know Tuff Luck. 2012. (ENG.). 55p. pap. 8.95 *(978-1-4327-9739-3(5))* Outskirts Pr., Inc.

Rhodes, Jewell Parker. Towers Falling. 2016. (ENG., Illus.). 240p. (J). (gr. 3-7). 16.99 *(978-0-316-26222-4(6))* Little, Brown Bks. for Young Readers.

Rhodes, Tamika. Francis & His Barnyard Friends. 2005. (J). pap. 8.00 *(978-0-8059-6752-4(4))* Dorrance Publishing Co., Inc.

Rhone, Alexus D. Secret Shame 2003. 237p. (YA). pap. 12.95 *(978-0-9708688-1-7(2))* Unshackled Publishing.

Rhuday-Perkovich, Olugbemisola & Vernick, Audrey. Two Naomis. 2016. 208p. (J). (gr. 3-7). 16.99 *(978-0-06-241425-0(9))* HarperCollins Pubs.

Riad, Hala. Twinkie Has a New Home. 2011. 24p. pap. 14.93 *(978-1-4269-7120-4(6))* Trafford Publishing.

Ribay, Randy. An Infinite Number of Parallel Universes. 2015. (ENG.). 240p. (YA). 17.99 *(978-1-4405-8814-3(7),* Simon Pulse) Simon Pulse.

Ribeiro, Nelson. Jughead with Archie in Power Play. Gorelick, Victor, illus. 2007. (Jughead with Archie Ser.). (ENG.). 80p. (J). (gr. 3-6). 24.21 *(978-1-59961-275-1(5))* Spotlight.

Ricahrdson, Larry. Metal Mike. Ricahrdson, Brittany, illus. 2010. 24p. (J). pap. 9.95 *(978-1-935706-26-7(8))* Wiggles Pr.

Ricard, Anouk. Fore! Dascher, Helge, tr. from FRE. 2015. (Anna & Froga Ser.). (ENG., Illus.). 40p. (J). (gr. k-4). 14.95 *(978-1-77046-204-5(X),* 9781770462045) Drawn & Quarterly Pubns. CAN. Dist: Macmillan.

Ricchiazzi, Lisa Gail. The Adventures of Fella & Dawn: Help One Another. 2012. 20p. pap. 13.77 *(978-1-4669-7170-7(3))* Trafford Publishing.

—Fella Finds a Friend: (You Are Never Alone) 2012. 24p. pap. 14.93 *(978-1-4669-2985-2(5))* Trafford Publishing.

Ricci, Christine. Best Friends Forever. 2007. (Illus.). (J). pap. *(978-1-4127-8920-2(6))* Publications International, Ltd.

Rice, Cindy & Stolarski, Jerry. Mr. Mahaffy on Wisdom Pond: The Beginning. 2007. (ENG.). 84p. per. 19.95 *(978-1-4241-3097-9(2))* America Star Bks.

Rice, James. Lyn & the Fuzzy, 1 vol. Rice, James, illus. 2007. (ENG., Illus.). 40p. (J). (gr. k-3). 17.99 *(978-1-58980-508-8(9))* Pelican Publishing Co., Inc.

Rice, June K. The Little Blue Tree. 2009. 20p. pap. 10.99 *(978-1-4389-4806-5(9))* AuthorHouse.

Rice, Morgan. A Charge of Valor. 2013. (Sorcerer's Ring Ser.: 6). 250p. (YA). pap. 14.99 *(978-1-939416-18-6(3),* Morgan Rice) Morgan Rice Bks.

Rice, Sheila. The Night Watchers. 2005. 88p. pap. 19.95 *(978-1-4137-7663-8(9))* America Star Bks.

Rich, Carol Bak. The Running Nose Book. Rich, Bobbie, illus. 2013. (ENG.). 41p. (J). pap. 9.95 *(978-1-4787-0062-3(9))* Outskirts Pr., Inc.

Richards, Barnaby. Blip! Toon Level 1. 2016. (ENG., Illus.). 40p. (J). (gr. -1-k). 12.95 *(978-1-935179-98-6(5))* TOON Books / RAW Junior, LLC.

Richards, Brenda. A Woodland Tale. 2011. 32p. pap. 21.99 *(978-1-4568-5708-0(8))* Xlibris Corp.

Richards, C. J. Battle of the Bots. Fujita, Goro, illus. (Robots Rule Ser.: 3). (ENG.). 240p. (J). (gr. 2-5). 2017. pap. 6.99 *(978-0-544-93524-2(1))* 2015. 13.99 *(978-0-544-33932-3(0))* Houghton Mifflin Harcourt Publishing Co. (HMH Books For Young Readers).

—Battle of the Bots. 2017. (Robots Rule Ser.: 3). (ENG.). (J). (gr. 2-5). lib. bdg. 17.20 ***(978-0-606-39811-4(2))*** Turtleback Bks.

—The Junkyard Bot, Bk. 7. Fujita, Goro, illus. 2014. (Robots Rule Ser.: 1). (ENG.). 208p. (J). (gr. 5-7). 13.99 *(978-0-544-33936-1(3),* HMH Books For Young Readers) Houghton Mifflin Harcourt Publishing Co.

—The Junkyard Bot. 2016. (Robots Rule Ser.: 1). lib. bdg. 17.20 *(978-0-606-37980-9(0))* Turtleback Bks.

—The Junkyard Bot: Robots Rule, Book 1. Fujita, Goro, illus. 2016. (Robots Rule Ser.). (ENG.). 208p. (J). (gr. 5-7). pap. 6.99 *(978-0-544-66843-0(X),* HMH Books For Young Readers) Houghton Mifflin Harcourt Publishing Co.

—Lots of Bots. Fujita, Goro, illus. 2016. (Robots Rule Ser.: 2). (ENG.). 224p. (J). (gr. 2-5). pap. 6.99 *(978-0-544-81082-2(1),* HMH Books For Young Readers) Houghton Mifflin Harcourt Publishing Co.

Richards, Dan. The Problem with Not Being Scared of Kids. Neubecker, Robert, illus. 2015. (ENG.). 32p. (J). (gr. -1-3). 16.95 *(978-1-62979-102-9(4))* Boyds Mills Pr.

Richards, J. Kirk. I'll Be There with Belzon. 2004. (Illus.). 32p. (J). per. 19.95 *(978-0-9752553-0-8(4))* Bright-Brights Media Co., The.

Richards, Jasmine. The Book of Wonders. 2012. (ENG.). 416p. (J). (gr. 3-7). 16.99 *(978-0-06-201007-0(7))* HarperCollins Pubs.

Richardson, Bernard. Freddy Weller's Holiday. 2011. 50p. 24.99 *(978-1-4628-9548-9(4));* pap. 15.99 *(978-1-4628-9547-2(6))* Xlibris Corp.

Richardson, Larry. Metal Mike. 2010. (Illus.). 32p. (J). pap. 9.95 *(978-1-935706-33-5(0))* Wiggles Pr.

Richardson, Lilith. TORO Special Edition Paperback. 2010. 63p. pap. 24.00 *(978-0-578-04792-8(6))* Richardson, Lilith.

Richardson, Nikki. A Beautiful Lie, 1 vol. 2009. 168p. pap. 24.95 *(978-1-61582-927-9(X))* America Star Bks.

Richardson, Timariay A. Billy Bean & the Chocolate Dragon. 2013. 44p. pap. 11.95 *(978-0-9840456-7-9(8))* Universal Publishing LLC.

Richens, Carol & Smith, Lori. Lori's Summer Fun with Tamara! 2009. 33p. 16.40 *(978-1-4357-1113-6(0))* Lulu Pr., Inc.

Richler, Mordecai. Jacob Two-Two's First Spy Case. Petricic, Dusan, illus. 2009. (Jacob Two-Two Ser.). (ENG.). 168p. (J). (gr. 4-7). 10.95 *(978-0-88776-927-6(6))* Tundra Bks. CAN. Dist: Random Hse., Inc.

Richman, Karyn. The Land Where All Things Become Beautiful. 2011. 204p. pap. 15.99 *(978-1-61215-926-3(5))* Salem Author Services.

Richmond, Lori. Pax & Blue. Richmond, Lori, illus. 2017. (ENG., Illus.). 32p. (J). (gr. -1-3). 17.99 *(978-1-4814-5132-1(4),* Simon & Schuster/Paula Wiseman Bks.) Simon & Schuster/Paula Wiseman Bks.

Richter, Murray. Lucky Rocks. 2014. (ENG.). 168p. (J). pap. 11.99 *(978-0-9916348-8-0(8))* Ten Story Bks., LLC.

Rickabus, Ted. Ookle. 2009. 32p. pap. 21.99 *(978-1-4415-3389-0(3))* Xlibris Corp.

Rickerty, Simon. The Crayon: A Colorful Tale about Friendship. Rickerty, Simon, illus. 2014. (ENG., Illus.). 32p. (J). (gr. -1-2). 15.99 *(978-1-4814-0475-4(X),* Aladdin) Simon & Schuster Children's Publishing.

Riddle, A. Yogi & Me. 2006. 48p. pap. 16.95 *(978-1-4241-0565-6(X))* PublishAmerica, Inc.

Ridell, Chris. Ottoline va al colegio/ Ottolina Goes To School. 2008. (SPA.). 172p. (J). 13.95 *(978-84-263-6833-1(6))* Vives, Luis Editorial (Edelvives) ESP. Dist: Baker & Taylor Bks.

Rideout, Henry. Dragons Blood. 2006. 144p. per. 11.95 *(978-1-59818-051-0(7));* 24.95 *(978-1-59818-548-5(9))* Aegypan.

Ridgers, Denise J. Elspeth's Great Adventure. 2007. (Illus.). 60p. (J). pap. 9.00 *(978-0-8059-7471-3(7))* Dorrance Publishing Co., Inc.

Riding, Gale. Milo Is Not So Different after All. 2009. 20p. pap. 12.49 *(978-1-4490-1976-1(5))* AuthorHouse.

Riedl, Sheila. Elijah & the Elephant. 2011. 24p. pap. 15.99 *(978-1-4653-5796-0(3))* Xlibris Corp.

Ries, Lori. Good Dog, Aggie. Dormer, Frank W., illus. 2012. (ENG.). 48p. (J). (gr. -1-3). pap. 5.95 *(978-1-57091-646-5(2))* Charlesbridge Publishing, Inc.

Rifkin, L. Life Four. 2008. (Nine Lives of Romeo Crumb Ser.). (Illus.). 201p. (gr. 6-8). per. 8.95 *(978-0-9743221-9-3(9))* Sunrise Publishing Co.

—The Nine Lives of Romeo Crumb: Life Seven. 2011. 218p. (J). pap. 8.95 *(978-0-9835480-0-3(5))* Sunrise Publishing Co.

Rifkin, L. (Lauren). The Nine Lives of Romeo Crumb: Life Five. Hartman, Kurt, illus. 2009. 169p. (YA). pap. 8.95 *(978-0-9743221-7-9(2))* Sunrise Publishing Co.

Rifkin, Lauren I. The Nine Lives of Romeo Crumb: Life Eight. 2013. (ENG.). 224p. (YA). pap. 8.95 *(978-0-9886853-8-3(8))* Sunrise Publishing Co.

Rigby Education Staff. Flying High. (Illus.). (J). suppl. ed. 20.00 *(978-0-7635-6505-3(9),* 765059C99) Rigby Education.

—Tom Sawyer: Jumbled Tumble. (gr. k-2). 26.00 *(978-0-7635-2424-1(7))* Rigby Education.

Riggs, Jon & Evanoff, Corrine R. Little Blue Planet. Nazar, Alexandria, illus. 2014. (ENG.). 24p. (J). (-5). 16.95 *(978-1-939621-07-8(0))* ORO Editions.

Riggs, Mary L. Dragon Forge the Ballad of Beighn. 2009. 110p. pap. 9.95 *(978-1-60860-499-9(3),* Strategic Bk. Publishing) Strategic Book Publishing & Rights Agency (SBPRA).

Rihani, Ina. Song to the Sun. 2012. 56p. pap. 31.99 *(978-1-4653-1123-8(8))* Xlibris Corp.

Riley, D. H. The Mysterians, 1 vol. 2009. 54p. pap. 16.95 *(978-1-60836-374-2(0))* America Star Bks.

Riley, Kellee, illus. Tolee's Rhyme Time. 2009. (Ni Hao, Kai-Lan Ser.). (ENG.). 24p. (J). pap. 3.99 *(978-1-4169-9024-6(0),* Simon Spotlight/Nickelodeon) Simon Spotlight/Nickelodeon.

Riley, Penelope A. Duckie Dan the Traveling Man. 2009. 44p. pap. 16.99 *(978-1-4490-4634-7(7))* AuthorHouse.

Riley, Zach. Surprise Kick. Ricci, Andrés, illus. 2012. (Zach Riley Ser.). 80p. (J). (gr. 3-6). lib. bdg. 27.07 *(978-1-61783-536-0(6))* Magic Wagon.

Rinaldi, Ann. My Vicksburg. 2011. (ENG.). 160p. (YA). (gr. 7). pap. 11.95 *(978-0-547-55000-8(6))* Houghton Mifflin Harcourt Publishing Co.

—An Unlikely Friendship: A Novel of Mary Todd Lincoln & Elizabeth Keckley. 2008. (ENG., Illus.). 256p. (J). (gr. 5-7). pap. 7.99 *(978-0-15-206398-6(6))* Houghton Mifflin Harcourt Publishing Co.

Rinck, Maranke. Hush Little Turtle. Van Der Linden, Martijn, illus. 2011. (ENG.). 24p. (J). (gr. -1). bds. 8.95 *(978-1-935954-06-4(7),* 9781935954064) Lemniscaat USA.

Riordan, Rick. The Lightning Thief. (Percy Jackson & the Olympians Ser.: Bk. 1). (ENG.). (J). (gr. 5-9). 2005. 384p. 17.99 *(978-0-7868-5629-9(7))*Bk. 1. 2006. 416p. reprint ed. per. 7.99 *(978-0-7868-3865-3(5))* Disney Publishing Worldwide.

—The Lightning Thief. 2008. (J). 54.99 *(978-0-7393-7113-8(4))* Findaway World, LLC.

—The Lightning Thief. 2006. (Percy Jackson & the Olympians Ser.: Bk. 1). 377p. (J). (gr. 5-12). 15.65 *(978-0-7569-6603-4(5))* Perfection Learning Corp.

—The Lightning Thief. rev. l.t. ed. 2006. (Percy Jackson & the Olympians Ser.: 1). (ENG.). 483p. (gr. 5-18). 22.95 *(978-0-7862-8225-8(8))* Thorndike Pr.

—The Lightning Thief. 2006. (Percy Jackson & the Olympians Ser.: 1). (J). lib. bdg. 18.40 *(978-1-4177-3247-0(4),* Turtleback) Turtleback Bks.

—The Sea of Monsters, Bk. 2. Tk, illus. 2nd rev. ed. 2007. (Percy Jackson & the Olympians Ser.: Bk. 2). (ENG.). 320p. (J). (gr. 5-9). pap. 7.99 *(978-1-4231-0334-9(3))* Disney Publishing Worldwide.

—The Sea of Monsters. l.t. ed. 2006. (Percy Jackson & the Olympians Ser.: Bk. 2). 361p. (J). (gr. 5-9). 22.95 *(978-0-7862-9074-1(9))* Thorndike Pr.

E F G

—The Sea of Monsters. 2007. (Percy Jackson & the Olympians Ser.: 2). 279p. (J). (gr. 4-7). lib. bdg. 18.40 (978-1-4177-7612-2(9), Turtleback) Turtleback Bks.

Riordan, Rick & Venditti, Robert. The Lightning Thief. Futaki, Attila & Villarrubia, Jose, illus. 2010. (Percy Jackson & the Olympians Ser.). (ENG.). 128p. (J). (gr. 5-9). 21.99 (978-1-4231-1696-7(8)); pap. 12.99 (978-1-4231-1710-0(7)) Hyperion Pr.

Rios, Yuri M. The Kingdom of Ice. Rios, Margarita, tr. 2012. 26p. pap. 9.99 (978-1-61897-223-1(5), Strategic Bk. Publishing) Strategic Book Publishing & Rights Agency (SBPRA).

Rippin, Sally. The Best Party Ever. Spartels, Stephanie, illus. 2014. (ENG.). 48p. (J). pap. 4.99 (978-1-61067-261-0(5)) Kane Miller.

—The Copycat Kid. Fukuoka, Aki, illus. 2015. 42p. (J). (978-1-61067-449-2(9)) Kane Miller.

—The New Friend: Hey Jack! Spartels, Stephanie, illus. 2014. (ENG.). 48p. (J). pap. 4.99 (978-1-61067-125-5(2)) Kane Miller.

—The Night Fright. Fukuoka, Aki, illus. 2015. 43p. (J). (978-1-61067-451-5(0)) Kane Miller.

—The Night Fright: Billie B Brown. Fukuoka, Aki, illus. 2016. (ENG.). 48p. (J). pap. 4.99 (978-1-61067-391-4(3)) Kane Miller.

—The Playground Problem. Spartels, Stephanie, illus. 2015. (ENG.). 48p. (J). pap. 4.99 (978-1-61067-260-3(7)) Kane Miller.

—The Scary Solo. Spartels, Stephanie, illus. 2013. (ENG.). 48p. (J). pap. 4.99 (978-1-61067-122-4(8)) Kane Miller.

—The Second-Best Friend: Billie B. Brown. Fukuoka, Aki, illus. 2014. (ENG.). 48p. (J). pap. 4.99 (978-1-61067-098-2(1)) Kane Miller.

—Spooky House. Fukuoka, Aki, illus. (J). 2015. (ENG.). 96p. pap. 4.99 (978-1-61067-311-2(5)) 2014. 89p. (978-1-61067-332-7(8)) Kane Miller.

—The Top Team. Spartels, Stephanie, illus. 2014. 42p. (J). (978-1-61067-293-1(3)) Kane Miller.

—The Worst Sleepover: Hey Jack! Spartels, Stephanie, illus. 2014. (ENG.). 48p. (J). pap. 4.99 (978-1-61067-185-9(6)) Kane Miller.

Rissi, Anica Mrose. Anna, Banana, & the Big-Mouth Bet. Park, Meg, illus. 2016. (Anna, Banana Ser.: 3). (ENG.). 128p. (J). (gr. 1-5). pap. 5.99 (978-1-4814-1612-2(X), Simon & Schuster Bks. For Young Readers) Simon & Schuster Bks. For Young Readers.

—Anna, Banana, & the Friendship Split. Park, Meg, illus. 2015. (Anna, Banana Ser.: 1). (ENG.). 128p. (J). (gr. 1-5). 16.99 (978-1-4814-1605-4(7), Simon & Schuster Bks. For Young Readers) Simon & Schuster Bks. For Young Readers.

—Anna, Banana, & the Monkey in the Middle. Park, Meg, illus. 2015. (Anna, Banana Ser.: 2). (ENG.). 128p. (J). (gr. 1-5). 15.99 (978-1-4814-1608-5(1), Simon & Schuster Bks. For Young Readers) Simon & Schuster Bks. For Young Readers.

—Anna, Banana, & the Puppy Parade. Park, Meg, illus. 2017. (Anna, Banana Ser.: 4). (ENG.). 144p. (J). (gr. 1-5). pap. 5.99 (978-1-4814-1615-3(4), Simon & Schuster Bks. For Young Readers) Simon & Schuster Bks. For Young Readers.

Rissman, Angelica. Julius & the Lost Letter to Santa. 2003. (J). 7.99 (978-1-59384-019-8(5)) Parklane Publishing.

Ritchey, Carmil White. The Adventures of Pine Cone the Cat. 2012. 24p. pap. 17.99 (978-1-4685-9470-6(2)) AuthorHouse.

Ritchey, Kate. A Perfect Picnic. 2013. (Mickey & Friends World of Reading Ser.). (J). lib. bdg. 13.55 (978-0-606-31753-5(8), Turtleback) Turtleback Bks.

Ritchie, Janet. Remember That I Love You. 2008. (ENG.). 40p. 18.99 (978-1-4389-3155-5(7)) AuthorHouse.

Ritter, Joshua & Ellis-Ritter, Karen. Be It Every Day! 2012. 40p. pap. 20.99 (978-1-4634-5231-5(4)) AuthorHouse.

Ritter, Philip. Tales in Rhyme from Three Little Mischief Maker's Country Time: The Escapades of Three Little Mischief Makers. 2005. (J). pap. 10.00 (978-0-8059-6928-3(4)) Dorrance Publishing Co., Inc.

Rivadeneira, Alexa. Confessions from the Heart of a Teenage Girl. 2007. 248p. per. 16.95 (978-0-595-42432-0(5)) iUniverse, Inc.

Rive, Myrtle. Sam's Adventures. 2009. (Illus.). 154p. pap. 38.99 (978-1-4490-0821-5(6)) AuthorHouse.

Rivers, Karen. Before We Go Extinct: A Novel. 2016. (ENG.). 256p. (YA). 17.99 (978-0-374-30240-5(5), 9780374302405, Farrar, Straus & Giroux (BYR)) Farrar, Straus & Giroux.

—Love, Ish. 2017. (ENG.). 288p. (J). (gr. 4-8). 16.95 (978-1-61620-570-6(9)) Algonquin Bks. of Chapel Hill.

Rivers-Moore, Debbie. Five Little Snowmen. Everitt-Stewart, Andrew, illus. 2015. (ENG.). 10p. (J). (gr. -1 — 1). bds. 8.99 (978-1-4998-0170-5(X)) Little Bee Books Inc.

—Pig. Larranaga, Ana Martin, illus. 2012. (Come Out & Play Bks.). (ENG.). 10p. (J). bds. 2.99 (978-0-7641-6519-1(4)) Barron's Educational Series, Inc.

Rivers, Phoebe. Moment of Truth. 2012. (Saranormal Ser.: 5). (ENG.). 160p. (J). (gr. 3-7). 15.99 (978-1-4424-6127-7(6)); pap. 5.99 (978-1-4424-6125-3(X)) Simon Spotlight. (Simon Spotlight).

—Playing with Fire. 2013. (Saranormal Ser.: 9). (ENG., Illus.). 160p. (J). (gr. 3-7). 15.99 (978-1-4424-8306-4(7)); pap. 5.99 (978-1-4424-8305-7(9)) Simon Spotlight. (Simon Spotlight).

Rixon, Denise. The Owl That Barked: Tammy, 1 vol. 2009. 203p. pap. 24.95 (978-1-4489-8472-5(6)) America Star Bks.

Rizzo, Cynthia Marie. Julie & the Unicorn. 2003. 49p. pap. 16.95 (978-1-4137-0785-4(8)) PublishAmerica, Inc.

Roach, Hesta. The Friendship Thief. Dillingham, Charlene, illus. (J). (gr. k-5). pap. 9.99 (978-0-9660583-3-8(X)) Sakura Pr.

Roba, Jean. Friends First. Roba, Jean, illus. 2012. (Billy & Buddy Ser.: 3). (ENG., Illus.). 48p. (J). (gr. 3-12). pap. 11.95 (978-1-84918-124-2(1)) CineBook GBR. Dist: National Bk. Network.

Robar, Serena. Giving up the V. 2009. (ENG.). 272p. (YA). (gr. 9-18). pap. 8.99 (978-1-4169-7558-8(6), Simon Pulse) Simon Pulse.

Robbins, Dean. Two Friends: Susan B. Anthony & Frederick Douglass: Susan B. Anthony & Frederick Douglass. Qualls, Sean & Alko, Selina, illus. 2016. (ENG.). 32p. (J). (gr. -1-3). 17.99 (978-0-545-39996-8(3), Orchard Bks.) Scholastic, Inc.

Robbins, Jacqui. The New Girl... & Me. Phelan, Matt, illus. 2006. (ENG.). 32p. (J). (gr. -1-2). 17.99 (978-0-689-86468-1(X), Atheneum/Richard Jackson Bks.) Simon & Schuster Children's Publishing.

—Two of a Kind. Phelan, Matt, illus. 2009. (ENG.). 32p. (J). (gr. -1-2). 17.99 (978-1-4169-2437-1(X), Atheneum Bks. for Young Readers) Simon & Schuster Children's Publishing.

Robbins, James L. Aristotle & Burgoo & the Ditto-Flake-Flu. 2012. 44p. pap. 21.99 (978-1-4771-3551-8(0)) Xlibris Corp.

Robert, Bulla Clyde & Bulla. Shoeshine Girl. 2014. (Trophy Chapter Bks). (ENG.). 96p. (J). (gr. 2-5). 9.24 (978-1-63245-292-4(8)) Lectorum Pubns., Inc.

(Robert Thompson), Pau Pau. Santa's Secret Helpers, 1 vol. 2009. 55p. pap. 16.95 (978-1-60836-859-4(9)) America Star Bks.

Roberts, Carmen. Inseparable: The Tale of the Amulet. 2009. 120p. 21.49 (978-1-4490-3394-1(6)); pap. 10.99 (978-1-4490-3396-5(2)) AuthorHouse.

Roberts, D. W. Pep Squad Mysteries Book 1: Cavern in the Hills. 2009. 71p. pap. 8.99 (978-0-557-05513-5(X)) Lulu Pr., Inc.

—Pep Squad Mysteries Book 2:the Haunting of Townsand Hall. 2009. 77p. pap. 8.95 (978-0-557-05289-9(0)) Lulu Pr., Inc.

Roberts, Daniel. Boy & Dinosaur. 2010. 86p. pap. 8.99 (978-0-557-28024-7(9)) Lulu Pr., Inc.

—Harrison & His Dinosaur Robot. 2009. (Illus.). 32p. pap. 14.95 (978-1-4389-2846-3(7)) AuthorHouse.

—Harrison & His Dinosaur Robot & the Purple Spotted Sea Monster. 2012. 36p. pap. 20.99 (978-1-4772-6979-4(7)) AuthorHouse.

—The Penguin & the Polar Bear. 2009. 32p. pap. 14.95 (978-1-4389-2845-6(9)) AuthorHouse.

—Young Pep Squad Mysteries. 2011. 36p. pap. 16.99 (978-1-4567-9640-2(2)) AuthorHouse.

Roberts, Dw. Pep Squad Mysteries Book: Cavern in the Hills. 2008. (Illus.). 68p. pap. 9.96 (978-0-557-02446-9(3)) Lulu Pr., Inc.

Roberts, Esyllt Nest & Owen, Carys Eurwen. Elidir A'r Tylwyth Teg. 2005. (WEL., Illus.). 36p. pap. (978-0-86381-530-0(8)) Gwasg Carreg Gwalch.

Roberts, Ken. Thumb & the Bad Guys. 2013. 104p. pap. (978-1-4596-6491-3(4)) ReadHowYouWant.com, Ltd.

Roberts, LaDawna. The Haunted Birthday Party. 2007. 48p. per. 16.95 (978-1-4241-8723-2(0)) America Star Bks.

Roberts, Patricia Gaskins. My Friend Tommy Has a Daddy & a Mommy. 2012. 20p. pap. 17.99 (978-1-4772-3273-6(7)) AuthorHouse.

Roberts, Pauline. He Shined on Me. 2010. 20p. pap. 9.95 (978-0-9841991-6-7(0)) Beckham Pubns. Group, Inc.

Roberts, Rachel. All That Glitters. (gr. 3-6). 2008. (Avalon: Web of Magic Ser.: 2). (ENG., Illus.). 216p. (YA). pap. 6.95 (978-1-933164-67-0(0), 9781933164670) 2007. (Avalon Ser.: Bk. 2). 175p. (J). 9.99 (978-1-933164-65-6(4)) Seven Seas Entertainment, LLC.

Roberts, Scott. Patty Cake & Friends. 2006. (ENG., Illus.). 96p. pap. 12.95 (978-1-59362-030-1(6), 9781593620301) Slave Labor Bks.

Roberts, Trina. The Lonley Little Birch. 2005. 9.00 (978-0-8059-8053-0(9)) Dorrance Publishing Co., Inc.

Robertson, Betsey. Frisky's Forest Friends: Robin Rescue. 2009. 28p. pap. 12.49 (978-1-4389-1906-5(9)) AuthorHouse.

Robertson, Elysia Hill. Toley's Sleep over Learning Party. Robertson, Elysia Hill, illus. 2005. (Illus.). 118p. (J). per. 12.95 (978-0-9764444-4-2(5), EJWV-005) E. J. Publishing.

Robertson, Kathy & Hooker, Jennifer. Jasmine & Chad Make New Friends. 2012. 28p. pap. 15.99 (978-1-4797-1656-2(1)) Xlibris Corp.

Robertson, Sadie. Life Just Got Real. 2016. (Live Original Fiction Ser.). (ENG.). 288p. (gr. 6-14). 17.99 (978-1-5011-2646-8(6), Howard Bks.) Howard Books.

Robins, E. The Easy Way. 2004. (Carter High Chronicles (High-Interest Readers) Ser.). (Illus.). 48p. (J). per. 4.95 (978-1-56254-683-0(X), SP683X) Saddleback Educational Publishing, Inc.

Robins, Eleanor. Boy of Their Dreams, 1 vol. unabr. ed. 2011. (Carter High Chronicles Ser.). (ENG.). 51p. (YA). (gr. 9-12). pap. 7.95 (978-1-61651-305-4(5)) Saddleback Educational Publishing, Inc.

—Broken Promise, 1 vol. unabr. ed. 2011. (Choices Ser.). (ENG.). 50p. (YA). (gr. 9-12). 7.95 (978-1-61651-591-1(0)) Saddleback Educational Publishing, Inc.

—Double-Cross, 1 vol. unabr. ed. 2011. (Choices Ser.). (ENG.). 51p. (YA). (gr. 9-12). 7.95 (978-1-61651-595-9(3)) Saddleback Educational Publishing, Inc.

—The Easy Way, 1 vol. unabr. ed. 2011. (Carter High Chronicles Ser.). (ENG.). 51p. (YA). (gr. 9-12). pap. 7.95 (978-1-61651-307-8(1)) Saddleback Educational Publishing, Inc.

—No Limits, 1 vol. unabr. ed. 2011. (Choices Ser.). (ENG.). 52p. (YA). (gr. 9-12). 7.95 (978-1-61651-598-0(8)) Saddleback Educational Publishing, Inc.

—Trust Me, 1 vol. unabr. ed. 2011. (Choices Ser.). (ENG.). 52p. (YA). (gr. 9-12). 7.95 (978-1-61651-599-7(6)) Saddleback Educational Publishing, Inc.

Robinson, Arlene. The Adventures of Wheelie Weenie & His Friends: A Brave & Wonderful Little Friend. 2011. (Illus.). 43p. pap. 12.95 (978-1-4327-6861-4(1)) Outskirts Pr., Inc.

Robinson, Barbara. The Best School Year Ever. 2005. (Trophy Bk.). (ENG.). 176p. (J). (gr. 3-18). pap. 5.99 (978-0-06-440492-1(7)) HarperCollins Pubs.

Robinson, Dierdre. I Don't Look Like You & That's Ok. 2011. 12p. (gr. 1-2). pap. 8.32 (978-1-4567-4466-3(6)) AuthorHouse.

Robinson, Donnell. Where's My L D ? 2008. 24p. pap. 12.95 (978-1-4327-1825-1(8)) Outskirts Pr., Inc.

Robinson, Keith. Valley of Monsters. 2013. 212p. pap. (978-0-9843906-6-3(9)) Roxby Media Ltd.

Robinson, Mary. Days of Terriers. 2008. 32p. pap. 13.50 (978-1-60693-481-4(3), Eloquent Bks.) Strategic Book Publishing & Rights Agency (SBPRA).

Robinson, Nikki Slade. Muddle & Mo. 2017. (ENG., Illus.). 32p. (J). (gr. -1-3). 14.99 (978-0-544-71612-4(4)) Houghton Mifflin Harcourt Publishing Co.

Robinson, Sharon. The Hero Two Doors Down: A Story of Friendship Between a Boy & a Baseball Legend. (ENG.). 208p. (J). (gr. 3-7). 2017. pap. 6.99 (978-0-545-80452-3(3), Scholastic Paperbacks) 2016. 16.99 (978-0-545-80451-6(5), Scholastic Pr.) Scholastic, Inc.

Robinson, T. J. The Academy Defenders. 2012. 326p. pap. 14.99 (978-1-936850-46-4(X)) Rhemalda Publishing.

Robson, Samantha Eliza. Jack & the Cats. 2011. 24p. pap. 16.95 (978-1-4475-0178-7(0)) Lulu Pr., Inc.

Rocha, K. E. Battle for Bearhaven. 2017. (Secrets of Bearhaven Ser.: 4). (ENG.). 240p. (J). (gr. 3-7). 14.99 (978-0-545-81306-8(9), Scholastic Pr.) Scholastic, Inc.

—Mission to Moon Farm. 2016. (J). (978-0-545-81316-7(6), Scholastic Pr.) Scholastic, Inc.

—Mission to Moon Farm (Secrets of Bearhaven #2) 2016. (Secrets of Bearhaven Ser.: 2). (ENG.). 224p. (J). (gr. 3-7). 14.99 (978-0-545-81304-4(2), Scholastic Pr.) Scholastic, Inc.

—Secrets of Bearhaven. 2016. (Bearhaven Ser.: 1). (ENG.). 256p. (J). (gr. 3-7). 14.99 (978-0-545-81303-7(4), Scholastic Pr.) Scholastic, Inc.

Rocheleau, Nicole. Ollie Ollie in Come Free! 2006. 76p. pap. 16.95 (978-1-4241-0433-8(5)) PublishAmerica, Inc.

Rochester, Andre, illus. The Sunflower & Rose. 2010. (ENG.). 36p. (J). 22.95 (978-0-9817291-1-4(8)) Metaphors 4 Life.

Rochman, Hazel & McCampbell, Darlene Z., eds. Who do you Think you Are? 2005. 176p. (YA). 23.00 (978-0-8446-7269-4(6), 3585) Smith, Peter Pub., Inc.

Rocklin, Joanne. Fleabrain Loves Franny. (ENG.). 288p. (J). (gr. 3-7). 2015. pap. 8.95 (978-1-4197-1676-8(X)) 2014. 16.95 (978-1-4197-1068-1(0)) Abrams, Inc. (Amulet Bks.).

—One Day & One Amazing Morning on Orange Street. 2012. (ENG., Illus.). 240p. (J). (gr. 3-7). pap. 8.95 (978-1-4197-0181-8(9), Amulet Bks.) Abrams, Inc.

Rodda, Emily. Dead End. 2006. (Raven Hill Mysteries Ser.: 6). (ENG., Illus.). 128p. (J). (gr. 3-7). pap. 4.99 (978-0-439-79572-2(9), Scholastic Paperbacks) Scholastic, Inc.

Roddie, Shen & Quarto Generic Staff. Best of Friends! Lamb, Sally Ann, illus. 2004. (ENG.). 25p. (J). (gr. -1-2). pap. 7.95 (978-1-84507-172-1(7), Frances Lincoln) Quarto Publishing Group UK GBR. Dist: Hachette Bk. Group.

Roddy, Lee. The City Bear's Adventures. 2008. (D. J. Dillon Adventure Ser.: No. 2). (J). 7.99 (978-0-88062-266-0(0)) Mott Media.

Röder, Marlene. In the River Darkness. Reichel, Tammi, tr. 2014. 224p. 18.95 (978-1-62324-010-3(7)) Enslow Pubs., Inc.

Rodman, Mary Ann. My Best Friend. Lewis, E. B., illus. 2007. (ENG.). 32p. (J). (gr. -1-3). pap. 5.99 (978-0-14-240806-3(9), Puffin Books) Penguin Young Readers Group.

—My Best Friend. Lewis, E. B., illus. 2007. (gr. -1-3). 16.00 (978-0-7569-8151-8(4)) Perfection Learning Corp.

—Yankee Girl. 2008. (ENG.). 240p. (J). (gr. 4-6). pap. 9.99 (978-0-312-53576-6(7), 9780312535766) Square Fish.

Rodriguez, AJ. Cycle of Life. 2009. 20p. pap. 12.49 (978-1-4389-5528-5(6)) AuthorHouse.

Rodriguez, Béatrice. Rooster's Revenge. 2011. (Stories Without Words Ser.). (ENG., Illus.). 32p. (J). (gr. -1). 14.95 (978-1-59270-112-4(4)) Enchanted Lion Bks., LLC.

Rodriguez, Béatrice, illus. Fox & Hen Together. 2011. (Stories Without Words Ser.). (ENG.). 32p. (J). (gr. -1-3). 14.95 (978-1-59270-109-4(4)) Enchanted Lion Bks., LLC.

Rodriguez, Marisela. Violet's Sweater. 2012. (ENG.). 27p. (J). pap. 12.95 (978-1-4787-1806-2(4)) Outskirts Pr., Inc.

Roe, Robin. A List of Cages. 2017. (ENG.). 320p. (YA). (gr. 7-12). 17.99 (978-1-4847-6380-3(7)) Hyperion Bks. for Children.

Roesser, Griffin. Digger Makes a Friend. 2006. (Neighborhood Readers Ser.). (ENG.). 8p. (gr. -1-3). pap. 5.15 (978-1-4042-5774-0(8), Rosen Classroom) Rosen Publishing Group, Inc., The.

Roesti, Delores Anne. Mareena Maree Mulligan & the Flying Wheelchair Book #3: Temptation's Talking, 1 vol. 2010. 93p. pap. 16.95 (978-1-4489-6692-9(2)) PublishAmerica, Inc.

Rogers, Amy Keating. The Journal of the Two Sisters: The Official Chronicles of Celestia & Luna. 2014. (ENG., Illus.). 192p. (J). (gr. 3-17). 14.99 (978-0-316-28224-6(3)) Little, Brown Bks. for Young Readers.

Rogers, Anne. Sooty Wooty Is a Cat. 2008. 32p. pap. 23.95 (978-1-4092-2565-2(8)) Lulu Pr., Inc.

Rogers, Blessing. Gabby & Ralph Meet Their New Teacher. 2010. 24p. 11.49 (978-1-4520-5447-6(9)) AuthorHouse.

Rogers, Bud & Krueger, Jim. The Battle for Argon Falls, 1 vol. Padilla, Ariel, illus. 2012. (Z Graphic Novels / Tomo Ser.). (ENG.). 160p. (J). pap. 6.99 (978-0-310-71307-4(2)) Zondervan.

—Secret Alliance, 1 vol. Padilla, Ariel, illus. 2008. (Z Graphic Novels / Tomo Ser.). (ENG.). 160p. (J). pap. 6.99 (978-0-310-71304-3(8)) Zondervan.

Rogers, Bud & Martin, Gary. The Witch of Endor, 1 vol. Cariello, Sergio, illus. 2008. (Z Graphic Novels / Son of Samson Ser.). (ENG.). 160p. (J). pap. 6.99 (978-0-310-71283-1(1)) Zonderkidz.

Rogers-Busboom, Kimberly. My Secret Best Friend. Dee, Kati, illus. 2009. 24p. lib. bdg. 16.99 (978-0-9823145-2-4(3)) Dirks Publishing, LLC.

Rogers, Carol J. The Adventures of Buttonballs' Trails. 2012. 28p. pap. 19.99 (978-1-4772-4481-4(6)) AuthorHouse.

Rogers, Jacqueline. Jack Jones off to the Post Office. 2012. 20p. pap. 13.77 (978-1-4669-0808-6(4)) Trafford Publishing.

Rogers, Jewels. The Princess & the Dolphin. 2011. 28p. 12.50 (978-1-4567-3278-3(1)) AuthorHouse.

—The Princess & the Dolphin. 2010. 28p. pap. 16.99 (978-1-4269-3966-2(3)) Trafford Publishing.

Rogers, Lauren. Skyler & the Se. Sexton, Jessa, ed. Keaggy, Sarah, illus. 2012. 36p. pap. 8.00 (978-0-9860150-1-4(6)) O'More Publishing.

Rogers, Martha. Bernie Finds a Friend. 2013. 36p. pap. 15.99 (978-1-4497-8288-7(4), WestBow Pr.) Author Solutions, Inc.

Rohmann, Eric. My Friend Rabbit. Rohmann, Eric, illus. 2011. (ENG., Illus.). 36p. (J). (gr. -1-3). bds. 7.99 (978-1-59643-641-1(7), 9781596436411) Roaring Brook Pr.

—My Friend Rabbit. Rohmann, Eric, illus. 2007. (ENG., Illus.). 32p. (J). (gr. -1-3). per. 7.99 (978-0-312-36752-7(X), 9780312367527) Square Fish.

Rokker, H. M. The Adventures of Ralph in the Search for Blackbeard's Gold, 1 vol. 2009. 41p. pap. 24.95 (978-1-60474-259-6(3)) America Star Bks.

Rolli. Kabungo, 1 vol. Pavlovic, Milan, illus. 2016. (ENG.). 176p. (J). (gr. 1-5). 14.95 (978-1-55498-804-4(7)) Groundwood Bks. CAN. Dist: Publishers Group West (PGW).

Rollins, Danielle. Breaking. 2017. (ENG.). 304p. (YA). 17.99 (978-1-61963-740-5(5), 9781619637405, Bloomsbury USA Childrens) Bloomsbury Publishing USA.

—Burning. 2017. (ENG.). 368p. (YA). pap. 9.99 (978-1-68119-205-5(5), 9781681192055, Bloomsbury USA Childrens) Bloomsbury Publishing USA.

Rollins, James. Jake Ransom & the Skull King's Shadow. 2010. (Jake Ransom Ser.: 1). (ENG.). 432p. (J). (gr. 5). pap. 7.99 (978-0-06-147381-4(2)) HarperCollins Pubs.

Rollins, Janice. Bunny's Dream. 2009. 56p. pap. 23.99 (978-1-4389-9146-7(0)) AuthorHouse.

Roman Saint-Pierre, Erika. Hoppa's Big Move. Newman, J. Heidi, ed. 2009. (Mimi's Kids Ser.: vol. 1). (ENG., Illus.). 32p. (J). pap. 12.95 (978-0-9712383-5-0(9)) Culturatti Ink.

Romanek, Trudee. Raising the Stakes, 1 vol. 2015. (Orca Limelights Ser.). (ENG.). 160p. (J). (gr. 6-9). pap. 9.95 (978-1-4598-0779-2(0)) Orca Bk. Pubs. USA.

Romano, Juliana. First There Was Forever. 2016. (ENG.). 416p. (YA). (gr. 9). pap. 10.99 (978-0-14-751391-5(X), Speak) Penguin Young Readers Group.

Romay, Alexis, tr. OLIVIA Vende Galletas (OLIVIA Sells Cookies) Spaziante, Patrick, illus. 2013. (Olivia TV Tie-In Ser.). (SPA.). 24p. (J). (gr. -1-2). pap. 3.99 (978-1-4424-5967-0(0), Libros Para Ninos) Libros Para Ninos.

Romeu, Emma. Gregorio Vuelve a Mexico. 2003. (SPA., Illus.). 148p. (J). (gr. 5-8). pap. 9.95 (978-968-19-0367-1(6)) Santillana USA Publishing Co., Inc.

Romito, Dee. The BFF Bucket List. 2016. (Mix Ser.). (ENG., Illus.). 240p. (J). (gr. 4-8). pap. 7.99 (978-1-4814-4642-6(8), Aladdin) Simon & Schuster Children's Publishing.

The Rootfriends. 2004. (J). mass mkt. (978-0-9749170-0-9(1)) Dazsling Inc.

Roques, Dominique. Sleep Tight, Anna Banana! Dormal, Alexis, illus. 2014. (Anna Banana Ser.). (ENG.). 28p. (J). (gr. -1-2). 15.99 (978-1-62672-019-0(3), 9781626720190, First Second Bks.) Roaring Brook Pr.

Rorby, Ginny. Lost in the River of Grass. (Carolrhoda YA Ser.). (ENG.). 264p. (YA). (gr. 7-12). 2012. pap. 9.95 (978-0-7613-8498-4(7)) 2011. 17.95 (978-0-7613-5685-1(1)) Lerner Publishing Group. (Carolrhoda Lab™).

Rosa, Guy. The Friends. 2014. (ENG.). 192p. (YA). 10.75 (978-1-63245-201-6(4)) Lectorum Pubns., Inc.

Roscoe, Charlie. The Red Prince. Cole, Tom Clohosy, illus. 2016. (ENG.). 32p. (J). (-k). 16.99 (978-0-7636-8912-4(2), Templar) Candlewick Pr.

Rose, C. T. Don't Play with the Craft, 1 vol. 2009. 82p. pap. 19.95 (978-1-61582-871-5(0)) America Star Bks.

Rose, Caroline Starr & McPike, Elizabeth. Blue Birds. 2015. (ENG., Illus.). 400p. (J). (gr. 5). bds. 16.99 (978-0-399-16810-9(9), G.P. Putnam's Sons Books for Young Readers) Penguin Young Readers Group.

Rose, D. M. A Tail of Friendship: The Psychiatrist Is In. 2012. 34p. 24.95 (978-1-4626-5240-2(9)) America Star Bks.

Rose, Jasmine. The Last Caterpillar Princess. 2011. 16p. pap. 8.64 (978-1-4634-1953-0(8)) AuthorHouse.

Rose, Melanie M. Zak Makes a New Friend: Zak's World Book One. 2012. 24p. pap. 17.99 (978-1-4772-2446-5(7)) AuthorHouse.

Rose, Nancy. Merry Christmas, Squirrels! 2015. (ENG., Illus.). 32p. (J). (gr. -1-3). 17.00 (978-0-316-30257-9(0)) Little, Brown Bks. for Young Readers.

Rose, Tammy Marie. Munchkin. 2012. 24p. 24.95 (978-1-4626-6095-7(9)) America Star Bks.

Rosebrock, Katie. Tabitha & Dundee: A Story of Friendship. 2013. 16p. pap. 15.99 (978-1-4817-1257-6(8)) AuthorHouse.

Roseman-Mendoza, Natalie. Maritza's Garden Path. 2009. 32p. pap. 24.95 (978-1-60749-386-0(1)) America Star Bks.

Rosen, Lucy. Bots' Best Friend. 2015. (Transformers Passport to Reading Ser.). (J). lib. bdg. 13.55 (978-0-606-37227-5(X)) Turtleback Bks.

—Meet the Teen Titans. 2014. (Passport to Reading Level 2 Ser.). (J). lib. bdg. 13.55 (978-0-606-35934-4(6)) Turtleback Bks.

—My Little Pony - Meet the Princess of Friendship. 2014. (Passport to Reading Level 1 Ser.). (ENG., Illus.). 32p. (J). (gr. -1-3). pap. 4.99 (978-0-316-28230-7(8)) Little, Brown Bks. for Young Readers.

—My Little Pony: Cutie Map Quest: Punch Out & Play. 2016. (ENG., Illus.). 36p. (J). (gr. 1-5). pap. 12.99 (978-0-316-39293-8(6)) Little, Brown Bks. for Young Readers.

—ParaNorman: Meet the Ghosts. movie tie-in ed. 2012. (Passport to Reading Level 2 Ser.). (ENG., Illus.). 32p. (J). (gr. -1-3). pap. 3.99 (978-0-316-20982-3(1)) Little, Brown Bks. for Young Readers.

Rosen, Michael. Bear's Day Out. Reynolds, Adrian, illus. (ENG.). (J). 2009. 26p. (gr. -1 — 1). bds. 7.99 (978-1-59990-391-0(1), 9781599903910) 2007. 32p. (gr. k-3). 16.95 (978-1-59990-007-0(6), 9781599900070) Bloomsbury Publishing USA. (Bloomsbury USA Childrens).

Rosenberg, Liz. What James Said. Myers, Matthew, illus. 2015. (ENG.). 32p. (J). (gr. k-3). 16.99 (978-1-59643-908-5(4), 9781596439085) Roaring Brook Pr.

Rosenberg, Madelyn & Shang, Wendy Wan-Long. This Is Just a Test: A Novel. 2017. (ENG.). 256p. (J). (gr. 3-7). 17.99 (978-1-338-03772-2(2), Scholastic Pr.) Scholastic, Inc.

Rosenberg, Michael. The Story of Bendalot. 2008. 40p. pap. 16.99 (978-1-4343-9932-8(X)) AuthorHouse.

—The Story of Bendalot Part: The Return Home. 2009. (Illus.). 36p. pap. 15.49 (978-1-4389-8294-6(1)) AuthorHouse.

Rosenbluth, Roz. Getting to Know Ruben Plotnick. Manning, Maurie J., illus. 2005. (ENG.). 32p. (J). (gr. k-2). 15.95 (978-0-9729225-5-5(5)) Flashlight Pr.

Rosenlund, Ranee Mercier. Benny the Frog & His New Friends. 2012. 20p. pap. 17.99 (978-1-4772-9630-1(1)) AuthorHouse.

Rosenthal, Amy Krouse. Exclamation Mark. Lichtenheld, Tom, illus. 2013. (ENG.). 56p. (J). 17.99 (978-0-545-43679-3(6), Scholastic Pr.) Scholastic, Inc.

—Friendshape. Lichtenheld, Tom, illus. 2015. (ENG.). 40p. (J). (gr. -1-k). 16.99 *(978-0-545-43682-3(6),* Scholastic Pr.) Scholastic, Inc.
Rosenthal, Amy Krouse & Lichtenheld, Tom. Exclamation Mark. 2013. 56p. (J). (gr. k-3). pap. 6.95 *(978-0-545-63130-3(0),* Scholastic) Scholastic, Inc.
Rosin, Lindsey. Cherry. 2016. (ENG., Illus.). 400p. (YA). (gr. 9). 17.99 *(978-1-4814-5908-2(2),* Simon Pulse) Simon Pulse.
Roske, Melissa. Kat Greene Comes Clean. 2017. (ENG.). 224p. (J). (gr. 4-7). lib. bdg. 16.99 *(978-1-58089-776-1(2))* Charlesbridge Publishing, Inc.
Rosman, Yitz. Jerry Sets Sail. 2013. 40p. pap. 16.46 *(978-1-4669-8202-4(0))* Trafford Publishing.
Ross, Chudney. Lone Bean. 2012. (ENG.). 208p. (J). (gr. 3-7). 16.99 *(978-0-06-166011-5(6),* Amistad) HarperCollins Pubs.
Ross, Donald. The Scribble Squad in the Weird Weird West. 2016. (ENG., Illus.). 256p. (J). 13.99 *(978-1-4494-6921-4(3))* Andrews McMeel Publishing.
Ross, Patrick. Oliver: The Great Escape. Burcham, David, illus. 2009. 34p. pap. 24.95 *(978-1-60749-151-4(6))* America Star Bks.
—Runt River Rat's Wild Ride, 1 vol. Burcham, David, illus. 2010. 24p. 24.95 *(978-1-4512-0067-6(6))* PublishAmerica, Inc.
Ross, Susan. Kiki & Jacques. 2015. (ENG.). 128p. (J). (gr. 3-7). 16.95 *(978-0-8234-3427-5(3))* Holiday Hse., Inc.
Ross, Tony & Tony, Ross). I Want a Friend! Ross, Tony, illus. 2017. (ENG., Illus.). 32p. (J). (gr. -1-3). 17.99 *(978-1-5124-0555-2(8))* Andersen Pr. GBR. Dist: Lerner Publishing Group.
Rosselson, Leon. Tom the Whistling Wonder. Haslam, John, illus. 2005. (ENG.). 24p. (J). lib. bdg. 23.65 *(978-1-59646-758-3(4))* Dingles & Co.
Rossi, Rich, illus. Pillow Fight. 2005. (I'm Going to Read(r) Ser.). (ENG.). 32p. (J). (gr. k-1). per. 3.95 *(978-1-4027-2719-1(4))* Sterling Publishing Co., Inc.
Røssland, Ingelin. Minus Me. Dawkin, Deborah, tr. from NOR. 2015. (ENG.). 288p. (gr. 4-9). pap. 10.99 *(978-1-78074-694-4(6))* Oneworld Pubns. GBR. Dist: Publishers Group West (PGW).
Roth, David. The Adventures of the Magnificent Seven. 2009. 347p. pap. 26.88 *(978-0-557-09999-3(4))* Lulu Pr., Inc.
Roth, Judith L. & Rothshank, Brooke, illus. Julia's Words. 2008. (J). (gr. -1-3). pap. 12.99 *(978-0-8361-9417-3(9))* Herald Pr.
Roth, Matthue. Candy in Action: A Novel. 2009. (ENG., Illus.). 208p. (gr. 8). pap. *(978-1-59376-228-5(3))* Ebury Publishing.
Roth, Megan. Bright Books: Bubble's Ocean Friends. Hayashi, Emiri, illus. 2016. (Bright Bks.). (ENG.). 12p. (J). bds. 14.99 *(978-1-62686-716-1(X),* Silver Dolphin Bks.) Readerlink Distribution Services, LLC.
Rothenberg, B. Annye. I Want to Make Friends: A Story for Kids in Preschool & Kindergarten & a Guidance Section for Parents. Bright, Bonnie, illus. 2012. 48p. (J). pap. 9.95 *(978-0-9790420-4-1(6))* Perfecting Parenting Pr.
Rothenberger, Charlene. Kara's Kapers with Katy Pillar. Rothenberger, Boyd & Bays, Gail, illus. 2006. 64p. per. 9.99 *(978-0-9776260-6-9(7))* Bearhead Publishing, LLC.
Rothstein, Evelyn. Evelyn & the Two Evas. Uhlig, Elizabeth, illus. 2013. 63p. (YA). pap. 12.95 *(978-0-9834030-5-0(8))* Marble Hse. Editions.
Rotter, Laura. Terratorv. 2009. 32p. pap. 12.99 *(978-1-4490-3092-6(0))* AuthorHouse.
Rottgen, Barbara. A Friend Like You. Julian, Sean, illus. 2016. (ENG.). 32p. (J). (gr. -1-2). 16.99 *(978-1-68010-031-0(9))* Tiger Tales.
Rouse, Walt. The Adventures of Clever Kitty. Bowker, Margie, illus. 2013. 56p. pap. *(978-1-4602-1254-7(1))* FriesenPress.
Rouss, Sylvia A. Sammy Spider's New Friend. Kahn, Katherine, illus. 2012. (Kar-Ben Favorites Ser.). (ENG.). 32p. (J). (gr. -1-2). lib. bdg. 17.95 *(978-0-7613-6663-8(6),* Kar-Ben Publishing) Lerner Publishing Group.
Rouss, Sylvia A. Sammy Spider's Passover Shapes. Kahn, Katherine Janus, illus. 2017. (Passover Ser.). (ENG.). 12p. (gr. -1 — 1). 23.99 ***(978-1-5124-2727-1(6),*** Kar-Ben Publishing) Lerner Publishing Group.
Rouss, Sylvia A. & Janus Kahn, Katherine. Sammy Spider's New Friend. 2012. (Kar-Ben Favorites Ser.). (ENG., Illus.). 32p. (J). (gr. -1-3). 7.95 *(978-0-7613-6664-5(4),* Kar-Ben Publishing) Lerner Publishing Group.
Rousselow, Jeff. Bury the Dead. 2009. 244p. pap. 15.26 *(978-0-557-07129-6(1))* Lulu Pr., Inc.
Rowe, Eva McKenzie & Hodge, Darren. Harrison Bean. 2012. 28p. pap. 24.95 *(978-1-4626-6503-7(9))* America Star Bks.
Rowe, W. W. Jerry's Madness. 2015. (ENG., Illus.). 98p. (J). (gr. 3-7). pap. 8.95 *(978-1-936012-68-8(5))* Larson Pubns.
—Jerry's Mystery. 2016. (ENG., Illus.). 96p. (J). (gr. 6-9). pap. 8.95 *(978-1-936012-70-1(7))* Larson Pubns.
Rowles, Louis. Ida Claire Decorates with Flair. Brownlee, Sunny, illus. 2004. 24p. (J). pap. *(978-0-9708748-1-8(2))* Rowles, Louis.
Roy, Alene Adele. The Legend of Dragonfly Pond: Coloring Book. 2008. 56p. pap. 11.99 *(978-1-4343-4628-5(5))* AuthorHouse.
Roy, James. Chaz & the Missing Mayo. Gorissen, Dean, illus. 2015. (J). pap. *(978-1-4966-0245-9(5))* Capstone Classroom.
—Max Quigley: Technically Not a Bully. 2009. (ENG., Illus.). 208p. (J). (gr. 2-5). 14.99 *(978-0-547-15263-9(9))* Houghton Mifflin Harcourt Publishing Co.
Roy, Ron. A to Z Mysteries Collection, No. 1. Gurney, John Steven, illus. 2010. (to Z Mysteries Ser.: Nos. 1-4). (ENG.). 384p. (J). (gr. 1-4). 9.99 *(978-0-375-85946-5(2),* Random Hse. Bks. for Young Readers) Random Hse. Children's Bks.
A Royal Tea. 2014. (Mermaid Tales Ser.: 9). (ENG., Illus.). 112p. (J). (gr. 1-4). pap. 5.99 *(978-1-4814-0254-5(4),* Aladdin) Simon & Schuster Children's Publishing.
Roys, Julie. Outside the Window. 2012. 24p. pap. 21.00 *(978-1-4669-3092-6(6))* Trafford Publishing.
Roza, Greg. Out & About. 2006. (Neighborhood Readers Ser.). (ENG.). 8p. (gr. -1-3). pap. 5.15 *(978-1-4042-5680-4(6),* Rosen Classroom) Rosen Publishing Group, Inc., The.
Rozman, Jennifer Blue. With You Forever. 2011. 24p. pap. 11.95 *(978-1-4520-9941-5(3))* AuthorHouse.
Rubens, Michael. Emily & the Spellstone. 2017. (ENG.). 288p. (J). (gr. 5-7). 16.99 *(978-0-544-79086-5(3))* Houghton Mifflin Harcourt Publishing Co.
Rubin, Bruce Joel & Michaels, Julie. Stuart Little 2 Vol. 2: El Libro de la Película. 2003. (SPA., Illus.). 60p. (J). (gr. 3-5). 14.95 *(978-84-204-6503-6(8))* Santillana USA Publishing Co., Inc.
Rubin, Diana. King Choco the Great. 2009. 45p. (J). pap. 10.95 *(978-1-4327-2972-1(1))* Outskirts Pr., Inc.
Rucker, Mike. Terry & the Earthquake. 2006. (Terry the Tractor Ser.: Vol. 14). 72p. (J). (gr. k-4). pap. 4.95 *(978-0-9711659-5-3(5))* Univ. Editions.
Rud, Jeff. High & Inside, 1 vol. 2006. (ENG.). 180p. (J). (gr. 3-7). per. 7.95 *(978-1-55143-532-9(2))* Orca Bk. Pubs. USA.
Rudetsky, Seth. My Awesome - Awful Popularity Plan. 2013. (ENG.). 224p. (YA). (gr. 7). pap. 8.99 *(978-0-375-89997-3(9),* Ember) Random Hse. Children's Bks.
Ruditis, Paul. Entrances & Exits. 2008. (Drama! Ser.). (ENG.). 256p. (YA). (gr. 9). pap. 12.99 *(978-1-4169-5906-9(8),* Simon Pulse) Simon Pulse.
Rue, Ginger. Aleca Zamm Is a Wonder. Persico, Zoe, illus. 2017. (Aleca Zamm Ser.: 1). (ENG.). 160p. (J). (gr. 2-5). 16.99 ***(978-1-4814-7061-2(2),*** Aladdin) Simon & Schuster Children's Publishing.
Rue, Nancy N. Sophie Steps Up, 1 vol. 2009. (Faithgirlz! Ser.: No. 4). (ENG.). 128p. (J). pap. 6.99 *(978-0-310-71841-3(4))* Zonderkidz.
Ruggieri, J. G. Weather Changes, Mountains Move, & Islands Disappear. 2012. 168p. pap. 15.00 *(978-0-9860300-0-0(7))* Alabaster Bk. Pub.
Ruiz-Flores, Lupe. The Battle of the Snow Cones/La Guerra de las Raspas. 2010. (SPA.). 32p. (J). (gr. -1-3). 16.95 *(978-1-55885-575-5(0),* Piñata Books) Arte Publico Pr.
Rule, Rebecca. The Iciest, Diciest, Scariest Sled Ride Ever!, 1 vol. Thermes, Jennifer, illus. 2012. (ENG.). 36p. (J). 17.95 *(978-1-934031-88-9(7),* 7e0b5554-6142-497e-ae8f-c0cb24d9743a) Islandport Pr., Inc.
Rundell, Katherine. The Explorer. 2017. (ENG., Illus.). 336p. (J). (gr. 3-7). 16.99 ***(978-1-4814-1945-1(5),*** Simon & Schuster Bks. For Young Readers) Simon & Schuster Bks. For Young Readers.
Rundstrom, T. S. Baribold Jones & Big Big Booger Grabber. 2004. (Illus.). per. *(978-1-932062-43-4(2))* Hability Solution Services, Inc.
Runholt, Susan. The Mystery of the Third Lucretia. 2009. (Kari & Lucas Mystery Ser.). (ENG.). 304p. (J). (gr. 5-18). pap. 6.99 *(978-0-14-241338-8(0),* Puffin Books) Penguin Young Readers Group.
—Rescuing Seneca Crane. 2009. (Kari & Lucas Mystery Ser.). (ENG.). 288p. (J). (gr. 5-18). 16.99 *(978-0-670-06291-1(X),* Viking Books for Young Readers) Penguin Young Readers Group.
Runkle, Toni & Webb, Stephen. Glitter Girl. 2013. (ENG.). 256p. (J). (gr. 4-7). pap. 7.99 *(978-1-4022-8557-8(4),* Sourcebooks Jabberwocky) Sourcebooks, Inc.
Running Press Staff. Berry Best Friends. 2009. (Miniature Editions Ser.). (ENG.). 128p. 5.95 *(978-0-7624-3589-0(5),* Running Pr.) Running Pr. Bk. Pubs.
Running Press Staff & Hello Kitty Staff. Hello Kitty: A Little Book of Happiness. 2009. (Miniature Editions Ser.). (ENG.). 96p. 5.95 *(978-0-7624-3594-4(1))* Running Pr. Bk. Pubs.
Runton, Andy. Owly & Wormy, Bright Lights & Starry Nights. Runton, Andy, illus. 2012. (ENG., Illus.). 40p. (J). (gr. -1-3). 17.99 *(978-1-4169-5775-1(8),* Atheneum Bks. for Young Readers) Simon & Schuster Children's Publishing.
Rupert, Rona. Straw Sense. 2013. (ENG., Illus.). 36p. (J). (gr. k-3). 17.99 *(978-1-4814-0151-7(3),* Simon & Schuster Bks. For Young Readers) Simon & Schuster Bks. For Young Readers.
Rusch, Elizabeth. Muddy Max: The Mystery of Marsh Creek. Lawrence, Mike, illus. 2014. (ENG.). 224p. (J). pap. 9.99 *(978-1-4494-3561-5(0))* Andrews McMeel Publishing.
Rusch, Elizabeth & Lawrence, Mike. Muddy Max: The Mystery of Marsh Creek. 2016. (ENG., Illus.). (J). (gr. 2-6). 37.99 ***(978-1-4494-7388-4(1))*** Andrews McMeel Publishing.
Rushford, Betty. Best Buddies: And the Fruit of the Spirit. 2003. 41p. pap. 24.95 *(978-1-59286-746-2(4))* America Star Bks.
Rushford, Patricia H. Secrets of Ghost Island. 2007. (J). *(978-88-02-46255-4(0))* Moody Pubs.
Russell, B. M. My Friend Bianca. 2010. 32p. 13.95 *(978-1-4497-0168-0(X),* WestBow Pr.) Author Solutions, Inc.
Russell, David O. & Auseon, Andrew. Alienated. 2010. (ENG.). 352p. (J). (gr. 3-7). pap. 5.99 *(978-1-4169-8299-9(X),* Aladdin) Simon & Schuster Children's Publishing.
Russell, Maureen Annette. MR & Mrs Universe & Their Four Best Friends. Caiafa, Laura, illus. 2017. (ENG.). (J). (gr. k-2). ***(978-1-84327-934-1(7))*** Electric Bk. Co.
Russell, Natalie. Brown Rabbit in the City. 2010. (ENG.). 40p. (J). (gr. -1-k). 16.99 *(978-0-670-01234-3(3),* Viking Books for Young Readers) Penguin Young Readers Group.
—Home Sweet Hamish. 2008. (Bloomsbury Paperbacks Ser.). (ENG., Illus.). 32p. (J). (gr. -1-2). pap. 10.95 *(978-0-7475-8319-6(6))* Bloomsbury Publishing Plc GBR. Dist: Independent Pubs. Group.
Russell, P. M. The Wormhole Adventures: Travel Is Relative. 2007. 57p. pap. 16.95 *(978-1-60441-426-4(X))* America Star Bks.
Russell, Paul. Immaculate Blue: A Novel. 2015. (ENG., Illus.). 340p. pap. 16.95 *(978-1-62778-095-7(5))* Cleis Pr.
Russell, Rachel Renée. Dork Diaries Set, Set. Russell, Rachel Renée, illus. 2011. (Dork Diaries: Nos. 1-3). (ENG., Illus.). 928p. (J). (gr. 4-8). 41.99 *(978-1-4424-2662-7(4),* Aladdin) Simon & Schuster Children's Publishing.
—How to Dork Your Diary. Russell, Rachel Renée, illus. 2011. (Dork Diaries: No. 3.5). (ENG., Illus.). 288p. (J). (gr. 4-8). 13.99 *(978-1-4424-2233-9(5),* Aladdin) Simon & Schuster Children's Publishing.
—Tales from a Not-So-Dorky Drama Queen, 3 vols. unabr. ed. 2015. (Dork Diaries: 8). (ENG.). 320p. (gr. 4-8). audio compact disk 14.99 *(978-1-4423-7023-4(8))* Simon & Schuster Audio.
—Tales from a Not-So-Dorky Drama Queen. Russell, Rachel Renée, illus. 2015. (Dork Diaries: Bk. 9). (ENG., Illus.). 352p. (J). (gr. 4-8). 13.99 *(978-1-4424-8769-7(0),* Aladdin Paperbacks) Simon & Schuster Children's Publishing.
—Tales from a Not-So-Fabulous Life. Russell, Rachel Renée, illus. 2009. (Dork Diaries: 1). (ENG., Illus.). 304p. (J). (gr. 4-8). 13.99 *(978-1-4169-8006-3(7),* Aladdin) Simon & Schuster Children's Publishing.
—Tales from a Not-So-Fabulous Life. 2009. (Dork Diaries: 1). lib. bdg. 25.75 *(978-0-606-32419-9(4),* Turtleback) Turtleback Bks.
—Tales from a Not-So-Friendly Frenemy. Russell, Rachel Renée, illus. 2016. (Dork Diaries: 11). (ENG., Illus.). 288p. (J). (gr. 4-8). 13.99 *(978-1-4814-7920-2(2),* Aladdin) Simon & Schuster Children's Publishing.
—Tales from a Not-So-Glam TV Star. Russell, Rachel Renée, illus. 2014. (Dork Diaries: 7). (ENG., Illus.). 336p. (J). (gr. 4-8). 13.99 *(978-1-4424-8767-3(4),* Aladdin) Simon & Schuster Children's Publishing.
—Tales from a Not-So-Glam TV Star. 2014. (Dork Diaries: 7). lib. bdg. 25.75 *(978-0-606-36240-5(1))* Turtleback Bks.
—Tales from a Not-So-Graceful Ice Princess. Russell, Rachel Renée, illus. 2012. (Dork Diaries: 4). (ENG., Illus.). 368p. (J). (gr. 4-8). 13.99 *(978-1-4424-1192-0(9),* Aladdin) Simon & Schuster Children's Publishing.
—Tales from a Not-So-Happy Heartbreaker. 2013. (Dork Diaries: 6). lib. bdg. 25.75 *(978-0-606-32424-3(0),* Turtleback) Turtleback Bks.
—Tales from a Not-So-Popular Party Girl. Russell, Rachel Renée, illus. 2010. (Dork Diaries: 2). (ENG., Illus.). 288p. (J). (gr. 4-8). 13.99 *(978-1-4169-8008-7(3),* Aladdin) Simon & Schuster Children's Publishing.
—Tales from a Not-So-Popular Party Girl. 2010. (Dork Diaries: 2). lib. bdg. 25.75 *(978-0-606-32420-5(8),* Turtleback) Turtleback Bks.
—Tales from a Not-So-Smart Miss Know-It-All. Russell, Rachel Renée, illus. 2012. (Dork Diaries: 5). (ENG., Illus.). 368p. (J). (gr. 4-8). 13.99 *(978-1-4424-4961-9(6),* Aladdin) Simon & Schuster Children's Publishing.
—Tales from a Not-So-Talented Pop Star. Russell, Rachel Renée, illus. 2011. (Dork Diaries: 3). (ENG., Illus.). 336p. (J). (gr. 4-8). 13.99 *(978-1-4424-1190-6(2),* Aladdin) Simon & Schuster Children's Publishing.
Russell, Rachel Renée, et al. Tales from a Not-So-Popular Party Girl. 2010. (ENG.). pap. *(978-1-4424-4042-5(2),* Aladdin Paperbacks) Simon & Schuster Children's Publishing.
Russo, Marisabina. Sophie Sleeps Over. Russo, Marisabina, illus. 2014. (ENG., Illus.). 32p. (J). (gr. -1-2). 16.99 *(978-1-59643-933-7(5),* 9781596439337) Roaring Brook Pr.
Russo, Richard. Bridge of Sighs. 2007. *(978-0-7393-2751-7(8))* Random Hse. Large Print.
Rustrian, Edvin E. The Adventures of Timmy & Jay. 2010. 24p. pap. 15.99 *(978-1-4535-3792-3(9))* Xlibris Corp.
Ruth, Nick. The Breezes of Inspire. Concannon, Sue, illus. 2005. (Remin Chronicles: 2). (ENG.). 264p. (J). (gr. 3-7). 16.95 *(978-0-9745603-3-5(2))* Imaginator Pr.
Ruzima, Keza. Girl Power: The Adventures of a Teenage Circle. 2009. 112p. pap. 23.75 *(978-1-60860-647-4(3),* Eloquent Bks.) Strategic Book Publishing & Rights Agency (SBPRA).
Ruzzier, Sergio. The Little Giant. 2004. (Illus.). 32p. (J). (gr. -1-2). 16.89 *(978-0-06-052952-9(0),* Geringer, Laura Book) HarperCollins Pubs.
—Too Busy. Ruzzier, Sergio, illus. 2014. (Bear & Bee Ser.). (ENG., Illus.). 48p. (J). (gr. -1-k). 14.99 *(978-1-4231-5961-2(6))* Disney Pr.
Ryan, Carrie & Davis, John Parke. City of Thirst. (Map to Everywhere Ser.: 2). (ENG., Illus.). (J). (gr. 3-7). 2016. 416p. pap. 7.99 *(978-0-316-24082-6(6))* 2015. 400p. 17.00 *(978-0-316-24084-0(2))* Little, Brown Bks. for Young Readers.
Ryan, Darlene. Cuts Like a Knife, 1 vol. 2012. (Orca Soundings Ser.). (ENG.). 128p. (YA). (gr. 8-12). 16.95 *(978-1-4598-0120-2(2));* pap. 9.95 *(978-1-4598-0119-6(9))* Orca Bk. Pubs. USA.
—Pieces of Me, 1 vol. 2012. (ENG.). 240p. (YA). (gr. 8-12). pap. 12.95 *(978-1-4598-0080-9(X))* Orca Bk. Pubs. USA.
—Responsible, 1 vol. 2007. (Orca Soundings Ser.). (ENG.). (YA). (gr. 8-12). 128p. pap. 9.95 *(978-1-55143-685-2(X));* 112p. lib. bdg. 14.95 *(978-1-55143-687-6(6))* Orca Bk. Pubs. USA.
Ryan, Margaret. Littlest Dragon. Smith, Jamie, illus. 2011. (ENG.). 80p. (J). (gr. 2-4). pap. 5.99 *(978-0-00-714163-0(7),* HarperCollins Children's Bks.) HarperCollins Pubs. Ltd. GBR. Dist: HarperCollins Pubs.
Ryan, Matthew. The Box. 2012. (ENG.). pap. *(978-1-4675-2638-8(X))* Independent Pub.
Ryan, Nancy. The Bookworm & His New Book. 2012. 32p. pap. 24.95 *(978-1-4626-6492-4(X))* America Star Bks.
Ryan, P. E. Saints of Augustine. 2007. 308p. (YA). (gr. 7-18). 16.99 *(978-0-06-085810-0(9));* lib. bdg. 17.89 *(978-0-06-085811-7(7))* HarperCollins Pubs. (HarperTeen).
Ryan, Pam Muñoz. Tony Baloney: Pen Pal. Fotheringham, Ed, illus. 2014. 39p. (J). pap. *(978-0-545-69227-4(X),* Scholastic Pr.) Scholastic, Inc.
—Tony Baloney: Pen Pal. Fotheringham, Edwin, illus. 2015. (Tony Baloney Ser.). (ENG.). 40p. (J). (gr. k-2). 6.99 *(978-0-545-65037-3(2),* Scholastic Pr.) Scholastic, Inc.
Ryan, Tom. Way to Go, 1 vol. 2012. (ENG.). 224p. (YA). (gr. 8-12). pap. 12.95 *(978-1-4598-0077-9(X))* Orca Bk. Pubs. USA.
Rycroft, Frederick. Young World: Book Two - Friends 'Til the End. 2012. 568p. pap. 23.99 *(978-1-4797-1311-0(2))* Xlibris Corp.
Ryder, Chloe. Best Friends Forever! 2015. (Princess Ponies Ser.). (ENG., Illus.). 128p. (YA). (gr. 2-4). pap. 5.99 *(978-1-61963-405-3(8),* 9781619634053, Bloomsbury USA Childrens) Bloomsbury Publishing USA.
—A Dream Come True. 2014. (Princess Ponies Ser.). (ENG., Illus.). 128p. (YA). (gr. 1-3). pap. 5.99 *(978-1-61963-167-0(9),* 9781619631670, Bloomsbury USA Childrens) Bloomsbury Publishing USA.
—A Magical Friend. 2014. (Princess Ponies Ser.). (ENG., Illus.). 128p. (J). (gr. 1-3). pap. 5.99 *(978-1-61963-165-6(2),* 9781619631656, Bloomsbury USA Childrens) Bloomsbury Publishing USA.
—Princess Ponies 7: a Special Surprise. 2015. (Princess Ponies Ser.). (ENG., Illus.). 128p. (J). (gr. 2-4). pap. 5.99 *(978-1-61963-565-4(8),* 9781619635654, Bloomsbury USA Childrens) Bloomsbury Publishing USA.
Rylander, Chris. The Fourth Stall. 2011. (Fourth Stall Ser.: 1). (ENG.). 320p. (J). (gr. 3-7). 16.99 *(978-0-06-199496-8(0),* Waldon Pond Pr.) HarperCollins Pubs.
Rylant, Cynthia. Annie & Snowball & the Magical House. Stevenson, Suçie, illus. (Annie & Snowball Ser.: 7). (ENG.). 40p. (J). (gr. k-2). 2011. pap. 3.99 *(978-1-4169-3949-8(0))* 2010. 16.99 *(978-1-4169-3945-0(8))* Simon Spotlight. (Simon Spotlight).
—Annie & Snowball & the Prettiest House. Stevenson, Suçie, illus. (Annie & Snowball Ser.: 2). (ENG.). 40p. (J). (gr. k-2). 2008. pap. 3.99 *(978-1-4169-1460-0(9))* 2007. 16.99 *(978-1-4169-0939-2(7))* Simon Spotlight. (Simon Spotlight).
—Annie & Snowball & the Thankful Friends. 2012. (Annie & Snowball Ready-To-Read Ser.). lib. bdg. 13.55 *(978-0-606-26917-9(7),* Turtleback) Turtleback Bks.
—A Fine White Dust. 2006. (ENG.). 112p. (J). (gr. 5-9). pap. 6.99 *(978-1-4169-2769-3(7),* Atheneum Bks. for Young Readers) Simon & Schuster Children's Publishing.
—The High-Rise Private Eyes Series. Karas, G. Brian, illus. 2003. pap. 61.95 incl. audio *(978-1-59112-430-6(1));* pap. 68.95 incl. audio compact disk *(978-1-59112-858-8(7))* Live Oak Media.
—Mr. Putter & Tabby Hit the Slope. Howard, Arthur, illus. 2016. (Mr. Putter & Tabby Ser.). (ENG.). 40p. (J). (gr. 1-4). 14.99 *(978-0-15-206427-3(3),* HMH Books For Young Readers) Houghton Mifflin Harcourt Publishing Co.
—Poppleton. Teague, Mark, illus. 2015. 56p. pap. 4.00 *(978-1-61003-551-4(8))* Center for the Collaborative Classroom.
—Poppleton in Winter. Teague, Mark, illus. 2008. 48p. (gr. -1-3). 14.00 *(978-0-7569-8910-1(8))* Perfection Learning Corp.
—Poppleton in Winter, Level 3. Teague, Mark, illus. 2008. (Scholastic Reader Level 3 Ser.). (ENG.). 56p. (J). (gr. -1-3). pap. 3.99 *(978-0-545-06823-9(1),* Cartwheel Bks.) Scholastic, Inc.
—Poppleton Se Divierte. Teague, Mark, illus. 2006. (Poppleton Ser.). (SPA.). 48p. pap. 11.73 *(978-0-15-356487-1(3))* Harcourt Children's Bks.
—Puppy Mudge Finds a Friend. Stevenson, Suçie, illus. 2005. (Puppy Mudge Ser.). (ENG.). 32p. (J). (gr. -1-k). pap. 3.99 *(978-1-4169-0369-7(0),* Simon Spotlight) Simon Spotlight.
—Thimbleberry Stories. Kneen, Maggie, illus. 2006. (ENG.). 64p. (J). (gr. -1-3). reprint ed. pap. 8.99 *(978-0-15-205645-2(9))* Houghton Mifflin Harcourt Publishing Co.
S. P. Glynn, Annie S. P. Glynn. Jodie's Adventures with Aunty Ann. 2016. (ENG.). 26p. (J). (gr. 3-4). mass mkt. 10.95 *(978-1-78612-838-6(1),* 66ce91c5-aae4-4fb3-864f-1d2ff1cbc8b5) Austin, Stan AUS. Dist: Bookmasters Distribution.
Sachar, Louis. Buchi nel Deserto. (ITA.). pap. 16.95 *(978-88-384-3651-2(7))* Edizioni PIEMME spa ITA. Dist: Distribooks, Inc.
—Buracos. pap. 29.95 *(978-85-336-1280-8(X))* Livraria Martins Editora BRA. Dist: Distribooks, Inc.
—Holes. 2008. (KOR., Illus.). 334p. (J). pap. *(978-89-364-5602-3(4))* Chang-jag and Bipyeong Co.
—Holes. 10th ed. 2008. (ENG., Illus.). 272p. (J). (gr. 4-8). 18.99 *(978-0-374-33266-2(5),* 9780374332662, Farrar, Straus & Giroux (BYR)) Farrar, Straus & Giroux.
—Holes. 2008. (ENG.). (J). 39.99 *(978-0-7393-7103-9(7))* Findaway World, LLC.
—Holes. 2014. (CHI & ENG.). 246p. (J). (gr. 4-8). pap. *(978-7-5442-7158-5(7))* Fukuinkan Shoten.
—Holes. 2009. 9.14 *(978-0-7848-1394-2(9),* Everbind) Marco Bk. Co.
—Holes. 240p. (J). (gr. 4-6). pap. 5.99 *(978-0-8072-8073-7(9),* Listening Library) Random Hse. Audio Publishing Group.
—Holes, 4 vols. (J). 2006. 46.75 *(978-1-4193-6136-4(8))* 2004. 1.25 *(978-1-4025-6758-2(8))* Recorded Bks., Inc.
—Holes. l.t. ed. 2003. 288p. pap. 10.95 *(978-0-7862-6190-1(0))* Thorndike Pr.
—Marvin Redpost #8: a Magic Crystal? Record, Adam, illus. 2015. (Marvin Redpost Ser.: 8). (ENG.). 96p. (J). (gr. 1-4). lib. bdg. 12.99 *(978-0-553-53546-4(3),* Random Hse. Bks. for Young Readers) Random Hse. Children's Bks.
—Le Passage. pap. 22.95 *(978-2-211-05287-0(8))* Archimede Editions FRA. Dist: Distribooks, Inc.
Sackanay, Kathleen. Adventures in the Forest. Wood, Morgan, illus. 2007. 24p. (J). pap. 8.45 *(978-0-9791276-2-5(9))* Athanatos Publishing Group.
The Sacrament Series. 2005. (J). *(978-0-9772007-0-2(1))* Layne Morgan Media, Inc.
Saddleback Educational Publishing Staff, ed. Dark Suspicions. 2012. (Urban Underground Ser.). (ENG.). 16p. (YA). (gr. 9-12). tchr. ed. 6.50 incl. cd-rom *(978-1-61651-968-1(1))* Saddleback Educational Publishing, Inc.
—Don't Blame Me. 2011. (Carter High Chronicles Ser.). (ENG.). 16p. (YA). (gr. 9-12). tchr. ed. 7.95 incl. cd-rom *(978-1-61651-317-7(9))* Saddleback Educational Publishing, Inc.
—The Easy Way. 2011. (Carter High Chronicles Ser.). (ENG.). 16p. (YA). (gr. 9-12). tchr. ed. 7.95 incl. cd-rom *(978-1-61651-316-0(0))* Saddleback Educational Publishing, Inc.
—The Fastest Runner. 2011. (Carter High Chronicles Ser.). (ENG.). 16p. (YA). (gr. 9-12). cd-rom 7.95 *(978-1-61651-318-4(7))* Saddleback Educational Publishing, Inc.
—It Does Matter. 2011. (Carter High Senior Year Ser.). (ENG.). 16p. (YA). (gr. 9-12). tchr. ed. 7.95 incl. cd-rom *(978-1-61651-334-4(9))* Saddleback Educational Publishing, Inc.
—It Is Not a Date. 2011. (Carter High Chronicles Ser.). (ENG.). 16p. (YA). (gr. 9-12). cd-rom 7.95 *(978-1-61651-319-1(5))* Saddleback Educational Publishing, Inc.
—Just Be Yourself. 2011. (Carter High Senior Year Ser.). (ENG.). 16p. (YA). (gr. 9-12). cd-rom 7.95 *(978-1-61651-335-1(7))* Saddleback Educational Publishing, Inc.
—One Date Too Many. 2011. (Carter High Chronicles Ser.). (ENG.). 16p. (YA). (gr. 9-12). tchr. ed. 7.95 incl. cd-rom *(978-1-61651-320-7(9))* Saddleback Educational Publishing, Inc.
—One More Chance. 2011. (Carter High Senior Year Ser.). (ENG.). 16p. (YA). (gr. 9-12). cd-rom 7.95 *(978-1-61651-337-5(3))* Saddleback Educational Publishing, Inc.

EFG

—Right Kind of Win. 2011. (Carter High Chronicles Ser.). (ENG.). 16p. (YA). (gr. 9-12). cd-rom 7.95 *(978-1-61651-321-4(7))* Saddleback Educational Publishing, Inc.

—Someone to Count On. 2011. (Carter High Senior Year Ser.). (ENG.). 16p. (YA). (gr. 9-12). cd-rom 7.95 *(978-1-61651-338-2(1))* Saddleback Educational Publishing, Inc.

—Time to Move. 2011. (Carter High Senior Year Ser.). (ENG.). 16p. (YA). (gr. 9-12). tchr. ed. 7.95 incl. cd-rom *(978-1-61651-339-9(X))* Saddleback Educational Publishing, Inc.

—Too Late. 2011. (Carter High Chronicles Ser.). (ENG.). 16p. (YA). (gr. 9-12). cd-rom 7.95 *(978-1-61651-322-1(5))* Saddleback Educational Publishing, Inc.

Sadler, Marilyn. Alice from Dallas. Hoyt, Ard, illus. 2014. (ENG.). 40p. (J). (gr. k-2). 16.95 *(978-1-4197-0790-2(6),* Abrams Bks. for Young Readers) Abrams, Inc.

Sáenz, Benjamin Alire. Aristotle & Dante Discover the Secrets of the Universe. (ENG., Illus.). 368p. (YA). (gr. 7). 2014. pap. 12.99 *(978-1-4424-0893-7(6))* 2012. 21.99 *(978-1-4424-0892-0(8))* Simon & Schuster Bks. For Young Readers. (Simon & Schuster Bks. For Young Readers).

—Aristotle & Dante Discover the Secrets of the Universe. 2014. lib. bdg. 23.30 *(978-0-606-35117-1(5))* Turtleback Bks.

—He Forgot to Say Goodbye. 2010. (ENG.). 352p. (YA). (gr. 7). pap. 12.99 *(978-1-4169-9434-3(3),* Simon & Schuster Bks. For Young Readers) Simon & Schuster Bks. For Young Readers.

—The Inexplicable Logic of My Life. 2017. (ENG.). 464p. (gr. 7). 17.99 *(978-0-544-58650-5(6))* Houghton Mifflin Harcourt Publishing Co.

Safran, Sheri. The Magic Carousel: A Book & Removable 3-D Play Carousel. Safran, Sheri, illus. 2011. (ENG., Illus.). 6p. (J). (gr. -1-k). 24.99 *(978-1-85707-800-8(4))* Tango Bks. GBR. Dist: Independent Pubs. Group.

Saft, Lauren. Those Girls. 2016. (ENG.). 336p. (YA). (gr. 10-17). pap. 9.99 *(978-0-316-26016-9(9),* Poppy) Little, Brown Bks. for Young Readers.

Sagar, Marie. Princess Samantha? 2009. 20p. pap. 12.49 *(978-1-4389-5297-0(X))* AuthorHouse.

Sage, Angie. Todhunter Moon: Sandrider. Zug, Mark, illus. 2016. (Septimus Heap: TodHunter Moon Ser.: 2). (ENG.). 496p. (J). (gr. 3-7). 18.40 *(978-0-606-39255-6(6))* Turtleback Bks.

Sage, Cathryn. Destiny's Secret. 2012. 44p. (-18). pap. 21.99 *(978-1-4389-1530-2(6))* AuthorHouse.

Said, Taunya D. Smart Alec- Alex: The 5th Grade Schedule Change. 2009. 53p. (YA). pap. 10.95 *(978-1-4327-4167-7(X))* Outskirts Pr., Inc.

Sakai, Komako. Emily's Balloon. 2015. (ENG., Illus.). 44p. (J). (gr. -1-7). pap. 7.99 *(978-1-4521-4567-9(9))* Chronicle Bks. LLC.

Salas-Tristan, M. U. Rocky's ABC Book with His Friends: Photographic Bilingual. 2012. (ENG.). 32p. (J). pap. 29.95 *(978-1-4327-9381-4(0))* Outskirts Pr., Inc.

Saldana, Rene. The Whole Sky Full of Stars. 2008. (ENG.). 144p. (YA). (gr. 7-11). mass mkt. 5.99 *(978-0-440-23791-4(2),* Laurel Leaf) Random Hse. Children's Bks.

Saldana, Theresa. The Almost Murder & Other Stories. 2008. (ENG.). 144p. (YA). (gr. 6-18). pap. 10.95 *(978-1-55885-507-6(6),* Piñata Books) Arte Publico Pr.

Saldivar, Jose A. The Adventures of Oskar: Oskar's New School. Nilsson, Janet Busbey, ed. Jasnoch, Dorothy, illus. 2013. (ENG.). 32p. pap. 13.99 *(978-1-937752-07-1(0))* Owl About Bks. Pub., Inc.

Saleem-Muhammad, Rasheedah. My Friend Michael: A Short Story about Autism - A Pedro Collection. Harris, - Crystal, illus. 2011. 30p. 19.95 *(978-1-4575-0295-8(X));* pap. 14.95 *(978-1-4575-0037-4(X))* Dog Ear Publishing, LLC.

Salerno, Tony. Dog Tired: A Learning Adventure in Perseverance. 4 vols. 2005. 56p. (J). 14.99 *(978-0-89221-605-5(0))* New Leaf Pub. Group.

—A Sticky Situation: A Learning Adventure in Honesty. 2005. 56p. (J). 14.99 *(978-0-89221-606-2(9))* New Leaf Pub. Group.

—Wise Quacks: A Learning Adventure in Self-Control. 4 vols. 2005. 56p. (J). 14.99 *(978-0-89221-604-8(2))* New Leaf Pub. Group.

Sales, Leila. Mostly Good Girls. (ENG.). 368p. (YA). (gr. 9). 2011. pap. 9.99 *(978-1-4424-0680-3(1))* 2010. 17.99 *(978-1-4424-0679-7(8))* Simon Pulse. (Simon Pulse).

—Once Was a Time: An Alliteration Adventure. 2016. (ENG., Illus.). 272p. (J). (gr. 5-17). 16.99 *(978-1-4521-4009-4(X))* Chronicle Bks. LLC.

Salisbury, Graham. House of the Red Fish. 2014. (ENG.). 318p. (YA). (gr. 7). pap. 9.99 *(978-0-385-38657-9(5),* Ember) Random Hse. Children's Bks.

Salisbury, Linda G. Mudd Saves the Earth: Booger Glue, Cow Diapers & Other Good Ideas. 2009. (Illus.). 96p. (J). pap. 8.95 *(978-1-881539-47-6(4))* Tabby Hse. Bks.

—The Mysterious Jamestown Suitcase: A Bailey Fish Adventure. Grotke, Christopher A., illus. 2006. (Bailey Fish Adventures Ser.). 191p. (J). (gr. 3-7). per. 8.95 *(978-1-881539-43-8(1))* Tabby Hse. Bks.

—The Thief at Keswick Inn: A Bailey Fish Adventure. Grotke, Christopher A., illus. 2006. (Bailey Fish Adventures Ser.). 191p. (J). (gr. 3-7). per. 8.95 *(978-1-881539-41-4(5))* Tabby Hse. Bks.

Salmon, Casey. The Adventures of Mabel & Stinky: Mabel, Stinky, & the Terrified Toad. 2009. 44p. pap. 19.99 *(978-1-4389-7454-5(X))* AuthorHouse.

Salomon, Peter Adam. All Those Broken Angels. 2014. (ENG.). 240p. (YA). pap. 11.99 *(978-0-7387-4079-9(9),* Flux) North Star Editions.

Salter, Helen. Does Snogging Count as Exercise? 2011. (ENG.). 256p. (YA). (gr. 7). pap. 12.99 *(978-1-4424-3111-9(3),* Simon Pulse) Simon Pulse.

Salter, Michelle Lewis. The Kitty Who Found His Meeooww. Stone, Jonny, illus. 2011. 40p. pap. 24.95 *(978-1-4560-5953-8(X))* America Star Bks.

Salter, Sydney. My Big Nose & Other Natural Disasters. 2009. (ENG., Illus.). 352p. (J). (gr. 7-18). pap. 19.95 *(978-0-15-206643-7(8))* Houghton Mifflin Harcourt Publishing Co.

Saltzberg, Barney. Redbird: Friends Come in Different Sizes. 2015. (ENG., Illus.). 22p. (J). bds. 5.95 *(978-0-7611-8190-3(3))* Workman Publishing Co., Inc.

Salyers, Rita. Wood's New Collar. Stafford, Rosalee, illus. 2006. (J). per. 11.95 *(978-0-9760129-3-1(6))* The Publishing Place LLC.

Sam Finds a Friend: Social/Emotional Lap Book. (Pebble Soup Explorations Ser.). (gr. -1-18). 16.00 *(978-0-7635-7564-9(X))* Rigby Education.

Sam tiene una Amiga: Social/Emotional Lap Book. (Pebble Soup Exploraciones Ser.). (SPA.). (gr. -1-18). 16.00 *(978-0-7578-1785-4(8))* Rigby Education.

Samarasinghe, Sara. Dalaina. 2007. 352p. pap. 18.95 *(978-0-9798997-2-0(9))* ITeenBooks Inc.

Samarripas, Gloria. In Search for Lucky's Lost Toys. 2006. 17.00 *(978-0-8059-7329-7(X))* Dorrance Publishing Co., Inc.

Sampson, Jeff. Havoc: A Deviants Novel. 2012. (Deviants Ser.: 2). (ENG.). 352p. (YA). (gr. 8). 17.99 *(978-0-06-199278-0(X))* HarperCollins Pubs.

—Ravage: A Deviants Novel. 2013. (Deviants Ser.: 3). (ENG.). 400p. (YA). (gr. 8). 17.99 *(978-0-06-199280-3(1))* HarperCollins Pubs.

—Vesper. 2011. (Deviants Ser.: 1). (ENG.). 304p. (YA). (gr. 8-18). 16.99 *(978-0-06-199276-6(3))* HarperCollins Pubs.

—Vesper: A Deviants Novel. 2011. (Deviants Ser.: 1). (ENG.). 320p. (YA). (gr. 8). pap. 8.99 *(978-0-06-199277-3(1))* HarperCollins Pubs.

Samuels, Jack. The Town of Masquerade. Snider, K. C., illus. 2012. 20p. pap. 9.95 *(978-1-61633-329-4(4))* Guardian Angel Publishing, Inc.

Samuels, Vallerie. The Village of Time. 2005. 9.00 *(978-0-8059-9709-5(1))* Dorrance Publishing Co., Inc.

San Souci, Robert D. Six Foolish Fishermen. 1 vol. Kennedy, Doug, illus. 2011. (ENG.). 32p. (J). (gr. k-3). 16.99 *(978-1-4556-1473-8(4))* Pelican Publishing Co., Inc.

Sanchez, Alex. Getting It. Mehta, Sangeeta, ed. 2007. (ENG., Illus.). 240p. (YA). (gr. 7-12). pap. 8.99 *(978-1-4169-0898-2(6),* Simon & Schuster Bks. For Young Readers) Simon & Schuster Bks. For Young Readers.

—The God Box. Del Rosario, Michael, ed. 2009. (ENG., Illus.). 272p. (YA). (gr. 7). pap. 10.99 *(978-1-4169-0900-2(1),* Simon & Schuster Bks. For Young Readers) Simon & Schuster Bks. For Young Readers.

Sanchez, Pete. A Friend for Petro. 2008. 73p. pap. 19.95 *(978-1-60474-902-1(4))* America Star Bks.

Sand-Eveland, Cyndi. Dear Toni. 2008. (ENG., Illus.). 136p. (J). (gr. 3-7). 14.95 *(978-0-88776-876-7(8),* Tundra Bks.) Tundra Bks. CAN. Dist: Penguin Random Hse. LLC.

Sandall, Ellie. Copycat Bear! Sandall, Ellie, illus. 2013. (ENG., Illus.). 32p. (J). (gr. -1-k). 14.99 *(978-1-58925-120-5(2))* Tiger Tales.

Sandberg, Winter. Private Display of Affection. 2016. (ENG., Illus.). (YA). (gr. 8-12). 24.99 ***(978-1-63533-065-6(3),*** Harmony Ink Pr.) Dreamspinner Pr.

Sandberg, Winter. Private Display of Affection [Library Edition]. 2014. 210p. pap. 14.99 *(978-1-62798-537-6(9),* Harmony Ink Pr.) Dreamspinner Pr.

Sander, Sonia, adapted by. Dragon's Snowy Day. 2005. (Scholastic Reader Ser.). (Illus.). 32p. (J). pap. *(978-0-439-80163-8(X))* Scholastic, Inc.

Sanders, Addie Meyer. I Don't Want to Go. I.t. ed. 2012. 43p. (J). pap. *(978-1-4596-3449-7(7))* ReadHowYouWant.com, Ltd.

Sanders, D. m. & Sanders, D. M. Fin the Godsend. 2010. 36p. pap. 25.49 *(978-1-4343-7864-4(0))* AuthorHouse.

Sanders, Russell J. Colors. 2016. (ENG., Illus.). (J). 24.99 ***(978-1-63477-956-2(8),*** Harmony Ink Pr.) Dreamspinner Pr.

Sanders, Stephanie S. Villain School: Good Curses Evil. 2011. (ENG.). 240p. (YA). (gr. 3-12). pap. 6.99 *(978-1-59990-848-9(4),* 9781599908489, Bloomsbury USA Childrens) Bloomsbury Publishing USA.

—Villain School: Hero in Disguise. 2012. (ENG.). 240p. (YA). (gr. 5-8). 15.99 *(978-1-59990-907-3(3),* 9781599909073, Bloomsbury USA Childrens) Bloomsbury Publishing USA.

Sandoval, Lynda. Father Knows Best. 2010. (ENG.). 264p. (J). (gr. 7). pap. 13.95 *(978-1-60282-147-7(X))* Bold Strokes Bks.

Sandra De Mos. Cleo's Playground Adventure. 2009. 40p. pap. 16.99 *(978-1-4389-2049-8(0))* AuthorHouse.

Sands, Kevin. The Blackthorn Key. (Blackthorn Key Ser.: 1). (ENG., Illus.). (J). (gr. 5-9). 2016. 400p. pap. 7.99 *(978-1-4814-4652-5(5))* 2015. 384p. 18.99 *(978-1-4814-4651-8(7))* Simon & Schuster Children's Publishing. (Aladdin).

—Mark of the Plague. (Blackthorn Key Ser.: 2). (ENG.). (J). (gr. 5-9). 2017. 560p. pap. 7.99 ***(978-1-4814-4675-4(4))*** 2016. (Illus.). 544p. 17.99 *(978-1-4814-4674-7(6))* Simon & Schuster Children's Publishing. (Aladdin).

Sands, Maria. Sanjee & Her Delightful Hats. 2008. 20p. pap. 24.95 *(978-1-60563-700-6(9))* America Star Bks.

Sandu, Anca. Churchill's Tale of Tails. 1 vol. Sandu, Anca, illus. (ENG., Illus.). 32p. (J). (gr. -1-3). 2016. pap. 7.95 *(978-1-56145-782-3(5))* 2013. 16.95 *(978-1-56145-738-0(8))* Peachtree Pubs.

Sandusky, Thomas & Hill, Kathy. Gracie, the Glass Tree Frog. Johnson, Gretchen, illus. 2008. 24p. pap. 12.95 *(978-0-9820479-2-7(4))* Peppertree Pr., The.

—Spidy the Spider Monkey. Johnson, Gretchen, illus. 2009. 32p. pap. 12.95 *(978-0-9823002-5-1(5))* Peppertree Pr., The.

Sanrio. Best Friends: Hello Kitty & Me. 2014. (ENG., Illus.). 32p. (J). (-2). 9.99 *(978-1-4022-9645-1(2),* Sourcebooks Jabberwocky) Sourcebooks, Inc.

—Hello Kitty, Hello Love! 2014. (ENG., Illus.). 24p. (J). (gr. k-2). pap. 6.99 *(978-1-4197-1249-4(7),* Abrams Bks. for Young Readers) Abrams, Inc.

—Merry Christmas, Hello Kitty! 2014. (ENG., Illus.). 24p. (J). (gr. k-2). 6.95 *(978-1-4197-1376-7(0),* Abrams Bks. for Young Readers) Abrams, Inc.

—Trick or Treat: Hello Kitty & Me. 2014. (ENG.). 32p. (J). (-2). 9.99 *(978-1-4022-9665-9(7),* 9781402296659) Sourcebooks, Inc.

Sanschagrin, Joceline. Caillou: It's Mine! Brignaud, Pierre, illus. 3rd ed. 2013. (Step by Step Ser.). (ENG.). 24p. (J). (gr. -1-k). bds. 5.99 *(978-2-89718-059-1(5))* Caillouet, Gerry.

Sansone, V. K. Katie Bear & Friends (Book One) 2009. 36p. pap. 16.97 *(978-0-557-09358-8(9))* Lulu Pr., Inc.

—Katie Bear & Friends (Book Three) 2009. 36p. pap. 16.97 *(978-0-557-09331-1(7))* Lulu Pr., Inc.

—Katie Bear & Friends (Book Two) 2009. 40p. pap. 18.00 *(978-0-557-09393-9(7))* Lulu Pr., Inc.

Sant, Sharon. Runners. 2013. 286p. pap. *(978-1-907737-52-7(9))* Immanion Pr.

Santat, Dan. The Adventures of Beekle: The Unimaginary Friend. 2014. (ENG., Illus.). 40p. (J). (gr. -1-3). 17.99 *(978-0-316-19998-8(2))* Little, Brown Bks. for Young Readers.

—The Guild of Geniuses. 2004. (ENG., Illus.). 40p. (J). (gr. -1-3). 17.99 *(978-0-439-43096-8(8),* Levine, Arthur A. Bks.) Scholastic, Inc.

Santat, Dan & Willems, Mo. The Cookie Fiasco. Santat, Dan & Willems, Mo, illus. 2016. (Elephant & Piggie Like Reading! Ser.). (ENG., Illus.). 64p. (J). (gr. 1-3). 9.99 *(978-1-4847-2636-5(7))* Hyperion Bks. for Children.

Santiago, Brianna A. Why Is the Moon Following Us? 2008. 16p. pap. 24.95 *(978-1-60474-944-1(X))* America Star Bks.

Santillo, LuAnn. The Dog. Santillo, LuAnn, ed. 2003. (Half-Pint Kids Readers Ser.). (Illus.). 7p. (J). (gr. -1-1). pap. 1.00 *(978-1-59256-065-3(2))* Half-Pint Kids, Inc.

—The Wet Dock. Santillo, LuAnn, ed. 2003. (Half-Pint Kids Readers Ser.). (Illus.). 7p. (J). (gr. -1-1). pap. *(978-1-59256-089-9(X))* Half-Pint Kids, Inc.

Santini, Philip. Harvey's Adventures. Chambers, Z., illus. 2011. 44p. pap. 24.95 *(978-1-4626-2078-4(7))* America Star Bks.

Santomero, Angela C., adapted by. You Are Special, Daniel Tiger! 2014. (Daniel Tiger's Neighborhood Ser.). (ENG., Illus.). 26p. (J). (gr. -1-2). 12.99 *(978-1-4814-1915-4(3),* Simon Spotlight) Simon Spotlight.

Santopolo, Jill. Fashion Disaster. Mingus, Cathi, illus. 2016. (Sparkle Spa Ser.: 9). (ENG.). 96p. (J). (gr. 2-5). pap. 5.99 *(978-1-4814-6391-1(8),* Aladdin) Simon & Schuster Children's Publishing.

—Fashion Disaster. Mingus, Cathi, illus. 2016. (Sparkle Spa Ser.: 9). (ENG.). 96p. (J). (gr. 2-5). 16.99 *(978-1-4814-6392-8(6),* Simon & Schuster/Paula Wiseman Bks.) Simon & Schuster/Paula Wiseman Bks.

Santopolo, Jill. Glam Opening! Mingus, Cathi, illus. 2017. (Sparkle Spa Ser.: 10). (ENG.). 112p. (J). (gr. 2-5). pap. 5.99 ***(978-1-4814-6395-9(0),*** Aladdin) Simon & Schuster Children's Publishing.

Santos, Penelope. Peas for Pat. 2015. (Rosen REAL Readers: STEM & STEAM Collection). (ENG.). 12p. (gr. 1-2). pap. 6.33 *(978-1-4994-9517-1(X),* Rosen Classroom) Rosen Publishing Group, Inc., The.

Santucci, Barbara. Abby's Chairs. Santini, Debrah L., illus. 2004. 32p. 16.00 *(978-0-8028-5205-2(X))* Eerdmans, William B. Publishing Co.

Sapre, Reshme. The Unfortunate Tale of Kachuva the Tortoise: As Told by Chukwa Sulcata. Robinson, Jayme, illus. 2012. (ENG.). 40p. 16.95 *(978-0-9829362-0-7(6))* Hathi Chiti Bks. for Kids.

Sarah, Linda. Big Friends. Davies, Benji, illus. 2016. (ENG.). 32p. (J). 16.99 *(978-1-62779-330-8(5),* 9781627793308, Holt, Henry & Co. Bks. For Young Readers) Holt, Henry & Co.

Sargent, Dave & Sargent, Pat. Bobby Bobcat: Be a Friend, 15 vols., Vol. 10. Huff, Jeane, illus. 2nd rev. ed. 2003. (Animal Pride Ser.: No. 10). 42p. (J). pap. 6.95 *(978-1-56763-778-6(7));* lib. bdg. 20.95 *(978-1-56763-777-9(9))* Ozark Publishing.

—Young Billy: A New Beginning!, Vol. 2. Woodward, Elaine, illus. 2003. (Young Animal Pride Ser.: 2). 24p. (J). pap. 10.95 *(978-1-56763-866-0(X));* lib. bdg. 20.95 *(978-1-56763-865-3(1))* Ozark Publishing.

—Young Redi: Friendship!, Vol. 3. Woodward, Elaine, illus. 2003. (Young Animal Pride Ser.: 3). 24p. (J). pap. 10.95 *(978-1-56763-868-4(6));* lib. bdg. 20.95 *(978-1-56763-867-7(8))* Ozark Publishing.

Sargent, Mandy And Ben. Best Ted & Ben. 2012. (Illus.). 40p. pap. 20.99 *(978-1-4678-8532-4(0))* AuthorHouse.

Sarmiento-Waring, D. Meet the One Race Kids. 2010. 20p. pap. 17.99 *(978-1-60957-899-2(6))* Salem Author Services.

Sarn, Amélie & Trouillot, Virgile. The Audition. 2009. (Groove High Ser.). (Illus.). 112p. (YA). (gr. 5-8). 31.95 *(978-1-60754-203-2(X),* 1293913); pap. 15.25 *(978-1-60754-204-9(8),* 1293913) Windmill Bks.

—Looking for Trouble. 2009. (Groove High Ser.). (Illus.). 112p. (YA). (gr. 5-8). 31.95 *(978-1-60754-206-3(4),* 1293914); pap. 15.25 *(978-1-60754-207-0(2),* 1293914) Windmill Bks.

—Love Is in the Air. Ducrest, Olivier, illus. 2009. (Groove High Ser.). 112p. (YA). (gr. 5-8). 31.95 *(978-1-60754-212-4(9),* 1293915); pap. 15.25 *(978-1-60754-213-1(7),* 1293915) Windmill Bks.

Saseen, Sharon, illus. Patience & the Flower Girl. 2004. *(978-0-9748425-0-9(8))* Saseen, Sharon.

Sateren, Shelley Swanson. The Lunchroom Fight. Sullivan, Mary, illus. 2013. (Max & Zoe Ser.). (ENG.). 32p. (gr. k-2). lib. bdg. 21.32 *(978-1-4048-7199-1(3),* Max & Zoe) Picture Window Bks.

—Max & Zoe. Sullivan, Mary, illus. (Max & Zoe Ser.). (ENG.). 32p. (gr. k-2). 2014. pap. 19.80 *(978-1-4795-5043-2(4))* 2013. 85.28 *(978-1-4795-1694-0(5))* 2013. 255.84 *(978-1-4795-1695-7(3))* 2013. pap. 19.80 *(978-1-4048-8064-1(X))* Picture Window Bks. (Max & Zoe).

—Max & Zoe at Recess. 1 vol. Sullivan, Mary, illus. 2012. (Max & Zoe Ser.). (ENG.). 32p. (gr. k-2). lib. bdg. 21.32 *(978-1-4048-7200-4(0),* Max & Zoe) Picture Window Bks.

—Max & Zoe at School. 1 vol. Sullivan, Mary, illus. 2011. (Max & Zoe Ser.). (ENG.). 32p. (gr. k-2). lib. bdg. 21.32 *(978-1-4048-6211-1(0),* Max & Zoe) Picture Window Bks.

—Max & Zoe at Soccer Practice. 1 vol. Sullivan, Mary, illus. 2012. (Max & Zoe Ser.). (ENG.). 32p. (gr. k-2). lib. bdg. 21.32 *(978-1-4048-6213-5(7),* Max & Zoe) Picture Window Bks.

—Max & Zoe at the Dentist. 1 vol. Sullivan, Mary, illus. 2011. (Max & Zoe Ser.). (ENG.). 32p. (gr. k-2). lib. bdg. 21.32 *(978-1-4048-6206-7(4),* Max & Zoe) Picture Window Bks.

—Max & Zoe at the Doctor. 1 vol. Sullivan, Mary, illus. 2011. (Max & Zoe Ser.). (ENG.). 32p. (gr. k-2). lib. bdg. 21.32 *(978-1-4048-6212-8(9),* Max & Zoe) Picture Window Bks.

—Max & Zoe at the Library. 1 vol. Sullivan, Mary, illus. 2011. (Max & Zoe Ser.). (ENG.). 32p. (gr. k-2). lib. bdg. 21.32 *(978-1-4048-6210-4(2),* Max & Zoe) Picture Window Bks.

—Max & Zoe: the Lunchroom Fight. 1 vol. Sullivan, Mary, illus. 2013. (Max & Zoe Ser.). (ENG.). 32p. (gr. k-2). pap. 5.19 *(978-1-4795-2328-3(3),* Max & Zoe) Picture Window Bks.

—Max & Zoe: the Science Fair. 1 vol. Sullivan, Mary, illus. 2013. (Max & Zoe Ser.). (ENG.). 32p. (gr. k-2). pap. 5.19 *(978-1-4795-2330-6(5),* Max & Zoe) Picture Window Bks.

—Max & Zoe: Too Many Tricks. 1 vol. Sullivan, Mary, illus. 2013. (Max & Zoe Ser.). (ENG.). 32p. (gr. k-2). pap. 5.19 *(978-1-4795-2327-6(5),* Max & Zoe) Picture Window Bks.

—The School Concert. Sullivan, Mary, illus. 2012. (Max & Zoe Ser.). (ENG.). 32p. (gr. k-2). lib. bdg. 21.32 *(978-1-4048-7198-4(5),* Max & Zoe) Picture Window Bks.

—The Science Fair. Sullivan, Mary, illus. 2013. (Max & Zoe Ser.). (ENG.). 32p. (gr. k-2). lib. bdg. 21.32 *(978-1-4048-7202-8(7),* Max & Zoe) Picture Window Bks.

—Too Many Tricks. Sullivan, Mary, illus. 2013. (Max & Zoe Ser.). (ENG.). 32p. (gr. k-2). lib. bdg. 21.32 *(978-1-4048-7197-7(7),* Max & Zoe) Picture Window Bks.

—The Very Best Art Project. Sullivan, Mary, illus. 2013. (Max & Zoe Ser.). (ENG.). 32p. (gr. k-2). lib. bdg. 21.32 *(978-1-4048-7201-1(9),* Max & Zoe) Picture Window Bks.

Sather, Connie. Sadie the Sled Dog? 2009. 44p. (J). pap. 13.95 *(978-1-4327-4164-6(0))* Outskirts Pr., Inc.

Satterfield, April. Leah Bug & Her Flying Friends. Guthrie, Lewis, illus. 2011. 20p. pap. 24.95 *(978-1-4560-8422-6(4))* America Star Bks.

Sattler, Jennifer. A Chick 'n' Pug Christmas. 2014. (ENG., Illus.). 32p. (J). (gr. -1-1). 16.99 *(978-1-59990-602-7(3),* 9781599906027, Bloomsbury USA Childrens) Bloomsbury Publishing USA.

—Chick 'n' Pug: the Love Pug. 2015. (ENG., Illus.). 32p. (J). (gr. -1-1). 16.99 *(978-1-61963-672-9(7),* 9781619636729, Bloomsbury USA Childrens) Bloomsbury Publishing USA.

—Who's That Pig? 2015. (Pig Kahuna Ser.). (ENG., Illus.). 32p. (J). (gr. -1-1). 16.99 *(978-1-61963-632-3(8),* 9781619636323, Bloomsbury USA Childrens) Bloomsbury Publishing USA.

Sattler, Jennifer Gordon, illus. A Chick 'n' Pug Christmas. 2014. (J). *(978-1-61963-463-3(5))* Bloomsbury Pr.

Sauer, Drake & Sauer, Katheryn. Betsy the Brachiosaurus. 2012. 32p. pap. *(978-1-105-68969-7(7))* Lulu.com.

Sauer, Tammi. I Love Cake! Starring Rabbit, Porcupine, & Moose. Rozelaar, Angie, illus. 2016. 40p. (J). (gr. -1-3). 17.99 *(978-0-06-227894-4(0),* Tegen, Katherine Bks) HarperCollins Pubs.

—Nugget & Fang. 2015. lib. bdg. 17.20 *(978-0-606-36825-4(6))* Turtleback Bks.

—Nugget & Fang: Friends Forever - Or Snack Time? Slack, Michael, illus. 2013. (ENG.). 40p. (J). (gr. -1-3). 16.99 *(978-0-547-85285-0(1))* Houghton Mifflin Harcourt Publishing Co.

—Nugget & Fang: Friends Forever — Or Snack Time? Slack, Michael, illus. 2015. (ENG.). 40p. (J). (gr. -1-3). 6.99 *(978-0-544-48171-8(2),* HMH Books For Young Readers) Houghton Mifflin Harcourt Publishing Co.

—Roar! Starin, Liz, illus. 2015. (ENG.). 32p. (J). (gr. -1-3). 17.99 *(978-1-4814-0224-8(2),* Simon & Schuster Bks. For Young Readers) Simon & Schuster Bks. For Young Readers.

—Your Alien. Fujita, Goro, illus. 2015. (ENG.). 32p. (J). (gr. -1). 14.95 *(978-1-4549-1129-6(8))* Sterling Publishing Co., Inc.

Saugstad, Edward. Oakee Doakee & the Ego Bomb. 2008. 108p. pap. 19.95 *(978-0-9551503-9-5(6))* Checkpoint Pr. IRL. Dist: Printondemand-worldwide.com.

Saunders, Brianna. The Magic Marble. 2013. 32p. pap. 24.95 *(978-1-63004-598-2(5))* America Star Bks.

Saunders, Karen. Suzy P. & the Trouble with Three. 2014. (Suzy P. Ser.). (ENG.). 352p. (J). (gr. 4-7). pap. 10.99 *(978-1-84877-369-1(2))* Bonnier Publishing GBR. Dist: Independent Pubs. Group.

Saunders, Kate. The Little Secret. Carman, William, illus. 2012. (ENG.). 240p. (J). (gr. 3-6). pap. 10.99 *(978-0-312-67427-4(9),* 9780312674274) Square Fish.

Saundra Luchs. Wait for the Sunrise. 2010. 172p. pap. 13.95 *(978-1-4401-9190-9(5))* iUniverse, Inc.

Sava, Scott Christian. Ed's Terrestrials. 2006. 84p. 19.95 *(978-0-9789168-1-7(6))* Blue Dream Studios.

Savage, Bridgette Z. Fly Like the Wind. Savage, Charles J., ed. Savage, Bridgette Z., illus. Savage, Charles J., photos by. 2005. (ENG., Illus.). 112p. (YA). (gr. 5). per. 16.99 *(978-0-9771494-0-7(4))* Buckbeech Studios.

Savage, J. Scott. Evil Twins. Holgate, Doug, illus. (Case File 13 Ser.: 3). (ENG.). (J). (gr. 3-7). 2015. 288p. pap. 6.99 *(978-0-06-213338-0(1))* 2014. 272p. 14.99 *(978-0-06-213337-3(3))* HarperCollins Pubs.

—Making the Team. Holgate, Doug, illus. 2013. (Case File 13 Ser.: 2). (ENG.). 272p. (J). (gr. 3-7). 14.99 *(978-0-06-213331-1(4))* HarperCollins Pubs.

—Zombie Kid. Holgate, Doug, illus. (Case File 13 Ser.: 1). (ENG.). (J). (gr. 3-7). 2013. 304p. pap. 6.99 *(978-0-06-213327-4(6))* 2012. 288p. 14.99 *(978-0-06-213325-0(X))* HarperCollins Pubs.

Savage, Kim. After the Woods. 2016. (ENG.). 304p. (YA). 17.99 *(978-0-374-30055-5(0),* 9780374300555, Farrar, Straus & Giroux (BYR)) Farrar, Straus & Giroux.

Savage, Melissa. Lemons. 2017. (ENG.). 320p. (J). (gr. 3-7). 16.99 ***(978-1-5247-0012-6(6));*** lib. bdg. 19.99 ***(978-1-5247-0013-3(4))*** Random Hse. Children's Bks. (Crown Books For Young Readers).

Savitsky, Steve, illus. Dora's Pirate Treasure Hunt. 2010. (Dora the Explorer Ser.). (ENG.). 12p. (J). (gr. -1-1). 6.99 *(978-1-4169-9927-0(2),* Simon Spotlight/Nickelodeon) Simon Spotlight/Nickelodeon.

Sawyer, Kim Vogel. Katy's New World. 1 vol. 2010. (Katy Lambright Ser.: No. 1). (ENG.). 208p. (YA). (gr. 8-11). pap. 9.99 *(978-0-310-71924-3(0))* Zondervan.

Sax, Anita. One Step at a Time. Jasuna, Aija, illus. 2013. 24p. (J). 17.95 *(978-1-60131-152-8(4),* Castlebridge Bks.) Big Tent Bks.

Sayers, Mary. Franky: The Cranky Crab. 2012. 40p. pap. 20.99 *(978-1-4772-6040-1(4))* AuthorHouse.

Scaglione, Rebecca L. Jack: The trilogy ... the Truth. 2007. 204p. per. 14.95 *(978-0-595-47331-1(8))* iUniverse, Inc.

Scala, Vincent. Beep Beep Goes the Bus Driver. 1 vol. 2013. (ENG., Illus.). 32p. (J). 16.99 *(978-0-7643-4493-0(5),* 9780764344930) Schiffer Publishing, Ltd.

Scaletta, Jane. Kimbo's First Horse Show, 1 vol. 2008. (ENG., Illus.). 52p. pap. 24.95 *(978-1-60474-480-4(4))* America Star Bks.
Scanlon, Liz Garton. The Great Good Summer. 2015. (ENG., Illus.). 224p. (J). (gr. 3-7). 16.99 *(978-1-4814-1147-9(0),* Beach Lane Bks.) Beach Lane Bks.
—Noodle & Lou. Howard, Arthur, illus. 2011. (ENG.). 32p. (J). (gr. -1-1). 15.99 *(978-1-4424-0288-1(1),* Beach Lane Bks.) Beach Lane Bks.
Scattergood, Augusta. Making Friends with Billy Wong. 2016. (ENG.). 224p. (J). (gr. 3-7). 16.99 *(978-0-545-92425-2(1),* Scholastic Pr.) Scholastic, Inc.
Scelsa, Greg & Debney, John. Friends Forever. Faulkner, Stacey, ed. Mahan, Benton, illus. 2006. (J). pap. 2.99 *(978-1-59198-322-4(3))* Creative Teaching Pr., Inc.
Scelsa, Kate. Fans of the Impossible Life. 368p. (YA). (gr. 9). 2017. pap. 9.99 *(978-0-06-233176-2(0))* 2015. (ENG.). 17.99 *(978-0-06-233175-5(2))* HarperCollins Pubs.
Schachner, Judy. Dewey Bob. Schachner, Judy, illus. 2015. (ENG., Illus.). 32p. (J). (gr. k-3). 17.99 *(978-0-8037-4120-1(0),* Dial Bks) Penguin Young Readers Group.
Schaefer, Carole Lexa. Monkey & Elephant. Bernstein, Galia, illus. 2013. (Candlewick Sparks Ser.). (ENG.). 48p. (J). (gr. k-4). pap. 3.99 *(978-0-7636-6261-5(5))* Candlewick Pr.
—Monkey & Elephant & a Secret Birthday Surprise. Bernstein, Galia, illus. 2016. (Candlewick Sparks Ser.). (ENG.). 48p. (J). (gr. k-4). pap. 3.99 *(978-0-7636-8744-1(8))* Candlewick Pr.
—Monkey & Elephant & the Babysitting Adventure. Bernstein, Galia, illus. 2016. (ENG.). 48p. (J). (gr. k-4). 14.99 *(978-0-7636-6535-7(5))* Candlewick Pr.
—Monkey & Elephant Get Better. Bernstein, Galia, illus. (Candlewick Sparks Ser.). (ENG.). 48p. (J). (gr. k-4). 2014. pap. 3.99 *(978-0-7636-7180-8(0))* 2013. 14.99 *(978-0-7636-4841-1(8))* Candlewick Pr.
Schaefer, Laura. The Secret Ingredient. Rim, Sujean, illus. (ENG.). 240p. (J). (gr. 4-8). 2012. pap. 6.99 *(978-1-4424-1960-5(1))* 2011. 15.99 *(978-1-4424-1959-9(8))* Simon & Schuster/Paula Wiseman Bks. (Simon & Schuster/Paula Wiseman Bks.).
—The Teashop Girls. Rim, Sujean, illus. (ENG.). (J). 2009. 272p. (gr. 4-9). pap. 6.99 *(978-1-4169-6794-1(X))* 2008. 256p. (gr. 3-9). 15.99 *(978-1-4169-6793-4(1))* Simon & Schuster/Paula Wiseman Bks. (Simon & Schuster/Paula Wiseman Bks.).
Schaefer, Lola M. Frankie Stein Starts School, 0 vols. Atteberry, Kevan, illus. 2010. (ENG.). 32p. (J). (gr. k-3). 15.99 *(978-0-7614-5656-8(2),* 9780761456568, Amazon Children's Publishing) Amazon Publishing.
Schanen, Adriana Brad. Partners in Slime. Santoso, Charles, illus. (Quinny & Hopper Ser.). (ENG.). 272p. (J). (gr. 3-7). 2017. pap. 6.99 ***(978-1-4847-7822-7(7))*** 2016. 15.99 *(978-1-4847-7506-6(6))* Hyperion Bks. for Children.
Schanen, Adriana Brad. Quinny & Hopper. Swearingen, Greg, illus. 2014. (ENG.). 240p. (J). (gr. 3-7). 15.99 *(978-1-4231-7829-3(7))* Hyperion Bks. for Children.
Scheffler, Axel & Nosy Crow Staff. Pip & Posy: the Snowy Day. Scheffler, Axel, illus. 2013. (Pip & Posy Ser.). (ENG., Illus.). 32p. (J). (-k). 12.99 *(978-0-7636-6607-1(6),* Nosy Crow) Candlewick Pr.
Scheffrin-Falk, Gladys. Another Celebrated Dancing Bear. Garrison, Barbara, illus. (J). 2007. 32p. (gr. -1-3). 18.95 *(978-1-930900-35-6(X))* 20th ed. 2011. 28p. 18.95 *(978-1-930900-50-9(3))* Purple Hse. Pr.
Scheier, Leah. Your Voice Is All I Hear. 2015. (ENG.). 336p. (YA). (gr. 8-12). pap. 9.99 *(978-1-4926-1441-8(6))* Sourcebooks, Inc.
Schertle, Alice. El Camioncito Azul. McElmurry, Jill, illus. 2013. (Little Blue Truck Ser.).Tr. of Little Blue Truck. (SPA & ENG.). 30p. (J). (— 1). bds. 7.99 *(978-0-547-98397-4(2))* Houghton Mifflin Harcourt Publishing Co.
—Little Blue Truck. McElmurry, Jill, illus. (Little Blue Truck Ser.). (ENG.). (J). 2015. 30p. (— 1). bds. 12.99 *(978-0-544-05685-5(X),* HMH Books For Young Readers) 2010. 32p. (gr. -1-3). 26.99 *(978-0-547-48248-4(5))* 2008. 32p. (gr. -1-3). 17.99 *(978-0-15-205661-2(0))* 2015. 30p. (— 1). bds. 7.99 *(978-0-544-56803-7(6),* HMH Books For Young Readers) Houghton Mifflin Harcourt Publishing Co.
Schield, Allie Schield. Solomon & Lily. Jerome, Barb, illus. 2003. 34p. (J). per. 11.99 *(978-0-9743948-0-0(7))* One Little Miracle.
Schirmer, Jodi L. Dear Deer Friend. 2008. 24p. pap. 11.95 *(978-1-4327-2540-2(8))* Outskirts Pr., Inc.
Schizas, Lea. Bubba & Giganto: Odds Against Us. 2008. 68p. (J). pap. *(978-0-9797513-6-3(5))* 4RV Publishing, LLC.
Schlegl, Stacey Lynn. Little Frog. 2008. (J). per. 8.95 *(978-0-9801504-0-7(X))* Jan-Carol Publishing, INC.
Schlegl, Stacey Lynn & Schlegl, Abigail. MerMountain. 2012. 84p. (J). pap. 11.95 *(978-0-9850272-2-3(3))* Jan-Carol Publishing, INC.
Schliewen, Richard D. Paulina, Girl of the Pacific. 2011. 104p. pap. 19.95 *(978-1-4626-3614-3(4))* America Star Bks.
Schlitt, Jayme & Schlitt, Ron. Rags, Riches & the Robe. 2010. 32p. 17.25 *(978-1-4269-4666-0(X))* Trafford Publishing.
Schlitz, Laura Amy. The Night Fairy. Barrett, Angela, illus. (ENG.). 128p. (J). (gr. 2-5). 2011. pap. 6.99 *(978-0-7636-5295-1(4))* 2010. 16.99 *(978-0-7636-3674-6(6))* Candlewick Pr.
—The Night Fairy, 2 vols. unabr. ed. 2010. (J). (gr. 1-4). 54.75 *(978-1-4407-6983-2(4))* Recorded Bks., Inc.
Schmickl, Angela. The Matador Who Ran Away from the Spider. 2013. 24p. pap. 10.96 *(978-1-4251-9190-0(8))* Trafford Publishing.
Schmidt, Gary D. Orbiting Jupiter. (ENG.). 192p. (gr. 7). 2017. (YA). pap. 9.99 *(978-0-544-93839-7(9),* HMH Books For Young Readers) 2015. (J). 17.99 *(978-0-544-46222-9(X),* Clarion Bks.) Houghton Mifflin Harcourt Publishing Co.
—Orbiting Jupiter. 2017. (ENG.). (YA). (gr. 7). lib. bdg. 20.85 ***(978-0-606-39818-3(X))*** Turtleback Bks.
Schmidt, René. Leaving Fletchville, 1 vol. 2008. (ENG.). 168p. (J). (gr. 3-7). pap. 9.95 *(978-1-55143-945-7(X))* Orca Bk. Pubs. USA.
Schmitt, H. D. Pee Wee Pickle Goes to Kinder-Garden. Spears, Sheri, illus. 2008. 20p. pap. 24.95 *(978-1-60672-731-7(1))* America Star Bks.
Schneider, Rosemary. Bully Paws. 2011. 40p. pap. 18.46 *(978-1-4567-6294-0(X))* AuthorHouse.
Schoene, Kerstin & Gunetsreiner, Nina. Milo Is Not a Dog Today. 2015. (Illus.). 32p. (J). *(978-1-4896-3867-0(9))* Weigl Pubs., Inc.
—Milo Is Not a Dog Today. Schoene, Kerstin & Gunetsreiner, Nina, illus. 2014. (ENG., Illus.). 32p. (J). (gr. -1-3). 16.99 *(978-0-8075-4793-9(X))* Whitman, Albert & Co.
Schoenherr, Ian. Pip & Squeak. Schoenherr, Ian, illus. 2007. (Illus.). 32p. (J). (gr. -1-k). 18.89 *(978-0-06-087254-0(3))* HarperCollins Pubs.
Scholastic. The Pokémon School Challenge. 2017. (Pokémon Ser.: 1). (ENG.). 96p. (J). (gr. 2-5). pap. 4.99 ***(978-1-338-14861-9(3))*** Scholastic, Inc.
Scholastic Editors. Peppa Plays Soccer. 2016. (Peppa Pig 8X8 Ser.). lib. bdg. 14.75 *(978-0-606-38825-2(7))* Turtleback Bks.
—Peppa's Halloween Party. 2016. (Peppa Pig 8X8 Ser.). lib. bdg. 14.75 *(978-0-606-38827-6(3))* Turtleback Bks.
Scholastic, Inc. Staff. Best Friends (Peppa Pig) Eone, illus. 2015. (Peppa Pig Ser.). (ENG.). 32p. (J). (gr. -1-k). 8.99 *(978-0-545-84232-7(8))* Scholastic, Inc.
—Dolphin Rescue. 2014. (LEGO Friends Ser.). (ENG., Illus.). 64p. (J). (gr. 2-5). pap. 4.99 *(978-0-545-51655-6(2))* Math Solutions.
—Friends Forever. 2012. (Lalaloopsy Ser.). (ENG.). 10p. (J). (gr. -1-k). bds. 12.99 *(978-0-545-46223-5(1))* Scholastic, Inc.
Scholastic, Inc. Staff, contrib. by. Class Trip. 2013. (Peppa Pig Ser.). (ENG., Illus.). 24p. (J). (gr. -1-k). pap. 3.99 *(978-0-545-52402-5(4))* Scholastic, Inc.
—A Day in Heartlake City. 2013. (LEGO Friends Ser.). (ENG.). 16p. (J). (gr. 1-3). 6.99 *(978-0-545-51757-7(5))* Scholastic, Inc.
—Fun with Friends. 2013. (Peppa Pig Ser.). (ENG.). 16p. (J). (gr. -1-k). 6.99 *(978-0-545-49861-6(9))* Scholastic, Inc.
—Johto Handbook. 2010. (Pokemon Ser.). (ENG., Illus.). 96p. (J). (gr. 2-5). pap. 7.99 *(978-0-545-15132-0(5),* Scholastic Paperbacks) Scholastic, Inc.
—LEGO Friends: Meet the Friends. 2013. (LEGO Friends Ser.). (ENG.). 32p. (J). (gr. 2-5). pap. 3.99 *(978-0-545-59943-6(1))* Scholastic, Inc.
—Olivia's Great Idea. 2013. (LEGO Friends Ser.). (ENG.). 32p. (J). (gr. 2-5). pap., act. bk. ed. 8.99 *(978-0-545-51759-1(1))* Scholastic, Inc.
—Stats & Facts on over 150 Brand-New Pokémon! 2011. (Pokemon Ser.). (ENG.). 112p. (J). (gr. 2-5). pap., instr.'s hndbk. ed. 7.99 *(978-0-545-31652-1(9),* Scholastic Paperbacks) Scholastic, Inc.
Scholastic, Inc. Staff & Hooks, Gwendolyn. Three's a Crowd. Walker, Sylvia, illus. 2004. (Just for You Ser.). (ENG.). 32p. (gr. k-3). pap. 3.99 *(978-0-439-56865-4(X),* Teaching Resources) Scholastic, Inc.
Scholastic, Inc. Staff, et al. Don't Hit Me! Grier, Gary, illus. 2004. (Just for You Ser.). (ENG.). 32p. (gr. k-1). pap. 3.99 *(978-0-439-56860-9(9),* Teaching Resources) Scholastic, Inc.
Schonzeit, Miriam. The Sweetest Song & other Stories. 2006. 304p. (YA). 16.95 *(978-1-932443-42-4(8),* SWSH) Judaica Pr., Inc., The.
Schoombee, Cherese. Frilly Lilly. 2009. 28p. 16.95 *(978-1-84799-435-6(0))* Lulu Pr., Inc.
Schories, Pat, illus. Biscuit Visits the Farm. 2012. (J). *(978-1-4351-4383-8(3),* HarperFestival) HarperCollins Pubs.
Schotter, Roni. Doo-Wop Pop. Collier, Bryan, illus. 2008. 40p. (J). (gr. -1-3). lib. bdg. 17.89 *(978-0-06-057974-6(9),* Amistad) HarperCollins Pubs.
Schraff, Anne. A Boy Called Twister, 1 vol. unabr. ed. 2010. (Urban Underground Ser.). (ENG.). 180p. (YA). (gr. 9-12). pap. 9.95 *(978-1-61651-002-2(1))* Saddleback Educational Publishing, Inc.
—A Boy Called Twister. 2010. (Urban Underground — Harriet Tubman High School Ser.). (YA). lib. bdg. 20.80 *(978-0-606-14271-7(1),* Turtleback) Turtleback Bks.
—Gingerbread Heart. 2008. 114p. (J). (gr. 4-7). 13.95 *(978-0-7569-8406-9(8))* Perfection Learning Corp.
—Hurting Time, 1 vol. unabr. ed. 2012. (Urban Underground Ser.). (ENG.). 204p. (YA). (gr. 9-12). pap. 9.95 *(978-1-61651-959-9(2))* Saddleback Educational Publishing, Inc.
—The Hyena Laughs at Night. 2008. (Passages 2000 Ser.). 111p. lib. bdg. 13.95 *(978-0-7569-8407-6(6))* Perfection Learning Corp.
—I Am Underdog. 2014. (Red Rhino Ser.). (J). lib. bdg. 18.40 *(978-0-606-36198-9(7))* Turtleback Bks.
—If You Really Loved Me. 2010. (Urban Underground — Harriet Tubman High School Ser.). (YA). lib. bdg. 20.80 *(978-0-606-14270-0(3),* Turtleback) Turtleback Bks.
—Just Another Name for Lonely. 2008. (Passages 2000 Ser.). 107p. (J). lib. bdg. 13.95 *(978-0-7569-8402-1(5));* (gr. 4-7). pap. 8.50 *(978-0-7891-7560-1(6))* Perfection Learning Corp.
—Memories Are Forever. 2008. (Passages Ser.). 135p. lib. bdg. 13.95 *(978-0-7569-8405-2(X))* Perfection Learning Corp.
—The Price of Friendship. 2008. (Passages Ser.). 138p. (J). (gr. 4-6). lib. bdg. 13.95 *(978-0-7569-8373-4(8))* Perfection Learning Corp.
—Something Dreadful down Below, 1 vol. unabr. ed. 2010. (Q Reads Ser.). (ENG.). 32p. (YA). (gr. 9-12). pap. 6.95 *(978-1-61651-205-7(9))* Saddleback Educational Publishing, Inc.
Schraff, Anne E. Bad Blood. 2014. (Urban Underground — Cesar Chavez High School Ser.). (YA). lib. bdg. 20.80 *(978-0-606-35591-9(X))* Turtleback Bks.
—Dark Suspicions, 1 vol. unabr. ed. 2012. (Urban Underground Ser.). (ENG.). 204p. (YA). (gr. 9-12). pap. 9.95 *(978-1-61651-958-2(4))* Saddleback Educational Publishing, Inc.
—Guilt Trip. 2014. (Urban Underground — Cesar Chavez High School Ser.). (YA). lib. bdg. 20.80 *(978-0-606-35592-6(8))* Turtleback Bks.
Schrecengost, Maity. High above the Hippodrome. 2007. (J). (gr. 3-6). pap. 13.95 *(978-0-9771079-7-1(3),* Chapin Hse. Bks.) Florida Historical Society.
Schroeder, Lisa. All We Have Is Now. 2015. (ENG.). 272p. (J). (gr. 7). 17.99 *(978-0-545-80253-6(9))* Scholastic, Inc.
—Caitlin's Lucky Charm. 2014. (Charmed Life Ser.: 1). lib. bdg. 16.00 *(978-0-606-35849-1(8))* Turtleback Bks.
—Charmed Life #1: Caitlin's Lucky Charm. 2014. (Charmed Life Ser.: 1). (ENG.). 192p. (J). (gr. 3-7). pap. 5.99 *(978-0-545-60372-0(2))* Scholastic, Inc.
—Charmed Life #2: Mia's Golden Bird. 2014. (Charmed Life Ser.: 2). (ENG.). 192p. (J). (gr. 3-7). pap. 5.99 *(978-0-545-60377-5(3))* Scholastic, Inc.
—Charmed Life #4: Hannah's Bright Star. 2014. (Charmed Life Ser.: 4). (ENG.). 192p. (J). (gr. 3-7). pap. 5.99 *(978-0-545-60379-9(X),* Scholastic Paperbacks) Scholastic, Inc.
—Frosting & Friendship. 2013. (ENG., Illus.). 224p. (J). (gr. 3-7). 15.99 *(978-1-4424-7396-6(7),* Aladdin) Simon & Schuster Children's Publishing.
—Keys to the City. 2017. (ENG.). 240p. (J). (gr. 3-7). 16.99 ***(978-0-545-90738-5(1),*** Scholastic Pr.) Scholastic, Inc.
—Libby's Sweet Surprise. 2014. (Charmed Life Ser.: 3). lib. bdg. 16.00 *(978-0-606-35851-4(X))* Turtleback Bks.
—Mia's Golden Bird. 2014. (Charmed Life Ser.: 2). lib. bdg. 16.00 *(978-0-606-35850-7(1))* Turtleback Bks.
—Sprinkles & Secrets. 2012. (ENG.). 240p. (J). (gr. 3-7). pap. 7.99 *(978-1-4424-2264-3(5),* Aladdin) Simon & Schuster Children's Publishing.
Schroeder, Lisa & Dion, Nathalie. Sprinkles & Secrets. 2011. (ENG.). 224p. (J). (gr. 3-7). 15.99 *(978-1-4424-2263-6(7),* Aladdin) Simon & Schuster Children's Publishing.
Schronk, Julie. The Grass Grows Green. 2007. 208p. per. 24.95 *(978-1-60441-057-0(4))* America Star Bks.
Schubert, Ingrid & Schubert, Dieter. Ophelia. 2009. (ENG.). 32p. (J). (gr. -1-1). 16.95 *(978-1-59078-659-8(9),* 9781590786598) Lemniscaat USA.
Schueler, M. A. Penny the Beach Westie Big Trouble for a Little Dog. 2009. 24p. pap. 16.50 *(978-1-60860-424-1(1),* Eloquent Bks.) Strategic Book Publishing & Rights Agency (SBPRA).
Schultz, Caleb. Keela & Capone's Take That Dog Back! 2012. 24p. pap. 17.99 *(978-1-4772-3718-2(6))* AuthorHouse.
Schultz, Edward L. Pix, 1 vol. 2009. 48p. pap. 16.95 *(978-1-60749-393-8(4))* PublishAmerica, Inc.
Schultz, Jan Neubert. Battle Cry. Allen, Rick, illus. 2006. (ENG.). 240p. (YA). (gr. 6-12). 15.95 *(978-1-57505-928-0(2),* Carolrhoda Bks.) Lerner Publishing Group.
Schultz, Leslie & Braulick, J. J. M. And Sometimes Y. Newman, Heather, illus. 2013. 302p. pap. 12.99 *(978-1-937848-07-1(8))* Do Life Right, Inc.
Schultz Nicholson, Lorna. Northern Star, 1 vol. 2006. (Lorimer Sports Stories Ser.). (ENG.). 112p. (J). (gr. 4-8). 16.95 *(978-1-55028-911-4(X),* 9781550289114); 9.95 *(978-1-55028-910-7(1),* 9781550289107) Lorimer, James & Co., Ltd., Pubs. CAN. Dist: Casemate Pubs. & Bk. Distributors, LLC.
Schulz, Charles. Charlie Brown Thanksgiving, 1 vol. 2013. (Peanuts Picture Bks.). (ENG.). 24p. (J). (gr. -1-4). lib. bdg. 24.21 *(978-1-61479-030-3(2))* ABDO Publishing Co.
—I Need All the Friends I Can Get. 2006. (Peanuts(r) Ser.). (ENG., Illus.). 72p. 5.95 *(978-1-933662-39-8(5))* Cider Mill Pr. Bk. Pubs., LLC.
—Von der Rolle. Herbst, Gabriele & Rolle, Ekkehard, trs. from ENG. (Snoopy & die Peanuts Ser.: Vol. 29). (GER., Illus.). 96p. (J). pap. *(978-3-8105-1879-8(4))* Kruger, Wolfgang Verlag, GmbH DEU. Dist: International Bk. Import Service, Inc.
Schulz, Charles. Charlie Brown Seasonal. Schulz, Charles, . Date not set. (J). pap. 93.60 *(978-0-590-39601-1(3))* Scholastic, Inc.
Schulz, Charles M. A Charlie Brown Christmas: With Sound & Music. 2011. (ENG.). 48p. (J). (gr. -1-3). 22.95 *(978-0-7624-4005-4(8))* Running Pr. Bk. Pubs.
—Peanuts: Be Friends. 2013. (ENG., Illus.). 72p. (J). (gr. -1-17). 7.95 *(978-0-7624-5044-2(4),* Running Pr. Kids) Running Pr. Bk. Pubs.
Schulz, Heidi. Giraffes Ruin Everything. Robertson, Chris, illus. 2016. (ENG.). 40p. (J). 16.99 *(978-1-61963-475-6(9),* 9781619634756, Bloomsbury USA Childrens) Bloomsbury Publishing USA.
Schusterman, Michelle. Crushes, Codas, & Corsages. Kote, Geneviève, illus. 2014. (I Heart Band Ser.: 4). (ENG.). 208p. (J). (gr. 3-7). 6.99 *(978-0-448-45686-7(9),* Grosset & Dunlap) Penguin Young Readers Group.
—Friends, Fugues, & Fortune Cookies. Kote, Genevieve, illus. 2014. (I Heart Band Ser.: 2). (ENG.). 208p. (J). (gr. 3-7). 6.99 *(978-0-448-45684-3(2),* Grosset & Dunlap) Penguin Young Readers Group.
—I Heart Band #1. Kote, Genevieve, illus. 2014. (I Heart Band Ser.: 1). (ENG.). 208p. (J). (gr. 3-7). 6.99 *(978-0-448-45683-6(4),* Grosset & Dunlap) Penguin Young Readers Group.
Schusterman, Michelle & Kote, Geneviève. Sleepovers, Solos, & Sheet Music. 2014. (I Heart Band Ser.: 3). (ENG.). 208p. (J). (gr. 3-7). 6.99 *(978-0-448-45685-0(0),* Grosset & Dunlap) Penguin Young Readers Group.
Schwab, Victoria. Last Wishes. 2014. (Everyday Angel Ser.: 3). (ENG.). 208p. (J). (gr. 3-7). pap. 6.99 *(978-0-545-52848-1(8),* Scholastic Paperbacks) Scholastic, Inc.
—New Beginnings. 2014. (Everyday Angel Ser.: 1). (J). (ENG.). 208p. (gr. 3-7). pap. 6.99 *(978-0-545-52846-7(1),* Scholastic Paperbacks); 195p. pap. *(978-0-545-68443-9(9))* Scholastic, Inc.
Schwartz, Amy. I Can't Wait! Schwartz, Amy, illus. 2015. (ENG., Illus.). 40p. (J). (gr. k-3). 17.99 *(978-1-4424-8231-9(1),* Beach Lane Bks.) Beach Lane Bks.
Schwartz, B. J. The Adventures of Max & I. 2011. 54p. pap. 24.99 *(978-1-4670-2434-1(1))* AuthorHouse.
—The Adventures of Max & I: Dream Pirates. 2011. 32p. pap. 15.99 *(978-1-4670-2435-8(X))* AuthorHouse.
Schwartz, Ellen. Abby's Birds, 1 vol. Shefrin, Sima Elizabeth, illus. 2007. (ENG.). 32p. (J). (gr. 1-4). 16.95 *(978-1-896580-86-9(6))* Tradewind Bks. CAN. Dist: Orca Bk. Pubs. USA.
Schwartz, Joel. The Extraordinary Pupfish of Calaveras County. 2008. 216p. 25.95 *(978-1-4401-0892-1(7))* iUniverse, Inc.
Schwartz, Suzanne & Schwartz, Robert. The Christmas Palm Tree: A Storybook to Color. Schwartz, Suzanne & Schwartz, Robert, illus. l.t. ed. 2005. (Illus.). 22p. (J). spiral bd. 3.99 *(978-0-9764152-3-7(2))* Seascay Productions.
—My Friend Hibby: A Tropical Adventure. Schwartz, Suzanne & Schwartz, Robert, illus. 2005. (Illus.). 20p. (J). spiral bd. 6.00 *(978-0-9764152-0-6(8))* Seascay Productions.
Schwarz, Viviane. How to Find Gold. Schwarz, Viviane, illus. 2016. (ENG., Illus.). 32p. (J). (-k). 16.99 *(978-0-7636-8104-3(0))* Candlewick Pr.
Schwiebert, Pat & DeKlyen, Chuck. Tear Soup: A Recipe for Healing after Loss. Bills, Taylor, illus. 2nd rev. l.t. ed. 2004. (ENG.). 56p. (gr. -1-12). reprint ed. 19.95 *(978-0-9615197-6-6(2),* 798) Grief Watch.
Schwind, Beverly Lahote. Patches & Her Backpack Adventures. 2013. (Illus.). 142p. 14.00 *(978-0-9745810-8-8(9))* Potters Publishing LLC.
Scieszka, Jon. Domingo, el Día del Vikingo. (SPA.). (J). 7.95 *(978-958-04-7448-7(6))* Norma S.A. COL. Dist: Distribuidora Norma, Inc.
—Spaceheadz. Prigmore, Shane, illus. (Spaceheadz Ser.: 3). (ENG.). 224p. (J). (gr. 2-5). 2012. pap. 7.99 *(978-1-4169-7956-2(5))* 2011. 15.99 *(978-1-4169-7955-5(7))* Simon & Schuster Bks. For Young Readers. (Simon & Schuster Bks. For Young Readers).
—SPHDZ 4 Life! Prigmore, Shane, illus. 2013. (Spaceheadz Ser.: 4). (ENG.). 192p. (J). (gr. 2-5). pap. 5.99 *(978-1-4169-7958-6(1));*Bk. 4. 16.99 *(978-1-4169-7957-9(3))* Simon & Schuster Bks. For Young Readers. (Simon & Schuster Bks. For Young Readers).
—Welcome to Trucktown! Shannon, David et al, illus. 2010. (Jon Scieszka's Trucktown Ser.). (ENG.). 40p. (J). (gr. -1-3). pap. 3.99 *(978-1-4424-1271-2(2),* Simon & Schuster Bks. For Young Readers) Simon & Schuster Bks. For Young Readers.
Scillian, Devin. Memoirs of a Goldfish. Bowers, Tim, illus. 2010. (ENG.). 32p. (J). (gr. -1-3). 15.95 *(978-1-58536-507-4(6))* Sleeping Bear Pr.
—Memoirs of a Parrot. Bowers, Tim, illus. 2016. (ENG.). 32p. (J). (gr. k-3). 16.99 *(978-1-58536-962-1(4),* 204036) Sleeping Bear Pr.
Scipio, Laurise. I Wish. 2012. 16p. pap. 12.68 *(978-1-4669-3948-6(6))* Trafford Publishing.
Scoggins, Terry. Electric Ellie & Lightning Lucy: Firefly Friends Forever. 2008. 16p. pap. 8.99 *(978-1-4389-1254-7(4))* AuthorHouse.
Scollon, Bill. Disney*Pixar Finding Dory: Friends Forever. 2016. (ENG.). 12p. (J). (gr. -1-k). 8.99 *(978-0-7944-3670-4(6),* Reader's Digest Children's Bks.) Studio Fun International.
—Super Adventure. Disney Book Group Staff & Disney Storybook Artists Staff, illus. 2013. (ENG.). 24p. (J). (gr. -1-k). pap. 4.99 *(978-1-4231-8657-1(5))* Disney Pr.
Scollon, William & Disney Book Group Staff. The Case of the Missing Sparkle-Izer, Level Pre-1. Disney Storybook Art Team, illus. 2013. (World of Reading Ser.). (ENG.). 32p. (J). (gr. -1-k). pap. 3.99 *(978-1-4231-8482-9(3))* Disney Pr.
Scott, Brandon James, illus. The Big Pet Story. 2013. (Justin Time Ser.). (ENG.). 36p. (J). (gr. -1-3). 15.95 *(978-1-59702-041-1(9))* Immedium.
Scott, Elizabeth. Love You Hate You Miss You. (ENG.). (YA). (gr. 8). 2010. 304p. pap. 8.99 *(978-0-06-112285-9(8))* 2009. 288p. 16.99 *(978-0-06-112283-5(1))* HarperCollins Pubs. (HarperTeen).
—Perfect You. 2008. (ENG.). 304p. (YA). (gr. 9-12). pap. 9.99 *(978-1-4169-5355-5(8),* Simon Pulse) Simon Pulse.
—Stealing Heaven. 2009. (ENG.). 336p. (YA). (gr. 8). pap. 8.99 *(978-0-06-112282-8(3),* HarperTeen) HarperCollins Pubs.
—The Unwritten Rule. (ENG.). (YA). (gr. 9). 2011. 240p. pap. 9.99 *(978-1-4169-7892-3(5))* 2010. 224p. 16.99 *(978-1-4169-7891-6(7))* Simon Pulse. (Simon Pulse).
Scott, Elizabeth M. Adventures with Mama Scottie & the Kids. Jackson, Kay Whytock, illus. 2008. 60p. pap. 8.95 *(978-0-595-51760-2(9))* iUniverse, Inc.
Scott, Jerry. Chillax. Borgman, Jim, illus. 2013. (Zits Ser.: 1). (ENG.). 256p. (YA). (gr. 8). pap. 9.99 *(978-0-06-222851-2(X),* HarperTeen) HarperCollins Pubs.
—Zits Vol. 7: Carretera y Manta. 2007. (SPA., Illus.). 128p. reprint ed. pap. 19.95 *(978-1-59497-337-6(7))* Public Square Bks.
Scott, Kieran. What Waits in the Woods. 2017. (ENG.). 288p. (J). (gr. 7). pap. 9.99 ***(978-0-545-83763-7(4))*** Scholastic, Inc.
Scott, Rosanna. Peter & Friends at Camp. Fargo, Todd, illus. l.t. ed. 2006. (Turtle Books). 32p. (J). (gr. k-4). pap. 9.95 *(978-0-944727-51-5(4));* lib. bdg. 15.95 *(978-0-944727-52-2(2))* Jason & Nordic Pubs. (Turtle Bks.).
Scott, Shirley A. The Adventures of Jack & Dobbie: Traveling Buddies. 2012. 30p. pap. 18.99 *(978-1-4772-7851-2(6))* AuthorHouse.
Scott, Victoria. Titans. 2016. (ENG.). 320p. (J). (gr. 7). 17.99 *(978-0-545-80601-5(1),* Scholastic Pr.) Scholastic, Inc.
Scott, William. Bouncy Bear. 2013. 32p. pap. 24.95 *(978-1-4626-9757-1(7))* America Star Bks.
Scotton, Rob. The Name of the Game. 2012. (Splat the Cat: I Can Read Ser.). (J). lib. bdg. 13.55 *(978-0-606-26281-1(4),* Turtleback) Turtleback Bks.
—Splat & Seymour, Best Friends Forevermore. 2014. (Splat the Cat: I Can Read Ser.). (J). lib. bdg. 13.55 *(978-0-606-35960-3(5))* Turtleback Bks.
—Splat the Cat. Scotton, Rob, illus. 2008. (Splat the Cat Ser.). (Illus.). 40p. (J). (gr. -1-3). (ENG.). 17.99 *(978-0-06-083154-7(5));* lib. bdg. 17.89 *(978-0-06-083155-4(3))* HarperCollins Pubs.
—Splat the Cat. 2011. (J). (gr. -1-2). 29.95 *(978-0-545-23794-9(7))* Weston Woods Studios, Inc.
—Splat the Cat: Splat & Seymour, Best Friends Forevermore. Scotton, Rob, illus. 2014. (I Can Read Level 1 Ser.). (ENG., Illus.). 32p. (J). (gr. -1-3). pap. 3.99 *(978-0-06-211601-7(0))* HarperCollins Pubs.
—Splat the Cat Goes to the Doctor. Scotton, Rob, illus. 2014. (Splat the Cat Ser.). (ENG., Illus.). 24p. (J). (gr. -1-3). pap. 4.99 *(978-0-06-211588-1(X),* HarperFestival) HarperCollins Pubs.
—Splish, Splash, Splat! Scotton, Rob, illus. 2011. (Splat the Cat Ser.). (ENG., Illus.). 40p. (J). (gr. -1-3). 16.99 *(978-0-06-197868-5(X))* HarperCollins Pubs.
—Up in the Air at the Fair. Scotton, Rob, illus. 2014. (I Can Read Level 1 Ser.). (ENG., Illus.). 32p. (J). (gr. -1-3). 16.99 *(978-0-06-211596-6(0));* pap. 3.99 *(978-0-06-211595-9(2))* HarperCollins Pubs.
—A Whale of a Tale. Scotton, Rob, illus. 2013. (I Can Read Level 1 Ser.). (ENG., Illus.). 32p. (J). (gr. -1-3). pap. 3.99 *(978-0-06-209022-5(4))* HarperCollins Pubs.

Scriber, Christian. The Adventures of Almighty Mouse: And Tales of His Friends. 2009. 112p. pap. 10.99 *(978-1-4389-4313-8(X))* AuthorHouse.
Scripture Teachers: Solomon & Friends Learn about Forgiveness. 2003. pap. *(978-0-9712894-1-3(7))* Lighthouse Christian Products Co.
Scripture Teachers: Solomon & Friends Learn about Prayer. 2003. pap. *(978-0-9712894-0-6(9))* Lighthouse Christian Products Co.
Scruggs, Sheldon. Tyler: The Strongest Boy on the Block. 2012. 140p. pap. 12.95 *(978-1-4575-1355-8(2))* Dog Ear Publishing, LLC.
Searl, Duncan. The Jamie & Angus Stories: A Study Guide. Friedland, Joyce & Kessler, Rikki, eds. 2008. (Novel-Ties Ser.). (Illus.). 23p. pap. 16.95 *(978-0-7675-1485-9(8))* Learning Links Inc.
Sebra, Diane. Making Mountains Out of Moles. 2003. 120p. pap. 9.95 *(978-1-55517-712-6(3),* 77123) Cedar Fort, Inc./CFI Distribution.
Secret in the Stable. 2008. (Illus.). 32p. *(978-0-545-02924-7(4))* Scholastic, Inc.
Seddon, Jane. Tales of Berry Wood, 1 vol. 2010. 64p. pap. 19.95 *(978-1-4489-2195-9(3))* America Star Bks.
Seeger, Laura Vaccaro. Dog & Bear: Tricks & Treats. Seeger, Laura Vaccaro, illus. 2014. (Dog & Bear Ser.). (ENG., Illus.). 32p. (J). (gr. -1-3). 14.99 *(978-1-59643-632-9(8),* 9781596436329) Roaring Brook Pr.
—Dog & Bear, Level 2: Two Friends, Three Stories. Seeger, Laura Vaccaro, illus. 2012. (My Readers Ser.). (ENG., Illus.). 32p. (J). (gr. k-2). pap. 3.99 *(978-0-312-54799-8(4),* 9780312547998) Square Fish.
—Two Friends, Three Stories. Seeger, Laura Vaccaro, illus. 2007. (Dog & Bear Ser.). (ENG., Illus.). 32p. (J). (gr. -1-3). 15.99 *(978-1-59643-053-2(2),* 9781596430532) Roaring Brook Pr.
Segal, Andrew. Roberto the Robot. Scott, Peter & JessT, Grant, illus. 2007. 32p. per. *(978-1-905823-26-0(6))* Panoma Pr. Ltd.
Segal, Zoe. Confessions of a Tenth-Grade Social Climber. 2005. 290p. (YA). *(978-0-618-44981-1(7))* Houghton Mifflin Harcourt Publishing Co.
Seiss, Ellie. Best Friends: A Chock-a-Block Book. Scanlon, Michael, illus. 2010. (Yo Gabba Gabba! Ser.). (ENG.). 12p. (J). 5.99 *(978-1-4424-0970-5(3),* Simon Spotlight) Simon Spotlight.
Seitz, Melissa. Stewie Meets New Friends. Accrocco, Anthony, illus. 2012. 26p. pap. 12.95 *(978-1-61244-079-8(7))* Halo Publishing International.
Seki, Sunny. The Last Kappa of Old Japan: A Magical Journey of Two Friends. rev. ed. 2016. (ENG & JPN., Illus.). 32p. (J). (gr. k-8). 12.95 *(978-4-8053-1399-2(4))* Tuttle Publishing.
Self, Jeffery. Drag Teen. 2016. (ENG.). 272p. (YA). (gr. 9). 17.99 *(978-0-545-82993-9(3),* PUSH) Scholastic, Inc.
Sell, Jeff. The Quarry Cave. 2006. 51p. pap. 16.95 *(978-1-4241-1188-6(9))* PublishAmerica, Inc.
Sellers, Kathy Lacey. Willie Chaff. 2010. pap. 10.95 *(978-0-7414-6080-6(7))* Infinity Publishing.
Sellers, Sandra. Gran's Story IV: Gathering Wild Violets. 2011. 24p. (gr. -1). pap. 15.99 *(978-1-4269-5707-9(6))* Trafford Publishing.
Sempé, Jean-Jacques & Bell, Anthea. Raoul Taburin Keeps a Secret. 2010. (ENG., Illus.). 96p. (gr. 7-17). 29.95 *(978-0-7148-4979-9(0))* Phaidon Pr., Inc.
Sempebwa, Christina. Tales of Zindan. 2012. 154p. pap. *(978-1-908895-48-6(9))* FeedARead.com.
Seo, Kaila Eunhye, illus. Fred. 2015. (ENG.). 40p. (J). 15.99 *(978-1-4413-1731-5(7),* 9781441317315) Peter Pauper Pr. Inc.
Serafin, Michael. 4 Seasons of Baghdad. 2007. (ENG.). 60p. per. 16.95 *(978-1-4241-2303-2(8))* PublishAmerica, Inc.
Sergeyeva, Marina. Nikki & Nick Are Great Friends to Pick. Sergeyeva, Marina, illus. 2012. (Illus.). 34p. 19.95 *(978-0-9834735-4-1(4))* Leo Publishing.
Serino, Robert. The Adventures of Pea-Shooter: Into the Forbidden Forest. Lally, Cory, illus. 2012. 32p. pap. 24.95 *(978-1-4626-8019-1(4))* America Star Bks.
Seroney, Kibny'aanko Arap. Cheebtabuut, Blue Berries & the Monsters Den. 2013. 36p. pap. *(978-1-909204-28-7(5))* BookPublishingWorld.
Serrano, Tina. Urban Scavenger Hunt, 1 vol. 2010. 50p. pap. 16.95 *(978-1-4489-4451-4(1))* America Star Bks.
Serros, Michele. Honey Blonde Chica. 2007. (ENG.). 320p. (YA). (gr. 9-12). pap. 14.99 *(978-1-4169-1592-8(3),* Simon Pulse) Simon Pulse.
—¡Scandalosa! A Honey Blonde Chica Novel. 2008. (ENG.). 320p. (YA). (gr. 9). pap. 14.99 *(978-1-4169-1594-2(X),* Simon Pulse) Simon Pulse.
Serwacki, Kevin & Pallace, Chris. Joey & Johnny - The Ninjas - Get Mooned. Serwacki, Kevin & Pallace, Chris, illus. 2015. (Joey & Johnny, the Ninjas Ser.: 1). (ENG., Illus.). 320p. (J). (gr. 3-7). 12.99 *(978-0-06-229933-8(6))* HarperCollins Pubs.
—Joey & Johnny, the Ninjas: Epic Fail. Serwacki, Kevin & Pallace, Chris, illus. 2016. (Joey & Johnny, the Ninjas Ser.: 2). (Illus.). 384p. (J). (gr. 3-7). 12.99 *(978-0-06-229935-2(2))* HarperCollins Pubs.
Sesame Workshop. All Tucked in on Sesame Street! 2014. (Sesame Street Scribbles Ser.: 0). (ENG., Illus.). 32p. (J). (-3). 10.99 *(978-1-4022-9725-0(4),* Sourcebooks Jabberwocky) Sourcebooks, Inc.
—Happy Halloween! 2014. (Sesame Street Scribbles Elmo Ser.: 0). (ENG., Illus.). 32p. (J). (-3). 10.99 *(978-1-4022-9750-2(5),* 9781402297502, Sourcebooks Jabberwocky) Sourcebooks, Inc.
Sesame Workshop Staff. Let's Make a Friend! 2016. (Sesame Street Scribbles Ser.: 0). (ENG., Illus.). 32p. (J). (-2). 10.99 *(978-1-4926-4139-1(1),* 9781492641391, Sourcebooks Jabberwocky) Sourcebooks, Inc.
—Sesame Street I Can Do It! A Treasury of Stories. 2017. (ENG., Illus.). 288p. (J). (gr. -1-17). 14.99 *(978-0-7624-6163-9(2),* Running Pr.) Running Pr. Bk. Pubs.
Sesso, Karen A. Off They Swam, 1 vol. 2009. 37p. pap. 19.95 *(978-1-61546-453-1(0))* PublishAmerica, Inc.
Seuling, Barbara. Robert & the Great Escape. Brewer, Paul, illus. 2003. (Robert Bks.). (ENG.). 120p. (J). 15.95 *(978-0-8126-2700-8(8))* Cricket Bks.
—Robert & the Practical Jokes. Brewer, Paul, illus. 2006. (Robert Bks.). (ENG.). 150p. (J). (gr. k-4). 16.95 *(978-0-8126-2741-1(5))* Cricket Bks.
—Robert Goes to Camp. Brewer, Paul, illus. 2007. (Robert Bks.). (ENG.). 160p. (J). (gr. k-4). 16.95 *(978-0-8126-2753-4(9))* Cricket Bks.
Seuss, Dr. Come over to My House. Kath, Katie, illus. 2016. (Beginner Books(R) Ser.). (ENG.). 64p. (J). (gr. k-4). 9.99 *(978-0-553-53665-2(6),* Random Hse. Bks. for Young Readers) Random Hse. Children's Bks.
Sévigny, Eric, illus. Caillou: the Doodle Artist. 2014. (ENG.). 128p. (J). (gr. -1-1). 7.95 *(978-2-89718-126-0(5))* Caillouet, Gerry.
S.E.W. The Year at Widows' Creek: The Beginning. 2009. 44p. pap. 17.49 *(978-1-4389-5546-9(4))* AuthorHouse.
Sewell, Kele. Beewee & Meager to the Rescue! the Underbed Entertainment Network. 2008. 28p. pap. 12.50 *(978-1-60693-326-8(4),* Eloquent Bks.) Strategic Book Publishing & Rights Agency (SBPRA).
Sexton, Jessa Rose. Eldy & Ohi. Miele, Brianna, illus. 2012. 36p. pap. 8.00 *(978-0-9860150-9-0(1))* O'More Publishing.
Seyderhelm, Amanda. Isaac & the Red Jumper. Scott, Ann, illus. 2013. 26p. pap. *(978-0-9572146-1-3(8))* HARK Pubns.
Seykora, Teresa. The Case of the Missing Peanut Butter: The Adventures of Peanut Butter Bob. Drewes, Dan, illus. 2010. 32p. 12.99 *(978-1-4520-2678-7(5))* AuthorHouse.
Seymour, Kristen. No Thank You, I'm Allergic: A Story Agout Food Allergy Awareness. 2011. 27p. (J). pap. 12.95 *(978-1-4327-3293-6(5))* Outskirts Pr., Inc.
Seyvos, Florence. Pockety: The Tortoise Who Lived As She Pleased. Provata-Carlone, Mika, tr. from FRE. Ponti, Claude, illus. 2014. (ENG.). 64p. (J). (gr. 2-4). pap. 9.99 *(978-1-78269-025-2(5),* Pushkin Press) Steerforth Pr.
Shaddix, M. K. Aisling's Summer Diary. 2012. 200p. pap. 6.99 *(978-0-9567500-8-2(7))* BeActive Publishing Co.
Shahan, Sherry. Skin & Bones. 2014. (ENG.). 272p. (YA). (gr. 8-12). 16.99 *(978-0-8075-7397-6(3))* Whitman, Albert & Co.
Shahbaz, Zak Iman. Ameerah's First Day. 2012. (ENG.). (J). pap. 8.95 *(978-1-4675-2269-4(4))* Independent Pub.
Shahbaz, Zakia. Ramadan & the Three R's. 2013. 26p. 19.95 *(978-1-61863-464-1(X))* Bookstand Publishing.
Shalant, Phyllis. Beware of Kissing Lizard Lips. 2010. 196p. pap. 13.95 *(978-1-4401-8339-3(2))* iUniverse, Inc.
—When Pirates Came to Brooklyn. 2010. 224p. pap. 14.95 *(978-1-4401-8338-6(4))* iUniverse, Inc.
Shally, Celeste. Since We're Friends: An Autism Picture Book. Harrington, David, illus. 2007. 32p. (J). (gr. -1-3). per. 8.99 *(978-0-9794713-0-8(3))* Awaken Specialty Pr.
—Since We're Friends: An Autism Picture Book. Harrington, David, illus. 2012. (ENG.). 32p. (J). (gr. -1-3). 12.95 *(978-1-61608-656-5(4),* 608656, Sky Pony Pr.) Skyhorse Publishing Co., Inc.
Shank, Diane S. Minnow Kisses. Bailey, Terri L., illus. 2011. 34p. pap. 12.95 *(978-1-936343-60-7(6))* Peppertree Pr., The.
Shankman, Ed. Champ & Me by the Maple Tree. O'Neill, Dave, illus. 2010. (Shankman & O'Neill Ser.). (ENG.). 32p. (gr. -1-3). 14.95 *(978-0-9819430-5-3(5),* Commonwealth Editions) Applewood Bks.
Shanks, Melanie. The Squints. 2007. 116p. per. 10.95 *(978-0-595-44849-4(6))* iUniverse, Inc.
Shann, Taylor. Strange Day. 2003. (J). 13.00 *(978-0-9679552-4-7(6))* Mushroom Cloud Pr. of Orlando.
Shannon, David. A Bad Case of Stripes. Shannon, David, illus. 2004. (Scholastic Bookshelf Ser.). (ENG., Illus.). 32p. (J). (gr. -1-3). reprint ed. pap. 6.99 *(978-0-439-59838-5(9),* Scholastic Paperbacks) Scholastic, Inc.
Shannon Simmons. The Community Club: #1 Aubrey & the Fight for Life. 2009. 112p. pap. 10.95 *(978-1-4401-7616-6(7))* iUniverse, Inc.
Shannon, Star Erian. Erian's Friend Jeremiah the Owl. 2003. (J). pap. 9.00 *(978-0-8059-6068-6(6))* Dorrance Publishing Co., Inc.
Sharifi, David & Sharifi, Jason. Moonlight Valley: The Great Race. 2008. 28p. pap. 13.99 *(978-1-4389-1865-5(8))* AuthorHouse.
Sharkey, Niamh. I'm a Happy Hugglewug: Laugh & Play the Hugglewug Way. Sharkey, Niamh, illus. 2008. (ENG., Illus.). 34p. (J). (gr. k-k). bds. 6.99 *(978-0-7636-3981-5(8))* Candlewick Pr.
Sharmat, Marjorie Weinman & Sharmat, Mitchell. The Green Toenails Gang. Brunkus, Denise, illus. 2nd ed. 2005. (Olivia Sharp: Agent for Secrets Ser.). (ENG.). 80p. (J). (gr. 3-7). per. 5.99 *(978-0-440-42063-7(6),* Yearling) Random Hse. Children's Bks.
—The Pizza Monster. Brunkus, Denise, illus. 2nd ed. 2005. (Olivia Sharp: Agent for Secrets Ser.). (ENG.). 80p. (J). (gr. 3-7). reprint ed. 5.99 *(978-0-440-42059-0(8),* Yearling) Random Hse. Children's Bks.
Sharp, Andre L. I Don't Talk Funny, I Stutter: A Children's Motivational Book. 2011. 28p. pap. 15.99 *(978-1-4628-9685-1(5))* Xlibris Corp.
Sharp, Euan. Diggedy Dozer in Ned at Night. 2009. 32p. pap. 13.90 *(978-0-557-04447-4(2))* Lulu Pr., Inc.
Sharpe, Gerald. Tommy's Tales. Moya, Patricia, illus. 2006. (Tommy's Tales Ser.). 300p. (J). per. 7.00 *(978-1-933894-00-3(8))* IJN Publishing, Inc.
—What Lies Beneath the Bed: Tommy's Tales (Revised) 2nd rev. ed. 2008. 320p. pap. 7.95 *(978-1-933894-04-1(0))* IJN Publishing, Inc.
Sharpe, Tess. Far from You. 2014. (ENG.). 352p. (YA). (gr. 9-17). 17.99 *(978-1-4231-8462-1(9))* Hyperion Bks. for Children.
Shaskan, Trisha Speed. Punk Skunks. Shaskan, Stephen, illus. 2016. 40p. (J). (gr. -1-3). 17.99 *(978-0-06-236396-1(4))* HarperCollins Pubs.
Shava, Ryder. Chen's Friends, 01 vols., 1. 2016. (Rosen REAL Readers: Social Studies Nonfiction / Fiction: Family, Community, & the World Ser.). (ENG.). 12p. (J). pap. 6.33 *(978-1-5081-1931-9(7),* Rosen Classroom) Rosen Publishing Group, Inc., The.
Shaw, Gina. Oh My! Ginny Fry! Barton, Patrice, illus. 2010. 48p. (J). *(978-0-545-24384-1(X))* Scholastic, Inc.
Shaw, J. D. The Secrets of Loon Lake. 2010. (ENG.). 338p. (J). (gr. 5). pap. 16.95 *(978-0-9845318-0-6(7))* Tiny Stachel Pr.
Shaw, Mary. Brady Brady & the B Team, 12 vols. Temple, Chuck, illus. l.t. ed. 2006. 32p. (J). per. *(978-1-897169-09-4(4))* Brady Brady, Inc.
Shaw, Natalie. A Guide to Being a Friend. 2014. (Olivia 8x8 Ser.). lib. bdg. 16.00 *(978-0-606-36117-0(0))* Turtleback Bks.
—I'm Feeling Happy. Fruchter, Jason, illus. 2016. (Daniel Tiger's Neighborhood Ser.). (ENG.). 14p. (J). (gr. -1 — 1). bds. 5.99 *(978-1-4814-6178-8(8),* Simon Spotlight) Simon Spotlight.
—I'M Feeling Silly. Fruchter, Jason, illus. 2016. (Daniel Tiger's Neighborhood Ser.). (ENG.). 14p. (J). (gr. -1 — 1). bds. 5.99 *(978-1-4814-6815-2(4),* Simon Spotlight) Simon Spotlight.
—It's Nice to Meet You. Giles, Mike, illus. 2010. (Yo Gabba Gabba! Ser.). (ENG.). 24p. (J). (gr. -1-2). pap. 3.99 *(978-1-4169-9721-4(0),* Simon Spotlight) Simon Spotlight.
—Meet the Neighbors! Style Guide Staff, illus. 2014. (Daniel Tiger's Neighborhood Ser.). (ENG.). 16p. (J). (gr. -1-k). bds. 7.99 *(978-1-4424-9837-2(4),* Simon Spotlight) Simon Spotlight.
—OLIVIA & the Perfect Valentine. Johnson, Shane L., illus. 2013. (Olivia TV Tie-In Ser.). (ENG.). 24p. (J). (gr. -1-2). pap. 4.99 *(978-1-4424-8484-9(5),* Simon Spotlight) Simon Spotlight.
Shaw, Susan. Safe. 2007. (ENG.). 176p. (YA). (gr. 9-18). pap. 14.00 *(978-0-525-47829-4(9),* Dutton Books for Young Readers) Penguin Young Readers Group.
Shaw, Tucker. The Girls. 2010. (ENG.). 224p. (YA). (gr. 7-11). pap. 7.95 *(978-0-8109-8991-7(3),* Amulet Bks.) Abrams, Inc.
—Oh Yeah, Audrey! 2014. (ENG., Illus.). 256p. (YA). (gr. 8-17). 16.95 *(978-1-4197-1223-4(3),* Amulet Bks.) Abrams, Inc.
Shaw, Tucker & Luce, Clare Boothe. The Girls. 2009. (ENG.). 208p. (YA). (gr. 7-11). 17.95 *(978-0-8109-8348-9(6),* Amulet Bks.) Abrams, Inc.
Shaw Wolf, Jennifer. Dead Girls Don't Lie. 2013. 336p. pap. 17.99 *(978-0-8027-3450-1(2))* Walker & Co.
Shay, Kenley. Marsha Mellow Goes Missing: An Unofficial Story for Shopkins Collectors. 2015. (Unofficial Shopkins Collectors Ser.). (ENG.). 112p. (J). (gr. 1-7). pap. 7.99 *(978-1-5107-0251-6(2),* Sky Pony Pr.) Skyhorse Publishing Co., Inc.
—Prommy Meets Her Match: An Unofficial Story for Shopkins Collectors. 2015. (Unofficial Shopkins Collectors Ser.). (ENG.). 112p. (J). (gr. 1-7). pap. 7.99 *(978-1-5107-0374-2(8),* Sky Pony Pr.) Skyhorse Publishing Co., Inc.
Shay, Mary Bernard. A Friend for Bobby. 2012. 24p. pap. 24.95 *(978-1-4626-6007-0(X))* America Star Bks.
Shea, Bob. Ballet Cat: The Totally Secret Secret. Shea, Bob, illus. 2015. (Ballet Cat Ser.). (ENG., Illus.). 56p. (J). (gr. 1-3). 9.99 *(978-1-4847-1378-5(8))* Disney Pr.
—Unicorn Thinks He's Pretty Great. Shea, Bob, illus. 2013. (ENG., Illus.). 40p. (J). (gr. -1-k). 15.99 *(978-1-4231-5952-0(7))* Hyperion Pr.
Shea, Lisa. Littlest Pet Shop: Sugar & Spice: Starring Pepper Clark. 2016. (ENG.). 144p. (J). (gr. 3-7). pap. 5.99 *(978-0-316-39523-6(4))* Little, Brown Bks. for Young Readers.
Shearer, Alex. Wilmot & Chips. 167p. (J). pap. *(978-0-340-72740-9(3))* Hodder & Stoughton.
—Wilmot & Chips. movie tie-in ed. 167p. pap. 7.99 *(978-0-340-80557-2(9))* Hodder & Stoughton GBR. Dist: Trafalgar Square Publishing.
—Wilmot & the Pops. (Illus.). 184p. (J). pap. *(978-0-340-71641-0(X))* Hodder & Stoughton.
Sheath, Irene. Lippy Lime Juice. 2004. 144p. (J). per. *(978-1-904502-48-7(2))* MediaWorld/BestBooks.
Sheehan, Jennifer E. Miss Bumples Lands on Earth. 2003. (Illus.). 32p. (J). 15.95 *(978-0-9700952-5-1(2))* Bumples.
Sheehy-Culhane, Roisin. WHEN MAMA GOES to WORK: DEVIN's STORY. 2006. (ENG.). 32p. per. 19.99 *(978-1-4257-0596-1(0))* Xlibris Corp.
Sheets, Katherine. Captured by Henrey, 1 vol. 2010. 48p. pap. 16.95 *(978-1-4489-4538-2(0))* America Star Bks.
Shefelman, Janice J. & Shefelman, Tom, illus. Son of Spirit Horse. 2004. 74p. (J). *(978-1-57168-833-0(1),* Eakin Pr.) Eakin Pr.
Sheinmel, Alyssa. Faceless. 2015. (ENG.). 352p. (J). (gr. 7). 18.99 *(978-0-545-67601-4(0),* Scholastic Pr.) Scholastic, Inc.
Sheinmel, Courtney. All the Things You Are. (ENG.). 256p. (J). (gr. 4-8). 2012. pap. 6.99 *(978-1-4169-9718-4(0))* 2011. 15.99 *(978-1-4169-9717-7(2))* Simon & Schuster Bks. For Young Readers. (Simon & Schuster Bks. For Young Readers).
—Broken Birthday. Bell, Jennifer A., illus. 2017. (Stella Batts Ser.). (ENG.). 160p. (J). (gr. 2-3). 9.99 *(978-1-58536-921-8(7),* 204228) Sleeping Bear Pr.
—The Kindness Club. 2016. (Kindness Club Ser.). (ENG.). 224p. (J). 15.99 *(978-1-68119-091-4(5),* 9781681190914, Bloomsbury USA Childrens) Bloomsbury Publishing USA.
—My So-Called Family. (ENG.). 208p. (J). (gr. 4-7). 2009. pap. 6.99 *(978-1-4169-7942-5(5))* 2008. 15.99 *(978-1-4169-5785-0(5))* Simon & Schuster Bks. For Young Readers. (Simon & Schuster Bks. For Young Readers).
—Positively. 2010. (ENG.). 240p. (J). (gr. 4-9). pap. 6.99 *(978-1-4424-0622-3(4),* Simon & Schuster Bks. For Young Readers) Simon & Schuster Bks. For Young Readers.
—Sincerely: Sincerely, Sophie; Sincerely, Katie. 2010. (ENG.). 400p. (J). (gr. 3-7). 15.99 *(978-1-4169-4010-4(3),* Simon & Schuster Bks. For Young Readers) Simon & Schuster Bks. For Young Readers.
—Sincerely: Sincerely, Sophie, Sincerely, Katie. 2011. (ENG.). 416p. (J). (gr. 3-7). pap. 7.99 *(978-1-4169-4022-7(7),* Simon & Schuster Bks. For Young Readers) Simon & Schuster Bks. For Young Readers.
—Stella Batts: Pardon Me. Bell, Jennifer A., illus. 2012. (Stella Batts Ser.: 3). (ENG.). 160p. (J). (gr. 1-3). 9.99 *(978-1-58536-193-9(3),* 202270); pap. 5.99 *(978-1-58536-194-6(1),* 202271) Sleeping Bear Pr.
Sheinmel, Courtney & Bell, Jennifer A. Stella Batts: Hair Today, Gone Tomorrow. 2012. (Stella Batts Ser.). (ENG., Illus.). (J). (gr. 1-3). 152p. pap. 5.99 *(978-1-58536-191-5(7),* 202269); 160p. lib. bdg. 9.99 *(978-1-58536-189-2(5),* 202268) Sleeping Bear Pr.
Sheldon, Dyan. Confessions of a Teenage Drama Queen. movie tie-in ed. 2004. (J). 107.82 *(978-0-7636-2538-2(8))* Candlewick Pr.
—My Worst Best Friend. 2010. (ENG., Illus.). 304p. (YA). (gr. 7-18). 15.99 *(978-0-7636-4555-7(9))* Candlewick Pr.
Sheley, Kristen. Partners in Time #4: Family Matters. 2008. 216p. pap. 15.95 *(978-0-595-51850-0(8))* iUniverse, Inc.
—Partners in Time #5: A Change of Course. 2010. 236p. 25.95 *(978-1-4502-6658-1(4));* pap. 15.95 *(978-1-4502-6657-4(6))* iUniverse, Inc.
ShelFish. Dots Dots Polka Dots, 1 vol. 2010. 46p. 24.95 *(978-1-4512-1427-7(8))* PublishAmerica, Inc.
Shell, S. E. Coffee with Orange Sherbert: Friendship Can Be Found Where Eyes & Hearts Are Open. Smith, Mary Elizabeth, illus. 2012. (ENG.). 42p. (J). pap. 14.99 *(978-0-9885461-2-7(4))* Osherbert Bks., LLC.
Shelley Ann Boutcher-Caldwell. The Naughty Little Birdie & the Surprise Cake. 2009. 40p. pap. 16.99 *(978-1-4389-4896-6(4))* AuthorHouse.
Shelly's Outdoor Adventure. 2013. (ENG.). 28p. pap. 8.00 *(978-0-9851845-0-6(7))* Shelly's Adventures LLC.
Shelton, Donna. Breaking Dawn. 2008. (Cutting Edge Ser.). (ENG.). 176p. pap. *(978-1-84167-699-9(3))* Ransom Publishing Ltd.
—Breaking Dawn, 1 vol. unabr. ed. 2012. (Cutting Edge Ser.). (ENG.). 170p. (YA). (gr. 9-12). pap. 9.95 *(978-1-61651-758-8(1))* Saddleback Educational Publishing, Inc.
Shelton, Rick. Hoggle's Christmas. Gates, Donald, illus. 2007. 80p. (J). pap. 11.95 *(978-1-60306-026-4(X))* NewSouth, Inc.
Shemtov, Yael. Sadie's Funny Feeling. 2009. 24p. pap. 16.99 *(978-1-4389-6023-4(9))* AuthorHouse.
Shepard, Sara. Burned. 2013. (Pretty Little Liars Ser.: 12). (ENG.). 352p. (YA). (gr. 9). pap. 9.99 *(978-0-06-208193-3(4))* HarperCollins Pubs.
—Burned. 2013. (Pretty Little Liars Ser.: 12). (YA). lib. bdg. 20.85 *(978-0-606-32177-8(2),* Turtleback) Turtleback Bks.
—Crushed. 2014. (Pretty Little Liars Ser.: 13). (YA). lib. bdg. 20.85 *(978-0-606-35497-4(2))* Turtleback Bks.
—Deadly. (Pretty Little Liars Ser.: 14). (ENG.). (YA). (gr. 9). 2014. 336p. pap. 10.99 *(978-0-06-219975-1(7))* 2013. 320p. 17.99 *(978-0-06-219974-4(9),* HarperTeen) HarperCollins Pubs.
—Deadly. 2014. (Pretty Little Liars Ser.: 14). (YA). lib. bdg. 20.85 *(978-0-606-35972-6(9))* Turtleback Bks.
—Flawless. (Pretty Little Liars Ser.: 2). (ENG.). (YA). (gr. 9-12). 2008. 352p. pap. 10.99 *(978-0-06-088735-3(4))* 2007. 352p. 16.99 *(978-0-06-088733-9(8))* 2010. 368p. pap. 8.99 *(978-0-06-205987-1(4))* HarperCollins Pubs. (HarperTeen).
—Flawless. 2008. (Pretty Little Liars Ser.: 2). (YA). lib. bdg. 20.85 *(978-0-606-12267-2(2),* Turtleback) Turtleback Bks.
—Heartless. 2010. (Pretty Little Liars Ser.: 7). (ENG.). (YA). (gr. 9-18). 304p. pap. 10.99 *(978-0-06-156616-5(0));* 288p. 16.99 *(978-0-06-156614-1(4))* HarperCollins Pubs. (HarperTeen).
—Killer. (Pretty Little Liars Ser.: 6). (ENG.). (YA). (gr. 9). 2010. 352p. pap. 9.99 *(978-0-06-156613-4(6))*No. 6. 2009. 336p. 16.99 *(978-0-06-156611-0(X))* HarperCollins Pubs. (HarperTeen).
—Killer. 2010. (Pretty Little Liars Ser.: 6). (YA). lib. bdg. 20.85 *(978-0-606-12278-8(8),* Turtleback) Turtleback Bks.
—Perfect. (Pretty Little Liars Ser.: No. 3). (ENG.). (YA). (gr. 9-12). 2007. 320p. 16.99 *(978-0-06-088736-0(2))*No. 3. 2008. 336p. pap. 9.99 *(978-0-06-088738-4(9))* HarperCollins Pubs. (HarperTeen).
—Pretty Little Liars. (Pretty Little Liars Ser.: 1). (YA). (gr. 9-12). 2007. (ENG.). 304p. pap. 9.99 *(978-0-06-088732-2(X))* 2006. (ENG.). 304p. 16.99 *(978-0-06-088730-8(3))* 2010. (ENG.). 304p. pap. 9.99 *(978-0-06-200954-8(0))*Set, Bks. 1-4. 2009. pap. 29.99 *(978-0-06-180131-0(3))* HarperCollins Pubs. (HarperTeen).
—Pretty Little Liars #16: Vicious. 2016. (Pretty Little Liars Ser.: 16). 368p. (YA). (gr. 9). pap. 10.99 *(978-0-06-228705-2(2),* HarperTeen) HarperCollins Pubs.
—Pretty Little Liars Bind-Up #1: Pretty Little Liars & Flawless. 2014. (Pretty Little Liars Ser.). (ENG.). 656p. (YA). (gr. 9). pap. 10.99 *(978-0-06-232292-0(3),* HarperTeen) HarperCollins Pubs.
—Pretty Little Liars Bind-Up #2: Perfect & Unbelievable. 2014. (Pretty Little Liars Ser.). (ENG.). 672p. (YA). (gr. 9). pap. 10.99 *(978-0-06-232293-7(1),* HarperTeen) HarperCollins Pubs.
—Pretty Little Secrets. (Pretty Little Liars Companion Novel Ser.). (ENG.). (YA). (gr. 9). 2013. 480p. pap. 9.99 *(978-0-06-212592-7(3))* 2012. 464p. 17.99 *(978-0-06-212591-0(5))* HarperCollins Pubs. (HarperTeen).
—Ruthless. (Pretty Little Liars Ser.: 10). (ENG.). (YA). (gr. 9). 2012. 368p. pap. 10.99 *(978-0-06-208187-2(X))* 2011. 352p. 17.99 *(978-0-06-208186-5(1))* HarperCollins Pubs. (HarperTeen).
—Ruthless. 2012. (Pretty Little Liars Ser.: 10). (YA). lib. bdg. 20.85 *(978-0-606-26873-8(1),* Turtleback) Turtleback Bks.
—Stunning. 2013. (Pretty Little Liars Ser.: 11). (ENG.). 336p. (YA). (gr. 9). pap. 10.99 *(978-0-06-208190-2(X),* HarperTeen) HarperCollins Pubs.
—Stunning. 2013. (Pretty Little Liars Ser.: 11). (YA). lib. bdg. 20.85 *(978-0-606-31813-6(5),* Turtleback) Turtleback Bks.
—Toxic. 2014. (Pretty Little Liars Ser.: 15). (ENG.). 352p. (J). (gr. 9). 17.99 *(978-0-06-228701-4(X),* HarperTeen) HarperCollins Pubs.
—Twisted. (Pretty Little Liars Ser.: 9). (ENG.). (YA). (gr. 9). 2012. 336p. pap. 10.99 *(978-0-06-208102-5(0))* 2011. 320p. 16.99 *(978-0-06-208101-8(2))* HarperCollins Pubs. (HarperTeen).
—Twisted. 2012. (Pretty Little Liars Ser.: 9). (YA). lib. bdg. 20.85 *(978-0-606-26288-0(1),* Turtleback) Turtleback Bks.
—Unbelievable. 2008. (Pretty Little Liars Ser.: 4). (ENG.). (gr. 9). 368p. (YA). pap. 9.99 *(978-0-06-088741-4(9));* 352p. (J). 16.99 *(978-0-06-088739-1(7))* HarperCollins Pubs. (HarperTeen).
—Vicious. 2014. (Pretty Little Liars Ser.: 16). (ENG.). 352p. (YA). (gr. 9). 17.99 *(978-0-06-228704-5(4))* HarperCollins Pubs.
—Wanted. (Pretty Little Liars Ser.: 8). (ENG.). (YA). (gr. 9). 2011. 288p. pap. 9.99 *(978-0-06-156619-6(5))* 2010. 272p. 16.99 *(978-0-06-156617-2(9))* HarperCollins Pubs. (HarperTeen).
—Wicked. 2009. (Pretty Little Liars Ser.: 5). (ENG.). 336p. (YA). (gr. 9). pap. 9.99 *(978-0-06-156610-3(1),* HarperTeen) HarperCollins Pubs.

Shepherd, Donna J. Chizzy's Topsy Tale. Collier, Kevin Scott, illus. 2008. 20p. pap. 10.95 (978-1-935137-10-8(7)) Guardian Angel Publishing, Inc.

—Dotty's Topsy Tale. Collier, Kevin Scott, illus. 2009. 16p. pap. 9.95 (978-1-935137-55-9(7)) Guardian Angel Publishing, Inc.

—Sully's Topsy Tale. Collier, Kevin Scott, illus. 2010. 20p. pap. 10.95 (978-1-61633-047-7(3)) Guardian Angel Publishing, Inc.

Shepherd, JaiLeen. Anan: Lea's Special Friend — Part II of the Lea Trilogy. 2006. (J). per. 15.95 (978-1-889743-55-4(0)) Robbie Dean Pr.

Shepherd, Jodie. Sesame Street Elmo Goes to School. Moroney, Christopher, illus. 2012. (Lift-The-Flap Ser.: 1). (ENG.). 10p. (J). (gr. -1-k). bds. 10.99 (978-0-7944-2585-2(2), Reader's Digest Children's Bks.) Studio Fun International.

Shepherd, Sandra. Kangapoo & the Monster at Kakadu. 2012. 40p. pap. 32.70 (978-1-4691-6123-5(0)) Xlibris Corp.

Shepperson, Jacqueline. Martins of the Everglades. 2007. (ENG.). 152p. per. 24.95 (978-1-4241-5446-3(4)) America Star Bks.

Sher, Emil. Young Man with Camera. Wyman, David, photos by. 2015. (ENG., Illus.). 240p. (J). (gr. 7). 17.99 (978-0-545-54131-2(X), Levine, Arthur A. Bks.) Scholastic, Inc.

Sherman, M. Zachary. Fall Line, Vol. 3. Majado, Caio & Emery, Thomas, illus. 2011. (Tony Hawk's 900 Revolution Ser.). (ENG.). 128p. (gr. 3-4). pap. 7.19 (978-1-4342-3453-7(3)); lib. bdg. 26.65 (978-1-4342-3204-5(2)) Stone Arch Bks. (Tony Hawk's 900 Revolution).

—Fighting Phantoms, 1 vol. Casas, Fritz, illus. 2011. (Bloodlines Ser.). (ENG.). 88p. (gr. 4-8). lib. bdg. 26.65 (978-1-4342-2560-3(7)) Stone Arch Bks.

—Impulse, Vol. 2. Majado, Caio et al, illus. 2011. (Tony Hawk's 900 Revolution Ser.). (ENG.). 128p. (gr. 3-4). pap. 7.19 (978-1-4342-3452-0(5)); lib. bdg. 26.65 (978-1-4342-3203-8(4)) Stone Arch Bks. (Tony Hawk's 900 Revolution).

—Unchained, Vol. 4. Majado, Caio & Emery, Thomas J., illus. 2011. (Tony Hawk's 900 Revolution Ser.). (ENG.). 128p. (gr. 3-4). pap. 7.19 (978-1-4342-3454-4(1)); lib. bdg. 26.65 (978-1-4342-3215-1(8)) Stone Arch Bks. (Tony Hawk's 900 Revolution).

Sherrard, Valerie. Searching for Yesterday: A Shelby Belgarden Mystery. 2008. (ENG.). 224p. (YA). (gr. 6-10). pap. 12.99 (978-1-55002-788-4(3), Boardwalk Bks.) Dundurn CAN. Dist: Ingram Publisher Services.

—Speechless. 2007. (ENG.). 176p. (YA). (gr. 6). pap. 12.99 (978-1-55002-701-3(8), Boardwalk Bks.) Dundurn CAN. Dist: Ingram Publisher Services.

Sherrell, Deborah. Baby Lauren & Theodore,hardcover. 2007. (Illus.). (J). bds. 17.95 (978-0-9779643-5-2(3)) Healing Tree Arts.

Sherry, Kevin. Monsters on the Run. 2015. (Yeti Files Ser.: 2). (ENG., Illus.). 128p. (J). (gr. 2-5). 8.99 (978-0-545-55619-4(8), Scholastic Pr.) Scholastic, Inc.

—Turtle Island. 2014. (ENG.). 40p. (J). (gr. -1-k). 16.99 (978-0-8037-3391-6(7), Dial Bks) Penguin Young Readers Group.

Sherwood, K. C. Midnight at Moonglow's. 2011. 204p. (gr. 4-6). 33.95 (978-1-4582-0085-3(X)); pap. 17.95 (978-1-4582-0084-6(1)) Author Solutions, Inc. (Abbott Pr.).

Sherwood, Lance. Grandpa Tales. 2012. 54p. pap. 14.95 (978-0-615-72525-3(2)) Spitzer, Lance.

Shevah, Emma. Dream on, Amber. Crawford-White, Helen, illus. 2016. (ENG.). 272p. (J). (gr. 3-7). 18.40 (978-0-606-39305-8(6)) Turtleback Bks.

Shields, Gillian. Eternal. (Immortal Ser.: 3). (ENG.). (YA). (gr. 8). 2012. 384p. pap. 9.99 (978-0-06-200040-8(3)) 2011. 368p. 16.99 (978-0-06-200039-2(X)) HarperCollins Pubs. (Tegen, Katherine Bks).

—Holly Takes a Risk. Turner, Helen, illus. 2008. (Mermaid S. O. S. Ser.: 4). (ENG.). 96p. (J). (gr. 1-4). pap. 4.50 (978-1-59990-214-2(1), 9781599902142, Bloomsbury USA Childrens) Bloomsbury Publishing USA.

—Library Lily. Chessa, Francesca, illus. 2011. (ENG.). 26p. (YA). 16.00 (978-0-8028-5401-8(X)) Eerdmans, William B. Publishing Co.

—Sophie Makes a Splash. Turner, Helen, illus. 2008. (Mermaid S. O. S. Ser.: 3). (ENG.). 96p. (J). (gr. 1-4). pap. 4.50 (978-1-59990-212-8(5), 9781599902128, Bloomsbury USA Childrens) Bloomsbury Publishing USA.

Shiell, Trevor. Pete's Journey. 2015. (ENG., Illus.). 378p. (J). pap. (978-0-9943491-0-1(6)) Port Campbell Pr.

Shimokawa, Melanie. A Family for Madison. 2008. 53p. pap. 16.95 (978-1-60672-701-0(X)) America Star Bks.

Shinn, Sharon. The Dream-Maker's Magic. 2008. (ENG.). 288p. (YA). (gr. 7-18). pap. 8.99 (978-0-14-241096-7(9), Speak) Penguin Young Readers Group.

Shire, Poppy. Jewel the Midnight Pony. Berg, Ron, illus. 2008. (Magic Pony Carousel Ser.: 4). (ENG.). 96p. (J). (gr. 2-5). pap. 3.99 (978-0-06-083788-4(8)) HarperCollins Pubs.

Shireen, Nadia. Yeti & the Bird. Shireen, Nadia, illus. 2015. (ENG., Illus.). 32p. (J). (gr. -1-3). 17.99 (978-1-4814-0389-4(3), Atheneum Bks. for Young Readers) Simon & Schuster Children's Publishing.

Shirer, Priscilla & Detwiler, Gina. The Prince Warriors. 2016. (Prince Warriors Ser.). (ENG.). 288p. (J). (gr. 3-7). 12.99 (978-1-4336-9019-8(5), B&H Kids) B&H Publishing Group.

Shirley, Alice. The Gentle Lion & the Little Owlet. Shirley, Alice, illus. 2013. Orig. Title: Owlet & Pussycat. (ENG., Illus.). 32p. (J). (gr. -1-k). pap. 8.99 (978-1-84365-199-4(8), Pavilion) Pavilion Bks. GBR. Dist: Independent Pubs. Group.

Shoemaker, Tim. Below the Surface, 1 vol. 2015. (Code of Silence Novel Ser.). (ENG.). 416p. (J). pap. 9.99 (978-0-310-73765-0(6)) Zonderkidz.

Shon. Henry Boothill: The Return of Nidagall, 1 vol. 2010. 52p. pap. 16.95 (978-1-4512-8700-4(3)) America Star Bks.

Shores, Lloyd. The Adventures of Mr. Ant. 2013. 28p. pap. 13.95 (978-1-4497-9747-8(4), WestBow Pr.) Author Solutions, Inc.

Shoshan, Beth. If You Can...we Can! Brown, Petra, illus. 2013. (J). (978-1-4351-4800-0(2)) Barnes & Noble, Inc.

Shotz, Jennifer Li. Max: Best Friend. Hero. Marine. 2017. 256p. (J). (gr. 3-7). 12.99 **(978-0-06-279138-2(9))** HarperCollins Pubs.

Shreeve, Elizabeth. Hector Finds a Fortune. Levy, Pamela R., illus. 2004. 68p. (J). lib. bdg. 15.00 (978-1-4242-0903-3(X)) Fitzgerald Bks.

—Hector Finds a Fortune. Levy, Pamela R., illus. 2004. (Adventures of Hector Fuller Ser.). 68p. (J). (gr. 1-4). 11.65 (978-0-7569-5527-4(0)) Perfection Learning Corp.

Shreve, Susan Richards. Kiss Me Tomorrow. 2006. 220p. (J). (978-1-4156-5592-4(8), Levine, Arthur A. Bks.) Scholastic, Inc.

Shuert, Randy. Randy Ray & Easy Jay: The Wood House Adventure. 2011. 28p. pap. 21.99 (978-1-4568-8395-9(X)) Xlibris Corp.

Shuff, Lana Tanaka. Kira Helps A Friend. l.t. ed. 2007. (ENG., Illus.). 28p. (J). per. 9.95 (978-1-4327-0810-8(4)) Outskirts Pr., Inc.

Shultz, Charles M. & Katschke, Judy. It's a Home Run, Charlie Brown!, 1 vol. Lo Bianco, Nick, illus. 2011. (Peanuts Ready-To-Reads Ser.). (ENG.). 32p. (gr. -1-2). lib. bdg. 24.21 (978-1-59961-801-2(X)) Spotlight.

—Lucy's Advice, 1 vol. Lo Bianco, Peter, illus. 2011. (Peanuts Ready-To-Reads Ser.). (ENG.). 32p. (gr. -1-2). lib. bdg. 24.21 (978-1-59961-805-0(2)) Spotlight.

Shultz, D. B. The World Adventures of Sahara the Mummy: The Magical Exploration of Ancient Egypt. 2012. 28p. pap. 17.99 (978-1-4772-3310-8(5)) AuthorHouse.

Shusterman, Neal. Downsiders. 2009. (ENG.). 272p. (YA). (gr. 7). pap. 10.99 (978-1-4169-9747-4(4), Simon & Schuster Bks. For Young Readers) Simon & Schuster Bks. For Young Readers.

—Dread Locks. 2006. (Dark Fusion Ser.: 1). (ENG.). 176p. (YA). (gr. 7-18). 7.99 (978-0-14-240599-4(X), Speak) Penguin Young Readers Group.

—The Schwa Was Here. 2006. (ENG.). 240p. (YA). (gr. 7-18). reprint ed. 6.99 (978-0-14-240577-2(9), Puffin Books) Penguin Young Readers Group.

Sica, Diane. The Adventures of Sammy & Vinney. 2012. 48p. pap. 11.95 (978-1-4685-6883-7(3)) AuthorHouse.

Sicks, Linda. How Different Is Good: Nick the Wise Old Cat. Messing, Dave, illus. 2010. (Importance of Friendship Ser.). 40p. (J). 18.95 (978-1-936193-04-2(3)) Nick The Cat, LLC.

Sidney, Margaret. Five Little Peppers Abroad. 2008. 212p. (gr. 4-7). 26.95 (978-1-60664-996-1(5)); per. 14.95 (978-1-60312-546-8(9)) Aegypan.

Siegal, Ida. Party Drama! (Emma Is on the Air #2) 2015. (Emma Is on the Air Ser.: 2). (ENG.). 128p. (J). (gr. 2-5). pap. 4.99 (978-0-545-68695-2(4), Scholastic Paperbacks) Scholastic, Inc.

—Showtime! 2015. (Emma Is on the Air Ser.: 3). (ENG., Illus.). 128p. (J). (gr. 2-5). pap. 4.99 (978-0-545-68702-7(0), Scholastic Paperbacks) Scholastic, Inc.

Siems, Dorthy R. A Fairy's Wings: Set 1. 2007. (Illus.). 50p. (J). spiral bd. 15.00 net. (978-0-9794483-3-1(6)) Siems, D.R.

Sif, Birgitta. Oliver. Sif, Birgitta, illus. 2012. (ENG., Illus.). 40p. (J). (gr. -1-3). 16.99 (978-0-7636-6247-9(X)) Candlewick Pr.

Sigmon-Heck, Christina. The Birthday Wish. 2012. 24p. pap. 24.95 (978-1-4626-6207-4(2)) America Star Bks.

Signorino, John. Billy & the Aliens of Alpha-C, 1 vol. 2008. (ENG.). 36p. pap. 24.95 (978-1-60474-882-6(6)) America Star Bks.

Silberberg, Alan. Milo: Sticky Notes & Brain Freeze. Silberberg, Alan, illus. (ENG., Illus.). 288p. (J). (gr. 4-8). 2011. pap. 7.99 (978-1-4169-9431-2(9)) 2010. 15.99 (978-1-4169-9430-5(0)) Simon & Schuster Children's Publishing. (Aladdin).

Sills, Elizabeth & Patrice, Elena. Nana Star. Saker, Linda, illus. 2007. 32p. (J). (gr. -1-3). 15.95 (978-0-9753843-5-0(X)) ee publishing & productions, inc.

—Nana Star & the Moonman. Saker, Linda, illus. 2008. 32p. (J). (gr. -1-3). 15.95 (978-0-9753843-6-7(8)) ee publishing & productions, inc.

Silver, Connie. A Story Book for Beginning Readers. 2007. 124p. 20.95 (978-0-595-70501-6(4)); per. 10.95 (978-0-595-46524-8(2)) iUniverse, Inc.

Silver Dolphin en Español Editors. Girlfriends Imanes Magicos. 2006. (Illus.). 8p. (J). (gr. -1). bds. (978-970-718-371-1(3), Silver Dolphin en Español) Advanced Marketing, S. de R. L. de C. V.

Silvera, Adam. They Both Die at the End. 2017. 384p. (YA). (gr. 9). 17.99 **(978-0-06-245779-0(9))** HarperCollins Pubs.

Silvera, Elvia. Candida. Peli, Peli, illus. 2005. (SPA.). (J). (gr. 2-3). pap. 7.95 (978-980-257-281-6(0)) Ekare, Ediciones VEN. Dist: Iaconi, Mariuccia Bk. Imports.

Silverberg, Beth. The Adventures of Mattie Mae: Life Lessons Through the Eyes of A Puppy. 2009. 76p. pap. 12.99 (978-1-4389-4587-3(6)) AuthorHouse.

Silverberry, A. R. Wyndano's Cloak. 2010. 424p. 21.95 (978-0-9841037-6-8(7)) Tree Tunnel Pr.

Silvermetz, Marcia A. Gertrude the Albino Frog & Her Friend Rupert the Turtle. Doyel, Ginger, illus. 2003. 48p. (J). (gr. 2-3). 19.95 (978-0-9718724-0-0(6)) Hiccup Cottage Pubns.

Silvestri, Enzo & Silvestri, Karen Hamilton. War in the Heavens: Episode 6. 2013. 84p. pap. 6.59 (978-0-9899318-1-6(1)) Karenzo Media.

Simard, Remy. Monsieur Iletaitunefois. 2004. (FRE.). (J). (gr. k-3). spiral bd. (978-0-616-01843-9(6)) Canadian National Institute for the Blind/Institut National Canadien pour les Aveugles.

Siminovich, Lorena. Alex & Lulu: Two of a Kind. Siminovich, Lorena, illus. 2009. (ENG., Illus.). 32p. (J). (gr. -1-3). 14.99 (978-0-7636-4423-9(4), Templar) Candlewick Pr.

Simmons, Cari & Alexander, Heather. Bending over Backwards. 2015. (Picture Perfect Ser.: 1). (ENG.). 224p. (J). (gr. 3-7). pap. 6.99 (978-0-06-231022-4(4)) HarperCollins Pubs.

Simmons, Cari & Burns, Laura J. Picture Perfect #5: All Together Now. Mingus, Cathi, illus. 2016. (Picture Perfect Ser.: 5). 192p. (J). (gr. 3-7). pap. 6.99 (978-0-06-233676-7(2)) HarperCollins Pubs.

Simmons, Cari & Douglas, Lola. You First. 2015. (Picture Perfect Ser.: 2). (ENG.). 256p. (J). (gr. 3-7). pap. 6.99 (978-0-06-231058-3(5)) HarperCollins Pubs.

Simmons, Cari & Metz, Melinda. Between Us. 2015. (Picture Perfect Ser.: 4). (ENG.). 224p. (J). (gr. 3-7). pap. 6.99 (978-0-06-233674-3(6)) HarperCollins Pubs.

Simmons, Cari & Zulkey, Claire. Best Frenemies. 2015. (Picture Perfect Ser.: 3). (ENG., Illus.). 224p. (J). (gr. 3-7). pap. 6.99 (978-0-06-231845-9(4)) HarperCollins Pubs.

Simmons, H. J. The Little House on the Corner. 2004. 63p. pap. 19.95 (978-1-4137-2934-4(7)) America Star Bks.

Simmons, Jane. Ship's Cat Doris. Simmons, Jane, illus. 2011. (ENG., Illus.). 176p. (J). (gr. k-2). pap. 8.99 (978-1-4083-0896-7(7)) Hodder & Stoughton GBR. Dist: Hachette Bk. Group.

Simmons, John M. Katya's Prayer. 2006. 15p. 4.95 (978-0-9725916-2-1(1), 21206) White Knight Printing and Publishing.

Simmons, Mary Louise. The Little Fir Tree Who Wanted a Friend. 2008. 28p. per. 24.95 (978-1-60441-391-5(3)) America Star Bks.

Simon, Coco. Alexis & the Missing Ingredient. 2013. (Cupcake Diaries: 16). (ENG., Illus.). 160p. (J). (gr. 3-7). 17.99 (978-1-4424-8588-4(4)); pap. 5.99 (978-1-4424-8587-7(6)) Simon Spotlight. (Simon Spotlight).

—Alexis Cool As a Cupcake. 2013. (Cupcake Diaries: 8). (ENG., Illus.). 160p. (J). (gr. 3-7). 16.99 (978-1-4424-8569-3(8), Simon Spotlight) Simon Spotlight.

—Alexis Cool as a Cupcake. 2012. (Cupcake Diaries: 8). lib. bdg. 16.00 (978-0-606-26334-4(9), Turtleback) Turtleback Bks.

—The Cupcake Diaries Collection: Katie & the Cupcake Cure; Mia in the Mix; Emma on Thin Icing; Alexis & the Perfect Recipe. 2012. (Cupcake Diaries). (ENG.). 640p. (J). (gr. 3-7). pap. 23.99 (978-1-4424-8445-0(4), Simon Spotlight) Simon Spotlight.

—Emma: Lights! Camera! Cupcakes! 2014. (Cupcake Diaries: 19). lib. bdg. 17.20 (978-0-606-35437-0(9)) Turtleback Bks.

—Emma on Thin Icing. 2013. (Cupcake Diaries: 3). (ENG., Illus.). 160p. (J). (gr. 3-7). 15.99 (978-1-4424-7492-5(0), Simon Spotlight) Simon Spotlight.

—Emma on Thin Icing. 2011. (Cupcake Diaries: 3). lib. bdg. 17.20 (978-0-606-23734-5(8), Turtleback) Turtleback Bks.

—Emma, Smile & Say "Cupcake!" 2014. (Cupcake Diaries: 11). (ENG., Illus.). 160p. (J). (gr. 3-7). 17.99 (978-1-4424-9611-8(8), Simon Spotlight) Simon Spotlight.

—Emma Sugar & Spice & Everything Nice. 2013. (Cupcake Diaries: 15). (ENG., Illus.). 160p. (J). (gr. 3-7). 15.99 (978-1-4424-7488-8(2)); pap. 5.99 (978-1-4424-7481-9(5)) Simon Spotlight. (Simon Spotlight).

—Katie & the Cupcake Cure. (Cupcake Diaries: 1). (ENG., 160p. (J). (gr. 3-7). 2013. Illus.). 15.99 (978-1-4424-7490-1(4)) 2011. pap. 6.99 (978-1-4424-2275-9(0)) Simon Spotlight. (Simon Spotlight).

—Katie & the Cupcake Cure; Mia in the Mix; Emma on Thin Icing, 3 in 1 bks. 2015. (Cupcake Diaries). (ENG., Illus.). 480p. (J). (gr. 3-7). pap. 8.99 (978-1-4814-5756-9(X), Simon Spotlight) Simon Spotlight.

—Katie & the Cupcake War. (Cupcake Diaries: 9). (ENG., 160p. (J). (gr. 3-7). 2014. Illus.). 17.99 (978-1-4424-9609-5(6)) 2012. pap. 6.99 (978-1-4424-5373-9(7)) Simon Spotlight. (Simon Spotlight).

—Katie & the Cupcake War. 2012. (Cupcake Diaries: 9). lib. bdg. 17.20 (978-0-606-26335-1(7), Turtleback) Turtleback Bks.

—Katie, Batter Up! (Cupcake Diaries: 5). (ENG., 160p. (J). (gr. 3-7). 2013. Illus.). 17.99 (978-1-4424-8564-8(7)) 2011. pap. 6.99 (978-1-4424-4611-3(0)) Simon Spotlight. (Simon Spotlight).

—Katie Sprinkled Secrets. 2015. (Cupcake Diaries: 25). (ENG., Illus.). 160p. (J). (gr. 3-7). pap. 6.99 (978-1-4814-2919-1(1), Simon Spotlight) Simon Spotlight.

—Katie Sprinkles & Surprises. 2013. (Cupcake Diaries: 17). (ENG., Illus.). 160p. (J). (gr. 3-7). 17.99 (978-1-4424-8591-4(4)); pap. 6.99 (978-1-4424-8590-7(6)) Simon Spotlight. (Simon Spotlight).

—Katie Sprinkles & Surprises. 2013. (Cupcake Diaries: 17). lib. bdg. 17.20 (978-0-606-32327-7(9), Turtleback) Turtleback Bks.

—Katie Starting from Scratch. 2014. (Cupcake Diaries: 21). (ENG., Illus.). 160p. (J). (gr. 3-7). pap. 5.99 (978-1-4814-0471-6(7), Simon Spotlight) Simon Spotlight.

—Katie's New Recipe. (Cupcake Diaries: 13). (ENG., Illus.). 160p. (J). (gr. 3-7). 2014. 16.99 (978-1-4814-0379-5(6)) 2013. pap. 5.99 (978-1-4424-7168-9(9)) Simon Spotlight. (Simon Spotlight).

—Mia: Fashion Plates & Cupcakes. 2014. (Cupcake Diaries: 18). lib. bdg. 16.00 (978-0-606-35436-3(0)) Turtleback Bks.

—Mia in the Mix. (Cupcake Diaries: 2). (ENG., 160p. (J). (gr. 3-7). 2013. Illus.). 15.99 (978-1-4424-7491-8(2)) 2011. pap. 6.99 (978-1-4424-2277-3(7)) Simon Spotlight. (Simon Spotlight).

—Mia Measures Up. 2017. (Cupcake Diaries: 30). lib. bdg. 17.20 **(978-0-606-40209-5(8))** Turtleback Bks.

—Mia's Baker's Dozen. 2013. (Cupcake Diaries: 6). (ENG., Illus.). 160p. (J). (gr. 3-7). 17.99 (978-1-4424-8566-2(3), Simon Spotlight) Simon Spotlight.

—Mia's Baker's Dozen. 2012. (Cupcake Diaries: 6). lib. bdg. 17.20 (978-0-606-26570-6(8), Turtleback) Turtleback Bks.

—Mia's Recipe for Disaster. 2014. (Cupcake Diaries: 22). lib. bdg. 17.20 (978-0-606-36098-2(0)) Turtleback Bks.

Simon, Elizabeth. Tyler Adams & the Adventures of Bravura: the First Quest. 2009. 49p. pap. 19.95 (978-0-557-06290-4(X)) Lulu Pr., Inc.

Simon, Jenne. Double Trouble. 2014. (Illus.). 32p. (J). (978-1-4844-2319-6(4)) Scholastic, Inc.

—The Double Trouble. 2015. (ENG.). 32p. (J). (gr. -1-k). 8.99 (978-0-545-85023-0(1)) Scholastic, Inc.

—Lalaloopsy: School Day! Hill, Prescott, illus. 2012. (Lalaloopsy Ser.). (ENG.). 32p. (J). (gr. -1-3). pap. 3.99 (978-0-545-40321-4(9)) Scholastic, Inc.

—Lalaloopsy: the Ballet Recital. 2012. (Lalaloopsy Ser.). (ENG.). 32p. (J). (gr. -1-3). pap. 3.99 (978-0-545-39216-7(0)) Scholastic, Inc.

—LEGO Friends: Andrea's New Horse. Ku, Min Sung, illus. 2014. (LEGO Friends Ser.). (ENG.). 24p. (J). (gr. -1-3). pap. 3.99 (978-0-545-78391-0(7)) Scholastic, Inc.

—The Magic Charm Chase. 2016. (ENG.). 24p. (J). (gr. -1-k). 3.99 (978-0-545-94302-4(7)) Scholastic, Inc.

—Meet the Little Charmers (Little Charmers) 2015. (ENG.). 24p. (J). (gr. -1-k). 3.99 (978-0-545-85021-6(5)) Scholastic, Inc.

—Snow Day!, Level 2. Hill, Prescott, illus. 2013. (Lalaloopsy Ser.). (ENG.). 32p. (J). (gr. -1-3). pap. 3.99 (978-0-545-58123-3(0)) Scholastic, Inc.

Simon, Jenne & Rusu, Meredith. Santa Sparkle. 2016. (Little Charmers Ser.). (ENG.). 24p. (J). (gr. -1-1). pap. 4.99 (978-1-338-09764-1(4)) Scholastic, Inc.

Simon, Mary Manz. Puppy Makes Friends. Couri, Kathy & Clearwater, Linda, illus. 2006. (First Virtues for Toddlers Ser.). 20p. (J). 5.99 (978-0-7847-1414-0(2), 04066) Standard Publishing.

Simone, Ni-Ni. No Boyz Allowed. 2012. lib. bdg. 20.80 (978-0-606-26377-1(2), Turtleback) Turtleback Bks.

Simone, Val Edward. Proton Gator & Friends Coloring Book. McGill, Joshua, illus. 2011. 32p. (J). pap. 5.99 (978-1-935296-27-0(2)) Morningside Publishing, LLC.

Simone, Yve. Little Valentine. 2013. 72p. pap. 28.99 (978-1-4817-0496-0(6)) AuthorHouse.

Simpkins, Debra Burke. The Luna Tuna. 2010. 32p. 12.99 (978-1-4520-0213-2(4)) AuthorHouse.

Simpson, Dana. A Heavenly Nostrils Chronicle. 2014. (Phoebe & Her Unicorn Ser.: 1). (ENG., Illus.). 224p. (J). 9.99 (978-1-4494-4620-8(5)) Andrews McMeel Publishing.

—Phoebe & Her Unicorn: A Heavenly Nostrils Chronicle. 2014. (Phoebe & Her Unicorn Ser.: 1). (Illus.). 222p. (J). lib. bdg. 20.85 (978-0-606-36144-6(8)) Turtleback Bks.

—Unicorn on a Roll. 2015. (Phoebe & Her Unicorn Ser.: 2). lib. bdg. 20.85 (978-0-606-36985-5(6)) Turtleback Bks.

Simpson, Wanda. Jupiter the Space Donkey, 1 vol. 2009. 17p. pap. 24.95 (978-1-61582-733-6(1)) PublishAmerica, Inc.

Sims, Anthony. Princess Zoe. 2012. (Illus.). 44p. pap. 24.40 (978-1-4772-2365-9(7)) AuthorHouse.

Sims, Janet G. Cristy & Her Amazing Friends. 2010. 36p. pap. 13.95 (978-1-60860-728-0(3), Eloquent Bks.) Strategic Book Publishing & Rights Agency (SBPRA).

Sinclair, Gardine. Keira at Stageschool. 2013. 186p. (J). pap. (978-1-78299-387-2(8)) FeedARead.com.

—Stageschool by the Sea. 2013. 176p. (J). pap. (978-1-78299-389-6(4)) FeedARead.com.

Singhose, Rose & StGermain, Annetta. Gramma's Sure Fire Cure for Insomnia in the Very Young. 2010. 67p. pap. 27.50 (978-0-557-08697-9(3)) Lulu Pr., Inc.

Singleton, David & Martin, Loyce. Us Mail. 2008. 132p. pap. 11.95 (978-0-595-52437-2(0)) iUniverse, Inc.

Singleton, Linda Joy. The Curious Cat Spy Club. 2015. (Curious Cat Spy Club Ser.: 1). (ENG.). 256p. (J). (gr. 3-7). 14.99 (978-0-8075-1376-7(8)) Whitman, Albert & Co.

—Kelsey the Spy. 2016. (Curious Cat Spy Club Ser.: 3). (ENG.). (J). (gr. 3-7). 304p. pap. 9.99 (978-0-8075-1384-2(9)); 288p. 14.99 (978-0-8075-1380-4(6)) Whitman, Albert & Co.

—The Mystery of the Zorse's Mask. (Curious Cat Spy Club Ser.: 2). (ENG.). (J). (gr. 3-7). 2016. 272p. pap. 9.99 (978-0-8075-1383-5(0)) 2015. 256p. 14.99 (978-0-8075-1378-1(4)) Whitman, Albert & Co.

—The Secret of the Shadow Bandit. (Curious Cat Spy Club Ser.). (ENG.). (J). (gr. 3-7). 2017. 296p. pap. 9.99 **(978-0-8075-1387-3(3))** 2016. 288p. 14.99 (978-0-8075-1385-9(7)) Whitman, Albert & Co.

Singleton, Linda Joy. Witch Ball. 2006. (Seer Ser.: 3). (ENG.). 216p. (YA). (gr. 3-7). pap. 9.95 (978-0-7387-0821-8(6), Flux) North Star Editions.

Sirowy, Alexandra. First We Were IV. 2017. (ENG., Illus.). 448p. (YA). (gr. 7). 18.99 **(978-1-4814-7842-7(7)**, Simon & Schuster Bks. For Young Readers) Simon & Schuster Bks. For Young Readers.

Sisco, Joann Ellen. Bonnie from Blue Mountain: 1. 2012. 88p. pap. 13.95 (978-1-4772-7070-7(1)) AuthorHouse.

—Midnight at Faraway Farm. 2008. 79p. pap. 19.95 (978-1-60474-777-5(3)) America Star Bks.

Sisler, Celeste. Disney Fairies: Meet Rosetta. 2015. (Passport to Reading Level 1 Ser.). (J). lib. bdg. 13.55 (978-0-606-37212-1(1)) Turtleback Bks.

—My Little Pony: the Rainbow Power Sticker Book. 2014. (ENG., Illus.). 12p. (J). (gr. -1-3). pap. 6.99 (978-0-316-37631-0(0)) Little, Brown Bks. for Young Readers.

Sit Beside the Gnomon. 2013. 108p. pap. (978-0-9874166-3-6(4)) Pagendam, Gladys.

Sivier, Janet. Charlotte & Jackson: The Butterfly. 2012. 28p. pap. 16.09 (978-1-4669-4555-5(9)) Trafford Publishing.

Skeffington, Miranda. My Little Pony: Friendship Is Magic: Collectible Poster Book. 2014. (ENG., Illus.). 40p. (J). (gr. 1-17). pap. 20.00 (978-0-316-32331-4(4)) Little, Brown Bks. for Young Readers.

Skidmore, Marlene. Wesley's Swoo-Foo. 2008. 28p. pap. 9.99 (978-0-9821408-5-7(1)) Faithful Life Pubs.

Skinner, Daphne. Palapalooza. Smath, Jerry, illus. 2006. (Social Studies Connects). 32p. (J). (gr. -1-3). pap. 5.95 (978-1-57565-163-7(7)) Kane Press, Inc.

Skipper, Cecil. The Deer Lick. 2004. 166p. (YA). pap. 12.95 (978-0-595-30949-8(6)) iUniverse, Inc.

Skofield, James. Bear & Bird. Thermes, Jennifer, illus. 2014. (ENG.). 40p. (J). (gr. 1-3). 15.99 (978-1-58536-835-8(0), 203012) Sleeping Bear Pr.

Skolsky, Mindy Warshaw. Love from Your Friend, Hannah. 256p. (J). (gr. 4-6). pap. 5.95 (978-0-8072-1546-3(5), Listening Library) Random Hse. Audio Publishing Group.

Skotnicki, Jill. Ham & Beans: Have You Seen the Color Green? 2010. 28p. pap. 12.49 (978-1-4520-6452-9(0)) AuthorHouse.

Skrbina, Daniel William. A Knight to Remember: Gulliver's Journey Continues, 1 vol. 2009. 74p. pap. 19.95 (978-1-60836-737-5(1)) America Star Bks.

Skurnick, Lizzie. The Girls' Life Big Book of Friendship Fiction. 2004. (Illus.). 124p. (978-0-439-44985-4(5)) Scholastic, Inc.

Skurzynski, Gloria. Good-Bye, Billy Radish. 2013. (ENG., Illus.). 152p. (J). (gr. 3-7). pap. 13.99 (978-1-4814-0158-6(0), Simon & Schuster Bks. For Young Readers) Simon & Schuster Bks. For Young Readers.

Skuse, C. J. Rockoholic. 2012. (YA). (978-0-545-44251-0(6)); (ENG.). 368p. (J). (gr. 9). 18.99 (978-0-545-42960-3(9)) Scholastic, Inc.

Sky Koster, Amy & Patrick, Ella. Ariel & the Big Baby/Rapunzel Finds a Friend (Disney Princess) Thomas, Jeffrey, illus. 2017. (Pictureback(R) Ser.). (ENG.). 48p. (J). (gr. -1-2). pap. 5.99 **(978-0-7364-3747-9(9)**, RH/Disney) Random Hse. Children's Bks.

Slagle, Clark. Axel Cecil & the Rising Sun Adventures: the Janwah. 2009. 105p. pap. 9.95 (978-0-615-24135-7(2)) Wold Creative Group.

Slate, Joseph. Miss Bindergarten & the Best Friends. Wolff, Ashley, illus. 2014. (Penguin Young Readers, Level 2 Ser.). (ENG.). 32p. (J). (gr. 1-2). pap. 3.99 *(978-0-448-48132-6(4)*, Penguin Young Readers) Penguin Young Readers Group.

—Miss Bindergarten & the Secret Bag. Wolff, Ashley, illus. 2013. (Penguin Young Readers, Level 2 Ser.). (ENG.). 32p. (J). (gr. 1-2). pap. 3.99 *(978-0-448-46803-7(4))*; 14.99 *(978-0-8037-3988-8(5))* Penguin Young Readers Group. (Penguin Young Readers).

Slater, Barbara B. When Wishes Come True. 2009. 165p. (J). 19.95 *(978-1-4327-2220-3(4))* Outskirts Pr., Inc.

Slater, David Michael. Missy Swiss, 1 vol. Reibeling, Brandon, illus. 2007. (Missy Swiss & More Ser.). (ENG.). 32p. (gr. -1-4). 28.50 *(978-1-60270-010-9(9)*, Looking Glass Library) ABDO Publishing Co.

—Seven Ate Nine, 1 vol. Trover, Zachary, illus. 2007. (Missy Swiss & More Ser.). (ENG.). 32p. (gr. -1-4). 28.50 *(978-1-60270-012-3(5)*, Looking Glass Library) ABDO Publishing Co.

Slater, Teddy, text. I Love Korky. 2008. (ENG., Illus.). 32p. (J). (gr. -1-k). 14.95 *(978-1-905417-81-0(0))* Boxer Bks., Ltd. GBR. Dist: Sterling Publishing Co., Inc.

Slater, Teddy & Springer, Sally. Trouble for Trudy. 2007. (No Bullies Allowed Ser.). (Illus.). (J). *(978-0-439-89709-9(2))* Scholastic, Inc.

Slavin, John Mark. My Friend Dad. 2010. 14p. 10.49 *(978-0-557-61038-9(9))* Lulu Pr., Inc.

Sleepover Girls. 2015. (Sleepover Girls Ser.). (ENG.). 128p. (gr. 3-5). 181.20 *(978-1-4965-2023-4(8))* Stone Arch Bks.

Slegers, Liesbet. A Puppy for Kevin. Slegers, Liesbet, illus. 2013. (Kevin & Katie Ser.). (ENG., Illus.). 32p. (J). (— 1). 13.95 *(978-1-60537-144-3(0))* Cobblestone Publishing Co.

Slider-Baker, Belinda. Lost Stripes, Please Return. 2008. 32p. pap. 24.95 *(978-1-60813-075-7(4))* America Star Bks.

Slivensky, Katie. The Countdown Conspiracy. 2017. 336p. (J). (gr. 3-7). 16.99 ***(978-0-06-246255-8(5))*** HarperCollins Pubs.

Sloan, Brian. Tale of Two Summers. 2014. (ENG., Illus.). 256p. (YA). (gr. 7). pap. 12.99 *(978-1-4169-5794-2(4)*, Simon & Schuster Bks. For Young Readers) Simon & Schuster Bks. For Young Readers.

Slobodkina, Esphyr & Sayer, Ann Marie Mulhearn. Caps for Sale & the Mindful Monkeys. Slobodkina, Esphyr, illus. 2017. (Illus.). 48p. (J). (gr. -1-3). 17.99 ***(978-0-06-249988-2(2))*** HarperCollins Pubs.

Sloniker, Phyllis. The Quest for the Golden Flower. 2005. 11.00 *(978-0-8059-9399-8(1))* Dorrance Publishing Co., Inc.

Sloyer, Elliot. The Safety Pin: Summer Camp Stories. Guiza, Victor, illus. 2014. (ENG.). 32p. (J). 16.95 *(978-1-60131-182-5(6)*, Castlebridge Bks.) Big Tent Bks.

Small, Lily. Poppy the Pony. 2016. (Fairy Animals of Misty Wood Ser.). (ENG., Illus.). 144p. (J). pap. 5.99 *(978-1-62779-734-4(3)*, 9781627797344, Holt, Henry & Co. Bks. For Young Readers) Holt, Henry & Co.

Small, Wylie J. The Great Prune Caper. 2009. 94p. pap. 9.98 *(978-1-84728-350-4(0))* Lulu Pr., Inc.

Smallman, Steve. Bear's Big Bottom, 1 vol. Yarlett, Emma, illus. 2014. (ENG.). 32p. (gr. -1-2). 14.95 *(978-1-62370-118-5(X))* Capstone Young Readers of Coughlan Cos.

—The Lamb Who Came for Dinner. Dreidemy, Joëlle, illus. 2007. 32p. (J). (gr. -1-2). 15.95 *(978-1-58925-067-3(2))* Tiger Tales.

—Troll Two — Three — Four. Temairik, Jaime, illus. 2014. (J). *(978-1-4723-2925-7(2))* Parragon Bk. Service Ltd.

—A Very Special Hug. Warnes, Tim, illus. 2008. 32p. pap. 6.95 *(978-1-58925-410-7(4))* Tiger Tales.

Smelser, Lynne M. Noodles & Goo: All over Baby. 2013. 34p. pap. 9.99 *(978-0-9789631-2-5(1))* Three Socks Publishing.

Smiley, Jane. Gee Whiz, Bk. 5. 2014. (Horses of Oak Valley Ranch Ser.: Bk. 5). (ENG.). 272p. (J). (gr. 5). 7.99 *(978-0-375-87132-0(2)*, Yearling) Random Hse. Children's Bks.

Smirl, Mike. Crysta Lun. 2012. 48p. pap. 14.95 *(978-0-615-43657-9(9))* crysta luna studios.

Smith, Alex. Home. Smith, Alex, illus. 2011. (ENG., Illus.). 32p. pap. 7.95 *(978-1-58925-433-6(3))* Tiger Tales.

Smith, Andrew. Ghost Medicine. 2010. (ENG.). 384p. (YA). (gr. 8-13). pap. 18.99 *(978-0-312-62912-0(5))* Square Fish.

—Grasshopper Jungle. 2015. (ENG.). 416p. (YA). (gr. 9). pap. 10.99 *(978-0-14-242500-8(1)*, Speak) Penguin Young Readers Group.

—The Marbury Lens. 2010. (ENG.). 368p. (YA). (gr. 9-12). 17.99 *(978-0-312-61342-6(3)*, 9780312613426) Feiwel & Friends.

—100 Sideways Miles. 2014. (ENG., Illus.). 288p. (YA). (gr. 9). 17.99 *(978-1-4424-4495-9(9)*, Simon & Schuster Bks. For Young Readers) Simon & Schuster Bks. For Young Readers.

Smith, Andrew Christopher John. Soi. 2009. (Illus.). 40p. pap. 16.99 *(978-1-4490-3591-4(4))* AuthorHouse.

Smith Annie, Laura. Whispers in the Wind. 2006. 144p. pap. 12.95 *(978-1-59113-914-0(7))* Booklocker.com, Inc.

Smith-Armand, Kristie. Diamond in the Rough: More Fun Adventures with Abby Diamond. 2010. 256p. pap. 16.95 *(978-1-4502-4618-7(4))* iUniverse, Inc.

Smith Bresciani, Cathleen & Eldredge, Richard. Sassafrass Jones & the Search for a Forever Home. 2013. 54p. 24.99 *(978-0-578-12084-3(4))* Misfit Mouse.

Smith, Carol & Quest, Suzanne. Dr Daphne & Nurse Moira Stories. 2015. (ENG.). 44p. (J). mass mkt. 13.95 *(978-1-78455-086-8(8)*, 62d0eae0-42aa-4e24-9576-96dd0967e0f5) Austin, Stan AUS. Dist: Bookmasters Distribution.

Smith, Cheryl Jean. The Journal. 2006. (ENG.). 164p. per. 11.95 *(978-0-7414-3491-3(1))* Infinity Publishing.

Smith, Clara Batton. Elliott & Anastaci. Smith, Clara Batton, illus. 2012. (Illus.). 16p. pap. 9.95 *(978-1-61633-233-4(6))* Guardian Angel Publishing, Inc.

Smith, D. K. Sock 'n Boots - Share. 2010. 32p. pap. 13.60 *(978-0-557-52614-7(0))* Lulu Pr., Inc.

Smith, Daniel. My Friend the Enemy. 2014. (ENG.). 288p. (J). (gr. 3-7). 17.99 *(978-0-545-66542-1(6)*, Chicken Hse., The) Scholastic, Inc.

Smith, David Thomas. Frenchie the Grass Seed's Journey Around the World to Learn How to Sow a Lawn. 2012. 28p. pap. 24.95 *(978-1-4626-8112-9(3))* America Star Bks.

Smith, Dianne M. Cyanne Rose & Sherbet Are Best Friends. l.t. ed. 2004. 22p. (YA). per. *(978-1-59196-678-4(7))* Instant Pub.

Smith Dinbergs, Holly. Diary Disaster. Stewart, Chantal, illus. 2005. (Girlz Rock! Ser.). (J). pap. *(978-1-59336-700-8(7))* Mondo Publishing.

—Pool Pals. Maddock, Monika, illus. 2005. (Girlz Rock! Ser.). (J). pap. *(978-1-59336-705-3(8))* Mondo Publishing.

Smith, Doris Buchanan. Un Sabor a Moras. Rioja, Alberto Jimenez, tr. Wimmer, Mike, illus. (SPA.). (YA). (gr. 3-18). 14.95 *(978-1-930332-25-6(4)*, LC31160) Lectorum Pubns., Inc.

Smith, Evelyn. The First Fifth Form. Wiles, Frank, illus. 2013. 176p. pap. *(978-1-909423-05-3(X))* Bks. to Treasure.

Smith, Gloria. Annie Elf & Bo Bo Robin. 2012. 24p. 24.95 *(978-1-62709-650-8(7))* America Star Bks.

Smith, Greg Leitich. Ninjas, Piranhas, & Galileo. 2013. 178p. (J). pap. 14.95 *(978-1-62352-029-8(0))* IntoPrint Publishing LLC.

Smith, Holly C. Tyler the Monkey & Andy the Mouse. 2012. 28p. (-18). pap. 24.95 *(978-1-4626-9501-0(9))* America Star Bks.

Smith, Ivy. Sully's New Home. 2011. (Illus.). 28p. (J). 19.95 *(978-0-9635757-5-3(9))*; pap. 11.95 *(978-0-9635757-6-0(7))* Red Tail Publishing.

Smith, J. L. The Abominators: And My Amazing Panty Wanty Woos! Hearn, Sam, illus. 2013. (ENG.). 144p. (J). (gr. 2-4). pap. 7.99 *(978-1-907411-62-5(3))* Little, Brown Book Group Ltd. GBR. Dist: Hachette Bk. Group.

Smith, James J. Mikey's Monster. 2013. (Step into Reading Level 4 Ser.). lib. bdg. 13.55 *(978-0-606-32223-2(X)*, Turtleback) Turtleback Bks.

Smith, James J. & James, Hollis. Mikey's Monster (Teenage Mutant Ninja Turtles) Spaziante, Patrick, illus. 2013. (Step into Reading Ser.). (ENG.). 48p. (J). (gr. k-3). 3.99 *(978-0-449-81826-8(8)*, Random Hse. Bks. for Young Readers) Random Hse. Children's Bks.

Smith, Jane. It's the First Day of Kindergarten, Chloe Zoe! Smith, Jane, illus. 2016. (Chloe Zoe Ser.). (ENG., Illus.). 32p. (J). (gr. -1-3). 12.99 *(978-0-8075-2458-9(1))* Whitman, Albert & Co.

Smith, Jennifer E. Windfall. 2017. (ENG.). 432p. (YA). (gr. 7). 18.99 *(978-0-399-55937-2(X)*, Delacorte Pr.) Random Hse. Children's Bks.

Smith, Joseph K. The Substitute Kid. 2008. 54p. pap. 16.95 *(978-1-60672-272-5(7))* America Star Bks.

Smith, Keeley. First Soul. 2013. 204p. pap. *(978-1-78299-452-7(1))* FeedARead.com.

Smith, Kourtney. The Adventures of Stanley the Staple. 2013. 28p. pap. 24.95 *(978-1-63004-276-9(5))* America Star Bks.

Smith, L. J. The Passion. 2008. (Dark Visions Ser.: Bk. 3). (ENG.). 224p. (YA). (gr. 7). pap. 10.99 *(978-1-4169-8483-2(6)*, Simon Pulse) Simon Pulse.

Smith, Lane. Return to Augie Hobble. 2015. (ENG., Illus.). 288p. (J). (gr. 3-7). 16.99 *(978-1-62672-054-1(1)*, 9781626720541) Roaring Brook Pr.

—Return to Augie Hobble. 2017. (J). lib. bdg. 18.40 *(978-0-606-38550-3(9))* Turtleback Bks.

Smith, Lauren. Ashley Enright & the Mystery at Miller's Pond. 2006. (ENG.). 60p. per. 16.95 *(978-1-4241-5268-1(2))* America Star Bks.

Smith, Lauren E. Ashley Enright & the Darnell Diamonds, 1 vol. 2009. 90p. pap. 19.95 *(978-1-60836-332-2(5))* America Star Bks.

—Ashley Enright Investigations. 2006. 48p. pap. 16.95 *(978-1-4241-2963-8(X))* America Star Bks.

Smith-Leckie, Nina. The Fall & Rise of Abuse-a-Saurus Rex. Gordon, Danny, illus. 2003. 28p. (YA). (gr. 5-18). pap. 6.95 *(978-0-9702582-0-6(8))* Prairie Arts, Inc.

Smith, Leone. Jasmine Finds a Doctor. Smith, Marcelle, illus. 2011. 30p. pap. 12.50 *(978-1-61204-042-4(X)*, Strategic Bk. Publishing) Strategic Book Publishing & Rights Agency (SBPRA).

Smith, Linda. Mrs. Biddlebox: Her Bad Day & What She Did about It. Frazee, Marla, illus. Date not set. 32p. (J). (gr. -1-3). pap. 5.99 *(978-0-06-443620-5(9))* HarperCollins Pubs.

Smith, Lisa. Makini, the Impala with a Crooked Horn. 2011. 24p. pap. 24.95 *(978-1-4626-2608-3(4))* America Star Bks.

Smith, Marvelyn A. The Kangaroo & the Crocodile. 2008. 28p. pap. 12.49 *(978-1-4343-9650-1(9))* AuthorHouse.

Smith, Maudie. Opal Moonbaby & the Best Friend Project. 2016. (Opal Moonbaby Ser.). (ENG.). 192p. (J). (gr. 2-4). 7.99 *(978-1-4440-1580-5(X)*, Orion Children's Bks.) Hachette Children's Group GBR. Dist: Hachette Bk. Group.

—The Summer Secret. 2016. (Opal Moonbaby Ser.). (ENG.). 304p. (J). (gr. 2-4). 7.99 *(978-1-4440-1584-3(2)*, Orion Children's Bks.) Hachette Children's Group GBR. Dist: Hachette Bk. Group.

—The Out of This World Adventure. 2016. (Opal Moonbaby Ser.). (ENG.). 304p. (J). (gr. 2-4). 7.99 *(978-1-4440-1582-9(6)*, Orion Children's Bks.) Hachette Children's Group GBR. Dist: Hachette Bk. Group.

Smith, Mike. Catch the Cuddle. 2015. (ENG., Illus.). 18p. (J). (gr. -1-k). pap. 11.99 *(978-1-4052-7190-5(6))* Egmont Bks., Ltd. GBR. Dist: Independent Pubs. Group.

Smith, Nerissia. Prince de'Mario's Adventure, 1 vol. Dartes, Staci, illus. 2009. 29p. pap. 24.95 *(978-1-61582-972-9(5))* America Star Bks.

Smith, Roger. The Adventures of Xavier Winfield & His Pal Oggie, the Great Camping Adventure. 2013. 184p. pap. 7.99 *(978-0-9854439-0-0(1))* Backpack Pubs.

Smith, Rosemarie. Meet the Bubblechomps - & the Bubblechomps Go Skiing. 2010. (Illus.). 36p. pap. *(978-1-907652-00-4(0))* Grosvenor Hse. Publishing Ltd.

Smith, Sandra. Dilemm. 2011. 28p. pap. 15.99 *(978-1-4628-6213-9(6))* Xlibris Corp.

Smith, Sarah. The Butterfly House. 2014. (ENG., Illus.). 32p. (gr. -1-3). 19.95 *(978-1-84976-205-2(8))* Tate Publishing, Ltd. GBR. Dist: Abrams, Inc.

Smith, Sindy. Charlie the Chipmunk & the Lost Goldmine. Smith, Sindy, illus. 2012. (Illus.). 38p. 29.95 *(978-1-4626-9865-3(4))* America Star Bks.

—Charlie the Chipmunk & the Lost Goldmine. 2012. 40p. pap. 24.95 *(978-1-4626-8590-5(0))* America Star Bks.

—Indy the Unicorn Prince. Smith, Sindy, illus. 2012. (Illus.). 46p. 29.95 *(978-1-4626-9864-6(6))* America Star Bks.

—Indy the Unicorn Prince. 2012. 48p. pap. 24.95 *(978-1-4626-7519-7(0))* America Star Bks.

Smith, Tamara Ellis. Another Kind of Hurricane. 2015. (ENG.). 336p. (J). (gr. 4-7). 16.99 *(978-0-553-51193-2(9))*; 19.99 *(978-0-553-51194-9(7))* Random Hse. Children's Bks. (Schwartz & Wade Bks.).

Smith, Tiffany Nicole. Bex Carter: Middle School Disaster (and Reluctant Fairy Protector) 2013. 148p. pap. 6.99 *(978-0-9893075-8-1(1))* Twisted Spice.

Smith, Tina. The Secret Love of Lone Wolf & Sarah. 2008. 55p. pap. 13.95 *(978-1-4357-4550-6(7))* Lulu Pr., Inc.

Smith, William. Frankie & Earnie Meet, 1 vol. 2009. pap. 24.95 *(978-1-60749-333-4(0))* America Star Bks.

Smithem, Beth. Cocoa Bean & Squirt. 2010. 68p. pap. 10.49 *(978-1-4520-1929-1(0))* AuthorHouse.

Smythe, Theresa. Chester's Colorful Easter Eggs. Smythe, Theresa, illus. 2013. (ENG., Illus.). 24p. (J). (gr. -1-k). 12.99 *(978-0-8050-9326-1(5)*, 9780805093261, Holt, Henry & Co. Bks. For Young Readers) Holt, Henry & Co.

Snadowsky, Daria. Anatomy of a Single Girl. 2014. (ENG.). 240p. (YA). (gr. 9). pap. 8.99 *(978-0-385-73799-9(8)*, Ember) Random Hse. Children's Bks.

Snell, Roy J. Little White Fox & His Arctic Friends. 2008. 108p. 22.95 *(978-1-60664-935-0(3))* Aegypan.

Snider, Ann. The Giant Sea & Me. 2008. (Illus.). 24p. pap. 14.99 *(978-1-4389-1720-7(1))* AuthorHouse.

Snider, Cindy Gay. Finding Anna Bee. Chambers, Mary, illus. 2007. 163p. (J). (gr. 3-7). per. 9.99 *(978-0-8361-9392-3(X))* Herald Pr.

Snider, Kc. Silence. Snider, Kc, illus. 2013. (Illus.). 28p. 19.95 *(978-1-61633-437-6(1))* Guardian Angel Publishing, Inc.

Sniegoski, Thomas E. & Golden, Christopher. Battle for Arcanum. 2013. (Magic Zero Ser.: 4). (ENG., Illus.). 240p. (J). (gr. 3-7). pap. 6.99 *(978-1-4424-7315-7(0)*, Aladdin) Simon & Schuster Children's Publishing.

—Battle for Arcanum. 2013. (Magic Zero Ser.: 4). (ENG., Illus.). 240p. (J). (gr. 3-7). 17.99 *(978-1-4424-7316-4(9)*, Simon & Schuster/Paula Wiseman Bks.) Simon & Schuster/Paula Wiseman Bks.

Snow, Carol. The Last Place on Earth. 2016. (ENG.). 304p. (YA). (gr. 7). 16.99 *(978-1-62779-039-0(X)*, 9781627790390, Holt, Henry & Co. Bks. For Young Readers) Holt, Henry & Co.

Snowballs & Coconuts. 2006. 56p. pap. 7.75 *(978-0-8341-2295-6(2)*, 083-412-2952) Beacon Hill Pr. of Kansas City.

Snyder, Laurel. The Forever Garden. Cotterill, Samantha, illus. 2017. (ENG.). 40p. (J). (gr. -1-3). 17.99 ***(978-0-553-51273-1(0))***; lib. bdg. 20.99 ***(978-0-553-51274-8(9))*** Random Hse. Children's Bks. (Schwartz & Wade Bks.).

Snyder, Laurel. Up & down the Scratchy Mountains. Dorman, Brandon & Call, Greg, illus. 2010. (ENG.). 272p. (J). (gr. 3-7). 7.99 *(978-0-375-84720-2(0)*, Yearling) Random Hse. Children's Bks.

Snyder, Maria V. Storm Watcher. 2013. 228p. (gr. 4-8). pap. 9.99 *(978-1-61603-033-9(X))* Leap Bks.

Sobat, Gail Sidonie. A Winter's Tale. 2004. (Ingamald Ser.: 2). (ENG.). 176p. pap. 16.95 *(978-1-894283-45-8(7))* Great Plains Pubns. CAN. Dist: Publishers Group Canada.

Sobel Frieder, Barbara. My Friend Penelope. 2009. 36p. pap. 16.99 *(978-1-4389-5232-1(5))* AuthorHouse.

Sobel, Gerrie. Jacob & His Magical Flying Bears. Torres, Dottie, illus. 2009. 32p. pap. 12.95 *(978-1-936051-16-8(8))* Peppertree Pr., The.

Soenen, Chantal. Sally: And the Wheel of the Year. 2012. (Illus.). 124p. (gr. 4-6). 27.45 *(978-1-4772-3038-1(6))*; pap. 15.18 *(978-1-4772-3037-4(8))* AuthorHouse.

Sola, Lawrence H. Jeremy's Adventures: Miracle on Main Street. 2012. 88p. *(978-1-77097-843-0(7))*; pap. *(978-1-77097-598-9(5))* FriesenPress.

Solheim, James. The Only Alex Addleston in All These Mountains. Ebbeler, Jeffrey, illus. 2014. (ENG.). 32p. (J). (gr. -1-3). lib. bdg. 17.95 *(978-1-4677-0346-8(X)*, Carolrhoda Bks.) Lerner Publishing Group.

Soli, Doris. Jango the Little Dragon: The Wondrous Adventures of Little Dragon. 2011. (Illus.). 36p. pap. 17.07 *(978-1-4567-8487-4(0))* AuthorHouse.

Soliano, Carolyn. Tree Top Angels. 2010. 56p. (gr. 4-6). pap. 8.95 *(978-1-4502-2276-1(5))* iUniverse, Inc.

Solod, Margo. Coyote Summer: A Summerhood Island Book. 2014. 1. (Illus.). 118p. (J). pap. 15.00 *(978-1-939930-18-7(9))* Brandylane Pubs., Inc.

Soman, David. The Monster Next Door. 2016. (ENG., Illus.). 40p. (J). (-k). 17.99 *(978-0-525-42783-4(X)*, Dial Bks) Penguin Young Readers Group.

Soman, David & Davis, Jacky. Who Can Play? 2013. (Penguin Young Readers Level 1 Ser.). lib. bdg. 13.55 *(978-0-606-32148-8(9)*, Turtleback) Turtleback Bks.

Sommer, Carl. King of the Pond. Budwine, Greg, illus. 2014. (J). pap. *(978-1-57537-956-2(2))* Advance Publishing, Inc.

—You Move You Lose. 2003. (Another Sommer-Time Story Ser.). (Illus.). 48p. (J). (gr. 1-4). 16.95 incl. audio *(978-1-57537-554-0(0))* Advance Publishing, Inc.

—You Move You Lose. James, Kennon, illus. 2003. (Another Sommer-Time Story Ser.). (ENG.). 48p. (J). (gr. 1-4). 16.95 incl. audio compact disk *(978-1-57537-505-2(2))* Advance Publishing, Inc.

Sommer, Isabell & Reinhardt, Swen. CHIP CHIPS JAM - 4: Der Schatz in der Elbe. 2010. 86p. pap. *(978-3-8391-0219-0(7))* Books on Demand GmbH.

Sommers, Jackie Lea. Truest. 2015. (ENG.). 384p. (YA). (gr. 8). 17.99 *(978-0-06-234825-8(6)*, Tegen, Katherine Bks) HarperCollins Pubs.

Somoskey, Rebecca. Summer of the Buckeye Whistle. 2004. (J). 5.00 *(978-0-9768514-0-0(7))* Bearwallow Blessings Ministries.

Sones, Sonya. Saving Red. 2016. 448p. (YA). (gr. 8). 17.99 *(978-0-06-237028-0(6)*, HarperTeen) HarperCollins Pubs.

Song & Juniper. 2006. (Song @ Juniper Ser.). (Illus.). 32p. (J). 17.95 *(978-0-9771990-0-6(2))* Big Kid Bks.

Sonnenblick, Jordan. After Ever After. (ENG.). 272p. (J). 2014. pap. 9.99 *(978-0-545-72287-2(X))* 2010. (gr. 7-12). 17.99 *(978-0-439-83706-4(5)*, Scholastic Pr.) Scholastic, Inc.

—Are You Experienced? 2015. (ENG.). 304p. (YA). (gr. 7). pap. 9.99 *(978-1-250-06304-5(3)*, 9781250063045) Square Fish.

—Dodger & Me. 2009. (Dodger & Me Ser.: 1). (ENG.). 192p. (J). (gr. 3-7). pap. 8.99 *(978-0-312-56122-2(9)*, 9780312561222) Square Fish.

—Notes from the Midnight Driver. 2009. 265p. 18.00 *(978-1-60686-516-3(1))* Perfection Learning Corp.

—Notes from the Midnight Driver. 2007. (ENG.). 288p. (J). (gr. 7-12). pap. 9.99 *(978-0-439-75781-2(9)*, Scholastic Paperbacks) Scholastic, Inc.

Sonnenblick, Jordan. The Secret Sheriff of Sixth Grade. 2017. (ENG.). 208p. (J). (gr. 4-7). 16.99 ***(978-0-545-86320-9(1)***, Scholastic Pr.) Scholastic, Inc.

Sontag, Mary G. Bruno's Adventures. 2009. 128p. pap. 38.49 *(978-1-4490-1769-9(X))* AuthorHouse.

Soo, Kean. Jellaby, 1 vol. 2014. (Jellaby Ser.). (ENG.). 184p. (gr. 4-6). 55.98 *(978-1-4342-9601-6(6))* Stone Arch Bks.

—The Lost Monster. 2014. (Jellaby Ser.). (ENG.). 160p. (gr. 4-8). 27.99 *(978-1-4342-9195-0(2))*; (Illus.). pap. 12.95 *(978-1-4342-6420-6(3))* Stone Arch Bks.

—Monster in the City. 2014. (Jellaby Ser.). (ENG., Illus.). 184p. (gr. 4-8). pap. 12.95 *(978-1-4342-6421-3(1))* Stone Arch Bks.

Sophia Hansen, Hansen & Hansen, Sophia. The Crow & the Raven. 2010. 20p. 9.50 *(978-1-4269-2752-2(5))* Trafford Publishing.

Soto, Gary. Mercy on These Teenage Chimps. 2008. (ENG., Illus.). 160p. (YA). (gr. 7-12). pap. 6.95 *(978-0-15-206215-6(7))* Houghton Mifflin Harcourt Publishing Co.

—Taking Sides. 2003. (ENG., Illus.). 176p. (J). (gr. 2-5). pap. 7.99 *(978-0-15-204694-1(1))* Houghton Mifflin Harcourt Publishing Co.

The Sound of Your Voice, Only Really Far Away. 2014. (Secret Language of Girl Trilogy Ser.). (ENG., Illus.). 256p. (J). (gr. 5-9). pap. 7.99 *(978-1-4424-3290-1(X)*, Atheneum Bks. for Young Readers) Simon & Schuster Children's Publishing.

Sourcebooks & Silverman, Laura. Girl Out of Water. 2017. (ENG.). 368p. (YA). (gr. 8-12). pap. 10.99 *(978-1-4926-4686-0(5)*, 9781492646860) Sourcebooks, Inc.

Sourcebooks, Inc. My Little Valentine: Coupons & Stickers for the Sweetest Girl I Know. 2013. (ENG.). 48p. (J). (-4). 7.99 *(978-1-4022-7959-1(0))* Sourcebooks, Inc.

Sowder, G. Wesley & Sowder, Joseph, told to. Hunter-Lee & the Toy Monster: Book One. 2008. 48p. pap. 16.95 *(978-1-60703-137-6(X))* America Star Bks.

Spaceboy Finds a Friend. 2003. (Spaceboy Set 1 Ser.). (J). 7.33 *(978-1-932570-01-4(2))* Pioneer Valley Bks.

Spaceboy Plays Hide & Seek. 2003. (Spaceboy Set 1 Ser.). (J). 7.33 *(978-1-932570-05-2(5))* Pioneer Valley Bks.

Spady, Angela & Thomas Nelson Publishing Staff. Channing O'Banning & the Rainforest Rescue, 1 vol. 2015. (ENG., Illus.). 112p. (J). pap. 6.99 *(978-0-7180-3262-3(4))* Nelson, Thomas Inc.

Spalding, Amy. Kissing Ted Callahan (and Other Guys) 2016. (ENG.). 336p. (YA). (gr. 10-17). pap. 9.99 *(978-0-316-37153-7(X)*, Poppy) Little, Brown Bks. for Young Readers.

—Kissing Ted Callahan (and Other Guys) 2015. (ENG.). 320p. (YA). (gr. 10-17). 18.00 *(978-0-316-37152-0(1))* Sports Illustrated For Kids.

Spalding, Andrea. Solomon's Tree, 1 vol. Wilson, Janet, illus. 2005. (ENG.). 32p. (J). (gr. -1-3). 10.95 *(978-1-55143-380-6(X))* Orca Bk. Pubs. USA.

Sparkes, Ali. Newt Nemesis. Collins, Ross, illus. 2014. (S. W. I. T. C. H. Ser.: 8). (ENG.). 88p. (J). (gr. 2-5). lib. bdg. 27.93 *(978-1-4677-3233-8(8)*, Darby Creek) Lerner Publishing Group.

Sparks, David. Flat-Top Sam & the Junkyard Elephant. Sparks, David, illus. 2008. (Illus.). 36p. pap. 12.95 *(978-1-59858-587-2(8))* Dog Ear Publishing, LLC.

Sparks, Favre. Agnes, the Eggless Quail. 2009. 28p. pap. 16.50 *(978-1-60693-491-3(0)*, Strategic Bk. Publishing) Strategic Book Publishing & Rights Agency (SBPRA).

Sparks, Kerry. Jen & the Frosted Friends: Book #2 of the Get Frosted Series. 2010. 84p. pap. 10.99 *(978-1-4520-5349-3(9))* AuthorHouse.

Sparks, Megan. Boot Camp Blues, 1 vol. 2014. (Roller Girls Ser.). (ENG.). 256p. (gr. 8-10). 12.95 *(978-1-62370-057-7(4))* Capstone Young Readers of Coughlan Cos.

—Falling Hard, 1 vol. 2013. (Roller Girls Ser.). (ENG.). 256p. (gr. 8-10). 12.95 *(978-1-62370-023-2(X))* Capstone Young Readers of Coughlan Cos.

—Hell's Belles, 1 vol. 2013. (Roller Girls Ser.). (ENG.). 256p. (gr. 8-10). 12.95 *(978-1-62370-024-9(8))* Capstone Young Readers of Coughlan Cos.

—Hell's Belles/By Megan Sparks. 2013. 255p. (YA). *(978-1-62370-022-5(1))* Capstone Young Readers of Coughlan Cos.

—In a Jam, 1 vol. 2014. (Roller Girls Ser.). (ENG.). 256p. (gr. 8-10). 12.95 *(978-1-62370-058-4(2))* Capstone Young Readers of Coughlan Cos.

Sparrow, Steve. The Wooden Tiger. 2009. 52p. pap. *(978-1-84923-773-4(5))* YouWriteOn.

Spaziante, Patrick, illus. OLIVIA Sells Cookies. 2013. (Olivia TV Tie-In Ser.). (ENG.). 24p. (J). (gr. -1-2). pap. 3.99 *(978-1-4424-5965-6(4)*, Simon Spotlight) Simon Spotlight.

Speakman, David. The Adventures of Sierra Rae: The Forgotten Map, 1 vol. 2009. 59p. pap. 16.95 *(978-1-4489-2657-2(2))* PublishAmerica, Inc.

Speare, Elizabeth George. The Sign of the Beaver. 2011. (ENG.). 144p. (J). (gr. 5-7). pap. 7.99 *(978-0-547-57711-1(7))* Houghton Mifflin Harcourt Publishing Co.

—The Sign of the Beaver. 135p. (J). (gr. 4-6). pap. 4.99 *(978-0-8072-1517-3(1)*, Listening Library) Random Hse. Audio Publishing Group.

Spears, Kat. The Boy Who Killed Grant Parker. 2016. (ENG.). 320p. (YA). 18.99 *(978-1-250-08886-4(0)*, 9781250088864, St. Martin's Griffin) St. Martin's Pr.

—Sway. 2014. (ENG.). 320p. (YA). (gr. 9-12). 18.99 *(978-1-250-05143-1(6)*, 9781250051431, St. Martin's Griffin) St. Martin's Pr.

Spector, Baron. Tracking Your Nightmare, 1 vol. Kneupper, Setch, illus. 2012. (Graveyard Diaries Ser.). (ENG.). 128p. (J). (gr. 3-8). lib. bdg. 27.07 *(978-1-61641-898-4(2)*, Calico Chapter Bks) Magic Wagon.

Spedding, Steven. Boriscat & the Quest for the Golden Carp. 2010. 136p. pap. 10.99 *(978-1-4520-5759-0(1))* AuthorHouse.

Spelman, Cornelia Maude. When I Feel Good about Myself. Parkinson, Kathy, illus. 2003. (Way I Feel Bks.). (ENG.). 24p. (J). (gr. -1-3). pap. 6.99 *(978-0-8075-8901-4(2))* Whitman, Albert & Co.

Spencer, Mignon. I'm Living My Dream: An inspirationsl Rhyme for all Ages in English & Spanish. Mack, Travis, illus. 2008.Tr. of Hago mi sueno Realidad. (ENG & SPA.). 32p. (J). 12.99 *(978-0-9763871-2-1(3))* Solomon's Bks.

Spendlove, Owen. Stanley Brambles & the Pirate's Treasure. 2007. 320p. per. 18.95 *(978-0-595-43792-4(3))* iUniverse, Inc.

Sperring, Mark & Teckentrup, Britta. Your Hand in My Hand. 2015. (ENG.). 32p. (J). (gr. -1-k). 15.99 *(978-0-545-80642-8(9),* Scholastic Pr.) Scholastic, Inc.

Spindler, Rebecca Williams & Spindler, Madelyn. Life According to Liz. 2012. 204p. pap. 12.95 *(978-0-9848050-5-1(2),* Little Creek Bks.) Jan-Carol Publishing, INC.

Spinelli, Eileen. When No One Is Watching. Johnson, David, illus. 2013. (ENG.). 26p. (J). 16.00 *(978-0-8028-5303-5(X),* Eerdmans Bks For Young Readers) Eerdmans, William B. Publishing Co.

Spinelli, Jerry. Eggs. 2008. (ENG., Illus.). 240p. (J). (gr. 3-7). pap. 8.99 *(978-0-316-16647-8(2))* Little, Brown Bks. for Young Readers.

—Fourth Grade Rats. 2012. (ENG.). 160p. (J). (gr. 2-5). pap. 5.99 *(978-0-545-46478-9(1),* Levine, Arthur A. Bks.) Scholastic, Inc.

—Fourth Grade Rats. 2012. lib. bdg. 16.00 *(978-0-606-26731-1(X),* Turtleback) Turtleback Bks.

—Jake & Lily. 2012. 352p. (J). (gr. 3-7). (ENG.). 16.99 *(978-0-06-028135-9(9));* lib. bdg. 16.89 *(978-0-06-028136-6(7))* HarperCollins Pubs.

—Smiles to Go. 2009. (ENG.). 272p. (J). (gr. 5). pap. 6.99 *(978-0-06-447197-8(7))* HarperCollins Pubs.

—Third Grade Angels. Bell, Jennifer, illus. 2014. (ENG.). 160p. (J). (gr. 2-5). pap. 5.99 *(978-0-545-38773-6(6),* Levine, Arthur A. Bks.) Scholastic, Inc.

Spires, Ashley. Binky: License to Scratch. Spires, Ashley, illus. 2013. (Binky Adventure Ser.). (ENG., Illus.). 64p. (J). (gr. 2-5). pap. 7.95 *(978-1-55453-964-2(1))* Kids Can Pr., Ltd. CAN. Dist: Hachette Bk. Group.

—Binky Takes Charge. Spires, Ashley, illus. 2012. (Binky Adventure Ser.: 4). (ENG., Illus.). 64p. (J). (gr. 2-5). 7.95 *(978-1-55453-768-6(1));* 16.95 *(978-1-55453-703-7(7))* Kids Can Pr., Ltd. CAN. Dist: Hachette Bk. Group.

Spires, Sharlene. The Grandsisters. 2010. 56p. pap. 15.99 *(978-1-4535-3004-7(5))* Xlibris Corp.

Spizman, Robyn Freedman & Johnston, Mark. The Secret Agents Strike Back. 2012. (ENG.). 160p. (YA). (gr. 4-7). pap. 8.99 *(978-1-4424-8189-3(7),* Atheneum Bks. for Young Readers) Simon & Schuster Children's Publishing.

Spooner, M. Entrapment. 2010. (ENG.). 320p. (YA). (gr. 8). pap. 8.99 *(978-1-4424-0366-6(7),* McElderry, Margaret K. Bks.) McElderry, Margaret K. Bks.

—Entr@pment: A High School Comedy in Chat. 2009. (ENG.). 320p. (YA). (gr. 8-18). 16.99 *(978-1-4169-5889-5(4),* McElderry, Margaret K. Bks.) McElderry, Margaret K. Bks.

Spoonmore, Scott. Seymour the Semi- Space Truckin' Sponaugle, Kim, illus. 2012. 24p. 19.95 *(978-1-61633-282-2(4));* pap. 11.95 *(978-1-61633-283-9(2))* Guardian Angel Publishing, Inc.

Spring, Melanie. Practice Makes Perfect. 2014. (Varsity Novel Ser.: 3). (ENG.). 192p. (YA). (gr. 7-17). pap. 10.00 *(978-0-316-22733-9(1),* Poppy) Little, Brown Bks. for Young Readers.

—Turn It Up. 2014. (Varsity Novel Ser.: 2). (ENG.). 208p. (YA). (gr. 7-17). pap. 10.00 *(978-0-316-22724-7(2))* Little Brown & Co.

Springer, Kristina. My Fake Boyfriend Is Better Than Yours. 2013. (ENG.). 208p. (YA). (gr. 6-9). pap. 6.99 *(978-0-312-64159-7(1),* 9780312641597) Square Fish.

Springer, Nancy. Wild Boy. 2005. (Tales of Rowan Hood Ser.). 115p. (J). (gr. 3). 13.65 *(978-0-7569-5490-1(8))* Perfection Learning Corp.

Springstubb, Tricia. Cody & the Mysteries of the Universe. Wheeler, Eliza, illus. 2016. (ENG.). 144p. (J). (gr. 2-5). 14.99 *(978-0-7636-5858-8(8))* Candlewick Pr.

—Cody & the Rules of Life. Wheeler, Eliza, illus. 2017. (ENG.). 176p. (J). (gr. 2-5). 14.99 *(978-0-7636-7920-0(8))* Candlewick Pr.

—Every Single Second. Sudyka, Diana, illus. 2016. 368p. (J). (gr. 3-7). 16.99 *(978-0-06-236628-3(9))* HarperCollins Pubs.

—Moonpenny Island. Ford, Gilbert, illus. (J). (gr. 3-7). 2016. 320p. pap. 6.99 *(978-0-06-211294-1(5))* 2015. (ENG.). 304p. 16.99 *(978-0-06-211293-4(7))* HarperCollins Pubs.

—Moonpenny Island. 2016. (J). lib. bdg. 17.20 *(978-0-606-38742-2(0))* Turtleback Bks.

—What Happened on Fox Street. Ross, Heather, illus. 2011. (Fox Street Ser.: 1). (ENG.). 240p. (J). (gr. 3-7). pap. 6.99 *(978-0-06-198636-9(4))* HarperCollins Pubs.

Spurgeon, S. The Great Kitten Mystery. 2008. 73p. pap. 19.95 *(978-1-60610-798-0(4))* America Star Bks.

Spurling, Wesley. Books for Jacob. 2009. 24p. pap. 14.79 *(978-1-4389-2231-7(0))* AuthorHouse.

Spurlock, Cathy. Toby, the Two-Toed Tiger. 2008. 24p. pap. 24.95 *(978-1-60563-108-0(6))* America Star Bks.

Spyri, Johanna. Veronica. 2006. 120p. (gr. 4-7). per. 10.95 *(978-1-59818-863-9(1))* Aegypan.

—Veronica & Other Friends. 2006. pap. *(978-1-4068-0697-7(8))* Echo Library.

Squiers, Connie. The Copper Colt. 2013. 94p. pap. 7.95 *(978-1-937829-78-0(2),* Total Publishing & Media) Yorkshire Publishing Group.

Sretaw. Aussie Animal Friends. 2010. 36p. pap. 32.70 *(978-1-4500-7415-5(4))* Xlibris Corp.

St. Anthony, Jane. Isabelle Day Refuses to Die of a Broken Heart. 2015. (ENG.). 152p. (J). 14.95 *(978-0-8166-9799-1(X))* Univ. of Minnesota Pr.

St. James, Leah. Lights of Imani. Morse, Nessa Neilson, illus. 2013. 28p. pap. 9.99 *(978-0-9853123-6-7(X))* Allen, Edward Publishing, LLC.

St. Jean, Alan. The Legend of OinkADoodleMoo. St. Jean, Alan, ed. Krock, Libby Carruth, illus. 2013. 32p. 19.95 *(978-0-9777272-9-2(7))* Oren Village, LLC.

St. John, Lauren. Kentucky Thriller. Dean, David, illus. 2014. (Jóvenes Lectores. Los Misterios de Laura Ser.). (SPA.). 248p. (J). (gr. 4-7). pap. 8.95 *(978-84-8343-271-6(4),* Bambu, Editorial) Combel Editorial, S.A. ESP. Dist: Independent Pubs. Group.

—The Last Leopard. 2010. (ENG.). 224p. (J). (gr. 3-7). 6.99 *(978-0-14-241515-3(4),* Puffin Books) Penguin Young Readers Group.

St-Onge, Donna Na-Tasa Katherine. The Eye of Isis, 1 vol. 2009. 155p. pap. 24.95 *(978-1-60836-986-7(2))* America Star Bks.

Staake, Bob. Beachy & Me. 2016. (ENG., Illus.). 40p. (J). (gr. -1-2). 16.99 *(978-0-385-37314-2(7));* lib. bdg. 19.99 *(978-0-375-97198-3(X))* Random Hse. Children's Bks. (Random Hse. Bks. for Young Readers).

—Bluebird. Staake, Bob, illus. 2013. (ENG., Illus.). 40p. (J). (gr. -1-3). 17.99 *(978-0-375-87037-8(7),* Schwartz & Wade Bks.) Random Hse. Children's Bks.

—My Pet Book. 2014. (ENG., Illus.). 40p. (J). (gr. -1-2). lib. bdg. 20.99 *(978-0-375-97195-2(5),* Random Hse. Bks. for Young Readers) Random Hse. Children's Bks.

Stacey, Tom. The First Dog to Be Somebody's Best Friend: A Likely Story in Two Bits & a Decide. Landels, Angela, illus. 2007. (ENG.). 46p. 15.95 *(978-1-905299-34-8(6),* Stacey International) Stacey Publishing GBR. Dist: Casemate Pubs. & Bk. Distributors, LLC.

Stafford, Liliana. Snow Bear. Davis, Lambert, illus. 32p. (J). pap. *(978-0-88899-441-7(9))* Groundwood Bks.

Stagliano, Michael F. Wesley's Stories: Afterschool Adventures. 2008. 208p. 24.95 *(978-0-595-50215-8(6));* pap. 14.95 *(978-0-595-50637-8(2))* iUniverse, Inc.

Stahl, Hilda. Big Trouble for Roxie. 2003. (Best Friends Ser.: No. 2). 160p. (YA). (gr. 4-7). pap. 4.99 *(978-0-89107-658-2(1))* Crossway.

Stahl, Matt. Fuzzy Winkerbane: The Boy Who Would Never Change. 2011. 28p. pap. 14.50 *(978-1-4634-0758-2(0))* AuthorHouse.

Stahler, David, Jr. Spinning Out. 2011. (ENG.). 288p. (YA). (gr. 7-17). 16.99 *(978-0-8118-7780-0(9))* Chronicle Bks. LLC.

Staller, Mary J. Meet Sandy Gull. 2013. 20p. pap. 10.00 *(978-1-4251-3171-5(9))* Trafford Publishing.

Stamp, Jeffrey. Red & Slim: One Hot Day. Bohrer, Joe, illus. 2008. 40p. (J). 16.99 *(978-0-9794543-0-1(1))* Syllabets, LLC.

Stamp, Jørgen & Buckley, William F., Jr. Flying High. 2009. (ENG., Illus.). 32p. (J). (gr. -1-2). 16.95 *(978-1-59270-089-6(6))* Enchanted Lion Bks., LLC.

Stampler, Ann Redisch. Afterparty. 2013. (ENG., Illus.). 416p. (YA). (gr. 9). 17.99 *(978-1-4424-2324-4(2),* Simon Pulse) Simon Pulse.

Stamps, Paula. Learning Makes Friends Fun, 1 vol. 2010. 22p. 24.95 *(978-1-4512-8765-3(8))* PublishAmerica, Inc.

Standiford, Natalie. How to Say Goodbye in Robot. 2009. (ENG.). 288p. (J). (gr. 7-18). 17.99 *(978-0-545-10708-2(3),* Scholastic Pr.) Scholastic, Inc.

—The Secret Tree. (J). 2014. (ENG.). 256p. (gr. 3-7). pap. 6.99 *(978-0-545-33480-8(2),* Scholastic Paperbacks) 2012. 245p. pap. *(978-0-545-48976-8(8),* Scholastic Pr.) Scholastic, Inc.

—Switched at Birthday. 2014. (ENG.). 240p. (J). (gr. 3-7). 16.99 *(978-0-545-34650-4(9),* Scholastic Pr.) Scholastic, Inc.

Standish, Ali. The Ethan I Was Before. 2017. 368p. (J). (gr. 3-7). 16.99 *(978-0-06-243338-1(5))* HarperCollins Pubs.

Standish, Burt L. Frank Merriwell's College Chums. Rudman, Jack, ed. 2003. (Frank Merriwell Ser.). 29.95 *(978-0-8373-9337-7(X));* pap. 9.95 *(978-0-8373-9037-6(0))* Merriwell, Frank Inc.

—Frank Merriwell's False Friend. Rudman, Jack, ed. 2003. (Frank Merriwell Ser.). 29.95 *(978-0-8373-9370-4(1));* pap. 9.95 *(978-0-8373-9070-3(2))* Merriwell, Frank Inc.

Stanek, Gerald. Sarah 'n' Dippity. Stanek, Joyce Huntington, illus. 2004. (ENG.). 28p. (J). 14.95 *(978-0-9747417-0-3(1))* Shiver Hill Bks.

Stanek, Robert, pseud. Bugville Critters & Every Day Is Different. 2011. (Illus.). 32p. pap. 4.99 *(978-1-57545-263-0(4),* Reagent Pr. Bks. for Young Readers) RP Media.

—The Bugville Critters Go on Vacation. 2008. (ENG., Illus.). (J). 32p. per. 9.95 *(978-1-57545-148-0(4));* 52p. per. 19.95 *(978-1-57545-125-1(5))* RP Media.

—The Bugville Critters Go to School. 2007. (ENG.). 28p. (J). per. 9.99 *(978-1-57545-145-9(X))* RP Media.

—The Bugville Critters Have a Sleepover. 2008. (ENG.). 28p. (J). per. 9.99 *(978-1-57545-146-6(8))* RP Media.

—The Bugville Critters Make New Friends: Buster Bee's School Days #2. 2008. (ENG., Illus.). 60p. (J). per. 18.95 *(978-1-57545-168-8(9))* RP Media.

—The Bugville Critters Play Their First Big Game. 2008. (ENG., Illus.). (J). 32p. per. 9.95 *(978-1-57545-149-7(2));* 52p. per. 16.95 *(978-1-57545-127-5(1))* RP Media.

—The Bugville Critters Visit Dad & Mom at Work. 2007. (ENG.). (J). 28p. per. 9.99 *(978-1-57545-144-2(1));* (Illus.). 52p. per. 19.95 *(978-1-57545-121-3(2),* Reagent Pr. Bks. for Young Readers) RP Media.

—The Bugville Critters Visit Garden Box Farms. (ENG.). (J). 2008. 28p. per. 10.99 *(978-1-57545-147-3(6))* 2007. (Illus.). 52p. per. 19.95 *(978-1-57545-124-4(7))* RP Media.

—Have a Backyard Picnic. 2009. (Bugville Critters Ser.: No. 14). (ENG., Illus.). 52p. (J). 14.95 *(978-1-57545-210-4(3),* Reagent Pr. Bks. for Young Readers) RP Media.

—Robert Stanek's Bugville Critters Storybook Treasury Volume 2 (the Bugville Critters Storybook Collection, Volume 2), 4 vols., Vol. 2. 2008. (ENG., Illus.). 124p. (J). per. 24.95 *(978-1-57545-173-2(5))* RP Media.

—Stay after School. 2009. (Bugville Critters Ser.: No. 10). (ENG., Illus.). 52p. (J). 14.95 *(978-1-57545-206-7(5),* Reagent Pr. Bks. for Young Readers) RP Media.

—Visit the Library. 2010. 28p. pap. 8.99 *(978-1-57545-176-3(X),* Reagent Pr. Bks. for Young Readers) RP Media.

Staniszewski, Anna. The Truth Game. 2016. (Dirt Diary Ser.: 4). (ENG., Illus.). 224p. (J). (gr. 5-9). pap. 7.99 *(978-1-4926-3272-6(4),* 9781492632726, Sourcebooks Jabberwocky) Sourcebooks, Inc.

Stanley, Diane. Goldie & the Three Bears. Stanley, Diane, illus. 2007. (ENG., Illus.). 40p. (J). (gr. k-3). pap. 7.99 *(978-0-06-113611-5(5))* HarperCollins Pubs.

—Joplin, Wishing. 2017. 272p. (J). (gr. 3-7). 16.99 *(978-0-06-242370-2(3))* HarperCollins Pubs.

Stanley, Shalanda. Drowning Is Inevitable. 2015. (ENG.). 288p. (YA). (gr. 9). 17.99 *(978-0-553-50828-4(8),* Knopf Bks. for Young Readers) Random Hse. Children's Bks.

Stanton, Nicholas Sheridan. KK Undercover Mystery: The Cookie Caper. 2011. 80p. (gr. 4-6). pap. 26.01 *(978-1-4567-6597-2(3))* AuthorHouse.

Stapleton, Rhonda. Flirting with Disaster. 2010. (ENG.). 256p. (YA). (gr. 7-18). pap. 9.99 *(978-1-4169-7465-9(2),* Simon Pulse) Simon Pulse.

—Stupid Cupid. 2009. (ENG.). 272p. (YA). (gr. 7-18). pap. 9.99 *(978-1-4169-7464-2(4),* Simon Pulse) Simon Pulse.

star, celina. Paw Prints on the Road. 2008. 79p. pap. 9.96 *(978-0-557-02420-9(X))* Lulu Pr., Inc.

Stark, Barbara. Blue Dinosaur's Friends. l.t. ed. 2006. (Illus.). 24p. (J). E-Book 9.95 incl. cd-rom *(978-1-933090-20-7(0))* Guardian Angel Publishing, Inc.

Starkey, Scott. The Call of the Bully. 2013. (How to Beat the Bully Ser.). (ENG.). 272p. (J). (gr. 3-7). 15.99 *(978-1-4424-5674-7(4),* Simon & Schuster/Paula Wiseman Bks.) Simon & Schuster/Paula Wiseman Bks.

—The Call of the Bully: A Rodney Rathbone Novel. 2014. (How to Beat the Bully Ser.). (ENG., Illus.). 272p. (J). (gr. 3-7). pap. 6.99 *(978-1-4424-5675-4(2),* Simon & Schuster/Paula Wiseman Bks.) Simon & Schuster/Paula Wiseman Bks.

Starmer, Aaron. The Riverman. 2015. (Riverman Trilogy Ser.: 1). (ENG.). 336p. (YA). (gr. 5-9). pap. 8.99 *(978-1-250-05685-6(3),* 9781250056856) Square Fish.

—Spontaneous. 2016. (ENG.). 368p. (YA). (gr. 9). 17.99 *(978-0-525-42974-6(3),* Dutton Books for Young Readers) Penguin Young Readers Group.

—The Storyteller. 2016. (Riverman Trilogy Ser.: 3). (ENG.). 336p. (J). 16.99 *(978-0-374-36313-0(7),* 9780374363130, Farrar, Straus & Giroux (BYR)) Farrar, Straus & Giroux.

—The Whisper. 2015. (Riverman Trilogy Ser.: 2). (ENG.). 368p. (YA). (gr. 5-9). 16.99 *(978-0-374-36311-6(0),* 9780374363116, Farrar, Straus & Giroux (BYR)) Farrar, Straus & Giroux.

Stauffacher, Sue. Donuthead. 2005. (ENG.). 176p. (J). (gr. 3-7). reprint ed. per. 6.99 *(978-0-440-41934-1(4),* Yearling) Random Hse. Children's Bks.

Staunton, Ted. Accord de Puissance: (Power Chord), 1 vol. 2012. (FRE.). 128p. (J). (gr. 5-9). pap. 9.95 *(978-1-4598-0311-4(6))* Orca Bk. Pubs. USA.

—Morgan & the Dune Racer. Slavin, Bill, illus. 2011. (Formac First Novels Ser.). (ENG.). 64p. (J). (gr. 2-3). 14.95 *(978-0-88780-966-8(9),* 9780887809668); pap. 5.95 *(978-0-88780-965-1(0),* 9780887809651) Formac Publishing Co., Ltd. CAN. Dist: Casemate Pubs. & Bk. Distributors, LLC.

—Morgan & the Money. Slavin, Bill, illus. 2008. (First Novel Ser.). (ENG.). 64p. (J). (gr. 1-5). *(978-0-88780-776-3(3))* Formac Publishing Co., Ltd.

—Morgan & the Money, 1 vol. Shannon, Ben, illus. 2008. (Formac First Novels Ser.). (ENG.). 64p. (gr. 1-5). 4.95 *(978-0-88780-774-9(7),* 9780887807749) Formac Publishing Co., Ltd. CAN. Dist: Casemate Pubs. & Bk. Distributors, LLC.

—Morgan Makes a Deal. Slavin, Bill, illus. 2005. (Formac First Novels Ser.: 33). (ENG.). 64p. (J). (gr. 2-5). 14.95 *(978-0-88780-667-4(8),* 9780887806674) Formac Publishing Co., Ltd. CAN. Dist: Casemate Pubs. & Bk. Distributors, LLC.

—Morgan Makes a Deal, 1 vol. Slavin, Bill & Shannon, Ben, illus. 2005. (Formac First Novels Ser.: 33). (ENG.). 64p. (J). (gr. 2-5). 4.95 *(978-0-88780-666-7(X),* 9780887806667) Formac Publishing Co., Ltd. CAN. Dist: Casemate Pubs. & Bk. Distributors, LLC.

—Morgan Makes a Splash. Slavin, Bill, illus. 2004. (Formac First Novels Ser.: 28). (ENG.). 64p. (J). (gr. 1-5). 14.95 *(978-0-88780-623-0(6),* 9780887806230) Formac Publishing Co., Ltd. CAN. Dist: Casemate Pubs. & Bk. Distributors, LLC.

—Power Chord, 1 vol. 2011. (Orca Currents Ser.). (ENG.). 128p. (J). (gr. 5-9). pap. 9.95 *(978-1-55469-903-2(7));* lib. bdg. 16.95 *(978-1-55469-904-9(5))* Orca Bk. Pubs. USA.

—Super Move, Morgan! Slavin, Bill, illus. 2006. (Formac First Novels Ser.: 35). (ENG.). 64p. (J). (gr. 2-5). 14.95 *(978-0-88780-704-6(6),* 9780887807046); 4.95 *(978-0-88780-702-2(X),* 9780887807022) Formac Publishing Co., Ltd. CAN. Dist: Casemate Pubs. & Bk. Distributors, LLC.

Stave, Mel. How Harry Found the Meaning of Friendship. 2010. (Illus.). 40p. pap. 14.95 *(978-1-60911-147-2(8),* Eloquent Bks.) Strategic Book Publishing & Rights Agency (SBPRA).

Stead, Philip C. Hello, My Name Is Ruby. Stead, Philip C., illus. 2013. (ENG., Illus.). 36p. (J). (gr. -1-1). 16.99 *(978-1-59643-809-5(6),* 9781596438095) Roaring Brook Pr.

—Lenny & Lucy. Stead, Erin E., illus. 2015. (ENG.). 40p. (J). (gr. -1-2). 17.99 *(978-1-59643-932-0(7),* 9781596439320) Roaring Brook Pr.

—Samson in the Snow. 2016. (ENG., Illus.). 40p. (J). 17.99 *(978-1-62672-182-1(3),* 9781626721821) Roaring Brook Pr.

—A Sick Day for Amos McGee. Stead, Erin E., illus. 2010. (ENG.). 32p. (J). (gr. -1-1). 17.99 *(978-1-59643-402-8(3),* 9781596434028) Roaring Brook Pr.

—A Sick Day for Amos Mcgee: Book & CD Storytime Set. Stead, Erin E., illus. 2017. (ENG.). 32p. (J). 12.99 *(978-1-4272-8722-9(8),* 9781427287229) Macmillan Audio.

Stead, Rebecca. Goodbye Stranger. (ENG.). (J). (gr. 5). 2017. 320p. 7.99 *(978-0-307-98086-1(3),* Yearling) 2015. 304p. 16.99 *(978-0-385-74317-4(3),* Lamb, Wendy Bks.) 2015. 304p. lib. bdg. 19.99 *(978-0-375-99098-4(4),* Lamb, Wendy Bks.) Random Hse. Children's Bks.

—Goodbye Stranger. 2017. lib. bdg. 18.40 ***(978-0-606-39873-2(2))*** Turtleback Bks.

Stead, Vince. Rusty the Runaway Golden Retriever. 2007. 73p. 19.95 *(978-1-4241-5739-6(0))* America Star Bks.

Steedley-Tolan, Chopper. I'm Not Sick! Chopper's Tails of the Doctor. 2012. 32p. (-18). pap. 12.95 *(978-1-4772-8618-0(7))* AuthorHouse.

Steele, Michael Anthony. Fresh, 1 vol. Cano, Fernando, illus. 2014. (Tony Hawk: Live2Skate Ser.). (ENG.). 72p. (gr. 4-5). lib. bdg. 25.32 *(978-1-4342-9140-0(5))* Stone Arch Bks.

Steffen, Tim & Thornton, Susan Ann. The Golden Dragonfly: The Adventures of Baby Cat in Cherry Grove. Thornton, Susan Ann, illus. 2009. (Illus.). 76p. pap. 8.95 *(978-1-4401-4804-0(X))* iUniverse, Inc.

Steig, William. Amos & Boris. 2011. 8.30 *(978-0-7848-3427-5(X),* Everbind) Marco Bk. Co.

—Amos & Boris. Steig, William, illus. 2009. (ENG., Illus.). 32p. (J). (gr. k-3). pap. 7.99 *(978-0-312-53566-7(X),* 9780312535667) Square Fish.

—Amos & Boris. 2009. (J). (gr. -1-2). lib. bdg. 18.40 *(978-0-8085-2709-1(6),* Turtleback) Turtleback Bks.

—Potch & Polly. Date not set. (J). 15.89 *(978-0-06-205145-5(8))* HarperCollins Pubs.

—Potch & Polly. Agee, Jon, illus. Date not set. (J). 14.99 *(978-0-06-205144-8(X))* HarperCollins Pubs.

—The Real Thief. 2007. (SPA.). (J). 1.25 *(978-1-4193-9992-3(6))* Recorded Bks., Inc.

—The Real Thief. Steig, William, illus. 2007. (ENG., Illus.). 64p. (J). (gr. 2-5). per. 7.99 *(978-0-312-37145-6(4),* 9780312371456) Square Fish.

Steigvilas, Nemira. Mini Eva Lovvves Ballet. 2013. 44p. pap. 15.95 *(978-1-4525-7341-0(7),* Balboa Pr.) Author Solutions, Inc.

Stein, David Ezra. Cowboy Ned & Andy. Stein, David Ezra, illus. (ENG., Illus.). 32p. (J). (gr. -1-1). 2011. 6.99 *(978-1-4424-3619-0(0))* 2006. 16.99 *(978-1-4169-0041-2(1))* Simon & Schuster/Paula Wiseman Bks. (Simon & Schuster/Paula Wiseman Bks.).

Stein, Garth. Enzo - Races in the Rain! Alley, R. W., illus. 2014. (ENG.). 40p. (J). (gr. -1-3). 17.99 *(978-0-06-229533-0(0))* HarperCollins Pubs.

—Racing in the Rain: My Life as a Dog. 2011. (ENG., Illus.). 304p. (J). (gr. 3-7). 16.99 *(978-0-06-201574-7(5));* pap. 6.99 *(978-0-06-201576-1(1))* HarperCollins Pubs.

Stein, Renea. The Wise Old Owl & Those Tricky Times Tables. 2008. 36p. pap. 24.95 *(978-1-60474-228-2(3))* America Star Bks.

Stein, Tammar. High Dive. 2011. (ENG.). 208p. (YA). (gr. 7). pap. 7.99 *(978-0-440-23903-1(6),* Knopf Bks. for Young Readers) Random Hse. Children's Bks.

Steiner, Dawn. The Silver Squirrel & Friends: The Original Book. 2009. 16p. pap. 8.99 *(978-1-4389-2944-6(7))* AuthorHouse.

—Silver Squirrel & Friends I Can Read Edition: For Beginner Readers. 2009. 16p. pap. 8.99 *(978-1-4389-2916-3(1))* AuthorHouse.

Steiner, Matt. Mission Possible. 2011. 108p. (gr. 4-6). 20.95 *(978-1-4620-0028-9(2));* pap. 10.95 *(978-1-4620-0027-2(4))* iUniverse, Inc.

Steinhöfel, Andreas & Wright, Chantal. The Spaghetti Detectives. 2011. (ENG.). 176p. (J). (gr. 3-7). 16.99 *(978-0-545-28975-7(0),* Chicken Hse., The) Scholastic, Inc.

Steinkellner, Teddy. Two Roads from Here. 2017. (ENG., Illus.). 448p. (YA). (gr. 9). 17.99 ***(978-1-4814-3061-6(0),*** Simon & Schuster Bks. For Young Readers) Simon & Schuster Bks. For Young Readers.

Steinkraus, Kyla. Vamos a Acampar. 2012. (SPA & ENG.). 24p. (gr. 2-3). pap. 8.95 *(978-1-61810-549-3(3))* Rourke Educational Media.

Steinlage, Ben. Bird Boy. 2011. 290p. pap. 17.95 *(978-1-4327-6667-2(8))* Outskirts Pr., Inc.

Stellings, Caroline. The Contest, 1 vol. 2009. (ENG.). 160p. (J). (gr. 4-7). pap. 9.95 *(978-0-9779183-5-5(1),* 7th Generation) Book Publishing Co.

Stephens, Ann Marie. Cy Makes a Friend. Subisak, Tracy, illus. 2017. (ENG.). 32p. (J). (gr. -1-3). 16.95 *(978-1-62979-578-2(X))* Boyds Mills Pr.

—Scuba Dog. Golden, Jess, illus. 2016. (ENG.). 40p. (J). (gr. -1-3). 17.99 *(978-1-4998-0143-9(2))* Little Bee Books Inc.

—A Surprise for Ray. Bolan, Michael P., illus. 2003. 47p. (J). per. 11.95 *(978-0-9729285-1-9(0),* 0-9729285-1-0) Kinkachoo Pr., The.

Stephens, Helen. How to Hide a Lion. Stephens, Helen, illus. 2013. (ENG., Illus.). 32p. (J). (gr. -1-3). 16.99 *(978-0-8050-9834-1(8),* 9780805098341, Holt, Henry & Co. Bks. For Young Readers) Holt, Henry & Co.

Stephenson, Nancy Ann. The Ducks' New Friends. Coffin, Marilyn, illus. l.t. ed. 2006. 34p. (J). per. 9.99 *(978-1-59879-164-8(8))* Lifevest Publishing, Inc.

Stephenson, Susan. Monster Maddie. Snider, K. C., illus. 2010. 20p. pap. 10.95 *(978-1-61633-027-9(9))* Guardian Angel Publishing, Inc.

Stepp, Shirley. Pongo Penguin's Whale of a Tale. 2012. 24p. 24.95 *(978-1-4626-5478-9(9))* America Star Bks.

Steps To Literacy Staff, compiled by. The Mysterious Benedict Society Collection: Class Pack (3 titles, 6 Each) 2010. (ENG.). (J). pap. 125.82 *(978-1-61267-335-6(X))* Steps To Literacy, LLC.

—The Mysterious Benedict Society Collection: Variety Pack (3 titles, 1 Each) 2010. (ENG.). (J). pap. 20.97 *(978-1-61267-334-9(1))* Steps To Literacy, LLC.

Sterling, James Milton. Willy the Mountain Climber. 2012. 32p. pap. 24.95 *(978-1-4626-8242-3(1))* America Star Bks.

Stern, Ricki. Mission Impossible. Date not set. (Beryl E. Bean Ser.: Vol. 3). (Illus.). (J). lib. bdg. 15.89 *(978-0-06-028773-3(X),* Harper Trophy) HarperCollins Pubs.

Sternberg, Julie. Everything's Changed. Wright, Johanna, illus. 2017. (Top-Secret Diary of Celie Valentine Ser.). (ENG.). 160p. (J). (gr. 2-6). 16.95 *(978-1-62979-672-7(7))* Boyds Mills Pr.

—Friendship Over. Wright, Johanna, illus. (Top-Secret Diary of Celie Valentine Ser.). (ENG.). 160p. (J). 2014. (gr. 3-6). 15.95 *(978-1-59078-993-3(8))*Bk. 1. 2015. (gr. 2-6). pap. 6.95 *(978-1-62979-405-1(8))* Boyds Mills Pr.

—Like Carrot Juice on a Cupcake. Cordell, Matthew, illus. (Eleanor Ser.). (ENG.). (J). (gr. 1-4). 2017. 200p. pap. 6.95 *(978-1-4197-2384-1(7))* 2014. 192p. 15.95 *(978-1-4197-1033-9(8))* Abrams, Inc. (Amulet Bks.).

Stevens, Cara. Let's Save Pirate Day! (Dora & Friends) Aikins, David, illus. 2014. (Pictureback(R) Ser.). (ENG.). 24p. (J). (gr. -1-2). 4.99 *(978-0-385-37440-8(2),* Random Hse. Bks. for Young Readers) Random Hse. Children's Bks.

Stevens, Courtney. The Lies about Truth. 2017. 336p. (YA). (gr. 9). pap. 9.99 *(978-0-06-224542-7(2),* HarperTeen) HarperCollins Pubs.

Stevens, Courtney C. Faking Normal. 2014. (Faking Normal Ser.). (ENG.). 336p. (YA). (gr. 9). 17.99 *(978-0-06-224538-0(4),* HarperTeen) HarperCollins Pubs.

EFG

—The Lies about Truth. 2015. (ENG.). 336p. (YA). (gr. 9). 17.99 (978-0-06-224541-0(4), HarperTeen) HarperCollins Pubs.
Stevens, Janet & Stevens Crummel, Susan. My Big Dog. Stevens, Janet, illus. 2009. (Golden Classic Ser.). (ENG., Illus.). 32p. (J). (gr. -1-2). pap. 7.99 (978-0-375-85103-2(8), Dragonfly Bks.) Random Hse. Children's Bks.
Stevens, Linda M. Unlocking the Hidden Treasures. 2009. 28p. pap. 24.95 (978-1-61546-454-8(9)) America Star Bks.
Stevens, Robin. Murder Is Bad Manners. 2015. (Wells & Wong Mystery Ser.). (ENG., Illus.). 320p. (J). (gr. 5). 17.99 (978-1-4814-2212-3(X), Simon & Schuster Bks. For Young Readers) Simon & Schuster Bks. For Young Readers.
—Poison Is Not Polite. 2016. (Wells & Wong Mystery Ser.). (ENG., Illus.). 336p. (J). (gr. 5). 17.99 (978-1-4814-2215-4(4), Simon & Schuster Bks. For Young Readers) Simon & Schuster Bks. For Young Readers.
Stevens, Serita. The Adventure Begins. 2004. (Illus.). 182p. (978-0-9753548-1-0(7)) Palm Publishing LLC.
Stevens, Terry. The Battle at Longshore Causeway. 2006. 64p. pap. (978-1-84401-751-5(6)) Athena Pr.
Stevenson, Peggy. Meet the Spencers & the Smart Knots. 2009. 48p. pap. 16.95 (978-1-60813-517-2(9)) America Star Bks.
Stevenson, Robin. Ben the Inventor, 1 vol. Parkins, David, illus. 2011. (Orca Echoes Ser.). (ENG.). 64p. (J). (gr. 2-3). pap. 6.95 (978-1-55469-802-8(2)) Orca Bk. Pubs. USA.
—Impossible Things, 1 vol. 2008. (ENG.). 192p. (J). (gr. 4-8). pap. 8.95 (978-1-55143-736-1(8)) Orca Bk. Pubs. USA.
—Out of Order, 1 vol. 2007. (ENG.). 232p. (YA). (gr. 7-12). per. 9.95 (978-1-55143-693-7(0)) Orca Bk. Pubs. USA.
—The World Without Us. 2014. 240p. pap. (978-1-4598-0681-8(6)) Orca Bk. Pubs.
Stevenson, S. Roy. The Magic Act: A Mystery by S. Roy Stevenson. 2008. 108p. 20.95 (978-0-595-51841-8(9)); pap. 10.95 (978-0-595-53062-5(1)) iUniverse, Inc.
Stevenson, Tysheia E. Jude, 1 vol. 2009. 57p. pap. 12.95 (978-1-61582-624-7(6)) PublishAmerica, Inc.
Steveson, Nanci Turner. Swing Sideways. 2016. 288p. (J). (gr. 3-7). 16.99 (978-0-06-237454-7(0)) HarperCollins Pubs.
Stewart, Barbara. The In-Between. 2013. (ENG.). 256p. (YA). (gr. 9-12). pap. 9.99 (978-1-250-03016-0(1), 9781250030160, St. Martin's Griffin) St. Martin's Pr.
Stewart, Dianne C. Longitude - Zero Degrees. 2009. (ENG.). 200p. pap. 8.95 (978-0-9667359-4-9(3), BeanPole Bks.) Harren Communications, LLC.
—Quimbaya. 2008. (ENG.). 200p. (gr. 1-18). pap. 8.95 (978-0-9667359-8-7(6), BeanPole Bks.) Harren Communications, LLC.
Stewart-Goodair, Madonna. Key to the Golden Gates: The Mystic Soldier, Book 1, 1 vol. 2009. 48p. pap. 16.95 (978-1-61582-625-4(4)) PublishAmerica, Inc.
Stewart, H. E. Walrus's Gift, 1 vol. 2011. (ENG.). 32p. (J). (gr. -1-3). 18.00 (978-0-9693852-7-1(7)) Tudor Hse. GBR. Dist: Orca Bk. Pubs. USA.
Stewart, Jane L. A Campfire Girl's Test of Friendship. 2004. reprint ed. pap. 26.95 (978-1-4179-3874-2(9)) Kessinger Publishing, LLC.
Stewart, Jennifer J. Close Encounters of a Third World Kind. 2004. (ENG.). 128p. (J). (gr. 4-6). tchr. ed. 16.95 (978-0-8234-1850-3(2)) Holiday Hse., Inc.
—Close Encounters of a Third-World Kind. 2008. (ENG., Illus.). 181p. (J). (gr. 3-7). 6.95 (978-0-8234-2161-9(9)) Holiday Hse., Inc.
Stewart, Joel. Dexter Bexley & the Big Blue Beastie. Stewart, Joel, illus. 2007. (ENG., Illus.). 32p. (J). (gr. -1-3). 16.95 (978-0-8234-2068-1(X)) Holiday Hse., Inc.
Stewart, Maddie. Cinders. Spencer, Alison, illus. 2007. (Panda Cubs Ser.: 05). (ENG.). 48p. (J). pap. 9.95 (978-1-84717-027-9(7)) O'Brien Pr., Ltd., The IRL. Dist: Dufour Editions, Inc.
Stewart, Mark R. Malcolm's Cubby House. Swope, Brenda, illus. 2011. 28p. pap. 24.95 (978-1-4560-0958-8(3)) America Star Bks.
Stewart, Samara. Solomon's Smile. 2011. 24p. (gr. -1). pap. 11.32 (978-1-4567-3734-4(1)) AuthorHouse.
Stewart, Trenton Lee. The Mysterious Benedict Society. Tingley, Megan, ed. Sudyka, Diana, illus. 2010. (Mysterious Benedict Society Ser.: 3). (ENG.). 400p. (J). (gr. 3-7). pap. 8.99 (978-0-316-04550-6(0)) Little, Brown Bks. for Young Readers.
—The Mysterious Benedict Society. Ellis, Carson, illus. (Mysterious Benedict Society Ser.: 1). (ENG.). (J). (gr. 3-7). 2008. 512p. pap. 9.99 (978-0-316-00395-7(6)) 2007. 496p. 19.00 (978-0-316-05777-6(0), Tingley, Megan Bks.) 2015. 512p. 12.99 (978-0-316-26501-0(2)) Little, Brown Bks. for Young Readers.
—The Mysterious Benedict Society. unabr. ed. 2007. (Mysterious Benedict Society Ser.: Bk. 1). (ENG.). (J). (gr. 3-7). 25.50 (978-0-307-28440-2(9), Listening Library (Audio)) Penguin Random House Audio Publishing Group.
—The Mysterious Benedict Society. 2009. 17.45 (978-1-60686-527-9(7)) Perfection Learning Corp.
—The Mysterious Benedict Society. 2010. (Mysterious Benedict Society Ser.: 3). (J). lib. bdg. 19.65 (978-0-606-15117-7(6), Turtleback) Turtleback Bks.
—The Mysterious Benedict Society. Ellis, Carson, illus. 2008. (Mysterious Benedict Society Ser.: 1). 485p. (J). (gr. 3-7). lib. bdg. 19.65 (978-1-4178-1817-4(4), Turtleback) Turtleback Bks.
—The Mysterious Benedict Society & the Perilous Journey. Sudyka, Diana, illus. 2009. (Mysterious Benedict Society Ser.: 2). (ENG.). 464p. (J). (gr. 3-7). pap. 8.99 (978-0-316-03673-3(0)) Little Brown & Co.
—The Mysterious Benedict Society & the Perilous Journey. Sudyka, Diana, illus. 2008. (Mysterious Benedict Society Ser.: 2). (ENG.). 448p. (J). (gr. 3-7). 18.99 (978-0-316-05780-6(0)) Little, Brown Bks. for Young Readers.
—The Mysterious Benedict Society & the Perilous Journey. 2009. (Mysterious Benedict Society Ser.: 2). (J). lib. bdg. 19.65 (978-0-606-07462-9(7), Turtleback) Turtleback Bks.
—The Mysterious Benedict Society & the Prisoner's Dilemma. Sudyka, Diana, illus. 2009. (Mysterious Benedict Society Ser.: 3). (ENG.). 400p. (J). (gr. 3-7). 18.99 (978-0-316-04552-0(7)) Little, Brown Bks. for Young Readers.
Stick & Stone. 2016. (978-0-545-93814-3(7)) Weston Woods Studios, Inc.
Sticks Stones & Stumped. 2006. (Illus.). 26p. (J). 19.95 (978-0-9773738-0-2(0)) Bryson Taylor Publishing.
Still, Teresa Brooks. Tasha Lucele's Ordeals: Dolly's Dilemma. 2012. 66p. pap. 7.95 (978-0-9848050-4-4(4), Little Creek Bks.) Jan-Carol Publishing, INC.
Stilton, Geronimo. Geronimo's Valentine, No. 36. 2009. (Geronimo Stilton Ser.: 36). (ENG.). 128p. (J). (gr. 2-5). pap. 7.99 (978-0-545-02136-4(7), Scholastic Paperbacks) Scholastic, Inc.
—Mighty Mount Kilimanjaro. 2010. (Geronimo Stilton Ser.: 41). (ENG.). 128p. (J). (gr. 2-5). 7.99 (978-0-545-10371-8(1), Scholastic Paperbacks) Scholastic, Inc.
—The Peculiar Pumpkin Thief. 2010. (Geronimo Stilton Ser.: 42). (ENG.). 128p. (J). (gr. 2-5). 7.99 (978-0-545-10372-5(X), Scholastic Paperbacks) Scholastic, Inc.
—The Race Across America. 2009. (Geronimo Stilton Ser.: 37). (ENG.). 128p. (J). (gr. 2-5). pap. 7.99 (978-0-545-02137-1(5), Scholastic Paperbacks) Scholastic, Inc.
Stilton, Geronimo & Stilton, Thea. Thea Stilton & the Ice Treasure. 2011. (Thea Stilton Ser.: 9). (ENG., Illus.). 176p. (J). (gr. 2-5). pap. 8.99 (978-0-545-33134-0(X), Scholastic Paperbacks) Scholastic, Inc.
—Thea Stilton & the Mountain of Fire. 2009. (Thea Stilton Ser.: 2). (ENG.). 176p. (J). (gr. 2-5). pap. 8.99 (978-0-545-15060-6(4), Scholastic Paperbacks) Scholastic, Inc.
—Thea Stilton & the Mystery on the Orient Express. 2012. (Thea Stilton Ser.: 13). (ENG.). 176p. (J). (gr. 2-5). pap. 8.99 (978-0-545-34105-9(1), Scholastic Paperbacks) Scholastic, Inc.
—Thea Stilton & the Prince's Emerald. 2012. (Thea Stilton Ser.: 12). (ENG.). 176p. (J). (gr. 2-5). pap. 8.99 (978-0-545-34108-0(6), Scholastic Paperbacks) Scholastic, Inc.
Stilton, Thea. Big Trouble in the Big Apple. 2011. (Thea Stilton Ser.: 8). (ENG., Illus.). 176p. (J). (gr. 2-5). pap. 8.99 (978-0-545-22775-9(5), Scholastic Paperbacks) Scholastic, Inc.
—The Spanish Dance Mission. 2013. (Thea Stilton Ser.: 16). (ENG., Illus.). 176p. (J). (gr. 2-5). pap. 8.99 (978-0-545-55626-2(0), Scholastic Paperbacks) Scholastic, Inc.
—Thea Stilton & the Great Tulip Heist. 2014. (Thea Stilton Ser.: 18). (ENG.). 176p. (J). (gr. 2-5). pap. 8.99 (978-0-545-55628-6(7), Scholastic Paperbacks) Scholastic, Inc.
—Thea Stilton & the Great Tulip Heist. 2014. (Thea Stilton Ser.: 18). lib. bdg. 19.65 (978-0-606-35386-1(0)) Turtleback Bks.
—Thea Stilton & the Journey to the Lion's Den. 2013. (Thea Stilton Ser.: 17). lib. bdg. 19.65 (978-0-606-32382-6(1), Turtleback) Turtleback Bks.
—Thea Stilton & the Secret City. 2010. (Thea Stilton Ser.: 4). (ENG.). 176p. (J). (gr. 2-5). 8.99 (978-0-545-15061-3(2), Scholastic Paperbacks) Scholastic, Inc.
—Thea Stilton & the Spanish Dance Mission. 2013. (Thea Stilton Ser.: 16). lib. bdg. 19.65 (978-0-606-32381-9(3), Turtleback) Turtleback Bks.
Stine, R. L. The Best Friend. 2006. (Fear Street Ser.: Bk. 14). (ENG.). 160p. (YA). (gr. 7). mass mkt. 7.99 (978-1-4169-1376-4(9), Simon Pulse) Simon Pulse.
—How I Met My Monster. 2013. (Goosebumps Most Wanted Ser.: 3). (ENG.). 160p. (J). (gr. 3-7). pap. 6.99 (978-0-545-41800-3(3), Scholastic Paperbacks) Scholastic, Inc.
—How I Met My Monster. 2013. (Goosebumps Most Wanted Ser.: 3). lib. bdg. 17.20 (978-0-606-31534-0(9), Turtleback) Turtleback Bks.
—Midnight Games. 2005. (Fear Street Nights Ser.: No. 2). 183p. (YA). lib. bdg. 20.00 (978-1-4242-1119-7(0)) Fitzgerald Bks.
—The New Girl. 2006. (Fear Street Ser.: Bk. 1). (ENG., Illus.). 176p. (YA). (gr. 7-12). mass mkt. 7.99 (978-1-4169-1810-3(8), Simon Pulse) Simon Pulse.
—Party Games: A Fear Street Novel. 2014. (Fear Street Ser.). (ENG.). 288p. (YA). (gr. 7-12). 17.99 (978-1-250-05161-5(4), 9781250051615, St. Martin's Griffin) St. Martin's Pr.
—Say Cheese & Die. 2009. (Goosebumps Ser.: 8). lib. bdg. 17.20 (978-0-606-00247-9(2), Turtleback) Turtleback Bks.
—Wizard of Ooze. 2010. (Goosebumps Horrorland Ser.: 17). (ENG.). 160p. (J). (gr. 3-7). pap. 6.99 (978-0-545-16198-5(3), Scholastic Paperbacks) Scholastic, Inc.
Stingley, Tanya. Jonas & the Pride of Fiona. 2008. pap. 9.00 (978-0-8059-8685-3(5)) Dorrance Publishing Co., Inc.
Stinson, Aimee. The Championship Game, 1 vol. 2009. 52p. pap. 16.95 (978-1-60813-645-2(0)) PublishAmerica, Inc.
Stinson, Kathy. Fish House Secrets. 2007. (ENG.). 128p. mass mkt. 7.95 (978-1-895449-10-5(3)) Thistledown Pr., Ltd. CAN. Dist: Univ. of Toronto Pr.
—The Great Bike Race, 1 vol. 2005. (Lorimer Streetlights Ser.). (ENG.). 104p. (J). (gr. 2-5). 7.95 (978-1-55028-890-2(3), 9781550288902) Lorimer, James & Co., Ltd., Pubs. CAN. Dist: Casemate Pubs. & Bk. Distributors, LLC.
Stiver, Joan. The Door in the Floor: An Underground Railroad Adventure. 2008. 48p. pap. 4.99 (978-1-4343-2953-0(4)) AuthorHouse.
Stock, Lisa. Perfect Pets. 2014. (DK Reader Level 2 Ser.). lib. bdg. 13.55 (978-0-606-35731-9(9)) Turtleback Bks.
Stockdale, Stephanie. Sidney Visits Australi. 2009. 44p. pap. 18.99 (978-1-4389-8698-2(X)) AuthorHouse.
Stockham, Jess, illus. Making Friends! 2008. (Just Like Us! Ser.). (ENG.). 12p. (J). (gr. -1). bds. (978-1-84643-180-7(8)) Child's Play International Ltd.
Stockland, Patricia M. Peanut Picking, 1 vol. Haugen, Ryan, illus. 2008. (Safari Friends Ser.). (ENG.). 32p. (gr. -1-3). 28.50 (978-1-60270-085-7(0), Looking Glass Library) ABDO Publishing Co.
Stocks, David. Moon Rabbit. 2008. 276p. pap. (978-1-84747-838-2(7)) Chipmunkapublishing.
Stockton, Lucille. God in a Child's World & King Catfish Roonie & His Neighbors. 2003. 48p. (J). per. (978-1-932077-34-6(0)) Athena Pr.
Stoddard, Jeffery. Pete & Pillar: A Story of Friendship Based on John 15:13: the Big Rain. Stoddard, Jeffery, illus. 2007. (Pete & Pillar Ser.). (ENG., Illus.). 32p. (J). (gr. -1-2). 12.99 (978-1-59317-203-9(6)) Warner Pr., Inc.
Stoeke, Janet Morgan. Snow Hens. 2016. (Loopy Coop Hens Ser.). (ENG., Illus.). 32p. (J). (gr. 1-2). pap. 3.99 (978-0-448-48843-1(4), Penguin Young Readers) Penguin Young Readers Group.
Stoh, Emily. Roger Meets Sam. Stoh, Judy, illus. 2009. 24p. pap. 9.95 (978-1-935105-41-1(8)) Avid Readers Publishing Group.
Stoker, Bram. Drácula. Schuler, Susan, tr. Ruiz, Alfonso, illus. 2010. (Classic Fiction Ser.). (ENG & SPA.). 72p. (gr. 2-3). pap. 7.15 (978-1-4342-2277-0(2), Graphic Revolve en Español) Stone Arch Bks.
—Dracula. Schuler, Susan, tr. Ruiz, Alfonso, illus. 2010. (Classic Fiction Ser.). 72p. pap. 0.90 (978-1-4342-2985-4(8), Graphic Revolve) Stone Arch Bks.
Stokes, Paula. Liars, Inc. 2015. 384p. (YA). (gr. 8). pap. 9.99 (978-0-06-223844-3(2), HarperTeen) HarperCollins Pubs.
Stokholm, Susan Mary. Between a Shadow & the Moon. 2010. 252p. pap. 14.49 (978-1-4520-1752-5(2)) AuthorHouse.
Stone, Chuck. Squizzy the Black Squirrel: A Fabulous Fable of Friendship. Jackson, Jeannie, tr. Jackson, Jeannie, illus. 2003. 30p. (J). 16.95 (978-0-940880-71-9(7)) Open Hand Publishing, LLC.
Stone, Danika & Goble, Karin. All the Feels. 2016. (ENG., Illus.). 336p. (YA). pap. 9.99 (978-1-250-08409-5(1), 9781250084095) Feiwel & Friends.
Stone, Forrest. The Ant & Grasshopper Show. 2006. (J). pap. (978-1-4108-6183-2(X)) Benchmark Education Co.
Stone, Heather Duffy. This Is What I Want to Tell You. 2009. (ENG.). 240p. (YA). (gr. 7-18). pap. 9.95 (978-0-7387-1450-9(X), Flux) North Star Editions.
Stone, Jeff. Five Ancestors Out of the Ashes #2: Lion. 2014. (Five Ancestors Out of the Ashes Ser.). (ENG.). 256p. (J). (gr. 4-7). 6.99 (978-0-375-87099-6(7), Yearling) Random Hse. Children's Bks.
—Five Ancestors Out of the Ashes #3: Jackal. 2014. (Five Ancestors Out of the Ashes Ser.). (ENG.). 192p. (J). (gr. 4-7). 16.99 (978-0-375-87020-0(2), Random Hse. Bks. for Young Readers) Random Hse. Children's Bks.
Stone, Phoebe. The Boy on Cinnamon Street. 2012. 234p. (J). (978-0-545-43368-6(1), Levine, Arthur A. Bks.) Scholastic, Inc.
Stone, Tamara Ireland. Friendship, Coded, Bk. 1. 2017. (Click'd Ser.). (ENG.). 208p. (J). (gr. 3-7). 16.99 **(978-1-4847-8497-6(9))** Hyperion Bks. for Children.
Stones, Yvonne. Olivia's Magical Moment. 2010. 36p. pap. 16.99 (978-1-4490-8045-7(6)) AuthorHouse.
Stork, Francisco X. The Last Summer of the Death Warriors. 2010. (ENG.). 352p. (J). (gr. 9-7). 18.99 (978-0-545-15133-7(3), Levine, Arthur A. Bks.) Scholastic, Inc.
—The Memory of Light. 2016. (Arthur a Levine Novel Bks.). (ENG.). 336p. (YA). (gr. 7). 17.99 (978-0-545-47432-0(9)) Scholastic, Inc.
Storm, Raen. God's Palette. 2007. 16p. per. 24.95 (978-1-4137-1793-8(4)) America Star Bks.
Stormer, Kate. Casey's Unexpected Friend. Lowes, Tom, illus. l.t. ed. 2003. 38p. (J). 16.95 (978-0-9722099-7-7(2), CUF) Caseys World Bks.
Storybook Friends Book Set 800919, 3 vols. 2005. (J). pap. (978-1-59794-084-9(4)) Environments, Inc.
Stoudemire, Amar'e. Double Team. Jessell, Tim, illus. 2012. (STAT: Standing Tall & Talented Ser.: 2). lib. bdg. 16.00 (978-0-606-26762-5(X), Turtleback) Turtleback Bks.
—Slam Dunk. 2013. (STAT: Standing Tall & Talented Ser.: 3). lib. bdg. 16.00 (978-0-606-31531-9(4), Turtleback) Turtleback Bks.
—Slam Dunk: Standing Tall & Talented. Jessell, Tim, illus. 2013. (Stat Ser.: 3). (ENG.). 144p. (J). (gr. 3-7). pap. 5.99 (978-0-545-38761-3(2), Scholastic Paperbacks) Scholastic, Inc.
Stout, Shawn K. Fiona Finkelstein Meets Her Match!! Martini, Angela, illus. 2010. (ENG.). 160p. (J). (gr. 1-5). 14.99 (978-1-4169-7928-9(X), Simon & Schuster/Paula Wiseman Bks.) Simon & Schuster/Paula Wiseman Bks.
—Penelope Crumb Is Mad at the Moon. 2015. (Penelope Crumb Ser.: 4). (ENG., Illus.). 208p. (J). (gr. 2-4). pap. 6.99 (978-0-14-242638-8(5), Puffin Books) Penguin Young Readers Group.
—Penelope Crumb Never Forgets. Docampo, Valeria, illus. 2013. (Penelope Crumb Ser.: 2). (ENG.). 208p. (J). (gr. 2-5). pap. 5.99 (978-0-14-751009-9(0), Puffin Books) Penguin Young Readers Group.
Stout, Shawn K. & Docampo, Valeria. Penelope Crumb Finds Her Luck. 2014. (Penelope Crumb Ser.: 3). (ENG., Illus.). 240p. (J). (gr. 2-5). pap. 6.99 (978-0-14-242637-1(7), Puffin Books) Penguin Young Readers Group.
Stower, Adam. The Den. 2005. (Bloomsbury Paperbacks Ser.). (ENG., Illus.). 32p. (J). (gr. 3-7). pap. 12.99 (978-0-7475-7550-4(9)) Bloomsbury Publishing Plc GBR. Dist: Independent Pubs. Group.
Strachan, Linda. Hamish Mchaggis & the Edinburgh Adventure. Collins, Sally J., illus. 2005. (Hamish Mchaggis Ser.). 26p. (J). per. 9.00 (978-0-9546701-7-7(5)) GW Publishing GBR. Dist: Wilson & Assocs.
—Hamish Mchaggis & the Ghost of Glamis. Collins, Sally J., illus. 2005. (Hamish Mchaggis Ser.). 26p. (J). per. 9.00 (978-0-9546701-9-1(1)) GW Publishing GBR. Dist: Wilson & Assocs.
—Hamish Mchaggis & the Search for the Loch Ness Monster. Collins, Sally J., illus. 2005. 32p. (J). pap. 9.00 (978-0-9546701-5-3(9)) GW Publishing GBR. Dist: Wilson & Assocs.
—Hamish Mchaggis & the Skye Surprise. Collins, Sally J., illus. 2005. (Hamish Mchaggis Ser.). 26p. (J). pap. 9.00 (978-0-9546701-8-4(3)) GW Publishing GBR. Dist: Wilson & Assocs.
Stracher, Cameron. The Water Wars. 2011. (ENG.). 256p. (YA). (gr. 7-12). pap. 10.99 (978-1-4022-6759-8(2), 9781402267598) Sourcebooks, Inc.
Straffi, Iginio. Winx Club: Magic Collection. 2014. (ENG.). 832p. (J). pap. 19.99 (978-1-4215-7729-6(1)) Viz Media.
Strand, Kai. Save the Lemmings. 2012. 108p. pap. 8.99 (978-1-60820-710-7(2)) MLR Pr., LLC.
Strange, Jason. Faceless Friend, 1 vol. Parks, Phil, illus. 2011. (Jason Strange Ser.). (ENG.). 72p. (gr. 2-3). pap. 6.25 (978-1-4342-3431-5(2)); lib. bdg. 25.32 (978-1-4342-3232-8(8)) Stone Arch Bks.
—Text 4 Revenge, 1 vol. Parks, Phil & Dal Lago, Alberto, illus. 2011. (Jason Strange Ser.). (ENG.). 72p. (gr. 2-3). pap. 6.25 (978-1-4342-3432-2(0)); lib. bdg. 25.32 (978-1-4342-3233-5(6)) Stone Arch Bks.
—To Wake the Dead, 1 vol. Parks, Phil, illus. 2011. (Jason Strange Ser.). (ENG.). 72p. (gr. 2-3). pap. 6.25 (978-1-4342-3094-2(5)); 25.32 (978-1-4342-2963-2(7)) Stone Arch Bks.
Strangway, Melissa. 56 Water Street. 2008. 156p. pap. 8.95 (978-1-60528-031-8(3), iUniverse Star) iUniverse, Inc.
Strasnick, Lauren. Her & Me & You. (ENG.). 208p. (YA). (gr. 9). 2011. pap. 9.99 (978-1-4169-8267-8(1)) 2010. 16.99 (978-1-4169-8266-1(3)) Simon Pulse. (Simon Pulse).
—Nothing Like You. 2010. (ENG.). 240p. (YA). (gr. 9). pap. 8.99 (978-1-4169-8265-4(5), Simon Pulse) Simon Pulse.
—Then You Were Gone. (ENG., 272p. (YA). (gr. 9). 2014. Illus.). pap. 9.99 (978-1-4424-2716-7(7)) 2013. 16.99 (978-1-4424-2715-0(9)) Simon Pulse. (Simon Pulse).
Strasser, Todd. Con-Fidence. 2006. (ENG.). 164p. (J). (gr. 4-7). pap. 6.95 (978-0-8234-2061-2(2)) Holiday Hse., Inc.
—Is That an Unlucky Leprechaun in Your Lunch? Swearingen, Greg, illus. 2009. 184p. (J). (978-0-545-11034-1(3)) Scholastic, Inc.
Strasser, Todd & Thacker, Nola. The Shore: Shirt & Shoes Not Required; LB (Laguna Beach) 2011. (ENG.). 480p. (YA). (gr. 9). pap. 9.99 (978-1-4424-1970-4(9), Simon Pulse) Simon Pulse.
Stratheam, Chris. Marvel's Guardians of the Galaxy: Friends & Foes. 2014. (Passport to Reading Level 2 Ser.). (ENG., Illus.). 32p. (J). (gr. -1-3). pap. 3.99 (978-0-316-29318-1(0)) Little, Brown Bks. for Young Readers.
Strathie, Chae. Dear Dinosaur: With Real Letters to Read! O'Byrne, Nicola, illus. 2017. (ENG.). 28p. (J). (gr. -1-3). 11.99 **(978-0-7641-6898-7(3))** Barron's Educational Series, Inc.
Stratten, Lou. Hello, I'm Sir Frettirick! Let's Say Hello to Our New Friends! Bennett, Judy, ed. Denaro, Sal, illus. 2006. (J). (gr. -1-2). pap. 6.95 incl. audio compact disk (978-0-9747173-1-9(2)) Stratten, Lou.
Stratton, Allan. Borderline. 2010. (ENG., Illus.). 304p. (YA). (gr. 8-18). 16.99 (978-0-06-145111-9(8), HarperTeen) HarperCollins Pubs.
Stratton, Erin. There's Nothing Wrong with Boys. Gregeory, Vicki, illus. 2010. 26p. pap. 12.00 (978-1-60911-021-5(8), Eloquent Bks.) Strategic Book Publishing & Rights Agency (SBPRA).
Stratton-Porter, Gene. At the Foot of the Rainbow. 2007. 180p. 18.95 (978-1-934169-52-0(8)); pap. 7.95 (978-1-934169-53-7(6)) Norilana Bks.
Strauch, Brenda. Tragic Endings: The Unwritten Series. 2011. 292p. (gr. -1). 24.99 (978-1-4567-4176-1(4)); pap. 14.99 (978-1-4567-4177-8(2)) AuthorHouse.
Strauss, Joanne. Charlie & His Friends. 2011. 30p. pap. 16.95 (978-1-4626-4401-8(5)) America Star Bks.
Strauss, Linda Leopold. Best Friends Pretend. Munsinger, Lynn, illus. 2014. (ENG.). 14p. (J). (gr. -1 — 1). bds. 6.99 (978-0-545-45171-0(X), Cartwheel Bks.) Scholastic, Inc.
—The Elijah Door. Natchev, Alexi, illus. 2012. (ENG.). 32p. (J). 16.95 (978-0-8234-1911-1(8)) Holiday Hse., Inc.
Streblow, Mary. A Martian for Christmas. 2007. (ENG.). 32p. per. 23.95 (978-1-4303-0794-5(3)) Lulu Pr., Inc.
Street, Sharon & National Geographic Learning Staff. My Friend & I. 2007. (Windows on Literacy Ser.). (ENG., Illus.). 12p. (J). pap. 10.95 (978-0-7922-8949-4(8)) CENGAGE Learning.
Strepponi, Blanca. Claudia y Daniel. Muller, Cristina, illus. 2004. (SPA.). 28p. (J). pap. 7.99 (978-980-257-268-7(3)) Ekare, Ediciones VEN. Dist: Lectorum Pubns., Inc.
Stretton, Hesba. Cassy. Hymper, W. & Stacey, W. S., illus. 2006. (Golden Inheritance Ser.: Vol. 9). 117p. (J). pap. (978-0-921100-94-2(9)) Inheritance Pubns.
—Jessica's First Prayer. Doe, Charles J., ed. 2008. (ENG., Illus.). 54p. (YA). pap. 7.95 (978-0-9817505-2-1(4)) Curiosmith.
—Jessica's First Prayer. 2004. reprint ed. pap. 15.95 (978-1-4191-2751-9(9)); pap. 1.99 (978-1-4192-2751-6(3)) Kessinger Publishing, LLC.
Strohm, Stephanie Kate. Confederates Don't Wear Couture: A Tale of Heartache, Haunting, & Hoop Skirts. 2013. (ENG.). 240p. (YA). (gr. 7). pap. 13.99 (978-0-547-97258-9(X)) Houghton Mifflin Harcourt Publishing Co.
—The Taming of the Drew. 2016. (ENG.). 304p. (J). (gr. 6).. 17.99 (978-1-5107-0215-8(6), Sky Pony Pr.) Skyhorse Publishing Co., Inc.
Strohmeyer, Sarah. This Is My Brain on Boys. 2016. 352p. (YA). (gr. 8). 17.99 (978-0-06-225962-2(8)) HarperCollins Pubs.
Strom, Maria Diaz. Joe Arco Iris y Yo. Strom, Maria Diaz, illus. 2008.Tr. of Rainbow Joe & Me. (SPA., Illus.). 32p. (J). (gr. -1-3). pap. 9.95 (978-1-60060-278-8(9)) Lee & Low Bks., Inc.
—Rainbow Joe & Me. 2004. (J). (gr. k-3). spiral bd. (978-0-616-03097-4(5)) Canadian National Institute for the Blind/Institut National Canadien pour les Aveugles.
Stromberg, Ronica. Living It up to Live It Down. 2009. (J). lib. bdg. (978-0-88092-752-9(6)) Royal Fireworks Publishing Co.
—A Shadow in the Dark. 2009. (J). pap. (978-0-88092-751-2(8)); lib. bdg. (978-0-88092-750-5(X)) Royal Fireworks Publishing Co.
Stroud-Peace, Glenda. Pearlie. Larkin, Paige A., illus. 2009. 48p. pap. 16.95 (978-1-60844-033-7(8)) Dog Ear Publishing, LLC.
Struyk-Bonn, Chris. Nice Girls Endure. 2016. (ENG.). 256p. (gr. 9-12). 16.95 (978-1-63079-047-9(8)) Switch Pr.
Stuart & McArthur, Amanda. Humphry & the Tree. 2012. 24p. pap. 15.99 (978-1-4691-5082-6(4)) Xlibris Corp.
Stuart, Duncan. The Whole of the Moon. 200p. (YA). (gr. 8-18). pap. (978-1-877135-05-7(4), Longacre Pr.) Random Hse. New Zealand.
Stuart, Raff. A Roman Odyssey: Book One of the chronicles of Adam Black the Teenage Time Traveller. 2009. 228p. pap. 14.49 (978-1-4389-7407-1(8)) AuthorHouse.
Stuart-Russell, C. Playtime with the Animals. 2007. 61p. pap. 19.95 (978-1-4241-5473-9(1)) America Star Bks.

Stuart, Sam. Stuart & Sami Go Bowling: Stuart's Special Friend Sami. 2010. 24p. pap. 11.49 *(978-1-4520-4326-5(4))* AuthorHouse.

Stubbs, Lisa. Grumpy Feet. Stubbs, Lisa, illus. 2017. (Lily & Bear Ser.). (ENG., Illus.). 32p. (J). (gr. -1-3). 17.99 *(978-1-4814-7167-1(8)*, Simon & Schuster/Paula Wiseman Bks.) Simon & Schuster/Paula Wiseman Bks.

—Lily & Bear. Stubbs, Lisa, illus. 2015. (Lily & Bear Ser.). (ENG., Illus.). 32p. (J). (gr. -1-3). 17.99 *(978-1-4814-4416-3(6)*, Simon & Schuster Bks. For Young Readers) Simon & Schuster Bks. For Young Readers.

Stubbs, Tommy, illus. Thomas & Friends Little Golden Book Library (Thomas & Friends), 5 vols. 2013. (ENG.). 120p. (J). (-k). 24.95 *(978-0-449-81482-6(3)*, Golden Bks.) Random Hse. Children's Bks.

Studio Mouse, ed. Disney Preincess Best Friends: Flat Learn & Carry 4 Board Books & CD. rev. ed. 2008. 80p. (J). 12.99 *(978-1-59069-553-1(4))* Studio Mouse LLC.

Studio Mouse Staff. Pet Friends. rev. ed. 2008. (ENG.). 12p. (J). 12.99 *(978-1-59069-611-8(5))* Studio Mouse LLC.

—Pooh & Eeyore. 2008. (ENG., Illus.). 36p. (J). (gr. -1). 7.99 *(978-1-59069-418-3(X))* Studio Mouse LLC.

—Pooh & Eeyore, Pooh & Tigger. rev. ed. 2004. (Friends Collection). (ENG., Illus.). 36p. (J). (gr. -1-3). 15.99 *(978-1-59069-390-2(6)*, 1A302) Studio Mouse LLC.

—Pooh & Friends ABCs & 123s: First Concepts. rev. ed. 2007. (ENG., Illus.). 24p. (J). (gr. -1-3). 4.99 *(978-1-59069-606-4(9))* Studio Mouse LLC.

—Pooh & Piglet. 2008. (ENG., Illus.). 36p. (J). (gr. -1). 7.99 *(978-1-59069-419-0(8))* Studio Mouse LLC.

—Sesame Street Colors & Shapes. 2008. (ENG.). 36p. (J). (gr. -1). 12.99 *(978-1-59069-741-2(3))* Studio Mouse LLC.

—Sesame Street My First Instrument. 2008. (ENG.). 24p. (J). (gr. -1). 4.99 *(978-1-59069-737-5(5))* Studio Mouse LLC.

—Sesame Street Share & Care, It's Only Fair. 2009. (ENG.). 60p. (J). (gr. -1). 12.99 *(978-1-59069-739-9(1))* Studio Mouse LLC.

—Winnie Pooh y sus amigos Ejercicios: Puffy Book with CD. rev. ed. 2007. (ESP & ENG.). 36p. (J). 14.99 *(978-1-59069-528-9(3))* Studio Mouse LLC.

Sturm, James. Ape & Armadillo Take over the World: Toon Level 340. 2016. (ENG., Illus.). 40p. (J). (gr. k-4). 12.95 *(978-1-943145-09-6(1))* TOON Books / RAW Junior, LLC.

Sturtevant, Karen. The Adventures of Gert & Stu & Zippy Too. 2012. 36p. pap. 18.99 *(978-1-4772-9360-7(4))* AuthorHouse.

Stutson, Caroline. Blue Corn Soup. Weidner, Teri, illus. 2017. (ENG.). 32p. (J). (gr. k-2). 16.99 ***(978-1-58536-967-6(5)***, 204325) Sleeping Bear Pr.

Stutzman, D. J. The Promise Ring. 2007. (J). pap. 9.00 *(978-0-8059-7365-5(6))* Dorrance Publishing Co., Inc.

StVil, Lola. Girls Like Me. 2016. (ENG.). 320p. (YA). (gr. 7). 17.99 *(978-0-544-70674-3(9)*, HMH Books For Young Readers) Houghton Mifflin Harcourt Publishing Co.

Style Guide Staff, illus. I'm Thankful for You! 2014. (Yo Gabba Gabba! Ser.). (ENG.). 12p. (J). (gr. -1-k). bds. 5.99 *(978-1-4814-1723-5(1)*, Simon Spotlight) Simon Spotlight.

—Po's Secret Move. 2014. (Kung Fu Panda TV Ser.). (ENG.). 32p. (J). (gr. k-2). pap. 3.99 *(978-1-4424-9995-9(8)*, Simon Spotlight) Simon Spotlight.

Style Guide, Style, illus. School Is Awesome! 2014. (Yo Gabba Gabba! Ser.). (ENG.). 24p. (J). (gr. -1-1). pap. 3.99 *(978-1-4814-0930-8(1)*, Simon Spotlight) Simon Spotlight.

Subrina. Jacko the Monkey. 2013. 16p. pap. 24.95 *(978-1-63000-145-2(7))* America Star Bks.

Suchy, Julianne. Leaf Me Alone. 2009. 36p. pap. 13.95 *(978-1-60693-300-8(0)*, Eloquent Bks.) Strategic Book Publishing & Rights Agency (SBPRA).

Sudderth, Jean. The Incredible Edible Girl & Friends. 2011. 24p. pap. 15.99 *(978-1-4415-7489-3(1))* Xlibris Corp.

Suen, Anastasia. The Clubhouse. Eitzen, Allan, illus. 2003. (Penguin Young Readers, Level 3 Ser.). (ENG.). 32p. (J). (gr. 1-3). mass mkt. 3.99 *(978-0-14-250054-5(2)*, Penguin Young Readers) Penguin Young Readers Group.

—Helping Sophia, 1 vol. Ebbeler, Jeffrey, illus. 2007. (Main Street School - Kids with Character Ser.). (ENG.). 32p. (gr. -1-4). 28.50 *(978-1-60270-030-7(3)*, Looking Glass Library) ABDO Publishing Co.

—New Girl: An Up2U Character Education Adventure, 1 vol. Dippold, Jane, illus. 2013. (Up2U Adventures Ser.). (ENG.). 80p. (J). (gr. 2-5). lib. bdg. 27.07 *(978-1-61641-968-4(7)*, Calico Chapter Bks) Magic Wagon.

—Times Tables Cheat, 1 vol. Ebbeler, Jeffrey, illus. 2007. (Main Street School - Kids with Character Ser.). (ENG.). 32p. (gr. -1-4). 28.50 *(978-1-60270-034-5(6)*, Looking Glass Library) ABDO Publishing Co.

—Trust Me: A Loyalty Story, 1 vol. Ebbeler, Jeff, illus. 2008. (Main Street School - Kids with Character Ser.). (ENG.). 32p. (gr. -1-4). 28.50 *(978-1-60270-273-8(X)*, Looking Glass Library) ABDO Publishing Co.

Sugg, Zoe. Girl Online: The First Novel by Zoella. 2016. (Girl Online Book Ser.: 1). (ENG.). 352p. (gr. 7). pap. 11.99 *(978-1-4767-9976-6(8)*, Atria Bks.) Simon & Schuster.

Suguitan, Jazel A. We're Moving?! Shari Tucker's Wacky World #1. 2010. 124p. 20.95 *(978-1-4502-6874-5(9))*; pap. 10.95 *(978-1-4502-6871-4(4))* iUniverse, Inc.

Sulkowski, Jennifer Suzanne. A Pony Named Napoleon. 2013. 74p. 30.95 *(978-1-59299-979-8(4))*; pap. 22.95 *(978-1-59299-978-1(6))* Inkwater Pr.

Sullivan, Deirdre. Ming Goes to School. Löfdahl, Maja, illus. 2016. (ENG.). 32p. (J). (gr. -1-k). 16.99 *(978-1-5107-0050-5(1)*, Sky Pony Pr.) Skyhorse Publishing Co., Inc.

Sullivan, E. J. Bubba the Redneck Reindeer. Eldredge, Ernie, illus. 2007. 32p. (J). (gr. 4-7). 12.95 *(978-1-60261-008-8(8))* Cliff Road Bks.

Sullivan, Kevin & Goldman, Leslie. Anne's Babysitting Blues. 2010. (Anne of Green Gables for Young Readers Ser.). (ENG.). 64p. (J). (gr. 2-4). pap. 4.95 *(978-0-9736803-1-7(8))* Davenport Pr. CAN. Dist: Independent Pubs. Group.

Sullivan, Kiki. The Dolls. 2014. (Dolls Ser.: 1). (ENG.). 384p. (YA). (gr. 8). pap. 9.99 *(978-0-06-228148-7(8))* HarperCollins Pubs.

—Midnight Dolls. 2015. (Dolls Ser.: 2). (ENG.). 336p. (YA). (gr. 8). pap. 9.99 *(978-0-06-228150-0(X))* HarperCollins Pubs.

Sullivan, Silvia. Hip Hip Hurray We Found Teddy: A Book Series to Teach Children Practical Life Skills & Eco-Friendly Skills. 2008. 32p. pap. 15.48 *(978-1-4343-5897-4(6))* AuthorHouse.

Sullivan, Tara. The Bitter Side of Sweet. 2017. lib. bdg. 22.10 ***(978-0-606-39795-7(7))*** Turtleback Bks.

Summer of Dreaming. 2010. (Illus.). 157p. (YA). pap. *(978-1-936021-22-2(6)*, Banana Oil Bks.) Cyberwizard Productions.

Summers, Laura. The Summer of Telling Tales. 2013. (ENG.). 224p. (YA). (gr. 8). pap. 11.99 *(978-1-84812-231-4(4))* Bonnier Publishing GBR. Dist: Independent Pubs. Group.

Sumner Johnson, Janet. The Last Great Adventure of the PB & J Society. 2016. (Middle-Grade Novels Ser.). (ENG.). 256p. (gr. 4-7). lib. bdg. 26.65 *(978-1-4965-2695-3(3))* Stone Arch Bks.

Sumner, M. C. Lost Soul. 2013. (Extreme Zone Ser.: 7). (ENG., Illus.). 192p. (YA). (gr. 11). pap. 13.99 *(978-1-4814-2117-1(4)*, Simon Pulse) Simon Pulse.

Sundaram, Renuka. Sammy, the Galapagos Sea Lion. 2011. 32p. pap. 15.00 *(978-1-61286-015-2(X))* Avid Readers Publishing Group.

Sunderland, Margot & Hancock, Nicky. Ruby & the Rubbish Bin. Armstrong, Nicky, tr. Armstrong, Nicky, illus. 2017. (Helping Children with Feelings Ser.). (ENG.). 32p. (C). pap. 15.95 *(978-0-86388-462-7(6)*, Y329066, Routledge) Taylor & Francis Group GBR. Dist: Taylor & Francis Group.

—Teenie Weenie in a Too Big World, 2 vols. Armstrong, Nicky, tr. Armstrong, Nicky, illus. (ENG.). 32p. pap. *(978-0-86388-460-3(1)*, 002-5144, Routledge) Taylor & Francis Group.

Sunkuli, O. The Hero & the Dream. 2004. (Illus.). 28p. pap. *(978-9966-25-161-9(8))* Heinemann Kenya, Limited (East African Educational Publishers Ltd E.A.E.P.) KEN. Dist: Michigan State Univ. Pr.

Supeene, Shelagh Lynne. My Name Is Mitch, 1 vol. 2003. (ENG.). 176p. (J). (gr. 3-7). pap. 6.95 *(978-1-55143-255-7(2))* Orca Bk. Pubs. USA.

Super Why Staff. The Ghost Who Was Afraid of Halloween. 2009. 32p. pap. 3.99 *(978-0-448-45179-4(4)*, Grosset & Dunlap) Penguin Publishing Group.

Supplee, Audra. I Almost Love You, Eddie Clegg, 1 vol. 2004. (ENG.). 192p. (J). (gr. 3-7). 14.95 *(978-1-56145-308-5(0))* Peachtree Pubs.

Surman-Hobbs, Debbi. The Little Brown Moth, 1 vol. 2010. 34p. pap. 24.95 *(978-1-4489-8620-0(6))* PublishAmerica, Inc.

Surman, Susan. Max & Friends. Owings, Rae, illus. 150p. (J). (gr. k-3). 9.99 *(978-0-88092-452-8(7))* Royal Fireworks Publishing Co.

Surrisi, Cynthia & Surrisi, C. M. Vampires on the Run: A Quinnie Boyd Mystery. 2017. (Quinnie Boyd Mysteries Ser.: 2). (ENG.). 296p. (J). (gr. 4-8). 16.99 *(978-1-5124-1150-8(7)*, Carolrhoda Bks.) Lerner Publishing Group.

Susanne, Gervay & Gervay, Susanne. Being Jack. Wilcox, Cathy, illus. 2016. (ENG.). 192p. (J). pap. 5.99 *(978-1-61067-379-2(4))* Kane Miller.

Susko, Mark D. Sally Sassafras, the Girl with Monster Hair. 2011. 50p. pap. 16.95 *(978-1-4560-5521-9(6))* America Star Bks.

Sussman, Elissa. Stray. 2014. (Stray Ser.: 1). (ENG., Illus.). 384p. (YA). (gr. 8). 17.99 *(978-0-06-227455-7(4)*, Greenwillow Bks.) HarperCollins Pubs.

Sutcliffe, Charlie. Zubert. 2014. (ENG., Illus.). 32p. (J). (gr. -1-3). 18.95 *(978-1-84976-121-5(3))* Tate Publishing, Ltd. GBR. Dist: Abrams, Inc.

Sutherland, Suzanne. Something Wiki. 2015. (ENG.). 160p. (J). pap. 12.99 *(978-1-4597-2821-9(1))* Dundurn CAN. Dist: Ingram Publisher Services.

Sutherland, Tui T. Escaping Peril. (Wings of Fire Ser.: 8). (ENG.). 336p. (J). (gr. 3-7). 2017. pap. 6.99 ***(978-0-545-68545-0(1))*** 2015. (Illus.). 16.99 *(978-0-545-68544-3(3))* Scholastic, Inc. (Scholastic Pr.).

—Escaping Peril. 2017. (Wings of Fire Ser.: 8). lib. bdg. 17.20 ***(978-0-606-40142-5(3))*** Turtleback Bks.

Sutherland, Tui T. Winter Turning. 2015. (Wings of Fire Ser.: Bk. 7). (ENG., Illus.). 336p. (J). (gr. 3-7). 16.99 *(978-0-545-68537-5(0)*, Scholastic Pr.) Scholastic, Inc.

—Winter Turning. 2016. (Wings of Fire Ser.: 7). lib. bdg. 17.20 ***(978-0-606-39706-3(X))*** Turtleback Bks.

Sutherland, Tui T. & Sutherland, Kari H. The Menagerie. 2013. (Menagerie Ser.: 1). (ENG., Illus.). 288p. (J). (gr. 3-7). 16.99 *(978-0-06-078064-7(9))* HarperCollins Pubs.

Sutter, Daniel R. Is a Tattoo Right for You? 2012. (ENG.). pap. *(978-1-4675-1738-6(0))* Independent Pub.

Sutton, Jane. Esther's Hanukkah Disaster. Rowland, Andrew, illus. 2013. (Hanukkah Ser.). 32p. (J). (gr. -1-3). lib. bdg. 17.95 *(978-0-7613-9043-5(X)*, Kar-Ben Publishing) Lerner Publishing Group.

—Esther's Hanukkah Disaster. Rowland, Andy, illus. 2013. 32p. 17.95 *(978-1-4677-1638-3(3))*; (ENG.). (J). (gr. -1-3). 7.95 *(978-0-7613-9044-2(8)*, Kar-Ben Publishing) Lerner Publishing Group.

Sutton, Margaret. The Phantom Friend, No. 30. Doane, Pelagie, illus. 2008. (Judy Bolton Mysteries Ser.). (ENG.). 188p. (J). (gr. 4-7). pap. 14.95 *(978-1-4290-9050-6(2))* Applewood Bks.

Suzie Sheep & her Friends. 2004. (Play Pals Ser.). (Illus.). 12p. (J). bds. *(978-1-84229-649-3(3))* Top That! Publishing PLC.

Suzy, Kline. Horrible Harry in Room 2B. 2014. (Horrible Harry Ser. No. 1 Ser.). (ENG.). 64p. (J). (gr. 3-7). 8.24 *(978-1-63245-257-3(X))* Lectorum Pubns., Inc.

Swan, Bill. Road Rage, 1 vol. 2006. (Lorimer Sports Stories Ser.). (ENG.). 120p. (J). (gr. 4-8). 8.95 *(978-1-55028-916-9(0)*, 9781550289169) Lorimer, James & Co., Ltd., Pubs. CAN. Dist: Casemate Pubs. & Bk. Distributors, LLC.

Swanberg, Arvon & Spicer, Carolyn. The Big, Blue, Overstuffed Chair. 2013. 46p. pap. 17.99 *(978-1-4808-0432-6(0))* Archway Publishing.

Swarabi, Fatma Abdulla & El Amin, Khalid Hamid. Marim & Her Grandmother. 2010. 28p. pap. 13.99 *(978-1-4490-8156-0(8))* AuthorHouse.

Swedeen, Staci. The Rumor Report, the Big Jump. 2011. (Readers' & Writers' Genre Workshop Ser.). (YA). pap. *(978-1-4509-3013-0(1))* Benchmark Education Co.

Sweeney, Joyce. Waiting for June, 0 vols. 2006. (ENG.). 158p. (YA). (gr. 10-12). pap. 7.99 *(978-0-7614-5329-1(6)*, 9780761453291, Amazon Children's Publishing) Amazon Publishing.

Sweet, J. H. Foo & Friends Storybook. 2013. 290p. 26.94 *(978-1-936660-04-9(0))* Sweet, Joanne.

Swenson, Dianne. An Ended Friendship: And Other Short Stories. 2006. (Fast Track Ser.). (Illus.). 98p. (YA). (gr. 8-12). lib. bdg. 12.25 *(978-0-8124-0632-0(X))* Perfection Learning Corp.

Swift, John. Tea with a Vampire. 2007. pap. 9.00 *(978-0-8059-8963-2(3))* Dorrance Publishing Co., Inc.

Swift, K. Marie. The Adventures of Jake & George: Jake Gets a New Brother. Paul, Kate, illus. 2010. 26p. pap. 11.75 *(978-1-60693-863-8(0)*, Eloquent Bks.) Strategic Book Publishing & Rights Agency (SBPRA).

Swiger, Lenora. Colt under the Wire. 2004. 73p. per. 8.49 *(978-1-4116-0884-9(4))* Lulu Pr., Inc.

Swiney, Wendy D. Harvey's First Halloween. 2010. (Illus.). 28p. pap. 12.99 *(978-1-4520-0540-9(0))* AuthorHouse.

Sydor, Colleen. Timmerman Was Here. Debon, Nicolas, illus. 2009. (ENG.). 32p. (J). (gr. -1-1). 19.95 *(978-0-88776-890-3(3)*, Tundra Bks.) Tundra Bks. CAN. Dist: Penguin Random Hse. LLC.

Sykes, Tina . Elliot Makes a Friend. 2012. 26p. 24.95 *(978-1-4626-5980-7(2))* America Star Bks.

Sylvester, Sr. Land of the Angels, 1 vol. Morrison, Nancy, illus. 2009. 32p. pap. 24.95 *(978-1-60836-888-4(2))* America Star Bks.

Szcsesniak, Janet. The Frog Who Made Friends. 2012. (Illus.). 26p. pap. *(978-1-78132-000-6(4))* SilverWood Bks.

Taber, Kristen. Ærenden - the Child Returns. 2012. 382p. (YA). pap. 13.99 *(978-0-9851200-0-9(2))* Sean Tigh Pr.

Tabernik, John. Ricky the Picky Koala. Wise, Catlin, illus. 2005. (J). 14.95 *(978-0-9773936-0-2(7))* Little Munchkin Bks.

Tabor, Corey R. Fox & the Bike Ride. Tabor, Corey R., illus. 2017. (Illus.). 32p. (J). (gr. -1-3). 17.99 ***(978-0-06-239875-8(X))*** HarperCollins Pubs.

Tacang, Brian. Bully-Be-Gone: The Misadventures of Millicent Madding #1. 2006. (Illus.). 216p. (J). (gr. 3-7). 17.89 *(978-0-06-073912-6(6))* HarperCollins Pubs.

Tada, Hiroshi. Who's There. Perry, Mia, tr. 2009. 24p. 11.95 *(978-1-74126-350-3(6))* R.I.C. Pubns. AUS. Dist: SCB Distributors.

Taddonio, Lea. Book 2: First Date. 2016. (Head over Heels Ser.). (ENG.). (J). (gr. 2-8). lib. bdg. 28.50 ***(978-1-62402-193-0(X))*** ABDO Publishing Co.

Taekema, Sylvia. Ripple Effect, 1 vol. 2015. (ENG.). 144p. (J). (gr. 4-7). pap. 9.95 *(978-1-4598-0872-0(X))* Orca Bk. Pubs. USA.

Tagge, Mark. The Coma & Convulsion Club: The Retreat. 2008. 112p. pap. 13.99 *(978-1-4259-7221-9(7))* AuthorHouse.

Tahmaseb, Charity & Vance, Darcy. The Geek Girl's Guide to Cheerleading. 2009. (ENG.). 352p. (YA). (gr. 9-18). pap. 8.99 *(978-1-4169-7834-3(8)*, Simon Pulse) Simon Pulse.

Talbot, Amy. Deer & His Dear Friends: A Tale from India. 2006. (J). pap. *(978-1-4108-6173-3(2))* Benchmark Education Co.

Tamaki, Mariko. Saving Montgomery Sole. 2016. (ENG.). 240p. (YA). 17.99 *(978-1-62672-271-2(4)*, 9781626722712) Roaring Brook Pr.

—Saving Montgomery Sole. 2017. (ENG.). 240p. (YA). pap. 9.99 *(978-1-250-10440-3(8)*, 9781250104403) Square Fish.

—Saving Montgomery Sole. 2017. (YA). lib. bdg. 20.85 ***(978-0-606-39584-7(9))*** Turtleback Bks.

Tamaki, Mariko. This One Summer. Tamaki, Jillian, illus. 2014. (ENG.). 320p. (YA). (gr. 7). 21.99 *(978-1-62672-094-7(0)*, 9781626720947); pap. 18.99 *(978-1-59643-774-6(X)*, 9781596437746) Roaring Brook Pr. (First Second Bks.).

Tan, Shaun. Rules of Summer. 2014. (ENG.). 48p. (J). (gr. 3-7). 18.99 *(978-0-545-63912-5(3)*, Levine, Arthur A. Bks.) Scholastic, Inc.

Tan, Susan. Cilla Lee-Jenkins: Future Author Extraordinaire. Wulfekotte, Dana, illus. 2017. (Cilla Lee-Jenkins Ser.). (ENG.). 256p. (J). 16.99 *(978-1-62672-551-5(9)*, 9781626725515) Roaring Brook Pr.

Tanabe, Yellow. Kekkaishi, Vol. 6. Tanabe, Yellow, illus. 2006. (ENG., Illus.). 208p. pap. 9.99 *(978-1-4215-0487-2(1))* Viz Media.

Tanigawa, Nagaru. The Dissociation of Haruhi Suzumiya. 2013. (Haruhi Suzumiya Ser.: 9). (ENG., Illus.). 192p. (YA). (gr. 10-17). pap. 8.99 *(978-0-316-03894-2(6))* Little, Brown Bks. for Young Readers.

—The Surprise of Haruhi Suzumiya. 2013. (Haruhi Suzumiya Ser.: 10). (ENG., Illus.). 368p. (YA). (gr. 10-17). 24.00 *(978-0-316-03898-0(9))*; pap. 10.99 *(978-0-316-03897-3(0))* Little, Brown Bks. for Young Readers.

Tanner, Lian. Icebreaker. 2015. (Hidden Ser.: Bk. 1). (ENG.). 304p. (J). (gr. 4-7). 16.99 *(978-1-250-05216-2(5)*, 9781250052162) Feiwel & Friends.

—Sunker's Deep. 2016. (Icebreaker Trilogy Ser.: 2). (ENG.). 304p. (J). 16.99 *(978-1-250-05217-9(3)*, 9781250052179) Feiwel & Friends.

Tanner-Moore, Margie. What Noah Knows. 2010. 49p. pap. 10.00 *(978-0-557-45753-3(X))* Lulu Pr., Inc.

Tapia, Rayner. The Adventures of Tom Mcguire: The Bard of Typheousina. 2009. (Illus.). 112p. 21.49 *(978-1-4389-3905-6(1))*; pap. 12.49 *(978-1-4389-3906-3(X))* AuthorHouse.

Tarkoff, Sarah. Eye of the Beholder - Revelation. 2018. (Eye of the Beholder Ser.: 1). 304p. pap. 15.99 *(978-0-06-245638-0(5)*, Harper Voyager) HarperCollins Pubs.

Tarlow, Ellen. Mole Catches the Sky. Bogacki, Tomek, illus. 2014. (ENG.). (J). 16.99 *(978-1-59572-656-8(X))* Star Bright Bks., Inc.

—Pinwheel Days, 1 vol. Parker, Gretel, illus. 2007. (ENG.). 32p. (J). (gr. -1-3). pap. 6.95 *(978-1-59572-059-7(6))* Star Bright Bks., Inc.

Tarr, Rebecca M. My Cricket & Me. 2008. 32p. pap. 24.95 *(978-1-60474-622-8(X))* America Star Bks.

Tarshis, Lauren. I Survived the Eruption of Mount St. Helens, 1980. 2016. (I Survived Ser.: 14). (ENG.). 112p. (J). (gr. 2-5). pap. 4.99 *(978-0-545-65852-2(7)*, Scholastic Paperbacks) Scholastic, Inc.

Tarver, Monroe S. Tales from the Mapmaker: Imagia & the Magic Pearls. 2015. (ENG.). 100p. (J). (gr. k-4). pap. 6.99 *(978-0-9723936-5-2(X))* Wizarding World Pr.

Tarver, Whitney B. The Best Day Ever! 2010. 24p. 14.95 *(978-1-4269-4114-6(5))* Trafford Publishing.

Tash, Sarvenaz. The Geek's Guide to Unrequited Love. 2016. (ENG., Illus.). 256p. (YA). (gr. 9). 18.99 *(978-1-4814-5653-1(9)*, Simon & Schuster Bks. For Young Readers) Simon & Schuster Bks. For Young Readers.

Tashjian, Janet. My Life As a Joke. Tashjian, Jake, illus. 2014. (My Life Ser.: 4). (ENG.). 272p. (J). (gr. 4-7). 13.99 *(978-0-8050-9650-1(X)*, 9780805098501, Holt, Henry & Co. Bks. For Young Readers) Holt, Henry & Co.

Tashlikowich, Natasha. The Secret of the Seven Stones. 2009. 117p. pap. 18.97 *(978-0-557-03747-6(6))* Lulu Pr., Inc.

Tate, Eleanora E. A Blessing in Disguise. 2004. 192p. (J). pap. 6.95 *(978-0-940975-66-8(1)*, Sankofa Bks.) Just Us Bks., Inc.

Tate, N. F. The Witch of Hambone: Books 1 And 2. 2009. (Illus.). 120p. pap. 33.49 *(978-1-4490-0621-1(3))* AuthorHouse.

Tatro, MaryAnn. Milton the Square Shell Turtle. Lucas, Diane, illus. 2013. 24p. pap. 11.95 *(978-1-61244-106-1(8))* Halo Publishing International.

Tauiliili, Pemerika L. The Rat & the Bat: And Other Short Stories. 2009. 88p. pap. 16.99 *(978-1-4490-4389-6(5))*; pap. 32.49 *(978-1-4389-2700-8(2))* AuthorHouse.

Tavadze, Olesya. Bursunsul & Paskualina. Ivanov, Evgueni, illus. 2007. (POL & ENG.). 32p. (J). pap. 16.95 *(978-1-60195-095-6(0))* International Step by Step Assn.

Tavener, Carys. The Adventures of T. C & Friends. 2011. (Illus.). 132p. pap. 38.72 *(978-1-4567-7096-9(9))* AuthorHouse.

Taylor, Angela. Izzy's Quest for Gold. 2015. (ENG., Illus.). 92p. (J). pap. *(978-1-78222-415-0(7))* Paragon Publishing, Rothersthorpe.

Taylor-Butler, Christine. Who Needs Friends? Havice, Susan, illus. 2006. (Rookie Readers Ser.). (ENG.). 32p. (J). (gr. k-2). pap. 4.95 *(978-0-516-24997-1(5)*, Children's Pr.) Scholastic Library Publishing.

Taylor, Chloë. Cute As a Button. Zhang, Nancy, illus. 2014. (Sew Zoey Ser.: 5). (ENG.). 176p. (J). (gr. 3-7). pap. 5.99 *(978-1-4814-0248-4(X)*, Simon Spotlight) Simon Spotlight.

—Dressed to Frill. Zhang, Nancy, illus. 2015. (Sew Zoey Ser.: 12). (ENG.). 160p. (J). (gr. 3-7). pap. 6.99 *(978-1-4814-2930-6(2)*, Simon Spotlight) Simon Spotlight.

Taylor, Chloe. Lights, Camera, Fashion! Zhang, Nancy, illus. 2013. (Sew Zoey Ser.: 3). (ENG.). 176p. (J). (gr. 3-7). 15.99 *(978-1-4424-8980-6(4))*; pap. 5.99 *(978-1-4424-8979-0(0))* Simon Spotlight. (Simon Spotlight).

—On Pins & Needles. Christy, Jana & Zhang, Nancy, illus. 2013. (Sew Zoey Ser.: 2). (ENG.). 160p. (J). (gr. 3-7). 15.99 *(978-1-4424-7937-1(X))*; pap. 6.99 *(978-1-4424-7936-4(1))* Simon Spotlight. (Simon Spotlight).

—Stitches & Stones. Zhang, Nancy, illus. 2013. (Sew Zoey Ser.: 4). (ENG.). 176p. (J). (gr. 3-7). 16.99 *(978-1-4424-9803-7(X))*; Bk. 4. pap. 5.99 *(978-1-4424-9802-0(1))* Simon Spotlight. (Simon Spotlight).

Taylor, Derrick & Garnett, Kaila. Jessica & Madison: Being Beautiful. Peters, Rob, illus. 2012. 38p. pap. 8.00 *(978-1-62050-492-5(8))*; 14.95 *(978-1-61364-734-9(4))* DTaylor Bks.

Taylor, Melissa Utz. Sneaky Snake. 2011. 24p. (gr. 1-2). pap. 14.99 *(978-1-4567-5518-8(8))* AuthorHouse.

Taylor, Theodore. The Cay. 2003. (ENG.). 160p. (J). (gr. 5-7). mass mkt. 6.99 *(978-0-440-22912-4(X)*, Laurel Leaf) Random Hse. Children's Bks.

Taylor, Theodore & Taylor, Theodore. The Cay. 2003. (gr. 5-8). lib. bdg. 17.20 *(978-0-613-72282-7(5)*, Turtleback) Turtleback Bks.

Taylor, Whitney. Definitions of Indefinable Things. 2017. (ENG.). 336p. (YA). (gr. 9). 17.99 *(978-0-544-80504-0(6)*, HMH Books For Young Readers) Houghton Mifflin Harcourt Publishing Co.

Teague, Mark. The Three Little Pigs & the Somewhat Bad Wolf. 2013. (ENG., Illus.). 48p. (J). (gr. -1-k). 17.99 *(978-0-439-91501-4(5)*, Orchard Bks.) Scholastic, Inc.

Teague, Monica. Diary of a Teenager in Junior High. 2011. 32p. pap. 16.95 *(978-1-4560-8552-0(2))* America Star Bks.

Teckentrup, Britta. Grumpy Cat. 2013. (ENG., Illus.). 26p. (J). (— 1). bds. 6.95 *(978-1-907967-48-1(6))* Boxer Bks., Ltd. GBR. Dist: Sterling Publishing Co., Inc.

—Sleep Tight, Little Bear. 2014. (ENG., Illus.). 40p. (J). 17.95 *(978-0-7358-4180-2(2))* North-South Bks., Inc.

—Up & Down. Teckentrup, Britta, illus. 2014. (ENG., Illus.). 28p. (J). (-k). 17.99 *(978-0-7636-7129-7(0)*, Templar) Candlewick Pr.

Tegan-Olsen, Sandra, illus. Joey's adventures by the Sea: Jellyfish Everywhere! 2008. 20p. (J). per. 9.95 *(978-0-9801527-0-8(4))* Freefox Publishing.

Tegen, Katherine. Dracula & Frankenstein Are Friends. Cushman, Doug, illus. 2003. 32p. (J). (gr. -1-3). 15.99 *(978-0-06-000115-5(1))* HarperCollins Pubs.

Tel-Or, Nava. Tristan & the Magical Vegetable Stew. 2011. (Illus.). 36p. (gr. -1). pap. 22.24 *(978-1-4567-7024-2(1))* AuthorHouse.

Tela, Carl M. Squnky's Big Awakening. Tela, Donna L., illus. 2009. 140p. pap. 14.99 *(978-1-4251-8145-1(7))* Trafford Publishing.

Telford, Tony. Tramp Life: Part 1 of the Pearly James Chronicles. 2017. (ENG.). 168p. (J). (gr. -1-12). pap. 11.95 *(978-1-78535-177-8(X)*, Lodestone Bks.) Hunt, John Publishing Ltd. GBR. Dist: National Bk. Network.

Telgemeier, Raina. Drama. 2012. (ENG., Illus.). 240p. (J). (gr. 5-9). 24.99 *(978-0-545-32698-8(2))*; pap. 10.99 *(978-0-545-32699-5(0))* Scholastic, Inc. (Graphix).

Telle, Anita. Always Time for Kindness. 2012. (ENG.). (J). pap. *(978-1-4675-2560-2(X))* Independent Pub.

Tello, Jorge. Pookie & Tushka Find a Little Piano. Tello, Jorge, illus. 2004. (Illus.). 32p. (J). 15.89 incl. cd-rom *(978-1-932179-23-1(2))* Pers Publishing.

Tenbeth, Kate. Burly & Grum & the Birthday Surprise. Jones, Rob, illus. 2012. 108p. pap. *(978-0-9572119-9-5(6))* Magic Toy Bks.

Tengan, G. Shay. Marching Dinosaur Parade. 2012. (Illus.). 60p. 17.99 *(978-0-9883478-0-9(6))* Tengan, G. Shay Service Group.

Tennant, Linda. Polly & Meril & the Wicked Spell. 2009. (Illus.). 20p. pap. 15.49 *(978-1-4389-7471-2(X))* AuthorHouse.

Tennapel, Doug. The Battle for Amphibopolis. 2017. (Nnewts Ser.: 3). lib. bdg. 22.10 **(978-0-606-40194-4(6))** Turtleback Bks.

Tennapel, Doug. Tommysaurus Rex. 2013. lib. bdg. 22.10 (978-0-606-31965-2(4), Turtleback) Turtleback Bks.

Terada, Junzo. Animal Friends on Parade Puzzle. 2017. (ENG., Illus.). 12p. (J). (gr. -1-k). 14.99 **(978-1-4521-5190-8(3))** Chronicle Bks. LLC.

Terada, Junzo. A Good Home for Max. 2014. (ENG., Illus.). 40p. (J). (gr. -1-k). 16.99 (978-1-4521-2702-6(6)) Chronicle Bks. LLC.

TerKeurst, Lysa. It Will Be Okay: Trusting God Through Fear & Change, 1 vol. 2014. (ENG., Illus.). 32p. (J). 14.99 (978-1-4003-2419-4(X)) Nelson, Thomas Inc.

Ternes, Caroline. Will You Be My Friend? The Prancer & Button Story. 2010. 20p. 14.99 (978-1-4490-7731-0(5)) AuthorHouse.

Terrell, Brandon. The Cursed Stage. Epelbaum, Mariano, illus. 2017. (Snoops, Inc Ser.). (ENG.). 112p. (gr. 4-6). lib. bdg. 26.65 (978-1-4965-4346-2(7)) Stone Arch Bks.

—Flipside, Vol. 11. Majado, Caio, illus. 2013. (Tony Hawk's 900 Revolution Ser.). (ENG.). 128p. (gr. 3-4). lib. bdg. 26.65 (978-1-4342-3842-9(3)) Stone Arch Bks.

—Flipside: Volume Eleven, 1 vol. Majado, Caio, illus. 2013. (Tony Hawk's 900 Revolution Ser.). (ENG.). 128p. (gr. 3-4). pap. 7.19 (978-1-4342-4895-4(X), Tony Hawk's 900 Revolution) Stone Arch Bks.

—High Drama. 2015. (ENG.). 112p. (YA). (gr. 6-12). 27.99 (978-1-4677-5710-2(1)) Lerner Publishing Group.

—Horizon, 1 vol. Dal Bello, Thiago & Tortosa, Wilson, illus. 2013. (Tony Hawk's 900 Revolution Ser.). (ENG.). 128p. (gr. 3-4). pap. 7.19 (978-1-4342-6218-9(9)); lib. bdg. 26.65 (978-1-4342-6032-1(1)) Stone Arch Bks.

—Phantom of the Library. Epelbaum, Mariano, illus. 2017. (Snoops, Inc Ser.). (ENG.). 112p. (gr. 4-6). lib. bdg. 26.65 **(978-1-4965-5060-6(9))** Stone Arch Bks.

—Recharged, Vol. 12. Tortosa, Wilson, illus. 2013. (Tony Hawk's 900 Revolution Ser.). (ENG.). 128p. (gr. 3-4). lib. bdg. 26.65 (978-1-4342-3843-6(1)) Stone Arch Bks.

—Recharged: Volume Twelve, 1 vol. Tortosa, Wilson, illus. 2013. (Tony Hawk's 900 Revolution Ser.). (ENG.). 128p. (gr. 3-4). pap. 7.19 (978-1-4342-4896-1(8), Tony Hawk's 900 Revolution) Stone Arch Bks.

—Take Away. 2014. (Red Zone Ser.: 5). (ENG.). 104p. (YA). (gr. 6-12). pap. 7.95 (978-1-4677-4474-4(3), Darby Creek) Lerner Publishing Group.

—Tracking Champ. Epelbaum, Mariano, illus. 2017. (Snoops, Inc Ser.). (ENG.). 112p. (gr. 4-6). lib. bdg. 26.65 (978-1-4965-4348-6(3)) Stone Arch Bks.

—The Undercover Cheerleader. Epelbaum, Mariano, illus. 2017. (Snoops, Inc Ser.). (ENG.). 112p. (gr. 4-6). lib. bdg. 26.65 **(978-1-4965-5061-3(7))** Stone Arch Bks.

—Unearthed, Vol. 10. Tortosa, Wilson, illus. 2013. (Tony Hawk's 900 Revolution Ser.). (ENG.). 128p. (gr. 3-4). lib. bdg. 26.65 (978-1-4342-3841-2(5)) Stone Arch Bks.

—Unearthed: Volume Ten, 1 vol. Tortosa, Wilson, illus. 2013. (Tony Hawk's 900 Revolution Ser.). (ENG.). 128p. (gr. 3-4). pap. 7.19 (978-1-4342-4897-8(6), Tony Hawk's 900 Revolution) Stone Arch Bks.

—The Vanishing Treasure. Epelbaum, Mariano, illus. 2017. (Snoops, Inc Ser.). (ENG.). 112p. (gr. 4-6). lib. bdg. 26.65 (978-1-4965-4345-5(9)) Stone Arch Bks.

Terrell, Brandon & Majado, Caio. Tunnel Vision, Vol. 6. Ito, Leonardo, illus. 2012. (Tony Hawk's 900 Revolution Ser.). (ENG.). 128p. (gr. 3-4). pap. 7.19 (978-1-4342-3888-7(1)); lib. bdg. 26.65 (978-1-4342-3312-7(X)) Stone Arch Bks. (Tony Hawk's 900 Revolution).

Terrell, Brandon & Tortosa, Wilson. Exiled, Vol. 7. Ito, Leonardo, illus. 2012. (Tony Hawk's 900 Revolution Ser.). (ENG.). 128p. (gr. 3-4). pap. 7.19 (978-1-4342-3889-4(X)); lib. bdg. 26.65 (978-1-4342-3313-4(8)) Stone Arch Bks. (Tony Hawk's 900 Revolution).

Terrill Holdman, Shirley. The Adventures of Giggles & Owen: Adventure Three - Unlimited Pawsibilities. Leeds, Marjorie M., illus. 2013. 50p. pap. 17.95 (978-1-4575-2175-1(X)) Dog Ear Publishing, LLC.

Terry Anne. Honest Bob, the Dog, Plays Ball. 2013. 24p. pap. 9.52 (978-1-62884-441-2(8)) Speedy Publishing LLC.

—Honest Bob, the Dog, Tells the Truth. 2013. 26p. pap. 9.66 (978-1-63022-211-6(9)) Speedy Publishing LLC.

Terry, Elliah. I Am Calliope June. 2017. (ENG.). 336p. (J). 16.99 (978-1-250-09627-2(8), 9781250096272) Feiwel & Friends.

Tesh, Jane & Klein-Higger, Joni. Land of Lost Socks: A Children's Musical. 2013. 24p. pap. 7.95 (978-1-61633-397-3(9)) Guardian Angel Publishing, Inc.

Testa, Maggie. Daniel Gets Scared. 2015. (Daniel Tiger's Neighborhood Ready-To-Read Ser.). lib. bdg. 13.55 (978-0-606-38243-4(7)) Turtleback Bks.

—Friends Are the Best! Style Guide, Style & Fruchter, Jason, illus. 2014. (Daniel Tiger's Neighborhood Ser.). (ENG.). 12p. (J). (gr. -1-k). bds. 5.99 (978-1-4424-9547-0(2), Simon Spotlight) Simon Spotlight.

—Happy Halloween, Brobee! 2013. (Yo Gabba Gabba! Ser.). (ENG., Illus.). 12p. (J). (gr. -1-k). bds. 5.99 (978-1-4424-7407-9(6), Simon Spotlight) Simon Spotlight.

—The Power of Po. 2015. (Kung Fu Panda 8x8 Ser.). lib. bdg. 13.55 (978-0-606-38258-8(5)) Turtleback Bks.

Tetlow, Karin. Harry Goes Rowing. Guze, Tessa, illus. 2013. 32p. pap. 11.95 (978-0-615-75585-4(2)) Juping Horse Pr.

Tetzlaff, Wendy Jo. A Girl Named Frannie. 2008. 28p. pap. 24.95 (978-1-60703-055-3(1)) America Star Bks.

—Summertime: A Girl Named Frannie, 1 vol. 2010. 38p. pap. 24.95 (978-1-4489-2598-8(3)) PublishAmerica, Inc.

Tewkesbury, Alexa. Josie's Jazzy Journal. 2008. (ENG., Illus.). 128p. (J). (978-1-85345-457-6(5)) Crusade for World Revival.

—Paul's Potty Pages. 2008. (ENG., Illus.). 128p. (J). (978-1-85345-456-1(7)) Crusade for World Revival.

Thayer, Robert Scott. Kobee Manatee: Heading Home to Florida. Korman, Susan, ed. Gallegos, Lauren, illus. 2013. (Kobee Manatee Ser.). (ENG.). 32p. (J). (gr. k-2). 16.99 (978-0-9883269-2-7(2)) Thompson Mill Pr.

The Duda Family. The Adventures of Newo: Newo & Emma Visit Their Furry Friends. 2008. 28p. pap. 12.49 (978-1-4343-9766-9(1)) AuthorHouse.

The Library Fairy. The Magical Tree & Musical Wind. Faust, Laurie A., illus. 2008. 32p. pap. 16.95 (978-1-59858-604-6(1)) Dog Ear Publishing, LLC.

The Poet 174. The Ways of Life. 2011. 130p. pap. 15.95 (978-1-4327-5135-7(2)) Outskirts Pr., Inc.

Theer, Justine M. The Backwards Town, 1 vol. 2010. 82p. pap. 19.95 (978-1-4489-5361-5(8)) America Star Bks.

Theo. Oscar & Hoo. Dudok de Wit, Michael, illus. 2003. 32p. (J). (gr. -1-2). 17.99 (978-0-00-710793-3(5), HarperCollins Children's Bks.) HarperCollins Pubs. Ltd. GBR. Dist: Trafalgar Square Publishing.

Therriault - Bruder, Dovie G. Life on the Farm: Story One Adventure with the Chickens. 2011. 36p. pap. 15.14 (978-1-4670-3797-6(4)) AuthorHouse.

Thewes Nicolai, Susan. The Thirteenth Butterfly: A Lizzie's Life Novel. 2009. 192p. pap. 14.49 (978-1-4389-9975-3(5)) AuthorHouse.

Theys, Erchen. Birdie Hop: The True Story. 2011. (Illus.). 28p. 12.19 (978-1-4567-7522-3(7)) AuthorHouse.

Thiel, Annie. Danny Is Moving. Edwards, William M., illus. 2006. (Playdate Kids Ser.). 32p. (J). (gr. -1-3). 14.95 (978-1-933721-02-6(2)) Playdate Kids Publishing.

—Danny's Secret. Edwards, W M, illus. 2007. (Playdate Kids: Let's Be Friends! Ser.). 27p. (J). (gr. -1-3). per. 6.95 (978-1-933721-22-4(7)) Playdate Kids Publishing.

Thiele, Colin. Storm Boy. Ingpen, Robert R., illus. 2006. (ENG.). 1p. (J). (gr. -1-3). 7.95 (978-1-74110-187-4(5)); 40th anniv. ed. pap. 7.95 (978-1-86436-804-8(7)) New Holland Pubs. Pty. Ltd. AUS. Dist: Tuttle Publishing.

Thieman, Linda. Katie & Kimble: A Ghost Story. l.t. ed. 2007. (Illus.). 148p. (J). pap. 12.48 (978-0-9794396-0-5(4)) Pale Silver Rainpop Pr.

Thomas, Amy A. The Abominog. Williams, Gail, illus. 2013. 120p. pap. 6.99 (978-0-9898579-0-1(5)) Passionate Purpose.

Thomas, Amy T. The Story of Rocco on Satterwhite Ridge: Spring Surprises. Lester, Roseanna, illus. 2009. 16p. pap. 8.49 (978-1-4389-3142-5(5)) AuthorHouse.

Thomas, C. Gordon. The Adventures of Jack & Jim. 2008. 132p. 26.54 (978-1-4251-5909-2(5)) Trafford Publishing.

Thomas, Dale. Soot & Frogskin. 2008. 118p. pap. 12.50 (978-0-9559798-0-4(3)) Inane Blabbering Bks. GBR. Dist: Lulu Pr., Inc.

Thomas, Jan. A Birthday for Cow! 2008. (ENG., Illus.). 40p. (J). (gr. -1-3). 12.95 (978-0-15-206072-5(3)) Houghton Mifflin Harcourt Publishing Co.

Thomas, Jason. The Adventures of Bird & Gator: Best Friends. 2012. 24p. pap. 12.56 (978-1-4669-4973-7(2)) Trafford Publishing.

Thomas, Kara. The Darkest Corners. (ENG.). (YA). (gr. 9). 2017. 352p. pap. 9.99 **(978-0-553-52148-1(9)**, Ember) 2016. 336p. 17.99 (978-0-553-52145-0(4), Delacorte Pr.) Random Hse. Children's Bks.

Thomas, Leah. Because You'll Never Meet Me. (ENG.). (YA). 2017. 368p. pap. 9.99 (978-1-68119-021-1(4), 9781681190211) 2015. 352p. (gr. 9-12). 17.99 (978-1-61963-590-6(9), 9781619635906) Bloomsbury Publishing USA. (Bloomsbury USA Childrens).

—Because You'll Never Meet Me. 2017. (YA). lib. bdg. 20.85 **(978-0-606-40347-4(7))** Turtleback Bks.

Thomas, Leah. Nowhere near You. 2017. (ENG.). 400p. (YA). 17.99 (978-1-68119-178-2(4), 9781681191782, Bloomsbury USA Childrens) Bloomsbury Publishing USA.

Thomas, Lisa E. Friends of the Heart. 20p. (J). (gr. 1-6). pap. (978-1-885091-05-5(2)); pap. (978-1-885091-04-8(4)) Eco-Busters.

Thomas, M. L. Brut Mccloud & His Friends. 2012. 44p. pap. 18.99 (978-1-4670-4259-8(5)) AuthorHouse.

Thomas, Mike. The Mysterious Treasure of Jerry Lee Thorton. 2013. 154p. pap. 12.95 (978-0-578-12603-6(6)) Moss Press Publishing.

Thomas Nelson Publishing Staff. Camping the Bug-A-Boo Way: Go for the Gold Against Camp Hot Foot! 2008. cd-rom 19.95 (978-0-9754280-7-8(1)) Nelson, Thomas Inc.

Thomas-Ngabe, T-Imani. Who Stole the Nutz? From the Chronicles of Poems & Stories Mother Goose Forgot. 2013. 40p. pap. 19.57 (978-1-4907-0718-1(2)) Trafford Publishing.

Thomas, P. J. The Cloud & the Cat. 2012. 52p. pap. 24.95 (978-1-4626-7211-0(6)) America Star Bks.

Thomas, Roger B. The Accidental Marriage. 2014. (ENG.). 219p. 19.95 (978-1-58617-908-3(X)) Ignatius Pr.

Thomas, Scarlett. Dragon's Green. 2017. (Worldquake Ser.: 1). (ENG., Illus.). 384p. (J). (gr. 4-7). 17.99 **(978-1-4814-9784-8(7)**, Simon & Schuster Bks. For Young Readers) Simon & Schuster Bks. For Young Readers.

—Dragon's Green. 2017. (J). pap. **(978-1-4814-9785-5(5)**, Simon & Schuster Bks. For Young Readers) Simon & Schuster Bks. For Young Readers.

Thomas, Shelley Moore. Get Well, Good Knight. Plecas, Jennifer, illus. 2004. (Easy-to-Read Ser.). 44p. (gr. k-3). 14.00 (978-0-7569-2923-7(7)) Perfection Learning Corp.

—Get Well, Good Knight. 2004. (Penguin Young Readers Level 3 Ser.). 13.55 (978-0-613-97291-8(0), Turtleback) Turtleback Bks.

—Happy Birthday, Good Knight. Plecas, Jennifer, illus. 2014. (Penguin Young Readers, Level 3 Ser.). (ENG.). 48p. (J). (gr. 1-3). pap. 3.99 (978-0-448-46374-2(1), Penguin Young Readers) Penguin Young Readers Group.

Thomas, Terri. The Barge Ghost, 1 vol. unabr. ed. 2010. (Q Reads Ser.). (ENG.). 32p. (YA). (gr. 9-12). pap. 6.95 (978-1-61651-211-8(3)) Saddleback Educational Publishing, Inc.

—J Mac Is the Freestyle King! Sefcik, Wendy, illus. 2010. 38p. pap. 20.00 (978-1-60844-453-3(8)) Dog Ear Publishing, LLC.

Thomas the Tank Engine. 2012. (978-0-7948-3764-8(6)) Egmont Bks., Ltd.

Thomes, William Henry. The Bushrangers a Yankee's Adventures During His Second Visit to Australia by William H Thomes. 2006. 420p. per. 26.99 (978-1-4255-4567-3(X)) Michigan Publishing.

Thomey, Zedar. Red Star Red Tar. 2010. 66p. pap. 20.00 (978-1-60860-360-2(1), Eloquent Bks.) Strategic Book Publishing & Rights Agency (SBPRA).

Thompson, Aiyana M. Miranda Fishhook: Makes a New Friend. 2010. 24p. 16.00 (978-1-4520-2364-9(6)) AuthorHouse.

Thompson, Alicia. Psych Major Syndrome. 2010. (ENG.). 336p. pap. 8.99 (978-1-4231-1549-6(X)) Disney Pr.

Thompson, C. Michael. Twinsational. 2009. 120p. (YA). pap. 14.95 (978-1-4327-3033-8(9)) Outskirts Pr., Inc.

Thompson, Carol. I Like You the Best. Thompson, Carol, illus. 2011. (ENG., Illus.). 32p. (J). (gr. -1-1). 16.95 (978-0-8234-2341-5(7)) Holiday Hse., Inc.

Thompson, Carolyn. BJ S Bean Patch. 2013. 18p. pap. 9.99 (978-1-62419-724-6(8)) Salem Author Services.

Thompson, David. The Nine Clues of Christmas, 1 vol. 2009. 172p. pap. 24.95 (978-1-60813-410-6(5)) America Star Bks.

Thompson, Debra. The Crumb Snatchers. Dennis, Tammy D., illus. 2012. 24p. pap. 12.95 (978-1-61493-037-2(6)) Peppertree Pr., The.

Thompson, Emma. The Christmas Tale of Peter Rabbit. Taylor, Eleanor, illus. 2013. (Peter Rabbit Ser.). (ENG.). 72p. (J). (gr. -1-2). 20.00 (978-0-7232-7694-4(3), Warne) Penguin Young Readers Group.

Thompson, Gareth. Sunshine to the Sunless. 2008. (ENG.). 256p. (YA). (gr. 7). pap. 11.99 (978-1-86230-467-3(X)) Transworld Publishers Ltd. GBR. Dist: Independent Pubs. Group.

Thompson, Holly Sue. Molly, the Good Furry Friend. Thompson, Kristi June, illus. 2011. 36p. pap. 14.75 (978-1-60911-431-2(0), Eloquent Bks.) Strategic Book Publishing & Rights Agency (SBPRA).

Thompson, J. E. Disappearance at Hangman's Bluff. (Felony Bay Mysteries Ser.: 2). (ENG.). 336p. (J). (gr. 3-7). 2015. pap. 6.99 (978-0-06-210450-2(0)) 2014. (Illus.). 16.99 (978-0-06-210449-6(7)) HarperCollins Pubs. (Walden Pond Pr.).

Thompson, Jan & Sharpe, Jaime. Amara's Magical Playhouse: The Adventure Begins. 2010. 108p. pap. 37.99 (978-1-4520-8284-4(7)) AuthorHouse.

Thompson, Joan. Lucy Russell: Stardom & Stinkwater. 2003. 129p. (YA). pap. 10.95 (978-0-595-26867-2(6), Writers Club Pr.) iUniverse, Inc.

—Mudpack & Melt Isnt Easy Getting Gorge. 2006. pap. 11.95 (978-0-595-39905-5(3), Backinprint.com) iUniverse, Inc.

Thompson, Joan R. Terrible Tumoff & Me. 2006. pap. 11.95 (978-0-595-39902-4(9), Backinprint.com) iUniverse, Inc.

Thompson, Kimberly. Toulouse Tangled up in Lights. Easey, Chris, illus. 2011. 64p. (J). 19.95 (978-0-9818976-1-5(4)) Little Pigeon Bks.

Thompson, Lauren. Little Quack's New Friend. Anderson, Derek, illus. 2008. (Classic Board Bks.). (ENG.). 34p. (J). (gr. -1-1). bds. 7.99 (978-1-4169-4923-7(2), Little Simon) Little Simon.

—Little Quack's New Friend. Anderson, Derek, illus. 2006. (ENG.). 32p. (J). (gr. -1-3). 17.99 (978-0-689-86893-1(6), Simon & Schuster Bks. For Young Readers) Simon & Schuster Bks. For Young Readers.

—Polar Bear Morning. Savage, Stephen, illus. 2013. (ENG.). 32p. (J). (gr. -1-k). 16.99 (978-0-439-69885-6(5), Scholastic Pr.) Scholastic, Inc.

Thompson, Mary G. Amy Chelsea Stacie Dee. 2016. (ENG.). 304p. (YA). (gr. 9). 17.99 (978-1-101-99680-5(3), G.P. Putnam's Sons Books for Young Readers) Penguin Young Readers Group.

Thompson, Susan A. Katie the Christian Caterpillar: The Loss of a Loved One. 2012. 20p. pap. 10.99 (978-1-4624-0223-6(2), Inspiring Voices) Author Solutions, Inc.

Thompson, Teresa. The Adventures of Shasta & Nikki: A True Friendship. 2004. 34p. pap. 24.95 (978-1-4137-1967-3(8)) PublishAmerica, Inc.

Thompson, Tyler. Sneaker Freak, 1 vol. 2010. 164p. pap. 24.95 (978-1-4489-6191-7(2)) America Star Bks.

Thompson, Vinny. Vinny & Bud. 2009. 64p. pap. 11.99 (978-1-4490-2551-9(X)) AuthorHouse.

Thomson, Carly. Truth Seekers. 2013. 60p. pap. 9.99 (978-1-62839-189-3(8)) Salem Author Services.

Thomson, Melissa. Keena Ford & the Secret Journal Mix-Up. Morrison, Frank, illus. 2011. (Keena Ford Ser.). (ENG.). 128p. (J). (gr. 1-3). 5.99 (978-0-14-241937-3(0), Puffin Books) Penguin Young Readers Group.

Thor, Annika. The Lily Pond. Schenck, Linda, tr. 2012. (ENG.). 224p. (J). (gr. 4-7). 7.99 (978-0-385-74040-1(9), Yearling) Random Hse. Children's Bks.

Thor, Annika & Schenck, Linda. Deep Sea. 2015. (ENG.). 240p. (YA). (gr. 9). 20.99 (978-0-375-99132-5(8), Delacorte Pr.) Random Hse. Children's Bks.

Thornburg, Michael. The Monster Kids' Adventures: The Retur. 2005. pap. 19.95 (978-1-4137-8556-2(5)) PublishAmerica, Inc.

Thome, Jenn Marie. The Inside of Out. 2016. (ENG.). 400p. (YA). (gr. 7). 17.99 (978-0-8037-4058-7(1), Dial Bks) Penguin Young Readers Group.

Thornton, D. S. Scrap City. Bowater, Charlie, illus. 2015. (Middle-Grade Novels Ser.). (ENG.). 352p. (gr. 4-7). lib. bdg. 27.99 (978-1-4965-0475-3(5)) Stone Arch Bks.

Thornton, M. H. Kylee & Lexie: Mystery of the Gholdees. 2010. 64p. pap. 10.99 (978-1-4269-3713-2(X)) Trafford Publishing.

Thorpe, Kiki. Before the Bell. RH Disney Staff & Christy, Jana, illus. 2015. (Never Girls Ser.: 9). (ENG.). 128p. (J). (gr. 1-4). lib. bdg. 12.99 (978-0-7364-8167-0(2), RH/Disney) Random Hse. Children's Bks.

—Before the Bell. RH Disney Staff, illus. 2015. (Never Girls Ser.: No. 9). (ENG.). 128p. (J). (gr. 1-4). 5.99 (978-0-7364-3304-4(X), RH/Disney) Random Hse. Children's Bks.

—A Fairy's Gift (Disney: the Never Girls) Christy, Jana, illus. 2017. (Never Girls Ser.). (ENG.). 224p. (J). (gr. 1-4). 7.99 **(978-0-7364-3773-8(8)**, RH/Disney) Random Hse. Children's Bks.

—A Fairy's Gift (Disney: the Never Girls) RH Disney Staff, illus. 2015. (Never Girls Ser.). (ENG.). 224p. (J). (gr. 1-4). 14.99 (978-0-7364-3278-8(7), RH/Disney) Random Hse. Children's Bks.

—Into the Waves. Christy, Jana, illus. 2016. (Never Girls Ser.: 11). (ENG.). 128p. (J). (gr. 1-4). 5.99 (978-0-7364-3525-3(5), RH/Disney) Random Hse. Children's Bks.

—Into the Waves. 2016. (Never Girls Ser.: 11). lib. bdg. 16.00 (978-0-606-38467-4(7)) Turtleback Bks.

—The Never Girls Collection, 4 vols. Christy, Jana & RH Disney Staff, illus. 2014. (ENG.). 640p. (J). (gr. 1-4). 24.96 (978-0-7364-3184-2(5), RH/Disney) Random Hse. Children's Bks.

—On the Trail. Christy, Jana, illus. 2015. (Never Girls Ser.: No. 10). (ENG.). 128p. (J). (gr. 1-4). 5.99 (978-0-7364-3306-8(6), RH/Disney) Random Hse. Children's Bks.

—Under the Lagoon. Christy, Jana, illus. 2016. (Never Girls Ser.). (ENG.). 128p. (J). (gr. 1-4). 5.99 (978-0-7364-3529-1(8), RH/Disney) Random Hse. Children's Bks.

—The Woods Beyond. Christy, Jana, illus. 2014. (ENG.). 128p. (J). (gr. 1-4). (Never Girls Ser.: 6). lib. bdg. 12.99 (978-0-7364-8148-9(6)); (Stepping Stone Book Ser.: No. 6). 5.99 (978-0-7364-3096-8(2)) Random Hse. Children's Bks. (RH/Disney).

—The Woods Beyond. Christy, Jana, illus. 2014. (Never Girls Ser.: 6). lib. bdg. 16.00 (978-0-606-35545-2(6)) Turtleback Bks.

Thorpe, Kiki, adapted by. Broken Hearts. 2003. (Lizzie Mcguire Ser.). (Illus.). 138p. (J). 12.65 (978-0-7569-2718-9(8)) Perfection Learning Corp.

Thorpe, Roslyn C. Rayray's Amazing Dream: An Adventurous Week. 2012. 24p. pap. 15.99 (978-1-4771-5366-6(7)) Xlibris Corp.

Thrasher, Amanda M. A Fairy Match in the Mushroom Patch. 2013. (ENG., Illus.). 162p. (J). (gr. 2-4). pap. 7.99 (978-0-9888568-1-3(6)) Rising Phoenix Pr.

Thurmond, Joey. Nojoe Makes New Friends. 2009. 16p. pap. 10.99 (978-1-4490-4156-4(6)) AuthorHouse.

Thyroff, Brad. Albert & Freddie. Gillen, Rosemarie, illus. 2013. 24p. pap. 9.99 (978-1-61286-190-6(3)) Avid Readers Publishing Group.

Tia, Rocio. Maire & the Monster, 1 vol. 2010. 64p. pap. 19.95 (978-1-60749-724-0(7)) America Star Bks.

Tibbs, Ely. The Mouse under My House - Ingle & the Cats Meow. 2010. 73p. pap. 27.81 (978-0-557-39421-0(X)) Lulu Pr., Inc.

Tibo, Gilles. My Best Friend. Nadeau, Janice, illus. 2018. (ENG.). 52p. (J). (gr. k-4). 16.95 (978-1-77229-022-6(X)) Simply Read Bks. CAN. Dist: Ingram Publisher Services.

Tiernan, Cate. Eternally Yours. 2013. (Immortal Beloved Ser.: 3). (ENG.). 464p. (YA). (gr. 7-17). pap. 10.00 (978-0-316-03595-8(5), Poppy) Little, Brown Bks. for Young Readers.

Tilby, Ginny. You Should, You Should. 2013. (ENG.). 32p. (J). (gr. k-3). 16.95 (978-1-938301-70-4(6)) Familius LLC.

Till, Nan. Solomon Finds His Spots. 2009. 24p. (J). pap. 15.95 (978-1-4327-5134-0(4)) Outskirts Pr., Inc.

Tilley, Sophie. Sparkly Shoes & Picnic Parties. 2015. (ENG., Illus.). 32p. (J). (gr. -1-1). 18.99 (978-1-4088-3662-0(9), 9781408836620, Bloomsbury USA Childrens) Bloomsbury Publishing USA.

Tillson, M. C. Secret of Bete Grise Bay: A Michigan Lighthouse Adventure. Bailey, Lisa, illus. 2008. (ENG.). (J). (gr. 1-5). pap. 9.95 (978-0-9764824-2-0(8)) A & M Writing and Publishing,.

Tillworth, Mary. Boots & Dora Forever! (Dora & Friends) Aikins, David, illus. 2016. (Pictureback(R) Ser.). (ENG.). 16p. (J). (gr. -1-2). 4.99 (978-0-553-53836-6(5), Random Hse. Bks. for Young Readers) Random Hse. Children's Bks.

—A Friend at the Zoo/un Amigo en el Zoologico (Bubble Guppies) Gomez, Yuliana, tr. Random House Editors, illus. 2014. (Pictureback(R) Ser.). (ENG.). 24p. (J). (gr. -1-2). 3.99 (978-0-385-37928-1(5), Random Hse. Bks. for Young Readers) Random Hse. Children's Bks.

—Here Come the Bubble Guppies! (Bubble Guppies) Random House Staff, illus. 2013. (Friendship Box Ser.). (ENG.). 48p. (J). (-k). bds. 10.99 (978-0-449-81768-1(7), Random Hse. Bks. for Young Readers) Random Hse. Children's Bks.

—Meet My Friends! (Dora & Friends) Aikins, David, illus. 2014. (Step into Reading Ser.). (ENG.). 24p. (J). (gr. -1-1). 3.99 (978-0-385-38462-9(9), Random Hse. Bks. for Young Readers) Random Hse. Children's Bks.

—Show Your Love! (Shimmer & Shine) Golden Books Staff & Aikins, Dave, illus. 2016. (Big Golden Book Ser.). (ENG.). 32p. (J). (gr. -1-2). 9.99 (978-1-5247-1603-5(0), Golden Bks.) Random Hse. Children's Bks.

Tilly, Meg. First Time, 1 vol. 2008. (Orca Soundings Ser.). (ENG.). (YA). (gr. 8-12). 128p. pap. 9.95 (978-1-55143-944-0(1)); 112p. 16.95 (978-1-55143-946-4(8)) Orca Bk. Pubs. USA.

Tilson, Gina L. Patches: Adventures of a Country Cavalier. 2011. 48p. pap. 9.99 (978-1-4567-6386-2(5)) AuthorHouse.

Time for Your Mind. l.t. ed. 2006. (Illus.). 35p. (J). (978-0-9785480-1-8(9)) Mielcarek, David.

Time, Nicholas O. Stay a Spell. 2016. (In Due Time Ser.: 2). lib. bdg. 17.20 (978-0-606-38986-0(5)) Turtleback Bks.

Timmers, Leo. Franky. Timmers, Leo, illus. 2016. (ENG., Illus.). 40p. (gr. -1-2). 16.99 (978-1-927271-93-3(2)); 33.32 (978-1-77657-054-6(5)); 33.32 (978-1-77657-053-9(7)) Gecko Pr. NZL. Dist: Lerner Publishing Group.

Timmons, Robbie. Twoey & the Goat. 2008. (ENG., Illus.). 192p. (J). (gr. 1-7). 15.95 (978-1-58726-517-4(6), Mitten Pr.) Ann Arbor Editions LLC.

Timothy, Ering. Frog Belly Rat F & G. 2003. (J). bds. 16.99 (978-0-7636-2248-0(6)) Candlewick Pr.

Tims, Laura. The Best Thing about Pain. 2017. 336p. (YA). (gr. 8). 17.99 (978-0-06-231735-3(0), HarperTeen) HarperCollins Pubs.

Ting, Mary. Three Best Friends: Fabulous Day, 1 vol. 2010. 48p. pap. 16.95 (978-1-4489-4300-5(0)) America Star Bks.

Tingle, Tim. Crossing Bok Chitto: A Choctaw Tale of Friendship & Freedom. Bridges, Jeanne Rorex, illus. (ENG.). 40p. (J). 2008. (gr. 2-7). pap. 8.95 (978-1-933693-20-0(7)) 2006. (gr. 1-8). 17.95 (978-0-938317-77-7(6)) Cinco Puntos Pr.

Tinti, Natalie. Magic in Us. the Healing Circle, bks. 2, vol. 2. Tinti, Natalie, illus. 2013. (Sewing a Friendship Ser.). (ENG., Illus.). 96p. (J). 25.95 (978-0-9830884-4-8(6)) Tintinatie Publishing Hse.

—Magic in Us. the Healing Circle: The Healing Circle, bks. 2, vol. 2. Tinti, Natalie, illus. 2013. (Sewing a Friendship Ser.: 3). (ENG., Illus.). 96p. (J). pap. 12.95 (978-0-9830884-0-0(3)) Tintinatie Publishing Hse.

—Magic in Us. the Power of Imagination, bks. 1, vol. 2. Tinti, Natalie, illus. 2013. (Sewing a Friendship Ser.: 2). (ENG., Illus.). 116p. (J). 25.95 (978-0-9830884-1-7(1)) Tintinatie Publishing Hse.

—Magic in Us. the Power of Imagination: The Power of Imagination, bks. 1, vol. 2. T, N., illus. ed. 2013. (Sewing a

Friendship Ser.). (ENG.). 116p. (J). pap. 12.95 *(978-0-9842625-3-3(9))* Tintinatie Publishing Hse.

—Sewing a Friendship. Tinti, Natalie, illus. 2009. (Sewing a Friendship Ser.: 1). (ENG., Illus.). 88p. (J). pap. 12.95 *(978-0-9842625-1-9(2))* Tintinatie Publishing Hse.

Tirado, Margot A. New Friends. 2012. 48p. (gr. 1-2). pap. 9.89 *(978-1-4669-0508-5(5))* Trafford Publishing.

Tisdale, Towanda. Wallace Mack Has a Bug Attack! 2012. 28p. 24.95 *(978-1-4626-6071-1(1))* America Star Bks.

Tish, Aunty. Kiddiwink Kingdom. 2006. (Illus.). 58p. (J). per. 19.95 *(978-1-59800-587-5(1))* Outskirts Pr., Inc.

Titelman, Becky. The Wonky Witch & the Witching Well. 2009. 364p. pap. 19.99 *(978-1-4490-2673-8(7))* AuthorHouse.

Tjemagel, Shirley. Obee & the Great Bank Heist. 2011. 28p. pap. 12.99 *(978-1-4634-1913-4(9))* AuthorHouse.

To Keep Me SAFE! A Story for Children Affected by Military Deployments. 2003. (J). 12.00 *(978-0-9740289-0-3(8))* State of Growth Publishing Co.

Tobias, Anne B. Harry Meets a Bully. Tobias, Tom, illus. 2008. 16p. pap. 9.95 *(978-0-9822540-3-5(2))* Peppertree Pr., The.

Todd, Chelva E. Up from the Barber's Chair. 2012. 44p. pap. 17.49 *(978-1-4691-4476-4(X))* Xlibris Corp.

Tokarz, Brenda. Curious Jane's: A Balloon Adventure. 2012. (ENG.). (J). pap. 9.95 *(978-1-4507-7092-7(4))* Independent Pub.

Tokidoki. Tokidoki Cactus Pups. 2008. 5.99 *(978-1-59396-993-6(7))* Diamond Bk. Distributors.

Tokio, Marnelle. Room 207. Hendry, Linda, illus. 2006. (ENG.). 120p. (J). (gr. 4-7). pap. 8.95 *(978-0-88776-695-4(1)*, Tundra Bks.) Tundra Bks. CAN. Dist: Penguin Random Hse. LLC.

Tokyopop Staff, creator. Contents under Pressure, Vol. 3. 2005. (Lilo & Stitch Ser.). (Illus.). 89p. (gr. 3-7). pap. 14.99 *(978-1-59532-069-8(5)*, Tokyopop Kids) TOKYOPOP, Inc.

Tolan, Stephanie S. Wishworks, Inc. Bates, Amy June, illus. 2011. (ENG.). 160p. (J). (gr. 2-5). pap. 5.99 *(978-0-545-03155-4(9)*, Levine, Arthur A. Bks.) Scholastic, Inc.

Toliver, Wendy. Lifted. 2010. (ENG.). 352p. (YA). (gr. 9-18). pap. 9.99 *(978-1-4169-9048-2(8)*, Simon Pulse) Simon Pulse.

—Miss Match. 2009. (Romantic Comedies Ser.). (ENG.). 304p. (YA). (gr. 7-18). mass mkt. 6.99 *(978-1-4169-6413-1(4)*, Simon Pulse) Simon Pulse.

—The Secret Life of a Teenage Siren. 2012. (Romantic Comedies Ser.). (ENG.). 304p. (YA). (gr. 7). pap. 14.99 *(978-1-4424-7494-9(7)*, Simon Pulse) Simon Pulse.

Tolman, Marije & Tolman, Ronald. The Island. 2012. (ENG., Illus.). 32p. (J). (gr. -1). 17.95 *(978-1-935954-19-4(9)*, 9781935954194) Lemniscaat USA.

Tolson, Aaron J. Washington Putter. 2005. 248p. (YA). per. 22.00 *(978-1-58982-243-6(9)*, Bedside Bks.) American Bk. Publishing Group.

Tom, Kelley. Missing the Moon. 2013. 52p. pap. 10.00 *(978-1-4797-8104-1(5))* Xlibris Corp.

Tom Sawyer: 6 Small Books. (gr. k-2). 23.00 *(978-0-7635-8507-5(6))* Rigby Education.

Tomkins, Jasper, illus. Nimby: An Extraordinary Cloud Who Meets a Remarkable Friend. 2011. (ENG.). 60p. 15.95 *(978-1-59583-428-7(1)*, 9781595834287, Green Tiger Pr.) Laughing Elephant.

Tommy. Bubba & Cecil. 2009. 52p. pap. 16.95 *(978-1-60836-860-0(2))* America Star Bks.

Tomonari, Itsuko. The Adventures of Meow Meow & Friends. 2003. (Illus.). 82p. per. 15.95 *(978-1-59405-012-1(0))* New Age World Publishing.

Toms, Kate. Funny Faces Cloth Book Jogger Dog. 2006. (Funny Faces (Make Believe Ideas) Ser.). (Illus.). 4p. (gr. -1). *(978-1-84610-289-9(8))* Make Believe Ideas.

—Funny Faces Moo-Riel Cow. 2006. (Funny Faces (Make Believe Ideas) Ser.). (Illus.). 4p. (gr. -1). *(978-1-84610-288-2(X))* Make Believe Ideas.

Tong, Reia D. The Lonely Gourmet: Juan the Vegetarian Wolf. 2010. 44p. pap. 16.99 *(978-1-4490-9466-9(X))* AuthorHouse.

Tony Hawk's 900 Revolution. 2013. (Tony Hawk's 900 Revolution Ser.). (ENG.). 128p. (gr. 3-4). 319.80 *(978-1-4342-4110-8(6)*, Tony Hawk's 900 Revolution) Stone Arch Bks.

Top Secret Tiaras. 2009. (Princess Protection Program Ser.: No. 3). (ENG.). 144p. (gr. 3-7). pap. 4.99 *(978-1-4231-2392-7(1))* Disney Pr.

Top That Publishing Staff, ed. One Little Penguin & His Friends: A Pushing, Turning, Counting Book. Gévry, Claudine, illus. 2007. 10p. (J). (gr. -1-3). bds. *(978-1-84666-268-3(0)*, Tide Mill Pr.) Top That! Publishing PLC.

Toral, Miguel A. Babu Goes Back to the Zoo. 2009. 32p. pap. 15.70 *(978-1-4389-6330-3(0))* AuthorHouse.

Toreeva, Natalia G. Greg & the Sea Monster. 2011. 34p. pap. 14.50 *(978-1-61204-332-6(1)*, Eloquent Bks.) Strategic Book Publishing & Rights Agency (SBPRA).

Torgrimsen, Reidun. Timmy's Christmas, a Very Special Pig from Sugar Valley & His Best Friend. 2012. 30p. 24.95 *(978-1-62709-149-7(1))* America Star Bks.

Torres, Daniel. Tom Tu Gran Amigo: Juega al Fútbol, Vol. 5. 2005. (SPA., Illus.). 32p. 17.95 *(978-1-59497-120-4(X))* Public Square Bks.

—Tom Tu Gran Amigo en Paris, Vol. 4. 2005. (Tom Ser.). (SPA., Illus.). 32p. (J). (gr. -1-4). 19.95 *(978-1-59497-119-8(6))* Public Square Bks.

Torres, Jennifer. The Battle. 2014. (Briny Deep Mysteries Ser.: Bk. 3). (Illus.). 96p. (J). (gr. 4-9). 17.95 *(978-1-62285-186-7(2))*; pap. 10.95 *(978-1-62285-187-4(0))* Enslow Pubs., Inc.

—The Disappearing. 2014. (Briny Deep Mysteries Ser.). (Illus.). 96p. (J). (gr. 4-9). 17.95 *(978-1-62285-172-0(2))*; pap. 10.95 *(978-1-62285-173-7(0))* Enslow Pubs., Inc.

—The Return. 2014. (Briny Deep Mysteries Ser.: Bk. 2). (Illus.). 96p. (J). (gr. 4-9). 17.95 *(978-1-62285-181-2(1))*; pap. 10.95 *(978-1-62285-182-9(X))* Enslow Pubs., Inc.

—Stef Soto, Taco Queen. 2017. (ENG.). 176p. (J). (gr. 3-7). 16.99 *(978-0-316-30686-7(X))* Little Brown & Co.

Torrey, Richard. Ally-Saurus & the Very Bossy Monster. 2017. (Ally-Saurus Ser.). (ENG., Illus.). 40p. (J). (gr. -1-1). 16.95 ***(978-1-4549-2123-3(4))*** Sterling Publishing Co., Inc.

Toten, Teresa. Beware That Girl. 2016. (ENG.). 336p. (YA). (gr. 9). 17.99 *(978-0-553-50790-4(7)*, Delacorte Pr.) Random Hse. Children's Bks.

Tougas, Shelley. Finders Keepers. 2015. (ENG.). 288p. (J). (gr. 3-7). 16.99 *(978-1-59643-990-0(4)*, 9781596439900) Roaring Brook Pr.

Toulon, Juliette Bellot. An Amazing Friendship. 2011. 24p. pap. 12.77 *(978-1-4634-0330-0(5))* AuthorHouse.

Towle, Barbara E. How Timbo & Trevor Got Together. Spellman, Susan, illus. 2007. (ENG.). 38p. (J). (gr. -1-3). 19.95 *(978-1-933002-21-7(2))* PublishingWorks.

Towler, Grayson. The Dragon Waking. (ENG.). 288p. (J). (gr. 3-7). 2017. pap. 9.99 ***(978-0-8075-1706-2(2))*** 2016. 14.99 *(978-0-8075-1704-8(6))* Whitman, Albert & Co.

Town, Florida Ann. With a Silent Companion. 2003. (ENG.). 160p. (J). (gr. 9-18). pap. 4.95 *(978-0-88995-211-9(6))* Red Deer Pr. CAN. Dist: Ingram Publisher Services.

Toybox Innovations Staff & Toybox Innovations, creators. Disney Read along Little Mermaid Collection, 3 vols. 2009. (ENG., Illus.). (J). (gr. -1-1). *(978-0-7634-1202-9(3))* Walt Disney Records.

Toynton, Ian. Hooligan Bear Home. Dietrich, Andrea, illus. 2012. 32p. (J). 15.95 *(978-1-60131-108-5(7))* Big Tent Bks.

—Hooligan Bear New Friends. Dietrich, Andrea, illus. 2012. 34p. (J). 15.95 *(978-1-60131-107-8(9))* Big Tent Bks.

Toz, Karen Pokras. Millicent Marie Is Not My Name. 2012. (ENG.). (J). 162p. pap. 7.99 *(978-0-9848608-5-2(1))*; 2nd ed. mass mkt. 8.99 ***(978-0-9962843-4-9(6))*** Grand Daisy Pr.

Tracy, Kristen. Camille McPhee Fell under the Bus. 2010. (ENG.). 304p. (J). (gr. 3-7). 7.99 *(978-0-375-84546-8(1)*, Yearling) Random Hse. Children's Bks.

—Crimes of the Sarahs. 2008. (ENG.). 368p. (YA). (gr. 9). pap. 7.99 *(978-1-4169-5519-1(4)*, Simon Pulse) Simon Pulse.

—Hung Up. 2014. (ENG., Illus.). 288p. (YA). (gr. 9). 17.99 *(978-1-4424-6075-1(X)*, Simon Pulse) Simon Pulse.

—Project (un)Popular Book #1. (Project (un)Popular Ser.). (ENG.). 336p. (J). (gr. 5). 2017. 7.99 ***(978-0-553-51051-5(7)***, Yearling) 2016. 16.99 *(978-0-553-51048-5(7)*, Delacorte Bks. for Young Readers) Random Hse. Children's Bks.

—Project (un)Popular Book #2: Totally Crushed. 2017. (Project (un)Popular Ser.: 2). (ENG.). 224p. (J). (gr. 5). 16.99 ***(978-0-553-51052-2(5)***, Delacorte Bks. for Young Readers) Random Hse. Children's Bks.

—The Reinvention of Bessica Lefter. 2012. (ENG.). 320p. (J). (gr. 5). 7.99 *(978-0-375-84547-5(X)*, Yearling) Random Hse. Children's Bks.

—Too Cool for This School. 2015. (ENG.). 288p. (J). (gr. 5). 6.99 *(978-0-375-87296-9(5)*, Yearling) Random Hse. Children's Bks.

Tracy, Kristen. Totally Crushed. 2017. 211p. (J). ***(978-0-553-51053-9(3)***, Delacorte Pr) Random House Publishing Group.

Tran, Tommy. Forever & a Day. 2010. 124p. 20.95 *(978-1-4502-5125-9(0))*; pap. 10.95 *(978-1-4502-5124-2(2))* iUniverse, Inc.

Trantham, Cary Gordon. The Saving of Sophi: El Rescate de Sofia. 2012. 28p. pap. 19.99 *(978-1-4772-0799-4(6))* AuthorHouse.

Trapani, Iza. Gabe & Goon. Trapani, Iza, illus. 2016. (ENG., Illus.). 32p. (J). (gr. -1-1). lib. bdg. 16.95 *(978-1-58089-640-5(5))* Charlesbridge Publishing, Inc.

Trasi, Amita. The Color of Our Sky. 2017. 416p. pap. 15.99 *(978-0-06-247407-0(3)*, William Morrow Paperbacks) HarperCollins Pubs.

Trasler, Janee. Mimi & Bear Make a Friend. Trasler, Janee, illus. 2017. (Mimi & Bear Ser.). (ENG., Illus.). 32p. (J). 16.99 *(978-0-374-30360-0(6)*, 9780374303600, Farrar, Straus & Giroux (BYR)) Farrar, Straus & Giroux.

Trayer, Edward H. Struggles of Felicity Brady: Articulus Quest. 2005. (YA). per. 14.95 *(978-1-59571-091-8(4))* Word Association Pubs.

Treacy, Ann. The Search for the Homestead Treasure: A Mystery. 2016. (ENG., Illus.). 160p. 16.95 *(978-0-8166-9956-8(9))* Univ. of Minnesota Pr.

Treadway, Clifton. Benny & Bugsy. 2013. 36p. pap. 15.95 *(978-1-4624-0492-6(8)*, Inspiring Voices) Author Solutions, Inc.

Tregay, Sarah. Fan Art. DeJesus, Melissa, illus. 2014. (ENG.). 368p. (YA). (gr. 8). 17.99 *(978-0-06-224315-7(2)*, Tegen, Katherine Bks) HarperCollins Pubs.

Trembath, Don. Emville Confidential, 1 vol. 2007. (ENG.). 198p. (J). (gr. 4-8). per. 7.95 *(978-1-55143-671-5(X))* Orca Bk. Pubs. USA.

Tremblay, Alain Ulysse. Jeanne la Terrienne. Malepart, Celine, tr. 2003. (Roman Jeunesse Ser.). (FRE., Illus.). 96p. (J). (gr. 4-7). pap. *(978-2-89021-631-0(4))* Diffusion du livre Mirabel (DLM).

Tremblay, Marc. Le Petit Frere du Chaperon Rouge. Fil et al, illus. 2004. (était une Fois Ser.). (FRE.). 24p. (J). (gr. -1). pap. *(978-2-89021-698-3(5))* Diffusion du livre Mirabel (DLM).

Trent, Sandy Chase. Tommy's Amazing Journey: The Cat that Could Fly. 2011. 16p. pap. 24.95 *(978-1-4626-2363-1(8))* America Star Bks.

Trest, Candace D. Zack & Tripp & the Indian Village. 2007. 64p. per. 9.99 *(978-1-60477-526-6(2))* Salem Author Services.

Trevethan, Glenn A. The Adventures of Sammi Snake: Sammi's Coat. 2012. 24p. pap. 13.97 *(978-1-61897-926-1(4)*, Strategic Bk. Publishing) Strategic Book Publishing & Rights Agency (SBPRA).

Triana, Gaby. The Temptress Four. 2008. 247p. (YA). (gr. 7). lib. bdg. 17.89 *(978-0-06-088568-7(8)*, HarperTeen) HarperCollins Pubs.

Trilling, Richard J. More Stories of Stephanie & Friends: Volume 2 in the Stephanie Stories. 2011. 64p. pap. 19.50 *(978-1-61204-034-9(9)*, Eloquent Bks.) Strategic Book Publishing & Rights Agency (SBPRA).

—Still More Stories of Stephanie & Friends: Volume 3 in the Stephanie Series. 2011. 72p. pap. 21.00 *(978-1-61204-546-7(4)*, Strategic Bk. Publishing) Strategic Book Publishing & Rights Agency (SBPRA).

—Stories of Stephanie & Friends. 2010. 42p. pap. 15.50 *(978-1-60860-410-4(1)*, Eloquent Bks.) Strategic Book Publishing & Rights Agency (SBPRA).

Tripp, Valerie. Kit's Surprise. Rane, Walter & McAliley, Susan, illus. 2004. (American Girls Collection: Bk. 3). (ENG.). 71p. (gr. 2-18). 12.95 *(978-1-58485-021-2(3))* American Girl Publishing, Inc.

Trivette, Donna K. A Friend for Ringo & Girl. 2011. 24p. pap. 24.95 *(978-1-4626-1373-1(X))* America Star Bks.

—Ringo & Girl. 2011. 40p. pap. 24.95 *(978-1-4626-1369-4(1))* America Star Bks.

Tromly, Stephanie. Trouble Makes a Comeback. (ENG.). (YA). (gr. 7). 2017. 320p. pap. 10.99 ***(978-0-14-751544-5(0)***, Speak) 2016. 304p. 17.99 *(978-0-525-42841-1(0)*, Kathy Dawson Books) Penguin Young Readers Group.

Trottier, Maxine. Three Songs for Courage. 2008. (ENG.). 328p. (YA). (gr. 9). pap. 10.95 *(978-0-88776-831-6(8)*, Tundra Bks.) Tundra Bks. CAN. Dist: Penguin Random Hse. LLC.

Troupe, Thomas Kingsley. The Big Hairy Secret, 1 vol. Gilpin, Stephen, illus. 2013. (Furry & Flo Ser.). (ENG.). 128p. (gr. 2-3). 8.95 *(978-1-62370-033-1(7))*; lib. bdg. 25.32 *(978-1-4342-3858-0(X))* Stone Arch Bks.

—Blizzard: a Tale of Snow-Blind Survival. Fagan, Kirbi, illus. 2016. (Survive! Ser.). (ENG.). 56p. (gr. 4-6). lib. bdg. 25.32 *(978-1-4965-2554-3(X))* Stone Arch Bks.

—Darling Doll. Faber, Rudy, illus. 2016. (Hauntiques Ser.). (ENG.). 128p. (gr. 4-6). lib. bdg. 25.32 *(978-1-4965-3548-1(0))* Stone Arch Bks.

—Ghostly Goalie. Faber, Rudy, illus. 2016. (Hauntiques Ser.). (ENG.). 128p. (gr. 4-6). lib. bdg. 25.32 *(978-1-4965-3544-3(8))* Stone Arch Bks.

—The Misplaced Mummy, 1 vol. Gilpin, Stephen, illus. 2014. (Furry & Flo Ser.). (ENG.). 128p. (gr. 2-3). 25.32 *(978-1-4342-6396-4(7))* Stone Arch Bks.

—Phantom's Favorite. Faber, Rudy, illus. 2016. (Hauntiques Ser.). (ENG.). 128p. (gr. 4-6). lib. bdg. 25.32 *(978-1-4965-3546-7(4))* Stone Arch Bks.

—The Problems with Goblins, 1 vol. Gilpin, Stephen, illus. 2013. (Furry & Flo Ser.). (ENG.). 128p. (gr. 2-3). 8.95 *(978-1-62370-034-8(5))*; lib. bdg. 25.32 *(978-1-4342-5042-1(3))* Stone Arch Bks.

—The Skeletons in City Park, 1 vol. Gilpin, Stephen, illus. 2014. (Furry & Flo Ser.). (ENG.). 128p. (gr. 2-3). 25.32 *(978-1-4342-6397-1(5))* Stone Arch Bks.

—The Solemn Golem. Gilpin, Stephen, illus. 2015. (Furry & Flo Ser.). (ENG.). 128p. (gr. 2-3). lib. bdg. 25.32 *(978-1-4342-9646-7(6))* Stone Arch Bks.

—The Voiceless Vampire. Gilpin, Stephen, illus. 2015. (Furry & Flo Ser.). (ENG.). 128p. (gr. 2-3). lib. bdg. 25.32 *(978-1-4342-9645-0(8))* Stone Arch Bks.

—Wandering Wagon. Faber, Rudy, illus. 2016. (Hauntiques Ser.). (ENG.). 128p. (gr. 4-6). lib. bdg. 25.32 *(978-1-4965-3547-4(2))* Stone Arch Bks.

Troutt, Susan. Not As It Seems. 2012. 196p. (gr. 4-6). pap. 16.95 *(978-1-4685-8373-1(5))* AuthorHouse.

Trover, Zachary. The Spring Chicken! 2013. (Step into Reading Level 2 Ser.). lib. bdg. 13.55 *(978-0-606-26979-7(7)*, Turtleback) Turtleback Bks.

Trudel, Sylvain & Langlois, Suzane. Pourquoi le Monde Est Comme il Est? 2004. (Premier Roman Ser.). (FRE., Illus.). 64p. (J). (gr. 1-4). pap. *(978-2-89021-587-0(3))* Diffusion du livre Mirabel (DLM).

Trueit, Trudi. Scab for Treasurer? Paillot, Jim, illus. 2011. (Secrets of a Lab Rat Ser.). (ENG.). 160p. (J). (gr. 3-7). pap. 5.99 *(978-1-4169-6113-0(5)*, Aladdin) Simon & Schuster Children's Publishing.

—Scab for Treasurer? Paillot, Jim, illus. 2011. (Secrets of a Lab Rat Ser.). (ENG.). 160p. (J). (gr. 3-7). 15.99 *(978-1-4169-7594-6(2)*, Simon & Schuster/Paula Wiseman Bks.) Simon & Schuster/Paula Wiseman Bks.

Trusler, Heidi Jo. Firecracker the Miniature Donkey: Makes A Marvelous Choice! 2009. 25p. (J). pap. 13.95 *(978-1-4327-4153-2(5))* Outskirts Pr., Inc.

Tsahiridis, Van. Peree' & the Magic Fish: Fairy Tale from Pontos. 2010. 64p. pap. 10.16 *(978-1-4269-2335-7(X))* Trafford Publishing.

Tuchman, Lauryn & Silverhardt, Lauryn. A Visit to the Firehouse. Craig, Karen, illus. 2009. (Blue's Clues Ser.). (ENG.). 24p. (J). (gr. -1-2). pap. 3.99 *(978-1-4169-7193-1(9)*, Simon Spotlight/Nickelodeon) Simon Spotlight/Nickelodeon.

Tucker, David J. Stickman World. 2005. 36p. (J). pap. 8.40 *(978-1-4116-4275-1(9))* Lulu Pr., Inc.

Tucker, Sally A. Leo & Apollo: The Forbidden Land. 2012. 28p. pap. 15.00 *(978-1-105-60121-7(8))* Lulu Pr., Inc.

Tuey, Doug E Do. Martin, Susan, illus. 2006. 76p. pap. 16.95 *(978-1-4241-0295-2(2))* PublishAmerica, Inc.

Tukel, Onur. Little Friends, 0 vols. 2012. (ENG.). 64p. (J). (gr. 1-4). 14.99 *(978-0-7614-6260-6(0)*, 9780761462606, Amazon Children's Publishing) Amazon Publishing.

Tullson, Diane. Riot Act, 1 vol. 2012. (Orca Soundings Ser.). (ENG.). 128p. (YA). (gr. 8-12). 16.95 *(978-1-4598-0140-0(7))*; pap. 9.95 *(978-1-4598-0139-4(3))* Orca Bk. Pubs. USA.

—Zero. 2006. (ENG.). 185p. (J). (gr. 7-18). per. *(978-1-55041-950-4(1))* Fitzhenry & Whiteside, Ltd.

Tuorto, Diana. Janie's New Legs. 2008. (ENG.). 48p. pap. 11.99 *(978-1-4196-9142-3(2))* CreateSpace Independent Publishing Platform.

Tupera, Tupera. Polar Bear's Underwear. 2015. (ENG., Illus.). 32p. (J). (gr. -1-k). 16.99 *(978-1-4521-4199-2(1))* Chronicle Bks. LLC.

Turk, Cheri. The Stone Between Kings. Turk, Cheri, illus. 2012. (Illus.). 36p. pap. 12.99 *(978-0-9860024-0-3(2))* Specialty Greetings.

Turnbull, Ann. Deep Water. 3rd ed. 2013. 102p. pap. *(978-1-78132-160-7(4))* SilverWood Bks.

Turnbull, Elizabeth J. Janjak & Freda Go to the Iron Market. Turnbull, Wally R., tr. Jones, Mark, illus. 2013. 36p. pap. 12.95 *(978-1-61153-062-9(8))* Light Messages Publishing.

Turnbull, Kathie. Because Everyone Needs a Friend. 2009. 20p. pap. 12.50 *(978-1-60693-372-5(8)*, Eloquent Bks.) Strategic Book Publishing & Rights Agency (SBPRA).

Turnbull, Samantha. Cruise Control: The Anti-Princess Club 5. Davis, Sarah, illus. 2017. (Anti-Princess Club Ser.: 5). (ENG.). 192p. (J). (gr. 2-4). pap. 9.99 ***(978-1-76029-188-4(9))*** Allen & Unwin AUS. Dist: Independent Pubs. Group.

Turnbull, Victoria. The Sea Tiger. Turnbull, Victoria, illus. 2015. (ENG., Illus.). 40p. (J). (gr. -1-2). 16.99 *(978-0-7636-7986-6(0)*, Templar) Candlewick Pr.

Turner, Max. End of Days. 2010. (Night Runner Novels Ser.: 2). (ENG.). 304p. (YA). (gr. 8-12). pap. 20.99 *(978-0-312-59252-3(3)*, 9780312592523, St. Martin's Griffin) St. Martin's Pr.

Turner, Taquila Lanina. New Friends. 2011. 32p. pap. 21.99 *(978-1-4568-5670-0(7))* Xlibris Corp.

Tuvu. Tiny & Flat: Two Bestfriends. 2012. 32p. pap. 17.25 *(978-1-4669-3651-5(7))* Trafford Publishing.

Tuzee, John, creator. What A Grape Can Be. 2007. (Illus.). 32p. (J). 9.95 *(978-0-9755348-3-0(1))* Kids Life Pr.

Twain, Mark, pseud. The Adventures of Huckleberry Finn. Andreasen, Dan, illus. 2006. (Classic Starts(tm) Ser.). (ENG.). 160p. (J). (gr. 2-4). 6.95 *(978-1-4027-2499-2(3))* Sterling Publishing Co., Inc.

—Adventures of Huckleberry Finn. Powell, Eric, illus. 2012. (ENG.). 276p. 19.99 *(978-1-61377-086-3(3)*, 9781613770863) Idea & Design Works, LLC.

—The Adventures of Huckleberry Finn. Andreasen, Dan, illus. 2010. (Classic Starts(tm) Ser.). (ENG.). 160p. (J). (gr. 2-4). cd-rom 9.95 *(978-1-4027-7355-6(2))* Sterling Publishing Co., Inc.

—The Adventures of Huckleberry Finn: With a Discussion of Friendship. Lauter, Richard, tr. Lauter, Richard, illus. 2003. (Values in Action Illustrated Classics Ser.). (J). *(978-1-59203-042-2(4))* Learning Challenge, Inc.

—Las Aventuras de Huckleberry Finn. de Atauri, Ines & de Atauri, Juan Diaz, eds. 2006. (Clasicos Juveniles Ser.).Tr. of Adventures of Huckleberry Finn. (SPA., Illus.). 359p. pap. 17.95 *(978-84-263-5252-1(9))* Vives, Luis Editorial (Edelvives) ESP. Dist: Lectorum Pubns., Inc.

—Tom Sawyer. 2006. (Classic Retelling Ser.). (Illus.). 224p. (YA). (gr. 8-12). *(978-0-618-12053-6(X)*, 2-00218) Holt McDougal.

Twin Sister Produtions. Sesame Street What Did Elmo Say? 2008. (ENG.). 20p. (J). (gr. -1-3). 9.99 *(978-1-59069-657-6(3))* Studio Mouse LLC.

Twin Sister Produtions & Shepherd, Jodie. Sesame Street Rosita & the Beanstalk. 2010. (J). (gr. k-2). 14.99 *(978-1-59922-634-7(0))* Twin Sisters IP, LLC.

Twin Sister Produtions Staff & Shepherd, Jodie. Sesame Street Rosita & the Beanstalk. 2010. (J). (gr. k-2). 14.99 *(978-1-59922-525-8(5))* Twin Sisters IP, LLC.

Twitty, Mary F. Ashley Visits Urchin Village. 2008. 92p. pap. 51.99 *(978-1-4363-5578-0(8))* Xlibris Corp.

Two Sisters Circle. The Lady of the Lane. 2013. 116p. pap. 19.95 *(978-1-63004-330-8(3))* America Star Bks.

Twohy, Mike. Mouse & Hippo. Twohy, Mike, illus. 2017. (ENG., Illus.). 32p. (J). (gr. -1-3). 17.99 *(978-1-4814-5124-6(3)*, Simon & Schuster/Paula Wiseman Bks.) Simon & Schuster/Paula Wiseman Bks.

—Poindexter Makes a Friend. Twohy, Mike, illus. 2011. (ENG., Illus.). 32p. (J). (gr. -1-3). 15.99 *(978-1-4424-0965-1(7)*, Simon & Schuster/Paula Wiseman Bks.) Simon & Schuster/Paula Wiseman Bks.

Tym, Kate. Say Please. 2008. (Manners Ser.). (Illus.). 24p. (J). (gr. -1-1). lib. bdg. 16.95 *(978-1-59566-589-8(7))* QEB Publishing Inc.

Tyree, Omar R. 12 Brown Boys. 2008. 196p. (J). (gr. 3-7). pap. 9.95 *(978-1-933491-12-7(4))* Just Us Bks., Inc.

Tzvi, G. J. The Great Adventure of la Gang du Sept. 2008. 177p. pap. 14.95 *(978-1-4116-8291-7(2))* Lulu Pr., Inc.

U. S. National Geographic Society Staff. The Great Cheese Chase. 2008. (Toot & Puddle Ser.). (ENG., Illus.). 24p. (J). (gr. -1-2). lib. bdg. 11.90 *(978-1-4263-0371-5(8)*, National Geographic Children's Bks.) National Geographic Society.

Uglow, Loma. The Fairy in the Potting Shed. 2008. (Illus.). 100p. pap. 28.99 *(978-1-4389-0858-8(X))* AuthorHouse.

Ulerio, Michelle. Lily Finds Her Way Home. 2013. 24p. pap. 24.95 *(978-1-63000-956-4(3))* America Star Bks.

Ullrich, Hortense. La Prueba de Valor de Lorenzo. (SPA.). (J). 7.95 *(978-958-04-7069-4(3))* Norma S.A. COL. Dist: Distribuidora Norma, Inc.

Ulrich, Ann Carol. The Mystery at Hickory Hill: Annette Vetter Adventure #1. 2006. (Illus.). 196p. (YA). per. 9.95 *(978-0-944851-25-8(8))* Earth Star Pubns.

Umansky, Kaye. Solomon Snow & the Silver Spoon. Nash, Scott, illus. 2007. (ENG.). 304p. (J). (gr. 2-5). 12.99 *(978-0-7636-3218-2(X))* Candlewick Pr.

Umina, Lisa. Milo Finds His Best Friend. Thompson, Chad, illus. 2013. 30p. 15.95 *(978-1-61244-182-5(3))* Halo Publishing International.

Uncle Henry. The Vileburgers: With Friends Like This Who Needs Halloween? Uncle Henry, illus. 100th ed. 2004. (Illus.). 88p. pap. 6.99 *(978-1-932568-01-1(8)*, UHB002) Uncle Henry Bks.

Unger-Pengilly, Elaine. Rat. Trockstad, Marcy, illus. 2013. 120p. *(978-1-4602-2262-1(8))* FriesenPress.

Ungerer, Tomi. The Beast of Monsieur Racine. 2014. (ENG., Illus.). 32p. (gr. -1-3). 16.95 *(978-0-7148-6081-7(6))* Phaidon Pr., Inc.

Ungermann Marshall, Yana. Gilda Gets Wise. Ungermann Marshall, Yana, illus. 2008. (Illus.). 34p. (J). pap. *(978-0-9670982-6-5(2))* Yana's Kitchen.

Ungureanu, Dan. Nara & the Island. Ungureanu, Dan, illus. 2016. (ENG., Illus.). 32p. (J). (gr. -1-3). 17.99 *(978-1-5124-1793-7(9))* Andersen Pr. GBR. Dist: Lerner Publishing Group.

—Nara & the Island. Ungureanu, Dan, illus. 2016. (ENG., Illus.). 32p. (gr. -1-3). 35.99 *(978-1-5124-1794-4(7))* Lerner Publishing Group.

Ünlükoç, Müge. Real Race. 2013. 32p. pap. 17.99 *(978-1-105-98879-0(1))* Lulu Pr., Inc.

Unrau, Adela. A Big Change, 1 vol. Friesen, Anni, illus. 2010. 16p. pap. 24.95 *(978-1-4489-7672-0(3))* PublishAmerica, Inc.

Upperman, Katy. Kissing Max Holden. Brzozowski, Kat, ed. 2017. (ENG.). 304p. (YA). 17.99 *(978-1-250-11116-6(1)*, 9781250111166) Feiwel & Friends.

Upton, Robert Jesten. Milo & the Dragon Cross: A Novel. 2017. (YA). pap. ***(978-1-63293-177-1(X))*** Sunstone Pr.

Urbach, Jourdan. Leaving Jeremiah. 2003. (Illus.). 108p. (J). 19.95 *(978-1-930648-57-9(X)*, 207-832-6665); per. 10.95 *(978-1-930648-50-0(2)*, 207-832-6665) Goose River Pr.

Urban, Linda. The Center of Everything. (ENG.). 208p. (J). (gr. 5-7). 2015. pap. 7.99 *(978-0-544-34069-5(8)*, HMH Books For Young Readers) 2013. 15.99 *(978-0-547-76348-4(4))* Houghton Mifflin Harcourt Publishing Co.

E F G

Urbanovic, Jackie. Duck Soup. Urbanovic, Jackie, illus. 2008. (Max the Duck Ser.: 2). (Illus.). 32p. (J). (gr. -1-2). (ENG.). 17.99 *(978-0-06-121441-7(8))*; lib. bdg. 18.89 *(978-0-06-121442-4(6))* HarperCollins Pubs.
Ure, Jean. Fortune Cookie. 2009. (ENG.). 192p. (J). (gr. 4-7). pap. 9.95 *(978-0-00-722462-3(1)*, HarperCollins Children's Bks.) HarperCollins Pubs. Ltd. GBR. Dist: HarperCollins Pubs.
—The Friends Forever Collection. 2007. (Diary Ser.). (ENG., Illus.). 608p. (J). (gr. 4-7). pap. 19.95 *(978-0-00-724820-9(2))* HarperCollins Pubs. Ltd. GBR. Dist: Independent Pubs. Group.
—Hunky Dory. 2011. (ENG., Illus.). 192p. (J). pap. 7.99 *(978-0-00-722460-9(5)*, HarperCollins Children's Bks.) HarperCollins Pubs. Ltd. GBR. Dist: HarperCollins Pubs.
Uribe, Denise. My Best Friend Sarah. 2013. 24p. pap. 14.93 *(978-1-4669-4902-7(3))* Trafford Publishing.
Ursu, Anne. Breadcrumbs. McGuire, Erin, illus. (ENG.). (J). (gr. 3-7). 2013. 336p. pap. 6.99 *(978-0-06-201506-8(0))* 2011. 320p. 16.99 *(978-0-06-201505-1(2))* HarperCollins Pubs. (Waldon Pond Pr.).
—Breadcrumbs. McGuire, Erin, illus. 2012. 320p. 55.00 *(978-0-449-01400-4(2))* Random Hse., Inc.
—Breadcrumbs. 2013. (J). lib. bdg. 17.20 *(978-0-606-27130-1(9)*, Turtleback) Turtleback Bks.
—The Real Boy. McGuire, Erin, illus. 2013. (ENG.). 352p. (J). (gr. 3-7). 16.99 *(978-0-06-201507-5(9)*, Waldon Pond Pr.) HarperCollins Pubs.
Usera, Abe. The Pigs & Friends. 2012. 52p. pap. 21.99 *(978-1-4685-6152-4(9))* AuthorHouse.
Vadney, Jackie. Pokey's Promise: A Charming Tale of Telling Time. Balogh, Jared, illus. 2011. 28p. pap. 24.95 *(978-1-4560-2850-3(2))* America Star Bks.
Vagner, Bohdanka. Bullying, Change, Friendship & Trust. Montgomerie, Genevieve, illus. 2013. 106p. pap. *(978-1-921863-51-4(0)*, MBS Pr.) Pick-a-Woo Woo Pubs.
Vail, Rachel. Flabbersmashed about You. Heo, Yumi, illus. 2012. (ENG.). 32p. (J). (gr. -1-3). 16.99 *(978-0-312-61345-7(8)*, 9780312613457) Feiwel & Friends.
—If You Only Knew. 2014. (Friendship Ring Ser.: 1). (ENG.). 176p. (J). (gr. 5). pap. 7.99 *(978-0-14-751118-8(6)*, Puffin Books) Penguin Young Readers Group.
—Lucky. 2009. (Avery Sisters Trilogy Ser.: 1). (ENG.). 256p. (YA). (gr. 8). pap. 8.99 *(978-0-06-089045-2(2))* HarperCollins Pubs.
—Not That I Care. 2014. (Friendship Ring Ser.: 3). (ENG.). 176p. (J). (gr. 5). pap. 7.99 *(978-0-14-751120-1(8)*, Puffin Books) Penguin Young Readers Group.
—Please, Please, Please. 2014. (Friendship Ring Ser.: 2). (ENG.). 176p. (J). (gr. 5). pap. 7.99 *(978-0-14-751119-5(4)*, Puffin Books) Penguin Young Readers Group.
—School, Drool, & Other Daily Disasters. Cordell, Matthew, illus. 2011. (Justin Case Ser.: 1). (ENG.). 272p. (J). (gr. 2-4). pap. 7.99 *(978-0-312-56357-8(4)*, 9780312563578) Square Fish.
—Unfriended. (ENG.). (J). (gr. 5). 2015. 304p. 8.99 *(978-0-14-751154-6(2)*, Puffin Books) 2014. 288p. 16.99 *(978-0-670-01307-4(2)*, Viking Books for Young Readers) Penguin Young Readers Group.
—Well, That Was Awkward. 2017. (ENG.). 320p. (J). (gr. 5). 16.99 *(978-0-670-01308-1(0)*, Viking Books for Young Readers) Penguin Young Readers Group.
—What Are Friends For? 2014. (Friendship Ring Ser.: 4). (ENG.). 176p. (J). (gr. 5). pap. 7.99 *(978-0-14-751121-8(6)*, Puffin Books) Penguin Young Readers Group.
Valente, Catherynne M. The Girl Who Soared over Fairyland & Cut the Moon in Two. Juan, Ana, illus. 2013. (Fairyland Ser.: 3). (ENG.). 256p. (YA). (gr. 5-9). 16.99 *(978-1-250-02350-6(5)*, 9781250023506) Feiwel & Friends.
Valentine, Billy. Trust Love: A Tale of Angels. 2008. 176p. (J). 23.95 *(978-0-595-48801-8(3))*; pap. 13.95 *(978-0-595-44989-7(1))* iUniverse, Inc.
Valentine, Victoria. The Cutest Little Duckie. Tucker, Amanda, illus. 2007. 80p. (J). per. 15.00 *(978-0-9723493-4-5(0)*, Water Forest Pr.) Skyline Pubn.
Valentino, Amanda & Stolarz, Laurie Faria. Shattered, Bk. 3. 2011. (Amanda Project Ser.: 3). (ENG.). 272p. (YA). (gr. 8). pap. 8.99 *(978-0-06-174217-0(1)*, HarperTeen) HarperCollins Pubs.
Valko, Danna. Dee & Maya Are Best Friends. 2013. (Illus.). *(978-1-62510-726-8(9))*; *(978-1-62563-112-1(X))* Tate Publishing, Ltd.
Van Ark, Katie. The Boy Next Door. 2015. (ENG.). 368p. (YA). (gr. 7). pap. 9.99 *(978-1-250-06146-1(6))* Feiwel & Friends.
van de Vendel, Edward & van der Linden, Martijn. For You & No One Else. 2009. (ENG.). 32p. (J). (gr. -1-2). 16.95 *(978-1-59078-658-1(0)*, Lemniscaat) Boyds Mills Pr.
van Diepen, Allison. Raven. 2010. (ENG.). 304p. (YA). (gr. 9). pap. 8.99 *(978-1-4169-7468-0(7)*, Simon Pulse) Simon Pulse.
—Run the Risk. 2017. 288p. (YA). (gr. 9). 17.99 *(978-0-06-243335-0(0)*, HarperTeen) HarperCollins Pubs.
—The Vampire Stalker. 2011. (ENG.). 272p. (J). (gr. 7-7). 17.99 *(978-0-545-28375-5(2))* Scholastic, Inc.
Van Draanen, Wendelin. Confessions of a Serial Kisser. 2009. (ENG.). 304p. (YA). (gr. 7-18). pap. 9.99 *(978-0-375-84249-8(7)*, Ember) Random Hse. Children's Bks.
—Meet the Gecko. Biggs, Brian, illus. 2006. (Shredderman Ser.: Bk. 3). (ENG.). 176p. (J). (gr. 1-4). 5.99 *(978-0-440-41914-3(X)*, Yearling) Random Hse. Children's Bks.
—Sammy Keyes & the Killer Cruise. (Sammy Keyes Ser.). (ENG.). (J). (gr. 5). 2014. 352p. 7.99 *(978-0-307-93062-0(9)*, Yearling) 2013. 336p. 16.99 *(978-0-375-87054-5(7)*, Knopf Bks. for Young Readers) Random Hse. Children's Bks.
—Sammy Keyes & the Kiss Goodbye. 2014. 236p. (J). pap. *(978-0-307-93063-7(7))* Knopf, Alfred A. Inc.
—Sammy Keyes & the Kiss Goodbye. 2014. (Sammy Keyes Ser.). (ENG.). 240p. (J). (gr. 5). 16.99 *(978-0-375-87055-2(5)*, Knopf Bks. for Young Readers) Random Hse. Children's Bks.
Van Durme, Leen. Mo & Mac: Socks On! Van Durme, Leen, illus. 2013. (ENG., Illus.). 16p. (J). (— 1). 9.95 *(978-1-60537-176-4(9))* Cobblestone Publishing Co.
Van Dusen, Chris. Hattie & Hudson. Van Dusen, Chris, illus. 2017. (ENG., Illus.). 40p. (J). (gr. -1-3). 16.99 *(978-0-7636-6545-6(2))* Candlewick Pr.
van Galen, Maggie. The Adventures of Keeno & Ernest: The Diamond Mine. 2013. (ENG.). 28p. (J). 19.95 *(978-1-4787-1812-3(9))* Outskirts Pr., Inc.
van Genechten, Guido. Floppy's Friends. van Genechten, Guido, illus. 2004. (ENG & POL., Illus.). 28p. (J). bds. *(978-1-84444-659-9(X))* Mantra Lingua.
—Floppy's Friends. 2004. (J). (BEN & ENG.). 16.95 *(978-1-84444-649-0(2))*; (CHI & ENG.). 16.95 *(978-1-84444-650-6(6))*; (ENG & URD.). 16.95 *(978-1-84444-665-0(4))* Mantra Lingua GBR. Dist: Chinasprout, Inc.
—Moon Is Sad. 2010. (ENG.). 12p. (J). (gr. k — 1). bds. 8.95 *(978-1-60537-048-4(7))* Clavis Publishing.
—Ricky & Annie. van Genechten, Guido, illus. 2010. (Ricky Ser.). (ENG., Illus.). 30p. (J). (gr. -1-k). 16.95 *(978-1-60537-062-0(2))* Cobblestone Publishing Co.
—Ricky's Birthday. 2012. (ENG.). 24p. (J). (gr. -1-k). 16.95 *(978-1-60537-119-1(X))* Cobblestone Publishing Co.
van Genechten, Guido & Frippiat, Stéphanie. Ricky & Mia the Chicken. 2009. (ENG.). 24p. (J). (gr. -1-k). 16.95 *(978-1-60537-027-9(4))* Cobblestone Publishing Co.
Van Hout, Mies. Friends. 2013. (ENG., Illus.). 32p. (J). (gr. -1). 17.95 *(978-1-935954-23-1(7)*, 9781935954231) Lemniscaat USA.
Van Kersen, Elizabeth. Who's Riley. 2005. (Illus.). 50p. (J). per. 8.99 *(978-1-932338-90-4(X))* Lifevest Publishing, Inc.
—Whos' Riley? Stevens, Debra, illus. l.t. ed. 2006. 23p. (J). 15.99 *(978-1-59879-173-0(7))* Lifevest Publishing, Inc.
Van Stockum, Hilda. A Day on Skates: The Story of a Dutch Picnic. Van Stockum, Hilda, illus. 2007. (Illus.). 40p. (J). (gr. 1). 19.95 *(978-1-932350-18-0(7))* Bethlehem Bks.
Van Tol, Alex. Food Freak. 2017. (Orca Currents Ser.). lib. bdg. 20.80 ***(978-0-606-40452-5(X))*** Turtleback Bks.
Van Tol, Alex. Redline, 1 vol. 2011. (Orca Soundings Ser.). (ENG.). (YA). (gr. 8-12). 136p. pap. 9.95 *(978-1-55469-893-6(6))*; 128p. lib. bdg. 16.95 *(978-1-55469-894-3(4))* Orca Bk. Pubs. USA.
Vance, Alexander. Behind the Canvas. 2016. (ENG.). 336p. (J). 16.99 *(978-1-250-02970-6(8)*, 9781250029706) Feiwel & Friends.
VanCil, Marybelle. Sadie Fourpaws & the Magic Rocking Chair. 2009. (Illus.). 57p. pap. 26.95 *(978-1-4327-3642-2(6))* Outskirts Pr., Inc.
Vandereyken, Leen. Loulou in Love. 2008. (Girls Only Ser.). (ENG.). 155p. (YA). (gr. 4-18). 16.95 *(978-1-60537-025-5(8))* Clavis Publishing.
Vanderlaan, Karen. Special Friends. 2008. 28p. pap. 24.95 *(978-1-60813-353-6(2))* America Star Bks.
VanDyck, Lilian Claudine. The Mystery Fire. 2012. 56p. pap. *(978-1-77097-382-4(6))* FriesenPress.
Vanier, Jolie. Puwaii Adventures with Joliea & Friends. 2006. 16.95 *(978-0-9787949-1-0(5))* Puwaii International, LLC.
Vaniko, K. L. Why the Dog Chases the Cat & the Cat Chases the Mouse. 2006. 189p. 30.99 *(978-1-59926-863-7(9))* Xlibris Corp.
Vanover, Rita. Yellow Head the Cockatiel. 2011. 38p. pap. 16.95 *(978-1-4626-4493-3(7))* America Star Bks.
Varacchi, Barbara. Desiree's Adventures with Her Friends. 2009. 36p. pap. 16.99 *(978-1-4389-1603-3(5))* AuthorHouse.
Varon, Sara. Robot Dreams. Varon, Sara, illus. 2007. (ENG., Illus.). 208p. (J). (gr. 3-7). pap. 17.99 *(978-1-59643-108-9(3)*, 9781596431089, First Second Bks.) Roaring Brook Pr.
—Robot Dreams. Varon, Sara, illus. 2016. (ENG., Illus.). 224p. (J). pap. 9.99 *(978-1-250-07350-1(2)*, 9781250073501) Square Fish.
Vaught, Susan. Fat Tuesday. Hamilton, Dianne, ed. 2004. 249p. (YA). pap. 8.50 *(978-0-9700752-3-9(5))* Onstage Publishing, LLC.
—Footer Davis Probably Is Crazy. Reinhardt, Jennifer Black, illus. 2015. (ENG.). 240p. (J). (gr. 5-9). 16.99 *(978-1-4814-2276-5(6)*, Simon & Schuster Bks. For Young Readers) Simon & Schuster Bks. For Young Readers.
Vaupel, Robin. My Contract with Henry. 2003. (ENG.). 192p. (J). (gr. 4-6). tchr. ed. 16.95 *(978-0-8234-1701-8(8))* Holiday Hse., Inc.
Vega, Danielle. The Merciless. 2014. (Merciless Ser.: 1). (ENG.). 288p. (YA). (gr. 9). 17.99 *(978-1-59514-722-6(5)*, Razorbill) Penguin Young Readers Group.
Vega, Danielle & Loftin, Nikki. Survive the Night. 2015. (DUT & ENG.). 272p. (YA). (gr. 9). 17.99 *(978-1-59514-724-0(1)*, Razorbill) Penguin Young Readers Group.
Veggie Tales, Veggie. VeggieTales: Bob Is a Buddy! A Story about Friends. 2015. (Googly Eyes Ser.: 1). (ENG.). 10p. (J). (gr. -1 — 1). bds. 8.99 *(978-0-7944-3465-6(7)*, Reader's Digest Children's Bks.) Studio Fun International.
Veldmeyer, Michele E. Francine's Freckles. 2011. 24p. pap. 12.79 *(978-1-4567-1572-4(0))* AuthorHouse.
Velle, Tori. Jake the Snake. 2009. 40p. pap. 16.99 *(978-1-4490-4431-2(X))* AuthorHouse.
Venable, Colleen Af. Mervin the Sloth Is about to Do the Best Thing in the World. Chan, Ruth, illus. 2016. 40p. (J). (gr. -1-3). 17.99 *(978-0-06-233847-1(1)*, Greenwillow Bks.) HarperCollins Pubs.
Venable Jr, Al B. Captain Tom, the Sea Adventurer. 2013. 40p. pap. 16.95 *(978-1-63004-037-6(1))* America Star Bks.
Vento, Anthony. Holes Are Us: A Worm's Tale about Friendship & Trust. 2009. 40p. pap. 21.99 *(978-1-4415-3446-0(6))* Xlibris Corp.
Ventura, Marne. Anxious Adam Braves the Test. Trinidad, Leo, illus. 2016. (Worry Warriors Ser.). (ENG.). 96p. (gr. 2-4). pap. 5.95 *(978-1-4965-3650-1(9))*; lib. bdg. 25.99 *(978-1-4965-3611-2(8))* Stone Arch Bks.
—Edgy Estella Aces the Sleepover Party. Trinidad, Leo, illus. 2016. (Worry Warriors Ser.). (ENG.). 96p. (gr. 2-4). lib. bdg. 25.99 *(978-1-4965-3610-5(X))* Stone Arch Bks.
—Jittery Jake Conquers Stage Fright. Trinidad, Leo, illus. 2016. (Worry Warriors Ser.). (ENG.). 96p. (gr. 2-4). lib. bdg. 25.99 *(978-1-4965-3612-9(6))* Stone Arch Bks.
Verde, Susan. You & Me. Reynolds, Peter H., illus. 2015. (ENG.). 32p. (J). (gr. k-2). 14.95 *(978-1-4197-1197-8(0)*, Abrams Bks. for Young Readers) Abrams, Inc.
Verhoosky, Michele. Molly Marie & the Amazing Jimmy. Verhoosky, Michele, illus. 2012. (Illus.). 34p. pap. 10.95 *(978-1-937260-22-4(4))* Sleepytown Pr.
Vermazen, Eve. Dogtales: Sebastian & the Destiny Stone. 2012. 36p. pap. 32.70 *(978-1-4797-4032-1(2))* Xlibris Corp.
Vermeulen, Mariska. Anton & Boris Finger Puppet Book. van de Liejgraaf, Deborah, illus. 2016. (My Best Friend & Me Ser.). (ENG.). 10p. (J). (gr. -1-k). bds., bds. 6.99 *(978-0-7641-6831-4(2))* Barron's Educational Series, Inc.
—Bella & Clara Finger Puppet Book. van de Liejgraaf, Deborah, illus. 2016. (My Best Friend & Me Ser.). (ENG.). 10p. (J). (gr. -1-k). bds. 6.99 *(978-0-7641-6829-1(0))* Barron's Educational Series, Inc.
—James & Cooper Finger Puppet Book. van de Liejgraaf, Deborah, illus. 2016. (My Best Friend & Me Ser.). (ENG.). 10p. (J). (gr. -1-k). bds. 6.99 *(978-0-7641-6830-7(4))* Barron's Educational Series, Inc.
—Kaila & Kahuna Finger Puppet Book. van de Liejgraaf, Deborah, illus. 2016. (My Best Friend & Me Ser.). (ENG.). 10p. (J). (gr. -1-k). bds. 6.99 *(978-0-7641-6832-1(0))* Barron's Educational Series, Inc.
Vermeulen, Thomas. Gabangani Guinea Fowl & Huzu the Bird Eating Spider. 2009. 50p. pap. 19.50 *(978-1-60693-741-9(3)*, Eloquent Bks.) Strategic Book Publishing & Rights Agency (SBPRA).
Vernick, Audrey. Unlike Other Monsters. Jack, Colin, illus. 2016. (ENG.). 48p. (J). (gr. -1-k). 16.99 *(978-1-4231-9959-5(6))* Disney Pr.
—Water Balloon. 2011. (ENG.). 320p. (J). (gr. 5-7). 16.99 *(978-0-547-59554-2(9)*, Clarion Bks.) Houghton Mifflin Harcourt Trade & Reference Pubs.
Vernick, Shirley Reva. Remember Dippy. 2013. (ENG.). 176p. (J). (gr. 5-10). 16.95 *(978-1-935955-48-1(9))*; pap. 9.95 *(978-1-935955-58-0(6))* Cinco Puntos Pr.
Vernon, Ursula. Attack of the Ninja Frogs. 2nd ed. (Dragonbreath Ser.: 2). (ENG.). 208p. (J). (gr. 3-7). 2012. pap. 6.99 *(978-0-14-242066-9(2)*, Puffin Books) 2010. 12.99 *(978-0-8037-3365-7(8)*, Dial Bks) Penguin Young Readers Group.
—Attack of the Ninja Frogs. 2012. (Dragonbreath Ser.: 2). lib. bdg. 17.20 *(978-0-606-26666-6(6)*, Turtleback) Turtleback Bks.
—Nightmare of the Iguana. 2013. (Dragonbreath Ser.: 8). (ENG., Illus.). 208p. (J). (gr. 3-7). 12.99 *(978-0-8037-3846-1(3)*, Dial Bks) Penguin Publishing Group.
Verrone, Patric C. W. Sharktooth. 2009. 229p. pap. 14.76 *(978-0-557-09535-3(2))* Lulu Pr., Inc.
Verstraete, Majanka. Valentina & the Whackadoodle Witch: Valentina's Spooky Adventures. Giffin, Noelle, illus. l.t. ed. 2013. 2. (ENG.). 46p. (gr. k-4). pap. 10.95 *(978-1-62253-059-5(4))* Evolved Publishing.
Verville, Claudia J. Little Duckie Doodle. 2013. 26p. pap. 14.25 *(978-1-4817-0407-6(9))* AuthorHouse.
Vetsch, Rita Kaye. The Many Colors of Friendship. 2009. 40p. pap. 16.50 *(978-1-60693-756-3(1)*, Eloquent Bks.) Strategic Book Publishing & Rights Agency (SBPRA).
Via, Jennifer Welsh. The Foggy Meadow Discovery. 2007. 216p. per. 14.95 *(978-0-595-44680-3(9))* iUniverse, Inc.
Vickers, Elaine. Like Magic. Not, Sara, illus. (J). (gr. 3-7). 2017. 288p. pap. 6.99 ***(978-0-06-241432-8(1))*** 2016. 272p. 16.99 *(978-0-06-241431-1(3))* HarperCollins Pubs.
—Paper Chains. Not, Sara, illus. 2017. 304p. (J). (gr. 3-7). 16.99 ***(978-0-06-241434-2(8))*** HarperCollins Pubs.
Vickers, Tamara. Mr. Green & the Animal Kingdom: (Imagine That!) You Draw the Picture! 2007. 228p. per. 24.95 *(978-1-4241-8256-5(5))* America Star Bks.
Vickery-Bharadwaj, Janice. Valentino & His Friends: It's Magic! 2012. 28p. pap. 12.99 *(978-1-4691-7709-0(9))* Xlibris Corp.
Vigilante, Danette. The Trouble with Half a Moon. 2015. (ENG.). 208p. (J). (gr. 5). 7.99 *(978-0-14-751550-6(5)*, Puffin Books) Penguin Young Readers Group.
Viguié, Debbie. The Fall of Candy Corn, 1 vol. 2008. (Sweet Seasons Novel Ser.). (ENG.). 224p. (YA). (gr. 8-11). pap. 9.99 *(978-0-310-71559-7(8))* Zondervan.
—The Spring of Candy Apples, 1 vol. 2009. (Sweet Seasons Novel Ser.). (ENG.). 208p. (YA). (gr. 8-11). pap. 9.99 *(978-0-310-71753-9(1))* Zondervan.
—The Summer of Cotton Candy, 1 vol. 2008. (Sweet Seasons Novel Ser.). (ENG., Illus.). 224p. (YA). (gr. 8-11). pap. 9.99 *(978-0-310-71558-0(X))* Zondervan.
Vil, Steve. Arvid & Hornschwatz Go Skunk Scoffing. Witt, Eddie, illus. 2011. 32p. pap. 24.95 *(978-1-4560-6043-5(0))* America Star Bks.
Vilarrubias, Pia & Vilarrubias Codina, Pia. Cua, el Amigo de Tona. (SPA.). 36p. 11.95 *(978-84-207-1256-7(6))* Grupo Anaya, S.A. ESP. Dist: Distribooks, Inc.
Vili, Fane. Mano: The Awakening. Frakes, Clint, ed. 2006. (Illus.). (YA). per. 19.95 *(978-0-9774074-0-8(3))* Plankton Pr.
Villa, Leesan. The Angel on Top of the Tree. 2011. 68p. pap. 31.99 *(978-1-4628-7837-6(7))* Xlibris Corp.
Villareal, Ray. Don't Call Me Hero. 2011. (J). pap. 10.95 *(978-1-55885-711-7(7)*, Piñata Books) Arte Publico Pr.
—Who's Buried in the Garden? 2009. 160p. (YA). (gr. 6-18). pap. 10.95 *(978-1-55885-546-5(7)*, Piñata Books) Arte Publico Pr.
Vipont, Elfrida. The Lark in the Morn. Freeman, T. R., illus. 2007. 196p. (YA). pap. 12.95 *(978-1-932350-22-7(5))* Bethlehem Bks.
Virant, Janice. T-Bone the Flying Horse. 2013. (ENG.). 26p. (J). pap. 10.95 *(978-1-4327-5951-3(5))* Outskirts Pr., Inc.
Vischer, Frans. Fuddles & Puddles. Vischer, Frans, illus. 2016. (ENG., Illus.). 32p. (J). (gr. -1-3). 17.99 *(978-1-4814-3839-1(5)*, Aladdin) Simon & Schuster Children's Publishing.
Visitors, 6 Packs. (Literatura 2000 Ser.). (gr. k-1). 28.00 *(978-0-7635-0069-6(0))* Rigby Education.
Vitale, Jill. Freddie: The Free-Range Chicken. 2007. (ENG., Illus.). 28p. (J). (gr. 1-2). 15.95 *(978-0-9767269-6-8(3))* WND Bks, Inc.
Viva, Frank. Sea Change. Viva, Frank, illus. 2016. (ENG., Illus.). 120p. (J). (gr. 2-7). 18.95 *(978-1-935179-92-4(6))* TOON Books / RAW Junior, LLC.
Vivian, Siobhan. The Last Boy & Girl in the World. 2016. (ENG., Illus.). 432p. (YA). (gr. 9). 17.99 *(978-1-4814-5229-8(0)*, Simon & Schuster Bks. For Young Readers) Simon & Schuster Bks. For Young Readers.
—The List. (ENG.). 336p. (J). (gr. 9). 2014. pap. 9.99 *(978-0-545-16918-9(6)*, Scholastic Paperbacks) 2012. 17.99 *(978-0-545-16917-2(8)*, PUSH) Scholastic, Inc.
—Not That Kind of Girl. 2010. (ENG.). 336p. (J). (gr. 9-9). 17.99 *(978-0-545-16915-8(1)*, PUSH) Scholastic, Inc.
—Same Difference. 2014. (ENG.). 304p. (J). pap. 9.99 *(978-0-545-75802-4(5))* Scholastic, Inc.
VIZ Media Staff. WINX Club, Vol. 1. 2012. (ENG.). 96p. (J). pap. 6.99 *(978-1-4215-4159-4(9))* Viz Media.
—WINX Club, Vol. 3. 2012. (ENG.). 96p. (J). pap. 6.99 *(978-1-4215-4161-7(0))* Viz Media.
VIZ Media Staff & Straffi, Iginio. WINX Club, Vol. 2. 2012. (ENG.). 96p. (J). pap. 6.99 *(978-1-4215-4160-0(2))* Viz Media.
Vizzi, Maria. Morely: The Mouse in the Bakery. 2011. 24p. (gr. 1-2). pap. 13.33 *(978-1-4567-4621-6(9))* AuthorHouse.
Vlahos, Len. The Scar Boys. 2014. (ENG.). 256p. (J). (gr. 9). 17.99 *(978-1-60684-439-7(3))* Lerner Publishing Group.
—Scar Girl. 2016. (ENG.). 280p. (YA). (gr. 9-12). 17.99 *(978-1-60684-607-0(8))*; 35.99 *(978-1-5124-0164-6(1))* Lerner Publishing Group. (Carolrhoda Lab™).
Voake, Steve. Daisy Dawson & the Secret Pond. Meserve, Jessica, illus. 2010. (Daisy Dawson Ser.: 2). (ENG.). 96p. (J). (gr. 1-4). pap. 5.99 *(978-0-7636-4730-8(6))* Candlewick Pr.
Vogel, Peter C. Mike Duffy & His Adventure Witht the World's Smallest Person. 2008. 112p. pap. 9.95 *(978-1-59526-796-2(4)*, Llumina Pr.) Aeon Publishing Inc.
Vogel, Rob & Azarov, Max. Garry the Groundhog l.t. ed. 2005. (Illus.). 10p. (J). spiral bd. 19.95 incl. DVD *(978-0-9768455-0-8(4)*, N/A) Vogel, Robert.
Voigt, Cynthia. The Tale of Elske. 2015. (Tales of the Kingdom Ser.: 4). (ENG., Illus.). 368p. (YA). (gr. 7). 19.99 *(978-1-4814-2189-8(1)*, Atheneum Bks. for Young Readers) Simon & Schuster Children's Publishing.
—Teddy & Co. Zakimi, Paola, illus. 2016. (ENG.). 192p. (J). (gr. 2-5). 16.99 *(978-0-553-51160-4(2)*, Knopf Bks. for Young Readers) Random Hse. Children's Bks.
Voigt, Cynthia & Marcus, Barry David. Bad Girls in Love. 2004. (ENG., Illus.). 240p. (J). (gr. 4-8). pap. 11.99 *(978-0-689-86620-3(8)*, Atheneum Bks. for Young Readers) Simon & Schuster Children's Publishing.
Voigtsberger, Sandra A. Jack's Pockets. 2008. 17p. pap. 24.95 *(978-1-60563-546-0(4))* America Star Bks.
Volker, Kerstin. Suzie Goes to Sleep. 2003. (Funny Friends Lift-and-Learn Bks.). (Illus.). 14p. (J). 5.99 *(978-1-59384-024-2(1))* Parklane Publishing.
Volkov, Alexander. Tales of Magic Land 1. 2010. 360p. pap. 22.95 *(978-0-557-44825-8(5))* Lulu Pr., Inc.
Volponi, Paul. Rucker Park Setup. 2008. (ENG.). 160p. (YA). (gr. 7-18). 6.99 *(978-0-14-241207-7(4)*, Speak) Penguin Young Readers Group.
Volta, A. Patulous, the Different Caterpillar. 2008. (Illus.). 28p. (J). 17.99 *(978-0-9711040-0-6(X))* Working Parents, LLC.
Von Bergen, Ingri. Friend to Friend. 2006. (J). 12.95 *(978-1-59354-177-4(5))* Blue Apple Bks.
von Rosenberg, Byron. Dale the Uniclyde: An adventure in Friendship. Parrott, Heather, illus. 2007. 22p. (J). 11.95 *(978-0-9759858-6-1(8))* Red Mountain Creations.
Von Schlichten, David. H-E-Double Hockey Stick. 2011. 124p. pap. 19.95 *(978-1-4560-9019-7(4))* America Star Bks.
Vorster, Nicola. A Monkeys' Wedding. 2012. (Illus.). 24p. pap. 21.35 *(978-1-4772-3126-5(9))* AuthorHouse.
Voss, Fonda. The Bossy Girl. 2005. (Illus.). (J). 31p. per. 9.99 *(978-1-932338-96-6(9))*; 30p. 15.95 *(978-1-932338-44-7(6))* Lifevest Publishing, Inc.
Votruba, Erik C. The Cowboy Mile. 2009. 231p. pap. 14.99 *(978-0-557-09002-0(4))* Lulu Pr., Inc.
Voutila, Ritva, illus. The Nutcracker. 2016. (ENG.). 32p. (J). (gr. k-3). 18.99 *(978-1-74297-778-2(2))* Little Hare Bks. AUS. Dist: Independent Pubs. Group.
Vrabel, Beth. Pack of Dorks. (Pack of Dorks Ser.). (ENG.). 240p. (J). (gr. 2-7). 2016. 16.99 *(978-1-63450-181-1(0))* 2015. pap. 7.99 *(978-1-5107-0179-3(6))* 2014. 15.95 *(978-1-62914-623-2(4))* Skyhorse Publishing Co., Inc. (Sky Pony Pr.).
Vrettos, Adrienne Maria. Best Friends for Never. 2016. (ENG.). 240p. (J). (gr. 3-7). 16.99 *(978-0-545-56149-5(3)*, Scholastic Pr.) Scholastic, Inc.
Waber, Bernard. Quique Duerme Fuera de Casa. Mlawer, Teresa, tr. 2003. (SPA., Illus.). (J). (gr. k-2). pap. *(978-968-6579-15-4(X)*, SI6510) Sistemas Tecnicos de Edicion, S.A. de C.V. MEX. Dist: Lectorum Pubns., Inc.
Wachtel, Shirley Russak. Brad Sureshot — Coach-Detective: The Baffling Case of the Disappearing Dribbler. 2007. 76p. per. 8.95 *(978-0-595-47266-6(4))* iUniverse, Inc.
Wacker, Eileen. Black Tortoise & the Dynasty Dragon. Low, Alan M., illus. 2012. (Fujimini Adventure Ser.: Vol. 5). (ENG.). 40p. (J). (gr. -1-3). 10.99 *(978-1-4675-1741-6(0))* Oncekids.
Waddilove, Guy. Dancing with the Dragleon. 2013. (Illus.). 222p. pap. *(978-1-78036-196-3(3))* Peach Publishing.
Wagner, Linda. Lady Flatterley. 2008. 44p. pap. 22.95 *(978-1-4327-3233-2(1))* Outskirts Pr., Inc.
Wagner, Mckenzie. Casters of Doovik. 2015. 298p. (YA). pap. 17.99 *(978-1-4621-1757-4(0))* Cedar Fort, Inc./CFI Distribution.
—Keys to the Dream World. 2014. pap. 8.99 *(978-1-4621-1435-1(0))* Cedar Fort, Inc./CFI Distribution.
Waits, Kristine. Sweet Sam Shares. 2008. 36p. pap. 14.98 *(978-0-557-01679-2(7))* Lulu Pr., Inc.
Wakefield, Beth. The Cleaner. 2010. 151p. pap. 14.50 *(978-1-4457-6809-0(7))* Lulu Pr., Inc.
Wakefield, Nelida. Little Flathead & the Black Pearl. Smith, Nathan, illus. 2009. 36p. pap. 12.99 *(978-1-59858-828-6(1))* Dog Ear Publishing, LLC.
Waldman, Alan/A. Erica from America & the Start of the Gang of Four. Scobie, Andrea, illus. 2013. 44p. pap. *(978-0-9840514-2-7(2))* Roxby Media Ltd.
Waldman, Debby. Addy's Race, 1 vol. 2011. (Orca Young Readers Ser.). (ENG.). 136p. (J). (gr. 3-6). pap. 7.95 *(978-1-55469-924-7(X))* Orca Bk. Pubs. USA.
Waldman, Maya, illus. To-Do List. 2007. (ENG.). 48p. (J). (gr. k). 12.95 *(978-0-9741319-5-5(4))* 4N Publishing LLC.
Waldron, Douglas E. Cody Sackett of Montana: Tales of Adventure. 2008. 188p. per. 24.95 *(978-1-4241-9781-1(3))* America Star Bks.
Wales, Amy S. Fiona & the Fiddle Tree. 2012. 32p. pap. 21.99 *(978-1-4691-5485-5(4))* Xlibris Corp.

Wales, Dirk. Jack London's Dog. Moser, Barry, illus. 2008. 64p. (YA). (gr. 5-9). 17.95 *(978-0-9632459-3-9(7))* Great Plains Pr.
Walker, Jorge. Little Winston's Desire. 2011. 20p. pap. 9.49 *(978-1-4567-2396-5(0))* AuthorHouse.
Walker, Kristin. A Match Made in High School. 2010. (ENG.). 288p. (YA). (gr. 7-18). 9.99 *(978-1-59514-257-3(6)*, Razorbill) Penguin Young Readers Group.
Walker, Landry Q. Secret Entity! #4, 1 vol. Jones, Eric, illus. 2013. (Supergirl: Cosmic Adventures in the 8th Grade Ser.). (ENG.). 32p. (gr. 2-3). 22.60 *(978-1-4342-4720-9(1))* Stone Arch Bks.
—Super Hero School: #3, 1 vol. Jones, Eric, illus. 2013. (Supergirl: Cosmic Adventures in the 8th Grade Ser.). (ENG.). 32p. (gr. 2-3). 22.60 *(978-1-4342-4719-3(8))* Stone Arch Bks.
Walker, Melissa. Let's Pretend We Never Met. 2017. 240p. (J). (gr. 3-7). 16.99 *(978-0-06-256716-1(0))* HarperCollins Pubs.
—Unbreak My Heart. (ENG., (YA). (gr. 7). 2013. Illus.). 256p. pap. 9.99 *(978-1-61963-007-9(9)*, 9781619630079) 2012. 240p. 16.99 *(978-1-59990-528-0(0)*, 9781599905280) Bloomsbury Publishing USA. (Bloomsbury USA Childrens).
Walker, Nan. Otto & the New Girl: Symmetry. Wummer, Amy, illus. 2017. (Math Matters (r) Ser.). (ENG.). 32p. (J). (gr. k-3). 5.95 *(978-1-57565-864-3(X))* Kane Press, Inc.
Walker, Nan. Otto & the New Girl: Symmetry. Wummer, Amy, illus. 2017. (Math Matters (r) Ser.). (ENG.). 32p. (gr. k-3). 23.99 ***(978-1-57565-867-4(4))*** Kane Press, Inc.
Walker, Peter. The Magic Airplane. 2006. (ENG.). 160p. per. 12.95 *(978-1-59526-416-9(7))* Aeon Publishing Inc.
Walker, Whitney. Doubting Destiny. 2006. 56p. per. 10.95 *(978-0-9774833-4-1(7))* Magic Valley Pubs.
Walko. Amigos: Friends Forever. 2012. (ENG., Illus.). 28p. (J). (gr. -1-k). 16.95 *(978-1-61608-388-5(3)*, 608388, Sky Pony Pr.) Skyhorse Publishing Co., Inc.
Wall, Julia & McKenzie, Heather. Nico's List. 2008. (Rigby Focus Forward: Level M Ser.). (Illus.). 24p. (J). (gr. 4-7). pap. *(978-1-4190-3829-7(X)*, Rigby) Pearson Education Australia.
Wall, Laura. Goose. Wall, Laura, illus. 2015. (ENG., Illus.). 48p. (J). (gr. -1-3). 12.99 *(978-0-06-232435-1(7))* HarperCollins Pubs.
—Goose Goes to the Zoo. Wall, Laura, illus. 2016. (Illus.). 48p. (J). (gr. -1-3). 12.99 *(978-0-06-232441-2(1))* HarperCollins Pubs.
—Goose on the Farm. Wall, Laura, illus. 2016. (Illus.). 48p. (J). (gr. -1-3). 12.99 *(978-0-06-232439-9(X))* HarperCollins Pubs.
Wallace, Bill. The Final Freedom. 2009. (ENG.). 176p. (J). (gr. 3-7). pap. 9.99 *(978-1-4169-9421-3(1)*, Simon & Schuster/Paula Wiseman Bks.) Simon & Schuster/Paula Wiseman Bks.
—No Dogs Allowed! 2004. (ENG.). 214p. (J). (gr. 4-6). tchr. ed. 16.95 *(978-0-8234-1818-3(9))* Holiday Hse., Inc.
Wallace, Carol. One Nosy Pup. Björkman, Steve, illus. 2004. (ENG.). 40p. (J). 15.95 *(978-0-8234-1917-3(7))* Holiday Hse., Inc.
Wallace, Dianne. Jungle in the Sky. 2012. (ENG.). 27p. (J). pap. 16.95 *(978-1-4327-4527-1(1))* Outskirts Pr., Inc.
Wallace, G. Ira. Bunny Tales: The Journey Begins. 2009. 24p. pap. 12.00 *(978-1-60860-869-0(7)*, Strategic Bk. Publishing) Strategic Book Publishing & Rights Agency (SBPRA).
Wallace, Ian. Mavis & Merna, 1 vol. 2005. (ENG., Illus.). 40p. (J). (gr. k-3). 16.95 *(978-0-88899-647-3(0))* Groundwood Bks. CAN. Dist: Publishers Group West (PGW).
Wallace, Karen. Raspberries on the Yangtze. 2013. (ENG.). 160p. (J). pap. 8.99 *(978-1-4711-2122-7(4)*, Simon & Schuster Children's) Simon & Schuster, Ltd. GBR. Dist: Simon & Schuster, Inc.
Wallace, Kim. Erik & Isabelle Freshman Year at Foresthill High. 2004. (Foresthill High Ser.). 225p. (YA). (gr. 9). per. 12.00 *(978-0-9755848-0-4(4))* Foglight Pr.
Wallace, Nancy Elizabeth. Water! Water! Water!, 0 vols. 2014. (ENG.). 40p. (J). (gr. -1-k). 17.99 *(978-1-4778-4730-5(8)*, 9781477847305, Amazon Children's Publishing) Amazon Publishing.
Wallace, Nancy K. Movie Mishaps, 1 vol. Chronister, Amanda, illus. 2013. (Abby & the Book Bunch Ser.). (ENG.). 80p. (J). (gr. 2-5). 27.07 *(978-1-61641-914-1(8))* Magic Wagon.
Wallace, Rich. Chasing the Baton, 1 vol. Heitz, Tim, illus. 2016. (Game Face Ser.). (ENG.). 112p. (J). (gr. 3-7). 27.07 *(978-1-62402-133-6(6))* Magic Wagon.
—Game Face. 2016. (Game Face Ser.: 4). (ENG.). 112p. (J). (gr. 3-7). lib. bdg. 108.28 *(978-1-62402-131-2(X)*, Calico Chapter Bks.) ABDO Publishing Co.
—Second-String Center. 2008. (Winning Season Ser.: 10). (ENG.). 128p. (J). (gr. 3-7). 5.99 *(978-0-14-241216-9(3)*, Puffin Books) Penguin Young Readers Group.
—Shots on Goal. 2005. (ENG.). 160p. (YA). (gr. 7-11). per. 5.99 *(978-0-679-88671-6(0)*, Laurel Leaf) Random Hse. Children's Bks.
Wallach, Tommy. We All Looked Up. 2015. (ENG., Illus.). 384p. (YA). (gr. 9). 17.99 *(978-1-4814-1877-5(7)*, Simon & Schuster Bks. For Young Readers) Simon & Schuster Bks. For Young Readers.
Wallen, Virginia. Sonny & Sammy. 2006. 17.00 *(978-0-8059-9809-2(8))* Dorrance Publishing Co., Inc.
Walley, Keith. An Angel to Guide Me. 2012. 62p. pap. 12.99 *(978-1-105-68254-4(4))* Lulu Pr., Inc.
Walling, Lani. Clyde-Fred & the Color of Friendship. 2005. 23p. (J). 9.98 *(978-1-4116-6091-5(9))* Lulu Pr., Inc.
Walsh, Ann. By the Skin of His Teeth. 2005. (Illus.). 144p. (YA). pap., tchr. ed. 6.95 *(978-0-88878-448-3(1))* Beach Holme Pubs., Ltd. CAN. Dist: Literary Pr. Group of Canada.
Walsh, Bill. The Dog Show. 2010. 32p. pap. 19.95 *(978-0-557-24059-3(X))* Lulu Pr., Inc.
Walsh, Franny. Who Cat: A Louisiana Tale. 2013. (ENG.). 32p. (J). pap. 16.95 *(978-1-4787-0280-1(X))* Outskirts Pr., Inc.
Walsh, Sheila. God's Little Princess Treasury, 1 vol. Johnson, Meredith, illus. 2009. (ENG.). 128p. (gr. -1-2). 19.99 *(978-1-4003-1472-0(0))* Nelson, Thomas Inc.
—Meet My Best Friend. 2015. (Bible Is My Best Friend Ser.). (ENG.). 32p. (J). (gr. -1-3). 14.99 *(978-1-4336-8805-8(0)*, B&H Kids) B&H Publishing Group.
Walsh, Stephen & O'Donovan, Marita. Vinnie Goes to Vegas. Le Feyer, Diane, illus. 2017. (ENG.). 32p. (J). pap. 13.00 ***(978-1-84717-724-7(7))*** O'Brien Pr., Ltd., The IRL. Dist: Dufour Editions, Inc.
Walsh, Susanne. My Very Favorite Time of Year: Featuring the Whimsy Kids. 2007. 34p. pap. 24.95 *(978-1-4241-9090-4(8))* America Star Bks.
Walsh, Vivian. June & August. McCauley, Adam, illus. 2009. (ENG.). 32p. (J). (gr. k-2). 16.95 *(978-0-8109-8410-3(5)*, Abrams Bks. for Young Readers) Abrams, Inc.
Walter, Debbie. Introducing Russell. Walter, Debbie, illus. 2007. (Illus.). 68p. (J). per. 6.95 *(978-0-9766315-2-1(0))* Moose Run Productions.
Walter-Goodspeed, Dee Dee. Friends Will Be There Forever. Jones, Ayanna, illus. 2012. 26p. (J). (-18). pap. 15.99 *(978-1-933846-36-1(4))* Fairwood Pr.
Walters, Celeste. The Glass Mountain. 2003. 280p. (YA). pap. *(978-0-7022-3297-8(1))* Univ. of Queensland Pr.
—Treading the Boards. 2007. 208p. *(978-1-921049-80-4(4))* Little Hare Bks. AUS. Dist: HarperCollins Pubs. Australia.
Walters, Eric. In a Flash, 1 vol. 2008. (Orca Currents Ser.). (ENG.). 112p. (J). (gr. 5-9). pap. 9.95 *(978-1-55469-034-3(X))* Orca Bk. Pubs. USA.
Walters, Gregory. Fouling Out, 1 vol. 2008. (ENG.). 176p. (J). (gr. 5-10). pap. 8.95 *(978-1-55143-714-9(7))* Orca Bk. Pubs. USA.
Walters, Nicole Y. Charis: A Journey to Pandora's Jar. Conard, Vincent, illus. 2013. 214p. 32.95 *(978-1-62015-318-5(1)*, Booktrope Editions) Booktrope.
Walton, Ann. Something to Do. Hinrichsen, Natalie, illus. 2010. (ENG.). 24p. (J). (gr. k-2). pap. 6.00 *(978-1-77009-706-3(6))* Jacana Media ZAF. Dist: Independent Pubs. Group.
Walton, Jess. Introducing Teddy. MacPherson, Dougal, illus. 2016. (ENG.). 32p. (J). 16.99 *(978-1-68119-210-9(1)*, 9781681192109, Bloomsbury USA Childrens) Bloomsbury Publishing USA.
Walton, Rick. Girl & Gorilla. Berger, Joe, illus. 2016. 32p. (J). (gr. -1-3). 17.99 *(978-0-06-227891-3(6))* HarperCollins Pubs.
Walton, Will. Anything Could Happen. 2015. (ENG.). 288p. (J). (gr. 7). 17.99 *(978-0-545-70954-5(7)*, PUSH) Scholastic, Inc.
Wampol, Pam & Woodard, Heather. Oscar's Dreamzz: The Story of Santa's First Elf. 2013. 40p. pap. *(978-1-4602-0414-6(X))* FriesenPress.
Wan, Joyce. Owl & Friends. Wan, Joyce, illus. 2013. (ENG., Illus.). 14p. (J). (gr. -1-k). bds. 6.99 *(978-0-8431-7275-1(4)*, Price Stern Sloan) Penguin Young Readers Group.
Wandless, David. Natural Magic. 2010. 344p. pap. 27.50 *(978-1-4461-4163-2(2))* Lulu Pr., Inc.
—Natural Magic Book 3 - the Milk Stone & the Tauren. 2010. 134p. pap. 20.95 *(978-1-4461-5162-4(X))* Lulu Pr., Inc.
Ward, Heather P. I Promise I'll Find You. McGraw, Sheila, illus. 2005. (ENG.). 32p. (J). (gr. -1-2). pap. 6.95 *(978-1-55209-094-7(9)*, 9781552090947) Firefly Bks., Ltd.
Ward, Helen. Moon Dog. 2005. (Illus.). 40p. (J). *(978-1-84011-864-3(4))* Templar Publishing.
Ward, Kari. Marley & Maverick & the Haunted Maze. 2012. 34p. (-18). pap. *(978-1-897512-61-6(9))* Saga Bks.
Ward, M. P. Sam & the Sea Witch. 2013. 158p. pap. *(978-1-77127-397-8(6))* MuseItUp Publishing.
Ward, Marcia. The Girl Who Found Her Voice. 2013. (ENG.). 276p. pap. 14.99 *(978-1-939927-28-6(5))* Telemachus Pr., LLC.
Ward, Nick. The Ice Child. Bailey, Peter, illus. 2004. 32p. (J). *(978-1-84458-038-5(5)*, Pavilion Children's Books) Pavilion Bks.
Wardale, David. Psico. 2013. 302p. (J). pap. *(978-1-78299-172-4(7))* FeedARead.com.
Wardell, Joe. Doodey the Combat Camel. Bane, T. Glenn, illus. 2012. 20p. pap. 12.95 *(978-0-615-58866-7(2))* Little Clive Pr.
Wardlaw, Lee. Coreys Fire. 2006. pap. 12.95 *(978-0-595-40170-3(8)*, Backinprint.com) iUniverse, Inc.
Wardlow, Lynn. Friends with My Brother. 2012. 28p. pap. 9.95 *(978-1-4787-1384-5(4))* Outskirts Pr., Inc.
Warne. Be My Friend. 2014. (Peter Rabbit Animation Ser.). (ENG.). 32p. (J). (gr. -1-k). 3.99 *(978-0-14-135506-1(9)*, Warne) Penguin Young Readers Group.
—The Peter Rabbit Club. 2014. (Peter Rabbit Animation Ser.). (ENG.). 32p. (J). (gr. -1-k). 3.99 *(978-0-14-135319-7(8)*, Warne) Penguin Young Readers Group.
Warner, Liz. El Conejito Grande. 2007. 40p. per. 21.32 *(978-1-4257-5616-1(6))* Xlibris Corp.
Warner, Sally. EllRay Jakes & the Beanstalk. Biggs, Brian, illus. 2013. (EllRay Jakes Ser.: 5). (ENG.). (J). (gr. 1-3). 128p. 14.99 *(978-0-670-78499-8(0)*, Viking Books for Young Readers); 144p. pap. 5.99 *(978-0-14-242359-2(9)*, Puffin Books) Penguin Young Readers Group.
—EllRay Jakes & the Beanstalk. 2013. (EllRay Jakes Ser.: 5). lib. bdg. 16.00 *(978-0-606-32137-2(3)*, Turtleback) Turtleback Bks.
—EllRay Jakes the Recess King! Biggs, Brian, illus. 2015. (EllRay Jakes Ser.: 8). (ENG.). 176p. (J). (gr. 1-3). 5.99 *(978-0-14-751252-9(2)*, Puffin Books); 14.99 *(978-0-451-46911-3(9)*, Viking Books for Young Readers) Penguin Young Readers Group.
—Not-So-Weird Emma. Harper, Jamie, illus. 2007. (Emma Ser.). (ENG.). 144p. (J). (gr. 3-7). 6.99 *(978-0-14-240807-0(7)*, Puffin Books) Penguin Young Readers Group.
Warnes, Tim. Can't You Sleep, Dotty? Warnes, Tim, illus. 2003. (Illus.). 32p. (J). pap. 5.95 *(978-1-58925-376-6(0))* Tiger Tales.
—Chalk & Cheese. Warnes, Tim, illus. 2008. (ENG., Illus.). 32p. (J). (gr. -1-3). 18.99 *(978-1-4169-1378-8(5)*, Simon & Schuster Bks. For Young Readers) Simon & Schuster Bks. For Young Readers.
Warren, Dotti M. Dreama Lynn & the Magic Tu Tu. 2008. 16p. pap. 9.49 *(978-1-4389-2983-5(8))* AuthorHouse.
Wartik, David J. The Vonnesta Project. 2006. 140p. (J). (gr. 3-6). pap. 12.95 *(978-1-59113-938-6(4))* Booklocker.com, Inc.
Wasenius, Richard. Friends. 2010. 88p. pap. 9.95 *(978-1-4502-6862-2(5))* iUniverse, Inc.
Washer, Mark Gregory. Blue Bonnie Butterfly: Tale of Two Tails. 2013. 36p. pap. 18.41 *(978-1-4669-8434-9(1))* Trafford Publishing.
Washington, Donna L. & Washington, Donna. A Big Spooky House: Picture Book. Rogers, Jacqueline, illus. 2006. (ENG.). 32p. (J). (gr. k-4). 4.99 *(978-0-7868-1231-8(1))* Hyperion Pr.
Wasserman, Robin. Envy. 2006. (Seven Deadly Sins Ser.: 2). (ENG.). 256p. (YA). (gr. 9-12). pap. 9.99 *(978-0-689-87783-4(8)*, Simon Pulse) Simon Pulse.
—Greed. 2007. (Seven Deadly Sins Ser.: 7). (ENG.). 256p. (YA). (gr. 9). pap. 8.99 *(978-1-4169-0720-6(3)*, Simon Pulse) Simon Pulse.
—Hacking Harvard. 2007. (ENG.). 336p. (YA). (gr. 9-12). pap. 9.99 *(978-1-4169-3633-6(5)*, Simon Pulse) Simon Pulse.
—Life, Starring Me! 2009. (Candy Apple Ser.). 182p. (J). *(978-0-545-19777-9(5))* Scholastic, Inc.
Waszak, Madonna. Mason's Mashed Potato Tree. Johnston, Lisa Harp, illus. 2011. 34p. pap. 14.95 *(978-1-4575-0159-3(7))* Dog Ear Publishing, LLC.
Waterfield, Susan. Spunkie's Magical Garden. 2012. 32p. pap. 14.95 *(978-1-257-77576-7(6))* Lulu Pr., Inc.
Waterman, Diana. Don't Bite, Dwight. 2012. 24p. pap. 24.95 *(978-1-4626-6452-8(0))* PublishAmerica, Inc.
Waters, Cassie. Cool Down. 2012. (Pool Girls Ser.: 3). (ENG.). 160p. (J). (gr. 3-7). 15.99 *(978-1-4424-5377-7(X))*; pap. 5.99 *(978-1-4424-4709-7(5))* Simon Spotlight. (Simon Spotlight).
—Dive In! 2012. (Pool Girls Ser.: 1). (ENG.). 160p. (J). (gr. 3-7). pap. 5.99 *(978-1-4424-4144-6(5)*, Simon Spotlight) Simon Spotlight.
Waters, Michael. Tommy & his Flying Saucer of Milk. 2009. 32p. 18.95 *(978-1-4092-8450-5(6))* Lulu Pr., Inc.
Waters, Summer. River Rescue, 10. 2010. (Silver Dolphins Ser.: 10). (ENG.). 176p. (J). (gr. 2-4). pap. 7.99 *(978-0-00-736750-4(3)*, HarperCollins Children's Bks.) HarperCollins Pubs. Ltd. GBR. Dist: HarperCollins Pubs.
Watkins, Constance L. That Was, the Kitten, That Was. 2010. 32p. pap. 13.49 *(978-1-4520-0037-4(9))* AuthorHouse.
Watkins, Elaine. Billy Bobbin at Mystery Farm. 2014. (ENG.). 56p. (J). (gr. 3-4). pap. 8.95 *(978-1-84963-823-4(3)*, f1c1638b-abbd-4463-9b5b-9133593e7447) Austin, Stan AUS. Dist: Bookmasters Distribution.
Watkins, Greg. A Big Beaked, Big Bellied Bird Named Bill, 1 vol. Watkins, Greg, illus. 2006. (Big Bill & Buddies Ser.). (ENG., Illus.). 32p. (J). (gr. k-3). 16.99 *(978-1-58980-441-8(4))* Pelican Publishing Co., Inc.
Watson, Andi. Princess Decomposia & Count Spatula. 2015. (ENG., Illus.). 176p. (YA). (gr. 8). 19.99 *(978-1-62672-275-0(7)*, 9781626722750, First Second Bks.) Roaring Brook Pr.
Watson-Dubisch, Carolyn. Bug-a-boo, 1. I.t. ed. 2006. (Illus.). 32p. (J). per. 9.95 *(978-0-9779295-1-1(5))* Medusa Road Pr.
Watson, K. R. Little Gabby Meets Her New Family. 2008. 44p. pap. 17.99 *(978-1-4389-1767-2(8))* AuthorHouse.
Watson, Myrtle. Kite Flying in the Village: A Guyanese Girl's Story. 2011. 20p. 10.03 *(978-1-4520-8632-3(X))* AuthorHouse.
Watson, Peter. The Heart of the Lion. Watson, Mary, illus. 2005. (ENG.). 32p. (J). (gr. 4-7). 15.95 *(978-0-9726614-1-6(7))* Shenanigan Bks.
Watson, Renée. This Side of Home. 2015. (ENG.). 336p. (YA). (gr. 7). 17.99 *(978-1-59990-668-3(6)*, 9781599906683, Bloomsbury USA Childrens) Bloomsbury Publishing USA.
Watson, Richard Jesse. The Magic Rabbit. Watson, Richard Jesse, illus. 2005. (ENG., Illus.). 40p. (J). (gr. -1-3). 16.99 *(978-0-590-47964-6(4)*, Blue Sky Pr., The) Scholastic, Inc.
Watson, Stephanie Elaine. Elvis & Olive: Super Detectives. 2010. (ENG.). 288p. (J). (gr. 3-7). 15.99 *(978-0-545-15148-1(1)*, Scholastic Pr.) Scholastic, Inc.
Watson, Tom. Stick Dog Dreams of Ice Cream. 2015. (Stick Dog Ser.: 4). (ENG., Illus.). 224p. (J). (gr. 3-7). 12.99 *(978-0-06-227807-4(X))* HarperCollins Pubs.
—Stick Dog Slurps Spaghetti. Long, Ethan, illus. 2016. (Stick Dog Ser.: 6). 240p. (J). (gr. 3-7). 12.99 *(978-0-06-234322-2(X))* HarperCollins Pubs.
Watson, Tom & Long, Ethan, illus. Stick Dog Dreams of Ice Cream. 2015. 216p. (J). *(978-0-06-238092-0(3))* Harper & Row Ltd.
Watson, Vicki. Bob & the Alien Escapade. 2013. 226p. pap. *(978-0-9574062-2-3(3))* Green, Callisto.
Watt, Fiona. Little Children's Christmas Music Book. 2012. (Little Children's Music Book Ser.). 24p. (J). bds. 18.99 *(978-0-7945-3328-1(0)*, Usborne) EDC Publishing.
Watt, Mélanie. Scaredy Squirrel Makes a Friend. Watt, Mélanie, illus. 2007. (ENG., Illus.). 32p. (J). (gr. -1-3). 16.95 *(978-1-55453-181-3(0))* Kids Can Pr., Ltd. CAN. Dist: Hachette Bk. Group.
Watts, Julia. Kindred Spirits. 2008. (ENG.). 147p. (gr. 3-18). pap. 8.95 *(978-0-9667359-9-4(4))* Harren Communications, LLC.
Watts, Katherine. Tiger Tails. 2008. 76p. pap. 35.95 *(978-0-9556878-0-8(2))* Watts, Katherine GBR. Dist: Lulu Pr., Inc.
Watts, Leslie. Just Leah. 2013. 28p. 16.99 *(978-0-9894748-5-6(2))* Mindstir Media.
Watts, Robin Queen. The Adventures of Beauty & Sam. 2009. 20p. pap. 10.50 *(978-1-4269-1286-3(2))* Trafford Publishing.
Wax, Wendy. Sugar & Spice. Perrett, Lisa, illus. 2007. (ENG.). 24p. (J). (gr. 1-4). per. 3.99 *(978-1-58476-614-8(X)*, IKIDS) Innovative Kids.
Weakley, David. Rowley to the Rescue. 2009. 72p. pap. 24.00 *(978-1-60860-295-7(8)*, Eloquent Bks.) Strategic Book Publishing & Rights Agency (SBPRA).
Weatherall, Barry. Jay & the Worm Save the Day. 2005. 40p. 14.28 *(978-1-4116-4717-6(3))* Lulu Pr., Inc.
Weatherbee, Tabatha. Dream Sharers: Love/Hate. 2013. 336p. (J). pap. 19.00 *(978-1-62212-978-2(4)*, Strategic Bk. Publishing) Strategic Book Publishing & Rights Agency (SBPRA).
Weatherstone, Hollie. When the Pandas Came to Scotland. 2012. (Illus.). 20p. pap. 19.82 *(978-1-4772-3528-7(0))* AuthorHouse.
Weaver, Amy Garrett. Zoe the Zebra. Schneider, Robin, illus. 2009. 33p. pap. 24.95 *(978-1-60749-552-9(X))* PublishAmerica, Inc.
Weaver, Anna E. Birds at My Window. 2004. (Illus.). 231p. 9.35 *(978-0-7399-2301-6(3)*, 2138) Rod & Staff Pubs., Inc.
Weaver, Greg & Weaver, Allie. Mickey the Monkey Makes a Friend. 2013. 24p. pap. 24.95 *(978-1-63000-802-4(8))* America Star Bks.
Webb, Derek & Webb, Arthur. Is. 2011. (ENG., Illus.). 182p. (J). (gr. 7). pap. 11.95 *(978-1-906998-11-0(6))* Parthian Bks. GBR. Dist: Independent Pubs. Group.
Webb, Dirk. A Warm Summer's Day. 2010. 37p. 17.00 *(978-0-578-01867-6(5))* Webb, Dirk E.
Webb, Heather. The Frog & the Fly. Sanderson, Constance, illus. 2008. 29p. pap. 24.95 *(978-1-60441-380-9(8))* America Star Bks.
Webb Quest, Sara. Angel's Shore. 2009. 36p. pap. 7.00 *(978-0-557-09386-1(4))* Lulu Pr., Inc.
—Aydil Vice & Her Disgustin' Hair Knots. 2008. 72p. pap. 7.00 *(978-1-4357-5150-7(7))* Lulu Pr., Inc.
Webb, Sarah. Ask Amy Green: Love & Other Drama-Ramas! 2012. (Ask Amy Green Ser.: 4). (ENG., Illus.). 224p. (YA). (gr. 7). 15.99 *(978-0-7636-5582-2(1))* Candlewick Pr.
—Ask Amy Green: Dancing Daze. 2013. (Ask Amy Green Ser.: 5). (ENG.). 256p. (J). (gr. 5). 16.99 *(978-0-7636-5583-9(X))* Candlewick Pr.
—Ask Amy Green: Wedding Belles. 2014. (Ask Amy Green Ser.: 6). (ENG.). 240p. (YA). (gr. 7). 16.99 *(978-0-7636-5584-6(8))* Candlewick Pr.
Weber, David & Lindskold, Jane. Fire Season. 2013. (Star Kingdom (Weber) Ser.: 2). (ENG., Illus.). 304p. (YA). (gr. 7). pap. 9.99 *(978-1-4516-3921-6(X))* Baen Bks.
Weber, John. Orphan. 2010. 266p. (YA). (gr. 7-18). 16.95 *(978-1-934813-38-6(9))* Westside Bks.
Weber, Judith Eichler. Seeking Safety. Martin, John F., illus. 2006. (Adventures in America Ser.). (J). *(978-1-893110-46-5(X))* Silver Moon Pr.
Weber, Lori. Picture Me, 1 vol. 2013. (ENG.). 168p. (YA). (gr. 8-12). pap. 12.95 *(978-1-4594-0510-3(2)*, 9781459405103) Lorimer, James & Co., Ltd., Pubs. CAN. Dist: Casemate Pubs. & Bk. Distributors, LLC.
Webster, Christy. Anna's Best Friends. 2014. (Disney Princess Step into Reading Ser.). lib. bdg. 13.55 *(978-0-606-35547-6(2))* Turtleback Bks.
—Barbie in a Mermaid Tale. Random House Editors, illus. 2010. (Step into Reading Ser.). (ENG.). 32p. (J). (gr. -1-1). pap. 3.99 *(978-0-375-86450-6(4)*, Random Hse. Bks. for Young Readers) Random Hse. Children's Bks.
—Barbie in a Mermaid Tale. 2010. (Barbie Step into Reading Level 2 Ser.). lib. bdg. 13.55 *(978-0-606-07031-7(1)*, Turtleback) Turtleback Bks.
Webster, Christy. Thomas' Opposites Book (Thomas & Friends) Courtney, Richard, illus. 2017. (Pictureback(R) Ser.). (ENG.). 24p. (J). (gr. -1-2). pap. 4.99 ***(978-1-5247-1604-2(9)***, Random Hse. Bks. for Young Readers) Random Hse. Children's Bks.
Webster-Tyson, Paulette L. I Gotta Get a Nickname! 2011. 32p. (gr. -1-2). pap. 17.25 *(978-1-4269-5625-6(8))* Trafford Publishing.
Wedding, Linda. The Blue-Eyed, Tri-Colored American Paint: A Lesson in Trust for Baby. 2008. 44p. pap. 24.95 *(978-1-4241-9925-9(5))* America Star Bks.
Weddle, Steve & Weddle, Nikki. Can Hedgehogs Jump? 2011. (Illus.). 28p. pap. 12.52 *(978-1-4520-5751-4(6))* AuthorHouse.
Wedgeworth, Anthony G. Nums of Shoreview: Unfair Trade. 2008. 87p. pap. 9.98 *(978-0-615-26007-5(1))* Wedgeworth, Anthony G.
Weeks, Sarah. As Simple as It Seems. (ENG.). 192p. (J). (gr. 3-7). 2011. pap. 5.99 *(978-0-06-084665-7(8))* 2010. 15.99 *(978-0-06-084663-3(1))* HarperCollins Pubs.
—Cheese: A Combo of Oggie Cooder & Oggie Cooder, Party Animal. 2016. (ENG.). 352p. (J). (gr. 2-5). pap. 8.99 *(978-0-545-93957-7(7))* Scholastic, Inc.
—If I Were a Lion. Solomon, Heather M., illus. 2007. (ENG.). 40p. (J). (gr. -1-2). 7.99 *(978-1-4169-3837-8(0)*, Atheneum Bks. for Young Readers) Simon & Schuster Children's Publishing.
—Mac & Cheese. Manning, Jane K., illus. 2010. (I Can Read Level 1 Ser.). (ENG.). 32p. (J). (gr. -1-3). 16.99 *(978-0-06-117079-9(8))*; pap. 3.99 *(978-0-06-117081-2(X))* HarperCollins Pubs.
—Mac & Cheese & the Perfect Plan. Manning, Jane, illus. 2012. 32p. (J). lib. bdg. 17.89 *(978-0-06-117083-6(6))*; (ENG.). 16.99 *(978-0-06-117082-9(8))*; (ENG.). pap. 3.99 *(978-0-06-117084-3(4))* HarperCollins Pubs.
—Oggie Cooder. 2009. (Oggie Cooder Ser.: Vol. 1). (ENG.). 176p. (J). (gr. 2-5). 5.99 *(978-0-439-92794-9(3)*, Scholastic Paperbacks) Scholastic, Inc.
—Oggie Cooder - Party Animal! 2011. (Oggie Cooder Ser.). (ENG.). 176p. (J). (gr. 2-5). pap. 6.99 *(978-0-439-92796-3(X)*, Scholastic Paperbacks) Scholastic, Inc.
—Pip Squeak. Manning, Jane K., illus. (I Can Read Level 1 Ser.). 32p. (J). 2008. (ENG.). (gr. k-3). pap. 3.99 *(978-0-06-075638-3(1))* 2007. (gr. -1-3). lib. bdg. 16.89 *(978-0-06-075637-6(3)*, Geringer, Laura Book) HarperCollins Pubs.
Weeks, Sarah & Varadarajan, Gita. Save Me a Seat. 2016. (ENG.). 240p. (J). (gr. 3-7). 16.99 *(978-0-545-84660-8(9)*, Scholastic Pr.) Scholastic, Inc.
Weeks, Timothy A. Goldie's Search for Silver: The Wise Mullet Finale! Weeks, Timothy A. & Weeks, Jeanne G., illus. 2009. (ENG.). 48p. (J). pap. 14.99 *(978-0-9779928-2-9(9))* Foolosophy Media.
Wegelius, Jakob. The Murderer's Ape. 2017. (ENG.). 624p. (YA). (gr. 7). 17.99 *(978-1-101-93175-2(2)*, Delacorte Pr.) Random Hse. Children's Bks.
Wegelius, Jakob & Graves, Peter. The Murderer's Ape. 2017. (YA). lib. bdg. *(978-1-101-93176-9(0)*, Delacorte Pr) Random House Publishing Group.
Wehrmeijer, Annelien. Anik & Yukon. van de Liejgraaf, Deborah, illus. 2015. (My Best Friend & Me Ser.). (ENG.). 10p. (J). (gr. -1-k). bds. 6.99 *(978-0-7641-6763-8(4))* Barron's Educational Series, Inc.
—Jacob & Rex. van de Liejgraaf, Deborah, illus. 2014. (My Best Friend & Me Ser.). 10p. (J). (gr. -1 — 1). bds. 7.99 *(978-0-7641-6663-1(8))* Barron's Educational Series, Inc.
—Kato & Simba. van de Liejgraaf, Deborah, illus. 2015. (My Best Friend & Me Ser.). (ENG.). 10p. (J). (gr. -1-k). bds. 6.99 *(978-0-7641-6762-1(6))* Barron's Educational Series, Inc.
—Mimi & Ling. van de Liejgraaf, Deborah, illus. 2015. (My Best Friend & Me Ser.). (ENG.). 10p. (J). (gr. -1-k). bds. 6.99 *(978-0-7641-6765-2(0))* Barron's Educational Series, Inc.
—Sophie & Daisy. van de Liejgraaf, Deborah, illus. 2014. (My Best Friend & Me Ser.). (ENG.). 10p. (J). (gr. -1 — 1). bds.

E
F
G

7.99 (978-0-7641-6664-8(6)) Barron's Educational Series, Inc.
—Tariq & Mika. van de Liejgraaf, Deborah, illus. 2015. (My Best Friend & Me Ser.). (ENG.). 10p. (J). (gr. -1-k). bds. 6.99 (978-0-7641-6764-5(2)) Barron's Educational Series, Inc.
Weigl Publishers, creator. The Lion & the Mouse: Can Little Friends Be Great Friends? 2013. (AV2 Animated Storytime Ser.: Vol. 15). (ENG., Illus.). 32p. (J). (gr. -1-3). lib. bdg. 29.99 (978-1-62127-919-8(7), AV2 by Weigl) Weigl Pubs., Inc.
Wein, Elizabeth. Code Name Verity. (ENG.). (YA). (gr. 9-17). 2013. 368p. pap. 9.99 (978-1-4231-5288-0(3)) 2012. 352p. 16.99 (978-1-4231-5219-4(0)) Hyperion Pr.
—Code Name Verity. 2013. (YA). lib. bdg. 20.85 (978-0-606-31760-3(0), Turtleback) Turtleback Bks.
Weinberg, Jennifer Liberts. Christmas Toys. 2012. (Step into Reading Level 2 Ser.). lib. bdg. 13.55 (978-0-606-26796-0(4), Turtleback) Turtleback Bks.
—Happy Birthday, Mike! 2014. (Step into Reading Level 2 Ser.). lib. bdg. 13.55 (978-0-606-36006-7(9)) Turtleback Bks.
Weinberg, Steven. Fred & the Lumberjack. Weinberg, Steven, illus. 2017. (ENG., Illus.). 40p. (J). (gr. -1-3). 17.99 **(978-1-4814-2983-2(3)**, McElderry, Margaret K. Bks.) McElderry, Margaret K. Bks.
Weinberg, Steven. You Must Be This Tall. Weinberg, Steven, illus. 2016. (ENG., Illus.). 40p. (J). (gr. -1-3). 17.99 (978-1-4814-2981-8(7), McElderry, Margaret K. Bks.) McElderry, Margaret K. Bks.
Weinberger, Justin. Reformed. 2017. (ENG.). 208p. (J). (gr. 3-7). 16.99 (978-0-545-90252-6(5), Scholastic Pr.) Scholastic, Inc.
Weinbrecht, William. Stories for Amand. 2009. 48p. pap. 15.50 (978-1-60693-150-9(4), Eloquent Bks.) Strategic Book Publishing & Rights Agency (SBPRA).
Weinbrenner, Darlene. Hannah, Mable, & the Moving Van. 2007. 76p. per. 19.95 (978-1-4241-6563-6(6)) America Star Bks.
Weiner, Brian. Toad Catchers' Creek. Weintraub, Claudia & Frederick, Robin, eds. Cannon, Martin, illus. 2005. 40p. (J). lib. bdg. 17.99 (978-1-932949-58-2(5)) Illusion Factory, The.
Weiner, Jennifer. The Littlest Bigfoot. 2017. (Littlest Bigfoot Ser.: 1). (ENG.). 352p. (J). (gr. 3-7). pap. 7.99 **(978-1-4814-7075-9(2)**, Aladdin) Simon & Schuster Children's Publishing.
—The Littlest Bigfoot. Mulvanny, Sara, illus. 2016. (Littlest Bigfoot Ser.: 1). (ENG.). 304p. (J). (gr. 3-7). 16.99 (978-1-4814-7074-2(4), Aladdin) Simon & Schuster Children's Publishing.
—The Littlest Bigfoot. 2017. lib. bdg. 18.40 **(978-0-606-40206-4(3))** Turtleback Bks.
Weingarten, Lynn. Suicide Notes from Beautiful Girls. (ENG., Illus.). 336p. (YA). (gr. 9). 2016. pap. 10.99 (978-1-4814-1858-4(0)) 2015. 17.99 (978-1-4814-1853-9(X)) Simon Pulse. (Simon Pulse).
—Suicide Notes from Beautiful Girls. 2016. (ENG.). (YA). (gr. 9). lib. bdg. 22.10 **(978-0-606-39882-4(1))** Turtleback Bks.
Weinmann, Julianne. The Mis-Adventures of Frissue the Tissue. 2005. 48p. (J). pap. 15.69 (978-1-4116-5310-8(6)) Lulu Pr., Inc.
Weir, Liz. Boom Chicka Boom. Lizatovic, Josip, illus. 2009. (ENG.). 80p. (J). pap. 11.95 (978-0-86278-417-1(4)) O'Brien Pr., Ltd., The IRL. Dist: Dufour Editions, Inc.
Weisman, Greg. Rain of the Ghosts. 2013. (Rain of the Ghosts Ser.: 1). (ENG., Illus.). 240p. (YA). (gr. 6-13). pap. 9.99 (978-1-250-02979-9(1), 9781250029799, St. Martin's Griffin) St. Martin's Pr.
Weiss, Ellen. Fruit Salad: A Touch-and-Learn Book. Bennett, Andy, illus. 2006. (PBS Kids Ser.). 8p. (J). (gr. -1-k). bds. 6.95 (978-1-57791-314-6(0)) Brighter Minds Children's Publishing.
Weiss, Ellen & Friedman, Mel. Porky & Bess. Winborn, Marsha, illus. 2011. (Step into Reading Ser.). (ENG.). 48p. (J). (gr. 2-4). pap. 3.99 (978-0-375-86113-0(0), Random Hse. Bks. for Young Readers) Random Hse. Children's Bks.
Weissman, Elissa Brent. The Short Seller. (ENG.). (J). (gr. 3-7). 2014. 272p. pap. 8.99 (978-1-4424-5256-5(0)) 2013. (Illus.). 256p. 15.99 (978-1-4424-5255-8(2)) Simon & Schuster Children's Publishing.
Wejrmeijer, Annelien. Emma & Bo. van de Liejgraaf, Deborah, illus. 2013. (My Best Friend & Me Ser.). (ENG.). 10p. (J). (gr. -1 — 1). bds. 6.99 (978-0-7641-6635-8(2)) Barron's Educational Series, Inc.
—Lily & Dolly. van de Liejgraaf, Deborah, illus. 2013. (My Best Friend & Me Ser.). (ENG.). 10p. (J). (gr. -1 — 1). bds. 6.99 (978-0-7641-6636-5(0)) Barron's Educational Series, Inc.
—Mason & Buddy. van de Liejgraaf, Deborah, illus. 2013. (My Best Friend & Me Ser.). (ENG.). 10p. (J). (gr. -1 — 1). bds. 6.99 (978-0-7641-6637-2(9)) Barron's Educational Series, Inc.
Welch, Michelle Rose. Country Hands. Harris, Patrick O'Neil, illus. 2013. 24p. pap. 24.95 (978-1-63000-898-7(2)) America Star Bks.
Welch, Pastor Clarence. My Friend the Lizzard. 2011. 20p. pap. 15.99 (978-1-61379-957-4(8)) Salem Author Services.
Welles, Lee. Enter the Earth. Hameister, Ann, illus. 2006. (Gaia Girls Ser.: 1). (ENG.). 336p. (YA). (gr. 4-7). 18.95 (978-1-933609-00-3(1)) Chelsea Green Publishing.
Welling, Martin. Eston Discovers Home: A Dog Discovers Freedom, Fear and, Finally, Family. 2011. (Illus.). 42p. (J). 29.95 (978-1-4327-7038-9(1)) Outskirts Pr., Inc.
—Guardian of the Stones: Nat & Mateo Discover the Two Forces of Magic Stones. 2012. (ENG.). 40p. (J). 29.95 (978-1-4327-7692-3(4)) Outskirts Pr., Inc.
Wells, Carolyn. Patty at Home. 2007. (ENG.). 204p. per. 12.95 (978-1-4218-3321-7(2)) 1st World Publishing, Inc.
—Patty in Paris. 2011. 148p. 24.95 (978-1-4638-9969-1(6)); pap. 12.95 (978-1-4638-0166-3(1)) Rodgers, Alan Bks.
—Patty's Butterfly Days. 2005. 28.95 (978-1-4218-0309-8(7), 1st World Library - Literary Society) 1st World Publishing, Inc.
Wells, Carolyn & E. C. CASWELL. Two Little Women on a Holiday. l.t. ed. 2006. 178p. pap. 21.99 (978-1-4264-2807-4(3)) Creative Media Partners, LLC.
Wells, Misty. Hank the Horse. 2012. 20p. pap. 15.99 (978-1-4685-7968-0(1)) AuthorHouse.
Wells, Pamela. The Crushes. 2009. (ENG.). 352p. (J). (gr. 7). pap. 8.99 (978-0-439-92560-0(6)) Scholastic, Inc.
Wells, Rosemary. Felix Stands Tall. Wells, Rosemary, illus. 2017. (Felix & Fiona Ser.). (ENG., Illus.). 32p. (J). (gr. k-3). 4.99 (978-0-7636-9418-0(5)) Candlewick Pr.
—Felix Stands Tall. Wells, Rosemary, illus. 2017. (Felix & Fiona Ser.). (ENG., Illus.). (J). (gr. k-3). lib. bdg. 14.75 **(978-0-606-39838-1(4))** Turtleback Bks.
—McDuff's New Friend with Plush Box Set. 2003. (Illus.). 28p. (J). 14.99 (978-0-7868-1866-2(2), Disney Editions) Disney Pr.
—Stella's Starliner. Wells, Rosemary, illus. 2014. (ENG., Illus.). 32p. (J). (gr. -1-3). 15.99 (978-0-7636-1495-9(5)) Candlewick Pr.
Wells, Rosemary & Rosemary, Wells. Yoko. Varela, Sandra Lopez, tr. Wells, Rosemary, illus. 2003. (SPA., Illus.). 34p. (J). (gr. k-2). pap. 8.50 (978-84-241-8034-8(8)) Everest Editora ESP. Dist: Lectorum Pubns., Inc.
Wells, Tina. Friends Forever? (Mackenzie Blue Ser.: 3). (ENG.). 208p. (J). (gr. 3-7). 2013. pap. 6.99 (978-0-06-158316-2(2)) 2010. (Illus.). 12.99 (978-0-06-158314-8(6)) HarperCollins Pubs.
—Mackenzie Blue. 2013. (Mackenzie Blue Ser.: 1). (ENG.). 224p. (J). (gr. 3-7). pap. 6.99 (978-0-06-158310-0(3)) HarperCollins Pubs.
—Mackenzie Blue. Segawa, Michael, illus. 2009. (Mackenzie Blue Ser.: 1). (ENG.). 224p. (J). (gr. 3-7). 12.99 (978-0-06-158308-7(1)) HarperCollins Pubs.
—The Secret Crush. 2013. (Mackenzie Blue Ser.: 2). (ENG.). 240p. (J). (gr. 3-7). pap. 6.99 (978-0-06-158313-1(8)) HarperCollins Pubs.
—The Secret Crush. Segawa, Michael, illus. 2009. (Mackenzie Blue Ser.: 2). (ENG.). 240p. (J). (gr. 3-7). 10.99 (978-0-06-158311-7(1)) HarperCollins Pubs.
Welsh, Karen Leis. Frolicking Friends. 2012. (Illus.). 44p. pap. 21.99 (978-1-4685-6422-8(6)) AuthorHouse.
Welsh, Lisa. Sammy Swan: The Big Storm. 2010. 24p. pap. 14.49 (978-1-4490-7234-6(8)) AuthorHouse.
Weltman, June. Mystery of the Missing Candlestick. 2004. (ENG.). 216p. (J). (gr. 4-7). 23.95 (978-1-878044-98-3(2)) Mayhaven Publishing, Inc.
Wemple, Sabrina. Gumby & Beanie. 2008. 32p. per. 13.95 (978-1-4327-0780-4(9)) Outskirts Pr., Inc.
Wendling, Peter. Caterpillars Never Lie, 1 vol. 2010. 26p. pap. 24.95 (978-1-4489-4676-1(X)) PublishAmerica, Inc.
Wenger, Brahm. Dewey Doo-It at the Jingle Jangle Jamboree: A Musical Storybook Inspired by Arnold Schwarzenegger to Benefit Inner-City Games. 2006. (ENG.). 32p. (J). (gr. -1-3). 18.95 (978-0-9745143-4-5(9)) RandallFraser Publishing.
—Dewey's Helping Heart: To Beneift the Larry King Cardiac Foundation. 2009. (ENG.). (J). (gr. -1-2). 18.95 incl. cd-rom (978-0-9745143-7-6(3)) RandallFraser Publishing.
Wenger, Brahm & Green, Alan. Dewey Doo-It Builds a House: A Children's Story about Habitat for Humanity. 2006. (ENG., Illus.). 32p. (J). (gr. -1-2). 17.95 incl. lp (978-0-9745143-2-1(2)) RandallFraser Publishing.
—Dewey Doo-It Feeds a Friend. Gillmore, Jean, illus. 2004. (J). (978-0-9745143-0-7(6)) RandallFraser Publishing.
Wenisch, Tanja, illus. Friends Always. 2014. (J). (978-1-4338-1639-0(3), Magination Pr.) American Psychological Assn.
Wentz, Tim. Dark Secret at Twenty-Five Feet. 2012. 220p. 24.95 (978-1-62709-663-8(9)) America Star Bks.
Wenxuan, Cao. Bronze & Sunflower. Wang, Helen, tr. So, Meilo, illus. 2017. (ENG.). 400p. (J). (gr. 4-7). 16.99 (978-0-7636-8816-5(9)) Candlewick Pr.
Werlin, Nancy. Extraordinary. 2011. (ENG.). 416p. (YA). (gr. 7-18). 9.99 (978-0-14-241974-8(5), Speak) Penguin Young Readers Group.
Werner, Jane. Cinderella's Friends (Disney Classic) Dempster, Al, illus. 2017. (Little Golden Book Ser.). (ENG.). 24p. (J). (-k). 4.99 **(978-0-7364-3713-4(4)**, Golden/Disney) Random Hse. Children's Bks.
Wesolick, Trenton. Why the Life of a Dinosaur Is Hard. 2013. 24p. pap. 14.95 (978-1-4669-8233-8(0)) Trafford Publishing.
West, C. The Adventures of Ice Cream & Honey Buns: A Day in the Park. 2012. 28p. pap. 16.09 (978-1-4669-4700-9(4)) Trafford Publishing.
—The Adventures of Ice Cream & Honey Buns: It's a Party. 2012. 24p. pap. 14.93 (978-1-4669-4665-1(2)) Trafford Publishing.
—The Adventures of Ice Cream & Honey Buns: Ready to Learn. 2012. 28p. pap. 16.09 (978-1-4669-4739-9(X)) Trafford Publishing.
West, Kasie. By Your Side. 2017. 352p. (YA). (gr. 8). pap. 9.99 (978-0-06-245586-4(9), HarperTeen) HarperCollins Pubs.
West, Robert. There's a Spaceship in My Tree!, 1 vol. 2008. (Star-Fighters of Murphy Street Ser.). (ENG., Illus.). 144p. (J). (gr. 4-7). pap. 6.99 (978-0-310-71425-5(7)) Zonderkidz.
Westall, Robert. The Machine Gunners. 2010. (KOR., Illus.). 287p. (J). pap. (978-89-522-1325-9(4)) Salrim Pubn.
Westera, Marleen. Sheep & Goat. Forest-Flier, Nancy, tr. from DUT. Van Ommen, Sylvia, illus. 2006. (ENG.). 99p. (J). 16.95 (978-1-932425-81-9(0), Lemniscaat) Boyds Mills Pr.
Westerfeld, Scott. Uglies. 2009. (Uglies Ser.: Bk. 1). 10.36 (978-0-7848-3338-4(9), Everbind) Marco Bk. Co.
—Uglies. Fournier, Guillaume, tr. 2007. (Uglies Trilogy). (FRE.). 432p. (YA). (gr. 7-12). pap. (978-2-266-15924-1(0)) Presses Pocket.
—Uglies. (Uglies Ser.: 1). (J). 2008. 80.49 (978-1-4281-8028-4(1)) 2007. 199.75 (978-1-4281-1334-3(7)) 2007. 1.25 (978-1-4281-1330-5(4)) 2006. 127.75 (978-1-4281-1337-4(1)) 2006. 97.75 (978-1-4281-1333-6(9)) 2006. 124.75 (978-1-4281-1339-8(8)) 2006. 94.75 (978-1-4281-1335-0(5)) Recorded Bks., Inc.
—Uglies. 2011. (Uglies Ser.). (ENG.). 432p. (YA). (gr. 7). pap. 12.99 (978-1-4424-1981-0(4)); (Illus.). 19.99 (978-1-4169-3638-1(6)) Simon Pulse. (Simon Pulse).
—Uglies: Uglies; Pretties; Specials; Extras. 2012. (Uglies Ser.). (ENG.). 1600p. (YA). (gr. 7). pap. 47.99 (978-1-4424-7939-5(6), Simon Pulse) Simon Pulse.
Westerfeld, Scott & Grayson, Devin. Cutters. 2012. (Uglies Graphic Novel Ser.: 2). lib. bdg. 22.10 (978-0-606-26828-8(6), Turtleback) Turtleback Bks.
—Shay's Story. 2012. (Uglies Graphic Novel Ser.: 1). lib. bdg. 24.50 (978-0-606-26475-4(2), Turtleback) Turtleback Bks.
Western, Foley. To Be Young: Alex, 75 Lilymeg Lane, Billy Goat & Bassey. 2012. (Illus.). 80p. (gr. 4-6). pap. 13.66 (978-1-4772-2678-0(8)) AuthorHouse.
Westheimer, Ruth K. Leopold. 2015. (ENG., Illus.). 34p. (J). 23.99 (978-1-63026-918-0(2)) Turner Publishing Co.
Westling, Vicki Diane. Cats Keep Out: Sam & Friends. 2009. 40p. pap. 16.99 (978-1-4490-3623-2(6)) AuthorHouse.
—Finders Keepers: Sam & Friends. 2010. 40p. pap. 16.99 (978-1-4520-2215-4(1)) AuthorHouse.
—Hannibal Breaks His Promise: Sam & Friends. 2009. 32p. pap. 15.99 (978-1-4490-4711-5(4)) AuthorHouse.
—Hannibal Goes to the Hospital: A Sam & Friends Book. 2011. 32p. pap. 15.99 (978-1-4634-0997-5(4)) AuthorHouse.
—Rudie & the Blue Van: Sam & Friends. 2010. 36p. pap. 15.99 (978-1-4490-8270-3(X)) AuthorHouse.
Westlund, Emmaline. Fatim. 2012. 42p. pap. 16.95 (978-1-4626-9660-4(0)) America Star Bks.
Weston, Avalon. All the Sky. 2013. 138p. pap. (978-1-78407-151-6(X)) FeedARead.com.
Weston, Carol. Ava XOX. 2016. (Ava & Pip Ser.: 3). (ENG.). 208p. (J). (gr. 5-8). 15.99 (978-1-4926-2077-8(7), 9781492620778, Sourcebooks Jabberwocky) Sourcebooks, Inc.
Weston, Greg. Ocean View Terrace & the Blue Pirate Eater. 2008. 232p. pap. 14.95 (978-1-4092-0278-3(X)) Lulu Pr., Inc.
Weston Woods Staff, creator. Fletcher & the Snowflake Christmas. 2011. 29.95 (978-0-545-42619-0(7)) Weston Woods Studios, Inc.
—Henry Hikes to Fitchburg. 2011. 18.95 (978-0-439-90696-8(2)); 38.75 (978-0-439-90698-2(9)) Weston Woods Studios, Inc.
—The Island of the Skog. 2011. 38.75 (978-0-545-23367-5(4)); 18.95 (978-0-545-23366-8(6)); 29.95 (978-0-545-23365-1(8)) Weston Woods Studios, Inc.
—A Weeekend with Wendell. 2004. 29.95 (978-1-55592-129-3(9)); (J). 18.95 (978-1-55592-116-3(7)) Weston Woods Studios, Inc.
—A Weekend with Wendell. 2004. (J). 38.75 (978-1-55592-647-2(9)) Weston Woods Studios, Inc.
—Will I Have a Friend? 2011. 38.75 (978-0-439-72970-3(X)) Weston Woods Studios, Inc.
—Wings: A Tale of Two Chickens. 2011. 18.95 (978-0-439-72920-8(3)); 38.75 (978-0-439-72921-5(1)) Weston Woods Studios, Inc.
Weyn, Suzanne. The Diamond Secret. 2009. (Once upon a Time Ser.). (ENG.). 240p. (YA). (gr. 7-18). mass mkt. 7.99 (978-1-4169-7530-4(6), Simon Pulse) Simon Pulse.
—The Haunted Museum #2: the Phantom Music Box: (a Hauntings Novel) 2014. (Haunted Museum Ser.: 2). (ENG.). 208p. (J). (gr. 3-7). pap. 6.99 (978-0-545-58845-4(6), Scholastic Paperbacks) Scholastic, Inc.
—The Phantom Music Box. 2014. (Hauntings: the Haunted Museum Ser.: 2). lib. bdg. 17.20 (978-0-606-36036-4(0)) Turtleback Bks.
Whaley, John Corey. Highly Illogical Behavior. 2016. (ENG.). 256p. (YA). (gr. 9). 17.99 (978-0-525-42818-3(6), Dial Bks) Penguin Young Readers Group.
—Highly Illogical Behavior. 2017. lib. bdg. 22.10 **(978-0-606-40099-2(0))** Turtleback Bks.
Whaley, John Corey. Where Things Come Back. (ENG., Illus.). (YA). (gr. 9). 2012. 256p. pap. 11.99 (978-1-4424-1334-4(4)) 2011. 240p. 16.99 (978-1-4424-1333-7(6)) Simon & Schuster Children's Publishing. (Atheneum Bks. for Young Readers).
Whamhower, Shogun. Nerdy Ninjas vs the Really Really Bad Guys. McKenzie, Heath, illus. 2012. 137p. (J). (978-0-545-53736-0(3)) Scholastic, Inc.
Whamond, Dave & Owlkids Books Inc. Staff. Oddrey & the New Kid. 2013. (Oddrey Ser.: 2). (ENG., Illus.). 32p. (J). (gr. -1-3). 16.95 (978-1-926973-90-6(9), Owlkids) Owlkids Bks. Inc. CAN. Dist: Publishers Group West (PGW).
What Tommy Did: Individual Title, 6 packs. (Literatura 2000 Ser.). (gr. 1-2). 28.00 (978-0-7635-0152-5(2)) Rigby Education.
Wheatley, Steven. Jack's Little Angel. 2012. 32p. pap. 19.99 (978-1-4685-9445-4(1)) AuthorHouse.
Wheatonnovember. The Little Hermit Ant. 2011. 28p. pap. 24.95 (978-1-4626-3805-5(8)) America Star Bks.
Wheeler-Cribb, Peggy. Madeline Becomes a Star. Bensch, April, illus. 2013. 50p. 29.95 (978-0-9886194-1-8(5)) ProsePress.
Wheeler, J. D. Gummery & Lubber. 2008. 56p. pap. 16.95 (978-1-60563-432-6(8)) America Star Bks.
Wheeler, Lisa. Invasion of the Pig Sisters. Ansley, Frank, illus. 2006. (Fitch & Chip Ser.: 4). (ENG.). 48p. (J). (gr. 1-3). 16.99 (978-0-689-84953-4(2)); pap. 3.99 (978-0-689-84958-9(3)) Simon Spotlight. (Simon Spotlight).
—New Pig in Town. Ansley, Frank, illus. 2003. (Fitch & Chip Ser.: 1). (ENG.). 48p. (J). (gr. 1-3). 16.99 (978-0-689-84950-3(8), Atheneum/Richard Jackson Bks.) Simon & Schuster Children's Publishing.
—One Dark Night. Bates, Ivan, illus. 2006. (ENG.). 32p. (J). (gr. -1-3). reprint ed. pap. 6.99 (978-0-15-205888-3(5)) Houghton Mifflin Harcourt Publishing Co.
Wheeler, Mary A. Over the Edge. 2010. 373p. pap. 16.95 (978-1-4327-5994-0(9)) Outskirts Pr., Inc.
Wheelie, P. The Fishing Trip: The tales of Tommy the tortoise & Friends. 2009. (Illus.). 32p. pap. 12.99 (978-1-4389-6414-0(5)) AuthorHouse.
Whelan, Gloria. A Time to Keep Silent. 2004. 144p. (J). pap. 8.00 (978-0-8028-5255-7(6)) Eerdmans, William B. Publishing Co.
When Aunt Mattie Got Her Wings. 2014. (ENG., Illus.). 32p. (J). (gr. -1-3). 17.99 (978-1-4814-1044-1(X), Beach Lane Bks.) Beach Lane Bks.
Whipple, Natalie. House of Ivy & Sorrow. 2014. (ENG.). 368p. (YA). (gr. 8). pap. 9.99 (978-0-06-212018-2(2), HarperTeen) HarperCollins Pubs.
Whitaker, Alecia. The Queen of Kentucky. 2013. (ENG.). 384p. (YA). (gr. 7-17). pap. 8.99 (978-0-316-12494-2(X), Poppy) Little, Brown Bks. for Young Readers.
Whitaker, Jimmy. Lilly & Twinkle Eyes, 1 vol. 2010. 100p. pap. 19.95 (978-1-4489-3032-6(4)) America Star Bks.
Whitaker, Nathan. Snap Decision, 1 vol. 2015. (Game Face Ser.). (ENG.). 272p. (J). pap. 8.99 (978-0-310-73703-2(6)) Zonderkidz.
White, Alexis. Three Peas in a Pod. 2008. 56p. pap. 11.95 (978-1-4327-1869-5(X)) Outskirts Pr., Inc.
White, Andrea. Window Boy. 2008. (ENG.). 256p. (J). (gr. 4-7). 17.95 (978-1-933979-14-4(3), 9781933979144) Bright Sky Pr.
White, Becky. PawPrints on Your Heart. Cranford, Darren, illus. 2013. 64p. (J). 18.95 (978-0-9860169-0-5(X)) Vision Chapters Publishing Co.
White, E. B. Charlotte's Web. Williams, Garth, illus. 2005. (Charming Classics). 192p. (J). pap. 7.99 (978-0-06-084594-0(5), HarperFestival) HarperCollins Pubs.
—Charlotte's Web. movie tie-in ed. 2006. (Charlotte's Web Ser.). (ENG., Illus.). 192p. (J). (gr. 4-7). per. 7.99 (978-0-06-112026-8(X)) HarperCollins Pubs.
—Charlotte's Web. Williams, Garth, illus. movie tie-in ed. 2006. (Charlotte's Web Ser.). (J). 192p. mass mkt. 7.99 (978-0-06-122874-2(5), Harper Trophy);Set. pap. 19.99 (978-0-06-121502-5(3)) HarperCollins Pubs.
—Charlotte's Web. Williams, Garth, illus. 2004. (CHI.). 158p. (YA). pap. (978-957-08-2568-8(5)) Linking Publishing Co., Ltd.
—Charlotte's Web. Williams, Garth, illus. 184p. (J). pap. 5.95 (978-0-8072-8305-9(3), Listening Library) Random Hse. Audio Publishing Group.
—Charlotte's Web. unabr. ed. 2004. 184p. (J). (gr. 3-7). pap. 36.00 incl. audio (978-0-8072-8304-2(5), YYA156SP, Listening Library) Random Hse. Audio Publishing Group.
—Charlotte's Web. 2012. (J). (gr. 3-6). 18.40 (978-0-8085-3772-4(5), Turtleback) Turtleback Bks.
—Wilbur's Adventure: A Charlotte's Web Picture Book. Kneen, Maggie, illus. 2008. (Charlotte's Web Ser.). 32p. (J). (gr. k-2). lib. bdg. 17.89 (978-0-06-078165-1(3)) HarperCollins Pubs.
White, E. B. & DiCamillo, Kate. Charlotte's Web. Williams, Garth, illus. (ENG.). 192p. (J). (gr. 3-7). 2012. 8.99 (978-0-06-112495-2(8)) 2012. 16.99 (978-0-06-026385-0(7)) 2012. pap. 8.99 (978-0-06-440055-8(7)) 2006. 16.99 (978-0-06-088261-7(1)) HarperCollins Pubs.
White, E. B. & DiCamillo, Kate. Charlotte's Web: a Harper Classic. Williams, Garth, illus. 2017. (Harper Classic Ser.). 208p. (J). (gr. 3-7). 16.99 **(978-0-06-265875-3(1))** HarperCollins Pubs.
White, Janet. Tales of Leafy Lane. White, Lee et al, illus. 2007. 88p. per. (978-1-84748-196-2(5)) Athena Pr.
White, K. B. Adrianna*Angelica*Andrea Mystery Stories: The Case of the Missing Dog. 2012. 20p. pap. 17.99 (978-1-4772-4549-1(9)) AuthorHouse.
White, Marcia. The Adventures of Ragpatch: Love Lost & Found. 2012. 28p. pap. 13.99 (978-1-4624-0150-5(3), Inspiring Voices) Author Solutions, Inc.
White, Marco. Freddy's Fishbowl. 2006. (Neighborhood Readers Ser.). (ENG.). 8p. (gr. -1-3). pap. 5.15 (978-1-4042-6702-2(6), Rosen Classroom) Rosen Publishing Group, Inc., The.
White, Pauline. Jewel Baxter & Friends, 1 vol. 2009. 48p. pap. 16.95 (978-1-60813-541-7(1)) America Star Bks.
Whitehead, Jenny. You're a Crab! A Moody Day Book. Whitehead, Jenny, illus. 2015. (ENG., Illus.). 32p. (J). (gr. -1-2). 16.99 (978-0-8050-9361-2(3), 9780805093612, Holt, Henry & Co. Bks. For Young Readers) Holt, Henry & Co.
Whitesides, Tyler. Heroes of the Dustbin. 2015. (Janitors Ser.: Bk. 5). (Illus.). vii, 408p. (J). 18.99 (978-1-62972-065-4(8), Shadow Mountain) Deseret Bk. Co.
—Strike of the Sweepers. 2014. (Janitors Ser.: 4). (ENG., Illus.). 400p. (J). (gr. 5). 18.99 (978-1-60907-907-9(8), Shadow Mountain) Shadow Mountain Publishing.
Whitfield, Willie. Big Pigpen Willie's Inheritance. 2006. (Illus.). 40p. (J). (gr. -1-3). pap. 12.95 (978-1-56167-958-4(5)) American Literary Pr.
Whitman, David L. Friends. 2012. 32p. pap. 14.51 (978-1-4669-6317-7(4)) Trafford Publishing.
Whitman, Sylvia. The Milk of Birds. (ENG., Illus.). 384p. (YA). (gr. 9). 2014. pap. 10.99 (978-1-4424-4683-0(8)) 2013. 16.99 (978-1-4424-4682-3(X), Atheneum Bks. for Young Readers) Simon & Schuster Children's Publishing.
Whitmore, Gary. Prince Luna & the Space Dreamers. 2011. (ENG.). 204p. pap. 8.50 (978-1-4565-8438-2(3)) CreateSpace Independent Publishing Platform.
Whitmore, Hugh. The Three Madelines. Wilson, Raylene Jenee & Gibbons, Deanna, illus. 2012. 124p. pap. 15.95 (978-0-9848314-4-9(4)) Sincerity Publishing.
Whitney, A. D. T. Sights & Insights: Patience Strong's Story of over the Way. Vol. 1. 2006. 356p. per. 26.99 (978-1-4255-3625-1(5)) Michigan Publishing.
—Sights & Insights: Patience Strong's Story of over the Way. Vol. 2. 2006. 344p. per. 23.99 (978-1-4255-3480-6(5)) Michigan Publishing.
Whittemore, Jo. Brooke's Bad Luck. 2017. (Confidentially Yours Ser.: 5). 288p. (J). (gr. 3-7). pap. 6.99 (978-0-06-235901-8(0)) HarperCollins Pubs.
—Brooke's Not-So-Perfect Plan. 2016. (Confidentially Yours Ser.: 1). (Illus.). 320p. (J). (gr. 3-7). pap. 6.99 (978-0-06-235893-6(6)) HarperCollins Pubs.
Whittemore, Jo. Confidentially Yours #3: Heather's Crush Catastrophe. 2016. (Confidentially Yours Ser.: 3). 288p. (J). (gr. 3-7). 6.99 **(978-0-06-235897-4(9))** HarperCollins Pubs.
Whybrow, Ian. Miss Wire's Christmas Surprise. Chichester Clark, Emma, illus. 2007. 45p. (J). (gr. -1-3). pap. 3.95 (978-0-7534-6136-5(6), Kingfisher) Roaring Brook Pr.
—The Unvisibles. 2006. 184p. (J). (gr. 4-7). 16.95 (978-0-8234-1972-2(X)) Holiday Hse., Inc.
Whyman, Matt. Boy Kills Man. 2005. 160p. (J). 15.99 (978-0-06-074663-6(7), HarperTeen) HarperCollins Pubs.
Whytock, Cherry. My Scrumptious Scottish Dumplings: The Life of Angelica Cookson Potts. Whytock, Cherry, illus. 2006. (ENG., Illus.). 192p. (YA). mass mkt. 5.99 (978-0-689-86552-7(X), Simon Pulse) Simon Pulse.
Wickham, Kimberly, illus. Summer of Magic Horses. 2007. 134p. 12.85 (978-1-4251-3012-1(7)) Trafford Publishing.
Widgen, Susan. A Caring Deed for Becky. Novak, Steven, illus. 2012. 36p. pap. 8.99 (978-1-60820-579-0(7)) MLR Pr., LLC.
Wiechman, Kathy Cannon. Like a River. 2015. (ENG.). 336p. (J). (gr. 5). 17.95 (978-1-62979-209-5(8), Calkins Creek) Boyds Mills Pr.
Wientge, Kristi. Karma Khullar's Mustache. 2017. (ENG., Illus.). 272p. (J). (gr. 3-7). 16.99 **(978-1-4814-7770-3(6)**, Simon & Schuster Bks. For Young Readers) Simon & Schuster Bks. For Young Readers.

—Karma Khullar's Mustache. 2017. (J). pap. **(978-1-4814-7771-0(4)**, Simon & Schuster Bks. For Young Readers) Simon & Schuster Bks. For Young Readers.
Wiersbitzky, Shannon. What Flowers Remember. 2014. 158p. (J). 18.95 *(978-1-60898-166-3(5))* namelos llc.
Wiesner, David. Tuesday. 2011. (gr. -1-2). lib. bdg. 18.40 *(978-0-613-03614-6(X)*, Turtleback) Turtleback Bks.
Wiess, Laura. Leftovers. 2008. (ENG.). 256p. (gr. 8-18). pap. 12.99 *(978-1-4165-4662-7(6)*, MTV Bks.) MTV Books.
Wigden, Susan & Salem, I. A Mitzva for Zelda. 2008. 32p. 12.95 *(978-1-934440-54-4(X)*, Pitspopany Pr.) Simcha Media Group.
Wigglesworth, Penny. Penny Bear's Gift of Love: A Story of Friendship Between a Grieving Young Boy & a Magical Little Bear. Eager, Michiko, illus. l.t. ed. 2004. 84p. (J). pap. 7.95 *(978-0-9675532-5-2(3))* Quality of Life Publishing Co.
Wightman, Jillian C. The Adventures of Erin Mctavitt. 2008. 68p. pap. 19.95 *(978-1-4327-3164-9(5))* Outskirts Pr., Inc.
Wilce, Colin. The Valley & Daffodils (Rabbit Brook T. 2007. 80p. pap. 11.34 *(978-1-4116-8792-9(2))* Lulu Pr., Inc.
Wilce, Ysabeau S. Flora's Dare: How a Girl of Spirit Gambles All to Expand Her Vocabulary, Confront a Bouncing Boy Terror, & Try to Save Califa from a Shaky Doom (Despite Being Confined to Her Room) 2010. (ENG.). 528p. (YA). (gr. 7). pap. 7.99 *(978-0-15-205403-8(0))* Houghton Mifflin Harcourt Publishing Co.
Wilcut-Bledsoe, Robin. The Imagination of Hollie Mason. 2008. 88p. pap. 19.95 *(978-1-60703-804-7(8))* America Star Bks.
Wild, Margaret. Fox. Brooks, Ron, illus. 2006. (ENG.). 32p. (J). (gr. 1). pap. 7.99 *(978-1-933605-15-9(4))* Kane Miller.
Wilde, Jen. Queens of Geek. 2017. (ENG.). 288p. (YA). pap. 10.99 *(978-1-250-11139-5(0)*, 9781250111395) Feiwel & Friends.
The Wildlife Adventures of Mugwa & Washtucna. 2008. (Illus.). 54p. (J). 19.95 *(978-0-9799493-0-2(0))* Carol Kalhagen-Tamanaha.
Wiles, Deborah. Freedom Summer. Lagarrigue, Jerome, illus. 50th anniv. ed. 2014. (ENG.). 32p. (J). (gr. -1-3). 17.99 *(978-1-4814-2298-7(7)*, Atheneum Bks. for Young Readers) Simon & Schuster Children's Publishing.
Wilhelm, Doug. The Revealers. 2011. (ENG.). 240p. (YA). (gr. 5-9). pap. 7.99 *(978-0-312-56374-5(4)*, 9780312563745) Square Fish.
Wilhelm, Hans. Seamos Amigos Otra Vez. (SPA.). (J). 13.95 *(978-84-261-2514-9(X))* Juventud, Editorial ESP. Dist: AIMS International Bks., Inc.
Wilhite, Becca. Bright Blue Miracle. 2009. 176p. (J). pap. 8.99 *(978-1-60641-031-8(8)*, Shadow Mountain) Shadow Mountain Publishing.
Wilkerson, Dawn. Katie & Katoa Travel down the River. 2009. 48p. pap. 16.95 *(978-1-61582-862-3(1))* America Star Bks.
Wilkins, Phil Cole. Dragog & the Seven Weeks of Summer. 2012. 164p. (gr. -1). pap. 15.60 *(978-1-4567-8998-5(8))* AuthorHouse.
Will Mcallister. Sam Rivers & the Night Rustlers. 2009. 88p. pap. 9.95 *(978-0-595-46287-2(1))* iUniverse, Inc.
Willard, Hugh. The Goodwill Vultures Club. Holjes, Kerry, ed. Eason, D. M., illus. 2013. 122p. pap. 9.99 *(978-1-935711-26-1(1))* Peak City Publishing, LLC.
—The Goodwill Vultures Club: No Time for Play. Holjes, Kerry, ed. Eason, D. M., illus. 2013. 140p. pap. 9.99 *(978-1-935711-30-8(X))* Peak City Publishing, LLC.
—The Goodwill Vultures Club: The Gift of the Vulture. Dozier, Dolly, ed. Eason, D. M., illus. 2013. 128p. pap. 9.99 *(978-1-935711-34-6(2))* Peak City Publishing, LLC.
Willems, Mo. A Big Guy Took My Ball! Willems, Mo, illus. 2013. (Elephant & Piggie Ser.). (ENG., Illus.). 64p. (J). (gr. 1-3). 9.99 *(978-1-4231-7491-2(7))* Hyperion Bks. for Children.
—Can I Play Too? 2012. (Elephant & Piggie Bks.). (CHI & JPN.). (J). (gr. -1-3). pap. **(978-986-189-329-7(6))** Grimm Cultural Ent., Co., Ltd.
—Can I Play Too? Willems, Mo, illus. 2010. (Elephant & Piggie Book Ser.). (ENG., Illus.). 64p. (J). (gr. -1-k). 9.99 *(978-1-4231-1991-3(6))* Hyperion Pr.
—Cat the Cat Who Is That? Willems, Mo, illus. 2010. (Illus.). 32p. (J). (gr. -1-3). (ENG.). 10.99 *(978-0-06-172840-2(3))*; lib. bdg. 14.89 *(978-0-06-172841-9(1))* HarperCollins Pubs.
—City Dog, Country Frog. Muth, Jon J., illus. 2010. (ENG.). 64p. (J). (gr. -1-k). 17.99 *(978-1-4231-0300-4(9))* Hyperion Pr.
—Happy Pig Day! Willems, Mo, illus. 2011. (Elephant & Piggie Book Ser.). (ENG., Illus.). 64p. (J). (gr. -1-k). 9.99 *(978-1-4231-4342-0(6))* Hyperion Pr.
—Hooray for Amanda & Her Alligator! Willems, Mo, illus. 2011. (ENG., Illus.). 72p. (J). (gr. -1-3). 17.99 *(978-0-06-200400-0(X))* HarperCollins Pubs.
—I Am Going! Willems, Mo, illus. 2010. (Elephant & Piggie Book Ser.). (ENG., Illus.). 64p. (J). (gr. -1-k). 9.99 *(978-1-4231-1990-6(8))* Hyperion Pr.
—I Really Like Slop! Willems, Mo, illus. 2015. (Elephant & Piggie Book Ser.). (ENG., Illus.). 64p. (J). (gr. 1-3). 9.99 *(978-1-4847-2262-6(0))* Hyperion Bks. for Children.
—I Will Surprise My Friend! Willems, Mo, illus. 2008. (Elephant & Piggie Book Ser.). (ENG., Illus.). 64p. (J). (gr. -1-k). 9.99 *(978-1-4231-0962-4(7))* Hyperion Pr.
—I Will Take a Nap! Willems, Mo, illus. 2015. (Elephant & Piggie Ser.). (ENG., Illus.). 64p. (J). (gr. 1-3). 9.99 *(978-1-4847-1630-4(2))* Hyperion Bks. for Children.
—I'm a Frog! Willems, Mo, illus. 2013. (Elephant & Piggie Ser.). (ENG., Illus.). 64p. (J). (gr. 1-3). 9.99 *(978-1-4231-8305-1(3))* Hyperion Pr.
—Listen to My Trumpet! Willems, Mo, illus. 2012. (Elephant & Piggie Book Ser.). (ENG., Illus.). 64p. (J). (gr. -1-k). 9.99 *(978-1-4231-5404-4(5))* Hyperion Pr.
—My Friend Is Sad. Willems, Mo, illus. 2007. (Elephant & Piggie Book Ser.). (ENG., Illus.). 64p. (J). (gr. -1-k). 9.99 *(978-1-4231-0297-7(5))* Hyperion Pr.
—My New Friend Is So Fun! Willems, Mo, illus. 2014. (Elephant & Piggie Ser.). (ENG., Illus.). 64p. (J). (gr. 1-3). 9.99 *(978-1-4231-7958-0(7))* Hyperion Bks. for Children.
—Pigs Make Me Sneeze! Willems, Mo, illus. 2009. (Elephant & Piggie Book Ser.). (ENG., Illus.). 64p. (J). (gr. -1-k). 9.99 *(978-1-4231-1411-6(6))* Hyperion Pr.
—Should I Share My Ice Cream? Willems, Mo, illus. 2011. (Elephant & Piggie Book Ser.). (ENG., Illus.). 64p. (J). (gr. -1-k). 9.99 *(978-1-4231-4343-7(4))* Hyperion Pr.
—The Story of Diva & Flea. DiTerlizzi, Tony, illus. 2015. (ENG.). 80p. (J). (gr. 1-3). 14.99 *(978-1-4847-2284-8(1))* Disney Pr.
—The Thank You Book. Willems, Mo, illus. 2016. (Elephant & Piggie Book Ser.). (ENG., Illus.). 64p. (J). (gr. 1-3). 9.99 *(978-1-4231-7828-6(9))* Hyperion Bks. for Children.
—¡Tienes un Pájaro en la Cabeza! Willems, Mo, illus. 2017. (Elephant & Piggie Book Ser.). (ENG & SPA., Illus.). 64p. (J). (gr. 1-3). 9.99 *(978-1-4847-8697-0(1))* Hyperion Bks. for Children.
—Today I Will Fly! Willems, Mo, illus. 2007. (Elephant & Piggie Book Ser.). (ENG., Illus.). 64p. (J). (gr. -1-k). 9.99 *(978-1-4231-0295-3(9))* Hyperion Pr.
—Who Flies, Cat the Cat? Willems, Mo, illus. 2014. (ENG., Illus.). 22p. (J). (gr. -1 — 1). bds. 6.99 *(978-0-06-230652-4(9))* HarperCollins Pubs.
—Who Is That, Cat the Cat? Willems, Mo, illus. 2014. (ENG., Illus.). 22p. (J). (gr. -1 — 1). bds. 6.99 *(978-0-06-230653-1(7))* HarperCollins Pubs.
—Who Sleeps, Cat the Cat? Willems, Mo, illus. 2014. (ENG., Illus.). 22p. (J). (gr. -1 — 1). bds. 6.99 *(978-0-06-230655-5(3))* HarperCollins Pubs.
Willems, Mo, narrated by. Leonardo, the Terrible Monster. 2011. (Illus.). (J). (gr. -1-3). 29.95 *(978-0-439-02766-3(7)*, WHCD801) Weston Woods Studios, Inc.
Willems, Mo & Campoy, F. Isabel. ¿Debo Compartir Mi Helado? Willems, Mo, illus. 2015. (Elephant & Piggie Book Ser.). (SPA., Illus.). 64p. (J). (gr. -1-k). 9.99 *(978-1-4847-2291-6(4))* Disney Publishing Worldwide.
—¡Hoy Volaré! Willems, Mo, illus. 2015. (Elephant & Piggie Book Ser.). (SPA., Illus.). 64p. (J). (gr. 1-3). 9.99 *(978-1-4847-2287-9(6))* Disney Publishing Worldwide.
—¡Un Tipo Grande Se Llevó Mi Pelota! Willems, Mo, illus. 2015. (Elephant & Piggie Book Ser.). (SPA., Illus.). 64p. (J). (gr. 1-3). 9.99 *(978-1-4847-2285-5(X))* Disney Publishing Worldwide.
Willems, Mo & Willems, Trixie, narrated by. Knuffle Bunny Too: A Case of Mistaken Identity. 2011. (J). (gr. -1-2). 29.95 *(978-0-545-13456-9(0))* Weston Woods Studios, Inc.
Willey, Margaret. Four Secrets. Hauser, Bill, illus. (ENG.). 288p. (YA). (gr. 7-12). 2014. pap. 9.95 *(978-1-4677-1626-0(X)*, Carolrhoda Lab™) 2012. 17.95 *(978-0-7613-8535-6(5))* Lerner Publishing Group.
Williams, Allix Elise. The Adventures of Prince Thaddeus: The Glamorous Guest. 2010. 56p. pap. 11.49 *(978-1-4520-5437-7(1))* AuthorHouse.
Williams, Annik. Mr. Mole's Day Off: With Goodnight Little Birdie. 2010. 20p. 15.78 *(978-1-4520-3756-1(6))* AuthorHouse.
Williams, Avery. The Impossibility of Tomorrow. 2014. (ENG., Illus.). 384p. (YA). (gr. 7). pap. 11.99 *(978-1-4424-4320-4(0)*, Simon & Schuster Bks. For Young Readers) Simon & Schuster Bks. For Young Readers.
Williams, Carol Lynch. Pretty Like Us, 1 vol. 2008. (ENG., Illus.). 224p. (J). (gr. 3-7). 15.95 *(978-1-56145-444-0(3))* Peachtree Pubs.
Williams, Dawn. Very Little Venus & the Very Friendly Fly. Chou, Joey, illus. 2007. 48p. (J). 15.00 *(978-0-9770783-2-5(9))* SunriseHouse Pubs.
Williams, Emma Louise. Harry the Hedgehog Loses His Favorite Sock. 2012. 20p. pap. 7.99 *(978-1-939076-00-7(5))* Wiggies, Piggy.
Williams, Geoffrey T. The Devil Fish. Artful Doodlers, illus. Campbell, Tom, photos by. 2008. (Save Our Seas Adventure Bks.). (ENG.). 64p. (J). (gr. 4-7). 8.95 *(978-0-9800444-1-6(3))* Save Our Seas, Ltd.
—The Hammerheads of Treasure Island. 2010. (ENG., Illus.). 64p. (J). (gr. 3-7). 8.95 *(978-0-9800444-2-3(1))* Save Our Seas, Ltd.
Williams, Greg. Cuddie the Cut Throat Trout. 2011. 28p. pap. 19.00 *(978-1-60746-981-0(2))* FastPrncil, Inc.
—Salty the Sea Gull. 2011. 38p. pap. 19.00 *(978-1-60746-205-7(2))* FastPrncil, Inc.
Williams-Hines, Jacqueline. Joshua, That's Sooo Slimming! 2009. 28p. pap. 13.99 *(978-1-4389-0342-2(1))* AuthorHouse.
Williams, Jason & Felt, Jeremy. The Adventures of Sam & Rowdy: Two Best Friends. 2013. 16p. pap. 15.99 *(978-1-4817-1268-2(3))* AuthorHouse.
Williams, Josie. Hoppy Finds Friends. 2004. 33p. pap. 24.95 *(978-1-4137-1461-6(7))* PublishAmerica, Inc.
Williams, Karen Lynn. Lubuto Means Light. Grifalconi, Ann, illus. 2010. (ENG.). 32p. 16.95 *(978-1-59078-716-8(1))* Boyds Mills Pr.
Williams, Kristen. Sheepy Sue & the Bedtime Blues. 2012. 28p. pap. 12.95 *(978-1-105-48819-1(5))* Lulu.com GBR. Dist: Lulu Pr., Inc.
Williams, Larry. The League of Clique. Williams, Larry, illus. 2007. (ENG., Illus.). 80p. per. 19.95 *(978-1-4241-5976-5(8))* America Star Bks.
Williams, Lori. Henrietta Peddles Her Eggs. 2010. 36p. pap. 15.49 *(978-1-4490-6810-3(3))* AuthorHouse.
Williams, Patricia de Belloy. Pioneers-1937. 2003. (Illus.). 409p. (J). per. 14.99 *(978-1-932176-00-1(4))* Beluga-Duga Pr.
Williams, Raymond. The House of Useful Things. 2012. (Illus.). 44p. pap. 13.50 *(978-1-78035-396-8(0)*, Fastprint Publishing) Upfront Publishing Ltd. GBR. Dist: Printondemand-worldwide.com.
Williams, Rozanne Lanczak. Two Stories, Two Friends. Allen, Joy, illus. 2006. (Learn to Write Ser.). 16p. (J). (gr. k-2). pap. 3.49 *(978-1-59198-295-1(2)*, 6186) Creative Teaching Pr., Inc.
Williams, Sam. I'm the Boss. Dufalla, Anita, illus. 2012. (ENG.). 24p. (gr. k-1). pap. 8.95 *(978-1-61810-297-3(4))* Rourke Educational Media.
Williams, Sean. Twinmaker. 2013. (Twinmaker Ser.: 1). (ENG.). 496p. (YA). (gr. 8). 17.99 *(978-0-06-220321-2(5)*, HarperTeen) HarperCollins Pubs.
Williams, Suzanne. The Gigantic, Genuine Genie. Gonzales, Chuck, illus. 2007. (Princess Power Ser.: No. 6). 128p. (J). 15.99 *(978-0-06-078309-9(5))* HarperCollins Pubs.
—The Mysterious, Mournful Maiden. Gonzales, Chuck, illus. 2007. 112p. (J). 15.99 *(978-0-06-078305-1(2))* HarperCollins Pubs.
Williams, Teresa Ann. Friends of Wildwood, 1 vol. 2009. 48p. pap. 16.95 *(978-1-4489-9419-9(5))* America Star Bks.
Williams, Teri. I Got Bank! What My Granddad Taught Me about Money. 2010. (ENG., Illus.). 88p. (J). pap. 14.95 *(978-0-9827943-7-1(1))* Beckham Pubns. Group, Inc.
Williamson, Lisa. The Art of Being Normal. 2016. (ENG.). 352p. (YA). 17.99 *(978-0-374-30237-5(5)*, 9780374302375, Farrar, Straus & Giroux (BYR)) Farrar, Straus & Giroux.
Williamson, Stafford. Puppyfish. 2005. 48p. (J). pap. 18.49 *(978-1-4116-3836-5(0))* Lulu Pr., Inc.
Willie's Reflection: A Story of Grief, Hope & Healing. 2008. (Illus.). 32p. (J). 15.95 *(978-0-9799021-0-9(X))* Aspire Publishing.
Willis, Jeanne. Lucinda Belinda Melinda Mccool. Ross, Tony, illus. 2016. (ENG.). 32p. (J). (-k). 16.99 *(978-1-78344-202-7(6))* Andersen Pr. GBR. Dist: Independent Pubs. Group.
Willis, Jeanne & Jossen, Penélope. When Stephanie Smiled... 2003. (ENG., Illus.). 32p. (J). 16.00 *(978-1-84270-075-4(8))* Andersen Pr. GBR. Dist: Trafalgar Square Publishing.
Willis, Tacey Lynn. Ellie, Tellie & Mellie: Best Jungle Friends Forever. 2010. 28p. pap. 12.49 *(978-1-4520-1903-1(7))* AuthorHouse.
Willner-Pardo, Gina. The Hard Kind of Promise. 2011. (ENG.). 204p. (J). (gr. 5-7). pap. 12.99 *(978-0-547-55017-6(0))* Houghton Mifflin Harcourt Publishing Co.
Willow, Tirissa & the Necklace of Nulidor. 2009. 338p. pap. 17.95 *(978-1-4327-4013-9(X))* Outskirts Pr., Inc.
Willsea, Hedley. The Heath of the Graves. 2009. 371p. pap. 31.50 *(978-1-4092-2226-2(8))* Lulu Pr., Inc.
Wilson, A. c. & Wilson, A. C. Ambersil - the Legacy of Mr Harrison. 2011. 496p. pap. *(978-1-908105-45-5(3))* Grosvenor Hse. Publishing Ltd.
Wilson, Alexandria M. Happy Birthday Gideon. 2013. 24p. pap. 24.95 *(978-1-62709-808-3(9))* America Star Bks.
Wilson, Angela. Frog Makes a Friend. Wilson, Whitleigh & Wilson, John, illus. 2013. 28p. pap. 24.95 *(978-1-63004-048-2(7))* America Star Bks.
—Tara the Terrified Turtle. Basta, Stormie, illus. 2012. 28p. pap. 24.95 *(978-1-4626-7454-1(2))* America Star Bks.
Wilson, Barbara. Jack & His Pal Max. Caracino, Leah, illus. 2012. (ENG.). 16p. (gr. k-3). pap. 9.00 *(978-1-56778-540-1(9))* Wilson Language Training.
Wilson, Barbara E. Small Enough Tall Enough. Gospodinov, George, illus. 2012. 46p. pap. 14.95 *(978-0-9838964-0-1(2))* Simply Silly Stories.
Wilson, Budge. Friendships. 2006. (ENG.). 224p. (J). (gr. 7-18). 11.99 *(978-0-14-301766-0(7)*, Puffin Canada) Penguin Random House Canada Young Readers CAN. Dist: Penguin Random Hse. LLC.
Wilson, David. The Adventures of Jack Bennett James Bay or Bust. 2013. 190p. pap. *(978-0-9919509-1-1(7))* Wilson, David.
—The Adventures of Jack Bennett Winter Rescue. 2013. 116p. pap. *(978-0-9919509-0-4(9))* Wilson, David.
Wilson, David Cramb. The Day that the Fairies stole Badger! 2008. 40p. pap. 9.95 *(978-0-557-00247-4(8))* Lulu Pr., Inc.
Wilson, David Lloyd. Some Dogs Fly, 1 vol. 2009. 89p. pap. 19.95 *(978-1-61582-968-2(7))* America Star Bks.
Wilson, Jacqueline. Best Friends. Sharratt, Nick, illus. 2009. (ENG.). 256p. (J). (gr. 4-7). pap. 8.99 *(978-0-312-58144-2(0)*, 9780312581442) Square Fish.
—Candyfloss. Sharratt, Nick, illus. 2008. (ENG.). 352p. (J). (gr. 4-7). pap. 9.99 *(978-0-312-38418-0(1)*, 9780312384180) Square Fish.
Wilson, Jenine. My Familiar. 2007. (YA). per. 9.99 *(978-0-9794414-0-0(4))* Jensonbooks.
Wilson, Karma. Bear Counts. Chapman, Jane, illus. 2015. (Bear Bks.). (ENG.). 32p. (J). (gr. -1-2). 16.99 *(978-1-4424-8092-6(0)*, McElderry, Margaret K. Bks.) McElderry, Margaret K. Bks.
—Bear Feels Scared. Chapman, Jane, illus. 2011. (Bear Bks.). (ENG.). 34p. (J). (gr. -1 — 1). bds. 7.99 *(978-1-4424-2755-6(8)*, Little Simon) Little Simon.
—Bear Feels Scared. Chapman, Jane, illus. 2008. (Bear Bks.). (ENG.). 40p. (J). (gr. -1-3). 17.99 *(978-0-689-85986-1(4)*, McElderry, Margaret K. Bks.) McElderry, Margaret K. Bks.
—Bear Sees Colors. Chapman, Jane, illus. 2014. (Bear Bks.). (ENG.). 32p. (J). (gr. -1-2). 16.99 *(978-1-4424-6536-7(0)*, McElderry, Margaret K. Bks.) McElderry, Margaret K. Bks.
—Bear's New Friend. Chapman, Jane, illus. 2009. (Bear Bks.). (ENG.). 34p. (J). (gr. -1-2). bds. 7.99 *(978-1-4169-5438-5(4)*, Little Simon) Little Simon.
—Dormouse Dreams. Liwska, Renata, illus. 2017. (ENG.). 40p. (J). (gr. -1-k). 16.99 *(978-1-4231-7874-3(2))* Disney Pr.
Wilson, Kevin. Brown Spot. 2006. 60p. (J). pap. 12.00 *(978-1-4116-8059-3(6))* Lulu Pr., Inc.
Wilson, Nathaniel. Jessie's Big Move. Shoopik, Marina, illus. 2010. (ENG.). 54p. (J). 16.95 *(978-0-9744935-7-2(0))* AllWrite Advertising & Publishing.
Wilson, Norah & Doherty, Heather. Embrace the Night. 2013. 226p. pap. *(978-1-927651-09-4(3)*, Something Shiny Pr.) Wilson, Norah.
Wilson, Patricia. The Rocking Horse & the Fighting Fish. 2012. 24p. (-18). 24.95 *(978-1-4626-9665-9(1))* America Star Bks.
Wilson, Patricia P. The Rocking Horse & the Fighting Fish. 2012. 24p. pap. 24.95 *(978-1-4626-8162-4(X))* America Star Bks.
Wilson, Robert. Pippy: The Miracle of A Dream. 2011. 136p. pap. 11.95 *(978-1-4620-6633-9(X))* iUniverse, Inc.
Wilson, Steve. Hedgehugs. Tapper, Lucy, illus. 2015. (Hedgehugs Ser.). (ENG.). 32p. (J). (gr. -1-3). 16.99 *(978-1-62779-404-6(2)*, 9781627794046, Holt, Henry & Co. Bks. For Young Readers) Holt, Henry & Co.
Wilson, W. Shane. Gavin the Gnome. 2010. 100p. pap. 11.99 *(978-0-557-50370-4(1))* Lulu Pr., Inc.
—Little Monsters. 2009. 99p. pap. 11.96 *(978-0-557-20687-2(1))* Lulu Pr., Inc.
—The sprite Adventure. 2010. 97p. pap. 12.99 *(978-0-557-42603-4(0))* Lulu Pr., Inc.
—War for Ice. 2010. 158p. pap. 13.99 *(978-0-557-23572-8(3))* Lulu Pr., Inc.
Wilson, Wayne L. Kate, the Ghost Dog: Coping with the Death of a Pet. Soud, illus. 2009. 48p. (J). (gr. 3-8). 14.95 *(978-1-4338-0554-7(5))*; pap. 9.95 *(978-1-4338-0555-4(3))* American Psychological Assn. (Magination Pr.).
Winborne, Mamie Pearl. Sweet Sugar I Got Your Back. 2012. 150p. pap. 13.95 *(978-0-615-58624-3(4))* Professional Publishing Hse. LLC.
Windhorst, Brenda. Do You Want a Henry Story? 2011. 24p. pap. 15.99 *(978-1-4628-8796-5(1))* Xlibris Corp.
Windsor, M. L. Jack Death. Ewald, Chris, illus. 2016. (ENG.). 165p. (J). (gr. 2-7). 12.99 *(978-1-939547-28-6(8))* Creston Bks.
Wineinger, Cherylann. Corgy & His Friends: A Trip to the Unknown. 2011. 24p. pap. 12.79 *(978-1-4520-0349-8(1))* AuthorHouse.
Wing, Natasha. The Night Before First Grade. Zemke, Deborah, illus. (Night Before Ser.). (ENG.). 32p. (J). (gr. k-1). 2014. 12.99 *(978-0-448-48256-9(8))* 2005. pap. 4.99 *(978-0-448-43747-7(3))* Penguin Young Readers Group. (Grosset & Dunlap).
Winget, Susan. Tucker's Four-Carrot School Day. Winget, Susan, illus. 2005. (ENG., Illus.). 40p. (J). (gr. -1-k). 12.99 *(978-0-06-054642-7(5))* HarperCollins Pubs.
Winick, Judd. The Boy Who Crashed to Earth. 2015. (Hilo Ser.: 1). (ENG., Illus.). 208p. (J). (gr. 3-7). 16.99 *(978-0-385-38618-0(4)*, Random Hse. Bks. for Young Readers) Random Hse. Children's Bks.
—The Great Big Boom. 2017. (Hilo Ser.: 3). (ENG., Illus.). 208p. (J). (gr. 3-7). 13.99 *(978-0-385-38620-3(6))*; lib. bdg. 16.99 *(978-0-385-38621-0(4))* Random Hse. Children's Bks. (Random Hse. Bks. for Young Readers).
—Saving the Whole Wide World. 2016. (Hilo Ser.: 2). (ENG., Illus.). 208p. (J). (gr. 3-7). 16.99 *(978-0-385-38624-1(9))*;Bk. 2. 13.99 *(978-0-385-38623-4(0))* Random Hse. Children's Bks. (Random Hse. Bks. for Young Readers).
Winkler, Henry & Oliver, Lin. Always Dance with a Hairy Buffalo. 2013. (Ghost Buddy Ser.: 4). (ENG.). 192p. (J). (gr. 3-7). pap. 5.99 *(978-0-545-29885-8(7)*, Scholastic Paperbacks) Scholastic, Inc.
—Barfing in the Backseat: How I Survived My Family Road Trip. Watson, Jesse Joshua, illus. 2007. (Hank Zipzer Ser.: 12). (ENG.). 160p. (J). (gr. 3-7). pap. 5.99 *(978-0-448-44328-7(7)*, Grosset & Dunlap) Penguin Young Readers Group.
—Day of the Iguana. 2006. (Hank Zipzer Ser.: No. 3). 154p. (J). (gr. 3-9). 24.21 *(978-1-59961-102-0(3))* Spotlight.
—Ghost Buddy: Always Dance with a Hairy Buffalo. 2013. (Ghost Buddy Ser.: 4). (ENG.). 192p. (J). (gr. 3-7). 17.99 *(978-0-545-29890-2(3)*, Scholastic Pr.) Scholastic, Inc.
—The Life of Me (Enter at Your Own Risk) 2008. (Hank Zipzer Ser.: No. 14). (Illus.). 186p. (gr. 3-7). 16.00 *(978-0-7569-8819-7(5))* Perfection Learning Corp.
—My Secret Life as a Ping-Pong Wizard, 9 vols. 2005. (Hank Zipzer Ser.: 9). (ENG., Illus.). 160p. (J). (gr. 3-7). 13.99 *(978-0-448-43877-1(1)*, Grosset & Dunlap) Penguin Young Readers Group.
—My Secret Life as a Ping-Pong Wizard, 9 vols. Heyer, Carol & Watson, Jesse Joshua, illus. 2005. (Hank Zipzer Ser.: 9). (ENG.). 160p. (J). (gr. 3-7). pap. 5.99 *(978-0-448-43749-1(X)*, Grosset & Dunlap) Penguin Young Readers Group.
—Who Ordered This Baby? Definitely Not Me! Watson, Jesse Joshua & Heitz, Tim, illus. 2007. (Hank Zipzer Ser.: 13). (ENG.). 160p. (J). (gr. 3-7). pap. 5.99 *(978-0-448-44374-4(0)*, Grosset & Dunlap) Penguin Young Readers Group.
Winn, Christine M. & Walsh, David. Clover's Secret. Winn, Christine M., illus. 2004. (Illus.). 28p. (J). (gr. k-4). reprint ed. 15.00 *(978-0-7567-7653-4(8))* DIANE Publishing Co.
Winnick, Karen B. Lucy's Cave: A Story of Vicksburg 1863. 2008. (ENG.). 32p. (J). (gr. 4-6). 16.95 *(978-1-59078-194-4(5))* Boyds Mills Pr.
Winnie the Pooh. Goodbye, Honeypot! 2010. 12p. 6.99 *(978-1-4231-3098-7(7))* Disney Pr.
—Spring Cleaning. 2010. 32p. pap. 4.99 *(978-1-4231-3072-7(3))* Disney Pr.
Winnie the Pooh: Party in the Wood. 2011. 32p. pap. 4.99 *(978-1-4231-5386-3(3))* Disney Pr.
Winslade, Jayn E. Emily & Jen Dance for Deeron. 2010. 352p. pap. *(978-1-907211-48-5(9))* Grosvenor Hse. Publishing Ltd.
Winslow, Barbara. Fancy & Francis. 2012. 32p. (-18). pap. 21.99 *(978-1-4797-4580-7(4))* Xlibris Corp.
Winslow, Theresa. Katie the Bear & Her Adventure for Honey, 1 vol. 2009. 20p. pap. 24.95 *(978-1-60836-893-8(9))* America Star Bks.
Winston, Sherri. President of the Whole Sixth Grade. 2015. (ENG.). 320p. (J). (gr. 3-7). 17.00 *(978-0-316-37723-2(6))* Little Brown & Co.
Winter, P. K. Back at Eagle Lake: More Eagle Lake Giant Stories. Winter, P. K., illus. 2009. (Illus.). 182p. pap. 18.50 *(978-1-4251-8831-3(1))* Trafford Publishing.
Winthrop, Elizabeth. Counting on Grace. 2007. 232p. (gr. 4-7). 17.00 *(978-0-7569-8205-8(7))* Perfection Learning Corp.
—Counting on Grace. 2007. (ENG., Illus.). 240p. (J). (gr. 3-7). 6.99 *(978-0-553-48783-1(3)*, Yearling) Random Hse. Children's Bks.
—Maia & the Monster Baby. Haley, Amanda, illus. 2012. (ENG.). 32p. (J). 16.95 *(978-0-8234-2518-1(5))* Holiday Hse., Inc.
Wirt, Mildred A. Swamp Island. 2011. 176p. pap. 12.99 *(978-1-935774-85-3(9)*, Resurrected Pr.) Intrepid Ink, LLC.
Wisbauer, Cortney. Rodney, the Ice Dragon. Wisbauer, Cortney, illus. 2006. (Illus.). 48p. (J). 22.95 *(978-1-59879-215-7(6))* Lifevest Publishing, Inc.
Wisdom, Gail Ann. Trouble with Bullies. 2013. 48p. pap. 20.45 *(978-1-4908-0026-4(3)*, WestBow Pr.) Author Solutions, Inc.
Wise, Alicia. Myrtle's True Friend. Wise, Jesse D., illus. 2008. 15p. pap. 24.95 *(978-1-60610-626-6(0))* America Star Bks.
Wise, Anna. The Vala of Trinity: Book One Norse Series, 1 vol. 2009. 195p. pap. 24.95 *(978-1-61582-763-3(3))* America Star Bks.
Wise, Keith. Isabella's Playmate. 2011. 278p. pap. 27.95 *(978-1-4560-7320-6(6))* America Star Bks.
Wise, Rachel. Breaking News. 2013. (Dear Know-It-All Ser.: 10). (ENG., Illus.). 160p. (J). (gr. 3-7). 15.99 *(978-1-4424-8965-3(0))*; pap. 6.99 *(978-1-4424-8964-6(2))* Simon Spotlight. (Simon Spotlight).
—Cast Your Ballot! 2013. (Dear Know-It-All Ser.: 9). (ENG., Illus.). 160p. (J). (gr. 3-7). 15.99 *(978-1-4424-8793-2(3))*; pap. 5.99 *(978-1-4424-8792-5(5))* Simon Spotlight. (Simon Spotlight).
—Late Edition. 2014. (Dear Know-It-All Ser.: 11). (ENG., Illus.). 160p. (J). (gr. 3-7). pap. 5.99 *(978-1-4424-9724-5(6)*, Simon Spotlight) Simon Spotlight.

—Old Story, New Twist. 2012. (Dear Know-It-All Ser.: 4). (ENG.). 160p. (J). (gr. 3-7). 15.99 *(978-1-4424-5385-2(0))*; pap. 5.99 *(978-1-4424-5328-9(1))* Simon Spotlight. (Simon Spotlight).
—Texting 1, 2, 3. 2013. (Dear Know-It-All Ser.: 8). (ENG., Illus.). 160p. (J). (gr. 3-7). 16.99 *(978-1-4424-7520-5(X))*; pap. 6.99 *(978-1-4424-7519-9(6))* Simon Spotlight. (Simon Spotlight).
Wishinsky, Frieda. A Bee in Your Ear. Laliberte, Louise-Andree, illus. 2004. 64p. (J). lib. bdg. 20.00 *(978-1-4242-1255-2(3))* Fitzgerald Bks.
—Dimples Delight, 1 vol. Laliberté, Louise-Andrée, illus. 2005. (Orca Echoes Ser.). (ENG.). 64p. (J). (gr. 2-3). per. 6.95 *(978-1-55143-362-2(1))* Orca Bk. Pubs. USA.
—Each One Special. 2004. (Illus.). (J). (gr. k-3). spiral bd. *(978-0-616-01815-6(0))*; spiral bd. *(978-0-616-01814-9(2))* Canadian National Institute for the Blind/Institut National Canadien pour les Aveugles.
—A Frog in My Throat, 1 vol. Laliberté, Louise-Andrée, illus. 2008. (Orca Echoes Ser.). (ENG.). 64p. (J). (gr. 2-3). pap. 6.95 *(978-1-55143-632-6(9))* Orca Bk. Pubs. USA.
—Jennifer Jones Won't Leave Me Alone. Layton, Neal, illus. 2005. (Carolrhoda Picture Bks.). 32p. (J). (gr. -1-3). per. 6.95 *(978-1-57505-921-1(5))*; (gr. k-2). 15.95 *(978-0-87614-921-8(2))* Lerner Publishing Group.
—Make It Fair!, No. 15. Lewis-MacDougall, Patricia Ann & Owlkids Books Inc. Staff, illus. 2010. (Canadian Flyer Adventures Ser.: 15). (ENG.). 96p. (J). (gr. 1-4). pap. 7.95 *(978-1-897349-99-1(8)*, Maple Tree Pr.) Owlkids Bks. Inc. CAN. Dist: Publishers Group West (PGW).
—Nothing Scares Us. Layton, Neal, illus. (Carolrhoda Picture Books Ser.). 32p. (J). 2004. (gr. 1-4). pap. 6.25 *(978-1-57505-669-2(0))* 2003. (gr. -1-3). 15.95 *(978-1-57505-490-2(6)*, Carolrhoda Bks.) Lerner Publishing Group.
Wismer, C. L. The Missing Chocolate Chip Oatmeal Peanut Butter Raisin Cookie. 2011. 28p. pap. 24.95 *(978-1-4626-3395-1(1))* America Star Bks.
Withers, Pam. Daredevil Club, 1 vol. 2006. (Orca Currents Ser.). (ENG.). 112p. (J). (gr. 5-9). per. 9.95 *(978-1-55143-614-2(0))* Orca Bk. Pubs. USA.
Witkowski, Teri. Bitty Bear's New Friend. Ackley, Peggy Jo, illus. 2005. (J). *(978-1-59369-021-2(5))* American Girl Publishing, Inc.
Wittlinger, Ellen. Razzle. 2003. (ENG.). 256p. (YA). (gr. 7). pap. 12.99 *(978-0-689-85600-6(8)*, Simon & Schuster Bks. For Young Readers) Simon & Schuster Bks. For Young Readers.
—Sandpiper. 2007. (ENG.). 288p. (YA). (gr. 7-12). pap. 6.99 *(978-1-4169-3651-0(3)*, Simon & Schuster Bks. For Young Readers) Simon & Schuster Bks. For Young Readers.
—This Means War! 2010. (ENG.). 224p. (J). (gr. 5-9). 16.99 *(978-1-4169-7101-6(7)*, Simon & Schuster Bks. For Young Readers) Simon & Schuster Bks. For Young Readers.
Wofford, Sherry Lynn. Introducing the Adventures of Jerry Giraffe & Feather Bird. 2011. 36p. pap. 16.95 *(978-1-4560-3238-8(0))* America Star Bks.
Wojciechowska, Maia & Manna, Sal. A Kingdom in a Horse. 2012. (ENG.). 160p. (J). (gr. 2-7). pap. 9.95 *(978-1-61608-481-3(2)*, 608481, Sky Pony Pr.) Skyhorse Publishing Co., Inc.
Wojciechowski, Susan. Beany & the Magic Crystal. Natti, Susanna, illus. 2005. (Beany Adventures Ser.). 87p. (J). lib. bdg. 13.65 *(978-0-7569-5836-7(9))* Perfection Learning Corp.
—Beany Goes to Camp. Natti, Susanna, illus. 2005. (Beany Adventures Ser.). 104p. (J). (gr. 4-7). 13.65 *(978-0-7569-6499-3(7))* Perfection Learning Corp.
—Beany (Not Beanhead) Natti, Susanna, illus. 2005. (Beany Adventures Ser.). 68p. (J). lib. bdg. 12.65 *(978-0-7569-5835-0(0))* Perfection Learning Corp.
—The Christmas Miracle of Jonathan Toomey. Lynch, P. J., illus. 2015. (ENG.). 40p. (J). (gr. 1-4). 17.99 *(978-0-7636-7822-7(8))* Candlewick Pr.
Wold, Justin And Janet. This Thing I Made Can Make Anything but Can't Make Friends & Family. 2013. 24p. pap. 14.93 *(978-1-4669-9572-7(6))* Trafford Publishing.
Wolf, Carla. Moving Towards a Dream. 2006. 91p. pap. 19.95 *(978-1-4241-5444-9(8))* America Star Bks.
Wolf, Jennifer Shaw. Dead Girls Don't Lie. 2014. (ENG.). 368p. (YA). (gr. 9). pap. 9.99 *(978-0-8027-3753-3(6)*, 9780802737533, Bloomsbury USA Childrens) Bloomsbury Publishing USA.
Wolfe, Carolyn. The Unhappy Little Dragon: Lessons Begin. Mathis, Leslie, illus. 2009. 38p. pap. 12.99 *(978-1-935105-42-8(6))* Avid Readers Publishing Group.
Wolfe, Frances. The Little Toy Shop. Wolfe, Frances, illus. 2008. (ENG., Illus.). 32p. (J). (gr. -1-2). 19.95 *(978-0-88776-865-1(2)*, Tundra Bks.) Tundra Bks. CAN. Dist: Penguin Random Hse. LLC.
Wolfe, Jack & Wolfe, Jennifer. The Tales of Spy Dogs Archie & Hazel. 2011. 44p. pap. 16.59 *(978-1-4567-6244-5(3))* AuthorHouse.
Wolfe, Susan Markle. The Deer from Ponchatoula, 1 vol. Welch, Gracie, illus. 2009. 24p. pap. 24.95 *(978-1-60813-519-6(5))* America Star Bks.
Wolff, Ferida & Savitz, Harriet May. The Story Blanket, 1 vol. Odriozola, Elena, illus. 2008. (ENG.). 32p. (J). (gr. -1-3). 16.95 *(978-1-56145-466-2(4)*, Peachtree Junior) Peachtree Pubs.
Wolff, Susan. Quackers Wants to Fly. Currie, Justin, illus. 2013. 32p. pap. 8.95 *(978-1-60653-074-0(7))* High Hill Pr.
Wolff, Virginia Euwer. Make Lemonade. unabr. ed. 2004. (Make Lemonade Trilogy: No. 1). 200p. (J). (gr. 7-18). pap. 36.00 incl. audio *(978-0-8072-0793-2(4)*, S YA 348 SP, Listening Library) Random Hse. Audio Publishing Group.
—This Full House. (ENG.). 496p. (YA). (gr. 9). 2011. pap. 9.99 *(978-0-06-158306-3(5))* 2009. (Make Lemonade Trilogy: No. 3). 17.99 *(978-0-06-158304-9(9))* HarperCollins Pubs. (HarperTeen).
—True Believer. 2004. (Make Lemonade Trilogy: No. 2). 272p. (J). (gr. 7-18). pap. 38.00 incl. audio *(978-0-8072-2283-6(6)*, Listening Library) Random Hse. Audio Publishing Group.
Wolford, Margo. The Moinks Collection Presents: Sami's Big Day. 2009. (Illus.). 39p. (J). pap. 18.95 *(978-1-4327-3980-5(8))* Outskirts Pr., Inc.
Wolitzer, Meg. Belzhar. (ENG.). 272p. (YA). (gr. 9). 2015. 10.99 *(978-0-14-242629-6(6)*, Speak) 2014. 17.99 *(978-0-525-42305-8(2)*, Dutton Books for Young Readers) Penguin Young Readers Group.
Woloson, Eliza. My Friend Isabelle. Gough, Bryan, tr. Gough, Bryan, illus. 2003. (ENG.). 28p. (J). 14.95 *(978-1-890627-50-8(X))* Woodbine Hse.
Woltz, Anna. A Hundred Hours of Night. Watkinson, Laura, tr. from DUT. 2016. (ENG.). 256p. (YA). (gr. 9). 17.99 *(978-0-545-84828-2(8)*, Levine, Arthur A. Bks.) Scholastic, Inc.
Won, Brian. Hooray for Books! 2017. (ENG., Illus.). 40p. (J). (gr. -1-3). 16.99 ***(978-0-544-74802-6(6)***, HMH Books For Young Readers) Houghton Mifflin Harcourt Publishing Co.
—Hooray for Hat! Big Book. 2016. (ENG., Illus.). 40p. (J). (gr. -1-3). 26.99 *(978-0-544-66831-7(6)*, HMH Books For Young Readers) Houghton Mifflin Harcourt Publishing Co.
—Hooray for Hat! (Board Book) 2016. (ENG., Illus.). 32p. (J). (— 1). bds. 7.99 *(978-0-544-78988-3(1)*, HMH Books For Young Readers) Houghton Mifflin Harcourt Publishing Co.
—Hooray for Today! 2016. (ENG., Illus.). 40p. (J). (gr. -1-3). 16.99 *(978-0-544-74803-3(4)*, HMH Books For Young Readers) Houghton Mifflin Harcourt Publishing Co.
Wong, Janet S. Minn & Jake's Almost Terrible Summer. Côté, Geneviève, illus. 2008. (ENG.). 112p. (J). (gr. 2-5). 15.99 *(978-0-374-34977-6(0)*, 9780374349776, Farrar, Straus & Giroux (BYR)) Farrar, Straus & Giroux.
Wong, Janet S. & Wong, Janet G. Minn & Jake. Cote, Genevieve, illus. 2008. (ENG.). 160p. (J). (gr. 2-5). pap. 9.99 *(978-0-374-40021-7(0)*, 9780374400217, Farrar, Straus & Giroux (BYR)) Farrar, Straus & Giroux.
Wood, David & Wood, Aimee. The Beautiful Swan. 2008. 24p. pap. 14.95 *(978-1-59858-624-4(6))* Dog Ear Publishing, LLC.
Wood, Gail. Lizzie & the Big Lake Mystery. 2015. (Illus.). ix, 93p. (J). pap. *(978-1-57249-416-9(6)*, White Mane Kids) White Mane Publishing Co., Inc.
—Lizzie, Light Feather & the Quarry Bluff Storm. 2015. (Illus.). viii, 88p. (J). pap. *(978-1-57249-415-2(8)*, White Mane Kids) White Mane Publishing Co., Inc.
Wood, Kate. Twinkle. 2013. (Illus.). 60p. (J). pap. 20.00 *(978-0-9837334-9-2(X))* Digi-Tall Media.
Wood, Lena. Elijah Creek & the Armor of Gift Set. 2006. 576p. (J). Bks. 1-3. 17.99 *(978-0-7847-1966-4(7))*Bks. 4-6. 17.99 *(978-0-7847-1967-1(5))* Standard Publishing.
Woodcock, Fiona. Hiding Heidi. 2016. (ENG., Illus.). 32p. (J). (gr. -1-3). 16.99 *(978-1-4998-0350-1(8))* Little Bee Books Inc.
Woodell, Rejoice. Kohara, the White Veiled City. 2011. 138p. pap. 19.99 *(978-1-4568-7969-3(3))* Xlibris Corp.
Wooding, Chris. Velocity. 2017. (ENG.). 336p. (J). (gr. 7). 18.99 *(978-0-545-94494-6(5)*, Scholastic Pr.) Scholastic, Inc.
Woodman, Melissa. Lessons with Our Jungle Friends. 2011. 32p. pap. 24.95 *(978-1-4626-1902-3(9))* America Star Bks.
Woodrow, Allan. Unschooled. 2017. (ENG.). 288p. (J). (gr. 3-7). 16.99 ***(978-1-338-11688-5(6)***, Scholastic Pr.) Scholastic, Inc.
Woods, Candy Godwin. Shimmer Finds Her Gift. 2009. 32p. pap. 13.00 *(978-1-60860-840-9(9)*, Eloquent Bks.) Strategic Book Publishing & Rights Agency (SBPRA).
Woods, Dawn. The Best Day Ever! 2010. 36p. pap. 16.44 *(978-1-4269-0331-1(6))* Trafford Publishing.
Woods, Elizabeth. Choker. (ENG.). 240p. (YA). (gr. 9). 2012. pap. 9.99 *(978-1-4424-1234-7(8))* 2011. (Illus.). 16.99 *(978-1-4424-1233-0(X))* Simon & Schuster Bks. For Young Readers. (Simon & Schuster Bks. For Young Readers).
Woods, Emily. Thingamafig B Quaxindehouse: Best Friends. 2011. 24p. pap. 12.99 *(978-1-4634-4853-0(8))* AuthorHouse.
Woodson, Jacqueline. After Tupac & D Foster. (ENG.). (J). (gr. 5-18). 2010. 192p. pap. 7.99 *(978-0-14-241399-9(2)*, Speak) 2008. 160p. 17.99 *(978-0-399-24654-8(1)*, G.P. Putnam's Sons Books for Young Readers) Penguin Young Readers Group.
—After Tupac & D Foster. 2010. lib. bdg. 18.40 *(978-0-606-10720-4(7)*, Turtleback) Turtleback Bks.
—Each Kindness. Lewis, E. B., illus. 2012. (ENG.). 32p. (J). (gr. k-3). 17.99 *(978-0-399-24652-4(5)*, Nancy Paulsen Books) Penguin Young Readers Group.
—Feathers. 2007. (ENG.). 128p. (J). (gr. 5-7). 16.99 *(978-0-399-23989-2(8)*, G.P. Putnam's Sons Books for Young Readers) Penguin Young Readers Group.
—Feathers. 2010. lib. bdg. 19.65 *(978-0-606-14654-8(7)*, Turtleback) Turtleback Bks.
—I Hadn't Meant to Tell You This. 2010. (ENG.). 160p. (YA). (gr. 7-18). 7.99 *(978-0-14-241704-1(1)*, Puffin Books) Penguin Young Readers Group.
—I Hadn't Meant to Tell You This. 2006. 114p. (YA). (gr. 7-12). 13.65 *(978-0-7569-6730-7(9))* Perfection Learning Corp.
Woodson, Rick. Poodles & Thunderchicken. 2012. 40p. pap. 24.95 *(978-1-4626-7531-9(X))* America Star Bks.
Woodson, Vera. Lady Bug, Beetle Boy, & Friends: Bullies Be Gone! 2013. (ENG., Illus.). (J). 14.95 *(978-1-62086-049-6(X))* Mascot Bks., Inc.
Woody, John. Ernie Tales. Byars, Bob M., illus. 2012. pap. 13.95 *(978-0-9848019-9-2(5))* Inkwell Books LLC.
Woolley, Barbara B. Freedom West. 2006. 22.99 *(978-1-4257-0124-6(8))*; pap. 15.99 *(978-1-4257-0123-9(X))* Xlibris Corp.
Wooten, Arthur. Wise Bear William: A New Beginning. Santora, Bud, illus. 2012. 44p. pap. 12.99 *(978-0-9850529-1-1(0))* Galaxias Productions.
Worcester, Sue. Ernesto Nia Lakeru. 2011. 28p. pap. 28.03 *(978-1-4568-8257-0(0))* Xlibris Corp.
Worley, Roger A. 14 Wishes, 1 vol. 2009. 164p. pap. 24.95 *(978-1-61582-419-9(7))* America Star Bks.
Worth, Bonnie. Way to Go, Chipmunk Cheeks. (Full House Ser.). 96p. (J). (gr. 4-6). pap. 3.25 *(978-0-938753-57-5(6)*, PP1) Parachute Publishing, LLC.
Wrecks, Billy. Batman! (DC Super Friends) Schoening, Dan & Beavers, Ethen, illus. 2012. (Little Golden Book Ser.). (ENG.). 24p. (J). (gr. k-k). 4.99 *(978-0-307-93103-0(X)*, Golden Bks.) Random Hse. Children's Bks.
—In the Lead! (Disney Planes) Random House Disney Staff, illus. 2014. (3-D Pictureback Ser.). (ENG.). 16p. (J). (gr. -1-2). 4.99 *(978-0-7364-2992-4(1)*, RH/Disney) Random Hse. Children's Bks.
—Shark Attack! 2017. (Step into Reading Level 2 Ser.). lib. bdg. 14.75 ***(978-0-606-39852-7(X))*** Turtleback Bks.
—Wonder Woman & Her Super Friends! (DC Super Friends) Random House, illus. 2016. (Tabbed Board Book Ser.). (ENG.). 16p. (J). (-k). bds. 7.99 *(978-1-101-93992-5(3)*, Random Hse. Bks. for Young Readers) Random Hse. Children's Bks.
—X-Ray Vision! (DC Super Friends) Borkowski, Michael, illus. 2014. (Pictureback Ser.). (ENG.). 16p. (J). (gr. -1-2). 4.99 *(978-0-385-38718-7(0)*, Random Hse. Bks. for Young Readers) Random Hse. Children's Bks.
Wrecks, Billy & Shealy, Dennis. T. Rex Trouble! Random House Staff et al, illus. 2011. (Step into Reading Ser.). (ENG.). 32p. (J). (gr. -1-1). pap. 3.99 *(978-0-375-86777-4(5)*, Random Hse. Bks. for Young Readers) Random Hse. Children's Bks.
Wrench, Peter. The Web She Wove. 2013. 186p. pap. *(978-1-78299-872-3(1))* FeedARead.com.
Wright, Barbara. Crow. 2013. (ENG.). 320p. (J). (gr. 5-7). pap. 7.99 *(978-0-375-87367-6(8)*, Yearling) Random Hse. Children's Bks.
Wright, Deana. The Playground. 2009. 48p. pap. 9.95 *(978-1-60693-680-1(8)*, Eloquent Bks.) Strategic Book Publishing & Rights Agency (SBPRA).
Wright, Jason F. Penny's Christmas Jar Party. Sowards, Ben, illus. 2009. 32p. (J). 17.95 *(978-1-60641-167-4(5)*, Shadow Mountain) Shadow Mountain Publishing.
Wright, Kiyah. Joshua's Surprise. 2010. 28p. pap. 16.95 *(978-1-4490-8234-5(3))* AuthorHouse.
Wright, Lanikka. The Fab Four 2: Eva's Obsession. 2012. (ENG.). 244p. pap. 13.95 *(978-1-4327-9846-8(4))* Outskirts Pr., Inc.
Wright, Lloyd. More Stories for Gramp's Little Friends. 2004. 180p. (J). 23.95 *(978-0-595-66836-6(4))* iUniverse, Inc.
Wright, Lynda. Flowers for Addison. 2012. 24p. pap. 24.95 *(978-1-4626-5787-2(7))* America Star Bks.
Wright, Olivia. Malarie Jane Learns to Help. 2010. 36p. pap. 20.00 *(978-0-557-23776-0(9))* Lulu Pr., Inc.
Wright, Peter M. The Stone Prince, 1 vol. 2009. 48p. pap. 16.95 *(978-1-4489-2591-9(6))* America Star Bks.
Wright, Sharrie. Wee Friends. 2011. (Illus.). 32p. (gr. -1). pap. 14.50 *(978-1-4567-7621-3(5))* AuthorHouse.
Written By Pamela McFarland; Illustrated. Guide Me Home, Sunny. Bates, Bill, illus. 2011. 44p. pap. 24.95 *(978-1-4560-8890-3(4))* America Star Bks.
Wrong Way, Mallory! 2015. (Mallory Ser.: 23). (ENG., Illus.). 160p. (J). (gr. 2-5). 15.95 *(978-1-4677-0923-1(9))* Lerner Publishing Group.
Wunder, Wendy. The Museum of Intangible Things. 2015. (ENG.). 256p. (YA). (gr. 7). pap. 9.99 *(978-1-59514-576-5(1)*, Razorbill) Penguin Young Readers Group.
Wyatt, Edwina. In the Evening. Chapman, Gaye, illus. 2016. (ENG.). 32p. (J). (gr. -1-k). 16.99 *(978-1-74297-528-3(3))* Little Hare Bks. AUS. Dist: Independent Pubs. Group.
—Together Always. Masciullo, Lucia, illus. 2017. (ENG.). 48p. (J). (gr. -1-3). 14.95 *(978-1-4549-2326-8(1))* Sterling Publishing Co., Inc.
Wynne-Jones, Tim. The Maestro, 1 vol. 2nd ed. 2004. (ENG.). 224p. (J). (gr. 5-9). pap. 8.95 *(978-0-88899-637-4(3))* Groundwood Bks. CAN. Dist: Publishers Group West (PGW).
Wyre, Yvonne. The Further Adventures of Cuthbert the Coal Lorry & all His Friends. 2007. (Illus.). 204p. pap. *(978-1-84401-801-7(6))* Athena Pr.
Yabroff, Jennie. If You Were Here. 2017. (ENG.). 272p. (YA). 17.99 *(978-1-5072-0002-5(1)*, Simon Pulse) Simon Pulse.
Yaccarino, Dan. Rainy Day: A Little Moral Story about Worry. 2016. (Dan Yaccarino's Happyland Ser.). (ENG., Illus.). 22p. (J). (gr. -1 — 1). bds. 5.95 *(978-0-7611-8735-6(9))* Workman Publishing Co., Inc.
—Unlovable. Yaccarino, Dan, illus. rev. ed. 2004. (ENG., Illus.). 32p. (J). (gr. -1-1). reprint ed. pap. 7.99 *(978-0-8050-7532-8(1)*, 9780805075328) Square Fish.
—Zorgoochi Intergalactic Pizza: Delivery of Doom. Yaccarino, Dan, illus. 2014. (ENG., Illus.). 336p. (J). (gr. 3-7). 16.99 *(978-1-250-00844-2(1)*, 9781250008442) Feiwel & Friends.
Yackle, Deanne. Jenny & Me. 2005. (J). lib. bdg. *(978-0-9725485-4-0(8))* Waterfall Ridge.
Yacobi, Lily & Yacobi, Diana. The Aleph Bet Story: Featuring Sarah & David & Friends. 2004. 22p. (J). per. 10.95 *(978-0-9761648-0-7(9))* Sarah & David LLC.
Yager, Karen & Williams, Kiersten. Krickle Forest Adventures, Wizbet's Notebook. Walsh, Jennifer, illus. 2012. 60p. pap. 7.95 *(978-0-9855997-0-6(7))* Krickle Forest Adventures.
Yang, Angela. Out of the Dark. 2012. 166p. pap. 12.85 *(978-0-578-09356-7(1))* Yang, Jennifer.
Yang, Belle. Foo, the Flying Frog of Washtub Pond. Yang, Belle, illus. 2009. (ENG., Illus.). 32p. (J). (gr. -1-2). 16.99 *(978-0-7636-3615-9(0))* Candlewick Pr.
Yang, James. Puzzlehead. Yang, James, illus. 2015. (ENG., Illus.). 32p. (J). (gr. -1-1). 13.99 *(978-1-4814-7507-5(X)*, Atheneum Bks. for Young Readers) Simon & Schuster Children's Publishing.
Yarbray Brucke, Candice & Moore, Dawnyelle. Wrappers Wanted: A Mathematical Adventure in Surface Area. 2009. 32p. pap. 15.00 *(978-1-4389-7468-2(X))* AuthorHouse.
Yardley Hastings Primary School. Tim & Holly's Olympic Adventure. 2012. 74p. pap. *(978-1-909039-52-0(7))* Legend Pr.
Yardley, Liz. The Firefly Legacy - Book Vii. Yardley, Liz, illus. 2013. (Illus.). 314p. pap. *(978-0-9872013-2-4(8))* BlueFlower Bks.
Yaseen, Mohammed. The Colour Blind Boy. 2017. (ENG., Illus.). 32p. (J). 7.95 ***(978-0-86037-384-1(3))*** Kube Publishing Ltd. GBR. Dist: Consortium Bk. Sales & Distribution.
Yasko, Carmen R. Buddy & His Buddies. 2012. 40p. pap. 22.65 *(978-1-4797-4710-8(6))* Xlibris Corp.
Yasuda, Anita. The Crazy Clues, 1 vol. Harpster, Steve, illus. 2013. (Dino Detectives Ser.). (ENG.). 32p. (gr. 1-2). lib. bdg. 22.65 *(978-1-4342-5971-4(4))* Stone Arch Bks.
—Crazy Clues. Harpster, Steve, illus. 2013. (Dino Detectives Ser.). (ENG.). 32p. (gr. 1-2). pap. 5.95 *(978-1-4342-6200-4(6))* Stone Arch Bks.
Yasuda, Anita & Harpster, Steve. The Crazy Clues. 2013. (Dino Detectives Ser.). (ENG.). 32p. (gr. 1-2). pap. 29.70 *(978-1-4342-6226-4(X))* Stone Arch Bks.
Yates, Patty Fee, told to. Friends. 2004. pap. 8.00 *(978-0-8059-6459-2(2))* Dorrance Publishing Co., Inc.
Yatscoff, Edward R. Archie's Gold. 2013. 200p. pap. *(978-0-9869678-7-0(4))* Yatscoff, Edward R.
Yayo. The Tales of Pop & Grace: The Burglar. 2013. 94p. (gr. 2-4). pap. 10.67 *(978-1-4817-8108-4(1))* AuthorHouse.
Yeager, Graham. Diablo: The Third Millersburg Novel. 2006. 145p. (YA). per. 7.99 *(978-0-9765478-4-6(8))* Stone Acres Publishing Co.
The Year of Shadows. 2014. (ENG., Illus.). 416p. (J). (gr. 3-7). pap. 7.99 *(978-1-4424-4295-5(6)*, Simon & Schuster Bks. For Young Readers) Simon & Schuster Bks. For Young Readers.
Yee, Lisa. Bobby vs. Girls (Accidentally) Santat, Dan, illus. 2010. (ENG.). 176p. (J). (gr. 2-5). pap. 5.99 *(978-0-545-05593-2(8)*, Levine, Arthur A. Bks.) Scholastic, Inc.
—The Kidney Hypothetical: or How to Ruin Your Life in Seven Days:Or How to Ruin Your Life in Seven Days. 2015. (ENG.). 272p. (J). (gr. 7). 17.99 *(978-0-545-23094-0(2))* Scholastic, Inc.
—The Kidney Hypothetical, or, How to Ruin Your Life in Seven Days. 2016. (ENG.). 272p. (J). (gr. 7). pap. 9.99 *(978-0-545-23095-7(0))* Scholastic, Inc.
—Millicent Min, Girl Genius. 2004. 248p. (gr. 3-7). 17.00 *(978-0-7569-3919-9(4))* Perfection Learning Corp.
—Millicent Min, Girl Genius. 2004. (Millicent Min Trilogy Ser.: 1). (ENG.). 256p. (J). (gr. 4-7). reprint ed. pap. 6.99 *(978-0-439-42520-9(4)*, Levine, Arthur A. Bks.) Scholastic, Inc.
—Stanford Wong Flunks Big-Time. 2007. (Apple Signature Edition Ser.). (ENG., Illus.). 320p. (J). (gr. 3-7). per. 6.99 *(978-0-439-62248-6(4)*, Levine, Arthur A. Bks.) Scholastic, Inc.
Yee, Paul. Shu-Li & Tamara, 1 vol. Wang, Shaoli, illus. 2008. (ENG.). 72p. (J). (gr. 1-4). per. 7.95 *(978-1-896580-93-7(9))* Tradewind Bks. CAN. Dist: Orca Bk. Pubs. USA.
Yee, Wong Herbert. A Brand-New Day with Mouse & Mole. (Mouse & Mole Story Ser.). (ENG., Illus.). 48p. (J). (gr. 1-4). 2012. pap. 3.99 *(978-0-547-72209-2(5))* 2008. 15.00 *(978-0-618-96676-9(5))* Houghton Mifflin Harcourt Publishing Co.
—A Brand-New Day with Mouse & Mole. 2012. (Green Light Readers — Level 3 Ser.). lib. bdg. 13.55 *(978-0-606-24437-4(9)*, Turtleback) Turtleback Bks.
—Did You See Chip? Ovresat, Laura, illus. 2004. (Green Light Readers Level 2 Ser.). (ENG.). 24p. (J). (gr. -1-3). pap. 3.95 *(978-0-15-205096-2(5))* Houghton Mifflin Harcourt Publishing Co.
—Mouse & Mole, a Winter Wonderland. Yee, Wong Herbert, illus. 2011. (Mouse & Mole Story Ser.). (ENG., Illus.). 48p. (J). (gr. 1-4). pap. 3.99 *(978-0-547-57697-8(8))* Houghton Mifflin Harcourt Publishing Co.
—A Perfect Halloween. 2011. (Mouse & Mole Story Ser.). (ENG., Illus.). 48p. (J). (gr. 1-4). 14.99 *(978-0-547-55152-4(5))* Houghton Mifflin Harcourt Publishing Co.
—Secret Valentine. Yee, Wong Herbert, illus. 2013. (Mouse & Mole Story Ser.). (ENG., Illus.). 48p. (J). (gr. 1-4). 15.99 *(978-0-547-88719-7(1))* Houghton Mifflin Harcourt Publishing Co.
Yeh, Kat. The Friend Ship. Groenink, Chuck, illus. 2016. (ENG.). 32p. (J). (gr. -1-k). 16.99 *(978-1-4847-0726-5(5))* Disney Pr.
Yeh, Kat. The Way to Bea. 2017. (ENG.). 352p. (J). (gr. 3-7). 16.99 ***(978-0-316-23667-6(5))*** Little, Brown Bks. for Young Readers.
Yelchin, Eugene & Kuryla, Mary. The Next Door Bear. Yelchin, Eugene & Kuryla, Mary, illus. 2011. (ENG., Illus.). 40p. (J). (gr. -1-3). 16.99 *(978-0-06-125925-8(X))* HarperCollins Pubs.
Yellowknife, Jessica. Spring Break Adventure. 2011. 84p. pap. 11.11 *(978-1-4269-6952-2(X))* Trafford Publishing.
Yep, Laurence. The Traitor. 2004. (Golden Mountain Chronicles). 310p. (J). (gr. 5). 14.65 *(978-0-7569-3457-6(5))* Perfection Learning Corp.
Yep, Laurence & Ryder, Joanne. A Dragon's Guide to the Care & Feeding of Humans. GrandPré, Mary, illus. 2015. (Dragon's Guide Ser.). (ENG.). 160p. (J). (gr. 3-7). 15.99 *(978-0-385-39228-0(1)*, Crown Books For Young Readers) Random Hse. Children's Bks.
Yi-K'lun, F. Los Cuatro Amigos. 2003. (SPA.). 24p. *(978-84-246-1923-7(4)*, GL30509) La Galera, S.A. Editorial ESP. Dist: Lectorum Pubns., Inc.
Ylvisaker, Anne. Button Down. (ENG.). 192p. (J). (gr. 3-7). 2013. pap. 6.99 *(978-0-7636-6463-3(4))* 2012. (Illus.). 15.99 *(978-0-7636-5396-5(9))* Candlewick Pr.
—Little Klein. 2009. (ENG.). 192p. (J). (gr. 3-7). pap. 6.99 *(978-0-7636-4338-6(6))* Candlewick Pr.
—The Luck of the Buttons. 2012. (ENG., Illus.). 240p. (J). (gr. 3-7). pap. 6.99 *(978-0-7636-6061-1(2))* Candlewick Pr.
Yolen, Jane. How Do Dinosaurs Stay Friends? Teague, Mark, illus. 2016. (ENG.). 40p. (J). (gr. -1-k). 16.99 *(978-0-545-82934-2(8)*, Exhibit A) Scholastic, Inc.
Yoon, Nicola. Everything, Everything. (ENG.). (YA). (gr. 7). 2017. 352p. pap. 10.99 ***(978-0-553-49667-3(0)***, Ember) 2015. (Illus.). 320p. 18.99 *(978-0-553-49664-2(6)*, Delacorte Pr.) 2017. 336p. 18.99 ***(978-1-5247-6980-2(0)***, Delacorte Pr.) Random Hse. Children's Bks.
—Everything, Everything. 2017. lib. bdg. 22.10 ***(978-0-606-40341-2(8))*** Turtleback Bks.
Yoon, Salina. Be a Friend. 2016. (ENG.). 40p. (J). 17.99 *(978-1-61963-951-5(3)*, 9781619639515, Bloomsbury USA Childrens) Bloomsbury Publishing USA.
—My Kite Is Stuck! & Other Stories. 2017. (Duck, Duck, Porcupine Book Ser.). (ENG.). 64p. (J). 9.99 *(978-1-61963-887-7(8)*, 9781619638877, Bloomsbury USA Childrens) Bloomsbury Publishing USA.
—Penguin & Pinecone. Yoon, Salina, illus. (Penguin Ser.). (ENG., Illus.). (J). (gr. -1-1). 2014. 32p. bds. 7.99 *(978-0-8027-3731-1(5)*, 9780802737311) 2012. 40p. 14.99 *(978-0-8027-2843-2(X)*, 9780802728432) Bloomsbury Publishing USA. (Bloomsbury USA Childrens).
—Penguin on Vacation. Yoon, Salina, illus. 2013. (Penguin Ser.). (ENG., Illus.). 40p. (J). (gr. -1-1). 14.99 *(978-0-8027-3397-9(2)*, 9780802733979, Bloomsbury USA Childrens) Bloomsbury Publishing USA.
—Penguin's Big Adventure. 2015. (Penguin Ser.). (ENG., Illus.). 40p. (J). (gr. -1-1). 14.99 *(978-0-8027-3828-8(1)*,

9780802738288, Bloomsbury USA Childrens) Bloomsbury Publishing USA.

Yost-Filgate, Susan. A Good Day for Abbey. Filgate, Leonard, illus. 2009. (ENG.). 12p. (J). (gr. -1-12). 6.99 *(978-1-934960-45-5(4),* Raven Tree Pr.,Csi) Continental Sales, Inc.

—Rip Squeak & His Friends. Filgate, Leonard, illus. 2009. (ENG.). 32p. (J). (gr. -1-3). 16.95 *(978-1-934960-40-0(3),* Raven Tree Pr.,Csi) Continental Sales, Inc.

—The Treasure. 2009. (ENG.). 32p. (J). (gr. -1-3). 16.95 *(978-1-934960-41-7(1),* Raven Tree Pr.,Csi) Continental Sales, Inc.

You Can Make a Difference, Maddie Morrison. 2008. 123p. (J). pap. 7.99 *(978-0-9786117-1-2(3))* Neal Morgan Publishing.

You My Friend. 2007. (J). bds. 21.95 *(978-0-9745191-4-2(6))* Lynn Tyner Mitchum & James Rogers.

Young, A. From Chicago to the Canyon, 1 vol. 2010. 54p. pap. 16.95 *(978-1-4489-8148-9(4))* America Star Bks.

Young, Amy. A New Friend for Sparkle. 2017. (ENG., Illus.). 40p. (J). 16.99 *(978-0-374-30553-6(6),* 9780374305536, Farrar, Straus & Giroux (BYR)) Farrar, Straus & Giroux.

Young, Beryl. Follow the Elephant. 2010. (ENG., Illus.). 248p. pap. 10.95 *(978-1-55380-098-9(2))* Ronsdale Pr. CAN. Dist: SPD-Small Pr. Distribution.

Young, Billy. Teddy the Bear. 2007. 27p. 19.95 *(978-1-84799-068-6(1))* Lulu Pr., Inc.

Young, Chris. Boko & the Big Red Bag. 2012. 36p. pap. 18.41 *(978-1-4669-6497-6(9))* Trafford Publishing.

Young, Diane. See No Evil, 1 vol. 2006. (Orca Currents Ser.). (ENG.). 128p. (J). (gr. 5-9). per. 9.95 *(978-1-55143-619-7(1))* Orca Bk. Pubs. USA.

Young, Elizabeth L. Dozens & Dozens of Cousins & Cousins. Perkins, Ruth, illus. 2012. 30p. 20.95 *(978-1-61633-353-9(7));* pap. 12.95 *(978-1-61633-352-2(9))* Guardian Angel Publishing, Inc.

Young, Heather. Norman. 2012. 36p. pap. 21.99 *(978-1-4797-1356-1(2))* Xlibris Corp.

Young, Jessica. Art-Rageous. Secheret, Jessica, illus. 2015. (Finley Flowers Ser.). (ENG.). 128p. (gr. 2-3). 8.95 *(978-1-4795-5960-2(1),* Finley Flowers) Picture Window Bks.

—Fin-Tastic Fashion. Secheret, Jessica, illus. 2017. (Finley Flowers Ser.). (ENG.). 128p. (gr. 2-3). lib. bdg. 25.32 ***(978-1-4795-9804-5(6),*** Finley Flowers) Picture Window Bks.

—Nature Calls. Secheret, Jessica, illus. 2015. (Finley Flowers Ser.). (ENG.). 128p. (gr. 2-3). 8.95 *(978-1-4795-5879-7(6),* Finley Flowers) Picture Window Bks.

—Original Recipe. Secheret, Jessica, illus. 2015. (Finley Flowers Ser.). (ENG.). 128p. (gr. 2-3). 8.95 *(978-1-4795-5878-0(8),* Finley Flowers) Picture Window Bks.

—Room to Bloom. Secheret, Jessica, illus. 2017. (Finley Flowers Ser.). (ENG.). 128p. (gr. 2-3). lib. bdg. 25.32 ***(978-1-4795-9806-9(2),*** Finley Flowers) Picture Window Bks.

—Super Spooktacular. Secheret, Jessica, illus. 2017. (Finley Flowers Ser.). (ENG.). 128p. (gr. 2-3). lib. bdg. 25.32 ***(978-1-4795-9807-6(0),*** Finley Flowers) Picture Window Bks.

Young, Judy. Minnow & Rose: An Oregon Trail Story. Farnsworth, Bill, illus. 2009. (Tales of Young Americans Ser.). (ENG.). 32p. (J). (gr. 1-5). 17.95 *(978-1-58536-421-3(5))* Sleeping Bear Pr.

Young, Julie. The Defeat of Gullvieg: Dragon Cliff Trilogy, Book Three. 2012. 132p. (gr. 4-6). pap. 11.95 *(978-1-4759-2585-2(9))* iUniverse, Inc.

—Dragon Stone: Dragon Cliff Trilogy Book Two. 2011. 160p. (gr. 4-6). pap. 12.95 *(978-1-4620-0682-3(5))* iUniverse, Inc.

Young, Karen. A Chimpanzee Tale. 2009. (Illus.). 36p. pap. 16.99 *(978-1-4389-2448-9(8))* AuthorHouse.

Young, Karen Romano. Hundred Percent. 2016. (ENG., Illus.). 256p. (J). (gr. 3-7). 16.99 *(978-1-4521-3890-9(7))* Chronicle Bks. LLC.

Young, Kristi. The Secret Club - the Powder Puff Club Book 1. 2007. (ENG.). 140p. (J). per. 12.95 *(978-1-59594-070-4(7),* Wingspan Pr.) WingSpan Publishing.

Young, Lauren. Ally M. & Ally G. Rooney, Sandra, illus. 2006. 20p. (J). 9.95 *(978-1-4120-8518-2(7))* Trafford Publishing.

Young, Leslie. Plaid: A Tale of Compassion. 2006. (Illus.). 15p. 9.00 *(978-1-4120-2793-9(4))* Trafford Publishing.

Young, Martha & McQuilkin, John A. The Legend of the Land of Caelumen, Pt. 1. 2005. per. 29.95 *(978-0-9773523-0-2(7))* Whimble Designs.

Young, Norene. Cathy, the Castaway Cat. Woodyard, Sandy Lilly, illus. 2012. 34p. 24.95 *(978-1-4626-6111-4(4))* America Star Bks.

Young, Paige. The Homework Dilemm. 2011. 26p. pap. 16.95 *(978-1-4626-2366-2(2))* America Star Bks.

Young, Pershail Catherine. Rusty & Mr. Earlie. 2010. 28p. pap. 12.49 *(978-1-4520-4514-6(3))* AuthorHouse.

Young, Valerie. The Adventures of Todd & Friends. 2009. 20p. pap. 12.49 *(978-1-4389-3196-8(4))* AuthorHouse.

Younger, David. Spanky, the Brave Space Mouse, 1 vol. 2010. 18p. 24.95 *(978-1-4489-4661-7(1))* PublishAmerica, Inc.

Youree, Barbara. Senegal Sleuths. 2006. 56p. 7.75 *(978-0-8341-2226-0(X))* Beacon Hill Pr. of Kansas City.

Yu, Jennifer. Four Weeks, Five People. 2017. (ENG.). 352p. 18.99 *(978-0-373-21230-9(5),* Harlequin Teen) Harlequin Enterprises, Ltd. CAN. Dist: HarperCollins Pubs.

Yu, Melissa. Ever after High. 2014. (ENG., Illus.). 12p. (J). (gr. 1-4). pap. 6.99 *(978-0-316-37736-2(8))* Little, Brown Bks. for Young Readers.

Yue, Gui & Farrow, Clare. Little Leap Forward: A Boy in Beijing. Cann, Helen, illus. 2011. (ENG.). 120p. (J). (gr. 3-6). pap. 12.99 *(978-1-84686-539-8(5))* Barefoot Bks., Inc.

Yue, Guo & Farrow, Clare. Little Leap Forward: A Boy in Beijing. Cann, Helen, illus. 2008. (ENG.). 128p. (YA). (gr. 4-7). 16.99 *(978-1-84686-114-7(4))* Barefoot Bks., Inc.

Yumoto, Kazumi. The Friends. Hirano, Cathy, tr. 2005. (ENG.). 176p. (J). (gr. 4-8). pap. 9.99 *(978-0-374-42461-9(6),* 9780374424619, Farrar, Straus & Giroux (BYR)) Farrar, Straus & Giroux.

Yurksaitis, Anne. The Ingle Bingle. Yurksaitis, Stephanie, illus. 2012. 16p. pap. 24.95 *(978-1-4626-7687-3(1))* America Star Bks.

Zadunajsky, Donna M. Help Me! Bowman Stevens, Deborah, ed. 2016. (Help Me! Ser.: Vol. 1). (ENG., Illus.). (YA). (gr. 7-12). 14.99 ***(978-1-938037-62-7(6));*** pap. 6.99 ***(978-1-938037-57-3(X))*** Zadunajsky, Donna M.

Zagarenski, Pamela. Henry & Leo. 2016. (ENG., Illus.). 40p. (J). (gr. -1-3). 17.99 *(978-0-544-64811-1(0),* HMH Books For Young Readers) Houghton Mifflin Harcourt Publishing Co.

Zaglada, Vladimir. Gymmy the Owl & His Friends. 2012. 52p. pap. 24.99 *(978-1-4772-0226-5(9))* AuthorHouse.

—Gymmy the Owl & His Friends: Tales in Rhyme about the Animal Kingdom's Natural Gymnasts. 2012. 52p. pap. 24.99 *(978-1-4685-6011-4(5))* AuthorHouse.

Zahler, Diane. A True Princess. (ENG.). (J). (gr. 3-7). 2012. 208p. pap. 6.99 *(978-0-06-182503-3(4))* 2011. 192p. 15.99 *(978-0-06-182501-9(8))* HarperCollins Pubs.

Zaionz, Ruth. Morris the Friendly Dinosaur. 2010. 24p. pap. 12.99 *(978-1-4490-6981-0(9))* AuthorHouse.

Zajac, Kristen. Chasing the Spirit of Service. Tucker, Julie, illus. 2013. 24p. 19.95 *(978-1-61633-393-5(6))* Guardian Angel Publishing, Inc.

Zak, Faith. Naptime Adventures: Christmas Tree. 2012. 24p. pap. 24.95 *(978-1-4626-5279-2(4))* America Star Bks.

Zalben, Jane Breskin. A Moon for Moe & Mo. Quraishi, Mariam, illus. 2017. (J). lib. bdg. *(978-1-58089-727-3(4))* Charlesbridge Publishing, Inc.

Zambak Çucok Publishing Staff, ed. Lost: Niloya 3. 2016. (J). pap. 4.99 *(978-1-4621-1864-9(X),* Horizon Pubs.) Cedar Fort, Inc./CFI Distribution.

—The Onion: Niloya 2. 2016. (J). pap. 4.99 *(978-1-4621-1863-2(1),* Horizon Pubs.) Cedar Fort, Inc./CFI Distribution.

Zameenzad, Adam. Pepsi & Maria. 2004. (ENG.). 317p. per. 16.95 *(978-1-904559-06-1(9),* 9781904559061) Arcadia Bks. Ltd. GBR. Dist: Bookmasters Distribution.

Zamora, Peter. A Story about Kandie Cole. 2010. 28p. pap. 13.99 *(978-1-4520-5632-6(3))* AuthorHouse.

Zann, Tara. Wild Child: Forest's First Birthday Party. Belleza, Rhoda, ed. Widdowson, Dan, illus. 2017. (Wild Child Ser.: 3). (ENG.). 128p. (J). pap. 5.99 *(978-1-250-10389-5(4),* 9781250103895) Imprint IND. Dist: Macmillan.

—Wild Child: Forest's First Day of School. Ermos, George & Widdowson, Dan, illus. 2017. (Wild Child Ser.: 2). (ENG.). 144p. (J). pap. 5.99 *(978-1-250-10387-1(8),* 9781250103871) Imprint IND. Dist: Macmillan.

—Wild Child: Forest's First Home. Ermos, George & Widdowson, Dan, illus. 2017. (Wild Child Ser.: 1). (ENG.). 144p. (J). pap. 5.99 *(978-1-250-10383-3(5),* 9781250103833) Imprint IND. Dist: Macmillan.

Zappa, Shana Muldoon & Zappa, Ahmet. Star Darlings Adora Finds a Friend. Disney Storybook Art Team, illus. 2016. (Star Darlings Ser.: 10). (ENG.). 176p. (J). (gr. 3-7). pap. 6.99 *(978-1-4847-1429-4(6))* Disney Pr.

—Star Darlings Clover's Parent Fix. Disney Storybook Art Team, illus. 2016. (Star Darlings Ser.: 11). (ENG.). 176p. (J). (gr. 3-7). pap. 6.99 *(978-1-4847-1430-0(X))* Disney Pr.

—Wish Cards. Disney Storybook Art Team, illus. 2016. (Star Darlings Ser.). (ENG.). 160p. (J). (gr. 3-7). 15.99 *(978-1-4847-9918-5(6))* Disney Pr.

Zappia, Francesca. Eliza & Her Monsters. 2017. 400p. (YA). (gr. 9). 17.99 *(978-0-06-229013-7(4),* Greenwillow Bks.) HarperCollins Pubs.

Zarr, Sara. Sweethearts. 2009. (ENG.). 224p. (YA). (gr. 7-17). pap. 10.99 *(978-0-316-01456-4(7))* Little, Brown Bks. for Young Readers.

Zarr, Sara & Altebrando, Tara. Roomies. 2013. (ENG.). 288p. (YA). (gr. 7-17). 18.00 *(978-0-316-21749-1(2))* Little, Brown Bks. for Young Readers.

Zeitlin, Meredith. Freshman Year & Other Unnatural Disasters. 2013. (ENG.). 288p. (YA). (gr. 7). pap. 8.99 *(978-0-14-242421-6(8),* Speak) Penguin Young Readers Group.

Zelaya, Carol. Caring for Emily's Family. 2008. (Illus.). 24p. (J). (gr. 2-3). 14.95 *(978-0-9796265-1-7(X))* Richlee Publishing.

Zemke, Deborah. The Curse of Einstein's Pencil. 2017. (Bea Garcia Ser.: 2). (ENG., Illus.). 144p. (J). (gr. 1-4). 15.99 *(978-0-8037-4155-3(3),* Dial Bks) Penguin Young Readers Group.

—My Life in Pictures. 2016. (Bea Garcia Ser.). (ENG., Illus.). 144p. (J). (gr. 1-3). 14.99 *(978-0-8037-4154-6(5),* Dial Bks) Penguin Young Readers Group.

—My Life in Pictures. 2017. (Bea Garcia Ser.: 1). lib. bdg. 18.40 ***(978-0-606-40083-1(4))*** Turtleback Bks.

Zenatti, Valerie. A Bottle in the Gaza Sea. Hunter, Adriana, tr. from FRE. 2008. (ENG.). 160p. (YA). (gr. 7-13). 17.99 *(978-1-59990-200-5(1),* 9781599902005, Bloomsbury USA Childrens) Bloomsbury Publishing USA.

Zentner, Jeff. Goodbye Days. 2017. (ENG.). 416p. (YA). (gr. 9). 17.99 *(978-0-553-52406-2(2),* Crown Books For Young Readers) Random Hse. Children's Bks.

—The Serpent King. 2016. (ENG.). 384p. (YA). (gr. 9). 17.99 *(978-0-553-52402-4(X),* Crown Books For Young Readers) Random Hse. Children's Bks.

Zera, Beata. Little Puppy Swifty & Elle. 2008. 64p. pap. 21.99 *(978-1-4257-6703-7(6))* Xlibris Corp.

Zevin, Gabrielle. Memoirs of a Teenage Amnesiac. 2011. 9.46 *(978-0-7848-3492-3(X),* Everbind) Marco Bk. Co.

—Memoirs of a Teenage Amnesiac. 2009. (ENG.). 304p. (YA). (gr. 9-13). pap. 10.99 *(978-0-312-56128-4(8),* 9780312561284) Square Fish.

Zhang, Amy. This Is Where the World Ends. 2016. 304p. (J). (gr. 9). 17.99 *(978-0-06-238304-4(3),* Greenwillow Bks.); (YA). *(978-0-06-241787-9(8),* Collins Design) HarperCollins Pubs.

—This Is Where the World Ends. 2017. (ENG.). (YA). (gr. 9). lib. bdg. 20.85 ***(978-0-606-40051-0(6))*** Turtleback Bks.

Zia, Farhana. Child of Spring, 1 vol. 2016. (ENG., Illus.). 192p. (J). (gr. 3-6). 16.95 *(978-1-56145-904-9(6))* Peachtree Pubs.

Ziegesar, Cecily von. Love the One You're With. 2009. (Gossip Girl: the Carlyles Ser.: 4). (ENG.). 240p. (YA). (gr. 10-17). pap. 10.99 *(978-0-316-02067-1(2),* Poppy) Little, Brown Bks. for Young Readers.

Ziglar, Christy. Must-Have Marvin! Martin, Luanne, illus. 2014. (Shine Bright Kids Ser.). 32p. (J). 14.99 *(978-0-8249-5657-8(5),* Ideal Pubns.) Worthy Publishing.

Zimmerman, Amanda. The Spring Snowman. 2011. 48p. pap. 9.95 *(978-1-4502-9816-2(8))* iUniverse, Inc.

Zimmerman, Dorothy. Why Am I Different? 2008. 128p. pap. 9.95 *(978-1-4327-2555-6(6))* Outskirts Pr., Inc.

Zimmerman, George G. Dougie & the Dane: Chelsea the Great Dane. 2004. (Illus.). 36p. 21.99 *(978-1-4134-4139-0(4))* Xlibris Corp.

Zimmerman, Virginia. The Rosemary Spell. (ENG.). (J). (gr. 5-7). 2017. 288p. pap. 7.99 *(978-0-544-93699-7(X),* HMH Books For Young Readers) 2015. 280p. 16.99 *(978-0-544-44537-6(6))* Houghton Mifflin Harcourt Publishing Co.

Zimmermann, Andreas. Shard. 2012. 302p. 28.95 *(978-1-4620-8351-0(X));* pap. 18.95 *(978-1-4620-8350-3(1))* iUniverse, Inc.

Zindel, Paul. The Pigman. 2005. (ENG., Illus.). 224p. (YA). (gr. 9-18). pap. 8.99 *(978-0-06-075735-9(3),* HarperTeen) HarperCollins Pubs.

—The Pigman. Date not set. (Scholastic Bookfiles Ser.). 64p. (J). pap. 4.99 *(978-0-439-53831-2(9))* Scholastic, Inc.

Zindel, Paul & Zindel, Paul. Pigman's Legacy. 2005. (ENG.). 176p. (YA). (gr. 8-18). pap. 8.99 *(978-0-06-075970-4(4),* HarperTeen) HarperCollins Pubs.

Zoellick, Todd. Daniel Harrington Fairbanks the Third & a Day on the Farm. 2012. 40p. pap. 18.58 *(978-1-4772-8408-7(7))* AuthorHouse.

—Daniel Harrington Fairbanks the Third & the Dog That Wouldn't Bark. 2009. 52p. pap. 20.49 *(978-1-4490-1047-8(4))* AuthorHouse.

Zoller, Jayson D. The Laziest Duck. l.t. ed. 2004. (Illus.). 13p. (J). lib. bdg. 12.95 *(978-1-932338-55-3(1));* per. 7.99 *(978-1-932338-52-2(7))* Lifevest Publishing, Inc.

Zolotow, Charlotte. If It Weren't for You. Karas, G. Brian, illus. 2006. 32p. (J). (gr. -1-3). 16.89 *(978-0-06-027876-2(5))* HarperCollins Pubs.

—The Three Funny Friends. Bronson, Linda, illus. 2006. 27p. (J). (gr. k-4). reprint ed. 16.00 *(978-0-7567-9860-4(4))* DIANE Publishing Co.

—A Tiger Called Thomas. 2017. (J). *(978-1-4926-0171-5(3))* Sourcebooks, Inc.

Zolty, H. Calli the Bear: the Story of a Little Bear Who Teaches Children about the Power of Friendship. 2005. 36p. 16.19 *(978-1-4116-7135-5(X))* Lulu Pr., Inc.

Zorn, Claire. Protected. 2017. (ENG.). 288p. (YA). (gr. 6-12). 17.99 ***(978-1-4926-5213-7(X))*** Sourcebooks, Inc.

Zuniga, Elisabeth. A Friend for Bo. 2016. (ENG., Illus.). 40p. (J). (gr. -1-2). 16.99 *(978-0-553-50998-4(5),* Random Hse. Bks. for Young Readers) Random Hse. Children's Bks.

FRIENDSHIP—POETRY

Fandel, Jennifer, et al. Trust, Truth, & Ridiculous Goofs: Reading & Writing Friendship Poems, 1 vol. Smith, Simon et al, illus. 2014. (Poet in You Ser.). (ENG.). 32p. (gr. 2-4). lib. bdg. 27.32 *(978-1-4795-2199-9(X))* Picture Window Bks.

Grimes, Nikki. My Man Blue. Lagarrigue, Jerome, illus. 2015. 32p. pap. 7.00 *(978-1-61003-533-0(X))* Center for the Collaborative Classroom.

Holbrook, Sara E. Weird? (Me, Too!) Let's Be Friends. Sandstrom, Karen, illus. 2011. (ENG.). 56p. (J). (gr. 4-6). 16.95 *(978-1-59078-821-9(4),* Wordsong) Boyds Mills Pr.

Lea, Synne. Night Guard. Hole, Stian, illus. 2016. (ENG.). 82p. (J). (-13). 17.00 *(978-0-8028-5458-2(3),* Eerdmans Bks For Young Readers) Eerdmans, William B. Publishing Co.

Lee, Dennis. The Cat & the Wizard. Johnson, Gillian, illus. 2013. (ENG.). 32p. (J). 15.99 *(978-1-4434-1175-2(2))* HarperCollins Pubs.

Martin, Tamara & Quebodeaux, Vernice. The Flea & the Ant. 2009. (J). pap. *(978-0-9789446-9-8(0))* Little Red Tree Publishing LLC.

Reynolds, Jason & Griffin, Jason. My Name Is Jason. Mine Too: Our Story. Our Way. Griffin, Jason, illus. 2009. (ENG., Illus.). 96p. (J). (gr. 8-18). pap. 12.99 *(978-0-06-154788-1(3),* HarperTeen) HarperCollins Pubs.

FROG AND TOAD (FICTITIOUS CHARACTERS)—FICTION

Book Company Staff. Hoppity Hop. 2003. (Novelty Bks.). (Illus.). (J). 15.95 *(978-1-74047-233-3(0))* Book Co. Publishing Pty, Ltd., The AUS. Dist: Penton Overseas, Inc.

Lobel, Arnold. Frog & Toad Are Friends. Lobel, Arnold, illus. 2003. (I Can Read Book 2 Ser.). (ENG., Illus.). 64p. (J). (gr. -1-3). pap. 3.99 *(978-0-06-444020-2(6))* HarperCollins Pubs.

—Sapo y Sepo, Inseparables. Lobel, Arnold, illus. 2003.Tr. of Frog & Toad Together. (SPA., Illus.). 68p. (J). (gr. -1-3). 12.95 *(978-84-204-3047-8(1))* Ediciones Alfaguara ESP. Dist: Lectorum Pubns., Inc., Santillana USA Publishing Co., Inc.

Shepherd-Harvey, M. Neville the Froad. 2011. 32p. pap. 14.95 *(978-1-4634-4651-2(9))* AuthorHouse.

FROGMEN

see Skin Diving

FROGS

see also Tadpoles

Affleck, Judith & Letchford, Clive. Aristophanes: Frogs. 2014. (Cambridge Translations from Greek Drama Ser.). (ENG., Illus.). 127p. pap. 14.34 *(978-0-521-17257-8(8))* Cambridge Univ. Pr.

Aimee Bakken, Aimee. Explore a Frog. 2017. (Explore Ser.). (ENG., Illus.). 16p. (J). (gr. 2). 21.99 *(978-1-62686-825-0(5),* Silver Dolphin Bks.) Readerlink Distribution Services, LLC.

Allen, Kathy. Deformed Frogs: A Cause & Effect Investigation, 1 vol. 2010. (Animals on the Edge Ser.). (ENG.). 32p. (gr. 3-4). lib. bdg. 27.32 *(978-1-4296-4533-1(4),* Fact Finders) Capstone Press of Coughlan Cos.

Aloian, Molly & Kalman, Bobbie. Endangered Frogs. 2006. (Earth's Endangered Animals Ser.). (ENG., Illus.). 32p. (J). (gr. 4-7). pap. *(978-0-7787-1918-2(9))* Crabtree Publishing Co.

Amstutz, L. J. F Is for Frog: ABCs of Endangered Amphibians. 2016. (E for Endangered Ser.). (ENG., Illus.). 32p. (gr. 1-2). lib. bdg. 27.32 *(978-1-4914-8033-5(5),* Aplus Bks.) Capstone Press of Coughlan Cos.

Appleby, Alex. I See a Frog. 2013. (In My Backyard Ser.). (Illus.). 24p. (J). (gr. k-2). pap. 8.15 *(978-1-4339-8552-2(7));* lib. bdg. 22.60 *(978-1-4339-8551-5(9))* Stevens, Gareth Publishing LLLP.

—I See a Frog: Puedo Ver una Rana. 2013. (In My Backyard / en Mi Jardin Ser.). (SPA & ENG., Illus.). 24p. (J). (gr. k-2). lib. bdg. 22.60 *(978-1-4339-8796-0(1))* Stevens, Gareth Publishing LLLP.

Arlon, Penelope & Kosara, Tori. Fantastic Frogs. 2013. (Scholastic Discover More Reader Ser.). (ENG.). 32p. (J). (gr. 1-2). pap. 3.99 *(978-0-545-57271-2(1),* Scholastic Reference) Scholastic, Inc.

AZ Books Staff. Frog's Pond. Potapenko, Olga, ed. 2012. (Talking Plush Animals Ser.). (ENG.). 10p. (J). (gr. -1-k). bds. 10.95 *(978-1-61889-113-6(8))* AZ Bks. LLC.

Bailer, Darice. How Do Tadpoles Become Frogs? 2010. (Tell Me Why, Tell Me How 4 Ser.). 32p. (gr. 3-5). 29.93 *(978-0-7614-4824-2(1))* Marshall Cavendish Corp.

Barnard, Edward S. Frogs. 2009. (Amazing Animals Ser.). 48p. (gr. 2-6). pap. 10.50 *(978-1-4339-2024-0(7),* Gareth Stevens Learning Library); (YA). (gr. 3-6). lib. bdg. 28.00 *(978-0-8368-9107-2(4))* Stevens, Gareth Publishing LLLP.

—Frogs. 2006. (Illus.). 45p. (J). *(978-1-59939-074-1(4),* Reader's Digest Young Families, Inc.) Studio Fun International.

Bekkering, Annalise. Frogs. 2010. pap. 9.95 *(978-1-60596-926-8(5));* 24p. (J). (gr. 2-4). lib. bdg. 25.70 *(978-1-60596-925-1(7))* Weigl Pubs., Inc.

Benton, Celia. How a Frog Grows, 6 vols., Set. 2003. (Phonics Readers 1-36 Ser.). (ENG.). 8p. (gr. k-1). pap. 29.70 *(978-0-7368-3196-3(7),* Phonics Readers) Capstone Press of Coughlan Cos.

Berger, Melvin & Berger, Gilda. De Renacuajo a Rana: Tadpole to Frog. 2006. (SPA & ENG., Illus.). (J). *(978-0-439-82864-2(3))* Scholastic, Inc.

—Frogs Live on Logs. 2003. (Illus.). 16p. (J). *(978-0-439-47176-3(1))* Scholastic, Inc.

Berne, Emma Carlson. Wood Frogs: Back from the Dead! 2013. (Animal Superpowers Ser.). 24p. (J). (gr. k-5). pap. 8.25 *(978-1-4777-0843-9(X));* pap. 49.50 *(978-1-4777-0844-6(8));* lib. bdg. 22.60 *(978-1-4777-0751-7(4))* Rosen Publishing Group, Inc., The. (PowerKids Pr.).

Bishop, Nic. Frogs. 2015. (Scholastic Reader Level 2 Ser.). (ENG., Illus.). 32p. (J). (gr. k-2). pap. 3.99 *(978-0-545-60570-0(9))* Scholastic, Inc.

—Frogs. Bishop, Nic, photos by. 2008. (Nic Bishop Ser.). (ENG., Illus.). 48p. (J). (gr. -1-3). 18.99 *(978-0-439-87755-8(5))* Scholastic, Inc.

Bluemel Oldfield, Dawn. Horned Lizard. 2017. (Weirder & Cuter Ser.). (ENG.). 24p. (J). (gr. -1-3). 17.95 ***(978-1-68402-260-1(6))*** Bearport Publishing Co., Inc.

Bodden, Valerie. Frogs. 2016. (Amazing Animals Ser.). 24p. (J). (ENG.). (gr. 1-3). pap. 8.99 *(978-1-62832-217-0(9),* Creative Paperbacks); (Illus.). 28.50 *(978-1-60818-611-2(3),* Creative Education) Creative Co., The.

Book Company Staff. Frog Gets Lost. 2004. (Pond Sparkle Bks.). (Illus.). 10p. (J). bds. 4.95 *(978-1-74047-493-1(7))* Book Co. Publishing Pty, Ltd., The AUS. Dist: Penton Overseas, Inc.

Bowman, Chris. Tree Frogs. 2015. (Animal Safari Ser.). (ENG., Illus.). 24p. (J). (gr. k-3). lib. bdg. 25.95 *(978-1-62617-166-4(1),* Blastoff! Readers) Bellwether Media.

Bredeson, Carmen. Fun Facts about Frogs! 2007. (I Like Reptiles & Amphibians! Ser.). (Illus.). 24p. (J). (gr. 1-3). lib. bdg. 22.60 *(978-0-7660-2788-6(0),* Enslow Elementary) Enslow Pubs., Inc.

—Poison Dart Frogs up Close. (Zoom in on Animals! Ser.). (Illus.). 24p. (J). 2012. (gr. k-18). pap. 7.95 *(978-1-59845-420-8(X))* 2008. (gr. 1-3). lib. bdg. 22.60 *(978-0-7660-3077-0(6))* Enslow Pubs., Inc. (Enslow Elementary).

Calhoun, Kelly. Spotted Singers: Leopard Frog. 2015. (Guess What Ser.). (ENG., Illus.). 24p. (J). (gr. k-2). pap. 12.79 *(978-1-63362-720-8(9),* 206705) Cherry Lake Publishing.

Cardenas, Ernesto A. Frogs & Toads. 2009. 19.95 *(978-1-60698-005-7(X));* pap. 3.95 *(978-1-60698-003-3(3))* Milo Educational Bks. & Resources.

Carney, Elizabeth. Frogs! 2009. (Readers Ser.). (ENG., Illus.). 32p. (J). (gr. -1-1). lib. bdg. 13.90 *(978-1-4263-0393-7(9),* National Geographic Children's Bks.) National Geographic Society.

—Frogs. 2009. (Readers Ser.). (ENG., Illus.). 32p. (J). (gr. -1-1). 3.99 *(978-1-4263-0392-0(0),* National Geographic Children's Bks.) National Geographic Society.

Carr, Aaron. Frog. 2014. (Illus.). 24p. (J). *(978-1-62127-293-9(1))* Weigl Pubs., Inc.

Carraway, Rose. Fun Frogs. 2012. (Pet Corner Ser.). (ENG.). 24p. (J). (gr. k-2). pap. 8.15 *(978-1-4339-6287-5(X));* lib. bdg. 22.60 *(978-1-4339-6285-1(3))* Stevens, Gareth Publishing LLLP.

—Fun Frogs: Ranas Saltarinas. 2012. (Pet Corner / RincóN de Las Mascotas Ser.). (SPA & ENG.). 24p. (J). (gr. k-3). lib. bdg. 22.60 *(978-1-4339-6637-8(9))* Stevens, Gareth Publishing LLLP.

Ciletti, Barbara. Cane Toads. 2017. (Invasive Species Takeover Ser.). (ENG., Illus.). 32p. (J). (gr. 3-7). 31.35 ***(978-1-68072-018-1(X),*** Bolt) Black Rabbit Bks.

Clark, Willow. Poison Dart Frog! 2010. (Animal Danger Zone Ser.). (ENG.). 24p. (J). (gr. k-3). lib. bdg. 22.60 *(978-1-60754-961-1(1));* (Illus.). pap. 8.15 *(978-1-60754-972-7(7))* Windmill Bks.

Collard, Sneed B. & Collard, Sneed B., III. Australia's Cane Toads: Overrun! 2015. (They Don't Belong: Tracking Invasive Species Ser.). (ENG., Illus.). 32p. (J). (gr. 2-7). lib. bdg. 26.60 *(978-1-62724-828-0(5))* Bearport Publishing Co., Inc.

Craats, Rennay. Caring for Your Frog. 2005. (Caring for Your Pet Ser.). (Illus.). 32p. (J). (gr. 4-7). per. 9.95 *(978-1-59036-218-1(7));* lib. bdg. 26.00 *(978-1-59036-198-6(9))* Weigl Pubs., Inc.

—Frog. 2010. (J). pap. 9.95 *(978-1-61690-071-7(7));* 32p. (gr. 3-5). lib. bdg. 27.13 *(978-1-61690-070-0(9))* Weigl Pubs., Inc.

Crump, Marty. The Mystery of Darwin's Frog. Jenkins, Steve & Rodriguez, Edel, illus. 2013. (ENG.). 40p. (J). (gr. 2-5). 16.95 *(978-1-59078-864-6(8))* Boyds Mills Pr.

Davies, Caroline, illus. Frog. 2017. (Shake & Play Bath Bks.). (ENG.). 8p. (J). (gr. -1 — 1). 5.99 ***(978-1-4380-7841-0(2))*** Barron's Educational Series, Inc.

De la Bédoyère, Camilla. Tadpole to Frog. 2012. (Illus.). 24p. (gr. 1-3). pap. 7.95 *(978-1-926853-41-3(5))* Saunders Bk. Co. CAN. Dist: RiverStream Publishing.

—The Wild Life of Frogs, 1 vol. 2015. (ENG., Illus.). 24p. (J). lib. bdg. 23.60 *(978-1-4777-5518-1(7),* Windmill Bks.) Rosen Publishing Group, Inc., The.

Delano, Marfe Ferguson. Explore My World Frogs. 2014. (Explore My World Ser.). (ENG.). 32p. (J). (gr. -1-2). pap.

E
F
G

4.99 (978-1-4263-1697-5(6), National Geographic Children's Bks.) National Geographic Society.

Dickmann, Nancy. A Frog's Life, 1 vol. 2010. (Watch It Grow Ser.). (ENG.). 24p. (gr. -1-1). 22.65 (978-1-4329-4140-6(2)); pap. 6.29 (978-1-4329-4149-9(6)) Heinemann-Raintree. (Acorn).

—La Vida de la Rana, 1 vol. 2011. (¡Mira Cómo Crece! Ser.). 24p. (gr. -1-1). (SPA & ENG.). 22.65 (978-1-4329-5273-0(0)); (ENG & SPA.). pap. 6.29 (978-1-4329-5285-3(4)) Heinemann-Raintree. (Bellota).

Dominquez, Amalia. Happy, Hopping Frog. 2004. (Illus.). 24p. bds. 8.95 (978-1-932915-00-6(1)) Sandvik Publishing.

Dorling Kindersley Publishing Staff. Everything You Need to Know about Frogs & Other Slippery Creatures. 2011. (Everything You Need to Know Ser.). (ENG., Illus.). 80p. (J). (gr. 2-5). 15.99 (978-0-7566-8232-3(0), DK Children) Dorling Kindersley Publishing, Inc.

Dorling Kindersley Publishing Staff & Gersh, Camilla. Frogs & Toads. 2014. (DK Readers Ser.). (ENG.). 32p. (J). (gr. -1-1). 14.99 (978-1-4654-2011-4(8)); pap. 3.99 (978-1-4654-2010-7(X)) Dorling Kindersley Publishing, Inc. (DK Children).

Duffey, Gary. Windows. 2012. 16p. pap. 7.95 (978-1-4582-0512-4(6), Abbott Pr.) Author Solutions, Inc.

Dussling, Jennifer. Deadly Poison Dart Frogs. 2008. (Gross-Out Defenses Ser.). (Illus.). 24p. (J). (gr. k-3). lib. bdg. 21.28 (978-1-59716-720-8(7), 1284312) Bearport Publishing Co., Inc.

Dyan, Penelope. Jump Frog, Funny Frog — -Because Frogs Are Funny. Dyan, Penelope, illus. 2008. (Illus.). 44p. pap. 11.95 (978-1-935118-19-0(6)) Bellissima Publishing, LLC.

Earley, Chris. Weird Frogs. 2014. (ENG., Illus.). 64p. (J). (gr. 5-12). pap. 9.95 (978-1-77085-361-4(8), 9781770853614) Firefly Bks., Ltd.

Eggleton. Sail Blu Nf Fantastic Frogs. 2004. (Rigby Sails Early Ser.). (ENG.). 16p. (gr. 1-2). pap. 6.95 (978-0-7578-9952-2(8)) Rigby Education.

Flynn, Wes. Horned Toads Are Not Toads! 2014. (Confusing Creature Names Ser.). 24p. (J). (gr. 1-3). 22.60 (978-1-4824-0956-7(9)) Stevens, Gareth Publishing LLLP.

French, Vivian. Growing Frogs. Bartlett, Alison, illus. 2003. (Read & Wonder Ser.). (ENG.). 32p. (J). (gr. -1-3). pap. 6.99 (978-0-7636-2052-3(1)) Candlewick Pr.

—Growing Frogs Big Book: Read & Wonder Big Book. Bartlett, Alison, illus. 2003. (Read & Wonder Ser.). (ENG.). 32p. (J). (gr. k-3). pap. 24.99 (978-0-7636-2232-9(X)) Candlewick Pr.

Frisch, Aaron. Frogs. 2014. (J). (978-1-60818-458-3(7), Creative Education) Creative Co., The.

—Seedlings: Frogs. 2015. (Seedlings Ser.). (ENG.). 24p. (J). (gr. -1-1). pap. 7.99 (978-1-62832-042-8(7), Creative Paperbacks) Creative Co., The.

Frog. 2004. (Peek-A-Boo Coloring Pads Ser.). 48p. (J). act. bk. ed. 3.99 (978-1-85997-394-3(9)) Byeway Bks.

Frogs: Level M, 6 vols. (Wonder Worldtm Ser.). 16p. 34.95 (978-0-7802-4573-0(3)) Wright Group/McGraw-Hill.

Frost, Helen. Tree Frogs [Scholastic]. 2011. (Rain Forest Animals Ser.). 24p. pap. 0.50 (978-1-4296-6310-6(3), Pebble Bks.) Capstone Press of Coughlan Cos.

Gail, Gibbons. Frogs. 2014. (ENG.). 32p. (J). (gr. k-3). 12.24 (978-1-63245-304-4(5)) Lectorum Pubns., Inc.

Ganeri, Anita. Frogs & Tadpoles. Axworthy, Anni, illus. 2010. (Animal Families Ser.). (ENG.). 14p. (J). bds. 10.99 (978-1-84089-642-8(6)) Evans Brothers, Ltd. GBR. Dist: Independent Pubs. Group.

—Poison Dart Frog, 1 vol. 2010. (Day in the Life: Rain Forest Animals Ser.). (ENG.). 24p. (gr. k-2). 23.32 (978-1-4329-4104-8(6)); pap. 6.79 (978-1-4329-4115-4(1)) Heinemann-Raintree. (Heinemann Read & Learn).

Gareth Stevens Publishing Staff, contrib. by. Frogs. 2004. (All about Wild Animals Ser.). (Illus.). 32p. (gr. k-4). lib. bdg. 26.00 (978-0-8368-4184-8(0), Gareth Stevens Learning Library) Stevens, Gareth Publishing LLLP.

Gerstein, Sherry. See-Thru Frogs. 2016. (See-Thru Bks.). (ENG., Illus.). 28p. (gr. 2-4). spiral bd. 12.99 (978-1-60684-587-5(X), Millbrook Pr.) Lerner Publishing Group.

Gish, Melissa. Frogs. 2013. (Illus.). 46p. (J). 35.65 (978-1-60818-287-9(8), Creative Education) Creative Co., The.

—Living Wild: Frogs. 2014. (Living Wild Ser.). (ENG., Illus.). 48p. (J). (gr. 4-7). pap. 12.00 (978-0-89812-840-6(4), Creative Paperbacks) Creative Co., The.

Godwin, Sam. The Trouble with Tadpoles: A First Look at the Life Cycle of a Frog. Abel, Simone, illus. 2004. (First Look: Science Ser.). (ENG.). 32p. (gr. -1-2). 26.65 (978-1-4048-0654-2(7)) Picture Window Bks.

Goldish, Meish. Amazing Water Frogs. 2010. (Amphibiana Ser.). (Illus.). 24p. (YA). (gr. k-3). lib. bdg. 22.61 (978-1-936087-34-1(0)) Bearport Publishing Co., Inc.

—Warty Toads. 2010. (Amphibiana Ser.). (Illus.). 24p. (YA). (gr. k-3). lib. bdg. 22.61 (978-1-936087-36-5(7)) Bearport Publishing Co., Inc.

Graham, Pamela, et al. A Frog Has a Sticky Tongue. 2007. (Rise & Shine Ser.). (ENG., Illus.). 24p. (J). (gr. k-2). pap. 13.95 (978-0-7922-8928-9(5)) CENGAGE Learning.

Gravel, Elise. The Toad. 2016. (Disgusting Critters Ser.). (ENG., Illus.). 32p. (J). (gr. 1-4). 10.99 (978-1-77049-667-5(X), Tundra Bks.) Tundra Bks. CAN. Dist: Penguin Random Hse. LLC.

Gray, Leon. Cane Toad: The World's Biggest Toad. 2013. (Even More SuperSized! Ser.). 24p. (J). (gr. k-3). lib. bdg. 23.93 (978-1-61772-727-6(X)) Bearport Publishing Co., Inc.

Gray, Susan H. Bullfrog. 2009. (21st Century Skills Library: Animal Invaders Ser.). (ENG.). 32p. (gr. 4-8). lib. bdg. 28.50 (978-1-60279-327-9(1), 200223) Cherry Lake Publishing.

Green, Emily. Frogs. 2010. (Backyard Wildlife Ser.). (ENG., Illus.). 24p. (J). (gr. k-3). lib. bdg. 25.95 (978-1-60014-442-4(X), Blastoff! Readers) Bellwether Media.

Guiberson, Brenda Z. Frog Song. Spirin, Gennady, illus. 2013. (ENG.). 40p. (J). (gr. -1-3). 17.99 (978-0-8050-9254-7(4), 9780805092547, Holt, Henry & Co. Bks. For Young Readers) Holt, Henry & Co.

Guidone, Julie. Frogs. 2009. (Animals That Live in the Rain Forest Ser.). 24p. (J). (gr. -1-3). pap. 8.15 (978-1-4339-0107-2(2)); lib. bdg. 22.60 (978-1-4339-0025-9(4)) Stevens, Gareth Publishing LLLP. (Weekly Reader Leveled Readers).

—Frogs (Ranas) 2009. (Animals That Live in the Rain Forest/Animales de la selva Ser.). (SPA & ENG.). 24p. (gr. -1-3). pap. 8.15 (978-1-4339-0114-0(5)); lib. bdg. 22.60 (978-1-4339-0064-8(5)) Stevens, Gareth Publishing LLLP. (Weekly Reader Leveled Readers).

Hamilton, Garry. Frog Rescue: Changing the Future for Endangered Wildlife. 2004. (Firefly Animal Rescue Ser.). (ENG., Illus.). 64p. (J). (gr. 5-8). pap. 9.95 (978-1-55297-596-1(7), 9781552975961) Firefly Bks., Ltd.

Haney, Johannah. Frogs. 2009. (Great Pets 3 Ser.). 48p. (gr. 3). 29.93 (978-0-7614-4151-9(4)) Marshall Cavendish GBR. Dist: Marshall Cavendish Corp.

Harris, Tim. Frogs. 2008. (Nature's Children Ser.). (Illus.). 52p. (J). (978-0-7172-6224-3(3)) Grolier, Ltd.

Hayes, Amy. A Tadpole Becomes a Frog. 2016. (Transformations in Nature Ser.). (ENG.). 24p. (J). (gr. 1-1). pap. 8.22 (978-1-5026-0818-5(9)) Cavendish Square Publishing.

Herrington, Lisa M. Frogs & Toads. 2015. (Rookie Read-About(tm) Science: What's the Difference? Ser.). (ENG., Illus.). 32p. (J). lib. bdg. 25.00 (978-0-531-21484-8(2), Children's Pr.) Scholastic Library Publishing.

—Tadpole to Frog. 2014. (Rookie Read-About(tm) Science -- Life Cycles Ser.). (ENG.). 32p. (J). lib. bdg. 25.00 (978-0-531-21057-4(X)) Scholastic Library Publishing.

Hewitt, Sally. Life Cycles from Tadpole to Frog, 8 vols. 2005. (QEB Readers). (Illus.). 24p. (J). (gr. -1-3). lib. bdg. 15.95 (978-1-59566-068-8(2)) QEB Publishing Inc.

Himmelman, John. Noisy Frog Sing-Along. Himmelman, John, illus. 2013. (ENG., Illus.). 32p. (J). (gr. -1-4). 16.95 (978-1-58469-339-0(8)); pap. 8.95 (978-1-58469-340-6(1)) Dawn Pubns.

Ho, Cammie. Tadpole Tadpole. 2016. (Life Cycle Bks.). (ENG., Illus.). 31p. (J). (gr. k-2). pap. 7.99 (978-1-943241-01-9(5)) Phonic Monic.

Holden, Pam. From Tadpole to Frog. 2015. (ENG., Illus.). 16p. (-1). pap. (978-1-77654-142-3(1), Red Rocket Readers) Flying Start Bks.

—From Tadpole to Frog - BIG BOOK. 2016. (ENG.). 16p. (-1). Beta (978-1-77654-165-2(0), Red Rocket Readers) Flying Start Bks.

Holzer, Angela. Fat Freddy. Tucker, Barclay, illus. 2009. 36p. (J). lib. bdg. 8.99 (978-0-9821563-4-6(0)) Good Sound Publishing.

Hopper, Whitney. The Life Cycle of a Frog. 2015. (Watch Them Grow! Ser.). (ENG., Illus.). 24p. (J). (gr. 1-1). pap. 8.25 (978-1-4994-0668-9(1), PowerKids Pr.) Rosen Publishing Group, Inc., The.

Hunt, Joni Phelps. A Chorus of Frogs: The Risky Life of an Ancient Amphibian. Leon, Vicki, ed. 2nd ed. 2005. (Jean-Michel Cousteau Presents Ser.). (ENG., Illus.). 48p. (J). (gr. 4). per. 7.95 (978-0-9766134-1-1(7)) London Town Pr.

Hurley, Jorey. Ribbit. Hurley, Jorey, illus. 2017. (ENG., Illus.). 40p. (J). (gr. -1-3). 16.99 (978-1-4814-3274-0(5), Simon & Schuster/Paula Wiseman Bks.) Simon & Schuster/Paula Wiseman Bks.

Huseby, Victoria. Frog. 2008. (J). 25.65 (978-1-59920-176-4(3)) Black Rabbit Bks.

James, Lincoln. Deadly Poison Dart Frogs. 2011. (Small but Deadly Ser.). (Illus.). 24p. (J). (gr. 2-5). pap. 8.15 (978-1-4339-5744-4(2)); lib. bdg. 22.60 (978-1-4339-5742-0(6)) Stevens, Gareth Publishing LLLP. (Gareth Stevens Learning Library).

Jenkins, Martin. Fabulous Frogs. Hopgood, Tim, illus. 2016. (ENG.). 32p. (J). (gr. k-3). 16.99 (978-0-7636-8100-5(8)) Candlewick Pr.

Johnson, Jinny. Frog. Rosewarne, Graham, illus. 2010. (J). 28.50 (978-1-59920-355-3(3)) Black Rabbit Bks.

Jones, Kadeem. Look Out for the Poison Dart Frog! 2015. (Surprisingly Scary! Ser.). (ENG.). 24p. (J). (gr. 2-3). 23.60 (978-1-4994-0944-4(3), PowerKids Pr.) Rosen Publishing Group, Inc., The.

Jordan, Apple. Guess Who Changes. 2nd rev. ed. 2011. (Bookworms 2nd Edition: Guess Who Ser.). (Illus.). 24p. (J). (gr. k-2). 21.36 (978-1-60870-425-5(4)) Marshall Cavendish Corp.

Kalman, Bobbie. Frogs & Other Amphibians. 2005. (What Kind of Animal Is It? Ser.). (Illus.). 32p. (J). (978-978-077-872-9(1)); (ENG., pap. (978-0-7787-2217-5(1)) Crabtree Publishing Co.

—The Life Cycle of a Frog. 2007. (ENG.). 32p. (J). (978-0-7787-7702-1(2)) Crabtree Publishing Co.

—Ranas y Otros Anfibios. 2007. (Que Tipo de Animal Es? Ser.). (SPA., Illus.). 32p. (J). (gr. 1-2). lib. bdg. (978-0-7787-8837-9(7)); (gr. k-4). pap. (978-0-7787-8873-7(3)) Crabtree Publishing Co.

—Tadpoles to Frogs. 2008. (It's Fun to Learn about Baby Animals Ser.). (ENG., Illus.). 24p. (J). (gr. k-3). pap. (978-0-7787-3975-3(9)) Crabtree Publishing Co.

Kalman, Bobbie & Smithyman, Kathryn. Les Grenouilles. Briere, Marie-Josee, tr. from ENG. Rouse, Bonna, illus. 2006. (Petit Monde Vivant Ser.). (FRE.). 32p. (J). (gr. -1-3). pap. 9.95 (978-2-89579-080-8(9)) Bayard Canada Livres CAN. Dist: Crabtree Publishing Co.

Kenan, Tessa. It's a Red-Eyed Tree Frog! 2017. (Bumba Books (tm) — Rain Forest Animals Ser.). (ENG.). 24p. (J). (gr. -1-1). 12.99 **(978-1-5124-3759-1(X)**, Lerner Pubns.); 38.65 **(978-1-5124-3758-4(1)**, Lerner Pubns.); 38.65 **(978-1-5124-2761-5(6)**, Lerner Pubns.); (Illus.). 25.32 (978-1-5124-2569-7(9)) Lerner Publishing Group.

Kingston, Anna. The Life Cycle of the Poison Dart Frog. 2011. (Nature's Life Cycles Ser.). (Illus.). 24p. (J). (gr. 2-5). pap. 8.15 (978-1-4339-4692-9(0)); lib. bdg. 22.60 (978-1-4339-4691-2(2)) Stevens, Gareth Publishing LLLP. (Gareth Stevens Learning Library).

Knudsen, Shannon. From Tadpole to Frog. 2012. (Start to Finish, Second Series: Nature's Cycles Ser.). (ENG., Illus.). 24p. (gr. k-3). lib. bdg. 23.93 (978-0-7613-6565-5(6)) Lerner Publishing Group.

Kralovansky, Susan. Frog or Toad?, 1 vol. 2014. (This or That? Ser.). (ENG.). 24p. (gr. 5-10). lib. bdg. 25.65 (978-1-62403-286-8(9), Super SandCastle) ABDO Publishing Co.

Lawrence, Ellen. A Frog's Life. (Animal Diaries: Life Cycles Ser.). 24p. (J). 2016. (ENG.). (gr. k-3). pap. 7.95 (978-1-944998-40-0(3)) 2012. (gr. -1-3). lib. bdg. 23.93 (978-1-61772-412-1(2)) Bearport Publishing Co., Inc.

Lunis, Natalie. Green Tree Frogs: Colorful Hiders. 2010. (Disappearing Acts Ser.). (Illus.). 24p. (J). (gr. k-3). lib. bdg. 22.61 (978-1-936087-44-0(8)) Bearport Publishing Co., Inc.

—Tricky Tree Frogs. (Amphibiana Ser.). 24p. (J). 2016. (ENG.). (gr. 1-6). pap. 7.95 (978-1-944998-56-1(X)) 2010. (Illus.). (gr. k-3). lib. bdg. 22.61 (978-1-936087-33-4(2)) Bearport Publishing Co., Inc.

Markle, Sandra. The Case of the Vanishing Golden Frogs. 2011. (Exceptional Science Titles for Intermediate Grades Ser.). (ENG., Illus.). 48p. (gr. 4-6). lib. bdg. 29.27 (978-0-7613-5108-5(6)) Lerner Publishing Group.

—Toad Weather, 1 vol. González, Thomas, illus. 2015. (ENG.). 32p. (J). (gr. 1-3). 16.95 (978-1-56145-818-9(X)) Peachtree Pubs.

Markovics, Joyce. My Eyes Are Big & Red (Tree Frog) 2014. (Zoo Clues Ser.). 24p. (J). (gr. -1-3). lib. bdg. 23.93 (978-1-62724-110-6(8)) Bearport Publishing Co., Inc.

Markovics, Joyce L. Las Ranas de la Madera. 2014. (¿a dónde Van en Invierno? Ser.). (SPA.). 24p. (J). (gr. -1-3). lib. bdg. 23.93 (978-1-62724-461-9(1)) Bearport Publishing Co., Inc.

—MIS Ojos Son Grandes y Rojos. 2015. (Pistas de Animales Ser.). (SPA.). 24p. (J). (gr. -1-3). lib. bdg. 23.93 (978-1-62724-579-1(0)) Bearport Publishing Co., Inc.

—Wood Frogs. 2015. (Illus.). 24p. (J). lib. bdg. (978-1-62724-319-3(4)) Bearport Publishing Co., Inc.

Marsico, Katie. American Bullfrogs. 2012. (Nature's Children Ser.). (ENG., Illus.). 48p. (J). pap. 6.95 (978-0-531-25477-6(1)); lib. bdg. 28.00 (978-0-531-26832-2(2)) Scholastic Library Publishing.

McCarthy, Cecilia Pinto. Poison Dart Frogs, 1 vol. 2011. (Colorful World of Animals Ser.). (ENG.). 24p. (gr. k-1). 26.65 (978-1-4296-6050-1(3), Pebble Plus) Capstone Press of Coughlan Cos.

McNab, Chris. Frogs, Toads, & Salamanders. 2006. (Nature's Monsters Ser.). (Illus.). 32p. (gr. 2-6). lib. bdg. 26.00 (978-0-8368-6172-3(8), Gareth Stevens Learning Library) Stevens, Gareth Publishing LLLP.

Meachen Rau, Dana. Adivina Quién Brinca. 2008. (Adivina Quién Ser.). (SPA.). 32p. (gr. k-2). lib. bdg. 15.95 (978-0-7614-3457-3(7), Benchmark Bks.) Marshall Cavendish Corp.

—The Frog in the Pond. (Benchmark Rebus). (Illus.). 2007. 23p. (J). (gr. -1-3). pap. 6.99 (978-0-7614-3245-6(0), Cavendish Children's Bks.) 2006. (SPA., 24p. (gr. k-1). lib. bdg. 15.95 (978-0-7614-2310-2(9), Benchmark Bks.) Marshall Cavendish Corp.

—La Rana en el Estanque. Vargus, Nanci R., ed. 2006. (Naturaleza Ser.). (SPA., Illus.). 24p. (gr. k-1). lib. bdg. 15.95 (978-0-7614-2415-4(6), Benchmark Bks.) Marshall Cavendish Corp.

Meadows, Graham & Vial, Claire. Fascinating Frogs & Toads. 2004. (ENG., Illus.). 24p. (J). (gr. 2-3). pap. 7.47 net. (978-0-7685-1634-0(X), Dominie Elementary) Pearson Schl.

Merritt, Robin. The Life Cycle of a Frog. 2011. (Life Cycles Ser.). (ENG., Illus.). 32p. (J). (gr. k-3). lib. bdg. 29.93 (978-1-60973-150-2(6), 201173) Child's World, Inc., The.

Michele, Tracey. The Life Cycle of a Frog. 2011. (Learn-Abouts Ser.). (Illus.). 16p. (J). pap. 7.95 (978-1-59920-627-1(7)) Black Rabbit Bks.

Milbourne, A. Tadpoles & Frogs. 2004. (Beginners Ser.). (J). (gr. 1-18). 32p. lib. bdg. 12.95 (978-1-58086-465-7(1)); (ENG., Illus.). 1p. pap. 4.95 (978-0-7945-0164-8(8), Usborne) EDC Publishing.

Milbourne, Anna. Tadpoles & Frogs. Donaera, Patrizia & Wray, Zoe, illus. 2007. (Usborne Beginners Ser.). 32p. (J). 4.99 (978-0-7945-1345-0(X), Usborne) EDC Publishing.

Miller, Amanda & Mayer, Sandra. I Love Frogs. 2017. (Rookie Toddler(tm) Ser.). (ENG.). 12p. (J). bds. 6.95 (978-0-531-22976-7(9), Children's Pr.) Scholastic Library Publishing.

Miller, Dave. Dogs, Frogs, & Hogs. 2006. (ENG., Illus.). (J). 3.00 (978-0-932859-88-4(7)) Apologetics Pr., Inc.

Mitchell, Melanie S. Frogs. (First Step Nonfiction Ser.). (Illus.). 24p. (gr. k-2). 2005. lib. bdg. 17.27 (978-0-8225-4600-9(0)) 2003. (ENG., pap. 6.95 (978-0-8225-4601-6(9), Lerner Pubns.) Lerner Publishing Group.

Moffett, Mark W. Face to Face with Frogs. 2010. (Face to Face with Animals Ser.). (ENG., Illus.). 32p. (J). (gr. 2-5). pap. 6.95 (978-1-4263-0626-6(1), National Geographic Children's Bks.) National Geographic Society.

Morgan, Sally. Frogs & Toads: Animal Lives Series. 2008. 32p. (J). lib. bdg. 18.95 (978-1-59566-538-6(2)) QEB Publishing Inc.

Murphy, Patricia J. A Frog's Life: Learning Sequential Order Using a Timeline. (PowerMath: Beginning Ser.). 16p. 2009. (gr. 2-2). 37.50 (978-1-60851-371-0(8), PowerKids Pr.) 2006. (Illus.). (J). (gr. 3-7). lib. bdg. 13.25 (978-1-4042-3334-8(2), PowerKids Pr.) 2004. (ENG.). (gr. 2-3). 37.95 (978-0-8239-7637-9(8)) Rosen Publishing Group, Inc., The.

Murray, Julie. Frogs, 1 vol. (Life Cycles Ser.). (ENG.). 24p. 2007. (gr. -1-3). 25.65 (978-1-59928-707-2(2)) 2005. (Illus.). (J). (gr. k-4). 25.65 (978-1-59197-315-7(5)) ABDO Publishing Co. (Buddy Bks.).

—Toads, 1 vol. 2003. (Animal Kingdom Ser.). (ENG.). 24p. (gr. k-4). 25.65 (978-1-57765-719-4(5), Buddy Bks.) ABDO Publishing Co.

National Geographic Editors. Creepy Crawly Collection. 2012. lib. bdg. 18.40 (978-0-606-26822-6(7), Turtleback) Turtleback Bks.

Nelson, Robin. Pet Frog. 2003. (First Step Nonfiction). (Illus.). 24p. (J). (gr. k-2). lib. bdg. 18.60 (978-0-8225-1271-4(8)) Lerner Publishing Group.

O'Brien, Lindsy. Frogs. 2016. (Illus.). 24p. (J). (978-1-60818-698-3(9), Creative Education) Creative Co., The.

O'Brien, Lindsy J. Frogs. 2017. (In My Backyard Ser.). (ENG., Illus.). 24p. (J). (gr. 1-3). pap. 8.99 (978-1-62832-294-1(2), Creative Paperbacks) Creative Co., The.

O'Connor, Rebecca K. Frogs & Toads. 2003. (Endangered Animals & Habitats Ser.). (Illus.). 112p. (J). 29.95 (978-1-56006-919-5(8), Lucent Bks.) Cengage Gale.

Oldfield, Dawn Bluemel. Leaping Ground Frogs. 2010. (Amphibiana Ser.). (Illus.). 24p. (YA). (gr. k-3). lib. bdg. 22.61 (978-1-936087-35-8(9)) Bearport Publishing Co., Inc.

—Water Frog Polliwogs. 2012. (Water Babies Ser.). 24p. (J). (gr. -1-3). lib. bdg. 21.32 (978-1-61772-606-4(0)) Bearport Publishing Co., Inc.

Orr, Tamra B. Poison Dart Frog. 2015. (21st Century Skills Library: Exploring Our Rainforests Ser.). (ENG., Illus.). 32p. (J). (gr. 3-6). 29.93 (978-1-63188-977-6(X), 205820) Cherry Lake Publishing.

—Red-Eyed Tree Frog. 2015. (21st Century Skills Library: Exploring Our Rainforests Ser.). (ENG., Illus.). 32p. (J). (gr. 3-6). 29.93 (978-1-63188-978-3(8), 205824) Cherry Lake Publishing.

Owen, Leslie E. Pacific Tree Frogs, 1 vol. Juhasz, George, illus. 2003. (ENG.). 32p. (J). (gr. 2-5). pap. 7.95 (978-1-896580-42-5(4)) Tradewind Bks. CAN. Dist: Orca Bk. Pubs. USA.

Owings, Lisa. Poison Dart Frogs. 2011. (Nature's Deadliest Ser.). (ENG., Illus.). 24p. (YA). (gr. 3-8). lib. bdg. 25.95 (978-1-60014-668-8(6), Pilot Bks.) Bellwether Media.

Parker, Steve. Frog's Diary: A Year in My Life. 2016. (ENG., Illus.). 32p. 9.99 (978-1-86147-656-2(6), Armadillo) Anness Publishing GBR. Dist: National Bk. Network.

Patent, Dorothy Hinshaw. Flashy Fantastic Rain Forest Frogs. Jubb, Kendahl Jan, illus. 2015. 32p. pap. 8.00 (978-1-61003-544-6(5)) Center for the Collaborative Classroom.

Pfeffer, Wendy. From Tadpole to Frog. Keller, Holly, illus. 2015. (Let's-Read-And-Find-Out Science 1 Ser.). (ENG.). 32p. (J). (gr. -1-3). pap. 6.99 (978-0-06-238186-6(5)) HarperCollins Pubs.

Phillips, Dee. Tree Frog. 2013. (Science Slam: Treed-Animal Life in the Trees Ser.). 24p. (J). (gr. -1-3). lib. bdg. 23.93 (978-1-61772-915-7(9)) Bearport Publishing Co., Inc.

Plattner, Josh. Poison Dart Frog: Master of Poison, 1 vol. 2016. (ENG., Illus.). 24p. (J). (978-1-62403-739-9(9)) ABDO Publishing Co.

Pringle, Laurence. Frogs! Strange & Wonderful. Henderson, Meryl, illus. 2012. (Strange & Wonderful Ser.). (ENG.). 32p. (J). (gr. 1-4). 16.95 (978-1-59078-371-9(9)) Boyds Mills Pr.

Pugliano-Martin, Carol. Watch a Frog Grow. 2006. (Early Explorers Ser.). (J). pap. (978-1-4108-6098-9(1)) Benchmark Education Co.

Quick, Gunner. Itty Bitty Tree Frogs, Vol. 1. 2014. (Itty Bitty Animals Ser.). 24p. (J). (gr. k-k). (ENG.). pap. 8.15 (978-1-4339-9896-6(3)); 22.60 (978-1-4339-9894-2(7)) Stevens, Gareth Publishing LLLP.

Las Ranas y los Sapos. (Fascinante Mundo de... Ser.).Tr. of Fascinating World of Frogs & Toads. (Illus.). 8.95 (978-958-04-2597-7(3)) Norma S.A. COL. Dist: Distribuidora Norma, Inc.

Rau, Dana Meachen. Guess Who Jumps/Adivina Quién Brinca. 2007. (Guess Who/Adivina Quién Ser.). (SPA & ENG.). 32p. (gr. k-2). 15.95 (978-0-7614-3482-5(8)) Marshall Cavendish Corp.

Raum, Elizabeth. Poison Dart Frogs. 2015. (Poisonous Animals Ser.). (ENG., Illus.). 32p. (J). (gr. 2-4). 19.95 (978-1-60753-787-8(7)) Amicus Publishing.

Reher, Matt. Frogs & Toads. 2016. (1G Science Ser.). (ENG., Illus.). 28p. (J). pap. 5.99 **(978-1-63437-569-6(6))** American Reading Co.

Rice, Dona Herweck. A Frog's Life, 1 vol. 2nd rev. ed. 2013. (Nonfiction Readers Ser.). (ENG., Illus.). 20p. (J). (gr. 1-1). pap. 19.96 (978-1-4807-1019-1(9)) Shell Educational Publishing.

—A Frog's Life, 1 vol. 2nd rev. ed. 2011. (TIME for KIDS(r) Nonfiction Readers Ser.). (ENG.). 20p. (J). (gr. 1-1). 4.99 (978-1-4333-3586-0(7)) Teacher Created Materials, Inc.

—La Vida de Una Rana, 1 vol. 2nd rev. ed. 2012. (Nonfiction Readers Ser.).Tr. of Frog's Life. (SPA.). 20p. (J). (gr. 1-1). pap. 4.99 (978-1-4333-4419-0(X)) Teacher Created Materials, Inc.

Riggs, Kate. Grow with Me: Frog. 2013. (Grow with Me Ser.). (ENG.). 32p. (J). (gr. 1-3). pap. 9.99 (978-0-89812-769-0(6), Creative Paperbacks) Creative Co., The.

Robbins, Lynette. Tree Frogs. 2012. (J). 49.50 (978-1-4488-5168-3(8), PowerKids Pr.); pap. 8.25 (978-1-4488-5167-6(X), PowerKids Pr.); lib. bdg. 22.60 (978-1-4488-5017-4(7)) Rosen Publishing Group, Inc., The.

Rockwood, Leigh. Tell Me the Difference Between a Frog & a Toad. 2013. (How Are They Different? Ser.). (ENG., Illus.). 24p. (J). (gr. k-5). pap. 8.25 (978-1-4488-9730-8(0)); lib. bdg. 22.60 (978-1-4488-9636-3(3)) Rosen Publishing Group, Inc., The. (PowerKids Pr.).

Ross, Dev. We Both Read Bilingual Edition-Frank & the Giant/Sapi y el Globo. Reinhart, Larry, illus. 2011. (ENG & SPA.). 44p. (J). pap. 4.99 (978-1-60115-042-4(3)) Treasure Bay, Inc.

Ross, Dev & Canetti, Yanitzia. Frank & the Balloon: Sapi y el Globo. Reinhart, Larry, illus. 2010. (SPA & ENG.). 41p. (J). (978-1-60115-041-7(5)) Treasure Bay, Inc.

Rustad, Martha E. H. Bullfrogs. 2013. (ENG., Illus.). 24p. (J). lib. bdg. 25.65 (978-1-62031-073-1(2)) Jump! Inc.

Ryndak, Rob. Frog or Toad? 2015. (Animal Look-Alikes Ser.). (ENG., Illus.). 24p. (J). (gr. 1-2). 22.60 (978-1-4824-2718-9(4)) Stevens, Gareth Publishing LLLP.

Salazar, Sydney. Being a Bullfrog, Vol. 1. 2014. (Can You Imagine? Ser.). (ENG.). 32p. (J). (gr. 2-3). 25.25 (978-1-4339-9858-4(0)) Stevens, Gareth Publishing LLLP.

Santillo, LuAnn. Mole. Santillo, LuAnn, ed. 2003. (Half-Pint Kids Readers Ser.). (Illus.). 7p. (J). (gr. -1-1). pap. (978-1-59256-111-7(X)) Half-Pint Kids, Inc.

Saunders-Smith, Gail. Frogs. 2016. (Animals: Life Cycles Ser.). (ENG.). 24p. (gr. k-1). pap. 6.29 (978-1-5157-4225-8(3), Pebble Bks.) Capstone Press of Coughlan Cos.

Scheunemann, Pam. Frogs Croak!, 1 vol. 2011. (Animal Sounds Set 2 Ser.). (ENG., Illus.). 24p. (J). (gr. k-3). lib. bdg. 24.21 (978-1-61613-572-0(7), SandCastle) ABDO Publishing Co.

Schuepbach, Lynnette. Froggy Hollow. Schuepbach, Lynnette, illus. l.t. ed. 2004. (Illus.). 32p. (J). 7.00 net. (978-0-9759613-0-8(6)) Creative Sources.

Schuetz, Kari. Toads. 2012. (Backyard Wildlife Ser.). (ENG., Illus.). 24p. (J). (gr. k-3). lib. bdg. 25.95 (978-1-60014-724-1(0), Blastoff! Readers) Bellwether Media.

Schuh, Mari. Tree Frogs. 2014. (Illus.). 24p. (J). lib. bdg. 25.65 *(978-1-62031-114-1(3)*, Bullfrog Bks.) Jump! Inc.

Sexton, Colleen. The Life Cycle of a Frog. 2010. (Life Cycles Ser.). (ENG., Illus.). 24p. (J). (gr. k-3). lib. bdg. 25.95 *(978-1-60014-308-3(3)*, Blastoff! Readers) Bellwether Media.

Shea, Therese. Attack of the Bullfrogs. 2016. (Animal Invaders: Destroying Native Habitats Ser.). 00024p. (J). pap. 8.15 ***(978-1-4824-5657-8(5))*** Stevens, Gareth Publishing LLLP.

Silverman, Buffy. Can You Tell a Frog from a Toad? 2011. (Lightning Bolt Books (tm) — Animal Look-Alikes Ser.). (ENG.). 32p. (gr. k-2). pap. 7.95 *(978-0-7613-7845-7(6))*; (Illus.). lib. bdg. 26.60 *(978-0-7613-6732-1(2))* Lerner Publishing Group.

—Can You Tell A Frog from A Toad? 2011. (Animal Look-Alikes Ser.). pap. 45.32 *(978-0-7613-8386-4(7))* Lerner Publishing Group.

Silverstein, Alvin, et al. Poison Dart Frogs: Cool Pets! Kelley, Gerald, illus. 2012. (Far-Out & Unusual Pets Ser.). 48p. (J). (gr. 3-4). pap. 8.95 *(978-1-4644-0126-8(8))*; 25.27 *(978-0-7660-3881-3(5))* Enslow Pubs., Inc. (Enslow Elementary).

Simon, Seymour. Frogs. 2015. (ENG., Illus.). 40p. (J). (gr. 1-5). pap. 6.99 *(978-0-06-228911-7(X))* HarperCollins Pubs.

Stewart, David. How a Tadpole Grows into a Frog. Franklin, Carolyn, illus. 2008. (Amaze Ser.). (ENG.). 32p. (J). (gr. k-3). 27.00 *(978-0-531-20443-6(X))*; pap. 8.95 *(978-0-531-20454-2(5))* Scholastic Library Publishing. (Children's Pr.).

Stewart, Melissa. Frog or Toad? How Do You Know? 2011. (Which Animal Is Which? Ser.). (Illus.). 24p. (J). (gr. k-18). pap. 7.95 *(978-1-59845-236-5(3)*, Enslow Elementary); lib. bdg. 22.60 *(978-0-7660-3682-6(0))* Enslow Pubs., Inc.

—A Place for Frogs, 1 vol. Bond, Higgins, illus. 2010. (ENG.). 32p. (J). (gr. 1-5). 16.95 *(978-1-56145-521-8(0))* Peachtree Pubs.

—Place for Frogs, 1 vol. Bond, Higgins, illus. rev. ed. 2016. (Place For... Ser.). (ENG.). 32p. (J). (gr. 1-5). 16.95 *(978-1-56145-901-8(1))* Peachtree Pubs.

Stone, Tanya Lee. Frogs. 2003. (Wild Wild World Ser.). 24p. (YA). 24.94 *(978-1-56711-813-1(5)*, Blackbirch Pr., Inc.) Cengage Gale.

Storm, Marysa. Frogs. 2017. (Spot Backyard Animals Ser.). (ENG.). 16p. (gr. k-3). 17.95 ***(978-1-68151-091-0(X))*** Amicus Publishing.

—La Rana (Frogs) 2017. (Spot Backyard Animals Ser.). (ENG & SPA.). 16p. (J). (gr. k-3). 17.95 ***(978-1-68151-271-6(8)***, Amicus Readers) Amicus Publishing.

Sullivan, Laura L. The Poison Dart Frog. 2017. (J). ***(978-1-5026-2578-6(4))*** Cavendish Square Publishing.

Sundance/Newbridge LLC Staff. Leaping Frogs. 2007. (Early Science Ser.). (gr. k-3). 18.95 *(978-1-4007-6305-4(3))*; pap. 6.10 *(978-1-4007-6301-6(0))* Sundance/Newbridge Educational Publishing.

Swanson, Diane. Frogs & Toads. 2004. (Welcome to the World of Animals Ser.). (Illus.). 32p. (gr. 1-4). lib. bdg. 24.00 *(978-0-8368-4023-0(2)*, Gareth Stevens Learning Library) Stevens, Gareth Publishing LLLP.

Sweeney, Alyse. Frogs, 1 vol. 2010. (Amphibians Ser.). (ENG.). 24p. (gr. k-1). pap. 7.29 *(978-1-4296-4849-3(X))*; pap. 41.70 *(978-1-4296-5088-5(5))*; lib. bdg. 26.65 *(978-1-4296-3987-3(3))* Capstone Press of Coughlan Cos. (Pebble Plus).

—Toads, 1 vol. 2010. (Amphibians Ser.). (ENG.). 24p. (gr. k-1). pap. 7.29 *(978-1-4296-4850-9(3))*; pap. 41.70 *(978-1-4296-5092-2(3))*; lib. bdg. 26.65 *(978-1-4296-3991-0(1))* Capstone Press of Coughlan Cos. (Pebble Plus).

Swift, Christine, illus. Croak, Frog! 2014. (Shake, Rattle, Splash Ser.). (ENG.). 8p. (J). (gr. -1 — 1). 6.99 *(978-1-4380-0422-8(2))* Barron's Educational Series, Inc.

Thomson, Ruth. A Frog's Life Cycle. 2010. (Let's Look at Life Cycles Ser.). 24p. (J). (ENG.). pap. 8.25 *(978-1-61532-224-4(8)*, PowerKids Pr.); lib. bdg., E-Book 42.50 *(978-1-4488-0358-3(6))*; (Illus.). 49.50 *(978-1-61532-225-1(6)*, PowerKids Pr.); (Illus.). lib. bdg. 22.60 *(978-1-61532-218-3(3)*, PowerKids Pr.) Rosen Publishing Group, Inc., The.

—The Life Cycle of a Frog. 2007. (Learning about Life Cycles Ser.). (Illus.). 24p. (J). (gr. 4-7). lib. bdg. 22.60 *(978-1-4042-3711-7(9)*, PowerKids Pr.) Rosen Publishing Group, Inc., The.

Time for Kids Editors. Frogs! 2006. (Time for Kids Science Scoops Ser.). (ENG., Illus.). 32p. (J). (gr. 1-3). 14.99 *(978-0-06-078222-1(6))* HarperCollins Pubs.

Tracy, Kathleen. The Frog in Our Class. 2011. (Randy's Corner Ser.). (Illus.). 32p. (J). (gr. -1-2). lib. bdg. 25.70 *(978-1-58415-977-3(4))* Mitchell Lane Pubs., Inc.

Trueit, Trudi Strain. Frogs & Toads. 2011. (Backyard Safari Ser.). (Illus.). 32p. (J). (gr. 3). 28.50 *(978-1-60870-245-9(6))* Marshall Cavendish Corp.

Turner, Pamela S. The Frog Scientist. Comins, Andy, illus. 2011. (Scientists in the Field Ser.). (ENG.). 64p. (J). (gr. 5-7). pap. 9.99 *(978-0-547-57698-5(6))* Houghton Mifflin Harcourt Publishing Co.

Twinn, M. Metamorphoses: Egg, Tadpole, Frog. 2006. (Metamorphoses Ser.). (ENG., Illus.). 16p. (J). (gr. 1-5). bds. *(978-1-84643-012-1(7))* Child's Play International Ltd.

Underwood, Gary. Frogs. 2010. (Weird, Wild, & Wonderful Ser.). (Illus.). 24p. (J). (gr. 2-5). lib. bdg. 22.00 *(978-1-4339-3578-7(3)*, Gareth Stevens Learning Library) Stevens, Gareth Publishing LLLP.

Vasilyeva, Anastasiya. Frog. 2017. (See Them Grow Ser.). (ENG., Illus.). 24p. (J). (gr. -1-3). 17.95 ***(978-1-68402-040-9(9))*** Bearport Publishing Co., Inc.

Vern, Alex. Where Do Frogs Come From? 2012. (ENG., Illus.). 24p. (C). (gr. -1-3). pap. 6.95 *(978-0-15-204844-0(8))* National Geographic School Publishing, Inc.

Watts, Barrie. Frog. 2004. (Illus.). 32p. (J). (gr. -1-17). lib. bdg. 24.25 *(978-1-58340-233-7(0))* Black Rabbit Bks.

Wechsler, Doug. Bullfrogs. 2009. (Really Wild Life of Animals Ser.). 24p. (gr. 3-4). 42.50 *(978-1-60854-184-3(3)*, PowerKids Pr.) Rosen Publishing Group, Inc., The.

—Glass Frogs. 2009. (Really Wild Life of Animals Ser.). 24p. (gr. 3-4). 42.50 *(978-1-60854-193-5(2)*, PowerKids Pr.) Rosen Publishing Group, Inc., The.

—The Hidden Life of the Toad. 2017. (ENG., Illus.). 48p. (J). (gr. -1-3). lib. bdg. 17.99 *(978-1-58089-738-9(X))* Charlesbridge Publishing, Inc.

—Leopard Frogs. 2009. (Really Wild Life of Animals Ser.). 24p. (gr. 3-4). 42.50 *(978-1-60854-197-3(5)*, PowerKids Pr.) Rosen Publishing Group, Inc., The.

—Really Wild Life of Frogs, 3 vols., set. (Illus.). 80.70 *(978-0-8239-7186-2(4))* Rosen Publishing Group, Inc., The.

—Wood Frogs. 2009. (Really Wild Life of Animals Ser.). 24p. (gr. 3-4). 42.50 *(978-1-60854-213-0(0)*, PowerKids Pr.) Rosen Publishing Group, Inc., The.

Whiting, Jim. Frogs in Danger. 2007. (On the Verge of Extinction Ser.). (Illus.). 32p. (YA). (gr. 2-5). lib. bdg. 25.70 *(978-1-58415-585-0(X))* Mitchell Lane Pubs., Inc.

Wildlife Education, compiled by. Frogs. 2007. (ENG., Illus.). 12p. (J). 5.99 *(978-1-932396-37-9(3)*, Critters Up Close) Wildlife Education, Ltd.

Williams, Zella. Coqui Frogs & Other Latin American Frogs. 2009. (Animals of Latin America / Animales de Latinoamérica Ser.). (SPA & ENG., Illus.). 24p. pap. 8.25 *(978-1-4358-3382-1(1)*, PowerKids Pr.) Rosen Publishing Group, Inc., The.

—Coqui Frogs & Other Latin American Frogs/Coquies y Otras Ranas de Latinoamerica. 2009. (Animals of Latin America / Animales de Latinoamérica Ser.). (SPA & ENG., Illus.). 24p. (J). (gr. 1-3). lib. bdg. 22.60 *(978-1-4042-8148-6(7)*, PowerKids Pr.) Rosen Publishing Group, Inc., The.

Winer, Yvonne. Frogs Sing Songs. Oliver, Tony, illus. 2003. 32p. (J). pap. 6.95 *(978-1-57091-549-9(0))*; (gr. -1-4). 16.95 *(978-1-57091-548-2(2))* Charlesbridge Publishing, Inc.

World Book, Inc. Staff, contrib. by. Frogs & Other Amphibians. 2005. (World Book's Animals of the World Ser.). (Illus.). 64p. (J). *(978-0-7166-1269-8(0))* World Bk., Inc.

Yarrow, Peter, et al. I'm in Love with a Big Blue Frog. Brunet, Joshua S., illus. 2013. (ENG.). 28p. (J). (gr. -1-3). 17.95 *(978-1-936140-37-4(3))* Charlesbridge Publishing, Inc.

Zemlicka, Shannon. Del Renacuajo a la Rana. Translations.com Staff, tr. from ENG. 2006. (De Principio a Fin (Start to Finish) Ser.). (SPA., Illus.). 24p. (J). (gr. 3-5). lib. bdg. 19.93 *(978-0-8225-6497-3(1)*, Ediciones Lerner) Lerner Publishing Group.

—Del renaucajo a la rana (from Tadpole to Frog) 2006. (De Principio a Fin (Start to Finish) Ser.). (Illus.). 24p. (J). (gr. -1-3). per. 5.95 *(978-0-8225-6634-2(6)*, Ediciones Lerner) Lerner Publishing Group.

—From Tadpole to Frog. 2012. (Start to Finish, Second Series: Nature's Cycles Ser.). (ENG.). 24p. (gr. k-3). pap. 39.62 *(978-0-7613-9296-5(3))*; pap. 6.95 *(978-0-7613-8577-6(0))* Lerner Publishing Group.

Zoehfeld, Kathleen Weidner. From Tadpole to Frog. 2011. (Scholastic Reader Level 1 Ser.). (ENG.). 32p. (J). (gr. -1-2). pap. 3.99 *(978-0-545-27337-4(4)*, Scholastic Paperbacks) Scholastic, Inc.

Zubal, Lynn. Sonoran Desert Frog. Zubal, Lynn, illus. 2011. (ENG., Illus.). 22p. (J). pap. 16.95 *(978-1-59299-600-1(0))* Inkwater Pr.

FROGS—FICTION

A Caribbean Experience Con Amor. There's a Coqui in My Shoe! 2007. (Illus.). 66p. (J). 21.99 *(978-0-9797641-0-3(6))* Chi Chi Rodriguez Bks.

Aesop. The Frog & the Ox. 2012. (J). *(978-1-61913-104-0(8))* Weigl Pubs., Inc.

Alexander, Kwame. Surf's Up. Miyares, Daniel, illus. 2016. (ENG.). 32p. (J). 17.95 *(978-0-7358-4220-5(5))* North-South Bks., Inc.

Allchin, Rosalind. The Frog Princess. 2004. (Illus.). (J). (gr. k-3). spiral bd. *(978-0-616-14557-9(8))* Canadian National Institute for the Blind/Institut National Canadien pour les Aveugles.

—The Frog Princess. Allchin, Rosalind, illus. 2003. (ENG., Illus.). 32p. (J). (gr. k-3). pap. 5.95 *(978-1-55337-526-5(2))* Kids Can Pr., Ltd. CAN. Dist: Hachette Bk. Group.

Allen, Katherine. Gloves down Under. Allen, Katherine, illus. 2005. (Illus.). 32p. (J). 15.95 *(978-0-9747278-9-9(X))* Diakonia Publishing.

Alvord, Larry. Down by Ol' Chooster's Pond. 2011. 56p. pap. 21.99 *(978-1-4628-7652-5(8))* Xlibris Corp.

Anderson, Peggy Perry. I Can Help! 2015. (Green Light Readers Level 1 Ser.). (ENG., Illus.). 32p. (J). (gr. 1-4). pap. 3.99 *(978-0-544-52801-7(8)*, HMH Books For Young Readers) Houghton Mifflin Harcourt Publishing Co.

—Joe on the Go. 2012. (Green Light Readers Level 1 Ser.). (ENG., Illus.). 32p. (J). (gr. -1-3). pap. 3.99 *(978-0-547-74563-3(X))* Houghton Mifflin Harcourt Publishing Co.

—Joe on the Go. 2012. (Green Light Readers — Level 1 Ser.: 1). lib. bdg. 13.55 *(978-0-606-24018-5(7)*, Turtleback) Turtleback Bks.

—Let's Clean Up! 2012. (Green Light Readers Level 1 Ser.). (ENG., Illus.). 32p. (J). (gr. -1-3). pap. 3.99 *(978-0-547-74562-6(1))* Houghton Mifflin Harcourt Publishing Co.

—Let's Clean Up! 2012. (Green Light Readers — Level 1 Ser.). lib. bdg. 13.55 *(978-0-606-24024-6(1)*, Turtleback) Turtleback Bks.

—Out to Lunch. 2015. (Green Light Readers Level 1 Ser.). (ENG., Illus.). 32p. (J). (gr. 1-4). pap. 3.99 *(978-0-544-52858-1(1)*, HMH Books For Young Readers) Houghton Mifflin Harcourt Publishing Co.

—Time for Bed, the Babysitter Said. 2012. (Green Light Readers Level 1 Ser.). (ENG., Illus.). 32p. (J). (gr. -1-3). pap. 3.99 *(978-0-547-85061-0(1))* Houghton Mifflin Harcourt Publishing Co.

—Time for Bed, the Babysitter Said. 2012. (Green Light Readers — Level 1 Ser.). lib. bdg. 13.55 *(978-0-606-26607-9(0)*, Turtleback) Turtleback Bks.

—To the Tub. 2012. (Green Light Readers Level 1 Ser.). (ENG., Illus.). 32p. (J). (gr. -1-3). pap. 3.99 *(978-0-547-85053-5(0))* Houghton Mifflin Harcourt Publishing Co.

—To the Tub. Anderson, Peggy Perry, illus. 2004. (Illus.). 52p. (gr. -1-3). 17.00 *(978-0-7569-4258-8(6))* Perfection Learning Corp.

—To the Tub. 2012. (Green Light Readers — Level 1 Ser.). lib. bdg. 13.55 *(978-0-606-26608-6(9)*, Turtleback) Turtleback Bks.

Anderson, Steven. Leap & Twirl. DeAnguelo Hout, Sarah, illus. 2012. 34p. (J). pap. 10.99 *(978-0-692-01667-1(8))* BalletMet Dance Centre.

Animal I Can Hear S/s -Frog. 2005. (J). bds. *(978-1-4194-0058-2(4))* Paradise Pr., Inc.

Ann, Sharrie. Granddaughter & King Green Warts. 2008. 24p. pap. 12.99 *(978-1-4343-9470-5(0))* AuthorHouse.

Armstrong, Tony. The Water Troll. 2008. (ENG.). 16p. 8.49 *(978-1-4389-1925-6(5))* AuthorHouse.

Arnold, Karen. Leaper Joins the Choir. 2011. 28p. pap. 15.99 *(978-1-4568-6535-1(8))* Xlibris Corp.

Arnold, Lobel. Frog & Toad Are Friends. 2014. (I Can Read Book 2 Ser.). (ENG.). 64p. (J). (gr. 7-12). 8.24 *(978-1-63245-259-7(6))* Lectorum Pubns., Inc.

—Frog & Toad Together. 2014. (I Can Read Book 2 Ser.). (ENG.). 64p. (J). (gr. 3-7). 8.24 *(978-1-63245-246-7(4))* Lectorum Pubns., Inc.

Arnold, Tedd. Green Wilma, Frog in Space. Arnold, Tedd, illus. 2009. (ENG., Illus.). 32p. (J). (gr. -1-3). 16.99 *(978-0-8037-2698-7(8)*, Dial Bks) Penguin Young Readers Group.

Asher, Sandy. Too Many Frogs! Graves, Keith, illus. 2005. (ENG.). 32p. (J). (gr. -1-k). 16.99 *(978-0-399-23978-6(2)*, Philomel Bks.) Penguin Young Readers Group.

August, Elaine. Fira Gani: An Earthly Fable. 2012. 38p. 24.95 *(978-1-4626-9437-2(3))*; 40p. pap. 24.95 *(978-1-4626-7589-0(1))* America Star Bks.

Austin, K. B. Old Mother Turtle & the Three Frogs. 2005. (J). lib. bdg. *(978-0-9772027-0-6(4))* Dream Star Productions.

AZ Books, creator. Frog the Hopper. 2012. (Curious Eyes Ser.). (ENG., Illus.). 12p. (J). (gr. -1 — 1). bds. 12.95 *(978-1-61889-104-4(9))* AZ Bks. LLC.

Azore, Barbara. Wanda & the Frogs. Graham, Georgia, illus. 2007. (ENG.). 32p. (J). (gr. -1-1). 18.95 *(978-0-88776-761-6(3)*, Tundra Bks.) Tundra Bks. CAN. Dist: Penguin Random Hse. LLC.

Bail, Willow & Fields, April. Is the World Bigger Than a Pond? 2013. 24p. 14.95 *(978-1-940911-00-7(1)*, Pixelated Publishing) Faithful Publishing.

Baker, E. D. The Frog Princess, 4 vols. 2005. (Frog Princess Ser.: 1). (J). 57.75 *(978-1-4193-2955-5(3)*, 42014) Recorded Bks., Inc.

—A Prince among Frogs. 2nd ed. 2015. (Tales of the Frog Princess Ser.). (ENG.). 240p. (YA). (gr. 3-6). pap. 8.99 *(978-1-61963-624-8(7)*, 9781619636248, Bloomsbury USA Childrens) Bloomsbury Publishing USA.

Baker, Harriet Lila. Boyduck Goose: His Life & Times, Bk. II. 2005. (J). pap. 9.00 *(978-0-8059-6694-7(3))* Dorrance Publishing Co., Inc.

Baker, Tyrone. Joey & Hoppy, 1 vol. 2009. 23p. pap. 24.95 *(978-1-60836-036-9(9))* America Star Bks.

Banta, Susan, illus. La Leyenda del Coqui. 2005. (SPA.). 29p. (J). (gr. k-12). 12.95 *(978-1-58173-256-6(2))* Sweetwater Pr.

Barry, Maureen. Freddie the Frog's Adventure. 2007. (J). pap. 10.00 net. *(978-1-60402-177-6(2))* Independent Pub.

Bartles, Veronica. The Princess & the Frogs. Palacios, Sara, illus. 2016. 40p. (J). (gr. -1-3). 17.99 *(978-0-06-236591-0(6))* HarperCollins Pubs.

Beardshaw, Rosalind, illus. Kiss the Frog. 2013. (J). *(978-1-4351-4925-0(4))* Barnes & Noble, Inc.

Beiser, Tim. Bradley McGogg: The Very Fine Frog. Berman, Rachel, illus. (ENG.). 24p. (J). (gr. k-k). 2011. pap. 7.95 *(978-1-77049-276-9(3))* 2009. 17.95 *(978-0-88776-864-4(4))* Tundra Bks. CAN. (Tundra Bks.). Dist: Penguin Random Hse. LLC.

—Little Chicken Duck. Slavin, Bill, illus. 2013. (ENG.). 24p. (J). (gr. -1-2). 17.95 *(978-1-77049-392-6(1)*, Tundra Bks.) Tundra Bks. CAN. Dist: Penguin Random Hse. LLC.

Bell, Anthea. Frog in Love. Velthuijs, Max, illus. 2015. (J). *(978-1-4351-5750-7(8))* Barnes & Noble, Inc.

Bell, Cece. Rabbit & Robot & Ribbit. Bell, Cece, illus. 2016. (ENG., Illus.). 48p. (J). (gr. k-4). 14.99 *(978-0-7636-7935-4(6))* Candlewick Pr.

Bennett, Debra J. Hip, Hop & Flop's Many Adventures. 2007. (ENG.). 60p. per. 16.95 *(978-1-4241-6564-3(4))* America Star Bks.

Bennett, Gretchen. Gina's Great Day. 2011. 28p. pap. 24.95 *(978-1-4626-0938-3(4))* America Star Bks.

Bentley, Dawn. Three Stretchy Frogs. Wallis, Becky, illus. 2010. (Stretchies Book Ser.). 16p. (J). 8.99 *(978-0-8249-1459-2(7))* Hinkler Bks. Pty, Ltd. AUS. Dist: Ideals Pubns.

Berkes, Marianne. Marsh Music. Noreika, Robert, illus. 2011. (ENG.). 32p. (J). (gr. k-3). pap. 6.95 *(978-0-7613-7461-9(2)*, Millbrook Pr.) Lerner Publishing Group.

Bickta, Brenda L. Tad's Life in the Lily Pond. 2008. 74p. pap. 19.95 *(978-1-60672-647-1(1))* America Star Bks.

Billout, Guy, creator. The Frog Who Wanted to See the Sea. 2014. (ENG., Illus.). 32p. (J). (gr. 1-3). 16.99 *(978-1-56846-267-7(0)*, Creative Editions) Creative Co., The.

Bills, Sherry. Flippy the Frog. 2008. 16p. per. 24.95 *(978-1-60441-578-0(9))* America Star Bks.

Birney, Betty G. Friendship According to Humphrey. (Humphrey Ser.: 2). (ENG.). (J). (gr. 3-7). 2006. 176p. 5.99 *(978-0-14-240633-5(3)*, Puffin Books) 2005. 160p. 15.99 *(978-0-399-24264-9(3)*, G.P. Putnam's Sons Books for Young Readers) Penguin Young Readers Group.

—Friendship According to Humphrey. 2007. (Humphrey Ser.). 150p. (gr. 4-7). 16.00 *(978-0-7569-8277-5(4))* Perfection Learning Corp.

—School Days According to Humphrey. (Humphrey Ser.: 7). (ENG.). (J). (gr. 3-7). 2012. 176p. pap. 5.99 *(978-0-14-242106-2(5)*, Puffin Books) 2011. 160p. 15.99 *(978-0-399-25413-0(7)*, G.P. Putnam's Sons Books for Young Readers) Penguin Young Readers Group.

—School Days According to Humphrey. 2012. (According to Humphrey Ser.: 7). lib. bdg. 16.00 *(978-0-606-26085-5(4)*, Turtleback) Turtleback Bks.

Bishop, Michael. Mr Toad Comes Home, 4 vols. Cloke, Rene, illus. 2012. (ENG.). 30p. (J). 4.95 *(978-1-84135-787-4(1))* Award Pubns. Ltd. GBR. Dist: Parkwest Pubns., Inc.

—Mr Toad in Trouble, 4 vols. Cloke, Rene, illus. 2012. (ENG.). 30p. (J). 4.95 *(978-1-84135-786-7(3))* Award Pubns. Ltd. GBR. Dist: Parkwest Pubns., Inc.

Blahitka, Vira. Joad the Toad. 2013. 32p. pap. *(978-1-4602-1881-5(7))* FriesenPress.

Blair, Eric. The Frog Prince: A Retelling of the Grimm's Fairy Tale, 1 vol. Ouren, Todd, illus. 2013. (My First Classic Story Ser.). (ENG.). 32p. (gr. k-3). pap. 7.10 *(978-1-4795-1853-1(0)*, My First Classic Story) Picture Window Bks.

—El Principe Encantado. Abello, Patricia, tr. from ENG. Ouren, Todd, illus. 2006. (Read-It! Readers en Español: Cuentos de Hadas Ser.).Tr. of Frog Prince. (SPA.). 32p. (gr. k-3). 21.32 *(978-1-4048-1631-2(3)*, Easy Readers) Picture Window Bks.

Blake. The Adventures of Libby the Leaping Learner. 2011. 92p. (gr. -1). pap. 13.95 *(978-1-4620-1499-6(2))* iUniverse, Inc.

Bodrogi, Michael. Herbert the Tadpole in the Big Change. La Beree, Brian, illus. 2003. 48p. (J). (gr. -1-4). 15.95 *(978-1-878398-61-1(X)*, Blue Note Bks.) Blue Note Pubns.

Bollen, Christine. Frogs by the Dozen. Matyschenko, Tanya, illus. l.t. ed. 2006. 24p. (J). per. 9.99 *(978-1-59879-115-0(X))* Lifevest Publishing, Inc.

Bonnell, Kris. Frog Fun. 2006. (J). pap. 5.95 *(978-1-933727-39-4(X))* Reading Reading Bks., LLC.

Book Buddy: Frog with Story Book. Orig. Title: Child's Play. (Illus.). 10p. (J). (gr. -1-3). reprint ed. *(978-1-881469-80-3(8))* Safari, Ltd.

Book Company Staff. Are You a Frog? 2003. (Novelty Bks.). (Illus.). (J). 12.95 *(978-1-74047-318-7(3))* Book Co. Publishing Pty, Ltd., The AUS. Dist: Penton Overseas, Inc.

—Froggy & Friends. 2003. (Novelty Bks.). (J). 15.95 *(978-1-74047-323-1(X))* Book Co. Publishing Pty, Ltd., The AUS. Dist: Penton Overseas, Inc.

—Who Am I: Frog. 2003. (Board Bks.). (Illus.). (J). bds. 10.95 *(978-1-74047-306-4(X))* Book Co. Publishing Pty, Ltd., The AUS. Dist: Penton Overseas, Inc.

Borland, Jerre Shadrick. Ferdinand the Frog. Bayard, Janie Domengeaux, illus. 2011. 32p. pap. 24.95 *(978-1-4560-6116-6(X))* America Star Bks.

Boyd, Lizi. I Love Daddy: Super Sturdy Picture Books. Boyd, Lizi, illus. 2004. (Super Sturdy Picture Bks.). (ENG., Illus.). 24p. (J). (gr. -1 — 1). 8.99 *(978-0-7636-2217-6(6))* Candlewick Pr.

Bradman, Tony. The Frog Prince Hops to It, 1 vol. Warburton, Sarah, illus. (After Happily Ever After Ser.). (ENG.). 56p. (gr. 2-3). 2014. pap. 5.05 *(978-1-4342-7962-0(6))* 2009. 25.32 *(978-1-4342-1303-7(X))* Stone Arch Bks. (After Happily Ever After).

Bradshaw, T.S. The Goodees. 2009. 36p. pap. 17.99 *(978-1-4389-3557-7(9))* AuthorHouse.

Brandon, Wendy. The Frog Prince: Board Book & Puppet Theater. Beckes, Shirley V., illus. 2004. (J). *(978-1-883043-46-9(8))* Straight Edge Pr., The.

—The Frog Prince: Imagination in a Box. Beckes, Shirley, illus. 2004. 10p. (J). bds. 17.99 *(978-1-883043-49-0(2))* Straight Edge Pr., The.

Brannock, Martha Lee. Freddie, the Frumpy, Grumpy Frog. 2006. (ENG.). 32p. per. 15.99 *(978-1-4257-2741-3(7))* Xlibris Corp.

Brantley, Meg. Love Family Adventures. 2009. 116p. pap. 11.99 *(978-1-60791-786-1(6))* Salem Author Services.

Braun, Sebastien. Who Can Jump? Braun, Sebastien, illus. 2014. (ENG., Illus.). 14p. (J). (— 1). bds. 6.99 *(978-0-7636-6753-5(6))* Candlewick Pr.

Breen, Steve. Stick. 2009. (ENG.). 48p. (J). (gr. -1-k). pap. 6.99 *(978-0-14-241303-6(8)*, Puffin Books) Penguin Young Readers Group.

Brenning, Juli. Maggi & Milo. Burris, Priscilla, illus. 2014. (ENG.). 32p. (J). (gr. -1-k). 16.99 *(978-0-8037-3795-2(5)*, Dial Bks) Penguin Young Readers Group.

Brewin, Barbara. Sidney Snail's Wonderful World of Adventure. 2009. (Illus.). 32p. pap. 14.49 *(978-1-4389-4100-4(5))* AuthorHouse.

Brightwood, Laura, illus. I Am A Frog. Brightwood, Laura, . 2007. (J). DVD *(978-1-934409-02-2(2))* 3-C Institute for Social Development.

Bronson, Tammy Carter. Polliwog. Bronson, Tammy Carter, illus. 2006. (ENG & SPA., Illus.). (J). 7.99 *(978-0-9678167-5-3(0))* Bookaroos Publishing, Inc.

—Polliwog. Davi, Annou, tr. Bronson, Tammy Carter, illus. 2004. (SPA & ENG., Illus.). 32p. (J). lib. bdg. 17.00 *(978-0-9678167-4-6(2))* Bookaroos Publishing, Inc.

Brown, Grandma. Does He Have to Be My Cousin Forever? 2010. 88p. pap. 15.99 *(978-1-4500-1372-7(4))* Xlibris Corp.

Brown, Jeff Allan. Floom Shroom the Battling Mushroom. 2009. 100p. pap. 28.99 *(978-1-60693-485-2(6)*, Strategic Bk. Publishing) Strategic Book Publishing & Rights Agency (SBPRA).

Bruner, Elizabeth. Henry, the Frog. 2012. 20p. pap. 12.95 *(978-1-937912-18-5(3))* Cordon Pubns.

Bucher, Charlotte. Cecil Learns to Smile. 26p. 2011. (Illus.). 16.95 *(978-1-4327-4619-3(7))* 2010. (J). pap. 19.95 *(978-1-4327-4992-7(7))* Outskirts Pr., Inc.

Bunting, Eve. Frog & Friends. 2012. (I AM a READER! Frog & Friends Ser.: 4). (ENG., Illus.). 48p. (J). (gr. 1-3). pap. 3.99 *(978-1-58536-806-8(7))* Sleeping Bear Pr.

—Frog & Friends. Masse, Josée, illus. 2011. (I Am A Reader! Ser.). (ENG.). 40p. (gr. k-3). pap. 3.99 *(978-1-58536-689-7(7))*; lib. bdg. 9.95 *(978-1-58536-548-7(3))* Sleeping Bear Pr.

—Frog & Friends: Frog's Flying Adventure. 2012. (I AM a READER! Frog & Friends Ser.: 4). (ENG., Illus.). 48p. (J). (gr. 1-3). 9.95 *(978-1-58536-805-1(9))* Sleeping Bear Pr.

—Frog & Friends: Outdoor Surprises. Masse, Josée, illus. 2013. (I AM a READER!: Frog & Friends Ser.). (ENG.). 48p. (J). (gr. 1-2). 9.95 *(978-1-58536-807-5(5)*, 202361); pap. 3.99 *(978-1-58536-808-2(3)*, 202370) Sleeping Bear Pr.

—Frog & Friends: Party at the Pond. 2011. (I am A Reader! Ser.). (ENG., Illus.). 40p. (gr. k-3). lib. bdg. 9.95 *(978-1-58536-549-4(1))* Sleeping Bear Pr.

—Frog & Friends: The Best Summer Ever. 2012. (I Am A Reader!, Frog & Friends Ser.). (ENG., Illus.). 48p. (J). (gr. k-3). pap. 3.99 *(978-1-58536-691-0(9))*; lib. bdg. 9.95 *(978-1-58536-550-0(5))* Sleeping Bear Pr.

—Frog & Friends Celebrate Thanksgiving, Christmas, & New Year's Eve. Masse, Josée, illus. 2015. (I AM a READER!: Frog & Friends Ser.). (ENG.). 40p. (J). (gr. 1-2). 9.99 *(978-1-58536-897-6(0)*, 203949) Sleeping Bear Pr.

—Frog's Lucky Day. Masse, Josée, illus. 2014. (I Am a Reader!: Frog & Friends Ser.). (ENG.). 40p. (J). (gr. 1-2). 9.99 *(978-1-58536-892-1(X)*, 203014) Sleeping Bear Pr.

Burch, Sharon. Freddie the Frog & the Bass Clef Monster. Harris, Tiffany, illus. 2010. (ENG.). 44p. (gr. -1-4). 24.99 incl. audio compact disk *(978-0-9747454-8-0(0),* 0974745480) Mystic Publishing.

—Freddie the Frog & the Mysterious Wahooooo: 3rd Adventure: Tempo Island. 2010. (ENG.). 34p. 24.99 incl. audio compact disk *(978-0-9747454-7-3(2),* 0974745472) Mystic Publishing.

—Freddie the Frog & the Mysterious Wahooooo (DIGITAL EDITION) Digital Storybook with Step-By-Step Lessons for Interactive Whiteboard. 2015. (ENG.). 2p. pap. 29.99 *(978-1-4950-1092-7(9),* 1495010929) Leonard, Hal Corp.

—Freddie the Frog & the Thump in the Night: 1st Adventure - Treble Clef Island. 2010. (ENG., Illus.). 46p. 24.99 incl. audio compact disk *(978-0-9747454-9-7(9),* 0974745499) Mystic Publishing.

Burch, Sharon, et al. Freddie the Frog & the Secret of Crater Island: 4th Adventure: Crater Island. 2010. (ENG.). 48p. 24.99 incl. audio compact disk *(978-0-9747454-6-6(4),* 0974745464) Mystic Publishing.

Burfoot, Ella, illus. Don't Kiss the Frog! Princess Stories with Attitude. 2013. (ENG.). 80p. (YA). (gr. 1-5). pap. 8.99 *(978-0-7534-6946-0(4),* 9780753469460, Kingfisher) Roaring Brook Pr.

Burgess, Thornton W. The Adventures of Grandfather Frog. 2007. 108p. (gr. -1-3). per. 9.95 *(978-1-60312-154-5(4));* 22.95 *(978-1-60312-837-7(9))* Aegypan.

—The Adventures of Grandfather Frog. 2011. 108p. 23.95 *(978-1-4638-9570-9(4))* Rodgers, Alan Bks.

—The Adventures of Old Mr Toad. 2007. 140p. per. 11.95 *(978-1-60312-379-2(2))* Aegypan.

—The Adventures of Old Mr Toad. 2011. 138p. 25.95 *(978-1-4638-9561-7(5))* Rodgers, Alan Bks.

—Big Book of Animal Stories. 2011. (Dover Children's Classics Ser.). (ENG., Illus.). 272p. (J). (gr. 3-8). 9.95 *(978-0-486-41980-0(0))* Dover Pubns., Inc.

—Mother West Wind 'Why' Stories. 2007. 108p. (gr. -1-3). per. 9.95 *(978-1-60312-004-3(1))* Aegypan.

Burns, Joanne. Frog's Dog Days. 2005. 30p. 9.99 *(978-1-4116-4829-6(3))* Lulu Pr., Inc.

Burris, Priscilla. Five Green & Speckled Frogs - A Count-and-Sing Book. Burris, Priscilla, illus. 2016. (ENG., Illus.). 16p. (J). (— 1). bds. 6.99 *(978-0-545-82505-4(9),* Cartwheel Bks.) Scholastic, Inc.

Busch, Jean. Aiden & the Frog Prince, 1 vol. 2009. 48p. pap. 16.95 *(978-1-60836-892-1(0))* America Star Bks.

Butterworth, MyLinda & Day, Linda S. Frogazoom! Day, Linda S., illus. I.t. ed. 2003. (Illus.). 32p. (J). (gr. k-3). pap. 16.95 *(978-1-890905-03-3(8),* Writers Collective, The) Day to Day Enterprises.

Caldecott, Randolph. A Frog He Would A-Wooing Go. 2006. pap. *(978-1-4065-1224-3(9))* Dodo Pr.

Callies, Debi. Frog Mill. 2008. 20p. pap. 24.95 *(978-1-60703-091-1(8))* America Star Bks.

Calmenson, Stephanie. The Frog Principal. Brunkus, Denise, illus. 2006. (ENG.). 32p. (J). pap. 5.99 *(978-0-439-81217-7(8),* Scholastic Paperbacks) Scholastic, Inc.

Cannella, Nicole DeRosa. The Ribbit Exhibit: One frog's tale of a leap of Faith. 2011. 28p. pap. 13.59 *(978-1-4634-2435-0(3))* AuthorHouse.

Cardoso, Kelly. Thomas & the Toad King. DeBroeck, Sarah, illus. 2011. 28p. pap. 24.95 *(978-1-4560-0956-4(7))* America Star Bks.

Carle, Eric. Rooster Is off to See the World. 2013. (Eric Carle Ready-To-Read Ser.). lib. bdg. 13.55 *(978-0-606-32063-4(6),* Turtleback) Turtleback Bks.

Carlson, Lavelle. The Frog Who Could Not Croak: Phonemic Awareness Tale #4. 2004. (Illus.). 32p. (J). per. 16.95 *(978-0-9725803-3-5(6))* Children's Publishing.

Carlson, Nancy. Smile a Lot! Carlson, Nancy, illus. (Nancy Carlson Picture Bks). (Illus.). 32p. (J). (gr. k-2). 2012. 56.72 *(978-0-7613-9310-8(2))* 2012. (ENG.). 9.95 *(978-0-7613-9173-9(8))* 2003. 15.95 *(978-0-87614-869-3(0))* Lerner Publishing Group. (Carolrhoda Bks.).

—¡Sonríe! Translations.com Staff, tr. from ENG. Carlson, Nancy, illus. 2007. (Ediciones Lerner Single Titles Ser.).Tr. of Smile a Lot! (SPA., Illus.). 32p. (J). (gr. k-2). 15.95 *(978-0-8225-7817-8(4),* Ediciones Lerner) Lerner Publishing Group.

Carroll, Kathy. Rabbit & the Amazing Hopping Contest. 2007. (Illus.). 16p. (J). 9.99 *(978-0-9791401-6-7(1))* Abecedarian Bks.

Carsonie, Diane Lynn. Silly Frog. Bullen, Marjorie, illus. 2008. 16p. per. 24.95 *(978-1-4241-9253-3(6))* America Star Bks.

Cartwright, Ran. The Adventures of Billy Space Boy, 1 vol. 2010. 208p. pap. 24.95 *(978-1-4489-3901-5(1))* America Star Bks.

Cecil, Randy. Horsefly & Honeybee. Cecil, Randy, illus. 2012. (ENG., Illus.). 32p. (J). (gr. -1-3). 16.99 *(978-0-8050-9300-1(1),* 9780805093001, Holt, Henry & Co. Bks. For Young Readers) Holt, Henry & Co.

Chandler Goldstein. Georgette: A Little Frog Discovers the Value in Revealing Her True Self! 2012. 20p. pap. 15.99 *(978-1-4772-0835-9(6))* AuthorHouse.

Charles, Faustin. The Selfish Crocodile Book of Words. Terry, Michael, illus. 2012. (Selfish Crocodile Ser.). (ENG.). 12p. (J). (gr. -1-k). bds. 10.99 *(978-1-4088-1452-9(8),* 9781408814529, Bloomsbury USA Childrens) Bloomsbury Publishing USA.

Charlesworth, Liza. Dog & Frog: An Animal Friends Reader. Smith, Ian, illus. 2015. 16p. (J). ***(978-0-545-85962-2(X))*** Scholastic, Inc.

Children's Press, contrib. by. The Frog in the Pond & Other Animal Stories. 2008. (Rookie Reader Treasury Ser.). (ENG., Illus.). 128p. (J). 11.95 *(978-0-531-21727-6(2),* Children's Pr.) Scholastic Library Publishing.

Chima, Ahiru & Misu, Max. Ellenâ_- Ellen meets Frog King - 2005. 32p. pap. 14.99 *(978-1-4116-4050-4(0))* Lulu Pr., Inc.

Chusid-Shur, Lauren, ed. The Golden Friendship. 2012. (ENG.). (J). pap. *(978-1-4675-4581-5(3))* Independent Pub.

Clark, Darrel. The Happy Frog. 2012. 28p. pap. 18.65 *(978-1-4653-9527-6(X))* Xlibris Corp.

Clarke, Jane. Only Tadpoles Have Tails. Gray, Jane, illus. 2003. (Flying Foxes Ser.). (ENG.). 48p. (J). lib. bdg. *(978-0-7787-1484-2(5))* Crabtree Publishing Co.

Cobb, Thomas J. Polly & His Frog Tale: Forbidden Meadow, 1 vol. 2010. 48p. pap. 24.95 *(978-1-61546-494-4(8))* PublishAmerica, Inc.

Cocca-Leffler, Maryann. Rain Brings Frogs: A Little Book of Hope. Cocca-Leffler, Maryann, illus. 2011. (ENG., Illus.). 32p. (J). (gr. -1-2). 9.99 *(978-0-06-196106-9(X))* HarperCollins Pubs.

Coccia. The Adventures of Itsy Bitsy Franny Frog: I Like What I Can Do When I Try! 2012. 34p. pap. 14.95 *(978-1-4575-0946-9(6))* Dog Ear Publishing, LLC.

Cofreros, Felipe A. The Hungry Frog. 2005. (J). per. *(978-0-9768251-6-6(3))* Dramatic Improvements Publishing.

Cohlene, Terri. Something Special. Keith, Doug, illus. 2005. 32p. (J). (gr. -1-k). 15.95 *(978-0-9740190-1-7(1))* Illumination Arts Publishing Co., Inc.

Colby, Rebecca. It's Raining Bats & Frogs. Henry, Steven, illus. 2015. (ENG.). 40p. (J). (gr. -1-k). 16.99 *(978-1-250-04992-6(X),* 9781250049926) Feiwel & Friends.

Collins, Diana Sue. Elfin, the Elf. 2011. 44p. pap. 24.95 *(978-1-4560-8493-6(3))* America Star Bks.

Collins, Rachel. Fiddle Faddle Frog & Piddle Paddle Polliwog. 2010. 32p. pap. 16.95 *(978-0-557-53411-1(9))* Lulu Pr., Inc.

Comer, Brigitte Renee. The Little Hopping Frog. 2012. 24p. pap. 24.95 *(978-1-4626-8243-0(X))* America Star Bks.

Conners, Lauren. The Stuffed Frog in Santa's Sack. 2009. 28p. pap. 12.49 *(978-1-4490-4623-1(1))* AuthorHouse.

Cooper, Bernice Soroka. The Little Elf-Frog. 2012. 24p. pap. 17.99 *(978-1-4772-9525-0(9))* AuthorHouse.

Cope, Steven R. The Frogville Skits. 2011. 214p. pap. 16.00 *(978-1-936138-39-5(5))* Wind Pubns.

Coplans, Peta & Williams, Dylan. Syniad Da Gwenlli Gwydd. 2005. (WEL., Illus.). 28p. *(978-1-84512-015-3(9))* Cymdeithas Lyfrau Ceredigion.

Corazza, Joe, illus. The Frog Prince: A Story about Keeping Your Word. 2006. (J). 6.99 *(978-1-59939-008-6(6))* Cornerstone Pr.

Coudakpo, Agrey Emile A. The Malignant & a Malignant One & Half: The Story of the Baby Frog & the Vicious Viper. 2013. 44p. pap. 20.72 *(978-1-4669-8247-5(0))* Trafford Publishing.

Courtney, Suzanne Gene. Rainfrog. 2011. 34p. pap. 14.50 *(978-1-61204-189-6(2),* Eloquent Bks.) Strategic Book Publishing & Rights Agency (SBPRA).

Coville, Bruce. Jennifer Murdley's Toad. Lippincott, Gary A., illus. 2007. (Magic Shop Book Ser.: 3). (ENG.). 176p. (J). (gr. 5-7). pap. 7.99 *(978-0-15-206246-0(7))* Houghton Mifflin Harcourt Publishing Co.

—Jennifer Murdley's Toad. (Magic Shop Bks.). 159p. (J). pap. 3.99 *(978-0-8072-1483-1(3),* Listening Library) Random Hse. Audio Publishing Group.

Cowan, Charlotte. Peeper Has a Fever. Banta, Susan, illus. 2007. (ENG.). 32p. (J). (gr. 3-7). 17.95 *(978-0-9753516-2-8(1))* Hippocratic Pr., The.

Cox, Phil Roxbee. Frog on a Log. Tyler, Jenny, ed. Cartwright, Stephen, illus. rev. ed. 2006. (Phonics Readers Ser.). 16p. (J). (gr. -1). pap. 6.99 *(978-0-7945-1504-1(5),* Usborne) EDC Publishing.

—Toad Makes a Road. Tyler, Jenny, ed. Cartwright, Stephen, illus. rev. ed. 2006. (Phonics Readers Ser.). 16p. (J). (gr. -1-k). pap. 6.99 *(978-0-7945-1512-6(6),* Usborne) EDC Publishing.

Cox, Phil Roxbee & Cartwright, S. Toad Makes a Road. 2004. (Phonics Board Bks.). (ENG.). 1p. (J). bds. 4.99 *(978-0-7945-0062-7(5),* Usborne) EDC Publishing.

Cox, Phil Roxbee & Cartwright, Stephen. Frog on a Log. 2004. (Easy Words to Read Ser.). (Illus.). 16p. (J). (gr. 1-18). pap. 6.95 *(978-0-7945-0114-3(1),* Usborne) EDC Publishing.

—Ted's Shed. 2004. (Phonics Board Bks.). (Illus.). 10p. (J). 4.95 *(978-0-7945-0304-8(7),* Usborne) EDC Publishing.

Cox, Tiffany. Amy, the Frog Who Loved to Sing. 2006. 9.00 *(978-0-8059-8806-2(8))* Dorrance Publishing Co., Inc.

Coyle, Carmela Lavigna. Do Princesses Really Kiss Frogs? Gordon, Mike & Gordon, Carl, illus. 2014. (ENG.). 96p. (J). (gr. -1-2). 15.95 *(978-1-58979-946-2(1))* Taylor Trade Publishing.

Crow, Melinda Melton. Little Lizard's New Friend, 1 vol. Rowland, Andrew, illus. 2011. (Little Lizards Ser.). (ENG.). 32p. (gr. -1-1). pap. 6.25 *(978-1-4342-3048-5(1))* Stone Arch Bks.

Crowther, Kitty, creator. Scritch Scratch Scraww Plop. 2015. (ENG., Illus.). 40p. (J). (gr. -1-3). 16.95 *(978-1-59270-179-7(5))* Enchanted Lion Bks., LLC.

Curtis, Jennifer Keats & Jensen, Laura. Trudy the Tree Frog, 1 vol. 2015. (ENG., Illus.). 32p. (J). 16.99 *(978-0-7643-4997-3(X),* 9780764349973) Schiffer Publishing, Ltd.

Cutler, Henry T. King Mork. 2011. 48p. (gr. -1). pap. 12.95 *(978-1-4678-7320-8(9))* AuthorHouse.

Cuzzone, Beth. Two Lily Pads & One Froggie Family. 2009. 36p. pap. 16.95 *(978-1-4490-2179-5(4))* AuthorHouse.

Dad's Bathtime: Individual Title Six-Packs. (Literatura 2000 Ser.). (gr. 1-2). 28.00 *(978-0-7635-0128-0(X))* Rigby Education.

Dahl, Michael. The Fantastic Flexy Frog, 1 vol. Baltazar, Art, illus. 2012. (DC Super-Pets Ser.). (ENG.). 56p. (gr. 2-2). pap. 4.95 *(978-1-4048-7666-8(9));* 23.99 *(978-1-4048-6494-8(6))* Picture Window Bks. (DC Super-Pets).

Dakos, Kalli. Why Am I Blue? A Story about Being Yourself. Garófoli, Viviana, illus. 2017. 32p. (J). 15.95 ***(978-1-4338-2734-1(4),*** Magination Pr.) American Psychological Assn.

Dalmatian Press Staff. The Icky Sticky Frog. 2008. (ENG.). 8p. (J). bds. 4.95 *(978-1-58117-712-1(7),* Intervisual/Piggy Toes) Bendon, Inc.

Davenport, Eddie. Bunnyburg: The Newcomers. 2013. (ENG.). 30p. (J). pap. 14.95 *(978-1-4787-2062-1(X))* Outskirts Pr., Inc.

Davidson, Susanna. The Frog Prince. 2005. 48p. (J). (gr. 2-18). 8.95 *(978-0-7945-0969-9(X),* Usborne) EDC Publishing.

Davis, Izzy. The Croaks at Roaring River, 1 vol. 2009. 40p. pap. 24.95 *(978-1-60813-245-4(5))* America Star Bks.

Davis, Julie. Philip the Frog Who Barked Like a Dog. 2011. 24p. pap. 12.99 *(978-1-4634-4926-1(7))* AuthorHouse.

Davis, Marshall L. Og the Magical Green Frog. 2012. (ENG.). (J). pap. *(978-1-4675-4055-1(2))* Independent Pub.

Day, Robert O. & Day, Linda S. There's a Frog on a Log in the Bog. Day, Linda S., illus. 2003. (Illus.). (J). (gr. 3-6). 212p. pap. 8.95 *(978-1-890905-50-7(X),* Writers Collective, The); (Just So Wild Ser.: Vol. 1). 14.95 *(978-1-890905-51-4(8),* Eco Fiction Bks.) Day to Day Enterprises.

De Audrade, Norma. The Frog, the Princess, the Purpurine, & the Silk Threads. 2005. (J). pap. 8.00 *(978-0-8059-6524-7(6))* Dorrance Publishing Co., Inc.

De Jesus, Opal. The Magical Purple-Blue Frog, 1 vol. Pagona, Aurora, illus. 2010. 16p. pap. 24.95 *(978-1-4489-5925-9(X))* PublishAmerica, Inc.

Dean, Janice. Freddy the Frogcaster. (ENG., Illus.). 40p. (J). (gr. -1-3). 2016. 7.99 *(978-1-62157-508-5(X))* 2013. 16.99 *(978-1-62157-084-4(3))* Regnery Publishing, Inc., An Eagle Publishing Co. (Regnery Kids).

—Freddy the Frogcaster & the Big Blizzard. 2014. (Freddy the Frogcaster Ser.). (ENG., Illus.). 40p. (J). (gr. -1-3). 16.99 *(978-1-62157-254-1(4),* Regnery Kids) Regnery Publishing, Inc., An Eagle Publishing Co.

—Freddy the Frogcaster & the Huge Hurricane. 2015. (Freddy the Frogcaster Ser.). (ENG., Illus.). 40p. (J). (gr. -1-3). 16.99 *(978-1-62157-260-2(9),* Regnery Kids) Regnery Publishing, Inc., An Eagle Publishing Co.

—Freddy the Frogcaster & the Terrible Tornado. 2016. (Freddy the Frogcaster Ser.). (ENG., Illus.). 40p. (J). (gr. -1-3). 16.99 *(978-1-62157-469-9(5),* Regnery Kids) Regnery Publishing, Inc., An Eagle Publishing Co.

Debose, Alison. Lenny & Di in the Frog & the Fly. 2011. 28p. pap. 24.95 *(978-1-4626-0394-7(7))* PublishAmerica, Inc.

deGennaro, Sue. The Pros & Cons of Being a Frog. deGennaro, Sue, illus. 2016. (ENG., Illus.). 40p. (J). (gr. -1-3). 17.99 *(978-1-4814-7130-5(9),* Simon & Schuster/Paula Wiseman Bks.) Simon & Schuster/Paula Wiseman Bks.

Delacre, Lulu. Rafi & Rosi. 2004. (Illus.). 64p. (J). lib. bdg. 13.85 *(978-1-4242-0596-7(4))* Fitzgerald Bks.

—Rafi & Rosi. Delacre, Lulu, illus. 2005. (I Can Read Bks.). (Illus.). 64p. (J). (gr. k-3). pap. 3.99 *(978-0-06-009897-1(X),* Rayo) HarperCollins Pubs.

—Rafi & Rosi. Delacre, Lulu, illus. 2016. (Rafi & Rosi Ser.). (ENG., Illus.). 63p. (J). (gr. k-3). pap. 8.95 *(978-0-89239-377-0(7))* Lee & Low Bks., Inc.

—Rafi & Rosi Carnival!, 1 vol. 2016. (Rafi & Rosi Ser.). (ENG., Illus.). 64p. (J). (gr. k-3). pap. 8.95 *(978-0-89239-379-4(3))* Lee & Low Bks., Inc.

—Rafi y Rosi. Delacre, Lulu, illus. 2016. (Rafi & Rosi Ser.).Tr. of Rafi & Rosi. (SPA., Illus.). (J). pap. 8.95 *(978-0-89239-378-7(5))* Lee & Low Bks., Inc.

—Rafi y Rosi ¡Carnaval!, 1 vol. 2016. (Rafi & Rosi Ser.).Tr. of Rafi & Rosi Carnival. (SPA & ENG., Illus.). 64p. (J). pap. 8.95 *(978-0-89239-380-0(7))* Lee & Low Bks., Inc.

Dell'Oro, Suzanne Paul. Hiding Toads. 2003. (Pull Ahead Bks.). (Illus.). 32p. (J). (gr. k-2). pap. 5.95 *(978-0-8225-3630-7(7))* Lerner Publishing Group.

Deloach, Pam. Shauna's Frog. 2012. 24p. 24.95 *(978-1-4626-5989-0(6))* America Star Bks.

Dennard, Deborah. Bullfrog at Magnolia Circle. Kest, Kristin, illus. 2005. (Smithsonian's Backyard Ser.). (ENG.). 32p. (J). (gr. -1-2). 9.95 *(978-1-931465-09-0(6),* PB5072); pap. 6.95 *(978-1-931465-39-7(8),* S5022); 15.95 *(978-1-931465-04-5(5),* B5022) Soundprints.

dePaola, Tomie. Four Friends at Christmas. dePaola, Tomie, illus. 2009. (ENG., Illus.). 32p. (J). (gr. -1-1). 12.99 *(978-1-4169-9175-5(1),* Aladdin) Simon & Schuster Children's Publishing.

deRubertis, Barbara. Frances Frog's Forever Friend. Alley, R. W., illus. 2010. (Animal Antics A to Z Ser.). 32p. (J). (gr. -1-3). (ENG.). pap. 7.95 *(978-1-57565-310-5(9));* lib. bdg. 22.60 *(978-1-57565-317-4(6))* Kane Press, Inc.

deRubertis, Barbara & DeRubertis, Barbara. Frances Frog's Forever Friend. Alley, R. W., illus. 2012. (Animal Antics A to Z Ser.). 32p. (J). (gr. 2 — 1). cd-rom 7.95 *(978-1-57565-399-0(0))* Kane Press, Inc.

Desjardins, Dawn. Leopold's Long Awaited Leap Year Birthday. 2008. (Illus.). 32p. (J). 18.95 *(978-0-9771495-2-0(8));* per. 10.95 *(978-0-9771495-3-7(6))* Artistic Ventures LLC. (Artistic Ventures Publishing).

Destra, Ronald. Hoppy the Frog. 2012. 32p. pap. 21.99 *(978-1-4691-8474-6(5))* Xlibris Corp.

Devol, Laura. To Be a Frog. Boone, Patti, illus. 2010. 20p. pap. 12.95 *(978-1-60910-278-4(9))* Booklocker.com, Inc.

Diego, Rapi. El Sapo Hechizado. (SPA.). (J). pap. *(978-968-7791-20-3(9))* SM Ediciones ESP. Dist: Lectorum Pubns., Inc.

Disney Book Group. The Princess & the Frog: The Story of Tiana. Disney Storybook Art Team, illus. 2016. (ENG.). 112p. (J). (gr. -1-k). 12.99 *(978-1-4847-6729-0(2))* Disney Pr.

Donaldson, Julia. The Giant Jumperee. Oxenbury, Helen, illus. 2017. (ENG.). 32p. (J). (-k). 17.99 *(978-0-7352-2797-2(7),* Dial Bks) Penguin Young Readers Group.

Dooley, Sarah. Wilfred & Harold's Dinner Party Disaster . 2004. 35p. pap. 17.95 *(978-1-4137-1585-9(0))* PublishAmerica, Inc.

Drachman, Eric. A Frog Thing. Muscarello, James, illus. 2006. (ENG.). 32p. (J). (gr. -1-2). 18.95 incl. audio compact disk *(978-0-9703809-3-7(3))* Kidwick Bks.

Drobeck, Ronald D. My Name Is Prince Albert. 2012. 152p. (gr. 4-6). 30.95 *(978-1-4582-0205-5(4));* pap. 12.99 *(978-1-4582-0203-1(8))* Author Solutions, Inc. (Abbott Pr.).

Du Plessis, Claire. Rebit's Rainbow. 2013. 44p. pap. 17.45 *(978-1-4525-7600-8(9),* Balboa Pr.) Author Solutions, Inc.

Ducharme, Huguette. Enquete Tres Speciale. Caron, Romi, illus. 2004. (Collection des 6 Ans: Vol. 32). (FRE.). 68p. (YA). 7.95 *(978-2-922565-94-2(7))* Editions de la Paix CAN. Dist: World of Reading, Ltd.

Dudley, Marie Luther. Tennessee Ocean Frogs. Primm, Patricia, illus. 2008. 24p. pap. 24.95 *(978-1-60474-261-9(5))* America Star Bks.

Dyan, Penelope. Mikey & Me & the Frogs — -the Continuing Story of a Girl & Her Dog. Dyan, Penelope, illus. 2010. (Illus.). 50p. pap. 14.95 *(978-1-935118-93-0(5))* Bellissima Publishing, LLC.

Eagle, Golden. It's Okay to Cry (Frog Medicine) I.t. ed. 2004. (Illus.). 16p. (J). per. 12.99 *(978-1-932338-37-9(3))* Lifevest Publishing, Inc.

Eberle, Melissa. Fricka the Flying Frog. 2009. 20p. pap. 11.59 *(978-1-4389-7514-6(7))* AuthorHouse.

Edwards, M. J. Dontayan. 2008. 62p. pap. 19.95 *(978-1-60610-026-4(2))* America Star Bks.

Emmett, Jonathan. Prince Ribbit, 1 vol. Bernatene, Poly, illus. 2017. (ENG.). 32p. (J). (gr. -1-2). 16.95 *(978-1-56145-761-8(2))* Peachtree Pubs.

Enos, Barbara. When George Stopped Talking. Kinney, Jo Hannah, illus. 2011. 20p. pap. 24.95 *(978-1-4626-4254-0(3))* America Star Bks.

Enriquez, Jose. Saving the Mango Farm. 2006. 23p. (J). 10.98 *(978-1-4116-5917-9(1))* Lulu Pr., Inc.

Erickson, Russell. A Toad for Tuesday. 64p. (J). (gr. 1-3). pap. 3.99 *(978-0-8072-1329-2(2),* Listening Library) Random Hse. Audio Publishing Group.

Esbaum, Jill. Teeny Tiny Toady. Yamaguchi, Keika, illus. 2016. (ENG.). 40p. (J). (gr. -1-2). 14.95 *(978-1-4549-1454-9(8))* Sterling Publishing Co., Inc.

Eskye, Tony. The Adventures of Fojo the Frog. 2009. (Illus.). 224p. pap. 14.49 *(978-1-4389-9530-4(X))* AuthorHouse.

Esperanza, Charles George, illus. Red, Yellow, Blue, & a Dash of White, Too! 2015. (ENG.). 40p. (J). (gr. -1-k). 16.99 *(978-1-62914-624-9(2),* Sky Pony Pr.) Skyhorse Publishing Co., Inc.

Ethan Finds a Frog. 2003. (Illus.). per. 14.95 *(978-0-9721948-5-3(1))* New Dawn Publishing.

Everett, George W. G. W. Frog & the Circus Lion. 2010. 32p. 16.95 *(978-1-4497-0443-8(3),* WestBow Pr.) Author Solutions, Inc.

—G. W. Frog & the Haunted House in Misty Meadows. 2010. 44p. 16.95 *(978-1-4497-0752-1(1),* WestBow Pr.) Author Solutions, Inc.

—G W Frog & the Pickle-Barrel Time MacHine. 2012. 30p. pap. 16.95 *(978-1-4497-4342-0(0),* WestBow Pr.) Author Solutions, Inc.

—G. W. Frog & the Pumpkin Patch Bandit. 2010. 40p. 16.95 *(978-1-4497-0759-0(9),* WestBow Pr.) Author Solutions, Inc.

Fear, E. G. Just a Medium Size Frog. 2013. (Illus.). 66p. (gr. 2-4). pap. 13.66 *(978-1-4817-8028-5(X))* AuthorHouse.

Fettig, Pamela. Leelah at the Lake. Strecker, Darren, illus. 2010. 28p. pap. 9.99 *(978-1-60844-697-1(2))* Dog Ear Publishing, LLC.

Feuer, Bonnie. Goliaths's Secret. Platt, Sharai, illus. 2013. (ENG.). 38p. (J). 18.50 *(978-0-9825468-8-8(2))* Connecticut Pr., The.

Few, Valerie. Filbert & Friends. 2008. 56p. pap. *(978-1-84748-346-1(1))* Athena Pr.

Flodin, Louise E. Sherman the Frog Meets the Snow Princess. I.t. ed. 2006. (Illus.). 24p. (J). (gr. -1-3). 15.95 *(978-0-9745052-5-1(0),* 1) Tree Of Life Publishing.

Flores, Eileen. To All a Good Knight. 2008. 92p. pap. 12.50 *(978-1-4389-2267-6(1))* AuthorHouse.

Fogerty, Ramona. Froggie Sang Tenor. Nurullah, Seitu, illus. 2005. (FRE.). (J). per. 15.00 *(978-0-9759889-0-9(5))* Potential Psychotherapy Counseling & Remedial Service.

Fontinalis. The Far Shore. 2011. 76p. pap. 6.99 *(978-1-61667-309-3(5))* Raider Publishing International.

Foreman, Michael. Superfrog & the Big Stink! Foreman, Michael, illus. 2014. (ENG., Illus.). 32p. (J). (gr. -1-k). pap. 9.99 *(978-1-78344-030-6(9))* Andersen Pr. GBR. Dist: Independent Pubs. Group.

Fox, Donna L. Willie the Toad. 2011. 16p. pap. 24.95 *(978-1-4626-2577-2(0))* America Star Bks.

Fox, Julie. Ugly As a Toad. Chamberlain-Pecorino, Sarah, illus. 2008. 24p. pap. 12.99 *(978-1-4389-0002-5(3))* AuthorHouse.

Fox, Stephen. Kim the Frog. Bowman, Brent, illus. 2003. (Little Lagoon Ser.). 22p. (J). bds. 6.95 *(978-0-9729197-0-8(8),* Gom Foxtail) Gom Publishing, LLC.

Franco, Betsy. Why the Frog Has Big Eyes. 2003. (Green Light Readers — Level 2 Ser.). (gr. -1-2). lib. bdg. 13.50 *(978-0-613-64618-5(5),* Turtleback) Turtleback Bks.

Franco, Betsy & Franco-Feeney, Betsy. Why the Frog Has Big Eyes. Kim, Joung Un, illus. 2003. (Green Light Readers Level 2 Ser.). (ENG.). 24p. (J). (gr. -1-3). pap. 3.95 *(978-0-15-204834-1(0))* Houghton Mifflin Harcourt Publishing Co.

Freddie the Frog: Set C Individual Title Six-Packs. (Supersonic Phonics Ser.). (gr. k-3). 29.00 *(978-0-7635-0545-5(5))* Rigby Education.

Freddy the Frog. Date not set. 5.95 *(978-0-89868-311-0(4))* ARO Publishing Co.

Freedman, Deborah. By Mouse & Frog. Freedman, Deborah, illus. 2015. (ENG., Illus.). 32p. (J). (gr. -1-k). 16.99 *(978-0-670-78490-5(7),* Viking Books for Young Readers) Penguin Young Readers Group.

Frick, Lisa. "Evie" the Little Jack Russell with Brown Around Her Eyes. 2009. 64p. pap. 31.99 *(978-1-4415-2911-4(X))* Xlibris Corp.

A Frog on a Log. 2004. (J). per. *(978-1-57657-471-3(7))* Paradise Pr., Inc.

The Frog Prince: 6 Small Books. (gr. k-2). 23.00 *(978-0-7635-8511-2(4))* Rigby Education.

The Frog Who Thought He Was a Horse: Individual Title Six-Packs. (Literatura 2000 Ser.). (gr. 2-3). 33.00 *(978-0-7635-0225-6(1))* Rigby Education.

Furie, Matt. The Night Riders. 2012. (ENG., Illus.). 48p. 17.95 *(978-1-936365-56-2(1))* McSweeney's Publishing.

Furie, Matt, illus. The Night Riders. 2013. (ENG.). 48p. (J). (gr. -1-3). 8.95 *(978-1-938073-72-4(X))* McSweeney's Publishing.

Galloway, Fhiona, illus. Where's Frog? 2012. (Squeaky Bath Bks.). (ENG.). 8p. (J). (— 1). 9.99 *(978-0-230-75868-1(1))* Pan Macmillan GBR. Dist: Independent Pubs. Group.

Gardner, Carol. Princess Zelda & the Frog. Young, Shane, photos by. 2011. (ENG., Illus.). 40p. (J). (gr. -1-3). 16.99 *(978-0-312-60325-0(8),* 9780312603250) Feiwel & Friends.

Garis, Howard Roger. Buddy & Brighteyes Pigg. 2004. reprint ed. pap. 1.99 *(978-1-4192-1107-2(2));* pap. 15.95 *(978-1-4191-1107-5(8))* Kessinger Publishing, LLC.

—Bully & Bawly No-Tail: (the Jumping Frogs) 2007. (ENG.). 140p. per. 18.99 *(978-1-4346-2971-5(6));* 144p. per. 19.99 *(978-1-4346-2989-0(9))* Creative Media Partners, LLC.

Geraghty, Paul. Hoppameleon. Geraghty, Paul, illus. 2014. (ENG., Illus.). 32p. (J). (gr. -1-k). pap. 9.99 *(978-1-84939-773-5(2))* Andersen Pr. GBR. Dist: Independent Pubs. Group.

Gershator, Phillis, illus. Little Lenty. 2014. (J). pap. *(978-1-934370-48-3(7))* Editorial Campana.

Gidwitz, Adam. In a Glass Grimmly. Santat, Dan, illus. 2013. (ENG.). 352p. (J). (gr. 5). pap. 7.99 *(978-0-14-242506-0(0),* Puffin Books) Penguin Young Readers Group.

—In a Glass Grimmly. D'Andrade, Hugh, illus. 2012. (ENG.). 336p. (J). (gr. 5). 16.99 *(978-0-525-42581-6(0),* Dutton Books for Young Readers) Penguin Young Readers Group.

—In a Glass Grimmly. 2013. (Grimm Ser.: 2). lib. bdg. 18.40 *(978-0-606-32135-8(7),* Turtleback) Turtleback Bks.

Gitau, Terri. Annie & Kindness the Frog. 2012. 16p. pap. 15.99 *(978-1-4634-4021-3(9))* AuthorHouse.

Glass, Sue. Helping Hop. 2nd ed. 2004. Orig. Title: What's Wrong with Hop? (J). spiral bd. 10.99 *(978-0-9763593-0-2(8))* Closer Looks Bks.

Gleitzman, Morris. Toad Rage. 2005. (Toad Bks.). (ENG.). 176p. (J). (gr. 3-7). per. 6.99 *(978-0-375-82763-1(3),* Yearling) Random Hse. Children's Bks.

Golden Books. Frog Fight! (Teenage Mutant Ninja Turtles) Lambe, Steve, illus. 2016. (Little Golden Book Ser.). (ENG.). 24p. (J). (-k). 4.99 *(978-0-553-53907-3(8),* Golden Bks.) Random Hse. Children's Bks.

Gologan, Trena. Alexandru's Gift. 2008. 35p. pap. 17.00 *(978-1-4357-3486-9(6))* Lulu Pr., Inc.

Goodnight, Macy. The Toad & the Dragonfly. 2008. 24p. pap. 24.95 *(978-1-60474-785-0(4))* America Star Bks.

Gorbachev, Valeri. Ms. Turtle the Babysitter. Gorbachev, Valeri, illus. 2005. (I Can Read Bks.). (Illus.). 64p. (J). (gr. k-3). (ENG.). 15.99 *(978-0-06-058073-5(9));* lib. bdg. 16.89 *(978-0-06-058074-2(7))* HarperCollins Pubs.

Gordon, Jennifer. Terrible Tales 2: The Bloodcurdling Truth about the Frog Prince, Jack & the Beanstalk, A Very Fowl Duckling, the Ghoulishly Ghoulish Snow White, A Really Crabby Princess, & A Very Squashed Pea. 2011. 110p. (gr. -1-12). 20.95 *(978-1-4620-0941-1(7));* pap. 10.95 *(978-1-4620-0940-4(9))* iUniverse, Inc.

Gordon, Mike, illus. The Frog Prince. rev. ed. 2007. (Young Reading CD Packs Ser.). 48p. (J). (gr. -1-3). 9.99 incl. audio compact disk *(978-0-7945-1868-4(0),* Usborne) EDC Publishing.

Graham-Morgan, Ivet. Grandma's Garden. 2009. 24p. pap. 12.99 *(978-1-4389-2733-6(9))* AuthorHouse.

Grahame, Kenneth. The Wind in the Willows. Roberts, David, illus. 2013. (ENG.). 256p. (J). (gr. 5). 24.99 *(978-0-7636-6526-5(6))* Candlewick Pr.

Grandma Poo Poo. Tessie the Toad. Oien, Jennifer, illus. 2008. 28p. pap. 24.95 *(978-1-60610-325-8(3))* America Star Bks.

Grandpa Dennis, as told by. George Washington's Smallest Army: The Miracle Before Trenton. 2009. 216p. (J). pap. 17.49 *(978-1-4389-3147-0(6))* AuthorHouse.

Gravett, Emily. Spells. Gravett, Emily, illus. 2009. (ENG., Illus.). 32p. (J). (gr. -1-3). 16.99 *(978-1-4169-8270-8(1),* Simon & Schuster Bks. For Young Readers) Simon & Schuster Bks. For Young Readers.

Gray, Kes. Frog on a Log? Field, Jim, illus. 2015. (ENG.). 32p. (J). (gr. -1-k). 16.99 *(978-0-545-68791-1(8),* Scholastic Pr.) Scholastic, Inc.

Gray, Kes & Gray, Claire. Dog on a Frog? Field, Jim, illus. 2017. (ENG.). 32p. (J). (gr. -1-k). 16.99 ***(978-1-338-11695-3(9),*** Scholastic Pr.) Scholastic, Inc.

Green, Poppy. The Clover Curse. Bell, Jennifer A., illus. 2016. (Adventures of Sophie Mouse Ser.: 7). (ENG.). 128p. (J). (gr. k-4). 16.99 *(978-1-4814-5184-0(7),* Little Simon) Little Simon.

—The Emerald Berries. Bell, Jennifer A., illus. 2015. (Adventures of Sophie Mouse Ser.: 2). (ENG.). 128p. (J). (gr. k-4). pap. 5.99 *(978-1-4814-2835-4(7),* Little Simon) Little Simon.

—Forget-Me-Not Lake. Bell, Jennifer A., illus. 2015. (Adventures of Sophie Mouse Ser.: 3). (ENG.). 128p. (J). (gr. k-4). 16.99 *(978-1-4814-3000-5(9),* Little Simon) Little Simon.

Greenberg, Penny. The Adventures of Toby the Turtle & Mighty Magoo. 2008. 16p. pap. 8.49 *(978-1-4389-1014-7(2))* AuthorHouse.

Grimm, J. & W. & Grimm, J. The Frog Prince: Or Iron Henry. Hager, Christian & Schroeder, Binette, illus. 2013. (ENG.). 32p. (J). (gr. -1-3). 17.95 *(978-0-7358-4140-6(3))* North-South Bks., Inc.

Grimm, Jacob & Grimm, Wilhelm K. The Frog Prince/ El Principe Sapo. 2004. (Illus.). (J). *(978-1-933530-21-5(9))* Bingo Bks., Inc.

Gross, S. D. Blue Frog. l.t. ed. 2006. (Illus.). 24p. (J). per. 11.99 *(978-1-59879-207-2(5))* Lifevest Publishing, Inc.

Grout, Claire. Emil & Ordi: Friends for All Time. 2012. 24p. pap. 15.99 *(978-1-4691-6279-9(2))* Xlibris Corp.

Guardado, Maria. The Frog That Went to the Moon. Valentin, Jeannette, illus. 32p. (J). (gr. 3-18). 16.00 *(978-0-9710860-6-7(0))* Libros, Encouraging Cultural Literacy.

Gudeon, Adam. Peep & Zeep. 2017. (I Like to Read(r) Ser.). (ENG.). 24p. (J). (gr. -1-3). 14.95 *(978-0-8234-3674-3(8))* Holiday Hse., Inc.

Guess, R. J. The Frog That Would Not Jump. 2011. 20p. pap. 24.95 *(978-1-4560-0977-9(X))* America Star Bks.

Guillain, Charlotte. The Frog Prince Saves Sleeping Beauty. Widdowson, Dan, illus. 2016. (Fairy Tale Mix-Ups Ser.). (ENG.). 24p. (gr. k-2). lib. bdg. 23.32 *(978-1-4109-8302-2(1))* Heinemann-Raintree.

Guillot, Angela K. The Day Frasier the Frog Jumped High. Ashley Comeaux-Foret, illus. 2011. 20p. pap. 24.95 *(978-1-4626-2312-9(3))* PublishAmerica, Inc.

Guinn, Dolores Hollyfield. Frederick Frog & His Family: Being a Bully. 2008. 16p. per. 24.95 *(978-1-4241-9223-6(4))* America Star Bks.

—Stubborn & Disobedient, 1 vol. Box, Paul, illus. 2009. 19p. pap. 24.95 *(978-1-4489-0902-5(3))* America Star Bks.

Gump, Granny. The Giraffe Who Went to School. 2011. 48p. pap. 21.99 *(978-1-4568-5805-6(X))* Xlibris Corp.

Hahn, Jan. Albert & the Milk Pail. 2012. 118p. (gr. -1). pap. 12.19 *(978-1-4669-7409-8(5))* Trafford Publishing.

Hall, Susan & Hall, Susan, illus. Diego Saves the Tree Frogs. 2006. (Go, Diego, Go! Ser.). (ENG.). 24p. (J). (gr. -1-1). pap. 3.99 *(978-1-4169-1574-4(5),* Simon Spotlight/Nickelodeon) Simon Spotlight/Nickelodeon.

Hamilton, Martha & Weiss, Mitch. A Tale of Two Frogs. Wrenn, Tom, illus. 2006. (Story Cove Ser.). (ENG.). 32p. (J). (gr. -1-3). pap. 4.95 *(978-0-87483-812-1(6))* August Hse. Pubs., Inc.

Hammon, Darrel L. Christmas Beneath the Lake: From the Adventures of Bob the Bullfrog. 2012. (ENG.). (J). (-18). 35p. pap. 17.95 *(978-1-4787-1910-6(9));* 25p. pap. 23.95 *(978-1-4327-7916-0(8))* Outskirts Pr., Inc.

Hannah Lane, illus. A Frog Named Dude. 2007. 16p. (J). *(978-0-9800870-0-0(7))* Robillard, Kristy.

Happy Books. Little Frog. 2013. (Mini-Creatures Ser.). (ENG., Illus.). 10p. (J). (gr. -1 — 1). bds. 4.99 *(978-0-7641-6597-9(6))* Barron's Educational Series, Inc.

Harbo, Gary. The Northern Woods Adventure: Early Reader. Harbo, Gary, illus. l.t. ed. 2004. (If You Want to Succeed, You Need to Read! Ser.: 6). (Illus.). 33p. (J). 10.95 *(978-1-884149-16-0(2))* Kutie Kari Bks., Inc.

Harcrow, Melissa. Where're Your Manners, William? 2008. 26p. pap. 24.95 *(978-1-60563-470-8(0))* America Star Bks.

Harper, Jamie. Miss Mingo & the First Day of School. Harper, Jamie, illus. 2009. (ENG., Illus.). 32p. (J). (gr. -1-3). pap. 6.99 *(978-0-7636-4134-4(0))* Candlewick Pr.

Harvey, Damian. Snail's Legs. Paul, Korky, illus. 2015. (ENG.). 32p. (J). (gr. -1-2). pap. 8.99 *(978-1-84780-712-0(7),* Frances Lincoln) Quarto Publishing Group UK GBR. Dist: Hachette Bk. Group.

Hauser, Sheri. Frog Frey Fun. 2011. (Illus.). (J). spiral bd. 5.95 *(978-1-60789-218-2(9))* Glorybound Publishing.

Hayes, J. B. Freddy the Frog's First Christmas. 2012. 44p. pap. 21.99 *(978-1-4772-2870-8(5))* AuthorHouse.

HB Staff. Frog's Day. 97th ed. 2003. (Signatures Ser.). (gr. 1-18). pap. 16.50 *(978-0-15-308149-1(X))* Harcourt Schl. Pubs.

Hedgman, Janis. Party in the Garden. 2009. (Illus.). 52p. pap. *(978-1-84748-514-4(6))* Athena Pr.

Heer, Dusty Rhoades. The Forest That Rains Frogs. 2012. (ENG.). 58p. pap. 19.95 *(978-1-4327-9303-6(9))* Outskirts Pr., Inc.

Henderson, Mary Anne. The Adventures of Linda's Little Frog. 2004. 252p. 29.50 *(978-1-4184-1576-1(6))* AuthorHouse.

Heo, Yumi. The Green Frogs: A Korean Folktale. 2004. (ENG., Illus.). 32p. (J). (gr. -1-3). reprint ed. 6.95 *(978-0-618-43228-8(0))* Houghton Mifflin Harcourt Publishing Co.

Hepola, Catherine R. The Great Toadie. 2009. 60p. pap. 23.99 *(978-1-4389-3451-8(3))* AuthorHouse.

Hiebert, Elfrieda H. & Juel, Connie. Little Frog's Monster Story. (Little Book Practice Reader Ser.). (J). *(978-0-8136-0807-5(4))* Modern Curriculum Pr.

Hilliard, Regina Foster. Tim & Tom: Frog Friends. 2011. (Illus.). 19p. (J). pap. 14.95 *(978-1-4327-5917-9(5))* Outskirts Pr., Inc.

Himes, John. Everyone Is Special. 2012. 24p. pap. 24.95 *(978-1-4626-7462-6(3))* America Star Bks.

Hinkler Books Staff, ed. The Hungry Frog. 2009. (ENG.). 12p. (J). bds. 12.99 *(978-1-74183-542-7(9),* Ideal Pubns.) Worthy Publishing.

Hinton, Maureen. William's Troublesome Tongue. 2010. 36p. pap. 13.95 *(978-1-60911-396-4(9),* Eloquent Bks.) Strategic Book Publishing & Rights Agency (SBPRA).

Hodgson, Karen J. Boris the Boastful Frog. Cox, Steve, illus. 2015. (ENG.). 32p. (J). (gr. -1-1). pap. 9.99 *(978-1-907432-10-1(8))* Hogs Back Bks. GBR. Dist: Independent Pubs. Group.

Hoffmire, Baird, illus. The Big Wide-Mouth Frog. 2009. (J). pap. *(978-0-87483-890-9(8),* August House Story Cove) August Hse. Pubs., Inc.

Holmes, Harold H. The Tale of the Purple Chicken & Orange Frog. 2010. 26p. pap. 12.00 *(978-1-60911-653-8(4),* Eloquent Bks.) Strategic Book Publishing & Rights Agency (SBPRA).

Hood, Karen Jean Matsko. There's a Toad in the Hole: A Big Fat Toad in the Hole, Bk.2. Whispering Pine Press International, ed. Artistic Design Service Staff, illus. 2014. (Hood Poetry Ser.). (J). 29.95 *(978-1-930948-24-2(7))* Whispering Pine Pr. International, Inc.

Hood, Susan. Leaps & Bounce. Cordell, Matthew, illus. 2016. (ENG.). 32p. (J). (gr. -1-k). 16.99 *(978-1-4231-5234-7(4))* Disney Pr.

Horender, Philip M. The Mighty Maximilian: Samuel Clemens's Traveling Companion, 1 vol. Wolek, Guy, illus. 2013. (Maximilian P. Mouse, Time Traveler Ser.). (ENG.). 112p. (J). (gr. 3-6). lib. bdg. 27.07 *(978-1-61641-960-8(1),* Calico Chapter Bks) Magic Wagon.

Horowitz, Jeanine. Toady Toad's Move. 2006. (Illus.). 32p. (J). lib. bdg. 17.95 *(978-1-934190-03-6(9))* Ocean Front Bk. Publishing, Inc.

How Clarence Found Harmony. 2004. (J). pap. 5.00 *(978-0-9747734-5-2(X))* Neal, Ann-Marie F.

Hulst, W. G. van de & Hulst, Willem G. van de, illus. The Secret in the Box. 2014. (J). *(978-1-928136-17-0(6))* Inheritance Pubns.

Hung, Yating. Where Is Mama? A Pop-Up Story. 2013. (ENG., Illus.). 24p. (J). (gr. -1-k). 19.95 *(978-1-4197-0718-6(3),* Abrams Appleseed) Abrams, Inc.

Hurd, Thacher. Bad Frogs. Hurd, Thacher, illus. 2009. (ENG., Illus.). 40p. (J). (gr. -1-2). 15.99 *(978-0-7636-3253-3(8))* Candlewick Pr.

Hutton, Gaila. Frank the Colorful Frog. Knox, Anna Mae, illus. 2011. 28p. pap. 24.95 *(978-1-4560-5607-0(7))* America Star Bks.

The Icky Sticky Frog. 2005. (ENG., Illus.). 17p. (J). 4.95 *(978-1-58117-219-5(2),* Intervisual/Piggy Toes) Bendon, Inc.

Irani, Dinaz. The Indigo Fairy & the Frogs. 2014. 28p. pap. 17.99 *(978-1-4828-2060-7(9))* Partridge Pub.

Irvin, Christine. Isaac the Frog. Less, Sally, illus. 2004. 14p. (J). 7.95 *(978-0-9706654-9-2(0))* Sprite Pr.

Ivo. Charles & Amand: The Adventuresome Frogs. 2012. 40p. pap. 14.95 *(978-1-61897-129-6(8),* Strategic Bk. Publishing) Strategic Book Publishing & Rights Agency (SBPRA).

Jackson's Plan: Evaluation Guide. 2006. (J). *(978-1-55942-410-3(9))* Witcher Productions.

Jacob, Bill & Fosnot, Catherine Twomey. The California Frog-Jumping Contest - Algebra. 2008. (ENG.). 80p. (gr. 4-5). pap. 31.25 *(978-0-325-01024-3(2),* E01024, Firsthand) Heinemann.

Jefferson, E. Louis. The Little Tadpole-A Story of Friendship: Companion Coloring Book. 2012. 48p. pap. 7.00 *(978-1-105-61123-0(X))* Lulu.com GBR. Dist: Lulu Pr., Inc.

Jefferson, Patti Brassard. How Long Will You Love Me? Jefferson, Patti Brassard, illus. 2013. (Illus.). 28p. pap. 12.95 *(978-1-61244-178-8(5))* Halo Publishing International.

Jenkins, Henry A. The Adventures of Monkey Squirrel & Frogman: Sand Trap. 2009. 16p. pap. 8.49 *(978-1-4343-7827-9(6))* AuthorHouse.

Jentsch, R. D. Froggy & Friends Go to the Creek, 1 vol. Jentsch, Joyce Harp, illus. 2009. 41p. pap. 24.95 *(978-1-60836-966-9(8))* America Star Bks.

Jeremy Fisher Rocks Out. 2015. (Illus.). (J). *(978-1-4844-5560-9(6),* Warne, Frederick Pubs.) Penguin Bks., Ltd.

Johnson, Amy. The Princess & the Frog. 2010. 24p. 14.93 *(978-1-4269-3712-5(1))* Trafford Publishing.

Johnson, Cindy B. Frantic the Frog. Lane, Cody R., illus. 2004. 27p. pap. 24.95 *(978-1-4137-2954-2(1))* America Star Bks.

Johnson, Rebecca. Tree Frog Hears a Sound. Parish, Steve, illus. 2005. (Animal Storybooks Ser.). 24p. (gr. k-3). lib. bdg. 22.00 *(978-0-8368-5976-8(6),* Gareth Stevens Learning Library) Stevens, Gareth Publishing LLLP.

Jones, Anna, illus. Scrub-a-Dub Froggy: Bath Mitt & Book Set. 2013. (ENG.). 8p. (J). (gr. -1 — 1). 9.99 *(978-1-4380-7439-9(5))* Barron's Educational Series, Inc.

Jones, Elwynn. Frank's Frantic Friday. 2010. 40p. pap. 16.95 *(978-1-60911-750-4(6),* Eloquent Bks.) Strategic Book Publishing & Rights Agency (SBPRA).

Jordan, Annie Laurie. Bogwaddle Pond. La Grange, Myrtle, illus. 2004. 25p. pap. 24.95 *(978-1-4137-2013-6(7))* PublishAmerica, Inc.

Jules. Bubble's World: Book Five Frogs & Fairies. 2011. 40p. pap. 16.59 *(978-1-4567-6730-3(5))* AuthorHouse.

Kalan, Robert. Jump, Frog, Jump! Barton, Byron, illus. 2003.Tr. of Salta, Ranita, Salta! (ENG.). 34p. (J). (gr. -1-3). bds. 7.99 *(978-0-06-008819-4(2),* Greenwillow Bks.) HarperCollins Pubs.

—Jump, Frog, Jump! Barton, Byron, illus. 2004.Tr. of Salta, Ranita, Salta! (J). (gr. -1-2). 28.95 incl. audio compact disk *(978-1-59112-728-4(9))* Live Oak Media.

Kale, Ann Stephanian. Artie - The Ugly Frog. Kale, Ann Stephanian, illus. 2004. (Illus.). 20p. (J). pap. 10.00 *(978-0-9704131-6-1(5))* Abril BookStore & Publishing.

Kalinowski, Delphine. Frog's Fruit Stand. 2006. (Neighborhood Readers Ser.). (ENG.). 8p. (gr. 1-3). pap. 5.15 *(978-1-4042-6807-4(3),* Rosen Classroom) Rosen Publishing Group, Inc., The.

Kang, Anna. Can I Tell You a Secret? Weyant, Christopher, illus. 2016. 40p. (J). (gr. -1-3). 17.99 *(978-0-06-239684-6(6))* HarperCollins Pubs.

Kellogg, Steven. The Mysterious Tadpole. Kellogg, Steven, illus. 25th anniv. ed. 2004. (ENG., Illus.). 40p. (J). (gr. k-3). reprint ed. pap. 6.99 *(978-0-14-240140-8(4),* Puffin Books) Penguin Young Readers Group.

Kelsey-Livin, Barbara. The Monkey & the Frog. 2012. 30p. 24.95 *(978-1-4626-6161-9(0))* America Star Bks.

Kendall, Carolyn. Phibby & Ribby. 2013. 32p. pap. *(978-1-4602-0387-3(9))* FriesenPress.

Kennedy, J. Aday. Juggerum. Morris, Alexander, illus. 2012. 16p. pap. 9.95 *(978-1-61633-348-5(0))* Guardian Angel Publishing, Inc.

Kilkka, Mary. Meet the Nydees, 1 vol. 2010. 28p. 24.95 *(978-1-4512-1495-6(2))* America Star Bks.

Killaire, B. M. The Adventures of Betty & Bo-Bob: A Tale of One & a Half Frogs. Kwik, Penny Shannon, ed. Killaire, B. M., illus. 2012. (Illus.). 32p. pap. 24.95 *(978-1-4626-6621-8(3))* America Star Bks.

Kim the Frog. 2004. (J). 7.95 *(978-0-9729197-5-3(9),* Gom Foxtail) Gom Publishing, LLC.

Kimura, ken. 999 Frogs Wake Up. 2013. (ENG., Illus.). 48p. (J). (gr. -1-3). 17.95 *(978-0-7358-4108-6(X))* North-South Bks., Inc.

Kimura, ken & Murakami, Yasunari. 999 Tadpoles. 2011. (ENG., Illus.). 40p. (J). (gr. -1-3). 17.95 *(978-0-7358-4013-3(X))* North-South Bks., Inc.

Kline, Trish & Donev, Mary. Coming Home: KA Reader 8. 2007. (Illus.). 32p. (J). per. 20.00 *(978-1-934307-01-4(7))* Ghost Hunter Productions.

Knudsen, Michelle. Fish & Frog: Brand New Readers. Petrone, Valeria, illus. 2005. (Brand New Readers Ser.). (ENG.). 8p. (J). (gr. -1-3). pap. 5.99 *(978-0-7636-2457-6(8))* Candlewick Pr.

—Fish & Frog Big Book: Brand New Readers. Petrone, Valeria, illus. 2010. (Brand New Readers Ser.). (ENG.). 48p. (J). (gr. -1-3). pap. 24.99 *(978-0-7636-4810-7(8))* Candlewick Pr.

Kobus, Joanne. Mr Frog's Bad Day. 2009. 40p. pap. 16.99 *(978-1-4389-7513-9(9))* AuthorHouse.

Kompelien, Tracy. Leap Frog, 1 vol. Haberstroh, Anne, illus. (Critter Chronicles Ser.). 24p. (J). (gr. k-3). 2007. (ENG.). lib. bdg. 24.21 *(978-1-59928-448-4(0),* SandCastle) 2006. 48.42 *(978-1-59928-449-1(9))* ABDO Publishing Co.

Konigsburg, E. L. Jennifer, Hecate, Macbeth, William McKinley, & Me, Elizabeth. 2011. 8.32 *(978-0-7848-3469-5(5),* Everbind) Marco Bk. Co.

Kratz, Jessica R. Sleigh Bells in Springtime: Frogs Calling. 2010. 48p. pap. 17.49 *(978-1-4490-8138-6(X))* AuthorHouse.

Krepela, Rebecca, Vernon, Drake & Chomp. 2013. 20p. pap. 24.95 *(978-1-62709-841-0(0))* America Star Bks.

Krosoczka, Jarrett J. The Frog Who Croaked. Krosoczka, Jarrett J., illus. 2013. (Platypus Police Squad Ser.: 1). (ENG., Illus.). 240p. (J). (gr. 3-7). 12.99 *(978-0-06-207164-4(5),* Walden Pond Pr.) HarperCollins Pubs.

Kurd, Tariq. Gordon the Goblin in Oh My! Is That a Pork Pie? Robertson, Laura, illus. 2012. 36p. pap. *(978-1-907762-10-9(8))* Malt Publishing.

Lagonegro, Melissa. Big Friend, Little Friend. 2010. (Disney Princess Step into Reading Ser.). lib. bdg. 13.55 *(978-0-606-07043-0(5),* Turtleback) Turtleback Bks.

Larson, Angela. Bobbie Burple: Frog Song. 2012. pap. *(978-1-4507-7997-5(2))* Independent Pub.

Laurel, Hylton. The Cowboy Frog. Laurel, Hylton, illus. 2003. (ENG., Illus.). 24p. (J). (gr. k-5). pap. 5.95 *(978-1-875641-85-7(8))* Magabala Bks. AUS. Dist: Independent Pubs. Group.

Lawson, Barbara Spilman, retold by. Two Frogs a Japanese Folktale. 2016. (Spring Forward Ser.). (J). (gr. 2). *(978-1-4900-9445-8(8))* Benchmark Education Co.

Lawson, Brandi. The Soap Bubble Frog. Kinra, Richa, illus. 2012. 32p. pap. 14.50 *(978-1-61897-784-7(9),* Strategic Bk. Publishing) Strategic Book Publishing & Rights Agency (SBPRA).

Layden, Joseph Lyon. The Other Side of Yore. 2007. 156p. pap. 14.95 *(978-1-60145-122-4(9))* Booklocker.com, Inc.

Lebrun, Jessica. Rainbow's Mist. 2008. 17p. pap. 24.95 *(978-1-60563-242-1(2))* America Star Bks.

Ledbetter, Penny. Frog's Lily Pad. 2006. (J). 9.95 *(978-1-59712-048-7(0))* Catawba Publishing Co.

Lee, George Douglas. Oppy Stops the Hopping Popper. Lee, Brenda Donaloio, ed. Lee, George Douglas, illus. 2012. (Illus.). 30p. pap. 10.95 *(978-0-9848486-1-4(4))* Electric Theatre Radio Hour.

LeLeu, Lisa. Frenchy the Frog Story Starter: Puppet Show Book Story Starter. 2004. (Puppet Show Bks.). (Illus.). 14p. 1.50 *(978-0-9710537-7-9(4))* LeLeu, Lisa Studios! Inc.

Lemberger, Evelyn. Furmin & Clyde Think Positive. 2012. 28p. pap. 16.09 *(978-1-4669-2195-5(1))* Trafford Publishing.

Levy, Janice. Flip-Flop & the Absolutely Awful New Baby, 1 vol. Madden, Colleen M., illus. 2011. (Flip-Flop Adventure Ser.). (ENG.). 32p. (J). (gr. k-3). 28.50 *(978-1-61641-651-5(3))* Magic Wagon.

—Flip-Flop & the BFFs, 1 vol. Madden, Colleen M., illus. 2011. (Flip-Flop Adventure Ser.). (ENG.). 32p. (J). (gr. k-3). 28.50 *(978-1-61641-652-2(1))* Magic Wagon.

—Flip-Flop & the Bully Frogs Gruff, 1 vol. Madden, Colleen M., illus. 2011. (Flip-Flop Adventure Ser.). (ENG.). 32p. (J). (gr. k-3). 28.50 *(978-1-61641-653-9(X))* Magic Wagon.

—Showtime for Flip-Flop, 1 vol. Madden, Colleen M., illus. 2011. (Flip-Flop Adventure Ser.). (ENG.). 32p. (J). (gr. k-3). 28.50 *(978-1-61641-654-6(8))* Magic Wagon.

Lewis, Elfyn. Scruff & Friends. 2012. (Illus.). 12p. pap. 18.30 *(978-1-4772-1449-7(6))* AuthorHouse.

Lewis, Paul Owen. Frog Girl. 2004. (Illus.). 38p. (J). tchr. ed., tchr.'s planning gde. ed. 2.95 *(978-1-58246-009-3(4),* Tricycle Pr.) Ten Speed Pr.

—Frog Girl. (ENG., Illus.). 32p. (J). (gr. -1-5). 18.95 *(978-1-55110-658-8(2));* pap. 8.95 *(978-1-55285-193-7(1))* Whitecap Bks., Ltd. CAN. Dist: Graphic Arts Ctr. Publishing Co.

Lin, Joyce, tr. The frog in the Well. Caprio, Pattie, illus. 2008. (ENG & CHI.). 36p. (J). 14.95 *(978-0-9801305-1-5(4))* CE Bilingual Bks. LLC.

Lionni, Leo. An Extraordinary Egg. 2014. (ENG., Illus.). 40p. (J). (gr. -1-2). 17.99 *(978-0-679-85840-9(7),* Knopf Bks. for Young Readers) Random Hse. Children's Bks.

—Fish Is Fish. 2015. (Step into Reading Ser.). (ENG., Illus.). 40p. (J). (gr. -1-2). 3.99 *(978-0-553-52218-1(3),* Random Hse. Bks. for Young Readers) Random Hse. Children's Bks.

—It's Mine! 2015. 32p. pap. 7.00 *(978-1-61003-547-7(X))* Center for the Collaborative Classroom.

Little Frog, Big Pond: Short Vowel review: Level C, 6 vols. (Wright Skills Ser.). 16p. (gr. k-3). 26.50 *(978-0-322-01492-3(1))* Wright Group/McGraw-Hill.

Livingston, Irene. Finklehopper Frog. Lies, Brian, illus. 2008. (ENG.). 32p. (J). (gr. -1-2). pap. 7.95 *(978-1-58246-234-9(8),* Tricycle Pr.) Random Hse. Children's Bks.

Lobel, Arnold. Days with Frog & Toad. Lobel, Arnold, illus. 2004. (I Can Read Level 2 Ser.). (ENG., Illus.). 64p. (J). (gr. -1-3). pap. 3.99 *(978-0-06-444058-5(3));* 25th ed. 16.99 *(978-0-06-023963-3(8))* HarperCollins Pubs.

—Days with Frog & Toad. 2004. (I Can Read! Level 2 Ser.). (J). (gr. k-3). lib. bdg. 13.55 *(978-0-8085-3378-8(9),* Turtleback) Turtleback Bks.

—Frog & Toad Are Friends. Lobel, Arnold, illus. (I Can Read Level 2 Ser.). (Illus.). (J). (gr. -1-3). 2017. 72p. 9.99 *(978-0-06-257273-8(3))* 2003. (ENG., 64p. pap. 3.99 *(978-0-06-444020-2(6))* HarperCollins Pubs.

—The Frog & Toad Collection, Set. Lobel, Arnold, illus. 2004. (I Can Read Level 2 Ser.). (Illus.). 13p. (J). (gr. k-3). pap. 11.99 *(978-0-06-058086-5(0))* HarperCollins Pubs.

—Frog & Toad Storybook Treasury. Lobel, Arnold, illus. 2013. (I Can Read Level 2 Ser.). (ENG., Illus.). 256p. (J). (gr. -1-3). 11.99 *(978-0-06-229258-2(7))* HarperCollins Pubs.

—Sapo y Sepo, Inseparables. Lobel, Arnold, illus. 2003.Tr. of Frog & Toad Together. (SPA., Illus.). 68p. (J). (gr. -1-3). 12.95 *(978-84-204-3047-8(1))* Ediciones Alfaguara ESP. Dist: Lectorum Pubns., Inc., Santillana USA Publishing Co., Inc.

Lobel, Arnold & Lobel, Adrianne. The Frogs & Toads All Sang. Lobel, Arnold & Lobel, Adrianne, illus. 2009. (ENG., Illus.). 32p. (J). (gr. -1-2). 16.99 *(978-0-06-180022-1(8))* HarperCollins Pubs.

Lobel, Gill. Little Bear's Special Wish. Hansen, Gaby, illus. 2004. 32p. (J). tchr. ed. 16.95 *(978-1-58925-034-5(6))* Tiger Tales.

Lombardi, Kristine A. Mr. Biddles. Lombardi, Kristine A., illus. 2017. (Illus.). 40p. (J). (gr. -1-3). 17.99 ***(978-0-06-244114-0(0))*** HarperCollins Pubs.

London, Jonathan. Froggy Builds a Tree House. 2013. (Froggy Ser.). (ENG.). 32p. (J). (-k). pap. 6.99 *(978-0-14-242533-6(8),* Puffin Books) Penguin Young Readers Group.

—Froggy Builds a Tree House. 2013. (Froggy Ser.). lib. bdg. 17.20 *(978-0-606-30518-1(1),* Turtleback) Turtleback Bks.

—Froggy Eats Out. 2004. (Illus.). (J). (gr. -1-18). spiral bd. *(978-0-616-11117-8(7));* spiral bd. *(978-0-616-11118-5(5))* Canadian National Institute for the Blind/Institut National Canadien pour les Aveugles.

—Froggy Eats Out. Remkiewicz, Frank, illus. 2003. (Froggy Ser.). (ENG.). 32p. (J). (gr. -1-k). pap. 6.99 *(978-0-14-250061-3(5),* Puffin Books) Penguin Young Readers Group.

—Froggy Eats Out. Remkiewicz, Frank, illus. 2003. (Froggy Ser.). 13.65 *(978-0-7569-1464-6(7))* Perfection Learning Corp.

—Froggy Eats Out. 2003. (Froggy Ser.). (gr. k-3). lib. bdg. 17.20 *(978-0-613-67453-9(7),* Turtleback) Turtleback Bks.

—Froggy Gets a Doggy. Remkiewicz, Frank, illus. (Froggy Ser.). (ENG.). 32p. (J). (gr. -1-k). 2015. 6.99 *(978-0-14-242230-4(4),* Puffin Books) 2014. 16.99 *(978-0-670-01428-6(1),* Viking Books for Young Readers) Penguin Young Readers Group.

—Froggy Gets Dressed, 1 vol. Remkiewicz, Frank, illus. 2007. (Froggy Ser.). (ENG.). 15p. (J). (gr. -1-k). 9.99 *(978-0-14-240870-4(0),* Puffin Books) Penguin Young Readers Group.

E
F
G

—Froggy Goes to Camp. Remkiewicz, Frank, illus. 2010. (Froggy Ser.). (ENG.). 32p. (J). (gr. -1-k). pap. 6.99 *(978-0-14-241604-4(5),* Puffin Books) Penguin Young Readers Group.
—Froggy Goes to Grandma's. 2017. (Froggy Ser.). (ENG., Illus.). 32p. (J). (-k). 16.99 *(978-1-101-99964-6(0),* Viking Books for Young Readers) Penguin Young Readers Group.
—Froggy Goes to Hawaii. Remkiewicz, Frank, illus. 2012. (Froggy Ser.). (ENG.). 32p. (J). (gr. -1-k). pap. 6.99 *(978-0-14-242119-2(7),* Puffin Books) Penguin Young Readers Group.
—Froggy Goes to Hawaii. 2012. (Froggy Ser.). lib. bdg. 17.20 *(978-0-606-26083-1(8),* Turtleback) Turtleback Bks.
—Froggy Goes to School. Remkiewicz, Frank, illus. 2006. (Froggy Ser.). 28p. (gr. -1-1). 16.00 *(978-0-7569-6986-8(7))* Perfection Learning Corp.
—Froggy Goes to the Doctor. 2004. (Illus.). (J). (gr. k-3). spiral bd. *(978-0-616-14585-2(3));* spiral bd. *(978-0-616-14586-9(1))* Canadian National Institute for the Blind/Institut National Canadien pour les Aveugles.
—Froggy Goes to the Doctor. Remkiewicz, Frank, illus. 2004. (Froggy Ser.). (ENG.). 32p. (J). (gr. -1-k). pap. 6.99 *(978-0-14-240193-4(5),* Puffin Books) Penguin Young Readers Group.
—Froggy Goes to the Doctor. 2004. (Froggy Ser.). (J). (gr. -1-18). 1.25 *(978-1-4025-3420-1(5))* Recorded Bks., Inc.
—Froggy Goes to the Library. Remkiewicz, Frank, illus. 2016. (Froggy Ser.). (ENG.). 32p. (J). (gr. -1-k). 16.99 *(978-0-670-01573-3(3),* Viking Books for Young Readers) Penguin Young Readers Group.
—Froggy Goes to the Library. 2017. (Froggy Ser.). lib. bdg. 17.20 ***(978-0-606-39799-5(X))*** Turtleback Bks.
—Froggy Plays in the Band. Remkiewicz, Frank & Frank, Remkiewicz, illus. 2004. (Froggy Ser.). (ENG.). 32p. (J). (gr. -1-k). 6.99 *(978-0-14-240051-7(3),* Puffin Books) Penguin Young Readers Group.
—Froggy Plays in the Band. Remkiewicz, Frank, illus. 2004. (Froggy Ser.). (J). (gr. -1-3). 13.65 *(978-0-7569-2955-8(5))* Perfection Learning Corp.
—Froggy's Baby Sister. Remkiewicz, Frank, illus. 2005. (Froggy Ser.). (ENG.). 32p. (J). (gr. -1-k). pap. 6.99 *(978-0-14-240342-6(3),* Puffin Books) Penguin Young Readers Group.
—Froggy's Best Babysitter. Remkiewicz, Frank, illus. 2011. (Froggy Ser.). (ENG.). 32p. (J). (gr. -1-k). pap. 6.99 *(978-0-14-241899-4(4),* Puffin Books) Penguin Young Readers Group.
—Froggy's Birthday Wish. Remkiewicz, Frank, illus. 2016. (Froggy Ser.). (ENG.). 32p. (J). (-k). 6.99 *(978-0-14-751799-9(0),* Puffin Books) Penguin Young Readers Group.
—Froggy's Day with Dad. Remkiewicz, Frank, illus. 2006. (Froggy Ser.). (ENG.). 32p. (J). (gr. -1-k). pap. 6.99 *(978-0-14-240634-2(1),* Puffin Books) Penguin Young Readers Group.
—Froggy's Halloween. Remkiewicz, Frank, illus. 2010. lib. bdg. 16.10 *(978-0-7569-8999-6(X))* Penguin Publishing Group.
—Froggy's Sleepover. Remkiewicz, Frank, illus. 2007. (Froggy Ser.). (ENG.). 32p. (J). (gr. -1-k). pap. 6.99 *(978-0-14-240750-9(X),* Puffin Books) Penguin Young Readers Group.
—Froggy's Worst Playdate. Remkiewicz, Frank, illus. (Froggy Ser.). (ENG.). 32p. (J). (gr. -1-k). 2015. pap. 6.99 *(978-0-14-242229-8(0),* Puffin Books) 2013. 16.99 *(978-0-670-01427-9(3),* Viking Books for Young Readers) Penguin Young Readers Group.
London, Jonathan & Bader, Bonnie. Froggy Is the Best. Remkiewicz, Frank, illus. 2015. (Froggy Ser.). (ENG.). 32p. (J). (gr. 1-2). 3.99 *(978-0-448-48380-1(7),* Penguin Young Readers) Penguin Young Readers Group.
London, Jonathan & Remkiewicz, Frank. Froggy Plays T-Ball. Remkiewicz, Frank, illus. 2009. (Froggy Ser.). (ENG., Illus.). 32p. (J). (gr. -1-k). pap. 6.99 *(978-0-14-241304-3(6),* Puffin Books) Penguin Young Readers Group.
—Froggy Rides a Bike. Remkiewicz, Frank & Remkiewicz, F., illus. 2008. (Froggy Ser.). (ENG.). 32p. (J). (gr. -1-k). pap. 6.99 *(978-0-14-241067-7(5),* Puffin Books) Penguin Young Readers Group.
London, Jonathan & Wells, Rosemary. Froggy's Birthday Wish. Remkiewicz, Frank, illus. 2015. (Froggy Ser.). (ENG.). 32p. (J). (gr. -1-k). bds. 16.99 *(978-0-670-01572-6(5),* Viking Books for Young Readers) Penguin Young Readers Group.
Long, Ethan. The Croaky Pokey! Long, Ethan, illus. 2012. (ENG., Illus.). 32p. (J). pap. 6.95 *(978-0-8234-2429-0(4))* Holiday Hse., Inc.
Lopatina, Irina. Tales from the Frog Forest. Lopatin, Dmitry, tr. Shapiro, Alla, illus. 2012. (ENG.). 48p. (J). 18.00 *(978-1-61153-022-3(9))* Light Messages Publishing.
Lowvorn, Ann R. Chocolate Puddles. Reece, James A., illus. 2010. 36p. pap. 15.49 *(978-1-4520-5158-1(5))* AuthorHouse.
Lutz II, William. A Frog from Anoratum. 2008. 124p. pap. 11.00 *(978-0-615-18287-2(9))* Lutz, William G.
Lyles, Tanya. The Frog That Needed an Umbrella. 2006. 17.00 *(978-0-8059-9906-8(X))* Dorrance Publishing Co., Inc.
Lynne, Kimberlee, illus. The Frog & the Mouse. 2011. (First Steps in Music Ser.). (ENG.). 32p. (J). (gr. k-2). 16.95 *(978-1-57999-802-8(X))* G I A Pubns., Inc.
Mack, Jeff. Ah Ha! 2013. (ENG., Illus.). 40p. (J). (gr. -1-k). 16.99 *(978-1-4521-1265-7(7))* Chronicle Bks. LLC.
—Frog & Fly. 2012. (ENG.). 40p. (J). (gr. -1-k). 12.99 *(978-0-399-25617-2(2),* Philomel Bks.) Penguin Young Readers Group.
MacKenzie-Krysko, Claudia & Krysko, Kenneth L. The Adventures of Granville, Coming to America. Cotton, Sue Lynn, illus. 2013. 24p. pap. 12.95 *(978-1-61493-227-7(1))* Peppertree Pr., The.
MacIver, Juliette. The Frog Who Lost His Underpants. Chapman, Cat, illus. 2014. (ENG.). 32p. (J). (gr. -1-1). 14.99 *(978-0-7636-6782-5(X))* Candlewick Pr.
Macmillan, Sue. Hoppy Frog's Fly Spy. Ward, Sarah, illus. 2014. (Cheery Chasers Ser.). (ENG.). 8p. (J). (gr. -1 — 1). bds. 4.99 *(978-0-7641-6700-3(6))* Barron's Educational Series, Inc.
Magic Wagon Staff. A Flip-Flop Adventure, 1 vol. 2011. (Flip-Flop Adventure Ser.). (ENG., Illus.). 32p. 114.00 *(978-1-61641-650-8(5),* Looking Glass Library) Magic Wagon.
Marie, Dani. The Tale of Prince George. 2012. 28p. pap. 24.95 *(978-1-4626-8264-5(2))* America Star Bks.
Markle, Sandra. The Case of the Vanishing Golden Frogs: A Scientific Mystery. 2015. (ENG., Illus.). 48p. (gr. 4-6). 34.65 *(978-1-4677-5925-0(2),* Lerner Digital) Lerner Publishing Group.
Martin, David Lozell. Lucy & Bob: Brand New Readers. Martin, David Lozell, illus. 2006. (Brand New Readers Ser.). (ENG., Illus.). 48p. (J). (gr. -1-3). pap. 5.99 *(978-0-7636-2722-5(4))* Candlewick Pr.
Martin, Tamra. My Wish, Our Little Oat. Tinker, Jason, illus. 2007. 36p. (J). 21.99 *(978-1-59879-522-6(8),* Lifevest) Lifevest Publishing, Inc.
Marzollo, Jean. Funny Frog. 2012. (I Spy — Scholastic Ser.). lib. bdg. 13.55 *(978-0-606-23969-1(3),* Turtleback) Turtleback Bks.
Mather, David. A Frog in the House. 2011. 32p. (gr. 1-2). 16.95 *(978-0-9819307-9-4(4));* pap. 9.95 *(978-0-9819307-8-7(6))* Raven Productions, Inc.
Mayer, Marianna. One Frog Too Many. Mayer, Marianna, illus. 2003. (Boy, a Dog, & a Frog Ser.). (ENG., Illus.). 32p. (J). (gr. -1-k). 6.99 *(978-0-8037-2885-1(9),* Dial Bks) Penguin Young Readers Group.
Mayer, Marvin. Ferdinand Frog's Flight. Macquignon, Stephen, illus. 2011. 32p. pap. 15.55 *(978-0-9832740-0-1(2))* 4RV Publishing, LLC.
Mayer, Mercer. A Boy, a Dog, & a Frog. Mayer, Mercer, illus. 2003. (Boy, a Dog, & a Frog Ser.). (ENG., Illus.). 32p. (J). (gr. -1-k). 6.99 *(978-0-8037-2880-6(8),* Dial Bks) Penguin Young Readers Group.
—Frog Goes to Dinner. Mayer, Mercer, illus. 2003. (Boy, a Dog, & a Frog Ser.). (ENG., Illus.). 32p. (J). (gr. -1-k). 6.99 *(978-0-8037-2884-4(0),* Dial Bks) Penguin Young Readers Group.
—Frog on His Own. Mayer, Mercer, illus. 2003. (Boy, a Dog, & a Frog Ser.). (ENG., Illus.). 32p. (J). (gr. -1-k). 6.99 *(978-0-8037-2883-7(2),* Dial Bks) Penguin Young Readers Group.
—Frog, Where Are You? Mayer, Mercer, illus. 2003. (Boy, a Dog, & a Frog Ser.). (ENG., Illus.). 32p. (J). (gr. -1-k). 6.99 *(978-0-8037-2881-3(6),* Dial Bks) Penguin Young Readers Group.
Mcallister, Herb West. Doo West to Toadstool. 2011. 44p. pap. 21.99 *(978-1-4628-5530-8(X))* Xlibris Corp.
McClure, Brian D. The Birds & the Frogs. Plumlee, Buddy, illus. 2009. (Brian D. Mcclure Childrens Book Collection). 37p. (J). (gr. -1-3). 16.95 *(978-1-933426-13-6(6))* Universal Flag Publishing.
McDaniel, Carren. Fresh Air Friends: The Dangers of Secondhand Smoke. 2012. (ENG.). 33p. (J). pap. 14.95 *(978-1-4327-9818-5(9))* Outskirts Pr., Inc.
McDonald, Megan. Stink & the Freaky Frog Freakout. Reynolds, Peter H., illus. 2013. (Stink Ser.: 8). (ENG.). 160p. (J). (gr. 1-4). 12.99 *(978-0-7636-6140-3(6))* Candlewick Pr.
—Stink & the Freaky Frog Freakout. 2014. (Stink Ser.: 8). lib. bdg. 14.75 *(978-0-606-35164-5(7))* Turtleback Bks.
Mcfarland, Jewel. Zach & His Frog. 2010. 16p. 9.95 *(978-1-4520-4504-7(6))* AuthorHouse.
Mcgee, Cotton. Bookman's Adventures: The Valley of the Frogs. 2011. 52p. pap. 22.28 *(978-1-4389-4771-6(2))* AuthorHouse.
McGinnis, Chelsea. Mk Frogg & the Lily Pad Adventures, 1 vol. 2009. 48p. pap. 24.95 *(978-1-60813-548-6(9))* America Star Bks.
McGuckin, Mitchelle. Bullfrog Henry. 2010. 60p. pap. 23.99 *(978-1-4490-9547-5(X))* AuthorHouse.
McLellan, Stephanie Simpson. Leon's Song. Bonder, Dianna, illus. 2004. (ENG.). 32p. (J). (gr. -1-3). *(978-1-55041-813-2(0))* Fitzhenry & Whiteside, Ltd.
McNamee, Kevin. My Brother the Frog. Morris, Alexander, illus. 2011. 24p. 19.95 *(978-1-61633-167-2(4));* pap. 10.95 *(978-1-61633-159-7(3))* Guardian Angel Publishing, Inc.
McOmber, Rachel B., ed. McOmber Phonics Storybooks: Boe E. Toad. rev. ed. (Illus.). (J). *(978-0-944991-54-1(8))* Swift Learning Resources.
Merriweather-Beech, Myrtle. The Unfroggettable Fiona Fayetta Froggee: A Green Pond Memoir. Sanda-Ebosh, Mary, illus. 2009. 52p. pap. 24.99 *(978-1-4389-2585-1(9))* AuthorHouse.
Miah, Esmail. I Once Knew... 2012. (Illus.). 25p. pap. 8.49 *(978-1-78035-333-3(2),* Fastprint Publishing) Upfront Publishing Ltd. GBR. Dist: Printondemand-worldwide.com.
Michaels, J. C. Firebelly: A Journey into the Heart of Thinking. 2005. 254p. pap. 18.00 *(978-0-9726173-1-4(0));* 50.00 *(978-0-9726173-0-7(2))* Cascade, Inc. (Philograph).
Michaels, Kat. Willow's Bend. 2006. (Illus.). 24p. (J). (gr. -1-3). 15.95 *(978-0-9745052-6-8(9))* Tree Of Life Publishing.
Mike, Grandpa. Hoppy the Happy Frog: A Grandpa Mike Tale. 2011. 29p. (J). pap. 16.95 *(978-1-4327-5872-1(1))* Outskirts Pr., Inc.
Miles, Brenda. Stickley Makes a Mistake! A Frog's Guide to Trying Again. Mack, Steve, illus. 2016. 32p. (J). *(978-1-4338-2264-3(4),* Magination Pr.) American Psychological Assn.
—Stickley Sticks to It! A Frog's Guide to Getting Things Done. Mack, Steve, illus. 2014. 27p. (J). *(978-1-4338-1910-0(4),* Magination Pr.) American Psychological Assn.
Milton, Cathlene. The Wonders of Billy Sniggles: Billy Sniggles Sees a Frog. 2013. 20p. pap. 9.99 *(978-1-62509-778-1(6))* Salem Author Services.
Missing Hog. 2004. (J). per. *(978-1-57657-374-7(5))* Paradise Pr., Inc.
Mitton, Tony. Down by the Cool of the Pool (a StoryPlay Book) Parker-Rees, Guy, illus. 2017. (StoryPlay Ser.). (ENG.). 32p. (J). (gr. -1-k). 5.99 ***(978-1-338-15841-0(4),*** Cartwheel Bks.) Scholastic, Inc.
Mlynowski, Sarah. Once upon a Frog. (Whatever After Ser.: 8). (ENG.). 176p. (J). (gr. 3-7). 2017. pap. 5.99 ***(978-0-545-74663-2(9))*** 2015. (Illus.). 14.99 *(978-0-545-74660-1(4))* Scholastic, Inc. (Scholastic Pr.).
Montes, Graciela. Cuentos del Sapo. 2003. (SPA.). *(978-950-07-1900-1(2),* SA31240) Editorial Sudamericana S.A. ARG. Dist: Lectorum Pubns., Inc.
Moore, Alison. What the Pond Frog Said. 2011. 60p. pap. 28.04 *(978-1-4568-2758-8(8))* Xlibris Corp.
Mora, Pat. Wiggling Pockets (Los Bolsillos Saltarines) Suarez, Maribel, illus. 2009. (My Family: Mi Familia Ser.). (SPA & ENG.). 24p. (J). (gr. -1-1). 12.99 *(978-0-06-085047-0(7),* Rayo) HarperCollins Pubs.
Moss, Patricia Crocker. Dillie & the Dragonfly. 2012. 32p. pap. 21.99 *(978-1-4691-7821-9(4))* Xlibris Corp.
Murakami, Yasanuri & Kimura, ken, illus. 999 Frogs & a Little Brother. 2015. (ENG.). 40p. (J). 17.95 *(978-0-7358-4202-1(7))* North-South Bks., Inc.
Nakagawa, Masafumi. Dr. Mouse's Mission. Perry, Mia Lynn, tr. Yamawaki, Yuriko, illus. 2007. (R. I. C. Story Chest Ser.). 27p. (J). (gr. -1-1). 14.95 incl. audio compact disk *(978-1-74126-051-9(5))* R.I.C. Pubns. AUS. Dist: SCB Distributors.
Nanette. Blue the Frog. 2004. (Life on Granny's Farm Ser.). (J). 12.95 *(978-0-9741269-2-0(6))* St. Bernard Publishing, LLC.
Nevis, Lance. The Pollywog Prince. Laible MBA, Steve William, ed. Piper, Tom, illus. 2012. 46p. pap. 10.99 *(978-0-9850142-8-5(8))* Kodel Group, LLC, The.
Nilsson, Ulf. Detective Gordon - The First Case. Spee, Gitte, illus. 2015. (Detective Gordon Ser.). (ENG.). 96p. (J). (gr. k-5). 16.99 *(978-1-927271-49-0(5))* Gecko Pr. NZL. Dist: Lerner Publishing Group.
El Nino y las Ranas. (SPA.). pap. 5.95 incl. audio compact disk *(978-88-8148-796-7(9))* EMC/Paradigm Publishing.
Nosy Crow Staff. Little Bubba Looks for His Elephant. Ho, Jannie, illus. 2014. (ENG.). 8p. (J). (— 1). bds. 7.99 *(978-0-7636-7401-4(X),* Nosy Crow) Candlewick Pr.
Nourse, Audrey S. & Shelton, Giulia M. Timothy Tree Frog. 2010. 44p. pap. 18.99 *(978-1-4490-5462-5(5))* AuthorHouse.
O'Boyle, Laurel. Froggy & Bug, 1 vol. 2010. 28p. pap. 24.95 *(978-1-4489-7068-1(7))* PublishAmerica, Inc.
O'Connor, Barbara. The Fantastic Secret of Owen Jester. 2010. (ENG.). 176p. (J). (gr. 3-7). 15.99 *(978-0-374-36850-0(3),* 9780374368500, Farrar, Straus & Giroux (BYR)) Farrar, Straus & Giroux.
—The Fantastic Secret of Owen Jester. 2011. (ENG.). 192p. (J). (gr. 3-7). pap. 7.99 *(978-0-312-67430-4(9),* 9780312674304) Square Fish.
O'Donnell, Kerri. King of the Swamp. 2006. (Neighborhood Readers Ser.). (ENG.). 16p. (gr. 1-3). pap. 6.50 *(978-1-4042-7216-3(X),* Rosen Classroom) Rosen Publishing Group, Inc., The.
Oldaugh, Charles. The Frog Knight. 2011. 28p. (gr. 1-2). pap. 16.99 *(978-1-4567-6198-1(6))* AuthorHouse.
Oneto, Maria Teresa. Liliana, la Iguan. 2012. 52p. pap. 25.00 *(978-1-4389-8241-0(0))* AuthorHouse.
O'Rourke, Molly. The Adventures of Gleeson & Cormac: Why Do People Cry? 2013. 28p. pap. 12.50 *(978-1-62212-880-8(X),* Strategic Bk. Publishing) Strategic Book Publishing & Rights Agency (SBPRA).
Osborn, D. W. Why Can't I Ribbit?, 1 vol. 2009. 48p. pap. 16.95 *(978-1-61582-641-4(6))* America Star Bks.
Pakalne, Violeta. A Motorcyclist Croaker Lee. 2010. 80p. pap. 29.49 *(978-1-4520-9578-3(7))* AuthorHouse.
Parenteau, Shirley. One Frog Sang. Jabar, Cynthia, illus. 2007. (ENG.). 32p. (J). (gr. -1-2). 15.99 *(978-0-7636-2394-4(6))* Candlewick Pr.
Parker, Emma. The Frog That Did Not Like Water. 2010. (Illus.). pap. *(978-1-877547-93-5(X))* First Edition Ltd.
Parker, Vic, ed. The Frog & the Ox & Other Fables. 2014. (Aesop's Fables Ser.). 40p. (J). (gr. 2-5). pap. 84.95 *(978-1-4824-1256-7(X))* Stevens, Gareth Publishing LLLP.
Patton, Jack. The Poison Frog Assault (Battle Bugs #3) 2015. (Battle Bugs Ser.: 3). (ENG.). 128p. (J). (gr. 2-5). pap. 4.99 *(978-0-545-70744-2(7),* Scholastic Paperbacks) Scholastic, Inc.
Peakler, Nicole Danette. Tayno Ti & the Legend of the Coqui. 2012. 28p. 24.95 *(978-1-4626-5940-1(3))* America Star Bks.
Penecale Jr., Richard P. The Luckiest Frog. 2009. 33p. (J). pap. 24.95 *(978-1-4327-3023-9(1))* Outskirts Pr., Inc.
Pepin, Rebecca. Bobby Dog & the Flying Frog. Fuller, Cari, illus. 2004. (J). (gr. 4-18). 16.99 *(978-0-9760684-0-2(0));* pap. 11.99 *(978-0-9760684-1-9(9))* FullofPep Pubns.
Perry, Dave, et al. Thwacked! A Fractured Fable of Frogs, Folks & Falling Skies. 2011. (ENG.). 260p. pap. 19.99 *(978-1-4234-9857-5(7),* 1423498577); 72p. pap. 19.99 *(978-1-4234-9856-8(9),* 1423498569) Shawnee Pr., Inc.
Petty, Dev. I Don't Want to Be a Frog. Boldt, Mike, illus. (ENG.). 32p. (J). (gr. -1-2). 2016. 16.99 *(978-1-101-93920-8(6))* 2015. lib. bdg. 19.99 *(978-0-375-97334-5(6))* Random Hse. Children's Bks. (Doubleday Bks. for Young Readers).
Petty, Dev. There's Nothing to Do! Boldt, Mike, illus. 2017. (ENG.). 32p. (J). (gr. -1-2). 16.99 ***(978-0-399-55803-0(9));*** lib. bdg. 19.99 ***(978-0-399-55804-7(7))*** Random Hse. Children's Bks. (Doubleday Bks. for Young Readers).
Pigman, Shari. Little Frog Finds Jesus. 2005. 23p. (J). 12.67 *(978-1-4116-5779-3(9))* Lulu Pr., Inc.
Pinkwater, Daniel M. Bear & Bunny. Hillenbrand, Will, illus. 2015. (ENG.). 40p. (J). 15.99 *(978-0-7636-7153-2(3))* Candlewick Pr.
Pixton, Kaaren. Plip, Plop, Pond! Hey Baby! Look at These Animals in the Pond! 2010. (Indestructibles Ser.). (ENG., Illus.). 12p. (J). (gr. k — 1). pap. 5.95 *(978-0-7611-5857-8(X),* 15857) Workman Publishing Co., Inc.
Plitt, Kay. Why Isn't Bobby Like Me, Mom? 2010. 32p. 14.75 *(978-1-4269-4038-5(6))* Trafford Publishing.
Plonk, Michelle. Fritz, the Forgetful Frog. 2009. 40p. pap. 18.50 *(978-1-60860-123-3(4),* Eloquent Bks.) Strategic Book Publishing & Rights Agency (SBPRA).
Pockat, Alison A. Adam's Bubble. 2010. 76p. pap. 10.49 *(978-1-4490-9287-0(X))* AuthorHouse.
Police, Gerard. Herbert the Frog Goes to the Store. 2008. 20p. pap. 13.50 *(978-1-60693-066-3(4),* Eloquent Bks.) Strategic Book Publishing & Rights Agency (SBPRA).
Pope, Stephanie L. Fedo the Frog Flew the Coop. 2012. 16p. pap. 15.99 *(978-1-4772-1656-9(1))* AuthorHouse.
Post, Jim. Frog in the Kitchen Sink. Vasconcellos, Daniel, illus. 2015. (ENG.). 26p. (J). bds. 9.99 *(978-1-4494-6709-8(1))* Andrews McMeel Publishing.
Potter, Beatrix. The Classic Tale of Mr. Jeremy Fisher. Santore, Charles, illus. 2015. (ENG.). 22p. (J). bds. 8.95 *(978-1-60433-548-4(3),* Applesauce Pr.) Cider Mill Pr. Bk. Pubs., LLC.
—The Tale of Mr. Jeremy Fisher, 1 vol. Jorgensen, David, illus. 2005. (Rabbit Ears: A Classic Tale Ser.). (ENG.). 28p. (gr. 2-7). 25.65 *(978-1-59197-753-7(3))* Spotlight.
—The Tale of Mr. Jeremy Fisher. (Beatrix Potter Bookmark Board Book Ser.). (Illus.). 6p. (J). bds. 3.95 *(978-1-58989-202-6(X))* Thurman Hse., LLC.
Powell, Patricia Hruby. Ch'at to Yinilo'/Frog Brings Rain. Thomas, Peter A., tr. Benally, Kendrick, illus. 2006. (NAV & ENG.). 32p. (J). (gr. 4-7). 17.95 *(978-1-893354-08-1(3))* Salina Bookshelf Inc.
Powell, Richard. Frog. Gardner, Louise, illus. 2014. (Bathing Beauties Ser.). (ENG.). 8p. (J). (gr. -1 — 1). 7.99 *(978-1-4380-7443-6(3))* Barron's Educational Series, Inc.
Prelutsky, Jack. The Frogs Wore Red Suspenders. Mathers, Petra, illus. 2005. (ENG.). 64p. (J). (gr. k-5). reprint ed. pap. 6.99 *(978-0-06-073776-4(X),* Greenwillow Bks.) HarperCollins Pubs.
Price, Mathew. Polo y la Rana. (SPA.). pap. 7.95 *(978-950-07-1979-7(7))* Editorial Sudamericana S.A. ARG. Dist: Distribooks, Inc.
Princess & Frog. (Ladybird Bks.). (Illus.). 52p. (J). 12.95 incl. audio *(978-0-86685-634-8(X))* International Bk. Ctr., Inc.
Proud, Amy. Izzy the Very Bad Burglar. 2016. (ENG., Illus.). 32p. (J). (gr. -1-k). 16.99 *(978-1-63450-174-3(8),* Sky Pony Pr.) Skyhorse Publishing Co., Inc.
Pryce, Trevor. Amphibians' End. Greene, Sanford, illus. 2016. (Kulipari Ser.). (ENG.). 304p. (J). (gr. 3-7). pap. 8.95 *(978-1-4197-2194-6(1),* Amulet Bks.) Abrams, Inc.
—An Army of Frogs. Greene, Sanford, illus. 2013. (Kulipari Ser.). (ENG.). 288p. (J). (gr. 3-7). 15.95 *(978-1-4197-0172-6(X),* Amulet Bks.) Abrams, Inc.
Pryce, Trevor & Naftali, Joel. Amphibians' End. 2015. (Kulipari Ser.). (ENG., Illus.). 304p. (J). (gr. 3-7). 15.95 *(978-1-4197-1648-5(4),* Amulet Bks.) Abrams, Inc.
—An Army of Frogs. Greene, Sanford, illus. 2014. (Kulipari Ser.). (ENG.). 304p. (J). (gr. 3-7). pap. 8.95 *(978-1-4197-1381-1(7),* Amulet Bks.) Abrams, Inc.
—The Rainbow Serpent. Greene, Sanford, illus. 2014. (Kulipari Ser.). (ENG.). 304p. (J). (gr. 3-7). 15.95 *(978-1-4197-1309-5(4),* Amulet Bks.) Abrams, Inc.
Publications International Ltd. Staff, ed. Little Sound the Princess & the Frog. 2009. 24p. (J). bds. 10.98 *(978-1-4127-6446-9(7))* Publications International, Ltd.
—The Princess & the Frog. 2009. 24p. (J). 16.98 *(978-1-4127-6421-6(1))* Publications International, Ltd.
Pugliano-Martin, Carol. A Frog Someday. 2006. (Early Explorers Ser.). (J). pap. *(978-1-4108-6099-6(X))* Benchmark Education Co.
Quinton, Sasha. Hoppity-Hop: A Phonics Reader. 2009. (Illus.). pap. *(978-1-936199-02-0(5))* Book Shop, Ltd., The.
Rae, Jennifer. Gilbert de la Frogponde: A Swamp Story. braille ed. 2004. (Illus.). (J). (gr. k-3). spiral bd. *(978-0-616-03054-7(1));* spiral bd. *(978-0-616-04561-9(1))* Canadian National Institute for the Blind/Institut National Canadien pour les Aveugles.
Rai, Lori. Princess Sheron & the Frog. l.t. ed. 2004. (Illus.). 20p. (J). 10.00 *(978-0-9717419-5-9(6))* Law Offices of Harry Glick.
Ramirez, Martha. The Fabulous Adventures of Fred the Frog. 2008. 48p. pap. 24.95 *(978-1-60474-799-7(4))* America Star Bks.
Ramos, Odalys Q. Allow Me to Introduce Myself. Graham, Michael, illus. 2012. 24p. (-18). pap. 12.95 *(978-1-61493-121-8(6))* Peppertree Pr., The.
Randall, Marilyn. Inside Out. 2009. 26p. 18.95 *(978-0-557-15699-3(8))* Lulu Pr., Inc.
Randolph, Joanne. Frankie: A Frog's Story. 2009. (Nature Stories Ser.). (Illus.). 24p. (J). (gr. -1-2). pap. 8.15 *(978-1-60754-096-0(7));* lib. bdg. 22.60 *(978-1-60754-095-3(9))* Windmill Bks.
Rankine-Van Wassenhoven, Jacqueline. A Frog Named Waldor. Zhang, Annie, illus. 2008. 20p. per. 24.95 *(978-1-4241-9926-6(3))* America Star Bks.
Ratcliff, Charline. The Princess, the Toad & the Whale. 2012. (ENG.). 36p. (J). (-18). pap. 12.95 *(978-1-4787-1672-3(X))* Outskirts Pr., Inc.
Reasoner, Charles. I'm Just a Frog. 2008. *(978-1-84666-159-4(5))* Top That! Publishing PLC.
Rees, Gwyneth. Cosmo & the Secret Spell, 1. Hearn, Samuel, illus. unabr. ed. 2010. (Cosmo Ser.: 3). (ENG.). 208p. (J). (gr. 2-4). pap. 7.99 *(978-0-330-44216-9(3))* Macmillan Pubs., Ltd. GBR. Dist: Independent Pubs. Group.
Reid, James. This Is My Story by Frederick G. Frog, 1 vol. rev. ed. 2013. (Fiction Readers Ser.). (ENG., Illus.). 20p. (J). (gr. 1-1). pap. 15.96 *(978-1-4807-1140-2(3));* pap. 4.99 *(978-1-4333-5484-7(5))* Shell Educational Publishing.
RH Disney Staff. The Princess & the Frog. RH Disney Staff, illus. 2009. (Little Golden Book Ser.). (ENG., Illus.). 24p. (J). (gr. -1-2). 4.99 *(978-0-7364-2628-2(0),* Golden/Disney) Random Hse. Children's Bks.
Richemont, Enid. Princess Frog. 2014. (ENG., Illus.). 32p. (J). *(978-0-7787-0443-0(2));* pap. *(978-0-7787-0452-2(1))* Crabtree Publishing Co.
Richter, Debra A. Two Frogs & the Lost Wedding Band. 2012. 32p. 24.95 *(978-1-4626-4343-1(4))* America Star Bks.
Rigby Education Staff. A Frog at Home. (Illus.). 16p. (J). pap. 30.00 *(978-0-7635-6470-4(2),* 764702C99) Rigby Education.
—Frog Prince: Jumbled Tumble. (gr. k-2). 26.00 *(978-0-7635-2417-3(4))* Rigby Education.
Rimes, Rebecca. Hippie Hippopotamus. 2011. 24p. (gr. 10-12). pap. 12.74 *(978-1-4634-0855-8(2))* AuthorHouse.
Roberts, Daniel. The Ghost of Froggy's Swamp. 2012. 36p. pap. 18.99 *(978-1-4772-0316-3(8))* AuthorHouse.
Roberts, Sarah E. Lunch with Sam & Max. 2012. 20p. pap. 17.99 *(978-1-4772-9053-8(2))* AuthorHouse.
Robleda, Margarita. Sana Ranita, Sana. Suarez, Maribel, illus. (Rana, Rema, Rimas Ser.).Tr. of Kiss Away My Boo-Boo. (SPA.). 16p. (J). (gr. k-3). 7.95 *(978-1-59437-820-1(7))* Santillana USA Publishing Co., Inc.
Rodriguez, Ed. Kiki Koki: La Leyenda Encantada del Coquí. 2015.Tr. of Kiki Koki - The Enchanted Legend of the Coquí Frog. (SPA & ENG., Illus.). 40p. (J). (gr. -1-3). 17.99 *(978-1-62672-104-3(1),* 9781626721043) Roaring Brook Pr.
—Kiki Koki: La Leyenda Encantada Del Coquí (Kiki Koki: the Enchanted Legend of the Coquí Frog) 2015. (SPA., Illus.). 40p. (J). (gr. -1-3). 8.99 *(978-1-62672-132-6(7),* 9781626721326) Roaring Brook Pr.

Rogers, Wanda. Polliwog Pete. 2013. 24p. pap. (978-1-77097-968-0(9)) FriesenPress.

Rose, Chloe Gayle & Rose, Tammy Marie. The Snake That Eats Cake. 2012. 28p. pap. 24.95 (978-1-4626-9882-0(4)) America Star Bks.

Rose, Jeremy. The Frog & the Fly. 2013. 28p. pap. 16.99 (978-1-4624-0517-6(7), Inspiring Voices) Author Solutions, Inc.

Rosenlund, Ranee. Benny the Frog's Leap of Faith. 2010. 16p. 8.49 (978-1-4490-5408-3(0)) AuthorHouse.

Rosenlund, Ranee Mercier. Benny the Frog & His New Friends. 2012. 20p. pap. 17.99 (978-1-4772-9630-1(1)) AuthorHouse.

Rosenthal, Michele Marie. The Frog & the Tadpole's Great Swamp Adventure, 1 vol. 2009. 22p. pap. 24.95 (978-1-61546-178-3(7)) America Star Bks.

Rosenthal, Sally. Matzo Frogs. Sheldon, David, illus. 2014. (ENG.). 32p. (J). 17.95 (978-1-58838-302-0(4), NewSouth Bks.) NewSouth, Inc.

Rosno, Connie. This Is My Lucky Day. 2011. 16p. pap. 9.49 (978-1-4567-5534-8(X)) AuthorHouse.

Ross, Dev. We Both Read Bilingual Edition-Frank & the Tiger/Sapi y el Tigre. Canetti, Yanitzia, tr. from ENG. Reinhart, Larry, illus. 2014. (We Both Read - Level K-1 (Quality) Ser.). (ENG & SPA.). 44p. (J). (gr. k-1). pap. 4.99 (978-1-60115-058-5(X)) Treasure Bay, Inc.

—We Both Read-Frank & the Balloon: Level K-1. Reinhart, Larry, illus. (We Both Read Ser.). 44p. (J). (gr. -1-2). 2008. per. 4.99 (978-1-60115-012-7(1)) 2007. 7.99 (978-1-60115-011-0(3)) Treasure Bay, Inc.

—We Both Read-Frank & the Giant. 2005. (We Both Read Ser.). (Illus.). 44p. (J). (gr. -1-2). 7.99 (978-1-891327-59-9(3)); per. 4.99 (978-1-891327-60-5(7)) Treasure Bay, Inc.

—We Both Read-Frank & the Giant (Picture Book) Reinhart, Larry, illus. 2007. (We Both Read Ser.). 44p. (J). (gr. -1-2). lib. bdg. 14.95 (978-1-60115-006-6(7)) Treasure Bay, Inc.

—We Both Read-Frank & the Tiger. Reinhart, Larry, illus. 44p. (J). 2012. pap. 4.99 (978-1-60115-260-2(4)) 2011. 9.95 (978-1-60115-259-6(0)) Treasure Bay, Inc.

Ross, Margaret Clark. Jumpy the Frog Learns the Meaning of Love, 1 vol. McNeely, William, illus. 2010. 20p. pap. 24.95 (978-1-4489-8370-4(3)) PublishAmerica, Inc.

Rossbacher, John R. T. O. A. D. Trombone Ollie & Dyslexia. 2011. 124p. (gr. 4-6). 21.49 (978-1-4567-3941-6(7)); pap. 12.49 (978-1-4567-3942-3(5)) AuthorHouse.

Rouss, Sylvia A. The Littlest Frog. Hannon, Holly, illus. 2005. 32p. (J). pap. 9.95 (978-1-930143-13-5(3)); (gr. -1-1). 14.95 (978-1-930143-12-8(5)) Simcha Media Group. (Devora Publishing).

Rovetch, L. Bob. Frog Went A-Dancing. Berry, Holly, illus. 2006. (J). (978-1-58987-008-6(5)) Kindermusik International.

Roy, Alene Adele. The Legend of Dragonfly Pond: Volume One. 2008. 60p. pap. 24.99 (978-1-4343-6824-9(6)) AuthorHouse.

Ruddock, Evie. Mozart the Singing Frog. 2006. 7p. (J). 10.58 (978-1-4116-8530-7(X)) Lulu Pr., Inc.

Rudnick, Arnold. Little Green. Gorenman, Marcelo, illus. 2012. 32p. (J). pap. 9.99 (978-0-9815879-7-4(6)) Paraphrase, LLC.

Russell-Gilmer, Phyllis A. Where Do Crickets Go When Winter Comes? Jones, Chamira, illus. 2009. 32p. (J). 16.95 (978-1-934363-10-2(3)) Zoe Life Publishing.

Sage, Angie. Frognapped. Pickering, Jimmy, illus. 2008. (Araminta Spookie Ser.: 3). (ENG.). 224p. (J). (gr. 2-5). pap. 6.99 (978-0-06-077489-9(4), Tegen, Katherine Bks) HarperCollins Pubs.

Saito, Taeko. Kiss the Frog. 2010. (Princess & the Frog Ser.). (JPN., Illus.). (J). bds. (978-4-06-262548-7(2)) Kodansha America, Inc.

Sakmar-Sullivan, Eva M. The Silly Looking Thing, 1 vol. 2012. (ENG., Illus.). 40p. (J). 16.99 (978-0-7643-4144-1(8), 9780764341441) Schiffer Publishing, Ltd.

Salmon, Casey. The Adventures of Mabel & Stinky: Mabel, Stinky, & the Terrified Toad. 2009. 44p. pap. 19.99 (978-1-4389-7454-5(X)) AuthorHouse.

Sampson, Brent. One Wacky Wasp: The Perfect Children's Book for Kids Ages 3-6 Who Are Learning to Read. 2010. 24p. (J). 14.95 (978-1-4327-6217-9(6)); pap. 9.95 (978-1-4327-0465-0(6)) Outskirts Pr., Inc.

Sandusky, Thomas. The Frogs Stopped Singing. 2011. pap. 8.95 (978-0-7414-6450-7(0)) Infinity Publishing.

Sandusky, Thomas & Hill, Kathy. Gracie, the Glass Tree Frog. Johnson, Gretchen, illus. 2008. 24p. pap. 12.95 (978-0-9820479-2-7(4)) Peppertree Pr., The.

—Peter the Poison Dart Frog, Stories of the Rainforest. Johnson, Gretchen, illus. 2011. 24p. pap. 12.95 (978-1-936343-85-0(1)) Peppertree Pr., The.

Sang, Franchesca Ho, compiled by. Wisdom of Frogs. 2006. (Wisdom of Animals Ser.). (Illus.). 128p. (J). (gr. k). (978-1-59258-251-8(6)) Hylas Publishing.

Sanrio Company, LTD. Hello Kitty Presents the Storybook Collection: Thumbelina. 2017. (Hello Kitty Storybook Ser.). (ENG., Illus.). 32p. (J). (gr. -1-k). pap. 6.95 (978-1-4197-2489-3(4), Abrams Appleseed) Abrams, Inc.

Santillo, LuAnn. The Kiss. Santillo, LuAnn, ed. 2003. (Half-Pint Kids Readers Ser.). (Illus.). 7p. (J). (gr. -1-1). pap. 1.00 (978-1-59256-053-0(9)) Half-Pint Kids, Inc.

—Look at Me. Santillo, LuAnn, ed. 2003. (Half-Pint Kids Readers Ser.). (Illus.). 7p. (J). (gr. -1-1). pap. 1.00 (978-1-59256-052-3(0)) Half-Pint Kids, Inc.

—Mole. Santillo, LuAnn, ed. 2003. (Half-Pint Kids Readers Ser.). (Illus.). 7p. (J). (gr. -1-1). pap. (978-1-59256-111-7(X)) Half-Pint Kids, Inc.

—Toad. Santillo, LuAnn, ed. 2003. (Half-Pint Kids Readers Ser.). (Illus.). 7p. (gr. -1-1). pap. 1.00 (978-1-59256-107-0(1)) Half-Pint Kids, Inc.

Santore, Charles, illus. William the Curious: Knight of the Water Lilies. 2012. (J). (978-1-60464-034-2(0)) Appleseed Pr. Bk. Pub. LLC.

El sapo que fue a la Luna. (SPA.). (J). (978-0-9710860-7-4(9)) Libros, Encouraging Cultural Literacy.

Sargent, Dave & Sargent, Pat. Do Frogs Have Tails?, 10 vols., Vol. 15. Robinson, Laura, illus. 2004. (Learn to Read Ser.: 10).Tr. of Tienen Colas las Ranas? 18p. (J). pap. 10.95 (978-1-56763-826-4(0)); lib. bdg. 20.95 (978-1-56763-825-7(2)) Ozark Publishing.

—Do Frogs Have Tails?/Tienen Colas las Ranas?, 10 vols. Robinson, Laura, illus. 2004. (Learn to Read Ser.: 10).Tr. of Tienen Colas las Ranas? (ENG & SPA.). 18p. (J). lib. bdg. 20.95 (978-1-56763-989-6(5));15. pap. 9.95 (978-1-56763-990-2(9)) Ozark Publishing.

Scheffler, Axel. Freddy the Frog. Scheffler, Axel, illus. 2014. (Noisy Bath Bks.). (ENG., Illus.). 12p. (J). (— 1). 13.99 (978-1-4472-6804-8(0)) Pan Macmillan GBR. Dist: Independent Pubs. Group.

Scheffler, Axel, illus. Freddy the Frog. 2015. (Buggy Buddies Ser.). (ENG.). 12p. (J). (— 1). bds. 7.99 (978-0-230-75614-4(X)) Pan Macmillan GBR. Dist: Independent Pubs. Group.

Schlegl, Stacey Lynn. Little Frog. 2008. (J). per. 8.95 (978-0-9801504-0-7(X)) Jan-Carol Publishing, INC.

Schnetzler, Pattie L. Fast 'n Snappy. Manning, Jane K., tr. Manning, Jane K., illus. 2004. (Carolrhoda Picture Books Ser.). 32p. (J). (gr. k-3). 16.95 (978-1-57505-539-8(2)) Lerner Publishing Group.

Schofield Sr., Derrick. A Frog's Tale. 2012. 20p. pap. 13.77 (978-1-4669-2009-5(2)) Trafford Publishing.

Scieszka, Jon. The Frog Prince, Continued. 2003. (Live Oak Readalong Ser.). (Illus.). (J). 28.95 incl. audio compact disk (978-1-59112-515-0(4)); 25.95 incl. audio (978-1-59112-229-6(5)) Live Oak Media.

—The Frog Prince, Continued. Johnson, Steve, illus. 2003. pap. 39.95 incl. audio compact disk (978-1-59112-522-8(7)) Live Oak Media.

—The Frog Prince, Continued, 4 bks. 2003. (Live Oak Readalong Ser.). (J). pap. 37.95 incl. audio (978-1-59112-230-2(9)) Live Oak Media.

Sellers, Melonie. Harry the Happy Frog. 2008. 16p. per. 24.95 (978-1-4241-9723-1(6)) America Star Bks.

Shankman, Ed. The Bourbon Street Band Is Back. O'Neill, Dave, illus. 2011. (Shankman & O'Neill Ser.). (ENG.). 32p. (gr. -1-3). 14.95 (978-1-933212-79-1(9), Commonwealth Editions) Applewood Bks.

Shaskan, Stephen. Toad on the Road: A Cautionary Tale. Shaskan, Stephen, illus. 2017. (Illus.). 32p. (J). (gr. -1-3). 17.99 (978-0-06-239347-0(2)) HarperCollins Pubs.

Shea, Bob. The Happiest Book Ever. Shea, Bob, illus. 2016. (ENG., Illus.). 40p. (J). (gr. 1-3). 16.99 (978-1-4847-3045-4(3)) Hyperion Bks. for Children.

Shooter, Darlene D. The Adventures of the Tree Frog Family: My Favorite Little Critters. 2009. 19p. (J). pap. 16.95 (978-1-4327-3483-1(0)) Outskirts Pr., Inc.

Shumway, Gail. Stripey Follows His Dream. 2010. 60p. (J). 19.95 (978-0-9824611-7-4(8)) Snow In Sarasota Publishing.

Silvermetz, Marcia A. Gertrude the Albino Frog & Her Friend Rupert the Turtle. Doyel, Ginger, illus. 2003. 48p. (J). (gr. 2-3). 19.95 (978-0-9718724-0-0(6)) Hiccup Cottage Pubns.

Simpson, Patricia Ann. The Frog, the Birds & the Trout. 2007. (J). per. 24.95 (978-0-9795460-3-7(6)) Creative Bk. Pubs.

Slate, Joseph. Miss Bindergarten & the Secret Bag. Wolff, Ashley, illus. 2013. (Penguin Young Readers, Level 2 Ser.). (ENG.). 32p. (J). (gr. 1-2). pap. 3.99 (978-0-448-46803-7(4)); 14.99 (978-0-8037-3988-8(5)) Penguin Young Readers Group. (Penguin Young Readers).

Small, David. Eulalie & the Hopping Head. Small, David, illus. 2003. (Illus.). pap. 35.95 incl. audio compact disk (978-1-59112-520-4(0)) Live Oak Media.

Smith, Brian W. Tree Mail. 2016. (ENG., Illus.). 120p. (J). (gr. 3-7). pap. 12.99 (978-1-5067-0096-0(9)) Dark Horse Comics.

Smith, Clyde R. The Bully of Glendale Pond. Perin, Pauline, illus. 2012. 24p. (-18). pap. 24.95 (978-1-4626-7795-5(9)) America Star Bks.

Smith, Joshua T. Frog's Van. 2010. 36p. pap. 15.95 (978-0-557-72956-2(4)) Lulu Pr., Inc.

Smith, Mary L. The Ramblings of Clyde Frog & Jasmine. Bermejo, Hilbert, illus. 2013. 30p. pap. 11.99 (978-1-61286-156-2(3)) Avid Readers Publishing Group.

Smith, Mildred M. Louie the Blue Frog. 2012. 24p. pap. 24.95 (978-1-62709-122-0(X)) America Star Bks.

Smith, William. Frankie & Earnie Meet, 1 vol. 2009. pap. 24.95 (978-1-60749-333-4(0)) America Star Bks.

Smithrud, Norma. The Mucky Yucky Swamp. Miles, Peregrine B., illus. 2011. 28p. pap. 24.95 (978-1-4560-8790-6(8)) America Star Bks.

Snow, Dorothea J. The Secret of the Stone Frog. Burns, Raymond, illus. 2011. 214p. 44.95 (978-1-258-08002-0(8)) Literary Licensing, LLC.

Snyder, Susan. There's a Frog Trapped in the Bathroom. Johanson, Anna, illus. 2005. 23p. (J). (gr. 1-3). 9.95 (978-0-9715411-0-8(8)) Kotzig Publishing, Inc.

Sommer, Carl. King of the Pond. Budwine, Greg, illus. 2014. (J). pap. (978-1-57537-956-2(2)) Advance Publishing, Inc.

—King of the Pond(El Rey Del Estanque) Budwine, Greg, illus. 2009. (Another Sommer-Time Story Bilingual Ser.). (SPA & ENG.). 48p. (J). lib. bdg. 16.95 (978-1-57537-156-6(1)) Advance Publishing, Inc.

Sonneborn, Scott. Pete Bogg: King of the Frogs. Aburtov, illus. 2013. (Pete Bogg Ser.). (ENG.). 48p. (gr. 1-3). pap. 5.95 (978-1-4342-3872-6(5)); lib. bdg. 23.99 (978-1-4342-3284-7(0)) Stone Arch Bks.

Sowards, Ellen. Ellie Lou Leaves the Ditch. 2011. 28p. pap. 12.03 (978-1-4634-3600-1(9)) AuthorHouse.

Sparkes, Ali. Frog Freakout. Collins, Ross, illus. 2014. (S. W. I. T. C. H. Ser.: 7). (ENG.). 88p. (J). (gr. 2-5). lib. bdg. 27.93 (978-1-4677-2111-0(5), Darby Creek) Lerner Publishing Group.

Spika, Jana. Locket & the Mask. 2004. 12.99 (978-0-9727103-0-5(2)) Tree of Life Pr.

Sprecher, John. Eric & the Angrry Frog, Vol. 2. Forrest, James, illus. l.t. ed. Date not set. (Special Kids "Special Message" Book Ser.). 32p. (J). (gr. k-4). pap. 10.00 (978-1-892186-01-0(2)) Anythings Possible, Inc.

Stacy, Heidi. Hoppy Feelings. 2013. 28p. pap. 13.99 (978-1-4525-8451-5(6), Balboa Pr.) Author Solutions, Inc.

Stadler, Kristina. Frog on my Head. Stader, Kristina & Stroede, Paul, illus. 2011. 24p. (J). lib. bdg. 11.95 (978-1-59598-138-7(1), Goblin Fern Pr.) HenschelHAUS Publishing.

Star, Nancy. The Case of the April Fool's Frogs. 2006. 77p. (978-0-439-67266-5(X)) Scholastic, Inc.

Stasco, Raymond. The Adventures of Mr Mccroak. 2009. 48p. pap. 21.99 (978-1-4363-4244-5(9)) Xlibris Corp.

Stead, Philip C. A Home for Bird. Stead, Philip C., illus. 2012. (ENG., Illus.). 32p. (J). (gr. -1-3). 17.99 (978-1-59643-711-1(1), 9781596437111) Roaring Brook Pr.

Stein, David Ezra. Tad & Dad. Stein, David Ezra, illus. 2015. (ENG., Illus.). 40p. (J). (gr. -1-k). 16.99 (978-0-399-25671-4(7), Nancy Paulsen Books) Penguin Young Readers Group.

Stillman, Norma. Forest Adventures: Book # 1 - Digger the Gopher & Hoppity the Frog. 2010. 20p. 12.77 (978-1-4520-1693-1(3)) AuthorHouse.

Stockham, Jess, et al, illus. The Frog Prince. 2007. (Flip-Up Fairy Tales Ser.). (ENG.). 24p. (J). (gr. 2-2). pap. (978-1-84643-077-0(1)) Child's Play International Ltd.

Stockham, Jess, illus. The Frog Prince. 2007. (Flip-Up Fairy Tales Ser.). (ENG.). 24p. (J). audio compact disk (978-1-84643-143-2(3)) Child's Play International Ltd.

Stratford, Ann. Tara Toad Meets Roman the Robot Soldier. 2005. (ENG., Illus.). pap. (978-1-84401-465-1(7)) Athena Pr.

Suttles, B. Mr Frog. 2011. 20p. pap. 24.95 (978-1-4560-6668-0(4)) America Star Bks.

Swann, Tammy & Benchmark Education Co., LLC Staff. Stop! It's a Frog! 2015. (BuildUp Ser.). (J). (gr. 1). (978-1-4900-0720-5(2)) Benchmark Education Co.

Swedeen, Staci. Phoebe & the Flame-Bellied Toad: An Original Fairy Tale. 2006. (J). pap. (978-1-4108-7153-4(3)) Benchmark Education Co.

—The Toad Bridegroom: A Fairy Tale from Korea. 2006. (J). pap. (978-1-4108-7152-7(5)) Benchmark Education Co.

—Tombi-Ende & the Frog: A Fairy Tale from Southern Africa. 2006. (J). pap. (978-1-4108-7151-0(7)) Benchmark Education Co.

Tahir "Z", Zarghuna. The Lazy Froggies. 2012. 28p. (-18). pap. 19.99 (978-1-4772-8907-5(0)) AuthorHouse.

Tarver, Whitney B. The Best Day Ever! 2010. 24p. 14.95 (978-1-4269-4114-6(5)) Trafford Publishing.

Teddy Bear Frog. 2003. (J). per. (978-1-57657-161-3(0)) Paradise Pr., Inc.

Terry, Will, illus. The Frog with the Big Mouth. 2012. (J). 34.28 (978-1-61913-146-0(3)) Weigl Pubs., Inc.

—The Frog with the Big Mouth, 1 vol. 2008. (ENG.). 32p. (J). (gr. k-3). 16.99 (978-0-8075-2621-7(5)) Whitman, Albert & Co.

Tessin, Kit Elaine. Never Enough Frogs, 1 vol. Whitman, Jennifer, illus. 2009. 19p. pap. 24.95 (978-1-60836-185-4(3)) America Star Bks.

Thomas, Jan. Can You Make a Scary Face? Thomas, Jan, illus. 2009. (ENG., Illus.). 40p. (J). (gr. -1-3). 15.99 (978-1-4169-8581-5(6), Beach Lane Bks.) Beach Lane Bks.

Thomas Nelson. Five Little Speckled Frogs. 2017. (ENG.). (gr. -1-2). bds. **(978-1-78598-944-5(8))** Make Believe Ideas.

Thomas-Ngabe, T-Imani. Once upon a Frog: From the Chronicles Of. 2012. 44p. pap. 20.72 (978-1-4669-5974-3(6)) Trafford Publishing.

Thomas, Peggy. Joshua the Giant Frog, 1 vol. Smith, Cat Bowman, illus. 2005. (ENG.). 32p. (J). (gr. k-3). 16.99 (978-1-58980-267-4(5)) Pelican Publishing Co., Inc.

Thomas The Toad. Willie the Frog Learns to Fly. 2009. 68p. pap. 27.49 (978-1-4389-6997-8(X)) AuthorHouse.

Thompson, Lauren. Leap Back Home to Me. Cordell, Matthew, illus. 2011. (ENG.). 32p. (J). (gr. -1-1). 17.99 (978-1-4169-0664-3(9), McElderry, Margaret K. Bks.) McElderry, Margaret K. Bks.

—Little Quack's New Friend. Anderson, Derek, illus. 2008. (Classic Board Bks.). (ENG.). 34p. (J). (gr. -1-1). bds. 7.99 (978-1-4169-4923-7(2), Little Simon) Little Simon.

—Little Quack's New Friend. Anderson, Derek, illus. 2006. (ENG.). 32p. (J). (gr. -1-3). 17.99 (978-0-689-86893-1(6), Simon & Schuster Bks. For Young Readers) Simon & Schuster Bks. For Young Readers.

Thompson, Tamara. Before You Were Born. 2010. 28p. pap. (978-1-84991-205-1(X)) Chipmunkapublishing.

Toad, please use your Manners! 2005. (YA). per. (978-1-59872-302-1(2)) Instant Pub.

Tobey, Carole. If Frogs Could Talk. 2003. (Illus.). 74p. (J). per. 12.00 (978-0-9773648-2-4(8)) Legend eXpress Publishing.

Tobey, Carole A. The Frog Olympics. 2005. (Illus.). 70p. (J). per. 12.00 (978-0-9773648-3-1(6)) Legend eXpress Publishing.

Tripp, Paul. Tubby the Tuba. Cole, Henry, illus. 2006. (ENG.). 32p. (J). (gr. -1-3). 16.99 (978-0-525-47717-4(9), Dutton Books for Young Readers) Penguin Young Readers Group.

Turchan, Monique. Mydoit. Turchan, Monique, illus. 2013. (Illus.). 24p. pap. 11.95 (978-1-61244-144-3(0)) Halo Publishing International.

Turner, Dannie E. You Don't Know Beans: the Great Frog Adventure. 2008. 28p. pap. 24.95 (978-1-60474-711-9(0)) America Star Bks.

Tyrrell, Kevin. Froggy Kisses. Tyrrell, Kayla, illus. 2008. 22p. pap. 24.95 (978-1-60672-066-0(X)) America Star Bks.

Ulrich, George. Mrs. Picasso's Polliwog: A Mystery. Ulrich, George, illus. 2003. (Illus.). 32p. pap. 7.95 (978-1-891577-84-0(0)); (J). (gr. -1-7). lib. bdg. 15.95 (978-1-891577-83-3(2)) Images Pr.

Urbanovic, Jackie. Prince of a Frog. 2015. (ENG., Illus.). 32p. (J). (gr. -1-k). 17.99 (978-0-545-63652-0(3), Orchard Bks.) Scholastic, Inc.

Van Fleet, Matthew. Monday the Bullfrog. Van Fleet, Matthew, illus. 2010. (ENG., Illus.). 20p. (J). (gr. -1). 24.99 (978-1-4424-0958-3(4), Simon & Schuster/Paula Wiseman Bks.) Simon & Schuster/Paula Wiseman Bks.

Vande Velde, Vivian. Frogged. 2013. (ENG., Illus.). 208p. (J). (gr. 5-7). 16.99 (978-0-547-94215-5(X)) Houghton Mifflin Harcourt Publishing Co.

Velthuijs, Max. Frog & Hare. (ENG., Illus.). 8p. (J). 6.99 (978-0-86264-995-1(1)) Andersen Pr. GBR. Dist: Trafalgar Square Publishing.

—Frog & the Stranger. 2014. (ENG., Illus.). 32p. (J). (-k). pap. 12.95 (978-1-78344-143-3(7)) Andersen Pr. GBR. Dist: Independent Pubs. Group.

—Frog Is Frog. 2005. (Frog Ser.). (SOM, ENG, BEN & URD., Illus.). 40p. (J). 13.50 (978-1-84059-212-2(5)) Milet Publishing.

Velthuijs, Max. Where Is Frog? 2017. (ENG., Illus.). 14p. (J). (gr. -1-k). bds. 8.95 **(978-0-2281-0002-7(X)**, 9780228100027) Firefly Bks., Ltd.

Vickers, Tamara. Mr. Green & the Animal Kingdom: (Imagine That!) You Draw the Picture! 2007. 228p. per. 24.95 (978-1-4241-8256-5(5)) America Star Bks.

Vine, Joshua M. Gnomey & Froggie. 2012. 46p. pap. 21.99 (978-1-4772-7529-0(0)) AuthorHouse.

Viviani, Luisa. There Is Something Special Inside of Me. 2004. 25p. pap. 24.95 (978-1-4137-2372-4(1)) PublishAmerica, Inc.

Walker, Raynn. Toadina: The Story of a Lady Toad. 2005. (J). pap. 15.00 (978-0-8059-6726-5(5)) Dorrance Publishing Co., Inc.

Walls, Robert D. Tiny's Second-Grade Field Trip. 2010. 40p. 19.99 (978-1-4490-9011-1(7)) AuthorHouse.

Walsh, Ellen Stoll. Hop Jump. 2010. (Rise & Shine Ser.). (ENG., Illus.). 32p. (C). (gr. -1-3). pap. 11.95 (978-0-15-201375-2(X)) National Geographic School Publishing, Inc.

Walton, Rick. Bullfrog Pops!, 1 vol. McAllister, Chris, illus. 2005. (ENG.). 32p. (J). (gr. 3-3). pap. 7.99 (978-1-58685-840-7(8)) Gibbs Smith, Publisher.

Waltz, Dan Hall. Freckles the Frog: A Read-a-Long/Sing-a-Long Story Book. Waltz, Dan Hall, illus. l.t. ed. 2003. (Illus.). 24p. (J). 19.95 (978-0-9741774-0-3(7)) D. W. Publishing.

Wamsley, Jody. What Am I Gonna Do? Turchan, Monique, illus. 2013. 24p. pap. 11.95 (978-1-61244-070-5(3)) Halo Publishing International.

Wan, Joyce. Frog & Friends. Wan, Joyce, illus. 2013. (ENG., Illus.). 14p. (J). (gr. -1-k). bds. 6.99 (978-0-8431-7277-5(0), Price Stern Sloan) Penguin Young Readers Group.

Waring, Geoff. Oscar & the Frog: A Book about Growing. Waring, Geoff, illus. (Start with Science Ser.). (ENG., Illus.). 32p. (J). (gr. -1-3). 2008. pap. 6.99 (978-0-7636-4030-9(1)) 2007. 11.99 (978-0-7636-3558-9(8)) Candlewick Pr.

Watson, Jacqueline. Six Frogs on a Log! 2004. 43p. pap. 24.95 (978-1-4137-2986-3(X)) PublishAmerica, Inc.

Watt, Fiona. That's Not My Frog. Wells, Rachel, illus. 2009. (Touchy-Feely Board Bks). 10p. (J). bds. 8.99 (978-0-7945-2505-7(9), Usborne) EDC Publishing.

Weare, Tim. I'm a Little Frog. 2004. (Illus.). 12p. (J). (gr. -1-3). 6.95 (978-1-904613-08-4(X), Buster Bks.) O'Mara, Michael Bks., Ltd. GBR. Dist: Ingram Publisher Services.

Webb, Heather. The Frog & the Fly. Sanderson, Constance, illus. 2008. 29p. pap. 24.95 (978-1-60441-380-9(8)) America Star Bks.

Weddle, Steve & Weddle, Nikki. Can Hedgehogs Jump? 2011. (Illus.). 28p. pap. 12.52 (978-1-4520-5751-4(6)) AuthorHouse.

Weiner, Brian. Toad Catchers' Creek. Weintraub, Claudia & Frederick, Robin, eds. Cannon, Martin, illus. 2005. 40p. (J). lib. bdg. 17.99 (978-1-932949-58-2(5)) Illusion Factory, The.

Weingarth, Poss. Gurgle, Gurgle Splash: I'm Always in a Hurry. 2012. 36p. pap. 32.70 (978-1-4771-4435-0(8)) Xlibris Corp.

Welch, Christopher Shiveley. Christopher Bullfrog Catcher. 2006. (J). pap. (978-1-894936-46-0(9)) Saga Bks.

Werner, Michael. Aspey's Adventures with Asperger's. 2012. 32p. pap. 21.99 (978-1-4771-0800-0(9)) Xlibris Corp.

Weston Woods Staff, creator. There Was an Old Lady Who Swallowed a Fly. 2011. 29.95 (978-0-439-87200-3(6)) Weston Woods Studios, Inc.

Whirlwhim. The Baffelgagging Blundernagging Brothers: In Curse of the Bog Frog. 2008. (Illus.). 192p. (YA). 29.95 (978-0-9800274-0-2(3)) Whirlwhim.

Wiesner, David. Tuesday. 2011. (ENG., Illus.). 32p. (J). (gr. -1-3). pap. 7.99 (978-0-395-87082-2(8)) Houghton Mifflin Harcourt Publishing Co.

Wilcut-Bledsoe, Robin. The Imagination of Hollie Mason. 2008. 88p. pap. 19.95 (978-1-60703-804-7(8)) America Star Bks.

Willems, Mo. City Dog, Country Frog. Muth, Jon J., illus. 2010. (ENG.). 64p. (J). (gr. -1-k). 17.99 (978-1-4231-0300-4(9)) Hyperion Pr.

Willems, Mo, illus. Nanette's Baguette. 2016. (ENG.). 40p. (J). (gr. -1-k). 17.99 (978-1-4847-2286-2(8)) Disney Pr.

Williams, Allen. Claude the Backward Jumping Bullfrog. 2008. 20p. pap. 24.95 (978-1-60672-550-4(5)) America Star Bks.

—Claude the Backward-Jumping Bullfrog: Space Shuttle Commander. 2009. 32p. pap. 17.99 (978-1-4490-0479-8(2)) AuthorHouse.

—Claude the Backward Jumping Bullfrog - Firefighter: Buster's Great Adventure. 2009. 36p. pap. 16.99 (978-1-4389-7817-8(0)) AuthorHouse.

Williams, James. Edna's Creek. 2009. 20p. pap. 12.49 (978-1-4490-1175-8(6)) AuthorHouse.

Williams, Noele. The Little Red Frog. Kern, Debb, illus. 2012. 54p. pap. 14.99 (978-1-61807-066-1(5), Little Blue Flower Pr.) Grey Gate Media, LLC.

Williams, Rufus. The Frog & the Butterfly. 2012. 88p. pap. 10.00 (978-1-61897-380-1(0), Strategic Bk. Publishing) Strategic Book Publishing & Rights Agency (SBPRA).

Wilsdon, Christina. A New York Sailing Adventure. Hockerman, Dennis, illus. 2006. 26p. (J). 7.99 (978-1-59939-014-7(0)) Cornerstone Pr.

Wilson, Angela. Frog Makes a Friend. Wilson, Whitleigh & Wilson, John, illus. 2013. 28p. pap. 24.95 (978-1-63004-048-2(7)) America Star Bks.

Wilson, Hannah & Parrish, Emma. Hoppity Frog: A Hide-and-Seek Book. 2015. (Slide-And-Seek Ser.). (ENG., Illus.). 10p. (J). (gr. -1-k). 8.99 (978-1-4998-0030-2(4)) Little Bee Books Inc.

Wilson, Karma. A Frog in the Bog. Rankin, Joan, illus. (ENG.). 32p. (J). (gr. -1-3). 2007. 7.99 (978-1-4169-2727-3(1)) 2003. 17.99 (978-0-689-84081-4(0)) McElderry, Margaret K. Bks. (McElderry, Margaret K. Bks.).

Winkler, Henry & Oliver, Lin. Stop That Frog! Garrett, Scott, illus. 2014. (Here's Hank Ser.: 3). (ENG.). 128p. (J). (gr. 1-3). 5.99 (978-0-448-48152-4(9)); 14.99 (978-0-448-48241-5(X)) Penguin Young Readers Group. (Grosset & Dunlap).

—Stop That Frog! 2014. (Here's Hank Ser.: 3). lib. bdg. 16.00 (978-0-606-36161-3(8)) Turtleback Bks.

Wisher, Mark. Don't kiss the Prince. 2010. 33p. pap. 21.50 (978-1-4457-7238-7(8)) Lulu Pr., Inc.

Witkowski, Teri. Wait Your Turn, Bitty Froggy! Ackley, Peggy Jo, illus. 2008. (J). (978-1-59369-285-8(4)) American Girl Publishing, Inc.

Wolfe, Jane. Cheeky Frog. Benham, Tors, illus. 2016. (ENG.). 8p. (J). (gr. -1-12). bds. 6.99 (978-1-84322-718-2(5),

Armadillo) Anness Publishing GBR. Dist: National Bk. Network.
Woods, Dawn. The Best Day Ever! 2010. 36p. pap. 16.44 *(978-1-4269-0331-1(6))* Trafford Publishing.
Woods, Emmett L. The Black Frog. 2004. 38p. (J). (gr. k-7). 6.95 *(978-0-615-12589-3(1))* Woods, Emmett L.
Wu, Nicholas. Tiddalick, the Greedy Frog: An Aboriginal Dreamtime Story. 1 vol. rev. ed. 2013. (Fiction Readers Ser.). (ENG., Illus.). 32p. (J). (gr. 3-3). pap. 8.99 *(978-1-4333-5636-0(8))* Shell Educational Publishing.
Yang, Belle. Foo, the Flying Frog of Washtub Pond. Yang, Belle, illus. 2009. (ENG., Illus.). 32p. (J). (gr. -1-2). 16.99 *(978-0-7636-3615-9(0))* Candlewick Pr.
Yang, Gladys. The Frog Rider & Other Folktales from Chin. 2008. 116p. 19.95 *(978-1-59654-569-4(0))* Disruptive Publishing.
Yeoman, John. The Bear's Water Picnic. Blake, Quentin, illus. 2011. (ENG.). 40p. (J). (gr. k-k). pap. 12.99 *(978-1-84939-004-0(5))* Andersen Pr. GBR. Dist: Independent Pubs. Group.
Yogananda, Paramahansa. Due Rane Nei Guai. 2011. 30p. 22.00 *(978-0-87612-125-2(3))* Self-Realization Fellowship Pubs.
Yogananda, Paramhansa. Two Frogs in Trouble: Based on a Fable Told by Paramahansa Yogananda. (Illus.). 30p. (J). (gr. -1-3). pap. 6.50 *(978-0-87612-351-5(5))* Self-Realization Fellowship Pubs.
Yost-Filgate, Susan. A Good Day for Abbey. Filgate, Leonard, illus. 2009. (ENG.). 12p. (J). (gr. -1-12). 6.99 *(978-1-934960-45-5(4),* Raven Tree Pr.,Csi) Continental Sales, Inc.
—Rip Squeak & His Friends. Filgate, Leonard, illus. 2009. (ENG.). 32p. (J). (gr. -1-3). 16.95 *(978-1-934960-40-0(3),* Raven Tree Pr.,Csi) Continental Sales, Inc.
—Rip Squeak & His Friends. Filgate, Leonard, illus. 2004. 32p. (J). 16.95 *(978-1-59384-058-7(6))* Parklane Publishing.
—The Treasure. 2009. (ENG.). 32p. (J). (gr. -1-3). 16.95 *(978-1-934960-41-7(1),* Raven Tree Pr.,Csi) Continental Sales, Inc.
—The Treasure: A Rip Squeak Book. Filgate, Leonard, illus. 2005. (Rip Squeak Ser.). (ENG.). 32p. (J). (gr. -1-3). 16.95 *(978-0-9747825-1-5(3),* Raven Tree Pr.,Csi) Continental Sales, Inc.
Young, Amy. The Mud Fairy. Young, Amy, illus. 2010. (ENG., Illus.). 40p. (J). (gr. -1-1). 16.99 *(978-1-59990-104-6(8),* 9781599901046, Bloomsbury USA Childrens) Bloomsbury Publishing USA.
Younger, David. The Mysterious Moat Maiden: A Wandering Firefly Fairy Adventure. 1 vol. 2009. 15p. pap. 24.95 *(978-1-61546-213-1(9))* America Star Bks.
Zabel, Randy & Broesch, Valerie, illus. Al-the-Gator & Freddy Frog. 2007. 48p. (J). per. 18.99 *(978-0-9797513-0-1(6))* 4RV Publishing, LLC.
Zimmerschied, P. Grampa Paul's Adventure Stories for Children. 2011. 112p. (gr. -1). 23.99 *(978-1-4634-2885-3(5));* pap. 13.99 *(978-1-4634-2883-9(9))* AuthorHouse.

FRONTIER AND PIONEER LIFE

see also Cowboys; Indian Captivities; Overland Journeys to the Pacific; Pioneers; Ranch Life

Adil, Janeen. Johnny Appleseed. 2003. (Folk Heroes Ser.). (Illus.). 24p. (J). lib. bdg. 24.45 *(978-1-59036-075-0(3))* Weigl Pubs., Inc.
Adkins, Jan. What If You Met a Cowboy? Adkins, Jan, illus. 2013. (ENG., Illus.). 48p. (J). (gr. 1-4). 17.99 *(978-1-59643-149-2(0),* 9781596431492) Roaring Brook Pr.
Adler, David A. & Adler, Michael S. A Picture Book of Daniel Boone. Collins, Matt, illus. 2013. (ENG.). 32p. (J). (gr. -1-3). 17.95 *(978-0-8234-2748-2(X))* Holiday Hse., Inc.
Allen, Charles F. David Crockett: Scout, Small Boy, Pilgrim, Mountaineer, Soldier, Bear-Hunter, & Congressman, Defender of the Alamo. (Illus.). 308p. reprint ed. lib. bdg. 98.00 *(978-0-7222-4856-0(3))* Library Reprints, Inc.
Alphin, Elaine Marie. Davy Crockett. 2003. (History Maker Bios Ser.). (Illus.). 48p. (J). (gr. 3-5). lib. bdg. 26.60 *(978-0-8225-0393-4(X))* Lerner Publishing Group.
Altsheler, Joseph A. The Young Trailers: A Story of Early Kentucky. l.t. ed. 2007. (Young Trailers Ser.: Vol. 1). 222p. (J). reprint ed. pap. 22.99 *(978-1-4346-3289-0(X))* Creative Media Partners, LLC.
Anderson, William. Laura Ingalls Wilder: A Biography. 2007. (Little House Nonfiction Ser.). (ENG., Illus.). 256p. (J). (gr. 3-7). pap. 6.99 *(978-0-06-088552-6(1),* Collins) HarperCollins Pubs.
Andra-Warner, Elle. Hudson's Bay Company Adventures: Tales of Canada's Early Fur Traders. 2006. (Amazing Stories Ser.). (ENG.). 96p. (J). pap. 9.95 *(978-1-55439-700-6(6),* 9781554397006) Lorimer, James & Co., Ltd., Pubs. CAN. Dist: Casemate Pubs. & Bk. Distributors, LLC.
Arnéz, Lynda. My Life As a Pioneer. 2016. (My Place in History Ser.). (ENG., Illus.). 24p. (J). (gr. 2-3). pap. 8.15 *(978-1-4824-3988-5(3))* Stevens, Gareth Publishing LLLP.
Aronin, Miriam. How Many People Traveled the Oregon Trail? And Other Questions about the Trail West. 2012. (Six Questions of American History Ser.). (ENG.). 48p. (gr. 4-6). pap. 56.72 *(978-0-7613-9237-8(8));* pap. 9.95 *(978-0-7613-8566-0(5))* Lerner Publishing Group.
Bair, Diane. Western Legends & Leyendas del Oeste: 6 English, 6 Spanish Adaptations. 2011. (ENG & SPA.). (J). 101.00 net. *(978-1-4108-5735-4(2))* Benchmark Education Co.
Barkan, Joanne. A Western Activity Book & Libro de actividades del Oeste: 6 English, 6 Spanish Adaptations. 2011. (ENG & SPA.). (J). 101.00 net. *(978-1-4108-5734-7(4))* Benchmark Education Co.
Bearce, Stephanie. Top Secret Files: the Wild West: Secrets, Strange Tales, & Hidden Facts about the Wild West. rev. ed. 2015. (Top Secret Files of History Ser.: 0). (ENG., Illus.). 125p. (J). (gr. 4-7). pap. 8.95 *(978-1-61821-462-1(4))* Prufrock Pr.
Beckwith, Cheryl. William Bent: Frontiersman. 2011. (ENG & SPA., Illus.). 60p. (J). pap. 8.95 *(978-0-86541-117-3(4))* Filter Pr., LLC.
Benge, Janet & Benge, Geoff. Heroes of History - Daniel Boone: Frontiersman. 2004. (ENG.). 224p. (YA). pap. 9.99 *(978-1-932096-09-5(4))* Emerald Bks.
Benjamin, Margaret. Johnny Appleseed. 2014. (Illus.). 31p. (J). pap. *(978-1-62712-278-8(8))* Cavendish Square Publishing.
Berne, Emma Carlson. Laura Ingalls Wilder. 1 vol. 2007. (Essential Lives Set 1 Ser.). (ENG., Illus.). 112p. (J). (gr. 6-12). lib. bdg. 35.64 *(978-1-59928-843-7(5))* ABDO Publishing Co.
Blair, Eric. Daniel Boone. 1 vol. Chambers-Goldberg, Micah, illus. 2013. (My First Classic Story Ser.). (ENG.). 32p. (gr. k-3). pap. 7.10 *(978-1-4795-1859-3(X),* My First Classic Story) Picture Window Bks.
—Johnny Appleseed. 1 vol. Muehlenhardt, Amy Bailey, illus. 2011. (My First Classic Story Ser.).Tr. of Johnny Appleseed. (ENG.). 32p. (gr. k-3). pap. 7.10 *(978-1-4048-7367-4(8),* My First Classic Story) Picture Window Bks.
Blashfield, Jean F. The California Gold Rush & The '49ers. 2017. (Landmarks in U. S. History Ser.). (ENG.). 32p. (gr. 3-4). lib. bdg. 27.32 ***(978-1-5157-7116-6(4),*** Fact Finders) Capstone Press of Coughlan Cos.
Boom, Rosie. Where Lions Roar at Night. 2nd ed. 2013. (Illus.). 240p. *(978-1-921161-18-6(3))* Boom Tree Publishing.
Brandt, Keith & Macken, JoAnn Early. Daniel Boone: Frontier Explorer. Lawn, John, illus. 2008. 55p. (J). pap. *(978-0-439-02020-6(4))* Scholastic, Inc.
Braun, Eric & Meister, Cari. American Folk Legends. 1 vol. 2014. (American Folk Legends Ser.). (ENG.). 32p. (gr. k-2). 109.28 *(978-1-4795-5531-4(2))* Picture Window Bks.
Brown, Don. Gold! Gold from the American River! January 24, 1848: the Day the Gold Rush Began. Brown, Don, illus. 2014. (Actual Times Ser.: 3). (ENG., Illus.). 64p. (J). (gr. 1-5). 8.99 *(978-1-250-04060-2(4),* 9781250040602) Square Fish.
Buffalo Bill Cody. 2010. (Legends of the Wild West Ser.). (Illus.). 136p. (gr. 6-12). 35.00 *(978-1-60413-528-2(X),* Chelsea Hse.) Facts On File, Inc.
Burkes-Larrañaga, Dustin, illus. Johnny Appleseed Plants Trees Across the Land. 1 vol. 2014. (American Folk Legends Ser.). (ENG.). 32p. (gr. k-2). lib. bdg. 27.32 *(978-1-4795-5428-7(6))* Picture Window Bks.
Burton, K. Melissa. Kentucky's Boone: The Pioneer Spirit. Asher, James, illus. 2008. 30p. (J). (gr. 4-7). pap. 14.95 *(978-1-934898-03-1(1))* McClanahan Publishing Hse., Inc.
Carlson, Lisa, illus. Calamity Jane. 2007. (On My Own Folklore Ser.). 48p. (J). (gr. -1-3). per. 6.95 *(978-0-8225-6480-5(7),* First Avenue Editions) Lerner Publishing Group.
Caswell, Max. My Life During the Gold Rush. 2017. (My Place in History Ser.). 24p. (J). (gr. 2-3). pap. 8.15 ***(978-1-5382-0297-5(2))*** Stevens, Gareth Publishing LLLP.
Codell, Esmé Raji. Seed by Seed: The Legend & Legacy of John Appleseed Anniversary. Perkins, Lynne Rae, illus. 2012. 32p. (J). (gr. -1-3). 17.89 *(978-0-06-145516-2(4),* Greenwillow Bks.) HarperCollins Pubs.
—Seed by Seed: The Legend & Legacy of John Appleseed Chapman. Perkins, Lynne Rae, illus. 2012. (ENG.). 32p. (J). (gr. -1-3). 16.99 *(978-0-06-145515-5(6),* Greenwillow Bks.) HarperCollins Pubs.
Collard, Sneed B., III. David Crockett: Fearless Frontiersman. 2006. (American Heroes Ser.). (Illus.). 40p. (J). (gr. 3-7). lib. bdg. 28.50 *(978-0-7614-2160-3(2),* Benchmark Bks.) Marshall Cavendish Corp.
Collins, Terry. Stake a Claim! Nickolas Flux & the California Gold Rush. 1 vol. Ginevra, Dante, illus. 2014. (Nickolas Flux History Chronicles Ser.). (ENG.). 32p. (gr. 3-4). lib. bdg. 30.65 *(978-1-4765-3944-7(8),* Graphic Library) Capstone Press of Coughlan Cos.
Cook, Diane. Pathfinders of the American Frontier. 2004. (Exploration & Discovery Ser.). (Illus.). 64p. (YA). (gr. 5-18). lib. bdg. 19.95 *(978-1-59084-045-0(3))* Mason Crest.
Cooke, Tim. Go West with Cowboys & Ranchers. 2016. (ENG.). 32p. (J). *(978-0-7787-2322-6(4))* Crabtree Publishing Co.
—Life on the Front Lines. 1 vol. 2014. (Life on the Front Lines Ser.). (ENG.). 32p. (gr. 3-4). 139.95 *(978-1-4914-0890-2(1),* Edge Bks.) Capstone Press of Coughlan Cos.
Corrigan, Kathleen. Pioneer Life. 2016. (Canada Through Time Ser.). (ENG., Illus.). 32p. (gr. 1-4). lib. bdg. 29.99 *(978-1-4109-8118-9(5),* Read Me!) Heinemann-Raintree.
Craats, Rennay. The Blacksmith: Pioneers of Canada. 2011. 24p. (YA). (gr. 2-4). *(978-1-77071-681-0(5));* pap. *(978-1-77071-685-8(8))* Weigl Educational Pubs. Ltd.
—Le Forgeron: Le Début de la Colonie. Karvonen, Tanjah, tr. from ENG. 2011. (FRE., Illus.). 24p. (gr. 3-6). *(978-1-77071-418-2(9))* Weigl Educational Pubs. Ltd.
—Le Magasin Général: Le Début de la Colonie. Karvonen, Tanjah, tr. from ENG. 2011. (FRE., Illus.). 24p. (gr. 3-6). *(978-1-77071-420-5(0))* Weigl Educational Pubs. Ltd.
Crowley Conn, Kathe. Juliette Kinzie: Frontier Storyteller. 2015. (Badger Biographies Ser.). (ENG., Illus.). 123p. (J). (gr. 4-6). pap. 12.95 *(978-0-87020-701-3(6))* Wisconsin Historical Society.
Davies, Monika. The Gold Rush. 2017. (Primary Source Readers Ser.). 32p. (gr. 4-4). 9.99 ***(978-1-4258-3238-4(5))*** Teacher Created Materials, Inc.
Davis, Kenneth C. Don't Know Much about the Pioneers & Indians. 48p. (J). Date not set. (gr. 1-4). pap. 5.99 *(978-0-06-446232-7(3))* 2003. (Picture Bks.: No. 6). (Illus.). (gr. -1-1). 16.89 *(978-0-06-028618-7(0))* HarperCollins Pubs.
Davy Crockett. 2010. (Legends of the Wild West Ser.). (Illus.). 120p. (gr. 6-12). 35.00 *(978-1-60413-592-3(1),* Chelsea Hse.) Facts On File, Inc.
Dean, Arlan. The Mormon Pioneer Trail: From Nauvoo, Illinois to the Great Salt Lake, Utah. (Famous American Trails Ser.). 24p. 2009. (gr. 3-3). 42.50 *(978-1-61512-488-6(8))* 2003. (Illus.). (J). lib. bdg. 22.60 *(978-0-8239-6476-5(0))* Rosen Publishing Group, Inc., The. (PowerKids Pr.)
—The Old Spanish Trail: From Santa Fe, New Mexico to Los Angeles, California. 2009. (Famous American Trails Ser.). 24p. (gr. 3-3). 42.50 *(978-1-61512-489-3(6),* PowerKids Pr.) Rosen Publishing Group, Inc., The.
—The Oregon Trail: From Independence, Missouri to Oregon City, Oregon. (Famous American Trails Ser.). 24p. 2009. (gr. 3-3). 42.50 *(978-1-61512-490-9(X))* 2003. (Illus.). (J). lib. bdg. 22.60 *(978-0-8239-6478-9(7))* Rosen Publishing Group, Inc., The. (PowerKids Pr.)
—The Overland Trail: From Atchison, Kansas, to Fort Bridger, Wyoming. 2003. (Famous American Trails Ser.). (Illus.). 24p. (J). lib. bdg. 22.60 *(978-0-8239-6479-6(5),* PowerKids Pr.) Rosen Publishing Group, Inc., The.
—The Overland Trail: From Atchison, Kansas to Ft. Bridger, Wyoming. 2009. (Famous American Trails Ser.). 24p. (gr. 3-3). 42.50 *(978-1-61512-491-6(8),* PowerKids Pr.) Rosen Publishing Group, Inc., The.
—The Wilderness Road: From the Shenandoah Valley to the Ohio River. 2003. (Famous American Trails Ser.). (Illus.). 24p. (J). lib. bdg. 22.60 *(978-0-8239-6477-2(9),* PowerKids Pr.) Rosen Publishing Group, Inc., The.
—The Wilderness Trail: From the Shenandoah Valley to the Ohio River. 2009. (Famous American Trails Ser.). 24p. (gr. 3-3). 42.50 *(978-1-61512-493-0(4),* PowerKids Pr.) Rosen Publishing Group, Inc., The.
Demuth, Patricia Brennan. Who Was Laura Ingalls Wilder? 2013. (Who Was? Ser.). (ENG., Illus.). 112p. (J). (gr. 3-7). 5.99 *(978-0-448-46706-1(2),* Grosset & Dunlap) Penguin Young Readers Group.
Domnauer, Teresa. Westward Expansion. 2010. (True Book Ser.). (ENG., Illus.). 48p. (J). pap. 6.95 *(978-0-531-21249-3(1))* Scholastic Library Publishing.
Downie, Mary Alice. A Pioneer Alphabet. Gerber, Mary Jane, illus. 2009. (ABC Our Country Ser.). (ENG.). 32p. (J). (gr. k-3). pap. 7.95 *(978-0-88776-961-0(6),* Tundra Bks.) Tundra Bks. CAN. Dist: Penguin Random Hse. LLC.
Dunn, Joeming W. The Oregon Trail. 1 vol. Smith, Tim, illus. 2008. (Graphic History Ser.). (ENG.). 32p. 28.50 *(978-1-60270-183-0(0),* Graphic Planet- Nonfiction) ABDO Publishing Co.
Durbin, William & Durbin, Barbara. Dead Man's Rapids. 2017. (J). pap. ***(978-1-5179-0224-7(X))*** Univ. of Minnesota Pr.
Edmondson, J. R. Jim Bowie: Frontier Legend, Alamo Hero. 2009. (Library of American Lives & Times Ser.). 112p. (gr. 5-5). 69.20 *(978-1-60853-488-3(X))* Rosen Publishing Group, Inc., The.
Fein, Eric. Outnumbered: Davy Crockett's Final Battle at the Alamo. 2009. (Great Moments in American History Ser.). 32p. (gr. 3-3). 47.90 *(978-1-61513-148-8(5))* Rosen Publishing Group, Inc., The.
Feinstein, Stephen. Read about Johnny Appleseed. 2006. (I Like Biographies! Ser.). (Illus.). 24p. (J). (gr. 1-3). lib. bdg. 22.60 *(978-0-7660-2599-8(3),* Enslow Elementary) Enslow Pubs., Inc.
Fischer, Jeff, illus. Johnny Appleseed. 2006. (Famous Fables Ser.). (J). 6.99 *(978-1-59939-028-4(0))* Cornerstone Pr.
Foran, Jill. La Petite école: Le Début de la Colonie. Karvonen, Tanjah, tr. from ENG. 2011. (FRE., Illus.). 24p. (gr. 3-6). *(978-1-77071-421-2(9))* Weigl Educational Pubs. Ltd.
—The School House: Pioneers of Canada. 2011. 24p. (YA). (gr. 2-4). *(978-1-77071-680-3(7));* pap. *(978-1-77071-684-1(X))* Weigl Educational Pubs. Ltd.
—La Vie de Famille: Le Début de la Colonie. Karvonen, Tanjah, tr. from ENG. 2011. (FRE., Illus.). 24p. (gr. 3-6). *(978-1-77071-419-9(7))* Weigl Educational Pubs. Ltd.
Franck, Irene M. & Brownstone, David M. Frontier America. 10 vols. 2004. (Illus.). (J). 369.00 *(978-0-7172-5990-8(0),* Grolier) Scholastic Library Publishing.
Fredericks, Anthony D. P Is for Prairie Dog: A Prairie Alphabet. Bowles, Doug, illus. 2011. (Sleeping Bear Alphabets Ser.). (ENG.). 32p. (J). (gr. k-6). 16.95 *(978-1-58536-508-1(4))* Sleeping Bear Pr.
Friedman, Mel. The Oregon Trail. 2010. (ENG.). 48p. (J). pap. 6.95 *(978-0-531-21247-9(5),* Children's Pr.); (Illus.). (gr. 2-5). 29.00 *(978-0-531-20584-6(3))* Scholastic Library Publishing.
Furbee, Mary Rodd. Anne Bailey: Frontier Scout. 2004. (Women of the Frontier Ser.). (Illus.). 112p. (J). (gr. 3-18). 21.95 *(978-1-883846-70-1(6))* Reynolds, Morgan Inc.
—Shawnee Captive: The Story of Mary Draper Ingles. 2003. (Illus.). 112p. (YA). per. 9.95 *(978-1-891852-29-9(9))* Quarrier Pr.
—Shawnee Captive: The Story of Mary Draper Ingles. 2004. (Women of the Frontier Ser.). (Illus.). 112p. (J). (gr. 6-12). 23.95 *(978-1-883846-69-5(2),* First Biographies) Reynolds, Morgan Inc.
Garland, Sherry. Voices of the Western Frontier. 1 vol. Buckner, Julie Dupre, illus. 2016. (ENG.). 40p. (J). (gr. -1-6). 17.99 *(978-1-4556-1961-0(2))* Pelican Publishing Co., Inc.
Giff, Patricia Reilly. Laura Ingalls Wilder. 2014. (Women of Our Time Ser.). (ENG., Illus.). 80p. (J). (gr. 3-7). pap. 7.99 *(978-0-14-751364-9(2),* Puffin Books) Penguin Young Readers Group.
Golden, Nancy. Life with the Comanches: The Kidnapping of Cynthia Ann Parker. 2009. (Great Moments in American History Ser.). 32p. (gr. 3-3). 47.90 *(978-1-61513-146-4(9))* Rosen Publishing Group, Inc., The.
Graham, Amy. The Oregon Trail & the Daring Journey West by Wagon. 2006. (Wild History of the American West Ser.). (Illus.). 128p. (J). (gr. 5-9). lib. bdg. 34.60 *(978-1-59845-021-7(2),* MyReportLinks.com Bks.) Enslow Pubs., Inc.
Graves, Karen M. School in Pioneer Times. 2016. (It's Back to School ... Way Back! Ser.). (ENG., Illus.). 32p. (gr. 3-4). lib. bdg. 27.32 *(978-1-5157-2096-6(9),* Fact Finders) Capstone Press of Coughlan Cos.
Gregory, Josh. If You Were a Kid on the Oregon Trail. Farré, Lluís, illus. 2016. (If You Were a Kid Ser.). (ENG.). 32p. (J). lib. bdg. 26.00 *(978-0-531-21970-6(4),* Children's Pr.) Scholastic Library Publishing.
Gunderson, Jessica & Gunderson, Mary. Pioneer Farm Cooking. 2016. (Exploring History Through Food Ser.). (ENG., Illus.). 32p. (gr. 3-4). lib. bdg. 27.32 *(978-1-5157-2355-4(0))* Capstone Press of Coughlan Cos.
Haley, James. Stephen Austin & the Founding of Texas. 2009. (Library of American Lives & Times Ser.). 112p. (gr. 5-5). 69.20 *(978-1-60853-506-4(1))* Rosen Publishing Group, Inc., The.
Haley, James L. Stephen F. Austin & the Founding of Texas. 2005. (Library of American Lives & Times). (Illus.). 112p. (YA). (gr. 4-8). lib. bdg. 34.60 *(978-0-8239-5738-5(1))* Rosen Publishing Group, Inc., The.
Hall, Brianna. Strike It Rich! The Story of the California Gold Rush. 1 vol. 2014. (Adventures on the American Frontier Ser.). (ENG.). 32p. (gr. 3-4). 27.32 *(978-1-4914-0184-2(2),* Fact Finders) Capstone Press of Coughlan Cos.
Hall, Brianna, et al. Adventures on the American Frontier. 1 vol. 2014. (Adventures on the American Frontier Ser.). (ENG.). 32p. (gr. 3-4). pap. 31.80 *(978-1-4914-0201-6(6),* Fact Finders) Capstone Press of Coughlan Cos.
Harasymiw, Mark. The Legend of Johnny Appleseed. 2017. (Famous Legends Ser.). 32p. (J). (gr. 2-3). pap. 10.50 ***(978-1-5382-0372-9(3))*** Stevens, Gareth Publishing LLLP.
Harness, Cheryl. The Tragic Tale of Narcissa Whitman & a Faithful History of the Oregon Trail. Harness, Cheryl, illus. 2006. (Cheryl Harness Histories Ser.). (ENG., Illus.). 144p. (J). (gr. 5-9). 16.95 *(978-0-7922-5920-6(3),* National Geographic Children's Bks.) National Geographic Society.
Herman, Gail. Who Was Davy Crockett? 2013. (Who Was... ? Ser.). lib. bdg. 16.00 *(978-0-606-32133-4(0),* Turtleback) Turtleback Bks.
Hill, Pamela Smith. Laura Ingalls Wilder: A Writer's Life. 2007. (South Dakota Biography Ser.). (Illus.). 244p. per. *(978-0-9777955-6-7(X),* South Dakota State Historical Society Pr.) South Dakota State Historical Society Pr.
Huey, Lois Miner. American Archaeology Uncovers the Westward Movement. 2009. (American Archaeology Ser.). (Illus.). 64p. (J). (gr. 5-6). 31.36 *(978-0-7614-4265-3(0))* Marshall Cavendish Corp.
Ichord, Loretta Frances & Millbrook Press. Skillet Bread, Sourdough, & Vinegar Days: Cooking in Pioneer Days. Ellis, Jan Davey, illus. 2005. 64p. (J). (gr. 4-8). per. 8.95 *(978-0-7613-9521-8(0),* First Avenue Editions) Lerner Publishing Group.
Jarnow, Jesse. Davy Crockett: Defensor de la frontera (Davy Crockett: Frontier Hero) 2009. (Grandes personajes en la historia de los Estados Unidos (Famous People in American History) Ser.). (SPA.). 32p. (gr. 2-3). 47.90 *(978-1-61512-797-9(6),* Editorial Buenas Letras) Rosen Publishing Group, Inc., The.
—Davy Crockett: Frontier Hero / Defensor de la Frontera. 2009. (Famous People in American History/Grandes personajes en la historia de los Estados Unidos Ser.). (ENG & SPA.). 32p. (gr. 2-3). 47.90 *(978-1-61512-543-2(4),* Editorial Buenas Letras) Rosen Publishing Group, Inc., The.
Johnson, Robin. California Gold Rush! 2013. (ENG., Illus.). 48p. (J). *(978-0-7787-1170-4(6));* pap. *(978-0-7787-1178-0(1))* Crabtree Publishing Co.
Johnston, Charles H. L. Famous Frontiersmen & Heroes of the Border: Their Adventurous. 2006. (ENG.). 420p. per. 34.95 *(978-1-4286-4118-1(1))* Kessinger Publishing, LLC.
Johnston, Marianne. Davy Crockett. 2009. (American Legends Ser.). 24p. (gr. 3-3). 42.50 *(978-1-61511-381-1(9),* PowerKids Pr.) Rosen Publishing Group, Inc., The.
—Johnny Appleseed. 2009. (American Legends Ser.). 24p. (gr. 3-3). 42.50 *(978-1-61511-383-5(5),* PowerKids Pr.) Rosen Publishing Group, Inc., The.
Kalman, Bobbie. My Community Long Ago. 2010. (My World Ser.). (ENG.). 24p. (J). (gr. k-3). *(978-0-7787-9517-9(9));* pap. *(978-0-7787-9542-1(X))* Crabtree Publishing Co.
—A Visual Dictionary of a Pioneer Community. 2007. (Visual Dictionaries Ser.). (ENG., Illus.). 32p. (J). (gr. 3-7). pap. *(978-0-7787-3524-3(9))* Crabtree Publishing Co.
Kanefield, Teri. The Extraordinary Suzy Wright: A Colonial Woman on the Frontier. 2016. (ENG., Illus.). 64p. (J). (gr. 3-7). 19.95 *(978-1-4197-1866-3(5),* Abrams Bks. for Young Readers) Abrams, Inc.
Kennedy, Emily. Daniel Boone. 2014. (Illus.). 31p. (J). lib. bdg. *(978-1-62712-280-1(X))* Cavendish Square Publishing.
Knowlton, MaryLee. La Colonia de Jamestown. 2006. (Hitos de la historia de Estados Unidos (Landmark Events in American History) Ser.). (SPA.). 48p. (gr. 5-12). pap. 11.70 *(978-0-8368-7470-9(6),* Gareth Stevens Learning Library) Stevens, Gareth Publishing LLLP.
Knudsen, Anders. Antoine de la Mothe Cadillac: French Settlements at Detroit & Louisiana. 2006. (In the Footsteps of Explorers Ser.). (ENG., Illus.). 32p. (J). (gr. 3-9). lib. bdg. *(978-0-7787-2429-2(8));* (gr. 4-7). pap. *(978-0-7787-2465-0(4))* Crabtree Publishing Co.
Kramer, Sydelle. Who Was Daniel Boone? Ulrich, George, illus. 2006. (Who Was? Ser.). (ENG.). 112p. (J). (gr. 3-7). pap. 5.99 *(978-0-448-43902-0(6),* Grosset & Dunlap) Penguin Young Readers Group.
—Who Was Daniel Boone? Ulrich, George, illus. 2006. (Who Was... ? Ser.). 108p. (gr. 2-6). 15.00 *(978-0-7569-6951-6(4))* Perfection Learning Corp.
—Who Was Daniel Boone? 2006. (Who Was... ? Ser.). 16.00 *(978-1-4177-8317-5(6),* Turtleback) Turtleback Bks.
Kravitz, Danny. Surviving the Journey: The Story of the Oregon Trail. 1 vol. 2014. (Adventures on the American Frontier Ser.). (ENG.). 32p. (gr. 3-4). 27.32 *(978-1-4914-0187-3(7),* Fact Finders) Capstone Press of Coughlan Cos.
Krensky, Stephen. Calamity Jane. 2008. pap. 40.95 *(978-0-8225-9291-4(6))* Lerner Publishing Group.
Kunstler, James Howard. Johnny Appleseed. Olson, Stan, illus. 2005. (Rabbit Ears-A Classic Tale Ser.). 36p. (J). (gr. k-5). 25.65 *(978-1-59197-765-0(7))* Spotlight.
Kurtz, Jane. Johnny Appleseed. Haverfield, Mary, illus. 2004. (Ready-To-Reads Ser.). (ENG.). 32p. (J). (gr. -1-1). pap. 3.99 *(978-0-689-85958-8(9),* Simon Spotlight) Simon Spotlight.
Landau, Elaine. The Oregon Trail. 2006. (True Bks.). (ENG., Illus.). 48p. (J). (gr. 3-7). pap. 6.95 *(978-0-516-27903-9(3),* Children's Pr.) Scholastic Library Publishing.
Lange, Karen. 1607: A New Look at Jamestown. Block, Ira, photos by. 2007. (ENG., Illus.). 48p. (J). (gr. 4-7). 17.95 *(978-1-4263-0012-7(3));* 27.90 *(978-1-4263-0013-4(1))* National Geographic Society. (National Geographic Children's Bks.).
Lappi, Megan. The Church: Pioneers of Canada. 2011. 24p. (YA). (gr. 2-4). *(978-1-77071-678-0(5));* pap. *(978-1-77071-682-7(3))* Weigl Educational Pubs. Ltd.
Lassieur, Allison. Westward Expansion: An Interactive History Adventure. 2016. (You Choose: History Ser.). (ENG.). 112p. (gr. 3-4). pap. 6.95 *(978-1-5157-4259-3(8),* You Choose Bks.) Capstone Press of Coughlan Cos.
Lemke, Donald B. The Schoolchildren's Blizzard. 2007. (Disasters in History Ser.). (ENG., Illus.). 32p. (gr. 3-4). 30.65 *(978-1-4296-0157-3(4),* Graphic Library) Capstone Press of Coughlan Cos.
Levy, Janey. The Battle of the Alamo. 2009. (Real Life Readers Ser.). 32p. (gr. 4-5). pap. 10.00 *(978-1-4358-0167-7(9),* Rosen Classroom); (gr. 4-4). 47.90 *(978-1-61511-369-9(X),* PowerKids Pr.); (J). (gr. 3-4). lib. bdg. 25.25 *(978-1-4358-2991-6(3),* PowerKids Pr.) Rosen Publishing Group, Inc., The.
Linde, Barbara M. The Price of a Pioneer Journey: Adding & Subtracting Two-Digit Dollar Amounts. 2009. (PowerMath: Beginning Ser.). 16p. (gr. 2-2). 37.50 *(978-1-60851-376-5(9),* PowerKids Pr.) Rosen Publishing Group, Inc., The.

Lowery, Linda. Aunt Clara Brown: Official Pioneer. Porter, Janice Lee, illus. 2006. (On My Own Biographies Ser.). 48p. 16.95 *(978-0-7569-6699-7(X))* Perfection Learning Corp.

Lowery, Linda & Porter, Janice Lee. Tia Clara Brown. 2005. (Yo Solo (On My Own) Ser.).Tr. of Aunt Clara Brown. (SPA., Illus.). 48p. (J). (gr. 2-5). 23.93 *(978-0-8225-3128-9(3),* Ediciones Lerner) Lerner Publishing Group.

Madsen, Susan Arrington. I Walked to Zion: True Stories of Young Pioneers on the Mormon Trail. 2008. 192p. pap. 9.95 *(978-1-59038-930-0(1))* Deseret Bk. Co.

Matzke, Ann H. My Life As a Pioneer. 2012. (ENG.). 24p. (gr. k-2). pap. 8.95 *(978-1-61810-280-5(X))* Rourke Educational Media.

Maynard, Charles W. Fort Clatsop. 2009. (Famous Forts Throughout American History Ser.). 24p. (gr. 3-4). 42.50 *(978-1-61512-515-9(9),* PowerKids Pr.) Rosen Publishing Group, Inc., The.

—Fort Laramie. 2009. (Famous Forts Throughout American History Ser.). 24p. (gr. 3-4). 42.50 *(978-1-61512-516-6(7),* PowerKids Pr.) Rosen Publishing Group, Inc., The.

McGill, Jordan. Farm Life: Pioneers of Canada. 2011. 24p. (YA). (gr. 2-4). *(978-1-77071-679-7(3));* pap. *(978-1-77071-683-4(1))* Weigl Educational Pubs. Ltd.

Mead, James R., et al. Hunting & Trading in Kansas, 1859-1875. 2015. (J). *(978-1-929731-25-1(6))* Rowfant Pr.

Meloche, Renee Taft. Daniel Boone: Bravery on the Frontier. Pollard, Bryan, illus. 2009. (Heroes of History for Young Readers Ser.). 32p. (J). (gr. 1). 8.99 *(978-1-932096-61-3(2))* Emerald Bks.

Micklos, John, Jr., et al. Adventures on the American Frontier. (Adventures on the American Frontier Ser.). (ENG.). 32p. (gr. 3-4). 2015. pap. 63.60 *(978-1-4914-7281-1(2),* Fact Finders) 2015. (Illus.). pap. 31.80 *(978-1-4914-7280-4(4))* 2014. 109.28 *(978-1-4914-0188-0(5),* Fact Finders) Capstone Press of Coughlan Cos.

Miller, Dean & Talbot, Jeffrey. Johnny Appleseed. 2014. (Illus.). 32p. (J). 28.50 *(978-1-62712-277-1(X))* Cavendish Square Publishing.

Moriarty, J. T. Davy Crockett: Defensor de la Frontera. 2004. (Grandes personajes en la historia de los Estados Unidos Ser.). (SPA.). 32p. (gr. 3-6). pap. 10.00 *(978-0-8239-4226-8(0),* Rosen Classroom) Rosen Publishing Group, Inc., The.

—Davy Crockett: Frontier Hero. 2009. (Primary Sources of Famous People in American History Ser.). 32p. (gr. 2-3). 47.90 *(978-1-60851-670-4(9))* Rosen Publishing Group, Inc., The.

Murphy, Patricia J. Journey of a Pioneer. 2008. (DK Readers Ser.). (ENG.). 32p. (J). (gr. 1-3). 3.99 *(978-0-7566-4005-7(9),* DK Children) Dorling Kindersley Publishing, Inc.

Nelson, Sheila. From the Atlantic to the Pacific: Canadian Expansion, 1867-1909. 2007. (How Canada Became Canada Ser.). (Illus.). 87p. (YA). (gr. 3-7). lib. bdg. 21.95 *(978-1-4222-0005-6(1),* 1247971) Mason Crest.

Nelson, Vaunda Micheaux. Bad News for Outlaws: The Remarkable Life of Bass Reeves, Deputy U. S. Marshall. Christie, R. Gregory, illus. 2009. (Exceptional Social Studies Titles for Intermediate Grades). (ENG.). 40p. (J). (gr. 3-6). lib. bdg. 17.95 *(978-0-8225-6764-6(4))* Lerner Publishing Group.

Nemerson, Roy. Daniel Boone. 2005. (Heroes of America Ser.). 239p. (gr. 3-8). 27.07 *(978-1-59679-256-2(6),* Abdo & Daughters) ABDO Publishing Co.

Nichols, Kaitlyn. Davey Crockett. 2009. pap. 13.25 *(978-1-60559-057-8(6))* Hameray Publishing Group, Inc.

Oachs, Emily Rose. Death in the Donner Party: A Cause-And-Effect Investigation. 2016. (Cause-And-Effect Disasters Ser.). (ENG., Illus.). 40p. (J). (gr. 4-6). 30.65 *(978-1-5124-1115-7(9))* Lerner Publishing Group.

Olson, Steven. The Oregon Trail: A Primary Source History of the Route to the American West. 2009. (Primary Sources in American History Ser.). 64p. (gr. 5-8). 58.50 *(978-1-60851-501-1(X))* Rosen Publishing Group, Inc., The.

O'Maley, Elizabeth. Bones on the Ground. 2014. (J). *(978-0-87195-362-9(5))* Indiana Historical Society.

Onsgard, Bethany. Life on the Frontier, 1 vol. 2014. (Daily Life in US History Ser.). (ENG., Illus.). 48p. (J). (gr. 3-6). lib. bdg. 32.79 *(978-1-62403-631-6(7))* ABDO Publishing Co.

Pacheco, Robert, illus. Trade on the Taos Mountain Trail. 2010. (ENG.). 48p. (J). pap. 16.99 *(978-0-9823445-0-7(3))* Vanishing Horizons.

Parker, Lewis K. Dutch Colonies in the Americas. (European Colonies in the Americas Ser.). 24p. 2009. (gr. 2-2). 42.50 *(978-1-61512-316-2(4))* 2003. (Illus.). (J). lib. bdg. 22.60 *(978-0-8239-6472-7(8))* Rosen Publishing Group, Inc., The. (PowerKids Pr.).

—English Colonies in the Americas. (European Colonies in the Americas Ser.). 24p. 2009. (gr. 2-2). 42.50 *(978-1-61512-317-9(2))* 2003. (Illus.). (J). lib. bdg. 22.60 *(978-0-8239-6475-8(2))* Rosen Publishing Group, Inc., The. (PowerKids Pr.).

—French Colonies in the Americas. (European Colonies in the Americas Ser.). 24p. 2009. (gr. 2-2). 42.50 *(978-1-61512-318-6(0))* 2003. (Illus.). (J). lib. bdg. 22.60 *(978-0-8239-6473-4(6))* Rosen Publishing Group, Inc., The. (PowerKids Pr.).

—Russian Colonies in the Americas. 2009. (European Colonies in the Americas Ser.). 24p. (gr. 2-2). 42.50 *(978-1-61512-319-3(9),* PowerKids Pr.) Rosen Publishing Group, Inc., The.

—Spanish Colonies in the Americas. (European Colonies in the Americas Ser.). 24p. 2009. (gr. 2-2). 42.50 *(978-1-61512-320-9(2))* 2003. (Illus.). (J). lib. bdg. 22.60 *(978-0-8239-6471-0(X))* Rosen Publishing Group, Inc., The. (PowerKids Pr.).

Patent, Dorothy Hinshaw. Homesteading: Settling America's Heartland. Munoz, William, photos by. 2013. (Illus.). 48p. (J). pap. 12.00 *(978-0-87842-605-8(1))* Mountain Pr. Publishing Co., Inc.

Peppas, Lynn. Why Charles Goodnight Matters to Texas. 2014. (Illus.). 32p. (J). lib. bdg. 26.25 *(978-1-4777-0907-8(X))* Rosen Publishing Group, Inc., The.

Peterson, Cris. Birchbark Brigade: A Fur Trade History. 2009. (ENG.). 136p. (J). (gr. 4-18). 18.95 *(978-1-59078-426-6(X),* Calkins Creek) Boyds Mills Pr.

Petrick, Neila Skinner. Jane Wilkinson Long: Texas Pioneer, 1 vol. Haynes, Joyce, illus. 2004. (ENG.). 32p. (J). (gr. k-3). 16.99 *(978-1-58980-147-9(4))* Pelican Publishing Co., Inc.

Petrie, Kristin. Daniel Boone, 1 vol. 2004. (Explorers Set 1 Ser.). (ENG.). 32p. (gr. k-6). 27.07 *(978-1-59197-592-2(1),* Checkerboard Library) ABDO Publishing Co.

Raabe, Emily. The Gold Rush: California or Bust! 2003. (Westward Ho! Ser.). (Illus.). 24p. (J). lib. bdg. 22.60 *(978-0-8239-6494-9(9),* PowerKids Pr.) Rosen Publishing Group, Inc., The.

—Pioneers: Life as a Homesteader. 2003. (Westward Ho! Ser.). (Illus.). 24p. (J). lib. bdg. 22.60 *(978-0-8239-6498-7(1),* PowerKids Pr.) Rosen Publishing Group, Inc., The.

Rajczak, Kristen. Life As a Pioneer. 2013. (What You Didn't Know about History Ser.). (Illus.). 24p. (J). (gr. 2-5). pap. 8.15 *(978-1-4339-8420-4(2));* lib. bdg. 22.60 *(978-1-4339-8419-8(9))* Stevens, Gareth Publishing LLLP.

Randolph, Ryan. A Bank Robber's End: The Death of Jesse James. 2009. (Great Moments in American History Ser.). 32p. (gr. 3-3). 47.90 *(978-1-61513-138-9(8))* Rosen Publishing Group, Inc., The.

Randolph, Ryan P. Black Cowboys. 2009. (Library of the Westward Expansion Ser.). 24p. (gr. 3-4). 42.50 *(978-1-60853-933-8(4),* PowerKids Pr.) Rosen Publishing Group, Inc., The.

Ransom, Candice. Daniel Boone. 2005. (History Maker Biographies Ser.). (ENG., Illus.). 48p. (gr. 3-6). lib. bdg. 27.93 *(978-0-8225-2941-5(6),* Lerner Pubns.) Lerner Publishing Group.

—Why Did English Settlers Come to Virginia? And Other Questions about the Jamestown Settlement. 2011. (Six Questions of American History Ser.). (ENG.). 48p. (gr. 4-6). 30.60 *(978-0-7613-5228-0(7));* pap. 56.72 *(978-0-7613-7301-8(2))* Lerner Publishing Group.

Raum, Elizabeth. Cutting a Path: Daniel Boone & the Cumberland Gap. 2015. (Adventures on the American Frontier Ser.). (ENG., Illus.). 32p. (gr. 3-4). pap. 7.95 *(978-1-4914-4909-7(8))* Capstone Press of Coughlan Cos.

Rauzi, Kelly Emerling. Fearless John: The Legend of John Beargrease. Horak, Mila, illus. 2006. 32p. 19.95 *(978-0-9774831-3-6(4))* Singing River Pubns.

Rea, Thelma. Pioneer Families. 2006. (Rosen Real Readers Big Bookstm Ser.). (ENG.). 16p. (gr. 2-3). 37.95 *(978-1-4042-6222-5(9))* Rosen Publishing Group, Inc., The.

Rice, Dona. Chicas y Chicos Malos Del Lejano Oeste. 2016. (TIME for Kids en Español - Level 5 Ser.). (SPA.). 64p. (gr. 5-5). lib. bdg. 31.99 *(978-1-5157-2954-9(0))* Time for Kids Inc AUS. Dist: Capstone Pub.

Riehecky, Janet & Knowlton, MaryLee. La Colonia de Jamestown. 2006. (Hitos de la historia de Estados Unidos (Landmark Events in American History) Ser.). (SPA., Illus.). 48p. (gr. 5-12). lib. bdg. 27.00 *(978-0-8368-7463-1(3),* Gareth Stevens Secondary Library) Stevens, Gareth Publishing LLLP.

Roberts, Russell. The Life & Times of Stephen F. Austin. 2007. (Profiles in American History Ser.). (Illus.). 48p. (J). (gr. 4-7). lib. bdg. 29.95 *(978-1-58415-531-7(0))* Mitchell Lane Pubs., Inc.

Robertson, James. The Wild West: 1804-1890. Kunstler, Mort, illus. 2016. (See American History Ser.). (ENG.). 48p. (J). (gr. 2). 13.95 *(978-0-7892-1260-3(9),* Abbeville Kids) Abbeville Pr., Inc.

Robertson, Theda Robinson. Journey to a Free Land: The Story of Nicodemus, the First All Black Town West of the Mississippi. 2006. (Illus.). (J). *(978-0-9705721-6-5(6))* Written Images, Inc.

Russell, Greta. Olive Boone: Frontier Woman. Hare, John, illus. 2014. (Notable Missourians Ser.). (ENG.). 48p. (J). lib. bdg. 24.00 *(978-1-61248-118-0(3))* Truman State Univ. Pr.

Saddleback Educational Publishing Staff, ed. Davy Crockett, 1 vol. unabr. ed. 2008. (Graphic Biographies Ser.). (ENG., Illus.). 25p. (YA). (gr. 9-12). pap. 7.95 *(978-1-59905-220-5(2))* Saddleback Educational Publishing, Inc.

Sammons, Sandra Wallus. Marjorie Kinnan Rawlings & the Florida Crackers. 2010. (Pineapple Press Biography Ser.). (ENG., Illus.). 72p. (Orig.). (J). (gr. 4-7). pap. 8.95 *(978-1-56164-473-5(0));* 11.95 *(978-1-56164-472-8(2))* Pineapple Pr., Inc.

Sanford, William R. & Green, Carl R. Daniel Boone: Courageous Frontiersman. 2012. (Courageous Heroes of the American West Ser.). (Illus.). 48p. (J). pap. 8.95 *(978-1-4644-0085-8(7));* (gr. 5-18). 22.60 *(978-0-7660-4002-1(X))* Enslow Pubs., Inc.

Savage, Jeff. American Cowboys: True Tales of the Wild West. 2012. (True Tales of the Wild West Ser.). (Illus.). 48p. (J). (gr. 5-18). pap. 8.95 *(978-1-4644-0027-8(X))* Enslow Pubs., Inc.

Saviola, Ava. The Story of Johnny Appleseed. 2009. (Real Life Readers Ser.). 12p. (gr. 1-2). pap. 5.90 *(978-1-4042-7927-8(X),* Rosen Classroom) Rosen Publishing Group, Inc., The.

Schiel, Katy. The Whiskey Rebellion: An Early Challenge to America's New Government. 2009. (Life in the New American Nation Ser.). 32p. (gr. 4-4). 47.90 *(978-1-61514-289-7(4))* Rosen Publishing Group, Inc., The.

Schwartz, Heather E. The Foul, Filthy American Frontier: The Disgusting Details about the Journey Out West. 2011. (Disgusting History Ser.). (ENG.). 32p. (gr. 3-4). pap. 47.70 *(978-1-4296-6478-3(9),* Fact Finders) Capstone Press of Coughlan Cos.

—Outlaws, Gunslingers, & Thieves. (ShockZone (tm) — Villains Ser.). (ENG., Illus.). 32p. (gr. 5-8). 2015. 21.32 *(978-1-4677-6004-1(8),* Lerner Digital) 2013. pap. 8.95 *(978-1-4677-0899-9(2))* Lerner Publishing Group.

Sechrist, Darren. Taming the West. 2008. (ENG.). 32p. (J). pap. *(978-0-7787-4215-9(6))* Crabtree Publishing Co.

—Westward, Ho! 2008. (ENG.). 32p. (J). pap. *(978-0-7787-4217-3(2))* Crabtree Publishing Co.

Shoup, Kate. The California Gold Rush. 2016. (Expanding America Ser.). (ENG., Illus.). 96p. (J). (gr. 8-8). lib. bdg. 42.79 *(978-1-5026-0968-7(1))* Cavendish Square Publishing.

Signature Lives - Reformation Era. 2006. (Signature Lives: Reformation Era Ser.). (ENG., Illus.). 112p. (gr. 6-7). 70.64 *(978-0-7565-1712-0(5))* Compass Point Bks.

Signature Lives - Revolutionary War Era, 13 bks. 2006. (Signature Lives: Revolutionary War Era Ser.). (ENG., Illus.). 112p. (gr. 6-7). 176.60 *(978-0-7565-1711-3(7))* Compass Point Bks.

Signature Lives: Colonial America. 2006. (Signature Lives: Colonial America Ser.). (ENG., Illus.). 112p. (gr. 6-7). 70.64 *(978-0-7565-1710-6(9))* Compass Point Bks.

Sioux, Tracee. Immigrants & the Westward Expansion. 2004. (Primary Sources of Immigration & Migration in America Ser.). (Illus.). 24p. (ENG.). (gr. 4-8). pap. 9.40 *(978-0-8239-8950-8(X));* (J). lib. bdg. 22.60 *(978-0-8239-6824-4(3))* Rosen Publishing Group, Inc., The. (PowerKids Pr.).

Smith, Andrea P. Daniel Boone. 2012. (Illus.). 24p. (J). 63.60 *(978-1-4488-5227-7(7));* pap. 10.60 *(978-1-4488-5226-0(9));* lib. bdg. 25.25 *(978-1-4488-5194-2(7))* Rosen Publishing Group, Inc., The. (PowerKids Pr.).

—Davy Crockett. 2012. (Illus.). 24p. (J). 63.60 *(978-1-4488-5223-9(4));* pap. 10.60 *(978-1-4488-5222-2(6));* lib. bdg. 25.25 *(978-1-4488-5192-8(0))* Rosen Publishing Group, Inc., The. (PowerKids Pr.).

—Jim Bowie. 2012. (Illus.). 24p. (J). 63.60 *(978-1-4488-5231-4(5));* pap. 10.60 *(978-1-4488-5230-7(7));* lib. bdg. 25.25 *(978-1-4488-5196-6(3))* Rosen Publishing Group, Inc., The. (PowerKids Pr.).

—Johnny Appleseed. 2012. (Illus.). 24p. (J). 63.60 *(978-1-4488-5225-3(0));* pap. 10.60 *(978-1-4488-5224-6(2));* lib. bdg. 25.25 *(978-1-4488-5193-5(9))* Rosen Publishing Group, Inc., The. (PowerKids Pr.).

Smith-Llera, Danielle, et al. Adventures on the American Frontier, 4 vols. 2015. (Adventures on the American Frontier Ser.). (ENG., Illus.). 32p. (gr. 3-4). 109.28 *(978-1-4914-6689-6(8))* Capstone Press of Coughlan Cos.

Spalding, Arthur W. Pioneer Stories. fac. rev. ed. 2010. (Illus.). 286p. per. 15.95 *(978-1-57258-042-8(9),* 945-5908) TEACH Services, Inc.

Spinner, Stephanie. Who Was Annie Oakley? Day, Larry, illus. 2003. (Who Was... ? Ser.). 109p. (gr. 4-7). 15.00 *(978-0-7569-1588-9(0))* Perfection Learning Corp.

Stanley, George Edward. The European Settlement of North America (1492-1754) 2005. (Primary Source History of the United States Ser.). (Illus.). 48p. (gr. 5-12). pap. 14.05 *(978-0-8368-5833-4(6));* lib. bdg. 31.00 *(978-0-8368-5824-2(7))* Stevens, Gareth Publishing LLLP. (Gareth Stevens Secondary Library).

Steele, Christy. Famous Wagon Trails. 2005. (America's Westward Expansion Ser.). (Illus.). 48p. (gr. 5-12). pap. 14.05 *(978-0-8368-5795-5(X));* lib. bdg. 31.00 *(978-0-8368-5788-7(7))* Stevens, Gareth Publishing LLLP. (Gareth Stevens Secondary Library).

—Pioneer Life in the American West. 2005. (America's Westward Expansion Ser.). (Illus.). 48p. (gr. 5-12). pap. 14.05 *(978-0-8368-5797-9(6));* lib. bdg. 31.00 *(978-0-8368-5790-0(9))* Stevens, Gareth Publishing LLLP. (Gareth Stevens Secondary Library).

Stefoff, Rebecca. Exploration & Settlement. 2007. (ENG., Illus.). 96p. (C). (gr. 6-18). lib. bdg. 158.00 *(978-0-7656-8108-9(0),* Y182272) Routledge.

—Surviving the Oregon Trail. 2012. (Stories in American History Ser.). (Illus.). 128p. (J). (gr. 5-18). 33.27 *(978-0-7660-3955-1(2))* Enslow Pubs., Inc.

—Surviving the Oregon Trail: Stories in American History. 2012. (Stories in American History Ser.). (Illus.). 128p. (J). (gr. 5-18). pap. 10.95 *(978-1-4644-0025-4(3))* Enslow Pubs., Inc.

Stokes, Betty Southard. Postcards from George, 1763-1781: George Rogers Clark Writes Home to Virginia from the Kentucky Wilderness. Cable, Annette, illus. 2010. (J). *(978-1-935497-12-7(X))* Butler Bk. Publishing.

Townsley, Janet Howe. Dakota Dreams: Fannie Sabra Howe's Own Story, 1881-1884. 2003. (Illus.). 77p. (J). 19.95 *(978-0-9715171-4-1(2))* South Dakota State Historical Society Pr.

Turner, Glennette Tilley. Fort Mosé: And the Story of the Man Who Built the First Free Black Settlement in Colonial America. 2010. (ENG., Illus.). 48p. (J). (gr. 3-7). 18.95 *(978-0-8109-4056-7(6),* Abrams Bks. for Young Readers) Abrams, Inc.

Unlocking the Secrets of Science: Set of 10 Pioneers. (Illus.). 31p. (gr. 4-10). lib. bdg. *(978-1-58415-234-7(6))* Mitchell Lane Pubs., Inc.

Wade, Mary Dodson. Jane Long: Choosing Texas. Roeder, Virginia Marsh, illus. 2009. (ENG.). 24p. (J). (gr. k-2). 16.95 *(978-1-933979-38-0(0),* 9781933979380) Bright Sky Pr.

—Jane Long: Texas Journey. Roeder, Virginia, illus. 2009. (ENG.). 64p. (J). (gr. 4-7). 16.95 *(978-1-933979-39-7(9),* 9781933979397) Bright Sky Pr.

—Stephen F. Austin: Keeping Promises. 2012. (Texas Heroes for Young Readers Ser.). (ENG.). 24p. (J). (gr. k-2). 16.95 *(978-1-933979-11-3(9))* Bright Sky Pr.

Wadsworth, Ginger. Survival in the Snow. Orback, Craig, illus. 2009. (On My Own History Ser.). (ENG.). 48p. (gr. 2-4). 25.26 *(978-0-8225-7892-5(1))* Lerner Publishing Group.

Waldman, Scott. Gunfight at the O. K. Corral: Wyatt Earp Upholds the Law. 2009. (Great Moments in American History Ser.). 32p. (gr. 3-3). 47.90 *(978-1-61513-143-3(4))* Rosen Publishing Group, Inc., The.

Warren, Andrea. Pioneer Girl: A True Story of Growing up on the Prairie. 2009. (ENG., Illus.). 104p. pap. 14.95 *(978-0-8032-2526-8(1),* Bison Bks.) Univ. of Nebraska Pr.

Welvaert, Scott R. & Welvaert, Scott R. The Donner Party, 1 vol. Frenz, Ron et al, illus. 2006. (Disasters in History Ser.). (ENG.). 32p. (gr. 3-4). 30.65 *(978-0-7368-5479-5(7),* Graphic Library) Capstone Press of Coughlan Cos.

Whiting, Jim. Jim Beckwourth: The Man Who Opened the West. 2007. (Illus.). 144p. (YA). (gr. 6-18). lib. bdg. 25.95 *(978-1-59556-027-8(0))* OTTN Publishing.

Wild Bill Hickok. 2010. (Legends of the Wild West Ser.). (Illus.). 112p. (gr. 6-12). 35.00 *(978-1-60413-593-0(X),* Chelsea Hse.) Facts On File, Inc.

Williams, Jack S. Sailors, Merchants, & Muleteers of the California Mission Frontier. 2009. (People of the California Missions Ser.). 64p. (gr. 4-4). 58.50 *(978-1-60851-159-4(6),* PowerKids Pr.) Rosen Publishing Group, Inc., The.

—Soldiers & Their Families of the California Mission Frontier. 2009. (People of the California Missions Ser.). 64p. (gr. 4-4). 58.50 *(978-1-60851-160-0(X),* PowerKids Pr.) Rosen Publishing Group, Inc., The.

Winders, Richard Bruce. Davy Crockett: The Legend of the Wild Frontier. (Library of American Lives & Times Ser.). 112p. 2009. (gr. 5-5). 69.20 *(978-1-60853-476-0(6))* 2005. (Illus.). (YA). (gr. 4-8). lib. bdg. 34.60 *(978-0-8239-5747-7(0))* Rosen Publishing Group, Inc., The.

Winters, Kay. John Appleseed: A Trail of Trees. Pullen, Zachary, illus. 2007. (J). *(978-1-4263-0101-8(4))* National Geographic Society.

Worth, Richard. Independence for Latino America. 2006. (Latino-American History Ser.). 112p. (YA). (gr. 5-9). 35.00 *(978-0-8160-6441-0(5))* Facts On File, Inc.

—Johnny Appleseed: Select Good Seeds & Plant Them in Good Ground. 2010. (Americans—the Spirit of a Nation Ser.). (Illus.). 128p. (J). lib. bdg. 33.27 *(978-0-7660-3352-8(X))* Enslow Pubs., Inc.

Yolen, Jane. Johnny Appleseed: The Legend & the Truth. Burke, Jim, illus. (ENG.). 32p. (J). (gr. 1-4). 2011. pap. 6.99 *(978-0-06-059137-3(4))* 2008. 16.99 *(978-0-06-059135-9(8))* HarperCollins Pubs.

Zronik, John Paul & Zronik, John. Daniel Boone: Woodsman of Kentucky. 2006. (In the Footsteps of Explorers Ser.). (ENG., Illus.). 32p. (J). (gr. 4-7). pap. *(978-0-7787-2464-3(6),* 1253442); lib. bdg. *(978-0-7787-2428-5(X),* 1253442) Crabtree Publishing Co.

FRONTIER AND PIONEER LIFE—ALASKA

Murphy, Claire Rudolf & Haigh, Jane G. Children of the Gold Rush. 2012. (Illus.). 96p. pap. 15.95 *(978-0-9627530-4-6(1))* Hillside Pr.

Parker, Lewis K. Russian Colonies in the Americas. 2003. (European Colonies in the Americas Ser.). (Illus.). 24p. (J). lib. bdg. 22.60 *(978-0-8239-6470-3(1),* PowerKids Pr.) Rosen Publishing Group, Inc., The.

FRONTIER AND PIONEER LIFE—CALIFORNIA

Benoit, Peter. The California Gold Rush. 2012. (Cornerstones of Freedom, Third Ser.). (ENG., Illus.). 64p. (J). pap. 8.95 *(978-0-531-28153-6(1));* lib. bdg. 30.00 *(978-0-531-23053-4(8))* Scholastic Library Publishing.

Blake, Kevin & Sturdivant, Brad. Bodie: The Town That Belongs to Ghosts. 2015. (Abandoned: Towns Without People Ser.). (ENG.). 32p. (J). (gr. 2-7). lib. bdg. 26.60 *(978-1-62724-524-1(3))* Bearport Publishing Co., Inc.

Brown, Don. Gold! Gold from the American River! January 24 1848 - The Day the Gold Rush Began. Brown, Don, illus. 2011. (Actual Times Ser.: 3). (ENG., Illus.). 64p. (J). (gr. 1-5). 17.99 *(978-1-59643-223-9(3),* 9781596432239) Roaring Brook Pr.

Brown, Rachel K. Sacramento: Daily Life in Western Mining Town. 2003. (J). lib. bdg. *(978-1-58417-015-0(8))* Lake Street Pubs.

Craats, Rennay. Gold Rush. 2003. (Real Life Stories Ser.). (Illus.). 24p. (J). lib. bdg. 24.45 *(978-1-59036-078-1(8))* Weigl Pubs., Inc.

Crewe, Sabrina & Uschan, Michael V. La Fiebre del Oro en California. 2006. (Hitos de la historia de Estados Unidos (Landmark Events in American History) Ser.). (SPA., Illus.). 48p. (gr. 5-12). lib. bdg. 27.00 *(978-0-8368-7466-2(8),* Gareth Stevens Secondary Library) Stevens, Gareth Publishing LLLP.

—La Fiebre del oro en California. 2006. (Hitos de la historia de Estados Unidos (Landmark Events in American History) Ser.). (SPA.). 48p. (gr. 5-12). pap. 11.70 *(978-0-8368-7473-0(0),* Gareth Stevens Learning Library) Stevens, Gareth Publishing LLLP.

Crewe, Sabrina, et al. The California Gold Rush. 2010. (ENG., Illus.). 32p. (C). (gr. 3-6). lib. bdg. 41.95 *(978-0-8368-3393-5(7))* National Geographic School Publishing, Inc.

Flores, Mina. The Gold Rush: Gold Seekers, Miners, & Merchants. 2016. (Spotlight on American History Ser.). (Illus.). 24p. (J). (gr. 6-4). 26.25 *(978-1-5081-4942-2(9),* PowerKids Pr.) Rosen Publishing Group, Inc., The.

George, Lynn. What Do You Know about the Gold Rush? (20 Questions: History Ser.). 24p. (gr. 2-3). 2009. 42.50 *(978-1-60854-959-7(3),* PowerKids Pr.) 2008. (J). lib. bdg. 22.60 *(978-1-4042-4188-6(4))* Rosen Publishing Group, Inc., The.

Goff, Elizabeth Hudson & Uschan, Michael V. The California Gold Rush. 2006. (Graphic Histories Ser.). (Illus.). 32p. (gr. 5-8). pap. 10.50 *(978-0-8368-6254-6(6))* Stevens, Gareth Publishing LLLP.

Goff, Elizabeth Hudson, et al. The California Gold Rush. Floor, Guus, illus. 2006. (Graphic Histories Ser.). 32p. (gr. 5-8). lib. bdg. 27.00 *(978-0-8368-6202-7(3))* Stevens, Gareth Publishing LLLP.

—La Fiebre Del Oro en California. 2007. (Historias Graficas (Graphic Histories) Ser.). (SPA., Illus.). 32p. (gr. 5-8). pap. 10.50 *(978-0-8368-7903-2(1));* lib. bdg. 27.00 *(978-0-8368-7896-7(5))* Stevens, Gareth Publishing LLLP.

Hayhurst, Chris. John Sutter: California Pioneer / Pionero de California. 2009. (Famous People in American History/Grandes personajes en la historia de los Estados Unidos Ser.). (ENG & SPA.). 32p. (gr. 2-3). 47.90 *(978-1-61512-549-4(3),* Editorial Buenas Letras) Rosen Publishing Group, Inc., The.

—John Sutter: Pionero de California (John Sutter: California Pioneer) 2009. (Grandes personajes en la historia de los Estados Unidos (Famous People in American History) Ser.). (SPA.). 32p. (gr. 2-3). 47.90 *(978-1-61512-803-7(4),* Editorial Buenas Letras) Rosen Publishing Group, Inc., The.

Holub, Joan. What Was the Gold Rush? Tomkinson, Tim, illus. 2013. (What Was? Ser.). (ENG.). 112p. (J). (gr. 3-7). pap. 5.99 *(978-0-448-46289-9(3),* Penguin Workshop) Penguin Young Readers Group.

—What Was the Gold Rush? 2013. (What Was... ? Ser.). lib. bdg. 16.00 *(978-0-606-29972-5(6),* Turtleback) Turtleback Bks.

Jordan, Shirley. California Gold Rush: Moments in History. 2003. (Cover-To-Cover Books). (Illus.). 64p. pap. 9.00 *(978-0-7891-5554-2(0));* (J). (gr. 4-7). lib. bdg. 17.95 *(978-0-7569-0633-7(4))* Perfection Learning Corp.

Landau, Elaine. The California Gold Rush: Would You Go for the Gold? (What Would You Do? Ser.). (Illus.). 48p. (J). 2010. pap. 8.95 *(978-1-59845-193-1(6))* 2008. (gr. 3-4). lib. bdg. 25.27 *(978-0-7660-2901-9(8))* Enslow Pubs., Inc. (Enslow Elementary).

—The Gold Rush in California: Would You Catch Gold Fever? 2015. (What Would You Do? Ser.). 48p. (J). (gr. 3-4). 25.27 *(978-0-7660-6300-6(3));* pap. 8.95 *(978-0-7660-6301-3(1),* Enslow Elementary) Enslow Pubs., Inc.

E F G

Levy, Janey. Life During the Gold Rush. 2013. (What You Didn't Know about History Ser.). (Illus.). 24p. (J). (gr. 2-5). pap. 8.15 *(978-1-4339-8430-3(X))*; lib. bdg. 22.60 *(978-1-4339-8429-7(6))* Stevens, Gareth Publishing LLLP.

Lynette, Rachel. The Gold Rush. 2013. (Pioneer Spirit: the Westward Expansion Ser.). 24p. (J). (gr. 3-6). 22.60 *(978-1-4777-0784-5(0))*; pap. 49.50 *(978-1-4777-0902-3(9))*; (ENG., Illus.). pap. 8.25 *(978-1-4777-0901-6(0))* Rosen Publishing Group, Inc., The. (PowerKids Pr.).

Madison, Amelia & Shoup, Kate. Life As a Prospector in the California Gold Rush. 2016. (Life As... Ser.). (ENG., Illus.). 32p. (J). (gr. 3-3). 28.50 *(978-1-5026-1780-4(3))* Cavendish Square Publishing.

Micklos, John, Jr. The Gold Rush. 2016. (Primary Source History Ser.). (ENG., Illus.). 32p. (gr. 3-4). lib. bdg. 27.32 *(978-1-4914-8486-9(1)*, Fact Finders) Capstone Press of Coughlan Cos.

Morlock, Theresa. The Gold Rush. 2017. (J). ***(978-1-5383-0050-3(8))***; pap. ***(978-1-68048-788-6(4))*** Rosen Publishing Group, Inc., The. (Britannica Educational Publishing).

Onsgard, Bethany. Life During the California Gold Rush, 1 vol. 2014. (Daily Life in US History Ser.). (ENG., Illus.). 48p. (J). (gr. 3-6). lib. bdg. 32.79 *(978-1-62403-624-8(4))* ABDO Publishing Co.

Quasha, Jennifer. Gold Rush: Hands-on Projects about Mining the Riches of California. 2009. (Great Social Studies Projects Ser.). 24p. (gr. 3-3). 42.50 *(978-1-61513-209-6(0)*, PowerKids Pr.) Rosen Publishing Group, Inc., The.

Raabe, Emily. The Gold Rush: California or Bust! 2009. (Westward Ho! Ser.). 24p. (gr. 2-3). 42.50 *(978-1-60854-762-3(0)*, PowerKids Pr.) Rosen Publishing Group, Inc., The.

Schuetz, Kari. Bodie: The Gold-Mining Ghost Town. 2017. (Abandoned Places Ser.). (ENG., Illus.). 24p. (J). (gr. 3-7). lib. bdg. 25.95 ***(978-1-62617-694-2(9)***, Torque Bks.) Bellwether Media.

Shoup, Kate. The Gold Rush. 2017. (J). ***(978-1-5026-2640-0(3))*** Cavendish Square Publishing.

Thompson, Gare. When the Mission Padre Came to the Rancho: The Early California Adventures of Rosalinda & Simon Delgado. 2004. (I Am American Ser.). (ENG., Illus.). 40p. (J). (gr. 3-7). pap. 6.99 *(978-0-7922-6945-8(4)*, National Geographic Children's Bks.) National Geographic Society.

Thompson, Gare & National Geographic Learning Staff. Missions & Ranchos. 2007. (Reading Expeditions Ser.). (ENG., Illus.). 40p. (J). pap. 19.95 *(978-0-7922-4548-3(2))* CENGAGE Learning.

Uschan, Michael V. The California Gold Rush. 2003. (Landmark Events in American History Ser.). (Illus.). 48p. (gr. 5-12). pap. 14.05 *(978-0-8368-5402-2(0))*; lib. bdg. 31.00 *(978-0-8368-5374-2(1))* Stevens, Gareth Publishing LLLP. (Gareth Stevens Secondary Library).

Van Meter, Larry A. Yerba Buena. 2007. (Colonial Settlements in America Ser.). (Illus.). 100p. (YA). (gr. 5-9). lib. bdg. 30.00 *(978-0-7910-9338-2(7))* Facts On File, Inc.

Wadsworth, Ginger. Survival in the Snow. Orback, Craig, illus. 2011. 48p. (J). pap. 6.95 *(978-0-7613-3941-0(8)*, First Avenue Editions) Lerner Publishing Group.

Williams, Jack S. Townspeople & Ranchers of the California Mission Frontier. 2009. (People of the California Missions Ser.). 64p. (gr. 4-4). 58.50 *(978-1-60851-161-7(8)*, PowerKids Pr.) Rosen Publishing Group, Inc., The.

Williams, Jack S. & Davis, Thomas L. Sailors, Merchants, & Muleteers. 2004. (People of the California Missions Ser.). (Illus.). 64p. (J). lib. bdg. 26.50 *(978-0-8239-6282-2(2))* Rosen Publishing Group, Inc., The.

—Soldiers & Their Families of the California Mission Frontier. 2004. (People of the California Missions Ser.). (Illus.). 64p. (J). lib. bdg. 26.50 *(978-0-8239-6285-3(7))* Rosen Publishing Group, Inc., The.

—Townspeople & Ranchers of the California Mission Frontier. 2004. (People of the California Missions Ser.). (Illus.). 64p. (J). lib. bdg. 26.50 *(978-0-8239-6284-6(9)*, PowerKids Pr.) Rosen Publishing Group, Inc., The.

FRONTIER AND PIONEER LIFE—FICTION

Aaron, Chester. An American Ghost. 2011. (YA). pap. *(978-1-936144-28-0(X))* Zumaya Pubns. LLC.

Abbott, E. F. Mary Jemison: Native American Captive. 2016. (Based on a True Story Ser.). (ENG., Illus.). 224p. (J). 15.99 *(978-1-250-06838-5(X)*, 9781250068385) Feiwel & Friends.

Aksomitis, Linda. Adeline's Dream, 1 vol. 2005. (From Many Peoples Ser.). (ENG.). 216p. (J). (gr. 4-7). per. 7.95 *(978-1-55050-323-4(5))* Coteau Bks. CAN. Dist: Orca Bk. Pubs. USA.

Alice, Dalgliesh. The Courage of Sarah Noble. 2nd rev. ed. 2014. (ENG.). 64p. (J). (gr. 2-5). 9.24 *(978-1-63245-307-5(X))* Lectorum Pubns., Inc.

Alter, Judy. Sam Houston Is My Hero. 2003. (Chaparral Bks.). (ENG.). 130p. (J). pap. 11.95 *(978-0-87565-277-1(8))* Texas Christian Univ. Pr.

Altsheler, Joseph A. The Border Watch: A Story of the Great Chief's Last Stand. 2008. 320p. pap. *(978-1-4099-0579-0(9))* Dodo Pr.

—The Border Watch: A Story of the Great Chief's Last Stand. 2008. 232p. pap. *(978-1-84830-132-0(4))* Echo Library.

—The Border Watch: A Story of the Great Chief's Last Stand. 2010. (Young Trailers Ser.: Vol. 8). (Illus.). 206p. (J). (gr. 4-7). reprint ed. pap. 20.31 *(978-1-153-78841-0(1))* General Bks. LLC.

—The Border Watch: A Story of the Great Chief's Last Stand. 2012. (Young Trailers Ser.: Vol. 8). 340p. (J). (gr. 4-7). reprint ed. pap. *(978-3-8472-2486-0(7))* Tredition GmbH.

—The Colonial Frontier Novels Vol. 1: The Young Trailers & The Forest Runners. 2009. (Young Trailers Ser.). 376p. (J). reprint ed. *(978-0-85706-002-0(3))*; pap. *(978-0-85706-001-3(5))* Leonaur Ltd.

—The Colonial Frontier Novels Vol. 2: The Keepers of the Trail & The Eyes of the Woods. 2009. (Young Trailers Ser.). 400p. (J). reprint ed. *(978-0-85706-004-4(X))*; pap. *(978-0-85706-003-7(1))* Leonaur Ltd.

—The Colonial Frontier Novels Vol. 3: The Free Rangers & The Riflemen of the Ohio. 2009. (Young Trailers Ser.). 468p. (J). reprint ed. *(978-0-85706-006-8(6))*; pap. *(978-0-85706-005-1(8))* Leonaur Ltd.

—The Colonial Frontier Novels Vol. 4: The Scouts of the Valley & The Border Watch. 2009. (Young Trailers Ser.). 536p. (J). reprint ed. *(978-0-85706-008-2(2))*; pap. *(978-0-85706-007-5(4))* Leonaur Ltd.

—The Eyes of the Woods: A Story of the Ancient Wilderness. (Young Trailers Ser.: Vol. 4). (J). reprint ed. 25.95 *(978-0-8488-1235-5(2))* Amereon Ltd.

—The Eyes of the Woods: A Story of the Ancient Wilderness. 2009. 284p. reprint ed. pap. *(978-1-84902-181-4(3))*; *(978-1-84902-180-7(5))* Benediction Classics.

—The Eyes of the Woods: A Story of the Ancient Wilderness. Hutchison, D. C., illus. 2008. (Young Trailers Ser.: Vol. 4). 256p. (J). reprint ed. pap. *(978-1-4065-4512-8(0))* Dodo Pr.

—The Eyes of the Woods: A Story of the Ancient Wilderness. 2008. (Young Trailers Ser.: Vol. 4). 160p. (J). reprint ed. pap. *(978-1-4068-6669-8(5))* Echo Library.

—The Eyes of the Woods: A Story of the Ancient Wilderness. 2010. (Young Trailers Ser.: Vol. 4). (Illus.). 144p. (J). (gr. 4-7). reprint ed. pap. 19.99 *(978-1-153-78508-2(0))* General Bks. LLC.

—The Eyes of the Woods: A Story of the Ancient Wilderness. 2012. (Young Trailers Ser.: Vol. 4). 230p. (J). (gr. 4-7). reprint ed. pap. 14.45 *(978-3-8472-2166-1(3))* Tredition GmbH.

—The Forest Runners: A Story of the Great War Trail in Early Kentucky. (Young Trailers Ser.: Vol. 2). (J). 25.95 *(978-0-8488-1236-2(0))* Amereon Ltd.

—The Forest Runners: A Story of the Great War Trail in Early Kentucky. l.t. ed. (Young Trailers Ser.: Vol. 2). (J). 2007. 178p. pap. 22.99 *(978-1-4264-8301-1(5))* 2010. 386p. reprint ed. pap. 33.75 *(978-1-149-35494-0(1)*, BiblioLife) 2008. 248p. reprint ed. 24.99 *(978-0-554-34443-0(2))* 2008. 248p. reprint ed. 27.99 *(978-0-554-25140-0(X))* 2007. (ENG.). 218p. reprint ed. pap. 20.99 *(978-1-4264-8264-9(7))* Creative Media Partners, LLC.

—The Forest Runners: A Story of the Great War Trail in Early Kentucky. 2010. (Young Trailers Ser.: Vol. 2). (Illus.). 142p. (J). (gr. 4-7). reprint ed. pap. 19.99 *(978-1-153-70291-1(6))* General Bks. LLC.

—The Free Rangers. 2007. (Young Trailers Ser.: Vol. 5). 244p. reprint ed. per. 14.45 *(978-1-60424-038-2(5)*, Book Jungle) Standard Pubns., Inc.

—The Free Rangers: A Story of the Early Days along the Mississippi. 2005. (Young Trailers Ser.: Vol. 5). 312p. (J). reprint ed. pap. 14.95 *(978-1-4218-1577-0(X)*, 1st World Library - Literary Society) 1st World Publishing, Inc.

—The Free Rangers: A Story of the Early Days along the Mississippi. 2009. (Young Trailers Ser.: Vol. 4). 294p. (J). reprint ed. 27.99 *(978-1-60512-311-0(0))*; pap. 14.99 *(978-1-60512-411-7(7))* Akasha Publishing, LLC. (Akasha Classics).

—The Free Rangers: A Story of the Early Days along the Mississippi. (Young Trailers Ser.: Vol. 5). (J). 2008. 280p. 25.99 *(978-0-554-36420-9(4))* 2008. 280p. 28.99 *(978-0-554-27117-0(6))* 2007. (ENG.). 278p. (gr. 4-7). reprint ed. pap. 23.99 *(978-1-4346-2560-1(5))* 2010. (ENG.). 382p. (gr. 4-7). reprint ed. pap. 33.75 *(978-1-176-61076-7(7))* 2007. (ENG.). 254p. reprint ed. pap. 21.99 *(978-1-4346-2518-2(4))* Creative Media Partners, LLC.

—The Free Rangers: A Story of the Early Days along the Mississippi. 2010. (Young Trailers Ser.: Vol. 5). (J). 170p. pap. 13.87 *(978-1-152-24703-1(4))*; 162p. (gr. 4-7). reprint ed. pap. 19.99 *(978-1-4432-1506-0(6))* General Bks. LLC.

—The Free Rangers: A Story of the Early Days along the Mississippi. (Young Trailers Ser.: Vol. 5). (J). 2010. 232p. pap. *(978-1-4076-1356-7(1))* 2012. 388p. (gr. 4-7). reprint ed. pap. *(978-1-290-66522-3(2))* HardPr.

—The Free Rangers: A Story of the Early Days along the Mississippi. 2012. (Young Trailers Ser.: Vol. 5). 220p. (J). (gr. 4-7). pap. 14.95 *(978-1-60444-735-4(4))* IndoEuropeanPublishing.com.

—The Free Rangers: A Story of the Early Days along the Mississippi. (Young Trailers Ser.: Vol. 5). (J). reprint ed. 2010. 248p. (gr. 4-7). 33.56 *(978-1-169-30153-5(3))* 2010. 41.95 *(978-1-161-46378-1(X))* 2004. pap. 1.99 *(978-1-4192-6302-6(1))* 2004. pap. 26.95 *(978-1-4191-6302-9(7))* Kessinger Publishing, LLC.

—The Free Rangers: A Story of the Early Days along the Mississippi. 2012. (Young Trailers Ser.: Vol. 5). 256p. (J). (gr. 4-7). reprint ed. *(978-3-8491-6283-2(4))*; pap. *(978-3-8491-5398-4(3))* Tredition GmbH.

—The Keepers of the Trail: A Story of the Great Woods. (Young Trailers Ser.: Vol. 3). 323p. (J). reprint ed. lib. bdg. 24.95 *(978-0-88411-948-7(3))* Amereon Ltd.

—The Keepers of the Trail: A Story of the Great Woods. 2010. (Young Trailers Ser.: Vol. 3). (J). reprint ed. (ENG.). 346p. (gr. 4-7). pap. 32.75 *(978-1-176-75334-1(7))*; 348p. pap. 32.75 *(978-1-142-54723-3(X))* Creative Media Partners, LLC.

—The Keepers of the Trail: A Story of the Great Woods. 2008. (Young Trailers Ser.: Vol. 3). 256p. (J). reprint ed. pap. *(978-1-4099-1719-9(3))* Dodo Pr.

—The Keepers of the Trail: A Story of the Great Woods. 2008. (Young Trailers Ser.: Vol. 3). 168p. (J). pap. *(978-1-84830-139-9(1))* Echo Library.

—The Keepers of the Trail: A Story of the Great Woods. (Young Trailers Ser.: Vol. 3). (J). reprint ed. 2010. (Illus.). 150p. (gr. 4-7). pap. 19.99 *(978-1-153-79160-1(9))* 2009. 176p. pap. 11.61 *(978-1-150-39028-9(X))* General Bks. LLC.

—The Keepers of the Trail: A Story of the Great Woods. 2012. (Young Trailers Ser.: Vol. 3). 352p. (J). reprint ed. pap. *(978-1-290-20366-1(0))* HardPr.

—The Keepers of the Trail: A Story of the Great Woods. 2009. (Young Trailers Ser.: Vol. 3). 224p. (gr. 4-7). reprint ed. pap. 15.45 *(978-1-4385-1899-2(4)*, Book Jungle) Standard Pubns., Inc.

—The Keepers of the Trail: A Story of the Great Woods. 2012. (Young Trailers Ser.: Vol. 3). 240p. (J). reprint ed. pap. *(978-3-8472-2195-1(7))* Tredition GmbH.

—The Riflemen of the Ohio: A Story of Early Days along the Beautiful River. (Young Trailers Ser.: Vol. 6). (J). reprint ed. 25.95 *(978-0-8488-1239-3(5))* Amereon Ltd.

—The Riflemen of the Ohio: A Story of Early Days along the Beautiful River. 2009. (Young Trailers Ser.: Vol. 6). 312p. (J). reprint ed. pap. *(978-1-4099-2567-5(6))* Dodo Pr.

—The Riflemen of the Ohio: A Story of Early Days along the Beautiful River. 2008. (Young Trailers Ser.: Vol. 6). 192p. (J). reprint ed. pap. *(978-1-4068-2807-8(6))* Echo Library.

—The Riflemen of the Ohio: A Story of Early Days along the Beautiful River. 2010. (Young Trailers Ser.: Vol. 6). (Illus.). 180p. (J). (gr. 4-7). reprint ed. pap. 19.99 *(978-1-153-79466-4(7))* General Bks. LLC.

—The Riflemen of the Ohio: A Story of Early Days along the Beautiful River. 2012. (Young Trailers Ser.: Vol. 6). 340p. (J). (gr. 4-7). pap. *(978-3-8472-2473-0(5))* Tredition GmbH.

—The Scouts of the Valley. (Young Trailers Ser.: Vol. 7). reprint ed. 2008. 272p. pap. 11.45 *(978-1-60597-237-4(1))* 2007. 276p. per. 14.95 *(978-1-60424-040-5(7))* Standard Pubns., Inc. (Book Jungle).

—The Scouts of the Valley: A Story of Wyoming & the Chemung. 2005. (Young Trailers Ser.: Vol. 7). (J). reprint ed. 29.95 *(978-1-4218-1054-6(9))*; 344p. pap. 14.95 *(978-1-4218-1154-3(5))* 1st World Publishing, Inc. (1st World Library - Literary Society).

—The Scouts of the Valley: A Story of Wyoming & the Chemung. 2009. (Young Trailers Ser.: Vol. 7). 274p. (J). 27.99 *(978-1-60512-310-3(2))*; reprint ed. pap. 14.99 *(978-1-60512-410-0(9))* Akasha Publishing, LLC. (Akasha Classics).

—The Scouts of the Valley: A Story of Wyoming & the Chemung. (Young Trailers Ser.: Vol. 7). (J). reprint ed. 26.95 *(978-0-8488-1241-6(7))* Amereon Ltd.

—The Scouts of the Valley: A Story of Wyoming & the Chemung. (Young Trailers Ser.: Vol. 7). (J). reprint ed. 2008. 320p. 28.99 *(978-0-554-35353-1(9))* 2008. 320p. 29.99 *(978-0-554-26050-1(6))* 2007. (ENG.). 284p. pap. 21.99 *(978-1-4346-0327-2(X))* Creative Media Partners, LLC.

—The Scouts of the Valley: A Story of Wyoming & the Chemung. 2006. (Young Trailers Ser.: Vol. 7). (J). reprint ed. pap. *(978-1-4065-0821-5(7))* Dodo Pr.

—The Scouts of the Valley: A Story of Wyoming & the Chemung. 2007. (Young Trailers Ser.: Vol. 7). 208p. (J). reprint ed. per. *(978-1-4068-1685-3(X))* Echo Library.

—The Scouts of the Valley: A Story of Wyoming & the Chemung. 2010. (Young Trailers Ser.: Vol. 7). (Illus.). 184p. (J). (gr. 4-7). reprint ed. pap. 19.99 *(978-1-153-72010-6(8))* General Bks. LLC.

—The Scouts of the Valley: A Story of Wyoming & the Chemung. 2010. (Young Trailers Ser.: Vol. 7). 250p. (J). pap. *(978-1-4076-0985-0(8))* HardPr.

—The Scouts of the Valley: A Story of Wyoming & the Chemung. (Young Trailers Ser.: Vol. 7). (J). reprint ed. 2010. 268p. (gr. 4-7). 34.36 *(978-1-169-30757-5(4))* 2010. 268p. (gr. 4-7). pap. 22.36 *(978-1-162-70769-3(0))* 2010. 42.95 *(978-1-161-47633-0(4))* 2004. pap. 27.95 *(978-1-4191-8163-4(7))* 2004. pap. 1.99 *(978-1-4192-8163-1(1))* Kessinger Publishing, LLC.

—The Scouts of the Valley (Webster's French Thesaurus Edition) 2008. (Young Trailers Ser.: Vol. 7). (FRE & ENG.). 360p. pap. 28.95 *(978-0-497-97888-4(1))* Icon Group International, Inc.

—The Scouts of the Valley (Webster's Korean Thesaurus Edition) 2008. (Young Trailers Ser.: Vol. 7). (KOR & ENG.). 379p. pap. 28.95 *(978-0-546-54127-4(5))* Icon Group International, Inc.

—The Young Trailers. 2007. (Young Trailers Ser.: Vol. 1). 248p. reprint ed. per. 12.45 *(978-1-60424-031-3(8)*, Book Jungle) Standard Pubns., Inc.

—The Young Trailers: A Story of Early Kentucky. 2006. (Young Trailers Ser.: Vol. 1). (J). 27.95 *(978-1-4218-2970-8(3))*; reprint ed. pap. 12.95 *(978-1-4218-3070-4(1))* 1st World Publishing, Inc.

—The Young Trailers: A Story of Early Kentucky. (Young Trailers Ser.: Vol. 1). (J). reprint ed. 25.95 *(978-0-89190-824-1(2))* Amereon Ltd.

—The Young Trailers: A Story of Early Kentucky. (Young Trailers Ser.: Vol. 1). (J). reprint ed. 2008. 224p. 27.99 *(978-0-554-27469-0(8))* 2008. 224p. 24.99 *(978-0-554-36772-9(6))* 2007. (ENG.). 202p. pap. 20.99 *(978-1-4346-3288-3(1))* Creative Media Partners, LLC.

—The Young Trailers: A Story of Early Kentucky. 2007. (Young Trailers Ser.: Vol. 1). 228p. (J). reprint ed. per. *(978-1-4065-6553-9(9))* Dodo Pr.

—The Young Trailers: A Story of Early Kentucky. 2007. (Young Trailers Ser.: Vol. 1). 144p. (J). reprint ed. per. *(978-1-4068-1694-5(9))* Echo Library.

—The Young Trailers: A Story of Early Kentucky. (Young Trailers Ser.: Vol. 1). (J). reprint ed. 2010. 180p. (gr. 4-7). 30.36 *(978-1-169-27791-5(8))* 2010. 180p. (gr. 4-7). pap. 18.36 *(978-1-162-71336-6(4))* 2010. 37.95 *(978-1-161-48200-3(8))* 2004. pap. 1.99 *(978-1-4192-8924-8(1))* 2004. pap. 22.95 *(978-1-4191-8924-1(7))* Kessinger Publishing, LLC.

—The Young Trailers: A Story of Early Kentucky. 2012. (Young Trailers Ser.: Vol. 1). 200p. (J). (gr. 4-7). reprint ed. pap. *(978-3-8472-3210-0(X))* Tredition GmbH.

—The Young Trailers - A Story of Early Kentucky. 2008. (Young Trailers Ser.: Vol. 1). 244p. reprint ed. pap. 14.45 *(978-1-60597-191-9(X)*, Book Jungle) Standard Pubns., Inc.

Anderson, Rian B. A Christmas Prayer. 2004. pap. 2.95 *(978-1-57734-900-6(8))* Covenant Communications, Inc.

Applegate, Katherine. The Buffalo Storm. Ormerod, Jan, illus. 2014. (ENG.). 32p. (J). (gr. -1-3). pap. 7.99 *(978-0-544-33921-7(5)*, HMH Books For Young Readers) Houghton Mifflin Harcourt Publishing Co.

Auch, Mary Jane. Journey to Nowhere. 2004. (Illus.). 202p. (gr. 5-9). 16.00 *(978-0-7569-4144-4(X))* Perfection Learning Corp.

Aviation Publications Staff & National Geographic Learning Staff. Hard Gold: The Colorado Gold Rush of 1859. 2010. (Rise & Shine Ser.). (ENG.). 240p. (C). (gr. 3-7). pap. 10.95 *(978-1-4231-0520-6(6))* National Geographic School Publishing, Inc.

Ballantyne, R. M. Silver Lake. 2004. reprint ed. pap. 19.95 *(978-1-4191-4729-6(3))*; pap. 1.99 *(978-1-4192-4729-3(8))* Kessinger Publishing, LLC.

Barker, Jane Valentine. Building Up. pap. 7.95 *(978-1-878611-07-9(0))* Silver Rim Pr.

Bayle, B. J. Red River Rising. 2012. (ENG., Illus.). 280p. (YA). (gr. 6). pap. 12.99 *(978-1-4597-0228-8(X))* Dundurn CAN. Dist: Ingram Publisher Services.

—Red River Rising: A Novel (Large Print 16pt) 2013. 332p. (gr. 5-8). pap. *(978-1-4596-6330-5(6))* ReadHowYouWant.com, Ltd.

The Bears of Blue River. 2008. 100p. pap. 10.95 *(978-1-60459-531-4(0))* Wilder Pubns., Corp.

Belaney, Archibald Stansfeld. On the Trail: Pages from the Writings of Grey Owl. Reynolds, E. E., ed. 2011. (ENG.). 130p. pap. 21.99 *(978-1-107-60015-7(4))* Cambridge Univ. Pr.

Bell, Cathleen Davitt. Little Blog on the Prairie. 2011. (ENG.). 288p. (YA). (gr. 7). pap. 9.99 *(978-1-59990-677-5(5)*, 9781599906775, Bloomsbury USA Childrens) Bloomsbury Publishing USA.

Bender, Esther. Elisabeth & the Windmill. 2003. (ENG.). 112p. (J). (gr. 3-7). pap. 6.99 *(978-0-8361-9204-9(4))* Herald Pr.

Bethel, Ellie & Patterson, Ellie. Michael Recycle Meets Bootleg Peg. Colombo, Alexandra, illus. 2014. (Michael Recycle Ser.). (ENG.). 28p. (J). (gr. 2-5). 17.99 *(978-1-61377-708-4(6)*, 9781613777084) Idea & Design Works, LLC.

Blakeslee, Ann R. A Different Kind of Hero, 1 vol. 2005. (ENG.). 32p. (YA). pap. 5.95 *(978-0-7614-5147-1(1))* Marshall Cavendish Corp.

Blanc, Esther Silverstein & Eagle, Godeane. Long Johns for a Small Chicken. Dixon, Tennessee, illus. 2003. (J). 16.95 *(978-1-884244-23-0(8))* volcano pr.

Bloomfield, Susanne George & Reed, Eric Melvin, eds. Adventures in the West: Stories for Young Readers. 2007. (ENG., Illus.). 302p. (gr. 3-7). pap. 19.95 *(978-0-8032-5974-4(3)*, Bison Bks.) Univ. of Nebraska Pr.

Blos, Joan W. Brothers of the Heart: A Story of the Old Northwest, 1837-1838. 2008. (ENG.). 176p. (J). (gr. 3-7). pap. 5.99 *(978-1-4169-7561-8(6)*, Simon & Schuster/Paula Wiseman Bks.) Simon & Schuster/Paula Wiseman Bks.

Bly, Stephen A. The Lost Wagon Train. 2005. (Retta Barre's Oregon Trail Ser.: Vol. 1). 110p. pap. 5.99 *(978-1-58134-391-5(4)*, Crossway Bibles) Crossway.

Bollen, Christina. An Angel in My Garden, 1 vol. Matyuschenko, Tanya, illus. 2009. 47p. pap. 24.95 *(978-1-60813-661-2(2))* America Star Bks.

Breault, Christie Merriman. Logan West, Printer's Devil. Archambault, Matthew, illus. 2006. 142p. (J). pap. *(978-1-59336-762-6(7))* Mondo Publishing.

Brink, Carol Ryrie. Caddie Woodlawn. 2006. (ENG., Illus.). 288p. (J). (gr. 3-7). pap. 7.99 *(978-1-4169-4028-9(6)*, Aladdin) Simon & Schuster Children's Publishing.

Browning, Diane. Signed, Abiah Rose. Browning, Diane, illus. 2010. (ENG., Illus.). 32p. (J). (gr. -1-2). 15.99 *(978-1-58246-311-7(5)*, Tricycle Pr.) Random Hse. Children's Bks.

Bunting, Eve. Wash Day. Sneed, Brad, illus. 2014. (ENG.). 32p. (J). (gr. -1-3). 16.95 *(978-0-8234-2868-7(0))* Holiday Hse., Inc.

Byars, Betsy. Golly Sisters Go West. Truesdell, Sue, illus. 2003. (I Can Read Level 3 Ser.). (ENG.). 64p. (J). (gr. k-3). pap. 3.99 *(978-0-06-444132-2(6))* HarperCollins Pubs.

—Trouble River. l.t. ed. 2004. (Beeler Mystery Ser.). 28.95 *(978-1-58118-120-3(5))* LRS.

Byars, Betsy & Byars, B. The Golly Sisters Go West. 2003. (I Can Read! Level 3 Ser.). (J). (gr. k-3). lib. bdg. 13.55 *(978-0-8335-4709-5(7)*, Turtleback) Turtleback Bks.

Calvert, Patricia. Bigger. Minor, Wendell, illus. 2003. (ENG.). 144p. (J). (gr. 3-7). pap. 8.95 *(978-0-689-86003-4(X)*, Simon & Schuster/Paula Wiseman Bks.) Simon & Schuster/Paula Wiseman Bks.

Cannon, A. E. Charlotte's Rose. 2011. (ENG., Illus.). 256p. (J). (gr. 4). pap. 9.95 *(978-1-60781-141-1(3))* Univ. of Utah Pr.

Carr, Mary Jane. Children of the Covered Wagon. 2007. (Illus.). 266p. per. 9.95 *(978-1-932971-50-7(5))* Christian Liberty Pr.

Clifton Wisler, G. All for Texas. 2004. 140p. (J). lib. bdg. 16.92 *(978-1-4242-0767-1(3))* Fitzgerald Bks.

Coats, J. Anderson. The Many Reflections of Miss Jane Deming. 2017. (ENG., Illus.). 288p. (J). (gr. 5-7). 16.99 *(978-1-4814-6496-3(5)*, Atheneum Bks. for Young Readers) Simon & Schuster Children's Publishing.

Coerr, Eleanor. The Josefina Story Quilt. Degen, Bruce, illus. 2003. (I Can Read Level 3 Ser.). (ENG.). 64p. (J). (gr. k-3). pap. 3.99 *(978-0-06-444129-2(6))* HarperCollins Pubs.

Connor, Leslie. Miss Bridie Chose a Shovel. Azarian, Mary, illus. unabr. ed. 2005. (J). (gr. k-3). 29.95 incl. audio compact disk *(978-0-8045-4135-0(3)*, SACD4135); 27.95 incl. audio *(978-0-8045-6936-1(3)*, SAC6936) Spoken Arts, Inc.

Cooper, James Fenimore. The Last of the Mohicans. Wyeth, N. C., illus. 2013. (Scribner Classics Ser.). (ENG.). 368p. (J). (gr. 5). 24.99 *(978-1-4424-8130-5(7)*, Atheneum Bks. for Young Readers) Simon & Schuster Children's Publishing.

—The Leatherstocking Saga. (J). (gr. 5-6). 44.95 *(978-0-8488-0059-8(1))* Amereon Ltd.

Couloumbis, Audrey. Maude March on the Run! Or Trouble Is Her Middle Name. 2008. (Maude March Ser.). (ENG., Illus.). 320p. (J). (gr. 3-7). pap. 7.99 *(978-0-375-83248-2(3)*, Yearling) Random Hse. Children's Bks.

—The Misadventures of Maude March: Or Trouble Rides a Fast Horse. 2007. (Illus.). 295p. (gr. 3-7). 18.00 *(978-0-7569-7770-2(3))* Perfection Learning Corp.

—The Misadventures of Maude March: Or Trouble Rides a Fast Horse. 2007. (Maude March Ser.). (ENG., Illus.). 320p. (J). (gr. 3-7). 7.99 *(978-0-375-83247-5(5)*, Yearling) Random Hse. Children's Bks.

Crawford, Neil. The Journeyers. 2006. (ENG.). 248p. (J). per. *(978-0-9778205-4-2(8))* Helm Publishing.

Crook, Connie Brummel. Meyers' Creek, 1 vol. 2nd ed. 2014. (ENG.). 212p. pap. *(978-1-55455-351-8(2))* Fitzhenry & Whiteside, Ltd.

Cullen, Lynn. Diary of Nelly Vandorn. Date not set. 128p. (gr. 3-18). mass mkt. 4.99 *(978-0-06-440926-1(0))* HarperCollins Pubs.

Dagg, Carole Estby. Sweet Home Alaska. 2016. (ENG.). 304p. (J). (gr. 5). 16.99 *(978-0-399-17203-8(3)*, Nancy Paulsen Books) Penguin Young Readers Group.

Dallas, Sandra. The Quilt Walk. (ENG.). 216p. (J). 2013. (gr. 4-7). pap. 9.95 *(978-1-58536-799-3(0)*, 202373) 2012. 18.95 *(978-1-58536-800-6(8))* Sleeping Bear Pr.

Dell, Pamela. Tag-along Tay: A Story about Annie Oakley & Buffalo Bill's Wild West Show. 2003. (Scrapbooks of America Ser.). (ENG., Illus.). 48p. (J). (gr. 3-6). 32.79 *(978-1-59187-039-5(9)*, 200812) Child's World, Inc., The.

Dueck, Adele. Racing Home, 1 vol. 2011. (ENG.). 200p. (J). (gr. 4-8). pap. 8.95 *(978-1-55050-450-7(9))* Coteau Bks. CAN. Dist: Orca Bk. Pubs. USA.

Durbin, William. Blackwater Ben. 2014. (Fesler-Lampert Minnesota Heritage Ser.). (ENG., Illus.). 216p. pap. 11.95 *(978-0-8166-9192-0(4))* Univ. of Minnesota Pr.

Ellis, Edward Sylvester & Coghlan, John. The Hunters of the Ozark. 2004. (Illus.). 224p. (J). pap. 19.95 *(978-0-9713470-2-1(6))* Phoenix International, Inc.

Ellsworth, Loretta. The Shrouding Woman. 2007. (ENG., Illus.). 160p. (YA). (gr. 4-9). pap. 17.99 *(978-0-8050-8185-5(2),* 9780805081855, Holt, Henry & Co. Bks. For Young Readers) Holt, Henry & Co.

Erdman, Loula G. The Wind Blows Free. 2006. (Living History Library). 271p. (YA). (gr. 6). pap. 12.95 *(978-1-932350-09-8(8))* Bethlehem Bks.

Erdman, Loula Grace. The Good Land. 2008. (Living History Library). 185p. (YA). (gr. 6). pap. 12.95 *(978-1-932350-13-5(6))* Bethlehem Bks.

Ernst, Kathleen. Whistler in the Dark. 2009. (Mysteries Through Time Ser.). 144 - 176p. (YA). (gr. 4-8). 31.95 *(978-1-60754-429-6(6));* pap. 15.25 *(978-1-60754-432-6(6))* Windmill Bks.

Finley, Martha. Elsie Dinsmore. 2006. (ENG.). pap. 13.95 *(978-1-4218-3092-6(2))* 1st World Publishing, Inc.

Finley, Mary Peace. Meadow Lark. 2003. (Santa Fe Trail Trilogy Ser.). (Illus.). 199p. (J). 15.95 *(978-0-86541-070-1(4))* Filter Pr., LLC.

Frazier, Neta. The Stout-Hearted Seven: Orphaned on the Oregon Trail. 2017. (Great Leaders & Events Ser.). (ENG.). (J). (gr. 4-8). lib. bdg. 35.99 ***(978-1-942875-43-7(6))*** Quarto Publishing Group USA.

Frazier, Neta Lohnes. The Stout-Hearted Seven: Orphaned on the Oregon Trail. 2016. (Young Voyageur Ser.). (ENG., Illus.). 224p. (J). (gr. 4-9). pap. 12.99 *(978-0-7603-5224-3(0),* Voyageur Pr.) Quarto Publishing Group USA.

—The Stout-Hearted Seven: Orphaned on the Oregon Trail. 2006. (Sterling Point Books(r) Ser.). (ENG., Illus.). 208p. (J). (gr. 4-7). pap. 6.95 *(978-1-4027-3617-9(7))* Sterling Publishing Co., Inc.

Frost, Helen. Salt: A Story of Friendship in a Time of War. 2013. (ENG.). 160p. (J). (gr. 5-9). 17.99 *(978-0-374-36387-1(0),* 9780374363871, Farrar, Straus & Giroux (BYR)) Farrar, Straus & Giroux.

Furman, A. L., ed. Pioneer Stories: Young Readers. Geer, Charles, illus. 2011. 190p. 42.95 *(978-1-258-09907-7(1))* Literary Licensing, LLC.

—Teenage Frontier Stories. Prezio, Victor, illus. 2011. 256p. 47.95 *(978-1-258-09865-0(2))* Literary Licensing, LLC.

Galbraith, Kathryn O. Arbor Day Square, 1 vol. Moore, Cyd, illus. 2016. (ENG.). 32p. (J). (gr. -1-3). pap. 7.95 *(978-1-56145-922-3(4))* Peachtree Pubs.

Galbraith, Kathryn Osebold. Arbor Day Square, 1 vol. Moore, Cyd, illus. 2010. (ENG.). 32p. (J). (gr. -1-3). 16.95 *(978-1-56145-517-1(2))* Peachtree Pubs.

Garinger, Alan K. Alone: The Journey of the Boy Sims. 2008. (J). 15.95 *(978-0-87195-266-0(1));* pap. 7.95 *(978-0-87195-267-7(X))* Indiana Historical Society.

Gray, Dianne & Gray, Dianne E. Holding up the Earth. 2006. (ENG.). 210p. (J). (gr. 5-7). pap. 12.95 *(978-0-618-73747-5(2))* Houghton Mifflin Harcourt Publishing Co.

Gregory, Kristiana. My Darlin' Clementine. 2009. (ENG.). 192p. (J). (gr. 5-18). 16.95 *(978-0-8234-2198-5(8))* Holiday Hse., Inc.

Grossman, Bill. Cowboy Ed. Wint, Florence, illus. 2004. 28p. (J). (gr. -1-3). reprint ed. *(978-0-7567-7851-4(4))* DIANE Publishing Co.

Hartson. Willa's New World: The Novel Study. 124p. stu. ed. 29.95 *(978-1-55378-058-8(2))* Edmonton Public Schls. Centre for Education CAN. Dist: Coteau Bks.

Hemphill, Kris. Ambush in the Wilderness. 2003. (Adventures in America Ser.). (Illus.). 90p. (gr. 4). 14.95 *(978-1-893110-34-2(6))* Silver Moon Pr.

Henty, George Alfred. In the Heart of the Rockies. l.t. ed. 2006. 322p. pap. 24.99 *(978-1-4264-3253-8(4))* Creative Media Partners, LLC.

—In the Heart of the Rockies. 2004. reprint ed. pap. 27.95 *(978-1-4191-2600-0(8));* pap. 1.99 *(978-1-4192-2600-7(2))* Kessinger Publishing, LLC.

—A Tale of the Western Plains. Pearse, Alfred, illus. 2006. (Dover Children's Classics Ser.). (ENG.). 352p. (YA). (gr. 3-8). per. 8.95 *(978-0-486-45261-6(1))* Dover Pubns., Inc.

Higgins, Joanna. Waiting for the Queen: A Novel of Early America. 2013. (ENG.). 256p. (J). (gr. 4-10). 16.95 *(978-1-57131-700-1(7))* Milkweed Editions.

Holm, Jennifer L. An Adventure. 2010. (Boston Jane Ser.: No. 1). (ENG.). 272p. (J). (gr. 3-7). 7.99 *(978-0-375-86204-5(8),* Yearling) Random Hse. Children's Bks.

—The Claim. 2010. (Boston Jane Ser.: No. 2). (ENG.). 224p. (J). (gr. 3-7). pap. 7.99 *(978-0-375-86206-9(4),* Yearling) Random Hse. Children's Bks.

—Our Only May Amelia. unabr. ed. 2004. 253p. (J). (gr. 5-9). pap. 36.00 incl. audio *(978-0-8072-8366-0(5),* YA191SP, Listening Library) Random Hse. Audio Publishing Group.

—The Trouble with May Amelia. Gustavson, Adam, illus. (ENG.). 224p. (J). (gr. 3-7). 2012. pap. 5.99 *(978-1-4169-1374-0(2))* 2011. 15.99 *(978-1-4169-1373-3(4))* Simon & Schuster Children's Publishing. (Atheneum Bks. for Young Readers).

—Wilderness Days. 2004. (Boston Jane Ser.: No. 2). 256p. (J). (gr. 5-18). pap. 5.99 *(978-0-06-440881-3(7),* Harper Trophy) HarperCollins Pubs.

—Wilderness Days. unabr. ed. 2004. (Boston Jane Ser.: No. 2). 288p. (J). (gr. 5-9). pap. 38.00 incl. audio *(978-0-8072-0787-1(X),* S YA 307 SP, Listening Library) Random Hse. Audio Publishing Group.

—Wilderness Days. 2010. (Boston Jane Ser.: No. 2). (ENG.). 256p. (J). (gr. 3-7). pap. 7.99 *(978-0-375-86205-2(6),* Yearling) Random Hse. Children's Bks.

Hopkinson, Deborah. Apples to Oregon. 2014. 17.00 *(978-1-63419-642-0(2))* Perfection Learning Corp.

—Apples to Oregon: Being the (Slightly) True Narrative of How a Brave Pioneer Father Brought Apples, Peaches, Pears, Plums, Grapes, & Cherries (and Children) Across the Plains. Carpenter, Nancy, illus. 2008. (ENG.). 40p. (J). (gr. -1-3). 7.99 *(978-1-4169-6746-0(X),* Aladdin) Simon & Schuster Children's Publishing.

—Our Kansas Home. Faricy, Patrick, illus. 2003. (Prairie Skies Ser.). 69p. (J). 11.65 *(978-0-7569-3448-4(6))* Perfection Learning Corp.

Hopkinson, Deborah & Carpenter, Nancy. Apples to Oregon: Being the (Slightly) True Narrative of How a Brave Pioneer Father Brought Apples, Peaches, Pears, Plums, Grapes, & Cherries (and Children) Across the Plains. 2004. (ENG., Illus.). 40p. (J). (gr. -1-3). 17.99 *(978-0-689-84769-1(6),* Atheneum Bks. for Young Readers) Simon & Schuster Children's Publishing.

Horender, Philip M. Head West, Young Mouse: Transcontinental Railroad Traveler, 1 vol. Wolek, Guy, illus. 2013. (Maximilian P. Mouse, Time Traveler Ser.). (ENG.). 112p. (J). (gr. 3-6). lib. bdg. 27.07 *(978-1-61641-959-2(6),* Calico Chapter Bks) Magic Wagon.

Howard, Ellen. The Log Cabin Wedding. Himler, Ronald, illus. 2006. (ENG.). 64p. (J). (gr. -1-3). 15.95 *(978-0-8234-1989-0(4))* Holiday Hse., Inc.

Hughes, Dean. As Wide As the River. 2005. 156p. (J). pap. *(978-1-59038-450-3(4))* Deseret Bk. Co.

—Facing the Enemy. 2005. (Illus.). 153p. (J). pap. *(978-1-59038-449-7(0))* Deseret Bk. Co.

—Under the Same Stars. 2005. viii, 152p. (J). pap. *(978-1-59038-448-0(2))* Deseret Bk. Co.

Hughes, Holly. Hoofbeats of Danger. 2009. (Mysteries Through Time Ser.). 144p. (YA). (gr. 4-8). 31.95 *(978-1-60754-176-9(9));* pap. 15.25 *(978-1-60754-177-6(7))* Windmill Bks.

Hulet, Debra. Independence Rock. 2011. 208p. pap. 13.99 *(978-1-59955-441-9(0),* Bonneville Bks.) Cedar Fort, Inc./CFI Distribution.

Hulme, Joy N. Climbing the Rainbow. 2004. 224p. (J). 15.99 *(978-0-380-81572-2(9))* HarperCollins Pubs.

Ingle, Sheila. Courageous Kate: A Daughter of the American Revolution. 2006. (ENG.). 130p. pap. 11.95 *(978-1-891885-52-5(9))* Hub City Pr.

Ingold, Jeanette. The Big Burn: Teddy Roosevelt & the Fire That Saved America. 2003. (Illus.). 301p. (YA). (gr. 8-12). 14.60 *(978-0-7569-4283-0(7))* Perfection Learning Corp.

—Mountain Solo. 2005. (ENG.). 320p. (YA). (gr. 7-12). pap. 15.95 *(978-0-15-205358-1(1))* Houghton Mifflin Harcourt Publishing Co.

Ingold, Jeanette & Egan, Timothy. The Big Burn: Teddy Roosevelt & the Fire That Saved America. 2003. (ENG., Illus.). 320p. (YA). (gr. 7-12). pap. 6.95 *(978-0-15-204924-9(X))* Houghton Mifflin Harcourt Publishing Co.

James, Will. Cowboy in the Making. rev. ed. (Illus.). 104p. (J). (gr. 4-6). pap. 15.00 *(978-0-87842-439-9(3),* 811) Mountain Pr. Publishing Co., Inc.

Kastner, Janet. The Snake Fence: A Novel. 2012. (J). pap. 14.95 *(978-1-937768-13-3(9))* QuakerPress.

Kay, Verla. Hornbooks & Inkwells. Schindler, S. D., illus. 2011. (ENG.). 32p. (J). (gr. -1-3). 16.99 *(978-0-399-23870-3(0),* G.P. Putnam's Sons Books for Young Readers) Penguin Young Readers Group.

Kelso, Mary Jean. The Christmas Angel. Snider, K. C., illus. 2007. 32p. (J). 11.95 *(978-1-933090-58-0(8))* Guardian Angel Publishing, Inc.

Kimmel, E. Cody. In the Eye of the Storm. Snow, Scott, illus. 2003. (Adventures of Young Buffalo Bill Ser.). (ENG.). 144p. (J). (gr. 3-7). 15.99 *(978-0-06-029115-0(X))* HarperCollins Pubs.

Kimmel, Elizabeth Cody. In the Eye of the Storm. Snow, Scott, illus. 2003. (Adventures of Young Buffalo Bill Ser.). 144p. (J). (gr. 3-7). lib. bdg. 16.89 *(978-0-06-029116-7(8))* HarperCollins Pubs.

LaFaye, A. Worth. unabr. ed. 2006. (Live Oak Histories Ser.). (J). (gr. 3-6). pap. 24.95 incl. audio *(978-1-59519-766-5(4));* pap. 28.95 incl. audio compact disk *(978-1-59519-767-2(2))* Live Oak Media.

—Worth. 2006. 144p. (J). (gr. 4-7). 13.65 *(978-0-7569-6614-0(0))* Perfection Learning Corp.

—Worth. (ENG., 160p. (J). 2004. Illus.). (gr. 3-7). 17.99 *(978-0-689-85730-0(6))* 2006. (gr. 4-7). reprint ed. pap. 7.99 *(978-1-4169-1624-6(5))* Simon & Schuster Bks. For Young Readers. (Simon & Schuster Bks. For Young Readers).

Larson, Kirby. Hattie Big Sky. (ENG.). (YA). (gr. 7-7). 2008. 304p. 7.99 *(978-0-385-73595-7(2),* Yearling) 2007. 320p. pap. 8.99 *(978-0-440-23941-3(9),* Ember) Random Hse. Children's Bks.

—Hattie Big Sky. l.t. ed. 2007. (Literacy Bridge Young Adult Ser.). 381p. (YA). (gr. 7-12). 23.95 *(978-0-7862-9697-2(6))* Thorndike Pr.

Lawton, Wendy G. Ransom's Mark: A Story Based on the Life of the Pioneer Olive Oatman. 2003. (Daughters of the Faith Ser.: Bk. 4). (ENG.). 144p. (J). (gr. 3-3). pap. 7.99 *(978-0-8024-3638-2(2))* Moody Pubs.

Leet, Karen M. Sarah's Courage: A Kentucky Frontier Kidnapping. 2014. (ENG., Illus.). 144p. (gr. 4-7). 14.99 *(978-1-62619-477-9(7),* History Pr., The) Arcadia Publishing.

Levinson, Nancy Smiler. Prairie Friends. Schuett, Stacey, illus. 2003. (I Can Read Bks.). 64p. (J). (gr. k-3). 15.99 *(978-0-06-028001-7(8))* HarperCollins Pubs.

Levitin, Sonia. Boom Town. Smith, Cat Bowman, illus. 2004. 30p. (J). (gr. -1-3). 14.65 *(978-0-7569-3185-8(1))* Perfection Learning Corp.

Lunsford, Russell. Benjamin Nathan Tuggle: Adventurer: Daniel Boone & the Settlement of Boonesborough, Kentucky. 2010. 112p. (gr. 4-6). 20.95 *(978-1-4502-3361-3(9));* pap. 10.95 *(978-1-4502-3360-6(0))* iUniverse, Inc.

MacBride, Roger Lea. Little Farm in the Ozarks. 2007. (Little House Ser.). 157p. (J). (gr. 2-5). per. 5.99 *(978-0-06-114810-1(5),* Harper Trophy) HarperCollins Pubs.

MacLachlan, Patricia. More Perfect Than the Moon. 2004. (Sarah, Plain & Tall Ser.). 96p. (J). (gr. 3-5). 14.99 *(978-0-06-027558-7(8),* Cotler, Joanna Books) HarperCollins Pubs.

—More Perfect Than the Moon. 2005. 16.00 *(978-0-7569-5437-6(1))* Perfection Learning Corp.

—Sarah, Plain & Tall. 30th anniv. ed. 2015. (Sarah, Plain & Tall Ser.: 1). (ENG.). 112p. (J). (gr. 1-5). pap. 6.99 *(978-0-06-239952-6(7),* Tegen, Katherine Bks) HarperCollins Pubs.

Manley, Candace. Skeeter's Dream. 2010. (ENG.). 192p. (J). (gr. 7-18). pap. 14.95 *(978-0-9785634-8-6(4))* La Frontera Publishing.

Martin, Rebecca. Blossoms on the Roof. 2015. (Amish Frontier Ser.). (ENG.). 160p. (J). (gr. 2-7). pap. 8.99 *(978-0-7369-6367-1(7))* Harvest Hse. Pubs.

—The Treasure Hunt. 2015. (Amish Frontier Ser.). (ENG., Illus.). 160p. (J). (gr. 2-7). pap. 8.99 *(978-0-7369-6369-5(3))* Harvest Hse. Pubs.

Mazer, Harry. My Brother Abe: Sally Lincoln's Story. 2009. (ENG.). 208p. (J). (gr. 3-7). pap. 5.99 *(978-1-4169-3894-1(X));* 15.99 *(978-1-4169-3884-2(2))* Simon & Schuster Bks. For Young Readers. (Simon & Schuster Bks. For Young Readers).

Mazzio, Joann. Leaving Eldorado. 2014. (ENG.). 176p. (YA). (gr. 7). pap. 10.99 *(978-0-544-33613-1(5),* HMH Books For Young Readers) Houghton Mifflin Harcourt Publishing Co.

McCabe, James Dabney, Jr. Planting the Wilderness or, the Pioneer Boys: a Story of Frontier Life. 2007. pap. 27.95 *(978-1-4304-8187-4(0))* Kessinger Publishing, LLC.

McCaughrean, Geraldine. Stop the Train! 2003. (ENG.). 304p. (J). (gr. 5-18). 16.99 *(978-0-06-050749-7(7))* HarperCollins Pubs.

McKernan, Victoria. The Devil's Paintbox. (ENG.). (YA). (gr. 9). 2013. 384p. pap. 9.99 *(978-0-449-81655-4(9),* Ember) 2010. 368p. mass mkt. 8.99 *(978-0-440-23962-8(1),* Laurel Leaf) Random Hse. Children's Bks.

McKinney-Whitaker, Courtney. The Last Sister: A Novel. 2014. (Young Palmetto Bks.). (ENG.). 232p. (YA). 39.95 *(978-1-61117-429-8(5))* Univ. of South Carolina Pr.

McMullan, Kate. For This Land Bk. 2: Meg's Prairie Diary. 2003. (My America Ser.). (ENG., Illus.). 112p. (J). 10.95 *(978-0-439-37059-2(0),* Scholastic Pr.) Scholastic, Inc.

McNeely, Marian Hurd. The Jumping-off Place. Siegel, William, illus. 2008. 321p. (J). 15.95 *(978-0-9798940-4-6(2),* South Dakota State Historical Society Pr.) South Dakota State Historical Society Pr.

Meigs, Cornelia & Holm, Jennifer L. Swift Rivers. Orr, Forrest W., illus. 2004. (Newbery Honor Book Ser.). (ENG.). 288p. (YA). (gr. 5). pap. 8.99 *(978-0-8027-7703-4(1),* 9780802777034, Bloomsbury USA Childrens) Bloomsbury Publishing USA.

Melton, Marcia. Joe Henry's Journey. 2014. (Illus.). 169p. (J). pap. 12.00 *(978-1-937849-20-7(1))* Raven Publishing Inc. of Montana.

Mitchell, Saundra. The Springsweet. 2013. (ENG.). 304p. (YA). (gr. 7). pap. 8.99 *(978-0-544-00327-9(6))* Houghton Mifflin Harcourt Publishing Co.

Moeri, Louise. The Devil in Ol' Rosie. 2009. (ENG.). 208p. (J). (gr. 3-6). pap. 10.99 *(978-1-4424-0202-7(4),* Atheneum Bks. for Young Readers) Simon & Schuster Children's Publishing.

Monson, Marianne. Pioneer Puzzle. 2010. (J). *(978-1-60641-669-3(3))* Deseret Bk. Co.

Morey, Walt. Year of the Black Pony. 2006. (Living History Library). 171p. (J). (gr. 4-7). pap. 11.95 *(978-1-932350-08-1(X))* Bethlehem Bks.

Morrow, Sherry. Woman of the Mountains. 268p. (YA). pap. 22.00 *(978-1-58982-611-3(6))* American Bk. Publishing Group.

Moser, Lisa. Kisses on the Wind. Brown, Kathryn, illus. 2009. (ENG.). 32p. (J). (gr. -1-2). 16.99 *(978-0-7636-3110-9(8))* Candlewick Pr.

Newman, Pamela Lillie. Lissie at Lincoln Lake: Book 2 of Lissie's Series. 2003. 92p. (J). per. 6.95 *(978-1-59196-234-2(X))* Instant Pub.

Ormerod, Jan. Lizzie Nonsense. 2006. (Illus.). 32p. pap. *(978-1-877003-93-6(X))* Little Hare Bks. AUS. Dist: HarperCollins Pubs. Australia.

Osborne, Mary Pope. Ghost Town at Sundown. unabr. ed. 2004. (Magic Tree House Ser.: No. 10). 73p. (J). (gr. k-3). pap. 17.00 incl. audio *(978-0-8072-0535-8(4),* Listening Library) Random Hse. Audio Publishing Group.

—Twister on Tuesday. 2004. (Magic Tree House Ser.: No. 23). 70p. (J). (gr. k-3). pap. 17.00 incl. audio *(978-0-8072-9932-6(4),* Listening Library) Random Hse. Audio Publishing Group.

Otis, James. Stephen of Philadelphi: A Story of Penn's Colony. 2007. 144p. per. 9.95 *(978-0-9790876-5-3(1))* Living Bks. Pr.

Otten, Charlotte F. Home in a Wilderness Fort: Copper Harbor 1844. 2006. (Illus.). 232p. (J). (gr. 2-7). per. 14.95 *(978-0-9766104-5-8(0))* Arbutus Pr.

Parramore, Helen. Maudie's Promise: A Girl on the Florida Frontier. 2008. 36p. pap. 20.99 *(978-1-4389-0226-5(3))* AuthorHouse.

Patchin, Frank Gee. The Pony Rider Boys in New Mexico. 2005. 28.95 *(978-1-4218-1429-2(3));* 252p. pap. 13.95 *(978-1-4218-1529-9(X))* 1st World Publishing, Inc. (1st World Library - Literary Society).

Patricia, MacLachlan. Sarah, Plain & Tall. 2014. (Sarah, Plain & Tall Ser.). (ENG.). 96p. (J). 10.24 *(978-1-63245-125-5(5))* Lectorum Pubns., Inc.

Patron, Susan. Behind the Masks: The Diary of Angeline Reddy - Bodie, California 1880. 2012. (Dear America Ser.). (ENG.). 304p. (J). (gr. 3-7). 12.99 *(978-0-545-30437-5(7))* Scholastic, Inc.

Paulsen, Gary. Woods Runner. 2011. (ENG.). 176p. (YA). (gr. 7). pap. 7.99 *(978-0-375-85908-3(X),* Lamb, Wendy Bks.) Random Hse. Children's Bks.

Pearce, Jonathan. The Far Side of the Moon: A California Story. 2nd ed. 2004. 150p. (J). pap. 15.95 *(978-1-59411-011-5(5))* Writers' Collective, The.

Pearsall, Shelley. Crooked River. 2007. 249p. (gr. 5-9). 17.00 *(978-0-7569-7771-9(1))* Perfection Learning Corp.

—Crooked River. 2007. (ENG.). 272p. (J). (gr. 3-7). 7.99 *(978-0-440-42101-6(2),* Yearling) Random Hse. Children's Bks.

Pearson, Carol Lynn. Summer of Truth. 2007. 104p. per. 9.99 *(978-1-59955-046-6(6))* Cedar Fort, Inc./CFI Distribution.

Peterson, Esther Allen. The House That Cared. 2010. (J). pap. *(978-0-88092-505-1(1))* Royal Fireworks Publishing Co.

—Will Spring Come? 2009. (Illus.). 157p. (J). *(978-0-88092-768-0(2))* Royal Fireworks Publishing Co.

Pfitsch, Patricia Curtis. Riding the Flume. 2004. (Aladdin Historical Fiction Ser.). 232p. (gr. 5-9). 15.00 *(978-0-7569-2938-1(5))* Perfection Learning Corp.

Pryor, Bonnie. Lottie's Dream. 2013. (ENG.). 36p. (J). (gr. -1-3). 14.99 *(978-1-4424-8878-6(6),* Atheneum Bks. for Young Readers) Simon & Schuster Children's Publishing.

Randall, Alison L. The Wheat Doll, 1 vol. Farnsworth, Bill, illus. 2008. (ENG.). 32p. (J). (gr. k-3). 16.95 *(978-1-56145-456-3(7))* Peachtree Pubs.

Rees, Celia. Witch Child. unabr. ed. 2004. (Young Adult Cassette Librariestm Ser.). 304p. (J). (gr. 5-9). pap. 40.00 incl. audio *(978-0-8072-1198-4(2),* S YA 343 SP, Listening Library) Random Hse. Audio Publishing Group.

Reiss, Kathryn. Riddle of the Prairie Bride. 2009. (Mysteries Through Time Ser.). 144 - 176p. (YA). (gr. 4-8). 31.95 *(978-1-60754-421-0(0));* pap. 15.25 *(978-1-60754-420-3(2))* Windmill Bks.

Reynolds, E. E. Behind the Ranges: Tales of Explorers, Pioneers & Travellers. Tresilian, S., illus. 2011. (ENG.). 128p. pap. 15.99 *(978-0-521-13526-9(5))* Cambridge Univ. Pr.

Richter, Conrad. The Light in the Forest. (YA). (gr. 7-18). 21.95 *(978-0-89190-333-8(X))* Amereon Ltd.

Risteen, H. L. Montana Gold: Frontier Stories. 2011. 222p. 44.95 *(978-1-258-02080-4(7))* Literary Licensing, LLC.

Ritter, John H. Desperado Who Stole Baseball. 2010. (ENG.). 288p. (J). (gr. 5-18). 7.99 *(978-0-14-241507-8(3),* Puffin Books) Penguin Young Readers Group.

Robinette, Joseph. Sarah, Plain & Tall. 2003. 84p. (YA). (gr. 6-18). pap. 6.50 *(978-1-58342-161-1(0),* SG8) Dramatic Publishing Co.

Rocan, Susan. Withershins. 2008. (Spirit Quest Ser.: 1). (ENG.). 225p. (YA). (gr. 12-14). pap. 14.95 *(978-1-894283-75-5(9))* Great Plains Pubns. CAN. Dist: Publishers Group Canada.

Rose, Caroline Starr. May B. 2012. (ENG.). 240p. (J). (gr. 3-7). 15.99 *(978-1-58246-393-3(X),* Schwartz & Wade Bks.) Random Hse. Children's Bks.

Rylant, Cynthia. Old Town in the Green Groves. 2007. (Little House Ser.). (ENG.). 192p. (J). (gr. 3-7). pap. 6.99 *(978-0-06-088546-5(7))* HarperCollins Pubs.

Sanders, Scott Russell. Floating House. Cogancherry, Helen, illus. 2011. 40p. (J). lib. bdg. 18.00 *(978-1-59098-425-3(0))* Wooster Bk. Co., The.

Santillo, LuAnn. Pioneer Days, 6 vols. Santillo, LuAnn, ed. 2003. (Half-Pint Kids Readers Ser.). (Illus.). 42p. (J). (gr. -1-1). pap. 6.95 *(978-1-59256-070-7(9))* Half-Pint Kids, Inc.

Sargent, Dave & Sargent, Pat. Pete: (Pink-skinned Palomino) Be a Hero, 30 vols., Vol. 46. Lenoir, Jane, illus. 2003. (Saddle up Ser.: Vol. 46). 42p. (J). lib. bdg. 23.60 *(978-1-56763-707-6(8))* Ozark Publishing.

—Pete: Pink-skinned Palomino) Be a Hero, 30 vols., Vol. 46. Lenoir, Jane, illus. 2003. (Saddle up Ser.: Vol. 46). 42p. (J). pap. 10.95 *(978-1-56763-708-3(6))* Ozark Publishing.

Schultz, Jan Neubert. Battle Cry. Allen, Rick, illus. 2006. (ENG.). 240p. (YA). (gr. 6-12). 15.95 *(978-1-57505-928-0(2),* Carolrhoda Bks.) Lerner Publishing Group.

Scillian, Devin. Johnny Kaw: A Tall Tale. Sneed, Brad, illus. 2013. (ENG.). 32p. (J). (gr. 1-4). 15.95 *(978-1-58536-791-7(5),* 202353) Sleeping Bear Pr.

—Pappy's Handkerchief. Ellison, Chris, illus. rev. ed. 2007. (Tales of Young Americans Ser.). (ENG.). 32p. (J). (gr. 3-7). 17.95 *(978-1-58536-316-2(2))* Sleeping Bear Pr.

Scillian, Devin & Young, Judy. Westward Journeys. Ellison, Chris et al, illus. 2013. (American Adventures Ser.). (ENG.). 96p. (J). (gr. 3-6). pap. 6.99 *(978-1-58536-860-0(1),* 202367) Sleeping Bear Pr.

Shaw, Janet. Kirsten Story Collection. Graef, Renee, illus. 2008. 380p. 29.95 *(978-1-59369-454-8(7))* American Girl Publishing, Inc.

—Kirsten's Short Story Collection. Lewis, Kim & Graef, Renee, illus. 2006. (American Girls Collection). 213p. (J). (gr. 3-8). 12.95 *(978-1-59369-323-7(0))* American Girl Publishing, Inc.

Shaw, Marilyn Bishop. Solomon. 2006. (Florida Historical Fiction for Youth Ser.). (ENG.). 204p. (J). (gr. 4-9). 14.95 *(978-1-56164-349-3(1))* Pineapple Pr., Inc.

Sibley, Linda. David Joins the California Gold Rush. 2004. 96p. pap. 6.65 *(978-0-7891-6002-7(1))* Perfection Learning Corp.

Silverthorne, Judith. The Secret of Sentinel Rock. 2007. (From Many Peoples Ser.). (Illus.). 159p. (J). (gr. 3-5). per. *(978-1-55050-386-9(3))* Coteau Bks.

—The Secret of the Stone House, 1 vol. 2005. (From Many Peoples Ser.). (ENG., Illus.). 224p. (J). (gr. 4-7). pap. 7.95 *(978-1-55050-325-8(1))* Coteau Bks. CAN. Dist: Orca Bk. Pubs. USA.

Skinner, Constance Lindsay. Becky Landers: Frontier Warrior. 2006. (Living History Library). 198p. (YA). (gr. 10). per. 12.95 *(978-1-932350-06-7(3))* Bethlehem Bks.

Smith, Debra. Hattie Marshall & the Dangerous Fire, 1 vol. 2007. (Hattie Marshall Ser.). (ENG.). 128p. (J). (gr. 3-6). per. 7.95 *(978-1-58980-492-0(9))* Pelican Publishing Co., Inc.

Snow, Dorothea J. Roy Rogers' Favorite Western Stories. Ushler, John, illus. 2011. 250p. 46.95 *(978-1-258-04169-4(3))* Literary Licensing, LLC.

Sommer, Carl. Light Your Candle. 2003. (Another Sommer-Time Story Ser.). (Illus.). 48p. (J). (gr. k-4). lib. bdg. 23.95 incl. audio compact disk *(978-1-57537-768-1(3));* 16.95 incl. audio *(978-1-57537-567-0(2))* Advance Publishing, Inc.

—Light Your Candle. James, Kennon, illus. 2003. (Another Sommer-Time Story Ser.). 48p. (J). (ENG.). 16.95 incl. audio compact disk *(978-1-57537-518-2(4));* lib. bdg. 23.95 incl. audio compact disk *(978-1-57537-718-6(7))* Advance Publishing, Inc.

Sommerdorf, Norma. Red River Girl. 2006. (ENG., Illus.). 192p. (J). (gr. 3-7). 16.95 *(978-0-8234-1903-6(7))* Holiday Hse., Inc.

Speare, Elizabeth George. The Sign of the Beaver. 2011. (ENG.). 144p. (J). (gr. 5-7). pap. 7.99 *(978-0-547-57711-1(7))* Houghton Mifflin Harcourt Publishing Co.

—The Sign of the Beaver. 135p. (J). (gr. 4-6). pap. 4.99 *(978-0-8072-1517-3(1),* Listening Library) Random Hse. Audio Publishing Group.

Spence, Eleanor. The Switherby Pilgrims: A Tale of the Australian Bush. 2005. (Living History Library). 195p. (YA). (gr. 8-12). pap. 12.95 *(978-1-883937-99-7(X))* Bethlehem Bks.

Sperry, Armstrong. Wagons Westward: The Old Trail to Santa Fe. Sperry, Armstrong, illus. 2005. (Illus.). 200p. (YA). (gr. 6-11). reprint ed. pap. 15.00 *(978-0-7567-9693-8(8))* DIANE Publishing Co.

Steele, William O. The Buffalo Knife. 2004. (ENG., Illus.). 144p. (J). (gr. 2-5). pap. 11.95 (978-0-15-205215-7(1)) Houghton Mifflin Harcourt Publishing Co.

—Flaming Arrows. 2004. (ENG., Illus.). 160p. (J). (gr. 2-5). pap. 11.95 (978-0-15-205213-3(5)) Houghton Mifflin Harcourt Publishing Co.

—Winter Danger. 2004. (ENG., Illus.). 144p. (J). (gr. 2-5). pap. 10.95 (978-0-15-205206-5(2)) Houghton Mifflin Harcourt Publishing Co.

Steig, Jeanne. Tales from Gizzard's Grill. Turner, Sandy, illus. 2004. 80p. (J). 17.89 (978-0-06-000960-1(8), Cotler, Joanna Books) HarperCollins Pubs.

Stites, Clara. Lixia of Gold Mountain: A Story of Early California. 2015. (ENG., Illus.). 100p. (J). pap. 8.95 (978-1-56474-421-0(3), Fithian Pr) Daniel & Daniel, Pubs., Inc.

Stone, B. J. Girl on the Bluff. (Illus.). 160p. 8.95 (978-1-57168-297-0(X)) Eakin Pr.

Stumpff, April D. & Johnston, Cassandra. Frontier Fun. 2007. (ENG., Illus.). 96p. pap., act. bk. ed. 9.95 (978-1-933337-21-0(4)) State Hse. Pr.

Stutson, Caroline. Prairie Primer: A to Z. Lamb, Susan Condie, illus. 2006. 29p. (J). (gr. -1-2). reprint ed. 16.00 (978-1-4223-5585-5(3)) DIANE Publishing Co.

Suen, Anastasia. Johnny Appleseed. Myer, Ed, illus. 2012. (ENG.). 24p. (gr. k-1). pap. 8.95 (978-1-61810-301-7(6)) Rourke Educational Media.

Thomas, Carroll. The Town on Rambling Creek: A Matty Trescott Novel. 2004. (Illus.). ix, 185p. (J). (978-1-57525-376-3(3)) Smith & Kraus Pubs., Inc.

Thompson, Gare. Our Journey West: An Adventure on the Oregon Trail. 2003. 40p. (J). pap. 6.99 (978-0-7922-5199-6(7)) CENGAGE Learning.

Timberlake, Amy. One Came Home. 2013. (ENG., Illus.). 272p. (J). (gr. 4-7). 16.99 (978-0-375-86925-9(5), Knopf Bks. for Young Readers) Random Hse. Children's Bks.

Toni Eubanks. Journey Home. 2010. 52p. pap. 8.95 (978-1-4401-8246-4(9)) iUniverse, Inc.

Turner, Ann Warren. Sewing Quilts. Allen, Thomas B., illus. 2012. (ENG.). 32p. (J). (gr. k-3). pap. 16.99 (978-1-4424-6042-3(3), Simon & Schuster Bks. For Young Readers) Simon & Schuster Bks. For Young Readers.

Van Leeuwen, Jean. Cabin on Trouble Creek. 2008. (ENG.). 224p. (J). (gr. 3-7). 7.99 (978-0-14-241164-3(7), Puffin Books) Penguin Young Readers Group.

Waggoner, Sandra. Son of an Honest Man. 2013. 136p. (J). pap. 10.95 (978-0-9890667-2-3(X)) Sable Creek Pr. LLC.

Waldron, Douglas Edward. Pathway to Montan: The Settlers Rest, 1 vol. 2009. 104p. pap. 19.95 (978-1-60836-313-1(9)) America Star Bks.

Warring, Molly-Ann. Paradise Acres. 2005. 518p. (978-0-88887-312-5(3)) Borealis Pr.

Weston Woods Staff, creator. Johnny Appleseed. 2011. 38.75 (978-0-439-72733-4(2)); 18.95 (978-0-439-72731-0(6)) Weston Woods Studios, Inc.

Wilder, Laura Ingalls. By the Shores of Silver Lake. (Little House Ser.). (J). (gr. 3-6). lib. bdg. 23.95 (978-0-8488-2117-3(3)) Amereon Ltd.

—By the Shores of Silver Lake. Williams, Garth, illus. (Little House Ser.: 5). (ENG.). 304p. (J). (gr. 3-7). 2008. pap. 7.99 (978-0-06-440005-3(0)) 2004. pap. 8.99 (978-0-06-058184-8(0)) HarperCollins Pubs.

—The First Four Years. Williams, Garth, illus. (Little House Ser.: 9). (ENG.). 160p. (J). (gr. 3-7). 2008. pap. 7.99 (978-0-06-440031-2(X)) 2004. pap. 8.99 (978-0-06-058188-6(3)) HarperCollins Pubs.

—A Little House Christmas Treasury: Festive Holiday Stories. Williams, Garth, illus. 2005. (Little House Ser.). (ENG.). 144p. (J). (gr. 3-7). 14.99 (978-0-06-076918-5(1)) HarperCollins Pubs.

—The Little House Collection, Set. Williams, Garth, illus. 2004. (Little House Ser.). (J). (gr. 3-7). pap. 44.99 (978-0-06-075428-0(1)) HarperCollins Pubs.

—Little House in the Big Woods. Williams, Garth, illus. 2008. (Little House Ser.: 1). (ENG.). 256p. (J). (gr. 3-7). pap. 7.99 (978-0-06-440001-5(8)) HarperCollins Pubs.

—Little House in the Big Woods. 2007. (Little House Ser.). 224p. (J). (gr. 3-7). pap. 6.99 (978-0-06-088537-3(8), Harper Trophy) HarperCollins Pubs.

—Little House in the Big Woods. Williams, Garth, illus. 2004. (Little House Ser.: 1). (ENG.). 256p. (J). (gr. 3-7). pap. 8.99 (978-0-06-058180-0(8)) HarperCollins Pubs.

—Little House on the Prairie. Williams, Garth, illus. 2008. (Little House Ser.: 3). (ENG.). 352p. (J). (gr. 3-7). pap. 7.99 (978-0-06-440002-2(6)) HarperCollins Pubs.

—Little House on the Prairie. 2007. (Little House Ser.). 336p. (J). (gr. 3-7). pap. 6.99 (978-0-06-088539-7(4), Harper Trophy) HarperCollins Pubs.

—Little House on the Prairie. Williams, Garth, illus. (Little House Ser.: 3). (ENG.). (J). (gr. 3-7). 2004. 352p. pap. 8.99 (978-0-06-058181-7(6)) 75th anniv. ed. 2010. 368p. 16.99 (978-0-06-195827-4(1)) HarperCollins Pubs.

—Little House on the Prairie. 2008. (Little House Bks.: 2). (J). 17.20 (978-1-4177-7357-2(X), Turtleback) Turtleback Bks.

—Little Town on the Prairie. Williams, Garth, illus. 2008. (Little House Ser.: 7). (ENG.). 320p. (J). (gr. 3-7). pap. 8.99 (978-0-06-440007-7(7)) HarperCollins Pubs.

—Little Town on the Prairie. 2007. (Little House Ser.). 320p. (J). (gr. 3-7). pap. 6.99 (978-0-06-088543-4(2), Harper Trophy) HarperCollins Pubs.

—Little Town on the Prairie. Williams, Garth, illus. (Little House Ser.: 7). 320p. (J). 2004. (ENG.). (gr. 3-7). pap. 8.99 (978-0-06-058186-2(7)) 2003. pap. 5.99 (978-0-06-052242-1(9)) HarperCollins Pubs.

—The Long Winter. Williams, Garth, illus. (Little House Ser.: 6). (ENG.). 352p. (J). (gr. 3-7). 2008. pap. 8.99 (978-0-06-440006-0(9)) 2004. pap. 8.99 (978-0-06-058185-5(9)) HarperCollins Pubs.

—On the Banks of Plum Creek. Williams, Garth, illus. 2008. (Little House Ser.: 4). (ENG.). 352p. (J). (gr. 3-7). pap. 7.99 (978-0-06-440004-6(2)) HarperCollins Pubs.

—On the Banks of Plum Creek. 2007. (Little House Ser.). 384p. (J). (gr. 3-7). pap., pap., pap. 6.99 (978-0-06-088540-3(8), Harper Trophy) HarperCollins Pubs.

—On the Banks of Plum Creek. Williams, Garth, illus. 2004. (Little House Ser.: 4). (ENG.). 352p. (J). (gr. 3-7). pap. 9.99 (978-0-06-058183-1(2)) HarperCollins Pubs.

—Pioneer Sisters. Kim, Ji-Hyuk, illus. 2017. (Little House Chapter Book Ser.: 2). 112p. (J). (gr. 1-5). pap. 4.99 (978-0-06-237710-4(8)) HarperCollins Pubs.

—These Happy Golden Years. 2007. (Little House Ser.). (ENG.). 304p. (J). (gr. 3-7). pap., pap. 6.99 (978-0-06-088544-1(0), Harper Trophy) HarperCollins Pubs.

—These Happy Golden Years. Williams, Garth, illus. (Little House Ser.: 8). (ENG.). 304p. (J). (gr. 3-7). 2004. pap. 8.99 (978-0-06-058187-9(5)) 2008. pap. 7.99 (978-0-06-440008-4(5)) HarperCollins Pubs.

—These Happy Golden Years. l.t. ed. (J). (gr. 3-6). 35.95 (978-1-58118-102-9(7)) LRS.

Wilder, Laura Ingalls & Videbeck, Sheila. Little House on the Prairie. Williams, Garth, illus. 7th rev. ed. 2016. (Charming Classics). (ENG.). 544p. pap. 75.99 (978-0-06-000046-2(5)) Lippincott Williams & Wilkins.

Wilkes, Maria D. Little House in Brookfield. abr. ed. 2007. (Little House Ser.). (ENG.). 144p. (J). (gr. 3-7). pap. 6.99 (978-0-06-114821-7(0)) HarperCollins Pubs.

—Little Town at the Crossroads. 2007. (Little House Ser.). 159p. (J). (gr. 3-7). per. 5.99 (978-0-06-114822-4(9), Harper Trophy) HarperCollins Pubs.

Williams, Heather. Nellie Oleson Meets Laura Ingalls. 2007. (Little House Ser.). 234p. (J). (gr. 3-7). lib. bdg. 16.89 (978-0-06-124249-6(7)) HarperCollins Pubs.

Wilson, Diane Lee. Black Storm Comin' 2006. (ENG.). 240p. (J). (gr. 5-9). pap. 7.99 (978-0-689-87138-2(4), McElderry, Margaret K. Bks.) McElderry, Margaret K. Bks.

—Black Storm Comin' 2006. (Illus.). 291p. (gr. 5-9). 17.00 (978-0-7569-6908-0(5)) Perfection Learning Corp.

Wilson, Laura. How I Survived the Oregon Trail: The Journal of Jesse Adams. 2006. (Illus.). 37p. (J). (gr. 4-8). reprint ed. pap. 10.00 (978-0-7567-9925-0(2)) DIANE Publishing Co.

Winters, Kay. Voices from the Oregon Trail. Day, Larry, illus. 2014. (ENG.). 48p. (J). (gr. 2-4). 17.99 (978-0-8037-3775-4(0), Dial Bks) Penguin Young Readers Group.

Wishinsky, Frieda. Pioneer Kids. Griffiths, Dean & Owlkids Books Inc. Staff, illus. 2007. (Canadian Flyer Adventures Ser.: 6). (ENG.). 96p. (J). (gr. 1-4). per. 9.95 (978-1-897349-05-2(X), Maple Tree Pr.) Owlkids Bks. Inc. CAN. Dist: Publishers Group West (PGW).

—Stop That Stagecoach! Eid, Jean-Paul & Owlkids Books Inc. Staff, illus. 2009. (Canadian Flyer Adventures Ser.: 13). (ENG.). 96p. (J). (gr. 1-4). pap. 7.95 (978-1-897349-63-2(7), Maple Tree Pr.) Owlkids Bks. Inc. CAN. Dist: Publishers Group West (PGW).

Wood, Gail. Lizzie, Light Feather & the Quarry Bluff Storm. 2015. (Illus.). viii, 88p. (J). pap. (978-1-57249-415-2(8), White Mane Kids) White Mane Publishing Co., Inc.

Yep, Laurence. When the Circus Came to Town. Wang, Suling, illus. 2004. 112p. (J). (gr. 3-5). 13.65 (978-0-7569-2969-5(5)) Perfection Learning Corp.

Yolen, Jane. Elsie's Bird. Small, David, illus. 2010. (ENG.). 40p. (J). (gr. k-3). 17.99 (978-0-399-25292-1(4), Philomel Bks.) Penguin Young Readers Group.

Young, Judy. A Book for Black-Eyed Susan. Ettlinger, Doris, illus. 2011. (Tales of Young Americans Ser.). (ENG.). 32p. (J). (gr. k-6). lib. bdg. 16.95 (978-1-58536-463-3(0)) Sleeping Bear Pr.

—Minnow & Rose: An Oregon Trail Story. Farnsworth, Bill, illus. 2009. (Tales of Young Americans Ser.). (ENG.). 32p. (J). (gr. 1-5). 17.95 (978-1-58536-421-3(5)) Sleeping Bear Pr.

FRONTIER AND PIONEER LIFE—SOUTHWEST

Brown, Rachel K. Santa Fe: Daily Life in a Western Trading Center. 2003. (J). lib. bdg. (978-1-58417-011-2(5)) Lake Street Pubs.

Dean, Arlan. The Old Spanish Trail: From Santa Fe, New Mexico to Los Angeles, California. 2003. (Famous American Trails Ser.). (Illus.). 24p. (J). lib. bdg. 22.60 (978-0-8239-6480-2(9)) Rosen Publishing Group, Inc., The.

Randolph, Ryan P. The Santa Fe Trail. (Library of the Westward Expansion Ser.). 24p. 2009. (gr. 3-4). 42.50 (978-1-60853-940-6(7)) 2003. (Illus.). (J). lib. bdg. 22.60 (978-0-8239-6292-1(X)) Rosen Publishing Group, Inc., The. (PowerKids Pr.).

Rubin, Donna. Log Cabin Kitty. Halbower, Susan J., illus. 2012. 56p. pap. 20.00 (978-0-87565-503-1(3)) Texas Christian Univ. Pr.

Waldman, Scott. Gunfight at the O. K. Corral: Wyatt Earp Upholds the Law. 2009. (Great Moments in American History Ser.). 32p. (gr. 3-3). 47.90 (978-1-61513-143-3(4)) Rosen Publishing Group, Inc., The.

FRONTIER AND PIONEER LIFE—WEST (U.S.)

Arnez, Lynda. My Wagon Train Adventure. 2016. (My Place in History Ser.). (ENG., Illus.). 24p. (J). (gr. 2-3). pap. 8.15 (978-1-4824-4002-7(4)) Stevens, Gareth Publishing LLLP.

Aronin, Miriam. How Many People Traveled the Oregon Trail? And Other Questions about the Trail West. 2012. (Six Questions of American History Ser.). (ENG.). 48p. (gr. 4-6). lib. bdg. 30.60 (978-0-7613-5332-4(1)) Lerner Publishing Group.

Arruda, Suzanne Middendorf. The Girl He Left Behind: The Life & Times of Libbie Custer. 2004. (Avisson Young Adult Ser.). (Illus.). 136p. (J). pap. 19.95 (978-1-888105-67-4(4)) Avisson Pr., Inc.

Aston, Claire. The Wild West Through Time. 2009. (Fast Forward Ser.). 32p. (YA). (gr. 2-5). lib. bdg. 25.25 (978-1-4358-2799-8(6)) Rosen Publishing Group, Inc., The.

Bailey Publishing Staff & McEvoy, Anne. The American West. 2009. (Costume Source Bks). (Illus.). 32p. (gr. 6-12). 35.00 (978-1-60413-382-0(1), Chelsea Hse.) Facts On File, Inc.

Baker, Brynn. Buffalo Soldiers: Heroes of the American West. 2015. (Military Heroes Ser.). (ENG., Illus.). 32p. (gr. 3-4). lib. bdg. 27.32 (978-1-4914-4838-0(5)) Capstone Press of Coughlan Cos.

Blassingame, Wyatt & Glendinning, Richard. The Mountain Men. 2011. 176p. 42.95 (978-1-258-00523-8(9)) Literary Licensing, LLC.

Bliss, John. Pioneers to the West, 1 vol. 2011. (Children's True Stories: Migration Ser.). (ENG.). 32p. (gr. 3-3). pap. 8.29 (978-1-4109-4082-7(9), Raintree Perspectives) Heinemann-Raintree.

Bork, Rhoda. Pioneering: Activities to Live History. 2007. (J). (978-0-9786018-6-7(6)) Sparrow Media Group, Inc.

Britton, Arthur K. Life in the Wild West. 2013. (What You Didn't Know about History Ser.). (Illus.). 24p. (J). (gr. 2-5). pap. 8.15 (978-1-4339-8440-2(7)); lib. bdg. 22.60 (978-1-4339-8439-6(3)) Stevens, Gareth Publishing LLLP.

Brook, Henry. Wild West. 2008. (True Stories Ser.). 160p. (YA). pap. 4.99 (978-0-7945-2197-4(5), Usborne) EDC Publishing.

Bryant, Jill. John Henry Holliday. 2003. (Folk Heroes Ser.). (Illus.). 24p. (J). lib. bdg. 24.45 (978-1-59036-077-4(X)) Weigl Pubs., Inc.

—Wagon Train. 2003. (Real Life Stories Ser.). (Illus.). 24p. (J). lib. bdg. 24.45 (978-1-59036-082-8(6)) Weigl Pubs., Inc.

—Women in the West. 2003. (Real Life Stories Ser.). (Illus.). 24p. (J). lib. bdg. 24.45 (978-1-59036-083-5(4)) Weigl Pubs., Inc.

Burger, James P. Mountain Men of the West. 2009. (Library of the Westward Expansion Ser.). 24p. (gr. 3-4). 42.50 (978-1-60853-937-6(7), PowerKids Pr.) Rosen Publishing Group, Inc., The.

Burlingame, Jeff. Jesse James: I Will Never Surrender. 2010. (Americans—the Spirit of a Nation Ser.). (Illus.). 128p. (J). lib. bdg. 33.27 (978-0-7660-3353-5(8)) Enslow Pubs., Inc.

Byers, Ann. Life As a Homesteader in the American West. 2016. (Life As... Ser.). (Illus.). 32p. (J). (gr. 3-3). 28.50 (978-1-5026-1787-3(0)) Cavendish Square Publishing.

Calvert, Patricia. Kit Carson: He Led the Way. 2006. (Great Explorations Ser.). (Illus.). 80p. (gr. 6-7). lib. bdg. 22.95 (978-0-7614-2223-5(4), Benchmark Bks.) Marshall Cavendish Corp.

Collins, Kathleen. Jesse James: Bank Robber of the American West. 2009. (Primary Sources of Famous People in American History Ser.). 32p. (gr. 2-3). 47.90 (978-1-60851-690-2(3)) Rosen Publishing Group, Inc., The.

—Jesse James: Bank Robber of the American West / Legendario bandido del oeste Americano. 2009. (Famous People in American History/Grandes personajes en la historia de los Estados Unidos Ser.). (ENG & SPA.). 32p. (gr. 2-3). 47.90 (978-1-61512-547-0(7), Editorial Buenas Letras) Rosen Publishing Group, Inc., The.

—Jesse James: Legendario Bandido del Oeste Americano. 2004. (Grandes personajes en la historia de los Estados Unidos Ser.). (SPA.). 32p. (gr. 3-6). pap. 10.00 (978-0-8239-4230-5(9), Rosen Classroom) Rosen Publishing Group, Inc., The.

—Jesse James: Legendario bandido del oeste americano (Jesse James: Bank Robber of the American West) 2009. (Grandes personajes en la historia de los Estados Unidos (Famous People in American History) Ser.). (SPA.). 32p. (gr. 2-3). 47.90 (978-1-61512-801-3(8), Editorial Buenas Letras) Rosen Publishing Group, Inc., The.

—Jesse James: Western Bank Robber. 2004. (Famous People in American History Ser.). (ENG., Illus.). 32p. (gr. 4-8). pap. 10.00 (978-0-8239-4184-1(1)) Rosen Publishing Group, Inc., The.

Cooke, Tim. Jesse James: A Notorious Bank Robber of the Wild West. 2016. (Wanted! Famous Outlaws Ser.). (ENG., Illus.). 48p. (J). (gr. 6-8). pap. 14.05 (978-1-4824-4259-5(0)) Stevens, Gareth Publishing LLLP.

Crewe, Sabrina & Uschan, Michael V. The Oregon Trail. 2004. (Events That Shaped America Ser.). (Illus.). 32p. (gr. 3-6). lib. bdg. 26.00 (978-0-8368-3405-5(4), Gareth Stevens Learning Library) Stevens, Gareth Publishing LLLP.

Cunningham, Meghan Engsberg. Jesse James. Lapegüe, Matias, illus. 2016. (American Legends & Folktales Ser.). 32p. (J). 28.50 (978-1-5026-2197-9(5)) Cavendish Square Publishing.

Demund, Tom. From Slave to Superstar of the Wild West: The Awesome Story of Jim Beckwourth. 2007. (Illus.). 154p. (J). 18.95 (978-0-9786904-0-3(0)) Legends of the West Publishing Co.

Dickinson, Rachel. Great Pioneer Projects. Braley, Shawn, illus. 2007. (Build It Yourself Ser.: 1). (ENG.). 128p. (J). (gr. 3-7). pap. 15.95 (978-0-9785037-6-5(7)) Northern Trails Pr.

DiVito, Anna. Annie Oakley Saves the Day. DiVito, Anna, illus. 2004. (Ready-To-read COFA Ser.). (ENG., Illus.). 32p. (J). (gr. k-2). pap. 3.99 (978-0-689-86520-6(1), Simon Spotlight) Simon Spotlight.

Doeden, Matt. Oregon Trail: An Interactive History Adventure. 2013. (You Choose: History Ser.). (ENG.). 112p. (gr. 3-4). pap. 6.95 (978-1-4765-3607-1(4)); 31.99 (978-1-4765-0254-0(4)) Capstone Press of Coughlan Cos. (You Choose Bks.).

Domnauer, Teresa. Life in the West. 2010. (True Book Ser.). (ENG., 48p. (J). Illus.). pap. 6.95 (978-0-531-21246-2(7)); (gr. 2-5). 29.00 (978-0-531-20583-9(5)) Scholastic Library Publishing.

—Westward Expansion. 2010. (True Book Ser.). (ENG., Illus.). 48p. (J). (gr. 2-5). 29.00 (978-0-531-20586-0(X)) Scholastic Library Publishing.

Ellis, Edward Sylvester. The Life of Kit Carson: The Life of Kit Carson. 2007. (ENG.). 180p. pap. 19.99 (978-1-4264-5784-5(7)) Creative Media Partners, LLC.

Evan-Moor. History Pockets: Moving West, Grades 4-6. 2003. (History Pockets Ser.). (ENG., Illus.). 96p. (J). (gr. 4-6). pap., suppl. ed. 14.99 (978-1-55799-902-3(3), EMC 3704) Evan-Moor Educational Pubs.

Expansionism. 2010. (Key Concepts in American History Ser.). (Illus.). 128p. (gr. 6-12). 45.00 (978-1-60413-221-2(3), Chelsea Hse.) Facts On File, Inc.

Favor, Lesli J. A Historical Atlas of America's Manifest Destiny. (United States: Historical Atlases of the Growth of a New Nation Ser.). 64p. 2009. (gr. 5-5). 61.20 (978-1-60854-250-5(5)) 2005. (Illus.). (J). (gr. 7-12). lib. bdg. 31.95 (978-1-4042-0201-6(3)) Rosen Publishing Group, Inc., The.

Fein, Eric. High Noon: Wild Bill Hickok & the Code of the Old West. 2009. (Great Moments in American History Ser.). 32p. (gr. 3-3). 47.90 (978-1-61513-145-7(0)) Rosen Publishing Group, Inc., The.

Figley, Marthy Rhodes. Clara Morgan & the Oregon Trail Journey. Orback, Craig, illus. 2011. (History Speaks: Picture Books Plus Reader's Theater Ser.). 48p. pap. 56.72 (978-0-7613-7631-6(3)) Lerner Publishing Group.

Figley, Marthy Rhodes & Figley, Marty Rhodes. Clara Morgan & the Oregon Trail Journey. Orback, Craig, illus. 2011. (History Speaks: Picture Books Plus Reader's Theater Ser.). (ENG.). 48p. (gr. 2-4). pap. 9.95 (978-0-7613-7115-1(X)) Lerner Publishing Group.

Flynn, Jean. Annie Oakley: Sharpshooter & Entertainer. 2015. (J). pap. (978-0-7660-6441-6(7)) Enslow Pubs., Inc.

Foran, Jill. Homesteading. 2003. (Real Life Stories Ser.). (Illus.). 24p. (J). lib. bdg. 24.45 (978-1-59036-079-8(6)) Weigl Pubs., Inc.

Freedman, Jeri. Life As a Pioneer on the Oregon Trail. 2016. (Life As... Ser.). (ENG., Illus.). 32p. (J). (gr. 3-3). pap. 10.58 (978-1-5026-1075-1(2)) Cavendish Square Publishing.

Friedman, Mel. The Oregon Trail. 2012. (Cornerstones of Freedom, Third Ser.). (ENG., Illus.). 64p. (J). pap. 8.95 (978-0-531-28163-5(9)); lib. bdg. 30.00 (978-0-531-23063-3(5)) Scholastic Library Publishing.

Frisch, Aaron. Jesse James. 2005. (Legends of the West (Creative Education) Ser.). (Illus.). 48p. (J). (gr. 5-9). lib. bdg. 21.95 (978-1-58341-338-8(3), Creative Education) Creative Co., The.

George, Lynn. What Do You Know about Westward Expansion? (20 Questions: History Ser.). 24p. (gr. 2-3). 2009. 42.50 (978-1-60854-960-3(7), PowerKids Pr.) 2008. (Illus.). (J). lib. bdg. 22.60 (978-1-4042-4189-3(2)) Rosen Publishing Group, Inc., The.

Gibbons, Gail. Cowboys & Cowgirls. Gibbons, Gail, illus. 2003. (ENG., Illus.). 32p. (J). (gr. 1-4). pap. 8.00 (978-0-316-16859-5(9)) Little, Brown Bks. for Young Readers.

—Cowboys & Cowgirls. Gibbons, Gail, illus. 2003. (Illus.). (J). (gr. 1-4). 18.45 (978-0-613-71749-6(X), Turtleback) Turtleback Bks.

Glaser, Jason. The Buffalo Soldiers & the American West. Smith, Tod G. et al, illus. 2005. (Graphic History Ser.). (ENG.). 32p. (gr. 3-4). 30.65 (978-0-7368-4966-1(1), Graphic Library) Capstone Press of Coughlan Cos.

Goodman, Michael E. Buffalo Bill. 2005. (Legends of the West (Creative Education) Ser.). (Illus.). 48p. (J). (gr. 5-9). lib. bdg. 21.95 (978-1-58341-336-4(7), Creative Education) Creative Co., The.

Green, Carl R. & Sanford, William R. Belle Starr. rev. ed. 2008. (Outlaws & Lawmen of the Wild West, Revised Edition Ser.). (Illus.). 48p. (J). (gr. 5-18). lib. bdg. 25.27 (978-0-7660-3176-0(4)) Enslow Pubs., Inc.

—Jesse James. rev. ed. 2008. (Outlaws & Lawmen of the Wild West, Revised Edition Ser.). (Illus.). 48p. (J). (gr. 5-18). lib. bdg. 25.27 (978-0-7660-3172-2(1)) Enslow Pubs., Inc.

—Wild Bill Hickok. rev. ed. 2008. (Outlaws & Lawmen of the Wild West, Revised Edition Ser.). (Illus.). 48p. (J). (gr. 5-18). lib. bdg. 25.27 (978-0-7660-3177-7(2)) Enslow Pubs., Inc.

Gunderson, Jessica. Your Life As a Pioneer on the Oregon Trail. Dougherty, Rachel, illus. 2012. (Way It Was Ser.). (ENG.). 32p. (gr. 2-3). pap. 8.95 (978-1-4048-7250-9(7)); lib. bdg. 26.65 (978-1-4048-7157-1(8)) Picture Window Bks.

Hale, Nathan. Donner Dinner Party. 2013. (Nathan Hale's Hazardous Tales Ser.). (ENG., Illus.). 128p. (J). (gr. 3-7). 12.99 (978-1-4197-0856-5(2), Amulet Bks.) Abrams, Inc.

Harkins, Susan Sales & Harkins, William H. The Donner Party. 2008. (What's So Great About... ? Ser.). (Illus.). 32p. (J). (gr. 2-4). lib. bdg. 25.70 (978-1-58415-669-7(4)) Mitchell Lane Pubs., Inc.

Harris, Irene. The Homestead ACT & Westward Expansion: Settling the Western Frontier. 2016. (Spotlight on American History Ser.). (Illus.). 24p. (gr. 6-4). 26.25 (978-1-5081-4943-9(7), PowerKids Pr.) Rosen Publishing Group, Inc., The.

Hester, Sallie. Diary of Sallie Hester: A Covered Wagon Girl, 1 vol. 2014. (First-Person Histories Ser.). (ENG.). 32p. (gr. 3-4). lib. bdg. 27.32 (978-1-4765-4193-8(0), Fact Finders) Capstone Press of Coughlan Cos.

Hicks, Peter. You Wouldn't Want to Live in a Wild West Town! Dust You'd Rather Not Settle. Antram, David, illus. 2013. (ENG.). (J). 32p. 29.00 (978-0-531-27106-3(4)); 40p. pap. 9.95 (978-0-531-23857-8(1)) Scholastic Library Publishing. (Watts, Franklin).

Hooker, Forrestine Cooper. Child of the Fighting Tenth: On the Frontier with the Buffalo Soldiers. Wilson, Steve, ed. 2011. (ENG., Illus.). 296p. pap. 19.95 (978-0-8061-4080-3(1)) Univ. of Oklahoma Pr.

Jeffrey, Gary. The Oregon Trail. Poluzzi, Allesandro, illus. 2012. (Graphic History of the American West Ser.). (ENG.). 24p. (J). (gr. 3-8). pap. 8.15 (978-1-4339-6745-0(6), Gareth Stevens Learning Library); (gr. 4-7). lib. bdg. 23.95 (978-1-4339-6743-6(X)) Stevens, Gareth Publishing LLLP.

Jesse James. 2010. (Legends of the Wild West Ser.). (Illus.). 128p. (gr. 6-12). 35.00 (978-1-60413-598-5(0), Chelsea Hse.) Facts On File, Inc.

Jones, Charlotte Foltz. Westward Ho! Eleven Explorers of the American West. 2005. (ENG., Illus.). 240p. (J). (gr. 4-6). tchr. ed. 22.95 (978-0-8234-1586-1(4)) Holiday Hse., Inc.

King, David C. Westward Expansion. 2012. (American Heritage, American Voices Ser.). (ENG.). 144p. (J). (gr. 5-9). pap. 22.95 (978-1-118-43608-0(3), Wiley) Wiley, John & Sons, Inc.

Koestler-Grack, Rachel A. Daily Life in a Southwestern Settlement: San Antonio. 2003. (J). (978-1-58417-012-9(3)); pap. (978-1-58417-075-4(1)) Lake Street Pubs.

Kovacs, Vic. Outlaws & Sheriffs. 2015. (True History of the Wild West Ser.). (ENG., Illus.). 32p. (J). (gr. 5-5). pap. 10.00 (978-1-4994-1178-2(2), PowerKids Pr.) Rosen Publishing Group, Inc., The.

Krohn, Katherine E. Calico Dresses & Buffalo Robes: American West Fashions from the 1840s to the 1890s. 2011. (Dressing a Nation: the History of U. S. Fashion Ser.). (ENG., Illus.). 64p. (gr. 5-12). lib. bdg. 31.93 (978-0-7613-5890-9(0), Twenty-First Century Bks.) Lerner Publishing Group.

—Women of the Wild West. 2003. (Biography Ser.). (Illus.). 112p. (YA). (gr. 6-18). pap. 7.95 (978-0-8225-9690-5(3), Carolrhoda Bks.) Lerner Publishing Group.

Langley, Andrew. 100 Things You Should Know about the Wild West. 2004. (Mosaic of Magical Information Ser.). (Illus.). 48p. (YA). (gr. 3-18). lib. bdg. 19.95 (978-1-59084-458-8(0)) Mason Crest.

Levy, Janey. Life on a Wagon Train. 2003. (Rosen Real Readers Big Bookstm Ser.). (ENG.). 16p. (gr. 2-3). 37.95 (978-1-4042-6224-9(5)) Rosen Publishing Group, Inc., The.

Link, Theodore. Annie Oakley: Wild West Sharpshooter. 2004. (Primary Sources of Famous People in American History

Ser.). (ENG., Illus.). 32p. (gr. 4-8). pap. 10.00 *(978-0-8239-4174-2(4))* Rosen Publishing Group, Inc., The.

Lusted, Marcia Amidon. The Oregon Trail, 1 vol. 2011. (Essential Events Set 7 Ser.). (ENG., Illus.). 112p. (J). (gr. 6-12). lib. bdg. 35.64 *(978-1-61783-102-7(6))* ABDO Publishing Co.

Lynette, Rachel. The Oregon Trail. 2013. (Pioneer Spirit: the Westward Expansion Ser.). 24p. (J). (gr. 3-6). 22.60 *(978-1-4777-0786-9(7))*; (ENG., Illus.). pap. 8.25 *(978-1-4777-0905-4(3))* Rosen Publishing Group, Inc., The. (PowerKids Pr.).

Manheimer, Ann S. James Beckwourth: Legendary Mountain Man. 2005. (Trailblazer Biographies Ser.). (ENG., Illus.). 112p. (gr. 5-9). lib. bdg. 31.93 *(978-1-57505-892-4(8))*, Twenty-First Century Bks.) Lerner Publishing Group.

Marciniak, Kristin. The Oregon Trail & Westward Expansion: A History Perspectives Book. 2013. (Perspectives Library). (ENG., Illus.). 32p. (J). (gr. 4-8). 28.50 *(978-1-62431-419-3(8))*, 202796); pap. 14.21 *(978-1-62431-495-7(3))*, 202798) Cherry Lake Publishing.

Markel, Rita J. Your Travel Guide to America's Old West. 2005. (Passport to History Ser.). (Illus.). 96p. (YA). (gr. 5-9). lib. bdg. 26.60 *(978-0-8225-3074-9(0))* Lerner Publishing Group.

Maynard, Charles W. Fort Laramie. 2009. (Famous Forts Throughout American History Ser.). 24p. (gr. 3-4). 42.50 *(978-1-61512-516-6(7))*, PowerKids Pr.) Rosen Publishing Group, Inc., The.

—Jedediah Smith: Mountain Man of the American West. 2009. (Famous Explorers of the American West Ser.). 24p. (gr. 3-4). 42.50 *(978-1-61512-501-2(9))*, PowerKids Pr.) Rosen Publishing Group, Inc., The.

—Jim Bridger: Frontiersman & Mountain Guide. (Famous Explorers of the American West Ser.). 24p. 2009. (gr. 3-4). 42.50 *(978-1-61512-502-9(7))* 2003. (Illus.). (J). lib. bdg. 22.60 *(978-0-8239-6288-4(1))* Rosen Publishing Group, Inc., The. (PowerKids Pr.).

McCarthy, Pat. Heading West: Life with the Pioneers, 21 Activities. 2009. (For Kids Ser.). (ENG., Illus.). 144p. (J). (gr. 4-7). pap. 16.95 *(978-1-55652-809-5(4))* Chicago Review Pr., Inc.

McIntosh, Kenneth. Saloons, Shootouts, & Spurs: The Wild West in The 1800's. 2009. (Daily Life in America in the 1800s Ser.). 64p. (YA). (gr. 7-18). pap. 9.95 *(978-1-4222-1862-4(7))*; lib. bdg. 22.95 *(978-1-4222-1789-4(2))* Mason Crest.

McNeese, Tim. The Donner Party: A Doomed Journey. 2009. (Milestones in American History Ser.). (Illus.). 160p. (gr. 6-12). 35.00 *(978-1-60413-025-6(3))*, Chelsea Hse.) Facts On File, Inc.

—The Oregon Trail. 2009. (Milestones in American History Ser.). (Illus.). 152p. (gr. 6-12). 35.00 *(978-1-60413-027-0(X))*, Chelsea Hse.) Facts On File, Inc.

Morley, Jacqueline. You Wouldn't Want to... Be an American Pioneer! Antram, David, illus. rev. ed. 2012. (ENG.). (J). 40p. pap. 9.95 *(978-0-531-28025-6(X))*; 32p. lib. bdg. 29.00 *(978-0-531-27500-9(0))* Scholastic Library Publishing.

Morretta, Alison. Homesteading & Settling the Frontier. 2017. (J). ***(978-1-5026-2641-7(1))*** Cavendish Square Publishing.

Musolf, Nell. The Split History of Westward Expansion in the United States: A Perspectives Flip Book, 1 vol. 2012. (Perspectives Flip Bks.). (ENG.). 64p. (gr. 5-6). pap. 8.95 *(978-0-7565-4596-3(X))*; lib. bdg. 33.99 *(978-0-7565-4571-0(4))* Compass Point Bks.

The New South & the Old West, 1866-1890. 2010. (Discovering U. S. History Ser.). (Illus.). 136p. (gr. 5-8). 35.00 *(978-1-60413-354-7(6))*, Chelsea Hse.) Facts On File, Inc.

Nolan, Frederick W. Gunslingers & Cowboys. 2015. (Wild West Ser.). (Illus.). 64p. (J). (gr. 9-12). 39.95 *(978-1-78404-078-9(9))* Arcturus Publishing GBR. Dist: Black Rabbit Bks.

—Outlaws & Rebels. 2015. (Wild West Ser.). (Illus.). 64p. (J). (gr. 9-12). 39.95 *(978-1-78404-080-2(0))* Arcturus Publishing GBR. Dist: Black Rabbit Bks.

Oachs, Emily Rose. Death in the Donner Party: A Cause-And-Effect Investigation. 2016. (Cause-And-Effect Disasters Ser.). (ENG., Illus.). 40p. (J). (gr. 4-6). 46.65 *(978-1-5124-1126-3(4))*, Lerner Pubns.) Lerner Publishing Group.

O'Brien, Cynthia. Go West with Merchants & Traders. 2016. (ENG.). 32p. (J). *(978-0-7787-2326-4(7))* Crabtree Publishing Co.

—Go West with Miners, Prospectors, & Loggers. 2016. (ENG.). 32p. (J). *(978-0-7787-2328-8(3))* Crabtree Publishing Co.

Olson, Steven P. The Oregon Trail. 2004. (Primary Sources in American History Ser.). (Illus.). 64p. (gr. 5-8). lib. bdg. 31.95 *(978-0-8239-4512-2(X))*, Rosen Reference) Rosen Publishing Group, Inc., The.

Olson, Tod. How to Get Rich on a Texas Cattle Drive: In Which I Tell the Honest Truth about Rampaging Rustlers, Stampeding Steers & Other Fateful Hazards on the Wild Chisolm Trail. Allred, Scott & Proch, Gregory, illus. 2010. (How to Get Rich Ser.). (ENG.). 48p. (J). (gr. 3-7). 18.95 *(978-1-4263-0524-5(9))*; 27.90 *(978-1-4263-0525-2(7))* National Geographic Society. (National Geographic Children's Bks.).

The Oregon Trail. 2013. (Pioneer Spirit: the Westward Expansion Ser.). 24p. (J). (gr. 3-6). pap. 49.50 *(978-1-4777-0906-1(1))*, PowerKids Pr.) Rosen Publishing Group, Inc., The.

Phillips, Larissa. Wild Bill Hickok: Legend of the American Wild West / Leyenda del oeste Americano. 2009. (Famous People in American History/Grandes personajes en la historia de los Estados Unidos Ser.). (ENG & SPA.). 32p. (gr. 2-3). 47.90 *(978-1-61512-557-9(4))*, Editorial Buenas Letras) Rosen Publishing Group, Inc., The.

—Wild Bill Hickok: Legend of the Wild West. 2009. (Primary Sources of Famous People in American History Ser.). 32p. (gr. 2-3). 47.90 *(978-1-60851-740-4(3))* Rosen Publishing Group, Inc., The.

—Wild Bill Hickok: Leyenda del oeste Americano. 2004. (Grandes personajes en la historia de los Estados Unidos Ser.). (SPA.). 32p. (gr. 3-6). pap. 10.00 *(978-0-8239-4240-4(6))*, Rosen Classroom) Rosen Publishing Group, Inc., The.

—Wild Bill Hickok: Leyenda del oeste americano (Wild Bill Hickok: Legend of the American Wild West) 2009. (Grandes personajes en la historia de los Estados Unidos (Famous People in American History) Ser.). (SPA.). 32p. (gr. 2-3). 47.90 *(978-1-61512-810-5(7))*, Editorial Buenas Letras) Rosen Publishing Group, Inc., The.

Porterfield, Jason. Annie Oakley: Tiradora del Lejano Oeste (Annie Oakley: Wild West Sharpshooter) 2009. (Grandes personajes en la historia de los Estados Unidos (Famous People in American History) Ser.). 32p. (gr. 2-3). 47.90 *(978-1-61512-789-4(5))*, Editorial Buenas Letras) Rosen Publishing Group, Inc., The.

—Annie Oakley: Wild West Sharpshooter / Tiradora del Lejano Oeste. 2009. (Famous People in American History/Grandes personajes en la historia de los Estados Unidos Ser.). 32p. (gr. 2-3). 47.90 *(978-1-61512-537-1(X))*, Editorial Buenas Letras) Rosen Publishing Group, Inc., The.

—The Homestead Act of 1862. 2005. (Primary Sources in American History Ser.). (Illus.). 64p. (J). (gr. 5-8). lib. bdg. 31.95 *(978-1-4042-0178-1(5))* Rosen Publishing Group, Inc., The.

—The Homestead Act Of 1862: A Primary Source History of the Settlement of the American Heartland in the Late 19th Century. 2009. (Primary Sources in American History Ser.). 64p. (gr. 5-8). 58.50 *(978-1-60851-496-0(X))* Rosen Publishing Group, Inc., The.

Quasha, Jennifer. Covered Wagons: Hands-on Projects about America's Westward Expansion. 2009. (Great Social Studies Projects Ser.). 24p. (gr. 3-3). 42.50 *(978-1-61513-208-9(2))*, PowerKids Pr.) Rosen Publishing Group, Inc., The.

Raabe, Emily. Buffalo Soldiers & the Western Frontier. (Westward Ho! Ser.). 24p. 2009. (gr. 2-3). 42.50 *(978-1-60854-759-3(0))* 2003. (Illus.). (J). lib. bdg. 22.60 *(978-0-8239-6495-6(7))* Rosen Publishing Group, Inc., The. (PowerKids Pr.).

—Pioneers: Life as a Homesteader. 2009. (Westward Ho! Ser.). 24p. (gr. 2-3). 42.50 *(978-1-60854-761-6(2))*, PowerKids Pr.) Rosen Publishing Group, Inc., The.

Rae, Thelma. Pioneer Families. 2009. (Reading Room Collection 1 Ser.). 16p. (gr. 2-3). 37.50 *(978-1-60851-948-4(1))*, PowerKids Pr.) Rosen Publishing Group, Inc., The.

Rajczak, Kristen. The Donner Party. 2015. (Doomed! Ser.). (ENG., Illus.). 32p. (J). (gr. 4-5). pap. 10.50 *(978-1-4824-2928-2(4))* Stevens, Gareth Publishing LLLP.

—Life on a Wagon Train. 2013. (What You Didn't Know about History Ser.). (Illus.). 24p. (J). (gr. 2-5). pap. 8.15 *(978-1-4339-8445-7(8))*; lib. bdg. 22.60 *(978-1-4339-8444-0(X))* Stevens, Gareth Publishing LLLP.

—20 Fun Facts about Pioneer Women. 2015. (Fun Fact File: Women in History Ser.). (ENG., Illus.). 32p. (J). (gr. 2-3). 25.25 *(978-1-4824-2806-3(7))* Stevens, Gareth Publishing LLLP.

Randolph, Ryan P. Black Cowboys. 2003. (Library of the Westward Expansion Ser.). (Illus.). (J). lib. bdg. 22.60 *(978-0-8239-6294-5(6))* Rosen Publishing Group, Inc., The.

—Frontier Schools & Schoolteachers. (Library of the Westward Expansion Ser.). 24p. 2009. (gr. 3-4). 42.50 *(978-1-60853-935-2(0))* 2003. (Illus.). (J). lib. bdg. 22.60 *(978-0-8239-6295-2(4))* Rosen Publishing Group, Inc., The. (PowerKids Pr.).

—Frontier Women Who Helped Shape the American West. (Library of the Westward Expansion Ser.). 24p. 2009. (gr. 3-4). 42.50 *(978-1-60853-936-9(9))* 2003. (Illus.). (J). lib. bdg. 22.60 *(978-0-8239-6297-6(0))* Rosen Publishing Group, Inc., The. (PowerKids Pr.).

—Wild West Lawmen & Outlaws. (Library of the Westward Expansion Ser.). 24p. 2009. (gr. 3-4). 42.50 *(978-1-60853-944-4(X))* 2003. (Illus.). (J). lib. bdg. 22.60 *(978-0-8239-6293-8(8))* Rosen Publishing Group, Inc., The. (PowerKids Pr.).

Rea, Thelma. Pioneer Families. 2006. (Reading Room Collection: Social Studies). (Illus.). 16p. (J). (gr. 3-7). lib. bdg. 17.25 *(978-1-4042-3346-1(6))*, PowerKids Pr.) Rosen Publishing Group, Inc., The.

Rice, Dona Herweck. Bad Guys & Gals of the Wild West, 1 vol. 2nd rev. ed. 2013. (Nonfiction Readers Ser.). (ENG., Illus.). 64p. (J). (gr. 5-5). pap. 31.96 *(978-1-4333-7426-5(9))* Teacher Created Materials, Inc.

Rice, Katelyn. The Great Leap Westward. 2017. (J). pap. *(978-1-4938-3791-5(5))* Teacher Created Materials, Inc.

Rice, Katelyn. Settling & Unsettling the West (America in The 1800s) 2017. (Primary Source Readers Ser.). (Illus.). 32p. (J). (gr. 4-5). pap. 8.99 ***(978-1-4938-3797-7(4))*** Teacher Created Materials, Inc.

Roza, Greg. Westward Expansion. 2011. (Story of America Ser.). (Illus.). 32p. (J). (gr. 4-6). pap. 10.50 *(978-1-4339-4781-0(1))*; lib. bdg. 26.60 *(978-1-4339-4780-3(3))* Stevens, Gareth Publishing LLLP. (Gareth Stevens Learning Library).

Ruffin, Frances E. Annie Oakley. 2009. (American Legends Ser.). 24p. (gr. 3-3). 42.50 *(978-1-61511-378-1(9))*, PowerKids Pr.) Rosen Publishing Group, Inc., The.

Sandler, Martin W. Who Were the American Pioneers? And Other Questions about Westward Expansion. Barrett, Robert, illus. 2014. (Good Question! Ser.). (ENG.). 32p. (J). pap. 5.95 *(978-1-4027-9047-8(3))* Sterling Publishing Co., Inc.

Sanford, William R. & Green, Carl R. Kit Carson: Courageous Mountain Man. 2012. (Courageous Heroes of the American West Ser.). 48p. (J). pap. 8.95 *(978-1-4644-0094-0(6))*; (Illus.). (gr. 5-18). 22.60 *(978-0-7660-4011-3(9))* Enslow Pubs., Inc.

Schwartz, Heather E. Outlaws, Gunslingers, & Thieves. 2013. (ShockZone (tm) — Villains Ser.). (ENG.). 32p. (gr. 5-8). lib. bdg. 26.60 *(978-1-4677-0605-6(1))*, Lerner Pubns.) Lerner Publishing Group.

Sioux, Tracee. Immigrants & the Westward Expansion. 2009. (Primary Sources of Immigration & Migration in America Ser.). 24p. (gr. 3-4). 42.50 *(978-1-60851-776-3(4))*, PowerKids Pr.) Rosen Publishing Group, Inc., The.

Smith-Llera, Danielle. Stranded in the Sierra Nevada: The Story of the Donner Party. 2015. (Adventures on the American Frontier Ser.). (ENG., Illus.). 32p. (gr. 3-4). pap. 7.95 *(978-1-4914-4912-7(8))* Capstone Press of Coughlan Cos.

Solomon, Sharon. Cathy Williams, Buffalo Soldier, 1 vol. Lorenzetti, Doreen, illus. 2010. (ENG.). 32p. (J). (gr. k-3). 16.99 *(978-1-58980-801-0(0))* Pelican Publishing Co., Inc.

Streissguth, Thomas. Perspectives on Westward Expansion. 2018. (ENG.). 32p. (gr. 3-6). ***(978-1-63235-404-4(7))***, 12-Story Library) Pr. Room Editions LLC.

Stuckey, Rachel. Go West with Settlers & Farmers. 2016. (ENG.). 32p. (J). *(978-0-7787-2330-1(5))* Crabtree Publishing Co.

—Wagon Trains Heading West. 2015. (True History of the Wild West Ser.). (ENG., Illus.). 32p. (J). (gr. 5-5). pap. 10.00 *(978-1-4994-1179-9(0))*, PowerKids Pr.) Rosen Publishing Group, Inc., The.

Sullivan, Laura L. Life As a Cowboy in the American West. 2016. (Life As... Ser.). (ENG., Illus.). 32p. (J). (gr. 3-3). pap. 10.58 *(978-1-5026-1072-0(8))* Cavendish Square Publishing.

Tieck, Sarah. Oregon Trail, 1 vol. 2008. (All Aboard America Ser.). (ENG.). 24p. (J). (gr. 1-4). 25.65 *(978-1-59928-939-7(3))* ABDO Publishing Co.

Torr, James D., ed. Westward Expansion. 2003. (Interpreting American History Through Primary Documents Ser.x). (Illus.). 208p. (J). 32.45 *(978-0-7377-1134-9(5))*, Greenhaven Pr., Inc.) Cengage Gale.

Vann, Donna. Wild West Adventures. 2006. (Adventure Ser.). (ENG., Illus.). 96p. (J). per. 8.99 *(978-1-84550-065-8(2))*, 9f994332-def5-4d9f-abc1-2f97eaba348d) Christian Focus Pubns. GBR. Dist: Bookmasters Distribution.

Wadsworth, Ginger. Survival in the Snow. Orback, Craig, illus. 2011. 48p. (J). pap. 6.95 *(978-0-7613-3941-0(8))*, First Avenue Editions) Lerner Publishing Group.

Waldman, Nomi J. Deadwood, South Dakota: A Frontier Community: Text Pairs. 2008. (Bridges/Navigators Ser.). (J). (gr. 3). 81.00 *(978-1-4108-8358-2(2))* Benchmark Education Co.

Warren, Andrea. The Boy Who Became Buffalo Bill: Growing up Billy Cody in Bleeding Kansas, 0 vols. 2015. (ENG., Illus.). 256p. (J). 19.99 *(978-1-4778-2718-5(8))*, 9781477827185, Two Lions) Amazon Publishing.

Winter, Jonah. Wild Women of the Wild West. Morgan, Mary & Guevara, Susan, illus. 2011. (ENG.). 40p. (J). 16.95 *(978-0-8234-1601-1(1))* Holiday Hse., Inc.

Woog, Adam & Triplett, Frank. Jesse James: The Wild West for Kids. 2014. (ENG., Illus.). 128p. (J). (gr. 2-7). pap. 12.95 *(978-1-62636-160-7(6))*, 263160, Sky Pony Pr.) Skyhorse Publishing Co., Inc.

Yasuda, Anita. Explore the Wild West! With 25 Great Projects. Kim, Alex & Stone, Bryan, illus. 2012. (Explore Your World Ser.). (ENG.). 96p. (J). (gr. k-4). pap. 12.95 *(978-1-936749-71-3(8))* Open City Bks.

FROST, ROBERT, 1874-1963

Bober, Natalie S. Papa Is a Poet: A Story about Robert Frost. Gibbon, Rebecca, illus. 2013. (ENG.). 40p. (J). (gr. -1-3). 17.99 *(978-0-8050-9407-7(5))*, 9780805094077, Holt, Henry & Co. Bks. For Young Readers) Holt, Henry & Co.

Deep Woods: The Story of Robert Frost. 2006. (World Writers Ser.). (Illus.). 176p. (gr. 6-12). lib. bdg. 28.95 *(978-1-931798-92-1(3))* Reynolds, Morgan Inc.

Kesselring, Susan Temple. Robert Frost, 1 vol. 2013. (Great American Authors Ser.). (ENG.). 48p. (J). (gr. 3-6). lib. bdg. 32.79 *(978-1-61783-717-3(2))* ABDO Publishing Co.

Kirk, Connie Ann. Reading & Interpreting the Works of Robert Frost. 2016. (Lit Crit Guides). (ENG., Illus.). 176p. (J). (gr. 8-8). lib. bdg. 39.93 *(978-0-7660-7350-0(5))* Enslow Pubs., Inc.

Whiting, Jim. Blue Banner Biographies-Pop Entertainers III. 2006. (J). lib. bdg. 282.70 *(978-1-58415-428-0(4))* Mitchell Lane Pubs., Inc.

Wooten, Sara McIntosh. Robert Frost: The Life of America's Poet. 2006. (People to Know Today Ser.). (Illus.). 128p. (J). (gr. 4-7). lib. bdg. 33.27 *(978-0-7660-2627-8(2))* Enslow Pubs., Inc.

FRUIT

see also Fruit Culture

also names of fruits, e.g. Apple, etc.

Aboff, Marcie. The Fantastic Fruit Group, 1 vol. Swift, Gary, illus. 2011. (First Graphics: Myplate & Healthy Eating Ser.). (ENG.). 24p. (gr. 1-2). lib. bdg. 23.99 *(978-1-4296-6090-7(2))* Capstone Press of Coughlan Cos.

Adams, Julia. Fruits. 2011. (Good Food Ser.). (ENG.). 24p. (J). lib. bdg. 22.60 *(978-1-4488-3271-2(3))*, PowerKids Pr.) Rosen Publishing Group, Inc., The.

AZ Books. Fruits. 2013. (Guess What? Ser.). (ENG.). 10p. (J). (— 1). bds. 5.95 *(978-1-61889-318-5(1))* AZ Bks. LLC.

AZ Books Staff. Fruits & Vegetables. Slusar, Julia, ed. 2012. (Pull It Out Ser.). (ENG.). 10p. (J). (— 1). 7.95 *(978-1-61889-192-1(8))* AZ Bks. LLC.

Bass, Jennifer Vogel. Edible Colors. Bass, Jennifer Vogel, photos by. (ENG., Illus.). (J). 2016. 30p. bds. 7.99 *(978-1-62672-284-2(6))*, 9781626722842) 2014. 32p. (gr. -1-k). 12.99 *(978-1-62672-002-2(9))*, 9781626720022) Roaring Brook Pr.

—Edible Numbers. (ENG., Illus.). (J). 2016. 30p. bds. 8.99 *(978-1-62672-285-9(4))*, 9781626722859) 2015. 32p. (gr. -1-k). 12.99 *(978-1-62672-003-9(7))*, 9781626720039) Roaring Brook Pr.

Benduhn, Tea. Fruit. 2007. (Find Out about Food Ser.). (Illus.). 24p. (gr. k-3). lib. bdg. 22.00 *(978-0-8368-8251-3(2))*, Weekly Reader Leveled Readers) Stevens, Gareth Publishing LLLP.

—Fruit: Fruta. 2007. (Find Out about Food/ Conoce la comida Ser.). (SPA & ENG.). 24p. (gr. k-3). pap. 8.15 *(978-0-8368-8462-3(0))*, Weekly Reader Leveled Readers) Stevens, Gareth Publishing LLLP.

—Fruit/Fruta. 2007. (Find Out about Food/Conoce la Comida Ser.). (SPA & ENG., Illus.). 24p. (gr. k-3). lib. bdg. 22.00 *(978-0-8368-8455-5(8))*, Weekly Reader Leveled Readers) Stevens, Gareth Publishing LLLP.

Bishop, Celeste. ¿Por Qué Las Plantas Tienen Frutas? / Why Do Plants Have Fruits?, 01 vols., 1. 2016. (Partes de la Planta / Plant Parts Ser.). (ENG & SPA., Illus.). 24p. (J). 23.60 *(978-1-5081-4740-4(X))*, PowerKids Pr.) Rosen Publishing Group, Inc., The.

—Why Do Plants Have Fruits?, 01 vols., 1. 2016. (Plant Parts Ser.). (ENG., Illus.). 24p. (J). pap. 8.25 *(978-1-5081-4217-1(3))*, PowerKids Pr.) Rosen Publishing Group, Inc., The.

Blanch, Xavier. Frutas. 2003. (SPA.). (J). *(978-84-246-0692-3(2))*, GL30334) La Galera, S.A. Editorial ESP. Dist: Lectorum Pubns., Inc.

Bodden, Valerie. Fruits. 2015. (J). *(978-1-60818-509-2(5))*, Creative Education) Creative Co., The.

—Healthy Plates: Fruits. 2015. (Healthy Plates Ser.). (ENG.). 24p. (J). (gr. 1-3). pap. 9.99 *(978-1-62832-109-8(1))*, Creative Paperbacks) Creative Co., The.

Borgert-Spaniol, Megan. Fruit Group. 2012. (Eating Right with Myplate Ser.). (ENG., Illus.). 24p. (J). (gr. k-3). lib. bdg. 25.95 *(978-1-60014-755-5(0))*, Blastoff! Readers) Bellwether Media.

Brannon, Cecelia H. Bananas. 2017. (All about Food Crops Ser.). 24p. (gr. k-1). lib. bdg. 22.60 ***(978-0-7660-8577-0(5))*** Enslow Pubs., Inc.

Brash, Lorna. Professor Cook's Fruity Desserts. 2013. (Professor Cook's... Ser.). 32p. (J). lib. bdg. 23.94 *(978-0-7660-4302-2(9))*; (gr. 4-12). pap. 7.95 *(978-1-4644-0549-5(2))* Enslow Pubs., Inc.

Burstein, John. Fabulous Fruits. 2009. (Slim Goodbody's Nutrition Edition Ser.). (ENG., Illus.). 24p. (J). (gr. k-3). pap. *(978-0-7787-5057-4(4))*; lib. bdg. *(978-0-7787-5042-0(6))* Crabtree Publishing Co.

Burton, Margie, et al. Peaches all the Time. 2011. (Early Connections Ser.). (J). *(978-1-61672-534-1(6))* Benchmark Education Co.

Byers, Ann. Fruits & Vegetables: From the Garden to Your Table. 2012. (Truth about the Food Supply Ser.). (ENG., Illus.). 48p. (J). (gr. 5-8). lib. bdg. 27.95 *(978-1-4488-6799-8(1))*, Rosen Reference) Rosen Publishing Group, Inc., The.

Byrd, Tracy. Fruits & Vegetables & How They Grow: A to Z. 2012. 60p. pap. 24.99 *(978-1-4772-4897-3(8))* AuthorHouse.

Cardenas, Ernesto A. Where Does Fruit Come From? 2009. 23.95 *(978-1-60698-056-9(4))*; pap. 4.95 *(978-1-60698-054-5(8))* Milo Educational Bks. & Resources.

Carter, Denzel T. All about Grapes. 2015. (Rosen REAL Readers: STEM & STEAM Collection). (ENG.). 8p. pap. 5.46 *(978-1-4994-9645-1(1))*, Rosen Classroom) Rosen Publishing Group, Inc., The.

Charney, Steve & Goldbeck, David. The ABC's of Fruits & Vegetables & Beyond: Delicious Alphabet Poems Plus Food, Facts & Fun for Everyone. Larson, Maria Burgaleta, illus. 2007. 112p. (J). (gr. -1-4). per. 16.95 *(978-1-886101-07-4(8))* Ceres Pr.

Cleary, Brian P. Apples, Cherries, Red Raspberries: What Is in the Fruits Group? Goneau, Martin, illus. 2011. (Food Is CATegorical Ser.). (ENG.). 32p. (gr. k-3). pap. 7.95 *(978-0-7613-6385-9(8))* Lerner Publishing Group.

Cleary, Brian P. & Nelson, Jennifer K. Apples, Cherries, Red Raspberries: What Is in the Fruits Group? Goneau, Martin, illus. 2010. (Food Is CATegorical Ser.). (ENG.). 32p. (gr. k-3). lib. bdg. 25.26 *(978-1-58013-589-4(7))* Lerner Publishing Group.

Dalmatian Press Staff. Pop & Sniff Fruit. 2008. (ENG.). 12p. (J). 10.95 *(978-1-58117-676-6(7))*, Intervisual/Piggy Toes) Bendon, Inc.

Deal, Darlene. Play with Your Food & Learn How to Eat Right: Nutritional Book about Fruits & Vegetables. 2004. (ENG & SPA., Illus.). 22p. (J). (gr. 1-4). pap. 9.95 *(978-0-9747299-0-9(6))* Deal, Darlene.

DePrisco, Dorothea. Orange. Taxali, Gary, illus. 2005. (Plush Learning Books Ser.). 10p. (J). bds. 6.95 *(978-1-58117-192-1(7))*, Intervisual/Piggy Toes) Bendon, Inc.

Derkazarian, Susan. Fruits & Vegetables. (Rookie Read-About Health Ser.). (ENG., Illus.). 32p. (J). (gr. k-2). 2006. pap. 5.95 *(978-0-516-25926-0(1))* 2005. lib. bdg. 20.50 *(978-0-516-23673-5(3))* Scholastic Library Publishing. (Children's Pr.).

Dickmann, Nancy. Fruits. 2012. (Healthy Eating with Myplate Ser.). (ENG.). 24p. (gr. -1-1). pap. 6.29 *(978-1-4329-6980-6(3))*; lib. bdg. 22.65 *(978-1-4329-6973-8(0))* Heinemann-Raintree. (Acorn).

Dilkes, D. H. Fruit. 2011. (All about Good Foods We Eat Ser.). (Illus.). 24p. (J). (gr. -1-18). pap. 7.95 *(978-1-59845-257-0(6))*, Enslow Elementary); (gr. k-3). lib. bdg. 22.60 *(978-0-7660-3927-8(7))* Enslow Pubs., Inc.

Driscoll, Laura. Apples: And How They Grow. Smith, Tammy, illus. 2003. (Penguin Young Readers, Level 2 Ser.). (ENG.). 32p. (J). (gr. 1-2). mass mkt. 3.99 *(978-0-448-43275-5(7))*, Penguin Young Readers) Penguin Young Readers Group.

Dwyer, Jacqueline. Fruits. 2009. (Nature Bks). 24p. (gr. 1-2). 37.50 *(978-1-61514-814-1(0))*, PowerKids Pr.) Rosen Publishing Group, Inc., The.

Edwards, Nicola. Fruits. 2007. (See How Plants Grow Ser.). (Illus.). 24p. lib. bdg. 22.60 *(978-1-4042-3701-8(1))*, PowerKids Pr.) Rosen Publishing Group, Inc., The.

Ehlert, Lois. Eating the Alphabet: Fruits & Vegetables from A to Z. alt. ed. 2006. (ENG., Illus.). 28p. (J). (gr. -1 — 1). bds. 11.99 *(978-0-15-205688-9(2))* Houghton Mifflin Harcourt Publishing Co.

Farndon, John. Fruits. 2006. (World of Plants (Blackbirch) Ser.). (ENG., Illus.). 24p. (J). (gr. 2-6). lib. bdg. 26.65 *(978-1-4103-0424-7(8))*, Blackbirch Pr., Inc.) Cengage Gale.

Flowers & Fruit Sets: 1 Each of 3 Big Books. (Sunshinetm Science Ser.). (gr. 1-2). 111.50 *(978-0-7802-2818-4(9))* Wright Group/McGraw-Hill.

Flowers & Fruit Sets: 1 Each of 3 Student Books. (Sunshinetm Science Ser.). (gr. 1-2). 20.95 *(978-0-7802-2819-1(7))* Wright Group/McGraw-Hill.

Fruit: 6 Each of 1 Student Book, 6 vols. (Sunshinetm Science Ser.). 24p. (gr. 1-2). 41.95 *(978-0-7802-2682-1(8))* Wright Group/McGraw-Hill.

Fruit: Big Book. (Sunshinetm Science Ser.). 24p. (gr. 1-2). 37.50 *(978-0-7802-2775-0(1))* Wright Group/McGraw-Hill.

Fruits & Vegetables I Like to Eat - English Take Home Book. 2007. (Journeys Ser.). (J). pap. 15.00 *(978-1-4042-5462-6(5))*, Rosen Classroom) Rosen Publishing Group, Inc., The.

Fruits & Vegetables I Like to Eat - Spanish Take Home Book. 2007. (Journeys Ser.). (J). pap. 49.95 *(978-1-4042-5513-5(3))*, Rosen Classroom) Rosen Publishing Group, Inc., The.

Gibbons, Gail. The Fruits We Eat. Gibbons, Gail, illus. 2016. (ENG., Illus.). 32p. (J). (gr. -1-3). 7.99 *(978-0-8234-3571-5(7))* Holiday Hse., Inc.

—The Fruits We Eat. 2015. (ENG.). 32p. (J). (gr. -1-3). 17.95 *(978-0-8234-3204-2(1))* Holiday Hse., Inc.

Green, Emily K. Fruits. 2006. (Blastoff! Readers Ser.). (ENG., Illus.). 24p. (J). (gr. k-3). lib. bdg. 24.95

E
F
G

(978-1-60014-005-1(X), Blastoff! Readers) Bellwether Media.

Hartley, Jill, photos by. Fruits of India. 2010. (ENG., Illus.). 24p. (J). (gr. k — 1). bds. 7.95 (978-81-907546-8-2(8)) Tara Books Agency IND. Dist: Publishers Group West (PGW).

Helenek, Sophie. My First Book FRUITS: GOLD Mom's Choice Awards. 2014. (My First Book Ser.). (ENG., Illus.). 16p. (J). (gr. -1-k). bds. 5.99 (978-0-9894505-0-8(3)) Nursery Bks.

Heos, Bridget. From Grapes to Jelly. Coleman, Stephanie Fizer, illus. 2017. (Who Made My Lunch? Ser.). (ENG.). 24p. (gr. 1-4). 20.95 **(978-1-68151-122-1(3))** Amicus Publishing.

Hewitt, Sally. Fruit. 2008. (Good for Me Ser.). (Illus.). 24p. (J). (gr. -1-3). lib. bdg. 22.60 (978-1-4042-4267-8(8), PowerKids Pr.) Rosen Publishing Group, Inc., The.

Hoffmann, Sara. Kinds of Fruits. 2012. (First Step Nonfiction - Kinds of Plants Ser.). (ENG., Illus.). 8p. (gr. -1-1). pap. 4.95 (978-1-4677-0491-5(1), Lerner Pubns.) Lerner Publishing Group.

Holden, Pam. Fruit for You, 6 pack. Cooper, Jenny, illus. 2009. (Red Rocket Readers Ser.). (ENG.). 16p. (gr. -1-1). pap. (978-1-877363-01-6(4), Red Rocket Readers) Flying Start Bks.

How Fruits & Vegetables Grow. (How Fruits & Vegetables Grow Ser.). (ENG.). 24p. (gr. k-1). 2011. pap. 178.50 (978-1-4296-6358-8(8)) 2010. pap. 29.75 (978-1-4296-6189-8(5)) Capstone Press of Coughlan Cos. (Pebble Bks.).

Jones, Bryony. Fabulous Fruit. 2011. (ENG., Illus.). 14p. (J). (gr. -1-k). bds. (978-1-84089-614-5(0)) Zero to Ten, Ltd.

Jones, Tammy. We Have Fruit. 2009. (Sight Word Readers Set A Ser.). (J). (978-1-60719-136-0(9)) Newmark Learning LLC.

Kalz, Jill. Fruits. 2003. 24p. (J). lib. bdg. 21.35 (978-1-58340-299-3(3)) Black Rabbit Bks.

Kesselring, Susan. Eat a Rainbow: Healthy Foods, 1 vol. Avakyan, Tatevik, illus. 2012. (Move & Get Healthy Ser.). (ENG.). 32p. (J). (gr. k-3). 28.50 (978-1-61641-858-8(3)) Magic Wagon.

Klepeis, Alicia. Fruits & Vegetables Explained. 2016. (Distinctions in Nature Ser.). 32p. (J). (gr. 3-3). 28.50 (978-1-5026-1744-6(7)) Cavendish Square Publishing.

Konicek-Moran, Richard. From Flower to Fruit. Konicek-Moran, Kathleen, illus. 2017. (ENG.). 30p. (J). (gr. k-2). pap. 11.95 (978-1-941316-34-4(4)) National Science Teachers Assn.

Lanz, Helen. Grow Your Own Strawberries. 2012. (Grow Your Own Ser.). (Illus.). 32p. (gr. 3-6). lib. bdg. 28.50 (978-1-59771-313-9(9)) Sea-To-Sea Pubns.

Lassieur, Allison. Fruits. 2015. (Illus.). 32p. (J). lib. bdg. 28.50 (978-1-60753-495-2(9)) Amicus Publishing.

Lee, Jackie. Coconut. 2015. (See It Grow Ser.). (ENG.). 24p. (J). (gr. -1-3). lib. bdg. 23.93 (978-1-62724-842-6(0)) Bearport Publishing Co., Inc.

Maile, Ruby. Why Should I Eat Fruit? 2014. (Little Books of Answers: Level a Ser.). (Illus.). 16p. (gr. k-2). pap. 7.95 (978-1-927136-03-4(2)) Three Crows Media NZL. Dist: RiverStream Publishing.

Marsico, Katie. Your Healthy Plate - Fruits. 2012. (21st Century Basic Skills Library: Your Healthy Plate Ser.). (ENG., Illus.). 24p. (J). (gr. k-3). lib. bdg. 22.79 (978-1-61080-346-5(9), 201292) Cherry Lake Publishing.

—Your Healthy Plate: Fruits. 2012. (21st Century Basic Skills Library: Your Healthy Plate Ser.). (ENG., Illus.). 24p. (J). (gr. k-3). pap. 12.79 (978-1-61080-400-4(7), 201335) Cherry Lake Publishing.

Martineau, Susan & James, Hel. Fruits & Vegetables. 2012. (Healthy Eating Ser.). (Illus.). 32p. (gr. 2-6). pap. 8.95 (978-1-59920-243-3(3)) Black Rabbit Bks.

Matthews, Colin. I Know Fruits & Vegetables. 2017. (What I Know Ser.). 24p. (J). (gr. k-k). pap. 8.15 **(978-1-4824-6293-7(1))** Stevens, Gareth Publishing LLLP.

McManus, Lori. Producing Fruits, 1 vol. 2012. (Technology of Farming Ser.). (ENG.). 48p. (gr. 4-6). lib. bdg. 33.32 (978-1-4329-6408-5(9), Heinemann InfoSearch) Heinemann-Raintree.

Meredith, Susan Markowitz. Fruit Salad. 2011. (Early Connections Ser.). (J). (978-1-61672-352-1(1)) Benchmark Education Co.

Milet Publishing Staff. Fruit. 2011. (My First Bilingual Book Ser.). (ENG., Illus.). 24p. (J). (gr. k — 1). bds. 7.99 (978-1-84059-625-0(2)) Milet Publishing.

—Fruit - My First Bilingual Book. 2011. (My First Bilingual Book Ser.). (ENG., Illus.). 24p. (J). (gr. k — 1). bds. 7.99 (978-1-84059-637-3(6)); bds. 8.99 (978-1-84059-630-4(9)); bds. 7.99 (978-1-84059-634-2(1)); bds. 7.99 (978-1-84059-632-8(5)); bds. 7.99 (978-1-84059-624-3(4)) Milet Publishing.

—Fruit (English-French) 2011. (My First Bilingual Book Ser.). (FRE & ENG., Illus.). 24p. (J). (gr. k — 1). bds. 7.99 (978-1-84059-628-1(7)) Milet Publishing.

—My First Bilingual Book - Fruit. 2011. (My First Bilingual Book Ser.). (ENG., Illus.). 24p. (J). (gr. k — 1). bds. 7.99 (978-1-84059-627-4(9)); bds. 7.99 (978-1-84059-631-1(7)); bds. 7.99 (978-1-84059-629-8(5)); bds. 8.99 (978-1-84059-633-5(3)); bds. 8.99 (978-1-84059-626-7(0)) Milet Publishing.

—My First Bilingual Book-Fruit (English-Somali) 2011. (My First Bilingual Book Ser.). (ENG., Illus.). 24p. (J). (gr. k — 1). bds. 7.99 (978-1-84059-635-9(X)) Milet Publishing.

—My First Bilingual Book-Fruit (English-Spanish) 2011. (My First Bilingual Book Ser.). (SPA & ENG., Illus.). 24p. (J). (gr. k — 1). bds. 7.99 (978-1-84059-636-6(8)) Milet Publishing.

—My First Bilingual Book-Fruit (English-Urdu) 2011. (My First Bilingual Book Ser.). (ENG., Illus.). 24p. (J). (gr. k — 1). bds. 7.99 (978-1-84059-638-0(4)) Milet Publishing.

El mural de Frutas: 6 Softcover Books. (Saludos Ser.: Vol. 1). (SPA.). (gr. 3-5). 31.00 (978-0-7635-1799-1(2)) Rigby Education.

Nelson, Maria. I'm Allergic to Strawberries. 2014. (I'm Allergic Ser.). 24p. (J). (gr. 1-3). 22.60 (978-1-4824-0984-0(4)) Stevens, Gareth Publishing LLLP.

Nelson, Robin. Fruits. 2003. (First Step Nonfiction Ser.). (Illus.). 24p. (J). (gr. k-2). lib. bdg. 18.60 (978-0-8225-4624-5(8)) Lerner Publishing Group.

—Las Frutas. Castañer, Mercedes & Fitzpatrick, Julia, trs. 2003. (Mi Primer Paso Al Mundo Real - Los Grupos de Alimentos (First Step Nonfiction - Food Groups) Ser.).Tr. of Fruits. (SPA., Illus.). 24p. (gr. k-2). lib. bdg. 23.93 (978-0-8225-5062-4(8)) Lerner Publishing Group.

—Strawberries. 2009. pap. 34.95 (978-0-7613-4120-8(X)) Lerner Publishing Group.

Nugent, Samantha. Fruit. 2015. (Let's Learn about Food Ser.). (ENG.). (J). lib. bdg. 27.13 (978-1-4896-3995-0(0), AV2 by Weigl) Weigl Pubs., Inc.

Owings, Lisa. From Strawberry to Jam. 2015. (Start to Finish, Second Ser.). (ENG.). 24p. (J). (gr. k-3). lib. bdg. 23.93 (978-1-4677-6022-5(6), Lerner Pubns.) Lerner Publishing Group.

Pettiford, Rebecca. Fruits. Fretland VanVoorst, Jenny, ed. 2015. (J). lib. bdg. 25.65 (978-1-62031-232-2(8)) Jump! Inc.

¿Qué Fruta es ésa? 2004. (SPA.). 16p. (J). (978-968-494-160-1(9)) Centro de Informacion y Desarrollo de la Comunicacion y la Literatura MEX. Dist: Iaconi, Mariuccia Bk. Imports.

Quinn, Lauren D. Fruits. 2016. (Illus.). 24p. (J). (978-1-5105-1409-6(0)) SmartBook Media, Inc.

Rajczak, Kristen. Fantastic Fruit Recipes. 2014. (Ingredients for a Healthy Life Ser.). (Illus.). 24p. (J). (gr. 2-5). 22.60 (978-1-4824-0565-1(2)) Stevens, Gareth Publishing LLLP.

Richards, Jean. A Fruit Is a Suitcase for Seeds. Harlton, Anca, illus. 2006. (ENG.). 32p. (J). (gr. -1-3). pap. 6.95 (978-0-8225-5991-7(9), First Avenue Editions) Lerner Publishing Group.

Ripley, Mark. Picking Fruit. 2017. (Plants in My World Ser.). 24p. (gr. 4-6). pap. 8.25 **(978-1-5081-6163-9(1)**, PowerKids Pr.) Rosen Publishing Group, Inc., The.

Rondeau, Amanda. Fruits Are Fun, 1 vol. 2003. (What Should I Eat? Ser.). (ENG., Illus.). 24p. (J). (gr. k-3). lib. bdg. 24.21 (978-1-57765-834-4(5), SandCastle) ABDO Publishing Co.

Rosa-Mendoza, Gladys, creator. Fruits & Vegetables. 2004. (English-Spanish Foundations Ser.: Vol. 10).Tr. of Frutas y Vegetales. (SPA & ENG., Illus.). 22p. (J). bds. 6.95 (978-1-931398-10-7(0)) Me+Mi Publishing.

Schaefer, Lola M. Pick, Pull, Snap! Where Once a Flower Bloomed. George, Lindsay Barrett, illus. 2003. (ENG.). 32p. (J). (gr. k-5). 17.99 (978-0-688-17834-5(0), Greenwillow Bks.) HarperCollins Pubs.

Schuette, Sarah L. Eating Pairs (Comer Pares) Counting Fruits & Vegetables by Two (Contar Frutas y Vegetales de DOS en DOS) 2012. (Vamos a Contar / Counting Bks.). (ENG, SPA & MUL.). 32p. (gr. 1-2). lib. bdg. 27.32 (978-1-4296-8251-0(5), A+ Bilingue/Bilingual) Capstone Press of Coughlan Cos.

Schuh, Mari. Fruits on Myplate, 1 vol. 2012. (What's on Myplate? Ser.). (ENG., 24p. (gr. k-1). Illus.). pap. 7.29 (978-1-4296-9412-4(2)); pap. 41.70 (978-1-4296-9413-1(0)); (Illus.). lib. bdg. 26.65 (978-1-4296-8741-6(X)) Capstone Press of Coughlan Cos. (Pebble Plus).

Schuh, Mari C. From Seed to Strawberry. 2016. (Start to Finish, Second Ser.). (ENG., Illus.). 24p. (J). (gr. k-3). 23.99 (978-1-5124-0913-0(8)) Lerner Publishing Group.

—How Fruits & Vegetables Grow, 5 vols., Set. Incl. Blueberries Grow on a Bush. Saunders-Smith, Gail, contrib. by. lib. bdg. 21.99 (978-1-4296-5282-7(9)); Lettuce Grows on the Ground. Saunders-Smith, Gail. lib. bdg. 21.99 (978-1-4296-5281-0(0)); Tomatoes Grow on a Vine. Saunders-Smith, Gail. lib. bdg. 21.99 (978-1-4296-5278-0(0)); (gr. k-1). (How Fruits & Vegetables Grow Ser.). (ENG.). 24p. 2010. Set lib. bdg. 65.97 (978-1-4296-5283-4(7), Pebble Bks.) Capstone Press of Coughlan Cos.

Scratch N Sniff Staff. Scratch N Sniff Fruit. 2005. 12p. 6.95 (978-0-9762524-7-4(3)) Gimme Gimme Toys & Games, Inc.

Shea, Therese. Watch Pine Trees Grow. 2011. (Watch Plants Grow! Ser.). 24p. (gr. k-2). 69.20 (978-1-4339-6158-8(X)) Stevens, Gareth Publishing LLLP.

—Watch Pine Trees Grow / ¡Mira cómo crecen los Pinos! 2011. (Watch Plants Grow! / ¡Mira cómo crecen las plantas! Ser.). (ENG & SPA., Illus.). 24p. (J). (gr. -1-2). 22.60 (978-1-4339-4843-5(5)) Stevens, Gareth Publishing LLLP.

Smucker, Anna Egan. Golden Delicious: A Cinderella Apple Story. Kemly, Kathleen, illus. 2008. (ENG.). 32p. (J). (gr. 1-3). 16.99 (978-0-8075-2987-4(7)) Whitman, Albert & Co.

Staniford, Linda. Where Does Fruit Come From? 2016. (From Farm to Fork: Where Does My Food Come From? Ser.). (ENG.). 24p. (J). (gr. k-2). lib. bdg. 23.99 (978-1-4846-3352-6(0)) Heinemann-Raintree.

Stone, Lynn. Fruit. 2007. (Plant Parts Ser.). (Illus.). 24p. (J). (gr. 2-4). per. 7.95 (978-1-60044-692-4(2)) Rourke Educational Media.

Taylor, Steve. Fruit Facts. 2008. (Rosen Real Readers: Upper Emergent Ser.). (ENG., Illus.). 12p. (gr. 1-2). pap. 5.90 (978-0-8239-8134-2(7)) Rosen Publishing Group, Inc., The.

Tometich, Annabelle. The Fruits Group. 2013. (Healthy Eating with Myplate Ser.). (ENG.). 24p. (J). (gr. 1-4). 28.50 (978-1-62323-603-8(7), 206405) Child's World, Inc., The.

Tropical Twist, 6 vols. (Let's Read about... Ser.). (Illus.). 10p. (J). (978-2-7643-0030-5(1)) Phidal Publishing, Inc./Editions Phidal, Inc.

Vize, Dania. Fruity Fun. 2006. (High Chair Buddy Ser.). (Illus.). 10p. (gr. -1 — 1). bds. (978-1-84610-015-4(1)) Make Believe Ideas.

Waldron, Melanie. Seeds & Fruits, 1 vol. 2014. (Plant Parts Ser.). (ENG.). 32p. (gr. 2-4). lib. bdg. 30.65 (978-1-4109-5423-7(4), Raintree Perspectives) Heinemann-Raintree.

Waters, Rosa. My Daily Diet: Fruits. Prock, Lisa Albers, ed. 2014. (On My Plate Ser.: 6). 48p. (J). (gr. 5-18). 20.95 (978-1-4222-3097-8(X)) Mason Crest.

Weiss, Ellen. From Pit to Peach Tree. 2007. (Scholastic News Nonfiction Readers Ser.). (ENG., Illus.). 24p. (J). (gr. 1-4). 22.00 (978-0-531-18538-4(9)) Scholastic Library Publishing.

Yummy Yummy Fruits. 2004. (J). per. 15.99 (978-0-9744205-3-0(0)) Golden Eagle Publishing Hse., Inc.

Zemlicka, Shannon. From Fruit to Jelly. 2004. (Start to Finish Ser.). (J). pap. 5.95 (978-0-8225-0748-2(X)); (Illus.). 24p. 18.60 (978-0-8225-0942-4(3), Lerner Pubns.) Lerner Publishing Group.

FRUIT—CANNING

see Canning and Preserving

FRUIT—MARKETING

see Farm Produce—Marketing

FRUIT CULTURE

see also Plant Propagation

Clark, Rosalyn. A Visit to the Orchard. 2017. (Bumba Books (tm) — Places We Go Ser.). (ENG., Illus.). 24p. (J). (gr. -1-1). 25.32 **(978-1-5124-3375-3(6))** Lerner Publishing Group.

Collier, Elise. What Grows in an Orchard? 2017. (Plants in My World Ser.). 24p. (gr. 4-6). pap. 8.25 **(978-1-5081-6159-2(3)**, PowerKids Pr.) Rosen Publishing Group, Inc., The.

Dwyer, Jacqueline. Fruits. 2009. (Nature Bks). 24p. (gr. 1-2). 37.50 (978-1-61514-814-1(0), PowerKids Pr.) Rosen Publishing Group, Inc., The.

Esseltine, Bruce. At the Orchard. 2016. (Fun on the Farm Ser.). 00024p. (J). pap. 8.15 (978-1-4824-5528-1(5)) Stevens, Gareth Publishing LLLP.

Hubbell, Patricia. Every Orchard Tree. Broxon, Janet, illus. 2008. (J). (978-1-55971-986-5(9), NorthWord Bks. for Young Readers) T&N Children's Publishing.

La Huerta: Individual Title Two-Packs. (Chiquilibros Ser.). (SPA.). (gr. -1-1). 12.00 (978-0-7635-8558-7(0)) Rigby Education.

Letts, Amelia. What Happens at an Orchard? Perform Multi-Digit Arithmetic. 2014. (Rosen Common Core Math Readers Ser.). (ENG., Illus.). 24p. (J). (gr. 3-4). pap. 8.25 (978-1-4777-4933-3(0), PowerKids Pr.) Rosen Publishing Group, Inc., The.

McDougall, Nancy & Hendy, Jenny. 300 Step-By-Step Cooking & Gardening Projects for Kids: The Ultimate Book for Budding Gardeners & Super Chefs with Amazing Things to Grow & Cook Yourself, Shown in over 2300 Photographs. 2012. (ENG., Illus.). 512p. 25.00 (978-0-7548-2383-4(0)) Anness Publishing GBR. Dist: National Bk. Network.

—300 Step-By-Step Cooking & Gardening Projects for Kids: The Ultimate Book for Budding Gardeners & Super Chefs, with Amazing Things to Grow & Cook Yourself, Shown in over 2300 Photographs. 2015. (ENG., Illus.). 512p. pap. 14.99 (978-1-86147-707-1(4), Armadillo) Anness Publishing GBR. Dist: National Bk. Network.

McManus, Lori. Producing Fruits, 1 vol. 2012. (Technology of Farming Ser.). (ENG.). 48p. (gr. 4-6). lib. bdg. 33.32 (978-1-4329-6408-5(9), Heinemann InfoSearch) Heinemann-Raintree.

Minden, Cecilia. Gardening by the Numbers. 2007. (21st Century Skills Library: Real World Math Ser.). (ENG., Illus.). 32p. (gr. 4-8). lib. bdg. 28.50 (978-1-60279-008-7(6), 200064) Cherry Lake Publishing.

Wolfman, Judy. Life on an Apple Orchard. Winston, David Lorenz, illus. Winston, David Lorenz, photos by. 2004. (Life on a Farm Ser.). (ENG.). 48p. (gr. 2-5). lib. bdg. 23.93 (978-1-57505-193-2(1)) Lerner Publishing Group.

FRUIT CULTURE—FICTION

Amore, Joanne. Joe's Fruit Store, 1 vol. 2009. 19p. pap. 24.95 (978-1-60749-331-0(4)) America Star Bks.

Atwood, Megan. Ice Cream Summer. Andrewson, Natalie, illus. 2017. (Orchard Novel Ser.: 1). (ENG.). 272p. (J). (gr. 2-6). 12.99 **(978-1-4814-9047-4(8)**, Aladdin) Simon & Schuster Children's Publishing.

Bob, Hippie. Juicy Lucy a Happy Strawberry: A Hippie Bob Tale. 2011. 28p. pap. 14.99 (978-1-4490-6093-0(5)) AuthorHouse.

Brightwood, Laura. The Banana Fairy Fuss. Pifer, Kimberly, ed. Brightwood, Laura, illus. 2012. (Illus.). (J). (978-1-934409-34-3(0)) 3-C Institute for Social Development.

Brooke, Samantha. Apple-Picking Day! Durk, Jim, illus. 2007. (Clifford's Puppy Days Ser.). (J). (978-0-545-02841-7(8)) Scholastic, Inc.

Bui, Chris Van. Yummy Yummy for My Tummy, 1 vol. 2009. 14p. pap. 24.95 (978-1-61582-826-5(5)) America Star Bks.

Dean, James. Pete the Cat & the Bad Banana. Dean, James, illus. 2014. (My First I Can Read Ser.). (ENG., Illus.). 32p. (J). (gr. -1-3). pap. 3.99 (978-0-06-230382-0(1)) HarperCollins Pubs.

DeGregorio, Linda. Ned the Banana. 2011. 20p. 11.99 (978-1-4520-0916-2(3)) AuthorHouse.

Doyen, Denise. The Pomegranate Witch. Moser, Barry, illus. 2013. (J). (978-0-375-87057-6(1)); lib. bdg. (978-0-375-97057-3(6)) Random Hse., Inc.

Duff, Justin. Alex Goes Apple Picking. 2012. 32p. pap. 21.99 (978-1-4771-2845-9(X)) Xlibris Corp.

Going, K. L. The Garden of Eve. 2009. (ENG., Illus.). 240p. (J). (gr. 2-5). pap. 14.95 (978-0-15-206614-7(4)) Houghton Mifflin Harcourt Publishing Co.

Hawes, Alison. The Enormous Watermelon. Rodriguez, Elba, illus. 2016. (Cambridge Reading Adventures Ser.). (ENG.). 16p. pap. 6.56 (978-1-107-54924-1(8)) Cambridge Univ. Pr.

Hawkins, Aaron. The Year Money Grew on Trees. 2011. (ENG.). 304p. (J). (gr. 5-7). pap. 6.99 (978-0-547-57716-6(8)) Houghton Mifflin Harcourt Publishing Co.

Hemingway, Edward. Bad Apple: A Tale of Friendship. Hemingway, Edward, illus. 2012. (ENG., Illus.). 32p. (J). (gr. -1-k). 16.99 (978-0-399-25191-7(X), G.P. Putnam's Sons Books for Young Readers) Penguin Young Readers Group.

Holloway, Jamie. A Day at the Strawberry Patch. 2015. (Rosen REAL Readers: STEM & STEAM Collection). (ENG.). 8p. pap. 5.46 (978-1-4994-9480-8(7), Rosen Classroom) Rosen Publishing Group, Inc., The.

Holub, Joan. Apple Countdown. Smith, Jan, illus. 2012. (J). (978-1-61913-117-0(X)) Weigl Pubs., Inc.

—Apple Countdown. Smith, Jan, illus. 2009. (ENG.). 32p. (J). (gr. -1-3). 16.99 (978-0-8075-0398-0(3)) Whitman, Albert & Co.

Hopkinson, Deborah. Apples to Oregon. 2014. 17.00 (978-1-63419-642-0(2)) Perfection Learning Corp.

Hyman, Teisha Lashe'. Uh Oh! a Human. 2011. 16p. pap. 15.99 (978-1-4634-3019-1(1)) AuthorHouse.

Janosch. Just One Apple. 2014. (ENG., Illus.). 32p. (J). 17.95 (978-0-7358-4151-2(9)) North-South Bks., Inc.

Jones, Elwynn. Frank's Frantic Friday. 2010. 40p. pap. 16.95 (978-1-60911-750-4(6), Eloquent Bks.) Strategic Book Publishing & Rights Agency (SBPRA).

McNamara, Margaret. The Apple Orchard Riddle. Karas, G. Brian, illus. 2013. (Mr. Tiffin's Classroom Ser.). (ENG.). 40p. (J). (gr. -1-3). 17.99 (978-0-375-84744-8(8), Schwartz & Wade Bks.) Random Hse. Children's Bks.

Metzger, Steve. Under the Apple Tree. Girasole, Alessia, illus. 2009. (J). (978-0-545-14200-7(8)) Scholastic, Inc.

Oginga, Effua. The Little Red Apple. 2011. 16p. pap. 10.99 (978-1-4634-0218-1(X)) AuthorHouse.

Paikai, Tammy. Too Many Mangos. Robinson, Don, illus. 2009. 28p. (J). (gr. -1). 11.95 (978-1-59700-758-0(7)) Island Heritage Publishing.

Parker, Emma. The Fruity Girls. 2010. (Illus.). pap. (978-1-877561-11-5(8)) First Edition Ltd.

Perelman, Helen. The Coconut Clue. Waters, Erica-Jane, illus. 2015. (Candy Fairies Ser.: 17). (ENG.). 128p. (J). (gr. 2-5). pap. 5.99 (978-1-4814-0616-1(7), Aladdin) Simon & Schuster Children's Publishing.

Ponko, Cindy A. Olive Fingers. 2006. (Illus.). (J). (978-0-9768230-0-1(4)) Some Kids I Know.

Ransom, Candice. Apple Picking Day! Meza, Erika, illus. 2016. (Step into Reading Ser.). (ENG.). 32p. (J). (gr. -1-1). pap. 3.99 (978-0-553-53858-8(6), Random Hse. Bks. for Young Readers) Random Hse. Children's Bks.

Raven's Orchard. 2017. (Raven's Orchard Ser.). 24p. (gr. 4-6). 70.80 **(978-1-5081-6188-2(7))**; pap. 24.75 **(978-1-5081-6190-5(9))** Rosen Publishing Group, Inc., The. (PowerKids Pr.).

Reed, Liz & Reed, Jimmy. Sweet Competition. Reed, Liz & Reed, Jimmy, illus. 2016. (Illus.). 40p. (J). (gr. -1-3). 17.99 (978-0-06-240359-9(1)) HarperCollins Pubs.

Rex, Adam. Nothing Rhymes with Orange. 2017. (ENG., Illus.). 48p. (J). (gr. k-3). 16.99 **(978-1-4521-5443-5(0))** Chronicle Bks. LLC.

Rey, H. A. Apple Harvest: Curious about Harvest Time. 2012. (Curious George TV Tie-In 8x8 Ser.). lib. bdg. 13.55 (978-0-606-23984-4(7), Turtleback) Turtleback Bks.

—Curious George Apple Harvest. 2012. (Curious George Ser.). (ENG., Illus.). 24p. (J). (gr. -1-3). pap. 4.99 (978-0-547-51705-6(X)) Houghton Mifflin Harcourt Publishing Co.

Rockwell, Anne. Apples & Pumpkins. Rockwell, Lizzy, illus. 2014. (Classic Board Bks.). (ENG.). 28p. (J). (gr. -1-k). bds. 7.99 (978-1-4424-9977-5(X), Little Simon) Little Simon.

Sacre, Antonio. A Mango in the Hand: A Story Told Through Proverbs. Serra, Sebastia, illus. 2011. (ENG.). 32p. (J). (gr. k-2). 16.95 (978-0-8109-9734-9(7), Abrams Bks. for Young Readers) Abrams, Inc.

Schaub, Michelle. The Bee Puzzle. 2006. (Early Explorers Ser.). (J). pap. (978-1-4108-6123-8(6)) Benchmark Education Co.

Shenhav. Raspberry Juice. Date not set. (Illus.). 32p. (J). (gr. -1-3). 14.99 (978-0-06-027292-0(9)); lib. bdg. 15.89 (978-0-06-027293-7(7)) HarperCollins Pubs.

Shipton, Paul. Get the Fruit! Dunton, Trevor, illus. 2004. (Collins Big Cat Ser.). (ENG.). 24p. (J). (gr. -1-k). pap. 5.99 (978-0-00-718529-0(4)) HarperCollins Pubs. Ltd. GBR. Dist: Independent Pubs. Group.

Stoklasa, JoAnne. Oliver & I: The Long Way Home. 2012. 20p. pap. 11.59 (978-1-4669-5287-4(3)) Trafford Publishing.

Wellington, Monica. Ana Cultiva Manzanas/Apple Farmer Annie. Del Risco, Eida & del Risco, Eida, trs. from ENG. Wellington, Monica, illus. 2004. (ENG & SPA., Illus.). 32p. (J). (gr. -1-2). 16.99 (978-0-525-47252-0(5), Dutton Books for Young Readers) Penguin Young Readers Group.

White, Pam. Buddy's Trip to the Blueberry Farm. 2009. 16p. pap. 8.95 (978-1-4389-7931-1(2)) AuthorHouse.

Wilkenstanley, Ellen. Berryville Bully. 2011. 24p. pap. 11.50 (978-1-61204-527-6(8), Strategic Bk. Publishing) Strategic Book Publishing & Rights Agency (SBPRA).

Wilkes, Ruth. Dancing Fruit Put on a Show! Cross, James, illus. 2013. 48p. 18.99 (978-1-62314-797-6(2)) Willow Publishing.

Williams, Gladys. What Do Apples Have? Special Steven Series. 2009. 24p. pap. 13.49 (978-1-4389-3658-1(3)) AuthorHouse.

FRUSTRATION

see Attitude (Psychology); Emotions

FRY, ELIZABETH GURNEY, 1780-1845

Benge, Janet and Geoff. Elizabeth Fry. 2015. (ENG., Illus.). 189p. (YA). pap. 9.99 (978-1-62486-064-5(8)) Emerald Bks.

FUDGE (FICTITIOUS CHARACTER)—FICTION

Blume, Judy. Tales of a Fourth Grade Nothing. 2009. 8.32 (978-0-7848-3046-8(0)); 8.32 (978-0-7848-0332-5(3)) Marco Bk. Co. (Everbind).

—Tales of a Fourth Grade Nothing. 2007. 17.00 (978-0-7569-7937-9(4)) 2004. (ENG.). 144p. (J). (gr. 3-7). 7.99 (978-0-425-19379-2(9), Berkley) Penguin Publishing Group.

—Tales of a Fourth Grade Nothing. 2007. (ENG.). 160p. (J). (gr. 3-7). 7.99 (978-0-14-240881-0(6), Puffin Books) Penguin Young Readers Group.

—Tales of a Fourth Grade Nothing. (Fudge Ser.). 120p. (J). (gr. 3-5). pap. 4.99 (978-0-8072-1496-1(5), Listening Library) Random Hse. Audio Publishing Group.

—Tales of a Fourth Grade Nothing. 2003. pap. (978-0-439-57779-3(9), Scholastic) Scholastic, Inc.

FUEL

see also Petroleum As Fuel; Wood

Bang, Molly & Chisholm, Penny. Buried Sunlight: How Fossil Fuels Have Changed the Earth. Bang, Molly, illus. 2014. (ENG., Illus.). 48p. (J). (gr. -1-3). 18.99 (978-0-545-57785-4(3)) Scholastic, Inc.

Bayden, Maya. What Is Chemical Energy? 2017. (Let's Find Out! Forms of Energy Ser.). 32p. (gr. 6-8). pap. 12.90 **(978-1-68048-693-3(4)**, Britannica Educational Publishing) Rosen Publishing Group, Inc., The.

Benduhn, Tea. Etanol y Otros Combustibles Nuevos. 2008. (Energía para el presente (Energy for Today) Ser.). (SPA.). 24p. (gr. 2-6). (J). lib. bdg. 22.00 (978-0-8368-9266-6(6)); pap. 8.15 (978-0-8368-9365-6(4)) Stevens, Gareth Publishing LLLP. (Weekly Reader Leveled Readers).

—Ethanol & Other New Fuels. 2008. (Energy for Today Ser.). 24p. (gr. 2-6). (J). lib. bdg. 22.00 (978-0-8368-9260-4(7)); pap. 8.15 (978-0-8368-9359-5(X)) Stevens, Gareth Publishing LLLP. (Weekly Reader Leveled Readers).

—Oil, Gas, & Coal. 2008. (Energy for Today Ser.). 24p. (gr. 2-6). (J). lib. bdg. 22.00 (978-0-8368-9261-1(5)); (SPA & ENG.). pap. 8.15 (978-0-8368-9360-1(3)) Stevens, Gareth Publishing LLLP. (Weekly Reader Leveled Readers).

Bickerstaff, Linda. Oil Power of the Future: New Ways of Turning Petroleum into Energy. 2009. (Library of Future Energy Ser.). 64p. (gr. 5-5). 58.50 *(978-1-60853-628-3(9))* Rosen Publishing Group, Inc., The.

Chambers, Catherine. How Harmful Are Fossil Fuels? 2015. (Earth Debates Ser.). (ENG.). 48p. (gr. 4-6). 33.32 *(978-1-4846-0997-2(2),* Heinemann InfoSearch) Heinemann-Raintree.

Currie-McGhee, L. K. Biofuels: By Leanne Currie-Mcghee. 2009. (Compact Research Ser.). (YA). (gr. 7-12). 25.95 *(978-1-60152-078-4(6))* ReferencePoint Pr., Inc.

Doeden, Matt. Finding Out about Coal, Oil, & Natural Gas. 2014. (Searchlight Books — What Are Energy Sources? Ser.). (Illus.). 40p. (gr. 3-4). (J). lib. bdg. 27.93 *(978-1-4677-3654-1(6),* Lerner Pubns.); pap. 8.95 *(978-1-4677-4553-6(7))* Lerner Publishing Group.

Dudley, William. Biofuels. 2015. (ENG., Illus.). 80p. (J). lib. bdg. *(978-1-60152-816-2(7))* ReferencePoint Pr., Inc.

Faust, Daniel R. Energy Crisis: The Future of Fossil Fuels. (Jr. Graphic Environmental Dangers Ser.). (ENG., 24p. 2009. Illus.). (gr. 3-8). pap. 10.60 *(978-1-4042-4598-3(7))* 2008. (J). 47.90 *(978-1-61532-101-8(2),* PowerKids Pr.) 2008. (Illus.). (J). (gr. 3-6). lib. bdg. 25.25 *(978-1-4042-4231-9(7))* Rosen Publishing Group, Inc., The.

Fridell, Ron. Earth-Friendly Energy. 2008. (Saving Our Living Earth Ser.). 72p. (YA). (gr. 4-7). lib. bdg. 30.60 *(978-0-8225-7563-4(9))* Lerner Publishing Group.

Friedman, Lauri S. Fossil Fuels. 2009. (Compact Research Ser.). (YA). (gr. 7-12). 25.95 *(978-1-60152-079-1(4))* ReferencePoint Pr., Inc.

Gogerly, Liz. Fossil Fuels. 2013. (World After Ser.). (ENG., Illus.). 56p. (gr. 7-8). 34.65 *(978-1-4329-7619-4(2));* pap. 9.95 *(978-1-4329-7624-8(9))* Heinemann-Raintree.

Goodman, Polly. Understanding Fossil Fuels. 2010. (World of Energy Ser.). (ENG.). 48p. (J). (gr. 6-8). lib. bdg. 31.95 *(978-1-4339-4118-4(X),* Gareth Stevens Learning Library) Stevens, Gareth Publishing LLLP.

Gorman, Jacqueline Laks. Fossil Fuels. 2009. (What If We Do Nothing? Ser.). 48p. (YA). (gr. 4-7). lib. bdg. 31.00 *(978-1-4339-0087-7(4))* Stevens, Gareth Publishing LLLP.

Grady, Colin. Fossil Fuels. 2016. (Saving the Planet Through Green Energy Ser.). 24p. (J). pap. 9.35 *(978-0-7660-8276-2(8))* Enslow Pubs., Inc.

Hansen, Amy. Fossil Fuels: Buried in the Earth. 2010. (Powering Our World Ser.). 24p. (J). (ENG.). pap. 8.25 *(978-1-4358-9738-0(2));* (Illus.). 49.50 *(978-1-4358-9739-7(0),* 1307107) Rosen Publishing Group, Inc., The. (PowerKids Pr.).

Hansen, Amy S. Fossil Fuels: Buried in the Earth. 2010. (Powering Our World Ser.). 24p. (J). (gr. 2-5). E-Book 42.50 *(978-1-4488-0195-4(8));* (Illus.). lib. bdg. 22.60 *(978-1-4358-9325-2(5),* PowerKids Pr.) Rosen Publishing Group, Inc., The.

Hartman, Eve & Meshbesher, Wendy. Fossil Fuels. 2016. (Sci-Hi: Earth & Space Science Ser.). (ENG.). 48p. (gr. 4-4). pap. 8.99 *(978-1-4109-8537-8(7),* Sci-Hi) Heinemann-Raintree.

Hock, Peggy. Clean Energy. 2008. (ENG.). 24p. (J). pap. 6.95 *(978-0-531-20433-7(2),* Children's Pr.) Scholastic Library Publishing.

Horn, Geoffrey M., et al. Biofuels. 2010. (Energy Today Ser.). 48p. (J). (gr. 3-6). 30.00 *(978-1-60413-782-8(7))* Facts On File, Inc.

Iyer, Rani. Endangered Energy: Investigating the Scarcity of Fossil Fuels. 2015. (Endangered Earth Ser.). (ENG.). 32p. (gr. 3-4). lib. bdg. 27.32 *(978-1-4914-2037-9(5),* Fact Finders) Capstone Press of Coughlan Cos.

Johanson, Paula. Biofuels: Sustainable Energy in the 21st Century. 2010. (In the News Ser.). 64p. (YA). (ENG.). pap. 12.95 *(978-1-4358-8550-9(3));* (Illus.). (gr. 7-12). lib. bdg. 31.95 *(978-1-4358-3584-9(0))* Rosen Publishing Group, Inc., The.

Kortemeier, Todd & Smibert, Angie. Finding an Energy Solution. 2016. (Science Frontiers Ser.). (ENG., Illus.). 32p. (J). pap. 9.95 *(978-1-63235-395-5(4))* Pr. Room Editions LLC.

Lepetit, Angie. Three Cheers for Trees! A Book about Our Carbon Footprint. 2013. (Earth Matters Ser.). (ENG.). 32p. (gr. 1-2). pap. 47.70 *(978-1-62065-742-3(2));* pap. 8.10 *(978-1-62065-741-6(4));* lib. bdg. 27.32 *(978-1-62065-048-6(7))* Capstone Press of Coughlan Cos. (Aplus Bks.).

Lippman, David & Muschal, Frank. Energy from Hydrogen. 2007. (21st Century Skills Library: Power Up! Ser.). (ENG.). 32p. (gr. 4-8). pap. 14.21 *(978-1-60279-095-7(7),* 200656); lib. bdg. 28.50 *(978-1-60279-048-3(5),* 200055) Cherry Lake Publishing.

Macken, JoAnn Early. Take a Closer Look at Oil. 2016. (Core Content Science — Take a Closer Look Ser.). (ENG., Illus.). 40p. (J). (gr. 2-4). lib. bdg. 26.65 *(978-1-63440-051-0(8))* Red Chair Pr.

mooney, carla. What Is the Future of Biofuels? 2012. (Illus.). 80p. (J). lib. bdg. *(978-1-60152-272-6(X))* ReferencePoint Pr., Inc.

Morris, Neil. Fossil Fuels. 2006. (Energy Sources Ser.). (Illus.). 32p. (YA). (gr. 4-7). lib. bdg. 28.50 *(978-1-58340-905-3(X))* Black Rabbit Bks.

—Fossil Fuels: Now & in the Future. 2010. (J). 34.25 *(978-1-59920-339-3(1))* Black Rabbit Bks.

Pipe, Jim. Biofuels. 2010. (J). 28.50 *(978-1-59604-209-4(5))* Black Rabbit Bks.

Raum, Elizabeth. Fossil Fuels & Biofuels. 2016. (Fueling the Future Ser.). (ENG.). 32p. pap. 8.29 *(978-1-4846-3817-0(4),* Heinemann InfoSearch) Heinemann-Raintree.

Reynoldson, Fiona. Geothermal Energy & Bioenergy. 2010. (World of Energy Ser.). (ENG.). 48p. (J). (gr. 6-8). lib. bdg. 31.95 *(978-1-4339-4121-4(X),* Gareth Stevens Learning Library) Stevens, Gareth Publishing LLLP.

Rice, William B. The Story of Fossil Fuels. 2015. (Science Readers: Content & Literacy Ser.). (ENG., Illus.). 32p. (gr. 4-4). pap. 8.99 *(978-1-4807-4690-9(8))* Teacher Created Materials, Inc.

Riddle, John. Coal Power of the Future: New Ways of Turning Coal into Energy. 2009. (Library of Future Energy Ser.). 64p. (gr. 5-5). 58.50 *(978-1-60853-624-5(6))* Rosen Publishing Group, Inc., The.

Rockwell, Anne F. What's So Bad about Gasoline? Fossil Fuels & What They Do. Meisel, Paul, illus. 2009. (Let's-Read-And-Find-Out Science 2 Ser.). (ENG.). 40p. (J). (gr. k-4). pap. 5.99 *(978-0-06-157527-3(5),* Collins) HarperCollins Pubs.

Rodger, Ellen. Is There a Future for Fossil Fuels? 2010. (ENG., Illus.). 32p. (J). pap. *(978-0-7787-2937-2(0));* lib. bdg. *(978-0-7787-2923-5(0))* Crabtree Publishing Co.

Somervill, Barbara A. The Story Behind Coal, 1 vol. 2011. (True Stories Ser.). (ENG.). 32p. (gr. 3-3). 30.65 *(978-1-4329-5434-5(2),* NA-h) Heinemann-Raintree.

Spilsbury, Richard & Spilsbury, Louise. Fossil Fuel Power. 2012. (Let's Discuss Energy Resources Ser.). (Illus.). 32p. (YA). (gr. 4-7). lib. bdg. 26.50 *(978-1-4488-5261-1(7))* Rosen Publishing Group, Inc., The.

Stefoff, Rebecca. The Pros & Cons of Coal. 2014. (Economics of Energy Ser.). 80p. (YA). (gr. 7-10). lib. bdg. 35.64 *(978-1-62712-918-3(9))* Cavendish Square Publishing.

Walker, Niki. Biomass: Fueling Change. 2006. (Energy Revolution Ser.). (ENG., Illus.). 32p. (J). (gr. 4-7). pap. *(978-0-7787-2928-0(1),* 1259460) Crabtree Publishing Co.

—Hydrogen: Running on Water. 2006. (Energy Revolution Ser.). (ENG., Illus.). 32p. (J). (gr. 3-7). pap. *(978-0-7787-2929-7(X));* lib. bdg. *(978-0-7787-2915-0(X))* Crabtree Publishing Co.

Wang, Andrea. How Can We Reduce Fossil Fuel Pollution? 2016. (Searchlight Books — What Can We Do about Pollution? Ser.). (ENG., Illus.). 40p. (J). (gr. 3-5). 30.65 *(978-1-4677-9513-5(5))* Lerner Publishing Group.

Weakland, Mark. Onion Juice, Poop, & Other Surprising Sources of Alternative Energy, 1 vol. 2011. (Nasty (but Useful!) Science Ser.). (ENG.). 32p. (gr. 3-4). pap. 8.10 *(978-1-4296-6347-2(2));* pap. 47.70 *(978-1-4296-6473-8(8))* Capstone Press of Coughlan Cos. (Fact Finders).

Zappa, Marcia. Fossil Fuels, 1 vol. 2010. (Big Buddy Bks.). (ENG.). 32p. (J). (gr. 2-5). 28.50 *(978-1-61613-492-1(5))* ABDO Publishing Co.

FUEL, LIQUID

see Gasoline; Petroleum As Fuel

FUEL OIL

see Petroleum As Fuel

FULTON, ROBERT, 1765-1815

Boothroyd, Jennifer. Robert Fulton: A Life of Innovation. 2007. (Pull Ahead Bks.). (Illus.). 32p. (J). (gr. 3-7). lib. bdg. 22.60 *(978-0-8225-6458-4(0),* Lerner Pubns.) Lerner Publishing Group.

Ford, Carin T. Robert Fulton: The Steamboat Man. 2004. (Famous Inventors Ser.). (Illus.). 32p. (J). lib. bdg. 23.94 *(978-0-7660-2248-5(X))* Enslow Pubs., Inc.

McLeese, Don. Robert Fulton. 2005. (Rourke Discovery Library). (Illus.). 24p. (J). (gr. 2-5). lib. bdg. *(978-1-59515-434-7(5),* 1244323) Rourke Educational Media.

Morrison, William. Robert Fulton: American Inventor. 2013. (InfoMax Readers Ser.). (ENG.). 24p. (J). (gr. 3-4). pap. 49.50 *(978-1-4777-2650-1(0));* (Illus.). pap. 8.25 *(978-1-4777-2649-5(7))* Rosen Publishing Group, Inc., The. (Rosen Classroom).

Parks, Peggy J. Robert Fulton: Innovator with Steam Power. 2003. (Giants of Science Ser.). (ENG., Illus.). 64p. (J). 28.35 *(978-1-56711-492-8(X),* Blackbirch Pr., Inc.) Cengage Gale.

Pierce, Morris A. Robert Fulton & the Development of the Steamboat. (Library of American Lives & Times Ser.). 112p. 2009. (gr. 5-5). 69.20 *(978-1-60853-502-6(9))* 2005. (Illus.). (YA). (gr. 4-8). lib. bdg. 34.60 *(978-0-8239-5737-8(3))* Rosen Publishing Group, Inc., The.

Roberts, Steven. Robert Fulton. 2013. (Jr. Graphic American Inventors Ser.). (ENG., Illus.). 24p. (J). (gr. 3-6). pap. 10.60 *(978-1-4777-0139-3(7));* lib. bdg. 25.25 *(978-1-4777-0077-8(3))* Rosen Publishing Group, Inc., The. (PowerKids Pr.).

Rogers, Kate. Robert Fulton Invents the Steamboat. 2013. (Rosen Readers Ser.). (ENG.). 24p. (J). (gr. 3-4). pap. 8.25 *(978-1-4777-2603-7(9));* pap. 49.50 *(978-1-4777-2604-4(7))* Rosen Publishing Group, Inc., The. (Rosen Classroom).

Rosenberg, Pam. Robert Fulton: Engineer & Inventor. 2003. (Our People Ser.). (ENG., Illus.). 32p. (J). (gr. 3-6). 29.93 *(978-1-56766-448-5(2),* 200651) Child's World, Inc., The.

Royston, Angela. Robert Fulton & the Steamboat, 01 vols., 1. 2016. (Inventions That Changed the World Ser.). (ENG.). 32p. (J). pap. 10.00 *(978-1-5081-4635-3(7),* PowerKids Pr.) Rosen Publishing Group, Inc., The.

Whiting, Jim. Robert Fulton. 2006. (What's So Great About... ? Ser.). (Illus.). 32p. (J). (gr. 2-4). lib. bdg. 25.70 *(978-1-58415-478-5(0))* Mitchell Lane Pubs., Inc.

FUND RAISING

Harper, Leslie. Cómo Recaudar Fondos para una Causa. 2014. (Sé un líder de la Comunidad (Be a Community Leader) Ser.). (SPA.). 32p. (J). (gr. 4-6). lib. bdg. 26.25 *(978-1-4777-6901-0(3),* PowerKids Pr.) Rosen Publishing Group, Inc., The.

—How to Raise Money for a Cause. 2014. (Be a Community Leader Ser.). 32p. (J). (gr. 4-6). pap. 60.00 *(978-1-4777-6681-1(2),* PowerKids Pr.) Rosen Publishing Group, Inc., The.

Kent, Renee Holmes. Robyn to the Rescue, Vol. 5. 2004. (Adventures in Misty Falls Ser.: Vol. 5). (Illus.). 100p. (J). (gr. 4-7). pap. 4.99 *(978-1-56309-451-4(7),* N007109) New Hope Pubs.

Loh-Hagan, Virginia. Bake Sale. 2016. (D. I. Y. Make It Happen Ser.). (ENG., Illus.). 32p. (J). (gr. 4-8). 29.93 *(978-1-63471-101-2(7),* 208515, 45th Parallel Press) Cherry Lake Publishing.

Loughran, Donna. Toy Tally: How Many Toys Are There? 2013. (IMath Ser.). (Illus.). 24p. (J). (gr. k-2). pap. 11.94 *(978-1-60357-492-1(1));* lib. bdg. 21.27 *(978-1-59953-553-1(X))* Norwood Hse. Pr.

Rajan, Bilaal. Making Change: Tips from an Underage Overachiever, 1 vol. 2008. (ENG.). 176p. (J). (gr. 4-8). pap. 14.00 *(978-1-55469-001-5(3))* Orca Bk. Pubs. USA.

FUNDS

see Finance

FUNERAL RITES AND CEREMONIES

Bower, Tamara. The Mummy-Makers of Egypt. 2016. (ENG., Illus.). 42p. (J). (gr. 2-5). 17.95 *(978-1-60980-600-2(X),* Triangle Square) Seven Stories Pr.

Casterline, L. C. & Packard, Mary. Beyond the Grave: Ripley's Believe It or Not! 2005. (Illus.). 62p. (J). *(978-1-884270-29-1(8))* Ripley Entertainment, Inc.

Digging up the Dead. 2014. (Digging up the Dead Ser.). 32p. (J). (gr. 4-6). 159.60 *(978-1-4824-1174-4(1))* Stevens, Gareth Publishing LLLP.

Ganeri, Anita. Remembering the Dead Around the World. 2015. (Cultures & Customs Ser.). (ENG., Illus.). 32p. (gr. 3-3). 30.65 *(978-1-4109-8018-2(9))* Heinemann-Raintree.

Griffey, Harriet. Secrets of the Mummies. 2013. (DK Reader Level 4 Ser.). lib. bdg. 13.55 *(978-0-606-32438-0(0),* Turtleback) Turtleback Bks.

Hall, Brianna. Mummies of Ancient Egypt. 2012. (Ancient Egyptian Civilization Ser.). (ENG.). 32p. (gr. 3-4). pap. 47.70 *(978-1-4296-8403-3(8));* pap. 8.10 *(978-1-4296-7978-7(6));* lib. bdg. 27.32 *(978-1-4296-7629-8(9))* Capstone Press of Coughlan Cos. (Fact Finders).

Henningfield, Diane Andrews. Disposal of the Dead. 2008. (At Issue Ser.). (ENG., Illus.). 128p. (gr. 10-12). 39.40 *(978-0-7377-4092-9(2));* pap. 27.80 *(978-0-7377-4093-6(0))* Cengage Gale. (Greenhaven Pr., Inc.).

Lace, William W. Mummification & Death Rituals of Ancient Egypt. 2012. (ENG., Illus.). 80p. (J). lib. bdg. *(978-1-60152-254-2(1))* ReferencePoint Pr., Inc.

Lange, Sarah, et al, eds. Contextualising Grave Inventories in the Ancient near East: Proceedings of a Workshop at the London 7th ICAANE in April 2010 & an International Symposium in Tubingen in November 2010, Both Organised by the Tubingen Post-Graduate School 'Symbols of the Dead' 2014. (Qatna-Studien. Supplementa Ser.: 3). (ENG., Illus.). 312p. (C). 125.00 *(978-3-447-10237-7(3))* Harrassowitz DEU. Dist: ISD.

Machajewski, Sarah. Death Rituals. 2014. (Digging up the Dead Ser.). 32p. (J). (gr. 4-6). pap. 63.00 *(978-1-4824-1228-4(4))* Stevens, Gareth Publishing LLLP.

Mundy, Michaelene. What Happens When Someone Dies? A Child's Guide to Death & Funerals. 2009. (Illus.). 32p. (J). pap. 7.95 *(978-0-87029-424-2(5))* Abbey Pr.

Nagelhout, Ryan. Preserving the Dead. 2014. (Digging up the Dead Ser.). 32p. (J). (gr. 4-6). pap. 63.00 *(978-1-4824-1234-5(9))* Stevens, Gareth Publishing LLLP.

SargentBrian. THE TRADITIONS OF DEATH INTERMEDIATE BOOK WITH ONLINE ACCESS. 2014. (ENG.). 28p. (J). pap. 9.50 *(978-1-107-63578-4(0))* Cambridge Univ. Pr.

Shea, Therese. Crypts & Tombs. 2014. (Digging up the Dead Ser.). 32p. (J). (gr. 4-6). pap. 63.00 *(978-1-4824-1225-3(X))* Stevens, Gareth Publishing LLLP.

World Book, Inc. Staff, contrib. by. End-of-Life Rituals. 2003. (World Book's Celebrations & Rituals Around the World Ser.). (Illus.). 46p. (J). *(978-0-7166-5014-0(2))* World Bk., Inc.

World Book, Inc Staff, contrib. by. End-Of-Life Rituals. 2009. (Illus.). 46p. (J). *(978-0-7166-5048-5(7))* World Bk., Inc.

FUNGI

see also Bacteriology; Mushrooms

Behnke, Alison. Can Rats Swim from Sewers into Toilets? And Other Questions about Your Home. 2010. (Is That a Fact? Ser.). (ENG.). 40p. (gr. 4-6). lib. bdg. 26.60 *(978-0-7613-4914-3(6))* Lerner Publishing Group.

Billups, Carla & Cusick, Dawn. It's a Fungus among Us: The Good, the Bad & the Downright Scary. 2017. (ENG., Illus.). 80p. (J). (gr. 3-7). 14.95 *(978-1-63322-154-3(7),* Moondance) Quarto Publishing Group USA.

Brock, David. Infectious Fungi. Alcamo, I. Edward, ed. 2006. (Deadly Diseases & Epidemics Ser.). (Illus.). 112p. (C). (gr. 9-12). lib. bdg. 34.95 *(978-0-7910-8680-3(1),* Chelsea Hse.) Facts On File, Inc.

Ciletti, Barbara. Asian Carp. 2016. (Invasive Species Takeover Ser.). (ENG., Illus.). 32p. (J). pap. 9.95 *(978-1-68072-277-2(8))* RiverStream Publishing.

Cohn, Jessica. Pest Control Worker. 2010. (Benchmark Rockets: Dirty & Dangerous Jobs Ser.). 32p. (J). (gr. 3-6). 28.50 *(978-1-60870-176-6(X))* Marshall Cavendish GBR. Dist: Marshall Cavendish Corp.

Eaton, Louise & Rogers, Kara. Examining Fungi & Protists. 2017. (J). lib. bdg. ***(978-1-5383-0008-4(7))*** Rosen Publishing Group, Inc., The.

Encyclopedia Britannica Staff, creator. Plants, Algae, & Fungi. 2011. (Britannica Illustrated Science Library Ser.). 104p. (J). 37.44 *(978-1-61535-461-0(1))* Encyclopaedia Britannica, Inc.

Gareth Stevens Publishing Staff, contrib. by. Protists & Fungi. 2003. (Discovery Channel School Science Ser.). (Illus.). 32p. (gr. 4-8). lib. bdg. 26.00 *(978-0-8368-3371-3(6),* Gareth Stevens Learning Library) Stevens, Gareth Publishing LLLP.

Holt, Rinehart and Winston Staff. Holt Science & Technology Chapter 11: Life Science: Protists & Fungi. 5th ed. 2004. (Illus.). pap. 12.86 *(978-0-03-030211-4(0))* Holt McDougal.

Nagle, Frances. Zombie Ants. 2015. (Zombie Animals: Parasites Take Control! Ser.). (ENG.). 24p. (J). (gr. 2-3). pap. 8.15 *(978-1-4824-2828-5(8))* Stevens, Gareth Publishing LLLP.

Snedden, Robert. Fungi. 2009. (Living Things Ser.). (Illus.). 32p. (J). (gr. -1-3). pap. 7.95 *(978-1-59920-196-2(8))* Black Rabbit Bks.

Stefoff, Rebecca. The Fungus Kingdom. 2007. (Family Trees Ser.). (Illus.). 95p. (J). (gr. 4-7). lib. bdg. 32.79 *(978-0-7614-2696-7(5),* Benchmark Bks.) Marshall Cavendish Corp.

Viegas, Jennifer. Fungi & Molds. (Germs: the Library of Disease-Causing Organisms Ser.). 48p. 2009. (gr. 5-5). 53.00 *(978-1-61512-715-3(1))* 2004. (Illus.). (gr. 7-12). lib. bdg. 29.25 *(978-0-8239-4492-7(1))* Rosen Publishing Group, Inc., The.

Viegas, Jennifer & Baum, Margaux. Fungi & Molds. 2016. (Germs: Disease Causing Organisms Ser.). 48p. (J). (gr. 5-5). pap. 11.75 *(978-1-4777-8840-0(9),* Rosen Reference) Rosen Publishing Group, Inc., The.

Wearing, Judy. Fungi: Classifying Mushrooms, Toadstools, Molds, Yeasts, & Other Fungi. 2010. (Class of Their Own Ser.). (ENG., Illus.). 48p. (J). (gr. 5-8). pap. *(978-0-7787-5389-6(1));* lib. bdg. *(978-0-7787-5375-9(1))* Crabtree Publishing Co.

FUNNIES

see Comic Books, Strips, etc.

FUR SEALS

see Seals (Animals)

FUR TRADE

Andra-Warner, Elle. Hudson's Bay Company Adventures: Tales of Canada's Early Fur Traders. 2006. (Amazing Stories Ser.). (ENG.). 96p. (J). pap. 9.95 *(978-1-55439-700-6(6),* 9781554397006) Lorimer, James & Co., Ltd., Pubs. CAN. Dist: Casemate Pubs. & Bk. Distributors, LLC.

Bailey, Katharine. Radisson & des Groseilliers: Fur Traders of the North. 2006. (In the Footsteps of Explorers Ser.). (ENG., Illus.). 32p. (J). (gr. 3-7). lib. bdg. *(978-0-7787-2422-3(0),* 1253444); (gr. 4-7). pap. *(978-0-7787-2458-2(1),* 1253444) Crabtree Publishing Co.

Blassingame, Wyatt & Glendinning, Richard. The Mountain Men. 2011. 176p. 42.95 *(978-1-258-00523-8(9))* Literary Licensing, LLC.

Graubart, Norman D. Beavers in American History. 2014. (How Animals Shaped History Ser.). (Illus.). 24p. (J). (gr. k-5). pap. 8.25 *(978-1-4777-6754-2(1),* PowerKids Pr.) Rosen Publishing Group, Inc., The.

Peterson, Cris. Birchbark Brigade: A Fur Trade History. 2009. (ENG.). 136p. (J). (gr. 4-18). 18.95 *(978-1-59078-426-6(X),* Calkins Creek) Boyds Mills Pr.

Prechtel, Jeff. Mountain Men — the History of Fur Trapping Coloring Book. 2015. (Dover History Coloring Book Ser.). (ENG.). 30p. (J). (gr. 3-6). pap. 3.99 *(978-0-486-79968-1(9))* Dover Pubns., Inc.

FUR TRADERS

Burger, James P. Mountain Men of the West. 2009. (Library of the Westward Expansion Ser.). 24p. (gr. 3-4). 42.50 *(978-1-60853-937-6(7),* PowerKids Pr.) Rosen Publishing Group, Inc., The.

O'Brien, Cynthia. Go West with Merchants & Traders. 2016. (ENG.). 32p. (J). *(978-0-7787-2326-4(7))* Crabtree Publishing Co.

FUR TRADERS—FICTION

Ballantyne, Robert Michael. Fort Desolation: Red Indians & Fur Traders of Rupert's Land. 2007. (ENG.). 60p. pap. 16.99 *(978-1-4346-3669-0(0));* 64p. pap. 18.99 *(978-1-4346-3717-8(4))* Creative Media Partners, LLC.

Ernst, Kathleen. Trouble at Fort la Pointe. 2009. (Mysteries Through Time Ser.). 144 - 176p. (YA). (gr. 4-8). 31.95 *(978-1-60754-426-5(1));* pap. 15.25 *(978-1-60754-427-2(X))* Windmill Bks.

Hossfeld, Harald. Rapacious Kings Sagacious Kids. 2010. 186p. pap. *(978-3-8391-4994-2(0))* Books on Demand GmbH.

Pendziwol, Jean E. The Red Sash, 1 vol. Debon, Nicolas, illus. 2005. (ENG.). 40p. (J). (gr. k-3). 18.95 *(978-0-88899-589-6(X))* Groundwood Bks. CAN. Dist: Publishers Group West (PGW).

Pinkerton, Robert E. The Fourth Norwood. 2011. 350p. 51.95 *(978-1-258-09433-1(9))* Literary Licensing, LLC.

Wallace, Dillon. Ungava Bob. 2007. (ENG.). 196p. pap. 19.99 *(978-1-4346-0196-4(X));* 216p. pap. 22.99 *(978-1-4346-0270-1(2))* Creative Media Partners, LLC.

Wargin, Kathy-jo. The Voyageur's Paddle. Geister, David & Van Frankenhuyzen, Gijsbert, illus. rev. ed. 2007. (Myths, Legends, Fairy & Folktales Ser.). (ENG.). 40p. (J). (gr. 1-4). 19.99 *(978-1-58536-007-9(4),* 201942) Sleeping Bear Pr.

FURNITURE

see also Cabinetwork; Wood-Carving

also names of articles of furniture, e.g. Chairs; Mirrors; etc.

Braithwaite, Jill. From Tree to Table. 2003. (Start to Finish Ser.). (ENG., Illus.). 24p. (gr. k-3). 19.93 *(978-0-8225-0947-9(4),* Lerner Pubns.) Lerner Publishing Group.

Clyde, Addie M. Sophie the Sofa. l.t. ed. 2004. 40p. (J). per. *(978-1-59196-744-6(9))* Instant Pub.

Greathead, Helen. My Bed & Other Home Furniture. 2016. (Well Made, Fair Trade Ser.). (ENG., Illus.). 32p. (J). (gr. 5-8). *(978-0-7787-2713-2(0))* Crabtree Publishing Co.

FUTURE LIFE

Bohlmann, Katharine. Grandpa, Is There a Heaven? Erickson, David, illus. 2008. 32p. pap. 7.49 *(978-0-7586-1478-0(0))* Concordia Publishing Hse.

Green, Carl R. & Sanford, William R. Discovering Past Lives. Kelley, Gerald, illus. 2011. (Investigating the Unknown Ser.). 48p. (J). (gr. 5-18). pap. 8.95 *(978-1-59845-308-9(4));* lib. bdg. 25.27 *(978-0-7660-3818-9(1))* Enslow Pubs., Inc.

Holford, Karen. I Miss Grandpa: A Story to Help Your Child Understand Death — & Eternal Life. 2004. (Illus.). 32p. (J). 4.97 *(978-0-8163-2030-1(6))* Pacific Pr. Publishing Assn.

MacKenzie, Catherine. What God Says: Resurrection. 2006. (Bible Art Ser.). (ENG.). 16p. (J). pap. 1.99 *(978-1-84550-218-8(3),* e8deff6e-314a-430c-82a4-8f17c4d053fc) Christian Focus Pubns. GBR. Dist: Bookmasters Distribution.

Oral, Osman. I Believe in the Hereafter. 2013. (J). *(978-1-59784-306-5(7))* Tughra Bks.

FUTURE LIFE—FICTION

Abedí, Isabel. Farewell, Grandpa Elephant: What Happens When a Loved One Dies? Cordes, Miriam, illus. 2012. (ENG.). 28p. (J). (gr. -1-k). 16.95 *(978-1-61608-655-8(6),* 608655, Sky Pony Pr.) Skyhorse Publishing Co., Inc.

Akatsuki, Natsume. God's Blessing on This Wonderful World! You are Being Summoned Darkness. Mishima, Kurone, illus. 2017. (Konosuba (light Novel) Ser.: 3). (ENG.). 192p. (YA). (gr. 8-17). pap. 14.00 ***(978-0-316-46873-2(8),*** Yen Pr.) Orbit.

Akatsuki, Natsume & Steinbach, Kevin. Konosuba, God's Blessing on This Wonderful World! Mishima, Kurone, illus. 2017. (YA). ***(978-0-316-46880-0(0)); (978-0-316-46885-5(1)); (978-0-316-46882-4(7))*** Yen Pr. LLC.

Almond, David. Slog's Dad. McKean, Dave, illus. 2011. (ENG.). 64p. (J). (gr. 5-18). 15.99 *(978-0-7636-4940-1(6))* Candlewick Pr.

Anderson, Jodi Lynn. Among the Stars. 2014. (May Bird Ser.: 2). (ENG., Illus.). 304p. (J). (gr. 3-7). pap. 6.99 *(978-1-4424-9578-4(2),* Aladdin) Simon & Schuster Children's Publishing.

—Among the Stars. 2014. (May Bird Ser.: 2). (ENG., Illus.). 304p. (J). (gr. 3-7). 17.99 *(978-1-4424-9579-1(0),* Simon & Schuster/Paula Wiseman Bks.) Simon & Schuster/Paula Wiseman Bks.

—The Ever After. 2014. (May Bird Ser.: 1). (ENG., Illus.). 368p. (J). (gr. 3-7). pap. 7.99 *(978-1-4424-9576-0(6),* Aladdin) Simon & Schuster Children's Publishing.

—The May Bird Trilogy: The Ever after; among the Stars; Warrior Princess. 2014. (May Bird Ser.). (ENG., Illus.). 960p. (J). (gr. 3-7). pap. 22.99 *(978-1-4814-1673-3(1),* Aladdin) Simon & Schuster Children's Publishing.
—Warrior Princess. 2014. (May Bird Ser.: 3). (ENG., Illus.). 288p. (J). (gr. 3-7). pap. 6.99 *(978-1-4424-9580-7(4),* Aladdin) Simon & Schuster Children's Publishing.
Appelhans, Lenore. Level 2 Bk. 1: There Has to Be More to the Afterlife Than This. 2013. (Memory Chronicles Ser.: 1). (ENG.). 288p. (YA). (gr. 7). 17.99 *(978-1-4424-4185-9(2),* Simon & Schuster Bks. For Young Readers) Simon & Schuster Bks. For Young Readers.
—Memory of After. 2013. (Memory Chronicles Ser.: 1). (ENG.). 304p. (YA). (gr. 7). pap. 9.99 *(978-1-4424-4186-6(0),* Simon & Schuster Bks. For Young Readers) Simon & Schuster Bks. For Young Readers.
Applegate, Anne. The Last Academy. 2013. (ENG.). 320p. (J). (gr. 7). 17.99 *(978-0-545-50204-7(7))* Scholastic, Inc.
Ashton, Brodi. Everbound. 2013. (Everneath Ser.: 2). (ENG.). (YA). (gr. 8). 384p. pap. 9.99 *(978-0-06-207117-0(3));* 368p. 17.99 *(978-0-06-207116-3(5))* HarperCollins Pubs.
—Everneath. 2012. (Everneath Ser.: 1). (ENG.). 384p. (YA). (gr. 9). 17.99 *(978-0-06-207113-2(0))* HarperCollins Pubs.
—Evertrue. 2014. (Everneath Ser.: 3). (ENG.). 368p. (YA). (gr. 8). 17.99 *(978-0-06-207119-4(X))* HarperCollins Pubs.
Auseon, Andrew. Jo-Jo & the Fiendish Lot. 2009. 473p. (YA). lib. bdg. 18.89 *(978-0-06-113924-6(6),* HarperTeen) HarperCollins Pubs.
Babbitt, Natalie. Tuck Everlasting. 2008. (J). 39.99 *(978-0-7393-7111-4(8))* Findaway World, LLC.
—Tuck Everlasting. 2007. 148p. (J). 17.20 *(978-1-4177-9367-9(8),* Turtleback) Turtleback Bks.
Barry, William J. Forever Awakening. 2014. 242p. pap. 18.50 *(978-1-61213-113-9(1))* Writer's Coffee Shop, The.
Basye, Dale E. Blimpo Vol. 3: The Third Circle of Heck. Dob, Bob, illus. 2011. (Heck Ser.). (ENG.). 464p. (J). (gr. 3-7). pap. 7.99 *(978-0-375-85677-8(3),* Yearling) Random Hse. Children's Bks.
—Fibble. Dob, Bob, illus. 2012. (Heck Ser.). (ENG.). 384p. (J). (gr. 4-7). pap. 6.99 *(978-0-375-85679-2(X),* Yearling) Random Hse. Children's Bks.
—Precocia: the Sixth Circle of Heck. Dob, Bob, illus. 2013. (Heck Ser.). (ENG.). 432p. (J). (gr. 3-7). 6.99 *(978-0-375-86807-8(0),* Yearling) Random Hse. Children's Bks.
—Rapacia. Dob, Bob, illus. 2010. (Heck Ser.). (ENG.). 384p. (J). (gr. 3-7). pap. 6.99 *(978-0-375-84078-4(8),* Yearling) Random Hse. Children's Bks.
—Snivel: the Fifth Circle of Heck. Dob, Bob, illus. 2013. (Heck Ser.). (ENG.). 448p. (J). (gr. 4-7). 8.99 *(978-0-375-86806-1(2),* Yearling) Random Hse. Children's Bks.
—Where the Bad Kids Go. Dob, Bob, illus. 2009. (Heck Ser.). (ENG.). 304p. (J). (gr. 3-7). 6.99 *(978-0-375-84076-0(1),* Yearling) Random Hse. Children's Bks.
—Wise Acres: the Seventh Circle of Heck. Dob, Bob, illus. 2013. (Heck Ser.). (ENG.). 448p. (J). (gr. 4-7). 16.99 *(978-0-307-98185-1(1),* Random Hse. Bks. for Young Readers) Random Hse. Children's Bks.
Berk, Ari. Lych Way. 2014. (Undertaken Trilogy Ser.: 3). (ENG., Illus.). 336p. (YA). (gr. 7). 17.99 *(978-1-4169-9119-9(0),* Simon & Schuster Bks. For Young Readers) Simon & Schuster Bks. For Young Readers.
Black, Robert A. Lunar Pioneers. 2008. 280p. (YA). pap. 14.99 *(978-1-59092-397-9(9))* Blue Forge Pr.
Booraem, Ellen. Texting the Underworld. 2013. (ENG.). 320p. (J). (gr. 5). 16.99 *(978-0-8037-3704-4(1),* Dial Bks) Penguin Young Readers Group.
Breese, K. Ryer. Past Continuous. 2011. (ENG.). 304p. (YA). (gr. 9-13). pap. 20.99 *(978-0-312-54772-1(2),* 9780312547721, St. Martin's Griffin) St. Martin's Pr.
Brian, Kate. Endless (a Shadowlands Novel) 2014. (Shadowlands Ser.). (ENG.). 336p. (YA). (gr. 7-12). 17.99 *(978-1-4231-6485-2(7))* Hyperion Bks. for Children.
—Hereafter (a Shadowlands Novel) 2014. (Shadowlands Ser.). (ENG.). 336p. (YA). (gr. 9-17). pap. 9.99 *(978-1-4231-6526-2(8))* Hyperion Bks. for Children.
Cabot, Meg. Underworld. 2012. (Abandon Ser.). (ENG.). 336p. (J). (gr. 9). 17.99 *(978-0-545-28411-0(2))* Scholastic, Inc.
Catanese, P. W. Donny's Inferno. 2016. (Donny's Inferno Ser.: 1). (ENG.). 320p. (J). (gr. 3-7). 16.99 *(978-1-4814-3800-1(X),* Aladdin) Simon & Schuster Children's Publishing.
—Down in Flames. 2017. (Donny's Inferno Ser.: 2). (ENG., Illus.). 336p. (J). (gr. 3-7). 16.99 *(978-1-4814-3803-2(4),* Simon & Schuster/Paula Wiseman Bks.) Simon & Schuster/Paula Wiseman Bks.
Chasing Before. 2014. (Memory Chronicles Ser.: 2). (ENG., Illus.). 368p. (YA). (gr. 7). 19.99 *(978-1-4424-4188-0(7),* Simon & Schuster Bks. For Young Readers) Simon & Schuster Bks. For Young Readers.
Clifford, Leah. A Touch Menacing. 2013. (Touch Mortal Trilogy Ser.: 3). (ENG.). 320p. (YA). (gr. 9). 17.99 *(978-0-06-200505-2(7),* Greenwillow Bks.) HarperCollins Pubs.
—A Touch Morbid. 2012. (Touch Mortal Trilogy Ser.: 2). (ENG.). 304p. (YA). (gr. 9). 16.99 *(978-0-06-200502-1(2),* Greenwillow Bks.) HarperCollins Pubs.
—A Touch Mortal. 2011. (Touch Mortal Trilogy Ser.: 1). (ENG.). 432p. (YA). (gr. 8-18). 17.99 *(978-0-06-200499-4(9),* Greenwillow Bks.) HarperCollins Pubs.
Colin, Thompson. How to Live Forever. 2008. 32p. 16.99 *(978-0-681-49757-3(2),* State Street Pr.) Borders Pr.
Cooper, Rose. I Text Dead People. 2015. (Dead Serious Ser.). (ENG.). 240p. (J). (gr. 3-7). 15.99 *(978-0-375-99138-7(7),* Delacorte Bks. for Young Readers) Random Hse. Children's Bks.
Crutcher, Chris. The Sledding Hill. 2006. (ENG.). 256p. (YA). (gr. 8-12). pap. 9.99 *(978-0-06-050245-4(2),* Greenwillow Bks.) HarperCollins Pubs.
Dalton, Annie. Budding Star: Mission - Rescue a Pop Princess. 2008. (Mel Beeby Agent Angel Ser.). (ENG.). 208p. (J). (gr. 4-7). pap. 6.95 *(978-0-00-720478-6(7))* HarperCollins Pubs. Ltd. GBR. Dist: Independent Pubs. Group.
Damico, Gina. Croak. 2012. (ENG.). 320p. (YA). (gr. 7). pap. 8.99 *(978-0-547-60832-7(2))* Houghton Mifflin Harcourt Publishing Co.
—Croak. 2012. (Croak Ser.: 1). lib. bdg. 19.65 *(978-0-606-24776-4(9),* Turtleback) Turtleback Bks.
—Rogue. 2013. (ENG.). 336p. (YA). (gr. 7). pap. 8.99 *(978-0-544-10884-4(1))* Houghton Mifflin Harcourt Publishing Co.
—Scorch. 2012. (Croak Ser.: 2). lib. bdg. 19.65 *(978-0-606-26627-7(5),* Turtleback) Turtleback Bks.
Downer, Denise. Soul Mates. Frampton, Otis, illus. 2013. (Tombstone Twins Ser.). (ENG.). 48p. (gr. 1-3). lib. bdg. 23.99 *(978-1-4342-2248-0(9))* Stone Arch Bks.
—Tombstone Twins: Soul Mates, 1 vol. Frampton, Otis, illus. 2013. (Tombstone Twins Ser.). (ENG.). 48p. (gr. 1-3). pap. 5.95 *(978-1-4342-3873-3(3))* Stone Arch Bks.
—Tombstone Twins Package: Soul Mates. Frampton, Otis, illus. 2013. (ENG.). 41p. (J). (gr. 2-4). pap. 35.70 *(978-1-4342-3955-6(1))* Stone Arch Bks.
Evans, Alfreda. The Little Boy in Blue. 2009. 24p. pap. *(978-1-55452-399-3(0),* Guardian Bks.) Essence Publishing.
Evans, Alfreda Lockett. The Little Boy in Blue. 2009. 24p. pap. *(978-1-55452-402-0(4))* Essence Publishing.
Fine, Sarah. Chaos, 0 vols. 2014. (Guards of the Shadowlands Ser.: 3). (ENG.). 368p. (J). (gr. 9-12). 17.99 *(978-1-4778-4781-7(2),* 9781477847817, Skyscape) Amazon Publishing.
France, Emily. Signs of You. (ENG.). 240p. (YA). (gr. 9). 2017. pap. 10.99 *(978-1-61695-815-2(4))* 2016. 18.99 *(978-1-61695-657-8(7))* Soho Pr., Inc. (Soho Teen).
Garvey, Amy. Cold Kiss. 2012. (Cold Kiss Ser.: 1). (ENG.). 336p. (YA). (gr. 8). pap. 8.99 *(978-0-06-199623-8(8),* HarperTeen) HarperCollins Pubs.
Gibsen, Cole. Senshi. 2013. (Katana Novel Ser.: 2). (ENG.). 384p. (YA). pap. 9.99 *(978-0-7387-3261-9(3),* Flux) North Star Editions.
Guarente, Gabe. Satan's Prep: A Graphic Novel. 2014. (ENG., Illus.). 112p. (J). (gr. 6). 17.95 *(978-1-62873-592-5(9),* Sky Pony Pr.) Skyhorse Publishing Co., Inc.
Halpern, Jake & Kujawinski, Peter. Edgeland. 2017. (ENG., Illus.). 272p. (J). (gr. 5). 17.99 *(978-0-399-17581-7(4),* G.P. Putnam's Sons Books for Young Readers) Penguin Young Readers Group.
Hannon, Rose. Finding Agate: An Epic Story of a Poodle's Heart & His Will to Survive. 2010. 268p. pap. 16.99 *(978-1-4490-8986-3(0))* AuthorHouse.
Harrison, Kim, pseud. Early to Death, Early to Rise. 2011. (Madison Avery Ser.: 2). (ENG., Illus.). 256p. (YA). (gr. 9). pap. 8.99 *(978-0-06-144169-1(4))* HarperCollins Pubs.
—Something Deadly This Way Comes. (Madison Avery Ser.: 3). (ENG.). (YA). (gr. 9). 2012. 288p. pap. 9.99 *(978-0-06-144170-7(8))* 2011. 256p. 16.99 *(978-0-06-171819-9(X))* HarperCollins Pubs.
Higgins, Jane. The Bridge. 2012. (ENG.). 352p. (YA). (gr. 7). 17.95 *(978-1-77049-437-4(5),* Tundra Bks.) Tundra Bks. CAN. Dist: Penguin Random Hse. LLC.
Hole, Stian. Anna's Heaven. 2014. (ENG., Illus.). 42p. (J). 17.00 *(978-0-8028-5441-4(9),* Eerdmans Bks For Young Readers) Eerdmans, William B. Publishing Co.
Hosie, Donna. The Devil's Banshee. 2016. (ENG.). 336p. (YA). 17.95 *(978-0-8234-3650-7(0))* Holiday Hse., Inc.
—The Devil's Dreamcatcher. (ENG.). (YA). (gr. 10). 2016. 272p. pap. 7.99 *(978-0-8234-3693-4(4))* 2015. 288p. 16.95 *(978-0-8234-3390-2(0))* Holiday Hse., Inc.
—The Devil's Intern. 2014. (ENG.). 288p. (YA). (gr. 10-12). 16.95 *(978-0-8234-3195-3(9))* Holiday Hse., Inc.
Hudson, Tara. Arise. (Hereafter Trilogy Ser.: 2). (ENG.). (YA). (gr. 8). 2013. 432p. pap. 9.99 *(978-0-06-202680-4(1))* 2012. 416p. 17.99 *(978-0-06-202679-8(8))* HarperCollins Pubs. (HarperTeen).
—Elegy. 2013. (Hereafter Trilogy Ser.: 3). (ENG.). 400p. (YA). (gr. 8). 17.99 *(978-0-06-202681-1(X),* HarperTeen) HarperCollins Pubs.
—Hereafter. 2012. (Hereafter Trilogy Ser.: 1). (ENG.). 432p. (YA). (gr. 8). pap. 8.99 *(978-0-06-202678-1(X),* HarperTeen) HarperCollins Pubs.
Hurley, Tonya. Ghostgirl. 2010. (Ghostgirl Ser.: 1). (ENG.). 336p. (YA). (gr. 7-17). pap. 9.99 *(978-0-316-03635-1(8))* Little, Brown Bks. for Young Readers.
—Ghostgirl. Frieyro, Alicia, tr. Impey, Allison & Phillips, Craig, illus. 2009. (SPA.). 1200p. (YA). (gr. 8-12). pap. 19.99 *(978-607-11-0185-3(9),* Alfaguara Juvenil) Santillana USA Publishing Co., Inc.
—Homecoming. 2010. (Ghostgirl Ser.: 2). (ENG.). 304p. (YA). (gr. 7-17). pap. 10.00 *(978-0-316-08943-2(5))* Little, Brown Bks. for Young Readers.
—Lovesick. 2011. (Ghostgirl Ser.: 3). (ENG.). 320p. (YA). (gr. 7-17). pap., pap. 9.99 *(978-0-316-13316-6(7))* Little, Brown Bks. for Young Readers.
Jones, Gareth P. Constable & Toop. 2013. (ENG.). 416p. (J). (gr. 3-7). 17.95 *(978-1-4197-0782-7(5),* Amulet Bks.) Abrams, Inc.
Kain, Jamie. The Good Sister. 2015. (ENG.). 304p. (YA). (gr. 9-12). pap. 9.99 *(978-1-250-04774-8(9),* 9781250047748, St. Martin's Griffin) St. Martin's Pr.
Kazmi, Ummul Baneen. Alisha's Heavenly Adventures: It's Magic! 2012. 28p. pap. 19.99 *(978-1-4685-5803-6(X))* AuthorHouse.
Keay, Ben. Perfect Solution. Hsu, Florence, illus. 2009. (YA). *(978-1-933791-09-8(8))* Finial Publishing.
Kwaymullina, Ambelin. The Interrogation of Ashala Wolf. 2014. (ENG.). 384p. (YA). (gr. 7). 17.99 *(978-0-7636-6988-1(1))* Candlewick Pr.
Leigh, Kyra. Reaper. 2017. (ENG., Illus.). 256p. (YA). (gr. 7). 18.99 ***(978-1-4814-7196-1(1),*** Simon & Schuster/Paula Wiseman Bks.) Simon & Schuster/Paula Wiseman Bks.
Lethcoe, Jason. Der Geheimnisvolle Mr. Spines - Wings. Altmann, Scott, illus. 2009. (Mysterious Mr. Spines Ser.: 1). (ENG.). 256p. (J). (gr. 5-18). pap. 7.99 *(978-0-448-44653-0(7),* Grosset & Dunlap) Penguin Young Readers Group.
Lindsey, Mary. Fragile Spirits. 2014. (ENG.). 320p. (YA). (gr. 7). 17.99 *(978-0-399-16186-5(4),* Philomel Bks.) Penguin Young Readers Group.
—Shattered Souls. 2012. (ENG.). 356p. (YA). (gr. 9). pap. 8.99 *(978-0-14-242190-1(1),* Speak) Penguin Young Readers Group.
Marino, Andy. The Door. 2014. (ENG.). 304p. (J). (gr. 3-7). 17.99 *(978-0-545-55137-3(4),* Scholastic Pr.) Scholastic, Inc.
Markowitz, Krista. Mrs Tipperwillow's Afterlife Adventures. 2008. 316p. 28.95 *(978-0-595-49079-0(4));* pap. 18.95 *(978-0-595-44671-1(X))* iUniverse, Inc.
Maschari, Jennifer. The Remarkable Journey of Charlie Price. 2016. 304p. (J). (gr. 3-7). 16.99 *(978-0-06-238010-4(9))* HarperCollins Pubs.
McEntire, K. D. Lightbringer. 2011. (ENG.). 319p. (YA). (gr. 7). 16.99 *(978-1-61614-539-2(0))* Prometheus Bks., Pubs.
—Never. 2013. (Lightbringer Ser.). (ENG.). 311p. (J). (gr. 7). 17.99 *(978-1-61614-771-6(7))* Prometheus Bks., Pubs.
—Reaper. 2012. (ENG.). 342p. (YA). (gr. 7). 16.95 *(978-1-61614-632-0(X))* Prometheus Bks., Pubs.
Meloy, Maile. The After-Room. Schoenherr, Ian, illus. 2015. (Apothecary Ser.: 3). (ENG.). 432p. (J). (gr. 5). 17.99 *(978-0-399-17544-2(X),* G.P. Putnam's Sons Books for Young Readers) Penguin Young Readers Group.
Mickelson, Marcia. The Huaca. 2013. (J). pap. 16.99 *(978-1-4621-1190-9(4),* Horizon Pubs.) Cedar Fort, Inc./CFI Distribution.
Mizielinska, Aleksandra & Mizielinski, Daniel. The World of Mamoko in the Year 3000. 2014. (ENG.). 16p. (J). (gr. k-3). 17.99 *(978-0-7636-7125-9(8),* Big Picture Press) Candlewick Pr.
Nevins, Paul. Dante's War. 2003. 168p. (YA). pap. 12.95 *(978-0-595-26743-9(2),* Writers Club Pr.) iUniverse, Inc.
Noël, Alyson. Radiance. unabr. ed. 2011. (ENG.). 208p. pap. *(978-0-330-52691-3(X),* Macmillan Children's Bks.) Pan Macmillan.
—Radiance. 2011. pap. *(978-0-545-34095-3(0))* Scholastic, Inc.
—Radiance. 2010. (Riley Bloom Book Ser.: 1). (ENG.). 192p. (J). (gr. 4-7). pap. 8.99 *(978-0-312-62917-5(6),* 9780312629175) Square Fish.
—Radiance. 2010. (Riley Bloom Ser.: 1). (J). lib. bdg. 19.65 *(978-0-606-15131-3(1),* Turtleback) Turtleback Bks.
—Shadowland. 2009. (Immortals Ser.: 3). (ENG.). 368p. (YA). (gr. 8-12). 17.99 *(978-0-312-59044-4(X),* 9780312590444, St. Martin's Griffin) St. Martin's Pr.
—Shimmer. 2011. pap. *(978-0-545-39923-4(8))* Scholastic, Inc.
—Shimmer. 2011. (Riley Bloom Book Ser.: 2). (ENG.). 208p. (J). (gr. 4-7). pap. 9.99 *(978-0-312-64825-1(1),* 9780312648251) Square Fish.
—Shimmer. 2011. (Riley Bloom Ser.: 2). (J). lib. bdg. 20.85 *(978-0-606-21683-8(9),* Turtleback) Turtleback Bks.
—Whisper, Bk. 4. 2012. (Riley Bloom Book Ser.: 4). (ENG.). 240p. (J). (gr. 4-7). pap. 8.99 *(978-0-312-64156-6(7),* 9780312641566) Square Fish.
—Whisper. 2012. (Riley Bloom Ser.: 4). (J). lib. bdg. 19.65 *(978-0-606-23786-4(0),* Turtleback) Turtleback Bks.
Oliver, Lauren. Liesl & Po. Acedera, Kei, illus. (ENG.). (J). (gr. 3-7). 2012. 336p. pap. 6.99 *(978-0-06-201452-8(8))* 2011. 320p. 16.99 *(978-0-06-201451-1(X))* HarperCollins Pubs.
—Liesl & Po. 2012. (J). lib. bdg. 17.20 *(978-0-606-26853-0(7),* Turtleback) Turtleback Bks.
Plante, Raymond. Marilou Forecasts the Future, 1 vol. Cummins, Sarah, tr. from FRE. Favreau, Marie-Claude, illus. 2003. (Formac First Novels Ser.: 49). (ENG.). 64p. (J). (gr. 1-5). 4.95 *(978-0-88780-614-8(7),* 9780887806148); (gr. 2-5). 14.95 *(978-0-88780-615-5(5),* 9780887806155) Formac Publishing Co., Ltd. CAN. Dist: Casemate Pubs. & Bk. Distributors, LLC.
Rothenberg, Jess. The Catastrophic History of You & Me. 2013. (ENG.). 400p. (YA). (gr. 7). pap. 9.99 *(978-0-14-242390-5(4),* Speak) Penguin Young Readers Group.
Russell, Randy. Dead Rules. 2011. (ENG.). 384p. (YA). (gr. 8-18). 16.99 *(978-0-06-198670-3(4),* HarperTeen) HarperCollins Pubs.
Sabatini, Kimberly. Touching the Surface. (ENG., 352p. (YA). (gr. 9). 2013. Illus.). pap. 9.99 *(978-1-4424-4003-6(1))* 2012. 16.99 *(978-1-4424-4002-9(3))* Simon Pulse. (Simon Pulse).
Schmitt, Sarah. It's a Wonderful Death. 2015. (ENG.). 320p. (J). (gr. 6). 17.99 *(978-1-63450-173-6(X),* Sky Pony Pr.) Skyhorse Publishing Co., Inc.
Schwab, Victoria. The Archived. 2014. (Archived Ser.). (ENG., Illus.). 352p. (YA). (gr. 7-12). pap. 9.99 *(978-1-4231-7108-9(X))* Hyperion Bks. for Children.
Shepard, Sara. Never Have I Ever. (Lying Game Ser.: 2). (ENG.). (YA). (gr. 9). 2012. 336p. pap. 9.99 *(978-0-06-186973-0(2))* 2011. 320p. 16.99 *(978-0-06-186972-3(4))* HarperCollins Pubs. (HarperTeen).
Showalter, Gena. Lifeblood. 2017. (Everlife Novel Ser.). (ENG.). 448p. 18.99 *(978-0-373-21219-4(4),* Harlequin Teen) Harlequin Enterprises, Ltd. CAN. Dist: HarperCollins Pubs.
Shusterman, Neal. Everfound. (Skinjacker Trilogy Ser.: 3). (ENG.). (YA). (gr. 7). 2012. 528p. pap. 11.99 *(978-1-4169-9050-5(X))* 2011. 512p. 17.99 *(978-1-4169-9049-9(6))* Simon & Schuster Bks. For Young Readers. (Simon & Schuster Bks. For Young Readers).
—Everlost. (Skinjacker Trilogy Ser.: 1). (ENG.). (YA). (gr. 7). 2009. 336p. pap. 11.99 *(978-1-4169-9749-8(0))* 2006. 320p. 19.99 *(978-0-689-87237-2(2))* Simon & Schuster Bks. For Young Readers. (Simon & Schuster Bks. For Young Readers).
—Everlost. rev. l.t. ed. 2007. (Skinjacker Trilogy: Bk. 1). 413p. (YA). (gr. 8-12). 22.95 *(978-0-7862-9365-0(9))* Thorndike Pr.
—Everwild. (Skinjacker Trilogy Ser.: 2). (ENG.). (YA). (gr. 7). 2010. 448p. pap. 11.99 *(978-1-4169-5864-2(9))* 2009. (Illus.). 432p. 18.99 *(978-1-4169-5863-5(0))* Simon & Schuster Bks. For Young Readers. (Simon & Schuster Bks. For Young Readers).
—The Skinjacker Trilogy: Everlost; Everwild; Everfound. 2013. (Skinjacker Trilogy Ser.). (ENG., Illus.). 1312p. (YA). (gr. 7). pap. 35.99 *(978-1-4424-9903-4(6),* Simon & Schuster Bks. For Young Readers) Simon & Schuster Bks. For Young Readers.
Singleton, Linda Joy. Dead Girl Walking. 2008. (Dead Girl Ser.: 1). (ENG.). 312p. (YA). (gr. 8-18). pap. 9.95 *(978-0-7387-1405-9(4),* Flux) North Star Editions.
Snicket, Lemony, pseud. Goldfish Ghost. Brown, Lisa, illus. 2017. (ENG.). 40p. (J). 17.99 *(978-1-62672-507-2(1),* 9781626725072) Roaring Brook Pr.
Van Dyke, Henry. The Mansion: 100th Anniversary Edition. 100th ed. 2011. 32p. (J). 18.99 *(978-1-60641-845-1(9),* Shadow Mountain) Shadow Mountain Publishing.
Walker, Melissa. Ashes to Ashes. (ENG.). (YA). (gr. 8). 2015. 352p. pap. 9.99 *(978-0-06-207735-6(X))* 2013. 336p. 17.99 *(978-0-06-207734-9(1))* HarperCollins Pubs. (Tegen, Katherine Bks).
—Dust to Dust. 320p. (YA). (gr. 8). 2016. pap. 9.99 *(978-0-06-207738-7(4))* 2015. (ENG.). 17.99 *(978-0-06-207737-0(6))* HarperCollins Pubs. (Tegen, Katherine Bks).
Westerfeld, Scott. Afterworlds. 2014. (ENG., Illus.). 608p. (YA). (gr. 9). 19.99 *(978-1-4814-2234-5(0),* Simon Pulse) Simon Pulse.
—Afterworlds. 2015. lib. bdg. 24.50 *(978-0-606-37860-4(X))* Turtleback Bks.
Westwood, Chris. Graveyard Shift. (Hauntings Ser.: bk.1). (ENG.). 304p. (J). (gr. 3-7). 2014. pap. 6.99 *(978-0-545-39920-3(3))* 2012. 17.99 *(978-0-545-39919-7(X))* Scholastic, Inc. (Scholastic Pr.).
Whitcomb, Laura. A Certain Slant of Light. 2005. (ENG.). 288p. (YA). (gr. 7-18). pap. 8.99 *(978-0-618-58532-8(X))* Houghton Mifflin Harcourt Publishing Co.
—The Fetch. 2010. (ENG.). 384p. (YA). (gr. 7). pap. 20.99 *(978-0-547-41163-7(4))* Houghton Mifflin Harcourt Publishing Co.
Zevin, Gabrielle. Elsewhere. 2007. 288p. (gr. 7). 20.00 *(978-0-7569-8191-4(3))* Perfection Learning Corp.
—Elsewhere. 2007. (ENG.). 304p. (YA). (gr. 7). per. 9.99 *(978-0-312-36746-6(5),* 9780312367466) Square Fish.

G

G.I.S

see Soldiers—United States

GAGARIN, YURI ALEKSEEVICH, 1934-1968

Feldman, Heather. Yuri Gagarin: The First Man in Space. 2003. (Space Firsts Ser.). (Illus.). 24p. (J). lib. bdg. 22.60 *(978-0-8239-6245-7(8),* PowerKids Pr.) Rosen Publishing Group, Inc., The.

GALAPAGOS ISLANDS

Banting, Erinn. The Galapagos Islands. 2006. (Natural Wonders Ser.). (Illus.). 32p. (gr. 3-7). 17.95 *(978-0-7569-6994-3(8))* Perfection Learning Corp.
—The Galapagos Islands. 2006. (Natural Wonders Ser.). (Illus.). 32p. (J). (gr. 3-7). per. 9.95 *(978-1-59036-455-0(4))* Weigl Pubs., Inc.
—The Galapagos Islands: A Unique Ecosystem. 2006. (Natural Wonders Ser.). (Illus.). 32p. (J). (gr. 3-7). lib. bdg. 26.00 *(978-1-59036-449-9(X))* Weigl Pubs., Inc.
Chin, Jason. Island: A Story of the Galápagos. Chin, Jason, illus. 2012. (ENG., Illus.). 40p. (J). (gr. k-3). 17.99 *(978-1-59643-716-6(2),* 9781596437166) Roaring Brook Pr.
Harper, Judith E. Unique Places. 2005. (Real Deal Ser.). (Illus.). 32p. (J). pap. *(978-0-7608-9635-8(6))* Sundance/Newbridge Educational Publishing.
Henzel, Cynthia Kennedy. Galápagos Islands, 1 vol. 2011. (Troubled Treasures: World Heritage Sites Ser.). (ENG., Illus.). 32p. (YA). (gr. 3-6). 27.07 *(978-1-61613-563-8(8))* ABDO Publishing Co.
Kras, Sara Louise. The Galapagos Islands. 2008. (Nature's Wonders Ser.). 96p. (gr. 6-18). lib. bdg. 35.64 *(978-0-7614-2856-5(9),* Benchmark Bks.) Marshall Cavendish Corp.
Roza, Greg. The Galapagos Islands. (Reading Room Collection 2 Ser.). 24p. 2009. (gr. 3-4). 42.50 *(978-1-60851-993-4(7),* PowerKids Pr.) 2003. (Illus.). (J). lib. bdg. 22.60 *(978-0-8239-3714-1(3))* Rosen Publishing Group, Inc., The.
Stine, Megan. Where Are the Galapagos Islands? Hinderliter, John, illus. 2017. (Where Is? Ser.). (ENG.). 112p. (J). (gr. 3-7). pap. 5.99 *(978-0-451-53387-6(9),* Grosset & Dunlap) Penguin Young Readers Group.
—Where Are the Galapagos Islands? 2017. (Where Is... ? Ser.). lib. bdg. 16.00 ***(978-0-606-40103-6(2))*** Turtleback Bks.
Tagliaferro, Linda. Galapagos Islands: Nature's Delicate Balance at Risk. 2005. (Discovery! Ser.). (Illus.). 120p. (gr. 5-12). lib. bdg. 27.93 *(978-0-8225-0648-5(3))* Lerner Publishing Group.
Wallis, Ginger. Finch Discoveries: An Inspiring Tale of Adaptation to a Changing Environment. Dodson, Bert, illus. 2013. 34p. pap. 12.95 *(978-0-9847662-2-2(7))* Dancing Journey Pr.
Wojahn, Rebecca Hogue & Wojahn, Donald. A Galápagos Island Food Chain: A Who-Eats-What Adventure. 2009. (Follow That Food Chain Ser.). (ENG.). 64p. (gr. 3-5). 30.60 *(978-0-8225-7613-6(9))* Lerner Publishing Group.

GALES

see Winds

GALILEI, GALILEO, 1564-1642

Bach, Nancy. Galileo Galilei e la Torre Di Pisa - Galileo Galilei & the Pisa Tower: A Bilingual Picture Book about the Italian Astronomer (Italian-English Text) Lätti, Leo, illus. 2013. 26p. pap. *(978-1-938712-07-4(2))* Roxby Media Ltd.
Bailey, Gerry & Foster, Karen. Galileo's Telescope. Noyes, Leighton & Radford, Karen, illus. 2008. (Stories of Great People Ser.). (ENG.). 40p. (J). (gr. 3-6). lib. bdg. *(978-0-7787-3694-3(6));* pap. *(978-0-7787-3716-2(0))* Crabtree Publishing Co.
Boekhoff, P. M. Galileo. 2003. (Inventors & Creators Ser.). (Illus.). 48p. (J). 23.70 *(978-0-7377-1891-1(9),* Greenhaven Pr., Inc.) Cengage Gale.
Boothroyd, Jennifer. Galileo Galilei: A Life of Curiosity. 2007. (Pull Ahead Bks.). (Illus.). 32p. (J). (gr. 3-7). lib. bdg. 22.60 *(978-0-8225-6460-7(2),* Lerner Pubns.) Lerner Publishing Group.
Brezina, Corona. Galileo Galilei. 2017. (Leaders of the Scientific Revolution Ser.). 112p. (J). (gr. 12-13). 37.10 ***(978-1-5081-7468-4(7),*** Rosen Young Adult) Rosen Publishing Group, Inc., The.
Christensen, Bonnie. I, Galileo. 2012. (ENG., Illus.). 40p. (J). (gr. 3-7). 20.99 *(978-0-375-96753-5(2));* 17.99

(978-0-375-86753-8(8)) Random Hse. Children's Bks. (Knopf Bks. for Young Readers).

De Almeida, Guilherme, et al. Galileo Galilei. 2010. (Me Llamo... Ser.). (SPA., Illus.). 63p. (J). pap. (978-84-342-3617-2(6)) Parramon Ediciones S.A.

Demuth, Patricia Brennan. Who Was Galileo? 2015. (Who Was... ? Ser.). lib. bdg. 16.00 (978-0-606-36594-9(X)) Turtleback Bks.

Demuth, Patricia Brennan & dePaola, Tomie. Who Was Galileo? O'brien, John & Harrison, Nancy, illus. 2015. (Who Was? Ser.). (ENG.). 112p. (J). (gr. 3-7). 5.99 (978-0-448-47985-9(0), Grosset & Dunlap) Penguin Young Readers Group.

Dickmann, Nancy. Galileo: Conqueror of the Stars. 2015. (Superheroes of Science Ser.). (ENG., Illus.). 48p. (J). (gr. 6-6). pap. 14.05 (978-1-4824-3137-7(8)) Stevens, Gareth Publishing LLLP.

Don Nardo. The Trial of Galileo. 2003. (Famous Trials Ser.). (ENG., Illus.). 112p. (J). 29.95 (978-1-59018-423-3(8)) Cengage Gale.

Foelker, Rita. Erase Una Vez Galileo Galilei. Abs, Renata, illus. 2004. 24p. pap. 2.95 (978-85-7416-192-1(6)) Callis Editora Ltda BRA. Dist: Independent Pubs. Group.

Hightower, Paul. Galileo: Astronomer & Physicist. rev. ed. 2008. (Great Minds of Science Ser.). (Illus.). 128p. (J). (gr. k-5). lib. bdg. 33.27 (978-0-7660-3008-4(3)) Enslow Pubs., Inc.

Hightower, Paul W. Galileo: Genius Astronomer. 2015. (Genius Scientists & Their Genius Ideas Ser.). 96p. (J). (gr. 5-12). 27.94 (978-0-7660-6560-4(X)); pap. 10.95 (978-0-7660-6561-1(8)) Enslow Pubs., Inc.

Hilliam, Rachel. Galileo Galilei: Father of Modern Science. (Rulers, Scholars, & Artists of the Renaissance Ser.). 112p. 2009. (gr. 5-8). 66.50 (978-1-60852-941-4(X), Rosen Reference) 2004. (Illus.). (J). lib. bdg. 34.60 (978-1-4042-0314-3(1)) Rosen Publishing Group, Inc., The.

Kessler, Colleen & Benchmark Education Co. Staff. Gallileo's Gift. 2014. (Text Connections Ser.). (J). (gr. 5). (978-1-4900-1371-8(7)) Benchmark Education Co.

Lin, Yoming S. Galileo & the Telescope. 2012. (Eureka! Ser.). (Illus.). 24p. (J). (gr. 3-6). lib. bdg. 22.60 (978-1-4488-5030-3(4)) Rosen Publishing Group, Inc., The.

O'Donnell, Kerri. Galileo: Man of Science. (Reading Room Collection 2 Ser.). 24p. 2009. (gr. 3-4). 42.50 (978-1-60851-964-4(3), PowerKids Pr.) 2003. (Illus.). (J). lib. bdg. 22.60 (978-0-8239-3700-4(3), Reading Room Collection) Rosen Publishing Group, Inc., The.

Panchyk, Richard. Galileo for Kids: His Life & Ideas, 25 Activities. 2005. (For Kids Ser.). (ENG., Illus.). 184p. (J). (gr. 4). pap. 18.95 (978-1-55652-566-7(4)) Chicago Review Pr., Inc.

Puerta, Germán. Galileo Galilei - Y Sin Embargo se Mueve. 2005. (SPA.). 108p. (YA). (978-958-30-1700-1(0)) Panamericana Editorial.

Ridley, Sarah. Galileo Galilei. 2017. (Super Scientists Ser.). (ENG., Illus.). 24p. (J). (gr. 1-3). pap. 9.99 **(978-1-4451-5358-2(0)**, Franklin Watts) Hachette Children's Group GBR. Dist: Hachette Bk. Group.

Steele, Philip. Galileo: The Genius Who Faced the Inquisition. (National Geographic World History Biographies Ser.). (ENG., Illus.). 64p. (J). (gr. 3-7). 2008. pap. 7.99 (978-1-4263-0295-4(9)) 2005. 17.95 (978-0-7922-3656-6(4)) 2005. lib. bdg. 27.90 (978-0-7922-3657-3(2)) National Geographic Society. (National Geographic Children's Bks.).

Whiting, Jim. Galileo. 2007. (What's So Great About... ? Ser.). (Illus.). 32p. (YA). (gr. 2-4). lib. bdg. 25.70 (978-1-58415-575-1(2)) Mitchell Lane Pubs., Inc.

GALLERIES (ART)

see Art Museums

GAMA, VASCO DA, 1469-1524

Bailey, Katharine. Vasco Da Gama: Quest for the Spice Trade. 2007. (In the Footsteps of Explorers Ser.). (ENG., Illus.). 32p. (J). (gr. 3-7). lib. bdg. (978-0-7787-2421-6(2)); pap. (978-0-7787-2457-5(3)) Crabtree Publishing Co.

Calvert, Patricia. Vasco Da Gama: So Strong a Spirit. 2004. (Great Explorations Ser.). (Illus.). 80p. (gr. 6). 22.95 (978-0-7614-1611-1(0), Benchmark Bks.) Marshall Cavendish Corp.

Draper, Allison Stark. Vasco da Gama: The Portuguese Quest for a Sea Route from Europe to India. rev. ed. (Library of Explorers & Explorationtm Ser.). (Illus.). 112p. (YA). (gr. 5-8). lib. bdg. 31.95 (978-1-4042-0637-3(X), Rosen Reference) Rosen Publishing Group, Inc., The.

Koestler-Grack, Rachel A. Vasco Da Gama & the Sea Route to India. Goetzmann, William H., ed. 2005. (Explorers of New Lands Ser.). (Illus.). 168p. (gr. 5-8). lib. bdg. 30.00 (978-0-7910-8611-7(9)) Facts On File, Inc.

Landau, Jennifer. Vasco Da Gama. 2016. (Spotlight on Explorers & Colonization Ser.). 48p. (J). (gr. 6-6). pap. 11.75 (978-1-4777-8825-7(5)) Rosen Publishing Group, Inc., The.

Morey, Allan. Vasco Da Gama. 2003. (Explorers of the Unknown Ser.). (J). (978-1-58417-033-4(6)); pap. (978-1-58417-096-9(4)) Lake Street Pubs.

Napoli, Tony. Vasco Da Gama: Discovering the Sea Route to India. 2010. (Great Explorers of the World Ser.). (Illus.). 112p. (J). (gr. 7-12). 33.27 (978-1-59845-127-6(8)) Enslow Pubs., Inc.

Petrie, Kristin. Vasco Da Gama, 1 vol. 2004. (Explorers Set 1 Ser.). (ENG., Illus.). 32p. (gr. k-6). 27.07 (978-1-59197-603-5(0), Checkerboard Library) ABDO Publishing Co.

Worth, Richard. Vasco da Gama. 2009. (Great Explorers Ser.). (Illus.). 104p. (gr. 6-12). 30.00 (978-1-60413-423-0(2), Chelsea Hse.) Facts On File, Inc.

GAME AND GAME BIRDS

see also Falconry; Game Protection; Hunting; Trapping

also names of animals and birds, e.g. Deer; Pheasants; etc.

Hemstock, Annie Wendt. Know Your Quarry. 2014. (Open Season Ser.). 32p. (J). (gr. 4-6). lib. bdg. 26.25 (978-1-4777-6720-7(7), PowerKids Pr.) Rosen Publishing Group, Inc., The.

MacRae, Sloan. Small-Game Hunting: Squirrels, Rabbits, & Other Small Animals. 2010. (Open Season Ser.). (ENG.). 32p. (J). pap. 10.00 (978-1-4488-1375-9(1)); lib. bdg. 25.25 (978-1-4488-0707-9(7)) Rosen Publishing Group, Inc., The. (PowerKids Pr.).

McDowell, Pamela. Birds. 2012. (J). (978-1-61913-505-5(1)); pap. (978-1-61913-509-3(4)) Weigl Pubs., Inc.

Peterson, Judy Monroe. Small Game Hunting. 2011. (Hunting: Pursuing Wild Game! Ser.). 64p. (YA). (ENG.). pap. 12.95 (978-1-4488-2272-0(6), Rosen Reference); (Illus.). (gr. 5-9). lib. bdg. 31.95 (978-1-4488-1242-4(9)) Rosen Publishing Group, Inc., The.

GAME PROTECTION

Gibson, Brylee. Wildlife Detectives. 2007. (Connectors Ser.). (gr. 2-5). pap. (978-1-877453-18-2(8)) Global Education Systems Ltd.

Jackson, Donna M. The Wildlife Detectives: How Forensic Scientists Fight Crimes Against Nature. Shattil, Wendy & Rozinski, Bob, photos by. 2005. (Scientists in the Field Ser.). (Illus.). 47p. (gr. 3-7). 20.00 (978-0-7569-5191-7(7)) Perfection Learning Corp.

Watkins, Sue. Getting Involved! A Guide to Hunting & Conservation for Kids. 2011. (ENG.). 128p. pap. 12.95 (978-1-57157-377-3(1)) Safari Pr., Inc.

GAME PROTECTION—FICTION

St. John, Lauren. The White Giraffe. 2008. (ENG., Illus.). 208p. (J). (gr. 2-5). 7.99 (978-0-14-241152-0(3), Puffin Books) Penguin Young Readers Group.

GAME WARDENS

see Game Protection

GAMES

see also Amusements; Bible Games and Puzzles; Cards; Games for Travelers; Kindergarten; Olympics; Play; Singing Games; Sports

also names of games, e.g. Chess; Tennis; etc.

Aaseng, Nathan. Business Builders in Toys. 2003. (Business Builders Ser.). (Illus.). 160p. (gr. 5-18). lib. bdg. 22.95 (978-1-881508-81-6(1)) Oliver Pr., Inc.

Accord Publishing Staff. Flip & Click Sports Bingo. 2012. (ENG.). 72p. (J). pap. 4.99 (978-1-4494-1044-5(8)) Andrews McMeel Publishing.

—Flip & Click Sports Hangman. 2012. (ENG.). 72p. (J). pap. 4.99 (978-1-4494-1102-2(9)) Andrews McMeel Publishing.

—Flip & Click Sports Memory Match. 2012. (ENG.). 72p. (J). pap. 4.99 (978-1-4494-1103-9(7)) Andrews McMeel Publishing.

Acorn's Gold Mine. 2004. (J). cd-rom 39.00 (978-1-890265-12-0(8)) Janelle Pubns., Inc.

Alipio, Byron P. Jambo Nation Board Game 1st Edition: The game of wild animal Football. 2006. (Illus.). (YA). 25.00 (978-0-9794647-0-6(6)) Idyllworks, LLC.

Allen, Miles. Christmas Lore & Legend. 2003. 40p. 10.99 (978-0-9710448-3-8(X), 1) Momentpoint Media.

Allen, Toi Lynn. Game Day/Test Day: Who's Keeping Score? l.t. ed. 2004. (Illus.). (YA). pap. 14.95 (978-0-9753787-0-0(8)) Allen, Toi Operations.

Allyson, Jackie. Antonio the Magician Esfandiari. 2009. (Superstars of Poker Ser.). (Illus.). 64p. (YA). (gr. 3-7). lib. bdg. 22.95 (978-1-4222-0217-3(8)) Mason Crest.

—Howard the Professor Lederer. 2009. (Superstars of Poker Ser.). (Illus.). 64p. (YA). (gr. 3-7). lib. bdg. 22.95 (978-1-4222-0223-4(2)) Mason Crest.

—Phil Unabomber Laak. 2009. (Superstars of Poker Ser.). (Illus.). 64p. (YA). (gr. 3-7). lib. bdg. 22.95 (978-1-4222-0222-7(4)) Mason Crest.

Alvarez O'Neill, Juan, illus. ¡Vamos a Jugar! 2005. (SPA.). 28p. (J). 8.95 (978-0-8477-1553-4(1)) Univ. of Puerto Rico Pr.

Amazing Card Tricks & Games. 2004. (How 2 Kits Ser.). (Illus.). 48p. (J). (978-1-84229-934-0(4)) Top That! Publishing PLC.

Ambrosek, Renee. Team Roping. 2006. (World of Rodeo Ser.). (Illus.). 48p. (YA). (gr. 4-7). lib. bdg. 29.25 (978-1-4042-0548-2(9)) Rosen Publishing Group, Inc., The.

American Heritage Dictionary Editors, ed. Qué Juego? Zagarenski, Pamela, illus. 2004. (Good Beginnings Ser.).Tr. of What Am I Playing? (SPA & ENG.). 8p. (J). (gr. k — 1). bds. 3.95 (978-0-618-44375-8(4)) Houghton Mifflin Harcourt Publishing Co.

Anastasio, Dina. The Magic Turtle. 2011. (Early Connections Ser.). (J). (978-1-61672-603-4(2)) Benchmark Education Co.

—Number Games. 2011. (Early Connections Ser.). (J). (978-1-61672-591-4(5)) Benchmark Education Co.

Ancona, George. Mis Juegos/My Games. 2005. (Somos Latinos (We Are Latinos) Ser.). (ENG & SPA., Illus.). 32p. (J). (gr. 1-3). lib. bdg. 21.00 (978-0-516-25293-3(3), Children's Pr.) Scholastic Library Publishing.

Anderson, Lindsay. My Spy Adventure. 2013. (Funny Fill-Ins Ser.). (ENG., Illus.). 48p. (J). (gr. 3-7). pap. 4.99 (978-1-4263-1644-9(5), National Geographic Children's Bks.) National Geographic Society.

Andrews McMeel Publishing, LLC Staff & Cole, Jeff. Flip & Click Big Book of Games: 100 Games. 2009. (ENG.). 208p. (J). (gr. -1). pap. 11.99 (978-0-7407-8154-4(5)) Andrews McMeel Publishing.

Angel, R. P. G. Angel: Investigator's Casebook. 2005. 160p. (YA). 30.00 (978-1-891153-43-3(9)) Eden Studios, Inc.

Arkham, Thomas. You're It! Tag, Red Rover, & Other Folk Games. 2013. (Illus.). 48p. (J). pap. (978-1-4222-2507-3(0)) Mason Crest.

—You're It! Tag, Red Rover, & Other Folk Games. Jabbour, Alan, ed. 2012. (North American Folklore for Youth Ser.). (Illus.). 48p. (J). (gr. 4). 19.95 (978-1-4222-2496-0(1)) Mason Crest.

Astacio, Mrinali Alvarez, illus. Pon, Pon: A Jugar con el Bebé! 2007. (SPA.). 28p. 14.95 (978-0-8477-1575-6(2)) Univ. of Puerto Rico Pr.

Atlantic, Leonard. We Play with Things Around the House! 2017. (Ways to Play Ser.). 24p. (J). (gr. k-k). pap. 8.15 **(978-1-4824-6361-3(X))** Stevens, Gareth Publishing LLLP.

Attainment Company, prod. Budget City Game. 2005. (gr. 3-6). suppl. ed. 39.00 (978-1-57861-059-4(1), BC-01E, IEP Resources) Attainment Co., Inc.

—BudgetTown: Budget Town. 2005. (J). mass mkt. 29.00 (978-0-934731-67-6(5), IEP Resources) Attainment Co., Inc.

Austin, Michael Allen. London Bridge Is Falling Down. Austin, Michael Allen, illus. 2011. (Favorite Children's Songs Ser.). (ENG., Illus.). 16p. (J). (gr. -1-2). lib. bdg. 25.64 (978-1-60954-292-4(4), 200096) Child's World, Inc., The.

Author, Oxford. Number Challenge Games Interactive: Champion. 2014. (ENG.). 1p. audio compact disk 191.00 (978-1-874099-91-8(X)) Oxford Univ. Pr., Inc.

—Number Challenge Interactive: Ace. 2014. (ENG.). 1p. audio compact disk 191.00 (978-1-906224-60-8(9)) Oxford Univ. Pr., Inc.

—Number Challenge Interactive: Brainbox. 2014. (ENG.). 1p. audio compact disk 191.00 (978-1-874099-90-1(1)) Oxford Univ. Pr., Inc.

—Number Challenge Interactive Cool, Vol. 3. 2014. (ENG.). 1p. audio compact disk 191.00 (978-1-906224-62-2(5)) Oxford Univ. Pr., Inc.

AZ Books Staff. Colors & Shapes. Petrovskaya, Olga, ed. 2012. (Matching Game Ser.). (ENG.). 18p. (J). (gr. -1-k). spiral bd. 4.95 (978-1-61889-201-0(0)) AZ Bks. LLC.

—Counting. Petrovskaya, Olga, ed. 2012. (Matching Game Ser.). (ENG.). 18p. (J). (gr. -1-k). spiral bd. 4.95 (978-1-61889-200-3(2)) AZ Bks. LLC.

Baker, Sue. Peep-O! Stockham, Jess, illus. 2006. (Blanket Babies Ser.). (ENG.). 12p. (J). (gr. -1-k). bds. (978-1-904550-88-4(6)) Child's Play International Ltd.

Ballantine Books Staff & Jelley, Craig. Minecraft: Exploded Builds: Medieval Fortress: An Official Mojang Book. 2016. (ENG., Illus.). 80p. (gr. 3-7). 18.99 (978-0-399-59321-5(7), Del Rey) Random House Publishing Group.

Bama & White, Sherrie. What Am I? 2011. (Illus.). 43p. (J). pap. (978-1-4620-6149-5(4)) iUniverse, Inc.

Barber, Irene. All about Hurling. 2003. (ENG., Illus.). 32p. pap. 15.95 (978-0-86278-808-7(0)) O'Brien Pr., Ltd., The IRL. Dist: Dufour Editions, Inc.

Barber, Nicola. Ancient Roman Sports & Pastimes. 2010. (Ancient Communities: Roman Life Ser.). 32p. (J). (ENG.). pap. 10.60 (978-1-61532-315-9(5)); (Illus.). (gr. 3-6). lib. bdg. 26.50 (978-1-61532-306-7(6)) Rosen Publishing Group, Inc., The. (PowerKids Pr.).

Barceló, Josefina. Vamos a Jugar. Álvarez, Mrinalí, illus. 2006. (SPA.). (J). 8.95 (978-0-8477-1560-2(4)) Univ. of Puerto Rico Pr.

Barkan, Joanne. Games We Play. 2005. (Real Deal Ser.). (Illus.). 32p. (J). pap. (978-0-7608-9632-7(1)) Sundance/Newbridge Educational Publishing.

Barker, Cicely Mary. How to Host a Flower Fairy Tea Party. 2004. (Flower Fairies Ser.). (ENG., Illus.). 48p. (J). (gr. -1-2). pap. 7.99 (978-0-7232-5360-0(9), Warne) Penguin Young Readers Group.

Barner, Bob. Animals! Matching Game. 2011. (ENG.). 72p. (J). (gr. -1-17). bds. 14.99 (978-1-4521-0055-5(1)) Chronicle Bks. LLC.

Bartl, Allison. 101 Pep-Up Games for Children: Refreshing, Recharging, Refocusing. Puth, Klaus, illus. 2007. (SmartFun Activity Bks.). (ENG.). 160p. pap. 14.95 (978-0-89793-495-4(4)); spiral bd. 19.95 (978-0-89793-496-1(2)) Turner Publishing Co. (Hunter Hse.).

—101 Relaxation Games for Children: Finding a Little Peace & Quiet in Between. Puth, Klaus, illus. 2007. (SmartFun Activity Bks.). (ENG.). 160p. (J). (gr. 3). per. 14.95 (978-0-89793-493-0(8), 1293019, Hunter Hse.) Turner Publishing Co.

Beeson, Sam. White Lies. 2009. 9.99 (978-1-59955-343-6(0)) Cedar Fort, Inc./CFI Distribution.

Bell-Rehwoldt, Sheri. The Kids' Guide to Jumping Rope, 1 vol. 2010. (Kids' Guides). (ENG.). 32p. (gr. 3-4). 27.99 (978-1-4296-5443-2(0), Edge Bks.) Capstone Press of Coughlan Cos.

Benedetti, Debra. Season of Play. Teets, Ashley, illus. 2011. 32p. (J). (978-0-929915-99-9(2)) Headline Bks., Inc.

Bennett, Carson. A Dozen Ways to Play Baseball Without the Ball & Bat. 2007. 48p. 7.56 (978-1-4116-3102-1(1)) Lulu Pr., Inc.

Berendes, Mary. Sports & Games/Los Deportes y Los Juegos. Petelinsek, Kathleen, illus. 2007. (WordBooks/Libros de Palabras Ser.). (SPA & ENG.). 24p. (J). (gr. k-3). 25.64 (978-1-59296-802-2(3), 201099) Child's World, Inc., The.

Berger, Loretta Oleck. Calm down & Play: Activities to Help Impulsive Children. 2003. 76p. (J). pap. 17.95 (978-1-58815-055-4(0), 63565) Childswork/Childsplay.

Berrie, Christine, illus. Bird Bingo. 2012. (ENG.). 160p. (gr. 1-17). bds. 29.95 (978-1-85669-917-4(X)) King, Laurence Publishing GBR. Dist: Hachette Bk. Group.

Beylon, Cathy. Camping Fun Sticker Activity Book. 2003. (Dover Little Activity Books Stickers Ser.). (ENG., Illus.). 4p. (J). (gr. k-3). pap. 1.99 (978-0-486-42626-6(2)) Dover Pubns., Inc.

Big Blue Bubble Inc., Big Blue. My Singing Monsters Search & Find. 2015. (My Singing Monsters Ser.). (ENG., Illus.). 24p. (J). (gr. 1). pap. 11.99 (978-1-4052-7686-3(X)) Egmont Bks., Ltd. GBR. Dist: Independent Pubs. Group.

Binkow, Howard. Howard B. Wigglebottom Learns about Sportsmanship: Winning Isn't Everything. Cornelison, Susan F., illus. 2012. (Howard B. Wigglebottom Ser.). 32p. (J). (gr. -1-2). 15.00 (978-0-9826165-6-7(2), We Do Listen) We Do Listen Foundation.

Birchall, Lorrie L. Word Family Game Boards. 2012. 86p. pap. 12.95 (978-0-9857816-1-3(0)) Birchall Publishing.

The Birthday Bug, 6 Pack. (Story Steps Ser.). (gr. k-2). 29.00 (978-0-7635-9575-3(6)) Rigby Education.

Boase, Petra. Games I Can Play: Loads of Fun Things for Kids to Do, Shown Step by Step. 2016. (ENG., Illus.). 48p. (J). (gr. -1 — 1). 7.99 (978-1-86147-405-6(9), Armadillo) Anness Publishing GBR. Dist: National Bk. Network.

Bodach, Vijaya Khisty. Pictografías. 2010. (Hacer Gráficas/Making Graphs Ser.). (MUL, SPA & ENG.). 32p. (gr. 1-2). lib. bdg. 27.32 (978-1-4296-6101-0(1), A+ Bilingue/Bilingual) Capstone Press of Coughlan Cos.

Bone, Emily. 50 Brain Games. 2008. (Activity Cards Ser.). (Illus.). 50p. (J). (gr. -1-3). 9.99 (978-0-7945-2075-5(8), Usborne) EDC Publishing.

—50 Secret Codes. 2008. (Activity Cards Ser.). 50p. pap. 9.99 (978-0-7945-2074-8(X), Usborne) EDC Publishing.

Boothroyd, Jennifer. From Marbles to Video Games: How Toys Have Changed. 2011. (Comparing Past & Present Ser.). pap. 45.32 (978-0-7613-8391-8(3)); pap. 7.95 (978-0-7613-7841-9(3)); (ENG., Illus.). 32p. lib. bdg. 26.60 (978-0-7613-6746-8(2)) Lerner Publishing Group.

Boyd, Anne, ed. Games 411. 2003. 200p. spiral bd. 49.00 (978-1-931625-21-0(2)) Reed Business Information.

Bozzo, Linda & Library. At Play in the Past, Present, & Future. 2010. (Imagining the Future Ser.). (Illus.). 24p. (J). lib. bdg. 22.60 (978-0-7660-3436-5(4), Enslow Elementary) Enslow Pubs., Inc.

BradyGames Staff & Deats, Adam. Prince of Persia: Warrior Within Official Strategy Guide. 2004. (Signature Ser.). (ENG., Illus.). 176p. pap. 15.99 (978-0-7440-0482-3(9)) Pearson Education.

Brian, Sarah Jane. Brainiac's Mindbenders: Fun Activities for Geniuses of All Ages. 2005. (Activity Journal Ser.). (Illus.). 128p. (J). act. bk. ed. 12.99 (978-0-88088-591-1(2)) Peter Pauper Pr. Inc.

Brilliant Board Games. 2004. (How 2 Kits Ser.). (Illus.). 48p. (J). (978-1-84229-930-2(1)) Top That! Publishing PLC.

Brooks, Felicity. Finger Rhymes. Gregorio, Giuliana, illus. 2010. (Rhyming Look & Say Ser.). 12p. (J). bds. 8.99 (978-0-7945-2780-8(9), Usborne) EDC Publishing.

—Messy Baby. 2005. (Busy Baby Board Books Ser.). 10p. (J). 8.95 (978-0-7945-0964-4(9), Usborne) EDC Publishing.

—Playtime Baby. 2005. (Busy Baby Board Books Ser.). 10p. (J). 8.95 (978-0-7945-0965-1(7), Usborne) EDC Publishing.

Bryant, Nick & Summers, Rowan. Amazing Spot What! (Illus.). 32p. (J). (978-1-86515-727-6(9)) Hinkler Bks. Pty, Ltd. AUS. Dist: Hinkler Bks. Pty, Ltd.

—Spectacular Spot What. (Illus.). 32p. (J). (978-1-86515-916-4(6)) Hinkler Bks. Pty, Ltd. AUS. Dist: Hinkler Bks. Pty, Ltd.

Bucken, Hajo. Button, Button, Who's Got the Button? (ENG., Illus.). 80p. pap. 15.95 (978-0-86315-214-6(7), 1915) Floris Bks. GBR. Dist: SteinerBooks, Inc.

Buckingham, Gabriella, illus. The Wheels on the Bus & Other Action Rhymes. 2013. (ENG.). 16p. (J). (gr. -1-12). bds. 7.99 (978-1-84322-830-1(0), Armadillo) Anness Publishing GBR. Dist: National Bk. Network.

Buffy, R. P. G. Military Monster Squad: Initiative Sourcebook. 2005. 128p. (YA). pap. 27.00 (978-1-891153-69-3(2)) Eden Studios, Inc.

Bussell, Linda. Probabilidad con Juegos y Diversión. 2008. (Matemáticas en Nuestro Mundo - Nivel 3 (Math in Our World - Level 3) Ser.). (SPA.). 24p. (gr. 2-5). (J). lib. bdg. 22.00 (978-0-8368-9298-7(4)); pap. 8.15 (978-0-8368-9397-7(2)) Stevens, Gareth Publishing LLLP. (Weekly Reader Leveled Readers).

—Probability with Fun & Games. 2008. (Math in Our World - Level 3 Ser.). 24p. (gr. 2-5). (J). lib. bdg. 22.00 (978-0-8368-9290-1(9)); pap. 8.15 (978-0-8368-9389-2(1)) Stevens, Gareth Publishing LLLP. (Weekly Reader Leveled Readers).

Butterfield, Moira. Toys & Games Around the World. 2016. (Children Like Us Ser.). (ENG., Illus.). 32p. (J). (gr. 3-3). pap. 10.58 (978-1-5026-0850-5(2), 1399892) Cavendish Square Publishing.

Calaboose. 2005. 12.95 (978-0-9764394-2-4(5)) Live Oak Games.

Campaign Map Packs: Village. 2005. (YA). 9.95 (978-0-9770071-7-2(0)) Paizo Inc.

Candyland Surprize Ink! Book & Marker. 2004. 24p. (J). 5.99 (978-1-932125-81-8(7)) Giddy Up, LLC.

Canetti, Yanitzia. ABeCedario Musical. 2010. (SPA.). 40p. (J). pap. 8.99 (978-1-59835-222-1(9), BrickHouse Education) Cambridge BrickHouse, Inc.

—Adivina, Adivinador: ¿Quién está Escondido? 2010. (SPA.). 24p. (J). pap. (978-1-59835-126-2(5), BrickHouse Education) Cambridge BrickHouse, Inc.

—De quien es esta Sombra? Adivina Adivinador. 2010. (J). pap. 8.99 (978-1-59835-129-3(X), BrickHouse Education) Cambridge BrickHouse, Inc.

—Guess Who? Who Crosses Here? 2010. (ENG.). 24p. (J). pap. 8.99 (978-1-59835-136-1(2), BrickHouse Education) Cambridge BrickHouse, Inc.

—Guess Who? Who's Hiding? 2010. (ENG.). 24p. (J). pap. 8.99 (978-1-59835-137-8(0), BrickHouse Education) Cambridge BrickHouse, Inc.

—Guess Who? Who's Looking at Me? 2010. (ENG.). (J). pap. 8.99 (978-1-59835-138-5(9), BrickHouse Education) Cambridge BrickHouse, Inc.

—Guess Who? Who's Shadow Is This? 2010. (ENG.). 24p. (J). pap. 8.99 (978-1-59835-140-8(0)) Cambridge BrickHouse, Inc.

—Guess Who? Whose Skin Is This? 2010. (ENG.). (J). pap. 8.99 (978-1-59835-142-2(7), BrickHouse Education) Cambridge BrickHouse, Inc.

—Guess Who? Whose Tracks Are These? 2010. (ENG.). 24p. (J). pap. 8.99 (978-1-59835-141-5(9), BrickHouse Education) Cambridge BrickHouse, Inc.

—Musical ABCs. 2010. 40p. (J). pap. 8.99 (978-1-59835-221-4(0), BrickHouse Education) Cambridge BrickHouse, Inc.

—Quien cruza por Aqui? Adivina, Adivinador. 2010. (SPA.). 24p. (J). pap. 8.99 (978-1-59835-125-5(7), BrickHouse Education) Cambridge BrickHouse, Inc.

—Quien deja esta Huella? Adivina, Adivinador. 2010. (SPA.). 24p. (J). pap. 8.99 (978-1-59835-130-9(3), BrickHouse Education) Cambridge BrickHouse, Inc.

—¿Quién se oculta tras la Luz? 2010. (SPA.). 24p. (J). pap. 8.99 (978-1-59835-128-6(1), BrickHouse Education) Cambridge BrickHouse, Inc.

—¿Quién tiene esta Piel? 2010. (SPA.). 24p. (J). pap. 8.99 (978-1-59835-131-6(1), BrickHouse Education) Cambridge BrickHouse, Inc.

—Rhyming Tongue Twisters Animals. 2010. 32p. (J). 6.99 (978-1-59835-269-6(5), BrickHouse Education) Cambridge BrickHouse, Inc.

—Rhyming Tongue-Twisters Art. 2010. pap. 6.99 (978-1-59835-261-0(X), BrickHouse Education) Cambridge BrickHouse, Inc.

—Rhyming Tongue-Twisters Math. 2010. 32p. (J). pap. 6.99 (978-1-59835-263-4(6), BrickHouse Education) Cambridge BrickHouse, Inc.

—Rhyming Tongue Twisters Science: Science. 2010. 32p. (J). pap. 6.99 (978-1-59835-265-8(2), BrickHouse Education) Cambridge BrickHouse, Inc.

—Trabalenguas Cientificos. 2010. 32p. (J). pap. 6.99 (978-1-59835-264-1(4), BrickHouse Education) Cambridge BrickHouse, Inc.

—Trabalenguas Zoológicos. 2010. (SPA.). 32p. (J). pap. 6.99 *(978-1-59835-159-0(1)*, BrickHouse Education) Cambridge BrickHouse, Inc.

Care Bears: Caring & Sharing. 2005. (Illus.). 100p. (YA). *(978-1-59524-046-0(2))* Giddy Up, LLC.

Care Bears Water Wow! Book. 2005. (J). per. 6.99 *(978-1-59524-055-2(1))* Giddy Up, LLC.

Carney, Elizabeth & National Geographic Kids Staff. Angry Birds Playground - Atlas: A Global Geography Adventure. 2016. (ENG., Illus.). 128p. (J). (gr. -1-3). pap. 9.99 *(978-1-4263-2459-8(6)*, National Geographic Children's Bks.) National Geographic Society.

Carson-Dellosa Publishing Staff. Puzzles & Games for Math, Grade 1. 2010. (Home Workbooks Ser.). (ENG.). 64p. (gr. 1-1). pap. 4.49 *(978-1-60418-791-5(3))* Carson-Dellosa Publishing, LLC.

—Puzzles & Games for Math, Grade 3. 2010. (Home Workbooks Ser.). (ENG.). 64p. (gr. 3-3). pap. 4.49 *(978-1-60418-803-5(0))* Carson-Dellosa Publishing, LLC.

—Puzzles & Games, Grade 1. 2010. (Home Workbooks Ser.). (ENG.). 64p. (gr. 1-1). pap. 4.49 *(978-1-60418-793-9(X))* Carson-Dellosa Publishing, LLC.

Carson-Dellosa Publishing Staff, compiled by. Puzzles & Games for Beginners, Grade K. 2010. (Home Workbooks Ser.). (ENG.). 64p. (gr. k-k). pap. 4.49 *(978-1-60418-778-6(6))* Carson-Dellosa Publishing, LLC.

—Puzzles & Games for Math, Grade 2. 2010. (Home Workbooks Ser.). (ENG.). 64p. (gr. 2-2). pap. 4.49 *(978-1-60418-798-4(0))* Carson-Dellosa Publishing, LLC.

—Puzzles & Games, Grade 2. 2010. (Home Workbooks Ser.). (ENG.). 64p. (gr. 2-2). pap. 4.49 *(978-1-60418-799-1(9))* Carson-Dellosa Publishing, LLC.

Carter, David A. Blue 2: A Pop-Up Book for Children of All Ages. Carter, David A., illus. ltd. ed. 2006. (ENG., Illus.). 18p. (J). 250.00 *(978-1-4169-2717-4(4)*, Little Simon) Little Simon.

—Blue 2 Vol. 2: A Pop-Up Book for Children of All Ages. Carter, David A., illus. 2006. (ENG., Illus.). 18p. (J). (gr. 2-5). 29.99 *(978-1-4169-1781-6(0)*, Little Simon) Little Simon.

Cartwright, Stephen, illus. Ludo. 2004. (Farmyard Tales Card Games Ser.). (J). 12.95 *(978-0-7945-0310-9(1)*, Usborne) EDC Publishing.

Cartwright, Stephen & Blundell, Kim, illus. Snakes & Ladders. 2004. (Farmyard Tales Card Games Ser.). (J). 12.95 *(978-0-7945-0312-3(8)*, Usborne) EDC Publishing.

Cassidy, Maura A. Go Ask Your Father! 2003. (YA). mass mkt. *(978-0-9742866-0-0(5))* Go Ask Anyone, Inc.

Cassone, Chris, creator. The Great Central Park Treasure Hunt: Interactive Orienteering Map of NYC's Famous Park. 2004. (YA). 24.95 *(978-0-9749809-0-4(0))* Treasure Hunt Adventures, Inc.

Castellano Boyum, Marie. More Simply Super Storytimes: Programming Ideas for Ages 3-6. 2006. (Illus.). 172p. (J). (gr. -1-1). per. 16.95 *(978-1-932146-29-5(6)*, Upstart Bks.) Highsmith Inc.

Caulson, Kathleen. Power Reading: Games. Caulson, Kathleen, illus. 2005. (Illus.). (J). 76p. (gr. 2-4). 29.95 *(978-1-883186-98-2(6)*, PPMXG2-3); 88p. (gr. 4-5). 79.95 *(978-1-883186-99-9(4)*, PPMXG45) National Reading Styles Institute, Inc.

—Power Reading: Games/Mixed P1. 2005. (Illus.). 76p. (J). (gr. k-2). 29.95 *(978-1-883186-97-5(8)*, PPMXGP1) National Reading Styles Institute, Inc.

Cernek, Kim. Preschool Songs & Fingerplays: Building Language Experience Through Rhythm & Movement. 2006. (Early Learning Ser.). (Illus.). 128p. (J). (gr. -1-1). per. 13.99 *(978-1-59198-223-4(5))* Creative Teaching Pr., Inc.

Chambers, Veronica. Double Dutch: A Celebration of Jump Rope, Rhyme, & Sisterhood. 2007. (Illus.). 64p. (J). 19.00 *(978-1-4223-6701-8(0))* DIANE Publishing Co.

Changing Seasons Matching Game. 2005. (J). 14.99 *(978-0-7353-0623-3(0))* Galison.

Chanko, Pamela & Michael, Joan. What Hat Goes with That? 2017. (Rookie Toddler(tm) Ser.). (ENG.). 12p. (J). bds. 6.95 *(978-0-531-22979-8(3)*, Children's Pr.) Scholastic Library Publishing.

Chase, Sherry. Matthew Loves to Play Nintendo Game Cube. 2011. 20p. pap. 10.03 *(978-1-4634-4460-0(5))* AuthorHouse.

Chevat, Richie. The Marble Book. Cooper, Martha, photos by. 2004. (Illus.). 186p. (J). (gr. k-4). reprint ed. pap. 10.00 *(978-0-7567-7776-0(3))* DIANE Publishing Co.

Chronicle Books Staff. Around the World Matching Game. Player, Micah, illus. 2013. (ENG.). 72p. (J). (gr. -1-1). bds. 14.99 *(978-1-4521-1699-0(7))* Chronicle Bks. LLC.

—Fantastical Fairies Matching Game. Medeiros, Giovana, illus. 2015. (ENG.). 36p. (J). (gr. -1-1). bds. 14.99 *(978-1-4521-3083-5(3))* Chronicle Bks. LLC.

—Star Wars Lightsaber Thumb Wrestling. 2013. (ENG., Illus.). 16p. (J). (gr. 1-17). 12.99 *(978-1-4521-2574-9(0))* Chronicle Bks. LLC.

Chutes & Ladders Suprize Ink! Book & Marker. 2004. 24p. (J). 5.99 *(978-1-932125-80-1(9))* Giddy Up, LLC.

Ciencin, Scott. Cry of the Banshee! Francavilla, Francesco, illus. 2008. 48p. (J). pap. *(978-0-545-03981-9(9))* Scholastic, Inc.

—Escape from Blackbeard's Curse! Francavilla, Francesco, illus. 2007. 48p. (J). pap. *(978-0-545-03767-9(0))* Scholastic, Inc.

Clark, Diane C., et al. A Kid's Guide to Washington, D. C. Brown, Richard, illus. rev. ed. 2008. (ENG.). 160p. (J). (gr. 1-4). pap. 15.99 *(978-0-15-206125-8(8))* Houghton Mifflin Harcourt Publishing Co.

Clarke, Phillip. Seas & Oceans Game Kid Kit. 2004. (Kid Kits Ser.). 64p. (J). 15.99 *(978-1-58086-730-6(8))*; 15.99 *(978-1-58086-728-3(6)*, Usborne) EDC Publishing.

Cloud 9. 2003. mass mkt. 9.95 *(978-1-932359-06-0(0))* Out of the Box Publishing, Inc.

Coast-to-Coast Games. (Backseat Bks.). 80p. (J). pap. 3.95 *(978-0-528-96548-7(4))* Rand McNally.

Correr, Saltar y Brincar. (SPA., Illus.). (J). pap. 6.95 *(978-950-11-0123-2(1)*, SGM123) Sigmar ARG. Dist: Continental Bk. Co., Inc.

Corrie, William E., 3rd & Corrie, Linda D. Another Man's Treasure: A Guide to Shadazar. Breed, Jessica & Corrie, Linda D., eds. 2003. (Illus.). 64p. (YA). per. 15.00 *(978-0-9740096-1-2(X)*, HWE1100) HinterWelt Enterprises, LLC.

—Shades of Earth: Earth History with a Twist Breed, Jessica & Corrie, Linda D., eds. 2003. (Illus.). 240p. (YA). per. 30.00 *(978-0-9740096-2-9(8)*, HWE2000) HinterWelt Enterprises, LLC.

Crabtree Publishing Company Staff & Iorizzo, Carrie. Gambling. 2012. (ENG., Illus.). 48p. (J). *(978-0-7787-2184-0(1))*; pap. *(978-0-7787-2191-8(4))* Crabtree Publishing Co.

Creative Team of Weldon Owen. 101 Things to Do Before You Grow Up: Fun Activities for You to Check off Your List. 2015. (101 Things Ser.). (ENG.). 144p. (J). (gr. 3-7). spiral bd. 12.95 *(978-1-63322-003-4(6))* Quarto Publishing Group USA.

Crick, Stephanie. Peek-a-Boo Moon. DeFazio, Deborah, illus. 2004. 16p. (J). per. 9.95 *(978-0-9746397-3-4(7))* Pinefield Publishing.

Crook, Lydia. Paper Play. Running Press Staff, ed. 2013. (ENG., Illus.). 112p. (J). (gr. -1-17). pap. 12.95 *(978-0-7624-4957-6(8)*, Running Pr. Kids) Running Pr. Bk. Pubs.

Crossingham, John & Kalman, Bobbie. Pass It Lacrosse. 2008. (Sports Starters Ser.). (ENG., Illus.). 32p. (J). (gr. 3-7). pap. *(978-0-7787-3173-3(1))* Crabtree Publishing Co.

Curry, Don, ed. Jungle Fun: Puzzles & Games. 2008. 10p. (J). bds. 9.99 *(978-0-696-23491-0(2))* Meredith Bks.

Dahlstrom, Kathryn. Street Games. Date not set. (Good News Club Ser.). (J). pap. 4.99 *(978-1-55976-829-0(0))* CEF Pr.

Danks, Fiona, et al. Nature's Playground: Activities, Crafts, & Games to Encourage Children to Get Outdoors. 2007. (ENG., Illus.). 192p. (J). (gr. 2-4). pap. 19.95 *(978-1-55652-723-4(3))* Chicago Review Pr., Inc.

Daronco, Mickey & Ohanesian, Diane. The Game: Set Of 6. 2nd rev. ed. 2004. (BuildUp Ser.). (J). pap. 27.00 net. *(978-1-4108-1533-0(1))* Benchmark Education Co.

De Ballon, N. V., contrib. by. Alphabet Dot to Dot. 2004. (ENG., Illus.). 64p. (J). pap. 4.95 *(978-1-4027-1835-9(7))* Sterling Publishing Co., Inc.

Dennis, Yvonne Wakim & Hirschfelder, Arlene. A Kid's Guide to Native American History: More Than 50 Activities. 2009. (Kid's Guide Ser.). (ENG.). 256p. (J). (gr. 2-4). pap. 16.95 *(978-1-55652-802-6(7))* Chicago Review Pr., Inc.

Dever, Joe. Caverns of Kalte. 2007. (ENG., Illus.). 320p. (YA). pap. 14.95 *(978-1-906103-20-0(8))* Mongoose Publishing GBR. Dist: Diamond Bk. Distributors.

Dewberry, Melba. Rainy Day Fun. 2016. (We Love Spring! Ser.). 00024p. (J). pap. 8.15 ***(978-1-4824-5503-8(X))*** Stevens, Gareth Publishing LLLP.

Disney Enterprises Staff, ed. Cars Stuck on Stories. 2013. *(978-2-7643-2070-9(1))* Phidal Publishing, Inc./Editions Phidal, Inc.

Do You Want to Play? (Pebble Soup Explorations Ser.). 16p. (gr. -1-18). 31.00 *(978-0-7578-1655-0(X))* Rigby Education.

Do You Want to Play? Small Book. (Pebble Soup Explorations Ser.). 16p. (gr. -1-18). 5.00 *(978-0-7578-1695-6(9))* Rigby Education.

Dodd, Lynley. Gold Star First Readers, 21 bks. Incl. Schnitzel Von Krumm, Dogs Never Climb Trees. (Illus.). 32p. (gr. -1-3). 2004. lib. bdg. 23.00 *(978-0-8368-4092-6(5)*, Gareth Stevens Learning Library); (Illus.). Set lib. bdg. 418.00 o.p. *(978-0-8368-4167-1(0))* Stevens, Gareth Publishing LLLP.

Dolby, Karen & Fischel, Emma. Spooks' Surprise. 2004. (Young Puzzle Adventures Ser.). (Illus.). 32p. (J). (gr. 2-18). pap. 4.95 *(978-0-7945-0234-8(2)*, Usborne) EDC Publishing.

Dorling Kindersley Publishing Staff. LEGO City: Build Your Own Adventure. 2016. (ENG.). 80p. (J). (gr. 2-4). 24.99 *(978-1-4654-5046-3(7)*, DK Children) Dorling Kindersley Publishing, Inc.

—Mind Benders. 2013. (ENG.). 32p. (J). (gr. 2-5). 19.99 *(978-1-4654-1456-4(8)*, DK Children) Dorling Kindersley Publishing, Inc.

—Playtime. 2012. (Touch & Feel Ser.). (ENG.). 12p. (J). (gr. -1-k). bds. 6.99 *(978-1-4654-0166-3(0)*, DK Children) Dorling Kindersley Publishing, Inc.

Douglas, Peter. Lacrosse: Facing off on the Field. 2017. (Preparing for Game Day Ser.: Vol. 10). (ENG.). (YA). (gr. 7-12). 24.95 ***(978-1-4222-3918-6(7))*** Mason Crest.

Doyle, Richard. Fairyland Notebook. 2003. (Dover Little Activity Bks.). (ENG.). 64p. (J). (gr. 3-5). pap. 1.50 *(978-0-486-42643-3(2))* Dover Pubns., Inc.

Drake, Jane & Love, Ann. Get Outside: The Kids Guide to Fun in the Great Outdoors. Collins, Heather, illus. 2012. (ENG.). 176p. (J). (gr. 1-5). 16.95 *(978-1-55453-802-7(5))* Kids Can Pr., Ltd. CAN. Dist: Hachette Bk. Group.

Drew, David. Mystery Monsters: A Game for Two or More Players. 2007. (Informazing Ser.). (Illus.). 16p. (J). (gr. -1). pap. *(978-0-947328-53-5(X)*, Rigby) Pearson Education Australia.

Drimmer, Stephanie Warren. Brain Bogglers: Over 100 Games & Puzzles to Reveal the Mysteries of Your Mind. 2017. (ENG., Illus.). 176p. (J). (gr. 3-7). pap. 12.99 *(978-1-4263-2423-9(5)*, National Geographic Children's Bks.) National Geographic Society.

Dunn, Phoebe, illus. Guess Who I Am... gif. ed. 2005. 10p. (J). (gr. -1). per., bds. 7.99 *(978-1-57791-175-3(X))* Brighter Minds Children's Publishing.

Eckdahl, Judith & Eckdahl, Kathryn. A Collection of Street Games. O'Regan, Lucy, ed. Miranda, Pedro, illus. 2005. 42p. pupil's gde. ed. 13.95 *(978-0-9767200-0-3(0))* Lesen Pub.

Eden Odyssey D20 Staff. Waysides: The Book of Taverns. 2005. (YA). pap. 30.00 *(978-1-891153-54-9(4))* Eden Studios, Inc.

Edley, Joe, et al. Bananagrams! For Kids. 2010. (ENG., Illus.). 156p. (J). (gr. 2-12). pap. 10.95 *(978-0-7611-5844-8(8)*, 15844) Workman Publishing Co., Inc.

Egmont UK, Egmont. My Singing Monsters. 2015. (My Singing Monsters Ser.). (ENG., Illus.). 96p. (J). (gr. 1). pap. 12.99 *(978-1-4052-7685-6(1))* Egmont Bks., Ltd. GBR. Dist: Independent Pubs. Group.

Einon, D. Juegos para Aprender. (SPA.). 178p. *(978-84-95456-37-3(0)*, 86756) Ediciones Oniro S.A.

Eisenberg, Rebecca & Frailey, Cheris. Webber Functional Communication Games: Gb146. 2006. (J). 69.95 *(978-1-58650-689-6(7))* Super Duper Pubns.

Elliott, Lynne. Children & Games in the Middle Ages. 2004. (Medieval World Ser.). (ENG., Illus.). 32p. (J). pap. *(978-0-7787-1381-4(4))*; lib. bdg. *(978-0-7787-1349-4(0))* Crabtree Publishing Co.

Elton, Richard & Elton, Candice. Every Kid Needs a Rubber Band Launcher. 2007. (J). *(978-1-4236-0268-2(4))* Gibbs Smith, Publisher.

Esbaum, Jill. Angry Birds Playground - Animals: An Around-the-World Habitat Adventure. 2012. (ENG.). 128p. (J). (gr. -1-3). lib. bdg. 21.90 *(978-1-4263-1323-3(3)*, National Geographic Children's Bks.) National Geographic Society.

Esbaum, Jill & National Geographic Kids Staff. Angry Birds Playground: Rain Forest: A Forest Floor to Treetop Adventure. 2016. (ENG., Illus.). 128p. (J). (gr. -1-3). pap. 9.99 *(978-1-4263-2458-1(8)*, National Geographic Children's Bks.) National Geographic Society.

—Animals: An Around-the-World Habitat Adventure. 2012. (ENG., Illus.). 128p. (J). (gr. -1-3). 14.95 *(978-1-4263-1266-3(0)*, National Geographic Children's Bks.) National Geographic Society.

—Dinosaurs: A Prehistoric Adventure! Tempesta, Franco, illus. 2016. (ENG.). 128p. (J). (gr. -1-3). pap. 9.99 *(978-1-4263-2460-4(X)*, National Geographic Children's Bks.) National Geographic Society.

Esparza, Thomas, Jr., prod. Esther's Playhouse, 2 Disk Set. 2004. (Illus.). (J). cd-rom 39.95 *(978-1-879817-49-4(7)*, Children) Star Light Pr.

—Esther's Playhouse, Disk 1. 2004. (J). cd-rom 39.95 *(978-1-879817-40-1(3)*, Children) Star Light Pr.

—Esther's Playhouse, Disk 2. 2004. (Illus.). (J). cd-rom *(978-1-879817-41-8(1)*, Children) Star Light Pr.

—Esther's Playhouse, Disk D. 2004. (Illus.). (J). cd-rom *(978-1-879817-45-6(4)*, Children) Star Light Pr.

Eubanks, Toni & Lombardi, Janet. Let's Play! 2005. (Illus.). 80p. (J). *(978-0-88441-691-3(7))* Girl Scouts of the USA.

Evans, Lory. One-Page Math Games: 30 Super-Easy, Super-Fun, Reproducible Games for Seatwork, Centers, Homework, & More! 2011. (ENG.). 48p. pap. 10.99 *(978-0-545-31475-6(5)*, Teaching Resources) Scholastic, Inc.

Falconer, C. J. Where Is Kitty? 2012. 20p. (-18). pap. 13.77 *(978-1-4669-6094-7(9))* Trafford Publishing.

Familyarcade — Cracking the Character Code. 2003. (J). (gr. 1-6). cd-rom 12.99 *(978-0-633-09040-1(9))* LifeWay Christian Resources.

Feiwel & Friends & Stead, Emily. Fantastic Fidget Spinners. 2017. (ENG., Illus.). 96p. (J). pap. 7.99 ***(978-1-250-18034-6(1)***, 9781250180346) Feiwel & Friends.

Felix, Rebecca. Cool Board Games: Crafting Creative Toys & Amazing Games, 1 vol. 2016. (Cool Toys & Games Ser.). (ENG., Illus.). 32p. (J). (gr. 3-6). lib. bdg. 28.50 *(978-1-68078-046-8(8)*, Checkerboard Library) ABDO Publishing Co.

Felix the Cat/el Gato Felix: A Fun Surprise. 2005. 32p. (J). pap. *(978-0-9762071-1-5(7))* Big City Publishing.

Ferguson, Melissa. Suzanne Collins: Author of the Hunger Games Trilogy. 2016. (Famous Female Authors Ser.). (ENG., Illus.). 32p. (gr. 3-4). pap. 7.95 *(978-1-5157-1334-0(2)*, Snap Bks.) Capstone Press of Coughlan Cos.

Ferri, Francesca. Peek-A-Boo Sea. 2014. (ENG., Illus.). 12p. (J). (gr. -1 — 1). 8.99 *(978-0-7641-6724-9(3))* Barron's Educational Series, Inc.

Ferri, Francesca, illus. Peek-A-Boo. 2005. (ENG.). 10p. (J). 8.99 *(978-0-7641-5851-3(1))* Barron's Educational Series, Inc.

Feyyaz. Das F Prinzip, 1 vol. aut. ltd. num. ed. 2008. (ENG, FRE & GER.). 60p. 115.00 *(978-3-937718-91-0(5))* DAAB Media Gmbh DEU. Dist: Innovative Logistics.

Filella, Nacho, et al. Los Juegos. 2005. (El Juego de Leer Ser.). (SPA.). 6p. 5.99 *(978-84-272-6683-4(9))* Molino, Editorial ESP. Dist: Santillana USA Publishing Co., Inc.

Fish Eat Fish. 2003. mass mkt. 19.95 *(978-1-932359-11-4(7))* Out of the Box Publishing, Inc.

Fisher, David. Cool Jump-Rope Tricks You Can Do! A Fun Way to Keep Kids 6 to 12 Fit Year-'Round. 2014. (ENG., Illus.). 160p. (J). (gr. 1-7). pap. 11.99 *(978-1-4814-1231-5(0))* Meadowbrook Pr.

Four Ace Reverse. 2004. (Formula Fun Ser.). (Illus.). 48p. (J). *(978-1-84229-583-0(7))* Top That! Publishing PLC.

Francis, Suzanne. How to Survive When (You Think) There's Nothing to Do. 2004. (Illus.). 80p. (J). pap. *(978-0-439-57906-3(6))* Scholastic, Inc.

Frank, Paul. Matching Game. 2008. (ENG., Illus.). 72p. (J). (gr. -1-17). bds. 14.95 *(978-0-8118-6352-0(2))* Chronicle Bks. LLC.

Free Spirit Publishing Staff & Stein, Deborah Jiang. More Feelings. 2009. (In a Jar(r) Ser.). (ENG.). (J). 9.99 *(978-1-57542-912-0(8))* Free Spirit Publishing, Inc.

Fremont, Victoria, et al. Nutcracker. 2012. (Dover Little Activity Bks.). (ENG., Illus.). 64p. (J). (gr. k-3). pap., act. bk. ed. 1.99 *(978-0-486-40494-3(3))* Dover Pubns., Inc.

Frost & Fur: The Explorer's Guide to the Frozen Lands. 2004. (Illus.). (YA). lib. bdg. 32.95 *(978-0-9728197-5-6(4)*, MKY2201) MonkeyGod Enterprises.

Fullman, Joe. Origami Games. 2016. (Amazing Origami Ser.). (ENG.). 32p. (J). (gr. 2-3). pap. 10.50 *(978-1-4824-4159-8(4))* Stevens, Gareth Publishing LLLP.

Games: KinderWords Individual Title Six-Packs. (Kinderstarters Ser.). 8p. (gr. -1-1). 21.00 *(978-0-7635-8692-8(7))* Rigby Education.

Gannon, Joe. Fun & Games: How to Play More Than 70 of the World's Greatest Games for Two or More Players. 2006. (Illus.). 80p. pap. *(978-1-59412-154-8(0))* Mud Puddle, Inc.

Garrett, Joseph. Stampy's Lovely Book. 2016. (ENG., Illus.). 72p. (J). (gr. 2-5). 9.99 *(978-0-399-55543-5(9)*, Random Hse. Bks. for Young Readers) Random Hse. Children's Bks.

Gave, Marc. Number Games Around the World & Juegos de números alrededor del Mundo: 6 English, 6 Spanish Adaptations 2011. (Navigators Ser.). (ENG & SPA.). (J). instr.'s gde. ed. 97.00 net. *(978-1-4108-1765-5(2))* Benchmark Education Co.

Gavitt's Stock Exchange. 2003. mass mkt. 12.95 *(978-1-932359-10-7(9))* Out of the Box Publishing, Inc.

Gelinas, Ben, et al. The World of Thedas, Vol. 1. Marshall, Dave, ed. 2013. (ENG., Illus.). 184p. 39.99 *(978-1-61655-115-5(1))* Dark Horse Comics.

Get Outdoors, 4 vols., Set 2. Incl. Camping & Hiking. Champion, Neil. lib. bdg. 25.25 *(978-1-4488-3295-8(0))*; Mountain Biking. Mason, Paul. lib. bdg. 25.25 *(978-1-4488-3296-5(9))*; Sailing. Porter, Suzie. lib. bdg. 25.25 *(978-1-4488-3297-2(7))*; Skiing. Gifford, Clive. lib. bdg. 25.25 *(978-1-4488-3298-9(5))*; (J). (gr. 4-6). (Get Outdoors Ser.). (Illus.). 32p. 2011. Set lib. bdg. 95.80 *(978-1-4488-3308-5(6)*, PowerKids Pr.) Rosen Publishing Group, Inc., The.

Gibson, R. Juggling. 2009. (How to Make Ser.). 32p. (J). pap. 7.99 *(978-0-7945-2476-0(1)*, Usborne) EDC Publishing.

Gibson, Ray. I Can Cut & Stick, I Can Crayon, I Can Finger Paint, I Can Draw Animals, I Can Count, I Can Add up & Fun with Numbers. 2004. (Playtime Ser.). (Illus.). 224p. (J). pap., act. bk. ed. 17.95 *(978-0-7945-0369-7(1)*, Usborne) EDC Publishing.

—Things That Move Kid Kit. 2004. (Playtime Ser.). 32p. (J). lib. bdg. 12.95 *(978-1-58086-593-7(3))* EDC Publishing.

Giddy Up Staff. Transformers Gears & Games. 2009. (Color-n-Carry Ser.). (J). 5.99 *(978-1-59524-265-5(1))* Giddy Up, LLC.

Giddy Up Staff, contrib. by. Dora the Explorer ColorBlast. 2009. 24p. 7.99 *(978-1-932125-98-6(1))* Giddy Up, LLC.

—Dora Water Wow! Book. 2009. 6.99 *(978-1-59524-088-0(8))* Giddy Up, LLC.

—Hello Kitty ColorBlast. 2009. 24p. (J). 7.99 *(978-1-932125-96-2(5))* Giddy Up, LLC.

—My Little Pony Water Wow! Book. 2009. 6.99 *(978-1-59524-056-9(X))* Giddy Up, LLC.

—Sesame Street Water Wow! Book. 2005. 6.99 *(978-1-59524-089-7(6))* Giddy Up, LLC.

—Spongebob Water Wow! Book. 2005. 6.99 *(978-1-59524-053-8(5))* Giddy Up, LLC.

Girard, Alexander. Alexander Girard Memory Game. 2012. (ENG.). 15.95 *(978-1-934429-76-1(7))* AMMO Bks., LLC.

Glenn, Joshua & Larsen, Elizabeth Foy. Unbored Games: Serious Fun for Everyone. Leone, Tony et al, illus. 2014. (ENG.). 176p. pap. 16.00 *(978-1-62040-706-6(X)*, 9781620407066) Bloomsbury Publishing USA.

Gob of Games. Date not set. (J). Vol. 1. pap. 2.95 *(978-1-57122-062-2(3))* Vol. 2. pap. 2.95 *(978-1-57122-063-9(1))* Nickel Pr.

Golding, Julia. Cat's Cradle. 2004. (Whizz Kits Ser.). (Illus.). 48p. (J). *(978-1-84229-949-4(2))* Top That! Publishing PLC.

Goldsack, Gaby. The Ultimate Sleepover Pack. Reeves, Sue, illus. 24p. (J). 79.60 *(978-0-7641-7662-3(5))* Barron's Educational Series, Inc.

Gordon, Lynn. 52 Fun Things to Do in the Car. Johnson, Karen & Synarski, Susan, illus. rev. ed. 2009. (ENG.). 54p. (J). (gr. -1-17). 6.95 *(978-0-8118-6371-1(9))* Chronicle Bks. LLC.

—52 Fun Things to Do on the Plane. Johnson, Karen & Synarski, Susan, illus. rev. ed. 2009. (ENG.). 54p. (J). (gr. -1-17). 6.95 *(978-0-8118-6372-8(7))* Chronicle Bks. LLC.

Gorman, Carol. Games. 2007. (ENG.). 288p. (J). (gr. 5-7). 17.99 *(978-0-06-057027-9(X))* HarperCollins Pubs.

Gow, Kailin. Activities Guide for 365 Days of the Year! Fun Things to Do for Kids & Grown-Ups That'll Help Develop Creativity, Social Skills, & Self-confidence! 2003. (Gifted Girls Ser.). 167p. (YA). pap., act. bk. ed. 19.95 *(978-0-9714776-6-7(3))* Sparklesoup LLC.

Grée, Alain. Alain Grée Animals Matching Game. 2016. (ENG., Illus.). 36p. (J). (gr. -1 — 1). 14.99 *(978-1-4521-3854-1(0))* Chronicle Bks. LLC.

Green, Sara. Minecraft. (Minecraft Ser.). 24p. (J). (gr. 3-8). 2017. pap. 7.99 ***(978-1-61891-269-5(0))*** 2016. (ENG., Illus.). 25.95 *(978-1-62617-410-8(5))* Bellwether Media. (Pilot Bks.).

—Parker Brothers. 2017. (Brands We Know Ser.). (ENG., Illus.). 24p. (J). (gr. 3-8). lib. bdg. 25.95 ***(978-1-62617-654-6(X)***, Pilot Bks.) Bellwether Media.

Gregory, Josh. Minecraft: Guide to Animals. 2017. (21st Century Skills Innovation Library: Unofficial Guides). (ENG., Illus.). 32p. (J). (gr. 4-8). lib. bdg. 29.93 *(978-1-63472-194-3(2)*, 209348) Cherry Lake Publishing.

Gryski, Camilla. Camilla Gryski's Favorite String Games. Sankey, Tom, illus. 2005. 48p. *(978-0-439-77939-5(1))* Scholastic, Inc.

Guicciardini, Desideria & McNicholas, Shelagh, illus. Hop, Skip & Jump. 2008. (Usborne Baby Board Bks.). 8p. (J). (gr. -1). bds. 15.99 incl. audio compact disk *(978-0-7945-1914-8(8)*, Usborne) EDC Publishing.

Gunzi, Christiane. Pigs in Pink. 2004. (Animal Pairs Ser.). (Illus.). 12p. (J). (gr. -1-k). 5.95 *(978-1-58728-240-9(2)*, Two-Can Publishing) T&N Children's Publishing.

Gunzl, Christiane & Gunzl, Christiane. Colours. 2014. (ENG., Illus.). 20p. 8.95 *(978-1-907604-24-9(3))* Award Pubns. Ltd. GBR. Dist: Parkwest Pubns., Inc.

Hall, Godfrey. Games: Traditions Around the World. 2007. (Illus.). 48p. (J). reprint ed. 17.00 *(978-1-4223-6682-0(0))* DIANE Publishing Co.

Handford, Martin. Where's Waldo? the Coloring Book. Handford, Martin, illus. 2016. (Where's Waldo? Ser.). (ENG., Illus.). 64p. (J). (gr. -1-3). pap. 12.00 *(978-0-7636-8844-8(4))* Candlewick Pr.

Hannah, Waldron & Magma Books Staff. Magic & Fairy-Tale Dice. 2012. (ENG., Illus.). 14.95 *(978-1-85669-919-8(6))* King, Laurence Publishing GBR. Dist: Hachette Bk. Group.

Hanrahan, Abigail & McSweeny, Catherine. 50 Quick Play Reading Games. 2004. (J). per. 34.95 *(978-0-7606-0535-6(1))* LinguiSystems, Inc.

Hansen, Dustin. Game On! Video Game History from Pong to Pac-Man to Mario, Minecraft, & Beyond. 2016. (Game On Ser.). (ENG., Illus.). 368p. (YA). 19.99 *(978-1-250-08095-0(9)*, 9781250080950) Feiwel & Friends.

Hanson, Sue & Hanson, Jon. All about Mancala: Its History & How to Play. 2003. (Illus.). pap. 17.95 *(978-0-9740175-0-1(7))* Happy Viking Crafts.

Harpster, Steve. 1-100 Dot-to-Dots. 2003. (ENG., Illus.). 64p. (J). pap. 4.95 *(978-1-4027-0714-8(2))* Sterling Publishing Co., Inc.

Harvey, Ken. The 'Fridge Games. Hermes, Mary Sue, illus. 2003. (Life in the 'Fridge Ser.). (J). *(978-1-930093-20-1(9))* Brookfield Reader, Inc., The.

Haws, Ileen. Nothin' 2 Do. 2008. 67p. pap. 9.90 *(978-1-4357-3654-2(0))* Lulu Pr., Inc.

Hazan, Maurice, creator. Resto Presto French. (FRE.). (J). 169.95 *(978-1-932770-58-2(5)*, FC3) Symtalk, Inc.

Head, Jason. Sui Companion Set. 2003. 241p. (YA). per. 14.99 *(978-1-4116-0371-4(0))* Lulu Pr., Inc.

Hello Kitty Water Wow! Book. 2005. (J). per. 6.99 *(978-1-59524-054-5(3))* Giddy Up, LLC.

Henley, Ralph. Action Rhymes & Active Games: Over 200 Bible Story Activities for Ages 2 To 5. 2004. (J). tchr. ed., per. 19.99 *(978-1-933803-02-9(9))* Child Sensitive Communication, LLC.

Hermansson, Casie. Parental Guidance Ratings. 2013. (Hot Topics in Media EBook Ser.). (ENG.). 48p. (J). pap. 15.64 *(978-1-61783-784-5(9))*; (gr. 3-6). lib. bdg. 32.79 *(978-1-61783-734-0(2))* ABDO Publishing Co.

Hodgson, Julie. Fun with Number Rhymes for the Early Years. 2005. (Illus.). 96p. pap. *(978-1-903853-72-6(9))* Brilliant Pubns.

Honig, Bruce. In Pursuit of the Aha! & Ha! Ha! Ha!: Games & Activities for Kids & Their Parents. 2009. 97p. pap. 12.90 *(978-1-4116-2959-2(0))* Lulu Pr., Inc.

Hovanec, Helene & Merrell, Patrick. The Great Outdoors Games & Puzzles: Bring the Outdoors Inside with 100 Mazes, Word Games, Picture Puzzles, Jokes & Riddles, Brainteasers, & Fun-Packed Activities. 2007. (Storey's Games & Puzzles Ser.). (ENG., Illus.). 144p. (J). (gr. 3-8). pap. 9.95 *(978-1-58017-679-8(8)*, 67679) Storey Publishing, LLC.

Huber, Joe M., des. Ice Cream. 2004. (DUT, FRE, GER, JPN & KOR.). (J). 18.00 *(978-0-9761156-0-1(3))* Face 2 Face Games Publishing.

Hudak, Heather C. MotoX. 2015. (J). *(978-1-5105-0002-0(2))* SmartBook Media, Inc.

Human Body Systems Bingo Game. 2008. (Journeys Ser.). 46.60 *(978-1-4042-9532-2(1)*, Rosen Classroom) Rosen Publishing Group, Inc., The.

Human Body Systems Word-picture match cards, Memory game cards, Labeled picture Cards. 2008. (Journeys Ser.). 46.60 *(978-1-4042-9531-5(3)*, Rosen Classroom) Rosen Publishing Group, Inc., The.

Hunt, Rhian G. Acrohelion Campaign Setting. 2004. (Illus.). 284p. per. 24.99 *(978-0-9759166-0-5(2)*, GMC-04-1) Great Mastiff Corp.

Hurley, Jo. Scooby-Doo's Super Fun Book. 2005. (Illus.). 64p. (J). *(978-0-439-70864-7(8))* Scholastic, Inc.

Ice Lake: Skate Circles Around Your Friends. 2003. (YA). 19.95 *(978-0-9764394-0-0(9))* Live Oak Games.

IllusionWorks Staff. Amazing Optical Illusions. 2004. (ENG., Illus.). 32p. (J). (gr. 1-3). 16.95 *(978-1-55297-961-7(X)*, 9781552979617); pap. 6.95 *(978-1-55297-962-4(8)*, 9781552979624) Firefly Bks., Ltd.

Isaac, Dawn. 101 Things for Kids to Do Outside. 2016. (ENG., Illus.). 224p. pap. 19.95 *(978-1-77085-711-7(7)*, 9781770857117) Firefly Bks., Ltd.

Jackson, Demi. Paintball. 2015. (Daredevil Sports Ser.). (ENG., Illus.). 32p. (J). (gr. 1-1). pap. 10.50 *(978-1-4824-2992-3(6))* Stevens, Gareth Publishing LLLP.

Jackson, Stephen. Mirrorworld: The World's Most Addictive Adventure Game Ever! 2004. (ENG., Illus.). 32p. (J). (gr. 3-7). 16.99 *(978-0-09-176929-1(9))* Transworld Publishers Ltd. GBR. Dist: Independent Pubs. Group.

Jasheway, Leigh Anne. 101 Comedy Games for Children & Grown-Ups. 2014. (SmartFun Activity Bks.). (ENG., Illus.). 168p. (gr. 1). pap. 14.95 *(978-0-89793-700-9(7)*, Hunter Hse.) Turner Publishing Co.

Jenkins, Emily S. Quicketty Splits, Original Edition. 2007. (J). spiral bd. 12.95 *(978-0-9752657-0-3(9))* Wisecracker Press, Inc.

John, Scott, text. Becoming A Student of the Game. 2004. (YA). pap. 60.00 *(978-1-879498-84-6(7))* SportAmerica.

Johnson, Paul F. & Halfman, Patti. 50 Quick Play Vocabulary Games. 2004. (YA). per. 34.95 *(978-0-7606-0539-4(4))* LinguiSystems, Inc.

Johnson, Robin. Toys & Games in Different Places. 2017. 24p. (J). ***(978-0-7787-3662-2(8))*** Crabtree Publishing Co.

Jones, Jen. Game Night Parties: Planning a Bash That Makes Your Friends Say Yeah!, 1 vol. 2014. (Perfect Parties Ser.). (ENG.). 32p. (gr. 3-4). lib. bdg. 27.99 *(978-1-4765-4006-1(3)*, Snap Bks.) Capstone Press of Coughlan Cos.

Jones, Stephanie, des. 1-2-3 Look & Say Chunky Flashcards. 2007. (Look & Say Flashcards Ser.). (Illus.). 30p. (J). (gr. -1-k). 9.99 *(978-0-7945-1462-4(6)*, Usborne) EDC Publishing.

Juegos Recreativos para Ninos. 2003.Tr. of Fun Activities for Children. (SPA.). 184p. 35.00 *(978-84-494-2464-9(X)*, GML07104-192212) Oceano Grupo Editoria, S.A. ESP. Dist: Cengage Gale.

KaBOOM! Go Out & Play! Favorite Outdoor Games from KaBOOM! Rose, Julianna, illus. 2012. (ENG.). 104p. (J). (gr. k-4). pap. 11.99 *(978-0-7636-5530-3(9))* Candlewick Pr.

Kadair, Deborah. I Spy in the Louisiana Sky, 1 vol. Kadair, Deborah, illus. 2011. (ENG., Illus.). 32p. (J). (gr. k-3). 16.99 *(978-1-58980-885-0(1))* Pelican Publishing Co., Inc.

Kadair, Deborah Ousley. I Spy in the Texas Sky, 1 vol. Kadair, Deborah Ousley, illus. 2009. (ENG., Illus.). 32p. (J). (gr. k-3). 16.99 *(978-1-58980-654-2(9))* Pelican Publishing Co., Inc.

Kalman, Bobbie. Toys & Games Then & Now. 2013. (ENG., Illus.). 24p. (J). *(978-0-7787-0128-6(X))*; pap. *(978-0-7787-0210-8(3))* Crabtree Publishing Co.

—What Is It? 2011. (ENG., Illus.). 16p. (J). pap. *(978-0-7787-9572-8(1))*; lib. bdg. *(978-0-7787-9547-6(0))* Crabtree Publishing Co.

Kalnes, Stephanie, creator. Viking Adventure: History-in-a-Box-Board-Game, 2. 2004. (Illus.). (YA). 69.95 *(978-0-9761274-0-6(7))* Great Lakes Design.

Kalvitis, David R. The Greatest Dot-to-Dot Super Challenge Book 8. 2010. 48p. (YA). 7.95 *(978-0-9799753-1-8(X))* Monkeying Around.

Kärcher, Gabriele. Games for Kids on Horseback: 13 Ideas for Fun & Safe Horseplay. 2014. (ENG., Illus.). 32p. (gr. 1-5). *(978-1-57076-652-7(5))* Verlhac Editions.

Katz, Karen. ¿Dónde Está el Ombliguito? Ziegler, Argentina Palacios, tr. Katz, Karen, illus. 2004. (SPA., Illus.). 14p. (J). (gr. -1-1). bds. 6.99 *(978-0-689-86977-8(0)*, Libros Para Ninos) Libros Para Ninos.

Kearney, Tom. Buckeyes Big Game. 2005. (Illus.). (J). bds. 10.95 *(978-0-9745454-5-5(7))* Timberwood Pr.

Keith, Sarah A. Chalk-It-up: 22 Awesome Outdoor Games Kids Draw with Chalk. MacLeod, Kit, ed. 2004. (Illus.). (J). mass mkt. 12.00 *(978-0-9665124-1-0(3)*, 014) SundaySchoolNetwork.com.

Kemp, Marion, et al. All Together. Barnes-Murphy, Rowan, illus. Date not set. (Whizz Bang Bumper Bk.). 63p. (J). pap. 129.15 *(978-0-582-18258-5(1))* Addison-Wesley Longman, Ltd. GBR. Dist: Trans-Atlantic Pubns., Inc.

Kennedy, Michelle. The Big Book of Happy: 500 Games & Activities for Ages 2 to 6. 2008. (Illus.). 360p. (J). *(978-1-4351-0544-7(3))* Metro Bks.

Kenney, Karen Latchana. Cool International Parties: Perfect Party Planning for Kids, 1 vol. 2012. (Cool Parties Ser.). (ENG., Illus.). 32p. (J). (gr. 3-6). 28.50 *(978-1-61714-975-7(6))* ABDO Publishing Co.

Kern. Kern Alphabet Deck & Book Set. (Illus.). 15.00 *(978-1-57281-115-7(3)*, AZS99) U.S. Games Systems, Inc.

Kids: Bays & Estuaries. 2005. (J). *(978-1-888631-33-3(3))* Project WET Foundation.

Klutz Editors, creator. Magnetic A to Z. 2005. (Chicken Socks Ser.). (ENG., Illus.). 12p. (J). (gr. -1-3). 12.95 *(978-1-59174-359-0(1))* Klutz.

Klutz Editors, ed. The Most Incredible, Outrageous, Packed-to-The Gills, Bulging-at-the-Seams Sticker Book You've Ever Seen. 2010. (ENG., Illus.). 30p. (J). (gr. -1-3). 12.99 *(978-1-57054-117-9(5))* Klutz.

—TRIPtivities. 2009. (ENG.). 120p. (J). (gr. 3). 9.95 *(978-1-59174-659-1(0))* Klutz.

Knizia, Reiner, des. Rhëinlander. 2005. (FRE, GER, JPN, KOR & SPA.). (YA). *(978-0-9761156-1-8(1))* Face 2 Face Games Publishing.

Kovacs, Vic. Get into Minecraft. 2016. (Get-Into-It Guides). (ENG., Illus.). 32p. (J). (gr. 3-6). *(978-0-7787-2642-5(8))* Crabtree Publishing Co.

Kranowitz, Carol & Newman, Joye. In Sync Activity Cards: Simple, Fun Activity Cards to Help Every Child Develop, Learn, & Grow! 2012. (ENG.). 112p. 29.95 *(978-1-935567-35-6(7))* Sensory Resources.

Kruse, Nancy. Treasure Hunt: A Book of Clues for Parties. 2008. 116p. pap. 12.95 *(978-1-60145-565-9(8))* Booklocker.com, Inc.

Kumon Publishing, creator. My Book of Alphabet Games Ages 4, 5, 6. 2007. (Kumon Workbooks Ser.). (Illus.). 80p. per. 7.95 *(978-1-933241-36-4(5))* Kumon Publishing North America, Inc.

Kumon Publishing, ed. My Book of Number Games 1-150. 2004. (ENG., Illus.). 82p. (J). per. 7.95 *(978-4-7743-0760-2(2))* Kumon Publishing North America, Inc.

Kvale, Anthony, creator & concept. Head1Liners board Game. Kvale, Anthony, concept. 2006. 38.99 *(978-0-9793583-0-2(2)*, H1L) Kvale Good Natured Games LLC.

Laden, Nina. Peek-A Who? Matching Game. 2014. (ENG., Illus.). 36p. (J). (gr. -1-k). bds. 14.99 *(978-1-4521-3359-1(X))* Chronicle Bks. LLC.

Laredo, Elizabeth. The Jump Rope Book. Cooper, Martha, photos by. 2004. (Illus.). 284p. (J). (gr. k-4). reprint ed. pap. 10.00 *(978-0-7567-7775-3(5))* DIANE Publishing Co.

Larsen, Elizabeth Foy & Glenn, Joshua. Unbored: The Essential Field Guide to Serious Fun. Leone, Tony et al, illus. 2012. (ENG.). 352p. 28.00 *(978-1-60819-641-8(0)*, 9781608196418) Bloomsbury Publishing USA.

Laval, Thierry. Look & Find on Vacation. 2017. (Mini Look & Find Ser.). (ENG.). 14p. (J). 9.95 ***(978-0-531-23083-1(X)***, Children's Pr.) Scholastic Library Publishing.

Lawrence, Ellen. Time to Play. 2015. (My World Your World Ser.). (ENG.). 24p. (J). (gr. -1-3). lib. bdg. 23.93 *(978-1-910549-06-3(1))* Bearport Publishing Co., Inc.

Lawson, Julia & Goodman, Polly. Games. 2011. (Little Steps Ser.). (ENG., Illus.). 14p. (J). (gr. -1-k). bds. *(978-1-84089-592-6(6))* Zero to Ten, Ltd.

Ledbetter, Mary Ellen. You Say I Say. 2005. per. 19.95 *(978-1-888237-61-0(9))* Baxter Pr.

Levete, Sarah. Games Around the World. 2010. (Big Picture: People & Culture Ser.). (ENG.). 24p. (gr. 1-2). pap. 41.70 *(978-1-4296-5820-1(7)*, First Facts) Capstone Press of Coughlan Cos.

Lewis, Alexandra. The Ultimate Jump Rope Book. 2010. (ENG., Illus.). 80p. (J). pap. 12.95 *(978-1-60433-102-8(X))* Cider Mill Pr. Bk. Pubs., LLC.

Lewis, Clare. Games Around the World, 1 vol. 2014. (Around the World Ser.). (ENG., Illus.). 24p. (gr. -1-1). 22.65 *(978-1-4846-0371-0(0)*, Acorn) Heinemann-Raintree.

Libal, Joyce. Folk Games. 2004. (North American Folklore Ser.). (Illus.). 112p. (J). (gr. 7-18). lib. bdg. 22.95 *(978-1-59084-339-0(8))* Mason Crest.

Lingo, Susan L. Collect-n-Play Games for Kids. Stoker, Bruce, ed. Carter, Paula Becker, illus. 2006. 112p. (YA). (gr. 1-7). 15.99 *(978-0-7847-1199-6(2)*, 02433) Standard Publishing.

Littlefield, Cindy A. Sea Life Games & Puzzles: 100 Brainteasers, Word Games, Jokes & Riddles, Picture Puzzles, Matches & Logic Tests. Kline, Michael et al, illus. 2006. (Storey's Games & Puzzles Ser.). (ENG.). 144p. (J). (gr. 3-8). pap. 9.95 *(978-1-58017-624-8(0)*, 67624) Storey Publishing, LLC.

Lluch, Alex A. Kindergarten Learning While Having Fun! 2013. (ENG., Illus.). 126p. (J). (gr. k). pap. 9.95 *(978-1-61351-073-5(X))* WS Publishing.

—Pre-K Learning While Having Fun! 2013. (ENG., Illus.). 126p. (J). (gr. -1). pap. 9.95 *(978-1-61351-072-8(1))* WS Publishing.

Loh-Hagan, Virginia. Extreme Base Jumping. 2015. (Nailed It! Ser.). (ENG., Illus.). 32p. (J). (gr. 4-8). pap. 14.21 *(978-1-63470-049-8(X)*, 206717) Cherry Lake Publishing.

Lonely Planet Publications Staff, et al. Boredom Buster, 1 vol. 2016. (Lonely Planet Kids Ser.). (ENG., Illus.). 128p. (J). pap. 11.99 *(978-1-76034-106-0(1)*, 5190) Lonely Planet Pubns.

Lupo, Tamar. Moto X: X Games. 2008. (Extreme Ser.). (Illus.). 32p. (J). (gr. 4-6). lib. bdg. 26.00 *(978-1-59036-914-2(9))* Weigl Pubs., Inc.

Lupo, Tamar & Hudak, Heather C. Moto X: X Games. 2008. (Extreme Ser.). (Illus.). 32p. (J). (gr. 4-6). pap. 9.95 *(978-1-59036-915-9(7))* Weigl Pubs., Inc.

Macmillan Children's Books Staff & Pan MacMillan Staff. Bin Weevils - The Official Guide. rev. unabr. ed. 2013. (ENG., Illus.). 160p. (J). (gr. 2). pap. 10.99 *(978-1-4472-3230-8(5))* Pan Macmillan GBR. Dist: Independent Pubs. Group.

Manderly, Lorin. Lilith Celebrates Lammas. Drewes, Dan, illus. 2010. 36p. pap. 15.50 *(978-1-4520-2689-3(0))* AuthorHouse.

Marquardt, Meg. E-Sports Competitions. 2017. (ESports: Game On! Ser.). (ENG.). 48p. (J). (gr. 5-8). 29.27 ***(978-1-59953-893-8(8))*** Norwood Hse. Pr.

Marrion, Thom & Ward, Kyla. Buffy the Vampire Slayer: Welcome to Sunnydale Supplement. 2005. 128p. (YA). pap. 27.00 *(978-1-891153-95-2(1))* Eden Studios, Inc.

Marsh, Carole. Alaska Wheel of Fortune: Game Book. (Orig.). pap. 9.95 *(978-0-7933-9621-4(2))* Gallopade International.

—Arkansas Jeopardy! Answers & Questions about Our State! 2004. (Illus.). 32p. (J). (gr. 3-8). pap. 7.95 *(978-0-7933-9792-1(8))* Gallopade International.

—Arkansas "Jography" A Fun Run Thru Our State! 2004. (Carole Marsh Arkansas Bks.). (Illus.). 32p. (J). (gr. 3-8). pap. 7.95 *(978-0-7933-9821-8(5))* Gallopade International.

—Kansas Jeopardy! Answers & Questions about Our State! 2004. (Carole Marsh Kansas Bks.). (Illus.). 32p. (J). (gr. 3-8). pap. 7.95 *(978-0-7933-9798-3(7))* Gallopade International.

—Kansas "Jography" A Fun Run Thru Your State! 2004. 32p. (J). (gr. 3-8). pap. 7.95 *(978-0-7933-9827-0(4))* Gallopade International.

—Tennessee Jeopardy! Answers & Questions about Our State! Line Art Staff, illus. 2004. 32p. (J). (gr. 3-8). pap. 7.95 *(978-0-7933-9812-6(6))* Gallopade International.

—Washington D. C. Millionaire. (GameBook Ser.). (Illus.). 32p. (J). pap., act. bk. ed. 9.95 *(978-0-635-00864-0(5))* Gallopade International.

—Washington D. C. Survivor. (GameBook Ser.). (Illus.). 32p. (J). pap., act. bk. ed. 9.95 *(978-0-635-00866-4(1))* Gallopade International.

—Washington D. C. Wheel of Fortune. (GameBook Ser.). (Illus.). 32p. (J). pap., act. bk. ed. 9.95 *(978-0-635-00865-7(3))* Gallopade International.

Martin, Chris. Minecraft: The Business Behind the Makers of Minecraft. 2016. (Big Brands Ser.). (ENG., Illus.). 32p. (J). (gr. 4-6). 26.65 *(978-1-5124-0589-7(2))*; 39.99 *(978-1-5124-0594-1(9))* Lerner Publishing Group. (Lerner Pubns.).

Martin, Rob & Sellmeyer, Mark, des. Seasons: The Calendar Rummy Game. 2004. mass mkt. 24.95 *(978-0-9747833-0-7(7))* Dust Bunny Games LLC.

Mattern, Joanne. Playing at School. 2006. (My Day at School Ser.). (Illus.). 24p. (gr. k-3). pap. 8.15 *(978-0-8368-6795-4(5))*; lib. bdg. 22.00 *(978-0-8368-6788-6(2))* Stevens, Gareth Publishing LLLP. (Weekly Reader Leveled Readers).

—Playing at School: Juego en la Escuela. 2006. (My Day at School/ Mi dia en la escuela Ser.). (ENG & SPA., Illus.). 24p. (gr. k-3). pap. 8.15 *(978-0-8368-7369-6(6)*, Weekly Reader Leveled Readers) Stevens, Gareth Publishing LLLP.

—Playing at School (Juego en la Escuela) 2006. (My Day at School/ Mi dia en la escuela Ser.). (SPA., Illus.). 24p. (gr. k-3). lib. bdg. 22.00 *(978-0-8368-7362-7(9)*, Weekly Reader Leveled Readers) Stevens, Gareth Publishing LLLP.

McCoy, M. M. Where Is Cecil? Maximilian Press Publishers Staff, ed. Brunner, Terry, illus. unabr. l.t. ed. 2005. 28p. (J). lib. bdg. 12.50 *(978-1-930211-68-1(6))* Maximilian Pr. Pubs.

McGillian, Jamie Kyle. Sidewalk Chalk: Outdoor Fun & Games. Sims, Blanche, illus. 2006. 80p. (J). (gr. k-4). reprint ed. 18.00 *(978-1-4223-5580-0(2))* DIANE Publishing Co.

Meachen Rau, Dana. Juegos y Diversiones en la Historia de América. 2006. (Como era la vida en America (How People Lived in America) Ser.). (SPA., Illus.). 24p. (gr. 1-4). lib. bdg. 22.00 *(978-0-8368-7429-7(3)*, Weekly Reader Leveled Readers) Stevens, Gareth Publishing LLLP.

—Juegos y diversiones en la historia de America (Toys, Games, & Fun in American History) 2006. (Como era la vida en America (How People Lived in America) Ser.). (SPA.). 24p. (gr. 1-4). pap. 8.15 *(978-0-8368-7436-5(6)*, Weekly Reader Leveled Readers) Stevens, Gareth Publishing LLLP.

—Toys, Games, & Fun in American History. 2006. (How People Lived in America Ser.). (Illus.). 24p. (gr. 1-4). pap. 8.15 *(978-0-8368-7216-3(9))*; lib. bdg. 22.00 *(978-0-8368-7209-5(6))* Stevens, Gareth Publishing LLLP. (Weekly Reader Leveled Readers).

Mercado, Nancy E. Boredom Busters! Activities to Do for Kids Like You! 2003. (Illus.). 38p. (J). *(978-0-439-52312-7(5))* Scholastic, Inc.

Michaels, Sarah, et al. Extra Ring Bling Rings: Rb67. 2013. 9.95 *(978-1-60723-093-9(3))* Super Duper Pubns.

—Ring Bling Extra Hands: Rb69. 2013. pap. 14.95 *(978-1-60723-092-2(5))* Super Duper Pubns.

Michele, Tracey. Games Around the World. 2011. (Learn-Abouts Ser.). (Illus.). 16p. (J). pap. 7.95 *(978-1-59920-621-9(8))* Black Rabbit Bks.

Miko, Christopher & Romines, Garrett. The Unofficial Holy Bible for Minecrafters: A Children's Guide to the Old Testament. 2016. (ENG.). 330p. (J). (gr. k). pap. 19.99 *(978-1-5107-0225-7(3)*, Sky Pony Pr.) Skyhorse Publishing Co., Inc.

Miles Kelly Staff. Animals: Family Flip Quiz. 2003. (Flip Quiz Ser.). (Illus.). 152p. (J). spiral bd. 12.95 *(978-1-84236-099-6(X))* Miles Kelly Publishing, Ltd. GBR. Dist: Independent Pubs. Group.

—Animals: Flip Quiz. 2003. (Flip Quiz Ser.). (Illus.). 38p. (J). spiral bd. 5.95 *(978-1-84236-079-8(5))*; spiral bd. 5.95 *(978-1-84236-076-7(0))*; spiral bd. 5.95 *(978-1-84236-078-1(7))*; spiral bd. 5.95 *(978-1-84236-077-4(9))* Miles Kelly Publishing, Ltd. GBR. Dist: Independent Pubs. Group.

—Bible: Family Flip Quiz. 2003. (Flip Quiz Ser.). (Illus.). 152p. (J). spiral bd. 12.95 *(978-1-84236-124-5(4))* Miles Kelly Publishing, Ltd. GBR. Dist: Independent Pubs. Group.

—Geography. 2003. (Flip Quiz Ser.). (Illus.). 152p. (J). spiral bd. 12.95 *(978-1-84236-146-7(5))* Miles Kelly Publishing, Ltd. GBR. Dist: Independent Pubs. Group.

—Geography Age 10-11: Flip Quiz. 2003. (Flip Quiz Ser.). (Illus.). 38p. (J). spiral bd. 5.95 *(978-1-84236-102-3(3))* Miles Kelly Publishing, Ltd. GBR. Dist: Independent Pubs. Group.

—Geography Age 11-12: Flip Quiz. 2003. (Flip Quiz Ser.). (Illus.). 38p. (J). spiral bd. 5.95 *(978-1-84236-103-0(1))* Miles Kelly Publishing, Ltd. GBR. Dist: Independent Pubs. Group.

—Geography Age 7-9: Flip Quiz. 2003. (Flip Quiz Ser.). (Illus.). 38p. (J). spiral bd. 5.95 *(978-1-84236-100-9(7))* Miles Kelly Publishing, Ltd. GBR. Dist: Independent Pubs. Group.

—Geography Age 9-10: Flip Quiz. 2003. (Flip Quiz Ser.). (Illus.). 38p. (J). spiral bd. 5.95 *(978-1-84236-101-6(5))* Miles Kelly Publishing, Ltd. GBR. Dist: Independent Pubs. Group.

—History. 2003. (Flip Quiz Ser.). (Illus.). 38p. (J). spiral bd. 5.95 *(978-1-902947-65-5(7))*; spiral bd. 5.95 *(978-1-902947-68-6(1))*; spiral bd. 5.95 *(978-1-902947-70-9(3))* Miles Kelly Publishing, Ltd. GBR. Dist: Independent Pubs. Group.

—History: Family Flip Quiz. 2003. (Flip Quiz Ser.). (Illus.). 152p. (J). spiral bd. 12.95 *(978-1-84236-052-1(3))* Miles Kelly Publishing, Ltd. GBR. Dist: Independent Pubs. Group.

—History Age. 2003. (Flip Quiz Ser.). (Illus.). 38p. (J). spiral bd. 5.95 *(978-1-902947-69-3(X))* Miles Kelly Publishing, Ltd. GBR. Dist: Independent Pubs. Group.

—Mix-Ups. 2003. (Illus.). 14p. 9.95 *(978-1-902947-83-9(5))* Miles Kelly Publishing, Ltd. GBR. Dist: Independent Pubs. Group.

—Noises: Let's Learn. Nilsen, Anna, ed. 2003. (Let's Learn Ser.). (Illus.). 20p. (J). 7.95 *(978-1-84236-139-9(2))* Miles Kelly Publishing, Ltd. GBR. Dist: Independent Pubs. Group.

—Opposites: Let's Learn. Nilsen, Anna, ed. 2003. (Let's Learn Ser.). (Illus.). 20p. (J). 7.95 *(978-1-84236-138-2(4))* Miles Kelly Publishing, Ltd. GBR. Dist: Independent Pubs. Group.

—Rock & Pop. 2003. (Flip Quiz Ser.). (Illus.). 152p. (J). spiral bd. 12.95 *(978-1-84236-145-0(7))* Miles Kelly Publishing, Ltd. GBR. Dist: Independent Pubs. Group.

—Science: Family Flip Quiz. 2003. (Family Flip Quiz Ser.). (Illus.). 152p. (J). spiral bd. 12.95 *(978-1-84236-073-6(6))* Miles Kelly Publishing, Ltd. GBR. Dist: Independent Pubs. Group.

—Science & Maths. 2003. (Flip Quiz Ser.). (Illus.). 38p. (J). (gr. 10-11). spiral bd. 5.95 *(978-1-84236-032-3(9))*; (gr. 11-12). spiral bd. 5.95 *(978-1-84236-033-0(7))*; (gr. 7-9). spiral bd. 5.95 *(978-1-84236-030-9(2))*; (gr. 9-10). spiral bd. 5.95 *(978-1-84236-031-6(0))* Miles Kelly Publishing, Ltd. GBR. Dist: Independent Pubs. Group.

Miles Kelly Staff & Nilsen, Anna. Actions: Let's Learn. 2003. (Let's Learn Ser.). (Illus.). 20p. (J). 7.95 *(978-1-84236-137-5(6))* Miles Kelly Publishing, Ltd. GBR. Dist: Independent Pubs. Group.

—Numbers: Let's Learn. 2003. (Let's Learn Ser.). (Illus.). 20p. (J). 7.95 *(978-1-84236-018-7(3))* Miles Kelly Publishing, Ltd. GBR. Dist: Independent Pubs. Group.

—Shapes: Let's Learn. 2003. (Let's Learn Ser.). (Illus.). 20p. (J). 7.95 *(978-1-84236-016-3(7))* Miles Kelly Publishing, Ltd. GBR. Dist: Independent Pubs. Group.

Miles, Liz. Games: From Dice to Gaming. 2010. (Timeline History Ser.). (ENG.). 32p. (gr. 3-5). 29.99 *(978-1-4329-3807-9(X)*, NA-h) Heinemann-Raintree.

Miller, Amanda. This Is the Way We Play. 2009. (Scholastic News Nonfiction Readers Ser.). (ENG.). 24p. (J). (gr. 1-2). pap. 6.95 *(978-0-531-21442-8(7)*, Children's Pr.); lib. bdg. 22.00 *(978-0-531-21342-1(0))* Scholastic Library Publishing.

Miller, Brandon Marie. Benjamin Franklin, American Genius: His Life & Ideas with 21 Activities. 2009. (For Kids Ser.). (ENG., Illus.). 144p. (J). (gr. 4-7). pap. 16.95 *(978-1-55652-757-9(8))* Chicago Review Pr., Inc.

Miller, Connie Colwell. Moto X Freestyle [Scholastic]. 2011. (X Games Ser.). 32p. pap. 1.00 *(978-1-4296-6486-8(X)*, Blazers) Capstone Press of Coughlan Cos.

Miller, John & Scott, Chris. Unofficial Minecraft Lab for Kids: Family-Friendly Projects for Exploring & Teaching Math, Science, History, & Culture Through Creative Building. 2016. (Hands-On Family Ser.). (ENG.). 144p. (J). (gr. 1-17). pap. 22.99 *(978-1-63159-117-4(7)*, Quarry Bks.) Quarto Publishing Group USA.

Miller, Megan. The Big Book of Hacks for Minecrafters: The Biggest Unofficial Guide to Tips & Tricks That Other Guides Won't Teach You. 2015. (ENG., Illus.). 400p. (J). (gr. 1-7). pap. 24.99 *(978-1-63450-211-5(6)*, Sky Pony Pr.) Skyhorse Publishing Co., Inc.

—Hacks for Minecrafters: The Unofficial Guide to Tips & Tricks That Other Guides Won't Teach You. 2014. (ENG., Illus.). 128p. (J). (gr. 1). 12.99 *(978-1-63450-101-9(2)*, Sky Pony Pr.) Skyhorse Publishing Co., Inc.

—Hacks for Minecrafters: The Unofficial Guide to Tips & Tricks the Official Guides Won't Teach You. 2014. (ENG., Illus.). 160p. (J). (gr. 1). 12.99 *(978-1-63220-440-0(1)*, Sky Pony Pr.) Skyhorse Publishing Co., Inc.

—Hacks for Minecrafters - Master Builder: The Unofficial Guide to Tips & Tricks That Other Guides Won't Teach You. 2014. (ENG., Illus.). 128p. (J). (gr. 1). 12.99 *(978-1-63450-043-2(1)*, Sky Pony Pr.) Skyhorse Publishing Co., Inc.

—Hacks for Minecrafters Box Set: 6 Unofficial Guides to Tips & Tricks That Other Guides Won't Teach You. 2016. (ENG., Illus.). 800p. (J). (gr. 1-7). 29.99 *(978-1-5107-0699-6(2)*, Sky Pony Pr.) Skyhorse Publishing Co., Inc.

—Mini Hacks for Minecrafters: The Unofficial Guide to the Combat Update. 2016. (ENG., Illus.). 104p. (J). (gr. 1-7). 9.99 *(978-1-5107-1797-8(8)*, Sky Pony Pr.) Skyhorse Publishing Co., Inc.

Miller, Ray, et al. Beat the Clock Sports. Thorp, Cameron, illus. 2007. 48p. (J). *(978-0-439-02189-0(8))* Scholastic, Inc.

Mitchell, Loretta. One, Two, Three... Echo Me! Ready-to-Use Songs, Games & Activities to Help Children Sing in Tune. 2003. (Illus.). 203p. pap. 29.95 *(978-0-89328-157-1(3)*, 30/1800H) Heritage Music Pr.

Mitchem, James. The Big Book of Things to Make. 2013. (ENG.). 128p. (J). (gr. 2-5). 16.99 *(978-1-4654-0255-4(1)*, DK Children) Dorling Kindersley Publishing, Inc.

Modern Publishing Staff, ed. No Place Like Celesteville. 2005. 12p. pap. 3.99 *(978-0-7666-1944-9(3))* Modern Publishing.

—Welcome to the Kingdom. 2005. 12p. pap. 3.99 *(978-0-7666-1943-2(5))* Modern Publishing.

Monsen, John, et al. Pirate's Log: A Handbook for Aspiring Swashbucklers. Ford, Gilbert, illus. 2008. (ENG.). 172p. (J). (gr. 3-5). 15.95 *(978-0-8118-6435-0(9))* Chronicle Bks. LLC.

Montaldo, Stuart. Cogno: The Alien Adventure Game. 2003. (J). 29.95 *(978-0-9742558-0-4(7))* DoubleStar, LLC.

—Cogno: the Alien Legends: Synapse. 2004. (Cogno the Alien Legends Ser.: Bk. 1). (Illus.). 238p. (J). per. 7.99 *(978-0-9742558-2-8(3))* DoubleStar, LLC.

Montaldo, Stuart, creator. Cogno: Deep Worlds. 2004. (J). 29.95 *(978-0-9742558-1-1(5))* DoubleStar, LLC.

Moog, Bob. Made You Laugh for Kids: Truth or Dare! 2005. (Illus.). 96p. pap. *(978-1-57528-927-4(X))* Univ. Games.

—Spinner Books: Two-Book Set. 2006. (Spinner Bks.). (ENG.). pap. 18.95 *(978-1-57528-970-0(9))* Univ. Games.

—Spinner Books for Kids 20-Copy Counter Display. 2004. (ENG.). (J). pap. 160.00 (978-1-57528-925-0(3)) Spinner Bks.

Moog, Robert. Spinner Books Junior: 20 Questions for Kids. 2004. (Spinner Books for Kids). (ENG., Illus.). 160p. (J). (gr. 3-6). pap. 7.95 (978-1-57528-918-2(0)) Univ. Games.

—Spinner Books Junior: 30 Second Mysteries for Kids. 2004. (Spinner Books for Kids). (ENG., Illus.). 158p. (J). (gr. -1-12). pap. 7.95 (978-1-57528-919-9(9)) Univ. Games.

—Spinner Books Junior: Kids Battle the Grown-Ups. 2004. (Spinner Books for Kids). (ENG., Illus.). 160p. pap. 7.95 (978-1-57528-921-2(0)) Univ. Games.

—Spinner Books Junior: Totally Gross. 2004. (Spinner Books for Kids Ser.). (ENG., Illus.). 160p. (J). (gr. 4-7). pap. 7.95 (978-1-57528-920-5(2)) Univ. Games.

Moon, Alan R. & Borg, Richard. Dragon Hordes: Warrior's Expansion 1. 2005. (JPN & KOR., Illus.). 19.95 (978-0-9728197-9-4(7)) Face 2 Face Games Publishing.

—Warriors: It's Monsters, Myth, & Mayhem! 2005. (JPN & KOR., Illus.). 19.95 (978-0-9728197-8-7(9)) Face 2 Face Games Publishing.

More Time for Bible Puzzles & Games. (Illus.). 32p. (YA). (gr. 5-18). pap. 2.25 (978-0-87162-664-6(0), E9706) Warner Pr., Inc.

Morgan, Gaby. My Christmas. rev. ed. 2007. 24p. pap., act. bk. ed. 7.99 (978-0-230-01546-3(8), Macmillan Children's Bks.) Pan Macmillan GBR. Dist: Trans-Atlantic Pubns., Inc.

Morley, Jacqueline. How to Be an Ancient Greek Athlete. Antram, David, illus. 2008. (How to Be Ser.). (ENG.). 32p. (J). (gr. 3-7). pap. 5.95 (978-1-4263-0278-7(9), National Geographic Children's Bks.) National Geographic Society.

Mosher, Geraldine. A Madcap Mother Goose. Rocque, Rose, illus. 2003. pap. 9.95 (978-0-9726311-4-3(3)) Top Quality Pubns.

Museum of Modern Art Staff. Topsy-Turvy Stacking Blocks. 2011. (ENG.). 10p. (J). (gr. -1-1). 19.99 (978-0-8118-7713-8(2)) Chronicle Bks. LLC.

My Little Pony Surprize Ink! Clipboard I. 2004. 24p. (J). 9.99 (978-1-932125-92-4(2)) Giddy Up, LLC.

National Geographic Editors & Esbaum, Jill. Angry Birds Playground - Dinosaurs. Tempesta, Franco, illus. 2013. (ENG.). 128p. (J). (gr. -1-3). lib. bdg. 21.90 (978-1-4263-1325-7(X), National Geographic Children's Bks.) National Geographic Society.

National Geographic Kids Staff. Colors! 2012. (ENG., Illus.). 24p. (J). (gr. k-k). bds. 6.99 (978-1-4263-0929-8(5), National Geographic Children's Bks.) National Geographic Society.

—Same & Different. 2012. (ENG., Illus.). 24p. (J). (gr. k-k). bds. 6.99 (978-1-4263-0928-1(7), National Geographic Children's Bks.) National Geographic Society.

—Shapes! 2012. (Look & Learn Ser.). (ENG., Illus.). 24p. (J). (gr. k-k). bds. 6.99 (978-1-4263-1042-3(0), National Geographic Children's Bks.) National Geographic Society.

National Geographic Kids Staff & Esbaum, Jill. Angry Birds Playground: Rain Forest: A Forest Floor to Treetop Adventure. 2014. (ENG., Illus.). 128p. (J). (gr. -1-3). 14.95 (978-1-4263-1685-2(2), National Geographic Children's Bks.) National Geographic Society.

—Dinosaurs: A Prehistoric Adventure! Tempesta, Franco, illus. 2013. (ENG.). 128p. (J). (gr. -1-3). 14.95 (978-1-4263-1324-0(1), National Geographic Children's Bks.) National Geographic Society.

Nicholaus, Bret & Lowrie, Paul. KidChat: 222 Creative Questions to Spark Conversations. 2nd rev. ed. 2004. (Illus.). 128p. (J). pap. 9.95 (978-0-9755801-0-3(8), KCR) Questmarc Publishing.

—KidChat Too! All-New Questions to Fuel Young Minds & Mouths. 2004. (Illus.). 128p. (J). pap. 9.95 (978-0-9755801-1-0(6), KCT) Questmarc Publishing.

Nicholls, Shawn. Sports Gamer: The Best Games, Gear, & Tips. 2004. (YA). 3.99 (978-1-930623-36-1(4)) Sports Illustrated For Kids.

Nilson, Anna. Art Shark: Collect Great Art, Auction It, Hide It, Steal It! 2006. (Illus.). (J). (gr. 2). 24.95 (978-1-889613-88-8(6)) Birdcage Pr.

Nitz, Kristin Wolden. Play-by-Play Track. 2004. (Play-by-Play Ser.). (Illus.). 80p. (J). (gr. 4-8). lib. bdg. 23.93 (978-0-8225-3936-0(5)) Lerner Publishing Group.

Norton, Frances Maree. The Victorian Tea Spirit: A Girl's Guide to Her Secret Self. 1. 100th ed. 2003. (Illus.). 230p. (YA). per. 19.95 (978-0-9632938-1-7(8)) Norton, Frances M.

Null Petersen, Casey. Games Around the World, 1 vol. 2nd rev. ed. 2014. (TIME for KIDS(r) Nonfiction Readers Ser.). (ENG., Illus.). 28p. (J). (gr. 3-3). pap. 25.96 (978-1-4807-1068-9(7)) Shell Educational Publishing.

—Games Around the World, 1 vol. 2nd rev. ed. 2011. (Nonfiction Readers Ser.). (ENG.). 28p. (J). (gr. 3-3). pap. 8.99 (978-1-4333-3653-9(7)) Teacher Created Materials, Inc.

Null Petersen, Christine. Juegos Alrededor Del Mundo. 2017. (TIME for Kids en Español - Level 3 Ser.). (SPA.). 32p. (gr. 3-3). lib. bdg. 31.99 **(978-1-5157-5165-6(1))** Time for Kids Inc AUS. Dist: Capstone Pub.

O'Connor, Jim. Where Is the Colosseum? O'brien, John & Groff, David, illus. 2017. (Where Is? Ser.). (ENG.). 112p. (J). (gr. 3-7). 5.99 (978-0-399-54190-2(X), Grosset & Dunlap) Penguin Young Readers Group.

Odom, Mel. Unlock the Secrets of Oddworld: Official Strategy Guide. (J). pap. 12.95 (978-1-56893-960-5(4)) GT Interactive Software.

Oh, H. Too. The Super Duper Water Balloon Launcher Kit: Ready! Aim! Splash! 2013. (ENG.). 64p. (J). (gr. 5). 19.95 (978-1-60433-222-3(0), Applesauce Pr.) Cider Mill Pr. Bk. Pubs., LLC.

Okido Staff. Color Me In! An Activity Book. 2013. (ENG., Illus.). 128p. (J). (gr. k-3). pap. 14.95 (978-0-500-65017-2(9), 565017) Thames & Hudson.

—My Animal Book: Facts & Fun, Questions & Answers, Things to Make & Do. 2014. (ENG., Illus.). 64p. (J). (gr. k-2). 18.95 (978-0-500-65024-0(1), 565024) Thames & Hudson.

Onyefulu, Ifeoma. Look at This! - Play. 2013. (ENG., Illus.). 32p. (J). (gr. -1-k). 17.99 (978-1-84780-267-5(2), Frances Lincoln) Quarto Publishing Group UK GBR. Dist: Hachette Bk. Group.

O'Reilly, Wenda. Amazing places natl Parks. 2007. n/ap. pap. 119.40 (978-1-59960-014-7(5)) Birdcage Pr.

—American Art Ditto. 2006. 24.95 (978-1-889613-84-0(3)) Birdcage Pr.

—Go fish wildlife Mammals. 2007. n/ap. pap. 119.40 (978-1-59960-016-1(1)) Birdcage Pr.

—GO FISH WILDLIFE REPTILES & AMPHIBIANS. 2007. n/ap. pap. 119.40 (978-1-59960-018-5(8)) Birdcage Pr.

—Go fish wildlife sea Creatures. 2007. n/ap. pap. 119.40 (978-1-59960-020-8(X)) Birdcage Pr.

—Wild Cards. 2007. n/ap. pap. 119.40 (978-1-59960-012-3(9)) Birdcage Pr.

Osborne, Mary Pope & Boyce, Natalie Pope. Animal Games & Puzzles. Murdocca, Sal, illus. 2015. (Magic Tree House Ser.). (ENG.). 256p. (J). (gr. 2-5). 6.99 (978-0-553-50840-6(7), Random Hse. Bks. for Young Readers) Random Hse. Children's Bks.

Otfinoski, Steven. Extreme Paintball. 2013. (Illus.). 48p. (J). (gr. 4-8). 29.93 (978-1-60870-226-8(X)); pap. 12.93 (978-1-62712-135-4(8)) Cavendish Square Publishing.

Oxlade, Chris. Gaming Technology. 2010. (New Technology Ser.). (ENG., Illus.). 48p. (J). 23.99 (978-0-237-54076-2(2)) Evans Brothers, Ltd. GBR. Dist: Independent Pubs. Group.

Pack, Linda Hager. Appalachian Toys & Games from a to Z. Banks, Pat, illus. 2013. (ENG.). 56p. 17.95 (978-0-8131-4104-6(4)) Univ. Pr. of Kentucky.

Painter, Lucy. The Outrageously Big Activity, Play & Project Book: Cookery, Painting, Crafts, Science, & Much More. 2014. (ENG., Illus.). 512p. (J). (gr. k-6). pap. 18.99 (978-1-84309-192-9(5)) Anness Publishing GBR. Dist: National Bk. Network.

Parker, Katie. Gone Extinct! Maydak, Mike, illus. 2009. (ENG.). 24p. (J). (gr. k-17). 19.99 (978-1-58476-941-5(6)) Innovative Kids.

Parkes, Lois. Paper Sport: Activities, Games & Puzzles for Sporty Kids. 2012. 44p. pap. 21.99 (978-1-4771-2582-3(5)) Xlibris Corp.

Parmalee, Thomas. Legalized Gambling, 1 vol. 2010. (Essential Viewpoints Set 5 Ser.). (ENG., Illus.). 112p. (J). (gr. 6-12). lib. bdg. 35.64 (978-1-61613-522-5(0), Essential Library) ABDO Publishing Co.

Pearson, Mary R. Bible Learning Games: Reproducible Activities. 2004. (Illus.). 64p. (J). pap. 9.95 (978-0-937282-72-4(3), RB36251); (gr. -1-k). pap. 9.95 (978-0-937282-73-1(1), RB36252); (gr. 1-2). pap. 9.95 (978-0-937282-74-8(X), RB36253); (gr. 3-4). pap. 9.95 (978-0-937282-75-5(8), RB36254) Rainbow Pubs. & Legacy Pr.

Peirce, Lincoln. Big Nate: Fun Blaster: Cheezy Doodles, Crazy Comix, & Loads of Laughs! Peirce, Lincoln, illus. 2012. (Big Nate Activity Book Ser.: 2). (ENG., Illus.). 224p. (J). (gr. 3-7). 10.99 (978-0-06-209045-4(3)) HarperCollins Pubs.

—Big Nate Fun Blaster. 2012. (Illus.). 198p. (J). 6.99 (978-0-06-219962-1(5)) HarperCollins Pubs.

Pence, Shari A. Games Galore for Children's Parties & More: 80 Fun Games & Activities for Parties, Classroom, Youth Groups, Carnivals, Company Picnics, Rainy Days & Special Occasions. Stearns, Debra & Kohout, Rosemary, eds. Burris, Priscilla, illus. 2nd rev. ed. 2005. (ENG.). 121p. (J). (gr. -1-7). pap. 12.00 (978-0-9645771-1-4(9)) Funcastle Pubns.

Penton Overseas, Inc. Staff. U. S. Presidents. 2006. (ENG., Illus.). (J). pap. 7.95 (978-1-59125-165-1(6)) Penton Overseas, Inc.

Perez, Jessica. Spin & Spell: A Book & Game in One! Gévry, Claudine, illus. 2005. 12p. (J). 14.95 (978-1-58117-332-1(6), Intervisual/Piggy Toes) Bendon, Inc.

Pétronille, Marc & Audureau, William. The History of Sonic the Hedgehog. 2014. (ENG., Illus.). 300p. (YA). pap. 34.99 (978-1-926778-96-9(0), 9781926778969) URON Entertainment Corp. CAN. Dist: Diamond Comic Distributors, Inc.

Petty, Kate. Playtime. 2006. (World Show-And-Tell Ser.). (ENG., Illus.). 32p. (J). (gr. -1-1). 14.95 (978-1-58728-549-3(5)); pap. 8.95 (978-1-58728-546-2(0)) Cooper Square Publishing Llc.

Phillips, Karen. The Truth about My Name: And What It Reveals about Me! 2010. (ENG.). 50p. (J). (gr. 3-18). 16.99 (978-1-59174-855-7(0)) Klutz.

Pinnington, Andrea. Princess Pocket Activity Fun & Games: Includes Games, Cutouts, Foldout Scenes, Textures, Stickers, & Stencils. 2013. (Pocket Activity Fun & Games Ser.). (ENG.). 96p. (J). (gr. 1-4). pap. 7.99 (978-1-4380-0313-9(7)) Barron's Educational Series, Inc.

Play the Game You Know. 2005. (Book Treks Ser.). (J). 37.95 (978-0-7652-3258-8(8)) Celebration Pr.

Player, Micah, illus. Sports Matching Game. 2011. (ENG.). 72p. (J). (gr. -1-3). bds. 14.99 (978-0-8118-7796-1(5)) Chronicle Bks. LLC.

Polydoros, Lori. Fascinating Role-Playing Games. 2017. (Cool Competitions Ser.). (ENG.). 32p. (gr. 1-2). lib. bdg. 26.65 **(978-1-5157-7351-1(5)**, Blazers) Capstone Press of Coughlan Cos.

Porterfield, Jason. Angry Birds & Rovio Entertainment, 1 vol. 2015. (ENG.). 128p. (YA). 35.60 (978-1-4777-7919-4(1), Rosen Young Adult) Rosen Publishing Group, Inc., The.

Power, Bob & Roza, Greg. Sports Tips, Techniques, & Strategies: An Insider's Guide to Paintball, 1 vol. 2015. (ENG.). 48p. (J). 30.25 (978-1-4777-8093-0(9), Rosen Reference) Rosen Publishing Group, Inc., The.

Press, Applesauce & Rhatigan, Joe. The Super Concentrated Brain De-Clogger Book: Hundreds of Games, Puzzles & Other Fun Activites That Are Positively Guaranteed to Remove Brain Sludge, Liquidate Blocked Brain Cells, & Stomp Out Boredom! Owsley, Anthony, illus. 2012. (ENG.). 528p. (J). (gr. 3). pap. 14.95 (978-1-60433-228-5(X), Applesauce Pr.) Cider Mill Pr. Bk. Pubs., LLC.

Pressnall, Debra Olson. Colorful File Folder Games: Skill-Building Center Activities for Language Arts & Math. 2006. (ENG., Illus.). 160p. (gr. -1 — 1). per. 22.99 (978-0-88724-268-7(5), CD-104047); (gr. k-k). per. 22.99 (978-0-88724-269-4(3), CD-104048) Carson-Dellosa Publishing, LLC.

Price, Roger & Stern, Leonard. Family Guy Mad Libs. 2007. (Mad Libs Ser.). (ENG., Illus.). 48p. (J). (gr. 3-7). 3.99 (978-0-8431-2190-2(4), Mad Libs) Penguin Young Readers Group.

—Halloween Mad Libs Junior. 2005. (Mad Libs Junior Ser.). (ENG.). 48p. (J). (gr. k-3). 4.99 (978-0-8431-1589-5(0), Mad Libs) Penguin Young Readers Group.

—Happy Birthday Mad Libs. 2008. (Mad Libs Ser.). (ENG.). 48p. (J). (gr. 3-7). 4.99 (978-0-8431-3311-0(2), Mad Libs) Penguin Young Readers Group.

—Sports Star Mad Libs Junior. 2004. (Mad Libs Junior Ser.). (ENG.). 48p. (J). (gr. k-3). 4.99 (978-0-8431-0770-8(7), Mad Libs) Penguin Young Readers Group.

—Summer Fun Mad Libs Junior. 2004. (Mad Libs Junior Ser.). (ENG.). 48p. (J). (gr. k-3). 4.99 (978-0-8431-0759-3(6), Mad Libs) Penguin Young Readers Group.

—Super Silly Mad Libs Junior. 2004. (Mad Libs Junior Ser.). (ENG.). 48p. (J). (gr. k-3). 4.99 (978-0-8431-0758-6(8), Mad Libs) Penguin Young Readers Group.

—Winter Games Mad Libs. 2005. (Mad Libs Ser.). (ENG.). 48p. (J). (gr. 3-7). 3.99 (978-0-8431-1651-9(X), Mad Libs) Penguin Young Readers Group.

Priddy, Roger. Easter Egg Hunt. 2014. (Shaped Board Bks.). (ENG.). 6p. (J). (gr. -1-k). bds. 6.99 (978-0-312-51669-7(X), 9780312516697, Priddy Bks.) St. Martin's Pr.

Privateer Press, creator. Warmachine Escalation. 2006. (Warmachine Ser.). (Illus.). 240p. per. 34.99 (978-0-9706970-8-0(2), PIP 1002) Privateer Pr., Inc.

—Warmachine: Prime: Steam Powered Miniatures Combat. 2006. (Iron Kingdoms Ser.). (Illus.). 200p. per. 19.99 (978-0-9706970-7-3(4)) Privateer Pr., Inc.

Publications International Ltd. Staff. Lion King Look & Find. (J). pap. 6.98 (978-0-7853-1189-8(0)) Publications International, Ltd.

Publications International Ltd. Staff, ed. Brain Games Kids: Mazes. 2011. 192p. (J). spiral bd. 13.98 (978-1-4508-1617-5(7)) Phoenix International Publications, Inc.

—The Incredibles: Look & Find. 2004. (Look & Find Books). (Illus.). 24p. (J). 7.98 (978-1-4127-3223-9(9), 7235900) Publications International, Ltd.

Pulver, David L. & MacKinnon, Mark C. Big Eyes, Small Mouth Third Edition Core Rulebook. 2005. 256p. (YA). 39.95 (978-1-894938-21-1(6)) Guardians of Order CAN. Dist: PSI (Publisher Services, Inc.).

Pulver, David L., et al. CyborGladiators. 2003. per. 14.95 (978-0-9747671-0-9(7)) Firefly Games.

Puzzle Society Staff. Mom's Pocket Posh: 100 Puzzles & Games to Play with Your Kids Ages 4 to 6. 2012. (ENG.). 128p. pap. 7.99 (978-1-4494-1822-9(8)) Andrews McMeel Publishing.

—Mom's Pocket Posh: 100 Puzzles & Games to Play with Your Kids Ages 7 to 12. 2012. (ENG.). 128p. pap. 7.99 (978-1-4494-1823-6(6)) Andrews McMeel Publishing.

Pyne, Lynette & Pressnall, Debra Olson. Colorful File Folder Games: Skill-Building Center Activities for Language Arts & Math. Neville, Bill, illus. 2005. (ENG.). 160p. (gr. 1-1). per. 22.99 (978-1-59441-089-5(5), CD-104049) Carson-Dellosa Publishing, LLC.

—File Folder Games Grade 2: Skill-Building Center Activities for Language Arts & Math. 2005. (ENG., Illus.). 160p. (gr. 2-2). per. 22.99 (978-0-88724-270-0(7), CD-104050) Carson-Dellosa Publishing, LLC.

Ragsdale, Susan & Saylor, Ann. Brain Boosters for Groups in Jar: Brain-Enhancing Games to Get Teens Moving & Connecting. 2016. (In a Jar(r) Ser.). (ENG.). (J). 11.99 (978-1-63198-076-3(9)) Free Spirit Publishing, Inc.

Rainbow Publishers Staff. Bible Games: Reproducible Activities. 2004. (Illus.). 64p. (J). (gr. -1-k). pap. 9.95 (978-0-937282-30-4(8), RB36209); (gr. 1-2). pap. 9.95 (978-0-937282-13-7(8), RB36210); (gr. 3-4). pap. 9.95 (978-0-937282-31-1(6), RB36211); (gr. 5-6). pap. 9.95 (978-0-937282-32-8(4), RB36216) Rainbow Pubs. & Legacy Pr.

Rand McNally. Kids' Road Atlas: Kra. 2015. (ENG.). pap. 6.99 (978-0-528-01341-6(6)) Rand McNally.

Rand McNally Staff. Are We There Yet? (Backseat Bks.). 64p. (J). pap. 3.95 (978-0-528-96543-2(3)) Rand McNally.

—Kids' Road Atlas. (Backseat Bks.). 80p. (J). pap. 3.95 (978-0-528-96544-9(1)) Rand McNally.

RBA, et al. El libro del aprendiz de Brujo. (SPA.). 144p. 21.95 (978-84-7901-783-5(X)) RBA Libros, S.A. ESP. Dist: Santillana USA Publishing Co., Inc.

Redmond, Lea. Connexio: A Game of Infinite Associations & Imagination. 2013. (ENG.). 1p. (gr. 13-17). bds. 24.95 (978-1-4521-1532-0(X)) Chronicle Bks. LLC.

Reilly, Cherie Brooks, et al. Animal Tales & Tracks: The Feathered & Furry Friends at Reilly's Summer Seat Farm. 2009. (Illus.). 106p. 13.17 (978-1-4251-4734-1(8)) Trafford Publishing.

Rhatigan, Joe. Super Duper Most Ginormous Bubble Kit. 2013. (ENG.). 64p. (J). 19.95 (978-1-60433-327-5(8), Applesauce Pr.) Cider Mill Pr. Bk. Pubs., LLC.

Rhodes, Immacula A. Addition & Subtraction: 10 Ready-to-Go Games That Motivate Children to Practice & Strengthen Essential Math Skills-Independently! 2010. (File-Folder Games in Color Ser.). (ENG.). 144p. (gr. k-2). pap. 19.99 (978-0-545-22609-7(0), Teaching Resources) Scholastic, Inc.

Rhodes, Immacula A. & Julio, Susan. Science: 10 Ready-to-Go Games That Help Children Learn Key Science Concepts & Vocabulary — Independently. 2009. (File-Folder Games in Color Ser.). (ENG.). 144p. pap. 19.99 (978-0-439-51764-5(8), Teaching Resources) Scholastic, Inc.

—Social Studies: 10 Ready-to-Go Games That Help Children Learn Key Social Studies Concepts & Vocabulary - Independently. 2009. (File-Folder Games in Color Ser.). (ENG.). 144p. pap. 19.99 (978-0-439-51763-8(X), Teaching Resources) Scholastic, Inc.

Rhodes, Judith & Hodgson, Julie, eds. Games for the Early Years: 26 Games to Make & Play. 2005. (Illus.). 88p. pap. (978-1-903853-55-9(9)) Brilliant Pubns.

Rickards, Lynne. Games Pink a Band. 2016. (Cambridge Reading Adventures Ser.). (ENG.). 16p. pap. 6.56 (978-1-316-60084-9(X)) Cambridge Univ. Pr.

Rigby, Christopher & Sail, Nicola. Let's Have a Christmas: Flip Quiz. 2003. (Family Flip Quiz Ser.). (Illus.). 152p. (J). spiral bd. 12.95 (978-1-902947-96-9(7)) Miles Kelly Publishing, Ltd. GBR. Dist: Independent Pubs. Group.

Ripley Entertainment Staff, contrib. by. Fun & Games. 2010. (Ripley's Believe It or Not Ser.). 36p. (YA). (gr. 3-18). lib. bdg. 19.95 (978-1-4222-1534-0(2)) Mason Crest.

Ripley's Believe It or Not, 16 vols., Set. Incl. All Consuming. Ripley Entertainment. (YA). (gr. 3-18). lib. bdg. 19.95 (978-1-4222-1536-4(9)); Amazing Earth. Ripley Entertainment. (YA). (gr. 3-18). lib. bdg. 19.95 (978-1-4222-1539-5(3)); Animal Antics. Ripley Entertainment Staff, contrib. by. (YA). (gr. 3-18). lib. bdg. 19.95 (978-1-4222-1535-7(0)); Arts & Entertainment. Ripley's Entertainment Inc Staff, contrib. by. (J). (gr. 5-18). lib. bdg. 19.95 (978-1-4222-1530-2(X)); Beyond Belief. Ripley Entertainment. (YA). (gr. 3-18). lib. bdg. 19.95 (978-1-4222-1537-1(7)); Beyond Understanding. Ripley Entertainment. (YA). (gr. 3-18). lib. bdg. 19.95 (978-1-4222-1531-9(8)); Body & Mind. Ripley Entertainment Staff, contrib. by. (YA). (gr. 3-18). lib. bdg. 19.95 (978-1-4222-1532-6(6)); Extraordinary Animals. Ripley Entertainment Staff, contrib. by. (YA). (gr. 3-18). lib. bdg. 19.95 (978-1-4222-1533-3(4)); Fun & Games. Ripley Entertainment Staff, contrib. by. (YA). (gr. 3-18). lib. bdg. 19.95 (978-1-4222-1534-0(2)); Life in the Fast Lane. Ripley Entertainment. (YA). (gr. 3-18). lib. bdg. 19.95 (978-1-4222-1538-8(5)); Off the Wall. Ripley Entertainment. (YA). (gr. 3-18). lib. bdg. 19.95 (978-1-4222-1542-5(3)); Taking Life to Extremes. Ripley Entertainment. (YA). (gr. 3-18). lib. bdg. 19.95 (978-1-4222-1540-1(7)); Totally Obsessed. Ripley Entertainment. (YA). (gr. 3-18). lib. bdg. 19.95 (978-1-4222-1541-8(5)); Was That a Good Idea? Ripley Entertainment. (YA). (gr. 3-18). lib. bdg. 19.95 (978-1-4222-1543-2(1)); What Are You Like? Ripley Entertainment. (YA). (gr. 3-18). lib. bdg. 19.95 (978-1-4222-1544-9(X)); Wonders of Science. Ripley Entertainment. (YA). (gr. 3-18). lib. bdg. 19.95 (978-1-4222-1545-6(8)); 36p. 2010. 2010. 319.20 (978-1-4222-1529-6(6)) Mason Crest.

Ripoll & Rovira. Hace un Buen Día? Ideal Para Jugar! 2004. (SPA.). 36p. (978-84-272-6143-3(8)) Molino, Editorial.

Rissman, Rebecca. Playing with Friends: Comparing Past & Present, 1 vol. 2014. (Comparing Past & Present Ser.). (ENG., Illus.). 24p. (gr. -1-1). lib. bdg. 22.65 (978-1-4329-8993-4(6), Acorn) Heinemann-Raintree.

Roberts, Laura. Careers in Gaming. 2017. (ENG.). 80p. (YA). (gr. 5-12). (978-1-68282-112-1(9)) ReferencePoint Pr., Inc.

Roehlkepartain, Jolene L. 101 Great Games for Infants, Toddlers, & Preschoolers: Active, Bible-Based Fun for Christian Education. 2004. (Illus.). 168p. pap. 18.99 (978-0-687-00814-8(X)) Abingdon Pr.

Rohrer, Neal. Rohrer's Fun Coloring & Games. Rohrer, Neal, illus. 2003. (Illus.). 28p. 3.95 (978-0-9721138-0-9(0)) Rohrer Design.

Romines, Garrett & Miko, Christopher. The Unofficial Holy Bible for Minecrafters: A Children's Guide to the Old & New Testament. 2015. (ENG.). 288p. (J). (gr. k-8). pap. 19.99 (978-1-63220-730-2(3), Sky Pony Pr.) Skyhorse Publishing Co., Inc.

Rose, Alexa. Spy Games. 2014. (PACKtivities Ser.: 3). (ENG.). 48p. (J). 11.99 (978-1-935703-38-9(2)) Downtown Bookworks.

Rosen Publishing Group. Get Outdoors, 8 vols., Sets 1-2. Incl. Set 1. 2009. lib. bdg. 95.80 (978-1-4358-3231-2(0)); Set 2. 2011. lib. bdg. 95.80 (978-1-4488-3308-5(6)); (J). (gr. 4-6). (Get Outdoors Ser.). (Illus.). 32p. 2011. Set lib. bdg. 191.60 (978-1-4488-3309-2(4), PowerKids Pr.) Rosen Publishing Group, Inc., The.

Rossignoli, Marco. The Complete Pinball Book: Collecting the Game & Its History, 1 vol. 2nd rev. ed. 2007. (Schiffer Book for Collectors Ser.). (ENG., Illus.). 320p. (gr. 10-13). 59.95 (978-0-7643-1586-2(2)) Schiffer Publishing, Ltd.

Roycroft, Mitch. Jennifer Harman. 2009. (Superstars of Poker Ser.). (Illus.). 64p. (YA). (gr. 3-7). lib. bdg. 22.95 (978-1-4222-0227-2(5)) Mason Crest.

—Johnny Orient Express Chan. 2009. (Superstars of Poker Ser.). (Illus.). 64p. (YA). (gr. 4-7). lib. bdg. 22.95 (978-1-4222-0224-1(0)) Mason Crest.

—Phil the Poker Brat Hellmuth. 2009. (Superstars of Poker Ser.). (Illus.). 64p. (YA). (gr. 4-7). lib. bdg. 22.95 (978-1-4222-0220-3(8)) Mason Crest.

—Phil Tiger Woods of Poker Ivey. 2009. (Superstars of Poker Ser.). (Illus.). 64p. (YA). (gr. 4-7). lib. bdg. 22.95 (978-1-4222-0221-0(6)) Mason Crest.

Roza, Greg. Paintball: Rules, Tips, Strategy, & Safety. 2009. (Sports from Coast to Coast Ser.). 48p. (gr. 6-6). 53.00 (978-1-60853-128-8(7), Rosen Reference) Rosen Publishing Group, Inc., The.

S. I. Artists Staff, illus. Fun & Games. 2003. 40p. (J). 3.95 (978-0-9729026-1-8(9)) Midwest Cylinder Management, Inc.

—Fun & Games. 2003. (J). per. (978-1-57657-854-4(2)) Paradise Pr., Inc.

Sach, Jacqueline. The Wham-O Hacky Sack Handbook: The Tips & Tricks for Becoming an Expert Shredder! 2008. (ENG.). 78p. (J). (gr. 5-18). pap. 14.95 (978-1-60433-002-1(3), Applesauce Pr.) Cider Mill Pr. Bk. Pubs., LLC.

Sacks, Janet. The Optical Illusion Pack. 2013. (ENG.). 36p. (J). 12.99 (978-0-7641-6617-4(4)) Barron's Educational Series, Inc.

Samuel, Charlie. Entertainment in Colonial America. 2003. (Primary Sources of Everyday Life in Colonial America Ser.). (Illus.). 24p. (J). lib. bdg. 22.60 (978-0-8239-6600-4(3), PowerKids Pr.) Rosen Publishing Group, Inc., The.

Sandler, Michael. Mighty MotoXers. 2009. (X-Moves Ser.). (Illus.). 24p. (J). (gr. 2-5). lib. bdg. 22.61 (978-1-59716-951-6(X)) Bearport Publishing Co., Inc.

Sanna, Lindsey. The Game. 2009. (Hip-Hop Ser.). (Illus.). 64p. (YA). (gr. 3-7). pap. 7.95 (978-1-4222-0329-3(8)) Mason Crest.

Santillo, LuAnn. Fun with Phonemes. Santillo, LuAnn, ed. 2004. (Half-Pint Readers Ser.). (Illus.). 36p. (J). (gr. -1-1). pap. 11.95 (978-1-59256-129-2(2)) Half-Pint Kids, Inc.

—Lots More Fun with Phonemes. Santillo, LuAnn, ed. 2004. (Half-Pint Readers Ser.). (Illus.). 36p. (J). (gr. -1-1). pap. 11.95 (978-1-59256-131-5(4)) Half-Pint Kids, Inc.

—More Fun with Phonemes. Santillo, LuAnn, ed. 2004. (Half-Pint Readers Ser.). (Illus.). 36p. (J). (gr. -1-1). pap. 11.95 (978-1-59256-130-8(6)) Half-Pint Kids, Inc.

Sarma, Kamya Subramanian & Fontichiaro, Kristin. Designing Board Games. 2017. (21st Century Skills Innovation Library: Makers As Innovators Junior Ser.). (ENG., Illus.). 24p. (J).

(gr. 2-5). lib. bdg. 28.50 *(978-1-63472-188-2(8)*, 209324) Cherry Lake Publishing.

Samat, Marjorie. Creativity Unhinged. 2013. 62p. pap. 8.79 *(978-0-9893189-0-7(7))* Jr Imagination.

Scarbro, Maxine. One Room Schoolgames: Children's Games of Yesteryear. 2003. (Illus.). 64p. per. 9.95 *(978-0-938985-05-1(1)*, Mountain Memories Bks.) Quarrier Pr.

Scholastic. The World of the Hunger Games: The Official Coloring Book. 2016. (ENG.). 96p. (J). (gr. 7). pap. 15.99 *(978-1-338-09619-4(2))* Scholastic, Inc.

Scholastic & Imagine Publishing Staff. Gaming Live. 2016. (ENG., Illus.). 128p. (J). (gr. 3-7). pap. 8.99 *(978-1-338-03273-4(9))* Scholastic, Inc.

Scholastic, Inc. Staff. Brain Play Preschool-1st. 2008. (J). 29.99 *(978-0-439-81350-1(6))* Scholastic, Inc.

—Vowel Sounds. 2010. (ENG.). (gr. k-2). 14.99 *(978-0-545-21376-9(2))* Teacher's Friend Pubns., Inc.

Scholastic, Inc. Staff & DreamWorks Animation Staff, contrib. by. Over the Hedge: Animal Antics. 2006. (Illus.). 16p. (J). *(978-1-4156-7542-7(2))* Scholastic, Inc.

Scholastic, Inc. Staff, et al. Alphabet: 10 Ready-to-Go Games That Help Children Learn & Practice Letter-Recognition Skills-Independently. 2009. (File-Folder Games in Color Ser.). (ENG.). 144p. pap. 19.99 *(978-0-439-46591-5(5)*, Teaching Resources) Scholastic, Inc.

—Minecraft: the Complete Handbook Collection (Updated Edition) An Official Mojang Book. 2015. (Minecraft Ser.). (ENG.). (J). (gr. 3-7). 35.96 *(978-0-545-82328-9(5))* Scholastic, Inc.

School Zone. Wonder Words Flash Action Software. 2007. 128p. pap. 15.99 *(978-1-58947-112-2(1))* School Zone Publishing Co.

School Zone Publishing Co. Make-A-Word Bingo Game. 2006. (ENG.). (J). 5.99 *(978-1-58947-496-3(1))* School Zone Publishing Co.

School Zone Staff. Old Maid. 2004. (ENG.). (J). 2.79 *(978-1-58947-992-0(0))* School Zone Publishing Co.

Schuette, Sarah L. Birthday Party Games, 1 vol. 2010. (Happy Birthday! Ser.). (ENG.). 24p. (gr. k-1). lib. bdg. 26.65 *(978-1-4296-4000-8(6)*, Pebble Plus) Capstone Press of Coughlan Cos.

Scott, Foresman and Company Staff. Up & over, Thrills & Spills. (J). 31.63 *(978-0-673-21375-4(7)*, Scott Foresman) Addison Wesley Schl.

Scratch N Sniff Staff. Scratch N Sniff Gang. 2005. 12p. 6.95 *(978-0-9762524-9-8(X))* Gimme Gimme Toys & Games, Inc.

Sesame Street Staff, creator. Sesame Street: Elmo & Me! Boxed Set. 2011. 40p. (J). bds. 12.99 *(978-1-60745-166-2(2))* Flying Frog Pubs.

Sévigny, Eric, illus. Caillou, Where Is My Cat? - Beginner Reader. 2016. (Read with Caillou Ser.). (ENG.). 32p. (J). (gr. -1-k). 3.99 *(978-2-89718-342-4(X))* Caillouet, Gerry.

Sharky & George. Don't You Dare. 2013. (Sharky & George Ser.). (ENG., Illus.). 96p. (J). (gr. -1). pap. 19.99 *(978-1-4052-5829-6(2))* Egmont Bks., Ltd. GBR. Dist: Independent Pubs. Group.

Shaw-Russell, Susan. Cinderella Activity Book. 2012. (Dover Little Activity Bks.). (ENG., Illus.). 32p. (J). (gr. -1-5). pap. 1.50 *(978-0-486-47517-2(4))* Dover Pubns., Inc.

Sherman, Michael. Suction Cup Critters. 2005. (ENG.). 20p. (J). 89.70 *(978-1-57054-269-5(4))* Klutz.

Sherman, Michael & Klutz Editors. Me vs. You: Head to Head Pencil Puzzles! 2011. (ENG.). 50p. (J). (gr. 3-7). 10.99 *(978-1-59174-929-5(8))* Klutz.

SiegeStones. 2004. (YA). 24.95 *(978-0-9764394-1-7(7)*, LOG002) Live Oak Games.

Sjonger, Rebecca. Maker Projects for Kids Who Love Games. 2016. (ENG., Illus.). 32p. (J). *(978-0-7787-2248-9(1))* Crabtree Publishing Co.

Slater, Lee. Board Game Builder: Milton Bradley, 1 vol. 2016. (Toy Trailblazers Ser.). (ENG., Illus.). 32p. (J). (gr. 3-6). lib. bdg. 27.07 *(978-1-62403-975-1(8)*, Checkerboard Library) ABDO Publishing Co.

Sleeping Bear Press. Diary of a Pennsylvania Kid. 2011. (State Journal Ser.). (ENG.). 128p. (J). (gr. 4-8). pap. 9.95 *(978-1-58536-610-1(2)*, 202226) Sleeping Bear Pr.

Sloan, Price Stern, et al. Flip, Sip, or Mad Libs. 2014. (Adult Mad Libs Ser.). (ENG.). 48p. (gr. 13). 4.99 *(978-0-8431-8236-1(9)*, Mad Libs) Penguin Young Readers Group.

Snape, Charles & Snape, Juliet. Brain Busters: Games, Puzzles & More! 2012. (Dover Children's Activity Bks.). (ENG., Illus.). 64p. (J). (gr. 3-5). pap. 9.99 *(978-0-486-48779-3(2))* Dover Pubns., Inc.

—Mind Twisters: Games, Puzzles & More! 2012. (Dover Children's Activity Bks.). (ENG., Illus.). 64p. (J). (gr. 3-5). pap. 9.99 *(978-0-486-48780-9(6))* Dover Pubns., Inc.

Snider, Brandon T. This or That? 2. 2017. (ENG., Illus.). 208p. (J). (gr. 3-5). pap. 8.95 *(978-1-4549-2103-5(X))* Sterling Publishing Co., Inc.

Snorta. 2003. mass mkt. 19.95 *(978-1-932359-14-5(1))* Out of the Box Publishing, Inc.

Solomon, Iris L. & Solomon, Ron. Friendz Pakz: Showbiz. 2003. (YA). (gr. 3-18). 4.99 *(978-1-930680-06-7(6)*, SSP-08SB) Swingset Pr., LLC.

Spiderman: Heroes & Adventures. 2009. (Illus.). (YA). 5.99 *(978-1-59524-044-6(6))* Giddy Up, LLC.

Spivet, Bonnie. Playing Games Online. 2011. (CyberSmarts: Staying Safe Online Ser.). (ENG.). 24p. (J). (gr. 4-6). pap. 10.00 *(978-1-4488-6423-2(2))*; lib. bdg. 21.25 *(978-1-4488-6414-0(3))* Rosen Publishing Group, Inc., The. (PowerKids Pr.).

Spot It. 2010. (Spot It Ser.). (ENG & ABK.). 32p. (gr. 1-2). lib. bdg. 54.64 *(978-1-4296-5263-6(2)*, Aplus Bks.) Capstone Press of Coughlan Cos.

Squareman, Clarence. My Book of Indoor Games. 2006. pap. *(978-1-4068-0699-1(4))* Echo Library.

Stadther, Michael. 101 New Puzzles Clues, Maps, Tantalizing Tales: And Stories of Real Treasure. Stadther, Michael, illus. 2006. (Treasure's Trove Ser.). (ENG., Illus.). 112p. (J). pap. 12.99 *(978-1-4169-2655-9(0))* Treasure Trove, Inc.

Stagnitti, Karen. Playthings: 101 Used for Everyday Objects. Treffry, Teresa, illus. (J). (gr. k-3). pap. *(978-1-876367-61-9(X))* Wizard Bks.

Standke, Linda. Play & Learn Bible Games: 16 Reproducible Games to Help Children Grow in Their Faith. 2003. 160p. (J). per. 12.99 *(978-0-88724-873-3(X))* Carson-Dellosa Publishing, LLC.

Staples, Edna. Wolf over the Ridge: Games We Used to Play. 2003. (Illus.). 228p. per. 15.00 *(978-1-932621-16-7(4))* Open Bk. Publishing.

Starzinsky, Inca & Williams, Ruth. DIY Board Games. 2014. (ENG.). (J). (gr. -1-3). 29.95 *(978-1-85669-951-8(X))* King, Laurence Publishing GBR. Dist: Hachette Bk. Group.

Steele-Saccio, Eva & Klutz Editors. Thumb Wars: The Ultimate Guide. 2011. (ENG.). 32p. (J). (gr. 3-7). 12.99 *(978-1-59174-938-7(7))* Klutz.

Stein, David & Klutz Editors. How to Make Monstrous, Huge, Unbelievably Big Bubbles. 2005. (ENG., Illus.). 38p. (J). (gr. 3-7). 16.95 *(978-1-57054-257-2(0))* Klutz.

Sterling Children's, Sterling. M. A. S. H. What Does Your Future Hold? 2017. (ENG., Illus.). 96p. (J). (gr. 2-6). pap. 6.95 ***(978-1-4549-2278-0(8))*** Sterling Publishing Co., Inc.

Stotter, Ruth. A Loop of String: String Stories & String Stunts: Traditional & Original String Figures & Stories. Coffey, Kevin, illus. 2009. 110p. (J). pap. 22.95 *(978-1-58790-170-6(6))* Regent Pr.

Stuttering Foundation, The. Trouble at Recess, No. 34. 2008. (Illus.). 29p. (J). pap. 5.00 *(978-0-933388-60-4(8))* Stuttering Foundation, The.

Sullivan, Carolyn Rose, illus. The Music Box: Songs, Rhymes, & Games for Young Children, 1 box. 2006. 200p. (J). 49.95 *(978-0-9772717-1-9(4))* ELZ Publishing.

Sutherland, Jon & Chalk, Gary. Bridgewater FC - 5-3-2. 2004. (Football Fantasy S. Ser.). (ENG., Illus.). 304p. pap. 9.50 *(978-1-84046-609-6(X)*, Wizard Books) Icon Bks., Ltd. GBR. Dist: Publishers Group Canada.

—Medway United - 4-5-1. 2004. (Football Fantasy S. Ser.). (ENG., Illus.). 272p. pap. 9.50 *(978-1-84046-599-0(9)*, Wizard Books) Icon Bks., Ltd. GBR. Dist: Publishers Group Canada.

—Mersey City - 4-4-2. 2004. (Football Fantasy S. Ser.). (ENG., Illus.). 272p. pap. 9.50 *(978-1-84046-597-6(2)*, Wizard Books) Icon Bks., Ltd. GBR. Dist: Publishers Group Canada.

—Thames United. 2004. (Football Fantasy S. Ser.). (ENG., Illus.). 272p. pap. 9.50 *(978-1-84046-598-3(0)*, Wizard Books) Icon Bks., Ltd. GBR. Dist: Publishers Group Canada.

—Trent Albion. 2004. (Football Fantasy S. Ser.). (ENG., Illus.). 272p. pap. 9.50 *(978-1-84046-590-7(5)*, Wizard Books) Icon Bks., Ltd. GBR. Dist: Publishers Group Canada.

Swain, Heather. Play These Games: 101 Delightful Diversions Using Everyday Items. 2012. (ENG.). 256p. (gr. 12). 14.00 *(978-0-399-53744-8(9)*, TarcherPerigee) Penguin Publishing Group.

Swaine, Meg. Career Building Through Alternate Reality Gaming. 2009. (Digital Career Building Ser.). 64p. (gr. 6-6). 58.50 *(978-1-61512-162-5(5))* Rosen Publishing Group, Inc., The.

Swartz, Clay. Who Wins? 100 Historical Figures Go Head-to-Head & You Decide the Winner! Booth, Tom, illus. 2016. (Who Wins? Ser.). (ENG.). 104p. (J). (gr. 3-6). spiral bd. 14.95 *(978-0-7611-8544-4(5))* Workman Publishing Co., Inc.

Taggar, Sam & Williamson, Susan. Great Games! Old & New, Indoor-Outdoor, Board, Card, Ball, & Word. 2004. (Kids Can Bks.). (ENG., Illus.). 128p. (J). (gr. 2-9). pap. 12.95 *(978-1-885593-72-6(4)*, Ideal Pubns.) Worthy Publishing.

Takemiya, Masaki. Imagination of a Go Master: Logic-Shattering Cosmic Style. Bianchi, Leslie, ed. Terry, Robert J., tr. 2004.Tr. of Japanese language edition Isbn 4-576=94060-0. (ENG., Illus.). 222p. spiral bd. 23.95 *(978-0-9713230-0-1(3)*, 323003) NEMESIS Enterprises, L.P.

Tango Books Staff. The Book of Dragon Myths. Wade, Gini, illus. 2011. (Pop-Up Board Games Ser.). (ENG.). 10p. (J). (gr. -1-2). 29.99 *(978-1-85707-720-9(2))* Tango Bks. GBR. Dist: Independent Pubs. Group.

Teckentrup, Britta. Where's the Pair? Teckentrup, Britta, illus. 2015. (ENG., Illus.). 52p. (J). (-k). 14.99 *(978-0-7636-7772-5(8)*, Big Picture Press) Candlewick Pr.

Teora, creator. 400 Funny Games for Smart Kids. 2005. (Illus.). 136p. (J). per. 7.95 *(978-1-59496-008-6(9))* Teora USA LLC.

—500 Games for Smart Kids. 2005. (Illus.). 112p. (J). per. 7.95 *(978-1-59496-006-2(2))* Teora USA LLC.

Teora, ed. Activity & Game BK. 2004. 96p. Vol. 1. pap. 7.95 *(978-1-59496-030-7(5))* Vol. 2. pap. 7.95 *(978-1-59496-031-4(3))* Vol. 3. pap. 7.95 *(978-1-59496-004-8(6))* Vol. 4. pap. 7.95 *(978-1-59496-005-5(4))* Teora USA LLC.

—Amazing Games. 2005. 108p. pap. 7.95 *(978-1-59496-007-9(0))* Teora USA LLC.

Thomas Nelson Publishing Staff. Original Dance Praise: Game Only, 0 vols. 2008. cd-rom 29.95 *(978-1-4003-1340-2(6))* Nelson, Thomas Inc.

Thomson, Ruth. The Science & Inventions Creativity Book: Games, Models to Make, High-Tech Craft Paper, Stickers, & Stencils. 2013. (Creativity Bks.). (ENG., Illus.). 80p. (J). (gr. 1-6). pap. 12.99 *(978-1-4380-0251-4(3))* Barron's Educational Series, Inc.

Time for Bible Puzzles & Games. (Illus.). 32p. (YA). (gr. 5-18). pap. 2.25 *(978-0-87162-662-2(4)*, E9705) Warner Pr., Inc.

Titus, David. Native Alaskan String Figures. 2007. (Illus.). 32p. (J). 5.99 *(978-0-9744562-7-0(6))* WRDSMTH Productions.

TNT Ministries Staff. God's Miracle Maker: Elisha. 2007. (King of Clubs Ser.). (ENG.). 96p. (J). pap. 17.99 *(978-1-84550-291-1(4)*, 9781845502911) Christian Focus Pubns. GBR. Dist: Bookmasters Distribution.

Tomljanovic, Tatiana. Rallying. 2009. (Extreme Ser.). (Illus.). 32p. (J). (gr. 4-6). pap. 9.95 *(978-1-60596-133-0(7))*; lib. bdg. 26.00 *(978-1-60596-132-3(9))* Weigl Pubs., Inc.

Top That Publishing Staff, ed. Rude Cocktails. 2004. 48p. pap. *(978-1-84510-215-9(0))* Top That! Publishing PLC.

—Strip Poker. 2004. (Naughty Shenanigans Ser.). (Illus.). 48p. *(978-1-84510-214-2(2))* Top That! Publishing PLC.

Torma, Patrick. Alphabet for American Children Coloring Book. 2010. 88p. pap. 12.99 *(978-1-4520-5231-1(X))* AuthorHouse.

Torpie, Kate. Knights & Castles. Denmark, Thomas, illus. 2008. (ENG.). 24p. (J). (gr. 2-17). 19.99 *(978-1-58476-726-8(X))* Innovative Kids.

Toth, Carolyn. Where Is Baby? 2012. 24p. pap. 10.99 *(978-1-4497-6302-2(2)*, WestBow Pr.) Author Solutions, Inc.

Touch & Feel Playtime. braille ed. 2004. (J). (gr. -1-18). bds. *(978-0-616-14614-9(0))* Canadian National Institute for the Blind/Institut National Canadien pour les Aveugles.

Travel Games Pad. 2017. (Tear-Off Pads Ser.). (ENG.). (J). pap. 5.99 ***(978-0-7945-3739-5(1)***, Usborne) EDC Publishing.

Tudhope, Simon. Pencil & Paper Games. 2015. (Tear-Off Pads Ser.). (ENG.). 204p. (J). (gr. k-5). pap. 5.99 *(978-0-7945-2183-7(5)*, Usborne) EDC Publishing.

Tukey, Paul & Rowell, Victoria. Tag, Toss & Run: 40 Classic Lawn Games. 2012. (ENG., Illus.). 208p. pap. 14.95 *(978-1-60342-560-5(8)*, 62560) Storey Publishing, LLC.

Tullet, Hervé. The Ball Game. 2014. (ENG., Illus.). 14p. 12.95 *(978-0-7148-6688-8(1))* Phaidon Pr., Inc.

—The Countryside Game. 2013. (ENG., Illus.). 14p. 12.95 *(978-0-7148-6074-9(3))* Phaidon Pr., Inc.

—The Eyes Game. 2014. (ENG., Illus.). 14p. 12.95 *(978-0-7148-6689-5(X))* Phaidon Pr., Inc.

—The Finger Circus Game. Oceano Editorial Staff, ed. 2013. (ENG., Illus.). 14p. 12.95 *(978-0-7148-6531-7(1))* Phaidon Pr., Inc.

—The Fnger Sport Game. 2015. (ENG., Illus.). 14p. (gr. -1 — 1). 12.95 *(978-0-7148-6979-7(1))* Phaidon Pr., Inc.

—The Game of Finger Worms. 2011. (ENG., Illus.). 14p. (gr. -1 — 1). 12.95 *(978-0-7148-6071-8(9))* Phaidon Pr., Inc.

—The Game of Light. Children's Publication Company Staff, ed. 2011. (ENG., Illus.). 14p. (gr. -1 — 1). 12.95 *(978-0-7148-6189-0(8))* Phaidon Pr., Inc.

—The Game of Lines. 2015. (ENG., Illus.). 14p. (gr. -1-17). 12.95 *(978-0-7148-6873-8(6))* Phaidon Pr., Inc.

—The Game of Shadows. 2013. (ENG., Illus.). 14p. 12.95 *(978-0-7148-6532-4(X))* Phaidon Pr., Inc.

—The Game of Tops & Tails. 2015. (ENG., Illus.). 14p. (gr. -1-17). 12.95 *(978-0-7148-6874-5(4))* Phaidon Pr., Inc.

—The Good Morning Game. 2015. (ENG., Illus.). 14p. (gr. -1-17). 12.95 *(978-0-7148-6875-2(2))* Phaidon Pr., Inc.

—Press Here Game. 2014. (ENG., Illus.). 1p. (J). (gr. -1-1). bds. 19.99 *(978-1-4521-3736-0(6))* Chronicle Bks. LLC.

—The Trail Game. 2015. (ENG., Illus.). 14p. (gr. -1-17). 12.95 *(978-0-7148-6876-9(0))* Phaidon Pr., Inc.

Turnbull, Stephanie. Fun & Games. 2016. (Sleepover Secrets Ser.). 24p. (gr. 2-6). 28.50 *(978-1-62588-380-3(3)*, Smart Apple Media) Black Rabbit Bks.

—Fun with Friends: Style Secrets for Girls. 2013. (Girl Talk Ser.). 32p. (gr. 4-7). 31.35 *(978-1-59920-946-3(2))* Black Rabbit Bks.

Tutankhamen. 2003. mass mkt. 9.95 *(978-1-932359-07-7(9))* Out of the Box Publishing, Inc.

Tuxworth, Nicola. Mix & Match. 2016. (Learn-a-Word Book Ser.). (ENG., Illus.). 20p. (J). (gr. -1-2). bds. 6.99 *(978-1-84322-862-2(9)*, Armadillo) Anness Publishing GBR. Dist: National Bk. Network.

Tyler, Jenny. Duck's Bathtime. Cartwright, Stephen, illus. 2005. 4p. (J). (gr. -1-3). 7.95 *(978-0-7945-0570-7(8)*, Usborne) EDC Publishing.

U. S. National Geographic Society Staff. NG Kids Big Book of Fun. 2010. (ENG., Illus.). 80p. (J). (gr. 1-4). pap. 6.99 *(978-1-4263-0661-7(X)*, National Geographic Children's Bks.) National Geographic Society.

Ubberball, R. The Wham-O Superball. Copeland, Cynthia L., illus. 2008. (ENG.). 80p. (J). (gr. 3). pap. 12.95 *(978-1-60433-049-6(X)*, Applesauce Pr.) Cider Mill Pr. Bk. Pubs., LLC.

UFlipp. You & Your Military Hero: Building Positive Thinking Skills During Your Hero's Deployment. 2009. 72p. (J). pap. 19.95 *(978-1-59298-268-4(9))* Beaver's Pond Pr., Inc.

Unisystem Staff. Eden Studios Presents, Vol. 3. 2005. 69p. (YA). pap. 15.00 *(978-1-891153-64-8(1))* Eden Studios, Inc.

United States Bingo. 2005. (J). pap. *(978-1-59461-069-1(X))* eeBoo Corp.

University Games Staff, compiled by. Made You Laugh for Kids! Books So Fun You'll Pee Your Pants! 2005. (ENG., Illus.). 224p. (J). (gr. -1-3). pap. 14.95 *(978-1-57528-995-3(4))* Univ. Games.

Valenti, Joseph. NERO Rule Book: 8th Edition. 8th ed. 2009. (ENG., Illus.). 148p. (YA). (gr. 9-18). pap. 24.95 *(978-0-9700563-0-6(3))* NERO International Holding Co., Inc.

van Genechten, Guido. Guess What? 2012. (Guess Along Ser.). (ENG.). 16p. (J). (gr. k — 1). 9.95 *(978-1-60537-116-0(5))* Cobblestone Publishing Co.

van Lieshout, Maria. Traffic Jam Matching Game. 2014. (ENG., Illus.). 36p. (J). (gr. -1-k). bds. 14.99 *(978-1-4521-3356-0(5))* Chronicle Bks. LLC.

Van Rynbach, Iris. Pilgrim House Sticker Activity Book. 2003. (Dover Little Activity Books Stickers Ser.). (ENG., Illus.). 4p. (J). (gr. k-3). 1.99 *(978-0-486-42628-0(9))* Dover Pubns., Inc.

Vecchione, Glen. Kids' Games. 2007. (ENG., Illus.). 352p. (J). (gr. 3-7). pap. 6.95 *(978-1-4027-4989-6(9))* Sterling Publishing Co., Inc.

Volke, Gordon, et al, illus. Panda Patrol Big Activity Book. 2004. 24p. 6.00 *(978-1-84161-111-2(5))* Ravette Publishing, Ltd. GBR. Dist: Parkwest Pubns., Inc.

—Panda Patrol Travel Games with Stickers. 2004. 16p. pap., act. bk. ed. 6.00 *(978-1-84161-110-5(7))* Ravette Publishing, Ltd. GBR. Dist: Parkwest Pubns., Inc.

Wai, Joan. 100+ Baby Shower Games. 2006. (100+ Ser.). (ENG., Illus.). 128p. pap. 14.00 *(978-0-9728354-1-1(5))* Brainstorm Co., The.

Waldron, Hannah, illus. Pirate Adventure Dice. 2014. (ENG.). 16p. (J). (gr. 1-4). 14.95 *(978-1-85669-938-9(2))* King, Laurence Publishing GBR. Dist: Hachette Bk. Group.

Walker, Niki & Dann, Sarah. Badminton in Action. 2003. (Sports in Action Ser.). (ENG., Illus.). 32p. (J). (gr. 1-4). pap. *(978-0-7787-0354-9(1))*; lib. bdg. *(978-0-7787-0334-1(7))* Crabtree Publishing Co.

Walsh, Doug. Viewtiful Joe 2 Official Strategy Guide. 2004. (ENG., Illus.). 112p. pap. 14.99 *(978-0-7440-0489-2(6))* Pearson Education.

Walsh, Liza Gardner. Muddy Boots: Outdoor Activities for Children. 2015. (ENG., Illus.). 136p. (J). (gr. -1-5). 16.95 *(978-1-60893-370-9(9)*, 1388618) Down East Bks.

Walter Foster Jr. Creative Team. Learn to Draw Angry Birds: Bad Piggies: Featuring All Your Favorite Crafty, Crazy Pigs, Including King Pig, Foreman Pig, Corporal Pig, & More! 2014. (Licensed Learn to Draw Ser.). (ENG., Illus.). 64p. (J). (gr. 1-17). pap. 9.95 *(978-1-60058-448-0(9))* Quarto Publishing Group USA.

Walton, Sally, et al. Fun Projects & Amazing Things to Make, Do, Play & Give: Two Fantastic Books in a Box - the Ultimate Rainy-Day Collection with 220 Exciting Step-By-Step Projects Shown in over 3000 Photographs, 2 vols. 2013. (ENG., Illus.). 265p. 25.00 *(978-1-84322-960-5(9))* Anness Publishing GBR. Dist: National Bk. Network.

Ward, Jennifer. Let's Go Outside! Outdoor Activities & Projects to Get You & Your Kids Closer to Nature. 2009. (ENG., Illus.). 144p. (gr. 3-7). pap. 14.00 *(978-1-59030-698-7(8)*, Roost Books) Shambhala Pubns., Inc.

Warmachine: Prime. 2004. (GER.). 224p. (YA). per. *(978-0-9706970-9-7(0))* Privateer Pr., Inc.

Waschak, Jay, et al. Wars of the Boltians & Kuissians. Watson, Travis & Lohr, Tyrel, illus. 2004. per. 25.00 *(978-0-9764048-1-1(8))* Victory by Any Means Games.

Webber, Sharon & Bradburn, Ryan, concepts. Holiday & Seasonal Chipper Chat: Cc99. 2007. (J). 64.95 *(978-1-58650-789-3(3))* Super Duper Pubns.

Wechsler, Kimberly. 303 Kid-Approved Exercises & Active Games. Sleva, Michael, illus. 2013. (SmartFun Activity Bks.). (ENG.). (gr. k-3). 144p. pap. 14.95 *(978-0-89793-619-4(1))*; 168p. spiral bd. 19.95 *(978-0-89793-624-8(8))* Turner Publishing Co. (Hunter Hse.).

—303 Preschooler-Approved Exercises & Active Games. Sleva, Michael, illus. 2013. (SmartFun Activity Bks.). (ENG.). 168p. (gr. k-k). pap. 14.95 *(978-0-89793-618-7(3))*; spiral bd. 19.95 *(978-0-89793-623-1(X))* Turner Publishing Co. (Hunter Hse.).

—303 Tween-Approved Exercises & Active Games. Sleva, Michael, illus. 2013. (SmartFun Activity Bks.). (ENG.). 168p. (gr. 3-6). pap. 14.95 *(978-0-89793-620-0(5))*; spiral bd. 19.95 *(978-0-89793-625-5(6))* Turner Publishing Co. (Hunter Hse.).

Wee Sing Staff. Games, Games, Games. (J). 7.98 incl. audio NewSound, LLC.

Weedin, Chris. Horror Worlds. 2006. (ENG., Illus.). 107p. (YA). (gr. 5-18). per. 19.99 *(978-0-9778263-0-8(9))* Crucifiction Games.

Weiss, Bobbi & Weiss, David. Monsters: The Hunt & the Capture. Deen, David, illus. 2008. (ENG.). 24p. (J). (gr. 2-17). 19.99 *(978-1-58476-727-5(8))* Innovative Kids.

Wells, H. G. Little Wars & Floor Games (A companion piece to Little Wars) 2006. 56p. pap. *(978-1-84637-799-0(4))* Echo Library.

Wendorff, Anne. Paintball. 2008. (Action Sports Ser.). (ENG., Illus.). 24p. (J). (gr. 3-7). lib. bdg. 25.95 *(978-1-60014-198-0(6))* Bellwether Media.

West, Tracey. Yu-Gi-Oh! 2016. (Yu-Gi-Oh! Ser.). (ENG., Illus.). 144p. (J). (gr. 3-7). pap. 8.99 *(978-0-545-94075-7(3))* Scholastic, Inc.

Western New York Trivia Quotient. 7.95 *(978-0-9620314-0-3(2))* Western New York Wares, Inc.

Whad Ya Know? 2003. mass mkt. 19.95 *(978-1-932359-02-2(8))* Out of the Box Publishing, Inc.

Whiting, Jim. BMX. 2016. (J). *(978-1-60818-691-4(1)*, Creative Education) Creative Co., The.

Wilcox, Christine. Gambling Addiction. 2015. (ENG., Illus.). 96p. (J). lib. bdg. *(978-1-60152-758-5(6))* ReferencePoint Pr., Inc.

WildSide! 2003. mass mkt. 9.95 *(978-1-932359-05-3(2))* Out of the Box Publishing, Inc.

Williams, Robert & Wood, Robert. Stacked Deck: A Program to Prevent Problem Gambling: Facilitator's Guide. 2010. (ENG., Illus.). 112p. (J). 59.95 *(978-1-59285-893-4(7))* Hazelden.

Willis Hudson, Cheryl. Hands Can. Bourke, John-Francis, illus. 2013. (ENG.). 32p. (J). (-k). 4.99 *(978-0-7636-6336-0(0))* Candlewick Pr.

Wilson, Deborah A. What's Your Number? 3 Digit Lottery Tracker. 2007. 196p. per. 12.95 *(978-1-4327-0863-4(5))* Outskirts Pr., Inc.

Wiseman, Blaine. Surfing. 2015. (J). *(978-1-4896-4299-8(4))* Weigl Pubs., Inc.

Woods, Christopher & McClintic, Ben, illus. Where's Hanuman? 2009. (ENG.). 32p. (J). (gr. 3-18). 9.95 *(978-0-9779785-8-8(3))* Torchlight Publishing.

World Book-Childcraft International Staff, contrib. by. Brain Games: A Supplement to Childcraft — The How & Why Library. 2010. (J). *(978-0-7166-0624-6(0))* World Bk., Inc.

Worth, Richard. Gambling: Winner or Loser? 2009. (Controversy! Ser.). 112p. (gr. 7). 37.07 *(978-0-7614-4233-2(2))* Marshall Cavendish GBR. Dist: Marshall Cavendish Corp.

Wyldeck, Kathi. Grammar & Vocabulary Games for Children. 2007. 83p. pap. 12.95 *(978-1-84799-930-6(1))*; 81p. pap. 12.95 *(978-1-84753-579-5(8))* Lulu Pr., Inc.

Young, Judy. Lazy Days of Summer. O'Malley, Kathy, illus. rev. ed. 2007. (ENG.). 32p. (J). (gr. k-6). 15.95 *(978-1-58536-241-7(7))* Sleeping Bear Pr.

Younie, Bradford. Now Playing: Roleplaying in Every TV Genre 2004. (Illus.). 224p. (YA). 35.00 *(978-0-9749150-0-5(9)*, CAR1000) Carnivore Games.

Zaslavsky, Claudia. More Math Games & Activities from Around the World. 2003. (ENG.). 176p. (J). (gr. 4). pap. 16.95 *(978-1-55652-501-8(X))* Chicago Review Pr., Inc.

Zeiger, Jennifer. The Making of Minecraft. 2017. (21st Century Skills Innovation Library: Unofficial Guides). (ENG., Illus.). 32p. (J). (gr. 4-8). lib. bdg. 29.93 *(978-1-63472-193-6(4)*, 209344) Cherry Lake Publishing.

Zuckerman, Andrew, photos by. Creature Matching Game. 2014. (ENG., Illus.). 36p. (J). (gr. -1-k). bds. 14.99 *(978-1-4521-1723-2(3))* Chronicle Bks. LLC.

10 Days in Africa. 2003. mass mkt. 19.95 *(978-1-932359-08-4(7))* Out of the Box Publishing, Inc.

10 Days in the USA. 2003. mass mkt. 19.95 *(978-1-932359-09-1(5))* Out of the Box Publishing, Inc.

1000 Games for Smart Kids. 2004. (Illus.). 384p. (J). pap. 14.95 *(978-1-59496-001-7(1))* Teora USA LLC.

43 Degrees North LLC Staff. Tailgate Trivia National Parks 2003. (Illus.). 60p. (YA). ring bd. 6.99 *(978-0-9744444-0-6(5))* 43 Degrees North LLC.

GAMES—FICTION

Aceti, Jerome & ASF, Jerome. Bacca & the Riddle of the Diamond Dragon: An Unofficial Minecrafter's Adventure. 2015. (ENG.). 224p. (J). (gr. 2). pap. 9.99 *(978-1-5107-0398-8(5)*, Sky Pony Pr.) Skyhorse Publishing Co., Inc.

Ackelsberg, Amy. Easter Surprise. Thomas, Laura, illus. 2011. (Strawberry Shortcake Ser.). (ENG.). 24p. (J). (gr. -1-k). mass mkt. 4.99 *(978-0-448-45547-1(1),* Grosset & Dunlap) Penguin Young Readers Group.

Aggs, Patrice. Strawberry Squirt. 2004. (Pandas Ser.: 27). (ENG., Illus.). 64p. (J). pap. 9.95 *(978-0-86278-805-6(6))* O'Brien Pr., Ltd., The IRL. Dist: Dufour Editions, Inc.

Albee, Sarah. Elmo Says... Leigh, Tom, illus. 2009. (Big Bird's Favorites Board Bks.). (ENG.). 24p. (J). (gr. k — 1). bds. 4.99 *(978-0-375-84540-6(2),* Random Hse. Bks. for Young Readers) Random Hse. Children's Bks.

—Trevor el Ingenioso; Clever Trevor. 2008. pap. 34.95 *(978-0-7613-3868-0(3))* Kane Press, Inc.

Albee, Sarah & Hood, Susan. Blue's Opposites Game. 2006. (Blue's Room Ser.). (ENG., Illus.). 26p. (J). (gr. -1-k). bds. 5.99 *(978-1-4169-0663-6(0),* Simon Spotlight/Nickelodeon) Simon Spotlight/Nickelodeon.

Alfonsi, Alice. The Playing Card Cases. Harrington, Rich, illus. 2007. 96p. (J). *(978-0-545-01087-0(X))* Scholastic, Inc.

Allen, Crystal. How Lamar's Bad Prank Won a Bubba-Sized Trophy. (ENG.). (J). (gr. 3-7). 2012. 304p. pap. 6.99 *(978-0-06-199273-5(9))* 2011. 288p. 16.99 *(978-0-06-199272-8(0))* HarperCollins Pubs.

Altebrando, Tara. The Best Night of Your (Pathetic) Life. 2013. (ENG.). 256p. (YA). (gr. 9). pap. 8.99 *(978-0-14-242640-1(7),* Speak) Penguin Young Readers Group.

Amerikaner, Susan. Game On! 2012. (Step into Reading Level 2 Ser.). lib. bdg. 13.55 *(978-0-606-26799-1(9),* Turtleback) Turtleback Bks.

Anastasio, Dina. The Magic Turtle & la tortuga Mágica: 6 English, 6 Spanish Adaptations. 2011. (ENG & SPA.). (J). 75.00 net. *(978-1-4108-5650-0(X))* Benchmark Education Co.

Anders, Lou. Nightborn. 2015. (Thrones & Bones Ser.). (ENG.). 368p. (J). (gr. 3-7). 16.99 *(978-0-385-39036-1(X),* Crown Books For Young Readers) Random Hse. Children's Bks.

—Skyborn. (Thrones & Bones Ser.: 3). (ENG., Illus.). (J). (gr. 3-7). 2017. 400p. 7.99 ***(978-0-385-39043-9(2),*** Yearling) 2016. 384p. 16.99 *(978-0-385-39040-8(8),* Crown Books For Young Readers) Random Hse. Children's Bks.

Anderson, John David. Insert Coin to Continue. (ENG.). 336p. (J). (gr. 3-7). 2017. pap. 7.99 ***(978-1-4814-4705-8(X))*** 2016. (Illus.). 16.99 *(978-1-4814-4704-1(1))* Simon & Schuster Children's Publishing. (Aladdin).

Anderson, M. T. The Game of Sunken Places. 2005. (Norumbegan Quartet: No. 1). 260p. (J). (gr. 4-7). 13.65 *(978-0-7569-5253-2(0))* Perfection Learning Corp.

Anderson, Suzette. Cybertreks: Wildest West. 2004. 196p. pap. 13.95 *(978-0-595-30840-8(6))* iUniverse, Inc.

Arena, Felice & Kettle, Phil. Battle of the Games. Gordon, Gus, illus. 2004. (J). pap. *(978-1-59336-372-7(9))* Mondo Publishing.

Arena, Felice, et al. Battle of the Games. Gordon, Gus & Vane, Mitch, illus. 2004. 48p. (J). pap. *(978-0-7329-9254-5(0))* Mondo Publishing.

Arnold, Tedd. I Spy Fly Guy! Arnold, Tedd, illus. 2009. (Fly Guy Ser.: 7). (Illus.). lib. bdg. 17.20 *(978-0-606-07098-0(2),* Turtleback) Turtleback Bks.

Awdry, W. & Berrios, Frank. Thomas & Friends Puzzle Book. Random House Staff, illus. 2010. (Puzzle Book Ser.). (ENG.). 10p. (J). (gr. -1-2). 8.99 *(978-0-375-86168-0(8),* Random Hse. Bks. for Young Readers) Random Hse. Children's Bks.

Axelrod, Amy & McGinley-Nally, Sharon. Pigs at Odds: Fun with Math & Games. McGinley-Nally, Sharon, illus. 2003. (ENG., Illus.). 40p. (J). (gr. -1-4). 7.99 *(978-0-689-86144-4(3),* Aladdin) Simon & Schuster Children's Publishing.

Barbour, Ralph Henry. Left Tackle Thayer. 2006. (ENG.). 196p. pap. 19.99 *(978-1-4264-7077-6(0));* 216p. pap. 22.99 *(978-1-4264-7153-7(X))* Creative Media Partners, LLC.

Barchers, Suzanne I. Kip Wins!, 1 vol. 2011. (Targeted Phonics Ser.). (ENG., Illus.). 16p. (J). (gr. k-2). pap. 5.99 *(978-1-4333-2411-6(3))* Teacher Created Materials, Inc.

—Main Street Game Day, 1 vol. 2011. (Targeted Phonics Ser.). (ENG.). 16p. (J). (gr. k-2). pap. 5.99 *(978-1-4333-2922-7(0))* Teacher Created Materials, Inc.

Barnett, Penny. Matilda & Puppy's Beach Adventure. 2012. 24p. pap. 15.99 *(978-1-4797-1106-2(3))* Xlibris Corp.

Beckwith, Kathy & Lyon, Lea. Playing War, 1 vol. 2005. (ENG., Illus.). 32p. (J). (gr. 2-6). 16.95 *(978-0-88448-267-3(7),* 884267) Tilbury Hse. Pubs.

Beil, Michael D. The Secret Cellar. 2013. (Red Blazer Girls Ser.). (ENG., Illus.). 288p. (J). (gr. 5). pap. 8.99 *(978-0-375-86495-7(4),* Yearling) Random Hse. Children's Bks.

Bender, Albert C. More 'Kids in the Alley' Tales. 2011. (Illus.). 200p. pap. 16.95 *(978-1-4327-7174-4(4))* Outskirts Pr., Inc.

Benjamin, Rick A. The Hunt for Lost Treasure, 1 vol. 2010. 56p. pap. 16.95 *(978-1-4489-6417-8(2))* America Star Bks.

Benton, Jim. Okay, So Maybe I Do Have Superpowers. Benton, Jim, illus. 2011. (Dear Dumb Diary Ser.: 11). (ENG., Illus.). 160p. (J). (gr. 3-7). pap. 6.99 *(978-0-545-11615-2(5),* Scholastic Paperbacks) Scholastic, Inc.

Berenstain, Stan & Berenstain, Jan. The Berenstain Bears Play T-Ball. Berenstain, Stan & Berenstain, Jan, illus. Berenstain, Mike, illus. (I Can Read Level 1 Ser.). (ENG.). 32p. (J). (gr. k-3). 2005. 16.99 *(978-0-06-058337-8(1))* 2004. pap. 3.99 *(978-0-06-058338-5(X))* HarperCollins Pubs.

Bergen, Lara. Buzzy Bee Plays Hide & Seek. 2010. 12p. (J). (gr. -1). 9.95 *(978-1-60747-720-4(3),* Pickwick Pr.) Phoenix Bks., Inc.

Berlin, Eric. The Potato Chip Puzzles. 2010. (Puzzling World of Winston Breen Ser.: 2). (ENG.). 272p. (J). (gr. 3-7). 7.99 *(978-0-14-241637-2(1),* Puffin Books) Penguin Young Readers Group.

Birney, Betty G. Humphrey's Treasure Hunt Trouble. Burris, Priscilla, illus. 2017. (Humphrey's Tiny Tales Ser.: 6). (ENG.). 96p. (J). (gr. k-3). 4.99 ***(978-0-14-751462-2(2),*** Puffin Books); 14.99 ***(978-0-399-17231-1(9),*** G.P. Putnam's Sons Books for Young Readers) Penguin Young Readers Group.

Blake, Stephanie J. The Marble Queen, 0 vols. 2012. (ENG.). 192p. (YA). (gr. 5-9). 16.99 *(978-0-7614-6227-9(9),* 9780761462279, Amazon Children's Publishing) Amazon Publishing.

Bloom, Suzanne. Treasure. 2007. (Goose & Bear Stories Ser.). (ENG., Illus.). 32p. (J). (gr. -1-1). 15.95 *(978-1-59078-457-0(X))* Boyds Mills Pr.

Blume, Erma Hill. Tattle-Tale Pete. 2012. 28p. pap. 24.95 *(978-1-62709-097-1(5))* America Star Bks.

Bond, Gwenda. Fallout. 2016. (Lois Lane Ser.). (ENG.). 304p. (gr. 9-12). pap. 9.95 *(978-1-63079-006-6(0))* Switch Pr.

Boone, Stewart. What in the World Is A Palindrome? 2010. 24p. 13.95 *(978-1-4269-2255-8(8))* Trafford Publishing.

Bowe, Julie. My Best Frenemy. 2011. (Friends for Keeps Ser.). (ENG.). 256p. (J). (gr. 3-7). 6.99 *(978-0-14-241880-2(3),* Puffin Books) Penguin Young Readers Group.

Bowen, Anne. Tooth Fairy's First Night. Berkeley, Jon, illus. 2005. (Carolrhoda Picture Bks.). 32p. (J). (gr. -1-3). 15.95 *(978-1-57505-753-8(0))* Lerner Publishing Group.

Brasch, Nicolas & Dawson, Amanda. The Chalk Circle. 2008. (Rigby Focus Forward: Level G Ser.). (Illus.). 24p. (J). (gr. 4-7). pap. *(978-1-4190-3713-9(7),* Rigby) Pearson Education Australia.

Brege, K. B. Ghost Board Posse London Screaming! 2008. (Ghost Board Posse Ser.: No. 1). (Illus.). 207p. (YA). pap. 6.99 *(978-0-9774119-6-2(6))* Team B Creative LLC.

Brezenoff, Steve. Guy in Real Life. (ENG.). 400p. (YA). (gr. 9). 2015. pap. 9.99 *(978-0-06-226684-2(5))* 2014. 17.99 *(978-0-06-226683-5(7))* HarperCollins Pubs.

Brouwer, Sigmund. Sewer Rats. 2006. (Orca Currents Ser.). 106p. (gr. 4-7). 19.95 *(978-0-7569-6872-4(0))* Perfection Learning Corp.

Bruel, Nick. Bad Kitty Does Not Like Video Games. 2016. (Bad Kitty Ser.). (ENG., Illus.). 24p. (J). pap. 4.99 *(978-1-62672-582-9(9),* 9781626725829) Roaring Brook Pr.

—Bad Kitty Does Not Like Video Games. 2016. (Bad Kitty Picture Bks.). (ENG.). 24p. (J). (gr. -1-k). 14.75 *(978-0-606-39297-6(1))* Turtleback Bks.

Bryant-Mole, Karen & Tyler, Jenny. Dot-to-Dot Book: Combined Volume. Round, Graham, illus. 2004. (Dot to Dot Ser.). 168p. (J). pap. 12.95 *(978-0-7945-0699-5(2),* Usborne) EDC Publishing.

Burningham, John. Tug-of-War. Burningham, John, illus. 2013. (ENG., Illus.). 32p. (J). (gr. k-3). 16.99 *(978-0-7636-6575-3(4))* Candlewick Pr.

Butcher, Kristin. Caching In, 1 vol. 2013. (Orca Currents Ser.). (ENG.). 128p. (J). (gr. 5-9). 16.95 *(978-1-4598-0233-9(0));* pap. 9.95 *(978-1-4598-0232-2(2))* Orca Bk. Pubs. USA.

Byrne, Marlene. Follow the Leader. Graber, Jesse, illus. 2009. (ENG.). 39p. (J). 14.99 *(978-0-9777135-1-6(2))* Celtic Marketing Inc.

—Kick the Can. Graber, Jesse, illus. 2009. 61p. pap. 9.99 *(978-0-9777135-3-0(9))* Celtic Marketing Inc.

Byrne, Marlene F. Ghost in the Graveyard. Graber, Jesse, illus. 2010. 57p. (J). pap. 9.99 *(978-0-9777135-4-7(7))* Celtic Marketing Inc.

—Treasure Hunt. Graber, Jesse, illus. 2009. 36p. (J). 14.99 *(978-0-9777135-0-9(4))* Celtic Marketing Inc.

Campbell, Matt. Unlocked. 2012. 82p. pap. *(978-1-909395-06-0(4))* Legend Pr.

Capucilli, Alyssa Satin. Biscuit Plays Ball. Schories, Pat, illus. 2012. (My First I Can Read Ser.). (ENG.). 32p. (J). (gr. -1-2). 16.99 *(978-0-06-193503-9(4));* pap. 3.99 *(978-0-06-193502-2(6))* HarperCollins Pubs.

—Biscuit Plays Ball. 2012. (Biscuit: My First I Can Read! Ser.). (J). lib. bdg. 13.55 *(978-0-606-23583-9(3),* Turtleback) Turtleback Bks.

Carman, Debby. Kittywimpuss Got Game. Carman, Debby, illus. 2007. (Illus.). 28p. (J). (gr. -1-1). 14.99 *(978-0-9777340-4-7(8))* Faux Paw Media Group.

Cascone, Annette & Cascone, Gina. The Witching Game. 2012. (Deadtime Stories Ser.: 2). (ENG.). 192p. (J). (gr. 3-7). mass mkt. 5.99 *(978-0-7653-6972-7(9),* 9780765369727, Starscape) Doherty, Tom Assocs., LLC.

Cecil, Lauren. Lalaloopsy: Here Come the Little Sisters! Hill, Prescott, illus. 2013. (Lalaloopsy Ser.). (ENG.). 5p. (J). (gr. -1-k). bds. 9.99 *(978-0-545-44266-4(4))* Scholastic, Inc.

Chambliss Bertman, Jennifer. Book Scavenger. 2015. (Book Scavenger Ser.). (ENG., Illus.). 368p. (J). (gr. 4-9). 16.99 *(978-1-62779-115-1(9),* 9781627791151, Holt, Henry & Co. Bks. For Young Readers) Holt, Henry & Co.

—Book Scavenger. 2016. (Book Scavenger Ser.). (ENG.). 368p. (J). pap. 7.99 *(978-1-250-07980-0(2),* 9781250079800) Square Fish.

Chapman, Jane. Hands off My Honey! Warnes, Tim, illus. 2013. (ENG.). 32p. (J). (gr. -1-1). 12.95 *(978-1-58925-142-7(3))* Tiger Tales.

Charles, Antoinette. My Favorite Island Games. 2012. 20p. pap. 17.99 *(978-1-4685-5678-0(9))* AuthorHouse.

Chaud, Benjamin, illus. The Bear's Song Matching Game. 2015. (ENG.). 60p. (J). (gr. -1-1). bds. 14.99 *(978-1-4521-4183-1(5))* Chronicle Bks. LLC.

Cheverton, Mark. Gameknight999 vs. Herobrine. 2016. (ENG.). 240p. (J). (gr. 3). pap. 9.99 *(978-1-5107-0010-9(2),* Sky Pony Pr.) Skyhorse Publishing Co., Inc.

—The Gameknight999 vs. Herobrine Box Set: Six Unofficial Minecrafter's Adventures. 2016. (Gameknight999 Ser.). (ENG.). 1488p. (J). (gr. 3). 29.99 *(978-1-5107-0993-5(2),* Sky Pony Pr.) Skyhorse Publishing Co., Inc.

—The Great Zombie Invasion: The Birth of Herobrine Book One: a Gameknight999 Adventure: an Unofficial Minecrafter's Adventure. 2016. (Gameknight999 Ser.). (ENG.). 248p. (J). (gr. 3). pap. 9.99 *(978-1-5107-0994-2(0),* Sky Pony Pr.) Skyhorse Publishing Co., Inc.

—Herobrine's War. 2017. (Birth of Herobrine Ser.: 3). lib. bdg. 20.85 ***(978-0-606-40305-4(1))*** Turtleback Bks.

—The Phantom Virus. 2016. (Gameknight999 Ser.: Bk. 1). (ENG.). 240p. (J). (gr. 3). pap. 9.99 *(978-1-5107-0683-5(6),* Sky Pony Pr.) Skyhorse Publishing Co., Inc.

—Saving Crafter. 2015. (ENG.). 304p. (J). (gr. 3). pap. 9.99 *(978-1-5107-0014-7(5),* Sky Pony Pr.) Skyhorse Publishing Co., Inc.

—System Overload. 2016. (Gameknight999 Ser.: Bk. 3). (ENG.). 272p. (J). (gr. 3). pap. 9.99 *(978-1-5107-0682-8(8),* Sky Pony Pr.) Skyhorse Publishing Co., Inc.

Child, Lauren. I've Won, No I've Won, No I've Won. 2006. (Charlie & Lola Ser.). (ENG., Illus.). 32p. (J). (gr. -1-2). mass mkt. 6.99 *(978-0-448-44350-8(3),* Grosset & Dunlap) Penguin Young Readers Group.

Childrens Press Staff & Scholastic, Inc. Staff, contrib. by. Hide-and-Peek. 2010. (Rookie Toddler: First Concepts Ser.). (ENG.). 12p. (J). bds. 6.95 *(978-0-531-25235-2(3),* Children's Pr.) Scholastic Library Publishing.

Chimeno del Campo, Ana Belén. El Preste Juan: Mito y Leyenda en la Literatura Infantil y Juvenil Contemporánea. 2009. (Europäische Hochschulschriften. Reihe 24: Ibero-Romanische Sprachen und Literaturen Ser.). (SPA & POR., Illus.). 128p. pap. 33.95 *(978-3-631-58935-9(2))* Lang, Peter GmbH, Internationaler Verlag der Wissenschaften DEU. Dist: Lang, Peter.

Christenson, Lisa. Harley Hippo & the Crane Game. Christenson, Lisa, illus. 2005. (Illus.). (J). per. *(978-0-9725311-0-8(6),* Pickled Eggs Press (TM)) Lisa Loucks Christenson Publishing, LLC.

Christopher, Lucy. The Killing Woods. 2014. (ENG.). 384p. (J). (gr. 9). pap. 10.99 *(978-0-545-46101-6(4));* 17.99 *(978-0-545-46100-9(6))* Scholastic, Inc. (Chicken Hse., The).

Christopher, Matt. Lacrosse Face-Off. 2010. (Matt Christopher Sports Library). 128p. (J). (gr. 4-6). lib. bdg. 26.60 *(978-1-59953-355-1(3))* Norwood Hse. Pr.

Ciencin, Scott. Point-Blank Paintball, 1 vol. Aburtov, illus. 2010. (Sports Illustrated Kids Graphic Novels Ser.). (ENG.). 32p. pap. 1.00 *(978-1-4342-2137-7(7))* Stone Arch Bks.

Ciencin, Scott, et al. Point-Blank Paintball, 1 vol. Aburto, Jesus, illus. 2010. (Sports Illustrated Kids Graphic Novels Ser.). (ENG.). 56p. (gr. 2-3). pap. 7.19 *(978-1-4342-2293-0(4));* 26.65 *(978-1-4342-1914-5(3))* Stone Arch Bks.

Clark, Leslie Ann. Peepsqueak Wants a Friend! Clark, Leslie Ann, illus. 2013. (ENG., Illus.). 32p. (J). (gr. -1-3). 15.99 *(978-0-06-207804-9(6))* HarperCollins Pubs.

Clark, Sherryl. Kim's Tug of War. McKenzie, Heath, illus. 2015. (J). pap. *(978-1-4966-0244-2(7))* Capstone Classroom.

Cohn, Rachel & Levithan, David. Dash & Lily's Book of Dares. 2011. (ENG.). 288p. (YA). (gr. 7). pap. 9.99 *(978-0-375-85955-7(1),* Ember) Random Hse. Children's Bks.

Costa, T. L. Playing Tyler. 2013. (ENG.). 304p. (J). (gr. 9). pap. 9.99 *(978-1-908844-61-3(2),* Strange Chemistry) Watkins Media Limited GBR. Dist: Penguin Random Hse. LLC.

Coulson, Art. The Creator's Game: A Story of Baaga'adowe/Lacrosse. Desjarlait, Robert, illus. 2013. (ENG.). 48p. (J). (gr. 3-6). pap. 6.95 *(978-0-87351-909-0(4))* Minnesota Historical Society Pr.

Cousins, Lucy. Maisy's Field Day. Cousins, Lucy, illus. 2016. (Maisy Ser.). (ENG., Illus.). 32p. (J). (-k). 12.99 *(978-0-7636-8441-9(4))* Candlewick Pr.

Craddock, Erik. Dragon Boogie. Craddock, Erik, illus. 2012. (Stone Rabbit Ser.: Vol. 7). (ENG., Illus.). 96p. (J). (gr. 2-5). pap. 6.99 *(978-0-375-86912-9(3),* Random Hse. Bks. for Young Readers) Random Hse. Children's Bks.

—Dragon Boogie. 2012. (Stone Rabbit Ser.: 7). lib. bdg. 17.20 *(978-0-606-23868-7(9),* Turtleback) Turtleback Bks.

Crimi, Carolyn. Where's My Mummy? Manders, John, illus. 2009. (ENG.). 32p. (J). (gr. -1-3). 7.99 *(978-0-7636-4337-9(8))* Candlewick Pr.

Curriculum Corporation. Tai Hao Le! 2005. pap. 79.95 incl. audio compact disk *(978-1-86366-402-8(5))* Education Services Australia Ltd. AUS. Dist: Cheng & Tsui Co.

Dahl, Michael. The Boy Who Was It: And Other Scary Tales. Bonet, Xavier, illus. 2016. (Michael Dahl's Really Scary Stories Ser.). (ENG.). 72p. (gr. 2-3). lib. bdg. 25.32 *(978-1-4965-3772-0(6))* Stone Arch Bks.

Davidson, Danica. Attack on the Overworld: The Overworld Adventures, Book 2. 2015. (Unofficial Overworld Adventure Ser.). (ENG.). 112p. (J). (gr. 1-7). pap. 7.99 *(978-1-5107-0276-9(8),* Sky Pony Pr.) Skyhorse Publishing Co., Inc.

de Brunhoff, Laurent & Rose, Phyllis. Babar's Celesteville Games. 2011. (ENG., Illus.). 48p. (J). (gr. k-2). 18.95 *(978-1-4197-0006-4(5),* Abrams Bks. for Young Readers) Abrams, Inc.

Dee, Barbara. Truth or Dare. (ENG.). (J). (gr. 4-8). 2017. 272p. pap. 7.99 ***(978-1-4814-5969-3(4))*** 2016. (Illus.). 256p. 16.99 *(978-1-4814-5968-6(6))* Simon & Schuster Children's Publishing. (Aladdin).

Derrick, David G., Jr. Play with Your Food. 2014. (ENG., Illus.). 36p. (J). (gr. -1-3). 15.95 *(978-1-59702-102-9(4))* Immedium.

Disney Book Group & Ritchey, Kate. Mickey & Friends Huey, Dewey, & Louie's Rainy Day. Loter, Inc. Staff, illus. 2014. (World of Reading Ser.). (ENG.). 32p. (J). (gr. 1-3). pap. 3.99 *(978-1-4231-6965-9(4))* Disney Pr.

Disney Book Group Staff & Hapka, Cathy. Sofia the First the Royal Games. Disney Storybook Artists Staff, illus. 2014. (ENG.). 24p. (J). (gr. -1-k). pap. 3.99 *(978-1-4231-6409-8(1))* Disney Pr.

Disney Publishing Staff. A Sense of Fun, 15 vols. 2003. (It's Fun to Learn Ser.). (Illus.). 32p. (J). (gr. -1-3). 3.99 *(978-1-57973-140-3(6))* Advance Pubs. LLC.

Dixon, Franklin W. The Missing Playbook. David, Matt, illus. 2016. (Hardy Boys Clue Book Ser.: 2). (ENG.). 96p. (J). (gr. 1-4). pap. 5.99 *(978-1-4814-5177-2(4),* Aladdin) Simon & Schuster Children's Publishing.

—The Video Game Bandit. David, Matt, illus. 2016. (Hardy Boys Clue Book Ser.: 1). (ENG.). 96p. (J). (gr. 1-4). 16.99 *(978-1-4814-5053-9(0));* pap. 5.99 *(978-1-4814-5052-2(2))* Simon & Schuster Children's Publishing. (Aladdin).

—Warehouse Rumble. 2004. (Hardy Boys Ser.: 183). (ENG., Illus.). 160p. (J). (gr. 3-7). pap. 4.99 *(978-0-689-86455-1(8),* Aladdin) Simon & Schuster Children's Publishing.

Doctorow, Cory. For the Win. 2010. (ENG.). 480p. (YA). (gr. 8-13). 17.99 *(978-0-7653-2216-6(1),* 9780765322166, Tor Teen) Doherty, Tom Assocs., LLC.

Dolby, Karen. Dragon in the Cupboard. 2004. (Young Puzzle Adventures Ser.). 32p. (J). (gr. 2-18). pap. 4.95 *(978-0-7945-0232-4(6));* lib. bdg. 12.95 *(978-1-58086-461-9(9))* EDC Publishing.

Druckman, Michael. Memory Emory & His Hiding Places. Druckman, Joan, illus. 2006. 24p. (gr. -1-3). per. 10.99 *(978-1-59858-060-0(4))* Dog Ear Publishing, LLC.

Duckett, Brenda. Casey's Shadow. 2008. pap. 10.96 *(978-0-615-17289-7(X))* Duckett, Brenda.

Durand, Hallie. Catch That Cookie! 2014. *(978-0-8037-3960-4(5),* Dial) Penguin Publishing Group.

—Catch That Cookie! Small, David, illus. 2014. (ENG.). 32p. (J). (gr. -1-k). 17.99 *(978-0-525-42835-0(6),* Dial Bks) Penguin Young Readers Group.

—Mitchell Goes Bowling. Fucile, Tony, illus. 2013. (ENG.). 40p. (J). (gr. -1-2). 15.99 *(978-0-7636-6049-9(3))* Candlewick Pr.

Duvall, Deborah L. Rabbit Goes to Kansas. Jacob, Murv, illus. 2007. (ENG.). 32p. (J). (gr. 1-18). 16.95 *(978-0-8263-4181-5(0))* Univ. of New Mexico Pr.

Eagle, Kim. It's Raining, It's Pouring. Davenier, Christine & Gilbert, Rob, illus. 2012. (ENG.). 32p. (J). (-k). 17.95 *(978-1-936140-77-0(2))* Charlesbridge Publishing, Inc.

Earhart, Kristin. Great Reef Games. 2015. (Race the Wild Ser.: 2). lib. bdg. 14.75 *(978-0-606-37043-1(9))* Turtleback Bks.

Ebl, Donna. The Adventures of Salamander Sam. 2004. (J). pap. 9.00 *(978-0-8059-6165-2(8))* Dorrance Publishing Co., Inc.

Ecks. Riddle in the Middle. 2008. 32p. pap. 14.99 *(978-1-4389-3506-5(4))* AuthorHouse.

Eddy, Catherine J. Sandbox Sandshoes. Krupnek, Joann J., illus. 2009. 38p. pap. 10.95 *(978-0-9818488-5-3(0))* Ajoyin Publishing, Inc.

Einhorn, Edward. A Very Improbable Story. Gustavson, Adam, illus. 2008. (ENG.). 32p. (J). (gr. 2-5). pap. 7.95 *(978-1-57091-872-8(4))* Charlesbridge Publishing, Inc.

Eliopoulos, Chris. Yo Gabba Gabba: Gabba Ball: Gabba Ball. 2010. 16p. bds. 7.99 *(978-1-934964-55-2(7))* Oni Pr., Inc.

Emerson, Carl. Monster Boy's Gym Class, 1 vol. Levin, Lon, illus. 2010. (Monster Boy Set 2 Ser.). (ENG.). 32p. (J). (gr. k-3). 28.50 *(978-1-60270-781-8(2))* ABDO Publishing Co.

Enderle, Dotti. Book 15: Rock & Roll!, 1 vol. 2014. (Ghost Detectors Set 3 Ser.). (ENG., Illus.). 80p. (J). (gr. 2-5). lib. bdg. 27.07 *(978-1-62402-003-2(8),* Calico Chapter Bks) Magic Wagon.

Faircloth, Carson. Games. 2011. 260p. 26.95 *(978-1-4620-1029-5(6));* pap. 16.95 *(978-1-4620-1027-1(X))* iUniverse, Inc.

Fairlie, Emily. The Magician's Bird. 2013. (Tuckernuck Mysteries Ser.: 2). (ENG.). 288p. (J). (gr. 3-7). 16.99 *(978-0-06-211893-6(5),* Tegen, Katherine Bks) HarperCollins Pubs.

Feldman, Jody. The Gollywhopper Games. Jamieson, Victoria, illus. (Gollywhopper Games Ser.: 1). (ENG.). (J). (gr. 3-7). 2013. 336p. pap. 6.99 *(978-0-06-121452-3(3))* 2008. 320p. 16.99 *(978-0-06-121450-9(7))* HarperCollins Pubs. (Greenwillow Bks.).

—The Gollywhopper Games. 2013. (Gollywhopper Games Ser.: 1). (J). lib. bdg. 17.20 *(978-0-606-35508-7(1))* Turtleback Bks.

—The Gollywhopper Games - Friend or Foe. Jamieson, Victoria, illus. 2015. (Gollywhopper Games Ser.: 3). (ENG.). 432p. (J). (gr. 3-7). 16.99 *(978-0-06-221128-6(5),* Greenwillow Bks.) HarperCollins Pubs.

—The Gollywhopper Games - The New Champion. Jamieson, Victoria, illus. 2015. (Gollywhopper Games Ser.: 2). (ENG.). 400p. (J). (gr. 3-7). pap. 6.99 *(978-0-06-221126-2(9),* Greenwillow Bks.) HarperCollins Pubs.

—The New Champion. Jamieson, Victoria, illus. 2014. (Gollywhopper Games Ser.: 2). (ENG.). 400p. (J). (gr. 3-7). 16.99 *(978-0-06-221125-5(0),* Greenwillow Bks.) HarperCollins Pubs.

—The Seventh Level. 2010. (ENG.). 304p. (J). (gr. 5-18). 16.99 *(978-0-06-195105-3(6),* Greenwillow Bks.) HarperCollins Pubs.

Flam, Charlie. Make Believe. (Goldie Gold Board Book Ser.: Vol. 3). (Illus.). (J). (gr. -1-1). bds. 4.95 *(978-1-58330-027-5(9))* Feldheim Pubs.

Flintham, Thomas. Game over, Super Rabbit Boy! 2016. (Press Start! Ser.: 1). lib. bdg. 14.75 ***(978-0-606-39712-4(4))*** Turtleback Bks.

—Super Rabbit Boy Powers up! a Branches Book (Press Start! #2) 2017. (Press Start! Ser.: 2). (ENG.). 80p. (J). (gr. k-2). pap. 4.99 ***(978-1-338-03473-8(1))*** Scholastic, Inc.

Flying Frog Pub, creator. ABC Fun with Elmo & Friends. 2011. (Sesame Street (Publications International) Ser.). (ENG., Illus.). 14p. (J). (gr. -1). bds. 3.99 *(978-1-60745-030-6(5))* Flying Frog Publishing.

—Big & Small Fun with Elmo & Friends. 2011. (ENG., Illus.). 14p. (gr. -1-k). bds. 3.99 *(978-1-60745-033-7(X))* Flying Frog Publishing.

Foxworthy, Jeff. Hide!!! Björkman, Steve, illus. 2010. (ENG.). 32p. (J). (gr. -1-2). 17.99 *(978-0-8253-0554-2(3))* Beaufort Bks., Inc.

Freeze Tag: Individual Title Six-Packs. (gr. -1-2). 27.00 *(978-0-7635-9449-7(0))* Rigby Education.

Frino, Michael G. Welcome to Waycool School: Where Learning Is Fun & Lessons are Learned by Everyone! 2010. 32p. pap. 17.25 *(978-1-4269-4048-4(3))* Trafford Publishing.

Fuchs, Menucha. Hide & Go Sleep. 2004. (Illus.). 20p. (J). 6.95 *(978-1-932443-13-4(4),* HGSH) Judaica Pr., Inc., The.

Gates, J. F. The Children of the White Tree: Brady Barrett & the Firstlings Assignment. 2011. 284p. (gr. -1). 35.95 *(978-1-4497-1716-2(0),* WestBow Pr.) Author Solutions, Inc.

Gellman, Ellie. Jeremy's Dreidel. Mola, Maria, illus. 2012. (Hanukkah Ser.). 32p. (J). (gr. k-3). (ENG.). lib. bdg. 17.95 *(978-0-7613-7507-4(4));* (SPA & ENG.). 7.95 *(978-0-7613-7508-1(2))* Lerner Publishing Group. (Kar-Ben Publishing).

Gipson, Crash. Sheldon's Favorite Game. 2011. 36p. pap. 24.95 *(978-1-4626-4578-7(X))* America Star Bks.

Golant, Galina & Grant, Lisa. Play Checkers with Me. Golant, Evgenia, illus. 2003. 32p. (J). pap. 6.95 *(978-1-932133-01-1(1))* Writers' Collective, The.

Gould, Jacqueline. The Guessing Book: For 3 to 7 Year Olds. 2013. (Illus.). 20p. pap. 19.82 *(978-1-4817-8301-9(7))* AuthorHouse.

Grabenstein, Chris. Escape from Mr. Lemoncello's Library. (ENG.). (J). (gr. 3-7). 2014. 336p. 7.99 *(978-0-307-93147-4(1),* Yearling) 2013. 304p. 17.99 *(978-0-375-87089-7(X),* Random Hse. Bks. for Young Readers) 2013. 304p. lib. bdg. 19.99 *(978-0-375-97089-4(4),* Random Hse. Bks. for Young Readers) 2017. 336p. 7.99 ***(978-0-525-58037-9(9),*** Yearling) Random Hse. Children's Bks.

—Escape from Mr. Lemoncello's Library. 2014. lib. bdg. 18.40 *(978-0-606-37114-8(1))* Turtleback Bks.

Grant, Michael. Messenger of Fear. 2014. (Messenger of Fear Ser.: 1). (ENG.). 272p. (YA). (gr. 9). 17.99 *(978-0-06-220740-1(7),* Tegen, Katherine Bks) HarperCollins Pubs.

—The Tattooed Heart. 2015. (Messenger of Fear Ser.: 2). (ENG.). 400p. (YA). (gr. 9). 17.99 *(978-0-06-220743-2(1))* HarperCollins Pubs.

Gratz, Alan. Something Wicked. 2009. (ENG.). 288p. (YA). (gr. 7-18). 7.99 *(978-0-14-241496-5(4),* Puffin Books) Penguin Young Readers Group.

Groethe, Kd. The Virtual Adventures of Megan & Timmy. 2012. 230p. (gr. 4-6). 27.99 *(978-1-4685-5050-4(0));* pap. 16.95 *(978-1-4685-5049-8(7))* AuthorHouse.

Grosset and Dunlap Staff, contrib. by. We Play Outside. 2005. (Dick & Jane Ser.). (ENG., Illus.). 144p. (J). (gr. -1-1). 8.99 *(978-0-448-43616-6(7),* Grosset & Dunlap) Penguin Young Readers Group.

Gutman, Dan. Back to School, Weird Kids Rule! Paillot, Jim, illus. 2014. (My Weird School Special Ser.). 144p. (J). (gr. 1-5). lib. bdg. 16.89 *(978-0-06-220686-2(9))* HarperCollins Pubs.

Gym Shoe Salad. 2007. (J). pap. 15.00 *(978-0-9779207-7-8(1))* Text 4m Publishing.

Hall, Kirsten. Tug-of-War: All about Balance. Luedecke, Bev, illus. 2004. (Beastieville Ser.). 31p. (J). 19.50 *(978-0-516-22899-0(4),* Children's Pr.) Scholastic Library Publishing.

Haneberg, Janet. Mighty Mitt. 2006. 36p. (J). pap. 14.99 *(978-1-4116-4168-6(X))* Lulu Pr., Inc.

Hapka, Cathy, pseud. The Royal Games. 2014. (Sofia the First Ser.). (J). lib. bdg. 13.55 *(978-0-606-34098-4(X),* Turtleback) Turtleback Bks.

Harris, Patricia. Rosalina Learns Magic Games. 2017. (Rosalina's Flower Garden Ser.). 24p. (gr. 4-6). pap. 8.25 ***(978-1-5383-2113-3(0),*** PowerKids Pr.) Rosen Publishing Group, Inc., The.

Harrison, Kevin. I Know a Rhino. Blue, Buster, illus. 2nd rev. ed. 2006. 37p. (J). (gr. -1-3). per. 10.99 *(978-1-59092-223-1(9))* Blue Forge Pr.

Hautman, Pete. All-In. 2012. (ENG.). 208p. (YA). (gr. 7). pap. 8.99 *(978-1-4424-3335-9(3),* Simon & Schuster Bks. For Young Readers) Simon & Schuster Bks. For Young Readers.

—No Limit. 2012. (ENG.). 224p. (YA). (gr. 7). pap. 8.99 *(978-1-4424-3338-0(8),* Simon & Schuster Bks. For Young Readers) Simon & Schuster Bks. For Young Readers.

—No Limit. 2007. (ENG.). 224p. (YA). (gr. 7). pap. 11.95 *(978-1-4169-6820-7(2),* Simon Pulse) Simon Pulse.

Hawley, Mabel C. Four Little Blossoms on Apple Tree Island. 2007. 80p. per. *(978-1-4068-1704-1(X))* Echo Library.

Heidbreder, Robert. Crocodiles Play! Mate, Rae, illus. 2009. (ENG.). 32p. (J). (gr. -1-3). 16.95 *(978-1-894965-86-6(8))* Simply Read Bks. CAN. Dist: Ingram Publisher Services.

Higginson, Sheila Sweeny. Drip, Drop! the Rain Won't Stop! Your Turn, My Turn Reader. Yee, Josie, illus. 2010. (Playskool Ser.). (ENG.). 24p. (J). (gr. -1-k). pap. 3.99 *(978-1-4169-9046-8(1),* Simon Spotlight) Simon Spotlight.

Hillert, Margaret. The Ball Book. Billin-Fry, Paige, illus. 2016. (BeginningtoRead Ser.). (ENG.). 32p. (J). (gr. -1-2). pap. 11.94 *(978-1-60357-935-3(4));* (gr. k-2). 22.60 *(978-1-59953-794-8(X))* Norwood Hse. Pr.

Holczer, Tracy. The Secret Hum of a Daisy. 2014. (ENG.). 320p. (J). (gr. 5). 16.99 *(978-0-399-16393-7(X),* G.P. Putnam's Sons Books for Young Readers) Penguin Young Readers Group.

Holden, Pam. The Paper Trail, 6 pack. Hawley, Kelvin, illus. 2009. (Red Rocket Readers Ser.). (ENG.). 16p. (gr. 2-2). pap. *(978-1-877363-69-6(3))* Flying Start Bks.

—Pass It On, 6 pack. Hawley, Kelvin, illus. 2009. (Red Rocket Readers Ser.). (ENG.). 16p. (gr. 2-2). pap. *(978-1-877363-66-5(9),* Red Rocket Readers) Flying Start Bks.

—Pin the Tail on the Donkey, 6 pack. Hawley, Kelvin, illus. 2009. (Red Rocket Readers Ser.). (ENG.). 16p. pap. *(978-1-877363-78-8(2))* Flying Start Bks.

Holm, Jennifer L. & Holm, Matthew. Game On! Holm, Jennifer L. & Holm, Matthew, illus. 2013. (Squish Ser.: No. 5). (ENG., Illus.). 96p. (J). (gr. 2-5). lib. bdg. 12.99 *(978-0-307-98300-8(5));*No. 5. pap. 6.99 *(978-0-307-98299-5(8))* Random Hse. Children's Bks. (Random Hse. Bks. for Young Readers).

—Game On! 2013. (Squish Ser.: 5). lib. bdg. 17.20 *(978-0-606-31946-1(8),* Turtleback) Turtleback Bks.

Holub, Joan & Williams, Suzanne. The Girl Games: Super Special. 2012. (Goddess Girls Ser.). (ENG.). 320p. (J). (gr. 3-7). pap. 7.99 *(978-1-4424-4933-6(0),* Aladdin) Simon & Schuster Children's Publishing.

Hrdlitschka, Shelley. Gotcha!, 1 vol. 2008. (ENG.). 272p. (YA). (gr. 7-12). pap. 9.95 *(978-1-55143-737-8(6))* Orca Bk. Pubs. USA.

Iorillo, Kristin. The Wacko Baby. 2011. 28p. pap. 15.99 *(978-1-4628-5792-0(2))* Xlibris Corp.

Isaacs, Latricia. Mason & Hayden Visit Grandma. 2011. 16p. 8.32 *(978-1-4567-0170-3(3))* AuthorHouse.

Jackson, Richard. In Plain Sight. Pinkney, Jerry, illus. 2016. (ENG.). 40p. (J). 17.99 *(978-1-62672-255-2(2),* 9781626722552) Roaring Brook Pr.

Jacobs, Evan. Clan Castles, 1 vol. 2014. (Red Rhino Ser.). (ENG.). 68p. (J). (gr. 4-6). pap. 7.95 *(978-1-62250-921-8(8))* Saddleback Educational Publishing, Inc.

—Clan Castles 2: Upgrade Pack. 2016. (Red Rhino Ser.). (J). lib. bdg. 18.40 *(978-0-606-38948-8(2))* Turtleback Bks.

—Clan Castles 2: Upgrade Pack, 1 vol. 2016. (Red Rhino Ser.). (ENG.). 70p. (J). (gr. 3-6). pap. 7.95 *(978-1-62250-977-5(3))* Saddleback Educational Publishing, Inc.

Jakubowski, Michele. Party Pooper. Waters, Erica-Jane, illus. 2014. (Perfectly Poppy Ser.). (ENG.). 32p. (gr. k-2). lib. bdg. 22.65 *(978-1-4795-2282-8(1))* Picture Window Bks.

James, Simon. Little One Step. James, Simon, illus. 2007. (ENG., Illus.). 24p. (J). (— 1). bds. 6.99 *(978-0-7636-3520-6(0))* Candlewick Pr.

Johns, Geoff, et al. Teen Titans, Vol. 1. rev. ed. 2004. (Teen Titans Go! Ser.: Vol. 1). (ENG., Illus.). 192p. pap. 16.99 *(978-1-4012-0308-5(6))* DC Comics.

Johnson, Kevin D. Around Every Corner. 2011. 24p. (gr. 1-2). pap. 11.32 *(978-1-4567-4869-2(6))* AuthorHouse.

Jones, Jasmine, adapted by. The Importance of Being Gordo. 2005. (Illus.). 138p. (J). *(978-1-4155-7362-4(X))* Disney Pr.

—Importance of Being Gordo. 2005. 138p. (J). lib. bdg. 16.92 *(978-1-4242-0688-9(X))* Fitzgerald Bks.

Jordan, Apple. Fast Kart, Slow Kart. 2013. (Step into Reading Level 1 Ser.). lib. bdg. 13.55 *(978-0-606-26980-3(0),* Turtleback) Turtleback Bks.

Jordan, Apple & Amerikaner, Susan. Game On! Random House Disney Staff, illus. 2012. (Step into Reading Ser.). (ENG.). 32p. (J). (gr. -1-1). pap. 3.99 *(978-0-7364-2889-7(5),* RH/Disney) Random Hse. Children's Bks.

Kattan, Peter & Kattan, Nicola. More Kindergarten Sudoku: 4x4 Classic Sudoku Puzzles for Kids. 2008. 48p. pap. 7.50 *(978-0-615-18718-1(8))* Kattan, Peter I.

Katz, Karen. Where Is Baby's Belly Button? Katz, Karen, illus. anniv. ed. 2009. (ENG., Illus.). 14p. (J). (gr. -1 — 1). bds. 12.99 *(978-1-4169-8733-8(9),* Little Simon) Little Simon.

—Where Is Baby's Belly Button? 2005. (CHI.). 12p. (J). 6.95 *(978-986-7517-72-2(5))* Shan Jen Publishing Co., Ltd. TWN. Dist: Chinasprout, Inc.

Kawahara, Reki. Sword Art Online 11: Alicization Turning. 2017. (Sword Art Online Ser.: 11). (ENG., Illus.). 208p. (YA). (gr. 8-17). pap. 14.00 ***(978-0-316-39044-6(5),*** Yen Pr.) Orbit.

Keene, Carolyn. Treasure Trouble. Pamintuan, Macky, illus. 2009. (Nancy Drew & the Clue Crew Ser.: 20). (ENG.). 112p. (J). (gr. 1-4). pap. 4.99 *(978-1-4169-7809-1(7),* Aladdin) Simon & Schuster Children's Publishing.

Kennedy, Linda. I Love You More... 2010. 17p. (J). pap. 13.95 *(978-1-4327-5196-8(4))* Outskirts Pr., Inc.

Kincaid, S. J. Insignia. 2013. (Insignia Ser.: 1). (ENG.). 480p. (YA). (gr. 8). pap. 9.99 *(978-0-06-209300-4(2),* Tegen, Katherine Bks) HarperCollins Pubs.

—Vortex. 2013. (Insignia Ser.: 2). (ENG.). 400p. (YA). (gr. 8). 17.99 *(978-0-06-209302-8(9),* Tegen, Katherine Bks) HarperCollins Pubs.

Kinney, Jeff. Double Down. 2016. (Diary of a Wimpy Kid Ser.: Bk. 11). (ENG., Illus.). 224p. (J). (gr. 3-7). 13.95 *(978-1-4197-2344-5(8));* E-Book 12.56 *(978-1-61312-992-0(0))* Abrams, Inc. (Amulet Bks.).

—Double Down. 2016. (Diary of a Wimpy Kid Ser.: 11). (J). lib. bdg. 25.70 *(978-0-606-38998-3(9))* Turtleback Bks.

Knudsen, Michelle. Fish & Frog Big Book: Brand New Readers. Petrone, Valeria, illus. 2010. (Brand New Readers Ser.). (ENG.). 48p. (J). (gr. -1-3). pap. 24.99 *(978-0-7636-4810-7(8))* Candlewick Pr.

Kondrat, Lauren. Mischievous Mort. 2010. 40p. pap. 17.91 *(978-0-557-43708-5(3))* Lulu Pr., Inc.

Korda, Lerryn. It's Vacation Time. Korda, Lerryn, illus. 2010. (Playtime with Little Nye Ser.). (ENG., Illus.). 26p. (J). (— 1). 8.99 *(978-0-7636-4813-8(2))* Candlewick Pr.

Kredensor, Diane. Ollie & Moon: Aloha! 2013. (Step into Reading Ser.). (ENG., Illus.). 48p. (J). (gr. 1-4). 3.99 *(978-0-307-97950-6(4),* Random Hse. Bks. for Young Readers) Random Hse. Children's Bks.

Krilanovich, Nadia. Chicken, Chicken, Duck! Krilanovich, Nadia, illus. (ENG., Illus.). (J). (gr. -1-2). 2016. 26p. bds. 7.99 *(978-0-553-53806-9(3))* 2011. 32p. 14.99 *(978-1-58246-385-8(9))* Random Hse. Children's Bks. (Tricycle Pr.).

Krosoczka, Jarrett J. Lunch Lady & the Video Game Villain. 2013. (Lunch Lady Ser.). (ENG.). 96p. (J). (gr. 2-5). pap. 6.99 *(978-0-307-98079-3(0));* lib. bdg. 12.99 *(978-0-307-98080-9(4))* Random Hse. Children's Bks. (Knopf Bks. for Young Readers).

—Lunch Lady & the Video Game Villain. 2013. (Lunch Lady Ser.: 9). lib. bdg. 17.20 *(978-0-606-27003-8(5),* Turtleback) Turtleback Bks.

Landers, Ace. Darth Maul's Mission. White, David A., illus. 2011. (Lego Star Wars Ser.). (ENG.). 24p. (J). (gr. -1-3). pap. 3.99 *(978-0-545-30441-2(5))* Scholastic, Inc.

Leigh, Susan K. God I Need to Talk to you About Video Games. 2011. 16p. pap. 1.19 *(978-0-7586-2659-2(2))* Concordia Publishing Hse.

Levine, Abby. This Is the Dreidel. Billin-Frye, Paige, illus. 2012. (J). 34.28 *(978-1-61913-134-7(X))* Weigl Pubs., Inc.

Levy, Janey. Play Ball! 2006. (Neighborhood Readers Ser.). (ENG.). 8p. (gr. -1-3). pap. 5.15 *(978-1-4042-5659-0(8),* Rosen Classroom) Rosen Publishing Group, Inc., The.

Lewison, Wendy Cheyette. Silly Milly. Westcott, Nadine Bernard, illus. 2010. (Scholastic Reader Level 1 Ser.). (ENG.). 32p. (J). (gr. -1-3). pap. 3.99 *(978-0-545-06859-8(2))* Scholastic, Inc.

—Silly Milly. 2010. (Scholastic Reader Level 1 Ser.). lib. bdg. 13.55 *(978-0-606-10556-9(5),* Turtleback) Turtleback Bks.

Little, Robert. Fun Day in Mrs. Walker's Class. Galey, Chuck, illus. 2005. 32p. (J). *(978-0-9701863-6-2(3))* Reide Publishing.

Lubar, David. Wizards of the Game. 2004. (ENG.). 176p. (J). (gr. 3-7). 6.99 *(978-0-14-240215-3(X),* Puffin Books) Penguin Young Readers Group.

MacHado, Ana Maria & Machado, Ana Maria. El Juego del Cambia-Cambia. Valverde, Mikel, illus. 2004.Tr. of Change-Change Game. (SPA.). (J). 6.50 *(978-84-348-8716-9(9))* SM Ediciones ESP. Dist: Lectorum Pubns., Inc.

Maddox, Jake. Disc Golf Drive, 1 vol. Tiffany, Sean, illus. 2009. (Jake Maddox Sports Stories Ser.). (ENG.). 72p. (gr. 2-3). 25.32 *(978-1-4342-1599-4(7))* Stone Arch Bks.

—Geocache Surprise, 1 vol. Tiffany, Sean, illus. 2011. (Jake Maddox Sports Stories Ser.). (ENG.). 72p. (gr. 2-3). lib. bdg. 25.32 *(978-1-4342-2600-6(X))* Stone Arch Bks.

—Paintball Blast. Tiffany, Sean, illus. 2007. (Jake Maddox Sports Stories Ser.). (ENG.). 72p. (gr. 2-3). pap. 5.95 *(978-1-59889-417-2(X));* lib. bdg. 25.32 *(978-1-59889-322-9(X))* Stone Arch Bks.

—Paintball Boss. 2016. (Jake Maddox JV Ser.). (ENG.). 96p. (gr. 3-4). lib. bdg. 25.99 *(978-1-4965-3982-3(6))* Stone Arch Bks.

—Paintball Invasion, 1 vol. Tiffany, Sean, illus. 2008. (Jake Maddox Sports Stories Ser.). (ENG.). 72p. (gr. 2-3). lib. bdg. 25.32 *(978-1-4342-0466-0(9));* per. 5.95 *(978-1-4342-0516-2(9))* Stone Arch Bks.

—Paintball Problems. 2013. (Jake Maddox Sports Stories Ser.). (ENG.). 72p. (gr. 2-3). pap. 35.70 *(978-1-4342-6237-0(5))* Stone Arch Bks.

—Paintball Problems, 1 vol. Aburtov, Jesus Aburto, illus. 2013. (Jake Maddox Sports Stories Ser.). (ENG.). 72p. (gr. 2-3). lib. bdg. 25.32 *(978-1-4342-5974-5(9))* Stone Arch Bks.

—Skateboard Idol. 2016. (Jake Maddox JV Ser.). (ENG.). 96p. (gr. 3-4). lib. bdg. 25.99 *(978-1-4965-2631-1(7))* Stone Arch Bks.

Mancusi, Mari. Gamer Girl. 2010. (ENG.). 256p. (YA). (gr. 7-18). 7.99 *(978-0-14-241509-2(X),* Speak) Penguin Young Readers Group.

Martín Anguita, Carmen & Carmen, Martín Anguita. Una Tarde en el Circo. Cortazar, Alicia Canas, illus. 2008. (SPA.). 32p. (J). 10.99 *(978-84-241-5459-2(2))* Everest Editora ESP. Dist: Lectorum Pubns., Inc.

Martin, R. Safe Zone. 2017. (Level Up Ser.). (ENG.). (YA). (gr. 6-12). 112p. pap. 7.99 ***(978-1-5124-5360-7(9));*** lib. bdg. 26.65 ***(978-1-5124-3986-1(X))*** Lerner Publishing Group. (Darby Creek).

Matthew, Anna. Hide & Seek, 1 vol. Heyworth, Heather, illus. 2013. (Start Reading Ser.). (ENG.). 24p. (gr. k-1). pap. 7.95 *(978-1-4765-3204-2(4));* pap. 41.94 *(978-1-4765-3217-2(6))* Capstone Press of Coughlan Cos.

—Hopscotch, 1 vol. Heyworth, Heather, illus. 2013. (Start Reading Ser.). (ENG.). 24p. (gr. k-1). pap. 7.95 *(978-1-4765-3205-9(2));* pap. 41.94 *(978-1-4765-3218-9(4))* Capstone Press of Coughlan Cos.

McBratney, Sam. Let's Play in the Snow. Jeram, Anita, illus. 2012. (Guess How Much I Love You Ser.). (ENG.). 24p. (J). (gr. k — 1). bds. 4.99 *(978-0-7636-6121-2(X))* Candlewick Pr.

McCauley, Adam & Shulman, Mark. Mom & Dad Are Palindromes. 2014. (ENG., Illus.). 36p. (J). (gr. 1-4). 7.99 *(978-1-4521-3643-1(2))* Chronicle Bks. LLC.

McDonald, Megan. Judy Moody & Stink: La Loca, Loca Busqueda del Tesoro. Reynolds, Peter, illus. 2011. (SPA.). 256p. (J). (gr. 2-5). pap. 14.95 *(978-1-61605-137-2(X))* Ediciones Alfaguara ESP. Dist: Two Rivers Distribution.

—Judy Moody & Stink: The Mad, Mad, Mad, Mad Treasure Hunt. Reynolds, Peter H., illus. 2009. (Judy Moody Ser.: No. 2). (ENG.). 128p. (J). (gr. 1-4). 14.99 *(978-0-7636-3962-4(1))* Candlewick Pr.

—The Mad, Mad, Mad, Mad Treasure Hunt. Reynolds, Peter H., illus. 2010. (Judy Moody Ser.: Bk. 2). (ENG.). 128p. (J). (gr. 1-4). pap. 7.99 *(978-0-7636-4351-5(3))* Candlewick Pr.

—The Mad, Mad, Mad, Mad Treasure Hunt. 2010. (Judy Moody & Stink Ser.: 2). lib. bdg. 18.40 *(978-0-606-01311-6(3),* Turtleback) Turtleback Bks.

—Stink & the Shark Sleepover. Reynolds, Peter H., illus. (Stink Ser.: 9). (ENG.). 176p. (J). (gr. 1-4). 2014. 12.99 *(978-0-7636-6474-9(X))*Bk. 9. 2015. pap. 4.99 *(978-0-7636-7678-0(0))* Candlewick Pr.

McGee, Barbi. The Jumping Game. 2011. 32p. pap. 21.99 *(978-1-4628-6804-9(5))* Xlibris Corp.

McKay, Kirsty. The Assassin Game. 2016. (ENG.). 336p. (YA). (gr. 6-12). pap. 10.99 *(978-1-4926-3275-7(9),* 9781492632757) Sourcebooks, Inc.

Meister, Cari. T-Ball Trouble, 1 vol. Ho, Jannie, illus. 2009. (My First Graphic Novel Ser.). (ENG.). 32p. (gr. k-2). pap. 6.25 *(978-1-4342-1413-3(3));* lib. bdg. 24.65 *(978-1-4342-1300-6(5))* Stone Arch Bks. (My First Graphic Novel).

Michaels, Rune. Genesis Alpha. 2011. (ENG.). 224p. (YA). (gr. 7). pap. 8.99 *(978-1-4169-6500-8(9),* Atheneum Bks. for Young Readers) Simon & Schuster Children's Publishing.

Michalak, Jamie. Fizzy's Lunch Lab: Escape from Greasy World. Lunch Lab, LLC., Llc., illus. 2015. (Fizzy's Lunch Lab Ser.). (ENG.). 48p. (J). (gr. 1-4). pap. 5.99 *(978-0-7636-7546-2(6),* Candlewick Entertainment) Candlewick Pr.

Miller, Jeff. The Nerdy Dozen. 2015. (Nerdy Dozen Ser.: 1). (ENG.). 320p. (J). (gr. 3-7). pap. 6.99 *(978-0-06-227263-8(2))* HarperCollins Pubs.

—The Nerdy Dozen #3 - 20,000 Nerds under the Sea. 2015. (Nerdy Dozen Ser.: 3). (ENG.). 208p. (J). (gr. 3-7). 16.99 *(978-0-06-227268-3(3))* HarperCollins Pubs.

Millett, Peter & Scales, Simon. The Game. 2008. (Rigby Focus Forward: Level H Ser.). (Illus.). 24p. (J). (gr. 4-7). pap. *(978-1-4190-3723-8(4),* Rigby) Pearson Education Australia.

Moncure, Jane Belk. Where Is Baby Bear? A Book about Animal Homes. Billin-Frye, Paige, illus. 2013. (Magic Castle Readers Ser.). (ENG.). 32p. (J). (gr. -1-2). 25.64 *(978-1-62323-585-7(5),* 206320) Child's World, Inc., The.

Moosmann, Heidi. Winter Games with Woodland Will. 2010. 28p. (J). 24.99 *(978-1-4415-6506-8(X))* Xlibris Corp.

Morgan, Winter. Battle in the Overworld: The Unofficial Minecrafters Academy Series, Book Three. 2016. (Unofficial Minecrafters Academy Ser.). (ENG.). 112p. (J). (gr. 1-7). pap. 7.99 *(978-1-5107-0596-8(1),* Sky Pony Pr.) Skyhorse Publishing Co., Inc.

—Creeper Invasion: An Unofficial Minetrapped Adventure, #5. 2016. (Unofficial Minetrapped Adventure Ser.: 5). (ENG., Illus.). 112p. (J). (gr. 1-7). pap. 7.99 *(978-1-5107-0601-9(1),* Sky Pony Pr.) Skyhorse Publishing Co., Inc.

—An Explorer's Guide to the Nether: Lost Minecraft Journals, Book Two. 2015. (Lost Minecraft Journals Ser.). (ENG.). 112p. (J). (gr. 1-7). pap. 7.99 *(978-1-5107-0351-3(9),* Sky Pony Pr.) Skyhorse Publishing Co., Inc.

—Six Thrilling Stories for Minecrafters. 2015. (ENG.). 668p. (J). (gr. 1-7). 29.99 *(978-1-63450-212-2(4),* Sky Pony Pr.) Skyhorse Publishing Co., Inc.

—Trapped in the Overworld: An Unofficial Minetrapped Adventure, #1. 2016. (Unofficial Minetrapped Adventure Ser.: 1). (ENG.). 112p. (J). (gr. 1-7). pap. 7.99 *(978-1-5107-0597-5(X),* Sky Pony Pr.) Skyhorse Publishing Co., Inc.

—Zombie Invasion: The Unofficial Minecrafters Academy Series, Book One. 2016. (Unofficial Minecrafters Academy Ser.). (ENG.). 112p. (J). (gr. 1-7). pap. 7.99 *(978-1-5107-0594-4(5),* Sky Pony Pr.) Skyhorse Publishing Co., Inc.

Morpurgo, Michael. Conker. Brown, Petra, illus. 2016. (Reading Ladder Ser.). (ENG.). 48p. (J). (gr. k-2). pap. 7.99 *(978-1-4052-8254-3(1))* Egmont Bks., Ltd. GBR. Dist: Independent Pubs. Group.

Most, Bernard. Catch Me If You Can! 2003. (Green Light Readers Level 2 Ser.). (ENG., Illus.). 24p. (J). (gr. -1-3). pap. 3.95 *(978-0-15-204839-6(1))* Houghton Mifflin Harcourt Publishing Co.

—Catch Me If You Can! 2003. (Green Light Readers — Level 2 Ser.). (gr. k-3). 13.50 *(978-0-613-64465-5(4),* Turtleback) Turtleback Bks.

Murphy, Sally. Toppling. James, Rhian Nest, illus. 2012. (ENG.). 128p. (J). (gr. 3-7). 15.99 *(978-0-7636-5921-9(5))* Candlewick Pr.

Murphy, Stuart J. Tally O'Malley. Jabar, Cynthia, illus. 2004. (MathStart Ser.). 40p. (J). (gr. 1-18). 15.99 *(978-0-06-053162-1(2));* (ENG.). pap. 5.99 *(978-0-06-053164-5(9))* HarperCollins Pubs.

Murray, Laura. The Gingerbread Man Loose at the Zoo. Lowery, Mike, illus. 2016. (ENG.). 32p. (J). (gr. k-3). 16.99 *(978-0-399-16867-3(2),* G.P. Putnam's Sons Books for Young Readers) Penguin Young Readers Group.

Nelson, Peter. Herbert's Wormhole. Rao, Rohitash, illus. 2010. (Herbert's Wormhole Ser.: 1). (ENG.). 304p. (J). (gr. 3-7). pap. 6.99 *(978-0-06-168870-6(3))* HarperCollins Pubs.

Newman, Lesléa. Where Is Bear? Gorbachev, Valeri, illus. 2006. (ENG.). 44p. (J). (gr. -1 — 1). pap. 6.99 *(978-0-15-205918-7(0))* Houghton Mifflin Harcourt Publishing Co.

Nickel, Scott. Egg Hunt. Fentz, Mike & Barker, Lori, illus. 2005. 22p. (J). *(978-0-439-67211-5(2))* Scholastic, Inc.

Nielsen, Susin. Word Nerd. (ENG.). (J). (gr. 4-7). 2010. 264p. pap. 12.95 *(978-0-88776-990-0(X))* 2008. 256p. 18.95 *(978-0-88776-875-0(X))* Tundra Bks. CAN. (Tundra Bks.). Dist: Penguin Random Hse. LLC.

Nordling, Lee. Andrew the Seeker. Roberts, Scott, illus. 2017. (Game for Adventure Ser.). (ENG.). 32p. (J). (gr. k-3). 25.32 *(978-1-5124-1330-4(5),* Graphic Universe™) Lerner Publishing Group.

—Belinda the Unbeatable. Roberts, Scott, illus. 2017. (Game for Adventure Ser.). (ENG.). 32p. (J). (gr. k-3). pap. 6.99 ***(978-1-5124-5413-0(3));*** lib. bdg. 25.32 ***(978-1-5124-1331-1(3))*** Lerner Publishing Group. (Graphic Universe™).

—The Bramble. Zick, Bruce, illus. 2013. (ENG.). 32p. (J). (gr. k-3). 16.95 *(978-0-7613-5856-5(0),* Carolrhoda Bks.) Lerner Publishing Group.

—SheHeWe. Bosch, Meritxell, illus. 2015. (ENG.). 32p. (J). (gr. k-3). pap. 6.95 *(978-1-4677-4578-9(2));* lib. bdg. 25.26 *(978-1-4677-4574-1(X))* Lerner Publishing Group. (Graphic Universe™).

Nosy Crow Staff. Pookie Pop Plays Hide-And-Seek: A Tiny Tab Book. Ho, Jannie, illus. 2015. (Tiny Tab Ser.). (ENG.). 8p. (J). (— 1). bds. 7.99 *(978-0-7636-7600-1(4),* Nosy Crow) Candlewick Pr.

O'Donnell, Liam. Max Finder Mystery, Vol. 2. Cho, Michael & Owlkids Books Inc. Staff, illus. 2007. (Max Finder Mystery Collected Casebook Ser.: 2). (ENG.). 96p. (J). (gr. 3-6). 9.95 *(978-2-89579-121-8(X))* Owlkids Bks. Inc. CAN. Dist: Publishers Group West (PGW).

—Max Finder Mystery Collected Casebook, Vol. 1. Cho, Michael & Owlkids Books Inc. Staff, illus. 2006. (Max Finder Mystery Collected Casebook Ser.: 1). (ENG.). 96p. (J). (gr. 3-6). pap. 9.95 *(978-2-89579-116-4(3),* Owlkids) Owlkids Bks. Inc. CAN. Dist: Publishers Group West (PGW).

—Max Finder Mystery Collected Casebook Vol. 3, Vol. 3. Cho, Michael & Owlkids Books Inc. Staff, illus. 2007. (Max Finder Mystery Collected Casebook Ser.: 3). (ENG.). 96p. (J). (gr. 3-6). pap. 9.95 *(978-2-89579-149-2(X),* Owlkids) Owlkids Bks. Inc. CAN. Dist: Publishers Group West (PGW).

Ofanansky, Allison. Sukkot Treasure Hunt. Alpern, Eliyahu, illus. Alpern, Eliyahu, photos by. 2009. (Sukkot & Simchat Torah Ser.). (ENG.). 32p. (J). (gr. -1-5). 15.95 *(978-0-8225-8763-7(7),* Kar-Ben Publishing) Lerner Publishing Group.

Oliver, Lauren. Panic. 2015. (ENG.). 432p. (YA). (gr. 9). pap. 9.99 *(978-0-06-201456-6(0))* 2014. (J). 137.91 *(978-0-06-230092-8(X))* 2014. (ENG.). 400p. (J). (gr. 9). 17.99 *(978-0-06-201455-9(2))* HarperCollins Pubs.

—Panic. 2015. (YA). lib. bdg. 20.85 *(978-0-606-36509-3(5))* Turtleback Bks.

O'Malley, Kevin. Lucky Leaf. O'Malley, Kevin, illus. 2007. (ENG., Illus.). 32p. (J). (gr. -1-2). 7.99 *(978-0-8027-9647-9(8),* 9780802796479, Bloomsbury USA Childrens) Bloomsbury Publishing USA.

O'Ryan, Ellie. The Case of the Digital Deception. 2013. (Club CSI Ser.: 5). (ENG.). 160p. (J). (gr. 3-7). 15.99 *(978-1-4424-7258-7(8));* pap. 6.99 *(978-1-4424-7257-0(X))* Simon Spotlight. (Simon Spotlight).

Osa, Nancy. The Battle of Zombie Hill: Defenders of the Overworld #1. 2015. (Defenders of the Overworld Ser.). (ENG.). 272p. (J). (gr. 6). pap. 9.99 *(978-1-63450-996-1(X),* Sky Pony Pr.) Skyhorse Publishing Co., Inc.

Ottersley, Martha T. Dora & the Winter Games (Dora the Explorer) Hall, Susan, illus. 2013. (Pictureback(R) Ser.). (ENG.). 24p. (J). (gr. -1-2). 3.99 *(978-0-385-37930-4(7),* Random Hse. Bks. for Young Readers) Random Hse. Children's Bks.

Papp, Robert, illus. The Great Detective Race. 2008. (Boxcar Children Mysteries Ser.: 115). (ENG.). 128p. (J). (gr. 1-5). 14.99 *(978-0-8075-5573-6(8))* Whitman, Albert & Co.

—The Great Detective Race. 2008. (Boxcar Children Mysteries Ser.: 115). (ENG.). 128p. (J). (gr. 1-5). pap. 5.99 *(978-0-8075-5574-3(6))* Whitman, Albert & Co.

—The Spy Game. 2009. (Boxcar Children Mysteries Ser.: 118). (ENG.). 128p. (J). (gr. 1-5). pap. 5.99 *(978-0-8075-7604-5(2))* Whitman, Albert & Co.

Park, Linda Sue. Trust No One. 2012. (39 Clues: Cahills vs. Vespers Ser.: 5). (ENG.). 192p. (J). (gr. 3-7). 12.99 *(978-0-545-29843-8(1))* Scholastic, Inc.

Parker, Emma. The Lightning Game. 2010. (Illus.). 24p. pap. *(978-1-877561-55-9(X))* First Edition Ltd.

Paul, Ruth. Stomp! 2013. pap. *(978-0-545-52940-2(9))* Scholastic, Inc.

Paul, Ruth & Lombana, J. P. Stomp! la Marchar! 2013. (SPA & ENG., Illus.). *(978-0-545-52795-8(3))* Scholastic, Inc.

Paz, Veronica. Play Pretend with Muno. 2009. (Yo Gabba Gabba! Ser.). (ENG.). 12p. (J). (gr. -1-1). bds. 6.99 *(978-1-4169-8508-2(5),* Simon Spotlight) Simon Spotlight.

Peck, Jan. Pirate Treasure Hunt!, 1 vol. Tans, Adrian, illus. 2008. (ENG.). 32p. (J). (gr. k-3). 16.99 *(978-1-58980-549-1(6))* Pelican Publishing Co., Inc.

Petrillo, Genevieve & Lyon, Lea. Keep Your Ear on the Ball, 1 vol. Lyon, Lea, illus. 2007. (ENG., Illus.). 32p. (J). (gr. -1-3). 16.95 *(978-0-88448-296-3(0))* Tilbury Hse. Pubs.

Peyo. The Smurf Championship Games. Peyo, illus. 2012. (Smurfs Classic Ser.). (ENG., Illus.). 32p. (J). (gr. k-2). pap. 3.99 *(978-1-4424-4993-0(4),* Simon Spotlight) Simon Spotlight.

Pingry, Patricia A. Noses & Toes. Rose, Drew, illus. 2005. (J). *(978-0-8249-6594-5(9),* Ideal Pubns.) Worthy Publishing.

Polan, Alex. Following Meowth's Footprints: PokéStop Stories, Book Two. 2016. (ENG.). 112p. (J). (gr. 1-7). pap. 7.99

E
F
G

(978-1-5107-2158-6(4), Sky Pony Pr.) Skyhorse Publishing Co., Inc.
—Welcome to Camp Pikachu. 2016. (Unofficial Stories for Pokémon Collectors Ser.). (ENG.). 112p. (J). (gr. 2-7). pap. 7.99 (978-1-5107-0378-0(0), Sky Pony Pr.) Skyhorse Publishing Co., Inc.
Popalis, Amy. Everyone Plays Games. 2015. (ENG.). 24p. (gr. k-3). 28.50 (978-1-63430-360-6(1)) Rourke Educational Media.
Posner, Richard. Sparrows Flight. 2014. (ENG.). 222p. (J). (gr. 7-10). pap. 14.95 (978-1-59077-316-1(0)) Evans, M. & Co., Inc.
Priddy, Roger. Best Friends: We Are Better Together. 2016. (Best Friends Ser.). (ENG., Illus.). 20p. (J). bds. 9.99 (978-0-312-51964-3(8), 9780312519643, Priddy Bks.) St. Martin's Pr.
Publications International Ltd. Staff, ed. First Look & Find Hello Kitty. 2013. (gr. -1-1). bds. 7.98 (978-1-4508-6378-0(7), 900f7270-d27c-4dbf-8614-52373c31c3df) Phoenix International Publications, Inc.
—Look & Find: Disney Pixar Cars. 2013. 24p. (J). 7.98 (978-1-4508-7916-3(0), 1450879160) Phoenix International Publications, Inc.
Quigley, Michael. A Monkey's Riddle. 2013. 24p. pap. 24.95 (978-1-63000-506-1(1)) America Star Bks.
Rancourt, Cheryle. The Puff Family: Volume 1. 2009. 28p. pap. 12.99 (978-1-4389-4442-5(X)) AuthorHouse.
Random House Disney Staff. Wreck-It Ralph (Disney Wreck-It Ralph) Random House Disney Staff, illus. 2012. (Big Golden Book Ser.). (ENG., Illus.). 64p. (J). (gr. -1-2). 9.99 (978-0-7364-2954-2(9), Golden/Disney) Random Hse. Children's Bks.
—Wreck-It Ralph Little Golden Book (Disney Wreck-It Ralph) Random House Disney Staff, illus. 2012. (Little Golden Book Ser.). (ENG., Illus.). 24p. (J). (gr. k-k). 3.99 (978-0-7364-2972-6(7), Golden/Disney) Random Hse. Children's Bks.
Raschka, Chris. Whaley Whale. 2014. (Thingy Things Ser.). (ENG., Illus.). 24p. (J). (gr. -1-k). 6.95 (978-1-4197-1058-2(3), Abrams Appleseed) Abrams, Inc.
Reichs, Kathy & Reichs, Brendan. Code. 2013. (Virals Ser.: 3). lib. bdg. 19.65 (978-0-606-32140-2(3), Turtleback) Turtleback Bks.
Riley, Zach. Sacred Stick. Ricci, Andrés, illus. 2012. (Zach Riley Ser.). 80p. (J). (gr. 3-6). lib. bdg. 27.07 (978-1-61783-535-3(8)) Magic Wagon.
Rippy, Patricia J. Here Comes the Tornado. 2012. 20p. pap. 17.99 (978-1-4772-4905-5(2)) AuthorHouse.
Ritchey, Kate. Huey, Dewey, & Louie's Rainy Day. 2014. (Mickey & Friends World of Reading Ser.). (J). lib. bdg. 13.55 (978-0-606-34122-6(6), Turtleback) Turtleback Bks.
Robinson, Gary. Little Brother of War. 2013. (PathFinders Ser.). (ENG.). 113p. (YA). pap. 9.95 (978-1-939053-02-2(1), 7th Generation) Book Publishing Co.
Rodkey, Geoff. The Tapper Twins Go to War (with Each Other) 2015. (Tapper Twins Ser.: 1). (ENG., Illus.). 240p. (J). (gr. 3-7). 13.99 (978-0-316-29779-0(8)) Little Brown & Co.
—The Tapper Twins Tear up New York. 2015. (Tapper Twins Ser.: 2). (ENG., Illus.). 288p. (J). (gr. 3-7). 13.99 (978-0-316-29783-7(6)) Little Brown & Co.
—The Tapper Twins Tear up New York. 2016. (Tapper Twins Ser.: 2). (ENG., Illus.). 288p. (J). (gr. 3-7). pap. 5.99 (978-0-316-31601-9(6)) Little, Brown Bks. for Young Readers.
Rohr, Rebecca. Flocks: A Buster Bird Adventure. 2011. pap. 8.95 (978-0-7414-6735-5(6)) Infinity Publishing.
Rosen, Lev Ac. The Memory Wall. 2016. (ENG.). 368p. (J). (gr. 4-7). 16.99 (978-1-101-93323-7(2), Knopf Bks. for Young Readers) Random Hse. Children's Bks.
Roy, Ron. April Adventure. Gurney, John Steven, illus. 2010. (Calendar Mysteries Ser.: 4). (ENG.). 80p. (J). (gr. 1-4). 4.99 (978-0-375-86116-1(5), Random Hse. Bks. for Young Readers) Random Hse. Children's Bks.
—April Adventure. 2010. (Calendar Mysteries Ser.: 4). lib. bdg. 14.75 (978-0-606-12465-2(9), Turtleback) Turtleback Bks.
Russo, David Anson. The Great Treasure Hunt. Russo, David Anson, illus. 2011. (ENG., Illus.). 28p. (J). (gr. k-3). pap. 14.99 (978-1-4424-4342-6(1), Simon & Schuster Bks. For Young Readers) Simon & Schuster Bks. For Young Readers.
Ryan, Jeanne. Nerve. (ENG.). (YA). (gr. 9). 2012. 304p. 17.99 (978-0-8037-3832-4(3), Dial Bks) 2016. 320p. pap. 10.99 (978-0-14-242283-0(5), Speak) Penguin Young Readers Group.
Ryan, Matthew. The Box. 2012. (ENG.). pap. (978-1-4675-2638-8(X)) Independent Pub.
Rylant, Cynthia. The Case of the Fidgety Fox. Karas, G. Brian, illus. 2004. (High-Rise Private Eyes Ser.). 58p. (J). (gr. 1-3). 11.65 (978-0-7569-3210-7(6)) Perfection Learning Corp.
Sachar, Louis. The Cardturner. 2011. (ENG.). 352p. (YA). (gr. 7). pap. 9.99 (978-0-385-73663-3(0), Ember) Random Hse. Children's Bks.
—The Cardturner. 2011. lib. bdg. 20.85 (978-0-606-23428-3(4), Turtleback) Turtleback Bks.
Sanschagrin, Joceline. Le Visage Masqué. Brignaud, Pierre, illus. 2004. (Mon Roman Ser.). (FRE.). 160p. (J). (gr. 2). pap. (978-2-89021-651-8(9)) Diffusion du livre Mirabel (DLM).
Scholastic. Ratchet & Clank. 2016. (Ratchet & Clank Ser.). (ENG.). 112p. (J). (gr. 2-5). pap. 7.99 (978-1-338-04549-9(0)) Scholastic, Inc.
Scholastic, Inc. Staff. Pokemon: Kalos Region Handbook. 2014. lib. bdg. 19.65 (978-0-606-35861-3(7)) Turtleback Bks.
Scholastic, Inc. Staff, contrib. by. Cahills vs. Vespers, Pack. 2012. (39 Clues: Cahills vs. Vespers Ser.). (ENG.). (J). (gr. 3-7). 6.99 (978-0-545-31644-6(8)) Scholastic, Inc.
Schreiber, Joe. Game over, Pete Watson. Rash, Andy, illus. 2014. (ENG.). 224p. (J). (gr. 5-7). 16.99 (978-0-544-15756-9(7), HMH Books For Young Readers) Houghton Mifflin Harcourt Publishing Co.
Scieszka, Jon. Me Oh Maya. McCauley, Adam, illus. 2005. (Time Warp Trio Ser.: No. 13). 69p. (gr. 2-6). 15.00 (978-0-7569-5060-6(0)) Perfection Learning Corp.
Scotton, Rob. The Name of the Game. 2012. (Splat the Cat: I Can Read Ser.). (J). lib. bdg. 13.55 (978-0-606-26281-1(4), Turtleback) Turtleback Bks.
Seibers, Elexis. Zoac Moves to Jugabh. 2011. 36p. pap. 21.99 (978-1-4568-1585-1(7)) Xlibris Corp.
Shulman, Mark. Mom & Dad Are Palindromes. 2014. (J). lib. bdg. 18.40 (978-0-606-36539-0(7)) Turtleback Bks.
Smith, L. J. The Forbidden Game: The Hunter - The Chase - The Kill. 2010. (Forbidden Game Ser.: Bks. 1-3). (ENG.). 768p. (YA). (gr. 7). pap. 10.99 (978-1-4169-8940-0(4), Simon Pulse) Simon Pulse.
Snyder, Zilpha Keatley. The Egypt Game. 2014. (ENG.). 240p. (J). (gr. 3-7). 11.24 (978-1-63245-327-3(4)) Lectorum Pubns., Inc.
—The Egypt Game. 2011. 9.00 (978-0-7848-3470-1(9), Everbind) Marco Bk. Co.
—The Egypt Game. Raible, Alton, illus. (ENG.). (J). (gr. 3-7). 2009. 240p. pap. 8.99 (978-1-4169-9051-2(8)) 2007. 224p. 17.99 (978-1-4169-6065-2(1)) Simon & Schuster Children's Publishing. (Atheneum Bks. for Young Readers).
Sparks, John. The Game. 2009. 76p. pap. 15.99 (978-1-4363-8935-8(6)) Xlibris Corp.
Stadther, Michael. Secrets of the Alchemist Dar. Stadther, Michael, illus. 2006. (Treasure's Trove Ser.). (ENG., Illus.). 144p. (J). 21.99 (978-1-4169-2653-5(4)); 39.99 (978-1-4169-2661-0(5)) Treasure Trove, Inc.
Stainton, Sue. Christmas Magic. Melhuish, Eva, illus. 2007. 32p. (J). (gr. -1-1). lib. bdg. 16.89 (978-0-06-078572-7(1), Tegen, Katherine Bks) HarperCollins Pubs.
Stanek, Robert, pseud. Play Their First Big Game. 2008. (ENG., Illus.). 32p. (J). pap. 5.59 (978-1-57545-193-0(X)) RP Media.
Stern, Leonard. The Mad Libs Worst-Case Scenario Survival Handbook. 2004. (Mad Libs Ser.). (ENG., Illus.). 48p. (J). (gr. 3-7). 4.99 (978-0-8431-1033-3(3), Mad Libs) Penguin Young Readers Group.
Stewart, Kenneth. The Kickball Kid. 2012. 24p. pap. 24.95 (978-1-4626-7683-5(9)) America Star Bks.
Stine, R. L. Hide & Shriek & Who's Been Sleeping in My Grave? Twice Terrifying Tales. 2009. (R. L. Stine's Ghosts of Fear Street Ser.). (ENG.). 256p. (J). (gr. 3-7). pap. 7.99 (978-1-4169-9134-2(4), Aladdin) Simon & Schuster Children's Publishing.
Strange, Jason. The Demon Card, 1 vol. Evergreen, Nelson & Kendall, Bradford, illus. 2012. (Jason Strange Ser.). (ENG.). 72p. (gr. 2-3). pap. 6.25 (978-1-4342-3884-9(9)); lib. bdg. 25.32 (978-1-4342-3296-0(4)) Stone Arch Bks.
Street, Sesame. Elmo's Guessing Game about Colors/Elmo y Su Juego de Adivinar Los Colores. 2006. (Elmo's Guessing Game about Colors / Elmo y Su Juego de Adivinar Los Colores Ser.). (SPA, ENG & MUL., Illus.). 10p. (J). (gr. -1 — 1). bds. 5.95 (978-0-87358-905-5(X)) Cooper Square Publishing Llc.
Suen, Anastasia. Dino Hunt: A Robot & Rico Story. Laughead, Mike, illus. 2010. (Robot & Rico Ser.). (ENG.). 32p. (gr. 1-2). pap. 6.25 (978-1-4342-2300-5(0)) Stone Arch Bks.
Sullivan, Erin Ash. Counting Clues. 2011. (Early Connections Ser.). (J). (978-1-61672-578-5(8)) Benchmark Education Co.
Swan, Bill. Man-to-Man, 1 vol. 2009. (Lorimer Sports Stories Ser.). (ENG.). 144p. (J). (gr. 4-8). 16.95 (978-1-55277-443-4(0), 9781552774434); 8.95 (978-1-55277-442-7(2), 9781552774427) Lorimer, James & Co., Ltd., Pubs. CAN. Dist: Casemate Pubs. & Bk. Distributors, LLC.
—Mud Run, 1 vol. 2003. (Lorimer Sports Stories Ser.). (ENG.). 104p. (J). (gr. 4-8). 8.95 (978-1-55028-786-8(9), 9781550287868); 16.95 (978-1-55028-787-5(7), 9781550287875) Lorimer, James & Co., Ltd., Pubs. CAN. Dist: Casemate Pubs. & Bk. Distributors, LLC.
Takhar, Jodi. What Can I Do Today? Takhar, Jodi & Jones, Paul, illus. 14p. (J). (gr. -1-3). 19.95 (978-1-886000-03-2(4)) Takhar's, Jodi Spilt Milk Collection.
Tashjian, Janet. My Life As a Gamer. Tashjian, Jake, illus. 2015. (My Life Ser.: 5). (ENG.). 272p. (J). (gr. 4-7). 13.99 (978-0-8050-9851-8(8), 9780805098518, Holt, Henry & Co. Bks. For Young Readers) Holt, Henry & Co.
Taylor, Dereen. The Mermaid's Treasure Hunt. East, Jacqueline, illus. 2012. (ENG.). 12p. (J). (gr. -1-12). 16.99 (978-1-84322-762-5(2)) Anness Publishing GBR. Dist: National Bk. Network.
Teitelbaum, Clancy. Queens of Cyberspace. 2016. (Queens of Cyberspace Ser.: 6). (ENG.). 200p. (YA). (gr. 6-12). lib. bdg. 162.78 (978-1-68076-196-2(X), Epic Pr.) ABDO Publishing Co.
Thaler, Mike. The School Carnival from the Black Lagoon. Lee, Jared, illus. 2005. 64p. (J). pap. (978-0-439-80075-4(7)) Scholastic, Inc.
—The School Carnival from the Black Lagoon, 1 vol. Lee, Jared, illus. 2012. (Black Lagoon Adventures Ser.: No. 2). (ENG.). 64p. (J). (gr. 2-5). 24.21 (978-1-59961-962-0(8)) Spotlight.
Thomas Nelson Publishing Staff. The Pirates Who Don't Do Anything - Veggietales Movie: Squawk-Along Songs & Games. 2008. (Adventures in Odyssey Activity Pack Ser.). 48p. (J). pap. 12.99 (978-1-4003-1235-1(3)) Nelson, Thomas Inc.
—The Pirates Who Don't Do Anything: A VeggieTales Movie: Whipcrack Island Games. 2008. 64p. (J). pap. 12.99 (978-1-4003-1229-0(9)) Nelson, Thomas Inc.
Thompson, Lauren & Anderson, Derek. Little Quack's Hide & Seek. 2004. (ENG., Illus.). 32p. (J). (gr. -1-3). 17.99 (978-0-689-85722-5(5), Simon & Schuster Bks. For Young Readers) Simon & Schuster Bks. For Young Readers.
Thompson, Nina C. The Puzzle King. 2009. 56p. pap. 9.95 (978-1-60860-149-3(8), Eloquent Bks.) Strategic Book Publishing & Rights Agency (SBPRA).
The three-legged Race, 6 Packs. (gr. 1-2). 25.00 (978-0-7635-9131-1(9)) Rigby Education.
Timmers, Leo. Oops! Timmers, Leo, illus. 2011. (ENG., Illus.). 32p. (J). (gr. k — 1). 15.95 (978-1-60537-105-4(X)) Cobblestone Publishing Co.
Top That Publishing Staff, ed. The Midnight Fairies. Atkins, Alison, illus. 2007. (Sparkling Jigsaw Book Ser.). 10p. (J). (gr. -1). bds. (978-1-84666-278-2(8), Tide Mill Pr.) Top That! Publishing PLC.
Torres, J. Yo Gabba Gabba: Good Night, Gabbaland: Good Night, Gabbaland. 2010. 16p. bds. 7.99 (978-1-934964-56-9(5)) Oni Pr., Inc.
Treasure Map. 2008. (Looney Tunes 8*8 Ser.). 24p. pap. (978-1-4075-2634-8(0)); pap. (978-1-4075-2644-7(8)) Parragon, Inc.
The Tug of War: Individual Title Six-Pack. (Story Steps Ser.). (gr. k-2). 23.00 (978-0-7635-9620-0(5)) Rigby Education.
Tulien, Sean & Maese, Fares. Paintball Punk, 1 vol. Aburto, Jesus & Esparza, Andres, illus. 2010. (Sports Illustrated Kids Graphic Novels Ser.). (ENG.). 56p. (gr. 2-3). 26.65 (978-1-4342-2219-0(5)); pap. 7.19 (978-1-4342-2788-1(X)) Stone Arch Bks.
Upton, Robert Jesten. Milo & the Dragon Cross: A Novel. 2017. (YA). pap. **(978-1-63293-177-1(X))** Sunstone Pr.
Valentine, Stephen J. The Lazarus Game. 2015. 311p. (YA). pap. 19.99 (978-1-4621-1554-9(3)) Cedar Fort, Inc./CFI Distribution.
Van Lemon, M. Champions of the Garden Games: Winter Fun for Everyone. 2009. 48p. pap. 20.95 (978-1-4490-3580-8(9)) AuthorHouse.
Voss, Fonda. The Bossy Girl. 2005. (Illus.). 31p. (J). per. 9.99 (978-1-932338-96-6(9)) Lifevest Publishing, Inc.
Walker, Nan. Follow That Clue! Palmisciano, Diane, illus. 2008. (Social Studies Connects Ser.). 32p. (J). (gr. -1-3). pap. 5.95 (978-1-57565-274-0(9)) Kane Press, Inc.
—Follow That Clue! Palmisciano, Diane, illus. 2009. (Social Studies Connects (r) Ser.). (ENG.). (gr. k-2). pap. 33.92 (978-0-7613-4805-4(0)) Lerner Publishing Group.
Ward, Terri & Ward, Tom. Aunt Tami's Strawberry Farm. Kindt, Rita, illus. 2010. 38p. pap. 14.50 (978-1-60693-935-2(1), Eloquent Bks.) Strategic Book Publishing & Rights Agency (SBPRA).
Watson, Stephanie. The Club. 2010. (Night Fall Ser.). (ENG.). 112p. (YA). (gr. 6-12). pap. 7.95 (978-0-7613-6162-6(6)) Lerner Publishing Group.
Wayne, Matt. Attack of the Virtual Villains. Moy, Philip, illus. 2012. (Batman: the Brave & the Bold Ser.). (ENG.). 32p. (gr. 2-3). lib. bdg. 22.60 (978-1-4342-4546-5(2)) Stone Arch Bks.
Webster, Christy. Toy Box Heroes! RH Disney Staff, illus. 2014. (Step into Reading Ser.). (ENG.). 32p. (J). (gr. -1-1). 4.99 (978-0-7364-3270-2(1), RH/Disney) Random Hse. Children's Bks.
Welvaert, Scott R. The 13th Floor. 2015. (ENG., Illus.). 96p. (J). (978-1-63235-056-5(4)) Pr. Room Editions LLC.
West, Tracey. Mario & the Incredible Rescue. 2006. 76p. (J). pap. (978-0-439-84366-9(9)) Scholastic, Inc.
West, Tracey, adapted by. A New Hero. 2007. (Illus.). 105p. (J). pap. (978-0-439-88836-3(0)) Scholastic, Inc.
Weston Woods Staff, creator. Pete's a Pizza. 2011. 29.95 (978-0-439-74519-2(5)) Weston Woods Studios, Inc.
Whitaker, Joan. Cartwheeling. Cusack, Elizabeth, illus. 2013. 24p. 22.95 (978-1-61493-189-8(5)); pap. 12.95 (978-1-61493-188-1(7)) Peppertree Pr., The.
Williams, Dylan, et al. Pawb Yn Cuddio. 2005. (WEL., Illus.). 16p. (978-1-84512-021-4(3)) Cymdeithas Lyfrau Ceredigion.
Willson, Sarah. Simon Says. Ulrich, George, illus. 2006. (Step-By-Step Readers Ser.). (J). pap. (978-1-59939-057-4(4), Reader's Digest Young Families, Inc.) Studio Fun International.
Winburn, William B. Hide-And-Peek. 2010. (J). (978-85-312-5235-8(0)) Children's Pr., Ltd.
Wolfe, Sean Fay. The New Order. 2015. (Elementia Chronicles Ser.: 2). (ENG.). 496p. (J). (gr. 3-7). pap. 9.99 (978-0-06-241634-6(0)) HarperCollins Pubs.
—Quest for Justice. 2015. (Elementia Chronicles Ser.: 1). (ENG.). 512p. (J). (gr. 3-7). pap. 9.99 (978-0-06-241632-2(4)) HarperCollins Pubs.
Wolitzer, Meg. The Fingertips of Duncan Dorfman. 2012. (ENG.). 304p. (J). (gr. 3-7). pap. 7.99 (978-0-14-242204-5(5), Puffin Books) Penguin Young Readers Group.
Wood, Audrey & Wood, Don. Piggies. 2016. (ENG., Illus.). 30p. (J). (— 1). bds. 7.99 (978-0-544-79114-5(2), HMH Books For Young Readers) Houghton Mifflin Harcourt Publishing Co.
Worrell, Maryellen. The Accidental Hero. 2008. 101p. pap. 19.95 (978-1-60672-145-2(3)) America Star Bks.
Yang, Gene Luen. Level Up. Pham, Thien, illus. 2011. (ENG.). 160p. (YA). (gr. 7). 19.99 (978-1-59643-714-2(6), 9781596437142, First Second Bks.) Roaring Brook Pr.
Yoon, Salina. Tap to Play! 2014. (ENG.). 40p. (J). (gr. -1-3). 15.99 (978-0-06-228684-0(6)) HarperCollins Pubs.
—Where's Boo? 2013. (ENG., Illus.). 18p. (J). (— 1). bds. 6.99 (978-0-307-97808-0(7), Random Hse. Bks. for Young Readers) Random Hse. Children's Bks.
York, Carol Beach. Takers & Returners: A Novel of Suspense. 2005. (ENG.). 128p. (J). (gr. 4-7). pap. 11.95 (978-0-929093-18-5(6), Taylor Productions) G R M Assocs.
Zepeda, Gwendolyn. Level up / Paso de Nivel. Baeza Ventura, Gabriela, tr. from ENG. Torrecilla, Pablo, illus. 2012. (SPA & ENG.). (J). (gr. 5-9). 16.95 (978-1-55885-747-6(8), Piñata Books) Arte Publico Pr.

GAMES FOR TRAVELERS

Calkhoven, Laurie & Laskey, Shannon. Miles of Smiles: Travel Games & Quizzes to Go. Hunt, Sara, ed. 2007. (ENG., Illus.). 80p. (gr. 4-7). spiral bd. 9.95 (978-1-59369-170-7(X), Pleasant Co.) American Girl Publishing, Inc.
Clarke, Catriona. 100 Things for Little Children to Do on a Trip. 2008. (Activity Cards Ser.). (Illus.). 50p. (J). 9.99 (978-0-7945-2122-6(3), Usborne) EDC Publishing.
Corporate Contributor, ed. Diary of a Texas Kid. 2011. (State Journal Ser.). (ENG.). 128p. (J). (gr. 4-8). pap. 9.95 (978-1-58536-608-8(0), 202225) Sleeping Bear Pr.
Galvin, Laura Gates. Learning Pack - First Concepts. rev. ed. 2005. (ENG., Illus.). 10p. (J). (gr. -1-3). 12.99 (978-1-59069-479-4(1)) Studio Mouse LLC.
Hill, Taven. My Travel Book. 2006. (Illus.). 105p. (J). 19.95 (978-0-9765321-1-8(5)) Taven Hill Studio.
Klutz Editors. Books-in-a-Cup: Orange. 2005. (Klutz to Go Ser.). 20p. (J). pap. 9.95 (978-1-57054-271-8(6)) Klutz.
Lonely Planet Publications Staff. Adventures in Smelly Places: Packed Full of Activities & over 250 Stickers, 1 vol. 2015. (Lonely Planet Kids Ser.). (ENG.). 48p. (J). pap. 9.99 (978-1-74360-781-7(4), 4984) Lonely Planet Pubns.
Pryor, Joanne. I Spy... the Next Stop: Kids Camping the Coast from Maine to Georgia. 2004. (Illus.). 164p. (J). spiral bd. (978-0-9735907-1-5(8)) Destination Publishing.
Rand McNally Staff. Kids' Road Atlas. (Backseat Bks.). 80p. (J). pap. 3.95 (978-0-528-96544-9(1)) Rand McNally.
Rhatigan, Joe. Don't Unravel When You Travel: Hold It Together with Goofy Games, Peculiar Puzzles, Atypical Activites, Droll Doodling, Fun Facts & Much More! 2010. (ENG.). 260p. (J). (gr. 3). pap. 14.95 (978-1-60433-154-7(2), Applesauce Pr.) Cider Mill Pr. Bk. Pubs., LLC.
Schiller, David. All American Car-I-Oke. 2003. (ENG., Illus.). 64p. (J). 14.95 (978-0-7611-3068-0(3), 13068) Workman Publishing Co., Inc.
Sleeping Bear Editor, ed. Diary of an American Kid. 2011. (Country Journal Ser.). (ENG.). 128p. (J). (gr. 4-8). pap. 9.95 (978-1-58536-171-7(2), 202262) Sleeping Bear Pr.
Thompson, Helen. Travel Math. 2013. (Math 24/7 Ser.: 10). 48p. (J). (gr. 5-18). 19.95 (978-1-4222-2911-8(4)) Mason Crest.
Usborne Books Staff, creator. 50 Travel Games & Activities. 2006. (Activity Cards Ser.). 50p. (J). 9.99 (978-0-7945-1319-1(0), Usborne) EDC Publishing.

GAMES, OLYMPIC

see Olympics

GANDALF (FICTITIOUS CHARACTER)—FICTION

Tolkien, J. R. R. El Hobbit. 2003. (Lord of the Rings Ser.). (SPA.). 320p. (YA). 17.95 (978-84-450-7141-0(6), MQ9001) Minotauro Ediciones ESP. Dist: Distribooks, Inc.
—The Hobbit. Tolkien, J. R. R., illus. 70th anniv. ed. 2011. (ENG., Illus.). 400p. mass mkt. (978-0-261-10221-7(4)) HarperCollins Pubs. Ltd.

GANDHI, INDIRA, 1917-1984

Prasad, H.Y. Sharada. Indira Gandhi. 2013. 56p. 10.00 (978-0-14-333288-6(0)) Penguin Group India IND. Dist: Penguin Publishing Group.
Schupack, Sara. Indira Gandhi. 2013. (Leading Women 2 Ser.). 96p. (gr. 7-12). (YA). pap. 19.99 (978-1-62712-113-2(7)); (Illus.). (J). 39.93 (978-0-7614-4955-3(8)) Cavendish Square Publishing.

GANDHI, MAHATMA, 1869-1948

Cook, Diane. Mohandas Gandhi: Spiritual Leader. 2013. (People of Importance Ser.: 21). (Illus.). 32p. (J). (gr. 4-18). 19.95 (978-1-4222-2852-4(5)) Mason Crest.
de Lambilly, Elisabeth. Gandhi: His Life, His Struggles, His Words. Cordier, Severine, illus. 2010. (Great Spiritual Figures of Modern Times Ser.). (ENG.). 72p. (J). (gr. 3-6). 16.95 (978-1-59270-094-3(2)) Enchanted Lion Bks., LLC.
Doeden, Matt. Darkness Everywhere: The Assassination of Mohandas Gandhi. 2013. 80p. pap. 31.93 (978-1-4677-1659-8(6)) Lerner Publishing Group.
—Mohandas Gandhi. 2011. (J). lib. bdg. (978-0-7613-5483-3(2)) Twenty First Century Bks.
Dorling Kindersley Publishing Staff. Gandhi. 2014. (DK Eyewitness Bks.). (ENG., Illus.). 72p. (J). (gr. 3-7). lib. bdg. 19.99 (978-1-4654-2698-7(1), DK Children) Dorling Kindersley Publishing, Inc.
Dorling Kindersley Publishing Staff & Walker, Richard. Human Body. 2014. (DK Eyewitness Bks.). (ENG.). 72p. (J). (gr. 3-7). pap. 9.99 (978-1-4654-2617-8(5), DK Children) Dorling Kindersley Publishing, Inc.
Gandhi, Arun & Hegedus, Bethany. Be the Change: A Grandfather Gandhi Story. Turk, Evan, illus. 2016. (ENG.). 48p. (J). (gr. -1-3). 18.99 (978-1-4814-4265-7(1)) Simon & Schuster Children's Publishing.
—Grandfather Gandhi. Turk, Evan, illus. 2014. (ENG.). 48p. (J). (gr. -1-3). 17.99 (978-1-4424-2365-7(X)) Simon & Schuster Children's Publishing.
Gandhi, Mahatma. My Experiments with Truth. Chougule, Shailja Jain, illus. 2016. (ENG.). 64p. pap. 6.95 (978-1-906230-88-3(9)) Real Reads Ltd. GBR. Dist: Casemate Pubs. & Bk. Distributors, LLC.
Green, Jen. Gandhi & the Quit India Movement: Days of Decision, 1 vol. 2013. (Days of Decision Ser.). (ENG.). 64p. (gr. 7-8). 35.99 (978-1-4329-7635-4(4)); pap. 10.95 (978-1-4329-7642-2(7)) Heinemann-Raintree.
Harmon, Daniel E. Ayatollah Ruhollah Khomeini. 2004. (Spiritual Leaders & Thinkers Ser.). (Illus.). 120p. (J). (gr. 9-13). 30.00 (978-0-7910-7865-5(5), Chelsea Hse.) Facts On File, Inc.
Kudlinski, Kathleen V. & Kudlinski, Kathleen. Gandhi: Young Nation Builder. 2006. (Childhood of World Figures Ser.). (ENG.). 192p. (J). (gr. 3-7). pap. 9.99 (978-1-4169-1283-5(5), Simon & Schuster/Paula Wiseman Bks.) Simon & Schuster/Paula Wiseman Bks.
Kuhn, Betsy. The Force Born of Truth: Mohandas Gandhi & the Salt March, India, 1930. 2010. (Civil Rights Struggles around the World Ser.). (ENG., Illus.). 160p. (J). (gr. 9-12). lib. bdg. 38.60 (978-0-8225-8968-6(0)) Lerner Publishing Group.
Lucas, Eileen. Mahatma Gandhi: Fighting for Indian Independence. 2017. (Rebels with a Cause Ser.). 128p. (J). (gr. 8-8). lib. bdg. 37.27 **(978-0-7660-8513-8(9))** Enslow Pubs., Inc.
Mahoney, Ellen. Gandhi for Kids: His Life & Ideas, with 21 Activities. 2016. (For Kids Ser.). (ENG., Illus.). 144p. (J). (gr. 9). pap. 17.99 (978-1-61373-122-2(1)) Chicago Review Pr., Inc.
Malaspina, Ann. Mahatma Gandhi & India's Independence. 2016. (People & Events That Changed the World Ser.). (ENG., Illus.). 128p. (J). (gr. 7-8). lib. bdg. 37.27 (978-0-7660-7262-6(2)) Enslow Pubs., Inc.
McGinty, Alice B. Gandhi: The March to the Sea, 0 vols. González, Thomas, illus. 2013. (ENG.). 40p. (J). (gr. 4-7). 17.99 (978-1-4778-1644-8(5), 9781477816448, Amazon Children's Publishing) Amazon Publishing.
O'Neill, John R. Mahatma Gandhi, Nelson Mandela. 2011. (Readers' & Writers' Genre Workshop Ser.). (YA). pap. (978-1-4509-3024-6(7)) Benchmark Education Co.
Pastan, Amy, et al. Gandhi: A Photographic Stroy of Life. 2006. (DK Biography Ser.). (ENG., Illus.). 128p. (J). (gr. 5-12). pap. 6.99 (978-0-7566-2111-7(9), DK Children) Dorling Kindersley Publishing, Inc.
The Power of Ghandi. 2003. (Illus.). pap. 5.60 (978-0-7398-7512-4(4)) Steck-Vaughn.
Rau, Dana Meachen. Who Was Gandhi? Hoare, Jerry & Harrison, Nancy, illus. 2014. (Who Was? Ser.). (ENG.). 112p. (J). (gr. 3-7). pap. 5.99 (978-0-448-48235-4(5), Grosset & Dunlap) Penguin Young Readers Group.
—Who Was Gandhi? 2014. (Who Was...? Ser.). lib. bdg. 16.00 (978-0-606-36177-4(4)) Turtleback Bks.
Rice, Dona. Mohandas Gandhi, 1 vol. 2nd rev. ed. 2014. (TIME for KIDS(r) Nonfiction Readers Ser.). (ENG., Illus.). 32p. (J). (gr. 3-3). pap. 25.96 (978-1-4807-1091-7(1)) Shell Educational Publishing.

—Mohandas Gandhi, 1 vol. 2nd rev. ed. 2012. (Nonfiction Readers Ser.). (ENG.). 32p. (J). (gr. 3-3). pap. 8.99 *(978-1-4333-3682-9(0))* Teacher Created Materials, Inc.

Rice, William & Rice, Dona. Mohandas Gandhi. 2017. (TIME for Kids en Español - Level 3 Ser.). (SPA.). 32p. (gr. 3-3). lib. bdg. 31.99 ***(978-1-5157-5189-2(9))*** Time for Kids Inc AUS. Dist: Capstone Pub.

Rivera, Sheila. Mohandas Gandhi: A Life of Integrity. 2006. (Pull Ahead Bks.). (Illus.). 32p. (J). (gr. 3-7). lib. bdg. 22.60 *(978-0-8225-6383-9(5)*, Lerner Pubns.) Lerner Publishing Group.

—Mohandas Ghandi: A Life of Integrity. 2007. (Pull Ahead Books-Biographies Ser.). (ENG., Illus.). 32p. (gr. k-3). pap. 7.95 *(978-0-8225-6432-4(7))* Lerner Publishing Group.

Rollason, Jane & Pearson Education Staff. Gandhi. 2nd ed. 2008. (ENG., Illus.). 32p. pap. 11.99 *(978-1-4058-7693-3(X))* Pearson Education.

Sawyer, Kem Knapp. Mohandas Gandhi. 2011. (Champion of Freedom Ser.). 144p. (gr. 7-12). 28.95 *(978-1-59935-166-7(8))* Reynolds, Morgan Inc.

Schuldt, Lori Meek. Martin Luther King, Jr. With Profiles of Mohandas K. Gandhi & Nelson Mandela. 2006. (Biographical Connections Ser.). (Illus.). 112p. (J). *(978-0-7166-1822-5(2))* World Bk., Inc.

Shaw, Maura D. Gandhi: India's Great Soul. Marchesi, Stephen, illus. 2003. (ENG.). 32p. (J). (gr. 1-3). 12.95 *(978-1-893361-91-1(8)*, 9781893361911, Skylight Paths Publishing) LongHill Partners, Inc.

Todd, Anne M. Mohandas Gandhi. 2004. (Spiritual Leaders & Thinkers Ser.). (Illus.). 120p. (C). (gr. 9-13). 30.00 *(978-0-7910-7864-8(7)*, Chelsea Hse.) Facts On File, Inc.

Trussell-Cullen, Alan. Mahatma Gandhi. 2009. pap. 13.25 *(978-1-60559-064-6(9))* Hameray Publishing Group, Inc.

Vander Hook, Sue. Mahatma Gandhi: Proponent of Peace, 1 vol. 2010. (Essential Lives Set 5 Ser.). (ENG.). 112p. (J). (gr. 6-12). lib. bdg. 35.64 *(978-1-61613-515-7(8))* ABDO Publishing Co.

Vescia, Monique & Nicholson, Michael. Mahatma Gandhi: Champion of the Indian Independence Movement. 2017. (J). ***(978-1-5383-8084-0(6))***; pap. ***(978-1-5383-8083-3(8))*** Rosen Publishing Group, Inc., The. (Rosen Young Adult).

Wheeler, Jill C. Gandhi. 2003. (Breaking Barriers Ser.). 64p. (gr. 3-8). 27.07 *(978-1-57765-906-8(6)*, Abdo & Daughters) ABDO Publishing Co.

Wilkinson, Philip. Gandhi: The Young Protester Who Founded a Nation. 2007. (National Geographic World History Biographies Ser.). (ENG., Illus.). 64p. (J). (gr. 3-7). pap. 7.99 *(978-1-4263-0132-2(4)*, National Geographic Children's Bks.) National Geographic Society.

—Gandhi: The Young Protestor Who Founded a Nation. 2005. (National Geographic World History Biographies Ser.). (ENG., Illus.). 64p. (J). (gr. 3-7). 17.95 *(978-0-7922-3647-4(5))*; lib. bdg. 27.90 *(978-0-7922-3648-1(3))* National Geographic Society. (National Geographic Children's Bks.).

GANDHI, MAHATMA, 1869-1948—FICTION

Benchimol, Brigitte. Jadyn & the Magic Bubble: I Met Gandhi. Adams, Mark Wayne, illus. 2008. (J). 24.95 *(978-0-9799339-7-4(8))* East West Discovery Pr.

GANDHI, MOHANDAS KARAMCHAND, 1869-1948

see Gandhi, Mahatma, 1869-1948

GANGES RIVER (INDIA AND BANGLADESH)

Aloian, Molly. The Ganges: India's Sacred River. 2010. (Rivers Around the World Ser.). (ENG., Illus.). 32p. (J). (gr. 5-8). pap. *(978-0-7787-7466-2(X))*; lib. bdg. *(978-0-7787-7443-3(0))* Crabtree Publishing Co.

The Ganges. 2011. (River Journey Ser.). (ENG.). 48p. (YA). (gr. 5-8). 27.95 *(978-1-4488-6011-1(3)*, Rosen Reference) Rosen Publishing Group, Inc., The.

Manning, Paul. The Ganges. 2014. (River Adventures Ser.). (J). lib. bdg. 31.35 *(978-1-59920-915-9(2))* Black Rabbit Bks.

Rice Jr., Earle. The Ganges River. 2012. (J). lib. bdg. 29.95 *(978-1-61228-295-4(4))* Mitchell Lane Pubs., Inc.

Simon, Charnan. The Sacred Ganges. 2004. (Geography of the World Ser.). (ENG., Illus.). 32p. (J). (gr. 3-6). 28.50 *(978-1-59296-338-6(2)*, 200273) Child's World, Inc., The.

GANGS

see also Juvenile Delinquency

Becnel, Barbara, ed. Gangs & Drugs: Stanley Tookie Williams Street Peace Series, 8 bks., Vol. 1, Bk. 1. 2008. 24p. (J). 6.95 *(978-0-9753584-2-9(1))* Damamli Publishing Co.

—Gangs & Friends: Stanley Tookie Williams Street Peace Series, 8 bks., Vol. 1, Bk. 5. 2008. 24p. (J). 6.95 *(978-0-9753584-5-0(6))* Damamli Publishing Co.

—Gangs & Self-Esteem: Stanley Tookie Williams Street Peace Series, 8 bks., Vol. 1, Bk. 4. 2008. 24p. (J). 6.95 *(978-0-9753584-1-2(3))* Damamli Publishing Co.

—Gangs & the Abuse of Power: Stanley Tookie Williams Street Peace Series, 8 bks., Vol. 1, Bk. 7. 2008. 24p. (J). 6.95 *(978-0-9753584-7-4(2))* Damamli Publishing Co.

—Gangs & Violence: Stanley Tookie Williams Street Peace Series, 8 bks., Vol. 1, Bk. 3. 2008. 24p. (J). 6.95 *(978-0-9753584-4-3(8))* Damamli Publishing Co.

—Gangs & Wanting to Belong: Stanley Tookie Williams Street Peace Series, 8 bks., Vol. 1, Bk. 6. 2008. 24p. (J). 6.95 *(978-0-9753584-6-7(4))* Damamli Publishing Co.

—Gangs & Weapons: Stanley Tookie Williams Street Peace Series, 8 bks., Vol. 1, Bk. 3. 2008. 24p. (J). *(978-0-9753584-3-6(X))* Damamli Publishing Co.

—Gangs & Your Neighborhood: Stanley Tookie Williams Street Peace Series, 8 bks., Vol. 1, Bk. 8. 2008. 24p. (J). 6.95 *(978-0-9753584-8-1(0))* Damamli Publishing Co.

Byers, Ann. Frequently Asked Questions about Gangs & Urban Violence. 2011. (FAQ: Teen Life Ser.). (ENG.). 64p. (YA). lib. bdg. 31.95 *(978-1-4488-1325-4(5))* Rosen Publishing Group, Inc., The.

Crabtree Publishing Company Staff & Bow, James. Gangs. 2012. (ENG., Illus.). 48p. (J). *(978-0-7787-2185-7(X))*; pap. *(978-0-7787-2192-5(2))* Crabtree Publishing Co.

Gangs. 2012. (Introducing Issues with Opposing Viewpoints Ser.). (ENG., Illus.). 144p. (gr. 7-10). lib. bdg. 36.95 *(978-0-7377-5679-1(9)*, Greenhaven Pr., Inc.) Cengage Gale.

Gifford, Clive. Gangs. 2010. (Voices Ser.). (Illus.). 48p. pap. *(978-0-237-54217-7(X))* Evans Brothers, Ltd.

Gitlin, Martin. I'm Being Targeted by a Gang. Now What? 2016. (Teen Life 411 Ser.). 00112p. (J). (gr. 7-7). 37.10 *(978-1-5081-7191-1(2)*, Rosen Young Adult) Rosen Publishing Group, Inc., The.

Hiber, Amanda. Gangs. 2013. (Issues That Concern You Ser.). (ENG., Illus.). 144p. (gr. 7-10). lib. bdg. 42.00 *(978-0-7377-6294-5(2)*, Greenhaven Pr., Inc.) Cengage Gale.

Hile, Lori. Gangs, 1 vol. 2012. (Teen Issues Ser.). (ENG.). 56p. (gr. 6-10). pap. 9.99 *(978-1-4329-6540-2(9))*; lib. bdg. 34.65 *(978-1-4329-6535-8(2))* Heinemann-Raintree.

Latchana Kenney, Karen. The Hidden Story of Gangs & Crime, 1 vol., 1. 2014. (Undercover Story Ser.). (ENG.). 48p. (J). (gr. 5-8). 30.25 *(978-1-4777-2799-7(X)*, Rosen Reference) Rosen Publishing Group, Inc., The.

Lindsay, Jabari. Gangs: Deal with It Before Wrong Seems Right, 1 vol. 2012. (Lorimer Deal with It Ser.). (ENG., Illus.). 32p. (YA). (gr. 4-6). 24.95 *(978-1-55277-920-0(3)*, 9781552779200) Lorimer, James & Co., Ltd., Pubs. CAN. Dist: Casemate Pubs. & Bk. Distributors, LLC.

MacKay, Jennifer, ed. Gangs. 2010. (Hot Topics Ser.). (ENG., Illus.). 128p. (gr. 7-10). 39.40 *(978-1-4205-0343-2(X))* Cengage Gale.

Marcovitz, Hal. Gangs, 1 vol. 2010. (Essential Issues Set 1 Ser.). (ENG.). 112p. (J). (gr. 6-12). lib. bdg. 35.64 *(978-1-60453-954-7(2)*, Essential Library) ABDO Publishing Co.

Parks, Peggy J. Gangs. 2010. (Compact Research Ser.). (YA). (gr. 7-12). lib. bdg. 26.95 *(978-1-60152-114-9(6))* ReferencePoint Pr., Inc.

Porterfield, Jason. Careers in Undercover Gang Investigation. 2013. (Extreme Law Enforcement Ser.). 112p. (YA). (gr. 7-12). 34.60 *(978-1-4777-1712-7(9))* Rosen Publishing Group, Inc., The.

Robbins-Turner, Darlene. Wake up & Recognize: Life of a Stepdaughter. Hendricks, Tracey, illus. Date not set. (YA). 16.95 *(978-1-889506-09-8(5))* Kendar Publishing, Inc.

Swift, Richard. Gangs, 1 vol. 2012. (Groundwork Guides). (ENG., Illus.). 144p. (gr. 8). pap. 10.00 *(978-0-88899-978-8(X))* Groundwood Bks. CAN. Dist: Publishers Group West (PGW).

Watkins, Christi, ed. How Can Gang Violence Be Prevented? 2006. (At Issue Ser.). (ENG., Illus.). 128p. (gr. 10-12). 39.40 *(978-0-7377-2380-9(7)*, Greenhaven Pr., Inc.) Cengage Gale.

Watkins, Christine. How Can Gang Violence Be Prevented? 2006. (At Issue Ser.). (ENG., Illus.). 97p. (J). (gr. 3-7). 24.45 *(978-0-7377-2381-6(5)*, Greenhaven Pr., Inc.) Cengage Gale.

Wolny, Philip. Defeating Gangs in Your Neighborhood & Online, 01 vols., 1. 2016. (Effective Survival Strategies Ser.). (ENG.). 64p. (J). 32.95 *(978-1-4994-6151-0(8)*, Rosen Young Adult) Rosen Publishing Group, Inc., The.

GANGS—FICTION

Allen, Justin. The American. 2008. (ENG.). 320p. (gr. 12). 21.95 *(978-1-59020-100-8(0))* Overlook Pr., The.

Anderson, Natalie C. City of Saints & Thieves. 2017. (ENG.). 432p. (YA). (gr. 7). 18.99 *(978-0-399-54758-4(4)*, G.P. Putnam's Sons Books for Young Readers) Penguin Young Readers Group.

Avi. City of Orphans. Ruth, Greg, illus. (ENG.). 368p. (J). (gr. 5-9). 2012. pap. 8.99 *(978-1-4169-7108-5(4)*, Atheneum Bks. for Young Readers) 2011. 17.99 *(978-1-4169-7102-3(5)*, Atheneum/Richard Jackson Bks.) Simon & Schuster Children's Publishing.

Benavidez, Max. Historia de Carlito/ Carlito's Story. 2008. 121p. pap. 8.95 *(978-1-60448-004-7(1))* Lectura Bks.

Benyo, Richard. The South Street Gang vs. the Coalcracker Cyclops. 2010. (ENG.). 151p. pap. 8.00 *(978-1-58966-208-7(3))* Univ. of Scranton Pr.

Big Bad Bully. 2006. (ENG.). 32p. (J). pap. 12.99 *(978-0-9758709-1-4(2))* Send The Light Distribution LLC.

Billingsley, ReShonda Tate. Friends 'Til the End. 2009. (Good Girlz Ser.: 6). (ENG., Illus.). 208p. pap. 11.00 *(978-1-4165-5877-4(2)*, Gallery Bks.) Gallery Bks.

Bock, Suzanne, illus. Meet the Angels l.t. ed. 2004. 10p. (J). bds. 12.99 *(978-0-9758709-4-5(7)*, 13401) Journey Stone Creations, LLC.

Bostick, B. k. Huber Hill & the Golden Staff of Cibola. 2013. (J). pap. 14.99 *(978-1-4621-1098-8(3)*, Horizon Pubs.) Cedar Fort, Inc./CFI Distribution.

Bowkett, Stephen. Passenger & Other Adventures. 2003. (ENG., Illus.). 162p. *(978-1-85539-162-8(7)*, Network Continuum Education) Bloomsbury Publishing Plc.

Bowler, Tim. Playing Dead. 2010. (Blade Ser.: 1). (ENG.). 256p. (YA). (gr. 9-18). 7.99 *(978-0-14-241600-6(2)*, Speak) Penguin Young Readers Group.

Brouwer, Sigmund. Hurricane Power, 1 vol. 2007. (Orca Sports Ser.). (ENG.). 176p. (YA). (gr. 6-10). per. 9.95 *(978-1-55143-865-8(8))* Orca Bk. Pubs. USA.

—Sewer Rats, 1 vol. 2006. (Orca Currents Ser.). (ENG.). 128p. (J). (gr. 5-9). per. 9.95 *(978-1-55143-488-9(1))* Orca Bk. Pubs. USA.

Butcher, Kristin. El Plan de Zee, 1 vol. 2008. (Spanish Soundings Ser.).Tr. of Zee's Way. (SPA.). 112p. (YA). (gr. 8-12). pap. 9.95 *(978-1-55469-057-2(9))* Orca Bk. Pubs. USA.

—Zee's Way. 2004. (Orca Soundings Ser.). 104p. (gr. 7-12). 19.95 *(978-0-7569-4360-8(4))* Perfection Learning Corp.

Butterworth, Nick. The Whisperer. Butterworth, Nick, illus. 2005. (ENG., Illus.). 32p. (J). (gr. k-3). pap. 15.95 *(978-0-00-712018-5(4)*, HarperCollins Children's Bks.) HarperCollins Pubs. Ltd. GBR. Dist: HarperCollins Pubs.

Buxton, Jamie. Temple Boys. 2015. (ENG.). 288p. (YA). (gr. 7). 17.99 *(978-1-62672-036-7(3))* Roaring Brook Pr.

Cannella, Marco & Marron, Jose Luis, illus. Tattoo of Death. 2007. (Choose Your Own Adventure Ser.: No. 22). 113p. (J). (gr. 4-7). pap. 6.99 *(978-1-933390-22-2(0))* Chooseco LLC.

Cohen, Marina. Mind Gap. 2011. (ENG.). 168p. (YA). (gr. 9-18). pap. 9.99 *(978-1-55488-801-6(8))* Dundurn CAN. Dist: Ingram Publisher Services.

Collard, Sneed B., III. Dog 4491. 2013. (Illus.). 256p. (J). 13.99 *(978-0-9844460-4-9(4))* Bucking Horse Bks.

Collard, Sneed B., 3rd. Dog 4491. 2013. (ENG., Illus.). 256p. (J). pap. 8.00 *(978-0-9844460-5-6(2))* Mountain Pr. Publishing Co., Inc.

Cooper, Susan. Dawn of Fear. Gill, Margery, illus. 2007. (ENG.). 176p. (J). (gr. 5-7). pap. 7.99 *(978-0-15-206106-7(1))* Houghton Mifflin Harcourt Publishing Co.

Crocker, Carter & Swift, Jonathan. The Last of the Gullivers. 2012. (ENG.). 224p. (J). (gr. 4-7). 16.99 *(978-0-399-24231-1(7)*, Philomel Bks.) Penguin Young Readers Group.

Dean, Myers Walter. Scorpions. 2014. (Trophy Bk Ser.). (ENG.). 240p. (J). (gr. 7-12). 13.24 *(978-1-63245-216-0(2))* Lectorum Pubns., Inc.

Delgado, Alvin. Spirit of the Gang. 2007. 192p. pap. 12.95 *(978-1-4303-1334-2(X))* Lulu Pr., Inc.

Doder, Joshua. Grk Smells a Rat. 2009. (J). *(978-0-385-90654-8(4)*, Delacorte Pr) Random House Publishing Group.

Elkeles, Simone. Chain Reaction. 2015. (Perfect Chemistry Novel Ser.). (ENG.). 336p. (YA). (gr. 9). pap. 9.99 *(978-1-61963-703-0(0)*, 9781619637030, Bloomsbury USA Childrens) Bloomsbury Publishing USA.

—Perfect Chemistry. 2015. (Perfect Chemistry Novel Ser.). (ENG.). 384p. (YA). (gr. 9). pap. 9.99 *(978-1-61963-701-6(4)*, 9781619637016, Bloomsbury USA Childrens) Bloomsbury Publishing USA.

Elster, Jean Alicia. I'll Do the Right Thing. Tadgell, Nicole, illus. 2010. (ENG.). 32p. (J). pap. 11.99 *(978-0-8170-1658-6(9))* Judson Pr.

Ewing, Lynne. The Lure. 2014. (ENG.). 288p. (YA). (gr. 9). 17.99 *(978-0-06-220688-6(5))* HarperCollins Pubs.

Fernández, Leandro, illus. The Punisher. 2006. (ENG.). 144p. (gr. 13-17). pap. 15.99 *(978-0-7851-1899-2(3))* Marvel Worldwide, Inc.

Fogelin, Adrian. Summer on the Moon, 1 vol. (ENG.). 256p. (J). 2014. (gr. 3-6). pap. 7.95 *(978-1-56145-785-4(X))* 2012. 15.95 *(978-1-56145-626-0(8))* Peachtree Pubs.

Gaines, Pat. O. O. Octopus: Sheriff of Blue Ribbon Sound. 2008. (Illus.). 24p. (J). lib. bdg. *(978-0-9801376-4-4(0))*; per. *(978-0-9801376-5-1(9))* Dragonfly Publishing, Inc.

Gates, J. Gabriel & Keel, Charlene. Ghost Crown. 2012. (Tracks Ser.). (ENG.). 456p. (YA). (gr. 6-12). pap. 9.95 *(978-0-7573-1594-7(1)*, HCI Teens) Health Communications, Inc.

Giles, Mike, illus. Halloween Is Fun! 2009. (Yo Gabba Gabba! Ser.). (ENG.). 16p. (J). (gr. -1-1). pap. 6.99 *(978-1-4169-7824-4(0)*, Simon Spotlight) Simon Spotlight.

Gottesfeld, Jeff. The Bank of Badness, 1 vol. 2013. (Robinson's Hood Ser.). (ENG.). (J). (gr. 5-8). pap. 8.95 *(978-1-62250-001-7(6))* Saddleback Educational Publishing, Inc.

—The Bank of Badness. 2013. (Robinson's Hood Ser.: 2). lib. bdg. 19.60 *(978-0-606-27019-9(1)*, Turtleback) Turtleback Bks.

—Chopped!, 1 vol. 2013. (Robinson's Hood Ser.). (ENG.). (gr. 5-8). pap. 8.95 *(978-1-62250-002-4(4))* Saddleback Educational Publishing, Inc.

—Robinson's Hood, 1 vol. 2013. (Robinson's Hood Ser.). (ENG.). 128p. (gr. 5-8). pap. 8.95 *(978-1-62250-000-0(8))* Saddleback Educational Publishing, Inc.

—Robinson's Hood. 2013. (Robinson's Hood Ser.: 1). lib. bdg. 19.60 *(978-0-606-27018-2(3)*, Turtleback) Turtleback Bks.

Grant, Sheryl. The Gumnut Gully Gang: Billy's Bright Idea. 2012. 32p. pap. 32.70 *(978-1-4771-5323-9(3))* Xlibris Corp.

Green, Jim. Shadows of the Moon... Dancing. 2007. (YA). pap. 14.95 *(978-1-59705-872-8(6))* Wings ePress, Inc.

Greg, Neri. Yummy: The Last Days of a Southside Shorty. 2014. (ENG.). 94p. (YA). (gr. k-3). 21.20 *(978-1-63245-250-4(2))* Lectorum Pubns., Inc.

Halliday, Keith. Aurore of the Yukon: A Girl's Adventure in the Klondike Gold Rush. 2006. 134p. (J). (gr. 1-1). pap. 11.95 *(978-0-595-39546-0(5))* iUniverse, Inc.

Harris, Loretta. Who Did It & Why? 2007. 26p. (YA). 1.99 *(978-0-9786681-2-1(1))* Triumphant Living Enterprises, Inc.

Henighan, Tom. Demon in My View. 2007. (ENG.). 176p. (J). (gr. 4). pap. 12.99 *(978-1-55002-656-6(9)*, Boardwalk Bks.) Dundurn CAN. Dist: Ingram Publisher Services.

Hinton, S. E. The Outsiders. 2006. (ENG.). 224p. (YA). (gr. 7-7). 10.00 *(978-0-14-240733-2(X)*, Speak) Penguin Young Readers Group.

—The Outsiders. 156p. (YA). (gr. 7-18). pap. 5.99 *(978-0-8072-1430-5(2)*, Listening Library) Random Hse. Audio Publishing Group.

—The Outsiders. 2006. (ENG.). 160p. (gr. 12-18). 15.00 *(978-0-14-303985-3(7)*, Penguin Classics) Penguin Publishing Group.

—The Outsiders. 50th anniv. ed. 2016. (ENG.). 224p. (YA). (gr. 7). 20.00 *(978-0-425-28829-0(3)*, Penguin Books) Penguin Young Readers Group.

—The Outsiders. l.t. ed. 2005. (ENG.). 253p. pap. 10.95 *(978-0-7862-7362-1(3)*, Large Print Pr.) Thorndike Pr.

—Rumble Fish. 2013. (ENG.). 144p. (YA). (gr. 7). pap. 7.99 *(978-0-385-37568-9(9)*, Delacorte Pr.) Random Hse. Children's Bks.

—Rumble Fish. 2006. 21.50 *(978-0-8446-7283-0(1))* Smith, Peter Pub., Inc.

Holm, Jennifer L. Full of Beans. 2016. (ENG.). 208p. (J). (gr. 3-7). 16.99 *(978-0-553-51036-2(3))*; lib. bdg. 19.99 *(978-0-553-51037-9(1))* Random Hse. Children's Bks. (Random Hse. Bks. for Young Readers).

Hutton, Sam. Kiss & Kill. 2004. (Special Agents Ser.: 4). (ENG.). 240p. (J). (gr. 4-7). pap. 9.99 *(978-0-00-714845-5(3))* HarperCollins Pubs. Ltd. GBR. Dist: HarperCollins Pubs.

Inagaki, Riichiro. Eyeshield 21, Vol. 12. Murata, Yusuke, illus. 2007. (ENG.). 208p. pap. 9.99 *(978-1-4215-1061-3(8))* Viz Media.

—Eyeshield 21, Vol. 13. Murata, Yusuke, illus. 2007. (ENG.). 216p. pap. 7.99 *(978-1-4215-1062-0(6))* Viz Media.

Jones, Patrick. Target. 2014. (Alternative Ser.). (ENG.). 128p. (YA). (gr. 6-12). pap. 7.95 *(978-1-4677-4485-0(9)*, Darby Creek) Lerner Publishing Group.

Jones, Patrick & Clark, Marshunna. Duty or Desire. 2016. (Unbarred Ser.). (ENG.). 112p. (YA). (gr. 6-12). 42.65 *(978-1-5124-0090-8(4)*, Darby Creek) Lerner Publishing Group.

Key, Watt. Dirt Road Home. 2011. (Alabama Moon Ser.: 2). (ENG.). 240p. (J). (gr. 5-9). pap. 8.99 *(978-0-312-67435-9(X)*, 9780312674359) Square Fish.

Kilpatrick, Irene. Meet the Gabba Gang. 2009. (Yo Gabba Gabba! Ser.: 1). (ENG.). 24p. (J). (gr. -1-2). pap. 3.99 *(978-1-4169-7097-2(5)*, Simon Spotlight) Simon Spotlight.

Kline, Trish. The Fang Gang: KA Reader 4. 2007. (Illus.). 32p. (J). per. 20.00 *(978-0-9717234-6-7(X))* Ghost Hunter Productions.

Kroll, Steven. Sweet America: An Immigrant's Story. 2004. 172p. (J). lib. bdg. 16.92 *(978-1-4242-0773-2(8))* Fitzgerald Bks.

Kropp, Alex. Turf Wars. 2007. (HIP Edge Ser.). (Illus.). 112p. (YA). (gr. 7-18). pap. *(978-1-897039-29-8(8))* High Interest Publishing (HIP).

Lake, Nick. In Darkness. (ENG.). (YA). (gr. 9). 2014. 368p. pap. 10.99 *(978-1-61963-122-9(9)*, 9781619631229) 2012. 352p. 17.99 *(978-1-59990-743-7(7)*, 9781599907437) Bloomsbury Publishing USA. (Bloomsbury USA Childrens).

Lariviere, Sarah. The Bad Kid. 2016. (ENG., Illus.). 304p. (J). (gr. 3-7). 16.99 *(978-1-4814-3581-9(7)*, Simon & Schuster Bks. For Young Readers) Simon & Schuster Bks. For Young Readers.

The Lazy Genie. 2008. (Lazy Town Ser.). (Illus.). 40p. pap. *(978-1-4052-3760-4(0))* Egmont Bks., Ltd.

Leonard, Niall. Shredder. 2015. (ENG.). 384p. (YA). (gr. 9). 17.99 *(978-0-385-74365-5(3)*, Delacorte Pr.) Random Hse. Children's Bks.

Macgoye, Marjorie Oludhe. The Black Hand Gang. 2003. (Illus.). 64p. (gr. 4-7). pap. *(978-9966-46-016-5(0))* Heinemann Kenya, Limited (East African Educational Publishers Ltd E.A.E.P.) KEN. Dist: Michigan State Univ. Pr.

MacPhail, Catherine. Hide & Seek. 2012. (Stoke Books Titles Ser.). 72p. (J). (gr. 5-8). pap. 45.32 *(978-0-7613-9219-4(X))*; pap. 7.95 *(978-1-78112-024-8(2))*; lib. bdg. 22.60 *(978-1-78112-023-1(4))* Stoke Bks.

Malton, Mel. The Drowned Violin. 2006. (Alan Nearing Mystery Ser.: 1). (ENG.). 168p. (J). (gr. 3-7). pap. 8.95 *(978-1-894917-23-0(5)*, Napoleon & Co.) Dundurn CAN. Dist: Ingram Publisher Services.

Marks, Burton. Tanya Tinker & the Gizmo Gang. Smath, Jerry, illus. 2003. 20p. (J). (gr. -1-3). reprint ed. 22.00 *(978-0-7567-6760-0(1))* DIANE Publishing Co.

Marquardt, Marie. The Radius of Us. 2017. (ENG., Illus.). 304p. (YA). 18.99 *(978-1-250-09689-0(8)*, 9781250096890, St. Martin's Griffin) St. Martin's Pr.

McClintock, Norah. Truth & Lies. 2014. (Mike & Riel Mysteries Ser.: 2). (ENG.). 216p. (YA). (gr. 6-12). pap. 8.95 *(978-1-4677-2613-9(3)*, Darby Creek) Lerner Publishing Group.

McGowan, Anthony. The Knife That Killed Me. 2011. (ENG.). 224p. (YA). (gr. 9). pap. 8.99 *(978-0-375-85516-0(5)*, Ember) Random Hse. Children's Bks.

Miles, Lisa & Chown, Xanna Eve. The Backyardigans Gang: Follow the Reader Level 1. 2008. (Backyardigans Ser.). (ENG.). 24p. (J). 24.99 *(978-1-4169-5844-4(4)*, Simon Scribbles) Simon Scribbles.

Moore, Wes & Goodman, Shawn. This Way Home. 2015. (ENG.). 256p. (YA). (gr. 9). 20.99 *(978-0-375-99019-9(4)*, Delacorte Pr.) Random Hse. Children's Bks.

Moriarty, Chris. The Inquisitor's Apprentice. Geyer, Mark Edward, illus. (ENG.). 352p. (J). (gr. 5-7). 2013. pap. 7.99 *(978-0-547-85084-9(0))* 2011. 16.99 *(978-0-547-58135-4(1))* Houghton Mifflin Harcourt Publishing Co.

Mowry, Jess. Voodu Dawgz. 2007. 253p. pap. 14.99 *(978-1-59092-359-7(6))* Blue Forge Pr.

Muchamore, Robert. Brigands M. C. 2016. (Cherub Ser.: 11). (ENG., Illus.). 416p. (YA). (gr. 9). 17.99 *(978-1-4814-5671-5(7)*, Simon Pulse) Simon Pulse.

Murphy, Barbara Beasley & Wolkoff, Judie. Ace Hits Rock Bottom. 2003. (Can't Stop Ace Ser.: No. 2). 204p. (J). pap. 16.95 *(978-0-86534-408-2(6))* Sunstone Pr.

—Ace Hits the Big Time. 2003. (Can't Stop Ace Ser.: No. 1). 184p. (J). pap. 16.95 *(978-0-86534-407-5(8))* Sunstone Pr.

Murray, Guillermo. Te Dije Que No Miraras. rev. ed. 2005. (Ediciones Castillo Castillo Del Terror Ser.). (SPA & ENG.). 100p. (J). (gr. -1-7). pap. 6.95 *(978-970-20-0308-3(3))* Castillo, Ediciones, S. A. de C. V. MEX. Dist: Macmillan.

Myers, Walter Dean. Autobiography of My Dead Brother. Myers, Christopher, illus. 2006. (ENG.). 224p. (YA). (gr. 9). pap. 9.99 *(978-0-06-058293-7(6)*, Amistad) HarperCollins Pubs.

—Autobiography of My Dead Brother. 2006. 20.00 *(978-0-7569-6388-0(5))* Perfection Learning Corp.

—Los Escorpiones.Tr. of Scorpions. (SPA.). (YA). (gr. 5-8). pap. *(978-958-04-4381-0(5)*, NR8278); 258p. (gr. 7-9). 9.95 *(978-958-04-1505-3(6)*, 10266247) Norma S.A. COL. Dist: Lectorum Pubns., Inc., Distribuidora Norma, Inc.

—Scorpions. 2013. (Trophy Bk.). (ENG.). 240p. (YA). (gr. 8-18). pap. 8.99 *(978-0-06-447066-7(0))*; 25th anniv. ed. pap. 9.99 *(978-0-06-440623-9(7))* HarperCollins Pubs. (Amistad).

—Scorpions. 2013. 216p. (YA). (gr. 7-12). lib. bdg. 19.65 *(978-0-8335-4233-5(8)*, Turtleback) Turtleback Bks.

Neri, G. Knockout Games. 2014. (ENG.). 304p. (YA). (gr. 8-12). 17.95 *(978-1-4677-3269-7(9)*, Carolrhoda Lab™) Lerner Publishing Group.

Nutrition Adventures with the Nutri Gang, Race Day, Issue #1: The Nutri Gang. 2007. (J). 2.99 *(978-0-9792383-0-7(7))* KJ Pubns.

O'Donnell, Liam. Ramp Rats: A Graphic Guide Adventure, 1 vol. Deas, Mike, illus. 2008. (Graphic Guides). (ENG.). 64p. (J). (gr. 3-7). pap. 9.95 *(978-1-55143-880-1(1))* Orca Bk. Pubs. USA.

Omaya, Tam. Passion & Pain. 2010. 216p. pap. 14.49 *(978-1-4520-1444-9(2))* AuthorHouse.

Parker, Ron. Teen Wars. 2010. 170p. pap. 9.42 *(978-1-4452-5000-7(4))* Lulu Pr., Inc.

Pérez, Ashley Hope. The Knife & the Butterfly. 2012. (Carolrhoda YA Ser.). (ENG.). 216p. (YA). (gr. 9-12). 17.95 *(978-0-7613-6156-5(1)*, Carolrhoda Lab™) Lerner Publishing Group.

Publications International Ltd. Staff, ed. Toy Story 3: New Friends. 2010. 12p. (J). bds. 10.98 *(978-1-4127-4584-0(5)*, PIL Kids) Publications International, Ltd.

Pullman, Philip. Two Crafty Criminals! And How They Were Captured by the Daring Detectives of the New Cut Gang. (ENG.). 288p. (J). (gr. 3-7). 2013. 7.99 *(978-0-307-93035-4(1)*, Yearling) 2012. (Illus.). 16.99

E
F
G

(978-0-375-87029-3(6), Knopf Bks. for Young Readers) Random Hse. Children's Bks.

Pyron, Bobbie. The Dogs of Winter. 2014. (ENG.). 320p. (J). (gr. 5-9). pap. 7.99 *(978-0-545-39931-9(9),* Levine, Arthur A. Bks.) Scholastic, Inc.

Robert, Na'ima B. Black Sheep. 2014. (ENG., Illus.). 272p. (J). (gr. 8-11). pap. 8.99 *(978-1-84780-235-4(4),* Frances Lincoln) Quarto Publishing Group UK GBR. Dist: Hachette Bk. Group.

Rodda, Emily. Dead End. 2006. (Raven Hill Mysteries Ser.: 6). (ENG., Illus.). 128p. (J). (gr. 3-7). pap. 4.99 *(978-0-439-79572-2(9),* Scholastic Paperbacks) Scholastic, Inc.

Sandoval, Victor. Roll over, Big Toben. 2003. 128p. (J). pap. 9.95 *(978-1-55885-401-7(0),* Piñata Books) Arte Publico Pr.

Schraff, Anne. Shadows of Guilt. 2010. (Urban Underground — Harriet Tubman High School Ser.). (YA). lib. bdg. 20.80 *(978-0-606-14272-4(X),* Turtleback) Turtleback Bks.

Schuh, Eileen. The Traz. 2012. 148p. pap. *(978-1-926997-61-2(1))* Imajin Bks.

Scrimger, Richard. Ink Me, 1 vol. 2012. (Seven (the Series) Ser.). (ENG., Illus.). 224p. (J). (gr. 5-10). pap. 9.95 *(978-1-4598-0016-8(8))* Orca Bk. Pubs. USA.

Sedgwick, Julian. The Black Dragon. Moffett, Patricia, illus. 2016. (Mysterium Ser.: 1). (ENG.). 352p. (gr. 4-8). 18.99 *(978-1-4677-7567-0(3));* 38.65 *(978-1-4677-9555-5(0))* Lerner Publishing Group. (Carolrhoda Bks.).

Shusterman, Neal. Red Rider's Hood. 2006. (Dark Fusion Ser.: 3). (ENG.). 192p. (YA). (gr. 7-18). 6.99 *(978-0-14-240678-6(3),* Speak) Penguin Young Readers Group.

Sommer, Carl. Dare to Dream! Martinez, Jorge et al, illus. 2007. (Another Sommer-Time Story Ser.). (ENG.). 48p. (J). (gr. -1-3). 16.95 incl. audio compact disk *(978-1-57537-523-6(0))* Advance Publishing, Inc.

Spencer, James. Sally Small & the Judith-Situation. 2011. 86p. pap. *(978-1-908147-61-5(X))* YouWriteOn.

Strasser, Todd. If I Grow Up. 2009. (ENG.). 240p. (YA). (gr. 7-18). 17.99 *(978-1-4169-2523-1(6),* Simon & Schuster Bks. For Young Readers) Simon & Schuster Bks. For Young Readers.

Sutcliffe, William. Concentr8. 2016. (ENG.). 256p. (YA). 17.99 *(978-1-61963-919-5(X),* 9781619639195, Bloomsbury USA Childrens) Bloomsbury Publishing USA.

Sutton, Laurie S. The Case of the Clown Carnival. Neely, Scott, illus. 2017. (You Choose Stories: Scooby-Doo Ser.). (ENG.). 112p. (gr. 2-3). lib. bdg. 32.65 *(978-1-4965-4333-2(5),* You Choose Bks.) Capstone Press of Coughlan Cos.

Tagged. 2015. (ENG.). 288p. (YA). (gr. 7). lib. bdg. 16.95 *(978-1-58089-583-5(2))* Charlesbridge Publishing, Inc.

Thomas, Lex. The Loners. (Quarantine Ser.: No. 1). (ENG.). 416p. (gr. 9). 2013. (J). pap. 9.99 *(978-1-60684-438-0(5))* 2012. 17.99 *(978-1-60684-329-1(X))* Lerner Publishing Group. (Carolrhoda Lab™).

—Quarantine: The Saints Book 2. 2014. (Quarantine Ser.: No. 2). (ENG.). 400p. (J). (gr. 9). pap. 9.99 *(978-1-60684-540-0(3))* Lerner Publishing Group.

Tullson, Diane. Foolproof, 1 vol. 2015. (Orca Soundings Ser.). (ENG.). 120p. (YA). (gr. 8-12). pap. 9.95 *(978-1-4598-1034-1(1))* Orca Bk. Pubs. USA.

van Diepen, Allison. Light of Day. 2015. (ENG.). 320p. (YA). (gr. 9). 17.99 *(978-0-06-230347-9(3))* HarperCollins Pubs.

—Snitch. 2013. (ENG., Illus.). 320p. (YA). (gr. 9). pap. 11.99 *(978-1-4424-8165-7(X),* Simon Pulse) Simon Pulse.

Van Draanen, Wendelin. Sammy Keyes & the Search for Snake Eyes. 2008. (Sammy Keyes Ser.: Bk. 7). (J). 64.99 *(978-1-60640-645-8(0))* Findaway World, LLC.

—Sammy Keyes & the Search for Snake Eyes. Van Draanen, Wendelin, illus. 2003. (Sammy Keyes Ser.: Bk. 7). (Illus.). pap. 36.95 incl. audio *(978-1-59112-273-9(2));* pap. 54.95 incl. audio compact disk *(978-1-59112-281-4(3))* Live Oak Media.

—Sammy Keyes & the Search for Snake Eyes. 2003. (Sammy Keyes Ser.: Bk. 7). (Illus.). 277p. (gr. 5-9). 17.00 *(978-0-7569-1445-5(0))* Perfection Learning Corp.

—Sammy Keyes & the Search for Snake Eyes. 2003. (Sammy Keyes Ser.: 7). (ENG.). 320p. (J). (gr. 5-7). 7.99 *(978-0-440-41900-6(X),* Yearling) Random Hse. Children's Bks.

Weber, Richard D. Elvis & Me. 2004. 511p. (YA). per. 17.41 *(978-1-4116-0549-7(7))* Lulu Pr., Inc.

Wicke, Ed. Mattie & the Highwaymen. 2012. 216p. (J). per. 9.99 *(978-0-9677652-1-1(8),* BlacknBlue Pr. UK) Blacknblue Pr.

Wiggins, Thalia. Greg's Game Dilemma, 1 vol. Tate, Don, illus. 2012. (Making Choices: the Mcnair Cousins Ser.). (ENG.). 64p. 27.07 *(978-1-61641-632-4(7),* Calico Chapter Bks) Magic Wagon.

—James Makes a Choice, 1 vol. Tate, Don, illus. 2012. (Making Choices: the Mcnair Cousins Ser.). (ENG.). 64p. 27.07 *(978-1-61641-634-8(3),* Calico Chapter Bks) Magic Wagon.

Wright, Richard. Rite of Passage. 2014. (Trophy Bk Ser.). (ENG.). 160p. (J). (gr. 8-12). 13.24 *(978-1-63245-325-9(8))* Lectorum Pubns., Inc.

Young, Diane. See No Evil, 1 vol. 2006. (Orca Currents Ser.). (ENG.). 128p. (J). (gr. 5-9). per. 9.95 *(978-1-55143-619-7(1))* Orca Bk. Pubs. USA.

Zephaniah, Benjamin. Gangsta Rap. 2004. (ENG.). 336p. (YA). (gr. 9-13). pap. 8.99 *(978-1-58234-886-5(3),* 9781582348865, Bloomsbury USA Childrens) Bloomsbury Publishing USA.

GANNETS—FICTION

Pryse-Phillips, William. Free Flight. 2013. 24p. pap. *(978-1-4602-0671-3(1))* FriesenPress.

GANNETT, DEBORAH SAMPSON, 1760-1827

McDonnell, Peter. A Soldier in Disguise. Tormey, Carlotta, illus. 2005. 16p. (J). pap. *(978-0-7367-2909-3(7))* Zaner-Bloser, Inc.

GARAGES

Carlson Berne, Emma. Run Your Own Yard Sale, 1 vol., 1. 2014. (Young Entrepreneurs Ser.). (ENG.). 32p. (J). (gr. 4-6). 26.25 *(978-1-4777-2919-9(4),* PowerKids Pr.) Rosen Publishing Group, Inc., The.

Wildot Press. David's Garage. 2008. (Illus.). 50p. (J). spiral bd. 14.95 *(978-0-9797933-1-8(9))* Wildot Pr.

GARAGES—FICTION

Crow, Melinda Melton. Let's Paint the Garage!, 1 vol. Thompson, Chad, illus. 2012. (Wonder Wheels Ser.). (ENG.). 32p. (gr. -1-1). pap. 6.25 *(978-1-4342-4238-9(2));* lib. bdg. 22.65 *(978-1-4342-4016-3(9))* Stone Arch Bks.

Fosse, Mika. Garage People. 2008. 84p. pap. 9.95 *(978-1-60693-500-2(3),* Eloquent Bks.) Strategic Book Publishing & Rights Agency (SBPRA).

Helmer, Marilyn. The Great Garage Sale, 1 vol. Deas, Mike, illus. 2013. (Orca Echoes Ser.). (ENG.). 64p. (J). (gr. 2-3). pap. 6.95 *(978-1-4598-0060-1(5))* Orca Bk. Pubs. USA.

Holcomb, Carrie E., ed. Monster Nation JR. 2007. (Illus.). 32p. (J). per. 6.99 *(978-0-696-23688-4(5))* Meredith Bks.

Naylor, Phyllis Reynolds. Boys in Control. 2005. (Boys Against Girls Ser.: No. 9). 143p. (J). (gr. 4-7). 13.65 *(978-0-7569-5094-1(5))* Perfection Learning Corp.

Shealy, Dennis R. The Noisy Garage. 2016. (Little Golden Book Ser.). (ENG., Illus.). 24p. (J). (-k). 4.99 *(978-1-101-93439-5(5),* Golden Bks.) Random Hse. Children's Bks.

Sterling Publishing Co., Inc. Staff. Garage. Finn, Rebecca, illus. 2015. (Busy Bks.). (ENG.). 10p. (J). (— 1). bds. 8.95 *(978-1-4549-1734-2(2))* Sterling Publishing Co., Inc.

GARBAGE

see Refuse and Refuse Disposal

GARDEN DESIGN

see Landscape Gardening

GARDEN PESTS

see Insect Pests

GARDENING

Here are entered works on the practical operations in the cultivation of fruits, vegetables, flowers and ornamental plants.

see also Flower Gardening; Fruit Culture; Gardens; Insect Pests; Landscape Gardening; Organic Gardening; Plant Propagation; Plants; Vegetable Gardening; Weeds

Abdo Publishing. A Green Kid's Guide to Gardening!, 1 vol. 2013. (Green Kid's Guide to Gardening! Ser.: 6). (ENG.). 24p. (J). (gr. -1-4). lib. bdg. 162.42 *(978-1-61641-942-4(3),* Looking Glass Library) Magic Wagon.

Aldrich, William & Williamson, Don. Gardening Month by Month in Illinois, 1 vol., Vol. 1. rev. ed. 2004. (ENG., Illus.). 160p. (gr. 4). pap. 15.95 *(978-1-55105-375-2(6),* 1551053756) Lone Pine Publishing USA.

—Tree & Shrub Gardening for Illinois, 1 vol., Vol. 1. rev. ed. 2004. (ENG., Illus.). 352p. (gr. 4). pap. 18.95 *(978-1-55105-404-9(3),* 1551054043) Lone Pine Publishing USA.

Amstutz, Lisa J. Creative Gardening: Growing Plants Upside down, in Water, & More. 2016. (Gardening Guides). (ENG., Illus.). 32p. (gr. 3-4). lib. bdg. 27.99 *(978-1-4914-8237-7(0),* Snap Bks.) Capstone Press of Coughlan Cos.

—Enchanted Gardening: Growing Miniature Gardens, Fairy Gardens, & More. 2016. (Gardening Guides). (ENG., Illus.). 32p. (gr. 3-4). lib. bdg. 27.99 *(978-1-4914-8234-6(6),* Snap Bks.) Capstone Press of Coughlan Cos.

—Gardening Guides. 2016. (Gardening Guides). (ENG.). 32p. (gr. 3-4). 111.96 *(978-1-4914-8698-6(8),* Snap Bks.) Capstone Press of Coughlan Cos.

—Indoor Gardening: Growing Air Plants, Terrariums, & More. 2016. (Gardening Guides). (ENG., Illus.). 32p. (gr. 3-4). lib. bdg. 27.99 *(978-1-4914-8236-0(2),* Snap Bks.) Capstone Press of Coughlan Cos.

—The Ultimate Guide to Gardening: Grow Your Own Indoor, Vegetable, Fairy, & Other Great Gardens. 2016. (Craft It Yourself Ser.). (ENG., Illus.). 112p. (gr. 3-4). pap. 12.95 *(978-1-62370-649-4(1))* Capstone Young Readers of Coughlan Cos.

Ancona, George. It's Our Garden: From Seeds to Harvest in a School Garden. Ancona, George, illus. 2015. (ENG., Illus.). 48p. (J). (gr. k-3). pap. 6.99 *(978-0-7636-7691-9(8))* Candlewick Pr.

—Nuestro Huerto: De la Semilla a la Cosecha en el Huerto Del Colegio. Ancona, George, illus. 2016. (ENG & SPA., Illus.). 48p. (J). (gr. k-3). 6.99 *(978-0-7636-8771-7(5))* Candlewick Pr.

Ashman, Sarah & Parent, Nancy. Holly Bloom's Garden. Mitchell, Lori, illus. 2008. (ENG.). 32p. (J). (gr. k-3). pap. 7.95 *(978-0-9799746-0-1(7))* Flashlight Pr.

Azarian, Mary. A Gardener's Alphabet. 2005. (ENG., Illus.). 32p. (J). (gr. -1-3). reprint ed. 7.99 *(978-0-618-54881-1(5))* Houghton Mifflin Harcourt Publishing Co.

Bearce, Stephanie. A Kid's Guide to Container Gardening. 2009. (Gardening for Kids Ser.). (Illus.). 48p. (J). (gr. 3-6). lib. bdg. 29.95 *(978-1-58415-814-1(X))* Mitchell Lane Pubs., Inc.

Beck, Alison & Kelbaugh, Duncan. Gardening Month by Month in the Maritimes, 1 vol., Vol. 1. rev. ed. 2004. (ENG., Illus.). 160p. (gr. 4). pap. 18.95 *(978-1-55105-408-7(6),* 1551054086) Lone Pine Publishing USA.

Beck, Alison & Knapke, Debra. Gardening Month by Month in Ohio, 1 vol., Vol. 1. rev. ed. 2004. (ENG., Illus.). 160p. (gr. 4). pap. 15.95 *(978-1-55105-406-3(X),* 155105406X) Lone Pine Publishing USA.

Beck, Alison & Wood, Tim. Gardening Month by Month in Michigan, 1 vol., Vol. 1. rev. ed. 2004. (ENG., Illus.). 160p. (gr. 4). pap. 15.95 *(978-1-55105-363-9(2),* 1551053632) Lone Pine Publishing USA.

Beck, Alison, et al. Gardening Month by Month in Washington & Oregon, 1 vol., Vol. 1. rev. ed. 2003. (ENG., Illus.). 160p. (gr. 4). pap. 16.95 *(978-1-55105-359-2(4),* 1551053594) Lone Pine Publishing USA.

Benjamin, Tina. Let's Dig in the Garden. 2015. (Let's Go Outdoors! Ser.). (ENG.). 24p. (J). (gr. k-k). pap. 8.15 *(978-1-4824-2613-7(7))* Stevens, Gareth Publishing LLLP.

Betanzos, Sue, illus. My New Backyard Garden. 2006.Tr. of Mi Nuevo Jardín del Traspatio. (SPA & ENG.). (J). *(978-0-9792253-0-7(2))* Tucson Botanical Gardens.

Blackaby, Susan. Growing Things, 6 vols. DeLage, Charlene, illus. Incl. Green & Growing: A Book about Plants. 26.65 *(978-1-4048-0107-3(3));* Plant Plumbing: A Book about Roots & Stems. 26.65 *(978-1-4048-0109-7(X));* (gr. -1-2). (Growing Things Ser.). (ENG., Illus.). 24p. 2003. 77.97 *(978-1-4048-0106-6(5))* Picture Window Bks.

Buczacki, Stefan & Buczacki, Beverly. Young Gardener. Sieveking, Anthea, photos by. 2006. (ENG., Illus.). 120p. (J). (gr. 2-5). 19.95 *(978-1-84507-295-7(2),* Frances Lincoln) Quarto Publishing Group UK GBR. Dist: Hachette Bk. Group.

Burns, Monique. Cool Careers Without College for People Who Love to Make Things Grow. 2009. (Cool Careers Without College Ser.). 144p. (gr. 6-6). 66.50 *(978-1-61511-975-2(2))* Rosen Publishing Group, Inc., The.

Bussell, Linda. Using Division Facts in the Garden. 2008. (Math in Our World - Level 3 Ser.). (Illus.). 24p. (J). (gr. 2-5). pap. 8.15 *(978-0-8368-9385-4(9));* lib. bdg. 22.00 *(978-0-8368-9286-4(0))* Stevens, Gareth Publishing LLLP. (Weekly Reader Leveled Readers).

—Vamos a Usar Datos de División en el Jardín. 2008. (Matemáticas en Nuestro Mundo - Nivel 3 (Math in Our World - Level 3) Ser.). (SPA.). 24p. (gr. 2-5). (J). lib. bdg. 22.00 *(978-0-8368-9294-9(1));* pap. 8.15 *(978-0-8368-9393-9(X))* Stevens, Gareth Publishing LLLP. (Weekly Reader Leveled Readers).

Chronicle Books Staff. Sprout Your Own Leafy Wonders. 2009. (ENG.). 32p. (J). (gr. -1-7). 18.99 *(978-0-8118-6107-6(4))* Chronicle Bks. LLC.

CICO Kidz Staff, compiled by. My First Gardening Book: 35 Easy & Fun Projects for Budding Gardeners: Planting, Growing, Maintaining, Gardencrafts. 2016. (ENG., Illus.). 112p. (J). (gr. 7-11). pap. 14.95 *(978-1-78249-333-4(6),* 1782493336, CICO Books) Ryland Peters & Small GBR. Dist: WIPRO.

Clay, Kathryn. Planting Seeds. 2016. (Celebrate Spring Ser.). (ENG., Illus.). 24p. (gr. k-1). lib. bdg. 21.99 *(978-1-4914-8305-3(9),* Pebble Bks.) Capstone Press of Coughlan Cos.

Colby, Jennifer. Growing New Plants. 2014. (21st Century Junior Library: Plants Ser.). (ENG., Illus.). 24p. (J). (gr. 2-5). 25.64 *(978-1-63188-036-0(5),* 205551) Cherry Lake Publishing.

Collier, Elise. I Help in the Garden. 2017. (Ways I Help Ser.). 24p. (gr. 4-6). 23.60 ***(978-1-5081-5738-0(3),*** PowerKids Pr.) Rosen Publishing Group, Inc., The.

Collins, Chris & Lia, Leendertz. Grow Your Own: For Kids! 2012. (ENG., Illus.). 112p. (gr. -1-17). 14.99 *(978-1-84533-606-6(2),* Mitchell Beazley) Octopus Publishing Group GBR. Dist: Hachette Bk. Group.

Comer, Arthur L., Jr. The Beginner's Guide to Successfully Growing Tillandsias - Commonly known as Air Plants. 2003. (Illus.). 10p. (YA). 3.95 *(978-0-9752760-0-6(X))* ALCJR Enterprises.

Cornell, Kari A. The Nitty-Gritty Gardening Book: Fun Projects for All Seasons. Larson, Jennifer S., photos by. 2015. (ENG., Illus.). 48p. (J). (gr. 4-8). lib. bdg. 26.65 *(978-1-4677-2647-4(8),* Millbrook Pr.) Lerner Publishing Group.

Cosneau, Olivia. In the Vegetable Garden: My Nature Sticker Activity Book. 2017. (ENG.). 24p. (J). (gr. k-3). pap. 7.99 *(978-1-61689-571-6(3))* Princeton Architectural Pr.

Cox, Martyn & Woram, Catherine. Gardening with Kids. Wreford, Polly, photos by. 2008. (ENG., Illus.). 128p. *(978-1-84597-590-6(1),* CICO Books) Ryland Peters & Small.

Davis, Tina. Sow & Grow: A Gardening Book for Children. 2008. (ENG., Illus.). 144p. (gr. 8-17). 21.95 *(978-1-58479-673-2(1))* Stewart, Tabori & Chang.

Dickinson, Becky. The Gardening Year. 2015. (Collins Big Cat Ser.). (ENG.). 24p. (J). (gr. 2-2). pap. 6.95 *(978-0-00-759107-7(1))* HarperCollins Pubs. Ltd. GBR. Dist: Independent Pubs. Group.

Duncan, Frances. When Mother Lets Us Garden: A Book for Little Folk Who Want to Make Gardens. 2009. (Gardening in America Ser.). (ENG., Illus.). 128p. (J). (gr. 4-7). pap. 10.95 *(978-1-4290-1479-3(2))* Applewood Bks.

Dunn-Georgiou, Elisha. Everything You Need to Know about Organic Foods. 2009. (Need to Know Library). 64p. (gr. 5-5). 58.50 *(978-1-60854-079-2(0))* Rosen Publishing Group, Inc., The.

Dybvik, Tina. Sadie's Seed Adventures: Learning about Seeds, 1 vol. Record, Adam, illus. 2013. (Take It Outside Ser.). (ENG.). 24p. (gr. k-2). 27.32 *(978-1-4048-8316-1(9));* pap. 8.95 *(978-1-4795-1937-8(5))* Picture Window Bks.

Dyer, Hadley. Potatoes on Rooftops: Farming in the City. 2012. (ENG., Illus.). 84p. (J). (gr. 4-7). 2nd ed. pap. 14.95 *(978-1-55451-424-3(X),* 9781554514243) 3rd ed. 24.95 *(978-1-55451-425-0(8),* 9781554514250) Annick Pr., Ltd. CAN. Dist: Publishers Group West (PGW).

Ely, Lisa & Glassman, Michael. Kinder Gardens: Growing Inspiration for Children, 1 vol. 2010. (ENG., Illus.). 64p. (J). pap. 12.99 *(978-0-7643-3453-5(0),* 9780764334535) Schiffer Publishing, Ltd.

Engel, Christiane. Little Green Helpers Grow! 2011. (Little Green Helpers Ser.). (ENG., Illus.). 10p. (J). (gr. -1-k). bds. 7.99 *(978-0-230-74356-4(0))* Pan Macmillan GBR. Dist: Independent Pubs. Group.

Engel, Cynthia. Granny's Garden. 2010. 16p. pap. 8.49 *(978-1-4490-7549-1(5))* AuthorHouse.

Floyd, Amy. A Little Perspective: Gardening with Grandma & Grandpa. 2012. 20p. pap. 12.95 *(978-1-4497-2447-4(7),* WestBow Pr.) Author Solutions, Inc.

Fortuna, Lois. Growing Plants. 2016. (We Can Do It! Ser.). (ENG., Illus.). 24p. (J). (gr. k-k). pap. 8.15 *(978-1-4824-3803-1(8))* Stevens, Gareth Publishing LLLP.

Forward, Megan. A Patch from Scratch. 2016. (ENG.). 32p. (J). (gr. -1-k). 23.99 ***(978-0-670-07829-5(8))*** Random Hse. Australia AUS. Dist: Independent Pubs. Group.

Fretland VanVoorst, Jenny. Gardens in Spring. 2015. (Illus.). 24p. (J). lib. bdg. *(978-1-62031-236-0(0))* Jump! Inc.

—Los Jardines en la Primavera. 2015.Tr. of Gardens in Spring. (SPA., Illus.). 24p. (J). lib. bdg. *(978-1-62031-242-1(5),* Bullfrog Bks.) Jump! Inc.

Garden Squad! 2015. (Garden Squad! Ser.). (ENG.). 24p. (J). (gr. 3-4). pap., pap., pap. 297.00 *(978-1-4994-1294-9(0),* PowerKids Pr.) Rosen Publishing Group, Inc., The.

Gardening for Kids, 6 vols., Set. Incl. Backyard Flower Garden for Kids. Leavitt, Amie Jane. (Illus.). lib. bdg. 29.95 *(978-1-58415-633-8(3));* Backyard Vegetable Garden for Kids. Leavitt, Amie. lib. bdg. 29.95 *(978-1-58415-634-5(1));* Design Your Own Butterfly Garden. Harkins, Susan Sales & Harkins, William H. (Illus.). lib. bdg. 29.95 *(978-1-58415-638-3(4));* Design Your Own Pond & Water Garden. Harkins, Susan Sales & Harkins, William H. (Illus.). lib. bdg. 29.95 *(978-1-58415-635-2(X));* Kid's Guide to Landscape Design. Kjelle, Marylou Morano. (Illus.). lib. bdg. 29.95 *(978-1-58415-637-6(6));* Kid's Guide to Perennial Gardens. Orr, Tamra. (Illus.). lib. bdg. 29.95 *(978-1-58415-636-9(8));* (YA). (gr. 1-4). (Illus.). 48p. 2008. Set lib. bdg. 179.70 *(978-1-58415-639-0(2))* Mitchell Lane Pubs., Inc.

Gerardi, Jan. The Little Gardener. 2012. (Teenie Greenies Ser.). (ENG., Illus.). 16p. (J). (gr. k — 1). bds. 6.99 *(978-0-307-93041-5(6),* Random Hse. Bks. for Young Readers) Random Hse. Children's Bks.

Gibson, R. What Shall I Grow? 2004. (What Shall I Do Today? Ser.). 32p. (J). pap. 7.95 *(978-0-7945-0388-8(8))* EDC Publishing.

Gibson, Ray. What Shall I Grow? Watt, Fiona, ed. Lane, Kim, illus. Allman, Howard, photos by. 2006. (What Shall I Do Today? Ser.). 32p. (J). (gr. 2). lib. bdg. 15.95 *(978-1-58086-548-7(8))* EDC Publishing.

Giulieri, Anne. The School Garden, 1 vol. Fleming, Garry, illus. 2012. (Engage Literacy Yellow Ser.). (ENG.). 32p. (gr. k-2). pap. 5.99 *(978-1-4296-8958-8(7),* Engage Literacy) Capstone Press of Coughlan Cos.

Glassman, Michael & Ely, Lisa. Kinder Gardens: Games & Adventures, 1 vol. 2011. (ENG., Illus.). 64p. (J). pap. 12.99 *(978-0-7643-3811-3(0),* 9780764338113, Schiffer Publishing Ltd) Schiffer Publishing, Ltd.

Gleisner, Jenna Lee. Planting a Garden in Spring. 2014. (21st Century Basic Skills Library: Let's Look at Spring Ser.). (ENG.). 24p. (J). (gr. k-3). 22.79 *(978-1-62431-655-5(7),* 203132); pap. 12.79 *(978-1-62431-682-1(4),* 203133) Cherry Lake Publishing.

Greg's Guide to Common Sense Gardening in the Northwest. 2004. 29.95 *(978-0-9639495-8-5(6))* Moore, Greg Publishing.

Greve, Tom. How to Grow a Garden. 2015. (ENG.). 24p. (gr. k-3). 28.50 *(978-1-63430-352-1(0))* Rourke Educational Media.

Hand, Carol. Community, Urban, & Home Gardens. 2016. (Growing Green Ser.). (ENG.). 64p. (J). (gr. 6-8). 51.99 *(978-1-4677-9709-2(X),* Lerner Pubns.) Lerner Publishing Group.

Hanneman, Monika, et al. Gardening with Children. Tomasello, Sam, illus. 2011. (BBG Guides for a Greener Planet Ser.). (ENG.). 120p. pap. 12.95 *(978-1-889538-78-5(7))* Brooklyn Botanic Garden.

Harkins, Susan Sales & Harkins, William H. Design Your Own Butterfly Garden. 2008. (Gardening for Kids Ser.). (Illus.). 48p. (YA). (gr. 1-4). lib. bdg. 29.95 *(978-1-58415-638-3(4))* Mitchell Lane Pubs., Inc.

Hendy, Jenny. The Best-Ever Step-by-Step Kid's First Gardening: Fantastic Gardening Ideas for 5-12 Year Olds, from Growing Fruit & Vegetables & Fun with Flowers to Wildlife Gardening & Outdoor Crafts. 2017. (ENG., Illus.). 256p. (J). (gr. -1-12). pap. 11.99 ***(978-1-78214-191-4(X),*** Southwater) Anness Publishing GBR. Dist: National Bk. Network.

—Fun Gardening for Kids - 30 Creative Outdoor Projects: Imaginative Ideas for Great Activities for 5-12 Year Olds, Shown in 500 Fantastic Step-By-Step Pictures. 2012. (ENG., Illus.). 128p. pap. 16.99 *(978-1-78019-136-2(7))* Anness Publishing GBR. Dist: National Bk. Network.

—Gardening Projects for Kids: Fantastic Ideas for Making Things, Growing Plants & Flowers & Attracting Wildlife, with 60 Practical Projects & 175 Photographs. 2012. (ENG., Illus.). 128p. pap. 17.99 *(978-1-78019-019-8(0))* Anness Publishing GBR. Dist: National Bk. Network.

Heos, Bridget. So You Want to Grow a Pie? Fabbri, Daniele, illus. 2015. (Grow Your Food Ser.). (ENG.). 24p. (gr. 1-3). 19.95 *(978-1-60753-739-7(7))* Amicus Publishing.

—So You Want to Grow a Pizza? Fabbri, Daniele, illus. 2015. (Grow Your Food Ser.). (ENG.). 24p. (gr. 1-3). 19.95 *(978-1-60753-740-3(0))* Amicus Publishing.

—So You Want to Grow a Taco? Fabbri, Daniele, illus. 2015. (Grow Your Food Ser.). (ENG.). 24p. (gr. 1-3). 19.95 *(978-1-60753-742-7(7))* Amicus Publishing.

Higgins, Myrta. Little Gardens for Boys & Girls. 2008. (Gardening in America Ser.). (ENG.). 184p. (J). (gr. 4-7). pap. 13.95 *(978-1-4290-9098-8(7))* Applewood Bks.

Horticultural Science: Compentency-Based Student Handbook & Planning Guide. 2003. 52p. (YA). pap., stu. ed. 12.95 *(978-0-913163-34-4(1),* 978) Hobar Pubns.

Houle, Michelle E. Lindsey Williams: Gardening for Impoverished Families. 2007. (Young Heroes Ser.). (ENG., Illus.). 48p. (J). (gr. 3-7). lib. bdg. 28.75 *(978-0-7377-3867-4(7),* Kidhaven) Cengage Gale.

Innovative Kids Staff. In the Garden. Phillips, Jillian, illus. 2009. (ENG.). 20p. (J). (gr. -1-1). 8.99 *(978-1-58476-810-4(X))* Innovative Kids.

Johnson, S. & Evans, C. Starting Gardening. 2004. (First Skills Ser.). (ENG., Illus.). 32p. (J). (gr. k-2). pap. 4.95 *(978-0-7945-0445-8(0),* Usborne) EDC Publishing.

Johnson, Sue & Evans, Cheryl. Starting Gardening. Gower, Teri, illus. Allman, Howard, photos by. 2006. (First Skills Ser.). 32p. (J). (gr. 1). lib. bdg. 12.95 *(978-1-58086-543-2(7))* EDC Publishing.

Johnson, Terry. Growing New Plants. 2008. (21st Century Junior Library: Plants Ser.). (ENG., Illus.). 24p. (gr. 2-5). lib. bdg. 25.64 *(978-1-60279-279-1(8),* 200183) Cherry Lake Publishing.

Kent, Lorna, illus. In the Garden. 2004. 8p. (J). bds. 3.99 *(978-1-85854-088-7(7))* Brimax Books Ltd. GBR. Dist: Byeway Bks.

Kopp, Megan. Maker Projects for Kids Who Love Greening up Spaces. 2017. (Be a Maker! Ser.). (ENG., Illus.). 32p. (J). (gr. 4-7). ***(978-0-7787-2881-8(1))*** Crabtree Publishing Co.

Krezel, Cindy. Kids' Container Gardening: Year-Round Projects for Inside & Out. Curtis, Bruce, photos by. 2nd ed. 2010. (ENG., Illus.). 88p. (J). (gr. 1-6). pap. 14.95 *(978-1-883052-75-1(0))* Ball Publishing.

Kuskowski, Alex. Super Simple Butterfly Gardens: A Kid's Guide to Gardening, 1 vol. 2014. (Super Simple Gardening Ser.). (ENG.). 32p. (gr. k-4). 27.07 *(978-1-62403-521-0(3))* ABDO Publishing Co.

—Super Simple Gardening, 1 vol. 2014. (Super Simple Gardening Ser.: 6). (ENG.). 32p. (gr. k-4). lib. bdg. 162.42

(978-1-62403-520-3(5), Super SandCastle) ABDO Publishing Co.

—Super Simple Hanging Gardens: A Kid's Guide to Gardening, 1 vol. 2014. (Super Simple Gardening Ser.). (ENG.). 32p. (gr. k-4). 27.07 (978-1-62403-523-4(X)) ABDO Publishing Co.

—Super Simple Indoor Gardens: A Kid's Guide to Gardening, 1 vol. 2014. (Super Simple Gardening Ser.). (ENG.). 32p. (gr. k-4). 27.07 (978-1-62403-524-1(8)) ABDO Publishing Co.

Lang, Elizabeth. In the Garden. 2013. (Healthy Kids Ser.). (ENG.). 24p. (J). (gr. 1-4). 28.50 (978-1-62323-542-0(1), 206271) Child's World, Inc., The.

Lang, Gail M. Horticulture. 2007. (Green World Ser.). (Illus.). 125p. (gr. 6-12). lib. bdg. 37.50 (978-0-7910-8961-3(4), Chelsea Hse.) Facts On File, Inc.

Lay, Richard & Zarrinnaal, Laura Nienhaus. A Green Kid's Guide to Soil Preparation, 1 vol. 2013. (Green Kid's Guide to Gardening! Ser.). (ENG.). 24p. (J). (gr. -1-4). 27.07 (978-1-61641-947-9(4)) Magic Wagon.

—A Green Kid's Guide to Watering Plants, 1 vol. 2013. (Green Kid's Guide to Gardening! Ser.). (ENG.). 24p. (J). (gr. -1-4). 27.07 (978-1-61641-948-6(2)) Magic Wagon.

Lendroth, Susan. Old Manhattan Has Some Farms: (E-I-E-I-Grow!) Endle, Kate, illus. 2014. (ENG.). 32p. (J). (gr. -1-2). lib. bdg. 16.95 (978-1-58089-572-9(7)) Charlesbridge Publishing, Inc.

Lendroth, Susan & Endle, Kate. Old Manhattan Has Some Farms: (E-I-E-I-Grow!) 2017. (ENG., Illus.). 28p. (J). (— 1). bds. 7.99 (978-1-58089-573-6(5)) Charlesbridge Publishing, Inc.

Lindley, Nancy & Peters, Laura. Roses for Michigan, 1 vol., Vol. 1. rev. ed. 2004. (ENG., Illus.). 272p. (gr. 4). pap. 18.95 (978-1-55105-367-7(5), 1551053675) Lone Pine Publishing USA.

Loreno, Rose, et al. In the Garden. 2007. (Windows on Literacy Ser.). (ENG., Illus.). 12p. (J). pap. 10.95 (978-0-7922-8492-5(5)) CENGAGE Learning.

Loughran, Donna & Brunner-Jass, Renata. The Garden Club: Operations with Fractions. 2013. (IMath Ser.). (Illus.). 48p. (J). (gr. 5-6). pap. 11.94 (978-1-60357-509-6(X)); lib. bdg. 23.94 (978-1-59953-570-8(X)) Norwood Hse. Pr.

Mack, Molly. Bugs, Pests, & Plants. 2015. (Garden Squad! Ser.). (ENG.). 24p. (J). (gr. 3-4). pap. 8.25 (978-1-4994-0941-3(9), PowerKids Pr.) Rosen Publishing Group, Inc., The.

Marika. Mary's Garden. 2012. (Illus.). 32p. 16.50 (978-1-4120-7765-1(6)) Trafford Publishing.

Marsico, Katie. Garden Math. 2015. (ENG., Illus.). 32p. (J). (gr. 3-4). 26.65 (978-1-4677-1887-5(4)) Lerner Publishing Group.

Messner, Kate. Up in the Garden & down in the Dirt. Neal, Christopher Silas, illus. 2017. (ENG.). 56p. (J). pap. 7.99 (978-1-4521-6136-5(4)) Chronicle Bks. LLC.

—Up in the Garden & down in the Dirt. 2015. (ENG., Illus.). 52p. (J). (gr. k-3). 16.99 (978-1-4521-1936-6(8)) Chronicle Bks. LLC.

Mitchell Lane Publishers Inc. Staff. Gardening for Kids, 9 vols., Set. 2009. (J). (gr. 3-6). lib. bdg. 269.95 (978-1-58415-816-5(6)) Mitchell Lane Pubs., Inc.

Muse, Elizabeth St. Cloud. A Child's Garden: Introducing Your Child to the Joys of the Garden. Saull, Eve, illus. 2007. 45p. reprint ed. 15.00 (978-1-4223-6638-7(3)) DIANE Publishing Co.

National Geographic Kids & Musgrave, Ruth. In My Garden. 2017. (Look & Learn Ser.). (ENG., Illus.). 24p. (J). (-k). bds. 6.99 (**978-1-4263-2844-2(3)**, National Geographic Children's Bks.) National Geographic Society.

The New Gardener. Date not set. (Essential Gardening Ser.). 96p. 6.98 (978-0-7525-9645-7(4)) Parragon, Inc.

Orr, Tamra. A Kid's Guide to Perennial Gardens. 2008. (Gardening for Kids Ser.). (Illus.). 48p. (YA). (gr. 1-4). lib. bdg. 29.95 (978-1-58415-636-9(8)) Mitchell Lane Pubs., Inc.

Orr, Tamra B. Growing Nutritious Food. 2015. (Explorer Library: Science Explorer Ser.). (ENG., Illus.). 32p. (J). (gr. 4-8). 29.93 (978-1-63362-392-7(0), 206988) Cherry Lake Publishing.

Papazoglu, Paula. I Plant a Garden with My Mom. Gumm, Susan Kathleen, illus. 2005. (J). per. 15.00 (978-0-9754298-9-1(2), Ithaca Pr.) Authors & Artists Publishers of New York, Inc.

Paris, Stephanie. Garden Invasion. 2015. (Building Fluency Through Reader's Theater Ser.). (ENG., Illus.). 32p. (gr. 5-5). pap. 7.99 (978-1-4938-1293-6(9)) Teacher Created Materials, Inc.

Peters, Laura. Indoor Plants for Canada, 1 vol., Vol. 1. rev. ed. 2004. (ENG., Illus.). 264p. (gr. 4). pap. 21.95 (978-1-55105-389-9(6), 1551053896) Lone Pine Publishing USA.

Peters, Laura & Didur, Dean. Gardening Month by Month in Manitoba, 1 vol., Vol. 1. rev. ed. 2003. (ENG., Illus.). 160p. (gr. 4). pap. 18.95 (978-1-55105-400-1(0), 1551054000) Lone Pine Publishing USA.

Peters, Laura & Hanbidge, Patricia. Gardening Month by Month in Saskatchewan, 1 vol., Vol. 1. rev. ed. 2003. (ENG., Illus.). 160p. (gr. 4). pap. 18.95 (978-1-55105-398-1(5), 1551053985) Lone Pine Publishing USA.

Pettiford, Rebecca. Planting. Fretland VanVoorst, Jenny, ed. 2015. (J). lib. bdg. 25.65 (978-1-62031-228-5(X)) Jump! Inc.

Quattlebaum, Mary. Jo MacDonald Had a Garden. Bryant, Laura J., illus. 2013. (ENG.). 26p. (J). (gr. -1 — 1). bds. 7.95 (978-1-58469-225-6(1)) Dawn Pubns.

Quin, Caroline & Pearce, Sue. Gardening. 2004. (Activities for 3-5 Year Olds Ser.). (Illus.). 32p. pap. 11.00 (978-1-897675-40-3(2)) Brilliant Pubns. GBR. Dist: Parkwest Pubns., Inc.

Radtke, Becky. Keep the Scene Green! Earth-Friendly Activities. 2010. (Dover Children's Activity Bks.). (ENG., Illus.). 30p. (J). (gr. 1-5). pap. 3.99 (978-0-486-47534-9(4)) Dover Pubns., Inc.

Rau, Dana Meachen. Making Butterfly Gardens. 2012. (How-To Library). (ENG.). 32p. (gr. 3-6). 28.50 (978-1-61080-472-1(4), 202082); pap. 14.21 (978-1-61080-646-6(8), 202256) Cherry Lake Publishing.

Ray, Christie Jones & Ray, Christie Jones. Goat's Milk & Gardening. 2013. (Illus.). 42p. pap. 15.00 (978-0-9853223-9-7(X)) Rose Water Cottage Pr.

Rees, Rob. Backyard Cookbook. 2010. (Crabtree Connections Ser.). (ENG.). 24p. (J). (gr. 3-6). (978-0-7787-9939-9(5)); pap. (978-0-7787-9961-0(1)) Crabtree Publishing Co.

Rein, Mary B., ed. The Budding Gardener. 2011. (Budding Ser.). (ENG., Illus.). 64p. (gr. -1-5). pap. 9.95 (978-0-87659-373-8(2), Gryphon House Inc) Gryphon Hse., Inc.

Reynolds, Alison. Let's Grow a Garden. Hopgood, Andrew, illus. 2009. (Save Our Planet! Ser.). 12p. (J). (gr. -1-3). bds. 11.40 (978-1-60754-412-8(1)) Windmill Bks.

Rhatigan, Joe. Grow Your Own Giant Pumpkin. 2013. (ENG.). 64p. (J). 18.95 (978-1-60433-301-5(4), Applesauce Pr.) Cider Mill Pr. Bk. Pubs., LLC.

Rich, Steve. Mrs. Carter's Butterfly Garden. 2014. (ENG., Illus.). 32p. (J). (gr. k-3). pap. 12.95 (978-1-941316-08-5(5)) National Science Teachers Assn.

RIGBY. What Fine Gardeners: Second Grade. 2003. (Rigby on Our Way to English Ser.). (ENG.). 24p. (gr. 2-2). pap. 50.70 (978-0-7578-1419-8(0)) Rigby Education.

Scheunemann, Pam. Cool Jobs for Yard-Working Kids: Ways to Make Money Doing Yard Work, 1 vol. 2011. (Cool Kid Jobs Ser.). (ENG.). 32p. (J). (gr. 3-6). 28.50 (978-1-61613-198-2(5), Checkerboard Library) ABDO Publishing Co.

—Cool Stuff for Your Garden: Creative Projects for Kids, 1 vol. 2012. (Cool Stuff Ser.). (ENG., Illus.). 32p. (J). (gr. 3-6). 28.50 (978-1-61714-984-9(5)) ABDO Publishing Co.

Schuh, Mari. All Kinds of Gardens, 1 vol. 2010. (Gardens Ser.). (ENG.). 24p. (gr. k-1). lib. bdg. 21.99 (978-1-4296-3981-1(4), Pebble Bks.) Capstone Press of Coughlan Cos.

—Growing a Garden. 2010. (Gardens Ser.). (ENG.). 24p. (gr. k-1). pap. 35.70 (978-1-4296-5153-0(9), Pebble Bks.) Capstone Press of Coughlan Cos.

—Growing a Garden [Scholastic]. 2011. (Gardens Ser.). 24p. pap. 0.50 (978-1-4296-6307-6(3), Pebble Bks.) Capstone Press of Coughlan Cos.

—Tools for the Garden. 2010. (Gardens Ser.). (ENG.). 24p. (gr. k-1). pap. 35.70 (978-1-4296-5154-7(7)); lib. bdg. 21.99 (978-1-4296-3983-5(0)) Capstone Press of Coughlan Cos. (Pebble Bks.).

—Tools for the Garden [Scholastic]. 2011. (Gardens Ser.). 24p. pap. 0.50 (978-1-4296-6308-3(1), Pebble Bks.) Capstone Press of Coughlan Cos.

Schuh, Mari C. From Soil to Garden. 2016. (Start to Finish, Second Ser.). (ENG., Illus.). 24p. (J). (gr. k-3). 23.99 (978-1-5124-0946-8(4)) Lerner Publishing Group.

Shah, Kieran. Math in the Garden. 2016. (Math Is Everywhere! Ser.). 00024p. (J). pap. 8.15 (978-1-4824-5441-3(6)) Stevens, Gareth Publishing LLLP.

Shepherd, Matthew, et al. Pollinator Conservation Handbook: A Guide to Understanding, Protecting, & Providing Habitat for Native Pollinator Insects 2003. (Illus.). 145p. pap. 19.95 (978-0-9744475-0-6(1)) Xerces Society, The.

Shofner, Melissa Raé. A Trip to the Community Garden. 2016. (PowerKids Readers: My Community Ser.). 00024p. (J). (gr. k-k). pap. 8.25 (978-1-4994-2781-3(6), PowerKids Pr.) Rosen Publishing Group, Inc., The.

Spohn, Rebecca. Ready Set Grow. 2007. 96p. pap. 12.95 (978-1-59647-132-0(8)) Good Year Bks.

Tanem, Bob & Williamson, Don. Gardening Month by Month in Northern California, 1 vol., Vol. 1. rev. ed. 2004. (ENG., Illus.). 160p. (gr. 4). pap. 16.95 (978-1-55105-365-3(9), 1551053659) Lone Pine Publishing USA.

Taylor, "Grandma" Mary. Randy Grows a Garden for Julia. Lawson, Keri, photos by. 2005. (Illus.). (J). 12.50 (978-1-58597-321-7(1)) Leathers Publishing.

Totilo, Rebecca Park. The Christian Kids' Gardening Guide: Cool Stuff for You to Make & Grow. 2004. (Illus.). 168p. (J). pap. 12.99 (978-1-58411-034-7(1), Legacy Pr.) Rainbow Pubs. & Legacy Pr.

Turnbull, Stephanie. Cool Stuff to Grow. 2015. (ENG., Illus.). 32p. (J). pap. 9.95 (978-1-77092-222-8(9)) RiverStream Publishing.

—Gardening. 2015. (Try This! Ser.). (ENG., Illus.). 24p. (J). (gr. 2-6). 27.10 (978-1-62588-372-8(2), 1389460) Black Rabbit Bks.

Turnbull, Stephaniel & Turnbull, Stephanie. Cool Stuff to Grow. 2014. (Cool Stuff Ser.). (Illus.). 32p. (gr. 2-5). 31.35 (978-1-62588-188-5(6)) Black Rabbit Bks.

Urban Gardening & Farming for Teens. 2013. (Urban Gardening & Farming for Teens Ser.). 64p. (YA). (gr. 7-12). 166.25 (978-1-4777-1788-2(9)) Rosen Publishing Group, Inc., The.

Walton, Sally & Donaldson, Stephanie. Show Me How: I Can Grow Things. 2014. (ENG., Illus.). 48p. (J). (gr. 2-8). 7.99 (978-1-84322-756-4(8), Armadillo) Anness Publishing GBR. Dist: National Bk. Network.

Wellington, Monica. Little Gardener's Stickers. 2011. (Dover Little Activity Books Stickers Ser.). (ENG., Illus.). 4p. (J). (gr. k-3). 1.99 (978-0-486-48188-3(3)) Dover Pubns., Inc.

Who Lives in the Garden? 2004. (Who Lives... Ser.). 12p. (J). bds. 4.99 (978-1-85854-643-8(5)) Brimax Books Ltd. GBR. Dist: Byeway Bks.

Wilde, Kim. Harry's Garden. 2006. (Collins Big Cat Ser.). (ENG., Illus.). 96p. (J). (gr. 1-1). pap. 5.99 (978-0-00-718676-1(2)) HarperCollins Pubs. Ltd. GBR. Dist: Independent Pubs. Group.

Williamson, Don. Lawns for Canada: Natural & Organic, 1 vol. rev. ed. 2005. (ENG., Illus.). 160p. (gr. 4). pap. 19.95 (978-1-55105-485-8(X), 155105485X) Lone Pine Publishing USA.

Winckler, Suzanne. Planting the Seed: A Guide to Gardening. (Illus.). 64p. 2005. (gr. 5-12). 25.76 (978-0-8225-0081-0(7)) 2003. (J). (gr. 6-12). pap. 7.95 (978-0-8225-0471-9(5)) Lerner Publishing Group.

Wright, Mabel Osgood. The Garden You & I. 2007. (ENG.). 264p. pap. 21.99 (978-1-4346-1154-3(X)); 288p. pap. 23.99 (978-1-4346-1225-0(2)) Creative Media Partners, LLC.

GARDENING—FICTION

Aardvark, E. Gartner Jake. 2005. Orig. Title: Jake, the Gardener. (DAN.). 18.95 (978-0-9766859-6-8(5)) Macaronic Pr.

—Giacco il Giardiniere. 2005. Orig. Title: Jake, the Gardener. (ITA.). 18.95 (978-0-9766859-3-7(0)) Macaronic Pr.

—Jakke, den Traedgaardaren. 2005. (SWE.). 18.95 (978-0-9766859-7-5(3)) Macaronic Pr.

Aardvark, E. S. Jakke Puutarhurina. 2005. (FIN.). 18.95 (978-0-9766859-8-2(1)) Macaronic Pr.

—Joao o Jardineiro. 2005. (POR.). 18.95 (978-0-9766859-5-1(7)) Macaronic Pr.

Aardvark, Esperanza. Jaap de Tuinman. Zimmer, Dirk, illus. 2006. (DUT.). 14.95 (978-0-9766859-9-9(X)) Macaronic Pr.

Abbott, Jacob. Rollo at Work. 2009. 124p. 23.95 (978-1-60664-636-6(2)); pap. 10.95 (978-1-60664-261-0(8)) Rodgers, Alan Bks.

Anstee, Ashlyn. No, No, Gnome! Anstee, Ashlyn, illus. 2016. (ENG., Illus.). 40p. (J). (gr. -1-3). 17.99 (978-1-4814-3091-3(2), Simon & Schuster Bks. For Young Readers) Simon & Schuster Bks. For Young Readers.

Argueta, Jorge. Xochitl & the Flowers. Angel, Carl, illus. 2013. (ENG.). 32p. (J). (gr. k). pap. 9.95 (978-0-89239-224-7(X)) Lee & Low Bks., Inc.

—Xochitl & the Flowers (Xochitl, la Nina de Las Flores) Angel, Carl, illus. 2003.Tr. of Xochitl, la Nina de Las Flores. (ENG & SPA.). 32p. (J). 16.95 (978-0-89239-181-3(2)) Lee & Low Bks., Inc.

Ash. The Thrush's Song. 2011. 20p. pap. 24.95 (978-1-4626-3720-1(5)) America Star Bks.

Awad, Shelley. The Greenhouse Kids: Dan Delion's Secret. Zonta, Rose, illus. 2009. 127p. (J). pap. (978-0-88887-379-8(4)) Borealis Pr.

Ayres, Katherine. Up, down, & Around. Westcott, Nadine Bernard, illus. 2008. (Big Bks.). (ENG.). 32p. (J). (-k). pap. 24.99 (978-0-7636-4018-7(2)); 6.99 (978-0-7636-4017-0(4)) Candlewick Pr.

Bess, Stacey. Planting More Than Pansies: A Fable about Love. Ricks, Melissa, illus. 2003. (J). 14.95 (978-1-57008-893-3(4), Shadow Mountain) Shadow Mountain Publishing.

Birkett, Georgie, illus. Grow It!/¡A Sembrar! 2009. (Helping Hands English/Spanish Edition Ser.). (ENG & SPA.). 24p. (J). (gr. -1-k). pap. (978-1-84643-570-6(6)) Child's Play International Ltd.

Blair, Marion E. Just Beyond a Finger's Reach. 2013. (ENG.). 54p. (YA). pap. 21.95 (978-1-4787-1396-8(8)) Outskirts Pr., Inc.

Bracken, Beth. Henry Helps Plant a Garden, 1 vol. Busby, Ailie, illus. 2012. (Henry Helps Ser.). (ENG.). 24p. (gr. -1 — 1). pap. 5.95 (978-1-4048-7670-5(7)); lib. bdg. 22.65 (978-1-4048-7305-6(8)) Picture Window Bks. (Henry Helps).

Brennan, Martin. I Saw It in the Garden. Monroe, Michael Glenn, illus. 2006. 32p. (J). (gr. -1-3). 17.95 (978-1-58726-296-8(7), Mitten Pr.) Ann Arbor Editions LLC.

Bronn, Charles Heil. The Sun, the Moon, & the Gardener's Son. Kami, Y. Z., illus. 2006. 30p. (J). (gr. 4-12). reprint ed. 16.00 (978-1-4223-5222-9(6)) DIANE Publishing Co.

Brown, Peter. The Curious Garden. 2009. (ENG., Illus.). 40p. (J). (gr. -1-3). 18.99 (978-0-316-01547-9(4)) Little Brown & Co.

—The Curious Garden. 2010. (J). 194.75 (978-1-4407-7739-4(X)); 39.75 (978-1-4407-7738-7(1)); 39.75 (978-1-4407-7742-4(X)); 37.75 (978-1-4407-7744-8(6)); 37.75 (978-1-4407-7740-0(3)) Recorded Bks., Inc.

Brunsvold, Eric. Gardening with Grandma. Mueller, Miranda, illus. 2010. 24p. pap. 9.95 (978-0-615-38944-8(9)) Specialized Printing, LLC.

Bunting, Eve. Flower Garden. Hewitt, Kathryn, illus. 2004. 28p. (gr. -1-2). 17.00 (978-0-7569-4113-0(X)) Perfection Learning Corp.

Castellucci, Cecil. Grandma's Gloves. Denos, Julia, illus. 2010. (ENG.). 32p. (J). (gr. k-3). 15.99 (978-0-7636-3168-0(X)) Candlewick Pr.

Cayce, Jw & Guy, K. T. Miss Milli's Adventure: Garden Adventure Series. Moore, Elyse, illus. 2011. 26p. pap. 13.95 (978-1-4575-0002-2(7)) Dog Ear Publishing, LLC.

Cheng, Andrea. The Year of the Garden. Barton, Patrice, illus. 2017. (Anna Wang Novel Ser.: 5). (ENG.). 128p. (J). (gr. 1-4). 15.99 (978-0-544-66444-9(2), HMH Books For Young Readers) Houghton Mifflin Harcourt Publishing Co.

Christensen, Bonnie. Plant a Little Seed. Christensen, Bonnie, illus. 2012. (ENG., Illus.). 32p. (J). (gr. -1-2). 18.99 (978-1-59643-550-6(X), 9781596435506) Roaring Brook Pr.

Colburn, Cherie Foster. Our Shadow Garden. 2010. (ENG., Illus.). 32p. (J). 19.95 (978-1-933979-69-4(0), 2a670c16-6bf1-4046-9b18-a6f621294483) Bright Sky Pr.

Cole, Henry. Jack's Garden. 2014. 17.00 (978-1-63419-714-4(3)) Perfection Learning Corp.

Collins, Peggy. In the Garden. 2012. (ENG., Illus.). 40p. bds. 6.99 (978-1-60433-150-9(X), Applesauce Pr.) Cider Mill Pr. Bk. Pubs., LLC.

—In the Garden. Collins, Peggy, illus. 2009. (ENG., Illus.). 40p. (J). 14.95 (978-1-60433-026-7(0), Applesauce Pr.) Cider Mill Pr. Bk. Pubs., LLC.

Corderoy, Tracey. Magical Snow Garden. Chapman, Jane, illus. 2014. (ENG.). 32p. (J). (gr. -1-3). 16.99 (978-1-58925-162-5(8)) Tiger Tales.

Cory, Kim Delmar. Tending Ben's Garden. 2009. (J). pap. (978-0-88092-778-9(X)) Royal Fireworks Publishing Co.

Cousins, Lucy. Maisy Grows a Garden. 2013. (Maisy Ser.). (ENG., Illus.). 16p. (J). (-k). 14.99 (978-0-7636-6242-4(9)) Candlewick Pr.

De Anda, Diane. The Patchwork Garden. Ventura, Gabriela Baeza, tr. Kemarskaya, Oksana, illus. 2013.Tr. of Pedacitos de Huerto. (ENG & SPA.). 32p. (J). 16.95 (978-1-55885-763-6(X), Piñata Books) Arte Publico Pr.

Deák, Erzsi. Pumpkin Time! Cushman, Doug, illus. 2014. (ENG.). 32p. (J). (-3). 14.99 (978-1-4022-9526-3(X), 9781402295263, Sourcebooks Jabberwocky) Sourcebooks, Inc.

Dharma Publishing Staff. The Spade Sage: The Story about Finding Happiness. 2nd ed. 2013. (ENG.). 36p. (gr. -1-7). pap. 8.95 (978-0-89800-522-6(1)) Dharma Publishing.

Diesen, Deborah. Bloom. Lundquist, Mary, illus. 2017. (ENG.). 32p. (J). 16.99 (978-0-374-30250-4(2), 9780374302504, Farrar, Straus & Giroux (BYR)) Farrar, Straus & Giroux.

Dillard, Sarah. Mouse Scouts. 2016. (Mouse Scouts Ser.). (ENG., Illus.). 128p. (J). (gr. 2-5). 12.99 (978-0-385-75599-3(6), Knopf Bks. for Young Readers) Random Hse. Children's Bks.

Donaldson, Julia. One Mole Digging a Hole, 2. Sharratt, Nick, illus. 2010. (ENG.). 32p. (J). (gr. k-k). pap. 8.99 (978-0-230-70647-7(9)) Macmillan Pubs., Ltd. GBR. Dist: Independent Pubs. Group.

Duke, Kate. Ready for Pumpkins. 2012. (ENG., Illus.). 40p. (J). (gr. k-3). 16.99 (978-0-375-87068-2(7), Knopf Bks. for Young Readers) Random Hse. Children's Bks.

Ehlert, Lois. Growing Vegetable Soup. 2004. (ENG., Illus.). 32p. (J). (gr. k — 1). bds. 6.95 (978-0-15-205055-9(8)) Houghton Mifflin Harcourt Publishing Co.

—Planting a Rainbow. Ehlert, Lois, illus. 2003. (ENG., Illus.). 32p. (J). (gr. k — 1). bds. 7.99 (978-0-15-204633-0(X)) Houghton Mifflin Harcourt Publishing Co.

—Planting a Rainbow: Lap-Sized Board Book. 2008. (ENG., Illus.). 32p. (J). (gr. -1 — 1). bds. 11.99 (978-0-15-206304-7(8)) Houghton Mifflin Harcourt Publishing Co.

Elvgren, Jennifer. Josias, Hold the Book. Tadgell, Nicole, illus. 2011. (ENG.). 32p. (J). (gr. 2-4). pap. 10.95 (978-1-59078-856-1(7)) Boyds Mills Pr.

Enos, Deanna. The Wooden Garden of Romano Gabriel, 1 vol. 2008. (ENG.). 36p. 24.95 (978-1-60563-234-6(1)) America Star Bks.

Evans, Cordelia, adapted by. Doozers Have Green Thumbs. 2015. (Doozers Ser.). (ENG., Illus.). 32p. (J). (gr. -1-1). pap. 3.99 (978-1-4814-3220-7(6), Simon Spotlight) Simon Spotlight.

Ewing, Juliana Horatia. Mary's Meadow: And Other Tales of Fields & Flowers. 2007. (ENG.). 154p. pap. 19.99 (978-1-4346-3334-7(9)); 168p. pap. 21.99 (978-1-4346-3335-4(7)) Creative Media Partners, LLC.

Falconer, Ian, et al. Olivia & Her Great Adventures. Osterhold, Jared & Johnson, Shane L., illus. 2012. (J). (978-1-4351-4316-6(7), Simon Spotlight) Simon Spotlight.

Fan, Terry & Fan, Eric. The Night Gardener. Fan, Terry & Fan, Eric, illus. 2016. (ENG., Illus.). 48p. (J). (gr. -1-3). 17.99 (978-1-4814-3978-7(2)) Simon & Schuster, Inc.

Fenn, G. Manville. Brownsmith's Boy. 2008. 260p. pap. 15.95 (978-1-60664-154-5(9)) Aegypan.

Fisch, Sarah. The Little Flower Seed. Roper, Robert, illus. 2007. (J). pap. (978-0-439-90899-3(X)) Scholastic, Inc.

Fleischman, Paul. Weslandia. braille ed. 2004. (Illus.). (J). (gr. k-3). spiral bd. (978-0-616-01641-1(7)) Canadian National Institute for the Blind/Institut National Canadien pour les Aveugles.

—Weslandia. Hawkes, Kevin, illus. 2006. (gr. -1-3). 17.00 (978-0-7569-6566-2(7)) Perfection Learning Corp.

Fleming, Candace. Muncha! Muncha! Muncha! Karas, G. Brian, illus. pap. incl. audio (978-1-59112-465-8(4)); pap. 18.95 incl. audio compact disk (978-1-59112-923-3(0)); pap. incl. audio compact disk (978-1-59112-925-7(7)); pap. 16.95 incl. audio (978-1-59112-463-4(8)) Live Oak Media.

—Ñam! Ñam! Ñam! Schmidt, Alejandra, tr. from ENG. Karas, G. Brian, illus. 2007. (SPA.). 32p. (J). (gr. -1-2). 15.95 (978-1-933032-35-1(9)) Lectorum Pubns., Inc.

French, Vivian. Yucky Worms. Ahlberg, Jessica, illus. 2012. (Read & Wonder Ser.). (ENG.). 32p. (J). (gr. -1-3). pap. 6.99 (978-0-7636-5817-5(0)) Candlewick Pr.

—Yucky Worms. 2012. (Read & Wonder Ser.). lib. bdg. 17.20 (978-0-606-23803-8(4), Turtleback) Turtleback Bks.

Fry, Stella. Grandpa's Garden. Jago & Moxley, Sheila, illus. 2012. (ENG.). 40p. (J). 16.99 (978-1-84686-053-9(9)) Barefoot Bks., Inc.

—Grandpa's Garden. 2012. lib. bdg. 19.65 (978-0-606-23824-3(7), Turtleback) Turtleback Bks.

Fry, Stella & Moxley, Sheila. Grandpa's Garden. Moxley, Sheila, illus. 2012. (ENG., Illus.). 40p. (J). (gr. -1-2). pap. 8.99 (978-1-84686-809-2(2)) Barefoot Bks., Inc.

Garland, Sarah. Eddie's Garden: And How to Make Things Grow. 2009. (ENG., Illus.). 40p. (J). (gr. -1-2). pap. 8.95 (978-1-84507-089-2(5), Frances Lincoln) Quarto Publishing Group UK GBR. Dist: Hachette Bk. Group.

Geras, Adèle. Lizzie's Wish. 2009. (Historical House Ser.). 144p. (YA). (gr. 5-18). pap. 5.99 (978-0-7945-2337-4(4), Usborne) EDC Publishing.

Ghigna, Charles. Little Seeds, 1 vol. Jatkowska, Ag, illus. 2012. (My Little Planet Ser.). (ENG.). 24p. (gr. -1 — 1). 6.95 (978-1-4048-7226-4(4)); lib. bdg. 22.65 (978-1-4048-6790-1(2)) Picture Window Bks. (My Little Planet).

Gibson, B. J. Grannie's World Record Collard Greens. 2004. (J). pap. 10.00 (978-0-8059-5951-2(3)) Dorrance Publishing Co., Inc.

Giff, Patricia Reilly. The Garden Monster. Palmisciano, Diane, illus. (Fiercely & Friends Ser.). (J). (gr. k-2). 2014. (ENG.). 40p. 16.99 (978-0-545-43379-2(7)) 2013. (978-0-545-24460-2(9)) Scholastic, Inc. (Orchard Bks.).

Grant, Judyann. Chicken Said, "Cluck!" Truesdell, Sue, illus. 2008. (My First I Can Read Bks.). 32p. (J). (gr. -1-3). lib. bdg. 16.89 (978-0-06-028724-5(1)) HarperCollins Pubs.

Grant, Judyann Ackerman. Chicken Said, "Cluck!" Truesdell, Sue, illus. 2010. (My First I Can Read Ser.). (ENG.). 32p. (J). (gr. -1-3). pap. 3.99 (978-0-06-444276-3(4)) HarperCollins Pubs.

—Chicken Said, "Cluck!" Truesdell, Sue, illus. 2008. (My First I Can Read Ser.). (ENG.). 32p. (J). (gr. -1-3). 16.99 (978-0-06-028723-8(3)) HarperCollins Pubs.

Grey, Mini. Three by the Sea. 2011. (ENG.). 32p. (J). (gr. k-3). 17.99 (978-0-375-86784-2(8), Knopf Bks. for Young Readers) Random Hse. Children's Bks.

Grigsby, Susan. First Peas to the Table: How Thomas Jefferson Inspired a School Garden. Tadgell, Nicole, illus. 2012. (ENG.). 32p. (J). (gr. 1-3). 16.99 (978-0-8075-2452-7(2)) Whitman, Albert & Co.

—In the Garden with Dr. Carver. Tadgell, Nicole, illus. 2012. (J). (978-1-61913-157-6(9)) Weigl Pubs., Inc.

—In the Garden with Dr. Carver. Tadgell, Nicole, illus. 2010. (ENG.). 32p. (J). (gr. 2-3). 16.99 (978-0-8075-3630-8(X)) Whitman, Albert & Co.

H & T Imaginations Unlimited, Inc. Professor Woodpecker's Strawberry Patch! Wholesome, Fun children's story with Professor Woodpecker. 2008. 20p. pap. 12.49 (978-1-4389-1304-9(4)) AuthorHouse.

—Vegetable Gardening with Professor Woodpecker. 2009. 16p. pap. 8.49 (978-1-4389-5402-8(6)) AuthorHouse.

Hapka, Catherine, pseud & Disney Book Group Staff. Pooh's Secret Garden. Disney Storybook Art Team, illus. 2012. (ENG.). 24p. (J). (gr. -1-k). pap. 4.99 (978-1-4231-4845-6(2)) Disney Pr.

Harrod-Eagles, Cynthia. The Biggest Pumpkin Ever! Woodruff, Liza, illus. 2007. (J). pap. *(978-0-545-00232-5(X))* Scholastic, Inc.
Harrod-Eagles, Cynthia. Hello Kitty: Garden Party. Hino, Sachiho, illus. 2015. 22p. (J). **(978-0-545-73447-9(9))** Scholastic, Inc.
Havill, Juanita. Grow, 1 vol. Kodman, Stansislawa, illus. 2011. (ENG.). 160p. (J). (gr. 3-7). pap. 7.95 *(978-1-56145-575-1(X))* Peachtree Pubs.
—Grow, 1 vol. Kodman, Stanislawa, illus. 2008. (ENG.). 144p. (J). (gr. 3-7). 14.95 *(978-1-56145-441-9(9))* Peachtree Pubs.
Hearn, Diane Dawson. Anna in the Garden. 2006. (Illus.). 29p. (J). (gr. k-4). reprint ed. 15.00 *(978-1-4223-5087-4(8))* DIANE Publishing Co.
Henderson, Kathy. And the Good Brown Earth. Henderson, Kathy, illus. 2008. (ENG., Illus.). 40p. (J). (gr. -1-2). per. 6.99 *(978-0-7636-3841-2(2))* Candlewick Pr.
Hensdill, Norma Mae. I'm Granny's Little Mess, Just Look at the Rest. 2009. 36p. pap. 17.99 *(978-1-4389-5054-9(3))* AuthorHouse.
Higgs, Liz Curtis. The Sunflower Parable, 1 vol. Munger, Nancy, illus. 10th anniv. ed. 2007. (Parable Ser.). (ENG.). 32p. (gr. -1-2). 7.99 *(978-1-4003-0845-3(3))* Nelson, Thomas Inc.
Hillert, Margaret. Dear Dragon Grows a Garden. Schimmell, David, illus. rev. ed. 2014. (BeginningtoRead Ser.). (ENG.). 32p. (J). (gr. k-2). pap. 11.94 *(978-1-60357-414-3(X))* Norwood Hse. Pr.
Hoffman, Alice. Green Heart. 2012. (ENG.). 272p. (J). (gr. 7-7). pap. 10.99 *(978-0-545-14196-3(6)*, Scholastic Paperbacks) Scholastic, Inc.
—Green Heart. 2012. lib. bdg. 22.10 *(978-0-606-23954-7(5)*, Turtleback) Turtleback Bks.
Holub, Joan. Spring Is Here! A Story about Seeds. Terry, Will, illus. 2008. (Ant Hill Ser.). (ENG.). 24p. (J). (gr. -1-k). lib. bdg. 13.89 *(978-1-4169-5132-2(6)*, Simon & Schuster/Paula Wiseman Bks.) Simon & Schuster/Paula Wiseman Bks.
—Spring Is Here! A Story about Seeds. Terry, Will, illus. 2008. (Ant Hill Ser.). (ENG.). 24p. (J). (gr. -1-k). pap. 3.99 *(978-1-4169-5131-5(8)*, Simon Spotlight) Simon Spotlight.
Hughes, Emily, illus. The Little Gardener. 2015. (ENG.). 40p. (J). (gr. -1-2). 17.95 *(978-1-909263-43-7(5))* Flying Eye Bks. GBR. Dist: Consortium Bk. Sales & Distribution.
Hurd, Edith Thacher & Brown, Margaret Wise. Two Little Gardeners. Elliot, Gertrude, illus. 2006. (Little Golden Book Ser.). (ENG.). 24p. (J). (gr. -1-2). 4.99 *(978-0-375-83529-2(6)*, Golden Bks.) Random Hse. Children's Bks.
Icanberry, Mark & Mount, Arthur. Super Salads. 2010. (Look, Learn & Do Ser.). (Illus.). 48p. (J). (gr. 3-5). 14.95 *(978-1-893327-01-6(9))* Look, Learn & Do Pubns.
Irene's Wish. 2014. (ENG., Illus.). 32p. (J). (gr. k-4). 17.99 *(978-0-689-86300-4(4)*, Simon & Schuster/Paula Wiseman Bks.) Simon & Schuster/Paula Wiseman Bks.
Jeffers, Dawn. Vegetable Dreams/Huerto Sonado. de La Vega, Eida, tr. Schneider, Claude, illus. 2006. (SPA & ENG.). 32p. (J). (gr. -1-3). 16.95 *(978-0-9741992-9-0(X)*, 626999, Raven Tree Pr.,Csi) Continental Sales, Inc.
Johnson, Jacqueline & Young, Jeanna Stolle. Princess Faith's Mysterious Garden, 1 vol. Aranda, Omar, illus. 2012. (Princess Parables Ser.). (ENG.). 32p. (J). 14.99 *(978-0-310-72703-3(0))* Zonderkidz.
Johnson, Marion. Caillou: The Carrot Patch. Sevigny, Eric, illus. 2017. (Read with Caillou Ser.). (ENG.). 32p. (J). (gr. -1-k). 3.99 *(978-2-89718-367-7(5))* Caillouet, Gerry.
Kellogg, Catherine Berry. The Moose Who Ate My Fort: Stories from Bella Sage. 2008. 36p. pap. 24.95 *(978-1-60441-696-1(3))* America Star Bks.
Kephart, Beth. Nothing but Ghosts. 2009. (ENG.). 288p. (J). (gr. 8-18). 17.99 *(978-0-06-166796-1(X)*, HarperTeen) HarperCollins Pubs.
Ketchum, Sally. Bread Garden. Harvey, Michael C., illus. 2008. 164p. pap. 12.95 *(978-0-595-52862-2(7))* iUniverse, Inc.
Krauss, Ruth. The Carrot Seed. Johnson, Crockett, illus. 60th anniv. ed. 2004. (ENG.). 32p. (J). (gr. -1-3). 16.99 *(978-0-06-023350-1(8))* HarperCollins Pubs.
—The Carrot Seed. 2004. (J). (gr. -1-2). 17.20 *(978-0-8335-1041-9(X)*, Turtleback) Turtleback Bks.
Kunce, Craig. Spring Is for Gardening. 2011. (Edrick the Inventor Ser.: 2). (ENG., Illus.). 24p. (J). (gr. k-2). 16.00 *(978-0-9844828-1-8(4))* Windhill Bks. LLC.
Kurtz, Jane. Lanie's Real Adventures. Papp, Robert, illus. 2010. (American Girl Today Ser.). (ENG.). 112p. (YA). (gr. 3-18). 12.95 *(978-1-59369-685-6(X))* American Girl Publishing, Inc.
Lasser, Jon & Foster-Lasser, Sage. Grow Happy. Lyles, Christopher, illus. 2017. 32p. (J). 15.95 *(978-1-4338-2331-2(4)*, Magination Pr.) American Psychological Assn.
Lindman, Maj. Flicka, Ricka, Dicka Go to Market. Lindman, Maj, illus. 2012. (ENG., Illus.). 32p. (J). (gr. -1-3). 9.99 *(978-0-8075-2478-7(6))*; (gr. k-3). 9.99 *(978-0-8075-2479-4(4))* Whitman, Albert & Co.
Manning, Ella L. Ashleigh's Rainbow Garden. 2012. 16p. pap. 15.99 *(978-1-4685-6601-7(6))* AuthorHouse.
Mannone, Christine. Flowers for Pudding Street. Carolan, Christine, illus. 2009. (ENG.). 32p. (J). 15.95 *(978-1-934860-02-1(6))* Shenanigan Bks.
Marshall, Linda Elovitz. Talia & the Rude Vegetables. Assirelli, Francesca, illus. 2011. (High Holidays Ser.). (ENG.). 24p. (J). (gr. k-3). pap. 6.95 *(978-0-7613-5218-1(X)*, Kar-Ben Publishing) Lerner Publishing Group.
Mattern, Joanne. The Tricky Garden. 2005. (J). pap. *(978-1-4108-4191-9(X))* Benchmark Education Co.
Matthies, Jana. The Goodbye Cancer Garden, 1 vol. Valiant, Kristi, illus. 2011. (ENG.). 32p. (J). (gr. 1-3). 16.99 *(978-0-8075-2994-2(X))* Whitman, Albert & Co.
May, Kyla. Coco: My Delicious Life. 2013. (Lotus Lane Ser.: 2). (ENG., Illus.). 96p. (J). (gr. 1-3). 15.99 *(978-0-545-49615-5(2))*; pap. 4.99 *(978-0-545-44514-6(0))* Scholastic, Inc.
—Coco: My Delicious Life. 2013. (Lotus Lane Ser.: 2). lib. bdg. 14.75 *(978-0-606-31978-2(6)*, Turtleback) Turtleback Bks.
Mayer, Mercer. A Green, Green Garden. Mayer, Mercer, illus. 2011. (My First I Can Read Ser.). (ENG., Illus.). 32p. (J). (gr. -1-3). 16.99 *(978-0-06-083562-0(1))*; pap. 3.99 *(978-0-06-083561-3(3))* HarperCollins Pubs.
McNamara, Margaret. The Garden Project. Gordon, Mike, illus. 2010. (Robin Hill School Ser.). (ENG.). 32p. (J). (gr. -1-1). pap. 3.99 *(978-1-4169-9171-7(9)*, Simon Spotlight) Simon Spotlight.
McQuinn, Anna. Lola Plants a Garden. Beardshaw, Rosalind, illus. 2014. (ENG.). 28p. (J). (-k). 15.95 *(978-1-58089-694-8(4))* Charlesbridge Publishing, Inc.
McQuinn, Anna & Calvo, Carlos E. Lola Planta un Jardin. Beardshaw, Rosalind, illus. 2017. (SPA.). 28p. (J). (-k). pap. 7.99 *(978-1-58089-786-0(X))* Charlesbridge Publishing, Inc.
McQuinn, Anna, et al. Lola Plants a Garden: Lola Planta un Jardin. Beardshaw, Rosalind, illus. 2017. (SPA & ENG.). (J). pap. **(978-1-63289-027-6(5))** Charlesbridge Publishing, Inc.
Meyerhoff, Jenny. Green Thumbs-Up! Chatelain, Éva, illus. 2015. (Friendship Garden Ser.: 1). (ENG.). 176p. (J). (gr. 2-5). pap. 5.99 *(978-1-4814-3904-6(9))*, Aladdin) Simon & Schuster Children's Publishing.
—Project Peep. Chatelain, Éva, illus. 2016. (Friendship Garden Ser.: 3). (ENG.). 144p. (J). (gr. 2-5). pap. 5.99 *(978-1-4814-3913-8(8)*, Aladdin) Simon & Schuster Children's Publishing.
—Pumpkin Spice. Chatelain, Éva, illus. 2015. (Friendship Garden Ser.: 2). (ENG.). 144p. (J). (gr. 2-5). pap. 5.99 *(978-1-4814-3909-1(X)*, Aladdin) Simon & Schuster Children's Publishing.
—Pumpkin Spice. 2015. (Friendship Garden Ser.: 2). lib. bdg. 16.00 *(978-0-606-37833-8(2))* Turtleback Bks.
—Sweet Peas & Honeybees. 2016. (Friendship Garden Ser.: 4). lib. bdg. 16.00 *(978-0-606-38978-5(4))* Turtleback Bks.
Mills, Susan & Shara, Diana. Frankie & Her Little Pals - Save the Watermelons. 2007. 32p. (J). *(978-0-9790690-3-1(3))* Lucky Red Pr., LLC.
Minger, Janet. How Do Strawberries & Green Beans Sleep at Night? 2011. 28p. pap. 13.54 *(978-1-4567-2239-5(5))* AuthorHouse.
Miranda, Patti. Sonny's Flower Garden. 2012. 24p. 24.95 *(978-1-4626-4619-7(0))* America Star Bks.
Mockford, Caroline. What's This? A Seed's Story. Mockford, Caroline, illus. 2007. (ENG., Illus.). 32p. (J). (gr. -1-2). pap. 7.99 *(978-1-84686-071-3(7))* Barefoot Bks., Inc.
Mortimer, Anne. Pumpkin Cat. Mortimer, Anne, illus. 2011. (ENG., Illus.). 24p. (J). (gr. -1-2). 14.99 *(978-0-06-187485-7(X)*, Tegen, Katherine Bks) HarperCollins Pubs.
Murphy, Stuart J. Great Choice, Camille! 2013. (I See I Learn Ser.). (ENG., Illus.). 32p. (J). (-k). pap. 6.95 *(978-1-58089-477-7(1))*; lib. bdg. 14.95 *(978-1-58089-476-0(3))* Charlesbridge Publishing, Inc.
Nelson, Kadir. If You Plant a Seed. Nelson, Kadir, illus. 2015. (ENG., Illus.). 32p. (J). (gr. -1-3). 18.99 *(978-0-06-229889-8(5))* HarperCollins Pubs.
Nettrour, Nelani. Jodi's Garden. 2006. (Illus.). 100p. (J). per. 14.95 *(978-1-932657-63-0(0))* Third Millennium Pubns.
Ochiltree, Dianne. Sunflowers Measure Up! 2003. (Hello Math Reader Ser.). (Illus.). (J). *(978-0-439-24228-8(2))* Scholastic, Inc.
O'Neal, Shaquille. Little Shaq. Taylor, Theodore, illus. 2015. 73p. (J). *(978-1-68119-119-5(9))* Bloomsbury Pr.
—Little Shaq. Taylor, Theodore, illus. (ENG.). 80p. (J). 2016. pap. 6.99 *(978-1-61963-722-1(7)*, 9781619637221) 2015. 9.99 *(978-1-61963-721-4(9)*, 9781619637214) Bloomsbury Publishing USA. (Bloomsbury USA Childrens).
Osterhold, Jared, illus. OLIVIA Plants a Garden. 2011. (Olivia TV Tie-In Ser.). (ENG.). 24p. (J). (gr. -1-1). pap. 3.99 *(978-1-4424-1675-8(0)*, Simon Spotlight) Simon Spotlight.
Pappas, Peter. Stu the Rabbit. 2007. (J). *(978-0-9801439-3-5(4))* Town & Country Reprographics.
Patton, Donna Alice. The Gift of Summer Snow: A Tale from the Garden of Mysteries. 2010. (Illus.). ix, 133p. (J). *(978-0-9826867-3-7(0))* Philothea Pr.
Pattou, Edith. Mrs. Spitzer's Garden. Tusa, Tricia, illus. gif. ed. 2007. (ENG.). 32p. (J). (gr. -1-3). 12.99 *(978-0-15-205802-9(8))* Houghton Mifflin Harcourt Publishing Co.
Paulsen, Gary. Notes from the Dog. 2011. (ENG.). 144p. (YA). (gr. 7). pap. 6.99 *(978-0-375-85542-9(4)*, Ember) Random Hse. Children's Bks.
Pearson, J. J. Anita & Ing: Garden Adventure. 2012. 24p. pap. 12.95 *(978-1-4525-4248-5(1))* Balboa Pr.
Perelman, Helen. Jelly Bean Jumble. Waters, Erica-Jane, illus. 2013. (Candy Fairies Ser.: 10). (ENG.). 128p. (J). (gr. 2-5). pap. 5.99 *(978-1-4424-5297-8(8)*, Aladdin) Simon & Schuster Children's Publishing.
—Jelly Bean Jumble. Waters, Erica-Jane, illus. 2013. (Candy Fairies Ser.: 10). (ENG.). 128p. (J). (gr. 2-5). 15.99 *(978-1-4424-6000-3(8)*, Simon & Schuster/Paula Wiseman Bks.) Simon & Schuster/Paula Wiseman Bks.
Prochovnic, Dawn Babb. See the Colors: Sign Language for Colors, 1 vol. Bauer, Stephanie, illus. 2009. (Story Time with Signs & Rhymes Ser.). (ENG.). 32p. (gr. -1-3). 28.50 *(978-1-60270-671-2(9)*, Looking Glass Library) ABDO Publishing Co.
Pryor, Katherine. Zora's Zucchini. Raff, Anna, illus. 2015. (ENG.). 32p. (J). (gr. -1-5). 16.95 *(978-0-9836615-7-3(X))* READERS to EATERS.
—Zora's Zucchini (1 Hardcover/1 CD) 2016. (ENG.). (J). (gr. -1-2). audio compact disk 29.95 *(978-1-4301-2183-1(1))* Live Oak Media.
Puttock, Simon & Bartlett, Alison. Pig's Prize. 2004. (ENG., Illus.). 28p. (J). (gr. -1-k). 17.99 *(978-1-4052-0538-2(5))* Egmont Bks., Ltd. GBR. Dist: Independent Pubs. Group.
Quattlebaum, Mary. Jackson Jones & the Curse of the Outlaw Rose. 2008. (ENG.). 112p. (J). (gr. 3-7). 5.99 *(978-0-440-42138-2(1)*, Yearling) Random Hse. Children's Bks.
Ray, Mary Lyn. Christmas Farm. Root, Barry, illus. (ENG.). 40p. (J). (gr. -1-3). 2008. 17.99 *(978-0-15-216290-0(9))* 2013. 6.99 *(978-0-544-10509-6(5))* Houghton Mifflin Harcourt Publishing Co.
Remkiewicz, Frank. Gus Grows a Plant. 2012. (Illus.). (J). pap. *(978-0-545-34052-6(7))* Scholastic, Inc.
Rey, H. A. Curious George Grows a Garden. 2012. (Curious George Ser.). (ENG., Illus.). 48p. (J). (gr. -1-3). pap. 4.99 *(978-0-547-64304-5(7))* Houghton Mifflin Harcourt Publishing Co.
Rock, Maria. MiMi's Garden, It's a Kid Thing! A Guide for Beginning Gardeners. l.t. ed. 2003. (Illus.). 45p. (J). 12.95 *(978-0-9726979-0-3(X))* Rock Ink.
Roper, Shannon L. Mommy's Garden. 2012. 26p. 24.95 *(978-1-4626-5327-0(8))* America Star Bks.
Ross, Thea. Molly Mole Loves to Garden. 2004. (Lift-the-Flap Surprise on Every Spread! Ser.). 12p. (J). 5.99 *(978-1-59384-044-0(6))* Parklane Publishing.
Ruth, Krauss & Krauss. The Carrot Seed. 60th rev. ed. 2014. (Trophy Picture Bks). (ENG.). 32p. (J). (gr. k-3). 11.24 *(978-1-63245-275-7(8))* Lectorum Pubns., Inc.
Ryder, Joanne. My Father's Hands. Graham, Mark, illus. 2014. 32p. pap. 8.00 *(978-1-61003-330-5(2))* Center for the Collaborative Classroom.
Sander, Sonia. Plant a Garden. Moore, Saxton & McGee, Warner, illus. 2008. (Care Bears Ser.). (ENG.). 24p. (J). (gr. -1-3). pap. 3.99 *(978-0-545-00908-9(1)*, Scholastic) Scholastic, Inc.
Schneider, Antonie & Maccarone, Grace. Mr. Happy & Miss Grimm. Strasser, Susanne, illus. 2015. (ENG.). 32p. (J). (gr. -1-3). 16.95 *(978-0-8234-3198-4(3))* Holiday Hse., Inc.
Segal, John. Carrot Soup. Segal, John, illus. 2006. (ENG., Illus.). 32p. (J). (gr. -1-3). 17.99 *(978-0-689-87702-5(1)*, McElderry, Margaret K. Bks.) McElderry, Margaret K. Bks.
—Sopa de Zanahoria. Mlawer, Teresa, tr. from ENG. 2006. (Illus.). (gr. -1-k). 12.99 *(978-1-933032-13-9(8))* Lectorum Pubns., Inc.
Sloan, Holly Goldberg. Counting by 7s. 2015. (CHI.). 392p. (J). pap. *(978-986-6104-68-8(0))* Daskovik, Izdatel'sko-torgovaja korporacija.
—Counting by 7s. 2013. (ENG.). 384p. (YA). (gr. 5). 17.99 *(978-0-8037-3855-3(2)*, Dial Bks) Penguin Publishing Group.
—Counting by 7s. 2014. (ENG.). 400p. (J). (gr. 5). 8.99 *(978-0-14-242286-1(X)*, Puffin Books) Penguin Young Readers Group.
—Counting by 7s. 2014. (ENG.). (J). (gr. 5). lib. bdg. 19.60 **(978-1-62765-616-0(2))** Perfection Learning Corp.
—Counting by 7s. 2014. (gr. 5-8). lib. bdg. 19.65 *(978-0-606-36583-3(4))* Turtleback Bks.
Smith, Shelli. Grammy Goes Green. 2012. 24p. pap. 12.45 *(978-1-4624-0104-8(X)*, Inspiring Voices) Author Solutions, Inc.
Snyder, Laurel. The Forever Garden. Cotterill, Samantha, illus. 2017. (ENG.). 40p. (J). (gr. -1-3). 17.99 **(978-0-553-51273-1(0))**; lib. bdg. 20.99 **(978-0-553-51274-8(9))** Random Hse. Children's Bks. (Schwartz & Wade Bks.).
Sollinger, Emily. OLIVIA Plants a Garden. Osterhold, Jared, illus. 2011. (Olivia TV Tie-In Ser.). (ENG.). 24p. (J). (gr. -1-1). 16.99 *(978-1-4424-2011-3(1)*, Simon Spotlight) Simon Spotlight.
Spurr, Elizabeth. In the Garden, 1 vol. Oliphant, Manelle, illus. 2012. (ENG.). 22p. (J). bds. 6.95 *(978-1-56145-581-2(4))* Peachtree Pubs.
Stewart, Sarah. The Gardener. Small, David, illus. 2003. (J). (gr. -1-2). 28.95 incl. audio compact disk *(978-1-59112-531-0(6))* Live Oak Media.
—The Gardener. Small, David, illus. 2007. (ENG.). 40p. (J). (gr. -1-2). per. 8.99 *(978-0-312-36749-7(X)*, 9780312367497) Square Fish.
Stockton, Frank Richard. John Gayther's Garden & the Stories Told Therein. 2008. 220p. 26.95 *(978-1-60664-746-2(6))* Rodgers, Alan Bks.
Taylor, W. Y. This Little Piggy Goes Green. 2009. (ENG.). 12p. bds. 3.95 *(978-1-58117-925-5(1)*, Intervisual/Piggy Toes) Bendon, Inc.
Thomas, Patricia. Green Bean! Green Bean! Hunner, Trina L., illus. 2016. 32p. (J). (gr. k-4). 16.95 *(978-1-58469-543-1(9))* Dawn Pubns.
Titherington, Jeanne. Pumpkin Pumpkin. 2015. 24p. pap. 7.00 *(978-1-61003-615-3(8))* Center for the Collaborative Classroom.
Townsend, Brenda. The Toad S Trilogy. 2013. pap. 9.99 *(978-1-62509-709-5(3))* Salem Author Services.
Waddell, Martin. Something So Big. Canty, Charlotte, illus. 2004. (ENG.). 24p. (J). lib. bdg. 23.65 *(978-1-59646-706-4(1))* Dingles & Co.
Warner, Gertrude Chandler, creator. The Garden Thief. 2012. (Boxcar Children Mysteries Ser.: 130). (ENG., Illus.). 128p. (J). (gr. 1-5). 5.99 *(978-0-8075-2752-8(1))* Whitman, Albert & Co.
—The Garden Thief 2012. (Boxcar Children Mysteries Ser.: 130). (ENG., Illus.). 128p. (J). (gr. 1-5). 15.99 *(978-0-8075-2751-1(3))* Whitman, Albert & Co.
Wellington, Monica. Zinnia's Flower Garden. Wellington, Monica, illus. 2007. (ENG., Illus.). 32p. (J). (gr. -1-2). pap. 5.99 *(978-0-14-240787-5(9)*, Puffin Books) Penguin Young Readers Group.
—Zinnia's Flower Garden. 2007. (Illus.). 28p. (gr. k-3). 16.00 *(978-0-7569-8171-6(9))* Perfection Learning Corp.
Weston Woods Staff, creator. Planting a Rainbow. 2011. 38.75 *(978-0-439-80645-9(3))*; 18.95 *(978-0-439-80643-5(7))*; 29.95 *(978-0-439-80436-3(1))* Weston Woods Studios, Inc.
Wiersbitzky, Shannon. What Flowers Remember. 2014. 158p. (J). 18.95 *(978-1-60898-166-3(5))* namelos llc.
Wilbur, Helen. Lily's Victory Garden. Steele, Robert, illus. 2010. (Tales of Young Americans Ser.). (ENG.). 32p. (J). (gr. 2-4). 16.95 *(978-1-58536-450-3(9))* Sleeping Bear Pr.
Wilson, Karma. Mortimer's First Garden. Andreasen, Dan, illus. 2009. (ENG.). 32p. (J). (gr. -1-3). 17.99 *(978-1-4169-4203-0(3)*, McElderry, Margaret K. Bks.) McElderry, Margaret K. Bks.
Wood, Douglas. Aunt Mary's Rose. Shed, Greg & Pham, LeUyen, illus. 2010. (ENG.). 32p. (J). (gr. -1-3). 16.99 *(978-0-7636-1090-6(9))* Candlewick Pr.
Young, Judy. Digger & Daisy Plant a Garden. Sullivan, Dana, illus. 2016. (I AM a READER: Digger & Daisy Ser.). (ENG.). 32p. (J). (gr. k-2). 9.99 *(978-1-58536-931-7(4)*, 204030) Sleeping Bear Pr.
Zepeda, Gwendolyn & Ventura, Gabriela Baeza. Sunflowers/Girasoles. Gambino, Alisha Ann Guadalupe, illus. 2009. (SPA & ENG.). 32p. (J). (gr. -1-2). 16.95 *(978-1-55885-267-9(0)*, Piñata Books) Arte Publico Pr.
Zibart, Rosemary. I Have a Grandma Who ... Herzlich, Valori, illus. 2014. (J). *(978-1-929115-25-9(3))* Azro Pr., Inc.

GARDENING—POETRY

Gordon, Elizabeth. Flower Children: The Little Cousins of the Field & Garden. Ross, M. T., illus. 2008. (ENG.). 96p. (J). (gr. -1-3). pap. 14.95 *(978-1-55709-086-7(6))* Applewood Bks.

GARDENING—VOCATIONAL GUIDANCE

Ferguson. Careers in Focus: Landscaping & Horticulture. 2008. (Careers in Focus Ser.). 184p. (gr. 6-12). 32.95 *(978-0-8160-7280-4(9)*, Ferguson Publishing Co.) Facts On File, Inc.

GARDENS

Agria, Mary A. Second Leaves. 2012. 24p. pap. 11.99 *(978-1-105-32509-0(1))* Lulu Pr., Inc.
Amstutz, Lisa J. Enchanted Gardening: Growing Miniature Gardens, Fairy Gardens, & More. 2016. (Gardening Guides). (ENG., Illus.). 32p. (gr. 3-4). lib. bdg. 27.99 *(978-1-4914-8234-6(6)*, Snap Bks.) Capstone Press of Coughlan Cos.
Ancona, George. It's Our Garden: From Seeds to Harvest in a School Garden. Ancona, George, illus. 2015. (ENG., Illus.). 48p. (J). (gr. k-3). pap. 6.99 *(978-0-7636-7691-9(8))* Candlewick Pr.
Appel, Dee. The Friends in My Garden. Francour, Kathleen, photos by. Date not set. (Tiny Times Board Book Ser.). (Illus.). 10p. (J). bds. 5.99 *(978-0-7369-0564-0(2))* Harvest Hse. Pubs.
Avery, Sebastian. The School Garden: Reason with Shapes & Their Attributes. 2014. (Rosen Common Core Math Readers Ser.). (ENG.). 24p. (J). (gr. 3-4). pap. 8.25 *(978-1-4777-4875-6(X)*, Rosen Classroom) Rosen Publishing Group, Inc., The.
Barlowe, Dot. Flower Gardens to Paint or Color. 2007. (Dover Art Coloring Book Ser.). (ENG., Illus.). 48p. (gr. 3-5). 5.99 *(978-0-486-46204-2(8))* Dover Pubns., Inc.
Basford, Johanna. Secret Garden: An Inky Treasure Hunt & Coloring Book. 2013. (J). lib. bdg. 28.10 *(978-0-606-37119-3(2))* Turtleback Bks.
Bearce, Stephanie. A Kid's Guide to Making a Terrarium. 2009. (Gardening for Kids Ser.). (Illus.). 48p. (J). (gr. 3-6). lib. bdg. 29.95 *(978-1-58415-813-4(1))* Mitchell Lane Pubs., Inc.
Bell, Samantha S. Build a Compact Garden. Stewart, Roger, illus. 2016. (Earth-Friendly Projects Ser.). (ENG.). 24p. (J). (gr. 2-5). 28.50 *(978-1-5038-0784-6(3)*, 210620) Child's World, Inc., The.
Björk, Christina. Linnea in Monet's Garden. Sandin, Joan, tr. Anderson, Lena, illus. 2012. (ENG.). 48p. (J). (-3). 16.99 *(978-1-4022-7729-0(6))*, Sourcebooks Jabberwocky) Sourcebooks, Inc.
Burns Chong, Susan. Community Gardens. 2013. (Urban Gardening & Farming for Teens Ser.). 64p. (YA). (gr. 7-12). 33.25 *(978-1-4777-1777-6(3))* Rosen Publishing Group, Inc., The.
Cole, Katelyn. The Class Terrarium. 2013. (InfoMax Readers Ser.). (ENG.). 24p. (J). (gr. 3-4). pap. 49.50 *(978-1-4777-2585-6(7))*; (Illus.). pap. 8.25 *(978-1-4777-2583-2(0))* Rosen Publishing Group, Inc., The. (Rosen Classroom).
Dee, Gabrielle. Planting a Community Garden: Reason with Shapes & Their Attributes, 1 vol. 2015. (InfoMax Common Core Math Readers Ser.). (ENG.). 24p. (J). pap. 8.25 *(978-1-4777-4576-2(9)*, Rosen Classroom) Rosen Publishing Group, Inc., The.
Dorling Kindersley Publishing Staff. Garden Friends, Pre-Level 1. 2010. (DK Readers Ser.). (ENG.). 32p. (J). (gr. -1-1). 3.99 *(978-0-7566-6167-0(6)*, DK Children) Dorling Kindersley Publishing, Inc.
Dunn, L. Kerr. Dreaming with Animals: Anna Hyatt Huntington & Brookgreen Gardens. Wyrick, Monica, illus. 2017. (Young Palmetto Bks.). (ENG.). 40p. (J). 18.99 *(978-1-61117-820-3(7))* Univ. of South Carolina Pr.
Ely, Lisa & Glassman, Michael. Kinder Gardens: Autumn Fun, 1 vol. 2011. (ENG., Illus.). 64p. (J). pap. 16.99 *(978-0-7643-3853-3(6)*, 9780764338533, Schiffer Publishing Ltd) Schiffer Publishing, Ltd.
Emberley, Rebecca. My Garden/ Mi Jardin. 2005. (SPA & ENG., Illus.). 10p. (J). (gr. -1 — 1). bds. 6.99 *(978-0-316-00049-9(3))* Little, Brown Bks. for Young Readers.
Eubank, Lorie. How Does Your Garden Grow? 2010. 40p. pap. 18.95 *(978-1-4520-6833-6(X))* AuthorHouse.
Forward, Megan. A Patch from Scratch. 2016. (ENG.). 32p. (J). (gr. -1-k). 23.99 **(978-0-670-07829-5(8))** Random Hse. Australia AUS. Dist: Independent Pubs. Group.
Fretland VanVoorst, Jenny. Gardens in Spring. 2015. (Illus.). 24p. (J). lib. bdg. *(978-1-62031-236-0(0))* Jump! Inc.
—Los Jardines en la Primavera. 2015.Tr. of Gardens in Spring. (SPA., Illus.). 24p. (J). lib. bdg. *(978-1-62031-242-1(5)*, Bullfrog Bks.) Jump! Inc.
Fronczak, Emerson. There's a Food Chain in Your Garden! 2013. (InfoMax Readers Ser.). (ENG.). 24p. (J). (gr. 2-3). pap. 8.25 *(978-1-4777-2360-9(9))*; pap. 49.50 *(978-1-4777-2362-3(5))* Rosen Publishing Group, Inc., The. (Rosen Classroom).
Gardens, 4 vols. 2010. (Gardens Ser.). (ENG.). 24p. (gr. k-1). lib. bdg. 65.97 *(978-1-4296-4412-9(5)*, Pebble Bks.) Capstone Press of Coughlan Cos.
Gardens [Capstone Sole Source]. 2010. (Gardens Ser.). 24p. lib. bdg. 82.60 *(978-1-4296-5859-1(2)*, Pebble Bks.) Capstone Press of Coughlan Cos.
Gardiner, Lisa. In the Garden. Flowerpot Press, ed. 2012. (Illus.). 20p. (J). *(978-1-926988-08-5(6))* Flowerpot Children's Pr. Inc.
Harkins, Susan Sales & Harkins, William H. Design Your Own Pond & Water Garden. 2008. (Gardening for Kids Ser.). (Illus.). 48p. (YA). (gr. 1-4). lib. bdg. 29.95 *(978-1-58415-635-2(X))* Mitchell Lane Pubs., Inc.
In the Garden Pack [Scholastic]. 2011. (Gardens Ser.). 24p. pap. 2.00 *(978-1-4296-6309-0(X)*, Pebble Bks.) Capstone Press of Coughlan Cos.
Jordan, Ashley. Gabriella's Butterfly Garden. 2013. (Core Math Skills: Operations & Algebraic Thinking Ser.). 24p. (J). (gr. 1-2). 22.60 *(978-1-4777-2209-1(2))*; (ENG.). pap. 8.25 *(978-1-4777-2025-7(1))* Rosen Publishing Group, Inc., The. (Rosen Classroom).
—Gabriella's Butterfly Garden: Understand & Apply Properties of Operations. 2013. (Rosen Math Readers Ser.). (ENG.). 24p. (J). (gr. 1-2). pap. 49.50 *(978-1-4777-2026-4(X)*, Rosen Classroom) Rosen Publishing Group, Inc., The.

Kalman, Bobbie. My Backyard Community. 2010. (My World Ser.). (ENG., Illus.). 24p. (J). (gr. k-2). *(978-0-7787-9448-6(2))*; pap. *(978-0-7787-9492-9(X))* Crabtree Publishing Co.

King, Zelda. Examining Backyard Habitats. 2009. (Graphic Organizers: Habitats Ser.). 24p. (gr. 2-4). (Illus.). (J). pap. 8.25 *(978-1-4358-3124-7(1))*; 42.50 *(978-1-61513-088-7(8))*; (J). lib. bdg. 22.60 *(978-1-4358-2720-2(1))* Rosen Publishing Group, Inc., The. (PowerKids Pr.).

Krezel, Cindy. Kids' Container Gardening: Year-Round Projects for Inside & Out. Curtis, Bruce, photos by. 2nd ed. 2010. (ENG., Illus.). 88p. (J). (gr. 1-6). pap. 14.95 *(978-1-883052-75-1(0))* Ball Publishing.

—101 Kid-Friendly Plants: Fun Plants & Family Garden Projects. 2008. (ENG., Illus.). 160p. (J). (gr. 1-7). pap. 19.95 *(978-1-883052-54-6(8))* Chicago Review Pr., Inc.

Kuskowski, Alex. Super Simple Butterfly Gardens: A Kid's Guide to Gardening, 1 vol. 2014. (Super Simple Gardening Ser.). (ENG.). 32p. (gr. k-4). 27.07 *(978-1-62403-521-0(3))* ABDO Publishing Co.

—Super Simple Indoor Gardens: A Kid's Guide to Gardening, 1 vol. 2014. (Super Simple Gardening Ser.). (ENG.). 32p. (gr. k-4). 27.07 *(978-1-62403-524-1(8))* ABDO Publishing Co.

Leavitt, Amie. A Backyard Vegetable Garden for Kids. 2008. (Gardening for Kids Ser.). 48p. (YA). (gr. 1-4). lib. bdg. 29.95 *(978-1-58415-634-5(1))* Mitchell Lane Pubs., Inc.

Leavitt, Amie Jane. A Backyard Flower Garden for Kids. 2008. (Gardening for Kids Ser.). (Illus.). 48p. (YA). (gr. 1-4). lib. bdg. 29.95 *(978-1-58415-633-8(3))* Mitchell Lane Pubs., Inc.

Loreno, Rose, et al. In the Garden. 2007. (Windows on Literacy Ser.). (ENG., Illus.). 12p. (J). pap. 10.95 *(978-0-7922-8492-5(5))* CENGAGE Learning.

Mary, Mary: 6 Small Books. (gr. k-2). 23.00 *(978-0-7635-8499-3(1))* Rigby Education.

McKendry, Sam. A Little Whale Tale. Castillon, Carly, illus. 2005. (Stories to Share Ser.). 18p. (J). (gr. -1-k). 9.95 *(978-1-58117-146-4(3)*, Intervisual/Piggy Toes) Bendon, Inc.

Messner, Kate. Up in the Garden & down in the Dirt. Neal, Christopher Silas, illus. 2017. (ENG.). 56p. (J). pap. 7.99 *(978-1-4521-6136-5(4))* Chronicle Bks. LLC.

—Up in the Garden & down in the Dirt. 2015. (ENG., Illus.). 52p. (J). (gr. k-3). 16.99 *(978-1-4521-1936-6(8))* Chronicle Bks. LLC.

Moonlight Publishing Ltd Staff & Allaire, Caroline. Let's Look at the Garden. 2013. (ENG.). 36p. (J). (gr. 1-4). pap. 11.99 *(978-1-85103-340-9(8))* Moonlight Publishing, Ltd. GBR. Dist: Independent Pubs. Group.

Mr Kean's Garden: Fourth Grade Guided Comprehension Level O. (On Our Way to English Ser.). (gr. 4-18). 34.50 *(978-0-7578-7166-5(6))* Rigby Education.

National Geographic Kids & Musgrave, Ruth. In My Garden. 2017. (Look & Learn Ser.). (ENG., Illus.). 24p. (J). (-k). bds. 6.99 ***(978-1-4263-2844-2(3)***, National Geographic Children's Bks.) National Geographic Society.

Nichol, Barbara. One Small Garden. Moser, Barry, illus. 2004. (ENG.). 56p. (J). (gr. 3-7). pap. 9.95 *(978-0-88776-687-9(0)*, Tundra Bks.) Tundra Bks. CAN. Dist: Penguin Random Hse. LLC.

Rich, Steve. My School Yard Garden. 2014. (ENG., Illus.). 32p. (J). (gr. k-3). pap. 12.95 *(978-1-938946-21-9(9))* National Science Teachers Assn.

Rissman, Rebecca. Parks, 1 vol. 2013. (Picture This! Ser.). (ENG.). 24p. (gr. -1-k). pap. 9.95 *(978-1-4109-5259-2(2)*, NA-r) Heinemann-Raintree.

RSPB Garden Nature Colouring Book. 2013. (ENG., Illus.). 48p. pap. 7.95 *(978-1-4081-9250-4(0)*, 9781408192504, A&C Black Childrens & Educational) Bloomsbury Publishing Plc GBR. Dist: Macmillan.

Sarkisian, K. I Go to the Garden: Learning the Hard G Sound. 2009. (PowerPhonics Ser.). 24p. (gr. 1-1). 39.90 *(978-1-60851-448-9(X)*, PowerKids Pr.) Rosen Publishing Group, Inc., The.

Scheunemann, Pam. Cool Stuff for Your Garden: Creative Projects for Kids, 1 vol. 2012. (Cool Stuff Ser.). (ENG., Illus.). 32p. (J). (gr. 3-6). 28.50 *(978-1-61714-984-9(5))* ABDO Publishing Co.

Schuh, Mari. All Kinds of Gardens. 2010. (Gardens Ser.). (ENG.). 24p. (gr. k-1). pap. 35.70 *(978-1-4296-5151-6(2))*; lib. bdg. 21.99 *(978-1-4296-3981-1(4))* Capstone Press of Coughlan Cos. (Pebble Bks.).

—All Kinds of Gardens [Scholastic]. 2011. (Gardens Ser.). 24p. pap. 0.50 *(978-1-4296-6305-2(7)*, Pebble Bks.) Capstone Press of Coughlan Cos.

—Animals in the Garden. 2010. (Gardens Ser.). (ENG.). 24p. (gr. k-1). pap. 35.70 *(978-1-4296-5152-3(0)*, Pebble Bks.) Capstone Press of Coughlan Cos.

—Animals in the Garden [Scholastic]. 2011. (Gardens Ser.). 24p. pap. 0.50 *(978-1-4296-6306-9(5)*, Pebble Bks.) Capstone Press of Coughlan Cos.

—Tools for the Garden [Scholastic]. 2011. (Gardens Ser.). 24p. pap. 0.50 *(978-1-4296-6308-3(1)*, Pebble Bks.) Capstone Press of Coughlan Cos.

Schuh, Mari C. From Soil to Garden. 2016. (Start to Finish, Second Ser.). (ENG., Illus.). 24p. (J). (gr. k-3). 23.99 *(978-1-5124-0946-8(4))* Lerner Publishing Group.

Shava, Ryder. Garden Fun with Mrs. Ochoa, 01 vols., 1. 2016. (Rosen REAL Readers: STEM & STEAM Collection). (ENG.). 12p. (J). pap. 6.33 *(978-1-5081-1563-2(X)*, Rosen Classroom) Rosen Publishing Group, Inc., The.

Spilsbury, Louise. How Community Gardens Work. 2013. (EcoWorks Ser.). 32p. (J). (gr. 3-5). pap. 63.00 *(978-1-4339-9558-3(1))*; pap. 10.50 *(978-1-4339-9557-6(3))*; (ENG., Illus.). lib. bdg. 26.60 *(978-1-4339-9556-9(5))* Stevens, Gareth Publishing LLLP.

Steffora, Tracey. Measuring in the Garden, 1 vol. 2011. (Math Around Us Ser.). (ENG.). 24p. (gr. -1-1). 22.65 *(978-1-4329-4926-6(8))*; pap. 6.29 *(978-1-4329-4934-1(9))* Heinemann-Raintree. (Acorn).

Wellington, Monica. My Garden. 2011. (Dover Sticker Bks.). (ENG., Illus.). 6p. (J). (gr. k-5). 7.99 *(978-0-486-48381-8(9))* Dover Pubns., Inc.

—My Garden Stickers. 2011. (Dover Sticker Bks.). (ENG., Illus.). 4p. (J). (gr. k-3). pap. 5.99 *(978-0-486-48374-0(6))* Dover Pubns., Inc.

Wild Garden. 2017. (ENG.). (J). 19.99 ***(978-0-7945-3957-3(2)***, Usborne) EDC Publishing.

Wood, Alix. Fairy Garden Design. 2017. (Design It! Ser.). 32p. (gr. 3-4). pap. 63.00 ***(978-1-5382-0780-2(X))*** Stevens, Gareth Publishing LLLP.

GARDENS—FICTION

Ackland, Nick. Little Lion in the Garden. Walshaw, Sam, illus. 2017. (Little Explorers Ser.). (ENG.). 10p. (J). (gr. -1 — 1). bds. 6.99 *(978-0-7641-6895-6(9))* Barron's Educational Series, Inc.

Akley, Jason. Sweet Pea & the Bumblebee. 2007. (ENG.). 36p. (J). per. 16.95 *(978-1-4327-0341-7(2))* Outskirts Pr., Inc.

Aldrick, Shirley H. F. Gordon, the Great Gobbley Grasshopper. 2011. 32p. pap. 13.00 *(978-1-60976-643-6(1)*, Strategic Bk. Publishing) Strategic Book Publishing & Rights Agency (SBPRA).

Alemagna, Beatrice. Bugs in the Garden. 2011. (ENG.). 40p. (gr. -1-2). 12.95 *(978-0-7148-6238-5(X))* Phaidon Pr., Inc.

Alexander, Carmen. Garden Stories: Rosemarie's Garden, Rosemarie's Roof Garden & Rosemarie Returns to Her Garden. Roswell, Stacey, illus. 2006. 60p. (J). pap. 14.99 *(978-1-886383-55-5(3))* Blue Forge Pr.

Aliki. Quiet in the Garden. Aliki, illus. 2009. (ENG., Illus.). 32p. (J). (gr. -1-2). 17.99 *(978-0-06-155207-6(0)*, Greenwillow Bks.) HarperCollins Pubs.

Anderson, Debra. The Seed Sower, Walter's Special Garden. Lucas, Diane, illus. 2012. 24p. pap. 11.95 *(978-1-61244-097-2(5))* Halo Publishing International.

Anderson, Virginia Lynn. The Flying Phlox. 2009. (Illus.). 24p. pap. 13.95 *(978-1-60844-151-8(2))* Dog Ear Publishing, LLC.

—The Very Lonely Garden. 2011. (Illus.). 34p. 24.99 *(978-1-4575-0526-3(6))*; pap. 14.99 *(978-1-4575-0518-8(5))* Dog Ear Publishing, LLC.

Anholt, Laurence. The Magical Garden of Claude Monet. (Anholt's Artists Books for Children Ser.). (ENG., Illus.). 32p. (J). 2007. (gr. -1-3). *(978-0-7641-3855-3(3))* 2003. 16.99 *(978-0-7641-5574-1(1))* Barron's Educational Series, Inc.

Anna. The Magic Money Tree. 2009. (Illus.). 20p. pap. 15.49 *(978-1-4389-0472-6(X))* AuthorHouse.

Arno. A Tiger in My Garden: A Do-It-Yourself Pop-Up Book. 2014. (ENG.). 32p. (J). (gr. 2-5). 19.95 *(978-3-7913-7193-1(2))* Prestel Verlag GmbH & Co KG. DEU. Dist: Penguin Random Hse. LLC.

Arthur, Peggy Ann. Come & Look in Grandma's Garden. 2012. 26p. 24.95 *(978-1-4560-3988-2(1))* America Star Bks.

Ashman, Sarah & Parent, Nancy. Holly Bloom's Garden. Mitchell, Lori, illus. 2004. (ENG.). 32p. (J). (gr. k-3). 15.95 *(978-0-9729225-0-0(4))* Flashlight Pr.

Bailey, Lori Gayle. The Dog Who Loved Cucumbers. 2009. 24p. pap. 11.95 *(978-1-4490-2457-4(2))* AuthorHouse.

Baker, Amanda, illus. Zack's Zany Zucchiniland. 2012. 32p. (J). 17.95 *(978-0-9832383-1-7(6))* Black Garnet Pr.

Balian, Lorna. A Garden for a Groundhog, 1 vol. Balian, Lorna, illus. 2011. (ENG., Illus.). 32p. (J). pap. 6.95 *(978-1-59572-296-6(3))* Star Bright Bks., Inc.

Ballou, Bert. Anthony's Amazing Garden. 2011. 20p. pap. 9.99 *(978-1-936750-12-2(0))* Yorkshire Publishing Group.

Barker, Cicely Mary & Potter, Beatrix. Magical Secret Garden. 2010. (Flower Fairies Ser.). (ENG.). 24p. (J). (gr. k-3). 16.99 *(978-0-7232-6440-8(6)*, Warne) Penguin Young Readers Group.

Barner, Bob. I Have a Garden. Barner, Bob, illus. (I Like to Read(r) Ser.). (ENG., Illus.). 24p. (J). (gr. -1-3). 2014. 6.99 *(978-0-8234-3056-7(1))* 2013. 14.95 *(978-0-8234-2527-3(4))* Holiday Hse., Inc.

Barnes, Ben. Don't Eat My Garden. Barnes, Page, illus. 2007. 28p. per. 24.95 *(978-1-4241-8964-9(0))* America Star Bks.

Bauer, Linda. Fruits & Flowers & Footprints OH MY!!! 2007. (Illus.). 29p. (J). 13.99 *(978-0-9798146-0-0(X))* Bauer, Linda.

Beach, Kathy Ann. Helping a Garden Grow, 1 vol. 2010. 20p. pap. 24.95 *(978-1-4489-8836-5(5))* PublishAmerica, Inc.

Beharrell, Gayle. The Adventures of Charlie. 2008. 36p. pap. 16.99 *(978-1-4389-2546-2(8))* AuthorHouse.

Benchmark Education Co., LLC. Mrs. MacDonald's Garden Big Book. 2014. (Shared Reading Foundations Ser.). (J). (gr. -1). *(978-1-4509-9450-7(4))* Benchmark Education Co.

Berrow, G. M. My Little Pony: Princess Cadance & the Spring Hearts Garden. 2016. (Princess Collection). (ENG., Illus.). 160p. (J). (gr. 3-7). 9.99 *(978-0-316-38930-3(7))* Little, Brown Bks. for Young Readers.

Berry, Eileen M. Buttercup Hill. Harrald-Pilz, Marilee, illus. 2006. 39p. (J). (gr. -1-3). pap. *(978-1-59166-667-7(8))* BJU Pr.

Betances, Brendan. Granny's Garden. 2006. (Neighborhood Readers Ser.). (ENG., Illus.). 12p. (gr. 1-3). pap. 5.90 *(978-1-4042-7022-0(1)*, Rosen Classroom) Rosen Publishing Group, Inc., The.

Beyers, Andrea. Johnny Joins the Army. LeTourneau, Anthony Alex, illus. 2008. (Flower Kingdom Ser.: Vol. 2). 40p. (J). 16.95 *(978-0-9800754-1-0(6))* RockTuff.

Blackshaw, Win. David's Dinosaur. 2009. 104p. pap. 17.55 *(978-1-4092-3704-4(4))* Lulu Pr., Inc.

Bogacki, Tomek. Mi Primer Jardin. 2003. (Picture Bks.). (SPA., Illus.). (J). *(978-970-690-649-6(5))* Planeta Mexicana Editorial S. A. de C. V.

Bond, Michael. Paddington in the Garden. Alley, R. W., illus. 2015. (Paddington Ser.). (ENG.). 32p. (J). (gr. -1-3). 17.99 *(978-0-06-231844-2(6))* HarperCollins Pubs.

Bonnell, Kris. A Garden Is Fun. 2006. (J). pap. 5.95 *(978-1-933727-37-0(3))* Reading Reading Bks., LLC.

Bowlby, Linda S. The Rock Garden. Helms, Dana, illus. 2008. 29p. (J). (gr. -1-3). pap. 9.95 *(978-0-9779993-4-7(3))* Red Earth Publishing.

Braun, Sebastien. Who's Hiding? 2013. (ENG., Illus.). 16p. (J). (gr. -1 — 1). bds. 6.99 *(978-0-7636-5932-5(0))* Candlewick Pr.

Brenner, Barbara. Good Morning, Garden. Ortakales, Denise, illus. 2004. (ENG.). 32p. (J). (gr. -1-k). 15.95 *(978-1-55971-888-2(9))* Cooper Square Publishing Llc.

Brezenoff, Steve. The Disappearing Fruit: An Interactive Mystery Adventure. Calo, Marcos, illus. 2017. (You Choose Stories: Field Trip Mysteries Ser.). (ENG.). 112p. (gr. 3-7). lib. bdg. 32.65 *(978-1-4965-2643-4(0))* Stone Arch Bks.

Brightwood, Laura. The Cheery Garden. Pifer, Kimberly, ed. Brightwood, Laura, illus. 2012. (Illus.). (J). *(978-1-934409-38-1(3))* 3-C Institute for Social Development.

Brodhead, Kimberly Renee. The Seedling: The Osarian Tales. 2008. 232p. pap. 24.95 *(978-1-60703-814-6(5))* America Star Bks.

Brown, E.A. Gossamer. 2012. 24p. pap. 24.95 *(978-1-4626-5043-9(0))* America Star Bks.

Brown, Jr. Jimmy's Alphabet Garden. 2013. 32p. pap. 13.50 *(978-1-4575-1797-6(3))* Dog Ear Publishing, LLC.

Bug in the Garden. Date not set. (Illus.). (J). bds. 1.98 *(978-0-7525-9839-0(2))* Parragon, Inc.

Burick, Rebecca. Little Daisy Tutu. Burick, Rebecca & Burick Jr., Michael, illus. 2012. 28p. pap. 24.95 *(978-1-4560-6883-7(0))* America Star Bks.

Burnett, Frances Hodgson. Geheidie Garten.Tr. of Secret Garden. (GER.). pap. 18.95 *(978-3-423-07317-2(9))* Deutscher Taschenbuch Verlag GmbH & Co KG DEU. Dist: Distribooks, Inc.

—The Secret Garden. McKowen, Scott, illus. 2004. (Sterling Unabridged Classics Ser.). (ENG.). 248p. (J). (gr. 5). 9.95 *(978-1-4027-1459-7(9))* Sterling Publishing Co., Inc.

—The Secret Garden. 2012. (Illus.). 304p. *(978-1-4351-4212-1(8))* Barnes & Noble, Inc.

—The Secret Garden. Robinson, Charles, illus. 2011. 304p. (J). *(978-1-4351-3344-0(7))* Barnes & Noble, Inc.

—The Secret Garden. Moore, Inga, illus. 2008. (ENG.). 272p. (J). (gr. 1-4). 22.99 *(978-0-7636-3161-1(2))* Candlewick Pr.

—The Secret Garden. 2014. (Oxford Children's Classics Ser.). (ENG.). 352p. pap. 9.95 *(978-0-19-273827-1(5))* Oxford Univ. Pr., Inc.

—The Secret Garden. 2011. (ENG.). 288p. *(978-1-904633-31-0(5)*, Collector's Library, The) Pan Macmillan.

—The Secret Garden. 2003. (ENG., Illus.). 288p. (gr. 12-18). mass mkt. 5.95 *(978-0-451-52883-4(2)*, Signet) Penguin Publishing Group.

—The Secret Garden. Lawrie, Robin, illus. 2008. (Puffin Classics Ser.). (ENG.). 368p. (J). (gr. 3-7). 5.99 *(978-0-14-132106-6(7)*, Puffin Books) Penguin Young Readers Group.

—The Secret Garden. 2003. (Modern Library Classics Ser.). (ENG.). 288p. (J). (gr. 3-7). pap. 7.95 *(978-0-8129-6998-6(7)*, Modern Library) Random House Publishing Group.

—The Secret Garden. 2013. (ENG.). 384p. (J). (gr. 4-7). pap. 11.99 *(978-0-09-957295-4(8))* Random Hse. GBR. Dist: Independent Pubs. Group.

—The Secret Garden. 2011. (ENG., Illus.). (J). (gr. 3-7). 15.99 ***(978-1-61382-911-0(6))*** Simon & Brown.

—The Secret Garden. Ingpen, Robert R., illus. 2011. (Sterling Illustrated Classics Ser.). (ENG.). 240p. (J). (gr. 5-18). 19.95 *(978-1-4027-7872-8(4))* Sterling Publishing Co., Inc.

—The Secret Garden. Moore, Inga, illus. 2010. (ENG.). 272p. (J). (gr. 1-4). pap. 16.99 *(978-0-7636-4732-2(2))* Candlewick Pr.

—The Secret Garden, 1 vol. Simon, Ute, illus. 2011. (Calico Illustrated Classics Ser.: No. 3). (ENG.). 112p. (J). (gr. 3-6). 27.07 *(978-1-61641-108-4(2))* Magic Wagon.

—The Secret Garden. Corvino, Lucy, illus. 2005. (Classic Starts(tm) Ser.). (ENG.). 160p. (J). (gr. 2-4). 6.95 *(978-1-4027-1319-4(3))* Sterling Publishing Co., Inc.

—The Secret Garden. Tudor, Tasha, illus. 100th anniv. ed. 2010. (Trophy Bk.). (ENG.). 384p. (J). (gr. 4-18). reprint ed. pap. 6.99 *(978-0-06-440188-3(X))* HarperCollins Pubs.

—The Secret Garden. Hunt, Peter, ed. 2011. (Oxford World's Classics Ser.). (ENG.). 304p. (gr. 7-18). pap. 8.95 *(978-0-19-958822-0(8))* Oxford Univ. Pr., Inc.

—The Secret Garden: A Young Reader's Edition of the Classic Story. 2005. 332p. 29.95 *(978-1-4218-0619-8(3)*, 1st World Library - Literary Society) 1st World Publishing, Inc.

—The Secret Garden: A Young Reader's Edition of the Classic Story. (J). 22.95 *(978-0-8488-0692-7(1))* Amereon Ltd.

—The Secret Garden: A Young Reader's Edition of the Classic Story. 2004. (Illus.). (J). (gr. 1-4). spiral bd. *(978-0-616-14565-4(9))*; spiral bd. *(978-0-616-14566-1(7))* Canadian National Institute for the Blind/Institut National Canadien pour les Aveugles.

—The Secret Garden: A Young Reader's Edition of the Classic Story. 2005. 132p. per. 5.95 *(978-1-4209-2229-5(7))* Digireads.com Publishing.

—The Secret Garden: A Young Reader's Edition of the Classic Story. 2004. reprint ed. pap. 28.95 *(978-1-4179-2544-5(2))*; pap. 1.99 *(978-1-4192-8193-8(3))* Kessinger Publishing, LLC.

—The Secret Garden: A Young Reader's Edition of the Classic Story. (English As a Second Language Bk.). (Illus.). 92p. pap. 4.46 net. *(978-0-582-53417-9(8))* Longman Publishing Group.

—The Secret Garden: A Young Reader's Edition of the Classic Story. 304p. (J). (gr. 3-5). pap. 4.95 *(978-0-8072-1412-1(4)*, Listening Library) Random Hse. Audio Publishing Group.

—The Secret Garden: A Young Reader's Edition of the Classic Story. 2005. (ENG.). 24.95 *(978-1-55742-519-5(1))*; pap. 15.95 *(978-1-55742-524-9(8))* Wildside Pr., LLC.

—The Secret Garden: With a Discussion of Compassion. Lauter, Richard, illus. 2003. (Values in Action Illustrated Classics Ser.). 191p. (J). *(978-1-59203-037-8(8))* Learning Challenge, Inc.

—The Secret Garden Book & Charm. Tudor, Tasha, illus. deluxe ed. 2005. (Charming Classics). 368p. (J). 9.99 *(978-0-06-075771-7(X)*, HarperFestival) HarperCollins Pubs.

Burnett, Frances Hodgson & Naxos of America Staff. The Secret Garden. 3rd ed. 2008. (Hear It Read It Classics Ser.: 0). (ENG., Illus.). 144p. (J). (gr. 2-4). 9.95 *(978-1-4022-1244-4(5)*, Sourcebooks Jabberwocky) Sourcebooks, Inc.

Burnette, Margarette. Counting in the Crazy Garden. Henson, Brooke, illus. 2008. (Chipper Kids Ser.). 30p. (J). (gr. -1-2). 15.95 *(978-0-9653791-3-7(2))* JenPrint Pubns., LLC.

Buxton, Jane. In My Garden. Teo, Ali, illus. 2010. (ENG.). 8p. (gr. k-1). pap. 7.95 *(978-1-61181-033-2(7)*, Kaeden Bks.) Kaeden Corp.

Cabral, Jeane. Kitty in the Grass. 2009. (Jeane Cabral Bks.). (Illus.). (J). bds. 12.99 *(978-1-934650-06-6(4))* Just For Kids Pr., LLC.

Calarco, Donald Charles. In a Dandelion's World: A Small Book with a Big Story! 2009. 40p. pap. 17.95 *(978-1-4327-1167-2(9))* Outskirts Pr., Inc.

Candlewick Press Editors. Peppa Pig & the Vegetable Garden. 2015. (Peppa Pig Ser.). lib. bdg. 16.00 *(978-0-606-36856-8(6))* Turtleback Bks.

Capucilli, Alyssa Satin. Biscuit in the Garden. Schories, Pat, illus. 2013. (My First I Can Read Ser.). (ENG.). 32p. (J). (gr. -1-3). 16.99 *(978-0-06-193505-3(0))*; pap. 3.99 *(978-0-06-193504-6(2))* HarperCollins Pubs.

—Biscuit in the Garden. 2013. (Biscuit: My First I Can Read! Ser.). (J). lib. bdg. 13.55 *(978-0-606-27157-8(0)*, Turtleback) Turtleback Bks.

Carbone, Elisa & Wells, Rosemary. Diana's White House Garden. Hill, Jen, illus. 2016. (ENG.). 44p. (J). (gr. k-3). bds. 17.99 *(978-0-670-01649-5(7)*, Viking Books for Young Readers) Penguin Young Readers Group.

Carlson, Nancy. Harriet & the Garden. 2nd rev. ed. 2004. (ENG., Illus.). 32p. (J). (gr. k-2). pap. 6.95 *(978-1-57505-612-8(7))* Lerner Publishing Group.

Carlson, Nancy, tr. & illus. Harriet & the Garden. Carlson, Nancy, illus. 2nd rev. ed. 2005. (Nancy Carlson's Neighborhood Ser.). 32p. (gr. k-2). 15.95 *(978-1-57505-710-1(7))* Lerner Publishing Group.

Carriger, Candace. Inside My Garden. Allen, Cassandra, illus. 2011. 46p. (J). pap. 11.95 *(978-0-9816047-5-6(7))* Sadie Bks.

Casey, Mark. An African Princess: Deasha's Wild Adventure. 2010. (Illus.). 54p. pap. 11.95 *(978-1-4327-3864-8(X))* Outskirts Pr., Inc.

Chambers, Melinda. The Day the Snapdragons Snapped Back. Spiker, Sue Ann, illus. 2007. 32p. (J). 16.95 *(978-0-929915-72-2(0))* Headline Bks., Inc.

A City Garden, 6 Packs. (gr. -1-2). 27.00 *(978-0-7635-9441-1(5))* Rigby Education.

Cohn, Diana. Mr Goethes Garden. Mirocha, Paul, illus. 2003. (ENG.). 32p. (J). 17.95 *(978-0-88010-521-7(6))* SteinerBooks, Inc.

Colburn, Cherie Foster. Our Shadow Garden. 2010. (ENG., Illus.). 32p. (J). 19.95 *(978-1-933979-69-4(0)*, 2a670c16-6bf1-4046-9b18-a6f621294483) Bright Sky Pr.

Collesano, Melissa J. Pheobe Mckeeby's Garden Apartment. 2011. 44p. pap. 21.99 *(978-1-4628-5506-3(7))* Xlibris Corp.

Collins, Peggy. In the Garden. 2012. (ENG., Illus.). 40p. bds. 6.99 *(978-1-60433-150-9(X)*, Applesauce Pr.) Cider Mill Pr. Bk. Pubs., LLC.

—In the Garden. Collins, Peggy, illus. 2009. (ENG., Illus.). 40p. (J). 14.95 *(978-1-60433-026-7(0)*, Applesauce Pr.) Cider Mill Pr. Bk. Pubs., LLC.

Colorful Garden: A Feelings Coloring Book. 2005. (Illus.). 17p. (J). 6.99 *(978-0-9769150-0-3(6))* Bright Spots.

Cooper, Jayda. My Mother's Garden. 2016. (Rosen REAL Readers: STEM & STEAM Collection). 8p. (gr. 1-k). pap. 5.46 *(978-1-5081-2589-1(9)*, Rosen Classroom) Rosen Publishing Group, Inc., The.

Corderoy, Tracey. Magical Snow Garden. Chapman, Jane, illus. 2014. (ENG.). 32p. (J). (gr. -1-3). 16.99 *(978-1-58925-162-5(8))* Tiger Tales.

Crespeno, John. Toby: The Mouse Who Lived in a Pumpkin. 2011. 84p. pap. 28.68 *(978-1-4634-1632-4(6))* AuthorHouse.

Cronick, Mitch. In the Garden. 2005. (Big Cat Ser.). (gr. k-2). pap. 6.50 *(978-1-60457-007-6(5))* Pacific Learning, Inc.

Cureton-Helfner, Donna Lynn. The Adventures of Itsy & Willy Wabbit: In Search of Lillian the Ladybug. 2012. 16p. pap. 24.95 *(978-1-4626-8547-9(1))* America Star Bks.

Curry, Peter. Millie in the Garden. 2004. (First Words with Millie Ser.). (Illus.). 12p. (J). bds. 3.99 *(978-1-85854-507-3(2))* Brimax Books Ltd. GBR. Dist: Byeway Bks.

Dalmatian Press Staff. Maggie's Colorful Garden. 2008. (ENG.). 5p. bds. 4.95 *(978-1-58117-727-5(5)*, Intervisual/Piggy Toes) Bendon, Inc.

Dalmatian Press Staff, adapted by. The Secret Garden. (Illus.). (J). 9.95 *(978-1-56156-312-8(9))* Kidsbooks, LLC.

Davidson, Susanna, retold by. Secret Garden (Picture Book) 2008. (Picture Book Classics Ser.). 24p. (J). 9.99 *(978-0-7945-2232-2(7)*, Usborne) EDC Publishing.

Davis, Caroline. Sparkly Garden. Davis, Caroline, illus. 2008. (Tiger Tales Ser.). (Illus.). 8p. (J). (gr. -1). bds. 6.95 *(978-1-58925-830-3(4))* Tiger Tales.

Davis, Chasta. Maggie's Little Strawberry, 1 vol. 2010. 20p. pap. 24.95 *(978-1-4489-5486-5(X))* PublishAmerica, Inc.

Davis, Maggie Steincrohn. A Garden of Whales. O'Connell, Jennifer Barrett, illus. 2008. (ENG.). 32p. (J). (gr. -1-2). reprint ed. pap. 6.95 *(978-0-944475-35-5(3)*, 9780944475355) Firefly Bks., Ltd.

Deluca, Laura. Flora & the Silver Coins. Manni, Mia (Maio), illus. 2011. 40p. pap. 24.95 *(978-1-4560-7752-5(X))* America Star Bks.

Dickens, Sara Jo. Karner's Quest for Blue Lupine. Nancy, Scheibe, illus. 2014. (J). 18.95 *(978-1-59298-923-2(3))* Beaver's Pond Pr., Inc.

Dinardo, Jeff. Worm & Farmer Maguire: Teamwork/Working Together. Joven, John, illus. 2014. (Funny Bone Readers: Being a Friend Ser.). 24p. (gr. -1-1). pap. 4.99 *(978-1-939656-07-0(9))* Red Chair Pr.

Dodee & Dodee. That Big Old Round Orange Thing: A Mrs. Tockalocka Adventure. 2006. (Illus.). 60p. (J). per. 9.95 *(978-1-60002-129-9(8)*, 3931) Mountain Valley Publishing, LLC.

Domingos, Fernanda Feitosa Rosas. O Jardim / the Garden. 2012. 20p. pap. 11.59 *(978-1-4669-6606-2(8))* Trafford Publishing.

Dompierre, Judith E. Wow, What's That? 2012. 48p. pap. 24.95 *(978-1-4626-9332-0(6))* America Star Bks.

Dozier, Mike. Zack & the Bean Stalk. 2009. pap. 10.00 *(978-1-61584-582-8(8))* Independent Pub.

Dyan, Penelope. Adam. 2011. 34p. pap. 11.96 *(978-1-935630-94-4(6))* Bellissima Publishing, LLC.

Ebel, Sherry. Cassie's Magic Doors the Butterfly Garden. 2012. 36p. pap. 21.99 *(978-1-4797-0108-7(4))* Xlibris Corp.

Erlich, Bev. Pink Roses Everywhere. gif. ed. 2004. (Illus.). 64p. (J). 14.95 *(978-0-9743913-0-4(1))* Snojoy Publishing.

Eves, Sue. Hic. 2003. (Illus.). 32p. (J). 19.99 *(978-0-370-32645-0(8))* Random Hse. GBR. Dist: Trafalgar Square Publishing.

Fairy Gardens Magic Painting Book. 2017. (Magic Painting Bks.). (ENG.). (J). pap. 9.99 ***(978-0-7945-3798-2(7)***, Usborne) EDC Publishing.

E
F
G

Falconer, Ian, et al. Olivia & Her Great Adventures. Osterhold, Jared & Johnson, Shane L., illus. 2012. (J). (978-1-4351-4316-6(7), Simon Spotlight) Simon Spotlight.

Falwell, Cathryn. Mystery Vine. Falwell, Cathryn, illus. 2009. (Illus.). 32p. (J). lib. bdg. 17.89 (978-0-06-177197-2(X), Greenwillow Bks.) HarperCollins Pubs.

Ficklin, Jonene H. The Garden Gate. 2005. (YA). 14.95 (978-0-9761188-2-4(3)) Victor's Crown Publishing.

Finch, Keith. Poppy Cat's Garden. Jones, Lara, illus. 2008. (ENG.). 8p. (J). (gr. 3-6). bds. 16.95 (978-0-230-01715-3(0), Macmillan) Pan Macmillan GBR. Dist: Trans-Atlantic Pubns., Inc.

Fine, Maureen. My Two Shepherds in the Garden: A Lesson in Listening. 2012. 24p. pap. 14.93 (978-1-4669-1991-4(4)) Trafford Publishing.

Fiona Fox Staff, ed. The Secret Garden. 2012. (ENG., Illus.). 64p. 15.00 (978-1-84135-837-6(1)) Award Pubns. Ltd. GBR. Dist: Parkwest Pubns., Inc.

Fitzl, Richelle Kristi, illus. Grandma's Garden. 2004. (J). (978-0-9741657-1-4(9)) Galaxia Publishing Group, LLC.

Fleischman, Paul. Seedfolks. Pedersen, Judy, illus. 2004. (Joanna Cotler Bks.). (ENG.). 112p. (YA). (gr. 8-18). pap. 8.99 (978-0-06-447207-4(8), HarperTeen) HarperCollins Pubs.

—Seedfolks. Pedersen, Judy, illus. 2004. (Joanna Colter Bks.). 102p. (YA). (gr. 5-9). 19.65 (978-0-613-18276-8(6), Turtleback) Turtleback Bks.

Fogliano, Julie. And Then It's Spring. Stead, Erin E., illus. 2012. (ENG.). 32p. (J). (gr. -1-2). 17.99 (978-1-59643-624-4(7), 9781596436244) Roaring Brook Pr.

—And Then It's Spring. 2013. (J). (gr. k-3). (978-0-545-57133-3(2)) Weston Woods Studios, Inc.

Fogwill, Joyce Graham. Bubs the Bumblebee & Her Most Unfortunate Fortunate Adventure. 2009. 24p. pap. 12.99 (978-1-4490-5042-9(5)) AuthorHouse.

—Bubs the Bumblebee & the Spider's Web. 2012. (ENG.). 24p. (J). pap. 12.95 (978-1-4327-9586-3(4)) Outskirts Pr., Inc.

Foreman, Michael. Evie & the Man Who Helped God. 2003. (ENG., Illus.). 32p. (J). 18.00 (978-1-84270-219-2(X)) Andersen Pr. GBR. Dist: Independent Pubs. Group.

—El Jardin del Nino: Una Historia de Esperanza. Diego, Rapi & Flores, Martha, illus. 2009. (SPA.). 30p. (J). (gr. 1-3). 14.99 (978-1-933032-56-6(1)) Lectorum Pubns., Inc.

Fortune, Tracy. Kaila's Garden. 2009. 32p. pap. 14.98 (978-0-557-02254-0(1)) Lulu Pr., Inc.

Francis, Pauline & Burnett, Frances Hodgson. The Secret Garden. 2003. (Fast Track Classics Ser.). (Illus.). 48p. (YA). pap. (978-0-237-52535-4(6)) Evans Brothers, Ltd.

Funk, Lynda. The Snake, the Humming Bird & Me. 2013. 44p. pap. 19.99 (978-1-4685-3329-3(0)) AuthorHouse.

Gabbitas, Jay. A Smell in the Air. 2011. (Illus.). 20p. (gr. 2-4). pap. 12.12 (978-1-4520-3220-7(3)) AuthorHouse.

Galvin, Laura Gates. My First Garden. 2009. (Sesame Street Carry-a-Tune Ser.). 24p. (J). (gr. -1). pap. 4.99 incl. audio compact disk (978-1-59069-864-8(9)) Studio Mouse LLC.

Garis, Howard Roger. Daddy takes us to the Garden. 2005. 25.95 (978-1-4218-1462-9(5)); 124p. pap. 10.95 (978-1-4218-1562-6(1)) 1st World Publishing, Inc. (1st World Library - Literary Society).

—Daddy Takes Us to the Garden. 2007. (Illus.). 132p. per. (978-1-4065-2766-7(1)) Dodo Pr.

Geddes, Anne. This Little Baby. 2014. (ENG., Illus.). 24p. (J). bds. 8.99 (978-1-4022-9828-8(5)) Sourcebooks, Inc.

George, Lindsay Barrett & George, Lindsay B. In the Garden: Who's Been Here? George, Lindsay Barrett, illus. 2006. (ENG., Illus.). 48p. (J). (gr. -1-3). 17.99 (978-0-06-078762-2(7), Greenwillow Bks.) HarperCollins Pubs.

Geras, Adèle. Lizzie's Wish. 2009. (Historical House Ser.). 144p. (YA). (gr. 5-18). pap. 5.99 (978-0-7945-2337-4(4), Usborne) EDC Publishing.

Gershator, Phillis. Who's in the Garden? McDonald, Jill, illus. 2010. (ENG.). 24p. (J). (gr. -1-k). 14.99 (978-1-84686-403-2(8)) Barefoot Bks., Inc.

Gilbert, Frances. The Secret Garden. Barrager, Brigette, illus. 2017. (Little Golden Book Ser.). (ENG.). 24p. (J). (-k). 4.99 (978-0-399-55225-0(1), Golden Bks.) Random Hse. Children's Bks.

Gilkey, Gail. Seashell Garden. 2005. (J). per. 9.95 (978-0-9662983-6-9(5)) Windy Hill Pr.

Gilmore, Rachna. Roses for Gita. Priestley, Alice, illus. 2004. 24p. (J). (978-1-85269-369-5(X)); (978-1-85269-367-1(3)) Mantra Lingua.

Golden Books Staff. Bunny's Garden. Golden Books Staff, illus. 2010. (Shaped Board Book Ser.). (ENG., Illus.). 12p. (J). (gr. -1 — 1). bds. 7.99 (978-0-375-85788-1(5), Golden Bks.) Random Hse. Children's Bks.

Gopinath, Karin Ursula. Friends in the Garden. Sutanto, Tommy, illus. 2008. 34p. (J). per. 19.95 (978-0-9800637-0-7(1)) Lotus Art Works Inc.

Gordon, Judy Ann. Grammie's Magical Garden: Beyond the Gate. 2012. 68p. pap. 28.99 (978-1-4772-7973-1(3)) AuthorHouse.

Gordon, Michele Lynne. The Springing Singing Sprout: Little Tales of a Little Sprout. 2008. 54p. pap. 19.95 (978-1-4241-8942-7(X)) America Star Bks.

Graham-Morgan, Ivet. Grandma's Garden. 2009. 24p. pap. 12.99 (978-1-4389-2733-6(9)) AuthorHouse.

Granados, Lucia, illus. Bemba's Secret Garden. 2006. (ENG.). 57p. (J). per. 16.95 (978-0-9790110-0-9(0)) Tpprince Esquire International.

Grandma Poo Poo. Tessie the Toad. Olen, Jennifer, illus. 2008. 28p. pap. 24.95 (978-1-60610-325-8(3)) America Star Bks.

Greenburg, J. C. In the Garden. Palen, Debbie, illus. 2003. (Andrew Lost Ser.: 4). (ENG.). 96p. (J). (gr. 1-4). 3.99 (978-0-375-81280-4(6), Random Hse. Bks. for Young Readers) Random Hse. Children's Bks.

Griffith, Diane. Granny's Magic Garden. 2010. 66p. pap. 19.95 (978-1-60693-925-3(4), Eloquent Bks.) Strategic Book Publishing & Rights Agency (SBPRA).

Grout, Claire. Emil & Ordi: Friends for All Time. 2012. 24p. pap. 15.99 (978-1-4691-6279-9(2)) Xlibris Corp.

Guerin, F. A. The Witch at NO46: Verbrola. 2011. (Illus.). 140p. pap. 14.69 (978-1-4567-7118-8(3)) AuthorHouse.

Gugler, Laurel Dee. There's a Billy Goat in the Garden. Beaton, Clare, illus. 2003. 32p. (J). (gr. -1-2). 14.99 (978-1-84148-089-3(4)) Barefoot Bks., Inc.

Hafiz, Caroline Owen. The Return of the Fossil. 2007. 76p. per. (978-1-897312-26-1(1)) Adlibbed Ltd.

Hall, Rosemary. The Kids Knee Garden from the Adventures with Lamb E. Boy Series. 2008. (ENG.). 30p. pap. 9.13 (978-1-4196-8967-3(3)) CreateSpace Independent Publishing Platform.

Hamilton, George. Seeing Red: Story Seeds Vol 1. Hazel, Andrew, illus. 2008. 20p. pap. 13.99 (978-1-4343-8004-3(1)) AuthorHouse.

Hanton, Sophie. First Words in the Garden. 2009. (Mag-NUT-Tics! Ser.). (Illus.). (J). bds. 9.99 (978-1-934650-75-2(7)) Just For Kids Pr., LLC.

Harris, Donna. Lucie & the Garden Fairies. 2008. (Illus.). 40p. pap. 18.49 (978-1-4389-1312-4(5)) AuthorHouse.

Harris, Patricia. Raven's Garden. 2017. (Raven's Orchard Ser.). 24p. (gr. 4-6). pap. 8.25 **(978-1-5081-6151-6(8)**, PowerKids Pr.) Rosen Publishing Group, Inc., The.

Harshman, Marc & Ryan, Cheryl. Red Are the Apples. Zahares, Wade, illus. 2007. (ENG.). 32p. (J). (gr. -1-3). pap. 6.99 (978-0-15-206065-7(0)) Houghton Mifflin Harcourt Publishing Co.

Hatton, Laura. The Fairy's Garden. 2012. 64p. pap. 26.52 (978-1-4669-3961-5(3)) Trafford Publishing.

Henkes, Kevin. My Garden. Henkes, Kevin, illus. 2010. (Illus.). 40p. (J). (gr. -1-2). (ENG.). 17.99 (978-0-06-171517-4(4)); lib. bdg. 18.89 (978-0-06-171518-1(2)) HarperCollins Pubs. (Greenwillow Bks.).

Hill, Eric. Spot en el Jardin. (SPA.). pap. 4.95 (978-950-07-1967-4(3)) Editorial Sudamericana S.A. ARG. Dist: Distribooks, Inc.

Höhn, Jessica. Please Don't Pick the Flowers I Am Watching You. 2012. 24p. pap. 17.99 (978-1-4685-9573-4(3)) AuthorHouse.

Holland, Karen. The Garden Gang. 2010. (Illus.). 32p. pap. 12.99 (978-1-4490-6532-4(5)) AuthorHouse.

Howell, Julie. The Pepper Tree, How the Seeds Were Planted! LaGrange, Tiffany, illus. 2007. 28p. per. 12.95 (978-1-934246-51-1(4)) Peppertree Pr., The.

Howell, Julie Ann. The Pepper Tree, How the Seeds Were Planted. LaGrange, Tiffany, illus. 2012. 28p. 24.95 (978-1-61493-059-4(7)) Peppertree Pr., The.

Hruby, Patrick & Hruby, Emily. Counting in the Garden. 2011. (ENG., Illus.). 58p. (J). bds. 14.95 (978-1-934429-70-9(8)) AMMO Bks., LLC.

Huckin, Amanda. Grandma¡ S Garden. 2012. 32p. pap. 23.36 (978-1-4797-0813-0(5)) Xlibris Corp.

Hudson-Monger, Nadine. Brooke-Lynn's Trip to the Botanical Gardens with Grandm. 2012. 24p. pap. 15.99 (978-1-4691-8418-0(4)) Xlibris Corp.

Huxley, Sheila M. One Lovely Summer: The Stories of One Little Butterfly & His Friends. 2009. (Illus.). 48p. pap. 19.49 (978-1-4389-2987-3(0)) AuthorHouse.

In the Garden: Individual Title Six-Packs. (Sails Literacy Ser.). 16p. (gr. k-18). 27.00 (978-0-7635-4416-4(7)) Rigby Education.

Ingersoll, Donna. Grandpa's Garden. 2011. 28p. pap. 24.95 (978-1-4626-3214-5(9)) America Star Bks.

Innocenti, Jane. Aunt Jane's Summer Garden. 2012. 20p. pap. 24.95 (978-1-62709-103-9(3)) America Star Bks.

Island, Fiona. Wishbone's Magic Garden. 2006. (Illus.). 120p. pap. (978-1-84401-733-1(8)) Athena Pr.

Jane, Sarah. Hope's Garden. Ferrigno, Angela, illus. 2008. (ENG.). 32p. (J). (gr. -1-2). lib. bdg. 16.95 (978-0-9790962-0-4(0)) Tri Valley Children's Publishing.

Janowski, Alice & Boyer, Colleen McKinnon. Dakota & the Magical Gardens. 2008. 28p. pap. 12.95 (978-1-59858-711-0(0)) Dog Ear Publishing, LLC.

Jeanne Taylor Thomas Illustrator: Pr. Austin & Harlow's First Adventure. Hardy, Pris, illus. 2011. 28p. pap. 24.95 (978-1-4560-8383-0(X)) America Star Bks.

Jenson-Elliott, Cindy. Dig In! Peterson, Mary, illus. 2016. (ENG.). 40p. (J). (gr. -1-3). 17.99 (978-1-4424-1261-3(5), Beach Lane Bks.) Beach Lane Bks.

Johnson, Esther A. The Princess & the Garden. Taylor, Carolyn, illus. 2012. 34p. pap. 19.99 (978-1-62419-614-0(4)) Salem Author Services.

Johnson, Jacqueline & Young, Jeanna Stolle. Princess Faith's Mysterious Garden, 1 vol. Aranda, Omar, illus. 2012. (Princess Parables Ser.). (ENG.). 32p. (J). 14.99 (978-0-310-72703-3(0)) Zonderkidz.

Johnson, Mo. Noah's Garden: When Someone You Love Is in the Hospital. Josse, Annabelle, illus. 2010. (ENG.). 32p. (J). (gr. -1-2). 15.99 (978-0-7636-4782-7(9)) Candlewick Pr.

Johnson, Rhonda & Paladin, Frank. The Little Garden. Amber, Holly & Davidsson, Ashton, illus. Lt. ed. 2004. 48p. (J). per. 16.95 (978-0-9763635-7-6(7), TLG01) Beyond the Stars Pubns.

Jordan, Claire. Fanakapan & the Fairies - a Children's Fairy Story. Skou, Nick, illus. 2013. 52p. pap. (978-1-78148-648-1(4)) Grosvenor Hse. Publishing Ltd.

Jordan's Zoo: Individual Title, 6 packs. (gr. -1-2). 27.00 (978-0-7635-9456-5(3)) Rigby Education.

Joyce, William. The Leaf Men: And the Brave Good Bugs. Joyce, William, illus. 2017. (World of William Joyce Ser.). (ENG., Illus.). 40p. (J). (gr. -1-3). 17.99 **(978-1-4814-8955-3(0)**, Atheneum/Caitlyn Dlouhy Books) Simon & Schuster Children's Publishing.

Kananen, Barbara L. Fairies in My Garden. 2007. 106p. (YA). (gr. 2-2). per. 10.95 (978-0-595-45082-4(2)) iUniverse, Inc.

—Fairies in My Garden. 2007. 106p. (YA). (gr. 2-2). 20.95 (978-0-595-91014-4(9)) iUniverse, Inc.

Kennedy, Pamela. Easter in the Garden. Wenzel, David T., illus. 2008. (ENG.). 32p. (J). (gr. -1-3). 12.99 (978-0-8249-5577-9(3), Ideal Pubns.) Worthy Publishing.

Kerline, Joni M. Sebastian Breaks for Freedom. 1. 2006. (Illus.). 30p. (J). 19.95 (978-0-9776772-0-7(6)) KidBookInk Publishing, LLC.

King, Diane. Elijah & the Talking Tree. 2012. (Illus.). 32p. pap. 21.99 (978-1-4691-4862-5(5)) Xlibris Corp.

Kladstrup, Kristin. Garden Princess. (ENG.). 272p. (J). (gr. 5). 2015. pap. 7.99 (978-0-7636-7668-1(3)) 2013. (Illus.). 15.99 (978-0-7636-5685-0(2)) Candlewick Pr.

Korda, Lerryn. Into the Wild. Korda, Lerryn, illus. 2010. (Playtime with Little Nye Ser.). (ENG., Illus.). 26p. (J). (gr. -1 — 1). 8.99 (978-0-7636-4812-1(4)) Candlewick Pr.

Kruusval, Catarina. Ellen's Apple Tree. Sandin, Joan, tr. from SWE. 2008. (Illus.). 32p. (J). (gr. -1-3). 16.00 (978-91-29-66905-3(7)) R & S Bks. SWE. Dist: Macmillan.

Lamba, Marie & Lamba, Baldev. Green, Green: A Community Gardening Story. Sanchez, Sonia, illus. 2017. (ENG.). 32p. (J). 17.99 (978-0-374-32797-2(1), 9780374327972, Farrar, Straus & Giroux (BYR)) Farrar, Straus & Giroux.

Lappano, Jon-Erik. Tokyo Digs a Garden, 1 vol. Hatanaka, Kellen, illus. 2016. (ENG.). 32p. (J). (gr. -1-2). 18.95 (978-1-55498-798-6(9)) Groundwood Bks. CAN. Dist: Publishers Group West (PGW).

Larsen, Andrew. The Imaginary Garden. Luxbacher, Irene, illus. 2009. (ENG.). 32p. (J). (gr. -1-2). 16.95 (978-1-55453-279-7(5)) Kids Can Pr., Ltd. CAN. Dist: Hachette Bk. Group.

Lascurain, Anna. Apollo in the Moon House. 2006. Orig. Title: The Moonboy. (J). per. 7.99 (978-0-9769612-3-9(7)) Darker Intentions Pr.

Lawson-Goins, Helen. Surprise in the Garden. 2012. 40p. pap. 21.99 (978-1-4771-1258-8(8)) Xlibris Corp.

Leppard, Lois Gladys. The Secret Garden. 2003. 160p. (J). mass mkt. 4.99 (978-1-889893-04-4(8), Ambassador-Emerald, International) Emerald Hse. Group, Inc.

Lin, Grace. Ugly Vegetables. 2014. 16.95 (978-1-63419-748-9(8)) Perfection Learning Corp.

Lobel, Anita. 10 Hungry Rabbits: Counting & Color Concepts. Bowers, Tim, illus. 2012. (ENG.). 24p. (J). (gr. k-k). 9.99 (978-0-375-86864-1(X), Knopf Bks. for Young Readers) Random Hse. Children's Bks.

Longo, Kaitlin. The Secret in Olivia's Garden. 2012. 36p. pap. 20.99 (978-1-4685-5222-5(8)) AuthorHouse.

Look at the Garden: Individual Title, 6 Packs. (gr. 1-2). 22.00 (978-0-7635-9112-0(2)) Rigby Education.

López Narváez, Concha. El Arbol de los Pajaros Sin Vuelo. (SPA.). 128p. (YA). (gr. 5-8). (978-84-207-2905-3(1)) Grupo Anaya, S.A. ESP. Dist: Lectorum Pubns., Inc.

Lorraine, Nancy. The Butterfly Adventure. Herron, Dorothy, illus. 2nd ed. 2013. 50p. 22.50 (978-0-9886194-9-4(0)) ProsePress.

Loye, David. Grandfather's Garden: Bedtime Stories for Little & Big Folk. 2008. (J). pap. 18.95 (978-0-9795257-7-3(2)) Benjamin Franklin Pr.

Malone, Ladawn. The Master's Garden. 2009. 32p. pap. 14.49 (978-1-4490-3860-1(3)) AuthorHouse.

Mandy and Ness Staff, et al. George's Garden. 2005. (Senses Ser.). (URD, ENG, VIE, CHI & BEN., Illus.). 16p. (J). pap. 9.95 (978-1-84059-168-2(4)) Milet Publishing.

Martin-Larranaga, Ana, illus. Butterfly in the Garden. 2007. (Butterfly Bks.). (J). bds. 5.95 (978-1-58925-803-7(7)) Tiger Tales.

Matthies, Jana. The Goodbye Cancer Garden, 1 vol. Valiant, Kristi, illus. 2011. (ENG.). 32p. (J). (gr. 1-3). 16.99 (978-0-8075-2994-2(X)) Whitman, Albert & Co.

Mayer, Mercer. A Green, Green Garden. Mayer, Mercer, illus. 2011. (My First I Can Read Ser.). (ENG., Illus.). 32p. (J). (gr. -1-3). 16.99 (978-0-06-083562-0(1)); pap. 3.99 (978-0-06-083561-3(3)) HarperCollins Pubs.

McGinnis, Chelsea. Mk Frogg & the Lily Pad Adventures, 1 vol. 2009. 48p. pap. 24.95 (978-1-60813-548-6(9)) America Star Bks.

McGuire, Heather Ridgway. The Vegetable Garden. 2006. 17.00 (978-0-8059-9093-5(3)) Dorrance Publishing Co., Inc.

McQuinn, Anna. Lola Plants a Garden. Beardshaw, Rosalind, illus. 2017. (ENG.). 28p. (J). (-k). pap. 6.99 (978-1-58089-695-5(2)) Charlesbridge Publishing, Inc.

Meadows, Daisy. Edie the Garden Fairy. 2014. (Rainbow Magic — the Earth Fairies Ser.). lib. bdg. 14.75 (978-0-606-35832-3(3)) Turtleback Bks.

Menconi, James Pasqual. Queen Mariella & the Fable of the Peony. 2011. 24p. (gr. -1). pap. 13.50 (978-1-4567-3934-8(4)) AuthorHouse.

Miller, Olive Beaupr. The Magic Garden of My Book House. 2005. reprint ed. pap. 24.95 (978-1-4191-4169-0(4)) Kessinger Publishing, LLC.

Miller, S. L. Yellow Kitty, Life in the Garden. 2008. 316p. pap. 18.95 (978-0-615-22038-3(X)) Polar Club Publishing.

Mora, Pat & Ventura, Gabriela Baeza. The Remembering Day / el Día de Los Muertos. Casilla, Robert, illus. 2015. (SPA & ENG.). 32p. (J). (gr. k-3). 17.95 (978-1-55885-805-3(9), Piñata Books) Arte Publico Pr.

Morales, Rebecca Lynn. Walter Plume & the Dehydrated Imagination. 2016. (ENG.). viii, 150p. (J). pap. 11.99 (978-1-4621-1780-2(5), Sweetwater Bks.) Cedar Fort, Inc./CFI Distribution.

More Than a Meal. (Early Intervention Levels Ser.). 28.56 (978-0-7362-1049-2(0)) CENGAGE Learning.

Morrison, Blake. The Yellow House. Craig, Helen, illus. 2011. (ENG.). 32p. (J). (gr. -1-2). 15.99 (978-0-7636-4959-3(7)) Candlewick Pr.

Moser, Lisa. Stories from Bug Garden. Millward, Gwen, illus. 2016. (ENG.). 32p. (J). (gr. -1-3). 16.99 (978-0-7636-6534-0(7)) Candlewick Pr.

Mun-Ensor, Michelle. The Angel's Garden. 2011. 48p. pap. 24.95 (978-1-4560-5596-7(8)) America Star Bks.

My Vegetable Garden. 2003. (J). per. (978-1-57657-896-4(8)) Paradise Pr., Inc.

Navarro-Talavera, Carmen. The Ant Lucy & the Hurricane. 2009. 48p. pap. 17.49 (978-1-4389-7788-1(3)) AuthorHouse.

Nesbit, E. The Rainbow & the Rose. 2007. 108p. per. (978-1-4065-3084-1(0)) Dodo Pr.

Neumann, A. C. The Drawer's Gift. 2010. 60p. pap. 25.95 (978-1-935340-62-1(X)) Worthy Shorts.

Nigro Heroux, Regina. Grandma's Butterfly Garden. 2009. 28p. pap. 13.99 (978-1-4490-3054-4(8)) AuthorHouse.

Noguchi, Rick & Jenks, Deneen. Flowers from Mariko. Kumata, Michelle Reiko, illus. 2013. (ENG.). 32p. (J). (gr. 1-18). 16.95 (978-1-58430-032-8(9)) Lee & Low Bks., Inc.

—Flowers from Mariko, 1 vol. Kumata, Michelle Reiko, illus. 2016. (ENG.). 32p. (J). pap. 9.95 (978-1-62014-315-5(1)) Lee & Low Bks., Inc.

Northfield, Gary. Gary's Garden. Northfield, Gary, illus. 2016. (ENG., Illus.). 64p. (J). (gr. 2-5). pap. 7.99 (978-0-545-86183-0(7)) Scholastic, Inc.

Novis, Jovita. The Tiny Ballerina in the Garden. 2013. 40p. pap. 15.95 (978-1-4497-9104-9(2), WestBow Pr.) Author Solutions, Inc.

Oechsli, Helen. In My Garden. 2013. (ENG., Illus.). 32p. (J). (gr. -1-3). 16.99 (978-1-4814-2169-0(7), Simon & Schuster Bks. For Young Readers) Simon & Schuster Bks. For Young Readers.

Oru, Gideon. The Walking Garden. 2012. 36p. pap. 24.95 (978-1-4626-9315-3(6)) America Star Bks.

Osterhold, Jared, illus. OLIVIA Plants a Garden. 2011. (Olivia TV Tie-In Ser.). (ENG.). 24p. (J). (gr. -1-1). pap. 3.99 (978-1-4424-1675-8(0), Simon Spotlight) Simon Spotlight.

Page, Lynda. Caley's Secret Garden. 2012. 28p. pap. 32.70 (978-1-4771-0605-1(7)) Xlibris Corp.

Parent, Nancy. A Surprise Garden, 15 vols. Harchy, Atelier Philippe, illus. 2003. (It's Fun to Learn Ser.). 32p. (J). (gr. -1-3). 3.99 (978-1-57973-126-7(0)) Advance Pubs. LLC.

Parker, Deborah. In the Garden (Cj) 2008. 24p. 7.95 (978-1-60231-000-1(9), Cub Bks.) Global Business Information Strategies, Inc.

Paul, Fleischman. Seedfolks. 2014. (Joanna Cotler Bks). (ENG.). 112p. (J). (gr. 12-12). 13.24 (978-1-63245-070-8(4)) Lectorum Pubns., Inc.

Pepper, Lily. In the Garden at Granddad's. 2012. (Illus.). 24p. pap. 19.82 (978-1-4772-2642-1(7)) AuthorHouse.

Pierce, Terry. My Busy Green Garden, 1 vol. Schwartz, Carol, illus. 2017. (Tilbury House Nature Book Ser.: 0). (ENG.). 36p. (gr. -1-1). 16.95 (978-0-88448-495-0(5), 884495) Tilbury Hse. Pubs.

Pitt, Sarah. Peek a Boo! Garden. 2009. (Little Peek a Boo Bks.). (Illus.). (J). bds. 9.99 (978-1-934650-60-8(9)) Just For Kids Pr., LLC.

Poole, Amy Lowry, illus. & retold by. The Pea Blossom. Poole, Amy Lowry, retold by. 2006. (ENG.). 32p. (J). reprint ed. 6.95 (978-0-8234-2018-6(3)) Holiday Hse., Inc.

Potter, Beatrix. The Tale of Peter Rabbit. Hague, Michael, illus. 2003. 29p. (J). (gr. 2-5). reprint ed. 16.00 (978-0-7567-6968-0(X)) DIANE Publishing Co.

—The Tale of Peter Rabbit. McPhail, David, illus. 2014. (ENG.). 28p. (J). (gr. -1 — 1). bds. 6.99 (978-0-545-65096-0(8), Cartwheel Bks.) Scholastic, Inc.

—The Tale of Peter Rabbit. (Illus.). 12p. 4.95 (978-1-58989-271-2(2)) Thurman Hse., LLC.

Potter, Ellen. The Humming Room. 2012. (ENG.). 192p. (J). (gr. 4-7). 16.99 (978-0-312-64438-3(8), 9780312644383) Feiwel & Friends.

—The Humming Room. 2013. (ENG.). 208p. (J). (gr. 4-7). pap. 6.99 (978-1-250-01666-9(5), 9781250016669) Square Fish.

Powell, Kathy Bingham. Save the Seeds. 2010. (Illus.). 24p. pap. 14.99 (978-1-4490-5936-1(8)) AuthorHouse.

Pratt, Sally. The Adventures of Bernie the Bee in Sally's Garden. 2013. 46p. pap. 21.99 (978-1-4772-9759-9(6)) AuthorHouse.

Ramos, Odalys Q. Allow Me to Introduce Myself. Graham, Michael, illus. 2012. 24p. (-18). pap. 12.95 (978-1-61493-121-8(6)) Peppertree Pr., The.

Random House Staff. The Great Train Mystery (SpongeBob SquarePants) Random House Staff, illus. 2013. (Step into Reading Ser.). (ENG., Illus.). 32p. (J). (gr. -1-1). pap. 3.99 (978-0-449-81441-3(6), Random Hse. Bks. for Young Readers) Random Hse. Children's Bks.

Ratcliff, Carol J. Grannie's Secret Garden: (Somewhere in England) 2009. (Illus.). 48p. pap. 19.49 (978-1-4490-4355-1(0)) AuthorHouse.

Raven's Orchard. 2017. (Raven's Orchard Ser.). 24p. (gr. 4-6). 70.80 **(978-1-5081-6188-2(7)**, PowerKids Pr.) Rosen Publishing Group, Inc., The.

Ray, Jane. Adán y Eva y el Jardín Del Edén. Rodríguez, Maite, tr. 2005. (SPA & ENG., Illus.). 32p. (J). (gr. k-2). 12.95 (978-84-95939-84-5(3)) Blume ESP. Dist: Independent Pubs. Group.

Ready Reader Staff. The City Cat & the Country Cat, 6 bks., set. Level 8, Bk. 18. 2003. (J). (gr. -1-3). pap. 33.50 (978-0-8136-2038-1(4)) Modern Curriculum Pr.

Reynolds, Peter H. Rose's Garden. Reynolds, Peter H., illus. 2009. (ENG., Illus.). 40p. (J). (gr. k-12). 15.99 (978-0-7636-4641-7(5)) Candlewick Pr.

Richards, Claire. Mai's Garden: Mickamoo's Rescue. 2011. (Illus.). 56p. (gr. -1). pap. 12.51 (978-1-4567-7559-9(6)) AuthorHouse.

Rist, Stephen. Ladybirds Don't Like Scrambled Eggs. 2010. (Illus.). 36p. 15.49 (978-1-4490-6614-7(3)) AuthorHouse.

Rivoal, Marine, creator. Three Little Peas. 2014. (ENG., Illus.). 48p. (J). (gr. -1-3). 16.95 (978-1-59270-155-1(8)) Enchanted Lion Bks., LLC.

Robert, Bulla Clyde. The Chalk Box Kid. 10th rev. ed. 2014. (Stepping Stone Book Ser.). (ENG.). 64p. (J). (gr. 12-12). 8.24 (978-1-63245-220-7(0)) Lectorum Pubns., Inc.

The rock Garden: Individual Title Six-Packs. (gr. 1-2). 25.00 (978-0-7635-9195-3(5)) Rigby Education.

Rosalina's Flower Garden. 2017. (Rosalina's Flower Garden Ser.). 24p. (gr. 4-6). 70.80 **(978-1-5081-6191-2(7))**; pap. 24.75 **(978-1-5081-6193-6(3))** Rosen Publishing Group, Inc., The. (PowerKids Pr.).

Roy, Ron. June Jam. Gurney, John Steven, illus. 2011. (Calendar Mysteries Ser.: 6). (ENG.). 80p. (J). (gr. 1-4). 4.99 (978-0-375-86112-3(2), Random Hse. Bks. for Young Readers) Random Hse. Children's Bks.

Roys, Julie. Outside the Window. 2012. 24p. pap. 21.00 (978-1-4669-3092-6(6)) Trafford Publishing.

Running Press Staff & Hello Kitty Staff. Hello Kitty: A Little Book of Happiness. 2009. (Miniature Editions Ser.). (ENG.). 96p. 5.95 (978-0-7624-3594-4(1)) Running Pr. Bk. Pubs.

Rushton, Jenna. A Simple Flower. 2012. 24p. pap. 14.50 (978-1-4772-0295-1(1)) AuthorHouse.

Rylant, Cynthia. Annie & Snowball & the Pink Surprise. Stevenson, Sucie, illus. (Annie & Snowball Ser.: 4). (ENG.). 40p. (J). (gr. k-2). 2010. pap. 3.99 (978-1-4169-1462-4(5)) 2008. 16.99 (978-1-4169-0941-5(9)) Simon Spotlight. (Simon Spotlight).

Sandoval, Anna. Tickle a Daisy. 2007. 28p. per. 24.95 (978-1-4241-8470-5(3)) America Star Bks.

Santos, Penelope. Peas for Pat. 2015. (Rosen REAL Readers: STEM & STEAM Collection). (ENG.). 12p. (gr. 1-2). pap.

6.33 *(978-1-4994-9517-1(X),* Rosen Classroom) Rosen Publishing Group, Inc., The.

Sawyer, J. Scott. The Broccoli Bush. Bozeman, Gary, illus. 2012. 36p. pap. 24.95 *(978-1-4626-2501-7(0))* America Star Bks.

Schaefer, Carole Lexa. The Children's Garden: Growing Food in the City. Morgan, Pierr, illus. 2017. (ENG.). 32p. (J). (gr. -1-3). 16.99 *(978-1-57061-984-7(0),* Little Bigfoot) Sasquatch Bks.

Schwarz, Evelyn. The Hummingbird Garden. Quinn, Kitty, illus. 2012. (ENG.). 34p. (J). pap. 16.95 *(978-1-4327-9815-4(4))* Outskirts Pr., Inc.

Scott, Nathan Kumar. Mangoes & Bananas. Balaji, T., illus. 2nd ed. 2006. (ENG.). 32p. (J). *(978-81-86211-06-9(3))* Temmen, Edition, Horst Temmen.

Scraper, Katherine. Garden Lunch. 2006. (Early Explorers Ser.). (J). pap. *(978-1-4108-6027-9(2))* Benchmark Education Co.

Scratch & Sniff: Garden. braille ed. 2004. (J). spiral bd., bds. *(978-0-616-11141-3(X))* Canadian National Institute for the Blind/Institut National Canadien pour les Aveugles.

Seabag-Montefiore, Mary. Secret Garden. 2009. (Young Reading Ser. 2 Ser.). 64p. (J). 6.99 *(978-0-7945-2481-4(8),* Usborne) EDC Publishing.

The Secret Garden. 2008. (Charm Book Classics Ser.). 32p. *(978-1-4075-2072-8(5))* Parragon, Inc.

Seider, Sharon J. The Door in the Garden Wall. 2003. 139p. (J). pap. 13.95 *(978-0-7414-1712-1(X))* Infinity Publishing.

The Selfish Giant: Individual Title Six-Packs. (Literatura 2000 Ser.). (gr. 2-3). 33.00 *(978-0-7635-0239-3(1))* Rigby Education.

Shamane, Aunty. Grandma of the Gardens. 2011. 20p. pap. 11.50 *(978-1-4634-3119-8(8))* AuthorHouse.

Shaw, Irene. Cosy Cottage. 2006. (Illus.). 48p. pap. *(978-1-84401-792-8(3))* Athena Pr.

Siminovich, Lorena, illus. You Are My Baby: Garden. 2014. (ENG.). 10p. (J). (gr. -1 — 1). bds. 8.99 *(978-1-4521-2649-4(6))* Chronicle Bks. LLC.

Slater, Dashka. Dangerously Ever After. Docampo, Valeria, illus. 2012. (ENG.). 40p. (J). (gr. k-3). 16.99 *(978-0-8037-3374-9(7),* Dial Bks) Penguin Young Readers Group.

Small World Creations. In the Garden. 2016. (Crinkle Cloth Bks.). (ENG.). 8p. (J). (gr. -1 — 1). 9.99 *(978-1-4380-7753-6(X))* Barron's Educational Series, Inc.

Smith, Lane. Grandpa Green. Smith, Lane, illus. 2011. (ENG., Illus.). 32p. (J). (gr. k-4). 16.99 *(978-1-59643-607-7(7),* 9781596436077) Roaring Brook Pr.

Smith-Rogers & Smith, Brady A. The Culinary Capers of Canon & Lily: Canon Grows a Garden. 2009. 20p. pap. 11.49 *(978-1-4490-1305-9(8))* AuthorHouse.

Smith, Shelli. Grammy Goes Green. 2012. 24p. pap. 12.45 *(978-1-4624-0104-8(X),* Inspiring Voices) Author Solutions, Inc.

Smith, Sherry Weaver. Search for the Hidden Garden: A Discovery with Saint Thérèse. Thornburgh, Rebecca McKillip, illus. 2016. 128p. (J). pap. 9.95 *(978-0-8198-9050-4(2))* Pauline Bks. & Media.

Snoozy Sam, 6 Packs. (Literatura 2000 Ser.). (gr. 1-2). 28.00 *(978-0-7635-0138-9(7))* Rigby Education.

Sollinger, Emily. OLIVIA Plants a Garden. Osterhold, Jared, illus. 2011. (Olivia TV Tie-In Ser.). (ENG.). 24p. (J). (gr. -1-1). 16.99 *(978-1-4424-2011-3(1),* Simon Spotlight) Simon Spotlight.

Spalding, Brenda M. Hayden's Garden. 2012. pap. 13.95 *(978-0-7414-7961-7(3))* Infinity Publishing.

Spurr, Elizabeth. In the Garden. 1 vol. Oliphant, Manelle, illus. 2012. (ENG.). 22p. (J). bds. 6.95 *(978-1-56145-581-2(4))* Peachtree Pubs.

Starr, Ringo, pseud. Octopus's Garden. Cort, Ben, illus. 2014. (ENG.). 32p. (J). (gr. -1-3). 17.99 *(978-1-4814-0362-7(1),* Aladdin) Simon & Schuster Children's Publishing.

Stewart, Lizzy. There's a Tiger in the Garden. 2016. (ENG., Illus.). 40p. (J). pap. 9.99 *(978-1-84780-807-3(7),* Frances Lincoln Children's Bks.) Quarto Publishing Group UK GBR. Dist: Littlehampton Bk Services, Ltd.

Stuefloten, Helen. There's A Giant in the Garden. Janguay, Patricia, illus. l.t. ed. 2006. 35p. (J). per. 11.99 *(978-1-59879-161-7(3))* Lifevest Publishing, Inc.

Sullivan, Kathryn. Michael & the Elf. Dunningham, Jo, illus. 2nd ed. 2012. 24p. pap. 10.95 *(978-1-61633-356-0(1))* Guardian Angel Publishing, Inc.

Talwar, Ankoor & Talwar, Abhinav. The Children's Garden. Chatterjee, Susnata, illus. 2009. 32p. pap. 16.49 *(978-1-4389-9309-6(9))* AuthorHouse.

Tani, Branca. Beth's Butterfly Garden. 2015. (Rosen REAL Readers: STEM & STEAM Collection). (ENG.). 8p. pap. 5.46 *(978-1-4994-9586-7(2),* Rosen Classroom) Rosen Publishing Group, Inc., The.

Tazewell, Lora A. Jelly Bread & Water Juice. 2009. 48p. pap. 17.49 *(978-1-4389-1973-7(5))* AuthorHouse.

Thomas, Jan. There's a Pest in the Garden! 2017. (Giggle Gang Ser.). (ENG., Illus.). 48p. (J). (gr. -1-3). 9.99 *(978-0-544-94165-6(9),* HMH Books For Young Readers) Houghton Mifflin Harcourt Publishing Co.

Ticktock Media, Ltd. Staff. In the Garden with the Hungry Little Snail. 2009. (Touch & Feel Fun Ser.). (ENG.). 10p. (J). (gr. k — 1). bds. 5.95 *(978-1-84696-810-5(0),* TickTock Books) Octopus Publishing Group GBR. Dist: Independent Pubs. Group.

Tildes, Phyllis L. The Garden Wall. Tildes, Phyllis L., illus. 2005. (Illus.). (J). per. 7.95 *(978-0-9723729-1-6(1))* Imagination Stage, Inc.

Tomio, Stacy. Cathy's Animal Garden: Enter at Your Own Risk. Bell, Samantha, illus. 2010. (J). *(978-1-934617-04-5(0),* Alma Little) Elva Resa Publishing, LLC.

Tower, Cory L. The Adventures of Courtney, Morgan & the Magic Toy Bears Book 2: In the Beginning. 2012. 24p. pap. 24.95 *(978-1-4626-8395-6(9))* America Star Bks.

Townsend, Vanessa Jane. What's in Molly's... Garden? 2012. (Illus.). 24p. pap. 15.99 *(978-1-4691-5781-8(0))* Xlibris Corp.

Travers, Georgia. The Wily Woodchucks. Gag, Flavia, illus. 2009. (Fesler-Lampert Minnesota Heritage Ser.). (ENG.). 32p. 14.95 *(978-0-8166-6548-8(6))* Univ. of Minnesota Pr.

Trooboff, Rhoda. Ben, the Bells & the Peacocks. Bucher, Cecile, illus. 2006. (ENG.). 36p. (J). per. 15.00 *(978-0-9773536-0-6(5))* Univ. of Toledo Pr.

Tulip, Jenny, illus. Who's Hiding in the Garden? 2008. 10p. (gr. -1-k). bds. 6.99 *(978-1-57755-785-2(9))* Gardner Pubns.

Tuxford, Jenny & Brazier, Jenny. Fred Boggitt & the Great Garden Centre Plot. 2012. 128p. (gr. 2-4). pap. 15.18 *(978-1-4678-9703-7(5))* AuthorHouse.

U. S. National Geographic Society Staff. How Does Your Garden Grow? 2009. (Toot & Puddle Ser.). (ENG., Illus.). 24p. (J). (gr. -1-2). pap. 3.99 *(978-1-4263-0482-8(X));* lib. bdg. 11.90 *(978-1-4263-0483-5(8))* National Geographic Society. (National Geographic Children's Bks.).

Ungerer, Tomi. The Beast of Monsieur Racine. 2014. (ENG., Illus.). 32p. (gr. -1-3). 16.95 *(978-0-7148-6081-7(6))* Phaidon Pr., Inc.

van Genechten, Guido. Crinkle Animals - Garden. 2011. (Crinkle Animals Ser.). (ENG.). 8p. (J). (gr. k — 1). 9.95 *(978-1-60537-081-1(9))* Cobblestone Publishing Co.

Vigneault, Gilles. A Treasure in My Garden. Jorisch, Stéphane, illus. 2007. (ENG & FRE.). 36p. (J). (gr. -1-2). 16.95 *(978-2-923163-14-7(1))* La Montagne Secrete CAN. Dist: Independent Pubs. Group.

Vollbracht, James. Mishan's Garden. Brooke, Janet, illus. 2013. (ENG.). 32p. (J). (gr. k-9). 16.95 *(978-1-61429-112-1(8))* Wisdom Pubns.

Wagner, Rachel A. Bogie the Boxer: Gardens. 2012. 24p. pap. 9.99 *(978-0-9885180-4-9(X))* Mindstir Media.

Wallace, T. M. Under a Fairy Moon. 2012. 224p. pap. *(978-0-9868657-4-9(5))* Brownridge Publishing.

Warner, Gertrude Chandler, creator. The Garden Thief. 2012. (Boxcar Children Mysteries Ser.: 130). (ENG., Illus.). 128p. (J). (gr. 1-5). 5.99 *(978-0-8075-2752-8(1))* Whitman, Albert & Co.

—The Garden Thief. 2012. (Boxcar Children Mysteries Ser.: 130). (ENG., Illus.). 128p. (J). (gr. 1-5). 15.99 *(978-0-8075-2751-1(3))* Whitman, Albert & Co.

—The Mystery of the Traveling Tomatoes. 2008. (Boxcar Children Mysteries Ser.: 117). (ENG.). 128p. (J). (gr. 1-5). 14.99 *(978-0-8075-5579-8(7));* pap. 6.99 *(978-0-8075-5580-4(0))* Whitman, Albert & Co.

Waterfield, Susan. Spunkie's Magical Garden. 2012. 32p. pap. 14.95 *(978-1-257-77576-7(6))* Lulu Pr., Inc.

Wayne, Viv. Bloom Where You Are Planted: A garden story about overcoming your Challenges. 2012. 28p. pap. 19.99 *(978-1-4685-4791-7(7))* AuthorHouse.

Webb, Holly. Return to the Secret Garden. 2016. (ENG.). 224p. (J). (gr. 3-7). 16.99 *(978-1-4926-3909-1(5),* 9781492639091) Sourcebooks, Inc.

Welch, Lance. Counting with the Fairies of Willow Garden. Welch, Mark, illus. 2012. 16p. pap. 24.95 *(978-1-62709-544-0(6))* America Star Bks.

Wellington, Monica. Zinnia's Flower Garden. Wellington, Monica, illus. 2007. (ENG., Illus.). 32p. (J). (gr. -1-2). pap. 5.99 *(978-0-14-240787-5(9),* Puffin Books) Penguin Young Readers Group.

—Zinnia's Flower Garden. 2007. (Illus.). 28p. (gr. k-3). 16.00 *(978-0-7569-8171-6(9))* Perfection Learning Corp.

West, William. The Gardener: The Tale of Toby the Tumbleweed. 2012. 28p. pap. 16.95 *(978-1-4497-6886-7(5),* WestBow Pr.) Author Solutions, Inc.

Weston, Laura. The Butterfly Garden. Weston, Laura, illus. 2017. (ENG., Illus.). 12p. (J). (-k). bds. 14.99 *(978-0-7636-9317-6(0),* Big Picture Press) Candlewick Pr.

What's in the Garden? 2003. (J). pap. *(978-1-57657-931-2(X))* Paradise Pr., Inc.

Wheat, Tiffany. There's a Gopher in My Garden! 2013. (ENG., Illus.). (J). (gr. -1-3). pap. 9.95 *(978-1-62086-463-0(0))* Mascot Bks., Inc.

Wilbur, Helen. Lily's Victory Garden. Steele, Robert, illus. 2010. (Tales of Young Americans Ser.). (ENG.). 32p. (J). (gr. 2-4). 16.95 *(978-1-58536-450-3(9))* Sleeping Bear Pr.

Wilkie, E. m. The Garden of Eden Adventure. Wilkie, E. m., illus. 2012. (Illus.). 42p. (J). pap. 9.99 *(978-0-9846685-7-1(8),* Indie Christian Book Group) IndieGo Publishing LLC.

Williams, Raymond. Tales from the Willow Tree. 2012. (Illus.). 28p. pap. 8.50 *(978-1-78035-343-2(X),* Fastprint Publishing) Upfront Publishing Ltd. GBR. Dist: Printondemand-worldwide.com.

Williams, Walter. The Bicycle Garden. 2013. 40p. pap. 6.99 *(978-0-9890698-0-9(X))* Fernwood & Hedges Bks.

Wimbiscus, Robin. Somewhere in the Garden. 2007. (ENG.). 72p. (J). (gr. k-2). 19.95 *(978-0-9772692-9-7(9))* Birch Island.

Winningham, Barbara. The Turtle Pit. 2013. 36p. 24.95 *(978-1-62709-875-5(5));* pap. 24.95 *(978-1-62709-493-1(8))* America Star Bks.

Wirth, Margie & Sherfinski, Julie. BF: the Carrot Monster. 2010. 36p. 15.50 *(978-0-557-27308-9(0))* Lulu Pr., Inc.

Wood, Maryrose & Duchess of Northumberland Staff. The Poison Diaries. 2010. (Poison Diaries: 1). (ENG.). 288p. (YA). (gr. 8-18). 16.99 *(978-0-06-180236-2(0))* HarperCollins Pubs.

Worth, Sharon. Jacob's Garden, 1 vol. 2009. 132p. pap. 19.95 *(978-1-60813-963-7(8))* America Star Bks.

Worthen, Diane. Oliver's Wish: A Tale from the Garden. 2012. 36p. pap. 20.99 *(978-1-4685-4005-5(X))* AuthorHouse.

Wyman, Susan. Pipsqueak's Puny Peepholes. 2013. 40p. pap. 15.99 *(978-1-4908-0412-5(9),* WestBow Pr.) Author Solutions, Inc.

Young, Annemarie. In the Garden. Redshaw, Louise, illus. 2013. (Start Reading Ser.). (ENG.). 24p. (gr. k-1). pap. 41.94 *(978-1-4765-3220-2(6));* pap. 7.95 *(978-1-4765-3192-2(7))* Capstone Press of Coughlan Cos.

Young, Valerie. The Adventures of Todd & Friends. 2009. 20p. pap. 12.49 *(978-1-4389-3196-8(4))* AuthorHouse.

Zera, Annette & Szekeres, Vivienne. Grandma Gets a Fright. 2013. (Illus.). 20p. pap. 9.50 *(978-1-78035-634-1(X),* Fastprint Publishing) Upfront Publishing Ltd. GBR. Dist: Printondemand-worldwide.com.

GARDENS, MINIATURE

Kuskowski, Alex. Super Simple Fairy Gardens: A Kid's Guide to Gardening, 1 vol. 2014. (Super Simple Gardening Ser.). (ENG.). 32p. (gr. k-4). 27.07 *(978-1-62403-522-7(1))* ABDO Publishing Co.

GARFIELD, JAMES A. (JAMES ABRAM), 1831-1881

Brunelli, Carol. James A. Garfield. 2008. (Presidents of the U. S. A. Ser.). (ENG., Illus.). 48p. (J). (gr. 3-6). 32.79 *(978-1-60253-049-2(1),* 200688) Child's World, Inc., The.

Feldman, Ruth Tenzer. James A. Garfield. 2005. (Presidential Leaders Ser.). (Illus.). 112p. (J). (gr. 6-12). 29.27 *(978-0-8225-1398-8(6))* Lerner Publishing Group.

Gunderson, Megan M. James A. Garfield, 1 vol. (ENG., Illus.). 40p. 2016. (J). *(978-1-68078-094-9(8))* 2009. (YA). (gr. 3-6). 27.07 *(978-1-60453-452-8(4))* ABDO Publishing Co.

Kent, Deborah. James A. Garfield. 2004. (Encyclopedia of Presidents Ser.). (ENG., Illus.). 110p. (YA). (gr. 5-9). 34.00 *(978-0-516-22886-0(2))* Scholastic Library Publishing.

Kingsbury, Robert. The Assassination of James A. Garfield. 2009. (Library of Political Assassinations Ser.). 64p. (gr. 5-5). 58.50 *(978-1-60853-825-6(7))* Rosen Publishing Group, Inc., The.

Mara, Wil. James Garfield. 2011. (Presidents & Their Times 5 Ser.). 96p. (gr. 6). 34.21 *(978-1-60870-183-4(2))* Marshall Cavendish GBR. Dist: Marshall Cavendish Corp.

Parker, Lewis. How to Draw the Life & Times of James A. Garfield. 2009. (Kid's Guide to Drawing the Presidents of the United States of America Ser.). 32p. (gr. 4-4). 50.50 *(978-1-61511-145-9(X),* PowerKids Pr.) Rosen Publishing Group, Inc., The.

Parker, Lewis K. How to Draw the Life & Times of James A. Garfield. 2006. (Kid's Guide to Drawing the Presidents of the United States of America Ser.). (YA). (gr. 2-5). 26.50 *(978-1-4042-2997-6(3))* Rosen Publishing Group, Inc., The.

Venezia, Mike. James A. Garfield. Venezia, Mike, illus. 2006. (Getting to Know the U. S. Presidents Ser.). (ENG., Illus.). 32p. (J). (gr. 3-7). lib. bdg. 28.00 *(978-0-516-22625-5(8),* Children's Pr.) Scholastic Library Publishing.

Young, Jeff C. James A. Garfield: A MyReportLinks.com Book. 2003. (Presidents Ser.). (Illus.). 48p. (J). (gr. 5-10). lib. bdg. 25.26 *(978-0-7660-5100-3(5),* MyReportLinks.com Bks.) Enslow Pubs., Inc.

GARFIELD, JAMES A. (JAMES ABRAM), 1831-1881—FICTION

Alger, Horatio. From Canal Boy to President. 2006. pap. *(978-1-4068-0665-6(X))* Echo Library.

—From Canal Boy to President: Or the Boyhood & Manhood of James A. Garfield. 2007. (ENG.). 196p. pap. 19.99 *(978-1-4346-2511-3(7));* 208p. pap. 22.99 *(978-1-4346-2553-3(2))* Creative Media Partners, LLC.

GARMENT MAKING

see Dressmaking

GARRISON, WILLIAM LLOYD, 1805-1879

Esty, Amos. The Liberator: The Story of William Lloyd Garrison. 2011. (Civil Rights Leaders Ser.). 144p. 28.95 *(978-1-59935-137-7(4))* Reynolds, Morgan Inc.

Morretta, Alison. Frederick Douglass & William Garrison. 2015. (Primary Sources of the Abolitionist Movement Ser.). (ENG., Illus.). 64p. (J). (gr. 6-6). lib. bdg. 34.21 *(978-1-5026-0532-0(5))* Cavendish Square Publishing.

Thomas, William David. William Lloyd Garrison: A Radical Voice Against Slavery. 2009. (Voices for Freedom Ser.). (ENG.). 64p. (J). (gr. 5-8). pap. *(978-0-7787-4841-0(3));* lib. bdg. *(978-0-7787-4825-0(1))* Crabtree Publishing Co.

GAS AND OIL ENGINES

see Internal Combustion Engines

GAS COMPANIES

see Public Utilities

GAS ENGINES

see Internal Combustion Engines

GASES

Bailey, Diane. Natural Gas Power. 2014. (J). *(978-1-60818-409-5(9),* Creative Education) Creative Co., The.

Bjorklund, Ruth. The Pros & Cons of Natural Gas & Fracking. 2014. (Economics of Energy Ser.). 80p. (YA). (gr. 7-10). lib. bdg. 35.64 *(978-1-62712-921-3(9))* Cavendish Square Publishing.

Bloom, Chrissa. In the Kitchen with Solids, Liquids, & Gases. 2009. (Real Life Readers Ser.). 12p. (gr. 1-2). pap. 5.90 *(978-1-4042-7897-4(4),* Rosen Classroom) Rosen Publishing Group, Inc., The.

Boothroyd, Jennifer. What Is a Gas? 2007. (First Step Nonfiction - States of Matter Ser.). (ENG., Illus.). 24p. (gr. k-2). pap. 6.95 *(978-0-8225-6818-6(7));* lib. bdg. 23.93 *(978-0-8225-6837-7(3),* Lerner Pubns.) Lerner Publishing Group.

Brannon, Barbara. Discover Gases. 2005. (J). pap. *(978-1-4108-5119-2(2))* Benchmark Education Co.

Braun, Eric. Joe-Joe the Wizard Brews up Solids, Liquids, & Gases, 1 vol. Boyden, Robin, illus. 2012. (In the Science Lab Ser.). (ENG.). 24p. (gr. 2-3). pap. 9.95 *(978-1-4048-7238-7(8))* Picture Window Bks.

Cesa, Irene, ed. Chemistry of Gases, 28 vols., Vol. 8. 2003. (ChemTopic Labs Ser.: 8). (Illus.). 84p. (YA). 11.95 *(978-1-877991-76-9(7))* Flinn Scientific, Inc.

—The Gas Laws, 26 vols., Vol. 9. 2003. (ChemTopic Labs Ser.: 9). (Illus.). 96p. (YA). pap. 11.95 *(978-1-877991-77-6(5))* Flinn Scientific, Inc.

Crabtree Publishing Company Staff & Jackson, Tom. Gases & Their Properties. 2012. (ENG., Illus.). 32p. (J). *(978-0-7787-4229-6(6));* pap. *(978-0-7787-4233-3(4))* Crabtree Publishing Co.

Doudna, Kelly. Super Simple Things to Do with Bubbles: Fun & Easy Science for Kids, 1 vol. 2011. (Super Simple Science Ser.). (ENG., Illus.). 24p. (J). (gr. k-3). 25.65 *(978-1-61714-673-2(0))* ABDO Publishing Co.

Duke, Shirley. Science Lab: Gases. 2011. (Explorer Library: Language Arts Explorer Ser.). (ENG.). 32p. (gr. 4-8). pap. 14.21 *(978-1-61080-292-5(6),* 201214); lib. bdg. 28.50 *(978-1-61080-203-1(9),* 201182) Cherry Lake Publishing.

Gases & Their Properties. 2011. (Science Made Simple Ser.). (ENG.). 64p. (YA). pap. 12.95 *(978-1-4488-2243-0(2),* Rosen Reference) Rosen Publishing Group, Inc., The.

Hasan, Heather. Nitrogen. 2005. (Understanding the Elements of the Periodic Table Ser.). (Illus.). 48p. (J). (gr. 5-8). lib. bdg. 29.25 *(978-1-4042-0158-3(0))* Rosen Publishing Group, Inc., The.

Hoffman, Sara E. Gases. 2012. (First Step Nonfiction - Kinds of Matter Ser.). (ENG., Illus.). 8p. (gr. -1-1). pap. 4.95 *(978-1-4677-0519-6(5))* Lerner Publishing Group.

Holt, Rinehart and Winston Staff. Holt Chemistry Chptr. 12: Gases. 4th ed. Date not set. pap. 11.20 *(978-0-03-068137-0(5))* Holt McDougal.

Hurd, Will. Changing States: Solids, Liquids, & Gases. 2016. (Do It Yourself Ser.). (ENG.). 48p. (gr. 3-6). pap. 8.99 *(978-1-4846-3818-7(2),* NA-h) Heinemann-Raintree.

Jakab, Cheryl. Greenhouse Gases. 2010. (Environment in Focus Ser.). 32p. (gr. 4). 28.50 *(978-1-60870-091-2(7))* Marshall Cavendish Corp.

Kiesbye, Stefan. The Alaska Gas Pipeline. 2010. (At Issue Ser.). (ENG.). 128p. (gr. 10-12). 39.40 *(978-0-7377-4864-2(8));* pap. 27.80 *(978-0-7377-4865-9(6))* Cengage Gale. (Greenhaven Pr., Inc.).

Kjelle, Marylou Morano. The Properties of Gases. (Library of Physical Science Ser.). 24p. 2009. (gr. 4-4). 42.50 *(978-1-60853-790-7(0))* 2007. (ENG., Illus.). (gr. 4-8). pap. 7.05 *(978-1-4042-2170-3(0))* 2006. (Illus.). (J). (gr. 3-7). lib. bdg. 22.60 *(978-1-4042-3423-9(3))* Rosen Publishing Group, Inc., The. (PowerKids Pr.).

Lankford, Ronald D. & Lankford, Ronnie D. Greenhouse Gases. 2008. (At Issue Ser.). (ENG., Illus.). 128p. (gr. 10-12). pap. 27.80 *(978-0-7377-4101-8(5),* Greenhaven Pr., Inc.) Cengage Gale.

Lankford, Ronnie D., Jr., ed. Greenhouse Gases. 2008. (At Issue Ser.). (ENG., Illus.). 128p. (gr. 10-12). 39.40 *(978-0-7377-4100-1(7),* Greenhaven Pr., Inc.) Cengage Gale.

Masters, Nancy Robinson. How Did That Get to My House? Natural Gas. 2009. (Community Connections: How Did That Get to My House? Ser.). (ENG.). 24p. (gr. 2-5). lib. bdg. 25.64 *(978-1-60279-479-5(0),* 200248) Cherry Lake Publishing.

Merrill, Amy French. Everyday Physical Science Experiments with Gases. 2009. (Science Surprises Ser.). 24p. (gr. 3-3). 42.50 *(978-1-60853-059-5(0),* PowerKids Pr.) Rosen Publishing Group, Inc., The.

Metz, Lorijo. What Can We Do about Global Warming? 2009. (Protecting Our Planet Ser.). (Illus.). 24p. (ENG.). (J). pap. 8.25 *(978-1-4358-2479-9(2));* (YA). (gr. 2-5). lib. bdg. 22.60 *(978-1-4042-8079-3(0))* Rosen Publishing Group, Inc., The.

Meyer, Susan. Gases & Their Properties. 2011. (Science Made Simple Ser.). (Illus.). 64p. (YA). (gr. 5-8). lib. bdg. 31.95 *(978-1-4488-1233-2(X),* Rosen Reference) Rosen Publishing Group, Inc., The.

Mezzanotte, Jim. Gases. 2006. (States of Matter Ser.). (Illus.). 24p. (gr. 1-4). pap. 8.15 *(978-0-8368-6802-9(1));* lib. bdg. 22.00 *(978-0-8368-6797-8(1))* Stevens, Gareth Publishing LLLP. (Weekly Reader Leveled Readers).

Michele, Tracey. Gas & Air. 2011. (Learn-Abouts Ser.). (Illus.). 16p. (J). pap. 7.95 *(978-1-59920-644-8(7))* Black Rabbit Bks.

Morano-Kjelle, Marylou. Gases, 1 vol., 1. 2014. (Ultimate Science: Physical Science Ser.). (ENG.). 24p. (gr. 3-6). 23.60 *(978-1-4777-6081-9(4),* PowerKids Pr.) Rosen Publishing Group, Inc., The.

Nagelhout, Ryan. How Natural Gas Is Formed. 2016. (From the Earth: How Resources Are Made Ser.). 32p. (J). (gr. 4-3). pap. 10.50 *(978-1-4824-4716-3(9))* Stevens, Gareth Publishing LLLP.

Nelson, Robin. Gases. 2005. (First Step Nonfiction Ser.). (J). (Illus.). 23p. (gr. 3-7). lib. bdg. 18.60 *(978-0-8225-2616-2(6),* Lerner Pubns.); pap. 5.95 *(978-0-8225-5378-6(3))* Lerner Publishing Group.

Parker, Steve. Oil & Gas. 2004. (Science Files Ser.). (Illus.). 32p. (gr. 2-6). lib. bdg. 26.00 *(978-0-8368-4031-5(3),* Gareth Stevens Learning Library) Stevens, Gareth Publishing LLLP.

Peppas, Lynn. What Is a Gas? 2012. (ENG.). 24p. (J). *(978-0-7787-0769-1(5));* (Illus.). pap. *(978-0-7787-0776-9(8))* Crabtree Publishing Co.

Pipe, Jim. Gas. 2011. (J). 28.50 *(978-1-59604-214-8(1))* Black Rabbit Bks.

Randolph, Joanne. Gases in My World. (My World of Science Ser.). 24p. 2009. (gr. 2-2). 37.50 *(978-1-61514-721-2(7),* PowerKids Pr.) 2007. (ENG.). (gr. k-8). pap. 7.05 *(978-1-4042-8419-7(2),* Rosen Classroom) 2006. (Illus.). (J). (gr. 3-7). lib. bdg. 18.75 *(978-1-4042-3284-6(2),* PowerKids Pr.) Rosen Publishing Group, Inc., The.

—Gases in My World / Los Gases en Mi Mundo. Brusca, Maria Cristina, tr. from ENG. 2006. (My World of Science/ Mi mundo y la Ciencia Ser.). (ENG & SPA., Illus.). 24p. (J). (gr. k-3). lib. bdg. 16.00 *(978-1-4042-3315-7(6))* Rosen Publishing Group, Inc., The.

—Gases in My World/Los gases en mi Mundo. 2009. (My World of Science/la ciencia en mi mundo Ser.). (ENG & SPA.). 48p. (gr. 2-2). 37.50 *(978-1-61514-733-5(0),* Editorial Buenas Letras) Rosen Publishing Group, Inc., The.

—Gears in My World. 2009. (My World of Science Ser.). 24p. (gr. 2-2). 37.50 *(978-1-61514-722-9(5),* PowerKids Pr.) Rosen Publishing Group, Inc., The.

—Gears in My World/Engranajes en mi Mundo. 2009. (My World of Science/la ciencia en mi mundo Ser.). (ENG & SPA.). 48p. (gr. 2-2). 37.50 *(978-1-61514-734-2(9),* Editorial Buenas Letras) Rosen Publishing Group, Inc., The.

Rockwell, Anne F. What's So Bad about Gasoline? Fossil Fuels & What They Do. Meisel, Paul, illus. 2009. (Let's-Read-And-Find-Out Science 2 Ser.). (ENG.). 40p. (J). (gr. k-4). pap. 5.99 *(978-0-06-157527-3(5),* Collins) HarperCollins Pubs.

Rodriguez, Cindy. Gases. 2013. (SPA.). (J). *(978-1-62127-601-2(5))* Weigl Pubs., Inc.

—Gases, with Code. 2012. (What Is Matter? Ser.). (ENG., Illus.). 24p. (J). (gr. -1-3). pap. 12.95 *(978-1-61913-604-5(X),* AV2 by Weigl) Weigl Pubs., Inc.

—Gases with Code. 2012. (What Is Matter? Ser.). (ENG., Illus.). 24p. (J). (gr. -1-3). lib. bdg. 27.13 *(978-1-61913-602-1(3),* AV2 by Weigl) Weigl Pubs., Inc.

Rodriguez, Cindy & Siemens, Jared. Gas. 2016. (J). ***(978-1-4896-5752-7(5))*** Weigl Pubs., Inc.

Rowell, Rebecca. Natural Gas. 2013. (J). *(978-1-61080-970-2(X));* (ENG.). 32p. (gr. 4-8). 28.50 *(978-1-61080-895-8(9),* 202559); (ENG.). 32p. (gr. 4-8). pap. 14.21 *(978-1-61080-920-7(3),* 202561) Cherry Lake Publishing.

Saucerman, Linda. Hydrogen. 2009. (Understanding the Elements of the Periodic Table Ser.). 48p. (gr. 6-6). 53.00 *(978-1-60854-656-5(X),* Rosen Reference) Rosen Publishing Group, Inc., The.

Sian Gases. 2004. (J). *(978-1-59242-035-3(4))* Delta Education, LLC.

Simon, Chaman & Kazunas, Ariel. Super Cool Science Experiments: Water. 2009. (Explorer Library: Science

EFG

Explorer Ser.). (ENG., Illus.). 32p. (gr. 4-8). lib. bdg. 28.50 (978-1-60279-529-7(0), 200298) Cherry Lake Publishing.

Spilsbury, Louise & Spilsbury, Richard. Solids, Liquids, & Gases, 1 vol. (Essential Physical Science Ser.). (ENG., Illus.). 48p. (gr. 4-6). 2014. lib. bdg. 33.32 (978-1-4329-8151-8(X)) 2013. pap. 9.95 (978-1-4329-8160-0(9)) Heinemann-Raintree. (Heinemann InfoSearch).

Sullivan, Erin Ash. Liquids & Gases: Set Of 6. 2010. (Navigators Ser.). (J). pap. 44.00 net. (978-1-4108-5071-3(4)) Benchmark Education Co.

—Liquids & Gases: Text Pairs. 2008. (Bridges/Navigators Ser.). (J). (gr. 3). 89.00 (978-1-4108-8366-7(3)) Benchmark Education Co.

Thomas, Michele. Oxygen. 2009. (Understanding the Elements of the Periodic Table Ser.). 48p. (gr. 6-6). 53.00 (978-1-60854-674-9(8), Rosen Reference) Rosen Publishing Group, Inc., The.

Tocci, Salvatore. Oxygen. 2005. (True Bks.). (ENG., Illus.). 48p. (J). (gr. 3-5). pap. 6.95 (978-0-516-27851-3(7), Children's Pr.) Scholastic Library Publishing.

Weakland, Mark. Bubbles Float, Bubbles Pop. 2011. (Science Starts Ser.). (ENG.). 32p. (gr. 1-2). pap. 47.70 (978-1-4296-6142-3(9), Aplus Bks.) Capstone Press of Coughlan Cos.

—Las Burbujas Flotan, Las Burbujas Explotan/Bubbles Float, Bubbles Pop. 2012. (Comienza la Ciencia/Science Starts Ser.). (MUL.). 32p. (gr. 1-2). pap. 7.99 (978-1-4765-0065-2(7), A+ Bilingue/Bilingual) Capstone Press of Coughlan Cos.

—The Solid Truth about Matter. Lum, Bernice, illus. 2012. (LOL Physical Science Ser.). (ENG.). 32p. (gr. 3-4). pap. 47.70 (978-1-4296-9303-5(7), Fact Finders) Capstone Press of Coughlan Cos.

Wheeler-Toppen, Jodi. Science Experiments That Fizz & Bubble: Fun Projects for Curious Kids, 1 vol. 2010. (Kitchen Science Ser.). (ENG.). 32p. (gr. 3-4). lib. bdg. 27.99 (978-1-4296-5425-8(2), Edge Bks.) Capstone Press of Coughlan Cos.

Willett, Edward. Neon. 2007. (Understanding the Elements of the Periodic Table Ser.). (ENG., Illus.). 48p. (YA). (gr. 3-7). lib. bdg. 29.25 (978-1-4042-1008-0(3)) Rosen Publishing Group, Inc., The.

Williams, Zella. Experiments with Solids, Liquids, & Gases. 2007. (Do-It-Yourself Science Ser.). (Illus.). 24p. (J). (gr. 2-5). lib. bdg. 25.25 (978-1-4042-3658-5(9)) Rosen Publishing Group, Inc., The.

Zoehfeld, Kathleen Weidner. What Is the World Made Of? Meisel, Paul, illus. 2015. (Let's-Read-And-Find-Out Science 2 Ser.). (ENG.). 32p. (J). (gr. -1-3). pap. 6.99 (978-0-06-238195-8(4)) HarperCollins Pubs.

GASOLINE

Cunningham, Kevin. Gasoline. 2008. (21st Century Skills Library: Global Products Ser.). (ENG.). 32p. (gr. 4-8). lib. bdg. 28.50 (978-1-60279-121-3(X), 200097) Cherry Lake Publishing.

Miller, Debra A. Gasoline. 2012. (Current Controversies Ser.). (ENG.). 224p. (gr. 10-12). lib. bdg. 46.40 (978-0-7377-6227-3(6), Greenhaven Pr., Inc.) Cengage Gale.

Murray, Julie. Oil to Gas, 1 vol. 2006. (Beginning to End Set 1 - 8 Titles Ser.). (ENG.). 24p. (gr. k-4). 25.65 (978-1-59679-913-4(7), Buddy Bks.) ABDO Publishing Co.

Rockwell, Anne F. What's So Bad about Gasoline? Fossil Fuels & What They Do. Meisel, Paul, illus. 2009. (Let's-Read-And-Find-Out Science 2 Ser.). (ENG.). 40p. (J). (gr. k-4). pap. 5.99 (978-0-06-157527-3(5), Collins) HarperCollins Pubs.

Zemlicka, Shannon. From Oil to Gas. 2013. (Start to Finish, Second Series: Everyday Products Ser.). (ENG., Illus.). 24p. (gr. k-3). pap. 6.95 (978-1-4677-0796-1(1)); lib. bdg. 23.93 (978-0-7613-9185-2(1), Lerner Pubns.) Lerner Publishing Group.

GASOLINE ENGINES

see Internal Combustion Engines

GASTRONOMY

see Cooking; Food; Menus

GAUCHOS

see Cowboys

GAUGUIN, PAUL, 1848-1903

Anderson, Robert. Paul Gauguin. 2003. (Artists in Their Time Ser.). (ENG., Illus.). 48p. (J). (gr. 5-7). pap. 6.95 (978-0-531-16647-5(3), Watts, Franklin) Scholastic Library Publishing.

Cook, Diane. Paul Gauguin: 18th Century French Painter. 2013. (People of Importance Ser.: 21). (Illus.). 32p. (J). (gr. 4-18). 19.95 (978-1-4222-2854-8(1)) Mason Crest.

De Magalhaes, Roberto Carvalho. Paul Gauguin. 2003. (Great Artists Ser.). (Illus.). 40p. (J). 15.95 (978-1-59270-010-3(1)) Enchanted Lion Bks., LLC.

de Salvia, Maria Siponta. Paul Gauguin. 2005. (Great Artists Ser.). (Illus.). 40p. (J). (gr. 5). per. 7.95 (978-1-59270-051-6(9)) Enchanted Lion Bks., LLC.

Haynes, Sara. Gauguin, Vol. 7. 2015. (Great Artists Collection). (Illus.). 64p. (J). (gr. 7). lib. bdg. 23.95 (978-1-4222-3259-0(X)) Mason Crest.

Klein, Adam G. Paul Gauguin, 1 vol. 2007. (Great Artists Set 2 Ser.). (ENG., Illus.). 32p. (gr. -1-3). 27.07 (978-1-59679-729-1(0), Checkerboard Library) ABDO Publishing Co.

Merberg, Julie & Bober, Suzanne. On an Island with Gauguin. 2007. (Mini Masters Ser.: MINI). (ENG., Illus.). 22p. (J). (gr. -1 — 1). bds. 6.99 (978-0-8118-5711-6(5)) Chronicle Bks. LLC.

Roddam, George. The Life & Art of Paul Gauguin. Harasymowicz, Slawa, illus. 2016. (Lives of Great Artists Ser.). 00080p. (J). (gr. 8-8). 35.75 (978-1-4994-6581-5(5), Rosen Young Adult) Rosen Publishing Group, Inc., The.

Spence, David. Gauguin. 2010. (Great Artists & Their World Ser.). (Illus.). 48p. (YA). 32.80 (978-1-84898-316-8(6)) Black Rabbit Bks.

Venezia, Mike. Paul Gauguin. 2016. (Getting to Know the World's Greatest Artists Ser.). (ENG., Illus.). 40p. (J). pap. 7.95 (978-0-531-22105-1(9), Children's Pr.) Scholastic Library Publishing.

—Paul Gauguin (Revised Edition) 2016. (Getting to Know the World's Greatest Artists Ser.). (ENG., Illus.). 40p. (J). lib. bdg. 29.00 (978-0-531-21666-8(7), Children's Pr.) Scholastic Library Publishing.

Wood, Alix. Paul Gauguin, 1 vol. 2015. (ENG., Illus.). 32p. (J). lib. bdg. 26.25 (978-1-4777-5405-4(9), Windmill Bks.) Rosen Publishing Group, Inc., The.

GAUTAMA BUDDHA

Carew-Miller, Anna. Buddha. 2004. (Great Names Ser.). (Illus.). 32p. (J). (gr. 3-18). lib. bdg. 19.95 (978-1-59084-137-2(9)) Mason Crest.

—Buddha: Father of Buddhism. 2013. (People of Importance Ser.: 21). (Illus.). 32p. (J). (gr. 4-18). 19.95 (978-1-4222-2842-5(8)) Mason Crest.

Dharma, A. M. Teacher Resource Guide Set: Teacher Resource Guide boxed with 12 Jataka Tales. 2008. (SPA.). 524p. (J). (gr. 4-7). pap. 123.00 (978-0-89800-280-5(X)) Dharma Publishing.

Duran, Magdalena. La Joya de la Amistad. 2009. (SPA.). 32p. (J). (gr. -1-3). pap. 8.95 (978-0-89800-429-8(2)) Dharma Publishing.

Foran, Jill. Buddha Day. 2003. (Celebrating Cultures Ser.). (Illus.). 24p. (J). lib. bdg. 24.45 (978-1-59036-090-3(7)) Weigl Pubs., Inc.

Gagne, Tammy. Buddha. 2017. (Junior Biography From Ancient Civilization Ser.). (gr. 4-6). 29.95 (978-1-68020-014-0(3)) Mitchell Lane Pubs., Inc.

Gedney, Mona K. The Life & Times of Buddha. 2005. (Biography from Ancient Civilizations Ser.). (Illus.). 48p. (J). (gr. -1-7). lib. bdg. 29.95 (978-1-58415-342-9(3)) Mitchell Lane Pubs., Inc.

Hsuan Hua. Buddha's Wisdom. Yeh, Alicia, illus. 2004. (ENG & CHI.). (J). (978-0-88139-867-0(5)) Buddhist Text Translation Society.

Jan, Emily. Monedas de Oro. 2009. (SPA.). 32p. (J). (gr. -1-3). pap. 8.95 (978-0-89800-433-5(0)) Dharma Publishing.

—Pieces of Gold. 2009. (ENG.). 32p. (J). (gr. -1-3). pap. 8.95 (978-0-89800-432-8(2)) Dharma Publishing.

Landaw, Jonathan. Prince Siddhartha: The Story of Buddha. Brooke, Janet, illus. 2nd rev. ed. 2011. (ENG.). 144p. (J). (gr. 2-7). pap. 22.95 (978-0-86171-653-1(1)) Wisdom Pubns.

Nestorowich, Sherry. Wisdom of the Golden Goose. 2009. (ENG.). 32p. (J). (gr. k-3). pap. 8.95 (978-0-89800-434-2(9)) Dharma Publishing.

Rawding, F. W. The Buddha. (Cambridge Topic Bks.). (Illus.). 52p. (J). (gr. 5-10). lib. bdg. 8.95 (978-0-8225-1212-7(2), Lerner Pubns.) Lerner Publishing Group.

Seth, Shantum. Siddhartha Gautama: The Life of the Buddha - Based on Original Sources. Mukherjee, Aniruddha, illus. adapted ed. 2014. (ENG.). 64p. pap. 6.95 (978-1-906230-61-6(7)) Real Reads Ltd. GBR. Dist: Casemate Pubs. & Bk. Distributors, LLC.

Zamosky, Lisa. Siddhartha Gautama: The Buddha, 1 vol. 2007. (Primary Source Readers Ser.). (ENG., Illus.). 32p. (J). (gr. 4-4). pap. 8.99 (978-0-7439-0431-5(1)) Shell Educational Publishing.

GAZELLES

Borgert-Spaniol, Megan. Gazelles. 2012. (Animal Safari Ser.). (ENG., Illus.). 24p. (J). (gr. k-3). lib. bdg. 25.95 (978-1-60014-768-5(2), Blastoff! Readers) Bellwether Media.

Doudna, Kelly. It's a Baby Gazelle!, 1 vol. 2009. (Baby African Animals Ser.). (ENG., Illus.). 24p. (J). (gr. k-3). lib. bdg. 24.21 (978-1-60453-153-4(3), SandCastle) ABDO Publishing Co.

Meinking, Mary. Lion vs. Gazelle, 1 vol. 2011. (Predator vs. Prey Ser.). (ENG., Illus.). 32p. (gr. 1-2). 29.99 (978-1-4109-3934-0(0)); pap. 8.29 (978-1-4109-3943-2(X)) Heinemann-Raintree. (Read Me!).

—Predator vs. Prey, 8 vols., Set. Incl. Crocodile vs. Wildebeest. (Illus.). pap. 8.29 (978-1-4109-3944-9(8)); Dolphin vs. Fish. (Illus.). pap. 8.29 (978-1-4109-3949-4(9)); Lion vs. Gazelle. (Illus.). pap. 8.29 (978-1-4109-3943-2(X)); Owl vs. Mouse. (Illus.). pap. 8.29 (978-1-4109-3945-6(6)); Polar Bear vs. Seal. (Illus.). pap. 8.29 (978-1-4109-3948-7(0)); Shark vs. Penguin. pap. 8.29 (978-1-4109-3946-3(4)); Tarantula vs. Bird. (Illus.). pap. 8.29 (978-1-4109-3947-0(2)); Wolf vs. Elk. (Illus.). pap. 8.29 (978-1-4109-3950-0(2)); (gr. 1-2). (Predator vs. Prey Ser.). (ENG.). 32p. 2011. Set pap. 63.92 (978-1-4109-3951-7(0)); Set lib. bdg. 119.96 (978-1-4109-3942-5(1)) Heinemann-Raintree. (Read Me!).

Robbins, Lynette. Gazelles. 2012. (J). 49.50 (978-1-4488-5162-1(9), PowerKids Pr.); pap. 8.25 (978-1-4488-5161-4(0), PowerKids Pr.); lib. bdg. 22.60 (978-1-4488-5014-3(2)) Rosen Publishing Group, Inc., The.

GAZELLES—FICTION

deRubertis, Barbara. Gertie Gorilla's Glorious Gift. Alley, R. W., illus. 2010. (Animal Antics A to Z Ser.). 32p. (J). (gr. -1-3). pap. 7.95 (978-1-57565-311-2(7)); lib. bdg. 22.60 (978-1-57565-318-1(4)) Kane Press, Inc.

deRubertis, Barbara & DeRubertis, Barbara. Gertie Gorilla's Glorious Gift. Alley, R. W., illus. 2012. (Animal Antics A to Z Ser.). 32p. (J). (gr. 2 — 1). cd-rom 7.95 (978-1-57565-400-3(8)) Kane Press, Inc.

Rex, Adam. XO, OX: A Love Story. Campbell, Scott, illus. 2017. (ENG.). 40p. (J). 17.99 (978-1-62672-288-0(9), 9781626722880) Roaring Brook Pr.

Rhodes, Genee M. & Travers, Jasmine. Gloria Gets Glasses. 2013. 32p. pap. 11.00 (978-2-01-300710-8(8)) Rhodes, EL. Bks., LLC.

Wilson, George H. The Legend of Thompson the Gazelle. 2010. (Illus.). 50p. (J). 15.00 (978-0-9778477-4-7(8)) A Story Plus Children Bks.

GEESE

Bailer, Darice. Geese. 2010. (Animals Animals 11 Ser.). 48p. (gr. 3). 23.95 (978-0-7614-4840-2(3)) Marshall Cavendish Corp.

Beer, Amy-Jane. Canada Goose. 2008. (Nature's Children Ser.). (Illus.). 52p. (J). (978-0-7172-6251-9(0)) Grolier, Ltd.

Beylon, Cathy. BOOST Mother Goose Coloring Book. 2013. (BOOST Educational Ser.). (ENG.). 32p. (J). (gr. 1-2). pap. 4.99 (978-0-486-49414-2(4)) Dover Pubns., Inc.

Borgert-Spaniol, Megan. Canada Geese. 2016. (North American Animals Ser.). (ENG., Illus.). 24p. (J). (gr. k-3). 25.95 (978-1-62617-401-6(6), Blastoff! Readers) Bellwether Media.

—Geese. 2012. (Backyard Wildlife Ser.). (ENG., Illus.). 24p. (J). (gr. k-3). lib. bdg. 25.95 (978-1-60014-722-7(4), Blastoff! Readers) Bellwether Media.

Bradley, James V. The Canada Goose. 2006. (Nature Walk Ser.). (Illus.). 64p. (gr. 4-6). lib. bdg. 28.00 (978-0-7910-9113-5(9), Chelsea Hse.) Facts On File, Inc.

Burrows, Jennifer S. The Canada Goose & You. Day, Margery, illus. 2009. 32p. pap. 15.95 (978-0-9791606-9-1(3)) E & E Publishing.

Cain, Marie Mowery. From Eggs to Geese. 2013. (Big Books, Red Ser.). (ENG & SPA., Illus.). 16p. pap. 33.00 (978-1-59246-217-9(0)) Big Books, by George!

Carr, Aaron. Goose. 2014. (Illus.). 24p. (J). (978-1-62127-231-1(1)) Weigl Pubs., Inc.

Dunrea, Olivier. Say Good Night. 2017. (Gossie & Friends Ser.). (ENG., Illus.). 18p. (J). (— 1). bds. 8.99 (978-0-544-91503-9(8), HMH Books For Young Readers) Houghton Mifflin Harcourt Publishing Co.

Hills, Tad. What's up, Duck? A Book of Opposites. Hills, Tad, illus. 2008. (Duck & Goose Ser.). (ENG., Illus.). 22p. (J). (gr. k — 1). bds. 6.99 (978-0-375-84738-7(3), Schwartz & Wade Bks.) Random Hse. Children's Bks.

Kallgren, Beverly H. A Duck Named Goose. 2004. (Illus.). 48p. (J). per. 10.00 (978-1-930648-90-6(1)) Goose River Pr.

Kozlowski, Bryan. Cook Me a Rhyme: In the Kitchen with Mother Goose. 2017. (Cook Me A... Ser.). (ENG., Illus.). 80p. (J). (gr. k-6). spiral bd. 16.95 (978-1-63322-218-2(7), Walter Foster Jr) Quarto Publishing Group USA.

Metz, Lorijo. Geese: Geese, Ganders, & Goslings. 2010. (On the Farm Ser.). (ENG.). 24p. (J). pap. 8.25 (978-1-4488-1345-2(X)); lib. bdg. 22.60 (978-1-4488-0692-8(5)) Rosen Publishing Group, Inc., The.

Sherk, Beth Larson. The Three Sisters. 2012. (Illus.). 35p. (J). 14.95 (978-1-62086-091-5(0)) Mascot Bks., Inc.

Stockland, Patricia M. In the Goose Pen, 1 vol. Ouren, Todd, illus. 2009. (Barnyard Buddies Set 2 Ser.). (ENG.). 24p. (gr. -1-2). 27.07 (978-1-60270-643-9(3), Looking Glass Library-Nonfiction) Magic Wagon.

GEESE—FICTION

Allen, Constance. Elmo's Mother Goose Rhymes (Sesame Street) Swanson, Maggie, illus. 2017. (Little Golden Book Ser.). (ENG.). 24p. (J). (-k). 4.99 (978-1-101-93994-9(X), Golden Bks.) Random Hse. Children's Bks.

Allen, Pat. The Field by the Sea. 2010. 20p. 21.50 (978-1-4457-3405-7(2)) Lulu Pr., Inc.

Award, Anna, et al. The Boy Who Cried Wolf & the Goose That Laid the Golden Eggs. 2014. (ENG.). 24p. (J). pap. 6.95 (978-1-84135-957-1(2)) Award Pubns. Ltd. GBR. Dist: Parkwest Pubns., Inc.

Baker, Harriet Lila. Book III: Boyduck Goose: His Life & Times. 2005. (J). pap. 9.00 (978-0-8059-6803-3(2)) Dorrance Publishing Co., Inc.

Baker, Michelle M. The Geese of Belle Isle: Volume I. 2011. 28p. pap. 24.95 (978-1-4626-3715-7(9)) America Star Bks.

Barchers, Suzanne I. On My Stoop, 1 vol. 2011. (Targeted Phonics Ser.). (ENG., Illus.). 16p. (J). (gr. k-2). pap. 5.99 (978-1-4333-2920-3(4)) Teacher Created Materials, Inc.

Bea, Holly. Lucy Goose Goes to Texas. Boddy, Joe, illus. 2005. (ENG.). 32p. (J). (gr. -1-5). 15.95 (978-1-932073-15-7(9)) New World Library.

Bedtime with Mothergoose. 2005. (J). bds. (978-1-4194-0089-6(4)) Paradise Pr., Inc.

Benton, Doug. The Hummingbird Goose, 1 vol. 2009. 64p. pap. 19.95 (978-1-61546-746-4(7)) America Star Bks.

Binks. Don't Be a Chicken. Begonia, Ruby, illus. 2013. 32p. 15.95 (978-1-935448-22-8(6)) Lost Coast Pr.

Bloom, Suzanne. Alone Together. Bloom, Suzanne, illus. 2014. (Goose & Bear Stories Ser.). (ENG., Illus.). 32p. (J). (gr. -1-k). 16.95 (978-1-62091-736-7(X)) Boyds Mills Pr.

—Fox Forgets. Bloom, Suzanne, illus. 2013. (Goose & Bear Stories Ser.). (ENG., Illus.). 32p. (J). (gr. -1-1). 16.95 (978-1-59078-996-4(2)) Boyds Mills Pr.

—Oh! What a Surprise! 2012. (Goose & Bear Stories Ser.). (ENG.). 32p. (J). (gr. -1-k). 16.95 (978-1-59078-892-9(3)) Boyds Mills Pr.

—A Splendid Friend, Indeed. Bloom, Suzanne, illus. 2009. (Goose & Bear Stories Ser.). (ENG., Illus.). 32p. (J). (gr. -1-k). pap. 7.95 (978-1-59078-488-4(X)) Boyds Mills Pr.

—A Splendid Friend, Indeed. 2005. (Goose & Bear Stories Ser.). (ENG., Illus.). 32p. (J). (gr. -1-k). 16.95 (978-1-59078-286-6(0)) Boyds Mills Pr.

—Treasure. (Goose & Bear Stories Ser.). (ENG.). 32p. (J). (gr. -1-1). 2012. pap. 7.95 (978-1-59078-920-9(2)) 2007. (Illus.). 15.95 (978-1-59078-457-0(X)) Boyds Mills Pr.

—What about Bear? (Goose & Bear Stories Ser.). (ENG., Illus.). 32p. (J). (gr. -1-1). 2012. pap. 7.95 (978-1-59078-913-1(X)) 2010. 16.95 (978-1-59078-528-7(2)) Boyds Mills Pr.

Bloom, Suzanne, illus. Bear Can Dance! 2015. (Goose & Bear Stories Ser.). (ENG.). 40p. (J). (-k). 16.95 (978-1-62979-442-6(2)) Boyds Mills Pr.

—A Splendid Friend, Indeed. 2015. (Goose & Bear Stories Ser.). (ENG.). 32p. (J). (— 1). bds. 7.99 (978-1-62979-408-2(2)) Boyds Mills Pr.

Boll, Katherine. Dante the Dancing Goose. 2009. 20p. pap. 9.95 (978-1-60844-278-2(0)) Dog Ear Publishing, LLC.

Bollen, Christine. Flying with the Geese, 1 vol. Matyuschenko, Tanya, illus. 2010. 34p. 24.95 (978-1-4489-4401-9(5)) PublishAmerica, Inc.

Bond, Rebecca. Pig & Goose & the First Day of Spring. Bond, Rebecca, illus. 2017. (ENG., Illus.). 48p. (J). (gr. k-3). lib. bdg. 12.99 (978-1-58089-594-1(8)) Charlesbridge Publishing, Inc.

Bonnet, Rosalinde. Daddy Honk Honk! Bonnet, Rosalinde, illus. 2017. (ENG., Illus.). 32p. (J). (-k). 16.99 (978-0-399-18676-9(X), Dial Bks) Penguin Young Readers Group.

Brennan-Nelson, Denise & Brennan-Nelson, Dense. Grady the Goose. Monroe, Michael Glenn, illus. rev. ed. 2006. (ENG.). 32p. (J). (gr. k-6). 16.95 (978-1-58536-282-0(4)) Sleeping Bear Pr.

Brenner, Tom. And Then Comes Halloween. Meade, Holly, illus. 2009. (ENG.). 32p. (J). (gr. -1-3). 16.99 (978-0-7636-3659-3(2)) Candlewick Pr.

Carter, Angela C. Momma, Why Do We Have to Take a Bath? 2012. 36p. pap. 24.95 (978-1-4626-7547-0(6)) America Star Bks.

Childress, Mildred Tickfer. Esmerelda the Silly Goose. Zipperer, Susan Johnson, illus. 2004. 52p. (J). (gr. -1-3). 11.95 (978-1-887774-17-8(3), Wynden) Canmore Pr.

Christensen, Bob. Gaylord Goose. Marsh, Bobbi, illus. 2011. 28p. pap. 12.95 (978-1-61493-014-3(7)) Peppertree Pr., The.

Colfer, Chris. Adventures from the Land of Stories Boxed Set: The Mother Goose Diaries & Queen Red Riding Hood's Guide to Royalty. 2015. (Land of Stories Ser.). (ENG.). 256p. (J). (gr. 3-7). 22.00 (978-0-316-26151-7(3)) Little, Brown Bks. for Young Readers.

—The Mother Goose Diaries. Dorman, Brandon et al, illus. 2015. 121p. (J). (978-0-316-38332-5(5)) Little Brown & Co.

Coplans, Peta & Williams, Dylan. Syniad Da Gwenlli Gwydd. 2005. (WEL., Illus.). 28p. (978-1-84512-015-3(9)) Cymdeithas Lyfrau Ceredigion.

Cox, Phil Roxbee & Cartwright, S. Goose on the Loose. 2004. (Easy Words to Read Ser.). 16p. (J). (gr. 1-18). pap. 6.95 (978-0-7945-0036-8(6), Usborne) EDC Publishing.

Cox, Phil Roxbee & Cartwright, Stephen. Goose on the Loose. 2004. (Phonics Board Bks.). (Illus.). 10p. (J). 4.99 (978-0-7945-0305-5(5), Usborne) EDC Publishing.

—Ted's Shed. 2004. (Phonics Board Bks.). (Illus.). 10p. (J). 4.95 (978-0-7945-0304-8(7), Usborne) EDC Publishing.

Cummings, Priscilla. Autumn Journey, 1 vol. Ben-Ami, Doron, illus. 2009. (ENG.). 120p. (J). pap. 12.95 (978-0-87033-606-5(1), 9780870336065, Cornell Maritime Pr./Tidewater Pubs.) Schiffer Publishing, Ltd.

Deedy, Carmen Agra. Un Colchón de Plumas para Ágata, 1 vol. De la Torre, Cristina, tr. from ENG. Seeley, Laura L., illus. 2007. (SPA.). 32p. (J). (gr. k-3). 15.95 (978-1-56145-426-6(5)) Peachtree Pubs.

dePaola, Tomie. My First Mother Goose. 2009. (ENG.). 14p. (J). (gr. -1-k). bds. 5.99 (978-0-448-45199-2(9), Grosset & Dunlap) Penguin Young Readers Group.

Devine, Ginger. The Missing Goose Egg: A Sam the Lamb Mystery. 2009. 32p. pap. 14.95 (978-1-4389-8839-9(7)) AuthorHouse.

Doudna, Kelly. Goose Down, 1 vol. Haberstroh, Anne, illus. 2006. (Animal Tales Ser.). 24p. (J). (gr. k-3). (ENG.). lib. bdg. 24.21 (978-1-59679-941-7(2), SandCastle); pap. 48.42 (978-1-59679-942-4(0)) ABDO Publishing Co.

Dreher, Gidge. Gus, Scruffy, Clara & Friends. 2007. 80p. per. 9.95 (978-1-933912-24-0(3)) Westview Publishing Co., Inc.

Dunrea, Olivier. BooBoo. 2008. (Gossie & Friends Ser.). (ENG., Illus.). 32p. (J). (gr. k — 1). bds. 6.95 (978-0-618-75505-9(5)) Houghton Mifflin Harcourt Publishing Co.

—Gansi y Gerti/Gossie & Gertie Bilingual Board Book. 2013. (Gossie & Friends Ser.). (SPA & ENG., Illus.). 32p. (J). (gr. -1-3). bds., bds. 4.99 (978-0-544-07773-7(3)) Houghton Mifflin Harcourt Publishing Co.

—Gemma & Gus. (Gossie & Friends Ser.). (ENG., Illus.). 32p. (J). (— 1). 2016. bds. 6.99 (978-0-544-65647-5(4), HMH Books For Young Readers) 2015. lib. bdg. 9.99 (978-0-547-86851-6(0)) Houghton Mifflin Harcourt Publishing Co.

—Gemma & Gus (reader) 2017. (Gossie & Friends Ser.). (ENG., Illus.). 32p. (J). (gr. -1-3). 12.99 (978-0-544-93680-5(9), HMH Books For Young Readers) Houghton Mifflin Harcourt Publishing Co.

—Gideon. 2012. (Gossie & Friends Ser.). (ENG., Illus.). 32p. (J). (gr. k — 1). 9.99 (978-0-618-43661-3(8)) Houghton Mifflin Harcourt Publishing Co.

—Gideon: It's Play Time, Not Naptime! 2013. (Gossie & Friends Ser.). (ENG., Illus.). 32p. (J). (— 1). bds. 6.99 (978-0-547-98399-8(9)) Houghton Mifflin Harcourt Publishing Co.

—Gideon & Otto. 2012. (Gossie & Friends Ser.). (ENG., Illus.). 32p. (J). (gr. k — 1). 9.99 (978-0-618-43662-0(6)) Houghton Mifflin Harcourt Publishing Co.

—Gideon & Otto: Best Friends, Lost & Found. 2013. (Gossie & Friends Ser.). (ENG., Illus.). 32p. (J). (— 1). bds. 6.99 (978-0-547-98398-1(0)) Houghton Mifflin Harcourt Publishing Co.

—Gossie. (Gossie & Friends Ser.). (ENG., Illus.). 32p. (J). (gr. -1 — 1). 2007. bds. 6.99 (978-0-618-74791-7(5)) 2011. bds. 4.99 (978-0-547-51072-9(1)) Houghton Mifflin Harcourt Publishing Co.

—Gossie & Gertie. Dunrea, Olivier, illus. 2007. (Gossie & Friends Ser.). (ENG., Illus.). 16p. (J). (gr. -1 — 1). bds. 6.99 (978-0-618-74793-1(1)) Houghton Mifflin Harcourt Publishing Co.

—Gossie & Gertie. 2014. (Gossie & Friends — Green Light Readers Ser.). lib. bdg. 13.55 (978-0-606-33981-0(7), Turtleback) Turtleback Bks.

—Gossie & Gertie Padded Board Book. 2015. (Gossie & Friends Ser.). (ENG., Illus.). 32p. (J). (— 1). bds. 8.99 (978-0-544-50644-2(8), HMH Books For Young Readers) Houghton Mifflin Harcourt Publishing Co.

—Gossie & Gertie (Reader) 2014. (Gossie & Friends Ser.). (ENG., Illus.). 32p. (J). (gr. -1-3). pap. 3.99 (978-0-544-10535-5(4)) Houghton Mifflin Harcourt Publishing Co.

—Gossie Padded Board Book. 2015. (Gossie & Friends Ser.). (ENG., Illus.). 32p. (J). (— 1). bds. 8.99 (978-0-544-50637-4(5), HMH Books For Young Readers) Houghton Mifflin Harcourt Publishing Co.

—Gossie (Reader) 2014. (Gossie & Friends Ser.). (ENG., Illus.). 32p. (J). (gr. -1-3). pap. 3.99 (978-0-544-10573-7(7)) Houghton Mifflin Harcourt Publishing Co.

—Gus. (Gossie & Friends Ser.). (ENG., Illus.). 32p. (J). 2017. (gr. -1-3). 12.99 (978-0-544-93723-9(6)) 2015. (— 1). 9.99 (978-0-547-86761-8(1)) Houghton Mifflin Harcourt Publishing Co. (HMH Books For Young Readers).

—Gus (board Book) 2016. (Gossie & Friends Ser.). (ENG., Illus.). 32p. (J). (— 1). bds. 6.99 (978-0-544-64102-0(7), HMH Books For Young Readers) Houghton Mifflin Harcourt Publishing Co.

—Jasper & Joop. 2013. (Gossie & Friends Ser.). (ENG., Illus.). 32p. (J). (— 1). 9.99 (978-0-547-86762-5(X)) Houghton Mifflin Harcourt Publishing Co.

—Jasper & Joop (Reader) 2015. (Gossie & Friends Ser.). (ENG., Illus.). 32p. (J). (gr. -1-3). pap. 3.99 (978-0-544-50381-6(3), HMH Books For Young Readers) Houghton Mifflin Harcourt Publishing Co.

—Merry Christmas, Ollie! (Gossie & Friends Ser.). (ENG., Illus.). (J). (gr. k — 1). 2011. 30p. bds. 6.99 (978-0-547-37016-3(4)) 2008. 32p. 12.95

(978-0-618-53242-1(0)) Houghton Mifflin Harcourt Publishing Co.
—Merry Christmas, Ollie (Reader) 2015. (Gossie & Friends Ser.). (ENG., Illus.). 32p. (J). (gr. -1 — 1). pap. 3.99 *(978-0-544-55394-1(2)*, HMH Books For Young Readers) Houghton Mifflin Harcourt Publishing Co.
—Oli/Ollie Bilingual Board Book. 2015. (Gossie & Friends Ser.). (ENG & SPA., Illus.). 32p. (J). (— 1). bds. 4.99 *(978-0-544-31684-3(3)*, HMH Books For Young Readers) Houghton Mifflin Harcourt Publishing Co.
—Ollie. 2007. (Gossie & Friends Ser.). (ENG., Illus.). 32p. (J). (gr. -1 — 1). bds. 6.99 *(978-0-618-75503-5(9))* Houghton Mifflin Harcourt Publishing Co.
—Ollie. Dunrea, Olivier, illus. 2003. (Gossie & Friends Ser.). (ENG., Illus.). 32p. (J). (gr. -1 — 1). tchr. ed. 9.95 *(978-0-618-33928-0(0))* Houghton Mifflin Harcourt Publishing Co.
—Ollie (Reader) 2014. (Gossie & Friends Ser.). (ENG., Illus.). 32p. (J). (gr. -1 — 1). pap. 3.99 *(978-0-544-14671-6(9)*, HMH Books For Young Readers) Houghton Mifflin Harcourt Publishing Co.
—Ollie the Stomper. 2007. (Gossie & Friends Ser.). (ENG., Illus.). 32p. (J). (gr. -1-k). bds. 6.95 *(978-0-618-75504-2(7))* Houghton Mifflin Harcourt Publishing Co.
—Ollie the Stomper (Reader) 2014. (Gossie & Friends Ser.). (ENG., Illus.). 32p. (J). (gr. -1-3). pap. 3.99 *(978-0-544-14676-1(X)*, HMH Books For Young Readers) Houghton Mifflin Harcourt Publishing Co.
—Ollie's Easter Eggs. 2010. (Gossie & Friends Ser.). (ENG., Illus.). 32p. (J). (gr. -1 — 1). 9.99 *(978-0-618-53243-8(9))* Houghton Mifflin Harcourt Publishing Co.
—Ollie's Easter Eggs Board Book. 2013. (Gossie & Friends Ser.). (ENG., Illus.). 30p. (J). (gr. k — 1). bds. 6.99 *(978-0-547-85918-7(X))* Houghton Mifflin Harcourt Publishing Co.
—Ollie's Easter Eggs (reader) 2017. (Gossie & Friends Ser.). (ENG., Illus.). 32p. (J). (gr. -1-3). pap. 3.99 *(978-0-544-80911-6(4)*, HMH Books For Young Readers) Houghton Mifflin Harcourt Publishing Co.
—Ollie's Halloween (reader) 2016. (Gossie & Friends Ser.). (ENG., Illus.). 32p. (J). (gr. -1-3). 12.99 *(978-0-544-64052-8(7)*, HMH Books For Young Readers) Houghton Mifflin Harcourt Publishing Co.
—Ollie's Valentine. 2015. (Gossie & Friends Ser.). (ENG., Illus.). 14p. (J). (— 1). bds. 6.99 *(978-0-544-50269-7(8)*, HMH Books For Young Readers) Houghton Mifflin Harcourt Publishing Co.
—Peedie. 2008. (Gossie & Friends Ser.). (ENG., Illus.). 32p. (J). (gr. -1 — 1). bds. 6.95 *(978-0-618-75506-6(3))* Houghton Mifflin Harcourt Publishing Co.
Dutton, Maude Barrows. The Tortoise & the Geese & Other Fables of Bidpai. Smith, E. Boyd, illus. 2008. 104p. pap. 7.95 *(978-1-59915-249-3(5))* Yesterday's Classics.
Duvoisin, Roger. Petunia. 2015. (ENG., Illus.). 32p. (J). (gr. -1-2). 6.99 *(978-0-553-50849-9(0)*, Dragonfly Bks.) Random Hse. Children's Bks.
Earnhardt, Heather L. The Wandering Goose: A Modern Fable of How Love Goes. Clements, Frida, illus. 2013. (ENG.). 64p. 15.95 *(978-1-57061-881-9(X))* Sasquatch Bks.
Ellis, Sue. Gorgeous Gwendolen Goose & Other Stories. 2015. (ENG.). 49p. (J). (gr. 3-4). mass mkt. 13.95 *(978-1-78455-571-9(1)*, 32f7fc86-9367-414f-b0a7-4ad5f341c9cb) Austin, Stan AUS. Dist: Bookmasters Distribution.
Etcheberry-Morton, Mary Jean. Oui Oui Oui of the Pyrenees. 2012. (Illus.). 125p. (J). pap. 10.95 *(978-1-935709-26-8(7))* Ctr. for Basque Studies.
Fey, Jaki. The Last Goose Concert. Hubenthal, Dayna, illus. 2012. 126p. pap. 12.99 *(978-1-938282-02-7(7))* Koho Pono, LLC.
Fisher, Annabelle. Pixie Piper & the Matter of the Batter. 2017. (Pixie Piper Ser.: 2). 336p. (J). (gr. 3-7). 16.99 *(978-0-06-239380-7(4)*, Greenwillow Bks.) HarperCollins Pubs.
Freedman, Claire. Gooseberry Goose. Cabban, Vanessa, illus. 2005. 32p. (J). (gr. -1-2). 6.95 *(978-1-58925-392-6(2))* Tiger Tales.
Freedman, Claire & Cabban, Vanessa. Gooseberry Goose. 2003. (Illus.). 32p. (J). (gr. -1-2). tchr. ed. 15.95 *(978-1-58925-030-7(3))* Tiger Tales.
Gage, Wilson. A Wild Goose Tale. Rounds, Glen, illus. 2012. 114p. 39.95 *(978-1-258-25188-8(4))*; pap. 24.95 *(978-1-258-25729-3(7))* Literary Licensing, LLC.
Garis, Howard R. Uncle Wiggily & Old Mother Hubbard. 2008. 116p. 22.95 *(978-1-60664-970-1(1))* Aegypan.
Gehrmann, Katja, illus. Goose the Bear. 2014. (ENG.). 40p. (J). (gr. -1-3). 16.95 *(978-1-62636-384-7(6)*, Sky Pony Pr.) Skyhorse Publishing Co., Inc.
George, Jean Craighead. Goose & Duck. Lamont, Priscilla, illus. 2008. (I Can Read Level 2 Ser.). (ENG.). 48p. (J). (gr. k-3). 16.99 *(978-0-06-117076-8(3))* HarperCollins Pubs.
Ghigna, Charles. Lucy Goose. East, Jacqueline, illus. 2015. (Tiny Tales Ser.). (ENG.). 64p. (gr. -1-2). lib. bdg. 23.99 *(978-1-4795-6529-0(6))* Tiny Tales.
Goodspeed, Judy. Perky Turkey Finds a Friend. (Illus.). 24p. (J). 2007. per. 11.99 *(978-0-9797574-2-6(8))* 2006. lib. bdg. 24.95 *(978-0-9778651-2-3(6))* Dragonfly Publishing, Inc.
Graves, Peter, tr. from SWE. Nils Holgersson's Wonderful Journey Through Sweden, 2 vols. 2013. (ENG., Illus.). 360p. pap. 32.00 *(978-1-870041-96-6(8))*; 382p. pap. 32.00 *(978-1-870041-97-3(6))* Norvik Pr. GBR. Dist: Dufour Editions, Inc.
Griffin Mims, Nancy. The Christmas Geese. 2013. 42p. 16.95 *(978-1-940224-05-3(5))* Taylor and Seale Publishing, LLC.
Grimm, Jacob & Grimm, Wilhelm K. The Golden Goose / La Oca de Oro. 2004. (Illus.). (J). *(978-1-933530-22-2(7))* Bingo Bks., Inc.
Gummer, Chiele. A Family of Geese. 2013. 34p. pap. 16.95 *(978-1-4808-0026-7(0))* Archway Publishing.
Hader, Berta and Elmer. Mother Goose Picture Book. 2014. (ENG., Illus.). 160p. (J). (gr. -1). 25.00 *(978-1-60660-054-2(0))* Dover Pubns., Inc.
Halfmann, Janet. Canada Goose at Cat Tail Lane. Stegos, Daniel, illus. 2006. (ENG.). 32p. (J). (gr. -1-2). 9.95 *(978-1-59249-499-6(4)*, PB5079) Soundprints.
—Canada Goose at Cattail Lane. Stegos, Daniel J., illus. (Smithsonian's Backyard Ser.). (ENG.). 32p. (J). 2011. (gr. -1-3). 19.95 *(978-1-60727-632-6(1))* 2011. (gr. -1-3). pap. 8.95 *(978-1-60727-633-3(X))* 2006. (gr. -1-2). 8.95 *(978-1-59249-498-9(6)*, SC5029) 2006. (gr. -1-2). pap. 6.95 *(978-1-59249-495-8(1)*, S5029) 2006. (gr. k-2). 19.95 *(978-1-59249-497-2(8))* 2005. (gr. k-2). 15.95 *(978-1-59249-494-1(3)*, B5029) Soundprints.
Halfmann, Janet & Stegos, Daniel. Canada Goose at Cattail Lane. 2005. (ENG., Illus.). 32p. (J). (gr. -1-2). 4.95 *(978-1-59249-496-5(X)*, B5079) Soundprints.
Hall, Kirsten. Duck, Duck, Goose! 2004. (My First Reader Ser.). (ENG., Illus.). 32p. (J). (gr. k-1). pap. 3.95 *(978-0-516-24627-7(5)*, Children's Pr.) Scholastic Library Publishing.
Hamilton, Martha & Weiss, Mitch. How Fox Became Red. O'Malley, Kathy, illus. 2005. (ENG.). 12p. (J). 5.75 *(978-1-57274-717-3(X)*, 2749, Bks. for Young Learners) Owen, Richard C. Pubs., Inc.
Hardinge, Frances. Fly by Night. (J). (gr. 5-9). 2008. 512p. per. 7.99 *(978-0-06-087630-2(1))* 2006. 487p. 16.99 *(978-0-06-087627-2(1))* HarperCollins Pubs.
—Fly Trap. 2012. 592p. (J). (gr. 5). pap. 7.99 *(978-0-06-088046-0(5))* HarperCollins Pubs.
Hay, Jerry M. & Pollema-Cahill, Phyllis. A Goose Named Gilligan. 2004. (ENG., Illus.). 32p. (J). 15.95 *(978-1-932073-09-6(4))* Kramer, H.J. Inc.
Higgins, Ryan T. Mother Bruce. Higgins, Ryan T., illus. 2015. (Mother Bruce Ser.). (ENG., Illus.). 48p. (J). (gr. -1-k). 17.99 *(978-1-4847-3088-1(7))* Disney Pr.
Hills, Tad. Duck & Goose. Hills, Tad, illus. 2006. (Duck & Goose Ser.). (ENG., Illus.). 40p. (J). (gr. -1-2). 17.99 *(978-0-375-83611-4(X)*, Schwartz & Wade Bks.) Random Hse. Children's Bks.
—Duck & Goose, 1, 2, 3. Hills, Tad, illus. 2008. (Duck & Goose Ser.). (ENG., Illus.). 22p. (J). (gr. k — 1). bds. 7.99 *(978-0-375-85621-1(8)*, Schwartz & Wade Bks.) Random Hse. Children's Bks.
—Duck & Goose Go to the Beach. 2014. (Duck & Goose Ser.). (ENG., Illus.). 40p. (J). (gr. -1-2). 17.99 *(978-0-385-37235-0(3)*, Schwartz & Wade Bks.) Random Hse. Children's Bks.
—Duck & Goose, Goose Needs a Hug. Hills, Tad, illus. 2012. (Duck & Goose Ser.). (ENG., Illus.). 22p. (J). (-k). bds. 6.99 *(978-0-307-98293-3(9)*, Schwartz & Wade Bks.) Random Hse. Children's Bks.
—Duck & Goose, Here Comes the Easter Bunny! Hills, Tad, illus. 2012. (Duck & Goose Ser.). (ENG., Illus.). 22p. (J). (gr. k-k). bds. 7.99 *(978-0-375-87280-8(9)*, Schwartz & Wade Bks.) Random Hse. Children's Bks.
—Duck & Goose, How Are You Feeling? Hills, Tad, illus. 2009. (Duck & Goose Ser.). (ENG., Illus.). 22p. (J). (gr. -1 — 1). bds. 7.99 *(978-0-375-84629-8(8)*, Schwartz & Wade Bks.) Random Hse. Children's Bks.
—Duck, Duck, Goose. Hills, Tad, illus. 2007. (Duck & Goose Ser.). (ENG., Illus.). 40p. (J). (gr. -1-2). 17.99 *(978-0-375-84068-5(0)*, Schwartz & Wade Bks.) Random Hse. Children's Bks.
—Find a Pumpkin. Hills, Tad, illus. 2009. (Duck & Goose Ser.). (ENG., Illus.). 22p. (J). (gr. k — 1). bds. 7.99 *(978-0-375-85813-0(X)*, Schwartz & Wade Bks.) Random Hse. Children's Bks.
—It's Time for Christmas! Hills, Tad, illus. (Duck & Goose Ser.). (ENG., Illus.). 22p. (J). 2011. (gr. -1 — 1). bds. 10.99 *(978-0-375-87112-2(8))* 2010. (gr. k — 1). bds. 7.99 *(978-0-375-86484-1(9))* Random Hse. Children's Bks. (Schwartz & Wade Bks.).
Hills, Tad & Hills, Tad. Duck & Goose, Honk! Quack! Boo! 2017. (Duck & Goose Ser.). (ENG., Illus.). 40p. (J). (gr. -1-2). 16.99 ***(978-1-5247-0175-8(0))***; lib. bdg. 19.99 ***(978-1-5247-0176-5(9))*** Random Hse. Children's Bks. (Schwartz & Wade Bks.).
Holzer, Angela. Gooey Gummy Geese. Smith, Ashley, illus. 2008. (ENG.). (J). lib. bdg. 8.99 *(978-0-9821563-1-5(6))* Good Sound Publishing.
Homan, Michael. Grendel Gander the Sinister Goose. Duggins, Peat, illus. 2012. 48p. pap. 14.95 *(978-1-60808-049-6(8)*, WriteLife Publishing) Boutique of Quality Books Publishing Co., Inc.
Hopkins, Lee Bennett. Mother Goose & Her Children. Fehlau, Dagmar et al, illus. 2005. (Lee Bennett Hopkins Mother Goose Ser.). (YA). (gr. -1-1). 76.50 *(978-0-8215-0460-4(6))* Sadlier, William H. Inc.
—Mother Goose Around the World. Fehlau, Dagmar et al, illus. 2005. (Lee Bennett Hopkins Mother Goose Ser.). (YA). (gr. -1-1). 76.50 *(978-0-8215-0490-1(8))* Sadlier, William H. Inc.
Horácek, Petr. Silly Suzy Goose. Horácek, Petr, illus. 2009. (ENG., Illus.). 32p. (J). (— 1). bds. 7.99 *(978-0-7636-4141-2(3))* Candlewick Pr.
—Suzy Goose & the Christmas Star. Horácek, Petr, illus. 2009. (ENG., Illus.). 32p. (J). (gr. -1-2). 15.99 *(978-0-7636-4487-1(0))* Candlewick Pr.
—Suzy Goose & the Christmas Star: Midi Edition. Horácek, Petr, illus. 2010. (ENG., Illus.). 32p. (J). (gr. -1-2). 7.99 *(978-0-7636-5000-1(5))* Candlewick Pr.
How the Geese Saved Rome: Individual Title Six-Packs. (Story Steps Ser.). (gr. k-2). 32.00 *(978-0-7635-9801-3(1))* Rigby Education.
Howard, Velma Swanston, tr. Wonderful Adventures of Nils. 2013. 354p. pap. *(978-1-78139-369-7(9))* Benediction Classics.
Howarth, Daniel, illus. The Goose That Laid the Golden Eggs. 2006. (First Reading Level 3 Ser.). 48p. (J). (gr. 1-4). 8.99 *(978-0-7945-1378-8(6)*, Usborne) EDC Publishing.
Jensen, Lillian. A Treasury of Modern Mother Goose Rhymes, Vol. 1. 2003. 54p. pap. 9.00 *(978-0-8059-5981-9(5))* Dorrance Publishing Co., Inc.
Kasza, Keiko. Silly Goose's Big Story. Kasza, Keiko, illus. 2012. (ENG., Illus.). 32p. (J). (gr. -1-k). 16.99 *(978-0-399-25542-7(7)*, G.P. Putnam's Sons Books for Young Readers) Penguin Young Readers Group.
Keith, Patty J. Hank the Honking Goose Learns to Listen. Wright, Brent A., illus. Keith, Patty J., photos by. 2013. 36p. pap. 12.95 *(978-0-9893303-1-2(1))* Patty's Blooming Words.
Keller, Holly. Farfallina & Marcel. Keller, Holly, illus. 2005. (ENG., Illus.). 32p. (J). (gr. -1-4). reprint ed. pap. 6.99 *(978-0-06-443872-8(4)*, Greenwillow Bks.) HarperCollins Pubs.
—Farfallina & Marcel. Keller, Holly, illus. 2005. (Illus.). (gr. -1-3). 17.00 *(978-0-7569-5785-8(0))* Perfection Learning Corp.
Kent, Jennifer McGrath. Gadzooks: The Christmas Goose, 1 vol. Murphy, Ivan, illus. 2011. (ENG.). 32p. (J). (gr. -1-2). 19.95 *(978-1-55109-794-7(X))* Nimbus Publishing, Ltd. CAN. Dist: Orca Bk. Pubs. USA.
Kerr, Judith. Goose in a Hole. Kerr, Judith, illus. 2006. (ENG., Illus.). 40p. (J). (gr. k-2). pap. 9.99 *(978-0-00-720794-7(8)*, HarperCollins Children's Bks.) HarperCollins Pubs. Ltd. GBR. Dist: Independent Pubs. Group.
—Goose in a Hole. 2005. (ENG., Illus.). 100p. (J). (gr. k-2). 15.99 *(978-0-00-720793-0(X))* HarperCollins Pubs. Ltd. GBR. Dist: Independent Pubs. Group.
Kick, J. D. A Goose Tale — Downside up. Just, John, illus. 2nd l.t. ed. 2003. 80p. (J). per. 16.95 *(978-1-929424-13-9(2)*, Owl Creek Farm Bks.) Owl Tree Pr.
Kindl, Patrice. Goose Chase. 2010. (ENG.). 240p. (J). (gr. 5-7). pap. 6.99 *(978-0-547-33164-5(9))* Houghton Mifflin Harcourt Publishing Co.
King-smith, Dick. The Golden Goose. Kronheimer, Ann, illus. 2006. (ENG.). 128p. (J). (gr. 3-7). 5.99 *(978-0-440-42030-9(X)*, Yearling) Random Hse. Children's Bks.
Korba, Joanne. Two Golden Geese. 2005. (J). pap. *(978-1-4108-4201-5(0))* Benchmark Education Co.
Kubik, Dorothy. The Adventures of Elbert & Leopoldina. James, Annie, illus. 2006. 104p. (J). per. 15.00 *(978-0-9790775-1-7(6))* Touchstone Communications.
Lagerlöf, Selma. The Wonderful Adventures of Nils. 2004. reprint ed. pap. 34.95 *(978-1-4191-8845-9(3))*; pap. 1.99 *(978-1-4192-8845-6(8))* Kessinger Publishing, LLC.
—The Wonderful Adventures of Nils. 2009. 360p. (gr. 4-7). pap. 10.99 *(978-1-60459-624-3(4))* Wilder Pubns., Corp.
—The Wonderful Adventures of Nils. Howard, Velma Swanston, tr. 2003. 284p. pap. 14.95 *(978-1-59224-322-8(3))* Wildside Pr., LLC.
—The Wonderful Adventures of Nils. 2003. 32.95 *(978-1-59224-745-5(8))* Wildside Pr., LLC.
Langton, Jane. The Fledgling. unabr. ed. 2004. 192p. (J). (gr. 4-7). pap. 36.00 incl. audio *(978-0-8072-8779-8(2)*, YA265SP, Listening Library) Random Hse. Audio Publishing Group.
Lewis, Cindy (Didas). Time to Head South with Cindy the Canadian Goose, 1 vol. 2010. 56p. pap. 16.95 *(978-1-4489-3879-7(1))* America Star Bks.
Lindwall, Erika. The Moose & the Goose. Lindwall, Erika, illus. 2013. (Illus.). 32p. pap. 11.95 *(978-1-940728-01-8(0)*, Simple Faith Bks.) Sunrise Mountain Bks.
Long, Sylvia, illus. Sylvia Long's Mother Goose: Four Classic Board Books. 2016. (ENG.). 48p. (J). (gr. -1 — 1). bds. 14.99 *(978-1-4521-3818-3(4))* Chronicle Bks. LLC.
Macy-Mills, Phyllis. Murphy Moose & Garrett Goose. Russell, Kay, illus. 2003. (J). spiral bd. *(978-1-932303-48-3(0)*, Llumina Pr.) Aeon Publishing Inc.
Manning, Vicky. Lucy Goose & the Flying Seeds. 2005. (ENG.). 40p. per. 20.50 *(978-1-4208-1876-5(7))* AuthorHouse.
Martin, Mary. Grandma's Goose. Hoover, Charity, illus. 2012. 188p. *(978-0-7399-2452-5(4))* Rod & Staff Pubs., Inc.
Matthews, Penny. Pudding & Chips, 1 vol. Dawson, Janine, illus. 2005. (ENG.). 40p. (J). (gr. k-3). *(978-0-86315-496-6(4))* Floris Bks.
Mayer, Mercer. Mercer Mayer's Little Monster Word Book with Mother Goose. 2012. (Classic Collectible Ser.: 4). (ENG.). 96p. (J). 12.95 *(978-1-60746-688-8(0)*, Premiere) FastPrncil, Inc.
McWilliams Pittard, Irene. Goose Dreams. Kiplinger Pandy, Lori, illus. 2005. (J). 10.00 *(978-1-59971-142-3(7))* Aardvark Global Publishing.
Mother Goose. The Three Little Kittens. Winter, Milo, illus. 2009. (Shape Bks.). (ENG.). 16p. (J). (gr. -1-1). pap. 9.95 *(978-1-59583-374-7(9)*, 9781595833747, Green Tiger Pr.) Laughing Elephant.
Mother Goose Barnyard. 2003. (J). per. *(978-1-57657-164-4(5))* Paradise Pr., Inc.
Mothergoose-Feathered. 2003. (J). per. *(978-1-57657-165-1(3))* Paradise Pr., Inc.
O'Kelley, Jeff. Sam Finds the Way. 2006. (Early Explorers Ser.). (J). pap. *(978-1-4108-6107-8(4))* Benchmark Education Co.
Parker, Vic, ed. The Goose That Laid the Golden Egg & Other Fables. 2014. (Aesop's Fables Ser.). 40p. (J). (gr. 2-5). pap. 84.95 *(978-1-4824-1257-4(8))* Stevens, Gareth Publishing LLLP.
Parrish, Edith. Sarah the Purple Goose Gets Lost. Odom, Kelly, illus. 2011. 34p. 23.95 *(978-1-60844-930-9(0))* Dog Ear Publishing, LLC.
Parrish, Edith E. It's Not Easy Being a Purple Goose. Odom, Kelly, illus. 2011. 44p. pap. 24.95 *(978-1-4626-4207-6(1))* America Star Bks.
Prentice, Amy. The Gray Goose's Story. 2004. reprint ed. pap. 15.95 *(978-1-4191-6454-5(6))*; pap. 1.99 *(978-1-4192-6454-2(0))* Kessinger Publishing, LLC.
Publications International Ltd. Staff, creator. Mother Goose. 2007. (Pop-up Treasury Ser.). (Illus.). 16p. (J). (gr. -1-3). 12.98 *(978-1-4127-8833-5(1))* Publications International, Ltd.
Pyle, Howard. Twilight Land. 2004. reprint ed. pap. 22.95 *(978-1-4191-9142-8(X))*; pap. 1.99 *(978-1-4192-9142-5(4))* Kessinger Publishing, LLC.
Rapson, Helen. One Lucky Goose, 1 vol. 2005. (ENG.). 32p. 24.95 *(978-1-4137-2852-1(9))* PublishAmerica, Inc.
Reasoner, Charles. Number Munch! 2009. (Bite Bks.). (Illus.). (J). bds. 7.99 *(978-1-934650-14-1(5))* Just For Kids Pr., LLC.
Renaud, Anne. Missuk's Snow Geese. Côté, Geneviève, illus. 2008. (ENG.). 36p. (J). (gr. -1-3). 16.95 *(978-1-894965-82-8(5))* Simply Read Bks. CAN. Dist: Ingram Publisher Services.
Rice, Dona Herwick & Bradley, Kathleen. The Goose That Laid the Golden Eggs, 1 vol. 2008. (Building Fluency Through Reader's Theater Ser.). (ENG., Illus.). 24p. (J). (gr. 1-3). pap. 6.99 *(978-1-4333-0291-6(8))* Teacher Created Materials, Inc.
Robertson, Jean. My Name Is Not... Dufalla, Anita, illus. 2012. (ENG.). 24p. (gr. 1-2). pap. 8.95 *(978-1-61810-320-8(2))* Rourke Educational Media.
Rohmann, Eric, creator. My Friend Rabbit & the Snow Geese. 2013. (My Readers Ser.). (ENG., Illus.). 32p. (J). (gr. -1-1). pap. 3.99 *(978-1-250-01661-4(4)*, 9781250016614) Square Fish.
Roxbee Cox, Phil. Phonics Stories for Young Readers, Vol. 2. 2009. (Phonics Readers Ser.). 96p. (J). 14.99 *(978-0-7945-1887-5(7)*, Usborne) EDC Publishing.
Rubino, M. Gayle. The Truth about Scuttlebutt. 2012. 32p. pap. 19.95 *(978-1-4772-0348-4(6))* AuthorHouse.
Rylant, Cynthia. Henry & Mudge & the Wild Goose Chase. Bracken, Carolyn, illus. 2005. (Henry & Mudge Ser.). 40p. (J). lib. bdg. 15.00 *(978-1-59054-946-9(5))* Fitzgerald Bks.
—Henry & Mudge & the Wild Goose Chase. Bracken, Carolyn, illus. 2004. (Henry & Mudge Ser.). 40p. (gr. k-2). 14.00 *(978-0-7569-3366-1(8))* Perfection Learning Corp.
—Henry & Mudge & the Wild Goose Chase. Bracken, Carolyn, illus. 2004. (Henry & Mudge Ready-To-Read Ser.: 26). 40p. (gr. k-2). lib. bdg. 13.55 *(978-1-4176-4340-0(4)*, Turtleback) Turtleback Bks.
Rylant, Cynthia & Bracken, Carolyn. Henry & Mudge & the Wild Goose Chase. 2004. (Henry & Mudge Ser.: 23). (ENG., Illus.). 40p. (J). (gr. k-2). pap. 3.99 *(978-0-689-83450-9(0)*, Simon Spotlight) Simon Spotlight.
—Henry & Mudge & the Wild Goose Chase. Bracken, Carolyn, illus. 2003. (Henry & Mudge Ser.: 23). (ENG., Illus.). 40p. (J). (gr. k-2). 16.99 *(978-0-689-81172-2(1)*, Simon Spotlight) Simon Spotlight.
Sauer, Tammi. Truck, Truck, Goose! Waring, Zoe, illus. 2017. 40p. (J). (gr. -1-3). 14.99 ***(978-0-06-242153-1(0))*** HarperCollins Pubs.
Sheets, Katherine. Captured by Henrey, 1 vol. 2010. 48p. pap. 16.95 *(978-1-4489-4538-2(0))* America Star Bks.
Smith, J. Albert. Goosey Green. 2011. 24p. pap. 24.95 *(978-1-4626-3392-0(7))* America Star Bks.
Soundprints Staff. Humpty Dumpty: And Other Favorites. 2005. (Meet Mother Goose Ser.). (ENG., Illus.). 36p. (J). 14.95 *(978-1-931465-49-6(5)*, MPD1101) Soundprints.
—Humpty Dumpty: And Other Favorites. 2005. (Meet Mother Goose Ser.). (ENG., Illus.). 36p. (J). 10.95 *(978-1-931465-29-8(0)*, MD1101) Soundprints.
Spinelli, Eileen. Silly Tilly, 0 vols. Slonim, David, illus. 2012. (ENG.). 32p. (J). (gr. -1-2). pap. 9.99 *(978-0-7614-5990-3(1)*, 9780761459903, Amazon Children's Publishing) Amazon Publishing.
Tafuri, Nancy. Blue Goose. Tafuri, Nancy, illus. 2008. (ENG., Illus.). 32p. (J). (gr. -1-3). 17.99 *(978-1-4169-2834-8(0)*, Simon & Schuster Bks. For Young Readers) Simon & Schuster Bks. For Young Readers.
Van Scoyoc, Pam. The Ballerina with Webbed Feet/la Bailarina Palmipeda. Teichman, Diane E., tr. from ENG. Lewis, R. J., illus. l.t. ed. 2004. (ENG & SPA.). 40p. (J). (gr. k-2). lib. bdg. 16.98 *(978-0-9663629-2-3(6))* By Grace Enterprises.
Vande Velde, Vivian. Three Good Deeds. 2007. (ENG., Illus.). 160p. (J). (gr. 5-7). pap. 7.99 *(978-0-15-205455-7(3))* Houghton Mifflin Harcourt Publishing Co.
Wall, Laura. Goose. Wall, Laura, illus. 2015. (ENG., Illus.). 48p. (J). (gr. -1-3). 12.99 *(978-0-06-232435-1(7))* HarperCollins Pubs.
—Goose Goes to School. Wall, Laura, illus. 2015. (ENG., Illus.). 48p. (J). (gr. -1-3). 12.99 *(978-0-06-232437-5(3))* HarperCollins Pubs.
—Goose Goes to the Zoo. Wall, Laura, illus. 2016. (Illus.). 48p. (J). (gr. -1-3). 12.99 *(978-0-06-232441-2(1))* HarperCollins Pubs.
—Goose on the Farm. Wall, Laura, illus. 2016. (Illus.). 48p. (J). (gr. -1-3). 12.99 *(978-0-06-232439-9(X))* HarperCollins Pubs.
—Goose on the Farm Board Book. Wall, Laura, illus. 2017. (Illus.). 36p. (J). (gr. -1 — 1). bds. 7.99 *(978-0-06-232440-5(3)*, HarperFestival) HarperCollins Pubs.
Wallace, Karen. Stolen Egg. Harland, Jackie, illus. 2013. (Start Reading Ser.). (ENG.). 24p. (gr. k-1). pap. 7.95 *(978-1-4765-4141-9(8))* Capstone Press of Coughlan Cos.
Wegwerth, A. L. Little Bo Peep & Her Bad, Bad Sheep: A Mother Goose Hullabaloo. Flowers, Luke, illus. 2016. (Fiction Picture Bks.). (ENG.). 40p. (gr. -1-2). lib. bdg. 22.65 *(978-1-4795-6483-5(4)*, Fiction Picture Bks.) Picture Window Bks.
Weigl Publishers, creator. The Goose & the Golden Egg: What Happens When You Are Greedy? 2013. (AV2 Animated Storytime Ser.: Vol. 14). (ENG., Illus.). 32p. (J). (gr. -1-3). lib. bdg. 29.99 *(978-1-62127-918-1(9)*, AV2 by Weigl) Weigl Pubs., Inc.
Weston Woods Staff, creator. Petunia. 2011. 38.75 *(978-0-439-72868-3(1))*; 29.95 *(978-0-439-73509-4(2))*; 18.95 *(978-0-439-72867-6(3))* Weston Woods Studios, Inc.
Whitaker, Margaret. Stacie's Geese at Goose Lake. Whitaker, Margaret, illus. 2005. (Illus.). 36p. (J). pap. 12.00 *(978-0-9768051-0-6(3))* RoseFountain Pr., LLC.
Wiggin, Kate Douglas. The Diary of a Goose Girl. 2007. 108p. per. 9.95 *(978-1-60312-330-3(X))*; 22.95 *(978-1-60312-748-6(8))* Aegypan.
—The Diary of a Goose Girl. 2004. reprint ed. pap. 1.99 *(978-1-4192-5922-7(9))* Kessinger Publishing, LLC.
—The Diary of a Goose Girl. Shepperson, Claude A., illus. 2004. reprint ed. pap. 20.95 *(978-1-4179-1501-9(3))* Kessinger Publishing, LLC.
Willems, Mo. That Is Not a Good Idea! Willems, Mo, illus. 2013. (ENG., Illus.). 48p. (J). (gr. k-3). 17.99 *(978-0-06-220309-0(6))* HarperCollins Pubs.
Wolff, Susan. Quackers Wants to Fly. Currie, Justin, illus. 2013. 32p. pap. 8.95 *(978-1-60653-074-0(7))* High Hill Pr.
Wright, Blanche Fisher, illus. The Real Mother Goose. 2017. (First Avenue Classics Ser.). (ENG.). 214p. (gr. -1-4). 19.99 ***(978-1-5124-2603-8(2)***, First Avenue Editions) Lerner Publishing Group.
Yolen, Jane. Grumbles from Town: Mother-Goose Voices with a Twist. 2016. (ENG.). 40p. (J). (gr. k-4). 17.95 *(978-1-59078-922-3(9)*, Wordsong) Boyds Mills Pr.
Young, Elizabeth L. Dozens & Dozens of Cousins & Cousins. Perkins, Ruth, illus. 2012. 30p. 20.95 *(978-1-61633-353-9(7))*; pap. 12.95 *(978-1-61633-352-2(9))* Guardian Angel Publishing, Inc.

GEESE—MIGRATION

Best, B. J. Geese. 2016. (Migrating Animals Ser.). 24p. (J). pap. 8.22 *(978-1-5026-2098-9(7))*; lib. bdg. 24.21 *(978-1-5026-2100-9(2))* Cavendish Square Publishing.

E
F
G

GEHRIG, LOU, 1903-1941

Abramovitz, Melissa. Lou Gehrig's Disease. 2008. (Disorders & Diseases Ser.). (ENG., Illus.). 112p. (YA). (gr. 7-10). lib. bdg. 33.45 *(978-1-59018-676-3(1)*, Lucent Bks.) Cengage Gale.

Boothroyd, Jennifer. Lou Gehrig. 2008. pap. 40.95 *(978-0-8225-9473-4(0))* Lerner Publishing Group.

—Lou Gehrig: A Life of Dedication. 2008. (Pull Ahead Bks.). 32p. (Illus.). (J). (gr. -1-3). lib. bdg. 22.60 *(978-0-8225-8587-9(1)*, Lerner Pubns.); (ENG.). (gr. k-3). pap. 7.95 *(978-0-8225-8620-3(7))* Lerner Publishing Group.

Greenberger, Robert. Lou Gehrig. (Baseball Hall of Famers Ser.). 112p. (gr. 5-8). 2009. 63.90 *(978-1-61511-512-9(9))* 2004. (Illus.). lib. bdg. 34.60 *(978-0-8239-3781-3(X))* Rosen Publishing Group, Inc., The. (Rosen Reference).

Moss, Marissa. Mighty Jackie: The Strike-Out Queen. Payne, C. F., tr. Payne, C. F., illus. 2004. (ENG.). 32p. (J). (gr. k-3). 18.99 *(978-0-689-86329-5(2)*, Simon & Schuster/Paula Wiseman Bks.) Simon & Schuster/Paula Wiseman Bks.

Patrick, Jean L. S. The Baseball Adventure of Jackie Mitchell, Girl Pitcher vs. Babe Ruth. Hammond, Ted & Carbajal, Richard, illus. 2011. (History's Kid Heroes Ser.). 32p. pap. 51.02 *(978-0-7613-7635-4(6))*; (ENG.). (gr. 3-5). pap. 8.95 *(978-0-7613-7072-7(2))* Lerner Publishing Group. (Graphic Universe™).

—The Baseball Adventure of Jackie Mitchell, Girl Pitcher vs. Babe Ruth. Trover, Zachary et al, illus. 2011. (History's Kid Heroes Ser.). (ENG.). 32p. (gr. 3-5). 26.60 *(978-0-7613-6180-0(4))* Lerner Publishing Group.

—La Nina Que Poncho A Babe Ruth. Reeves, Jeni, illus. 2007. (Yo Solo - Historia (on My Own - History) Ser.). 48p. (J). (gr. 4-7). per. 6.95 *(978-0-8225-7788-1(7))* Lerner Publishing Group.

—La Niña Que Ponchó a Babe Ruth. Translations.com Staff, tr. from ENG. Reeves, Jeni, illus. 2007. (Yo Solo - Historia (on My Own - History) Ser.).Tr. of Girl Who Struck Out Babe Ruth. (SPA.). 48p. (gr. 2-4). lib. bdg. 25.26 *(978-0-8225-7785-0(2))* Lerner Publishing Group.

—La Nina Que Poncho a Babe Ruth; the Girl Who Struck Out Babe Ruth. 2008. pap. 40.95 *(978-0-8225-9725-4(X))* Lerner Publishing Group.

Reis, Ronald A. Lou Gehrig. (Baseball Superstars Ser.). 2009. 136p. (gr. 6-12). pap. 11.95 *(978-0-7910-9898-1(2)*, Checkmark Bks.) 2007. (Illus.). 130p. (YA). (gr. 7-12). lib. bdg. 30.00 *(978-0-7910-9423-5(5))* Facts On File, Inc.

Viola, Kevin. Lou Gehrig. (Sports Heroes & Legends Ser.). (J). 2005. (Illus.). 112p. (gr. 6-12). lib. bdg. 27.93 *(978-0-8225-1794-8(9))* 2004. pap. 9.95 *(978-0-8225-5311-3(2))* Lerner Publishing Group.

GEMINI PROJECT

see Project Gemini (U.S.)

GEMS

Here are entered antiquarian or artistic works on engraved stones and jewels. Mineralogical and technological works on potential and actual engraved stones and jewels are entered under Precious Stones.

see also Precious Stones

Cole, Tayler. Aquamarine. 2015. (Gems: Nature's Jewels Ser.). (ENG., Illus.). 24p. (J). (gr. 2-3). pap. 8.15 *(978-1-4824-2860-5(1))* Stevens, Gareth Publishing LLLP.

Cole, Taylor. Aquamarine. 2015. (Gems: Nature's Jewels Ser.). (ENG., Illus.). 24p. (J). (gr. 2-3). 22.60 *(978-1-4824-2862-9(8))* Stevens, Gareth Publishing LLLP.

Connolly, Lorraine. Bad, Bad Germs - Stay Away!!! 2010. 20p. pap. 10.95 *(978-1-4490-4696-5(7))* AuthorHouse.

Dorling Kindersley Publishing Staff. The Rock & Gem Book. 2016. (ENG., Illus.). 192p. (J). (gr. 3-7). 22.99 *(978-1-4654-5070-8(X)*, DK Children) Dorling Kindersley Publishing, Inc.

Farndon, John. Rocks, Gems, Minerals. 2016. (ENG., Illus.). 120p. (J). (gr. 6-10). 24.95 *(978-1-77085-740-7(0)*, 9781770857407) Firefly Bks., Ltd.

Gems: Nature's Jewels: Set 2. 2015. (Gems: Nature's Jewels Ser.). (ENG.). 24p. (J). (gr. 2-3). 135.60 *(978-1-4824-2550-5(5))*; pap., pap., pap. 293.40 *(978-1-4824-3475-0(X))*; pap., pap., pap. 48.90 *(978-1-4824-3476-7(8))* Stevens, Gareth Publishing LLLP.

Hansen, Grace. Gems, 1 vol. 2016. (ENG., Illus.). 24p. (J). *(978-1-62970-906-2(9)*, 1391185) ABDO Publishing Co.

—Piedras Preciosas. 2016. (¡Súper Geologíal Ser.). (SPA.). 24p. (J). (gr. 1-6). pap. 7.95 *(978-1-4966-0679-2(5))* Capstone Classroom.

Hayes, Amy. Garnets. 2015. (Gems: Nature's Jewels Ser.). (ENG., Illus.). 24p. (J). (gr. 2-3). pap. 8.15 *(978-1-4824-2864-3(4))* Stevens, Gareth Publishing LLLP.

Hoffman, Steven M. Gems, Crystals, & Precious Rocks. 2011. (Rock It! Ser.). (Illus.). 24p. (J). 22.60 *(978-1-4488-2561-5(X))*; pap. 8.25 *(978-1-4488-2708-4(6))* Rosen Publishing Group, Inc., The. (PowerKids Pr.).

Keppeler, Jill. How Gems Are Formed. 2016. (From the Earth: How Resources Are Made Ser.). (Illus.). 32p. (J). (gr. 4-3). pap. 10.50 *(978-1-4824-4709-5(6))* Stevens, Gareth Publishing LLLP.

Martin, Bobi. What Are Gems?, 01 vols., 1. 2016. (Junior Geologist Ser.). (ENG., Illus.). 32p. (J). pap. 12.90 *(978-1-5081-0050-8(0)*, Britannica Educational Publishing) Rosen Publishing Group, Inc., The.

McConnell, William. Crystals & Gems. 2009. (Real Life Readers Ser.). 16p. (gr. 1-3). pap. 7.05 *(978-1-4358-0107-3(5)*, Rosen Classroom) Rosen Publishing Group, Inc., The.

Petersen, Christine. Groovy Gems, 1 vol. 2010. (Rock on!: a Look at Geology Ser.). (ENG.). 32p. (YA). (gr. 3-6). 27.07 *(978-1-60453-743-7(4))* ABDO Publishing Co.

—Jade, 1 vol. 2013. (Earth's Treasures Ser.). (ENG.). 32p. (J). (gr. 3-6). lib. bdg. 27.07 *(978-1-61783-872-9(1)*, Checkerboard Library) ABDO Publishing Co.

Phelan, Glen. Rocks & Minerals. 2007. (Nonfiction Reading & Writing Workshops Ser.). (ENG., Illus.). 32p. (J). pap. 17.95 *(978-0-7922-4571-1(7))* CENGAGE Learning.

Reynolds, Toby & Calver, Paul. Rocks, Crystals, & Gems. 2016. (Visual Explorers Ser.). (ENG., Illus.). 32p. (J). (gr. 3-7). pap. 6.99 *(978-1-4380-0828-8(7))* Barron's Educational Series, Inc.

Symes, R. F. Crystal & Gem. 2014. (DK Eyewitness Bks.). (ENG., Illus.). 72p. (J). (gr. 3-7). pap. 9.99 *(978-1-4654-2052-7(5)*, DK Children) Dorling Kindersley Publishing, Inc.

VanVoorst, Jenny Fretland. Gems, 1 vol. 2014. (Rocks & Minerals Ser.). (ENG.). 48p. (gr. 8-12). lib. bdg. 32.79 *(978-1-62403-386-5(5))* ABDO Publishing Co.

GENDARMERIE ROYALE DU CANADA

see Royal Canadian Mounted Police

GENEALOGY

see also Biography; Heraldry

Beller, Susan Provost. Roots for Kids: A Genealogy Guide for Young People. 2nd ed. 2007. (Illus.). 104p. 19.95 *(978-0-8063-1777-9(9))* Genealogical.com.

Benchmark Education Company, compiled by. Our Family Stories & Las Historias de Nuestras Familias. 2005. (J). 62.00 net. *(978-1-4108-4493-4(5))* Benchmark Education Co.

Benchmark Education Company, LLC Staff, compiled by. Family Album & Ancestors. 2005. spiral bd. 225.00 *(978-1-4108-5821-4(9))* Benchmark Education Co.

Burton, Margie, et al. Then & Now. 2011. (Early Connections Ser.). (J). *(978-1-61672-543-3(5))* Benchmark Education Co.

Day, Reed B. Two Families: A History of the Lives & Times of the Families of Isaac Newton Day & Lucilla Caroline Blachly 1640-1940. 2004. (Illus.). 296p. per. 29.95 *(978-0-9760563-1-7(3)*, 7796) Mechling Bookbindery.

EchoHawk, Terry. Call Me Little Echo Hawk. 2005. (Illus.). 22p. (J). 15.99 *(978-1-55517-804-8(9))* Cedar Fort, Inc./CFI Distribution.

Forest, Anne. Our Family Album. 2013. (InfoMax Readers Ser.). (ENG.). 24p. (J). (gr. 2-3). pap. 49.50 *(978-1-4777-2352-4(8))*; pap. 8.25 *(978-1-4777-2351-7(X))* Rosen Publishing Group, Inc., The. (Rosen Classroom).

Gallagher, Debbie. Family Members. 2008. (Families Ser.). 32p. (gr. 1-2). lib. bdg. 18.56 *(978-0-7614-3139-8(X)*, Benchmark Bks.) Marshall Cavendish Corp.

—Family Stories. 2008. (Families Ser.). 32p. (gr. 1-2). lib. bdg. 18.56 *(978-0-7614-3142-8(X)*, Benchmark Bks.) Marshall Cavendish Corp.

Harrell, Antoinette. Nurturing My Family Tree: Genealogy for Children. 2010. 52p. pap. 28.99 *(978-1-4490-6541-6(4))* AuthorHouse.

Hill, George. The Fall of Irish Chiefs & Clans & the Plantation of Ulster: Including the Names of Irish Catholics, & Protestant Settlers. 2004. Orig. Title: An Historical Account of the Plantation in Ulster at the Commencement of the 17th Century. (Illus.). 276p. lib. bdg. 39.00 *(978-0-940134-42-3(X))* Irish Genealogical Foundation.

Hinman, Bonnie. Basic Genealogy for Kids. 2011. (Kid's Guide to Genealogy Ser.). (Illus.). (J). (gr. 3-6). lib. bdg. 29.95 *(978-1-58415-949-0(9))* Mitchell Lane Pubs., Inc.

Hirschmann, Kris. Are You Related to a Rock Star? A Guide to Unlocking Your Secret Family History. 2011. (Illus.). 103p. (J). pap. *(978-0-545-28223-9(3))* Scholastic, Inc.

Hunter, Nick. Finding Out about Your Family History, 1 vol. 2014. (History at Home Ser.). (ENG., Illus.). 32p. (gr. 1-3). pap. 7.99 *(978-1-4846-0235-5(8)*, Heinemann First Library) Heinemann-Raintree.

—Talking about the Past, 1 vol. 2014. (History at Home Ser.). (ENG., Illus.). 32p. (gr. 1-3). 27.32 *(978-1-4846-0232-4(3))*; pap. 7.99 *(978-1-4846-0236-2(6))* Heinemann-Raintree. (Heinemann First Library).

Johnson, Mary J. Super Smart Information Strategies: Your Fascinating Family History. 2011. (Explorer Library: Information Explorer Ser.). (ENG.). 32p. (gr. 4-8). pap. 14.21 *(978-1-61080-268-0(3)*, 201229); lib. bdg. 28.50 *(978-1-61080-122-5(9)*, 201130) Cherry Lake Publishing.

Leavitt, Amie Jane. Design Your Family Tree. 2011. (Kid's Guide to Genealogy Ser.). (Illus.). 48p. (J). (gr. 3-6). lib. bdg. 29.95 *(978-1-58415-952-0(9))* Mitchell Lane Pubs., Inc.

MacDonald, Margaret. A Family Tree. 2011. (Learn-Abouts Ser.). (Illus.). 16p. (J). pap. 9.95 *(978-1-59920-613-4(7))* Palgrave Macmillan.

Ollhoff, Jim. Beginning Genealogy, 1 vol. 2010. (Your Family Tree Ser.). (ENG.). 32p. (gr. 4-7). 27.07 *(978-1-61613-460-0(7)*, Abdo & Daughters) ABDO Publishing Co.

—Collecting Primary Records, 1 vol. 2010. (Your Family Tree Ser.). (ENG.). 32p. (gr. 4-7). 27.07 *(978-1-61613-461-7(5)*, Abdo & Daughters) ABDO Publishing Co.

—DNA: Window to the Past, 1 vol. 2010. (Your Family Tree Ser.). (ENG.). 32p. (gr. 4-7). 27.07 *(978-1-61613-462-4(3)*, Abdo & Daughters) ABDO Publishing Co.

—Exploring Immigration, 1 vol. 2010. (Your Family Tree Ser.). (ENG.). 32p. (gr. 4-7). 27.07 *(978-1-61613-463-1(1)*, Abdo & Daughters) ABDO Publishing Co.

—Filling the Family Tree, 1 vol. 2010. (Your Family Tree Ser.). (ENG.). 32p. (gr. 4-7). 27.07 *(978-1-61613-464-8(X)*, Abdo & Daughters) ABDO Publishing Co.

—Using Your Research, 1 vol. 2010. (Your Family Tree Ser.). (ENG.). 32p. (gr. 4-7). 27.07 *(978-1-61613-465-5(8)*, Abdo & Daughters) ABDO Publishing Co.

Orr, Tamra. How to Research Your Ancestry. 2011. (Kid's Guide to Genealogy Ser.). (Illus.). 48p. (J). (gr. 3-6). lib. bdg. 29.95 *(978-1-58415-950-6(2))* Mitchell Lane Pubs., Inc.

Petriéié, Duÿan. My Family Tree & Me. Petriéié, Duÿan, illus. 2015. (ENG., Illus.). 24p. (J). (gr. -1-2). 16.95 *(978-1-77138-049-2(7))* Kids Can Pr., Ltd. CAN. Dist: Hachette Bk. Group.

Peyton, Denyce Porter. Learn to Harvest Your Family History. 2005. 41p. spiral bd. 14.96 *(978-1-4116-3350-6(4))* Lulu Pr., Inc.

Shea, Therese. Around the Globe: Where Are Your Ancestors From? 2009. (Real Life Readers Ser.). 16p. (gr. 2-3). pap. 7.05 *(978-1-4358-0073-1(7)*, Rosen Classroom) Rosen Publishing Group, Inc., The.

Thompson, Aron. Grammy & Me: The Family Tree. 2012. 32p. pap. 21.99 *(978-1-4691-3933-3(2))* Xlibris Corp.

Vickers, Rebecca. Every Person Has a History, 1 vol. 2014. (Everything Has a History Ser.). (ENG., Illus.). 64p. (gr. 7-8). pap. 10.95 *(978-1-4329-9589-8(8))*; lib. bdg. 35.99 *(978-1-4329-9584-3(7))* Heinemann-Raintree.

Vickers, Rebecca & Langley, Andrew. Everything Has a History, 1 vol. 2014. (Everything Has a History Ser.). (ENG.). 64p. (gr. 7-8). lib. bdg. 143.96 *(978-1-4329-9587-4(1))* Heinemann-Raintree.

Williams, Jeffrey Lewis. The Cheek Family Chronicles: Of America, England & Australia, a 700 Year History. 2004. (Illus.). 1104p. lib. bdg. 79.95 *(978-0-9712564-5-3(4))* Kinfolk Research Pr.

GENERALS

Abbott, Jacob. Alexander the Great. 2009. (J). pap. 12.00 *(978-1-59128-058-3(3))* Canon Pr.

—Alexander the Great. 2009. 212p. pap. 10.95 *(978-1-59915-132-8(4))* Yesterday's Classics.

—Hannibal. 2009. (J). pap. 12.00 *(978-1-59128-059-0(1))* Canon Pr.

—Julius Caesar. 2009. (J). pap. 12.00 *(978-1-59128-060-6(5))* Canon Pr.

—Julius Caesar. 2009. 206p. pap. 10.95 *(978-1-59915-141-0(3))* Yesterday's Classics.

Abnett, Dan. George Washington y la Guerra de Independencia. 2009. (Historietas Juveniles: Biografías (Jr. Graphic Biographies) Ser.). (SPA & ENG., Illus.). 24p. (YA). (gr. 2-5). 25.25 *(978-1-4358-8564-6(3))*; (gr. 3-8). pap. 10.60 *(978-1-4358-3322-7(8))* Rosen Publishing Group, Inc., The.

Adams, Simon. World History Biographies: Alexander: The Boy Soldier Who Conquered the World. 2013. (National Geographic World History Biographies Ser.). (ENG., Illus.). 64p. (J). (gr. 3-7). pap. 7.99 *(978-1-4263-1449-0(3)*, National Geographic Children's Bks.) National Geographic Society.

Allen, Thomas B. George Washington, Spymaster: How the Americans Outspied the British & Won the Revolutionary War. Harness, Cheryl, illus. 2007. (ENG.). 192p. (J). (gr. 5-7). per. 7.95 *(978-1-4263-0041-7(7)*, National Geographic Children's Bks.) National Geographic Society.

Aller, Susan Bivin. Ulysses S. Grant. 2006. (History Maker Bios Ser.). (Illus.). 48p. (J). (gr. 3-7). lib. bdg. 26.60 *(978-0-8225-2438-0(4)*, Lerner Pubns.) Lerner Publishing Group.

Anderson, Dale. Leaders of the American Revolution. 2005. (World Almanac Library of the American Revolution Ser.). 48p. (gr. 5-12). pap. 14.05 *(978-0-8368-5940-9(5))*; lib. bdg. 31.00 *(978-0-8368-5931-7(6))* Stevens, Gareth Publishing LLLP. (Gareth Stevens Secondary Library).

—The Patriots Win the American Revolution. 2005. (World Almanac Library of the American Revolution Ser.). 48p. (gr. 5-12). pap. 14.05 *(978-0-8368-5937-9(5))*; lib. bdg. 31.00 *(978-0-8368-5928-7(6))* Stevens, Gareth Publishing LLLP. (Gareth Stevens Secondary Library).

Anderson, Paul C. George Armstrong Custer: The Indian Wars & the Battle of the Little Bighorn. 2009. (Library of American Lives & Times Ser.). 112p. (gr. 5-5). 69.20 *(978-1-60853-483-8(9))* Rosen Publishing Group, Inc., The.

Antonio Lopez de Santa Anna. 2010. (Great Hispanic Heritage Ser.). (Illus.). 104p. (gr. 6-12). 35.00 *(978-1-60413-734-7(7)*, Chelsea Hse.) Facts On File, Inc.

Archer, Jules. A House Divided: The Lives of Ulysses S. Grant & Robert E. Lee. rev. ed. 2015. (Jules Archer History for Young Readers Ser.). (ENG., Illus.). 176p. (J). (gr. 6). 16.99 *(978-1-63220-604-6(8)*, Sky Pony Pr.) Skyhorse Publishing Co., Inc.

Aronson, Billy. Ulysses S. Grant. 2007. (Presidents & Their Times Ser.). (Illus.). 96p. (J). (gr. 3-7). lib. bdg. 34.21 *(978-0-7614-2430-7(X)*, Benchmark Bks.) Marshall Cavendish Corp.

Ashby, Ruth. Lee vs. Grant. Great Battles of the Civil War. 2016. (Civil War Chronicles Ser.: Vol. 4). (ENG., Illus.). (J). (gr. 5-6). 23.95 ***(978-1-59687-514-2(3)**, ipicturebooks)* ibooks, Inc.

Bader, Bonnie. Who Was Robert E. Lee? Harrison, Nancy & O'brien, John, illus. 2014. (Who Was? Ser.). (ENG.). 112p. (J). (gr. 3-7). 5.99 *(978-0-448-47909-5(5)*, Grosset & Dunlap) Penguin Young Readers Group.

Bailey, Diane. General George Thomas: The Rock of Chickamauga. 2011. (J). *(978-1-59556-045-2(9))*; pap. *(978-1-59556-051-3(3))* OTTN Publishing.

Bailey, Gerry & Foster, Karen. Julius Caesar's Sandals. Noyes, Leighton, illus. 2008. (Stories of Great People Ser.). (ENG.). 40p. (J). (gr. 3-6). pap. *(978-0-7787-3717-9(9))*; lib. bdg. *(978-0-7787-3695-0(4))* Crabtree Publishing Co.

Bankston, John. Alexander the Great. 2013. (ENG.). 48p. (J). (gr. 3-6). lib. bdg. 29.95 *(978-1-61228-431-6(0))* Mitchell Lane Pubs., Inc.

—The Life & Times of Alexander the Great. 2004. (Biography of Ancient Civilizations Ser.). (Illus.). 48p. (J). lib. bdg. *(978-1-58415-235-4(4))* Mitchell Lane Pubs., Inc.

Baum, Margaux & Thorne, James. Julius Caesar. 2016. (Leaders of the Ancient World Ser.). 00112p. (J). (gr. 6-6). 37.10 *(978-1-5081-7248-2(X))* Rosen Publishing Group, Inc., The.

Behnke, Alison. The Conquests of Alexander the Great. 2007. (Pivotal Moments in History Ser.). (ENG., Illus.). 160p. (gr. 9-12). lib. bdg. 38.60 *(978-0-8225-5920-7(X))* Lerner Publishing Group.

Benge, Janet & Benge, Geoff. Heroes of History - Douglas MacArthur: What Greater Honor. 2005. (ENG., Illus.). 205p. (YA). pap. 9.99 *(978-1-932096-15-6(9))* Emerald Bks.

Bodie, Idella. Light-Horse Harry. 2004. (Illus.). 86p. (J). pap. 6.95 *(978-0-87844-172-3(7))* Sandlapper Publishing Co., Inc.

—The Wizard Owl. 2003. (Illus.). 86p. (J). pap. 6.95 *(978-0-87844-167-9(0))* Sandlapper Publishing Co., Inc.

Boomhower, Ray E. The Sword & the Pen: A Life of Lew Wallace. 2005. (Illus.). x, 164p. (J). 15.95 *(978-0-87195-185-4(1))* Indiana Historical Society.

Brager, Bruce L. There He Stands: The Story of Stonewall Jackson. 2005. (Civil War Leaders Ser.). (Illus.). 176p. (J). (gr. 6-12). 26.95 *(978-1-931798-44-0(3))* Reynolds, Morgan Inc.

Brooks, Philip. Hannibal. rev. ed. 2015. (Wicked History Ser.). (ENG., Illus.). 144p. (J). lib. bdg. 33.00 *(978-0-531-22122-8(9)*, Children's Pr.) Scholastic Library Publishing.

—Hannibal: Rome's Worst Nightmare. 2008. (Wicked History Ser.). (ENG., Illus.). 128p. (J). 31.00 *(978-0-531-18553-7(2)*, Watts, Franklin) Scholastic Library Publishing.

Cawthorne, Nigel. Military Commanders: The 100 Greatest Throughout History. 2004. (Illus.). 208p. 18.95 *(978-1-59270-029-5(2))* Enchanted Lion Bks., LLC.

—Victory: 100 Great Military Commanders. 2012. (Illus.). 208p. (J). *(978-1-4351-4242-8(X))* Metro Bks.

Chambers, Catherine. Fierce Fighters. Bustamante, Maryin & Juta, Jason, illus. 2016. (Warriors! Ser.). (ENG.). 32p. (J). (gr. 3-6). 26.65 *(978-1-4677-9357-5(4))* Lerner Publishing Group.

Chorlian, Meg & Hale, Sarah Elder, eds. Ulysses S. Grant: Confident Leader & Hero. 2005. (ENG., Illus.). 48p. (J). (gr. 3-9). 17.95 *(978-0-8126-7906-9(7))* Cobblestone Publishing Co.

Coleman, Wim & Perrin, Pat. George Washington: Creating a Nation. 2004. (America's Founding Fathers Ser.). (Illus.). 128p. (J). lib. bdg. 26.60 *(978-0-7660-2290-4(0))* Enslow Pubs., Inc.

Collier, Peter. Choosing Courage: Inspiring Stories of What It Means to Be a Hero. (ENG., Illus.). (J). 2016. 272p. (gr. 4-6). pap. 8.95 *(978-1-57965-705-5(2))* 2015. 240p. 18.95 *(978-1-57965-596-9(3))* Artisan.

Collins, Kathleen. El Marques de Lafayette: Heroe Frances de la Guerra de Independencia. 2004. (Grandes personajes en la historia de los Estados Unidos Ser.). (SPA.). 32p. (gr. 3-6). pap. 10.00 *(978-0-8239-4233-6(3)*, Rosen Classroom) Rosen Publishing Group, Inc., The.

—Marquis de Lafayette: French Hero of the American Revolution. 2009. (Primary Sources of Famous People in American History Ser.). 32p. (gr. 2-3). 47.90 *(978-1-60851-703-9(9))* Rosen Publishing Group, Inc., The.

—Marquis de Lafayette / el Marques de Lafayette: French Hero of the American Revolution / Héroe francés de la Revolución Estadounidense. 2009. (Famous People in American History/Grandes personajes en la historia de los Estados Unidos Ser.). (ENG & SPA.). 32p. (gr. 2-3). 47.90 *(978-1-61512-550-0(7)*, Editorial Buenas Letras) Rosen Publishing Group, Inc., The.

Collins, Terry. Robert E. Lee: The Story of the Great Confederate General. Mallea, Cristian, illus. (American Graphic Ser.). (ENG.). 32p. (gr. 3-4). 2011. pap. 47.70 *(978-1-4296-6436-3(3))* 2010. lib. bdg. 30.65 *(978-1-4296-5475-3(9))* Capstone Press of Coughlan Cos. (Graphic Library).

Conklin, Wendy. Robert E. Lee, 1 vol. 2005. (Primary Source Readers Ser.). (ENG.). 24p. (J). (gr. 4-4). pap. 8.99 *(978-0-7439-8918-3(X))* Shell Educational Publishing.

Cooper, Meghan. Sun Tzu. 2017. (J). ***(978-1-5026-2867-1(8))*** Cavendish Square Publishing.

Corrigan, Jim. General George G. Meade: Victor at Gettysburg. 2011. (J). *(978-1-59556-044-5(0))*; pap. *(978-1-59556-050-6(5))* OTTN Publishing.

—General James Longstreet: Lee's "Old War Horse" 2012. (J). *(978-1-59556-043-8(2))*; pap. *(978-1-59556-049-0(1))* OTTN Publishing.

Crannell, Karl. John Stark: Live Free or Die. 2006. (Forgotten Heroes of the American Revolution Ser.). (Illus.). 80p. (J). (gr. 5-11). lib. bdg. 23.95 *(978-1-59556-016-2(5))* OTTN Publishing.

—John Stark: Live Free or Die! 2006. (J). pap. *(978-1-59556-021-6(1))* OTTN Publishing.

Crompton, Samuel Willard. Alexander the Great. 2003. (Ancient World Leaders Ser.). (Illus.). 112p. (J). (gr. 6-12). 30.00 *(978-0-7910-7219-6(3)*, Chelsea Hse.) Facts On File, Inc.

—Ariel Sharon. 2nd rev. ed. 2007. (Modern World Leaders Ser.). (Illus.). 111p. (J). (gr. 7-12). lib. bdg. 30.00 *(978-0-7910-9263-7(1))* Facts On File, Inc.

—Julius Caesar. 2003. (Ancient World Leaders Ser.). (Illus.). 112p. (J). (gr. 6-12). 30.00 *(978-0-7910-7220-2(7)*, Chelsea Hse.) Facts On File, Inc.

Darby, Jean. Dwight D. Eisenhower. 2004. (Presidential Leaders Ser.). (Illus.). 112p. (J). (gr. 6-12). lib. bdg. 29.27 *(978-0-8225-0813-7(3))* Lerner Publishing Group.

Demi Staff & Marshall Cavendish Corporation Staff. Alexander the Great, 0 vols. 2010. (ENG., Illus.). 64p. (J). (gr. 3-7). 19.99 *(978-0-7614-5700-8(3)*, 9780761457008, Amazon Children's Publishing) Amazon Publishing.

Doyle, William. Napoleon Bonaparte: Emperor. 2016. (History Makers Ser.). 144p. (J). 45.64 *(978-1-5026-2447-5(8))* Cavendish Square Publishing.

Dugan, Christine. Marquis de Lafayette & the French (Alexander Hamilton) 2017. (Primary Source Readers Focus On Ser.). (Illus.). 32p. (J). (gr. 4-8). pap. 8.99 ***(978-1-4258-6353-1(1))*** Teacher Created Materials, Inc.

Earl, Sari. Benjamin O. Davis, Jr.: Air Force General & Tuskegee Airmen Leader, 1 vol. 2010. (Military Heroes Ser.). (ENG.). 112p. (J). (gr. 6-12). lib. bdg. 35.64 *(978-1-60453-961-5(5))* ABDO Publishing Co.

—George Washington: Revolutionary Leader & Founding Father, 1 vol. 2010. (Military Heroes Ser.). (ENG.). 112p. (J). (gr. 6-12). lib. bdg. 35.64 *(978-1-60453-967-7(4))* ABDO Publishing Co.

Edwards, Roberta. Who Was George Washington? Kelley, True & Harrison, Nancy, illus. 2009. (Who Was? Ser.). (ENG.). 112p. (J). (gr. 3-7). pap. 5.99 *(978-0-448-44892-3(0)*, Grosset & Dunlap) Penguin Young Readers Group.

—Who Was George Washington? 2009. (Who Was... ? Ser.). lib. bdg. 16.00 *(978-0-606-04042-6(0)*, Turtleback) Turtleback Bks.

Egan, Tracie. George Washington: Padre de la Patria. 2004. (Grandes personajes en la historia de los Estados Unidos Ser.). (SPA.). 32p. (gr. 3-6). pap. 10.00 *(978-0-8239-4229-9(5)*, Rosen Classroom) Rosen Publishing Group, Inc., The.

—George Washington: The Father of the American Nation. 2009. (Primary Sources of Famous People in American History Ser.). 32p. (gr. 2-3). 47.90 *(978-1-60851-683-4(0))* Rosen Publishing Group, Inc., The.

Ellis, Catherine. Key Figures of World War II. 2015. (Biographies of War Ser.). (ENG., Illus.). 112p. (J). (gr. 7-8). 32.90 *(978-1-68048-057-3(X)*, Britannica Educational Publishing) Rosen Publishing Group, Inc., The.

Finkelstein, Norman H. Ariel Sharon. 128p. (J). (gr. 6-18). 20.95 *(978-1-58013-205-3(7)*, Kar-Ben Publishing); 2005. (Illus.). 112p. (YA). (gr. 7-12). lib. bdg. 29.27 *(978-0-8225-2370-3(1)*, Lerner Pubns.) Lerner Publishing Group.

Firth, Rachel. Julius Caesar. 2007. (Famous Lives Gift Bks). (Illus.). 64p. (J). 8.99 *(978-0-7945-1595-9(9)*, Usborne) EDC Publishing.

Fryer, Mary Beacock. Bold, Brave, & Born to Lead: Major General Isaac Brock & the Canadas. 2004. (ENG., Illus.). 264p. (YA). pap. 9.99 *(978-1-55002-501-9(5))* Dundurn CAN. Dist: Ingram Publisher Services.

Galford, Ellen. Julius Caesar: The Boy Who Conquered an Empire. 2007. (National Geographic World History Biographies Ser.). (ENG., Illus.). 64p. (J). (gr. 3-7). 17.95 *(978-1-4263-0064-6(6))*; lib. bdg. 27.90 *(978-1-4263-0065-3(4))* National Geographic Society. (National Geographic Children's Bks.).

Gallagher, Jim. Daniel Morgan: Fighting Frontiersman. 2006. (J). pap. *(978-1-59556-020-9(3))*; (Illus.). 88p. (gr. 5-11). lib. bdg. 23.95 *(978-1-59556-015-5(7))* OTTN Publishing.

Ganeri, Anita. Alexander the Great: The Life of a King & Conqueror. 2005. (Graphic Nonfiction Biographies Ser.). (ENG., Illus.). 48p. (J). (gr. 4-7). lib. bdg. 31.95 *(978-1-4042-0238-2(2)*, 1241094) Rosen Publishing Group, Inc., The.

Gimpel, Lee. Fighting Wars, Planning for Peace: The Story of George C. Marshall. 2005. (World Leaders Ser.). (Illus.). 176p. (J). (gr. 6-12). lib. bdg. 26.95 *(978-1-931798-66-2(4))* Reynolds, Morgan Inc.

Gitlin, Martin. George S. Patton: World War II General & Military Innovator, 1 vol. 2010. (Military Heroes Ser.). (ENG.). 112p. (J). (gr. 6-12). lib. bdg. 35.64 *(978-1-60453-964-6(X))* ABDO Publishing Co.

Goddu, Krystyna Poray. George Washington's Presidency. 2016. (Presidential Powerhouses Ser.). (ENG., Illus.). 104p. (J). (gr. 6-12). 35.99 *(978-1-4677-7924-1(5))*; 53.32 *(978-1-4677-8598-3(9)*, Lerner Pubns.) Lerner Publishing Group.

Greenblatt, Miriam. Julius Caesar & the Roman Republic. 2005. (Rulers & Their Times Ser.). (Illus.). 96p. (J). (gr. 3-7). lib. bdg. 29.93 *(978-0-7614-1836-8(9)*, Benchmark Bks.) Marshall Cavendish Corp.

Gunderson, Jessica. Benedict Arnold: Battlefield Hero or Selfish Traitor?, 1 vol. 2013. (Perspectives on History Ser.). (ENG.). 32p. (gr. 3-4). 27.32 *(978-1-4765-0243-4(9))*; pap. 7.95 *(978-1-4765-3407-7(1))* Capstone Press of Coughlan Cos. (Fact Finders).

Hale, Sarah Elder, ed. Robert E. Lee: Duty & Honor. 2005. (ENG., Illus.). 48p. (J). (gr. 3-9). 17.95 *(978-0-8126-7905-2(9))* Cobblestone Publishing Co.

—Stonewall Jackson: Spirit of the South. 2005. (ENG., Illus.). 48p. (J). (gr. 3-9). 17.95 *(978-0-8126-7907-6(5))* Cobblestone Publishing Co.

Hamilton, John. Leaders & Generals of the American Revolution. 2013. (American Revolution Ser.). 32p. (J). (gr. 5-9). lib. bdg. 27.07 *(978-1-61783-681-7(8)*, Abdo & Daughters) ABDO Publishing Co.

Harness, Cheryl. The Adventurous Life of Myles Standish & the Amazing-but-True Survival Story of Plymouth Colony: Barbary Pirates, the Mayflower, the First Thanksgiving, & Much, Much More. 2006. (Cheryl Harness Histories Ser.). (ENG., Illus.). 144p. (J). (gr. 5-9). 9.95 *(978-1-4263-0284-8(3)*, National Geographic Children's Bks.) National Geographic Society.

Hart, Paul. Emiliano Zapata: Mexico's Social Revolutionary. 2017. (World in a Life Ser.). (ENG.). 320p. (C). pap. 19.95 ***(978-0-19-068808-0(4))*** Oxford Univ. Pr., Inc.

Havelin, Kate. Ulysses S. Grant. 2004. (Presidential Leaders Ser.). (Illus.). 112p. (J). 29.27 *(978-0-8225-0814-4(1)*, Lerner Pubns.) Lerner Publishing Group.

Hollar, Sherman, contrib. by. George Washington. 2012. (Pivotal Presidents: Profiles in Leadership Ser.). (ENG., Illus.). 80p. (YA). (gr. 7-12). 65.80 *(978-1-61530-956-6(X))* Rosen Publishing Group, Inc., The.

Hoogenboom, Lynn. William Tecumseh Sherman: The Fight to Preserve the Union. (Library of American Lives & Times Ser.). 112p. 2009. (gr. 5-5). 69.20 *(978-1-60853-511-8(8))* 2005. (Illus.). (J). (gr. 4-8). lib. bdg. 34.60 *(978-0-8239-6625-7(9))* Rosen Publishing Group, Inc., The.

Hosein, Ann. Key Figures of World War I. 2015. (Biographies of War Ser.). (ENG., Illus.). 112p. (J). (gr. 7-8). 32.90 *(978-1-68048-054-2(5)*, Britannica Educational Publishing) Rosen Publishing Group, Inc., The.

Hunter, Nick. Alexander the Great, 1 vol. 2013. (Hero Journals). (ENG.). 48p. (gr. 4-6). 33.32 *(978-1-4109-5357-5(2)*, NA-r) Heinemann-Raintree.

—Julius Caesar, 1 vol. Edwards, Mat, illus. 2013. (Hero Journals). (ENG.). 48p. (gr. 4-6). pap. 9.95 *(978-1-4109-5363-6(7)*, NA-r) Heinemann-Raintree.

—Julius Caesar, 1 vol. 2013. (Hero Journals). (ENG., Illus.). 48p. (gr. 4-6). 33.32 *(978-1-4109-5356-8(4)*, NA-r) Heinemann-Raintree.

Hunter, Nick & Faure, Florence. Alexander the Great, 1 vol. 2013. (Hero Journals). (ENG.). 48p. (gr. 4-6). pap. 9.95 *(978-1-4109-5364-3(5)*, NA-r) Heinemann-Raintree.

Jeffrey, Gary. Julius Caesar: The Life of a Roman General. 2009. (Graphic Nonfiction Biographies Ser.). (ENG.). 48p. (YA). (gr. 4-5). 58.50 *(978-1-61513-020-7(9)*, Rosen Reference) Rosen Publishing Group, Inc., The.

Jeffrey, Gary & Petty, Kate. Julius Caesar: The Life of a Roman General. 2005. (Graphic Nonfiction Biographies Ser.). (ENG., Illus.). 48p. (J). (gr. 4-7). lib. bdg. 31.95 *(978-1-4042-0239-9(0)*, 1241097) Rosen Publishing Group, Inc., The.

Kajencki, AnnMarie Francis. Count Casimir Pulaski: From Poland to America, a Hero's Fight for Liberty. (Library of American Lives & Times Ser.). 112p. 2009. (gr. 5-5). 69.20 *(978-1-60853-475-3(8))* 2005. (Illus.). (YA). (gr. 4-7). lib. bdg. 34.60 *(978-1-4042-2646-3(X))* Rosen Publishing Group, Inc., The.

Kauffman, Scott. Francis Marion: Swamp Fox of South Carolina. 2006. (Forgotten Heroes of the American Revolution Ser.). (Illus.). 88p. (YA). (gr. 5-11). lib. bdg. 23.95 *(978-1-59556-014-8(9))* OTTN Publishing.

Kawa, Katie. 20 Fun Facts about George Washington. 2017. (Fun Fact File: Founding Fathers Ser.). 32p. (gr. 2-3). pap. 63.00 ***(978-1-5382-0272-2(7))*** Stevens, Gareth Publishing LLLP.

Kent, Zachary. Julius Caesar: Ruler of the Roman World. 2006. (Rulers of the Ancient World Ser.). (Illus.). 160p. (YA). (gr. 6-9). lib. bdg. 29.27 *(978-0-7660-2563-9(2))* Enslow Pubs., Inc.

Kerby, Mona. Robert E. Lee: Commander of the Confederate Army. 2015. (Legendary American Biographies Ser.). 96p. (J). (gr. 6-12). 27.94 *(978-0-7660-6490-4(5))*; pap. 10.95 *(978-0-7660-6491-1(3))* Enslow Pubs., Inc.

Kirkman, Marissa. The Life & Times of George Washington & the American Revolution. 2016. (Life & Times Ser.). (ENG., Illus.). 24p. (gr. 1-2). lib. bdg. 25.32 *(978-1-5157-2476-6(X)*, First Facts) Capstone Press of Coughlan Cos.

Knapp, Ron. Fighting U. S. Generals of World War II. 2013. (Inspiring Collective Biographies Ser.). 112p. (J). (gr. 5-12). pap. 10.95 *(978-1-4644-0249-4(3))*; 33.27 *(978-0-7660-4164-6(6))* Enslow Pubs., Inc.

Koestler-Grack, Rachel A. Stonewall Jackson. 2009. (Leaders of the Civil War Era Ser.). (Illus.). 136p. (gr. 6-12). 35.00 *(978-1-60413-299-1(X)*, Chelsea Hse.) Facts On File, Inc.

—William Tecumseh Sherman. 2009. (Leaders of the Civil War Era Ser.). (Illus.). 149p. (gr. 6-12). 35.00 *(978-1-60413-300-4(7)*, Chelsea Hse.) Facts On File, Inc.

Kravitz, Danny. The Untold Story of Henry Knox: The Man Who Saved Boston. 2015. (What You Didn't Know about the American Revolution Ser.). (ENG., Illus.). 64p. (gr. 4-8). 34.65 *(978-0-7565-4972-5(8))* Compass Point Bks.

Link, Theodore. George Armstrong Custer: General de la caballería Estadounidense. 2004. (Grandes personajes en la historia de los Estados Unidos Ser.). (SPA.). 32p. (gr. 3-6). pap. 10.00 *(978-0-8239-4228-2(7)*, Rosen Classroom) Rosen Publishing Group, Inc., The.

—George Armstrong Custer: General de la caballería estadounidense (George Armstrong Custer: General of the U. S. Cavalry) 2009. (Grandes personajes en la historia de los Estados Unidos (Famous People in American History) Ser.). (SPA.). 32p. (gr. 2-3). 47.90 *(978-1-61512-799-3(2)*, Editorial Buenas Letras) Rosen Publishing Group, Inc., The.

—George Armstrong Custer: General of the U. S. Cavalry. 2009. (Primary Sources of Famous People in American History Ser.).Tr. of George Armstrong Custer: General de la Caballeria Estadounidense. 32p. (gr. 2-3). 47.90 *(978-1-60851-680-3(6))* Rosen Publishing Group, Inc., The.

—George Armstrong Custer: General of the U. S. Cavalry / General de la caballería Estadounidense. 2009. (Famous People in American History/Grandes personajes en la historia de los Estados Unidos Ser.). (ENG & SPA.). 32p. (gr. 2-3). 47.90 *(978-1-61512-545-6(0)*, Editorial Buenas Letras) Rosen Publishing Group, Inc., The.

Marsh, Carole. General Colin Powell. 2003. 12p. (gr. k-4). 2.95 *(978-0-635-02359-9(8))* Gallopade International.

—John C. Fremont. 2004. 12p. (gr. k-4). 2.95 *(978-0-635-02380-3(6))* Gallopade International.

Marsico, Katie. Alexander the Great: Ancient King & Conqueror, 1 vol. 2009. (Essential Lives Set 3 Ser.). (ENG., Illus.). 112p. (J). (gr. 6-12). lib. bdg. 35.64 *(978-1-60453-520-4(2))* ABDO Publishing Co.

Mattern, Joanne. Julius Caesar. 2017. (Junior Biography From Ancient Civilization Ser.). (gr. 4-6). 29.95 *(978-1-68020-024-9(0))* Mitchell Lane Pubs., Inc.

Maynard, Charles W. John Charles Fremont: The Pathfinder. 2003. (Famous Explorers of the American West Ser.). (Illus.). 24p. (J). lib. bdg. 22.60 *(978-0-8239-6289-1(X)*, PowerKids Pr.) Rosen Publishing Group, Inc., The.

McCarthy, Pat. Famous Union Generals & Leaders of the North: A MyReportLinks. com Book. 2004. (American Civil War Ser.). (Illus.). 48p. (J). lib. bdg. 26.60 *(978-0-7660-5188-1(9)*, MyReportLinks.com Bks.) Enslow Pubs., Inc.

McElroy, Lisa Tucker. Alberto Gonzalez. 2006. (J). pap. 8.95 *(978-0-8225-6058-6(5)*, First Avenue Editions) Lerner Publishing Group.

McGowen, Tom. Alexander the Great: Conqueror of the Ancient World. 2006. (Rulers of the Ancient World Ser.). (Illus.). 160p. (YA). (gr. 6-12). lib. bdg. 29.27 *(978-0-7660-2560-8(8))* Enslow Pubs., Inc.

McLeese, Don. Stonewall Jackson. 2005. (Civil War Military Leaders Ser.). (Illus.). 32p. (J). (gr. 3-6). lib. bdg. 19.95 *(978-1-59515-477-4(9))* Rourke Educational Media.

McNeese, Tim. Robert E. Lee. 2009. (Leaders of the Civil War Era Ser.). (Illus.). 152p. (gr. 6-12). lib. bdg. 35.00 *(978-1-60413-304-2(X)*, Chelsea Hse.) Facts On File, Inc.

McPherson, Stephanie Sammartino. Douglas MacArthur. 2005. (History Maker Bios Ser.). (Illus.). 48p. (J). 26.60 *(978-0-8225-2434-2(1))* Lerner Publishing Group.

Meltzer, Brad. I Am George Washington. Eliopoulos, Christopher, illus. 2016. (Ordinary People Change the World Ser.). (ENG.). 40p. (J). (gr. k-3). 14.99 *(978-0-525-42848-0(8)*, Dial Bks) Penguin Young Readers Group.

Mierka, Gregg A. Nathanael Greene: The General Who Saved the Revolution. 2006. (J). pap. *(978-1-59556-017-9(3))*; (Illus.). 88p. (gr. 5-11). lib. bdg. 23.95 *(978-1-59556-012-4(2))* OTTN Publishing.

Miller, Brandon Marie. George Washington for Kids: His Life & Times - 21 Activities. 2007. (For Kids Ser.). (ENG., Illus.). 144p. (J). (gr. 4-7). pap. 16.95 *(978-1-55652-655-8(5))* Chicago Review Pr., Inc.

Miller, Roger G. Billy Mitchell: Evangelist of Airpower. 2007. (Illus.). 152p. (J). (gr. 10-18). lib. bdg. 25.95 *(978-1-59556-025-4(4))* OTTN Publishing.

Murphy, Frank. George Washington & the General's Dog. Walz, Richard, illus. 2015. 48p. pap. 5.00 *(978-1-61003-605-4(0))* Center for the Collaborative Classroom.

—George Washington & the General's Dog. 2003. (J). 1.25 *(978-1-4025-4103-2(1))* Recorded Bks., Inc.

Nardo, Don. Alexander the Great: Conqueror of the Known World. 2009. (World Leaders Ser.). (Illus.). 100p. (J). 28.95 *(978-1-59935-126-1(9))* Reynolds, Morgan Inc.

Newsome, Joel. Hannibal. 2017. (J). ***(978-1-5026-2869-5(4))*** Cavendish Square Publishing.

North, Sterling. George Washington: Frontier Colonel. (Great Leaders & Events Ser.). (ENG.). (J). (gr. 4-8). 2017. 208p. lib. bdg. 35.99 ***(978-1-942875-24-6(X))*** 2016. (Illus.). 175p. pap. 12.99 *(978-0-7603-5229-8(1))* Quarto Publishing Group USA. (Voyageur Pr.).

Olesen, Andrew. George Washington: The First President of the United States. 2015. (Spotlight on American History Ser.). (ENG., Illus.). 24p. (J). (gr. 4-6). pap. 10.00 *(978-1-4994-1751-7(9)*, PowerKids Pr.) Rosen Publishing Group, Inc., The.

Otfinoski, Steven. Patriots & Redcoats: Stories of American Revolutionary War Leaders. 2015. (Revolutionary War Ser.). (ENG.). 48p. (gr. 3-4). pap. 8.95 *(978-1-4914-2158-1(4))* Capstone Press of Coughlan Cos.

Peerson, Marie Graham. Joseph Wheeler: The Fearless 'Fightin' Joe' 2003. (Alabama Roots Biography Ser.). (Illus.). 120p. (J). *(978-1-878561-40-4(5))* Seacoast Publishing, Inc.

Petrie, Kristin. John C. Fremont, 1 vol. 2004. (Explorers Set 1 Ser.). (ENG., Illus.). 32p. (gr. k-6). 27.07 *(978-1-59197-602-8(2)*, Checkerboard Library) ABDO Publishing Co.

Pflueger, Lynda. Stonewall Jackson: General of the Confederate Army. 2015. (J). *(978-0-7660-6495-9(6))* Enslow Pubs., Inc.

Pingry, Patricia A. Meet Robert E. Lee. Johnson, Meredith, illus. 2004. (J). 9.95 *(978-0-8249-5465-9(3)*, Ideal Pubns.) Worthy Publishing.

Powell, Walter L. Benedict Arnold: Revolutionary War Hero & Traitor. (Library of American Lives & Timestm Ser.). (Illus.). 112p. (J). (gr. 4-8). lib. bdg. 31.95 *(978-1-4042-6627-8(5))* Rosen Publishing Group, Inc., The.

Power, J. Tracey. Stonewall Jackson: Hero of the Confederacy. 2009. (Library of American Lives & Times Ser.). 112p. (gr. 5-5). 69.20 *(978-1-60853-507-1(X))* Rosen Publishing Group, Inc., The.

Price, Sean. Hannibal of Carthage, 1 vol. 2013. (Hero Journals). (ENG., Illus.). 48p. (gr. 4-6). 33.32 *(978-1-4109-5359-9(9))*; pap. 9.95 *(978-1-4109-5366-7(1))* Heinemann-Raintree. (NA-r).

Publishers, Chelsea House, creator. Leaders of the American Revolution Set, 11-Volumes. 2006. (Leaders of the American Revolution Ser.). 100p. (gr. 5-8). 270.00 *(978-0-7910-9320-7(4)*, Chelsea Hse.) Facts On File, Inc.

Randolph, Joanne. The Call of Liberty: Marquis de Lafayette & the American Revolution. 2009. (Great Moments in American History Ser.). 32p. (gr. 3-3). 47.90 *(978-1-61513-152-5(3))* Rosen Publishing Group, Inc., The.

Redgrave, Roy. The Adventures of Colonel Daffodil: Balkan Beginnings, Memorable Travels & Forgotten Conflicts. 2007. (Illus.). 202p. (J). 45.00 *(978-1-84415-525-5(0))* Pen & Sword Bks. Ltd. GBR. Dist: Casemate Pubs. & Bk. Distributors, LLC.

Rice, Earle. The Life & Times of the Brothers Custer: Galloping to Glory. 2008. (Profiles in American History Ser.). (Illus.). 48p. (J). (gr. 4-8). lib. bdg. 29.95 *(978-1-58415-665-9(1))* Mitchell Lane Pubs., Inc.

Rice, Earle, Jr. Ulysses S. Grant: Defender of the Union. 2005. (Civil War Leaders Ser.). (Illus.). 176p. (gr. 6-12). 28.95 *(978-1-931798-48-8(6))* Reynolds, Morgan Inc.

Rinaldo, Denise. Julius Caesar: Dictator for Life. (Wicked History Ser.). (ENG.). 128p. (J). 2010. (gr. 6-12). pap. 5.95 *(978-0-531-22822-7(3)*, Watts, Franklin) 2009. (gr. 5-9). 31.00 *(978-0-531-21276-9(9))* Scholastic Library Publishing.

Robertson, James I., Jr. Robert E. Lee: Virginian Soldier, American Citizen. 2005. (ENG., Illus.). 176p. (YA). (gr. 7-12). 29.99 *(978-0-689-85731-7(4)*, Atheneum Bks. for Young Readers) Simon & Schuster Children's Publishing.

Rockliff, Mara. Gingerbread for Liberty! How a German Baker Helped Win the American Revolution. Kirsch, Vincent X., illus. 2015. (ENG.). 32p. (J). (gr. 1-4). 17.99 *(978-0-544-13001-2(4)*, HMH Books For Young Readers) Houghton Mifflin Harcourt Publishing Co.

Roppelt, Donna J. & DeAngelis, Therese. General A.P. Hill: Light Division Leader. 2011. (J). *(978-1-59556-042-1(4))*; pap. *(978-1-59556-048-3(3))* OTTN Publishing.

Rumsch, BreAnn. Ulysses S. Grant, 1 vol. 2009. (United States Presidents Ser.). (ENG., Illus.). 40p. (YA). (gr. 3-6). 27.07 *(978-1-60453-453-5(2))* ABDO Publishing Co.

Sanford, William R. & Green, Carl R. John C. Frémont: Courageous Pathfinder of the Wild West. 2012. (Courageous Heroes of the American West Ser.). (Illus.). 48p. (J). pap. 8.95 *(978-1-4644-0091-9(1))*; (gr. 5-18). 22.60 *(978-0-7660-4008-3(9))* Enslow Pubs., Inc.

Santillian, Beatriz & Randall, Bernard. Alexander the Great: Macedonian King & Conqueror. 2017. (Leaders of the Ancient World Ser.). 112p. (J). (gr. 12-11). 37.10 ***(978-1-5081-7482-0(2)***, Rosen Young Adult) Rosen Publishing Group, Inc., The.

Sapp, Richard. Ulysses S. Grant & the Road to Appomattox. 2006. (In the Footsteps of American Heroes Ser.). (Illus.). 64p. (gr. 5-12). pap. 14.05 *(978-0-8368-6436-6(0))*; lib. bdg. 34.00 *(978-0-8368-6431-1(X))* Stevens, Gareth Publishing LLLP. (Gareth Stevens Secondary Library).

Schanzer, Rosalyn. George vs. George: The American Revolution as Seen from Both Sides. 2007. (ENG., Illus.). 64p. (J). (gr. 4-7). per. 6.95 *(978-1-4263-0042-4(5)*, National Geographic Children's Bks.) National Geographic Society.

Seabrook, Lochlainn. The Quotable Nathan Bedford Forrest: Selections from the Writings & Speeches of the Confederacy's Most Brilliant Cavalryman. 2012. (Illus.). 130p. pap. 12.95 *(978-0-9838185-5-7(X))* Sea Raven Pr.

Shecter, Vicky Alvear. Alexander the Great Rocks the World. Naughton, Terry, illus. 2006. 128p. (J). (gr. 5-7). lib. bdg. 18.95 *(978-1-58196-045-7(X)*, Darby Creek) Lerner Publishing Group.

Sheinkin, Steve. The Notorious Benedict Arnold: A True Story of Adventure, Heroism & Treachery. 2010. (ENG., Illus.). 352p. (YA). (gr. 6-9). 19.99 *(978-1-59643-486-8(4)*, 9781596434868) Roaring Brook Pr.

—The Notorious Benedict Arnold: A True Story of Adventure, Heroism & Treachery. 2013. (ENG., Illus.). 368p. (YA). (gr. 6-9). pap. 9.99 *(978-1-250-02460-2(9)*, 9781250024602) Square Fish.

—The Notorious Benedict Arnold: A True Story of Adventure, Heroism & Treachery. 2013. (YA). lib. bdg. 20.85 *(978-0-606-28487-5(7)*, Turtleback) Turtleback Bks.

Shone, Rob. Alexander the Great: The Life of a King & Conqueror. 2009. (Graphic Nonfiction Biographies Ser.). (ENG.). 48p. (YA). (gr. 4-5). 58.50 *(978-1-61513-012-2(8)*, Rosen Reference) Rosen Publishing Group, Inc., The.

Souza, D. M. John C. Fremont. 2004. (Watts Library). (ENG., Illus.). 64p. (J). (gr. 5-7). pap. 8.95 *(978-0-531-16652-9(X)*, Watts, Franklin) Scholastic Library Publishing.

Spivey, Mark. A Spot in the Road: My Personal Adventu. 2005. 52p. pap. 16.95 *(978-1-4137-8806-8(8))* PublishAmerica, Inc.

Stanley, George E. George S. Patton: War Hero. Henderson, Meryl, illus. 2007. (Childhood of Famous Americans Ser.). (ENG.). 192p. (J). (gr. 3-7). pap. 6.99 *(978-1-4169-1547-8(8)*, Simon & Schuster/Paula Wiseman Bks.) Simon & Schuster/Paula Wiseman Bks.

Stein, R. Conrad. Emiliano Zapata & the Mexican Revolution. 2011. (Story of Mexico Ser.). (Illus.). 144p. (gr. 7-12). 28.95 *(978-1-59935-163-6(3))* Reynolds, Morgan Inc.

Sterngass, Jon. John Brown. 2009. (Leaders of the Civil War Era Ser.). (Illus.). 144p. (gr. 6-12). 35.00 *(978-1-60413-305-9(8)*, Chelsea Hse.) Facts On File, Inc.

Stine, Megan. Who Was Ulysses S. Grant? Harrison, Nancy & Geyer, Mark Edward, illus. 2014. (Who Was? Ser.). (ENG.). 112p. (J). (gr. 3-7). 5.99 *(978-0-448-47894-4(3)*, Grosset & Dunlap) Penguin Young Readers Group.

Stokes, Betty Southard. Postcards from George, 1763-1781: George Rogers Clark Writes Home to Virginia from the Kentucky Wilderness. Cable, Annette, illus. 2010. (J). *(978-1-935497-12-7(X))* Butler Bk. Publishing.

Stotts, Stuart. Lucius Fairchild: Civil War Hero. 2011. (Badger Biographies Ser.). (ENG., Illus.). 112p. (J). pap. 12.95 *(978-0-87020-460-9(2))* Wisconsin Historical Society.

Strazzabosco, Jeanne M. Learning about Responsibility from the Life of Colin Powell. 2009. (Character Building Book Ser.). 24p. (gr. 2-3). 42.50 *(978-1-61511-003-2(8)*, PowerKids Pr.) Rosen Publishing Group, Inc., The.

Strum, Richard. Henry Knox: Washington's Artilleryman. 2006. (Forgotten Heroes of the American Revolution Ser.). (Illus.). 88p. (J). (gr. 5-11). lib. bdg. 23.95 *(978-1-59556-013-1(0))* OTTN Publishing.

Strum, Richard M. Henry Knox: Washington's Artilleryman. 2006. (J). pap. *(978-1-59556-018-6(1))* OTTN Publishing.

Sutcliffe, Jane. George S. Patton JR. 2006. (History Maker Bios Ser.). (Illus.). 48p. (J). (gr. 3-7). lib. bdg. 26.60 *(978-0-8225-2436-6(8)*, Lerner Pubns.) Lerner Publishing Group.

Turner, Pamela S. Samurai Rising: The Epic Life of Minamoto Yoshitsune. Hinds, Gareth, illus. 2016. (ENG.). 256p. (YA). (gr. 7-12). 16.95 *(978-1-58089-584-2(0))* Charlesbridge Publishing, Inc.

Vander Hook, Sue. Colin Powell: General & Statesman, 1 vol. 2010. (Military Heroes Ser.). (ENG.). 112p. (J). (gr. 6-12). lib. bdg. 35.64 *(978-1-60453-965-3(8))* ABDO Publishing Co.

Venezia, Mike. Ulysses S. Grant. Venezia, Mike, illus. 2005. (Getting to Know the U. S. Presidents Ser.). (ENG., Illus.). 32p. (J). (gr. 3-7). lib. bdg. 28.00 *(978-0-516-22623-1(1)*, Children's Pr.) Scholastic Library Publishing.

Warrick, Karen Clemens. Hannibal: Great General of the Ancient World. 2006. (Rulers of the Ancient World Ser.). (Illus.). 160p. (J). (gr. 6-12). lib. bdg. 27.93 *(978-0-7660-2564-6(0))* Enslow Pubs., Inc.

Waterfield, Robin H., et al. Who Was Alexander the Great? Thomson, Andrew, illus. 2016. (Who Was? Ser.). (ENG.). 112p. (J). (gr. 3-7). lib. bdg. 15.99 *(978-0-399-54235-0(3)*, Grosset & Dunlap) Penguin Young Readers Group.

Waxman, Laura Hamilton. Colin Powell. 2005. (History Maker Bios Ser.). 48p. (J). pap. 8.95 *(978-0-8225-5463-9(1))*; (ENG., Illus.). (gr. 3-6). lib. bdg. 27.93 *(978-0-8225-2433-5(3)*, Lerner Pubns.) Lerner Publishing Group.

Welch, Catherine A. George C. Marshall. (History Maker Bios Ser.). 48p. (J). 2006. (Illus.). (gr. 3-7). lib. bdg. 26.60 *(978-0-8225-2435-9(X)*, Lerner Pubns.) 2005. pap. 8.95 *(978-0-8225-5460-8(7))* Lerner Publishing Group.

Whiting, Jim. The Life & Times of Julius Caesar. 2005. (Biography from Ancient Civilizations Ser.). (Illus.). 48p. (J). (gr. -1-7). lib. bdg. 29.95 *(978-1-58415-337-5(7))* Mitchell Lane Pubs., Inc.

Wilhelm, Doug. Alexander the Great. rev. ed. 2015. (Wicked History Ser.). (ENG., Illus.). 144p. (J). lib. bdg. 33.00 *(978-0-531-22124-2(5)*, Children's Pr.) Scholastic Library Publishing.

—Alexander the Great: Master of the Ancient World. (Wicked History Ser.). (ENG.). 128p. (J). 2010. (gr. 6-12). pap. 5.95 *(978-0-531-22821-0(5)*, Watts, Franklin) 2009. (gr. 5-9). 31.00 *(978-0-531-21275-2(0))* Scholastic Library Publishing.

Worth, Richard. Toussaint L'Ouverture: Fighting for Haitian Independence. 2017. (Rebels with a Cause Ser.). 128p. (J). (gr. 8-8). lib. bdg. 37.27 ***(978-0-7660-8521-3(X))*** Enslow Pubs., Inc.

Young, Jeff C. Dwight D. Eisenhower: Soldier & President. 2004. (Notable Americans Ser.). (Illus.). 128p. (YA). (gr. 6-12). 23.95 *(978-1-883846-76-3(5)*, First Biographies) Reynolds, Morgan Inc.

GENERATION

see Reproduction

GENERATORS, ELECTRIC

see Electric Generators

GENETIC ENGINEERING

see also Biotechnology; Cloning

Anderson, Michael. A Closer Look at Genes & Genetic Engineering. 2011. (Illus.). 87p. (J). lib. bdg. 31.70 *(978-1-61530-527-8(0))* Rosen Publishing Group, Inc., The.

Barber, Nicola. Cloning & Genetic Engineering. 2012. (Both Sides of the Story Ser.). (ENG., Illus.). 48p. (J). (gr. 5-8). lib. bdg. 29.25 *(978-1-4488-7187-2(5)*, Rosen Reference) Rosen Publishing Group, Inc., The.

Berlatsky, Noah. Genetic Engineering. 2012. (Global Viewpoints Ser.). (ENG., Illus.). 224p. (gr. 10-12). pap. 31.70 *(978-0-7377-6441-3(4)*, Greenhaven Pr., Inc.) Cengage Gale.

Berlatsky, Noah, ed. Genetic Engineering. 2012. (Global Viewpoints Ser.). (ENG., Illus.). 224p. (J). (gr. 10-12). lib. bdg. 40.45 *(978-0-7377-6265-5(9)*, Greenhaven Pr., Inc.) Cengage Gale.

Bortz, Fred. The Laws of Genetics & Gregor Mendel. 2013. (Revolutionary Discoveries of Scientific Pioneers Ser.). (Illus.). 80p. (J). (gr. 7-12). 33.25 *(978-1-4777-1806-3(0))* Rosen Publishing Group, Inc., The.

Burgan, Michael. Genetic Engineering: Science, Technology, & Engineering. 2016. (Calling All Innovators: a Career for You Ser.). (ENG., Illus.). 64p. (J). lib. bdg. 32.00 *(978-0-531-23001-5(5)*, Children's Pr.) Scholastic Library Publishing.

Canini, Mikko. Genetic Engineering. (History of Issues Ser.). 192-240p. (gr. 10-12). pap. 23.70 *(978-0-7377-1908-6(7)*, Greenhaven Pr., Inc.) Cengage Gale.

Carmichael, L. E. Gene Therapy, 1 vol. 2013. (Medical Marvels Ser.). (ENG.). 112p. (J). (gr. 6-12). lib. bdg. 35.64 *(978-1-61783-902-3(7)*, Essential Library) ABDO Publishing Co.

EFG

Claybourne, Anna. Introduction to Genes & DNA. 2004. (Genes & Dna Ser.). (ENG., Illus.). 64p. (J). pap. 11.95 (978-0-7945-0444-1(2), Usborne) EDC Publishing.

Cohen, Marina. Genetic Engineering. 2009. (Let's Relate to Genetics Ser.). (ENG., Illus.). 48p. (J). (gr. 5-8). lib. bdg. (978-0-7787-4950-9(9)); (gr. 6-9). pap. (978-0-7787-4967-7(3)) Crabtree Publishing Co.

Cothran, Helen & Canini, Mikko, eds. Genetic Engineering. 2004. (History of Issues Ser.). (ENG.). 240p. (YA). (gr. 10-13). pap. 39.70 (978-0-7377-1907-9(9), Greenhaven Pr., Inc.) Cengage Gale.

Dowswell, Paul. Genetic Engineering. 2004. (21st Century Issues Ser.). (Illus.). 48p. (gr. 5-12). lib. bdg. 31.00 (978-0-8368-5643-9(0), Gareth Stevens Secondary Library) Stevens, Gareth Publishing LLLP.

Forman, Lillian E. Genetically Modified Foods, 1 vol. 2009. (Essential Viewpoints Set 4 Ser.). (ENG., Illus.). 112p. (J). (gr. 6-12). lib. bdg. 35.64 (978-1-60453-531-0(8)) ABDO Publishing Co.

Fridell, Ron. Genetic Engineering. 2005. (Cool Science Ser.). (Illus.). 48p. (J). (gr. 3-7). lib. bdg. 26.60 (978-0-8225-2633-9(6), Lerner Pubns.) Lerner Publishing Group.

Friedman, Lauri S. Genetic Engineering. 2007. (Writing the Critical Essay Ser.). (ENG., Illus.). 128p. (YA). (gr. 7-12). lib. bdg. 33.75 (978-0-7377-3857-5(X), LML02109-234654) Cengage Gale.

Friedman, Lauri S., ed. Genetic Engineering. 2011. (Introducing Issues with Opposing Viewpoints Ser.). (Illus.). 144p. (YA). (gr. 9-12). 36.95 (978-0-7377-5680-7(2)) Cengage Gale.

Fritz, Sandy. Genomics & Cloning. 2003. (Hot Science Ser.). (J). lib. bdg. 28.50 (978-1-58340-365-5(5)) Black Rabbit Bks.

Genetic Engineering. 2005. (Introducing Issues with Opposing Viewpoints Ser.). (ENG., Illus.). 126p. (YA). (gr. 7-10). lib. bdg. 35.75 (978-0-7377-3223-8(7), Greenhaven Pr., Inc.) Cengage Gale.

Goodnough, David. The Debate over Human Cloning. 2003. (Hot Pro/Con Issues Ser.). (Illus.). 64p. (YA). (gr. 6-12). lib. bdg. 27.93 (978-0-7660-1818-1(0)) Enslow Pubs., Inc.

Gray, Leon. Genetic Modification: Should Humans Control Nature? 2013. (Ask the Experts Ser.). (Illus.). 48p. (gr. 6-8). 31.95 (978-1-4339-8635-2(3)); pap. 14.05 (978-1-4339-8636-9(1)) Stevens, Gareth Publishing LLLP. (Gareth Stevens Secondary Library).

Hartman, Eve & Meshbesher, Wendy. What Are the Issues with Genetic Technology?, 1 vol. 2012. (Sci-Hi: Science Issues Ser.). (ENG., Illus.). 48p. (gr. 4-4). pap. 9.95 (978-1-4109-4471-9(9), Sci-Hi) Heinemann-Raintree.

Henneberg, Susan, ed. Genetic Engineering. 2017. (Current Controversies Ser.). 224p. (YA). (gr. 10-12). pap. 32.00 **(978-1-5345-0038-9(3))**; lib. bdg. 46.40 **(978-1-5345-0017-4(0))** Greenhaven Publishing LLC. (Greenhaven Publishing).

Hunnicutt, Susan C. World Hunger. 2006. (At Issue Ser.). (ENG., Illus.). 128p. (gr. 10-12). 39.40 (978-0-7377-2761-6(6), Greenhaven Pr., Inc.) Cengage Gale.

Hunnicutt, Susan C., ed. World Hunger. 2006. (At Issue Ser.). (ENG., Illus.). 91p. (gr. 3-7). pap. 24.45 (978-0-7377-2762-3(4), Greenhaven Pr., Inc.) Cengage Gale.

Kafka, Tina. Genetic Engineering. 2009. (Hot Topics Ser.). (ENG.). 128p. 39.40 (978-1-4205-0148-3(8), Lucent Bks.) Cengage Gale.

Kovacs, Vic. Gene Therapy. 2016. (Miracles of Medicine Ser.). 00048p. (J). pap. 14.05 **(978-1-4824-6099-5(8))** Stevens, Gareth Publishing LLLP.

Marquardt, Meg. Curing Cancer. 2016. (Science Frontiers Ser.). (ENG., Illus.). 32p. (J). pap. 9.95 (978-1-63235-392-4(X)) Pr. Room Editions LLC.

Merino, Noel. Genetic Engineering. 2013. (Opposing Viewpoints Ser.). (ENG., Illus.). 224p. (gr. 10-12). pap. 33.80 (978-0-7377-6425-3(2), Greenhaven Pr., Inc.) Cengage Gale.

Merino, Noël, ed. Genetic Engineering. 2013. (Opposing Viewpoints Ser.). (ENG., Illus.). 224p. (gr. 10-12). lib. bdg. 48.80 (978-0-7377-6424-6(4), Greenhaven Pr., Inc.) Cengage Gale.

Parmalee, Thomas. Genetic Engineering, 1 vol. 2008. (Essential Viewpoints Set 2 Ser.). (ENG., Illus.). 112p. (J). (gr. 6-12). lib. bdg. 35.64 (978-1-60453-057-5(X)) ABDO Publishing Co.

Rice, Elizabeth. Genetic Engineering. 2012. (Illus.). 64p. (J). 32.79 (978-0-7614-4972-0(8)) Marshall Cavendish Corp.

Rogers, Kara. Cloning. 2015. (Biotechnology Revolution Ser.). (ENG., Illus.). 128p. (J). (gr. 10-10). 38.75 (978-1-62275-576-9(6), Britannica Educational Publishing) Rosen Publishing Group, Inc., The.

Roleff, Tamara L. Genetic Engineering. 2008. (Compact Research Ser.). (Illus.). 112p. (YA). (gr. 3-7). lib. bdg. (978-1-60152-038-8(7)) ReferencePoint Pr., Inc.

Rooney, Anne. Genetic Engineering & Developments in Biotechnology. 2016. (Engineering in Action Ser.). (ENG., Illus.). 32p. (J). (gr. 5-8). (978-0-7787-7538-6(0)) Crabtree Publishing Co.

Smith, Terry L. Modern Genetic Science: New Technology, New Decisions. 2009. (Science & Society Ser.). 64p. (gr. 5-6). 58.50 (978-1-60853-009-0(4)) Rosen Publishing Group, Inc., The.

Spangenburg, Ray & Moser, Diane. Genetic Engineering. 2003. (Open for Debate Ser.). (Illus.). 128p. (gr. 7-18). lib. bdg. 42.79 (978-0-7614-1586-2(6), Benchmark Bks.) Marshall Cavendish Corp.

Stille, Darlene R. Altering the Biological Blueprint: The Science of Genetic Engineering, 1 vol. 2010. (Headline Science Ser.). (ENG.). 48p. (gr. 7-8). lib. bdg. 29.32 (978-0-7565-4049-4(6), Headline Science) Compass Point Bks.

Thompson, Martin. Critical World Issues: Genetic Engineering, Vol. 16. 2016. (Critical World Issues Ser.: Vol. 16). (ENG., Illus.). 112p. (J). (gr. 7-12). 25.95 (978-1-4222-3655-0(2)) Mason Crest.

Yount, Lisa. Modern Genetics: Engineering Life. 2nd rev. ed. 2006. (Milestones in Discovery & Invention Ser.). (Illus.). 224p. (YA). (gr. 7-12). 35.00 (978-0-8160-5744-3(3)) Facts On File, Inc.

GENETICS

see also Adaptation (Biology); Evolution; Life (Biology); Natural Selection; Reproduction

Anders, Mason. Heredity. 2017. (Genetics Ser.). (ENG.). 32p. (gr. 3-4). lib. bdg. 27.32 **(978-1-5157-7257-6(8))** Capstone Press of Coughlan Cos.

Arbuthnott, Gill. What Makes You You? Mones, Marc, illus. 2016. (ENG.). 64p. (J). (978-0-7787-2239-7(2)) Crabtree Publishing Co.

Ballen, Karen Gunnison. Decoding Our DNA: Craig Venter vs the Human Genome Project. 2012. (Scientific Rivalries & Scandals Ser.). (ENG.). 64p. (gr. 6-12). lib. bdg. 33.27 (978-0-7613-5489-5(1)) Lerner Publishing Group.

Bankston, John. Gregor Mendel & the Discovery of the Gene. 2004. (Uncharted, Unexplored, & Unexplained Ser.). (Illus.). 48p. (J). (gr. 4-8). lib. bdg. 29.95 (978-1-58415-266-8(4)) Mitchell Lane Pubs., Inc.

Bardoe, Cheryl. Gregor Mendel: The Friar Who Grew Peas. 2015. (J). lib. bdg. 20.80 (978-0-606-37418-7(3)) Turtleback Bks.

Bjorklund, Ruth. Sickle Cell Anemia. 2010. (Health Alert 7 Ser.). 64p. (YA). (gr. 4-7). 32.79 (978-0-7614-4821-1(7)) Marshall Cavendish GBR. Dist: Marshall Cavendish Corp.

Boothroyd, Jennifer. Eye Color: Brown, Blue, Green, & Other Hues. 2012. (Lightning Bolt Books (tm) — What Traits Are in Your Genes? Ser.). (Illus.). 32p. (gr. k-2). (SPA & ENG.). pap. 7.95 (978-1-58013-954-0(X)); (ENG., lib. bdg. 26.60 (978-0-7613-8938-5(5)) Lerner Publishing Group.

Bortz, Fred. The Laws of Genetics & Gregor Mendel. 2013. (Revolutionary Discoveries of Scientific Pioneers Ser.). (Illus.). 80p. (J). (gr. 7-12). 33.25 (978-1-4777-1806-3(0)) Rosen Publishing Group, Inc., The.

Boskey, Elizabeth. America Debates Genetic DNA Testing. 2009. (America Debates Ser.). 64p. (gr. 5-6). 58.50 (978-1-61511-332-3(0), Rosen Reference) Rosen Publishing Group, Inc., The.

Butterfield, Moira. Genetics. 2003. (21st Century Science Ser.). 48p. (J). lib. bdg. 27.10 (978-1-58340-350-1(7)) Black Rabbit Bks.

Christie, Lee. Basic Heredity: Text Pairs. 2008. (Bridges/Navigators Ser.). (J). (gr. 6). 89.00 (978-1-4108-8431-2(7)) Benchmark Education Co.

Claybourne, A. Introduction to Genes & DNA. 2004. (Genes & Dna Ser.). (Illus.). 64p. (J). lib. bdg. 19.95 (978-1-58086-546-3(1)) EDC Publishing.

Claybourne, Anna. The Story of You. 2016. (ENG., Illus.). 48p. (J). (gr. 4-6). 16.99 (978-0-7502-9685-4(2), Wayland) Hachette Children's Group GBR. Dist: Hachette Bk. Group.

Conklin, Wendy. DNA. 2015. (Science Readers: Content & Literacy Ser.). (Illus.). 32p. (gr. 5-5). pap. 8.99 (978-1-4807-4719-7(X)) Teacher Created Materials, Inc.

Cullen, J. Heather. Barbara McClintock. 2003. (Women in Science Ser.). (Illus.). 112p. (gr. 6-12). 30.00 (978-0-7910-7248-6(7), Chelsea Hse.) Facts On File, Inc.

Day, Trevor. Genetics: Investigating the Function of Genes & the Science of Heredity. 2012. (Scientific Pathways Ser.). (ENG., Illus.). 48p. (YA). (gr. 5-8). 27.95 (978-1-4488-7199-5(9), Rosen Reference) Rosen Publishing Group, Inc., The.

Day, Trevor, rev. Genetics. 2004. (Routes of Science Ser.). (Illus.). 40p. (J). (gr. 4-7). 24.95 (978-1-4103-0301-1(2), Blackbirch Pr., Inc.) Cengage Gale.

Dlugos, Jenn & Hatton, Charlie. Mystifying Mutants. 2016. (Things That Make You Go Yuck! Ser.: 0). (ENG., Illus.). 88p. (J). (gr. 4-7). pap. 7.95 (978-1-61821-564-2(7), 9781618215642) Prufrock Pr.

Doak, Robin. Genetic Disorders: Set Of 6. 2011. (Navigators Ser.). (J). pap. 50.00 net. (978-1-4108-6239-6(9)) Benchmark Education Co.

Doeden, Matthew. Advances in Genetics: Set Of 6. 2010. (Navigators Ser.). (J). pap. 50.00 net. (978-1-4108-6240-2(2)) Benchmark Education Co.

—Advances in Genetics: Text Pairs. 2008. (Bridges/Navigators Ser.). (J). (gr. 6). 81.00 (978-1-4108-8426-8(0)) Benchmark Education Co.

Duke, Shirley Smith. You Can't Wear These Genes. 2010. (ENG., Illus.). 48p. (gr. 4-6). pap. 10.95 (978-1-61590-563-8(4)) Rourke Educational Media.

Eason, Sarah, ed. Reproduction & Genetics. 2011. (FAYFT: Introducing Biology Ser.). 64p. (gr. 4-10). lib. bdg. 39.95 (978-1-936333-00-4(7)) Brown Bear Bks.

Encyclopaedia Britannica, Inc. Staff. Britannica Illustrated Science Library Series (18 Title Series), 18 vols. 2010. 599.00 (978-1-61535-423-8(9)) Encyclopaedia Britannica, Inc.

Encyclopaedia Britannica, Inc. Staff, compiled by. Britannica Illustrated Science Library: Evolution & Genetics, 16 vols. 2008. (Illus.). (J). 29.95 (978-1-59339-388-5(1)) Encyclopaedia Britannica, Inc.

Fridell, Ron. Decoding Life: Unraveling the Mysteries of the Genome. 2005. (Discovery! Ser.). (Illus.). 112p. (J). (gr. 3-7). lib. bdg. 29.27 (978-0-8225-1196-0(7)) Lerner Publishing Group.

Friedman, Lauri S. Stem Cell Research. 2011. (Writing the Critical Essay: an Opposing Viewpoints Guide Ser.). (ENG.). 128p. 33.75 (978-0-7377-5025-6(1), Greenhaven Pr., Inc.) Cengage Gale.

Fritz, Sandy. Genomics & Cloning. 2003. (Hot Science Ser.). (J). lib. bdg. 28.50 (978-1-58340-365-5(5)) Black Rabbit Bks.

Gardner, Robert. Genetics & Evolution Science Fair Projects: Using Skeletons, Cereal, Earthworms, & More. 2005. (Biology! Best Science Projects Ser.). (Illus.). 128p. (J). (gr. 6-13). lib. bdg. 27.94 (978-0-7660-1175-5(5)) Enslow Pubs., Inc.

—Genetics & Evolution Science Fair Projects, Revised & Expanded Using the Scientific Method. LaBaff, Stephanie, illus. 2010. (Biology Science Projects Using the Scientific Method Ser.). 160p. (J). (gr. 5-18). 35.94 (978-0-7660-3422-8(4)) Enslow Pubs., Inc.

Genetik: Fachliche Inhalte und Uebungsaufgaben. 2nd ed. (Duden Abiturhilfen Ser.). (GER.). 112p. (YA). (gr. 12-13). (978-3-411-05472-5(7)) Bibliographisches Institut & F. A. Brockhaus AG DEU. Dist: International Bk. Import Service, Inc.

Gerdes, Louise I. Human Genetics. 2014. (Opposing Viewpoints Ser.). (ENG., Illus.). 224p. (gr. 7-12). pap. 33.80 (978-0-7377-6954-8(8)); lib. bdg. 48.80 (978-0-7377-6953-1(X)) Cengage Gale. (Greenhaven Pr., Inc.).

Gleason, Katherine. Awesome Science: A Chapter Book. 2004. (True Tales Ser.). (ENG., Illus.). 48p. (J). 22.50 (978-0-516-23727-5(6), Children's Pr.) Scholastic Library Publishing.

Glimm, Adele. Gene Hunter: The Story of Neuropsychologist Nancy Wexler. 2006. (ENG., Illus.). 128p. (gr. 7-9). per. 19.95 (978-0-309-09558-7(1), Joseph Henry Pr.) National Academies Pr.

Green, Jen. Inheritance & Reproduction, 1 vol. 2013. (Essential Life Science Ser.). (ENG.). 48p. (gr. 4-6). 33.32 (978-1-4329-7808-2(X), Heinemann InfoSearch) Heinemann-Raintree.

—Inheritance of Traits: Why Is My Dog Bigger Than Your Dog?, 1 vol. 2014. (Show Me Science Ser.). (ENG.). 32p. (gr. 3-5). lib. bdg. 30.65 (978-1-4329-8747-3(X), Raintree Perspectives) Heinemann-Raintree.

Guttman, Burton S. Genetics: The Code of Life. 2011. (Contemporary Issues Ser.). (Illus.). 309p. (YA). (gr. 9-12). lib. bdg. 37.95 (978-1-4488-1863-1(X)) Rosen Publishing Group, Inc., The.

Hamilton, Sue L. DNA Analysis: Forensic Fluids & Follicles, 1 vol. 2008. (Crime Scene Investigation Ser.). (ENG.). 32p. (gr. 4-8). 27.07 (978-1-59928-987-8(3), Abdo & Daughters) ABDO Publishing Co.

Hand, Carol. Introduction to Genetics. 2010. (Understanding Genetics Ser.). (ENG.). 80p. (YA). lib. bdg. 33.25 (978-1-4358-9531-7(2)) Rosen Publishing Group, Inc., The.

Heos, Bridget. The Human Genome. 2010. (Understanding Genetics Ser.). (ENG.). 80p. (YA). lib. bdg. 33.25 (978-1-4358-9533-1(9)) Rosen Publishing Group, Inc., The.

—Stronger Than Steel: Spider Silk DNA & the Quest for Better Bulletproof Vests, Sutures, & Parachute Rope. Comins, Andy, illus. 2017. (Scientists in the Field Ser.). (ENG.). 80p. (J). (gr. 5-7). pap. 9.99 (978-0-544-93247-0(1), HMH Books For Young Readers) Houghton Mifflin Harcourt Publishing Co.

Hodge, Russ. Genetics & Evolution, 6 vols., Set. 2010. (Genetics & Evolution Ser.). (C). (gr. 9). 237.00 (978-0-8160-8300-8(2)) Facts On File, Inc.

Holt, Rinehart and Winston Staff. Holt Science & Technology Chapter 6: Life Science: Genes & DNA. 5th ed. 2004. (Illus.). pap. 12.86 (978-0-03-030186-5(6)) Holt McDougal.

Hunter, William. DNA Analysis. Noziglia, Carla Miller & Siegel, Jay A., eds. 2013. (Solving Crimes with Science: Forensics Ser.: 12). (Illus.). 112p. (J). (gr. 7-18). 22.95 (978-1-4222-2864-7(9)) Mason Crest.

Hyde, Natalie. Traits & Attributes. 2009. (Let's Relate to Genetics Ser.). (ENG.). 48p. (J). (gr. 5-8). lib. bdg. (978-0-7787-4949-3(5)); (gr. 6-9). pap. (978-0-7787-4966-0(5)) Crabtree Publishing Co.

Johnson, Rebecca L. Genetics. 2005. (Great Ideas of Science Ser.). (ENG., Illus.). 80p. (gr. 8-12). lib. bdg. 27.93 (978-0-8225-2910-1(6)) Lerner Publishing Group.

Johnson, Rebecca L. & National Geographic Learning Staff. You & Your Genes. 2007. (Reading Expeditions Ser.). (ENG., Illus.). 32p. (J). pap. 17.95 (978-0-7922-8866-4(1)) CENGAGE Learning.

Keyser, Amber J., et al. Decoding Genes with Max Axiom, Super Scientist, 1 vol. 2010. (Graphic Science Ser.). (ENG.). 32p. (gr. 3-4). lib. bdg. 30.65 (978-1-4296-3976-7(8), Graphic Library) Capstone Press of Coughlan Cos.

Kidd, Renee A. New Genetics: The Study of Lifelines. 2nd rev. ed. 2006. (Science & Society Ser.). (Illus.). 176p. (gr. 6-12). 35.00 (978-0-8160-5604-0(8)) Facts On File, Inc.

Knowles, Johanna. Huntington's Disease. 2006. (Genetic Diseases & Disorders Ser.). (Illus.). 64p. (YA). (gr. 5-9). lib. bdg. 31.95 (978-1-4042-0694-6(9)) Rosen Publishing Group, Inc., The.

Kyi, Tanya Lloyd. DNA Detective. Crump, Lil, illus. 2015. (ENG.). 120p. (YA). (gr. 5-8). 24.95 (978-1-55451-774-9(5), 9781554517749) Annick Pr., Ltd. CAN. Dist: Publishers Group West (PGW).

Larson, Kirsten W. Mutants in Nature. 2015. (Freaky Nature Ser.). (ENG., Illus.). 32p. (J). (gr. 2-4). 19.95 (978-1-60753-780-9(X)) Amicus Publishing.

Leech, Bonnie. Gregor Mendel's Genetic Theory: Understanding & Applying Concepts of Probability. (PowerMath: Advanced Proficiency Plus Ser.). 2009. 32p. (gr. 5-5). 47.90 (978-1-60851-356-7(4)) 2007. 36p. pap. 23.95 (978-1-4358-3820-8(3)) Rosen Publishing Group, Inc., The. (PowerKids Pr.).

Leech, Bonnie Coulter. Gregor Mendel's Genetic Theory: Understanding & Applying Concepts of Probability. (Math for the Real World Ser.). (Illus.). 32p. 2009. (ENG.). (gr. 6-7). pap. 10.00 (978-1-4042-6063-4(3)) 2006. (YA). (gr. 5-9). lib. bdg. 25.25 (978-1-4042-3355-3(5)) Rosen Publishing Group, Inc., The.

Lokere, Jillian. Genetics: Unlocking the Secrets of Life, 1 vol. 2014. (History of Science Ser.). (ENG., Illus.). 112p. (YA). (gr. 6-12). lib. bdg. 35.64 (978-1-62403-562-3(0), Essential Library) ABDO Publishing Co.

Lundgren, Julie K. I Look Like My Mother. 2012. (ENG.). 24p. (gr. 4-5). pap. 8.95 (978-1-61810-233-1(8)) Rourke Educational Media.

Meredith, Susan. Genes & Dna - Internet Linked. rev. ed. 2006. 64p. (J). pap. 11.99 (978-0-7945-1562-1(2), Usborne) EDC Publishing.

Merino, Noël. Human Genetics. 2010. (Current Controversies Ser.). (Illus.). 240p. 40.95 (978-0-7377-4707-2(2)); pap. 28.45 (978-0-7377-4708-9(0)) Cengage Gale. (Greenhaven Pr., Inc.).

Nardo, Don. DNA Evidence. 2007. (Crime Scene Investigations Ser.). (ENG., Illus.). 104p. (YA). (gr. 7-12). lib. bdg. 33.45 (978-1-59018-951-1(5)) Cengage Gale.

O'Neal, Claire. Projects in Genetics. 2010. (Life Science Projects for Kids Ser.). (Illus.). 48p. (J). (gr. 4-8). lib. bdg. 29.95 (978-1-58415-877-6(8)) Mitchell Lane Pubs., Inc.

Parker, Lew. Genetics. Krasnow, David, ed. 2003. (Discovery Channel School Science Ser.). (Illus.). 32p. (gr. 4-8). lib. bdg. 26.00 (978-0-8368-3370-6(8), Gareth Stevens Learning Library) Stevens, Gareth Publishing LLLP.

Pezzi, Bryan. David Suzuki. 2010. (Illus.). 24p. (978-1-77071-595-0(9)); pap. (978-1-77071-601-8(7)) Weigl Educational Pubs. Ltd.

Powell, Jillian. Explaining Cystic Fibrosis. 2009. (Explaining... Ser.). 48p. (gr. 7-12). 37.10 (978-1-59920-312-6(X)) Black Rabbit Bks.

Quinn, Lauren D. Heredity. 2016. (Illus.). 32p. (J). (978-1-5105-1186-6(5)) SmartBook Media, Inc.

Rainis, Kenneth G. Blood & DNA Evidence: Crime-Solving Science Experiments. 2006. (Forensic Science Projects Ser.). (Illus.). 104p. (J). (gr. 3-7). lib. bdg. 33.27 (978-0-7660-1958-4(6)) Enslow Pubs., Inc.

Rice, Dona. All in the Family, 1 vol. rev. ed. 2014. (Science Readers: Content & Literacy Ser.). (ENG., Illus.). 24p. (gr. 1-1). pap. 8.99 (978-1-4807-4563-6(4)) Teacher Created Materials, Inc.

Rogers, Kara. Cloning. 2015. (Biotechnology Revolution Ser.). (ENG., Illus.). 128p. (J). (gr. 10-10). 38.75 (978-1-62275-576-9(6), Britannica Educational Publishing) Rosen Publishing Group, Inc., The.

Sandvold, Lynnette Brent. Genetics. 2009. (Big Ideas in Science Ser.). 48p. (gr. 5). 31.36 (978-0-7614-4396-4(7)) Marshall Cavendish Corp.

Schacter, Bernice. Genetics in the News. 2007. (Science News Flash Ser.). (Illus.). 102p. (YA). (gr. 7-12). lib. bdg. 31.95 (978-0-7910-9255-2(0)) Facts On File, Inc.

Schafer, Susan. DNA & Genes. 2009. (ENG., Illus.). 96p. (C). (gr. 6-18). lib. bdg. 158.00 (978-0-7656-8135-5(8), Y181927) Routledge.

—Heredity. 2009. (ENG., Illus.). 96p. (C). (gr. 6-18). lib. bdg. 158.00 (978-0-7656-8136-2(6), Y182755) Routledge.

The Science of Life. 2016. (Illus.). 48p. (J). (978-1-4222-3514-0(9)) Mason Crest.

Science Readers Staff & Van Gorp, Lynn. The World of Genetics, 1 vol. 2007. (Science Readers Ser.). (ENG., Illus.). 32p. (J). (gr. 4-4). pap. 8.99 (978-0-7439-0597-8(0)) Shell Educational Publishing.

Sheen, Barbara. Birth Defects. 2005. (Diseases & Disorders Ser.). (Illus.). 112p. (YA). (gr. 7-10). lib. bdg. 32.45 (978-1-59018-406-6(8), Lucent Bks.) Cengage Gale.

Sian revision one&only You. 2004. (Science in A Nutshell Ser.). (J). (978-1-59242-051-3(6)) Delta Education, LLC.

Silverman, Buffy. Hair Traits: Color, Texture, & More. 2012. (Lightning Bolt Books (tm) — What Traits Are in Your Genes? Ser.). (Illus.). 32p. (gr. k-2). (SPA & ENG.). pap. 7.95 (978-1-58013-956-4(6)); (ENG., lib. bdg. 26.60 (978-0-7613-8941-5(5), Lerner Pubns.) Lerner Publishing Group.

—Unusual Traits: Tongue Rolling, Special Taste Sensors, & More. 2012. (Lightning Bolt Books (tm) — What Traits Are in Your Genes? Ser.). (ENG., Illus.). 32p. (gr. k-2). pap. 7.95 (978-1-58013-957-1(4)); lib. bdg. 26.60 (978-0-7613-8943-9(1), Lerner Pubns.) Lerner Publishing Group.

Simpson, Kathleen. Genetics: From DNA to Designer Dogs. 2008. (National Geographic Investigates Science Ser.). (ENG., Illus.). 64p. (J). (gr. 5). 27.90 (978-1-4263-0327-2(0), National Geographic Children's Bks.) National Geographic Society.

Simpson, Kathleen & National Geographic Kids Staff. Genetics: From DNA to Designer Dogs. 2008. (National Geographic Investigates Science Ser.). (ENG., Illus.). 64p. (J). (gr. 5). 17.95 (978-1-4263-0361-6(0), National Geographic Children's Bks.) National Geographic Society.

Smith, Terry L. Modern Genetic Science: New Technology, New Decisions. 2009. (Science & Society Ser.). 64p. (gr. 5-6). 58.50 (978-1-60853-009-0(4)) Rosen Publishing Group, Inc., The.

Solway, Andrew. Genetics. 2010. (CC: 21st Century Science Ser.). 112p. (gr. 6-12). 42.80 (978-1-933834-73-3(0)) Brown Bear Bks.

—Genetics in Medicine. 2007. (Cutting Edge Medicine Ser.). (Illus.). 64p. (gr. 6-12). lib. bdg. 34.00 (978-0-8368-7865-3(5), Gareth Stevens Secondary Library) Stevens, Gareth Publishing LLLP.

Taylor-Butler, Christine. Genetics. 2016. (True Book(tm), a — Greatest Discoveries & Discoverers Ser.). (ENG., Illus.). 48p. (J). lib. bdg. 31.00 (978-0-531-21861-7(9), Children's Pr.) Scholastic Library Publishing.

Toriello, James. The Human Genome Project. (Library of Future Medicine Ser.). 64p. 2009. (gr. 5-5). 58.50 (978-1-60853-632-0(7)) 2005. (Illus.). (YA). (gr. 7-12). lib. bdg. 31.95 (978-0-8239-3671-7(6)) Rosen Publishing Group, Inc., The.

Vaughan, Jenny. Genetics. 2010. (J). 34.25 (978-1-59920-317-1(0)) Black Rabbit Bks.

Walker, Pamela & Wood, Elaine. Genetics Experiments. 2010. (Facts on File Science Experiments Ser.). (Illus.). 158p. (gr. 6-12). 40.00 (978-0-8160-8173-8(5)) Facts On File, Inc.

Wanjie, Anne, ed. The Basics of Genetics. 2013. (Core Concepts Ser.). 96p. (YA). (gr. 7-12). 34.60 (978-1-4777-0552-0(X)) Rosen Publishing Group, Inc., The.

Watson, Stephanie, ed. The Mechanisms of Genetics: An Anthology of Current Thought. (Contemporary Discourse in the Field of Biology Ser.). 2009. 224p. (gr. 10-12). 63.90 (978-1-61511-914-1(0)) 2005. (Illus.). 206p. (YA). (gr. 7-12). lib. bdg. 35.95 (978-1-4042-0402-7(4)) Rosen Publishing Group, Inc., The.

Wolfe, James. Genetic Testing & Gene Therapy. 2015. (Biotechnology Revolution Ser.). (ENG., Illus.). 128p. (J). (gr. 10-10). 38.75 (978-1-62275-572-1(3), Britannica Educational Publishing) Rosen Publishing Group, Inc., The.

World Book, Inc Staff, contrib. by. Traits & Heredity. 2014. (Illus.). 32p. (J). (978-0-7166-2827-9(9)) World Bk., Inc.

Yount, Lisa. Modern Genetics: Engineering Life. 2nd rev. ed. 2006. (Milestones in Discovery & Invention Ser.). (Illus.). 224p. (YA). (gr. 7-12). 35.00 (978-0-8160-5744-3(3)) Facts On File, Inc.

GENGHIS KHAN, 1162-1227

Behnke, Alison. The Conquests of Genghis Khan. 2008. (Pivotal Moments in History Ser.). (ENG., Illus.). 160p. (gr. 9-12). lib. bdg. 38.60 (978-0-8225-7519-1(1)) Lerner Publishing Group.

Boeheme, Gerry. Genghis Khan. 2017. (J). **(978-1-5026-2787-2(6))** Cavendish Square Publishing.

Demi. Genghis Khan, 0 vols. 2009. (ENG.). 64p. (J). (gr. 3-7). 19.99 (978-0-7614-5547-9(7), 9780761455479, Amazon Children's Publishing) Amazon Publishing.

Kent, Zachary. Genghis Khan: Invincible Ruler of the Mongol Empire. 2007. (Rulers of the Middle Ages Ser.). (Illus.). 160p.

(YA). (gr. 6-12). lib. bdg. 35.94 *(978-0-7660-2715-2(5))* Enslow Pubs., Inc.

Knight, P. V. Genghis Khan: Fierce Mongolian Conqueror. 2016. (History's Most Murderous Villains Ser.). (Illus.). 32p. (J). (gr. 5-4). pap. 10.50 *(978-1-4824-4790-3(8))* Stevens, Gareth Publishing LLLP.

Lange, Brenda. Genghis Khan. 2003. (Ancient World Leaders Ser.). (Illus.). 112p. (gr. 6-12). 30.00 *(978-0-7910-7222-6(3),* Chelsea Hse.) Facts On File, Inc.

Medina, Nico. Who Was Genghis Khan? Thomson, Andrew & Harrison, Nancy, illus. 2014. (Who Was? Ser.). (ENG.). 112p. (J). (gr. 3-7). pap. 5.99 *(978-0-448-48260-6(6),* Grosset & Dunlap) Penguin Young Readers Group.

—Who Was Genghis Khan? 2014. (Who Was... ? Ser.). lib. bdg. 16.00 *(978-0-606-36178-1(2))* Turtleback Bks.

Nardo, Don. Genghis Khan & the Mongol Empire. 2010. (World History Ser.). (ENG.). 128p. 34.95 *(978-1-4205-0326-5(X),* Lucent Bks.) Cengage Gale.

Rice, Earle, Jr. Empire in the East: The Story of Genghis Khan. 2005. (World Leaders Ser.). (Illus.). 160p. (gr. 3-7). 28.95 *(978-1-931798-62-4(1))* Reynolds, Morgan Inc.

Sepahban, Lois. Mongol Warriors. 2015. (Ancient Warriors Ser.). (ENG.). 32p. (J). (gr. 2-5). 28.50 *(978-1-63143-756-4(9),* 208588) Child's World, Inc., The.

Whiting, Jim. The Life & Times of Genghis Khan. 2005. (Biography from Ancient Civilizations Ser.). (Illus.). 48p. (J). (gr. 4-8). lib. bdg. 29.95 *(978-1-58415-348-1(2))* Mitchell Lane Pubs., Inc.

GENGHIS KHAN, 1162-1227—FICTION

Kerr, P. B., pseud. The Grave Robbers of Genghis Khan. 2011. (Children of the Lamp Ser.: Vol. 7). (ENG.). 448p. (J). (gr. 3-7). 18.99 *(978-0-545-12660-1(6),* Orchard Bks.) Scholastic, Inc.

GENIUS—FICTION

Banks, Piper. Geek Abroad, 2 vols. 2008. (Geek High Ser.: 2). (ENG.). 256p. (YA). (gr. 9-18). 9.99 *(978-0-451-22393-7(4),* Berkley) Penguin Publishing Group.

—Summer of the Geek. 2010. (Geek High Ser.: 3). (ENG.). 256p. (YA). (gr. 5-18). 9.99 *(978-0-451-22984-7(3),* Berkley) Penguin Publishing Group.

Benton, Jim. Let's Do a Thing! 2017. (Victor Shmud, Total Expert Ser.: 1). (ENG.). 128p. (J). (gr. 2-5). pap. 5.99 ***(978-0-545-93229-5(7))***; lib. bdg. 16.99 ***(978-0-545-93233-2(5))*** Scholastic, Inc. (Scholastic Paperbacks).

Clements, Andrew. The Report Card. (ENG., Illus.). (J). (gr. 3-7). 2004. 176p. 18.99 *(978-0-689-84515-4(4))* 2006. 192p. reprint ed. pap. 7.99 *(978-0-689-84524-6(3))* Simon & Schuster Children's Publishing. (Atheneum Bks. for Young Readers).

Colfer, Eoin. The Last Guardian. 2012. (Artemis Fowl Ser.). (ENG.). 336p. (J). (gr. 5-9). 18.99 *(978-1-4231-6161-5(0))* Hyperion Pr.

—The Last Guardian. 2014. (Artemis Fowl Ser.: 8). (J). lib. bdg. 19.65 *(978-0-606-32288-1(4),* Turtleback) Turtleback Bks.

Draper, Sharon M. Out of My Mind. 2009. 9.00 *(978-0-7848-3780-1(5),* Everbind) Marco Bk. Co.

—Out of My Mind. (ENG., Illus.). (J). (gr. 5). 2012. 320p. pap. 9.99 *(978-1-4169-7171-9(8))* 2010. 304p. 18.99 *(978-1-4169-7170-2(X))* Simon & Schuster Children's Publishing. (Atheneum Bks. for Young Readers).

—Out of My Mind. 2012. lib. bdg. 20.85 *(978-0-606-25672-8(5),* Turtleback) Turtleback Bks.

Elish, Dan. The School for the Insanely Gifted. 2011. (ENG.). 304p. (J). (gr. 3-7). 15.99 *(978-0-06-113873-7(8))* HarperCollins Pubs.

Evans, Richard. Hunt for Jade Dragon. 2015. (Michael Vey Ser.: 4). (ENG., Illus.). 336p. (YA). (gr. 7). pap. 11.99 *(978-1-4814-2439-4(4))* Simon & Schuster, Inc.

—Michael Vey 5. 2015. (Michael Vey Ser.: 5). (ENG., Illus.). 288p. (YA). (gr. 7). 18.99 *(978-1-4814-4410-1(7),* Simon Pulse/Mercury Ink) Simon Pulse/Mercury Ink.

Forester, Victoria. The Boy Who Knew Everything. 2015. (ENG.). 416p. (J). (gr. 4-7). 16.99 *(978-0-312-62600-6(2),* 9780312626006) Feiwel & Friends.

Gout, Leopoldo. Genius: The Game. 2016. (Genius Ser.: 1). (ENG., Illus.). 304p. (YA). 17.99 *(978-1-250-04581-2(9),* 9781250045812) Feiwel & Friends.

—Genius: The Game. 2017. (Genius Ser.: 1). (ENG., Illus.). 320p. (YA). pap. 10.99 *(978-1-250-11527-0(2),* 9781250115270) Square Fish.

—Genius: the Con. 2017. (Genius Ser.: 2). (ENG.). 288p. (YA). 18.99 *(978-1-250-04582-9(7),* 9781250045829) Feiwel & Friends.

Graff, Lisa. Sophie Simon Solves Them All. Beene, Jason, illus. 2010. (ENG.). 112p. (J). (gr. 3-5). 14.99 *(978-0-374-37125-8(3),* 9780374371258, Farrar, Straus & Giroux (BYR)) Farrar, Straus & Giroux.

—Sophie Simon Solves Them All. Beene, Jason, illus. 2012. (ENG.). 112p. (J). (gr. 3-5). pap. 6.99 *(978-1-250-02898-3(1),* 9781250028983) Square Fish.

Greenland, Shannon. The Winning Element, Vol. 3. 2008. (Specialists Ser.). (ENG.). 224p. (YA). (gr. 7-18). 6.99 *(978-0-14-241052-3(7),* Speak) Penguin Young Readers Group.

Gutman, Dan. From Texas with Love. 2014. (ENG.). (J). (gr. 3-7). (Genius Files Ser.: 4). 304p. pap. 6.99 *(978-0-06-182775-4(4))*; (Genius Files Ser.: Bk. 4). (Illus.). 288p. 16.99 *(978-0-06-182773-0(8))* HarperCollins Pubs.

—From Texas with Love. 2014. (Genius Files Ser.: 4). (J). lib. bdg. 17.20 *(978-0-606-36462-1(5))* Turtleback Bks.

—The Genius Files #4: from Texas with Love. 2014. (Genius Files Ser.: 4). 288p. (J). (gr. 3-7). lib. bdg. 17.89 *(978-0-06-182774-7(6))* HarperCollins Pubs.

—The Genius Files #5: License to Thrill. 2016. (Genius Files Ser.: 5). (Illus.). 272p. (J). (gr. 3-7). pap. 6.99 *(978-0-06-223633-3(4))* HarperCollins Pubs.

—Mission Unstoppable. 2011. (Genius Files Ser.: 1). (ENG.). 304p. (J). (gr. 3-7). pap. 6.99 *(978-0-06-182766-2(5))*; (Illus.). 16.99 *(978-0-06-182764-8(9))* HarperCollins Pubs.

—Mission Unstoppable. 2011. (Genius Files Ser.: 1). (J). lib. bdg. 17.20 *(978-0-606-23559-4(0),* Turtleback) Turtleback Bks.

—Never Say Genius. 2012. (Genius Files Ser.: 2). (J). (gr. 3-7). (ENG.). 304p. pap. 6.99 *(978-0-06-182769-3(X))*; (ENG.). 288p. 16.99 *(978-0-06-182767-9(3))*; 288p. lib. bdg. 17.89 *(978-0-06-182768-6(1))* HarperCollins Pubs.

—You Only Die Twice. 2013. (Genius Files Ser.: 3). (J). (gr. 3-7). (ENG.). 320p. pap. 6.99 *(978-0-06-182772-3(X))*; (ENG., Illus.). 304p. 16.99 *(978-0-06-182770-9(3))*; (Illus.). 304p. lib. bdg. 17.89 *(978-0-06-182771-6(1))* HarperCollins Pubs.

—You Only Die Twice. 2013. (Genius Files Ser.: 3). (J). lib. bdg. 17.20 *(978-0-606-35043-3(8),* Turtleback) Turtleback Bks.

Haynes, Marilee. A. K. A. Genius. 2013. (ENG.). 208p. (YA). 9.95 *(978-0-8198-0830-1(X))* Pauline Bks. & Media.

—Genius under Construction. 2014. (ENG.). (YA). pap. *(978-0-8198-3126-2(3))* Pauline Bks. & Media.

Hunt for Jade Dragon. 2014. (Michael Vey Ser.: No. 4). (ENG., Illus.). 336p. (YA). (gr. 7). 19.99 *(978-1-4814-2438-7(6),* Simon Pulse/Mercury Ink) Simon Pulse/Mercury Ink.

Ishida, S. E. M. Nick Newton Is Not a Genius. 2016. (Illus.). 151p. (J). *(978-1-62856-235-4(8))* BJU Pr.

Ivanoff, George & Quarmby, Toby. My Best Friend Thinks I'm a Genius. 2008. (Rigby Focus Forward Ser.). (ENG., Illus.). 24p. (gr. 3-8). pap. 11.20 *(978-1-4190-3849-5(4))* Houghton Mifflin Harcourt Publishing Co.

Jinks, Catherine. Evil Genius. 2007. 486p. (J). *(978-1-4287-3510-1(0))* Harcourt Trade Pubs.

—Evil Genius. 2008. (ENG., Illus.). 496p. (YA). (gr. 7). pap. 9.99 *(978-0-15-206185-2(1))* Houghton Mifflin Harcourt Publishing Co.

—Genius Squad. 2009. (ENG., Illus.). 448p. (J). (gr. 7). pap. 8.99 *(978-0-15-206650-5(0))* Houghton Mifflin Harcourt Publishing Co.

—The Genius Wars. 2011. (ENG.). 384p. (YA). (gr. 7). pap. 8.99 *(978-0-547-57727-2(3))* Houghton Mifflin Harcourt Publishing Co.

Kennedy, Katie. Learning to Swear in America. 2017. (ENG.). 368p. (YA). pap. 9.99 *(978-1-61963-911-9(4),* 9781619639119, Bloomsbury USA Childrens) Bloomsbury Publishing USA.

Lieb, Josh. I Am a Genius of Unspeakable Evil & I Want to Be Your Class President. 2010. (ENG.). 304p. (J). (gr. 5-7). 8.99 *(978-1-59514-354-9(8),* Razorbill) Penguin Young Readers Group.

Lithgow, John & Payne, C. F. The Remarkable Farkle McBride. 2003. (ENG., Illus.). 40p. (J). (gr. -1-3). pap. 7.99 *(978-0-689-83541-4(8),* Simon & Schuster Bks. For Young Readers) Simon & Schuster Bks. For Young Readers.

Mann, Jennifer Ann. Sunny Sweet Can So Get Lost. 2015. (Sunny Sweet Ser.). (ENG., Illus.). 208p. (YA). (gr. 3-6). 15.99 *(978-1-61963-505-0(4),* 9781619635050, Bloomsbury USA Childrens) Bloomsbury Publishing USA.

—Sunny Sweet Is So Dead Meat. (Sunny Sweet Ser.). (ENG., Illus.). 208p. (YA). (gr. 3-6). 2015. pap. 6.99 *(978-1-61963-563-0(1),* 9781619635630) 2014. 15.99 *(978-1-59990-978-3(2),* 9781599909783) Bloomsbury Publishing USA. (Bloomsbury USA Childrens).

—Sunny Sweet Is So Not Scary. 2015. (Sunny Sweet Ser.). (ENG.). 192p. (YA). (gr. 3-6). 15.99 *(978-1-61963-507-4(0),* 9781619635074, Bloomsbury USA Childrens) Bloomsbury Publishing USA.

—Sunny Sweet Is So Not Sorry. 2013. (Sunny Sweet Ser.). (ENG., Illus.). 208p. (YA). (gr. 3-6). 15.99 *(978-1-59990-977-6(4),* 9781599909776, Bloomsbury USA Childrens) Bloomsbury Publishing USA.

McCranie, Stephen. Mal & Chad - The Biggest, Bestest Time Ever! McCranie, Stephen, illus. 2011. (Mal & Chad Ser.: 1). (ENG., Illus.). 224p. (J). (gr. 3-7). 9.99 *(978-0-399-25221-1(5),* Philomel Bks.) Penguin Young Readers Group.

Mezrich, Ben. Bringing down the Mouse. 2014. (ENG., Illus.). 336p. (J). (gr. 3-7). 16.99 *(978-1-4424-9626-2(6),* Simon & Schuster Bks. For Young Readers) Simon & Schuster Bks. For Young Readers.

Offit, Sidney. Adventures of Homer Fink. Galdone, Paul, illus. 2016. (ENG.). 192p. pap. 11.99 *(978-1-5040-3621-4(2))* Open Road Integrated Media, Inc.

Pennypacker, Sara. Waylon! One Awesome Thing. Frazee, Marla, illus. 2016. (Waylon Ser.). (ENG.). 204p. (J). (gr. 1-3). 15.99 *(978-1-4847-0152-2(6))* Disney Pr.

Roy, Jennifer. Mindblind, 0 vols. unabr. ed. 2013. (ENG.). 254p. (J). (gr. 7-9). pap. 9.99 *(978-1-4778-1712-4(3),* 9781477817124, Amazon Children's Publishing) Amazon Publishing.

Shade, Jeff. An Unusual Education. 2010. (J). pap. *(978-0-88092-317-0(2))* Royal Fireworks Publishing Co.

Sloan, Holly Goldberg. Counting by 7s. 2015. (CHI.). 392p. (J). pap. *(978-986-6104-68-8(0))* DaskoviK, Izdatel'sko-torgovaja korporacija.

—Counting by 7s. 2013. (ENG.). 384p. (YA). (gr. 5). 17.99 *(978-0-8037-3855-3(2),* Dial Bks) Penguin Publishing Group.

—Counting by 7s. 2014. (ENG.). 400p. (J). (gr. 5). 8.99 *(978-0-14-242286-1(X),* Puffin Books) Penguin Young Readers Group.

—Counting by 7s. 2014. (ENG.). (J). (gr. 5). lib. bdg. 19.60 ***(978-1-62765-616-0(2))*** Perfection Learning Corp.

—Counting by 7s. 2014. (J). (gr. 5-8). lib. bdg. 19.65 *(978-0-606-36583-3(4))* Turtleback Bks.

Spratt, R. A. Friday Barnes, Girl Detective. Gosier, Phil, illus. 2016. (Friday Barnes Mysteries Ser.: Bk. 1). (ENG.). 272p. (J). 13.99 *(978-1-62672-297-2(8),* 9781626722972) Roaring Brook Pr.

—Under Suspicion. Gosier, Phil, illus. 2016. (Friday Barnes Mysteries Ser.). (ENG.). 288p. (J). 13.99 *(978-1-62672-299-6(4),* 9781626722996) Roaring Brook Pr.

Stewart, Trenton Lee. The Extraordinary Education of Nicholas Benedict. Sudyka, Diana, illus. (Mysterious Benedict Society Ser.). (ENG.). (J). (gr. 3-7). 2013. 496p. pap. 9.99 *(978-0-316-17620-0(6))* 2012. 480p. 18.99 *(978-0-316-17619-4(2))* Little, Brown Bks. for Young Readers.

—The Extraordinary Education of Nicholas Benedict. 2013. (Mysterious Benedict Society Ser.: 0). (J). lib. bdg. 19.65 *(978-0-606-31743-6(0),* Turtleback) Turtleback Bks.

Tobin, Paul. The Genius Factor - How to Capture an Invisible Cat. Lafontaine, Thierry, illus. 2016. (ENG.). 272p. (J). 16.99 *(978-1-61963-840-2(1),* 9781619638402, Bloomsbury USA Childrens) Bloomsbury Publishing USA.

—The Genius Factor: How to Capture an Invisible Cat. Lafontaine, Thierry, illus. 2017. (ENG.). 288p. (J). pap. 7.99 *(978-1-68119-278-9(0),* 9781681192789, Bloomsbury USA Childrens) Bloomsbury Publishing USA.

—How to Outsmart a Billion Robot Bees. Lafontaine, Thierry & Abey, Katie, illus. 2017. (ENG.). 320p. (J). 16.99 *(978-1-61963-897-6(5),* 9781619638976, Bloomsbury USA Childrens) Bloomsbury Publishing USA.

Valentine, Stephen J. The Lazarus Game. 2015. 311p. (YA). pap. 19.99 *(978-1-4621-1554-9(3))* Cedar Fort, Inc./CFI Distribution.

Walden, Mark. Dreadnought. (H. I. V. E. Ser.: 4). (ENG.). (J). (gr. 3-7). 2012. 320p. pap. 8.99 *(978-1-4424-1368-9(9))* 2011. 304p. 16.99 *(978-1-4424-2186-8(X))* Simon & Schuster Bks. For Young Readers. (Simon & Schuster Bks. For Young Readers).

—Escape Velocity. (H. I. V. E. Ser.: 3). (ENG.). (J). (gr. 3-7). 2012. 368p. pap. 8.99 *(978-1-4424-1367-2(0))* 2011. 352p. 16.99 *(978-1-4424-2185-1(1))* Simon & Schuster Bks. For Young Readers. (Simon & Schuster Bks. For Young Readers).

—H. I. V. E. Higher Institute of Villainous Education. 2007. (H. I. V. E. Ser.: 1). (ENG., Illus.). 320p. (J). (gr. 3-7). 17.99 *(978-1-4169-3571-1(1),* Simon & Schuster Bks. For Young Readers) Simon & Schuster Bks. For Young Readers.

—The Higher Institute of Villainous Education. 2008. (H. I. V. E. Ser.: 1). (ENG.). 320p. (J). (gr. 3-7). pap. 8.99 *(978-1-4169-3572-8(X),* Simon & Schuster Bks. For Young Readers) Simon & Schuster Bks. For Young Readers.

—The Overlord Protocol. (H. I. V. E. Ser.: 2). (ENG.). 384p. (J). (gr. 3-7). 2009. pap. 7.99 *(978-1-4169-3574-2(6))* 2008. 18.99 *(978-1-4169-3573-5(8))* Simon & Schuster Bks. For Young Readers. (Simon & Schuster Bks. For Young Readers).

—Rogue. (H. I. V. E. Ser.: 5). (ENG.). (J). (gr. 3-7). 2012. 320p. pap. 8.99 *(978-1-4424-1369-6(7))* 2011. 304p. 16.99 *(978-1-4424-2187-5(8))* Simon & Schuster Bks. For Young Readers. (Simon & Schuster Bks. For Young Readers).

—Zero Hour. (H. I. V. E. Ser.: 6). (ENG.). 304p. (J). (gr. 3-7). 2013. pap. 7.99 *(978-1-4424-1373-3(5))* 2012. 18.99 *(978-1-4424-2188-2(6))* Simon & Schuster Bks. For Young Readers. (Simon & Schuster Bks. For Young Readers).

Yee, Lisa. Millicent Min, Girl Genius. 2004. 248p. (gr. 3-7). 17.00 *(978-0-7569-3919-9(4))* Perfection Learning Corp.

—Millicent Min, Girl Genius. 2004. (Millicent Min Trilogy Ser.: 1). (ENG.). 256p. (J). (gr. 4-7). reprint ed. pap. 6.99 *(978-0-439-42520-9(4),* Levine, Arthur A. Bks.) Scholastic, Inc.

GENOCIDE

see also Holocaust, Jewish (1939-1945)

Altman, Linda Jacobs. Genocide: The Systematic Killing of a People. rev. ed. 2008. (Issues in Focus Today Ser.). (Illus.). 128p. (J). (gr. k-6). lib. bdg. 33.27 *(978-0-7660-3358-0(9))* Enslow Pubs., Inc.

Bearing Witness: Genocide & Ethnic Cleansing in the Modern World. 2016. (Bearing Witness: Genocide & Ethnic Cleansing in the Modern World Ser.). 64p. (gr. 6-6). 241.15 *(978-1-4777-8551-5(5),* Rosen Young Adult) Rosen Publishing Group, Inc., The.

Berlatsky, Noah. Darfur. Greenhaven Press Staff, ed. 2015. (Genocide & Persecution Ser.). (ENG.). 240p. (gr. 10-12). lib. bdg. 42.00 *(978-0-7377-7231-9(X),* Greenhaven Pr., Inc.) Cengage Gale.

—Sri Lanka. Greenhaven Press Editors & Gale Editors, eds. 2014. (Genocide & Persecution Ser.). (ENG., Illus.). 240p. (gr. 10-12). lib. bdg. 42.00 *(978-0-7377-6900-5(9),* Greenhaven Pr., Inc.) Cengage Gale.

Friedman, Mark D. Genocide, 1 vol. 2012. (Hot Topics Ser.). (ENG.). 64p. (gr. 7-8). 34.65 *(978-1-4329-6034-6(2),* NA-h) Heinemann-Raintree.

Genocide & International Justice. 2009. (Global Issues Ser.). 400p. (C). (gr. 9-18). 45.00 *(978-0-8160-7310-8(4))* Facts On File, Inc.

Greenhaven Press Editors. Genocide. 2012. (Global Viewpoints Ser.). (ENG., Illus.). 224p. (gr. 10-12). lib. bdg. 40.45 *(978-0-7377-5652-4(7),* Greenhaven Pr., Inc.) Cengage Gale.

Greenhaven Press Editors & Haerens, Margaret. Genocide. 2012. (Global Viewpoints Ser.). (ENG., Illus.). 224p. (gr. 10-12). pap. 31.70 *(978-0-7377-5653-1(5),* Greenhaven Pr., Inc.) Cengage Gale.

Hay, Jeff. Tibet. Greenhaven Press Editors & Gale Editors, eds. 2014. (Genocide & Persecution Ser.). (ENG., Illus.). 240p. (gr. 10-12). lib. bdg. 42.00 *(978-0-7377-6901-2(7),* Greenhaven Pr., Inc.) Cengage Gale.

Levy, Janey. Genocide in Darfur. 2009. (Genocide in Modern Times Ser.). 64p. (gr. 6-6). 58.50 *(978-1-61512-673-6(2))* Rosen Publishing Group, Inc., The.

Lowery, Zoe & Levy, Janey. The Darfur Genocide. 2016. (Bearing Witness: Genocide & Ethnic Cleansing in the Modern World Ser.). 64p. (J). (gr. 6-6). 34.45 *(978-1-4994-6306-4(5))* Rosen Publishing Group, Inc., The.

Lowery, Zoe & Spalding, Frank. The Rwandan Genocide. 2016. (Bearing Witness: Genocide & Ethnic Cleansing in the Modern World Ser.). 64p. (J). (gr. 6-6). 34.45 *(978-1-4777-8570-6(1))* Rosen Publishing Group, Inc., The.

Nardo, Don. The Rwanda Genocide. 2011. (World History Ser.). 128p. (J). lib. bdg. 34.95 *(978-1-4205-0567-2(X),* Lucent Bks.) Cengage Gale.

Perl, Lila. Genocide: Standby or Intervene? 2010. (Controversy! 2 Ser.). 112p. (gr. 7-18). 37.07 *(978-0-7614-4900-3(0))* Marshall Cavendish Corp.

Spalding, Frank. Genocide in Rwanda. (Genocide in Modern Times Ser.). 64p. 2009. (gr. 6-6). 58.50 *(978-1-61512-674-3(0))* 2008. (Illus.). (YA). (gr. 9-12). lib. bdg. 31.95 *(978-1-4042-1823-9(8))* Rosen Publishing Group, Inc., The.

Springer, Jane. Genocide, 1 vol. 2007. (Groundwork Guides). (ENG., Illus.). 144p. (gr. 8). pap. 10.00 *(978-0-88899-682-4(9))* Groundwood Bks. CAN. Dist: Publishers Group West (PGW).

Torres, John Albert. The Guatemalan Genocide of the Maya People. 2017. (J). ***(978-1-5081-7736-4(8))*** Rosen Publishing Group, Inc., The.

Ward, Albert. Critical World Issues: Genocide, Vol. 16. 2016. (Critical World Issues Ser.: Vol. 16). (ENG., Illus.). 112p. (J). (gr. 7-12). 25.95 *(978-1-4222-3656-7(0))* Mason Crest.

Winckelmann, Thom. Genocide. 2008. (Man's Inhumanities Ser.). (YA). (gr. 7-12). 23.95 *(978-1-60217-975-2(1))* Erickson Pr.

Wolny, Philip. Holodomor: The Ukrainian Famine-Genocide. 2017. (J). ***(978-1-5081-7732-6(5),*** Rosen Young Adult) Rosen Publishing Group, Inc., The.

Woolf, Alex. Genocide. (Illus.). 64p. (YA). (gr. 5-18). lib. bdg. 29.95 *(978-1-931983-81-5(X))* Chrysalis Education.

GEODESY

see also Surveying

Graf, Mike & Snedden, Robert. Mapping Earth from Space, 1 vol. 2011. (Science Missions Ser.). (ENG.). 56p. (gr. 3-3). 34.65 *(978-1-4109-3994-4(4))*; pap. 9.95 *(978-1-4109-4001-8(2))* Heinemann-Raintree. (Raintree Freestyle Express).

GEOGRAPHICAL ATLASES

see Atlases

GEOGRAPHICAL DISTRIBUTION OF ANIMALS AND PLANTS

see Animal Distribution; Plant Distribution

GEOGRAPHICAL DISTRIBUTION OF HUMANS

see Ethnology; Human Geography

GEOGRAPHICAL NAMES

see Names, Geographical

GEOGRAPHY

Here are entered works on geography as a branch of learning. Works limited to descriptive information including those derived from travel narratives or intended to assist travelers are entered under the names of countries, cities, etc. with the subdivision Description and Travel or Guidebooks.

see also Atlases; Discoveries in Geography; Ethnology; Human Geography; Maps; Physical Geography; Surveying; Voyages and Travels

also subdivision Maps under names of countries, cities, etc.

ABDO Publishing Company. Explore the Countries: Set Of 16. 2013. (Explore the Countries Ser.: 16). (ENG.). 40p. (J). (gr. 2-5). lib. bdg. 478.88 *(978-1-61783-803-3(9),* Big Buddy Bks.) ABDO Publishing Co.

Abramovitz, Melissa. World's Smallest Country & Other Geography Records. 2013. (Wow! Ser.). (ENG.). 24p. (gr. k-1). 26.65 *(978-1-4765-0241-0(2),* Pebble Plus) Capstone Press of Coughlan Cos.

Adams, Simon, et al. Geography of the World. 2006. (ENG., Illus.). 304p. (J). (gr. 5-12). pap. 24.99 *(978-0-7566-1952-7(1),* DK Children) Dorling Kindersley Publishing, Inc.

Alexander, Heather. A Child's Introduction to the World: Geography, Cultures, & People - From the Grand Canyon to the Great Wall of China. Hamilton, Meredith, illus. 2010. (ENG.). 96p. (J). (gr. -1-17). 19.99 *(978-1-57912-832-6(7),* 81832, Black Dog & Leventhal Pubs. Inc.) Hachette Bks.

Arden, Carolyn. Mountains & Valleys. 2009. (Restless Earth Ser.). (Illus.). 112p. (YA). (gr. 5-9). 35.00 *(978-0-7910-9707-6(2))* Facts On File, Inc.

Arganello, Lisa. Henry the Navigator: Prince of Portuguese Exploration. 2006. (In the Footsteps of Explorers Ser.). (ENG., Illus.). 32p. (J). (gr. 4-7). pap. *(978-0-7787-2469-8(7))*; lib. bdg. *(978-0-7787-2433-9(6))* Crabtree Publishing Co.

Atlas del mundo para niveles Primarios. 2003. (MacMillan/McGraw-Hill. Estudios Sociales Ser.). (ENG & SPA.). (gr. k-3). *(978-0-02-149475-0(4))* Macmillan/McGraw-Hill Schl. Div.

Babcock, Denise L., et al, texts. Student Activity Book. 2008. (World of Communities - Student Activity Book Ser.). (ENG., Illus.). (J). (gr. 3-5). pap., stu. ed. 16.00 *(978-1-4103-0747-7(6),* Blackbirch Pr., Inc.) Cengage Gale.

Babcock, Denise L., et al. A World of Communities. 2008. (World of Communities - Student Edition Ser.). (ENG., Illus.). (J). (gr. 3-5). stu. ed. 35.35 *(978-1-4103-0745-3(X))*; pap., stu. ed. 22.50 *(978-1-4103-0746-0(8))* Cengage Gale. (Blackbirch Pr., Inc.).

Beck, Roger B. World History: Patterns of Interaction: Pupil's Edition. l.t. ed. 2005. (YA). (gr. 9-12). 86.64 *(978-0-618-18774-4(X),* 2-01396) Holt McDougal.

Benchmark Education Co., LLC. The Geography of Africa. 2014. (PRIME Ser.). (J). (gr. 6-8). pap. *(978-1-4509-9503-0(9))* Benchmark Education Co.

—The Geography of Asia & Australia. 2014. (PRIME Ser.). (J). (gr. 6-8). pap. *(978-1-4509-9504-7(7))* Benchmark Education Co.

—The Geography of Europe. 2014. (PRIME Ser.). (J). (gr. 6-8). pap. *(978-1-4509-9506-1(3))* Benchmark Education Co.

—The Geography of North & South America. 2014. (PRIME Ser.). (J). (gr. 6-8). pap. *(978-1-4509-9505-4(5))* Benchmark Education Co.

Benchmark Education Company, LLC Staff, compiled by. Engish Explorers Social Studies Levels 2, 3, 4 (CAN) 2006. spiral bd. 95.00 *(978-1-4108-6045-3(0))* Benchmark Education Co.

—Geography. 2006. (J). 91.00 *(978-1-4108-7045-2(6))* Benchmark Education Co.

—Geography: Theme Set. 2006. (J). 131.00 *(978-1-4108-7114-5(2))* Benchmark Education Co.

—Native Land & Geography. 2005. spiral bd. 225.00 *(978-1-4108-5811-5(1))* Benchmark Education Co.

—This State Is Mine & Geography. 2005. spiral bd. 110.00 *(978-1-4108-5818-4(9))* Benchmark Education Co.

—World Geography: Theme Set. 2006. (J). 135.00 *(978-1-4108-7141-1(X))* Benchmark Education Co.

Bennett, Doraine. Lower Coastal Plain. 2009. (J). 20.60 *(978-1-935077-49-7(X))*; pap. 10.60 *(978-1-935077-50-3(3))* State Standards Publishing, LLC.

Blain, Theresa A. Visualize World Geography in 7 Minutes a Day: Let Pictography Take You from Clueless to Knowing the World. Blain, Theresa A., illus. 2003. (Illus.). 302p. per. 19.95 *(978-0-9741401-0-0(4))* Tender Heart Pr.

Bluthenthal, Todd. Continents. 2017. (Where on Earth? Mapping Parts of the World Ser.). 24p. (gr. 1-2). pap. 48.90 ***(978-1-4824-6414-6(4))*** Stevens, Gareth Publishing LLLP.

Boddy, Alan, et al. Geography for the Australian Curriculum Year 7. 2013. (ENG.). pap. *(978-1-107-69012-7(9))* Cambridge Univ. Pr.

E
F
G

Boehm, Richard G., et al. Daily Geography: Grades K-2. 2003. (Harcourt Brace Social Studies). (gr. k-2). 33.90 (978-0-15-310426-8(0)) Harcourt Schl. Pubs.

—World Geography & Cultures. 2007. (Illus.). 853p. (J). 98.00 (978-0-07-874529-4(2), 9780078745294) Glencoe/McGraw-Hill.

Boone, Melvin, Jr. JD Mc Doil What's up with Oil. l.t. ed. 2003. (Illus.). 32p. (J). 19.95 (978-0-9741750-0-3(5)) Never Stop Reading Never Stop Learning.

Bowman, John S. Exploration in the World of the Ancients, Revised Edition. 2nd rev. ed. 2009. (Discovery & Exploration Ser.). (Illus.). 112p. (gr. 5-8). 35.00 (978-1-60413-191-8(8), Chelsea Hse.) Facts On File, Inc.

Boyle, Deborah A. Your Geography. Date not set. (Illus.). 48p. (J). Bk. A. pap. 129.15 (978-0-582-18799-3(0))Bk. B. pap. 129.15 (978-0-582-18800-6(8)) Addison-Wesley Longman, Ltd. GBR. Dist: Trans-Atlantic Pubns., Inc.

Brett, Anna. Maze Hop: Around the World. Woolley, Tom, illus. 2016. (ENG.). 64p. (J). (gr. 2). pap. 14.95 (978-1-78312-134-2(3)) Carlton Kids GBR. Dist: Sterling Publishing Co., Inc.

Burnett, Lindy, illus. I Live Here! 2010. (My World Ser.).Tr. of Yo Vivo Aqui! (ENG.). 24p. (J). (gr. -1-1). pap. 8.15 (978-1-61533-033-1(X)); lib. bdg. 22.60 (978-1-60754-950-5(6)) Windmill Bks.

Butler, David, et al. Geography for the Australian Curriculum Year 10. 2014. (ENG.). pap., stu. ed. (978-1-107-69696-9(8)) Cambridge Univ. Pr.

—Geography for the Australian Curriculum Year 9. 2013. (ENG.). pap. (978-1-107-64717-6(7)) Cambridge Univ. Pr.

—Geography for the Australian Curriculum Year 9 Bundle 1 Textbook & Interactive Textbook. 2014. (ENG.). pap. (978-1-107-66478-4(0)) Cambridge Univ. Pr.

Cane, Ella. Countries in My World, 1 vol. 2013. (My World Ser.). (ENG.). 24p. (gr. k-1). 21.99 (978-1-4765-3122-9(6)); pap. 6.95 (978-1-4765-3464-0(0)) Capstone Press of Coughlan Cos. (Pebble Bks.).

Carney, Elizabeth & National Geographic Kids Staff. Little Kids First Big Book of the World. 2015. (National Geographic Little Kids First Big Bks.). (ENG., Illus.). 128p. (J). (gr. -1-3). 14.99 (978-1-4263-2050-7(7), National Geographic Children's Bks.) National Geographic Society.

Chambers, Catherine. Stickmen's Guide to Cities in Layers. Dean, Venitia & De Quay, John Paul, illus. 2016. (Stickmen's Guides to This Incredible Earth Ser.). (ENG.). 32p. (J). (gr. 3-6). 26.65 (978-1-5124-0620-7(1)) Lerner Publishing Group.

Claybourne, A. Encyclopedia of Planet Earth. 2004. (Geography Ser.). (Illus.). 160p. (J). 19.95 (978-0-7945-0534-9(1)) EDC Publishing.

Cleveland, Will & Alvarez, Mark. Yo, Sacramento! (And All Those Other State Capitals You Don't Know) - Memorize Them All (Forever) in 20 Minutes-Without Trying! Nation, Tate, illus. 2011. (ENG.). 128p. (J). (gr. 3-7). pap. 7.95 (978-1-935212-38-6(9), Prospecta Pr.) Easton Studio Pr., LLC.

Clifford, Clive. Atlas of Oddities. Worrall, Tracy, illus. 2016. (ENG.). 96p. (J). (gr. 2). 16.95 (978-1-4549-2176-9(5)) Sterling Publishing Co., Inc.

Clinch, Mike, et al. Allwedd Daearyddiaeth: Cyfnod Allweddol 3. 2005. (WEL., Illus.). 176p. pap. (978-1-85644-677-8(8)) CAA.

Clissold, Caroline. Extreme Earth. 2007. (Trackers-Math Ser.). (gr. 2-5). pap. 5.00 (978-1-59055-912-3(6)) Pacific Learning, Inc.

Cole, Sonja. Booktalking Around the World: Great Global Reads for Ages 9-14. 2010. (ENG.). 178p. E-Book (978-1-59884-614-0(0), Libraries Unlimited) ABC-CLIO, LLC.

Coleman-Smith, Charlotte. Women in the Skies. 2017. (ENG.). 32p. (J). pap. 8.99 **(978-0-00-820879-0(4))** HarperCollins Pubs. Ltd. GBR. Dist: Independent Pubs. Group.

Collins. Collins Fascinating Facts - The World. rev. ed. 2016. (Collins Fascinating Facts Ser.). (ENG., Illus.). 72p. (J). (gr. 1-3). pap. 10.99 (978-0-00-816920-6(9)) HarperCollins Pubs. Ltd. GBR. Dist: Independent Pubs. Group.

Collins Maps Staff. Atlas for the Middle East. 2014. (Collins Primary Geography Ser.). (ENG.). 72p. (J). pap. 14.99 (978-0-00-756370-8(1)) HarperCollins Pubs. Ltd. GBR. Dist: Independent Pubs. Group.

Collins Publishers Staff. KS3 Geography. 2014. (ENG., Illus.). 144p. (YA). (gr. 6-9). pap. 12.95 (978-0-00-756286-2(1)) HarperCollins Pubs. Ltd. GBR. Dist: Independent Pubs. Group.

Collins Publishers Staff & Collins KS3 Staff. KS3 Geography. 2014. (ENG., Illus.). 216p. (YA). (gr. 6-9). pap. 16.95 (978-0-00-756287-9(X)) HarperCollins Pubs. Ltd. GBR. Dist: Independent Pubs. Group.

Continentes: Atlas de Geografia e Historia. (SPA.). (J). 25.00 (978-958-04-6482-2(0)) Norma S.A. COL. Dist: Distribuidora Norma, Inc.

Continents & Countries. 2008. (Question & Answers Ser.). 320p. (978-1-4075-2528-0(X)) Parragon, Inc.

Cooke, Rex, et al. Geography for the Australian Curriculum Year 8. 2014. (ENG.). pap. (978-1-107-66606-1(6)) Cambridge Univ. Pr.

Countries of the World: A Primary Source Journey: Set 3. (Illus.). (J). (gr. k-5). 119.70 (978-1-4042-2952-5(3)) Rosen Publishing Group, Inc., The.

Countries of the World: A Primary Source Journey: Set 4. (Illus.). (J). (gr. k-5). 119.70 (978-1-4042-2951-8(5)) Rosen Publishing Group, Inc., The.

Cowling, Dan. Color Yourself Smart: Geography. Franklin, Mark, illus. 2012. (Color Yourself Smart Ser.). (ENG.). 128p. 19.95 (978-1-60710-216-8(1), Thunder Bay Pr.) Readerlink Distribution Services, LLC.

Crespi, Jess. Exploring Jamaica with the Five Themes of Geography. 2005. (Library of the Western Hemisphere Ser.). (Illus.). 24p. (J). lib. bdg. 22.60 (978-1-4042-2674-6(5), PowerKids Pr.); (ENG., (gr. 3-8). pap. 8.25 (978-0-8239-4634-1(7)) Rosen Publishing Group, Inc., The.

Cunha, Stephen F. How to Ace the National Geographic Bee. 4th ed. 2012. (ENG., Illus.). 128p. (J). (gr. 4-7). pap., pupil's gde. ed. 9.95 (978-1-4263-0986-1(4)); lib. bdg., pupil's gde. ed. 18.90 (978-1-4263-0985-4(6)) National Geographic Society. (National Geographic Children's Bks.).

—National Geographic Bee. 3rd ed. 2008. (ENG., Illus.). 128p. (J). (gr. 4-7). per., pupil's gde. ed. 9.95 (978-1-4263-0198-8(7), National Geographic Children's Bks.) National Geographic Society.

—National Geographic Bee Official Study Guide. 2005. (National Geographic Ser.). (ENG., Illus.). 128p. (J). (gr. 4-7). 26.90 (978-0-7922-7997-6(2), National Geographic Children's Bks.) National Geographic Society.

Cunningham, Patricia. Making Places. 2005. (Four-Blocks Ser.). (J). per. 24.99 (978-1-59441-199-1(9), CD-104108) Four Blocks.

De Capua, Sarah. Massachusetts. 2003. (Rookie Read-about Science Ser.). (Illus.). 31p. (J). (gr. -1-3). 13.60 (978-0-7569-7153-3(5)) Perfection Learning Corp.

Dell, Pamela. Show Me the Continents: My First Picture Encyclopedia, 1 vol. 2013. (My First Picture Encyclopedias Ser.). (ENG.). 32p. (gr. 1-2). 27.32 (978-1-4765-0114-7(9)); pap. 8.10 (978-1-4765-3348-3(2)) Capstone Press of Coughlan Cos. (Aplus Bks.).

Doherty, Gillian. Encyclopedia of World Geography: With Complete World Atlas. 2004. (Geography Encyclopedias Ser.). (Illus.). 400p. (J). 39.99 (978-0-7945-0108-2(7), Usborne); lib. bdg. 47.99 (978-1-58086-390-2(6)) EDC Publishing.

—Encyclopedia of World Geography II (Reduced) 2010. (Geography Ser.). 400p. (J). pap. 19.99 (978-0-7945-2698-6(5), Usborne) EDC Publishing.

Dolphin, Colleen. Alcatraz to Zanzibar: Famous Places from A to Z, 1 vol. 2009. (Let's Learn A to Z Ser.). (ENG., Illus.). 32p. (J). (gr. -1-2). 27.07 (978-1-60453-492-4(3)) ABDO Publishing Co.

Donaldson, Madeline. Europe. 2005. (Pull Ahead Bks.). (Illus.). 32p. (gr. k-3). (J). lib. bdg. 22.60 (978-0-8225-4719-8(8)); (ENG., pap. 7.95 (978-0-8225-2493-9(7)) Lerner Publishing Group.

Dorion, Christiane. How the World Works: A Hands-On Guide to Our Amazing Planet. Young, Beverley, illus. 2010. (Explore the Earth Ser.). (ENG.). 18p. (J). (gr. 2-5). 18.99 (978-0-7636-4801-5(9), Templar) Candlewick Pr.

Dorling Kindersley Publishing Staff. DK Workbooks: Geography, Fifth Grade. 2016. (ENG., Illus.). 60p. (J). (gr. 4-7). pap. 6.99 (978-1-4654-4424-0(6), DK Children) Dorling Kindersley Publishing, Inc.

—DK Workbooks: Geography, First Grade: Geography, First Grade. 2015. (ENG.). 60p. (J). (gr. k-4). pap. 6.99 (978-1-4654-2847-9(X), DK Children) Dorling Kindersley Publishing, Inc.

—DK Workbooks: Geography, Fourth Grade. 2016. (ENG., Illus.). 60p. (J). (gr. 4-7). pap. 6.99 (978-1-4654-4423-3(8), DK Children) Dorling Kindersley Publishing, Inc.

—DK Workbooks: Geography, Kindergarten: Geography, Kindergarten. 2015. (ENG., Illus.). 60p. (J). (gr. -1-1). pap. 6.99 (978-1-4654-2850-9(X), DK Children) Dorling Kindersley Publishing, Inc.

—DK Workbooks: Geography, Pre-K: Geography, Pre-K. 2015. (ENG., Illus.). 60p. (J). (gr. -1-k). pap. 6.99 (978-1-4654-2851-6(8), DK Children) Dorling Kindersley Publishing, Inc.

—DK Workbooks: Geography, Second Grade: Geography, Second Grade. 2015. (ENG., Illus.). 60p. (J). (gr. 1-3). pap. 6.99 (978-1-4654-2848-6(8), DK Children) Dorling Kindersley Publishing, Inc.

—DK Workbooks: Geography, Sixth Grade. 2016. (ENG., Illus.). 60p. (J). (gr. 4-7). pap. 6.99 (978-1-4654-4425-7(4), DK Children) Dorling Kindersley Publishing, Inc.

—DK Workbooks: Geography, Third Grade: Geography, Third Grade. 2015. (ENG.). 60p. (J). (gr. 2-4). pap. 6.99 (978-1-4654-2849-3(6), DK Children) Dorling Kindersley Publishing, Inc.

—Geography: a Visual Encyclopedia: A Visual Encyclopedia. 2013. (Visual Encyclopedia Ser.). (ENG.). 304p. (J). (gr. 3-7). 29.99 (978-1-4654-1218-8(2), DK Children) Dorling Kindersley Publishing, Inc.

—Smithsonian Geography. 2013. (Visual Encyclopedia Ser.). (ENG.). 304p. (J). (gr. 3-7). pap. 19.99 (978-1-4654-0885-3(1), DK Children) Dorling Kindersley Publishing, Inc.

—Where on Earth? Atlas. 2017. (ENG., Illus.). 160p. (J). (gr. 3-7). 19.99 (978-1-4654-5864-3(6), DK Children) Dorling Kindersley Publishing, Inc.

Doucet, Bob, illus. Fact & Fable: State Stories, 6 vols., Set 2. Incl. Buster's Trip to Cape Cod: A Story about Massachusetts. Gaarder-Juntti, Oona. 25.65 (978-1-60453-921-9(6)); Frenchy's Float: A Story about Louisiana. Scheunemann, Pam. 25.65 (978-1-60453-922-6(4)); Great Lei Race: A Story about Hawaii. Salzmann, Mary Elizabeth. 25.65 (978-1-60453-923-3(2)); Leaping Lily: A Story about Georgia. Dolphin, Colleen. 25.65 (978-1-60453-924-0(0)); Monty's Ice Pick: A Story about Alaska. Hengel, Katherine. 25.65 (978-1-60453-925-7(9)); Rupert & the Liberty Bell: A Story about Pennsylvania. Hengel, Katherine. 25.65 (978-1-60453-926-4(7)); (J). (gr. -1-3). (Fact & Fable: State Stories Set 2 Ser.). (Illus.). 24p. 2010. 153.90 (978-1-60453-920-2(8)); 153.90 (978-1-61714-678-7(1)) ABDO Publishing Co. (Super SandCastle).

Doyle, James. Where on Earth? Geography Without the Boring Bits. 2017. (Buster Reference Ser.). (ENG., Illus.). 128p. (J). (gr. 3-7). pap. 8.99 **(978-1-78055-468-6(0))** O'Mara, Michael Bks., Ltd. GBR. Dist: Independent Pubs. Group.

Dusek, Jiri, et al. World Atlas. Hikadova, Katerina et al, illus. 2014. (ENG.). 42p. (J). (gr. 3-5). 16.95 (978-1-4549-1235-4(9)) Sterling Publishing Co., Inc.

Enciclopedia Mega - Benjamin. (SPA.). 159p. 12.95 (978-970-607-203-0(9), LA039) Larousse, Ediciones, S. A. de C. V. MEX. Dist: Continental Bk. Co., Inc.

Evan-Moor. Geography Centers, Grades 1-2. 2005. (Take It to Your Seat Ser.). (ENG., Illus.). 192p. (J). (gr. 1-2). pap. 21.99 (978-1-55799-995-5(3), EMC 3716) Evan-Moor Educational Pubs.

—Geography Centers, Grades 2-3. 2005. (Take It to Your Seat Ser.). (ENG.). 192p. (J). (gr. 2-3). pap. 21.99 (978-1-55799-996-2(1), EMC 3717) Evan-Moor Educational Pubs.

—Geography Centers, Grades 3-4. 2005. (Take It to Your Seat Ser.). (ENG.). 192p. (J). (gr. 3-4). pap. 21.99 (978-1-55799-997-9(X), EMC 3718) Evan-Moor Educational Pubs.

—Geography Centers, Grades 4-5. 2005. (Take It to Your Seat Ser.). (ENG., Illus.). 192p. (J). (gr. 4-5). pap. 21.99 (978-1-55799-998-6(8), EMC 3719) Evan-Moor Educational Pubs.

F, Professor Charles, ed. Geography of Extreme Environments Set, 3-Volumes. 2007. (Geography of Extreme Environments Ser.). (gr. 6-12). 90.00 (978-0-7910-9459-4(6), Chelsea Hse.) Facts On File, Inc.

Feldman, Jean R. & Karapetkova, Holly. Continents Together (Tune, He's Got the Whole World in His Hands) Lap Book. 2010. (ENG., Illus.). 12p. (gr. -1-k). 9.95 (978-1-61590-194-4(9)) Rourke Educational Media.

Fisher, Douglas & McGraw-Hill Book Company Staff. Glencoe World Geography, Active Reading Note-Taking Guide. 8th ed. 2004. (Glencoe World Geography Ser.). (ENG., Illus.). 406p. (gr. 9-12). stu. ed., per., wbk. ed. 12.80 (978-0-07-867989-6(3), 0078679893) McGraw-Hill Higher Education.

Galè. Junior Worldmark Encyclopedia of the Nations, 10 vols. 6th ed. 2012. (Junior Worldmark Encyclopedia of the Nations Ser.). (ENG., Illus.). 3200p. lib. bdg. 819.00 (978-1-4144-6313-1(8), UXL) Cengage Gale.

Gallagher, Aileen. Prince Henry the Navigator: Pioneer of Modern Exploration. rev. ed. (Library of Explorers & Explorationtm Ser.). (Illus.). 112p. (YA). (gr. 5-8). lib. bdg. 31.95 (978-1-4042-0636-6(1), Rosen Reference) Rosen Publishing Group, Inc., The.

Ganeri, Anita. Country Guides, with Benjamin Blog & His Inquisitive Dog, 1 vol. Isik, Semur, illus. 2014. (Country Guides, with Benjamin Blog & His Inquisitive Dog Ser.). (ENG.). 32p. (gr. 1-3). 239.92 (978-1-4109-6669-8(0), Read Me!) Heinemann-Raintree.

Gardner, David, et al. Geography, 11-14. 2005. (Geography 11-14 Ser.). (Illus.). 260p. (J). pap. 257.50 incl. cd-rom (978-0-7487-9055-5(1)) Nelson Thornes Ltd. GBR. Dist: Trans-Atlantic Pubns., Inc.

Garton, Keith & Cutler, Nelida Gonzalez, eds. Time for Kids World Atlas. 2007. (Illus.). 176p. (J). reprint ed. pap. 11.00 (978-1-4223-6807-7(6)) DIANE Publishing Co.

Die Geographie. (Duden-Schuelerduden Ser.). (GER., Illus.). 468p. (YA). (978-3-411-04223-4(0)) Bibliographisches Institut & F. A. Brockhaus AG DEU. Dist: International Bk. Import Service, Inc.

Geography, Set. 2004. (Illus.). (gr. 9-12). pap. 23.95 (978-0-86717-682-7(2), ES3015, Lifepac) Alpha Omega Pubns., Inc.

Geography Wise, 4 vols., Set. Incl. Coasts. Green, Jen. lib. bdg. 26.50 (978-1-4488-3279-8(9)); Deserts. Gray, Leon. lib. bdg. 26.50 (978-1-4488-3280-4(2)); Mountains. Green, Jen. lib. bdg. 26.50 (978-1-4488-3281-1(0)); Rivers. Gray, Leon. lib. bdg. 26.50 (978-1-4488-3282-8(9)); (YA). (gr. 2-5). (Geography Wise Ser.). (Illus.). 32p. 2011. Set lib. bdg. 101.00 (978-1-4488-3305-4(1), PowerKids Pr.) Rosen Publishing Group, Inc., The.

Gildea, Ray Y. Letters Home: Children Learn Geography Through Communication with Parents Traveling/Working Abroad. 2005. (J). per. (978-0-9721032-4-4(4)) Parlance Publishing.

Glencoe McGraw-Hill Staff. World Geography & Cultures, Interactive Tutor Self-Assessment. 2007. (Glencoe World Geography Ser.). (ENG.). (gr. 9-12). cd-rom 107.12 (978-0-07-878573-3(1), 0078785731) McGraw-Hill Higher Education.

—World Geography & Cultures, Standardized Test Practice Workbook. 2007. (Glencoe World Geography Ser.). (ENG.). (gr. 9-12). pap. 9.00 (978-0-07-878564-1(2), 0078785642) McGraw-Hill Higher Education.

Glencoe McGraw-Hill Staff & McGraw-Hill Education Editors. Exploring Our World, Student Edition. 3rd ed. 2008. (WORLD & ITS PEOPLE EASTERN Ser.). (ENG.). 960p. (gr. 6-8). 106.04 (978-0-07-880310-9(1), 0078803101) McGraw-Hill Education.

Golden, Nancy. Exploring the United States with the Five Themes of Geography. 2009. (Library of the Western Hemisphere Ser.). 24p. (gr. 4-4). 42.50 (978-1-60853-932-1(6), PowerKids Pr.) Rosen Publishing Group, Inc., The.

Graham, Leland & McCoy, Isabelle. World Geography, Grades 4-6: Where in the World Are You? 2004. (Skills for Success Ser.). (ENG., Illus.). 128p. (gr. 4-6). per. 16.99 (978-0-88724-255-7(3), CD-4347) Carson-Dellosa Publishing, LLC.

Green, Jen. Slide & Discover: World Atlas. 2013. (Slide & Discover Ser.). (ENG., Illus.). 24p. (J). (gr. 2). 19.95 (978-1-60710-584-8(5), Silver Dolphin Bks.) Readerlink Distribution Services, LLC.

Griffiths, Rachel. What's the Address? 2004. (ENG., Illus.). 16p. (J). (gr. 1-1). pap. 10.92 (978-0-7652-5163-3(9), Celebration Pr.) Pearson Schl.

Group/McGraw-Hill, Wright. Canada Coast to Coast, 6 vols. (Book2WebTM Ser.). (gr. 4-8). 36.50 (978-0-322-04444-9(8)) Wright Group/McGraw-Hill.

Gutman, Dan. My Weird School Fast Facts: Geography. Paillot, Jim, illus. 2016. (My Weird School Fast Facts Ser.). 176p. (J). (gr. 1-5). pap. 5.99 (978-0-06-230620-3(0)) HarperCollins Pubs.

Hamilton, Robert. Encyclopedia of Amazing Places: Discover Famous Wonders of the World. 2012. (Illus.). 224p. (J). (978-1-4351-4347-0(7)) Barnes & Noble, Inc.

Harcourt School Publishers Staff. My World, Unit 6. 3rd ed. 2003. (Harcourt Brace Social Studies). pap. 76.00 (978-0-15-341063-5(9)) Harcourt Schl. Pubs.

Hart, Greg & Arundale, Jackie. Investigating Geography. 2003. (Illus.). 132p. pap. 33.50 (978-0-340-84634-6(8)); pap. 33.50 (978-0-340-84633-9(X)) Hodder Education Group GBR. (Hodder Education). Dist: Trans-Atlantic Pubns., Inc.

Hawes, Alison. Landscape Detective: Tracking Changes in Your Surroundings. 2010. (Crabtree Connections Ser.). (ENG.). 24p. (J). (gr. 3-6). (978-0-7787-9948-1(4)); pap. (978-0-7787-9970-2(0)) Crabtree Publishing Co.

Heinrichs, Ann. Continents. 2009. (21st Century Skills Library: Real World Math Ser.). (ENG.). 32p. (gr. 4-8). lib. bdg. 28.50 (978-1-60279-490-0(1), 200313) Cherry Lake Publishing.

Helgren, David M. World Geography Today: Online Edition. 3rd ed. 2003. 79.06 (978-0-03-072539-5(9)) Holt McDougal.

Hirsch, E. D., Jr., ed. Early Explorers & Settlers. 2003. tchr. ed. 9.95 (978-0-7690-5041-6(7)); stu. ed. 49.95 (978-0-7690-2946-7(9)) Pearson Learning.

—Geography of the Americas. 2003. stu. ed. 49.95 (978-0-7690-2959-7(0)) Pearson Learning.

—Geography of the United States, Level 5. tchr. ed. 9.95 (978-0-7690-5084-3(0)); stu. ed. 49.95 (978-0-7690-2849-1(7)) Pearson Learning.

History & Geography. 2004. (Switched on Schoolhouse Ser.). (YA). (gr. 7). cd-rom 69.95 (978-0-7403-0587-0(5));Set. (Illus.). (gr. 5). tchr. ed., stu. ed. 47.95 (978-1-58095-651-2(3), HIS05015, Lifepac) Alpha Omega Pubns., Inc.

History & Geography: Government & Economics. 2004. (Illus.). (gr. 12). tchr. ed., stu. ed. 47.95 (978-1-58095-672-7(6), HIS1215, Lifepac) Alpha Omega Pubns., Inc.

History & Geography: U. S. History, 12 vols., Set. 2004. (Illus.). (gr. 11-12). tchr. ed., stu. ed. 47.95 (978-1-58095-669-7(6), HIS1115, Lifepac) Alpha Omega Pubns., Inc.

Hogan & Wiggers. Ultimate Geography & Timeline. 2004. pap. 34.95 (978-0-9663722-0-5(4)) Coffee Hse. Ink.

Holiday, Jane. Exploring Argentina with the Five Themes of Geography. 2005. (Library of the Western Hemisphere Ser.). (Illus.). 24p. (J). (gr. -1-3). lib. bdg. 22.60 (978-1-4042-2678-4(8), PowerKids Pr.); (ENG., (gr. 3-8). pap. 8.25 (978-0-8239-4638-9(X)) Rosen Publishing Group, Inc., The.

—Exploring Brazil with the Five Themes of Geography. 2005. (Library of the Western Hemisphere Ser.). (Illus.). 24p. (J). 22.60 (978-1-4042-2679-1(6), PowerKids Pr.); (ENG., (gr. 3-8). pap. 8.25 (978-0-8239-4639-6(8)) Rosen Publishing Group, Inc., The.

Holt, Rinehart and Winston Staff. World Geography Today: Guided Reading Strategies. 5th ed. 2005. (World Geography Today Ser.). (ENG.). 104p. (gr. 9-12). pap. 4.90 (978-0-03-038874-3(0)) Houghton Mifflin Harcourt Publishing Co.

Hurst, Catherine. New Key Geography Interactions Teacher's Handbook. 2014. (ENG.). 136p. pap. 83.00 (978-1-4085-1788-8(4)) Oxford Univ. Pr., Inc.

James, Trisha. I Know Places Around Town. 2017. (What I Know Ser.). 24p. (gr. k-k). pap. 8.15 **(978-1-4824-6305-7(9))** Stevens, Gareth Publishing LLLP.

Jarrell, Jane & Saathoff, Deborah. Address: Planet Earth. 2004. 48p. pap., act. bk. ed. 6.99 (978-0-8054-0824-9(X)) B&H Publishing Group.

Jenkins, Noel, et al. This Is Geography Elearning Activities. unabr. ed. (Illus.). 2007. (J). cd-rom (978-0-340-90749-8(5)) 2006. cd-rom (978-0-340-90748-1(7)) 2006. cd-rom (978-0-340-90747-4(9)) Hodder & Stoughton.

Jenkins, Steve. Hottest, Coldest, Highest, Deepest. 2004. (ENG., Illus.). 32p. (J). (gr. -1-3). pap. 7.99 (978-0-618-49488-0(X)) Houghton Mifflin Harcourt Publishing Co.

Jennings, Ken. Maps & Geography. Lowery, Mike, illus. 2014. (Ken Jennings' Junior Genius Guides). (ENG.). 160p. (J). (gr. 3-5). pap. 7.99 (978-1-4424-7328-7(2), Little Simon) Little Simon.

Jones, David & Kimpton, Laurence. Quick Revision KS3 Geography. 2007. pap. 9.95 (978-0-340-94310-6(6), Hodder Education) Hodder Education Group GBR. Dist: Trans-Atlantic Pubns., Inc.

Juarez, Christine. Countries. 2013. (Countries Ser.). (ENG.). 24p. (gr. k-1). lib. bdg. 159.90 (978-1-4765-3693-4(7), Pebble Plus) Capstone Press of Coughlan Cos.

Kalman, Bobbie. The ABCs of Continents. 2009. (ENG., Illus.). 32p. (J). (gr. 2-4). lib. bdg. (978-0-7787-3414-7(5)) Crabtree Publishing Co.

—¿Dónde Estoy? 2010. (SPA & ENG.). 16p. (J). pap. (978-0-7787-8588-0(2)); lib. bdg. (978-0-7787-8562-0(9)) Crabtree Publishing Co.

—Explore Earth's Seven Continents. 2010. (Explore the Continents Ser.). (ENG., Illus.). 32p. (J). (gr. 1-5). pap. (978-0-7787-3092-7(1)) Crabtree Publishing Co.

—I Can Write a Book about Countries. 2012. (ENG.). 32p. (J). (978-0-7787-7988-9(2)); pap. (978-0-7787-7997-1(1)) Crabtree Publishing Co.

—I Can Write a Book about Landforms. 2012. (ENG.). 32p. (J). (978-0-7787-7992-6(0)); pap. (978-0-7787-8001-4(5)) Crabtree Publishing Co.

—Rapping about Directions on Earth. 2012. (ENG.). 24p. (J). (978-0-7787-2796-5(3)); pap. (978-0-7787-2803-0(X)) Crabtree Publishing Co.

—Where Am I? 2010. (My World Ser.). (ENG., Illus.). 16p. (J). (gr. k-2). (978-0-7787-9437-0(7)); pap. (978-0-7787-9481-3(4)) Crabtree Publishing Co.

Kaplan, Leslie C. Land & Resources in Ancient Egypt. 2004. (Primary Sources of Ancient Civilizations Ser.). (Illus.). 24p. (J). lib. bdg. 22.60 (978-0-8239-6781-0(6), PowerKids Pr.) Rosen Publishing Group, Inc., The.

—Land & Resources of Ancient Egypt. 2004. (Primary Sources of Ancient Civilizations Ser.). (ENG., Illus.). 24p. (gr. 4-8). pap. 8.25 (978-0-8239-8931-7(3), PowerKids Pr.) Rosen Publishing Group, Inc., The.

Kids, National Geographic. How to Ace the National Geographic Bee. 2017. (ENG.). 176p. (J). (gr. 3-7). pap. 13.99 **(978-1-4263-3080-3(4)**, National Geographic Children's Bks.) National Geographic Society.

Kitchen, Rebecca, et al. Geographical Enquiry, Bk. 1. 2015. (ENG., Illus.). 128p. (J). (gr. 2). pap., stu. ed. 26.95 (978-0-00-741103-0(0)) HarperCollins Pubs. Ltd. GBR. Dist: Independent Pubs. Group.

Kummer, Patricia K. Asia. 2014. (J). (978-0-7614-8090-7(0)) Marshall Cavendish Corp.

Lasseter, Rollin, ed. History: All Ye Lands. (Illus.). 360p. (J). (gr. 6). 55.00 (978-0-89870-944-5(X)) Ignatius Pr.

Lerner Publishing Group Staff. Continents: Classroom Set. 2005. (Pull Ahead Bks.). (Illus.). (J). (gr. 1-3). 40.95 (978-0-8225-2410-6(4)) Lerner Publishing Group.

LernerClassroom Editors. First Step Nonfiction-Geography Teaching Guide. 2009. pap. 7.95 (978-0-8225-5454-7(2)) Lerner Publishing Group.

Lewis, Siân. Dilyn Declan. 2005. (WEL.). 24p. pap. (978-1-901862-58-4(5)) FBA Pubns.

El Libro de los Acertijos Geograficos. (Coleccion Acertijos). (SPA.). (YA). (gr. 5-8). pap. (978-950-724-973-0(7), LMA6983) Lumen ARG. Dist: Lectorum Pubns., Inc.

Lindsey, Cameron. The 10 Most Dangerous Geographic Locations. 2008. 14.99 *(978-1-55448-539-0(8))* Scholastic Library Publishing.
little bee books, little bee. Listopia: Planet Earth. 2016. (ENG., Illus.). 208p. (J). (gr. 2-4). pap. 9.99 *(978-1-4998-0279-5(X))* Little Bee Books Inc.
Lonely Planet Publications Staff. You Rule! Create Your Own Country, 1 vol. 2015. (Lonely Planet Kids Ser.). (ENG., Illus.). 96p. (J). 14.99 *(978-1-74360-784-8(9),* 4988) Lonely Planet Pubns.
Lubawy, Susan. World View: A Global Study of Geography, History & Culture, Bk. 1. (J). stu. ed. 8.95 *(978-0-916591-30-4(1))* Linmore Publishing, Inc.
Macdonald, Margaret. Where Am I? 2014. (Little Books of Answers: Level a Ser.). (Illus.). 16p. (gr. k-2). pap. 7.95 *(978-1-927136-05-8(9))* Three Crows Media NZL. Dist: RiverStream Publishing.
Maile, Ruby. Why Do You Live Here? 2014. (Little Books of Answers: Level C Ser.). (Illus.). 16p. (gr. k-2). pap. 7.95 *(978-1-927136-25-6(3))* Three Crows Media NZL. Dist: RiverStream Publishing.
Mara, Wil. The Seven Continents. 2005. (Rookie Read-About Geography Ser.). (ENG., Illus.). 32p. (J). (gr. 1-2). pap. 5.95 *(978-0-516-22534-0(0),* Children's Pr.) Scholastic Library Publishing.
Marsh, Carole. Jography. 2004. (New York Experience! Ser.). 32p. (J). (gr. 3-8). pap. 7.95 *(978-0-635-00162-7(4))* Gallopade International.
Matthews, Colin. I Know People Around Town. 2017. (What I Know Ser.). 24p. (J). (gr. k-k). pap. 8.15 ***(978-1-4824-6301-9(6))***; pap. 48.90 ***(978-1-4824-6302-6(4))*** Stevens, Gareth Publishing LLLP.
McGraw-Hill Education. World Geography & Cultures, Spanish Reading Essentials & Note-Taking Guide. 2007. (Glencoe World Geography Ser.). (ENG & SPA.). (gr. 9-12). pap. 11.68 *(978-0-07-878391-3(7),* 0078783917) McGraw-Hill Higher Education.
McGraw-Hill Education Staff. Glencoe World Geography. 8th ed. 2004. (Glencoe World Geography Ser.). (ENG., Illus.). 291p. (gr. 9-12). stu. ed., per., wbk. ed. 12.80 *(978-0-07-865326-1(6),* 0078653266) McGraw-Hill Higher Education.
—World Geography: Spanish Reading Essentials. 8th ed. 2004. (Glencoe World Geography Ser.). (SPA.). (gr. 9-12). pap., stu. ed., wbk. ed. 18.72 *(978-0-07-865328-5(2),* 0078653282) McGraw-Hill Higher Education.
McGraw-Hill Staff. World Geography & Cultures, StudentWorks Plus. 2007. (Glencoe World Geography Ser.). (ENG.). (gr. 9-12). cd-rom 168.08 *(978-0-07-878394-4(1),* 0078783941) McGraw-Hill Higher Education.
McGraw-Hill Staff, creator. The World & Its People: Standardized Test Skills Practice. 2004. (GEOGRAPHY: WORLD & ITS PEOPLE Ser.). (ENG., Illus.). 59p. (gr. 6-9). pap., stu. ed., wbk. ed. 7.20 *(978-0-07-865523-4(4),* 0078655234) McGraw-Hill Education.
Miles Kelly Staff. Geography. 2003. (Info Bank Ser.). (Illus.). 96p. (J). 7.95 *(978-1-84236-055-2(8))* Miles Kelly Publishing, Ltd. GBR. Dist: Independent Pubs. Group.
—Geography Age 10-11: Flip Quiz. 2003. (Flip Quiz Ser.). (Illus.). 38p. (J). spiral bd. 5.95 *(978-1-84236-102-3(3))* Miles Kelly Publishing, Ltd. GBR. Dist: Independent Pubs. Group.
—Geography Age 11-12: Flip Quiz. 2003. (Flip Quiz Ser.). (Illus.). 38p. (J). spiral bd. 5.95 *(978-1-84236-103-0(1))* Miles Kelly Publishing, Ltd. GBR. Dist: Independent Pubs. Group.
—Geography Age 7-9: Flip Quiz. 2003. (Flip Quiz Ser.). (Illus.). 38p. (J). spiral bd. 5.95 *(978-1-84236-100-9(7))* Miles Kelly Publishing, Ltd. GBR. Dist: Independent Pubs. Group.
—Geography Age 9-10: Flip Quiz. 2003. (Flip Quiz Ser.). (Illus.). 38p. (J). spiral bd. 5.95 *(978-1-84236-101-6(5))* Miles Kelly Publishing, Ltd. GBR. Dist: Independent Pubs. Group.
Morter, Peter. Atlas Visual de los Descubrimientos. (SPA., Illus.). 412p. (YA). (gr. 5-8). *(978-84-216-1814-1(8),* BU4892) Bruño, Editorial ESP. Dist: Lectorum Pubns., Inc.
National Geographic Kids Staff. National Geographic Kids Ultimate Globetrotting World Atlas. 2014. (ENG., Illus.). 256p. (J). (gr. 4-7). pap. 13.99 *(978-1-4263-1488-9(4),* National Geographic Children's Bks.) National Geographic Society.
Nations of the World Series, 4 vols., Set. 2003. pap. 137.12 *(978-0-7398-7002-0(5))* Steck-Vaughn.
Nelson, Robin. Where Is My Continent? 2005. (First Step Nonfiction Ser.). (Illus.). 24p. (J). (gr. k-2). lib. bdg. 17.27 *(978-0-8225-0193-0(7))* Lerner Publishing Group.
Nelson, Robin & National Geographic Learning Staff. Where Is My State? 2012. (ENG.). 24p. (C). (gr. k-2). pap. 10.95 *(978-0-8225-1980-5(1))* National Geographic School Publishing, Inc.
Osbourne, David. The World of Waters or A Peaceful Progress O'er the Unpathed Sea. 2004. reprint ed. pap. 1.99 *(978-1-4192-8870-8(9))* Kessinger Publishing, LLC.
Our World. Date not set. (Questions & Answers Ser.). 176p. (J). 7.98 *(978-0-7525-9624-2(1))* Parragon, Inc.
Our World - A Look at Kenya. 2003. (Our World Ser.). (ENG.). 24p. (gr. k-1). lib. bdg. 42.64 *(978-1-4296-5680-1(8),* Pebble Bks.) Capstone Press of Coughlan Cos.
Our World Set. (gr. k-2). 346.95 *(978-0-7368-9396-1(2))* Red Brick Learning.
Owaki, Takashi. Dreams Around the World. 2012. (ENG., Illus.). 32p. 16.95 *(978-1-935548-11-9(5))* One Peace Bks., Inc.
Peacock, L. A. The Truth (and Myths) about Creepy Places. Wigsby, Nick, illus. 2015. 96p. (J). *(978-0-545-83026-3(5))* Scholastic, Inc.
Penn, Briony. The Kids Book of Canadian Geography. Penn, Briony, illus. 2008. (Kids Book Of Ser.). (ENG., Illus.). 56p. (J). (gr. 3-7). 19.95 *(978-1-55074-890-1(4))* Kids Can Pr., Ltd. CAN. Dist: Hachette Bk. Group.
Penton Overseas, Inc. Staff. States & Capitals. (Social Studies Ser.). (J). incl. audio. incl. audio NewSound, LLC.
—States & Capitals. 2006. (ENG., Illus.). (J). pap. 7.95 *(978-1-59125-164-4(8))* Penton Overseas, Inc.
Pettit, Loree & Mullins, Dari. Galloping the Globe: The Geography Unit Study for Young Learners: Kindergarten Through 4th Grade. 2007. (Illus.). 236p. per. 24.95 *(978-1-931397-38-4(4))* Geography Matters, Inc.
Probst, Jeff. Amazing Places: Weird Trivia & Unbelievable Facts to Test Your Knowledge about the Most Extreme Places on Earth! 2015. (Challenge Yourself Ser.: 2). (ENG., Illus.). 176p. (J). (gr. 3-7). 8.99 *(978-0-14-751376-2(6),* Puffin Books) Penguin Young Readers Group.
Proujan, Carl & National Geographic Learning Staff. South America - Geography & Environments. 2007. (Reading Expeditions Ser.). (ENG., Illus.). 64p. (J). pap. 25.95 *(978-0-7922-4382-3(X))* CENGAGE Learning.
Randall, Marisa. The Geographic Features of New York City. 2011. (My Community Ser.). 12p. (gr. 2-2). pap. 6.95 *(978-1-4488-5733-3(3))* Rosen Publishing Group, Inc., The.
Rassi, Lee. Capital Heroes. 2008. (Illus.). 56p. pap. 23.99 *(978-1-4343-8208-5(7))* AuthorHouse.
Rayner, David, et al. Geographical Enquiry, Bk. 2. 2015. (ENG., Illus.). 128p. (YA). (gr. 7). pap., stu. ed. 26.95 *(978-0-00-741116-0(2))* HarperCollins Pubs. Ltd. GBR. Dist: Independent Pubs. Group.
Readman, Jo & Roberts, Ley Honor. The World Came to My Place Today. 2003. (ENG., Illus.). 32p. 19.99 *(978-1-903919-01-9(0),* Eden Project Children's) Random House Children's Books GBR. Dist: Trafalgar Square Publishing.
Rice, Dona Herweck. Places Around the World, 1 vol. 2nd rev. ed. 2014. (TIME for KIDS(r) Nonfiction Readers Ser.). (ENG., Illus.). 20p. (J). (gr. 1-1). pap. 19.96 *(978-1-4807-1033-7(4))* Shell Educational Publishing.
Robins, Maureen Picard. What Are the Us Regions? 2012. (ENG., Illus.). 24p. (J). (gr. k-2). pap. 8.95 *(978-1-61810-278-2(8))* Rourke Educational Media.
Rockett, Paul. Mapping Australia & Oceania, & Antarctica. 2016. (Illus.). 32p. (J). *(978-0-7787-2614-2(2))* Crabtree Publishing Co.
Rockwood, Leigh. Ancient Egyptian Geography. 2013. (Spotlight on Ancient Civilizations: Egypt Ser.). (ENG., Illus.). 24p. (J). (gr. 3-4). pap. 10.00 *(978-1-4777-0867-5(7),* PowerKids Pr.) Rosen Publishing Group, Inc., The.
—V Ancient Egyptian Geography. 2013. (Spotlight on Ancient Civilizations: Egypt Ser.). (ENG.). 24p. (J). (gr. 3-4). 23.60 *(978-1-4777-0767-8(0),* PowerKids Pr.) Rosen Publishing Group, Inc., The.
Rookie Read-About Geography: States, 10 bks., Set. Incl. Hawaii. Taylor-Butler, Christine. 32p. 20.50 *(978-0-531-12571-7(8))*; Indiana. Hyde, Judith Jensen. 31p. 20.50 *(978-0-516-21846-5(8))*; Louisiana. Hyde, Judith Jensen. 32p. 20.50 *(978-0-516-21848-9(4))*; Mississippi. Trueit, Trudi Strain. 31p. 20.50 *(978-0-531-12572-4(6))*; Nebraska. Zollman, Pam. 31p. 20.50 *(978-0-516-25466-1(9))*; Nevada. Labella, Susan. 31p. 20.50 *(978-0-516-25467-8(7))*; Ohio. Taylor-Butler, Christine. 31p. 20.50 *(978-0-531-12573-1(4))*; Oklahoma. Labella, Susan. 31p. 20.50 *(978-0-516-25468-5(5))*; Utah. Trueit, Trudi Strain. 31p. 20.50 *(978-0-531-12574-8(2))*; Vermont. Taylor-Butler, Christine. 31p. 20.50 *(978-0-531-12593-9(9))*; (Illus.). (J). (gr. 1-2). 2007. 205.00 o.p. *(978-0-531-17737-2(8))*; 97.50 o.p. *(978-0-516-25415-9(4))* Scholastic Library Publishing. (Children's Pr.).
Rosa-Mendoza, Gladys. I Live Here!/Yo Vivo Aqui! Gonzalez, Margarita E. & Weber, Amy, eds. Burnett, Lindy, illus. 2007. (# 1 Bilingual Board Book Ser.). (ENG & SPA.). 20p. (J). (gr. -1-k). bds. 6.95 *(978-1-931398-19-0(4))* Me+Mi Publishing.
Rosen, Michael J. Urban Exploration. 2015. (ENG., Illus.). 72p. (J). (gr. 8-12). lib. bdg. 33.32 *(978-1-4677-2515-6(3),* Twenty-First Century Bks.) Lerner Publishing Group.
Rosenberg, Matthew T. The Handy Geography Answer Book. (Illus.). 462p. (YA). pap. *(978-1-57859-105-3(8))* Visible Ink Pr.
Ross, Simon. Exploring Geography in a Changing World. 2010. (Illus.). 144p. pap. 42.50 *(978-0-340-94606-0(7))* Hodder Education Group GBR. Dist: Trans-Atlantic Pubns., Inc.
Salzmann, Mary Elizabeth. Arctic Ocean to Zimbabwe: Geography from A to Z, 1 vol. 2008. (Let's Look A to Z Ser.). (ENG., Illus.). 32p. (gr. k-4). 27.07 *(978-1-60453-013-1(8),* Super SandCastle) ABDO Publishing Co.
Sapp, Eric. World Geography Student Activity Book. 2003. (Illus.). stu. ed., per., wbk. ed. *(978-1-931680-38-7(8),* Expert Systems for Teachers) Teaching Point, Inc.
Sasek, Miroslav. This Is New York, 16 vols. 2011. (Illus.). 287.20 *(978-0-7893-2415-3(6))* Universe Publishing.
Saunders-Smith, Gail. Countries. 2013. (Countries Ser.). (ENG.). 24p. (gr. k-1). pap. 35.70 *(978-1-4765-3691-0(0),* Pebble Bks.) Capstone Press of Coughlan Cos.
Scholastic Library Publishing. Rookie Read: About Geography—Continents. 2012. (J). 161.00 *(978-0-531-25499-8(2),* Children's Pr.) Scholastic Library Publishing.
—Rookie Read: About Geography—Map Skills. 2012. (J). 92.00 *(978-0-531-28525-1(1),* Children's Pr.) Scholastic Library Publishing.
Schwartz, Jaime. See the U. S. A. 2007. (Nonfiction Reading & Writing Workshops Ser.). (ENG., Illus.). 16p. (J). pap. 11.95 *(978-0-7922-8496-3(8))* CENGAGE Learning.
Scillian, Devin. P Is for Passport: A World Alphabet. Rose, Melanie, illus. 2003. (Discover the World Ser.). (ENG.). 48p. (J). (gr. 1-3). 19.95 *(978-1-58536-157-1(7),* 202017) Sleeping Bear Pr.
Scoffham, Stephen & Bridge, Colin. Change. 2014. (Collins Primary Geography Ser.). (ENG., Illus.). 64p. (J). (gr. 4). pap. 14.99 *(978-0-00-756361-6(2))* HarperCollins Pubs. Ltd. GBR. Dist: Independent Pubs. Group.
—Investigation, Bk. 3. 2014. (Collins Primary Geography Ser.). (ENG., Illus.). 64p. (J). (gr. 2). pap. 14.99 *(978-0-00-756359-3(0))* HarperCollins Pubs. Ltd. GBR. Dist: Independent Pubs. Group.
—Movement, Bk. 4. 2014. (Collins Primary Geography Ser.). (ENG., Illus.). 64p. (J). (gr. 3). pap. 14.99 *(978-0-00-756360-9(4))* HarperCollins Pubs. Ltd. GBR. Dist: Independent Pubs. Group.
—Primary Geography. 2014. (Collins Primary Geography Ser.). (ENG., Illus.). 64p. (J). (gr. 5). pap. 14.99 *(978-0-00-756362-3(0))* HarperCollins Pubs. Ltd. GBR. Dist: Independent Pubs. Group.
—World Around Us, Bk. 2 & 3. 2014. (Collins Primary Geography Ser.). (ENG., Illus.). 64p. (J). (gr. 1). pap. 14.99 *(978-0-00-756358-6(2))* HarperCollins Pubs. Ltd. GBR. Dist: Independent Pubs. Group.
Senker, Cath. Tropical Climates. 2017. (Focus on Climate Zones Ser.). (ENG., Illus.). 48p. (gr. 4-6). pap. 4.95 *(978-1-4846-3787-6(9))*; lib. bdg. 33.32 *(978-1-4846-3783-8(6))* Heinemann-Raintree. (Heinemann InfoSearch).
Sepehri, Sandy. Continents. 2007. (ENG., Illus.). 32p. (gr. 2-5). pap. 9.95 *(978-1-60694-910-8(1))* Rourke Educational Media.
Sepheri, Sandy. Continents. 2007. (Landforms Ser.). (Illus.). 32p. (J). (gr. 4-7). lib. bdg. 28.50 *(978-1-60044-548-4(9))* Rourke Educational Media.
Shariati, Karen Allison. Meet Arzeen, Citizen of the World. Kim, Jay Jiyeon, illus. 2006. 45p. (J). *(978-0-9770475-0-5(4))* Arzana, Inc.
Shattuck, Jason. Geography. 2016. (Study of Science Ser.). 00104p. (YA). (gr. 8-8). 36.25 *(978-1-5081-0428-5(X))* Rosen Publishing Group, Inc., The.
Sheehan, Nicholas, et al. Geographical Enquiry, Bk. 3. 2015. (ENG., Illus.). 112p. (YA). (gr. 7). pap., stu. ed. 26.95 *(978-0-00-741118-4(9))* HarperCollins Pubs. Ltd. GBR. Dist: Independent Pubs. Group.
Siegfried Holtz, Eric & Barenblat, Rachel. Texas. 2003. (World Almanac Biblioteca de los Estados). (SPA., Illus.). 48p. (gr. 4-9). pap. 14.05 *(978-0-8368-5554-8(X),* Gareth Stevens Learning Library) Stevens, Gareth Publishing LLLP.
Silver, Donald & Wynne, Patricia J. Geographic Terms: 15 Engaging Mini-Books That Students Read-And-Interact With-To Really Learn about Key Landforms. 2009. (ENG.). 72p. pap. 13.99 *(978-0-439-35527-8(3),* Teaching Resources) Scholastic, Inc.
Somervill, Barbara A. Australia. 2003. (Geography of the World Ser.). (ENG., Illus.). 32p. (J). (gr. 3-6). 28.50 *(978-1-59296-063-7(4),* 200257) Child's World, Inc., The.
Sullivan, Erin Ash. Math Around the Globe & Matemáticas alrededor del Mundo: 6 English, 6 Spanish Adaptations. 2011. (ENG & SPA.). (J). 97.00 net. *(978-1-4108-5689-0(5))* Benchmark Education Co.
Sumner, Ray, ed. World Geography, 8 vols., Vol. 8. Incl. World Geography, Volume 1 Vol. 1: The World. lib. bdg. 62.00 *(978-0-89356-276-2(9))*; World Geography, Volume 2 Vol. 2: North America & the Caribbean. lib. bdg. 62.00 *(978-0-89356-277-9(7))*; World Geography, Volume 3 Vol. 3: South & Central America. lib. bdg. 62.00 *(978-0-89356-335-6(8))*; World Geography, Volume 4 Vol. 4: Africa. lib. bdg. 62.00 *(978-0-89356-336-3(6))*; World Geography, Volume 5 Vol. 5: Europe. lib. bdg. 62.00 *(978-0-89356-399-8(4))*; World Geography, Volume 6 Vol. 6: Asia. lib. bdg. 62.00 *(978-0-89356-650-0(0))*; World Geography, Volume 7 Vol. 7: Antarctica, Australia, & the Pacific. lib. bdg. 62.00 *(978-0-89356-699-9(3))*; World Geography, Volume 8 Vol. 8: Glossary, Bibliography, Appendices. lib. bdg. 62.00 *(978-0-89356-723-1(X))*; (YA). 2001. (Illus.). 2048p. 2005. Set lib. bdg. 499.00 *(978-0-89356-024-9(3),* 608) Salem Pr., Inc.
Toth, J. A. Those Fabulous 50 States (Esos 50 Estados Fabulosos) (ENG & SPA.). (YA). (gr. 4-18). pap. 14.95 *(978-1-883986-04-9(4),* SPC6044) Imprints.
A True Book - Geography: Countries, 5 vols., Set. Incl. Brazil. Walters, Tara. 31.00 *(978-0-531-16851-6(4))*; China. Friedman, Mel. 31.00 *(978-0-531-16852-3(2))*; North Korea. Walters, Tara. 29.00 *(978-0-531-16854-7(9))*; South Korea. Walters, Tara. 31.00 *(978-0-531-16855-4(7))*; (Illus.). 48p. (J). (gr. 3-7). (True Bks.). 2008. Set lib. bdg. 319.00 *(978-0-531-20546-4(0),* Children's Pr.) Scholastic Library Publishing.
A True Book: Geography: Countries, 6 vols., Set. Incl. Egypt. Gutner, Howard. 31.00 *(978-0-531-16889-9(1))*; India. Apte, Sunita. 31.00 *(978-0-531-16890-5(5))*; Iraq. Friedman, Mel. 31.00 *(978-0-531-16891-2(3))*; Ireland. Koponen, Libby. 31.00 *(978-0-531-16892-9(1))*; Puerto Rico. Gutner, Howard. 31.00 *(978-0-531-16893-6(X))*; United Arab Emirates. Bryan, Antonia D. 31.00 *(978-0-531-16888-2(3))*; (Illus.). 48p. (J). (gr. 2-5). 2009. 2009. Set lib. bdg. 156.00 *(978-0-531-26134-7(4),* Children's Pr.) Scholastic Library Publishing.
U. S. National Geographic Society Staff. You Are the World! 3rd rev. ed. 2014. (ENG.). 144p. (J). (gr. 7-12). 17.20 *(978-1-63245-311-2(8))* Lectorum Pubns., Inc.
Unglick, Richard. Journey Around the World. 2016. (Playmobil Ser.). (ENG., Illus.). 64p. (J). (gr. 1-7). 19.95 *(978-1-63322-079-9(6),* Walter Foster Jr) Quarto Publishing Group USA.
Unidad 2 Superlibro: Geografía: Superlibros. 2003. (MacMillan/McGraw-Hill. Estudios Sociales Ser.). (ENG & SPA.). (gr. 1-18). *(978-0-02-149435-4(5))* Macmillan/McGraw-Hill Schl. Div.
Unidad 2 Superlibro: Geografía: Vivimos Juntos: Superlibros (Big Books) 2003. (MacMillan/McGraw-Hill. Estudios Sociales Ser.). (ENG & SPA.). (gr. 2-18). *(978-0-02-149442-2(8))* Macmillan/McGraw-Hill Schl. Div.
USA - UDSSR: Die Geographischen Aspekte der USA und der Ehemaligen zweiten Weltmacht UDSSR. (Duden Abiturhilfen Ser.). (GER.). 96p. (YA). (gr. 12-13). *(978-3-411-02626-5(X))* Bibliographisches Institut & F. A. Brockhaus AG DEU. Dist: International Bk. Import Service, Inc.
Volpe, Theresa. All about Continents. 2006. (Early Explorers Ser.). (J). pap. *(978-1-4108-6128-3(7))* Benchmark Education Co.
Waugh, David. The New Wider World. 2nd rev. ed. 2005. (ENG., Illus.). 328p. pap. 47.50 *(978-0-7487-7376-3(2))* Nelson Thornes Ltd. GBR. Dist: Trans-Atlantic Pubns., Inc.
The Western Hemisphere Through the Five Themes of Geography. 2006. (Western Hemisphere Through the Five Themes of Geography Ser.). 24p. 43.95 *(978-1-4042-6098-6(6),* Rosen Classroom) Rosen Publishing Group, Inc., The.
The Western Hemisphere Through the Five Themes of Geography Map Activities Book plus 5 Transparencies. 2005. (Western Hemisphere Through the Five Themes of Geography Ser.). 16p. 55.95 *(978-1-4042-5159-5(6),* Rosen Classroom) Rosen Publishing Group, Inc., The.
Widdowson, John. Geography for Common Entrance. 2003. (Illus.). 160p. pap. 36.50 *(978-0-7195-7572-3(9),* Hodder Education) Hodder Education Group GBR. Dist: Trans-Atlantic Pubns., Inc.
—This Is Geography, Bk. 1. 2006. (Illus.). 144p. (J). pap., pupil's gde. ed. *(978-0-340-91219-5(7))* Hodder & Stoughton.
—This is Geography, Vol. 2. 2006. (Illus.). 144p. (J). pap., pupil's gde. ed. *(978-0-340-90742-9(8))* Hodder & Stoughton.
—This Is Geography, Vol. 3. 2007. (Illus.). 144p. (J). pap., pupil's gde. ed. 39.50 *(978-0-340-90743-6(6))* Hodder Education Group GBR. Dist: Trans-Atlantic Pubns., Inc.
Williams, Brian. People & Places. 2010. (What About... Ser.). (Illus.). 40p. (J). (gr. 6-8). lib. bdg. 19.95 *(978-1-4222-1563-0(6))* Mason Crest.
Williams, Rachel. Atlas of Adventures: A Collection of Natural Wonders, Exciting Experiences & Fun Festivities from the Four Corners of the Globe. Letherland, Lucy, illus. 2015. (Atlas Of Ser.). (ENG.). 96p. (J). (gr. 2-5). 30.00 *(978-1-84780-695-6(3),* Wide Eyed Editions) Quarto Publishing Group UK GBR. Dist: Hachette Bk. Group.
Woodworth, Viki. World of Mazes. 2007. (Dover Children's Activity Bks.). (ENG., Illus.). 48p. (J). (gr. 3-5). per. 4.99 *(978-0-486-45640-9(4))* Dover Pubns., Inc.
World Book, Inc Staff, contrib. by. Explore & Learn — Atlas of the World. 2008. (J). *(978-0-7166-3022-7(2))* World Bk., Inc.
World Geography: EEdition Plus Online with purchase of print Pupil's Edition-1 Year. 2005. (gr. 6-12). *(978-0-618-25856-7(6),* 2-00435) Holt McDougal.
World View: A Global Study of Geography, History & Culture, Bk. 2. stu. ed. 21.95 *(978-0-916591-45-8(X))* Linmore Publishing, Inc.
Zárate, Antonio, et al. Atlas Geografico (Geographical Atlas) (SPA., Illus.). 160p. (J). (gr. 5-7). *(978-84-348-4114-7(2),* SM6162) SM Ediciones ESP. Dist: i. b. d., Ltd.
Zeman, Anne & Kelly, Kate. Everything You Need to Know about Geography Homework. 2011. (Illus.). vii, 138p. (J). *(978-0-545-37472-9(3))* Scholastic, Inc.
Zumbusch, Amelie von. Ancient Roman Geography. 2013. (Spotlight on Ancient Civilizations: Rome Ser.). (ENG., Illus.). 24p. (J). (gr. 3-4). pap. 10.00 *(978-1-4777-0891-0(X),* PowerKids Pr.) Rosen Publishing Group, Inc., The.
Zumbusch, Amelie Von & Von Zumbusch, Amelie. Ancient Roman Geography. 2013. (Spotlight on Ancient Civilizations: Rome Ser.). (ENG., Illus.). 24p. (J). (gr. 3-4). 23.60 *(978-1-4777-0779-1(4),* PowerKids Pr.) Rosen Publishing Group, Inc., The.

GEOGRAPHY, BIBICAL

see Bible—Geography

GEOGRAPHY—DICTIONARIES

Doherty, Gillian & Claybourne, Anna. Encyclopedia of World Geography Internet Linked. 2004. 400p. (J). pap. 19.95 *(978-0-7945-0805-0(7),* Usborne) EDC Publishing.
Ganeri, Anita. Esos Destructores Terremotos. (Coleccion Esa Horrible Geografia). (SPA.). 128p. (YA). (gr. 5-8). 9.95 *(978-84-272-2156-7(8),* ML31293) Molino, Editorial ESP. Dist: Lectorum Pubns., Inc.
Knowlton, Jack. Geography from A to Z: A Picture Glossary. 2004. (Illus.). (J). (gr. k-3). spiral bd. *(978-0-616-03042-4(8))* Canadian National Institute for the Blind/Institut National Canadien pour les Aveugles.
Wojtanik, Andrew. Afghanistan to Zimbabwe: Country Facts That Helped Me Win the National Geographic Bee. 2005. (ENG., Illus.). 384p. (J). (gr. 4-7). pap. 12.95 *(978-0-7922-7981-5(6),* National Geographic Children's Bks.) National Geographic Society.

GEOGRAPHY, ECONOMIC

see Economic Geography

GEOGRAPHY, HISTORICAL

see Historical Geography

GEOGRAPHY, PHYSICAL

see Physical Geography

GEOGRAPHY—PICTORIAL WORKS

see Views

GEOGRAPHY, SOCIAL

see Human Geography

GEOLOGICAL PHYSICS

see Geophysics

GEOLOGISTS

Gullo, Arthur. Volcanoes. 2015. (J). lib. bdg. *(978-1-62713-513-9(8))* Cavendish Square Publishing.
Letts, Amelia. A Day at Work with a Geologist, 01 vols., 1. 2016. (Super STEM Careers Ser.). (ENG., Illus.). 24p. (J). pap. 8.25 *(978-1-5081-4406-9(0),* PowerKids Pr.) Rosen Publishing Group, Inc., The.
Manatt, Kathleen. Volcanologist. 2007. (21st Century Skills Library: Cool Science Careers Ser.). (ENG.). 32p. (gr. 4-8). pap. 14.21 *(978-1-60279-085-8(X),* 200646) Cherry Lake Publishing.
Maynard, Charles W. John Wesley Powell: Soldier, Scientist, & Explorer. 2009. (Famous Explorers of the American West Ser.). 24p. (gr. 3-4). 42.50 *(978-1-61512-505-0(1),* PowerKids Pr.) Rosen Publishing Group, Inc., The.
Mullins, Matt. Geoscientist. 2013. (21st Century Skills Library: Cool STEM Careers Ser.). (ENG.). 32p. (J). (gr. 4-8). 28.50 *(978-1-62431-004-1(4),* 202467); pap. 14.21 *(978-1-62431-028-7(1),* 202469) Cherry Lake Publishing.
Nagelhout, Ryan. Be a Geologist. 2014. (Be a Scientist! Ser.). 32p. (J). (gr. 3-6). pap. 63.00 *(978-1-4824-1196-6(2))*; pap. 10.50 *(978-1-4824-1213-0(6))* Stevens, Gareth Publishing LLLP.
Owen, Ruth. Volcanologists & Seismologists. 2013. (Out of the Lab: Extreme Jobs in Science Ser.). 32p. (J). (gr. 3-6). 25.25 *(978-1-4777-1292-4(5))*; pap. 10.00 *(978-1-4777-1382-2(4))* Rosen Publishing Group, Inc., The. (PowerKids Pr.).
Person, Stephen. Devastated by a Volcano! 2010. (Disaster Survivors Ser.). (Illus.). 32p. (YA). (gr. 4-7). lib. bdg. 25.27 *(978-1-936087-50-1(2))* Bearport Publishing Co., Inc.
Peterson, Judy Monroe. Braving Volcanoes: Volcanologists. 2009. (Extreme Scientists Ser.). 24p. (gr. 2-3). 42.50 *(978-1-61512-449-7(7),* PowerKids Pr.) Rosen Publishing Group, Inc., The.
Ross, Michael Elsohn. Exploring the Earth with John Wesley Powell. Smith, Wendy, illus. 2005. (Naturalist's Apprentice Biographies Ser.). 48p. (gr. 3-6). lib. bdg. 19.93 *(978-1-57505-254-0(7))* Lerner Publishing Group.
Solway, Andrew. The Scientists Behind Earth's Processes, 1 vol. 2011. (Sci-Hi: Scientists Ser.). (ENG.). 48p. (gr. 4-4). pap. 9.95 *(978-1-4109-4051-3(9),* Sci-Hi) Heinemann-Raintree.
Souza, Dorothy M. John Wesley Powell. 2004. (Watts Library). (ENG., Illus.). 64p. (J). (gr. 5-7). pap. 8.95

E F G

(978-0-531-16653-6(8), Watts, Franklin) Scholastic Library Publishing.

Van Gorp, Lynn. Pioneers of Earth Science, 1 vol. 2007. (Science Readers Ser.). (ENG., Illus.). 32p. (J). (gr. 3-3). pap. 8.99 *(978-0-7439-0558-9(X))* Shell Educational Publishing.

Volcanologists & Seismologists. 2013. (Out of the Lab: Extreme Jobs in Science Ser.). 32p. (J). (gr. 3-6). pap. 60.00 *(978-1-4777-1383-9(2)*, PowerKids Pr.) Rosen Publishing Group, Inc., The.

GEOLOGY

see also Coral Reefs and Islands; Creation; Earth (Planet); Earthquakes; Glaciers; Mineralogy; Mountains; Oceanography; Physical Geography; Rocks; Submarine Geology; Volcanoes

Anderson, Michael. Investigating the History of Earth. 2011. (J). lib. bdg. 31.70 *(978-1-61530-498-1(3))* Rosen Publishing Group, Inc., The.

Anderson, Rane. Travel Adventures: The Grand Canyon: Data (Grade 3) 2017. (Mathematics Readers Ser.). (Illus.). 32p. (gr. 3-3). 8.99 ***(978-1-4807-5808-7(6))*** Teacher Created Materials, Inc.

Ball, Jacqueline A. & Ball, Jacqueline A. Earth's History. 2004. (Discovery Channel School Science Ser.). (Illus.). 32p. (gr. 4-8). lib. bdg. 26.00 *(978-0-8368-3379-9(1)*, Gareth Stevens Learning Library) Stevens, Gareth Publishing LLLP.

Behrens, Janice. Totally Cool Caves & Hot Volcanoes: + 10 More Epic Landforms! 2017. (Rookie Amazing America(tm) Ser.). (ENG., Illus.). 32p. (J). pap. 5.95 *(978-0-531-22589-9(5)*, Children's Pr.) Scholastic Library Publishing.

Benchmark Education Company, LLC Staff, compiled by. Our Environment: Theme Set. 2006. (J). 178.00 *(978-1-4108-7088-9(X))*; 121.00 *(978-1-4108-7102-2(9))* Benchmark Education Co.

Berger, Melvin & Berger, Gilda. Are Mountains Getting Taller? Questions & Answers about the Changing Earth. Carter, Robin, illus. 2003. (Question & Answer Ser.). (ENG.). 48p. (J). pap. 5.95 *(978-0-439-26673-4(4)*, Scholastic Reference) Scholastic, Inc.

Bethune, Helen. Why Do Glaciers Move? Level 6 Factbook. 2010. (Cambridge Young Readers Ser.). (ENG., Illus.). 24p. pap. 7.16 *(978-0-521-13743-0(8))* Cambridge Univ. Pr.

Blay, Chuck & Siemers, Robert. Kauai's Geologic History: A Simplified Guide. 2003. (Illus.). 15.00 *(978-0-9744723-0-0(1))* Siemers, Robert.

Brannon, Cecelia H. A Look at Sand, Silt, & Mud. 2016. (Rock Cycle Ser.). (ENG.). 32p. (J). (gr. 3-4). pap. 10.52 *(978-0-7660-7332-6(7))*; (Illus.). 25.27 *(978-0-7660-7334-0(3))* Enslow Pubs., Inc.

Brasch, Nicolas. Why Do Volcanoes Erupt? 2010. (Solving Science Mysteries Ser.). (Illus.). 24p. (J). pap. 8.25 *(978-1-4488-0401-6(9)*, PowerKids Pr.); (YA). (gr. 3-6). lib. bdg. 22.60 *(978-1-4488-0400-9(0))* Rosen Publishing Group, Inc., The.

—Why Do Volcanoes Erupt? All about Earth Science. 2010. (Illus.). 24p. (J). 49.50 *(978-1-4488-0402-3(7)*, 1307173, PowerKids Pr.) Rosen Publishing Group, Inc., The.

Brown, Cynthia Light & Brown, Nick. Explore Rocks & Minerals! 20 Great Projects, Activities, Experiments. Stone, Bryan, illus. 2010. (Explore Your World Ser.). (ENG.). 96p. (J). (gr. k-4). pap. 12.95 *(978-1-934670-61-3(8))* Octavio Publishing.

Brown, Don & Perfit, Michael R. Older Than Dirt. 2017. (ENG., Illus.). 112p. (J). (gr. 5-7). 18.99 *(978-0-544-80503-3(8)*, HMH Books For Young Readers) Houghton Mifflin Harcourt Publishing Co.

Bullard, Lisa. This Is My Continent. Becker, Paula, illus. 2016. (Cloverleaf Books (tm) — Where I Live Ser.). (ENG.). 24p. (J). (gr. k-2). 25.32 *(978-1-4677-9525-8(9)*, Millbrook Pr.) Lerner Publishing Group.

Bureau Of Land Management, et al. Junior Explorer Geology & Fossils Activity Book. 2012. 26p. pap. *(978-1-78266-060-6(7))* Military Studies Pr.

Charles Kingsley Staff. Madam How & Lady Why. 2005. pap. *(978-1-4065-0016-5(X))* Dodo Pr.

Ciocchi, Catherine. This Land Is Your Land, 1 vol. Morrison, Cathy, illus. 2015. (ENG.). 32p. (J). (gr. 1-4). 17.95 *(978-1-62855-557-8(2))* Arbordale Publishing.

Ciocchi, Catherine & Morrison, Cathy. Esta Tierra, Es Tu País. Morrison, Cathy, illus. 2015. (ENG & SPA., Illus.). 32p. (J). (gr. 1-4). pap. 9.95 *(978-1-62855-575-2(0))* Arbordale Publishing.

Cole, Joanna & Jackson, Tom. Planet Earth. Degen, Bruce & Bracken, Carolyn, illus. 2014. (Magic School Bus Presents Ser.). (ENG.). 32p. (J). (gr. 1-3). pap. 6.99 *(978-0-545-68012-7(3))* Scholastic, Inc.

Cook, Mauliola. Discover Hawaii's Volcanoes: Birth by Fire. Orr, Katherine, illus. rev. ed. 2010. (ENG.). 44p. pap. *(978-1-59700-849-5(4))* Island Heritage Publishing.

Cook, Mauliola & Orr, Katherine. Discover His Birth by Fire Volcanoes. 2010. 44p. 9.95 *(978-1-59700-830-3(3))* Island Heritage Publishing.

Culp, Jennifer. What Are Sedimentary Rocks?, 01 vols., 1. 2016. (Junior Geologist Ser.). (ENG., Illus.). 32p. (J). pap. 12.90 *(978-1-5081-0046-1(2)*, Britannica Educational Publishing) Rosen Publishing Group, Inc., The.

Dale, Jay. The Big Mud Puddle, 1 vol. Gulliver, Amanda, illus. 2012. (Engage Literacy Yellow Ser.). (ENG.). 32p. (gr. k-2). pap. 5.99 *(978-1-4296-8956-4(0)*, Engage Literacy) Capstone Press of Coughlan Cos.

Dayton, Connor. Rock Formations. (Rocks & Minerals Ser.). 24p. (gr. 2-3). 2009. 42.50 *(978-1-60852-502-7(3)*, PowerKids Pr.) 2007. (Illus.). (YA). lib. bdg. 22.60 *(978-1-4042-3690-5(2))* Rosen Publishing Group, Inc., The.

Denecke, Edward J., Jr. & Long, Lynette. Painless Earth Science. 2011. (Painless Ser.). (ENG., Illus.). 320p. pap. 11.99 *(978-0-7641-4601-5(7))* Barron's Educational Series, Inc.

Desonie, Dana. Geosphere: The Land & Its Uses. 2007. (Our Fragile Planet Ser.). (Illus.). 200p. (YA). (gr. 7-12). lib. bdg. 35.00 *(978-0-8160-6217-1(X))* Facts On File, Inc.

Dorion, Christiane. How the World Works: A Hands-On Guide to Our Amazing Planet. Young, Beverley, illus. 2010. (Explore the Earth Ser.). (ENG.). 18p. (J). (gr. 2-5). 18.99 *(978-0-7636-4801-5(9)*, Templar) Candlewick Pr.

Dorling Kindersley Publishing Staff. My Tourist Guide to the Centre of the Earth. 2013. (ENG., Illus.). 64p. (J). *(978-1-4093-2443-0(5))* Dorling Kindersley Publishing, Inc.

Earth. 2014. (Four Elements Ser.). 32p. (J). (gr. k-3). pap. 10.00 *(978-1-4777-9273-5(2))* Windmill Bks.

Elda, Doug & Elda, Dorry. Lyrical Earth Science: Geology. Raskauskas, Sally, illus. 2003. 116p. (YA). (gr. 5-10). pap. 25.50 incl. audio *(978-0-9741635-2-9(X))* Lyrical Learning.

Elda, Doug & Elda, Dory. Lyrical Earth Science: Geology. Raskauskas, Sally, illus. 2003. 116p. (YA). (gr. 5-10). pap. 19.95 incl. audio *(978-0-9741635-7-4(0))* Lyrical Learning.

Eldon, Doug & Eldon, Dorry. Lyrical Earth Science: Geology. Raskavskas, Sally, illus. 2003. 116p. (YA). (gr. 5-10). pap. 23.95 incl. audio compact disk *(978-0-9741635-8-1(9))* Lyrical Learning.

Encyclopaedia Britannica, Inc. Staff. Britannica Illustrated Science Library Series (18 Title Series), 18 vols. 2010. 599.00 *(978-1-61535-423-8(9))* Encyclopaedia Britannica, Inc.

Enz, Tammy. Dynamic Planet: Exploring Changes on Earth with Science Projects. 2015. (Discover Earth Science Ser.). (ENG., Illus.). 32p. (gr. 3-4). lib. bdg. 27.32 *(978-1-4914-4815-1(6))* Capstone Press of Coughlan Cos.

Estigarribia, Diana. Learning about Rocks, Weathering, & Erosion with Graphic Organizers. 2009. (Graphic Organizers in Science Ser.). 24p. (gr. 3-4). 42.50 *(978-1-61513-044-3(6)*, PowerKids Pr.) Rosen Publishing Group, Inc., The.

Famighetti, Robert, et al. How Do Islands Form? 2009. (Science in the Real World Ser.). (Illus.). 32p. (gr. 4-6). 28.00 *(978-1-60413-474-2(7)*, Chelsea Clubhouse) Facts On File, Inc.

Ferguson. Careers in Focus: Geology. 2nd rev. ed. 2011. (Careers in Focus Ser.). (Illus.). 201p. (gr. 6-12). 32.95 *(978-0-8160-8042-7(9)*, Ferguson Publishing Co.) Facts On File, Inc.

Forces of Nature. 2009. (Illus.). 47p. (J). *(978-0-7166-9822-7(6))* World Bk., Inc.

Ganeri, Anita. Shaky Ground. 2004. (Turbulent Planet Ser.). (Illus.). 48p. (J). 28.56 *(978-1-4109-0589-5(6))* Heinemann-Raintree.

Gerwitz, Felice & Whitlock, Jill. Creation Geology: A Study Guide to Fossils, Formations & the Flood. 2004. 206p. (YA). per. 18.95 *(978-1-931941-09-9(2))* Media Angels, Inc.

Gill, Maria. Under Your Feet. 2009. (ENG., Illus.). 24p. pap. 4.99 *(978-1-59198-709-3(1))* Creative Teaching Pr., Inc.

Gray, Susan H. Geology: The Study of Rocks. 2012. (True Book Ser.). (ENG., Illus.). 48p. (J). lib. bdg. 29.00 *(978-0-531-24676-4(0)*, Children's Pr.) Scholastic Library Publishing.

Gray, Susan Heinrichs. Geology: The Study of Rocks. 2012. (True Book Ser.). (ENG., Illus.). 48p. (J). (gr. 3-5). pap. 6.95 *(978-0-531-28270-0(8)*, Children's Pr.) Scholastic Library Publishing.

Green, Jen. Big Fantastic Earth. 2016. (Illus.). 96p. (J). *(978-1-5182-1730-2(3))* Dorling Kindersley Publishing, Inc.

—Geology: Investigating the Science of the Earth. 2012. (Scientific Pathways Ser.). (ENG., Illus.). 48p. (J). (gr. 5-8). lib. bdg. 27.95 *(978-1-4488-7200-8(6)*, Rosen Reference) Rosen Publishing Group, Inc., The.

Hicks, Terry Allan. How Do Mountains Form? 2009. (Tell Me Why, Tell Me How Ser.). 32p. (gr. 3-5). 29.93 *(978-0-7614-3992-9(7))* Marshall Cavendish Corp.

Higgins, Nadia. Sinkholes. 2015. (ENG.). 48p. (gr. 3-6). 35.64 *(978-1-63430-422-1(5))* Rourke Educational Media.

Hocker, Katherine M. Frozen in Motion: Alaska's Glaciers. Brubaker, Jill, ed. Lepley, Kathy, illus. 2006. 54p. (J). spiral bd. 8.95 *(978-0-930931-76-6(9))* Alaska Geographic Assn.

Hoffman, Steven M. Rocks & Soil. 2011. (Rock It! Ser.). (Illus.). 24p. (J). pap. 8.25 *(978-1-4488-2706-0(X))*; lib. bdg. 22.60 *(978-1-4488-2560-8(1))* Rosen Publishing Group, Inc., The. (PowerKids Pr.).

Holmes & Thom. Early Life: The Cambrian Period. 2008. (Prehistoric Earth Ser.). (Illus.). 224p. (YA). (gr. 9-12). 35.00 *(978-0-8160-5957-7(8))* Facts On File, Inc.

—Time of the Giants. 2008. (Prehistoric Earth Ser.). (Illus.). 155p. (YA). (gr. 9-12). 35.00 *(978-0-8160-5961-4(6))* Facts On File, Inc.

Holmes, Thom. Early Humans: The Pleistocene & Holocene Epochs. 2008. (Prehistoric Earth Ser.). (Illus.). 152p. (YA). (gr. 9-12). 35.00 *(978-0-8160-5966-9(7))* Facts On File, Inc.

Holt, Rinehart and Winston Staff. Holt Science & Technology Chapter 3: Earth Science: Minerals & Earth's Crust. 5th ed. 2004. (Illus.). pap. 12.86 *(978-0-03-030276-3(5))* Holt McDougal.

—Holt Science & Technology Chapter 4: Earth Science: Rocks - Mineral Mixtures. 5th ed. 2004. (Illus.). pap. 12.86 *(978-0-03-030281-7(1))* Holt McDougal.

—Holt Science & Technology Chapter 6: Earth Science: Rocks & Fossils. 5th ed. 2004. (Illus.). pap. 12.86 *(978-0-03-030291-6(9))* Holt McDougal.

—Holt Science & Technology Chapter 7: Earth Science: Plate Tectonics. 5th ed. 2004. (Illus.). pap. 12.86 *(978-0-03-030296-1(X))* Holt McDougal.

Hooper, Meredith. Pebble in My Pocket: A History of Our Earth. Coady, Chris, illus. rev. ed. 2015. (ENG.). 40p. (J). (gr. 2-5). pap. 9.99 *(978-1-84780-768-7(2)*, Frances Lincoln Children's Bks.) Quarto Publishing Group UK GBR. Dist: Hachette Bk. Group.

Hopping, Lorraine Jean. Space Rocks: The Story of Planetary Geologist Adriana Ocampo. 2006. (ENG., Illus.). 128p. (gr. 7-9). per. 19.95 *(978-0-309-09555-6(7)*, Joseph Henry Pr.) National Academies Pr.

Hunter, Rebecca. The Earth. 2010. (CC: 21st Century Science Ser.). 112p. (gr. 6-12). 42.80 *(978-1-933834-75-7(7))* Brown Bear Bks.

Interior Dept. (U.S.) & Land Management Bureau (U.S.), eds. Junior Explorer Geology & Fossils Activity Book. 2012. (ENG., Illus.). 25p. 7.00 *(978-0-16-091363-1(2)*, Interior Dept.) United States Government Printing Office.

James, Emily. The Simple Science of Rocks. 2017. (Simply Science Ser.). (ENG.). 32p. (gr. 1-2). lib. bdg. 27.32 ***(978-1-5157-7084-8(2)***, Aplus Bks.) Capstone Press of Coughlan Cos.

Johnson, Rebecca L. Plate Tectonics. 2005. (Great Ideas of Science Ser.). (Illus.). 80p. (YA). (gr. 9-12). lib. bdg. 27.93 *(978-0-8225-3056-5(2))* Lerner Publishing Group.

Keppeler, Jill. How Gems Are Formed. 2016. (From the Earth: How Resources Are Made Ser.). (Illus.). 32p. (J). (gr. 4-3). pap. 10.50 *(978-1-4824-4709-5(6))* Stevens, Gareth Publishing LLLP.

Kingsley, Charles. Madam How & Lady Why: Or First Lessons in Earth Lore for Children. 2007. 190p. pap. 19.99 *(978-1-4346-1518-3(9))*; (ENG.). 214p. pap. 22.99 *(978-1-4346-1612-8(6))* Creative Media Partners, LLC.

Koontz, Robin. The Science of a Sink Hole. 2015. (21st Century Skills Library: Disaster Science Ser.). (ENG., Illus.). 32p. (J). (gr. 4-8). pap. 14.21 *(978-1-63362-497-9(8)*, 206833) Cherry Lake Publishing.

Kovacs, Nicola. Digging Deep. 2007. (Action Numeracy Middle Primary Ser.). 32p. pap. 9.95 *(978-0-86431-694-3(1))* ACER Pr. AUS. Dist: ISBS Publisher Services.

Lawrence, Debbie & Lawrence, Richard. Our Planet Earth. 2004. (Illus.). vi, 134p. (gr. 1-6). pap. 18.00 *(978-0-9725365-3-0(1))* Boarding House Publishing.

Leavitt, Amie Jane. The Science Behind Wonders of the Earth: Cave Crystals, Balancing Rocks, & Snow Donuts. 2016. (Science Behind Natural Phenomena Ser.). (ENG., Illus.). 32p. (gr. 3-4). lib. bdg. 27.99 *(978-1-5157-0773-8(3)*, Edge Bks.) Capstone Press of Coughlan Cos.

Levy, Janey. Viaje Al Centro de la Tierra (a Trip to the Center of the Earth) 2015. (Maravillosos Viajes a Través de la Ciencia (Fantastic Science Journeys) Ser.). (SPA., Illus.). 32p. (J). (gr. 2-3). 25.25 *(978-1-4824-2025-8(2)*, 1384039) Stevens, Gareth Publishing LLLP.

Loeschnig, L. V. Experimentos Sencillos de Geologia y Biologia. 2004. (Juego de la Ciencia Ser.). (SPA.). 128p. (gr. 5-8). *(978-84-95456-60-1(5)*, 87804) Ediciones Oniro S.A.

Looye, Juliette, text. I Live on an Island. 2004. (Illus.). 16p. (J). pap. *(978-0-7367-1936-0(9))* Zaner-Bloser, Inc.

Loria, Laura. Volcanic Processes. 2017. (J). ***(978-1-5383-0030-5(3))*** Rosen Publishing Group, Inc., The.

Lunis, Natalie & White, Nancy. Investigating Rocks. Date not set. (Thinking Like a Scientist Ser.). (Illus.). 20p. (J). pap. 16.95 *(978-1-58273-081-3(4))* Sundance/Newbridge Educational Publishing.

Luongo, Charlotte. Plate Tectonics. 2009. (Big Ideas in Science Ser.). (Illus.). 48p. (gr. 5-8). 31.36 *(978-0-7614-4397-1(5))* Marshall Cavendish Corp.

Manning, Mick. Que Hay Debajo de la Cama? Cortes, Eunice, tr. Granström, Brita, illus. 2003. (Descubriendo Mi Mundo Ser.). (SPA.). 32p. (J). *(978-970-690-588-8(X))* Planeta Mexicana Editorial S. A. de C. V.

Marsh, Carole. Kentucky's Big Activity Book. 2004. (Kentucky Experience! Ser.). (Illus.). 96p. (J). (gr. 2-6). pap. 9.95 *(978-0-7933-9461-6(9))* Gallopade International.

Mattern, Joanne. Sand, Silt, & Mud & the Rock Cycle. (Shaping & Reshaping of Earth's Surface Ser.). 24p. (gr. 4-4). 2009. 42.50 *(978-1-60854-219-2(X)*, PowerKids Pr.) 2006. (Illus.). (YA). lib. bdg. 22.60 *(978-1-4042-3197-9(8))* Rosen Publishing Group, Inc., The.

Milford, Alison. A Finders' Guide to Rocks, Fossils & Soils. 2017. (ENG., Illus.). 32p. (J). pap. 8.99 ***(978-0-00-820877-6(8))*** HarperCollins Pubs. Ltd. GBR. Dist: Independent Pubs. Group.

Miller, Heather. A Changing Earth. 2009. (21st Century Skills Library: Real World Science Ser.). (ENG., Illus.). 32p. (J). (gr. 4-8). lib. bdg. 28.50 *(978-1-60279-465-8(0)*, 200232) Cherry Lake Publishing.

Morgan, Sally. The Rock Cycle. 2009. (Nature's Cycles Ser.). (J). (ENG., Illus.). 32p. (gr. 4-6). pap. 10.00 *(978-1-4358-2947-3(6))*; lib. bdg. 26.50 *(978-1-4358-2865-0(8))* Rosen Publishing Group, Inc., The. (PowerKids Pr.).

Morley, Catherine Weyerhaeuser. Where Do Mountains Come from, Momma? 2012. (Illus.). (J). *(978-0-87842-582-2(9))* Mountain Pr. Publishing Co., Inc.

Morris, John D. The Geology Book. 2006. (Wonders of Creation Ser.). 44p. pap. 3.99 *(978-1-893345-60-7(2))* Answers in Genesis Ministries.

Nagle, Frances. What Are Sedimentary Rocks? 2017. (Look at Earth's Rocks Ser.). 32p. (gr. 2-2). 26.60 ***(978-1-4824-6240-1(0))*** Stevens, Gareth Publishing LLLP.

—What Is the Rock Cycle? 2017. (Look at Earth's Rocks Ser.). 32p. (gr. 2-2). pap. 10.50 ***(978-1-4824-6019-3(X))*** Stevens, Gareth Publishing LLLP.

Nunn, Daniel. Pterodactyl, 1 vol. 2014. (All about Dinosaurs Ser.). (ENG., Illus.). 24p. (gr. -1-1). 22.65 *(978-1-4846-0205-8(6)*, Acorn) Heinemann-Raintree.

O'Neal, Claire. A Project Guide to Rocks & Minerals. 2010. (Earth Science Projects for Kids Ser.). (Illus.). 48p. (J). (gr. 4-7). lib. bdg. 29.95 *(978-1-58415-866-0(2))* Mitchell Lane Pubs., Inc.

O'Neill Grace, Catherine. Forces of Nature: The Awesome Power of Volcanoes, Earthquakes, & Tornadoes. 2004. (ENG., Illus.). 64p. (J). (gr. 3-7). 17.95 *(978-0-7922-6328-9(6)*, National Geographic Children's Bks.) National Geographic Society.

Orr, Tamra. Studying Sinkholes. 2015. (Explorer Library: Science Explorer Ser.). (ENG., Illus.). 32p. (J). (gr. 4-8). lib. bdg. 29.93 *(978-1-63362-391-0(2)*, 206984) Cherry Lake Publishing.

Ostopowich, Melanie. The Rock Cycle. 2016. (Illus.). 24p. (J). *(978-1-5105-1152-1(0))* SmartBook Media, Inc.

—The Rock Cycle. 2006. (Science Matters Ser.). (Illus.). 24p. (J). (gr. 3-7). lib. bdg. 24.45 *(978-1-59036-209-9(8))* Weigl Pubs., Inc.

—Rocks. 2004. (Science Matters Ser.). (Illus.). 24p. (J). lib. bdg. 24.45 *(978-1-59036-210-5(1))* Weigl Pubs., Inc.

Otfinoski, Steven. Quicksand. 2016. (True Book(tm), a — Extreme Earth Ser.). (ENG., Illus.). 48p. (J). lib. bdg. 31.00 *(978-0-531-22295-9(0)*, Children's Pr.) Scholastic Library Publishing.

Oxlade, Chris. Rocks. 2016. (Rock On! Ser.). (ENG., Illus.). 32p. (gr. 2-4). lib. bdg. 30.65 *(978-1-4109-8135-6(5)*, Raintree Perspectives) Heinemann-Raintree.

Parks, Peggy J. The Importance of Plate Tectonic Theory. 2015. (ENG., Illus.). 80p. (J). lib. bdg. *(978-1-60152-894-0(9))* ReferencePoint Pr., Inc.

Pendergast, George. The Rock Cycle at Work. 2015. (Cycles in Nature Ser.). (ENG., Illus.). 24p. (J). (gr. 1-2). 48.90 *(978-1-4824-1668-8(9))* Stevens, Gareth Publishing LLLP.

Peter, Carsten & Phelan, Glen. Extreme Planet: Carsten Peter's Wild Adventures in Volcanoes, Caves, Canyons, Deserts, & Ice! 2015. (ENG., Illus.). 112p. (J). (gr. 3-7). pap. 12.99 *(978-1-4263-2100-9(7)*, National Geographic Children's Bks.) National Geographic Society.

Peterson, Judy Monroe. What Are Metamorphic Rocks?, 01 vols., 1. 2016. (Junior Geologist Ser.). (ENG., Illus.). 32p. (J). pap. 12.90 *(978-1-5081-0048-5(9)*, Britannica Educational Publishing) Rosen Publishing Group, Inc., The.

Poynter, Margaret. Doomsday Rocks from Space. 2011. (Bizarre Science Ser.). (Illus.). 48p. (J). (gr. 5-18). pap. 8.95 *(978-1-59845-221-1(5))*; lib. bdg. 25.27 *(978-0-7660-3673-4(1))* Enslow Pubs., Inc.

Publishers, Chelsea House, creator. The Restless Earth Set, 6-Volumes. 2009. (Restless Earth Ser.). (gr. 5-8). 210.00 *(978-0-7910-9878-3(8)*, Chelsea Hse.) Facts On File, Inc.

Quinlan, Julia J. Plate Tectonics. 2017. (J). ***(978-1-5383-0029-9(X))***; pap. ***(978-1-68048-832-6(5))*** Rosen Publishing Group, Inc., The.

Richards, Jon & Simkins, Ed. The Natural World. 2016. 32p. (J). *(978-0-7787-2658-6(4))* Crabtree Publishing Co.

Riley, Joelle. Examining Erosion. 2013. (Searchlight Books (tm) — Do You Dig Earth Science? Ser.). (ENG., Illus.). 40p. (gr. 3-5). pap. 8.95 *(978-1-4677-0790-9(2))*; lib. bdg. 27.93 *(978-1-4677-0021-4(5))* Lerner Publishing Group.

Ripley's Believe It Or Not! Staff, et al. Extreme Earth: Fun, Facts, & Earth-Shattering Stories... 2010. (Twist Ser.: 7). (ENG., Illus.). 48p. (J). 12.95 *(978-1-893951-78-5(2))* Ripley Entertainment, Inc.

Rockett, Paul. Seven Quintillion, Five Hundred Quadrillion Grains of Sand on Planet Earth. Ruffle, Mark, illus. 2015. (Big Countdown Ser.). (ENG.). 32p. (gr. 3-5). 29.99 *(978-1-4109-6880-7(4)*, Raintree Perspectives) Heinemann-Raintree.

Romaine, Garret. Geology Lab for Kids: 52 Projects to Explore Rocks, Gems, Geodes, Crystals, Fossils, & Other Wonders of the Earth's Surface. 2017. (Lab Ser.). (ENG., Illus.). 144p. (J). (gr. 1-7). pap. 22.99 *(978-1-63159-285-0(8)*, Quarry Bks.) Quarto Publishing Group USA.

Ross, Michael. Earth Cycles. 2003. (Illus.). 32p. (J). (gr. 2-5). pap. 7.95 *(978-0-7613-1977-1(8)*, First Avenue Editions) Lerner Publishing Group.

Saunders, Craig. What Is the Theory of Plate Tectonics? 2010. (Shaping Modern Science Ser.). (ENG.). 64p. (J). (gr. 5-8). lib. bdg. *(978-0-7787-7202-6(0))* Crabtree Publishing Co.

Science stories foss spanish pebbles sand & silt ea Cr05. 2005. (J). *(978-1-59242-585-3(2))* Delta Education, LLC.

Shepherd, Jodie. To the Moon! Byrne, Mike, illus. 2017. (Cloverleaf Books (tm) — Space Adventures Ser.). (ENG.). 24p. (J). (gr. k-2). 25.32 *(978-1-5124-2536-9(2))*; 6.99 ***(978-1-5124-3894-9(4))***; 38.65 ***(978-1-5124-3893-2(6))***; 38.65 ***(978-1-5124-2833-9(7))*** Lerner Publishing Group. (Millbrook Pr.).

Solway, Andrew. The Scientists Behind Earth's Processes, 1 vol. 2011. (Sci-Hi: Scientists Ser.). (ENG.). 48p. (gr. 4-4). pap. 9.95 *(978-1-4109-4051-3(9)*, Sci-Hi) Heinemann-Raintree.

Sparrow, Giles. Destination Venus. 32p. (J). 2010. (Illus.). pap. 10.00 *(978-1-4358-3457-6(7))* 2009. (ENG.). lib. bdg. 25.25 *(978-1-4358-3442-2(9))* Rosen Publishing Group, Inc., The. (PowerKids Pr.).

Spilsbury, Louise & Spilsbury, Richard. Under the Ground. 2016. (Science on Patrol Ser.). 00048p. (J). pap. 14.05 ***(978-1-4824-5984-5(1))*** Stevens, Gareth Publishing LLLP.

Squire, Ann O. Sinkholes. 2016. (True Book(tm), a — Extreme Earth Ser.). (ENG.). 48p. (J). lib. bdg. 31.00 *(978-0-531-22296-6(9)*, Children's Pr.) Scholastic Library Publishing.

Strother, Ruth. B Is for Blue Planet: An Earth Science Alphabet. Marstall, Robert, illus. 2011. (Sleeping Bear Alphabets Ser.). (ENG.). 40p. (J). (gr. k-6). lib. bdg. 16.95 *(978-1-58536-454-1(1))* Sleeping Bear Pr.

Thompson, David. Processes That Shape the Earth. 2007. (Physics in Action Ser.). 120p. (YA). (gr. 9-12). 35.00 *(978-0-7910-8932-3(0))* Facts On File, Inc.

Tomecek, Stephen M. Plate Tectonics. 2009. (Science Foundations Ser.). (Illus.). 104p. (YA). (gr. 7-12). lib. bdg. 35.00 *(978-1-60413-014-0(8))* Facts On File, Inc.

Tomecek, Steve. Dirtmeister's Nitty Gritty Planet Earth: All about Rocks, Minerals, Fossils, Earthquakes, Volcanoes, & Even Dirt! Harper, Fred, illus. 2015. (ENG.). 128p. (J). (gr. 3-7). pap. 12.99 *(978-1-4263-1903-7(7)*, National Geographic Children's Bks.) National Geographic Society.

Twist, Clint. Extreme Earth. 2010. (Ripley Twists Ser.). (Illus.). 48p. (J). (gr. 3-18). lib. bdg. 19.95 *(978-1-4222-1829-7(5)*, 1318258) Mason Crest.

Twist, Clint, et al. Extreme Earth. 2009. (Ripley Twists Ser.). (Illus.). 48p. (J). (gr. 3-18). pap. 8.95 *(978-1-4222-2067-2(2)*, 1318258) Mason Crest.

Weakland, Mark. Yogi Bear's Guide to Rocks. Beach, Bryan, illus. 2015. (Yogi Bear's Guide to the Great Outdoors Ser.). (ENG.). 32p. (gr. 1-2). lib. bdg. 27.99 *(978-1-4914-6548-6(4))* Capstone Press of Coughlan Cos.

Weintraub, Aileen. The Grand Canyon: The Widest Canyon. 2009. (Great Record Breakers in Nature Ser.). 24p. (gr. 3-4). 42.50 *(978-1-61513-183-9(3)*, PowerKids Pr.) Rosen Publishing Group, Inc., The.

West, Krista. Hands-on Projects about Changes in the Earth. 2009. (Great Earth Science Projects Ser.). 24p. (gr. 3-3). 42.50 *(978-1-61513-110-5(8)*, PowerKids Pr.) Rosen Publishing Group, Inc., The.

Whiting, Jim. The Volcanic Eruption on Santorini, 1650 BCE. 2007. (Natural Disasters Ser.). (Illus.). 32p. (J). (gr. 1-4). lib. bdg. 25.70 *(978-1-58415-568-3(X))* Mitchell Lane Pubs., Inc.

Williams, Zella. Experiments on Rocks & the Rock Cycle. (Do-It-Yourself Science Ser.). 24p. (gr. 2-3). 2009. 47.90 *(978-1-61512-187-8(0)*, PowerKids Pr.) 2007. (Illus.). (YA). lib. bdg. 25.25 *(978-1-4042-3660-8(0))* Rosen Publishing Group, Inc., The.

Wilson, Steve. Erosion & Sediments. 2016. (Spotlight on Earth Science Ser.). 00024p. (J). (gr. 4-6). pap. 10.00 *(978-1-4994-2509-3(0)*, PowerKids Pr.) Rosen Publishing Group, Inc., The.

Wolny, Philip. Geologists at Work. 2017. (Scientists at Work Ser.). 32p. (gr. 6-8). pap. 12.90 ***(978-1-68048-760-2(4)***, Britannica Educational Publishing) Rosen Publishing Group, Inc., The.

Wolny, Philip, ed. Earth Science, 1 vol., 1. 2016. (Study of Science Ser.). (ENG.). 00104p. (YA). (gr. 8-8). 36.25

(978-1-68048-226-3(2), Britannica Educational Publishing) Rosen Publishing Group, Inc., The.
Woods, Michael & Woods, Mary B. Mudflows & Landslides. 2007. (Disasters up Close Ser.). (ENG., Illus.). 64p. (gr. 4-8). lib. bdg. 27.93 *(978-0-8225-6574-1(9),* Lerner Pubns.) Lerner Publishing Group.
Woolf, Alex. An Asteroid Strike. 2013. (World After Ser.). (ENG., Illus.). 56p. (gr. 7-8). 34.65 *(978-1-4329-7618-7(4));* pap. 9.95 *(978-1-4329-7623-1(0))* Heinemann-Raintree.
World Book, Inc Staff, contrib. by. Forces of Nature. 2007. (J). *(978-0-7166-9806-7(4))* World Bk., Inc.
Woyt, Barbara A. Geology. 2016. (Study of Science Ser.). 00104p. (YA). (gr. 8-8). 36.25 *(978-1-5081-0426-1(3))* Rosen Publishing Group, Inc., The.

GEOLOGY, DYNAMIC
see Geophysics

GEOLOGY, HISTORICAL
see Geology, Stratigraphic

GEOLOGY—NORTH AMERICA
Adams, Colleen. Exploring the Grand Canyon. 2009. (Reading Room Collection 2 Ser.). 24p. (gr. 3-4). 42.50 *(978-1-60851-963-7(5),* PowerKids Pr.) Rosen Publishing Group, Inc., The.
Alt, David D. & Hyndman, Donald W. Roadside Geology of Montana. rev. ed. (Roadside Geology Ser.). (Illus.). 435p. (J). (gr. 4). pap. 20.00 *(978-0-87842-202-9(1),* 212) Mountain Pr. Publishing Co., Inc.
Chin, Jason. Grand Canyon. 2017. (ENG., Illus.). 56p. (J). 19.99 *(978-1-59643-950-4(5),* 9781596439504) Roaring Brook Pr.
Frye, Keith. Roadside Geology of Virginia. Alt, David & Hyndman, Donald W., eds. Venkatakrishnan, Rames, illus. rev. ed. (Roadside Geology Ser.). 256p. (J). (gr. 4). pap. *(978-0-87842-199-2(8),* 211) Mountain Pr. Publishing Co., Inc.
Putnam, Jeff. National Monuments: Nature. 2004. (ZB Reads Trio Books). (Illus.). iii, 92p. (gr. 4-6). pap. 5.00 *(978-0-7367-1788-5(9))* Zaner-Bloser, Inc.

GEOLOGY, STRATIGRAPHIC
see also Fossils
Barker, Charles Ferguson. Under New England: The Story of New England's Rocks & Fossils. Barker, Charles Ferguson, illus. 2008. (ENG., Illus.). 72p. (J). (gr. 2-7). 12.95 *(978-1-58465-696-8(4))* Univ. Pr. of New England.
Dayton, Connor. Rock Formations. 2009. (Rocks & Minerals Ser.). 24p. (gr. 2-3). 42.50 *(978-1-60852-502-7(3),* PowerKids Pr.) Rosen Publishing Group, Inc., The.
Holmes, Thom. Primates & Human Ancestors: The Pliocene Epoch. 2008. (Prehistoric Earth Ser.). (Illus.). 160p. (YA). (gr. 9-12). 35.00 *(978-0-8160-5965-2(9))* Facts On File, Inc.
—Rise of the Mammals: The Paleocene & Eocene Periods. 2008. (Prehistoric Earth Ser.). (Illus.). 168p. (YA). (gr. 9-12). 35.00 *(978-0-8160-5963-8(2))* Facts On File, Inc.
Naish, Darren. Jurassic Record Breakers. 2015. (ENG., Illus.). 48p. (J). (gr. 3). pap. 7.95 *(978-1-78312-118-2(1))* Carlton Kids GBR. Dist: Sterling Publishing Co., Inc.
Petersen, Christine. Rockin' Rocks, 1 vol. 2010. (Rock on!: a Look at Geology Ser.). (ENG.). 32p. (YA). (gr. 3-6). 27.07 *(978-1-60453-746-8(9))* ABDO Publishing Co.
Prehistoric World - Group 1, 5 bks., Set. 128.21 *(978-0-7614-1021-8(X),* Benchmark Bks.) Marshall Cavendish Corp.
The Shaping & Reshaping of Earth's Surface. (Illus.). (J). (gr. k-6). 127.50 *(978-1-4042-3296-9(6))* Rosen Publishing Group, Inc., The.
Williams, Colleen Madonna Flood. My Adventure in the Mesozoic Period: Advanced My Adventure. 2009. (ENG.). 44p. (J). pap. 8.99 *(978-1-59092-437-2(1))* Blue Forge Pr.

GEOLOGY, SUBMARINE
see Submarine Geology

GEOLOGY—VOCATIONAL GUIDANCE
Cunningham, Kevin. Volcanologist. 2015. (21st Century Skills Library: Cool STEAM Careers Ser.). (ENG., Illus.). 32p. (J). (gr. 4-7). 29.93 *(978-1-63362-568-6(0),* 206456) Cherry Lake Publishing.
Firestone, Mary. Volcanologist. 2005. (Weird Careers in Science Ser.). (Illus.). 80p. (gr. 5-8). lib. bdg. 25.00 *(978-0-7910-8702-2(6),* Chelsea Hse.) Facts On File, Inc.
Latta, Sara L. Lava Scientist: Careers on the Edge of Volcanoes. 2009. (Wild Science Careers Ser.). (Illus.). 128p. (J). (gr. 5-9). lib. bdg. 33.27 *(978-0-7660-3049-7(0))* Enslow Pubs., Inc.
Letts, Amelia. A Day at Work with a Geologist, 01 vols., 1. 2016. (Super STEM Careers Ser.). (ENG., Illus.). 24p. (J). pap. 8.25 *(978-1-5081-4406-9(0),* PowerKids Pr.) Rosen Publishing Group, Inc., The.
Mullins, Matt. Geoscientist. 2013. (21st Century Skills Library: Cool STEM Careers Ser.). (ENG.). 32p. (J). (gr. 4-8). 28.50 *(978-1-62431-004-1(4),* 202467); pap. 14.21 *(978-1-62431-028-7(1),* 202469) Cherry Lake Publishing.
Nagelhout, Ryan. Be a Geologist. 2014. (Be a Scientist! Ser.). 32p. (J). (gr. 3-6). pap. 10.50 *(978-1-4824-1213-0(6))* Stevens, Gareth Publishing LLLP.

GEOMETRICAL DRAWING
see also Graphic Methods; Mechanical Drawing; Perspective
Pelli, Tammy. Constructions: Creating Geometric Figures. 2004. (Studies in Geometry Ser.). (ENG.). 64p. (YA). (gr. 7). pap., wbk. ed. 10.95 *(978-1-930820-43-2(7))* Garlic Pr.
Pomaska, Anna. 3-D Coloring Book — My First Geometric Designs. 2011. (Dover 3-D Coloring Book Ser.). (ENG., Illus.). 32p. (J). (gr. -1-2). pap. 5.99 *(978-0-486-48110-4(7))* Dover Pubns., Inc.
Randolph, Joanne. Let's Draw a Bird with Shapes: Vamos a Dibujar un Ave Usando Figuras. Muschinske, Emily, illus. 2005. (Let's Draw with Shapes / Vamos a Dibujar con Figuras Ser.). (J). 22.60 *(978-1-4042-7555-3(X),* PowerKids Pr.) Rosen Publishing Group, Inc., The.
Snozek, Lee Anne. Simply Square Designs. 2009. (Dover Design Coloring Bks.). (ENG., Illus.). 32p. (gr. 3-5). pap. 3.99 *(978-0-486-46992-8(1))* Dover Pubns., Inc.

GEOMETRY
see also Geometrical Drawing; Trigonometry
ABDO Publishing Company Staff. Shapes Everywhere. 2013. (Shapes Everywhere Ser.: 6). 24p. (gr. k-4). lib. bdg. 153.90 *(978-1-61783-410-3(6),* Super SandCastle) ABDO Publishing Co.
ABDO Publishing Company Staff & Hanson, Anders. 3-D Shapes, 1 vol. 2008. (3-D Shapes Ser.: 6). (ENG.). 24p. (J). (gr. k-3). lib. bdg. 145.26 *(978-1-59928-885-7(0),* SandCastle) ABDO Publishing Co.
Aboff, Marcie & Shaskan, Trisha Speed. Math Fun, 1 vol. Carabelli, Francesca & Dillard, Sarah, illus. 2009. (Math Fun Ser.). (ENG.). 192p. (gr. 2-4). pap. 14.95 *(978-1-4048-5611-0(0))* Picture Window Bks.
Accelerated Math West Virginia State Tagged Geometry Library. 2004. cd-rom 1199.00 *(978-1-59455-115-4(4))* Renaissance Learning, Inc.
Ackroyd, Patricia. Where's Polygon? 2013. 44p. pap. 7.00 *(978-0-9829811-8-4(X))* Spiritbuilding.
Adler, David A. Circles. Miller, Edward, illus. 2016. (ENG.). 32p. (J). 17.95 *(978-0-8234-3642-2(X))* Holiday Hse., Inc.
—Triangles. Miller, Edward, illus. 2014. (ENG.). 32p. (J). (gr. 1-5). 17.95 *(978-0-8234-2378-1(6))* Holiday Hse., Inc.
Alaina, Maria. Shapes, 1 vol. 2011. (Wonder Readers Early Level Ser.). (ENG.). (gr. -1-1). 32p. pap. 5.99 *(978-1-4296-7810-0(0));* 16p. pap. 35.94 *(978-1-4296-8145-2(4))* Capstone Press of Coughlan Cos. (Wonder Readers).
—Shapes in the City, 1 vol. 2013. (Wonder Readers Next Steps: Math Ser.). (ENG.). 20p. (gr. -1-1). lib. bdg. 22.65 *(978-1-4765-0035-5(5),* Wonder Readers) Capstone Press of Coughlan Cos.
Alexander, Emmett. Sort It by Shape. 2015. (Sort It Out! Ser.). (ENG., Illus.). 24p. (J). (gr. k-1). pap. 8.15 *(978-1-4824-2569-7(6),* 1390345) Stevens, Gareth Publishing LLLP.
Amazing Geogami. 2007. *(978-1-884270-10-9(7));* *(978-1-884270-11-6(5))* Hall, Nancy Inc.
Anderson, Jill. Finding Shapes with Sebastian Pig & Friends at the Museum. Amy Huntington, illus. 2013. (Math Fun with Sebastian Pig & Friends! Ser.). 32p. (J). (gr. k-3). pap. 7.95 *(978-0-7660-5981-8(2),* Enslow Elementary) Enslow Pubs., Inc.
—Finding Shapes with Sebastian Pig & Friends at the Museum. Huntington, Amy, illus. 2009. (Math Fun with Sebastian Pig & Friends! Ser.). 32p. (J). (gr. k-3). lib. bdg. 23.94 *(978-0-7660-3363-4(5))* Enslow Pubs., Inc.
Arias, Lisa. Galactic Geometry: Two-Dimensional Figures. 2014. (ENG.). 32p. (gr. 3-6). 32.79 *(978-1-62717-708-5(6))* Rourke Educational Media.
—Glorious Geometry: Lines, Angles & Shapes, Oh My! 2014. (ENG.). 32p. (gr. 3-6). 32.79 *(978-1-62717-713-9(2))* Rourke Educational Media.
Arvoy, Marsha & Nardi, Dorianne. Area. 2010. (ENG.). 24p. (J). *(978-0-7787-6780-0(9));* pap. *(978-0-7787-6789-3(2))* Crabtree Publishing Co.
Avery, Sebastian. The School Garden: Reason with Shapes & Their Attributes. 2014. (Rosen Common Core Math Readers Ser.). (ENG.). 24p. (J). (gr. 3-4). pap. 8.25 *(978-1-4777-4875-6(X),* Rosen Classroom) Rosen Publishing Group, Inc., The.
Avett, Harper. Go Fly a Kite! Reason with Shapes & Their Attributes. 2014. (Rosen Common Core Math Readers Ser.). (ENG., Illus.). 24p. (J). (gr. 3-4). pap. 8.25 *(978-1-4777-4881-7(4),* Rosen Classroom) Rosen Publishing Group, Inc., The.
Award, Anna. My First Shapes. 2012. (ENG., Illus.). 10p. (J). bds. 6.50 *(978-1-84135-564-1(X));* bds. 9.95 *(978-1-84135-565-8(8))* Award Pubns. Ltd. GBR. Dist: Parkwest Pubns., Inc.
Bailey, Gerry & Law, Felicia. Circles. Phillips, Mike, illus. 2014. (ENG.). 32p. (J). *(978-0-7787-0507-9(2))* Crabtree Publishing Co.
—Spheres. Phillips, Mike, illus. 2014. (ENG.). 32p. (J). lib. bdg. *(978-0-7787-0510-9(2))* Crabtree Publishing Co.
—Stone Age Geometry - Circles. Phillips, Mike, illus. 2014. (Stone Age Geometry Ser.). (ENG.). 32p. (J). pap. *(978-0-7787-0513-0(7))* Crabtree Publishing Co.
—Stone Age Geometry - Cubes. Phillips, Mike, illus. 2014. (Stone Age Geometry Ser.). (ENG.). 32p. (J). *(978-0-7787-0508-6(0));* pap. *(978-0-7787-0514-7(5))* Crabtree Publishing Co.
—Stone Age Geometry - Lines. Phillips, Mike, illus. 2014. (Stone Age Geometry Ser.). (ENG.). 32p. (J). *(978-0-7787-0509-3(9));* pap. *(978-0-7787-0515-4(3))* Crabtree Publishing Co.
—Stone Age Geometry - Squares. Phillips, Mike, illus. 2014. (Stone Age Geometry Ser.). (ENG.). 32p. (J). *(978-0-7787-0511-6(0));* pap. *(978-0-7787-0517-8(X))* Crabtree Publishing Co.
—Stone Age Geometry -Triangles. Phillips, Mike, illus. 2014. (Stone Age Geometry Ser.). (ENG.). 32p. (J). lib. bdg. *(978-0-7787-0512-3(9))* Crabtree Publishing Co.
Basher, Simon. Algebra & Geometry: Anything but Square! Basher, Simon, illus. 2011. (Basher Science Ser.). (ENG., Illus.). 128p. (J). (gr. 5-9). pap. 8.99 *(978-0-7534-6597-4(3),* 9780753465974, Kingfisher) Roaring Brook Pr.
Begin Smart Books Staff, contrib. by. What Shapes Do You See? 2010. (Illus.). 14p. (J). bds. *(978-1-60906-005-3(9))* Begin Smart LLC.
Benchmark Education Company, LLC Staff, compiled by. Geometry. 2005. spiral bd. 55.00 *(978-1-4108-3886-5(2));* spiral bd. 180.00 *(978-1-4108-3893-3(5));* spiral bd. 110.00 *(978-1-4108-3885-8(4));* spiral bd. 50.00 *(978-1-4108-3909-1(5));* spiral bd. 60.00 *(978-1-4108-3894-0(3));* spiral bd. 165.00 *(978-1-4108-4511-5(7));* spiral bd. 350.00 *(978-1-4108-5451-3(5));* spiral bd. 160.00 *(978-1-4108-5862-7(6))* Benchmark Education Co.
Berry, Minta. Perimeter. Crabtree Publishing Staff, ed. 2011. (My Path to Math Ser.: No. 35). (ENG.). 24p. (J). pap. *(978-0-7787-5265-3(8))* Crabtree Publishing Co.
Bienik, Stella. Sculpting with Clay: Reason with Shapes & Their Attributes. 2014. (Math Masters: Geometry Ser.). 24p. (J). (gr. 2-3). 23.60 *(978-1-4777-6444-2(5));* (ENG.). pap. 8.25 *(978-1-4777-4906-7(3))* Rosen Publishing Group, Inc., The. (Rosen Classroom).
Bishop, Celeste. Core Math Skills: Measurement & Geometry. 2013. (Core Math Skills: Measurement & Geometry Ser.). 24p. (J). (gr. 1-2). 135.60 *(978-1-4777-2236-7(X),* Rosen Classroom) Rosen Publishing Group, Inc., The.
Boothroyd, Jennifer. Cone. 2008. (First Step Nonfiction - Solid Shapes Ser.). (ENG.). 8p. (gr. -1-1). pap. 4.95 *(978-0-8225-8850-4(1))* Lerner Publishing Group.
—Cube. 2008. pap. 22.95 *(978-0-8225-9365-2(3));* (ENG.). 8p. (gr. -1-1). pap. 4.95 *(978-0-8225-8852-8(8))* Lerner Publishing Group.
—Cylinder. 2008. pap. 22.95 *(978-0-8225-9366-9(1));* (ENG.). 8p. (gr. -1-1). pap. 4.95 *(978-0-8225-8851-1(X))* Lerner Publishing Group.
—Pyramid. 2008. pap. 22.95 *(978-0-8225-9367-6(X));* (ENG.). 8p. (gr. -1-1). pap. 4.95 *(978-0-8225-8855-9(2))* Lerner Publishing Group.
—Rectangular Prism. 2008. pap. 22.95 *(978-0-8225-9369-0(6));* (ENG.). 8p. (gr. -1-1). pap. 4.95 *(978-0-8225-8854-2(4))* Lerner Publishing Group.
—Sphere. 2008. pap. 22.95 *(978-0-8225-9368-3(8));* (ENG.). 8p. (gr. -1-1). pap. 4.95 *(978-0-8225-8853-5(6))* Lerner Publishing Group.
Boyd, Cindy J., et al. Geometry. 2003. (GEOMETRY: CONCEPTS & APPLIC Ser.). (ENG., Illus.). 912p. (gr. 9-12). stu. ed. 115.64 *(978-0-07-829637-6(4),* 0078296374) McGraw-Hill Education.
Brocket, Jane. Circles, Stars, & Squares: Looking for Shapes. Brocket, Jane, photos by. 2012. (Jane Brocket's Clever Concepts Ser.). (ENG., Illus.). 32p. (gr. -1-2). lib. bdg. 26.60 *(978-0-7613-4611-1(2),* Millbrook Pr.) Lerner Publishing Group.
Brown, Margery W. Afro-Bets Book of Shapes. Blair, Culverson & Simpson, Howard, illus. 2nd ed. 2004. (Afro-Bets Ser.). 24p. (J). (gr. -1-1). pap. 3.95 *(978-0-940975-58-3(0),* Sankofa Bks.) Just Us Bks., Inc.
Brunner-Jass, Renata. Designer Digs: Finding Area & Surface Area. 2013. (IMath Ser.). (Illus.). 48p. (J). (gr. 5-6). pap. 11.94 *(978-1-60357-513-3(8))* Norwood Hse. Pr.
Brunner-Jass, Renata & Loughran, Donna. Designer Digs: Finding Area & Surface Area. 2013. (IMath Ser.). (Illus.). 48p. (J). (gr. 5-6). lib. bdg. 23.94 *(978-1-59953-574-6(2))* Norwood Hse. Pr.
Buchanan, Theo. Power of Patterns: Fractals. 2017. (Time for Kids Nonfiction Readers Ser.). lib. bdg. 20.85 ***(978-0-606-40283-5(7))*** Turtleback Bks.
Buchanan, Theodore. Fractals. 2017. (J). pap. 9.97 ***(978-1-4938-3626-0(9))*** Teacher Created Materials, Inc.
Burstein, John. Calculating Area: Space Rocket! 2003. (Weekly Reader Early Learning Library). (Illus.). 24p. (J). (gr. k-4). pap. 8.15 *(978-0-8368-3819-0(X),* Weekly Reader Leveled Readers) Stevens, Gareth Publishing LLLP.
Bussell, Linda. Exploring Solid Figures on the Web. 2008. (Math in Our World - Level 3 Ser.). 24p. (gr. 2-5). (J). lib. bdg. 22.00 *(978-0-8368-9287-1(9));* pap. 8.15 *(978-0-8368-9386-1(7))* Stevens, Gareth Publishing LLLP. (Weekly Reader Leveled Readers).
—Vamos a Explorar Cuerpos Sólidos en la Red. 2008. (Matemáticas en Nuestro Mundo - Nivel 3 (Math in Our World - Level 3) Ser.). (SPA.). 24p. (gr. 2-5). (J). lib. bdg. 22.00 *(978-0-8368-9295-6(X));* pap. 8.15 *(978-0-8368-9394-6(8))* Stevens, Gareth Publishing LLLP. (Weekly Reader Leveled Readers).
Campbell, Josette & Hayhurst, Chris. Euclid: The Father of Geometry. 2015. (Greatest Greek Philosophers Ser.). (ENG., Illus.). 112p. (J). (gr. 7-8). 35.60 *(978-1-4994-6128-2(3),* Rosen Young Adult) Rosen Publishing Group, Inc., The.
Canavan, Thomas. Shapes & Symmetry: 50 Math Super Puzzles. 2011. (Math Standards Workout Ser.). (ENG., Illus.). 48p. (YA). (gr. 5-8). pap. 11.75 *(978-1-4488-6683-0(9),* Rosen Reference); lib. bdg. 29.25 *(978-1-4488-6676-2(6))* Rosen Publishing Group, Inc., The.
Caron, Lucille & St. Jacques, Philip M. Geometry Smarts! 2011. (Math Smarts! Ser.). (Illus.). 64p. (J). (gr. 5-18). pap. 8.95 *(978-1-59845-316-4(5))* Enslow Pubs., Inc.
Caron, Lucille, et al. Geometry Smarts! 2011. (Math Smarts! Ser.). (Illus.). 64p. (J). (gr. 5-18). lib. bdg. 29.27 *(978-0-7660-3935-3(8))* Enslow Pubs., Inc.
Carr, Aaron. Diseños de Animales. 2012. (SPA.). (J). *(978-1-61913-204-7(4))* Weigl Pubs., Inc.
Carroll, Danielle. Tiling with Shapes. 2005. (Yellow Umbrella Fluent Level Ser.). (ENG., Illus.). 16p. (gr. k-1). pap. 35.70 *(978-0-7368-5323-1(5),* Yellow Umbrella Bks.) Capstone Press of Coughlan Cos.
Carrow, Ian. Jackson's Surprise Party. 2013. (InfoMax Math Readers Ser.). (ENG.). 24p. (J). (gr. 1-2). pap. 8.25 *(978-1-4777-2204-6(1),* Rosen Classroom) Rosen Publishing Group, Inc., The.
—Jackson's Surprise Party: Shapes & Their Attributes. 2013. (InfoMax Math Readers Ser.). (ENG.). 24p. (J). (gr. 1-2). pap. 49.50 *(978-1-4777-2205-3(X),* Rosen Classroom) Rosen Publishing Group, Inc., The.
Circulos, 4 vols. 2010. (Figuras Geométricas/Shapes Ser.).Tr. of Circles. (MUL & ENG.). 32p. (gr. 1-2). lib. bdg. 109.28 *(978-1-4296-4608-6(X),* A+ Bilingue/Bilingual) Capstone Press of Coughlan Cos.
Cohen, Marina. Polygons. 2010. (ENG.). 24p. (J). *(978-0-7787-6784-8(1));* pap. *(978-0-7787-6793-0(0))* Crabtree Publishing Co.
Colson, Rob. Get in Shape: Two-Dimensional & Three-Dimensional Shapes. 2017. (Math Everywhere Ser.). (ENG.). 32p. (J). pap. 8.95 ***(978-0-531-23318-4(9));*** lib. bdg. 27.00 ***(978-0-531-22882-1(7))*** Scholastic Library Publishing. (Children's Pr.).
Corcorane, Ann. Circles Everywhere, 1 vol. 2011. (Wonder Readers Emergent Level Ser.). (ENG.). 32p. (gr. -1-1). pap. 5.99 *(978-1-4296-7841-4(0),* Wonder Readers) Capstone Press of Coughlan Cos.
—Patterns Everywhere. 2011. (Wonder Readers Emergent Level Ser.). (ENG.). 16p. (gr. -1-1). pap. 35.94 *(978-1-4296-8137-7(3),* Wonder Readers) Capstone Press of Coughlan Cos.
Corporate Contributor Staff & West, David. Dinosaur Shapes. 2012. (ENG.). 24p. (J). *(978-0-7787-7456-3(2));* pap. *(978-0-7787-7461-7(9))* Crabtree Publishing Co.
Danielson, Christopher. Which One Doesn't Belong? 2016. (ENG., Illus.). 36p. (gr. k-12). stu. ed. 16.67 *(978-1-62531-080-4(3))* Stenhouse Pubs.
Deen, Marilyn. Tiling Shapes. 2011. (Wonder Readers Fluent Level Ser.). (ENG.). (gr. -1-2). 16p. pap. 35.94 *(978-1-4296-8188-9(8));* 32p. pap. 5.99 *(978-1-4296-7936-1(7))* Capstone Press of Coughlan Cos. (Wonder Readers).
Del Moral, Susana. El Juego de las Formas. Zaidi, Nadeem, illus. 2005. (Baby Einstein: Libros de Carton Ser.). (SPA.). 6p. (J). (gr. -1). bds. *(978-970-718-303-2(9),* Silver Dolphin en Español) Advanced Marketing, S. de R. L. de C. V.
Diggins, Julia E. String, Straightedge & Shadow: The Story of Geometry. Diggins, Julia E. & Bell, Corydon, illus. 2003. (J). per. 16.95 *(978-1-892857-07-1(3))* Whole Spirit Pr.
Dilkes, D. H. I See Ovals. 2010. (All about Shapes Ser.). (Illus.). 24p. (J). pap. 7.95 *(978-1-59845-151-1(0),* Enslow Elementary) Enslow Pubs., Inc.
Dingles, Molly. Rectangle Ranch. Dobson, Len, illus. 2005. (Community of Shapes Ser.). 32p. (J). pap. 10.95 *(978-1-59646-244-1(2));* lib. bdg. 21.65 *(978-1-59646-035-5(0));* per. 10.95 *(978-1-59646-245-8(0))* Dingles & Co.
—Rectangle Ranch/Rancho Rectangular. Dobson, Len, illus. 2005. (Community of Shapes Ser.).Tr. of Rancho Rectangular. (ENG & SPA.). 32p. (J). pap. 10.95 *(978-1-59646-246-5(9));* lib. bdg. 20.65 *(978-1-59646-036-2(9));* per. 10.95 *(978-1-59646-247-2(7))* Dingles & Co.
—Seaside Circles. Brodie, Neale, illus. 2006. (Community of Shapes Ser.). 32p. (J). pap. 10.95 *(978-1-59646-256-4(6));* lib. bdg. 21.65 *(978-1-59646-033-1(4));* per. 10.95 *(978-1-59646-257-1(4))* Dingles & Co.
—Seaside Circles/Circulos a la orilla del Mar. Brodie, Neale, illus. 2006. (Community of Shapes Ser.).Tr. of Circulos a la orilla del Mar. (ENG & SPA.). 32p. (J). pap. 10.95 *(978-1-59646-258-8(2));* lib. bdg. 21.65 *(978-1-59646-034-8(2))* Dingles & Co.
—Seaside Circles/Círculos a la orilla del Mar. Brodie, Neal, illus. 2006. (Community of Shapes Ser.).Tr. of Círculos a la orilla del Mar. (ENG & SPA.). 32p. (J). per. 10.95 *(978-1-59646-259-5(0))* Dingles & Co.
—Town Squares. Brodie, Neale, illus. 2006. (Community of Shapes Ser.). 32p. (J). pap. 10.95 *(978-1-59646-264-9(7));* lib. bdg. 21.65 *(978-1-59646-041-6(5));* per. 10.95 *(978-1-59646-265-6(5))* Dingles & Co.
—Town Squares/Cuadrados en la Plaza. Brodie, Neale, illus. 2006. (Community of Shapes Ser.).Tr. of Cuadrados en la Plaza. (ENG & SPA.). 32p. (J). pap. 10.95 *(978-1-59646-266-3(3));* lib. bdg. 21.65 *(978-1-59646-042-3(3));* per. 10.95 *(978-1-59646-267-0(1))* Dingles & Co.
—Triangle Trail: Sendero de Triángulos. 2005. (ENG & SPA., Illus.). 32p. (J). lib. bdg. 21.65 *(978-1-59646-046-1(6))* Dingles & Co.
Dowdy, Penny. Geometry. 2008. (My Path to Math Ser.). (ENG.). 24p. (J). (gr. k-3). lib. bdg. *(978-0-7787-4340-8(3));* (Illus.). pap. *(978-0-7787-4358-3(6))* Crabtree Publishing Co.
Dreyer, Kira. My New Bedroom: Estimate Lengths in Standard Units. 2014. (Math Masters: Measurement & Data Ser.). 24p. (J). (gr. 2-3). 23.60 *(978-1-4777-6438-1(0));* (ENG.). pap. 8.25 *(978-1-4777-4801-5(6))* Rosen Publishing Group, Inc., The. (Rosen Classroom).
Dugan, Christine. Landscape by Design. rev. ed. 2012. (Mathematics Readers Ser.). (ENG.). 32p. (J). (gr. 6-6). pap. 8.99 *(978-1-4333-3459-7(3))* Teacher Created Materials, Inc.
—A Sense of Art. rev. ed. 2012. (Mathematics Readers Ser.). (ENG.). 32p. (J). (gr. 6-6). pap. 8.99 *(978-1-4333-3458-0(5))* Teacher Created Materials, Inc.
Earle, Erin. Surprise Party! 2013. (Core Math Skills: Measurement & Geometry Ser.). 24p. (J). (gr. 1-2). 22.60 *(978-1-4777-2230-5(0));* (ENG.). pap. 8.25 *(978-1-4777-2103-2(7))* Rosen Publishing Group, Inc., The. (Rosen Classroom).
—Surprise Party! Shapes & Their Attributes. 2013. (Rosen Math Readers Ser.). (ENG.). 24p. (J). (gr. 1-2). pap. 49.50 *(978-1-4777-2104-9(5),* Rosen Classroom) Rosen Publishing Group, Inc., The.
Ellis, Julie. Pythagoras & the Ratios: A Math Adventure. Peacock, Phyllis Hornung, illus. 2010. (ENG.). 32p. (J). (gr. 2-5). 16.95 *(978-1-57091-775-2(2))* Charlesbridge Publishing, Inc.
—What's Your Angle, Pythagoras? A Math Adventure. Hornung, Phyllis, illus. 2004. (Math Adventures Ser.). (ENG.). 32p. (J). (gr. 2-5). pap. 7.95 *(978-1-57091-150-7(9))* Charlesbridge Publishing, Inc.
Encycbrita. Looking at an Angle Mic 2006 G. 6th ed. 2005. pap. 10.60 *(978-0-03-038569-8(5))* Harcourt Schl. Pubs.
—Packages & Polygons Mic 2006. 6th ed. 2005. pap. 10.60 *(978-0-03-039632-8(8))* Harcourt Schl. Pubs.
Evans, Henry. Cubeworld: An Adventure in Solid Geometry. 2004. (Illus.). 110p. per. 11.95 *(978-0-9754699-2-7(4))* Gross, H. H.
Faulkner, Nicholas & Hosch, William L. Geometry. 2017. (J). lib. bdg. ***(978-1-68048-776-3(0),*** Britannica Educational Publishing) Rosen Publishing Group, Inc., The.
Fisher, Valorie. Everything I Need to Know Before I'm Five. Fisher, Valorie, illus. 2011. (ENG., Illus.). 40p. (J). (gr. k-k). 17.99 *(978-0-375-86865-8(8),* Schwartz & Wade Bks.) Random Hse. Children's Bks.
Flippen, David. Where Is It? 2013. (InfoMax Math Readers Ser.). (ENG.). 16p. (J). (gr. k-1). pap. 7.00 *(978-1-4777-1937-4(7),* Rosen Classroom) Rosen Publishing Group, Inc., The.
—Where Is It? Identify & Describe Shapes. 2013. (InfoMax Math Readers Ser.). (ENG.). 16p. (J). (gr. k-1). pap. 42.00 *(978-1-4777-1938-1(5),* Rosen Classroom) Rosen Publishing Group, Inc., The.
Freeman, Christopher. Drawing Stars & Building Polyhedra. 2003. per. 11.95 *(978-1-883055-59-2(8),* 153) Dandy Lion Pubns.
Freudenthal. Triangles & Patchwork. 3rd ed. 2003. (Math in Context Ser.). (Illus.). 7.86 *(978-0-03-071711-6(6))* Holt McDougal.
Furstinger, Nancy. Cones. 2014. (3-D Shapes Ser.). (ENG.). 24p. (J). (gr. 1-4). 27.07 *(978-1-62323-981-7(8),* 206760) Child's World, Inc., The.
—Cubes. 2014. (3-D Shapes Ser.). (ENG.). 24p. (J). (gr. 1-4). 27.07 *(978-1-62323-982-4(6),* 206761) Child's World, Inc., The.
—Cylinders. 2014. (3-D Shapes Ser.). (ENG.). 24p. (J). (gr. 1-4). 27.07 *(978-1-62323-983-1(4),* 206762) Child's World, Inc., The.

—Discovering Cones. 2016. (J). *(978-1-4896-4971-3(9))* Weigl Pubs., Inc.
—Discovering Cubes. 2016. (J). *(978-1-4896-4974-4(3))* Weigl Pubs., Inc.
—Discovering Cylinders. 2016. (J). *(978-1-4896-4980-5(8))* Weigl Pubs., Inc.
—Discovering Prisms. 2016. (J). *(978-1-4896-4977-5(8))* Weigl Pubs., Inc.
—Discovering Pyramids. 2016. (J). *(978-1-4896-4983-6(2))* Weigl Pubs., Inc.
—Discovering Spheres. 2016. (J). *(978-1-4896-4986-7(7))* Weigl Pubs., Inc.
—Prisms. 2014. (3-D Shapes Ser.). (ENG.). 24p. (J). (gr. 1-4). 27.07 *(978-1-62323-984-8(2),* 206763) Child's World, Inc., The.
—Pyramids. 2014. (3-D Shapes Ser.). (ENG.). 24p. (J). (gr. 1-4). 27.07 *(978-1-62323-985-5(0),* 206764) Child's World, Inc., The.
—Spheres. 2014. (3-D Shapes Ser.). (ENG.). 24p. (J). (gr. 1-4). 27.07 *(978-1-62323-986-2(9),* 206765) Child's World, Inc., The.
Furstinger, Nancy & Willis, John. Cones. 2016. (J). ***(978-1-5105-1987-9(4))*** SmartBook Media, Inc.
—Cubes. 2016. (J). ***(978-1-5105-1989-3(0))*** SmartBook Media, Inc.
—Cylinders. 2016. (J). ***(978-1-5105-1991-6(2))*** SmartBook Media, Inc.
—Pyramids. 2016. (J). ***(978-1-5105-1993-0(9))*** SmartBook Media, Inc.
—Spheres. 2016. (J). ***(978-1-5105-1995-4(5))*** SmartBook Media, Inc.
Gateways to Algebra & Geometry, an Integrated Approach: Multi-Language Glossary. 2003. *(978-0-618-10650-9(2),* 2-61315) Holt McDougal.
Geometry: Concepts & Skills: EEdition. 2003. (gr. 6-12). cd-rom *(978-0-618-43975-1(7),* 2-05844) Holt McDougal.
George, Bobby & George, June. Montessori - Shape Work. Nassner, Alyssa, illus. 2013. (Montessori Ser.). (ENG.). 18p. (J). (gr. -1-k). bds. 9.95 *(978-1-4197-0935-7(6),* Abrams Appleseed) Abrams, Inc.
George, Lynn. Teotihuacan: Designing an Ancient Mexican City: Calculating Perimeters & Areas of Squares & Rectangles. (PowerMath Ser.). 32p. 2009. (ENG., Illus.). (gr. 4-5). pap. 10.00 *(978-0-8239-8876-1(7))* 2009. (gr. 4-5). 47.90 *(978-1-60851-400-7(5))* 2004. (Illus.). (J). lib. bdg. 25.25 *(978-0-8239-8983-6(6))* Rosen Publishing Group, Inc., The. (PowerKids Pr.).
Ginsburg, Herbert P., et al. Favorite Shapes. 2003. (Illus.). 9.95 *(978-0-7690-3043-2(2))* Seymour, Dale Pubns.
Gorini, Catherine A. The Geometry. 2nd rev. ed. 2009. (Science Handbks.). (Illus.). 342p. (gr. 6-12). instr.'s hndbk. ed. 40.00 *(978-0-8160-7389-4(9))* Facts On File, Inc.
Hall, Pamela. Rectangles, 1 vol. Holm, Sharon, illus. 2007. (Shapes Ser.). (ENG.). 24p. (gr. -1-2). 27.07 *(978-1-60270-046-8(X),* Looking Glass Library- Nonfiction) Magic Wagon.
—Squares, 1 vol. Holm, Sharon, illus. 2007. (Shapes Ser.). (ENG.). 24p. (gr. -1-2). 27.07 *(978-1-60270-047-5(8),* Looking Glass Library- Nonfiction) Magic Wagon.
Hamilton, Laura. Cones, 1 vol. Mitter, Kathryn, illus. 2012. (Everyday 3-D Shapes Ser.). (ENG.). 24p. (J). (gr. -1-2). lib. bdg. 27.07 *(978-1-61641-872-4(9),* Looking Glass Library) Magic Wagon.
—Cubes, 1 vol. Mitter, Kathryn, illus. 2012. (Everyday 3-D Shapes Ser.). (ENG.). 24p. (J). (gr. -1-2). lib. bdg. 27.07 *(978-1-61641-873-1(7),* Looking Glass Library) Magic Wagon.
—Cylinders, 1 vol. Mitter, Kathryn, illus. 2012. (Everyday 3-D Shapes Ser.). (ENG.). 24p. (J). (gr. -1-2). lib. bdg. 27.07 *(978-1-61641-874-8(5),* Looking Glass Library) Magic Wagon.
—Prisms, 1 vol. Mitter, Kathryn, illus. 2012. (Everyday 3-D Shapes Ser.). (ENG.). 24p. (J). (gr. -1-2). lib. bdg. 27.07 *(978-1-61641-875-5(3),* Looking Glass Library) Magic Wagon.
—Pyramids, 1 vol. Mitter, Kathryn, illus. 2012. (Everyday 3-D Shapes Ser.). (ENG.). 24p. (J). (gr. -1-2). lib. bdg. 27.07 *(978-1-61641-876-2(1),* Looking Glass Library) Magic Wagon.
—Spheres, 1 vol. Mitter, Kathryn, illus. 2012. (Everyday 3-D Shapes Ser.). (ENG.). 24p. (J). (gr. -1-2). lib. bdg. 27.07 *(978-1-61641-877-9(X),* Looking Glass Library) Magic Wagon.
Hanson, Anders. What in the World Is a Cone?, 1 vol. 2008. (3-D Shapes Ser.). (ENG., Illus.). 24p. (J). (gr. k-3). 24.21 *(978-1-59928-886-4(9),* SandCastle) ABDO Publishing Co.
—What in the World Is a Cube?, 1 vol. 2008. (3-D Shapes Ser.). (ENG., Illus.). 24p. (J). (gr. k-3). 24.21 *(978-1-59928-887-1(7),* SandCastle) ABDO Publishing Co.
—What in the World Is a Cylinder?, 1 vol. 2008. (3-D Shapes Ser.). (ENG., Illus.). 24p. (J). (gr. k-3). 24.21 *(978-1-59928-888-8(5),* SandCastle) ABDO Publishing Co.
—What in the World Is a Prism?, 1 vol. 2008. (3-D Shapes Ser.). (ENG., Illus.). 24p. (J). (gr. k-3). 24.21 *(978-1-59928-889-5(3),* SandCastle) ABDO Publishing Co.
—What in the World Is a Pyramid?, 1 vol. 2008. (3-D Shapes Ser.). (ENG., Illus.). 24p. (J). (gr. k-3). 24.21 *(978-1-59928-890-1(7),* SandCastle) ABDO Publishing Co.
—What in the World Is a Sphere?, 1 vol. 2008. (3-D Shapes Ser.). (ENG., Illus.). 24p. (J). (gr. k-3). 24.21 *(978-1-59928-891-8(5),* SandCastle) ABDO Publishing Co.
Hanson, Anders & Mann, Elissa. Cool Flexagon Art: Creative Activities That Make Math & Science Fun for Kids!, 1 vol. 2013. (Cool Art with Math & Science Ser.). (ENG.). 32p. (J). (gr. 3-6). lib. bdg. 28.50 *(978-1-61783-821-7(7),* Checkerboard Library) ABDO Publishing Co.
—Cool String Art: Creative Activities That Make Math & Science Fun for Kids!, 1 vol. 2013. (Cool Art with Math & Science Ser.). (ENG.). 32p. (J). (gr. 3-6). lib. bdg. 28.50 *(978-1-61783-824-8(1),* Checkerboard Library) ABDO Publishing Co.
—Cool Structures: Creative Activities That Make Math & Science Fun for Kids!, 1 vol. 2013. (Cool Art with Math & Science Ser.). (ENG.). 32p. (J). (gr. 3-6). lib. bdg. 28.50 *(978-1-61783-825-5(X),* Checkerboard Library) ABDO Publishing Co.
Harbo, Christopher L. Shapes. Banks, Timothy, illus. 2013. (Wizard of Oz Ser.). (ENG.). 24p. (gr. 1-2). 27.99 *(978-1-4765-3767-2(4))* Capstone Press of Coughlan Cos.
Harcourt, creator. I Know Shapes: Math Concept Reader. 2007. (Illus.). (J). pap. 31.53 *(978-0-15-379896-2(3))* Houghton Mifflin Harcourt School Pubs.
Harrison, Lorraine. Flat Shapes, Solid Shapes: Identify & Describe Shapes. 2013. (Rosen Math Readers Ser.). (ENG.). 16p. (J). (gr. k-1). pap. 42.00 *(978-1-4777-1615-1(7))*; (Illus.). pap. 7.00 *(978-1-4777-1614-4(9))* Rosen Publishing Group, Inc., The. (Rosen Classroom).
Harrison, Micah. Perimeters of Ancient Buildings: Recognize Perimeter. 2014. (Rosen Common Core Math Readers Ser.). (ENG.). 24p. (J). (gr. 3-4). pap. 8.25 *(978-1-4777-4888-6(1),* Rosen Classroom) Rosen Publishing Group, Inc., The.
Hayhurst, Chris. Euclid: The Great Geometer. 2009. (Library of Greek Philosophers Ser.). 112p. (gr. 6-6). 66.50 *(978-1-60853-659-7(9),* Rosen Reference) Rosen Publishing Group, Inc., The.
Hein, Marilyn B. Math Phonic(tm) Pre-Geometry. 2003. (Illus.). 96p. pap. 10.95 *(978-1-57310-406-7(X))* Teaching & Learning Co.
Heinze, Monica Bacon. A Day with Shapes. Dow, S. B., illus. 2004. (J). *(978-0-9761710-0-3(7))* Paisley Publishing.
Hightower, Paul. The Father of Geometry: Euclid & His 3-D World. 2010. (Great Minds of Ancient Science & Math Ser.). 112p. (J). 33.27 *(978-0-7660-3409-9(7))* Enslow Pubs., Inc.
Hoena, Blake. Circles & Crescents: A Song about Drawing with Shapes. Palin, Tim, illus. 2017. (Sing & Draw! Ser.). (ENG.). 24p. (gr. 1-3). 33.99 ***(978-1-68410-015-6(1))*** Cantata Learning.
—Rectangles & Triangles: A Song about Drawing with Shapes. Palin, Tim, illus. 2017. (Sing & Draw! Ser.). (ENG.). 24p. (gr. 1-3). 33.99 ***(978-1-68410-047-7(X))*** Cantata Learning.
Holt, Rinehart and Winston Staff. Holt Geometry 2003: South Carolina Practice Workbook. 3rd ed. 2003. pap. 9.60 *(978-0-03-069036-5(6))* Holt McDougal.
—Standart Test Practice Workbook: South Carolina Edition - Geometry. 3rd ed. 2003. pap. 13.26 *(978-0-03-069032-7(3))* Holt McDougal.
Hoover, Melanie. Name the Missing Shape: Analyze, Compare, Create, & Compose Shapes. 2013. (InfoMax Math Readers Ser.). (ENG.). 16p. (J). (gr. k-1). pap. 7.00 *(978-1-4777-1964-0(4))*; pap. 42.00 *(978-1-4777-1965-7(2))* Rosen Publishing Group, Inc., The. (Rosen Classroom).
Hudson, Finn. Mowing for Money: Relate Area to Multiplication & to Addition. 2014. (Rosen Common Core Math Readers Ser.). (ENG.). 24p. (J). (gr. 3-4). pap. 8.25 *(978-1-4777-4891-6(1),* Rosen Classroom) Rosen Publishing Group, Inc., The.
In Step with the Standards - Geometry Concept. 2005. (J). spiral bd. 15.95 *(978-1-58123-379-7(5))* Larson Learning, Inc.
Jednik, Alice. What Does It Look Like? 2012. (InfoMax Readers Ser.). (ENG., Illus.). 16 pp.p. (J). (gr. k-1). pap. 7.00 *(978-1-4488-8974-7(X),* Rosen Classroom) Rosen Publishing Group, Inc., The.
Johnson, Rebecca L. Sizing up Shapes. 2007. (Reading Expeditions Ser.). (ENG., Illus.). 24p. (J). pap. 14.95 *(978-0-7922-4589-6(X))* CENGAGE Learning.
Joyce, Jeffrey. Pablo's Paper Crafts. 2013. (Core Math Skills: Measurement & Geometry Ser.). (Illus.). 24p. (J). (gr. 1-2). 22.60 *(978-1-4777-2232-9(7),* 1359255, Rosen Classroom) Rosen Publishing Group, Inc., The.
—Pablo's Paper Crafts: Shapes & Their Attributes. 2013. (Rosen Math Readers Ser.). (ENG., Illus.). 24p. (J). (gr. 1-2). pap. 8.25 *(978-1-4777-2049-3(9),* 1359255); pap. 49.50 *(978-1-4777-2050-9(2),* 1359255) Rosen Publishing Group, Inc., The. (Rosen Classroom).
Kalman, Bobbie. My Toys Have Shapes. 2010. (ENG., Illus.). 16p. (J). (gr. k-2). *(978-0-7787-9413-4(X))*; pap. *(978-0-7787-9457-8(1))* Crabtree Publishing Co.
—¿Qué forma Tiene? 2008. (SPA & ENG., Illus.). 24p. (J). lib. bdg. *(978-0-7787-8728-0(1))* Crabtree Publishing Co.
—¿Qué Forma Tiene? 2008. (SPA & ENG., Illus.). 24p. (J). pap. *(978-0-7787-8737-2(0))* Crabtree Publishing Co.
Kautza, Jeremy. Geometry Student Activity Book. Matthews, Douglas L., ed. 2003. (Illus.). stu. ed., act. bk. ed. *(978-1-931680-49-3(3),* 25, Expert Systems for Teachers) Teaching Point, Inc.
Killian, Pat. Put It Together: Analyze, Compare, Create, & Compose Shapes. 2013. (Rosen Math Readers Ser.). (ENG.). 16p. (J). (gr. k-1). pap. 7.00 *(978-1-4777-1674-8(2))*; pap. 42.00 *(978-1-4777-1675-5(0))* Rosen Publishing Group, Inc., The. (Rosen Classroom).
King, Zelda. Try it with Triangles: Learning to Put Triangles Together to Form Other Shapes. 2004. (Math Big Bookstm Ser.). (ENG.). 16p. (gr. 2-3). 37.95 *(978-0-8239-7641-6(6))* Rosen Publishing Group, Inc., The.
—Try It with Triangles: Learning to Put Triangles Together to Form Other Shapes. 2009. (Math for the REAL World Ser.). 16p. (gr. 2-3). pap. 7.05 *(978-0-8239-8873-0(2),* Rosen Classroom) Rosen Publishing Group, Inc., The.
Kingfisher Editors, ed. Puzzling Puzzles: What Shape Is This? Book + 2004. (J). pap. 7.95 *(978-0-7534-5644-6(3))* Kingfisher Bks.
Kishel, Ann-Marie & Rivera, Sheila. Hexagon. 2007. (First Step Nonfiction - Shapes Ser.). (ENG.). 8p. (gr. -1-1). pap. 4.95 *(978-0-8225-6857-5(8))* Lerner Publishing Group.
—Oval. 2007. (First Step Nonfiction - Shapes Ser.). (ENG.). 8p. (gr. -1-1). pap. 4.95 *(978-0-8225-6858-2(6))* Lerner Publishing Group.
—Trapezoid. 2007. (First Step Nonfiction - Shapes Ser.). (ENG., Illus.). 8p. (gr. -1-1). pap. 4.95 *(978-0-8225-6856-8(X))* Lerner Publishing Group.
Koizim, Jessica. Geometry. 2004. (BrainBuilders Ser.). (ENG.). 48p. (gr. k-4). pap. 5.25 *(978-1-4042-8529-3(6))* Rosen Publishing Group, Inc., The.
Kompelien, Tracy. 2-D Shapes Are Behind the Drapes!, 1 vol. 2007. (Math Made Fun Ser.). (ENG., Illus.). 24p. (J). (gr. k-3). lib. bdg. 24.21 *(978-1-59928-507-8(X),* SandCastle) ABDO Publishing Co.
—3-D Shapes Are Like Green Grapes!, 1 vol. 2007. (Math Made Fun Ser.). (ENG., Illus.). 24p. (J). (gr. k-3). lib. bdg. 24.21 *(978-1-59928-509-2(6),* SandCastle) ABDO Publishing Co.
Lacey, Saskia. Art & Culture: The Stories of Constellations: Shapes (Grade 3) 2017. (Mathematics Readers Ser.). (Illus.). 32p. (J). (gr. 3-3). 8.99 ***(978-1-4807-5812-4(4))*** Teacher Created Materials, Inc.
Larson, Roland E. Passport to Algebra & Geometry: (c)2004. l.t. ed. 2004. (McDougal Littell Math Ser.). (YA). (gr. 6-9). stu. ed. *(978-0-618-37422-9(1),* 2-05530) Holt McDougal.
Lawrence, Elizabeth. I See Circles. 2015. (J). lib. bdg. *(978-1-62713-495-8(6))*; (ENG.). 24p. (gr. 1-1). pap. 8.22 *(978-1-5026-0263-3(6))* Cavendish Square Publishing.
—I See Ovals. 2015. (J). lib. bdg. *(978-1-62713-498-9(0))*; (ENG.). 24p. (gr. 1-1). 24.21 *(978-1-5026-0264-0(4))* Cavendish Square Publishing.
—I See Rectangles. 2015. (J). lib. bdg. *(978-1-62713-501-6(4))*; (ENG.). 24p. (gr. 1-1). pap. 8.22 *(978-1-5026-0259-6(8))* Cavendish Square Publishing.
Leech, Bonnie. Geometry's Great Thinkers: The History of Geometry. 2009. (PowerMath: Advanced Proficiency Plus Ser.). 32p. (gr. 5-5). 47.90 *(978-1-60851-355-0(6),* PowerKids Pr.) Rosen Publishing Group, Inc., The.
Leech, Bonnie Coulter. Circles & Spheres. 2009. (Exploring Shapes Ser.). 24p. (gr. 2-3). 42.50 *(978-1-61512-369-8(5),* PowerKids Pr.) Rosen Publishing Group, Inc., The.
—Geometry's Great Thinkers: The History of Geometry. (Math for the Real World Ser.). (Illus.). 32p. 2009. (ENG.). (gr. 6-7). pap. 10.00 *(978-1-4042-6073-3(0))* 2006. (YA). (gr. 5-9). lib. bdg. 25.25 *(978-1-4042-3360-7(1))* Rosen Publishing Group, Inc., The.
—Polygons. 2009. (Exploring Shapes Ser.). 24p. (gr. 2-3). 42.50 *(978-1-61512-370-4(9),* PowerKids Pr.) Rosen Publishing Group, Inc., The.
—Prisms. 2009. (Exploring Shapes Ser.). 24p. (gr. 2-3). 42.50 *(978-1-61512-371-1(7),* PowerKids Pr.) Rosen Publishing Group, Inc., The.
—Quadrilaterals. 2009. (Exploring Shapes Ser.). 24p. (gr. 2-3). 42.50 *(978-1-61512-375-9(X),* PowerKids Pr.) Rosen Publishing Group, Inc., The.
Levy, Janey. Islamic Art: Recognizing Geometric Ideas in Art. (Math for the Real World Ser.). 32p. 2009. (ENG., Illus.). (gr. 6-7). pap. 10.00 *(978-1-4042-6081-8(1))* 2009. (gr. 5-5). 47.90 *(978-1-60851-360-4(2),* PowerKids Pr.) 2006. (ENG.). (gr. 6-7). 47.50 *(978-1-4042-6367-3(5))* 2006. (Illus.). (YA). (gr. 5-9). lib. bdg. 25.25 *(978-1-4042-3364-5(4))* Rosen Publishing Group, Inc., The.
Linde, Barbara M. Origami: Identifying Right Angles in Geometric Figures. (PowerMath Ser.). 24p. 2009. (ENG., Illus.). (gr. 3-4). pap. 8.25 *(978-0-8239-8882-2(1))* 2009. (gr. 3-4). 45.00 *(978-1-60851-382-6(3))* 2004. (Illus.). (J). lib. bdg. 22.50 *(978-0-8239-8968-3(2))* Rosen Publishing Group, Inc., The. (PowerKids Pr.).
Long, Dorian. What Are Polygons? Reason with Shapes & Their Attributes. 2014. (Math Masters: Geometry Ser.). 24p. (J). (gr. 2-3). 23.60 *(978-1-4777-6409-1(7))*; (ENG.). pap. 8.25 *(978-1-4777-4882-4(2))* Rosen Publishing Group, Inc., The. (Rosen Classroom).
Long, Ethan. The Wing Wing Brothers Geometry Palooza! Long, Ethan, illus. 2014. (ENG., Illus.). 32p. (J). (gr. -1-1). 15.95 *(978-0-8234-2951-6(2))* Holiday Hse., Inc.
Long, Lynette. Painless Geometry. 2nd rev. ed. 2009. (Painless Ser.). (ENG., Illus.). 320p. pap. 9.99 *(978-0-7641-4230-7(5))* Barron's Educational Series, Inc.
Lorbiecki, Marybeth. Circles. (Shapes Site-based CD Ser.). 24p. (J). lib. bdg. 57.07 *(978-1-60270-491-6(0))* ABDO Publishing Co.
—Circles, 1 vol. Holm, Sharon, illus. 2007. (Shapes Ser.). (ENG.). 24p. (gr. -1-2). 27.07 *(978-1-60270-043-7(5),* Looking Glass Library- Nonfiction) Magic Wagon.
—Triangles, 1 vol. Holm, Sharon, illus. 2007. (Shapes Ser.). (ENG.). 24p. (gr. -1-2). 27.07 *(978-1-60270-048-2(6),* Looking Glass Library- Nonfiction) Magic Wagon.
Loughran, Donna. Look for Them. 2013. (IMath Ser.). (Illus.). 24p. (J). (gr. k-2). pap. 11.94 *(978-1-60357-489-1(1))* Norwood Hse. Pr.
—Look for Them: Where Are the Shapes? 2013. (IMath Ser.). (Illus.). 24p. (J). (gr. k-2). lib. bdg. 21.27 *(978-1-59953-550-0(5))* Norwood Hse. Pr.
—Ship Shape: Making Shapes Fly. 2013. (IMath Ser.). (Illus.). 24p. (J). (gr. k-2). pap. 11.94 *(978-1-60357-493-8(X))*; lib. bdg. 21.27 *(978-1-59953-554-8(8))* Norwood Hse. Pr.
Loughrey, Anita. Ciries. 2011. (ENG., Illus.). 24p. (J). pap. 8.95 *(978-1-77092-003-3(X))* Saunders Bk. Co. CAN. Dist: RiverStream Publishing.
—Rectangles. 2011. (ENG., Illus.). 24p. (J). pap. 8.95 *(978-1-77092-004-0(8))* Saunders Bk. Co. CAN. Dist: RiverStream Publishing.
—Squares. 2011. (ENG., Illus.). 24p. (J). 8.95 *(978-1-77092-005-7(6))* Saunders Bk. Co. CAN. Dist: RiverStream Publishing.
—Triangles. 2011. (ENG., Illus.). 24p. (J). pap. 8.95 *(978-1-77092-006-4(4))* Saunders Bk. Co. CAN. Dist: RiverStream Publishing.
Lucas, Bruce. Drawing Shapes: Shapes & Their Attributes. 2013. (InfoMax Math Readers Ser.). (ENG.). 24p. (J). (gr. 1-2). pap. 49.50 *(978-1-4777-2149-0(5))*; pap. 8.25 *(978-1-4777-2148-3(7))* Rosen Publishing Group, Inc., The. (Rosen Classroom).
Luz, Oscar. Payton's Plane Figures: Understand Concepts of Area. 2014. (Rosen Common Core Math Readers Ser.). (ENG.). 24p. (J). (gr. 3-4). pap. 8.25 *(978-1-4777-4898-5(9),* Rosen Classroom) Rosen Publishing Group, Inc., The.
Margaritas, Aki. Investigations in Geometry Using Cabri(r) Jr. & the Graphing Calculator. 2004. 50p. pap. 14.95 net. *(978-1-58108-048-3(4),* 1-58108-048-4) Pencil Point Pr., Inc.
Marrewa, Jennifer. Making a Model with Solid Figures. 2008. (Math in Our World - Level 2 Ser.). 24p. (gr. 1-4). pap. 8.15 *(978-0-8368-9014-3(0))*; (Illus.). lib. bdg. 22.00 *(978-0-8368-9005-1(1))* Stevens, Gareth Publishing LLLP. (Weekly Reader Leveled Readers).
—Vamos a Hacer una Maqueta con Figuras Solidas. 2008. (Las Matemáticas en Nuestro Mundo Ser.). (SPA.). 24p. (gr. 1-4). pap. 8.15 *(978-0-8368-9032-7(9))*; (Illus.). lib. bdg. 22.00 *(978-0-8368-9023-5(X))* Stevens, Gareth Publishing LLLP. (Weekly Reader Leveled Readers).
Math Forum Staff. Dr. Math Presents More Geometry: Learning Geometry Is Easy! Just Ask Dr. Math. 2004. (ENG., Illus.). 192p. pap. 17.00 *(978-0-471-22553-9(3),* Jossey-Bass) Wiley, John & Sons, Inc.
Mazurkiewicz, Jessica. Magnificent Mosaics. 2009. (Dover Design Coloring Bks.). (ENG., Illus.). 32p. (J). (gr. 1-5). pap. 3.99 *(978-0-486-46989-8(1))* Dover Pubns., Inc.
McDougal Littell Geometry: EEdition Plus Online with Print Purchase - 1 Year. 2004. (gr. 6-12). *(978-0-618-39820-1(1),* 2-05650) Holt McDougal.
McDougal Littell Geometry: EEdition Plus Online without print purchase - 6 Years. 2004. (gr. 6-12). *(978-0-618-39643-6(8),* 2-05630) Holt McDougal.
McDougal Littell Geometry: Exercises in Spanish. 2004. (McDougal Littell Math Ser.). (gr. 6-12). *(978-0-618-37053-5(6),* 2-06337) Holt McDougal.
McDougal-Littell Publishing Staff. Geometry: Concepts & Skills: Notetaking Guide. 2003. (Geometry: Concepts & Skills Ser.). (ENG.). 304p. (gr. 9-12). pap. 4.90 *(978-0-618-41063-7(5),* 2-05719) Great Source Education Group, Inc.
McGraw-Hill Education Staff. Geometry: Concepts & Applications. 2005. (GEOMETRY: CONCEPTS & APPLIC Ser.). (ENG., Illus.). 878p. (gr. 9-12). stu. ed. 110.72 *(978-0-07-868172-1(3),* 0078681723) McGraw-Hill Higher Education.
McGraw-Hill Staff. Glencoe Geometry: Concepts & Applications. 3rd ed. 2003. (GEOMETRY: CONCEPTS & APPLIC Ser.). (ENG.). 864p. (gr. 9-12). stu. ed. 109.80 *(978-0-07-845773-9(4),* 0078457734) McGraw-Hill Education.
McKay, Chelsea. A Tangram ABC: Shaping the Alphabet from an Ancient Chinese Puzzle. Firos, Daphne, illus. 2013. 60p. (J). pap. 13.95 *(978-1-939431-04-2(2))* MathWord Pr., LLC.
Meachen Rau, Dana. Circles. 2006. (Bookworms Ser.). (Illus.). 24p. (gr. k-1). lib. bdg. 15.95 *(978-0-7614-2280-8(3),* Benchmark Bks.) Marshall Cavendish Corp.
—Many-Sided Shapes. 2006. (Bookworms Ser.). (Illus.). 24p. (gr. k-1). lib. bdg. 15.95 *(978-0-7614-2279-2(X),* Benchmark Bks.) Marshall Cavendish Corp.
—Ovals. 2006. (Bookworms Ser.). (Illus.). 24p. (gr. k-1). lib. bdg. 15.95 *(978-0-7614-2281-5(1),* Benchmark Bks.) Marshall Cavendish Corp.
—Rectangles: The Shape of the World. 2006. (Bookworms Ser.). (Illus.). 24p. (gr. k-1). lib. bdg. 15.95 *(978-0-7614-2282-2(X),* Benchmark Bks.) Marshall Cavendish Corp.
—Squares. 2006. (Bookworms Ser.). (Illus.). 24p. (gr. k-1). lib. bdg. 15.95 *(978-0-7614-2284-6(6),* Benchmark Bks.) Marshall Cavendish Corp.
—Triangles. 2006. (Bookworms Ser.). (Illus.). 24p. (gr. k-1). lib. bdg. 15.95 *(978-0-7614-2286-0(2),* Benchmark Bks.) Marshall Cavendish Corp.
Measurement & Geometry. 2003. Level C. tchr. ed. 19.50 *(978-0-7652-1317-4(6))*Level C. stu. ed. 14.50 *(978-0-7652-1305-1(2))*Level D. tchr. ed. 19.50 *(978-0-7652-1321-1(4))*Level D. stu. ed. 14.50 *(978-0-7652-1309-9(5))*Level E. tchr. ed. 19.50 *(978-0-7652-1325-9(7))*Level E. stu. ed. 14.50 *(978-0-7652-1313-6(3))* Modern Curriculum Pr.
Migachyov, Dina & Migachyov, Larisa. Equations in Geometry: How to Make Your Child Successful in Math. Migachyov, Larisa, ed. 2004. (Illus.). 267p. per. 29.99 *(978-0-9672535-4-1(3))* Quaternion Pr.
Miller, Reagan & Berry, Minta. Perimeter. 2011. (ENG.). 24p. (J). lib. bdg. *(978-0-7787-5276-9(3))* Crabtree Publishing Co.
Minden, Cecilia. Shapes Everywhere. 2010. (21st Century Basic Skills Library: Measurements Ser.). (ENG.). 24p. (gr. k-3). lib. bdg. 22.79 *(978-1-60279-850-2(8),* 200566) Cherry Lake Publishing.
Mitten, Luana K. Three Dimensional Shapes: Cones. 2008. (Concepts Ser.). (Illus.). 24p. (J). (gr. -1-k). lib. bdg. 22.79 *(978-1-60472-415-8(3))* Rourke Educational Media.
Murphy, Stuart J. Hamster Champs. Martin, Pedro, illus. 2005. (MathStart 3 Ser.). (ENG.). 40p. (J). (gr. 2). pap. 5.99 *(978-0-06-055773-7(7))* HarperCollins Pubs.
Nelson, Robin. Playing Safely. 2005. (Pull Ahead Books: Health Ser.). (ENG., Illus.). 32p. (gr. k-3). lib. bdg. 22.60 *(978-0-8225-2632-2(8))* Lerner Publishing Group.
Nelson, Seth. We Love Art Class! Analyze, Compare, Create, & Compose Shapes. 2013. (InfoMax Math Readers Ser.). (ENG.). 16p. (J). (gr. k-1). pap. 7.00 *(978-1-4777-1934-3(2))*; pap. 42.00 *(978-1-4777-1935-0(0))* Rosen Publishing Group, Inc., The. (Rosen Classroom).
Neuschwander, Cindy. Sir Cumference & the Isle of Immeter. Geehan, Wayne, illus. 2006. (Math Adventures Ser.). (ENG.). 32p. (J). (gr. 3-7). per. 7.95 *(978-1-57091-681-6(0))* Charlesbridge Publishing, Inc.
Newland, Sonya. Doodle Yourself Smart... Geometry. 2012. (Doodle Bks.). (ENG., Illus.). 128p. pap. 12.95 *(978-1-60710-440-7(7),* Thunder Bay Pr.) Readerlink Distribution Services, LLC.
O'Donnell, Kerri. Space Circles: Learning about Radius & Diameter. 2004. (Math for the REAL World Ser.). (ENG.). 32p. (gr. 4-5). 47.50 *(978-0-8239-7651-5(3))* Rosen Publishing Group, Inc., The.
O'Donoghue, Sean. Create a Quilt: Understand Concepts of Area. 2014. (Rosen Common Core Math Readers Ser.). (ENG., Illus.). 24p. (J). (gr. 3-4). pap. 8.25 *(978-1-4777-4894-7(6),* Rosen Classroom) Rosen Publishing Group, Inc., The.
Olson, Nathan. Esferas/Spheres, 1 vol. Strictly Spanish, LLC., tr. 2012. (Figuras en 3-D/3-d Shapes Ser.). (MUL & ENG.). 32p. (gr. 1-2). lib. bdg. 27.32 *(978-1-4296-9211-3(1),* A+ Bilingue/Bilingual) Capstone Press of Coughlan Cos.
Passport to Algebra & Geometry. 2004. (gr. 6-12). stu. ed. *(978-0-618-18596-2(8),* 2-05508); stu. ed. *(978-0-395-87988-7(4),* 2-77610) Holt McDougal.
Passport to Algebra & Geometry: Practice Workbook. 2004. (gr. 6-12). (SPA.). *(978-0-395-90160-1(X),* 2-77865); stu. ed., wbk. ed. *(978-0-395-89670-9(3),* 2-77742) Holt McDougal.
Pelli, Tammy. Circles: Relationships with Segments & Angles. 2004. (Studies in Geometry Ser.). (ENG.). 64p. (YA). (gr. 7). pap., wbk. ed. 10.95 *(978-1-930820-45-6(3))* Garlic Pr.
—Proofs: Reasoning with Mathematics. 2004. (Studies in Geometry Ser.). (ENG.). 64p. (gr. 7). pap., wbk. ed. 11.95 *(978-1-930820-46-3(1))* Garlic Pr.
—Triangles: Calculating Measurements & Rations. 2004. (Studies in Geometry Ser.). (ENG.). 64p. (J). (gr. 4-7). pap., wbk. ed. 10.95 *(978-1-930820-44-9(5))* Garlic Pr.

Penn, M. W. 2 Lines. Firos, Daphne, illus. 2011. (ENG.). 32p. (J). pap. 11.95 (978-0-9840425-0-0(4)) MathWord Pr., LLC.
Penn, Shelly. The Geoma Tree. 2013. 24p. pap. 10.95 (978-1-4908-1007-2(2), WestBow Pr.) Author Solutions, Inc.
Perritano, John. Start the Game: Geometry in Sports. 2013. (IMath Ser.). (Illus.). 32p. (J). (gr. 3-4). lib. bdg. 22.60 (978-1-59953-563-0(7)) Norwood Hse. Pr.
—A Toy Store Summer: Finding Area. 2013. (IMath Ser.). 32p. (J). (gr. 3-4). lib. bdg. 22.60 (978-1-59953-565-4(3)) Norwood Hse. Pr.
Piddock, Claire. Lines, Segments, Rays, & Angles. 2010. (ENG., Illus.). 24p. (J). (978-0-7787-5245-5(3)); pap. (978-0-7787-5292-9(5)) Crabtree Publishing Co.
—Slides, Flips, & Turns. 2010. (ENG., Illus.). 24p. (J). (978-0-7787-5251-6(8)); pap. (978-0-7787-5298-1(4)) Crabtree Publishing Co.
Pistoia, Sara. Patterns. 2016. (J). (978-1-4896-5116-7(0)) Weigl Pubs., Inc.
—Shapes. 2013. (Simply Math Ser.). (ENG.). 24p. (J). (gr. -1-2). 27.07 (978-1-62323-534-5(0), 206340) Child's World, Inc., The.
—Shapes. 2016. (J). (978-1-4896-5119-8(5)) Weigl Pubs., Inc.
Pluckrose, Henry. What Shape Is It? 2006. (Let's Explore, Maths Set Ser.). (Illus.). 32p. (J). (gr. -1-3). lib. bdg. 27.10 (978-1-59771-039-8(3)) Sea-To-Sea Pubns.
Price, Justine. The Class Mural: Reason with Shapes & Their Attributes. 2014. (Math Masters: Geometry Ser.). 24p. (J). (gr. 2-3). 23.60 (978-1-4777-6443-5(7)); (ENG.). pap. 8.25 (978-1-4777-4903-6(9)) Rosen Publishing Group, Inc., The. (Rosen Classroom).
Puritz, Christian. Venture Mathematics Worksheet Geometry: Helping to Stretch the More Able 11 to 16 Year Olds. 2007. (ENG.). 32p. (J). pap. 21.00 (978-1-899618-71-2(6)) Parkwest Pubns., Inc.
Rapoport, Rebecca & Yoder, J. Math Lab for Kids: Fun Projects for Learning about Shapes & Numbers. 2017. (Lab Ser.). (ENG., Illus.). 144p. (J). (gr. 2-5). pap. 24.99 (978-1-63159-252-2(1), Quarry Bks.) Quarto Publishing Group USA.
Rau, Dana Meachen & Meachen, Dana. A Star in My Orange: Looking for Nature's Shapes. 2006. (ENG., Illus.). 32p. (J). (gr. k-2). pap. 6.95 (978-0-8225-5992-4(7), First Avenue Editions) Lerner Publishing Group.
Ribke, Simone T. The Shapes We Eat. 2004. (Rookie Read-About Math Ser.). (J). 20.50 (978-0-516-24431-0(0), Children's Pr.) Scholastic Library Publishing.
Richardson, Erik. Applying Geometry to Everyday Life. 2016. (Applied Mathematics Ser.). (ENG., Illus.). 128p. (J). (gr. 9-9). 45.64 (978-1-5026-1971-6(7)) Cavendish Square Publishing.
Rigby Education Staff. Shapes. (Illus.). 8p. (J). bds. 3.95 (978-0-7635-6440-7(0), 764400C99) Rigby Education.
Riley, Matt. Making Shapes: Analyze, Compare, Create, & Compose Shapes. 2013. (Rosen Math Readers Ser.). (ENG.). 16p. (J). (gr. k-1). pap. 42.00 (978-1-4777-1657-1(2)); (Illus.). pap. 7.00 (978-1-4777-1656-4(4)) Rosen Publishing Group, Inc., The. (Rosen Classroom).
Rivera, Sheila. Compass. 2007. (First Step Nonfiction - Simple Tools Ser.). (ENG., Illus.). 8p. (gr. -1-1). pap. 4.95 (978-0-8225-6852-0(7)) Lerner Publishing Group.
—Pentagon. 2007. (First Step Nonfiction - Shapes Ser.). (ENG.). 8p. (gr. -1-1). pap. 4.95 (978-0-8225-6859-9(4)) Lerner Publishing Group.
—Rhombus. 2007. (First Step Nonfiction - Shapes Ser.). (ENG., Illus.). 8p. (gr. -1-1). pap. 4.95 (978-0-8225-6860-5(8)) Lerner Publishing Group.
—What Shape Is It? 2005. (First Step Nonfiction - Properties of Matter Ser.). (ENG.). 8p. (gr. -1-1). pap. 4.95 (978-0-8225-5407-3(0), Lerner Pubns.) Lerner Publishing Group.
Robinson, C. L. MATH1on1 Geometry Foundation. 2006. (YA). per. 9.99 (978-0-9786767-6-6(9)) Robinson, Consuelo.
Robleda, Maria. Jugando con Geometria.Tr. of Playing with Geometry. (SPA.). (J). 4.95 (978-968-6579-18-5(4)) Sistemas Tecnicos de Edicion, S.A. de C.V. MEX. Dist: AIMS International Bks., Inc.
Ross, Catherine Sheldrick. Shapes in Math, Science & Nature: Squares, Triangles & Circles. Slavin, Bill, illus. 2014. (ENG.). 192p. (J). (gr. 4-9). 24.95 (978-1-77138-124-6(8)) Kids Can Pr., Ltd. CAN. Dist: Hachette Bk. Group.
Roy, Jennifer Rozines & Roy, Gregory. Shapes in Transportation. (Math All Around Ser.). (Illus.). 31p. (J). 2007. (gr. 4-7). pap. 6.99 (978-0-7614-3387-3(2)) 2006. (gr. 3-7). lib. bdg. 29.93 (978-0-7614-2265-5(X)) Marshall Cavendish Corp. (Benchmark Bks.).
Roza, Greg. Geometry. 2004. (BrainBuilders Ser.). (ENG.). 48p. (gr. k-4). pap. 9.35 (978-1-4042-8538-5(5)) Rosen Publishing Group, Inc., The.
—Where We Play Sports: Measuring the Perimeters of Polygons. 2009. (PowerMath Ser.). (ENG., Illus.). 24p. (gr. 3-4). pap. 8.25 (978-0-8239-8895-2(3), PowerKids Pr.) Rosen Publishing Group, Inc., The.
Rudenko, Dennis. Planning My Farm: Reason with Shapes & Their Attributes. 2014. (Rosen Common Core Math Readers Ser.). 24p. (J). (gr. 2-3). (ENG.). pap. 49.50 (978-1-4777-4895-4(4), Rosen Classroom); (ENG., Illus.). pap. 8.25 (978-1-4777-4887-9(3), PowerKids Pr.); (Illus.). lib. bdg. 23.60 (978-1-4777-6442-8(9), PowerKids Pr.) Rosen Publishing Group, Inc., The.
Schuette, Sarah L. Círculos: Círculos a Nuestro Alrededor. 2012. (Figuras Geométricas/Shapes Ser.).Tr. of Circles - Seeing Circles All Around Us. (MUL.). 32p. (gr. 1-2). pap. 47.70 (978-1-4296-8528-3(X)); pap. 8.10 (978-1-4296-8527-6(1)) Capstone Press of Coughlan Cos. (A+ Bilingue/Bilingual).
—Cuadrados: Cuadrados a Nuestro Alrededor. 2012. (Figuras Geométricas/Shapes Ser.).Tr. of Squares - Seeing Squares All Around Us. (MUL.). 32p. (gr. 1-2). pap. 47.70 (978-1-4296-8530-6(1)); pap. 8.10 (978-1-4296-8529-0(8)) Capstone Press of Coughlan Cos. (A+ Bilingue/Bilingual).
—Réctangulos: Réctangulos a Nuestro Alrededor. 2010. (Figuras Geométricas/Shapes Ser.).Tr. of Rectangles: Seeing Rectangles All Around Us. (MUL., SPA & ENG.). 32p. (gr. 1-2). lib. bdg. 27.32 (978-1-4296-4586-7(5), A+ Bilingue/Bilingual) Capstone Press of Coughlan Cos.
—Rectángulos: Rectángulos a Nuestro Alrededor. 2012. (Figuras Geométricas/Shapes Ser.).Tr. of Rectangles - Seeing Rectangles All Around Us. (MUL.). 32p. (gr. 1-2). pap. 47.70 (978-1-4296-8532-0(8)); pap. 8.10 (978-1-4296-8531-3(X)) Capstone Press of Coughlan Cos. (A+ Bilingue/Bilingual).
—Triángulos: Triángulos a Nuestro Alrededor. 2012. (Figuras Geométricas/Shapes Ser.).Tr. of Triangles - Seeing Rectangles All Around Us. (MUL.). 32p. (gr. 1-2). pap. 47.70 (978-1-4296-8534-4(4)); pap. 8.10 (978-1-4296-8533-7(6)) Capstone Press of Coughlan Cos. (A+ Bilingue/Bilingual).
Schuh, Mari C. The Crayola Shapes Book. 2017. (Crayola (r) Concepts Ser.). (ENG.). 24p. (J). (gr. -1-3). 26.65 **(978-1-5124-3284-8(9))** Lerner Publishing Group.
Schultz. Geometry: Premier Online Edition. 4th ed. 2003. 19.93 (978-0-03-040423-8(1)) Holt McDougal.
Shepard, Daniel. Solid Shapes. 2005. (Yellow Umbrella Fluent Level Ser.). (ENG.). 16p. (gr. k-1). pap. 35.70 (978-0-7368-5319-4(7), Yellow Umbrella Bks.) Capstone Press of Coughlan Cos.
Shumer, Christine. Can You Find It? Identify & Describe Shapes. 2013. (Rosen Math Readers Ser.). (ENG.). 16p. (J). (gr. k-1). pap. 42.00 (978-1-4777-1648-9(3)); (Illus.). pap. 7.00 (978-1-4777-1647-2(5)) Rosen Publishing Group, Inc., The. (Rosen Classroom).
Sidman, Joyce. Round. Yoo, Taeeun, illus. 2017. (ENG.). 32p. (J). (gr. -1-3). 17.99 (978-0-544-38761-4(9), HMH Books For Young Readers) Houghton Mifflin Harcourt Publishing Co.
Smallwood, Sally & Jones, Bryony. Circle. Fox, Rebecca, illus. 2011. (Shapes Are Fun Ser.). (ENG.). 24p. (J). (gr. k — 1). bds. (978-1-84089-610-7(8)) Zero to Ten, Ltd.
—Rectangle. Fox, Rebecca, illus. 2011. (Shapes Are Fun Ser.). (ENG.). 14p. (J). (gr. k — 1). bds. (978-1-84089-613-8(2)) Zero to Ten, Ltd.
—Triangle. Fox, Rebecca, illus. 2011. (Shapes Are Fun Ser.). (ENG.). 14p. (J). (gr. k — 1). bds. (978-1-84089-611-4(6)) Zero to Ten, Ltd.
Somervill, Barbara A. Distance, Area, & Volume, 1 vol. 2010. (Measure It! Ser.). (ENG., Illus.). 32p. (gr. 3-6). 33.32 (978-1-4329-3763-8(4)); pap. 8.29 (978-1-4329-3769-0(3)) Heinemann-Raintree. (Heinemann InfoSearch).
Stanley, Joseph. Is It Flat or Is It Solid? Identify & Describe Shapes. 2013. (InfoMax Math Readers Ser.). (ENG.). 16p. (J). (gr. k-1). pap. 42.00 (978-1-4777-2001-1(4)); (Illus.). pap. 7.00 (978-1-4777-2000-4(6)) Rosen Publishing Group, Inc., The. (Rosen Classroom).
Steck-Vaughn Staff. Focus on Math Level C: Geometry. 2005. pap. 2.99 (978-1-4190-0270-0(8)) Harcourt Schl. Pubs.
—Focus on Math Level C 10-pack: Geometry. 2005. pap. 29.95 (978-1-4190-0294-6(5)) Harcourt Schl. Pubs.
—Focus on Math Level D: Geometry. 2005. pap. 2.99 (978-1-4190-0276-2(7)) Harcourt Schl. Pubs.
—Focus on Math Level D 10-pack: Geometry. 2005. pap. 29.95 (978-1-4190-0300-4(3)) Harcourt Schl. Pubs.
—Focus on Math Level E: Geometry. 2005. pap. 2.99 (978-1-4190-0281-6(3)) Harcourt Schl. Pubs.
—Focus on Math Level E 10-pack: Geometry. 2005. pap. 29.95 (978-1-4190-0305-9(4)) Harcourt Schl. Pubs.
—Focus on Math Level F: Geometry. 2005. pap. 2.99 (978-1-4190-0286-1(4)) Harcourt Schl. Pubs.
—Focus on Math Level F 10-pack: Geometry. 2005. pap. 29.95 (978-1-4190-0310-3(0)) Harcourt Schl. Pubs.
—Measurement & Geometry. 2004. pap. 14.95 (978-0-7398-9855-0(8)) Harcourt Schl. Pubs.
—Top Line Math: Geometry. 2005. pap. 5.49 (978-1-4190-0373-8(9)) Steck-Vaughn.
Steffora, Tracey. Shapes in the Kitchen, 1 vol. 2011. (Math Around Us Ser.). (ENG.). 24p. (gr. -1-1). 22.65 (978-1-4329-4922-8(5)); pap. 6.29 (978-1-4329-4930-3(6)) Heinemann-Raintree. (Acorn).
—Shapes with Snakes, 1 vol. 2013. (Animal Math Ser.). (ENG.). 24p. (gr. -1-1). 22.65 (978-1-4329-7562-3(5), NA-h) Heinemann-Raintree.
Sterling, Kristin. Subtraction. 2008. (First Step Nonfiction - Early Math Set II Ser.). (ENG.). 8p. (gr. -1-1). pap. 4.95 (978-0-8225-8845-0(5)) Lerner Publishing Group.
Stich, Tim. Paper Crafts: Shapes & Their Attributes. 2013. (InfoMax Math Readers Ser.). (ENG.). 24p. (J). (gr. 1-2). pap. 49.50 (978-1-4777-2143-8(6)); pap. 8.25 (978-1-4777-2142-1(8)) Rosen Publishing Group, Inc., The. (Rosen Classroom).
Suppes, Patrick C. Angles, Bk. 6. Gearhart, George & Rasmussen, Peter, eds. 2012. (Key To... workbooks Ser.: Bk. 6). (ENG.). 56p. (gr. 6-8). spiral bd., wbk. ed. 5.64 (978-0-913684-76-4(7), 0913684767) McGraw-Hill Education.
Suppes, Patrick C. & Curriculum, Key. Key to Geometry - Circles, Bk. 2. Gearhart, George & Rasmussen, Peter, eds. 2012. (Key To... workbooks Ser.: Bk. 2). (ENG.). 56p. (gr. 6-8). spiral bd., wbk. ed. 5.64 (978-0-913684-72-6(4), 0913684724) McGraw-Hill Education.
—Key to Geometry - Perpendiculars, Bk. 4. Gearhart, George & Rasmussen, Peter, eds. 2012. (Key To... workbooks Ser.: Bk. 4). (ENG.). 56p. (gr. 6-8). spiral bd., wbk. ed. 5.64 (978-0-913684-74-0(0), 0913684740) McGraw-Hill Education.
—Key to Geometry - Squares & Rectangles, Bk. 5. Gearhart, George & Rasmussen, Peter, eds. 2012. (Key To... workbooks Ser.: Bk. 5). (ENG.). 56p. (gr. 6-8). spiral bd., wbk. ed. 5.64 (978-0-913684-75-7(9), 0913684759) McGraw-Hill Education.
—Lines & Segments, Bk. 1. Gearhart, George & Rasmussen, Peter, eds. 2012. (Key To... workbooks Ser.: Bk. 1). (ENG.). 56p. (gr. 6-8). spiral bd., wbk. ed. 5.64 (978-0-913684-71-9(6), 0913684716) McGraw-Hill Education.
Suppes, Patrick C. & Key Curriculum Press Staff. Constructions, Bk. 3. Gearhart, George & Rasmussen, Peter, eds. 2012. (Key To... workbooks Ser.: Bk. 3). (ENG.). 56p. (gr. 6-8). spiral bd., wbk. ed. 5.64 (978-0-913684-73-3(2), 0913684732) McGraw-Hill Education.
—Perpendiculars & Parallels, Chords & Tangents, Circles, Bk. 7. Gearhart, George & Rasmussen, Peter, eds. 2012. (Key To... workbooks Ser.: Bk. 7). (ENG.). 160p. (gr. 6-8). pap., wbk. ed. 14.20 (978-0-913684-77-1(5), 0913684775) McGraw-Hill Education.
—Triangles, Parallel Lines & Similar Polygons, Bk. 8. Gearhart, George & Rasmussen, Peter, eds. 2012. (Key To... workbooks Ser.: Bk. 8). (ENG.). 144p. (gr. 6-8). pap., wbk. ed. 14.20 (978-0-913684-78-8(3), 0913684783) McGraw-Hill Education.
Twine, Alice. My Favorite Book of Shapes. 2008. (Board Bks.). (Illus.). 14p. (J). (gr. -1-k). bds. 11.95 (978-1-4042-4255-5(4)) Rosen Publishing Group, Inc., The.
Valentine, Bridget. Building with Shapes: Analyze, Compare, Create, & Compose Shapes. 2013. (InfoMax Math Readers Ser.). (ENG.). 16p. (J). (gr. k-1). pap. 42.00 (978-1-4777-1947-3(4)); (Illus.). pap. 7.00 (978-1-4777-1946-6(6)) Rosen Publishing Group, Inc., The. (Rosen Classroom).
Visto, Joy. When Does a Line Become a Shape? 2015. (Illus.). 48p. (J). (978-1-60818-574-0(5), Creative Education) Creative Co., The.
—When Does a Line Become a Shape? Making Math Work. 2016. (Making Math Work Ser.). (ENG.). 48p. (J). (gr. 5-9). pap. 12.00 (978-1-62832-175-3(X), Creative Paperbacks) Creative Co., The.
Vogel, Julia. Crescents, 1 vol. Holm, Sharon, illus. 2007. (Shapes Ser.). (ENG.). 24p. (gr. -1-2). 27.07 (978-1-60270-044-4(3), Looking Glass Library- Nonfiction) Magic Wagon.
—Ovals, 1 vol. Holm, Sharon, illus. 2007. (Shapes Ser.). (ENG.). 24p. (gr. -1-2). 27.07 (978-1-60270-045-1(1), Looking Glass Library- Nonfiction) Magic Wagon.
Weekly Reader Editorial Staff. I Know Shapes: Las Figuras. 2006. (I'm Ready for Math/ Ya puedo aprender matematicas Ser.). (ENG & SPA., Illus.). 16p. (gr. -1-2). pap. 5.30 (978-0-8368-6492-2(1), Weekly Reader Leveled Readers) Stevens, Gareth Publishing LLLP.
—I Know Shapes (Las Figuras) 2006. (I'm Ready for Math/YA Puedo Aprender Matematicas Ser.). (ENG & SPA., Illus.). 16p. (gr. -1-2). lib. bdg. 19.00 (978-0-8368-6487-8(5), Weekly Reader Leveled Readers) Stevens, Gareth Publishing LLLP.
Weekly Reader Editorial Staff, contrib. by. I Know Shapes. 2006. (I'm Ready for Math Ser.). (Illus.). 16p. (gr. -1-2). pap. 5.30 (978-0-8368-6482-3(4)); lib. bdg. 19.00 (978-0-8368-6477-9(8)) Stevens, Gareth Publishing LLLP. (Weekly Reader Leveled Readers).
Wik, John & Coloring Books for Adults. Deco Tech: Geometric Coloring Book. 2010. (Dover Design Coloring Bks.). (ENG., Illus.). 32p. (J). (gr. 1-5). pap. 3.99 (978-0-486-47546-2(8)) Dover Pubns., Inc.
Wiltshire, Alan. Creativity Through Design: Challenges in Art & Mathematics Using the Anglemaster. 64p. pap. 12.50 (978-1-871098-25-9(4)) Claire Pubns. GBR. Dist: Parkwest Pubns., Inc.
Wingard-Nelson, Rebecca. Figuring Out Geometry. 2008. (Math Busters Ser.). (Illus.). 64p. (J). (gr. 3-7). lib. bdg. 29.27 (978-0-7660-2880-7(1)) Enslow Pubs., Inc.
—Geometry. 2012. (Ace Your Math Test Ser.). (Illus.). 104p. (J). (gr. 5-18). 33.27 (978-0-7660-3783-0(5)) Enslow Pubs., Inc.
—Geometry: Ace Your Math Test. 2012. (Ace Your Math Test Ser.). (Illus.). 104p. (J). (gr. 5-18). pap. 10.95 (978-1-4644-0010-0(5)) Enslow Pubs., Inc.
—Geometry: It's Easy. 2014. (Easy Genius Math Ser.). 64p. (J). pap. 8.95 (978-1-4644-0525-9(5)) Enslow Pubs., Inc.
—Geometry, It's Easy. 2014. (Easy Genius Math Ser.). 64p. (J). (gr. 4-18). 29.27 (978-0-7660-4288-9(X)) Enslow Pubs., Inc.
—Trigonometry. 2004. (Math Success Ser.). (Illus.). 64p. (J). lib. bdg. 23.94 (978-0-7660-2568-4(3)) Enslow Pubs., Inc.
Wingard-Nelson, Rebecca & Library. Geometry Word Problems: No Problem! 2010. (Math Busters Word Problems Ser.). (Illus.). 64p. (J). lib. bdg. 29.27 (978-0-7660-3368-9(6)) Enslow Pubs., Inc.
Wojick, Luke. I Can Draw Shapes. 2013. (Core Math Skills: Measurement & Geometry Ser.). (Illus.). 24p. (J). (gr. 1-2). 22.60 (978-1-4777-2231-2(9)); (ENG., pap. 8.25 (978-1-4777-2055-4(3)) Rosen Publishing Group, Inc., The. (Rosen Classroom).
—I Can Draw Shapes: Shapes & Their Attributes. 2013. (Rosen Math Readers Ser.). (ENG., Illus.). 24p. (J). (gr. 1-2). pap. 49.50 (978-1-4777-2056-1(1), Rosen Classroom) Rosen Publishing Group, Inc., The.
Woodford, Chris. Volume. 2012. (Measure up Math Ser.). (Illus.). 32p. (J). (gr. 4-6). pap. 10.50 (978-1-4339-7458-8(4)); lib. bdg. 26.60 (978-1-4339-7457-1(6)) Stevens, Gareth Publishing LLLP.
Zuravicky, Orli. Exploring Pyramids Around the World: Making Models of Geometric Solids. 2009. (PowerMath Ser.). (ENG., Illus.). 32p. (gr. 4-5). pap. 10.00 (978-0-8239-8908-9(9), PowerKids Pr.) Rosen Publishing Group, Inc., The.

GEOMETRY, ANALYTIC

Lechner, Judith. Our New Fish Tank: Learning to Estimate & Round Numbers to the Nearest Ones, Tens, & Hundreds Places. 2004. (Math Big Bookstm Ser.). (ENG.). 16p. (gr. 2-3). 37.95 (978-0-8239-7640-9(8)) Rosen Publishing Group, Inc., The.
Lineare Algebra und Analytische Geometrie I: Leistungskurs. (Duden Abiturhilfen Ser.). (GER.). 96p. (YA). (gr. 12-13). (978-3-411-04601-0(5)) Bibliographisches Institut & F. A. Brockhaus AG DEU. Dist: International Bk. Import Service, Inc.
Lineare Algebra und Analytische Geometrie II: Leistungskurs. (Duden Abiturhilfen Ser.). (GER.). 96p. (YA). (gr. 12-13). (978-3-411-04631-7(7)) Bibliographisches Institut & F. A. Brockhaus AG DEU. Dist: International Bk. Import Service, Inc.
Neuschwander, Cindy. Sir Cumference & the Viking's Map. Geehan, Wayne, illus. 2012. (ENG.). 32p. (J). (gr. 3-7). 16.95 (978-1-57091-791-2(4)); pap. 7.95 (978-1-57091-792-9(2)) Charlesbridge Publishing, Inc.

GEOMETRY, PLANE

see Geometry

GEOMETRY, SOLID

see Geometry

GEOPHYSICS

see also Meteorology; Oceanography

Bodden, Valerie. Northern Lights. 2010. (Big Outdoors Ser.). 24p. (J). (gr. k-3). 16.95 (978-1-58341-818-5(0)) Creative Co., The.
Bow, James. Earth's Secrets. 2010. (Invisible Worlds Ser.). 48p. (gr. 4). 28.50 (978-0-7614-4196-0(4)) Marshall Cavendish GBR. Dist: Marshall Cavendish Corp.
Dorling Kindersley Publishing Staff. Rainbow Colors Peekaboo! 2008. (ENG.). 12p. (J). (gr. -1-k). bds. 6.99 (978-0-7566-3760-6(0), DK Children) Dorling Kindersley Publishing, Inc.
Fleisher, Paul. Gases, Pressure, & Wind: The Science of the Atmosphere. 2010. (Weatherwise Ser.). (ENG., Illus.). 48p. (gr. 4-8). lib. bdg. 29.27 (978-0-8225-7537-5(X)) Lerner Publishing Group.
Ganeri, Anita. I Wonder Why the Wind Blows. 2011. (I Wonder Why Ser.). (ENG., Illus.). 32p. (J). (gr. k-3). pap. 6.99 (978-0-7534-6522-6(1), 9780753465226, Kingfisher) Roaring Brook Pr.
Gardner, Robert. Earth-Shaking Science Projects about Planet Earth. LaBaff, Tom, illus. 2007. (Rockin' Earth Science Experiments Ser.). 48p. (J). (gr. 3-4). lib. bdg. 25.27 (978-0-7660-2733-6(3), Enslow Elementary) Enslow Pubs., Inc.
Gosman, Gillian. What Do You Know about Plate Tectonics? 2013. (20 Questions: Earth Science Ser.). 24p. (J). (gr. 3-6). 22.60 (978-1-4488-9698-1(3), PowerKids Pr.) Rosen Publishing Group, Inc., The.
Gosman, Gillian & Houghton Gosman, Gillian. What Do You Know about Plate Tectonics? 2013. 24p. (J). (gr. 3-6). pap. 8.25 (978-1-4488-9854-1(4), PowerKids Pr.) Rosen Publishing Group, Inc., The.
Hunter, Nick. Northern Lights, 1 vol. 2013. (Night Sky: & Other Amazing Sights in Space Ser.). (ENG.). 32p. (gr. 1-3). 27.32 (978-1-4329-7516-6(1)); pap. 8.95 (978-1-4329-7521-0(8)) Heinemann-Raintree. (Heinemann First Library).
Mullins, Matt & Plummer, Todd. Super Cool Science Experiments: Planet Earth. 2009. (Explorer Library: Science Explorer Ser.). (ENG., Illus.). 32p. (gr. 4-8). lib. bdg. 28.50 (978-1-60279-515-0(0), 200302) Cherry Lake Publishing.
Nemeth, Jason D. Plate Tectonics. 2012. (Our Changing Earth Ser.). (ENG., Illus.). 24p. (J). (gr. 3-6). pap. 8.25 (978-1-4488-6294-8(9), PowerKids Pr.); lib. bdg. 22.60 (978-1-4488-6168-2(3)) Rosen Publishing Group, Inc., The.
Olien, Rebecca. Longitude & Latitude. 2012. (Rookie Read-About(tm) Geography — Map Skills Ser.). (ENG.). 32p. (J). lib. bdg. 25.00 (978-0-531-28963-1(X)); pap. 5.95 (978-0-531-29287-7(8)) Scholastic Library Publishing.
Piehl, Janet. Northern Lights. 2009. pap. 40.95 (978-0-7613-4771-2(2)) 2008. (ENG.). 32p. 22.60 (978-0-8225-8832-0(3), Lerner Pubns.) Lerner Publishing Group.
Rajczak, Kristen. The Northern Lights. 2012. (Nature's Light Show Ser.). (Illus.). 24p. (J). (gr. 2-5). pap. 8.15 (978-1-4339-7028-3(7)); lib. bdg. 22.60 (978-1-4339-7027-6(9)) Stevens, Gareth Publishing LLLP.
René, Ellen. Investigating Volcanic Eruptions. 2009. (Science Detectives Ser.). 24p. (gr. 2-3). 42.50 (978-1-60853-014-4(0), PowerKids Pr.) Rosen Publishing Group, Inc., The.
Saunders, Craig. What Is the Theory of Plate Tectonics? 2010. (Shaping Modern Science Ser.). (ENG.). 64p. (J). (gr. 5-8). pap. (978-0-7787-7209-5(8)) Crabtree Publishing Co.
Schneider, Herman & Schneider, Nina. Rocks, Rivers & the Changing Earth: A First Book about Geology. Herron, Edwin, illus. 2014. (ENG.). 192p. (J). (gr. 3-8). pap. 6.99 (978-0-486-78201-0(8)) Dover Pubns., Inc.
Silverstein, Alvin, et al. Plate Tectonics. rev. ed. 2009. (Science Concepts, Second Ser.). (ENG.). 120p. (gr. 6-8). 31.93 (978-0-7613-3936-6(1)) Lerner Publishing Group.
What Do You Know about Plate Tectonics? 2013. (20 Questions: Earth Science Ser.). 24p. (J). (gr. 3-6). pap. 49.50 (978-1-4488-9855-8(2), PowerKids Pr.) Rosen Publishing Group, Inc., The.
Whitfield, David. Northern Lights. (Illus.). 24p. (J). 2013. pap. (978-1-61913-545-1(0), 1346029) 2012. (ENG., (gr. 4-7). lib. bdg. 27.13 (978-1-61913-098-2(X), AV2 by Weigl) Weigl Pubs., Inc.
Young, Greg. Alfred Wegener: Uncovering Plate Tectonics, 1 vol. 2007. (Science Readers Ser.). (ENG.). 32p. (J). (gr. 3-3). pap. 8.99 (978-0-7439-0560-2(1)) Shell Educational Publishing.
—Investigating Plate Tectonics, 1 vol. 2007. (Science Readers Ser.). (ENG.). 32p. (J). (gr. 4-4). pap. 8.99 (978-0-7439-0559-6(8)) Shell Educational Publishing.

GEORGE, SAINT, -303—FICTION

Bilinsky, Cornelia Mary. The Saint Who Fought the Dragon: The Story of St. George. 2011. (J). 10.95 (978-0-8198-7161-9(3)) Pauline Bks. & Media.
Grahame, Kenneth. The Reluctant Dragon. Shepard, Ernest H., illus. 2013. (ENG.). 64p. (J). (gr. 1-5). 2nd ed. pap. 6.95 (978-0-8234-2821-2(4)) 75th ed. 16.95 (978-0-8234-2820-5(6)) Holiday Hse., Inc.
—The Reluctant Dragon (Illustrated Edition) 2015. (ENG., Illus.). 42p. pap. (978-1-5154-0330-2(0), Illustrated Bks.) Jorge Pinto Bks.
Hightman, Jason. The Saint of Dragons. 2004. 304p. (J). (gr. 7-18). (ENG.). 16.99 (978-0-06-054011-7(7)); lib. bdg. 17.89 (978-0-06-054012-8(5)) HarperCollins Pubs.

GEORGE WASHINGTON BRIDGE (NEW YORK, N.Y.)—FICTION

Swift, Hildegarde H. The Little Red Lighthouse & the Great Gray Bridge: Restored Edition. Ward, Lynd, illus. 2003. (ENG.). 64p. (J). (gr. -1-3). pap. 8.99 (978-0-15-204573-9(2)) Houghton Mifflin Harcourt Publishing Co.

GEORGIA

Bennett, Doraine. Atlantic Ocean. 2009. (J). (978-1-935077-34-3(1)); pap. (978-1-935077-39-8(2)) State Standards Publishing, LLC.
—Coast. 2009. (J). (978-1-935077-35-0(X)); pap. (978-1-935077-40-4(6)) State Standards Publishing, LLC.
—Coastal Plain. 2009. (J). (978-1-935077-51-0(1)); pap. (978-1-935077-52-7(X)) State Standards Publishing, LLC.
—Lower Coastal Plain. 2009. (J). 20.60 (978-1-935077-49-7(X)); pap. 10.60 (978-1-935077-50-3(3)) State Standards Publishing, LLC.

EFG

—Piedmont. 2009. (J). 22.60 *(978-1-935077-22-0(8))*; *(978-1-935077-38-1(4))*; pap. *(978-1-935077-43-5(0))* State Standards Publishing, LLC.
—Upper Coastal Plain. 2009. (J). 20.60 *(978-1-935077-21-3(X))*; pap. 10.60 *(978-1-935077-26-8(0))* State Standards Publishing, LLC.
—Valley & Ridge. 2009. (J). 20.60 *(978-1-935077-23-7(6))*; pap. 10.60 *(978-1-935077-28-2(7))* State Standards Publishing, LLC.
Berry, Carrie. Diary of Carrie Berry: A Confederate Girl, 1 vol. 2014. (First-Person Histories Ser.). (ENG.). 32p. (gr. 3-4). lib. bdg. 27.32 *(978-1-4765-4192-1(2)*, Fact Finders) Capstone Press of Coughlan Cos.
Boehm Jerome, Kate. Savannah & the State of Georgia: Cool Stuff Every Kid Should Know. 2011. (Arcadia Kids Ser.). (ENG., Illus.). 48p. (J). pap. 9.99 *(978-1-4396-0091-7(0))* Arcadia Publishing.
Bredeson, Carmen. Georgia. 2003. (Rookie Read-about Science Ser.). (Illus.). 31p. (J). (gr. -1-3). 13.60 Perfection Learning Corp.
Coleman, Wim & Perrin, Pat. Martin Luther King, Jr. National Historic Site: A MyReportLinks.com Book. 2005. (Virtual Field Trips Ser.). (Illus.). 48p. (J). (gr. 4-10). lib. bdg. 26.60 *(978-0-7660-5225-3(7)*, MyReportLinks.com Bks.) Enslow Pubs., Inc.
Crane, Carol. A Peck of Peaches: A Georgia Number Book. Braught, Mark, illus. rev. ed. 2007. (State Counting Ser.). (ENG.). 40p. (J). (gr. 1-3). 17.95 *(978-1-58536-177-9(1))* Sleeping Bear Pr.
Dolphin, Colleen. Leaping Lily: A Story about Georgia, 1 vol. Doucet, Bob, illus. 2010. (Fact & Fable: State Stories Set 2 Ser.). (ENG.). 24p. (J). (gr. -1-2). 25.65 *(978-1-60453-924-0(0))* ABDO Publishing Co.
Harmon, Daniel E. Lower Atlantic: Florida, Georgia, South Carolina, Vol. 19. 2015. (Let's Explore the States Ser.). (Illus.). 64p. (J). (gr. 5). 23.95 *(978-1-4222-3325-2(1))* Mason Crest.
Haywood, Karen Diane. Georgia. 2013. (It's My State 2nd Ed 4 Ser.). 80p. (J). (gr. 4-8). pap. 17.64 *(978-1-62712-092-0(0))* Cavendish Square Publishing.
—Georgia. 2005. (It's My State! Ser.). (Illus.). 79p. (J). (gr. 4-7). lib. bdg. 27.07 *(978-0-7614-1862-7(8)*, Benchmark Bks.) Marshall Cavendish Corp.
Herda, D. J. Furman V. Georgia: The Death Penalty Case. rev. ed. 2010. (Landmark Supreme Court Cases, Gold Edition Ser.). (Illus.). 112p. (J). (gr. 6-18). 33.27 *(978-0-7660-3428-0(3))* Enslow Pubs., Inc.
Hinman, Bonnie. Paula Deen. 2012. (J). *(978-1-61900-013-1(X))*; *(978-1-61900-015-5(6))*; *(978-1-61900-014-8(8))* Eldorado Ink.
Jackson, Edwin L. & Stakes, Mary E. The Georgia Studies Book: Our State & the Nation. 2nd ed. 2004. (J). *(978-0-89854-210-3(3))* Univ. of Georgia, Carl Vinson Institute of Government.
Kalman, Bobbie & Dyer, Hadley. Savanna Food Chains. 2006. (Food Chains Ser.). (ENG., Illus.). 32p. (J). (gr. -1-3). pap. *(978-0-7787-1998-4(7))* Crabtree Publishing Co.
Kalman, Bobbie & Sjonger, Rebecca. A Savanna Habitat. 2006. (Introducing Habitats Ser.). (ENG., Illus.). 32p. (J). (gr. 3-7). pap. *(978-0-7787-2980-8(X))* Crabtree Publishing Co.
Kirchner, Jason. Georgia. 2016. (States Ser.). (ENG., Illus.). 32p. (gr. 3-4). lib. bdg. 27.32 *(978-1-5157-0396-9(7))* Next Page Pr., The.
LaDoux, Rita. Georgia. 2012. (J). lib. bdg. 25.26 *(978-0-7613-4528-2(0)*, Lerner Pubns.) Lerner Publishing Group.
Lusted, Marcia Amidon. Georgia: The Peach State. (Illus.). 24p. (J). 2010. pap. 8.25 *(978-1-4358-3376-0(7))* 2009. lib. bdg. 22.60 *(978-1-4042-8149-3(5))* Rosen Publishing Group, Inc., The. (PowerKids Pr.).
Marsh, Carole. Georgia Current Events Projects: 30 Cool, Activities, Crafts, Experiments & More for Kids to Do to Learn about Your State! 2003. (Georgia Experience Ser.). 32p. (gr. k-5). pap. 5.95 *(978-0-635-02029-1(7)*, Marsh, Carole Bks.) Gallopade International.
—Georgia Geography Projects: 30 Cool, Activities, Crafts, Experiments & More for Kids to Do to Learn about Your State! 2003. (Georgia Experience Ser.). 32p. (gr. k-5). pap. 5.95 *(978-0-635-01829-8(2)*, Marsh, Carole Bks.) Gallopade International.
—Georgia Government Projects: 30 Cool, Activities, Crafts, Experiments & More for Kids to Do to Learn about Your State! 2003. (Georgia Experience Ser.). 32p. (gr. k-5). pap. 5.95 *(978-0-635-01929-5(9)*, Marsh, Carole Bks.) Gallopade International.
—Georgia People Projects: 30 Cool, Activities, Crafts, Experiments & More for Kids to Do to Learn about Your State! 2003. (Georgia Experience Ser.). 32p. (gr. k-5). pap. 5.95 *(978-0-635-01979-0(5)*, Marsh, Carole Bks.) Gallopade International.
—Georgia Symbols & Facts Projects: 30 Cool, Activities, Crafts, Experiments & More for Kids to Do to Learn about Your State! 2003. (Georgia Experience Ser.). 32p. (gr. k-5). pap. 5.95 *(978-0-635-01879-3(9)*, Marsh, Carole Bks.) Gallopade International.
—Georgia's Big Activity Book. 2004. (Georgia Experience! Ser.). (Illus.). 96p. (J). (gr. 2-6). pap. 9.95 *(978-0-7933-9459-3(7))* Gallopade International.
Murphy, Andrea. Georgia. 2005. (Portraits of the States Ser.). (Illus.). 32p. (gr. 2-6). pap. 10.50 *(978-0-8368-4642-3(7))*; lib. bdg. 26.00 *(978-0-8368-4623-2(0))* Stevens, Gareth Publishing LLLP. (Gareth Stevens Learning Library).
Murray, Julie. Georgia, 1 vol. 2006. (United States (BB) Ser.). (ENG., Illus.). 32p. (gr. k-4). 27.07 *(978-1-59197-669-1(3)*, Buddy Bks.) ABDO Publishing Co.
Otfinoski, Steven. Georgia. 2nd rev. ed. 2009. (Celebrate the States 9 Ser.). 144p. (gr. 6). 42.79 *(978-0-7614-4031-4(3))* Marshall Cavendish Corp.
Piddock, Charles. Republic of Georgia. 2006. (Nations in the News Ser.). (Illus.). 48p. (gr. 5-12). pap. 14.05 *(978-0-8368-6717-6(3))*; lib. bdg. 31.00 *(978-0-8368-6710-7(6))* Stevens, Gareth Publishing LLLP. (Gareth Stevens Secondary Library).
Prentzas, G. S. Georgia. 2014. (America the Beautiful Ser.: 3). (ENG.). 144p. (J). lib. bdg. 40.00 *(978-0-531-24881-2(X))* Scholastic Library Publishing.
Quasha, Jennifer. How to Draw Georgia's Sights & Symbols. 2009. (Kid's Guide to Drawing America Ser.). 32p. (gr. k-k). 50.50 *(978-1-61511-057-5(7)*, PowerKids Pr.) Rosen Publishing Group, Inc., The.
Savage, Jeff. Georgia: A MyReportLinks. Com Book. 2003. (States Ser.). (Illus.). 48p. (J). lib. bdg. 25.26 *(978-0-7660-5114-0(5)*, MyReportLinks.com Bks.) Enslow Pubs., Inc.
Shofner, Shawndra. Georgia. 2008. (This Land Called America Ser.). 32p. (YA). (gr. 3-6). 22.95 *(978-1-58341-635-8(8))* Creative Co., The.
Smith, Rich. Georgia, 1 vol. 2009. (United States Ser.). (ENG., Illus.). 48p. (YA). (gr. 2-5). 27.07 *(978-1-60453-645-4(4))* ABDO Publishing Co.
Spilling, Michael & Wong, Winnie. Georgia. 2nd rev. ed. 2008. (Cultures of the World Ser.). 144p. (gr. 6-18). lib. bdg. 42.79 *(978-0-7614-3033-9(4)*, Benchmark Bks.) Marshall Cavendish Corp.
Stefoff, Rebecca. Furman V. Georgia: Debating the Death Penalty. 2007. (Supreme Court Milestones Ser.). (Illus.). 128p. (gr. 7-18). lib. bdg. 42.79 *(978-0-7614-2583-0(7)*, Benchmark Bks.) Marshall Cavendish Corp.
Stout, Mary. Atlanta. 2005. (Great Cities of the World Ser.). (Illus.). 48p. (gr. 5-12). lib. bdg. 31.00 *(978-0-8368-5042-0(4)*, Gareth Stevens Secondary Library) Stevens, Gareth Publishing LLLP.
Sullivan, E. J. G Is for Georgia. Cross, Neal, illus. 2006. 24p. (J). *(978-1-58173-524-6(3))* Sweetwater Pr.
Watson, Stephanie. Georgia: Past & Present. 2009. (Illus.). 48p. (J). 70.50 *(978-1-4358-5583-0(3))*; pap. 11.75 *(978-1-4358-5582-3(5))*; (ENG., lib. bdg. 29.25 *(978-1-4358-5292-1(3))* Rosen Publishing Group, Inc., The. (Rosen Reference).
Weaver, Jack. Uga Hunkers down in Athens Town. Ingram, Glenda Brown, illus. 2004. (J). *(978-0-9773370-0-2(6))* Weaver, Jack R. Company.
William H. Sadlier Staff. Peach Tree Street, Vol. 2. 2005. (Early Library). (gr. k-2). 24.00 net. *(978-0-8215-8949-6(0))* Sadlier, William H. Inc.
Windham, Kathryn Tucker. 13 Georgia Ghosts & Jeffrey. 2nd ed. 2015. (ENG., Illus.). 160p. (gr. 4-12). 29.95 *(978-0-8173-1881-9(X))* Univ. of Alabama Pr.

GEORGIA—FICTION

Altsheler, Joseph A. The Rock of Chickamauga: A Story of the Western Crisis. 2006. (Civil War Ser.: Vol. 6). 292p. (J). reprint ed. 28.95 *(978-1-4218-1775-0(6))*; pap. 13.95 *(978-1-4218-1875-7(2))* 1st World Publishing, Inc. (1st World Library - Literary Society).
—The Rock of Chickamauga: A Story of the Western Crisis. (Civil War Ser.: Vol. 6). (J). reprint ed. 25.95 *(978-0-8488-0071-0(0))* Amereon Ltd.
—The Rock of Chickamauga: A Story of the Western Crisis. l.t. ed. (Civil War Ser.: Vol. 6). (J). reprint ed. 2007. (ENG.). 258p. pap. 23.99 *(978-1-4346-2064-4(6))* 2010. 360p. (gr. 4-7). pap. 32.75 *(978-1-177-86302-5(2))* 2010. 356p. pap. 32.75 *(978-1-142-78423-2(1))* 2008. 260p. 28.99 *(978-0-554-26869-9(8))* 2008. 260p. 25.99 *(978-0-554-36172-7(8))* 2007. (ENG.). 234p. pap. 20.99 *(978-1-4346-2035-4(2))* Creative Media Partners, LLC.
—The Rock of Chickamauga: A Story of the Western Crisis. 2006. (Civil War Ser.: Vol. 6). (J). reprint ed. pap. *(978-1-4065-0818-5(7))* Dodo Pr.
—The Rock of Chickamauga: A Story of the Western Crisis. 2007. (Civil War Ser.: Vol. 6). 176p. (J). reprint ed. per. *(978-1-4068-1682-2(5))* Echo Library.
—The Rock of Chickamauga: A Story of the Western Crisis. 2010. (Civil War Ser.: Vol. 6). (Illus.). 154p. (J). (gr. 4-7). reprint ed. pap. 19.99 *(978-1-153-71942-1(8))* General Bks. LLC.
—The Rock of Chickamauga: A Story of the Western Crisis. 2010. (Civil War Ser.: Vol. 6). 220p. (J). pap. *(978-1-4076-5409-6(8))* HardPr.
—The Rock of Chickamauga: A Story of the Western Crisis. (Civil War Ser.: Vol. 6). (J). reprint ed. 2010. 236p. (gr. 4-7). 33.56 *(978-1-169-29814-9(1))* 2010. 41.95 *(978-1-161-47572-2(9))* 2004. pap. 26.95 *(978-1-4191-8082-8(7))* 2004. pap. 1.99 *(978-1-4192-8082-5(1))* Kessinger Publishing, LLC.
—The Rock of Chickamauga: A Story of the Western Crisis. 2011. (Civil War Ser.: Vol. 6). 260p. (J). (gr. 4-7). reprint ed. pap. *(978-3-8424-7218-1(8))* Tredition GmbH.
Anderson, Jodi Lynn. Love & Peaches. 256p. (YA). 2009. (Peaches Ser.: 3). (ENG.). (gr. 8). pap. 8.99 *(978-0-06-073313-1(6))* 2008. (gr. 7-18). lib. bdg. 17.89 *(978-0-06-073312-4(8))* HarperCollins Pubs. (HarperTeen).
—Peaches. (ENG.). (YA). 2005. 320p. (gr. 7-12). 15.99 *(978-0-06-073305-6(5))* 2012. (Peaches Ser.: 1). 368p. (gr. 9-12). reprint ed. pap. 8.99 *(978-0-06-073307-0(1)*, HarperTeen) HarperCollins Pubs.
—The Secrets of Peaches. 2012. (Peaches Ser.: 2). (ENG.). 368p. (YA). (gr. 9-12). pap. 8.99 *(978-0-06-073310-0(1)*, HarperTeen) HarperCollins Pubs.
As Orange As Marmalade: Tan naranja como Mermelada. 2007. (ENG & SPA.). (J). per. 10.00 *(978-0-9749876-8-2(9))* Journey of a Dream Pr.
Bakewell, Lori. Savannah Adventure: Pirate's Treasure. 2007. 173p. (J). pap. 12.95 *(978-0-9799473-9-1(1))* Tailwind Press.
Ballard, Kim. Light at Summer's End. 2007. 116p. per. 15.95 *(978-1-60290-047-9(7))* OakTara Publishing Group LLC.
Bauer Mueller, Pamela. An Angry Drum Echoed: Mary Musgrove, Queen of the Creeks. 2007. (ENG., Illus.). 296p. (YA). (gr. 6-7). per. 13.95 *(978-0-9685097-8-4(9))*; 18.95 *(978-0-9685097-7-7(0))* Pinata Publishing CAN. Dist: Midpoint Trade Bks., Inc.
Blackstock, Terri. Southern Storm, 1 vol. 2014. (Cape Refuge Ser.). (ENG.). 400p. pap. 15.99 *(978-0-310-34280-9(5))* Zondervan.
Bovi, J. K. Wicked Haints: A Savannah Ghost Story, 1 vol. 2013. (ENG., Illus.). 128p. (J). pap. 16.99 *(978-0-7643-4383-4(1)*, 9780764343834) Schiffer Publishing, Ltd.
Brown, Jaye Robin. Georgia Peaches & Other Forbidden Fruit. 2016. 432p. (YA). (gr. 9). 17.99 *(978-0-06-227098-6(2)*, HarperTeen) HarperCollins Pubs.
Bundy, Tamara. Walking with Miss Millie. 2017. (ENG.). 240p. (J). (gr. 5). 16.99 ***(978-0-399-54456-9(9)***, Nancy Paulsen Books) Penguin Young Readers Group.
Burt, Vickie. Hot Dog or Egg Sandwich? Lindsey, Jessica, illus. 2013. 28p. pap. 13.99 *(978-1-937129-87-3(X))* Faithful Life Pubs.
Clare, Mimi St. The Fairbluffs of Pennington Island. 2013. 36p. pap. 12.99 *(978-1-935986-49-2(X))* Liberty University Press.
Cofer, Amadeus. Mystery of the Golden Pearls: A Halloween Adventure in Clarkesville, 1. l.t. ed. 2004. (Illus.). 36p. (J). 14.00 *(978-1-932957-02-0(2))* Legacy Pubs.
Coker, Rachel. Chasing Jupiter, 1 vol. 2013. (ENG.). 224p. (YA). 15.99 *(978-0-310-73293-8(X))* Zondervan.
Coleman, Evelyn. Freedom Train. 2012. (ENG.). 160p. (J). (gr. 3-7). pap. 7.99 *(978-1-4424-3652-7(2)*, McElderry, Margaret K. Bks.) McElderry, Margaret K. Bks.
—Freedom Train. Riley, David, illus. 2008. (ENG.). 160p. (J). (gr. 3-7). 17.99 *(978-0-689-84716-5(5)*, McElderry, Margaret K. Bks.) McElderry, Margaret K. Bks.
Crouch, Katie. The Magnolia League. 2012. (Magnolia League Ser.: 1). (ENG.). 384p. (YA). (gr. 10-17). pap. 8.99 *(978-0-316-07848-1(4)*, Poppy) Little, Brown Bks. for Young Readers.
—The White Glove War. 2013. (Magnolia League Ser.: 2). (ENG.). 320p. (YA). (gr. 10-17). pap. 9.00 *(978-0-316-18749-7(6)*, Poppy) Little, Brown Bks. for Young Readers.
Dawson, Delilah S. Servants of the Storm. 2014. (ENG., Illus.). 384p. (YA). (gr. 9). 17.99 *(978-1-4424-8378-1(4)*, Simon Pulse) Simon Pulse.
DeVilliers, Julia. Cleared for Takeoff. Pooler, Paige, illus. 2012. (Liberty Porter, First Daughter Ser.: 3). (ENG.). 224p. (J). (gr. 3-7). pap. 7.99 *(978-1-4169-9131-1(X)*, Simon & Schuster/Paula Wiseman Bks.) Simon & Schuster/Paula Wiseman Bks.
Dudley, David L. Caleb's Wars. 2011. (ENG.). 272p. (YA). (gr. 9). 17.99 *(978-0-547-23997-2(1))* Houghton Mifflin Harcourt Publishing Co.
Dunshee, Gloria Fjare. Will & the Magic Snowman. 2010. 32p. pap. 11.95 *(978-0-9828231-1-8(8))* WillGo Pr.
Eller, Sylvia Klope. The Squirrel Who Hitchhiked to Atlanta. 2007. (Illus.). 32p. (J). pap. 8.00 *(978-0-8059-7596-3(9))* Dorrance Publishing Co., Inc.
Eubanks, Jacquelyn R. The Last Summer. McTyre, Robert E., ed. 2012. 206p. pap. 9.99 *(978-0-9785900-3-1(1))* VG Publishing.
Gamble, Adam. Good Night Atlanta. Veno, Joe, illus. 2007. (Good Night Our World Ser.). (ENG.). 20p. (J). (gr. k — 1). bds. 9.95 *(978-0-60219-001-6(1))* Good Night Bks.
—Good Night Georgia. Rosen, Anne & Veno, Joe, illus. 2009. (Good Night Our World Ser.). (ENG.). 20p. (J). (gr. k — 1). bds. 9.95 *(978-1-60219-032-0(1))* Good Night Bks.
Gibbons, Faye. The Day the Picture Man Came. Meidell, Sherry, illus. 2003. (ENG.). 32p. (YA). (gr. k-2). 16.95 *(978-1-56397-161-7(5))* Boyds Mills Pr.
—Full Steam Ahead. Meidell, Sherry, illus. 2003. (ENG.). 32p. (J). (gr. k-2). 15.95 *(978-1-56397-858-6(X))* Boyds Mills Pr.
Gibson, Marley. The Awakening. 2009. (ENG.). 352p. (YA). (gr. 7-18). pap. 19.99 *(978-0-547-15093-2(8))* Houghton Mifflin Harcourt Publishing Co.
—The Discovery. 2011. (ENG.). 264p. (YA). (gr. 7-18). pap. 8.99 *(978-0-547-39308-7(3))* Houghton Mifflin Harcourt Publishing Co.
—The Guidance. 2009. (ENG.). 320p. (YA). (gr. 7-18). pap. 16.95 *(978-0-547-15094-9(6))* Houghton Mifflin Harcourt Publishing Co.
—The Reason, Bk. 3. 2010. (ENG.). 240p. (YA). (gr. 7-18). pap. 8.99 *(978-0-547-15095-6(4))* Houghton Mifflin Harcourt Publishing Co.
Green, Tim. The Big Time. (Football Genius Ser.: 4). (ENG.). (J). (gr. 3-7). 2011. 304p. pap. 6.99 *(978-0-06-168621-4(2))* 2010. 288p. 16.99 *(978-0-06-168619-1(0))* HarperCollins Pubs.
—Deep Zone. 2012. (Football Genius Ser.: 5). (J). lib. bdg. 17.20 *(978-0-606-26854-7(5)*, Turtleback) Turtleback Bks.
—Football Champ. (Football Genius Ser.: 3). (ENG.). (J). (gr. 3-7). 2010. 304p. pap. 6.99 *(978-0-06-162691-3(0))* 2009. (Illus.). 288p. 16.99 *(978-0-06-162689-0(9))* HarperCollins Pubs.
—Football Genius. 2008. (Football Genius Ser.: 1). (ENG.). 272p. (J). (gr. 5-9). pap. 6.99 *(978-0-06-112273-6(4))* HarperCollins Pubs.
—Football Genius. l.t. ed. 2008. (Thorndike Literacy Bridge Ser.). 291p. (YA). (gr. 8-12). 23.95 *(978-1-4104-0497-8(8))* Thorndike Pr.
Harkey, Faith. Genuine Sweet. (ENG.). 288p. (J). (gr. 5-7). 2016. pap. 6.99 *(978-0-544-66853-9(7)*, HMH Books For Young Readers) 2015. 16.99 *(978-0-544-28366-4(X))* Houghton Mifflin Harcourt Publishing Co.
Harris, Joel Chandler. Mingo. 2007. 108p. 22.95 *(978-1-60312-654-0(6))*; per. 9.95 *(978-1-60312-396-9(2))* Aegypan.
—Nights with Uncle Remus. 2008. 288p. 29.95 *(978-1-60664-915-2(9))* Aegypan.
Hegedus, Bethany. Between Us Baxters. 2009. 306p. (YA). (gr. 7-9). 17.95 *(978-1-934813-02-7(8))* 2011. 9.14 *(978-1-934813-18-8(4))* Westside Bks.
Holmes, Lynda. Spring Cleaning. 2006. 55p. pap. 16.95 *(978-1-4241-4324-5(1))* PublishAmerica, Inc.
Jabaley, Jennifer. Crush Control. 2011. (ENG.). 336p. (YA). (gr. 7-18). 9.99 *(978-1-59514-424-9(2)*, Razorbill) Penguin Young Readers Group.
Jacobs, Lily. The Littlest Bunny in Georgia: An Easter Adventure. 2015. (ENG.). 32p. (J). (-3). 9.99 *(978-1-4926-1072-4(0)*, Sourcebooks Jabberwocky) Sourcebooks, Inc.
James, Eric. A Halloween Scare in Georgia. Le Ray, Marina, illus. 2014. (ENG.). 32p. (J). (-5). 9.99 *(978-1-4926-0588-1(3)*, 9781492605881, Sourcebooks Jabberwocky) Sourcebooks, Inc.
—Santa's Sleigh Is on Its Way to Georgia. Dunn, Robert, illus. 2015. (ENG.). 32p. (J). (-2). 12.99 *(978-1-4926-2744-9(5)*, Sourcebooks Jabberwocky) Sourcebooks, Inc.
Jones, C. B. Kiss of the Snake. Green, Chris, illus. 2017. (Bog Hollow Boys Ser.). (ENG.). 72p. (gr. 4-5). lib. bdg. 25.32 *(978-1-4965-4056-0(5))* Stone Arch Bks.
Kadohata, Cynthia. Kira-Kira. (ENG., Illus.). (J). (gr. 5-9). 2004. 256p. 17.99 *(978-0-689-85639-6(3))* 2006. 272p. reprint ed. pap. 7.99 *(978-0-689-85640-2(7))* Simon & Schuster Children's Publishing. (Atheneum Bks. for Young Readers).
Kate, Lauren. Fallen. (Fallen Ser.: Bk. 1). (ENG.). (YA). (gr. 7). 2010. 480p. pap. 10.99 *(978-0-385-73913-9(3)*, Ember) 2009. 464p. 17.99 *(978-0-385-73893-4(5)*, Delacorte Pr.) Random Hse. Children's Bks.
—Fallen. 2010. (Fallen Ser.: 1). lib. bdg. 22.10 *(978-0-606-15168-9(0)*, Turtleback) Turtleback Bks.
—Fallen in Love. 2012. (Fallen Ser.). (ENG.). (YA). (gr. 7). 224p. pap. 8.99 *(978-0-385-74262-7(2)*, Ember); 256p. 15.99 *(978-0-385-74261-0(4)*, Delacorte Pr.) Random Hse. Children's Bks.
—Oscuros. 2011. (Vintage Espanol Ser.: Bk. 1).Tr. of Fallen. (SPA.). 416p. (YA). (gr. 5). pap. 9.95 *(978-0-307-74500-2(7)*, Vintage Espanol) Knopf Doubleday Publishing Group.
Kline, Lisa Williams. Write Before Your Eyes. 2010. (ENG.). 192p. (J). (gr. 3-7). 6.99 *(978-0-440-42251-8(5)*, Yearling) Random Hse. Children's Bks.
Lester, R. A. Clearview Stories, 1 vol. 2009. 238p. pap. 19.95 *(978-1-61582-913-2(X))* PublishAmerica, Inc.
Love, Judy. Praise Be & Rainbows. 2006. 51p. pap. 16.95 *(978-1-4241-0333-1(9))* PublishAmerica, Inc.
Malaspina, Ann. Touch the Sky: Alice Coachman, Olympic High Jumper. Velasquez, Eric, illus. 2012. (ENG.). 32p. (J). (gr. 1-3). 16.99 *(978-0-8075-8035-6(X))* Whitman, Albert & Co.
Marsh, Carole. The Ghosts of Pickpocket Plantation. 2009. (Pretty Darn Scary Mysteries Ser.). (Illus.). 109p. (YA). lib. bdg. 18.99 *(978-0-635-07019-7(7)*, Marsh, Carole Mysteries) Gallopade International.
—The Giggling Ghost Girl Scout Mystery. 2012. (ENG., Illus.). 158p. (J). pap. 7.99 *(978-0-635-10230-0(7)*, Marsh, Carole Mysteries) Gallopade International.
—The Mystery at Fort Thunderbolt. 2007. (Pretty Darn Scary Mysteries Ser.). (Illus.). 113p. (YA). lib. bdg. 18.99 *(978-0-635-07021-0(9)*, Marsh, Carole Mysteries) Gallopade International.
—The Secret of Eyesocket Island. 2009. (Pretty Darn Scary Mysteries Ser.). (Illus.). 113p. (J). lib. bdg. 18.99 *(978-0-635-07022-7(7)*, Marsh, Carole Mysteries) Gallopade International.
Martin, J. Marshall. The Bird. 2008. 88p. pap. 12.50 *(978-0-9801224-1-1(4))* Boys Read Bks.
McDaniel, Lurlene. Letting Go of Lisa. 2007. (ENG.). 192p. (YA). (gr. 7-12). mass mkt. 6.99 *(978-0-440-23868-3(4)*, Laurel Leaf) Random Hse. Children's Bks.
McGee, Anne Loader. Anni's Attic. 2012. 326p. (-18). pap. 12.99 *(978-1-936307-24-1(3))* Vendera Publishing.
McGurk, Monica. Dark Hope: Book 1 of the Archangel Prophecies. 2014. 410p. (YA). pap. *(978-1-938416-67-5(8))* River Grove Bks.
McVoy, Terra Elan. After the Kiss. (ENG.). (YA). (gr. 9). 2011. 416p. pap. 10.99 *(978-1-4424-0216-4(4))* 2010. 400p. 16.99 *(978-1-4424-0211-9(3))* Simon Pulse. (Simon Pulse).
Mickles Sr., Robert T. S. Blood Kin, a Savannah Story. 2007. 108p. per. 9.95 *(978-0-595-45129-6(2))* iUniverse, Inc.
Moore, Stephanie Perry. Forever Hot/Truly Fine. 2013. (Grovehill Giants Ser.). (YA). lib. bdg. 26.90 *(978-0-606-31877-8(1)*, Turtleback) Turtleback Bks.
Moore, Stephanie Perry & Moore, Derrick. Forever Hot/Truly Fine, 1 vol. 2013. (Grovehill Giants Ser.: Bk. 1). (ENG.). 318p. (YA). (gr. 9-12). pap. 14.95 *(978-1-62250-683-5(9))* Saddleback Educational Publishing, Inc.
Mosley, Walter. 47. 2006. (ENG., Illus.). 240p. (J). (gr. 7-17). reprint ed. per. 10.99 *(978-0-316-01635-3(7))* Little, Brown Bks. for Young Readers.
Moss, Patricia Crocker. Dillie's Ride to the Sea: A Visit to Savannah. 2011. 36p. (J). 31.99 *(978-1-4568-5325-9(2))*; pap. 17.49 *(978-1-4568-5321-1(X))* Xlibris Corp.
Myracle, Lauren. Bliss. 2008. (ENG.). 464p. (YA). (gr. 9-17). 16.95 *(978-0-8109-7071-7(6)*, Amulet Bks.) Abrams, Inc.
—The Infinite Moment of Us. 2014. (ENG.). 336p. (YA). (gr. 9-17). pap. 8.95 *(978-1-4197-1358-3(2)*, Amulet Bks.) Abrams, Inc.
—Peace, Love, & Baby Ducks. 2010. (ENG.). 304p. (YA). (gr. 7-18). 8.99 *(978-0-14-241527-6(8)*, Speak) Penguin Young Readers Group.
—Ten. 2011. (Winnie Years Ser.). (ENG.). 272p. (J). (gr. 3-7). 16.99 *(978-0-525-42356-0(7)*, Dutton Books for Young Readers) Penguin Young Readers Group.
—Thirteen. 2009. (Winnie Years Ser.). (ENG.). 272p. (J). (gr. 3-7). 7.99 *(978-0-14-241370-8(4)*, Puffin Books) Penguin Young Readers Group.
O'Connor, Barbara. The Fantastic Secret of Owen Jester. 2010. (ENG.). 176p. (J). (gr. 3-7). 15.99 *(978-0-374-36850-0(3)*, 9780374368500, Farrar, Straus & Giroux (BYR)) Farrar, Straus & Giroux.
—The Fantastic Secret of Owen Jester. 2011. (ENG.). 192p. (J). (gr. 3-7). pap. 7.99 *(978-0-312-67430-4(9)*, 9780312674304) Square Fish.
Oliver, Jana. Briar Rose, 1. unabr. ed. 2015. (ENG.). 480p. (YA). (gr. 8). pap. 9.99 *(978-1-4472-4109-6(6))* Pan Macmillan GBR. Dist: Independent Pubs. Group.
—The Demon Trapper's Daughter. 2011. (Demon Trappers Ser.: 1). (ENG.). 368p. (YA). (gr. 7-18). pap. 9.99 *(978-0-312-61478-2(0)*, 9780312614782, St. Martin's Griffin) St. Martin's Pr.
O'Neill, Elizabeth. Alfred Visits Georgia. 2007. (Illus.). 24p. (gr. -1-3). pap. 12.00 *(978-0-9799121-0-8(5))* Global Business Information Strategies, Inc.
Pandanas, Ms L. A. The Slinky Luminescence: Two Plus Who? 2013. 84p. pap. *(978-0-9870702-9-6(0))* Reed, Laura.
Rinaldi, Ann. The Ever-After Bird. 2010. (ENG.). 240p. (J). (gr. 5-7). pap. 8.99 *(978-0-547-25854-6(2))* Houghton Mifflin Harcourt Publishing Co.
—Leigh Ann's Civil War. 2011. (ENG.). 320p. (YA). (gr. 7). pap. 17.99 *(978-0-547-54999-6(7))* Houghton Mifflin Harcourt Publishing Co.
Salomon, Peter Adam. All Those Broken Angels. 2014. (ENG.). 240p. (YA). pap. 11.99 *(978-0-7387-4079-9(9)*, Flux) North Star Editions.
Salvati, Elizabeth A. Counting Your Way down the Toccoa River Canoe Trail. 2011. 24p. pap. 12.95 *(978-1-4567-5773-1(3))* AuthorHouse.
Scampering Through Savannah. 2007. (YA). lib. bdg., act. bk. ed. *(978-0-9787589-2-9(7))* ON Words Publishing, LLC.

Shulimson, Sarene. Lights Out Shabbat. Ebbeler, Jeff, illus. 2012. (Shabbat Ser.). (ENG.). 32p. (J). (gr. -1-2). pap. 7.95 *(978-0-7613-7565-4(1)*, Kar-Ben Publishing) Lerner Publishing Group.
—Lights Out Shabbat. Ebbeler, Jeffrey, illus. 2012. (Shabbat Ser.). (ENG.). 32p. (J). (gr. -1-2). lib. bdg. 17.95 *(978-0-7613-7564-7(3)*, Kar-Ben Publishing) Lerner Publishing Group.
Silvano, Wendi. Love Is All Around Georgia. Czernichowska, Joanna, illus. 2016. (ENG.). 32p. (J). (-6). 12.99 *(978-1-4926-2919-1(7)*, Sourcebooks Jabberwocky) Sourcebooks, Inc.
Smallman, Steve. Santa Is Coming to Atlanta. Dunn, Robert, illus. 2015. (ENG.). 32p. (J). (-3). 9.99 *(978-1-4926-2640-4(6)*, Sourcebooks Jabberwocky) Sourcebooks, Inc.
—Santa Is Coming to Georgia. Dunn, Robert, illus. 2013. (ENG.). 32p. (J). (-3). 9.99 *(978-1-4022-8794-7(1)*, Sourcebooks Jabberwocky) Sourcebooks, Inc.
—Santa Is Coming to Savannah. Dunn, Robert, illus. 2013. (ENG.). 32p. (J). (-3). 9.99 *(978-1-4022-8979-8(0)*, Sourcebooks Jabberwocky) Sourcebooks, Inc.
Spain, Susan Rosson. The Twelve Days of Christmas in Georgia. Dulemba, Elizabeth O., illus. 2010. (Twelve Days of Christmas in America Ser.). (ENG.). 40p. (J). (gr. k). 12.95 *(978-1-4027-7008-1(1))* Sterling Publishing Co., Inc.
Steveson, Nanci Turner. Georgia Rules. 2017. 272p. (J). (gr. 3-7). 16.99 *(978-0-06-237457-8(5))* HarperCollins Pubs.
Stinson, Aimee. The Championship Game, 1 vol. 2009. 52p. pap. 16.95 *(978-1-60813-645-2(0))* PublishAmerica, Inc.
Stroud, Bettye. The Patchwork Path: A Quilt Map to Freedom. Bennett, Erin Susanne, illus. 2007. (ENG.). 32p. (J). (gr. k-3). pap. 7.99 *(978-0-7636-3519-0(7))* Candlewick Pr.
Sully, Katherine. Night-Night Georgia. Kolanovic, Dubravka & Poole, Helen, illus. 2016. (ENG.). 20p. (J). (-1). bds. 9.99 *(978-1-4926-4216-9(9)*, 9781492642169, Sourcebooks Jabberwocky) Sourcebooks, Inc.
Wilkinson, Brenda. Ludell. 2014. (ENG., Illus.). 228p. (J). (-9). pap. 12.95 *(978-1-939601-16-2(9))* Ig Publishing, Inc.
Woods, Brenda. My Name Is Sally Little Song. 2007. (ENG.). 192p. (J). (gr. 3-7). 7.99 *(978-0-14-240943-5(X)*, Puffin Books) Penguin Young Readers Group.
—My Name Is Sally Little Song. 2007. (Illus.). 182p. (gr. 2-7). 17.00 *(978-0-7569-8156-3(5))* Perfection Learning Corp.
Woodsonrick. Poodles in Space. 2012. 24p. 24.95 *(978-1-4626-5333-1(2))* America Star Bks.
Zalonis, C. B. Strangers in the Forest. 2006. (J). pap. 8.00 *(978-0-8059-6820-0(2))* Dorrance Publishing Co., Inc.

GEORGIA—HISTORY

Alphin, Elaine. An Unspeakable Crime: The Prosecution & Persecution of Leo Frank. 2014. (ENG., Illus.). 152p. (gr. 9-12). pap. 9.95 *(978-1-4677-4630-4(4)*, Carolrhoda Bks.) Lerner Publishing Group.
Barger, Jeff. Atlanta. 2016. (Dropping In On Ser.). (ENG., Illus.). 32p. (gr. 2-4). 32.79 *(978-1-68191-404-6(2))* Rourke Educational Media.
Bennett, Doraine. Appalachian Plateau. 2009. (J). 22.60 *(978-1-935077-19-0(8))*; pap. 10.60 *(978-1-935077-24-4(4))* State Standards Publishing, LLC.
—Blue Ridge Mountains. 2009. (J). 20.60 *(978-1-935077-20-6(1))*; pap. 10.60 *(978-1-935077-25-1(2))* State Standards Publishing, LLC.
—Sequoyah. 2008. *(978-1-935077-05-3(8))*; pap. *(978-1-935077-12-1(0))* State Standards Publishing, LLC.
—Tomochichi. 2008. (J). *(978-1-935077-06-0(6))*; pap. *(978-1-935077-13-8(9))* State Standards Publishing, LLC.
Blackburn, Joyce. James Edward Oglethorpe. 2004. (ENG., Illus.). 192p. (J). per. 15.95 *(978-1-57736-332-3(9))* Turner Publishing Co.
Boehm Jerome, Kate. Atlanta, Ga: Cool Stuff Every Kid Should Know. 2010. (Arcadia Kids Ser.). (ENG., Illus.). 48p. (J). (gr. 3-6). pap. 9.99 *(978-1-4396-0062-7(7))* Arcadia Publishing.
Brown, Vanessa. Georgia. (Bilingual Library of the United States of America Ser.). (ENG & SPA.). 32p. 2009. (gr. 2-2). 47.90 *(978-1-60853-355-8(7)*, Editorial Buenas Letras) 2005. (Illus.). (J). (gr. 3-6). lib. bdg. 25.25 *(978-1-4042-3075-0(0))* Rosen Publishing Group, Inc., The.
Carr, Diane. Chattahoochee River. 2010. (Illus.). 24p. (J). *(978-1-935077-54-1(6))*; pap. *(978-1-935077-61-9(9))* State Standards Publishing, LLC.
Crane, Carol. Little Georgia. Knorr, Laura, illus. 2013. (Little State Ser.). (ENG.). 20p. (J). (gr. -1-k). 9.95 *(978-1-58536-203-5(4)*, 202355) Sleeping Bear Pr.
Crompton, Sam. The Colonial Period of Georgia's History. 2017. (Spotlight on Georgia Ser.). 32p. (gr. 9-10). pap. 11.75 ***(978-1-5081-6011-3(2)***, PowerKids Pr.) Rosen Publishing Group, Inc., The.
—Developments in Georgia after World War II. 2017. (Spotlight on Georgia Ser.). 32p. (gr. 9-10). pap. 11.75 ***(978-1-5081-6021-2(X)***, PowerKids Pr.) Rosen Publishing Group, Inc., The.
—Developments in Georgia During the Late 20th Century. 2017. (Spotlight on Georgia Ser.). 32p. (gr. 9-10). pap. 11.75 ***(978-1-5081-6006-9(6)***, PowerKids Pr.) Rosen Publishing Group, Inc., The.
—Georgia & the Modern Civil Rights Movement. 2017. (Spotlight on Georgia Ser.). 32p. (gr. 9-10). pap. 11.75 ***(978-1-5081-5976-6(9)***, PowerKids Pr.) Rosen Publishing Group, Inc., The.
—Georgia During Reconstruction. 2017. (Spotlight on Georgia Ser.). 32p. (gr. 9-10). pap. 11.75 ***(978-1-5081-5981-0(5)***, PowerKids Pr.) Rosen Publishing Group, Inc., The.
—Georgia During the New South Era. 2017. (Spotlight on Georgia Ser.). 32p. (gr. 9-10). pap. 11.75 ***(978-1-5081-6001-4(5)***, PowerKids Pr.) Rosen Publishing Group, Inc., The.
—Georgia During World War II. 2017. (Spotlight on Georgia Ser.). 32p. (gr. 9-10). pap. 11.75 ***(978-1-5081-5996-4(3)***, PowerKids Pr.) Rosen Publishing Group, Inc., The.
—Georgia from World War I Through the Great Depression. 2017. (Spotlight on Georgia Ser.). 32p. (gr. 9-10). pap. 11.75 ***(978-1-5081-5986-5(6)***, PowerKids Pr.) Rosen Publishing Group, Inc., The.
Crompton, Samuel. Georgia & the American Revolution. 2017. (Spotlight on Georgia Ser.). 32p. (gr. 9-10). 70.50 ***(978-1-5081-5972-8(6)***, PowerKids Pr.) Rosen Publishing Group, Inc., The.
—Georgia During the Civil War & Reconstruction. 2017. (Spotlight on Georgia Ser.). 32p. (gr. 9-10). pap. 11.75 ***(978-1-5081-5991-9(2)***, PowerKids Pr.) Rosen Publishing Group, Inc., The.
—Georgia During the ERA of Westward Expansion, 1789 to 1840. 2017. (Spotlight on Georgia Ser.). 32p. (gr. 9-10). pap. 11.75 ***(978-1-5081-6016-8(3)***, PowerKids Pr.) Rosen Publishing Group, Inc., The.
—Native American Cultures of Georgia. 2017. (Spotlight on Georgia Ser.). 32p. (gr. 9-10). 26.25 ***(978-1-5081-6029-8(5)***, PowerKids Pr.) Rosen Publishing Group, Inc., The.
Doak, Robin Santos. Georgia, 1521-1776. 2006. (National Geographic Voices from ColonialAmerica Ser.). (ENG., Illus.). 112p. (gr. k-3). 21.95 *(978-0-7922-6389-0(8))*; lib. bdg. 32.90 *(978-0-7922-6858-1(X))* National Geographic Society. (National Geographic Children's Bks.).
Doherty, Craig A. & Doherty, Katherine M. Georgia. 2005. (Thirteen Colonies Ser.). (Illus.). 144p. (gr. 5-8). 35.00 *(978-0-8160-5419-0(3))* Facts On File, Inc.
Durrie, Karen. Georgia: The Peach State. 2012. (J). *(978-1-61913-341-9(5))*; pap. *(978-1-61913-342-6(3))* Weigl Pubs., Inc.
Hall, Brianna. Exploring the Georgia Colony. 2016. (Exploring the 13 Colonies Ser.). (ENG., Illus.). 48p. (gr. 3-4). lib. bdg. 31.99 *(978-1-5157-2241-0(4))* Capstone Press of Coughlan Cos.
Hally, Ashleigh. Coretta Scott King. 2012. (Illus.). 24p. (J). *(978-1-935884-78-1(6))*; pap. *(978-1-935884-84-2(0))* State Standards Publishing, LLC.
—Jackie Cochran. 2012. (Illus.). 24p. (J). *(978-1-935884-75-0(1))*; pap. *(978-1-935884-81-1(6))* State Standards Publishing, LLC.
—Juliette Gordon Low. 2012. (Illus.). 24p. (J). *(978-1-935884-77-4(8))*; pap. *(978-1-935884-83-5(2))* State Standards Publishing, LLC.
—Lugenia Burns Hope. 2012. (Illus.). 24p. (J). lib. bdg. *(978-1-935884-76-7(X))* State Standards Publishing, LLC.
—Martha Berry. 2012. (Illus.). 24p. (J). *(978-1-935884-73-6(5))*; pap. *(978-1-935884-79-8(4))* State Standards Publishing, LLC.
—Rosalynn Carter. 2012. (Illus.). 24p. (J). *(978-1-935884-74-3(3))*; pap. *(978-1-935884-80-4(8))* State Standards Publishing, LLC.
Harkins, Susan Sales & Harkins, William H. Georgia: The Debtors Colony. 2006. (Building America Ser.). (Illus.). 48p. (J). (gr. 3-7). lib. bdg. 29.95 *(978-1-58415-465-5(9))* Mitchell Lane Pubs., Inc.
Haywood, Karen Diane. Georgia. 2nd ed. 2013. 80p. (J). (gr. 4-8). 31.36 *(978-1-60870-879-6(9))* Cavendish Square Publishing.
Hill, Christina. Georgia's Goods & Services. 2016. (Primary Source Readers Ser.). (Illus.). 32p. (gr. 2-2). 8.99 *(978-1-4938-2563-9(1))* Teacher Created Materials, Inc.
Jerome, Kate B. Lucky to Live in Georgia. 2017. (Arcadia Kids Ser.). (ENG., Illus.). 32p. (J). 16.99 ***(978-0-7385-2780-2(7))*** Arcadia Publishing.
King Farris, Christine. My Brother Martin: A Sister Remembers Growing up with the Rev. Dr. Martin Luther King Jr. Soentpiet, Chris K., illus. 2005. 35p. (J). (gr. 4-7). 15.65 *(978-0-7569-6552-5(7))* Perfection Learning Corp.
Kopp, Kathleen. Atlanta: The Big Peach. 2016. (Primary Source Readers Ser.). 32p. (gr. 2-2). 8.99 *(978-1-4938-2551-6(8))* Teacher Created Materials, Inc.
—Regions & Rivers of Georgia. 2016. (Primary Source Readers Ser.). (Illus.). 32p. (gr. 2-2). 8.99 *(978-1-4938-2550-9(X))* Teacher Created Materials, Inc.
Kurtz, Jane. Celebrating Georgia: 50 States to Celebrate. Canga, C. B., illus. 2015. (Green Light Readers Level 3 Ser.). (ENG.). 40p. (J). (gr. 1-4). pap. 3.99 *(978-0-544-41975-9(8)*, HMH Books For Young Readers) Houghton Mifflin Harcourt Publishing Co.
Maloof, Torrey. Mary Musgrove: Bringing People Together. 2016. (Primary Source Readers Ser.). (Illus.). 32p. (gr. 2-2). 8.99 *(978-1-4938-2557-8(7))* Teacher Created Materials, Inc.
Marsh, Carole. Exploring Georgia Through Project-Based Learning. 2016. (Georgia Experience Ser.). (ENG.). (J). pap. 9.99 *(978-0-635-12334-3(7))* Gallopade International.
—Georgia History Projects: 30 Cool, Activities, Crafts, Experiments & More for Kids to Do to Learn about Your State! 2003. (Georgia Experience Ser.). 32p. (gr. k-5). pap. 5.95 *(978-0-635-01779-6(2)*, Marsh, Carole Bks.) Gallopade International.
Mis, Melody S. The Colony of Georgia: A Primary Source History. (Primary Source Library of the Thirteen Colonies & the Lost Colony Ser.). 24p. (gr. 3-4). 2009. 42.50 *(978-1-60854-136-2(3))* 2006. (Illus.). (J). lib. bdg. 22.60 *(978-1-4042-3433-8(0))* Rosen Publishing Group, Inc., The. (PowerKids Pr.).
Nault, Jennifer. Georgia. 2011. (Guide to American States Ser.). (Illus.). 48p. (YA). (gr. 3-6). 29.99 *(978-1-61690-782-2(7))*; (J). *(978-1-61690-458-6(5))* Weigl Pubs., Inc.
—Georgia: The Peach State. 2016. (J). *(978-1-4896-4845-7(3))* Weigl Pubs., Inc.
Niland, Kurt, Sr. Gwinnett: Success Lives Here. 2003. 256p. bds. 64.95 *(978-0-9748034-0-1(5))* Intaglio, Inc.
Peters, Yvette. Tell Me about Georgia!!!! Facts about Georgia. 2010. 12p. 9.49 *(978-1-4520-0874-5(4))* AuthorHouse.
Pohl, Amelia E. Mary Musgrove: Georgia, My State Biographies. l.t. ed. 2008. (ENG., Illus.). 24p. (J). (gr. k-2). 22.60 *(978-1-935077-02-2(3)*, Everett Pr.) State Standards Publishing, LLC.
Pohl, Amelia J. Flint River. 2009. (J). *(978-1-935077-55-8(4))*; pap. *(978-1-935077-62-6(7))* State Standards Publishing, LLC.
—Ocmulgee River. 2009. (J). *(978-1-935077-56-5(2))*; pap. *(978-1-935077-63-3(5))* State Standards Publishing, LLC.
—Savannah River. 2009. (J). *(978-1-935077-58-9(9))*; pap. *(978-1-935077-65-7(1))* State Standards Publishing, LLC.
Publications International Ltd. Staff. Yesterday & Today Football Universary of Georgia. 2009. 144p. 15.95 *(978-1-4127-1657-4(8))* Publications International, Ltd.
Rice, Katelyn. Savannah: Hostess City of the South. 2016. (Primary Source Readers Ser.). (Illus.). 32p. (gr. 2-2). 8.99 *(978-1-4938-2558-5(5))* Teacher Created Materials, Inc.
Rich, Steve. Mrs. Carter's Butterfly Garden. 2014. (ENG., Illus.). 32p. (J). (gr. k-3). pap. 12.95 *(978-1-941316-08-5(5))* National Science Teachers Assn.
Schwartz, Heather E. Locked up for Freedom: Civil Rights Protesters at the Leesburg Stockade. 2017. (ENG., Illus.). 64p. (J). (gr. 5-8). lib. bdg. 33.32 ***(978-1-4677-8597-6(0)***, Millbrook Pr.) Lerner Publishing Group.
Schwartz, Heather E. Tomochichi: A Chief & a Friend. 2016. (Primary Source Readers Ser.). (Illus.). 32p. (gr. 2-2). 8.99 *(978-1-4938-2556-1(9))* Teacher Created Materials, Inc.
Sonneborn, Liz. A Primary Source History of the Colony of Georgia. (Primary Sources of the Thirteen Colonies & the Lost Colony Ser.). 64p. 2009. (gr. 5-8). 58.50 *(978-1-60851-878-4(7))* 2006. (Illus.). (YA). (gr. 4-7). lib. bdg. 31.95 *(978-1-4042-0426-3(1))* 2006. (ENG., Illus.). (gr. 4-8). per. 12.95 *(978-1-4042-0674-8(4))* Rosen Publishing Group, Inc., The.
Spotlight on Georgia. 2017. (Spotlight on Georgia Ser.). 32p. (gr. 9-10). 315.00 ***(978-1-5081-6031-1(7))***; pap. 141.00 ***(978-1-5081-6034-2(1))*** Rosen Publishing Group, Inc., The. (PowerKids Pr.).
Sullivan, Laura L., et al. Georgia. 2015. (It's My State! (r) Ser.). (ENG., Illus.). 80p. (J). (gr. 4-4). 34.21 *(978-1-62713-192-6(2))* Cavendish Square Publishing.
Thompson, Landy. Altamaha River. 2009. (J). *(978-1-935077-53-4(8))*; pap. *(978-1-935077-60-2(0))* State Standards Publishing, LLC.
Tieck, Sarah. Georgia, 1 vol. 2012. (Explore the United States Ser.). (ENG.). 32p. (J). (gr. 2-5). 28.50 *(978-1-61783-348-9(7))* ABDO Publishing Co.
Wang, Andrea. What's Great about Georgia? 2014. (Our Great States Ser.). (Illus.). 32p. (gr. 2-5). (J). lib. bdg. 26.60 *(978-1-4677-3337-3(7)*, Lerner Pubns.); (ENG., pap. 7.95 *(978-1-4677-4528-4(6))* Lerner Publishing Group.
Ward, Jill. The Cherokees. 2010. (J). *(978-1-935077-79-4(1))*; pap. *(978-1-935077-86-2(4))* State Standards Publishing, LLC.
—The Creeks. 2010. (J). *(978-1-935077-78-7(3))*; pap. *(978-1-935077-85-5(6))* State Standards Publishing, LLC.
—Creeks & Cherokees Today. 2010. (J). *(978-1-935077-80-0(5))*; pap. *(978-1-935077-87-9(2))* State Standards Publishing, LLC.
—Georgia's First People. 2010. (J). *(978-1-935077-74-9(0))*; pap. *(978-1-935077-81-7(3))* State Standards Publishing, LLC.
—Mississippian Indians. 2010. (J). *(978-1-935077-77-0(5))*; pap. *(978-1-935077-84-8(8))* State Standards Publishing, LLC.
—Oconee River. 2010. (J). *(978-1-935077-57-2(0))*; pap. *(978-1-935077-64-0(3))* State Standards Publishing, LLC.
—Shell Mound Builders. 2010. (J). *(978-1-935077-75-6(9))*; pap. *(978-1-935077-82-4(1))* State Standards Publishing, LLC.
—St. Marys River. 2009. (J). *(978-1-935077-59-6(7))*; pap. *(978-1-935077-66-4(X))* State Standards Publishing, LLC.
—Woodland Indians. 2010. (J). *(978-1-935077-76-3(7))*; pap. *(978-1-935077-83-1(X))* State Standards Publishing, LLC.

GEOSCIENCE

see Geology

GERBILS

Coppendale, Jean. Gerbils & Hamsters. 2004. (QEB You & Your Pet Ser.). (Illus.). 32p. (J). lib. bdg. 18.95 *(978-1-59566-055-8(0))* QEB Publishing Inc.
Ellis, Carol. Hamsters & Gerbils. 2008. (Great Pets Ser.). 48p. (gr. 3-18). lib. bdg. 29.93 *(978-0-7614-2999-9(9)*, Benchmark Bks.) Marshall Cavendish Corp.
Howell, Laura. Gerbils. Fox, Christyan, illus. Burton, Jane, photos by. 2005. (Usborne First Pets Ser.). 32p. (J). (gr. k-4). pap. 5.95 *(978-0-7945-1116-6(3)*, Usborne) EDC Publishing.
Johnson, Jinny. Hamster & Gerbil. 2014. (My New Pet Ser.). 24p. (gr. k-3). lib. bdg. 28.50 *(978-1-62588-030-7(8))* Black Rabbit Bks.
—Hamster & Gerbil. 2014. (My New Pet Ser.). (ENG., Illus.). 24p. (J). (gr. -1-3). pap. 8.95 *(978-1-77092-207-5(5))* Saunders Bk. Co. CAN. Dist: RiverStream Publishing.
Koopmans, Carol. Caring for Your Gerbil. 2006. (Caring for Your Pet Ser.). (Illus.). 32p. (J). (gr. 3-7). per. 9.95 *(978-1-59036-469-7(4))*; lib. bdg. 26.00 *(978-1-59036-468-0(6))* Weigl Pubs., Inc.
—Gerbil. 2010. (J). pap. 9.95 *(978-1-61690-074-8(1))*; 32p. (gr. 3-5). lib. bdg. 27.13 *(978-1-61690-073-1(3))* Weigl Pubs., Inc.
Morgan, Sally. Gerbils & Hamsters. 2012. (Pets Plus Ser.). (Illus.). 32p. (gr. 3-6). lib. bdg. 31.35 *(978-1-59920-701-8(X))* Black Rabbit Bks.
Northeast Editing, Inc Staff, contrib. by. Gerbils. 2008. (J). *(978-1-932904-28-4(X))* Eldorado Ink.
Roswell, Jackie. Gerbils, Vol. 12. 2016. (Understanding & Caring for Your Pet Ser.). (ENG., Illus.). 128p. (J). (gr. 5-8). 25.95 *(978-1-4222-3696-3(X))* Mason Crest.
Sjonger, Rebecca & Kalman, Bobbie. Gerbils. Crabtree, Marc, illus. Crabtree, Marc, photos by. 2003. (Pet Care Ser.). (ENG.). 32p. (J). lib. bdg. *(978-0-7787-1752-2(6))* Crabtree Publishing Co.
Sparling, Rebecca. Gerbils. 2009. (Illus.). 112p. (J). 14.95 *(978-1-932904-36-9(0))* Eldorado Ink.
Thomas, Isabel. Giggle's Guide to Caring for Your Gerbils, 1 vol. Peterson, Rick, illus. 2014. (Pets' Guides). (ENG.). 32p. (gr. 1-3). pap. 8.29 *(978-1-4846-0267-6(6))*; 27.32 *(978-1-4846-0260-7(9))* Heinemann-Raintree. (Heinemann First Library).

GERBILS—FICTION

Adler, David A. The Many Troubles of Andy Russell. Hillenbrand, Will, illus. 2005. (Andy Russell Ser.: 1). (ENG.). 144p. (J). (gr. 1-4). pap. 6.99 *(978-0-15-205440-3(5))* Houghton Mifflin Harcourt Publishing Co.
—The Many Troubles of Andy Russell. 2008. (J). (gr. 2-4). pap. 24.95 incl. audio *(978-1-4301-0479-7(1))* Live Oak Media.
Conrad, Cody And Ametta. The Gerbil & the Arabian Nights: Jamal's Night Trip for Water. 2012. 16p. pap. 15.99 *(978-1-4772-2430-4(0))* AuthorHouse.
Delaney, Michael. Obi, Gerbil on the Loose! 2008. (ENG.). 208p. (J). (gr. 5-18). 16.99 *(978-0-525-47890-4(6)*, Dutton Books for Young Readers) Penguin Young Readers Group.
Farrer, Vashti. Fearsome Creatures. Webb, Melissa, illus. 2004. iv, 36p. (J). pap. *(978-0-7608-6744-0(5))* Sundance/Newbridge Educational Publishing.
Fine, Anne. Countdown. 2006. (Yellow Bananas Ser.). (ENG., Illus.). 48p. (J). (gr. -1-3). lib. bdg. *(978-0-7787-0958-9(2))* Crabtree Publishing Co.
Jane, Pamela. Winky Blue Goes Wild! Tilley, Debbie, illus. 2003. 64p. (J). 13.95 *(978-1-59034-588-7(6))*; pap. *(978-1-59034-589-4(4))* Mondo Publishing.
Kebbe, Jonathan. Shredder. Nayler, Sarah, illus. 2014. (ENG.). 80p. (J). (gr. k-2). pap. 7.99 *(978-0-552-56898-2(8))* Transworld Publishers Ltd. GBR. Dist: Independent Pubs. Group.
Lang, Kathy. Spaced Out Gerbil. Cotton, Sue Lynn, illus. 2013. 20p. pap. 12.95 *(978-1-61493-190-4(9))* Peppertree Pr., The.
Lois, Lowry. Anastasia off Her Rocker. 2015. (Anastasia Krupnik Story Ser.). (ENG., Illus.). 160p. (J). (gr. 5-7). pap. 6.99 *(978-0-544-43959-7(7)*, HMH Books For Young Readers) Houghton Mifflin Harcourt Publishing Co.
Marbury, Stephanie. Off to the Moon! Leigh, Tom, illus. 2006. 20p. (J). *(978-1-59939-100-7(7)*, Reader's Digest Young Families, Inc.) Studio Fun International.
Stewart, Emma. The Adventures of Fillmore the Gerbil. 2008. 24p. pap. 13.50 *(978-1-60693-033-5(8)*, Eloquent Bks.) Strategic Book Publishing & Rights Agency (SBPRA).
Swallow, Pamela Curtis. Melvil & Dewey Gone Fishin', 1 vol. Eliasen, Lorena, ed. 2004. (Illus.). 56p. (C). pap. 14.00 *(978-1-59158-153-6(2)*, LU1532) Pearson Education GBR. Dist: ABC-CLIO, LLC.
—Melvil & Dewey in the Chips, 1 vol. Schroeder, Judith, ed. 2004. (Illus.). 48p. (C). (gr. 2-4). pap. 14.00 *(978-1-59158-150-5(8)*, LU1508, Libraries Unlimited) ABC-CLIO, LLC.
—Melvil & Dewey in the Fast Lane, 1 vol. Schroeder, Judith, ed. 2004. (Illus.). 48p. (C). (gr. 2-4). pap. 14.00 *(978-1-59158-151-2(6)*, LU1516, Libraries Unlimited) ABC-CLIO, LLC.

GERMAN LANGUAGE

Auf Deutsch! 2003. stu. ed., wbk. ed. *(978-0-618-02967-9(2))*;Level 3. stu. ed. *(978-0-618-02963-1(X))* Holt McDougal.
Daves-Schneider, Lida, et al. Auf Deutsch! 2006. (Illus.). 273p. stu. ed. *(978-0-618-02962-4(1))*; 273p. stu. ed. *(978-0-618-02961-7(3))*; 200p. stu. ed., per., wbk. ed. *(978-0-618-02968-6(0))* Holt McDougal.
Fedoruk, Dennis, prod. Bilingual Baby - Flashcard Set - German. 2013. (GER.). (J). 7.99 *(978-1-892703-76-7(9))* Small Fry Beginnings.
Funk, Hermann, et al. genial. A1 Intensivtrainer: Deutsch als Fremdsprache für Jugendliche. 2005. (GER & ENG.). (YA). Level A2. 94p. pap. 12.75 *(978-3-468-47579-5(9))*Level B1. pap. 12.75 *(978-3-468-47539-9(X))* Langenscheidt Publishing Group.
—genial. A2 Testheft mit CD: Deutsch als Fremdsprache für Jugendliche. 2005. (GER & ENG.). (YA). Level A1. 48p. pap. 27.50 *(978-3-468-47558-0(6))*Level B1. 56p. pap. 27.50 incl. audio compact disk *(978-3-468-47538-2(1))* Langenscheidt Publishing Group.
—geni@l B1: Zertifikatsniveau. (GER.). (YA). Level A1. 2005. pap. 22.95 *(978-3-468-96709-2(8))*Level A2. 2005. 192p. pap., tchr. ed. 34.95 *(978-3-468-47572-6(1))*Level A2. 2003. wbk. ed. 14.95 *(978-3-468-96712-2(8))*Level B1. 2005. pap., tchr. ed. 34.75 *(978-3-468-47532-0(2))*Level B1. 2005. pap., wbk. ed. 16.50 *(978-3-468-47536-8(5))* Langenscheidt Publishing Group.
Mayesky & Kalz, Jill. My First German Phrases, 1 vol. Translations.com Staff, tr. Fabbri, Daniele, illus. 2012. (Speak Another Language! Ser.). (ENG.). 32p. (gr. 1-3). lib. bdg. 26.65 *(978-1-4048-7154-0(3))* Picture Window Bks.
Milet Publishing Staff. My Bilingual Book-Hearing (English-German) 2014. (My Bilingual Book Ser.). (ENG & GER., Illus.). 28p. (J). (gr. -1-k). 9.95 *(978-1-84059-777-6(1))* Milet Publishing.
—My Bilingual Book-Sight (English-German) 2014. (My Bilingual Book Ser.). (ENG & GER., Illus.). 28p. (J). (gr. -1-k). 9.95 *(978-1-84059-793-6(3))* Milet Publishing.
—My Bilingual Book-Touch (English-German) 2014. (My Bilingual Book Ser.). (ENG & GER., Illus.). 28p. (J). (gr. -1-k). 9.95 *(978-1-84059-841-4(7))* Milet Publishing.
—Smell / Das Riechen. 2014. (My Bilingual Book Ser.). (ENG & GER., Illus.). 28p. (J). (gr. -1-k). 9.95 *(978-1-84059-809-4(3))* Milet Publishing.
Passport Books Staff, ed. German Picture Dictionary. Goodman, Marlene, illus. 2003. (Let's Learn... Picture Ser.). (GER.). (J). (gr. 4-7). pap. 9.95 *(978-0-8442-2167-0(8)*, 21678, Passport Bks.) McGraw-Hill Trade.
Pirz, Therese S. & Hobson, Mark. Kids Stuff German: Easy German Phrases to Teach Your Kids (and Yourself) 2003. (Bilingual Kids Ser.: Vol. 3). (ENG & GER., Illus.). 183p. (J). (gr. -1-8). pap. 29.95 *(978-0-9606140-4-2(4))* Chou Chou Pr.

GERMAN LANGUAGE—DICTIONARIES

Amery, Heather. First Hundred Words in German II. 2015. (First Hundred Words Ser.). (ENG.). 32p. (J). pap. 6.99 *(978-0-7945-3514-8(3)*, Usborne) EDC Publishing.
Bedeutungswoerterbuch. 3rd ed. (Duden-Schuelerduden Ser.). (GER.). 496p. (YA). 26.95 *(978-3-411-05963-8(X))* Bibliographisches Institut & F. A. Brockhaus AG DEU. Dist: International Bk. Import Service, Inc.
Collins Dictionaries. German School Dictionary. 2015. (GER & ENG.). 624p. (YA). 2nd rev. ed. (gr. 6-11). pap. 7.99 *(978-0-00-756932-8(7))* 4th rev. ed. (gr. 5-11). pap. 10.99 *(978-0-00-756934-2(3))* HarperCollins Pubs. Ltd. GBR. Dist: Independent Pubs. Group.
Davies, Helen. German Dictionary for Beginners. Irving, Nicole, ed. Shackell, John, illus. 2006. (Beginner's Dictionaries Ser.). (GER.). 128p. (J). (gr. 4). lib. bdg. 20.95 *(978-1-58086-487-9(2))* EDC Publishing.
Funk, Hermann, et al. Geni@l: Deutsch Fremdsprache fuer Jugendliche - Learning Glossary German-English. (GER & ENG.). (YA). 2005. 64p. pap. 11.50 *(978-3-468-47560-3(8))*Level A2. 2005. 64p. pap. 10.95 *(978-3-468-47580-1(2))*Level A2. 2003. 18.95 *(978-3-468-96711-5(X))*Level B1. 2004. 72p. 9.95 *(978-3-468-47540-5(3))* Langenscheidt Publishing Group.
Goodman, Marlene. Let's Learn German Picture Dictionary. 2003. (ENG & GER., Illus.). 80p. 13.00

E
F
G

(978-0-07-140824-0(X), 007140824X) McGraw-Hill Cos., The.

Hanson, Tracie, des. New World Baby - German. 2007. (ENG, GER, FRE, SPA & ITA., Illus.). 28p. (J). 14.00 (978-0-9799185-2-0(9)) Hanson, Tracie.

Hippocrene Books Staff. Children's Illustrated German Dictionary: English-German, German-English. 2003. (Hippocrene Children's Illustrated Foreign Language Dictionaries Ser.). (ENG & GER., Illus.). 122p. pap. 11.95 (978-0-7818-0986-3(X)) Hippocrene Bks., Inc.

Kudela, Katy R. My First Book of German Words, 1 vol. 2011. (Bilingual Picture Dictionaries Ser.). 32p. (gr. 1-2). (ENG & MUL.). pap. 8.10 (978-1-4296-6335-9(9)); (MUL.). pap. 47.70 (978-1-4296-6462-2(2)) Capstone Press of Coughlan Cos. (Apius Bks.).

Litchfield, J. & Brooks, F. Everyday Words in German. rev. ed. 2004. (What Shall I Do Today? Ser.). (GER.). 48p. (J). lib. bdg. 20.95 (978-1-58086-547-0(X)) EDC Publishing.

Milet Publishing Staff. Bilingual Visual Dictionary. 2011. (Milet Multimedia Ser.). (ENG & GER., Illus.). 1p. (J). (gr. k-2). cd-rom 19.95 (978-1-84059-585-7(X)) Milet Publishing.

—Milet Bilingual Visual Dictionary. 2012. (Milet Bilingual Visual Dictionary Ser.). (ENG & GER., Illus.). 148p. (J). (gr. k-2). 34.95 (978-1-84059-689-2(9)) Milet Publishing.

—Vegetables - My First Bilingual Book. 2011. (My First Bilingual Book Ser.). (ENG., Illus.). 24p. (J). (gr. k — 1). bds. 7.99 (978-1-84059-661-8(9)) Milet Publishing.

Rauenhorst, Linda. Frohliche Weihnachten: Learning Songs & Traditions in German. Collier, Roberta, illus. 2007. (Teach Me Ser.). (GER & ENG.). 32p. (J). (gr. -1-3). 19.95 (978-1-59972-063-0(9)) Teach Me Tapes, Inc.

Turhan, Sedat. New Bilingual Visual Dictionary (English-German) 2nd ed. 2017. (New Bilingual Visual Dictionary Ser.). (ENG & GER., Illus.). 144p. (J). (gr. k-2). 19.95 (978-1-78508-886-5(6)) Milet Publishing.

WrightGroup/McGraw-Hill. German. 2003. (Just Look 'n Learn Picture Dictionary Ser.). (GER & ENG., Illus.). 96p. (J). (gr. 4-7). 11.95 (978-0-8442-2058-1(2), 20582, Passport Bks.) McGraw-Hill Trade.

York, M. J. Learn German Words. Petelinsek, Kathleen, illus. 2014. (Foreign Language Basics Ser.). (ENG.). 24p. (J). (gr. 2-5). 27.07 (978-1-62687-375-9(5), 207122) Child's World, Inc., The.

GERMAN LANGUAGE—GRAMMAR

Amery, H. First Thousand Words in German. 2004. (First Thousand Words Ser.). 64p. (J). lib. bdg. 20.95 (978-1-58086-625-5(5), Usborne) EDC Publishing.

Derkow-Disselbeck, Barbara & Kirsch, Dieter. Anna, Schmidt und Oskar, Level 2. 2005. (GER.). 64p. (J). pap., tchr. ed. 19.25 (978-3-468-96853-2(1)) Langenscheidt Publishing Group.

Duden. Kennst du Das? Das ABC. (Duden Ser.). (GER., Illus.). 16p. (J). (978-3-411-70631-0(7)) Bibliographisches Institut & F. A. Brockhaus AG DEU. Dist: International Bk. Import Service, Inc.

—Kennst du Das? Lastwagen. (Duden Ser.). (GER., Illus.). 16p. (J). (978-3-411-70641-9(4)) Bibliographisches Institut & F. A. Brockhaus AG DEU. Dist: International Bk. Import Service, Inc.

Funk, Hermann, et al. genial. A1 Intensivtrainer: Deutsch als Fremdsprache für Jugendliche, Level A1. 2005. (GER.). 96p. pap. 10.95 (978-3-468-47559-7(4)) Langenscheidt Publishing Group.

—geni@l B1: Zertifikatsniveau. 2005. (GER & ENG.). (YA). pap. 16.50 (978-3-468-47555-9(1)); (YA). pap. 16.50 (978-3-468-47576-4(4));Level A1. 168p. pap., tchr. ed. 34.75 (978-3-468-47552-8(7));Level A1. (YA). pap. 22.50 (978-3-468-47553-5(5));Level A1. (YA). pap. 43.00 (978-3-468-47557-3(8));Level A1. (YA). pap. 16.50 (978-3-468-47556-6(X));Level A1. (YA). pap. 22.50 (978-3-468-47554-2(3));Level A2. (YA). pap. 16.50 (978-3-468-47575-7(6));Level A2. (YA). pap. 22.50 (978-3-468-47573-3(X));Level A2. (YA). pap. 22.50 (978-3-468-47574-0(8));Level B1. (YA). pap., tchr. ed. 22.50 (978-3-468-47534-4(9));Level B1. (YA). pap., tchr. ed. 22.50 (978-3-468-47533-7(0));Level B1. (YA). pap., wbk. ed. 16.50 (978-3-468-47535-1(7)) Langenscheidt Publishing Group.

Grammatik. (Duden-Schuelerduden Ser.). (GER.). 522p. (YA). (978-3-411-05634-7(7)); 96p. (J). (gr. 4-5). (978-3-411-04441-2(1)) Bibliographisches Institut & F. A. Brockhaus AG DEU. Dist: International Bk. Import Service, Inc.

Holt, Rinehart and Winston Staff. Komm Mit! Level 1: Grammatikheft. 3rd ed. 2003. (GER.). pap., tchr. ed. 21.46 (978-0-03-065009-3(7)) Holt McDougal.

—Komm Mit! Level 1: Ubungsheft. 3rd ed. 2003. (GER.). pap., tchr. ed. 22.66 (978-0-03-065012-3(7)) Holt McDougal.

Junge Leute: Deutsch Aktuell. 4th ed. (J). 19.95 (978-0-8219-1667-4(X), 45156) EMC/Paradigm Publishing.

Milet Publishing Staff. Home - My First Bilingual Book. 2011. (My First Bilingual Book Ser.). (ENG., Illus.). 24p. (J). (gr. k — 1). bds. 8.99 (978-1-84059-645-8(7)) Milet Publishing.

—Jobs - Berufe. 2012. (My First Bilingual Book Ser.). (ENG & GER., Illus.). 24p. (J). (gr. k — 1). bds. 7.99 (978-1-84059-705-9(4)) Milet Publishing.

—My First Bilingual Book - Fruit. 2011. (My First Bilingual Book Ser.). (ENG., Illus.). 24p. (J). (gr. k — 1). bds. 7.99 (978-1-84059-629-8(5)) Milet Publishing.

—My First Bilingual Book-Music (English-German) 2012. (My First Bilingual Book Ser.). (ENG & GER., Illus.). 24p. (J). (gr. k — 1). bds. 7.99 (978-1-84059-721-9(6)) Milet Publishing.

—My First Bilingual Book-Opposites. 2012. (My First Bilingual Book Ser.). (ENG & GER., Illus.). 24p. (J). (gr. k — 1). bds. 7.99 (978-1-84059-737-0(2)) Milet Publishing.

—My First Bilingual Book-Sports (English-German) 2012. (My First Bilingual Book Ser.). (ENG & GER., Illus.). 24p. (J). (gr. k — 1). bds. 7.99 (978-1-84059-753-0(4)) Milet Publishing.

Overton, Carrie. Was Ist das? Animals. 2012. 44p. pap. 11.98 (978-1-937571-02-3(5)) Huginn & Muninn.

Specht, Roland H., et al. Deutsch Aktuell 3: Junge Leute. 4th ed. (GER.). (YA). (gr. 10-12). pap. 198.95 incl. VHS (978-0-8219-1666-7(1), 45064Z) EMC/Paradigm Publishing.

Uebungen zur Deutschen Rechtschreibung I. (Duden-Schuelerduden Ser.). (GER.). 304p. (YA). (978-3-411-05243-1(0)) Bibliographisches Institut & F. A. Brockhaus AG DEU. Dist: International Bk. Import Service, Inc.

Uebungen zur Deutschen Rechtschreibung II. (Duden-Schuelerduden Ser.). (GER.). 160p. (YA). (978-3-411-05593-7(6)) Bibliographisches Institut & F. A. Brockhaus AG DEU. Dist: International Bk. Import Service, Inc.

GERMAN LANGUAGE—READERS

Die Abenteuer der Seefahrt.Tr. of Adventure of Seafares. (GER., Illus.). (YA). 31.95 (978-3-411-09141-6(X), MY9141E) Bibliographisches Institut & F. A. Brockhaus AG DEU. Dist: Continental Bk. Co., Inc.

Das Aegyptische Grab. (GER.). (978-3-411-09301-4(3)) Bibliographisches Institut & F. A. Brockhaus AG DEU. Dist: i. b. d., Ltd.

Am Himmel und im Weltall. (GER.). 19.95 (978-3-411-09311-3(0)) Bibliographisches Institut & F. A. Brockhaus AG DEU. Dist: Distribooks, Inc.

Aufsatz. (Duden-Schuelerhilfen Ser.). (GER.). 79p. (J). (gr. 2-3). (978-3-411-02616-6(2)) Bibliographisches Institut & F. A. Brockhaus AG DEU. Dist: International Bk. Import Service, Inc.

Aufsatz 2. (Duden-Schuelerhilfen Ser.). (GER.). 96p. (J). (gr. 3-4). (978-3-411-02633-3(2)) Bibliographisches Institut & F. A. Brockhaus AG DEU. Dist: International Bk. Import Service, Inc.

Aufsatz/Bericht. (Duden-Schuelerhilfen Ser.). (GER.). 112p. (YA). (gr. 8-10). (978-3-411-05731-3(9)) Bibliographisches Institut & F. A. Brockhaus AG DEU. Dist: International Bk. Import Service, Inc.

Aufsatz/Beschreibung. (Duden-Schuelerhilfen Ser.). (GER.). 112p. (YA). (gr. 7-10). (978-3-411-05761-0(0)) Bibliographisches Institut & F. A. Brockhaus AG DEU. Dist: International Bk. Import Service, Inc.

Aufsatz/Eroerterung. (Duden-Schuelerhilfen Ser.). (GER.). 112p. (YA). (gr. 8-10). (978-3-411-05741-2(6)) Bibliographisches Institut & F. A. Brockhaus AG DEU. Dist: International Bk. Import Service, Inc.

Aufsatz/Erzaehlen. (Duden-Schuelerhilfen Ser.). (GER.). 112p. (J). (gr. 5-7). (978-3-411-05821-1(8)) Bibliographisches Institut & F. A. Brockhaus AG DEU. Dist: International Bk. Import Service, Inc.

Aufsatz/Inhaltsangabe. (Duden-Schuelerhilfen Ser.). (GER.). 112p. (YA). (gr. 7-9). (978-3-411-05801-3(3)) Bibliographisches Institut & F. A. Brockhaus AG DEU. Dist: International Bk. Import Service, Inc.

Boldt. Politik und Gesellschaft. (Duden-Schuelerduden Ser.). (GER., Illus.). 460p. (YA). 27.95 (978-3-411-04723-9(2)) Bibliographisches Institut & F. A. Brockhaus AG DEU. Dist: Continental Bk. Co., Inc.

Bour, Laura. Am Fluss. 2005. (Meyers Klein Kinderbibliothek). (GER.). 24p. (J). spiral bd. 14.25 (978-3-411-08591-0(6)) Langenscheidt Publishing Group.

Bourgoing, Pascale de. Der Apfel. 2005. (Meyers Klein Kinderbibliothek).Tr. of Apple. (GER., Illus.). 24p. (J). spiral bd. 14.25 (978-3-411-08541-5(X)) Langenscheidt Publishing Group.

Bröger, Achim. Meyers Grosses Kinderlexikon. (GER., Illus.). 348p. (978-3-411-07693-2(3)) Bibliographisches Institut & F. A. Brockhaus AG DEU. Dist: i. b. d., Ltd.

Burke, David. Beauty & the Beast: Level 3: Learn German Through Fairy Tales. Sandoval, Migs, illus. 2006. (Learn German Through Fairy Tales Ser.). (ENG & GER.). 29p. (J). (gr. -1-3). pap. 14.95 incl. audio compact disk (978-1-891888-88-5(9)) Slangman Publishing.

—Goldilocks (English to German - Level 2) Learn GERMAN Through Fairy Tales. 2007. (Learn German Through Fairy Tales Ser.). (ENG & GER., Illus.). 29p. (J). pap. 14.95 incl. audio compact disk (978-1-891888-83-0(8)) Slangman Publishing.

de Harven, Emile. Gefahrliche Wege. (GER.). (J). tchr. ed. 95.00 (978-0-88436-636-2(7), 45018) EMC/Paradigm Publishing.

Delafosse, Claude. Das Haus. 2005. (Meyers Klien Kinderbibliothek). (GER.). 24p. (J). spiral bd. 14.25 (978-3-411-08561-3(4)) Langenscheidt Publishing Group.

Delafosse, Claude & Mettler, Rène. Die Maus. 2005. (Meyers Klien Kinderbibliothek). (GER., Illus.). 24p. (J). spiral bd. 14.25 (978-3-411-08551-4(7)) Langenscheidt Publishing Group.

—Der Vogel. 2005. (Meyers Klien Kinderbibliothek).Tr. of Bird. (GER.). 24p. (J). spiral bd. 14.25 (978-3-411-08531-6(2)) Langenscheidt Publishing Group.

Der Deutsche Aufsatz. (Duden Abiturhilfen Ser.). (GER.). 96p. (YA). (gr. 12-13). (978-3-411-04641-6(4)) Bibliographisches Institut & F. A. Brockhaus AG DEU. Dist: International Bk. Import Service, Inc.

Holt, Rinehart and Winston Staff. Elements of Literature: Terra Nova Test Preparation with Answer Key. 5th ed. 2005. pap. 13.46 (978-0-03-037789-1(7)) Harcourt Schl. Pubs.

—Komm Mit! Level 1: Storytelling Book. 3rd ed. 2003. (GER.). pap. 14.60 (978-0-03-065479-4(3)) Holt McDougal.

Im Zirkus. (GER.). (978-3-411-09341-0(2)) Bibliographisches Institut & F. A. Brockhaus AG DEU. Dist: i. b. d., Ltd.

In den Nestern der Insekten. (GER.). (978-3-411-09281-9(5)) Bibliographisches Institut & F. A. Brockhaus AG DEU. Dist: i. b. d., Ltd.

In Hoehlen und Grotten. (GER.). (978-3-411-09291-8(2)) Bibliographisches Institut & F. A. Brockhaus AG DEU. Dist: i. b. d., Ltd.

Kenkmann, Andrea. 1000 First Words in German. Lacome, Susie, illus. 2013. (ENG & GER.). 96p. (J). (gr. k-4). 12.99 (978-1-84322-958-2(7)) Anness Publishing GBR. Dist: National Bk. Network.

König, Hans J. Geheime Mission. (J). tchr. ed. 95.00 (978-0-88436-635-5(9), 45020) EMC/Paradigm Publishing.

Lenz, Siegfried. Lehmanns Erzählungen, Level C. (GER.). (J). pap. 9.99 (978-0-8219-0852-5(9), 45301) EMC/Paradigm Publishing.

Literatur. 3rd ed. (Duden-Schuelerduden Ser.). (GER.). 432p. (YA). (978-3-411-05403-9(4)) Bibliographisches Institut & F. A. Brockhaus AG DEU. Dist: International Bk. Import Service, Inc.

Mahoney, Judy. Teach Me Everyday German V. 1, Vol 1. Girouard, Patrick, illus. 2008. (GER & ENG.). 32p. (J). (gr. -1). 19.95 (978-1-59972-103-3(1)) Teach Me Tapes, Inc.

Meyer-Hullmann, Kerstin, illus. Das Grundschulwoerterbuch. (Duden Ser.). (GER.). 224p. (J). (978-3-411-06061-0(1)) Bibliographisches Institut & F. A. Brockhaus AG DEU. Dist: International Bk. Import Service, Inc.

Meyers Editors. Der Bauernhof. 2005. (Meyers Klien Kinderbibliothek). (GER.). 24p. (J). spiral bd. 14.25 (978-3-411-08581-1(9)) Langenscheidt Publishing Group.

—Das Schiff. 2005. (Meyers Klien Kinderbibliothek). (GER.). 24p. (J). spiral bd. 14.25 (978-3-411-08571-2(1)) Langenscheidt Publishing Group.

Milet Publishing Staff. Animals. 2011. (My First Bilingual Book Ser.). (ENG., Illus.). 24p. (J). (gr. k — 1). bds. 8.99 (978-1-84059-613-7(9)) Milet Publishing.

—Colours - My First Bilingual Book. 2010. (My First Bilingual Book Ser.). (ENG & GER., Illus.). 24p. (J). (gr. k — 1). bds. 8.99 (978-1-84059-536-9(1)) Milet Publishing.

—My First Bilingual Book - Numbers. 2010. (My First Bilingual Book Ser.). (ENG & GER., Illus.). 24p. (J). (gr. k — 1). bds. 7.99 (978-1-84059-542-0(6)) Milet Publishing.

Naoura, Salah. Auf dem Bauernhof. (GER., Illus.). 24p. pap. (978-3-411-08241-4(0)) Bibliographisches Institut & F. A. Brockhaus AG DEU. Dist: i. b. d., Ltd.

—Im Eis. (GER., Illus.). 24p. pap. (978-3-411-08251-3(8)) Bibliographisches Institut & F. A. Brockhaus AG DEU. Dist: i. b. d., Ltd.

—Im Regenwald. (GER., Illus.). 24p. pap. (978-3-411-08231-5(3)) Bibliographisches Institut & F. A. Brockhaus AG DEU. Dist: i. b. d., Ltd.

—In der Savanne. (GER., Illus.). 24p. pap. (978-3-411-08261-2(5)) Bibliographisches Institut & F. A. Brockhaus AG DEU. Dist: i. b. d., Ltd.

Nunn, Daniel. Families in German: Die Familien, 1 vol. 2013. (World Languages - Families Ser.). (ENG, MUL & GER.). 24p. (gr. 1-3). pap. 6.29 (978-1-4329-7181-6(6)); lib. bdg. 22.65 (978-1-4329-7174-8(3)) Heinemann-Raintree. (Acorn).

—Numbers in German: Die Zahlen - 1 2 3. 2012. (World Languages - Numbers Ser.). (ENG, GER & MUL.). 24p. (gr. 1-3). pap. 6.29 (978-1-4329-6681-2(2), Acorn) Heinemann-Raintree.

—Numbers in German (Die Zahlen) Eins, Zwei, Drei... 2012. (World Languages - Numbers Ser.). (ENG, GER & MUL.). 24p. (gr. 1-3). lib. bdg. 22.65 (978-1-4329-6674-4(X), Acorn) Heinemann-Raintree.

Rosler, O'Sullivan. It could be worse - oder? Eine deutsch-englische Geschichte. (GER.). 8.95 (978-3-499-20374-9(X), RW374E) Rowohlt Taschenbuch Verlag GmbH DEU. Dist: Continental Bk. Co., Inc.

Schaetze und Wracks. (GER.). (978-3-411-09331-1(5)) Bibliographisches Institut & F. A. Brockhaus AG DEU. Dist: i. b. d., Ltd.

Scholz, Barbara, illus. Der Abc-Duden. 2nd ed. (Duden Ser.). (GER.). 96p. (J). (978-3-411-70772-0(0)) Bibliographisches Institut & F. A. Brockhaus AG DEU. Dist: International Bk. Import Service, Inc.

Semper, Lothar. Auf einer Harley Davidson möchte ich sterben. 2005. (GER.). 104p. (YA). (gr. 7-12). pap. 9.00 (978-3-468-49697-4(4)) Langenscheidt Publishing Group.

Trim, John & Kohl, Katrin M. Deutsch Direkt. (J). (gr. 9-12). suppl. ed. 84.00 (978-0-8219-0227-1(X), 45033) EMC/Paradigm Publishing.

—Deutsch Direkt! (J). (gr. 9-12). wbk. ed. 19.95 (978-0-8219-0240-0(7), 45659) EMC/Paradigm Publishing.

—Deutsch Direkt! Answer Key. (J). (gr. 9-12). 11.95 (978-0-8219-0354-4(3), 45826) EMC/Paradigm Publishing.

Verdet, Jean-Pierre. Das Weltall. 2005. (Meyers Klien Kinderbibliothek Ser.). (GER.). (J). spiral bd. 14.25 (978-3-411-09791-3(4)) Langenscheidt Publishing Group.

GERMAN SHEPHERD DOG

Barnes, Nico. German Shepherds, 1 vol. 2014. (Dogs Ser.). (ENG.). 24p. (J). (gr. 4-8). lib. bdg. 28.50 (978-1-62970-030-4(4)) ABDO Publishing Co.

Beal, Abigail. I Love My German Shepherd. 2011. (Top Dogs Ser.). 24p. (J). (ENG.). pap. 8.25 (978-1-4488-2654-4(3)); (Illus.). lib. bdg. 22.60 (978-1-4488-2535-6(0)) Rosen Publishing Group, Inc., The. (PowerKids Pr.).

Bodden, Valerie. German Shepherds. 2014. (Illus.). 24p. (J). 25.65 (978-1-60818-362-3(9), Creative Education) Creative Co., The.

Bozzo, Linda. I Like German Shepherds! 2012. (Discover Dogs with the American Canine Association Ser.). (Illus.). 24p. (J). (gr. k-3). pap. 7.95 (978-1-4644-0119-0(5), Enslow Elementary) Enslow Pubs., Inc.

Fiedler, Julie. German Shepherd Dogs. (Tough Dogs Ser.). 24p. (gr. 3-4). 2009. 42.50 (978-1-60854-564-3(4)) 2006. (Illus.). (J). lib. bdg. 22.60 (978-1-4042-3121-4(8)) Rosen Publishing Group, Inc., The. (PowerKids Pr.).

Gray, Susan H. German Shepherds. 2008. (Domestic Dogs Ser.). (ENG., Illus.). 32p. (J). (gr. 2-5). 28.50 (978-1-59296-965-4(8), 200141) Child's World, Inc., The.

Gray, Susan Heinrichs. German Shepherds. 2016. (J). (978-1-4896-4591-3(8)) Weigl Pubs., Inc.

Johnson, Jinny. German Shepherd. 2013. (My Favorite Dogs Ser.). (Illus.). 24p. (gr. k-3). 28.50 (978-1-59920-842-8(3)) Black Rabbit Bks.

Loewen, Nancy. German Shepherds. 2003. (Dog Breeds Ser.). 24p. (J). lib. bdg. 21.35 (978-1-58340-313-6(2)) Black Rabbit Bks.

Lunis, Natalie. German Shepherd: Super Smart. 2011. (Big Dogs Rule! Ser.). 32p. (YA). (gr. 2-5). lib. bdg. 25.27 (978-1-61772-299-8(5)) Bearport Publishing Co., Inc.

Rajczak, Kristen. German Shepherds. 2011. (Great Big Dogs Ser.). (Illus.). 24p. (J). (gr. 2-5). pap. 8.15 (978-1-4339-5772-7(8), Gareth Stevens Learning Library); lib. bdg. 22.60 (978-1-4339-5770-3(1)) Stevens, Gareth Publishing LLLP.

Rustad, Martha E. H. German Shepherds. 2017. (Favorite Dog Breeds Ser.). (ENG.). 24p. (gr. 1-4). 20.95 (978-1-68151-127-6(4)) Amicus Publishing.

Shores, Erika L. All about German Shepherds, 1 vol. 2012. (Dogs, Dogs, Dogs Ser.). (ENG., Illus.). 24p. (gr. k-1). lib. bdg. 26.65 (978-1-4296-8725-6(8), Pebble Plus) Capstone Press of Coughlan Cos.

Ward, Gill. German Shepherd. 2017. (Dog Lover's Guides: Vol. 18). (ENG.). (YA). (gr. 7-12). 26.95 **(978-1-4222-3856-1(3))** Mason Crest.

World Book, Inc Staff, contrib. by. German Shepherds & Other Herding Dogs. 2009. (J). (978-0-7166-1373-2(5)) World Bk., Inc.

GERMANS—PENNSYLVANIA

see also Pennsylvania Dutch

Wall, Joanne. Anna of Allegheny. Wall, Joanne, ed. 2009. (Illus.). 110p. (YA). pap. 20.00 (978-0-9644283-9-3(3)) Wall, Mary Joanne.

GERMANS—UNITED STATES

Boyer Binns, Tristan. German Americans. 2003. (We Are America Ser.). (Illus.). 32p. (J). (gr. 2-4). lib. bdg. (978-1-4034-0165-6(9)) Heinemann-Raintree.

Moreno, Barry. The German Americans. 2007. (Major American Immigration Ser.). (YA). pap. 9.95 (978-1-4222-0674-4(2)) Mason Crest.

Moreno, Barry & Ashbrock, Peg. The German Americans. 2010. (Major American Immigration Ser.). (Illus.). 64p. (YA). (gr. 9-12). 22.95 (978-1-4222-0607-2(6)) Mason Crest.

Parker, Lewis K. Why German Immigrants Came to America. 2003. (Coming to America Ser.). (Illus.). 24p. (J). lib. bdg. 22.60 (978-0-8239-6458-1(2), PowerKids Pr.) Rosen Publishing Group, Inc., The.

Sonneborn, Liz. German Americans. 2003. (Immigrants in America Ser.). (Illus.). 112p. (gr. 6-12). 30.00 (978-0-7910-7127-4(8), Chelsea Hse.) Facts On File, Inc.

GERMANS—UNITED STATES—FICTION

Doty, Kathryn Adams. Wild Orphan. 2006. (ENG.). 144p. (gr. 3-7). per. 14.95 (978-1-889020-20-4(6)) Edinborough Pr.

Dudley, David L. Caleb's Wars. 2011. (ENG.). 272p. (YA). (gr. 9). 17.99 (978-0-547-23997-2(1)) Houghton Mifflin Harcourt Publishing Co.

O Little Town (Germans) 76p. (YA). (gr. 6-12). pap. 9.95 (978-0-8224-3681-2(7)) Globe Fearon Educational Publishing.

GERMANY

Bechstein, Ludwig. The Rabbit Catcher & Other Fairy Tales. Jarrell, Randall, tr. Fontana, Ugo, illus. 2011. 42p. 35.95 (978-1-258-08375-5(2)) Literary Licensing, LLC.

Byers, Ann. Germany: A Primary Source Cultural Guide. 2005. (Primary Sources of World Cultures Ser.). (Illus.). 128p. (J). (gr. 5-8). lib. bdg. 37.25 (978-1-4042-2910-5(8)) Rosen Publishing Group, Inc., The.

Carew-Miller, Anna. Ludwig Van Beethoven: Great Composer. 2013. (People of Importance Ser.: 21). (Illus.). 32p. (J). (gr. 4-18). 19.95 (978-1-4222-2849-4(5)) Mason Crest.

Cates, David. Karl Marx: Philosopher & Revolutionary, 1 vol. 2011. (Essential Lives Set 7 Ser.). (ENG., Illus.). 112p. (J). (gr. 6-12). lib. bdg. 35.64 (978-1-61783-005-1(4)) ABDO Publishing Co.

Dubois & Fuller, Barbara. Germany. 3rd ed. 2013. 144p. (J). (gr. 6-9). 47.07 (978-1-60870-868-0(3)) Cavendish Square Publishing.

Flint, David. Focus on Germany. 2006. (World in Focus Ser.). (Illus.). 64p. (gr. 5-12). (J). lib. bdg. 34.00 (978-0-8368-6218-8(X)); pap. 14.05 (978-0-8368-6237-9(6)) Stevens, Gareth Publishing LLLP. (Gareth Stevens Secondary Library).

Fuller, Barbara. Germany. 2013. (Cultures of the World 4 Ser.). 144p. (J). (gr. 6-9). pap. 23.51 (978-1-62712-159-0(5)) Cavendish Square Publishing.

Fuller, Barbara & Vossmeyer, Gabriele. Germany. 2nd rev. ed. 2003. (Cultures of the World Ser.). (Illus.). 144p. (gr. 6-18). lib. bdg. 42.79 (978-0-7614-1667-8(6), Marshall Cavendish Reference Bks.) Marshall Cavendish Corp.

Hamen, Susan E. Germany, 1 vol. 2011. (Countries of the World Set 1 Ser.). (ENG., Illus.). 144p. (J). (gr. 6-12). lib. bdg. 37.07 (978-1-61783-110-2(7)) ABDO Publishing Co.

Hardyman, Robyn. Celebrate: Germany. 2009. (Celebrate Country Ser.). 32p. (gr. 4-6). 28.00 (978-1-60413-266-3(3), Chelsea Clubhouse) Facts On File, Inc.

Horne, William Reginald. Germany. 2nd rev. ed. 2007. (Modern World Nations Ser.). (Illus.). 120p. (YA). (gr. 7-12). lib. bdg. 35.00 (978-0-7910-9512-6(6)) Facts On File, Inc.

Marsh, Carole. Germany: The Country of Fairytale Castles & Cutting Edge Science! 2009. (It's Your World Ser.). 48p. (J). (gr. 2-9). pap. 7.99 (978-0-635-06815-6(X)) Gallopade International.

Mills, Clifford W. Angela Merkel. 2007. (Modern World Leaders Ser.). (Illus.). 120p. (YA). (gr. 7-12). lib. bdg. 30.00 (978-0-7910-9496-9(0)) Facts On File, Inc.

Nagelhout, Ryan. The Hindenburg Disaster. 2015. (Doomed! Ser.). (ENG., Illus.). 32p. (J). (gr. 4-5). 26.60 (978-1-4824-2938-1(1)) Stevens, Gareth Publishing LLLP.

Obregón, José María. Germany: Alemania. 2009. (Great National Soccer Teams / Grandes selecciones del fútbol mundial Ser.). (SPA & ENG.). 24p. pap. 8.25 (978-1-4358-2493-5(8)) Rosen Publishing Group, Inc., The.

—Germany: Alemania. Benson, Megan, tr. 2009. (Great National Soccer Teams / Grandes Selecciones Del Fútbol Mundial Ser.). (SPA & ENG., Illus.). 24p. (J). (gr. 2-5). lib. bdg. 22.60 (978-1-4042-8087-8(1)) Rosen Publishing Group, Inc., The.

Otfinoski, Steven. The Hindenburg Explosion: Core Events of a Disaster in the Air, 1 vol. 2014. (What Went Wrong? Ser.). (ENG.). 32p. (gr. 3-4). lib. bdg. 27.32 (978-1-4765-4184-6(1)) Capstone Press of Coughlan Cos.

Pohl, Kathleen. Alemania. 2008. (Descubramos Países del Mundo Ser.). (SPA., Illus.). 32p. (gr. 1-5). pap. 10.50 (978-0-8368-8788-4(3)); lib. bdg. 26.00 (978-0-8368-8781-5(6)) Stevens, Gareth Publishing LLLP. (Gareth Stevens Learning Library).

Popper, Garry. Lena & Peter in Germany. Johnson, Andi, illus. 2004. 36p. (gr. -1-7). 4.00 (978-1-84161-060-3(7)) Ravette Publishing, Ltd. GBR. Dist: Parkwest Pubns., Inc.

Reed, Avery. Who Were the Brothers Grimm? O'brien, John, illus. 2015. 105p. (J). (978-1-4844-6177-8(0), Grosset & Dunlap) Penguin Publishing Group.

Robbins, Trina. Lily Renée, Escape Artist: From Holocaust Survivor to Comic Book Pioneer. Timmons, Anne & Oh, Mo, illus. 2011. (Single Titles Ser.). (ENG.). 96p. (J). (gr. 5-8). pap. 7.95 (978-0-7613-8114-3(7), Graphic Universe™) Lerner Publishing Group.

Roberts, Russell. The Evolution of Government & Politics in Germany. 2014. (gr. 4-8). 29.95 (978-1-61228-587-0(2)) Mitchell Lane Pubs., Inc.

Rössig, Wolfgang. Karl Marx. 2009. (Profiles in Economics Ser.). 112p. (YA). lib. bdg. 28.95 (978-1-59935-132-2(3)) Reynolds, Morgan Inc.

Schwartz, Simon. The Other Side of the Wall. Watkinson, Laura, tr. from GER. 2015. (ENG., Illus.). 112p. (J). (gr. 7-12). pap. 9.99 *(978-1-4677-6028-7(5))*; lib. bdg. 29.32 *(978-1-4677-5840-6(X))* Lerner Publishing Group. (Graphic Universe™).

Senker, Cath. Germany. 2008. (Costume Around the World Ser.). (Illus.). 32p. (gr. 4-6). 28.00 *(978-0-7910-9767-0(6))*, Chelsea Clubhouse) Facts On File, Inc.

Tecco, Betsy Dru. How to Draw Germany's Sights & Symbols. 2009. (Kid's Guide to Drawing the Countries of the World Ser.). 48p. (gr. 4-4). 53.00 *(978-1-61511-111-4(5))*, PowerKids Pr.) Rosen Publishing Group, Inc., The.

Throp, Claire. Angela Merkel, 1 vol. 2014. (Extraordinary Women Ser.). (ENG.). 48p. (gr. 6-6). pap. 9.95 *(978-1-4109-5951-5(1))* Heinemann-Raintree.

Trumbauer, Lisa. King Ludwig's Castle: Germany's Neuschwanstein. 2005. (Castles, Palaces, & Tombs Ser.). 32p. (J). lib. bdg. 25.27 *(978-1-59716-002-5(4))* Bearport Publishing Co., Inc.

Wukovits, John F. World War II in Europe. 2004. (World History Ser.). (ENG., Illus.). 112p. (gr. 7-10). 34.95 *(978-1-59018-185-0(9))*, Lucent Bks.) Cengage Gale.

Zocchi, Judy. In Germany. Brodie, Neale, illus. 2005. (Global Adventures II Ser.). 32p. (J). per. 10.95 *(978-1-59646-181-9(0))* Dingles & Co.

—In Germany/en Alemania. Brodie, Neale, illus. 2005. (Global Adventures II Ser.).Tr. of En Alemania. (ENG & SPA.). 32p. (J). per. 10.95 *(978-1-59646-183-3(7))* Dingles & Co.

Zuehlke, Jeffrey. Germany in Pictures. 2nd ed. 2003. (Visual Geography Series, Second Ser.). (ENG., Illus.). 80p. (gr. 5-12). 31.93 *(978-0-8225-4681-8(7))* Lerner Publishing Group.

GERMANY—FICTION

Alden-Tirrill, Anna. The Promise Box. 2013. 284p. pap. 14.95 *(978-1-885831-05-7(6))* Proclaim Publishing.

Alma, Ann. Skateway to Freedom. 2nd ed. 2008. (ENG.). 136p. (YA). (gr. 5-8). pap. 11.99 *(978-1-55002-719-8(0))* Dundurn CAN. Dist: Ingram Publisher Services.

Andersen, Hans Christian & Capstone Press Staff. Caperucita Roja. Rivas, Victor, illus. 2010. (Graphic Spin en Español Ser.). (SPA.). 40p. (gr. 1-3). lib. bdg. 25.32 *(978-1-4342-1903-9(8))*, Graphic Spin en Español) Stone Arch Bks.

Andersen, Hans Christian & Stone Arch Books Staff. Caperucita Roja. Rivas, Victor, illus. 2010. (Graphic Spin en Español Ser.). (SPA & ENG.). 40p. (gr. 1-3). pap. 5.95 *(978-1-4342-2315-9(9))*, Graphic Spin en Español) Stone Arch Bks.

Bailer, Darice & Domínguez, Madelca. La Bella Durmiente. Vila Delclòs, Jordi, illus. 2007. (SPA & ENG.). 28p. (J). *(978-0-545-03030-4(7))* Scholastic, Inc.

—El Flautista de Hamelín. Vila Delclòs, Jordi, illus. 2007. (SPA & ENG.). 28p. (J). *(978-0-545-02961-2(9))* Scholastic, Inc.

—El Lobo y Los Siete Cabritos. Montaña, Marta, illus. 2007. (SPA & ENG.). 28p. (J). *(978-0-545-02962-9(7))* Scholastic, Inc.

Bass, Karen. Summer of Fire, 1 vol. 2009. (ENG.). 295p. (YA). (gr. 9-12). pap. 12.95 *(978-1-55050-415-6(0))* Coteau Bks. CAN. Dist: Orca Bk. Pubs. USA.

Bauer, Sepp. The Christmas Rose. Wenz-Vietor, Else, illus. 2008. 48p. (J). (gr. -1-3). 12.95 *(978-1-58089-232-2(9))* Charlesbridge Publishing, Inc.

Bell, Michele Ashman. Spyhunt: A Heart-Pounding Adventure: A Novel. 2004. 187p. (J). *(978-1-59156-457-7(3))* Covenant Communications.

Blair, Eric. The Bremen Town Musicians: A Retelling of the Grimm's Fairy Tale, 1 vol. Dickson, Bill, illus. 2013. (My First Classic Story Ser.). (ENG.). 32p. (gr. k-3). pap. 7.10 *(978-1-4795-1848-7(4))*, My First Classic Story) Picture Window Bks.

—Rumpelstiltskin: A Retelling of the Grimm's Fairy Tale, 1 vol. Shaw, David, illus. 2013. (My First Classic Story Ser.). (ENG.). 32p. (gr. k-3). pap. 7.10 *(978-1-4795-1850-0(6))*, My First Classic Story) Picture Window Bks.

Blair, Eric & Peterson, Ben. The Pied Piper, 1 vol. 2010. (My First Classic Story Ser.). (ENG.). 32p. (gr. k-3). lib. bdg. 22.65 *(978-1-4048-6084-1(3))*, My First Classic Story) Picture Window Bks.

Blair, Eric, et al. The Brave Little Tailor: A Retelling of the Grimm's Fairy Tale, 1 vol. Shaw, David, illus. 2010. (My First Classic Story Ser.). (ENG.). 32p. (gr. k-3). lib. bdg. 22.65 *(978-1-4048-6074-2(6))*, My First Classic Story) Picture Window Bks.

—The Pied Piper. 2011. (My First Classic Story Ser.). (ENG.). 32p. (gr. k-3). pap. 7.10 *(978-1-4048-7362-9(7))*, My First Classic Story) Picture Window Bks.

—Sleeping Beauty: A Retelling of the Grimm's Fairy Tale, 1 vol. Ouren, Todd, illus. 2010. (My First Classic Story Ser.). (ENG.). 32p. (gr. k-3). lib. bdg. 22.65 *(978-1-4048-6080-3(0))*, My First Classic Story) Picture Window Bks.

Bolton, Violet. Heidi & Huber the Adventures Begin. 2011. (Illus.). 60p. pap. *(978-1-908447-90-6(7))* Grosvenor Hse. Publishing Ltd.

Bowling, Athena. Malice: The Magicka Barney Chronicles, 1 vol. 2010. 388p. pap. 29.95 *(978-1-4489-4066-0(4))* PublishAmerica, Inc.

Brandeis, Madeline. Mitz & Fritz of Germany. 2011. 164p. 41.95 *(978-1-258-10138-1(6))* Literary Licensing, LLC.

Brown, Carron, ed. Sleeping Beauty & Snow White & the Seven Dwarfs: Two Tales & Their Histories. 2009. (World of Fairy Tales Ser.). 32p. (J). (gr. -1-2). pap. 10.55 *(978-1-60754-635-1(3))*; lib. bdg. 22.60 *(978-1-60754-634-4(5))* Windmill Bks.

Capstone Press Staff. Rapunzel. Timmins, Jeffrey Stewart, illus. 2009. (Graphic Spin Ser.). (ENG.). 40p. (gr. 1-3). pap. 5.95 *(978-1-4342-1392-1(7))*, Graphic Revolve) Stone Arch Bks.

—Snow White. Valdez Y Alanis, Erik, illus. 2009. (Graphic Spin Ser.). (ENG.). 40p. (gr. 1-3). pap. 5.95 *(978-1-4342-1394-5(3))*, Graphic Revolve) Stone Arch Bks.

Carney, Larry, adapted by. Rapunzel. 2009. (ENG., Illus.). 24p. (J). 6.95 *(978-1-60072-113-7(3))* PC Treasures, Inc.

—Snow White. 2009. (ENG., Illus.). 24p. (J). 6.95 *(978-1-60072-117-5(6))* PC Treasures, Inc.

Cela, Jaume. The Pied Piper: El Flautista de Hamelín. Losantos, Cristina, illus. 2008. (Bilingual Fairy Tales Ser.: BIL). (SPA & ENG.). 32p. (J). (gr. -1-3). 14.95 *(978-0-8118-6028-4(0))* Chronicle Bks. LLC.

Christensen, Gerda. Troll Peter Discovers the Bog-Woman's Secret & Other Stories. 2010. 40p. pap. 18.27 *(978-1-4251-8822-1(2))* Trafford Publishing.

Christmas in Bavaria. 2005. (YA). per. 16.95 *(978-0-9763572-7-8(5))* English Garden Talk Pr.

Cole, Tom Clohosy. Wall. Cole, Tom Clohosy, illus. 2014. (ENG., Illus.). 32p. (J). (gr. -1-3). 16.99 *(978-0-7636-7560-8(1))*, Templar) Candlewick Pr.

Cooley, Danika. When Lightning Struck! The Story of Martin Luther. 2015. (ENG.). 264p. 16.99 *(978-1-5064-0583-4(5))*, Fortress Pr.) Augsburg Fortress, Pubs.

Crawford, Marie. Nutmeg, Ginger & Little Joan. 2012. 24p. pap. 17.99 *(978-1-62230-186-7(2))* Salem Author Services.

De La Ramee, Louise & Ouida. The Nurnberg Stove. 2009. 64p. pap. 7.95 *(978-1-60664-399-0(1))* Rodgers, Alan Bks.

Du Bist Spat Aufgewacht, Mein Schatz: Eine Abenteuergeschichte. 2003. (Illus.). 284p. (YA). 15.00 *(978-0-9712545-0-3(8))* Privatgaeste Verlag.

Dublin, Anne. The Baby Experiment. 2012. (ENG., Illus.). 160p. (YA). (gr. 7-9). pap. 9.99 *(978-1-4597-0135-9(6))* Dundurn CAN. Dist: Ingram Publisher Services.

—The Baby Experiment: A Novel (Large Print 16pt) 2013. 172p. pap. *(978-1-4596-6337-4(3))* ReadHowYouWant.com, Ltd.

Encyclopaedia Britannica, Inc. Staff, compiled by. Hansel & Gretel. 2008. 49.95 *(978-1-59339-687-9(2))* Encyclopaedia Britannica, Inc.

Florida-James, Mark. Berlin Wolf. 2013. (ENG.). 336p. pap. *(978-1-78306-005-4(0))* Troubador Publishing Ltd.

French, Simon. Where in the World. 2003. 208p. (J). (gr. 3-7). 14.95 *(978-1-56145-292-7(0))*, Q34443) Peachtree Pubs.

Galdone, Paul. Rumpelstiltskin, 1 vol. 2008. (Read along Book & CD Ser.). (ENG., Illus.). 32p. (J). (gr. -1-3). audio compact disk 10.99 *(978-0-547-18181-3(7))* Houghton Mifflin Harcourt Publishing Co.

Gallaz, Christophe. Rose Blanche. Innocenti, Roberto, illus. 2011. (ENG.). 32p. (J). (gr. 5-17). pap. 10.99 *(978-0-89812-385-2(2))* Creative Co., The.

Glatshteyn, Yankev. Emil & Karl. Shandler, Jeffrey, tr. 2008. (ENG.). 208p. (J). (gr. 4-9). per. 9.99 *(978-0-312-37387-0(2))*, 9780312373870) Square Fish.

Grimm, Jacob & Grimm, Wilhelm. Grimm's Fairy Tales. McKowen, Scott, illus. 2009. (Sterling Unabridged Classics Ser.). (ENG.). 288p. (J). (gr. 5). 9.95 *(978-1-4027-6702-9(1))* Sterling Publishing Co., Inc.

—The Story of Little Red Riding Hood. Bing, Christopher H., illus. 2010. (ENG.). 40p. (J). (gr. k-17). 18.99 *(978-0-8118-6986-7(5))* Chronicle Bks. LLC.

Grimm, Jacob & Grimm, Wilhelm K. Grimm's Fairy Tales, 1 vol. Canga, C. B., illus. 2011. (Calico Illustrated Classics Ser.: No. 3). (ENG.). 112p. (YA). (gr. 3-6). 27.07 *(978-1-61641-102-2(3))* Magic Wagon.

—Hans My Hedgehog: A Tale from the Brothers Grimm. Nickle, John, illus. 2012. (ENG.). 40p. (J). (gr. k-3). 16.99 *(978-1-4169-1533-1(8))*, Atheneum Bks. for Young Readers) Simon & Schuster Children's Publishing.

Grimm, Jakob & Grimm, Wilhelm K. Grimm's Fairy Tales. Freeberg, Eric, illus. 2011. (Classic Starts(tm) Ser.). (ENG.). 160p. (J). (gr. 2-4). 6.95 *(978-1-4027-7311-2(0))* Sterling Publishing Co., Inc.

Grimm, The Brothers, et al. The Complete Grimm's Fairy Tales. 2011. 262p. pap. 8.69 *(978-1-936041-79-4(0))* Simon & Brown.

Grimm, Wilhelm K. & Grimm, Jacob. Little Red Riding-Hood: A Grimm's Fairy Tale. Lawson, Polly, tr. from GER. Van Zeyl, Marjan, illus. 2008. (ENG.). 20p. (J). (gr. -1-3). *(978-0-86315-622-9(3))* Floris Bks.

Higgins, Nadia. Hansel & Gretel. Petelinsek, Kathleen, illus. 2013. (Fairy Tale Collection). (ENG.). 24p. (J). (gr. k-3). 28.50 *(978-1-62323-609-0(6))*, 206376) Child's World, Inc., The.

Hobeika, Noelia, tr. The Pied Piper of Hamelin. Baas, Thomas, illus. 2016. (ENG.). 48p. (J). (gr. -1-3). 19.95 *(978-3-89955-767-1(0))* Die Gestalten Verlag DEU. Dist: Penguin Random Hse. LLC.

Hoffman, Mary. The Twelve Dancing Princesses. Clara, Miss, illus. 2012. (ENG.). 64p. (J). (gr. 2-6). pap. 9.99 *(978-1-84686-838-2(6))* Barefoot Bks., Inc.

Holub, Joan. Little Red Writing. Sweet, Melissa, illus. 2016. (ENG.). 36p. (J). (gr. k-3). pap. 7.99 *(978-1-4521-5209-7(8))* Chronicle Bks. LLC.

Howell, Trisha Adelena. The Stinky Shepherd. Marshall, Jamie, illus. 2005. 32p. (J). 15.95 *(978-1-931210-25-6(X))* Howell Canyon Pr.

Huling, Jan. Ol Bloo's Boogie-Woogie Band & Blues Ensemble, 1 vol. Sørensen, Henri, illus. 2010. (ENG.). 32p. (J). (gr. 1-5). 16.95 *(978-1-56145-436-5(2))* Peachtree Pubs.

Jeffers, Susan. Hansel & Gretel. 2011. (ENG.). 32p. (J). (gr. -1-k). 18.99 *(978-0-525-42221-1(8))*, Dutton Books for Young Readers) Penguin Young Readers Group.

Jones, Christianne C. Rapunzel: A Retelling of the Grimms' Fairy Tale, 1 vol. Muehlenhardt, Amy Bailey, illus. 2013. (My First Classic Story Ser.). (ENG.). 32p. (gr. k-3). pap. 7.10 *(978-1-4795-1852-4(2))*, My First Classic Story) Picture Window Bks.

Kacer, Kathy. Stones on a Grave, 1 vol. 2015. (Secrets Ser.). (ENG.). 240p. (YA). (gr. 8-12). pap. 14.95 *(978-1-4598-0659-7(X))* Orca Bk. Pubs. USA.

Kemp, Kristin. The Boy in the Striped Pajamas: An Instructional Guide for Literature. 2015. (Great Works). (ENG., Illus.). 72p. (gr. 4-8). pap. 9.99 *(978-1-4807-8507-6(5))* Shell Educational Publishing.

Lang, George. Pixy's Holiday Journey. 2007. (ENG.). 146p. pap. 18.99 *(978-1-4264-9501-4(3))*; 164p. pap. 21.99 *(978-1-4264-9882-4(9))* Creative Media Partners, LLC.

Lessing, Edeltraut B. Amber & Flax. 2009. *(978-1-61623-777-6(5))* Independent Pub.

Lickel, Lisa J. The German Girl. Hendricks, Brenda K., illus. 2013. 38p. pap. 5.95 *(978-0-9856215-4-4(0))* Fox Ridge Pubns.

Magers, Ramona Hirsch. Walter's Discovery. Hirsch, Charmaine, illus. 2008. 26p. pap. 24.95 *(978-1-60563-623-8(1))* America Star Bks.

Marsh, Carole. The Mystery of the Crystal Castle: Bavaria, Germany. 2009. (Around the World in 80 Mysteries Ser.). 133p. (J). 18.99 *(978-0-635-07041-8(3))*, Marsh, Carole Mysteries) Gallopade International.

McFadden, Deanna, et al. Sleeping Beauty. Graegin, Stephanie, illus. 2013. (Silver Penny Stories Ser.). (ENG.). 48p. (J). (gr. -1-1). 4.95 *(978-1-4027-8341-8(8))* Sterling Publishing Co., Inc.

McGowan, Keith. The Witch's Guide to Cooking with Children. Tanaka, Yoko, illus. 2011. (ENG.). 192p. (J). (gr. 4-7). pap. 8.99 *(978-0-312-67486-1(4))*, 9780312674861) Square Fish.

Michaelis, Antonia. The Storyteller. 2012. (ENG.). 416p. (YA). (gr. 9-17). 19.95 *(978-1-4197-0047-7(2))*, Amulet Bks.) Abrams, Inc.

Morpurgo, Michael. The Pied Piper of Hamelin. Chichester Clark, Emma, illus. 2011. (ENG.). 64p. (J). (gr. k-4). 16.99 *(978-0-7636-4824-4(8))* Candlewick Pr.

Namm, Diane. The Frog Prince. Quarello, Maurizio A. C., illus. 2013. (Silver Penny Stories Ser.). (ENG.). 48p. (J). (gr. -1-1). 4.95 *(978-1-4027-8429-3(5))* Sterling Publishing Co., Inc.

Oppenlander, Annette. Escape from the Past: The Duke's Wrath. 2015. (ENG.). 299p. (YA). (gr. 8-17). pap. 12.95 *(978-1-84694-973-9(4))*, Lodestone Bks.) Hunt, John Publishing Ltd. GBR. Dist: National Bk. Network.

Optic, Oliver, pseud. Northern Lands: Or, Young America in Russia & Prussia; A Story of Travel & Adventure / by William T. Adams (Oliver Optic). 2006. 384p. per. 26.99 *(978-1-4255-4074-6(0))* Michigan Publishing.

—Northern Lands; or, Young America in Russia & Prussia a Story of Travel & Adventure. 2006. 376p. per. 26.99 *(978-1-4255-3923-8(8))* Michigan Publishing.

Osei, Leah. The Bremen Town Musicians: A Retelling of the Story by the Brothers Grimm, 1 vol. rev. ed. 2013. (Fiction Readers Ser.). (ENG., Illus.). 28p. (J). (gr. 3-3). pap. 8.99 *(978-1-4333-5601-8(5))* Shell Educational Publishing.

Parker, Emma. Little Red Riding Hood. 2010. (Illus.). pap. *(978-1-877561-01-6(0))* First Edition Ltd.

Parunia, Des. The Quest for the Magic Funnel. 2012. (Illus.). 196p. (gr. 4-6). pap. 18.24 *(978-1-4772-3508-9(6))* AuthorHouse.

Patterson, James & Grabenstein, Chris. Secret of the Forbidden City. Neufeld, Juliana, illus. 2015. (Treasure Hunters Ser.: 3). (ENG.). 448p. (J). (gr. 3-7). 14.99 *(978-0-316-28480-6(7))*, Jimmy Patterson) Little Brown & Co.

Pausewang, Gudrun. Traitor. (Carolrhoda YA Ser.). 2010. (ENG.). 224p. (YA). (gr. 7-12). pap. 9.95 *(978-0-7613-6571-6(0))*, Carolrhoda Lab™) 2006. (Illus.). 220p. (J). (gr. -1-7). 16.95 *(978-0-8225-6195-8(6))*, Carolrhoda Bks.) Lerner Publishing Group.

Phillips, Dee. Tail Gunner. 2014. (Yesterday's Voices Ser.). (YA). lib. bdg. 19.60 *(978-0-606-35579-7(0))* Turtleback Bks.

Pinkney, Jerry. Little Red Riding Hood. 2007. (ENG., Illus.). 40p. (J). (gr. -1-3). 18.99 *(978-0-316-01355-0(2))* Little, Brown Bks. for Young Readers.

Playmore Publishers. Blanca Nieves: Cuento Plegable. 2011. pap. 4.95 *(978-0-86611-656-5(7))* Waldman Publishing Corp.

Richter, Jutta. The Cat: Or, How I Lost Eternity. Brailovsky, Anna, tr. from GER. Berner, Rotraut Susanne, illus. 2007. (ENG.). 80p. (J). (gr. 1-6). 14.00 *(978-1-57131-676-9(0))* Milkweed Editions.

—The Summer of the Pike. Brailovsky, Anna, tr. from GER. Buchholz, Quint, illus. 2006. (ENG.). 132p. (J). (gr. 2-8). 16.95 *(978-1-57131-671-4(X))*; (gr. 8-12). per. 6.95 *(978-1-57131-672-1(8))* Milkweed Editions.

Robert L. Drake. The Boy Allies with the Victorious Fleets: The Fall of the German Navy. l.t. ed. 2007. 384p. pap. 21.99 *(978-1-4264-8195-6(0))* Creative Media Partners, LLC.

Rowley, Deborah. The Miracle of the Wooden Shoes. 2008. 32p. (J). 18.95 *(978-1-59038-990-4(5))* Deseret Bk. Co.

Schröder, Monika. The Dog in the Wood. 2009. (ENG.). 168p. (J). (gr. 5-9). 17.95 *(978-1-59078-701-4(3))*, Front Street) Boyds Mills Pr.

Smith, Annie Laura. The Legacy of Bletchley Park. 2004. (YA). mass mkt. 6.99 *(978-0-9753367-1-7(1))* Onstage Publishing, LLC.

Smith, Dan. My Brother's Secret. 2015. (ENG.). 304p. (J). (gr. 3-7). 16.99 *(978-0-545-77155-9(2))* Scholastic, Inc.

Snowe, Olivia. Cassie & the Woolf, 1 vol. Lamoreaux, Michelle, illus. 2013. (Twicetold Tales Ser.). (ENG.). 128p. (gr. 3-4). lib. bdg. 25.32 *(978-1-4342-3786-6(9))* Stone Arch Bks.

—The Girl & the Seven Thieves, 1 vol. Lamoreaux, Michelle, illus. 2014. (Twicetold Tales Ser.). (ENG.). 128p. (gr. 3-4). pap. 5.95 *(978-1-4342-9555-2(9))* Stone Arch Bks.

Sommer, Isabell & Reinhardt, Swen. CHIP CHIPS JAM - 4: Der Schatz in der Elbe. 2010. 86p. pap. *(978-3-8391-0219-0(7))* Books on Demand GmbH.

Spradlin, Michael P. The Enemy Above. 2016. (ENG.). 240p. (J). (gr. 3-7). 16.99 *(978-0-545-85782-6(1))*, Scholastic Pr.) Scholastic, Inc.

Steiner, Rudolf. Three Grimms' Fairy Tales. Wagner, Gerard, illus. 2010. 88p. (J). 25.00 *(978-0-88010-716-7(2))* SteinerBooks, Inc.

Steinhöfel, Andreas & Wright, Chantal. The Spaghetti Detectives. 2011. (ENG.). 176p. (J). (gr. 3-7). 16.99 *(978-0-545-28975-7(0))*, Chicken Hse., The) Scholastic, Inc.

StJohn, Amanda. The Pied Piper of Hamelin: A German Folktale. Bonder, Dianna, illus. 2011. (Folktales from Around the World Ser.). (ENG.). 24p. (J). (gr. k-3). 28.50 *(978-1-60973-142-7(5))*, 201146) Child's World, Inc., The.

Stone Arch Books Staff. Rumpelstiltskin: The Graphic Novel, 1 vol. Alanis, Erik Valdez Y., illus. 2008. (Graphic Spin Ser.). (ENG.). 40p. (gr. 1-3). pap. 5.95 *(978-1-4342-0864-4(8))*, Graphic Revolve) Stone Arch Bks.

Tarshis, Lauren. I Survived the Hindenburg Disaster 1937. 2016. (I Survived Ser.: 13). (ENG.). 112p. (J). (gr. 2-5). pap. 4.99 *(978-0-545-65850-8(0))*, Scholastic Paperbacks) Scholastic, Inc.

Taylor, Mary Ann. Spies: A Gander's Cove Mystery. Casteel, Kay, illus. 2006. (J). mass mkt. 5.99 *(978-0-9753367-7-9(0))* Onstage Publishing, LLC.

Theisen, Manfred. Ohne Fehl und Makel: Ein Junge im Lebensborn-Heim. 2010. (GER.). 285p. pap. *(978-3-570-40029-6(8))* Bertelsman, Verlagsgruppe C. GmbH.

Ungerer, Tomi. Otto: The Autobiography of a Teddy Bear. 2010. (ENG., Illus.). 36p. (gr. 7-17). 16.95 *(978-0-7148-5766-4(1))* Phaidon Pr., Inc.

Vagnozzi, Barbara. The Musicians of Bremen. 2007. (Flip-Up Fairy Tales Ser.). (ENG., Illus.). 24p. (J). (gr. 1-2). *(978-1-84643-115-9(8))* Child's Play International Ltd.

Vander Zee, Ruth. Erika's Story. Innocenti, Roberto, illus. 2013. (ENG.). 24p. (J). (gr. 1-3). pap. 10.99 *(978-0-89812-891-8(9))*, Creative Paperbacks) Creative Co., The.

Voremberg, Linda. Robbie: A Journey of Hope, 1 vol. 2009. 52p. pap. 16.95 *(978-1-60703-486-5(7))* America Star Bks.

Watts, Irene N. Good-Bye Marianne: A Story of Growing up in Nazi Germany. Shoemaker, Kathryn E., illus. 2008. (ENG.). 128p. (J). (gr. 4-7). pap. 12.95 *(978-0-88776-830-9(X))*, Tundra Bks.) Tundra Bks. CAN. Dist: Penguin Random Hse. LLC.

Weisleder, Stanley. Wings of the Panther. 2010. (ENG.). 224p. pap. 15.00 *(978-0-936783-38-3(9))* Merril Pr.

Wilson, John. Flames of the Tiger. 2003. (ENG., Illus.). 176p. (J). (gr. 13-18). 6.95 *(978-1-55337-619-4(6))* Kids Can Pr., Ltd. CAN. Dist: Hachette Bk. Group.

Winch, John. Run, Hare, Run. 2007. (Illus.). 40p. pap. *(978-1-921049-55-2(3))* Little Hare Bks. AUS. Dist: HarperCollins Pubs. Australia.

GERMANY—HISTORY

Altman, Linda Jacobs. Hitler, Goebbels, Himmler: The Nazi Holocaust Masterminds. 2014. (Remembering the Holocaust Ser.). 96p. (J). (gr. 6-12). pap. 10.95 *(978-0-7660-6198-9(1))* Enslow Pubs., Inc.

—Hitler, Goebbles, Himmler: The Nazi Holocaust Masterminds. 2014. (Remembering the Holocaust Ser.). (Illus.). 96p. (J). (gr. 6-12). 27.94 *(978-0-7660-6197-2(3))* Enslow Pubs., Inc.

Bascomb, Neal. The Nazi Hunters: How a Team of Spies & Survivors Captured the World's Most Notorious Nazi. 2013. (ENG., Illus.). 256p. (J). (gr. 7). 17.99 *(978-0-545-43099-9(2))*, Levine, Arthur A. Bks.) Scholastic, Inc.

Benoit, Peter. The Hindenburg Disaster. 2011. (Illus.). 48p. (J). pap. *(978-0-531-29025-5(5))* Children's Pr., Ltd.

—The Hindenburg Disaster. 2011. (True Book(tm), A — Disasters Ser.). (ENG.). 48p. (J). (gr. 3-5). lib. bdg. 31.00 *(978-0-531-20626-3(2))*; pap. 6.95 *(978-0-531-28995-2(8))* Scholastic Library Publishing. (Children's Pr.).

Beyer, Mark. Heinrich Muller: Gestapo Chief. 2005. (Holocaust Biographies Ser.). (Illus.). 112p. (YA). (gr. 7-12). lib. bdg. 34.60 *(978-0-8239-3376-1(8))* Rosen Publishing Group, Inc., The.

Blashfield, Jean F. Germany. 2013. (Enchantment of the World™, Second Ser.). (ENG.). 144p. (J). 40.00 *(978-0-531-25601-5(4))*, Children's Pr.) Scholastic Library Publishing.

Burgan, Michael. Germany in Our World. 2011. (Countries in Our World Ser.). (Illus.). 32p. (YA). (gr. 4-7). lib. bdg. 28.50 *(978-1-59920-387-4(1))* Black Rabbit Bks.

Byers, Ann. Germany: A Primary Source Cultural Guide. 2009. (Primary Sources of World Cultures Ser.). 128p. (gr. 4-5). 79.90 *(978-1-60851-921-7(X))* Rosen Publishing Group, Inc., The.

Colson, Mary. Germany, 1 vol. 2011. (Countries Around the World Ser.). (ENG.). 48p. (gr. 3-6). pap. 9.95 *(978-1-4329-5229-7(3))*; 33.32 *(978-1-4329-5204-4(8))* Heinemann-Raintree. (NA-h).

Corbett, Sean. Germany. 2016. (Illus.). 32p. (J). *(978-1-4896-4607-1(8))* Weigl Pubs., Inc.

Coy, Jason P. A Brief History of Germany. 2010. (Brief History Ser.). (Illus.). 304p. (C). (gr. 9). 49.50 *(978-0-8160-8142-4(5))* Facts On File, Inc.

Darman, Peter, ed. World War II Begins. 2012. (World War II Ser.). (ENG., Illus.). 64p. (J). (gr. 7-12). lib. bdg. 31.95 *(978-1-4488-9232-7(5))* Rosen Publishing Group, Inc., The.

De La B&apos, et al. Discover Germany. 2010. (Illus.). 32p. (J). pap. 10.60 *(978-1-61532-292-3(2))*, PowerKids Pr.) Rosen Publishing Group, Inc., The.

De la Bédoyère, Camilla. Discover Germany. 2010. (Illus.). 32p. (J). 63.60 *(978-1-61532-293-0(0))*, PowerKids Pr.); (gr. 3-5). lib. bdg. 26.50 *(978-1-61532-287-9(6))* Rosen Publishing Group, Inc., The.

DeCarlo, Carolyn. The Holy Roman Empire. 2017. (J). ***(978-1-68048-782-4(5))*** Rosen Publishing Group, Inc., The.

Dyan, Penelope. It's Medieval! a Kid's Guide to Nuremberg, Germany. Weigand, John D., photos by. 2013. (Illus.). 34p. pap. 11.95 *(978-1-61477-079-4(4))* Bellissima Publishing, LLC.

—Let It Snow! a Kid's Guide to Regensburg, Germany. Weigand, John D., photos by. 2013. (Illus.). 34p. pap. 11.95 *(978-1-61477-076-3(X))* Bellissima Publishing, LLC.

—Shoes & Ships & Sealing Wax — A Kids's Guide to Warnemünde, Germany. Weigand, John D., photos by. 2011. (Illus.). 34p. pap. 11.95 *(978-1-935630-99-9(7))* Bellissima Publishing, LLC.

Farrell, Courtney. Terror at the Munich Olympics, 1 vol. 2010. (Essential Events Set 4 Ser.). (ENG.). 112p. (J). (gr. 6-12). lib. bdg. 35.64 *(978-1-60453-945-5(3))* ABDO Publishing Co.

Franchino, Vicky. Germany. 2011. (Explorer Library: Social Studies Explorer Ser.). (ENG.). 48p. (gr. 4-8). lib. bdg. 31.36 *(978-1-61080-098-3(2))*, 201090) Cherry Lake Publishing.

Frank, Nicole & Lord, Richard A. Germany. 2010. (Welcome to My Country Ser.). 48p. (gr. 3). 28.50 *(978-1-60870-154-4(9))* Marshall Cavendish Corp.

Ganeri, Anita. Germany. Isik, Semur, illus. 2015. (Country Guides, with Benjamin Blog & His Inquisitive Dog Ser.). (ENG.). 32p. (gr. 1-3). 29.99 *(978-1-4109-7994-0(6))*, Read Me!) Heinemann-Raintree.

Hinds, Kathryn. Early Germans: Peoples of the North. 2009. (Barbarians! Ser.). 80p. (gr. 6-8). 35.64 *(978-0-7614-4064-2(X))* Marshall Cavendish Corp.

Jukes, Geoffrey & O'Neill, Robert John. World War II: The Eastern Front 1941-1945. 2010. (World War II: Essential Histories Ser.). (Illus.). 96p. (YA). (gr. 9-12). lib. bdg. 33.25 *(978-1-4358-9134-0(1))* Rosen Publishing Group, Inc., The.

Kacer, Kathy. The Magician of Auschwitz, 1 vol. Newland, Gillian, illus. 2014. (ENG.). 32p. (J). (gr. 3-5). 18.95 *(978-1-927583-46-3(2))* Second Story Pr. CAN. Dist: Orca Bk. Pubs. USA.

—To Hope & Back: The Journey of the St. Louis, 1 vol. 2011. (Holocaust Remembrance Ser.). (ENG., Illus.). 200p. (J). (gr. 6-8). pap. 14.95 *(978-1-897187-96-8(3))* Second Story Pr. CAN. Dist: Orca Bk. Pubs. USA.

E
F
G

Kacer, Kathy. To Look a Nazi in the Eye: A Teen's Account of a War Criminal Trial, 1 vol. 2017. (ENG.). 256p. (YA). (gr. 8-12). pap. 13.95 **(978-1-77260-040-7(7))** Second Story Pr. CAN. Dist: Orca Bk. Pubs. USA.

Kallmeyer-Mehlhorn, Margarete. The Wondrous Ball of Yarn: A Facsimile of the Previously Unpublished Manuscript. 2008.Tr. of Wunderknaul. (ENG & GER., Illus.). 40p. 41.00 (978-0-9745168-2-0(1)) Cotsen Occasional Pr.

Klar, Jeremy & Lily, Henrietta M. Josef Mengele, 01 vols., 1. 2016. (Holocaust Ser.). (ENG., Illus.). 112p. (J). 35.60 (978-1-5081-7047-1(9), Rosen Young Adult) Rosen Publishing Group, Inc., The.

Kleiner, Mariela. Meet Einstein. Garofoli, Viviana, illus. 2011. 28p. (J). (gr. -1-1). lib. bdg. (978-0-615-31579-9(8)) Meet Bks., LLC.

Knauf, Barbara. When I Was Little in the Old Country: Childhood Memories of a German Grandmother. 2008. (Illus.). 29p. (J). (gr. 4-7). pap. 8.95 (978-1-60702-244-2(3)) Independent Pub.

Krammer, Arnold. Hitler in Paris: How a Photograph Shocked a World at War, 1 vol. 2014. (Captured World History Ser.). (ENG.). 64p. (gr. 5-7). lib. bdg. 34.65 (978-0-7565-4733-2(4), CPB Grades 4-8) Compass Point Bks.

Lord, Richard. Germany. 2010. (Festivals of the World Ser.). 32p. (gr. 3). 28.50 (978-1-60870-100-1(X)) Marshall Cavendish GBR. Dist: Marshall Cavendish Corp.

Manning, Jack. Christmas in Germany, 1 vol. 2013. (Christmas Around the World Ser.). (ENG.). 24p. (gr. 1-2). 25.32 (978-1-4765-3099-4(8), First Facts) Capstone Press of Coughlan Cos.

Miller, Susan Hoskins. Germany. 2015. (One World, Many Countries Ser.). (ENG.). 32p. (J). (gr. 1-4). 28.50 (978-1-63407-044-7(5), 208874) Child's World, Inc., The.

Nardo, Don. Massacre in Munich: How Terrorists Changed the Oylmpics & the World. 2016. (Captured History Sports Ser.). (ENG., Ilus.). 64p. (gr. 5-7). lib. bdg. 34.65 (978-0-7565-5292-3(3), CPB Grades 4-8) Compass Point Bks.

Nelson, Robin. Germany. 2011. (Country Explorers Ser.). 48p. pap. 51.02 (978-0-7613-7623-1(2)); (ENG.). (gr. 2-4). pap. 9.95 (978-0-7613-7080-2(3)) Lerner Publishing Group.

Otfinoski, Steven. The Hindenburg Explosion: Core Events of a Disaster in the Air, 1 vol. 2014. (What Went Wrong? Ser.). (ENG.). 32p. (gr. 3-4). pap. 7.95 (978-1-4765-5133-3(2)) Capstone Press of Coughlan Cos.

Perritano, John. Germany, Vol. 12. 2015. (Major Nations in a Global World: Tradition, Culture, & Daily Life Ser.). (Illus.). 64p. (J). (gr. 7). 23.95 (978-1-4222-3344-3(8)) Mason Crest.

Pohl, Kathleen. Looking at Germany. 2008. (Looking at Countries Ser.). 32p. (gr. 1-5). pap. 10.50 (978-0-8368-8774-7(3)); (Illus.). lib. bdg. 26.00 (978-0-8368-8767-9(0)) Stevens, Gareth Publishing LLLP. (Gareth Stevens Learning Library).

Prien, Jochen & Stemmer, Gerhard. Jagdgeschwader 3 Udet in World War II: II. /JG 3 in Action with the Messerschmitt Bf 109, 1 vol. 2003. (ENG., Illus.). 464p. (gr. 10-13). 69.95 (978-0-7643-1774-3(1), 9780764317743) Schiffer Publishing, Ltd.

Ramen, Fred. Albert Speer: Hitler's Architect. 2009. (Holocaust Biographies Ser.). 112p. (gr. 7-12). 63.90 (978-1-61513-382-6(8)) Rosen Publishing Group, Inc., The.

—Hermann Goering: Hitler's Second in Command. 2005. (Holocaust Biographies Ser.). (Illus.). 112p. (YA). (gr. 7-12). lib. bdg. 34.60 (978-0-8239-3307-5(5), HBGORI) Rosen Publishing Group, Inc., The.

—Hermann Göring: Hitler's Second-in-Command. 2009. (Holocaust Biographies Ser.). 112p. (gr. 7-12). 63.90 (978-1-61513-387-1(9)) Rosen Publishing Group, Inc., The.

Ray, Michael, ed. Germany. 2013. (Britannica Guide to Countries of the European Union Ser.). 352p. (YA). (gr. 9-12). 53.00 (978-1-61530-965-8(9)) Rosen Publishing Group, Inc., The.

Robbins, Trina. Lily Renée, Escape Artist: From Holocaust Survivor to Comic Book Pioneer. Timmons, Anne & Oh, Mo, illus. 2011. (Single Titles Ser.). (ENG.). 96p. (J). (gr. 5-8). lib. bdg. 29.27 (978-0-7613-6010-0(7), Graphic Universe™) Lerner Publishing Group.

Rudolph, Jessica. Germany. 2017. (Countries We Come From Ser.). (ENG., Illus.). 32p. (J). (gr. -1-3). 19.95 (978-1-68402-053-9(0)) Bearport Publishing Co., Inc.

Rumford, James. From the Good Mountain: How Gutenberg Changed the World. Rumford, James, illus. 2012. (ENG., Illus.). 36p. (J). (gr. -1-3). 17.99 (978-1-59643-542-1(9), 9781596435421) Roaring Brook Pr.

Russell, Henry. National Geographic Countries of the World - Germany. 2007. (National Geographic Countries of the World Ser.). (ENG., Illus.). 64p. (J). (gr. 5-9). lib. bdg. 27.90 (978-1-4263-0059-2(X), National Geographic Children's Bks.) National Geographic Society.

Schiel, Katy. Inside Germany's BND: The Federal Intelligence Service. 2005. (Illus.). 63p. (YA). (gr. 4-8). reprint ed. 20.00 (978-0-7567-8669-4(X)) DIANE Publishing Co.

—Inside Germany's BND: The Federal Intelligence Service. (Inside the World's Most Famous Intelligence Agencies Ser.). 64p. 2009. (gr. 5-5). 58.50 (978-1-61513-570-7(7)) 2005. (Illus.). (YA). (gr. 7-12). lib. bdg. 31.95 (978-0-8239-3813-1(1)) Rosen Publishing Group, Inc., The.

Sexton, Colleen & Simmons, Walter. Germany. 2010. (Exploring Countries Ser.). (ENG., Illus.). 32p. (J). (gr. 3-7). lib. bdg. 26.95 (978-1-60014-481-3(0), Blastoff! Readers) Bellwether Media.

Tieck, Sarah. Germany, 1 vol. 2013. (Explore the Countries Ser.). (ENG.). 40p. (J). (gr. 2-5). lib. bdg. 29.93 (978-1-61783-811-8(X), Big Buddy Bks.) ABDO Publishing Co.

Uschan, Michael V. German Americans. 2006. (World Almanac Library of American Immigration). (Illus.). 48p. (gr. 5-12). pap. 14.05 (978-0-8368-7323-8(8)); lib. bdg. 31.00 (978-0-8368-7310-8(6)) Stevens, Gareth Publishing LLLP. (Gareth Stevens Secondary Library).

Walker, Ida. Germany. 2007. (European Union Ser.). (Illus.). 88p. (YA). (gr. 3-7). lib. bdg. 21.95 (978-1-4222-0048-3(5), 1248000) Mason Crest.

Walker, Ida & Indovino, Shaina C. Germany. Bruton, John, ed. 2012. (Major European Union Nations Ser.). 64p. (J). (gr. 7). 22.95 (978-1-4222-2243-0(8)) Mason Crest.

Walker, Ida & Indovino, Shaina Carmel. Germany. 2012. (J). pap. (978-1-4222-2274-4(8)) Mason Crest.

Zocchi, Judy. In Germany. Brodie, Neale, illus. 2005. (Global Adventures II Ser.). 32p. (J). pap. 10.95 (978-1-59646-180-2(2)); lib. bdg. 21.65 (978-1-59646-089-8(X)) Dingles & Co.

—In Germany/en Alemania. Brodie, Neale, illus. 2005. (Global Adventures II Ser.).Tr. of En Alemania. (ENG & SPA.). (J). 32p. pap. 10.95 (978-1-59646-182-6(9)); 28p. lib. bdg. 21.65 (978-1-59646-090-4(3)) Dingles & Co.

GERMANY—HISTORY—FICTION

Alcock, Deborah. The King's Service: A Story of the Thirty Years' War. 2008. (YA). (978-1-894666-06-0(2)) Inheritance Pubns.

Bartoletti, Susan Campbell. The Boy Who Dared. 2008. (ENG., Illus.). 192p. (J). (gr. 3-7). 17.99 (978-0-439-68013-4(1), Scholastic Pr.) Scholastic, Inc.

Bass, Karen. Graffiti Knight, 1 vol. 2014. (ENG., Illus.). 288p. (YA). (gr. 7-11). pap. 11.95 (978-1-927485-53-8(3)) Pajama Pr. CAN. Dist: Ingram Publisher Services.

Bessey, Siân Ann. Escape from Germany. 2004. 183p. (J). (978-1-59156-436-2(0)) Covenant Communications.

Blankman, Anne. Conspiracy of Blood & Smoke. 2015. (ENG.). 416p. (YA). (gr. 8). 17.99 (978-0-06-227884-5(3)) HarperCollins Pubs.

—Prisoner of Night & Fog. (ENG.). (YA). (gr. 8). 2015. 432p. pap. 9.99 (978-0-06-227882-1(7)) 2014. 416p. 17.99 (978-0-06-227881-4(9)) HarperCollins Pubs.

Chapman, Fern Schumer. Is It Night or Day? 2010. (ENG.). 224p. (J). (gr. 5-9). 17.99 (978-0-374-17744-7(9), 9780374177447, Farrar, Straus & Giroux (BYR)) Farrar, Straus & Giroux.

Chotjewitz, David. Daniel Half Human. Orgel, Doris, tr. from GER. 2006. (ENG., Illus.). 336p. (YA). (gr. 7). reprint ed. mass mkt. 8.99 (978-0-689-85748-5(9), Simon Pulse) Simon Pulse.

Chotjewitz, David & Orgel, Doris. Daniel, Half Human: And the Good Nazi. 2004. 298p. (J). (978-3-551-58045-0(6)) Carlsen Verlag DEU. Dist: Distribooks, Inc.

Cohen-Scali, Sarah. Max. Hueston, Penny, tr. from FRE. 2017. (ENG.). 432p. (YA). 21.99 (978-1-62672-071-8(1), 9781626720718) Roaring Brook Pr.

Davidson, Halsey. Navy Boys Behind the Big Guns or Sinking the German U-Boats. 2007. 108p. per. (978-1-4068-1847-5(X)) Echo Library.

Elmer, Robert. Life Behind the Wall: Candy Bombers, Hidden Bunkers, & Smugglers Treasure, 1 vol. rev. ed. 2014. (ENG.). 528p. (J). pap. 13.99 (978-0-310-74265-4(X)) Zonderkidz.

French, Jackie. Hitler's Daughter. 2003. (ENG.). 128p. (J). (gr. 3-7). 16.99 (978-0-06-008652-7(1)) HarperCollins Pubs.

Gallaz, Christophe. ROSA BLANCA. 2nd ed. 2003. (Rosa y Manzana Ser.). (SPA., Illus.). 32p. (978-84-85334-52-0(3), LG2811) Lóguez Ediciones ESP. Dist: Lectorum Pubns., Inc.

Gratz, Alan. Projekt 1065: A Novel of World War II. 2016. (ENG.). 320p. (J). (gr. 4-7). 16.99 (978-0-545-88016-9(5), Scholastic Pr.) Scholastic, Inc.

Ibbotson, Eva. The Star of Kazan. Hawkes, Kevin, illus. 2006. (ENG.). 416p. (J). (gr. 3-7). reprint ed. 8.99 (978-0-14-240582-6(5), Puffin Books) Penguin Young Readers Group.

Lasky, Kathryn. Ashes. 2010. (ENG.). 320p. (J). (gr. 5-18). 16.99 (978-0-670-01157-5(6), Viking Books for Young Readers) Penguin Young Readers Group.

Lawton, Wendy. A La Sombra de Su Mano, 1 vol. 2009. Orig. Title: Shadow of His Hand. (SPA.). 160p. pap. 4.99 (978-0-8254-1379-7(6), Editorial Portavoz) Kregel Pubns.

Lehman, Theodore H. Defying Odds. 2014. (YA). pap. (978-1-935604-63-1(5)) Gaon Bks.

Morpurgo, Michael. An Elephant in the Garden. 2013. (ENG.). 224p. (J). (gr. 5-9). pap. 7.99 (978-1-250-03414-4(0), 9781250034144) Square Fish.

Nelson, Suzanne. Serendipity's Footsteps. 2015. (ENG.). 368p. (YA). (gr. 7). 17.99 (978-0-385-39212-9(5), Knopf Bks. for Young Readers) Random Hse. Children's Bks.

Oakes, Stephanie. The Arsonist. 2017. (ENG.). 496p. (YA). (gr. 7). 17.99 **(978-0-8037-4071-6(9)**, Dial Bks) Penguin Young Readers Group.

Oppenlander, Annette. Escape from the Past: At Witches' End (Book 3) 2016. (ENG.). 312p. (J). (gr. -1-12). pap. 12.95 (978-1-78535-426-7(4), Lodestone Bks.) Hunt, John Publishing Ltd. GBR. Dist: National Bk. Network.

Ryan, Pam Muñoz. Echo. 2015. (ENG., Illus.). 512p. (J). (gr. 5-9). 19.99 (978-0-439-87402-1(5), Scholastic Pr.) Scholastic, Inc.

Schröder, Monika. The Dog in the Wood. 2009. (ENG.). 168p. (J). (gr. 5-9). 17.95 (978-1-59078-701-4(3), Front Street) Boyds Mills Pr.

Sharenow, Robert. The Berlin Boxing Club. (ENG.). (YA). (gr. 8). 2012. 432p. pap. 9.99 (978-0-06-157970-7(X)) 2011. 416p. 17.99 (978-0-06-157968-4(8)) HarperCollins Pubs. (HarperTeen).

—The Berlin Boxing Club. 2012. (YA). lib. bdg. 20.85 (978-0-606-26871-4(5), Turtleback) Turtleback Bks.

Skrypuch, Marsha Forchuk. Making Bombs for Hitler. 2017. (ENG.). 240p. (J). (gr. 3-7). 17.99 (978-0-545-93191-5(6), Scholastic Pr.) Scholastic, Inc.

Smith, Molly. Border Breakdown: The Fall of the Berlin Wall. 2011. (ENG.). (J). 9.95 (978-1-60727-113-0(3)) Soundprints.

Wein, Elizabeth. Rose under Fire. 2014. (ENG.). 384p. (YA). (gr. 9-17). pap. 9.99 (978-1-4231-8469-0(6)) Disney Pr.

Williams, Laura E. Behind the Bedroom Wall. Goldstein, A. Nancy, illus. 2006. 169p. (gr. -1-7). 17.45 (978-0-7569-6389-7(3)) Perfection Learning Corp.

Wilson, John. Germania. 2008. (ENG., Illus.). 280p. (YA). (gr. 7-18). (978-1-55470-112-4(0)) Me to We.

Wiviott, Meg. Benno & the Night of Broken Glass. Bisaillon, Josée, illus. 2010. (ENG.). 32p. (J). (gr. 2-5). pap. 7.95 (978-0-8225-9975-3(9)); lib. bdg. 17.95 (978-0-8225-9929-6(5)) Lerner Publishing Group. (Kar-Ben Publishing).

Wulffson, Don L. & Wulffson, Don. Soldier X. 2003. (ENG.). 240p. (YA). (gr. 7-18). 6.99 (978-0-14-250073-6(9), Speak) Penguin Young Readers Group.

Zusak, Markus. The Book Thief. 2014. (ENG.). 576p. (YA). 17.24 (978-1-63245-052-4(6)) Lectorum Pubns., Inc.

—The Book Thief. 2009. 12.64 (978-0-7848-1941-8(6), Everbind) Marco Bk. Co.

—The Book Thief. 2008. 552p. (gr. 7-12). 23.00 (978-0-7569-8440-3(8)) Perfection Learning Corp.

—The Book Thief. (ENG., Illus.). (YA). (gr. 7). 2016. 592p. lib. bdg. 22.99 (978-0-399-55652-4(4)) 2007. 592p. pap. 12.99 (978-0-375-84220-7(9)) 2013. 576p. pap. 12.99 (978-0-385-75472-9(8)) 2016. 592p. 19.99 (978-1-101-93418-0(2)) Random Hse. Children's Bks. (Knopf Bks. for Young Readers).

—The Book Thief. l.t. ed. 2006. (ENG.). 552p. 23.99 (978-1-4104-6806-2(2)); 757p. (YA). (gr. 7-12). 24.95 (978-0-7862-9021-5(8)) Thorndike Pr.

—The Book Thief. 2008. (ENG., Illus.). 560p. pap. (978-0-552-77389-8(1), Black Swan) Transworld Publishers Ltd.

—The Book Thief. 2007. 552p. lib. bdg. 24.50 (978-1-4177-9738-7(X)) 2013. lib. bdg. 24.50 (978-0-606-34656-6(2)) Turtleback Bks. (Turtleback).

—La Ladrona de Libros. 2010. (Vintage Espanol Ser.).Tr. of Book Thief. (SPA.). 544p. (YA). (gr. 7). pap. 12.99 (978-0-307-47573-2(5), Vintage Espanol) Knopf Doubleday Publishing Group.

GERMANY—HISTORY, MILITARY

Beyer, Mark. Heinrich Müller: Gestapo Chief. 2009. (Holocaust Biographies Ser.). 112p. (gr. 7-12). 63.90 (978-1-61513-386-4(0)) Rosen Publishing Group, Inc., The.

GERMANY—HISTORY—20TH CENTURY

Brezina, Corona. Nazi Architects of the Holocaust. 2014. (Documentary History of the Holocaust Ser.). 80p. (YA). (gr. 7-12). 34.25 (978-1-4777-7597-4(8)) Rosen Publishing Group, Inc., The.

Byers, Ann. Anti-Semitism & the Final Solution: The Holocaust Overview. 2014. (Remembering the Holocaust Ser.). 96p. (J). (gr. 6-12). pap. 10.95 (978-0-7660-6193-4(0)) Enslow Pubs., Inc.

La Bella, Laura. The Nuremberg Trials. 2014. (Documentary History of the Holocaust Ser.). (Illus.). 80p. (J). (gr. 7-12). 34.25 (978-1-4777-7607-0(9)) Rosen Publishing Group, Inc., The.

Peak, Doris-Jean. Wernher Von Braun: Alabama's Rocket Scientist. 2009. (Alabama Roots Biography Ser.). (Illus.). 112p. (J). (978-1-59421-044-0(6)) Seacoast Publishing, Inc.

Peppas, Lynn. Cultural Traditions in Germany. 2015. (ENG., Illus.). 32p. (J). (978-0-7787-8060-1(0)) Crabtree Publishing Co.

Shoup, Kate. Nazi Propaganda: Jews in Hitler's Germany. 2016. (Public Persecutions Ser.). 128p. (J). 45.64 (978-1-5026-2321-8(8)) Cavendish Square Publishing.

Thomson, Ruth. Terezin: Voices from the Holocaust. 2013. (ENG., Illus.). 64p. (YA). (gr. 5-9). pap. 9.99 (978-0-7636-6466-4(9)) Candlewick Pr.

Tracy, Kathleen. The Fall of the Berlin Wall. 2005. (Monumental Milestones Ser.). (Illus.). 48p. (YA). (gr. 4-7). lib. bdg. 29.95 (978-1-58415-405-1(5)) Mitchell Lane Pubs., Inc.

Vansant, Wayne. The Red Baron: The Graphic History of Richthofen's Flying Circus & the Air War in WWI. 2014. (Zenith Graphic Histories Ser.). (ENG., Illus.). 104p. pap. 19.99 (978-0-7603-4602-0(X), 076034602X, Zenith Pr.) Quarto Publishing Group USA.

GERMANY—HISTORY—1918-1933

Banham, Dale, et al. Germany, 1918-1945: A Study in Depth. 2004. (Illus.). 96p. pap., stu. ed. 32.50 (978-0-7195-7753-6(5), Hodder Education) Hodder Education Group GBR. Dist: Trans-Atlantic Pubns., Inc.

Clare, John D. Germany, 1918-45. 2nd rev. ed. 2004. (Illus.). 64p. pap. 26.50 (978-0-340-81478-9(0), Hodder Education) Hodder Education Group GBR. Dist: Trans-Atlantic Pubns., Inc.

Freeman, Charles. The Rise of the Nazis. 2005. (How Did It Happen? Ser.). (ENG., Illus.). 48p. (gr. 7-10). lib. bdg. 36.70 (978-1-59018-608-4(7), Lucent Bks.) Cengage Gale.

—Why Did the Rise of the Nazis Happen? 2010. (Moments in History Ser.). (Illus.). 48p. (YA). (gr. 5-9). lib. bdg. 31.95 (978-1-4339-4175-7(9)); (ENG., (J). (gr. 6-8). pap. 14.05 (978-1-4339-4176-4(7), Gareth Stevens Secondary Library) Stevens, Gareth Publishing LLLP.

Giblin, James Cross. The Life & Death of Adolf Hitler. 2015. (ENG., Illus.). 256p. (J). (gr. 5-7). pap. 9.99 (978-0-544-45591-7(6), HMH Books For Young Readers) Houghton Mifflin Harcourt Publishing Co.

—The Life & Death of Adolf Hitler. 2015. lib. bdg. 20.85 (978-0-606-36830-8(2)) Turtleback Bks.

Marcovitz, Hal. The Rise of the Nazis. 2014. (Understanding World History Ser.). (ENG., Illus.). 96p. (J). lib. bdg. (978-1-60152-654-0(7)) ReferencePoint Pr., Inc.

Woolf, Alex. The Rise of Nazi Germany. 2004. (Questioning History Ser.). (J). lib. bdg. 28.50 (978-1-58340-442-3(2)) Black Rabbit Bks.

GERMANY—HISTORY—1933-1945

Adolf Hitler & Nazi Germany. 2006. (World Leaders Ser.). (Illus.). 176p. (gr. 3-7). lib. bdg. 28.95 (978-1-931798-78-5(8)) Reynolds, Morgan Inc.

Altman, Linda Jacobs. Adolf Hitler: Evil Mastermind of the Holocaust. 2005. (Holocaust Heroes & Nazi Criminals Ser.). (Illus.). 160p. (YA). (gr. 7-13). lib. bdg. 29.27 (978-0-7660-2533-2(0)) Enslow Pubs., Inc.

—Adolf Hitler & the Rise of the Third Reich. 2016. (People & Events That Changed the World Ser.). (ENG., Illus.). 112p. (J). (gr. 7-8). 37.27 (978-0-7660-7175-9(8)) Enslow Pubs., Inc.

—Hitler's Rise to Power & the Holocaust. 2003. (Holocaust in History Ser.). (Illus.). 128p. (J). (gr. 5-12). lib. bdg. 26.60 (978-0-7660-1991-1(8)) Enslow Pubs., Inc.

—The Jewish Victims of the Holocaust. 2003. (Holocaust in History Ser.). (Illus.). 104p. (J). (gr. 5-12). lib. bdg. 27.94 (978-0-7660-1992-8(6)) Enslow Pubs., Inc.

—Resisters & Rescuers: Standing up Against the Holocaust. 2003. (Holocaust in History Ser.). (Illus.). 104p. (J). (gr. 5-12). lib. bdg. 27.94 (978-0-7660-1994-2(2)) Enslow Pubs., Inc.

Axelrod, Toby. Hans & Sophie Scholl: German Resisters of the White Rose. 2005. (Holocaust Biographies Ser.). (Illus.). 112p. (YA). (gr. 7-12). lib. bdg. 34.60 (978-0-8239-3316-7(4), HBHOBI) Rosen Publishing Group, Inc., The.

Banham, Dale, et al. Germany, 1918-1945: A Study in Depth. 2004. (Illus.). 96p. pap., stu. ed. 32.50 (978-0-7195-7753-6(5), Hodder Education) Hodder Education Group GBR. Dist: Trans-Atlantic Pubns., Inc.

Buckley, James, Jr. Adolf Hitler. 2017. (History's Worst Ser.). (ENG., Illus.). 208p. (J). (gr. 3-7). pap. 7.99 **(978-1-4814-7942-4(3)**, Aladdin) Simon & Schuster Children's Publishing.

Byers, Ann. Kristallnacht & Living in Nazi Germany. 2014. (Documentary History of the Holocaust Ser.). 80p. (YA). (gr. 7-12). 34.25 (978-1-4777-7595-0(1)) Rosen Publishing Group, Inc., The.

Clare, John D. Germany, 1918-45. 2nd rev. ed. 2004. (Illus.). 64p. pap. 26.50 (978-0-340-81478-9(0), Hodder Education) Hodder Education Group GBR. Dist: Trans-Atlantic Pubns., Inc.

Darman, Peter, ed. The Holocaust & Life under Nazi Occupation. 2012. (World War II Ser.). (ENG., Illus.). 64p. (YA). (gr. 7-12). lib. bdg. 31.95 (978-1-4488-9235-8(X)) Rosen Publishing Group, Inc., The.

Davenport, John. The Nuremberg Trials. 2006. (World History Ser.). (ENG., Illus.). 96p. (YA). (gr. 7-10). lib. bdg. 34.95 (978-1-59018-634-3(6), Lucent Bks.) Cengage Gale.

Dufner, Annette. The Rise of Adolf Hitler. 2003. (At Issue in History Ser.). (ENG., Illus.). 144p. (YA). 26.70 (978-0-7377-1519-4(7)); pap. 35.75 (978-0-7377-1518-7(9)) Cengage Gale. (Greenhaven Pr., Inc.).

Ellis, Catherine & Roberts, Jeremy. Adolf Hitler, 01 vols., 1. 2016. (Holocaust Ser.). (ENG., Illus.). 112p. (J). 35.60 (978-1-4994-6248-7(4), Rosen Young Adult) Rosen Publishing Group, Inc., The.

Garner, Eleanor Ramrath & Ramrath Garner, Eleanor. Eleanor's Story: An American Girl in Hitler's Germany, 1 vol. 2003. (ENG., Illus.). 288p. (YA). (gr. 7-18). pap. 9.95 (978-1-56145-296-5(3), Q19196) Peachtree Pubs.

Giblin, James Cross. The Life & Death of Adolf Hitler. 2015. (ENG., Illus.). 256p. (J). (gr. 5-7). pap. 9.99 (978-0-544-45591-7(6), HMH Books For Young Readers) Houghton Mifflin Harcourt Publishing Co.

—The Life & Death of Adolf Hitler. 2015. lib. bdg. 20.85 (978-0-606-36830-8(2)) Turtleback Bks.

Lowery, Zoe & Norton, James R. The Nazi Regime & the Holocaust. 2016. (Bearing Witness: Genocide & Ethnic Cleansing in the Modern World Ser.). 64p. (J). (gr. 6-6). 34.45 (978-1-5081-7163-8(7)) Rosen Publishing Group, Inc., The.

Marcovitz, Hal. Life in Nazi Germany. 2015. (ENG., Illus.). 96p. (J). lib. bdg. (978-1-60152-776-9(4)) ReferencePoint Pr., Inc.

McCormick, Patricia. The Plot to Kill Hitler: Dietrich Bonhoeffer: Pastor, Spy, Unlikely Hero. 2016. (Illus.). 192p. (J). (gr. 3). 18.99 (978-0-06-241108-2(X)) HarperCollins Pubs.

O'Reilly, Bill. Hitler's Last Days: The Death of the Nazi Regime & the World's Most Notorious Dictator. 2015. (Illus.). 320p. (J). pap. (978-1-62779-455-8(7)); (ENG., (gr. 5-9). 19.99 (978-1-62779-396-4(8), 9781627793964, Holt, Henry & Co. Bks. For Young Readers) Holt, Henry & Co.

—Hitler's Last Days: The Death of the Nazi Regime & the World's Most Notorious Dictator. Barcellona, Christine, ed. 2017. (ENG.). 336p. (J). pap. 12.99 (978-1-250-08859-8(3), 9781250088598) Square Fish.

Price, Sean Stewart. Adolf Hitler. 2010. (Wicked History Ser.). (ENG.). 128p. (J). (gr. 6-12). pap. 5.95 (978-0-531-22357-4(4)); (Illus.). 31.00 (978-0-531-20757-4(9)) Scholastic Library Publishing. (Watts, Franklin).

Ramen, Fred. Albert Speer: Hitler's Architect. 2005. (Holocaust Biographies Ser.). (Illus.). 112p. (YA). (gr. 7-12). lib. bdg. 34.60 (978-0-8239-3372-3(5)) Rosen Publishing Group, Inc., The.

—Reinhard Heydrich: Hangman of the Third Reich. (Holocaust Biographies Ser.). 112p. (gr. 7-12). 2009. 63.90 (978-1-61513-392-5(5)) 2005. (Illus.). (YA). lib. bdg. 34.60 (978-0-8239-3379-2(2)) Rosen Publishing Group, Inc., The.

Roscoe, Kelly & Roberts, Jeremy. Joseph Goebbels, 01 vols., 1. 2016. (Holocaust Ser.). (ENG., Illus.). 112p. (J). 35.60 (978-1-5081-7049-5(5), Rosen Young Adult) Rosen Publishing Group, Inc., The.

Soumerai, Eve Nussbaum & Schulz, Carol D. A Voice from the Holocaust, 1 vol. 2003. (Voices of Twentieth-Century Conflict Ser.). (Illus.). 144p. (C). 46.00 (978-0-313-32358-4(5), GR2358, Greenwood) ABC-CLIO, LLC.

Throp, Claire. Resisting the Nazis. 2015. (Heroes of World War II Ser.). (ENG., Illus.). 48p. (gr. 4-6). 32.65 (978-1-4109-8045-8(6)) Heinemann-Raintree.

Woolf, Alex. The Rise of Nazi Germany. 2004. (Questioning History Ser.). (J). lib. bdg. 28.50 (978-1-58340-442-3(2)) Black Rabbit Bks.

GERMANY—HISTORY—1945-

Doeden, Matt. The Berlin Wall: An Interactive Modern History Adventure, 1 vol. 2014. (You Choose: Modern History Ser.). (ENG.). 112p. (gr. 3-4). 31.99 (978-1-4914-0354-9(3), You Choose Bks.) Capstone Press of Coughlan Cos.

GERMS

see Bacteriology; Microorganisms

GERONIMO, 1829-1909

Dell, Pamela. Apache Resistance: Causes & Effects of Geronimo's Campaign. 2015. (Cause & Effect: American Indian History Ser.). (ENG., Illus.). 32p. (gr. 3-4). pap. 7.95 (978-1-4914-4904-2(7)) Capstone Press of Coughlan Cos.

Feinstein, Stephen. Read about Geronimo. 2006. (I Like Biographies! Ser.). (Illus.). 24p. (J). (gr. 1-3). lib. bdg. 21.26 (978-0-7660-2598-1(5), Enslow Elementary) Enslow Pubs., Inc.

Geronimo. 2010. (Legends of the Wild West Ser.). (Illus.). 128p. (gr. 6-12). 35.00 (978-1-60413-525-1(5), Chelsea Hse.) Facts On File, Inc.

Haugen, Brenda. Geronimo: The Inspiring Life Story of an Apache Warrior. 2016. (Inspiring Stories Ser.). (ENG., Illus.). 112p. (gr. 5-7). lib. bdg. 35.99 (978-0-7565-5162-9(5), CPB Grades 4-8) Compass Point Bks.

Hunt, Santana. Geronimo. 2015. (Native American Heroes Ser.). (ENG., Illus.). 24p. (J). (gr. 1-2). pap. 8.15 (978-1-4824-2685-4(4)) Stevens, Gareth Publishing LLLP.

Kjelgaard, Jim. The Story of Geronimo. Meadowcroft, Enid Lamonte, ed. Wilson, Charles Banks, illus. 2011. 192p. 42.95 (978-1-258-05298-0(9)) Literary Licensing, LLC.

Marsh, Carole. Geronimo. 2003. 12p. (gr. k-4). 2.95 (978-0-635-02381-0(4)) Gallopade International.

Moskal, Greg. An Apache Indian Community. 2009. (Reading Room Collection 2 Ser.). 24p. (gr. 3-4). 42.50 *(978-1-60851-956-9(2),* PowerKids Pr.) Rosen Publishing Group, Inc., The.

—Un pueblo apache (an Apache Indian Community) 2009. (Reading Room Collection: Spanish Ser.). (SPA.). 24p. (gr. 3-4). 42.50 *(978-1-60854-180-5(0),* Editorial Buenas Letras) Rosen Publishing Group, Inc., The.

Sanford, William R. Apache Chief Geronimo. 2013. (Native American Chiefs & Warriors Ser.). 48p. (J). (gr. 5-18). lib. bdg. 22.60 *(978-0-7660-4093-9(3));* pap. 8.95 *(978-1-4644-0253-1(1))* Enslow Pubs., Inc.

Spilsbury, Richard. Geronimo, 1 vol. Faure, Florence, illus. 2013. (Hero Journals). (ENG.). 48p. (gr. 4-6). pap. 9.95 *(978-1-4109-5367-4(X),* NA-r) Heinemann-Raintree.

—Geronimo, 1 vol. 2013. (Hero Journals). (ENG., Illus.). 48p. (gr. 4-6). 33.32 *(978-1-4109-5360-5(2),* NA-r) Heinemann-Raintree.

Weil, Ann. Geronimo, 1 vol. 2012. (American Biographies Ser.). (ENG.). 48p. (gr. 4-6). pap. 9.95 *(978-1-4329-6458-0(5));* lib. bdg. 32.65 *(978-1-4329-6447-4(X))* Heinemann-Raintree. (NA-h).

Welch, Catherine A. Geronimo. 2004. (History Maker Biographies Ser.). (ENG.). 48p. (gr. 3-6). pap. 8.95 *(978-0-8225-2069-6(9))* Lerner Publishing Group.

—Geronimo. Parlin, Tim, tr. Parlin, Tim, illus. 2004. (History Maker Bios Ser.). 47p. (J). 26.60 *(978-0-8225-0698-0(X),* Carolrhoda Bks.) Lerner Publishing Group.

GERONIMO, 1829-1909—FICTION

Stilton, Thea. Thea Stilton & the Madagascar Madness: A Geronimo Stilton Adventure. 2016. (Thea Stilton Ser.: 24). (ENG.). 176p. (J). (gr. 2-5). pap. 8.99 *(978-1-338-03269-5(5),* Scholastic Paperbacks) Scholastic, Inc.

Wallace, Bill. The Final Freedom. 2009. (ENG.). 176p. (J). (gr. 3-7). pap. 9.99 *(978-1-4169-9421-3(1),* Simon & Schuster/Paula Wiseman Bks.) Simon & Schuster/Paula Wiseman Bks.

GERONTOLOGY

see Old Age

GERSHWIN, GEORGE, 1898-1937

Ford, Carin T. George Gershwin: American Musical Genius. 2008. (People to Know Today Ser.). (Illus.). 112p. (J). (gr. k-6). lib. bdg. 33.27 *(978-0-7660-2887-6(9))* Enslow Pubs., Inc.

Reef, Catherine. George Gershwin: American Composer. 2004. (Masters of Music Ser.). (Illus.). 112p. (YA). (gr. 6-12). 23.95 *(978-1-883846-58-9(7),* First Biographies) Reynolds, Morgan Inc.

Venezia, Mike. George Gershwin (Revised Edition) 2017. (Getting to Know the World's Greatest Composers Ser.). (ENG.). 40p. (J). pap. 7.95 ***(978-0-531-23037-4(6));*** lib. bdg. 29.00 ***(978-0-531-22659-9(X))*** Scholastic Library Publishing. (Children's Pr.).

Whiting, Jim. The Life & Times of George Gershwin. 2004. (Masters of Music Ser.). (Illus.). 48p. (gr. 4-8). lib. bdg. 20.95 *(978-1-58415-279-8(6))* Mitchell Lane Pubs., Inc.

GETTYSBURG (PA.), BATTLE OF, 1863

see Gettysburg, Battle of, Gettysburg, Pa., 1863

GETTYSBURG, BATTLE OF, GETTYSBURG, PA., 1863

Abnett, Dan. The Battle of Gettysburg: Invasion of the North! 2007. (Graphic Battles: Civil War Ser.). (ENG., Illus.). 48p. (gr. 5-8). pap. 14.05 *(978-1-4042-6477-9(9),* Rosen Classroom) Rosen Publishing Group, Inc., The.

—The Battle of Gettysburg: Spilled Blood on Sacred Ground. 2009. (Graphic Civil War Battles Ser.). (ENG.). 48p. (YA). (gr. 4-5). 58.50 *(978-1-61512-899-0(9),* Rosen Reference) Rosen Publishing Group, Inc., The.

—The Battle of Gettysburg: Spilled Blood on Sacred Ground. Verma, Dheeraj, illus. 2007. (Graphic Battles of the Civil War Ser.). (ENG.). 48p. (YA). (gr. 4-7). lib. bdg. 31.95 *(978-1-4042-0777-6(5))* Rosen Publishing Group, Inc., The.

Anderson, Dale & O'Hern, Kerri. The Battle of Gettysburg. McHargue, D., illus. 2006. (Graphic Histories Ser.). 32p. (gr. 5-8). lib. bdg. 27.00 *(978-0-8368-6204-1(X))* Stevens, Gareth Publishing LLLP.

Anderson, Tanya. Tillie Pierce: Teen Eyewitness to the Battle of Gettysburg. (ENG., Illus.). 96p. (gr. 6-8). 2015. 34.65 *(978-1-4677-5927-4(9),* Lerner Digital) 2013. lib. bdg. 34.60 *(978-1-4677-0692-6(2),* Twenty-First Century Bks.) Lerner Publishing Group.

Bow, James. Gettysburg. 2012. (ENG.). 48p. (J). *(978-0-7787-7928-5(9));* pap. *(978-0-7787-7937-7(8))* Crabtree Publishing Co.

Burgan, Michael. The Battle of Gettysburg. Erwin, Steve et al, illus. 2006. (Graphic History Ser.). (ENG.). 32p. (gr. 3-4). per. 8.10 *(978-0-7368-6880-8(1),* Graphic Library) Capstone Press of Coughlan Cos.

Burgan, Michael & Hoena, Blake A. The Battle of Gettysburg, 1 vol. Erwin, Steve et al, illus. 2006. (Graphic History Ser.). (ENG.). 32p. (gr. 3-4). 30.65 *(978-0-7368-5491-7(6),* Graphic Library) Capstone Press of Coughlan Cos.

Butzer, C. M. The Gettysburg. Butzer, C. M., illus. (ENG., Illus.). 80p. 2009. (YA). (gr. 4-9). pap. 9.99 *(978-0-06-156175-7(4))* 2008. (J). (gr. 5-9). 16.99 *(978-0-06-156176-4(2))* HarperCollins Pubs.

Corrigan, Jim. General George G. Meade: Victor at Gettysburg. 2011. (J). *(978-1-59556-044-5(0));* pap. *(978-1-59556-050-6(5))* OTTN Publishing.

Dell, Pamela. Memoir of Tillie Pierce: An Eyewitness to the Battle of Gettysburg. 2017. (First-Person Histories Ser.). (ENG., Illus.). 32p. (gr. 3-4). lib. bdg. 27.32 *(978-1-5157-3355-3(6),* Fact Finders) Capstone Press of Coughlan Cos.

Doeden, Matt. Gettysburg Battlefield: A Chilling Interactive Adventure. 2017. (You Choose: Haunted Places Ser.). (ENG., Illus.). 112p. (gr. 3-4). lib. bdg. 31.99 *(978-1-5157-3649-3(0),* You Choose Bks.) Capstone Press of Coughlan Cos.

Dunn, Joeming. Graphic Warfare. 2016. (Graphic Warfare Ser.: 6). (ENG.). 32p. (J). (gr. 3-8). lib. bdg. 171.00 *(978-1-61641-977-6(6),* Graphic Planet) Magic Wagon.

Elish, Dan. The Battle of Gettysburg. 2005. (Cornerstones of Freedom Ser.). (ENG., Illus.). 48p. (YA). (gr. 4-7). 26.00 *(978-0-516-23623-0(7))* Scholastic Library Publishing.

Fitzgerald, Stephanie. Split History of the Battle of Gettysburg. 2013. (Perspectives Flip Bks.). (ENG.). 64p. (gr. 5-6). 33.99 *(978-0-7565-4695-3(8));* pap. 8.95 *(978-0-7565-4701-1(6))* Compass Point Bks. (CPB Grades 4-8).

Ford, Carin T. The Battle of Gettysburg & Lincoln's Gettysburg Address. 2004. (Civil War Library). (Illus.). 48p. (J). lib. bdg. 25.27 *(978-0-7660-2253-9(6))* Enslow Pubs., Inc.

—Lincoln's Gettysburg Address & the Battle of Gettysburg Through Primary Sources. 2013. (Civil War Through Primary Sources Ser.). 48p. (J). (gr. 4-18). lib. bdg. 25.27 *(978-0-7660-4126-4(3))* Enslow Pubs., Inc.

Fradin, Dennis Brindell. The Battle of Gettysburg. 2007. (Turning Points in U. S. History Ser.). (J). lib. bdg. 31.36 *(978-0-7614-2043-9(6),* Benchmark Bks.) Marshall Cavendish Corp.

Gregory, Josh. Gettysburg. 2011. (Cornerstones of Freedom, Third Ser.). 64p. (J). (ENG.). pap. 8.95 *(978-0-531-26559-8(5));* lib. bdg. 30.00 *(978-0-531-25034-1(2))* Scholastic Library Publishing. (Children's Pr.).

Johnson, Jennifer. Gettysburg: The Bloodiest Battle of the Civil War. 2017. (24/7 Goes to War Ser.). (ENG.). 64p. (J). (gr. 6-12). pap. 7.95 *(978-0-531-25453-0(4),* Watts, Franklin) Scholastic Library Publishing.

—Pickett's Charge at Gettysburg: A Bloody Clash in the Civil War. 2011. (J). pap. *(978-0-545-32941-5(8))* Scholastic, Inc.

Landau, Elaine. The Battle of Gettysburg: Would You Lead the Fight? (What Would You Do? Ser.). (Illus.). 48p. (J). 2010. pap. 8.95 *(978-1-59845-192-4(8))* 2008. (gr. 3-4). lib. bdg. 25.27 *(978-0-7660-2903-3(4))* Enslow Pubs., Inc. (Enslow Elementary).

—The Great Battle of Gettysburg: Would You Stand & Fight? 2015. (What Would You Do? Ser.). 48p. (J). (gr. 3-4). 25.27 *(978-0-7660-6295-5(3));* pap. 8.95 *(978-0-7660-6296-2(1),* Enslow Elementary) Enslow Pubs., Inc.

MacCarald, Clara. The Battle of Gettysburg: Bloodiest Battle of the Civil War. 2017. (Major Battles in US History (hardcover) Ser.). (ENG., Illus.). 32p. (J). (gr. 4-7). lib. bdg. 28.50 ***(978-1-63517-018-4(4),*** Focus Readers) North Star Editions.

Martin, Iain C. Gettysburg: The True Account of Two Young Heroes in the Greatest Battle of the Civil War. (ENG., Illus.). 208p. (gr. 6). 2015. (J). pap. 16.99 *(978-1-63220-438-7(X))* 2013. (YA). 16.95 *(978-1-62087-532-2(2),* 620532) Skyhorse Publishing Co., Inc. (Sky Pony Pr.).

McNamara, Margaret. The Battle of Gettysburg. 2006. (J). pap. *(978-1-4108-6445-1(6))* Benchmark Education Co.

—Discover the Battle of Gettysburg. 2006. (J). pap. *(978-1-4108-6448-2(0))* Benchmark Education Co.

Morris, Rob, et al. The Battle of Gettysburg Close Up. 2015. (War Chronicles Ser.). (ENG., Illus.). 72p. (YA). (gr. 9-9). 32.95 *(978-1-4994-6162-6(3),* Rosen Young Adult) Rosen Publishing Group, Inc., The.

O'Connor, Jim. What Was the Battle of Gettysburg? Mantha, John & Bennett, James, illus. 2013. (What Was? Ser.). (ENG.). 112p. (J). (gr. 3-7). pap. 5.99 *(978-0-448-46286-8(9),* Grosset & Dunlap) Penguin Young Readers Group.

—What Was the Battle of Gettysburg? 2013. (What Was... ? Ser.). lib. bdg. 16.00 *(978-0-606-29963-3(7),* Turtleback) Turtleback Bks.

O'Hern, Kerri & Anderson, Dale. The Battle of Gettysburg. 2006. (Graphic Histories Ser.). (Illus.). 32p. (gr. 5-8). pap. 10.50 *(978-0-8368-6256-0(2))* Stevens, Gareth Publishing LLLP.

O'Hern, Kerri, et al. La Batalla de Gettysburg. 2007. (Historias Graficas (Graphic Histories) Ser.). (SPA., Illus.). 32p. (gr. 5-8). pap. 10.50 *(978-0-8368-7901-8(5));* lib. bdg. 27.00 *(978-0-8368-7894-3(9))* Stevens, Gareth Publishing LLLP.

Olson, Kay Melchisedech. The Gettysburg Address in Translation: What It Really Means. 2016. (Kids' Translations Ser.). (ENG.). 32p. (gr. 3-4). pap. 8.10 *(978-1-5157-5168-7(6),* Fact Finders) Capstone Press of Coughlan Cos.

Olson, Steven P. Lincoln's Gettysburg Address: A Primary Source Investigation. (Great Historic Debates & Speeches Ser.). 64p. 2009. (gr. 5-8). 58.50 *(978-1-61513-115-0(9))* 2004. (Illus.). (J). lib. bdg. 31.95 *(978-1-4042-0151-4(3))* Rosen Publishing Group, Inc., The.

Pingry, Patricia A. The Story of Gettysburg. Britt, Stephanie, illus. 2003. (ENG.). 26p. (J). (gr. -1-k). bds. 7.69 *(978-0-8249-6503-7(5),* Ideal Pubns.) Worthy Publishing.

Rajczak, Michael. Haunted! Gettysburg. 2013. 32p. (J). (gr. 3-6). 26.60 *(978-1-4339-9248-3(5));* pap. 10.50 *(978-1-4339-9249-0(3));* pap. 63.00 *(978-1-4339-9250-6(7))* Stevens, Gareth Publishing LLLP.

Ray, Frederic. Gettysburg Sketches: A Concise & Illustrated History of the Battle of Gettysburg. 2012. 34p. (J). reprint ed. pap. 20.95 *(978-1-258-48954-0(6))* Literary Licensing, LLC.

RJF Publishing Staff & Todras, Ellen H. The Gettysburg Battlefield. 2009. (Symbols of American Freedom Ser.). 48p. (gr. 4-6). 30.00 *(978-1-60413-514-5(X),* Chelsea Clubhouse) Facts On File, Inc.

Roberts, Russell. Haunted Battlefields Gettysburg: Gettysburg. 2015. (ENG., Illus.). 48p. (J). 29.95 *(978-1-62469-112-6(9))* Purple Toad Publishing, Inc.

Sinnott, Susan. Charley Waters Goes to Gettysburg. Handelman, Dorothy, photos by. 2003. (Illus.). 48p. (J). (gr. 4-7). pap. 8.95 *(978-0-7613-1887-3(9),* Millbrook Pr.) Lerner Publishing Group.

Slepian, Curtis. You Are There! Gettysburg, July 1. 3 1863. 2017. (Time for Kids Nonfiction Readers Ser.). lib. bdg. 19.65 ***(978-0-606-40260-6(8))*** Turtleback Bks.

—You Are There! Gettysburg, July 1-3, 1863. 2nd ed. 2017. (TIME for KIDS(r) Nonfiction Readers Ser.). 32p. (gr. 8-8). 8.99 ***(978-1-4938-3927-8(6))*** Teacher Created Materials, Inc.

Stotts, Stuart. Lucius Fairchild: Civil War Hero. 2011. (Badger Biographies Ser.). (ENG., Illus.). 112p. (J). pap. 12.95 *(978-0-87020-460-9(2))* Wisconsin Historical Society.

Sutherland, Jonathan. The Battle of Gettysburg the Turning Point in the Civil War. 2017. (Civil War Ser.: Vol. 5). (ENG.). (YA). (gr. 7-12). 24.95 ***(978-1-4222-3884-4(9))*** Mason Crest.

Tanaka, Shelley. Gettysburg: The Legendary Battle & the Address That Inspired a Nation. Craig, David, illus. 2003. (Day That Changed America Ser.). (ENG.). 48p. 16.99 *(978-0-7868-1922-5(7))* Hyperion Pr.

Vierow, Wendy. The Battle of Gettysburg: The Civil War's Biggest Battle. (Headlines from History Ser.). 24p. 2009. (gr. 3-3). 42.50 *(978-1-61513-242-3(2),* PowerKids Pr.) 2004. (Illus.). (YA). (gr. 2-5). lib. bdg. 22.60 *(978-0-8239-6225-9(3))* Rosen Publishing Group, Inc., The.

Warrick, Karen Clemens. Gettysburg National Military Park: A MyReportLinks.com Book. 2005. (Virtual Field Trips Ser.). (Illus.). 48p. (J). (gr. 4-10). lib. bdg. 26.60 *(978-0-7660-5223-9(0),* MyReportLinks.com Bks.) Enslow Pubs., Inc.

Waryncia, Lou. Gettysburg: Bold Battle in the North. Hale, Sarah Elder, ed. 2005. (ENG., Illus.). 43p. (J). (gr. 3-9). 17.95 *(978-0-8126-7903-8(2))* Cobblestone Publishing Co.

Weber, Jennifer. Summer's Bloodiest Days: The Battle of Gettysburg as Told from All Sides. 2010. (ENG., Illus.). 64p. (J). (gr. 5-18). 27.90 *(978-1-4263-0707-2(1));* 17.95 *(978-1-4263-0706-5(3))* National Geographic Society. (National Geographic Children's Bks.).

GETTYSBURG, BATTLE OF, GETTYSBURG, PA., 1863—FICTION

Altsheler, Joseph A. The Star of Gettysburg: A Story of Southern High Tide. 2006. (Civil War Ser.: Vol. 5). 324p. (J). reprint ed. 29.95 *(978-1-4218-1780-4(2));* pap. 14.95 *(978-1-4218-1880-1(9))* 1st World Publishing, Inc. (1st World Library - Literary Society).

—The Star of Gettysburg: A Story of Southern High Tide. l.t. ed. (Civil War Ser.: Vol. 5). (J). reprint ed. 2007. (ENG.). 290p. per. 23.99 *(978-1-4346-7665-6(4))* 2008. 292p. 25.99 *(978-0-554-38764-2(6))* 2008. 292p. 28.99 *(978-0-554-29461-2(3))* 2007. (ENG.). 258p. per. 21.99 *(978-1-4346-7684-9(6))* Creative Media Partners, LLC.

—The Star of Gettysburg: A Story of Southern High Tide. 2006. (Civil War Ser.: Vol. 5). (J). reprint ed. pap. *(978-1-4065-0824-6(1))* Dodo Pr.

—The Star of Gettysburg: A Story of Southern High Tide. 2007. (Civil War Ser.: Vol. 5). 192p. (J). reprint ed. per. *(978-1-4068-1688-4(4))* Echo Library.

—The Star of Gettysburg: A Story of Southern High Tide. 2010. (Civil War Ser.: Vol. 5). 174p. (J). (gr. 4-7). reprint ed. pap. 19.99 *(978-1-153-72161-5(9))* General Bks. LLC.

—The Star of Gettysburg: A Story of Southern High Tide. (Civil War Ser.: Vol. 5). (J). reprint ed. 2010. 262p. (gr. 4-7). 34.36 *(978-1-169-30586-1(5))* 2010. 262p. (gr. 4-7). pap. 22.36 *(978-1-162-70899-7(9))* 2010. 42.95 *(978-1-161-47763-4(2))* 2004. pap. 1.99 *(978-1-4192-8344-4(8))* 2004. pap. 27.95 *(978-1-4191-8344-7(3))* Kessinger Publishing, LLC.

—The Star of Gettysburg: A Story of Southern High Tide. 2011. (Civil War Ser.: Vol. 5). 280p. (J). (gr. 4-7). reprint ed. pap. *(978-3-8424-5317-3(5))* Tredition GmbH.

—The Star of Gettysburg (Webster's Korean Thesaurus Edition) 2008. (Civil War Ser.: Vol. 5). (Illus.). 340p. (C). pap. 28.95 *(978-0-546-50036-3(6))* Icon Group International, Inc.

Calkhoven, Laurie. Will at the Battle of Gettysburg. 2012. (Boys of Wartime Ser.: 2). (ENG.). 256p. (J). (gr. 4-7). 7.99 *(978-0-14-241987-8(7),* Puffin Books) Penguin Young Readers Group.

Cregar, Elyse M. Hanna's Courage: A Story of Love & Betrayal at the Battle of Gettysburg. 2012. 212p. pap. 8.99 *(978-0-9621292-2-3(4))* Tamerac Publishing.

Crist-Evans, Craig. Moon over Tennessee: A Boy's Civil War Journal. Christensen, Bonnie, illus. 2003. (ENG.). 64p. (J). (gr. 5-7). pap. 8.95 *(978-0-618-31107-1(6))* Houghton Mifflin Harcourt Publishing Co.

Dunn, Joeming W. Gettysburg. Dunn, Ben, illus. 2016. (Graphic Warfare Ser.). (ENG.). 32p. (J). (gr. 3-8). 28.50 *(978-1-61641-981-3(4))* Magic Wagon.

Ernst, Kathleen. Retreat from Gettysburg. 2010. (White Mane Kids Ser.). (Illus.). 145p. (YA). pap. *(978-1-57249-403-9(4),* White Mane Kids) White Mane Publishing Co., Inc.

Garland, Sherry. Voices of Gettysburg, 1 vol. Hierstein, Judith, illus. 2010. (Voices of History Ser.). (ENG.). 40p. (J). (gr. 3-3). 17.99 *(978-1-58980-653-5(0))* Pelican Publishing Co., Inc.

Gutman, Dan. Abner & Me. 2007. (Baseball Card Adventures Ser.). (ENG., Illus.). 176p. (J). (gr. 5-9). pap. 5.99 *(978-0-06-053445-5(1))* HarperCollins Pubs.

—Abner & Me. 2007. (Baseball Card Adventures Ser.). (Illus.). 166p. (gr. 5-9). 16.00 *(978-0-7569-7920-1(X))* Perfection Learning Corp.

Hopkinson, Deborah. Billy & the Rebel: Based on a True Civil War Story. Floca, Brian, illus. 2005. 44p. (J). lib. bdg. 15.00 *(978-1-4242-1148-7(4))* Fitzgerald Bks.

—Billy & the Rebel: Based on a True Civil War Story. Floca, Brian, illus. 2006. (Ready-to-Read Ser.). 44p. (gr. 1-3). 14.00 *(978-0-7569-6390-3(7))* Perfection Learning Corp.

—Billy & the Rebel: Based on a True Civil War Story. Floca, Brian, illus. 2006. (Ready-To-Reads Ser.). (ENG.). 48p. (J). (gr. 1-3). pap. 3.99 *(978-0-689-83396-0(2),* Simon Spotlight) Simon Spotlight.

—Billy & the Rebel: Based on a True Civil War Story. Anderson, Bethanne & Floca, Brian, illus. 2005. (Ready-To-Reads Ser.). (ENG.). 48p. (J). (gr. 1-3). 16.99 *(978-0-689-83964-1(2),* Simon Spotlight) Simon Spotlight.

Kay, Alan N. Crossroads at Gettysburg. 2005. (Young Heroes of History Ser.: 6). (Illus.). 166p. (J). (gr. 3-7). per. 7.95 *(978-1-57249-359-9(3),* White Mane Kids) White Mane Publishing Co., Inc.

Malkus, Alida Sims. We Were There at the Battle of Gettysburg. Vosburgh, Leonard, illus. 2013. (ENG.). 192p. (J). (gr. 3-8). pap. 6.99 *(978-0-486-49261-2(3))* Dover Pubns., Inc.

Miller, Bobbi. The Girls of Gettysburg. 2014. (ENG.). 160p. (J). (gr. 2-7). 16.95 *(978-0-8234-3163-2(0))* Holiday Hse., Inc.

Papp, Lisa & Noble, Trinka Hakes. The Battles. Papp, Robert, illus. 2013. (American Adventures Ser.). (ENG.). 88p. (J). (gr. 3-6). pap. 9.99 *(978-1-58536-861-7(X),* 202368) Sleeping Bear Pr.

Perez, Norah A. The Slopes of War. 2008. (ENG., Illus.). 224p. (YA). (gr. 7-12). pap. 7.99 *(978-0-547-01614-6(X))* Houghton Mifflin Harcourt Publishing Co.

Potter, David. The Left Behinds: Abe Lincoln & the Selfie That Saved the Union. 2016. (Left Behinds Ser.). (ENG.). 304p. (J). (gr. 3-7). 16.99 *(978-0-385-39060-6(2),* Crown Books For Young Readers) Random Hse. Children's Bks.

Ruby, Lois. Rebel Spirits. 2013. (ENG.). 304p. (J). (gr. 7). 17.99 *(978-0-545-42623-7(5))* Scholastic, Inc.

Sykes, Shelley & Szymanski, Lois. The Soldier in the Cellar. 2011. (Gettysburg Ghost Gang Ser.: Vol. 5). 96p. (J). pap. 7.95 *(978-1-57249-299-8(6),* White Mane Kids) White Mane Publishing Co., Inc.

Tarshis, Lauren. I Survived the Battle of Gettysburg 1863. 2013. (I Survived Ser.: 7). (ENG.). 112p. (J). (gr. 2-5). pap. 4.99 *(978-0-545-45936-5(2),* Scholastic Pr.) Scholastic, Inc.

—I Survived the Battle of Gettysburg 1863. 2013. (I Survived ... Ser.: No. 7). lib. bdg. 14.75 *(978-0-606-31530-2(6),* Turtleback) Turtleback Bks.

Walter, Aaron T. Mr Lincoln's Hat. 2008. 75p. pap. 16.95 *(978-1-60672-852-9(0))* PublishAmerica, Inc.

GETTYSBURG ADDRESS

see Lincoln, Abraham, 1809-1865—Gettysburg Address

GHANA

Ashley, Bernard, et al. Angel Boy. 2009. (ENG.). 96p. (J). (gr. 3-7). pap. 7.95 *(978-1-84507-809-6(8),* Frances Lincoln) Quarto Publishing Group UK GBR. Dist: Hachette Bk. Group.

Bankston, John. We Visit Ghana. 2012. (J). lib. bdg. 33.95 *(978-1-61228-303-6(9))* Mitchell Lane Pubs., Inc.

Blauer, Ettagale & Lauré, Jason. Ghana. rev. ed. 2009. (Enchantment of the World Ser.). (ENG., Illus.). 144p. (J). (gr. 5-9). 40.00 *(978-0-531-20652-2(1))* Scholastic Library Publishing.

Conrad, David C. Empires of Medieval West Africa, Revised Edition. 2nd rev. ed. 2009. (Great Empires of the Past Ser.). (Illus.). 152p. (gr. 6-12). 35.00 *(978-1-60413-164-2(0),* Chelsea Hse.) Facts On File, Inc.

Discover Ghana. 2012. (Discover Countries Ser.). (ENG., Illus.). 32p. (J). (gr. 3-5). 25.25 *(978-1-4488-6621-2(9),* PowerKids Pr.) Rosen Publishing Group, Inc., The.

Galat, Joan Marie. Cultural Traditions in Ghana. 2017. 32p. (J). ***(978-0-7787-8095-3(3))*** Crabtree Publishing Co.

Klobuchar, Lisa. Africans of the Ghana, Mali, & Songhai Empires. 2009. (J). *(978-0-7166-2134-8(7))* World Bk., Inc.

La Pierre, Yvette. Ghana in Pictures. 2nd rev. expurg. ed. 2004. (Visual Geography Series, Second Ser.). (ENG., Illus.). 80p. (gr. 5-12). 31.93 *(978-0-8225-1997-3(6))* Lerner Publishing Group.

Larson, Lyn. Ghana. 2010. pap. 51.02 *(978-0-7613-6974-5(0))* Lerner Publishing Group.

Levy, Patricia & Wong, Winnie. Ghana. 2nd rev. ed. 2009. (Cultures of the World 18 Ser.). 144p. (gr. 6). 42.79 *(978-0-7614-4847-1(0))* Marshall Cavendish GBR. Dist: Marshall Cavendish Corp.

Poisson, Barbara Aoki. Ghana. Rotberg, Robert I., ed. 2012. (Evolution of Africa's Major Nations Ser.). (Illus.). 80p. (J). (gr. 7). 22.95 *(978-1-4222-2196-9(2))* Mason Crest.

—Ghana. 2011. (J). pap. *(978-1-4222-2224-9(1))* 2006. (Illus.). 79p. (YA). lib. bdg. 21.95 *(978-1-59084-814-2(4))* Mason Crest.

Sheen, Barbara, ed. Foods of Ghana. 2012. (Taste of Culture Ser.). (ENG., Illus.). 64p. (gr. 3-6). lib. bdg. 35.20 *(978-0-7377-5949-5(6),* Kidhaven) Cengage Gale.

GHANA—BIOGRAPHY

Currie-McGhee, Leanne K. Emmanuel Osofu Yeboah: Champion for Ghana's Disabled. 2006. (Young Heroes Ser.). (ENG., Illus.). 64p. (gr. 4-8). lib. bdg. 35.70 *(978-0-7377-3614-4(3),* Kidhaven) Cengage Gale.

Gordon, Nick. Kofi Kingston. 2012. (Pro Wrestling Champions Ser.). (ENG., Illus.). 24p. (J). (gr. 3-7). lib. bdg. 25.95 *(978-1-60014-784-5(4),* Torque Bks.) Bellwether Media.

Larson, Lyn. Ghana. 2010. (Country Explorers Ser.). (ENG.). 48p. (gr. 2-4). lib. bdg. 29.27 *(978-0-7613-5318-8(6))* Lerner Publishing Group.

Thompson, Laurie Ann. Emmanuel's Dream: The True Story of Emmanuel Ofosu Yeboah. Qualls, Sean, illus. 2015. (ENG.). 40p. (J). (gr. -1-3). 17.99 *(978-0-449-81744-5(X),* Schwartz & Wade Bks.) Random Hse. Children's Bks.

GHANA—CIVILIZATION

Cohen, Robert Z. Discovering the Empire of Ghana. 2013. (Exploring African Civilizations Ser.). 64p. (J). (gr. 5-8). 31.95 *(978-1-4777-1882-7(6),* Rosen Reference) Rosen Publishing Group, Inc., The.

GHANA—FICTION

Badoe, Adwoa. The Pot of Wisdom. Diakité, Baba Wagué, illus. 2008. (ENG.). 64p. (J). (gr. 1-5). pap. 12.95 *(978-0-88899-869-9(4))* Groundwood Bks. CAN. Dist: Publishers Group West (PGW).

Cooper, William Y. Nakai & the Red Shoes. 2011. 52p. (gr. 4-6). pap. 19.39 *(978-1-4269-6048-2(4))* Trafford Publishing.

Cudjoe, Dzagbe. Tales My Ghanaian Grandmother Told Me. 2008. 52p. pap. 19.95 *(978-1-934925-87-4(X),* Strategic Bk. Publishing) Strategic Book Publishing & Rights Agency (SBPRA).

Hewins, Shirley, illus. Rainy Brown & the Seven Midgets. l.t. ed. 2006. (J). (gr. k-3). pap. 11.95 *(978-1-884242-24-3(3),* RB1STED); 44p. lib. bdg. 19.95 *(978-1-884242-25-0(1),* RB1STED) Multicultural Pubns.

Jarman, Julia. The Magic Backpack. Gon, Adriano, illus. 2003. (Flying Foxes Ser.). (ENG.). 48p. (J). lib. bdg. *(978-0-7787-1487-3(X))* Crabtree Publishing Co.

Kittle, Katrina. Reasons to Be Happy. 2011. (ENG.). 288p. (J). (gr. 6-8). pap. 10.99 *(978-1-4022-6020-9(2),* Sourcebooks Jabberwocky) Sourcebooks, Inc.

Lokko, CNN. Adventures of Elizabeth Sam. 2012. 280p. pap. *(978-9964-70-151-2(9))* Afram Pubns. Ghana, Ltd.

Mitchard, Jacquelyn & Lewis, Michael S. Eagle Eyes. 2009. (ENG.). 128p. (gr. 4-7). pap. 9.99 *(978-0-9790072-2-4(4))* MAHVL Publishing.

Mussi, Sarah. The Door of No Return. 2009. (ENG.). 400p. (YA). (gr. 7). pap. 10.99 *(978-1-4169-6825-2(3),* McElderry, Margaret K. Bks.) McElderry, Margaret K. Bks.

Norfolk, Bobby & Norfolk, Sherry. Anansi & Turtle Go to Dinner. Hoffmire, Baird, illus. 2007. (Story Cove Ser.). (ENG.). 32p. (J). (gr. -1-3). pap. 4.95 *(978-0-87483-856-5(8))* August Hse. Pubs., Inc.

Onyefulu, Ifeoma. Deron Goes to Nursery School. Onyefulu, Ifeoma, photos by. 2010. (First Experiences Ser.). (ENG., Illus.). 32p. (J). (gr. -1-2). 17.95 *(978-1-84507-864-5(0),* Frances Lincoln) Quarto Publishing Group UK GBR. Dist: Hachette Bk. Group.

—Grandma Comes to Stay. Onyefulu, Ifeoma, photos by. 2010. (First Experiences Ser.). (ENG., Illus.). 32p. (J). (gr. -1-2). 17.99 *(978-1-84507-865-2(9),* Frances Lincoln) Quarto Publishing Group UK GBR. Dist: Hachette Bk. Group.

GHOST STORIES

Adler, David A. Mystery at the Haunted House, 13 vols. Natti, Susanna, illus. 2004. (Cam Jansen Ser.: 13). (ENG.). 64p.

EFG

(J). (gr. 2-5). 4.99 *(978-0-14-240210-8(9),* Puffin Books) Penguin Young Readers Group.

Alender, Katie. The Dead Girls of Hysteria Hall. 2015. (ENG.). 336p. (J). (gr. 7). 18.99 *(978-0-545-63999-6(9))* Scholastic, Inc.

—The Dead Girls of Hysteria Hall. 2016. (ENG.). 329p. (YA). (gr. 7). 20.85 *(978-0-606-39121-4(5))* Turtleback Bks.

Anderson, Jodi Lynn. Among the Stars. 2014. (May Bird Ser.: 2). (ENG., Illus.). 304p. (J). (gr. 3-7). 17.99 *(978-1-4424-9579-1(0),* Simon & Schuster/Paula Wiseman Bks.) Simon & Schuster/Paula Wiseman Bks.

Anzaldúa, Gloria. Prietita & the Ghost Woman: Prietita y la Llorona. Gonzalez, Maya Christina, illus. 2013. (ENG & SPA.). 32p. (J). (gr. 1-18). pap. 9.95 *(978-0-89239-167-7(7))* Lee & Low Bks., Inc.

—Prietita & the Ghost Woman: Prietita y la Llorona. 2004. (ENG & SPA., Illus.). (J). (gr. k-3). spiral bd. *(978-0-616-07273-8(2))* Canadian National Institute for the Blind/Institut National Canadien pour les Aveugles.

Armstrong, Kelley. The Summoning. (Darkest Powers Ser.: 1). (YA). (gr. 8). 2009. 416p. pap. 9.99 *(978-0-06-145054-9(5))* 2008. 400p. 17.99 *(978-0-06-166269-0(0))* HarperCollins Pubs.

—The Summoning, 7 vols. 2009. (Darkest Powers Ser.: 1). (J). 243.75 *(978-1-4361-9718-2(X))*; 81.75 *(978-1-4361-9717-5(1))* Recorded Bks., Inc.

Arnold, Louise. Golden & Grey: The Nightmares That Ghosts Have. 2007. (ENG.). 304p. (J). (gr. 3-7). pap. 5.99 *(978-0-689-87587-8(8),* McElderry, Margaret K. Bks.) McElderry, Margaret K. Bks.

Asch, Frank. The Ghost of P. S. 42. Kanzler, John, illus. 2014. (Class Pets Ser.). (ENG.). 96p. (J). (gr. 2-5). pap. 13.99 *(978-1-4814-3624-3(4),* Simon & Schuster/Paula Wiseman Bks.) Simon & Schuster/Paula Wiseman Bks.

Asfar, Dan & Banks, Sydney. Dear Liza, 1 vol. rev. ed. 2004. 28. (ENG., Illus.). 88p. 12.95 *(978-1-55105-332-5(2),* 1551053322) Lone Pine Publishing USA.

Auxier, Jonathan. The Night Gardener. (ENG.). (YA). (gr. 3-7). 2015. 384p. pap. 8.95 *(978-1-4197-1531-0(3))* 2014. 368p. 16.95 *(978-1-4197-1144-2(X))* Abrams, Inc. (Amulet Bks.).

—The Night Gardener. 2015. (J). lib. bdg. 19.60 *(978-0-606-36891-9(4))* Turtleback Bks.

Avi. The Seer of Shadows. 2009. (ENG.). 224p. (J). (gr. 4-7). pap. 6.99 *(978-0-06-000017-2(1))* HarperCollins Pubs.

Avila, Kat. Hanako Loves Monsters. 2008. 32p. 14.98 *(978-1-4357-0188-5(7))* Lulu Pr., Inc.

Barnett, Mac. Leo: A Ghost Story. Robinson, Christian, illus. 2015. (ENG.). 52p. (J). (gr. -1-k). 16.99 *(978-1-4521-3156-6(2))* Chronicle Bks. LLC.

Bass, Guy. The Ghost of Grotteskew, 1 vol. Williamson, Pete, illus. 2014. (Stitch Head Ser.). (ENG.). 208p. (gr. 3-4). 10.95 *(978-1-62370-030-0(2))* Capstone Young Readers of Coughlan Cos.

Baxter, Nicola. The Mystery of the Haunted House: Dare You Peek Through the 3-D Windows? Goulding, June, illus. 2013. (ENG.). 12p. 16.99 *(978-1-84322-754-0(1))* Anness Publishing GBR. Dist: National Bk. Network.

Bladek, John. Lost in Ghostville. 2016. (ENG.). 208p. (gr. 4-8). 10.95 *(978-1-62370-776-7(5))* Capstone Young Readers of Coughlan Cos.

Blake, Kendare. Anna Dressed in Blood. 2012. (Anna Dressed in Blood Ser.: 1). (YA). lib. bdg. 22.10 *(978-0-606-26252-1(0),* Turtleback) Turtleback Bks.

Blanchet, Deborah A. The Hat. 2009. 122p. 29.99 *(978-1-4415-4624-1(3))*; pap. 19.99 *(978-1-4415-4623-4(5))* Xlibris Corp.

Bougie, Matt. The Bell Witch: Ghost of Tennessee. Greenan, Amy, illus. 2016. (American Legends & Folktales Ser.). 32p. (J). pap. 10.58 *(978-1-5026-2220-4(3))* Cavendish Square Publishing.

Bradshaw, John. Fun Campfire Ghost Stories. 2009. 114p. pap. 13.98 *(978-0-557-11729-1(1))* Lulu Pr., Inc.

Bryant, Mark. Ghosts in the Cloisters: Clerical Tales of Mystery & Supernatural. (Illus.). x, 307p. (J). pap. 15.00 *(978-0-340-71376-1(3))* Hodder & Stoughton GBR. Dist: Trafalgar Square Publishing.

Bunce, Elizabeth C. A Curse Dark as Gold. 2010. (ENG.). 400p. (J). (gr. 7). 9.99 *(978-0-439-89577-4(4),* Scholastic Paperbacks) Scholastic, Inc.

Bunting, Eve. In the Haunted House. Meddaugh, Susan, illus. 2013. (ENG.). 16p. (J). (gr. -1-3). 6.99 *(978-0-544-06670-0(7))* Houghton Mifflin Harcourt Publishing Co.

Burchett, Janet & Vogler, Sara. Bones & Groans. 2003. (ENG., Illus.). 107p. (J). pap. *(978-0-330-36814-8(1),* Pan) Pan Macmillan.

—Creep from the Deep. Brown, Judy, illus. 10th ed. (ENG.). 96p. (J). pap. *(978-0-330-37607-5(1),* Pan) Pan Macmillan.

—Shiver & Deliver. Brown, Judy, illus. 7th ed. 2003. (ENG.). 87p. (J). pap. *(978-0-330-37604-4(7),* Pan) Pan Macmillan.

Butler, Dori H. The Ghost in the Tree House. 2016. (Haunted Library: 7). lib. bdg. 16.00 *(978-0-606-38402-5(2))* Turtleback Bks.

Butler, Dori Hillestad. The Hide-and-Seek Ghost. Damant, Aurore, illus. 2016. (Haunted Library: 8). (ENG.). 128p. (J). (gr. 1-3). 5.99 *(978-0-448-48942-1(2),* Grosset & Dunlap) Penguin Young Readers Group.

Butler, Dori Hillestad & dePaola, Tomie. The Secret Room. Damant, Aurore, illus. 2015. (Haunted Library: 5). (ENG.). 128p. (J). (gr. 1-3). 5.99 *(978-0-448-48332-0(7),* Grosset & Dunlap) Penguin Young Readers Group.

Cabot, Meg. Shadowland & Ninth Key. 2010. (Mediator Ser.). (ENG.). 544p. (YA). (gr. 8). pap. 9.99 *(978-0-06-204020-6(0),* HarperTeen) HarperCollins Pubs.

—Twilight. 2005. (Mediator Ser.: 6). (ENG.). 336p. (YA). (gr. 8-12). pap. 8.99 *(978-0-06-072469-6(2),* HarperTeen) HarperCollins Pubs.

Carroll, Jenny, pseud & Cabot, Meg. Shadowland. 2004. (Mediator Ser.: 1). (ENG.). 304p. (YA). (gr. 8-12). pap. 8.99 *(978-0-06-072511-2(7),* HarperTeen) HarperCollins Pubs.

Christensen, Jo-Anne. Haunted Halloween Stories Vol. 1: A Collection of Ghost Stories, 1 vol. Kubish, Shelagh, ed. rev. ed. 2003. (Ghost Stories Ser.). (ENG., Illus.). 208p. (gr. 4). pap. 12.95 *(978-1-894877-34-3(9),* 1894877349, Ghost Hse. Bks.) Lone Pine Publishing USA.

Clarke, Jane. Creaky Castle. Fox, Christyan, illus. 2013. *(978-1-4351-4951-9(3))* Barnes & Noble, Inc.

Coffey, Stephen. Rosemary Herbb & the Zodiac Ghosts. 2009. 148p. pap. 14.50 *(978-1-4092-9751-2(9))* Lulu Pr., Inc.

Cohen, Marina. The Inn Between. Watts, Sarah, illus. 2016. (ENG.). 208p. (J). 16.99 *(978-1-62672-202-6(1),* 9781626722026) Roaring Brook Pr.

Cooke, Tobias. The Secret of the Lost Soul: A Ben Street Mystery. 2011. 272p. pap. *(978-1-907499-80-7(6))* Pen Pr. Pubs., Ltd.

Cool, Kim. Ghost Stories of Clearwater & St. Petersburg. 2004. (YA). pap. 12.95 *(978-0-9721655-4-9(1))* Cool, Kim @ Historic Venice Pr.

Cooper, Louise. Short & Scary! 2014. (ENG., Illus.). 96p. (J). 10.95 *(978-0-19-278190-1(1))* Oxford Univ. Pr., Inc.

Cooper, Susan. Ghost Hawk. 2014. (ENG., Illus.). 352p. (J). (gr. 5-9). pap. 7.99 *(978-1-4424-8142-8(0),* McElderry, Margaret K. Bks.) McElderry, Margaret K. Bks.

Cooper, Susan, et al. Haunted. Andersen Press Staff, ed. 2013. (ENG.). 336p. (J). (gr. 4-7). pap. 8.99 *(978-1-84939-321-8(4))* Andersen Pr. GBR. Dist: Independent Pubs. Group.

Creech, Sharon. Pleasing the Ghost. Schuett, Stacey, illus. 2013. (Trophy Bk.). 112p. (J). (gr. 3-7). reprint ed. pap. 5.99 *(978-0-06-440686-4(5))* HarperCollins Pubs.

Crews, G. S. Ellen G Goes to the Haunted Planetarium. Designs, Marion, photos by. 2009. (Illus.). 50p. pap. 20.00 *(978-0-9795236-4-9(8))* Crews Pubns., LLC.

Cusick, Richie Tankersley. Overdue. 2013. (ENG., Illus.). 224p. (YA). (gr. 7). pap. 15.99 *(978-1-4814-0162-3(9),* Simon Pulse) Simon Pulse.

de Brunhoff, Laurent. Babar Raconte le Fantome. (Babar Ser.). (FRE., Illus.). 48p. (J). (gr. -1-3). 19.95 *(978-0-7859-8819-9(X))* French & European Pubns., Inc.

Dickens, Charles. A Christmas Carol. Sanchez Almara, Dono & Almara, Dono Sanchez, illus. 2015. (Graphic Revolve: Common Core Editions Ser.). (ENG.). 72p. (gr. 2-3). lib. bdg. 27.99 *(978-1-4965-0370-1(8))* Stone Arch Bks.

Disney Book Group Staff, et al. Doc Mcstuffins Boo to You! Disney Storybook Artists Staff, illus. 2014. (ENG.). 12p. (J). (gr. -1-k). bds. 7.99 *(978-1-4231-8388-4(6))* Disney Pr.

Downie, Mary Alice & Downie, John. Alison's Ghosts, 1 vol. 2008. (Lorimer Streetlights Ser.). (ENG.). 104p. (J). (gr. 2-4). 8.95 *(978-1-55277-013-9(3),* 9781552770139) Lorimer, James & Co., Ltd., Pubs. CAN. Dist: Casemate Pubs. & Bk. Distributors, LLC.

Eboch, Chris. The Knight in the Shadows. 2009. (Haunted Ser.). (ENG.). 192p. (J). (gr. 3-7). pap. 5.99 *(978-1-4169-7550-2(0),* Simon & Schuster/Paula Wiseman Bks.) Simon & Schuster/Paula Wiseman Bks.

Enderle, Dotti. Book 13: Yo Ho No!, 1 vol. 2014. (Ghost Detectors Set 3 Ser.). (ENG., Illus.). 80p. (J). (gr. 2-5). lib. bdg. 27.07 *(978-1-62402-001-8(1),* Calico Chapter Bks) Magic Wagon.

—Grow a Ghost!, 1 vol. McWilliam, Howard, illus. 2016. (ENG.). 80p. (J). *(978-1-62402-100-8(X))* Magic Wagon.

—Spaced Out!, 1 vol. McWilliam, Howard, illus. 2016. (ENG.). 80p. (J). *(978-1-62402-101-5(8))* Magic Wagon.

Falcone, L. M. The Ghost & Max Monroe, Case #1: The Magic Box. Smith, Kim, illus. 2014. (Ghost & Max Monroe Ser.). (ENG.). 88p. (J). (gr. 1-4). pap. 6.95 *(978-1-77138-017-1(9))* Kids Can Pr., Ltd. CAN. Dist: Hachette Bk. Group.

Farber, E. S. Fish Finelli (Book 3) Warrick, Jessica, illus. 2016. (Fish Finelli Ser.). (ENG.). 176p. (J). (gr. 3-7). 15.99 *(978-1-4521-3815-2(X))* Chronicle Bks. LLC.

Feldhahn, Cathy J. Nosam. 2009. 37p. pap. 8.50 *(978-1-4092-8290-7(2))* Lulu Pr., Inc.

Field, C. D. The Peculiar World of Billy Peanut. 2017. (ENG.). 136p. pap. 11.95 ***(978-1-78710-324-5(2),*** 761715a7-350b-426e-b9ac-f5e11430104d) Austin, Stan AUS. Dist: Bookmasters Distribution.

—Zackery Grimm Investigates: The Ghost of Agapantha Claypole. 2016. (ENG.). 91p. (J). 19.95 *(978-1-78612-531-6(5),* 189f44f5-9499-4f02-a614-3d6db5444361) Austin, Stan AUS. Dist: Bookmasters Distribution.

—Zackery Grimm Investigates: the Ghost of Agapantha Claypole. 2016. (ENG.). 91p. (J). pap. 10.95 *(978-1-78612-530-9(7),* bedfa740-2a75-4fd8-8f86-a12279b743bd) Austin, Stan AUS. Dist: Bookmasters Distribution.

Fields, Jan. Ghost Light Burning: An Up2U Mystery Adventure, 1 vol. Fabbretti, Valerio, illus. 2015. (ENG.). 80p. (J). *(978-1-62402-092-6(5))* Magic Wagon.

Fine, Sarah. Of Metal & Wishes. 2014. (ENG., Illus.). 336p. (YA). (gr. 9). 17.99 *(978-1-4424-8358-3(X),* McElderry, Margaret K. Bks.) McElderry, Margaret K. Bks.

Finn, Perdita. Monster High - Haunted. 2015. (ENG., Illus.). 144p. (J). (gr. 3-7). pap. 5.99 *(978-0-316-37739-3(2))* Little, Brown Bks. for Young Readers.

Fisher, Catherine. The Ghost Box. 2012. (Stoke Books Titles Ser.). 72p. (J). (gr. 5-8). pap. 45.32 *(978-0-7613-9218-7(1))* Stoke Bks.

Flora, James. Grandpa's Ghost Stories. Flora, James, illus. 2017. (ENG., Illus.). 32p. (J). (gr. -1). 17.95 ***(978-1-62731-052-9(5))*** Feral Hse.

Frade, B. A. Vampire Vacation. 2017. (Tales from the Scaremaster Ser.: 5). (ENG.). 160p. (J). (gr. 3-7). pap. 5.99 ***(978-0-316-46409-3(0))*** Little, Brown Bks. for Young Readers.

—Vampire Vacation. 2017. (Tales of the Scaremaster Ser.). (J). lib. bdg. 16.00 ***(978-0-606-40225-5(X))*** Turtleback Bks.

Francis, Pauline, retold by. The Turn of the Screw. 2010. (Essential Classics - Horror Ser.). (Illus.). 48p. pap. *(978-0-237-54110-1(6))* Evans Brothers, Ltd.

Gale Editors & Wilson, Sean Michael. The Canterville Ghost: The Graphic Novel. 2011. (Classic Graphic Novel Collection). (ENG.). 160p. (gr. 7-10). lib. bdg. 39.40 *(978-1-4205-0629-7(3))* Cengage Gale.

Garton, Kevan. The Cockleton Mystery. 2006. 68p. pap. *(978-1-84401-788-1(5))* Athena Pr.

Gelsey, James. Scooby-Doo! & the Carnival Creeper, 1 vol. 2013. (Scooby-Doo Mysteries Set 2 Ser.). (ENG.). 64p. (J). (gr. 3-6). lib. bdg. 24.21 *(978-1-61479-042-6(6))* ABDO Publishing Co.

—Scooby-Doo! & the Frankenstein Monster, 1 vol. 2013. (Scooby-Doo Mysteries Set 2 Ser.). (ENG.). 64p. (J). (gr. 3-6). lib. bdg. 24.21 *(978-1-61479-043-3(4))* ABDO Publishing Co.

—Scooby-Doo! & the Groovy Ghost, 1 vol. 2013. (Scooby-Doo Mysteries Set 2 Ser.). (ENG.). 64p. (J). (gr. 3-6). lib. bdg. 24.21 *(978-1-61479-044-0(2))* ABDO Publishing Co.

—Scooby-Doo! & the Howling Wolfman, 1 vol. 2013. (Scooby-Doo Mysteries Set 2 Ser.). (ENG.). 64p. (J). (gr. 3-6). lib. bdg. 24.21 *(978-1-61479-046-4(9))* ABDO Publishing Co.

—Scooby-Doo! & the Spooky Strikeout, 1 vol. 2013. (Scooby-Doo Mysteries Set 2 Ser.). (ENG.). 64p. (J). (gr. 3-6). lib. bdg. 24.21 *(978-1-61479-047-1(7))* ABDO Publishing Co.

Gelsey, James & Duendes Del Sur Staff. Scooby-Doo & the Sunken Ship, 1 vol. 2011. (Scooby-Doo Mysteries Ser.). (ENG., Illus.). 64p. (J). (gr. 3-6). 24.21 *(978-1-59961-893-7(1))* Spotlight.

Ghost of a Chance. 2014. (Girl Meets Ghost Ser.: 3). (ENG., Illus.). 240p. (J). (gr. 4-9). pap. 7.99 *(978-1-4424-2148-6(7),* Aladdin) Simon & Schuster Children's Publishing.

Gibson, Marley. The Reason, Bk. 3. 2010. (ENG.). 240p. (YA). (gr. 7-18). pap. 8.99 *(978-0-547-15095-6(4))* Houghton Mifflin Harcourt Publishing Co.

Gilligan, Shannon. Ghost Island. Newton, Keith, illus. 2008. (Dragonlarks Ser.). 80p. (J). (gr. k-3). pap. 7.99 *(978-1-933390-57-4(3))* Chooseco LLC.

Hahn, Mary Downing. Time for Andrew: A Ghost Story. 2007. (ENG.). 176p. (J). (gr. 5-7). pap. 6.99 *(978-0-618-87316-6(3))* Houghton Mifflin Harcourt Publishing Co.

Hansen, Tevin. Mr. Boggarty: The Halloween Grump. 2014. (ENG.). 154p. pap. 5.95 *(978-1-941429-04-4(1))* Handersen Publishing.

—Mr. Boggarty & the Haunted Hospital. 2015. 154p. (J). pap. 7.95 *(978-1-941429-09-9(2))* Handersen Publishing.

Harrowing Haunts, Set. 2016. (Harrowing Haunts Ser.). (ENG.). 256p. (J). (gr. 7-7). lib. bdg. 159.00 *(978-1-4994-6380-4(4))* Rosen Publishing Group, Inc., The.

Hastings, Rook. Nearly Departed. 2010. (ENG.). 272p. (J). (gr. 6-9). 8.99 *(978-0-00-725810-9(0),* HarperCollins Children's Bks.) HarperCollins Pubs. Ltd. GBR. Dist: HarperCollins Pubs.

Helquist, Brett, illus. Scary Stories 3: More Tales to Chill Your Bones. 2011. 109p. (J). pap. *(978-0-545-38507-7(5))* Scholastic, Inc.

Hesse, Laura. The Great Pumpkin Ride. 2004. ix, 133p. (J). *(978-0-9734013-1-8(1))* Running L. Productions.

Holland, Robert. The Ghost Who Came to Tea: A Novel of Sports & Mystery. 2006. (Illus.). 204p. (J). *(978-0-9794273-4-3(7))* Frost Hollow Pubs., LLC.

James, Henry. The Turn of the Screw. 310p. reprint ed. pap. 75.00 *(978-1-4047-3418-0(X))* Classic Textbooks.

Jepson, Gill. Out of Time: The Secret of the Swan. 2011. (ENG.). 144p. pap. *(978-1-84876-612-9(2))* Troubador Publishing Ltd.

—Out of Time 2: Raven's Hoard. 2012. (ENG., Illus.). 168p. pap. *(978-1-78088-322-9(6))* Troubador Publishing Ltd.

Jobling, Curtis. Haunt: Dead Scared. 2016. (ENG.). 256p. (J). pap. 7.99 *(978-1-4711-1577-6(1),* Simon & Schuster Children's) Simon & Schuster, Ltd. GBR. Dist: Simon & Schuster, Inc.

Johnson, Sandi. The Haunted Dog House. Brundige, Britt & Durant, Sybrina, eds. Stillwell, Heath, illus. 2014. (Spooky Ser.). 32p. (J). (gr. -1-6). pap. 12.99 *(978-1-929063-50-5(4),* 149) Moons & Stars Publishing For Children.

Johnson, Sandi, et al. Haunted Doghouse II: Halloween Night, 3 vols., bk. 2. Durant, Sybrina, ed. Stargeon, Bobbi, illus. l.t. ed. 2014. (ENG.). 36p. (J). (gr. k-5). pap. 12.99 *(978-1-929063-27-7(X),* 351) Moons & Stars Publishing For Children.

Jones, Marcia Thornton & Dadey, Debbie. Ghosts Do Splash in Puddles. Dreidemy, Joëlle, illus. 2006. 64p. (J). pap. *(978-0-439-87629-2(X))* Scholastic, Inc.

—Red, White, & Boo! Francis, Guy, illus. 2007. (Ghostville Elementary Ser.: Bk. 16). 64p. (J). *(978-0-439-88364-1(4))* Scholastic, Inc.

Jr. Graphic Ghost Stories. 2014. (Jr. Graphic Ghost Stories Ser.). 24p. (J). (gr. 3-6). pap. 381.60 *(978-1-4777-7209-6(X),* PowerKids Pr.) Rosen Publishing Group, Inc., The.

Kehret, Peg. The Ghost Followed Us Home. 2013. (Frightmares Ser.: No. 5). (J). 14.00 *(978-0-671-53521-6(8),* Simon & Schuster Bks. For Young Readers) Simon & Schuster Bks. For Young Readers.

Kimmel, Eric A. Hayyim's Ghost. 2005. (Illus.). 40p. (J). pap. 9.95 *(978-1-932687-03-3(3),* Devora Publishing) Simcha Media Group.

—Hayyim's Ghost. Binus, Ari, illus. 2005. 40p. (J). 16.95 *(978-1-932687-02-6(5),* Devora Publishing) Simcha Media Group.

Kirby, Matthew J. A Taste for Monsters. 2016. (ENG.). 352p. (YA). (gr. 7). 18.99 *(978-0-545-81784-4(6),* Scholastic Pr.) Scholastic, Inc.

Knutson, Lori. The Ghost of Northumberland Strait. 2008. (ENG.). 152p. (J). (gr. 5-9). pap. 9.95 *(978-1-894917-43-8(X),* Napoleon & Co.) Dundurn CAN. Dist: Ingram Publisher Services.

LeVitt, J. A. Ghsots of Whitner. LeVitt, Mike, illus. 2004. 84p. (J). per. 10.95 *(978-1-932196-47-4(1))* WordWright.biz, Inc.

Lockwood, Vicki. The Magnificent Lizzie Brown, 1 vol. 2014. (Magnificent Lizzie Brown Ser.). (ENG.). 200p. (gr. 5-9). 53.30 *(978-1-4342-9515-6(X))* Stone Arch Bks.

Loughead, Deb. Time & Again, 1 vol. 2005. (ENG.). 192p. (YA). (gr. 7-12). pap. *(978-1-894549-39-4(2),* Sumach Pr.) Canadian Scholars.

MacHale, D. J. The Blood. 2013. (Morpheus Road Ser.: 3). (ENG.). 384p. (J). (gr. 5-9). pap. 8.99 *(978-1-4169-6521-3(1),* Aladdin) Simon & Schuster Children's Publishing.

MacPhail, Catherine. Hide & Seek. 2012. (Stoke Books Titles Ser.). 72p. (J). (gr. 5-8). pap. 45.32 *(978-0-7613-9219-4(X))* Stoke Bks.

Mahy, Margaret, et al, contrib. by. Don't Read This! And Other Tales of the Unnatural. Date not set. 214p. (J). (gr. 5-10). pap. 9.95 *(978-0-88899-325-0(0),* Libros Tigrillo) Groundwood Bks. CAN. Dist: Publishers Group West (PGW).

Mann, Jennifer Ann. Sunny Sweet Is So Not Scary. 2015. (Sunny Sweet Ser.). (ENG.). 192p. (YA). (gr. 3-6). 15.99 *(978-1-61963-507-4(0),* 9781619635074, Bloomsbury USA Childrens) Bloomsbury Publishing USA.

Maria & the Ghosts of Barrengarry. 2016. (ENG.). 360p. (J). pap. 13.95 *(978-1-78612-253-7(7),* 36b04a6c-fb02-4ccc-a425-18166e95e7d6) Austin, Stan AUS. Dist: Bookmasters Distribution.

Matas, Carol & Nodelman, Perry. The Proof That Ghosts Exist. 2008. (Ghosthunters Ser.: Bk. 1). (ENG.). 216p. (J). (gr. 4-7). *(978-1-55470-014-1(0))* Me to We.

McCorkle, Michelle M. Voices from Beyond. 2011. (YA). pap. 14.95 *(978-1-936615-09-4(6))* Snowy Day Distribution & Publishing, A.

McKenzie, Paige. The Haunting of Sunshine Girl. (ENG.). 2016. 320p. (gr. 7-10). pap. 9.99 *(978-1-60286-302-6(4))* 2015. (Haunting of Sunshine Girl Ser.: Bk. 1). 304p. (YA). 16.00 *(978-1-60286-272-2(9))* Perseus Bks. Group. (Weinstein Bks.).

McKissack, Jenny & McKissack, Jennifer. Sanctuary. 2015. (ENG.). 320p. (J). (gr. 7). 17.99 *(978-0-545-58758-7(1),* Scholastic Pr.) Scholastic, Inc.

McKissack, Patricia C. The Dark-Thirty: Southern Tales of the Supernatural. Pinkney, Brian, illus. 2006. (ENG.). 128p. (J). (gr. 3-7). 18.95 *(978-0-679-81863-2(4),* Knopf Bks. for Young Readers) Random Hse. Children's Bks.

Miles, Cindy. Forevermore. 2013. (ENG.). 288p. (J). (gr. 7). pap. 9.99 *(978-0-545-42622-0(7))* Scholastic, Inc.

Moriarty, Jaclyn. The Ghosts of Ashbury High. 2010. (ENG.). 496p. (J). (gr. 7-18). 18.99 *(978-0-545-06972-4(6),* Levine, Arthur A. Bks.) Scholastic, Inc.

Mould, Chris. Dust 'n' Bones. 2008. (ENG., Illus.). 144p. (J). (gr. 4-6). 9.99 *(978-0-340-95070-8(6))* Hodder & Stoughton GBR. Dist: Hachette Bk. Group.

—Dust 'n' Bones: Ten Ghost Stories. 2011. (ENG., Illus.). 96p. (J). (gr. 4-6). pap. 12.99 *(978-1-4449-0617-2(8))* Hodder & Stoughton GBR. Dist: Hachette Bk. Group.

Nelson, Suzanne. The Ghoul Next Door. 2012. 186p. (J). *(978-0-545-48421-3(9))* Scholastic, Inc.

Night, P. J. Is She for Real? 2012. (You're Invited to a Creepover Ser.: 7). (ENG.). 160p. (J). (gr. 3-7). pap. 6.99 *(978-1-4424-5056-1(8),* Simon Spotlight) Simon Spotlight.

—It's All Downhill from Here. 2012. (Creepover Ser.: 10). lib. bdg. 16.00 *(978-0-606-26896-7(0),* Turtleback) Turtleback Bks.

—The Terror Behind the Mask. 2014. (You're Invited to a Creepover Ser.: 19). (ENG., Illus.). 160p. (J). (gr. 3-7). pap. 6.99 *(978-1-4814-0460-0(1),* Simon Spotlight) Simon Spotlight.

Noyes, Deborah. Plague in the Mirror. 2013. (ENG.). 272p. (YA). (gr. 9). 16.99 *(978-0-7636-5980-6(0))* Candlewick Pr.

Noyes, Deborah, ed. The Restless Dead: Ten Original Stories of the Supernatural. 2007. (ENG., Illus.). 272p. (YA). (gr. 7-12). 16.99 *(978-0-7636-2906-9(5))* Candlewick Pr.

Olin, Sean. Killing Britney. 2005. (ENG.). 240p. (YA). (gr. 9-12). pap. 9.99 *(978-0-689-87778-0(1),* Simon Pulse) Simon Pulse.

Olson, Norah. What the Dead Want. 2016. (Illus.). 304p. (YA). (gr. 8). 17.99 *(978-0-06-241011-5(3),* Tegen, Katherine Bks) HarperCollins Pubs.

Palmer, Michele. Ghosts & Golems: Haunting Tales of the Supernatural. Black, Theodor, illus. 2003. (ENG.). 128p. pap. 9.95 *(978-0-8276-0763-7(6))* Jewish Pubn. Society.

Parker, S. M. The Rattled Bones. 2017. (ENG., Illus.). 384p. (YA). (gr. 9). 17.99 ***(978-1-4814-8204-2(1),*** Simon Pulse) Simon Pulse.

Pearson, Maggie. Ghosts & Goblins: Scary Stories from Around the World. Greenwood, Francesca, illus. 2016. (World of Stories Ser.). (ENG.). 152p. (J). (gr. 2-6). 26.65 *(978-1-5124-1318-2(6))* Lerner Publishing Group.

Penn-Coughin, O. They're Coming for You: Scary Stories that Scream to be Read. 2009. (J). per. *(978-0-9816836-0-7(6))* You Come Too Publishing.

Penn, Tony. The Misadventures of Michael Mcmichaels: The Creepy Campers, vol. 3. Martin, Brian, illus. 2017. (Michael Mcmichaels Ser.: 3). (ENG.). 84p. (J). pap. 7.95 ***(978-1-944882-10-5(3))*** Boys Town Pr.

Pilling, Ann. Black Harvest. 2009. (Collins Modern Classics Ser.). (ENG., Illus.). 192p. (J). pap. 7.99 *(978-0-00-675426-8(0),* HarperCollins Children's Bks.) HarperCollins Pubs. Ltd. GBR. Dist: HarperCollins Pubs.

Poblocki, Dan. The Ghost of Graylock. (ENG.). 272p. (J). (gr. 5-9). 2014. pap. 7.99 *(978-0-545-40269-9(7),* Scholastic Paperbacks) 2012. 16.99 *(978-0-545-40268-2(9),* Scholastic Pr.) Scholastic, Inc.

—The House on Stone's Throw Island. 2015. (ENG.). 272p. (J). (gr. 5-9). 16.99 *(978-0-545-64556-0(5),* Scholastic Pr.) Scholastic, Inc.

Price, Susan. Cân Yr Ysbrydion. 2005. (WEL.). 172p. pap. *(978-1-85596-217-0(9))* Dref Wen.

Rand, Johnathan. American Chillers #15 Nebraska Nightcrawlers, Vol. 15. 2004. (American Chillers Ser.: 15). 208p. (J). pap. 5.99 *(978-1-893699-67-0(6))* AudioCraft Publishing, Inc.

Rees, Celia. A Is for Apparition. (Haunts Ser.: Vol. 2). 122p. (J). pap. *(978-0-340-71488-1(3))* Hodder & Stoughton.

—Haunts Vol. 4: N Is for Nightmare. 137p. (J). pap. *(978-0-340-71525-3(1))* Hodder & Stoughton.

Riddle, Waide Aaron. The Chocolate Man A Children's Horror Tale. Aragon Art Studio, illus. ed. 2010. (ENG.). 44p. pap. 15.00 *(978-0-615-38560-0(5))* Green Ghost Pr.

Rivers, Phoebe. Ghost Town. 2012. (Saranormal Ser.: 1). (ENG.). 160p. (J). (gr. 3-7). pap. 5.99 *(978-1-4424-4038-8(4),* Simon Spotlight) Simon Spotlight.

—Haunted Memories. 2012. (Saranormal Ser.: 2). (ENG.). 176p. (J). (gr. 3-7). 15.99 *(978-1-4424-5381-4(8))*; pap. 5.99 *(978-1-4424-4040-1(6))* Simon Spotlight. (Simon Spotlight).

—The Secrets Within. 2013. (Saranormal Ser.: 7). (ENG.). 160p. (J). (gr. 3-7). 15.99 *(978-1-4424-6850-4(5))*; pap. 5.99 *(978-1-4424-6849-8(1))* Simon Spotlight. (Simon Spotlight).

Roberts, David & Fletcher, Corina, illus. Ghoul School. 2003. 10p. (J). (gr. k-4). reprint ed. 18.00 *(978-0-7567-7028-0(9))* DIANE Publishing Co.

Rose, Dorothy. The Haunted House. Oechsli, Kelly, illus. 2014. (ENG.). 24p. (J). (gr. -1-k). pap. 13.99 *(978-1-4814-2646-6(X),* Little Simon) Little Simon.

Ruby, Laura. Lily's Ghosts. 2005. (Illus.). 258p. (J). (gr. 5-9). 13.65 *(978-0-7569-5115-3(1))* Perfection Learning Corp.

Ruby, Lois. Rebel Spirits. 2013. (ENG.). 304p. (J). (gr. 7). 17.99 *(978-0-545-42623-7(5))*; 292p. (YA). *(978-0-545-55282-0(6))* Scholastic, Inc.

Sala, Sharon. Lunatic Detective. 2011. 164p. (YA). pap. 11.95 *(978-1-61194-043-5(5))* BelleBks., Inc.

San Souci, Robert D. Even More Short & Shivery: Thirty Spine-Tingling Tales. Rogers, Jacqueline, illus. 2003. (ENG.). 176p. (J). (gr. 3-7). pap. 5.99 *(978-0-440-41877-1(1)*, Yearling) Random Hse. Children's Bks.

—Even More Short & Shivery: Thirty Spine-Tingling Tales. Rogers, Jacqueline, illus. 2003. 162p. (gr. 5-7). lib. bdg. 16.00 *(978-0-613-72191-2(8)*, Turtleback) Turtleback Bks.

Santoro, Christopher. It's Haunted! 2015. (ENG., Illus.). 12p. (J). (— 1). 7.99 *(978-0-553-52370-6(8)*, Random Hse. Bks. for Young Readers) Random Hse. Children's Bks.

Schoen, Robin. Grandmother's Guest: The Blue Lady of Wilton. Hoar, Gail, illus. 2013. 32p. 16.95 *(978-0-615-89154-5(3))* Hobby Horse Publishing, LLC.

Schusterman, Michelle. Dead Air #1. Olesh, Stephanie, illus. 2015. (Kat Sinclair Files Ser.: 1). (ENG.). 248p. (J). (gr. 3-7). 12.99 *(978-0-448-47980-4(X)*, Grosset & Dunlap) Penguin Young Readers Group.

Schwartz, Alvin. More Scary Stories to Tell in the Dark. Helquist, Brett, illus. 2010. (Scary Stories Ser.). (ENG.). 128p. (J). (gr. 4-18). 16.99 *(978-0-06-083521-7(4))*; pap. 5.99 *(978-0-06-083522-4(2))* HarperCollins Pubs.

—More Scary Stories to Tell in the Dark. 2010. (Scary Stories Ser.: 2). (J). lib. bdg. 16.00 *(978-0-606-14981-5(3)*, Turtleback) Turtleback Bks.

—Scary Stories Box Set, 3 vols. Helquist, Brett, illus. 2011. (Scary Stories Ser.). (ENG.). 128p. (J). (gr. 4). pap. 14.99 *(978-0-06-198093-0(5))* HarperCollins Pubs.

Schwartz, Alvin. More Scary Stories to Tell in the Dark. Gammell, Stephen, illus. 2017. (Scary Stories Ser.: 2). 112p. (J). (gr. 3-7). pap. 6.99 ***(978-0-06-268285-7(7))*** HarperCollins Pubs.

Shelton, Dave. Thirteen Chairs. (ENG.). 256p. (J). (gr. 7). 2016. pap. 9.99 *(978-1-338-03248-2(8))* 2015. (Illus.). 17.99 *(978-0-545-81665-6(3))* Scholastic, Inc.

Shults, Sylvia. Double Double Love & Trouble. 2013. 150p. pap. 12.99 *(978-0-9848931-3-3(X))* Dark Continents Publishing.

Shusterman, Neal. Full Tilt. 2009. (ENG.). 224p. (YA). (gr. 7). pap. 10.99 *(978-1-4169-9748-1(2)*, Simon & Schuster Bks. For Young Readers) Simon & Schuster Bks. For Young Readers.

Sierra, Judy. Never Kick a Ghost & Other Silly Chillers. Constantin, Pascale, illus. 2011. (I Can Read Level 2 Ser.). (ENG.). 32p. (J). (gr. k-3). pap. 3.99 *(978-0-06-143521-8(X))* HarperCollins Pubs.

Small, Cathleen. The Legend of Sleepy Hollow: The Headless Horseman. Antal, Lara, illus. 2016. (American Legends & Folktales Ser.). 32p. (J). pap. 10.58 *(978-1-5026-2206-8(8))* Cavendish Square Publishing.

Smith, Barbara. Ghost Stories of the Sea, 1 vol., Vol. 1. rev. ed. 2003. (Ghost Stories Ser.). (ENG., Illus.). 224p. (gr. 4). pap. 12.95 *(978-1-894877-23-7(3)*, 1894877233, Ghost Hse. Bks.) Lone Pine Publishing USA.

Smith, L. J. Strange Fate. 2014. (Night World Ser.: Vol. 10). (ENG.). 528p. (YA). (gr. 7-18). 18.99 *(978-1-4169-8677-5(4)*, Simon Pulse) Simon Pulse.

Soileau, Hodges, illus. The Mystery of the Haunted Boxcar. 2004. (Boxcar Children Mysteries Ser.: 100). (ENG.). 128p. (J). (gr. 1-5). mass mkt. 5.99 *(978-0-8075-5554-5(1))* Whitman, Albert & Co.

Specter, Baron. All in a Night's Work, 1 vol. Kneupper, Setch, illus. 2012. (Graveyard Diaries Ser.). (ENG.). 128p. (J). (gr. 3-8). 27.07 *(978-1-61641-903-5(2))* Magic Wagon.

—How Not to Be Killed by a Zombie, 1 vol. Kneupper, Setch, illus. 2012. (Graveyard Diaries Ser.). (ENG.). 128p. (J). (gr. 3-8). 27.07 *(978-1-61641-900-4(8))* Magic Wagon.

Spector, Baron. Approaching the Undead, 1 vol. Kneupper, Setch, illus. 2012. (Graveyard Diaries Ser.). (ENG.). 128p. (J). (gr. 3-8). lib. bdg. 27.07 *(978-1-61641-899-1(0)*, Calico Chapter Bks) Magic Wagon.

—Tracking Your Nightmare, 1 vol. Kneupper, Setch, illus. 2012. (Graveyard Diaries Ser.). (ENG.). 128p. (J). (gr. 3-8). lib. bdg. 27.07 *(978-1-61641-898-4(2)*, Calico Chapter Bks) Magic Wagon.

Stilton, Geronimo. The Thirteen Ghosts. 2011. (Creepella Von Cacklefur Ser.: 1). (ENG., Illus.). 128p. (J). (gr. 2-5). pap. 7.99 *(978-0-545-30742-0(2)*, Scholastic Paperbacks) Scholastic, Inc.

—This Hotel Is Haunted! 2012. (Geronimo Stilton Ser.: 50). lib. bdg. 18.40 *(978-0-606-26182-1(6)*, Turtleback) Turtleback Bks.

Stine, R. L. All-Night Party. 2005. (Fear Street Ser.: Bk. 44). (ENG.). 160p. (YA). (gr. 7). pap. 6.99 *(978-1-4169-0321-5(6)*, Simon Pulse) Simon Pulse.

—Fright Knight & the Ooze: Twice Terrifying Tales. 2010. (R. L. Stine's Ghosts of Fear Street Ser.). (ENG.). 240p. (J). (gr. 3-7). pap. 6.99 *(978-1-4169-9135-9(2)*, Aladdin) Simon & Schuster Children's Publishing.

—Ghost Beach. 2003. (Goosebumps Ser.: No. 22). (gr. 5-8). 14.75 *(978-0-613-70848-7(2)*, Turtleback) Turtleback Bks.

—Killer's Kiss. 2005. (Fear Street Ser.: Bk. 42). (ENG.). 160p. (YA). (gr. 7). pap. 7.99 *(978-1-4169-0320-8(8)*, Simon Pulse) Simon Pulse.

—Midnight Games. 2005. (Fear Street Nights Ser.: 2). (ENG.). 160p. (YA). (gr. 7). pap. 6.99 *(978-0-689-87865-7(6)*, Simon Pulse) Simon Pulse.

—The Stepsister. 2005. (Fear Street Ser.: Bk. 7). (ENG.). 176p. (YA). (gr. 7). pap. 7.99 *(978-1-4169-0029-0(2)*, Simon Pulse) Simon Pulse.

—When the Ghost Dog Howls. 2010. (Goosebumps Horrorland Ser.: 13). (ENG.). 160p. (J). (gr. 3-7). 6.99 *(978-0-545-16194-7(0)*, Scholastic Paperbacks) Scholastic, Inc.

Strange, Jason. To Wake the Dead, 1 vol. Parks, Phil, illus. 2011. (Jason Strange Ser.). (ENG.). 72p. (gr. 2-3). pap. 6.25 *(978-1-4342-3094-5(5))*; 25.32 *(978-1-4342-2963-2(7))* Stone Arch Bks.

—23 Crow's Perch, 1 vol. Evergreen, Nelson & Kendall, Bradford, illus. 2012. (Jason Strange Ser.). (ENG.). 72p. (gr. 2-3). pap. 6.25 *(978-1-4342-3885-6(7))*; lib. bdg. 25.32 *(978-1-4342-3297-7(2))* Stone Arch Bks.

Thuma, Cynthia & Lower, Catherine. Creepy Colleges & Haunted Universities: True Ghost Stories, 1 vol. 2003. (ENG., Illus.). 128p. (gr. 10-13). pap. 9.95 *(978-0-7643-1805-4(5)*, 9780764318054) Schiffer Publishing, Ltd.

Tingle, Tim. How I Became a Ghost: A Choctaw Trail of Tears Story, 1 vol. l.t. ed. 2013. (ENG., Illus.). 160p. (J). 18.95 *(978-1-937054-53-3(5))* RoadRunner Pr.

Tingle, Tim & Moore, Doc. More Spooky Texas Tales. Benas, Jeanne A., illus. 2010. (ENG.). 104p. (J). (gr. 4-7). lib. bdg. 18.95 *(978-0-89672-700-7(9))* Texas Tech Univ. Pr.

Triple-Decker, 3 vols., Set. pap. 20.00 *(978-0-9657367-4-9(1))* Less Pr.

Turnage, Sheila. The Ghosts of Tupelo Landing. 2015. (ENG.). 368p. (J). (gr. 5). 7.99 *(978-0-14-242571-8(0)*, Puffin Books) Penguin Young Readers Group.

Verday, Jessica. The Haunted. (ENG.). (YA). (gr. 9). 2011. 496p. pap. 11.99 *(978-1-4169-7896-1(8))* 2010. 480p. 17.99 *(978-1-4169-7895-4(X))* Simon Pulse. (Simon Pulse).

Verstraete, Majanka. The Doll Maker: Weirdville. l.t. ed. 2013. 1. (ENG.). 86p. (gr. 2-6). pap. 9.95 *(978-1-62253-065-6(9))* Evolved Publishing.

Wallace, Rich. Lost in the Dark. Volpari, Daniela, illus. 2016. (J). *(978-1-62402-148-0(4))* Magic Wagon.

—Phantom Flames. Volpari, Daniela, illus. 2016. 48p. (J). *(978-1-62402-150-3(6))* Magic Wagon.

—The Room of Woe: An Up2U Horror Adventure, 1 vol. Emroca Flores, Jose, illus. 2015. (ENG.). 80p. (J). *(978-1-62402-094-0(1))* Magic Wagon.

Warner, Gertrude Chandler, creator. The Mystery of the Haunted Boxcar. 2004. (Boxcar Children Mysteries Ser.: 100). (ENG., Illus.). 128p. (J). (gr. 1-5). 14.99 *(978-0-8075-5553-8(3))* Whitman, Albert & Co.

West, David. Ten of the Best Ghost Stories. 2014. (ENG., Illus.). 24p. (J). pap. *(978-0-7787-0819-3(5))* Crabtree Publishing Co.

Whiting, Sue. Portraits of Celina. 2015. (ENG.). 352p. 16.95 *(978-1-63079-024-0(9))* Switch Pr.

Wignall, K. J. Alchemy. Book Two of the Mercian Trilogy: Alchemy. 2012. (ENG.). 336p. (J). (gr. 7). 17.99 *(978-1-60684-265-2(X)*, Carolrhoda Lab™) Lerner Publishing Group.

Wilde, Oscar. El Fantasma de Canterville y Otros Cuentos. (Clasicos Juveniles Coleccion). (SPA.). (YA). (gr. 5-8). pap. *(978-950-11-1264-1(0)*, SG8742) Sigmar ARG. Dist: Lectorum Pubns., Inc.

Wilde, Oscar & O'Flahertie Wills Wilde, Oscar Fingal. El Fantasma de Canterville y Otros Cuentos. Ballesteros, Antonio, tr. (SPA., Illus.). 224p. pap. 12.95 *(978-84-414-0713-8(4))* Ediciones B ESP. Dist: Spanish Pubs., LLC.

Williams, Katie. Absent. 2013. (ENG.). 180p. (YA). (gr. 7-12). 16.99 *(978-0-8118-7150-1(9))* Chronicle Bks. LLC.

Wingo, W. Bruce. There Grows a Crooked Tree. 2003. 188p. 23.95 *(978-0-595-75271-3(3))*; pap. 13.95 *(978-0-595-28903-5(7))* iUniverse, Inc.

Winters, Kay. The Teeny Tiny Ghost & the Monster, Vol. 3. Munsinger, Lynn, illus. 2004. (ENG.). 32p. (J). (gr. -1-3). 14.99 *(978-0-06-028884-6(1))* HarperCollins Pubs.

Woodbury, Mary. The Ghost in the Machine. 2005. 222p. (J). (gr. 6-9). pap. 7.95 *(978-1-55050-227-5(1))* Coteau Bks. CAN. Dist: Fitzhenry & Whiteside, Ltd.

Yee, Paul. The Bone Collector's Son, 1 vol. 2012. (ENG., Illus.). 175p. (YA). (gr. 6-8). pap. 12.95 *(978-1-896580-50-0(5))* Tradewind Bks. CAN. Dist: Orca Bk. Pubs. USA.

—Dead Man's Gold & Other Stories, 1 vol. Chan, Harvey, illus. 2004. (ENG.). 112p. (YA). pap. 9.95 *(978-0-88899-587-2(3))* Groundwood Bks. CAN. Dist: Publishers Group West (PGW).

—Ghost Train. Chan, Harvey, illus. 2004. 29p. (J). (gr. k-4). reprint ed. 16.00 *(978-0-7567-9083-7(2))* DIANE Publishing Co.

Zenko, Darren. Ghost Stories of Pets & Animals, 1 vol., Vol. 1. rev. ed. 2004. (Ghost Stories Ser.). (ENG., Illus.). 208p. (gr. 4). pap. 12.95 *(978-1-894877-36-7(5)*, 1894877365, Ghost Hse. Bks.) Lone Pine Publishing USA.

13 Ghosts Strange but True. 2003. pap. 2.50 *(978-0-590-41690-0(1))* Scholastic, Inc.

GHOST TOWNS

see Extinct Cities

GHOSTS

see also Apparitions; Superstition

Asfar, Dan. Dear Liza, 1 vol., Vol. 1. Kubish, Shelagh, ed. rev. ed. 2003. (Ghost Stories Ser.). (ENG., Illus.). 216p. (gr. 4). pap. 12.95 *(978-1-894877-17-6(9)*, 1894877179, Ghost Hse. Bks.) Lone Pine Publishing USA.

Asfar, Dan, et al. Ghost Stories of America, 1 vol., Vol. 2. Kubish, Shelagh, ed. rev. ed. 2003. (Ghost Stories Ser.). (ENG., Illus.). 248p. (gr. 4). pap. 12.95 *(978-1-894877-31-2(4)*, 1894877314, Ghost Hse. Bks.) Lone Pine Publishing USA.

Axelrod-Contrada, Joan. Ghoulish Ghost Stories, 1 vol. 2010. (Scary Stories Ser.). (ENG.). 32p. (gr. 3-4). lib. bdg. 27.99 *(978-1-4296-4574-4(1)*, Edge Bks.) Capstone Press of Coughlan Cos.

—The World's Most Famous Ghosts, 1 vol. 2011. (Ghost Files Ser.). (ENG.). 32p. (gr. 3-4). lib. bdg. 27.99 *(978-1-4296-6516-2(5)*, Edge Bks.) Capstone Press of Coughlan Cos.

Bailey, Diane. Ghosts in America. 2011. (America's Supernatural Secrets Ser.). (ENG., Illus.). 48p. (YA). (gr. 5-8). pap. 11.75 *(978-1-4488-5572-8(1)*, Rosen Reference) Rosen Publishing Group, Inc., The.

Belanger, Jeff. Paranormal Encounters: A Look at the Evidence. 2011. (Haunted: Ghosts & the Paranormal Ser.). (Illus.). 224p. (J). lib. bdg. 37.95 *(978-1-4488-4839-3(3))* Rosen Publishing Group, Inc., The.

—Real-Life Ghost Encounters. 2013. 208p. (YA). (gr. 7-12). 37.25 *(978-1-4777-0678-7(X))* Rosen Publishing Group, Inc., The.

Bielski, Ursula. Creepy Chicago: A Ghosthunter's Tales of the City's Scariest Sites. Noble, Amy, illus. 2003. (ENG.). 136p. (J). (gr. 3-7). pap. 7.95 *(978-1-933272-28-3(7))* Thunder Bay Pr.

Bingham, Jane. Ghosts & Haunted Houses, 1 vol. King, Chris, illus. 2013. (Solving Mysteries with Science Ser.). (ENG.). 48p. (gr. 3-6). pap. 9.95 *(978-1-4109-5506-7(0))* Heinemann-Raintree.

—Ghosts & Haunted Houses, 1 vol. 2013. (Solving Mysteries with Science Ser.). (ENG.). 48p. (gr. 3-6). 29.99 *(978-1-4109-5500-5(1))* Heinemann-Raintree.

Bodden, Valerie. Haunted Houses. 2017. (J). *(978-1-60818-808-6(6)*, Creative Education) Creative Co., The.

Bolte, Mari. Encountering Ghosts: Eyewitness Accounts, 1 vol. Kako, Franco, illus. 2014. (Eyewitness to the Unexplained Ser.). (ENG.). 32p. (gr. 3-4). 30.65 *(978-1-4914-0245-0(8)*, Graphic Library) Capstone Press of Coughlan Cos.

Breman, Billy & Watkins, Graham. Searching for Ghosts & Poltergeists. 2011. (J). 77.70 *(978-1-4488-4778-5(8))*; pap. 12.95 *(978-1-4488-4770-9(2))*; lib. bdg. 31.95 *(978-1-4488-4762-4(1))* Rosen Publishing Group, Inc., The.

Brinker, Spencer. The Ghost of Skip-Count Castle. 2015. (Illus.). 32p. (J). lib. bdg. *(978-1-62724-332-2(1))* Bearport Publishing Co., Inc.

Brucken, Kelli M. Ghosts. 2006. (Encounters with Ser.). (ENG., Illus.). 48p. (J). (gr. 4-8). lib. bdg. 27.50 *(978-0-7377-3474-4(4)*, Greenhaven Pr., Inc.) Cengage Gale.

Burtinshaw, Julie. Romantic Ghost Stories, 1 vol., Vol. 1. Wangler, Chris, ed. rev. ed. 2003. (Ghost Stories Ser.). (ENG., Illus.). 224p. (gr. 4). pap. 12.95 *(978-1-894877-28-2(4)*, 1894877284, Ghost Hse. Bks.) Lone Pine Publishing USA.

Cassidy, Tam. The White Lady Ghost. 2014. (Jr. Graphic Ghost Stories Ser.). 24p. (J). (gr. 3-6). lib. bdg. 26.25 *(978-1-4777-7125-9(5)*, PowerKids Pr.) Rosen Publishing Group, Inc., The.

Chandler, Matt. Bachelor's Grove Cemetery & Other Haunted Places of the Midwest, 1 vol. 2014. (Haunted America Ser.). (ENG.). 32p. (gr. 3-4). lib. bdg. 27.99 *(978-1-4765-3913-3(8)*, Edge Bks.) Capstone Press of Coughlan Cos.

—Ghosts of the Alamo & Other Hauntings of the South, 1 vol. 2014. (Haunted America Ser.). (ENG.). 32p. (gr. 3-4). lib. bdg. 27.99 *(978-1-4765-3914-0(6)*, Edge Bks.) Capstone Press of Coughlan Cos.

Chandler, Matt & Garbe, Suzanne. Haunted America, 1 vol. 2014. (Haunted America Ser.). (ENG.). 32p. (gr. 3-4). lib. bdg. 111.96 *(978-1-4765-7925-2(3)*, Edge Bks.) Capstone Press of Coughlan Cos.

Chmielewski, Gary. The Fright Zone: Jokes, Riddles, Tongue Twisters & Daffynitions. Caputo, Jim, illus. rev. ed. 2009. (Funny Zone Ser.). (ENG.). 24p. (J). (gr. 2-4). lib. bdg. 22.60 *(978-1-59953-298-1(0))* Norwood Hse. Pr.

Cocca, Lisa Colozza. Sleepy Hollow. 2014. (Jr. Graphic Ghost Stories Ser.). (Illus.). 24p. (J). (gr. 3-6). lib. bdg. 26.25 *(978-1-4777-7084-9(4)*, PowerKids Pr.) Rosen Publishing Group, Inc., The.

Coddington, Andrew. Ghosts. 2016. (Creatures of Fantasy Ser.). (ENG., Illus.). 64p. (J). (gr. 6-6). 34.21 *(978-1-5026-0932-8(0))* Cavendish Square Publishing.

Collins, Terry Lee & Weakland, Mark Andrew. Scooby Doo Unmasks the Truth Behind Ghosts. 2016. (Illus.). 24p. (J). *(978-1-4062-8899-5(3))* Capstone Press of Coughlan Cos.

Cooley Peterson, Megan. Haunted Hotels Around the World. 2017. (It's Haunted! Ser.). (ENG., Illus.). 32p. (gr. 3-4). lib. bdg. 27.99 *(978-1-5157-3858-9(2)*, Snap Bks.) Capstone Press of Coughlan Cos.

—Haunted Objects from Around the World. 2017. (It's Haunted! Ser.). (ENG., Illus.). 32p. (gr. 3-4). lib. bdg. 27.99 *(978-1-5157-3859-6(0)*, Snap Bks.) Capstone Press of Coughlan Cos.

DeMolay, Jack. Amityville: La casa encantada (Ghosts in Amityville:the Haunted House) 2009. (Historietas Juveniles: Misterios (Jr. Graphic Mysteries) Ser.). (SPA.). 24p. (gr. 2-3). 47.90 *(978-1-61513-344-4(5)*, Editorial Buenas Letras) Rosen Publishing Group, Inc., The.

—Amityville: La Casa Encantada. Obregón, José María, tr. from ENG. 2008. (Historietas Juveniles: Misterios (Jr. Graphic Mysteries) Ser.). (SPA., Illus.). 24p. (J). (gr. 2-5). lib. bdg. 25.25 *(978-1-4358-2537-6(3))* Rosen Publishing Group, Inc., The.

—Ghosts in Amityville: The Haunted House. (Jr. Graphic Mysteries Ser.). (ENG.). 24p. 2009. (J). (gr. 2-3). 47.90 *(978-1-61513-843-2(9)*, PowerKids Pr.) 2007. (Illus.). (J). (gr. 2-5). lib. bdg. 25.25 *(978-1-4042-3402-4(0))* 2007. (Illus.). (gr. 3-8). pap. 10.60 *(978-1-4042-2155-0(7)*, PowerKids Pr.) Rosen Publishing Group, Inc., The.

DeYoe, Aaron. Biggest, Baddest Book of Ghosts, 1 vol. 2014. (Biggest, Baddest Books Set 2 Ser.). (ENG.). 24p. (gr. k-4). 25.65 *(978-1-62403-516-6(7))* ABDO Publishing Co.

Doak, Robin S. Investigating Hauntings, Ghosts, & Poltergeists, 1 vol. 2010. (Unexplained Phenomena Ser.). (ENG.). 48p. (gr. 3-4). lib. bdg. 31.99 *(978-1-4296-4814-1(7))* Capstone Press of Coughlan Cos.

Doeden, Matt. The Queen Mary: A Chilling Interactive Adventure. 2016. (You Choose: Haunted Places Ser.). (ENG., Illus.). 112p. (gr. 3-4). lib. bdg. 31.99 *(978-1-5157-2578-7(2)*, You Choose Bks.) Capstone Press of Coughlan Cos.

Dowswell, Paul & Allen, Troy. Ghosts. rev. ed. 2008. (True Stories Ser.). 122p. (J). pap. 4.99 *(978-0-7945-2196-7(7)*, Usborne) EDC Publishing.

Duffield, Katy. Poltergeists. 2007. (Mysterious Encounters Ser.). (ENG., Illus.). 48p. (gr. 4-8). lib. bdg. 33.60 *(978-0-7377-3665-6(8)*, LML02109-234128, Kidhaven) Cengage Gale.

Dunn, Dinah. Haunted Prisons. 2014. (Scary Places Ser.). 32p. (J). (gr. 4-8). lib. bdg. 25.27 *(978-1-62724-089-5(6))* Bearport Publishing Co., Inc.

Everett, J. H. & Scott-Waters, Marilyn. Haunted Histories: Creepy Castles, Dark Dungeons, & Powerful Palaces. 2012. (ENG., Illus.). 160p. (J). (gr. 4-7). 14.99 *(978-0-8050-8971-4(3)*, 9780805089714, Holt, Henry & Co. Bks. For Young Readers) Holt, Henry & Co.

—Haunted Histories: Creepy Castles, Dark Dungeons, & Powerful Palaces. Everett, J. H. & Scott-Waters, Marilyn, illus. 2013. (ENG., Illus.). 160p. (J). (gr. 4-7). pap. 8.99 *(978-1-250-02726-9(8)*, 9781250027269) Square Fish.

Everett, Lawrence. Ghosts & Legends of Southeastern Ohio & Beyond: Tales of Legends, Hauntings & the Unexplained, 2. 2003. 124p. (YA). pap. 11.95 *(978-0-7414-1760-2(X))* Infinity Publishing.

Farman, John. The Short & Bloody History of Ghosts. 2005. (Short & Bloody Histories Ser.). (Illus.). 96p. (gr. 6-12). lib. bdg. 19.93 *(978-0-8225-0837-3(0))* Lerner Publishing Group.

Felix, Rebecca. Ghosts: The Truth Behind History's Spookiest Spirits. 2015. (Monster Handbooks Ser.). (ENG., Illus.). 32p. (gr. 3-4). lib. bdg. 27.99 *(978-1-4914-4249-4(2))* Capstone Press of Coughlan Cos.

Ferut, Michael. Gettysburg. 2014. (Scariest Places on Earth Ser.). (ENG., Illus.). 24p. (J). (gr. 3-7). lib. bdg. 25.95 *(978-1-60014-995-5(2)*, Torque Bks.) Bellwether Media.

—RMS Queen Mary. 2014. (Scariest Places on Earth Ser.). (ENG., Illus.). 24p. (J). (gr. 3-7). lib. bdg. 25.95 *(978-1-60014-996-2(0)*, Torque Bks.) Bellwether Media.

—St. Louis Cemetery No. 1. 2014. (Scariest Places on Earth Ser.). (ENG., Illus.). 24p. (J). (gr. 3-7). lib. bdg. 25.95 *(978-1-60014-997-9(9)*, Torque Bks.) Bellwether Media.

—Winchester Mystery House. 2014. (Scariest Places on Earth Ser.). (ENG., Illus.). 24p. (J). (gr. 3-7). lib. bdg. 25.95 *(978-1-60014-998-6(7)*, Torque Bks.) Bellwether Media.

Finn, Denny Von. Stanley Hotel. 2013. (Scariest Places on Earth Ser.). (ENG., Illus.). 24p. (J). (gr. 3-7). lib. bdg. 25.95 *(978-1-60014-950-4(2)*, Torque Bks.) Bellwether Media.

Frisch, Aaron. Ghosts. 2013. (Illus.). 24p. (J). 25.65 *(978-1-60818-246-6(0)*, Creative Education) Creative Co., The.

—That's Spooky: Ghosts. 2013. (That's Spooky Ser.). (ENG., Illus.). 160p. (J). (gr. 1-3). pap. 7.99 *(978-0-89812-803-1(X)*, Creative Paperbacks) Creative Co., The.

—Zombies. 2013. (That's Spooky! Ser.). (ENG., Illus.). 24p. (J). (gr. 3-7). 25.65 *(978-1-60818-251-0(7)*, Creative Education) Creative Co., The.

Ganeri, Anita. Ghosts & Other Specters. West, David, illus. 2010. (Dark Side Ser.). 32p. (J). pap. 10.50 *(978-1-4488-1566-1(5))*; (ENG.). lib. bdg. 26.50 *(978-1-61531-897-1(6))* Rosen Publishing Group, Inc., The. (PowerKids Pr.).

Garbe, Suzanne. Ghostly Encounters, 1 vol. 2011. (Ghost Files Ser.). (ENG.). 32p. (gr. 3-4). lib. bdg. 27.99 *(978-1-4296-6515-5(7)*, Edge Bks.) Capstone Press of Coughlan Cos.

—Ghosts of Alcatraz & Other Hauntings of the West, 1 vol. 2014. (Haunted America Ser.). (ENG.). 32p. (gr. 3-4). lib. bdg. 27.99 *(978-1-4765-3915-7(4)*, Edge Bks.) Capstone Press of Coughlan Cos.

—Ghosts of Gettysburg & Other Hauntings of the East, 1 vol. 2014. (Haunted America Ser.). (ENG.). 32p. (gr. 3-4). lib. bdg. 27.99 *(978-1-4765-3916-4(2)*, Edge Bks.) Capstone Press of Coughlan Cos.

The Ghost Files. 2011. (Ghost Files Ser.). (ENG.). 32p. (gr. 3-4). lib. bdg. 83.97 *(978-1-4296-6519-3(X)*, Edge Bks.) Capstone Press of Coughlan Cos.

Ghost Sticker Book. 2003. (Illus.). 16p. (J). 2.98 *(978-1-84273-120-8(3)*, Exclusive Editions) Parragon, Inc.

Gordon, Nick. Edinburgh Castle. 2013. (Scariest Places on Earth Ser.). (ENG., Illus.). 24p. (J). (gr. 3-7). lib. bdg. 25.95 *(978-1-60014-948-1(0)*, Torque Bks.) Bellwether Media.

Graham, Stacey. Girls' Ghost Hunting Guide. 2012. (ENG., Illus.). 192p. (J). (gr. 4-7). pap. 9.99 *(978-1-4022-6612-6(X)*, Sourcebooks Jabberwocky) Sourcebooks, Inc.

Gudgeon, Chris. Ghost Trackers: The Unreal World of Ghosts, Ghost-Hunting, & the Paranormal. 2010. (ENG.). 80p. (J). (gr. 4-7). pap. 14.95 *(978-0-88776-950-4(0)*, Tundra Bks.) Tundra Bks. CAN. Dist: Penguin Random Hse. LLC.

Guiley, Rosemary Ellen. Ghosts & Haunted Places. 2008. (Mysteries, Legends, & Unexplained Phenomena Ser.). (Illus.). 144p. (YA). (gr. 7-12). 29.95 *(978-0-7910-9392-4(1))* Facts On File, Inc.

Guy, John. Ghosts. 2006. (Unexplained Ser.). (Illus.). 36p. (gr. 3-6). lib. bdg. 26.00 *(978-0-8368-6265-2(1)*, Gareth Stevens Learning Library) Stevens, Gareth Publishing LLLP.

Hamilton, S. L. Ghosts. 2010. (Xtreme Monsters Ser.). 32p. (gr. 3-9). 27.07 *(978-1-61613-468-6(2)*, A&D Xtreme) ABDO Publishing Co.

Hamilton, Sue. Ghosts & Goblins, 1 vol. 2007. (World of Horror Ser.). (ENG., Illus.). 32p. (gr. 4-8). 27.07 *(978-1-59928-767-6(6)*, Abdo & Daughters) ABDO Publishing Co.

Harmon, Daniel E. Haunted Places & Ghostly Encounters. 2015. (J). *(978-1-61900-066-7(0))* Eldorado Ink.

Haunted: Ghosts & the Paranormal: Set 3. 2013. (Haunted: Ghosts & the Paranormal Ser.). 208p. (YA). (gr. 7-12). 149.00 *(978-1-4777-0686-2(0))* Rosen Publishing Group, Inc., The.

Haunted: Ghosts & the Paranormal: Sets 1 - 3. 2013. (Haunted: Ghosts & the Paranormal Ser.). 208p. (YA). (gr. 7-12). 414.65 *(978-1-4777-0734-0(4))* Rosen Publishing Group, Inc., The.

Haunted! Alcatraz. 2013. (History's Most Haunted Ser.). 32p. (J). (gr. 3-6). pap. 63.00 *(978-1-4339-9245-2(0))* Stevens, Gareth Publishing LLLP.

Haunted! the Queen Mary. 2013. (History's Most Haunted Ser.). 32p. (J). (gr. 3-6). pap. 63.00 *(978-1-4339-9260-5(4))* Stevens, Gareth Publishing LLLP.

Hawkins, John. Hauntings. 2012. (Mystery Hunters Ser.). (ENG., Illus.). 32p. (J). (gr. 4-6). pap. 10.60 *(978-1-4488-6439-3(9))*; lib. bdg. 25.25 *(978-1-4488-6428-7(3))* Rosen Publishing Group, Inc., The. (PowerKids Pr.).

Hayes, Amy. Zombies. 2016. (Creatures of Fantasy Ser.). (ENG., Illus.). 64p. (J). (gr. 6-6). 34.21 *(978-1-5026-0926-7(6))* Cavendish Square Publishing.

Henneberg, Susan. Investigating Ghosts & the Spirit World, 1 vol. 2015. (ENG.). 48p. (YA). 25.85 *(978-1-62275-863-0(3)*, Britannica Educational Publishing) Rosen Publishing Group, Inc., The.

Hennessy, B. G. The Scary Places Map Book: Seven Terrifying Tours. Madrid, Erwin, illus. 2012. (ENG.). 32p. (J). (gr. k-4). 15.99 *(978-0-7636-4541-0(9))* Candlewick Pr.

Higgins, Nadia. Ghosts. 2014. (Unexplained Mysteries Ser.). (ENG., Illus.). 24p. (J). (gr. 3-7). lib. bdg. 25.95 *(978-1-62617-104-6(1)*, Epic Bks.) Bellwether Media.

Hile, Kevin. Ghost Ships. 2008. (Mysterious Encounters Ser.). (ENG., Illus.). 48p. (gr. 4-8). lib. bdg. 33.60 *(978-0-7377-4086-8(8)*, LML02109-242881, Kidhaven) Cengage Gale.

History's Most Haunted. 2013. (History's Most Haunted Ser.). 32p. (J). (gr. 3-6). 159.60 *(978-1-4339-9679-5(0))*; pap.

EFG

378.00 *(978-1-4339-9758-7(4))*; pap. 63.00 *(978-1-4339-9757-0(6))* Stevens, Gareth Publishing LLLP.

Houran, Lori Haskins. Spooky & Spookier: Four American Ghost Stories. Diaz, Viviana, illus. 2015. (Step into Reading Ser.). (ENG.). 48p. (J). (gr. 2-4). 3.99 *(978-0-553-53396-5(7)*, Random Hse. Bks. for Young Readers) Random Hse. Children's Bks.

Jones, Jen. Bone-Chilling Ghost Stories, 1 vol. 2013. (Scared! Ser.). (ENG.). 32p. (gr. 3-4). 27.99 *(978-1-4296-9981-5(7)*, Snap Bks.) Capstone Press of Coughlan Cos.

Kallen, Stuart A. Haunted Houses. 2007. (Mysterious & Unknown Ser.). (Illus.). 96p. (YA). (gr. 7-12). lib. bdg. 25.95 *(978-1-60152-026-5(3))* ReferencePoint Pr., Inc.

Klepeis, Alicia Z. Haunted Cemeteries Around the World. 2017. (It's Haunted! Ser.). (ENG., Illus.). 32p. (gr. 3-4). lib. bdg. 27.99 *(978-1-5157-3861-9(2)*, Snap Bks.) Capstone Press of Coughlan Cos.

Knudsen, Shannon. I'll Haunt You! - Meet a Ghost. Buccheri, Chiara, illus. 2014. (Monster Buddies Ser.). (ENG.). 24p. (gr. k-2). lib. bdg. 23.93 *(978-0-7613-9186-9(X)*, Millbrook Pr.) Lerner Publishing Group.

Krensky, Stephen. Ghosts. 2008. pap. 52.95 *(978-0-8225-9884-8(1))* 2007. (Illus.). 48p. (J). (gr. 4-8). lib. bdg. 26.60 *(978-0-8225-6762-2(8)*, Lerner Pubns.) Lerner Publishing Group.

Krohn, Katherine. Mystery of Haunted Houses. 2013. (Unexplained Mysteries Ser.). (ENG.). 24p. (gr. 1-2). 25.32 *(978-1-4765-3097-0(1)*, First Facts) Capstone Press of Coughlan Cos.

—The Unsolved Mystery of Haunted Houses. 2013. (Unexplained Mysteries Ser.). (ENG.). 24p. (gr. 1-2). pap. 7.95 *(978-1-4765-3442-8(X)*, First Facts) Capstone Press of Coughlan Cos.

Lake, G. G. Take Your Pick of Haunted Places. 2017. (Take Your (Equally Horrible) Pick! Ser.). (ENG., Illus.). 32p. (gr. 1-2). lib. bdg. 26.65 *(978-1-5157-4471-9(X)*, Blazers) Capstone Press of Coughlan Cos.

Lanigan-Schmidt, Therese. Ghosts of New York City, 1 vol. 2003. (ENG., Illus.). 224p. (gr. 10-13). pap. 12.99 *(978-0-7643-1714-9(8)*, 9780764317149) Schiffer Publishing, Ltd.

Leblanc, Catherine. How to Get Rid of Ghosts. Garrigue, Roland, illus. 2013. (ENG.). 32p. (J). (gr. -1). 14.99 *(978-1-60887-195-7(9))* Insight Editions.

Loh-Hagan, Virginia. Ghost Hunter: Odd Jobs. 2015. (Illus.). 32p. pap. 9.95 *(978-1-63470-055-9(4))* Cherry Lake Publishing.

Lunis, Natalie. Eerie Inns. 2014. (Scary Places Ser.). 32p. (J). (gr. 4-8). lib. bdg. 25.27 *(978-1-62724-090-1(X))* Bearport Publishing Co., Inc.

—Spooky Schools. (Scary Places Ser.). 32p. (J). (gr. 4-8). 2017. (ENG.). 8.95 ***(978-1-68402-605-0(9))*** 2013. lib. bdg. 25.27 *(978-1-61772-750-4(4))* Bearport Publishing Co., Inc.

Lunis, Natalie. Tragic Theaters. 2013. (Scary Places Ser.). 32p. (J). (gr. 4-8). lib. bdg. 25.27 *(978-1-61772-885-3(3))* Bearport Publishing Co., Inc.

Lunis, Natalie & Taylor, Troy. A Haunted Capital. 2015. (Illus.). 32p. (J). lib. bdg. *(978-1-62724-243-1(0))* Bearport Publishing Co., Inc.

MacKay, Jenny. Do Haunted Houses Exist? 2015. (ENG., Illus.). 80p. (J). lib. bdg. *(978-1-60152-858-2(2))* ReferencePoint Pr., Inc.

Marcovitz, Hal. Do Ghosts Exist? 2015. (ENG., Illus.). 80p. (J). lthr. *(978-1-60152-856-8(6))* ReferencePoint Pr., Inc.

—Poltergeists. 2009. (Library of Ghosts & Hauntings Ser.). (YA). (gr. 7-12). 25.95 *(978-1-60152-093-7(X))* ReferencePoint Pr., Inc.

Markovics, Joyce. Deadly Morgues. 2017. (Tiptoe into Scary Places Ser.). (ENG.). (J). (gr. k-3). lib. bdg. 18.95 ***(978-1-68402-270-0(3))*** Bearport Publishing Co., Inc.

Markovics, Joyce L. Haunted Gotham. 2017. (Scary Places Ser.). (ENG., Illus.). 32p. (J). (gr. 4-8). 19.95 *(978-1-68402-020-1(4))* Bearport Publishing Co., Inc.

Martin, Michael. The Unsolved Mystery of Ghosts. 2013. (Unexplained Mysteries Ser.). (ENG.). 24p. (gr. 1-2). pap. 41.70 *(978-1-62065-809-3(7)*, First Facts); pap. 7.95 *(978-1-62065-808-6(9))*; lib. bdg. 25.32 *(978-1-62065-136-0(X))* Capstone Press of Coughlan Cos.

McCollum, Sean. Handbook to Ghosts, Poltergeists, & Haunted Houses. 2016. (Paranormal Handbooks Ser.). (ENG., Illus.). 32p. (gr. 3-4). lib. bdg. 27.99 *(978-1-5157-1308-1(3)*, Edge Bks.) Capstone Press of Coughlan Cos.

McCullum, Kenya. 12 Notorious Ghosts. 2017. (Scary & Spooky Ser.). (ENG.). 32p. (J). (gr. 3-6). 21.95 *(978-1-63235-294-1(X))* Pr. Room Editions LLC.

Mendoza, Patrick M. Between Midnight & Morning: Historic Hauntings from the Frontier, Hispanic, & Native American Traditions. 2005. (ENG.). 128p. (J). (gr. 4-17). pap. 8.95 *(978-0-87483-607-3(7))* August Hse. Pubs., Inc.

Montgomerie, Adrienne. Ghost Ships. 2012. (ENG.). 32p. (J). *(978-0-7787-8008-3(2))*; pap. *(978-0-7787-8013-7(9))* Crabtree Publishing Co.

Morey, Allan. 12 Spooky Haunted Places. 2017. (Scary & Spooky Ser.). (ENG., Illus.). 32p. (J). (gr. 3-6). 21.95 *(978-1-63235-296-5(6))* Pr. Room Editions LLC.

Mott, A. S. Fireside Ghost Stories, 1 vol., Vol. 1. Kubish, Shelagh, ed. rev. ed. 2003. (Ghost Stories Ser.). (ENG.). 216p. (gr. 4). pap. 12.95 *(978-1-894877-40-4(3)*, 1894877403, Ghost Hse. Bks.) Lone Pine Publishing USA.

—Haunted Schools Vol. 1: Ghost Stories & Strange Tales, 1 vol., Vol. 1. Boer, Faye, ed. rev. ed. 2003. (Ghost Stories Ser.). (ENG., Illus.). 216p. (gr. 4). pap. 12.95 *(978-1-894877-32-9(2)*, 1894877322, Ghost Hse. Bks.) Lone Pine Publishing USA.

My Big Spooky Sticker Activity Book. 2003. (Illus.). 48p. (J). 5.98 *(978-1-4054-1219-3(4))* Parragon, Inc.

Nagelhout, Ryan. Haunted! Alcatraz. 2013. 32p. (J). (gr. 3-6). 26.60 *(978-1-4339-9243-8(4))*; pap. 10.50 *(978-1-4339-9244-5(2))* Stevens, Gareth Publishing LLLP.

Nagle, Jeanne. Haunted Houses, 01 vols., 1. 2016. (Role-Playing for Fun & Profit Ser.). (ENG.). 48p. (J). pap. 11.75 *(978-1-4994-3716-4(1)*, Rosen Central) Rosen Publishing Group, Inc., The.

Nelson, Drew. Haunted! the Tower of London. 2013. 32p. (J). (gr. 3-6). 26.60 *(978-1-4339-9263-6(9))*; pap. 10.50 *(978-1-4339-9264-3(7))*; pap. 63.00 *(978-1-4339-9265-0(5))* Stevens, Gareth Publishing LLLP.

Niver, Heather Moore. Are Ghosts Real? 2016. (I Want to Know Ser.). (Illus.). 32p. (J). pap. 10.52 *(978-0-7660-8236-6(9))* Enslow Pubs., Inc.

Noll, Elizabeth. Ghosts. 2017. (Strange ... but True? Ser.). (ENG.). 32p. (gr. 3-7). 31.35 ***(978-1-68072-024-2(4))*** Black Rabbit Bks.

—Haunted Places. 2017. (Strange ... but True? Ser.). (ENG.). 32p. (gr. 3-7). 31.35 ***(978-1-68072-025-9(2))*** Black Rabbit Bks.

O'Donnell, Kerri. Ghosts & Poltergeists. 2006. (Tony Stead Nonfiction Independent Reading Collection). (ENG.). 24p. (gr. 3-6). pap. 8.85 *(978-1-4042-5677-4(6))* Rosen Publishing Group, Inc., The.

O'Hearn, Michael. Ghosts vs. Witches: Tussle of the Tricksters. Moffet, Patricia, illus. 2011. (Monster Wars Ser.). (ENG.). 32p. (gr. 3-4). pap. 47.70 *(978-1-4296-7262-7(5))*; lib. bdg. 27.99 *(978-1-4296-6522-3(X))* Capstone Press of Coughlan Cos. (Edge Bks.).

Osborne, Mary Pope & Boyce, Natalie Pope. Ghosts: A Nonfiction Companion to a Good Night for Ghosts. Murdocca, Sal, illus. 2009. (Magic Tree House - Fact Tracker Ser.: 20). (ENG.). 128p. (J). (gr. 2-5). 6.99 *(978-0-375-84666-3(2)*, Random Hse. Bks. for Young Readers) Random Hse. Children's Bks.

—Ghosts: A Nonfiction Companion to a Good Night for Ghosts. 2009. (Magic Tree House Fact Tracker Ser.: 20). lib. bdg. 16.00 *(978-0-606-01833-3(6)*, Turtleback) Turtleback Bks.

Owen, Ruth. Ghosts & Other Spirits of the Dead. 2013. (Not near Normal: the Paranormal Ser.). 32p. (J). (gr. 3-8). lib. bdg. 26.60 *(978-1-61772-724-5(5))* Bearport Publishing Co., Inc.

Owings, Lisa. Ghosts at Sea. 2016. (Ghost Stories Ser.). (ENG., Illus.). 24p. (J). (gr. 3-7). 25.95 *(978-1-62617-425-2(3)*, Epic Bks.) Bellwether Media.

—Ghosts in Battlefields. 2016. (Ghost Stories Ser.). (ENG., Illus.). 24p. (J). (gr. 3-7). 25.95 *(978-1-62617-426-9(1)*, Epic Bks.) Bellwether Media.

—Ghosts in Cemeteries. 2016. (Ghost Stories Ser.). (ENG., Illus.). 24p. (J). (gr. 3-7). 25.95 *(978-1-62617-427-6(X)*, Epic Bks.) Bellwether Media.

—Ghosts in Hotels. 2016. (Ghost Stories Ser.). (ENG., Illus.). 24p. (J). (gr. 3-7). 25.95 *(978-1-62617-428-3(8)*, Epic Bks.) Bellwether Media.

—Ghosts in Mansions. 2016. (Ghost Stories Ser.). (ENG., Illus.). 24p. (J). (gr. 3-7). 25.95 *(978-1-62617-429-0(6)*, Epic Bks.) Bellwether Media.

—Ghosts in Palaces. 2016. (Ghost Stories Ser.). (ENG., Illus.). 24p. (J). (gr. 3-7). 25.95 *(978-1-62617-430-6(X)*, Epic Bks.) Bellwether Media.

—Ghosts in Prisons. 2016. (Ghost Stories Ser.). (ENG., Illus.). 24p. (J). (gr. 3-7). 25.95 *(978-1-62617-431-3(8)*, Epic Bks.) Bellwether Media.

—Ghosts in the White House. 2016. (Ghost Stories Ser.). (ENG., Illus.). 24p. (J). (gr. 3-7). 25.95 *(978-1-62617-432-0(6)*, Epic Bks.) Bellwether Media.

Page, Jason. Ghosts & Monsters. 2008. (Factastic Journey Ser.). (Illus.). 32p. (J). (gr. k-7). pap. 8.95 *(978-1-59905-240-3(7))* Saddleback Educational Publishing, Inc.

Parks, Peggy J. Ghosts. 2009. (Library of Ghosts & Hauntings Ser.). (YA). (gr. 7-12). 25.95 *(978-1-60152-090-6(5))* ReferencePoint Pr., Inc.

Pearce, Q. L. Ghost Hunters. 2011. (Mysterious Encounters Ser.). (ENG.). 48p. (gr. 8-8). lib. bdg. 33.60 *(978-0-7377-5290-8(4)*, Kidhaven) Cengage Gale.

Perritano, John. Amityville. 2014. (Jr. Graphic Ghost Stories Ser.). 24p. (J). (gr. 3-6). lib. bdg. 26.25 *(978-1-4777-7121-1(2)*, PowerKids Pr.) Rosen Publishing Group, Inc., The.

—The Ghosts of Civil War Soldiers. 2014. (Jr. Graphic Ghost Stories Ser.). 24p. (J). (gr. 3-6). lib. bdg. 26.25 *(978-1-4777-7133-4(6)*, PowerKids Pr.) Rosen Publishing Group, Inc., The.

Person, Stephen. Ghostly Alcatraz Island. 2010. (HorrorScapes Ser.). 32p. (YA). (gr. 4-7). lib. bdg. 25.27 *(978-1-936087-97-6(9))* Bearport Publishing Co., Inc.

Peterson, Megan Cooley. Super Scary Ghosts. 2016. (Super Scary Stuff Ser.). (ENG., Illus.). 24p. (gr. 1-2). lib. bdg. 25.32 *(978-1-5157-0276-4(6))* Capstone Press of Coughlan Cos.

—Super Scary Places. 2016. (Super Scary Stuff Ser.). (ENG., Illus.). 24p. (gr. 1-2). lib. bdg. 25.32 *(978-1-5157-0278-8(2))* Capstone Press of Coughlan Cos.

Pipe, Jim. Ghosts. 2013. (Twilight Realm Ser.). (Illus.). 32p. (J). (gr. 4-6). 26.60 *(978-1-4339-8751-9(1))*; pap. 10.50 *(978-1-4339-8752-6(X))* Stevens, Gareth Publishing LLLP. (Gareth Stevens Learning Library).

Raij, Emily. Ghosts of the Rich & Famous. 2015. (Spooked Ser.). (ENG.). 32p. (gr. 1-2). lib. bdg. 26.65 *(978-1-4914-4079-7(1))* Capstone Press of Coughlan Cos.

—The Most Haunted Places in the United States. 2015. (Spooked Ser.). (ENG., Illus.). 32p. (gr. 1-2). lib. bdg. 26.65 *(978-1-4914-4077-3(5))* Capstone Press of Coughlan Cos.

—The Most Haunted Places in the World. 2015. (Spooked Ser.). (ENG., Illus.). 32p. (gr. 1-2). lib. bdg. 26.65 *(978-1-4914-4076-6(7))* Capstone Press of Coughlan Cos.

—Tracking Ghosts. 2015. (Spooked Ser.). (ENG., Illus.). 32p. (gr. 1-2). lib. bdg. 26.65 *(978-1-4914-4078-0(3))* Capstone Press of Coughlan Cos.

Rajczak, Michael. Haunted! The White House. 2013. (History's Most Haunted Ser.). (Illus.). 32p. (J). (gr. 3-6). pap. 10.50 *(978-1-4339-9269-8(8))*; lib. bdg. 26.60 *(978-1-4339-9268-1(X))* Stevens, Gareth Publishing LLLP.

—Haunted! Gettysburg. 2013. 32p. (J). (gr. 3-6). 26.60 *(978-1-4339-9248-3(5))*; pap. 10.50 *(978-1-4339-9249-0(3))*; pap. 63.00 *(978-1-4339-9250-6(7))* Stevens, Gareth Publishing LLLP.

—Haunted! the White House. 2013. (History's Most Haunted Ser.). 32p. (J). (gr. 3-6). pap. 63.00 *(978-1-4339-9270-4(1))* Stevens, Gareth Publishing LLLP.

Raum, Elizabeth. Birth & Death of a City. 2007. (Illus.). 32p. (J). *(978-1-4062-0505-3(2))* Steck-Vaughn.

Rice, Earle, Jr. Haunted Battlefields Little Big Horn: Little Big Horn. 2015. (ENG., Illus.). 48p. (J). 29.95 *(978-1-62469-118-8(8))* Purple Toad Publishing, Inc.

—Haunted Battlefields Verdun: Verdun. 2015. (ENG., Illus.). 48p. (J). 29.95 *(978-1-62469-116-4(1))* Purple Toad Publishing, Inc.

Richard, Orlin. Ghosts. 2015. (Unsolved Mysteries Ser.). (ENG.). 24p. (J). (gr. 1-4). 28.50 *(978-1-63407-073-7(9)*, 208906) Child's World, Inc., The.

Ritchie, Scott. Ghouliest Ever Puzzle Book: Ghosts & Ghouls. 2008. 32p. (J). pap. *(978-1-921272-62-2(7))* Little Hare Bks. AUS. Dist: HarperCollins Pubs. Australia.

Roberts, Russell. Haunted Battlefields Antietam: Antietam. 2015. (ENG., Illus.). 48p. (J). 29.95 *(978-1-62469-114-0(5))* Purple Toad Publishing, Inc.

—Haunted Battlefields Gettysburg: Gettysburg. 2015. (ENG., Illus.). 48p. (J). 29.95 *(978-1-62469-112-6(9))* Purple Toad Publishing, Inc.

Roland, James. Frightful Ghost Ships. 2017. (Searchlight Books (tm) — Fear Fest Ser.). (ENG.). 32p. (J). (gr. 3-5). pap. 9.99 ***(978-1-5124-5605-9(5))***; (Illus.). 30.65 ***(978-1-5124-3402-6(7))*** Lerner Publishing Group.

Rooney, Anne. Strange Places. 2010. (Amazing Mysteries Ser.). (YA). (gr. 3-6). 28.50 *(978-1-59920-366-9(9))* Black Rabbit Bks.

—Zombies on the Loose. 2008. (Crabtree Contact Ser.). (ENG., Illus.). 32p. (J). (gr. 3-7). lib. bdg. *(978-0-7787-3767-4(5))* Crabtree Publishing Co.

Rudolph, Jessica. Ghost Houses. 2017. (Tiptoe into Scary Places Ser.). (ENG., Illus.). 24p. (J). (gr. k-3). 18.95 *(978-1-68402-045-4(X))* Bearport Publishing Co., Inc.

Rudolph, Jessica. Spooky Libraries. 2017. (Tiptoe into Scary Places Ser.). (ENG.). 24p. (J). (gr. k-3). 18.95 ***(978-1-68402-049-2(2))*** Bearport Publishing Co., Inc.

Scariest Places on Earth. 2014. (Scariest Places on Earth Ser.). 24p. (J). (gr. 2-5). 135.60 *(978-1-4824-1145-4(8))* Stevens, Gareth Publishing LLLP.

Shea, Therese. Haunted! the Queen Mary. 2013. (History's Most Haunted Ser.). 32p. (J). (gr. 3-6). 26.60 *(978-1-4339-9258-2(2))*; pap. 10.50 *(978-1-4339-9259-9(0))* Stevens, Gareth Publishing LLLP.

Simon, Seymour. Ghosts. 2012. (Dover Children's Science Bks.). (ENG., Illus.). 80p. (J). (gr. 3-5). pap. 5.99 *(978-0-486-48469-3(6))* Dover Pubns., Inc.

Smith, Barbara. Animal Phantoms Vol. 1: Fin, Fur & Feather Ghosts, 1 vol. rev. ed. 2004. (Haunted Kids Ser.). (ENG., Illus.). 144p. (J). (gr. 4). pap. 6.95 *(978-1-894877-52-7(7)*, 1894877527, Ghost Hse. Bks.) Lone Pine Publishing USA.

—Ghost Riders Vol. 1: Planes, Trains & Automobiles, 1 vol. rev. ed. 2004. (Haunted Kids Ser.). (ENG., Illus.). 144p. (J). (gr. 4-6). pap. 9.95 *(978-1-894877-56-5(X)*, 189487756X, Ghost Hse. Bks.) Lone Pine Publishing USA.

Smitten, Susan. Ghost Stories of New England, 1 vol., Vol. 1. Wangler, Chris, ed. rev. ed. 2003. (Ghost Stories Ser.). (ENG., Illus.). 224p. (gr. 4). pap. 12.95 *(978-1-894877-12-1(8)*, 1894877128, Ghost Hse. Bks.) Lone Pine Publishing USA.

Smitten, Susan, et al. Canadian Ghost Stories, 1 vol., Vol. 2. rev. ed. 2003. (Ghost Stories Ser.). (ENG., Illus.). 240p. (gr. 4). pap. 14.95 *(978-1-894877-24-4(1)*, 1894877241, Ghost Hse. Bks.) Lone Pine Publishing USA.

Stemple, Heidi E. Y. Witch Haunts. 2016. (Scary Places Ser.). (ENG.). 32p. (J). (gr. 4-8). 19.95 *(978-1-944102-39-5(6))* Bearport Publishing Co., Inc.

Stewart, Gail B. Hauntings. 2009. (Library of Ghosts & Hauntings Ser.). (YA). (gr. 7-12). 25.95 *(978-1-60152-092-0(1))* ReferencePoint Pr., Inc.

Stone, Adam. Ghosts. 2010. (Unexplained Ser.). (ENG., Illus.). 24p. (J). (gr. 3-7). lib. bdg. 25.95 *(978-1-60014-500-1(0)*, Torque Bks.) Bellwether Media.

Taylor, Troy. Creepy Libraries. (Scary Places Ser.). (ENG.). 32p. (J). (gr. 4-8). 2017. 8.95 ***(978-1-68402-604-3(0))*** 2015. lib. bdg. 26.60 *(978-1-62724-862-4(5))* Bearport Publishing Co., Inc.

Teitelbaum, Michael. Ghosts: And Real-Life Ghost Hunters. 2008. (24/7: Science Behind the Scenes Ser.). (ENG., Illus.). 64p. (J). (gr. 9-12). 29.00 *(978-0-531-12077-4(5))*; pap. 7.95 *(978-0-531-18740-1(3))* Scholastic Library Publishing. (Watts, Franklin).

Tieck, Sarah. Ghosts, 1 vol. 2015. (ENG.). 32p. (J). *(978-1-62403-765-8(8))* ABDO Publishing Co.

Top That Publishing Staff, ed. Freaky Fredas Ghost. 2004. (Wicked Tattoos Ser.). (Illus.). 16p. (J). pap. *(978-1-84510-110-7(3))* Top That! Publishing PLC.

True Ghost Stories of Alameda. 2005. (YA). per. *(978-1-59872-163-8(1))* Instant Pub.

Walker, Kathryn. The Mystery of the Ghosts of Flight 401. 2008. (ENG., Illus.). 32p. (J). (gr. 3-7). pap. *(978-0-7787-4155-8(9))*; lib. bdg. *(978-0-7787-4142-8(7))* Crabtree Publishing Co.

Walsh, Liza Gardner. Ghost Hunter's Handbook. 2016. (ENG., Illus.). 96p. (J). (gr. 1-6). 15.95 *(978-1-60893-570-3(1))* Down East Bks.

West, David. Ghosts & Poltergeists: Stories of the Supernatural. 2009. (Graphic Mysteries Ser.). (Illus.). 48p. (YA). (gr. 5-5). 58.50 *(978-1-61512-964-5(2)*, Rosen Reference) Rosen Publishing Group, Inc., The.

Wheeler-Toppen, Jodi. Ghosts & Atoms, 1 vol. Haus, Estudio, illus. 2011. (Monster Science Ser.). (ENG.). 32p. (gr. 3-4). pap. 8.10 *(978-1-4296-7329-7(X))*; pap. 47.70 *(978-1-4296-7330-3(3))* Capstone Press of Coughlan Cos. (Graphic Library).

Whiting, Jim. Scary Ghosts. 2010. (Really Scary Stuff Ser.). (ENG.). 24p. (gr. 1-2). lib. bdg. 25.32 *(978-1-4296-3967-5(9)*, First Facts) Capstone Press of Coughlan Cos.

—Scary Places. 2010. (Really Scary Stuff Ser.). (ENG.). 24p. (gr. 1-2). lib. bdg. 25.32 *(978-1-4296-3970-5(9)*, First Facts) Capstone Press of Coughlan Cos.

Wick, Walter. On a Scary Scary Night: Picture Puzzles to Search & Solve. Wick, Walter, illus. 2008. (Can You See What I See? Ser.). (ENG., Illus.). 40p. (J). (gr. -1-3). 13.99 *(978-0-439-70870-8(2))* Scholastic, Inc.

Williams, Dinah. Abandoned Amusement Parks. 2013. (Scary Places Ser.). 32p. (J). (gr. 4-8). lib. bdg. 25.27 *(978-1-61772-884-6(5))* Bearport Publishing Co., Inc.

—Creepy Islands. 2015. (Illus.). 32p. (J). lib. bdg. *(978-1-62724-294-3(5))* Bearport Publishing Co., Inc.

—Creepy Stations. 2013. (Scary Places Ser.). 32p. (J). (gr. 4-8). lib. bdg. 25.27 *(978-1-61772-749-8(0))* Bearport Publishing Co., Inc.

—Haunted Hollywood. 2015. (Scary Places Ser.). (ENG.). 32p. (J). (gr. 4-8). lib. bdg. 26.60 *(978-1-62724-519-7(7))* Bearport Publishing Co., Inc.

—Haunted Prisons. 2017. (Scary Places Ser.). (ENG.). 32p. (J). (gr. 4-8). 8.95 ***(978-1-68402-603-6(2))*** Bearport Publishing Co., Inc.

Williams, Dinah. Monstrous Morgues of the Past. (Scary Places Ser.). 32p. (gr. 4-8). 2017. (ENG.). (J). 8.95 ***(978-1-68402-606-7(7))*** 2011. (YA). lib. bdg. 25.27 *(978-1-61772-149-6(2))* Bearport Publishing Co., Inc.

Windham, Kathryn Tucker. Jeffrey Introduces 13 More Southern Ghosts: Commemorative Edition. 2nd ed. 2015. (ENG., Illus.). 136p. 29.95 *(978-0-8173-1873-4(9))* Univ. of Alabama Pr.

—Thirteen Tennessee Ghosts & Jeffrey: Commemorative Edition. 2nd ed. 2016. (ENG., Illus.). 168p. 29.95 *(978-0-8173-1901-4(8))* Univ. of Alabama Pr.

—13 Georgia Ghosts & Jeffrey. 2nd ed. 2015. (ENG., Illus.). 160p. (gr. 4-12). 29.95 *(978-0-8173-1881-9(X))* Univ. of Alabama Pr.

World's Scariest Places. 2016. (World's Scariest Places Ser.). 00032p. (J). lib. bdg. 159.60 ***(978-1-4824-5863-3(2))*** Stevens, Gareth Publishing LLLP.

Zoehfeld, Kathleen Weidner. Ghost Mysteries: Unraveling the World's Most Mysterious Hauntings. Hale, Nathan, illus. 2009. (ENG.). 128p. (J). (gr. 4-8). pap. 5.99 *(978-1-4169-6448-3(7)*, Aladdin) Simon & Schuster Children's Publishing.

GHOSTS—FICTION

Abnett, Dan. This Ghost Is Toast! Williams, Anthony, illus. 2007. (Real Ghostbusters Ser.). (ENG.). 96p. per. 8.95 *(978-1-84576-143-1(X)*, Titan Bks.) Titan Bks. Ltd. GBR. Dist: Penguin Random Hse. LLC.

Accord Publishing Staff & Stone, Kate. One Spooky Night: A Halloween Adventure. 2011. (ENG.). 36p. (J). pap. 11.99 *(978-1-4494-0330-0(1))* Andrews McMeel Publishing.

Adler, David A. The Ghostly Mystery, Vol. 16. Natti, Susanna, illus. 2005. (Cam Jansen Ser.: 16). (ENG.). 64p. (J). (gr. 2-5). 4.99 *(978-0-14-240287-0(7)*, Puffin Books) Penguin Young Readers Group.

Adornetto, Alexandra. Ghost Hour. 2017. 272p. 9.99 *(978-0-7322-9934-7(9))* HarperCollins Pubs. Australia AUS. Dist: HarperCollins Pubs.

Ahern, Cecelia. Perfect. 2017. (ENG.). (YA). (gr. 8-12). pap. 12.99 ***(978-1-250-14643-4(7))*** St. Martin's Pr.

Aikins, Dave. Haunted Houseboat. 2013. (SpongeBob Squarepants 8X8 Ser.). lib. bdg. 13.55 *(978-0-606-32220-1(5)*, Turtleback) Turtleback Bks.

Aldridge, Janet. Meadow Brook Girls Afloat. l.t. ed. 2006. (ENG.). 156p. pap. 21.99 *(978-1-4264-0859-5(5))* Creative Media Partners, LLC.

—Meadow Brook Girls Afloat: Or the Stormy Cruise of the Red Rover. 2006. 160p. pap. 19.99 *(978-1-4264-0878-6(1))* Creative Media Partners, LLC.

—The Meadow-Brook Girls under Canvas (Ill. 2006. pap. *(978-1-4065-0695-2(8))* Dodo Pr.

Alender, Katie. As Dead as It Gets. 2013. (Bad Girls Don't Die Ser.). (ENG.). 448p. (J). (gr. 7-17). pap. 9.99 *(978-1-4231-3778-8(7))* Hyperion Pr.

—From Bad to Cursed. 2012. (ENG.). 448p. (YA). (gr. 7-17). pap. 9.99 *(978-1-4231-3777-1(9))* Hyperion Pr.

—Marie Antoinette, Serial Killer. (ENG.). 304p. (J). (gr. 7). 2014. pap. 9.99 *(978-0-545-46810-7(8)*, Scholastic Paperbacks) 2013. 18.99 *(978-0-545-46809-1(4))* Scholastic, Inc.

Alexander, Michael. Until Wishes Are Fulfilled II: Alec's Story. 2007. 204p. per. 15.50 *(978-1-84426-468-1(8))* Upfront Publishing Ltd. GBR. Dist: Printondemand-worldwide.com.

Alexander, William. A Properly Unhaunted Place. Murphy, Kelly, illus. 2017. (ENG.). 192p. (J). (gr. 3-7). 16.99 ***(978-1-4814-6915-9(0)***, McElderry, Margaret K. Bks.) McElderry, Margaret K. Bks.

Allan, Tony. True Ghost Stories. rev. ed. 2004. (True Adventure Stories Ser.). 144p. (J). pap. 4.99 *(978-0-7945-0274-4(1)*, Usborne) EDC Publishing.

Allan, Tony & Dowswell, Paul. True Ghost Stories. 2004. (True Adventure Stories Ser.). (Illus.). 122p. (J). (gr. 5). lib. bdg. 12.95 *(978-1-58086-601-9(8))* EDC Publishing.

Allison, Jennifer. The Ghost Sonata. 2008. (Gilda Joyce Ser.). (ENG.). 352p. (J). (gr. 3-7). 8.99 *(978-0-14-241232-9(5)*, Puffin Books) Penguin Young Readers Group.

—Gilda Joyce, Psychic Investigator. 2006. (Gilda Joyce Ser.). (ENG.). 336p. (J). (gr. 5-18). reprint ed. 8.99 *(978-0-14-240698-4(8)*, Puffin Books) Penguin Young Readers Group.

—The Ladies of the Lake. 2007. (Gilda Joyce Ser.). (ENG.). 352p. (J). (gr. 5-18). 9.99 *(978-0-14-240907-7(3)*, Puffin Books) Penguin Young Readers Group.

Almond, David. Kit's Wilderness. unabr. ed. 2004. 240p. (J). (gr. 7-18). pap. 36.00 incl. audio *(978-0-8072-8216-8(2)*, Listening Library) Random Hse. Audio Publishing Group.

Amato, Carol J. The Secret of Blackhurst Manor. 2017. (ENG.). 232p. (J). pap. 9.95 *(978-1-933277-02-8(5))* Stargazer Publishing Co.

Anderson, Connie Kingrey. Haunted Cattle Drive. 2013. (Creepers Mysteries Ser.: Bk. 1). (ENG.). 112p. (J). pap. 7.99 *(978-1-935793-00-7(4))* Movies for the Ear, LLC.

Anderson, Jodi Lynn. Among the Stars. 2014. (May Bird Ser.: 2). (ENG., Illus.). 304p. (J). (gr. 3-7). pap. 6.99 *(978-1-4424-9578-4(2)*, Aladdin) Simon & Schuster Children's Publishing.

—The Ever After. 2014. (May Bird Ser.: 1). (ENG., Illus.). 368p. (J). (gr. 3-7). pap. 7.99 *(978-1-4424-9576-0(6)*, Aladdin) Simon & Schuster Children's Publishing.

—The May Bird Trilogy: The Ever after; among the Stars; Warrior Princess. 2014. (May Bird Ser.). (ENG., Illus.). 960p. (J). (gr. 3-7). pap. 22.99 *(978-1-4814-1673-3(1)*, Aladdin) Simon & Schuster Children's Publishing.

—The Vanishing Season. 2014. (ENG.). 272p. (YA). (gr. 9). 17.99 *(978-0-06-200327-0(5)*, HarperTeen) HarperCollins Pubs.

—Warrior Princess. 2014. (May Bird Ser.: 3). (ENG., Illus.). 288p. (J). (gr. 3-7). pap. 6.99 *(978-1-4424-9580-7(4)*, Aladdin) Simon & Schuster Children's Publishing.

Arcane, Amicus. Tales from the Haunted Mansion: Volume I: The Fearsome Foursome. Jones, Kelley, illus. 2016. (Tales from the Haunted Mansion Ser.: 1). (ENG.). 240p. (J). (gr. 3-7). 14.99 (978-1-4847-1329-7(X)) Disney Pr.

Armstrong, Kelley. The Awakening. (Darkest Powers Ser.: 2). (YA). (gr. 8). 2010. 384p. pap. 9.99 (978-0-06-145055-6(3)) 2009. 368p. 17.99 (978-0-06-166276-8(3)) HarperCollins Pubs.

—The Awakening, 7 vols. 2009. (Darkest Powers Ser.: 2). (YA). 133.75 (978-1-4407-3103-7(9)); 103.75 (978-1-4407-3099-3(7)) Recorded Bks., Inc.

—The Reckoning. (Darkest Powers Ser.: 3). (YA). (gr. 8). 2011. 416p. pap. 9.99 (978-0-06-145056-3(1)) 2010. 400p. 17.99 (978-0-06-166283-6(6)) HarperCollins Pubs.

Arnold, Louise. Golden & Grey: An Unremarkable Boy & a Rather Remarkable Ghost. 2006. (ENG., Illus.). 272p. (J). (gr. 3-7). reprint ed. pap. 6.99 (978-0-689-87585-4(1), McElderry, Margaret K. Bks.) McElderry, Margaret K. Bks.

—Golden & Grey - A Good Day for Haunting. 2009. (ENG.). 336p. (J). (gr. 3-7). pap. 6.99 (978-1-4169-0864-7(1), McElderry, Margaret K. Bks.) McElderry, Margaret K. Bks.

Arrigan, Mary. Grimstone's Ghost. 2003. 159p. (J). (gr. 3-6). pap. 6.99 (978-0-00-675480-0(5), HarperCollins Children's Bks.) HarperCollins Pubs. Ltd. GBR. Dist: Trafalgar Square Publishing.

Ashes to Ashes. 2014. (ENG., Illus.). 400p. (YA). (gr. 9). 18.99 (978-1-4424-4081-4(3), Simon & Schuster Bks. For Young Readers) Simon & Schuster Bks. For Young Readers.

Ashkenas, Bruce. Auntie's Ghost. 2007. 108p. 34.50 (978-1-4303-1929-0(1)) Lulu Pr., Inc.

Asquith, Ros. Trixie Ace Ghost Buster. 2008. (Trixie Ser.). (ENG., Illus.). 176p. (J). (gr. 3-6). pap. 7.99 (978-0-00-725909-0(3)) HarperCollins Pubs. Ltd. GBR. Dist: Independent Pubs. Group.

Atwater-Rhodes, Amelia. Token of Darkness. 2011. (ENG.). 208p. (YA). (gr. 7). pap. 8.99 (978-0-385-73751-7(3), Ember) Random Hse. Children's Bks.

Atwood, Megan. The Bridge of Death. 2012. (Paranormalists Ser.: 4). (ENG.). 104p. (YA). (gr. 6-12). pap. 7.95 (978-0-8225-9090-3(5), Darby Creek); lib. bdg. 27.93 (978-0-7613-8335-2(2)) Lerner Publishing Group.

—The Mayhem on Mohawk Avenue. 2012. (Paranormalists Ser.: 3). (ENG.). 104p. (YA). (gr. 6-12). pap. 7.95 (978-0-8225-9088-0(3), Darby Creek); lib. bdg. 27.93 (978-0-7613-8334-5(4)) Lerner Publishing Group.

—The Terror of Black Eagle Tavern. 2012. (Paranormalists Ser.: 2). (ENG.). 104p. (YA). (gr. 6-12). lib. bdg. 27.93 (978-0-7613-8333-8(6)) Lerner Publishing Group.

Auxier, Jonathan. The Night Gardener. (ENG.). (YA). (gr. 3-7). 2015. 384p. pap. 8.95 (978-1-4197-1531-0(3)) 2014. 368p. 16.95 (978-1-4197-1144-2(X)) Abrams, Inc. (Amulet Bks.).

—The Night Gardener. 2015. (J). lib. bdg. 19.60 (978-0-606-36891-9(4)) Turtleback Bks.

Avi. Something Upstairs. 2010. (ENG.). 144p. (J). (gr. 3-7). 5.99 (978-0-545-21491-9(2), Scholastic Pr.) Scholastic, Inc.

—Something Upstairs. 2010. lib. bdg. 16.00 (978-0-606-14682-1(2), Turtleback) Turtleback Bks.

Awdry, W. Runaway Engine! Stubbs, Tommy, illus. 2011. (Pictureback(R) Ser.). (ENG.). 16p. (J). (gr. -1-2). pap. 4.99 (978-0-375-87253-2(1), Random Hse. Bks. for Young Readers) Random Hse. Children's Bks.

AZ Books Staff & Evans, Olivia. Haunted Castle. Shumovich, Nadezhda, ed. 2012. (Terribly Funny Monsters Ser.). (ENG., Illus.). 10p. (J). bds. 15.95 (978-1-61889-134-1(0)) AZ Bks. LLC.

Babbitt, Natalie. Kneeknock Rise. 2007. (J). lib. bdg. 18.40 (978-1-4177-9310-5(4), Turtleback) Turtleback Bks.

Babcock, Lee L. Ghost of Sunday Creek. 2006. (Illus.). 104p. per. 13.95 (978-1-4251-0162-6(3)) Trafford Publishing.

Baguley, Elizabeth. Ready, Steady, Ghost! Lindsay, Marion, illus. 2014. (ENG.). 32p. (J). (gr. -1-k). 16.99 (978-1-4231-8039-5(9)) Hyperion Bks. for Children.

Baker, Kage. The Hotel under the Sand. Law, Stephanie Pui-Mun, illus. 2009. (ENG.). 179p. (J). (gr. 2-7). pap. (978-1-892391-89-6(9)) Temmen, Edition, Horst Temmen.

Bakewell, Lori. Savannah Adventure: Pirate's Treasure. 2007. 173p. (J). pap. 12.95 (978-0-9799473-9-1(1)) Tailwind Press.

Banks, Steven. The Big Halloween Scare. Martinez, Heather, illus. 2003. (SpongeBob SquarePants Ser.: Vol. 1). (ENG.). 32p. (J). (gr. k-2). pap. 3.99 (978-0-689-84196-5(5), Simon Spotlight/Nickelodeon) Simon Spotlight/Nickelodeon.

Bardhan-Quallen, Sudipta. Ghostly Horse. Random House Disney Staff & Gurihiru Staff, illus. 2016. (Stepping Stone Book(TM) Ser.). (ENG.). 128p. (J). (gr. 1-4). 9.99 (978-0-7364-3515-4(8), RH/Disney) Random Hse. Children's Bks.

Barnholdt, Lauren. Ghost of a Chance. 2014. (Girl Meets Ghost Ser.: 3). (ENG., Illus.). 240p. (J). (gr. 4-9). 15.99 (978-1-4424-4248-1(4), Aladdin) Simon & Schuster Children's Publishing.

—Girl Meets Ghost. 2013. (Girl Meets Ghost Ser.: 1). (ENG.). (J). (gr. 4-9). 240p. pap. 7.99 (978-1-4424-2146-2(0)); 224p. 15.99 (978-1-4424-4246-7(8)) Simon & Schuster Children's Publishing. (Aladdin).

—The Harder the Fall. (Girl Meets Ghost Ser.: 2). (ENG., (J). (gr. 4-9). 2014. Illus.). 256p. pap. 7.99 (978-1-4424-2147-9(9)) 2013. 240p. 16.99 (978-1-4424-4247-4(6)) Simon & Schuster Children's Publishing. (Aladdin).

Barrows, Annie. Ivy + Bean & the Ghost That Had to Go. Blackall, Sophie, illus. (Ivy & Bean Ser.: IVYB). (ENG.). 136p. (J). (gr. 1-5). 2007. pap. 5.99 (978-0-8118-4911-1(2))Bk. 2. 2006. 14.99 (978-0-8118-4910-4(4)) Chronicle Bks. LLC.

—Ivy & Bean & the Ghost That Had to Go. Blackall, Sophie, illus. 2007. (Ivy & Bean Ser.: 2). (J). lib. bdg. 16.00 (978-1-4177-9273-3(6), Turtleback) Turtleback Bks.

Barrows, Annie & Blackall, Sophie. Ivy + Bean & the Ghost That Had to Go, 1 vol. 2011. (Ivy & Bean Ser.). (ENG., Illus.). 136p. (J). (gr. 1-4). 24.21 (978-1-59961-929-3(6)) Spotlight.

Basic, Zdenko, illus. Steampunk Charles Dickens' a Christmas Carol. 2014. (ENG.). 204p. (gr. 7). 18.95 (978-0-7624-5090-9(8), Running Pr. Kids) Running Pr. Bk. Pubs.

Bass, Guy. The Ghost of Grotteskew, 1 vol. Williamson, Pete, illus. 2014. (Stitch Head Ser.). (ENG.). 208p. (gr. 3-4). 10.95 (978-1-62370-030-0(2)) Capstone Young Readers of Coughlan Cos.

Baudet, Stephanie. New Library of Horror: Dracula. 128p. (J). pap. 7.95 (978-0-233-99578-6(1)) Andre Deutsch GBR. Dist: Trans-Atlantic Pubns., Inc.

Bauer, Marion Dane. The Blue Ghost. Wang, Suling, illus. 2006. (Stepping Stone Book Ser.). (ENG.). 96p. (J). (gr. 1-4). 3.99 (978-0-375-83339-7(0), Random Hse. Bks. for Young Readers) Random Hse. Children's Bks.

Beard, Sarah. Beyond the Rising Tide. 2016. (YA). pap. 18.99 (978-1-4621-1874-8(7)) Cedar Fort, Inc./CFI Distribution.

Beaty, Andrea. Hush, Baby Ghostling. Lemaître, Pascal, illus. 2009. (ENG.). 32p. (J). (gr. -1-3). 14.99 (978-1-4169-2545-3(7), McElderry, Margaret K. Bks.) McElderry, Margaret K. Bks.

Beauregard, Lynda. The Whispering Lake Ghosts: A Mystery about Sound. Torres, German, illus. 2013. (Summer Camp Science Mysteries Ser.: 6). (ENG.). 48p. (gr. 3-6). pap. 6.95 (978-1-4677-0734-3(1), Graphic Universe™) Lerner Publishing Group.

Belanger, Jeff. Ghosts of War: Restless Spirits of Soldiers, Spies, & Saboteurs. 2009. (Haunted: Ghosts & the Paranormal Ser.). 235p. (YA). (gr. 7-12). lib. bdg. 37.95 (978-1-4358-5177-1(3)) Rosen Publishing Group, Inc., The.

Bell, Alex. Frozen Charlotte. 2016. (ENG.). 304p. (J). (gr. 7). 18.99 (978-0-545-94108-2(3), Scholastic Pr.) Scholastic, Inc.

Benedict, Nicholas & Benedict, Janet. My Mommy Is a Zombie. 2013. 36p. 17.99 (978-0-9883938-3-7(2)) Janik Pr.

Benson, Amber. Among the Ghosts. Grace, Sina, illus. 2011. (ENG.). 256p. (J). (gr. 3-7). pap. 6.99 (978-1-4169-9426-8(2), Aladdin) Simon & Schuster Children's Publishing.

—Among the Ghosts. Grace, Sina, illus. 2010. (ENG.). 256p. (J). (gr. 3-7). 15.99 (978-1-4169-9405-3(X), Simon & Schuster/Paula Wiseman Bks.) Simon & Schuster/Paula Wiseman Bks.

Benson, Donna. Ghost Finds 100ct Diamond in Little Rock. 2012. 36p. 19.95 (978-1-4626-6892-2(5)) America Star Bks.

Bentley, Cheryl. Petronella & the Trogot. 2012. (Petronella Ser.: 1). (ENG., Illus.). 192p. (YA). pap. 14.95 (978-1-907230-45-5(9)) Sparkling Bks. GBR. Dist: Silvermine International Bks., LLC.

Berenstain, Stan & Berenstain, Jan. The Berenstain Bears Go on a Ghost Walk. Berenstain, Jan, illus. 2005. (Berenstain Bears Ser.). (ENG., Illus.). 32p. (J). (gr. -1-2). 10.99 (978-0-06-057399-7(6)); pap. 3.99 (978-0-06-057383-6(X)) HarperCollins Pubs. (HarperFestival).

—The Berenstain Bears Happy Halloween! 2013. (First Time Books(R) Ser.). (ENG., Illus.). 96p. (J). (gr. -1-2). 9.99 (978-0-385-37191-9(8), Random Hse. Bks. for Young Readers) Random Hse. Children's Bks.

Berenstain, Stan, et al. The Berenstain Bears & the Haunted House. 2010. (Berenstain Bears Ser.). (ENG., Illus.). 16p. (J). (gr. -1-1). pap. 6.99 (978-0-06-057426-0(7), HarperFestival) HarperCollins Pubs.

Beresford, Elisabeth. The Ghost of Wimbledon Common. (Illus.). 15p. (J). (gr. k-6). pap. (978-0-340-73579-4(1)) Hodder & Stoughton.

Berk, Ari. Lych Way. 2014. (Undertaken Trilogy Ser.: 3). (ENG., Illus.). 336p. (YA). (gr. 7). 17.99 (978-1-4169-9119-9(0), Simon & Schuster Bks. For Young Readers) Simon & Schuster Bks. For Young Readers.

—Mistle Child. (Undertaken Trilogy Ser.: 2). (ENG., (YA). (gr. 7). 2014. Illus.). 368p. pap. 9.99 (978-1-4169-9118-2(2)) 2013. 352p. 17.99 (978-1-4169-9117-5(4)) Simon & Schuster Bks. For Young Readers. (Simon & Schuster Bks. For Young Readers).

Berry, Diane Lambright. Port City Pirates. 2008. 128p. pap. 12.95 (978-0-9815763-0-5(3)) Alabaster Bk. Pub.

Bial, Raymond. Shadow Island: A Tale of Lake Superior. 2006. 172p. (J). (gr. 3-7). 18.95 (978-1-883953-37-9(5)); per. 12.95 (978-1-883953-36-2(7)) Great Lakes Literary, LLC. (Blue Horse Books).

Biro, Val. Gumdrop Finds a Ghost. (Illus.). 27p. (J). (978-0-340-71062-3(4)); pap. (978-0-340-71063-0(2)) Hodder & Stoughton.

Black, Holly. Doll Bones. Wheeler, Eliza, illus. 2013. (ENG.). 256p. (J). (gr. 5-9). 18.99 (978-1-4169-6398-1(7), McElderry, Margaret K. Bks.) McElderry, Margaret K. Bks.

—Doll Bones. 2015. lib. bdg. 18.40 (978-0-606-36308-2(4)) Turtleback Bks.

Black, Holly & DiTerlizzi, Tony. The Wyrm King. DiTerlizzi, Tony, illus. 2009. (Beyond the Spiderwick Chronicles Ser.: 3). (ENG., Illus.). 224p. (J). (gr. 2-7). 11.99 (978-0-689-87133-7(3), Simon & Schuster Bks. For Young Readers) Simon & Schuster Bks. For Young Readers.

Bladek, John. Lost in Ghostville. 2016. (Middle-Grade Novels Ser.). (ENG.). 208p. (gr. 4-7). lib. bdg. 25.99 (978-1-4965-3360-9(7)) Stone Arch Bks.

Blake, Kendare. Girl of Nightmares. (Anna Dressed in Blood Ser.: 2). (ENG.). 336p. (YA). (gr. 8). 2014. pap. 9.99 (978-0-7653-2868-7(2), 9780765328687) 2012. 17.99 (978-0-7653-2866-3(6), 9780765328663) Doherty, Tom Assocs., LLC. (Tor Teen).

—Girl of Nightmares. l.t. ed. 2012. (ENG.). 412p. 23.99 (978-1-4104-5206-1(9)) Thorndike Pr.

Blevins, Wiley. Goldilocks & the Three Ghosts. Cox, Steve, illus. 2016. (Scary Tales Retold Ser.). (ENG.). 24p. (gr. k-3). lib. bdg. 23.99 (978-1-63440-093-0(3)) Red Chair Pr.

Bloom, Carol A. The Wishing Closet. (Magic Mansion Mystery Ser.: Bk. 2). 124p. (J). (gr. 3-6). 9.99 (978-0-88092-476-4(4)) Royal Fireworks Publishing Co.

Bloomfield, Charlotte. Corridor of Doors. 2013. 130p. pap. (978-1-909411-28-9(0)) Mauve Square Publishing.

Bloor, Edward. Story Time. 2005. (ENG., Illus.). 444p. (YA). (gr. 7-12). reprint ed. pap. 8.99 (978-0-15-205222-5(4)) Houghton Mifflin Harcourt Publishing Co.

Bodi, Sari. The Ghost in Allie's Pool. 2007. 192p. (J). (gr. 5-18). pap. 8.95 (978-0-9768126-6-1(5)) Brown Barn Bks.

Bonham, T. J. Spi: The Case of the Dark Shadow. 2012. (ENG.). 112p. (J). pap. 12.99 (978-0-7643-4132-8(4), 9780764341328) Schiffer Publishing, Ltd.

Borraga, Charles R. The Old Parson's House. 2008. 24p. pap. 11.49 (978-1-4389-0698-0(6)) AuthorHouse.

Bouton, Warren Hussey. Oliver's Ghost: A Spooky Tale from Nantucket. Locke, Barbara K., illus. 2003. (J). per. 5.95 (978-0-9700555-3-8(6)) Hither Creek Pr.

Bovi, J. K. Wicked Haints: A Savannah Ghost Story, 1 vol. 2013. (ENG., Illus.). 128p. (J). pap. 16.99 (978-0-7643-4383-4(1), 9780764343834) Schiffer Publishing, Ltd.

Bowvayne. A Turn in the Grave. Snow, Alan, illus. 2006. (Misadventures of Danny Cloke Ser.). 143p. (J). per. 4.99 (978-0-7945-1292-7(5), Usborne) EDC Publishing.

The Boy Who Tricked the Ghosts. 2003. (J). 14.95 (978-0-89610-769-4(8)) Island Heritage Publishing.

Bozik, Chrissy. The Ghosts Go Scaring. Storms, Patricia, illus. 2016. (ENG.). 24p. (J). (gr. -1-k). 14.99 (978-1-5107-1228-7(3), Sky Pony Pr.) Skyhorse Publishing Co., Inc.

Bradman, Tony. Final Cut. 2004. (Illus.). 87p. (978-0-439-79597-5(4)) Scholastic, Inc.

Brezenoff, Steve. The Case of the Soldier's Ghost. Weber, Lisa K., illus. 2016. (Museum Mysteries Ser.). (ENG.). 128p. (gr. 2-3). pap. 6.95 (978-1-4965-2523-9(X)); lib. bdg. 26.65 (978-1-4965-2519-2(1)) Stone Arch Bks. (Museum Mysteries).

—The Ghost Who Haunted the Capitol, 1 vol. Canga, C. B., illus. 2010. (Field Trip Mysteries Ser.). (ENG.). 88p. (gr. 2-3). 25.32 (978-1-4342-2140-7(7)); pap. 6.10 (978-1-4342-2772-0(3)) Stone Arch Bks.

—Lost Island, 1 vol. Pinelli, Amerigo, illus. 2013. (Ravens Pass Ser.). (ENG.). 96p. (gr. 2-3). pap. 6.15 (978-1-4342-6214-1(6)) Stone Arch Bks.

—Lost Island. 2013. (Ravens Pass Ser.). (ENG.). 96p. (gr. 2-3). pap. 35.70 (978-1-4342-6290-5(1)) Stone Arch Bks.

—Lost Island, 1 vol. Pinelli, Amerigo, illus. 2013. (Ravens Pass Ser.). (ENG.). 96p. (gr. 2-3). lib. bdg. 25.32 (978-1-4342-4614-1(0)) Stone Arch Bks.

Brezenoff, Steven. The Case of the Soldier's Ghost. Weber, Lisa K., illus. 2017. 120p. (J). pap. (978-1-4965-2531-4(0)) Stone Arch Bks.

Brightwood, Laura, illus. The Ghost House. Brightwood, Laura, . 2006. (J). (978-0-9779290-1-6(9)) 3-C Institute for Social Development.

Brodeur, Tom. Regina Silsby's Phantom Militia. 2005. (Illus.). 267p. (J). (gr. 3-7). 7.49 (978-1-59166-385-0(7)) BJU Pr.

—Regina Silsby's Secret War. 2004. 248p. (J). 7.49 (978-1-59166-235-8(4)) BJU Pr.

Brooks, Walter R. Jimmy Takes Vanishing Lessons. Bolognese, Don, illus. 2007. (ENG.). 26p. (gr. k-3). 16.95 (978-1-58567-895-2(3), 856895) Overlook Pr., The.

Brosgol, Vera. Anya's Ghost. Brosgol, Vera, illus. 2011. (ENG., Illus.). 224p. (YA). (gr. 7-12). 22.99 (978-1-59643-713-5(8), 9781596437135); pap. 17.99 (978-1-59643-552-0(6), 9781596435520) Roaring Brook Pr. (First Second Bks.).

—Anya's Ghost. Brosgol, Vera, illus. 2014. (ENG., Illus.). 240p. (YA). (gr. 7). pap. 10.99 (978-1-250-04001-5(9), 9781250040015) Square Fish.

Brown, Mick. From Round about Midnight until about Five! 2012. 60p. pap. 27.45 (978-1-4772-2701-5(6)) AuthorHouse.

Bryant, Annie. Ghost Town. 2009. (Beacon Street Girls Ser.: 11). (ENG.). 240p. (J). (gr. 4-8). pap. 7.99 (978-1-4169-6441-4(X), Aladdin) Simon & Schuster Children's Publishing.

Buckingham, Royce. The Dead Boys. 2010. (ENG.). 208p. (J). (gr. 5-18). 16.99 (978-0-399-25222-8(3), G.P. Putnam's Sons Books for Young Readers) Penguin Young Readers Group.

Buffie, Margaret. Who Is Frances Rain? 20th ed. 2007. (ENG.). 184p. (J). (gr. 7-9). 7.95 (978-1-55453-209-4(4)) Kids Can Pr., Ltd. CAN. Dist: Hachette Bk. Group.

Bunce, Elizabeth C. A Curse Dark as Gold. (ENG.). 400p. (J). (gr. 7). 2010. 9.99 (978-0-439-89577-4(4), Scholastic Paperbacks) 2008. 17.99 (978-0-439-89576-7(6), Levine, Arthur A. Bks.) Scholastic, Inc.

Bunting, Eve. Ghost Cat. Barry, Kevin M., illus. 2017. (ENG.). 32p. (J). (gr. k-2). 16.99 (978-1-58536-993-5(4), 204323) Sleeping Bear Pr.

Bunting, Eve. The Presence: A Ghost Story. 2010. (ENG.). 204p. (YA). (gr. 7). pap. 12.99 (978-0-547-48032-9(6)) Houghton Mifflin Harcourt Publishing Co.

Burchett, Janet & Vogler, Sara. Shiver & Deliver. Brown, Judy, illus. 7th ed. 2003. (ENG.). 87p. (J). pap. (978-0-330-37604-4(7), Pan) Pan Macmillan.

Burchett, Loni R. Bear & Katie in a Day with Friends, Vol. 3. l.t. ed. 2005. (Illus.). 68p. (J). per. 11.95 (978-0-9742815-2-0(2), bk003) Black Lab Publishing LLC.

Burgess, Melvin. El Fantasma tras la Pared. (SPA.). (J). 8.95 (978-958-04-6483-9(9)) Norma S.A. COL. Dist: Distribuidora Norma, Inc.

Burnham, Erik. Ghostbusters. Schoening, Dan, illus. 2016. (ENG.). 24p. (J). (978-1-61479-485-1(5)) Spotlight.

Burrows, Roger. The Haunted House. 2004. (Illus.). 10p. bds. 9.95 (978-1-932915-05-1(2)) Sandvik Publishing.

Butler, Dori H. The Ghost at the Fire Station. 2015. (Haunted Library: 6). lib. bdg. 16.00 (978-0-606-38401-8(4)) Turtleback Bks.

Butler, Dori Hillestad. The Ghost Backstage. Damant, Aurore, illus. 2014. (Haunted Library: 3). (ENG.). 128p. (J). (gr. 1-3). 5.99 (978-0-448-46246-2(X), Grosset & Dunlap) Penguin Young Readers Group.

—The Ghost in the Attic, No. 2. Damant, Aurore, illus. 2014. (Haunted Library: 2). (ENG.). 128p. (J). (gr. 1-3). 5.99 (978-0-448-46244-8(3), Grosset & Dunlap) Penguin Young Readers Group.

—The Ghosts at the Movie Theater. 2017. (Haunted Library: 9). lib. bdg. 16.00 (978-0-606-39772-8(8)) Turtleback Bks.

—The Haunted Library. 2014. (Haunted Library: 1). lib. bdg. 14.75 (978-0-606-35702-9(5)) Turtleback Bks.

—The Haunted Library #1. Damant, Aurore, illus. 2014. (Haunted Library: 1). (ENG.). 128p. (J). (gr. 1-3). 5.99 (978-0-448-46242-4(7), Grosset & Dunlap) Penguin Young Readers Group.

Butler, Dori Hillestad & dePaola, Tomie. The Five O'Clock Ghost, No. 4. Damant, Aurore, illus. 2015. (Haunted Library: 4). (ENG.). 144p. (J). (gr. 1-3). bds. 5.99 (978-0-448-46248-6(6), Grosset & Dunlap) Penguin Young Readers Group.

—The Ghost at the Fire Station, No. 6. Damant, Aurore, illus. 2015. (Haunted Library: 6). (ENG.). 128p. (J). (gr. 1-3). bds. 5.99 (978-0-448-48334-4(3), Grosset & Dunlap) Penguin Young Readers Group.

Butler, T. Lee. The Ghost on Tanner's Mountain. 2008. 96p. pap. 11.94 (978-1-4357-5963-3(X)) Lulu Pr., Inc.

Cabot, Meg. Haunted. 2004. (Mediator Ser.: No. 5). (ENG.). 288p. (J). (gr. 7-18). pap. 6.99 (978-0-06-447278-4(7), Harper Trophy) HarperCollins Pubs.

—Haunted. 2007. (Mediator Ser.: No. 5). 263p. 18.00 (978-0-7569-7831-0(9)) Perfection Learning Corp.

—Love You to Death. 2009. 1.00 (978-1-4074-4802-2(1)) Recorded Bks., Inc.

—Shadowland & Ninth Key. 2010. (Mediator Ser.). (ENG.). 544p. (YA). (gr. 8). pap. 9.99 (978-0-06-204020-6(0), HarperTeen) HarperCollins Pubs.

—Twilight. 2005. (Mediator Ser.: No. 6). (ENG.). 256p. (J). 15.99 (978-0-06-072467-2(6)) HarperCollins Pubs.

Campbell, Suzy. The Hidden Graveyard. 2011. 62p. pap. 19.95 (978-1-4560-4265-3(3)) America Star Bks.

Carlee: The Ghost of the Black Forest. 2004. per. 13.00 (978-0-8059-9996-9(5)) Dorrance Publishing Co., Inc.

Carman, Patrick. 3:15 Season One Things That Go Bump in the Night. 2011. (3:15 Ser.: 1). (ENG.). 176p. (J). (gr. 5-9). 12.99 (978-0-545-38475-9(3)) Scholastic, Inc.

Carpenter, Ray. The Adventures of Benny Bell. 2004. 252p. 26.45 (978-1-4140-8467-1(6)) AuthorHouse.

Carris, Joan D. A Ghost of a Chance. 2003. (Legends of the Carolinas Ser.). 155p. (J). 8.95 (978-1-928556-40-4(X)) Coastal Carolina Pr.

Carroll, Jenny, pseud & Cabot, Meg. Darkest Hour. 2004. (Mediator Ser.: 4). (ENG.). 336p. (YA). (gr. 8-18). pap. 7.99 (978-0-06-072514-3(1), HarperTeen) HarperCollins Pubs.

Carthage, Lynn. Haunted. 2015. (Arnaud Legacy Ser.: 1). (ENG.). 288p. (YA). (gr. 9). pap. 9.95 (978-1-61773-626-1(0)) Kensington Publishing Corp.

Cascone, Annette & Cascone, Gina. Grave Secrets. 2014. (Deadtime Stories Ser.). (ENG.). 192p. (J). (gr. 3-7). pap. 6.99 (978-0-7653-3071-0(7), 9780765330710, Starscape) Doherty, Tom Assocs., LLC.

Cazet, Denys. The Perfect Pumpkin Pie. Cazet, Denys, illus. 2005. (ENG., Illus.). 32p. (J). (gr. -1-1). 17.99 (978-0-689-86467-4(1), Atheneum/Richard Jackson Bks.) Simon & Schuster Children's Publishing.

Chandler, Elizabeth. The Deep End of Fear. 2008. (Dark Secrets Ser.: 4). (ENG.). 320p. (J). (gr. 7). pap. 13.99 (978-1-4169-7142-9(4), Simon Pulse) Simon Pulse.

Chapman, Linda. Starlight Surprise, Vol. 4. 4th ed. 2003. (ENG., Illus.). 144p. pap. (978-0-14-131344-3(7), Puffin) Penguin Bks., Ltd.

—Starlight Surprise. Hull, Biz, illus. 2003. (My Secret Unicorn Ser.). 130p. (J). (978-0-439-65275-9(8)) Scholastic, Inc.

A Christmas Carol. 2004. (J). cd-rom 7.99 (978-0-9740847-9-4(4)) GiGi Bks.

A Christmas Carol. 2003. (Illus.). 32p. (J). 4.98 (978-1-4054-0980-3(0)); 9.98 (978-1-4054-0997-1(5)) Parragon, Inc.

Chupeco, Rin. The Girl from the Well. 2014. (ENG.). 272p. (YA). (gr. 9-12). 16.99 (978-1-4022-9218-7(X), 9781402292187) Sourcebooks, Inc.

—The Suffering. 2015. (ENG.). 320p. (YA). (gr. 8-12). 16.99 (978-1-4926-2983-2(9), 9781492629832) Sourcebooks, Inc.

Ciccone, Tiziana. Taylor, Please Stop Talking! Cannavicci, Luigi A., illus. 2013. 32p. pap. 12.95 (978-1-62516-817-7(9), Strategic Bk. Publishing) Strategic Book Publishing & Rights Agency (SBPRA).

Citra, Becky. Never to Be Told, 1 vol. 2006. (ENG.). 224p. (J). (gr. 5-9). per. 8.95 (978-1-55143-567-1(5)) Orca Bk. Pubs. USA.

Clapp, Patricia. Jane-Emily: And Witches' Children. 2007. (ENG.). 304p. (gr. 7). pap. 12.99 (978-0-06-124501-5(1), Harper Paperbacks) HarperCollins Pubs.

Class 1-208. Pizza Place Ghost, 1 vol. 2013. (Scooby-Doo! Picture Clue Bks.). (ENG.). 24p. (J). (gr. -1-1). lib. bdg. 24.21 (978-1-61479-038-9(8), Essential Library) ABDO Publishing Co.

Clement-Moore, Rosemary. Spirit & Dust. 2014. (ENG.). 400p. (YA). (gr. 7). pap. 9.99 (978-0-385-74081-4(6), Ember) Random Hse. Children's Bks.

—Texas Gothic. 2012. (ENG.). 416p. (YA). (gr. 9). pap. 10.99 (978-0-385-73694-7(0), Ember) Random Hse. Children's Bks.

Clickard, Carrie. Magic for Sale. Shelley, John, illus. 2017. (ENG.). 32p. (J). 16.95 (978-0-8234-3559-3(8)) Holiday Hse., Inc.

Cobb, Rebecca. Spooky Sums & Counting Horrors. 2006. (ENG., Illus.). 32p. (J). (gr. -1-3). 14.95 (978-0-7145-3307-0(6)) Boyars, Marion Pubs., Inc.

Cole, Frank. Hashbrown Winters & the Phantom of Pordunce. 2010. 128p. (J). pap. 7.99 (978-1-59955-398-6(8)) Cedar Fort, Inc./CFI Distribution.

Collins, Lynette. The Round Door: The Willow Tree. 2017. (Round Door Ser.: Bk. 2). (ENG., Illus.). (J). pap. 28.22 (978-1-5245-6171-0(1)) Xlibris Corp.

Collins, Ross. The Elephantom. Collins, Ross, illus. 2015. (ENG., Illus.). 40p. (J). (gr. -1-2). 16.99 (978-0-7636-7591-2(1), Templar) Candlewick Pr.

Common, Gabriel. The Demon of Basile High: The Return of Cassius. 2007. 132p. per. 11.95 (978-1-4327-0664-7(0)) Outskirts Pr., Inc.

Compestine, Ying Chang. Boy Dumplings. Yamasaki, James, illus. 2009. (ENG.). 32p. (J). (gr. -1-3). 16.95 (978-0-8234-1955-5(X)) Holiday Hse., Inc.

—Boy Dumplings: A Chinese Food Tale. Yamaski, James, illus. 2016. (ENG & CHI.). 40p. (J). (gr. -1-3). 15.95 (978-1-59702-119-7(9)) Immedium.

Cook, Eileen. Unraveling Isobel. 2012. (ENG.). (YA). (gr. 9). 320p. pap. 9.99 (978-1-4424-1328-3(X)); 304p. 16.99 (978-1-4424-1327-6(1)) Simon Pulse. (Simon Pulse).

Cooper, Susan. Ghost Hawk. 2013. (ENG.). 336p. (J). (gr. 5-9). 16.99 (978-1-4424-8141-1(2), McElderry, Margaret K. Bks.) McElderry, Margaret K. Bks.

Cormier, Robert. El Sindrome de la Ternura. Palmer, Magdalena, tr. 2005. (Escritura desatada Ser.).Tr. of Tenderness. (SPA.). 208p. (YA). pap. 11.95 (978-84-666-0160-3(0)) Ediciones B ESP. Dist: Independent Pubs. Group.

Cosby, Sam & Metzger, Clancy. Ceruladons: Blue dreams rain to Tears. 2008. 304p. pap. 18.95 (978-0-595-52400-6(1)) iUniverse, Inc.

Craddock, Erik. Pirate Palooza. Craddock, Erik, illus. 2009. (Stone Rabbit Ser.: Bk. 2). (ENG., Illus.). 96p. (J). (gr. 3-7).

pap. 6.99 (978-0-375-85660-0(9), Random Hse. Bks. for Young Readers) Random Hse. Children's Bks.

Cramer, Jon. Ghost! The Adventures of Horace & His Jungle Friends. 2005. (Illus.). 48p. (978-1-86074-183-8(5)) Sanctuary Publishing, Ltd.

Crossley-Holland, Kevin. Storm. Marks, Alan, illus. (Red Bananas Ser.). (ENG.). 48p. (J). (gr. k-2). 2013. pap. 5.99 (978-1-4052-6264-4(8)) 2nd ed. 2016. 7.99 (978-1-4052-8236-9(3)) Egmont Bks., Ltd. GBR. Dist: Independent Pubs. Group.

Crowson, Andrew. Flip Flap Spooky. Crowson, Andrew, illus. 2003. (Illus.). 12p. (J). bds. (978-1-85602-475-4(X), Pavilion Children's Books) Pavilion Bks.

Culbertson, Jan E. The Legend of Dunsmoor Manor. 2006. 88p. pap. 13.95 (978-1-58909-348-5(8)) Bookstand Publishing.

Cunningham, Scott. Scooby-Doo & the Hungry Ghost. Duendes Del Sur Staff, illus. 2005. (Scooby Doo Ser.). (ENG.). 12p. (J). (gr. -1-3). 8.99 (978-0-439-74882-7(8)) Scholastic, Inc.

Curtin, Ann. Dreamcatcher. 2015. 201p. (YA). (978-1-61271-246-8(0)) Zumaya Pubns. LLC.

Cushman, Doug. Dirk Bones & the Mystery of the Haunted House. 2009. (I Can Read! Level 1 Ser.). (J). lib. bdg. 13.55 (978-0-606-04778-4(6), Turtleback) Turtleback Bks.

Cusick, Richie Tankersley. Walk of the Spirits. 2008. (ENG.). 336p. (YA). (gr. 7-18). 9.99 (978-0-14-241050-9(0), Speak) Penguin Young Readers Group.

Cuyler, Margery. Skeleton for Dinner. Terry, Will, illus. 2013. (ENG.). 32p. (J). (gr. -1-3). 16.99 (978-0-8075-7398-3(1)) Whitman, Albert & Co.

Cypess, Leah. Nightspell. 2011. (ENG.). 336p. (YA). (gr. 8-18). 16.99 (978-0-06-195702-4(X), Greenwillow Bks.) HarperCollins Pubs.

Damico, Gina. Rogue. 2013. (ENG.). 336p. (YA). (gr. 7). pap. 8.99 (978-0-544-10884-4(1)) Houghton Mifflin Harcourt Publishing Co.

D'Angelo, Elaina R. The Magic Book of E, 1 vol. 2010. 48p. pap. 16.95 (978-1-4489-3949-7(6)) America Star Bks.

Darke, J. A. The Screaming Bridge. Evergreen, Nelson, illus. 2015. (Spine Shivers Ser.). (ENG.). 128p. (gr. 3-4). lib. bdg. 26.65 (978-1-4965-0219-3(1)) Stone Arch Bks.

Davidson, Danica. The Rise of Herobrine: An Unofficial Overworld Adventure, Book Three. 2016. (Unofficial Overworld Adventure Ser.). (ENG.). 112p. (J). (gr. 1-7). pap. 7.99 (978-1-5107-0802-0(2), Sky Pony Pr.) Skyhorse Publishing Co., Inc.

Davies, Donna M. Bye, Bye Boogeyman. Bailin-Rembar, Jill, ed. Peters, Rob, illus. 2013. 32p. pap. 9.95 (978-0-9853082-5-4(7)) All Hallows Eve Pr.

de Brunhoff, Laurent. Babar & the Ghost. 2012. (ENG., Illus.). 40p. (J). (gr. k-2). 15.95 (978-1-4197-0380-5(3), Abrams Bks. for Young Readers) Abrams, Inc.

—Babar & the Ghost. 2004. (Illus.). (J). (gr. k-3). spiral bd. (978-0-616-14571-5(3)); spiral bd. (978-0-616-14570-8(5)) Canadian National Institute for the Blind/Institut National Canadien pour les Aveugles.

de Lint, Charles. The Blue Girl. 2006. (ENG.). 384p. (YA). (gr. 7-18). reprint ed. 7.99 (978-0-14-240545-1(0), Firebird) Penguin Young Readers Group.

DeFelice, Cynthia. The Ghost & Mrs. Hobbs. 2010. (Ghost Mysteries Ser.: 2). (ENG.). 208p. (J). (gr. 3-7). pap. 8.99 (978-0-312-62909-0(5), 9780312629090) Square Fish.

—The Ghost of Cutler Creek. 2011. (Ghost Mysteries Ser.: 3). (ENG.). 208p. (J). (gr. 3-7). pap. 9.99 (978-0-312-62967-0(2), 9780312629670) Square Fish.

DeFelice, Cynthia C. The Ghost of Cutler Creek. 2006. (Ghost Mysteries Ser.). 181p. (J). (gr. 3-7). 13.60 (978-0-7569-8185-3(9)) Perfection Learning Corp.

—The Ghost of Fossil Glen. 2010. (Ghost Mysteries Ser.: 1). (ENG.). 192p. (J). (gr. 3-7). pap. 7.99 (978-0-312-60213-0(8), 9780312602130) Square Fish.

deGroat, Diane. Good Night, Sleep Tight, Don't Let the Bedbugs Bite! deGroat, Diane, illus. 2008. (ENG., Illus.). 32p. (J). (gr. -1-3). pap. 6.99 (978-0-06-134061-1(8)) HarperCollins Pubs.

Del Negro, Janice M. Passion & Poison: Tales of Shape-Shifters, Ghosts, & Spirited Women, 0 vols. Natale, Vince, illus. 2013. (ENG.). 64p. (J). (gr. 5-7). pap. 9.99 (978-1-4778-1685-1(2), 9781477816851, Amazon Children's Publishing) Amazon Publishing.

Delaney, Joseph. Ghost Prison. (ENG.). 112p. (YA). (gr. 6-12). 2014. pap. 5.99 (978-1-4926-0174-6(8)) 2013. 12.99 (978-1-4022-9318-4(6), 9781402293184) Sourcebooks, Inc.

Denman, K. L. The Shade, 1 vol. 2008. (Orca Currents Ser.). (ENG.). (J). (gr. 5-9). 112p. lib. bdg. 16.95 (978-1-55143-933-4(6)); (Illus.). 128p. pap. 9.95 (978-1-55143-931-0(X)) Orca Bk. Pubs. USA.

DeStefano, Lauren. A Curious Tale of the In-Between. 2015. (ENG.). 240p. (YA). (gr. 3-6). 16.99 (978-1-61963-600-2(X), 9781619636002, Bloomsbury USA Childrens) Bloomsbury Publishing USA.

—The Girl with the Ghost Machine. 2017. (ENG.). 224p. (J). 16.99 (978-1-68119-444-8(9), 9781681194448, Bloomsbury USA Childrens) Bloomsbury Publishing USA.

Deutsch, Stacia. Ghostbusters Movie Novelization. 2016. lib. bdg. 17.20 (978-0-606-38993-8(8)) Turtleback Bks.

Dicerto, Mike. The Ghost of Winter Joy. 2013. 196p. pap. 12.99 (978-1-61271-111-9(1)) Zumaya Pubns. LLC.

Dickens, Charles. A Christmas Carol. 2003. (ENG.). 128p. (Orig.). (C). pap. 16.95 (978-0-7593-9886-3(0), Cengage Learning) CENGAGE Learning.

—A Christmas Carol. Lynch, P. J., illus. 2006. (ENG.). 160p. (Orig.). (J). (gr. 5-6). 19.99 (978-0-7636-3120-8(5)) Candlewick Pr.

—A Christmas Carol. 2009. (Foundation Classics Ser.). 56p. (J). (gr. 5-9). lib. bdg. 27.95 (978-1-60754-850-8(X)) Windmill Bks.

—A Christmas Carol. Sanchez Almara, Dono & Almara, Dono Sanchez, illus. 2015. (Graphic Revolve: Common Core Editions Ser.). (ENG.). 72p. (gr. 2-3). lib. bdg. 27.99 (978-1-4965-0370-1(8)) Stone Arch Bks.

—A Christmas Carol: Being a Ghost Story of Christmas. 2013. (Cambridge Library Collection - Fiction & Poetry Ser.). (ENG., Illus.). 186p. pap. 28.99 (978-1-108-05714-1(4)) Cambridge Univ. Pr.

Dickens, Charles & Wright, Brett. Scrooge #worstgiftever. 2016. (OMG Classics Ser.). (ENG., Illus.). 112p. (YA). (gr. 9). 9.99 (978-0-399-55064-5(X), Random Hse. Bks. for Young Readers) Random Hse. Children's Bks.

Diller, Janelle. Mystery of the Ballerina Ghost. Turner, Adam, illus. 2013. 104p. (J). pap. 5.99 (978-1-936376-00-1(8)) WorldTrek Publishing.

Dillon, Kimberly M. The Ghosts of Wolf Creek. 2008. 73p. pap. 19.95 (978-1-60563-996-3(6)) America Star Bks.

Disney Book Group. Tales from the Haunted Mansion: Volume II: Midnight at Madame Leota's. 2017. (Tales from the Haunted Mansion Ser.: 2). (ENG.). 208p. (J). (gr. 3-7). 14.99 **(978-1-4847-1471-3(7))** Disney Pr.

Disney Book Group, et al. Disney Parks Presents the Haunted Mansion: Purchase Includes a CD with Song! Disney Storybook Art Team, illus. 2016. (Disney Parks Presents Ser.). (ENG.). 32p. (J). (gr. -1-k). 17.99 (978-1-4847-2785-0(1)) Disney Pr.

Donaldson, Julia. Wake up Do, Lydia Lou!, 2. George, Karen, illus. 2nd ed. 2015. (ENG.). 24p. (J). (gr. -1-k). pap. 10.99 (978-1-4472-0957-7(5)) Pan Macmillan GBR. Dist: Independent Pubs. Group.

Donbavand, Tommy. Skull of the Skeleton, Bk. 5. Cartoon Saloon Staff, illus. 2010. (Scream Street Ser.: 5). (ENG.). 128p. (J). (gr. 3-7). pap. 5.99 (978-0-7636-4635-6(0)) Candlewick Pr.

—Skull of the Skeleton: Book 5, 1 vol. Cartoon Saloon, illus. 2012. (ENG.). 120p. (J). 24.21 (978-1-59961-996-5(2), Chapter Bks.) Spotlight.

Doyle, Patrick H. T. Edgar Font's Hunt for a House to Haunt: Adventure One: the Castle Tower Lighthouse. 2006. (Illus.). 213p. (J). (gr. -1). per. 6.99 (978-0-9786132-0-4(1)) Armadillo Bks.

—Edgar Font's Hunt for a House to Haunt: Adventure Three: the Flint Island Treehouse. 2008. (Illus.). 300p. (J). per. 7.99 (978-0-9786132-2-8(8)) Armadillo Bks.

—Edgar Font's Hunt for a House to Haunt: Adventure Two: the Fakersville Power Station. Doyle, Patrick H. T., illus. 2007. (Edgar Font's Hunt for a House to Haunt Ser.). (Illus.). 303p. (J). (gr. 4-7). per. 7.99 (978-0-9786132-1-1(X)) Armadillo Bks.

Duckworth, Michael. Voodoo Island. Oxford University Press Staff & Bassett, Jennifer, eds. 3rd ed. 2008. (ENG., Illus.). 64p. 10.00 (978-0-19-479075-8(4)) Oxford Univ. Pr., Inc.

Dunkle, Clare B. The House of Dead Maids. Arrasmith, Patrick, illus. 2011. (ENG.). 176p. (YA). (gr. 7-12). pap. 16.99 (978-0-312-55155-1(X), 9780312551551) Square Fish.

East, Bob. Tommy Cat & the Haunted Well, 1 vol. 2009. 42p. pap. 24.95 (978-1-60703-754-5(8)) America Star Bks.

Edwards, Nicholas. Dog Whisperer: the Ghost. 2012. (Dog Whisperer Ser.: 3). (ENG.). 224p. (J). (gr. 3-7). pap. 9.99 (978-0-312-37096-1(2), 9780312370961) Square Fish.

Eggleton, Hazel. Ghost of Widdecot Manor. 2013. 184p. pap. (978-1-909734-07-4(1)) ThornBerry Publishing UK.

Elliott, Rebecca. Eva Sees a Ghost. 2015. (Owl Diaries: 2). (ENG., Illus.). 80p. (J). (gr. k-2). 15.99 (978-0-545-78784-0(X)); pap. 4.99 (978-0-545-78783-3(1)) Scholastic, Inc.

—Eva Sees a Ghost. 2015. (Owl Diaries: 2). lib. bdg. 14.75 (978-0-606-37038-7(2)) Turtleback Bks.

Enderle, Dotti. Book 14: Plop!, 1 vol. 2014. (Ghost Detectors Set 3 Ser.). (ENG., Illus.). 80p. (J). (gr. 2-5). lib. bdg. 27.07 (978-1-62402-002-5(X), Calico Chapter Bks) Magic Wagon.

—Book 15: Rock & Roll!, 1 vol. 2014. (Ghost Detectors Set 3 Ser.). (ENG., Illus.). 80p. (J). (gr. 2-5). lib. bdg. 27.07 (978-1-62402-003-2(8), Calico Chapter Bks) Magic Wagon.

—Book 16: Abracadabra!, 1 vol. 2014. (Ghost Detectors Set 3 Ser.). (ENG., Illus.). 80p. (J). (gr. 2-5). lib. bdg. 27.07 (978-1-62402-004-9(6), Calico Chapter Bks) Magic Wagon.

—Book 17: Grow a Ghost! 2014. (Ghost Detectors Set 3 Ser.). 80p. (J). (gr. 2-5). lib. bdg. 27.07 (978-1-62402-005-6(4), Calico Chapter Bks) Magic Wagon.

—Book 18: Spaced Out! 2014. (Ghost Detectors Set 3 Ser.). 80p. (J). (gr. 2-5). lib. bdg. 27.07 (978-1-62402-006-3(2), Calico Chapter Bks) Magic Wagon.

—Ghost Detectors Volume 1: Let the Specter-Detecting Begin, Books 1-3. McWilliam, Howard, illus. 2013. (Ghost Detectors Ser.: 1). (ENG.). 192p. (gr. 2-7). pap. 8.95 (978-1-938063-28-2(7), Mighty Media Junior Readers) Mighty Media Pr.

—Grow a Ghost!, 1 vol. McWilliam, Howard, illus. 2016. (ENG.). 80p. (J). (978-1-62402-100-8(X)) Magic Wagon.

—Hidden, 1 vol. Gentry, T. Kyle, illus. 2007. (ENG.). 104p. (J). (gr. 3-7). per. 8.95 (978-1-58980-481-4(3)) Pelican Publishing Co., Inc.

—Spaced Out!, 1 vol. McWilliam, Howard, illus. 2016. (ENG.). 80p. (J). (978-1-62402-101-5(8)) Magic Wagon.

—Tell No One!, 1 vol. McWilliam, Howard, illus. 2010. (Ghost Detectors Ser.: No. 1). (ENG.). 80p. (J). (gr. 2-5). 27.07 (978-1-60270-692-7(1)) Magic Wagon.

Enderle, Dotti & McWilliam, Howard. Ghost Detectors Book 12: Monsters!, 1 vol. 2012. (Ghost Detectors Ser.). (ENG., Illus.). 80p. (J). (gr. 2-5). 27.07 (978-1-61641-628-7(9)) Magic Wagon.

—Ghost Detectors Book 7: Pop!, 1 vol. 2012. (Ghost Detectors Ser.). (ENG., Illus.). 80p. (J). (gr. 2-5). 27.07 (978-1-61641-623-2(8)) Magic Wagon.

—Ghost Detectors Book 9: Never! Never! Never!, 1 vol. 2012. (Ghost Detectors Ser.). (ENG., Illus.). 80p. (J). (gr. 2-5). 27.07 (978-1-61641-625-6(4)) Magic Wagon.

Escondete y Grita, Vol. II. (Fantasmas de Fear Street Coleccion: No. 1). (SPA.). (J). (gr. 4-7). pap. 7.95 (978-950-04-1999-4(8), EM4474) Emecé Editores S.A. ARG. Dist: Planeta Publishing Corp., Lectorum Pubns., Inc.

Escott, John & Pearson Education Staff. Ghost of Genny Castle. 2nd ed. 2008. (ENG., Illus.). 48p. pap. 11.99 (978-1-4058-6953-9(4)) Pearson Education.

Etshied, Karl Jeffrey. Eggplant Rufus: Amused Indifference on a Stupid Planet. 2008. 158p. pap. (978-0-9814627-3-8(1)) Great American Pr., The.

Eustace, Robert & Meade, L. T. A Master of Mysteries. Walton, J. Ambrose, illus. 2013. 106p. pap. 8.00 (978-1-927558-41-6(7)) Birch Tree Publishing.

Even Little Ghosts Get Boo-Boo's. 2005. (J). per. 8.95 (978-1-930154-17-9(8)) Whitline Ink, Inc.

Falcone, L. M. The Ghost & Max Monroe, Case #3: The Dirty Trick. Smith, Kim, illus. 2015. (Ghost & Max Monroe Ser.). (ENG.). 96p. (J). (gr. 1-4). 6.95 (978-1-77138-019-5(5)) Kids Can Pr., Ltd. CAN. Dist: Hachette Bk. Group.

Fallenstein, J. Graffiti. 2017. (Midnight Ser.). (ENG.). 88p. (YA). (gr. 6-12). 26.65 (978-1-5124-2767-7(5)); 12.99 **(978-1-5124-3489-7(2)**, Darby Creek); 39.99 **(978-1-5124-2787-5(X)**, Darby Creek); 39.99 **(978-1-5124-3488-0(4)**, Darby Creek) Lerner Publishing Group.

—S. O. S. 2017. (Midnight Ser.). (ENG.). 104p. (YA). (gr. 6-12). lib. bdg. 26.65 (978-1-5124-2770-7(5), Darby Creek) Lerner Publishing Group.

—S. O. S. 2017. (Midnight Ser.). (ENG.). 104p. (YA). (gr. 6-12). 12.99 **(978-1-5124-3492-7(2))**; 39.99 **(978-1-5124-2790-5(X))**; 39.99 **(978-1-5124-3491-0(4))** Lerner Publishing Group. (Darby Creek).

—The Witching Hour. 2017. (Midnight Ser.). (ENG.). 96p. (YA). (gr. 6-12). 26.65 (978-1-5124-2771-4(3)); 12.99 **(978-1-5124-3498-9(1)**, Darby Creek); 39.99 **(978-1-5124-3497-2(3)**, Darby Creek); 39.99 **(978-1-5124-2791-2(8)**, Darby Creek) Lerner Publishing Group.

Fama, Elizabeth. Monstrous Beauty. 2013. (ENG.). 352p. (YA). (gr. 7-12). pap. 9.99 (978-1-250-03425-0(6)) Square Fish.

El Fantasma: Individual Title Six-Packs. (Literatura 2000 Ser.). (SPA.). (gr. k-1). 28.00 (978-0-7635-1022-0(X)) Rigby Education.

Farren, Rick. Grandpa & the Pirate. 2007. 49p. (J). per. 9.95 (978-0-9794863-6-4(X)) Summerland Publishing.

Fennell, Emerald. The Creeper. 2014. (Shiverton Hall Ser.). (ENG.). 272p. (YA). (gr. 3-6). pap. 13.00 (978-1-4088-2779-6(4), 9781408827796, Bloomsbury USA Childrens) Bloomsbury Publishing USA.

Fenton, Joe. Boo! Fenton, Joe, illus. 2010. (ENG., Illus.). 32p. (J). (gr. -1-1). 12.99 (978-1-4169-7936-4(0), Simon & Schuster Bks. For Young Readers) Simon & Schuster Bks. For Young Readers.

Ferguson, Donald. Chums of Scranton High on the Cinder Pat. 2006. 25.95 (978-1-4218-2937-1(1)); pap. 10.95 (978-1-4218-3037-7(X)) 1st World Publishing, Inc.

—The Chums of Scranton High on the Cinder Path. 2007. 124p. per. (978-1-4065-2363-8(1)) Dodo Pr.

Ferrier, Florian & Ferrier, Katherine. The Ghosts in the Clouds. Ferrier, Katherine, illus. 2017. (Hotel Strange Ser.: 4). (ENG., Illus.). 40p. (gr. 2-5). 7.99 (978-1-5124-3066-0(8), Graphic Universe™) Lerner Publishing Group.

Ferrier, Florian, et al. The Ghosts in the Clouds. Ferrier, Katherine, illus. 2017. (Hotel Strange Ser.: 4). (ENG.). 40p. (gr. 2-5). 26.65 (978-1-4677-8587-7(3), Graphic Universe™) Lerner Publishing Group.

Ferrier, Katherine & Ferrier, Florian. The Ghosts in the Clouds. Ferrier, Katherine, illus. 2017. (Hotel Strange Ser.: 4). (ENG., Illus.). 40p. (J). (gr. 3-3). E-Book 19.99 **(978-1-5124-2704-2(7)**, 9781512427042, Graphic Universe™) Lerner Publishing Group.

Fields, Jan. The Calm Before the Storm: A Night in Sleepy Hollow, 1 vol. Altmann, Scott, illus. 2013. (Adventures in Extreme Reading Ser.). (ENG.). 112p. (J). (gr. 3-6). 27.07 (978-1-61641-920-2(2)) Magic Wagon.

—Ghost Light Burning: An Up2U Mystery Adventure, 1 vol. Fabbretti, Valerio, illus. 2015. (ENG.). 80p. (J). (978-1-62402-092-6(5)) Magic Wagon.

Fine, Sarah. Of Dreams & Rust. 2016. (ENG.). 304p. (YA). (gr. 9). pap. 11.99 (978-1-4424-8362-0(8), McElderry, Margaret K. Bks.) McElderry, Margaret K. Bks.

—Of Metal & Wishes. 2015. (ENG., Illus.). 352p. (YA). (gr. 9). pap. 11.99 (978-1-4424-8359-0(8), McElderry, Margaret K. Bks.) McElderry, Margaret K. Bks.

Fischel, Emma. The Midnight Ghosts. Kern, Adrienne, illus. 2005. (Young Reading Ser.: Vol. 2). 64p. (J). (gr. 2-18). lib. bdg. 13.95 (978-1-58086-777-1(4), Usborne) EDC Publishing.

Fisher, Catherine & Fisher, Catherine. The Ghost Box. 2012. (Stoke Books Titles Ser.). 72p. (J). (gr. 5-8). pap. 7.95 (978-1-78112-018-7(8)); lib. bdg. 22.60 (978-1-78112-017-0(X)) Stoke Bks.

Flanagan, Jim. The School of Scary Stories. 2006. (Illus.). 125p. (J). per. 12.95 (978-0-9766666-5-3(0)) Arcadian Hse.

Fleischman, Sid. The Entertainer & the Dybbuk. 2009. (ENG.). 192p. (J). (gr. 4-9). pap. 6.99 (978-0-06-177140-8(6), Greenwillow Bks.) HarperCollins Pubs.

Fleming, Candace. On the Day I Died: Stories from the Grave. 2012. (ENG.). 208p. (J). (gr. 5-9). 16.99 (978-0-375-86781-1(3), Schwartz & Wade Bks.) Random Hse. Children's Bks.

Flynn, M. H. The Shadow City Ghost Hunters Vol. 1: The Mystery of Mapleshade Manor. 2006. 48p. pap. 16.95 (978-1-4241-2002-4(0)) PublishAmerica, Inc.

Fontes, Justine & Fontes, Ron. Casebook: Ghosts & Poltergeists. 2009. (Top Secret Graphica Mysteries Ser.). (Illus.). 48p. (YA). (gr. 2-6). 29.25 (978-1-60754-597-2(7)); pap. 11.75 (978-1-60754-598-9(5)) Windmill Bks.

Fred, Anthony. Fred & Anthony Meet the Heinie Goblins from the Black Lagoon. Primavera, Elise, illus. rev. ed. 2008. 128p. 14.99 (978-0-7868-3681-9(4)) Hyperion Bks. for Children.

Freeman, Martha. Who Stole Halloween? 2005. (Chickadee Court Mystery Ser.). (ENG.). 224p. (J). (gr. 3-7). 16.95 (978-0-8234-1962-3(2)) Holiday Hse., Inc.

Freese, Thomas, reader. Fog Swirler & 11 Other Ghost Stories. 2006. (J). Pt. 1. cd-rom 13.95 (978-0-9789511-0-8(7))Pt. 2. cd-rom 13.95 (978-0-9789511-1-5(5))Pt. 3. cd-rom 13.95 (978-0-9789511-2-2(3)) Illumination Pubns.

—Shaker Ghost Stories from Pleasant Hill, KY Audio Book/cd. 2006. (J). cd-rom 17.95 (978-0-9789511-3-9(1)) Illumination Pubns.

Freese, Thomas & Riddell, Fran. Halloween Sleepwalker, 1 vol. 2013. (ENG., Illus.). 64p. (J). 16.99 (978-0-7643-4399-5(8), 9780764343995) Schiffer Publishing, Ltd.

Funke, Cornelia. Ghost Knight. 2013.Tr. of Geisterritter. (ENG., Illus.). 352p. (J). (gr. 3-7). pap. 7.99 (978-0-316-05616-8(2)) Little, Brown Bks. for Young Readers.

Furber, Rosemary. What You See Is What You Get. 208p. pap. 6.95 (978-0-86327-924-9(4)) Wolfhound Pr. IRL. Dist: Interlink Publishing Group, Inc.

Furie, Peter. Numchuks' Curse. 2005. (Cyber Screams Ser.). 189p. (YA). (gr. 8-12). per. 12.95 (978-0-9772927-0-7(3)) Bangzoom Pubs.

Gaiman, Neil. The Graveyard Book. McKean, Dave, illus. (J). 2014. (ENG.). 352p. (gr. 5-7). pap. 9.99 (978-0-06-234918-7(X)) 2010. (ENG.). 352p. (gr. 5). pap. 8.99 (978-0-06-053094-5(4)) 2008. 552p. pap. 17.99 (978-0-06-170912-8(3)) 2008. (ENG.). 320p. (gr. 5-7). 17.99 (978-0-06-053092-1(8)) 2008. 320p. (gr. 5-7). lib. bdg. 18.89 (978-0-06-053093-8(6)) HarperCollins Pubs.

—The Graveyard Book. 2009. 19.00 (978-1-60686-823-2(3)) Perfection Learning Corp.

—The Graveyard Book. 2011. (Literature Kit Ser.). (ENG., Illus.). 55p. pap. 12.95 (978-1-55319-559-7(0), Classroom Complete Pr.) Rainbow Horizons Publishing, Inc.

—The Graveyard Book, 7 vols. 2008. (J). 256.75 (978-1-4361-5882-4(6)); 100.75 (978-1-4361-5887-9(7)) Recorded Bks., Inc.

—The Graveyard Book. l.t. ed. 2009. (ENG.). 373p. (YA). 23.95 (978-1-4104-1441-0(8)) Thorndike Pr.

—The Graveyard Book. 2010. (J). lib. bdg. 19.65 (978-0-606-14883-2(3), Turtleback) Turtleback Bks.

—EL LIBRO DEL CEMENTERIO. (SPA.). 2010. 256p. pap. 20.95 (978-84-9918-146-2(5)) 2009. 306p. (YA). 20.95 (978-84-9918-030-4(2)) Roca Editorial ESP. Dist: Spanish Pubs., LLC.

Gaiman, Neil & Russell, P. Craig. The Graveyard Book Graphic Novel. Russell, P. Craig, illus. 2014. (ENG., Illus.). (J). (gr. 3-7). Vol. 1. 192p. 19.99 (978-0-06-219481-7(X)) Vol. 2. 176p. 19.99 (978-0-06-219483-1(6)) HarperCollins Pubs.

Galdone, Paul. The Teeny-Tiny Woman. 2016. (Folk Tale Classics Ser.). (ENG., Illus.). 40p. (J). (gr. -1-3). 8.99 (978-0-544-64105-1(1), HMH Books For Young Readers) Houghton Mifflin Harcourt Publishing Co.

Gale Editor, ed. A Christmas Carol: The Graphic Novel. 2011. (Classic Graphic Novel Collection Ser.). 160p. (YA). (gr. 7-12). lib. bdg. 34.80 (978-1-4205-0630-3(7)) Cengage Gale.

Gallego García, Laura & Peden, Margaret Sayers. The Valley of the Wolves. 2006. 247p. (J). pap. (978-0-439-58554-5(6), Levine, Arthur A. Bks.) Scholastic, Inc.

Gallo, Tina, adapted by. The Po Who Cried Ghost. 2014. (Kung Fu Panda TV Ser.). (ENG., Illus.). 24p. (J). (gr. -1-2). pap. 3.99 (978-1-4814-0491-4(1), Simon Spotlight) Simon Spotlight.

Gapanowicz, Delores. The Finchley House Mystery. 2005. 112p. (J). per. 13.95 (978-1-933449-06-7(3)) Nightengale Pr.

Garcia, Randolph. The Steamer Trunk Adventures #2: The Ghosts of Machu Picchu. 2006. (ENG.). 88p. per. 16.95 (978-1-4241-1843-4(3)) PublishAmerica, Inc.

Gardner, Faith. Perdita. 2015. (ENG.). 224p. (YA). 17.99 (978-1-4405-8811-2(2), Simon Pulse) Simon Pulse.

Gareth Stevens Editorial Staff, creator. Haunted. 2006. (Ghost Stories Ser.). (Illus.). 128p. (gr. 3-7). lib. bdg. 31.00 (978-0-8368-6824-1(2), Gareth Stevens Learning Library) Stevens, Gareth Publishing LLLP.

Gareth Stevens Publishing, creator. Cursed Creatures. 2006. (Ghost Stories Ser.). (Illus.). 128p. (gr. 3-7). lib. bdg. 31.00 (978-0-8368-6821-0(8), Gareth Stevens Learning Library) Stevens, Gareth Publishing LLLP.

—The Doomed & the Dead. 2006. (Ghost Stories Ser.). (Illus.). 128p. (gr. 3-7). lib. bdg. 31.00 (978-0-8368-6822-7(6), Gareth Stevens Learning Library) Stevens, Gareth Publishing LLLP.

—From the Grave. 2006. (Ghost Stories Ser.). (Illus.). 128p. (gr. 3-7). lib. bdg. 31.00 (978-0-8368-6823-4(4), Gareth Stevens Learning Library) Stevens, Gareth Publishing LLLP.

Garsee, Jeannine. The Unquiet. 2012. (ENG.). 400p. (YA). (gr. 9). 16.99 (978-1-59990-723-9(2), 9781599907239, Bloomsbury USA Childrens) Bloomsbury Publishing USA.

Gavagan, Cinda J. The Old Haunted House. 2011. 56p. pap. 16.95 (978-1-4560-8301-4(5)) PublishAmerica, Inc.

Gelsey, James. The Baseball Boogeyman. 2004. (Illus.). 44p. (J). (978-0-439-55713-9(5)) Scholastic, Inc.

Gensler, Sonia. Ghostlight. 2015. (ENG.). 256p. (J). (gr. 3-7). 16.99 (978-0-553-52214-3(0), Knopf Bks. for Young Readers) Random Hse. Children's Bks.

—The Revenant. 2013. (ENG.). 354p. (YA). (gr. 7). pap. 9.99 (978-0-375-86139-0(4), Ember) Random Hse. Children's Bks.

Ghost of a Chance. 2014. (Girl Meets Ghost Ser.: 3). (ENG., Illus.). 240p. (J). (gr. 4-9). pap. 7.99 (978-1-4424-2148-6(7), Aladdin) Simon & Schuster Children's Publishing.

Gibbons, Alan. The Dying Photo. 2012. (Stoke Books Titles Ser.). 64p. (J). (gr. 5-8). pap. 7.95 (978-1-78112-020-0(X)); lib. bdg. 22.60 (978-1-78112-019-4(6)) Stoke Bks.

Gibson, Jo. Obsessed. 2014. (ENG.). 384p. (YA). (gr. 13). pap. 9.95 (978-1-61773-238-6(9), K-Teen) Kensington Publishing Corp.

Gibson, Marley. The Awakening. 2009. (ENG.). 352p. (YA). (gr. 7-18). pap. 19.99 (978-0-547-15093-2(8)) Houghton Mifflin Harcourt Publishing Co.

—The Counseling. 2010. (ENG.). 264p. (YA). (gr. 7). pap. 8.99 (978-0-547-39307-0(5)) Houghton Mifflin Harcourt Publishing Co.

—The Discovery. 2011. (ENG.). 264p. (YA). (gr. 7-18). pap. 8.99 (978-0-547-39308-7(3)) Houghton Mifflin Harcourt Publishing Co.

—The Guidance. 2009. (ENG.). 320p. (YA). (gr. 7-18). pap. 16.95 (978-0-547-15094-9(6)) Houghton Mifflin Harcourt Publishing Co.

—The Reason, Bk. 3. 2010. (ENG.). 240p. (YA). (gr. 7-18). pap. 8.99 (978-0-547-15095-6(4)) Houghton Mifflin Harcourt Publishing Co.

Giff, Patricia Reilly. Gingersnap. 2014. (ENG.). 160p. (J). (gr. 3-7). 6.99 (978-0-440-42178-8(0), Yearling) Random Hse. Children's Bks.

Gil, Carmen. Un Fantasma con Asma. Webster, Sarah, illus. 2004. (Libros para Sonar Ser.). (SPA.). 40p. (J). 15.99 (978-84-8464-186-5(4)) Kalandraka Editora, S.L. ESP. Dist: Lectorum Pubns., Inc.

Gilmore, Grace. The Ghost of Juniper Creek. Brown, Petra, illus. 2015. (Tales from Maple Ridge Ser.: 4). (ENG.). 128p. (J). (gr. k-4). pap. 5.99 (978-1-4814-3009-8(2), Little Simon) Little Simon.

Goldie, Sonia. Ghosts. Boutavant, Marc, illus. 2013. (ENG.). 40p. (J). (gr. -1-3). 16.95 (978-1-59270-142-1(6)) Enchanted Lion Bks., LLC.

Goodwin, Anne. No Business Like Ghost Business. 2010. 60p. pap. 14.95 (978-1-4520-7593-8(X)) AuthorHouse.

Goodwin, Vincent. Moonlit Road, 1 vol. 2014. (Graphic Horror Set 3 Ser.). (ENG.). 32p. (J). (gr. 5-8). lib. bdg. 28.50 (978-1-62402-016-2(X), Graphic Planet) Magic Wagon.

Gosselin, Jake & Gosselin, Laura. The Pinkaboos: Belladonna & the Nightmare Academy. 2016. (Pinkaboos Ser.: 2). (ENG.). 96p. (J). pap. 7.99 (978-1-4494-7832-2(8)) Andrews McMeel Publishing.

Grabenstein, Chris. The Black Heart Crypt. 2012. (Haunted Mystery Ser.: 4). (ENG.). 336p. (J). (gr. 3-7). 7.99 (978-0-375-87301-0(5), Yearling) Random Hse. Children's Bks.

—The Crossroads. 2009. (Haunted Mystery Ser.: 1). (ENG.). 352p. (J). (gr. 3-7). 7.99 (978-0-375-84698-4(0), Yearling) Random Hse. Children's Bks.

—The Hanging Hill. 2010. (Haunted Mystery Ser.: 2). (ENG.). 336p. (J). (gr. 3-7). pap. 6.99 (978-0-375-84700-4(6), Yearling) Random Hse. Children's Bks.

Grabo, Carl. The Cat in Grandfather's House. 2008. 120p. 23.95 (978-1-60664-842-1(X)); pap. 10.95 (978-1-60664-087-6(9)) Aegypan.

Graham, Denise R. Curse of the Lost Grove. 2005. (Knights of the Silver Dragon Ser.: Bk. 10). (Illus.). 177p. (J). (978-1-4156-3841-5(1), Mirrorstone) Wizards of the Coast.

Grant, John & Stocks, Mike. Classic Horror. 2004. 432p. (J). 12.95 (978-0-7945-0616-2(X), Usborne) EDC Publishing.

Graves, Annie. Guinea Pig Killer. McElhinney, Glenn, illus. 2015. (Nightmare Club Ser.: 4). (ENG.). 64p. (J). (gr. 2-5). pap. 6.99 (978-1-4677-6044-7(7)); lib. bdg. 25.32 (978-1-4677-4351-8(8)) Lerner Publishing Group.

Graves, Damien. Shut Your Mouth. 2007. (Midnight Library). 159p. (J). (gr. 4-7). 13.65 (978-0-7569-8313-0(4)) Perfection Learning Corp.

Gray, Claudia. Afterlife. 2012. (Evernight Ser.: 4). (ENG.). 384p. (YA). (gr. 8). pap. 9.99 (978-0-06-128451-9(3), HarperTeen) HarperCollins Pubs.

—Hourglass. 2011. (Evernight Ser.: 3). (ENG.). 368p. (YA). (gr. 8). pap. 8.99 (978-0-06-128448-9(3), HarperTeen) HarperCollins Pubs.

Gray, Keith. Ghosting. 2012. (Stoke Books Titles Ser.). (ENG.). 72p. (YA). (gr. 8-12). pap. 6.95 (978-1-78112-103-0(6)); lib. bdg. 22.60 (978-1-78112-104-7(4)) Lerner Publishing Group.

Green, Jim. The Ghost Dancer. 2007. (YA). pap. 15.95 (978-1-59705-923-7(4)) Wings ePress, Inc.

Griffin, Adele. Tighter. (ENG.). (YA). (gr. 7). 2012. 240p. pap. 8.99 (978-0-375-85933-5(0), Ember) 2011. 224p. 16.99 (978-0-375-86645-6(0), Knopf Bks. for Young Readers) Random Hse. Children's Bks.

Grigsby, Cynthia. Hollow Creek: A Haunted Beginning, 01. 2006. 163p. (J). 14.95 (978-0-9786840-0-6(1)) Grigsby, Cynthia.

Guerra, Elisa Puricelli. The Legend of Black Bart, 1 vol. Pernigotti, Chiara, tr. from ITA. Bernstein, Gabo León, illus. 2014. (Minerva Mint Ser.). (ENG.). 160p. (gr. 2-4). pap. 7.99 (978-1-4342-6515-9(3)) Capstone Young Readers of Coughlan Cos.

—The Legend of Black Bart, 1 vol. Pernigotti, Chiara, tr. from ITA. Bernstein, Gabo León, illus. 2014. (Minerva Mint Ser.). (ENG.). 160p. (gr. 2-4). 25.32 (978-1-4342-6512-8(9)) Stone Arch Bks.

Gunther, Joseph. The Bluff, 1. Sabiston, Susan, illus. l.t. ed. 2006. 28p. (J). 14.95 (978-0-9789525-0-1(2)) Young Readers Publications.

Gurney, Stella. Mr. Bickle & the Ghost. Raga, Silvia, illus. 2009. (Get Ready (Windmill Books) Ser.). 32p. (J). (gr. k-2). lib. bdg. 22.60 (978-1-60754-260-5(9)) Windmill Bks.

Gutteridge, Alex. No Going Back. 2016. (ENG.). 368p. (YA). (gr. 8). pap. 11.99 (978-1-84877-927-3(5)) Bonnier Publishing GBR. Dist: Independent Pubs. Group.

Hadcroft, Will. Anne Droyd & the Ghosts of Winter Hill. 2013. 210p. pap. (978-0-9560537-2-5(6)) Nordic.

Hahn, Mary Downing. All the Lovely Bad Ones. 2009. (ENG.). 192p. (J). (gr. 2-5). pap. 7.99 (978-0-547-24878-3(4)) Houghton Mifflin Harcourt Publishing Co.

—Deep & Dark & Dangerous. 2008. (ENG.). 192p. (J). (gr. 5-7). pap. 7.99 (978-0-547-07645-4(2)) Houghton Mifflin Harcourt Publishing Co.

—Deep & Dark & Dangerous: A Ghost Story. 2007. (ENG.). 192p. (J). (gr. 5-7). 16.99 (978-0-618-66545-7(5)) Houghton Mifflin Harcourt Publishing Co.

—The Doll in the Garden; The Old Willis Place. 2009. pap. 11.90 (978-0-547-37542-7(5)) Houghton Mifflin Harcourt Trade & Reference Pubs.

—The Ghost of Crutchfield Hall. (ENG.). 160p. (J). (gr. 5-7). 2011. pap. 6.99 (978-0-547-57715-9(X)) 2010. 17.00 (978-0-547-38560-0(9)) Houghton Mifflin Harcourt Publishing Co.

—A Haunting Collection by Mary Downing Hahn: Deep & Dark & Dangerous, All the Lovely Bad Ones, & Wait till Helen Comes. 2016. (ENG.). 576p. (J). (gr. 5-7). 15.99 (978-0-544-85452-9(7), HMH Books For Young Readers) Houghton Mifflin Harcourt Publishing Co.

—Look for Me by Moonlight. 2008. (ENG.). 208p. (YA). (gr. 7). pap. 7.99 (978-0-547-07616-4(9)) Houghton Mifflin Harcourt Publishing Co.

—The Old Willis Place. 2007. (ENG.). 208p. (J). (gr. 5-7). pap. 7.99 (978-0-618-89741-4(0)) Houghton Mifflin Harcourt Publishing Co.

—One for Sorrow: A Ghost Story. 2017. (ENG.). 304p. (J). (gr. 5-7). 16.99 (978-0-544-81809-5(1)) Houghton Mifflin Harcourt Publishing Co.

—Wait till Helen Comes: A Ghost Story. 2008. (ENG., Illus.). 192p. (J). (gr. 5-7). pap. 7.99 (978-0-547-02864-4(4)) Houghton Mifflin Harcourt Publishing Co.

Halam, Ann. The Shadow on the Stairs. 2012. (Stoke Books Titles Ser.). 64p. (J). (gr. 5-8). pap. 7.95 (978-1-78112-016-3(1)); pap. 45.32 (978-0-7613-9222-4(X)); lib. bdg. 22.60 (978-1-78112-015-6(3)) Stoke Bks.

Hall, Annalisa. Blanket of Comfort. 2008. 20p. 11.95 (978-0-615-22113-7(0)) Hall, Annalisa.

Hamilton, Martha & Weise, Mutch. Scared Witless: Thirteen Eerie Tales to Tell. Pope, Kevin, illus. 2015. (ENG.). 64p. (J). (gr. 3-6). pap. 8.95 (978-1-939160-95-9(2)) August Hse. Pubs., Inc.

Hamilton, Martha & Weiss, Mitch. The Ghost Catcher: A Bengali Folktale. Balouch, Kristen, illus. 2007. (ENG.). 32p. (J). (gr. -1-3). 16.95 (978-0-87483-835-0(5)) August Hse. Pubs., Inc.

Hamley, Dennis. The Ghosts Who Waited. 2005. 172p. (gr. -1-7). per. (978-1-904529-15-6(1), Back to Front) Solidus.

Hand, Cynthia. The Afterlife of Holly Chase. 2017. 400p. (YA). (gr. 8). 17.99 **(978-0-06-231850-3(0)**, HarperTeen) HarperCollins Pubs.

Hapka, Cathy, pseud. Mystery in the Whispering Woods. 2013. (LEGO Friends Chapter Bks.: 3). lib. bdg. 14.75 (978-0-606-32394-9(5), Turtleback) Turtleback Bks.

Hardegree, Maureen. Haint Misbehavin' 2010. 222p. pap. 12.95 (978-1-935661-93-1(0), Bell Bridge Bks.) BelleBks., Inc.

—Haint She Sweet. 2013. 206p. pap. 12.95 (978-1-61194-325-2(6), Bell Bridge Bks.) BelleBks., Inc.

—Hainted Love. 2011. 184p. pap. 12.95 (978-1-61194-014-5(1), Bell Bridge Bks.) BelleBks., Inc.

—If It Haint Broke. 2015. (ENG., Illus.). 196p. (J). pap. 12.95 (978-1-61194-597-3(6)) BelleBks., Inc.

Harness, Cheryl. Ghosts of the Civil War. Harness, Cheryl, illus. 2004. (ENG., Illus.). 48p. (J). (gr. 2-5). 8.99 (978-0-689-86992-1(4), Simon & Schuster Bks. For Young Readers) Simon & Schuster Bks. For Young Readers.

Harper, Suzanne. A Gust of Ghosts. (ENG.). 320p. (J). (gr. 3-7). 2075. 6.99 (978-0-06-199612-2(2)) 2012. (Unseen World of Poppy Malone Ser.: 2). 16.99 (978-0-06-199610-8(6)) HarperCollins Pubs. (Greenwillow Bks.).

Harrington, Kim. The Dead & Buried. 2013. (ENG.). 304p. (J). (gr. 7). 17.99 (978-0-545-33302-3(4)) Scholastic, Inc.

Harris, Ashley Rae. The Prank. 2011. (Night Fall Ser.). (ENG.). 120p. (YA). (gr. 6-12). pap. 7.95 (978-0-7613-7814-3(6)); lib. bdg. 27.93 (978-0-7613-7747-4(6)) Lerner Publishing Group.

Harvey, Pam & Panckridge, Michael. Ghost of a Chance. 2007. 208p. (978-0-207-20063-2(7)) HarperCollins Pubs. Australia.

The Haunted House. 2007. (Choose Your Own Adventure Ser.). (Illus.). 80p. (J). (gr. 4-7). pap. 7.99 (978-1-933390-51-2(4)) Chooseco LLC.

Hawkins, Rachel. Demonglass. 2012. (ENG.). 384p. (YA). (gr. 6-17). pap. 8.99 (978-1-4231-2844-1(3)) Hyperion Pr.

Hayes, Denis. Silly Ghost Stories for Kids. 2014. 100p. pap. 36.15 (978-1-4828-9440-0(8)) Partridge Pub.

Hayes, Joe. Ghost Fever (Mal de Fantasma) 2006. (ENG & SPA., Illus.). 90p. (J). (gr. 4-6). pap. 8.95 (978-1-933693-03-3(7)) Cinco Puntos Pr.

—Ghost Fever (Mal de Fantasma) Pennypacker, Mona, illus. 2004. (ENG & SPA.). 80p. (J). (gr. 4-6). 14.95 (978-0-938317-83-8(0)) Cinco Puntos Pr.

Hegarty, Patricia. Five Little Ghosts. Woolf, Julia, illus. 2014. (ENG.). 22p. (J). (gr. -1-k). bds. 8.99 (978-1-58925-587-6(9)) Tiger Tales.

Hegarty, Shane. Darkmouth #1: the Legends Begin. 2016. (Darkmouth Ser.: 1). 432p. (J). (gr. 3-7). pap. 7.99 (978-0-06-231130-6(1)) HarperCollins Pubs.

—Darkmouth #2: Worlds Explode. de la Rue, James, illus. 2016. (Darkmouth Ser.: 2). 464p. (J). (gr. 3-7). 17.99 (978-0-06-231132-0(8)) HarperCollins Pubs.

Hendry, Diana. Harvey Angel y la Nina Fantasma. Alban, Rafael Segovia, tr. Morin, Mauricio Gomez, illus. 2003. (la Orilla Del Viento Ser.). (SPA.). 166p. (J). reprint ed. pap., pap. 7.50 (978-968-16-6723-8(9)) Fondo de Cultura Economica USA.

Henn, Pamela. Nick & Slim: The Legend of the Falcon Mine. 2006. (Illus.). 472p. (YA). 19.95 (978-0-9760654-0-1(1)) White Wolf Studio, Inc.

Hermes, Patricia. Emma Dilemma, the Nanny, & the Secret Ferret, 0 vols. Carter, Abby, illus. 2010. (Emma Dilemma Ser.: 5). (ENG.). 112p. (J). (gr. 3-6). 15.99 (978-0-7614-5650-6(3), 9780761456506, Amazon Children's Publishing) Amazon Publishing.

Heyliger, William. Jerry Hicks, Ghost Hunter. Salg, Bert, illus. 2011. 210p. 44.95 (978-1-258-08870-5(3)) Literary Licensing, LLC.

Hicks, Faith Erin. Friends with Boys. Hicks, Faith Erin, illus. 2012. (ENG., Illus.). 224p. (YA). (gr. 7-11). pap. 16.99 (978-1-59643-556-8(9), 9781596435568, First Second Bks.) Roaring Brook Pr.

Hicks, John B. The Ghost of Fire Company 18. 2005. 149p. (J). per. 6.50 (978-0-9742829-2-3(8)) Quiet Man Publishing.

Higgins, M. G. The Lost House. 2014. (Red Rhino Ser.). (J). lib. bdg. 18.40 (978-0-606-36202-3(9)) Turtleback Bks.

Higgins, Nadia. Pegleg Gets Stumped, 1 vol. Holder, Jimmy, illus. 2008. (Barnacle Barb & Her Pirate Crew Ser.). (ENG.). 32p. (gr. -1-3). 28.50 (978-1-60270-093-2(1), Looking Glass Library) ABDO Publishing Co.

High, Linda Oatman. Ghost Girl [3]. 2017. (TERL Boosters Ser.). (ENG.). 64p. (YA). (gr. 9-12). pap. 7.95 **(978-1-68021-158-0(7))** Saddleback Educational Publishing, Inc.

Hightman, J. P. Spirit. 2008. 224p. (gr. 7-18). (ENG.). (J). 16.99 (978-0-06-085063-0(9)); (YA). lib. bdg. 17.89 (978-0-06-085064-7(7)) HarperCollins Pubs. (HarperTeen).

Hilburn, Dora. Between. 2015. 247p. (YA). pap. (978-1-56825-175-2(0)) Rainbow Bks., Inc.

Hilson, R. Phantoms of the Fort. 2004. 164p. (J). 23.95 (978-0-595-66757-4(0)) iUniverse, Inc.

Hirschmann, Kris & Langdo, Bryan, illus. We're Going on a Ghost Hunt. 2011. (J). (978-0-545-34173-8(6)) Scholastic, Inc.

Hitchcock, Fleur. Ghosts on Board. (Shrunk! Adventure Ser.: 3). (ENG., Illus.). 192p. (J). 2016. (gr. 3-7). pap. 9.99 (978-1-84812-483-7(X)) 2015. (gr. 4-7). pap. 7.99 (978-1-4714-0346-0(7)) Bonnier Publishing GBR. Dist: Independent Pubs. Group.

Hodder, Beth. The Ghost of Schafer Meadows. 2007. (J). per. 7.99 (978-0-9793963-0-4(1)) Grizzly Ridge Publishing.

Hoena, Blake & Hoena, Blake A. The Ghost Trap. Bardin, Dave, illus. 2016. (Monster Heroes Ser.). (ENG.). 32p. (gr. 1-2). lib. bdg. 21.32 (978-1-4965-3757-7(2)) Stone Arch Bks.

Holder, Nancy. The Screaming Season. 3rd ed. 2011. (Possessions Ser.). (ENG.). 336p. (YA). (gr. 7-18). 9.99 (978-1-59514-333-4(5), Razorbill) Penguin Young Readers Group.

Holland, Robert. The Ghost Who Came to Tea: A Novel of Sports & Mystery. 2006. (Illus.). 204p. (J). (978-0-9794273-4-3(7)) Frost Hollow Pubs., LLC.

Holmes, Fay. The Happy Little Ghost: A Halloween Tale. Holmes, Fay, illus. 2003. (Illus.). 20p. (J). (gr. 1-3). pap. 5.00 (978-0-9674241-4-9(3)) IZA Publishing Co.

Hooper, Mary. The Ghoul at School. Harker, Lesley, illus. 2008. (Two Naughty Angels Ser.). (ENG.). 96p. (J). (gr. 2-4). pap. 11.95 (978-0-7475-9060-6(5)) Bloomsbury Publishing Plc GBR. Dist: Independent Pubs. Group.

Hope, Kathleen. Jack Eagle the Pirate & Other Mysterious Tales. 2012. (Illus.). 48p. pap. 24.40 (978-1-4678-9611-5(X)) AuthorHouse.

Hope, Laura. The Bobbsey Twins. 2005. pap. 14.95 (978-1-55742-523-2(X)) Wildside Pr., LLC.

Hope, Laura Lee. The Outdoor Girls in a Motor Car. 2007. 180p. 26.95 (978-1-4218-3284-5(4)); per. 11.95 (978-1-4218-3384-2(0)) 1st World Publishing, Inc. (1st World Library - Literary Society).

Hope, Lee Laura. The Outdoor Girls in a Motor Car: The Haunted Mansion of Shadow Valley. 2007. (ENG.). 134p. pap. 18.99 (978-1-4346-3200-5(8)); 150p. pap. 19.99 (978-1-4346-3201-2(6)) Creative Media Partners, LLC.

Hopkins, Howard. The Nightmare Club #2: the Deadly Dragon. 2009. 104p. pap. 9.98 (978-0-578-00320-7(1)) Golden Perils Pr.

Howe, James. The Fright Before Christmas. Mack, Jeff, illus. (Bunnicula & Friends Ser.: 5). (ENG.). 48p. (J). (gr. 1-3). 2007. pap. 3.99 (978-0-689-86941-9(X)) 2006. 16.99 (978-0-689-86939-6(8)) Simon Spotlight. (Simon Spotlight).

Howe, Katherine. The Appearance of Annie Van Sinderen. 2015. (ENG.). 400p. (YA). (gr. 7). 18.99 (978-0-399-16778-2(1), G.P. Putnam's Sons Books for Young Readers) Penguin Young Readers Group.

Howland, Ashley. Ghostnapped. 2009. 64p. pap. 9.99 (978-1-60860-145-5(5), Strategic Bk. Publishing) Strategic Book Publishing & Rights Agency (SBPRA).

Hudson, Tara. Hereafter. 2012. (Hereafter Trilogy Ser.: 1). (ENG.). 432p. (YA). (gr. 8). pap. 8.99 (978-0-06-202678-1(X), HarperTeen) HarperCollins Pubs.

Hummel, Jim. The Hunters. 2010. 36p. 15.49 (978-1-4269-4216-7(8)) Trafford Publishing.

Hunter, C. C. Taken at Dusk. 2012. (Shadow Falls Novel Ser.: 3). (ENG.). 400p. (YA). (gr. 7-12). pap. 10.99 (978-0-312-62469-9(7), 9780312624699, St. Martin's Griffin) St. Martin's Pr.

—Taken at Dusk: A Shadow Falls Novel. 2013. (Shadow Falls Novel Ser.: 3). (ENG.). 400p. (YA). (gr. 7-12). mass mkt. 9.99 (978-1-250-04681-9(5), 9781250046819, St. Martin's Paperbacks) St. Martin's Pr.

Hurley, Tonya. Ghostgirl. 2010. (Ghostgirl Ser.: 1). (ENG.). 336p. (YA). (gr. 7-17). pap. 9.99 (978-0-316-03635-1(8)) Little, Brown Bks. for Young Readers.

—Ghostgirl. Frieyro, Alicia, tr. Impey, Allison & Phillips, Craig, illus. 2009. (SPA.). 1200p. (YA). (gr. 8-12). pap. 19.99 (978-607-11-0185-3(9), Alfaguara Juvenil) Santillana USA Publishing Co., Inc.

—Homecoming. 2010. (Ghostgirl Ser.: 2). (ENG.). 304p. (YA). (gr. 7-17). pap. 10.00 (978-0-316-08943-2(5)) Little, Brown Bks. for Young Readers.

—Lovesick. 2011. (Ghostgirl Ser.: 3). (ENG.). 320p. (YA). (gr. 7-17). pap., pap. 9.99 (978-0-316-13316-6(7)) Little, Brown Bks. for Young Readers.

Hutchison, Dot. A Wounded Name. 2013. 320p. 17.95 (978-1-4677-1618-5(9)); (ENG.). (YA). (gr. 7-12). 17.95 (978-1-4677-0887-6(9), Carolrhoda Lab™) Lerner Publishing Group.

Hutton, Clare. Zombie Dog. 2012. (Rotten Apple Ser.: Vol. 2). (ENG.). 192p. (J). (gr. 3-7). pap. 5.99 (978-0-545-39824-4(X), Scholastic Paperbacks) Scholastic, Inc.

Ibbotson, Eva. Dial-a-Ghost. Hawkes, Kevin, illus. 2003. (ENG.). 224p. (J). (gr. 3-7). pap. 6.99 (978-0-14-250018-7(6), Puffin Books) Penguin Young Readers Group.

—The Great Ghost Rescue. Hawkes, Kevin, illus. 2003. (ENG.). 192p. (J). (gr. 3-7). pap. 6.99 (978-0-14-250087-3(9), Puffin Books) Penguin Young Readers Group.

Ikaris, Despoina. The Little Red Jacket: A True Almost Christmas Almost Mystery Almost Ghost Story for Children And Certain Grown-Ups. 2008. 48p. pap. 10.99 (978-1-60647-898-1(2)) Salem Author Services.

Imfeld, Robert. Baylor's Guide to the Other Side. 2016. (Beyond Baylor Ser.: 1). (ENG., Illus.). 320p. (J). (gr. 5-9). 16.99 (978-1-4814-6636-3(4), Aladdin) Simon & Schuster Children's Publishing.

Ireland, Kenneth. Noises in the Night. 2004. 126p. (J). 5.00 (978-1-84161-031-3(3)) Ravette Publishing, Ltd. GBR. Dist: Parkwest Pubns., Inc.

Irvine, Patricia McCune. Haunted Pavilion: And Other Short Stories. 2003. 144p. 21.95 (978-0-595-75249-2(7)) iUniverse, Inc.

Irving, Washington. The Legend of Sleepy Hollow. Van Nutt, Robert, illus. 2005. (Rabbit Ears Ser.). 36p. (J). (gr. k-5). 25.65 (978-1-59679-225-8(6)) Spotlight.

—Washington Irving. Hall, Tracy, illus. 2004. (Great American Short Stories Ser.). 80p. (gr. 4-7). lib. bdg. 24.00 (978-0-8368-4253-1(7), Gareth Stevens Learning Library) Stevens, Gareth Publishing LLLP.

Irving, Washington & Gutierrez, Dave. La Leyenda Del Jinete Sin Cabeza, 1 vol. Tobon, Sara, tr. from ENG. Smith, Tod G., illus. 2009. (Classic Fiction Ser.). (SPA.). 72p. (gr. 2-3). lib. bdg. 27.99 (978-1-4342-1688-5(8), Graphic Revolve en Español) Stone Arch Bks.

Isaacs, Anne. The Ghosts of Luckless Gulch. Santat, Dan, illus. 2008. (ENG.). 48p. (J). (gr. k-3). 18.99 (978-1-4169-0201-0(5), Atheneum Bks. for Young Readers) Simon & Schuster Children's Publishing.

J. Katyn. Boo & the Halloween Grin. 2011. 36p. pap. (978-1-4269-7197-6(4)) Trafford Publishing (UK) Ltd.

Jackson, A. H. The Adventures of Pinkin Rasbury, 1 vol. 2015. (ENG.). 160p. (YA). pap. 9.95 **(978-0-9866546-7-1(1)**, 9780986654671) Dragon Hill Publishing CAN. Dist: Lone Pine Publishing USA.

Jaffrey, Alizeh. The Silly Ghost 2004. (Illus.). 24p. (J). per. 10.00 (978-0-9753673-0-8(7)) Jaffrey, Kamal.

James, Henry. The Turn of the Screw. 2009. (Foundation Classics Ser.). (Illus.). 56p. (J). (gr. 5-9). lib. bdg. 27.95 (978-1-60754-851-5(8)) Windmill Bks.

Jenkins, A. M. Repossessed. 2007. 224p. (J). (gr. 7). lib. bdg. 16.89 (978-0-06-083569-9(9), HarperTeen) HarperCollins Pubs.

Jennings, Richard W. Scribble. 2004. (ENG.). 160p. (YA). (gr. 5-9). tchr. ed. 15.00 (978-0-618-43367-4(8)) Houghton Mifflin Harcourt Publishing Co.

Jennings, Sharon. Franklin's Pond Phantom. McIntyre, Sasha et al, illus. 2005. 32p. (J). lib. bdg. 15.38 (978-1-4242-1181-4(6)) Fitzgerald Bks.

Jensen, Michael & King, David Powers. Woven. 2015. (ENG., Illus.). 352p. (J). (gr. 7). 18.99 (978-0-545-68572-6(9), Scholastic Pr.) Scholastic, Inc.

Jessell, Tim, illus. The Return of the Graveyard Ghost. 2013. (Boxcar Children Mysteries Ser.: 133). (ENG.). 128p. (J). (gr. 1-5). 15.99 (978-0-8075-6935-1(6)); 5.99 (978-0-8075-6936-8(4)) Whitman, Albert & Co.

Jessup, VonDa. Wanda the Witch at the Happy Haunted House. 2008. (Illus.). 44p. pap. 18.50 (978-1-60693-149-3(0), Eloquent Bks.) Strategic Book Publishing & Rights Agency (SBPRA).

Jinks, Catherine. Eloise. 2007. (Allie's Ghost Hunters Ser.: Bk. 3). (ENG.). 180p. (Orig.). (J). (gr. 4-7). pap. 11.99 (978-1-74114-659-2(3)) Allen & Unwin AUS. Dist: Independent Pubs. Group.

—Eustace. 2007. (Allie's Ghost Hunters Ser.: Bk. 2). (ENG.). 168p. (J). (gr. 4-7). pap. 11.99 (978-1-74114-660-8(7)) Allen & Unwin AUS. Dist: Independent Pubs. Group.

Johnson, Maureen. The Madness Underneath. 2013. (Shades of London Ser.: 2). (ENG.). 304p. (YA). (gr. 7). pap. 9.99 (978-0-14-242754-5(3), Speak) Penguin Young Readers Group.

—The Name of the Star. (Shades of London Ser.: 1). (ENG.). (YA). (gr. 7). 2012. 400p. pap. 10.99 (978-0-14-242205-2(3), Speak) 2011. 368p. 16.99 (978-0-399-25660-8(1), G.P. Putnam's Sons Books for Young Readers) Penguin Young Readers Group.

Johnson, Sandi, et al. Haunted Doghouse II: Halloween Night, 3 vols., bk. 2. Durant, Sybrina, ed. Stargeon, Bobbi, illus. l.t. ed. 2014. (ENG.). 36p. (J). (gr. k-5). pap. 12.99 (978-1-929063-27-7(X), 351) Moons & Stars Publishing For Children.

Johnston, K. E. M. The Witness Tree & the Shadow of the Noose: Mystery, Lies, & Spies in Manassas. 2009. 111p. (J). (gr. 5-7). pap. 8.95 (978-1-57249-397-1(6), White Mane Kids) White Mane Publishing Co., Inc.

Jones, Gareth P. Constable & Toop. 2013. (ENG.). 416p. (J). (gr. 3-7). 17.95 (978-1-4197-0782-7(5), Amulet Bks.) Abrams, Inc.

Jones, Marcia Thornton. A Very Haunted Holiday. 2006. (Ghostville Elementary Ser.: Bk. 15). (Illus.). 67p. (J). pap. (978-0-439-88361-0(X)) Scholastic, Inc.

Jones, Marcia Thornton & Dadey, Debbie. Guys & Ghouls. Francis, Guy, illus. 2006. (Ghostville Elementary Ser.: Bk. 13). 81p. (978-0-439-79402-2(1)) Scholastic, Inc.

Kade, Stacey. The Ghost & the Goth. 2011. (ENG.). 304p. (J). (gr. 7-17). pap. 8.99 (978-1-4231-2487-0(1)) Hyperion Pr.

Kasischke, Laura. Boy Heaven. 2006. 275p. (YA). (gr. 9-12). 16.99 (978-0-06-081314-7(8)); lib. bdg. 17.89 (978-0-06-081315-4(6)) HarperCollins Pubs. (HarperTeen).

Keeley, Catherine. The Secrets of Phantom Valley. 2003. 101p. (YA). pap. 10.95 (978-0-7414-1831-9(2)) Infinity Publishing.

Keenan, Sheila & Stine, R. L. Scary Summer. Haspiel, Dean et al, illus. 2007. (Goosebumps Graphix Ser.: 3). (ENG.). 144p. (J). (gr. 3-7). pap. 9.99 (978-0-439-85782-6(1)) Scholastic, Inc.

Keene, Carolyn. The Ghost of Grey Fox Inn. 2016. (Nancy Drew Diaries: 13). (ENG., Illus.). 192p. (J). (gr. 3-7). pap. 6.99 (978-1-4814-6595-3(3), Aladdin) Simon & Schuster Children's Publishing.

—Ghost Stories. 2008. (Nancy Drew (All New) Girl Detective Ser.). (ENG.). 240p. (J). (gr. 3-7). pap. 5.99 (978-1-4169-5909-0(2), Aladdin) Simon & Schuster Children's Publishing.

Kehret, Peg. Ghost Dog Secrets. 2011. (ENG.). 192p. (J). (gr. 5-18). 6.99 (978-0-14-241964-9(8), Puffin Books) Penguin Young Readers Group.

—Ghost Followed Us Home. 2008. (ENG.). 128p. (J). (gr. 3-7). pap. 7.99 (978-1-4169-9110-6(7), Simon & Schuster/Paula Wiseman Bks.) Simon & Schuster/Paula Wiseman Bks.

—The Ghost's Grave. 2007. 224p. pap. 5.99 (978-0-14-280819-1(9), Puffin) Penguin Publishing Group.

—The Ghost's Grave. 2007. (ENG.). 224p. (J). (gr. 5-18). 6.99 (978-0-14-240819-3(0), Puffin Books) Penguin Young Readers Group.

Kelley, Jane. The Girl Behind the Glass. 2012. (ENG.). 192p. (J). (gr. 4-7). pap. 6.99 (978-0-375-86219-9(6), Yearling) Random Hse. Children's Bks.

Kelly, David A. The Pinstripe Ghost. Meyers, Mark, illus. 2011. (Ballpark Mysteries Ser.: 2). (ENG.). 112p. (J). (gr. 1-4). 4.99 (978-0-375-86704-0(X), Random Hse. Bks. for Young Readers) Random Hse. Children's Bks.

Kennedy, Kim. Misty Gordon & the Mystery of the Ghost Pirates. 2010. (ENG., Illus.). 240p. (YA). (gr. 3-7). 15.95 (978-0-8109-9357-0(0), Amulet Bks.) Abrams, Inc.

Kerbel, Deborah. Lure. 2010. (ENG.). 200p. (YA). (gr. 9). pap. 12.99 (978-1-55488-754-5(2)) Dundurn CAN. Dist: Ingram Publisher Services.

Kerns, Ann. I Date Dead People. Gorman, Mike & Görrissen, Janina, illus. 2012. (My Boyfriend Is a Monster Ser.: 5). (ENG.). 128p. (YA). (gr. 7-12). pap. 9.95 (978-0-7613-8549-3(5), Graphic Universe™) Lerner Publishing Group.

—I Date Dead People. Görrissen, Janina, illus. 2012. (My Boyfriend Is a Monster Ser.: 5). (ENG.). 128p. (YA). (gr. 7-12). lib. bdg. 29.27 (978-0-7613-6007-0(7)) Lerner Publishing Group.

Kerr, P. B., pseud. The Day of the Djinn Warriors. 2008. (Children of the Lamp Ser.: 4). (ENG.). 400p. (J). (gr. 3-7). 7.99 (978-0-439-93216-5(5), Scholastic Paperbacks) Scholastic, Inc.

Kerr, Philip. The Most Frightening Story Ever Told. 2016. (ENG.). 320p. (J). (gr. 3-7). 16.99 (978-0-553-52209-9(4), Knopf Bks. for Young Readers) Random Hse. Children's Bks.

Kimmel, Elizabeth Cody. Legend of the Ghost Dog. (J). 2014. (ENG.). 208p. (gr. 3-7). pap. 6.99 (978-0-545-39128-3(8))

2012. 200p. pap. (978-0-545-50705-9(7)) Scholastic, Inc. (Scholastic Pr.).

—ParaNormaN. 2012. (ENG.). (J). (gr. 4-7). 64.99 (978-1-61969-450-7(6)) Findaway World, LLC.

—ParaNorman: A Novel. 2013. (ENG., Illus.). 256p. (J). (gr. 3-7). pap. 6.99 (978-0-316-20987-8(2)) Little, Brown Bks. for Young Readers.

King, Daren. Frightfully Friendly Ghosties: School of Meanies. Roberts, David, illus. 2014. (ENG.). 128p. (J). (gr. k-3). 12.99 (978-1-62365-349-1(5), Quercus) Quercus NA.

Kline, C. A. The Fright Night Series. 2010. 88p. pap. 11.00 (978-1-4490-3795-6(X)) AuthorHouse.

—The Fright Night Series: Elizabeth Kind & the Strange Things. 2007. pap. 10.00 (978-0-8059-8619-8(7)) Dorrance Publishing Co., Inc.

Kline, Trish & Donev, Mary. The Ghost Hunter & the Ghost of the Amazon Warrior. Droney, John, illus. 2003. 96p. (J). per. 7.50 (978-0-9717234-1-2(9)) Ghost Hunter Productions.

Klise, Kate. Dying to Meet You. Klise, M. Sarah, illus. (43 Old Cemetery Road Ser.: Bk. 1). (ENG.). 160p. (J). (gr. 2-5). 2010. pap. 6.99 (978-0-547-39848-8(4)) 2009. 16.99 (978-0-15-205727-5(7)) Houghton Mifflin Harcourt Publishing Co.

—Greetings from the Graveyard. Klise, M. Sarah, illus. (43 Old Cemetery Road Ser.). (ENG.). 160p. (J). (gr. 2-5). 2015. pap. 6.99 (978-0-544-54010-1(7)) 2014. 15.99 (978-0-544-10567-6(2)) Houghton Mifflin Harcourt Publishing Co. (HMH Books For Young Readers).

—Hollywood, Dead Ahead. Klise, M. Sarah, illus. (43 Old Cemetery Road Ser.: 5). (ENG.). 144p. (J). (gr. 2-5). 2014. pap. 6.99 (978-0-544-33661-2(5), HMH Books For Young Readers) 2013. 15.99 (978-0-547-85283-6(5)) Houghton Mifflin Harcourt Publishing Co.

—The Loch Ness Punster. Klise, M. Sarah, illus. 2016. (43 Old Cemetery Road Ser.: 7). (ENG.). 144p. (J). (gr. 2-5). pap. 6.99 (978-0-544-81085-3(6), HMH Books For Young Readers) Houghton Mifflin Harcourt Publishing Co.

—Over My Dead Body. Klise, M. Sarah, illus. (43 Old Cemetery Road Ser.: Bk. 2). (ENG.). 128p. (J). (gr. 2-5). 2011. pap. 6.99 (978-0-547-57713-5(3)) 2009. 15.99 (978-0-15-205734-3(X)) Houghton Mifflin Harcourt Publishing Co.

—The Phantom of the Post Office. Klise, M. Sarah, illus. (43 Old Cemetery Road Ser.: 4). (ENG.). 160p. (J). (gr. 2-5). 2013. pap. 6.99 (978-0-544-02281-2(5)) 2012. 16.99 (978-0-547-51974-6(5)) Houghton Mifflin Harcourt Publishing Co.

—The Phantom of the Post Office. 2013. (43 Old Cemetery Road Ser.: 4). lib. bdg. 17.20 (978-0-606-31668-2(X), Turtleback) Turtleback Bks.

—Till Death Do Us Bark. 2012. (43 Old Cemetery Road Ser.: 3). lib. bdg. 17.20 (978-0-606-26543-0(0), Turtleback) Turtleback Bks.

Klise, Kate & Klise, M. Sarah. Till Death Do Us Bark. Klise, Kate & Klise, M. Sarah, illus. 2011. (43 Old Cemetery Road Ser.: 3). (ENG., Illus.). 144p. (J). (gr. 2-5). 16.99 (978-0-547-40036-5(5)) Houghton Mifflin Harcourt Publishing Co.

Kochalka, James. The Best Little Ghost in the World! 2008. (Johnny Boo Ser.: 1). (ENG., Illus.). 40p. (J). (gr. 2-5). 9.95 (978-1-60309-013-1(4), 9781603090131) Top Shelf Productions.

—Johnny Boo Meets Dragon Puncher. 2015. (Johnny Boo Ser.). (ENG., Illus.). 40p. (J). (gr. 2-5). 9.99 (978-1-60309-368-2(0), 9781603093682) Top Shelf Productions.

—The Mean Little Boy. 2010. (Johnny Boo Ser.: 4). (ENG., Illus.). 40p. (J). (gr. 2-5). 9.95 (978-1-60309-059-9(2), 9781603090599) Top Shelf Productions.

Kohara, Kazuno. Ghosts in the House! Kohara, Kazuno, illus. 2012. (ENG., Illus.). 26p. (J). (gr. -1 — 1). bds. 7.99 (978-1-59643-725-8(1), 9781596437258) Roaring Brook Pr.

—Ghosts in the House! Kohara, Kazuno, illus. 2010. (ENG., Illus.). 32p. (J). (gr. -1-1). pap. 7.99 (978-0-312-60886-6(1), 9780312608866) Square Fish.

Kooi, Jason. Hunter's Legacy: Cause. 2008. 256p. pap. 16.95 (978-0-595-52910-0(0)) iUniverse, Inc.

Kornher-Stace, Nicole. Archivist Wasp: A Novel. 2015. (ENG.). 256p. (YA). (gr. 6). pap. 14.00 (978-1-61873-097-8(5), Big Mouth Hse.) Small Beer Pr.

Kostro, Ed. Mystery of Madera Canyon. 2004. 108p. (gr. -1-7). per. 11.95 (978-1-59113-622-4(9)) Booklocker.com, Inc.

Krensky, Stephen. The Tale of la Llorona: A Mexican Folktale. 2009. pap. 40.95 (978-0-7613-4819-1(0)) Lerner Publishing Group.

Krishnaswami, Uma & Bhabha, Shiraaz. The Closet Ghosts. Bhabha, Shiraaz, illus. 2013. (ENG., Illus.). 32p. (J). (gr. 2). 16.95 (978-0-89239-208-7(8)) Lee & Low Bks., Inc.

Lachenmeyer, Nathaniel. The Boo! Book. Ceccoli, Nicoletta, illus. 2012. (ENG.). 46p. (J). (gr. -1-3). 17.99 (978-1-4169-3513-1(4), Atheneum Bks. for Young Readers) Simon & Schuster Children's Publishing.

Lambert, Shirley. Tales of Beaver Hollow: The Magic Flute, 1 vol. 2009. 31p. pap. 24.95 (978-1-60836-705-4(3)) America Star Bks.

Landry, Leo. Trick or Treat. 2012. (ENG., Illus.). 32p. (J). (gr. -1-3). 12.99 (978-0-547-24969-8(1)) Houghton Mifflin Harcourt Publishing Co.

Landy, Derek. Scepter of the Ancients. Percival, Tom, illus. 2009. (Skulduggery Pleasant Ser.: Bk. 1). (ENG.). 416p. (J). pap. 3.99 (978-0-06-173155-6(2), Harper Trophy) HarperCollins Pubs.

Langley, Jan. The Captain & Harry: A Trembling Tail of Thieves. Robinson, Susan, illus. 2006. 30p. (J). (gr. 4-7). pap. 10.95 (978-1-892384-23-2(X)) Avery Color Studios, Inc.

Larbalestier, Justine. Razorhurst. 2016. (ENG.). 336p. (YA). (gr. 9). pap. 10.99 (978-1-61695-625-7(9), Soho Teen) Soho Pr., Inc.

Larsen, Kirsten & National Geographic Learning Staff. The Ghost Town Mystery. Smath, Jerry, illus. 2010. (Rise & Shine Ser.). (ENG.). 32p. (C). (gr. -1-3). pap. 9.95 (978-1-57565-257-3(9)) National Geographic School Publishing, Inc.

Larson, Kirsten. The Ghost Town Mystery. 2008. pap. 34.95 (978-1-58013-773-7(3)) Kane Press, Inc.

Lasky, Kathryn. Double Trouble Squared. 2008. (ENG., Illus.). 240p. (J). (gr. 2-5). pap. 14.99 (978-0-15-205878-4(8)) Houghton Mifflin Harcourt Publishing Co.

—A Voice in the Wind. 2008. (ENG., Illus.). 272p. (J). (gr. 2-5). pap. 15.95 (978-0-15-205875-3(3)) Houghton Mifflin Harcourt Publishing Co.

Last, Mary. The Ghost of Dark Swamp Road. 2011. 108p. pap. 7.95 (978-1-257-13238-6(5)) Lulu Pr., Inc.

Le Fanu, J. Sheridan. Madam Crowl's Ghost & the Dead Sexton. 2004. reprint ed. pap. 1.99 (978-1-4192-3188-9(X)); pap. 15.95 (978-1-4191-3188-2(5)) Kessinger Publishing, LLC.

Legrand, Claire. The Year of Shadows. Kwasny, Karl, illus. 2013. (ENG.). 416p. (J). (gr. 3-7). 16.99 (978-1-4424-4294-8(8), Simon & Schuster Bks. For Young Readers) Simon & Schuster Bks. For Young Readers.

Leloup, Roger. The Prey & the Ghost. 2009. (Yoko Tsuno Ser.: 3). (ENG., Illus.). 48p. pap. 11.95 (978-1-905460-56-4(2)) CineBook GBR. Dist: National Bk. Network.

Leroux, Gaston. The Phantom of the Opera, 1 vol. Fisher, Scott, illus. 2011. (Calico Illustrated Classics Ser.). (ENG.). 112p. (J). (gr. 3-6). 27.07 (978-1-60270-749-8(9)) Magic Wagon.

Levithan, David. Marly's Ghost. Selznick, Brian, illus. 2007. (ENG.). 208p. (YA). (gr. 7-18). 7.99 (978-0-14-240912-1(X), Speak) Penguin Young Readers Group.

Lewman, David. Who You Gonna Call? 2016. (Simon & Schuster Ready-To-Read Level 3 Ser.). lib. bdg. 13.55 (978-0-606-38995-2(4)) Turtleback Bks.

Lim, Rebecca. Afterlight. 2016. (ENG., Illus.). 240p. (gr. 8). 11.95 (978-1-925240-49-8(5)) Text Publishing Co. AUS. Dist: Consortium Bk. Sales & Distribution.

Lindsey, Mary. Fragile Spirits. 2014. (ENG.). 320p. (YA). (gr. 7). 17.99 (978-0-399-16186-5(4), Philomel Bks.) Penguin Young Readers Group.

—Shattered Souls. 2012. (ENG.). 356p. (YA). (gr. 9). pap. 8.99 (978-0-14-242190-1(1), Speak) Penguin Young Readers Group.

Little, Kimberley Griffiths. Circle of Secrets. 2011. 326p. (J). (978-0-545-38523-7(7), Scholastic Pr.) Scholastic, Inc.

Lockwood, Vicki. The Magnificent Lizzie Brown & the Devil's Hound, 1 vol. 2014. (Magnificent Lizzie Brown Ser.). (ENG., Illus.). 200p. (gr. 5-9). lib. bdg. 26.65 (978-1-4342-7941-5(3)) Stone Arch Bks.

Loiske, Jennifer. Black Diamond. 2013. 246p. (J). pap. 13.61 (978-1-291-30145-8(3)) Lulu Pr., Inc.

Lord, Cynthia. Hot Rod Hamster & the Haunted Halloween Party. Anderson, Derek & Paprocki, Greg, illus. 2015. (Scholastic Reader, Level 2 Ser.). (ENG.). 32p. (J). (gr. k-2). pap. 3.99 (978-0-545-81528-4(2), Scholastic Pr.) Scholastic, Inc.

—Hot Rod Hamster & the Haunted Halloween Party! Anderson, Derek, illus. 2015. (ENG.). 32p. (J). (gr. -1-3). 16.99 (978-0-545-81529-1(0), Scholastic Pr.) Scholastic, Inc.

Lorimer, Janet. The Woman Who Loved a Ghost, 1 vol. unabr. ed. 2010. (Q Reads Ser.). (ENG.). 32p. (YA). (gr. 9-12). pap. 6.95 (978-1-61651-207-1(5)) Saddleback Educational Publishing, Inc.

Lowenstein, Sallie. Waiting for Eugene. Lowenstein, Sallie, illus. 2005. (Illus.). 208p. (J). 19.00 (978-0-9658486-5-7(5)) Lion Stone Bks.

Lowery, Linda. The Tale of la Llorona: A Mexican Folktale. 2008. 48p. (J). pap. 6.95 (978-0-8225-6743-1(1), First Avenue Editions) Lerner Publishing Group.

—Truth & Salsa, 1 vol. (ENG.). 176p. (J). 2009. pap. 7.95 (978-1-56145-498-3(2)) 2006. (gr. 3-7). 15.95 (978-1-56145-366-5(8)) Peachtree Pubs.

Lubar, David. Enter the Zombie. 2011. (Nathan Abercrombie, Accidental Zombie Ser.: 5). (ENG.). 192p. (J). (gr. 3-7). pap. 5.99 (978-0-7653-2672-0(8), 9780765326720, Starscape) Doherty, Tom Assocs., LLC.

—Ghost Attack (Monster Itch #1) 2017. (Monster Itch Ser.: 1). (ENG.). 128p. (J). (gr. 2-5). pap. 4.99 **(978-0-545-87348-2(7)**, Scholastic Paperbacks) Scholastic, Inc.

Lubar, David. The Gloomy Ghost. 2014. (Monsterrific Tales Ser.). (ENG., Illus.). 144p. (J). (gr. 3-7). 15.99 (978-0-7653-3080-2(6), 9780765330802, Starscape) Doherty, Tom Assocs., LLC.

Mac Iver, Kathi. Ghosts of the Mining District. 2003. (Illus.). 60p. 9.95 (978-0-9651272-1-9(4)) Columbine Pr.

MacDonald, George. Malcolm. 2008. 232p. 29.95 (978-1-60664-853-7(5)); pap. 15.95 (978-1-60664-099-9(2)) Aegypan.

MacHado, Ana Maria. Del otro Mundo. (SPA.). (YA). 8.95 (978-958-04-7071-7(5)) Norma S.A. COL. Dist: Distribuidora Norma, Inc.

MacHale, D. J. The Light. 2010. (Morpheus Road Ser.: 1). (ENG.). 352p. (J). (gr. 5-9). pap. 9.99 (978-1-4169-6519-0(X), Aladdin) Simon & Schuster Children's Publishing.

—The Light. 2010. (Morpheus Road Ser.: 1). (ENG.). 352p. (J). (gr. 5-18). 17.99 (978-1-4169-6516-9(5), Simon & Schuster/Paula Wiseman Bks.) Simon & Schuster/Paula Wiseman Bks.

MacPhail, Catherine. Hide & Seek. 2012. (Stoke Books Titles Ser.). 72p. (J). (gr. 5-8). pap. 7.95 (978-1-78112-024-8(2)); lib. bdg. 22.60 (978-1-78112-023-1(4)) Stoke Bks.

Madrzak, Carole. In the Shadows of Bington Manor. 2006. (ENG.). 132p. per. 24.95 (978-1-4241-5168-4(6)) America Star Bks.

Maher, Liam & May, Gin. Ghost Story. 2013. 20p. pap. 9.95 (978-1-61633-428-4(2)) Guardian Angel Publishing, Inc.

Mahy, Margaret. Don't Read This! And Other Tales of the Unnatural. 2004. (ENG., Illus.). 208p. (J). reprint ed. pap. 7.95 (978-1-932425-25-3(X), Lemniscaat) Boyds Mills Pr.

Manning, Matthew K. Secret of the Haunted Cave. Neely, Scott, illus. 2016. (Scooby-Doo Comic Chapter Bks.). (ENG.). 88p. (gr. 3-7). pap. 5.95 (978-1-4965-3589-4(8)) Capstone Press of Coughlan Cos.

Marciano, John Bemelmans. Madeline & the Old House in Paris. 2013. (Madeline Ser.). (ENG.). 48p. (J). (gr. -1-2). 17.99 (978-0-670-78485-1(0), Viking Books for Young Readers) Penguin Young Readers Group.

—Respect Your Ghosts. Blackall, Sophie, illus. 2017. (Witches of Benevento Ser.: 4). (ENG.). 128p. (J). (gr. 2-5). 13.99 (978-0-451-47183-3(0), Viking Books for Young Readers) Penguin Young Readers Group.

Margolis, Leslie. The Secrets at the Chocolate Mansion. 2013. (Maggie Brooklyn Mystery Ser.). (ENG.). 256p. (YA). (gr. 3-6). 16.99 (978-1-61963-036-9(2), 9781619630369, Bloomsbury USA Childrens) Bloomsbury Publishing USA.

—Secrets at the Chocolate Mansion. 2014. (Maggie Brooklyn Mystery Ser.). (ENG.). 272p. (YA). (gr. 3-6). pap. 7.99 (978-1-61963-493-0(7), 9781619634930, Bloomsbury USA Childrens) Bloomsbury Publishing USA.

Marie, Leann. The Ghost of Oberlin. 2008. pap. 16.95 (978-1-4241-9597-8(7)) America Star Bks.

Marin, Cheech. Cheech y el Autobus Fantasma. Fabiancic, Miriam, tr. Ramirez, Orlando L., illus. 2009. (SPA.). 32p. (J). (gr. -1-3). 17.99 (978-0-06-113214-8(4), Rayo) HarperCollins Pubs.

Mariotti, Celine Rose. Olivia Macallister, Who Are You? A Ghost Mystery Set in Maine. Tango-Schurmann, Ann, illus. 2004. 85p. (YA). (gr. 3-6). pap. 12.95 (978-0-9721389-6-3(X)) Rock Village Publishing.

Marr, Andrew. Born in the Darkest Time of Year: Stories for the Season of the Christ Child. 2004. 180p. (J). pap. 13.95 (978-0-595-32633-4(1)) iUniverse, Inc.

Marr Osb, Andrew. From Beyond to Here: Merendael's Gift & Other Stories. 2012. 320p. (gr. 4-6). 29.95 (978-1-4759-3460-1(2)); pap. 19.95 (978-1-4759-3458-8(0)) iUniverse, Inc.

Marrone, Amanda. Devoured. 2009. (ENG.). 304p. (YA). (gr. 9-18). pap. 9.99 (978-1-4169-7890-9(9), Simon Pulse) Simon Pulse.

—Uninvited. 2007. (ENG.). 224p. (YA). (gr. 9-12). pap. 8.99 (978-1-4169-3978-8(4), Simon Pulse) Simon Pulse.

Marsh, Carole. The Ghost of Pickpocket Plantation. 2006. (Pretty Darn Scary Mysteries Ser.). (Illus.). 109p. (YA). (gr. 7-14). 14.95 (978-0-635-06237-6(2)); (J). (gr. 3-5). per. 7.99 (978-0-635-06233-8(X)) Gallopade International.

—The Ghosts of Pickpocket Plantation. 2009. (Pretty Darn Scary Mysteries Ser.). (Illus.). 109p. (YA). lib. bdg. 18.99 (978-0-635-07019-7(7), Marsh, Carole Mysteries) Gallopade International.

—The Mystery at Fort Thunderbolt. 2007. (Pretty Darn Scary Mysteries Ser.). (Illus.). 113p. (J). (gr. 3-5). per. 5.99 (978-0-635-06235-2(6)); (YA). lib. bdg. 18.99 (978-0-635-07021-0(9), Marsh, Carole Mysteries); (YA). (gr. 7-14). 14.95 (978-0-635-06239-0(9)) Gallopade International.

—The Mystery of Blackbeard the Pirate. Marsh, Carole, photos by. 2009. (Real Kids, Real Places Ser.). (Illus.). 150p. (J). 18.99 (978-0-635-06992-4(X), Marsh, Carole Mysteries) Gallopade International.

—The Mystery of the Alamo Ghost. (Real Kids, Real Places Ser.). (J). 2009. (Illus.). 146p. lib. bdg. 18.99 (978-0-635-06993-1(8), Marsh, Carole Mysteries) 2003. 160p. (gr. 2-8). 14.95 (978-0-635-01654-6(0)) 2003. 160p. (gr. 2-8). pap. 7.99 (978-0-635-01652-2(4)) Gallopade International.

—The Mystery of the Haunted Ghost Town. 2009. (Real Kids, Real Places Ser.). 144p. (J). 18.99 (978-0-635-07044-9(8), Marsh, Carole Mysteries) Gallopade International.

Masters, Anthony. Ghost Stories to Tell in the Dark. 2012. (ENG.). 92p. pap. 12.99 (978-1-4482-0501-1(8), 9781448205011, Bloomsbury Reader) Bloomsbury Publishing Plc GBR. Dist: Macmillan.

Matas, Carol & Nodelman, Perry. The Curse of the Evening Eye. 2009. (Ghosthunters Ser.). (ENG.). 216p. (J). (gr. 3-7). pap. (978-1-55470-145-2(7)) Me to We.

Matthews, John. The Barefoot Book of Giants, Ghosts, & Goblins. Manna, Giovanni, illus. 2008. (ENG.). 80p. (J). 21.99 (978-1-84686-235-9(3)) Barefoot Bks., Inc.

Matthews, Rupert. Hide-And-Ghost Seek... Le Ray, Marina, illus. 2013. (J). (978-1-4351-4895-6(9)) Barnes & Noble, Inc.

Maxwell, Lisa. Sweet Unrest. 2014. (ENG.). 336p. (YA). pap. 11.99 (978-0-7387-4081-2(0), Flux) North Star Editions.

McCLure, Beverly Stowe. Listen to the Ghost. 2005. (J). per. 16.95 (978-1-933353-51-7(1), Paladin Timeless) Twilight Times Bks.

McClymer, Kelly. Must Love Black. 2008. (ENG.). 192p. (YA). (gr. 7-18). pap. 8.99 (978-1-4169-4903-9(8), Simon Pulse) Simon Pulse.

McCoy, Mimi, pseud. The Dead End. 2010. 174p. (J). (978-0-545-25838-8(3)) Scholastic, Inc.

McDonald, Fiona. Ghost Doll & Jasper. 2012. (ENG., Illus.). 112p. (J). (gr. 2-7). 12.95 (978-1-62087-174-4(2), 620174, Sky Pony Pr.) Skyhorse Publishing Co., Inc.

McEntire, K. D. Lightbringer. 2011. (ENG.). 319p. (YA). (gr. 7). 16.99 (978-1-61614-539-2(0)) Prometheus Bks., Pubs.

McKenzie, Paige. Sacrifice of Sunshine Girl. 2017. (Haunting of Sunshine Girl Ser.: 3). (ENG.). 336p. (gr. 7-17). 17.99 **(978-1-60286-298-2(2)**, Weinstein Bks.) Perseus Bks. Group.

McKissack, Patricia C. Ol' Clip-Clop: A Ghost Story. Velasquez, Eric, illus. (ENG.). 32p. (J). 2014. (gr. 1-4). 6.99 (978-0-8234-3186-1(X)) 2013. 16.95 (978-0-8234-2265-4(8)) Holiday Hse., Inc.

McLean, Alan C. Ghost of the Glen. Date not set. (Knockout Ser.). 123p. 44.77 (978-0-582-25082-6(X)) Addison-Wesley Longman, Ltd. GBR. Dist: Trans-Atlantic Pubns., Inc.

McMullan, Kate. The Ghost of Sir Herbert Dungeonstone, 1 vol. Basso, Bill, illus. 2006. (Dragon Slayers' Academy Ser.: No. 12). (ENG.). 112p. (gr. 1-7). 24.21 (978-1-59961-124-2(4)) Spotlight.

McMullen, Judy Benson, ed. Ghost in the Gazebo. 2012. (ENG.). (YA). pap. (978-1-4675-3218-1(5)) Independent Pub.

McNamee, Graham. Beyond: A Ghost Story. (ENG.). 240p. (YA). (gr. 9). 2013. pap. 8.99 (978-0-375-85165-0(8), Ember) 2012. 15.99 (978-0-385-73775-3(0), Lamb, Wendy Bks.) Random Hse. Children's Bks.

McNeal, Tom. Far Far Away. (ENG.). (YA). (gr. 7). 2014. 400p. pap. 9.99 (978-0-375-84329-7(9), Ember) 2013. 384p. 17.99 (978-0-375-84972-5(6), Knopf Bks. for Young Readers) Random Hse. Children's Bks.

McNeil, Gretchen. Ten. 2012. (ENG.). 304p. (YA). (gr. 8). 17.99 (978-0-06-211878-3(1)) HarperCollins Pubs.

McNish, Cliff. Breathe: A Ghost Story. (Exceptional Reading & Language Arts Titles for Intermediate Grades Ser.). (ENG.). 264p. (J). (gr. 4-8). 2009. pap. 6.95 (978-0-7613-4962-4(6), First Avenue Editions) 2006. lib. bdg. 15.95 (978-0-8225-6443-0(2), Carolrhoda Bks.) Lerner Publishing Group.

McRae, David. Blood of the Donnellys. 2007. (ENG.). 144p. (J). (gr. 8). pap. 11.99 (978-1-55002-754-9(9)) Dundurn CAN. Dist: Ingram Publisher Services.

Melling, David. The Ghost Library. Melling, David, illus. 2004. (ENG., Illus.). 32p. (J). (gr. -1-k). 16.99 (978-0-340-86088-5(X)) Hodder & Stoughton GBR. Dist: Hachette Bk. Group.

Mercer, Sienna. Spooktacular! 2015. (My Sister the Vampire Ser.: 17). (ENG.). 224p. (J). (gr. 4-6). pap. 6.99 (978-1-4052-7843-0(9)) Egmont Bks., Ltd. GBR. Dist: Independent Pubs. Group.

Messer, Celeste M. The Ghost of Piper's Landing. Hoeffner, Deb, illus. 2004. 82-92p. 4.95 (978-0-9702171-7-2(X)) AshleyAlan Enterprises.

Metz, Melinda. Raven's Point. 2005. pap. (978-0-06-052373-2(5)) HarperCollins Canada, Ltd.

Metzger, Steve. Five Spooky Ghosts Playing Tricks at School. Harrald-Pilz, Marilee, illus. 2005. (J). (978-0-439-80381-6(0)) Scholastic, Inc.

Milford, Kate. Ghosts of Greenglass House. 2017. (ENG., Illus.). 464p. (J). (gr. 5-7). 17.99 **(978-0-544-99146-0(X)**, Clarion Bks.) Houghton Mifflin Harcourt Trade & Reference Pubs.

Mills, Rachel. Wraiths. 2010. 269p. pap. 18.95 (978-1-4461-4326-1(0)) Lulu Pr., Inc.

Mills, Timothy. The Mystery Kids: the Mystery of Ghost Lake. 2009. 87p. pap. 14.96 (978-0-557-01282-4(1)) Lulu Pr., Inc.

Milord, Susan. The Ghost on the Hearth. Dabcovich, Lydia, illus. 2003. (Vermont Folklife Center Children's Book Ser.). (ENG.). 32p. (J). (gr. -1-3). 15.95 (978-0-916718-18-3(2)) Vermont Folklife Ctr.

Mind Grabber. 64p. (YA). (gr. 6-12). pap. (978-0-8224-2335-5(9)) Globe Fearon Educational Publishing.

Monahan, Hillary. Bloody Mary, Book 2 Mary: Unleashed. 2015. (Bloody Mary Ser.). (ENG.). 256p. (YA). (gr. 7-12). 17.99 (978-1-4231-8539-0(0)) Hyperion Bks. for Children.

—Mary: The Summoning. 2014. (Bloody Mary Ser.). (ENG.). 256p. (YA). (gr. 7-12). 16.99 (978-1-4231-8519-2(6)) Hyperion Bks. for Children.

—Summoning. 2015. (Bloody Mary Ser.). (ENG.). 272p. (YA). (gr. 7-12). pap. 9.99 (978-1-4231-8693-9(1)) Hyperion Bks. for Children.

Mooney, Ms Olive. The Chronicles of Cadaver College: Book of Ornis. 2013. 110p. pap. (978-0-9575130-1-3(1)) Olive Mooney.

Moore, Kelly, et al. Amber House. 2012. (Amber House Ser.: 1). (ENG.). 368p. (J). (gr. 9). 17.99 (978-0-545-43416-4(5), Levine, Arthur A. Bks.) Scholastic, Inc.

Morales, Yuyi. Just in Case: A Trickster Tale & Spanish Alphabet Book. Morales, Yuyi, illus. 2008. (ENG., Illus.). 40p. (J). (gr. -1-3). 18.99 (978-1-59643-329-8(9), 9781596433298) Roaring Brook Pr.

Moro, Robin, et al, illus. Read Aloud Spooky Stories. 2006. 320p. (J). (gr. 4-7). 15.98 (978-0-7853-6338-5(6), 7159100) Publications International, Ltd.

Morris, Paula. Dark Souls. 2011. (ENG.). 304p. (J). (gr. 7-7). 17.99 (978-0-545-25132-7(X)) Scholastic, Inc.

—Unbroken. (ENG.). 304p. (J). (gr. 7). 2014. pap. 9.99 (978-0-545-41642-9(6)) 2013. 17.99 (978-0-545-41641-2(8)) Scholastic, Inc.

Morton-Shaw, Christine. The Hunt for the Seventh. 2009. (ENG.). 288p. (J). (gr. 5). pap. 7.99 (978-0-06-072824-3(8), Tegen, Katherine Bks) HarperCollins Pubs.

Moses, Antoinette. The Girl at the Window. 2007. (Cambridge English Readers Ser.). (ENG., Illus.). 32p. pap. 8.50 (978-0-521-70585-1(1)) Cambridge Univ. Pr.

Mott, A. S. & Dean, Jessica Casey. Gothic Ghost Stories Vol. 1: Tales of Intrigue & Fantasy from Beyond the Grave, 1 vol. rev. ed. 2004. (Ghost Stories Ser.). (ENG., Illus.). 216p. (gr. 4). pap. 12.95 (978-1-894877-39-8(X), 189487739X, Ghost Hse. Bks.) Lone Pine Publishing USA.

Mould, Chris. The Icy Hand. Mould, Chris, illus. 2008. (Something Wickedly Weird Ser.: 2). (ENG., Illus.). 176p. (J). (gr. 5-9). 9.95 (978-1-59643-385-4(X), 9781596433854) Roaring Brook Pr.

Mowat, Diane. Pair of Ghostly Hands & Other Stories. 3rd ed. 2008. (ENG., Illus.). 80p. 9.38 (978-0-19-479125-0(4)) Oxford Univ. Pr., Inc.

Mowry, Jess. Voodu Dawgz. 2007. 253p. pap. 14.99 (978-1-59092-359-7(6)) Blue Forge Pr.

Mutis, Álvaro. La Mansión de Araucaíma: Diario de Lecumberri. (SPA.). (J). 8.00 (978-958-04-6975-9(X)) Norma S.A. COL. Dist: Distribuidora Norma, Inc.

Nardone, Frank. Something's Brewing in Salem. 2013. 164p. pap. 9.99 (978-0-9884024-1-6(6)) Dragon Tree Bks.

Naylor, Phyllis Reynolds. The Boys Return. 2003. (Boys Against Girls Ser.: No. 7). 132p. (gr. 4-7). 16.00 (978-0-7569-1381-6(0)) Perfection Learning Corp.

—The Boys Return. l.t. ed. 2003. (Boys Against Girls Ser.: No. 7). 170p. (J). 23.95 (978-0-7862-5822-2(5)) Thorndike Pr.

Nesbit, E. The Red House. 2006. 140p. per. 11.95 (978-1-59818-965-0(4)) Aegypan.

Newbound, Andrew. Ghoul Strike! 2010. (ENG.). 320p. (J). (gr. 3-7). 16.99 (978-0-545-22938-8(3), Chicken Hse., The) Scholastic, Inc.

Nichols, Lee. Deception. 2010. (Haunting Emma Ser.). (ENG.). 336p. (YA). (gr. 9-12). 16.99 (978-1-59990-308-8(3), 9781599903088); pap. 9.99 (978-1-59990-421-4(7), 9781599904214) Bloomsbury Publishing USA. (Bloomsbury USA Childrens).

—Surrender. 2011. (Haunting Emma Ser.). (ENG.). 272p. (YA). (gr. 9-12). pap. 9.99 (978-1-59990-423-8(3), 9781599904238, Bloomsbury USA Childrens) Bloomsbury Publishing USA.

Night, P. J. Is She for Real? 2012. (Creepover Ser.: 7). lib. bdg. 17.20 (978-0-606-26340-5(3), Turtleback) Turtleback Bks.

—It's All Downhill from Here. 2012. (You're Invited to a Creepover Ser.: 10). (ENG.). 160p. (J). (gr. 3-7). pap. 5.99 (978-1-4424-5285-5(4), Simon Spotlight) Simon Spotlight.

—Truth or Dare... 2011. (You're Invited to a Creepover Ser.: 1). (ENG., Illus.). 160p. (J). (gr. 3-7). pap. 6.99 (978-1-4424-2096-0(0), Simon Spotlight) Simon Spotlight.

—You're Invited to a Creepover Collection: Truth or Dare...; You Can't Come in Here!; Ready for a Scare?; the Show Must Go On! 2012. (You're Invited to a Creepover Ser.). (ENG.). 640p. (J). (gr. 3-7). pap. 23.99 *(978-1-4424-8444-3(6)*, Simon Spotlight) Simon Spotlight.

Nishi, Yoshiyuki. Muhyo & Roji's Bureau of Supernatural Investigation, Vol. 18. Nishi, Yoshiyuki, illus. 2010. (ENG., Illus.). 192p. pap. 9.99 *(978-1-4215-2840-3(1))* Viz Media.

Nixon, Audrey. Jennifer's Body. 2009. 208p. (J). (gr. 9-18). pap. 8.99 *(978-0-06-180892-0(X)*, Harper Entertainment) HarperCollins Pubs.

Noël, Alyson. Radiance. unabr. ed. 2011. (ENG.). 208p. pap. *(978-0-330-52691-3(X)*, Macmillan Children's Bks.) Pan Macmillan.

—Radiance. 2011. pap. *(978-0-545-34095-3(0))* Scholastic, Inc.

—Radiance. 2010. (Riley Bloom Book Ser.: 1). (ENG.). 192p. (J). (gr. 4-7). pap. 8.99 *(978-0-312-62917-5(6)*, 9780312629175) Square Fish.

—Radiance. 2010. (Riley Bloom Ser.: 1). (J). lib. bdg. 19.65 *(978-0-606-15131-3(1)*, Turtleback) Turtleback Bks.

—Shimmer. 2011. pap. *(978-0-545-39923-4(8))* Scholastic, Inc.

—Shimmer. 2011. (Riley Bloom Book Ser.: 2). (ENG.). 208p. (J). (gr. 4-7). pap. 9.99 *(978-0-312-64825-1(1)*, 9780312648251) Square Fish.

—Shimmer. 2011. (Riley Bloom Ser.: 2). (J). lib. bdg. 20.85 *(978-0-606-21683-8(9)*, Turtleback) Turtleback Bks.

—Whisper, Bk. 4. 2012. (Riley Bloom Book Ser.: 4). (ENG.). 240p. (J). (gr. 4-7). pap. 8.99 *(978-0-312-64156-6(7)*, 9780312641566) Square Fish.

—Whisper. 2012. (Riley Bloom Ser.: 4). (J). lib. bdg. 19.65 *(978-0-606-23786-4(0)*, Turtleback) Turtleback Bks.

Norriss, Andrew. Friends for Life. 2015. (ENG.). 240p. (J). (gr. 3-7). 17.99 *(978-0-545-85186-2(6))* Scholastic, Inc.

Noyes, Deborah. The Ghosts of Kerfol. 2010. (ENG., Illus.). 176p. (YA). (gr. 9). pap. 7.99 *(978-0-7636-4825-1(6))* Candlewick Pr.

Nugent, Matthew. Nightmares on Goose Rocks Beach in Kennebunkport, Maine: Book 4 of the Goose Rocks Tales. 2003. (Illus.). 204p. (J). per. 14.95 *(978-0-9705812-3-5(8))* CBI Pr.

Nye, Alex. Chill, 1 vol. 2006. (ENG., Illus.). 176p. (J). 11.95 *(978-0-86315-546-8(4))* Floris Bks. GBR. Dist: SteinerBooks, Inc.

Ogburn, Jacqueline K. The Bake Shop Ghost. Priceman, Marjorie, illus. 2008. (ENG.). 32p. (J). (gr. -1-3). pap. 6.99 *(978-0-547-07677-5(0))* Houghton Mifflin Harcourt Publishing Co.

Ohlin, Nancy. Always, Forever. 2014. (ENG., Illus.). 320p. (YA). (gr. 9). pap. 9.99 *(978-1-4424-6487-2(9)*, Simon Pulse) Simon Pulse.

—Thorn Abbey. 2013. (ENG.). 304p. (YA). (gr. 9). 16.99 *(978-1-4424-6486-5(0)*, Simon Pulse) Simon Pulse.

Oliver, Lauren. Liesl & Po. Acedera, Kei, illus. (ENG.). (J). (gr. 3-7). 2012. 336p. pap. 6.99 *(978-0-06-201452-8(8))* 2011. 320p. 16.99 *(978-0-06-201451-1(X))* HarperCollins Pubs.

—Liesl & Po. 2012. (J). lib. bdg. 17.20 *(978-0-606-26853-0(7)*, Turtleback) Turtleback Bks.

Olivia MacAllister, Who Are You? 2006. (J). 12.95 *(978-0-615-13155-9(7))* CRM Enterprises.

Onyefulu, Ifeoma & Quarto Generic Staff. The Girl Who Married a Ghost: And Other Tales from Nigeria. 2010. (ENG., Illus.). 112p. (J). (gr. 3-6). 15.95 *(978-1-84780-176-0(5)*, Frances Lincoln Children's Bks.) Quarto Publishing Group UK GBR. Dist: Hachette Bk. Group.

O'Reilly, Sean. Kade: Identity, 5 vols. 2005. (Illus.). (YA). 9.95 *(978-0-9763095-1-2(3))* Arcana Studio, Inc.

—Monster Mansion, 1 vol. 2010. (Mighty Mighty Monsters Ser.). (ENG.). 48p. (gr. 2-3). lib. bdg. 23.99 *(978-1-4342-2152-0(0))* Stone Arch Bks.

O'Ryan, Ray. A Haunted Halloween. Kraft, Jason, illus. 2015. (Galaxy Zack Ser.: 11). (ENG.). 128p. (J). (gr. k-4). 16.99 *(978-1-4814-3491-1(8)*, Little Simon) Little Simon.

Osborne, Mary Pope. A Good Night for Ghosts. Murdocca, Sal, illus. 2009. (Magic Tree House Merlin Mission Ser.: 42). (ENG.). 128p. (J). (gr. 2-5). 12.99 *(978-0-375-85648-8(X)*, Random Hse. Bks. for Young Readers) Random Hse. Children's Bks.

Papp, Robert, illus. The Ghost of the Chattering Bones. 2007. (Boxcar Children Ser.). 120p. 15.00 *(978-0-7569-7611-8(1))* Perfection Learning Corp.

—The Ghost of the Chattering Bones. 2005. (Boxcar Children Mysteries Ser.: 102). (ENG.). 128p. (J). (gr. 1-5). pap. 5.99 *(978-0-8075-0874-9(8))* Whitman, Albert & Co.

Paquette, Ammi-Joan. Ghost in the House. Record, Adam, illus. (ENG.). (J). (gr. -1-2). 2015. 20p. 9.99 *(978-0-7636-7622-3(5))* 2013. 32p. 15.99 *(978-0-7636-5529-7(5))* Candlewick Pr.

Parker, Natalie C. Behold the Bones. 2016. (Beware the Wild Ser.: 2). 368p. (YA). (gr. 8). 17.99 *(978-0-06-224155-9(9)*, HarperTeen) HarperCollins Pubs.

Pavanello, Roberto. The Ghost of Dr. Mold. Zeni, Marco, tr. from ITA. Pisapia, Blasco & Brughera, Pamela, illus. 2012. (Echo & the Bat Pack Ser.). (ENG.). 128p. (gr. 2-3). 25.32 *(978-1-4342-3834-4(2)*, Echo & the Bat Pack) Stone Arch Bks.

—The Pirate with the Golden Tooth, 1 vol. Zeni, Marco, tr. from ITA. Pisapia, Blasco & Brughera, Pamela, illus. (Echo & the Bat Pack Ser.). (ENG.). 128p. (gr. 2-3). 2013. 9.95 *(978-1-4342-4888-6(7))* 2012. 25.32 *(978-1-4342-3836-8(9)*, Echo & the Bat Pack) Stone Arch Bks.

Pearce, Bryony. The Weight of Souls. 2013. (ENG.). 288p. (YA). 17.99 *(978-1-908844-64-4(7)*, Strange Chemistry) Watkins Media Limited GBR. Dist: Penguin Random Hse. LLC.

Pearsall, John. Rodney's Room: Dr. Ghoul's Party Plans. 2009. 54p. pap. 8.95 *(978-1-4327-4780-0(0))* Outskirts Pr., Inc.

Pearson Education Staff. Room in the Tower & Other Stories. 2nd ed. 2008. (ENG., Illus.). 48p. pap. 11.99 *(978-1-4058-6962-1(3))* Pearson Education.

Pearson, Susan. We're Going on a Ghost Hunt, 0 vols. Schindler, S. D., illus. 2012. (ENG.). 32p. (J). (gr. -1-3). 16.99 *(978-0-7614-6307-8(0)*, 9780761463078, Amazon Children's Publishing) Amazon Publishing.

Peck, Richard. The Ghost Belonged to Me. 2005. 176p. (YA). 21.00 *(978-0-8446-7275-5(0)*, 3590) Smith, Peter Pub., Inc.

Peebles, Joseph. The Stickman & the Crow. 2004. (ENG.). (YA). pap. 10.95 *(978-0-9644758-4-7(7))* Peebco Publishing Hse., The.

Peifer, Meighan. The Chocolate Chip Ghost. French, Phyllis, illus. 2004. (J). 14.95 *(978-1-58597-245-6(2))* Leathers Publishing.

Penn, Audrey. Mystery at Blackbeard's Cove. Howard, Philip & Miller, Joshua, illus. 2004. (ENG.). 263p. (J). (gr. 2-7). per. 7.95 *(978-1-933718-09-5(9))* Tanglewood Pr.

—Mystery at Blackbeard's Cove. Howard, Philip & Miller, Josh, illus. 2004. (ENG.). 200p. (J). (gr. 3-7). 14.95 *(978-0-9749303-1-2(8))* Tanglewood Pr.

Peretti, Frank E. & Thomas Nelson & Sons Staff. The Legend of Annie Murphy, 1 vol. 2005. (Cooper Kids Adventure Ser.: 7). (ENG.). 160p. pap. 6.99 *(978-1-4003-0576-6(4))* Nelson, Thomas Inc.

Perkins, T. J. In the Grand Scheme of Things: A Kim & Kelly Mystery. 2007. (Illus.). 151p. (YA). 10.99 *(978-0-9777538-4-0(0))* GumShoe Press.

—Mystery of the Attic. 2006. (Illus.). 113p. (YA). 10.99 *(978-0-9777538-6-4(7))* GumShoe Press.

Peschke, Marci & Townson, H. The Ghost's Revenge, 1 vol. Garvey, Brann & O'Connor, Niamh, illus. 2006. (Vortex Bks.). (ENG.). 112p. (gr. 2-3). 7.19 *(978-1-59889-283-5(5)*, Vortex Bks.) Stone Arch Bks.

Peterson, Megan Cooley. Scooby-Doo! a Science of Chemical Reactions Mystery: The over-Reacting Ghost. Brizuela, Dario, illus. 2017. (Scooby-Doo Solves It with S. T. E. M. Ser.). (ENG.). 32p. (gr. 3-4). lib. bdg. 27.99 *(978-1-5157-3697-4(0))* Capstone Press of Coughlan Cos.

Petrucha, Stefan & Pendleton, Thomas. Wicked Dead: Skin. (Wicked Dead Ser.). 224p. (J). pap. 7.99 *(978-0-06-113854-6(1)*, HarperTeen) HarperCollins Pubs.

Peyton, K. M. Stealaway. Wyatt, David, illus. 2004. (ENG.). 96p. (J). 12.95 *(978-0-8126-2722-0(9))* Cricket Bks.

Phillips, Dee. Dare, 1 vol. unabr. ed. 2011. (Right Now! Ser.). (ENG.). 45p. (YA). (gr. 9-12). pap. 8.95 *(978-1-61651-246-0(6))* Saddleback Educational Publishing, Inc.

—Doomed on Death Row. 2016. (Cold Whispers II Ser.). (ENG.). 32p. (J). (gr. 2-6). 19.95 *(978-1-944102-35-7(3))* Bearport Publishing Co., Inc.

—The Ghostly Secret of Lakeside School. 2016. (Cold Whispers II Ser.). (ENG.). 32p. (J). (gr. 2-6). 19.95 *(978-1-944102-33-3(7))* Bearport Publishing Co., Inc.

—Terror in the Underground Tunnel. 2016. (Cold Whispers II Ser.). (ENG.). 32p. (J). (gr. 2-6). 19.95 *(978-1-944102-37-1(X))* Bearport Publishing Co., Inc.

Pike, Aprilynne. Life after Theft. 2013. (Life after Theft Ser.). (ENG.). 352p. (YA). (gr. 8). 17.99 *(978-0-06-199900-0(8)*, HarperTeen) HarperCollins Pubs.

Pike, Christopher, pseud. The Howling Ghost. 2014. (Spooksville Ser.: 2). (ENG., Illus.). 128p. (J). (gr. 3-7). pap. 6.99 *(978-1-4814-1052-6(0)*, Aladdin) Simon & Schuster Children's Publishing.

—Remember Me. 2007. (Remember Me Ser.: 1). (ENG.). 240p. (YA). (gr. 8). pap. 12.95 *(978-1-4169-6819-1(9)*, Simon Pulse) Simon Pulse.

Pinkwater, Daniel M. The Yggyssey: How Iggy Wondered What Happened to All the Ghosts, Found Out Where They Went, & Went There. 2010. (ENG., Illus.). 256p. (J). (gr. 5-7). pap. 6.99 *(978-0-547-32865-2(6))* Houghton Mifflin Harcourt Publishing Co.

Pirotta, Saviour. The Ghosts Who Danced: And Other Spooky Stories from Around the World. Hess, Paul, illus. 2015. (ENG.). 64p. (J). (gr. 1-5). 22.99 *(978-1-84780-435-8(7)*, Frances Lincoln) Quarto Publishing Group UK GBR. Dist: Hachette Bk. Group.

Plum-Ucci, Carol. The She. 2005. (ENG., Illus.). 372p. (YA). (gr. 9-12). reprint ed. pap. 19.99 *(978-0-15-205453-3(7))* Houghton Mifflin Harcourt Publishing Co.

Pluth, Lisa Anderson. A Haunting in Little River. 2011. 94p. pap. 19.95 *(978-1-4560-9700-4(8))* America Star Bks.

Poe, Edgar Allen. The Raven & Other Writings. 2003. (Aladdin Classics Ser.). (ENG.). 448p. (J). (gr. 4-7). pap. 7.99 *(978-0-689-86352-3(7)*, Aladdin) Simon & Schuster Children's Publishing.

Poskitt, Kjartan. Agatha Parrot & the Odd Street School Ghost. Hargis, Wes, illus. (ENG.). 160p. (J). (gr. 2-5). 2017. pap. 6.99 *(978-0-544-93530-3(6)*, HMH Books For Young Readers) 2016. 16.99 *(978-0-544-50672-5(3))* Houghton Mifflin Harcourt Publishing Co.

Potter, Ellen. Olivia Kidney & the Secret Beneath the City. 2009. (ENG.). 336p. (J). (gr. 3-7). 9.99 *(978-0-14-241263-3(5)*, Puffin Books) Penguin Young Readers Group.

Poulsen, David A. Shivers & Shakes. 2009. (Salt & Pepper Chronicles Ser.). (ENG.). 176p. (J). (gr. 3-7). pap. *(978-1-55470-144-5(9))* Me to We.

Powell, Jim S. The Mystery of the Totem Trees: A Plumroy Pack Adventure. 2009. 124p. pap. 10.95 *(978-1-4401-3921-5(0))* iUniverse, Inc.

Pratchett, Terry. I Shall Wear Midnight. (Tiffany Aching Ser.: 4). (YA). (gr. 8). 2015. (ENG.). 464p. pap. 9.99 *(978-0-06-243529-3(9))* 2011. 368p. pap. 9.99 *(978-0-06-143306-1(3))* 2010. 368p. 16.99 *(978-0-06-143304-7(7))* HarperCollins Pubs.

—Johnny & the Dead. 2006. (Johnny Maxwell Trilogy). 213p. (J). (gr. 3-7). 15.99 *(978-0-06-054188-0(1))*; lib. bdg. 16.89 *(978-0-06-054189-7(X))* HarperCollins Pubs.

Pray, Linda. Characters of the Dark. 2011. 36p. pap. 16.95 *(978-1-4626-0329-9(7))* America Star Bks.

Preller, James. The Case of the Groaning Ghost. Smith, Jamie & Alley, R. W., illus. 2008. (Jigsaw Jones Mysteries Ser.: Bk. 32). 89p. (gr. 1-5). 15.00 *(978-0-7569-8302-4(9))* Perfection Learning Corp.

—Home Sweet Horror. Bruno, Iacopo, illus. 2013. (Scary Tales Ser.: 1). (ENG.). 112p. (J). (gr. 2-5). pap. 5.99 *(978-1-250-01887-8(0)*, 9781250018878) Feiwel & Friends.

—Jigsaw Jones: The Case of the Glow in the Dark Ghost. 2017. (Jigsaw Jones Mysteries Ser.). (ENG.). 96p. (J). pap. 4.99 *(978-1-250-11020-6(3)*, 9781250110206) Feiwel & Friends.

Priddy, Roger. Spooky Bus. 2013. (Shaped Board Bks.). (ENG., Illus.). 6p. (J). (gr. -1-k). bds. 6.99 *(978-0-312-51618-5(5)*, 9780312516185, Priddy Bks.) St. Martin's Pr.

Priestley, Chris. The Dead of Winter. 2012. (ENG., Illus.). 224p. (YA). (gr. 7-12). 16.99 *(978-1-59990-745-1(3)*, 9781599907451, Bloomsbury USA Childrens) Bloomsbury Publishing USA.

Primavera, Elise. Fred & Anthony Meet the Heinie Goblins from the Black Lagoon. Primavera, Elise, illus. rev. ed. 2008. (ENG., Illus.). 128p. (J). (gr. 2-4). pap. 4.99 *(978-0-7868-3682-6(2))* Hyperion Bks. for Children.

Primavera, Elise & Arevamirp, Esile. Fred & Anthony Escape from the Netherworld. Primavera, Elise, illus. 2007. (ENG., Illus.). 128p. (J). (gr. 2-6). pap. 4.99 *(978-0-7868-3678-9(4))* Hyperion Pr.

Prime Time History, 4 vols., Set. Incl. Crusades: The Two Hundred Years War: The Clash Between the Cross & the Crescent in the Middle East 1096-1291. Harpur, James. 118p. lib. bdg. 42.60 *(978-1-4042-1367-8(8))*; Troy: The Myth & Reality Behind the Epic Legend. McCarty, Nick. 122p. lib. bdg. 42.60 *(978-1-4042-1365-4(1))*; (Illus.). (YA). (gr. 9-12). 2008. 2008. Set lib. bdg. 159.80 *(978-1-4042-1487-3(9))* Rosen Publishing Group, Inc., The.

Prins, Piet. The Flying Phantom. 2006. (Illus.). 142p. (J). pap. *(978-1-894666-45-9(3))* Inheritance Pubns.

Prisant, Guillermo Murray. Que Miedo! rev. ed. 2006. (Castillo del Terror Ser.). (SPA & ENG.). 112p. (J). (gr. 6-9). pap. 6.95 *(978-970-20-0338-0(5))* Castillo, Ediciones, S. A. de C. V. MEX. Dist: Macmillan.

Promitzer, Rebecca. The Pickle King. 2010. (ENG.). 416p. (J). (gr. 3-7). 17.99 *(978-0-545-17087-1(7)*, Chicken Hse., The) Scholastic, Inc.

Pulver, Robin. Never Say Boo! Lucke, Deb, illus. 2009. (ENG.). 32p. (J). (gr. -1-3). 16.95 *(978-0-8234-2110-7(4))* Holiday Hse., Inc.

Ranade, Soumitra. Tak-Tak! Suleman, Shilo Shiv, illus. 2013. (ENG.). 32p. (J). (gr. k). pap. 9.95 *(978-81-8190-183-5(5))* Karadi Tales Co. Pvt, Ltd. IND. Dist: Consortium Bk. Sales & Distribution.

Randall, Thomas. The Waking: A Winter of Ghosts. 2011. (YA). pap. 9.99 *(978-1-59990-252-4(4)*, Bloomsbury USA Childrens) Bloomsbury Publishing USA.

Random House Staff. Haunted Houseboat (SpongeBob SquarePants) Random House Staff & Aikins, Dave, illus. 2013. (Pictureback(R) Ser.). (ENG.). 24p. (J). (gr. -1-2). 3.99 *(978-0-449-81759-9(8)*, Random Hse. Bks. for Young Readers) Random Hse. Children's Bks.

Ransom, Candice. Key to the Griffon's Lair. Fiegenshuh, Emily, illus. 2005. (Knights of the Silver Dragon Ser.: Bk. 9). 182p. (J). *(978-1-4156-3032-7(1)*, Mirrorstone) Wizards of the Coast.

Rao, Cheryl. Mixed Score: Ghost & Other Stories. 2004. 122p. 15.00 *(978-81-291-0401-4(6))* Rupa & Co. IND. Dist: South Asia Bks.

Really Scary Stuff [Capstone Sole Source]. 2010. (Really Scary Stuff Ser.). 24p. lib. bdg. 95.96 *(978-1-4296-5877-5(0)*, First Facts) Capstone Press of Coughlan Cos.

Reasoner, Charles. Charles Reasoner Halloween Books. 2015. (Charles Reasoner Halloween Bks.). (ENG.). 12p. (gr. -1 — 1). bds. 23.96 *(978-1-4795-8505-2(X))* Picture Window Bks.

—Halloween Ghost, 1 vol. 2014. (Charles Reasoner Halloween Bks.). (ENG.). 12p. (gr. -1 — 1). bds. 5.99 *(978-1-4795-5971-8(7))* Picture Window Bks.

—Peek-A-Boo Ghosts. Le Ray, Marina & Jones, Anna, illus. 2013. (Charles Reasoner Peek-A-Boo Bks.). (ENG.). 10p. (gr. -1 — 1). bds. 9.99 *(978-1-4795-2359-7(3))*; bds. 4.99 *(978-1-4795-2360-3(7))* Picture Window Bks.

—The 3 Blind Mice Inside the Spooky Scary & Creepy Haunted House. Reasoner, Charles, illus. 2007. (Story Book Ser.). (Illus.). 10p. (J). (gr. -1-3). bds. *(978-1-84666-381-9(4)*, Tide Mill Pr.) Top That! Publishing PLC.

Reber, Jack. The Ghost form the Schenectady Massacre: A Haunting from the Dutch Settlers. 121p. (J). (gr. 4-5). 9.99 *(978-0-88092-547-1(7))* Royal Fireworks Publishing Co.

Redbank, Tennant. The Haunted Boardwalk. 2016. (Barbie Chapters Ser.). (ENG., Illus.). 64p. (J). (gr. 1-4). lib. bdg. 12.99 *(978-0-375-97412-0(1)*, Random Hse. Bks. for Young Readers) Random Hse. Children's Bks.

Rees, Celia. Haunts - Evil Lurks Under This City... 136p. (J). pap. *(978-0-340-71487-4(5))* Hodder & Stoughton.

—U Is for Unbeliever. 120p. (J). pap. *(978-0-340-71524-6(3))* Hodder & Stoughton.

Reiss, Kathryn. Sweet Miss Honeywell's Revenge: A Ghost Story. 2005. (ENG.). 444p. (YA). (gr. 7-12). pap. 22.95 *(978-0-15-205471-7(5))* Houghton Mifflin Harcourt Publishing Co.

Richter, Jeff, photos by. White Deer: Ghost of the Forest. 2007. (Illus.). 96p. pap. 19.95 *(978-0-9741883-1-7(X))* Nature's Pr.

Riddell, Andrew G. The Curse of Blackbeard's Ghost. 2010. 122p. (gr. 4-6). pap. 10.95 *(978-1-4502-6952-0(4))* iUniverse, Inc.

Riddell, J. H. The Open Door. 2004. reprint ed. pap. 1.99 *(978-1-4192-7623-1(9))* Kessinger Publishing, LLC.

Riddle, Waide. The Chocolate Man: A Children's Horror Tale. 2003. 24p. (J). 9.95 *(978-0-9724619-1-7(4))* Passage Publishing.

Ridell, Chris. Ottoline va al colegio/ Ottolina Goes To School. 2008. (SPA.). 172p. (J). 13.95 *(978-84-263-6833-1(6))* Vives, Luis Editorial (Edelvives) ESP. Dist: Baker & Taylor Bks.

Rivers, Phoebe. Giving up the Ghost. 2013. (Saranormal Ser.: 6). (ENG.). 160p. (J). (gr. 3-7). 15.99 *(978-1-4424-6616-6(2))*; pap. 5.99 *(978-1-4424-6617-3(0))* Simon Spotlight. (Simon Spotlight).

—Mischief Night. 2012. (Saranormal Ser.: 3). (ENG.). 160p. (J). (gr. 3-7). 15.99 *(978-1-4424-5380-7(X))*; pap. 5.99 *(978-1-4424-5221-3(8))* Simon Spotlight. (Simon Spotlight).

—Playing with Fire. 2013. (Saranormal Ser.: 9). (ENG., Illus.). 160p. (J). (gr. 3-7). 15.99 *(978-1-4424-8306-4(7))*; pap. 5.99 *(978-1-4424-8305-7(9))* Simon Spotlight. (Simon Spotlight).

Riviello, Linda. Werewolves, Vampires & Ghosts... Oh My! 2009. (J). pap. 12.95 *(978-1-61623-088-3(6))* Independent Pub.

Robbins, Trina. The Big Flush. Page, Tyler, illus. 2012. (Chicagoland Detective Agency Ser.: 4). (ENG.). 64p. (gr. 4-8). pap. 6.95 *(978-0-8225-9161-0(8))*; lib. bdg. 29.27 *(978-0-7613-8165-5(1))* Lerner Publishing Group. (Graphic Universe™).

Roberts, Jeyn. When They Fade. 2016. (ENG.). 352p. (YA). (gr. 9). 17.99 *(978-0-385-75413-2(2)*, Knopf Bks. for Young Readers) Random Hse. Children's Bks.

Roberts, Nancy. Ghosts of the Wild West. Roberts, Bruce, photos by. 2nd fac. ed. 2008. (Illus.). 110p. (J). (gr. 3-7). 24.95 *(978-1-57003-731-3(0))* Univ. of South Carolina Pr.

—Ghosts of the Wild West: Enlarged Edition Including Five Never-Before-Published Stories. Roberts, Bruce, photos by. 2nd enl. ed. 2008. (ENG., Illus.). 120p. (gr. 3-7). pap. 13.95 *(978-1-57003-732-0(9))* Univ. of South Carolina Pr.

Rocklin, Joanne. This Book Is Haunted. Adinolfi, JoAnn, illus. 2004. (I Can Read Bks.). 48p. (gr. k-3). 14.00 *(978-0-7569-3081-3(2))* Perfection Learning Corp.

Rodda, Emily. The Ghost of Raven Hill. 2005. (Illus.). 112p. (J). *(978-0-439-79770-2(5))* Scholastic, Inc.

Roddy, Lee. Ghost of the Moaning Mansion. 2008. (D. J. Dillon Adventure Ser.: No. 8). (J). 7.99 *(978-0-88062-272-1(5))* Mott Media.

Roland, Timothy. Monkey Me & the School Ghost. 2014. (Illus.). 90p. (J). *(978-1-4844-3840-4(X))* Scholastic, Inc.

—Monkey Me & the School Ghost. 2014. (Monkey Me Ser.: 4). lib. bdg. 14.75 *(978-0-606-36053-1(0))* Turtleback Bks.

Rosen, Lucy. Paranorman: Meet the Ghosts. 2012. (Passport to Reading Level 2 Ser.). (J). lib. bdg. 13.55 *(978-0-606-26155-5(9)*, Turtleback) Turtleback Bks.

—ParaNorman: Meet the Ghosts. movie tie-in ed. 2012. (Passport to Reading Level 2 Ser.). (ENG., Illus.). 32p. (J). (gr. -1-3). pap. 3.99 *(978-0-316-20982-3(1))* Little, Brown Bks. for Young Readers.

Ross, Tony. I Want My Light On! Ross, Tony, illus. 2010. (Andersen Press Picture Bks). (ENG., Illus.). 32p. (J). (gr. -1-3). 16.95 *(978-0-7613-6443-6(9))* Lerner Publishing Group.

Rouzer, Walter. Rebel Stone & the Ghost Whisperers. 2009. 304p. pap. 18.95 *(978-0-595-52313-9(7))* iUniverse, Inc.

Roy, Ron. The Ghost at Camp David. Bush, Timothy, illus. 2010. (Capital Mysteries Ser.: 12). (ENG.). 96p. (J). (gr. 1-4). pap. 4.99 *(978-0-375-85925-0(X)*, Random Hse. Bks. for Young Readers) Random Hse. Children's Bks.

—The Ghost at Camp David. 2010. (Capital Mysteries Ser.: 12). lib. bdg. 14.75 *(978-0-606-14010-2(7)*, Turtleback) Turtleback Bks.

Ruby, Laura. Lily's Ghosts. 2005. (ENG.). 272p. (J). (gr. 5-18). pap. 5.99 *(978-0-06-051831-8(6)*, Harper Trophy) HarperCollins Pubs.

Ruby, Lois. Rebel Spirits. 2013. (ENG.). 304p. (J). (gr. 7). 17.99 *(978-0-545-42623-7(5))*; 292p. (YA). *(978-0-545-55282-0(6))* Scholastic, Inc.

—The Secret of Laurel Oaks. 2009. (ENG.). 288p. (YA). (gr. 6-9). 5.99 *(978-0-7653-5229-3(X)*, 9780765352293, Starscape) Doherty, Tom Assocs., LLC.

Sage, Angie. Araminta Spookie: The Sword in the Grotto. Pickering, Jimmy, illus. 2006. (Araminta Spookie Ser.: Bk. 2). 160p. (J). (gr. 2-5). 8.99 *(978-0-06-077484-4(3)*, Tegen, Katherine Bks) HarperCollins Pubs.

—Frognapped. Pickering, Jimmy, illus. 2007. (Araminta Spookie Ser.: Bk. 3). (J). (gr. 2-5). 128p. 8.99 *(978-0-06-077487-5(8))*; 208p. lib. bdg. 14.89 *(978-0-06-077488-2(6))* HarperCollins Pubs. (Tegen, Katherine Bks).

—Ghostsitters. Pickering, Jimmy, illus. 2009. (Araminta Spookie Ser.: 5). (ENG.). 224p. (J). (gr. 1-5). pap. 6.99 *(978-0-06-144925-3(3)*, Tegen, Katherine Bks) HarperCollins Pubs.

—My Haunted House. Pickering, Jimmy, illus. (Araminta Spookie Ser.: 1). (ENG.). (J). (gr. 2-5). 2008. 160p. pap. 5.99 *(978-0-06-077483-7(5))* 2006. 144p. 8.99 *(978-0-06-077481-3(9))* HarperCollins Pubs. (Tegen, Katherine Bks).

—Skeleton Island. 2016. (Araminta Spookie Adventure Ser.: 2). (ENG.). 176p. (J). 16.99 *(978-1-61963-945-4(9)*, 9781619639454, Bloomsbury USA Childrens) Bloomsbury Publishing USA.

—The Sword in the Grotto. Pickering, Jimmy, illus. 2008. (Araminta Spookie Ser.: 2). (ENG.). 176p. (J). (gr. 2-5). pap. 5.99 *(978-0-06-077486-8(X)*, Tegen, Katherine Bks) HarperCollins Pubs.

—Vampire Brat. Pickering, Jimmy, illus. 2007. (Araminta Spookie Ser.: Bk. 4). 128p. (J). (gr. 2-5). 8.99 *(978-0-06-077490-5(8))* HarperCollins Pubs.

Salomon, Peter Adam. All Those Broken Angels. 2014. (ENG.). 240p. (YA). pap. 11.99 *(978-0-7387-4079-9(9)*, Flux) North Star Editions.

Sander, Sonia. Scooby-Doo & the International Express. 2009. (Illus.). 32p. (J). pap. *(978-0-545-16283-8(1))* Scholastic, Inc.

—Scooby-Doo in Shiver Me Timbers, 1 vol. 2016. (Scooby-Doo! Set 3 Ser.). (ENG., Illus.). 32p. (J). (gr. k-4). lib. bdg. 24.21 *(978-1-61479-408-0(1)*, 1401184) Spotlight.

Sargent, Dave, et al. Keeping Ghosts Away Vol. 8: (Creek) Be Respectful, 20 vols. Lenoir, Jane, illus. l.t. ed. 2003. (Story Keeper Ser.: Vol. 8). 42p. (J). pap. 10.95 *(978-1-56763-918-5(6)*, 1228135) Ozark Publishing.

Sauer, Cat. Gwendolyn the Ghost. Jankowski, Daniel, illus. l.t. ed. 2006. (Brown Bag Bedtime Bks.: 1). 29p. (J). (gr. -1-2). 16.95 incl. audio compact disk *(978-0-9704460-9-1(8))* Writer's Ink. Studios, Inc.

Saunders, Jami Lynn. Feral: Book I of the Werecat Saga. 2011. 86p. (YA). pap. 4.99 *(978-1-936307-15-9(4)*, 711Press) Vendera Publishing.

Sawka, Searra. Ghost Stories: John, Are You down There? 2012. 72p. (gr. 4-6). pap. 8.95 *(978-1-4759-4210-1(9))* iUniverse, Inc.

Saxena, Shalini. The Legend of Sleepy Hollow. 2015. (Famous Legends Ser.). (ENG., Illus.). 32p. (J). (gr. 2-3). pap. 10.50 *(978-1-4824-2752-3(4))* Stevens, Gareth Publishing LLLP.

Sazaklis, John. Ghostbusters 2016 Little Golden Book. Golden Books, illus. 2016. (Little Golden Book Ser.). (ENG.). 24p. (J). (gr. -1-2). 4.99 *(978-1-5247-1491-8(7)*, Golden Bks.) Random Hse. Children's Bks.

—Ghostbusters Little Golden Book. Golden Books, illus. 2016. (Little Golden Book Ser.). (ENG.). 24p. (J). (gr. -1-2). 4.99 *(978-1-5247-1489-5(5)*, Golden Bks.) Random Hse. Children's Bks.

—Ghostbusters/Ghostbusters 2016 Big Golden Book. Golden Books & Batson, Alan, illus. 2016. (Big Golden Book Ser.).

E F G

(ENG.). 48p. (J). (gr. -1-2). 9.99 (978-1-5247-1487-1(9), Golden Bks.) Random Hse. Children's Bks.

Scarry, Richard. Richard Scarry's Books on the Go. Scarry, Richard, illus. 2015. (ENG., Illus.). 24p. (J). (gr. k — 1). bds. 19.96 (978-0-375-87522-9(0), Golden Bks.) Random Hse. Children's Bks.

Scary Stories Treasury Lenticular Cover. 2007. 80p. (978-1-4054-9871-5(4)) Parragon, Inc.

Schkolnik, Saul. Cuentos de Terror, de Magia y de Otras Cosas Extranas. (SPA.). (YA). (gr. 5-8). pap. (978-956-13-1319-4(7), AB0160) Bello, Andres CHL. Dist: Lectorum Pubns., Inc.

Schlosser, S. E. Spooky Texas: Tales of Hauntings, Strange Happenings, & Other Local Lore. Hoffman, Paul G., illus. 2008. (Spooky Ser.). (ENG.). 200p. pap. 14.95 (978-0-7627-4853-2(2)) Globe Pequot Pr., The.

Schmid, Susan Maupin. Ghost of a Chance. Marlin, Lissy, illus. 2017. (100 Dresses Ser.: 2). (ENG.). 320p. (J). (gr. 3-7). 16.99 (978-0-553-53373-6(8), Random Hse. Bks. for Young Readers) Random Hse. Children's Bks.

Scholastic Editors. Day of the Departed. 2016. (Ninjago Readers Ser.). lib. bdg. 13.55 (978-0-606-39734-6(5)) Turtleback Bks.

Scholastic, Inc. Staff. Scooby-Doo: Frankencreepy Movie Reader. 2014. (Scooby Doo Reader Ser.). lib. bdg. 13.55 (978-0-606-36270-2(3)) Turtleback Bks.

Schusterman, Michelle. Theater of Forever & Ever. 2017. (ENG.). 224p. (J). (gr. 3-7). 16.99 (978-0-399-55066-9(6), Random Hse. Bks. for Young Readers) Random Hse. Children's Bks.

Schwartz, Alvin. Scary Stories to Tell in the Dark. Helquist, Brett, illus. 2010. (Scary Stories Ser.). (ENG.). 128p. (J). (gr. 4-18). 16.99 (978-0-06-083519-4(2)); pap. 5.99 (978-0-06-083520-0(6)) HarperCollins Pubs.

Schwartz, Alvin. Scary Stories to Tell in the Dark. Gammell, Stephen, illus. 2017. (Scary Stories Ser.: 1). 128p. (J). (gr. 3-7). pap. 6.99 (978-0-06-268282-6(2)) HarperCollins Pubs.

Schwarzkopf, Tom. The Ghost at Mahone Bay, 1 vol. 2007. (ENG., Illus.). 128p. (J). (gr. 4-7). pap. 10.95 (978-1-55109-526-4(2)) Nimbus Publishing, Ltd. CAN. Dist: Orca Bk. Pubs. USA.

Scieszka, Jon. The Spooky Tire. Shannon, David et al, illus. 2009. (Jon Scieszka's Trucktown Ser.). (ENG.). 24p. (J). (gr. -1-k). lib. bdg. 15.99 (978-1-4169-4153-8(3)); pap. 3.99 (978-1-4169-4142-2(8)) Simon Spotlight. (Simon Spotlight).

Sedgwick, Marcus. The Ghosts of Heaven. 2016. (ENG.). 360p. (YA). (gr. 7). 20.85 (978-0-606-39292-1(0)) Turtleback Bks.

Selzer, Adam. Just Kill Me. 2016. (ENG., Illus.). 336p. (YA). (gr. 9). 17.99 (978-1-4814-3494-2(2), Simon & Schuster Bks. For Young Readers) Simon & Schuster Bks. For Young Readers.

Sena, Keiko. Gracie Meets a Ghost. 2016. (Gracie Wears Glasses Book Ser.). (ENG.). 32p. (J). (gr. -1-k). 16.99 (978-1-940842-13-4(1)) Museyon.

Shea, Bob. The Scariest Book Ever. Shea, Bob, illus. 2017. (ENG., Illus.). 40p. (J). (gr. 1-3). 16.99 (978-1-4847-3046-1(1)) Hyperion Bks. for Children.

Shelton, Dave. Thirteen Chairs. (ENG.). 256p. (J). (gr. 7). 2016. pap. 9.99 (978-1-338-03248-2(8)) 2015. (Illus.). 17.99 (978-0-545-81665-6(3)) Scholastic, Inc.

Shepherd, Jodie. Olivia & the Haunted Hotel. Spaziante, Patrick, illus. 2010. (Olivia TV Tie-In Ser.). (ENG.). 24p. (J). (gr. -1-2). pap. 4.99 (978-1-4424-0182-2(6), Simon Spotlight) Simon Spotlight.

—Olivia & the Haunted Hotel. 2010. (Olivia 8x8 Ser.). lib. bdg. 14.75 (978-0-606-26573-7(2), Turtleback) Turtleback Bks.

Sholl, Anna. Faery Tales of Weir. 2006. 116p. 22.95 (978-1-59818-405-1(9)) Aegypan.

Shulman, Polly & Airgood, Ellen. The Poe Annex. 2015. (ENG.). 272p. (J). (gr. 5). 16.99 (978-0-399-16614-3(9), Nancy Paulsen Books) Penguin Young Readers Group.

Shusterman, Neal. Darkness Creeping: Twenty Twisted Tales. 2007. (ENG.). 304p. (J). (gr. 3-7). 7.99 (978-0-14-240721-9(6), Puffin Books) Penguin Young Readers Group.

Shutter. 2015. (ENG.). 384p. (YA). (gr. 8-12). 17.99 (978-1-250-04467-9(7)) Feiwel & Friends.

Simpson, Pat. A Compilation of Tales to Thrill & Chill. 2008. 103p. pap. 15.95 (978-1-4357-2976-6(5)) Lulu Pr., Inc.

Singleton, Linda Joy. Last Dance. 2005. (Seer Ser.: 2). (ENG.). 264p. (YA). pap. 9.95 (978-0-7387-0638-2(8), Flux) Llewellyn Pubns.

—Sword Play. 2006. (Seer Ser.: 4). (ENG.). 288p. (YA). (gr. 7). per. 9.99 (978-0-7387-0880-5(1), Flux) Llewellyn Pubns.

Sinykin, Sheri. Giving up the Ghost, 1 vol. (ENG.). (YA). 2011. 240p. pap. 7.95 (978-1-56145-572-0(5)) 2007. 224p. (gr. 4-7). pap. 14.95 (978-1-56145-423-5(0)) Peachtree Pubs.

Skogen, Jennifer. Forests of the Night #2. 2015. (Haunting of Grey Hills Ser.). (ENG.). 200-216p. (YA). (gr. 9-12). lib. bdg. 27.13 (978-1-68076-030-9(0), Epic Pr.) ABDO Publishing Co.

—Tyger, Tyger #6. 2015. (Haunting of Grey Hills Ser.). (ENG.). 200-216p. (YA). (gr. 9-12). lib. bdg. 27.13 (978-1-68076-034-7(3), Epic Pr.) ABDO Publishing Co.

—What Dread Hand #3. 2015. (Haunting of Grey Hills Ser.). (ENG.). 200-216p. (YA). (gr. 9-12). lib. bdg. 27.13 (978-1-68076-031-6(9), Epic Pr.) ABDO Publishing Co.

Sleator, William. The Boy Who Couldn't Die. 2005. (ENG.). 184p. (J). (gr. 7-17). pap. 8.95 (978-0-8109-8790-6(2)) Abrams, Inc.

Smith, Keeley. First Soul. 2013. 204p. pap. (978-1-78299-452-7(1)) FeedARead.com.

Smith-Ready, Jeri. Shade. (ENG.). (YA). (gr. 9). 2011. 336p. pap. 9.99 (978-1-4169-9407-7(6)) 2010. 320p. 17.99 (978-1-4169-9406-0(8)) Simon Pulse. (Simon Pulse).

—Shift. (ENG.). (YA). (gr. 9). 2012. 400p. pap. 9.99 (978-1-4169-9409-1(2)) 2011. 384p. 17.99 (978-1-4169-9408-4(4)) Simon Pulse. (Simon Pulse).

—Shine. 2012. (ENG.). 416p. (YA). (gr. 9). pap. 9.99 (978-1-4424-3946-7(7), Simon Pulse) Simon Pulse.

Smith, Sarah. The Other Side of Dark. (ENG., 320p. (YA). (gr. 7). 2011. Illus.). pap. 11.99 (978-1-4424-0281-2(4)) 2010. 16.99 (978-1-4424-0280-5(6)) Simon & Schuster Children's Publishing. (Atheneum Bks. for Young Readers).

Snell, Gordon & Askin, Corrina. The Supermarket Ghost. Byrne, Bob, illus. 2007. (ENG.). 80p. (J). pap. 10.95 (978-1-84717-049-1(8)) O'Brien Pr., Ltd., The IRL. Dist: Dufour Editions, Inc.

Snicket, Lemony, pseud. Goldfish Ghost. Brown, Lisa, illus. 2017. (ENG.). 40p. (J). 17.99 (978-1-62672-507-2(1), 9781626725072) Roaring Brook Pr.

Soileau, Hodges, illus. The Mystery of the Runaway Ghost. 2004. (Boxcar Children Mysteries Ser.: 98). (ENG.). 144p. (J). (gr. 1-5). pap. 5.99 (978-0-8075-5551-4(7)) Whitman, Albert & Co.

Specter, Baron. Chasing Whales Aboard the Charles W. Morgan, 1 vol., Bk. 2. Evans, Dustin, illus. 2010. (Ghostly Graphic Adventures Ser.). (ENG.). 32p. (gr. 4-6). 28.50 (978-1-60270-771-9(5), Graphic Planet- Fiction) ABDO Publishing Co.

—Dodging Danger on the Dartmouth, 1 vol., Bk. 1. Evans, Dustin, illus. 2010. (Ghostly Graphic Adventures Ser.). (ENG.). 32p. (J). (gr. 3-6). 28.50 (978-1-60270-770-2(7)) ABDO Publishing Co.

—Drama at Dungeon Rock: #6, 1 vol. Evans, Dustin, illus. 2010. (Ghostly Graphic Adventures Ser.). (ENG.). 32p. (J). (gr. 3-6). 28.50 (978-1-60270-775-7(8)) ABDO Publishing Co.

—The Lighthouse of Terror, 1 vol., Bk. 3. Evans, Dustin, illus. 2010. (Ghostly Graphic Adventures Ser.). (ENG.). 32p. (J). (gr. 3-6). 28.50 (978-1-60270-772-6(3)) ABDO Publishing Co.

—The Spooky Short Sands Shipwreck: #4, 1 vol. Evans, Dustin, illus. 2010. (Ghostly Graphic Adventures Ser.). (ENG.). 32p. (J). (gr. 3-6). 28.50 (978-1-60270-773-3(1)) ABDO Publishing Co.

—The Star Island Spirits: #5, 1 vol. Evans, Dustin, illus. 2010. (Ghostly Graphic Adventures Ser.). (ENG.). 32p. (J). (gr. 3-6). 28.50 (978-1-60270-774-0(X)) ABDO Publishing Co.

Spector, Baron. Tracking Your Nightmare, 1 vol. Kneupper, Setch, illus. 2012. (Graveyard Diaries Ser.). (ENG.). 128p. (J). (gr. 3-8). lib. bdg. 27.07 (978-1-61641-898-4(2), Calico Chapter Bks) Magic Wagon.

Spooky Stories Treasury Lenticular Cover. 2007. 80p. (978-1-4075-0127-7(5)) Parragon, Inc.

The Spooky Storybook: Full of Fearsome Fun! 2003. (ENG., Illus.). 128p. pap. (978-0-09-189305-7(4), Hutchinson) Random Hse.

St. George, Judith. The Ghost, the White House & Me. 2007. (ENG.). 128p. (J). (gr. 4-7). 16.95 (978-0-8234-2045-2(0)) Holiday Hse., Inc.

Stahler, David, Jr. Gathering of Shades. 2006. (ENG.). 256p. pap. (978-0-06-052296-4(8)) HarperCollins Canada, Ltd.

—A Gathering of Shades. 2005. (ENG.). 304p. (J). 15.99 (978-0-06-052294-0(1), HarperTeen) HarperCollins Pubs.

Steele, Michael Anthony. Creepy Cowboy Caper. Jeralds, Scott, illus. 2017. (Scooby-Doo! Beginner Mysteries Ser.). (ENG.). 112p. (gr. 2-3). lib. bdg. 22.65 (978-1-4965-4768-2(3)) Capstone Press of Coughlan Cos.

Stein, Mathilde. Mine! Van Hout, Mies, illus. 2007. (ENG.). 26p. (J). (gr. -1-3). 16.95 (978-1-59078-506-5(1)) Boyds Mills Pr.

Stern, Jacqueline. The Ghosts of Goliad. 2003. iii, 165p. (J). 17.95 (978-1-57168-785-2(8), Eakin Pr.) Eakin Pr.

Stevenson, Sarah Jamila. The Truth Against the World. 2014. (ENG.). 360p. (YA). pap. 9.99 (978-0-7387-4058-4(6), Flux) North Star Editions.

Stilton, Geronimo. Ghost Pirate Treasure. 2012. (Creepella Von Cacklefur Ser.: 3). (ENG.). 128p. (J). (gr. 2-5). pap. 7.99 (978-0-545-30744-4(9), Scholastic Paperbacks) Scholastic, Inc.

—Ghost Pirate Treasure. 2012. (Geronimo Stilton — Creepella Von Cacklefur Ser.: 3). lib. bdg. 18.40 (978-0-606-23931-8(6), Turtleback) Turtleback Bks.

—The Phantom of the Subway. Wolf, Matt, illus. 2004. (Geronimo Stilton Ser.: No. 13). 112p. (J). lib. bdg. 10.00 (978-1-4242-0282-9(5)) Fitzgerald Bks.

—Return of the Vampire. 2012. (Geronimo Stilton — Creepella Von Cacklefur Ser.: 4). lib. bdg. 18.40 (978-0-606-26180-7(X), Turtleback) Turtleback Bks.

—A Suitcase Full of Ghosts. 2015. (Creepella Von Cacklefur Ser.: 7). (ENG.). 128p. (J). (gr. 2-5). pap. 7.99 (978-0-545-74611-3(6), Scholastic Paperbacks) Scholastic, Inc.

Stine, R. L. The Attack of the Aqua Apes & Nightmare in 3-D: Twice Terrifying Tales. 2009. (R. L. Stine's Ghosts of Fear Street Ser.). (ENG.). 272p. (J). (gr. 3-7). pap. 12.99 (978-1-4169-9136-6(0), Aladdin) Simon & Schuster Children's Publishing.

—The Confession. 2005. (Fear Street Ser.: Bk. 39). (ENG.). 160p. (YA). (gr. 7). pap. 7.99 (978-1-4169-0322-2(4), Simon Pulse) Simon Pulse.

—Dudes, the School Is Haunted!, 1 vol. Park, Trip, illus. 2011. (Rotten School Ser.: No. 7). (ENG.). 128p. (gr. 2-5). 24.21 (978-1-59961-831-9(1)) Spotlight.

—Ghost Beach. 2010. (Classic Goosebumps Ser.: 15). (ENG.). 160p. (J). (gr. 3-7). 6.99 (978-0-545-17803-7(7), Scholastic Paperbacks) Scholastic, Inc.

—The Ghost Next Door. 2015. (Goosebumps Ser.: 29). lib. bdg. 17.20 (978-0-606-37072-1(2)) Turtleback Bks.

—Halloween Party. 2006. (Fear Street Ser.: Bk. 18). (ENG.). 160p. (YA). (gr. 7-12). mass mkt. 7.99 (978-1-4169-1811-0(6), Simon Pulse) Simon Pulse.

—The Haunter. 2016. (Goosebumps Most Wanted Ser.). lib. bdg. 18.40 (978-0-606-38784-2(6)) Turtleback Bks.

—Hide & Shriek & Who's Been Sleeping in My Grave? Twice Terrifying Tales. 2009. (R. L. Stine's Ghosts of Fear Street Ser.). (ENG.). 256p. (J). (gr. 3-7). pap. 7.99 (978-1-4169-9134-2(4), Aladdin) Simon & Schuster Children's Publishing.

—Midnight Games. 2005. (Fear Street Nights Ser.: No. 2). 183p. (YA). lib. bdg. 20.00 (978-1-4242-1119-7(0)) Fitzgerald Bks.

—The Perfect Date. 2005. (Fear Street Ser.). (ENG.). 160p. (YA). (gr. 7). pap. 7.99 (978-1-4169-0323-9(2), Simon Pulse) Simon Pulse.

—Revenge of the Living Dummy. 2008. (Goosebumps HorrorLand Ser.: No. 1). 128p. (J). (gr. 4-7). 13.65 (978-0-7569-8816-6(0)) Perfection Learning Corp.

—The Rich Girl. 2005. (Fear Street Ser.: Bk. 45). (ENG.). 144p. (YA). (gr. 7). pap. 6.99 (978-1-4169-0324-6(0), Simon Pulse) Simon Pulse.

—Rotten School - Dudes, the School Is Haunted! Park, Trip, illus. 2009. (Rotten School Ser.: No. 7). 128p. (J). pap. 4.99 (978-0-06-078820-9(8), Harper Trophy) HarperCollins Pubs.

—Secret Admirer. 2006. (Fear Street Ser.: Bk. 37). (ENG.). 160p. (YA). (gr. 7). mass mkt. 7.99 (978-1-4169-0820-3(X), Simon Pulse) Simon Pulse.

—Stay Away from the Tree House & Eye of the Fortuneteller: Twice Terrifying Tales. 2009. (R. L. Stine's Ghosts of Fear Street Ser.). (ENG., Illus.). 224p. (J). (gr. 3-7). pap. 7.99 (978-1-4169-9137-3(9), Aladdin) Simon & Schuster Children's Publishing.

—Terror Trips. Thompson, Jill et al, illus. 2007. (Goosebumps Graphix Ser.: 2). (ENG.). 144p. (J). (gr. 3-7). pap. 9.99 (978-0-439-85780-2(5), Graphix) Scholastic, Inc.

—Young Scrooge: A Very Scary Christmas Story. 2016. (ENG.). 192p. (J). 16.99 (978-1-250-07015-9(5), 9781250070159) Feiwel & Friends.

—Zombie Town, 0 vols. unabr. ed. 2012. (ENG.). 74p. (J). (gr. 3-7). pap. 4.99 (978-1-61218-329-9(8), 9781612183299, Amazon Children's Publishing) Amazon Publishing.

—The 12 Screams of Christmas. 2014. (Goosebumps Most Wanted Ser.). lib. bdg. 18.40 (978-0-606-36066-1(2)) Turtleback Bks.

Storrie, Paul D. Terror in Ghost Mansion. Carruthers, Sandy, illus. 2007. (Twisted Journeys (r) Ser.: 3). (ENG.). 112p. (J). (gr. 4-7). lib. bdg. 27.93 (978-0-8225-6776-9(8), Graphic Universe™) Lerner Publishing Group.

Strachan, Linda. Hamish Mchaggis & the Ghost of Glamis. Collins, Sally J., illus. 2005. (Hamish Mchaggis Ser.). 26p. (J). per. 9.00 (978-0-9546701-9-1(1)) GW Publishing GBR. Dist: Wilson & Assocs.

Strangway, Melissa. 56 Water Street. 2008. 156p. pap. 8.95 (978-1-60528-031-8(3), iUniverse Star) iUniverse, Inc.

Strasser, Todd. Nighttime: Too Dark to See. Cushman, Doug, illus. 2008. 79p. (J). (978-0-439-80068-6(4)) Scholastic, Inc.

—Too Dark to See. Cushman, Doug, illus. 2009. (Nighttime Ser.). (ENG.). 80p. (J). (gr. 2-5). 4.99 (978-0-545-12476-8(X), Scholastic Paperbacks) Scholastic, Inc.

Stroud, Jonathan. The Creeping Shadow. 2016. (Lockwood & Co Ser.). (ENG., Illus.). 464p. (J). (gr. 3-7). 16.99 (978-1-4847-0967-2(5)) Hyperion Bks. for Children.

—The Hollow Boy. 2015. (Lockwood & Co Ser.). (ENG.). 400p. (J). (gr. 3-7). 16.99 (978-1-4847-0968-9(3)) Hyperion Bks. for Children.

—Lockwood & Co. the Screaming Staircase. 2014. (Lockwood & Co Ser.). (ENG., Illus.). 416p. (J). (gr. 3-7). pap. 7.99 (978-1-4231-8692-2(3)) Hyperion Bks. for Children.

—The Screaming Staircase. 2013. (Lockwood & Co Ser.: Bk. 1). (ENG.). 400p. (J). (gr. 3-7). 16.99 (978-1-4231-6491-3(1)) Hyperion Pr.

—The Whispering Skull. (ENG.). (J). (gr. 3-7). 2015. (Lockwood & Co Ser.). 464p. pap. 7.99 (978-1-4231-9462-0(4)) 2014. (Lockwood & Co. Ser.: 2). 448p. 17.99 (978-1-4231-6492-0(X)) Hyperion Bks. for Children.

Sublime. 2014. (ENG., Illus.). 336p. (YA). (gr. 9). 17.99 (978-1-4814-1368-6(6), Simon & Schuster Bks. For Young Readers) Simon & Schuster Bks. For Young Readers.

Summersville: One Flight Fiction. 2007. 105p. per. (978-0-9773175-2-3(8), 004) Banda Pr. International, Inc.

Summy, Barrie. I So Don't Do Famous. 2012. (ENG.). 304p. (J). (gr. 5). 7.99 (978-0-385-73791-3(2), Yearling) Random Hse. Children's Bks.

—I So Don't Do Mysteries. 2009. (ENG.). 288p. (J). (gr. 3-7). 6.99 (978-0-385-73603-9(7), Yearling) Random Hse. Children's Bks.

—I So Don't Do Spooky. 2010. (ENG.). 304p. (J). (gr. 3-7). 7.99 (978-0-385-73605-3(3), Yearling) Random Hse. Children's Bks.

Sundell, Joanne. Arctic Shadow. 2015. (Watch Eyes Trilogy Ser.: 2). (ENG.). 278p. (YA). 25.95 (978-1-4328-3008-3(2), Five Star Trade) Cengage Gale.

—Arctic Will. 2016. (ENG.). 326p. (YA). 25.95 (978-1-4328-3175-2(5), Five Star) Cengage Gale.

Super Why Staff. The Ghost Who Was Afraid of Halloween. 2009. 32p. pap. 3.99 (978-0-448-45179-4(4), Grosset & Dunlap) Penguin Publishing Group.

Sutherland, Robert. Greysteel's Ghost. 2007. (ENG.). 208p. (J). mass mkt. 6.99 (978-0-00-639399-3(3), Harper Trophy) HarperCollins Pubs.

Sutton, Margaret. The Haunted Attic, No. 2. Doane, Pelagie, illus. 2008. (Judy Bolton Mysteries Ser.). (ENG.). 240p. (J). (gr. 4-7). pap. 14.95 (978-1-4290-9022-3(7)) Applewood Bks.

Syers, Rita Hsu. Mystery of the Crying Ghost. 2007. 155p. 9.95 (978-0-9779267-1-8(0)) Bronwen Publishing.

Sykes, Shelley & Szymanski, Lois. The Soldier in the Cellar. 2011. (Gettysburg Ghost Gang Ser.: Vol. 5). 96p. (J). pap. 7.95 (978-1-57249-299-8(6), White Mane Kids) White Mane Publishing Co., Inc.

—A Whisper of War. 2003. (J). 5.95 (978-1-57249-327-8(5), White Mane Kids) White Mane Publishing Co., Inc.

Taylor, Sean. Purple Class & the Skelington: And Other Stories. Bate, Helen & Dunbar, Polly, illus. 2006. (ENG.). 96p. (J). (gr. 2-5). per. 7.95 (978-1-84507-377-0(0), Frances Lincoln Children's Bks.) Quarto Publishing Group UK GBR. Dist: Hachette Bk. Group.

Taylor, Thomas. Haunters. 2013. (J). 327p. (978-0-545-50253-5(5)); (ENG.). 336p. (gr. 5-9). 17.99 (978-0-545-49644-5(6)) Scholastic, Inc.

Teitelbaum, Michael. The Ghost at the Grand Inn. 2015. (Cold Whispers Ser.). (ENG., Illus.). 32p. (J). (gr. 2-6). lib. bdg. 26.60 (978-1-62724-808-2(0)) Bearport Publishing Co., Inc.

—Night of the Gravedigger. 2015. (Cold Whispers Ser.). (ENG., Illus.). 32p. (J). (gr. 2-6). lib. bdg. 26.60 (978-1-62724-805-1(6)) Bearport Publishing Co., Inc.

—The Secret of the Tragic Theater. 2015. (Cold Whispers Ser.). (ENG., Illus.). 32p. (J). (gr. 2-6). lib. bdg. 26.60 (978-1-62724-809-9(9)) Bearport Publishing Co., Inc.

Telgemeier, Raina. Ghosts. Telgemeier, Raina, illus. 2016. (ENG., Illus.). 256p. (J). (gr. 3-7). 24.99 (978-0-545-54061-2(5), Graphix) Scholastic, Inc.

Tennapel, Doug. Ghostopolis. 2010. (ENG.). 272p. (J). (gr. 4-7). pap. 12.99 (978-0-545-21028-7(3), Graphix) Scholastic, Inc.

Terasaki, Stanley Todd. Ghosts for Breakfast. Shinjo, Shelly, illus. 2013. (ENG.). 32p. (J). (gr. k-4). 16.95 (978-1-58430-046-5(9)) Lee & Low Bks., Inc.

Thay, Edrick. Haunted Cemeteries, 1 vol., Vol. 1. rev. ed. 2004. (Ghost Stories Ser.). (ENG., Illus.). 200p. (gr. 4). pap. 12.95 (978-1-894877-60-2(8), 1894877608, Ghost Hse. Bks.) Lone Pine Publishing USA.

Theriault, Francis. Just Another Ghost Story: A critical thinking Novel. 2007. 68p. (J). per. 8.95 (978-0-595-45258-3(2)) iUniverse, Inc.

Thieman, Linda. Katie & Kimble: A Ghost Story. 2007. (Illus.). (J). 108p. pap. 8.95 (978-0-9794396-9-8(8)); 148p. pap. 12.48 (978-0-9794396-0-5(4)) Pale Silver Rainplop Pr.

—Katie & Kimble: The Magic Wish. 2008. 115p. (J). pap. 8.95 (978-0-9794396-6-7(3)) Pale Silver Rainplop Pr.

Thomas, Deborah Kadiar. Cemetery Jamboree, 1 vol. Thomas, Deborah Kadiar, illus. 2016. (ENG., Illus.). 32p. (J). (gr. k-5). pap. 9.95 (978-1-4556-2239-9(7)) Pelican Publishing Co., Inc.

Thomas, Jesse Lee. The Ghost House. Daily, Rick, illus. 2011. 30p. pap. 16.00 (978-1-4349-8472-2(9), RoseDog Bks.) Dorrance Publishing Co., Inc.

Thomas, Teri. The Barge Ghost. 2005. (Quickreads Ser.). (Illus.). 32p. (J). pap. 2.95 (978-1-56254-737-0(2), SP7372) Saddleback Educational Publishing, Inc.

Thompson, Kate. The Last of the High Kings. 2008. 323p. (YA). (gr. 7-18). lib. bdg. 17.89 (978-0-06-117596-1(X), HarperTeen) HarperCollins Pubs.

Thomson, Sarah L. Mercy: The Last New England Vampire, 1 vol. 2011. (ENG.). 178p. (J). pap. 16.95 (978-1-934031-36-0(4), 9caae975-eeb4-4b56-8673-b3abbf16fc2f) Islandport Pr., Inc.

Thrasher, Amanda M. The Ghost of Whispering Willow. Dunigan, Anne, ed. 2013. (ENG., Illus.). 258p. (J). (gr. 4-7). pap. 10.95 (978-0-615-74990-7(9)) Rising Phoenix Pr.

—The Ghost of Whispering Willow. 2012. 222p. 26.50 (978-1-61897-881-3(0)); pap. 13.95 (978-1-61897-630-7(3)) Strategic Book Publishing & Rights Agency (SBPRA). (Strategic Bk. Publishing).

Tibbetts, Peggy. The Road to Weird. 2003. 12.00 (978-1-869942-59-5(0)) Zumaya Pubns. LLC.

Ticktock Media, Ltd. Staff. The Unexplained: Encounters with Ghosts, Monsters, & Aliens. 2008. (ENG.). 96p. (J). (gr. 2-4). pap. 9.95 (978-1-84696-807-5(0), TickTock Books) Octopus Publishing Group GBR. Dist: Independent Pubs. Group.

Tingle, Tim & Moore, James W. Spooky Texas Tales. Miller, Gina, illus. 2005. x, 85p. (J). pap. (978-0-89672-566-9(9)) Texas Tech Univ. Pr.

Towell, Katy. Skary Childrin & the Carousel of Sorrow. 2013. (ENG.). 272p. (J). (gr. 3-7). pap. 8.99 (978-0-375-87240-2(X), Knopf Bks. for Young Readers) Random Hse. Children's Bks.

Townson, Hazel. Vanishing Village. 2008. (ENG.). 80p. (J). (gr. 4-7). pap. 9.95 (978-1-84270-472-1(9)) Andersen Pr. GBR. Dist: Independent Pubs. Group.

Trapani, Iza. Haunted Party. Trapani, Iza, illus. 2010. (ENG., Illus.). 28p. (J). (gr. -1-2). pap. 7.95 (978-1-58089-247-6(7)) Charlesbridge Publishing, Inc.

Trigiani, Adriana. Viola in Reel Life. (Viola Ser.: 1). (ENG.). (YA). (gr. 8). 2011. 304p. pap. 8.99 (978-0-06-145104-1(5)) 2009. 288p. 17.99 (978-0-06-145102-7(9)) HarperCollins Pubs. (HarperTeen).

Tucholke, April Genevieve. Between the Spark & the Burn. 2014. (ENG.). 336p. (YA). (gr. 7). 17.99 (978-0-8037-4047-1(6), Dial Bks) Penguin Young Readers Group.

Turnage, Sheila. The Ghosts of Tupelo Landing. 2014. (Mo & Dale Mysteries Ser.). (ENG.). 368p. (J). (gr. 5). 16.99 (978-0-8037-3671-9(1), Kathy Dawson Books) Penguin Young Readers Group.

—The Ghosts of Tupelo Landing. 2015. lib. bdg. 18.40 (978-0-606-36773-8(X)) Turtleback Bks.

Turner, Suzy. The Ghost of Josiah Grimshaw: A Morgan Sisters Novel. 2013. 286p. pap. (978-989-97348-6-9(1)) Turner, Suzanne.

Twigg, Aeres. The Green Hawk. 2003. (ENG., Illus.). 88p. (J). pap. 12.95 (978-1-85902-787-5(3)) Beekman Bks., Inc.

Ure, Jean. Daisy May. Donnelly, Karen, illus. 2011. (ENG.). 96p. (J). pap. 5.99 (978-0-00-713369-7(3), HarperCollins Children's Bks.) HarperCollins Pubs. Ltd. GBR. Dist: HarperCollins Pubs.

Vail, Emily Blake. The Grey Ghost of the Pharaoh. Barbra K. Mudd, illus. 2004. 176p. (YA). per. 8.99 (978-0-935087-27-7(3)) Wright Publishing, Inc.

Valdes, Alisa. Perdition: A Kindred Novel. 2013. (YA). pap. (978-0-06-202421-3(3), HarperTeen) HarperCollins Pubs.

—The Temptation. 2012. (ENG.). 320p. (YA). (gr. 9). pap. 8.99 (978-0-06-202420-6(5), HarperTeen) HarperCollins Pubs.

van Genechten, Guido. No Ghost under My Bed. 2010. (ENG.). 30p. (J). (gr. -1-k). 17.95 (978-1-60537-069-9(X)) Cobblestone Publishing Co.

Vande Velde, Vivian. Ghost of a Hanged Man, 1 vol. 2003. (ENG.). 32p. (J). (gr. 5). pap. 5.95 (978-0-7614-5154-9(4)) Marshall Cavendish Corp.

—There's a Dead Person Following My Sister Around. 2008. (ENG., Illus.). 160p. (J). (gr. 5-7). pap. 11.95 (978-0-15-206467-9(2)) Houghton Mifflin Harcourt Publishing Co.

Verday, Jessica. The Hidden. (ENG.). 400p. (YA). (gr. 9). 2012. pap. 12.99 (978-1-4169-7898-5(4)) 2011. 17.99 (978-1-4169-7897-8(6)) Simon Pulse. (Simon Pulse).

—The Hollow. (ENG.). (YA). (gr. 7). 2010. 528p. pap. 11.99 (978-1-4169-7894-7(1))No. 1. 2009. 544p. 17.99 (978-1-4169-7893-0(3)) Simon Pulse. (Simon Pulse).

Vernick, Shirley Reva. The Black Butterfly. 2014. (ENG.). 226p. (J). 19.95 (978-1-935955-79-5(9)) Cinco Puntos Pr.

Vernon, Ursula. No Such Thing as Ghosts. 5th ed. 2011. (Dragonbreath Ser.: 5). (ENG.). 208p. (J). (gr. 3-7). 12.99 (978-0-8037-3527-9(8), Dial Bks) Penguin Young Readers Group.

Verstraete, Majanka. Valentina & the Haunted Mansion (Valentina's Spooky Adventures - 1) Giffin, Noelle, illus. l.t. ed. 2013. (ENG.). 48p. 21.95 (978-1-62253-057-1(8)); pap. 10.95 (978-1-62253-056-4(X)) Evolved Publishing.

Viney, Peter. A Tidy Ghost, 17. 2013. (Garnet Oracle Readers Ser.). (Illus.). 40p. pap., stu. ed. 4.50 (978-1-907575-23-5(5)) Garnet Education GBR. Dist: Garnet Publishing, Ltd.

Waddell, Martin. The Orchard Book of Goblins Ghouls & Ghosts & Other Magical Stories. Ross, Tony, illus. 2006. (ENG.). 128p. (J). (gr. -1-k). 22.99 *(978-1-84121-922-6(3))* Hodder & Stoughton GBR. Dist: Hachette Bk. Group.

Wade, Rebecca. The Whispering House. 2012. (ENG.). 272p. (J). (gr. 3-7). 16.99 *(978-0-06-077497-4(5)*, Tegen, Katherine Bks) HarperCollins Pubs.

Wagner, Lloyd S. Ghosts at Gettysburg: An Oliver Family Adventure. 2007. 144p. 21.95 *(978-0-595-70995-3(8))*; per. 11.95 *(978-0-595-46877-5(2))* iUniverse, Inc.

Walker, Melissa. Ashes to Ashes. (ENG.). (YA). (gr. 8). 2015. 352p. pap. 9.99 *(978-0-06-207735-6(X))* 2013. 336p. 17.99 *(978-0-06-207734-9(1))* HarperCollins Pubs. (Tegen, Katherine Bks).

—Dust to Dust. 320p. (YA). (gr. 8). 2016. pap. 9.99 *(978-0-06-207738-7(4))* 2015. (ENG.). 17.99 *(978-0-06-207737-0(6))* HarperCollins Pubs. (Tegen, Katherine Bks).

Wallace, Carey. The Ghost in the Glass House. 2014. (ENG.). 240p. (YA). (gr. 7). pap. 13.99 *(978-0-544-33618-6(6)*, HMH Books For Young Readers) Houghton Mifflin Harcourt Publishing Co.

Wallace, Karen. Ghost Mouse. Blake, Beccy, illus. 2009. (Go! Readers Ser.). 48p. (J). (gr. 2-5). pap. 12.85 *(978-1-60754-273-5(0))*; lib. bdg. 29.25 *(978-1-60754-272-8(2))* Windmill Bks.

Wallace, Rich. A Deadly Fall. Volpari, Daniela, illus. 2016. 48p. (J). *(978-1-62402-147-3(6))* Magic Wagon.

—The Room of Woe: An Up2U Horror Adventure, 1 vol. Emroca Flores, Jose, illus. 2015. (ENG.). 80p. (J). *(978-1-62402-094-0(1))* Magic Wagon.

Warner, Gertrude Chandler. The Mystery of the Runaway Ghost. Soileau, Hodges, illus. 2004. (Boxcar Children Ser.). 135p. (J). 12.65 *(978-0-7569-3264-0(5))* Perfection Learning Corp.

Warner, Gertrude Chandler, creator. The Ghost at the Drive-In Movie. 2008. (Boxcar Children Mysteries Ser.: 116). (ENG.). 128p. (J). (gr. 1-5). pap. 5.99 *(978-0-8075-5578-1(9))* Whitman, Albert & Co.

Warren, Samuel. The Spectre Smitten. 2004. reprint ed. pap. 1.99 *(978-1-4192-8323-9(5))* Kessinger Publishing, LLC.

Waters, Daniel. Break My Heart 1,000 Times. 2013. (ENG., Illus.). 352p. (YA). (gr. 7-17). pap. 9.99 *(978-1-4231-2228-9(3))* Hyperion Pr.

Watkins, Steve. Awol in North Africa. 2016. (Ghosts of War Ser.: 3). (ENG.). 208p. (J). (gr. 3-7). pap. 5.99 *(978-0-545-83706-4(5))* Scholastic, Inc.

—The Secret of Midway. 2014. (Ghosts of War Ser.: 1). (ENG.). 208p. (J). (gr. 3-7). pap. 5.99 *(978-0-545-66585-8(X)*, Scholastic Paperbacks) Scholastic, Inc.

Watts, Julia. Free Spirits. 2009. (ENG.). 176p. (J). (gr. 1). pap. 8.95 *(978-0-9667359-2-5(7)*, BeanPole Bks.) Harren Communications, LLC.

—Kindred Spirits. 2008. (ENG.). 147p. (gr. 3-18). pap. 8.95 *(978-0-9667359-9-4(4))* Harren Communications, LLC.

—Revived Spirits. 2011. (ENG.). 170p. (J). (gr. 7). pap. 8.95 *(978-0-9831032-2-6(4)*, BeanPole Bks.) Harren Communications, LLC.

Weatherford, Carole Boston. The Library Ghost. White, Lee, illus. 2008. 22p. (J). (gr. -1-3). 17.95 *(978-1-60213-017-3(5)*, Upstart Bks.) Highsmith Inc.

Webb, Holly. Rose & the Silver Ghost. 2015. (Rose Ser.: 4). (ENG.). 224p. (J). (gr. 3-6). pap. 6.99 *(978-1-4926-0433-4(X)*, Sourcebooks Jabberwocky) Sourcebooks, Inc.

Weck, Peter. Lima Bear's Halloween. DiSalvo, Len, illus. 2012. (Lima Bear Stories Ser.). 40p. (J). 15.95 *(978-1-933872-16-2(0))* Lima Bear Pr LLC, The.

Weeks, Sarah. As Simple as It Seems. (ENG.). 192p. (J). (gr. 3-7). 2011. pap. 5.99 *(978-0-06-084665-7(8))* 2010. 15.99 *(978-0-06-084663-3(1))* HarperCollins Pubs.

Weisman, Greg. Rain of the Ghosts. 2013. (Rain of the Ghosts Ser.: 1). (ENG., Illus.). 240p. (YA). (gr. 6-13). pap. 9.99 *(978-1-250-02979-9(1)*, 9781250029799, St. Martin's Griffin) St. Martin's Pr.

Wells, Charity. The Trouble with the Supernatural, 1 vol. 2010. 84p. pap. 19.95 *(978-1-4489-2117-1(1))* America Star Bks.

Wells, Marcia. Mystery in Mayan Mexico. Calo, Marcos, illus. 2016. (Eddie Red Undercover Ser.: 2). (ENG.). 224p. (J). (gr. 5-7). pap. 7.99 *(978-0-544-66850-8(2)*, HMH Books For Young Readers) Houghton Mifflin Harcourt Publishing Co.

West, Tracey. The Audio Files. Harrington, Rich, illus. 2006. 96p. (J). pap. *(978-0-439-90719-4(5))* Scholastic, Inc.

Westcott, Jim. The Gift. 2014. (Red Rhino Ser.). (J). lib. bdg. 18.40 *(978-0-606-36201-6(0))* Turtleback Bks.

Westerfeld, Scott. Afterworlds. 2014. (ENG., Illus.). 608p. (YA). (gr. 9). 19.99 *(978-1-4814-2234-5(0)*, Simon Pulse) Simon Pulse.

—Afterworlds. 2015. lib. bdg. 24.50 *(978-0-606-37860-4(X))* Turtleback Bks.

Westwood, Chris. Graveyard Shift. (Hauntings Ser.: bk.1). (ENG.). 304p. (J). (gr. 3-7). 2014. pap. 6.99 *(978-0-545-39920-3(3))* 2012. 17.99 *(978-0-545-39919-7(X))* Scholastic, Inc. (Scholastic Pr.).

Weyn, Suzanne. The Titanic Locket. 2014. (Haunted Museum Ser.: 1). (ENG.). 208p. (J). (gr. 3-7). pap. 6.99 *(978-0-545-58842-3(1)*, Scholastic Paperbacks) Scholastic, Inc.

—The Titanic Locket. 2014. (Hauntings: the Haunted Museum Ser.: 1). lib. bdg. 17.20 *(978-0-606-35809-5(9))* Turtleback Bks.

Wharton, Edith. Edith Wharton. McConnell, James, illus. 2004. (Great American Short Stories Ser.). 80p. (gr. 4-7). lib. bdg. 24.00 *(978-0-8368-4256-2(1)*, Gareth Stevens Learning Library) Stevens, Gareth Publishing LLLP.

Wheeler, E. B. The Haunting of Springett Hall. 2015. (ENG.). 256p. (YA). (gr. 7-13). pap. 16.99 *(978-1-4621-1672-0(8)*, Sweetwater Bks.) Cedar Fort, Inc./CFI Distribution.

Whitcomb, Laura. A Certain Slant of Light. 2005. (ENG.). 288p. (YA). (gr. 7-18). pap. 8.99 *(978-0-618-58532-8(X))* Houghton Mifflin Harcourt Publishing Co.

—Under the Light. 2014. (ENG.). 256p. (YA). (gr. 7). pap. 8.99 *(978-0-544-30294-5(X)*, HMH Books For Young Readers) Houghton Mifflin Harcourt Publishing Co.

White, David. The Bad Luck Gang & the Ghost That Wasn't. 2007. 76p. per. 19.95 *(978-1-4241-7504-8(6))* America Star Bks.

Whiting, Jim. Really Scary Stuff, 4 vols., Set. Incl. Scary Ghosts. lib. bdg. 25.32 *(978-1-4296-3967-5(9))*; Scary Monsters. lib. bdg. 25.32 *(978-1-4296-3968-2(7))*; Scary Places. lib. bdg. 25.32 *(978-1-4296-3970-5(9))*; (gr. 1-2). (Really Scary Stuff Ser.). (ENG.). 24p. 2010. Set lib. bdg. 75.96 *(978-1-4296-4417-4(6)*, First Facts) Capstone Press of Coughlan Cos.

Whybrow, Ian. Little Wolf's Haunted Hall for Small Horrors. Ross, Tony, illus. (Middle Grade Fiction Ser.). (J). 2005. 132p. (gr. 3-6). 14.95 *(978-1-57505-412-4(4))* 2004. 125p. (gr. 4-7). per. 6.95 *(978-1-57505-794-1(8))* Lerner Publishing Group.

Wiesner, David, adapted by. Gonna Roll the Bones. 2004. (ENG., Illus.). 32p. (J). (gr. -1-12). 16.95 *(978-1-59687-176-2(8))* iBks., Inc.

Wigger, Sherry. Scary Stories for Brave Kids, 1 vol. 2009. 73p. pap. 16.95 *(978-1-61582-308-6(5))* PublishAmerica, Inc.

Wilde, Oscar. The Canterville Ghost. Date not set. (Nelson Readers Ser.). (J). pap. *(978-0-17-557035-5(3))* Addison-Wesley Longman, Inc.

—The Canterville Ghost. Marks, Alan, illus. 2005. (Young Reading Ser.: Vol. 2). 64p. (J). (gr. 2-18). lib. bdg. 13.95 *(978-1-58086-781-8(2)*, Usborne) EDC Publishing.

—The Canterville Ghost: Complete & Unabridged with Extensive Notes. annot. ed. 2013. (ENG.). 96p. pap. 4.99 *(978-93-5036-302-7(X))* Ratna, Sagar Pvt. Ltd. IND. Dist: Midpoint Trade Bks., Inc.

Wilde, Terry Lee. Ghostly Liaisons. 2006. (ENG.). 350p. (YA). pap. *(978-1-932815-37-5(6))* Medallion Pr., Inc.

Williams, Carol Lynch. Messenger. 2016. (ENG., Illus.). 288p. (YA). (gr. 7). 17.99 *(978-1-4814-5776-7(4)*, Simon & Schuster/Paula Wiseman Bks.) Simon & Schuster/Paula Wiseman Bks.

Williams, Katie. Absent. 2013. (ENG.). 180p. (YA). (gr. 7-12). 16.99 *(978-0-8118-7150-1(9))* Chronicle Bks. LLC.

Williams, Kethette. The Ghosts on the Hill. 2007. (ENG.). 56p. per. 16.95 *(978-1-4241-6767-8(1))* America Star Bks.

Wilson, John. Ghosts of James Bay. 2nd ed. 2009. (ENG.). 128p. (J). (gr. 6). pap. 11.99 *(978-1-55002-827-0(8)*, Sandcastle Bks.) Dundurn CAN. Dist: Ingram Publisher Services.

Wilson, Mark A. The Old Man's Secret Friend, 1 vol. 2009. 19p. pap. 19.95 *(978-1-61582-315-4(8))* PublishAmerica, Inc.

Winkler, Henry & Oliver, Lin. Zero to Hero. 2012. (Ghost Buddy Ser.: 1). (ENG.). 176p. (J). (gr. 3-7). pap. 5.99 *(978-0-545-29882-7(2)*, Scholastic Paperbacks) Scholastic, Inc.

Winters, Cat. In the Shadow of Blackbirds. 2013. (ENG., Illus.). 400p. (YA). (gr. 7-17). 17.95 *(978-1-4197-0530-4(X)*, Amulet Bks.) Abrams, Inc.

—The Steep & Thorny Way. (ENG.). (YA). (gr. 8-17). 2017. 368p. pap. 9.99 ***(978-1-4197-2350-6(2))*** 2016. (Illus.). 352p. 17.95 *(978-1-4197-1915-8(7))* Abrams, Inc. (Amulet Bks.).

Wolnik, Charlotte. The Chocolate Chip Ghost. 2008. 40p. pap. 24.95 *(978-1-4241-8896-3(2))* America Star Bks.

Wright, Betty Ren. Christina's Ghost. 2008. (ENG.). 149p. (J). (gr. 3-7). pap. 7.99 *(978-0-8234-2171-8(6))* Holiday Hse., Inc.

—Crandalls' Castle. 2005. (ENG.). 184p. (YA). (gr. 4-6). tchr. ed. 17.95 *(978-0-8234-1726-1(3))* Holiday Hse., Inc.

—Princess for a Week. Rogers, Jacqueline, illus. (ENG.). 160p. (J). (gr. 4-7). 2007. pap. 6.95 *(978-0-8234-2111-4(2))* 2006. 16.95 *(978-0-8234-1945-6(2))* Holiday Hse., Inc.

Wright, Susan. Grandma's Haunted House. 2007. 64p. per. 16.95 *(978-1-4241-0466-6(1))* PublishAmerica, Inc.

Yansky, Brian. Utopia, Iowa. 2015. (ENG.). 336p. (YA). (gr. 9). 17.99 *(978-0-7636-6533-3(9))* Candlewick Pr.

The Year of Shadows. 2014. (ENG., Illus.). 416p. (J). (gr. 3-7). pap. 7.99 *(978-1-4424-4295-5(6)*, Simon & Schuster Bks. For Young Readers) Simon & Schuster Bks. For Young Readers.

Young, Timothy. They're Coming!, 1 vol. 2012. (ENG., Illus.). 32p. (J). 16.99 *(978-0-7643-4225-7(8)*, 9780764342257) Schiffer Publishing, Ltd.

Youngquist, D. M. Ghosts of Interstate 80. 2007. (ENG., Illus.). 180p. per. 9.95 *(978-1-57166-459-4(9))* Quixote Pr.

Yovanoff, Brenna. Paper Valentine. 2013. (ENG.). 320p. (YA). (gr. 7). 17.99 *(978-1-59514-599-4(0)*, Razorbill) Penguin Young Readers Group.

Zullo, Allan. The Haunted Shortstop: True Ghostly Sports Stories. 2007. 128p. (J). pap. *(978-0-439-88618-5(X))* Scholastic, Inc.

The 13 Pet Geists. 2005. (Illus.). (J). 15.99 *(978-0-9755889-0-1(7))*; lib. bdg. 15.99 *(978-0-9755889-1-8(5))* RoseKnows, Inc.

GIANTS

Andreasen, Dan. The Giant of Seville: A Tall Tale Based on a True Story. 2007. (ENG., Illus.). 32p. (J). (gr. -1-3). 16.95 *(978-0-8109-0988-5(X)*, Abrams Bks. for Young Readers) Abrams, Inc.

Bowen, Carl. Thor vs. the Giants: A Viking Graphic Novel. Garcia, Eduardo, illus. 2016. (Norse Myths: a Viking Graphic Novel Ser.). (ENG.). 56p. (gr. 3-4). pap. 5.95 *(978-1-4965-3491-0(3))*; lib. bdg. 27.99 *(978-1-4965-3487-3(5))* Stone Arch Bks.

Bowen, Carl, et al. Gods & Thunder: A Graphic Novel of Old Norse Myths. Garcia, Eduardo et al, illus. 2017. (ENG.). 208p. (gr. 3-4). pap. 14.95 *(978-1-62370-848-1(6))* Capstone Young Readers of Coughlan Cos.

Broutin, Christian & Delafosse, Claude. Let's Look at Fairies, Witches, Giants & Dragons. 2012. (ENG., Illus.). 38p. (J). (gr. k-3). pap. 11.99 *(978-1-85103-358-4(0))* Moonlight Publishing, Ltd. GBR. Dist: Independent Pubs. Group.

Christopher, Neil. Arctic Giants, 1 vol. Widermann, Eva, illus. 2010. (ENG.). 128p. (J). (gr. 3). 24.95 *(978-1-926569-09-3(1))* Inhabit Media Inc. CAN. Dist: Independent Pubs. Group.

Hamilton, John. Ogres And Giants, 1 vol. 2004. (Fantasy & Folklore Ser.). (ENG., Illus.). 32p. (gr. 4-8). 27.07 *(978-1-59197-714-8(2)*, Abdo & Daughters) ABDO Publishing Co.

Haze, Xaviant. Ancient America's Lost Giants. 2017. (Discovering Ancient America Ser.). 200p. (J). (gr. 12-14). 39.75 ***(978-1-4994-6676-8(5)***, Rosen Young Adult) Rosen Publishing Group, Inc., The.

Jeffrey, Gary. Giants. 2011. (Graphic Mythical Creatures Ser.). 24p. (J). (gr. 3-5). pap. 8.15 *(978-1-4339-6035-2(4)*, Gareth Stevens Learning Library); lib. bdg. 23.95 *(978-1-4339-6034-5(6))* Stevens, Gareth Publishing LLLP.

Knudsen, Shannon. Giants, Trolls, & Ogres. 2009. (Fantasy Chronicles Ser.). (ENG., Illus.). 48p. (gr. 4-7). lib. bdg. 27.93 *(978-0-8225-9985-2(6))* Lerner Publishing Group.

Limke, Jeff. Thor & Loki. 2008. pap. 52.95 *(978-0-8225-9458-1(7))* Lerner Publishing Group.

—Thor Y Loki: En la Tierra de Los Gigantes; Thor & Loki: in the Land of Giants. 2008. pap. 52.95 *(978-0-8225-9675-2(X))* Lerner Publishing Group.

Stefoff, Rebecca. Giants. 2015. (Creatures of Fantasy Ser.). (ENG., Illus.). 64p. (J). (gr. 5-5). lib. bdg. 34.21 *(978-1-5026-0502-3(3))* Cavendish Square Publishing.

Susaeta, Equipo. LOS GIGANTES. (SPA.). 24p. (J). 3.48 *(978-84-305-9409-2(4))* Susaeta Ediciones, S.A. ESP. Dist: AIMS International Bks., Inc.

West, David & Ganeri, Anita. Giants & Ogres. West, David & Ganeri, Anita, illus. 2010. (Dark Side Ser.). (Illus.). 32p. (J). (ENG.). pap. 10.50 *(978-1-4488-1568-5(1))*; lib. bdg. 26.50 *(978-1-61531-898-8(4))* Rosen Publishing Group, Inc., The. (PowerKids Pr.).

Woog, Adam. Giants. 2011. 80p. (YA). lib. bdg. 37.27 *(978-1-60152-224-5(X))* ReferencePoint Pr., Inc.

GIANTS—FICTION

Adams, Alison. Jack & the Beanstalk: Classic Tales Edition. Magnuson, Diana, illus. 2011. (Classic Tales Ser.). (J). *(978-1-936258-68-0(4))* Benchmark Education Co.

Adventures in Flatfrost. 2014. (Kingdom of Wrenly Ser.: 5). (ENG., Illus.). 128p. (J). (gr. k-4). pap. 5.99 *(978-1-4814-1388-6(0)*, Little Simon) Little Simon.

Aguirre, Jorge. Giants Beware! Rosado, Rafael, illus. 2012. (Chronicles of Claudette Ser.). (ENG.). 208p. (J). (gr. 2-5). pap. 15.99 *(978-1-59643-582-7(8)*, 9781596435827, First Second Bks.) Roaring Brook Pr.

Ambrose, Sophie. The Lonely Giant. Ambrose, Sophie, illus. 2016. (ENG., Illus.). 32p. (J). (gr. -1-3). 16.99 *(978-0-7636-8225-5(X))* Candlewick Pr.

Anderson, Brian. The Adventures of Commander Zack Proton & the Red Giant. Holgate, Douglas, illus. 2006. (Adventures of Commander Zack Proton Ser.: 1). (ENG.). 128p. (J). (gr. 2-5). pap. 5.99 *(978-1-4169-1364-1(5)*, Simon & Schuster/Paula Wiseman Bks.) Simon & Schuster/Paula Wiseman Bks.

Appleton, Victor. Tom Swift in Captivity or A Daring Escap. 2006. pap. *(978-1-4065-0914-4(0))* Dodo Pr.

Arengo, Sue. Jack & the Beanstalk. Ratto, Cinzia, illus. 2006. (ENG.). 24p. 5.50 *(978-0-19-422538-0(0))* Oxford Univ. Pr. GBR. Dist: Oxford Univ. Pr., Inc.

Balian, Lorna. A Sweetheart for Valentine, 1 vol. Balian, Lorna, illus. 2005. (ENG., Illus.). 32p. (J). 15.95 *(978-1-932065-14-5(8))* Star Bright Bks., Inc.

Barchers, Suzanne I. The Princess & the Giant: A Tale from Scotland. Lafrance, Marie, illus. 2013. (Tales of Honor Ser.). (ENG.). 32p. (gr. 1-3). pap. 8.95 *(978-1-937529-61-1(4))* Red Chair Pr.

Beamish, Diane. Gentle Jack. 2006. 25p. (J). 10.25 *(978-1-4116-5553-9(2))* Lulu Pr., Inc.

Beer, Barbara Vagnozzi. Jack & the Beanstalk. Vagnozzi, Barbara, illus. 2005. (Flip-Up Fairy Tales Ser.). (ENG.). 24p. (J). pap. *(978-1-904550-20-4(7))* Child's Play International Ltd.

Bellows, Greg. The Giant. 2011. 24p. pap. 13.50 *(978-1-4634-3940-8(7))* AuthorHouse.

Bills, Taylor, illus. Jack & the Beanstalk. 2009. 24p. 12.95 *(978-0-9776845-3-3(9))* 3D Alley, Inc.

Bird, Betsy. Giant Dance Party. Dorman, Brandon, illus. 2013. (ENG.). 32p. (J). (gr. k-3). 17.99 *(978-0-06-196083-3(7)*, Greenwillow Bks.) HarperCollins Pubs.

Black, Holly & DiTerlizzi, Tony. A Giant Problem. DiTerlizzi, Tony, illus. 2008. (Beyond the Spiderwick Chronicles Ser.: 2). (ENG., Illus.). 176p. (J). (gr. 2-5). 12.99 *(978-0-689-87132-0(5)*, Simon & Schuster Bks. For Young Readers) Simon & Schuster Bks. For Young Readers.

Blevins, Wiley. Jack & the Bloody Beanstalk. Cox, Steve, illus. 2016. (Scary Tales Retold Ser.). (ENG.). 24p. (gr. k-3). lib. bdg. 23.99 *(978-1-63440-099-2(2))* Red Chair Pr.

Bradman, Tony. Mr. Giant & the Beastly Baron, 1 vol. Warburton, Sarah, illus. 2014. (After Happily Ever After Ser.). (ENG.). 56p. (gr. 2-3). lib. bdg. 25.32 *(978-1-4342-7949-1(9)*, After Happily Ever After) Stone Arch Bks.

Butler, Dave. The Giant's Seat (the Extraordinary Journeys of Clockwork Charlie) 2017. (Extraordinary Journeys of Clockwork Charlie Ser.: 2). (ENG.). 352p. (J). (gr. 3-7). 16.99 ***(978-0-553-51299-1(4)***, Knopf Bks. for Young Readers) Random Hse. Children's Bks.

Catlow, Nikalas. Spies vs. Giant Slugs in the Jungle. Wesson, Tim, illus. 2012. (Mega Mash-Up Ser.). (ENG.). 96p. (J). (gr. 2-5). pap. 6.99 *(978-0-7636-5902-8(9)*, Nosy Crow) Candlewick Pr.

Christopher, Neil. Way Back Then, 1 vol. Amaktauyok, Germaine, illus. 2015. (ENG.). 40p. (J). (gr. -1-k). 16.95 *(978-1-77227-021-1(0))* Inhabit Media Inc. CAN. Dist: Independent Pubs. Group.

Connelly, Peg. A Madman Hunts for Bigfoot. 2008. 110p. pap. 19.95 *(978-1-60672-322-7(7))* America Star Bks.

Courtauld, Sarah. Buckle & Squash: the Gigantic Giant Goof-Up. 2016. (Buckle & Squash Ser.). (ENG., Illus.). 192p. (J). 14.99 *(978-1-250-05279-7(3)*, 9781250052797) Feiwel & Friends.

Coville, Bruce. Thor's Wedding Day: By Thialfi, the Goat Boy. Cogswell, Matthew, illus. 2008. (ENG.). 144p. (J). (gr. 2-5). pap. 6.99 *(978-0-15-205872-2(9))* Houghton Mifflin Harcourt Publishing Co.

Cowley, Joy. The Hungry Giant's Baby. 2009. pap. 8.25 *(978-1-60559-221-3(8))* Hameray Publishing Group, Inc.

—The Hungry Giant's Shoe. 2009. pap. 8.25 *(978-1-60559-223-7(4))* Hameray Publishing Group, Inc.

—The Hungry Giant's Shoe Big Book. 2010. 48.25 *(978-1-60559-250-3(1))* Hameray Publishing Group, Inc.

—Poor Sore Hungry Giant. 2009. pap. 8.25 *(978-1-60559-237-4(4))* Hameray Publishing Group, Inc.

Cross, Frances. The Mystery of the Green Elephant. 2007. (Blobber Ser.). (ENG.). 84p. (J). per. *(978-1-84167-559-6(8))* Ransom Publishing Ltd.

Dahl, Roald. The BFG. 2016. (CHI.). 112p. (J). (gr. 3-6). pap. ***(978-986-479-012-8(9))*** Commonwealth Publishing Co., Ltd.

—The BFG. 30th rev. ed. 2014. (ENG.). 208p. (J). (gr. 2-12). 11.24 *(978-1-63245-341-9(X))* Lectorum Pubns., Inc.

—The BFG. 2009. 9.00 *(978-0-7848-2054-4(6)*, Everbind) Marco Bk. Co.

—The BFG. Dahl, Roald & Blake, Quentin, illus. 2007. 17.00 *(978-0-7569-8233-1(2))* Penguin Publishing Group.

—The BFG. movie tie-in ed. 2016. (ENG., Illus.). 224p. (J). (gr. 3-7). 7.99 *(978-1-101-99769-7(9)*, Puffin Books) Penguin Young Readers Group.

—The BFG. Blake, Quentin, illus. 30th anniv. ed. 2007. (ENG.). 224p. (J). (gr. 3-7). 7.99 *(978-0-14-241038-7(1)*, Puffin Books) Penguin Young Readers Group.

—The BFG. 2005. (J). 1.25 *(978-1-4193-5995-8(9))* Recorded Bks., Inc.

—The BFG. 2007. 18.40 *(978-1-4177-8612-1(4)*, Turtleback) Turtleback Bks.

—James y el Melocoton Gigante. Blake, Quentin, illus. 2003.Tr. of James & the Giant Peach. (SPA.). 184p. pap. 9.95 *(978-968-19-0625-2(X))* Aguilar, Altea, Taurus, Alfaguara, S.A. de C.V MEX. Dist: Santillana USA Publishing Co., Inc.

Daynes, Katie. Jack & the Beanstalk. Mounter, Paddy, illus. 2006. 48p. (J). 8.99 *(978-0-7945-1238-5(0)*, Usborne) EDC Publishing.

dela Pena, Alba. The Tales of Gorba the Crafty Giant of Loomsville. 2006. (J). 6.95 *(978-1-56167-925-6(9))* American Literary Pr.

DiTerlizzi, Tony & Black, Holly. The Nixies Song - A Giant Problem - The Wyrm King Set, Set. DiTerlizzi, Tony, illus. 2009. (Beyond the Spiderwick Chronicles Ser.: Nos. 1-3). (ENG., Illus.). 528p. (J). (gr. 2-5). 33.99 *(978-1-4169-9011-6(9)*, Simon & Schuster Bks. For Young Readers) Simon & Schuster Bks. For Young Readers.

Doherty, Berlie. Jack the Giant Killer. (Illus.). 139p. pap. 8.99 *(978-0-340-76452-7(X))* Hodder & Stoughton GBR. Dist: Trafalgar Square Publishing.

Dokey, Cameron. The World Above. 2010. (Once upon a Time Ser.). (ENG.). 208p. (YA). (gr. 7-18). pap. 6.99 *(978-1-4424-0337-6(3)*, Simon Pulse) Simon Pulse.

Donaldson, Julia. The Giants & the Joneses. Swearingen, Greg, illus. 2008. (ENG.). 224p. (J). (gr. 3-5). pap. 14.99 *(978-0-312-37961-2(7)*, 9780312379612) Square Fish.

Doyle, Malachy & Philpot, Graham. Jack the Giant-Killer. 2009. (Hopscotch Adventures Ser.). (Illus.). 31p. (J). (gr. 1). lib. bdg. 25.65 *(978-1-59771-184-5(5))* Sea-To-Sea Pubns.

Dussling, Jennifer. In a Dark, Dark House. Jones, Davy, illus. Date not set. (All Aboard Reading Ser.). 32p. (J). (gr. -1-k). pap. *(978-0-448-40974-0(7)*, Grosset & Dunlap) Penguin Publishing Group.

Eggleton, Jill. The Giant's Ice Cream: 3-in-1 Package. Hawley, Kelvin, illus. (Sails Literacy Ser.). 24p. (gr. k-18). 57.00 *(978-0-7578-3195-9(8))* Rigby Education.

—The Giant's Ice Cream: Big Book Only. Hawley, Kelvin, illus. (Sails Literacy Ser.). 24p. (gr. k-18). 27.00 *(978-0-7635-6986-0(0))* Rigby Education.

Evans, Latonya, adapted by. Jack & the Beanstalk. l.t. ed. 2005. (Fairy Tales of Special Children Ser.: Book 1). (Illus.). 25p. (J). *(978-0-9767258-0-0(0))* Diversity Ink Publishing.

Fairy Tales- Jack & the Beanstalk. 2005. (J). bds. *(978-1-4194-0040-7(1))* Paradise Pr., Inc.

Foxley, Janet. Muncle Trogg. 2012. (J). *(978-0-545-37801-7(X))* Scholastic, Inc.

—Muncle Trogg. O'Kif, illus. 2012. (ENG.). 224p. (J). (gr. 2-5). 14.99 *(978-0-545-37800-0(1)*, Chicken Hse., The) Scholastic, Inc.

Friedman, Joe. Boobela & the Belching Giant. Childs, Sam, illus. 2010. (ENG.). 128p. 12.99 *(978-1-4440-0046-7(2))* Orion Publishing Group, Ltd. GBR. Dist: Hachette Bk. Group.

—Boobela, Worm & Potion Power. Childs, Sam, illus. 2010. (ENG.). 128p. 12.99 *(978-1-4440-0045-0(4))* Orion Publishing Group, Ltd. GBR. Dist: Hachette Bk. Group.

Gaiman, Neil. Odd & the Frost Giants. Riddell, Chris, illus. 2016. 128p. (J). (gr. 3-7). 19.99 *(978-0-06-256795-6(0))* HarperCollins Pubs.

—Odd & the Frost Giants. Helquist, Brett, illus. 128p. (J). 2009. (ENG.). (gr. 3-18). 14.99 *(978-0-06-167173-9(8))* 2008. lib. bdg. 15.89 *(978-0-06-167175-3(4))* HarperCollins Pubs.

Galdone, Paul. Jack & the Beanstalk. 2013. (Folk Tale Classics Ser.). (ENG., Illus.). 40p. (J). (gr. -1-3). 8.99 *(978-0-544-06665-6(0))* Houghton Mifflin Harcourt Publishing Co.

Garcia Sanchez, J. L. El Nino Gigante (The Giant Child) (Derechos del Nino Ser.). (SPA., Illus.). 32p. (J). (gr. 3-5). pap. 8.95 *(978-1-56014-580-6(3))* Santillana USA Publishing Co., Inc.

Ghani, Samna. The Shoe, the Necklace, & the Giant. Williams, Nancy E., ed. Cappoen, Jennifer Tipton, illus. 2012. 48p. (J). pap. 9.95 *(978-1-938526-18-3(X))* Roxby Media Ltd. GBR. Dist: Laurus Co., The.

The Giant's Day Out: Set D Individual Title Six-Packs. (Smart Start Ser.). (gr. k-1). 23.00 *(978-0-7635-0454-0(8))* Rigby Education.

El gigante Egoista: Individual Title Six-Packs. (Literatura 2000 Ser.). (SPA.). (gr. 2-3). 33.00 *(978-0-7635-1261-3(3))* Rigby Education.

Glynn, Gower. Stories Told in the Wigwam. 2006. pap. 24.95 *(978-1-4254-9966-2(X))* Kessinger Publishing, LLC.

Grau, Sheila. The Boy with Seventeen Senses. 2016. (ENG.). 256p. (J). (gr. 3-7). 16.95 *(978-1-4197-2119-9(4)*, Amulet Bks.) Abrams, Inc.

Greene, Joshua M. The Littlest Giant: The Story of Vamana. Moore, Emma V., illus. 2014. (ENG.). 32p. (gr. -1). 16.99 *(978-1-60887-303-6(X))* Mandala Publishing.

Gregory, Manju. Jill & the Beanstalk. Anstey, David, illus. 2004. (ENG & TUR.). (J). *(978-1-84444-495-3(3))* Mantra Lingua.

Grindley, Sally. Shhh! 2008. (ENG.). 32p. (J). (gr. -1-3). 16.95 *(978-1-933718-19-4(6))* Tanglewood Pr.

Hale, Shannon & Hale, Dean. Calamity Jack. Hale, Nathan, illus. 2010. (ENG.). 144p. (YA). (gr. 6-18). pap. 15.99 *(978-1-59990-373-6(3)*, 9781599903736, Bloomsbury USA Childrens) Bloomsbury Publishing USA.

EFG

Hall, Amanda. Giant Tales from Around the World. Waters, Fiona, illus. 2004. 96p. (J). 17.95 (978-1-84458-143-6(8)) Avalon Publishing Group.

Hall, Amanda, tr. & illus. Giant Tales. Hall, Amanda, illus. 2003. 96p. (YA). (978-1-84365-017-1(7), Pavilion Children's Books) Pavilion Bks.

Hart, Caryl. The Princess & the Giant. Warburton, Sarah, illus. 2015. (ENG.). 32p. (J). (gr. -1-2). 16.99 (978-0-7636-8007-7(9), Nosy Crow) Candlewick Pr.

Haugen, Timothy A. The Castle of Gloom, 1 vol. 2009. (ENG.). 175p. pap. 24.95 (978-1-61546-106-6(X)) America Star Bks.

Hendry, Frances. Atlantis. l.t. ed. 2007. 228p. per. (978-1-905665-20-4(2)) Pollinger In Print.

The Heroes in Training Collection Books 1-4: Zeus & the Thunderbolt of Doom; Poseidon & the Sea of Fury; Hades & the Helm of Darkness; Hyperion & the Great Balls of Fire. 2014. (Heroes in Training Ser.). (ENG., Illus.). 512p. (J). (gr. 1-4). pap. 23.99 (978-1-4814-2200-0(6), Aladdin) Simon & Schuster Children's Publishing.

Higgins, Ryan. Wilfred. Higgins, Ryan, illus. 2013. (ENG., Illus.). 40p. (J). (gr. -1-k). 16.99 (978-0-8037-3732-7(7), Dial Bks) Penguin Young Readers Group.

Hillenbrand, Will, illus. Look Out, Jack! the Giant Is Back! 2003. (ENG.). 32p. (J). (gr. -1-3). 6.95 (978-0-8234-1776-6(X)) Holiday Hse., Inc.

Hillert, Margaret. The Magic Beans. Zaman, Farida, illus. 2016. (BeginningtoRead Ser.). (ENG.). 32p. (J). (gr. -1-2). pap. 11.94 (978-1-60357-910-0(9)) Norwood Hse. Pr.

Hoena, B. A. Jack & the Beanstalk: An Interactive Fairy Tale Adventure. Tayal, Amit, illus. 2015. (You Choose: Fractured Fairy Tales Ser.). (ENG.). 112p. (gr. 3-4). pap. 6.95 (978-1-4914-5930-0(1), You Choose Bks.) Capstone Press of Coughlan Cos.

Hoffmire, A. B., illus. & as told by. The Ogre Bully. Hoffmire, A. B., as told by. 2007. (Story Cove Ser.). (ENG.). 32p. (J). (gr. -1-3). 3.95 (978-0-87483-803-9(7)) August Hse. Pubs., Inc.

Holden, Pam. The Gentle Giant, 6 pack. Hatam, Samer, illus. 2009. (Red Rocket Readers Ser.). (ENG.). 16p. (gr. 2-2). pap. (978-1-877363-81-8(2)) Flying Start Bks.

Holt, Julie. Conner's Giant Secret. 2008. (Illus.). 52p. per. (978-1-84748-043-9(8)) Athena Pr.

Holub, Joan & Williams, Suzanne. Hades & the Helm of Darkness. Phillips, Craig, illus. 2013. (Heroes in Training Ser.: 3). (ENG.). 128p. (J). (gr. 1-4). 15.99 (978-1-4424-5725-6(2)); pap. 5.99 (978-1-4424-5267-1(6)) Simon & Schuster Children's Publishing. (Aladdin).

—Hades & the Helm of Darkness. 2013. (Heroes in Training Ser.: 3). lib. bdg. 16.00 (978-0-606-27041-0(8), Turtleback) Turtleback Bks.

—Typhon & the Winds of Destruction. Phillips, Craig, illus. 2013. (Heroes in Training Ser.: 5). (ENG.). 112p. (J). (gr. 1-4). 16.99 (978-1-4424-8844-1(1)); pap. 5.99 (978-1-4424-8842-7(5)) Simon & Schuster Children's Publishing. (Aladdin).

Impey, Rose. The Ginormous Giant, Bk. 5. McEwen, Katharine, illus. 2017. (Sir Lance-A-Little Ser.). (ENG.). 32p. (J). (gr. k-2). 9.99 (978-1-4083-2524-7(1), Orchard Bks.) Hachette Children's Group GBR. Dist: Hachette Bk. Group.

InSeon, Chae. Handy Mr. Hippo. YouDae, Kim, illus. rev. ed. 2014. (MySELF Bookshelf Ser.). (ENG.). 32p. (J). (gr. k-2). pap. 11.94 (978-1-60357-661-1(4)); lib. bdg. 25.27 (978-1-59953-652-1(8)) Norwood Hse. Pr.

Jack & The Beanstalk. 2008. (Read & Learn Sticker Books Ser.). 48p. pap. (978-1-4075-3195-3(6)) Parragon, Inc.

Jacques et le Haricot Magique.Tr. of Jack & the Bean Stalk. (FRE.). 48p. (J). pap. 12.95 incl. audio compact disk (978-2-89558-069-0(3)) Coffragants CAN. Dist: Penton Overseas, Inc.

Jarman, Julia. Molly & the Giant. Sholto, Walker, illus. 2005. (ENG.). 24p. (J). lib. bdg. 23.65 (978-1-59646-746-0(0)) Dingles & Co.

Jill & the Beanstalk. 2004. (J). (ENG & VIE.). (978-1-84444-496-0(1)); (ENG & URD.). (978-1-84444-485-4(6)); (ENG & TAM.). (978-1-84444-484-7(8)); (ENG & SPA.). (978-1-84444-490-8(2)); (ENG & SOM.). (978-1-84444-487-8(2)); (ENG & RUS.). (978-1-84444-482-3(1)); (ENG & POR.). (978-1-84444-481-6(3)); (ENG & PAN.). (978-1-84444-494-6(5)); (ENG & ITA.). (978-1-84444-480-9(5)); (ENG & GUJ.). (978-1-84444-479-3(1)); (ENG & FRE.). (978-1-84444-489-2(9)); (ENG & PER.). (978-1-84444-491-5(0)); (SBC & ENG.). (978-1-84444-483-0(X)); (CHI & ENG.). (978-1-84444-488-5(0)); (BEN & ENG.). (978-1-84444-478-6(3)); (ARA & ENG.). (978-1-84444-486-1(4)); (ALB & ENG.). (978-1-84444-492-2(9)); E-Book incl. cd-rom (978-1-84444-463-2(5)) Mantra Lingua.

Johnson, Paul Brett, illus. & adapted by. Jack Outwits the Giants. Johnson, Paul Brett, adapted by. 2008. (ENG.). 36p. (J). (gr. -1-3). 11.99 (978-1-4169-7861-9(5), Simon & Schuster/Paula Wiseman Bks.) Simon & Schuster/Paula Wiseman Bks.

Johnson, Richard, tr. & illus. Jack & the Beanstalk. Johnson, Richard, illus. 2004. 31p. (J). (978-1-84444-108-2(3)) Mantra Lingua.

Judge, Chris & Wickham, Mark. Brian & the Giant. 2016. (ENG., Illus.). 32p. (J). pap. 11.00 (978-1-84717-773-5(5)) O'Brien Pr., Ltd., The IRL. Dist: Dufour Editions, Inc.

Kasza, Keiko. The Mightiest. 2003. (ENG., Illus.). 32p. (J). (gr. -1-k). pap. 5.99 (978-0-14-250185-6(9), Puffin Books) Penguin Young Readers Group.

Keilty, Derek. Back up the Beanstalk. Myler, Terry, illus. 2003. (Chimps Ser.: 5). (ENG.). 64p. (J). pap. 10.95 (978-1-901737-45-5(4)) Anvil Bks., Ltd. IRL. Dist: Dufour Editions, Inc.

Ketteman, Helen. Waynetta & the Cornstalk: A Texas Fairy Tale. Greenseid, Diane, illus. 2012. (J). (978-1-61913-152-1(8)) Weigl Pubs., Inc.

Kimmel, Eric A. Big Sam: A Rosh Hashanah Tall Tale. Starr, Jim, illus. 2017. (J). **(978-1-68115-525-8(7))** Behrman Hse., Inc.

Kimmel, Eric A. Jack & the Giant Barbecue, 0 vols. Manders, John, illus. 2012. (ENG.). 32p. (J). (gr. 1-3). 17.99 (978-0-7614-6128-9(0), 9780761461289, Amazon Children's Publishing) Amazon Publishing.

Klise, Kate. Stand Straight, Ella Kate: The True Story of a Real Giant. Klise, M. Sarah, illus. 2010. (ENG.). 32p. (J). (gr. 1-3). 16.99 (978-0-8037-3404-3(2), Dial Bks) Penguin Young Readers Group.

Kurtz, John. JATS Fairytale Classics - Jack & the Beanstalk. Kurtz, John, illus. 2004. (Illus.). 24p. (J). lib. bdg. 8.00 (978-1-4242-0636-0(7)) Fitzgerald Bks.

Lairamore, Dawn. Ivy & the Meanstalk. 2011. (ENG.). 192p. (J). 16.95 (978-0-8234-2392-7(1)) Holiday Hse., Inc.

Larcombe, Jennifer Rees. The Terrible Giant. Björkman, Steve, illus. 2004. (Best Bible Stories Ser.). 24p. (gr. -1-3). 2.99 (978-1-58134-054-9(0)) Crossway.

Leedy, Loreen. Jack & the Hungry Giant: Eat Right with Myplate. 2013. (ENG., Illus.). 32p. (J). 17.95 (978-0-8234-2602-7(5)) Holiday Hse., Inc.

Lemke, Amy J. & Lemke, Donald B. Frank 'n' Beans, 1 vol. Bradley, Jessica, illus. 2013. (Comics Land Ser.). (ENG.). 32p. (gr. k-2). 7.95 (978-1-4342-6284-4(7)); lib. bdg. 25.32 (978-1-4342-4988-3(3)) Stone Arch Bks.

Lesynski, Loris. Boy Soup. Martchenko, Michael, illus. 2nd ed. 2008. (ENG.). 32p. (J). (gr. -1-2). 18.95 (978-1-55451-143-3(7), 9781554511433); pap. 6.95 (978-1-55451-142-6(9), 9781554511426) Annick Pr., Ltd. CAN. Dist: Publishers Group West (PGW).

Light, Steve. The Christmas Giant. Light, Steve, illus. 2010. (ENG., Illus.). 32p. (J). (gr. -1-2). 15.99 (978-0-7636-4692-9(X)) Candlewick Pr.

Limke, Jeff. Thor & Loki: In the Land of Giants - A Norse Myth. Randall, Ron, illus. 2007. (Graphic Myths & Legends Ser.). (ENG.). 48p. (gr. 4-8). per. 8.95 (978-0-8225-6481-2(5)) Lerner Publishing Group.

—Thor y Loki: en la Tierra de los Gigantes: Un Mito Escandinavo. Randall, Ron, illus. 2007. (Mitos y leyendas en viñetas (Graphic Myths & Legends) Ser.). (SPA.). 48p. (J). (gr. 4-7). per. 8.95 (978-0-8225-7969-4(3), Ediciones Lerner) Lerner Publishing Group.

The Lonely Giant: Individual Title Six-Packs. (Literatura 2000 Ser.). (gr. 2-3). 33.00 (978-0-7635-0175-4(1)) Rigby Education.

MacGregor, Doug, creator. Ochre the Smoker: A fantastic Fable. 2007. (Illus.). 48p. (J). per. 14.95 (978-0-9654843-2-9(7)) MacGregor, Doug.

MacKenzie, Robert, illus. Jack & the Beanstalk. 2008. (Classic Fairy Tale Collection). (ENG.). 32p. (J). (gr. -1-2). 14.95 (978-1-4027-3064-1(0)) Sterling Publishing Co., Inc.

Malaspina, Ann. Jack & the Beanstalk: An English Folktale. Manning, Mary, illus. 2013. (Folktales from Around the World Ser.). (ENG.). 24p. (J). (gr. k-3). 28.50 (978-1-62323-615-1(0), 206382) Child's World, Inc., The.

Manjula Padmanabhan, illus. Unprincess! 2005. 98p. (J). (978-0-14-333495-8(6), Puffin) Penguin Publishing Group.

Marks, Allison & Marks, Wayne. Og's Ark. Peluso, Martina, illus. 2016. (ENG.). 32p. (J). (gr. -1-3). 17.99 (978-1-4677-6149-9(4), Kar-Ben Publishing) Lerner Publishing Group.

Massenot, Véronique. The Dreaming Giant: A Children's Book Inspired by Wassily Kandinsky. Nille, Peggy, illus. 2017. (ENG.). 32p. (J). (gr. -1-3). 14.95 **(978-3-7913-7279-2(3))** Prestel Verlag GmbH & Co KG. DEU. Dist: Penguin Random Hse. LLC.

McCaughrean, Geraldine. Fig's Giant. (ENG., Illus.). 40p. (J). (gr. -1-2). 10.99 (978-0-19-279130-6(3)) Oxford Univ. Pr., Inc.

McMullan, Kate. Little Giant-Big Trouble. Basso, Bill, illus. 2007. (Dragon Slayers' Academy Ser.: 19). (ENG.). 112p. (J). (gr. 2-5). pap. 4.99 (978-0-448-44448-2(8), Grosset & Dunlap) Penguin Young Readers Group.

Meyer, Victoria. Dream Catcher, 1 vol. 2009. 48p. pap. 16.95 (978-1-61582-998-9(9)) PublishAmerica, Inc.

Mora, Pat. Doña Flor: A Tall Tale about a Giant Woman with a Great Big Heart. Colón, Raúl, illus. (ENG & SPA.). (J). (gr. -1-2). 2010. 32p. pap. 7.99 (978-0-375-86144-4(0), Dragonfly Bks.) 2005. 40p. 15.95 (978-0-375-82337-4(9), Knopf Bks. for Young Readers) Random Hse. Children's Bks.

Morgan, Gwyn & Owen, Dai. Babi Ben. 2005. (WEL., Illus.). 64p. pap. (978-1-85596-611-6(5)) Dref Wen.

Morpurgo, Michael. Gentle Giant. Foreman, Michael, illus. 2006. 28p. (J). (gr. 4-8). reprint ed. 19.00 (978-1-4223-5398-1(2)) DIANE Publishing Co.

—Gentle Giant. Foreman, Michael, illus. 2003. (ENG.). 32p. (J). 16.95 (978-0-00-711064-3(2), HarperCollins Children's Bks.) HarperCollins Pubs. Ltd. GBR. Dist: Trafalgar Square Publishing.

Myklusch, Matt. The Accidental Hero. 2011. (Jack Blank Adventure Ser.: 1). (ENG., Illus.). 496p. (J). (gr. 3-7). pap. 7.99 (978-1-4169-9562-3(5), Aladdin) Simon & Schuster Children's Publishing.

—Jack Blank & the Imagine Nation. 2010. (Jack Blank Adventure Ser.: Bk. 1). (ENG., Illus.). 480p. (J). (gr. 3-7). 16.99 (978-1-4169-9561-6(7), Aladdin) Simon & Schuster Children's Publishing.

Nesbit, E. Jack & the Beanstalk. Tavares, Matt, illus. 2006. (ENG.). 48p. (J). (gr. -1-2). 16.99 (978-0-7636-2124-7(2)) Candlewick Pr.

Nolen, Jerdine. Hewitt Anderson's Great Big Life. Nelson, Kadir, illus. (ENG.). 40p. (J). (gr. k-3). 2013. 7.99 (978-1-4424-6035-5(0)) 2005. 18.99 (978-0-689-86866-5(9)) Simon & Schuster/Paula Wiseman Bks. (Simon & Schuster/Paula Wiseman Bks.).

Norac, Carl. My Daddy Is a Giant: For Everyone Who Has the Best Daddy in the World. Godon, Ingrid, illus. 2004. (ENG & GLE.). 32p. (J). pap. (978-1-84444-719-0(7)) Mantra Lingua.

North, Laura. Jack & the Bean Pie. 2014. (ENG., Illus.). 32p. (J). (978-0-7787-0441-6(6)); pap. (978-0-7787-0449-2(1)) Crabtree Publishing Co.

Nosy Crow Staff. Jack & the Beanstalk: a Nosy Crow Fairy Tale. Bryan, Ed, illus. 2017. (ENG.). 32p. (J). (gr. -1-2). 9.99 (978-0-7636-9332-9(4), Nosy Crow) Candlewick Pr.

Odezi, Jesse. Little Sunny & the Giants: The World's Greatest. 2012. 76p. pap. 30.00 (978-1-4669-0270-1(1)) Trafford Publishing.

Offen, Hilda. There Might Be Giants. (Illus.). 25p. (J). pap. (978-0-340-68149-7(7)) Hodder & Stoughton.

O'Malley, Kevin. Once upon a Cool Motorcycle Dude. O'Malley, Kevin et al, illus. 2005. (ENG.). 32p. (J). (gr. 1-5). 16.99 (978-0-8027-8947-1(1), 9780802789471, Bloomsbury USA Childrens) Bloomsbury Publishing USA.

Oram, Hiawyn. The Giant Surprise: A Narnia Story. Humphries, Tudor, illus. 2005. (Step into Narnia Ser.). 40p. (J). (gr. -1-2). lib. bdg. 16.89 (978-0-06-001360-8(5)) HarperCollins Pubs.

Page, Nick & Page, Claire. David & Goliath. Loy, Nikki, illus. 2006. (Read with Me (Make Believe Ideas) Ser.). 31p. (J). (gr. k-2). (978-1-84610-173-1(5)) Make Believe Ideas.

—Read with Me Jack & the Beanstalk: Sticker Activity Book. Goodberry, Jo, illus. 2006. (Read with Me (Make Believe Ideas) Ser.). 12p. (J). (gr. k-2). pap. (978-1-84610-180-9(8)) Make Believe Ideas.

Parker, Emma. Jack & the Beanstalk. 2010. (Illus.). 24p. pap. (978-1-877561-49-8(5)) First Edition Ltd.

Pelley, Kathleen. The Giant King. Manning, Maurie J., tr. Manning, Maurie J., illus. 2003. (New Child & Family Press Titles Ser.). 32p. (gr. -1-4). 14.95 (978-0-87868-880-7(3), 8803, Child & Family Pr.) Child Welfare League of America, Inc.

Peyo. The Giant Smurf. Peyo, illus. 2013. (Smurfs Classic Ser.). (ENG., Illus.). 24p. (J). (gr. -1-2). pap. 3.99 (978-1-4424-6178-9(0), Simon Spotlight) Simon Spotlight.

Poo. A Giant Called Tiny. 2017. (ENG.). (J). pap. 13.95 **(978-1-78693-120-7(6)**, 6d599168-1ceb-4e25-ac0f-c81c1cbd761e) Austin, Stan AUS. Dist: Bookmasters Distribution.

Pope, Brennan & Pope, Janet. The Adventures of William Walkingstick. 2007. 132p. (gr. 2-2). per. 11.95 (978-0-595-45786-1(X)); Vol. 1. 21.95 (978-0-595-69866-0(2)) iUniverse, Inc.

Potter, Tony, des. Finn & the Magic Harp. 2004. (Illus.). 12p. (J). 10.95 (978-0-7171-3767-1(8)) M.H. Gill & Co. U. C. IRL. Dist: Dufour Editions, Inc.

Powell, Gary Allison. In That Land There Are Giants. Johnston, Jillian S., illus. 2011. 38p. pap. 14.50 (978-1-60860-891-1(3), Eloquent Bks.) Strategic Book Publishing & Rights Agency (SBPRA).

Rawson, C. Stories of Giants. 2004. (Young Reading Ser.: Vol. 1). 48p. (J). (gr. 2-18). pap. 5.95 (978-0-7945-0646-9(1)) EDC Publishing.

Riordan, Rick. The House of Hades, Bk. 4. 2015. (Heroes of Olympus Ser.). (ENG.). 720p. (J). (gr. 5-9). pap. 9.99 (978-1-4231-4677-3(8)) Hyperion Bks. for Children.

—The Mark of Athena. 2012. (Heroes of Olympus Ser.). (ENG.). 608p. (J). (gr. 5-17). 19.99 (978-1-4231-4060-3(5)) Hyperion Pr.

—The Mark of Athena. l.t. ed. 2012. (Heroes of Olympus Ser.: Bk. 3). (ENG.). 698p. 23.99 (978-1-4104-5205-4(0)) Thorndike Pr.

—The Mark of Athena. 2014. (Heroes of Olympus Ser.: 3). (J). lib. bdg. 20.85 (978-0-606-35255-0(4)) Turtleback Bks.

Roberts, Esyllt Nest & Owen, Carys Eurwen. Rhita Gawr. 2005. (WEL., Illus.). 36p. pap. (978-0-86381-624-6(X)) Gwasg Carreg Gwalch.

Ross, Dev. We Both Read-Frank & the Giant (Picture Book). Reinhart, Larry, illus. 2007. (We Both Read Ser.). 44p. (J). (gr. -1-2). lib. bdg. 14.95 (978-1-60115-006-6(7)) Treasure Bay, Inc.

Rubenstein, Lauri. My Friendly Giant. Adams, Mark W., illus. 2012. (ENG.). 36p. (J). 16.95 (978-0-9770391-6-6(1)) Growing Field Bks.

Russell, P. Craig. Fairy Tales of Oscar Wilde: The Selfish Giant & the Star Child, Vol. 1. Russell, P. Craig, illus. 2003. (Fairy Tales of Oscar Wilde Ser.: 1). (ENG., Illus.). 1111p. pap. 9.99 (978-1-56163-375-3(5)) NBM Publishing Co.

Ruzzier, Sergio. The Little Giant. 2004. (Illus.). 32p. (J). (gr. -1-2). 16.89 (978-0-06-052952-9(0), Geringer, Laura Book) HarperCollins Pubs.

Salan, Felipe Lopez, illus. Jack & the Beanstalk. 2006. (ENG.). 32p. (J). (gr. -1). 15.95 (978-1-933327-11-2(1)) Purple Bear Bks., Inc.

The Selfish Giant: Individual Title Six-Packs. (Literatura 2000 Ser.). (gr. 2-3). 33.00 (978-0-7635-0239-3(1)) Rigby Education.

Seomeng, Judah. Dimo & the Little Bush Doctor. 2004. (Illus.). 24p. pap. (978-99912-555-1-4(6)) Pyramid Publishing (PTY), Ltd. BWA. Dist: Michigan State Univ. Pr.

Snowe, Olivia. A Home in the Sky, 1 vol. Lamoreaux, Michelle, illus. (Twicetold Tales Ser.). (ENG.). 128p. (gr. 3-4). 2014. pap. 5.95 (978-1-4342-9554-5(0)) 2013. 8.95 (978-1-4342-6279-0(0)) 2013. lib. bdg. 25.32 (978-1-4342-5041-4(5)) Stone Arch Bks.

Solomon, Matt & Pauls, Chris. The Giant Smugglers. Roberto, Anna, ed. 2016. (ENG.). 288p. (J). 16.99 (978-1-250-06652-7(2), 9781250066527) Feiwel & Friends.

Stanley, Diane. The Giant & the Beanstalk. Stanley, Diane, illus. 2004. (ENG., Illus.). 32p. (J). (gr. k-3). 17.99 (978-0-06-000010-3(4)) HarperCollins Pubs.

Stockton, Frank Richard. Ting-a-Ling Tales. 2008. 88p. pap. 8.95 (978-1-60664-056-2(9)) Aegypan.

Strong, Jeremy. Giant Jim & the Hurricane. (Illus.). 96p. (J). pap. 7.95 (978-0-14-038248-8(8)) Penguin Bks., Ltd. GBR. Dist: Trafalgar Square Publishing.

Suzukaze, Ryo. Kuklo Unbound. Shibamoto, Thores, illus. 2015. (Attack on Titan Ser.). (ENG.). 298p. (J). (gr. 7). pap. 14.95 (978-1-939130-87-7(5), Vertical) Vertical, Inc.

Sweet, Susan D. & Miles, Brenda. Jacqueline & the Beanstalk: A Tale of Facing Giant Fears. Docampo, Valeria, illus. 2017. 32p. (J). 15.95 **(978-1-4338-2682-5(8)**, Magination Pr.) American Psychological Assn.

Tate, Suzanne. Teena Tortoise: A Tale of a Little Giant. Melvin, James, illus. 2012. 32p. (J). pap. 4.95 (978-1-878405-60-9(8)) Nags Head Art, Inc.

Tercio, Ricardo, illus. Jack & the Beanstalk: The Graphic Novel. 2008. (Graphic Spin Ser.). (ENG.). 40p. (gr. 1-3). 25.32 (978-1-4342-0766-1(8), Graphic Revolve) Stone Arch Bks.

Trafton, Jennifer. The Rise & Fall of Mount Majestic. Helquist, Brett, illus. 2011. (ENG.). 352p. (J). (gr. 3-7). 6.99 (978-0-14-241934-2(6), Puffin Books) Penguin Young Readers Group.

Umansky, Kaye. The Jealous Giant. Weir, Doffy, illus. 2005. 32p. (J). (gr. -1 — 1). pap. 6.95 (978-1-903015-41-4(3)) Barn Owl Bks, London GBR. Dist: Independent Pubs. Group.

Vagnozzi, Barbara, illus. Jack & the Beanstalk. 2011. (Classic Fairy Tales Ser.). (ENG.). 24p. (J). audio compact disk (978-1-84643-456-3(4)) Child's Play International Ltd.

Valois, Rob & Caravan Studios Staff. Spyro & the Giants. 2013. (Penguin Young Readers Level 3 Ser.). lib. bdg. 13.55 (978-0-606-31693-4(0), Turtleback) Turtleback Bks.

Vaughn, Royce, illus. Seymour Bluffs & Robert Wadlow, the Tallest Man in the World: A Story about Diversity & Tolerance. 2007. 28p. (J). 12.95 (978-0-9728538-4-2(7)) Arnica Publishing.

Walker, Raven. The Feather Giant. 2004. 92p. pap. 9.95 (978-0-595-30484-4(2)) iUniverse, Inc.

Walker, Richard. Jack & the Beanstalk. 2009. (ENG., Illus.). (J). 16.99 (978-1-84686-297-7(3)) Barefoot Bks., Inc.

—Juan y los Frijoles Magicos. 2008. (ENG & SPA., Illus.). 40p. (J). (gr. -1-1). 10.99 (978-1-84686-216-8(7)) Barefoot Bks., Inc.

Wallace, Karen. Stinky Giant. Brett, Cathy, illus. 2013. (Start Reading Ser.). (ENG.). 24p. (gr. k-1). pap. 7.95 (978-1-4765-4139-6(6)) Capstone Press of Coughlan Cos.

Watch Out! Individual Title Six-Packs. (Literatura 2000 Ser.). (gr. -1-1). 28.00 (978-0-7635-0016-0(X)) Rigby Education.

Webster, Christy. Bath Party! Random House Editors & VanTuyle, David, illus. 2015. (Step into Reading Ser.). (ENG.). 24p. (J). (gr. -1-1). pap. 4.99 (978-0-385-38767-5(9), Random Hse. Bks. for Young Readers) Random Hse. Children's Bks.

Weiss, Ellen & Friedman, Mel. The Stinky Giant. Girasole, Alessia, illus. 2012. (Step into Reading Level 3 Ser.). lib. bdg. 13.55 (978-0-606-23858-8(1), Turtleback) Turtleback Bks.

West, David. Ten of the Best Giant Stories. 2014. (ENG., Illus.). 24p. (J). pap. (978-0-7787-0821-6(7)) Crabtree Publishing Co.

Wilce, Ysabeau S. Flora's Dare: How a Girl of Spirit Gambles All to Expand Her Vocabulary, Confront a Bouncing Boy Terror, & Try to Save Califa from a Shaky Doom (Despite Being Confined to Her Room) 2010. (ENG.). 528p. (YA). (gr. 7). pap. 7.99 (978-0-15-205403-8(0)) Houghton Mifflin Harcourt Publishing Co.

Wilde, Oscar. The Selfish Giant: A Tale about Being Unselfish. Ebert, Len, illus. 2006. (J). (978-1-59939-085-7(X), Reader's Digest Young Families, Inc.) Studio Fun International.

Wilde, Oscar & Hollingsworth, Mary. The Selfish Giant. Bell, Bill, illus. 2013. (ENG.). 40p. (J). (gr. -1-1). 14.95 (978-1-62087-540-7(3), 620540, Sky Pony Pr.) Skyhorse Publishing Co., Inc.

Wisniewski, David. Golem. Wisniewski, David, illus. 2007. (ENG., Illus.). 32p. (J). (gr. 5-7). 7.99 (978-0-618-89424-6(1)) Houghton Mifflin Harcourt Publishing Co.

Zeman, Ludmila, retold by. Sindbad's Secret. 2003. (ENG., Illus.). 32p. (J). (gr. 1-4). 17.95 (978-0-88776-462-2(2), Tundra Bks.) Tundra Bks. CAN. Dist: Penguin Random Hse. LLC.

GIBRALTAR

Dyan, Penelope. The Comeback Kids — Book 9 — the Barbary Macaques of Gibraltar. Weigand, John D., photos by. 2012. (Illus.). 36p. pap. 14.95 (978-1-61477-036-7(0)) Bellissima Publishing, LLC.

—Rockin' the Rock, a Kid's Guide to the Rock of Gibraltar. Weigand, John D., photos by. 2012. (Illus.). 34p. pap. 11.95 (978-1-61477-037-4(9)) Bellissima Publishing, LLC.

GIBSON, ALTHEA, 1927-2003

Deans, Karen. Playing to Win: The Story of Althea Gibson. Brown, Elbrite, illus. 2007. (ENG.). 32p. (J). (gr. -1-3). 16.95 (978-0-8234-1926-5(6)) Holiday Hse., Inc.

Stauffacher, Sue. Nothing but Trouble: The Story of Althea Gibson. Couch, Greg, illus. 2011. (ENG.). 40p. (J). (gr. -1-2). pap. 7.99 (978-0-375-86544-2(6), Dragonfly Bks.) Random Hse. Children's Bks.

GIDEON, CLARENCE EARL, 1910-1972

Fridell, Ron. Gideon V. Wainwright: The Right to Free Counsel. 2006. (Supreme Court Milestones Ser.). (Illus.). 128p. (gr. 7). lib. bdg. 42.79 (978-0-7614-2146-7(7), Benchmark Bks.) Marshall Cavendish Corp.

Prentzas, G. S. Gideon V. Wainwright: The Right to Free Legal Counsel. 2007. (Great Supreme Court Decisions Ser.). (Illus.). 120p. (YA). (gr. 5-9). lib. bdg. 32.95 (978-0-7910-9383-2(2)) Facts On File, Inc.

Wroble, Lisa A. The Right to Counsel: From Gideon V. Wainwright to Gideon's Trumpet. 2009. (Famous Court Cases That Became Movies Ser.). (Illus.). 104p. (J). (gr. 7-12). lib. bdg. 33.27 (978-0-7660-3057-2(1)) Enslow Pubs., Inc.

GIFTED CHILDREN

Here are entered works on talented elementary and secondary school students.

Almukahhal, Raja. Physics Laboratory Experiments for the Gifted: Middle & High School. 2005. (Illus.). 90p. (978-0-910609-51-7(9)) Gifted Education Pr.

Delisle, James R. & Schultz, Robert. If I'm So Smart, Why Aren't the Answers Easy? Advice from Teens on Growing up Gifted. 2012. (ENG., Illus.). 208p. (YA). (gr. 6-10). pap. 14.95 (978-1-59363-960-0(0)) Prufrock Pr.

Fonseca, Christine. 101 Success Secrets for Gifted Kids: The Ultimate Handbook. 2011. (ENG.). 208p. (J). (gr. 3-7). pap. 16.95 (978-1-59363-544-2(3), 9781593635442) Prufrock Pr.

Galbraith, Judy. The Survival Guide for Gifted Kids. 2013. (ENG., Illus.). 128p. (J). (gr. 1-5). pap. 13.99 (978-1-57542-448-4(7)) Free Spirit Publishing, Inc.

Galbraith, Judy & Delisle, Jim. The Gifted Teen Survival Guide: Smart, Sharp, & Ready for (Almost) Anything. 4th rev. ed. 2011. (ENG., Illus.). 272p. (YA). (gr. 6). pap. 15.99 (978-1-57542-381-4(2), 1332008) Free Spirit Publishing, Inc.

Mitchell, Saundra. 50 Impressive Kids & Their Amazing (And True!) Stories. 2016. (They Did What? Ser.). (ENG., Illus.). 320p. (J). (gr. 5). 8.99 (978-0-14-751813-2(X), Puffin Books) Penguin Young Readers Group.

Sganga, Francis. Introducing Gifted Students to the Wonders of Mathematics: Preparation for High School & Higher Mathematics, Grades 4-8. 2004. (Illus.). 75p. (978-0-910609-47-0(0)) Gifted Education Pr.

Wood, Mark. Beyond Classroom Enrichment: Creative Units for Gifted Students. 2004. (Illus.). 80p. (978-0-910609-48-7(9)) Gifted Education Pr.

GIFTED CHILDREN—FICTION

Beard, Robert W. A Boy Named Shawn. 2009. (A Shawn Barton Adventure Ser.). 116p. (J). pap. 12.95 (978-1-935083-07-8(4)) CyPress Pubns.

—Halcyon. 2009. (J). pap. *(978-1-935083-08-5(2))* CyPress Pubns.

Besser, Kenneth/R. Amie Carver & the Plague of Demeverde. 2007. (Illus.). x, 338p. (J). *(978-1-934316-02-3(4))* RTMC Organization, LLC.

Blume, Judy. Here's to You, Rachel Robinson. 2010. (ENG.). 208p. (J). (gr. 5). pap. 8.99 *(978-0-385-73987-0(7),* Delacorte Bks. for Young Readers) Random Hse. Children's Bks.

Brown, Jennifer. Pennybaker School Is Headed for Disaster. Kissi, Marta, illus. 2017. (ENG.). 320p. (J). 16.99 *(978-1-68119-174-4(1),* 9781681191744, Bloomsbury USA Childrens) Bloomsbury Publishing USA.

Burton, Jennifer. Christopher's Dilemma. 2003. (Topeka Heights Ser.). (YA). (gr. 9-12). pap. 10.99 *(978-0-9724733-1-6(9))* ALEXZUS Bks.

Cody, Paul. Love Is Both Wave & Particle. 2017. (ENG.). 320p. (YA). 17.99 *(978-1-62672-688-8(4),* 9781626726888) Roaring Brook Pr.

de Vigan, Delphine. No & Me. Miller, George, tr. from FRE. 2010. (ENG.). 256p. (YA). (gr. 7-12). 16.99 *(978-1-59990-479-5(9),* 9781599904795, Bloomsbury USA Childrens) Bloomsbury Publishing USA.

Dee, Barbara. Solving Zoe. 2010. (Mix Ser.). (ENG.). 256p. (J). (gr. 4-8). pap. 7.99 *(978-1-4169-9159-5(X),* Aladdin) Simon & Schuster Children's Publishing.

Eliopoulis, Chris, text. Franklin Richards: Son of a Genius Ultimate Collection - Book 1. 2010. (ENG., Illus.). 208p. (J). (gr. -1-17). pap., pap. 19.99 *(978-0-7851-4924-8(4))* Marvel Worldwide, Inc.

Evans, Richard. Michael Vey 5. 2015. (Michael Vey Ser.: 5). (ENG., Illus.). 288p. (YA). (gr. 7). 18.99 *(978-1-4814-4410-1(7),* Simon Pulse/Mercury Ink) Simon Pulse/Mercury Ink.

Forester, Victoria. The Girl Who Could Fly. 2008. (ENG.). 336p. (J). (gr. 4-7). 16.95 *(978-0-312-37462-4(3),* 9780312374624) Feiwel & Friends.

—The Girl Who Could Fly. Barcellona, Christine, ed. 2015. (ENG.). 352p. (J). (gr. 4-7). pap. 7.99 *(978-1-250-07246-7(8),* 9781250072467) Square Fish.

Gutman, Dan. Ms. Coco Is Loco! Paillot, Jim, illus. 2007. (My Weird School Ser.: 16). (J). 14.75 *(978-1-4177-7428-9(2),* Turtleback) Turtleback Bks.

Haynes, Marilee. A. K. A. Genius. 2013. (ENG.). 208p. (YA). 9.95 *(978-0-8198-0830-1(X))* Pauline Bks. & Media.

—Genius under Construction. 2014. (ENG.). (YA). pap. *(978-0-8198-3126-2(3))* Pauline Bks. & Media.

Holmes, Sara Lewis. Letters from Rapunzel. 2007. 184p. (J). (gr. 3-7). lib. bdg. 16.89 *(978-0-06-078074-6(6))* HarperCollins Pubs.

Hunt for Jade Dragon. 2014. (Michael Vey Ser.: No. 4). (ENG., Illus.). 336p. (YA). (gr. 7). 19.99 *(978-1-4814-2438-7(6),* Simon Pulse/Mercury Ink) Simon Pulse/Mercury Ink.

Huws, Emily. Nid Fy Mai I. Lawrie, Robin, illus. 2005. (WEL.). 64p. pap. *(978-1-84512-025-2(6))* Cymdeithas Lyfrau Ceredigion.

Jacobson, Jennifer Richard. Paper Things. 2015. (ENG.). 384p. (J). (gr. 5). 16.99 *(978-0-7636-6323-0(9))* Candlewick Pr.

—Paper Things. 2017. (ENG.). (J). (gr. 5). lib. bdg. 19.65 ***(978-0-606-39841-1(4))*** Turtleback Bks.

Kiernan, Kristy. Catching Genius. 2007. (ENG.). 384p. (gr. 12-18). 15.00 *(978-0-425-21435-0(4),* Berkley) Penguin Publishing Group.

Korman, Gordon. Ungifted. 288p. (J). (gr. 5). 2014. pap. 7.99 *(978-0-06-174267-5(8))* 2012. 16.99 *(978-0-06-174266-8(X))* 2012. lib. bdg. 17.89 *(978-0-06-174268-2(6))* HarperCollins Pubs.

Le Clézio, J. M. G. Lullaby. Lemoine, Georges, illus. 2007. (FRE.). 72p. (J). (gr. 5-10). pap. *(978-2-07-061258-1(9))* Gallimard, Editions.

Marino, Nan. Hiding Out at the Pancake Palace. 2013. (ENG.). 256p. (J). (gr. 3-7). 16.99 *(978-1-59643-753-1(7),* 9781596437531) Roaring Brook Pr.

—Hiding Out at the Pancake Palace. 2014. (ENG.). 272p. (J). (gr. 3-7). pap. 7.99 *(978-1-250-04000-8(0),* 9781250040008) Square Fish.

McCranie, Stephen. Food Fight!, 2 vols. McCranie, Stephen, illus. 2nd ed. 2012. (Mal & Chad Ser.: 2). (ENG., Illus.). 224p. (J). (gr. 3-7). 9.99 *(978-0-399-25657-8(1),* Philomel Bks.) Penguin Young Readers Group.

Myers, Walter Dean. Checkmate. 2015. (News Crew Ser.). (ENG.). 144p. (J). (gr. 5-9). pap. 6.99 *(978-0-545-82875-8(9),* Scholastic Pr.) Scholastic, Inc.

—A Star Is Born. (J). 2015. (News Crew Ser.). (ENG.). 176p. (gr. 5-9). pap. 6.99 *(978-0-545-82876-5(7),* Scholastic Pr.) 2012. (Cruisers Ser.: Bk. 3). *(978-0-439-91631-8(3))* 2012. (Cruisers Ser.: Bk. 3). (ENG.). 176p. (gr. 5-9). 17.99 *(978-0-439-91628-8(3))* Scholastic, Inc.

Robinson, Craig & Mansbach, Adam. Jake the Fake Keeps It Real. Knight, Keith, illus. 2017. (Jake the Fake Ser.: 1). (ENG.). 144p. (J). (gr. 3-7). 13.99 *(978-0-553-52351-5(1),* Crown Books For Young Readers) Random Hse. Children's Bks.

Stewart, Trenton Lee. The Mysterious Benedict Society. Tingley, Megan, ed. Sudyka, Diana, illus. 2010. (Mysterious Benedict Society Ser.: 3). (ENG.). 400p. (J). (gr. 3-7). pap. 8.99 *(978-0-316-04550-6(0))* Little, Brown Bks. for Young Readers.

—The Mysterious Benedict Society. Ellis, Carson, illus. (Mysterious Benedict Society Ser.: 1). (ENG.). (J). (gr. 3-7). 2008. 512p. pap. 9.99 *(978-0-316-00395-7(6))* 2007. 496p. 19.00 *(978-0-316-05777-6(0),* Tingley, Megan Bks.) 2015. 512p. 12.99 *(978-0-316-26501-0(2))* Little, Brown Bks. for Young Readers.

—The Mysterious Benedict Society. unabr. ed. 2007. (Mysterious Benedict Society Ser.: Bk. 1). (ENG.). (J). (gr. 3-7). 25.50 *(978-0-307-28440-2(9),* Listening Library (Audio)) Penguin Random House Audio Publishing Group.

—The Mysterious Benedict Society. 2009. 17.45 *(978-1-60686-527-9(7))* Perfection Learning Corp.

—The Mysterious Benedict Society. 2010. (Mysterious Benedict Society Ser.: 3). (J). lib. bdg. 19.65 *(978-0-606-15117-7(6),* Turtleback) Turtleback Bks.

—The Mysterious Benedict Society. Ellis, Carson, illus. 2008. (Mysterious Benedict Society Ser.: 1). 485p. (J). (gr. 3-7). lib. bdg. 19.65 *(978-1-4178-1817-4(4),* Turtleback) Turtleback Bks.

—The Mysterious Benedict Society & the Prisoner's Dilemma. Sudyka, Diana, illus. 2009. (Mysterious Benedict Society Ser.: 3). (ENG.). 400p. (J). (gr. 3-7). 18.99 *(978-0-316-04552-0(7))* Little, Brown Bks. for Young Readers.

Turner, Blaine. Beastmasters. 2012. 164p. pap. 12.98 *(978-0-578-09035-1(X))* Turner, Blaine.

Yang, Gene Luen. Secret Coders. Holmes, Mike, illus. 2015. (Secret Coders Ser.: 1). (ENG.). 96p. (J). (gr. 3-7). 17.99 *(978-1-62672-276-7(5),* 9781626722767); pap. 9.99 *(978-1-62672-075-6(4),* 9781626720756) Roaring Brook Pr. (First Second Bks.).

Yee, Lisa. Millicent Min, Girl Genius. 2004. 248p. (gr. 3-7). 17.00 *(978-0-7569-3919-9(4))* Perfection Learning Corp.

—Millicent Min, Girl Genius. 2004. (Millicent Min Trilogy Ser.: 1). (ENG.). 256p. (J). (gr. 4-7). reprint ed. pap. 6.99 *(978-0-439-42520-9(4),* Levine, Arthur A. Bks.) Scholastic, Inc.

GIFTS

Ashour, Monica & Harrald-Pilz, Marilee. Everybody Has Something to Give. 2015. (Illus.). 29p. (J). pap. 12.95 *(978-0-8198-2389-2(9))* Pauline Bks. & Media.

Bixby, James F. The Mystery of the Christmas Dollhouse. 2010. 76p. pap. 11.95 *(978-1-4401-7141-3(6))* iUniverse, Inc.

Bolte, Mari. Eco Gifts: Upcycled Gifts You Can Make. 2015. (Make It, Gift It Ser.). (ENG., Illus.). 32p. (gr. 3-4). lib. bdg. 27.99 *(978-1-4914-5202-8(1),* Snap Bks.) Capstone Press of Coughlan Cos.

—From Me to You: Handmade Gifts for Your VIPs. 2015. (Make It, Gift It Ser.). (ENG., Illus.). 32p. (gr. 3-4). lib. bdg. 27.99 *(978-1-4914-5201-1(3),* Snap Bks.) Capstone Press of Coughlan Cos.

—Homemade Holiday: Gifts for Every Occasion. 2015. (Make It, Gift It Ser.). (ENG., Illus.). 32p. (gr. 3-4). lib. bdg. 27.99 *(978-1-4914-5199-1(8),* Snap Bks.) Capstone Press of Coughlan Cos.

—In Good Taste: Great Gifts to Make, Eat, & Share. 2015. (Make It, Gift It Ser.). (ENG., Illus.). 32p. (gr. 3-4). lib. bdg. 27.99 *(978-1-4914-5200-4(5),* Snap Bks.) Capstone Press of Coughlan Cos.

—Make It, Gift It. 2015. (Make It, Gift It Ser.). (ENG.). 32p. (gr. 3-4). 111.96 *(978-1-4914-6959-0(5),* Snap Bks.) Capstone Press of Coughlan Cos.

—Make It, Gift It: Handmade Gifts for Every Occasion. 2015. (Craft It Yourself Ser.). (ENG., Illus.). 144p. (gr. 3-4). pap. 14.95 *(978-1-62370-319-6(0))* Capstone Press of Coughlan Cos.

Bonnett, Rosalind, illus. Santa Flap Book. 2012. (Flap Bks). 10p. (J). bds. 7.99 *(978-0-7945-3316-8(7),* Usborne) EDC Publishing.

Deedy, Carmen Agra. 14 Cows for America, 1 vol. González, Thomas, illus. 2009. (ENG.). 36p. (J). (gr. 1-5). 17.95 *(978-1-56145-490-7(7))* Peachtree Pubs.

—14 Cows for America. Gonzalez, Thomas, illus. 2016. (ENG.). 36p. (J). (gr. -1-3). lib. bdg. 19.60 *(978-0-606-39065-1(0))* Turtleback Bks.

—14 Vacas para América, 1 vol. González, Thomas, illus. 2010.Tr. of 14 Cows for America. (SPA.). 36p. (J). pap. 8.95 *(978-1-56145-555-3(5))* Peachtree Pubs.

—14 Vacas para América, 1 vol. De la Torre, Cristina, tr. from ENG. González, Thomas, illus. 2010.Tr. of 14 Cows for America. (SPA.). 36p. (J). (gr. 1-5). 17.95 *(978-1-56145-550-8(4))* Peachtree Pubs.

Deedy, Carmen Agra & Naiyomah, Wilson Kimeli. 14 Cows for America, 1 vol. González, Thomas, illus. 2016. (ENG.). 36p. (J). (gr. 1-5). pap. 8.95 *(978-1-56145-961-2(5))* Peachtree Pubs.

Erlbach, Arlene & Erlbach, Herb. Fun Valentine's Day Crafts. 2015. (Kid Fun Holiday Crafts! Ser.). 32p. (J). (gr. 3-4). 23.94 *(978-0-7660-6255-9(4))* Enslow Pubs., Inc.

Hoard, Julia. God, What Is the Gift of Tongues? 2007. (ENG., Illus.). 32p. (gr. -1-3). 14.99 *(978-1-59979-076-3(9),* Creation Hse.) Charisma Media.

Hyman, Corine & Bryant, Julie. Why We Give Gifts at Christmas Time. 2013. 34p. pap. 12.00 *(978-0-9855423-9-9(X))* Teaching Christ's Children Publishing.

Johnson, Kristin & Cummins, Mimi. Christmas Cookies Are for Giving: Recipes, Stories & Tips for Making Heartwarming Gifts. 2003. (Illus.). 208p. 16.95 *(978-0-9723473-9-6(9))* Tyr Publishing.

Kallmeyer-Mehlhorn, Margarete. The Wondrous Ball of Yarn: A Facsimile of the Previously Unpublished Manuscript. 2008.Tr. of Wunderknaul. (ENG & GER., Illus.). 40p. 41.00 *(978-0-9745168-2-0(1))* Cotsen Occasional Pr.

Kruse, Nancy. Treasure Hunt: A Book of Clues for Parties. 2008. 116p. pap. 12.95 *(978-1-60145-565-9(8))* Booklocker.com, Inc.

Lodien, Jennie, des. Cat Tales. 2004. (Illus.). 48p. (YA). ring bd. 16.95 *(978-0-9746341-8-0(2))* Chin & A Pr.

Mecham, Janeal A. Christmas Gifts. Mecham, Janeal A., illus. l.t. unabr. ed. 2003. (Illus.). 32p. (J). (gr. k-3). 12.95 *(978-1-932280-16-6(2),* 80162) Granite Publishing & Distribution.

Mercier, Johanne. Caillou - Merry Christmas! Brignaud, Pierre, illus. 2nd ed. 2012. (Confetti Ser.). (ENG.). 24p. (J). (gr. -1-1). pap. 4.99 *(978-2-89718-020-1(X))* Caillouet, Gerry.

Owen, Ruth. Gifts. 2013. (From Trash to Treasure Ser.). 32p. (J). (gr. 3-6). 26.50 *(978-1-4777-1287-0(9));* pap. 70.50 *(978-1-4777-1369-3(7));* pap. 11.75 *(978-1-4777-1368-6(9))* Rosen Publishing Group, Inc., The. (PowerKids Pr.).

Saenz, Sandra C. The Precious Gift. 2011. 16p. (gr. -1). 9.50 *(978-1-4567-4708-4(8))* AuthorHouse.

Sévigny, Eric, illus. Caillou: The Birthday Party. 2014. (ENG.). 24p. (J). (gr. -1-1). pap. 4.99 *(978-2-89718-122-2(2))* Caillouet, Gerry.

Subramaniam, Manasi. The Story & the Song. Sankaranarayanan, Ayswarya, illus. 2013. (ENG.). 32p. (J). (gr. k). pap. 9.95 *(978-81-8190-273-3(4))* Karadi Tales Co. Pvt, Ltd. IND. Dist: Consortium Bk. Sales & Distribution.

Summerer, Marilyn. The First Christmas Present. van der Sterre, Johanna, illus. 2009. 32p. (J). (gr. -1). 14.99 *(978-0-7586-1663-0(5))* Concordia Publishing Hse.

Zimmerman, Andrea. Eliza's Cherry Trees: Japan's Gift to America, 1 vol. Chen, Ju-Hong, illus. 2011. (ENG.). 32p. (J). (gr. k-3). 16.99 *(978-1-58980-954-3(8))* Pelican Publishing Co., Inc.

GIFTS—FICTION

Acevedo, Jenny. Ginger's Grand Adventure. 2012. 36p. pap. 24.95 *(978-1-4626-2472-0(3))* America Star Bks.

Adair, Amy. Jay Jay's Special Delivery. 2003. (Illus.). (J). 15.98 *(978-0-7853-8625-4(4))* Publications International, Ltd.

Adler, David A. Bones & the Birthday Mystery, No. 5. Newman, Barbara Johansen, illus. 2009. (Bones Ser.: 5). (ENG.). 32p. (J). (gr. 1-3). mass mkt. 3.99 *(978-0-14-241432-3(8),* Penguin Young Readers) Penguin Young Readers Group.

Albert, Richard E. & National Geographic Learning Staff. Alejandro's Gift. Long, Sylvia, illus. 97th ed. 2010. (Rise & Shine Ser.). (ENG.). 40p. (C). (gr. -1-7). pap. 11.95 *(978-0-8118-1342-6(8))* National Geographic School Publishing, Inc.

Aldrick, Shirley H. F. Hazel, the Hoppity Kangaroo. 2010. 28p. pap. 12.50 *(978-1-60860-743-3(7),* Strategic Bk. Publishing) Strategic Book Publishing & Rights Agency (SBPRA).

Alpert, Barbara. The True Meaning of Christmas, the Greatest Gift of All. Zamboni, David, illus. 2009. 24p. pap. 12.95 *(978-1-936051-18-2(4))* Peppertree Pr., The.

Ameen, Judith. Harold & the Magic Books. 2005. 40p. pap. 8.95 *(978-1-933265-42-1(6))* Wasteland Pr.

Anderson, Shel. Spoofaloof's Adventures: Rainy Day Fun. Anderson, Shauna, illus. 2008. 52p. pap. 22.50 *(978-1-4389-1689-7(2))* AuthorHouse.

Andrews, Julie & Hamilton, Emma Walton. A Fairy Merry Christmas. 2012. (Passport to Reading Level 1 Ser.). (J). lib. bdg. 14.75 *(978-0-606-26692-5(5),* Turtleback) Turtleback Bks.

Antoine, Leon. Santa's Destiny: A Legend Reborn, 1 vol. 2010. 48p. pap. 16.95 *(978-1-4512-9281-7(3))* America Star Bks.

Appel, Cindy. The Best Christmas Gift. Collier, Kevin Scott, illus. 2005. (J). E-Book 6.00 incl. cd-rom *(978-1-933090-19-1(7))* Guardian Angel Publishing, Inc.

Appelt, Kathi. The Best Kind of Gift. 2003. (Illus.). 32p. (J). 17.89 *(978-0-688-15393-9(3))* HarperCollins Pubs.

Auger, Dale. Mwâkwa Talks to the Loon: A Cree Story for Children, 1 vol. Auger, Dale, illus. 2007. (ENG., Illus.). 32p. (J). (gr. k-3). pap. 12.95 *(978-1-894974-32-5(8))* Heritage Hse. CAN. Dist: Orca Bk. Pubs. USA.

Bailey, Tressie. The Little Box Kittens meet Santa Claus. 2009. 37p. pap. 24.10 *(978-0-557-03198-6(2))* Lulu Pr., Inc.

Bailey's Birthday - Evaluation Guide: Evaluation Guide. 2006. (J). *(978-1-55942-399-1(4))* Witcher Productions.

Bak, Jenny. Ten Gifts from Santa Claus: A Counting Book. Harding, Niall, illus. 2011. (ENG.). 22p. (J). (gr. -1-k). 14.99 *(978-1-4052-5127-3(1))* Egmont Bks., Ltd. GBR. Dist: Independent Pubs. Group.

Balfour, Melissa. The Magic Footprints. Julian, Russell, illus. 2005. (Green Bananas Ser.). (ENG.). 48p. (J). lib. bdg. *(978-0-7787-1023-3(8))* Crabtree Publishing Co.

Balfour, Melissa, et al. Yr Olion Traed Hud. 2005. (WEL., Illus.). 48p. pap. *(978-1-85596-677-2(8))* Dref Wen.

Barbera, Katia. Iron Horse, 1 vol. 2010. 16p. 24.95 *(978-1-4489-4634-1(4))* PublishAmerica, Inc.

Barchers, Suzanne I. A Box for Ross, 1 vol. 2011. (Targeted Phonics Ser.). (ENG., Illus.). 16p. (J). (gr. k-2). pap. 5.99 *(978-1-4333-2415-4(6))* Teacher Created Materials, Inc.

Barnhill, Carla. Rufus & the Very Special Baby: A Frolic Christmas Story. Barnhill, Carla, illus. 2016. (Frolic First Faith Ser.). (ENG., Illus.). 32p. (J). (gr. -1-3). 12.99 *(978-1-5064-1762-2(0),* Sparkhouse Family) Augsburg Fortress, Pubs.

Bass, William E. A Gift for Sant. Salazar, Vivian Rose, illus. 2012. 36p. pap. 24.95 *(978-1-4626-6731-4(7))* America Star Bks.

Bates, Janet. Seaside Dream, 1 vol. Davis, Lambert, illus. 2016. (ENG.). 32p. (J). pap. 9.95 *(978-1-62014-256-1(2))* Lee & Low Bks., Inc.

Bates, Janet Costa. Seaside Dream. Davis, Lambert, illus. 2013. (ENG.). 32p. (J). (gr. k-5). 17.95 *(978-1-60060-347-1(5))* Lee & Low Bks., Inc.

Batt Tanya Robyn. Faeries Gift. Ceccoli Nicoletta, illus. 2006. 0032p. pap. 6.99 *(978-1-905236-73-2(5))* Barefoot Bks., Inc.

Bauld, Jane S. The Gift of the Gold Coin. Carpenter, Christina D., ed. Newsome, Andy, illus. Date not set. 32p. (J). (gr. -1-5). 15.95 *(978-1-886440-03-6(4))* Portunus Publishing Co.

Beck, Glenn, et al. The Christmas Sweater. Dorman, Brandon, illus. 2009. (ENG.). 40p. (J). (gr. -1-2). 17.99 *(978-1-4169-9543-2(9),* Aladdin) Simon & Schuster Children's Publishing.

Bellingham, Brenda. Lilly's Special Gift. 2005. (Illus.). 59p. (J). lib. bdg. 12.00 *(978-1-4242-1204-0(9))* Fitzgerald Bks.

Benjamin, Ruth. My Little Pony: A Secret Gift. Middleton, Gayle, illus. 2006. 24p. (J). lib. bdg. 15.00 *(978-1-4242-1536-2(6))* Fitzgerald Bks.

—A Secret Gift/el Regalo Secreto. Abboud, Adela, tr. from ENG. Middleton, Gayle, illus. 2006. (I Can Read Bks.). (SPA & ENG.). 24p. (J). (gr. k-3). per. 3.99 *(978-0-06-112391-7(9),* Rayo) HarperCollins Pubs.

The Best Birthday Present: Individual Title Six-Packs. (Literatura 2000 Ser.). (gr. 2-3). 33.00 *(978-0-7635-0216-4(2))* Rigby Education.

Best, Cari. Three Cheers for Catherine the Great! Potter, Giselle, illus. 2003. (Catherine the Great Ser.). (ENG.). 32p. (J). (gr. -1-3). pap. 8.99 *(978-0-374-47551-2(2),* 9780374475512) Square Fish.

The Best Gift of All. 2003. (J). per. *(978-1-57657-803-2(8))* Paradise Pr., Inc.

Bishop, Jennie. The Three Gifts of Christmas. McDaniels, Preston, illus. 2009. 32p. (J). (gr. 3-18). 15.99 incl. audio compact disk *(978-1-59317-378-4(4))* Warner Pr., Inc.

Black, Birdie. Just Right for Christmas. Beardshaw, Rosalind, illus. 2014. (ENG.). 24p. (J). (-k). bds. 6.99 *(978-0-7636-7563-9(6),* Nosy Crow) Candlewick Pr.

Black, Sonia W. Jumping the Broom. Van Wright, Cornelius & Hu, Ying-Hwa, illus. 2004. 32p. (J). lib. bdg. 15.00 *(978-1-4242-0234-8(5))* Fitzgerald Bks.

Blair, Marcia L. Nana's Birthday Bubbles. 2012. 24p. pap. 24.95 *(978-1-4626-7880-8(7))* America Star Bks.

Bloom, Suzanne. Oh! What a Surprise! 2012. (Goose & Bear Stories Ser.). (ENG.). 32p. (J). (gr. -1-k). 16.95 *(978-1-59078-892-9(3))* Boyds Mills Pr.

Blount, Jill Rutland. Tara's Gift. 2010. 24p. pap. 11.99 *(978-1-4520-0507-2(9))* AuthorHouse.

Boggs, Danielle. The Snow Globe. 2008. 55p. pap. 16.95 *(978-1-60703-588-6(X))* America Star Bks.

Borden, Louise. The Last Day of School. Gustavson, Adam, illus. 2006. (ENG.). 40p. (J). (gr. 2-5). 17.99 *(978-0-689-86869-6(3),* McElderry, Margaret K. Bks.) McElderry, Margaret K. Bks.

Bright, Phoebe. Wish upon a Gift. 2012. (Lucky Stars Ser.: 6). (ENG.). 96p. (J). (gr. 2-5). pap. 5.99 *(978-0-545-42003-7(2),* Scholastic Paperbacks) Scholastic, Inc.

Bright, Rachel. Love Monster & the Perfect Present. 2014. (ENG., Illus.). 32p. (J). (gr. -1-k). 17.99 *(978-0-374-34648-5(8),* 9780374346485, Farrar, Straus & Giroux (BYR)) Farrar, Straus & Giroux.

Brookover, Brian D. Neddy & Little Roy Go to Town. 2013. 40p. pap. 20.99 *(978-1-4817-1185-2(7))* AuthorHouse.

Brown, Marc. D. W.'s Perfect Present. Brown, Marc, illus. 2004. (ENG., Illus.). 24p. (J). (gr. -1-1). pap. 3.99 *(978-0-316-73386-1(5),* Tingley, Megan Bks.) Little, Brown Bks. for Young Readers.

Brown, Palmer. Something for Christmas. Brown, Palmer, illus. 2011. (ENG., Illus.). 40p. (J). (gr. -1-2). 12.95 *(978-1-59017-462-3(3),* NYR Children's Collection) New York Review of Bks., Inc., The.

Bunting, Eve. The Mother's Day Mice. Brett, Jan, illus. 2017. (ENG.). 40p. (J). (gr. -1-3). 8.99 *(978-0-544-88033-7(1),* HMH Books For Young Readers) Houghton Mifflin Harcourt Publishing Co.

—Mr. Goat's Valentine. Zimmer, Kevin, illus. 2016. (ENG.). 32p. (J). (gr. k-2). 16.99 *(978-1-58536-944-7(6),* 204024) Sleeping Bear Pr.

Burkart, Tammy Jayne. Lillie, 1 vol. 2009. 48p. pap. 16.95 *(978-1-60813-680-3(9))* America Star Bks.

Burton, Lynne. Charlotte's Crocodile. 2012. 22p. pap. *(978-1-909395-00-8(5))* Legend Pr.

Callahan, Thera S. Un Regalo Bien Envuelto: All Wrapped Up. Gordon, Mike, illus. 2003. (Rookie Readers Spanish Ser.). (SPA.). (J). 19.50 *(978-0-516-25885-0(0),* Children's Pr.) Scholastic Library Publishing.

Calmenson, Stephanie. Birthday at the Panda Palace. Cushman, Doug, illus. 2007. 32p. (J). (gr. -1-3). 15.99 *(978-0-06-052663-4(7))* HarperCollins Pubs.

Campbell, Suzy. Pennies for Christmas, 1 vol. 2010. 24p. 24.95 *(978-1-4512-0553-4(8))* PublishAmerica, Inc.

Candlewick Press Staff. Peppa Pig & the Lost Christmas List. Ladybird Books Staff, illus. 2012. (Peppa Pig Ser.). (ENG.). 32p. (J). (gr. k-k). 12.99 *(978-0-7636-6276-9(3),* Candlewick Entertainment) Candlewick Pr.

Capucilli, Alyssa Satin. Biscuit Gives a Gift. Schories, Pat, illus. 2004. (ENG.). 16p. (J). (gr. -1-3). bds. 4.99 *(978-0-06-009467-6(2),* HarperFestival) HarperCollins Pubs.

Chamberlain, Karen, et al. A Feather for the Queen. 2009. 28p. pap. 13.95 *(978-1-4490-3903-5(0))* AuthorHouse.

Chandler, Elizabeth. The Back Door of Midnight. 2010. (Dark Secrets Ser.: Vol. 5). (ENG.). 320p. (YA). (gr. 7-18). pap. 9.99 *(978-1-4424-0626-1(7),* Simon Pulse) Simon Pulse.

Clark, Michelle. The Special Gift: Michelle Clark. 2010. 36p. 16.95 *(978-1-4490-3059-9(9))* AuthorHouse.

Clement-Davies, David. Fell. 2009. (ENG.). 544p. (YA). (gr. 7-11). pap. 10.95 *(978-0-8109-7266-7(2),* Amulet Bks.) Abrams, Inc.

Climo, Shirley. Pandora's Gift. Date not set. (Illus.). 64p. (J). (gr. 3-4). 15.99 *(978-0-06-028632-3(6))* HarperCollins Pubs.

Cocca-Leffler, Maryann. A Homemade Together Christmas. Cocca-Leffler, Maryann, illus. 2015. (ENG., Illus.). 32p. (J). (gr. -1-3). 16.99 *(978-0-8075-3366-6(1))* Whitman, Albert & Co.

Coffelt, Nancy. Uh-Oh, Baby! Nash, Scott, illus. 2013. (ENG.). 40p. (J). (gr. -1-3). 16.99 *(978-1-4169-9149-6(2),* Simon & Schuster/Paula Wiseman Bks.) Simon & Schuster/Paula Wiseman Bks.

Columbro, Judy. The Gift That Grows. Scottorosano, Deborah, illus. 2011. 28p. pap. 24.95 *(978-1-4626-1800-2(6))* America Star Bks.

Conroy, Christine. Mama Wants a Llam. 2012. 16p. pap. 15.99 *(978-1-4772-1605-7(7))* AuthorHouse.

Coon, Dianne. Nerual's Adventures & the Greatness of Agnes. 2010. 68p. pap. 11.49 *(978-1-4520-2321-2(2))* AuthorHouse.

Cregg, R. J. Best Sister Ever. 2017. (Olivia 8x8 Ser.). lib. bdg. 13.55 ***(978-0-606-40213-2(6))*** Turtleback Bks.

Curl, Terry J. Abby's Aunt Ate All the Apples. 2010. 56p. pap. 9.99 *(978-1-60911-393-3(4),* Eloquent Bks.) Strategic Book Publishing & Rights Agency (SBPRA).

Cuyler, Margery. That's Good! That's Bad! on Santa's Journey. 2015. (J). lib. bdg. 17.20 *(978-0-606-37582-5(1))* Turtleback Bks.

Danneberg, Julie. Last Day Blues. Love, Judy, illus. 2006. (Mrs. Hartwells Classroom Adventures Ser.). (ENG.). 32p. (J). (gr. k-3). 7.95 *(978-1-58089-104-2(7))* Charlesbridge Publishing, Inc.

David, E. L. The Christmas Gift. 2011. 28p. pap. 14.99 *(978-1-4634-2685-9(2))* AuthorHouse.

David, Jamie. Johann Sebastian Humpbach. David, Jamie, illus. 2009. (Illus.). 167p. pap. 14.95 *(978-0-615-31840-0(1))* Chai Yo Maui Pr.

Davis, Aubrey. Bagels from Benny. Petricic, Dusan, illus. 2005. (ENG.). 32p. (J). (gr. -1-3). 7.95 *(978-1-55337-749-8(4))* Kids Can Pr., Ltd. CAN. Dist: Hachette Bk. Group.

de Brunhoff, Laurent. Babar Raconte le Plus Beau Cadeau du Monde. (Babar Ser.). (FRE., Illus.). 48p. (J). (gr. -1-3). 19.95 *(978-0-7859-8821-2(1))* French & European Pubns., Inc.

deGroat, Diane. Happy Birthday to You, You Belong in a Zoo. deGroat, Diane, illus. 2007. (Gilbert & Friends Ser.). (ENG., Illus.). 32p. (J). (gr. -1-3). pap. 6.99 *(978-0-06-001029-4(0))* HarperCollins Pubs.

—Happy Birthday to You, You Belong in a Zoo. deGroat, Diane, illus. 2007. (Gilbert & Friends Ser.). (Illus.). (gr. -1-3). 17.00 *(978-0-7569-8108-2(5))* Perfection Learning Corp.

DePalma, Mary Newell. The Perfect Gift. 2010. (J). pap. *(978-0-545-15403-1(0),* Levine, Arthur A. Bks.) Scholastic, Inc.

Derubertis, Barbara. Gertie Gorilla's Glorious Gift. 2010. pap. 45.32 *(978-0-7613-6509-9(5))* Kane Press, Inc.

deRubertis, Barbara. Gertie Gorilla's Glorious Gift. Alley, R. W., illus. 2010. (Animal Antics A to Z Ser.). 32p. (J). (gr. -1-3).

pap. 7.95 *(978-1-57565-311-2(7))*; lib. bdg. 22.60 *(978-1-57565-318-1(4))* Kane Press, Inc.

deRubertis, Barbara & DeRubertis, Barbara. Gertie Gorilla's Glorious Gift. Alley, R. W., illus. 2012. (Animal Antics A to Z Ser.). 32p. (J). (gr. 2 — 1). cd-rom 7.95 *(978-1-57565-400-3(8))* Kane Press, Inc.

Di Santo, Melina. Mel & her Magic Journey. 2010. (Illus.). 32p. 14.49 *(978-1-4490-6889-9(8))* AuthorHouse.

Diaz, Katacha. Carolina's Gift: A Story of Peru. Landolt, Gredna, illus. 2005. (ENG.). 32p. (J). (gr. k-3). 8.95 *(978-1-56899-699-8(3)*, SC8005) Soundprints.

Diaz, Nelbaliz. Laura y Su Caja de Sorpresas. 2007. (SPA.). 48p. 14.95 *(978-0-8477-0452-1(1))* Univ. of Puerto Rico Pr.

Diesen, Deborah. The Not Very Merry Pout-Pout Fish. Hanna, Dan, illus. (Pout-Pout Fish Adventure Ser.). (ENG.). (J). 2017. 34p. bds. 7.99 *(978-0-374-30459-1(9)*, 9780374304591) 2015. 32p. (gr. -1-1). 16.99 *(978-0-374-35549-4(5)*, 9780374355494) Farrar, Straus & Giroux. (Farrar, Straus & Giroux (BYR)).

Dillard, Mary Gregory. Finding Betsyanna. 2006. (ENG.). 48p. per. 16.95 *(978-1-4241-5492-0(8))* America Star Bks.

Dipucchio, Kelly. Crafty Chloe. Ross, Heather, illus. 2012. (Crafty Chloe Ser.). (ENG.). 40p. (J). (gr. -1-3). 16.99 *(978-1-4424-2123-3(1)*, Atheneum Bks. for Young Readers) Simon & Schuster Children's Publishing.

Disney Book Group Staff & Higginson, Sheila Sweeny. Minnie: Minnie's Valentine. Disney Storybook Artists Staff, illus. 2013. 10p. 5.99 *(978-1-4231-8811-7(X))* Disney Pr.

—My Huggy Valentine. Disney Storybook Art Team, illus. 2013. (ENG.). 24p. (J). (gr. -1-k). pap. 5.99 *(978-1-4847-0425-7(8))* Disney Pr.

Dooley, Norah. Everybody Serves Soup. Thornton, Peter, illus. 2004. (Carolrhoda Picture Books Ser.). (ENG.). 40p. (J). (gr. -1-3). per. 6.95 *(978-1-57505-791-0(3))* Lerner Publishing Group.

—Everybody Serves Soup. Thornton, Peter J., illus. 2004. (Picture Bks.). 40p. (J). (gr. -1-3). 15.95 *(978-1-57505-422-3(1))* Lerner Publishing Group.

Dubinski, Lisa. A Gift to Give & Coloring Book. 2010. 32p. pap. 17.99 *(978-0-557-60224-7(6))* Lulu Pr., Inc.

Durrant, George D. Sam's Christmas Wish. Burr, Dan, illus. 2014. (ENG.). 32p. (J). (gr. 3). 17.99 *(978-1-60907-606-1(0)*, Shadow Mountain) Shadow Mountain Publishing.

Elliott, Rebecca. Warm Hearts Day: A Branches Book. Elliott, Rebecca, illus. 2016. (Owl Diaries: 5). (ENG., Illus.). 80p. (J). (gr. k-2). pap. 4.99 *(978-1-338-04260-1(7))* Scholastic, Inc.

Emmett, Jonathan. The Best Gift of All. Cabban, Vanessa, illus. 2008. (ENG.). 32p. (J). (gr. -1-2). 15.99 *(978-0-7636-3860-3(9))* Candlewick Pr.

Endacott, C. R. Afflatus. 2008. 232p. pap. 15.95 *(978-0-595-52418-1(4))* iUniverse, Inc.

Engelbreit, Mary. Queen of Christmas. Engelbreit, Mary, illus. 2003. (Ann Estelle Stories Ser.). (Illus.). (J). 32p. 16.99 *(978-0-06-058608-9(7))*; 159.90 *(978-0-06-056902-0(6))*; 127.92 *(978-0-06-056903-7(4))* HarperCollins Pubs.

Evans, Michael. Poggle & the Birthday Present. Evans, Michael, illus. 2011. (Poggle Ser.). (ENG., Illus.). 32p. (J). (gr. k — 1). pap. 8.99 *(978-1-4052-5359-8(2))* Egmont Bks., Ltd. GBR. Dist: Independent Pubs. Group.

Fagan, Cary. My New Shirt. Petricic, Dusan, illus. 2007. (ENG.). 32p. (J). (gr. -1-1). 18.95 *(978-0-88776-715-9(X)*, Tundra Bks.) Tundra Bks. CAN. Dist: Penguin Random Hse. LLC.

Faye Morningstar. Little Dream Athe: The Sand Prince. 2012. 20p. pap. 17.99 *(978-1-4772-9540-3(2))* AuthorHouse.

Fernandez, Joyce & Marsh, Laura. Un et Deux are One & Two. 2009. 22p. 15.95 *(978-0-615-26239-0(2))* My Second Language Publishing, USA.

—Uno Is One. 2009. 22p. 15.95 *(978-0-615-24460-0(2))* My Second Language Publishing, USA.

Ferry, Beth. Land Shark. Mantle, Ben, illus. 2015. (ENG.). 36p. (J). (gr. -1-k). 16.99 *(978-1-4521-2458-2(2))* Chronicle Bks. LLC.

Fisher, Kimball. Finding Baby Jesus. 2015. 12p. (J). pap. 3.99 *(978-1-4621-1698-0(1))* Cedar Fort, Inc./CFI Distribution.

Fox, R. J. Stuart & His Incredibly Obnoxious Magical Book: Soccer, 1 vol. 2009. 86p. pap. 19.95 *(978-1-4489-9833-3(6))* America Star Bks.

Frazee, Maria. Santa Claus the World's Number One Toy Expert. 2010. (ENG., Illus.). 32p. (J). (gr. -1-3). pap. 7.99 *(978-0-547-48074-9(1))* Houghton Mifflin Harcourt Publishing Co.

Frederick, Heather Vogel. A Little Women Christmas. Ibatoulline, Bagram, illus. 2014. (ENG.). 32p. (J). (gr. -1-3). 17.99 *(978-1-4424-1359-7(X)*, Simon & Schuster Bks. For Young Readers) Simon & Schuster Bks. For Young Readers.

Freeman, Tor. Olive & the Embarrassing Gift. Freeman, Tor, illus. 2014. (ENG., Illus.). 32p. (J). (gr. -1-3). 15.99 *(978-0-7636-7406-9(0)*, Templar) Candlewick Pr.

Froeb, Lori C. & Disney Storybook Artists Staff. Cinderella's Shining Moment. 2012. (Fold-Out Figure Ser.). (ENG., Illus.). 32p. (J). (gr. -1-2). 14.99 *(978-0-7944-2547-0(X)*, Reader's Digest Children's Bks.) Studio Fun International.

Fromental, Jean-Luc. 365 Penguins. Jolivet, Joëlle, illus. 2006. (ENG.). 48p. (J). (gr. -1-3). 19.95 *(978-0-8109-4460-2(X)*, Abrams Bks. for Young Readers) Abrams, Inc.

Gauthier, Gilles. Le Gros Cadeau du Petit Marcus. 2003. (Premier Roman Ser.). (FRE., Illus.). 64p. (J). (gr. 2-5). pap. *(978-2-89021-255-8(6))* Diffusion du livre Mirabel (DLM).

George, Kallie. The Lost Gift: A Christmas Story. Graegin, Stephanie, illus. 2016. (ENG.). 40p. (J). (gr. -1-3). 17.99 *(978-0-553-52481-9(X)*, Schwartz & Wade Bks.) Random Hse. Children's Bks.

George R. Cathcart Jr. Ernie's Clever Plan. 2012. 24p. 24.95 *(978-1-4626-6795-6(3))* America Star Bks.

Gerlach-Babb nee Maines, Mary & Gerlach, Susan. Best Christmas Gift. 2007. (ENG.). 52p. per. 16.95 *(978-1-4241-6389-2(7))* America Star Bks.

Gevry, C. C. A Christmas Kindness. Mabey, Coline, illus. 2012. 24p. pap. 11.99 *(978-0-9852661-4-1(7))* 4RV Publishing, LLC.

The Gift. l.t. ed. 2003. 360p. per. *(978-0-9725719-5-1(7))* 21st Century Pr.

The Gift, 6 vols. (Multicultural Programs Ser.). 16p. (gr. 1-6). 31.95 *(978-0-7802-8309-1(0))* Wright Group/McGraw-Hill.

Gilmore, Rachna. A Gift for Gita. Priestley, Alice, illus. 2004. 24p. (J). *(978-1-85269-409-8(2))*; *(978-1-85269-408-1(4))*; *(978-1-85269-403-6(3))*; *(978-1-85269-407-4(6))* Mantra Lingua.

Gilmore, Rachna & Priestley, Alice. A Gift for Gita, 1 vol. 2005. (Gita Ser.: 2). (ENG., Illus.). 24p. (gr. 2-6). pap. 7.95 *(978-0-88448-239-0(1)*, 884239) Tilbury Hse. Pubs.

Goldman, Dara. Boris & Stella & the Perfect Gift. 2013. (ENG.). (J). *(978-1-58536-859-4(8))* Sleeping Bear Pr.

Gordon, Fran & Tischler, Faye. Dutch Double. 2007. (Illus.). 88p. pap. 15.95 *(978-1-59299-242-3(0))* Inkwater Pr.

Gorgas, Paula Blais. The Perfect Purple Present. 2007. (Illus.). (J). 20p. per. 11.99 *(978-0-9797574-4-0(4))*; 24p. 24.99 *(978-0-9794660-4-5(0))*; 24p. per. 12.99 *(978-0-9794660-5-2(9))* Dragonfly Publishing, Inc.

Grace, Ann Marie. The Secret Gift. 2013. 18p. pap. 12.99 *(978-1-4808-0411-1(8))* Archway Publishing.

Gramp's Magic Gift. 2011. 98p. 24.99 *(978-1-4628-2980-4(5))*; pap. 15.99 *(978-1-4628-2979-8(1))* Xlibris Corp.

Graw, Christine Werts. The Day I Gave My Stuff Away: The Story of Ashley Mae. 2011. 28p. pap. 13.95 *(978-1-4497-0981-5(8)*, WestBow Pr.) Author Solutions, Inc.

Greenberger, Tehilla. Gifts to Treasure. Toron, Eli, illus. 2007. (Fun to Read Book). 224p. (J). per. 10.95 *(978-1-929628-32-2(3))* Hachai Publishing.

Grein, Josh. Petunia Bobbin & the Baby Robin: A Christmas Adventure. 2012. 48p. (-18). 28.95 *(978-1-4582-0614-5(9))*; pap. 20.95 *(978-1-4582-0615-2(7))* Author Solutions, Inc. (Abbott Pr.).

Griffin, Ramona Rorie. The Gift That Grandma Gave: Including Bloom's Leveled Questions Study Guide. Tunstel Jr., Robert L., illus. 2011. 44p. pap. 24.95 *(978-1-4560-1034-8(4))* America Star Bks.

Guiffre, William. The First Gift of Christmas. Baron, Cheri Ann, illus. 2008. 32p. (J). (gr. -1-3). pap. 9.95 *(978-1-931650-33-5(0))* Bks. for Children Publishing.

Gutman, Anne. Gaspard & Lisa's Christmas Surprise. Hallensleben, Georg, illus. 2012. lib. bdg. 17.20 *(978-0-606-26782-3(4)*, Turtleback) Turtleback Bks.

Hall, Donald. Lucy's Christmas. McCurdy, Michael, illus. 2007. (ENG.). 32p. (J). (gr. 1). pap. 10.95 *(978-1-56792-342-1(9))* Godine, David R. Pub.

Hallwood, Cheri L. The Curious Polka-Dot Present. Rose, Patricia M., illus. 2007. (ENG.). 32p. (J). 16.99 *(978-0-9774422-1-8(7))* Forever Young Pubs.

Hamilton, Martha & Weiss, Mitch. Priceless Gifts: A Tale from Italy. Kanzler, John, illus. 2006. (ENG.). 32p. (J). (gr. k-3). 16.95 *(978-0-87483-788-9(X))* August Hse. Pubs., Inc.

Hanson, Bonnie Compton. The Impossible Christmas Present. 2004. (Ponytail Girls Ser.). (Illus.). 208p. (J). pap. 7.99 *(978-1-58411-030-9(9)*, Legacy Pr.) Rainbow Pubs. & Legacy Pr.

Hardie, Jill. The Sparkle Box: The Story of a Very Special Christmas Gift. Kornacki, Christine, illus. 2012. 32p. (J). 19.99 *(978-0-8249-5647-9(8)*, Ideal Pubns.) Worthy Publishing.

Hardin, Holly. Aurora of the Northern Lights. 2009. 31p. (J). pap. 18.95 *(978-1-4327-2439-9(8))* Outskirts Pr., Inc.

Hargreaves, Roger. Mr. Christmas Sticker Activity Book. Hargreaves, Adam, illus. 2010. (Mr. Men & Little Miss Ser.). (ENG.). 24p. (J). (gr. -1-2). act. bk. ed. 4.99 *(978-0-8431-2670-9(1)*, Price Stern Sloan) Penguin Young Readers Group.

Harper, John. Time Lapse: Collapse. 2011. 184p. 24.99 *(978-1-4490-7045-8(0))*; pap. 17.99 *(978-1-4490-7044-1(2))* AuthorHouse.

Harry, Rebecca. Snow Bunny's Christmas Gift. 2015. (ENG., Illus.). 32p. (J). (gr. -1-3). 17.99 *(978-1-4998-0164-4(5))* Little Bee Books Inc.

Hart, Caryl. The Princess & the Presents. Warburton, Sarah, illus. 2014. (ENG.). 32p. (J). (gr. -1-2). 16.99 *(978-0-7636-7398-7(6)*, Nosy Crow) Candlewick Pr.

Harvey, Jacqueline. Clementine Rose & the Perfect Present. 2015. (Clementine Rose Ser.: 3). (ENG.). 160p. (J). (gr. 2-4). 8.99 *(978-1-74275-545-8(3))* Random Hse. Australia AUS. Dist: Independent Pubs. Group.

Hayn, Carter. The Class Gift. 2015. (Rosen REAL Readers: STEM & STEAM Collection). (ENG.). 8p. pap. 5.46 *(978-1-4994-9614-7(1)*, Rosen Classroom) Rosen Publishing Group, Inc., The.

Hayward, Jason. Teddy Bear Adventures. 2011. 40p. pap. 24.95 *(978-1-4560-4068-0(5))* America Star Bks.

Henry, O. The Gift of the Magi. Zwerger, Lisbeth, illus. 2006. (ENG.). 32p. (J). (gr. 1-4). 17.99 *(978-1-4169-3586-5(X)*, Simon & Schuster Bks. For Young Readers) Simon & Schuster Bks. For Young Readers.

—The Gift of the Magi: A Story about Giving. Jaekel, Susan M., illus. 2006. (J). *(978-1-59939-084-0(1)*, Reader's Digest Young Families, Inc.) Studio Fun International.

Higgs, Liz Curtis. The Parable of the Lily, 1 vol. Munger, Nancy, illus. 10th anniv. ed. 2007. (Parable Ser.). (ENG.). 32p. (gr. -1-2). 7.99 *(978-1-4003-0844-6(5))* Nelson, Thomas Inc.

Hillert, Margaret. The Birthday Car. Girouard, Patrick, illus. 2016. (BeginningtoRead Ser.). (ENG.). 32p. (J). (gr. -1-2). pap. 11.94 *(978-1-60357-936-0(2))* Norwood Hse. Pr.

Holden, Pam. Presents for Grace, 6 pack. Hawley, Kelvin, illus. 2009. (Red Rocket Readers Ser.). (ENG.). 16p. (gr. 2-2). pap. *(978-1-877363-61-0(8)*, Red Rocket Readers) Flying Start Bks.

Hollis, Ginger. The Pumpkin Gift. Scarborough, Casey, illus. 2006. (ENG.). 32p. (J). 16.95 *(978-1-933660-04-2(X)*, Tadpole Pr. 4 Kids) Smooth Sailing Pr., LLC.

Holm, Jennifer L. & Holm, Matthew. A Very Babymouse Christmas. Holm, Jennifer L. & Holm, Matthew, illus. 2011. (Babymouse Ser.: 15). (ENG., Illus.). 96p. (J). (gr. 2-5). 12.99 *(978-0-375-96779-5(6))*; pap. 6.99 *(978-0-375-86779-8(1))* Random Hse. Children's Bks. (Random Hse. Bks. for Young Readers).

Huffman, Jared. The Lost Piece. Huffman, Jared & Rampley, Leigh, illus. 2011. 36p. pap. 24.95 *(978-1-4626-1784-5(0))* America Star Bks.

Huppert, Susan. The Perfect Gift. White, Rachel, illus. 2007. 24p. (J). per. *(978-0-9799635-0-6(8))* Homegrown Pubns., LLC.

I Only Like Dogs. 2013. (Illus.). 36p. pap. 9.99 *(978-1-941037-01-0(1))* Gordon Rocket.

Immi's Gift, 1 vol. 2014. (ENG., Illus.). 32p. (J). (gr. -1-3). 7.95 *(978-1-56145-813-4(9))* Peachtree Pubs.

Iriyama, Satoshi. Happy Spring, Chirp! 2015. (Chirp the Chick Ser.). (ENG., Illus.). 32p. (J). (— 1). 8.99 *(978-0-544-36150-8(4)*, HMH Books For Young Readers) Houghton Mifflin Harcourt Publishing Co.

Jacono, Mary Kaye. Lenny's Gift. 2005. 27p. pap. 10.95 *(978-0-7414-2602-4(1))* Infinity Publishing.

Jaklich, Brian. The Fireflies' Christmas. 2010. 24p. pap. 11.32 *(978-1-4567-0075-1(8))* AuthorHouse.

James, Brian. Yo-Ho-Ho! Zivoin, Jennifer, illus. 2008. (Pirate School Ser.: 7). (ENG.). 64p. (J). (gr. 1-3). pap. 3.99 *(978-0-448-44887-9(4)*, Grosset & Dunlap) Penguin Young Readers Group.

Jarkins, Sheila. The Adventures of Marco Flamingo in the Jungle. Jarkins, Sheila, illus. 2012. (Illus.). 32p. (J). 1.99 *(978-1-936299-31-7(3)*, Raven Tree Pr.) Delta Systems Company, Inc.

Jeffers, Susan. The Twelve Days of Christmas. Jeffers, Susan, illus. 2013. (ENG., Illus.). 40p. (J). (gr. -1-3). 17.99 *(978-0-06-206615-2(3))* HarperCollins Pubs.

Jeffers, Susan, illus. The Twelve Days of Christmas. 2013. (J). *(978-0-06-206616-9(1))* Harper & Row Ltd.

Jerome, Louie. Peter & the Black Dog. 2009. 120p. 22.50 *(978-1-60693-737-2(5)*, Strategic Bk. Publishing) Strategic Book Publishing & Rights Agency (SBPRA).

Jitchotvisut, Donna M. Mittens for Christmas. 2009. 376p. 31.95 *(978-1-4401-0372-8(0))*; pap. 21.95 *(978-1-4401-0370-4(4))* iUniverse, Inc.

Johnson, Shane L., illus. OLIVIA & the Christmas Present. 2011. (Olivia TV Tie-In Ser.). (ENG.). 24p. (J). (gr. -1-2). 9.99 *(978-1-4424-3624-4(7)*, Simon Spotlight) Simon Spotlight.

Johnston, Camille. A Gifted Book. Donahue, Linda, illus. 2008. 19p. pap. 24.95 *(978-1-60563-329-9(1))* America Star Bks.

Jones, Stella J. The Perfect Present. Pedler, Caroline, illus. 2016. (ENG.). 32p. (J). (gr. -1-2). pap. 16.99 *(978-1-68010-036-5(X))* Tiger Tales.

Joyce, Kelley A. Amos the Elf & His Magical Pajamas. Beckman, Jeff & Aguirre, Diego, illus. 2012. 38p. pap. 9.95 *(978-0-9881822-0-2(3))* Elf Garb.

Kann, Victoria. Pinkalicious & the Perfect Present. 2014. (Pinkalicious I Can Read Ser.). (J). lib. bdg. 13.55 *(978-0-606-35054-9(3)*, Turtleback) Turtleback Bks.

Karevold, Alison. KenKarta: Battle of the Onoxmon. Malone, Susan Mary, ed. Polinko, Les, illus. 2011. 300p. (J). 25.98 *(978-0-9843166-3-2(9))* Artists' Orchard, LLC, The.

Kathleen, Judith. Attila's Wobbly Birthday Box, 1 vol. 2010. 20p. pap. 24.95 *(978-1-4489-2451-6(0))* PublishAmerica, Inc.

Katy Duck & the Secret Valentine. 2014. (Katy Duck Ser.). (ENG., Illus.). 24p. (J). (gr. -1-1). pap. 3.99 *(978-1-4424-9809-9(9)*, Simon Spotlight) Simon Spotlight.

Keane, Claire. Once upon a Cloud. 2015. (ENG., Illus.). 34p. (J). (gr. -1-k). 17.99 *(978-0-8037-3911-6(7)*, Dial Bks) Penguin Young Readers Group.

Kim, Cecil. Little Moon's Christmas: Imagination - Objects. Cowley, Joy, ed. Horácek, Petr, illus. 2015. (Step up - Creative Thinking Ser.). (ENG.). 32p. (J). (gr. -1-2). 26.65 *(978-1-925186-39-0(3))* Lerner Publishing Group.

Kim, YeShil. The Very Best Teacher. Moriuchi, Mique, illus. 2015. (ENG.). 24p. (J). (-3). 12.99 *(978-1-4926-0998-8(6))* Sourcebooks, Inc.

Kimmel, Elizabeth Cody. My Penguin Osbert. Lewis, H. B., illus. (ENG.). 40p. (J). (gr. -1-3). 2011. pap. 6.99 *(978-0-7636-5730-7(1))* 2008. 7.99 *(978-0-7636-3692-0(4))* 2004. 16.99 *(978-0-7636-1699-1(0))* Candlewick Pr.

Kimpton, Diana. Princess Ellie's Royal Jamboree No. 11. Finlay, Lizzie, illus. 11th ed. 2008. (ENG.). 96p. (gr. 1-4). pap. 3.99 *(978-1-4231-1531-1(7))* Hyperion Pr.

—Princess Ellie's Snowy Ride. Finlay, Lizzie, illus. 2007. (Pony-Crazed Princess Ser.). 90p. (J). 11.65 *(978-0-7569-8352-9(5))* Perfection Learning Corp.

Kleinberg, Naomi. Elmo's Mommy. Womble, Louis, illus. 2012. (ENG.). 12p. (J). (gr. k-k). bds. 4.99 *(978-0-307-92967-9(1)*, Random Hse. Bks. for Young Readers) Random Hse. Children's Bks.

Knudsen, Michelle. A Slimy Story. Billin-Frye, Paige, illus. 2004. 32p. (J). lib. bdg. 20.00 *(978-1-4242-1150-0(6))* Fitzgerald Bks.

—A Slimy Story. Billin-Frye, Paige, illus. 2004. (Science Solves It! Ser.). 32p. (J). (gr. -1-3). pap. 5.95 *(978-1-57565-144-6(0))* Kane Press, Inc.

Koch, Janet Marie. Hallie's Best Birthday. 2008. 48p. pap. 24.95 *(978-1-60610-812-3(3))* America Star Bks.

Koncerak, Veronica. The Bubble That Never Popped. 2010. 24p. 11.49 *(978-1-4520-3935-0(6))* AuthorHouse.

Kowen, Dorothy. The Gift of Gold. Mathew, Gillian, illus. 2011. (ENG.). 24p. 13.95 *(978-1-77009-796-4(1))* Jacana Media ZAF. Dist: Independent Pubs. Group.

Krackow, Eric T. The Lollipop Monster Meets Clem the Klutz, 1 vol. 2013. (ENG., Illus.). 64p. (J). 16.99 *(978-0-7643-4287-5(8)*, 9780764342875) Schiffer Publishing, Ltd.

Krensky, Stephen. The Magic Pomegranate: A Jewish Folktale. 2009. pap. 40.95 *(978-0-7613-4818-4(2))* Lerner Publishing Group.

Lafrance, Marie, illus. The First Gift. 2006. 24p. (J). (gr. 2). per. 6.95 *(978-1-58013-149-0(2)*, Kar-Ben Publishing) Lerner Publishing Group.

Laird, Elizabeth. Beautiful Bananas, 1 vol. Pichon, Liz, illus. 2013. (ENG.). 32p. pap. 7.95 *(978-1-56145-691-8(8))* Peachtree Pubs.

Langlois, Florence. The Extraordinary Gift. Goodman, John, tr. from FRE. Langlois, Florence, illus. 2005. (Illus.). 48p. (J). (gr. -1-2). reprint ed. 15.00 *(978-0-7567-8942-8(7))* DIANE Publishing Co.

Lee, HaeDa. Ida's Present. Kim, InHyeon, illus. 2014. (MySELF Bookshelf Ser.). (ENG.). 32p. (J). (gr. k-2). pap. 11.94 *(978-1-60357-694-9(0))*; lib. bdg. 25.27 *(978-1-59953-659-0(5))* Norwood Hse. Pr.

Legall, D. Antoinette. A Gift for God. 2013. 16p. pap. 12.68 *(978-1-4669-7568-2(7))* Trafford Publishing.

Levine, Anna. Jodie's Shabbat Surprise. Topaz, Ksenia, illus. 2015. (J). (gr. k-3). (ENG.). 32p. lib. bdg. 17.95 *(978-1-4677-3465-3(9))*; 6.99 *(978-1-4677-6204-5(0))* Lerner Publishing Group. (Kar-Ben Publishing).

Littlewood, Karin. Immi's Gift, 1 vol. Littlewood, Karin, illus. 2010. (ENG., Illus.). 32p. (J). (gr. -1-3). 15.95 *(978-1-56145-545-4(8))* Peachtree Pubs.

Litton, Jonathan. Surprise: A Book of Christmas Shapes. Galloway, Fhiona, illus. 2014. (ENG.). 16p. (J). (gr. -1-k). bds. 7.99 *(978-1-58925-567-8(4))* Tiger Tales.

Llewellyn, Claire. Is It for Me?, 1 vol. Lovsin, Polona, illus. 2013. (Start Reading Ser.). (ENG.). 24p. (gr. k-1). pap. 7.95 *(978-1-4765-3185-4(4))*; pap. 41.94 *(978-1-4765-3221-9(4))* Capstone Press of Coughlan Cos.

Lobel, Gill. Little Bear's Special Wish. Hansen, Gaby, illus. 2004. 32p. (J). tchr. ed. 16.95 *(978-1-58925-034-5(6))* Tiger Tales.

Lodding, Linda Ravin. A Gift for Mama. Jay, Alison, illus. 2014. (ENG.). 32p. (J). (gr. -1-3). 17.99 *(978-0-385-75331-9(4)*, Knopf Bks. for Young Readers) Random Hse. Children's Bks.

Long, Mary Evelyn Curton. The First Christmas Gift. 2012. 16p. (-18). pap. 15.99 *(978-1-4772-8836-8(8))* AuthorHouse.

Louie, Therese On & Wang, Suling. Raymond's Perfect Present, 1 vol. 2015. (ENG.). 32p. (J). pap. 9.95 *(978-1-62014-229-5(5))* Lee & Low Bks., Inc.

Lucado, Max. Punchinello & the Most Marvelous Gift. Martinez, Sergio, illus. 2004. (Max Lucado's Wemmicks Ser.: 5). 32p. (J). 15.99 *(978-1-58134-546-9(1))* 2003. 28p. bds. 6.99 *(978-1-58134-562-9(3))* Crossway.

—Punchinello & the Most Marvelous Gift: And, Your Special Gift. Martinez, Sergio, illus. 2007. (J). *(978-1-58134-877-4(0))* Crossway.

Lucado, Max, et al. Your Special Gift. Wenzel, David T. & Wenzel, David, illus. 2006. (Max Lucado's Wemmicks Ser.: 6). 32p. (J). (gr. -1-3). 16.99 *(978-1-58134-698-5(0))* Crossway.

Luces-Tucker, Max. Bobby & Chrissy: One Gift. 2008. 36p. pap. 17.99 *(978-1-4343-8199-6(4))* AuthorHouse.

Mackall, Dandi Daley. Gift Horse. 2003. (Winnie the Horse Gentler Ser.: 6). (ENG., Illus.). 224p. (J). mass mkt. 5.99 *(978-0-8423-5547-6(2))* Tyndale Hse. Pubs.

Macmillan, Sue. Bouncy, Pouncy Puppy. Ward, Sarah, illus. 2014. (Cheery Chasers Ser.). (ENG.). 8p. (J). (gr. -1 — 1). bds. 4.99 *(978-0-7641-6698-3(0))* Barron's Educational Series, Inc.

Mansfield, Katherine. PARTIES AND PRESENTS: THREE SHORT STORIES LEVEL 2 ELEMENTARY/LOWER-INTERMEDIATE. 2010. (ENG., Illus.). 62p. pap. 12.00 *(978-84-8323-836-3(5))* Cambridge Univ. Pr.

—PARTIES AND PRESENTS THREE SHORT STORIES LEVEL 2 ELEMENTARY/LOWER-INTERMEDIATE WITH CD-ROM/AUDIO CD, 1 vol. 2010. (ENG., Illus.). 62p. pap. 14.25 incl. cd-rom *(978-84-8323-684-0(2))* Cambridge Univ. Pr.

Manushkin, Fran. Katie's Happy Mother's Day. Lyon, Tammie, illus. 2015. (Katie Woo Ser.). (ENG.). 32p. (gr. k-2). 21.32 *(978-1-4795-6179-7(7))* Picture Window Bks.

Marcos, Teri. Bethlehem's Gift. 2013. 24p. pap. 12.45 *(978-1-4908-0901-4(5)*, WestBow Pr.) Author Solutions, Inc.

Marshall, Geraldine Ann. Spider's Gift: A Christmas Story. Sorge, Rebecca, illus. 2016. 40p. (J). pap. 14.95 *(978-0-8198-9058-0(8))* Pauline Bks. & Media.

Martin, Maria G. The Christmas Crown. Stratman, Kay, illus. 2010. 20p. pap. 10.95 *(978-1-60911-442-8(6)*, Eloquent Bks.) Strategic Book Publishing & Rights Agency (SBPRA).

Mauthe, Deb. The Bishop's Christmas Tree. 2011. 24p. pap. 12.74 *(978-1-4634-3572-1(X))* AuthorHouse.

McDaniel Hailey. The Amazing Angelina: And Her Hula Hoop. 2013. 38p. pap. 10.19 *(978-1-62884-794-9(8))* Speedy Publishing LLC.

McDonnell, Patrick. The Gift of Nothing. (ENG., Illus.). 56p. (gr. -1-3). 2005. (J). 15.99 *(978-0-316-11488-2(X))* 2009. 19.99 *(978-0-316-05441-6(0))* Little, Brown Bks. for Young Readers.

—The Little Gift of Nothing. 2016. (ENG., Illus.). 30p. (J). (gr. -1 — 1). bds. 7.99 *(978-0-316-39473-4(4))* Little, Brown Bks. for Young Readers.

McIntyre, Mel. The Legend of Lumpus & Ogols. McQuillan, David, illus. 2009. 28p. pap. 10.95 *(978-1-935137-96-2(4))* Guardian Angel Publishing, Inc.

McKee, David. El Principe Pedro y el oso de Peluche. (SPA.). (J). 7.95 *(978-958-04-6258-3(5))* Norma S.A. COL. Dist: Distribuidora Norma, Inc.

McNamara, Margaret. Secret Santa. Gordon, Mike, illus. 2012. (Robin Hill School Ser.). (ENG.). 32p. (J). (gr. -1-1). 15.99 *(978-1-4424-3649-7(2))*; pap. 3.99 *(978-1-4424-3648-0(4))* Simon Spotlight. (Simon Spotlight).

McOmber, Rachel B., ed. McOmber Phonics Storybooks: A Box. rev. ed. (Illus.). (J). *(978-0-944991-13-8(0))* Swift Learning Resources.

Meddaugh, Susan. Martha Says It with Flowers. 2010. (Martha Speaks Ser.). (ENG., Illus.). 32p. (J). (gr. -1-3). 12.99 *(978-0-547-21058-2(2))* Houghton Mifflin Harcourt Publishing Co.

Michiko Florence, Debbi. The Hunt for the Perfect Present. Roe, Monika, illus. 2016. (Dorothy & Toto Ser.). (ENG.). 40p. (gr. k-2). lib. bdg. 21.32 *(978-1-4795-8703-2(6))* Capstone Press of Coughlan Cos.

Moore, Diane. Aniville Tales Presents: O. C.'s Big Lesson. 2009. 15p. (J). pap. 12.95 *(978-1-4327-3630-9(2))* Outskirts Pr., Inc.

Mora, Pat. Una Cesta de Cumpleanos para Tia Abuela. Lang, Cecily, illus. (SPA.). (J). (gr. k-2). pap. 3.16 net. *(978-0-395-78817-2(X)*, HMS088) Houghton Mifflin Harcourt Publishing Co.

Morales, Yuyi. Just in Case: A Trickster Tale & Spanish Alphabet Book. Morales, Yuyi, illus. 2008. (ENG., Illus.). 40p. (J). (gr. -1-3). 18.99 *(978-1-59643-329-8(9)*, 9781596433298) Roaring Brook Pr.

Morro, Scott. Danni's Gift. 2008. pap. 24.95 *(978-1-4241-7540-6(2))* America Star Bks.

Mullarkey, Lisa. The Purr-Fect-O Present: Book 10, 1 vol. Harris, Phyllis, illus. 2012. (Katharine the Almost Great Ser.). (ENG.). 80p. (J). (gr. 1-4). 27.07 *(978-1-61641-831-1(1))* Magic Wagon.

Muncaster, Harriet. The Biggest Smallest Christmas Present. Muncaster, Harriet, illus. 2016. (ENG., Illus.). 32p. (J). (-k). 16.99 *(978-0-399-16432-3(4)*, G.P. Putnam's Sons Books for Young Readers) Penguin Young Readers Group.

Murail, Marie-aude & Murail, Elvire. Santa's Last Present. Blake, Quentin, illus. 2004. (ENG.). 32p. (J). (gr. 3-7). 12.95 (978-1-56145-319-1(6)) Peachtree Pubs.

Myers, Tim J. The Christmas Stick: A Children's Story. Yilmaz, Necdet, illus. 2014. (ENG.). 32p. (J). pap. 13.99 (978-1-61261-571-4(6)) Paraclete Pr., Inc.

Nancy Mann Israel. The Juggler & His Wife. 2009. 24p. pap. 12.95 (978-1-4389-5334-2(8)) AuthorHouse.

Nayar, Nandini. What Could It Be? Manetti, Francesco, illus. 2013. (ENG.). 28p. (J). (gr. -1). 11.95 (978-81-8190-285-6(8)) Karadi Tales Co. Pvt, Ltd. IND. Dist: Consortium Bk. Sales & Distribution.

Nielsen, Kelli & Benham, Kelly. You Will Always Be My Son. 2009. 36p. pap. 13.95 (978-1-60844-018-4(4)) Dog Ear Publishing, LLC.

Niemi, Renee. Riia's Dream Diary. 2012. 54p. pap. 16.95 (978-1-4626-9942-1(1)) America Star Bks.

Oceanak, Karla. Glitch: An Aldo Zelnick Comic Novel. Spanjer, Kendra, illus. 2016. (Aldo Zelnick Comic Novel Ser.: 7). (ENG.). 160p. (J). (gr. 1-8). pap. 8.95 (978-1-934649-71-8(6)) Bailiwick Pr.

—Jackpot: An Aldo Zelnick Comic Novel. Spanjer, Kendra, illus. 2016. (Aldo Zelnick Comic Novel Ser.: 10). (ENG.). 160p. (J). (gr. 1-8). pap. 8.95 (978-1-934649-74-9(0)) Bailiwick Pr.

Odgers, Sally. The Untold Story of Ms. Mirabella, 1 vol. 2013. (Fiction Readers Ser.). (ENG., Illus.). 28p. (J). (gr. 2-2). pap. 6.99 (978-1-4333-5571-4(X)) Shell Educational Publishing.

Osteen, Victoria. Gifts from the Heart. Palmisciano, Diane, illus. 2010. (ENG.). 32p. (J). (gr. -1-2). 17.99 (978-1-4169-5551-1(8), Little Simon Inspirations) Little Simon Inspirations.

Painter, Grace. The Harry Bear Story. Kacer, Stephen, illus. 2011. 28p. pap. 24.95 (978-1-4626-3327-2(7)) America Star Bks.

Park, Barbara. Jingle Bells, Batman Smells! Brunkus, Denise, illus. 2009. (Junie B. Jones Ser.: No. 8). (ENG.). 128p. (J). (gr. 1-4). 4.99 (978-0-375-82809-6(5), Random Hse. Bks. for Young Readers) Random Hse. Children's Bks.

Pau Pau. Bird Bandit, 1 vol. 2010. 56p. pap. 16.95 (978-1-4489-3991-6(7)) America Star Bks.

Paul, Ann Whitford. Fiesta Fiasco. Long, Ethan, illus. 2009. (ENG.). 32p. (J). (gr. -1-2). pap. 6.95 (978-0-8234-2275-3(5)) Holiday Hse., Inc.

—Fiesta Fiasco. Long, Ethan, illus. 2012. pap. 18.95 (978-1-4301-1099-6(6)) Live Oak Media.

Pearson, Carol Lynn. The Modern Magi. 2009. 80p. pap. 7.99 (978-1-59955-354-2(6)) Cedar Fort, Inc./CFI Distribution.

Pennington, Norma C. & Schuller, Sheldon V. The Unopened Gift, 1 vol. 2010. 18p. 24.95 (978-1-4489-7670-6(7)) PublishAmerica, Inc.

Perry, Salena Maria. Recipe for Chocolate Soup. 2011. 28p. 12.95 (978-1-4567-1640-0(9)) AuthorHouse.

Phillips, Shirley. The Best Gift. 2012. 20p. pap. 10.95 (978-1-4497-4229-4(7), WestBow Pr.) Author Solutions, Inc.

Pierce, Brian. The Little Red Present. Crowell, Helen, illus. 2007. 32p. (J). per. 8.00 (978-0-9793269-1-2(5)) Straub, Rick.

Pittar, Gill. Milly, Molly & the Secret Scarves. 2006. cd-rom (978-1-877337-68-0(4)) Milly Molly Bks.

—Milly, Molly & the Secret Scarves/CD-ROM. 2004. 28p. pap. incl. cd-rom (978-1-877337-67-3(6)) Milly Molly Bks.

Pokas, Dora. Muriel's Red Sweater. (J). 15.95 (978-0-8118-3771-2(8)) Chronicle Bks. LLC.

Polacco, Patricia. Gifts of the Heart. Polacco, Patricia, illus. 2013. (ENG., Illus.). 40p. (J). (gr. k-3). 17.99 (978-0-399-16094-3(9), G.P. Putnam's Sons Books for Young Readers) Penguin Young Readers Group.

Pollock, Beth. Harley's Gift, 1 vol. 2007. (Lorimer Streetlights Ser.). (ENG.). 128p. (J). (gr. 2-5). 7.95 (978-1-55028-992-3(6), 9781550289923) Lorimer, James & Co., Ltd., Pubs. CAN. Dist: Casemate Pubs. & Bk. Distributors, LLC.

Porrata, Mayra. The Day Kyle Met Nuf. Rice, Kaleb & Deasey, Kevin, illus. 2013. 28p. pap. 12.95 (978-0-9825480-2-8(8)) Sunny Day Publishing, LLC.

Posner-Sanchez, Andrea. The Christmas Party. Random House Disney Staff, illus. 2014. (Step into Reading Ser.). (ENG.). 24p. (J). (gr. -1-1). 4.99 (978-0-7364-3279-5(5), RH/Disney) Random Hse. Children's Bks.

The Presents: Individual Title Six-Packs. (Sails Literacy Ser.). 16p. (gr. k-18). 27.00 (978-0-7635-4444-7(2)) Rigby Education.

Price, Margaret Evans, illus. The Betty Fairy Book. 2006. (Shape Bks.). (ENG.). 16p. (J). pap. 9.95 (978-1-59583-092-0(8), Green Tiger Pr.) Laughing Elephant.

Provencio, Marta. The Christmas Dragon. 2013. 24p. pap. 12.99 (978-1-4808-0379-4(0)) Archway Publishing.

Ramsey, Grandma. The Surprise Birthday Gift. 2008. 16p. pap. 9.99 (978-1-4259-4459-9(0)) AuthorHouse.

Randolph, Joanne. A Rock for Mom. 2015. (Rosen REAL Readers: STEM & STEAM Collection). (ENG.). 8p. pap. 5.46 (978-1-4994-9533-1(1), Rosen Classroom) Rosen Publishing Group, Inc., The.

Rao, Lisa & Gallo, Tina. It's Nice to Be Nice! Giles, Mike, illus. 2009. (Yo Gabba Gabba! Ser.). (ENG.). 24p. (J). (gr. -1-2). pap. 3.99 (978-1-4169-7866-4(6), Simon Spotlight) Simon Spotlight.

Ray, Christie Jones & Ray, Christie Jones. Eliza & a Cottage Door. 2012. (Illus.). 40p. pap. 15.00 (978-0-9853223-0-4(6)) Rose Water Cottage Pr.

Reisner, Molly. Dora's Birthday Surprise! Aikins, David, illus. 2010. (Little Golden Book Ser.). (ENG.). 24p. (J). (gr. -1-2). 3.99 (978-0-375-86163-5(7), Golden Bks.) Random Hse. Children's Bks.

Remkiewicz, Frank. Gus Makes a Gift. 2012. (Scholastic Reader Pre-Level 1 Ser.). (ENG., Illus.). 24p. (J). (gr. k-1). pap. 3.99 (978-0-545-24469-5(2), Cartwheel Bks.) Scholastic, Inc.

Rempt, Fiona. Snail's Birthday Wish. Smit, Noelle, illus. 2007. (ENG.). 32p. (J). (gr. -1-1). 14.95 (978-1-905417-52-0(7)) Boxer Bks., Ltd. GBR. Dist: Sterling Publishing Co., Inc.

Rey, H. A. My First Words at the Farm, Set. gif. ed. 2010. (Curious Baby Curious George Ser.). (ENG., Illus.). 12p. (J). (gr. k — 1). 14.99 (978-0-547-24306-1(5)) Houghton Mifflin Harcourt Publishing Co.

Rey, H. A. & Rey, Margret. The Surprise Gift. gif. ed. 2008. (Curious George Ser.). (ENG., Illus.). 24p. (J). (gr. -1-3). pap. 4.99 (978-0-618-99864-7(0)) Houghton Mifflin Harcourt Publishing Co.

—Three Tales for a Winter's Night. 2012. (Curious George TV Tie-In 8x8 Ser.). lib. bdg. 18.40 (978-0-606-26603-1(8), Turtleback) Turtleback Bks.

Reynolds, Peter H. The Smallest Gift of Christmas. Reynolds, Peter H., illus. (ENG., Illus.). 40p. (J). (gr. -1-2). 2015. 10.00 (978-0-7636-7981-1(X)) 2013. 14.00 (978-0-7636-6103-8(1)) Candlewick Pr.

Reynolds, Peter H., illus. Star Bright: A Christmas Story. 2014. (ENG.). 40p. (J). (gr. -1-3). 17.99 (978-1-4169-5858-1(4), Atheneum Bks. for Young Readers) Simon & Schuster Children's Publishing.

Richardson, Linda. The Gift. 2003. (J). 6.95 (978-1-59094-021-1(0), Jawbreakers for Kids) Jawbone Publishing Corp.

Rinck, Maranke. The Prince Child. Linden, Martijn van der, illus. 2004. (ENG & GER.). 32p. (J). 16.95 (978-1-932425-15-4(2), Lemniscaat) Boyds Mills Pr.

Ritchie, Joseph R. Peter Cottontail's Easter Surprise. Halverson, Lydia, illus. 2006. (ENG.). 18p. (J). (gr. -1-k). bds. 9.95 (978-0-8249-6627-0(9), Ideal Pubns.) Worthy Publishing.

Rives, J. G. Where Are My Christmas Presents? Young, Dot, illus. 2007. 44p. (J). 17.95 (978-0-9790014-0-6(4)) Sterli Publishing.

Robertson, Amber. The Runaway Doll. 2009. 20p. pap. 10.49 (978-1-4343-9336-4(4)) AuthorHouse.

Roddy-Worsham, Clara. Bear Baby's Birthday Gift. 2013. 24p. 24.95 (978-1-4626-9940-7(5)) America Star Bks.

Rogers, Jewels. The Princess & the Puppy. 2010. 28p. pap. 16.99 (978-1-4269-4177-1(3)) Trafford Publishing.

Rogers, Lauren. Skyler & the Se. Sexton, Jessa, ed. Keaggy, Sarah, illus. 2012. 36p. pap. 8.00 (978-0-9860150-1-4(6)) O'More Publishing.

Rosciti, Donna. The Birthday Train: Book 1. 2013. (ENG.). 48p. (J). 24.95 (978-1-4787-2236-6(3)) Outskirts Pr., Inc.

Rovetch, L. Bob. TLC Grow with Me! McLeod, Chum, illus. 2005. (J). (978-1-58987-114-4(6)) Kindermusik International.

Roy, Ronald. Calendar Mysteries #12: December Dog. Gurney, John Steven, illus. 2014. (Calendar Mysteries Ser.: 12). (ENG.). 80p. (J). (gr. 1-4). 4.99 (978-0-385-37168-1(3), Random Hse. Bks. for Young Readers) Random Hse. Children's Bks.

—December Dog. 2014. (Calendar Mysteries Ser.: 12). lib. bdg. 14.75 (978-0-606-36019-7(0)) Turtleback Bks.

Ryan, Ann Marie. The Best Gift. Denis, Florencia, illus. 2011. (My Phonics Readers: Level 1 Ser.). 24p. (J). (gr. -1-1). 24.25 (978-1-84898-507-0(X)) Sea-To-Sea Pubns.

Ryles, Donald. The Magic Holiday Forest. 2008. 40p. pap. 8.95 (978-1-4357-4772-2(0)) Lulu Pr., Inc.

Sánchez-Korrol, Virginia. A Surprise for Teresita / una Sorpresa para Teresita. Flores, Carolyn Dee, illus. 2016. (ENG & SPA.). 32p. (J). (gr. k-3). 17.95 (978-1-55885-831-2(8), Piñata Books) Arte Publico Pr.

Santat, Dan. The Guild of Geniuses. 2004. (ENG., Illus.). 40p. (J). (gr. -1-3). 17.99 (978-0-439-43096-8(8), Levine, Arthur A. Bks.) Scholastic, Inc.

Sam, Amélie & Trouillot, Virgile. Happy Holidays. 2009. (Groove High Ser.). (Illus.). 112p. (YA). (gr. 5-8). 31.95 (978-1-60754-526-2(8)); pap. 15.25 (978-1-60754-527-9(6)) Windmill Bks.

Schneider, Josh. The Meanest Birthday Girl. (ENG., Illus.). 48p. (J). (gr. 1-4). 2015. pap. 5.99 (978-0-544-45597-9(5), HMH Books For Young Readers) 2013. 14.99 (978-0-547-83814-4(X)) Houghton Mifflin Harcourt Publishing Co.

Schoenherr, Ian. Pip & Squeak. Schoenherr, Ian, illus. 2007. (Illus.). 32p. (J). (gr. -1-k). 18.89 (978-0-06-087254-0(3)) HarperCollins Pubs.

Scholastic, Inc. Staff & Black, Sonia. Jumping the Broom. Hu, Ying-Hwa & Van Wright, Cornelius, illus. 2004. (Just for You Ser.). (ENG.). 32p. pap. 3.99 (978-0-439-56878-4(1), Teaching Resources) Scholastic, Inc.

Scieszka, Jon. Kat's Mystery Gift. Gordon, David et al, illus. 2009. (Jon Scieszka's Trucktown Ser.). (ENG.). 24p. (J). (gr. -1-1). pap. 3.99 (978-1-4169-4143-9(6), Simon Spotlight) Simon Spotlight.

—Kat's Mystery Gift. Shannon, David et al, illus. 2009. (Jon Scieszka's Trucktown Ser.). (ENG.). 24p. (J). (gr. -1-1). lib. bdg. 14.99 (978-1-4169-4154-5(1), Simon Spotlight) Simon Spotlight.

Scotto, Michael. Buck's Bad Dreams. Gabriel, Evette, illus. 2009. (J). (978-1-935193-46-3(5)) National Network of Digital Schls.

Scotton, Rob. The Perfect Present for Mom & Dad. Scotton, Rob, illus. 2012. (Splat the Cat Ser.). (ENG., Illus.). 24p. (J). (gr. k-3). pap. 4.99 (978-0-06-210009-2(2), HarperFestival) HarperCollins Pubs.

—The Perfect Present for Mom & Dad. 2012. (Splat the Cat 8X8 Ser.). (J). lib. bdg. 14.75 (978-0-606-23579-2(5), Turtleback) Turtleback Bks.

Scraper, Katherine. The Gift-Guessing Kid. 2005. (J). pap. (978-1-4108-4211-4(8)) Benchmark Education Co.

Seif Simpson, Martha. What NOT to Give Your Mom on Mother's Day, 0 vols. 2013. (ENG.). 24p. (J). (gr. -1-2). 12.99 (978-1-4778-1647-9(X), 9781477816479, Amazon Children's Publishing) Amazon Publishing.

Seymour, Jane & Keach, James. The Other One: You Make Me Happy. Planer, Geoffrey, illus. gif. ed. 2003. (This One & That One Ser.). (ENG.). 16p. (J). (gr. -1-3). 5.99 (978-1-932431-57-5(8)) Left Field,Angel Gate.

Shawver, Amanda Nicole. Lily's Rag Doll. 2012. 24p. pap. 17.99 (978-1-4772-7459-0(6)) AuthorHouse.

Sheard, Jean. A Chinese Fantasy - Cave in a Casket. 2007. 128p. 34.95 (978-1-84753-349-4(3)); (Illus.). pap. 10.50 (978-1-84753-249-7(7)) Lulu Pr., Inc.

Sheets, Judy. The Gift. Nausley, Kathy, illus. 2005. 40p. (J). lib. bdg. 24.00 (978-0-9726451-2-6(8)) Sheets, Judy.

Shein, Erik Daniel & Reker, Martin. The Forgotten Ornament. Safar, Lina, illus. 2010. (J). pap. 11.95 (978-0-578-05938-9(X)) Ark Watch Holdings LLC.

Shephard, H. Ferebee. Dad's Birthday Present. 2010. 24p. pap. 15.99 (978-1-4535-3496-0(2)) Xlibris Corp.

Simon, Coco. Emma's Not-So-Sweet Dilemma. 2014. (Cupcake Diaries: 23). lib. bdg. 17.20 (978-0-606-36102-6(2)) Turtleback Bks.

Smith, Jane. It's Valentine's Day, Chloe Zoe! Smith, Jane, illus. 2016. (Chloe Zoe Ser.). (ENG., Illus.). 32p. (J). (gr. -1-3). 12.99 (978-0-8075-2462-6(X)) Whitman, Albert & Co.

Smith, Sindy. Charlie the Chipmunk & the Lost Goldmine. Smith, Sindy, illus. 2012. (Illus.). 38p. 29.95 (978-1-4626-9865-3(4)) America Star Bks.

—Charlie the Chipmunk & the Lost Goldmine. 2012. 40p. pap. 24.95 (978-1-4626-8590-5(0)) America Star Bks.

Soderberg, Erin. The Quirks & the Quirkalicious Birthday. Light, Kelly, illus. 2015. (Quirks Ser.). (ENG.). 208p. (YA). (gr. 3-6). 13.99 (978-1-61963-370-4(1), 9781619633704, Bloomsbury USA Childrens) Bloomsbury Publishing USA.

Springer, Audrey. Rusty's Gift. Richards, Kris, illus. 2012. 28p. 24.95 (978-1-4626-6589-1(6)) America Star Bks.

St-Onge, Claire. Caillou: L'anniversaire. (FRE., Illus.). 32p. pap. 11.95 (978-2-89450-263-1(X)) Éditions Chouette CAN. Dist: Distribooks, Inc.

Stahel, Merry Kesner. Jennifer's Christmas Gift. 2005. 48p. pap. 8.93 (978-1-4116-4029-0(2)) Lulu Pr., Inc.

Steiner, Michaela & Steiner II, Michael. Mike Lost His Bike. 2012. 32p. pap. 19.99 (978-1-4772-7602-0(5)) AuthorHouse.

Stevens, Michael J. Silver Spitfire. 2010. 164p. pap. (978-1-907652-13-4(2)) Grosvenor Hse. Publishing Ltd.

Stewart, Paul. Un Regalo de Cumpleanos. Riddell, Chris, illus. (SPA.). 30p. (J). (gr. k-2). (978-84-348-6840-3(7), SM30935) SM Ediciones ESP. Dist: Lectorum Pubns., Inc.

Stine, R. L. The Birthday Party of No Return! 2012. (Goosebumps Hall of Horrors Ser.: 6). (ENG.). 160p. (J). (gr. 3-7). pap. 6.99 (978-0-545-28938-2(6), Scholastic Paperbacks) Scholastic, Inc.

—The Birthday Party of No Return. 2012. (Goosebumps HorrorLand: Hall of Horrors Ser.: 6). lib. bdg. 17.20 (978-0-606-23932-5(4), Turtleback) Turtleback Bks.

Stone, Julia. Little Bear's Sparkly Christmas. Muss, Angela, illus. 2014. (ENG.). 6p. (J). (gr. -1-k). 8.99 (978-0-7459-6262-7(9)) Lion Hudson PLC GBR. Dist: Independent Pubs. Group.

Strelitski, Mies & Hartog, Arnold. Woobie Dreams Hc. 2006. (ENG., Illus.). 32p. (J). 16.95 (978-1-59249-554-2(0)) Soundprints.

Surette, Janet H. The Prince & the Gift: A Tale of True Beauty. 2010. 44p. pap. 14.95 (978-1-4497-0662-3(2), WestBow Pr.) Author Solutions, Inc.

Sutton, Jane. Esther's Hanukkah Disaster. Rowland, Andrew, illus. 2013. (Hanukkah Ser.). 32p. (J). (gr. -1-3). lib. bdg. 17.95 (978-0-7613-9043-5(X), Kar-Ben Publishing) Lerner Publishing Group.

—Esther's Hanukkah Disaster. Rowland, Andy, illus. 2013. 32p. 17.95 (978-1-4677-1638-3(3)); (ENG.). (J). (gr. -1-3). 7.95 (978-0-7613-9044-2(8), Kar-Ben Publishing) Lerner Publishing Group.

Taylor, Jennifer. Dragon Sitter. 2005. 36p. (J). 14.99 (978-1-4116-6449-4(3)) Lulu Pr., Inc.

Tewkesbury, Alexa. The Perfect Christmas Present. 2008. (ENG.). 32p. (J). (978-1-85345-476-9(1)) Crusade for World Revival.

Thaler, Mike. The Christmas Party from the Black Lagoon. Lee, Jared, illus. 2006. 64p. (J). pap. (978-0-439-87160-0(3)) Scholastic, Inc.

Thomas, Shelley Moore. Happy Birthday, Good Knight. 2014. (Penguin Young Readers Level 3 Ser.). lib. bdg. 13.55 (978-0-606-35728-9(9)) Turtleback Bks.

Thompson, Don. Bunny World: Kindness Is the Key to Happiness. 2009. 28p. pap. 14.99 (978-1-4389-5475-2(1)) AuthorHouse.

Titonis, George, illus. The Gift of the Giggles. 2005. 24p. (J). 16.95 (978-0-9765398-0-3(2)) Bellaboozle Books, Inc.

Trotta-Gilbert, Susan. What Ever Happened to Puppy? 2009. 36p. pap. 16.75 (978-1-4490-4482-4(4)) AuthorHouse.

van de Vendel, Edward & van der Linden, Martijn. For You & No One Else. 2009. (ENG.). 32p. (J). (gr. -1-2). 16.95 (978-1-59078-658-1(0), Lemniscaat) Boyds Mills Pr.

van Genechten, Guido. Snowy's Special Secret. van Genechten, Guido, illus. 2005. (Illus.). 32p. (J). (gr. -1-2). 15.95 (978-1-58925-049-9(4)) Tiger Tales.

Van Lieshout, Elle & Van Os, Erik. Lovey & Dovey. Van Hout, Mies, illus. 2009. (ENG.). 32p. (J). (gr. k-2). 16.95 (978-1-59078-660-4(2), Lemniscaat) Boyds Mills Pr.

Varicak, Rebecca. The Journey of a Toys for Tots Toy! 2012. 24p. pap. 15.99 (978-1-4772-8601-2(2)) AuthorHouse.

Velasquez, Eric. Grandma's Gift. Velasquez, Eric, illus. 2013. (ENG., Illus.). 32p. (J). (gr. k-1). pap. 9.99 (978-0-8027-3536-2(3), 9780802735362, Bloomsbury USA Childrens) Bloomsbury Publishing USA.

Vigneault, Gilles. Un Cadeau Pour Sophie: Conte et Chansons. Jorisch, Stéphane, illus. 2013. (FRE.). 40p. (J). (gr. k-2). 16.95 (978-2-923163-38-3(9)) La Montagne Secrete CAN. Dist: Independent Pubs. Group.

—A Gift for Sophie. Jorisch, Stéphane, illus. 2013. (ENG.). 44p. (J). (gr. k-2). 16.95 (978-2-923163-98-7(2)) La Montagne Secrete CAN. Dist: Independent Pubs. Group.

Voskoboinikov, Valery & Linnamagi, Anne. The Icicle. 2007. (POL & ENG., Illus.). 32p. (J). pap. 16.95 (978-1-60195-100-7(0)) International Step by Step Assn.

Wallace, Adam. Only YOU Can Save Christmas! A Help-The-Elf Adventure. Bruner, Garth, illus. 2017. (ENG.). 40p. (J). (gr. 1-5). 16.99 **(978-1-4926-4136-0(7)**, Sourcebooks Jabberwocky) Sourcebooks, Inc.

Warne. Merry Christmas, Peter! 2014. (Peter Rabbit Animation Ser.). (ENG.). 32p. (J). (gr. -1-k). 9.99 (978-0-14-135173-5(X), Warne) Penguin Young Readers Group.

Warner, Larry. Chocolate Island, 1 vol. 2010. 42p. pap. 24.95 (978-1-4489-7372-9(4)) PublishAmerica, Inc.

Watts, Jeri Hanel. Keepers. Marshall, Felicia, illus. 2013. (ENG.). 32p. (J). (gr. -1-5). pap. 9.95 (978-1-58430-013-7(2)) Lee & Low Bks., Inc.

West, Tracey. The Birthday Surprise. 2014. (LEGO Friends Ser.: 4). (ENG.). 64p. (J). (gr. 2-5). pap. 4.99 (978-0-545-60589-2(X)) Scholastic, Inc.

—The Birthday Surprise. 2014. (LEGO Friends Chapter Bks.: 4). lib. bdg. 14.75 (978-0-606-35408-0(5)) Turtleback Bks.

Weston Woods Staff, creator. Mr. Rabbit & the Lovely Present. 2011. 38.75 (978-0-439-72860-7(6)); 18.95 (978-0-439-72859-1(2)) Weston Woods Studios, Inc.

—Mr Rabbit & the Lovely Present. 2011. 29.95 (978-0-439-73502-5(5)) Weston Woods Studios, Inc.

—Three Cheers for Catherine the Great! 2011. 38.75 (978-0-439-78620-1(7)) Weston Woods Studios, Inc.

Wheeler, Lance. Kula & the Old Ukulele. 2007. 32p. 12.95 (978-1-56647-844-1(8)) Mutual Publishing LLC.

Where Is Baby's Christmas Present? A Lift-The-Flap Book/Lap Edition. 2014. (ENG., Illus.). 14p. (J). (gr. -1 — 1). bds. 12.99 (978-1-4424-0363-5(2), Little Simon) Little Simon.

White, Jenny. A Surprise for Junior. 2013. 24p. pap. 17.99 (978-1-4817-0602-5(0)) AuthorHouse.

Whitford Paul, Ann. Fiesta Fiasco. 2012. 29.95 (978-1-4301-1100-9(3)) Live Oak Media.

Whybrow, Ian. It's Much Too Early! Watson, Laura, illus. 2016. (Cambridge Reading Adventures Ser.). (ENG.). 16p. pap. 6.56 (978-1-107-56032-1(2)) Cambridge Univ. Pr.

Wilkins, Nalini. Doby's First Christmas. Robb, Jonathan, illus. 2012. 28p. pap. 12.50 (978-1-62212-777-1(3), Strategic Bk. Publishing) Strategic Book Publishing & Rights Agency (SBPRA).

Wilkinson, Thomas M. Willie-off-the-Pickleboat. 2009. 71p. pap. 12.99 (978-0-557-06181-5(4)) Lulu Pr., Inc.

Williamson, K. E. Kayla & the Christmas Monkey. 2010. 28p. pap. 15.49 (978-1-4520-9749-7(6)) AuthorHouse.

Willis, Jeanne. Boa's Bad Birthday. Ross, Tony, illus. 2014. (ENG.). 32p. (J). (gr. -1-3). 16.95 (978-1-4677-3450-9(0)) Lerner Publishing Group.

Wooters, Duane. The Unnamed Manuscript. 2003. 70p. (YA). pap. 8.95 (978-0-595-29612-5(2)) iUniverse, Inc.

Worley, Roger A. 14 Wishes, 1 vol. 2009. 164p. pap. 24.95 (978-1-61582-419-9(7)) America Star Bks.

Wurst, Thomas Scott. Pearl's Christmas Present. Wurst, Thomas Scott, illus. 2006. (Illus.). 40p. (J). 20.00 (978-0-9772441-1-9(3)) Pearl & Dotty.

GILBRETH FAMILY

Gilbreth, Frank B., Jr. & Carey, Ernestine Gilbreth. Cheaper by the Dozen. 188p. (YA). (gr. 7-18). reprint ed. lib. bdg. 24.95 (978-0-88411-289-1(6)) Amereon Ltd.

—Cheaper by the Dozen. 180p. (YA). (gr. 7-18). pap. 5.50 (978-0-8072-8308-0(8)); 2004. (J). (gr. 4-7). pap. 38.00 incl. audio (978-0-8072-8307-3(X), YA157SP) Random Hse. Audio Publishing Group. (Listening Library).

GILDS

see Guilds

GILGAMESH

Zeman, Ludmila, illus. & narrated by. Gilgamesh. Zeman, Ludmila, narrated by. 2005. (SPA.). (J). 29.95 (978-968-7381-51-0(5)); pap. 21.95 (978-968-7381-47-3(7)) Tecolote, Ediciones, S.A. de C.V. MEX. Dist: Iaconi, Mariuccia Bk. Imports.

GIRAFFES

Ackland, Nick. Little Giraffe at the Beach. Walshaw, Sam, illus. 2017. (Little Explorers Ser.). (ENG.). 10p. (J). (gr. -1 — 1). bds. 6.99 (978-0-7641-6894-9(0)) Barron's Educational Series, Inc.

Albee, Sarah. Giraffes. 2006. (J). 7.99 (978-1-59939-034-5(5)) Cornerstone Pr.

—Giraffes. (Amazing Animals Ser.). 48p. 2009. (gr. 2-6). pap. 10.50 (978-1-4339-2014-1(X), Gareth Stevens Learning Library) 2008. (YA). (gr. 3-6). lib. bdg. 28.00 (978-0-8368-9097-6(3)) Stevens, Gareth Publishing LLLP.

Amstutz, Lisa J. Giraffes Are Awesome! 2015. (Awesome African Animals! Ser.). (ENG.). 32p. (gr. 1-2). lib. bdg. 27.32 (978-1-4914-1761-4(7)) Capstone Press of Coughlan Cos.

Anderson, Jill. Giraffes. 2005. (Wild Ones Ser.). (ENG., Illus.). 24p. (J). (gr. -1-1). 12.95 (978-1-55971-928-5(1)); pap. 8.95 (978-1-55971-929-2(X)) Cooper Square Publishing Llc.

Bell, Samantha S. Meet a Baby Giraffe. 2015. (ENG., Illus.). 32p. (J). (gr. k-2). 26.65 (978-1-4677-7975-3(X), Lerner Pubns.) Lerner Publishing Group.

Bodden, Valerie. Amazing Animals - Giraffes. 2009. (Amazing Animals Ser.). 24p. (J). (gr. 1-5). 24.25 (978-1-58341-714-0(1), Creative Education) Creative Co., The.

—Amazing Animals: Giraffes. 2011. (Amazing Animals Ser.). (ENG.). 24p. (J). (gr. 1-3). pap. 8.99 (978-0-89812-741-6(6), Creative Paperbacks) Creative Co., The.

Borgert-Spaniol, Megan. Baby Giraffes. 2015. (Super Cute! Ser.). (ENG., Illus.). 24p. (J). (gr. k-3). 25.95 (978-1-62617-216-6(1), Blastoff! Readers) Bellwether Media.

Bredeson, Carmen. Giraffes up Close. (Zoom in on Animals! Ser.). (Illus.). 24p. (J). 2012. (gr. k-18). pap. 7.95 (978-1-59845-414-7(5)) 2008. (gr. 1-3). lib. bdg. 22.60 (978-0-7660-3081-7(4)) Enslow Pubs., Inc. (Enslow Elementary).

Butterfield, Moira. Giraffe. (Who Am I? Ser.). (Illus.). 32p. (J). lib. bdg. 25.25 (978-1-930643-92-5(6)) Chrysalis Education.

Carr, Aaron. Giraffe. 2014. (Illus.). 24p. (J). (978-1-62127-282-3(6)) Weigl Pubs., Inc.

Craig, Diane. Giraffe, 1 vol. 2014. (Giant Animals Ser.). (ENG., Illus.). 24p. (J). (gr. -1-3). 24.21 (978-1-62403-058-1(0)) ABDO Publishing Co.

Dorling Kindersley Publishing Staff. Colors. 2013. (ENG.). 16p. (J). (gr. -1 — 1). bds. 6.99 (978-1-4654-0959-1(9), DK Children) Dorling Kindersley Publishing, Inc.

—Sophie's Busy Day. 2013. (Baby Touch & Feel Ser.). (ENG.). 14p. (J). (gr. -1 — 1). bds. 5.99 (978-1-4654-0967-6(X), DK Children) Dorling Kindersley Publishing, Inc.

Doudna, Kelly. It's a Baby Giraffe!, 1 vol. 2009. (Baby African Animals Ser.). (ENG., Illus.). 24p. (J). (gr. k-3). lib. bdg. 24.21 (978-1-60453-154-1(1), SandCastle) ABDO Publishing Co.

Dussling, Jennifer. Giraffes. 2016. (Penguin Young Readers, Level 3 Ser.). (ENG., Illus.). 32p. (J). (gr. 1-3). pap. 3.99 (978-0-448-48969-8(4), Penguin Young Readers) Penguin Young Readers Group.

Feldman, Thea. Dedan Saves the Day. 2006. (Illus.). (J). (978-0-696-23291-6(X)) Meredith Bks.

First Words. 2014. (ENG.). 16p. (J). (gr. -1 — 1). bds. 6.99 (978-1-4654-1832-6(6), DK Children) Dorling Kindersley Publishing, Inc.

Gareth Stevens Publishing Staff, contrib. by. Giraffes. 2004. (All about Wild Animals Ser.). (Illus.). 32p. (gr. k-4). lib. bdg.

26.00 (978-0-8368-4116-9(6), Gareth Stevens Learning Library) Stevens, Gareth Publishing LLLP.

Giant Giraffes. 2013. (Great Big Animals Ser.). 24p. (J). (gr. k-2). pap. 48.90 (978-1-4339-9430-2(5)) Stevens, Gareth Publishing LLLP.

Giraffes. 2007. (Nonfiction Collection). (ENG.). (J). pap. 8.00 (978-1-932570-92-2(6)) Pioneer Valley Bks.

Glaser, Rebecca Stromstad. Giraffes Stretch. 2016. (ENG., Illus.). 16p. (J). (gr. -1 — 1). bds. 7.99 (978-1-68152-069-8(9)) Amicus.

Goldish, Meish. Giraffe: The World's Tallest Mammal. 2007. (SuperSized! Ser.). (Illus.). 24p. (J). (gr. k-3). lib. bdg. 21.28 (978-1-59716-374-3(0), 1265932) Bearport Publishing Co., Inc.

Gray, Elizabeth. A Giraffe for a Pet, 1 vol. Valente, Christa, illus. 2010. 16p. 24.95 (978-1-4489-6515-1(2)) PublishAmerica, Inc.

Gregory, Josh. Giraffes. 2012. (21st Century Basic Skills Library: Baby Zoo Animals Ser.). (ENG.). 24p. (gr. k-3). 22.79 (978-1-61080-456-1(2), 202066); pap. 12.79 (978-1-61080-630-5(1), 202240) Cherry Lake Publishing.

Helget, Nicole Lea. Giraffes. 2008. (Living Wild Ser.). (Illus.). 46p. (J). (gr. 4-6). lib. bdg. 22.95 (978-1-58341-654-9(4), Creative Education) Creative Co., The.

Hewett, Richard, illus. & photos by. A Giraffe Calf Grows Up. Hewett, Richard, photos by. Hewett, Joan, photos by. 2004. (Baby Animals Ser.). 32p. (J). (gr. -1-2). pap. 6.95 (978-1-57505-630-2(5)); (gr. k-3). lib. bdg. 21.27 (978-1-57505-197-0(4)) Lerner Publishing Group.

Hofmeyr, Dianne & Quarto Generic Staff. Zeraffa Giraffa. Ray, Jane, illus. 2014. (ENG.). 40p. (J). (gr. -1-1). 17.99 (978-1-84780-344-3(X), Frances Lincoln) Quarto Publishing Group UK GBR. Dist: Hachette Bk. Group.

Ipcizade, Catherine. Giraffes. 2010. (African Animals Ser.). (ENG.). 24p. (gr. k-1). pap. 41.70 (978-1-4296-5080-9(X), Pebble Plus) Capstone Press of Coughlan Cos.

—Giraffes [Scholastic]. 2010. (African Animals Ser.). 24p. pap. 0.49 (978-1-4296-5791-4(X), Pebble Plus) Capstone Press of Coughlan Cos.

Kalman, Bobbie. Baby Giraffes. 2010. (ENG., Illus.). 24p. (J). (978-0-7787-3961-6(9)); pap. (978-0-7787-3980-7(5)) Crabtree Publishing Co.

Kalz, Jill. Giraffes. 2005. (Wild World of Animals Ser.). (Illus.). 32p. (J). (gr. 2-5). lib. bdg. 18.95 (978-1-58341-350-0(2), Creative Education) Creative Co., The.

Keller, Susanna. Meet the Giraffe. 2010. (At the Zoo Ser.). 24p. (J). (ENG.). pap. 8.25 (978-1-4358-9732-8(3)); (Illus.). 49.50 (978-1-4358-9733-5(1), 1307178); (Illus.). (gr. -1-1). lib. bdg. 22.60 (978-1-4358-9310-8(7)) Rosen Publishing Group, Inc., The. (PowerKids Pr.).

Leigh, A. Giant Giraffes: Learning the Soft G Sound. 2009. (PowerPhonics Ser.). 24p. (gr. 1-1). 39.90 (978-1-60851-443-4(9), PowerKids Pr.) Rosen Publishing Group, Inc., The.

Lindeen, Mary. Giraffes. 2013. (ENG., Illus.). 24p. (J). lib. bdg. 25.65 (978-1-62031-063-2(5)) Jump! Inc.

Marie, Christian. Little Giraffes. Lantier, Patricia, tr. from FRE. 2005. (Born to Be Wild Ser.). (Illus.). 24p. (gr. k-3). lib. bdg. 23.00 (978-0-8368-4436-8(X), Gareth Stevens Learning Library) Stevens, Gareth Publishing LLLP.

Markovics, Joyce L. My Tongue Is Long & Curved. 2016. (Zoo Clues 2 Ser.). (ENG.). 24p. (J). (gr. -1-3). lib. bdg. 17.95 (978-1-944102-59-3(0)) Bearport Publishing Co., Inc.

Marsico, Katie. Giraffes Have Long Necks. 2014. (Tell Me Why Library). (ENG., Illus.). 24p. (J). (gr. 2-5). 25.64 (978-1-63188-003-2(9), 205419) Cherry Lake Publishing.

Moldovo, Eustacia. Baby Giraffes at the Zoo. 2015. (All about Baby Zoo Animals Ser.). (ENG., Illus.). 24p. (J). (gr. -1-1). 22.60 (978-0-7660-7084-4(0)); pap. 9.35 (978-0-7660-7081-3(6)) Enslow Pubs., Inc.

Morgan, Sally. Giraffes. 2006. (QEB Animal Lives Ser.). (Illus.). 32p. (J). (gr. 4-7). lib. bdg. 19.95 (978-1-59566-201-9(4)) QEB Publishing Inc.

Murray, Julie. Giraffes, 1 vol. (ENG.). 2012. 32p. 28.50 (978-1-61783-219-2(7), Big Buddy Bks.) 2003. 24p. 25.65 (978-1-57765-722-4(5), Buddy Bks.) ABDO Publishing Co.

Nagelhout, Ryan. Giant Giraffes. 2013. (Great Big Animals Ser.). 24p. (J). (gr. k-2). pap. 8.15 (978-1-4339-9429-6(1)); (ENG., Illus.). lib. bdg. 22.60 (978-1-4339-9428-9(3)) Stevens, Gareth Publishing LLLP.

—Giant Giraffes / Jirafas Gigantes. 2013. (Great Big Animals / Superanimales Ser.). (SPA.). 24p. (J). (gr. k-2). 22.60 (978-1-4339-9444-9(5)) Stevens, Gareth Publishing LLLP.

National Geographic Kids. National Geographic Readers: Giraffes. 2016. (Readers Ser.). (ENG., Illus.). 32p. (J). (gr. -1-1). pap. 3.99 (978-1-4263-2448-2(0), National Geographic Children's Bks.) National Geographic Society.

National Geographic Kids Staff. Giraffes. 2016. (Readers Ser.). (ENG., Illus.). 32p. (J). (gr. -1-1). lib. bdg. 13.90 (978-1-4263-2449-9(9), National Geographic Children's Bks.) National Geographic Society.

Nosy Crow Staff. Where's the Giraffe? Arrhenius, Ingela P., illus. 2017. (ENG.). 10p. (J). (— 1). bds. 8.99 (978-0-7636-9334-3(0), Nosy Crow) Candlewick Pr.

Owen, Ruth. Giraffes. 2012. (Dr. Bob's Amazing World of Animals Ser.). (Illus.). 32p. (J). (gr. k-5). pap. 11.75 (978-1-61533-556-5(0)); lib. bdg. 26.50 (978-1-61533-548-0(X)) Windmill Bks.

Paige, Joy. The Giraffe: World's Tallest Animal. 2009. (Record-Breaking Animals Ser.). 24p. (gr. 1-1). 42.50 (978-1-60852-441-9(8), PowerKids Pr.) Rosen Publishing Group, Inc., The.

Parker, Barbara Keevil. Giraffes. (Early Bird Nature Bks.). (Illus.). 48p. 2005. (ENG.). (gr. 2-5). lib. bdg. 26.60 (978-0-8225-2419-9(8)) 2004. (J). 25.26 (978-1-57505-346-2(2), Carolrhoda Bks.) Lerner Publishing Group.

Pelusey, Michael. Giraffes & Zebras. 2008. (Zoo Animals Ser.). 32p. (gr. 2-3). lib. bdg. 18.56 (978-0-7614-3149-7(7), Benchmark Bks.) Marshall Cavendish Corp.

Pingry, Patricia A. Baby Giraffe. 2003. (San Diego Zoo Animal Library: Vol. 4). (ENG., Illus.). 26p. (J). bds. 6.95 (978-0-8249-6529-7(9), Ideal Pubns.) Worthy Publishing.

Raatma, Lucia. Giraffes. 2013. (ENG.). 48p. (J). 28.00 (978-0-531-23358-0(8)); pap. 6.95 (978-0-531-25156-0(X)) Scholastic Library Publishing.

Riggs, Kate. Giraffes. 2012. (Seedlings Ser.). (Illus.). 24p. (J). (gr. -1-3). 15.95 (978-1-60818-276-3(2), Creative Education) Creative Co., The.

—Seedlings: Giraffes. 2013. (Seedlings Ser.). (ENG.). 24p. (J). (gr. -1-k). pap. 7.99 (978-0-89812-783-6(1), Creative Paperbacks) Creative Co., The.

Sackett-Smith, Lucy. Giraffes: Towering Tall. 2009. (Mighty Mammals Ser.). (Illus.). 24p. (J). (gr. k-3). 22.60 (978-1-4042-8103-5(7)) Rosen Publishing Group, Inc., The.

Schuetz, Kari. Giraffes. 2011. (Animal Safari Ser.). (ENG., Illus.). 24p. (J). (gr. k-3). lib. bdg. 25.95 (978-1-60014-604-6(X), Blastoff! Readers) Bellwether Media.

Shea, Mary Molly. Giraffes. 2010. (Animals That Live in the Grasslands Ser.). (ENG.). 24p. (J). (gr. -1-3). pap. 8.15 (978-1-4339-3867-2(7)); lib. bdg. 22.60 (978-1-4339-3866-5(9)) Stevens, Gareth Publishing LLLP.

Smith, Lucy. Giraffes: Towering Tall. 2009. 24p. (YA). pap. 8.25 (978-1-4358-3267-1(1)) Rosen Publishing Group, Inc., The.

Soundprints, creator. New Baby Giraffe. 2011. (Let's Go to the Zoo! Ser.). (ENG., Illus.). 16p. (gr. -1). 5.95 (978-1-60727-454-4(X)) Soundprints.

Sweeney, Alyse. High-Rise Thriller. 2010. (Zoo Animal Mysteries Ser.). (ENG.). 24p. (gr. k-1). lib. bdg. 26.65 (978-1-4296-4501-0(6), Pebble Plus) Capstone Press of Coughlan Cos.

Turnbull, Stephanie. Giraffe. 2013. (Big Beasts Ser.). (Illus.). 24p. (gr. k-3). 28.50 (978-1-59920-834-3(2)) Black Rabbit Bks.

Von Zumbusch, Amelie. Giraffes. 2007. (Safari Animals Ser.). (Illus.). 24p. (J). (gr. 3-7). lib. bdg. 22.60 (978-1-4042-3615-8(5), PowerKids Pr.) Rosen Publishing Group, Inc., The.

von Zumbusch, Amelie. Giraffes. 2009. (Safari Animals Ser.). 24p. (gr. 1-1). 42.50 (978-1-60852-951-3(7), PowerKids Pr.) Rosen Publishing Group, Inc., The.

Von Zumbusch, Amelie. Giraffes/Jirafas. Sanz, Pilar, tr. from ENG. 2007. (Safari Animals / Animales de Safari Ser.: Vol. 1). (ENG & SPA., Illus.). 24p. (J). (gr. k-3). lib. bdg. 22.60 (978-1-4042-7606-2(8)) Rosen Publishing Group, Inc., The.

von Zumbusch, Amelie. Giraffes/Jirafas. 2009. (Safari Animals/Animales de safari Ser.). (ENG & SPA.). 24p. (gr. 1-1). 42.50 (978-1-60852-974-2(6), Editorial Buenas Letras) Rosen Publishing Group, Inc., The.

Waldendorf, Kurt. How Tall Is a Giraffe? 2017. (Comparison Fun Ser.). (ENG.). 24p. (J). (gr. -1-2). lib. bdg. 27.07 (978-1-5038-1682-4(6), 211517) Child's World, Inc., The.

Ward, Finn. Giraffes at the Zoo. 2015. (Zoo Animals Ser.). (ENG., Illus.). 24p. (J). (gr. k-k). pap. 8.15 (978-1-4824-2593-2(9)) Stevens, Gareth Publishing LLLP.

—Jirafas / Giraffes at the Zoo. 2015. (Animales Del Zoológico / Zoo Animals Ser.). (ENG & SPA.). 24p. (J). (gr. k-k). lib. bdg. 22.60 (978-1-4824-3229-9(3)) Stevens, Gareth Publishing LLLP.

Weingarten, Ethan. Graphs with Giraffes. 2013. (Animal Math Ser.). 24p. (J). (gr. 1-3). 22.60 (978-1-4339-9313-8(9)); pap. 48.90 (978-1-4339-9315-2(5)) Stevens, Gareth Publishing LLLP.

Weingarten, Ethan & Weingarten, E. T. Graphs with Giraffes. 2013. 24p. (J). (gr. 1-3). pap. 8.15 (978-1-4339-9314-5(7)) Stevens, Gareth Publishing LLLP.

Wexo, John Bonnett. Giraffes. 2003. (Illus.). 24p. (J). (gr. 1-7). 10.95 (978-1-888153-92-7(X), Zoo Bks.) Wildlife Education, Ltd.

—Jirafas. Rountree, Monica, tr. 2003. (Zoobooks Ser.). Orig. Title: Giraffes. (SPA., Illus.). 24p. (J). (gr. k-6). lib. bdg. 15.95 (978-1-888153-74-3(1)) Wildlife Education, Ltd.

Wicker, Jan Lee. Those Giant Giraffes. Weaver, Steve, illus. 2015. (Those Amazing Animals Ser.). (ENG.). 56p. (J). pap. 9.95 (978-1-56164-788-0(8)) Pineapple Pr., Inc.

Wildlife Education. Giraffes. 2006. (Critters Up Close Ser.). (J). bds. 5.99 (978-1-932396-16-4(0), Critters Up Close) Wildlife Education, Ltd.

GIRAFFES—FICTION

Allen, Alejandro & Rountree, Benjamín. El Jirafante Luis: The Giraffephant Luis. 2011. (SPA.). 40p. (gr. 1-2). pap. 18.99 (978-1-4567-3903-4(4)) AuthorHouse.

Andreae, Giles. Giraffes Can't Dance. Parker-Rees, Guy, illus. (J). (gr. -1-3). 2012. (ENG.). 32p. bds. 6.99 (978-0-545-39255-6(1), Cartwheel Bks.) 2008. (ENG.). 9.99 (978-0-545-09738-3(X)) 2007. 24.95 incl. audio (978-0-439-02733-5(0)) Scholastic, Inc.

—Giraffes Can't Dance. Parker-Rees, Guy, illus. unabr. ed. 2011. (J). (gr. -1-1). 29.95 (978-0-439-02734-2(9)) Weston Woods Studios, Inc.

—Giraffes Can't Dance: Number Rumba. Parker-Rees, Guy, illus. 2014. (ENG.). 12p. (J). (gr. -1 — 1). bds. 7.99 (978-0-545-63996-5(4), Cartwheel Bks.) Scholastic, Inc.

Averbeck, Jim. One Word from Sophia. Ismail, Yasmeen, illus. 2015. (ENG.). 40p. (J). (gr. -1-3). 17.99 (978-1-4814-0514-0(4)) Simon & Schuster Children's Publishing.

Baxter, Nicola. Josie the Giraffe & the Starry Night. Fox, Lisa, illus. 2016. (ENG.). 16p. (J). (gr. -1-12). 7.99 (978-0-85723-526-8(5), Armadillo) Anness Publishing GBR. Dist: National Bk. Network.

Bergmann, Andy. The Starry Giraffe. Bergmann, Andy, illus. 2017. (ENG., Illus.). 40p. (J). (gr. -1-3). 15.99 **(978-1-4814-9100-6(8)**, Aladdin) Simon & Schuster Children's Publishing.

Berresford, J. R. Gerald Giraffe's Garage. Parmelee, George, illus. 2013. (ENG.). 32p. (J). (gr. -1-3). 11.95 (978-0-9860321-0-3(7)) Tuscarora Publishing Company.

Blight, Peter. Lonely Giraffe. Matthewson, Emma, ed. Terry, Michael, illus. 2005. (ENG.). 32p. (J). 19.99 (978-0-7475-6894-0(4)) Bloomsbury Publishing Plc GBR. Dist: Independent Pubs. Group.

—The Lonely Giraffe. Terry, Michael, illus. 2006. (Bloomsbury Paperbacks Ser.). (ENG.). 32p. (J). (gr. -1-3). pap. 12.99 (978-0-7475-7144-5(9)) Bloomsbury Publishing Plc GBR. Dist: Trafalgar Square Publishing.

Boddy, Gary. Giraffe's Holiday in Sydney. 2007. 23p. 19.95 (978-1-84799-919-1(0)) Lulu Pr., Inc.

Brightwood, Laura. Giraffe's Shocking Surprise. Pifer, Kimberly, ed. Brightwood, Laura, illus. 2012. (Illus.). (J). (978-1-934409-30-5(8)) 3-C Institute for Social Development.

Brown, Bruce & Shelton, A. Gordon the Giraffe. 2013. (Illus.). 50p. pap. 5.95 (978-1-927424-53-7(4)) Arcana Studio, Inc.

Burach, Ross. I Am Not a Chair! Burach, Ross, illus. 2017. (Illus.). 40p. (J). (gr. -1-3). 17.99 (978-0-06-236016-8(7)) HarperCollins Pubs.

Buzzeo, Toni. Stay Close to Mama. Wohnoutka, Mike, illus. 2012. (ENG.). 32p. (J). (gr. -1-k). 15.99 (978-1-4231-3482-4(6)) Hyperion Pr.

Campbell, Susan. Little Jimmy: The Itty Bitty Fifty Foot Tall Giraffe. 2011. 24p. pap. 24.95 (978-1-4626-2929-9(6)) America Star Bks.

Carlson, Amie. The Giraffe That Was Afraid of Heights. 2016. (Who's Afraid? Ser.). (ENG.). 18p. (J). 15.99 (978-1-4964-1155-6(2)) Tyndale Hse. Pubs.

Carter, Herbert. The, Boy Scouts on Sturgeon Island. rev. ed. 2006. (ENG.). 212p. 27.95 (978-1-4218-2084-2(6), 1st World Library - Literary Society) 1st World Publishing, Inc.

Cefalo, Maria Raffaella. If Dreams Could Talk. 2012. (ENG.). 25p. (J). pap. 27.95 (978-1-4327-9708-9(5)); pap. 17.95 (978-1-4327-9623-5(2)) Outskirts Pr., Inc.

Cosmic Debris Etc., Inc. Staff, et al. Little Giraffe: Finger Puppet Book. 2009. (Little Finger Puppet Board Bks.). (ENG., Illus.). 12p. (J). (gr. -1 — 1). bds. 6.99 (978-0-8118-6787-0(0)) Chronicle Bks. LLC.

Cressey, Roger. The Talking Giraffe. Cressey, Roger, illus. 2013. (Illus.). 118p. pap. (978-1-78222-143-2(3)) Paragon Publishing, Rothersthorpe.

Cronin, Doreen. Rescue Bunnies. Menchin, Scott, illus. 2010. (ENG.). 32p. (J). (gr. -1-3). 16.99 (978-0-06-112871-4(6)) HarperCollins Pubs.

Dahl, Michael. Big Bed for Giraffe. Vidal, Oriol, illus. 2015. (Hello Genius Ser.). (ENG.). 20p. (gr. 1-2). bds. 7.99 (978-1-4795-5791-2(9)) Picture Window Bks.

Dahl, Roald. The Giraffe & the Pelly & Me. Blake, Quentin, illus. 2009. (ENG.). 96p. (Orig.). (J). (gr. 3-7). 7.99 (978-0-14-241384-5(4), Puffin Books) Penguin Young Readers Group.

—The Giraffe, the Pelly & Me. 2009. (Orig.). (gr. 3-6). 18.40 (978-0-8085-9436-9(2), Turtleback) Turtleback Bks.

Dartez, C. Jenny Giraffe Discovers the French Quarter. 2nd ed. 160p. (J). 17.95 (978-1-56554-819-0(1)) Pelican Publishing Co., Inc.

Del Riego, Erica. The Heart of Life. 2010. 36p. pap. 17.75 (978-1-4389-7572-6(4)) AuthorHouse.

Deliso, Chris & Dorling Kindersley Publishing Staff. Playtime with Sophie. 2014. (ENG., Illus.). 14p. (J). (gr. -1 — 1). bds. 5.99 (978-1-4654-2042-8(8), DK Children) Dorling Kindersley Publishing, Inc.

Dickens, Frank. Fly Away Peter. 2017. (ENG., Illus.). 32p. (J). (gr. k-2). pap. 9.99 **(978-1-84365-321-9(4)**, Pavilion) Pavilion Bks. GBR. Dist: Independent Pubs. Group.

Dominguez, Angela. How Do You Say? / ¿Cómo Se Dice? Dominguez, Angela, illus. 2016. (SPA & ENG., Illus.). 32p. (J). 17.99 (978-1-62779-496-1(4), 9781627794961, Holt, Henry & Co. Bks. For Young Readers) Holt, Henry & Co.

Dorling Kindersley Publishing Staff. Let's Get Counting! 2013. (My First Bks.). (ENG.). 36p. (J). (gr. -1 — 1). bds. 5.99 (978-1-4654-0958-4(0), DK Children) Dorling Kindersley Publishing, Inc.

—Peekaboo Sophie! 2013. (ENG.). 12p. (J). (gr. -1 — 1). bds. 6.99 (978-1-4654-0960-7(2), DK Children) Dorling Kindersley Publishing, Inc.

—Sophie la Girafe: Sophie's Big Noisy Day Book! 2015. (ENG., Illus.). 12p. (J). (— 1). bds. 14.99 (978-1-4654-3803-4(3), DK Children) Dorling Kindersley Publishing, Inc.

—Sophie la Girafe: Sophie's Little Library. 2015. (ENG., Illus.). 42p. (J). (— 1). bds. 19.99 (978-1-4654-4013-6(5), DK Children) Dorling Kindersley Publishing, Inc.

—Sophie Pop-Up Peekaboo! 2014. (ENG., Illus.). 12p. (J). (gr. -1 — 1). bds. 9.99 (978-1-4654-2041-1(X), DK Children) Dorling Kindersley Publishing, Inc.

Dyan, Penelope. Baylee's Giraffes! Sometimes Only a Giraffe Will Do. Dyan, Penelope, illus. 2013. (Illus.). 34p. pap. 11.95 (978-1-61477-085-5(9)) Bellissima Publishing, LLC.

Eaton, Kay A. Gleason & the Dewdrop's Dream. 2011. 24p. (gr. -1). pap. 15.00 (978-1-4567-4075-7(X)) AuthorHouse.

—Gleason, the Christmas Giraffe. 2009. 28p. pap. 12.50 (978-1-4389-3010-7(0)) AuthorHouse.

Eulate, Ana. Life Is Beautiful! 2013. (ENG., Illus.). 28p. (J). (gr. -1-k). 16.95 (978-84-15619-26-0(X)) Eastern National.

Flory, Neil. The Short Giraffe. 2015. (Illus.). 24p. (J). (978-1-4896-3885-4(7)) Weigl Pubs., Inc.

Galvin, Laura. New Baby Giraffe. Cohen, Jessie, photos by. 2003. (Let's Go to the Zoo! Ser.). (ENG., Illus.). 16p. (J). (gr. -1-k). 5.95 (978-1-56899-798-8(1), B9003) Soundprints.

Galvin, Laura Gates. Kakuda the Giraffe. Denman, Michael & Huiett, William, illus. (ENG.). 36p. (J). (gr. -1-2). 2006. 2.95 (978-1-59249-187-2(1), S6551) 2005. 8.95 (978-1-59249-206-0(1), SD6501) Soundprints.

—Kakuda the Giraffe. Denman, Michael L. & Huiett, William J., trs. Denman, Michael L. & Huiett, William J., illus. 2005. (Meet Africa's Animals Ser.). (ENG.). 36p. (J). (gr. -1-2). 14.95 (978-1-59249-185-8(5), H6501); pap. 6.95 (978-1-59249-186-5(3), S6501) Soundprints.

—Kakuda the Giraffe. Denman, Michael & Huiett, William, illus. 2003. (ENG.). 36p. (J). (gr. -1-2). 9.95 (978-1-59249-188-9(X), PS6551) Soundprints.

Gan, Jessie Low. How Giraffe Got Spots. 2012. 24p. pap. 15.99 (978-1-4797-1203-8(5)) Xlibris Corp.

Georgie Giraffe, the Detective. 2005. (Georgie Giraffe Set 1 Ser.). (J). 7.33 (978-1-932570-41-0(1)) Pioneer Valley Bks.

Glover, Matt. But It's True. 2012. (Illus.). 32p. pap. 13.50 (978-1-78035-330-2(8), Fastprint Publishing) Upfront Publishing Ltd. GBR. Dist: Printondemand-worldwide.com.

Gough, Simon. I Can'T Fly & I Can'T Swim. 2011. (Illus.). 24p. pap. 11.44 (978-1-4567-8063-0(8)) AuthorHouse.

Griffiths, Andy. Killer Koalas from Outer Space & Lots of Other Very Bad Stuff That Will Make Your Brain Explode! Denton, Terry, illus. 2012. (ENG.). 192p. (J). (gr. 3-7). pap. 7.99 (978-1-250-01017-9(9), 9781250010179) Square Fish.

Grindley, Sally. Archie's Amazing Adventure. Bendall-Brunello, John, tr. Bendall-Brunello, John, illus. 2003. 32p. (YA). (978-1-84365-026-3(6), Pavilion Children's Books) Pavilion Bks.

Gump, Granny. The Giraffe Who Went to School. 2011. 48p. pap. 21.99 (978-1-4568-5805-6(X)) Xlibris Corp.

Hadithi, Mwenye & Kennaway, Adrienne. Laughing Giraffe. 2009. (ENG., Illus.). 32p. (J). (gr. k-2). 8.99 (978-0-340-94520-9(6)) Hodder & Stoughton GBR. Dist: Hachette Bk. Group.

Haggis-On-Whey, Doris & Haggis-On-Whey, Benny. Giraffes? Giraffes! 2008. (How Ser.: 1). (ENG., Illus.). 64p. (gr. 4-7). 20.00 (978-1-932416-97-8(8)) McSweeney's Publishing.

Hagin, Karen. Jeremy, the Giraffe Who Was Afraid of Heights. 2005. (J). lib. bdg. 19.95 (978-0-9754728-8-0(7)) Big Ransom Studio.

Hamilton, Elizabeth L. Georgey Giraffe's Giant Respect: Character Critter Series #6. 2004. (Character Critters Ser.: No. 6). (Illus.). 32p. (J). per. 5.95 (978-0-9754629-1-1(1), Character-in-Action) Quiet Impact, Inc.

Harvey, Carol. Lulu, the Friendly Giraffe. 2008. (Illus.). 32p. pap. (978-1-84549-313-4(3), Swirl) arima publishing.

Hellings, Collete & Jacobs, Nadine. Un Bebe Caido del Cielo. Jacobs, Nadine, illus. 2003. (SPA., Illus.). 32p. (J). (gr. k-1). 16.95 (978-84-95150-10-3(7), COR4033) Corimbo, Editorial S.L. ESP. Dist: Distribooks, Inc.

Hofmeyr, Dianne. Zeraffa Giraffa. Ray, Jane, illus. 2015. (ENG.). 40p. (J). pap. 9.99 (978-1-84780-661-1(9), Frances Lincoln Children's Bks.) Quarto Publishing Group UK GBR. Dist: Littlehampton Bk Services, Ltd.

Holmes, Mary Tavener & Harris, John. A Giraffe Goes to Paris, 0 vols. Cannell, Jon, illus. 2010. (ENG.). 32p. (J). (gr. 1-4). 17.99 (978-0-7614-5595-0(7), 9780761455950, Amazon Children's Publishing) Amazon Publishing.

Horowitz, Dave. A Monkey among Us. Horowitz, Dave, illus. 2004. (Illus.). 40p. (J). (gr. -1-1). 14.99 (978-0-06-054335-8(3), HarperFestival) HarperCollins Pubs.

Huang, Yu-Hsuan, illus. Baby Giraffe: Finger Puppet Book. 2017. (ENG.). 12p. (J). (gr. -1 — 1). bds. 6.99 (978-1-4521-5611-8(5)) Chronicle Bks. LLC.

Iwasa, Megumi. Yours Sincerely, Giraffe. Takabatake, Jun, illus. 2017. (ENG.). 104p. (gr. k-3). 16.99 (978-1-927271-88-9(6)); 9.99 **(978-1-77657-114-7(2))** Gecko Pr. NZL. Dist: Lerner Publishing Group.

Jacobs, Leslie. The Adventure of the Tall giraffe & the Short Duck. 2009. (J). 14.99 (978-1-61584-646-7(8)) Independent Pub.

Jeremy Can't Drink Milk. 2006. (Illus.). 24p. (J). 5.99 (978-0-9725593-2-4(9)) by shayne.

Jiggly Giraffe Book & Soft Rattle. 2014. (Illus.). (J). (978-1-4723-3976-8(2)) Parragon Bk. Service Ltd.

Johns, Eric. The Giraffe Tree & Other Tall Stories. 2012. 180p. (-18). pap. 12.95 (978-1-291-03279-6(7)) Lulu Pr., Inc.

Kaiser, Lori. Gigi the Greedy Giraffe. Kaiser, Lori, illus. 2012. (Illus.). 28p. pap. (978-0-9836651-8-2(4)) Roxby Media Ltd.

Kayler, Ralph. The Tea Party in the Tree Tops. 2009. 48p. pap. 19.49 (978-1-4389-8000-3(0)) AuthorHouse.

Kelley, Louise. Stretch the Giraffe. 2012. 32p. pap. 19.99 (978-1-4772-2161-7(1)) AuthorHouse.

Keyworth, R. L. Gregory Giraffe's New Friends Adventure: Gregory Giraffe Is about to find some altogether different but new friends at his watering Hole. 2009. 20p. pap. 10.99 (978-1-4389-3284-2(7)) AuthorHouse.

Kraegel, Kenneth. The Song of Delphine. Kraegel, Kenneth, illus. 2015. (ENG., Illus.). 40p. (J). (gr. k-3). 15.99 (978-0-7636-7001-6(4)) Candlewick Pr.

Lane, Angela. Mommy, there's a giraffe in my Room. 2007. (Illus.). 32p. (J). 16.99 (978-0-9721142-3-3(8)) Soar Publishing, LLC.

Lannen, Jon Jon. The Giraffe That Taught Me How to Laugh. 2010. 28p. pap. 14.99 (978-1-4490-5930-9(9)) AuthorHouse.

Lenker, David "Papa". The Skin They're In. 2011. 28p. pap. 15.99 (978-1-4568-7294-6(X)) Xlibris Corp.

Lindgren, Barbro. Soda Pop. Adbage, Lisen, illus. 2017. (ENG.). 112p. (J). (gr. 3-5). 16.99 **(978-1-77657-010-2(3))** Gecko Pr. NZL. Dist: Lerner Publishing Group.

Litten, Kristyna. Blue & Bertie. Litten, Kristyna, illus. 2016. (ENG., Illus.). 32p. (J). (gr. -1-3). 17.99 (978-1-4814-6154-2(0), Simon & Schuster Bks. For Young Readers) Simon & Schuster Bks. For Young Readers.

Mattel. Bob the Builder: Lofty & the Giraffe. 2016. (Passport to Reading Level 1 Ser.). (ENG., Illus.). 32p. (J). (gr. -1-3). pap. 3.99 (978-0-316-35682-4(4)) Little, Brown Bks. for Young Readers.

Mayfield, Sue. I Can, You Can, Toucan! 2006. (Green Bananas Ser.). (ENG., Illus.). 48p. (J). (gr. -1-3). lib. bdg. (978-0-7787-1032-5(7)) Crabtree Publishing Co.

—I Can, You Can, Toucan! Padua, Rochelle, illus. 2005. (Green Bananas Ser.). (ENG.). 48p. (J). (gr. k-2). pap. 5.99 (978-1-4052-1793-4(6)) Egmont Bks., Ltd. GBR. Dist: Independent Pubs. Group.

McMaster, Alex. Giant George & Little Leo. 2012. 24p. pap. 14.95 (978-1-4669-5080-1(3)) Trafford Publishing.

McNamee, Kevin. My Brother the Frog. Morris, Alexander, illus. 2011. 24p. 19.95 (978-1-61633-167-2(4)); pap. 10.95 (978-1-61633-159-7(3)) Guardian Angel Publishing, Inc.

Michalak, Jamie. Joe & Sparky Get New Wheels. Remkiewicz, Frank, illus. 2013. (Candlewick Sparks Ser.). (ENG.). 48p. (J). (gr. k-4). pap. 3.99 (978-0-7636-6641-5(6)) Candlewick Pr.

—Joe & Sparky Go to School. Remkiewicz, Frank, illus. 2014. (Candlewick Sparks Ser.). (ENG.). 48p. (J). (gr. k-4). pap. 3.99 (978-0-7636-7181-5(9)) Candlewick Pr.

—Joe & Sparky, Superstars! Remkiewicz, Frank, illus. (Candlewick Sparks Ser.). (ENG.). 48p. (J). (gr. k-4). 2013. pap. 3.99 (978-0-7636-6642-2(4)) 2011. 15.99 (978-0-7636-4578-6(8)) Candlewick Pr.

Milton, Nancy. The Giraffe That Walked to Paris. Roth, Roger, illus. 2013. (ENG.). 32p. (J). (gr. -1-3). 18.95 (978-1-930900-67-7(8)) Purple Hse. Pr.

Morgan, Dennis W. Stubby the Giraffe Who Wouldn't Take Chances. 2013. 40p. pap. 14.99 (978-0-9892295-0-0(5)) Dreamstreet Studios, Inc. (A Div. of DSMV Industries, Inc.).

Murphy, Stuart J. Percy Gets Upset. 2011. (I See I Learn Ser.). (ENG., Illus.). 32p. (J). (gr. -1-k). 14.95 (978-1-58089-460-9(7)); pap. 6.95 (978-1-58089-461-6(5)) Charlesbridge Publishing, Inc.

—Percy Juega con Cuidado. 2011. (I See I Learn Ser.). (SPA & ENG., Illus.). 32p. (J). (-k). 14.95 (978-1-58089-484-5(4)); pap. 6.95 (978-1-58089-485-2(2)) Charlesbridge Publishing, Inc.

—Percy Listens Up. 2012. (I See I Learn Ser.). (ENG., Illus.). 32p. (J). (-k). 14.95 *(978-1-58089-468-5(2))*; pap. 6.95 *(978-1-58089-469-2(0))* Charlesbridge Publishing, Inc.
—Percy Se Enoja. 2012. (I See I Learn Ser.). (SPA & ENG., Illus.). 32p. (J). (-k). 14.95 *(978-1-58089-492-0(5))*; pap. 6.95 *(978-1-58089-493-7(3))* Charlesbridge Publishing, Inc.
Nirgad, Lia. A Kiss for Lily. Abulafia, Yossi, illus. 2006. (ENG.). 24p. (J). (gr. -1-1). *(978-1-59692-163-4(3))* MacAdam/Cage Publishing, Inc.
O'Donnell, Kerri. A Giraffe Can Laugh. 2006. (Neighborhood Readers Ser.). (ENG.). 12p. (gr. -1-3). pap. 5.90 *(978-1-4042-5762-7(4)*, Rosen Classroom) Rosen Publishing Group, Inc., The.
Opal, Paola. Ollie. 2010. (ENG., Illus.). 24p. (J). (gr. -1 — 1). bds. 7.95 *(978-1-897476-12-3(4))* Simply Read Bks. CAN. Dist: Ingram Publisher Services.
—Totty. 2009. (Simply Small Ser.). (ENG., Illus.). 24p. (J). (gr. -1 — 1). bds. 7.95 *(978-1-897476-06-2(X))* Simply Read Bks. CAN. Dist: Ingram Publisher Services.
Oron, Judie. Cry of the Giraffe. 2010. (ENG., Illus.). 208p. (YA). (gr. 9-12). 21.95 *(978-1-55451-272-0(7)*, 9781554512720); pap. 12.95 *(978-1-55451-271-3(9)*, 9781554512713) Annick Pr., Ltd. CAN. Dist: Publishers Group West (PGW).
Papineau, Lucie. Pas de Taches Pour une Girafe. 2004. (FRE., Illus.). (J). (gr. k-3). spiral bd. *(978-0-616-03075-2(4))* Canadian National Institute for the Blind/Institut National Canadien pour les Aveugles.
Piper, William Bowman. Giraffe of Montana, Volume 1, 1. 2005. (Giraffe of Montana Ser.). (Illus.). 152p. (J). 19.95 *(978-0-9763359-4-8(8)*, 0-9763359) Little Pemberley Pr.
Platt, Kin. Big Max & the Mystery of the Missing Giraffe. Cravath, Lynne Avril, illus. (I Can Read Level 2 Ser.). 64p. (J). 2006. (ENG.). (gr. k-3). pap. 3.99 *(978-0-06-009920-6(8))* 2005. (gr. -1). 15.99 *(978-0-06-009918-3(6))* 2005. (gr. -1 — 1). lib. bdg. 17.89 *(978-0-06-009919-0(4))* HarperCollins Pubs.
Power, Michael. The Zoo. 2009. 201p. pap. 13.75 *(978-1-60695-075-3(4))* EchoRoad, Inc.
Randel, Jackie. Calendar Friends. l.t. ed. 2005. (Illus.). 34p. (J). per. 9.99 *(978-1-59879-018-4(8))* Lifevest Publishing, Inc.
Random House. Thomas' Tall Friend (Thomas & Friends) 2016. (Step into Reading Ser.). (ENG., Illus.). 24p. (J). (gr. -1-1). 4.99 *(978-1-101-94034-1(4)*, Random Hse. Bks. for Young Readers) Random Hse. Children's Bks.
Random House Editors. Thomas' Tall Friend. 2016. (Step into Reading Level 2 Ser.). lib. bdg. 14.75 *(978-0-606-38883-2(4))* Turtleback Bks.
Rayner, Catherine. Abigail. Rayner, Catherine, illus. 2013. (ENG., Illus.). 32p. (J). 14.99 *(978-1-58925-147-2(4))* Tiger Tales.
—Counting Stars. Rayner, Catherine, illus. 2016. (ENG., Illus.). 28p. (J). (gr. -1-k). bds. 7.99 *(978-1-58925-225-7(X))* Tiger Tales.
Reginelli, Nina. Geraldine's Rainy Day. 2011. *(978-1-77069-281-7(9))* Word Alive Pr.
Rettore. Giraffe & Friends. 2014. (Friends Cloth Bks.). (ENG.). 8p. (J). (gr. -1 — 1). 9.99 *(978-1-4380-0528-7(8))* Barron's Educational Series, Inc.
Rey, H. A. & Rey, Margret. Cecily G. & the 9 Monkeys. 2007. (Curious George Ser.). (ENG., Illus.). 48p. (J). (gr. -1-3). 16.00 *(978-0-618-80066-7(2))* Houghton Mifflin Harcourt Publishing Co.
—Cecily G. & the 9 Monkeys. 2009. (Curious George Ser.). (ENG., Illus.). 48p. (J). (gr. -1-3). pap. 6.99 *(978-0-618-99794-7(6)*, HMH Books For Young Readers) Houghton Mifflin Harcourt Publishing Co.
Robertson, Donald. Mitford at the Fashion Zoo. 2015. (ENG., Illus.). 40p. (J). (gr. -1-2). 17.99 *(978-0-451-47542-8(9)*, Viking Books for Young Readers) Penguin Young Readers Group.
—Mitford at the Hollywood Zoo. 2017. (ENG., Illus.). 40p. (J). (gr. -1-2). 17.99 *(978-0-451-47543-5(7)*, Viking Books for Young Readers) Penguin Young Readers Group.
Rosario, Joann. Happy- Go -Lucky Giraffe!! Rosario, Joann, illus. 2004. (Illus.). 20p. (J). (gr. k-5). pap. 10.00 *(978-0-9758746-7-7(5)*, 1246169) J.G.R. Enterprises.
Sagerman, Evan. Giraffe Rescue Company. Chou, Joey, illus. 2016. (J). *(978-1-4424-1366-5(2))* Simon & Schuster Children's Publishing.
Schulz, Heidi. Giraffes Ruin Everything. Robertson, Chris, illus. 2016. (ENG.). (J). 16.99 *(978-1-61963-475-6(9)*, 9781619634756, Bloomsbury USA Childrens) Bloomsbury Publishing USA.
Soli, Doris. Jango the Little Dragon: The Wondrous Adventures of Little Dragon. 2011. (Illus.). 36p. pap. 17.07 *(978-1-4567-8487-4(0))* AuthorHouse.
Sophie & Friends. 2014. (ENG.). 12p. (J). (gr. -1 — 1). bds. 6.99 *(978-1-4654-1815-9(6)*, DK Children) Dorling Kindersley Publishing, Inc.
Spurling, Wesley. Gerry the Giraffe. 2009. 36p. pap. 16.99 *(978-1-4389-4223-0(0))* AuthorHouse.
St. John, Lauren. The White Giraffe. 2008. (ENG., Illus.). 208p. (J). (gr. 2-5). 7.99 *(978-0-14-241152-0(3)*, Puffin Books) Penguin Young Readers Group.
Stamp, Jørgen & Buckley, William F., Jr. Flying High. 2009. (ENG., Illus.). 32p. (J). (gr. -1-2). 16.95 *(978-1-59270-089-9(6))* Enchanted Lion Bks., LLC.
Tate, Cynthia Wagoner. Gordy's Grimy but Groovy Adventure. 2006. 24p. 12.98 *(978-1-4116-6297-1(0))* Lulu Pr., Inc.
Till, Nan. Solomon Finds His Spots. 2009. 24p. (J). pap. 15.95 *(978-1-4327-5134-0(4))* Outskirts Pr., Inc.
Trasacco, Christina. Indigo. 2012. (ENG.). 35p. (J). 26.95 *(978-1-4327-7722-7(X))* Outskirts Pr., Inc.
Trotter, Bob. Up the Wooden Hill: Bedtime Stories for Little Ones. Edgar, Barrie, illus. 2011. 98p. pap. 17.99 *(978-1-60976-139-4(1)*, Eloquent Bks.) Strategic Book Publishing & Rights Agency (SBPRA).
Ufer, David A. The Giraffe Who Was Afraid of Heights, 1 vol. Carlson, Kirsten, illus. 2006. (ENG.). 32p. (J). (gr. -1-3). 15.95 *(978-0-9768823-0-5(2))* Arbordale Publishing.
Underhill, Marjorie Fay. Jeremiah. Garrett, Caroline S., tr. Garrett, Caroline S., illus. 2003. (J). 12.00 *(978-1-887905-75-6(8))* Parkway Pubs., Inc.
Uvezian, Verne. The Day Benny Stuck His Neck Out. 2011. 12p. (gr. 1-2). 9.95 *(978-1-4567-3119-9(X))* AuthorHouse.
Vajda, Joseph. Michael Jones -. the First Encounter. 2015. (ENG., Illus.). 42p. (J). *(978-1-78222-417-4(3))* Paragon Publishing, Rothersthorpe.
Veerkamp, Misty J. Oh What I Could Do with a Neck Like a Giraffe. 2011. 16p. pap. 24.95 *(978-1-4560-7474-6(1))* America Star Bks.
Voyager, Beatrice Nambouy. Mama Minko: A Survival Quest. 2010. (Illus.). 28p. pap. 15.49 *(978-1-4490-5797-8(7))* AuthorHouse.
Wahl, Jan. The Long Tall Journey. Gapaillard, Laurent, illus. 2015. (ENG.). 48p. (J). (gr. 1-3). 18.99 *(978-1-56846-230-1(1)*, Creative Editions) Creative Co., The.
Weiss, Fred G. Mag-Nan-I-Mous Monkey & Gerald Giraffe. 2013. 28p. 18.99 *(978-0-9898820-5-7(5))* Mindstir Media.
Wilson, Veronica B. Aswald's ABC Adventure. 2008. 28p. pap. 24.95 *(978-1-60441-691-6(2))* America Star Bks.
Winnard, Rebecca Victoria & Winnard, Linda. Giraffe Liberation: An Act of Freedom. 2006. 53p. pap. 16.95 *(978-1-4241-0552-6(8))* PublishAmerica, Inc.
Wofford, Sherry Lynn. Introducing the Adventures of Jerry Giraffe & Feather Bird. 2011. 36p. pap. 16.95 *(978-1-4560-3238-8(0))* America Star Bks.
Woolf, Julia. Giraffe on a Bicycle. 2016. (ENG., Illus.). 32p. (J). (gr. -1-1). 17.99 ***(978-1-4472-8768-1(1))*** Pan Macmillan GBR. Dist: Independent Pubs. Group.
Yates, Gene, illus. The Giraffe Numbers Book. 2006. (J). *(978-1-58865-364-2(1))* Kidsbooks, LLC.
Yuly, Toni. The Jelly Bean Tree. Yuly, Toni, illus. 2017. (ENG., Illus.). 40p. (J). 17.99 *(978-1-250-09406-3(2)*, 9781250094063) Feiwel & Friends.

GIRL SCOUTS

Aller, Susan Bivin. Juliette Low. 2007. (History Maker Biographies Ser.). (Illus.). 48p. (J). (gr. 3-7). lib. bdg. 26.60 *(978-0-8225-6580-2(3)*, Lerner Pubns.) Lerner Publishing Group.
Corey, Shana. Here Come the Girl Scouts! Hooper, Hadley, illus. 2012. (ENG.). 40p. (J). (gr. -1-3). 17.99 *(978-0-545-34278-0(3)*, Scholastic Pr.) Scholastic, Inc.
Cox, Palmer. The Brownies: Their Book. Cox, Palmer, illus. 2011. (Dover Children's Classics Ser.). (ENG., Illus.). 144p. (Orig.). (J). (gr. 1-6). pap. 7.95 *(978-0-486-21265-4(3))* Dover Pubns., Inc.
Eubanks, Toni. Let's Celebrate! Girl Scout Ceremonies. 2004. (Illus.). 48p. (J). *(978-0-88441-688-3(7))* Girl Scouts of the USA.
Girl Scout Gold Award Insert. 2004. (YA). *(978-0-88441-674-6(7))* Girl Scouts of the USA.
Girl Scout Silver Award Insert. 2004. (YA). *(978-0-88441-675-3(5))* Girl Scouts of the USA.
Hally, Ashleigh. Juliette Gordon Low. 2012. (Illus.). 24p. (J). *(978-1-935884-77-4(8))*; pap. *(978-1-935884-83-5(2))* State Standards Publishing, LLC.
Parks Matter! 2004. (YA). *(978-0-88441-673-9(9))* Girl Scouts of the USA.
Studio 2b: Focus - Express It. 2004. (YA). pap. *(978-0-88441-671-5(2))* Girl Scouts of the USA.
Studio 2b Focus - Don't Sweat It. 2004. (YA). pap. *(978-0-88441-669-2(0))* Girl Scouts of the USA.
Studio 2b Focus - Express It. 2004. (YA). *(978-0-88441-670-8(4))* Girl Scouts of the USA.
Studio 2B Focus - On the Money. 2004. (YA). *(978-0-88441-687-6(9))* Girl Scouts of the USA.
STUDIO 2B Guide for Councils Phase II: Strategies & Models. 2004. (YA). *(978-0-88441-686-9(0))* Girl Scouts of the USA.
Welsh, Anne Marie & Tuchman, Laura. A World of Girls. Garcia, Helena, illus. 2010. 40p. (J). *(978-0-88441-750-7(6))* Girl Scouts of the USA.

GIRL SCOUTS—FICTION

Lubar, David. Curse of the Campfire Weenies: And Other Warped & Creepy Tales. 2008. (Weenies Stories Ser.). (ENG.). 208p. (J). (gr. 4-9). mass mkt. 5.99 *(978-0-7653-5771-7(2)*, 9780765357717, Starscape) Doherty, Tom Assocs., LLC.
McKenzie, Lyn. Betsy, Girl Scout of Woodward Center 1935. 2007. 244p. (YA). pap. 17.95 net. *(978-0-9722839-0-8(0))* Just Write Bks.
Roy, Lillian Elizabeth. Girl Scouts in Arizona & New Mexico. Lehman, A. C., illus. 2011. 250p. 46.95 *(978-1-258-05940-8(1))* Literary Licensing, LLC.
Warner, Penny. The Mystery of the Missing Mustangs. 2012. 107p. (J). *(978-0-88166-411-9(1))* Meadowbrook Pr.
Wirt, Mildred A. The Brownie Scouts at Silver Beach. 2011. 224p. 44.95 *(978-1-258-09299-3(9))* Literary Licensing, LLC.

GIRL SCOUTS—HANDBOOKS, MANUALS, ETC.

Girl Scouts of the USA, creator. The Ambassador Girl's Guide to Girl Scouting. 2011. ring bd. 22.50 *(978-0-88441-780-4(8))* Girl Scouts of the USA.
—The Senior Girl's Guide to Girl Scouting. 2011. spiral bd. 22.50 *(978-0-88441-779-8(4))* Girl Scouts of the USA.
Tuchman, Laura. Welcome to the Daisy Flower Garden. Kalis, Jennifer, illus. 2008. 88p. (J). *(978-0-88441-709-5(3))* Girl Scouts of the USA.
Welsh, Anne Marie & Fenly, Leigh. Wow! Wonders of Water. Garcia, Helena, illus. 2009. 112p. (J). pap. *(978-0-88441-732-3(8))* Girl Scouts of the USA.

GIRLS

Abingdon. Promises for Girls Living Faithfully with God & Neighbor. 2006. 64p. 4.00 *(978-0-687-49385-2(4))* Abingdon Pr.
Adelman, Penina, et al. The JGirl's Guide: The Young Jewish Woman's Handbook for Coming of Age. 2005. (ENG.). 240p. pap. 16.99 *(978-1-58023-215-9(9)*, 9781580232159, Jewish Lights Publishing) LongHill Partners, Inc.
AIO Team & Buchanan, Kathy. Candid Conversations with Connie Vol. 1: A Girl's Guide to Growing Up. 2014. (Adventures in Odyssey Bks.). (ENG., Illus.). 160p. (J). pap. 9.99 *(978-1-58997-792-1(0))* Focus on the Family Publishing.
Akana, Anna. So Much I Want to Tell You. 2017. (ENG., Illus.). 208p. pap. 16.00 ***(978-0-399-59493-9(0)***, Ballantine Bks.) Random House Publishing Group.
Alagna, Magdalena. Everything You Need to Know about the Dangers of Binge Drinking. 2009. (Need to Know Library). 64p. (gr. 5-5). 58.50 *(978-1-60854-091-4(X))* Rosen Publishing Group, Inc., The.
Allen, Laurie. Acting Duets for Young Women: Eight- to ten-minute duo scenes for practice & Competition, 1 vol. 2010. (ENG.). 216p. (J). pap. 17.95 *(978-1-56608-172-6(6))* Meriwether Publishing, Ltd.
American Girl, creator. You Can Do It! A Kit to Help You Do Just about Anything. 2006. (American Girl Library). (ENG., Illus.). 48p. 9.95 *(978-1-59369-155-4(6)*, American Girl) American Girl Publishing, Inc.
Barbour Publishing Staff & Biggers, Emily. Power Prayers for Girls. 2015. (ENG.). 224p. (J). pap. 7.99 *(978-1-63058-859-5(8))* Barbour Publishing, Inc.
Belfield, Annie. Stressed-Out Girl? Girls Dealing with Feelings. 2014. (ENG.). 64p. (J). (gr. 5-12). 15.95 *(978-1-62293-040-1(1))* Enslow Pubs., Inc.
Berkley, Elizabeth. Ask Elizabeth: Real Answers to Everything You Secretly Wanted to Ask about Love, Friends, Your Body... & Life in General. 2011. (ENG., Illus.). 240p. (YA). (gr. 7-18). 16.99 *(978-0-399-25449-9(8)*, G.P. Putnam's Sons Books for Young Readers) Penguin Young Readers Group.
Bialik, Mayim. Girling Up, 9 vols. 2017. (ENG.). (YA). 170.91 ***(978-0-525-48653-4(4))***; 192p. (gr. 7). 18.99 *(978-0-399-54860-4(2))* Penguin Young Readers Group. (Philomel Bks.).
Birkemoe, Karen. Strike a Pose: The Planet Girl Guide to Yoga. Collett, Heather, illus. 2007. (Planet Girl Ser.). (ENG.). 96p. (J). (gr. 5-9). 12.95 *(978-1-55337-004-8(X))* Kids Can Pr., Ltd. CAN. Dist: Hachette Bk. Group.
Bokram, Karen, ed. Head-to-Toe Guide to You. Thomas, Bill, illus. 2010. (ENG.). 128p. (J). (gr. 5-9). pap. 8.99 *(978-0-545-20236-7(1)*, Scholastic Paperbacks) Scholastic, Inc.
Bolte, Mari. Unique Accessories: You Can Make & Share. 2015. (Sleepover Girls Crafts Ser.). (ENG.). 64p. (gr. 3-4). pap. 9.95 *(978-1-62370-421-6(9))* Capstone Press of Coughlan Cos.
Bowen, Shane. Out of the Darkness. 2010. 220p. pap. 21.95 *(978-0-557-26249-6(6))* Lulu Pr., Inc.
Brereton, Erin. Real Girls' Guide to Everything: That Makes It Awesome to Be a Girl! Zalevskaya, Anastacia, illus. 2011. (ENG.). 192p. (J). pap. 12.95 *(978-1-60078-561-0(1))* Triumph Bks.
Brewer, Marie. For Smart Girls Only. 2010. pap. 12.95 *(978-0-7414-6184-1(6))* Infinity Publishing.
Brooks, E. S. Historic Girls. 2013. 140p. pap. *(978-3-95507-936-9(8))* DOGMA. in Europäischer Hochschulverlag GmbH & Co. KG.
Buchanan, Kathy. Candid Conversations with Connie, Volume 3: A Girl's Guide to Entertainment, Body Image, & Social Media. 2016. (Adventures in Odyssey Bks.). (ENG.). 192p. (J). pap. 9.99 *(978-1-58997-798-3(X))* Focus on the Family Publishing.
Burningham, Sarah O'Leary. Girl to Girl: Honest Talk about Growing up & Your Changing Body. Arnold, Alli, illus. 2013. (ENG.). 136p. (J). (gr. 3-7). 12.99 *(978-1-4521-0242-9(2))* Chronicle Bks. LLC.
Cabot, Meg. Princess Lessons. McLaren, Chesley, illus. 2003. (Princess Diaries Guidebook Ser.). (ENG.). 144p. (YA). (gr. 8-18). 15.99 *(978-0-06-052677-1(7)*, HarperTeen) HarperCollins Pubs.
Carlson, Melody & Rue, Nancy N. Dear Nancy: Answers to Letters from Girls Like You, 1 vol. 2008. (Faithgirlz Ser.). (ENG.). 160p. (J). pap. 7.99 *(978-0-310-71496-5(6))* Zonderkidz.
Carmindy. Bloom: A Girl's Guide to Growing up Gorgeous. 2014. (ENG., Illus.). 160p. (gr. k-12). pap. 20.00 *(978-0-399-16659-4(9)*, TarcherPerigee) Penguin Publishing Group.
Cassel, Katrina. Promises for God's Princesses. 2014. (ENG.). 224p. (J). 9.99 *(978-1-4143-9660-6(0))* Tyndale Hse. Pubs.
Clark, Travis & Belfield, Annie. A Guys' Guide to Stress. 2008. (Flip-It-Over Guides to Teen Emotions Ser.). (Illus.). 128p. (J). (gr. 8-13). lib. bdg. 33.27 *(978-0-7660-2857-9(7))* Enslow Pubs., Inc.
Countryman, Jack & Parker, Amy. God's Promises for Girls, 1 vol. 2010. (ENG.). 128p. (gr. 1-5). 12.99 *(978-1-4003-1591-8(3))* Nelson, Thomas Inc.
Courtney, Vicki. Reflect: Discovering the Beauty, Worth, & Wonderfulness of You. 2016. (ENG., Illus.). 208p. (J). (gr. 7-12). pap. 14.99 *(978-1-4336-9175-1(2)*, B&H Kids) B&H Publishing Group.
—Teenvirtue Confidential: Your Questions Answered about Guys, God, & Getting Older. 2007. (Illus.). 149p. (YA). per. 14.99 *(978-0-8054-4192-5(1)*, B&H Bks.) B&H Publishing Group.
—What about Me? Seeing Yourself the Way God Sees You. 2016. (ENG.). 208p. (J). (gr. 3-6). pap. 14.99 *(978-1-4336-9176-8(0)*, B&H Kids) B&H Publishing Group.
Criswell, Patti Kelley. Friendship Troubles. 2013. (Smart Girl's Guide Ser.). lib. bdg. 24.50 *(978-0-606-34732-7(1)*, Turtleback) Turtleback Bks.
—What Would You Do? Quizzes about Real-Life Problems. Chobanian, Elizabeth, ed. Bendell, Norm, illus. 2004. (ENG.). 64p. (J). (gr. 3-18). pap. 8.95 *(978-1-58485-874-4(5))* American Girl Publishing, Inc.
Daily Whispers of Wisdom for Girls Journal. 2014. (ENG.). 384p. (J). pap. 14.99 *(978-1-62836-945-8(0)*, Barbour Bks.) Barbour Publishing, Inc.
Decaire, Carmale, ed. Girls & Their Horses. Clar, David, illus. 2006. (ENG.). 64p. (J). (gr. 4-7). pap. 8.95 *(978-1-59369-209-4(9))* American Girl Publishing, Inc.
Dellasega, Cheryl & Sourcebooks, Inc Staff. The Girl's Friendship Journal. 2005. (ENG.). 128p. (J). (gr. 4-7). pap. 16.00 *(978-1-932783-59-9(8))* Sourcebooks, Inc.
Delmege, Sarah. Pink Pages. 2004. (Illus.). 158p. (J). *(978-0-439-67992-3(3))* Scholastic, Inc.
Devadasan, Rashmi Ruth. Kumari Loves a Monster. Kumariyin Ratcaca Katalan. Shyam, illus. 2010. (TAM & ENG.). 52p. pap. 17.95 *(978-93-80636-01-6(6))* Blaft Pubns.
Doak, Robin S. Malala Yousafzai. 2015. (True Book(tm), A — Biographies Ser.). (ENG., Illus.). 48p. (J). lib. bdg. 31.00 *(978-0-531-21191-5(6))* Scholastic Library Publishing.
Don, Katherine. Nujood Ali & the Fight Against Child Marriage. 2014. (J). *(978-1-59935-466-8(7))* Reynolds, Morgan Inc.
Dorling Kindersley Publishing Staff. The Adventure Guide. 2015. (ENG., Illus.). 96p. (J). (gr. k-4). lib. bdg. 16.99 *(978-1-4654-3623-8(5)*, DK Children) Dorling Kindersley Publishing, Inc.
Doudna, Kelly. Boys & Girls Around the World, 1 vol. 2004. (Around the World Ser.). (ENG., Illus.). 24p. (J). (gr. k-3). lib. bdg. 24.21 *(978-1-59197-564-9(6)*, SandCastle) ABDO Publishing Co.
Douglas, Tasha K. God's Beautiful Daughter: Discover the Love of Your Heavenly Father, 1 vol. 2015. (Faithgirlz Ser.). (ENG.). 192p. (J). pap. 8.99 *(978-0-310-74594-5(2))* Zonderkidz.
Dower, Laura. For Girls Only: Everything Great about Being a Girl. 2008. (ENG., Illus.). 208p. (J). (gr. 6-9). 15.99 *(978-0-312-38205-6(7)*, 9780312382056) Feiwel & Friends.
DuJardin, Rosamond & DuJardin, Judy. Junior Year Abroad. 2003. (YA). pap. 12.95 *(978-1-930009-80-6(1)*, 800-691-7779) Image Cascade Publishing.
Dunham, Kelli. The Girl's Body Book. 4th rev. ed. 2017. (ENG.). 148p. (J). pap. 12.95 ***(978-1-60433-714-3(1)***, Applesauce Pr.) Cider Mill Pr. Bk. Pubs., LLC.
—The Girls Body Book: Everything You Need to Know for Growing up YOU. Tallardy, Laura, illus. 2013. (ENG.). 116p. (J). pap. 11.95 *(978-1-60433-353-4(7)*, Applesauce Pr.) Cider Mill Pr. Bk. Pubs., LLC.
—The Girl's Body Book: Everything You Need to Know for Growing up You! Tallardy, Laura, illus. 3rd rev. ed. 2015. (ENG.). 132p. (J). pap. 12.95 *(978-1-60433-575-0(0)*, Applesauce Pr.) Cider Mill Pr. Bk. Pubs., LLC.
Eastwood, Kay. Women & Girls in the Middle Ages. 2003. (Medieval World Ser.). (ENG., Illus.). 32p. (J). (gr. 5). pap. *(978-0-7787-1378-4(4))* Crabtree Publishing Co.
Eckel, Jessie, illus. How to Be a Princess in 7 Days or Less. 2005. (How to be A Ser.). 32p. (J). (gr. 3-5). 12.95 *(978-0-7534-5921-8(3)*, Kingfisher) Roaring Brook Pr.
Etler, Cyndy. We Can't Be Friends. 2017. (ENG.). 304p. (YA). (gr. 8-12). 17.99 ***(978-1-4926-3576-5(6))*** Sourcebooks, Inc.
Falligant, Erin, ed. Just Mom & Me: The Tear-Out, Punch-Out, Fill-Out Book of Fun for Girls & Their Moms. Peterson, Stacy, illus. 2008. (ENG.). 96p. (J). (gr. 4-7). spiral bd. 10.95 *(978-1-59369-340-4(0))* American Girl Publishing, Inc.
Fargo, Donna. You Are in My Thoughts & Prayers. 2008. (ENG.). pap. 12.95 *(978-1-59842-352-5(5))* Blue Mountain Arts Inc.
Fast, Suellen M. America's Daughters. Fast, Suellen M., photos by. (Illus.). 100p. (Orig.). (J). (gr. k-18). pap. 19.00 *(978-0-935281-13-2(4))* Daughter Culture Pubns.
Faulkner, Nicholas & Sherman, Josepha. Soccer: Girls Rocking It, 01 vols., 1. 2016. (Title IX Rocks! Ser.). (ENG., Illus.). 64p. (J). 32.95 *(978-1-5081-7039-6(8)*, Rosen Young Adult) Rosen Publishing Group, Inc., The.
Finnis, Anne & Bond, Denis. It's a Boy/Girl Thing! The Truth... in Their Own Words. 2003. (ENG., Illus.). 144p. (J). pap. 10.95 *(978-0-09-943212-8(9)*, Red Fox) Random House Children's Books GBR. Dist: Random Hse. of Canada.
Foster, Juliana. The Girls' Book: How to Be the Best at Everything. Wingate, Philippa, ed. Enright, Amanda, illus. 2007. (Best at Everything Ser.). (ENG.). 128p. (J). (gr. 3-7). 9.99 *(978-0-545-01629-2(0)*, Scholastic Pr.) Scholastic, Inc.
Frankel, Alona. Mi Bacinica y Yo (para Ella) 2013. (SPA., Illus.). 44p. (J). (gr. -1 — 1). 7.95 *(978-1-77085-403-1(7)*, 9781770854031) Firefly Bks., Ltd.
—Once upon a Potty — Girl. 2014. (Once upon a Potty Ser.). (ENG., Illus.). 24p. (J). (gr. -1 — 1). bds. 6.95 *(978-1-77085-405-5(3)*, 9781770854055) Firefly Bks., Ltd.
Free Spirit Publishing. Questions & Quotes for Girls. 2nd rev. ed. 2015. (In a Jar(r) Ser.). (ENG.). (J). (gr. 5). 9.99 *(978-1-57542-488-0(6))* Free Spirit Publishing, Inc.
Friedman, Hannah. Everything Sucks: Losing My Mind & Finding Myself in a High School Quest for Cool. 2009. (ENG.). 264p. (YA). (gr. 8-12). pap. 12.95 *(978-0-7573-0775-1(2)*, HCI Teens) Health Communications, Inc.
Frier, Raphaële. Malala: Activist for Girls' Education. Fronty, Aurélia, illus. 2017. 45p. (J). ***(978-1-63289-592-9(7))*** Charlesbridge Publishing, Inc.
Frier, Raphaelle. Malala: Activist for Girls' Education. Fronty, Aurélia, illus. 2017. (ENG.). 48p. (J). (gr. 1-4). 17.99 *(978-1-58089-785-3(1))* Charlesbridge Publishing, Inc.
Gadeberg, Jeanette. Brave New Girls: Creative Ideas to Help Girls Be Confident, Healthy, & Happy. 2nd rev. ed. 2008. (ENG., Illus.). 256p. (J). (gr. 4-7). pap. 12.95 *(978-1-57749-179-8(3))* Taylor Trade Publishing.
Gagliardi, Tina. School Survival: Keeping Your Cool at School, 1 vol. 2008. (Essential Health: Strong Beautiful Girls Set 1 Ser.). (ENG.). 112p. (J). (gr. 6-12). lib. bdg. 35.64 *(978-1-60453-104-6(5))* ABDO Publishing Co.
Gallagher, Jim & Kavanaugh, Dorothy. A Guys' Guide to Conflict. 2008. (Flip-It-Over Guides to Teen Emotions Ser.). (Illus.). 128p. (J). (gr. 3-7). lib. bdg. 33.27 *(978-0-7660-2852-4(6))* Enslow Pubs., Inc.
George, Elizabeth. A Girl's Guide to Discovering Her Bible. 2015. (ENG.). 144p. (J). pap. 10.99 *(978-0-7369-6256-8(5))* Harvest Hse. Pubs.
Gerelds, Jennifer. Brave Girls: Beautiful You: A 90-Day Devotional, 1 vol. 2016. (ENG., Illus.). 144p. (J). pap. 8.99 *(978-0-7180-7611-5(7))* Nelson, Thomas Inc.
Gillespie, Sarah. Diary of Sarah Gillespie: A Pioneer Farm Girl, 1 vol. 2014. (First-Person Histories Ser.). (ENG.). 32p. (gr. 3-4). lib. bdg. 27.32 *(978-1-4765-4194-5(9)*, Fact Finders) Capstone Press of Coughlan Cos.
Girl Talk. 2013. (Girl Talk Ser.). 48p. (J). (gr. 5-8). 175.50 *(978-1-4777-0728-9(X))*; pap. 70.50 *(978-1-4777-2705-8(1))*; pap. 423.00 *(978-1-4777-2706-5(X))* Rosen Publishing Group, Inc., The. (Rosen Reference).
Girls' Guides. 2005. (Illus.). 48p. (gr. 5-8). lib. bdg. 215.40 *(978-0-8239-3919-0(7))* Rosen Publishing Group, Inc., The.
The Girls' Guides to Everything Unexplained, 6 vols., Set. Incl. Girls' Guide to Fairies: Everything Irresistible about the Fair Folk. Johnson, Sheri A. 2011. lib. bdg. 27.99 *(978-1-4296-6556-8(4))*; Girl's Guide to Mermaids: Everything Alluring about These Mythical Beauties. Johnson, Sheri A. 2011. lib. bdg. 27.99 *(978-1-4296-6557-5(2))*; Girls' Guide to Vampires: Everything Enchanting about These Immortal Creatures. Jones, Jen. 2010. lib. bdg. 27.99 *(978-1-4296-5452-4(X))*; Girls' Guide to Werewolves: Everything Charming about These Shape-Shifters. Jones, Jen. 2010. lib. bdg. 27.99 *(978-1-4296-5453-1(8))*; Girls' Guide to Wizards: Everything Magical about These Spellbinders. Jones, Jen. 2010. lib. bdg. 27.99

E
F
G

(978-1-4296-5454-8(6)); Girls Guide to Zombies: Everything Vital about These Undead Monsters. Jones, Jen. 2010. lib. bdg. 27.99 *(978-1-4296-5455-5(4))*; (gr. 3-4). (Girls' Guides to Everything Unexplained Ser.). (ENG.). 32p. 2011. Set lib. bdg. 167.94 *(978-1-4296-6559-9(9)*, Snap Bks.) Capstone Press of Coughlan Cos.

Gosselin, Suzanne Hadley. Faithgirlz Handbook, Updated & Expanded: How to Let Your Faith Shine Through, 1 vol. 2016. (Faithgirlz Ser.). (ENG.). 144p. (J). pap. 7.99 *(978-0-310-75440-4(2))* Zonderkidz.

Graham, Stacey. Girls' Ghost Hunting Guide. 2012. (ENG., Illus.). 192p. (J). (gr. 4-7). pap. 9.99 *(978-1-4022-6612-6(X)*, Sourcebooks Jabberwocky) Sourcebooks, Inc.

Gravelle, Karen & Gravelle, Jennifer. The Period Book: A Girl's Guide to Growing Up. Palen, Debbie, illus. 2017. (ENG.). 144p. (J). pap. 13.99 *(978-1-61963-662-0(X)*, 9781619636620, Bloomsbury USA Childrens) Bloomsbury Publishing USA.

Green, Mischa P. Sacred: 100 Affirmations for Girls. 2004. (YA). per. 12.00 *(978-0-9754191-3-7(7))* Morals & Values Pr.

Gresh, Dannah. It's Great to Be a Girl! A Guide to Your Changing Body. 2015. (Secret Keeper Girl(r) Ser.). (ENG., Illus.). 128p. (J). pap. 11.99 *(978-0-7369-6007-6(4))* Harvest Hse. Pubs.

Greven, Alec. How to Talk to Girls. Acedera, Kei, illus. 2008. (ENG.). 48p. (J). (gr. 1-5). 9.99 *(978-0-06-170999-9(9)*, Collins) HarperCollins Pubs.

Griffin, Starla. Girl, 13: A Global Snapshot of Generation E. 2004. (Illus.). 240p. (J). pap. *(978-1-59258-112-2(9))* Hylas Publishing.

Guest, Elissa Haden & Blackstone, Margaret. Girl Stuff: A Survival Guide to Growing Up. Pollak, Barbara, illus. 2006. (ENG.). 192p. (J). (gr. 5-7). pap. 8.95 *(978-0-15-205679-7(3))* Houghton Mifflin Harcourt Publishing Co.

Haberman, Lia. About Face: Beauty Tricks & Tips. 2005. (Illus.). 48p. (J). *(978-0-439-80297-0(0))* Scholastic, Inc.

Hadley, Margie. Looking Back in the Mirror. 2013. 36p. pap. 16.95 *(978-1-63004-529-6(2))* America Star Bks.

Hadley, Suzanne. Faithgirlz Handbook: How to Let Your Faith Shine Through. 2009. (Faithgirlz! Ser.). (ENG.). 96p. (J). (gr. 4-7). pap. 9.99 *(978-0-310-71966-3(6))* Zonderkidz.

Hamilton, Bethany. Ask Bethany, 1 vol. rev. ed. 2014. (Faithgirlz / Soul Surfer Ser.). (ENG., Illus.). 192p. (J). pap. 9.99 *(978-0-310-74572-3(1))* Zonderkidz.

—Rise Above: A 90-Day Devotional, 1 vol. (Faithgirlz / Soul Surfer Ser.). (ENG.). 192p. (J). 2014. pap. 9.99 *(978-0-310-74559-4(4))* 2011. pap. 9.99 *(978-0-310-72567-1(4))* Zonderkidz.

Handler, Daniel. Girls Standing on Lawns. Kalman, Maira, illus. 2014. (ENG.). 64p. (gr. 3-7). 14.95 *(978-0-87070-908-1(9))* Museum of Modern Art.

Hanna, Janice & Thompson, Janice. 3-Minute Devotions for Girls: 180 Inspirational Readings for Young Hearts. 2014. (3-Minute Devotions Ser.). (ENG.). 192p. (J). pap. 4.99 *(978-1-62836-638-9(9)*, Barbour Bks.) Barbour Publishing, Inc.

Hardy, Mary Smith. Uncle Hubbard & the Burlap Sack. 2012. 48p. (gr. 4-6). pap. 12.95 *(978-1-4759-0179-5(8))* iUniverse, Inc.

Harrison, Emma. From Head to Toe: The Girls' Life Guide to Taking Care of You. Montagna, Frank, illus. 2004. 124p. (J). *(978-0-439-44983-0(9))* Scholastic, Inc.

Heiman, Diane & Suneby, Liz. See What You Can Be: Explore Careers That Could Be for You! Wood, Tracey, illus. 2009. (ENG.). 108p. (gr. 4-7). spiral bd. 9.95 *(978-1-59369-277-3(3))* American Girl Publishing, Inc.

Hemmen, Lucie. The Teen Girl's Survival Guide: 10 Tips for Making Friends, Avoiding Drama & Coping with Social Stress. 2015. (Instant Help Solutions Ser.). (ENG.). 208p. (YA). (gr. 5-12). pap. 17.95 *(978-1-62625-306-3(4))* New Harbinger Pubns.

Hentges, Katie. Your First Boyfriend. 2012. (Relationships 101 Ser.). (ENG., Illus.). 48p. (J). (gr. 5-8). 27.95 *(978-1-4488-6829-2(7))*; pap. 11.75 *(978-1-4488-6833-9(5))* Rosen Publishing Group, Inc., The. (Rosen Reference).

Hester, Sallie. Diary of Sallie Hester: A Covered Wagon Girl, 1 vol. 2014. (First-Person Histories Ser.). (ENG.). 32p. (gr. 3-4). lib. bdg. 27.32 *(978-1-4765-4193-8(0)*, Fact Finders) Capstone Press of Coughlan Cos.

Holl, Kristi. Shine on Girl: Devotions to Keep You Sparkling, 1 vol. 2006. (Faithgirlz Ser.). (ENG., Illus.). 192p. (J). pap. 9.99 *(978-0-310-71144-5(4))* Zonderkidz.

—What's a Girl to Do? Finding Faith in Everyday Life, 1 vol. 2007. (Faithgirlz Ser.). (ENG.). 192p. (J). (gr. 3-7). pap. 9.99 *(978-0-310-71348-7(X))* Zonderkidz.

Holmes, Andy. My Princess Bible. Eliseev, Sergey, illus. 2010. (ENG.). 66p. (J). bds. 12.99 *(978-1-4143-3324-3(2))* Tyndale Hse. Pubs.

Holmes, Melisa & Hutchinson, M.D., Patricia. Girlology: A Girl's Guide to Stuff That Matters. 2005. (ENG., Illus.). 264p. (YA). (gr. 7-12). pap. 12.95 *(978-0-7573-0295-4(5)*, HCI Teens) Health Communications, Inc.

Holmes, Melisa & Hutchison, Patricia. Girlology's There's Something New about You: A Girl's Guide to Growing Up. 2010. (ENG., Illus.). 128p. (J). (gr. 7-11). pap. 12.95 *(978-0-7573-1526-8(7)*, HCI Teens) Health Communications, Inc.

Hoobler, Thomas & Hoobler, Dorothy. Real American Girls Tell Their Own Stories: Messages from the Heart & Heartland. 2012. (ENG.). 112p. (J). (gr. 5-9). pap. 6.99 *(978-1-4424-6043-0(1)*, Simon & Schuster Bks. For Young Readers) Simon & Schuster Bks. For Young Readers.

Hopper, Missy. Peggy Sue & the Pepper Patch. Bowden, Cecelia, illus. 2010. 32p. (J). *(978-1-57736-430-6(9))* Providence Hse Pubs.

Hovsepian, Ann-Margret. The One Year Designer Genes Devo. 2007. (ENG.). 320p. (J). (gr. 4-8). per. 13.99 *(978-1-4143-1359-7(4)*, Tyndale Kids) Tyndale Hse. Pubs.

Jeffrie, Sally. A Guide to Being a Goddess. 2009. (Best at Everything Ser.). (ENG.). 128p. (J). (gr. 3-7). 9.99 *(978-0-545-08537-3(3))* Scholastic, Inc.

Jensen, Diane Mastromarino. The Girl's Guide to Loving Yourself: A book about falling in love with the one person who matters most... you - UPDATED EDITION -, 1 vol. 2011. 64p. pap. 12.95 *(978-1-59842-600-7(1))* Blue Mountain Arts Inc.

Johnson, Sheri A. The Girls' Guides to Everything Unexplained. 2011. (Girls' Guides to Everything Unexplained Ser.). (ENG.). 32p. (gr. 3-4). lib. bdg. 55.98 *(978-1-4296-6558-2(0)*, Snap Bks.) Capstone Press of Coughlan Cos.

Johnston, Darcie. Is This Normal? More Girls' Questions, Answered by the Editors of the Care & Keeping of You. 2015. lib. bdg. 20.85 *(978-0-606-37238-1(5))* Turtleback Bks.

Jones, Jen. Planning Perfect Parties: The Girls' Guide to Fun, Fresh, Unforgettable Events. 2014. (Craft It Yourself Ser.). (ENG.). 128p. (gr. 3-4). pap. 14.95 *(978-1-62370-063-8(9))* Capstone Young Readers of Coughlan Cos.

Just for Girls. 2008. (Amazing Body Growing Up Ser.). 96p. *(978-1-4075-1571-7(3))* Parragon, Inc.

Kallmeyer-Mehlhorn, Margarete. The Wondrous Ball of Yarn: A Facsimile of the Previously Unpublished Manuscript. 2008.Tr. of Wunderknaul. (ENG & GER., Illus.). 40p. 41.00 *(978-0-9745168-2-0(1))* Cotsen Occasional Pr.

Kalman, Bobbie. Rapping about Being a Girl. 2012. (ENG.). 24p. (J). *(978-0-7787-2794-1(7))*; pap. *(978-0-7787-2801-6(3))* Crabtree Publishing Co.

Katz, Anne. Girl in the Know: Your Inside-and-Out Guide to Growing Up. Melnychuk, Monika, illus. 2010. (ENG.). 112p. (J). (gr. 5-9). 18.95 *(978-1-55453-303-9(1))* Kids Can Pr., Ltd. CAN. Dist: Hachette Bk. Group.

Kauchak, Therese. Real Beauty: 101 Ways to Feel Great about You. Yoshizumi, Carol, illus. 2008. (American Girl Library). (ENG.). 120p. (J). pap. 9.95 *(978-1-58485-908-6(3))* American Girl Publishing, Inc.

Kavanaugh, Dorothy. Hassled Girl? Girls Dealing with Feelings. 2014. (ENG.). 64p. (J). (gr. 5-12). 15.95 *(978-1-62293-035-7(5))* Enslow Pubs., Inc.

Kelly, Camryn, et al. Just Me & My Friends & Family. 2012. (Hot Chocolate with God Ser.: 2). (ENG.). 160p. (YA). (gr. 3-7). pap. 10.99 *(978-0-89296-844-2(3)*, Faithwords) Hachette Nashville.

Kelly, Dorothy A. Developing a Sense of Self: A Workbook of Tenets & Tactics for Adolescent Girls. 2006. (Illus.). 146p. (J). pap. 29.99 *(978-0-87101-366-8(5)*, NASW Pr.) National Assn. of Social Workers/NASW Pr.

Kenney, Karen Latchana. Boho Fashion. Kubley, Ashley Newsome, illus. 2014. (What's Your Style? Ser.). (ENG.). 48p. (gr. 5-8). lib. bdg. 30.60 *(978-1-4677-1470-9(4)*, Lerner Pubns.) Lerner Publishing Group.

King, Bart. The Big Book of Girl Stuff, 1 vol. Kalis, Jennifer, illus. 2014. (ENG.). 320p. pap. 19.99 *(978-1-4236-3762-2(3))* Gibbs Smith, Publisher.

Knowlton, Laurie Lazzaro. Cowgirl Alphabet, 1 vol. Knowlton, Charlotte & Coates, Kathy, illus. 2011. (ENG.). 32p. (J). (gr. k-3). 16.99 *(978-1-58980-669-6(7))* Pelican Publishing Co., Inc.

Larsen, Carolyn. For Girls Only! Devotions. Sutherland, Leah, illus. 2009. (ENG.). 256p. (J). pap. 9.99 *(978-1-4143-2209-4(7)*, Tyndale Kids) Tyndale Hse. Pubs.

—Prayers for Little Girls. Turk, Caron, illus. 2008. (Prayers For... Ser.). 131p. (J). (gr. -1-3). *(978-1-86920-526-3(X))* Christian Art Pubs.

—Princess Stories: Real Bible Stories of God's Princesses. Eliseev, Sergey, illus. 2012. (ENG.). 128p. (J). 14.99 *(978-1-4143-4811-7(8)*, Tyndale Kids) Tyndale Hse. Pubs.

Lazurek, Michelle S. Daddy, Am I Beautiful? Stott, Apryl, illus. 2015. 24p. (J). pap. *(978-0-8198-1905-5(0))* Pauline Bks. & Media.

Lecreux, Michele & Gallais, Celia. The Girl's Book of Adventure: The Little Guidebook for Smart & Resourceful Girls. Millet, Esao & Millet, Jocelyn, illus. 2013. (ENG.). 128p. (J). (gr. 3-7). 14.99 *(978-0-7641-6610-5(7))* Barron's Educational Series, Inc.

Legacy Press Staff. God's Girls! Fun & Faith for Ages 9-12. 2004. (God's Girls Ser.: Vol. 1). (Illus.). (J). (gr. 4-7). 176p. pap. 12.99 *(978-1-58411-020-0(1))*; Vol. 2. 192p. pap. 12.99 *(978-1-58411-021-7(X))* Rainbow Pubs. & Legacy Pr. (Legacy Pr.).

Lindsey, Brooklyn. Confessions of a Not-So-Supermodel: Faith, Friends, & Festival Queens, 1 vol. 2008. (Invert Ser.). (ENG., Illus.). 176p. (YA). (gr. 7-14). pap. 9.99 *(978-0-310-27753-8(1))* Zondervan.

Lluch, Isabel B. & Lluch, Emily. Girls' Guide to Caring for Your Body: Everything You Need to Know - Questions & Answers about Growing Up. 2012. (ENG.). 100p. (J). (gr. 6). pap. 6.95 *(978-1-936061-54-9(6))* WS Publishing.

Loewen, Nancy & Skelley, Paula. Girl Talk. Mora, Julissa, illus. 2015. (Girl Talk Ser.). (ENG.). 32p. (gr. 3-4). lib. bdg. 111.96 *(978-1-4914-1862-8(1)*, Snap Bks.) Capstone Press of Coughlan Cos.

—Girl Talk: Questions & Answers about Daily Dramas, Disasters, & Delights. Mora, Julissa, illus. 2015. (ENG.). 112p. (gr. 3-4). pap. 12.95 *(978-1-62370-218-2(6))* Capstone Young Readers of Coughlan Cos.

—Lunch Lines, Tryouts, & Making the Grade: Questions & Answers about School. Mora, Julissa, illus. 2015. (Girl Talk Ser.). (ENG.). 32p. (gr. 3-4). lib. bdg. 27.99 *(978-1-4914-1861-1(3)*, Snap Bks.) Capstone Press of Coughlan Cos.

—Tangles, Growth Spurts, & Being You: Questions & Answers about Growing Up. Mora, Julissa, illus. 2015. (Girl Talk Ser.). (ENG.). 32p. (gr. 3-4). lib. bdg. 27.99 *(978-1-4914-1860-4(5)*, Snap Bks.) Capstone Press of Coughlan Cos.

Lohmann, Raychelle Cassada & Raja, Sheela. The Sexual Trauma Workbook for Teen Girls: A Guide to Recovery from Sexual Assault & Abuse. 2016. (ENG.). 200p. (YA). (gr. 6-12). pap. 16.95 *(978-1-62625-399-5(4))* New Harbinger Pubns.

Long, Hayley. Being a Girl. Correll, Gemma, illus. 2016. (ENG.). 224p. (J). pap. 12.99 *(978-1-4494-7797-4(6))* Andrews McMeel Publishing.

Loulan, Joann & Worthen, Bonnie. Periodo: Guina de una Joven. Dyrud, Chris Wold & Quackenbush, Marcia, illus. 4th ed. 2003. (Lansky, Vicki Ser.). (SPA.). 92p. pap. 9.99 *(978-0-916773-99-1(X))* Book Peddlers.

Lucan, Dawn. Adventure Memories for Girls. 2010. 44p. pap. 16.95 *(978-0-557-52399-3(0))* Lulu Pr., Inc.

Lundsten, Apryl. The Girls' Life Guide to Being a Style Superstar! Parett, Lisa, illus. 2004. 124p. (J). *(978-0-439-44984-7(7))* Scholastic, Inc.

Lynch, Amy. A Smart Girl's Guide to Understanding Her Family: Feelings, Fighting & Figuring It Out. Scheuer, Lauren, illus. 2009. (ENG.). 64p. (J). (gr. 3-18). pap. 9.95 *(978-1-59369-617-7(5))* American Girl Publishing, Inc.

Madaras, Lynda & Davick, Linda. Ready, Set, Grow! A What's Happening to My Body? Book for Younger Girls. 2003. (What's Happening to My Body? Ser.). (ENG., Illus.). 128p. (gr. 4-6). pap. 12.99 *(978-1-55704-565-2(8)*, William Morrow Paperbacks) HarperCollins Pubs.

Madaras, Lynda & Madaras, Area. My Body, My Self for Girls. 3rd rev. ed. 2007. (What's Happening to My Body? Ser.). (ENG., Illus.). 160p. (gr. 4-6). pap. 12.99 *(978-1-55704-766-3(9)*, William Morrow Paperbacks) HarperCollins Pubs.

—¿Que Pasa en Mi Cuerpo? El Libro para Muchachos: La Guía de Mayor Venta Sobre el Desarrollo, Escrita para Adolescentes y Preadolescentes. 2012. (What's Happening to My Body? Ser.). (SPA., Illus.). 256p. (gr. 4-18). pap. 12.99 *(978-1-55704-940-7(8)*, William Morrow Paperbacks) HarperCollins Pubs.

—¿Que Pasa en Mi Cuerpo? Libro para Muchachas: La Guía de Mayor Venta Sobre el Desarrollo Escrita para Adolescentes y Preadolescentes. 2011. (What's Happening to My Body? Ser.). (SPA & ENG., Illus.). 288p. (gr. 4-18). pap. 12.95 *(978-1-55704-939-1(4)*, William Morrow Paperbacks) HarperCollins Pubs.

Madaras, Lynda, et al. "What's Happening to My Body?" Book for Girls. 3rd rev. ed. 2007. (What's Happening to My Body? Ser.). (ENG., Illus.). 288p. (gr. 7-9). pap. 14.99 *(978-1-55704-764-9(2)*, William Morrow Paperbacks) HarperCollins Pubs.

Marcovitz, Hal & Snyder, Gail. A Guys' Guide to Anger. 2008. (Flip-It-Over Guides to Teen Emotions Ser.). (Illus.). 128p. (J). (gr. 8-13). lib. bdg. 33.27 *(978-0-7660-2853-1(4))* Enslow Pubs., Inc.

—A Guys' Guide to Jealousy. 2008. (Flip-It-Over Guides to Teen Emotions Ser.). (Illus.). 128p. (J). (gr. k-5). lib. bdg. 33.27 *(978-0-7660-2854-8(2))* Enslow Pubs., Inc.

Martin, Dawn. Fast Girls Finish Last: A Girl's Guide to Becoming a Virgin with Attitude! 2nd rev. ed. 2006. (Illus.). 248p. (YA). (gr. 7-13). per. 19.95 *(978-0-9668718-0-7(4))* 20/20 Publishing.

McCann, Michelle Roehm & Welden, Amelie. Girls Who Rocked the World: Heroines from Joan of Arc to Mother Teresa. Hahn, Daniel & Hahn, David, illus. 2012. (ENG.). 256p. (J). (gr. 3-7). 19.99 *(978-1-58270-361-9(2))*; pap. 10.99 *(978-1-58270-302-2(7))* Aladdin/Beyond Words.

McCarney, Rosemary. Because I Am a Girl: I Can Change the World, 1 vol. 2014. (ENG., Illus.). 72p. (J). (gr. 6-8). pap. 16.95 *(978-1-927583-44-9(6))* Second Story Pr. CAN. Dist: Orca Bk. Pubs. USA.

—Dear Malala, We Stand with You. 2014. (ENG.). 32p. (J). (gr. -1-3). lib. bdg. 19.99 *(978-0-553-52121-4(7))*; 16.99 *(978-0-553-52120-7(9))* Random Hse. Children's Bks. (Crown Books For Young Readers).

Metzger, Julie & Lehman, Robert. Will Puberty Last My Whole Life? Real Answers to Real Questions from Preteens about Body Changes, Sex, & Other Growing-Up Stuff. 2012. (ENG., Illus.). 192p. (YA). (gr. 4-7). pap. 16.95 *(978-1-57061-739-3(2)*, Little Bigfoot) Sasquatch Bks.

Mihulka, Krystyna & Goddu, Krystyna Poray. Krysia: A Polish Girl's Stolen Childhood During World War II. 2017. (ENG., Illus.). 192p. (J). (gr. 5). 17.99 *(978-1-61373-441-4(7))* Chicago Review Pr., Inc.

Miles, Lisa. The Girls' Super Activity Book. 2013. (ENG.). 144p. (J). pap. 8.95 *(978-1-78212-060-5(2))* Arcturus Publishing GBR. Dist: Bookmasters Distribution.

Miles, Lisa & Chown, Xanna Eve. How to Survive Having a Crush. 2013. (Girl Talk Ser.). 48p. (J). (gr. 5-8). pap. 70.50 *(978-1-4777-0727-2(1)*, Rosen Reference); (ENG., Illus.). pap. 11.75 *(978-1-4777-0720-3(4)*, Rosen Reference); (ENG., Illus.). lib. bdg. 29.25 *(978-1-4777-0706-7(9)*, Rosen Classroom) Rosen Publishing Group, Inc., The.

—How to Survive Mean Girls. 2013. (Girl Talk Ser.). 48p. (J). (gr. 5-8). pap. 70.50 *(978-1-4777-0722-7(0)*, Rosen Reference); (ENG., Illus.). pap. 11.75 *(978-1-4777-0721-0(2)*, Rosen Classroom); (ENG., Illus.). lib. bdg. 29.25 *(978-1-4777-0707-4(7)*, Rosen Reference) Rosen Publishing Group, Inc., The.

—How to Survive Online Embarrassment. 2013. (Girl Talk Ser.). (Illus.). 48p. (J). (gr. 5-8). (ENG.). pap. 11.75 *(978-1-4777-0723-4(9)*, Rosen Classroom); pap. 70.50 *(978-1-4777-0726-5(3)*, Rosen Reference); (ENG., lib. bdg. 29.25 *(978-1-4777-0708-1(5)*, Rosen Reference) Rosen Publishing Group, Inc., The.

—How to Survive Zits & Bad Hair Days. 2013. (Girl Talk Ser.). 48p. (J). (gr. 5-8). pap. 70.50 *(978-1-4777-0725-8(5)*, Rosen Reference); (ENG., Illus.). pap. 11.75 *(978-1-4777-0724-1(7)*, Rosen Reference); (ENG., Illus.). lib. bdg. 29.25 *(978-1-4777-0709-8(3)*, Rosen Classroom) Rosen Publishing Group, Inc., The.

Miller, Kat & Manley, Claudia B. Volleyball: Girls Rocking It, 01 vols., 1. 2016. (Title IX Rocks! Ser.). (ENG., Illus.). 64p. (J). 32.95 *(978-1-5081-7045-7(2)*, Rosen Young Adult) Rosen Publishing Group, Inc., The.

Monaghan, Annabel & Wolfe, Elisabeth. Click! The Girl's Guide to Knowing What You Want & Making It Happen. 2007. (ENG.). 240p. (YA). (gr. 7). pap. 12.99 *(978-1-4169-5790-4(1)*, Simon Pulse) Simon Pulse.

Monckeberg, Paulina. Pascualina 2006. 2005. (Pascualina Family of Products Ser.). (ENG., Illus.). 272p. (J). spiral bd. 16.99 *(978-956-8222-28-4(6))* Pascualina Producciones S.A.

Mulcahy, Lisa, et al. Bye Bye Boredom! The Girl's Life Big Book of Fun. 2003. (Illus.). 124p. (J). *(978-0-439-44976-2(6))* Scholastic, Inc.

Mysko, Claire. You're Amazing! A No-Pressure Guide to Being Your Best Self. 2008. (ENG., Illus.). 176p. pap. 9.99 *(978-1-59869-713-1(7))* Adams Media Corp.

Naik, Anita. Bras, Boys & Bad Hair Days: A Girl's Guide to Living with Style. 2008. (ENG., Illus.). 172p. (J). (gr. 7-17). pap. 7.99 *(978-0-340-97057-7(X))* Hodder & Stoughton GBR. Dist: Hachette Bk. Group.

—Think Yourself Gorgeous: How to Feel Good - Inside & Out. 2012. (ENG., Illus.). 176p. (YA). (gr. 7). pap. 11.99 *(978-0-7499-5244-0(X)*, Piatkus Bkis.) Little, Brown Book Group Ltd. GBR. Dist: Independent Pubs. Group.

Natterson, Cara. The Care & Keeping of You 2: The Body Book for Older Girls. Masse, Josée, illus. 2013. lib. bdg. 24.50 *(978-0-606-31576-0(4)*, Turtleback) Turtleback Bks.

Norac, Carl & Dubois, Claude K. Las Palabras Dulces. 2003. (SPA.). 32p. *(978-84-95150-18-9(2))* Corimbo, Editorial S.L.

O'Dell, Nicole. Girl Talk: a Journal: ... for Life's Ups, Downs, & In-Betweens. 2014. (ENG.). 176p. (YA). pap. 12.99 *(978-1-62416-848-2(5)*, Barbour Bks.) Barbour Publishing, Inc.

Olsen, Mary-Kate & Olsen, Ashley. Mary-Kate & Ashley: Our Story. rev. ed. 2003. 96p. mass mkt. 4.99 *(978-0-06-056848-1(8)*, Harper Entertainment) HarperCollins Pubs.

Orr, Tamra. Playing Safe, Eating Right: Making Healthy Choices, 1 vol. 2008. (Essential Health: Strong Beautiful Girls Set 1 Ser.). (ENG.). 112p. (J). (gr. 6-12). lib. bdg. 35.64 *(978-1-60453-103-9(7))* ABDO Publishing Co.

Ottaviano, Patricia. Girl World: How to Ditch the Drama & Find Your Inner Amazing. 2015. (ENG.). 160p. (YA). (gr. 6-12). pap. 9.99 *(978-1-4926-0912-4(9)*, 9781492609124) Sourcebooks, Inc.

Parrish, MariLee. God Hearts Me: 3-Minute Devotions for Girls on the Go! 2015. (3-Minute Devotions Ser.). (ENG.). 160p. (J). pap. 4.99 *(978-1-63058-609-6(9)*, Barbour Bks.) Barbour Publishing, Inc.

Peters, Diane. Girlness: Body & Soul, 1 vol. Murray, Steven, illus. 2005. (Lorimer Deal with It Ser.). (ENG.). 32p. (J). (gr. 4-6). pap. 12.95 *(978-1-55028-891-9(1)*, 9781550288919) Lorimer, James & Co., Ltd., Pubs. CAN. Dist: Casemate Pubs. & Bk. Distributors, LLC.

Peters, Diane. Girlness: Deal with It Body & Soul. Murray, Steven, illus. 2017. (Lorimer Deal with It Ser.). (ENG.). 32p. (J). (gr. 4-9). lib. bdg. 22.65 ***(978-1-4594-1186-9(2)***, 9781459411869) Lorimer, James & Co., Ltd., Pubs. CAN. Dist: Casemate Pubs. & Bk. Distributors, LLC.

Pfeifer, Kate Gruenwald, et al. American Medical Association Girl's Guide to Becoming a Teen. Middleman, Amy B., ed. 2006. (ENG., Illus.). 128p. (gr. 5-8). per. 14.95 *(978-0-7879-8344-4(6)*, Jossey-Bass) Wiley, John & Sons, Inc.

Phidal Publishing Staff, ed. Girls World: My Best Friends. (Illus.). 64p. (J). pap. *(978-2-7643-0145-6(6))* Phidal Publishing, Inc./Editions Phidal, Inc.

Picone, Linda. My Changing Body. 2010. (ENG., Illus.). 150p. (J). (gr. 4-7). pap. 9.95 *(978-1-57749-187-3(4))* Taylor Trade Publishing.

Pitts, Wynter. For Girls Like You: A Devotional for Tweens. 2015. (ENG.). 144p. (J). pap. 10.99 *(978-0-7369-6175-2(5))* Harvest Hse. Pubs.

Plaisted, Caroline. Girl Talk: Girl Talk: A Survival Guide to Growing Up. 2011. (ENG., Illus.). 48p. (J). pap. 11.95 *(978-1-926853-91-8(1))* Saunders Bk. Co. CAN. Dist: RiverStream Publishing.

Reader, Jenny. Girl 2 Girl: The Swap Book You Share with Your Friends. Martin, Caroline & Davies, Nic, illus. 2003. 96p. (J). pap. *(978-0-439-56743-5(2))* Scholastic, Inc.

Rice, Ashley. Adelante, niñA... Sigue soñando (You Go, Girl Keep Dreaming) Un libro especial sobre Cómo. 2006. (SPA & ENG., Illus.). 64p. (J). pap. 9.95 *(978-1-59842-162-0(X)*, Blue Mountain Pr.) Blue Mountain Arts Inc.

—Friends Rule: A Very Special Book of Friendship Especially for Girls. 2003. (Illus.). 64p. (J). pap. *(978-0-88396-772-0(3)*, Blue Mountain Pr.) Blue Mountain Arts Inc.

—Girls Rule: A Very Special Book Created Especially for Girls. Rice, Ashley, illus. (Illus.). 64p. (J). pap. 9.95 *(978-0-88396-627-3(1)*, Blue Mountain Pr.) Blue Mountain Arts Inc.

—Girls Rule: A very special book created especially for girls — UPDATED EDITION —, 1 vol. 2011. 64p. pap. 12.95 *(978-1-59842-598-7(6))* Blue Mountain Arts Inc.

—Make Your Dreams Come True: A Girl's Guide to Always Believing in Yourself. 2015. 96p. pap. ***(978-1-59842-865-0(9)***, Blue Mountain Pr.) Blue Mountain Arts Inc.

—You Are an Amazing Girl: A Very Special Book about Being You & Making Your Dreams Come True. 2006. (Illus.). 64p. (J). (gr. 4-7). per. 9.95 *(978-1-59842-066-1(6)*, Blue Mountain Pr.) Blue Mountain Arts Inc.

—You Go, Girl... Keep Dreaming. 2006. (ENG., Illus.). 56p. 5.95 *(978-1-59842-101-9(8)*, Blue Mountain Pr.) Blue Mountain Arts Inc.

Rich, C. & Richardson, Carla R. Completely You: 12 Things Every Girl Needs to Know. 2008. 60p. pap. 9.95 *(978-0-595-51675-9(0))* iUniverse, Inc.

Rivadeneira, Caryn. Grit & Grace. Betz, Katy, illus. 2017. (ENG.). 144p. (J). (gr. 4-6). pap. 9.99 ***(978-1-5064-2495-8(3)***, Sparkhouse Family) Augsburg Fortress, Pubs.

Robertson, Sadie. Live Original Devotional. 2016. (Live Original Ser.). (ENG., Illus.). 256p. (gr. 7). 16.99 *(978-1-5011-2651-2(2)*, Howard Bks.) Howard Books.

Roderick, Stacey & Warwick, Ellen. Centsibility: The Planet Girl Guide to Money. Melnychuk, Monika, illus. 2008. (Planet Girl Ser.). (ENG.). 80p. (J). (gr. 5-9). 12.95 *(978-1-55453-208-7(6))* Kids Can Pr., Ltd. CAN. Dist: Hachette Bk. Group.

Rogers, Kate. Girls Play Lacrosse. 2016. (Girls Join the Team Ser.). 24p. (J). (gr. 3-3). pap. 8.25 *(978-1-4994-2101-9(X)*, PowerKids Pr.) Rosen Publishing Group, Inc., The.

Rothschild, Jennifer. Me, Myself, & Lies for Young Women: What to Say When You Talk to Yourself. 2017. (ENG.). 192p. (J). pap. 12.99 *(978-0-7369-6421-0(5))* Harvest Hse. Pubs.

Rue, Nancy N. Everybody Tells Me to Be Myself but I Don't Know Who I Am. 2007. (Faithgirlz! Ser.). (ENG., Illus.). 144p. (J). (gr. 3-7). pap. 7.99 *(978-0-310-71295-4(5))* Zonderkidz.

—The Fun-Finder Book: It's a God Thing!, 1 vol. 2003. (Lily Ser.). (ENG.). 112p. (J). pap. 7.99 *(978-0-310-70258-0(5))* Zondervan.

Rue, Nancy N., et al. The Beauty of Believing: 365 Devotions That Will Change Your Life, 1 vol. 2014. (Faithgirlz Ser.). (ENG.). 432p. (J). pap. 12.99 *(978-0-310-73617-2(X))* Zonderkidz.

Russell, Wendy Thomas & Goodman, Sarah. MEdia. 2010. (Illus.). 96p. (J). *(978-0-88441-752-1(2))* Girl Scouts of the USA.

Rutledge, Jill Zimmerman. Picture Perfect: What You Need to Feel Better about Your Body. 2007. (ENG.). 240p. (gr. 8-12).

pap. 14.95 *(978-0-7573-0607-5(1))* Health Communications, Inc.

Sawyer, Kem Knapp. Grace Akallo & the Pursuit of Justice for Child Soldiers. 2015. (J). *(978-1-59935-456-9(X))* Reynolds, Morgan Inc.

Schaefer, Valorie. The Care & Keeping of You Vol. 1: The Body Book for Younger Girls. 2013. lib. bdg. 24.50 *(978-0-606-31575-3(6),* Turtleback) Turtleback Bks.

Schoenberg, Jill. Journal Buddies: A Girl's Journal for Sharing & Celebrating Magnificence. 2nd ed. 2007. (J). per. 16.95 *(978-0-9768623-0-7(1))* Blue Sky at Night Publishing.

Scholastic, Inc. Staff. A Drama-Free Life. Bokram, Karen, ed. Thomas, Bill, illus. 2010. (ENG.). 128p. (J). (gr. 5-9). pap. 8.99 *(978-0-545-21493-3(9),* Scholastic Paperbacks) Scholastic, Inc.

—Girls' Life Guide to Being the Most Amazing You. Bokram, Karen, ed. Thomas, Bill, illus. 2010. (ENG.). 128p. (J). (gr. 5-9). pap. 8.99 *(978-0-545-21494-0(7),* Scholastic Paperbacks) Scholastic, Inc.

Schrier, Allyson Valentine. A Girl's Guide to Soccer, 1 vol. 2012. (Get in the Game Ser.). (ENG.). 32p. (gr. 3-4). lib. bdg. 27.99 *(978-1-4296-7671-7(X),* Snap Bks.) Capstone Press of Coughlan Cos.

Scollen, C. My Big Book for Girls. 2009. 80p. (J). 12.99 *(978-1-84879-046-9(5))* Make Believe Ideas GBR. Dist: Nelson, Thomas Inc.

Smith, Liz. A Girl's Guide to Growing up - Booklet, 10 per packet. Perry, Gala, illus. 2005. (J). 63.95 *(978-1-55942-207-9(6))* Witcher Productions.

Snyder, Gail. Angry Girl? Girls Dealing with Feelings. 2014. (ENG.). 64p. (J). (gr. 5-12). 15.95 *(978-1-62293-030-2(4))* Enslow Pubs., Inc.

—Jealous Girl? Girls Dealing with Feelings. 2014. (ENG.). 64p. (J). (gr. 5-12). 15.95 *(978-1-62293-045-6(2))* Enslow Pubs., Inc.

—Lonely Girl? Girls Dealing with Feelings. 2014. (ENG.). 64p. (J). (gr. 5-12). 15.95 *(978-1-62293-055-5(X))* Enslow Pubs., Inc.

Sokol, Dawn DeVries. The Doodle Circle: A Fill-In Journal for BFFs to Share. 2013. (ENG.). 160p. (J). (gr. 3-7). pap. 12.95 *(978-1-61769-053-2(8),* Amulet Bks.) Abrams, Inc.

Spector, Todd. How to Pee: Potty Training for Girls. Chung, Arree, illus. 2016. (ENG.). 40p. (J). 12.99 *(978-1-62779-297-4(X),* 9781627792974, Holt, Henry & Co. Bks. For Young Readers) Holt, Henry & Co.

Stillman, Sarah. Soul Searching: A Girl's Guide to Finding Herself. Gross, Susan, illus. 2012. (ENG.). 176p. (YA). (gr. 7). pap. 9.99 *(978-1-58270-303-9(5))* Simon Pulse/Beyond Words.

Stortz, Diane M. Sweetest Story Bible: Sweet Thoughts & Sweet Words for Little Girls, 1 vol. Bailey, Sheila, illus. 2010. (ENG.). 224p. (J). 16.99 *(978-0-310-71673-0(X))* Zonderkidz.

Strickland, Jennifer. Pretty from the Inside Out: Discover All the Ways God Made You Special. 2015. (ENG.). 128p. (J). pap. 10.99 *(978-0-7369-5634-5(4))* Harvest Hse. Pubs.

Stride, Lottie & Oliver, Martin. Girls Only: How to Survive Anything! Geremia, Daniela & Ecob, Simon, illus. 2012. (Best at Everything Ser.). (ENG.). 64p. (J). (gr. 3-7). pap. 6.99 *(978-0-545-43095-1(X),* Scholastic Paperbacks) Scholastic, Inc.

Swain, Claudia. What's a Girl to Do? 2004. 128p. pap. 6.99 *(978-1-56309-440-8(1))* New Hope Pubs.

Swann, Elaine. Girls Have Style... at School! A Glam Girl's Guide to Taking on the Day with Grace & Style. 2005. (Illus.). (YA). pap. 8.95 *(978-0-9773520-0-5(5))* W S Publishing.

Telgemeier, Raina. Smile. 2010. 21.00 *(978-1-60686-896-6(9))* Perfection Learning Corp.

—Smile. 2010. (ENG.). 224p. (J). (gr. 3-7). 24.99 *(978-0-545-13205-3(3));* (Illus.). pap. 10.99 *(978-0-545-13206-0(1))* Scholastic, Inc. (Graphix).

—Smile. 2010. lib. bdg. 22.10 *(978-0-606-14082-9(4),* Turtleback) Turtleback Bks.

Terp, Gail. Malala Yousafzai. 2017. (Women Who Rock Ser.). (ENG.). 32p. (gr. 3-7). 31.35 ***(978-1-68072-064-8(3))*** Black Rabbit Bks.

Thomas Nelson Publishing Staff. Brave Girls - Better Than Perfect: A 90-Day Devotional for Brave Girls Like You!, 1 vol. 2015. (ENG., Illus.). 144p. (J). pap. 7.99 *(978-0-7180-3052-0(4))* Nelson, Thomas Inc.

Thomas Nelson, Thomas. Brave Girls 365-Day Devotional, 1 vol. 2016. (ENG., Illus.). 416p. (J). 16.99 *(978-0-7180-8976-4(6))* Nelson, Thomas Inc.

Thrash, Maggie. Honor Girl: A Graphic Memoir. Thrash, Maggie, illus. 2015. (ENG., Illus.). 272p. (YA). (gr. 9). 19.99 *(978-0-7636-7382-6(X))* Candlewick Pr.

—Honor Girl: A Graphic Memoir. 2017. lib. bdg. 26.95 ***(978-0-606-39843-5(0))*** Turtleback Bks.

Tolstikova, Dasha. A Year Without Mom, 1 vol. 2015. (ENG., Illus.). 176p. (J). (gr. 4-9). 19.95 *(978-1-55498-692-7(3))* Groundwood Bks. CAN. Dist: Publishers Group West (PGW).

Turnbull, Stephanie. Fun with Friends: Style Secrets for Girls. 2013. (Girl Talk Ser.). 32p. (gr. 4-7). 31.35 *(978-1-59920-946-3(2))* Black Rabbit Bks.

—Health & Fitness: Style Secrets for Girls. 2013. (Girl Talk Ser.). 32p. (gr. 4-8). 28.50 *(978-1-59920-947-0(0))* Black Rabbit Bks.

—Health & Fitness: Style Secrets for Girls. 2014. (Girl Talk Ser.). (ENG., Illus.). 32p. (J). (gr. 4-8). pap. 9.95 *(978-1-77092-204-4(0))* Saunders Bk. Co. CAN. Dist: RiverStream Publishing.

—Looking Good: Style Secrets for Girls. 2013. (Girl Talk Ser.). 32p. (gr. 4-7). 31.35 *(978-1-59920-948-7(9))* Black Rabbit Bks.

—Looking Good: Style Secrets for Girls. 2014. (Girl Talk Ser.). (ENG., Illus.). 32p. (J). (gr. 4-8). pap. 9.95 *(978-1-77092-205-1(9))* Saunders Bk. Co. CAN. Dist: RiverStream Publishing.

Twin Sisters(r) Staff, et al. My First Bedtime Prayers for Girls. 2016. (Let's Share a Story Ser.). (Illus.). 14p. (J). bds. 5.99 *(978-1-63409-646-1(0))* Barbour Publishing, Inc.

Van Wagenen, Maya. Popular: A Memoir. 2015. (ENG.). 272p. (YA). (gr. 7). pap. 10.99 *(978-0-14-751254-3(9),* Speak) Penguin Young Readers Group.

—Popular: A Memoir. 2015. lib. bdg. 22.10 *(978-0-606-36796-7(9))* Turtleback Bks.

Vander Pluym, Andrea. Mission: Sisterhood. Waters, Susy Pilgrim, illus. 2010. 80p. (YA). *(978-0-88441-753-8(0))* Girl Scouts of the USA.

Varnadeau, Jeni. Chikchat(r) Workshop Manual. 2005. 92p. pap. 12.00 *(978-0-9766634-7-8(3))* ChikChat(r) Ink.

Wall, Joanne. Anna of Allegheny. Wall, Joanne, ed. 2009. (Illus.). 110p. (YA). pap. 20.00 *(978-0-9644283-9-3(3))* Wall, Mary Joanne.

Walsh, Sheila. You're Worth It for Girls: God Thinks You Rock! 2016. (ENG.). 112p. (J). 9.99 *(978-0-7369-6387-9(1))* Harvest Hse. Pubs.

Walton, Rick & Earl, Cheri. Psst... Secret Instructions Every Girl Should Know. 2009. (ENG.). 104p. (YA). spiral bd. 9.95 *(978-1-59369-489-0(X))* American Girl Publishing, Inc.

Weiss, S. I. Coping with the Beauty Myth: A Guide for Real Girls. 2009. (Coping Ser.). 192p. (gr. 7-12). 63.90 *(978-1-61512-014-7(9))* Rosen Publishing Group, Inc., The.

Weschler, Toni. Cycle Savvy: The Smart Teen's Guide to the Mysteries of Her Body. 2006. (ENG., Illus.). 240p. pap. 15.99 *(978-0-06-082964-3(8),* Harper Perennial) HarperCollins Pubs.

Weston, Carol. Girltalk: All the Stuff Your Sister Never Told You. 4th ed. 2004. (ENG.). 448p. pap. 14.99 *(978-0-06-058575-4(7),* Harper Perennial) HarperCollins Pubs.

Wheeler-Toppen, Jodi, et al. Girls Science Club. 2012. (Girls Science Club Ser.). (ENG.). 32p. (gr. 3-4). lib. bdg. 83.97 *(978-1-4296-8218-3(3),* Snap Bks.) Capstone Press of Coughlan Cos.

Whelan, Gloria. Waiting for the Owl's Call. Milelli, Pascal, illus. 2009. (Tales of the World Ser.). (ENG.). 32p. (J). (gr. 1-5). 17.95 *(978-1-58536-418-3(5))* Sleeping Bear Pr.

White, Anne. Lessons in Responsibility for Girls: Level One. 2006. Orig. Title: Home Economics for Home Schoolers Level One. (J). per., pupil's gde. ed. 18.95 *(978-0-9792446-2-9(5))* Messiah Publishing - Pearables.

—Lessons in Responsibility for Girls: Level Three, 3. 2005. Orig. Title: Home Economics for Home Schoolers Level Three. (J). per., pupil's gde. ed. *(978-0-9792446-4-3(1))* Messiah Publishing - Pearables.

—Lessons in Responsibility for Girls: Level Two, 2. 2006. Orig. Title: Home Economics for Home Schoolers Level Two. (J). per., pupil's gde. ed. 18.95 *(978-0-9792446-3-6(3))* Messiah Publishing - Pearables.

White, Kelly. The Girls' Life Guide to Being the Best You! Parett, Lisa, illus. 2003. 124p. (J). *(978-0-439-44978-6(2))* Scholastic, Inc.

White, Kelly & Stacy, Lori. Ask Lucky! The Girls'life Guide to Dealing with Dilemmas. 2003. (Illus.). 120p. (J). *(978-0-439-44982-3(0))* Scholastic, Inc.

Whiting, Karen & White, Rebecca. The Nature Girl: A Guide to Caring for God's Creation, 1 vol. 2014. (ENG.). 176p. (J). pap. 7.99 *(978-0-310-72500-8(3))* Zonderkidz.

Yan, Ma. The Diary of Ma Yan: The Life of a Chinese School Girl. Haski, Pierre, ed. 2006. (Illus.). 208p. reprint ed. pap. 22.00 *(978-1-4223-5712-5(0))* DIANE Publishing Co.

Yan, Ma & Haski, Pierre. The Diary of Ma Yan: The Struggles & Hopes of a Chinese Schoolgirl. 2009. (ENG.). 192p. (J). (gr. 5). pap. 5.99 *(978-0-06-076498-2(8),* Collins) HarperCollins Pubs.

Yolen, Jane & Stemple, Heidi E. Y. Bad Girls: Sirens, Jezebels, Murderesses, Thieves & Other Female Villains. Guay, Rebecca, illus. 2015. (ENG.). 128p. (J). (gr. 7-9). 18.95 *(978-1-4301-1785-8(0))* Live Oak Media.

GIRLS—EDUCATION

see Women—Education

GIRLS—EMPLOYMENT

see Child Labor

GIRLS—FICTION

Abbot, Belle K. Leah Mordecai. 2006. pap. *(978-1-4065-0341-8(X))* Dodo Pr.

Abbott, Ellen Jensen. Watersmeet, 0 vols. 2012. (Watersmeet Ser.: 1). (ENG.). 352p. (YA). (gr. 7-11). pap. 8.99 *(978-0-7614-5992-7(8),* 9780761459927, Amazon Children's Publishing) Amazon Publishing.

Abbott, Hailey. The Other Boy. 2008. (ENG.). 272p. (YA). (gr. 9-18). pap. 8.99 *(978-0-06-125383-6(9),* HarperTeen) HarperCollins Pubs.

Abbott, Jane. Janny. 2011. 286p. 48.95 *(978-1-258-08786-9(3))* Literary Licensing, LLC.

Abbott, Roz. A Bump in the Road. Seltzer, Jerry Joe, illus. 2013. 26p. (J). 16.95 *(978-1-60131-179-5(6))* Big Tent Bks.

Abdul-Rauf, Muhammad. The Story of Tawaddud: A Brilliant & Beautiful Girl & a Model of Good Moral Conduct. 2005. xx, 185p. *(978-983-9184-66-2(0))* Institut Perkembangan Minda.

Abegg, Rainbow. Mom, Are You There? 2004. (Illus.). (J). *(978-1-59156-437-9(9))* Covenant Communications.

Ackelsberg, Amy. Berry Bitty Bakers. MJ Illustrations Staff, illus. 2011. (Strawberry Shortcake Ser.). (ENG.). 24p. (J). (gr. -1-k). pap. 4.99 *(978-0-448-45695-9(8),* Grosset & Dunlap) Penguin Young Readers Group.

—The Sweetest Friends. 2013. (Lalaloopsy Ser.). (ENG., Illus.). 24p. (J). (gr. -1-3). 4.99 *(978-0-545-53366-9(X))* Scholastic, Inc.

Adams, Denise H. Annabelle's Angels. Adams, Denise H., illus. 2007. (Illus.). 24p. (J). (gr. -1-3). 11.99 *(978-1-59879-386-4(1))* Lifevest Publishing, Inc.

Adams, Jean Ekman. A Cowgirl & her Horse. 2011. (Illus.). 32p. (J). 15.95 *(978-1-933855-71-4(1))* Rio Nuevo Pubs.

Adams, Jennifer Lynn. For I Am Always with You: Valerie's True Fairy Tale. 2012. 46p. pap. 20.95 *(978-1-4497-4910-1(0),* WestBow Pr.) Author Solutions, Inc.

Adams, Laurie Gifford. Finding Atticus. 2009. 208p. pap. 14.95 *(978-1-4401-3779-2(X))* iUniverse, Inc.

Adams, Mark Wayne. Good NightMare. 2007. (ENG.). 32p. (J). (gr. -1-1). lib. bdg. 12.99 *(978-1-59616-001-9(2),* SYP Kids) Southern Yellow Pine (SYP) Publishing LLC.

Adler, Denise. Thank You for Looking for Me. 2010. 20p. 12.99 *(978-1-4520-2438-7(3))* AuthorHouse.

Agraso, Alberto & Dojeiji, Mony. I Am Happy. Agraso, Alberto, illus. 2013. (Illus.). 36p. pap. *(978-0-9878762-3-2(6))* Walking for Peace Publishing.

Aguirre, Ann. Horde. 2014. (Razorland Trilogy Ser.: 3). (ENG.). 464p. (YA). (gr. 7). pap. 10.99 *(978-1-250-05077-9(4),* 9781250050779) Square Fish.

Ahlberg, Allan. Miss Dirt the Dustman's Daughter. Ross, Tony, illus. (ENG.). 24p. (J). pap. 6.95 *(978-0-14-037882-5(0))* Penguin Bks., Ltd. GBR. Dist: Trafalgar Square Publishing.

Albin, Gennifer. Altered. 2014. (Crewel World Ser.: 2). (ENG.). 416p. (YA). (gr. 7). pap. 10.99 *(978-1-250-05073-1(1),* 9781250050731) Square Fish.

Alcott, Louisa May. Eight Cousins. 2005. 300p. pap. 14.95 *(978-1-59540-676-7(X),* 1st World Library - Literary Society) 1st World Publishing, Inc.

—Eight Cousins. 2005. 120p. per. 4.95 *(978-1-4209-2569-2(5))* Digireads.com Publishing.

—Eight Cousins. 2007. (Dover Children's Evergreen Classics Ser.). (ENG.). 224p. (J). (gr. 4-7). per. 5.99 *(978-0-486-45559-4(9))* Dover Pubns., Inc.

—Eight Cousins. 2004. reprint ed. pap. 1.99 *(978-1-4192-1740-1(2))* Kessinger Publishing, LLC.

—A Garland for Girls. 2006. pap. *(978-1-4065-0587-0(0))* Dodo Pr.

—A Garland for Girls. 2006. 300p. pap. 19.95 *(978-1-59462-405-6(4),* 441, Book Jungle) Standard Pubns., Inc.

—Kitty's Class Day. l.t. ed. 2005. 424p. pap. *(978-1-84637-055-7(8))* Echo Library.

—An Old-Fashioned Girl. 2013. (Works of Louisa May Alcott). 409p. reprint ed. lthr. 79.00 *(978-0-7812-1628-9(1))* Reprint Services Corp.

—Les Quatre Filles du Docteur March.Tr. of Little Women. (FRE.). (J). pap. 19.95 *(978-2-07-051516-5(8))* Gallimard, Editions FRA. Dist: Distribooks, Inc.

—Silver Pitchers & Independence. 2011. 208p. 26.95 *(978-1-4638-9587-7(9));* pap. 14.95 *(978-1-60664-548-2(X))* Rodgers, Alan Bks.

Aldridge, Janet. The Meadow-Brook Girls Afloat. rev. ed. 2006. 208p. 27.95 *(978-1-4218-1766-8(7));* pap. 12.95 *(978-1-4218-1866-5(3))* 1st World Publishing, Inc. (1st World Library - Literary Society).

Alexander, Dorothy. Ce Ce & Her Shadow. 2012. 24p. pap. 15.99 *(978-1-4691-9090-7(7))* Xlibris Corp.

Alexander, Sy. Pinksta & the Polka Dotted-Pinstriped-Pants-Wearing Princess. Young, Aviance, illus. 2005. (J). per. 9.00 *(978-0-9655726-2-0(5))* Proud 2-B Me Publishing!

Alfonsi, Alice, adapted by. Face-off. 2006. (Hannah Montana Ser.). (Illus.). 126p. (J). (gr. 3-7). 12.65 *(978-0-7569-8315-4(0))* Perfection Learning Corp.

Ali, Saleena. Behind My Eyes & Truly in Love Stories of Friendship & Love: Book Two. 2012. 76p. pap. 10.84 *(978-1-4669-2217-4(6))* Trafford Publishing.

Allen, Debbie. Winker & the Kitten. 2009. 28p. pap. 13.99 *(978-1-4389-8266-3(6))* AuthorHouse.

Allen-Vath, Ami. Prom Bitch. 2016. (ENG.). 240p. (J). (gr. 8). 16.99 *(978-1-63450-184-2(5),* Sky Pony Pr.) Skyhorse Publishing Co., Inc.

Alsius, Lourdes. Unos Padres Para Aruna. 2005. (SPA.). 32p. (J). 18.95 *(978-84-8418-096-8(4))* Zendrera Zariquiey, Editorial ESP. Dist: Iaconi, Mariuccia Bk. Imports.

Alsop - Jinks, A. G. Kylie & the Butterfly. 2011. 16p. pap. 8.32 *(978-1-4634-0859-6(5))* AuthorHouse.

Alvarado, I. J. The Adventures of Saleiah & Emm: Book 1. Zacker, Sandi, illus. 2009. 16p. pap. 11.99 *(978-1-4490-0515-3(2))* AuthorHouse.

Amato, Anne McCoy. Moving Shelly: A Novel. 2010. 148p. (gr. 4-6). pap. 12.95 *(978-1-4502-2584-7(5))* iUniverse, Inc.

American Girl Magazine: Jan/Feb 2004. (J). 19.75 *(978-1-58485-925-3(3))* American Girl Publishing, Inc.

American Girl Magazine: July/Aug 2004 Jumbo Issue. (J). 24.75 *(978-1-58485-928-4(8))* American Girl Publishing, Inc.

American Girl Magazine: March/April 2004. (J). 19.75 *(978-1-58485-926-0(1))* American Girl Publishing, Inc.

American Girl Magazine: May/June 2004. (J). 19.75 *(978-1-58485-927-7(X))* American Girl Publishing, Inc.

American Girl Magazine: Sept/Oct 2004. (J). 19.75 *(978-1-58485-929-1(6))* American Girl Publishing, Inc.

Andersen, Hans Christian. Hans Andersen's Fairy Tales. Lewis, Naomi, tr. from DAN. 2nd ed. 2010. (Puffin Classics Ser.). (ENG., Illus.). 176p. (J). (gr. 5-7). pap. 5.99 *(978-0-14-132901-7(7),* Puffin Books) Penguin Young Readers Group.

—The Little Match Seller. 2005. (SPA.). 12p. (J). pap. *(978-958-30-1509-0(1))* Panamericana Editorial.

Anderson, Alice. Penny's Love for Cats. 2012. 20p. pap. 17.99 *(978-1-4772-9245-7(4))* AuthorHouse.

Anderson, David. Emily's Imaginary Airplane. 2013. 24p. pap. 10.99 *(978-1-4808-0347-3(2))* Archway Publishing.

Anderson, Geraldine. Bev's Amazing Adventures Book Ii: The Girl from Peru. 2013. 20p. pap. 24.95 *(978-1-62709-129-9(7))* America Star Bks.

Anderson, Laurie Halse. Speak. 2011. (ENG.). 224p. (YA). (gr. 7-12). pap. 10.99 *(978-0-312-67439-7(2),* 9780312674397) Square Fish.

Anderson, Pamela. My New School: Brunette Girl. Lee, Han & Wu, Stacie, illus. 2004. (J). 12.95 *(978-1-932555-06-6(4))* Watch Me Grow Kids.

Anderson, R. J. Ultraviolet. 2013. (ENG.). 312p. (YA). (gr. 7-12). pap. 9.95 *(978-1-4677-0914-9(X),* Carolrhoda Lab™) Lerner Publishing Group.

Anderson, William. Hallie's Bad Day, 1 vol. 2009. 48p. pap. 16.95 *(978-1-60836-681-1(2))* America Star Bks.

Andrews, Carol. The Giggle Wind. 2003. (Illus.). 40p. 17.95 *(978-0-9725609-2-4(0))* Diakonia Publishing.

Andrews, Jackie. Goldilocks & the Three Bears. Taylor, Lawrie, illus. 2012. (ENG.). 32p. (J). pap. 6.50 *(978-1-84135-191-9(1))* Award Pubns. Ltd. GBR. Dist: Parkwest Pubns., Inc.

Andrews, V. C. Garden of Shadows. 2010. (ENG.). 368p. (YA). (gr. 9). pap. 9.99 *(978-1-4424-0643-8(7),* Simon Pulse) Simon Pulse.

Anfousse, Ginette. Mon Ami Pichou. 2004. (FRE.). (J). (gr. -1-1). spiral bd. *(978-0-616-01824-8(X))* Canadian National Institute for the Blind/Institut National Canadien pour les Aveugles.

Angel, Embracing. Miranda the Flying Mermaid. 2010. 36p. pap. 18.99 *(978-1-4490-9563-5(1))* AuthorHouse.

Angelina, Laura. A Little Girl's Wish. 2013. 32p. pap. 19.99 *(978-1-4772-9896-1(7))* AuthorHouse.

Angelique, Aj. Lady Cy. 2011. 108p. pap. 7.95 *(978-1-4583-5494-5(6))* Lulu Pr., Inc.

Anholt, Laurence. El Jardin Magico de Claude Monet. 2004.Tr. of Magical Garden of Claude Monet. (SPA., Illus.). 28p. (J). 19.99 *(978-84-8488-101-8(6))* Serres, Ediciones, S. L. ESP. Dist: Lectorum Pubns., Inc.

Anna. The Magic Money Tree. 2009. (Illus.). 20p. pap. 15.49 *(978-1-4389-0472-6(X))* AuthorHouse.

Anns, Lynn. Tent City Princess. 2013. 224p. pap. 9.99 *(978-1-939403-05-6(7))* PageSpring Publishing.

Anonymous. Calling Maggie May. 2015. (ENG., Illus.). 272p. (YA). (gr. 9). pap. 10.99 *(978-1-4814-3901-5(4),* Simon Pulse) Simon Pulse.

Answer Why for Mee Mee: Work & Play Book. 2006. (J). *(978-0-9748715-3-0(2))* Vision Harmony Publishing.

Antillano, Laura. Diana en la Tierra Wayuu. Armas, Lourdes, illus. 2003. (SPA.). 121p. (YA). (gr. 5-8). pap. 9.95 *(978-958-24-0180-1(X))* Santillana COL. Dist: Santillana USA Publishing Co., Inc.

Applegate, Katherine. Spring Break. 2010. (Summer Ser.). (ENG., Illus.). 240p. (YA). (gr. 9-18). pap. 8.99 *(978-1-4169-9094-9(1),* Simon Pulse) Simon Pulse.

Arai, Kiyoko. Beauty Pop, Vol. 1. 2006. (ENG., Illus.). 208p. pap. 8.99 *(978-1-4215-0575-6(4))* Viz Media.

Argueta, Jorge & Alvarez, Cecilia Concepcion. Moony Luna: Luna, Lunita Lunera. Gomez, Elizabeth, illus. 2005. (ENG & SPA.). 32p. (J). 16.95 *(978-0-89239-205-6(3))* Lee & Low Bks., Inc.

Arlen, Richard. Girls' Boarding School. 320p. pap. 6.95 *(978-0-7472-4039-6(6))* Headline Publishing Group GBR. Dist: Trafalgar Square Publishing.

Armstrong, Bill. Letters from Ozo, 1. 2005. (Illus.). 190p. (J). per. *(978-0-9771676-0-9(7))* Rubicon Bks.

Arnold, Shauna. Baa. Hines, Irene, illus. 2004. 19p. (J). (gr. -1-3). 12.00 *(978-0-9743669-0-6(0))* Trinity Bks.

Arrington, Linda. Ugly Trees. Arrington, Linda, photos by. 2012. (Illus.). 24p. pap. 24.95 *(978-1-4626-8925-5(6))* America Star Bks.

Asai, Carrie. The Book of the Pearl. Verhoye, Annabelle & Alarcao, Renato, illus. 2003. (Samurai Girl Ser.: 3). (ENG.). 240p. (YA). (gr. 11). pap. 6.99 *(978-0-689-86432-2(9),* Simon Pulse) Simon Pulse.

Asai, Carrie & Gray, Mitchel. The Book of the Wind. Verhoye, Annabelle & Alarcão, Renato, illus. 2003. (Samurai Girl Ser.: 4). (ENG.). 224p. (YA). (gr. 11). pap. 6.99 *(978-0-689-86433-9(7),* Simon Pulse) Simon Pulse.

Askew, Kim & Helmes, Amy. Tempestuous. Mitchard, Jacquelyn, ed. 2014. (Twisted Lit Ser.). (ENG.). 224p. (YA). pap. 9.99 *(978-1-4405-8283-7(1),* Simon Pulse) Simon Pulse.

Asner, Anne-Marie. Shluffy Girl l.t. ed. 2005. (Illus.). 32p. (J). (gr. -1-3). per. 6.95 *(978-0-9753629-2-1(5))* Matzah Ball Bks.

—Shmutzy Girl. Asner, Anne-Marie, illus. l.t. ed. 2004. (Illus.). 32p. (J). (gr. -1-3). per. 6.95 *(978-0-9753629-0-7(9))* Matzah Ball Bks.

Atkins, Carla. Kiara & the Butterfly. 2012. 52p. pap. 24.99 *(978-1-4685-2323-2(6))* AuthorHouse.

Atkins, Jeannine. Preparadas... Listas... Ya! 2004. (SPA., Illus.). (J). (gr. k-3). spiral bd. *(978-0-616-07274-5(0))* Canadian National Institute for the Blind/Institut National Canadien pour les Aveugles.

Aumann, Jane & Ladage, Cindy. The Christmas Tractor. Freitag, Charles, illus. 2003. 30p. (J). (gr. k-4). pap. 8.95 *(978-0-9703319-2-2(4))* Roots & Wings.

Aunt Fezzie. Happy-Feliz & Fatso's Heroic School Adventures: Heroes vs. Bullies. 2013. 32p. pap. 13.99 *(978-1-4808-0134-9(8))* Archway Publishing.

Austin, Rikey. Captain's Treasure: Alice's Bear Shop. 2012. 28p. pap. *(978-1-78092-149-5(7))* MX Publishing, Ltd.

—Cobby Goes for a Swim: Alice's Bear Shop. 2012. 28p. pap. *(978-1-78092-164-8(0))* MX Publishing, Ltd.

—Sandy Paints a Picture: Alice's Bear Shop. 2012. 28p. pap. *(978-1-78092-155-6(1))* MX Publishing, Ltd.

—Tat Gets a Patch: Alice's Bear Shop. 2012. 28p. pap. *(978-1-78092-161-7(6))* MX Publishing, Ltd.

—Tilly & the Magic Wand: Alice's Bear Shop. 2012. 28p. pap. *(978-1-78092-146-4(2))* MX Publishing, Ltd.

—Ting Finds a Bell: Alice's Bear Shop. 2012. 28p. pap. *(978-1-78092-158-7(6))* MX Publishing, Ltd.

—Woodroffe Growls Again: Alice's Bear Shop. 2012. (Illus.). 32p. pap. *(978-1-78092-085-6(7))* MX Publishing, Ltd.

Avi. The Secret School. 2003. (ENG., Illus.). 176p. (J). (gr. 2-5). pap. 7.99 *(978-0-15-204699-6(2),* 53582853) Houghton Mifflin Harcourt Publishing Co.

—The True Confessions of Charlotte Doyle. (EMC Masterpiece Series Access Editions). xvii, 187p. (J). 11.99 *(978-0-8219-1983-5(0))* EMC/Paradigm Publishing.

Avia. Sunshine & Ladybug: In Angel Balloons. 2013. 32p. pap. 17.25 *(978-1-4669-6380-1(8))* Trafford Publishing.

Ayer, Jacqueline, creator. The Paper-Flower Tree. 2017. (ENG.). 40p. (J). (gr. -1-3). 16.95 *(978-1-59270-224-4(4))* Enchanted Lion Bks., LLC.

Aylesworth, Jim. Goldilocks & the Three Bears. McClintock, Barbara, illus. 2003. (ENG.). 32p. (J). (gr. -1-3). 17.99 *(978-0-439-39545-8(3),* Scholastic Pr.) Scholastic, Inc.

Ayozie, Ben-EL. Ants Everywhere. 2011. 20p. 11.49 *(978-1-4520-3431-7(1))* AuthorHouse.

AZ Books, creator. Fashion Collection. 2013. (My Workshop Ser.). (ENG., Illus.). 46p. (J). (gr. 1-3). spiral bd. 14.95 *(978-1-61889-073-5(5))* AZ Bks. LLC.

—My Favorite Pet. 2013. (Velvet Fantasy Ser.). (ENG., Illus.). 16p. (J). (gr. k-3). pap. 4.95 *(978-1-61889-293-5(2))* AZ Bks. LLC.

AZ Books Staff. Fashion Ideas. Batan, Natalia, ed. 2012. (Fashion Ideas Ser.). (ENG.). 60p. (J). bds. 15.95 *(978-1-61889-075-7(1))* AZ Bks. LLC.

—Movie Star. Puzik, Uljana, ed. 2012. (Lovely Charmie Ser.). (ENG.). 16p. (J). (gr. 1-3). pap. 6.95 *(978-1-61889-184-6(7))* AZ Bks. LLC.

Azuma, Kiyohiko. Azumanga Daioh, Vol. 3. 2004. (Illus.). 172p. (YA). pap. 9.99 *(978-1-4139-0030-9(5))* ADV Manga.

Babiak, Alexandra Brittany. The Runaway Jacket, 1 vol. 2009. 40p. pap. 24.95 *(978-1-60749-332-7(2))* America Star Bks.

Babineaux, Jason James. That's What Big Girls Do! 2013. 32p. pap. 24.95 *(978-1-4489-2712-8(9))* America Star Bks.

Bacon, Josephine Daskam. While Caroline was Growing: Books about Children. 2007. (ENG.). 178p. pap. 19.99 *(978-1-4346-0447-7(0));* 196p. pap. 21.99 *(978-1-4346-0448-4(9))* Creative Media Partners, LLC.

Baicker, Karen & Chronicle Books Staff. I Can Do It Too! Wilson-Max, Ken, illus. 2010. (ENG.). (J). (gr. -1 — 1). bds. 9.99 *(978-0-8118-7560-8(1))* Chronicle Bks. LLC.

Bailey, Helen. Life at the Shallow End. 2010. (ENG., Illus.). 304p. (YA). (gr. 7-17). pap. 9.99 *(978-0-340-94538-4(9))* Hodder & Stoughton GBR. Dist: Hachette Bk. Group.

—Out of My Depth. 2010. (ENG.). 304p. (YA). (gr. 7-17). pap. 9.99 *(978-0-340-95029-6(3))* Hodder & Stoughton GBR. Dist: Hachette Bk. Group.

—Swimming Against the Tide. 2010. (ENG.). 320p. (YA). (gr. 7-17). pap. 9.99 *(978-0-340-95030-2(7))* Hodder & Stoughton GBR. Dist: Hachette Bk. Group.

Bailey, Mary. Vhan Zeely & the Time Prevaricators. 2009. 192p. 25.50 *(978-1-60693-477-7(5),* Eloquent Bks.) Strategic Book Publishing & Rights Agency (SBPRA).

Bailey, Mary R. Vhan Zeely & the Time Prevaricators. 2009. 188p. pap. 12.95 *(978-1-60911-003-1(X),* Eloquent Bks.) Strategic Book Publishing & Rights Agency (SBPRA).

Bajpai, Sneha. Grant Me a Wish: Sometimes... you do get exactly what you wish For. 2010. 28p. pap. 12.49 *(978-1-4490-9780-6(4))* AuthorHouse.

Balaskovits, A. A. Magic for Unlucky Girls: Stories. 2017. (SFWP Literary Awards Ser.). (ENG.). 230p. pap. 14.95 *(978-1-939650-66-5(6))* Santa Fe Writers Project.

Baliko, Janelle. It Doesn't Have to be Pink. Hackmann, Bethany, illus. 2007. 32p. (J). 14.95 *(978-0-9799012-0-1(0))* Baliko, Janelle A.

Ball, Duncan. An Eyeful of Emily. 2007. 336p. *(978-0-7322-8568-5(2))* HarperCollins Pubs. Australia.

Balzola, Asun. Munia y Sra. Piltronera (Munia & Mrs. Piltronera) (SPA.). 36p. (J). 16.95 *(978-84-233-1290-0(9))* Ediciones Destino ESP. Dist: AIMS International Bks., Inc.

Balzola, Asun & Asun, Balzola. Babi es Barbara. (SPA.). 72p. 8.95 *(978-84-392-8113-9(7))* Baker & Taylor Bks.

Bang, Molly. When Sophie Gets Angry - Really, Really Angry. 2004. (Scholastic Bookshelf Ser.). (Illus.). 36p. (gr. -1-3). 17.00 *(978-0-7569-3206-0(8))* Perfection Learning Corp.

Baniti, Nailah. Nana's Sweetie-Pie-Chicken. 2012. 32p. pap. 9.99 *(978-0-9853574-1-2(X))* Mountan Creek Pubns.

Banks, Anna. Of Poseidon. 2013. (Syrena Legacy Ser.: 1). (ENG.). 384p. (YA). (gr. 8-12). pap. 10.99 *(978-1-250-02736-8(5),* 9781250027368) Square Fish.

Banting, Celia. I only said I was telling the Truth. 2006. 240p. (YA). per. 14.99 *(978-0-9786648-4-8(1))* Wighita Pr.

—I Only Said Yes So That They'd Like Me. 2006. (Illus.). 224p. (YA). per. 14.99 *(978-0-9786648-1-7(7))* Wighita Pr.

Barbara Stathi. Sacrifice. 2009. 312p. pap. 18.95 *(978-1-4401-7699-9(X))* iUniverse, Inc.

Barber, Antonia. Dancing Shoes: Lucy's Next Step, Vol. 4. (Illus.). 96p. (J). 5.95 *(978-0-14-038685-1(8))* Penguin Bks., Ltd. GBR. Dist: Trafalgar Square Publishing.

Barber, Barbara E. Allie's Basketball Dream. Ligasan, Darryl, illus. 2013. (ENG.). 32p. (J). (gr. 2-2). pap. 9.95 *(978-1-880000-72-4(5))* Lee & Low Bks., Inc.

Barchers, Suzanne I. The Wounded Lion: A Tale from Spain. Joven, John, illus. 2013. (Tales of Honor Ser.). (ENG.). 32p. (gr. 1-3). pap. 8.95 *(978-1-937529-63-5(0))* Red Chair Pr.

Bardwell, Harrison. Roberta's Flying Courage. 2003. (ENG.). 248p. pap. 13.95 *(978-1-55753-335-7(0),* 9e38e2dc-8c18-49c1-8447-1205f9e2b108) Purdue Univ. Pr.

Barfield, Asia. My Inspiration. 2009. 14p. 10.70 *(978-0-557-05867-9(8))* Lulu Pr., Inc.

Barkley, Callie. Ellie the Flower Girl. Bishop, Tracy, illus. 2016. (Critter Club Ser.: 14). (ENG.). 128p. (J). (gr. k-4). pap. 5.99 *(978-1-4814-6718-6(2),* Little Simon) Little Simon.

—Ellie the Flower Girl. 2016. (Critter Club Ser.: 14). lib. bdg. 16.00 *(978-0-606-38965-5(2))* Turtleback Bks.

Barnaby, Hannah. Wonder Show. 2013. (ENG., Illus.). 288p. (YA). (gr. 7). pap. 8.99 *(978-0-544-10483-9(8))* Houghton Mifflin Harcourt Publishing Co.

Barnes, Charlotte. Stella Ducktropolis. 2008. 36p. pap. 11.95 *(978-1-4327-1806-0(1))* Outskirts Pr., Inc.

Barnes, Vivi. Olivia Twisted. 2013. (Olivia Twisted Ser.: 1). (ENG.). 352p. (J). (gr. 7-12). pap. 9.99 *(978-1-62266-028-5(5),* 9781622660285) Entangled Publishing, LLC.

Barnholdt, Lauren. Hailey Twitch & the Wedding Glitch. Beaky, Suzanne, illus. 2011. (Hailey Twitch Ser.: 4). (ENG.). 144p. (J). (gr. 2-4). pap. 6.99 *(978-1-4022-2447-8(8),* Sourcebooks Jabberwocky) Sourcebooks, Inc.

Barrett, Ms S. Moe. Mangoe & Marlie: Mangoe Takes Care of Marlie. 2013. 56p. pap. 11.93 *(978-0-9701289-5-9(9))* Moselle Productions, Inc.

Barrows, Annie. Ivy + Bean - What's the Big Idea? Blackall, Sophie, illus. 2011. (ENG.). 132p. (J). (gr. 1-5). pap. 5.99 *(978-1-4521-0236-8(8))* Chronicle Bks. LLC.

Barry, Debra R. Debbie's Eyes. Tessier, Beth Marie, photos by. 2011. (Illus.). 32p. pap. 24.95 *(978-1-4560-5272-0(1))* America Star Bks.

Barson, Kelly. 45 Pounds. 2014. (ENG.). 272p. (YA). (gr. 7). pap. 9.99 *(978-0-14-242265-6(7),* Speak) Penguin Young Readers Group.

—45 Pounds (More or Less) 2013. (ENG.). 272p. (YA). (gr. 7). 16.99 *(978-0-670-78482-0(6),* Viking Books for Young Readers) Penguin Young Readers Group.

Barta, Jeralyn. Rolling with Life. 2010. 24p. pap. 15.99 *(978-1-4490-6862-2(6))* AuthorHouse.

Baruch, M. P. Spend the Day with Me. Arscott, Dean, illus. 2009. 20p. pap. 10.95 *(978-1-936051-27-4(3))* Peppertree Pr., The.

Baskin, Nora Raleigh. The Summer Before Boys. (ENG.). 208p. (J). (gr. 4-7). 2012. pap. 6.99 *(978-1-4169-8674-4(X))* 2011. 16.99 *(978-1-4169-8673-7(1))* Simon & Schuster Bks. For Young Readers. (Simon & Schuster Bks. For Young Readers).

Bass, Karen. Drummer Girl, 1 vol. 2011. (ENG.). 192p. (YA). (gr. 8-12). pap. 14.95 *(978-1-55050-462-0(2))* Coteau Bks. CAN. Dist: Orca Bk. Pubs. USA.

Bassoff, Leah & DeLuca, Laura. Lost Girl Found, 1 vol. 2014. (ENG., Illus.). 192p. (J). (gr. 7). 16.95 *(978-1-55498-416-9(5))* Groundwood Bks. CAN. Dist: Publishers Group West (PGW).

Bates, Helen. A Girl Like Tilly. Li, Ellen, illus. 2016. (ENG.). 72p. (J). 15.95 *(978-1-78592-163-6(0),* 8435) Kingsley, Jessica Pubs. GBR. Dist: Macmillan Distribution Ltd.

Bates, Marni. Invisible. 2013. (Smith High Ser.). (ENG.). 288p. (YA). (gr. 9). pap. 9.95 *(978-0-7582-6938-6(2),* K-Teen) Kensington Publishing Corp.

Baum, L. Frank. Mary Louise & the Liberty Girls. 2007. (ENG.). 144p. pap. 18.99 *(978-1-4346-4333-9(6));* 160p. pap. 21.99 *(978-1-4346-4334-6(4))* Creative Media Partners, LLC.

—The Patchwork Girl of Oz. rev. ed. 2006. 272p. 28.95 *(978-1-4218-1793-4(4));* pap. 13.95 *(978-1-4218-1893-1(0))* 1st World Publishing, Inc. (1st World Library - Literary Society).

—The Patchwork Girl of Oz. 2004. reprint ed. pap. 22.95 *(978-1-4191-7678-4(1));* pap. 1.99 *(978-1-4192-7678-1(6))* Kessinger Publishing, LLC.

—The Patchwork Girl of Oz. 2004. (Twelve-Point Ser.). lib. bdg. 24.00 *(978-1-58287-275-9(9))* North Bks.

Baum, L. Frank & van Dyne, Edith. Mary Louise Solves a Mystery. 2011. 140p. 24.95 *(978-1-4638-9498-6(8))* Rodgers, Alan Bks.

Baumgartner, John Robert. Rori's Ghost: The Secret of the Stone Stairs. 2012. 296p. 27.95 *(978-1-4626-6310-1(9))* America Star Bks.

Beach, Kathleen H. & Weeber, Stephanie B. Madison's Mixed-up Flower Girl Magic & Aiden's Amazing Ring Bearer Act Aiden's Amazing Ring Bearer Act. Baisley, Maryann Leake, illus. 2009. 32p. pap. 19.95 *(978-1-4251-7059-2(5))* Trafford Publishing.

Beacon Street Girls Staff. Meet the Beacon Street Girls. 2004. (Illus.). 36p. (J). pap. 3.99 *(978-0-9746587-5-9(8),* Beacon Street Girls) B*tween Productions, Inc.

Beasley, Kate. Gertie's Leap to Greatness. Tamaki, Jillian, illus. 2016. (ENG.). 256p. (J). 16.99 *(978-0-374-30261-0(8),* 9780374302610, Farrar, Straus & Giroux (BYR)) Farrar, Straus & Giroux.

Because of Walter, 6 Packs. (Action Packs Ser.). 104p. (gr. 3-5). 44.00 *(978-0-7635-8402-3(9))* Rigby Education.

Becker, Aaron. Journey. Becker, Aaron, illus. 2013. (ENG., Illus.). 40p. (J). (gr. -1-3). 15.99 *(978-0-7636-6053-6(1))* Candlewick Pr.

Becker Holstein, Barbara. The Truth: I'm a Girl, I'm Smart, & I Know Everything! 2007. (Illus.). 91p. (J). per. 6.95 *(978-0-9798952-0-3(0))* Enchanted Self Pr.

Bee, Stevie J. Cross Your Heart. 2009. 216p. 25.50 *(978-1-60860-133-2(1),* Eloquent Bks.) Strategic Book Publishing & Rights Agency (SBPRA).

Beeke, Joel R. & Kleyn, Diana. How God Used a Snowdrift. Anderson, Jeff, illus. 2013. (Building on the Rock Ser.). (ENG.). 176p. (J). pap. 8.99 *(978-1-85792-817-4(2),* 9781857928174, CF4Kids) Christian Focus Pubns. GBR. Dist: Bookmasters Distribution.

Bell, Anita & Bell, Belinda. 'Twas Ever. 2011. 208p. 28.99 *(978-0-557-41894-7(1));* 210p. pap. 11.99 *(978-1-257-00131-6(0))* Lulu Pr., Inc.

Bell, Joanne. Juggling Fire, 1 vol. 2009. (ENG.). 184p. (YA). (gr. 7-12). pap. 12.95 *(978-1-55469-094-7(3))* Orca Bk. Pubs. USA.

Bell-Martin, Janelle. Mary Had a Little Lamb, 1 vol. 2011. (Early Childhood Themes Ser.). (ENG.). 16p. (J). (gr. -1-2). pap. 19.99 *(978-1-4333-2358-4(3));* pap. 6.99 *(978-1-4333-2357-7(5))* Teacher Created Materials, Inc.

Bell, Sophie. Power to the Purple! Battle, Christina, illus. 2013. (Ultra Violets Ser.: 2). (ENG.). 336p. (J). (gr. 3-7). 12.99 *(978-1-59514-647-2(4),* Razorbill) Penguin Young Readers Group.

Bellingham, Brenda. Lilly Takes the Lead. MacDonald, Clarke, illus. 2006. (Formac First Novels Ser.: 34). (ENG.). 64p. (gr. 2-5). 14.95 *(978-0-88780-703-9(8),* 9780887807039) Formac Publishing Co., Ltd. CAN. Dist: Casemate Pubs. & Bk. Distributors, LLC.

—Lilly's Special Gift. MacDonald, Clarke, illus. 2005. (Formac First Novels Ser.: 32). (ENG.). 64p. (gr. 2-5). 14.95 *(978-0-88780-665-0(1),* 9780887806650) Formac Publishing Co., Ltd. CAN. Dist: Casemate Pubs. & Bk. Distributors, LLC.

—Lilly's Special Gift, 1 vol. MacDonald, Clarke & Kaulbach, Kathy, illus. 2005. (Formac First Novels Ser.: 32). (ENG.). 64p. (gr. 2-5). 4.95 *(978-0-88780-664-3(3),* 9780887806643) Formac Publishing Co., Ltd. CAN. Dist: Casemate Pubs. & Bk. Distributors, LLC.

Beltran, Andrea. Juliet's Day. 2009. 34p. pap. 24.20 *(978-0-557-18983-0(7))* Lulu Pr., Inc.

Benchmark Education Co., LLC. Look at Me! Big Book. 2014. (Shared Reading Foundations Ser.). (J). (gr. -1). *(978-1-4509-9421-7(0))* Benchmark Education Co.

—Strawberry Girl Big Book. 2014. (Shared Reading Foundations Ser.). (J). (gr. -1). *(978-1-4509-9448-4(2))* Benchmark Education Co.

Bencomo, Martin. Paloma Padilla. 2010. 32p. (J). *(978-0-9790350-3-6(1))* Star Fire.

Benedis-Grab, Daphne. The Girl in the Wall. Mitchard, Jacquelyn, ed. (ENG.). 256p. (YA). 2014. pap. 9.99 *(978-1-4405-8282-0(3))* 2012. 17.95 *(978-1-4405-5270-0(3))* Simon Pulse. (Simon Pulse).

Bennett, Donna I. Jessica's Bear. Dippold, Jane, illus. 2003. (ENG.). 32p. (J). pap. 9.95 *(978-1-878044-57-0(5))* Mayhaven Publishing, Inc.

Bennett, Marilyn J. The Poinsettia Adventure. 2010. 60p. pap. 21.99 *(978-1-4490-7108-0(2))* AuthorHouse.

Bennett, Olivia. Who What Wear! The Allegra Biscotti Collection. 2011. (ENG., Illus.). 240p. (J). (gr. 5-7). pap. 8.99 *(978-1-4022-4392-9(8),* Sourcebooks Jabberwocky) Sourcebooks, Inc.

Benson, Ken. Leela's Great Life. 2012. 28p. pap. 15.99 *(978-1-4771-2713-1(5))* Xlibris Corp.

Benson, Patty. Pretty Little Gipsy. 2013. 24p. pap. 24.95 *(978-1-62709-505-1(5))* America Star Bks.

Bentley, Sue. A Forest Charm, 6 vols. Farley, Andrew & Swan, Angela, illus. 2010. (Magic Puppy Ser.: 6). (ENG.). 128p. (J). (gr. 1-3). pap. 5.99 *(978-0-448-45065-0(8),* Grosset & Dunlap) Penguin Young Readers Group.

Benton, Jim. What I Don't Know Might Hurt Me. 2013. (Dear Dumb Diary: Year Two Ser.: 4). lib. bdg. 16.00 *(978-0-606-32009-2(1),* Turtleback) Turtleback Bks.

Berg, R. J. Jenny Martin & the Unexpected Gift. 2004. (Illus.). 139p. (YA). per. 9.95 *(978-0-9666104-2-0(3))* Ziert, Paul Assocs., Inc.

Berger, Samantha. Princess Potty. Cartwright, Amy, illus. 2010. (ENG.). 24p. (J). (gr. -1 — 1). pap. 5.99 *(978-0-545-17296-7(9),* Cartwheel Bks.) Scholastic, Inc.

Bernard, Margaret Mitchell. Kate & the Family Tree. Duncan, Shirley, ed. Ciesinska, Izabela, illus. 2009. 24p. pap. 14.99 *(978-1-4251-7408-8(6))* Trafford Publishing.

Berne, Emma Carlson. Hard to Get. 2010. (Romantic Comedies Ser.). (ENG.). 288p. (YA). (gr. 7-18). mass mkt. 6.99 *(978-1-4169-8951-6(X),* Simon Pulse) Simon Pulse.

Bernstein, Danielle V. The Magic in a Mermaid's Tear. 2013. 28p. pap. 24.95 *(978-1-62709-604-1(3))* America Star Bks.

Berridge-Burley, Niamh. The Shoes That Couldn't Stop Dancing. 2010. 28p. pap. 15.99 *(978-1-4535-1415-3(5))* Xlibris Corp.

Bertling, Judy. There's Poo on My Shoe. 2010. 36p. 17.25 *(978-1-4269-4300-3(8))* Trafford Publishing.

Beth, Libby. There's a Rainbow in the Mud. 2013. 52p. pap. 23.04 *(978-1-4669-9641-0(2))* Trafford Publishing.

Bevin, Teresa. Tina Springs into Summer/Tina Se Lanza Al Verano. Rodriguez, Perfecto, illus. 2005. (ENG & SPA.). 114p. (J). pap. 21.00 *(978-1-928589-28-0(6))* Gival Pr., LLC.

Bevis, Brittany. Two Foals, a Dash of Sprinkles & a Cherry on Top! Talley, Pam, illus. 2011. 32p. (J). 18.47 *(978-0-9824766-7-3(1));* pap. 18.47 *(978-0-9824766-8-0(X))* Caballo Pr. of Ann Arbor. (Caballito Children's Bks.).

Bibi, Zarina. The Bright Night Sky. 2012. 24p. pap. 15.49 *(978-1-4685-4566-1(3))* AuthorHouse.

Big. The Very Best Me. 2012. 24p. pap. 15.99 *(978-1-4691-5294-3(0))* Xlibris Corp.

The Big Rain. 2003. (Illus.). 32p. (J). mass mkt. *(978-0-9740599-2-1(7),* 3) Omnibus Publishing.

Billingsley, ReShonda Tate. Drama Queens. 2010. (Good Girlz Ser.: 8). (ENG., Illus.). 256p. pap. 12.99 *(978-1-4391-5687-2(5),* Gallery Bks.) Gallery Bks.

—Fair-Weather Friends. 2008. (Good Girlz Ser.: 5). (ENG.). 224p. pap. 15.99 *(978-1-4165-5876-7(4),* Gallery Bks.) Gallery Bks.

—Getting Even: Good Girlz. 2008. (Good Girlz Ser.: 4). (ENG.). 208p. pap. 11.00 *(978-1-4165-5873-6(X),* Gallery Bks.) Gallery Bks.

Binks. The Girl with Chipmunk Hands. Begonia, Ruby, illus. 2013. 24p. (J). 15.95 *(978-1-935448-20-4(X))* Lost Coast Pr.

Birch, Kate Jarvik. Perfected. 2014. (Entangled Teen Ser.). (ENG.). 304p. (YA). (gr. 7-12). 16.99 *(978-1-62266-268-5(7),* 9781622662685) Entangled Publishing, LLC.

Bird, Helen. Party Time. 2008. (Siti's Sisters Ser.). (ENG.). 36p. *(978-1-84167-726-2(4))* Ransom Publishing Ltd.

Birdsall, Bridget. Double Exposure. 2014. (ENG.). 304p. (J). (gr. 6). 16.95 *(978-1-62914-606-5(4),* Sky Pony Pr.) Skyhorse Publishing Co., Inc.

Bishop, Benita. Escape from el Monte. 2005. 155p. pap. 7.64 *(978-1-4116-1415-4(1))* Lulu Pr., Inc.

Black, Natalie & Black, Melissa. Double Sided: A Teen Novel. 2010. 124p. 23.50 *(978-1-4520-7415-3(1));* pap. 12.99 *(978-1-4520-7416-0(X))* AuthorHouse.

Blackstone, Mick. Broken Wings Will Fly, 1 vol. Wharton, Jennifer Heyd, illus. 2009. (ENG.). 32p. (J). (gr. 7-18). 10.95 *(978-0-87033-439-9(5),* 9780870334399, Cornell Maritime Pr./Tidewater Pubs.) Schiffer Publishing, Ltd.

Blackwell North America Staff. Matilda. (FRE., Illus.). (J). pap. *(978-2-07-033555-8(0))* Gallimard, Editions.

Blair, Candice. Rosie's Pink House, 1 vol. Cato, Andrea, illus. 2010. 18p. 24.95 *(978-1-4489-4619-8(0))* America Star Bks.

Blegvad, Lenore. Ana Banana y Yo. Puncel, Maria & Blegvad, Erik, trs. Blegvad, Erik, illus. 2003.Tr. of Anna Banana & Me. (SPA.). 56p. (J). (gr. k-3). pap. 9.95 *(978-84-204-4375-1(1))* Santillana USA Publishing Co., Inc.

—Ana Banana y Yo. Blegvad, Erik, illus. 14th ed. 2003.Tr. of Anna Banana & Me. (SPA.). 56p. (gr. k-3). pap. 10.95 *(978-84-204-0083-9(1),* Alfaguara) Santillana USA Publishing Co., Inc.

Blevins, Wiley. Goldilocks & the Three Ghosts. Cox, Steve, illus. 2016. (Scary Tales Retold Ser.). (ENG.). 24p. (gr. k-3). lib. bdg. 23.99 *(978-1-63440-093-0(3))* Red Chair Pr.

—Little Dead Riding Hood. Cox, Steve, illus. 2016. (Scary Tales Retold Ser.). (ENG.). 24p. (gr. k-3). lib. bdg. 23.99 *(978-1-63440-102-9(6))* Red Chair Pr.

—The on-Again, off-Again Friend: Standing up for Friends. Alley, R. W., illus. 2015. (ENG.). 24p. (J). (gr. k-2). lib. bdg. 19.99 *(978-1-63440-015-2(1))* Red Chair Pr.

—Stella... Almost: Self-Confidence. Nez, John Abbott, illus. 2015. (ENG.). 24p. (J). (gr. k-2). lib. bdg. 19.99 *(978-1-63440-006-0(2),* 1392169) Red Chair Pr.

Bloomberg, Sandi. Veronica & the Magic Fountain. 2010. (Illus.). 32p. (J). pap. 13.95 *(978-1-935268-66-6(X))* Halo Publishing International.

Blossom, F. Blossom Kingdom: The Adventures of Emily. 2005. 189p. pap. 24.95 *(978-1-4241-1112-1(9))* PublishAmerica, Inc.

Blume, Judy. Blubber. unabr. ed. 2004. 153p. (J). (gr. 3-7). pap. 29.00 incl. audio *(978-0-8072-1709-2(3),* S YA 1016 SP, Listening Library) Random Hse. Audio Publishing Group.

—Deenie. 143p. (YA). (gr. 7-18). pap. 3.99 *(978-0-8072-1360-5(8),* Listening Library) Random Hse. Audio Publishing Group.

—Double Fudge. 2004. (ENG.). 192p. (J). (gr. 3-7). 5.99 *(978-0-425-19647-2(X),* Berkley) Penguin Publishing Group.

—Otherwise Known As Sheila the Great. (Fudge Ser.). 166p. (J). pap. 4.99 *(978-0-8072-1497-8(3),* Listening Library) Random Hse. Audio Publishing Group.

Blyton, Enid. The Naughtiest Girl Again. (Illus.). 176p. (J). mass mkt. 6.95 *(978-0-09-915911-7(2))* Random Hse. GBR. Dist: Trafalgar Square Publishing.

—The Naughtiest Girl Is a Monitor. (Illus.). 160p. (J). pap. 6.95 *(978-0-09-945490-8(4))* Random Hse. GBR. Dist: Trafalgar Square Publishing.

Boase, Wendy. Caperucita Roja. Puncel, Maria, tr. Philpot, Heather, illus. (Primeros Cuentos Ser.). (SPA.). 28p. (J). (gr. k-3). pap. 7.95 *(978-1-56014-458-8(0))* Santillana USA Publishing Co., Inc.

Bodin, Alexol. Puke. 2010. 133p. pap. 11.50 *(978-0-557-29424-4(X))* Lulu Pr., Inc.

Bogunya, Angels. El Maiz Amargo. 2004. (SPA.). 144p. (J). *(978-84-263-5237-8(5))* Vives, Luis Editorial (Edelvives) ESP. Dist: Lectorum Pubns., Inc.

Bolden-Thompson, Angela. When Company Comes. 2007. 254p. pap. 19.99 *(978-0-615-14774-1(7))* Thompson, Angela Bolden.

Bolme, Edward Sarah. Jesus Heals a Little Girl. Gillette, Tim, illus. l.t. ed. 2003. 20p. (J). bds. 6.99 *(978-0-9725546-1-9(0))* CREST Pubns.

Bompart, Juanita A. Anna Pinnepole Poolah. 2011. 32p. pap. 16.95 *(978-1-4497-2335-4(7),* WestBow Pr.) Author Solutions, Inc.

Bond, Gwenda. Girl in the Shadows, 0 vols. 2016. (Cirque American Ser.: 2). (ENG.). 380p. (YA). (gr. 9-13). pap. 9.99 *(978-1-5039-5393-2(9),* 9781503953932, Skyscape) Amazon Publishing.

Booth, Sara. Poppy. Home, Nathan, illus. 2012. 28p. pap. 12.50 *(978-1-61897-666-6(4),* Strategic Bk. Publishing) Strategic Book Publishing & Rights Agency (SBPRA).

Bortnick, Lori. A Straw Hat So Big. Santos, Carriel Ann, illus. 2013. 52p. pap. 11.95 *(978-0-9851492-6-0(4))* Flying Turtle Publishing.

Boucles d'Or et les Trois Ours.Tr. of Goldilocks & the Three Bears. (FRE.). 48p. pap. 12.95 incl. audio compact disk *(978-2-89558-061-4(8))* Coffragants CAN. Dist: Penton Overseas, Inc.

Bound, Samantha-Ellen. Rhythm & Blues. 2016. (Silver Shoes Ser.: 7). (ENG., Illus.). 144p. (J). (gr. 4-7). pap. 8.99 *(978-0-85798-907-9(3))* Random Hse. Australia AUS. Dist: Independent Pubs. Group.

Bourne, Tracey. Not Just a Dream! 2009. (Illus.). 52p. pap. 11.49 *(978-1-4389-4819-5(0))* AuthorHouse.

Bowe, Julie. Victoria Torres, Unfortunately Average. 2015. (Victoria Torres, Unfortunately Average Ser.). (ENG.). 160p. (gr. 4-4). 106.60 *(978-1-4965-2028-9(9))* Stone Arch Bks.

Boynton, Cara. Sam's Secret World. 2006. (ENG.). 48p. per. 16.95 *(978-1-4241-4529-4(5))* PublishAmerica, Inc.

Braden, Stephanie. The Wishing Well. 2012. 48p. pap. 16.95 *(978-1-62709-450-4(4))* America Star Bks.

Bradford, K. B. Grandma's Sunshine. 2011. 16p. 12.74 *(978-1-4567-3270-7(6))* AuthorHouse.

Bradley, Alex. 24 Girls in 7 Days. 2006. (ENG.). 272p. (YA). (gr. 7-18). reprint ed. 6.99 *(978-0-14-240543-7(4),* Speak) Penguin Young Readers Group.

Bradley, Debby. Sophie Wonders about Marriage. Guzman, Lula, illus. 2013. (Sophie Wonders about the Sacraments Ser.). (ENG.). 31p. (J). pap. 4.99 *(978-0-7648-2351-0(5))* Liguori Pubns.

Bragaw, Jennie M. The Marble Harvest. 2012. 60p. pap. 31.99 *(978-1-4691-8569-9(5))* Xlibris Corp.

Brahmachari, Sita. Mira in the Present Tense. 2013. (ENG.). 288p. (J). (gr. 3-7). 16.99 *(978-0-8075-5149-3(X))* Whitman, Albert & Co.

Braithwaite, Lisa. Lucy Goes into the Wild. 2012. 28p. pap. 15.99 *(978-1-4771-4341-4(6))* Xlibris Corp.

Braithwaite, Pamela. Missing Jessic. 2012. 44p. pap. *(978-1-105-74130-2(3))* Lulu.com.

Branford, Anna. Violet Mackerel's Outside-the-Box Set: Violet Mackerel's Brilliant Plot; Violet Mackerel's Remarkable Recovery; Violet Mackerel's Natural Habitat; Violet Mackerel's Personal Space. Allen, Elanna, illus. 2013. (Violet Mackerel Ser.). (ENG.). 464p. (J). (gr. 1-5). pap. 23.99 *(978-1-4424-8859-5(X),* Atheneum Bks. for Young Readers) Simon & Schuster Children's Publishing.

Brendler, Carol. Radio Girl. 2013. (ENG.). 224p. (J). (gr. 5-9). 16.95 *(978-0-8234-2861-8(3))* Holiday Hse., Inc.

Breshears, Alyce Park. Run, Girl, Run! Boyd, Shelby, illus. 2013. 36p. pap. 7.95 *(978-1-60414-742-1(3))* Fideli Publishing, Inc.

Brewer, Cristine S. Ilsa, Dad, & Ed. 2011. 60p. (gr. -1). pap. 9.99 *(978-1-4670-3756-3(7))* AuthorHouse.

Brewer, Jo Ann. The Little Girl No One Wanted. 2011. 48p. pap. 15.99 *(978-1-4568-6581-8(1))* Xlibris Corp.

Brian, Kate, pseud. Cruel Love. 2011. (Privilege Ser.). (ENG.). 224p. (YA). (gr. 9). pap. 9.99 *(978-1-4424-0788-6(3),* Simon & Schuster Bks. For Young Readers) Simon & Schuster Bks. For Young Readers.

—Vengeance. 2011. (Private Ser.). (ENG.). 240p. (YA). (gr. 9). pap. 9.99 *(978-1-4169-8473-3(9),* Simon & Schuster Bks. For Young Readers) Simon & Schuster Bks. For Young Readers.

Bright, Belle. Crash, Bang, Boom, Zing. Bright, Michael, illus. 2009. 12p. pap. 24.95 *(978-1-60749-383-9(7))* America Star Bks.

Bright, Phoebe. Lucky Stars #1: Wish upon a Friend. 2012. (Lucky Stars Ser.). (ENG.). 96p. (J). (gr. 2-5). pap. 5.99 *(978-0-545-41998-7(0),* Scholastic Paperbacks) Scholastic, Inc.

—Lucky Stars #5: Wish upon a Superstar. 2012. (Lucky Stars Ser.). (ENG.). 96p. (J). (gr. 2-5). pap. 5.99 *(978-0-545-42002-0(4),* Scholastic Paperbacks) Scholastic, Inc.

Britan, Denise G. Harry Meets Sam. 2011. 24p. pap. 12.99 *(978-1-4628-6756-1(1))* Xlibris Corp.

Brockenbrough, Martha. The Game of Love & Death. 2015. (ENG.). 336p. (J). (gr. 7). 17.99 *(978-0-545-66834-7(4))* Scholastic, Inc.

Brooke, Samantha. Makeover Madness. Thomas, Laura, illus. 2011. (Strawberry Shortcake Ser.). (ENG.). 24p. (J). (gr. -1-k). pap. 4.99 *(978-0-448-45720-8(2),* Grosset & Dunlap) Penguin Young Readers Group.

Brooks, Amy. Randy's Summer. 2011. 264p. 47.95 *(978-1-258-09855-1(5))* Literary Licensing, LLC.

Brooks, Charlie. Greystone Valley. Grundy, Jessica, illus. 2013. 166p. 17.99 *(978-1-938821-33-2(5));* 198p. pap. 9.99 *(978-1-938821-41-7(6))* Grey Gecko Pr.

Brooks, Robert. Sonrieta. Urban, Helle, illus. 2008. 40p. (YA). 17.95 *(978-0-9792294-0-4(5))* Mystic Jaguar Publishing.

Brophy, Mary-Beth. The Last Stop Before Home. 2004. 166p. (YA). pap. 12.95 *(978-0-595-30436-3(2))* iUniverse, Inc.

Brothers, Marilee. Moon Rise. 2009. (YA). pap. 14.95 *(978-0-9821756-9-9(8),* Bell Bridge Bks.) BelleBks., Inc.

—Moon Spun. 2010. 246p. pap. 14.95 *(978-1-935661-95-5(7),* Bell Bridge Bks.) BelleBks., Inc.

Brothers, Meagan. Weird Girl & What's His Name. 2015. (ENG.). 336p. (gr. 8). pap. 16.95 *(978-1-941110-27-0(4),* 1397530) Three Rooms Pr.

Brouwer, Sigmund. Justine Mckeen, Queen of Green, 1 vol. Whamond, Dave, illus. 2011. (Orca Echoes Ser.). (ENG.).

64p. (J). (gr. 2-3). pap. 6.95 (978-1-55469-927-8(4)) Orca Bk. Pubs. USA.

Brown, Carron, ed. The Three Little Pigs & Little Red Riding Hood: Two Tales & Their Histories. 2009. (World of Fairy Tales Ser.). (Illus.). 32p. (J). (gr. -1-2). pap. 10.55 (978-1-60754-641-2(8)); lib. bdg. 22.60 (978-1-60754-640-5(X)) Windmill Bks.

Brown, Kathryn. Adventures at Aaron Loch Farm. 2009. 50p. pap. 23.50 (978-1-4092-6961-8(2)) Lulu Pr., Inc.

Brown, Liz. The Bully. (Illus.). 90p. (978-1-897039-08-3(5)) High Interest Publishing (HIP).

Brown, Marc. D. W.'s Perfect Present. Brown, Marc, illus. 2004. (ENG., Illus.). 24p. (J). (gr. -1-1). pap. 3.99 (978-0-316-73386-1(5), Tingley, Megan Bks.) Little, Brown Bks. for Young Readers.

Bryant, Annie. Freestyle with Avery. 2007. (Beacon Street Girls Special Adventure Ser.: No. 2). 240p. (J). (gr. 4-8). pap. 7.99 (978-1-933566-01-6(9)) B*tween Productions, Inc.

—Freestyle with Avery. 2009. (Beacon Street Girls Ser.). (ENG.). 240p. (J). (gr. 4-8). pap. 8.99 (978-1-4169-6435-3(5), Aladdin) Simon & Schuster Children's Publishing.

—Ghost Town. 2009. (Beacon Street Girls Ser.: 11). (ENG.). 240p. (J). (gr. 4-8). pap. 7.99 (978-1-4169-6441-4(X), Aladdin) Simon & Schuster Children's Publishing.

—Out of Bounds. 2005. (Beacon Street Girls Ser.: No. 4). 255p. (J). 7.99 (978-0-9746587-9-7(0), Beacon Street Girls) B*tween Productions, Inc.

—Out of Bounds. 2008. (Beacon Street Girls Ser.: 4). (ENG., Illus.). 288p. (J). (gr. 4-8). pap. 8.99 (978-1-4169-6427-8(4), Aladdin) Simon & Schuster Children's Publishing.

—Time's Up. 2008. (Beacon Street Girls Ser.: 12). (ENG.). 208p. (J). (gr. 4-8). pap. 7.99 (978-1-4169-6422-3(3), Aladdin) Simon & Schuster Children's Publishing.

Buchanan, Pendella. Layers. 2011. (Illus.). 16p. pap. 12.52 (978-1-4567-8749-3(7)) AuthorHouse.

Buckey, Sarah Masters. The Stolen Sapphire: A Samantha Mystery. Tibbles, JeanPaul, illus. 2006. (ENG.). 192p. (J). (gr. 4-7). pap. 6.95 (978-1-59369-099-1(1), American Girl) American Girl Publishing, Inc.

Buckley, Kate. Choices: A Novel. 2009. 208p. (J). pap. 14.95 (978-1-935359-12-8(6)) Book Pubs. Network.

Bulla, Clyde Robert & Bulla. Shoeshine Girl. Grant, Leigh & Burke, Jim, illus. 2004. (Rise & Shine Ser.). (ENG.). 96p. (J). (gr. 2-5). reprint ed. pap. 4.99 (978-0-06-440228-6(2)) HarperCollins Pubs.

Burge, Constance M. Seasons of the Witch, Vol. 1. Simon and Schuster Children's Staff, ed. 2003. (Charmed Ser.). (ENG.). 192p. (YA). pap. (978-0-689-86545-9(7)) Gallery Pr., The.

Burkhart, Jessica. Elite Ambition. 2010. (Canterwood Crest Ser.: 10). (ENG.). 224p. (J). (gr. 4-8). pap. 7.99 (978-1-4424-0382-6(9), Aladdin) Simon & Schuster Children's Publishing.

—Jealousy. 2013. (Canterwood Crest Ser.: 17). lib. bdg. 17.20 (978-0-606-27032-8(9), Turtleback) Turtleback Bks.

—Little White Lies. 2009. (Canterwood Crest Ser.: 6). (ENG.). 240p. (J). (gr. 4-8). pap. 7.99 (978-1-4169-9038-3(0), Aladdin) Simon & Schuster Children's Publishing.

—Rival Revenge. 2010. (Canterwood Crest Ser.: 7). (ENG.). 240p. (J). (gr. 4-8). pap. 7.99 (978-1-4169-9039-0(9), Aladdin) Simon & Schuster Children's Publishing.

—Unfriendly Competition. 2011. (Canterwood Crest Ser.: 12). (ENG.). 192p. (J). (gr. 4-8). pap. 7.99 (978-1-4424-0386-4(1), Aladdin) Simon & Schuster Children's Publishing.

Burks, Megan. Sally the Circle. 2012. 28p. pap. 21.99 (978-1-4771-3343-9(7)) Xlibris Corp.

Burnham, Niki. Scary Beautiful. 2006. (Romantic Comedies Ser.). (ENG.). 272p. (YA). (gr. 9-12). mass mkt. 6.99 (978-0-689-87619-6(X), Simon Pulse) Simon Pulse.

—Sticky Fingers. 2005. (ENG.). 288p. (YA). (gr. 9-18). pap. 7.99 (978-0-689-87649-3(1), Simon Pulse) Simon Pulse.

Burnham, Niki & Saidens, Amy. Royally Jacked. 2003. (Romantic Comedies Ser.). (ENG.). 208p. (YA). mass mkt. 6.99 (978-0-689-86668-5(2), Simon Pulse) Simon Pulse.

Burns, Joanne. Abigail Is a Big Girl Now. 2005. 20p. (J). 8.99 (978-1-4116-2042-1(9)) Lulu Pr., Inc.

—Annibelle Is a Big Girl Now Weaning Two Year-Olds. 2005. 20p. 8.99 (978-1-4116-2044-5(5)) Lulu Pr., Inc.

Burns, Mary Gore. The Magic Room: Mandy & the Lily Pond. 2011. 48p. pap. 17.30 (978-1-4634-2642-2(9)) AuthorHouse.

Burt, Vicky. Eager Beavers. Lindsey, Jessica, illus. 2012. 28p. pap. 13.99 (978-1-937129-39-2(X)) Faithful Life Pubs.

Burton, Chanel & Burton, Chanel. Wildancer Takes First: Wildancer Wins First Place. 2012. 44p. pap. 15.00 (978-1-60976-164-6(2), Strategic Bk. Publishing) Strategic Book Publishing & Rights Agency (SBPRA).

Busch, Jean. Cheyenne & the Indian Spirit. 2011. 28p. pap. 16.95 (978-1-4560-5651-3(4)) America Star Bks.

Butcher, Kristin. Cheat, 1 vol. 2010. (Orca Currents Ser.). (ENG.). 128p. (J). (gr. 5-9). pap. 9.95 (978-1-55469-274-3(1)) Orca Bk. Pubs. USA.

Butler, Terrold B. Sharing. 2010. 24p. 11.49 (978-1-4490-6890-5(1)) AuthorHouse.

Byars, Betsy. Tarot Says Beware, No. 2. 2006. (Herculeah Jones Mystery Ser.). (ENG.). 160p. (J). (gr. 3-7). 5.99 (978-0-14-240593-2(0), Puffin Books) Penguin Young Readers Group.

Bybee, Linda & Lawless, Laura. Untwin. 2011. 32p. pap. 14.99 (978-1-4567-5365-8(7)) AuthorHouse.

Bynum, Betty. I'm a Pretty Little Black Girl! 2013. 32p. pap. 14.95 (978-0-615-78551-6(4)) Workhouse Road Productions.

Cabot, Meg. Teen Idol. 2005. (ENG., Illus.). 320p. (YA). (gr. 8-18). reprint ed. pap. 9.99 (978-0-06-009618-2(7), HarperTeen) HarperCollins Pubs.

Cadman, Mistie. Sophie's Summer Sombrero Adventure. 2012. 32p. pap. 24.95 (978-1-62709-289-0(7)) America Star Bks.

Caffee, Tammie Jenks. The Summer of Snail. 2007. (J). per. 12.95 (978-1-934345-24-5(5)) SouthWest Pubns.

Cage, Elizabeth. Covert Affairs: License to Thrill; Live & Let Spy; Nobody Does It Better. 2014. (ENG., Illus.). 704p. (YA). (gr. 7). pap. 12.99 (978-1-4424-8227-2(3), Simon Pulse) Simon Pulse.

—Covert Affairs 2: Spy Girls Are Forever; Dial V for Vengeance; If Looks Could Kill. 2014. (ENG., Illus.). 640p. (YA). (gr. 7). pap. 12.99 (978-1-4424-8229-6(X), Simon Pulse) Simon Pulse.

—Dial V for Vengeance. 2013. (Spy Girls Ser.: 5). (ENG., Illus.). 192p. (YA). (gr. 7). pap. 13.99 (978-1-4814-2084-6(4), Simon Pulse) Simon Pulse.

—If Looks Could Kill. 2013. (Spy Girls Ser.: 6). (ENG., Illus.). 192p. (YA). (gr. 7). pap. 13.99 (978-1-4814-2085-3(2), Simon Pulse) Simon Pulse.

—Nobody Does It Better. 2013. (Spy Girls Ser.: 3). (ENG., Illus.). 192p. (YA). (gr. 7). pap. 13.99 (978-1-4814-2080-8(1), Simon Pulse) Simon Pulse.

—Spy Girls Are Forever. 2013. (Spy Girls Ser.: 4). (ENG., Illus.). 192p. (YA). (gr. 7). pap. 13.99 (978-1-4814-2082-2(8), Simon Pulse) Simon Pulse.

Cai, Ning & Bosco, Don. Magicienne: A Novel. 2017. (ENG.). 192p. pap. 11.99 **(978-981-4771-40-5(6))** Marshall Cavendish International (Asia) Private Ltd. SGP. Dist: National Bk. Network.

Caligiuri, Susan. Haylie's Haunted Hamper. Baker, David, illus. 2011. 28p. pap. 24.95 (978-1-4560-0909-0(5)) America Star Bks.

Calkhoven, Laurie. Fork in the Trail. Studios, Arcana, illus. 2010. (ENG.). 120p. (J). (gr. 3-18). pap. 8.95 (978-1-59369-758-7(9)) American Girl Publishing, Inc.

Callahan, Thera S. All Wrapped Up. 2004. (Rookie Reader Español Ser.). (ENG., Illus.). 32p. (J). (gr. k-2). pap. 4.95 (978-0-516-21949-3(9), Children's Pr.) Scholastic Library Publishing.

—All Wrapped Up. Gordon, Mike, illus. 2003. (Rookie Readers Ser.). 32p. (J). 19.50 (978-0-516-22844-0(7), Children's Pr.) Scholastic Library Publishing.

Caloyeras, Jennifer. Strays: A Novel. 2015. (ENG.). 219p. (J). pap. 17.95 (978-1-61822-037-0(3), Ashland Creek Pr.) Byte Level Research.

Cammuso, Frank. Spelling Trouble. 2013. (Misadventures of Salem Hyde Ser.). (ENG., Illus.). 96p. (J). (gr. 1-3). 14.95 (978-1-4197-0803-9(1)); pap. 6.95 (978-1-4197-0804-6(X)) Abrams, Inc. (Amulet Bks.).

Campbell, Angella. Angel & Turkish. 2011. 32p. pap. 14.99 (978-1-4634-0372-0(0)) AuthorHouse.

—Engel und Turkish. 2012. 32p. pap. 19.99 (978-1-4772-2556-1(0)) AuthorHouse.

Campbell, Ellen Langas. Will Stephanie Get the Story?, 3 bks., No. 1. 2004. (Girls Know How Ser.: #1 - Journalism). (ENG., Illus.). 112p. (J). pap. 4.95 (978-0-9743604-0-9(6), GIRLS KNOW HOW) NouSoma Communications, Inc.

Campbell, H. David. Merribell: A Comforting Story. 2011. 218p. (gr. 2-2). 23.95 (978-1-4620-4477-1(8)); pap. 13.95 (978-1-4620-4476-4(X)) iUniverse, Inc.

Campbell, Todd M. Puppy Dog's New Friend. 2012. 24p. 24.95 (978-1-4626-6127-5(0)) America Star Bks.

Candybird Staff. My Book of Secrets. 2013. (ENG., Illus.). 144p. (J). (gr. 1). 12.95 (978-2-7338-2313-2(2)) Auzou, Philippe Editions FRA. Dist: Consortium Bk. Sales & Distribution.

Cann, Kate. Crow Girl. 2012. (Stoke Books Titles Ser.). (ENG.). 80p. (YA). (gr. 8-12). pap. 6.95 (978-1-78112-121-4(4)); lib. bdg. 22.60 (978-1-78112-122-1(2)) Lerner Publishing Group.

Capucilli, Alyssa Satin. Tulip Loves Rex. Massini, Sarah, illus. 2013. (ENG.). 32p. (J). (gr. -1-3). 17.99 (978-0-06-209413-1(0), Tegen, Katherine Bks) HarperCollins Pubs.

Carey, Rosa Nouchette. Esther: A Book for Girls. 2007. pap. (978-1-4065-1267-0(2)) Dodo Pr.

Carlson, Melody. Bad Connection. 2006. (Secret Life of Samantha Mcgregor Ser.: No. 1). (ENG.). 256p. (J). (gr. 7-12). per. 12.99 (978-1-59052-692-7(9), Multnomah) Doubleday Religious Publishing Group, The.

—Charlene's Grumpy Day: A Scoozie Tale about Patience. Fincher, Kathryn Andrews, illus. Date not set. 32p. (J). 9.99 (978-0-7369-0734-7(3)) Harvest Hse. Pubs.

—Just Ask. 2005. (Diary of a Teenage Girl Ser.: Bk. 10). (ENG.). 256p. (J). (gr. 7-12). per. 14.99 (978-1-59052-321-6(0), Multnomah Bks.) Crown Publishing Group.

Carol Hersh. Handy Sandy. Baker, David, illus. 2011. 28p. pap. 24.95 (978-1-4560-8991-7(9)) America Star Bks.

Carr, C. Hanna's Way. 2011. (Illus.). 112p. 28.31 (978-1-4567-8179-8(0)); pap. 14.11 (978-1-4567-8178-1(2)) AuthorHouse.

Carr, Suzanna & Crutchfield, Tylicia. Nosey Rosey. Illustrated by: Charles Duke, illus. 2011. 44p. pap. 24.95 (978-1-4560-7939-0(5)) America Star Bks.

Carriger, Candace. Inside My Garden. Allen, Cassandra, illus. 2011. 46p. (J). pap. 11.95 (978-0-9816047-5-6(7)) Sadie Bks.

Carroll, Jenny, pseud & Cabot, Meg. Code Name Cassandra. 2007. (1-800-Where-R-You Ser.: No. 2). (ENG., Illus.). 272p. (YA). (gr. 9-12). mass mkt. 6.99 (978-1-4169-2704-4(2), Simon Pulse) Simon Pulse.

—Sanctuary. 2007. (1-800-Where-R-You Ser.: No. 4). (ENG., Illus.). 240p. (YA). (gr. 9-12). mass mkt. 6.99 (978-1-4169-2707-5(7), Simon Pulse) Simon Pulse.

Carroll, Lewis, pseud. Alicia en el País de las Maravillas. (SPA., Illus.). (YA). 11.95 (978-84-7281-081-5(X), AF1081) Auriga, Ediciones S.A. ESP. Dist: Continental Bk. Co., Inc.

—Anya V Stranye Chudes. Nabokov, Vladimir, tr. from RUS. 2011. (Dover Dual Language Russian Ser.).Tr. of Alice in Wonderland. (RUS & ENG., Illus.). 128p. (J). reprint ed. pap. 10.95 (978-0-486-23316-1(2)) Dover Pubns., Inc.

Carroll, Lewis, pseud & Baker, Kyle. Through the Looking-Glass. (Classics Illustrated Ser.). (Illus.). 52p. (YA). pap. 4.95 (978-1-57209-002-6(2)) Classics International Entertainment, Inc.

Carroll, Lewis, pseud & Carroll. Alicia en el País de las Maravillas. (Coleccion Cuentos Universales). (SPA.). 128p. (YA). (gr. 4-18). (978-84-261-0267-6(0), JV30114) Juventud, Editorial ESP. Dist: Lectorum Pubns., Inc.

Carter, Aimée. The Goddess Inheritance. 2013. (Goddess Test Ser.: 3). lib. bdg. 20.85 (978-0-606-26948-3(7), Turtleback) Turtleback Bks.

—The Goddess Test. 2011. (Goddess Test Ser.: 1). lib. bdg. 20.85 (978-0-606-26943-8(6), Turtleback) Turtleback Bks.

Carter, Ally. United We Spy (10th Anniversary Edition) 2016. (Gallagher Girls Ser.). (ENG.). 320p. (YA). (gr. 5-9). pap. 9.99 (978-1-4847-8508-9(8)) Hyperion Bks. for Children.

Carter, Caela. My Life with the Liars. 2016. 288p. (J). (gr. 3-7). 16.99 (978-0-06-238571-0(2)) HarperCollins Pubs.

Carttar, Debra. Picturing Lucy. 2010. pap. 14.95 (978-0-7414-6195-7(1)) Infinity Publishing.

Cary. Rosa Nouchette. Esther: A book for Girls. 2007. (ENG.). 206p. pap. 20.99 (978-1-4264-5023-5(0)) 2006. 230p. pap. 22.99 (978-1-4264-5324-3(8)) Creative Media Partners, LLC.

Casanova, Mary. Jess. 2005. (American Girl Today Ser.). (ENG., Illus.). 136p. (J). (gr. 4-7). per. 6.95 (978-1-59369-016-8(9)) American Girl Publishing, Inc.

Cass, Kiera. The One. 2015. (Selection Ser.: 3). (YA). lib. bdg. 20.85 (978-0-606-36960-2(0)) Turtleback Bks.

Cast, P. C. & Cast, Kristin. Destined. 2013. (House of Night Novels Ser.: 9). (ENG.). 336p. (YA). (gr. 7-12). pap. 10.99 (978-0-312-38798-3(9), 9780312387983, St. Martin's Griffin) St. Martin's Pr.

—Tempted. 2013. (House of Night Novels Ser.: 6). (ENG.). 352p. (YA). (gr. 7-12). mass mkt. 9.99 (978-1-250-04698-7(X), 9781250046987, St. Martin's Paperbacks) St. Martin's Pr.

Castellucci, Cecil. Janes in Love. 2008. (Plain Janes Ser.). (ENG.). 176p. (YA). (gr. 7-10). pap. 9.99 (978-1-4012-1387-9(1), Minx) DC Comics.

Casten, Diane. The Christmas Doll. 2012. 46p. pap. 9.99 (978-1-62419-021-6(9)) Salem Author Services.

Castle, Jan And Kare. Gracey's Desire. LaFerriere, Suzanne, illus. 2008. 28p. pap. 17.99 (978-1-4389-2433-5(X)) AuthorHouse.

Caudill, Rebecca. Up & down the River. Merwin, Decie, illus. 2005. 143p. (J). (gr. -1-17). pap. 11.95 (978-1-883937-81-2(7)) Bethlehem Bks.

Cecil, Lauren & Scholastic, Inc. Staff. Party Time! Hill, Prescott, illus. 2011. (Lalaloopsy Ser.: 2). (ENG.). 24p. (J). (gr. -1-3). pap. 3.99 (978-0-545-37998-4(9)) Scholastic, Inc.

Cellucci, Lucy Lemay. True Colours. 2010. (ENG., Illus.). 240p. (YA). (gr. 7-10). pap. 9.95 (978-1-926607-13-9(9), Napoleon & Co.) Dundum CAN. Dist: Ingram Publisher Services.

Center for Learning Network Staff. The House on Mango Street: Curriculum Unit. 2005. (Novel Ser.). (YA). tchr. ed., spiral bd. 19.95 (978-1-56077-783-0(4)) Center for Learning, The.

Chacko, Miss Hannah. The Lie. 2009. 372p. pap. 25.50 (978-0-557-06829-6(0)) Lulu Pr., Inc.

Chandler, Andrew & Chandler, Amanda. Gertrude & Abigail: The Adventures Thereof. 2006. 35p. (J). 18.90 (978-1-4116-7572-8(X)) Lulu Pr., Inc.

Chandler, Elizabeth. The Back Door of Midnight. 2010. (Dark Secrets Ser.: Vol. 5). (ENG.). 320p. (YA). (gr. 7-18). pap. 9.99 (978-1-4424-0626-1(7), Simon Pulse) Simon Pulse.

Chapman, Brenda. Second Chances. 2013. 312p. pap. (978-1-4596-6332-9(2)) ReadHowYouWant.com, Ltd.

Chapmon, Rachelle. Mari. 2009. 148p. pap. 11.99 (978-1-4389-6310-5(6)) AuthorHouse.

Che, Dana. The Choice That Changed Her Life: ne Choice Can Change Everything! 2013. (ENG.). 300p. pap. 16.95 (978-1-4327-7614-5(2)) Outskirts Pr., Inc.

Chedekel, Evelyn. The Fake Doughnut. Le, Loanne, illus. 2013. 24p. 16.95 (978-0-9888974-0-3(7)) BugaBk. llc.

Cheva, Cherry. She's So Money. 2008. 304p. (gr. 7-12). (J). lib. bdg. 17.89 (978-0-06-128852-4(7)); (ENG.). (YA). 16.99 (978-0-06-128855-5(1)) HarperCollins Pubs. (HarperTeen).

Child, Lauren. Soy Demasiado Pequeña para Ir Al Colegio: Protagonizado Por Juan y Totola. 2004. (SPA., Illus.). (J). 17.99 (978-84-8488-111-7(3)) Serres, Ediciones, S. L. ESP. Dist: Lectorum Pubns., Inc.

Child, Lauren & Rubio, Esther. Nunca Jamás Comeré Tomates. 2003. (ESP & SPA., Illus.). 32p. (J). (gr. k-2). 20.99 (978-84-8488-092-9(3)) Serres, Ediciones, S. L. ESP. Dist: Lectorum Pubns., Inc.

Chima, Ahiru & Misu, Max. Ellenã__- Ellen meets Frog King - 2005. 32p. pap. 14.99 (978-1-4116-4050-4(0)) Lulu Pr., Inc.

Chime, Taffeta. The Last. 2011. 204p. 25.00 (978-0-9795020-3-3(9)); pap. 16.00 (978-0-9795020-2-6(0)) Broken Oak Publishing.

Chlebowski, Rachel. Better Together! (Shimmer & Shine) Golden Books, illus. 2017. (Color & Paint Plus Stickers Ser.). (ENG.). 128p. (J). (gr. -1-2). pap. 9.99 (978-0-399-55793-4(8), Golden Bks.) Random Hse. Children's Bks.

Choi, Haran. Why Me? 2011. 20p. pap. 11.99 (978-1-4634-2585-2(6)) AuthorHouse.

Chopra, Deepak. You with the Stars in Your Eyes: A Little Girl's Glimpse at Cosmic Consciousness. Zaboski, Dave, illus. 2010. (ENG & ABK.). 32p. 14.95 (978-1-4019-2711-0(4)) Hay Hse., Inc.

Christopher, Lawrence. The Tickle Fingers: Where Is Pinky? Christopher, Lawrence, illus. 2006. (ENG., Illus.). 24p. (J). (gr. -1-18). 9.95 (978-0-9712278-3-5(7)) MF Unlimited.

Chronicle Books Editors & Player, Micah. Lately Lily ABC Travel Flash Cards. 2014. (ENG., Illus.). 26p. (J). (gr. -1-17). 14.99 (978-1-4521-1524-5(9)) Chronicle Bks. LLC.

Circle of Blue. 2006. (J). (978-1-933343-37-2(0), PONY) Stabenfeldt Inc.

Clark, Carol. Eternity Express. 2009. 32p. pap. 10.95 (978-0-9818488-6-0(9)) Ajoyin Publishing, Inc.

Clark, Catherine. The Alison Rules. 2004. (ENG.). 272p. (J). 15.99 (978-0-06-055980-9(2), HarperTeen) HarperCollins Pubs.

Clark, Clara. Nellie Bishop. Shine, Andrea, illus. 2003. (ENG.). 128p. (YA). (gr. 4-6). pap. 12.95 (978-1-56397-642-1(0)) Boyds Mills Pr.

Clark, Maria. Lousy Luck Lucy. 2012. 32p. pap. 13.50 (978-1-61897-699-4(0), Strategic Bk. Publishing) Strategic Book Publishing & Rights Agency (SBPRA).

Clark, Philip. Little Red. 2010. 20p. 10.95 (978-1-4520-4843-7(6)) AuthorHouse.

Clark, Sherryl;Perry. Ellyse Perry 2: Magic Feet. 2017. (Ellyse Perry Ser.: 2). (ENG.). 160p. (J). (gr. 4-7). 12.99 **(978-0-14-378126-4(X))** Random Hse. Australia AUS. Dist: Independent Pubs. Group.

Claudine Sherels Johnson. Nire Goes to the Color Books Bookstore: Featuring God Is Awesome & Pink Carnation. 2009. 84p. pap. 10.49 (978-1-4389-5952-8(4)) AuthorHouse.

Claus, Fred J. You're Too Small, 1 vol. Webb, Sarah, illus. 2009. 20p. pap. 24.95 (978-1-60703-757-6(2)) America Star Bks.

Clausman, Rachel. Miriam, Come Sit. 2011. 24p. pap. 11.32 (978-1-4634-4812-7(0)) AuthorHouse.

Cleary, Beverly. Ellen Tebbits. Darling, Louis & Dockray, Tracy, illus. 2008. (Avon Camelot Bks.). (ENG.). 192p. (J). (gr. 3-7). pap. 6.99 (978-0-380-70913-7(9)) HarperCollins Pubs.

—Ellen Tebbits. 160p. (J). (gr. 2-4). pap. 4.99 (978-0-8072-1397-1(7), Listening Library) Random Hse. Audio Publishing Group.

—Ramona y Su Padre. 10th ed. 2003.Tr. of Ramona & Her Father. (SPA., Illus.). 136p. (J). (gr. 3-5). 15.95 (978-84-239-9020-7(6), EC1443) Espasa Calpe, S.A. ESP. Dist: Lectorum Pubns., Inc., Distribooks, Inc.

—Troton Mi Perro. 2nd ed. 2003. (Ramona Quimby Ser.).Tr. of Strider. (SPA., Illus.). 128p. (J). (gr. 5-8). 9.95 (978-84-239-9017-7(6), EC4693) Espasa Calpe, S.A. ESP. Dist: Planeta Publishing Corp., Lectorum Pubns., Inc.

—Viva Ramona. 4th ed. 2003. (Ramona Quimby Ser.: Vol. 23).Tr. of Ramona Forever. (SPA., Illus.). 152p. (J). (gr. 4-7). 15.95 (978-84-239-8877-8(5), EC3784) Espasa Calpe, S.A. ESP. Dist: Lectorum Pubns., Inc., Distribooks, Inc.

Cloci, Gabriella. Minda's Happily Ever After. 2003. (J). pap. 9.95 (978-0-7414-1501-1(1)) Infinity Publishing.

Clout, Susan. The Six Week Road Trip. 2011. 36p. pap. (978-1-4269-9459-3(1)) Trafford Publishing (UK) Ltd.

Cloyd, Suzy. Pippi's Silent Message: Adventures of Suzy Q & You Too. Barham, Timothy E., illus. 2012. 24p. 24.95 (978-1-4512-7832-3(2)) America Star Bks.

Cohen, Leah. Sophie. 2010. 24p. 11.49 (978-1-4520-1854-6(5)) AuthorHouse.

Colasanti, Susane. Forever in Love. 2017. (City Love Ser.: 3). 320p. (YA). (gr. 9). 17.99 (978-0-06-230776-7(2), Tegen, Katherine Bks) HarperCollins Pubs.

Cole, Brock. Celine. 2003. (ENG.). 224p. (YA). (gr. 7-12). pap. 16.99 (978-0-374-41082-7(8), 9780374410827, Farrar, Straus & Giroux (BYR)) Farrar, Straus & Giroux.

Colhoun, Sheelah. It's Fun to Feed the Little Lambs. Cotton, Sue Lynn, illus. 2013. 32p. pap. 14.95 (978-1-61493-185-0(2)) Peppertree Pr., The.

Collins, Lynette. Margie & Wolf: The Series. 2016. 260p. (gr. 1-1). 40.31 (978-1-5245-1645-1(7)); pap. 24.19 (978-1-5245-1644-4(9)) Xlibris Corp.

Collins, Lynette. Margie & Wolf: When They Were Free. 2017. (ENG., Illus.). pap. 32.25 **(978-1-5245-2168-4(X))** Xlibris Corp.

Collins, Michael. Anu & the Blue. 2009. 166p. pap. 16.68 (978-0-557-20316-1(3)) Lulu Pr., Inc.

Condon, Bill. The Human Calculator, 1 vol. 2013. (Fiction Readers Ser.). (ENG., Illus.). 28p. (J). (gr. 2-2). pap. 6.99 (978-1-4333-5565-3(5)) Shell Educational Publishing.

Coné, Robert. The Candy Bandit Strikes Again! Baker, David, illus. 2011. 28p. pap. 24.95 (978-1-4560-8019-8(9)) America Star Bks.

Conklin, Jennie Maria. Miss Prudence: A Story of Two Girls' Lives. l.t. ed. 2007. (ENG.). 414p. pap. 28.99 (978-1-4264-4100-4(2)) 2006. 308p. pap. 23.99 (978-1-4264-4041-0(3)) Creative Media Partners, LLC.

—Miss Prudence A Story of Two Girls' Lives. 2004. reprint ed. pap. 1.99 (978-1-4192-3464-4(1)) Kessinger Publishing, LLC.

Conlon, Linda L. Not Today. 2011. 32p. 14.39 (978-1-4343-9195-7(7)) AuthorHouse.

Connolly, Megan B. Mommy, Mommy! Is This for Me? Mundy, Jen, illus. 2013. (ENG.). (J). 14.95 (978-1-62086-356-5(1)) Mascot Bks., Inc.

Connor, Naomi. I Am. 2011. 52p. pap. 22.49 (978-1-4634-3673-5(4)) AuthorHouse.

Connors, Colleen. A Real Princess. 2009. 32p. pap. 12.99 (978-1-4389-6884-1(1)) AuthorHouse.

Cook, Eileen. Getting Revenge on Lauren Wood. 2010. (ENG.). (YA). (gr. 9). 288p. pap. 9.99 (978-1-4424-0976-7(2)); 272p. 15.99 (978-1-4169-7433-8(4)) Simon Pulse. (Simon Pulse).

Cook, Kacy. Nuts, 0 vols. 2012. (ENG.). 160p. (J). (gr. 3-7). pap. 7.99 (978-0-7614-6311-5(9), 9780761463115, Amazon Children's Publishing) Amazon Publishing.

Cooper, Nelle. Princess Lil. 2013. 82p. (J). pap. 9.00 (978-1-936442-16-4(7)) Fresh Ink Group.

Corey, Shana. Players in Pigtails. Gibbon, Rebecca, illus. 2003. (ENG.). 40p. (J). (gr. -1-3). 21.99 (978-0-439-18305-5(7)) Scholastic, Inc.

Cosby, Andrew. Mary Scary. Nixey, Troy, illus. 2007. (ENG.). 56p. (gr. 7). pap. 9.95 (978-1-59307-730-3(0)) Dark Horse Comics.

Costanza, Francine. Autumn's Indigo. Petru, Suzin, illus. 2012. 30p. 24.95 (978-1-4626-6523-5(3)) America Star Bks.

Coste, Marion. Wild Beach. Gray, Cissy, illus. 2005. 32p. (J). pap. 8.25 (978-0-89317-062-2(3), WW-623); lib. bdg. 17.95 (978-0-89317-061-5(5), WW-0615) Finney Co., Inc. (Windward Publishing).

Cotton, Connie. Crashing. 2009. 52p. pap. 16.95 (978-1-61546-198-1(1)) America Star Bks.

Courtney, Suzanne Gene. Dear Diary: My Brother Died Today. 2013. 32p. pap. 14.95 (978-1-62857-013-7(X), Strategic Bk. Publishing) Strategic Book Publishing & Rights Agency (SBPRA).

—Rainfrog. 2011. 34p. pap. 14.50 (978-1-61204-189-6(2), Eloquent Bks.) Strategic Book Publishing & Rights Agency (SBPRA).

Coven, Wanda. Heidi Heckelbeck Is a Flower Girl. Burris, Priscilla, illus. 2014. (Heidi Heckelbeck Ser.: 11). (ENG.). 128p. (J). (gr. k-2). pap. 4.99 (978-1-4814-0498-3(9), Little Simon) Little Simon.

Coville, Bruce. Juliet Dove, Queen of Love. 2005. (Magic Shop Book Ser.: 5). (ENG.). 208p. (J). (gr. 5-7). pap. 7.99 (978-0-15-205217-1(8)) Houghton Mifflin Harcourt Publishing Co.

Coville, Katherine. Ivy. 2017. (ENG.). 144p. (J). (gr. 2-5). 16.99 (978-0-553-53975-2(2), Knopf Bks. for Young Readers) Random Hse. Children's Bks.

Cowsert, Sami. Tammi & Her Dragon. 2006. 48p. pap. 16.95 (978-1-4241-5211-7(9)) America Star Bks.

Cox, Katherine. Scholastic Reader Level 2: Katie Fry, Private Eye #1: the Lost Kitten. Newton, Vanessa Brantley, illus.

2015. (Scholastic Reader Level 2 Ser.). (ENG.). 32p. (J). (gr. 1-3). pap. 3.99 *(978-0-545-66672-5(4))* Scholastic, Inc.
Crawford, Jaleesa. Teeny Tot. 2013. 28p. pap. 24.95 *(978-1-62709-372-9(9))* America Star Bks.
Creel, Ann Howard. Nicki. Bk. 1. Ben-Ami, Doron, illus. 2007. (ENG.). 136p. (J). (gr. 4-7). pap. 6.95 *(978-1-59369-259-9(5),* Pleasant Co.) American Girl Publishing, Inc.
Cresswell, Helen. Sophie & the Seawolf. (Illus.). 32p. (J). *(978-0-340-65608-2(5))* Hodder & Stoughton.
Crook, Connie Brummel. Meyers' Creek, 1 vol. (ENG.). 293p. (J). (gr. 3-6). mass mkt. 5.95 *(978-0-7736-7436-3(5))* Stoddart Kids CAN. Dist: Fitzhenry & Whiteside, Ltd.
Crowne, Alyssa. Green Princess Saves the Day. Alder, Charlotte, illus. 2010. (J). (Perfectly Princess Ser.: 3). (ENG.). 80p. (gr. 2-5). 4.99 *(978-0-545-20848-2(3),* Scholastic Paperbacks); 71p. *(978-0-545-23414-6(X))* Scholastic, Inc.
—Pink Princess Rules the School. Alder, Charlotte, illus. 2009. 80p. (J). pap. *(978-0-545-16077-3(4))* Scholastic, Inc.
Crystian, Carol Payne. Ebony Black & The 7. 2012. 28p. pap. 24.95 *(978-1-4626-9728-1(3))* America Star Bks.
Cummings, W. L. A Far West Texas Christmas, 1 vol. 2009. 25p. pap. 19.95 *(978-1-4489-9402-1(0))* PublishAmerica, Inc.
Cummins, Maria S. The Lamplighter. 2011. 308p. pap. 16.99 *(978-1-61203-228-3(1))* Bottom of the Hill Publishing.
Cunha, Francisco. My Very Own Lighthouse. Leal, Joao, tr. from POR. 2006. (Picture books from around the World Seri Ser.). (ENG., Illus.). 32p. (J). (gr. -1-k). 18.95 *(978-1-905341-01-6(6))* WingedChariot Pr. GBR. Dist: Independent Pubs. Group.
Cunningham, Karen. I See a Bug, 1 vol. 2010. 16p. 24.95 *(978-1-4489-4181-0(4))* PublishAmerica, Inc.
Curley, Marianne. Old Magic. 2009. (ENG.). 400p. (YA). (gr. 7-18). pap. 9.99 *(978-1-4169-8991-2(9),* Simon Pulse) Simon Pulse.
Currey, Anna. Albertine. (Illus.). 25p. (J). pap. *(978-0-340-68325-5(2))* Hodder & Stoughton.
Curtis, Kelli. Amber & the Fallen Bridge. 2009. 32p. pap. 13.00 *(978-1-60860-631-3(7),* Strategic Bk. Publishing) Strategic Book Publishing & Rights Agency (SBPRA).
Cushenberry, Lisa. No Tears for Teary. 2009. 84p. pap. 9.99 *(978-1-60860-556-9(6),* Strategic Bk. Publishing) Strategic Book Publishing & Rights Agency (SBPRA).
Cushman, Karen. Aprendiz de Comadrona. 2003.Tr. of Midwife's Apprentice. (SPA.). 96p. (YA). (gr. 5-8). *(978-84-236-4773-6(0),* ED3133) Edebé ESP. Dist: Lectorum Pubns., Inc.
Daines, Julie. Unraveled: A Tale of True Love. 2014. 192p. (J). pap. 14.99 *(978-1-62108-627-7(5))* Covenant Communications, Inc.
Dales, Cindy. Autumn's First Easter. 2009. 28p. pap. 12.99 *(978-1-4343-1433-8(2))* AuthorHouse.
Damerau, Diane Deci. The Petoskey Stones, 1 vol. 2009. 135p. pap. 24.95 *(978-1-60749-903-9(7))* America Star Bks.
Dancing Dilemma. 2005. 46p. (J). 3.99 *(978-0-9763213-1-6(9))* OHC Group LLC.
Darrows, Eva. Dead Little Mean Girl. 2017. (ENG.). 256p. 18.99 *(978-0-373-21241-5(0),* Harlequin Teen) Harlequin Enterprises, Ltd. CAN. Dist: HarperCollins Pubs.
Daughtrey, Patricia & Benson, Gary. Shanaya & Friends: Litter Bugs Turn Eco H. E. R. O. S. Balkovek, Jim, illus. 2011. 40p. pap. 14.95 *(978-1-60911-475-6(2),* Eloquent Bks.) Strategic Book Publishing & Rights Agency (SBPRA).
Davenport, Kathy. Holly's Chocolate Heart. 2011. 40p. 17.49 *(978-1-4567-1520-5(8))* AuthorHouse.
Davies, Nicola. Manatee Rescue. Wright, Annabel, illus. 2016. (Heroes of the Wild Ser.). (ENG.). 112p. (J). (gr. 2-5). 14.99 *(978-0-7636-7830-2(9))* Candlewick Pr.
Davis, Anita. Grandma, It's Beautiful. 2012. 16p. pap. 7.99 *(978-1-4624-0155-0(4),* Inspiring Voices) Author Solutions, Inc.
Davis, Carol Marie. The Adventures of Moon Spirit, a Girl from Florida's Past. Davis, Carol Marie, illus. 2008. (Illus.). 60p. pap. 8.95 *(978-0-9821654-2-3(0))* Peppertree Pr., The.
Davis, Daniel M. & Davis, Dawna Jo. Klawberry: Good Girl. Bad World. McClellan, Sara, ed. ltd. ed. 2007. (Illus.). per. 20.00 *(978-0-9774173-3-9(6))* Steam Crow Pr.
Davis, David Denton. Polly's Promise: A Story about Thriving Rather Than Simply Surviving... Turning Apparent Disability into Gifted Ability. 2013. 80p. pap. 21.95 *(978-1-4787-0275-7(3))* Outskirts Pr., Inc.
Davis, Deon M. Beanie & the Bully. 2012. 28p. pap. 19.99 *(978-1-4685-7483-8(3))* AuthorHouse.
Davis, Jacky. I Love You, Bingo. 2015. (Penguin Young Readers Level 2 Ser.). lib. bdg. 13.55 *(978-0-606-37578-8(3))* Turtleback Bks.
Davis, Jacky & Bader, Bonnie. I Love You, Bingo. Soman, David, illus. 2015. (Ladybug Girl Ser.). (ENG.). 32p. (J). (gr. 1-2). 3.99 *(978-0-448-48756-4(X),* Penguin Young Readers) Penguin Young Readers Group.
Davis, Jacky & Soman, David. Ladybug Girl Visits the Farm. Soman, David, illus. 2011. (Ladybug Girl Ser.). (ENG., Illus.). 16p. (J). (gr. -1-k). pap. 6.99 *(978-0-448-45598-3(6),* Grosset & Dunlap) Penguin Young Readers Group.
—Who Can Play? Soman, David, illus. 2013. (Ladybug Girl Ser.). (ENG., Illus.). 32p. (J). (gr. k-1). pap. 3.99 *(978-0-448-46501-2(9),* Penguin Young Readers) Penguin Young Readers Group.
Davis, Penny. Annabel's Yearnings. 2012. 274p. pap. *(978-1-78003-309-9(5))* Pen Pr. Pubs., Ltd.
Davis, Richard. The Red Cross Girl & Other Stories. 2004. reprint ed. pap. 1.99 *(978-1-4192-7996-6(3))* Kessinger Publishing, LLC.
Dawson, Jennifer. Silly Sally Sue. 2013. 24p. pap. 24.95 *(978-1-62709-938-7(7))* America Star Bks.
De Fonté, Desiree. Jazzy: A Story of Love. 2012. 26p. 24.95 *(978-1-4626-5106-1(2))* America Star Bks.
De Horne, George. Pixie O'shaughnessy. 2004. reprint ed. pap. 24.95 *(978-1-4191-4172-0(4))* Kessinger Publishing, LLC.
—Pixie O'Shaughnessy. 2004. reprint ed. pap. 1.99 *(978-1-4192-4172-7(9))* Kessinger Publishing, LLC.
De la Cruz, Melissa. Birthday Vicious. 2008. (Ashleys Ser.: Bk. 3). (ENG.). 256p. (J). (gr. 4-8). pap. 9.99 *(978-1-4169-3408-0(1),* Simon & Schuster Bks. For Young Readers) Simon & Schuster Bks. For Young Readers.
Debra Maymon. Debra Meets Her Best Friend in Kindergarten. Richa Kinra, illus. 2009. 36p. pap. 15.49 *(978-1-4389-6261-0(4))* AuthorHouse.
Deen, Ron. Annabelle Rides Her Bike on an Iowa Farm. 2005. (J). 6.95 *(978-1-57166-261-3(8))* Quixote Pr.
DEKELB-RITTENHOUSE, Diane. Immortal Longings. 2012. (ENG.). 340p. (J). (gr. 7). pap. 14.95 *(978-0-9845318-4-4(X))* Tiny Stachel Pr.
Delacroix, Sibylle. Blanche Hates the Night. Morelli, Christelle, tr. from FRE. 2016. (ENG., Illus.). 32p. (J). (gr. -1-2). 16.95 *(978-1-77147-158-9(1),* Owlkids) Owlkids Bks. Inc. CAN. Dist: Publishers Group West (PGW).
Deloza, Lara. Winning. 2016. 304p. (YA). (gr. 8). 17.99 *(978-0-06-239669-3(2),* HarperTeen) HarperCollins Pubs.
Dembkoski, Kacey. Believe. 2004. 60p. (YA). pap. 8.95 *(978-0-595-30549-0(0))* iUniverse, Inc.
Demers, Dominique. Today, Maybe, 1 vol. Grimard, Gabrielle, illus. 2011. (ENG.). 32p. (J). (gr. -1-3). 19.95 *(978-1-55469-400-6(0))* Orca Bk. Pubs. USA.
Demetrios, Heather. Something Real. 2014. (ENG.). 416p. (YA). (gr. 7). 17.99 *(978-0-8050-9794-8(5),* Holt, Henry & Co. Bks. For Young Readers) Holt, Henry & Co.
Denman, K. L. Destination Human, 1 vol. 2013. (Orca Currents Ser.). (ENG.). 136p. (J). (gr. 5-9). pap. 9.95 *(978-1-4598-0371-8(X));* lib. bdg. 16.95 *(978-1-4598-0372-5(8))* Orca Bk. Pubs. USA.
—Perfect Revenge, 1 vol. 2009. (Orca Currents Ser.). (ENG.). (J). (gr. 5-9). 112p. 16.95 *(978-1-55469-103-6(6));* 128p. pap. 9.95 *(978-1-55469-102-9(8))* Orca Bk. Pubs. USA.
—La Revanche Parfaite, 1 vol. 2011. (FRE.). 144p. (J). (gr. 5-9). pap. 9.95 *(978-1-55469-853-0(7))* Orca Bk. Pubs. USA.
—Stuff We All Get, 1 vol. 2011. (Orca Currents Ser.). (ENG.). 128p. (J). (gr. 5-9). pap. 9.95 *(978-1-55469-820-2(0));* lib. bdg. 16.95 *(978-1-55469-821-9(9))* Orca Bk. Pubs. USA.
Denos, Julia. Swatch: the Girl Who Loved Color. Denos, Julia, illus. 2016. (Illus.). 40p. (J). (gr. -1-3). 17.99 *(978-0-06-236638-2(6))* HarperCollins Pubs.
Derting, Kimberly. The Taking. 2015. (Taking Ser.: 1). (ENG.). 384p. (YA). (gr. 9). pap. 9.99 *(978-0-06-229361-9(3),* HarperTeen) HarperCollins Pubs.
Desmond, Elisabeth. God's Little Adventures Destiny & Dillon. 2010. 16p. pap. 15.99 *(978-1-60957-849-7(X))* Salem Author Services.
Dessen, Sarah. Keeping the Moon. 2004. (ENG.). 256p. (YA). (gr. 7-7). pap. 10.99 *(978-0-14-240176-7(5),* Speak) Penguin Young Readers Group.
—That Summer. (ENG.). (YA). (gr. 7-18). 2006. 208p. 17.99 *(978-0-670-06110-5(7),* Viking Books for Young Readers) 2004. 224p. 10.99 *(978-0-14-240172-9(2),* Speak) Penguin Young Readers Group.
Las Desventuras de Sofia. (SPA., Illus.). (YA). 14.95 *(978-84-7281-169-0(7),* AF1169) Auriga, Ediciones S.A. ESP. Dist: Continental Bk. Co., Inc.
Deutsch, Barry. Hereville: How Mirka Caught a Fish. 2015. (Hereville Ser.: 3). (ENG., Illus.). 144p. (J). (gr. 3-7). 17.95 *(978-1-4197-0800-8(7),* Amulet Bks.) Abrams, Inc.
—Hereville: How Mirka Got Her Sword. 2012. (Hereville Ser.). (ENG., Illus.). 144p. (J). (gr. 3-7). pap. 9.95 *(978-1-4197-0619-6(5),* Amulet Bks.) Abrams, Inc.
—Hereville: How Mirka Met a Meteorite. 2012. (Hereville Ser.). (ENG., Illus.). 128p. (J). (gr. 3-7). 17.95 *(978-1-4197-0398-0(6),* Amulet Bks.) Abrams, Inc.
Deutsch, Stacia. The Friendship Code. Fernandez, Andrea, illus. 2017. (Girls Who Code Ser.: 1). (ENG.). 144p. (J). (gr. 3-7). 12.99 ***(978-0-399-54251-0(5),*** Penguin Workshop) Penguin Young Readers Group.
Deutsch, Stacia & Cohon, Rhody. In the Stars. 2012. (Romantic Comedies Ser.). (ENG.). 304p. (YA). (gr. 9). pap. 14.99 *(978-1-4424-8293-7(1),* Simon Pulse) Simon Pulse.
—Lucky Phoo. 2013. 182p. pap. *(978-1-927792-28-5(2))* Imajin Bks.
Devereux, Jan. Poe the Crow. Devereux, Jan, ed. Vanslette, Roxy, illus. 2004. 139p. (J). per. *(978-0-9749677-0-7(X))* Lakeview Pr.
Devorsine, Sally. Now I Know... That I Wouldn't Be Who I Think I Am, Without Other People. 2012. (Now I Know Ser.). (ENG., Illus.). (J). (gr. -1-3). pap. 15.00 *(978-0-9740268-4-8(0))* Chocolate Sauce.
—Now I Know... That Silly Hopes & Fears Will Just Make Wrinkles on My Face. 2012. (Now I Know Ser.). (ENG., Illus.). 52p. (J). (gr. -1-3). pap. 15.00 *(978-0-9740268-1-7(6))* Chocolate Sauce.
Dewees-Gilger, Connie. Isia Saves Egypt. Bouthyette, Valerie, illus. 2013. (ENG.). (J). 14.95 *(978-1-62086-375-6(8))* Mascot Bks., Inc.
Diamond, Corinna. The Mystical Manifestations of Morgan. 2012. 16p. pap. 7.99 *(978-1-4525-6321-3(7))* Balboa Pr.
Diamond, Lorraine. I Want a Camel for a Pet, 1 vol. 2009. 13p. pap. 24.95 *(978-1-61546-425-8(5))* America Star Bks.
DiCamillo, Kate. Because of Winn-Dixie. braille ed. 2003. (J). (gr. 2). spiral bd. *(978-0-616-15263-8(9))* Canadian National Institute for the Blind/Institut National Canadien pour les Aveugles.
—Because of Winn-Dixie. aut. ed. 2010. (Because of Winn-Dixie Ser.). (ENG., Illus.). 192p. (J). (gr. 4-7). 15.99 *(978-0-7636-5007-0(2));* 50.00 *(978-0-7636-5185-5(0))* Candlewick Pr.
—Because of Winn-Dixie. unabr. ed. 2004. 192p. (J). (gr. 4-7). pap. 29.00 incl. audio *(978-0-8072-0707-9(1),* Listening Library) Random Hse. Audio Publishing Group.
—Flora & Ulysses: The Illuminated Adventures. Campbell, K. G., illus. (ENG.). (J). (gr. 3-7). 2016. pap. 6.99 *(978-0-7636-8764-9(2))* 2013. 240p. 17.99 *(978-0-7636-6040-6(X))* Candlewick Pr.
—Flora & Ulysses: The Illuminated Adventures. Campbell, K. G., illus. 2016. (ENG.). 256p. (J). (gr. 3-7). 17.20 *(978-0-606-39100-9(2))* Turtleback Bks.
—Flora & Ulysses: The Illuminated Adventures. 2015. lib. bdg. 19.65 *(978-0-606-36861-2(2))* Turtleback Bks.
—Gracias a Winn-Dixie. 2003.Tr. of Because of Winn-Dixie. (SPA.). 154p. (gr. 4-6). 16.99 *(978-84-279-5002-3(0))* Noguer y Caralt Editores, S. A. ESP. Dist: Lectorum Pubns., Inc.
Dickman, Jacqueline Rosett. God's Little Lake: Max & Me, 1 vol. 2009. 48p. pap. 16.95 *(978-1-61582-523-3(1))* America Star Bks.
Dickson, Julie A. Girl from the Shadows. 2011. 74p. pap. 19.95 *(978-1-4626-3473-6(7))* America Star Bks.
Dillon, Elizabeth. Forgetful Lucy Goes to the Ranch. 2012. 62p. pap. 19.50 *(978-1-60911-688-0(7),* Strategic Bk. Publishing) Strategic Book Publishing & Rights Agency (SBPRA).
Dinosaur Girl: Individual Title, 6 packs. (Action Packs Ser.). 120p. (gr. 3-5). 44.00 *(978-0-7635-8394-1(4))* Rigby Education.
Disney Book Group Staff. Doc Mcstuffins Dad's Favorite Toy. Disney Storybook Art Team, illus. 2015. (ENG.). 24p. (J). (gr. -1-k). pap. 4.99 *(978-1-4847-2164-3(0))* Disney Pr.
—Doc on Call. Disney Storybook Art Team, illus. 2015. (ENG.). 40p. (J). (gr. -1-k). 10.99 *(978-1-4847-2187-2(X))* Disney Pr.
Disney Storybook Art Team, illus. Moana Read-Along Storybook & CD. 2016. (Read-Along Storybook & CD Ser.). (ENG.). 32p. (J). (gr. 1-3). pap. 6.99 *(978-1-4847-4361-4(X))* Disney Pr.
Disney Storybook Artists Staff. Tangled, Rapunzel's Adventures: Storybook with Music Player. 2010. (Music Player Storybook Ser.). (ENG., Illus.). 32p. (J). (gr. -1-3). 24.99 *(978-0-7944-2029-1(X))* Reader's Digest Assn., Inc., The.
Ditchfield, Lily K. & Zielski, Julie A. The Witches That Saved the Dogs. 2009. 26p. pap. 12.95 *(978-1-60264-494-6(2))* Virtualbookworm.com Publishing, Inc.
Divine, L. Hustlin' 2009. (Drama High Ser.: 7). lib. bdg. 26.95 *(978-0-606-00156-4(5),* Turtleback) Turtleback Bks.
Dodd, Kelly. Gregarious Gabby & Her Gabbyful Life: Moving Day. 2011. 28p. 13.59 *(978-1-4567-2890-8(3))* AuthorHouse.
Doherty, Berlie. The Company of Ghosts. 2015. (ENG., Illus.). 272p. (YA). (gr. 7). 9.99 *(978-1-84939-729-2(5))* Andersen Pr. GBR. Dist: Independent Pubs. Group.
Dokey, Cameron. How Not to Spend Your Senior Year. 2012. (Romantic Comedies Ser.). (ENG.). 304p. (YA). (gr. 9). pap. 14.99 *(978-1-4424-6056-0(3),* Simon Pulse) Simon Pulse.
Dokey, Cameron & Burge, Constance M. Truth & Consequences. 2003. (Charmed Ser.). (ENG., Illus.). 208p. (YA). mass mkt. 6.99 *(978-0-689-85791-1(8))* Pocket Books.
Dompierre, Judith. Jennie's Search for Colors & Numbers. 2012. 38p. 29.95 *(978-1-4626-9277-4(X))* America Star Bks.
Dompierre, Judith E. Jennie's New Adventure Looking for Letters. 2012. 28p. pap. 24.95 *(978-1-4626-9330-6(X));* pap. 24.95 *(978-1-4626-9625-3(2));* 24.95 *(978-1-4626-6486-3(5))* America Star Bks.
—Jennie's Search for Colors & Numbers. 2012. 40p. pap. 24.95 *(978-1-4626-9331-3(8))* America Star Bks.
Don, Lari. Masha & the Bear: A Story from Russia. Williamson, Melanie, illus. 2013. (Animal Stories Ser.). (ENG.). 48p. (J). (gr. 1-4). pap. 8.99 *(978-1-84686-874-0(2))* Barefoot Bks., Inc.
Donnell, Annie Hamilton. Four Girls & a Compact. 2005. 76p. pap. 10.95 *(978-1-59540-606-4(9),* 1st World Library - Literary Society) 1st World Publishing, Inc.
—Four Girls & A Compact. 2004. reprint ed. pap. 1.99 *(978-1-4192-2048-7(9));* pap. 15.95 *(978-1-4191-2048-0(4))* Kessinger Publishing, LLC.
Donner, Candie. American Girl: Assembled: Meet Molly Lapbook. Kinney, Cyndi, ed. 2013. (J). pap. 35.99 *(978-1-61625-511-4(0))* Knowledge Box Central.
—American Girl: Meet Molly Lapbook. Kinney, Cyndi, ed. 2013. (J). pap. 25.99 *(978-1-61625-509-1(9));* cd-rom 19.99 *(978-1-61625-508-4(0))* Knowledge Box Central.
Donwerth-Chikamatsu, Annie. Somewhere Among. Chaghatzbanian, Sonia, illus. 2016. (ENG.). 448p. (J). (gr. 4-7). 16.99 *(978-1-4814-3786-8(0),* Atheneum/Caitlyn Dlouhy Books) Simon & Schuster Children's Publishing.
Dorris, Michael. Tainos. Escrivá, Vivi, illus. 97th ed. 2003.Tr. of Morning Girl. (SPA.). 112p. (gr. 5-8). pap. 26.30 *(978-84-204-4757-5(9),* AF1929) Harcourt Schl. Pubs.
Doscher, E. L. M. S. Emmy Sue & the Blue Moo. Doscher, Susan, illus. 2010. 20p. pap. 9.99 *(978-1-935125-92-1(3))* Robertson Publishing.
Dotlich, Rebecca Kai. One Day, the End: Short, Very Short, Shorter-Than-Ever Stories. Koehler, Fred, illus. 2015. (ENG.). 32p. (J). (gr. -1-3). 16.95 *(978-1-62091-451-9(4),* 1396728) Boyds Mills Pr.
Dowell, Frances O'Roark. The Secret Language of Girls. (Secret Language of Girl Trilogy Ser.). (ENG., Illus.). 256p. (J). (gr. 3-7). 2005. pap. 7.99 *(978-1-4169-0717-6(3))* 2004. 19.99 *(978-0-689-84421-8(2))* Simon & Schuster Children's Publishing. (Atheneum Bks. for Young Readers).
Dower, Laura. Give Me a Break. 2004. 166p. (J). lib. bdg. 16.92 *(978-1-4242-0649-0(9))* Fitzgerald Bks.
Downing, Erin. Best Friends (until Someone Better Comes Along) 2014. (Mix Ser.). (ENG., Illus.). 240p. (J). (gr. 4-8). pap. 6.99 *(978-1-4424-8519-8(1),* Aladdin) Simon & Schuster Children's Publishing.
Doyle, Brian. Up to Low, 1 vol. 3rd ed. 2004. (ENG.). 115p. (J). pap. 6.95 *(978-0-88899-622-0(5))* Groundwood Bks. CAN. Dist: Publishers Group West (PGW).
Doyle, Mary K. Saint Theodora & Her Promise to God. Velikan, Phil, illus. 2013. 34p. 16.99 *(978-0-9897397-0-2(8))* Sisters of Providence.
Drachman, Eric. It's Me! Isabelle, Decenciere, illus. 2005. (ENG.). 32p. (J). (gr. -1-2). 18.95 incl. audio compact disk *(978-0-9703809-2-0(5))* Kidwick Bks.
Drawson, Blair. Mary Margaret's Tree. (ENG., Illus.). 32p. (J). 16.95 *(978-0-88899-259-8(9))* Groundwood Bks. CAN. Dist: Publishers Group West (PGW).
Driscoll, Laura. We Are Twins. Campion, Pascal, illus. 2012. (Penguin Young Readers, Level 1 Ser.). (ENG.). 32p. (J). (gr. k-1). mass mkt. 3.99 *(978-0-448-46157-1(9),* Penguin Young Readers) Penguin Young Readers Group.
Du Jardin, Rosamond. Marcy Catches Up. 2003. (YA). pap. 12.95 *(978-1-930009-75-2(5),* 800-691-7779) Image Cascade Publishing.
Dubinski, Lisa. A Gift to Give & Coloring Book. 2010. 32p. pap. 17.99 *(978-0-557-60224-7(6))* Lulu Pr., Inc.
Dubuc, Marianne & Ghione, Yvette. The Bus Ride. Dubuc, Marianne, illus. 2015. (ENG., Illus.). 40p. (J). (gr. -1-2). 15.95 *(978-1-77138-209-0(0))* Kids Can Pr., Ltd. CAN. Dist: Hachette Bk. Group.
Duey, Kathleen. Lara & the Moon-Colored Filly, Bk. 2. 2nd ed. 2005. (Hoofbeats Ser.: 6). (ENG.). 136p. (J). (gr. 3-7). pap. 4.99 *(978-0-14-240231-3(1),* Puffin Books) Penguin Young Readers Group.
Dunn, Carrie. Gracie Goes to Grandma's, 1 vol. 2010. 36p. pap. 24.95 *(978-1-4489-5483-4(5))* PublishAmerica, Inc.
Dunn, Pintip. Before Tomorrow. 2016. (ENG., Illus.). (YA). pap. 12.99 ***(978-1-68281-336-2(3))*** Entangled Publishing, LLC.
Durrant, Sabine. Cross Your Heart, Connie Pickles. 2007. 263p. (YA). (gr. 7-12). lib. bdg. 17.89 *(978-0-06-085480-5(4),* HarperTeen) HarperCollins Pubs.
Dyan, Penelope. A Girl Named Dot. Dyan, Penelope, illus. 2013. (Illus.). 34p. pap. 11.95 *(978-1-61477-102-9(2))* Bellissima Publishing, LLC.
Eagan, Mary. Chelsea & the Swan. 2011. 48p. pap. 24.95 *(978-1-4560-8471-4(2))* America Star Bks.
East, Bob. Tommy Cat & the Haunted Well, 1 vol. 2009. 42p. pap. 24.95 *(978-1-60703-754-5(8))* America Star Bks.
Easton, Marilyn. New Girl in Town. 2013. (ENG., Illus.). 64p. (J). (gr. 2-5). pap. 4.99 *(978-0-545-54762-8(8))* Math Solutions.
—New Girl in Town. 2013. (LEGO Friends Chapter Bks.: 1). lib. bdg. 14.75 *(978-0-606-31548-7(9),* Turtleback) Turtleback Bks.
Echo of Hooves. 2005. (J). *(978-1-933343-10-5(9),* PONY) Stabenfeldt Inc.
Echols, Jennifer. The Boys Next Door. 2007. (Romantic Comedies Ser.). (ENG.). 336p. (YA). (gr. 9-12). mass mkt. 6.99 *(978-1-4169-1831-8(0),* Simon Pulse) Simon Pulse.
—Endless Summer: The Boys Next Door; Endless Summer. 2010. (ENG.). 624p. (YA). (gr. 7). mass mkt. 11.99 *(978-1-4424-0659-9(3),* Simon Pulse) Simon Pulse.
Edison-Clark, Gina. Arrione's Daddies!, 1 vol. Newkirk, Errol Q., illus. 2010. 24p. pap. 24.95 *(978-1-4489-6511-3(X))* PublishAmerica, Inc.
Edwards, Asasimone. What's a Mimi-Saurus? 2009. (Illus.). 36p. pap. 16.99 *(978-1-4389-7919-9(3))* AuthorHouse.
Edwards, Cindi. Imagination Rocks. Bruner, Justine, illus. 2009. 28p. pap. 13.99 *(978-1-4490-0386-9(9))* AuthorHouse.
Edwards, Jean E. Adventure Tales: For Kids Who Want to Become Better Readers. 2012. 102p. 24.99 *(978-1-4771-4118-2(9))* Xlibris Corp.
Edwards, Linda M. Emma & Topsy's Story: The Art of Loving & Letting Go. Maher, Bob, illus. 2010. 20p. pap. 10.95 *(978-1-60911-808-2(1),* Eloquent Bks.) Strategic Book Publishing & Rights Agency (SBPRA).
Egbert, Charles. The Story of Princess Olivia: Wherein an Optimistic Slip of a Girl Brings Sunshine into the Lives of Her Royal Parents, the Whiny King & the ... & His Magical Minion, the Mischi. 2013. (ENG.). 144p. (gr. 2-7). 14.95 *(978-1-59373-147-2(7))* Bunker Hill Publishing, Inc.
Eggleston, Margaret. Fireside Stories for Girls in Their Teen. 2005. pap. 20.95 *(978-1-885529-65-7(1))* Stevens Publishing.
Eglin, Lorna. A Girl of Two Worlds. 2014. (Flamingo Fiction 9-13s Ser.). (ENG., Illus.). 176p. (J). mass mkt. 8.99 *(978-1-85792-839-6(3),* 2636467c-3c6f-46ba-9b87-167b83d659f4) Christian Focus Pubns. GBR. Dist: Bookmasters Distribution.
Eifrig, Kate. Scary Monster. Graves, Dennis, illus. 2003. (ENG.). 8p. (gr. k-1). pap. 7.95 *(978-1-879835-29-0(0),* Kaeden Bks.) Kaeden Corp.
Eilers, Roxanne. The Chocolate Brown Coat, 1 vol. 2010. 44p. pap. 24.95 *(978-1-4489-8540-1(4))* PublishAmerica, Inc.
Elizabeth, Lauren. Far from Forgotten. 2013. 112p. pap. 10.00 *(978-1-4575-2316-8(7))* Dog Ear Publishing, LLC.
Elliot, Jessie. Girls' Dinner Club. 2005. (ENG.). 256p. (gr. 7-18). 15.99 *(978-0-06-059539-5(6))* HarperCollins Pubs.
—Girls Dinner Club. 2005. (Illus.). 256p. (J). (gr. 7-18). lib. bdg. 16.89 *(978-0-06-059540-1(X))* HarperCollins Pubs.
Ellis, Amanda & Block, Maggie. Jwenlapaix in the Bateyes. 2009. 52p. pap. 24.00 *(978-1-4389-4391-6(1))* AuthorHouse.
Ellis, Deborah. Parvana's Journey. 2013. 184p. pap. *(978-1-4596-6476-0(0))* ReadHowYouWant.com, Ltd.
Ellis, Tonya. Sophie Washington: Queen of the Bee. 2013. 100p. pap. 9.99 *(978-1-4575-1754-9(X))* Dog Ear Publishing, LLC.
Eloise French. (J). *(978-2-07-056179-7(8))* Gallimard, Editions.
England, Nora. The Witches of Dorkdom. 2013. 180p. pap. 9.95 *(978-0-9676344-4-9(X))* Penury Pr.
Epperson, Kathy. Belly Thumpers. 2012. 24p. pap. 24.95 *(978-1-4626-9251-4(6))* America Star Bks.
Epstein, Robin. First Pajama Party: Slumberrific Six. 2005. (Groovy Girls Ser.). (ENG., Illus.). 80p. (J). (gr. 2-5). 3.99 *(978-0-439-81431-7(6))* Scholastic, Inc.
—The Great Outdoors: Take a Hike. 2005. (Groovy Girls Sleepover Club Ser.: Vol. 6). 58p. (J). *(978-0-439-65794-5(6))* Scholastic, Inc.
—Pranks a Lot: The Girls vs. the Boys. 2005. (Groovy Girls Ser.). (ENG., Illus.). 80p. (J). (gr. 2-5). pap. 3.99 *(978-0-439-81432-4(4))* Scholastic, Inc.
—Rock & Roll: Divas Supreme. 2005. (Groovy Girls Ser.). (ENG.). 80p. (J). (gr. 2-5). 3.99 *(978-0-439-81434-8(0))* Scholastic, Inc.
—Sleepover Surprise: A Twin-Sational Birthday. 2005. (Groovy Girls Ser.). (ENG., Illus.). 80p. (J). (gr. 2-5). 3.99 *(978-0-439-81433-1(2))* Scholastic, Inc.
Ericson, Helen. Harriet Spies Again. 2004. 240p. (J). (gr. 3-7). pap. 36.00 incl. audio *(978-0-8072-2091-7(4),* Listening Library) Random Hse. Audio Publishing Group.
Ericson, Helen & Fitzhugh, Louise. Harriet Spies Again. 2003. (ENG.). 256p. (J). (gr. 3-7). mass mkt. 7.99 *(978-0-440-41688-3(4),* Yearling) Random Hse. Children's Bks.
Ernestine. Town Girl. 2011. 36p. pap. 21.99 *(978-1-4628-4649-8(1))* Xlibris Corp.
Ernst, Lisa Campbell. Sylvia Jean, the Drama Queen. 2005. (ENG., Illus.). 32p. (J). (gr. -1-3). 16.99 *(978-0-525-46962-9(1),* Dutton Books for Young Readers) Penguin Young Readers Group.
Esperanza, Charles George, illus. Red, Yellow, Blue, & a Dash of White, Too! 2015. (ENG.). 40p. (J). (gr. -1-k). 16.99 *(978-1-62914-624-9(2),* Sky Pony Pr.) Skyhorse Publishing Co., Inc.
Eswar, Smrithi. The Naboola Island. 2013. 44p. pap. 7.99 *(978-1-300-57554-2(9))* Lulu Pr., Inc.
Eulberg, Elizabeth. Revenge of the Girl with the Great Personality. 2014. (ENG.). 272p. (J). (gr. 7). pap. 10.99

(978-0-545-47700-0(X), Scholastic Paperbacks) Scholastic, Inc.

Evans, Leslie, illus. You Have to Be Smart If You're Going to Be Tall/Tienes Que Ser Inteligente Si Vas a Ser Alta. 2006. 46p. (J). (gr. -1-3). per. 16.99 (978-1-59879-217-1(2)) Lifevest Publishing, Inc.

Evans, Pamela. Tina Queen of the Dragons. 2006. 101p. pap. 16.95 (978-1-4241-3356-7(4)) PublishAmerica, Inc.

Faber, Polly. Mango & Bambang: The Not-a-Pig. Vulliamy, Clara, illus. 2016. (ENG.). 144p. (J). (gr. 1-4). 14.99 (978-0-7636-8226-2(8)) Candlewick Pr.

Facey, Paulet. Annie & the Washpan of Ripe Bananas. 2012. 24p. pap. 15.99 (978-1-4797-2659-2(1)) Xlibris Corp.

Falconer, Ian. Olivia. (Olivia Ser.). (FRE.). pap. 29.95 (978-2-02-041087-8(7)) Editions du Seuil FRA. Dist: Distribooks, Inc.

—Olivia. (Olivia Ser.). pap. 27.95 (978-85-250-3380-2(4)) Globo, Editora SA BRA. Dist: Distribooks, Inc.

—Olivia. (Olivia Ser.). (978-3-7891-6504-7(2)) Oetinger, Friedrich GmbH Verlag.

Falligant, Erin. Braving the Lake. Studios, Arcana, illus. 2010. (ENG.). 120p. (YA). (gr. 3-18). pap. 8.95 (978-1-59369-757-0(0)) American Girl Publishing, Inc.

—A Surprise Find. Studios, Arcana, illus. 2011. (ENG.). 120p. (J). pap. 8.95 (978-1-59369-908-6(5)) American Girl Publishing, Inc.

Fallin, Rachel. Little Blessings. 2012. 24p. pap. 17.99 (978-1-4685-6209-5(6)) AuthorHouse.

Famularo, Joe. Chiara's Bite of the Big Apple: A Happy Book. 2013. 28p. pap. 16.09 (978-1-4669-5274-4(1)) Trafford Publishing.

—Taco/Fatso: The Story of a Fat Dog, Too Fat to Fly. 2013. 32p. pap. 17.25 (978-1-4669-4926-3(0)) Trafford Publishing.

Fanning, Meghan. Mrs. Kisses. Judah, Nathan, illus. 2013. 28p. pap. 9.99 (978-1-61225-227-8(3)) Mirror Publishing.

Farley, Terri. Phantom Stallion Box Set: The Wild One; Mustang Moon; Dark Sunshine. Call, Greg, illus. 2004. (Phantom Stallion Ser.). 704p. (J). (gr. 5-18). pap. 14.99 (978-0-06-059504-3(3), HarperCollins) HarperCollins Pubs.

Feldman, Rachel S. The Pink Blanket. 2012. 24p. pap. 14.99 (978-1-4634-5297-1(7)) AuthorHouse.

Ferguson, Alex. Tiggie: A Story of Good & Evil Written for Young People. 2011. 112p. 28.31 (978-1-4520-7799-4(1)); pap. 13.32 (978-1-4520-7798-7(3)) AuthorHouse.

Ferguson, Jamianne. Lost in Past Remembrence. 2010. 265p. pap. 17.25 (978-0-557-52788-5(0)) Lulu Pr., Inc.

Ferrara, Gin. I'm Not Afraid of Snakes. 2009. 39p. pap. 22.95 (978-0-557-15979-6(2)) Lulu Pr., Inc.

Ferrell, Miralee. A Horse for Kate. 2015. (Horses & Friends Ser.: 1). (ENG.). 208p. (J). pap. 7.99 (978-0-7814-1114-1(9)) Cook, David C.

—Silver Spurs. 2015. (Horses & Friends Ser.: 2). (ENG.). 240p. (J). pap. 7.99 (978-0-7814-1113-4(0)) Cook, David C.

Ferrone, John M. Margo & the Secret Pond. Ferrone, John M., photos by. Date not set. (Illus.). 36p. (J). (gr. -1-5). pap. 16.95 (978-1-928811-03-9(5)) Story Stuff, Inc.

Fielding, Sarah. The Governess or the Little Female Academy. 2004. reprint ed. pap. 19.95 (978-1-4191-6442-2(2)); pap. 1.99 (978-1-4192-6442-9(7)) Kessinger Publishing, LLC.

Fifteen at Last. 2003. (J). pap. 2.75 (978-0-590-43526-0(4)) Scholastic, Inc.

Figueroa, Acton. So Not the Drama. 2005. (Illus.). 79p. (J). (978-1-4156-3929-0(9)) Disney Pr.

Figueroa, Juanita Kimberly. Kendra Gives a Birthday Party. 2012. 24p. pap. 24.95 (978-1-4626-6009-4(6)) PublishAmerica, Inc.

Finley, Martha. Elsie Dinsmore. 2006. (ENG.). pap. 13.95 (978-1-4218-3092-6(2)) 1st World Publishing, Inc.

Finneron, Karyn A. Susu of the Frufru. Provencher, Annemarie, illus. 2012. 32p. (-18). pap. 9.99 (978-0-9857362-0-0(8)) Nana's Stories.

Firth, Norma. Tasha a Fraidy Cat. 2012. 28p. pap. 15.99 (978-1-4685-6079-4(4)) AuthorHouse.

Fishman, Linda Charles. The Little Girl Who Loves Colors: Book Four of Grandma's Girls. 2012. 24p. pap. 17.99 (978-1-4772-9277-8(2)) AuthorHouse.

—The Little Girl Who Loves Make Believe: Book 2 of Grandma's Girls. 2012. 24p. pap. 17.99 (978-1-4685-4467-1(5)) AuthorHouse.

—The Little Girl Who Loves Music: Book Three of Grandma's Girls. 2012. 24p. pap. 17.99 (978-1-4772-6156-9(7)) AuthorHouse.

Fisk, Pauline. Midnight Blue. 2005. 217p. (gr. -1). 16.95 (978-0-7569-5683-7(8)) Perfection Learning Corp.

Fitzpatrick, Huntley. The Boy Most Likely To. 2015. (ENG.). 432p. (YA). (gr. 9). 17.99 (978-0-8037-4142-3(1), Dial Bks) Penguin Young Readers Group.

Flake, Sharon G. The Skin I'm In. Disney Press Staff, illus. rev. ed. 2007. (ENG.). 176p. (J). (gr. 5-9). pap. 8.99 (978-1-4231-0385-1(8), Jump at the Sun) Hyperion Bks. for Children.

Flambaum, Victor & Flambaum, Andrew. How to Make a Big Bang: A Cosmic Journey. 2012. (ENG.). 226p. (J). (gr. 7-10). pap. 14.95 (978-1-936782-72-7(3)) Salem Author Services.

Flint, Ann. Charlotte's Curtain Call. 2011. 190p. pap. (978-1-908105-51-6(8)) Grosvenor Hse. Publishing Ltd.

Flower, Graham Jessie. Grace Harlowe's Overland Riders on the Great American Desert. 2007. (ENG.). 132p. pap. 18.99 (978-1-4264-1676-7(8)) Creative Media Partners, LLC.

—Grace Harlowe's Overland Riders on the Great American Desert. 2004. reprint ed. pap. 20.95 (978-1-4191-2221-7(5)); pap. 1.99 (978-1-4192-2221-4(X)) Kessinger Publishing, LLC.

—Grace Harlowe's Return to Overton Campus. l.t. ed. 2007. (ENG.). 146p. pap. 19.99 (978-1-4264-3853-0(2)); 154p. pap. 19.99 (978-1-4264-3783-0(8)) Creative Media Partners, LLC.

Flower, Jessie Graham. Grace Harlowe's Return to Overton Campus. 2007. 260p. 29.95 (978-1-4344-9674-4(0)); per. 19.95 (978-1-4344-9673-7(2)) Wildside Pr., LLC.

—Grace Harlowe's Second Year at Overton Campus. 2007. 252p. 29.95 (978-1-4344-9676-8(7)); per. 19.95 (978-1-4344-9675-1(9)) Wildside Pr., LLC.

—Grace Harlowe's Sophomore Year at High School. 2007. 256p. 29.95 (978-1-4344-9678-2(3)) Wildside Pr., LLC.

—Grace Harlowe's Third Year at Overton College. 2007. 252p. 29.95 (978-1-4344-9680-5(5)); per. 19.95 (978-1-4344-9679-9(1)) Wildside Pr., LLC.

Foard, Judith P. Senior Year. 2013. 416p. pap. 16.95 (978-1-4759-6552-4(2)); (gr. 10-12). 26.95 (978-1-4759-6554-4(0)) iUniverse, Inc.

Foglio, Kaja & Foglio, Phil. Agatha Heterodyne & the Clockwork Princess: A Gaslamp Fantasy with Adventure, Romance & Mad Science. Foglio, Kaja & Foglio, Phil, eds. 2013. (ENG., Illus.). 112p. (YA). pap. 25.00 (978-1-890856-39-7(8), 9781890856397) Studio Foglio, LLC.

Foley, Jessie Ann. Neighborhood Girls. 2017. 368p. (YA). (gr. 9). 17.99 **(978-0-06-257185-4(0)**, HarperTeen) HarperCollins Pubs.

Ford, Lorry. Goodnight Red: A Lesson in Courage, 1 vol. 2009. 15p. pap. 24.95 (978-1-61582-421-2(9)) PublishAmerica, Inc.

Forte, Joyce. The Brave Little Girl. 2004. 37p. pap. 24.95 (978-1-4137-1833-1(7)) PublishAmerica, Inc.

Fosberry, Jennifer. Isabella: Girl on the Go. Litwin, Mike, illus. 2012. (ENG.). 32p. (J). (gr. k-3). 16.99 (978-1-4022-6648-5(0), Sourcebooks Jabberwocky) Sourcebooks, Inc.

—Isabella for President. Litwin, Mike, illus. 2016. (ENG.). 32p. (J). (-4). 16.99 (978-1-4926-4173-5(1), 9781492641735, Sourcebooks Jabberwocky) Sourcebooks, Inc.

—My Name Is Not Isabella. Litwin, Mike, illus. 2008. 32p. (J). (gr. -1-3). lib. bdg. 19.99 (978-0-9802000-7-2(5)) Monkey Barrel Pr.

—My Name Is Not Isabella: Just How Big Can a Little Girl Dream? Litwin, Mike, illus. 2010. (ENG.). 32p. (J). (gr. k-3). 16.99 (978-1-4022-4395-0(2), Sourcebooks Jabberwocky) Sourcebooks, Inc.

Foster, Claudie. Princess Vanilla of the Amazon Jungle. 2011. 48p. pap. 24.95 (978-1-60749-297-9(0)) America Star Bks.

Foster, T. e. & Foster, T. E. In These Veins. 2011. 184p. pap. 14.99 (978-1-257-01022-6(0)) Lulu Pr., Inc.

Fotso, Serge. The Little Girl & the Lost Bag. Woods, Michele, illus. 2011. 20p. pap. 24.95 (978-1-4626-1741-8(7)) America Star Bks.

Fower, C. A. The Bramblefrost Fairies. 2013. 116p. (978-1-909740-40-2(3)); pap. (978-1-909593-96-1(6)) Legend Pr.

Francis, Stella M. Campfire Girls in the Allegheny Mountains. rev. ed. 2006. (ENG.). 136p. 25.95 (978-1-4218-2100-9(1), 1st World Library - Literary Society) 1st World Publishing, Inc.

Francois, Rose Darlie. When You least Expect It. 2009. 41p. pap. 25.30 (978-0-557-07202-6(6)) Lulu Pr., Inc.

Franz, Kevin. The Princess Sisters & the Underwater City. Stigler, Marilyn, illus. 2004. 112p. (J). per. 7.99 (978-0-9747774-1-2(2)) Starbell Bks.

Frederick, Heather Vogel. Wish You Were Eyre. 2012. (Mother-Daughter Book Club Ser.). (ENG.). 464p. (J). (gr. 4-9). 16.99 (978-1-4424-3064-8(8), Simon & Schuster Bks. For Young Readers) Simon & Schuster Bks. For Young Readers.

Freeman, Tor. Olive & the Bad Mood. Freeman, Tor, illus. 2013. (ENG., Illus.). 32p. (J). (gr. -1-3). 15.99 (978-0-7636-6657-6(2), Templar) Candlewick Pr.

Freer, Ida. Panama Girl. 2011. 116p. (gr. 4-6). 20.95 (978-1-4620-3081-1(5)); pap. 10.95 (978-1-4620-3079-8(3)) iUniverse, Inc.

Frenkel, Yetti. Libby & the Cat. Frenkel, Yetti, illus. 2005. (Illus.). 32p. (J). 16.95 (978-0-9749006-2-9(1)) Snow Tree Bks.

Frey, Hildegard G. The Camp Fire Girls at School or the Woleho Weavers. 2004. reprint ed. pap. 21.95 (978-1-4191-5575-8(X)); pap. 1.99 (978-1-4192-5575-5(4)) Kessinger Publishing, LLC.

—The Camp Fire Girls Do Their Bit. 2004. reprint ed. pap. 1.99 (978-1-4192-5577-9(0)); pap. 20.95 (978-1-4191-5577-2(6)) Kessinger Publishing, LLC.

—The Camp Fire Girls Go Motoring. 2004. reprint ed. pap. 20.95 (978-1-4191-5583-3(0)); pap. 1.99 (978-1-4192-5583-0(5)) Kessinger Publishing, LLC.

Friesen, Gayle. For Now. 2007. (ENG.). 248p. (J). (gr. 5-9). 7.95 (978-1-55453-133-2(0)) Kids Can Pr., Ltd. CAN. Dist: Hachette Bk. Group.

Froud, Brian, illus. Chelsea Morning. 2004. (ENG.). 32p. (J). (gr. -1-3). 17.95 (978-1-59687-178-6(4)) IBks., Inc.

Fuchs, Michael. Keniff & Kieff. 2013. 28p. pap. 13.95 (978-1-4908-0002-8(6), WestBow Pr.) Author Solutions, Inc.

Fujieda, Toru, creator. Dragon Girl, 2 vols., Vol. 2. 2011. (Dragon Girl Ser.: 2). (ENG., Illus.). 464p. (J). (gr. 8-17). pap. 20.99 (978-0-7595-3167-3(6), Yen Pr.) Orbit.

Fyfe, Connie. Grandma's Christmas Candy. 2011. 24p. pap. 12.79 (978-1-4567-5437-2(8)) AuthorHouse.

Gág, Wanda. The Funny Thing. 2003. (Fesler-Lampert Minnesota Heritage Ser.). (ENG., Illus.). 32p. 14.95 (978-0-8166-4241-0(9)) Univ. of Minnesota Pr.

Gaiman, NEil. Blueberry Girl. Vess, Charles, illus. (ENG.). 32p. (J). (gr. -1-3). 2011. pap. 7.99 (978-0-06-083810-2(8)) 2009. 17.99 (978-0-06-083808-9(6)) HarperCollins Pubs.

—Blueberry Girl. 2011. (J). lib. bdg. 17.20 (978-0-606-15398-0(5), Turtleback) Turtleback Bks.

Gale, Emily. Just Josie & the Number 7. Byrne, Mike, illus. 2010. (Picture Books Ser.). 25p. (J). (gr. -1-1). (978-1-4075-9505-4(9)) Parragon, Inc.

Gallagher, Diana G. Homecoming, 1 vol. 2013. (Claudia & Monica: Freshman Girls Ser.). (ENG.). 144p. (gr. 3-6). 9.95 (978-1-4342-4887-9(9), Claudia & Monica: Freshman Girls) Stone Arch Bks.

Gallardo, Adam. 100 Girls Vol. 1: Vol 1: the First Girl, Vol. 1. Demong, Todd, illus. 2008. (YA). 9.95 (978-0-9763095-3-6(X)) Arcana Studio, Inc.

Gallaz, Christophe. ROSA BLANCA. 2nd ed. 2003. (Rosa y Manzana Ser.). (SPA., Illus.). 32p. (978-84-85334-52-0(3), LG2811) Lóguez Ediciones ESP. Dist: Lectorum Pubns., Inc.

Gallegos, Jacqueline C. The Night the Princesses Danced. 2009. 40p. pap. 18.00 (978-1-4389-4514-9(0)) AuthorHouse.

Gano, Debra. Beauty's Secret. Pitre, Dawn, illus. 2008. (Heartlight Girls Ser.). 54p. (J). 17.95 (978-0-9787689-0-4(6)) Heartlight Girls.

Ganz, Yaffa. Raise a Rabbit, Grow a Goose. Klineman, Harvey, illus. 2008. 30p. 14.99 (978-1-59826-235-3(1)) Feldheim Pubs.

Garis, Lilian C. The Girl Scout Pioneers; or, Winning the First B C. 2007. 148p. per. (978-1-4065-2775-9(0)) Dodo Pr.

Garza, Shelly S. Dancing Danica. Weinstein, Holly, illus. 2013. 24p. (J). 12.99 net. (978-1-61254-138-9(0)) Brown Books Publishing Group.

Gauch, Patricia Lee. Christina Katerina & the Box. 2012. (ENG.). 32p. (J). (gr. -1-3). 7.95 (978-1-59078-915-5(6)) Boyds Mills Pr.

Gayatri Stein, Mari. Puddle Moon. 2010. (ENG., Illus.). 32p. 17.95 (978-0-9793840-0-4(1), Riverwood Bks.) White Cloud Pr.

Geddes, Diana E. Let's Play Basketball. Kaeden Corp. Staff, ed. Palmer, Kate S., illus. 2005. (ENG.). 16p. (gr. k-1). pap. 7.95 (978-1-879835-55-9(X), Kaeden Bks.) Kaeden Corp.

Geldart, Thomas. Emilie the Peacemaker. 2004. reprint ed. pap. 15.95 (978-1-4191-1769-5(6)); pap. 1.99 (978-1-4192-1769-2(0)) Kessinger Publishing, LLC.

Gelfer, Regina. The Kiss Box. 2010. 24p. pap. 12.99 (978-1-4490-8838-5(4)) AuthorHouse.

Gelford, Inga. Sophie Ma's Magical Glasses. 2012. 48p. pap. 18.00 (978-1-4670-8180-1(9)) AuthorHouse.

Gentry, Jennifer Mills. Maria Loves to Dance. 2011. 24p. pap. 24.95 (978-1-4626-1869-9(3)) America Star Bks.

Gershman, Regina. Animals from My Window. 2011. 24p. pap. 16.44 (978-1-4634-2094-9(3)) AuthorHouse.

Gershtein, V. M. Two Stories about Nothing Significant. 2004. 104p. pap. 9.95 (978-0-595-30594-0(6)) iUniverse, Inc.

Gervay, Susanne. Butterflies. 2012. (Fiction Ser.). (ENG.). 256p. (J). pap. 4.99 (978-1-61067-043-2(4)) Kane Miller.

Get Together Girls - Fashion Show. 2005. (J). bds. (978-1-4194-0086-5(X)) Paradise Pr., Inc.

Get Together Girls - Girl Band. 2005. (J). bds. (978-1-4194-0084-1(3)) Paradise Pr., Inc.

Get Together Girls - Going to the Mall. 2005. (J). bds. (978-1-4194-0087-2(8)) Paradise Pr., Inc.

Get Together Girls - Hanging Out. 2005. (J). bds. (978-1-4194-0085-8(1)) Paradise Pr., Inc.

Getson, Denise. Dry Souls. 2011. (ENG.). 200p. (YA). (gr. 8-3). pap. 7.95 (978-1-933767-12-3(X)) CBAY Bks.

Giangregorio, Kimberly A. The Smelly Shoe. O'Toole, Julianne, illus. 2012. 24p. pap. 24.95 (978-1-4626-9387-0(3)) America Star Bks.

Gibbs, Anna. The Mystery of the Healing Waters. 2005. 55p. pap. 10.00 (978-1-4134-4533-6(0)) Xlibris Corp.

Gibbs, Gretchen. The Book of Maggie Bradstreet. 2012. (Bradstreet Chronicles). (ENG.). 183p. (YA). pap. 9.99 (978-0-9852948-0-9(9)) Glenmere Pr.

Gibsen, Cole. Life Unaware. 2015. 284p. (YA). **(978-1-62844-152-9(6))** Entangled Publishing, LLC.

Giff, Patricia Reilly. All about Stacy. 79p. (J). (gr. 1-2). pap. 3.99 (978-0-8072-1280-6(6), Listening Library) Random Hse. Audio Publishing Group.

—Stacy Says Good-Bye. 75p. (J). (gr. 1-2). pap. 3.99 (978-0-8072-1278-3(4), Listening Library) Random Hse. Audio Publishing Group.

Gillespie, Hollis. Unaccompanied Minor. 2014. (ENG.). 256p. (YA). 17.99 (978-1-4405-6773-5(5)) Adams Media Corp.

Gilligan, Shannon. Princess Island. 2015. (ENG.). (J). pap. 7.99 (978-1-937133-50-4(8)) Chooseco LLC.

Gilmore, Rachna. A Gift for Gita. Priestley, Alice, illus. 2004. 24p. (J). (978-1-85269-409-8(2)); (978-1-85269-408-1(4)); (978-1-85269-407-4(6)); (978-1-85269-403-6(3)) Mantra Lingua.

—When-I-Was-a-Little-Girl, 1 vol. Benoit, Renne, illus. 2007. (ENG.). 24p. (J). (gr. -1-2). 14.95 (978-1-897187-12-8(2)) Second Story Pr. CAN. Dist: Orca Bk. Pubs. USA.

Gilmore, Rachna & Priestley, Alice. A Gift for Gita, 1 vol. 2005. (Gita Ser.: 2). (ENG., Illus.). 24p. (gr. 2-6). pap. 7.95 (978-0-88448-239-0(1), 884239) Tilbury Hse. Pubs.

Girel, Stephane, illus. A Bird in Winter: A Children's Book Inspired by Pieter Breugel. 2011. (ENG.). 32p. (J). (gr. -1-3). 14.95 (978-3-7913-7080-4(4)) Prestel Verlag GmbH & Co KG. DEU. Dist: Penguin Random Hse. LLC.

A Girl Named Pants. 2004. (J). per. 7.99 (978-0-9755959-0-9(3)) Girl Named Pants, Inc., A.

Gitau, Terri. Annie & Kindness the Frog. 2012. 16p. pap. 15.99 (978-1-4634-4021-3(9)) AuthorHouse.

Gittemeier, Tausha. Hmmm, I was Thinking... What If? 2004. 20p. pap. 24.95 (978-1-4137-3429-4(4)) PublishAmerica, Inc.

Giuliani, Al. New Nanny. 2013. (Jessie Junior Novel Ser.). (ENG.). 128p. (J). (gr. 3-7). pap. 5.99 (978-1-4231-8369-3(X)) Disney Pr.

Glass, Lisa. Blue. 2015. (Blue Ser.: 1). (ENG.). 352p. (J). (gr. 7-17). 16.99 (978-1-62365-414-6(9), Quercus) Quercus NA.

Glasser, Sophie. I've Known since I Was Eight. 2003. 126p. (YA). pap. 10.95 (978-0-595-29333-9(6)) iUniverse, Inc.

Glatzer, Jenna. Hattie, Get a Haircut! Kendall, Monica, illus. 2005. (ENG.). 32p. (J). (gr. -1-3). lib. bdg. 19.95 (978-0-9724853-0-2(9)) Keene Publishing.

Glenn, Shelley. Gracie's Fall. 2011. 40p. pap. 21.99 (978-1-4568-8768-1(8)) Xlibris Corp.

Global Fund for Children Staff, contrib. by. Global Baby Girls. 2013. (ENG., Illus.). 16p. (J). (— 1). bds. 6.95 (978-1-58089-439-5(9)) Charlesbridge Publishing, Inc.

Glyn, Pamela. The green light in the Mountains. 2010. 32p. pap. 23.96 (978-1-4457-5153-5(4)) Lulu Pr., Inc.

Godbersen, Anna. Envy. 2009. (Luxe Ser.: 3). (ENG.). 432p. (YA). (gr. 9). pap. 9.99 (978-0-06-134574-6(1)) HarperCollins Pubs.

—The Lucky Ones. 2013. (Bright Young Things Ser.: 3). (ENG.). 400p. (YA). (gr. 9). pap. 9.99 (978-0-06-196271-4(6)) HarperCollins Pubs.

—Rumors. 2008. (Luxe Ser.: No. 2). (YA). (gr. 9-12). (ENG.). 304p. 17.99 (978-0-06-134569-2(5)); 423p. lib. bdg. 18.89 (978-0-06-134570-8(9)) HarperCollins Pubs. (HarperTeen).

Goerzen, Christy. The Big Apple Effect, 1 vol. 2014. (Orca Currents Ser.). (ENG.). 136p. (J). (gr. 5-9). pap. 9.95 (978-1-4598-0738-9(3)) Orca Bk. Pubs. USA.

Gold, Rachel. Being Emily. 2012. (ENG.). 264p. (gr. 9). pap. 15.95 (978-1-59493-283-0(2)) Bella Bks., Inc.

Golden Books Staff. Rainbow Adventure. Miller, Victoria, illus. 2010. (Super Color with Stickers Ser.). (ENG.). 96p. (J). (gr. -1-2). pap. 3.99 (978-0-375-86350-9(8), Golden Bks.) Random Hse. Children's Bks.

—Save the Unicorn King! Miller, Victoria, illus. 2011. (Paint Box Book Ser.). (ENG.). 48p. (J). (gr. -1-2). pap. 3.99 (978-0-375-87391-1(0), Golden Bks.) Random Hse. Children's Bks.

Goldilocks & the Three Bears. 2004. (My First Fairy Tales Ser.). (Illus.). 24p. (J). pap. 3.99 (978-1-85854-686-5(9)) Brimax Books Ltd. GBR. Dist: Byeway Bks.

Goldilocks & the Three Bears. (Ladybird Bks.). (ARA., Illus.). 52p. (J). 12.95 incl. audio (978-0-86685-254-8(9), LDL109C) International Bk. Ctr., Inc.

Gomolski, Mark F. Ginny's Adventures: Little Ginny. 2013. (ENG.). 72p. pap. 9.95 (978-1-4787-2490-2(0)) Outskirts Pr., Inc.

Goobie, Beth. Something Girl, 1 vol. 2005. (Orca Soundings Ser.). (ENG.). 128p. (YA). (gr. 8-12). per. 9.95 (978-1-55143-347-9(8)) Orca Bk. Pubs. USA.

Goodman, Hannah R. Fear of Falling. 2009. 168p. pap. 12.95 (978-1-4401-5645-8(X)) iUniverse, Inc.

Goodyear-Brown, Paris. Gabby the Gecko. 2003. per. (978-1-932203-54-7(0)) Sundog, Ltd.

Gordon, Lorell Cynthia. Tilly's Birthday: A Young Girl's Introduction to Menstruation. 2005. (Illus.). 64p. (J). per. 6.99 (978-0-9763961-0-9(6)) Learning All About Me, LLC.

Gordon, Meryl G. The Flower Girl Wore Celery. Clifton-Brown, Holly, illus. 2016. (ENG.). 32p. (J). (gr. -1-5). 17.99 (978-1-4677-7844-2(3), Kar-Ben Publishing) Lerner Publishing Group.

Gorman, Katie. Wondrous Adventures, 1 vol. 2009. 24p. pap. 24.95 (978-1-60749-878-0(2)) America Star Bks.

Gossler, Renate Von. The Little Weed. 2012. 24p. pap. 15.99 (978-1-4691-3866-4(2)) Xlibris Corp.

Gottesfeld, Jeff. Too Many Dogs, 1 vol. 2015. (Red Rhino Ser.). (ENG.). 68p. (J). (gr. 4-6). pap. 7.95 (978-1-62250-951-5(X)) Saddleback Educational Publishing, Inc.

Govan, Christine Noble. The Pink Maple House. Sari, illus. 2013. 292p. pap. 13.95 (978-1-61427-443-8(6)) Martino Fine Bks.

Gow, Kailin. Reborn #1: Queen B Superheroine Series. 2005. 168p. (YA). per. 7.99 (978-1-59748-855-6(0)) Sparklesoup LLC.

Graceland Book Publishers, as told by. A Little Girl by Chinyere Nwakanma. 2nd ed. 2010. (Illus.). 32p. (J). (978-0-9566210-0-9(7)) Graceland Book Publishing U.K.

Grami, B. Help! I Have Rats in My Hair! 2011. 22p. (J). pap. 17.95 (978-1-4327-5348-1(7)) Outskirts Pr., Inc.

Grant, Katy. Fearless. 2010. (Summer Camp Secrets Ser.). (ENG.). 240p. (J). (gr. 3-7). pap. 7.99 (978-1-4169-9162-5(X), Aladdin) Simon & Schuster Children's Publishing.

—Pranked. 2008. (Summer Camp Secrets Ser.). (ENG.). 240p. (J). (gr. 3-7). pap. 7.99 (978-1-4169-3576-6(2), Aladdin) Simon & Schuster Children's Publishing.

Grant, Ruthie. Oh, No! Fancy-Free Amy Gets Bad News. 2012. 24p. pap. 13.99 (978-1-4634-4700-7(0)) AuthorHouse.

Graves, Sue. Bad Luck, Lucy! Williams, Lisa, illus. 2008. (Tadpoles Ser.). (ENG.). 24p. (J). (gr. -1-3). pap. (978-0-7787-3882-4(5)); lib. bdg. (978-0-7787-3851-0(5)) Crabtree Publishing Co.

Gray, Amy. How to Be a Vampire: A Fangs-On Guide for the Newly Undead. Erwert, Scott, illus. 2009. (ENG.). 144p. (YA). (gr. 7-18). 14.99 (978-0-7636-4915-9(5)) Candlewick Pr.

Graziano, Alexandra Marie. The Colors of Rayne. 2012. 140p. pap. 19.99 (978-1-4771-0791-1(6)) Xlibris Corp.

Greathouse, Cindy. Robin the Abused Child. 2011. 28p. pap. 24.95 (978-1-60749-065-4(X)) America Star Bks.

—Sophie the Missing Bunny. 2011. 20p. pap. 24.95 (978-1-4489-5607-4(2)) America Star Bks.

Green, Jacqueline. Truth or Dare. 2014. (Truth or Dare Ser.: 1). (ENG.). 416p. (YA). (gr. 10-17). pap. 10.99 (978-0-316-22035-4(3), Poppy) Little, Brown Bks. for Young Readers.

Green, John. Terdellaine: A Free-Spirited, Energeti. 2005. 48p. pap. 16.95 (978-1-4137-9528-8(5)) PublishAmerica, Inc.

Green, Melissa J. & G., Melissa J. Mona Whine'ona: (the List) G., Ashley R., illus. 2007. 20p. per. 24.95 (978-1-4241-8451-4(7)) PublishAmerica, Inc.

Greenberg, Joanne. I Never Promised You a Rose Garden. 256p. (YA). (gr. 7-18). pap. 5.99 (978-0-8072-1362-9(4), Listening Library) Random Hse. Audio Publishing Group.

Greene, Brenda. Dog Gone: Boomer's Story. Cheryl H. Hahn, illus. 2005. 127p. (YA). per. 8.99 (978-0-9770279-0-3(2)) Three Willows Pr.

Greene, Constance C. A Girl Called Al. 127p. (J). (gr. 4-6). pap. 5.99 (978-0-8072-1410-7(8), Listening Library) Random Hse. Audio Publishing Group.

Greene, Jacqueline. Rebecca Story Collection. Hirsch, Jennifer, ed. Hunt, Robert, illus. 2009. (ENG.). 456p. (YA). (gr. 3-18). 29.95 (978-1-59369-626-9(4)) American Girl Publishing, Inc.

Greene, Reggie. The Adventures of Swami Somewhere- the Supermarket. Graham, Michael, illus. 2011. 32p. (J). 14.95 (978-1-60131-095-8(1)) Big Tent Bks.

Grennan, Michael F. The Adventures of E-Lane: Maple Syrul Heaven. 2012. 36p. (-18). pap. 20.99 (978-1-4772-8794-1(9)) AuthorHouse.

Gresh, Dannah. Secret Keeper Girl Pajama Party. 2014. (ENG.). 64p. (J). pap. 12.99 (978-0-7369-6002-1(3)) Harvest Hse. Pubs.

Gresham, Evelyn. Sweet Sweet Carabee. Sponaugle, Kim, illus. 2013. 24p. pap. 11.95 (978-1-61244-233-4(1)) Halo Publishing International.

Gribben, Valerie. The Fairytale Trilogy: Fairytale, the Emperor's Realm, & the Three Crowns. 2010. (ENG.). 320p. (YA). (gr. 5-10). 24.95 (978-1-58838-251-1(6), NewSouth Bks.) NewSouth, Inc.

Griffie, Sandra. The Snow Dancer. 2012. 28p. 24.95 (978-1-4626-6777-2(5)) America Star Bks.

Griffin, C. R. Runt & the Two Roses. 2011. 24p. pap. 15.99 (978-1-4628-4589-7(4)) Xlibris Corp.

Griffin, Marcia. Debbie's Letter to God. Davies, Michelle, illus. 2005. (J). pap. 8.00 (978-0-8059-6409-7(6)) Dorrance Publishing Co., Inc.

E F G

Griffith, Linda Hill, illus. Most Special Flower Girl. 2010. (ENG.). 24p. 10.99 *(978-1-4022-3817-8(7))* Sourcebooks, Inc.

Griffiths, Neil & Nash, Doug. Florence Was No Ordinary Fairy. 2015. (ENG., Illus.). 28p. (J). pap. 13.50 *(978-1-905434-03-9(0))* Award Pubns. Ltd. GBR. Dist: Parkwest Pubns., Inc.

Grimm, Jacob, et al. The Goose Girl. (Illus.). 32p. (J). 15.95 *(978-0-86315-182-8(5)*, 1751) Floris Bks. GBR. Dist: SteinerBooks, Inc.

Groenewald, Catherine. The Little Girl Who Didn't Want to Grow Up. 2011. (Best Loved Tales for Africa Ser.). (ENG., Illus.). 32p. (J). (gr. k-2). pap. 10.95 *(978-1-77009-819-0(4))* Jacana Media ZAF. Dist: Independent Pubs. Group.

Grover, Kuloa A. Charlie the Snake. 2012. 32p. pap. 19.99 *(978-1-4685-5568-4(5))* AuthorHouse.

Guerra, R. R. Gabirochi y la Isla de la Vid. 2010. 168p. pap. 31.90 *(978-1-59754-554-9(6))* Editorial Libros en Red.

Guerras, Safia. Lou Lou. 2012. (Illus.). 40p. *(978-1-78132-021-1(7))*; pap. *(978-1-78132-019-8(5))* SilverWood Bks.

Guerras Safia. Lou Lou. Kemble, Mai S., illus. 2013. (ENG.). 24p. (J). pap. 16.95 *(978-1-4787-2359-2(9))* Outskirts Pr., Inc.

Guillory, Sarah. Reclaimed. 2013. (ENG.). 296p. (YA). (gr. 7-9). pap. 9.95 *(978-1-937053-88-8(1)*, Spencer Hill Contemporary) Spencer Hill Pr.

Gunderson, Jessica. A Rebel among Redcoats: A Revolutionary War Novel. 2015. (Revolutionary War Ser.). (ENG., Illus.). 96p. (gr. 4-4). lib. bdg. 26.65 *(978-1-4342-9701-3(2))* Stone Arch Bks.

Guyot, Rebecca. Flyin' Ryan the Rescue Ranger: In: the Puzzleton Storm, 1 vol. 2009. 20p. pap. 24.95 *(978-1-60836-856-3(4))* America Star Bks.

Ha, Thu Huong. Hail Caesar. 2007. (Push Ser.). (ENG.). 304p. (J). (gr. 9-12). pap. 8.99 *(978-0-439-89026-7(8)*, PUSH) Scholastic, Inc.

Haas, Jessie. Bramble & Maggie: Snow Day. Friend, Alison, illus. 2016. (ENG.). 56p. (J). (gr. k-3). 14.99 *(978-0-7636-7364-2(1))* Candlewick Pr.

Hadley, Sally C. Little Sally Girl's Greatest Adventure Series. 2013. (ENG.). 38p. (J). 27.95 *(978-1-4787-2067-6(0))* Outskirts Pr., Inc.

Hager, Janet. Truly Julie. 2012. 26p. 14.95 *(978-1-4626-6121-3(1))* America Star Bks.

Hahn, Molly. Under the Sneep Tree: The Wamboozling of a Village. 2009. pap. *(978-1-61623-907-7(7))* Independent Pub.

Haldeman, Myrtle L. Cassie after Antietam. 2004. (Illus.). 109p. (J). pap. 7.99 *(978-0-8280-1782-4(4)*, 30-665) Review & Herald Publishing Assn.

Hale, Helen. Dale Evans & Danger in Crooked Canyon. Luhrs, Henry, illus. 2011. 280p. 47.95 *(978-1-258-02056-9(4))* Literary Licensing, LLC.

Hale, Linda. Activity Story Book: Sunshine & Her Big Blarney Smile. Liao, Yivian, illus. 2013. 26p. pap. *(978-1-927915-03-5(1))* Chase Enterprises.

—Sunshine & Her Big Blarney Smile. Liao, Yivian, illus. 2013. 26p. pap. *(978-1-927915-02-8(3))* Chase Enterprises.

Hall, Tara. Good Girls Do. Raluca, Cristina Cirti, illus. 2013. 36p. pap. 9.99 *(978-1-61286-192-0(X))* Avid Readers Publishing Group.

Hamblin, Hope. Kyl. 2012. 28p. pap. 17.99 *(978-1-4772-2084-9(4))* AuthorHouse.

Hamilton, Harriet. Ribbons of the Sun. 2006. 159p. (YA). (gr. 7-16). per. 8.95 *(978-0-9768126-2-3(2))* Brown Barn Bks.

Hankey, Sandy. Sweet Little Girl. Gay, Maria T., illus. 2004. 20p. pap. 24.95 *(978-1-4137-3329-7(8))* PublishAmerica, Inc.

Hapka, Catherine, pseud. Pony Crazy. Kennedy, Anne, illus. 2010. (I Can Read Level 2 Ser.). (ENG.). 32p. (J). (gr. -1-3). pap. 3.99 *(978-0-06-125535-9(1))* HarperCollins Pubs.

Hapka, Cathy, pseud. LEGO Friends: Mystery in the Whispering Woods (Chapter Book #3) 2013. (LEGO Friends Ser.). (ENG.). 64p. (J). (gr. 2-5). pap. 4.99 *(978-0-545-56669-8(X))* Scholastic, Inc.

—Lights, Camera, Girl Power! 2013. (ENG.). 64p. (J). (gr. 2-5). pap. 4.99 *(978-0-545-51654-9(4))* Math Solutions.

—Lights, Camera, Girl Power! 2013. (LEGO Friends Chapter Bks.: 2). lib. bdg. 14.75 *(978-0-606-31550-0(0)*, Turtleback) Turtleback Bks.

—My Sparkle Purse. 2003. (Sparkle Shape Bks.). (Illus.). 10p. (J). (gr. -1-18). bds. 6.99 *(978-1-57151-714-2(6))* Playhouse Publishing.

—Mystery in the Whispering Woods. 2013. (LEGO Friends Chapter Bks.: 3). lib. bdg. 14.75 *(978-0-606-32394-9(5)*, Turtleback) Turtleback Bks.

Harkes, Willy. Little Dutch Girl in World War II. Blair, Jocelyn, illus. l.t. ed. 2004. 22p. (J). pap. 13.95 *(978-0-9741627-1-3(X))* PricePoint+Publications.

Harnest, Faye. Girl Fight, 1 vol. 2011. (Lorimer SideStreets Ser.). (ENG.). 112p. (YA). (gr. 9-12). 16.95 *(978-1-55277-866-1(5)*, 9781552778661); pap. 9.95 *(978-1-55277-865-4(7)*, 9781552778654) Lorimer, James & Co., Ltd., Pubs. CAN. Dist: Casemate Pubs. & Bk. Distributors, LLC.

Harpster, Steve, illus. Debra Doesn't Take the Dare: An Emotional Literacy Book. 2004. 54p. (J). 14.95 *(978-0-9747789-3-8(1)*, 20705) CTC Publishing.

Harrington, Jenna. Katie Mcginty Wants a Pet! Simpson, Finn, illus. 2015. (ENG.). 32p. (J). (gr. -1-3). 16.99 *(978-1-58925-192-2(X))* Tiger Tales.

Harris, Amber. Black, White & Beautiful. Mamata, Sue, illus. 2007. 25p. pap. 24.95 *(978-1-4241-8932-8(2))* PublishAmerica, Inc.

Harris, Carol Gahara. My Name is Leona. Fujiwara, Kim, illus. 2013. 24p. (J). 19.95 *(978-0-9860324-0-0(9))* Snowy Night Pub.

Harris, Carrie. Sally Slick & the Steel Syndicate. Valentine, Amanda, ed. 2014. (Illus.). 200p. (YA). pap. 15.00 *(978-1-61317-063-2(7))* Evil Hat Productions LLC.

Harris, Joe. Narda. 2005. (J). *(978-0-9772259-0-3(9))* Character Arts.

Harris, Lee. Carla & the Great Talent Show. 2009. 80p. pap. 10.00 *(978-1-60860-515-6(9)*, Strategic Bk. Publishing) Strategic Book Publishing & Rights Agency (SBPRA).

Harris, Robert & Yolen, Jane. Girl in a Cage. 2004. (ENG.). 240p. (YA). (gr. 7-7). 6.99 *(978-0-14-240132-3(3)*, Speak) Penguin Young Readers Group.

Harris, Sally M. Color Me Happy. Paplinksie, Cecilia, illus. 2009. 24p. pap. 10.95 *(978-1-935137-75-7(1))* Guardian Angel Publishing, Inc.

Harris, Teresa E. American Girl: Girl of the Year 2017. 2017. (Girl of the Year 2017 Ser.: 2). (ENG.). 192p. (J). (gr. 3-7). pap. 9.99 *(978-1-338-13700-2(X))* Scholastic, Inc.

—American Girl: Girl of the Year: 2017, Novel 1. 2016. (American Girl Contempory Middle Grade Ser.: 1). lib. bdg. 20.85 ***(978-0-606-39986-9(0))*** Turtleback Bks.

—Gabriela. 2016. (American Girl: Girl of the Year Ser.: 1). (ENG.). 208p. (J). (gr. 3-7). pap. 9.99 *(978-1-338-13698-2(4))* Scholastic, Inc.

Harris, Teresa E. Girl of the Year - 2017 Novel 2. 2017. (American Girl Contempory Middle Grade Ser.: 2). lib. bdg. 20.85 ***(978-0-606-39987-6(9))*** Turtleback Bks.

Harrison, Emma. Phoebe Who? 2006. (Charmed Ser.). (ENG.). 208p. (YA). (gr. 8-12). mass mkt. 6.99 *(978-1-4169-2532-3(5))* Pocket Books.

Harrison, Jean & Cristnogol, Cymorth. Shompa o India. 2005. *(978-0-904379-43-3(4))* Christian Aid.

Harrison, Lisi. P. S. I Loathe You. 2009. (Clique Ser.: 10). (ENG.). 224p. (gr. 7-17). pap. 9.99 *(978-0-316-00681-1(5)*, Poppy) Little, Brown Bks. for Young Readers.

—The Pretty Committee Strikes Back, No. 5. 2006. (Clique Ser.: 5). (ENG.). 272p. (J). (gr. 7-17). per. 9.99 *(978-0-316-11500-1(2)*, Poppy) Little, Brown Bks. for Young Readers.

Harrison, Lisi, creator. Dylan. 2008. (Clique Ser.). (ENG.). 144p. (YA). (gr. 10-17). pap. 6.99 *(978-0-316-03565-1(3)*, Poppy) Little, Brown Bks. for Young Readers.

Hart, Alison. Dive Right In. Studios, Arcana, illus. 2011. (ENG.). 120p. (J). pap. 8.95 *(978-1-59369-909-3(3))* American Girl Publishing, Inc.

Hartley, Susan. Stephanie Investigates. 2004. (Shared Connections Ser.). (J). instr.'s gde. ed. 27.00 *(978-1-4108-1618-4(4))* Benchmark Education Co.

—Stephanie Investigates: Small Book. 2004. (Shared Connections Ser.). (J). pap. *(978-1-4108-1642-9(7))* Benchmark Education Co.

Hartley, Susan & Schieber, Jennifer. Red Riding Hood. 2004. (Shared Connections Ser.). (J). pap. *(978-1-4108-1635-1(4))*; instr.'s gde. ed. 27.00 *(978-1-4108-1611-5(7))* Benchmark Education Co.

Harvey, Jacqueline. Alice-Miranda Shows the Way. 2015. (Alice-Miranda Ser.: 6). (ENG.). 368p. (J). (gr. 3-7). 9.99 *(978-1-74275-117-7(2))* Random Hse. Australia AUS. Dist: Independent Pubs. Group.

—Clementine Rose & the Special Promise. 2016. (Clementine Rose Ser.: 11). (ENG.). 160p. (J). (gr. 1-3). pap. 8.99 *(978-0-85798-786-0(0))* Random Hse. Australia AUS. Dist: Independent Pubs. Group.

Hashimi, Nadia. One Half from the East. 2016. 272p. (J). (gr. 3-7). 16.99 *(978-0-06-242190-6(5))* HarperCollins Pubs.

Hatke, Ben. Zita the Spacegirl. Hatke, Ben, illus. 2011. (Zita the Spacegirl Ser.: 1). (ENG., Illus.). 192p. (J). (gr. 3-7). 19.99 *(978-1-59643-695-4(6)*, 9781596436954); pap. 12.99 *(978-1-59643-446-2(5)*, 9781596434462) Roaring Brook Pr. (First Second Bks.).

—Zita the Spacegirl. 2011. (Zita the Spacegirl Ser.: 1). (J). lib. bdg. 24.50 *(978-0-606-21623-4(5)*, Turtleback) Turtleback Bks.

Hawes, Louise. The Language of Stars. 2016. (ENG., Illus.). 368p. (J). (gr. 7). 17.99 *(978-1-4814-6241-9(5)*, McElderry, Margaret K. Bks.) McElderry, Margaret K. Bks.

Hawkins-Rodgers, Donzella. No Bulley Destroy's Chloe's Hairdo. Hewins, Shirley, illus. 2003. 32p. (J). (gr. 3-18). lib. bdg. 16.95 *(978-1-884242-56-4(1))* Multicultural Pubns.

Hawthorne, Rachel. Trouble from the Start: A Companion to the Boyfriend Project. 2015. (ENG.). 400p. (YA). (gr. 9). pap. 9.99 *(978-0-06-233071-0(3)*, HarperTeen) HarperCollins Pubs.

Hayatian, MaryAnn. The Flower Child. 2009. 32p. 20.00 *(978-0-557-06445-8(7))* Lulu Pr., Inc.

Hayden, Gwendolen Lampshire. Mary Martha's Really Truly Stories: Book 1. 2nd ed. 2013. 130p. pap. 11.95 *(978-1-4796-0099-1(7))* TEACH Services, Inc.

—Mary Martha's Really Truly Stories: Book 2. 2nd ed. 2013. (Illus.). 136p. pap. 11.95 *(978-1-4796-0102-8(0))* TEACH Services, Inc.

—Mary Martha's Really Truly Stories: Book 4. 2nd ed. 2013. 130p. pap. 11.95 *(978-1-4796-0108-0(X))* TEACH Services, Inc.

—Mary Martha's Really Truly Stories: Book 5. 2nd ed. 2013. 130p. pap. 11.95 *(978-1-4796-0111-0(X))* TEACH Services, Inc.

—Mary Martha's Really Truly Stories: Book 6. 2nd ed. 2013. 130p. pap. 11.95 *(978-1-4796-0114-1(4))* TEACH Services, Inc.

—Mary Martha's Really Truly Stories: Book 7. 2nd ed. 2013. 130p. pap. 11.95 *(978-1-4796-0117-2(9))* TEACH Services, Inc.

—Mary Martha's Really Truly Stories: Book 8. 2nd ed. 2013. 130p. pap. 11.95 *(978-1-4796-0120-2(9))* TEACH Services, Inc.

Hayes, Juliana. Ari Sylph Valley. 2012. 84p. 19.95 *(978-1-4626-6912-7(3))* America Star Bks.

Hayes, Paula. Lily in the Mirror. 2017. (ENG.). 200p. (J). (gr. 4-7). 9.95 ***(978-1-925163-87-2(3))*** Fremantle Pr. AUS. Dist: Independent Pubs. Group.

Hays, Anna. Portia's Ultra Mysterious Double Life. 2008. (Mix Ser.). (ENG.). 224p. (J). (gr. 4-8). pap. 5.99 *(978-1-4169-4893-3(7)*, Aladdin) Simon & Schuster Children's Publishing.

Hearne, Betsy. Seven Brave Women. Andersen, Bethanne, illus. 2006. (gr. -1-3). 17.00 *(978-0-7569-6669-0(8))* Perfection Learning Corp.

Heather Rose Brabant. The Moon Princess. 2009. 20p. pap. 11.95 *(978-1-4389-2980-4(3))* AuthorHouse.

Hébert, Marie-Francine. La Petite Fille Qui Detestait l'Heure du Dodo. 2004. (FRE., Illus.). (J). (gr. k-3). spiral bd. *(978-0-616-01834-7(7))* Canadian National Institute for the Blind/Institut National Canadien pour les Aveugles.

Hegerhorst, Bethany. The Soccer Princess: Josephina & the Gown Fashion Runway Show, 13 bks., bk. 1. Abbott, Kristin, illus. 2011. 32p. (J). 17.99 *(978-0-615-35488-0(2))* Leo Publishing Works, Inc.

—The Soccer Princess: Josephina & the Gown Fashion Runway Show, 12. Abbott, Kristin, illus. 2011. 32p. (J). *(978-0-9803829-6-9(3))* Murray Bks.

Heisler, H. T. A. The Innkeeper's Daughter: A Christmas Story & Music Score. 2013. 40p. pap. *(978-0-9917756-2-0(7))* Daisy Harriette Tina Anne Heisler.

Held, Kristen. Holding Court. 2016. (ENG.). 352p. (YA). pap. 9.99 *(978-1-63375-227-6(5)*, 9781633752276) Entangled Publishing, LLC.

Heller, Sarah & Reader's Digest Staff. Disney Fairies Music Player. 2008. (RD Innovative Book & Player Format Ser.). (ENG.). 36p. (J). 24.99 *(978-0-7944-1300-2(5))* Reader's Digest Assn., Inc., The.

Helmso, Candy Grant. Cakewalk. Taylor, Stephen, illus. 2003. (Books for Young Learners). (ENG.). 16p. (J). pap. 5.75 net. *(978-1-57274-250-5(X)*, 2727, Bks. for Young Learners) Owen, Richard C. Pubs., Inc.

Hemsworth, Jade. Project Mc2: Smart Is the New Cool. 2016. (Illus.). 144p. (J). ***(978-1-250-12632-0(0))*** ETT Imprint.

Hen, Ms. Lucky Lottie. 2012. 58p. pap. 6.99 *(978-1-300-09653-5(5))* Lulu Pr., Inc.

Henderson, Dianne. The Frightening Old Mansion. 2006. 116p. pap. 19.95 *(978-1-4241-2486-2(7))* PublishAmerica, Inc.

Henderson, Tim. Butterflies & Magic Dreams. Hansen, Melissa, illus. l.t. ed. 2003. 28p. (J). *(978-0-9728691-0-2(7))* Logan Bks.

Hendrix, Heather. What Should I Be for Halloween?, 1 vol. 2010. 16p. pap. 24.95 *(978-1-4489-8139-7(5))* PublishAmerica, Inc.

Henkes, Kevin. Lilly's Chocolate Heart. Henkes, Kevin, illus. 2003. (ENG., Illus.). 24p. (J). (gr. -1-k). bds. 6.99 *(978-0-06-056066-9(5)*, Greenwillow Bks.) HarperCollins Pubs.

Henry, James. The Cabinet of Curiosities. 2010. 240p. pap. 21.50 *(978-0-9559851-0-2(2))* Blue Cat GBR. Dist: Lulu Pr., Inc.

Henshon, Suzanna. Mildew on the Wall. (J). pap. 9.99 *(978-0-88092-484-9(5))* Royal Fireworks Publishing Co.

Henson, Heather. Here's How I See It — Here's How It Is. 2010. (ENG., Illus.). 304p. (J). (gr. 5-9). pap. 6.99 *(978-1-4169-9773-3(3)*, Atheneum Bks. for Young Readers) Simon & Schuster Children's Publishing.

Herman, Debbie. Carla's Sandwich. Bailey, Sheila, illus. 2004. (ENG.). 32p. (J). (gr. k-3). 17.95 *(978-0-9729225-2-4(0))* Flashlight Pr.

Herman, Gail. Flower Girl. Billin-Frye, Paige, illus. 2012. (Penguin Young Readers, L3 Ser.). (ENG.). 32p. (J). (gr. 1-4). 3.99 *(978-0-448-49487-6(6)*, Grosset & Dunlap) Penguin Publishing Group.

Hermes, Patricia. Emma Dilemma, the Nanny, & the Wedding, 0 vols. 2012. (Emma Dilemma Ser.: 7). (ENG.). 144p. (J). (gr. 3-6). 16.99 *(978-0-7614-6210-1(4)*, 9780761462101, Amazon Children's Publishing) Amazon Publishing.

Herren, Greg. Sorceress. 2010. (ENG.). 434p. (J). (gr. 6). pap. 18.95 *(978-0-9845318-1-3(5))* Tiny Stachel Pr.

Herring, Bruce D. The Wizard of Wonderland, 1 vol. 2010. 192p. pap. 24.95 *(978-1-4489-5844-3(X))* America Star Bks.

Hertz, Kellen. American Girl. 2017. (American Girl Contempory Middle Grade Ser.: 1). lib. bdg. 20.85 ***(978-0-606-39988-3(7))*** Turtleback Bks.

Hesse, Karen. The Cats in Krasinski Square. Watson, Wendy, illus. 2004. (ENG.). 32p. (J). (gr. 2-5). 18.99 *(978-0-439-43540-6(4)*, Scholastic Pr.) Scholastic, Inc.

Hest, Amy. When Jessie Came Across the Sea. Lynch, P. J., illus. 2003. (ENG.). 40p. (J). (gr. 1-4). pap. 6.99 *(978-0-7636-1274-0(X))* Candlewick Pr.

Hetherington, Sally. Where's Pa? Hetherington, Jan, illus. 2013. 28p. pap. 15.97 *(978-1-62516-299-1(5)*, Strategic Bk. Publishing) Strategic Book Publishing & Rights Agency (SBPRA).

Heyde, Christiane. The Happy Girl. Hawkins, Linda, illus. 2003. 48p. 14.95 *(978-0-87516-618-6(0)*, Devorss Pubns.) DeVorss & Co.

Heywood, Grandma Geny. Stegot: ... the Great. 2012. 44p. pap. 20.99 *(978-1-4685-5914-9(1))* AuthorHouse.

Higbee, Heidi. It Could Happen... on the Bus. Hezlep, Amber, illus. 2012. 32p. (J). pap. 16.95 *(978-0-9882940-0-4(1))* Bryson Taylor Publishing.

Higgins, M. G. I'm Just Me. 2014. (Gravel Road Ser.). (YA). lib. bdg. 20.80 *(978-0-606-35220-8(1))* Turtleback Bks.

Higginson, Sheila Sweeny. Chilly Catches a Cold. 2013. (Doc Mcstuffins 8X8 Ser.). (J). lib. bdg. 13.55 *(978-0-606-35109-6(4)*, Turtleback) Turtleback Bks.

Higginson, Sheila Sweeny & Disney Book Group Staff. Loud Louie. Disney Storybook Artists Staff, illus. 2013. (World of Reading Ser.). (ENG.). 32p. (J). (gr. -1-k). pap. 3.99 *(978-1-4231-6456-2(3))* Disney Pr.

Higginson, Sheila Sweeny, et al. Chilly Catches a Cold. 2013. (Illus.). 24p. (J). *(978-1-4844-1108-7(0))* Disney Pr.

High, Linda Oatman. A Heart Like Ringo Starr, 1 vol. 2015. (Gravel Road Verse Ser.). (ENG.). (YA). (gr. 9-12). pap. 10.95 *(978-1-62250-968-3(4))* Saddleback Educational Publishing, Inc.

Hill, Chelsie & Love, Jessica. Push Girl: A Novel. 2014. (ENG.). 240p. (YA). (gr. 7). 18.99 *(978-1-250-04591-1(6)*, 9781250045911, St. Martin's Griffin) St. Martin's Pr.

Hill, Janet Muirhead. Miranda & Starlight. 2013. (J). cd-rom 19.00 *(978-1-937849-08-5(2))* Raven Publishing Inc. of Montana.

Hillan, Pamela & Dyan, Penelope. The Discovery in the Old Mine. Weigand, John, photos by. 2013. (Illus.). 116p. pap. 8.95 *(978-1-61477-095-4(6))* Bellissima Publishing, LLC.

—The Mystery on Burgundy Street. 2013. 134p. pap. 8.95 *(978-1-61477-086-2(7))* Bellissima Publishing, LLC.

—The Secret at Fort Huachuca. 2013. 130p. pap. 8.95 *(978-1-61477-093-0(X))* Bellissima Publishing, LLC.

Hillert, Margaret. Little Red Riding Hood. (Illus.). (J). 6.00 *(978-0-87895-680-7(8))* Modern Curriculum Pr.

Hillyer, Rhonda. Butterfly Magic. Wood, Steve, illus. 2013. 84p. pap. 12.00 *(978-1-62212-306-3(9)*, Strategic Bk. Publishing) Strategic Book Publishing & Rights Agency (SBPRA).

Hitchcock, Shannon. Ruby Lee & Me. 2016. (ENG., Illus.). 272p. (J). (gr. 3-7). 16.99 *(978-0-545-78230-2(9)*, Scholastic Pr.) Scholastic, Inc.

Hobbs, Ellen Youngs. Oh ! Hannah. 2012. 24p. pap. 19.99 *(978-1-4685-9895-7(3))* AuthorHouse.

Hodgkins, Dorothy. Darlington's Margaret. 2009. 82p. pap. 12.20 *(978-1-4251-8668-5(8))* Trafford Publishing.

Hodgson, Karen J. I Don't Care! Said Claire. Rowe, Harriet, illus. 2010. (ENG.). 32p. (J). (gr. -1-2). pap. 9.99 *(978-1-907432-05-7(1))* Hogs Back Bks. GBR. Dist: Independent Pubs. Group.

Hoestlandt, Jo. Emile bille de Clown. pap. 14.95 *(978-2-7470-0822-8(3))* Bayard Editions FRA. Dist: Distribooks, Inc.

Hofmeister, Alan, et al. It Is Ann. (Reading for All Learners Ser.). (Illus.). (J). pap. *(978-1-56861-084-9(X))* Swift Learning Resources.

—Nan & the Man. (Reading for All Learners Ser.). (Illus.). (J). pap. *(978-1-56861-086-3(6))* Swift Learning Resources.

—Nan Sits. (Reading for All Learners Ser.). (Illus.). (J). pap. *(978-1-56861-092-4(0))* Swift Learning Resources.

Hogan, Mary. Perfect Girl. 2007. (YA). (gr. 7-12). 196p. lib. bdg. 17.89 *(978-0-06-084109-6(5))*; (ENG., Illus.). 208p. 16.99 *(978-0-06-084108-9(7))* HarperCollins Pubs. (HarperTeen).

Holden, Anthony. Massie. 2008. (ENG.). 144p. (YA). (gr. 7-17). pap. 6.99 *(978-0-316-02751-9(0)*, Poppy) Little, Brown Bks. for Young Readers.

Holliman, Lynn. The Best Day Ever!, 1 vol. 2009. 18p. pap. 24.95 *(978-1-60836-731-3(2))* America Star Bks.

Holm, Jennifer L. Wilderness Days. 2004. (Boston Jane Ser.: No. 2). 240p. (J). (gr. 5-18). 15.99 *(978-0-06-029045-0(5))*; lib. bdg. 16.89 *(978-0-06-029046-7(3))* HarperCollins Pubs.

Holmes, Katherine L. The Wide Awake Loons. 2013. 188p. pap. 9.95 *(978-1-938083-18-1(0))* Silver Knight Publishing, LLC.

Holub, Joan & Williams, Suzanne. Amphitrite the Bubbly. 2015. (Goddess Girls Ser.: 17). lib. bdg. 18.40 *(978-0-606-37137-7(0))* Turtleback Bks.

—Athena the Proud. 2014. (Goddess Girls Ser.: 13). lib. bdg. 18.40 *(978-0-606-35441-7(7))* Turtleback Bks.

—Cassandra the Lucky. 2013. (Goddess Girls Ser.: 12). lib. bdg. 18.40 *(978-0-606-32329-1(5)*, Turtleback) Turtleback Bks.

—Gretel Pushes Back (Grimmtastic Girls #8) 2016. (Grimmtastic Girls Ser.: 8). (ENG.). 192p. (J). (gr. 3-7). pap. 5.99 *(978-0-545-94535-6(6)*, Scholastic Paperbacks) Scholastic, Inc.

—Red Riding Hood Gets Lost. 2014. (Grimmtastic Girls Ser.: 2). lib. bdg. 16.00 *(978-0-606-35396-0(8))* Turtleback Bks.

Holzer, Angela. Lovely Lily. Hansen, Angela, illus. 2009. (ENG.). 36p. (J). lib. bdg. 8.99 *(978-0-9821563-2-2(4))* Good Sound Publishing.

Hornzie, Hillary. The Hot List. 2011. (Mix Ser.). (ENG.). 256p. (J). (gr. 4-8). pap. 6.99 *(978-1-4424-0657-5(7)*, Aladdin) Simon & Schuster Children's Publishing.

Hood, Cortney Thomas. Miss Sippi Sass: Seriously Southern. Seriously Sassy. 2011. 36p. pap. 16.95 *(978-1-4497-2132-9(X)*, WestBow Pr.) Author Solutions, Inc.

Hood, Karen Jean Matsko. Girls Can Do Journal: A Daily Journal, bk. 5. Whispering Pine Press International, ed. 2014. (Children's Journal Series). 164p. (J). 19.95 *(978-1-59649-421-3(2))* Whispering Pine Pr. International, Inc.

Hoole, Elissa Janine. Sometimes Never, Sometimes Always. 2013. (ENG.). 360p. (YA). pap. 9.99 *(978-0-7387-3722-5(4)*, Flux) North Star Editions.

Hope, Laura Lee. The Moving Picture Girls at Sea: Or A Pictured Shipwreck That Became Real. l.t. ed. 2007. (ENG.). 154p. pap. 21.99 *(978-1-4264-9792-6(X))* Creative Media Partners, LLC.

—The Outdoor Girls at Ocean View: Or the Box That Was Found in the Sand. 2007. 140p. pap. 18.99 *(978-1-4264-9639-4(7))*; (ENG.). 150p. pap. 19.99 *(978-1-4264-2712-1(3))* Creative Media Partners, LLC.

—The Outdoor Girls at the Hostess House: Or, doing their best for the Soldiers. 2006. (ENG.). 138p. pap. 18.99 *(978-1-4264-7589-4(6))* Creative Media Partners, LLC.

—The Outdoor Girls at Wild Rose Lodge. l.t. ed. 2007. (ENG.). 144p. pap. 19.99 *(978-1-4264-4399-2(4))* Creative Media Partners, LLC.

—The Outdoor Girls at Wild Rose Lodge: The Outdoor Girls at Wild Rose Lodge. 2007. (ENG.). 134p. pap. 18.99 *(978-1-4264-4361-9(7))* Creative Media Partners, LLC.

—The Outdoor Girls in a Motor Car. 2007. 180p. 26.95 *(978-1-4218-3284-5(4))*; per. 11.95 *(978-1-4218-3384-2(0))* 1st World Publishing, Inc. (1st World Library - Literary Society).

—The Outdoor Girls in Army Service: Or Doing Their Bit for the Soldier Boys. 2007. (ENG.). 134p. pap. 18.99 *(978-1-4264-9612-7(5))*; 148p. pap. 19.99 *(978-1-4264-9993-7(0))* Creative Media Partners, LLC.

—The Outdoor Girls in Florida: Or Wintering in the Sunny South. 2007. 130p. pap. 18.99 *(978-1-4264-9645-5(1))*; 144p. pap. 19.99 *(978-1-4264-4927-7(5))* Creative Media Partners, LLC.

—The Outdoor Girls in the Saddle: Or the Girl Miner of Gold Run. 2007. (ENG.). 138p. pap. 18.99 *(978-1-4264-9648-6(6))*; 150p. pap. 19.99 *(978-1-4264-6870-4(9))* Creative Media Partners, LLC.

—The Outdoor Girls on Pine Island: Or A Cave & What It Contained. 2007. (ENG.). 144p. pap. 18.99 *(978-1-4264-9638-7(9))*; 162p. pap. 21.99 *(978-1-4264-1870-9(1))* Creative Media Partners, LLC.

Hope, Lee Laura. The Outdoor Girls in a Motor Car or the Haunted Mansion of Shadow Valley. 2007. 156p. 41.99 *(978-1-4280-7518-4(6))*; per. 35.99 *(978-1-4280-7519-1(4))* IndyPublish.com.

—The Outdoor Girls in a Winter Camp or Glorious Days on Skates & Ice Boats. 2007. 156p. 41.99 *(978-1-4280-7498-9(8))*; per. 35.99 *(978-1-4280-7509-2(7))* IndyPublish.com.

Hopkins, Cathy. Mates, Dates, & Chocolate Cheats. 2011. (Mates, Dates Ser.). (ENG.). 224p. (YA). (gr. 7). pap. 10.99 *(978-1-4424-3081-5(8)*, Simon Pulse) Simon Pulse.

—Mates, Dates, & Great Escapes. 2011. (Mates, Dates Ser.). (ENG.). 224p. (YA). (gr. 7). pap. 10.99 *(978-1-4424-3080-8(X)*, Simon Pulse) Simon Pulse.

—Mates, Dates, & Inflatable Bras. 2011. (Mates, Dates Ser.). (ENG.). 176p. (YA). (gr. 7). pap. 9.99 *(978-1-4424-3113-3(X)*, Simon Pulse) Simon Pulse.

—Mates, Dates, & Mad Mistakes. 2014. (Mates, Dates Ser.). (ENG., Illus.). 224p. (YA). (gr. 7). pap. 12.99 *(978-1-4814-4494-1(8),* Simon Pulse) Simon Pulse.
—Mates, Dates, & Sleepover Secrets. 2010. (Mates, Dates Ser.). (ENG.). 208p. (YA). (gr. 7). pap. 10.99 *(978-1-4424-1421-1(9),* Simon Pulse) Simon Pulse.
—Mates, Dates, & Tempting Trouble. 2011. (Mates, Dates Ser.). (ENG.). 256p. (YA). (gr. 7). pap. 12.99 *(978-1-4424-3114-0(8),* Simon Pulse) Simon Pulse.
—The Princess of Pop. 2012. (Truth or Dare Ser.). (ENG.). 224p. (YA). (gr. 7). pap. 10.99 *(978-1-4424-6057-7(1),* Simon Pulse) Simon Pulse.
Hopkins, Cathy & Hopkins, Cathy. All Mates Together. 2007. (Truth or Dare Ser.: No. 8). (ENG.). 240p. (YA). (gr. 7-18). mass mkt. 11.99 *(978-1-4169-2722-8(0),* Simon Pulse) Simon Pulse.
Hopkinson, Deborah. Girl Wonder: A Baseball Story in Nine Innings. Widener, Terry, illus. 2006. (ENG.). 40p. (J). (gr. k-3). reprint ed. 7.99 *(978-1-4169-1393-1(9),* Aladdin) Simon & Schuster Children's Publishing.
Houghton Mifflin Harcourt Publishing Company Staff. Girl Power 5-Minute Stories. 2015. (5-Minute Stories Ser.). (ENG., Illus.). 224p. (J). (gr. -1-3). 12.99 *(978-0-544-33925-5(8),* HMH Books For Young Readers) Houghton Mifflin Harcourt Publishing Co.
Houston, Anna. Daisy's Bug. 2009. 32p. pap. 14.49 *(978-1-4389-6696-0(2))* AuthorHouse.
Howard, Jennifer. Lucy & the Land of Lost Socks. 2009. 56p. pap. 10.49 *(978-1-4389-5362-5(3))* AuthorHouse.
Howard, Josh. Dead@17: Blood of Saints. Howard, Josh, illus. 2004. (Illus.). 112p. (YA). per. 14.95 *(978-0-9754193-1-1(5))* Viper Comics.
Howard, Kate. Double Trouble. 2016. (LEGO NEXO Knights Ser.). (ENG.). 80p. (J). (gr. 2-5). pap. 4.99 *(978-1-338-03803-3(6))* Scholastic, Inc.
Howell, Gail L. Sarah's World: Sarah Meets her Cousins by the Sea. 2009. 24p. pap. 11.49 *(978-1-4389-4864-5(6))* AuthorHouse.
Hoyle, K. B. The Scroll. 2016. (ENG., Illus.). (J). 29.99 ***(978-1-61213-400-0(9))*** 2013. 266p. pap. 18.99 *(978-1-61213-169-6(7))* Writer's Coffee Shop, The.
Hrdlitschka, Shelley. Sun Signs, 1 vol. 2005. (ENG.). 208p. (YA). (gr. 8-12). pap. 14.95 *(978-1-55143-338-7(9))* Orca Bk. Pubs. USA.
Huber, Mike. Bree Finds a Friend. Cowman, Joseph, illus. 2014. (ENG.). 32p. (gr. -1). 15.95 *(978-1-60554-211-9(3))* Redleaf Pr.
Huddleston, Courtney & Zirkel, Scott. A Bit Haywire. Huddleston, Courtney, illus. 2006. (Illus.). 112p. per. 11.95 *(978-0-9777883-5-4(0))* Viper Comics.
Hudson, Lisa. Meet Lisa Jo: First Day of School & Words Can Hurt. 2013. 42p. pap. 17.45 *(978-1-4497-8463-8(1),* WestBow Pr.) Author Solutions, Inc.
Hughes, Jenny. Dark Horse. 2014. (ENG.). 224p. (J). (gr. 3-7). pap. 9.95 *(978-1-62124-010-5(X))* Breakaway Bks.
—A Horse by Any Other Name. 2014. (ENG.). 224p. (J). (gr. 3-7). pap. 9.95 *(978-1-62124-009-9(6))* Breakaway Bks.
—Horse in the Portrait. 2014. (ENG.). 128p. (J). (gr. 3-7). pap. 9.95 *(978-1-62124-013-6(4))* Breakaway Bks.
—Legend of the Island Horse. 2013. (ENG.). 224p. (J). (gr. 3-7). pap. 9.95 *(978-1-62124-007-5(X))* Breakaway Bks.
—Mystery at Black Horse Farm. 2013. (ENG.). 144p. (J). (gr. 3-7). pap. 9.95 *(978-1-62124-003-7(7))* Breakaway Bks.
—Sea Horses. 2013. (ENG., Illus.). 224p. (J). (gr. 3-7). pap. 9.95 *(978-1-62124-006-8(1))* Breakaway Bks.
Hughes, Sananjaleen June. Joanna's World. 44p. (J). spiral bd. *(978-1-880757-01-7(X))* Reverence for Life.
Hull, Norman. Joyce's Holiday in France. 2011. 96p. (gr. -1). pap. 9.99 *(978-1-4634-3694-0(7))* AuthorHouse.
Humphreys, Neil. Picking up a Penguin's Egg Really Got Me into Trouble. Cheng, Puay Koon, illus. 2014. (Abbie Rose & the Magic Suitcase Ser.). (ENG.). 24p. (J). (gr. -1-3). pap. 9.90 *(978-981-4484-18-3(0))* Marshall Cavendish International (Asia) Private Ltd. SGP. Dist: National Bk. Network.
Hunter, Kendall. Miff the Martian. 2009. 64p. pap. 6.98 *(978-0-578-03542-0(1))* Desert West Publishing.
Hurley, Tonya. Homecoming. 2010. (Ghostgirl Ser.: 2). (ENG.). 304p. (YA). (gr. 7-17). pap. 10.00 *(978-0-316-08943-2(5))* Little, Brown Bks. for Young Readers.
I Spy: Individual Title Six-Packs. (Story Steps Ser.). (gr. k-2). 29.00 *(978-0-7635-9571-5(3))* Rigby Education.
Ignatow, Amy. Love & Other Fiascos with Lydia Goldblatt & Julie Graham-Chang, Bk. 6. 2013. (Popularity Papers). (ENG., Illus.). 208p. (J). (gr. 3-7). 16.95 *(978-1-4197-0859-6(7),* Amulet Bks.) Abrams, Inc.
—The Popularity Papers: Book Four: the Rocky Road Trip of Lydia Goldblatt & Julie Graham-Chang. 2013. (Popularity Papers). (ENG., Illus.). 208p. (J). (gr. 3-7). pap. 8.95 *(978-1-4197-0972-2(0),* Amulet Bks.) Abrams, Inc.
—The Awesomely Awful Melodies of Lydia Goldblatt & Julie Graham-Chang. 2013. (Popularity Papers). (ENG., Illus.). 208p. (J). (gr. 3-7). 16.95 *(978-1-4197-0536-6(9),* Amulet Bks.) Abrams, Inc.
—Words of (Questionable) Wisdom from Lydia Goldblatt & Julie Graham-Chang, Bk. 3. 2011. (Popularity Papers). (ENG., Illus.). 208p. (J). (gr. 3-7). 16.95 *(978-1-4197-0063-7(4),* Amulet Bks.) Abrams, Inc.
Ikegwuonu, Patricia Ryan. I Love My Hair, Too! 2013. 20p. pap. 24.95 *(978-1-4626-7556-2(5))* PublishAmerica, Inc.
The Imaginer: Individual Title Six-Packs. (Bookweb Ser.). 32p. (gr. 6-18). 34.00 *(978-0-7578-0900-2(6))* Rigby Education.
Inches, Alison. School Gyrls POW Scrapbook. 2010. (School Gyrls Ser.). (ENG.). 64p. (J). pap. 7.99 *(978-1-4424-0865-4(0),* Simon Spotlight) Simon Spotlight.
Inoue, Kazurou. Midori Days. Inoue, Kazurou, illus. 2006. (Midori Days Ser.). (ENG., Illus.). 208p. Vol. 6. pap. 9.99 *(978-1-4215-0495-7(2))* Vol. 7. pap. 9.99 *(978-1-4215-0496-4(0))* Viz Media.
Iorillo, Kristin. The Wacko Baby. 2011. 28p. pap. 15.99 *(978-1-4628-5792-0(2))* Xlibris Corp.
Ireland, Cameron Robert. Say the 'K', Kay! 2012. 28p. pap. 24.95 *(978-1-4626-6139-8(4))* America Star Bks.
Izzo, Donna. Frilly Lilly. 2011. 28p. pap. 15.99 *(978-1-4628-7708-9(7))* Xlibris Corp.

Jackson, Bridgett. The Princess & the Pink Palace: Book Two of Tales from the Creek. 2008. 36p. pap. 16.99 *(978-1-4389-2038-2(5))* AuthorHouse.
Jackson, Gwendolyn. The Adventures of Super T: The Missing Blanket Scott-Daniel, Toni, illus. 2004. 32p. (J). lib. bdg. 15.95 *(978-0-9753434-0-1(8))* LeTay Publishing.
Jackson, Louise A. Exiled! From Tragedy to Triumph on the Missouri Frontier. 2007. (Illus.). 235p. (YA). (gr. 7-9). per. 16.95 *(978-1-57168-948-1(6),* Eakin Pr.) Eakin Pr.
Jacobs, Breena. Daddy's Girl. Austrew, Neva, illus. 2006. 32p. (J). (gr. -1-k). 15.95 *(978-0-9749423-2-2(4))* Bookworm Bks.
Jacobs, John. I Wanna Be. 2006. (Illus.). 144p. 9.95 *(978-0-9774659-6-5(9))* Cameo Pubns., LLC.
Jakobitz, Marilee. Martha Lu & the Whobegots. 2008. 32p. pap. 24.95 *(978-1-60441-482-0(0))* America Star Bks.
James, Annabelle. Abigail's Ballet Class. 2003. (J). per. *(978-1-57657-956-5(5))* Paradise Pr., Inc.
—Abigail's Ballet Class. Beckes, Shirley, illus. 2004. 10p. (J). (gr. -1-k). 12.49 *(978-1-883043-54-4(9))* Straight Edge Pr., The.
James, Catherine. Bobby Cottontail's Gift. Collier, Kevin Scott, illus. 2008. 28p. pap. 10.95 *(978-1-935137-07-8(7))* 2006. 32p. (J). E-Book 9.95 incl. cd-rom *(978-1-933090-24-5(3))* Guardian Angel Publishing, Inc.
James, Henry. Alexandra's Accident: A Little Girl Comes to Grief While Out with Her Pa. 2012. 24p. pap. 28.03 *(978-1-4797-5649-0(0))* Xlibris Corp.
James, Tina. Sarabeth Palmer: 1963-1964. 2010. 91p. (J). *(978-0-615-37484-0(0))* Afrolez Productions, LLC.
Jamison, Jo Lynn & Elliott, Lela Mae. Siren's Call of the Caves, 1 vol. 2009. 55p. pap. 16.95 *(978-1-4489-8627-9(3))* PublishAmerica, Inc.
Janni, Rebecca. Nellie Sue, Happy Camper. Avril, Lynne, illus. 2013. (Every Cowgirl Ser.). (ENG.). 32p. (J). (gr. 1-2). 14.99 *(978-0-448-46507-4(8));* mass mkt. 3.99 *(978-0-448-46387-2(3))* Penguin Young Readers Group. (Penguin Young Readers).
Jarman, Julia. Make Friends - Break Friends. Pankhurst, Kate, illus. 2015. (Friends Ser.: 1). (ENG.). 96p. (J). (gr. 2-4). pap. 6.99 *(978-1-84939-509-0(8))* Andersen Pr. GBR. Dist: Independent Pubs. Group.
Jeanne-Marie in Gay Paris. 2003. (Illus.). 32p. (J). mass mkt. 9.99 *(978-0-9740599-1-4(9),* 2) Omnibus Publishing.
Jeffs, Dixie. A Happy Lightning Bug. 2013. 24p. pap. 24.95 *(978-1-62709-633-1(7))* America Star Bks.
—The Little Pink Dress. 2012. 24p. 24.95 *(978-1-4626-5853-4(9))* America Star Bks.
Jenny's Yellow Ribbon. Date not set. 5.95 *(978-0-89868-365-3(3))* ARO Publishing Co.
Jensen, Marie-Louise. Between Two Seas. 2009. pap. 1.00 *(978-1-4074-4422-2(0))* Recorded Bks., Inc.
Jensen, Melissa. The Fine Art of Truth or Dare. 2012. (ENG.). 400p. (YA). (gr. 7-18). 8.99 *(978-0-14-242090-4(5),* Speak) Penguin Young Readers Group.
Jeremy Can't Drink Milk. 2006. (Illus.). 24p. (J). 5.99 *(978-0-9725593-2-4(9))* by shayne.
Jeune, Marie Carole. Rita & the Parrot. Saincilus, Larimer, illus. 2010. (HAT.). 32p. (J). pap. 16.95 *(978-1-60195-317-9(8))* International Step by Step Assn.
Jewell, Roe. Flight to Andolin: Journeys of a Reluctant Heroine. 2013. 170p. pap. 15.95 *(978-1-938208-11-9(0))* World Nouveau.
Jewett, Sarah Orne. Betty Leicester: A Story for Girls. 2004. reprint ed. pap. 1.99 *(978-1-4192-0978-9(7));* pap. 20.95 *(978-1-4191-0978-2(2))* Kessinger Publishing, LLC.
Jimenez, Angeles. Macarena la Anguila. Gil, Sabina, illus. 2004. 26p. pap. 8.00 *(978-84-931888-0-1(8))* Editorial Brief ESP. Dist: Independent Pubs. Group.
Johnson, Andi. Rollerskate Kate. 2004. (Illus.). 16p. 9.00 *(978-1-84161-115-0(8))* Ravette Publishing, Ltd. GBR. Dist: Parkwest Pubns., Inc.
Johnson, Denise Donna. The Veridical Circle. 2011. 78p. pap. 19.95 *(978-1-4626-0472-2(2))* America Star Bks.
Johnson, Gerald J. J. Misty's Christmas Present, 1 vol. Miltenberger, Jeri & Miltenberger, Dave, illus. 2010. 32p. 24.95 *(978-1-4512-1330-0(1))* PublishAmerica, Inc.
Johnson, Julia. Cheetah's Tale. Stacey International Staff, ed. Keeble, Susan, illus. 2004. (ENG.). 56p. 16.95 *(978-1-900988-87-2(9),* Stacey International) Stacey Publishing GBR. Dist: Casemate Pubs. & Bk. Distributors, LLC.
Johnson, Tina Marie. Heaven Dolly: Little Miss Attitude. 2012. pap. 8.95 *(978-0-7414-7470-4(0))* Infinity Publishing.
Johnston, Annie Fell. Georgina of the Rainbows (Illustrated Ed. 2006. pap. *(978-1-4065-1134-5(X))* Dodo Pr.
Johnston, Annie Fellows. The Giant Scissors. Barry, Etheldred B., illus. 2005. reprint ed. pap. 22.95 *(978-1-4179-0341-2(4))* Kessinger Publishing, LLC.
—The Little Colonel s Chum: Mary Ware. 2007. 184p. pap. 19.99 *(978-1-4264-9087-3(9))* Creative Media Partners, LLC.
—The Little Colonel's Chum: Mary Ware. l.t. ed. 2007. (ENG.). 206p. pap. 22.99 *(978-1-4264-9141-2(7))* Creative Media Partners, LLC.
—The Little Colonel's Hero. Barry, Etheldred B., illus. 2007. 180p. per. *(978-1-4065-3513-6(3))* Dodo Pr.
—The Little Colonel's House Party. Meynell, Louis, illus. 2007. 176p. per. *(978-1-4065-3514-3(1))* Dodo Pr.
Jones, Christianne C. Lacey Walker, Nonstop Talker, 1 vol. Watson, Richard, illus. 2013. (Little Boost Ser.). (ENG.). 32p. (gr. k-3). 14.95 *(978-1-4795-2156-2(6),* Little Boost) Picture Window Bks.
Jones, Elizabeth McDavid. Peril at King's Creek: A Felicity Mystery. Tibbles, JeanPaul, illus. 2006. (ENG.). 176p. (gr. 4-7). pap. 6.95 *(978-1-59369-101-1(7),* American Girl) American Girl Publishing, Inc.
Jones, Jen. Sleepover Girls. Franco, Paula, illus. 2014. (Sleepover Girls Ser.). (ENG.). 128p. (gr. 3-5). 90.60 *(978-1-4965-0316-9(3))* Stone Arch Bks.
Jones, Vickie E. The Many Worlds of Sachsawan. 2012. 62p. 19.95 *(978-1-4626-5957-9(8))* America Star Bks.
Joosse, Barbara M. Evermore Dragon. Cecil, Randy, illus. 2015. (ENG.). 32p. (J). (gr. -1-2). 15.99 *(978-0-7636-6882-2(6))* Candlewick Pr.
Jordan, Evora. Annie Love: A Hannah Gray Dog Story. 2003. (Hannah Gray Mysteries). (J). per. *(978-0-9725071-2-7(4))* EvoraBooks, LLC.

Joshi, Bhabika. Mortals: Hayden Roux Chronicles. 2009. 208p. 24.95 *(978-1-4401-5014-2(1));* pap. 14.95 *(978-1-4401-5016-6(8))* iUniverse, Inc.
Joven, John, illus. The Wounded Lion: A Tale from Spain. 2013. (Tales of Honor (Red Chair Press) Ser.). (ENG.). 32p. (J). (gr. 1-4). lib. bdg. 26.60 *(978-1-937529-79-6(7))* Red Chair Pr.
Judson, Clara Ingram. Mary Jane - Her Book. White, Frances, illus. 2007. 212p. 22.95 *(978-1-934671-13-9(4));* per. 12.95 *(978-1-934671-14-6(2))* Salem Ridge Press LLC.
Judybee. Queen Esther: Queens of Africa Book 4. LittlePinkPebble, illus. 2011. 28p. pap. *(978-1-908218-52-0(5))* MX Publishing, Ltd.
Jukes, Mavis. Es Cosa de Chicas. (SPA.). 120p. *(978-84-7927-422-1(0))* Robinbook, Ediciones S.L. ESP. Dist: Lectorum Pubns., Inc.
Justis, Jon. Pumpkin & the Great Dragon Caper. 2012. 32p. pap. 24.95 *(978-1-4626-9733-5(X))* America Star Bks.
Kaider, Azi Sabi. Angela's Sunflower. 2012. 24p. pap. 16.95 *(978-1-4772-9703-2(0))* AuthorHouse.
Kamio, Yoko. Boys over Flowers, Vol. 18. Kamio, Yoko, illus. 2006. (Boys over Flowers Ser.). (ENG., Illus.). 208p. pap. 9.99 *(978-1-4215-0532-9(0))* Viz Media.
Kaneyoshi, Izumi. Doubt!!, Vol. 4. Kaneyoshi, Izumi, illus. 2005. (Doubt Ser.: 4). (ENG., Illus.). 192p. pap. 9.99 *(978-1-59116-984-0(4))* Viz Media.
Kann, Victoria. Flower Girl. Kann, Victoria, illus. 2013. (Pinkalicious Ser.). (ENG., Illus.). 24p. (J). (gr. -1-3). pap. 3.99 *(978-0-06-218766-6(X),* HarperFestival) HarperCollins Pubs.
—Pinkalicious - The Pinkamazing Storybook Collection. 2013. (Pinkalicious Ser.). (J). lib. bdg. 23.30 *(978-0-606-31783-2(X),* Turtleback) Turtleback Bks.
—Pinkalicious & the Pinkatastic Zoo Day. Kann, Victoria, illus. 2012. (I Can Read Level 1 Ser.). (ENG., Illus.). 32p. (J). (gr. -1-3). 16.99 *(978-0-06-218780-2(5));* pap. 3.99 *(978-0-06-218779-6(1))* HarperCollins Pubs.
—Teeny Tiny Pinky Library, 4 vols. 2012. (Pinkalicious Ser.). (ENG., Illus.). 36p. (J). (gr. -1-3). 14.99 *(978-0-06-222724-9(6))* HarperCollins Pubs.
Kann, Victoria & Kann, Elizabeth. Pinkalicious, 1 vol. Kann, Victoria, illus. 2011. (Pinkalicious Ser.). (SPA., Illus.). 40p. (J). (gr. k-3). 17.99 *(978-0-06-179959-4(9))* HarperCollins Pubs.
Kaplan-Taylor, Maeve. At the Movies with Maeve. 2004. (Illus.). 36p. (J). 3.99 *(978-0-9746587-4-2(X),* Beacon Street Girls) B*tween Productions, Inc.
Kargbo, Ms Mariatu. Three Themne Titi Girls. 2013. 24p. (J). pap. 24.95 *(978-1-63004-790-0(2))* America Star Bks.
Katz, Jennifer A. The Era of Courting. 2006. 119p. pap. 19.95 *(978-1-4241-3321-5(1))* PublishAmerica, Inc.
Katz, Karen. My Big Girl Undies. 2012. (ENG.). 14p. (J). (gr. -1-k). bds. 7.99 *(978-0-448-45703-1(2),* Grosset & Dunlap) Penguin Young Readers Group.
Kay, Kimberly. Courage to Face an Ogre. 2012. 28p. pap. 21.99 *(978-1-4691-5436-7(6))* Xlibris Corp.
Kaye, Shelley. Saving Private Woods. 2012. (Illus.). 76p. pap. 8.50 *(978-1-78035-510-8(6),* Fastprint Publishing) Upfront Publishing Ltd. GBR. Dist: Printondemand-worldwide.com.
Kayla Taylor. Fatal Elements: Book 1. 2009. 368p. pap. 20.95 *(978-1-4401-8495-6(X))* iUniverse, Inc.
Keene, Carolyn. Action! 2005. (Nancy Drew Ser.: 6). 138p. (J). lib. bdg. 15.00 *(978-1-59054-809-7(4))* Fitzgerald Bks.
—Case of the Sneaky Snowman. Pamintuan, Macky, illus. 5th ed. 2006. (Nancy Drew & the Clue Crew Ser.: 5). (ENG.). 96p. (J). (gr. 1-4). pap. 4.99 *(978-1-4169-1254-5(1),* Aladdin) Simon & Schuster Children's Publishing.
—The Cinderella Ballet Mystery. Pamintuan, Macky, illus. 4th ed. 2006. (Nancy Drew & the Clue Crew Ser.: 4). (ENG.). 96p. (J). (gr. 1-4). pap. 5.99 *(978-1-4169-1256-9(8),* Aladdin) Simon & Schuster Children's Publishing.
—False Notes. 3rd ed. 2004. (Nancy Drew (All New) Girl Detective Ser.: 3). (ENG.). 160p. (J). (gr. 3-7). pap. 5.99 *(978-0-689-86568-8(6),* Aladdin) Simon & Schuster Children's Publishing.
—Framed. 15th ed. 2006. (Nancy Drew (All New) Girl Detective Ser.: 15). (ENG.). 160p. (J). (gr. 3-7). pap. 5.99 *(978-0-689-87863-3(X),* Aladdin) Simon & Schuster Children's Publishing.
—Green with Envy: Book Two in the Eco Mystery Trilogy. 2010. (Nancy Drew (All New) Girl Detective Ser.: 40). (ENG.). 160p. (J). (gr. 3-7). pap. 6.99 *(978-1-4169-7842-8(9),* Aladdin) Simon & Schuster Children's Publishing.
—Lights, Camera ... Cats! Pamintuan, Macky, illus. 8th ed. 2007. (Nancy Drew & the Clue Crew Ser.: 8). (ENG.). 96p. (J). (gr. 1-4). pap. 5.99 *(978-1-4169-3957-3(1),* Aladdin) Simon & Schuster Children's Publishing.
—The Perfect Escape, Bk. 3. 32nd ed. 2008. (Nancy Drew (All New) Girl Detective Ser.: 32). (ENG.). 160p. (J). (gr. 3-7). pap. 5.99 *(978-1-4169-5531-3(3),* Aladdin) Simon & Schuster Children's Publishing.
—Pit of Vipers. 18th ed. 2006. (Nancy Drew (All New) Girl Detective Ser.: 18). (ENG.). 160p. (J). (gr. 3-7). pap. 5.99 *(978-1-4169-1180-7(4),* Aladdin) Simon & Schuster Children's Publishing.
—A Race Against Time. 2005. (Nancy Drew Ser.: 2). 154p. (J). lib. bdg. 15.00 *(978-1-59054-808-0(6))* Fitzgerald Bks.
—Seeing Green: Book Three in the Eco Mystery Trilogy. 2010. (Nancy Drew (All New) Girl Detective Ser.: 41). (ENG.). 160p. (J). (gr. 3-7). pap. 6.99 *(978-1-4169-7845-9(3),* Aladdin) Simon & Schuster Children's Publishing.
—Serial Sabotage: Book Two in the Sabotage Mystery Trilogy. 2010. (Nancy Drew (All New) Girl Detective Ser.: 43). (ENG.). 144p. (J). (gr. 3-7). pap. 5.99 *(978-1-4169-9070-3(4),* Aladdin) Simon & Schuster Children's Publishing.
—The Singing Suspects. Jones, Jan Naimo, illus. Frost, Michael, photos by. 67th ed. 2005. (Nancy Drew Notebooks Ser.: 67). (ENG.). 80p. (J). (gr. 1-4). pap. 4.99 *(978-1-4169-0087-0(X),* Simon & Schuster/Paula Wiseman Bks.) Simon & Schuster/Paula Wiseman Bks.
—A Taste of Danger. 174th ed. 2003. (Nancy Drew Ser.: 174). (ENG.). 176p. (J). (gr. 3-7). pap. 5.99 *(978-0-689-86154-3(0),* Aladdin) Simon & Schuster Children's Publishing.
—Thanksgiving Thief. Pamintuan, Macky, illus. 2008. (Nancy Drew & the Clue Crew Ser.: 16). (ENG.). 96p. (J). (gr. 1-4). pap. 5.99 *(978-1-4169-6777-4(X),* Aladdin) Simon & Schuster Children's Publishing.
—Uncivil Acts. 10th ed. 2005. (Nancy Drew (All New) Girl Detective Ser.: 10). (ENG.). 160p. (J). (gr. 3-7). pap. 5.99 *(978-0-689-86937-2(1),* Aladdin) Simon & Schuster Children's Publishing.
—Valentine's Day Secret. Pamintuan, Macky, illus. 12th ed. 2007. (Nancy Drew & the Clue Crew Ser.: 12). (ENG.). 96p. (J). (gr. 1-4). pap. 5.99 *(978-1-4169-4944-2(5),* Aladdin) Simon & Schuster Children's Publishing.
Keller, Laurie. Birdy's Smile Book. Keller, Laurie, illus. 2010. (ENG., Illus.). 40p. (J). (gr. k-3). 16.99 *(978-0-8050-8883-0(0),* 9780805088830, Holt, Henry & Co. Bks. For Young Readers) Holt, Henry & Co.
Kellie, Kerrie. The Sleep over Adventure. 2011. 20p. pap. 24.95 *(978-1-4560-6884-4(9))* America Star Bks.
Kelly, Everett. Tiny Tom. 2007. 56p. (J). per. 15.95 *(978-1-58939-983-9(8))* Virtualbookworm.com Publishing, Inc.
Kelly, Karen. Angel Tree. 2012. (Illus.). 24p. pap. 19.82 *(978-1-4678-9637-5(3))* AuthorHouse.
Kelly, Kathy & Feder, Debbie. Jelly Bean's Art Museum Adventure. 2012. 40p. pap. 20.99 *(978-1-4772-4828-7(5))* AuthorHouse.
Kelly, Katy. Busy Like You Can't Believe. Rex, Adam, illus. 2007. (Lucy Rose Ser.). (ENG.). 192p. (J). (gr. 3-7). per. 6.99 *(978-0-440-42108-5(X),* Yearling) Random Hse. Children's Bks.
Kelly, Lisa. The Many Adventures of Elysse: Her Journey Begins. 2012. 36p. pap. 16.99 *(978-1-4525-5760-1(8))* Balboa Pr.
Kelso, Mary Jean & Snider, K. C. Rv Mouse. 2013. 24p. 19.95 *(978-1-61633-399-7(5))* Guardian Angel Publishing, Inc.
Kenneally, Miranda. Catching Jordan. 2011. (Hundred Oaks Ser.: Bk. 1). (ENG.). 288p. (YA). (gr. 7-12). pap. 9.99 *(978-1-4022-6227-2(2))* Sourcebooks, Inc.
Kennemore, Tim. Alice's World Record. 2006. (ENG., Illus.). 96p. (J). (gr. 3-4). pap. 8.99 *(978-1-84270-238-3(6))* Andersen Pr. GBR. Dist: Independent Pubs. Group.
—Alice's World Record. Spoor, Mike, illus. 2008. 85p. (J). (gr. 4-7). 12.00 *(978-0-8028-5336-3(6))* Eerdmans, William B. Publishing Co.
Kenny, Michael Daedalus. Little Miss Sunshine in: Here Comes the Sun!, Vol. 2. 2012. (ENG.). 80p. (J). pap. 6.99 *(978-1-4215-4071-9(1))* Viz Media.
Kensley, Karen. Gods in Pods. 2008. (ENG., Illus.). 122p. (J). (gr. 4-7). pap. *(978-1-85756-682-6(3))* Janus Publishing Co.
Keough, Kevin. Snoozy Dog: And Curly Cat Too! 2011. 24p. (gr. -1). pap. 12.98 *(978-1-4389-4794-5(1))* AuthorHouse.
Kess, Ollie Garrett. Cutie Curlie Claire. 2011. 28p. pap. 15.99 *(978-1-4628-7974-8(8))* Xlibris Corp.
Key, Janet Rhyme. Rosa in Bloom. 2013. 86p. (J). pap. 13.95 *(978-1-4817-1956-8(4))* AuthorHouse.
The Kicks Collection: Saving the Team; Sabotage Season; Win or Lose. 2014. (Kicks Ser.). (ENG., Illus.). 544p. (J). (gr. 3-7). pap. 20.99 *(978-1-4814-2478-3(5),* Simon & Schuster Bks. For Young Readers) Simon & Schuster Bks. For Young Readers.
Kidd, Dorothy. Tina's Tail, 1 vol. 2010. 20p. pap. 24.95 *(978-1-4489-5974-7(8))* PublishAmerica, Inc.
Kidd, Erin. Cowgirl. 2004. 32p. (J). per. 9.95 *(978-1-59094-072-3(5))* Jawbone Publishing Corp.
Kiefer, Janet Kennedy. Freckles. 2012. 40p. pap. *(978-1-77097-263-6(3))* FriesenPress.
Kilby, Tracie. Gymnastics Gina. 2010. 32p. pap. 16.00 *(978-1-4520-6277-8(3))* AuthorHouse.
Kilpatrick, Sheila. Anastasia's Rain. 2013. 1. (ENG.). 48p. (-4). pap. 9.95 *(978-1-61448-625-1(5))* Morgan James Publishing.
Kimmel, Elizabeth Cody. #1 Forever Four. Mingus, Cathi, illus. 2012. (Forever Four Ser.: 1). (ENG.). 224p. (J). (gr. 3-7). pap. 6.99 *(978-0-448-45548-8(X),* Grosset & Dunlap) Penguin Young Readers Group.
King, M. C. Truth or Dare. 2nd ed. 2008. (Hannah Montana Ser.). (Illus.). 126p. (gr. 3-7). 15.00 *(978-0-7569-8336-9(3))* Perfection Learning Corp.
King, Valerie. The Gift of Fate. 2012. 188p. (YA). pap. 12.99 *(978-1-105-52942-9(8))* Lulu Pr., Inc.
Kingsley, Kate. Pretty on the Outside. 2010. (Young, Loaded, & Fabulous Ser.: 1). (ENG.). 320p. (YA). (gr. 9-18). pap. 9.99 *(978-1-4169-9399-5(1),* Simon Pulse) Simon Pulse.
Kinsella, Sophie, pseud. Finding Audrey. (ENG.). 304p. (YA). (gr. 7). 2016. pap. 9.99 *(978-0-553-53653-9(2),* Ember) 2015. 18.99 *(978-0-553-53651-5(6),* Delacorte Pr.) Random Hse. Children's Bks.
—Finding Audrey. 2016. lib. bdg. 20.85 *(978-0-606-38874-0(5))* Turtleback Bks.
Kirby, Jessi. The Secret History of Us. 2017. 288p. (YA). (gr. 9). 17.99 ***(978-0-06-229946-8(8),*** HarperTeen) HarperCollins Pubs.
Kirchel, Karen. Irrepressible Lucie Archer. 2006. 147p. pap. 24.95 *(978-1-4241-3400-7(5))* PublishAmerica, Inc.
Kirk, Heather. A Drop of Rain. 2004. (ENG.). 224p. (YA). pap. 9.95 *(978-1-894917-10-0(3),* Napoleon & Co.) Dundurn CAN. Dist: Ingram Publisher Services.
Kirkland, Kim M. Mi Mi's Mini Tea Party. Swope, Brenda, illus. 2011. 28p. pap. 24.95 *(978-1-4512-8099-9(8))* America Star Bks.
Kisinger, E. Jean. Firebug & the Mind Spark. Marta, Diana M., illus. 2012. 42p. pap. 12.50 *(978-0-615-58954-1(5))* Firebug Fairy Tales.
Klages, Ellen. White Sands, Red Menace. 2010. (ENG.). 352p. (J). (gr. 5-18). 8.99 *(978-0-14-241518-4(9),* Puffin Books) Penguin Young Readers Group.
Kline, Christina Baker. Orphan Train Girl. 2017. 240p. (J). (gr. 3-7). 17.99 *(978-0-06-244594-0(4))* HarperCollins Pubs.
Klinkerman, Anthonette. Battle of the Grandmas. 2012. (ENG.). 34p. (J). pap. 13.95 *(978-1-4787-1930-4(3))* Outskirts Pr., Inc.
Knaggs, Robin A. I Am a Squirmy Wormy. 2012. 16p. pap. 9.99 *(978-1-60911-969-0(X),* Strategic Bk. Publishing) Strategic Book Publishing & Rights Agency (SBPRA).
Knisley, Lucy. Heart: Seed Snow Circuit. 2007. 20p. pap. 10.00 *(978-0-9789427-7-9(9),* Epigraph Bks.) Monkfish Bk. Publishing Co.

E
F
G

Knoebel, Suzanne B. Dr. Tootsie: A Young Girl's Dream. Armour, Steven & Kennard, Thomas, illus. 2003. 100p. (J). per. 12.97 (978-0-9679416-1-5(X)) Alexie Bks.

Kocek, Sara. Promise Me Something. 2013. (ENG.). 320p. (YA). (gr. 8-12). 16.99 (978-0-8075-6641-1(1)) Whitman, Albert & Co.

Konigsberg, Bill. The Porcupine of Truth. 2015. (ENG.). 336p. (J). (gr. 9). 17.99 (978-0-545-64893-6(9)) Scholastic, Inc.

Koraido, Beth S. On the Farm with Grandma Gert. 2008. 53p. pap. 16.95 (978-1-60474-400-2(6)) America Star Bks.

Korba, Joanna. Rough-Face Girl: A Native American Cinderella Tale. 2006. (J). pap. (978-1-4108-6163-4(5)) Benchmark Education Co.

Korda, Lerryn. Into the Wild. Korda, Lerryn, illus. 2010. (Playtime with Little Nye Ser.). (ENG., Illus.). 26p. (J). (gr. -1 — 1). 8.99 (978-0-7636-4812-1(4)) Candlewick Pr.

Koski, Mary B. Impatient Pamela Asks: Why Are My Feet So Huge? Brown, Dan, illus. 2003. (Impatient Pamela Ser.). 32p. (J). (gr. -1-3). pap. 4.95 (978-1-930650-02-2(7)) mTrellis Publishing, Inc.

—Impatient Pamela Calls 9-1-1. Brown, Dan, illus. 2003. (Impatient Pamela Ser.). 32p. (J). (gr. -1-3). 15.95 (978-0-9663281-9-6(1)) mTrellis Publishing, Inc.

Kozlowsky, M. P. Frost. 2016. (ENG.). 352p. (J). (gr. 9). 17.99 (978-0-545-83191-8(1), Scholastic Pr.) Scholastic, Inc.

Kraft, Andrea. Gracie Blue Knows a Secret. 1 vol. 2010. 24p. 24.95 (978-1-4512-1035-4(3)) PublishAmerica, Inc.

—Gracie Blue Knows a Secret. 1 vol. Kraft, Joe, illus. 2009. 23p. pap. 19.95 (978-1-61582-554-7(1)) PublishAmerica, Inc.

Kramer, Paul. Maggie Goes on a Diet. 2011. (ENG.). 44p. (J). (gr. 1-7). 15.95 (978-0-9819745-5-2(4)) Aloha Wellness Pubs.

Kratz, Jessica R. Sleigh Bells in Springtime: Frogs Calling. 2010. 48p. pap. 17.49 (978-1-4490-8138-6(X)) AuthorHouse.

Kravetz, Stacy. The Fosters: Keep Your Frenemies Close. 2015. (ENG.). 224p. (YA). (gr. 7-12). pap. 9.99 (978-1-4847-1620-5(5)) Hyperion Bks. for Children.

Kretzmer, Alissa. Brandy's Day at the Beach. 2013. 16p. pap. 12.97 (978-1-61897-357-3(6), Strategic Bk. Publishing) Strategic Book Publishing & Rights Agency (SBPRA).

Kristina Simmons. Winter Beauty. 2010. 192p. pap. 13.95 (978-1-4401-4449-3(4)) iUniverse, Inc.

Kroll, Virginia. She Is Born. 2010. (ENG.). 32p. (J). (gr. -1-3). 11.99 (978-1-4424-1656-7(4)) Aladdin/Beyond Words.

Krossing, Karen. Pure. 1 vol. 2006. (ENG.). 245p. (YA). (gr. 7-9). per. 10.95 (978-1-896764-96-2(7)) Second Story Pr. CAN. Dist: Orca Bk. Pubs. USA.

Krouskop, Adrienne. The Bakers Moon. 2013. 24p. pap. 10.50 (978-1-938743-92-4(X)) Reimann Bks.

Krulik, Nancy. Katie Kazoo, Switcheroo: A Collection of Katie. John and Wendy, illus. 2008. (Katie Kazoo, Switcheroo Ser.: Bks. 1-4). (ENG.). 320p. (J). (gr. 2-4). 10.99 (978-0-448-44910-4(2), Grosset & Dunlap) Penguin Young Readers Group.

—Who's Afraid of Fourth Grade? John and Wendy Staff, illus. 2004. (Katie Kazoo, Switcheroo Ser.: No. 1). (ENG.). 160p. (J). (gr. 2-4). mass mkt. 4.99 (978-0-448-43555-8(1), Grosset & Dunlap) Penguin Young Readers Group.

Kurchinski, Alessandra. Disney Story. 2010. 36p. pap. 17.30 (978-0-557-25447-7(7)) Lulu Pr., Inc.

Kyber, Manfred. The Three Candles of Little Veronica. 2003. (Illus.). 194p. pap. 19.95 (978-0-913098-84-4(1)) Orion Society, The.

Lacasse, Monique. Good Morning to You. 2012. 24p. pap. 15.99 (978-1-4691-8623-8(3)) Xlibris Corp.

Ladig, Kim. Ellie's Lake House. 2010. 48p. pap. 19.49 (978-1-4490-5641-4(5)) AuthorHouse.

Lafantasie, Shilo. House of Love. 2012. 32p. pap. 24.95 (978-1-4560-9404-1(1)) America Star Bks.

Laidlaw, S. J. Fifteen Lanes. 2016. (ENG., Illus.). 302p. (YA). (gr. 9). 17.99 (978-1-101-91780-0(6), Tundra Bks.) Tundra Bks. CAN. Dist: Penguin Random Hse. LLC.

Lalwani, Shalaka. Mrs. Mulberry's Winter. 1 vol. 2010. 32p. 24.95 (978-1-4512-2436-8(2)) PublishAmerica, Inc.

Lamere, Jill. Upside Down. Lamere, Jill, illus. 2005. (Illus.). (J). bds. 12.95 (978-0-9772320-0-0(X)) Minikin Pr.

—The Wishing Star. 2006. (Illus.). 4p. (J). bds. 16.95 (978-0-9772320-1-7(8)) Minikin Pr.

Lampman, Annette. Nicole's Wish. 2006. 23.00 (978-0-8059-9146-8(8)) Dorrance Publishing Co., Inc.

Lance, Charlotte. This Girl, That Girl. 2017. (ENG.). 32p. (J). (gr. -1-2). 18.99 **(978-1-76029-170-9(6))** Allen & Unwin AUS. Dist: Independent Pubs. Group.

Lancett, Peter. The Dark Side of Magic. 1 vol. unabr. ed. 2010. (Dark Man Ser.). (ENG.). 34p. (YA). (gr. 9-12). pap. 7.95 (978-1-61651-019-0(6)) Saddleback Educational Publishing, Inc.

Land, Linda C. The Mysterious Traveling Trunk. 2011. 156p. 23.50 (978-1-4269-6160-1(X)); pap. 13.50 (978-1-4269-6161-8(8)) Trafford Publishing.

Langill, Jill. Sweet Tea for Frankenstein. 2010. 212p. pap. 14.95 (978-1-4490-6480-8(9)) AuthorHouse.

Langlois, Annie. Victorine et la Pièce D'or. Beshwaty, Steve, tr. 2003. (Picture Bks.). (FRE., Illus.). 32p. (J). (gr. -1). pap. (978-2-89021-658-7(6)) Diffusion du livre Mirabel (DLM).

Lansky, Bruce, ed. Hidden Courage: 10 Inspiring Stories about Clever & Courageous Girls from Around the World. 2013. (Girls to the Rescue Ser.: 3). (ENG.). 112p. (J). (gr. 3-6). pap. 4.99 (978-1-4424-9195-3(7)) Meadowbrook Pr.

—Lion on the Prowl: 10 Inspiring Stories about Clever & Courageous Girls from Around the World. 2013. (Girls to the Rescue Ser.: 2). (ENG.). 112p. (J). (gr. 3-6). pap. 4.99 (978-1-4424-9194-6(9)) Meadowbrook Pr.

—The Royal Joust: 10 Inspiring Stories about Clever & Courageous Girls from Around the World. 2013. (Girls to the Rescue Ser.: 1). (ENG.). 112p. (J). (gr. 3-6). pap. 4.99 (978-1-4424-9193-9(0)) Meadowbrook Pr.

Lansky, Bruce & Johnson, Martha. Girls to the Rescue, Bk. 5. 108p. (J). pap. (978-0-88166-315-0(8)) Meadowbrook Pr.

Larose, Ella. The Best Rainbow Ever! 2012. 16p. pap. 15.99 (978-1-4685-4946-1(4)) AuthorHouse.

Larrypoet. Green, the Fairy: Cici & the Fairy. 2011. (Illus.). 48p. pap. 12.10 (978-1-4670-0090-1(6)) AuthorHouse.

Larson, Hope. Chiggers. Larson, Hope, illus. 2008. (ENG., Illus.). 176p. (J). (gr. 5-9). pap. 11.99 (978-1-4169-3587-2(8), Simon & Schuster/Paula Wiseman Bks.) Simon & Schuster Children's Publishing.

Larson, Kirby. Liberty. 2016. (Dogs of World War II Ser.). (ENG.). 240p. (J). (gr. 3-7). 16.99 (978-0-545-84071-2(6), Scholastic Pr.) Scholastic, Inc.

Larson, Rachel. Jesse Strong & Courageous Runaway: There Comes A Time When the Roads of Destiny Will No Longer Wait... 2011. 192p. (J). (gr. -1). pap. 14.03 (978-1-4520-0421-1(8)) AuthorHouse.

Larue, Ravyn. Sophie Browne Isn't Dead. 2011. 40p. pap. 19.95 (978-0-557-91717-4(4)) Lulu Pr., Inc.

Lascurain, Guadalupe Aleman. La Domadora de Miedos. Arte y Cultura, A.C Staff, illus. rev. ed. 2006. (Castillo de la Lectura Roja Ser.). (SPA & ENG.). 232p. (YA). (gr. 7). pap. 8.95 (978-970-20-0182-9(X)) Castillo, Ediciones, S. A. de C. V. MEX. Dist: Macmillan.

Lasser, Olivier. Charlotte et l'nie du Destin. 2004. (FRE., Illus.). (J). (gr. k-3). spiral bd. (978-0-616-07262-2(7)) Canadian National Institute for the Blind/Institut National Canadien pour les Aveugles.

Laubenstein, Sharon. Something about Sally. 2013. 24p. pap. 10.95 (978-1-4908-0723-2(3), WestBow Pr.) Author Solutions, Inc.

Laurens, Jennifer. Magic Hands. 2007. (YA). per. 12.95 (978-1-933963-97-6(2)) Grove Creek Publishing, LLC.

Lavender, William. Just Jane: A Daughter of England Caught in the Struggle of the American Revolution. 2005. (Great Episodes Ser.). (ENG.). 336p. (YA). (gr. 7-12). pap. 15.95 (978-0-15-205472-4(3)) Houghton Mifflin Harcourt Publishing Co.

Lawrence, Antoinette & Lewis, Terry. I Remember. 2011. (ENG.). 29p. (J). pap. 12.95 (978-1-4327-7342-7(9)) Outskirts Pr., Inc.

Lawrence, Dionne L. The Story of Her?! 2012. 28p. (-18). pap. 16.95 (978-1-62709-253-1(6)) America Star Bks.

Lawrence, Josephine. Rainbow Hill. 2005. pap. 30.95 (978-1-4179-9852-4(0)) Kessinger Publishing, LLC.

Lawrence, Mike. The Macaroni Disaster! 2006. 44p. pap. 12.00 (978-1-4116-8613-7(6)) Lulu Pr., Inc.

Lay, Eddie. Mystery of the Hats. 2006. 61p. pap. 16.95 (978-1-4241-2649-1(5)) PublishAmerica, Inc.

Leblanc, Avis Lyons. To Ride a Dragonfly. 2012. 94p. pap. 15.99 (978-1-4771-2222-8(2)) Xlibris Corp.

Leblanc, Louise. Ca Suffit, Sophie! 2003. (Premier Roman Ser.). (FRE.). 64p. (J). (gr. 2-5). pap. (978-2-89021-131-5(2)) Diffusion du livre Mirabel (DLM).

Lederhos, Lynn. Return to Her Roots: Revelations from a Young Girl's Journey Home. 2010. 40p. 20.99 (978-1-4520-3812-4(0)) AuthorHouse.

Lee, Amy Sue. Lou Lou & Lenny's Boat Ride. 2005. (Illus.). 28p. (J). (gr. -1-3). per. 19.99 (978-1-4208-6447-2(5)) AuthorHouse.

Lee, SangEun. 13th Boy, 12 vols., Vol. 5. 2010. (13th Boy Ser.: 5). (ENG., Illus.). 192p. (YA). (gr. 8-17). pap. 10.99 (978-0-7595-2998-4(1), Yen Pr.) Orbit.

Lee, Vanessa. The Beauty Queen & the School Nerd. 2007. 78p. (YA). (gr. 4-6). per. 8.95 (978-0-595-45936-0(6)) iUniverse, Inc.

Lehman, Barbara. The Red Book. Lehman, Barbara, illus. 2004. (ENG., Illus.). 32p. (J). (gr. -1-3). 16.99 (978-0-618-42858-8(5)) Houghton Mifflin Harcourt Publishing Co.

Leigh, Suzie. The Glitter Man. 2010. 164p. 22.95 (978-1-4520-1266-7(0)); pap. 12.95 (978-1-4520-1267-4(9)) AuthorHouse.

Leloup, Roger. The Time Spiral. 2008. (Yoko Tsuno Ser.: 2). (ENG., Illus.). 48p. pap. 11.95 (978-1-905460-43-4(0)) CineBook GBR. Dist: National Bk. Network.

Lemay, Violet. Isabella's Shoe Studio: Read! Doodle! Create! Lemay, Violet, illus. 2013. (Doodle Story Bks.). (ENG., Illus.). 120p. (J). (gr. 2-3). pap. 12.95 (978-1-938093-18-0(6)) Duo Pr. LLC.

L'Engle, Madeleine. Camilla. 278p. (YA). (gr. 7-18). pap. 4.95 (978-0-8072-1359-9(4), Listening Library) Random Hse. Audio Publishing Group.

Lepri, Nancy Carty. Tiny Angel. 2009. 104p. pap. 8.95 (978-1-935137-94-8(8)) Guardian Angel Publishing, Inc.

LernerClassroom Editors. Mallory Teaching Guide. 2009. pap. 7.95 (978-0-8225-7448-4(9)) Lerner Publishing Group.

Lester, Helen. La Mochila de Lin, Level 2. Flor Ada, Alma, tr. from ENG. Munsinger, Lynn, illus. 3rd ed. 2003. (Dejame Leer Ser.).Tr. of Lin's Backpack. (SPA.). 8p. (J). (gr. -1-1). 6.50 (978-0-673-36291-9(4), Good Year Bks.) Celebration Pr.

Levine, Gail Carson. Ella Enchanted. 2011. 238p. (J). (gr. 3-7). 18.40 (978-0-613-07691-3(5), Turtleback) Turtleback Bks.

Levine, Gail Carson & Levine, Gail C. Ella Enchanted. movie tie-in ed. 2004. (ENG.). 288p. (J). (gr. 3-7). pap. 6.99 (978-0-06-055886-4(5), HarperTeen) HarperCollins Pubs.

Levinson, Robin K. Shoshana & the Native Rose. Kehl, Drusilla, illus. 2006. 103p. (J). (gr. 3-5). per. 12.00 (978-0-9773673-2-0(0)) Gali Girls, Inc.

Lewis-Domenech, Shanty. Toot. 1 vol. 2010. 16p. pap. 24.95 (978-1-4489-5311-0(1)) PublishAmerica, Inc.

Lewis, Megan. The Girl Who Could Fly. l.t. ed. 2005. (Illus.). 30p. (J). per. 9.99 (978-1-59879-029-0(3)) Lifevest Publishing, Inc.

Lewis, Olive. Three Shades of Blackness. 2004. 246p. (YA). 25.95 (978-0-595-66311-8(7)) iUniverse, Inc.

Libhart, Virginia B. Carrie's Dream. 2005. (978-0-9652963-7-3(7)) Harborseal Publishing Co.

Licata, Rosemarie & Reizer, Edwina. Betsy & Her Buttons. 2008. 24p. 14.95 (978-1-4357-0697-2(8)) Lulu Pr., Inc.

Lichtman, Wendy. Secrets, Lies, & Algebra. 2007. (Do the Math Ser.: 1). (ENG., Illus.). 192p. (YA). (gr. 8-8). 16.99 (978-0-06-122955-8(5), Greenwillow Bks.) HarperCollins Pubs.

Lickel, Lisa J. The German Girl. Hendricks, Brenda K., illus. 2013. 38p. pap. 5.95 (978-0-9856215-4-4(0)) Fox Ridge Pubns.

Light, John. Julie's Problem. 2005. (Illus.). 24p. (978-1-897968-13-0(2)) Photon Pr.

Lillian's First Day. 2003. (J). 12.00 (978-0-9724442-3-1(8)) LightHouse Pr.

Limb, Sue. Girl, 15, Charming but Insane. 2005. (Girl, 15 Ser.). (ENG.). 240p. (YA). (gr. 7-12). reprint ed. pap. 8.99 (978-0-385-73215-4(5), Delacorte Bks. for Young Readers) Random Hse. Children's Bks.

Limon, Cyndi. Hello, My Name Is Boots. 2011. 20p. pap. 10.50 (978-1-4634-3670-4(X)) AuthorHouse.

Lindgren, Astrid. Pippi Longstocking. (Pippi Longstocking Ser.). 160p. (J). (gr. 3-5). pap. 4.99 (978-0-8072-1431-2(0), Listening Library) Random Hse. Audio Publishing Group.

Lindsay, Elizabeth. Dancing Magic. 2012. (Silverlake Fairy School Ser.). 100p. (J). pap. 4.99 (978-0-7945-3067-9(2), Usborne) EDC Publishing.

Linker, Julie. Disenchanted Princess. 2007. (ENG.). 240p. (YA). (gr. 9-18). pap. 11.99 (978-1-4169-3472-1(3), Simon Pulse) Simon Pulse.

Linklater, Eric. The Wind on the Moon. Bentley, Nicolas, illus. 2017. (New York Review Children's Collection). (ENG.). 376p. (J). (gr. 7). pap. 12.99 (978-1-68137-103-0(0), NYRB Kids) New York Review of Bks., Inc., The.

Lionheart, Amelia. The Dolphin Heptad. 2009. 200p. (gr. 4-6). pap. 14.95 (978-1-4401-8028-6(8)) iUniverse, Inc.

Lipson, Amy Kron & Laddy, Lee. Penelope Pratt's Hats: A Young Girl's Dilemma Turns Rhyme to Reason. 2012. (ENG.). 44p. (J). pap. 20.95 (978-1-4327-8173-6(1)) Outskirts Pr., Inc.

Lisa's Ices: Individual Title Six-Packs. (gr. -1-2). 27.00 (978-0-7635-9459-6(8)) Rigby Education.

Lisle, Chris. Bedtime Stories for Girls. 2011. 32p. pap. 13.10 (978-1-257-04108-4(8)) Lulu Pr., Inc.

Lisle, Janet Taylor. The Crying Rocks. 2017. (ENG., Illus.). 208p. (YA). (gr. 7). pap. 10.99 **(978-1-4814-7976-9(8)**, Atheneum Bks. for Young Readers) Simon & Schuster Children's Publishing.

Lisle, Rebecca. Amethyst. Hess, Paul, illus. 2007. (ENG.). 176p. (J). (gr. 4-7). per. 8.99 (978-1-84270-541-4(5)) Andersen Pr. GBR. Dist: Independent Pubs. Group.

Literature Connections English: My Antonia. 2004. (gr. 6-12). (978-0-395-77539-4(6), 2-80108) Holt McDougal.

Literature Connections English: Nervous Conditions. 2004. (gr. 6-12). (978-0-395-77560-8(4), 2-80129) Holt McDougal.

Little, Ashley. The New Normal. 1 vol. 2013. (ENG.). 232p. (YA). (gr. 8-12). pap. 12.95 (978-1-4598-0074-8(5)) Orca Bk. Pubs. USA.

Little China's Not So Mean after All. 2012. 28p. 24.95 (978-1-4137-7549-5(7)) America Star Bks.

The Little Girl & Her Beetle: Individual Title Six-Packs. (Literatura 2000 Ser.). (gr. 2-3). 33.00 (978-0-7635-0174-7(3)) Rigby Education.

Lizzy Anne's Adventures Staff & Zarrella, Sharon. Lizzy Anne's Adventures, Vol. 1. Vasudevan, Vidya, illus. 2011. 52p. (J). (gr. k-4). pap. 5.99 (978-0-9845887-2-5(8)) Lizzy Anne's Adventures.

Lockhart, E., et al. How to Be Bad. 2008. 325p. (YA). (gr. 9-12). lib. bdg. 17.89 (978-0-06-128423-6(8), HarperTeen) HarperCollins Pubs.

Lodding, Linda Ravin. The Busy Life of Ernestine Buckmeister. Beaky, Suzanne, illus. 2011. (ENG.). 32p. (J). (gr. -1-1). 16.95 (978-0-9799746-9-4(0)) Flashlight Pr.

London, Kelli. Beware of Boys. 2014. (Charly's Epic Fiascos Ser.). (ENG., Illus.). 240p. (YA). (gr. 9). pap. 9.95 (978-0-7582-8701-4(1)) Kensington Publishing Corp.

London, Victoria. Emily Cobbs & the Naked School Bk. 1: A Gifted Girls Series. 2005. (Gifted Girls Ser.). (J). per. 7.99 (978-1-59748-857-0(7)) Sparklesoup LLC.

—Emily Cobbs Collection Bk. 1 & Bk. 2: A Gifted Girls Series. 2005. (Gifted Girls Ser.). (J). per. 12.95 (978-1-59748-859-4(3)) Sparklesoup LLC.

Longo, Kaitlin. The Secret in Olivia's Garden. 2012. 36p. pap. 20.99 (978-1-4685-5222-5(8)) AuthorHouse.

Look Out the Window: Individual Title Six-Packs. (Story Steps Ser.). (gr. k-2). 29.00 (978-0-7635-9587-6(X)) Rigby Education.

Lopez, C. Pellicer. Julieta y Su Caja de Colores. (SPA., Illus.). (J). (gr. k-2). pap. 3.96 net. (978-0-395-79735-8(7), HMS033) Houghton Mifflin Harcourt Publishing Co.

López, Diana. Choke. 2012. (ENG.). 240p. (J). (gr. 7). 17.99 (978-0-545-41822-5(4)) Scholastic, Inc.

Lorimer, Janet. Ruby's Terrible Secret. (Quickreads Ser.). 32p. 2005. (Illus.). (J). pap. 2.95 (978-1-56254-744-8(5), SP7445) 2010. (ENG.). (YA). (gr. 9-12). pap. 6.95 (978-1-61651-218-7(0)) Saddleback Educational Publishing, Inc.

Lost in the Wilderness. 2006. (J). (978-1-933343-39-6(7), PONY) Stabenfeldt Inc.

Louis HéMon Staff. Maria Chapdelaine. 2005. pap. (978-1-4065-0017-2(8)) Dodo Pr.

Love, Emily. The Beginning of Freedom. 2010. 81p. pap. 9.00 (978-0-557-56598-6(7)) Lulu Pr., Inc.

Loveridge, Pamela. The Man in the Moon. 2012. 28p. pap. 32.70 (978-1-4797-5423-6(4)) Xlibris Corp.

Lowe, Lana. The Three Little Girls & the Giant Sea Turtle. Beaumont, Peter, illus. 2006. (J). (978-0-9777274-0-7(8)) Lone Star Publishing Co.

Lück, Stefanie. Carla's Worlds. 2010. 222p. pap. 20.90 (978-3-8391-4857-0(X)) Bks. on Demand.

Lueck, Andrew M. Chicabee. 2006. (Illus.). 32p. (J). (gr. -1-3). 16.95 (978-0-9774547-0-9(3)) Lueck Studios.

Luker, Penny. The Green Book. 2013. 68p. pap. (978-0-9559896-3-6(9)) Bindon Bks.

Lundquist, Jenny. Plastic Polly. 2013. (Mix Ser.). (ENG.). 256p. (J). (gr. 4-8). pap. 6.99 (978-1-4424-5248-0(X), Aladdin) Simon & Schuster Children's Publishing.

Lundstrom, Norma Niemi. The Chubby Girl. 2013. 12p. pap. 7.99 (978-1-4624-0556-5(8), Inspiring Voices) Author Solutions, Inc.

Lunsk, Robert. Kippy Berryfoote. 2012. (ENG.). (J). pap. (978-1-4675-4313-2(6)) Independent Pub.

Lux, Josephine Kei & Doerflinger, Marion. Daydreaming Daisy Part of the Daydreamer's Club Series. 2009. 40p. pap. 17.50 (978-1-60860-252-0(4), Eloquent Bks.) Strategic Book Publishing & Rights Agency (SBPRA).

Lyles, Whitney. Party Games. 2012. (Romantic Comedies Ser.). (ENG.). 304p. (YA). (gr. 7). pap. 14.99 (978-1-4424-6060-7(1), Simon Pulse) Simon Pulse.

Lyons, Suzanne. Oops! Why Did I Do That? Set Of 6. 2010. (Early Connections Ser.). (J). pap. 39.00 net. (978-1-4108-1550-7(1)) Benchmark Education Co.

M a, Stuck. Proulx, Denis, illus. 2011. (ENG.). 38p. (J). (gr. 1-5). 15.77 (978-1-935204-33-6(5)) Salem Author Services.

Macenski, Geraldine. Healthy, Happy Gigi! 2009. 28p. pap. 15.99 (978-1-4415-3644-0(2)) Xlibris Corp.

MacGregor, Helen & Chadwick, Stephen. Goldilocks & the Three Bears: An Impeccable Judged Musical. 1 vol. Lowe, Harriet et al, eds. Eccles, Jane, illus. 2005. (and C Black Musicals Ser.). (ENG.). 56p. (J). (gr. 2-6). pap. 42.95 **(978-0-7136-7085-1(1))** HarperCollins Pubs. Ltd. GBR. Dist: Independent Pubs. Group.

Mack, Winnie. After All, You're Callie Boone. 2013. (ENG.). 192p. (J). (gr. 4-7). pap. 14.99 (978-1-250-02735-1(7), 9781250027351) Square Fish.

MacLeod, Jean. At Home in This World: A China Adoption Story. Su, Qin, illus. 2nd ed. 2004. 32p. 15.95 (978-0-9726244-1-1(4)) EMK Pr.

Madden, Avery. Sport Talk with Avery. 2004. (Illus.). 36p. (J). 3.99 (978-0-9746587-2-8(3), Beacon Street Girls) B*tween Productions, Inc.

Maddox, Jake. Jake Maddox Girl Sport Stories. Wood, Katie, illus. 2013. (Jake Maddox Girl Sports Stories Ser.). (ENG.). 72p. (gr. 2-3). 101.28 (978-1-4342-4134-4(3)) Stone Arch Bks.

—Jake Maddox Girl Sports Stories. Wood, Katie, illus. 2013. (Jake Maddox Girl Sports Stories Ser.). (ENG.). 72p. (gr. 2-3). 708.96 (978-1-4342-4847-3(X)); pap. 71.40 (978-1-4342-4359-1(1)); pap. 23.80 (978-1-4342-4358-4(3)) Stone Arch Bks.

Madrid, Bo. The Lunar Express. 2010. (Illus.). 32p. 12.99 (978-1-4490-6949-0(5)) AuthorHouse.

Maizel, Rebecca. Infinite Days. 2010. (Vampire Queen Ser.: 1). (ENG.). 336p. (YA). (gr. 7-18). pap. 9.99 (978-0-312-64991-3(6), 9780312649913, St. Martin's Griffin) St. Martin's Pr.

Malik, Katherine. Giselle's Magical World. 1 vol. 2009. 150p. pap. 24.95 (978-1-4489-1902-4(9)) America Star Bks.

Man-Kong, Mary. Sensational Style. Golden Books Staff, illus. 2010. (Big Coloring Book Ser.). (ENG.). 48p. (J). (gr. -1-2). pap. 6.99 (978-0-375-86490-2(3), Golden Bks.) Random Hse. Children's Bks.

—Sparkling Style. Golden Books Staff, illus. 2010. (Deluxe Coloring Book Ser.). (ENG.). 96p. (J). (gr. -1-2). pap. 3.99 (978-0-375-86031-7(2), Golden Bks.) Random Hse. Children's Bks.

Mancil, Julie A. Anna's Decision. 2011. 68p. (gr. 4-6). pap. 9.95 (978-1-4497-1694-3(6), WestBow Pr.) Author Solutions, Inc.

Mann, Jennifer K. Two Speckled Eggs. Mann, Jennifer K., illus. 2014. (ENG., Illus.). 32p. (J). (gr. k-3). 14.99 (978-0-7636-6168-7(6)) Candlewick Pr.

Mann, Seymour. The Purple Automobile & the Newspaper Girl. 2003. 112p. 20.95 (978-0-595-66076-6(2)); pap. 10.95 (978-0-595-29907-2(5)) iUniverse, Inc.

Manning, Ella L. Ashleigh's Rainbow Garden. 2012. 16p. pap. 15.99 (978-1-4685-6601-7(6)) AuthorHouse.

Manos, John. Samantha Saves the Stream. 2006. (Early Explorers Ser.). (J). pap. (978-1-4108-6125-2(2)) Benchmark Education Co.

Manushkin, Fran. Big Girl Panties. Petrone, Valeria, illus. 2012. (ENG.). 24p. (J). (gr. k — 1). bds. 7.99 (978-0-307-93152-8(8), Robin Corey Bks.) Random Hse. Children's Bks.

—Katie Woo Collection. Lyon, Tammie, illus. 2016. (Katie Woo Ser.). (ENG.). 288p. (gr. k-2). 9.99 (978-1-4795-9318-7(4)) Picture Window Bks.

Marchessault, Sara J. Pinky the Dreamer & Her Silver Jet. 2009. 36p. pap. 15.49 (978-1-4389-9902-9(X)) AuthorHouse.

Margaret Bruce Clarke. Hunter's Marjory: A Story for Girls. 2007. (ENG.). 200p. pap. 19.99 (978-1-4264-8118-5(7)); 224p. pap. 22.99 (978-1-4346-3052-0(8)) Creative Media Partners, LLC.

Marie, E. The Porcupine Connection: The Story of a Young Girl's Journey from Tragedy to Healing, with the Help of Her Forest Friends. 2004. 48p. pap. 16.95 (978-1-4137-3480-5(4)) America Star Bks.

Marie, Tina. Isabella Learns Her Manners. 2011. 24p. 12.95 (978-1-4567-2000-1(7)) AuthorHouse.

—Isabella Learns the Value of Money. 2011. 24p. pap. 12.95 (978-1-4567-4537-0(9)) AuthorHouse.

Marino, Kellie A. Marcella's Angel. 2011. 20p. 10.95 (978-1-4520-9519-6(1)) AuthorHouse.

Markle, Sandra. The Fledglings. 2003. (ENG.). 144p. (YA). (gr. 4-6). pap. 9.95 (978-1-56397-696-4(X)) Boyds Mills Pr.

Marquis, Melanie. Bugbug & the Ants. 2013. 44p. pap. 12.99 (978-1-60820-841-8(9)) MLR Pr., LLC.

Marr, Melissa. Challenge. Xian Nu Studio Staff, illus. 2010. (Wicked Lovely: Desert Tales Ser.: 2). (ENG.). 176p. (YA). (gr. 8-18). pap. 9.99 (978-0-06-149349-2(X)) HarperCollins Pubs.

Marsh, Carole. The Puzzle of the Shark Surfer Girl. 2006. (Criss Cross Applesauce Ser.). (Illus.). 54p. (J). (gr. 1-3). 14.95 (978-0-635-06204-8(6)) Gallopade International.

—The Riddle of the Missing Puppies. 2006. (Criss Cross Applesauce Ser.). (Illus.). 54p. (J). (gr. 4-7). 14.95 (978-0-635-06203-1(8)) Gallopade International.

Marshall, Jill. Kave-Tina Rox. Childs, Sam, illus. 2010. (ENG.). 32p. (J). (978-0-340-95712-7(3), Hodder Children's Books) Hachette Children's Group GBR. Dist: Hachette Bk. Group.

Marshall, Peter, et al. Mercy Clifton: Pilgrim Girl. 2007. 208p. (J). pap. 9.99 (978-0-8054-4395-0(9), B&H Bks.) B&H Publishing Group.

Martin Ann, M. Claudia & Mean Janine. Telgemeier, Raina, illus. 2016. (Baby-Sitters Club Graphix Ser.: 4). (ENG.). 176p. (J). (gr. 3-7). 24.99 (978-0-545-88623-9(6), Graphix) Scholastic, Inc.

Martin, Ann M. Claudia & Mean Janine. Telgemeier, Raina, illus. rev. ed. 2016. (Baby-Sitters Club Graphix Ser.: 4). (ENG.). 176p. (J). (gr. 3-7). pap. 10.99 (978-0-545-88622-2(8), Graphix) Scholastic, Inc.

—Needle & Thread. Andreasen, Dan, illus. 2007. 205p. (J). pap. (978-0-545-03660-3(7)) Scholastic, Inc.

Martin, Caroline Jane. The Flow. 2013. (ENG.). 276p. pap. (978-0-9928101-0-8(8)) Lovell Pr.

Martin, Rebecca. Joanna's Journey. Yoder, Laura & Weaver, Lisa, illus. 2006. 168p. (YA). pap. 9.99 (978-1-933753-01-0(3)) Carlisle Pr.- Walnut Creek.

Martinez, Vendrell. Yo Las Queria (I Loved Them) (SPA.). 40p. (J). 18.95 (978-84-233-1289-4(5)) Ediciones Destino ESP. Dist: AIMS International Bks., Inc.

Mary Emme. Date not set. (978-0-517-80135-2(3)) Random Hse. Value Publishing.

Mary Mccowski Was Not a Pretty Girl: About a Girl Who Isn't Pretty, & Never Will Be Pretty but Finds Success Anyway. 2005. (J). 3.99 (978-0-9754420-0-5(7)) www.underdogpublishing.com.

Maslin, Mirabelle. Tracy. 2007. 210p. pap. (978-0-9549551-0-6(2)) Augur Pr.

Mason, Jane B. & Hines-Stephens, Sarah. Disguised & Dangerous. Phillips, Craig, illus. 2011. 92p. (J). (978-0-545-37469-9(3)) Scholastic, Inc.

Mason, Jane B. & Stephens, Sarah Hines. A Dog & His Girl Mysteries #3: Cry Woof. 2013. (ENG.). 208p. (J). (gr. 3-7). pap. 5.99 (978-0-545-43626-7(5), Scholastic Paperbacks) Scholastic, Inc.

Mason, Richard. The Red Scarf: A Country Boy's Christmas Story. 2011. (ENG.). 155p. (J). (gr. 3-7). pap. 11.95 (978-0-87483-954-8(8)) August Hse. Pubs., Inc.

Matthews, Caitlín. The Barefoot Book of Princesses. Whelan, Olwyn, illus. 2004. (ENG.). 64p. (J). (gr. k-4). 16.99 (978-1-84148-172-2(6)) Barefoot Bks., Inc.

Maxwell, Ruth H. Eighteen Roses Red: A Young Girl's Heroic Mission in the Revolutionary War. 2006. (American Revolution Adventures Ser.). 126p. (J). (gr. 3-7). per. 8.95 (978-1-57249-380-3(1), White Mane Kids) White Mane Publishing Co., Inc.

May, Kyla. Kyla Miss. Behaves Around the World. May, Kyla, illus. 2005. (Kyla May Miss. Behaves Ser.). (ENG., Illus.). 64p. (J). (gr. 2-5). pap. 5.99 (978-0-8431-1371-6(5), Price Stern Sloan) Penguin Young Readers Group.

May, Maggie. Times Three. L, Joe, illus. 2011. 36p. pap. 24.95 (978-1-4626-2504-8(5)) America Star Bks.

Mayfield, Sue. Hill of the Angels. 2016. (ENG., Illus.). pap. **(978-0-281-07641-3(3))** SPCK Publishing.

Mazer, Anne. Everything New under the Sun. 2003. (Amazing Days of Abby Hayes Ser.: Bk. 10). (Illus.). 105p. (J). (gr. 4-7). 12.65 (978-0-7569-3931-1(3)) Perfection Learning Corp.

—Good Things Come in Small Packages. 2003. (Amazing Days of Abby Hayes Ser.: Bk. 12). (Illus.). 101p. (J). (gr. 4-7). 12.65 (978-0-7569-3935-9(6)) Perfection Learning Corp.

—Now You See It, Now You Don't. 2005. (Amazing Days of Abby Hayes Ser.: Bk. 15). (Illus.). 126p. (J). (gr. 4-7). 12.65 (978-0-7569-5932-6(2)) Perfection Learning Corp.

—Some Things Never Change. 2004. (Amazing Days of Abby Hayes Ser.: Bk. 13). (Illus.). 101p. (J). (gr. 4-7). 12.65 (978-0-7569-5302-7(2)) Perfection Learning Corp.

Mbonu, Ngozi Elizabeth. Tatiana. Taylor, Kristen Michelle, illus. 2013. (ENG.). (J). 14.95 (978-1-62086-307-7(3)) Mascot Bks., Inc.

McAnulty, Stacy. Beautiful. Lew-Vriethoff, Joanne, illus. 2016. (ENG.). 32p. (J). (gr. -1-17). 16.95 (978-0-7624-5781-6(3), Running Pr. Kids) Running Pr. Bk. Pubs.

McBride, Alisha. No Way! 2013. 28p. pap. 24.95 (978-1-63000-545-0(2)) America Star Bks.

McBrier, Page. Beatrice's Goast. unabr. ed. 2005. (J). (gr. -1-3). 27.95 incl. audio (978-0-8045-6938-5(X)) Spoken Arts, Inc.

McBroom, Danielle Loiselle. A Painted Dream. 2008. 20p. pap. 24.95 (978-1-60441-694-7(7)) America Star Bks.

McCarthy, Peggy & Rivers, Julia. Not for the Meek. 2013. (ENG.). 130p. (J). pap. 10.95 (978-1-4327-9157-5(5)) Outskirts Pr., Inc.

—Tough Break: The Barn Girls. 2012. (ENG.). 132p. pap. 10.95 (978-1-4327-9122-3(2)) Outskirts Pr., Inc.

McCarthy, Terry. The Little Girl with a Loud Voice. McCarthy, Kate, illus. 2013. 26p. pap. (978-0-646-90439-9(6)) McCarthy, Kate.

McClintock, Norah. Back, 1 vol. 2009. (Orca Soundings Ser.). (ENG.). 112p. (YA). (gr. 8-12). 16.95 (978-1-55143-991-4(3)); pap. 9.95 (978-1-55143-989-1(1)) Orca Bk. Pubs. USA.

McCorkle, Mark & Schooley, Bob. Grudge Match. 2005. (Illus.). 80p. (J). (978-1-4155-9100-0(8)) Disney Pr.

McCoy, Tanya. If My Best Friend was an Elephant, 1 vol. 2010. 20p. 24.95 (978-1-4512-1063-7(9)) PublishAmerica, Inc.

McDaniel Hailey. The Amazing Angelina: And Her Hula Hoop. 2013. 38p. pap. 10.19 (978-1-62884-794-9(8)) Speedy Publishing LLC.

McDaniel, Lurlene. A Horse for Mandy. 2004. 80p. (J). (gr. 3-5). pap. 4.99 (978-1-58196-011-2(5), Darby Creek) Lerner Publishing Group.

—Sometimes Love Isn't Enough. 2007. (ENG.). 144p. (YA). (gr. 6-12). per. 4.99 (978-1-58196-048-8(4), Darby Creek) Lerner Publishing Group.

McDonald, Ann-Eve. I Can't Go to School Today, My Horses Might Escape. 2004. (J). (978-0-9770158-0-1(7)) BeachWalk Bks. Inc.

McGill, Justin. Friends Forever, Signed Jeremy E. 2007. 48p. per. 16.95 (978-1-4241-8794-2(X)) America Star Bks.

McGowan, Sharlene. Macaroni Monday. 2007. 112p. (YA). per. 10.95 (978-0-595-45984-1(6)) iUniverse, Inc.

McIntosh, Maria J. Florence Arnott; or, Is She Generous? by M J Mcintosh. 2006. 136p. per. 16.99 (978-1-4255-0994-1(0)) Michigan Publishing.

McKay, Hilary. The Terrible Time Without Tilly. Scott, Kimberley, illus. 2014. (Red Bananas Ser.). (ENG.). 48p. (J). (gr. k-2). pap. 5.99 (978-1-4052-6080-0(7)) Egmont Bks., Ltd. GBR. Dist: Independent Pubs. Group.

McKee, David. Charlotte's Piggy Bank. McKee, David, illus. 2004. (ENG., Illus.). 32p. (J). pap. 12.95 (978-1-84270-331-1(5)) Andersen Pr. GBR. Dist: Independent Pubs. Group.

McKenna, K. J. Take Three Girls. 2005. 96p. pap. 10.00 (978-1-4116-6290-2(3)) Lulu Pr., Inc.

McKenzie, Paige. The Haunting of Sunshine Girl. (ENG.). 2016. 320p. (gr. 7-10). pap. 9.99 (978-1-60286-302-6(4)) 2015. (Haunting of Sunshine Girl Ser.: Bk. 1). 304p. (YA). 16.00 (978-1-60286-272-2(9)) Perseus Bks. Group. (Weinstein Bks.).

McLaughlin, Emma & Kraus, Nicola. Over You. 2013. (ENG.). 304p. (YA). (gr. 9). pap. 9.99 (978-0-06-172045-1(3), HarperTeen) HarperCollins Pubs.

McLaughlin, Vicki. The Dancer of Her Dreams. 2006. 48p. pap. 16.95 (978-1-4241-2723-8(8)) PublishAmerica, Inc.

McMillen, Charlotte Palmer. The Little Sea Rock & His Friend Arena. 2005. (Illus.). 32p. (J). per. 14.95 (978-0-9771939-4-3(2), 003) New World Publishing.

McMullen, Judy. Stephanie & the Excellent E's. 2012. (ENG.). pap. (978-1-4675-4211-1(3)) Independent Pub.

McPhate, Paul. The Puggles: The Adventures of Carly & Vinigin. 2006. (ENG.). 48p. per. 16.95 (978-1-4241-4481-5(7)) PublishAmerica, Inc.

McPherson, Heather L. A. Sonja's Wish. Cartwright, Christina, illus. 2012. 26p. (J). pap. 11.95 (978-1-61863-394-1(5)) Bookstand Publishing.

Meade, L. T. A Modern Tomboy. 2011. 328p. 50.95 (978-1-258-06028-2(0)) Literary Licensing, LLC.

—Red Rose & Tiger Lily or in a Wider Wo. 2004. reprint ed. pap. 28.95 (978-0-7661-8345-2(9)) Kessinger Publishing, LLC.

Meadows, Daisy. Chloe Slipperside's Secret. 2016. (Magic Animal Friends Ser.: 11). (ENG., Illus.). 112p. (J). (gr. 2-5). pap. 4.99 (978-0-545-94078-8(8), Scholastic Paperbacks) Scholastic, Inc.

—Evie Scruffypup's Big Surprise. 2016. (Magic Animal Friends Ser.: 1). (ENG., Illus.). 112p. (J). (gr. 2-5). pap. 4.99 (978-0-545-94077-1(X), Scholastic Paperbacks) Scholastic, Inc.

—Evie Scruffypup's Surprise. 2016. (Magic Animal Friends Ser.: 10). lib. bdg. 14.75 (978-0-606-38800-9(1)) Turtleback Bks.

—Grace Woollyhop's Musical Mystery. 2016. (Magic Animal Friends Ser.: 12). lib. bdg. 14.75 (978-0-606-38802-3(8)) Turtleback Bks.

—Grace Woollyhop's Musical Mystery (Magic Animal Friends #12) 2016. (Magic Animal Friends Ser.: 12). (ENG., Illus.). 112p. (J). (gr. 2-5). pap. 4.99 (978-0-545-94079-5(6), Scholastic Paperbacks) Scholastic, Inc.

Medina, Meg. Yaqui Delgado Wants to Kick Your Ass. (ENG., 272p. (YA). (gr. 9). 2014. Illus.). pap. 7.99 (978-0-7636-7164-8(9)) 2013. 16.99 (978-0-7636-5859-5(6)) Candlewick Pr.

Meehan, Kelly. A Star Named Symphony. 2009. 24p. pap. 12.99 (978-1-4389-6652-6(0)) AuthorHouse.

Melrose, Laurie. Willow Wood. 2013. 238p. pap. 15.95 (978-1-62646-375-2(1)) Booklocker.com, Inc.

Melvin, Treva. Mr. Samuel's Penny. 2014. (Elizabeth Parrot Landers Mysteries Ser.: 1). (ENG.). 264p. (YA). pap. 10.95 (978-1-929345-04-5(6)) Poisoned Pen Pr.

Mendoza, Madeleine. Simply & the Shiny Quarter. Abasta, Mary, illus. 2011. 24p. pap. 24.95 (978-1-4560-3792-5(7)) America Star Bks.

Meredith, Susan Markowitz. A Happy Summer Day: Set Of 6. 2010. (Early Connections Ser.). (J). 37.00 net. (978-1-4108-1371-8(1)) Benchmark Education Co.

Merline, Sharlene. Sharlene & Her Animal Friends. Rongner, Bridget, ed. Murfield, Anna, illus. 2012. 106p. pap. 8.99 (978-1-937165-09-3(4)) Orange Hat Publishing.

Messersmith, Heather. Seasons. 2005. pap. 23.50 (978-1-4208-6698-8(2)) AuthorHouse.

Messier, Mireille. The Branch. Pratt, Pierre, illus. 2016. (ENG.). 32p. (J). (gr. -1-2). 16.95 (978-1-77138-564-0(2)) Kids Can Pr., Ltd. CAN. Dist: Hachette Bk. Group.

Metzger, Haley & Banks, Rayelynn. I Am Not Weird, 1 vol. 2010. 22p. pap. 24.95 (978-1-4489-7001-8(6)) PublishAmerica, Inc.

Meyer, L. A. Bloody Jack: Being an Account of the Curious Adventures of Mary "Jacky" Faber, Ship's Boy. 2nd ed. 2010. (Bloody Jack Adventures Ser.: 1). (ENG., Illus.). 304p. (YA). (gr. 7-12). reprint ed. pap. 9.99 (978-0-15-205085-6(X)) Houghton Mifflin Harcourt Publishing Co.

Meyer, Marissa. Cress. 2014. 552p. (YA). (978-1-250-05632-0(2)) Feiwel & Friends.

Meyerhoff, Jenny. Playing Cupid. 2016. 246p. (J). **(978-0-545-86780-1(0))** Scholastic, Inc.

Michener, Tara. 100% Real: A Who I Am Book. 2009. 48p. pap. 17.99 (978-1-4490-2027-9(5)) AuthorHouse.

Middendorf, Gay. The Little Girl Who Lived on the Countertop. 2011. 20p. pap. 10.99 (978-1-4634-4708-3(6)) AuthorHouse.

Midence, Dominica. Mary's Fairy Learns to Exercise. 2009. 28p. pap. 13.99 (978-1-4389-5003-7(9)) AuthorHouse.

Milan, D. S. A Year of Starless Nights. 2013. 154p. pap. 14.95 (978-1-62432-012-5(0)) Loose Leaves Publishing.

Milburn, Trish. White Witch. 2012. 188p. pap. 12.95 (978-1-61194-083-1(4), Bell Bridge Bks.) BelleBks., Inc.

Miles Kelly Publishing, creator. Stories for Girls. 2007. (Illus.). 512p. (J). pap. (978-1-84236-586-1(X)) Miles Kelly Publishing, Ltd.

Miller, Meredith. Little Wrecks. 2017. 368p. (YA). (gr. 9). 17.99 **(978-0-06-247425-4(1)**, HarperTeen) HarperCollins Pubs.

Miller, Mike. The Woodland Girls: Quest for the Rings. 2011. 120p. pap. 12.95 (978-1-4502-8934-4(7)) iUniverse, Inc.

Millman, M. C. Always Something Else: The whimsical adventures of Elisheva Raskin. 2005. (Illus.). 160p. (J). 14.95 (978-1-932443-23-3(1), ASEH) Judaica Pr., Inc., The.

—Always Something Else 2. 2006. (Illus.). 160p. (J). 14.95 (978-1-932443-43-1(6), ASE2H) Judaica Pr., Inc., The.

Millner, Denene. Early Sunday Morning. Brantley-Newton, Vanessa, illus. 2017. (Denene Millner Bks.). (ENG.). 40p. (J). 17.95 (978-1-57284-211-3(3)) Agate Publishing, Inc.

Mitchell, Tammy. Rachel & the Magical Butterfly. 2011. 36p. 15.14 (978-1-4520-8390-2(8)) AuthorHouse.

Mobley, Monica W. Moving Out. 2010. 12p. 8.49 (978-1-4490-8985-6(2)) AuthorHouse.

Moffitt, Debra. Girls in Charge. 2011. (Pink Locker Society Novels Ser.: 4). (ENG.). 208p. (J). (gr. 3-7). pap. 18.99 (978-0-312-64506-9(6), 9780312645069, St. Martin's Griffin) St. Martin's Pr.

Mohler, Marie. Swallow the Sun. 2008. 32p. 18.95 (978-1-4357-1340-6(0)) Lulu Pr., Inc.

Molesworth. The Cuckoo Clock. 2007. 172p. per. 12.99 (978-1-59986-835-6(0)) Filiquarian Publishing, LLC.

Molesworth, Mary Louisa. Carrots, Just a Little Boy. Oldham, Marion, illus. 2004. reprint ed. pap. 22.95 (978-1-4179-3800-1(5)) Kessinger Publishing, LLC.

—Rosy. 2004. reprint ed. pap. 1.99 (978-1-4192-4549-7(X)); pap. 15.95 (978-1-4191-4549-0(5)) Kessinger Publishing, LLC.

Molesworth, Mary Louisa S. & Molesworth. Rosy. 2008. 120p. 22.95 (978-1-60664-727-1(X)) Rodgers, Alan Bks.

Money, Mo. Little Sister. 2011. (School Gyrls Ser.). (ENG.). 112p. (J). pap. 5.99 (978-1-4424-0879-1(0), Simon & Schuster/Paula Wiseman Bks.) Simon & Schuster/Paula Wiseman Bks.

Mongredien, Sue. Star Girls. 2010. (Sleepover Club Ser.). (ENG.). 128p. (J). (gr. 2-6). pap. 6.99 (978-0-00-727706-3(7)) HarperCollins Pubs. Ltd. GBR. Dist: Independent Pubs. Group.

Montalbano, Andrea. Lily Out of Bounds. 2012. (ENG.). 132p. (J). pap. 8.99 (978-0-9858956-1-7(6)) In This Together Media.

Montgomery Gibson, Jane. Gracie Got Glasses. Montgomery Gibson, Jane, illus. 2005. (Illus.). (J). bds. 8.99 (978-1-4183-0039-5(X)) Christ Inspired, Inc.

Montgomery, L. M. Further Chronicles of Avonlea. 2004. 152p. (YA). pap. 7.95 (978-1-57646-892-0(5)) Quiet Vision Publishing.

—Kilmeny of the Orchard. 2004. 100p. (YA). pap. 7.95 (978-1-57646-894-4(1)) Quiet Vision Publishing.

—Rainbow Valley. 2004. 184p. (YA). pap. 8.95 (978-1-57646-890-6(9)) Quiet Vision Publishing.

Montgomery, Mykah. The Little Girl Who Wanted a Tail. 2012. 28p. pap. 21.99 (978-1-4797-1668-5(5)) Xlibris Corp.

Montijo, Rhode. Gum Luck. Montijo, Rhode, illus. 2017. (Gum Girl Novel Ser.). (ENG., Illus.). 160p. (J). (gr. 1-3). 14.99 (978-1-4231-6117-2(3)) Hyperion Bks. for Children.

Moore, Bradley. Introducing Serina K. , Ph. D. & Future Famous Person. 2006. (ENG.). 60p. per. 16.95 (978-1-4241-5631-3(9)) America Star Bks.

Moore, Deborah K. & Mulbah-Bondo, Gbolu. A Girl Like Me. 2013. 36p. pap. 15.99 (978-1-4497-9414-9(9), WestBow Pr.) Author Solutions, Inc.

Moore, Graeme. Ruin. 2009. 240p. pap. 21.50 (978-1-4092-8737-7(8)) Lulu Pr., Inc.

Moore, Natascha. Lost Verloren. 2013. 28p. pap. 19.99 (978-1-4817-0664-3(0)) AuthorHouse.

Moore, Stephanie Perry & Moore, Derrick. All in/Stand Firm. 2014. (Grovehill Giants Ser.). (YA). lib. bdg. 26.90 (978-0-606-31876-1(3), Turtleback) Turtleback Bks.

—Golden Heart/Deep Soul. 2013. (Grovehill Giants Ser.). (YA). lib. bdg. 26.90 (978-0-606-31878-5(X), Turtleback) Turtleback Bks.

Moore, Yvonne. The Listening Gift. 2012. 24p. pap. 17.99 (978-1-4772-9313-3(2)) AuthorHouse.

Morgan, Marlee. Soujon's Journey. 2010. 380p. (J). pap. 10.00 (978-0-9789247-6-8(2), INDI Best) INDI, LLC.

Morgan, Melissa J. Super Special. 2007. (Camp Confidential Ser.: 14). (ENG.). 256p. (J). (gr. 4-7). pap. 5.99 (978-0-448-44452-9(6), Grosset & Dunlap) Penguin Young Readers Group.

—Winter Games. 2006. (Camp Confidential Ser.: 12). (ENG.). 160p. (J). (gr. 3-7). pap. 4.99 (978-0-448-44392-8(9), Grosset & Dunlap) Penguin Young Readers Group.

Moriyama, Daisuke. Chrono Crusade. 2004. (Illus.). (YA). Vol. 2. 200p. pap. 9.99 (978-1-4139-0104-7(2)) Vol. 3. 198p. pap. 9.99 (978-1-4139-0045-3(3)) ADV Manga.

Morpurgo, Michael. Mimi & the Mountain Dragon. Stephens, Helen, illus. 2015. (ENG.). 48p. (J). (gr. 2-4). 9.99 (978-1-4052-6934-6(0)) Egmont Bks., Ltd. GBR. Dist: Independent Pubs. Group.

Morris, Robert. Grandma Ursu, Think Blue. 2003. (Illus.). 32p. (J). 15.95 (978-0-9741634-0-6(6)) Ursu Pubns.

Morris, Sandra. Willow & Her Grandm. 2011. 32p. pap. 21.99 (978-1-4628-8900-6(X)) Xlibris Corp.

Morrison, Danette W. & Johnson, Dana A. My Eyebrows Are Hiding. 2009. 48p. pap. 12.99 (978-1-4343-4029-0(5)) AuthorHouse.

Morrison, Gertrude W. The Girls of Central High Aiding the Red Cross. l.t. ed. 2007. (ENG.). 150p. pap. 19.99 (978-1-4264-2244-7(X)) Creative Media Partners, LLC.

Morrison, Glenda. Lilly Beans. 2013. 24p. pap. 24.95 (978-1-62709-712-3(0)) America Star Bks.

Morrison, Patricia. Shadow Girl. 2013. (ENG., Illus.). 218p. (YA). (gr. 4-7). pap. 10.95 (978-1-77049-290-5(9), Tundra Bks.) Tundra Bks. CAN. Dist: Penguin Random Hse. LLC.

Moses, Jennifer Anne. Tales from My Closet. 2014. 298p. (J). pap. (978-0-545-66811-8(5), Scholastic Pr.) Scholastic, Inc.

Moster, Jamey S. Fly, Fly Away. 2009. 28p. pap. 13.99 (978-1-4490-0140-7(8)) AuthorHouse.

Moulton, Mark Kimball. Twisted Sistahs. Good, Karen H., illus. 2006. (ENG.). 32p. (J). (gr. 2-3). 14.95 (978-0-8249-8676-6(8), Ideal Pubns.) Worthy Publishing.

Moyer, Bess. Gypsies of the Air. 2004. reprint ed. pap. 19.95 (978-1-4179-9112-9(7)) Kessinger Publishing, LLC.

Mun-Ensor, Michelle. The Angel's Garden. 2011. 48p. pap. 24.95 (978-1-4560-5596-7(8)) America Star Bks.

Muñoz, Isabel. Desastre en la Cocina. Mazali, Gustavo, illus. 2012. (Eric & Julieta Ser.). (SPA & ENG.). 24p. (J). (gr. -1-3). pap. 3.99 (978-0-545-35581-0(8), Scholastic en Espanol) Scholastic, Inc.

Murphy, Jennifer. The Storm. 2013. 26p. 24.95 (978-1-63004-419-0(9)) 2012. 28p. pap. 24.95 (978-1-4626-9846-2(8)) America Star Bks.

Murphy, Lisa. Little Vampire. 2009. 262p. pap. 16.95 (978-1-4092-9494-8(3)) Lulu Pr., Inc.

Murray, C. J. Shayna Gladstone: In Search of the Scientist. 2011. 148p. 22.95 (978-1-4502-8992-4(4)); pap. 12.95 (978-1-4502-8990-0(8)) iUniverse, Inc.

Murrell, Belinda. Lulu Bell's Best Friends Ever. 2017. (Lulu Bell Ser.). (ENG.). 384p. (J). (gr. 1-4). 16.99 **(978-0-14-378257-5(6))** Random Hse. Australia AUS. Dist: Independent Pubs. Group.

MUSS, Anon E. Time Portal. 2010. 221p. pap. 11.84 (978-0-557-46606-1(7)) Lulu Pr., Inc.

Mutcherson, Toni. The Adventures of Jett Antoinette: Where Does Time Go? 2013. 24p. pap. 15.99 (978-1-4797-8161-4(4)) Xlibris Corp.

Muthu, Antony M. Athim. 2008. 48p. pap. 19.49 (978-1-4389-3074-9(7)) AuthorHouse.

Myers, Sharon A. Slumber Party. 2009. 73p. 24.99 (978-1-4415-9854-7(5)); pap. 15.99 (978-1-4415-9853-0(7)) Xlibris Corp.

Myracle, Lauren. Wishing Day. McLaughlin, Julie, illus. 2016. (Wishing Day Ser.: 1). 336p. (J). (gr. 3-7). 16.99 (978-0-06-234206-5(1), Tegen, Katherine Bks) HarperCollins Pubs.

Mysak, Mary. Little Train! Stickley, Kelly, illus. 2004. 16p. (J). 7.50 (978-0-9762274-0-3(1)) Helping Hands Children's Bks.

Napoli, Donna Jo. Skin, 0 vols. 2013. (ENG.). 352p. (YA). (gr. 9-12). pap. 9.99 (978-1-4778-1690-5(9), 9781477816905, Amazon Children's Publishing) Amazon Publishing.

Natlie, Jeffrey Michael. Emily Gets Angry. 2006. (J). 9.95 (978-0-9779822-0-2(3)) ErieKIDS, Inc.

Neal, Allyson. Ava Lillian's Blessing. Bynum, Saran, illus. 2012. 24p. (J). pap. 10.00 (978-0-9714320-6-2(6)) A & L Communications, Inc.

Needham B.Ed, Louise. Flossie's Escape to Freedom. 2010. (Illus.). 44p. pap. 16.99 (978-1-4490-9385-3(X)) AuthorHouse.

Nelson, Suzanne. Cake Pop Crush. 2013. 247p. (J). (978-0-545-50389-1(2)) Scholastic, Inc.

Nelson, Suzanne. Hot Cocoa Hearts. 2015. 248p. (J). pap. **(978-0-545-83968-6(8))** Scholastic, Inc.

Newman, Patrice Tomasetti. Beautiful Colors. 2013. 24p. pap. 24.95 (978-1-63000-660-0(2)) America Star Bks.

—Where Oh Where? It's in My Hair! 2012. 26p. 24.95 (978-1-4626-6284-5(6)) America Star Bks.

Newmark, Rachel J. Fearless Faith: And the New School. Specialty Publishing Company, illus. 2006. (J). pap. 7.95 (978-0-9755199-4-3(8)) Specialty Publishing Co.

Newton, Samantha. Being Nine Isn't So Bad. 2006. 52p. pap. 16.95 (978-1-4241-1902-8(2)) PublishAmerica, Inc.

Nicholas, J. B. The Waving Girl, 1 vol. Waites, Joan C., illus. 2004. (ENG.). 32p. (J). (gr. k-3). pap. 8.99 (978-1-58980-185-1(7)) Pelican Publishing Co., Inc.

Nichols, C. D. Kids Courageous. 2010. 66p. pap. 9.99 (978-1-60911-809-9(X), Eloquent Bks.) Strategic Book Publishing & Rights Agency (SBPRA).

Night, P. J. Off the Wall. 2013. (You're Invited to a Creepover Ser.: 14). (ENG., Illus.). 160p. (J). (gr. 3-7). pap. 5.99 (978-1-4424-7238-9(3), Simon Spotlight) Simon Spotlight.

Nigrosh, Millicent. Camilla Makes a Choice. 2012. 36p. pap. 15.49 (978-1-4669-2223-5(0)) Trafford Publishing.

—'Huh' Is Not a Word. 2012. 40p. pap. 16.45 (978-1-4669-3550-1(2)) Trafford Publishing.

Nijssen, Elfi. Laurie. van Lindehuizen, Eline, illus. 2010. (ENG & DUT.). 24p. (J). (gr. -1-k). 16.95 (978-1-60537-072-9(X)) Cobblestone Publishing Co.

Nimble, Jacque. Prank Wars. 2011. (School Gyrls Ser.). (ENG.). 144p. (J). (gr. 3-7). pap. 5.99 (978-1-4424-0880-7(4), Simon & Schuster/Paula Wiseman Bks.) Simon & Schuster/Paula Wiseman Bks.

Nixon, Kareh. The Little Woman in My House. 2012. 24p. pap. 14.93 (978-1-4669-6302-3(6)) Trafford Publishing.

Norling, Beth. The Stone Baby. Norling, Beth, illus. 2004. (Illus.). 32p. (J). (gr. k-2). (978-0-7344-0353-7(4), Lothian Children's Bks.) Hachette Australia.

Normandin, Jeri. Nicole's Adventures in Her Wheelchair. 2013. 20p. pap. 24.95 (978-1-62709-683-6(3)) America Star Bks.

Nöstlinger, Christine. Rosalinde Tiene Ideas en la Cabeza. Balzola, Sofia, illus. 2003. (SPA.). 80p. (J). (gr. 3-5). 11.95 (978-84-204-4804-6(4)) Ediciones Alfaguara ESP. Dist: Santillana USA Publishing Co., Inc.

Nowak, Linda Y. Cinnamon: A Teen's Survival & Romance on the Appalachain Trail. 2005. 169p. (YA). per. 11.95 (978-0-9762392-0-8(5)) Harmony Spirit Publishing Co., Inc.

Nowra, Louis. Into That Forest, 0 vols. 2013. (ENG.). 160p. (YA). (gr. 7-9). 16.99 (978-1-4778-1725-4(5), 9781477817254, Amazon Children's Publishing) Amazon Publishing.

Numeroff, Laura Joffe. Si le das un Pastilito a un Gato, 1 vol. Bond, Felicia, illus. 2010. (If You Give... Ser.). (SPA & ENG.). 32p. (J). (gr. -1-2). 16.99 (978-0-06-180431-1(2)) HarperCollins Pubs.

Nunes, Bill. 301 Things a Bright St Louis Southern Illinois Girl Can Do. 2011. 344p. pap. 29.95 (978-0-9787994-6-5(1)) Nunes, H. William.

Nunes, Lygia Bojunga. La Cuerda Floja. (SPA.). 136p. (YA). (gr. 5-8). (978-84-204-3122-2(2), AF1749) Ediciones Alfaguara ESP. Dist: Lectorum Pubns., Inc.

Nunnery, Donna. The Leaf That Was Afraid to Fall, 1 vol. Scardina, Tom, illus. 2010. 26p. 24.95 (978-1-4489-5927-3(6)) PublishAmerica, Inc.

Nye, Donna Kight. Sammi & the Tree. 2011. 12p. pap. 8.32 (978-1-4634-4659-8(4)) AuthorHouse.

Oates, Joyce Carol. Big Mouth & Ugly Girl. 2003. (ENG.). 288p. (YA). (gr. 8). pap. 8.99 (978-0-06-447347-7(3), HarperTeen) HarperCollins Pubs.

Obioha, Natalie O. Emotions. 2010. 120p. pap. 19.99 (978-1-4500-2791-5(1)) Xlibris Corp.

O'Brien, Caragh M. Birthmarked. 2010. (Birthmarked Trilogy Ser.: 1). (ENG., Illus.). 368p. (YA). (gr. 7-18). 18.99 (978-1-59643-569-8(0), 9781596435698) Roaring Brook Pr.

Obrien, Elaime F. Anita of Rancho del Mar. 2005. 171p. (Orig.). (J). (gr. 5-6). reprint ed. pap. 995.00 (978-1-885375-14-8(X), Shore Line Pr.) Pacific Bks.

O'Connor, Jane. Every Day Is Earth Day. 2010. (Fancy Nancy - I Can Read! Ser.). (J). lib. bdg. 13.55 (978-0-606-12294-8(X), Turtleback) Turtleback Bks.

—Express Yourself! A Doodle & Draw Book. Glasser, Robin Preiss, illus. 2011. (Fancy Nancy Ser.). (ENG.). 64p. (J). (gr. -1-3). pap. 6.99 (978-0-06-188281-4(X), HarperFestival) HarperCollins Pubs.

—Fancy Nancy & the Late, Late, Late Night. Glasser, Robin Preiss, illus. 2010. (Fancy Nancy Ser.). (ENG.). 24p. (J). (gr. -1-3). pap. 3.99 (978-0-06-170377-5(X), HarperFestival) HarperCollins Pubs.

—Fancy Nancy & the Late, Late, Late Night. 2010. (Fancy Nancy Picture Bks.). (J). lib. bdg. 13.55 (978-0-606-12312-9(1), Turtleback) Turtleback Bks.

—Fancy Nancy & the Sensational Babysitter. Glasser, Robin Preiss et al, illus. 2010. (Fancy Nancy Ser.). (ENG.). 24p. (J). (gr. -1-3). pap. 3.99 (978-0-06-170378-2(8), HarperFestival) HarperCollins Pubs.

—Fancy Nancy & the Sensational Babysitter. 2010. (Fancy Nancy Picture Bks.). (J). lib. bdg. 13.55 (978-0-606-14840-5(X), Turtleback) Turtleback Bks.

—Fancy Nancy's Fabulously Fancy Treasury. Glasser, Robin Preiss, illus. 2012. (Fancy Nancy Ser.). (ENG.). 25p. (J). (gr. -1-3). 15.99 (978-0-06-218804-5(6), HarperFestival) HarperCollins Pubs.

—Fashionista. Glasser, Robin Preiss, illus. 2011. (Fancy Nancy Ser.). (ENG.). 32p. (J). (gr. -1-3). pap., act. bk. ed. 4.99 (978-0-06-188266-1(6), HarperFestival) HarperCollins Pubs.

—Hair Dos & Hair Don'ts. Glasser, Robin Preiss, illus. 2011. (I Can Read Level 1 Ser.). (ENG.). 32p. (J). (gr. -1-3). pap. 3.99 (978-0-06-200179-5(5)) HarperCollins Pubs.

—Hair DOS & Hair Don'ts. Glasser, Robin Preiss, illus. 2011. (I Can Read Level 1 Ser.). (ENG.). 32p. (J). (gr. -1-3). 16.99 *(978-0-06-200180-1(9))* HarperCollins Pubs.
—Haunted Mansion: A Reusable Sticker Book for Halloween. Glasser, Robin Preiss, illus. 2011. (Fancy Nancy Ser.). (ENG.). 12p. (J). (gr. -1-2). pap. 6.99 *(978-0-06-170388-1(5),* HarperFestival) HarperCollins Pubs.
—Puzzle-Palooza. Glasser, Robin Preiss, illus. 2011. (Fancy Nancy Ser.). (ENG.). 32p. (J). (gr. -1-3). pap. 4.99 *(978-0-06-188267-8(4),* HarperFestival) HarperCollins Pubs.
O'Dell, Kathleen. The Aviary. 2012. (ENG.). 352p. (J). (gr. 3-7). 7.99 *(978-0-375-85226-8(3),* Yearling) Random Hse. Children's Bks.
O'Dell, Scott. La Isla de los Delfines Azules. (SPA., Illus.). (YA). (gr. 5-8). 7.96 net. *(978-1-56137-541-7(1),* NU5722) Novel Units, Inc.
O'Donnell, Elizabeth. Maggie Does Not Want to Move. 2013. (ENG., Illus.). 32p. (J). (gr. -1-3). 13.99 *(978-1-4814-2150-8(6),* Simon & Schuster Bks. For Young Readers) Simon & Schuster Bks. For Young Readers.
Ogilvie, Yolanda. Nana: A Portrait of Inspiration. 2013. 28p. pap. 8.99 *(978-1-62697-503-3(5))* Salem Author Services.
Ogle-Graham, Laura. No-No Nona & No-No Nit. 2012. 30p. pap. 12.95 *(978-0-9853094-1-1(5))* Warren Publishing, Inc.
O'Kelley, Jeff. Sharing Our Stories. 2006. (Early Explorers Ser.). (J). pap. *(978-1-4108-6127-6(9))* Benchmark Education Co.
Oldfield, Jenny. Drop Dead, Danielle. Layton, Neal, illus. (ENG.). 112p. mass mkt. *(978-0-340-85106-7(6),* Coronet) Hodder & Stoughton.
—Get Lost, Lola. Layton, Neal, illus. (ENG.). 112p. mass mkt. 7.99 *(978-0-340-85104-3(X),* Coronet) Hodder & Stoughton GBR. Dist: Trafalgar Square Publishing.
—Sophie the Show-Off, Bk. 15. (Illus.). 121p. (J). pap. 7.99 *(978-0-340-69987-4(6))* Hodder & Stoughton GBR. Dist: Trafalgar Square Publishing.
—What's the Matter, Maya? Child, Lauren, illus. 106p. (J). pap. *(978-0-340-78503-4(9))* Hodder & Stoughton.
O'Leary, Sara. When I Was Small. Morstad, Julie, illus. 2012. (ENG.). 32p. (J). (gr. -1-3). 16.95 *(978-1-897476-38-3(8))* Simply Read Bks. CAN. Dist: Ingram Publisher Services.
Oliver, Veronica A. The Rainbow Colors: Learning Primary & Secondary Colors. 2011. 20p. 11.59 *(978-1-4269-4805-3(0))* Trafford Publishing.
Olsen, Mary-Kate & Olsen, Ashley. Secret Crush. 2003. (ENG., Illus.). 128p. *(978-0-00-714452-5(0),* HarperCollins Children's Bks.) HarperCollins Pubs. Ltd.
Olson, Cynthia J. Kiera's Cry, 1 vol. 2009. 151p. pap. 24.95 *(978-1-60749-280-1(6))* America Star Bks.
Olson, Mildred Thompson. Diamondola: A Little Diamond. 2003. (Illus.). 192p. reprint ed. pap. 11.95 *(978-1-57258-251-4(0),* 945-6106) TEACH Services, Inc.
On the Job: Individual Title Six-Packs. (gr. -1-2). 27.00 *(978-0-7635-9468-8(7))* Rigby Education.
Onus, Katie. Island of the Wolves. 2012. 180p. pap. 11.99 *(978-0-9823271-7-3(X))* Adventure Bks. of Seattle.
Optometrist: Individual Title Six-Packs. (Bookweb Ser.). 32p. (gr. 3-18). 34.00 *(978-0-7635-3946-7(5))* Rigby Education.
Orgel, Doris. Sarah's Room. Sendak, Maurice, illus. 2003. (Sendak Reissues Ser.). (ENG.). 48p. (J). (gr. -1-3). 15.95 *(978-0-06-029727-5(1))* HarperCollins Pubs.
Orliac, Catherine. Te Tumu o Rapa Nui: El Arbolito de Rapa Nui. the Little Tree of Rapa Nui. le Petit Arbre de Rapa Nui. Haoa Cardinali, Viki et al, trs. Willemin, Veronique, illus. 2005. (FRE, SPA & ENG.). 40p. (J). spiral bd. 12.00 *(978-1-880636-02-2(6))* Easter Island Foundation.
Orme, Helen. Horsing Around. 2008. (Siti's Sisters Ser.). (ENG., Illus.). 36p. pap. *(978-1-84167-685-2(3))* Ransom Publishing Ltd.
—Odd One Out. Brett, Cathy, illus. 2007. (Siti's Sisters Ser.). (ENG.). 36p. (J). per. *(978-1-84167-597-8(0))* Ransom Publishing Ltd.
—Stalker. Brett, Cathy, illus. 2007. (Siti's Sisters Ser.). (ENG.). 36p. (J). per. *(978-1-84167-595-4(4))* Ransom Publishing Ltd.
—Trouble with Teachers. Brett, Cathy, illus. 2007. (Siti's Sisters Ser.). (ENG.). 36p. (J). per. *(978-1-84167-599-2(7))* Ransom Publishing Ltd.
Oshima, Towa. High School Girls Volume 1-6 Set. 2007. (ENG., Illus.). 200p. pap. 44.95 *(978-1-59796-072-4(1))* DrMaster Pubns. Inc.
Osmer, Janice. Timmy & the Captain. 2009. 20p. pap. 10.49 *(978-1-4389-4683-2(X))* AuthorHouse.
Ostow, Micol. What Would My Cell Phone Do? 2011. (ENG.). 272p. (YA). (gr. 7-18). 7.99 *(978-0-14-241469-9(7),* Speak) Penguin Young Readers Group.
Ostrom, Gladys. Leggys in Number-land. Suits, Rosella, illus. 2011. 40p. (J). pap. 12.95 *(978-0-9841721-6-0(5))* Open Door Publishers, Inc.
Owen, Sarah. Sarah the Fairy Princess's Birthday Party. 2009. 32p. pap. 41.50 *(978-1-4452-5921-5(4))* Lulu Pr., Inc.
Ozmun, Lori. The Monster in Lulu's Head: The Tale of Two Spoons. 2013. 56p. pap. 31.99 *(978-1-4797-6780-9(8))* Xlibris Corp.
Pace, Renee. The Forsaken. 2013. 204p. pap. 10.99 *(978-1-939194-79-4(2))* Etopia Pr.
Packard, Robbi Anne. Two Daddies & Me. 2009. 32p. pap. 12.99 *(978-1-4389-5558-2(8))* AuthorHouse.
Pangalos, Carol B. Gabriella & the Magic Stars. 2011. 36p. (gr. -1). pap. 15.14 *(978-1-4634-1108-4(1))* AuthorHouse.
Pansy. Ester Ried. 2007. 206p. pap. 20.99 *(978-1-4264-6875-9(X))* 2006. (ENG.). 228p. pap. 22.99 *(978-1-4264-6957-2(8))* Creative Media Partners, LLC.
Pants Makes the Swim Team. 2004. (J). per. 7.99 *(978-0-9755959-2-3(X))* Girl Named Pants, Inc., A.
Papademetriou, Lisa. Save the Cupcake! 2012. (Confectionately Yours Ser.: 1). (J). (ENG.). 240p. (gr. 3-7). pap. 6.99 *(978-0-545-22228-0(1),* Scholastic Paperbacks); 231p. *(978-0-545-46039-2(5))* Scholastic, Inc.
—Taking the Cake! 2012. (Confectionately Yours Ser.: Bk. 2). 223p. (J). *(978-0-545-49391-8(9))* Scholastic, Inc.
Parent, Dan. Betty & Veronica: Best Friends Forever. 2012. (Archie & Friends All-Stars Ser.: 16). (ENG.). 128p. (J). (gr. 4-7). pap. 9.99 *(978-1-879794-76-4(4),* Archie Comics) Archie Comic Pubns., Inc.
Parish, Herman. Amelia Bedelia Chapter Book #10: Amelia Bedelia Ties the Knot. Avril, Lynne, illus. 2016. (Amelia Bedelia Ser.). 160p. (J). (gr. 1-5). pap. 4.99 *(978-0-06-233416-9(6),* Greenwillow Bks.) HarperCollins Pubs.
Parish, Peggy. Amelia Bedelia Helps Out. Sweat, Lynn, illus. 2005. (I Can Read Level 2 Ser.). (ENG.). 64p. (J). (gr. k-3). pap. 3.99 *(978-0-06-051111-1(7),* Greenwillow Bks.) HarperCollins Pubs.
—Teach Us, Amelia Bedelia. Sweat, Lynn, illus. 2004. (I Can Read Level 2 Ser.). (ENG.). 64p. (J). (gr. k-3). pap. 3.99 *(978-0-06-051114-2(1),* Greenwillow Bks.) HarperCollins Pubs.
Parisi, Bettie. The Quiet. 2009. 36p. pap. 15.00 *(978-1-4269-1015-9(0))* Trafford Publishing.
Park, Barbara. Junie B. Jones & That Meanie Jim's Birthday, Vol. 6. unabr. ed. 2004. (Junie B. Jones Ser.: No. 6). 85p. (J). (gr. k-3). pap. 17.00 incl. audio *(978-0-8072-0642-3(3),* Listening Library) Random Hse. Audio Publishing Group.
—Junie B. Jones & the Yucky Blucky Fruitcake. unabr. ed. 2004. (Junie B. Jones Ser.: No. 5). 71p. (J). (gr. k-3). pap. 17.00 incl. audio *(978-0-8072-0641-6(5),* Listening Library) Random Hse. Audio Publishing Group.
—Junie B. Jones Has a Monster under Her Bed. unabr. ed. 2004. (Junie B. Jones Ser.: No. 8). 69p. (J). (gr. k-3). pap. 17.00 incl. audio *(978-0-8072-0644-7(X),* Listening Library) Random Hse. Audio Publishing Group.
—Junie B. Jones Has a Peep in Her Pocket. unabr. ed. 2004. (Junie B. Jones Ser.: No. 15). 80p. (J). (gr. k-3). pap. 17.00 incl. audio *(978-0-8072-0336-1(X),* Listening Library) Random Hse. Audio Publishing Group.
—Junie B. Jones Is (Almost) a Flower Girl. unabr. ed. 2004. (Junie B. Jones Ser.: No. 13). 68p. (J). (gr. k-3). pap. 17.00 incl. audio *(978-0-8072-0334-7(3),* Listening Library) Random Hse. Audio Publishing Group.
—Junie B. Jones Is Captain Field Day. unabr. ed. 2004. (Junie B. Jones Ser.: No. 16). 80p. (J). (gr. k-3). pap. 17.00 incl. audio *(978-0-8072-0337-8(8),* Listening Library) Random Hse. Audio Publishing Group.
—Junie B. Jones Loves Handsome Warren. unabr. ed. 2004. (Junie B. Jones Ser.: No. 7). 71p. (J). (gr. k-3). pap. 17.00 incl. audio *(978-0-8072-0643-0(1),* Listening Library) Random Hse. Audio Publishing Group.
—Junie B. Jones Smells Something Fishy. unabr. ed. 2004. (Junie B. Jones Ser.: No. 12). 66p. (J). (gr. k-3). pap. 17.00 incl. audio *(978-0-8072-0533-4(8),* Listening Library) Random Hse. Audio Publishing Group.
Park, Barbara & Brunkus, Denise. Junie B. Jones & That Meanie Jim's Birthday. pap. *(978-0-439-13075-2(1))* Scholastic, Inc.
Parker, Danny. Lola's Toybox: on the Story Sea. 2017. (Lola's Toy Box Ser.: 2). (ENG.). 96p. (J). (gr. k-2). pap. 6.99 *(978-1-76012-437-3(0))* Hardie Grant Egmont Pty, Ltd. AUS. Dist: Independent Pubs. Group.
—Lola's Toybox: the Patchwork Picnic. 2017. (Lola's Toy Box Ser.: 1). (ENG.). 96p. (J). (gr. k-2). pap. 6.99 ***(978-1-76012-436-6(2))*** Hardie Grant Egmont Pty, Ltd. AUS. Dist: Independent Pubs. Group.
—Lola's Toybox: the Plastic Palace. Shield, Guy, illus. 2017. (Lola's Toy Box Ser.: 4). (ENG.). 96p. (J). (gr. k-2). pap. 6.99 ***(978-1-76012-439-7(7))*** Hardie Grant Egmont Pty, Ltd. AUS. Dist: Independent Pubs. Group.
—Lola's Toybox: the Treasure Trove. 2017. (Lola's Toy Box Ser.: 3). (ENG.). 96p. (J). (gr. k-2). pap. 6.99 ***(978-1-76012-438-0(9))*** Hardie Grant Egmont Pty, Ltd. AUS. Dist: Independent Pubs. Group.
Parker, Lisa L. Gray. Princesses Do Not Wear Tattoos. Logan, Desiree, illus. 2011. 48p. pap. 24.95 *(978-1-4560-3281-4(X))* America Star Bks.
Parra, Kelly. Graffiti Girl. 2007. (ENG.). 256p. (gr. 8-12). pap. 16.99 *(978-1-4165-3461-7(X),* MTV Bks.) MTV Books.
Pascal, Francine. Betrayed. 2011. (Fearless Ser.: 24). (ENG.). 256p. (YA). (gr. 11). pap. 12.99 *(978-1-4424-3108-9(3),* Simon Pulse) Simon Pulse.
—Esa Clase de Chica.Tr. of Wrong Kind of Girl. (SPA.). 168p. (J). 7.95 *(978-84-272-3880-0(0))* Molino, Editorial ESP. Dist: AIMS International Bks., Inc.
—Fearless: Fearless; Sam; Run. 2012. (Fearless Ser.). (ENG.). 608p. (YA). (gr. 9). pap. 12.99 *(978-1-4424-4631-1(5),* Simon Pulse) Simon Pulse.
—Fearless 2: Twisted; Kiss; Payback. 2013. (Fearless Ser.). (ENG.). 656p. (YA). (gr. 9). pap. 12.99 *(978-1-4424-6860-3(2),* Simon Pulse) Simon Pulse.
—Nueva Mirada de Jessica. Orig. Title: Jessica's New Look. (SPA.). 160p. (J). 6.95 *(978-84-272-4647-8(1))* Molino, Editorial ESP. Dist: AIMS International Bks., Inc.
Patterson, Francine. Koko's Kitten. 2010. (Rise & Shine Ser.). (ENG.). 32p. (C). (gr. -1-3). pap. 9.95 *(978-0-590-44425-5(5))* National Geographic School Publishing, Inc.
Paul & Lady Jan. Mako in My Backyard. Beeson, Jan, illus. 2013. 34p. pap. 12.99 *(978-0-9890482-3-1(3))* Beeson, Jan.
Pausewang, Gudrun. Traitor. 2010. (Carolrhoda YA Ser.). (ENG.). 224p. (YA). (gr. 7-12). pap. 9.95 *(978-0-7613-6571-6(0),* Carolrhoda Lab™) Lerner Publishing Group.
Payne, K. E. Another 365 Days. 2013. (ENG.). 264p. (J). (gr. 7). pap. 11.95 *(978-1-60282-775-2(3))* Bold Strokes Bks.
—365 Days. 2011. (ENG.). 280p. (J). (gr. 7). pap. 13.95 *(978-1-60282-540-6(8))* Bold Strokes Bks.
Payton, Belle. Twice the Talent. 2016. (It Takes Two Ser.: 11). (ENG., Illus.). 160p. (J). (gr. 3-7). pap. 6.99 *(978-1-4814-5263-2(0),* Simon Spotlight) Simon Spotlight.
Pearson, Luke, illus. Hilda & the Bird Parade. 2013. (Hildafolk Ser.). (ENG.). 44p. (J). (gr. k). 24.00 *(978-1-909263-06-2(0))* Flying Eye Bks. GBR. Dist: Consortium Bk. Sales & Distribution.
Pearson, S. & Ellis, Sarah. Next Door Neighbours, 1 vol. (ENG.). 123p. (J). pap. 7.95 *(978-0-88899-084-6(7))* Groundwood Bks. CAN. Dist: Publishers Group West (PGW).
Peep for Keeps. 2005. 43p. (J). 3.99 *(978-0-9763213-4-7(3))* OHC Group LLC.
Pelham, P.J. Hanna Searches for "Me!" 2004. 24p. (J). pap. 15.50 *(978-1-4120-3208-7(3))* Trafford Publishing.
Penn, Astor. All the Devils Here. 2016. (ENG., Illus.). (YA). (gr. 8-12). 24.99 ***(978-1-63477-933-3(9),*** Harmony Ink Pr.) Dreamspinner Pr.
Penrose, Margaret. Dorothy Dale. rev. ed. 2006. 196p. 26.95 *(978-1-4218-1801-6(9))*; pap. 11.95 *(978-1-4218-1901-3(5))* 1st World Publishing, Inc. (1st World Library - Literary Society).
—The Motor Girls. 2007. (ENG.). 152p. pap. 19.99 *(978-1-4264-1903-4(1))* Creative Media Partners, LLC.
—The Motor Girls. 2004. reprint ed. pap. 1.99 *(978-1-4192-7466-4(X))* Kessinger Publishing, LLC.
—The Motor Girls on the Coast or the Waif from the Se. 2011. 140p. pap. 9.99 *(978-1-61203-219-1(2))* Bottom of the Hill Publishing.
—The Motor Girls on Waters Blue. rev. ed. 2006. 228p. 27.95 *(978-1-4218-1802-3(7))*; pap. 12.95 *(978-1-4218-1902-0(3))* 1st World Publishing, Inc. (1st World Library - Literary Society).
—The Motor Girls on Waters Blue. 2007. (ENG.). 164p. pap. 19.99 *(978-1-4264-2184-6(2))* Creative Media Partners, LLC.
—The Motor Girls on Waters Blue. 2004. reprint ed. pap. 1.99 *(978-1-4192-7467-1(8))*; pap. 22.95 *(978-1-4191-7467-4(3))* Kessinger Publishing, LLC.
Perkins, Lynne Rae & Perkins, Lynne R. All Alone in the Universe. 2007. (ENG., Illus.). 224p. (J). (gr. 5-18). reprint ed. pap. 6.99 *(978-0-380-73302-6(1),* Greenwillow Bks.) HarperCollins Pubs.
Pernice, Clare. Circus Girl. 2014. (ENG., Illus.). 40p. (J). (gr. -1-3). 16.95 *(978-1-927018-36-1(6),* 9781927018361) Simply Read Bks. CAN. Dist: Ingram Publisher Services.
Perrow, Angeli. Many Hands: A Penobscot Indian Story. Austin, Heather, illus. 2011. (ENG.). 32p. (J). (gr. -1-3). pap. 10.95 *(978-1-60893-014-2(9))* Down East Bks.
Perry, Ellyse;Clark. Double Time. 2017. (Ellyse Perry Ser.: 4). (ENG.). 160p. (J). (gr. 4-7). 12.99 *(978-0-14-378130-1(8))* Random Hse. Australia AUS. Dist: Independent Pubs. Group.
—Ellyse Perry 1: Pocket Rocket. 2017. (Ellyse Perry Ser.: 1). (ENG.). 160p. (J). (gr. 4-7). 12.99 ***(978-0-14-378124-0(3))*** Random Hse. Australia AUS. Dist: Independent Pubs. Group.
Perry, Ellyse;Clark. Winning Touch. 2017. (Ellyse Perry Ser.: 3). (ENG.). 160p. (J). (gr. 4-7). 12.99 *(978-0-14-378128-8(6))* Random Hse. Australia AUS. Dist: Independent Pubs. Group.
Perry, Hailey. On the Move. 2010. 188p. pap. 12.00 *(978-1-60844-428-1(7))* Dog Ear Publishing, LLC.
Perry, Sarah Catherine. Clara's Test. 2006. (J). per. *(978-1-55452-022-0(3))* Essence Publishing.
Perry, Valerie J. Tribly Learns a Lesson. 2011. 26p. pap. 14.00 *(978-1-60976-659-7(8),* Eloquent Bks.) Strategic Book Publishing & Rights Agency (SBPRA).
Peschke, Marci. Kylie Jean, 1 vol. Mourning, Tuesday, illus. (Kylie Jean Ser.). (ENG.). 112p. (gr. 2-3). 2014. 317.10 *(978-1-4795-4545-2(7))* 2013. 271.80 *(978-1-4048-8051-1(8))* 2013. 90.60 *(978-1-4048-8050-4(X))* Picture Window Bks. (Kylie Jean).
Peschke, Marci. Kylie Jean Collection. Mourning, Tuesday, illus. 2017. (Kylie Jean Ser.). (ENG.). 304p. 9.99 ***(978-1-5158-1892-2(6),*** Kylie Jean) Picture Window Bks.
Peterson, J. D. R. & Reimer, Diana. Priscilla Bailey: A Story of the Great Depression. 2009. 196p. 24.95 *(978-1-4401-3929-1(6))*; pap. 14.95 *(978-1-4401-3927-7(X))* iUniverse, Inc.
Peterson, Lois J. Three Good Things, 1 vol. 2015. (Orca Currents Ser.). (ENG.). 144p. (J). (gr. 5-9). pap. 9.95 *(978-1-4598-0985-7(8))* Orca Bk. Pubs. USA.
Petroff, Shani. Love Struck. McKenney, J. David, illus. 2010. (Bedeviled Ser.: 4). (ENG.). 240p. (J). (gr. 5-18). pap. 7.99 *(978-0-448-45114-5(X),* Grosset & Dunlap) Penguin Young Readers Group.
Petrucha, Stefan. Writ in Stone. Murase, Sho, illus. 2005. (Nancy Drew: Girl Detective Ser.). 88p. (gr. 3-9). 24.21 *(978-1-59961-058-0(2))* Spotlight.
Pett, Mark & Rubinstein, Gary. The Girl Who Never Made Mistakes. Pett, Mark, illus. 2011. (ENG., Illus.). 32p. (J). (gr. k-3). 16.99 *(978-1-4022-5544-1(6),* Sourcebooks Jabberwocky) Sourcebooks, Inc.
Peymani, Christine. Super Starz Masquerade. 2007. (Illus.). 94p. (J). pap. *(978-0-439-91952-4(5))* Scholastic, Inc.
Pfister, Ashley. Cindy Makes A Difference. 2005. 21p. (J). 13.93 *(978-1-4116-3348-3(2))* Lulu Pr., Inc.
Phypers, Lisa Marie. My Favorite Little Girl. 2011. 28p. pap. 15.99 *(978-1-4628-6048-7(6))* Xlibris Corp.
Pilkons, Alyssa. Confessions of a Teenage Lima Bean. 2009. 232p. pap. 14.98 *(978-1-4303-1132-4(0))* Lulu Pr., Inc.
Pittar, Gill. Milly, Molly & the Runaway Bean. Morrell, Cris, illus. 2005. 28p. (J). (gr. -1). pap. *(978-1-86972-049-0(0))* Milly Molly Bks.
Pittar, Gill & Gill, Pittar. Basura No, Gracias! Rioja, Alberto Jimenez, tr. Morrell, Cris, illus. 2003. (Milly Molly Ser.). (SPA.). 24p. (J). pap. *(978-84-241-8695-1(8))* Everest Editora ESP. Dist: Lectorum Pubns., Inc.
—Las Ciruelas de Isa Bela. Rioja, Alberto Jimenez, tr. Morrell, Cris, illus. 2003. (Milly Molly Ser.). (SPA.). 24p. (J). pap. *(978-84-241-8687-6(7))* Everest Editora ESP. Dist: Lectorum Pubns., Inc.
—De Quien es Este Sombrero? Rioja, Alberto Jimenez, tr. Morrell, Cris, illus. 2003. (Milly Molly Ser.). (SPA.). 24p. (J). pap. *(978-84-241-8679-1(6))* Everest Editora ESP. Dist: Lectorum Pubns., Inc.
Pittman, Eddie. Red's Planet. 2016. (Red's Planet Ser.: 1). (J). lib. bdg. 20.80 *(978-0-606-38203-8(8))* Turtleback Bks.
Pixton, Amy. Mary Had a Little Lamb. 2010. (Indestructibles Ser.). (ENG., Illus.). 12p. (J). (gr. k — 1). pap. 5.95 *(978-0-7611-5860-8(X),* 15860) Workman Publishing Co., Inc.
Plaisted, Caroline. 10 Things to Do Before You're 16. 2010. (ENG.). 160p. (YA). (gr. 7). pap. 8.99 *(978-1-4424-1422-8(7),* Simon Pulse) Simon Pulse.
Plante, Raymond. Un Dromadaire Chez Marilou Polaire. Favreau, Marie-Claude, illus. 2003. (Premier Roman Ser.). (FRE.). 64p. (J). (gr. 1-4). pap. *(978-2-89021-608-2(X))* Diffusion du livre Mirabel (DLM).
Platt, Richard. Roman Diary: The Journal of Iliona, a Young Slave. Parkins, David, illus. 2014. (ENG.). 128p. (J). (gr. 4-7). pap. 6.99 *(978-0-7636-7053-5(7))* Candlewick Pr.
Plumberg, William. The Legend of Peggy Postue: The Girl with the Upturned Nose. 2011. 28p. pap. 15.99 *(978-1-4568-9635-5(0))* Xlibris Corp.
Poer, Nancy Jewel. Mia's Apple Tree. Poer, Nancy Jewel, illus. 2004. (Illus.). 34p. (J). 21.95 *(978-0-9740413-1-5(9))* White Feather Publishing.
Polak, Monique. On the Game, 1 vol. 2005. (Lorimer SideStreets Ser.). (ENG.). 184p. (YA). (gr. 9-12). 16.95 *(978-1-55028-877-3(6),* 9781550288773); 9.95 *(978-1-55028-876-6(8),* 9781550288766) Lorimer, James & Co., Ltd., Pubs. CAN. Dist: Casemate Pubs. & Bk. Distributors, LLC.
Polk, Douglas. Marie's Home, 1 vol. 2009. 48p. pap. 16.95 *(978-1-60749-454-6(X))* America Star Bks.
The Pony Winter. 2007. (J). *(978-1-933343-42-6(7),* PONY) Stabenfeldt Inc.
Poole-Carter, Rosemary. Juliette Ascending. 2007. (YA). pap. 14.00 *(978-1-929976-41-6(0),* TOP) Top Pubns., Ltd.
Pope, Cheryl Lynn. The Adventures of Princess Zari. Nyamor, Eric, illus. 2009. 34p. pap. 12.99 *(978-0-9840660-1-8(2))* Second Time Media & Communications.
Porcelli-Munisteri, Nadia. Who Are You Calling a Bully? 2013. (ENG.). 34p. (J). pap. 14.95 *(978-1-4787-1703-4(3))* Outskirts Pr., Inc.
Posner-Sanchez, Andrea. Bunny Magic! (Disney Junior: Sofia the First) RH Disney Staff, illus. 2014. (Little Golden Book Ser.). (ENG.). 24p. (J). (-k). 4.99 *(978-0-7364-3085-2(7),* Golden/Disney) Random Hse. Children's Bks.
—A Knight in Sticky Armor (Disney Junior: Doc Mcstuffins) Random House Disney Staff, illus. 2012. (Little Golden Book Ser.). (ENG.). 24p. (J). (-k). 4.99 *(978-0-7364-3030-2(X),* Golden/Disney) Random Hse. Children's Bks.
—The Perfect Tea Party (Disney Junior: Sofia the First) Random House Disney Staff, illus. 2013. (Little Golden Book Ser.). (ENG.). 24p. (J). (-k). 4.99 *(978-0-7364-3109-5(8),* Golden/Disney) Random Hse. Children's Bks.
—Shake Your Tail Feathers (Disney Junior: Doc Mcstuffins) Random House Disney Staff, illus. 2015. (Little Golden Book Ser.). (ENG.). 24p. (J). (-k). 3.99 *(978-0-7364-3274-0(4),* Golden/Disney) Random Hse. Children's Bks.
Potash, Mildred. Millie & Cupcake. 2013. (ENG.). 24p. (J). pap. 10.95 *(978-1-4787-0997-8(9))* Outskirts Pr., Inc.
Potts, Christiane Elenes. Lola & the Caterpillar. 2011. 28p. pap. 13.99 *(978-1-4520-2563-6(0))* AuthorHouse.
Poulin, Stephane. Agarren Esa Gata (Can You Catch Josephine?) (SPA., Illus.). 24p. (J). (gr. 1-4). pap. 8.95 *(978-980-257-116-1(4))* Ekare, Ediciones VEN. Dist: Kane Miller.
Poulin, Stephane & Poulin, Stéphane. Agarren Esa Gata! (SPA., Illus.). 24p. (J). (gr. 1-4). pap. 6.99 *(978-980-257-233-5(0))* Ekare, Ediciones VEN. Dist: Kane Miller.
Power, Michael. The Zoo. 2009. 201p. pap. 13.75 *(978-1-60695-075-3(4))* EchoRoad, Inc.
A Prairie Heart. 2007. (Illus.). (J). per. 19.95 *(978-0-9793668-0-2(1))* Prairie Heart Publishing.
Prasad, Sheela. Apocrit. 2012. 348p. 30.00 *(978-0-615-66700-3(7))* Silent Hse. Pr.
Pratts, Christine. Tabby Wise for School Secretary. 2005. 61p. pap. 8.99 *(978-1-4116-4935-4(4))* Lulu Pr., Inc.
Preble, Joy. Haunted. 2011. (ENG.). 304p. (YA). (gr. 7-12). pap. 9.99 *(978-1-4022-4468-1(1))* Sourcebooks, Inc.
Preston, Sarah. The, Adventures of Abby. 2011. (ENG.). 30p. (J). pap. 14.95 *(978-1-4327-7566-7(9))* Outskirts Pr., Inc.
Price, M. J. The Skin I'm In. 2013. 32p. pap. 24.95 *(978-1-63000-967-0(9))* America Star Bks.
Price, Roy. The Gnome Guardian: Polly's Adventure. 2012. 64p. pap. 13.66 *(978-1-4678-9701-3(9))* AuthorHouse.
Prom Girl. 2nd ed. 2003. (J). pap. 8.95 *(978-0-9726917-0-3(7))* Prom Girl Publishing, Inc.
Pugh, Tracey D. A Show & Tell Lesson. McCracken, Jaime, photos by. l.t. ed. 2006. (Illus.). 32p. (J). 12.95 *(978-1-59879-105-1(2))* Lifevest Publishing, Inc.
Pullman, Philip. Der goldene Kompass. (GER.). pap. 27.95 *(978-3-453-13744-8(2))* Verlag Wilhelm Heyne DEU. Dist: Distribooks, Inc.
Purdie, Kathryn. Burning Glass. (Burning Glass Ser.: 1). (YA). (gr. 9). 2017. 528p. pap. 9.99 *(978-0-06-241237-9(X))* 2016. (Illus.). 512p. 17.99 *(978-0-06-241236-2(1))* HarperCollins Pubs. (Tegen, Katherine Bks).
Pyatt, Sue. Call Me Madame President. Gaston, Keith A., illus. 2003. 31p. (J). 17.00 *(978-0-9742575-0-1(8))* Imagination Station Pr.
Quillen, Carl. Dragon Girl Myra. 2009. 53p. pap. 5.56 *(978-0-557-08268-1(4))* Lulu Pr., Inc.
Racaniello, P. Stella Asks What. 2011. 20p. pap. 9.99 *(978-1-257-03851-0(6))* Lulu Pr., Inc.
—Stella Asks When. 2011. 20p. pap. 9.99 *(978-0-557-69993-3(2))* Lulu Pr., Inc.
—Stella Asks Where. 2011. 20p. pap. 9.99 *(978-1-257-03918-0(0))* Lulu Pr., Inc.
—Stella Asks Who. 2011. 20p. pap. 9.99 *(978-0-557-87923-6(X))* Lulu Pr., Inc.
—Stella Asks Why. 2011. 20p. pap. 9.99 *(978-1-257-03920-3(2))* Lulu Pr., Inc.
Rackley, Beth Shaw. The Girl in the Blue & White Checked Dress. 2011. 24p. pap. 12.79 *(978-1-4520-9239-3(7))* AuthorHouse.
Rae, Angela. All of Us. 2009. 81p. pap. 12.99 *(978-0-557-05491-6(5))* Lulu Pr., Inc.
Rain, Mandy. Rock 'n' Roll. 2011. (School Gyrls Ser.). (ENG.). 128p. (J). pap. 5.99 *(978-1-4424-0878-4(2),* Simon & Schuster/Paula Wiseman Bks.) Simon & Schuster/Paula Wiseman Bks.
—Spring Fling. 2011. (School Gyrls Ser.). (ENG.). 144p. (J). (gr. 3-7). pap. 5.99 *(978-1-4424-0882-1(0),* Simon & Schuster/Paula Wiseman Bks.) Simon & Schuster/Paula Wiseman Bks.
Rainey, L. E. Sad Sam, Glad Sam. 2006. (Illus.). 32p. (J). 16.95 *(978-0-9785521-0-7(5))* Shoetree Publishers, Inc.
Rainville, Doris I., creator. The Girl Who Never Let Her Mother Brush Her Hair. l.t. ed. 2003. (Illus.). 24p. (J). per. 7.95 *(978-0-9744879-0-8(2))* Magical Creations.
Raitman, Ira. Amanda's Bunny. 2010. 16p. 8.99 *(978-1-4520-2021-1(3))* AuthorHouse.
Ramos, Dania. Who's Ju? 2015. (ENG.). 174p. (J). pap. 9.95 *(978-1-937997-61-8(8))* Northampton Hse.

Ramsey, Charlotte. Go Global with Charlotte. 2004. (Illus.). 36p. (J). 3.99 *(978-0-9746587-1-1(5),* Beacon Street Girls) B*tween Productions, Inc.

Randazzo, Dottie. The Blue Girl. 2008. 81p. pap. 10.95 *(978-0-615-18340-4(9))* Creative Dreaming Ltd.

Random House Disney Staff. Inside Out (Disney/Pixar Inside Out) Batson, Alan, illus. 2016. (Little Golden Book Ser.). (ENG.). 24p. (J). (-k). 4.99 *(978-0-7364-3629-8(4),* Golden/Disney) Random Hse. Children's Bks.

Rasheed, Leila. Chips, Beans, & Limousines. 2013. (Fantastic Diary of Bathsheba Claric de Trop Ser.). 197p. (J). pap. 5.99 *(978-0-7945-3028-0(1),* Usborne) EDC Publishing.

—Doughnuts, Dreams & Drama Queens. 2013. (Fantastic Diary of Bathsheba Claric de Trop Ser.). 299p. (J). pap. 5.99 *(978-0-7945-3030-3(3),* Usborne) EDC Publishing.

—Socks, Shocks & Secrets. 2013. (Fantastic Diary of Bathsheba Claric de Trop Ser.). 293p. (J). pap. 5.99 *(978-0-7945-3029-7(X),* Usborne) EDC Publishing.

Ray, Anna Chapin. Half A Dozen Girls. 2004. reprint ed. pap. 1.99 *(978-1-4192-2264-1(3));* pap. 24.95 *(978-1-4191-2264-4(9))* Kessinger Publishing, LLC.

Rayburn, Tricia. Maggie Bean in Love. 2009. (ENG.). 288p. (J). (gr. 4-8). pap. 6.99 *(978-1-4169-8700-0(2),* Aladdin) Simon & Schuster Children's Publishing.

Rea, Ba. Monarch! Come Play with Me. Rea, Ba, illus. 2006. (Illus.). 32p. (J). per. 10.95 *(978-0-9657472-5-7(5))* Bas Relief, LLC.

Read for a Smile. 2013. (Illus.). 106p. pap. 6.00 *(978-0-9912750-0-7(4))* Rodriguez, Raul.

RealBuzz Studios Staff. Girl Overboard Frankensteins Monster: Life Camera Action Book 4. 2007. 128p. (YA). pap. 4.97 *(978-1-59789-580-4(6),* Barbour Bks.) Barbour Publishing, Inc.

—Hits & Misses. 2007. 128p. (YA). No. 1. pap. 4.97 *(978-1-59789-569-9(5))*No. 2. pap. 4.97 *(978-1-59789-570-5(9))*No. 3. pap. 4.97 *(978-1-59789-571-2(7))*No. 4. pap. 4.97 *(978-1-59789-572-9(5))* Barbour Publishing, Inc. (Barbour Bks.).

Rebello, Kevin. Julia & Mckinley's Day at the Beach. 2009. 32p. pap. 12.99 *(978-1-4389-7330-2(6))* AuthorHouse.

Redmond, Valerie. Emma & the African Wishing Bead. Victoria, Kirton, illus. 2013. 28p. pap. 13.95 *(978-1-61244-115-3(7))* Halo Publishing International.

Reece, Julie. Crux. 2012. (ENG.). 298p. (YA). pap. 14.99 *(978-1-937744-06-9(X))* J. Taylor Publishing.

Reed, Jennifer Bond. Doodle Girl. Foster, Jack, illus. 2012. 20p. pap. 9.95 *(978-1-61633-341-6(3))* Guardian Angel Publishing, Inc.

Reekles, Beth. The Kissing Booth. 2013. (ENG.). 448p. (YA). (gr. 9). pap. 8.99 *(978-0-385-37868-0(8),* Ember) Random Hse. Children's Bks.

Reely, Mary Katharine. The Blue Mittens. Wiese, Kurt, illus. 2011. 164p. 41.95 *(978-1-258-10114-5(9))* Literary Licensing, LLC.

Regan, Dian. The World According to Kaley. 2005. (ENG., Illus.). 112p. (J). (gr. 2-5). 14.99 *(978-1-58196-039-6(5),* Darby Creek) Lerner Publishing Group.

Reichs, Kathy & Reichs, Brendan. Code. 2013. (Virals Ser.: 3). lib. bdg. 19.65 *(978-0-606-32140-2(3),* Turtleback) Turtleback Bks.

Reid, David. The Shade Girls Were Right. 2012. (ENG.). 23p. (J). pap. 14.95 *(978-1-4327-8179-8(0))* Outskirts Pr., Inc.

Renae, Cameo. Hidden Wings. 2013. 270p. pap. 13.99 *(978-1-939769-21-3(3))* Crushing Hearts and Black Butterfly Publishing.

Renner, Sarah. The Bouquet. 2012. 24p. pap. 17.99 *(978-1-4685-4273-8(7))* AuthorHouse.

Rennison, Louise. Away Laughing on a Fast Camel: Even More Confessions of Georgia Nicolson. (Confessions of Georgia Nicolson Ser.: No. 5). 2004. (Illus.). 288p. (J). lib. bdg. 16.89 *(978-0-06-058935-6(3))* 2006. (ENG.). 304p. (YA). (gr. 8). reprint ed. pap. 9.99 *(978-0-06-058936-3(1))* HarperCollins Pubs. (HarperTeen).

—The Taming of the Tights. 2013. (Misadventures of Tallulah Casey Ser.: 3). (ENG.). 320p. (YA). (gr. 8). 17.99 *(978-0-06-222620-4(7),* HarperTeen) HarperCollins Pubs.

Rentas, Donna. Leticia Goes to School. 2008. 16p. pap. 24.95 *(978-1-4241-8966-3(7))* America Star Bks.

Reyes, Shawntie L. I'm Two, So What Should I Do?, 1 vol. Taylor, Amber L., illus. 2010. 34p. 24.95 *(978-1-4489-7869-4(6))* PublishAmerica, Inc.

Reynolds, Caroline. Bead Street-the Fable of Red Clover. 2009. 116p. 22.50 *(978-1-60693-579-8(8),* Eloquent Bks.) Strategic Book Publishing & Rights Agency (SBPRA).

Reynolds, Peter H. El Punto. 2003. (SPA., Illus.). 32p. (J). (gr. k-2). 18.50 *(978-84-8488-110-0(5))* Serres, Ediciones, S. L. ESP. Dist: Lectorum Pubns., Inc.

Reza, Connie. Leah Ann Adopta un Perico. 2006. (SPA., Illus.). 32p. (J). 19.99 incl. audio compact disk *(978-0-9714533-2-6(2))* Yo Puedo Publishing.

RH Disney. Quest for the Heart. RH Disney, illus. 2016. (Step into Reading Ser.). (ENG., Illus.). 32p. (J). (gr. -1-1). lib. bdg. 12.99 *(978-0-7364-8226-4(1),* RH/Disney) Random Hse. Children's Bks.

Rice, Sheila. The Night Watchers. 2005. 88p. pap. 19.95 *(978-1-4137-7663-8(9))* America Star Bks.

Richards, Claire. Mai's Garden: Mickamoo's Rescue. 2011. (Illus.). 56p. (gr. -1). pap. 12.51 *(978-1-4567-7559-9(6))* AuthorHouse.

Richards, J. Kirk. I'll Be There with Belzon. 2004. (Illus.). 32p. (J). per. 19.95 *(978-0-9752553-0-8(4))* Bright-Brights Media Co., The.

Richards, Josie Aleardi. Grandma's Just Not Herself. Rowland, Lauri, illus. 2010. 36p. pap. 13.95 *(978-1-60911-236-3(9),* Eloquent Bks.) Strategic Book Publishing & Rights Agency (SBPRA).

Richards, Katherine. My Favorite Run. Fieldhouse, Vicky, illus. 2013. (ENG.). 32p. (J). 16.99 *(978-0-9895095-2-7(4))* Fit Kids Publishing.

Richardson, Nikki. A Beautiful Lie, 1 vol. 2009. 168p. pap. 24.95 *(978-1-61582-927-9(X))* America Star Bks.

Richens, Carol & Smith, Lori. Lori's Summer Fun with Tamara! 2009. 33p. 16.40 *(978-1-4357-1113-6(0))* Lulu Pr., Inc.

Richmond, Marianne. Big Girls Go Potty. Richmond, Marianne, illus. 2012. (ENG., Illus.). 32p. (J). 9.99 *(978-1-4022-6662-1(6),* Sourcebooks Jabberwocky) Sourcebooks, Inc.

Ridell, Chris. Ottoline y la gata amarilla/ Ottolina & the Yellow Cat. 2008. (SPA.). 172p. (J). 13.95 *(978-84-263-6832-4(8))* Vives, Luis Editorial (Edelvives) ESP. Dist: Baker & Taylor Bks.

Rigby Education Staff, ed. Going to the Doctor. (Illus.). 8p. (J). bds. 3.95 *(978-0-7635-6427-8(3),* 764273C99) Rigby Education.

Rippin, Sally. The Bad Butterfly. Fukuoka, Aki, illus. 2012. 44p. (J). *(978-1-61067-132-3(5))* Kane Miller.

—The Bad Butterfly: Billie B. Brown. Fukuoka, Aki, illus. 2013. (ENG.). 48p. (J). pap. 4.99 *(978-1-61067-095-1(7))* Kane Miller.

—The Copycat Kid: Billie B. Brown. Fukuoka, Aki, illus. 2016. (ENG.). 48p. (J). pap. 4.99 *(978-1-61067-389-1(1))* Kane Miller.

—The Midnight Feast. Fukuoka, Aki, illus. 2013. (ENG.). 48p. (J). pap. 4.99 *(978-1-61067-097-5(3))* Kane Miller.

—The Soccer Star. Fukuoka, Aki, illus. 2013. (ENG.). 48p. (J). pap. 4.99 *(978-1-61067-096-8(5))* Kane Miller.

Rizy, Brock, illus. Emily Edison: Volume 1. 2006. 139p. (gr. 8-18). pap. 12.95 *(978-0-9777883-2-3(6))* Viper Comics.

Roat, Sharon Huss. Between the Notes. 2015. (ENG.). 400p. (YA). (gr. 9). 17.99 *(978-0-06-229172-1(6),* HarperTeen) HarperCollins Pubs.

Roat, Sharon Huss. How to Disappear. 2017. 384p. (YA). (gr. 8). 17.99 ***(978-0-06-229175-2(0),*** HarperTeen) HarperCollins Pubs.

Roberts, Gaylia. Giant Feathered Monsters. 2008. 20p. pap. 24.95 *(978-1-60441-582-7(7))* America Star Bks.

Roberts, Justin. The Smallest Girl in the Smallest Grade. Robinson, Christian, illus. 2014. (ENG.). 32p. (J). (gr. -1-k). 16.99 *(978-0-399-25743-8(8),* G.P. Putnam's Sons Books for Young Readers) Penguin Young Readers Group.

Roberts, Pauline. He Shined on Me. 2010. 20p. pap. 9.95 *(978-0-9841991-6-7(0))* Beckham Pubns. Group, Inc.

Roberts, Tony. Turquie the Turkey. 2011. 28p. pap. 15.99 *(978-1-4568-5969-5(2))* Xlibris Corp.

Roberts, Willo Davis. Girl with the Silver Eyes. 2011. (ENG.). 192p. (J). (gr. 3-7). pap. 7.99 *(978-1-4424-2170-7(3),* Aladdin) Simon & Schuster Children's Publishing.

Robertson, Chris. My Yellow Umbrella. Robertson, Chris, illus. 2013. (Illus.). 32p. pap. 9.99 *(978-1-62395-543-4(2))* Xist Publishing.

Robertson, Elysia Hill. Toley's Sleep over Learning Party. Robertson, Elysia Hill, illus. 2005. (Illus.). 118p. (J). per. 12.95 *(978-0-9764444-4-2(5),* EJWV-005) E. J. Publishing.

Robinson, Aquila. Septic Zombie - a Short Story. 2012. 28p. pap. 4.99 *(978-0-9840423-6-4(9))* Breakneck Media.

Robinson, Barbara. The Best School Year Ever. 2005. (Trophy Bk.). (ENG.). 176p. (J). (gr. 3-18). pap. 5.99 *(978-0-06-440492-1(7))* HarperCollins Pubs.

Robinson, Timberly. Masterpiece Creation. 2009. 16p. pap. 8.99 *(978-1-4343-5462-4(8))* AuthorHouse.

Robleda, Margarita. Este Soy Yo. Suarez, Maribel, illus. 2006. (Rana, Rema, Rimas Ser.).Tr. of This Is Me. (SPA.). 12p. (J). (gr. -1-k). 7.95 *(978-1-59820-207-6(3),* Alfaguara) Santillana USA Publishing Co., Inc.

—Muneca de Trapo. Suarez, Maribel, illus. 2006. (Rana, Rema, Rimas Ser.). (SPA.). 12p. (J). (gr. -1-k). 7.95 *(978-1-59820-209-0(X),* Alfaguara) Santillana USA Publishing Co., Inc.

—Patito, Donde Estas? Suarez, Maribel, illus. 2006. (Rana, Rema, Rimas Ser.).Tr. of Where Are You Little Ducky? (SPA.). 12p. (J). (gr. -1-k). 7.95 *(978-1-59820-208-3(1),* Alfaguara) Santillana USA Publishing Co., Inc.

The Rocket, 6 Packs. (gr. -1-2). 27.00 *(978-0-7635-9471-8(7))* Rigby Education.

Rockwell, D. R. The Jessicas: The Adventures of Five City Girls. 2005. (J). pap. 9.95 *(978-0-9767711-0-4(1))* CLOJ Publishing.

Rodrigues, Carmen. Not Anything. 2008. (ENG.). 240p. (YA). (gr. 9-18). 9.99 *(978-0-425-21928-7(3),* Berkley) Penguin Publishing Group.

Rodriguez, Ashley. A Mermaid Tale. 2010. 60p. pap. 10.50 *(978-0-557-65601-1(X))* Lulu Pr., Inc.

Rodriguez, Edarissa. The Girl Who Took a Shower. Santiago, Claribel, ed. Rodriguez, Edarissa, illus. 2003. (Illus.). (J). pap. 13.99 *(978-0-9744726-0-7(3))* Santiago, Claribel.

Rodriguez, Robert, et al. The Day Dreamer. Toader, Alex, illus. 2005. (Shark Boy & Lava Girl Adventures Ser.: Bk. 1). 162p. (J). (gr. -1-7). per. *(978-1-933104-04-1(5))* Troublemaker Publishing, LP.

Roesti, Delores. Mareena Maree Mulligan & the Flying Wheelchair: Book 2: The Busybodies. 2008. 102p. pap. 10.95 *(978-0-7414-4477-6(1))* Infinity Publishing.

Roger, Marie-Sabine. Of Course They Do! Boys & Girls Can Do Anything. Sol, Anne, photos by. 2014. (ENG., Illus.). 40p. (J). (-k). lib. bdg. 9.95 *(978-1-58089-669-6(3))* Charlesbridge Publishing, Inc.

Rolli. Kabungo, 1 vol. Pavlovic, Milan, illus. 2016. (ENG.). 176p. (J). (gr. 1-5). 14.95 *(978-1-55498-804-4(7))* Groundwood Bks. CAN. Dist: Publishers Group West (PGW).

Romero, Sensi. La Familia de Nieve. Serra, Armando, illus. 2004. (Cuentos con miga Ser.). 47p. (J). (gr. 1-5). pap. 11.00 *(978-84-95895-22-6(6))* Editorial Brief ESP. Dist: Independent Pubs. Group.

Ron Cherney With Angel Logan. Coming Out of Her Shell. 2011. 72p. pap. 33.32 *(978-1-4568-7141-3(2))* Xlibris Corp.

Roper, Robert. Dora Goes to the Doctor. 2013. (Dora the Explorer 8X8 Ser.). lib. bdg. 14.75 *(978-0-606-32216-4(7),* Turtleback) Turtleback Bks.

Rosen, Marvin. Becca in Cyberland, 1 vol. 2010. 48p. pap. 16.95 *(978-1-4489-9831-9(X))* America Star Bks.

Rosen, Michael. Burping Bertha. Ross, Tony, illus. 2012. (ENG.). 64p. (J). (gr. -1-2). pap. 8.99 *(978-1-84939-406-2(7))* Andersen Pr. GBR. Dist: Independent Pubs. Group.

Rosenbaum, Andria Warmflash. Meg Goldberg on Parade. Lyles, Christopher, illus. 2015. (ENG.). 32p. (J). (gr. -1-3). 17.99 *(978-1-4677-3906-1(5),* Kar-Ben Publishing) Lerner Publishing Group.

Rosenstiehl, Agnes. Silly Lilly & the Four Seasons. Mouly, Francoise, ed. 2008. (ENG., Illus.). 36p. (J). (gr. -1-3). 12.95 *(978-0-9799238-1-4(6))* TOON Books / RAW Junior, LLC.

Rosenthal, S. L. Mama, Where Do Our Butterflies Go in the Winter? 2011. 40p. pap. 24.95 *(978-1-4560-7498-2(9))* America Star Bks.

Ross, K. N. Daughters of the Lost World. 2012. 132p. 29.99 *(978-1-4653-8397-6(2));* pap. 19.99 *(978-1-4653-8396-9(4))* Xlibris Corp.

Roter, Jordan. Camp Rules. 2007. 260p. (J). *(978-1-4287-4603-9(X),* Dutton Adult) Penguin Publishing Group.

Roth, Matthue. Candy in Action. 2007. (ENG.). 224p. (gr. 9-18). *(978-1-933368-63-4(2))* CSA Telltapes, Ltd.

Roth, Sarra J. Not the Quitting Kind. Bishop, Tracy, illus. 2014. 32p. pap. 16.99 *(978-1-4413-1415-4(6))* Peter Pauper Pr. Inc.

Rothberg, Kimmy. Saturdays with Daddy. 2010. 20p. 11.95 *(978-0-557-50036-9(2))* Lulu Pr., Inc.

Rotstein, Adira. Little Jane Silver. 2011. (Little Jane Silver Adventure Ser.: 1). (ENG., Illus.). 288p. (YA). (gr. 7). pap. 12.99 *(978-1-55488-878-8(6),* Dundurn Pr.) Dundurn CAN. Dist: Ingram Publisher Services.

Rousay II, Richard A. Choose the Right! Walk with Ruth. 2009. 101p. pap. 17.50 *(978-1-4092-5519-2(0))* Lulu Pr., Inc.

Roy, Lillian Elizabeth. Polly in Egypt: The Polly Brewster Series. Barbour, H. S., illus. 2011. 226p. 44.95 *(978-1-258-09808-7(3))* Literary Licensing, LLC.

—Polly's Southern Cruise: The Polly Brewster Series. Barbour, H. S., illus. 2011. 294p. 48.95 *(978-1-258-10514-3(4))* Literary Licensing, LLC.

Roy, Wendy. Kelly Confident Shows You Why... It's POWERFUL to be a GIRL! It's POWERFUL to be a GIRL! 2012. (ENG.). 34p. (J). pap. 10.95 *(978-0-615-59502-3(2))* Roy, Wendy.

Ruben, Pamela J. Don't Pick on Pepper! Take a Journey with Pepper as She Takes on a Schoolyard Bully with Brainpower, Humor, & a Dash of Spice! Ruben, Anthony R., ed. 2004. 31p. (J). 12.95 *(978-0-9764813-1-7(6))* Peppery Pr.

Ruditis, Paul. Ready to Glow. Choi Sung Hwan, Aragon Noel, illus. 2005. (Trollz Ser.). (ENG.). 80p. (J). pap. 5.99 *(978-0-439-80313-7(6))* Scholastic, Inc.

Rushton, Jenna. A Simple Flower. 2012. 24p. pap. 14.50 *(978-1-4772-0295-1(1))* AuthorHouse.

Russell, Rachel Renée. How to Dork Your Diary. Russell, Rachel Renée, illus. 2011. (Dork Diaries: No. 3.5). (ENG., Illus.). 288p. (J). (gr. 4-8). 13.99 *(978-1-4424-2233-9(5),* Aladdin) Simon & Schuster Children's Publishing.

—Tales from a Not-So-Dorky Drama Queen, 3 vols. unabr. ed. 2015. (Dork Diaries: 8). (ENG.). 320p. (gr. 4-8). audio compact disk 14.99 *(978-1-4423-7023-4(8))* Simon & Schuster Audio.

—Tales from a Not-So-Dorky Drama Queen. Russell, Rachel Renée, illus. 2015. (Dork Diaries: Bk. 9). (ENG., Illus.). 352p. (J). (gr. 4-8). 13.99 *(978-1-4424-8769-7(0),* Aladdin Paperbacks) Simon & Schuster Children's Publishing.

Russo, Angela B. Beautiful. 2013. 28p. pap. 24.95 *(978-1-62709-040-7(1))* America Star Bks.

Rutledge, Eddie. Amani's World: Amani Goes to Washington D. C. Anderson, Susan, illus. 2009. 16p. pap. 8.75 *(978-1-4490-2095-8(X))* AuthorHouse.

Ryan, Carrie. The Dead-Tossed Waves. 2010. (Forest of Hands & Teeth Ser.: Bk. 2). (ENG.). 416p. (YA). (gr. 9-18). 17.99 *(978-0-385-73684-8(3),* Delacorte Bks. for Young Readers) Random Hse. Children's Bks.

Ryherd, Tim. My Hurricane Book. 2006. (Illus.). (J). 12.95 *(978-0-9749974-1-4(2))* Ryherd, Tim Publishing.

Sackstein, Starr. Simply May. 2009. 162p. pap. 19.99 *(978-0-557-13275-1(4))* Lulu Pr., Inc.

Sala, Sharon. Lunatic Revenge. 2012. 186p. pap. 11.95 *(978-1-61194-179-1(2),* Bell Bridge Bks.) BelleBks., Inc.

Salant, Dawnelle. Smile. 2009. 112p. pap. 13.35 *(978-1-4251-3268-2(5))* Trafford Publishing.

Salmon, Sheryl. The Adventures of Kaptain Kristian. 2010. 68p. pap. 9.99 *(978-1-60911-829-7(4),* Eloquent Bks.) Strategic Book Publishing & Rights Agency (SBPRA).

Salti, Kim. Riley's Imagination Super Highway - Adventures in Dreamworld. 2012. 56p. pap. 12.00 *(978-1-105-81460-0(2))* Lulu Pr., Inc.

Salvatus, Mark & Olizon-Chikiamco, Norma. Pan de Sal Saves the Day: An Award-Winning ChildrenAEs Story from the Philippines [New Bilingual English & Tagalog Edition]. 2017. (ENG., Illus.). 28p. (J). (gr. -1-6). pap. 8.95 *(978-0-8048-4754-4(1))* Tuttle Publishing.

Santana, Sr. Stella. We Are the People of This World: Book One. Bear, Andrea, illus. 2011. 40p. pap. 14.95 *(978-1-61204-643-3(6),* Eloquent Bks.) Strategic Book Publishing & Rights Agency (SBPRA).

Sarah Bishop. 2003. pap. 2.50 *(978-0-590-41407-4(0))* Scholastic, Inc.

Sargent, Dave & Sargent, Pat. Amy Armadillo: Mind Your Mama, 15 vols. Huff, Jeane, illus. 2003. (Animal Pride Ser.: 15). 42p. (J). pap. 6.95 *(978-1-56763-788-5(4));* lib. bdg. 20.95 *(978-1-56763-787-8(6))* Ozark Publishing.

—Valley Oak Acorns: (Maidu) Be Helpful, 20 vols., Vol. 20. Lenoir, Jane, illus. l.t. ed. 2005. (Story Keeper Ser.: 20). 42p. (J). (gr. -1 — 1). lib. bdg. 23.60 *(978-1-56763-941-4(0))* Ozark Publishing.

Sargent, Dave, et al. The Bundle Keeper: (Pawnee) Be Responsible, 20 vols., Vol. 18. Lenoir, Jane, illus. l.t. ed. 2004. (Story Keeper Ser.: 18). 48p. (J). pap. 10.95 *(978-1-56763-938-4(0))* Ozark Publishing.

—On the Banks of the Wallowa River: (Nez Perce) Use Your Talent, 20 vols., Vol. 13. Lenoir, Jane, illus. l.t. ed. 2004. (Story Keeper Ser.: 13). 48p. (J). pap. 10.95 *(978-1-56763-928-5(3))* Ozark Publishing.

—Rays of the Sun Vol. 15: (shoshone) Learn Lessons, 20 vols. Lenoir, Jane, illus. l.t. ed. 2004. (Story Keeper Ser.: 15). 48p. (J). pap. 10.95 *(978-1-56763-932-2(1))* Ozark Publishing.

—Rays of the Sun Vol. 15: (Shoshone) Learn Lessons, 20 vols. Lenoir, Jane, illus. l.t. ed. 2004. (Story Keeper Ser.: 15). 48p. (J). lib. bdg. 23.60 *(978-1-56763-931-5(3))* Ozark Publishing.

—Valley Oaks Acorns Vol. 20: (Maidu) Be Helpful, 20 vols. Lenoir, Jane, illus. l.t. ed. 2004. (Story Keeper Ser.: 20). 48p. (J). pap. 10.95 *(978-1-56763-942-1(9))* Ozark Publishing.

Sataram, Nikita. Zatheria: The Hidden Realm. 2013. 194p. (gr. -1). 24.77 *(978-1-4907-0938-3(X));* pap. 14.77 *(978-1-4907-0936-9(3))* Trafford Publishing.

Satterfield, Barbara. Answer Why for Mee Mee. 2004. (Illus.). 32p. (J). pap. 11.50 *(978-0-9748715-1-6(6),* 314-004) Vision Harmony Publishing.

Satterfield, Mary & Satterfield, Nathaniel. The Leaping Lady: A Tall Tale from Mary & Nathaniel Satterfield. 2011. (Illus.). 24p. (J). pap. 11.95 *(978-1-58909-989-0(3))* Bookstand Publishing.

Savage, Tawanna. Anna Mischievous: The Early Years. 2005. Orig. Title: ANNA MISCHIEVOUS: the Early Years. (J). spiral bd. *(978-0-9754147-9-8(8))* ASP Corp. Entertainment Group, Inc.

Say, Allen. Allison. 2004. (ENG., Illus.). 32p. (J). (gr. -1-3). reprint ed. pap. 8.99 *(978-0-618-49537-5(1))* Houghton Mifflin Harcourt Publishing Co.

Schaeffer, Teresa. The Questions Within, 1 vol. unabr. ed. 2012. (Cutting Edge Ser.). (ENG.). 143p. (YA). (gr. 9-12). pap. 9.95 *(978-1-61651-760-1(3))* Saddleback Educational Publishing, Inc.

Scheffer, Stephanie. Elise the Patriot: A Revolutionary War Story. 2008. 108p. 20.95 *(978-0-595-51324-6(7));* pap. 10.95 *(978-0-595-52582-9(2))* iUniverse, Inc.

Scheidies, Carolyn R. My Summer Journel: the Rescue. 2007. 96p. pap. 14.99 *(978-0-615-16029-0(8))* C R Pubns.

Scheie, Jesse. Kisses to Heaven, 1 vol. Scheie, Jesse, illus. 2009. (Illus.). 16p. pap. 24.95 *(978-1-61582-707-7(2))* America Star Bks.

Schena, Maghan. When I Grow Up. 2011. (ENG.). 18p. (J). pap. 11.95 *(978-1-4327-8203-0(7))* Outskirts Pr., Inc.

Schliewen, Richard D. Paulina, Girl of the Pacific. 2011. 104p. pap. 19.95 *(978-1-4626-3614-3(4))* America Star Bks.

Schmidt, Kristina Edelkamp. Miss Flavia & the Cookie Cottage. Cologne, Starla, illus. 2009. 28p. pap. 7.99 *(978-1-935125-61-7(3))* Robertson Publishing.

Schnur, Dawn. Bailey's Tree House Adventures. 2013. 138p. pap. 12.99 *(978-1-62697-613-9(9))* Salem Author Services.

Scholastic, Inc. Staff. Dolphin Rescue. 2014. (LEGO Friends Ser.). (ENG., Illus.). 64p. (J). (gr. 2-5). pap. 4.99 *(978-0-545-51655-6(2))* Math Solutions.

Scholastic, Inc. Staff, contrib. by. A Day in Heartlake City. 2013. (LEGO Friends Ser.). (ENG.). 16p. (J). (gr. 1-3). 6.99 *(978-0-545-51757-7(5))* Scholastic, Inc.

—LEGO Friends: Meet the Friends. 2013. (LEGO Friends Ser.). (ENG.). 32p. (J). (gr. 2-5). pap. 3.99 *(978-0-545-59943-6(1))* Scholastic, Inc.

Scholastic, Inc. Staff & Bailey, Ellen. The Girls' Book of Secrets. Ryan, Nellie, illus. 2011. (Best at Everything Ser.). (ENG.). 128p. (J). (gr. 3-7). pap. 7.99 *(978-0-545-37356-2(5))* Scholastic, Inc.

Scholastic, Inc. Staff & Glass, Calliope. Annie - A True Family. 2014. (ENG., Illus.). 32p. (J). (gr. 1-3). pap. 3.99 *(978-0-545-79752-8(7))* Scholastic, Inc.

Schomer-Wendel, Gretchen & Schomer, Adam Anthony. All Around Town. 2009. (Becka & the Big Bubble Ser.). (Illus.). 32p. (J). (gr. -1-3). pap. 10.55 *(978-1-60754-105-9(X))* Windmill Bks.

Schoombee, Cherese. Frilly Lilly. 2009. 28p. 16.95 *(978-1-84799-435-6(0))* Lulu Pr., Inc.

Schraff, Anne. Like a Broken Doll, 1 vol. unabr. ed. 2011. (Urban Underground Ser.). (ENG.). 182p. (YA). (gr. 9-12). pap. 9.95 *(978-1-61651-005-3(6))* Saddleback Educational Publishing, Inc.

Schuette, Eva. The Kingdom of the Wild Gootsies: Meet the Wild Gootsies. 2010. 12p. 8.49 *(978-1-4490-8798-2(1))* AuthorHouse.

Schultz, Edward L. Pix, 1 vol. 2009. 48p. pap. 16.95 *(978-1-60749-393-8(4))* PublishAmerica, Inc.

Scollon, Bill & Nee, Chris. Engine Nine, Feelin' Fine! 2013. (Illus.). 24p. (J). *(978-1-4844-0835-3(7))* Disney Pr.

Scollon, William. Doc Mcstuffins: Starry, Starry Night. 2014. (World of Reading Ser.). (Illus.). 32p. (J). lib. bdg. 13.55 *(978-0-606-35257-4(0))* Turtleback Bks.

Scollon, William & Disney Book Group Staff. World of Reading: Doc Mcstuffins Starry, Starry Night: Level 1. Disney Storybook Art Team, illus. 2014. (World of Reading Ser.). (ENG.). 32p. (J). (gr. -1-k). pap. 3.99 *(978-1-4231-9419-4(5))* Disney Pr.

Scollon, William & Parent, Nancy. Blooming Bows. Disney Storybook Artists Staff, illus. 2013. (ENG.). 32p. (J). (gr. -1-1). pap. 3.99 *(978-1-4231-6691-7(4))* Disney Pr.

Scott, Elizabeth. Something, Maybe. 2010. (ENG.). 240p. (YA). (gr. 9). pap. 9.99 *(978-1-4169-5356-2(6),* Simon Pulse) Simon Pulse.

Scott, Gwen. In Between the Cracks: The Search for Zar. 2013. 20p. pap. 16.95 *(978-1-63000-080-6(9))* America Star Bks.

Scott, Ladena Mae. Bossy Rossy. 2013. 36p. pap. 18.41 *(978-1-4669-8965-8(3))* Trafford Publishing.

Scott, Michele. Dark Harmony: A Vivienne Taylor Horse Lover's Mystery, 0 vols. 2014. (Fairmont Riding Academy Ser.: 2). (ENG.). 384p. (YA). (gr. 7-12). pap. 9.99 *(978-1-4778-4726-8(X),* 9781477847268, Amazon Children's Publishing) Amazon Publishing.

—Perfect Harmony: A Vivienne Taylor Horse Lover's Mystery, 0 vols. 2014. (Fairmont Riding Academy Ser.). (ENG.). 274p. (YA). (gr. 7-9). pap. 9.99 *(978-1-4778-4779-4(0),* 9781477847794, Skyscape) Amazon Publishing.

—Silent Harmony, 0 vols. unabr. ed. 2013. (Fairmont Riding Academy Ser.: 1). (ENG.). 256p. (YA). (gr. 7-12). pap. 9.99 *(978-1-4778-1713-1(1),* 9781477817131, Amazon Children's Publishing) Amazon Publishing.

Scott, Sabrina & Scott, Brigett. What's That in Mom's Belly? 2012. 34p. pap. 15.99 *(978-1-105-60556-7(6))* Lulu Pr., Inc.

Scott, Victoria. The Liberator. 2013. (Dante Walker Ser.: 2). (ENG.). 352p. (YA). (gr. 7-12). pap. 9.99 *(978-1-62266-016-2(1),* 9781622660162) Entangled Publishing, LLC.

Scudamore, Beverly. Ready to Run, 1 vol. 2006. (Lorimer Sports Stories Ser.). (ENG.). 96p. (J). (gr. 4-8). 16.95 *(978-1-55028-915-2(2),* 9781550289152); 8.95 *(978-1-55028-914-5(4),* 9781550289145) Lorimer, James & Co., Ltd., Pubs. CAN. Dist: Casemate Pubs. & Bk. Distributors, LLC.

Seaman, John E. On the Road with Ruben Doyle. 2010. 170p. 29.99 *(978-1-4500-3196-7(X))* Xlibris Corp.

E
F
G

Seda, Gus. Sally & the Four Wizards. 2012. 28p. pap. 24.95 *(978-1-4626-7746-7(0))* America Star Bks.
Seroney, Kibny'aanko Arap. Cheebtabuut, Blue Berries & the Monsters Den. 2013. 36p. pap. *(978-1-909204-28-7(5))* BookPublishingWorld.
Settino, Erica. I Am Everything & Everything Is Me. 2011. 32p. pap. 19.95 *(978-1-4560-0275-6(9))* America Star Bks.
Sewell, Anna. Black Beauty. Aldous, Kate, illus. 2003. 288p. (J). 9.98 *(978-1-4054-1675-7(0))* Parragon, Inc.
Shah, Yasmin. Abby & the Feather Quest. 2010. (Illus.). 48p. pap. 10.49 *(978-1-4343-9839-0(0))* AuthorHouse.
Shannon, Molly. Tilly the Trickster. Hoyt, Ard, illus. 2011. (ENG.). 32p. (J). (gr. k-2). 16.95 *(978-1-4197-0030-9(8))*, Abrams Bks. for Young Readers) Abrams, Inc.
Sharafeddine, Fatima. The Servant. 2013. 160p. *(978-1-55498-309-4(6))* Groundwood Bks.
—The Servant, 1 vol. 2017. (ENG.). 160p. (J). (gr. 6). pap. 9.95 *(978-1-55498-308-7(8))* Groundwood Bks. CAN. Dist: Publishers Group West (PGW).
Shaw, Laura. Priscilla & the Big Red Ball, 1 vol. Shaw, Yvonne, illus. 2009. 19p. pap. 24.95 *(978-1-60749-523-9(6))* America Star Bks.
Shaw, Natalie. A Guide to Being a Big Sister. 2014. (Olivia 8x8 Ser.). lib. bdg. 16.00 *(978-0-606-35761-6(0))* Turtleback Bks.
Sheldon, Dyan. Confessions of a Teenage Drama Queen. braille ed. 2003. (J). (gr. 2). spiral bd. *(978-0-616-15873-9(4))* Canadian National Institute for the Blind/Institut National Canadien pour les Aveugles.
—The Truth about My Success. 2015. (ENG.). 352p. (J). (gr. 7). 16.99 *(978-0-7636-7272-0(6))* Candlewick Pr.
Shen-Chow, Lulu. Silly Girl Adventures. 2011. 24p. pap. 15.99 *(978-1-4628-6478-2(3))* Xlibris Corp.
Shepherd, Angela. Through the Lens #1: Ava's Big Surprise. 2009. 32p. pap. 14.95 *(978-0-557-23332-8(1))* Lulu Pr., Inc.
Sherman, Susan & Poryes, Michael. That's So Raven, 2 vols., Vol. 1. 2004. (Illus.). 192p. pap. 14.99 *(978-1-59182-806-8(6))*, Tokyopop Kids) TOKYOPOP, Inc.
Shimko, Bonnie. You Know What You Have to Do, 0 vols. 2013. (ENG.). 240p. (YA). (gr. 9-12). 17.99 *(978-1-4778-1642-4(9))*, 9781477816424, Amazon Children's Publishing) Amazon Publishing.
Shirin Yim, Bridges. Ruby's Wish. Blackall, Sophie, illus. 2015. (ENG.). 36p. (J). (gr. 3-7). 7.99 *(978-1-4521-4569-3(5))* Chronicle Bks. LLC.
Shore, Elayne. Candy Girl. 2013. 24p. pap. 24.95 *(978-1-63000-402-6(2))* America Star Bks.
Shrode, Donna. Fun with Nana: Let's Play. 2011. 28p. (gr. -1). pap. 12.03 *(978-1-4567-4600-1(6))* AuthorHouse.
Shull, Megan. Amazing Grace. 2006. (ENG.). 256p. (gr. 6-9). pap. 6.99 *(978-0-7868-5691-6(2))* Hyperion Pr.
—Penelope. 2007. (ENG.). (J). (gr. 6-9). 15.99 *(978-0-7868-3730-4(6))* Hyperion Pr.
Sidney's Saddest Sunday. 2007. (J). per. 14.95 *(978-0-9787913-4-6(7))* Urban Moon Publishing.
Sills, Elizabeth & Patrice, Elena. Nana Star. Saker, Linda, illus. 2004. 32p. (J). (gr. -1-3). *(978-0-9753843-0-5(9))* Elfstone Press.
Silver Dolphin en Español Editors. Girlfriends Imanes Magicos. 2006. (Illus.). 8p. (J). (gr. -1). bds. *(978-970-718-371-1(3))*, Silver Dolphin en Español) Advanced Marketing, S. de R. L. de C. V.
Silverberry, A. R. Wyndano's Cloak. 2010. 424p. 21.95 *(978-0-9841037-6-8(7))* Tree Tunnel Pr.
Silverman, Erica. Cowgirl Kate & Cocoa. Lewin, Betsy, illus. 2005. (Cowgirl Kate & Cocoa Ser.). (ENG.). 44p. (J). (gr. 1-4). 15.00 *(978-0-15-202124-5(8))* Houghton Mifflin Harcourt Publishing Co.
—Favorite Stories from Cowgirl Kate & Cocoa: Partners. Lewin, Betsy, illus. 2013. (Cowgirl Kate & Cocoa — Green Light Readers Ser.). (ENG.). 22p. (J). (gr. -1-3). lib. bdg. 13.55 *(978-0-606-33983-4(3))*, Turtleback) Turtleback Bks.
—Partners. Lewin, Betsy, illus. 2007. (Cowgirl Kate & Cocoa Ser.). (gr. 1-4). 15.95 *(978-0-7569-8042-9(9))* Perfection Learning Corp.
Simmons, Cari & Zulkey, Claire. Best Frenemies. 2015. (Picture Perfect Ser.: 3). (ENG., Illus.). 224p. (J). (gr. 3-7). pap. 6.99 *(978-0-06-231845-9(4))* HarperCollins Pubs.
Simmons, Kristen. The Glass Arrow. 2015. (ENG.). 336p. (YA). (gr. 8-12). 17.99 *(978-0-7653-3661-3(8))*, 9780765336613, Tor Teen) Doherty, Tom Assocs., LLC.
Simon, Coco. Alexis Gets Frosted. 2013. (Cupcake Diaries: 12). (ENG., Illus.). 160p. (J). (gr. 3-7). pap. 6.99 *(978-1-4424-6867-2(X))*, Simon Spotlight) Simon Spotlight.
—Alexis Gets Frosted. 2013. (Cupcake Diaries: 12). lib. bdg. 17.20 *(978-0-606-27026-7(4))*, Turtleback) Turtleback Bks.
—Emma: Sugar & Spice & Everything Nice. 2013. (Cupcake Diaries: 15). lib. bdg. 16.00 *(978-0-606-32052-8(0))*, Turtleback) Turtleback Bks.
—Emma on Thin Icing. 2011. (Cupcake Diaries: 3). (ENG.). 160p. (J). (gr. 3-7). pap. 6.99 *(978-1-4424-2279-7(3))*, Simon Spotlight) Simon Spotlight.
—Mia a Matter of Taste. 2013. (Cupcake Diaries: 14). (ENG., Illus.). 160p. (J). (gr. 3-7). 15.99 *(978-1-4424-7480-2(7))*; pap. 6.99 *(978-1-4424-7435-2(1))* Simon Spotlight. (Simon Spotlight).
—Mia Fashion Plates & Cupcakes. 2014. (Cupcake Diaries: 18). (ENG., Illus.). 160p. (J). (gr. 3-7). pap. 5.99 *(978-1-4424-9790-0(4))*, Simon Spotlight) Simon Spotlight.
—Mia's Boiling Point. 2012. (Cupcake Diaries: 10). (ENG., Illus.). 160p. (J). (gr. 3-7). pap. 6.99 *(978-1-4424-5396-8(6))*, Simon Spotlight) Simon Spotlight.
Simon, Elizabeth. Tyler Adams & the Adventures of Bravura: the First Quest. 2009. 49p. pap. 19.95 *(978-0-557-06290-4(X))* Lulu Pr., Inc.
Simon, Jenne. Double Trouble. 2014. (Illus.). 32p. (J). *(978-1-4844-2319-6(4))* Scholastic, Inc.
—Snow Day!, Level 2. Hill, Prescott, illus. 2013. (Lalaloopsy Ser.). (ENG.). 32p. (J). (gr. -1-3). pap. 3.99 *(978-0-545-58123-3(0))* Scholastic, Inc.
Simon, Margaret. Blessen. 2012. 120p. (J). pap. 15.00 *(978-0-9848915-2-8(8))* Border Pr.
Simon, Nadine. Flickers of True Destiny. 2010. 58p. pap. 11.95 *(978-1-60860-948-2(0))*, Eloquent Bks.) Strategic Book Publishing & Rights Agency (SBPRA).
Simpson, C. E. & Smith, C. E. Eighth Grade Witch. Utomo, Gabhor, illus. 2014. (ENG.). 144p. (J). mass mkt. 6.99 *(978-1-937133-45-0(1))* Chooseco LLC.
Simpson, Dana. Phoebe & Her Unicorn: A Heavenly Nostrils Chronicle. 2014. (Phoebe & Her Unicorn Ser.: 1). (Illus.). 222p. (J). lib. bdg. 20.85 *(978-0-606-36144-6(8))* Turtleback Bks.
—Unicorn on a Roll. 2015. (Phoebe & Her Unicorn Ser.: 2). lib. bdg. 20.85 *(978-0-606-36985-5(6))* Turtleback Bks.
Simpson, Dorothy. A Lesson for Janie. Date not set. 190p. (J). 20.95 *(978-0-8488-2617-8(5))* Amereon Ltd.
Simpson, N. J. Not So Random. 2011. 200p. pap. 13.67 *(978-0-557-83059-6(1))* Lulu Pr., Inc.
Sims, Lesley. Illustrated Classics for Girls. Mason, Conrad, illus. 2009. (Illustrated Stories Ser.). 384p. (YA). (gr. 3-18). 19.99 *(978-0-7945-2419-7(2))*, Usborne) EDC Publishing.
Singleton, Jennifer. That magnificent Medallion. 2009. 66p. pap. 13.95 *(978-1-4452-0639-4(0))* Lulu Pr., Inc.
Sinke, Janet Mary. Priscilla Mcdoodlenut Doodle Mcmae Asks, Why? Pennington, Craig, illus. 2007. 40p. (J). 17.95 *(978-0-9742732-8-0(7))* My Grandma & Me Pubs.
Skorlinski, Cynthia. My Little Erica. 2013. 28p. pap. 13.99 *(978-1-4808-0181-3(X))* Archway Publishing.
Slater, David Michael. Flour Girl: A Recipe for Disaster, 1 vol. Brooks, S. G., illus. 2007. (Missy Swiss & More Ser.). (ENG.). 32p. (gr. -1-4). 28.50 *(978-1-60270-009-3(5))*, Looking Glass Library) ABDO Publishing Co.
Sleepover Girls, 4 vols. 2015. (Sleepover Girls Ser.). (ENG.). 128p. (gr. 3-5). 90.60 *(978-1-4965-2022-7(X))* Stone Arch Bks.
Smith, Barbara Maxine. God Loves You & You Love Yourself -To God You Are Special. 2013. 38p. pap. 12.99 *(978-0-578-11939-7(0))* Smith, Barbara Maxine.
Smith, Evelyn. The Small Sixth Form. Wiles, Frank, illus. 2013. 200p. pap. *(978-1-909423-08-4(4))* Bks. to Treasure.
Smith, Heather. Baygirl, 1 vol. 2013. (ENG.). 288p. (YA). (gr. 8-12). pap. 12.95 *(978-1-4598-0274-2(8))* Orca Bk. Pubs. USA.
Smith, J. L. The Blue & Purple Egg. Baker, David, illus. 2012. 28p. pap. 24.95 *(978-1-4626-6789-5(9))* America Star Bks.
Smith, Jessica Gillis. Charlotte's Halloween. 2012. 28p. pap. 19.99 *(978-1-4772-0522-8(5))* AuthorHouse.
Smith, John C. Popee the Purple Pig-a-Saurus. 2010. 40p. pap. 16.99 *(978-1-4490-9285-6(3))* AuthorHouse.
Smith, Kirsten. The Geography of Girlhood. 2007. (ENG.). 192p. (YA). (gr. 7-17). per. 7.99 *(978-0-316-01735-0(3))* Little, Brown Bks. for Young Readers.
Smith, Lane. Abe Lincoln's Dream. Smith, Lane, illus. 2012. (ENG., Illus.). 32p. (J). (gr. k-4). 16.99 *(978-1-59643-608-4(5))*, 9781596436084) Roaring Brook Pr.
Smith, Richard G. Wanda Jean's Face. Date not set. 240p. (J). pap. 4.99 *(978-0-06-440826-4(4))* HarperCollins Pubs.
Smith, Sherwood. Over the Sea: CJ's First Notebook. 2007. (Illus.). 260p. (YA). pap. 12.95 *(978-1-934648-36-0(1))*, YA Angst) Norilana Bks.
Smucker, Anna. No Star Nights. Johnson, Steve & Fancher, Lou, illus. 2012. 40p. (J). pap. 8.95 *(978-1-891852-82-4(5))* Quarrier Pr.
Soci Et E de La Faune Et Des Parcs Du Qu Ebec. Sarah de Cordoba. Sanchez, Andres & Tagle, illus. 2003. (la Orilla del Viento Ser.). (SPA.). 136p. (J). per. 8.50 *(978-968-16-7020-7(5))* Fondo de Cultura Economica USA.
Soman, David & Davis, Jacky. Little Box of Ladybug Girl, 4 vols. Soman, David, illus. 2013. (Ladybug Girl Ser.). (ENG., Illus.). 14p. (J). (gr. -1-k). bds. 23.96 *(978-0-8037-4102-7(2))*, Dial Bks) Penguin Young Readers Group.
Sorensen, Virginia. Plain Girl. Geer, Charles, illus. 2003. (ENG.). 176p. (J). (gr. 2-5). pap. 6.95 *(978-0-15-204725-2(5))* Houghton Mifflin Harcourt Publishing Co.
Soto, Gary. The Afterlife. 2005. (ENG.). 176p. (YA). (gr. 7-12). reprint ed. pap. 7.99 *(978-0-15-205220-1(8))* Houghton Mifflin Harcourt Publishing Co.
Spalding, Andrea. Seal Song, 1 vol. Milelli, Pascal, illus. 2011. (ENG.). 32p. (J). (gr. -1-3). 19.95 *(978-1-55469-242-2(3))* Orca Bk. Pubs. USA.
Sparklington, Madame & Gurney, Stella. Princess: A Glittering Guide for Young Ladies. Allsop, Sophie et al, illus. 2006. (Genuine & Moste Authentic Guide Ser.: 2). (ENG.). 26p. (J). (gr. 1-4). 15.99 *(978-0-7636-3430-8(1))* Candlewick Pr.
Sparks, Favre. Katie. 2009. 28p. pap. 12.00 *(978-1-60860-413-5(6))*, Eloquent Bks.) Strategic Book Publishing & Rights Agency (SBPRA).
Sparks, Kerry. Jen & the Frosted Friends: Book #2 of the Get Frosted Series. 2010. 84p. pap. 10.99 *(978-1-4520-5349-3(9))* AuthorHouse.
Sparks, Megan. Hell's Belles/By Megan Sparks. 2013. 255p. (YA). *(978-1-62370-022-5(1))* Capstone Young Readers of Coughlan Cos.
Speer, Beth. LuLa. 2010. 24p. pap. 13.99 *(978-1-4520-1549-1(X))* AuthorHouse.
Spetzler, Carl. Goldilocks Meets Desidero. Meyers, Mark, illus. 2011. 36p. pap. 16.86 *(978-1-4634-2684-2(4))* AuthorHouse.
Spinelli, Jerry. The Warden's Daughter. 2017. (ENG.). 352p. (J). (gr. 4-7). 16.99 *(978-0-375-83199-7(1))*; lib. bdg. 19.99 *(978-0-375-93199-4(6))* Random Hse. Children's Bks. (Knopf Bks. for Young Readers).
Spinelli, Patti. Mackenzie & Emma Visit York Beach. Spinelli, Patti, illus. 2003. (Illus.). (J). *(978-0-9742328-0-5(7))* Spinelli, Patti.
Spring Break Safari. (Bratz Fiction Totally Awesome Tales Ser.). 128p. pap. *(978-1-4054-8739-9(9))* Parragon, Inc.
Spurlin, Barbara & Bernhardt, Michael J. Jellyfish on the Menu. 2011. (Illus.). 120p. (J). pap. *(978-0-692-01277-2(X))* Kan sasana Printer.
Spyri, Johanna. Heidi. (J). 24.95 *(978-0-8488-1179-2(8))* Amereon Ltd.
St-Onge, Julie-Ann. Passage to Fairywell. 2008. 80p. pap. 19.95 *(978-1-60441-172-0(4))* America Star Bks.
Stacy, Dorothy. Three Weeks in Utica. Stacy, Dorothy, illus. 2008. (Illus.). 120p. (J). pap. 9.95 *(978-0-9792947-1-6(1))* Blackberry Hill Pr.
Stanisha, Terésa (Tracey). Especially for Rachel - Butterflies Abound. 2009. 84p. pap. 16.97 *(978-0-557-04450-4(2))* Lulu Pr., Inc.
Stanley, Malaika Rose. Dance Dreams. 2013. (ENG., Illus.). 144p. (J). (gr. 3-6). pap. 8.99 *(978-1-84853-055-3(2))* Transworld Publishers Ltd. GBR. Dist: Independent Pubs. Group.
Stapleton, Rhonda. Flirting with Disaster. 2010. (ENG.). 256p. (YA). (gr. 7-18). pap. 9.99 *(978-1-4169-7465-9(2))*, Simon Pulse) Simon Pulse.
Stayer, Elizabeth. Get off My Corner!! 2012. 40p. pap. 16.99 *(978-1-4772-1297-4(3))* AuthorHouse.
Stegall, Billy Mark. Pat & Pea Soup. Archambault, Matthew, illus. 2003. (Books for Young Learners). (ENG.). 12p. (J). 5.75 net. *(978-1-57274-278-9(X))*, 2757, Bks. for Young Learners) Owen, Richard C. Pubs., Inc.
Steigvilas, Nemira. Mini Eva Lovvves Ballet. 2013. 44p. pap. 15.95 *(978-1-4525-7341-0(7))*, Balboa Pr.) Author Solutions, Inc.
Stein, Uriel Von. Gretta's & Graci's Bright, Bright, Moonlit Night. 2011. 24p. pap. 12.79 *(978-1-4634-0225-9(2))* AuthorHouse.
Stella M. Reese. The Princess of Topaz: An African American Saga. 2010. 20p. 13.95 *(978-1-4269-2432-3(1))* Trafford Publishing.
Stephenson, Kenniqueca. The Magical Land of Norms. 2010. 24p. pap. 12.99 *(978-1-4490-5146-4(4))* AuthorHouse.
Stern, A. J. Here Comes the... Trouble! Marts, Doreen Mulryan, illus. 2012. (Frankly, Frannie Ser.: 9). (ENG.). 128p. (J). (gr. 1-3). pap. 5.99 *(978-0-448-45752-9(0))*, Grosset & Dunlap) Penguin Young Readers Group.
Sternberg, Julie. Bedtime at Bessie & Lil's. Gudeon, Adam, illus. 2015. (ENG.). 32p. (J). (gr. -1-2). 16.95 *(978-1-59078-934-6(2))* Boyds Mills Pr.
Stevenson, Steve. The Curse of the Pharaoh. Turconi, Stefano, illus. 2013. (Agatha: Girl of Mystery Ser.: 1). (ENG.). 144p. (J). (gr. 2-5). pap. 6.99 *(978-0-448-46217-2(6))*, Grosset & Dunlap) Penguin Young Readers Group.
Stewart, Elizabeth. Blue Gold: A Novel. 2014. (ENG., Illus.). 304p. (YA). (gr. 7-12). 21.95 *(978-1-55451-635-3(8))*, 9781554516353) Annick Pr., Ltd. CAN. Dist: Publishers Group West (PGW).
Stewart, Jane L. The Camp Fire Girls at Long Lake. rev. ed. 2006. (ENG.). 140p. 25.95 *(978-1-4218-2057-6(9))*, 1st World Library - Literary Society) 1st World Publishing, Inc.
—The Camp Fire Girls at Long Lake or Bessie King in Summer Camp. 2004. reprint ed. pap. 15.95 *(978-1-4191-5574-1(1))*; pap. 1.99 *(978-1-4192-5574-8(6))* Kessinger Publishing, LLC.
—A Campfire Girl's Test of Friendship. 2004. reprint ed. pap. 26.95 *(978-1-4179-3874-2(9))* Kessinger Publishing, LLC.
Stewart, Vicky. Heide Loves to Cheer. 2012. 24p. pap. 17.99 *(978-1-62509-113-0(3))* Salem Author Services.
Stine, R. L. Dangerous Girls. 2004. (Dangerous Girls Ser.: 1). (ENG.). 320p. (YA). (gr. 8-18). pap. 6.99 *(978-0-06-053082-2(0))*, HarperTeen) HarperCollins Pubs.
—You Can't Scare Me! 2010. (Classic Goosebumps Ser.: 17). (ENG.). 160p. (J). (gr. 3-7). pap. 6.99 *(978-0-545-17796-2(0))*, Scholastic Paperbacks) Scholastic, Inc.
Stockdale, Stephanie. Sidney Visits Australi. 2009. 44p. pap. 18.99 *(978-1-4389-8698-2(X))* AuthorHouse.
Stokely, Ted. Yaya & Uncle Ted Go Walk! 2010. 20p. 11.99 *(978-1-4520-9198-3(6))* AuthorHouse.
Stokes, Paula. Girl Against the Universe. 2016. 400p. (YA). (gr. 8). 17.99 *(978-0-06-237996-2(8))*, HarperTeen) HarperCollins Pubs.
Stone, Laura. Little Lulu Learns a Lesson. 2010. 34p. pap. 16.95 *(978-0-557-33222-9(2))* Lulu Pr., Inc.
—Miss Clarissa & Her Musical Shoes. 2010. 32p. pap. 16.95 *(978-0-557-33226-7(5))* Lulu Pr., Inc.
The Story of Jacqueline. 2004. (Illus.). 36p. (J). per. 12.95 *(978-0-9762911-0-7(X))* Ameeramac Bks. Inc.
The Strange & Beautiful Sorrows of Ava Lavender. 2014. 320p. (J). (gr. 9). E-Book 8.99 *(978-0-7636-7034-4(0))* Candlewick Pr.
Strauss, Victoria. Color Song, 0 vols. 2014. (Passion Blue Novel Ser.: 2). (ENG.). 344p. (J). (gr. 7-9). pap. 9.99 *(978-1-4778-2504-4(5))*, 9781477825044, Skyscape) Amazon Publishing.
Stringham, Jean. Balance. 2011. 208p. (J). pap. 14.99 *(978-1-59955-518-8(2))*, Bonneville Bks.) Cedar Fort, Inc./CFI Distribution.
Strobel-Cort, Joanne. Emillee Kart & the Seven Saving Signs: The Tale of Beasley's Bonnet. 2007. 204p. per. 24.95 *(978-1-4241-8597-9(1))* America Star Bks.
Strohmeyer, Sarah. Smart Girls Get What They Want. 2013. (ENG.). 368p. (YA). (gr. 8). pap. 9.99 *(978-0-06-195341-5(5))* HarperCollins Pubs.
Strykowski, Marcia. Call Me Amy. 2013. (ENG.). 176p. (J). (gr. 3-10). 24.95 *(978-1-935462-76-7(8))*; pap. 14.95 *(978-1-935462-75-0(X))* Luminis Bks., Inc.
Suarez, Maribel, illus. Rebecca. (Rowing Frog's Rhymes Ser.). 16p. (J). (gr. k-3). 7.95 *(978-1-59437-840-9(1))* Santillana USA Publishing Co., Inc.
Sudderth, Jean. The Incredible Edible Girl & Friends. 2011. 24p. pap. 15.99 *(978-1-4415-7489-3(1))* Xlibris Corp.
Sugg, Zoe "Zoella". Girl Online. 2014. (ENG.). 352p. 17.99 *(978-1-4767-9745-8(5))*, Atria Bks.) Simon & Schuster.
Sullivan, Jenny. Magic Apostrophe. 2003. (ENG.). 216p. pap. 19.95 *(978-1-85902-116-3(6))* Beekman Bks., Inc.
Summers, Katani. Style in with Katani. 2004. (Illus.). 36p. (J). 3.99 *(978-0-9746587-3-5(1))*, Beacon Street Girls) B*tween Productions, Inc.
Sunderland, Margot & Hancock, Nicky. How Hattie Hated Kindness. Armstrong, Nicky, tr. Armstrong, Nicky, illus. 2017. (Helping Children with Feelings Ser.). (ENG.). 30p. (C). pap. 15.95 *(978-0-86388-461-0(X))*, Y328994, Routledge) Taylor & Francis Group GBR. Dist: Taylor & Francis Group.
Suneby, Elizabeth. Razia's Ray of Hope: One Girl's Dream of an Education. Verelst, Suana, illus. 2013. (CitizenKid Ser.). (ENG.). 32p. (J). (gr. 3-7). 18.95 *(978-1-55453-816-4(5))* Kids Can Pr., Ltd. CAN. Dist: Hachette Bk. Group.
Surget, Alain. Tirya y el Complot del Nilo. 2004.Tr. of Tirya & the Conspiracy in the Nile. (SPA.). 208p. (YA). 14.95 *(978-84-95618-50-4(8))*, Umbriel) Ediciones Urano S. A. ESP. Dist: Spanish Pubs., LLC.
Sutherland, Suzanne. When We Were Good, 1 vol. 2013. (ENG.). 240p. (YA). (gr. 9-12). pap. *(978-1-927513-11-8(1))*, Sumach Pr.) Canadian Scholars.
Sutton, Margaret. The Secret Quest: Judy Bolton. 2011. 182p. 42.95 *(978-1-258-10241-8(2))* Literary Licensing, LLC.
Swain, Gwenyth. I Wonder as I Wander. Himler, Ronald, illus. 2005. 32p. (J). (gr. k-3). pap. 8.00 *(978-0-8028-5298-4(X))*, Eerdmans Bks For Young Readers) Eerdmans, William B. Publishing Co.
Sweeney, Kathleen L. The Dream of a Little Farmer Girl. 2012. 24p. pap. 15.99 *(978-1-4653-7927-6(4))* Xlibris Corp.
Sweetser, Kate Dickinson. Boys & girls from Thackeray. l.t. ed. 2007. (ENG.). 264p. pap. 21.99 *(978-1-4264-3943-8(1))* Creative Media Partners, LLC.
Swensen, Karen, et al. Catherine the Great & Her Teatime Tagalongs, 1 vol. 2005. (ENG., Illus.). 32p. (J). (gr. k-3). 16.99 *(978-1-58980-343-5(4))* Pelican Publishing Co., Inc.
Sydor, Colleen. Smarty pants. Langlois, Suzane, illus. 2nd rev. ed. 2003. 32p. (J). (gr. 1-5). *(978-1-894222-62-4(8))* Lobster Pr.
Tabibi, Alexis Deeba. An Unusual World. 2011. 16p. pap. 8.32 *(978-1-4670-3798-3(2))* AuthorHouse.
Taborn, Deborah V. Donia & Her Marvelous Bag of Cents. 2011. 36p. pap. 16.99 *(978-1-4567-6934-5(0))* AuthorHouse.
Takahashi, Rumiko. Inuyasha Ani-Manga, Vol. 20. 2007. (Inuyasha Ser.: 20). (ENG., Illus.). 216p. pap. 11.99 *(978-1-4215-0904-4(0))* Viz Media.
Takemoto, Novala. Kamikaze Girls. Kanesata, Yukio, illus. 2006. (Kamikaze Girls Ser.). (ENG.). 208p. pap. 8.99 *(978-1-4215-0268-7(2))* Viz Media.
—Kamikaze Girls, Vol. 1. Wegmuller, Akemi, tr. from JPN. 2006. (Kamikaze Girls Ser.). (ENG.). 208p. (YA). (gr. 10). 17.99 *(978-1-4215-0269-4(0))* Viz Media.
Talley, Gigi T. Fairest Florabell. 2012. 34p. 24.95 *(978-1-4560-0628-0(2))* America Star Bks.
Tamaki, Mariko. This One Summer. Tamaki, Jillian, illus. 2014. (ENG.). 320p. (YA). (gr. 7). 21.99 *(978-1-62672-094-7(0))*, 9781626720947); pap. 18.99 *(978-1-59643-774-6(X))*, 9781596437746) Roaring Brook Pr. (First Second Bks.).
Tamang, Mayan, illus. Captain Remarkable; Girls can be Superheroes Too! 2009. 28p. (J). pap. 10.95 *(978-0-9823906-1-0(0))* Wiggles Pr.
Tan, Valerie Genevivie. Hello! I'm Sha Sha: Join Sha Sha in Her New School. 2009. (Illus.). 50p. (J). pap. 14.95 *(978-1-4327-4195-2(0))* Outskirts Pr., Inc.
Tarter, Mildred. Alexis Sets up Search Groups. 2013. 26p. pap. 16.49 *(978-1-4389-6881-0(7))* AuthorHouse.
Taylor-Bonds, Darlena. I Am Not Chocolate, It Melt's. 2008. 32p. pap. 10.00 *(978-0-557-01574-0(X))* Lulu Pr., Inc.
Taylor, R. W. The Curiosity of Sadie: A Collection of 35 Individual Stories about an Individual Little Girl & Her Puppy. 2011. 172p. (gr. 4-6). pap. 15.66 *(978-1-4567-8202-3(9))* AuthorHouse.
Taylor Sr., Anthony. I Pray. 2012. 20p. pap. 24.95 *(978-1-4626-8113-6(1))* America Star Bks.
Teacher Talk: Individual Title Six-Packs. (gr. -1-2). 27.00 *(978-0-7635-9477-0(6))* Rigby Education.
Telgemeier, Raina. Drama. 2012. lib. bdg. 22.10 *(978-0-606-26738-0(7))*, Turtleback) Turtleback Bks.
Terena Luvica Taff. Rising Sun. 2011. 40p. pap. 24.95 *(978-1-4560-2972-2(X))* America Star Bks.
Tewee, Laqaixit. Winterbloom & the Magical Swan: Book 1 Discovery of the Moon Treasure. 2012. 68p. pap. 31.99 *(978-1-4653-9933-5(X))* Xlibris Corp.
Tewkesbury, Alexa. Josie's Jazzy Journal. 2008. (ENG., Illus.). 128p. (J). *(978-1-85345-457-8(5))* Crusade for World Revival.
Thame, Val. Witches in Trouble. l.t. ed. 2006. 104p. per. *(978-1-905665-27-3(X))* Pollinger In Print.
This & That, 6 Packs. (gr. -1-2). 23.00 *(978-0-7635-8812-0(1))* Rigby Education.
Thomas, Cici. Give Me Some Sugar! 2011. 24p. pap. 12.50 *(978-1-4634-1316-3(5))* AuthorHouse.
Thomas, Laura Michelle. Polly Wants to Be a Writer - the Junior Authors Guide to Writing & Getting Published. 2013. 232p. pap. *(978-1-4602-2819-7(7))* FriesenPress.
Thompson, Jan & Sharpe, Jaime. Amara's Magical Playhouse: The Adventure Begins. 2010. 108p. pap. 37.99 *(978-1-4520-8284-4(7))* AuthorHouse.
Thompson, Lisa. The Goldfish Boy. 2017. (ENG.). 320p. (J). (gr. 3-7). 16.99 *(978-1-338-05392-0(2))*, Scholastic Pr.) Scholastic, Inc.
Thomson, Carly. Truth Seekers. 2013. 60p. pap. 9.99 *(978-1-62839-189-3(8))* Salem Author Services.
Thorp, Gloria J. & Ruotsala, Charity Aili. Anna's Hats: Anna has a hat for every Adventure. 2009. 40p. pap. 19.49 *(978-1-4389-8967-9(9))* AuthorHouse.
Thorpe, Kiki. The Never Girls Collection #2 (Disney: the Never Girls), 4 vols. Christy, Jana, illus. 2015. (ENG.). 512p. (J). (gr. 1-4). 23.96 *(978-0-7364-3462-1(3))*, RH/Disney) Random Hse. Children's Bks.
Thorpe, Kiki. The Never Girls Volume 3: Books 7-9 (Disney: the Never Girls) Christy, Jana, illus. 2017. (Never Girls Ser.). (ENG.). 384p. (J). (gr. 1-4). 15.99 ***(978-0-7364-3819-3(X))***, RH/Disney) Random Hse. Children's Bks.
Thurston, Alecia Frances. Shumalady's Butterfly Tree. 2010. 40p. pap. 18.49 *(978-1-4490-5609-4(1))* AuthorHouse.
Tiger Tales, ed. & compiled by. Stories for Girls. Tiger Tales, compiled by. 2015. (ENG.). 176p. (J). (gr. -1-3). 12.99 *(978-1-58925-536-4(4))* Tiger Tales.
Tillworth, Mary. Movie Night Magic! (Shimmer & Shine) Aikins, David, illus. 2016. (Step into Reading Ser.). (ENG.). 24p. (J). (gr. -1-1). 4.99 *(978-1-101-93704-4(1))*, Random Hse. Bks. for Young Readers) Random Hse. Children's Bks.
Ting, Mary. Three Best Friends: Fabulous Day, 1 vol. 2010. 48p. pap. 16.95 *(978-1-4489-4300-5(0))* America Star Bks.
Tinkler, David. Revenge of the Dinner Ladies. l.t. ed. 2005. (J). pap. *(978-0-7540-7804-3(3))*, CLP 185) AudioGo.
Tinti, Natalie. Magic in Us. the Power of Imagination: The Power of Imagination, bks. 1, vol. 2. T, N., illus. ed. 2013. (Sewing a Friendship Ser.). (ENG.). 116p. (J). pap. 12.95 *(978-0-9842625-3-3(9))* Tintinatie Publishing Hse.
Tisdell, Wendy & Takhar, Jodi. Angela Goes to Daycare. 14p. (J). (gr. -1-3). 19.95 *(978-1-886000-01-8(8))* Takhar's, Jodi Spilt Milk Collection.
Toliver, Wendy. Once upon a Time: Red's Untold Tale. 2015. (ENG., Illus.). 410p. (YA). (gr. 7-12). 16.99 *(978-1-4847-2746-1(0))* Hyperion Bks. for Children.
Tomasi, Joseph. Miss Wheezer Comes to Stay. 2006. 48p. pap. 16.95 *(978-1-4241-3703-9(9))* PublishAmerica, Inc.
Too Many Clothes: Individual Title Six-Packs. (Literatura 2000 Ser.). (gr. k-1). 28.00 *(978-0-7635-0068-9(2))* Rigby Education.

Torres, J. The Collected Alison Dare Little Miss Adventures. Bone, J., illus. 2005. (J). (gr. 4-7). pap. 19.95 *(978-1-4156-1359-7(1))* Oni Pr., Inc.
Townsend, Vanessa. What's in Molly's... . Bedroom? 2012. (Illus.). 24p. pap. 15.99 *(978-1-4797-3248-7(6))* Xlibris Corp.
Townsend, Wendy. Blue Iguana. 2014. 188p. 18.95 *(978-1-60898-157-1(6))* namelos llc.
Tracy, Kristen. Crimes of the Sarahs. 2014. (ENG., Illus.). 384p. (YA). (gr. 9). pap. 9.99 *(978-1-4424-8100-8(5),* Simon Pulse) Simon Pulse.
Traffic Jam: Individual Title Six-Packs. (gr. -1-2). 27.00 *(978-0-7635-9479-4(2))* Rigby Education.
Travitzky, Paul Joseph & Travitzky, Brianna Marie. Brianna Marie Wants to Be: A Cowgirl. 2009. 20p. pap. 11.95 *(978-1-4490-2110-8(7))* AuthorHouse.
Trayer, Edward H. Struggles of Felicity Brady: Articulus Quest. 2005. (YA). per. 14.95 *(978-1-59571-091-8(4))* Word Association Pubs.
Traylor, Marci. What Will I Be? 2008. 40p. pap. 19.50 *(978-1-4389-0247-0(6))* AuthorHouse.
Tremlin, Nathan, et al. Mookie: A Girl in Maximsubornia. Tremlin, Nathan & Chomiak, Joseph, illus. 2004. 48p. (J). (gr. 4-8). reprint ed. 18.00 *(978-0-7567-9081-3(6))* DIANE Publishing Co.
Tripp, Valerie. Brave Emily. England, Tamara, ed. Backes, Nick, illus. 2006. (ENG.). 96p. (J). (gr. 4-7). pap. 6.95 *(978-1-59369-210-0(2),* American Girl) American Girl Publishing, Inc.
—Very Funny, Elizabeth! England, Tamara, ed. Andreasen, Dan, illus. 2005. (ENG.). 96p. (gr. 3). pap. 6.95 *(978-1-59369-061-8(4),* American Girl) American Girl Publishing, Inc.
Trivas, Tracy. The Wish Stealers. 2011. (ENG.). 288p. (J). (gr. 3-7). pap. 7.99 *(978-1-4169-8726-0(6),* Aladdin) Simon & Schuster Children's Publishing.
Trombley, Cyndi. According to Abbey. 2005. (J). 22.00 *(978-1-59858-087-7(6));* (YA). per. 14.00 *(978-1-59858-014-3(0))* Dog Ear Publishing, LLC.
Troulis, Jennifer. Penelope & Prisilla & the Enchanted House of Whispers 2004. 240p. (YA). per. 13.95 *(978-0-9741805-5-7(6))* American LaserTechnic.
Troyer, Gloria Irene. Beatrice & the Snow People. 2013. 114p. pap. 14.95 *(978-1-62646-481-0(2))* Booklocker.com, Inc.
Tsukirino, Yumi. Stitch!, Vol. 2. 2017. (ENG.). 176p. (J). pap. 10.99 *(978-1-4278-5675-3(3),* 9781427856753) TOKYOPOP, Inc.
Tullgren, Tom. Journey to Imagiland. 2012. 320p. pap. 17.95 *(978-1-62141-272-4(5))* Booklocker.com, Inc.
Tuorto, Diana. Janie's New Legs. 2008. (ENG.). 48p. pap. 11.99 *(978-1-4196-9142-3(2))* CreateSpace Independent Publishing Platform.
Turley/Alber. And the Tide Comes In. 2012. (Long Term Ecological Research Ser.). (ENG., Illus.). 32p. (J). (gr. 3-7). 15.95 *(978-0-9817700-5-5(3))* Taylor Trade Publishing.
Turnbull, Samantha. Cruise Control: The Anti-Princess Club 5. Davis, Sarah, illus. 2017. (Anti-Princess Club Ser.: 5). (ENG.). 192p. (J). (gr. 2-4). pap. 9.99 ***(978-1-76029-188-4(9))*** Allen & Unwin AUS. Dist: Independent Pubs. Group.
Turner, Deirdre. Lilac Sky. 2005. 60p. pap. 16.95 *(978-1-4137-9316-1(9))* PublishAmerica, Inc.
Turtschaninoff, Maria. Maresi. 2017. (Red Abbey Chronicles Ser.). (ENG.). 256p. (J). (gr. 8-17). 17.95 *(978-1-4197-2269-1(7),* Amulet Bks.) Abrams, Inc.
Two Smart Cookies. 2005. 44p. (J). 3.99 *(978-0-9763213-5-4(1))* OHC Group LLC.
Tyler, Braxton. Chains of Whispers. 2012. 92p. pap. 34.64 *(978-1-4669-1271-7(5))* Trafford Publishing.
Tyler, Tanith. Aegis Rising. 2007. (Illus.). 179p. *(978-0-9800860-0-3(0))* TNT Publishing Co.
Universal. Agnes Loves Unicorns! 2017. (ENG., Illus.). 32p. (J). (gr. -1-3). 12.99 ***(978-0-316-50747-9(4))*** Little, Brown Bks. for Young Readers.
Unobagha, Uzo. Grandma, How Do You Say I Love You? Krassa, Victoria, illus. 2007. 28p. (J). 16.95 *(978-0-9773180-0-1(1))* Adonoke Inc.
Uram, Maggie. Good Night Good Knight. 2004. (Illus.). 39p. (J). per. *(978-1-932077-38-4(3))* Athena Pr.
USCCB Department of Justice, Peace, and Human Development. Drop by Drop. 2015. (ENG., Illus.). 40p. (J). (gr. 1-5). pap. 7.95 *(978-0-8294-4100-0(X))* Loyola Pr.
Uslan, Michael E. Chatterbox: The Bird Who Wore Glasses. Gurney, John Steven, illus. 2006. 34p. (J). *(978-0-9753843-2-9(5))* Egmont Bks., Ltd.
Vaizey, George de Horne. Etheldreda the Ready. Horrell, Charles, illus. 2007. 200p. per. *(978-1-4065-4688-0(7))* Dodo Pr.
—Tom & Some Other Girls. Tarrant, Percy, illus. 2007. 208p. per. *(978-1-4065-4698-9(4))* Dodo Pr.
Valente, Catherynne M. The Girl Who Circumnavigated Fairyland in a Ship of Her Own Making. Juan, Ana, illus. 2011. (Fairyland Ser.: 1). (ENG.). 256p. (YA). (gr. 5-9). 16.99 *(978-0-312-64961-6(4),* 9780312649616) Feiwel & Friends.
—The Girl Who Circumnavigated Fairyland in a Ship of Her Own Making. 2012. (CHI & ENG., Illus.). 304p. (J). (gr. 5-8). pap. *(978-986-6026-24-9(8))* Muses Publishing Hse.
—The Girl Who Circumnavigated Fairyland in a Ship of Her Own Making. Juan, Ana, illus. 2012. (Fairyland Ser.: 1). (ENG.). 288p. (YA). (gr. 5-9). pap. 7.99 *(978-1-250-01019-3(5),* 9781250010193) Square Fish.
—The Girl Who Fell Beneath Fairyland & Led the Revels There. Juan, Ana, illus. 2013. (Fairyland Ser.: 2). (ENG.). 304p. (YA). (gr. 5-9). pap. 7.99 *(978-1-250-03412-0(4),* 9781250034120) Square Fish.
Vallejo-Nagera, Alejandra. Los Bigotes de Chocolate. 2003.Tr. of Chocolate Mustache. (SPA., Illus.). 27p. (J). (gr. k-1). 8.95 *(978-968-19-1020-4(6))* Santillana USA Publishing Co., Inc.
Van Dusen, Chris. Hattie & Hudson. Van Dusen, Chris, illus. 2017. (ENG., Illus.). 40p. (J). (gr. -1-3). 16.99 *(978-0-7636-6545-6(2))* Candlewick Pr.
Van Dyne, Edith. Mary Louise. 2007. (ENG.). 148p. pap. 18.99 *(978-1-4264-1952-2(X));* 144p. pap. 19.99 *(978-1-4264-2063-4(3))* Creative Media Partners, LLC.
van Slyke, Lucille. Little Miss By-the-Day. 2007. 196p. per. *(978-1-4065-4735-1(2))* Dodo Pr.
Vandercook, Margaret. The Camp Fire Girls at Sunrise Hill. 2005. 26.95 *(978-1-4218-0977-9(X),* 1st World Library - Literary Society) 1st World Publishing, Inc.
—The Camp Fire Girls at Sunrise Hill. 2004. reprint ed. pap. 19.95 *(978-1-4191-5576-5(8));* pap. 1.99 *(978-1-4192-5576-2(2))* Kessinger Publishing, LLC.
—Camp Fire Girls at Sunrise Hill, the (Fi. 2006. pap. 55.99 *(978-1-4219-9140-5(3))* IndyPublish.com.
Verral, Charles Spain. Annie Oakley, Sharpshooter. Dreany, E. Joseph, illus. 2011. 28p. pap. 35.95 *(978-1-258-06762-5(5))* Literary Licensing, LLC.
Vestry, Annabelle. The Carlyles, Vol. 1. 2008. (Gossip Girl: the Carlyles Ser.: 1). (ENG.). 256p. (YA). (gr. 10-17). pap. 10.99 *(978-0-316-02064-0(8),* Poppy) Little, Brown Bks. for Young Readers.
Vickie A. Soman. The Sahara Desert Angel: Education & Nature Folktales 2. 2010. 208p. pap. 14.95 *(978-1-4502-1465-0(7))* iUniverse, Inc.
Vilcoq, Marianne. Espero un Hermanito. (SPA.). 24p. (J). *(978-84-8470-013-5(5))* Corimbo, Editorial S.L. ESP. Dist: Lectorum Pubns., Inc.
Vincent, Harris T. & Brewer, Mary. When Grandmother Was A Little Girl. 2010. 40p. 23.99 *(978-1-4520-7728-4(2))* AuthorHouse.
Vinsh, Aara J. Ben, the Miracle Horse, 1 vol. 2010. 193p. pap. 24.95 *(978-1-4489-7591-4(3))* America Star Bks.
Viorst, Judith. Earrings! Malone, Nola Langner, illus. 2010. (ENG.). 32p. (J). (gr. 1-5). 17.99 *(978-1-4424-1281-1(X),* Atheneum Bks. for Young Readers) Simon & Schuster Children's Publishing.
Vogl, Nancy & Strange, David. Grandma Loves Her Harley Too. Gibson, Nichoel, illus. 2006. (J). per. 16.95 *(978-0-9772771-1-7(9))* Cherry Tree Pr. LLC.
Voigt, Cynthia. Izzy, Willy-Nilly. unabr. ed. 2004. 280p. (J). (gr. 7-18). pap. 46.00 incl. audio *(978-0-8072-8763-7(6),* YA260SP, Listening Library) Random Hse. Audio Publishing Group.
Volk, Gretchen. The Amazing Adventures of Tristy Ruth, Raisin Girl. 2012. 258p. pap. *(978-1-105-51531-6(1))* Lulu.com.
Voss, Fonda. The Bossy Girl. l.t. ed. 2005. (Illus.). 30p. (J). 15.95 *(978-1-932338-44-7(6))* Lifevest Publishing, Inc.
Wales, Amy S. Fiona & the Fiddle Tree. 2012. 32p. pap. 21.99 *(978-1-4691-5485-5(4))* Xlibris Corp.
Walker, Landry Quinn. Supergirl Cosmic Adventures of the 8th Grade. 2016. (ENG., Illus.). 144p. (J). (gr. 4-7). pap. 12.99 *(978-1-4012-6320-1(8))* DC Comics.
Walker Perry, Kelley. Joy in the Darkness. 2008. pap. 13.50 *(978-0-615-20417-8(1))* Phoenix Publishing.
Wallace, Bonny. The Raymond Wikins' Adventures, Children of Straw. 2009. 70p. pap. 9.95 *(978-1-60860-699-3(6),* Eloquent Bks.) Strategic Book Publishing & Rights Agency (SBPRA).
Walsh, Suella. The Case of Erica's Weird Behavior. 79p. (J). (gr. 3-6). 9.99 *(978-0-88092-093-3(9))* Royal Fireworks Publishing Co.
Walter-Sereg, D. Bonnie Catches Lights in the Night Sky. 2013. 28p. 24.95 *(978-1-4137-9977-4(9))* America Star Bks.
—Bonnie, the Trapeze Artist. 2013. 30p. 24.95 *(978-1-4137-6032-3(5))* America Star Bks.
Walters, Eric. Elixir. 2006. (ENG.). 192p. (J). (gr. 3-7). 6.99 *(978-0-14-301641-0(5),* Puffin) Penguin Canada CAN. Dist: Penguin Random Hse. LLC.
—Prince for a Princess, 1 vol. Parkins, David, illus. 2012. (Orca Echoes Ser.). (ENG.). 64p. (J). (gr. 2-3). pap. 6.95 *(978-1-4598-0200-1(4))* Orca Bk. Pubs. USA.
—Skye Above, 1 vol. Parkins, David, illus. 2014. (Orca Echoes Ser.). (ENG.). 64p. (J). (gr. 2-3). pap. 6.95 *(978-1-4598-0701-3(4))* Orca Bk. Pubs. USA.
Walton, Leslye. The Strange & Beautiful Sorrows of Ava Lavender. (ENG.). 320p. (YA). (gr. 9). 2015. pap. 8.99 *(978-0-7636-8027-5(3))* 2014. 17.99 *(978-0-7636-6566-1(5))* Candlewick Pr.
—The Strange & Beautiful Sorrows of Ava Lavender. 2015. lib. bdg. 19.65 *(978-0-606-36879-7(5))* Turtleback Bks.
Walton, O. F. A Peep Behind the Scenes: A Little Girl's Journey of Discovery. 2015. (Classic Stories Ser.). (ENG.). 256p. (J). mass mkt. 8.99 *(978-1-85792-524-1(6),* 37143942-7c21-48e0-b651-a53c9e09b36c, Christian Heritage) Christian Focus Pubns. GBR. Dist: Bookmasters Distribution.
Warnus, Paul J. Sue's Zoo & the Magic Garden. 2012. pap. 11.95 *(978-0-7414-7200-7(7))* Infinity Publishing.
Warner, Sally. Hattie's Year. Date not set. 160p. (J). pap. 4.99 *(978-0-06-440793-9(4))* HarperCollins Pubs.
—Quinney Novel, 2. Date not set. 224p. (J). (gr. 3-7). 4.99 *(978-0-06-440763-2(2))* HarperCollins Pubs.
Warren, Jessica. Prime-Time Kid. 2013. 24p. pap. 12.99 *(978-1-4808-0142-4(9))* Archway Publishing.
Wash, Melissa. My Beautiful Girl Close Your Eyes. 2011. 28p. pap. 21.99 *(978-1-4628-5000-6(6))* Xlibris Corp.
Wasserman, Robin. Frozen. 2011. (Cold Awakening Ser.: 1). (ENG.). 384p. (YA). (gr. 9). pap. 12.99 *(978-1-4424-2038-0(3),* Simon Pulse) Simon Pulse.
—Life, Starring Me! 2009. (Candy Apple Ser.). 182p. (J). *(978-0-545-19777-9(5))* Scholastic, Inc.
Watase, Yuu. Fushigi Yûgi: Genbu Kaiden, Vol. 4. Watase, Yuu, illus. 2006. (ENG., Illus.). 208p. pap. 8.99 *(978-1-4215-0579-4(7))* Viz Media.
Watch Out, Sara! 2006. (J). *(978-1-933343-35-8(4),* PONY) Stabenfeldt Inc.
Waterton, Betty. Pettranella. Waterton, Betty & Blades, Ann, illus. 2003. (J). pap. 5.95 *(978-0-88899-108-9(8))* Groundwood Bks. CAN. Dist: Publishers Group West (PGW).
Watson, Lena. Noise in My Room: The Adventure of Jane Barnette, the Problem Solver. 2012. 32p. pap. 19.99 *(978-1-4685-8780-7(3))* AuthorHouse.
Watt, Fiona. That's Not My Baby (Girl) 2010. (Touchy Feely Board Book Ser.). 43p. (J). bds. 8.99 *(978-0-7945-2603-0(9),* Usborne) EDC Publishing.
Watts, Jeri. Kizzy Ann Stamps. 2013. (ENG., Illus.). 192p. (J). (gr. 4-7). pap. 5.99 *(978-0-7636-6976-8(8))* Candlewick Pr.
Watts, Leslie. Just Leah. 2013. 28p. 16.99 *(978-0-9894748-5-6(2))* Mindstir Media.
Weale, Andrew. Nora: The Girl Who Ate & Ate & Ate ... Cort, Ben, illus. 2012. (ENG.). 32p. (J). (gr. -1-k). pap. 13.99 *(978-1-84939-382-9(6))* Andersen Pr. GBR. Dist: Independent Pubs. Group.
Weaver, Lisa D. Praying with Our Feet. Hess, Ingrid, illus. 2005. 40p. (J). pap. 12.99 *(978-0-8361-9306-0(7))* Herald Pr.
Webster, Jean. Just Patty. 2011. 156p. 24.95 *(978-1-4638-9965-3(3));* pap. 12.95 *(978-1-60664-435-5(1))* Rodgers, Alan Bks.
Wedekind, Annie. A Horse of Her Own. 2009. (ENG.). 288p. (YA). (gr. 5-9). pap. 8.99 *(978-0-312-58146-6(7),* 9780312581466) Square Fish.
Weir, Jaime L. Out of Bed. 2008. 20p. pap. 24.95 *(978-1-60474-363-0(8))* America Star Bks.
Weis, Michael David. Diamond & the Fosters. Avant, Matthew, illus. 2013. 64p. 21.95 *(978-1-59663-635-4(1),* Castle Keep Pr.) Rock, James A. & Co. Pubs.
Welch, Teri. My New Dance. 2011. 20p. 10.99 *(978-1-4567-1514-4(3))* AuthorHouse.
Wells, Carolyn. Marjorie at Seacote. 2011. 296p. 48.95 *(978-1-258-08998-6(X))* Literary Licensing, LLC.
—Patty at Home. 2004. reprint ed. pap. 21.95 *(978-1-4191-4032-7(9));* pap. 1.99 *(978-1-4192-4032-4(3));* pap. 21.95 *(978-1-4191-4032-7(9))* Kessinger Publishing, LLC.
—Patty at Home. 2011. 182p. pap. 14.95 *(978-1-60664-589-5(7))* Rodgers, Alan Bks.
Wells, Rita. Janie Plants a Tree. 2013. 26p. pap. 16.95 *(978-1-4497-8903-9(X),* WestBow Pr.) Author Solutions, Inc.
Wells, Rosemary. Julieta, Estate Quieta! (SPA.). 43p. (J). 5.50 *(978-84-372-1523-5(4))* Santillana USA Publishing Co., Inc.
—Julieta, Estate Quieta! Wells, Rosemary, illus. 2003. (SPA., Illus.). 38p. (J). (gr. k-3). 5.95 *(978-0-88272-433-1(9))* Santillana USA Publishing Co., Inc.
Welshman, Kate. Anais Butt & the Hairy-Handed Gent. 2013. 164p. pap. 16.50 *(978-1-61213-187-0(5))* Writer's Coffee Shop, The.
West, Kathryn E. Garden of Roses. 2007. 328p. 29.95 *(978-0-595-70333-3(X));* per. 19.95 *(978-0-595-45295-8(7))* iUniverse, Inc.
Weyn, Suzanne. Daring to Dream. 2010. 163p. (J). *(978-0-545-23330-9(5))* Scholastic, Inc.
—The Titanic Locket. 2014. (Hauntings: the Haunted Museum Ser.: 1). lib. bdg. 17.20 *(978-0-606-35809-5(9))* Turtleback Bks.
Whamond, Dave. Oddrey. 2012. 32p. *(978-1-926973-52-4(6))* Owlkids Bks. Inc.
—Oddrey. 2017. (Oddrey Ser.: 1). (ENG., Illus.). 32p. (J). (gr. k-3). pap. 7.95 ***(978-1-77147-303-3(7))*** Owlkids Bks. Inc. CAN. Dist: Publishers Group West (PGW).
Whamond, Dave & Owlkids Books Inc. Staff. Oddrey. 2012. (Oddrey Ser.: 1). (ENG., Illus.). 32p. (J). (gr. k-3). 16.95 *(978-1-926973-45-6(3),* Owlkids) Owlkids Bks. Inc. CAN. Dist: Publishers Group West (PGW).
—Oddrey & the New Kid. 2013. (Oddrey Ser.: 2). (ENG., Illus.). 32p. (J). (gr. -1-3). 16.95 *(978-1-926973-90-6(9),* Owlkids) Owlkids Bks. Inc. CAN. Dist: Publishers Group West (PGW).
Whitaker, Joan. Cartwheeling. Cusack, Elizabeth, illus. 2013. 24p. 22.95 *(978-1-61493-189-8(5));* pap. 12.95 *(978-1-61493-188-1(7))* Peppertree Pr., The.
White, Melissa. Purple Frogs, Imagine High. 2009. 131p. pap. 13.24 *(978-0-557-02960-0(0))* Lulu Pr., Inc.
Whitehouse, Howard. The Strictest School in the World: Being the Tale of a Clever Girl, a Rubber Boy & a Collection of Flying Machines, Mostly Broken. Slavin, Bill, illus. 2006. (Mad Misadventures of Emmaline & Rubberbones Ser.). (ENG.). 256p. (J). (gr. 4-7). 16.95 *(978-1-55337-882-2(2))* Kids Can Pr., Ltd. CAN. Dist: Hachette Bk. Group.
Wick, Elaine. It's MY Future: Should I Be a Nurse Practitioner? Tremaine, Michele, illus. 2004. 64p. (J). lib. bdg. 12.95 *(978-0-9749769-0-7(3))* NAPNAP.
Wick, Kimberly. Katie's First Day of School: The Adventures of Mrs. Swirlie. 2009. 36p. pap. 15.49 *(978-1-4389-2257-7(4))* AuthorHouse.
Wiederblank. Save Our School. 2006. 144p. (J). 14.99 *(978-1-56871-392-2(4))* Targum Pr., Inc.
Wiersbitzky, Shannon. What Flowers Remember. 2014. 158p. (J). 18.95 *(978-1-60898-166-3(5))* namelos llc.
Wiggin, Kate Douglas. New Chronicles of Rebecca. 2007. 288p. (gr. 4-7). 35.00 *(978-1-4344-9021-6(1));* per. 19.95 *(978-1-4344-9020-9(3))* Wildside Pr., LLC.
—New Chronicles of Rebecca. 2006. 128p. pap. *(978-1-84637-648-1(3))* Echo Library.
—New Chronicles of Rebecca. 2004. reprint ed. pap. 28.95 *(978-1-4179-2096-9(3));* pap. 1.99 *(978-1-4179-9944-6(6));* pap. 15.95 *(978-1-4179-9994-1(2))* Kessinger Publishing, LLC.
—New Chronicles of Rebecca. 2006. (ENG.). 300p. per. 21.45 *(978-1-59462-367-7(8),* 403, Book Jungle) Standard Pubns., Inc.
—Rebecca of Sunnybrook Farm. 2013. 425p. reprint ed. lthr. 69.00 *(978-0-7426-1139-9(6))* Classic Bks.
Wilcox, Jean A. Diary of Sir Winston Loki, 1 vol. 2010. 34p. 24.95 *(978-1-4512-1813-8(3))* PublishAmerica, Inc.
Wilding, Valerie. The Grumpy Queen. Sanfilippo, Simona, illus. 2011. (ENG.). 32p. (J). (gr. -1-k). pap. *(978-1-84089-637-4(X))* Zero to Ten, Ltd.
Wiley, Melissa. Across the Puddingstone Dam. Andreasen, Dan, illus. 2004. (Little House Ser.: No. 4). 224p. (J). 16.99 *(978-0-06-027021-6(7))* HarperCollins Pubs.
Williams-Garcia, Rita. P. S. Be Eleven. 2013. 288p. (J). (gr. 3-7). lib. bdg. 17.89 *(978-0-06-193863-4(7),* Amistad) HarperCollins Pubs.
—P. S. Be Eleven. 2015. (J). lib. bdg. 17.20 *(978-0-606-36471-3(4))* Turtleback Bks.
Williams, Kelly Ann. Pye. 2010. 36p. pap. 11.50 *(978-1-4452-8438-5(3))* Lulu Pr., Inc.
Williams, Lori Aurelia. When Kambia Elaine Flew in from Neptune. unabr. ed. 2004. 246p. (J). (gr. 7-18). pap. 50.00 incl. audio *(978-0-8072-8851-1(9),* Listening Library) Random Hse. Audio Publishing Group.
Williams, Marilyn & Caspersen, Barbara. Peggy & Barbie on the Farm. 2013. 24p. pap. 24.95 *(978-1-63004-043-7(6))* America Star Bks.
Williams, Rozanne Lanczak. Emily Santos, Star of the Week. Burris, Priscilla, illus. 2006. (Learn to Write Ser.). 16p. (J). (gr. k-2). pap. 2.99 *(978-1-59198-298-2(7),* 6194) Creative Teaching Pr., Inc.
—Tess Builds a Snowman. Harris, Jenny B., illus. 2006. (Learn to Write Ser.). 8p. (J). (gr. k-2). pap. 3.49 *(978-1-59198-286-9(3),* 6180) Creative Teaching Pr., Inc.
Willner, Judy. How My Sun Got Its Smile: The Story of Deana Vega. 2010. 48p. pap. 20.99 *(978-1-4520-7720-8(7))* AuthorHouse.
Willow, Tirissa & the Necklace of Nulidor. 2009. 338p. pap. 17.95 *(978-1-4327-4013-9(X))* Outskirts Pr., Inc.
Wills, Morgan B. Mulright Island. 2004. (Illus.). 417p. (YA). per. 14.95 *(978-0-9762768-0-7(1))* Williams, Morgan.
Wilson, Debra. 65 Mustang: A Novel. 2011. 300p. pap. *(978-1-934922-47-7(1))* IBJ Custom Publishing.
Wilson, Elizabeth & de los Heros, Luis. Chifa Chi's Little Adventure in Cuzco & MacHu Picchu. 2012. 42p. pap. 21.99 *(978-1-105-20126-4(0))* Lulu Pr., Inc.
Wimberly, Nikisha. Hair Like That. Drewes, Dan, illus. 2010. 24p. 13.00 *(978-1-4520-0177-7(4))* AuthorHouse.
Winkler, Susan Elliott. Haylee & the Mud Puddle. 2013. 24p. pap. 24.95 *(978-1-4626-7862-4(9))* America Star Bks.
Wise, Rachel. Read All about It! 2012. (Dear Know-It-All Ser.: 1). (ENG.). 176p. (J). (gr. 3-7). 15.99 *(978-1-4424-5382-1(6));* pap. 5.99 *(978-1-4424-4402-7(9))* Simon Spotlight. (Simon Spotlight).
—Set the Record Straight! 2012. (Dear Know-It-All Ser.: 2). (ENG.). 160p. (J). (gr. 3-7). 15.99 *(978-1-4424-5383-8(4));* pap. 5.99 *(978-1-4424-4445-4(2))* Simon Spotlight. (Simon Spotlight).
Wittman, Patricia. Scrabble Creek. 2013. (ENG., Illus.). 32p. (J). (gr. -1-3). 16.99 *(978-1-4814-2145-4(X),* Simon & Schuster Bks. For Young Readers) Simon & Schuster Bks. For Young Readers.
Wiviott, Meg. Paper Hearts. 2016. (ENG.). 368p. (YA). (gr. 7). 22.10 *(978-0-606-39239-6(4))* Turtleback Bks.
Wood, Gail Ann. Lizzie & the Prairie Fire: Girl Pioneer in the American Midwest. 2006. (American Frontier Story Ser.). (Illus.). 115p. (YA). (gr. 8-12). per. 7.95 *(978-1-57249-381-0(X),* White Mane Kids) White Mane Publishing Co., Inc.
Wood Jr, Richard L. The Stick Family. 2011. 28p. pap. 15.00 *(978-1-4634-2564-7(3))* AuthorHouse.
Wood, Maryrose. What I Wore to Save the World. 2009. (ENG.). 288p. (YA). (gr. 9). pap. 9.99 *(978-0-425-22967-5(X),* Berkley) Penguin Publishing Group.
—Why I Let My Hair Grow Out. 2007. (ENG.). 224p. (YA). (gr. 9). 11.00 *(978-0-425-21380-3(3),* Berkley) Penguin Publishing Group.
Woodbury. Where in the World is Jenny Parker. (J). 6.95 *(978-0-88894-813-7(1))* Da Capo Pr., Inc.
Wooden, Thomas James, Jr. Four-Hundred Meter Champion. Winston, Dennis, illus. 2003. 103p. (J). mass mkt. 12.00 *(978-0-9740195-0-5(X))* New Castle Publishing Co.
Woollvin, Bethan. Little Red, 1 vol. Woollvin, Bethan, illus. 2016. (ENG., Illus.). 32p. (J). (gr. k-4). 16.95 *(978-1-56145-917-9(8))* Peachtree Pubs.
Worley, Roger A. 14 Wishes, 1 vol. 2009. 164p. pap. 24.95 *(978-1-61582-419-9(7))* America Star Bks.
Wormell, Chris. The Wild Girl. Wormell, Chris, illus. 2006. (Illus.). 32p. (J). (gr. -1). 17.00 *(978-0-8028-5311-0(0),* Eerdmans Bks For Young Readers) Eerdmans, William B. Publishing Co.
Wreggelsworth, Irene. Liv's Search for the Last Unicorn. Anderson, Anya, illus. 2011. (ENG.). 112p. pap. 26.99 *(978-1-4538-9270-1(2))* CreateSpace Independent Publishing Platform.
Wright, Lanikka. The Fab Four 2: Eva's Obsession. 2012. (ENG.). 244p. pap. 13.95 *(978-1-4327-9846-8(4))* Outskirts Pr., Inc.
Wright, Olivia. Malarie Jane Learns to Help. 2010. 36p. pap. 20.00 *(978-0-557-23776-0(9))* Lulu Pr., Inc.
Ye, Ting-Xing. White Lily. 2003. (ENG.). 64p. (J). (gr. 2-5). 4.99 *(978-0-7704-2931-7(9),* Seal Bks.) Penguin Random House Canada Young Readers CAN. Dist: Penguin Random Hse. LLC.
Yep, Laurence. Bravo, Mia! England, Tamara, ed. Papp, Robert, illus. 2008. (ENG.). 136p. (J). (gr. 3). pap. 6.95 *(978-1-59369-410-4(5))* American Girl Publishing, Inc.
—Mia, Bk. 1. England, Tamara, ed. Papp, Robert, illus. 2008. (ENG.). 136p. (gr. 3-18). pap. 6.95 *(978-1-59369-409-8(1))* American Girl Publishing, Inc.
Yolen, Jane. Sister Bear: A Norse Tale, 0 vols. Linda, Graves & Graves, Linda, illus. 2011. (ENG.). 32p. (J). (gr. k-3). 17.99 *(978-0-7614-5958-3(8),* 9780761459583, Amazon Children's Publishing) Amazon Publishing.
Yolen, Jane & Stemple, Heidi E. Y. Not All Princesses Dress in Pink. Lanquetin, Anne-Sophie, illus. 2010. (ENG.). 32p. (J). (gr. -1-3). 17.99 *(978-1-4169-8018-6(0),* Simon & Schuster Bks. For Young Readers) Simon & Schuster Bks. For Young Readers.
Young, Samantha. I Can't Wait. 2012. 12p. pap. 15.99 *(978-1-4772-6013-5(7))* AuthorHouse.
Yoxen, Jackie. Hannah's Sunday Hats. Francis, Lauren, illus. l.t. ed. 2006. 32p. (J). 19.95 *(978-1-59879-184-6(2))* Lifevest Publishing, Inc.
Yurksaitis, Anne. The Ingle Bingle. Yurksaitis, Stephanie, illus. 2012. 16p. pap. 24.95 *(978-1-4626-7687-3(1))* America Star Bks.
Zabel, Alanna. The Seven Doors. 2006. 59p. pap. 18.50 *(978-1-4116-4369-7(0))* Lulu Pr., Inc.
Zadunajsky, Donna M. Tayla Takes a Trip. Bicking, Judith, illus. 2013. (ENG.). 40p. pap. 9.99 *(978-1-938037-36-8(7))* Zadunajsky, Donna M.
—Tayla's Day at the Beach. Bicking, Judith, illus. 2013. (ENG.). 26p. pap. 6.99 *(978-1-938037-34-4(0))* Zadunajsky, Donna M.
Zakatchenko, Lilian. Girls from Brazil, 1 vol. 2010. 16p. 24.95 *(978-1-4489-3834-6(1))* PublishAmerica, Inc.
Zappa, Shana Muldoon & Zappa, Ahmet. Star Darlings Clover's Parent Fix. Disney Storybook Art Team, illus. 2016. (Star Darlings Ser.: 11). (ENG.). 176p. (J). (gr. 3-7). pap. 6.99 *(978-1-4847-1430-0(X))* Disney Pr.
Zdunich, Terrance. The Molting: Issue #1 Guilty Susie. 2009. pap. 7.99 *(978-1-61623-120-0(3))* Independent Pub.
Zeigler, Robbie. Down by the Se. 2011. 16p. pap. 13.99 *(978-1-4634-2056-7(0))* AuthorHouse.
Zendrera, Concepcion. Yaci y Su Muneca. (SPA.). 16p. (J). 9.95 *(978-84-261-5604-4(5),* JV3576) Juventud, Editorial ESP. Dist: AIMS International Bks., Inc., Lectorum Pubns., Inc.
Zerza, Safoora Z. Sophia V. Is Flower Girl. 2012. 24p. pap. 17.99 *(978-1-4685-5136-5(1))* AuthorHouse.

Zhang, Kat. Echoes of US. 2014. (Hybrid Chronicles Ser.: 3). (ENG.). 368p. (YA). (gr. 8). 17.99 *(978-0-06-211493-8(X))* HarperCollins Pubs.

Ziegesar, Cecily von. Adored. 2009. (It Girl Ser.: 8). (ENG.). 240p. (YA). (gr. 10-17). pap. 9.99 *(978-0-316-02509-6(7),* Tingley, Megan Bks.) Little, Brown Bks. for Young Readers.

—I Will Always Love You. 2010. (Gossip Girl Ser.: 12). (ENG.). 400p. (YA). (gr. 10-17). pap. 10.99 *(978-0-316-04359-5(1),* Poppy) Little, Brown Bks. for Young Readers.

Ziegesar, Cecily von, creator. Don't You Forget about Me. 2007. (Gossip Girl Ser.: 11). (ENG.). 304p. (YA). (gr. 10-17). per. 10.99 *(978-0-316-01184-6(3),* Poppy) Little, Brown Bks. for Young Readers.

Ziegler, Jennifer. Revenge of the Flower Girls. 2014. (ENG.). 240p. (J). (gr. 3-7). 16.99 *(978-0-545-56141-9(8),* Scholastic Pr.) Scholastic, Inc.

Zirkind, Chaya Sara. Bas Mitzvah X 3. 2008. 156p. (J). *(978-1-56871-448-6(3))* Targum Pr., Inc.

Zoboi, Ibi. American Street. 2017. 336p. (YA). (gr. 9). 17.99 *(978-0-06-247304-2(2))* HarperCollins Pubs.

Zuckerberg, Randi. Dot. Berger, Joe, illus. 2013. (ENG.). 32p. (J). (gr. -1-3). 17.99 *(978-0-06-228751-9(6))* HarperCollins Pubs.

Zusak, Markus. Underdogs. 2011. (ENG.). 512p. (J). (gr. 7-5). 19.99 *(978-0-545-35442-4(0),* Levine, Arthur A. Bks.) Scholastic, Inc.

GIRLS—POETRY

Block, Francesca Lia. How to (Un)Cage a Girl. 2008. 128p. (J). (gr. 9-18). lib. bdg. 16.89 *(978-0-06-135837-1(1),* Cotler, Joanna Books) HarperCollins Pubs.

Harjo, Joy. For a Girl Becoming. McDonald, Mercedes, illus. 2009. (Sun Tracks Ser.: 66). (ENG.). 36p. (gr. -1). 17.95 *(978-0-8165-2797-7(0))* University of Arizona Pr.

Kearney, Meg. The Secret of Me. 2007. (ENG.). 144p. (YA). (gr. 9-17). per. 13.95 *(978-0-89255-336-5(7),* 255336) Persea Bks., Inc.

Nye, Naomi Shihab. A Maze Me: Poems for Girls. Maher, Terre, illus. (ENG.). 128p. (YA). (gr. 8). 2014. pap. 8.99 *(978-0-06-058191-6(3))* 2005. 17.99 *(978-0-06-058189-3(1))* HarperCollins Pubs. (Greenwillow Bks.).

Richards, Beah E. Keep Climbing, Girls. Christie, R. Gregory, illus. 2006. (ENG.). 32p. (J). (gr. -1-3). 18.99 *(978-1-4169-0264-5(3),* Simon & Schuster Bks. For Young Readers) Simon & Schuster Bks. For Young Readers.

Yeagle, Gary. Angels Footprints. 2007. per. 24.95 *(978-1-59633-011-5(2))* Goose Creek Pubs., Inc.

GIRLS' CLUBS—FICTION

Alcott, Louisa May. A Garland for Girls. 2007. (ENG.). 182p. pap. 19.99 *(978-1-4264-2791-6(3));* 198p. pap. 21.99 *(978-1-4264-2829-6(4))* Creative Media Partners, LLC.

—A Garland for Girls. 2006. 300p. pap. 19.95 *(978-1-59462-405-6(4),* 441, Book Jungle) Standard Pubns., Inc.

Benson, Donna. Dog Gone Drama, the Cupcakes Club #2. 2008. 130p. (J). pap. 7.95 *(978-0-9799159-1-8(0))* Pink Lemonade, LLC.

—Spotlight on the Cupcakes: The Cupcakes Club #3. 2008. (ENG.). 115p. (J). pap. 7.95 *(978-0-9799159-2-5(9))* Pink Lemonade, LLC.

French, Vivian. The Tiara Club at Ruby Mansions No. 5: Princess Lauren & the Diamond Necklace. 2008. (Tiara Club Ser.). (ENG., Illus.). 80p. (J). (gr. 1-4). pap. 3.99 *(978-0-06-143488-4(4),* Tegen, Katherine Bks) HarperCollins Pubs.

Lewis, Linda. We Hate Everything but Boys. 2008. (ENG.). 160p. (YA). (gr. 7). pap. 8.95 *(978-1-4169-7537-3(3),* Simon Pulse) Simon Pulse.

Martin, Ann M. & Martin Ann, M. Claudia & Mean Janine. Telgemeier, Raina, illus. 2016. (Baby-Sitters Club Graphix Ser.: 4). (ENG.). 176p. (J). (gr. 3-7). lib. bdg. 22.10 *(978-0-606-38056-0(6))* Turtleback Bks.

Perry, Chrissie. The Secret Club. Oswald, Ash, illus. 2007. (Go Girl! Ser.: 7). (ENG.). 96p. (Orig.). (J). (gr. 2-4). per. 5.99 *(978-0-312-34652-2(2),* 9780312346522) Square Fish.

Polak, Monique. Forensics Squad Unleashed, 1 vol. 2016. (ENG.). 208p. (J). (gr. 3-6). pap. 9.95 *(978-1-4598-0979-6(3))* Orca Bk. Pubs. USA.

Price, Roger & Stern, Leonard, creators. Totally Pink Mad Libs. 2010. (Mad Libs Ser.). (ENG.). 48p. (J). (gr. 3-7). 4.99 *(978-0-8431-9898-0(2),* Mad Libs) Penguin Young Readers Group.

GLACIAL EPOCH

Donnelly, Karen. Ice Ages of the Past & the Future. 2009. (Earth's Changing Weather & Climate Ser.). 24p. (gr. 4-4). 42.50 *(978-1-61512-248-6(6),* PowerKids Pr.) Rosen Publishing Group, Inc., The.

Donnelly, Karen J. Ice Ages of the Past & the Future. 2003. (Earth's Changing Weather & Climate Ser.). (Illus.). 24p. (J). lib. bdg. 22.60 *(978-0-8239-6219-8(9),* PowerKids Pr.) Rosen Publishing Group, Inc., The.

Ferrett, Russell. Ice Ages: When the World Chills Out. 2010. (ENG., Illus.). 48p. 14.95 *(978-1-921073-56-4(X))* New Holland Pubs. Pty, Ltd. AUS. Dist: Midpoint Trade Bks., Inc.

George, Joshua. Ice Age. Myer, Ed, illus. 2016. (Sticker History Ser.). (ENG.). 38p. (J). (gr. 2-6). pap. 8.99 *(978-1-78445-860-7(0))* Top That! Publishing PLC GBR. Dist: Independent Pubs. Group.

Medina, Nicolas David. What Was the Ice Age? 2017. (What Was... ? Ser.). lib. bdg. 16.00 ***(978-0-606-40502-7(X))*** Turtleback Bks.

Meierhenry, Mark V. & Volk, David. The Mystery of the Round Rocks. Folkerts, Jason, illus. 2007. 44p. (J). (gr. 2-5). pap. 13.95 *(978-0-9777955-3-6(5),* South Dakota State Historical Society Pr.) South Dakota State Historical Society Pr.

Nemeth, Jason D. Ice Ages. 2012. (Our Changing Earth Ser.). (ENG., Illus.). 24p. (J). (gr. 3-6). pap. 8.25 *(978-1-4488-6292-4(2),* PowerKids Pr.); lib. bdg. 22.60 *(978-1-4488-6167-5(5))* Rosen Publishing Group, Inc., The.

Oard, Beverly & Oard, Michael. What Ever Happened to the Wooly Mammoth: Life at the End of the Great Ice Age. Looney, Bill, illus. 2007. 72p. (J). 15.99 *(978-0-89051-508-2(5))* Master Bks.

Osborne, Mary Pope & Boyce, Natalie Pope. Sabertooths & the Ice Age: A Nonfiction Companion to Sunset of the Sabertooth. Murdocca, Sal, illus. 2005. (Magic Tree House - Fact Tracker Ser.: 12). (ENG.). 128p. (J). (gr. 2-5). 6.99 *(978-0-375-82380-0(8),* Random Hse. Bks. for Young Readers) Random Hse. Children's Bks.

Parker, Steve. Ice Age Giants. 2011. (ENG., Illus.). 32p. (J). pap. 10.95 *(978-1-77092-012-5(9))* Saunders Bk. Co. CAN. Dist: RiverStream Publishing.

Spilsbury, Louise. Ice Age Animals. 2010. (Big Picture: Climate Ser.). (ENG.). 24p. (gr. 1-2). pap. 41.70 *(978-1-4296-5823-2(1),* First Facts) Capstone Press of Coughlan Cos.

Stein, Paul. Ice Ages of the Future. 2009. (Library of Future Weather & Climate Ser.). 64p. (gr. 5-5). 58.50 *(978-1-60853-647-4(5))* Rosen Publishing Group, Inc., The.

Worth, Bonnie. Once upon a Mastodon: All about Prehistoric Mammals. 2014. (Cat in the Hat's Learning Library). (ENG., Illus.). 48p. (J). (gr. k-3). 9.99 *(978-0-375-87075-0(X),* Random Hse. Bks. for Young Readers) Random Hse. Children's Bks.

GLACIAL EPOCH—FICTION

Bright, J. E. Best Friends - Continental Drift. 2012. (I Can Read Level 2 Ser.). (ENG.). 32p. (J). (gr. k-3). pap. 3.99 *(978-0-06-210483-0(7))* HarperCollins Pubs.

—Continental Drift: Manny's Big Adventure. 2012. (I Can Read Level 2 Ser.). (ENG.). 32p. (J). (gr. k-3). pap. 3.99 *(978-0-06-210481-6(0))* HarperCollins Pubs.

Gabriel, Andrea. Wandering Woolly, 1 vol. 2015. (ENG., Illus.). 32p. (J). (gr. 1-4). 17.95 *(978-1-62855-558-5(0))* Arbordale Publishing.

Greenburg, J. C. In the Ice Age. Gerardi, Jan, illus. 2005. (Andrew Lost Ser.: 12). (ENG.). 96p. (J). (gr. 1-4). 3.99 *(978-0-375-82952-9(0),* Random Hse. Bks. for Young Readers) Random Hse. Children's Bks.

Kirby, Matthew J. The Arctic Code. 2015. (Dark Gravity Sequence Ser.: 1). (ENG.). 336p. (J). (gr. 3-7). 16.99 *(978-0-06-222487-3(5))* HarperCollins Pubs.

Layton, Neal. Hot Hot Hot. Layton, Neal, illus. 2004. (ENG., Illus.). 32p. (J). (gr. -1-3). 15.99 *(978-0-7636-2148-3(X))* Candlewick Pr.

little bee books, little bee, et al. Ice Age - Collision Course. 2016. (Ice Age: Collision Course Ser.). (ENG., Illus.). 144p. (J). (gr. 2-5). pap. 6.99 *(978-1-4998-0309-9(5))* Little Bee Books Inc.

Mayer, Kirsten. The Pack Is Back! 2012. (Ice Age Ser.). (ENG.). 24p. (J). (gr. -1-3). pap. 3.99 *(978-0-06-210479-3(9),* HarperFestival) HarperCollins Pubs.

Russell, Jesse & Cohn, Ronald, eds. Ice Age: Continental Drift. 2012. 158p. pap. *(978-5-512-74544-1(1))* Books on Demand.

Weston, Martha. Dr. Clock-Sicle: A Holiday House Reader, Level 1. (ENG., Illus.). 32p. (J). (gr. k-3). tchr. ed. 14.95 *(978-0-8234-1825-1(1))* Holiday Hse., Inc.

Zeltser, David. Blast from the North. 2016. (Lug Ser.: 2). (ENG., Illus.). 160p. (gr. 3-6). 15.99 *(978-1-5124-0641-2(4));* 31.99 *(978-1-5124-0890-4(5))* Lerner Publishing Group. (Carolrhoda Bks.).

—Lug, Dawn of the Ice Age, No. 1. 2014. (ENG., Illus.). 182p. (J). (gr. 3-7). 15.99 *(978-1-60684-513-4(6),* Carolrhoda Bks.) Lerner Publishing Group.

GLACIER NATIONAL PARK (MONT.)

Aretha, David. Glacier National Park: Adventure, Explore, Discover. 2009. (America's National Parks Ser.). (Illus.). 128p. (J). (gr. 5-9). lib. bdg. 34.60 *(978-1-59845-088-0(3))* Enslow Pubs., Inc.

Christian, Peggy. Chocolate, a Glacier Grizzly. Cottone-Kolthoff, Carol, illus. (Humane Society of the United States Animal Tales Ser.). 32p. (J). (gr. 1-5). 34.95 incl. audio *(978-1-882728-64-0(5));* pap. 9.95 incl. audio *(978-1-882728-67-1(X));* pap. 19.95 incl. audio *(978-1-882728-69-5(6))* Benefactory, Inc., The.

Glastetter, KC & Hollman, Jeremie. Glacier National Park: An ABC Adventure. 2008. (J). pap. *(978-0-87842-552-5(7))* Mountain Pr. Publishing Co., Inc.

Leftridge, Alan. Going to Glacier National Park. 2006. (Illus.). 48p. (J). (gr. 4-7). pap. 12.95 *(978-1-56037-340-7(7))* Farcountry Pr.

Love, Donna. Totally Out There Gd Glacier Natl Park. Mihran, Turley Joyce, illus. 2010. 0096p. (J). pap. 15.00 *(978-0-87842-566-2(7))* Mountain Pr. Publishing Co., Inc.

Robinson, Gary D. Who Pooped in the Park: Glacier. 2004. (Illus.). 48p. (J). pap. 11.95 *(978-1-56037-279-0(6))* Farcountry Pr.

Wade, Linda R. & Hamilton, John. Glacier National Park, 1 vol. 2005. (National Parks Ser.). (ENG., Illus.). 32p. (gr. 3-8). 27.07 *(978-1-59197-425-3(9),* Abdo & Daughters) ABDO Publishing Co.

GLACIER NATIONAL PARK (MONT.)—FICTION

Skurzynski, Gloria & Ferguson, Alane. The Hunted. 2007. (Mysteries in Our National Park Ser.). (ENG., Illus.). 160p. (J). (gr. 3-7). per. 4.99 *(978-1-4263-0095-0(6),* National Geographic Children's Bks.) National Geographic Society.

Thomson, Sarah L. The Eagle's Quill. 2017. (Secrets of the Seven Ser.). (ENG.). 224p. (J). 16.99 *(978-1-61963-733-7(2),* 9781619637337, Bloomsbury USA Childrens) Bloomsbury Publishing USA.

GLACIERS

Allen, Patrick. A Look at Glaciers. 2009. (Real Life Readers Ser.). 32p. (gr. 4-5). (Illus.). (J). pap. 10.00 *(978-1-4358-0147-9(4),* Rosen Classroom); 47.90 *(978-1-60853-032-8(9),* PowerKids Pr.) Rosen Publishing Group, Inc., The.

Allen, Patrick D. A Look at Glaciers. 2009. (Science Kaleidoscope Ser.). (J). lib. bdg. 25.25 *(978-1-4358-2982-4(4),* PowerKids Pr.) Rosen Publishing Group, Inc., The.

Benchmark Education Company. Glaciers (Teacher Guide) 2005. *(978-1-4108-4655-6(5))* Benchmark Education Co.

Bethune, Helen. Why Do Glaciers Grind? 2010. (Solving Science Mysteries Ser.). (Illus.). 24p. (YA). (gr. 3-6). lib. bdg. 22.60 *(978-1-4488-0391-0(8))* Rosen Publishing Group, Inc., The.

Bodden, Valerie. Glaciers. 2006. (Our World Ser.). (Illus.). 24p. (J). (gr. -1-3). lib. bdg. 16.95 *(978-1-58341-462-0(2),* Creative Education) Creative Co., The.

Brannon, Barbara. Discover Glaciers. 2005. (J). pap. *(978-1-4108-5134-5(6))* Benchmark Education Co.

Coupe, Robert. Vanishing Ice. 2012. (Discovery Education: the Environment Ser.). (ENG., Illus.). 32p. (J). (gr. 3-6). pap. 10.00 *(978-1-4488-7980-9(9));* lib. bdg. 25.25 *(978-1-4488-7892-5(6))* Rosen Publishing Group, Inc., The. (PowerKids Pr.).

Espejo, Roman. Can Glacier & Icemelt Be Reversed? Greenhaven Press Editors, ed. 2014. (At Issue Ser.). (ENG.). 128p. (gr. 10-12). pap. 27.80 *(978-0-7377-6827-5(4),* Greenhaven Pr., Inc.) Cengage Gale.

—Can Glacier & Icemelt Be Reversed? Greenhaven Press Editors & Gale Editors, eds. 2014. (At Issue Ser.). (ENG.). 128p. (gr. 10-12). lib. bdg. 39.40 *(978-0-7377-6826-8(6),* Greenhaven Pr., Inc.) Cengage Gale.

Hand, Carol. The Creation of Glaciers. 2009. (J). 77.70 *(978-1-4358-5595-3(7),* Rosen Reference); (ENG.). 64p. (YA). pap. 12.95 *(978-1-4358-5594-6(9),* Rosen Reference); (ENG., Illus.). 64p. (YA). (gr. 5-9). lib. bdg. 31.95 *(978-1-4358-5298-3(2))* Rosen Publishing Group, Inc., The.

Harrison, David L. Glaciers: Nature's Icy Caps. Nathan, Cheryl, illus. 2006. (Earth Works). (ENG.). 32p. (J). (gr. 1-3). 15.95 *(978-1-59078-372-6(7))* Boyds Mills Pr.

Hocker, Katherine M. Frozen in Motion: Alaska's Glaciers. Brubaker, Jill, ed. Lepley, Kathy, illus. 2006. 54p. (J). spiral bd. 8.95 *(978-0-930931-76-6(9))* Alaska Geographic Assn.

Hotchkins, Dewayne. All about Glaciers. 2016. (Rosen REAL Readers: STEM & STEAM Collection). 12p. (gr. 1-k). pap. 6.33 *(978-1-5081-2467-2(1),* Rosen Classroom) Rosen Publishing Group, Inc., The.

Johnson, Rebecca L. & National Geographic Learning Staff. Surviving Volcanoes & Glaciers. 2007. (Reading Expeditions Ser.). (ENG., Illus.). 32p. (J). pap. 17.95 *(978-0-7922-8448-2(8))* CENGAGE Learning.

Kenney, Karen Latchana. The Science of Glaciers: How Temperature Works, 1 vol. 2016. (Science in Action Ser.). (ENG., Illus.). 32p. (J). (gr. 3-6). 27.07 *(978-1-62403-961-4(8))* ABDO Publishing Co.

Leathers, Dan. The Snows of Kilimanjaro. 2007. (On the Verge of Extinction Ser.). (Illus.). 32p. (YA). (gr. 2-5). lib. bdg. 25.70 *(978-1-58415-584-3(1))* Mitchell Lane Pubs., Inc.

Lindeen, Mary & Sexton, Colleen. Glaciers. 2007. (Learning about the Earth Ser.). (ENG., Illus.). 24p. (J). (gr. k-3). lib. bdg. 25.95 *(978-1-60014-113-3(7))* Bellwether Media.

Love, Donna. The Glaciers Are Melting!, 1 vol. Bersani, Shennen, illus. 2011. (ENG.). 32p. (J). (gr. -1-4). 16.95 *(978-1-60718-126-2(6));* pap. 8.95 *(978-1-60718-136-1(3))* Arbordale Publishing.

Mattern, Joanne. Antarctica: World's Biggest Glacier. 2009. (Nature's Greatest Hits Ser.). 24p. (gr. 2-2). 42.50 *(978-1-61514-838-7(8),* PowerKids Pr.) Rosen Publishing Group, Inc., The.

—Antartida: El glaciar más grande del mundo (Antarctica: World's Biggest Glacier) 2009. (Maravillas naturales (Natures Greatest Hits) Ser.). 24p. (gr. 2-2). 42.50 *(978-1-61514-360-3(2),* Editorial Buenas Letras) Rosen Publishing Group, Inc., The.

Mis, Melody S. Exploring Glaciers. 2009. (Geography Zone: Landforms Ser.). (Illus.). 24p. (J). (gr. 2-4). pap. 8.25 *(978-1-4358-3112-4(8));* 24p. (gr. 2-3). 42.50 *(978-1-61512-698-9(8));* (J). lib. bdg. 22.60 *(978-1-4358-2714-1(7))* Rosen Publishing Group, Inc., The. (PowerKids Pr.).

Nadeau, Isaac. Glaciers. 2006. (Library of Landforms Ser.). (Illus.). 24p. (J). (gr. 3-7). lib. bdg. 22.60 *(978-1-4042-3124-5(2),* PowerKids Pr.) Rosen Publishing Group, Inc., The.

—Water in Glaciers. (Water Cycle Ser.). 24p. 2009. (gr. 4-4). 42.50 *(978-1-60854-268-0(8))* 2003. (Illus.). (J). lib. bdg. 22.60 *(978-0-8239-6265-5(2))* Rosen Publishing Group, Inc., The. (PowerKids Pr.).

Osborne, Mary Pope & Boyce, Natalie Pope. Sabertooths & the Ice Age: A Nonfiction Companion to Sunset of the Sabertooth. Murdocca, Sal, illus. 2005. (Magic Tree House - Fact Tracker Ser.: 12). (ENG.). 128p. (J). (gr. 2-5). 6.99 *(978-0-375-82380-0(8),* Random Hse. Bks. for Young Readers) Random Hse. Children's Bks.

Prokos, Anna. Ice Queen: Exploring Icebergs & Glaciers. Tablason, Jamie, illus. 2017. (Imagine That! Ser.). (ENG.). 32p. (J). (gr. 2-4). lib. bdg. 26.65 *(978-1-63440-149-4(2));* 39.99 ***(978-1-63440-161-6(1))*** Red Chair Pr.

Schuh, Mari. Glaciers, 1 vol. 2010. (Natural Wonders Ser.). (ENG., 24p. (gr. k-1). Illus.). pap. 7.29 *(978-1-4296-5594-1(1));* pap. 41.70 *(978-1-4296-5595-8(X))* Capstone Press of Coughlan Cos. (Pebble Plus).

Sepheri, Sandy. Glaciers. 2007. (Landforms Ser.). (Illus.). 32p. (J). (gr. 4-7). lib. bdg. 28.50 *(978-1-60044-544-6(6))* Rourke Educational Media.

Sexton, Colleen. Glaciers. 2011. (Blastoff! Readers: Learning about the Earth: Level 3 Ser.). (ENG., Illus.). 24p. (J). (gr. 1). pap. 5.95 *(978-0-531-26029-6(1),* Children's Pr.) Scholastic Library Publishing.

Somervill, Barbara A. Glaciers. 2009. (21st Century Skills Library: Real World Math Ser.). (ENG.). 32p. (gr. 4-8). lib. bdg. 28.50 *(978-1-60279-495-5(2),* 200314) Cherry Lake Publishing.

Trumbauer, Lisa. Glaciers. 2005. (J). pap. *(978-1-4108-4607-5(5))* Benchmark Education Co.

Walker, Sally M. Glaciers. 2008. pap. 52.95 *(978-0-8225-9129-0(4))* 2007. (ENG., Illus.). 48p. (J). (gr. 2-5). lib. bdg. 26.60 *(978-0-8225-6737-0(7),* Lerner Pubns.) Lerner Publishing Group.

Webster, Christine. Glaciers. 2015. (Illus.). 24p. (J). *(978-1-5105-0050-1(2))* SmartBook Media, Inc.

—Glaciers. 2016. (J). ***(978-1-4896-5791-6(6))*** 2010. (Illus.). 24p. (J). (gr. 3-5). pap. 11.95 *(978-1-61690-006-9(7))* 2010. (Illus.). 24p. (YA). (gr. 3-6). lib. bdg. 25.70 *(978-1-61690-000-7(8))* 2005. (Illus.). 24p. (J). (gr. 3-7). pap. 9.95 *(978-1-59036-309-6(4))* 2005. (Illus.). 24p. (J). (gr. 3-7). lib. bdg. 24.45 *(978-1-59036-303-4(5))* Weigl Pubs., Inc.

Zappa, Marcia. Glaciers, 1 vol. 2010. (Big Buddy Bks.). (ENG.). 32p. (J). (gr. 2-5). 28.50 *(978-1-61613-493-8(3))* ABDO Publishing Co.

GLADSTONE, W. E. (WILLIAM EWART), 1809-1898

Lee, Stephen J. Gladstone & Disraeli. 2005. (Questions & Analysis in History Ser.). (ENG., Illus.). 208p. (C). 110.00 *(978-0-415-32356-7(8),* RU27027); per. 30.95 *(978-0-415-32357-4(6))* Routledge.

GLANDS

Burstein, John. The Exciting Endocrine System: How Do My Glands Work? 2009. (Slim Goodbody's Body Buddies Ser.). (ENG., Illus.). 32p. (J). (gr. 3-5). pap. *(978-0-7787-4432-0(9));* lib. bdg. *(978-0-7787-4418-4(3))* Crabtree Publishing Co.

Kim, Melissa. Learning about the Endocrine & Reproductive Systems. 2013. (Learning about the Human Body Systems Ser.). 48p. (J). (gr. 5-18). 25.27 *(978-0-7660-4158-5(1))* Enslow Pubs., Inc.

Kim, Melissa L. Learning about the Endocrine & Reproductive Systems. 2013. (Learning about the Human Body Systems Ser.). 48p. (J). (gr. 5-12). pap. 8.95 *(978-1-4644-0237-1(X))* Enslow Pubs., Inc.

Klosterman, Lorrie. Endocrine System. 2008. (Amazing Human Body Ser.). 80p. (gr. 5-18). lib. bdg. 34.21 *(978-0-7614-3055-1(5),* Benchmark Bks.) Marshall Cavendish Corp.

Rogers, Kara, ed. The Endocrine System. 2011. (Human Body Ser.). (ENG.). 176 ndash; 288p. (YA). (gr. 9-12). lib. bdg. 38.75 *(978-1-61530-675-6(7))* Rosen Publishing Group, Inc., The.

Verville, Kathleen. Testicular Cancer. 2009. (Biology of Cancer Ser.). (Illus.). 160p. (C). (gr. 9-18). 35.00 *(978-1-60413-166-6(7),* Chelsea Hse.) Facts On File, Inc.

Wilson, Michael R. The Endocrine System: Hormones, Growth, & Development. 2009. (Library of Sexual Health Ser.). 64p. (gr. 6-6). 58.50 *(978-1-60853-850-8(8));* (YA). (gr. 7-12). lib. bdg. 31.95 *(978-1-4358-5062-0(9))* Rosen Publishing Group, Inc., The.

GLASS

Capstone Publishing, creator. Exploring Materials: Glass Set. 2013. (ENG., Illus.). (J). (gr. -1-1). pap. 35.94 *(978-1-4329-8030-6(0),* Acorn) Heinemann-Raintree.

Colich, Abby. Glass, 1 vol. 2013. (Exploring Materials Ser.). (ENG., Illus.). 24p. (gr. -1-1). 22.65 *(978-1-4329-8014-6(9));* pap. 6.95 *(978-1-4329-8022-1(X))* Heinemann-Raintree. (Acorn).

Graham, Ian. You Wouldn't Want to Live Without Glass! Bergin, Mark, illus. 2016. (ENG.). 32p. (J). lib. bdg. *(978-0-531-22460-1(0))* Scholastic Library Publishing.

Heimberg, Justin. The Spirit Glass: A Book of Magically Hidden Images. 2011. (ENG., Illus.). 32p. (J). (gr. 2). 16.95 *(978-1-934734-49-0(7))* Seven Footer Pr.

Johnson, Jinny. Polar Sea Life. 2011. (Watery Worlds Ser.). (Illus.). 32p. (gr. 3-6). lib. bdg. 31.35 *(978-1-59920-505-2(X))* Black Rabbit Bks.

Kassinger, Ruth. Glass: From Cinderella's Slipper to Fiber Optics. 2003. (Material World Ser.). (Illus.). 80p. (gr. 6-8). lib. bdg. 25.90 *(978-0-7613-2109-5(8),* Twenty-First Century Bks.) Lerner Publishing Group.

Langley, Andrew. Glass. 2008. (ENG., Illus.). 24p. (J). (gr. k-3). pap. *(978-0-7787-4133-6(8))* Crabtree Publishing Co.

Lowery, Lawrence F. Rubber vs. Glass: I Wonder Why. Smith, Phil, illus. 2014. (I Wonder Why Ser.). (ENG.). 36p. (J). (gr. k-3). pap. 11.95 *(978-1-938946-50-9(2))* National Science Teachers Assn.

MacDonald, Margaret. Glass. 2011. (Learn-Abouts Ser.). (Illus.). 16p. (J). pap. 7.95 *(978-1-59920-636-3(6))* Black Rabbit Bks.

Morris, Neil. Glass. 2010. (Materials That Matter Ser.). 32p. (YA). (gr. 4-7). 28.50 *(978-1-60753-065-7(1))* Amicus Publishing.

Rau, Dana Meachen. Glass. 2011. (Bookworms Chapter Books: Use It! Reuse It! Ser.). 24p. (gr. 2-3). 22.79 *(978-1-60870-515-3(3))* Marshall Cavendish Corp.

Rivera, Sheila. Magnifying Glass. 2006. (First Step Nonfiction - Simple Tools Ser.). (ENG., Illus.). 8p. (gr. -1-1). pap. 4.95 *(978-0-8225-5713-5(4),* Lerner Pubns.) Lerner Publishing Group.

Royston, Angela. Glass: Let's Look at Marbles. 2005. (J). *(978-1-4109-1825-3(4))* Steck-Vaughn.

—Let's Look at Marbles, 1 vol. 2005. (ENG.). 24p. (J). pap. *(978-1-4109-1834-5(3))* Steck-Vaughn.

Somervill, Barbara A. The Story Behind Glass, 1 vol. 2011. (True Stories Ser.). (ENG.). 32p. (gr. 3-3). 30.65 *(978-1-4329-5437-6(7),* NA-h) Heinemann-Raintree.

Spielman, Madison. Craft It: Hand-Blown Glass, 1 vol. 2nd rev. ed. 2014. (TIME for KIDS(r) Nonfiction Readers Ser.). (ENG., Illus.). 28p. (J). (gr. 2-2). pap. 23.96 *(978-1-4807-1046-7(6))* Shell Educational Publishing.

Wallace, Holly. Glass. 2007. (How We Use Materials/Watts Ser.). (Illus.). 30p. (J). (gr. 4-7). lib. bdg. 28.50 *(978-1-59920-002-6(3))* Black Rabbit Bks.

GLASS, STAINED

see Glass Painting and Staining

GLASS MANUFACTURE

Branse, J. L. A Day in the Life of a Colonial Glassblower. 2009. (Library of Living & Working in Colonial Times Ser.). 24p. (gr. 3-3). 42.50 *(978-1-60853-731-0(5),* PowerKids Pr.) Rosen Publishing Group, Inc., The.

Hallock, Marilyn R. Central Glass Company: The First Thirty Years, 1863-1893, 1 vol. 2003. (ENG., Illus.). 176p. 39.95 *(978-0-7643-1762-0(8),* 9780764317620) Schiffer Publishing, Ltd.

Hayes, Amy. Turning Sand into Glass. 2015. (Step-By-Step Transformations Ser.). (ENG., Illus.). 24p. (J). (gr. 1-1). 24.21 *(978-1-5026-0452-1(3))* Cavendish Square Publishing.

Orr, Tamra. Careers in Glasswork, 01 vols., 1. 2016. (Essential Careers Ser.). (ENG.). 80p. (J). 34.25 *(978-1-4994-6211-1(5),* Rosen Young Adult) Rosen Publishing Group, Inc., The.

Ridley, Sarah. A Glass Jar. 2006. (How It's Made Ser.). (Illus.). 32p. (gr. 1-4). lib. bdg. 26.00 *(978-0-8368-6701-5(7),* Gareth Stevens Learning Library) Stevens, Gareth Publishing LLLP.

Zemlicka, Shannon. From Sand to Glass. 2003. (Start to Finish Ser.). (ENG., Illus.). 24p. (gr. k-3). 19.93 *(978-0-8225-0945-5(8),* Lerner Pubns.) Lerner Publishing Group.

GLASS MANUFACTURE—FICTION

Golding, Julia. The Glass Swallow, 0 vols. 2011. (ENG.). 320p. (gr. 7-12). 17.99 *(978-0-7614-5979-8(0),* 9780761459798, Amazon Children's Publishing) Amazon Publishing.

Hemphill, Stephanie. Sisters of Glass. 2013. (ENG.). 160p. (YA). (gr. 7). pap. 7.99 *(978-0-307-98141-7(X),* Ember) Random Hse. Children's Bks.

GLASS PAINTING AND STAINING

The Art of Glass Painting. 2004. (Classic Craft Cases Ser.). (Illus.). 64p. *(978-1-84229-801-5(1))* Top That! Publishing PLC.

Beylon, Cathy. Happy Halloween Stained Glass Jr. Coloring Book. 2012. (Dover Stained Glass Coloring Book Ser.). (ENG.). 32p. (J). (gr. -1-5). pap. 3.99 *(978-0-486-49872-0(7))* Dover Pubns., Inc.

Bloomenstein, Susan. Flower Power Stained Glass Coloring Book. 2012. (Dover Nature Stained Glass Coloring Book Ser.). (ENG.). 32p. (gr. 3-8). pap. 6.99 *(978-0-486-48389-4(4))* Dover Pubns., Inc.

Braden, Linda. Mason Jar Crafts for Kids: More Than 25 Cool, Crafty Projects to Make for Your Friends, Your Family, & Yourself! 2015. (ENG., Illus.). 160p. (J). (gr. 1). pap. 14.99 *(978-1-63220-413-4(4)*, Sky Pony Pr.) Skyhorse Publishing Co., Inc.

Crossling, Nick. Alhambra Stained Glass Coloring Book. 2008. (Dover Design Stained Glass Coloring Book Ser.). (ENG., Illus.). 32p. (gr. 3-8). per. 7.99 *(978-0-486-46531-9(4))* Dover Pubns., Inc.

Croyle, Anna. Mandala Stained Glass Pattern Book. 2008. (Dover Stained Glass Instruction Ser.). (ENG., Illus.). 64p. pap. 8.95 *(978-0-486-46605-7(1))* Dover Pubns., Inc.

Donahue, Peter. Classic Arabian Nights Stained Glass Coloring Book. 2011. (Dover Stained Glass Coloring Book Ser.). (ENG., Illus.). 32p. (J). (gr. 3-5). pap. 6.99 *(978-0-486-47609-4(X))* Dover Pubns., Inc.

Dover. Geometric Stained Glass Coloring Book: Deluxe Edition with 48 Stained Glass Sheets. 2010. (Dover Design Stained Glass Coloring Book Ser.). (ENG., Illus.). 96p. (J). (gr. 2-5). pap. 14.99 *(978-0-486-47549-3(2))* Dover Pubns., Inc.

Eaton, Connie Clough. Easy Victorian Florals Stained Glass Pattern Book. 2005. (Dover Stained Glass Instruction Ser.). (ENG., Illus.). 64p. pap. 8.95 *(978-0-486-44174-0(1))* Dover Pubns., Inc.

Elder, Jeremy. Hot Rod Tattoos Stained Glass Coloring Book. 2013. (Dover Stained Glass Coloring Book Ser.). (ENG., Illus.). 32p. (J). (gr. 3-8). pap. 6.99 *(978-0-486-48829-5(2))* Dover Pubns., Inc.

—Neon Lights Stained Glass Coloring Book. 2014. (Dover Stained Glass Coloring Book Ser.). (ENG., Illus.). 32p. (J). (gr. 3). pap. 6.99 *(978-0-486-48598-0(6))* Dover Pubns., Inc.

Elder, Jeremy & Coloring Books for Grownups Staff. In the Wild Stained Glass Coloring Book. 2013. (Dover Stained Glass Coloring Book Ser.). (ENG., Illus.). 32p. (J). (gr. 3-8). pap. 7.99 *(978-0-486-49942-0(1))* Dover Pubns., Inc.

Foldvary-Anderson, Carol. Heart to Heart Stained Glass Coloring Book. 2012. (Dover Stained Glass Coloring Book Ser.). (ENG., Illus.). 32p. (gr. 3-5). pap. 6.99 *(978-0-486-48648-2(6))* Dover Pubns., Inc.

Giannotta, Andres Bernardo. Manga Stained Glass Coloring Book. 2011. (Dover Stained Glass Coloring Book Ser.). (ENG., Illus.). 32p. (J). (gr. 3-5). pap. 6.99 *(978-0-486-47809-8(2))* Dover Pubns., Inc.

Green, John. Heavenly Snowflakes Stained Glass Coloring Book. 2006. (Dover Stained Glass Coloring Book Ser.). (ENG., Illus.). 8p. (J). (gr. k-3). 1.99 *(978-0-486-44923-4(8))* Dover Pubns., Inc.

—Samurai Stained Glass Coloring Book. 2008. (Dover Stained Glass Coloring Book Ser.). (ENG., Illus.). 32p. (gr. 3-8). 6.99 *(978-0-486-46558-6(X))* Dover Pubns., Inc.

Green, John, et al. Merry Christmas! Stained Glass Coloring Book. 2008. (Holiday Stained Glass Coloring Book Ser.). (ENG., Illus.). 96p. (gr. 1-5). pap. 12.99 *(978-0-486-46944-7(1))* Dover Pubns., Inc.

Hunter, Llyn. Sea Life GemGlow Stained Glass Coloring Book. 2009. (Dover Nature Stained Glass Coloring Book Ser.). (ENG., Illus.). 32p. (J). (gr. -1-5). pap. 7.99 *(978-0-486-47149-5(7))* Dover Pubns., Inc.

Kane, Barbara & Scholastic, Inc. Staff. Color in Stained Glass. 2016. (ENG.). 78p. (J). (gr. 3-7). 21.99 *(978-0-545-93966-9(6))* Klutz.

Klutz Editors, ed. Window Art. 4th ed. 2012. (ENG.). 56p. (J). (gr. 3). 21.99 *(978-0-545-45990-7(7))* Klutz.

LaFontaine, Bruce. Construction Trucks Stained Glass Coloring Book. 2004. (Dover Stained Glass Coloring Book Ser.). (ENG., Illus.). 8p. (J). pap. 1.50 *(978-0-486-44106-1(7))* Dover Pubns., Inc.

Levin, Freddie. ABC Stained Glass Coloring Book. 2010. (Dover Stained Glass Coloring Book Ser.). (ENG., Illus.). 32p. (J). (gr. -1-2). pap. 6.99 *(978-0-486-47334-5(1))* Dover Pubns., Inc.

Mazurkiewicz, Jessica. Coral Reef Stained Glass Coloring Book. 2008. (Dover Nature Stained Glass Coloring Book Ser.). (ENG., Illus.). 32p. (gr. 1-5). pap. 7.99 *(978-0-486-46789-4(9))* Dover Pubns., Inc.

—Out of This World Circular Designs Stained Glass Coloring Book. 2012. (Dover Design Stained Glass Coloring Book Ser.). (ENG., Illus.). 32p. (J). (gr. -1-2). pap. 6.99 *(978-0-486-49776-1(3))* Dover Pubns., Inc.

—Santa's Busy Workshop Stained Glass Jr. Coloring Book. 2012. (Dover Stained Glass Coloring Book Ser.). (ENG.). 32p. (J). (gr. -1-5). pap. 3.99 *(978-0-486-49870-6(0))* Dover Pubns., Inc.

Miller, Eileen Rudisill. Mermaids Stained Glass Coloring Book. 2008. (Dover Stained Glass Coloring Book Ser.). (ENG., Illus.). 32p. (J). (gr. 3-8). 6.99 *(978-0-486-46555-5(1))* Dover Pubns., Inc.

—Princess Stained Glass Jr. Coloring Book. 2012. (Dover Stained Glass Coloring Book Ser.). (ENG.). 32p. (J). (gr. -1-5). pap. 3.99 *(978-0-486-49871-3(9))* Dover Pubns., Inc.

Noble, Marty. Artful Eggs from Around the World Stained Glass Coloring Book. 2011. (Dover Design Stained Glass Coloring Book Ser.). (ENG., Illus.). 32p. (gr. 3-8). pap. 7.99 *(978-0-486-48025-1(9))* Dover Pubns., Inc.

—Christmas. 2011. (Build Window Stained Glass Coloring Book Ser.). (ENG., Illus.). 32p. (J). (gr. 3-5). pap. 6.99 *(978-0-486-48394-8(0))* Dover Pubns., Inc.

—Fairy Babies Stained Glass Coloring Book. 2006. (Dover Stained Glass Coloring Book Ser.). (ENG., Illus.). 8p. (J). (gr. -1-5). 1.50 *(978-0-486-44916-6(5))* Dover Pubns., Inc.

—Japanese Designs Stained Glass Coloring Book. 2006. (Dover Design Stained Glass Coloring Book Ser.). (ENG., Illus.). 16p. (gr. 6-8). 6.99 *(978-0-486-45175-6(5))* Dover Pubns., Inc.

—Mexican Designs Stained Glass Coloring Book. 2012. (Dover Stained Glass Coloring Book Ser.). (ENG., Illus.). 32p. (gr. 3-5). pap. 6.99 *(978-0-486-49008-3(4))* Dover Pubns., Inc.

—Wild Cards Stained Glass Coloring Book. 2010. (Dover Stained Glass Coloring Book Ser.). (ENG., Illus.). 32p. (gr. 3-8). pap. 6.99 *(978-0-486-47451-9(8))* Dover Pubns., Inc.

Noble, Marty & Coloring Books Staff. Day of the Dead (Dia de los Muertos) 2011. (Dover Stained Glass Coloring Book Ser.). (ENG., Illus.). 32p. (gr. 3-8). pap. 6.99 *(978-0-486-48033-6(X))* Dover Pubns., Inc.

Pomaska, Anna. Same & Different. 2007. (Dover Coloring Bks.). (ENG., Illus.). 32p. (J). (gr. k-3). pap. 3.99 *(978-0-486-46107-6(6))* Dover Pubns., Inc.

Rechlin, Ted. Superheroes Stained Glass Coloring Book. 2012. (Dover Stained Glass Coloring Book Ser.). (ENG., Illus.). 32p. (J). (gr. 2-5). pap. 6.99 *(978-0-486-49036-6(X))* Dover Pubns., Inc.

Roytman, Arkady. Build-a-Window Halloween Stained Glass Coloring Book. 2011. (Build Window Stained Glass Coloring Book Ser.). (ENG., Illus.). 32p. (J). (gr. 3-5). pap. 6.99 *(978-0-486-48391-7(6))* Dover Pubns., Inc.

—Fantasy Warriors Stained Glass Coloring Book. 2010. (Dover Stained Glass Coloring Book Ser.). (ENG., Illus.). 32p. (J). (gr. 3-5). pap. 6.99 *(978-0-486-47372-7(4))* Dover Pubns., Inc.

—Vampire Nights. 2010. (Dover Stained Glass Coloring Book Ser.). (ENG., Illus.). 32p. (J). (gr. 3-5). pap. 6.99 *(978-0-486-47638-4(3))* Dover Pubns., Inc.

Roytman, Arkady & Coloring Books Staff. Outer Space. 2011. (Build Window Stained Glass Coloring Book Ser.). (ENG., Illus.). 32p. (J). (gr. 3-5). pap. 6.99 *(978-0-486-48392-4(4))* Dover Pubns., Inc.

Schmidt, Carol. Butterfly Fairies Stained Glass Coloring Book. 2011. (Dover Stained Glass Coloring Book Ser.). (ENG., Illus.). 32p. (gr. 3-8). pap. 7.99 *(978-0-486-48034-3(8))* Dover Pubns., Inc.

—Witches Stained Glass Coloring Book. 2010. (Dover Stained Glass Coloring Book Ser.). (ENG., Illus.). 96p. (gr. 3-8). pap. 6.99 *(978-0-486-47654-4(5))* Dover Pubns., Inc.

Smith, A. G. Arabic Patterns Stained Glass Coloring Book. 2006. (Dover Design Stained Glass Coloring Book Ser.). (ENG., Illus.). 32p. (J). (gr. 3-8). pap. 6.99 *(978-0-486-44839-8(8))* Dover Pubns., Inc.

—Celtic Knotwork Stained Glass Colouring Book. 2006. (Dover Design Stained Glass Coloring Book Ser.). (ENG., Illus.). 32p. (gr. 3-8). 7.99 *(978-0-486-44816-9(9))* Dover Pubns., Inc.

—Decorative Chinese Designs. 2006. (Dover Design Stained Glass Coloring Book Ser.). (ENG., Illus.). 16p. (gr. 3-8). 6.99 *(978-0-486-45172-5(0))* Dover Pubns., Inc.

Soffer, Ruth & Coloring Books Staff. Beautiful Birds in Mated Pairs Stained Glass Coloring Book. 2012. (Dover Nature Stained Glass Coloring Book Ser.). (ENG., Illus.). 32p. (gr. 3-5). pap. 7.99 *(978-0-486-48680-2(X))* Dover Pubns., Inc.

Sovak, Jan. Fairy World. 2011. (Build Window Stained Glass Coloring Book Ser.). (ENG., Illus.). 32p. (J). (gr. 3-5). pap. 6.99 *(978-0-486-48393-1(2))* Dover Pubns., Inc.

Spilsbury, Richard. Stained Glass Windows. 2016. (ENG., Illus.). 32p. (J). (gr. 4-6). pap. 11.99 *(978-0-7502-9450-8(7)*, Wayland) Hachette Children's Group GBR. Dist: Hachette Bk. Group.

—Stained Glass Windows. 2009. (Stories in Art Ser.). (Illus.). 30p. (J). lib. bdg. 26.50 *(978-1-4042-4439-9(5)*, PowerKids Pr.) Rosen Publishing Group, Inc., The.

GLASSWARE

Blaxland, Wendy. Bottles & Jars. 2009. (How Are They Made? 2 Ser.). 32p. (gr. 4). lib. bdg. 18.56 *(978-0-7614-4752-8(0))* Marshall Cavendish GBR. Dist: Marshall Cavendish Corp.

Marsh, Thomas E. The Official Guide to Collecting Applied Color Soda Bottles, Vol. II. 105p. (J). (gr. -1-18). pap. *(978-0-9633682-1-8(4))* Marsh, Thomas E. Inc.

Spielman, Madison. Craft It: Hand-Blown Glass, 1 vol. 2nd rev. ed. 2011. (Nonfiction Readers Ser.). (ENG.). 28p. (J). (gr. 2-2). pap. 6.99 *(978-1-4333-3619-5(7))* Teacher Created Materials, Inc.

Walk, John. Fenton Special Orders: 1980-Present: QVC; Mary Walrath; Martha Stewart; Cracker Barrel; JC Penney; National Fenton Glass Society; & Fenton Art Glass Club of America, 1 vol. 2003. (ENG., Illus.). 239p. 29.95 *(978-0-7643-1813-9(6)*, 9780764318139) Schiffer Publishing, Ltd.

Walker, Kate. Glass. 2010. (Recycling Ser.). (Illus.). 32p. (J). (gr. 1). 28.50 *(978-1-60870-130-8(1))* Marshall Cavendish Corp.

Wight, Karol. Paperweight Pals. 2012. (Illus.). 22p. (J). *(978-0-87290-191-9(2))* Corning Museum of Glass.

GLENN, JOHN, 1921-2016

Ashby, Ruth. Rocket Man: The Mercury Adventure of John Glenn, 1 vol. Hunt, Robert, illus. 2004. (ENG.). 144p. (J). (gr. 2-5). 12.95 *(978-1-56145-323-8(4))* Peachtree Pubs.

Collard, Sneed B., III. John Glenn: Hooked on Flying. 2008. (American Heroes Ser.). (Illus.). 48p. (J). (gr. 3-18). lib. bdg. 29.93 *(978-0-7614-3066-7(0)*, Benchmark Bks.) Marshall Cavendish Corp.

Holden, Henry M. Trailblazing Astronaut John Glenn: A MyReportLinks.com Book. 2004. (Space Flight Adventures & Disasters Ser.). (Illus.). 48p. (J). lib. bdg. 26.60 *(978-0-7660-5166-9(8)*, MyReportLinks.com Bks.) Enslow Pubs., Inc.

Kupperberg, Paul. John Glenn. 2004. (Library of Astronaut Biographies Ser.). (Illus.). 112p. (J). (gr. 5-8). lib. bdg. 34.60 *(978-0-8239-4460-6(3)*, Rosen Reference) Rosen Publishing Group, Inc., The.

—John Glenn: The First American in Orbit & His Return to Space. 2009. (Library of Astronaut Biographies Ser.). 112p. (gr. 5-8). 63.90 *(978-1-60853-523-1(1)*, Rosen Reference) Rosen Publishing Group, Inc., The.

Mitchell, Don. Liftoff: A Photobiography of John Glenn. 2006. (Photobiographies Ser.). (ENG., Illus.). 64p. (J). (gr. 5-7). 17.95 *(978-0-7922-5899-5(1))*; lib. bdg. 27.90 *(978-0-7922-5900-8(9))* National Geographic Society. (National Geographic Children's Bks.).

Pierce, Philip N. & Schuon, Karl. John H Glenn, Astronaut. 2011. 234p. 46.95 *(978-1-258-00503-0(4))* Literary Licensing, LLC.

Streissguth, Thomas. John Glenn. 2003. (Biography Ser.). (Illus.). 112p. (J). (gr. 6-18). pap. 7.95 *(978-0-8225-9685-1(7))* Lerner Publishing Group.

Streissguth, Tom. John Glenn. 2004. (Just the Facts Biographies Ser.). (ENG., Illus.). 112p. (J). (gr. 5-12). lib. bdg. 27.93 *(978-0-8225-2274-4(8))* Lerner Publishing Group.

Zelon, Helen. The Mercury 6 Mission: The First American Astronaut to Orbit Earth. 2009. (Space Missions Ser.). 24p. (gr. 3-4). 42.50 *(978-1-60853-120-2(1)*, PowerKids Pr.) Rosen Publishing Group, Inc., The.

GLIDERS (AERONAUTICS)

Boothroyd, Jennifer. How Do Hang Gliders Work? 2013. (Lightning Bolt Books (tm) — How Flight Works). (ENG., Illus.). 32p. (gr. k-2). pap. 7.95 *(978-1-4677-0775-6(9))* Lerner Publishing Group.

Clark, Nancy Lawrence, ed. Gliders Soaring: The Sport of Motorless Flight with Pioneer Larry Lawrence. 2003. (Illus.). 120p. (J). pap. 15.00 *(978-0-9641197-2-7(2))* Clark Pubns.

Kelley, K. C. Gliding. 2012. (Extreme Sports Ser.). (ENG., Illus.). 32p. (J). (gr. 2-5). lib. bdg. 28.50 *(978-1-60973-207-3(3)*, 201125) Child's World, Inc., The.

Masters, Nancy Robinson. How Does It Fly? Glider. 2011. (Community Connections: How Does It Fly? Ser.). (ENG.). 24p. (gr. 2-5). lib. bdg. 25.64 *(978-1-61080-072-3(9)*, 201070) Cherry Lake Publishing.

GLIDERS (AERONAUTICS)—FICTION

Appleton, Victor. Tom Swift & his Air Glider. 2005. 26.95 *(978-1-4218-1500-8(1)*, 1st World Library - Literary Society) 1st World Publishing, Inc.

—Tom Swift & His Air Glider or Seeking. 2006. pap. *(978-1-4065-0895-6(0))* Dodo Pr.

McMullen, Brian & Jägel, Jason. Hang Glider & Mud Mask. 2012. (ENG., Illus.). 32p. (J). (gr. -1-3). 14.95 *(978-1-936365-83-8(9))* McSweeney's Publishing.

GLIDING AND SOARING

Boothroyd, Jennifer. How Do Hang Gliders Work? 2013. (Lightning Bolt Books (tm) — How Flight Works). (ENG., Illus.). 32p. (gr. k-2). pap. 7.95 *(978-1-4677-0775-6(9))* Lerner Publishing Group.

Clark, Nancy Lawrence, ed. Gliders Soaring: The Sport of Motorless Flight with Pioneer Larry Lawrence. 2003. (Illus.). 120p. (J). pap. 15.00 *(978-0-9641197-2-7(2))* Clark Pubns.

Kelley, K. C. Gliding. 2012. (Extreme Sports Ser.). (ENG., Illus.). 32p. (J). (gr. 2-5). lib. bdg. 28.50 *(978-1-60973-207-3(3)*, 201125) Child's World, Inc., The.

—Hang Gliding. 2011. (Extreme Sports Ser.). (ENG., Illus.). 32p. (J). (gr. 2-5). lib. bdg. 28.50 *(978-1-60973-208-0(1)*, 201126) Child's World, Inc., The.

Masters, Nancy Robinson. How Does It Fly? Glider. 2011. (Community Connections: How Does It Fly? Ser.). (ENG.). 24p. (gr. 2-5). lib. bdg. 25.64 *(978-1-61080-072-3(9)*, 201070) Cherry Lake Publishing.

Rigby Education Staff. Gliders & Sliders. (Sails Literacy Ser.). (Illus.). 16p. (gr. 1-2). 27.00 *(978-0-7635-9922-5(0)*, 699220C99) Rigby Education.

Schindler, John E. Hang Gliding & Parasailing. 2005. (Extreme Sports Ser.). (Illus.). 24p. (gr. 2-5). pap. 8.15 *(978-0-8368-4547-1(1))*; lib. bdg. 23.00 *(978-0-8368-4540-2(4))* Stevens, Gareth Publishing LLLP. (Gareth Stevens Learning Library).

Schuh, Mari C. Hang Gliders, 1 vol. 2013. (Aircraft Ser.). (ENG., Illus.). 24p. (gr. k-1). lib. bdg. 26.65 *(978-1-62065-112-4(2)*, Pebble Plus) Capstone Press of Coughlan Cos.

GLOBAL SATELLITE COMMUNICATIONS SYSTEMS

see Artificial Satellites in Telecommunication

GLOBAL WARMING

ABDO Publishing Company Staff. Climate Change. 2010. (ABDO & Daughters Ser.). 32p. 162.42 *(978-1-61613-452-5(6)*, Abdo & Daughters) ABDO Publishing Co.

Aitken, Stephen. Earth's Fever, 1 vol. 2011. (Climate Change Ser.). (ENG., Illus.). 32p. (YA). (gr. k-3). 28.50 *(978-1-61641-670-6(X))* Magic Wagon.

—Fever on the Land, 1 vol. 2011. (Climate Change Ser.). (ENG., Illus.). 32p. (J). (gr. k-3). 28.50 *(978-1-61641-673-7(4))* Magic Wagon.

Anderson, Dale. Al Gore: A Wake-Up Call to Global Warming. 2009. (Voices for Green Choices Ser.). (ENG., Illus.). 48p. (J). (gr. 5-9). pap. *(978-0-7787-4679-9(8))*; lib. bdg. *(978-0-7787-4666-9(6))* Crabtree Publishing Co.

Anderson, Michael. Global Warming. 2011. (J). lib. bdg. 31.70 *(978-1-61530-506-3(8))* Rosen Publishing Group, Inc., The.

Animal 911: Environmental Threats. 2013. (Animal 911: Environmental Threats Ser.). 48p. (J). (gr. 3-5). 191.70 *(978-1-4339-9726-6(6))*; pap. 84.30 *(978-1-4339-9798-3(3))*; pap. 505.80 *(978-1-4339-9799-0(1))* Stevens, Gareth Publishing LLLP.

Bermann, Flemming. Global Warming for Young Minds: A Global Warming & Sustainability Guide for Children. 2010. 46p. pap. 17.50 *(978-1-60911-468-8(X)*, Eloquent Bks.) Strategic Book Publishing & Rights Agency (SBPRA).

Bishop, Amanda. Climate Change. 2008. (Saving Our World Ser.). 32p. (gr. 4-18). lib. bdg. 28.50 *(978-0-7614-3219-7(1)*, Benchmark Bks.) Marshall Cavendish Corp.

Bishop, W. H. Meltin: The Iceberg. 2012. 20p. pap. 17.99 *(978-1-4772-5268-0(1))* AuthorHouse.

Biskup, Agnieszka. Understanding Global Warming with Max Axiom, Super Scientist, 1 vol. Martin, Cynthia & Anderson, Bill, illus. (Graphic Science Ser.). (ENG.). 32p. (gr. 3-4). 2008. per. 8.10 *(978-1-4296-1767-3(5))* 2007. 30.65 *(978-1-4296-0139-9(6))* Capstone Press of Coughlan Cos. (Graphic Library).

Biskup, Agnieszka, et al. Comprender el Calentamiento Global con Max Axiom, Supercientífico. Strictly Spanish Translation Services Staff, tr. from ENG. Martin, Cynthia & Anderson, Bill, illus. 2012. (Ciencia Gráfica Ser.). (SPA.). 32p. (gr. 3-4). lib. bdg. 30.65 *(978-1-4296-9235-9(9))* Capstone Press of Coughlan Cos.

Bow, James. Earth's Climate Change: Carbon Dioxide Overload. 2015. (Next Generation Energy Ser.). (ENG., Illus.). 32p. (J). *(978-0-7787-1978-6(2))* Crabtree Publishing Co.

Buchanan, Shelly. Global Warming. 2015. (Science Readers: Content & Literacy Ser.). (Illus.). 32p. (gr. 5-5). pap. 8.99 *(978-1-4807-4729-6(7))* Teacher Created Materials, Inc.

Casper, Julie Kerr. Global Warming, 7 vols., Set. 2010. (Global Warming Ser.). (C). (gr. 9). 280.00 *(978-0-8160-8297-1(9))* Facts On File, Inc.

Changing Climates. 2010. (Global Connections Ser.). (Illus.). 120p. (gr. 5-8). 35.00 *(978-1-60413-291-5(4)*, Chelsea Hse.) Facts On File, Inc.

Cheel, Richard. Global Warming Alert! 2007. (Disaster Alert! Ser.). (ENG., Illus.). 32p. (J). (gr. 3-7). lib. bdg. *(978-0-7787-1587-0(6))*; (gr. 2-9). pap. *(978-0-7787-1619-8(8))* Crabtree Publishing Co.

Chehoski, Robert, ed. Critical Perspectives on Climate Disruption. 2009. (Critical Anthologies of Nonfiction Writing Ser.). 184p. (gr. 8-8). 63.90 *(978-1-61512-074-1(2))* Rosen Publishing Group, Inc., The.

Cherry, Lynne. How We Know What We Know about Our Changing Climate: Scientists & Kids Explore Global Warming. Braasch, Gary, photos by. 2008. (Illus.). (J). pap. *(978-1-58469-104-4(2))* Dawn Pubns.

Cherry, Lynne & Braasch, Gary. How We Know What We Know about Our Changing Climate: Scientists & Kids Explore Global Warming, 1 vol. Braasch, Gary, illus. 2008. (ENG., Illus.). 66p. (J). (gr. 5-9). 17.95 *(978-1-58469-103-7(4))* Dawn Pubns.

Cohen, Judith Love & Friend, Robyn C. A Clean Sky: The Global Warming Story. Katz, David A., illus. 2007. (J). (gr. 4-8). 46p. pap. 7.00 *(978-1-880599-81-5(3))*; 42p. 13.95 *(978-1-880599-82-2(1))* Cascade Pass, Inc.

Cole, Joanna. The Magic School Bus & the Climate Challenge. Degen, Bruce, illus. 2014. (Magic School Bus Ser.). (ENG.). 40p. (J). (gr. 2-5). 6.99 *(978-0-545-65599-6(4))* Scholastic, Inc.

Colligan, L. H. Global Warming. 2011. (Debating the Issues Ser.). 64p. (gr. 6). 32.79 *(978-0-7614-4971-3(X))* Marshall Cavendish Corp.

Collins, Terry, et al. Getting to the Bottom of Global Warming: An Isabel Soto Investigation. 2010. (Graphic Expeditions Ser.). (ENG.). 32p. (gr. 3-4). pap. 47.70 *(978-1-4296-5143-1(1)*, Graphic Library) Capstone Press of Coughlan Cos.

—Getting to the Bottom of Global Warming: An Isabel Soto Investigation. Schulz, Barbara, illus. 2010. (Graphic Expeditions Ser.). (ENG.). 32p. (gr. 3-4). lib. bdg. 30.65 *(978-1-4296-3972-9(5)*, Graphic Library) Capstone Press of Coughlan Cos.

Confronting Global Warming, 5 vols., Set. Incl. Energy Production & Alternative Energy. Miller, Debra A. 112p. lib. bdg., lib. bdg. 38.95 *(978-0-7377-5106-2(1))*; Extreme Weather. Streissguth, Tom. 128p. 38.95 *(978-0-7377-4859-8(1))*; Health & Disease. Henningfeld, Diane Andrews. 136p. 38.95 *(978-0-7377-4858-1(3))*; Role of the Government. Langwith, Jacqueline. 128p. 38.95 *(978-0-7377-4860-4(5))*; Water & Ice. Berlatsky, Noah. (Illus.). 120p. 38.95 *(978-0-7377-4861-1(3))*; (YA). (gr. 10-12). 128p. 2010. Set lib. bdg. 194.75 o.s.i *(978-0-7377-5423-0(0)*, Greenhaven Pr., Inc.) Cengage Gale.

Coupe, Robert. Vanishing Ice. 2012. (Discovery Education: the Environment Ser.). (ENG., Illus.). 32p. (J). (gr. 3-6). pap. 10.00 *(978-1-4488-7980-9(9))*; lib. bdg. 25.25 *(978-1-4488-7892-5(6))* Rosen Publishing Group, Inc., The. (PowerKids Pr.).

Davis, Barbara J. Earth's Core & Crust. 2007. (Gareth Stevens Vital Science: Earth Science Ser.). (Illus.). 48p. (gr. 5-12). lib. bdg. 27.00 *(978-0-8368-7762-5(4)*, Gareth Stevens Secondary Library) Stevens, Gareth Publishing LLLP.

DeFrancesco, B. J. Rising above Global Warming. Myers, Shari, illus. 2007. 46p. (J). per. 19.95 *(978-0-9801555-0-1(9))* Argus Enterprises International, Inc.

Donnelly, Karen. Floods of the Past & the Future. 2009. (Earth's Changing Weather & Climate Ser.). 24p. (gr. 4-4). 42.50 *(978-1-61512-245-5(1)*, PowerKids Pr.) Rosen Publishing Group, Inc., The.

—Ice Ages of the Past & the Future. 2009. (Earth's Changing Weather & Climate Ser.). 24p. (gr. 4-4). 42.50 *(978-1-61512-248-6(6)*, PowerKids Pr.) Rosen Publishing Group, Inc., The.

—Rising Temperatures of the Past & Future. 2009. (Earth's Changing Weather & Climate Ser.). 24p. (gr. 4-4). 42.50 *(978-1-61512-249-3(4)*, PowerKids Pr.) Rosen Publishing Group, Inc., The.

—Rising Temperatures of the Past & the Future. 2003. (Earth's Changing Weather & Climate Ser.). (Illus.). 24p. (J). lib. bdg. 22.60 *(978-0-8239-6214-3(8)*, PowerKids Pr.) Rosen Publishing Group, Inc., The.

Donnelly, Karen J. Floods of the Past & Future. 2003. (Earth's Changing Weather & Climate Ser.). (Illus.). 24p. (J). lib. bdg. 22.60 *(978-0-8239-6218-1(0))* Rosen Publishing Group, Inc., The.

—Ice Ages of the Past & the Future. 2003. (Earth's Changing Weather & Climate Ser.). (Illus.). 24p. (J). lib. bdg. 22.60 *(978-0-8239-6219-8(9)*, PowerKids Pr.) Rosen Publishing Group, Inc., The.

Farrar, Amy. Global Warming, 1 vol. 2007. (Essential Viewpoints Set 1 Ser.). (ENG., Illus.). 112p. (J). (gr. 6-12). lib. bdg. 35.64 *(978-1-59928-859-8(1))* ABDO Publishing Co.

Farrington, Karen. A Cool Kid's Field Guide to Global Warming. Woollatt, Sue, illus. 2009. (Cool Kid's Field Guide Ser.). 26p. (J). (gr. 1-3). spiral bd. 6.99 *(978-0-8416-7146-1(X))* Hammond World Atlas Corp.

Faust, Daniel R. Cambio Climático: Los Gases de Efecto Invernadero y la Capa de Ozono. Obregón, José María, illus. 2009. (Historietas Juveniles: Peligros Del Medioambiente (Jr. Graphic Environmental Dangers) Ser.). (SPA.). 24p. (gr. 3-6). (YA). lib. bdg. 25.25 *(978-1-4358-8462-5(0))*; pap. 10.60 *(978-1-4358-8463-2(9))* Rosen Publishing Group, Inc., The.

—Global Warming: Greenhouse Gases & the Ozone Layer. (Jr. Graphic Environmental Dangers Ser.). (ENG., 24p. 2009. Illus.). (gr. 3-8). pap. 10.60 *(978-1-4042-4599-0(5))* 2008. (J). 47.90 *(978-1-61532-096-7(2)*, PowerKids Pr.) 2008. (Illus.). (J). (gr. 3-6). lib. bdg. 25.25 *(978-1-4042-4260-9(0))* Rosen Publishing Group, Inc., The.

Feinstein, Stephen. Critical Perspectives on Climate Change. 2016. (Analyzing the Issues Ser.). 208p. (J). (gr. 8-8). 47.93 *(978-0-7660-7670-9(9))* Enslow Pubs., Inc.

Ferguson, Rebecca. The Role of the Individual. 2011. (Confronting Global Warming Ser.). (ENG.). 128p. (gr.

E F G

12-12). 44.30 *(978-0-7377-4853-6(2)*, Greenhaven Pr., Inc.) Cengage Gale.

Flannery, Tim. We Are the Weather Makers: The History of Climate Change. 2010. (ENG., Illus.). 320p. (YA). (gr. 9). pap. 12.99 *(978-0-7636-4656-1(3))* Candlewick Pr.

Fretwell, Holly. The Sky's Not Falling! Why It's Ok to Chill about Global Warming. 2007. (ENG., Illus.). 128p. (J). (gr. 4-7). per. 17.95 *(978-0-9767269-4-4(7))* WND Bks, Inc.

Friedman, Lauri S., ed. Global Warming. 2012. (Introducing Issues with Opposing Viewpoints Ser.). (ENG., Illus.). 144p. (gr. 7-10). lib. bdg. 36.95 *(978-0-7377-5681-4(0)*, Greenhaven Pr., Inc.) Cengage Gale.

Goldstein, Natalie. Global Warming. 2009. (Global Issues Ser.). (Illus.). 352p. (YA). (gr. 9-12). 45.00 *(978-0-8160-6769-5(4))* Facts On File, Inc.

Gore, Al. An Inconvenient Truth: The Crisis of Global Warming. 2007. (ENG., Illus.). 192p. (J). (gr. 5-18). 16.00 *(978-0-670-06272-0(3)*, Viking Books for Young Readers) Penguin Young Readers Group.

Green, Robert. Global Warming. 2008. (21st Century Skills Library: Global Perspectives Ser.). (ENG.). 32p. (gr. 4-8). lib. bdg. 28.50 *(978-1-60279-123-7(6)*, 200099) Cherry Lake Publishing.

Gunderson, Jessica. Global Warming. 2010. (Earth Issues Ser.). 48p. (YA). (gr. 5-18). 23.95 *(978-1-58341-982-3(9)*, Creative Education) Creative Co., The.

Hall, Julie. A Hot Planet Needs Cool Kids: Understanding Climate Change & What You can do About it. 2007. 88p. (J). pap. 15.99 *(978-0-615-15585-2(5))* Green Goat Bks.

Hand, Carol. Climate Change: Our Warming Earth, 1 vol. 2014. (History of Science Ser.). (ENG.). 112p. (J). (gr. 6-12). lib. bdg. 35.64 *(978-1-62403-558-6(2)*, Essential Library) ABDO Publishing Co.

Harmon, Daniel E. Al Gore & Global Warming. (Celebrity Activists Ser.). 112p. 2009. (gr. 8-8). 66.50 *(978-1-61511-826-7(8))* 2008. (Illus.). (YA). (gr. 7-12). lib. bdg. 34.60 *(978-1-4042-1761-4(4))* Rosen Publishing Group, Inc., The.

Haugen, David M. Is Global Warming a Threat? 2007. (At Issue Ser.). (ENG., Illus.). 128p. (gr. 10-12). 39.40 *(978-0-7377-3687-8(9))*; pap. 27.80 *(978-0-7377-3688-5(7)*, Greenhaven Pr., Inc.) Cengage Gale.

Heos, Bridget. It's Getting Hot in Here: The Past, Present, & Future of Climate Change. 2016. (ENG., Illus.). 240p. (YA). (gr. 7). 17.99 *(978-0-544-30347-8(4)*, HMH Books For Young Readers) Houghton Mifflin Harcourt Publishing Co.

Hirsch, Rebecca E. Climate Migrants: On the Move in a Warming World. 2016. (ENG., Illus.). 88p. (YA). (gr. 7-12). 35.99 *(978-1-4677-9341-4(8)*, Twenty-First Century Bks.) Lerner Publishing Group.

Hodge, Susie. Global Warming. 2013. (21st Century Science Ser.). (ENG.). 64p. (J). (gr. 4-7). pap. 7.95 *(978-1-84898-191-1(0)*, TickTock Books) Octopus Publishing Group GBR. Dist: Independent Pubs. Group.

Johnson, Rebecca L. Understanding Global Warming. (Saving Our Living Earth Ser.). (gr. 4-7). 2009. (ENG.). pap. 56.72 *(978-0-7613-4698-2(8))* 2008. 72p. (YA). lib. bdg. 30.60 *(978-0-8225-7561-0(2))* Lerner Publishing Group.

Johnson, Rebecca L. & National Geographic Learning Staff. Global Warming. 2007. (Nonfiction Reading & Writing Workshops Ser.). (ENG., Illus.). 32p. (J). pap. 17.95 *(978-0-7922-8873-2(4))* CENGAGE Learning.

Juettner, Bonnie. Global Warming. 2008. (Ripped from the Headlines Ser.). (YA). (gr. 7-12). 23.95 *(978-1-60217-024-7(X))* Erickson Pr.

Kallen, Stuart A. How Should the World Respond to Global Warming? 2009. (In Controversy Ser.). (YA). (gr. 7-12). 25.95 *(978-1-60152-086-9(7))* ReferencePoint Pr., Inc.

Kallio, Jamie. 12 Things to Know about Climate Change. 2015. (ENG., Illus.). 32p. (J). *(978-1-63235-028-2(9))* Pr. Room Editions LLC.

Knauer, Kelly & Cadley, Patricia, eds. Time Global Warming. 2008. (Time Inc. Ser.). (Illus.). 122p. (YA). (gr. 8-12). lib. bdg. 33.27 *(978-0-8225-7276-3(1)*, Twenty-First Century Bks.) Lerner Publishing Group.

Kowalski, Kathiann M. Global Warming. 2003. (Open for Debate Ser.). (Illus.). 128p. (gr. 7-18). lib. bdg. 42.79 *(978-0-7614-1582-4(3)*, Benchmark Bks.) Marshall Cavendish Corp.

Langwith, Jacqueline. The Role of the Government. 2010. (Confronting Global Warming Ser.). 128p. (YA). (gr. 10-12). 38.95 *(978-0-7377-4860-4(5)*, Greenhaven Pr., Inc.) Cengage Gale.

Lawrence, Ellen. Global Warming. 2014. (Science Slam: Green World, Clean World Ser.). 24p. (J). (gr. -1-3). lib. bdg. 23.93 *(978-1-62724-104-5(3))* Bearport Publishing Co., Inc.

Leathers, Dan. The Snows of Kilimanjaro. 2007. (On the Verge of Extinction Ser.). (Illus.). 32p. (YA). (gr. 2-5). lib. bdg. 25.70 *(978-1-58415-584-3(1))* Mitchell Lane Pubs., Inc.

Lerner, Adrienne. Climate Change. 2009. (Global Viewpoints Ser.). (ENG., Illus.). 224p. (YA). (gr. 10-12). 27.95 *(978-0-7377-4157-5(0)*, LML02109-243057, Greenhaven Pr., Inc.); (gr. 9-12). pap. 40.45 *(978-0-7377-4156-8(2)*, LML02109-243051) Cengage Gale.

Levete, Sarah. Catastrophic Weather. 2010. (Protecting Our Planet Ser.). (ENG., Illus.). 32p. (J). (gr. 3-6). *(978-0-7787-5210-3(0))*; pap. *(978-0-7787-5227-1(5))* Crabtree Publishing Co.

Llewellyn, Bridget McGovern. One Child, One Planet: Inspiration for the Young Conservationist. Sams, Carl R., 2nd & Stoick, Jean, photos by. 2009. (Illus.). 48p. (J). 19.95 *(978-0-9841880-0-0(2))* Emerald Shamrock Pr. LLC.

Mack, Molly. Reducing Global Warming. 2016. (Global Guardians Ser.). 00024p. (J). (gr. 3-3). pap. 8.25 *(978-1-4994-2754-7(9)*, PowerKids Pr.) Rosen Publishing Group, Inc., The.

McCutcheon, Chuck. What Are Global Warming & Climate Change? Answers for Young Readers. 2010. (World's of Wonder Ser.). (ENG., Illus.). 114p. (J). (gr. 4-18). 34.95 *(978-0-8263-4745-9(2))* Univ. of New Mexico Pr.

McPherson, Stephanie Sammartino. Arctic Thaw: Climate Change & the Global Race for Energy Resources. 2014. (Illus.). 64p. (J). (gr. 6-12). lib. bdg. 34.60 *(978-1-4677-2043-4(7)*, Twenty-First Century Bks.) Lerner Publishing Group.

Metz, Lorijo. What Can We Do about Global Warming? 2009. (Protecting Our Planet Ser.). (Illus.). 24p. (ENG.). (J). pap. 8.25 *(978-1-4358-2479-9(2))*; (YA). (gr. 2-5). lib. bdg. 22.60 *(978-1-4042-8079-3(0))* Rosen Publishing Group, Inc., The.

Miller, Debra A. Confronting Global Warming, 5.0. 2011. (Confronting Global Warming Ser.). (ENG.). 128p. (gr. 12-12). lib. bdg. 221.50 *(978-0-7377-5457-5(5)*, Greenhaven Pr., Inc.) Cengage Gale.

—Conserving the Environment. 2010. (Current Controversies Ser.). (Illus.). 240p. (J). 40.95 *(978-0-7377-4661-7(0))*; pap. 28.45 *(978-0-7377-4662-4(9))* Cengage Gale. (Greenhaven Pr., Inc.).

—Global Warming. 2008. (Hot Topics Ser.). (ENG., Illus.). 128p. (gr. 7-10). lib. bdg. 39.40 *(978-1-4205-0049-3(X)*, LML02109-240037, Lucent Bks.) Cengage Gale.

Morris, Neil. Global Warming. 2007. (What If We Do Nothing? Ser.). (Illus.). 48p. (gr. 5-12). pap. 14.05 *(978-0-8368-8155-4(9))*; lib. bdg. 31.00 *(978-0-8368-7755-7(1))* Stevens, Gareth Publishing LLLP. (Gareth Stevens Secondary Library).

Nagle, Jeanne. Reducing Your Carbon Footprint at School. (Your Carbon Footprint Ser.). 48p. (gr. 5-5). 2009. 53.00 *(978-1-60854-911-5(9)*, Rosen Reference) 2008. (Illus.). (YA). lib. bdg. 29.25 *(978-1-4042-1774-4(6)*, 1284467) Rosen Publishing Group, Inc., The.

Nelson, John. Polar Ice Caps in Danger: Expedition to Antarctica. 2008. (Jr. Graphic Environmental Dangers Ser.). (ENG.). 24p. (J). 47.90 *(978-1-61532-097-4(0))*; (Illus.). (gr. 3-6). lib. bdg. 25.25 *(978-1-4042-4227-2(9))* Rosen Publishing Group, Inc., The. (PowerKids Pr.).

Nelson, John & Obregón, José María. Casquetes Polares en Riesgo: Expedición a la Antártida. 2009. (Historietas Juveniles: Peligros Del Medioambiente (Jr. Graphic Environmental Dangers) Ser.). (SPA., Illus.). 24p. (gr. 3-6). (YA). lib. bdg. 25.25 *(978-1-4358-8474-8(4))*; pap. 10.60 *(978-1-4358-8475-5(2))* Rosen Publishing Group, Inc., The.

Nemeth, Jason D. Climate Change. 2012. (Our Changing Earth Ser.). (ENG.). 24p. (J). (gr. 3-6). pap. 8.25 *(978-1-4488-6290-0(6)*, PowerKids Pr.); lib. bdg. 22.60 *(978-1-4488-6166-8(7))* Rosen Publishing Group, Inc., The.

Ollhoff, Jim. Living in a Warmer World, 1 vol. 2010. (ABDO & Daughters Ser.). (ENG.). 32p. 27.07 *(978-1-61613-453-2(4)*, Abdo & Daughters) ABDO Publishing Co.

—Myths & Controversies, 1 vol. 2010. (ABDO & Daughters Ser.). (ENG.). 32p. 27.07 *(978-1-61613-454-9(2)*, Abdo & Daughters) ABDO Publishing Co.

—The Science, 1 vol. 2010. (ABDO & Daughters Ser.). (ENG.). 32p. 27.07 *(978-1-61613-455-6(0)*, Abdo & Daughters) ABDO Publishing Co.

—Social Solutions, 1 vol. 2010. (ABDO & Daughters Ser.). (ENG.). 32p. 27.07 *(978-1-61613-456-3(9)*, Abdo & Daughters) ABDO Publishing Co.

—Technological Solutions, 1 vol. 2010. (ABDO & Daughters Ser.). (ENG.). 32p. 27.07 *(978-1-61613-457-0(7)*, Abdo & Daughters) ABDO Publishing Co.

—Water & Ice, 1 vol. 2010. (ABDO & Daughters Ser.). (ENG.). 32p. 27.07 *(978-1-61613-458-7(5)*, Abdo & Daughters) ABDO Publishing Co.

Orme, Helen. Climate Change. 2008. (Earth in Danger Ser.). (Illus.). 32p. (YA). (gr. 3-6). lib. bdg. 25.27 *(978-1-59716-723-9(1)*, 1284355) Bearport Publishing Co., Inc.

Parker, Russ. Climate Crisis. 2009. (Planet in Crisis Ser.). 32p. (gr. 5-8). (ENG., Illus.). (J). pap. 10.00 *(978-1-4358-0684-9(0))*; (YA). lib. bdg. 25.25 *(978-1-4358-5254-9(0))* Rosen Publishing Group, Inc., The. (Rosen Reference).

Perritano, John. Meltdown! Global Warming Puts the World on Thin Ice. 2009. (Current Science Ser.). (ENG.). 48p. (gr. 4-7). (YA). lib. bdg. 31.00 *(978-1-4339-2240-4(1))*; (J). pap. 8.95 *(978-1-4339-2244-2(4)*, Gareth Stevens Learning Library) Stevens, Gareth Publishing LLLP.

Reynolds, Toby & Calver, Paul. Global Warming. 2017. (Visual Explorers Ser.). (ENG.). 32p. (J). (gr. 3-7). pap. 6.99 ***(978-1-4380-1082-3(6))*** Barron's Educational Series, Inc.

Robinson, Matthew. America Debates Global Warming: Crisis or Myth? (America Debates Ser.). 64p. (gr. 5-6). 2009. 58.50 *(978-1-61511-333-0(9)*, Rosen Reference) 2007. (Illus.). (YA). lib. bdg. 31.95 *(978-1-4042-1925-0(0))* Rosen Publishing Group, Inc., The.

—America Debates-Global Warming: Crisis or Myth? Lt. ed. 2012. 81p. (J). pap. *(978-1-4596-3473-2(X))* ReadHowYouWant.com, Ltd.

Rockwell, Anne F. Why Are the Ice Caps Melting? The Dangers of Global Warming. Meisel, Paul, illus. 2006. (Let's-Read-And-Find-Out Science 2 Ser.). (ENG.). 40p. (J). (gr. k-4). pap. 5.99 *(978-0-06-054671-7(9)*, Collins) HarperCollins Pubs.

Royston, Angela. The Race to Survive Climate Change. 2014. (World in Crisis Ser.). 48p. (YA). (gr. 5-8). 30.25 *(978-1-4777-7848-7(9)*, Rosen Reference) Rosen Publishing Group, Inc., The.

—What Happens When an Ice Cap Melts? 2015. (Unstable Earth Ser.). (Illus.). 32p. (J). 31.35 *(978-1-62588-160-1(6))* Black Rabbit Bks.

Scholastic, Inc. Staff, contrib. by. Is It Hot Enough for You? Global Warming Heats Up. 2009. (24/7: Behind the Headlines Ser.). (ENG.). 64p. (J). (gr. 6-12). 29.00 *(978-0-531-21805-1(8)*, Watts, Franklin) Scholastic Library Publishing.

Shea, Nicole. Animals & Climate Change. 2013. (Animal 911: Environmental Threats Ser.). 48p. (J). (gr. 3-5). pap. 14.05 *(978-1-4339-9703-7(7))*; pap. 84.30 *(978-1-4339-9704-4(5))*; (ENG., Illus.). lib. bdg. 31.95 *(978-1-4339-9702-0(9))* Stevens, Gareth Publishing LLLP.

Silverstein, Alvin, et al. Global Warming. 2003. (Science Concepts Ser.). (ENG., Illus.). 64p. (gr. 5-9). lib. bdg. 26.60 *(978-0-7613-2256-6(6)*, Twenty-First Century Bks.) Lerner Publishing Group.

—Global Warming (Revised Edition) rev. ed. 2009. (Science Concepts, Second Ser.). (YA). (gr. 5-9). 31.93 *(978-0-7613-3935-9(3))* Lerner Publishing Group.

Simon, Seymour. Global Warming. 2014. 32p. pap. 7.00 *(978-1-61003-345-9(0))* Center for the Collaborative Classroom.

—Global Warming. (ENG., Illus.). 32p. (J). (gr. k-4). 2013. pap. 6.99 *(978-0-06-114252-9(2))* 2010. 17.99 *(978-0-06-114250-5(6))* HarperCollins Pubs. (Collins).

Simpson, Kathleen. Extreme Weather: Science Tackles Global Warming & Climate Change. 2008. (National Geographic Investigates Ser.). (ENG., Illus.). 64p. (J). (gr. 5). lib. bdg. 27.90 *(978-1-4263-0281-7(9)*, National Geographic Children's Bks.) National Geographic Society.

Simpson, Kathleen & National Geographic Kids Staff. Extreme Weather: Science Tackles Global Warming & Climate Change. 2008. (National Geographic Investigates Science Ser.). (ENG., Illus.). 64p. (J). (gr. 5). 17.95 *(978-1-4263-0359-3(9)*, National Geographic Children's Bks.) National Geographic Society.

Sivertsen, Linda & Sivertsen, Tosh. Generation Green: The Ultimate Teen Guide to Living an Eco-Friendly Life. 2008. (ENG.). 272p. (YA). (gr. 7-18). pap. 15.99 *(978-1-4169-6122-2(4)*, Simon Pulse) Simon Pulse.

Slade, Suzanne. The Structure of Atoms. 2006. (Library of Physical Science Ser.: Vol. 3). (Illus.). 24p. (J). (gr. 3-7). lib. bdg. 22.60 *(978-1-4042-3414-7(4))* Rosen Publishing Group, Inc., The.

Sommers, Michael A. Antarctic Melting: The Disappearing Antarctic Ice Cap. 2009. (Extreme Environmental Threats Ser.). 64p. (gr. 6-6). 58.50 *(978-1-61512-423-7(3))* Rosen Publishing Group, Inc., The.

Spalding, Frank. Catastrophic Climate Change & Global Warming. 2010. (Doomsday Scenarios: Separating Fact from Fiction Ser.). 64p. (YA). (gr. 5-8). E-Book 58.50 *(978-1-4488-1204-2(6))* Rosen Publishing Group, Inc., The.

Stein, Paul. Global Warming: A Threat to Our Future. 2009. (Library of Future Weather & Climate Ser.). 64p. (gr. 5-5). 58.50 *(978-1-60853-646-7(7))* Rosen Publishing Group, Inc., The.

—Storms of the Future. 2009. (Library of Future Weather & Climate Ser.). 64p. (gr. 5-5). 58.50 *(978-1-60853-651-1(3))* Rosen Publishing Group, Inc., The.

Streissguth, Tom. Extreme Weather. 2010. (Confronting Global Warming Ser.). 128p. (YA). (gr. 10-12). 38.95 *(978-0-7377-4859-8(1)*, Greenhaven Pr., Inc.) Cengage Gale.

Tara, Stephanie Lisa. Snowy White World to Save. Walton, Alex, illus. 2007. 32p. (J). (gr. -1-3). 16.95 *(978-1-933285-89-4(3))* Brown Books Publishing Group.

Vogel, Carole G. Human Impact. 2003. (Restless Sea Ser.). (ENG., Illus.). 96p. (J). (gr. 5-8). 30.50 *(978-0-531-12323-2(5)*, Watts, Franklin) Scholastic Library Publishing.

Wells, Robert E. Polar Bear, Why Is Your World Melting? Wells, Robert E., illus. 2008. (Wells of Knowledge Science Ser.). (ENG., Illus.). 32p. (J). (gr. 2-3). 16.99 *(978-0-8075-6598-8(9))*; pap. 7.99 *(978-0-8075-6599-5(7))* Whitman, Albert & Co.

World Book, Inc Staff, contrib. by. Understanding Climate Change. 2015. (Illus.). 48p. (J). *(978-0-7166-2706-7(X))* World Bk., Inc.

—Weather & Climate Change. 2015. (Illus.). 47p. (J). *(978-0-7166-2707-4(8))* World Bk., Inc.

Yomtov, Nelson. Polar Ice Caps in Danger: Expedition to Antarctica. 2009. (Jr. Graphic Environmental Dangers Ser.). (ENG., Illus.). 24p. (gr. 3-8). pap. 10.60 *(978-1-4042-4594-5(4)*, PowerKids Pr.) Rosen Publishing Group, Inc., The.

GLOBE THEATRE (SOUTHWARK, LONDON, ENGLAND)—FICTION

Blackwood, Gary. Shakespeare's Spy. 2005. 281p. (gr. 5-9). 17.00 *(978-0-7569-5216-7(6))* Perfection Learning Corp.

Blackwood, Gary L. Shakespeare's Spy. 2005. (ENG.). 288p. (J). (gr. 3-7). 6.99 *(978-0-14-240311-2(3)*, Puffin Books) Penguin Young Readers Group.

Mullarkey, Lisa & Mullarkey, John. Shakespeare Saves the Globe, 1 vol. Bernard, Courtney, illus. 2015. (ENG.). 128p. (J). *(978-1-62402-090-2(9))* Magic Wagon.

GLOBES

Bredeson, Carmen. Mapas y Globos Terraqueos. 2005. (Rookie Espanool Geografia Ser.). (ENG & SPA., Illus.). 32p. (J). (gr. k-2). lib. bdg. 19.50 *(978-0-516-25241-4(0)*, Children's Pr.) Scholastic Library Publishing.

Dalton, Kippy. Globes. 2016. (Spring Forward Ser.). (J). (gr. k). *(978-1-4900-2252-9(X))* Benchmark Education Co.

Edson, Ann & Insel, Eunice. Reading Maps, Globes, Charts, Graphs. (J). (gr. 4-6). stu. ed., instr.'s gde. ed. 39.00 incl. audio *(978-0-89525-175-6(2)*, AKC 356) Educational Activities, Inc.

Figorito, Juliet. How We Use Globes. 2009. (Real Life Readers Ser.). 12p. (gr. 1-2). pap. 5.90 *(978-1-4042-7909-4(1)*, Rosen Classroom) Rosen Publishing Group, Inc., The.

Greve, Meg. Maps Are Flat, Globes Are Round. 2009. (ENG., Illus.). 24p. (gr. k-2). pap. 8.95 *(978-1-60694-533-9(5))* Rourke Educational Media.

Hammond World Atlas Corporation Staff, ed. Globes in a Box. 2008. (Hammond Ser.). 64p. (J). (gr. 5-18). 19.95 *(978-0-8437-1825-6(0))* Hammond World Atlas Corp.

Nelson, Robin. Globes. 2005. (First Step Nonfiction - Geography Ser.). (ENG.). 8p. (gr. -1-1). pap. 4.95 *(978-0-8225-5391-5(0))* Lerner Publishing Group.

Olien, Rebecca. Looking at Maps & Globes. 2012. (Rookie Read-About(tm) Geography — Map Skills Ser.). (ENG., Illus.). 32p. (J). lib. bdg. 25.00 *(978-0-531-28964-8(8))*; (gr. -1-1). pap. 5.95 *(978-0-531-29288-4(6))* Scholastic Library Publishing.

Sundance/Newbridge LLC Staff. Maps & Globes. 2004. (Reading PowerWorks Ser.). (gr. 1-3). 37.50 *(978-0-7608-9747-8(6))*; pap. 6.10 *(978-0-7608-9748-5(4))* Sundance/Newbridge Educational Publishing.

GNOMES

see Fairies

GNUS

Bowman, Chris. Wildebeests. 2015. (Animal Safari Ser.). (ENG., Illus.). 24p. (J). (gr. k-3). lib. bdg. 25.95 *(978-1-62617-167-1(X)*, Blastoff! Readers) Bellwether Media.

Carmichael, L. E. Wildebeest Migration. 2012. (Animal Migrations Ser.). (ENG., Illus.). 32p. (J). (gr. 2-5). lib. bdg. 29.93 *(978-1-60973-626-2(5)*, 201203) Child's World, Inc., The.

Catt, Thessaly. Migrating with the Wildebeest. 2011. (Animal Journeys Ser.). (Illus.). 24p. (J). (gr. 1-4). lib. bdg. 22.60 *(978-1-4488-2544-8(X))* Rosen Publishing Group, Inc., The.

Meinking, Mary. Crocodile vs. Wildebeest, 1 vol. 2011. (Predator vs. Prey Ser.). (ENG., Illus.). 32p. (gr. 1-2). 29.99 *(978-1-4109-3935-7(9))*; pap. 8.29 *(978-1-4109-3944-9(8))* Heinemann-Raintree. (Read Me!).

Migrating with the Wildebeest. 2011. (Animal Journeys Ser.). (Illus.). 24p. (J). pap. 8.25 *(978-1-4488-2795-4(7)*, PowerKids Pr.) Rosen Publishing Group, Inc., The.

Scott, Jonathan & Scott, Angela. The Great Migration White Band. 2016. (Cambridge Reading Adventures Ser.). (ENG.). 32p. pap. 7.81 *(978-1-107-56065-9(9))* Cambridge Univ. Pr.

Shea, Mary Molly. Wildebeests. 2010. (Animals That Live in the Grasslands Ser.). (ENG.). 24p. (J). (gr. -1-3). pap. 8.15 *(978-1-4339-3885-6(5))*; lib. bdg. 22.60 *(978-1-4339-3884-9(7))* Stevens, Gareth Publishing LLLP.

Spilsbury, Louise. Wildebeest, 1 vol. 2011. (Day in the Life: Grassland Animals Ser.). (ENG., Illus.). 24p. (gr. k-2). 23.32 *(978-1-4329-4735-4(4)*, Heinemann Read & Learn) Heinemann-Raintree.

Walden, Katherine. Wildebeests. 2009. (Safari Animals Ser.). 24p. (Illus.). (J). (gr. k-3). pap. 8.25 *(978-1-4358-3066-0(0))*; (gr. 1-1). 42.50 *(978-1-60852-966-7(5))*; (J). (gr. -1-2). lib. bdg. 22.60 *(978-1-4358-2692-2(2))* Rosen Publishing Group, Inc., The. (PowerKids Pr.).

GO KARTS

see Karts and Karting

GOATS

Aspen-Baxter, Linda & Kissock, Heather. Cabras. 2012. (SPA.). (J). *(978-1-61913-188-0(9))* Weigl Pubs., Inc.

Berendes, Mary. Goats. 2016. (In the Barnyard Ser.). (ENG.). 24p. (J). (gr. k-3). 27.07 *(978-1-5038-0827-0(0)*, 210671) Child's World, Inc., The.

Borgert-Spaniol, Megan. Mountain Goats. 2017. (North American Animals Ser.). (ENG., Illus.). 24p. (J). (gr. k-3). lib. bdg. 25.95 ***(978-1-62617-638-6(8)**, Blastoff! Readers)* Bellwether Media.

Bregoli, Jane. The Goat Lady. Bregoli, Jane, illus. 2008. (ENG., Illus.). 32p. (gr. 2-6). pap. 8.95 *(978-0-88448-309-0(6)*, 884309) Tilbury Hse. Pubs.

Carmen, Indigo. Princess the Pygmy Goat. Nardi, Tisa, illus. 2009. 24p. pap. 24.95 *(978-1-60703-824-5(2))* America Star Bks.

Carraway, Rose. Goats on the Farm. 2012. (Farm Animals Ser.). (Illus.). 24p. (gr. k-2). 69.20 *(978-1-4339-8054-1(1))*; (J). 22.60 *(978-1-4339-7352-9(9))*; (J). pap. 8.15 *(978-1-4339-7353-6(7))* Stevens, Gareth Publishing LLLP.

—Goats on the Farm / Cabras de Granja. 2012. (Farm Animals / Animales de granja Ser.). (SPA & ENG., Illus.). 24p. (J). (gr. k-2). 22.60 *(978-1-4339-7398-7(7))* Stevens, Gareth Publishing LLLP.

Ciovacco, Justine. Goats. 2009. (Amazing Animals Ser.). (ENG.). 48p. (J). (gr. 2-6). pap. 10.50 *(978-1-4339-2122-3(7)*, Gareth Stevens Learning Library); (YA). (gr. 3-6). lib. bdg. 28.00 *(978-0-8368-9118-8(X))* Stevens, Gareth Publishing LLLP.

—Goats. 2007. (J). *(978-1-59939-121-2(X)*, Reader's Digest Young Families, Inc.) Studio Fun International.

Clay, Kathryn. Goats, 1 vol. 2012. (Farm Animals Ser.). (ENG., Illus.). 24p. (gr. k-1). lib. bdg. 26.65 *(978-1-4296-8649-5(9)*, Pebble Plus) Capstone Press of Coughlan Cos.

Dicker, Katie. Goats. 2014. (Farm Animals Ser.). (Illus.). 24p. (gr. 2-5). 28.50 *(978-1-62588-021-5(9))* Black Rabbit Bks.

Dobson, Starr. My Goat Gertrude, 1 vol. Dodwell, Dayle, illus. 2012. (ENG.). 32p. (J). (gr. -1-3). 18.95 *(978-1-55109-861-6(X))* Nimbus Publishing, Ltd. CAN. Dist: Orca Bk. Pubs. USA.

—My Goat Gertrude (pb), 1 vol. Dodwell, Dayle, illus. 2013. (ENG.). 32p. (J). (gr. -1-3). pap. 12.95 *(978-1-55109-920-0(9))* Nimbus Publishing, Ltd. CAN. Dist: Orca Bk. Pubs. USA.

Dolphin, Colleen. Gleeful Goats, 1 vol. 2011. (Farm Pets Ser.). (ENG., Illus.). 24p. (J). (gr. k-3). lib. bdg. 24.21 *(978-1-61613-371-9(6))* ABDO Publishing Co.

Gibbs, Maddie. Goats, 1 vol. 2015. (ENG., Illus.). 24p. (J). lib. bdg. 23.60 *(978-1-4994-0134-9(5)*, PowerKids Pr.) Rosen Publishing Group, Inc., The.

—Las Cabras / Goats, 1 vol. 2015. (Amigos de la Granja / Farmyard Friends Ser.). (ENG & SPA.). 24p. (J). 23.60 *(978-1-4994-0272-8(4)*, PowerKids Pr.) Rosen Publishing Group, Inc., The.

The Goat: KinderReaders Individual Title Six-Packs. (Kinderstarters Ser.). 8p. (gr. -1-1). 21.00 *(978-0-7635-8658-4(7))* Rigby Education.

The Goats: Individual Title Six-Packs. (Sails Literacy Ser.). 16p. (gr. k-18). 27.00 *(978-0-7635-4408-9(6))* Rigby Education.

Green, Emily K. Goats. 2007. (Farm Animals Ser.). (ENG., Illus.). 24p. (J). (gr. k-3). lib. bdg. 25.95 *(978-1-60014-066-2(1))* Bellwether Media.

Hudak, Heather C. Goats. 2006. (Farm Animals Ser.). (Illus.). 24p. (J). (gr. 3-7). lib. bdg. 24.45 *(978-1-59036-424-6(4))*; per. 8.95 *(978-1-59036-431-4(7))* Weigl Pubs., Inc.

Ketel, Debbie M. One Baby Mountain Goat. Horstman, Lisa, illus. 2006. (J). bds. 6.99 *(978-0-9752617-3-6(8))* Mount Rushmore Bookstores.

Kissock, Heather & Aspen-Baxter, Linda. Goats. 2011. (J). *(978-1-61690-573-6(5))*; *(978-1-61690-927-7(7))* Weigl Pubs., Inc.

Macken, JoAnn Early. Goats. 2nd rev. ed. 2009. (Animals That Live on the Farm Ser.). (ENG.). 24p. (J). (gr. -1-3). pap. 8.15 *(978-1-4339-2466-8(8))*; lib. bdg. 22.60 *(978-1-4339-2397-5(1))* Stevens, Gareth Publishing LLLP. (Weekly Reader Leveled Readers).

—Goats;Las Cabras. 2nd rev. ed. 2009. (Animals That Live on the Farm/Animales que viven en la granja Ser.). (ENG & SPA.). (J). (gr. -1-3). pap. 8.15 *(978-1-4339-2473-6(0))*; lib. bdg. 22.60 *(978-1-4339-2429-3(3))* Stevens, Gareth Publishing LLLP. (Weekly Reader Leveled Readers).

—Mountain Goats. 2nd rev. ed. 2009. (Animals That Live in the Mountains Ser.). 24p. (J). (gr. -1-3). (ENG.). pap. 8.15 *(978-1-4339-2497-2(8))*; lib. bdg. 22.60 *(978-1-4339-2414-9(5))* Stevens, Gareth Publishing LLLP. (Weekly Reader Leveled Readers).

Magby, Meryl. Mountain Goats. 2013. (American Animals Ser.). 24p. (J). (gr. k-5). pap. 8.25 *(978-1-4777-0952-8(5))*; pap. 49.50 *(978-1-4777-0953-5(3))*; lib. bdg. 22.60 *(978-1-4777-0790-6(5))* Rosen Publishing Group, Inc., The. (PowerKids Pr.).

Meister, Cari. Goats. 2012. (Illus.). 24p. (J). lib. bdg. 25.65 (978-1-62031-003-8(1)) Jump! Inc.

Mercer, Abbie. Goats on a Farm. 2009. (Barnyard Animals Ser.). (ENG.). 24p. (J). pap. 8.25 (978-1-4042-8056-4(1)); (Illus.). lib. bdg. 22.60 (978-1-4042-8049-6(9)) Rosen Publishing Group, Inc., The. (PowerKids Pr.).

Metz, Lorijo. Goats: Nannies, Billies, & Kids. 2010. (On the Farm Ser.). (ENG.). 24p. (J). pap. 8.25 (978-1-4488-1339-1(5)); lib. bdg. 22.60 (978-1-4488-0689-8(5)) Rosen Publishing Group, Inc., The. (PowerKids Pr.).

Minden, Cecilia. Farm Animals: Goats. 2009. (21st Century Junior Library: Farm Animals Ser.). (ENG., Illus.). 24p. (gr. 2-4). lib. bdg. 25.64 (978-1-60279-543-3(6), 200273) Cherry Lake Publishing.

Morgan, Sally. Goats. 2008. (Down on the Farm (N.Y.) Ser.). (ENG., Illus.). 24p. (J). (gr. 3-7). pap. (978-0-7787-4054-4(4)) Crabtree Publishing Co.

—Goats. 2007. (QEB Down on the Farm Ser.). (Illus.). 24p. (J). (gr. -1-3). lib. bdg. 15.95 (978-1-59566-389-4(4)) QEB Publishing Inc.

Murray, Julie. Goats, 1 vol. (ENG., 24p. 2015. Illus.). (J). 27.07 (978-1-62970-940-6(9), 1391179) 2003. 25.65 (978-1-57765-700-2(4), Buddy Bks.) ABDO Publishing Co.

Nelson, Robin. Goats. 2009. pap. 34.95 (978-0-7613-4092-8(0)); (ENG.). 24p. 23.93 (978-0-7613-4061-4(0), Lerner Pubns.); (ENG.). 24p. pap. 6.95 (978-0-7613-4098-0(X)) Lerner Publishing Group.

Owings, Lisa. From Goat to Cheese. 2015. (Start to Finish, Second Ser.). (ENG., Illus.). 24p. (J). (gr. k-3). pap. 6.95 (978-1-4677-6111-6(7)); lib. bdg. 23.93 (978-1-4677-6023-2(4), Lerner Pubns.) Lerner Publishing Group.

Pratt, Laura. Mountain Goats. 2011. (gr. 2-4). (J). pap. 12.95 (978-1-61690-629-0(4), AV2 by Weigl); (Illus.). 24p. (YA). 27.13 (978-1-61690-623-8(5)) Weigl Pubs., Inc.

Quinton, Sasha. Go-Go-Goat: A Phonics Reader. 2009. (Illus.). pap. (978-1-936199-09-9(2)) Book Shop, Ltd., The.

Salzmann, Mary Elizabeth. Baby Goats, 1 vol. 2014. (Baby Animals Set 2 Ser.). (ENG.). 24p. (J). (gr. -1-3). 24.21 (978-1-62403-509-8(4)) ABDO Publishing Co.

Schuetz, Kari. Baby Goats. 2013. (Super Cute! Ser.). (ENG., Illus.). 24p. (J). (gr. k-3). lib. bdg. 25.95 (978-1-60014-927-6(8), Blastoff! Readers) Bellwether Media.

Silverman, Buffy. Pygmy Goats. 2017. (J). **(978-1-5124-8303-1(6))** Lerner Publishing Group.

Stiefel, Chana. Goats on the Family Farm. 2013. (Animals on the Family Farm Ser.). 24p. (J). (gr. k-3). pap. 7.95 (978-1-4644-0355-2(4), Enslow Elementary); lib. bdg. 22.60 (978-0-7660-4206-3(5)) Enslow Pubs., Inc.

Stockland, Patricia M. In the Goat Yard, 1 vol. Ouren, Todd, illus. 2009. (Barnyard Buddies Set 2 Ser.). (ENG.). 24p. (gr. -1-2). 27.07 (978-1-60270-642-2(5), Looking Glass Library-Nonfiction) Magic Wagon.

Top That Publishing Staff, ed. Wacky Goat. 2004. (Wacky Animals Ser.). (Illus.). 10p. (J). pap. (978-1-84510-087-2(5)) Top That! Publishing PLC.

Wood, Alix. Pygmy Goats. 2016. (Mini Animals Ser.). 00032p. (J). (gr. 2-3). pap. 10.00 (978-1-4994-8164-8(0), Windmill Bks.) Rosen Publishing Group, Inc., The.

Wood, Ramona. The Goat Woman of Smackover: An Arkansas Legend. Wood, Ramona, . 2006. (Illus.). 32p. (J). 11.00 (978-0-9758622-1-6(9)) ABC Pr.

GOATS—FICTION

Abedí, Isabel & Neuendorf, Abedi -. No Quiero Verte Mas! Neuendorf, Silvio, illus. 2003. (SPA.). 196p. (J). (gr. -1-3). 17.99 (978-84-261-3303-8(7)) Juventud, Editorial ESP. Dist: Lectorum Pubns., Inc.

Adams, Alison. The Three Billy Goats Gruff: Classic Tales Edition. Harpster, Steve, illus. 2011. (Classic Tales Ser.). (J). (978-1-936258-62-8(5)) Benchmark Education Co.

Aizen, Marina, illus. Mary Had a Little Lamb. 2012. (Classic Books with Holes Board Book Ser.). (ENG.). (J). 14p. bds. (978-1-84643-512-6(9)); 16p. pap. (978-1-84643-501-0(3)) Child's Play International Ltd.

Alakija, Polly. Catch That Goat! A Market Day in Nigeria. Alakija, Polly, illus. 2007. (ENG., Illus.). 40p. (J). (gr. -1-3). 8.99 (978-1-84686-057-7(1)) Barefoot Bks., Inc.

Alakija, Polly, et al. Catch That Goat! 2004. (Avenues Ser.). (ENG., Illus.). 32p. (C). pap. 11.95 (978-1-84148-161-6(0)) National Geographic School Publishing, Inc.

Amery, Heather. Grumpy Goat. Cartwright, Stephen, illus. 2004. 16p. (J). pap. 5.95 (978-0-7945-0788-6(3), Usborne) EDC Publishing.

Anderson, Henry Morgan. Timmy the Goat: Spelunking Adventure. Falk, Wendy & Makepeace, Jonathan, eds. Funnell, Sonja, illus. 2011. (Adventures of Henry Ser.). 48p. 14.99 (978-1-936813-00-1(9)) Adventures of Henry, LLC.

Andrews, Julie & Hamilton, Emma Walton. Dumpy to the Rescue! Walton, Tony, illus. 2004. 24p. (J). lib. bdg. 13.85 (978-1-4242-0707-7(X)) Fitzgerald Bks.

Angleberger, Tom. The Goat Who Chewed Too Much. 2017. (Inspector Flytrap Ser.: 3). lib. bdg. 15.95 **(978-0-606-39682-0(9))** Turtleback Bks.

Angleberger, Tom. Inspector Flytrap. Bell, Cece, illus. (Inspector Flytrap Ser.). (ENG.). 112p. (J). (gr. 1-4). 2017. 14.95 (978-1-4197-0956-2(9)) 2016. 14.95 (978-1-4197-0955-5(0)) 2016. 14.95 (978-1-4197-0948-7(8)) 2016. pap. 5.95 (978-1-4197-0965-4(8)) Abrams, Inc. (Amulet Bks.).

Artigas de Sierra, Ione M. La Chivita del Cebollar. (Superbks./Superlibros). (J). (gr. k-1). 21.95 (978-0-88272-486-7(X));Big Book. (SPA.). 21.95 (978-0-88272-484-3(3)) Santillana USA Publishing Co., Inc.

—The Goat in the Onion Patch. (Superbks./Superlibros). (Illus.). 16p. (J). (gr. k-3). pap. 6.95 (978-0-88272-487-4(8)) Santillana USA Publishing Co., Inc.

Asbjømsen, Peter Christen. The Three Billy Goats Gruff. Sperling, Thomas, illus. 2005. (J). (978-0-7664-1054-1(4)) Abrams, Inc.

—The Three Billy Goats Gruff. Vohra, Sibi, illus. 2010. (J). (978-1-60617-149-3(6)) Teaching Strategies, LLC.

—The Three Billy Goats Gruff. Scott, Gavin, illus. 2014. (J). (978-1-4723-5209-5(2)) Parragon Bk. Service Ltd.

Barkow, Henriette. Three Billy Goats Gruff. Johnson, Richard, illus. 2004. (J). (SER & ENG.). 24p. (978-1-85269-620-7(6)); (ENG & POR.). 32p. pap. (978-1-85269-619-1(2)); (ENG & ALB.). 32p. pap. (978-1-85269-611-5(7)); (GER & ENG.). 32p. pap. (978-1-85269-785-3(7)); (ENG & CZE.). 32p. pap. (978-1-85269-627-6(3)); (ENG & URD.). 32p. pap. (978-1-85269-625-2(7)); (ENG & TUR.). 32p. pap. (978-1-85269-624-5(9)); (ENG & TAM.). 32p. pap. (978-1-85269-623-8(0)); (ENG & SPA.). 32p. pap. (978-1-85269-622-1(2)); (ENG & SOM.). 32p. pap. (978-1-85269-621-4(4)); (ARA & ENG.). 32p. pap. (978-1-85269-612-2(5)); (ENG & PAN.). 32p. pap. (978-1-85269-618-4(4)); (ENG & GUJ.). 32p. pap. (978-1-85269-617-7(6)); (FRE & ENG.). 32p. pap. (978-1-85269-616-0(8)); (ENG & PER.). 32p. pap. (978-1-85269-615-3(X)) Mantra Lingua.

—Three Billy Goats Gruff: English Big Book. Johnson, Richard, illus. 2004. (ENG.). 32p. (J). pap. (978-1-85269-784-6(9)) Mantra Lingua.

Bell, Phillip. Ken the Farmer & His Friend Herbie the Talking Goat. 2012. 26p. 24.95 (978-1-4626-6212-8(9)) America Star Bks.

Bellon-Fisher, Linda. Take Note of Tommy-Toe Goat. 2011. 28p. pap. 24.95 (978-1-4560-7323-7(0)) America Star Bks.

Berry, Lynne. What Floats in a Moat? Cordell, Matthew, illus. 2013. (ENG.). 48p. (J). (gr. k-4). 17.99 (978-1-4169-9763-4(6), Simon & Schuster Bks. For Young Readers) Simon & Schuster Bks. For Young Readers.

Bester, Maryanne. Three Friends & a Taxi. Bester, Shayle, illus. 2007. (Cool Nguni Ser.: 1). (ENG.). 24p. (J). (gr. k-2). 12.00 (978-1-77009-265-5(X)) Jacana Media ZAF. Dist: Independent Pubs. Group.

Bloch, Carole. The Hyena & the Seven Little Kids. Morris, Hannah, illus. 2012. (Best Loved Tales for Africa Ser.). (ENG.). 32p. (J). (gr. k-2). pap. 9.95 (978-1-77009-820-6(8)) Jacana Media ZAF. Dist: Independent Pubs. Group.

—The Three Billy Goats Gruff. Bester, Shayle, illus. 2011. (Best Loved Tales for Africa Ser.). (ENG.). 32p. (J). (gr. k-2). pap. 10.95 (978-1-77009-765-0(1)) Jacana Media ZAF. Dist: Independent Pubs. Group.

Blyton, Enid. Don't Be Silly Mr Twiddle! (ENG., Illus.). 111p. (J). pap. 7.95 (978-0-7475-3858-5(1)) Bloomsbury Publishing Plc GBR. Dist: Trafalgar Square Publishing.

Brewer, Dottie A. Jessie's Walk. Naenix, Robin, illus. 2004. 20p. (J). 4.95 (978-0-9707945-7-4(6)) Billion $ Baby Pubns.

Brightwood, Laura, illus. Bully Goat Grim. Brightwood, Laura, . 2006. (J). (978-0-9779290-2-3(7)) 3-C Institute for Social Development.

Bristol, P. L. & Branda, Barnabus. Fiona Faintly: A Goats Tale. Howard, Megz, illus. 2011. 32p. pap. 24.95 (978-1-4626-3362-3(5)) America Star Bks.

Brooks, Yvonne & Grant, Steven. The Goat Kids Explore the Woods. 2006. (Illus.). 32p. (J). 14.95 (978-0-9791021-1-0(1)) Lotus Pond Media.

—Meet the Goat Kids. l.t. ed. 2006. (Illus.). 32p. (J). 14.95 (978-0-9791021-0-3(3), 978-0-9791021-0-3) Lotus Pond Media.

Brown, Janet. The Three Billy Goats Gruff (Floor Book) Morton, Ken, illus. 2015. (ENG.). 24p. (J). (gr. -1-1). pap. 6.99 (978-1-86147-397-4(4), Armadillo) Anness Publishing GBR. Dist: National Bk. Network.

Bruno, Pep. THE SILLY NANNY GOAT. 2007. (ENG., Illus.). 36p. (J). 17.95 (978-84-96788-86-2(5)) OQO, Editora ESP. Dist: Baker & Taylor Bks.

Bryan, Jennifer Liu. Hilda, A Very Loyal Goat. 2009. 40p. (J). 15.95 (978-0-9816265-1-2(3)) Next Chapter Pr.

Bunting, Eve. Mr. Goat's Valentine. Zimmer, Kevin, illus. 2016. (ENG.). 32p. (J). (gr. k-2). 16.99 (978-1-58536-944-7(6), 204024) Sleeping Bear Pr.

Burks, James. Beep & Bah. Burks, James, illus. 2012. (Carolrhoda Picture Bks.). (ENG., Illus.). 32p. (J). (gr. k-3). lib. bdg. 16.95 (978-0-7613-6567-9(2)) Lerner Publishing Group.

Carr, Elias. Ava y el Picnic Raquitico. Garton, Michael, illus. 2016. (SPA.). (J). **(978-1-5064-2095-0(8))** Augsburg Fortress, Pubs.

—Hal y el Nuevo Compañero. Garton, Michael, illus. 2016. (SPA.). (J). **(978-1-5064-2098-1(2))** Augsburg Fortress, Pubs.

—Jo y la Sopa Lenta. Garton, Michael, illus. 2016. (SPA.). (J). **(978-1-5064-2097-4(4)**, Sparkhouse Pr.) Spark Hse.

Church, Caroline Jayne. Little Apple Goat. Church, Caroline Jayne, illus. 2007. (ENG., Illus.). 28p. (J). (gr. k-3). 16.00 (978-0-8028-5320-2(X), Eerdmans Bks For Young Readers) Eerdmans, William B. Publishing Co.

Cole, Henry. Trudy. Cole, Henry, illus. 2009. (ENG., Illus.). 32p. (J). (gr. -1-3). 17.99 (978-0-06-154267-1(9), Greenwillow Bks.) HarperCollins Pubs.

Cook, Sherry & Johnson, Terri. Gilbert Gas, 26 vols. Kuhn, Jesse, illus. l.t. ed. 2006. (Quirkles — Exploring Phonics through Science Ser.: 7). 32p. (J). 7.99 (978-1-933815-06-0(X), Quirkles, The) Creative 3, LLC.

Cooper, William Y. Nakai & the Red Shoes. 2011. 52p. (gr. 4-6). pap. 19.39 (978-1-4269-6048-2(4)) Trafford Publishing.

Corum, Stephanie J. Goats with Coats. 2008. 32p. pap. 12.99 (978-1-4343-9302-9(X)) AuthorHouse.

Coville, Bruce. Thor's Wedding Day: By Thialfi, the Goat Boy. Cogswell, Matthew, illus. 2008. (ENG.). 144p. (J). (gr. 2-5). pap. 6.99 (978-0-15-205872-2(9)) Houghton Mifflin Harcourt Publishing Co.

Cromwell, Daisy. Arthur, the Talking Goat. Paxton, Cameron L., illus. 2007. 52p. (J). pap. 18.99 (978-0-9800675-1-4(0)) Mirror Publishing.

Crummel, Susan Stevens. Ten-Gallon Bart, 0 vols. Donohue, Dorothy, illus. 2010. (ENG.). 32p. (J). (gr. k-3). pap. 9.99 (978-0-7614-5719-0(4), 9780761457190, Amazon Children's Publishing) Amazon Publishing.

Cunliffe, John. Postman Pat & the Goat's Supper. (Illus.). 20p. (J). (978-0-340-71437-9(9)) Hodder & Stoughton.

Davies, Stephen. The Goggle-Eyed Goats. Corr, Christopher, illus. 2012. (ENG.). 32p. (J). (gr. -1-k). 22.99 (978-1-84939-293-8(5)) Andersen Pr. GBR. Dist: Independent Pubs. Group.

Davies, Stephen & Corr, Christopher. The Goggle-Eyed Goats. 2013. (ENG., Illus.). 32p. (J). (gr. -1-k). pap. 12.99 (978-1-84939-312-6(5)) Andersen Pr. GBR. Dist: Independent Pubs. Group.

deRubertis, Barbara. Gertie Gorilla's Glorious Gift. Alley, R. W., illus. 2010. (Animal Antics A to Z Ser.). 32p. (J). (gr. -1-3). pap. 7.95 (978-1-57565-311-2(7)); lib. bdg. 22.60 (978-1-57565-318-1(4)) Kane Press, Inc.

deRubertis, Barbara & DeRubertis, Barbara. Gertie Gorilla's Glorious Gift. Alley, R. W., illus. 2012. (Animal Antics A to Z Ser.). 32p. (J). (gr. 2 — 1). cd-rom 7.95 (978-1-57565-400-3(8)) Kane Press, Inc.

Dewdney, Anna. Llama Llama & the Bully Goat. 2013. (Llama Llama Ser.). (ENG., Illus.). 40p. (J). (gr. -1-k). 17.99 (978-0-670-01395-1(1), Viking Books for Young Readers) Penguin Young Readers Group.

DiTaranto, Cynthia A. Kristmas Karol the Nigerian Dwarf Goat. 2010. 24p. 14.95 (978-1-4269-3016-4(X)) Trafford Publishing.

Dockery, Marie F. The Three Billy Goats Gruff Find Jesus & the Three Little Souls. 2008. 52p. pap. 12.99 (978-1-60647-605-5(X)) Salem Author Services.

Dolan, Penny. Little Troll. Smith, Lisa, illus. 2008. (Tadpoles Ser.). (ENG.). 24p. (J). (gr. -1-3). lib. bdg. (978-0-7787-3856-5(6)) Crabtree Publishing Co.

Las Dos Cabritas. (Coleccion Fabulas y Cuentos Populares). (SPA.). (J). (gr. 2-4). lib. bdg. (978-84-246-1554-3(9), GL3091) La Galera, S.A. Editorial ESP. Dist: Lectorum Pubns., Inc.

Doudna, Kelly. Goat Cheese, 1 vol. Haberstroh, Anne, illus. 2006. (Animal Tales Ser.). 24p. (J). (gr. k-3). (ENG.). lib. bdg. 24.21 (978-1-59679-937-0(4), SandCastle); pap. 48.42 (978-1-59679-938-7(2)) ABDO Publishing Co.

Dyson, Edward. Missing Link. 2006. pap. 11.95 (978-1-4218-3040-7(X)) 1st World Publishing, Inc.

Edgson, Alison, illus. Three Billy Goats Gruff. (Flip-Up Fairy Tales Ser.). (ENG.). 24p. (J). 2007. (gr. -1-2). audio compact disk (978-1-84643-089-3(5)) 2006. (gr. 1-2). (978-1-904550-72-3(X)) Child's Play International Ltd.

Emerson, Carl. Falling Freddy the Fainting Goat, 1 vol. Trover, Zachary, illus. 2007. (Animal Underdogs Ser.). (ENG.). 32p. (gr. -1-4). 28.50 (978-1-60270-015-4(X), Looking Glass Library) ABDO Publishing Co.

The Fight on the Hill: Individual Title Six-Pack. (Story Steps Ser.). (gr. k-2). 23.00 (978-0-7635-9837-2(2)) Rigby Education.

Florence, Nancy L. Harold the Goat. 2004. (ENG.). 30p. 24.95 (978-1-4137-3941-1(5)) PublishAmerica, Inc.

Ford, Bernette. No More Biting for Billy Goat! Williams, Sam, illus. 2013. (Ducky & Piggy Ser.). (ENG.). 32p. (J). (gr. -1-k). 14.95 (978-1-907967-31-3(1)) Boxer Bks., Ltd. GBR. Dist: Sterling Publishing Co., Inc.

Ford, Carolyn. The Paper Bag. Diez-Luckie, Cathy, illus. 2005. (ENG.). 8p. (J). 5.75 (978-1-57274-756-2(0), 2494, Bks. for Young Learners) Owen, Richard C. Pubs., Inc.

Fox, Mem. Let's Count Goats! Thomas, Jan, illus. 2010. (ENG.). 40p. (J). (gr. -1-1). 16.99 (978-1-4424-0598-1(8), Beach Lane Bks.) Beach Lane Bks.

French, Vivian. Mountain Mona: Band 09/Gold. Fisher, Chris, illus. 2006. (Collins Big Cat Ser.). (ENG.). 24p. (J). (gr. 2-2). pap. 7.99 (978-0-00-718700-3(9)) HarperCollins Pubs. Ltd. GBR. Dist: Independent Pubs. Group.

Galdone, Paul. The Three Billy Goats Gruff. 2011. (Folk Tale Classics Ser.). (ENG., Illus.). 40p. (J). (gr. -1-3). 8.99 (978-0-547-57655-8(2)) Houghton Mifflin Harcourt Publishing Co.

—The Three Billy Goats Gruff, 1 vol. Galdone, Paul, illus. 2008. (Paul Galdone Classics Ser.). (ENG., Illus.). 32p. (J). (gr. -1-3). audio compact disk 10.99 (978-0-618-89499-4(3)) Houghton Mifflin Harcourt Publishing Co.

—The Three Billy Goats Gruff. 2006. (Paul Galdone Classics Ser.). (ENG., Illus.). 32p. (J). (gr. -1-3). 26.99 (978-0-618-83685-7(3)) Houghton Mifflin Harcourt Publishing Co.

—Los Tres Chivitos Gruff. Fiol, María A., tr. 2003.Tr. of Three Billy Goats Gruff. (SPA., Illus.). (J). (gr. k-3). pap. 7.95 (978-1-880507-62-9(5), LC0249) Lectorum Pubns., Inc.

Garis, Howard R. The Curlytops & Their Pets. 2009. 120p. pap. 10.95 (978-1-60664-341-9(X)) Rodgers, Alan Bks.

Garland, Michael. King Puck. Garland, Michael, illus. 2009. (ENG., Illus.). 32p. (J). (gr. -1-3). pap. 6.99 (978-0-06-084811-8(1)) HarperCollins Pubs.

Glover, Dennis W. The Goat Farm. 2009. 32p. pap. 12.99 (978-1-4490-1532-9(8)) AuthorHouse.

Glover, Rosanne Harper. Chloe, the Very Special Goat. Sites, Jennifer, illus. 2012. (ENG.). 48p. (J). 16.95 (978-0-938467-53-3(0)) Headline Bks., Inc.

Grandma's Pie: Individual Title Six-Packs. (Story Steps Ser.). (gr. k-2). 32.00 (978-0-7635-9816-7(X)) Rigby Education.

Guillain, Adam & Guillain, Charlotte. The Three Frilly Goats Fluff. Littler, Phil, illus. 2015. (ENG.). 32p. (J). (978-0-7787-1935-9(9)) Crabtree Publishing Co.

Haines, Doris. 1 Goat, 2 Goat, 3 Goat, 4. 2013. 24p. pap. (978-1-4602-0527-3(8)) FriesenPress.

Hale, Dean. Scapegoat: The Story of a Goat Named Oat & a Chewed-Up Coat. Slack, Michael, illus. 2011. (ENG.). 32p. (J). (gr. -1-3). 16.99 (978-1-59990-468-9(3), 9781599904689, Bloomsbury USA Childrens) Bloomsbury Publishing USA.

Hamilton, Benny. The Goat in the Coat. 2010. 36p. (J). pap. 21.95 (978-1-4327-4884-5(X)) Outskirts Pr., Inc.

Hamilton, Martha & Weiss, Mitch. Two Fables of Aesop. MacDonald, Bruce, illus. 2005. (ENG.). 16p. (J). 5.75 (978-1-57274-718-0(8), 2788, Bks. for Young Learners) Owen, Richard C. Pubs., Inc.

Heeney, Bronwyn. Nibbles. Sayers, Rachel, illus. 2011. 26p. pap. 13.50 (978-1-60860-278-0(8), Eloquent Bks.) Strategic Book Publishing & Rights Agency (SBPRA).

Helquist, Brett. Grumpy Goat. Helquist, Brett, illus. 2013. (ENG., Illus.). 40p. (J). (gr. -1-3). 17.99 (978-0-06-113953-6(X)) HarperCollins Pubs.

Hiebert, Elfrieda H. & Juel, Connie. Eric & the Three Goats. (Little Book Practice Reader Ser.). (J). (978-0-8136-0987-4(9)) Modern Curriculum Pr.

—Nanny Goat's Nap. (Little Book Practice Reader Ser.). (J). (978-0-8136-0692-7(6)) Modern Curriculum Pr.

Hillert, Margaret. The Three Goats. Banks, Timothy, illus. 2016. (BeginningtoRead Ser.). (ENG.). 32p. (J). (gr. -1-2). pap. 11.94 (978-1-60357-914-8(1)) Norwood Hse. Pr.

Holden, Pam. Trip, Trap!, 6 pack. Hawley, Kelvin, illus. 2009. (Red Rocket Readers Ser.). (ENG.). 16p. (gr. 2-2). pap. (978-1-877363-62-7(6), Red Rocket Readers) Flying Start Bks.

Hudson, Judith. Bayo a Good African Boy. 2009. 28p. (J). pap. 12.95 (978-1-4327-4067-2(9)) Outskirts Pr., Inc.

Hulst, W. G. van de & Hulst, Willem G. van de, illus. Annie & the Goat. 2014. (J). (978-1-928136-06-4(0)) Inheritance Pubns.

The Hungry Goat. (Early Intervention Levels Ser.). 23.10 (978-0-7362-0010-3(X)) CENGAGE Learning.

Ippolito, Heidi. Bobo's New Home. 2009. 24p. pap. 11.50 (978-1-60860-220-9(6), Strategic Bk. Publishing) Strategic Book Publishing & Rights Agency (SBPRA).

Jacob, Annie. When I Was a Kid. 2013. 24p. pap. 14.93 (978-1-4669-9740-0(0)) Trafford Publishing.

Jarrett, Judy. Billy the Kid. 2004. 46p. (978-1-57168-988-7(5), Nortex Pr.) Eakin Pr.

Johnson, Phyllis. Four Baby Goats. 2013. 32p. 19.95 (978-1-4575-2260-4(8)) Dog Ear Publishing, LLC.

Jolivert, Immaculine. The Lamb Who Counted Clouds. Gillen, Rosemarie, illus. 2013. 24p. pap. 13.75 (978-1-937260-91-0(7)) Sleepytown Pr.

Jordan, Rosa. The Goatnappers. 2007. (ENG.). 224p. (J). (gr. 3-7). 14.95 (978-1-56145-400-6(1)) Peachtree Pubs.

—Lost Goat Lane, 1 vol. 2004. (ENG.). 192p. (J). (gr. 3-7). 14.95 (978-1-56145-325-2(0)) Peachtree Pubs.

Josiah, Iris. Tiny Goat. 2012. (Illus.). 28p. (J). pap. (978-0-9572728-2-8(0)) Tiny Island Pr.

Jupin, David Perez, illus. Love. 2013. 20p. pap. 11.95 (978-1-937504-67-0(0)) Worthy Shorts.

The Kids from Quiller's Bend: Individual Title Six-Packs. (Action Packs Ser.). 120p. (gr. 3-5). 44.00 (978-0-7635-8432-0(0)) Rigby Education.

Kimmel, Eric A. Los Tres Cabritos, 0 vols. Gilpin, Stephen, illus. 2012. (SPA & ENG.). 32p. (J). (gr. k-3). pap. 9.99 (978-0-7614-5961-3(8), 9780761459613, Amazon Children's Publishing) Amazon Publishing.

—The Three Cabritos, 0 vols. Gilpin, Stephen, illus. 2012. (ENG.). 32p. (J). (gr. -1-3). pap. 7.99 (978-0-7614-6309-2(7), 9780761463092, Amazon Children's Publishing) Amazon Publishing.

Kimmelman, Leslie. The Three Bully Goats. Terry, Will, illus. 2012. (J). (978-1-61913-136-1(6)) Weigl Pubs., Inc.

—The Three Bully Goats. Terry, Will, illus. 2011. (ENG.). 32p. (J). (gr. -1-3). 16.99 (978-0-8075-7900-8(9)) Whitman, Albert & Co.

Kimura & North, Lucy. One Stormy Night. Abe, Hiroshi, illus. 2005. 48p. (J). (gr. 1-3). 16.00 (978-4-7700-2970-6(5)) Kodansha International JPN. Dist: Cheng & Tsui Co.

—One Sunny Day, 2 vols., Vol. 2. Abe, Hiroshi, illus. 2005. 48p. (J). 16.00 (978-4-7700-2971-3(3)) Kodansha International JPN. Dist: Cheng & Tsui Co.

Kitamura, Satoshi. Por el Hilo se Saca el Ovillo. Kitamura, Satoshi, illus. 2003. (Picture Books Collection). (SPA., Illus.). 32p. (J). (gr. k-3). 14.95 (978-84-372-2357-5(1)) Altea, Ediciones, S.A. - Grupo Santillana ESP. Dist: Santillana USA Publishing Co., Inc.

Koontz, Robin. Cinderella Zelda. Koontz, Robin, illus. 2011. (ENG., Illus.). 24p. (gr. 2-3). pap. 8.95 (978-1-61236-027-0(0)) Rourke Educational Media.

—Los Tres Carneros y el Ogro / the Three Billy Goats & Gruff. 2012. (SPA & ENG.). 24p. (gr. 2-3). pap. 8.95 (978-1-61810-540-0(X)) Rourke Educational Media.

Laird, Lisa J. I'm the Only One Who Loves Cliff the Goat. 2009. 48p. pap. 19.49 (978-1-4389-5660-2(6)) AuthorHouse.

Lamb Ii, James. Jimmy Jimmy el Cordero Salto Cumple Phil el Pato. 2012. 28p. pap. 17.99 (978-1-4685-5036-8(5)) AuthorHouse.

Leite, Karen. A Miracle Named Angel. 2009. 24p. pap. 11.49 (978-1-4389-5246-8(5)) AuthorHouse.

Little Goat's Coat. (Sails Literacy Ser.). 24p. (gr. k-18). 27.00 (978-0-7635-6990-7(9)) Rigby Education.

Little Goat's Coat: 3-in-1 Package. (Sails Literacy Ser.). 24p. (gr. k-18). 57.00 (978-0-7578-3200-0(8)) Rigby Education.

Lochmandy, Sandy. Kids & Critters on an Adventure. 2009. 36p. pap. 14.95 (978-1-60860-387-9(3), Eloquent Bks.) Strategic Book Publishing & Rights Agency (SBPRA).

Lopez, Barbara J. Pepper's Wish. 2009. 32p. pap. 14.49 (978-1-4389-4976-5(6)) AuthorHouse.

Louise, Cristina & McIlroy, Michelle. Where Is Paco Now? Louise, Cristina & McIlroy, Michelle, illus. 2012. (SPA & ENG., Illus.). (J). (978-1-934370-26-1(6), Campanita Bks.) Editorial Campana.

Malone, Jean M. Dexter the Very Good Goat, 1 vol. Min Lin, Jia, illus. 2016. (ENG.). 32p. (J). 14.99 (978-0-7643-5051-1(X), 9780764350511) Schiffer Publishing, Ltd.

Marinaro, Stacy. Annabelle & the Meteor. 2008. 32p. pap. 8.95 (978-1-4357-2841-7(6)) Lulu Pr., Inc.

Martinez, Rene. The Journey of the Golden Sword. 2011. 64p. pap. 15.99 (978-1-4535-9187-1(7)) Xlibris Corp.

Mason, Jo-Anne. Paddy, the Goat That Saved Rainbow Island. 2003. 48p. (gr. -1-3). 13.95 (978-0-333-97062-1(4)) Macmillan Caribbean GBR. Dist: Interlink Publishing Group, Inc.

McBrier, Page. Beatrice's Goat. Lohstoeter, Lori, illus. 2004. (ENG.). 40p. (J). (gr. -1-3). reprint ed. 7.99 (978-0-689-86990-7(8), Aladdin) Simon & Schuster Children's Publishing.

MCP Staff. Nanny Goat's Nap, Level 3, Bk. 21. (J). (gr. -1-3). 24.50 (978-0-8136-0691-0(8)) Modern Curriculum Pr.

Mcwherter, Barbara. Oliver & His Mountain Climbing Adventures. McWherter, Shelley, illus. 2012. 34p. 24.95 (978-1-4626-7601-9(4)) America Star Bks.

Michaels, Dood. Tennyshoe Adventures: Treasure Hunters. 2010. 101p. pap. 12.95 (978-0-557-70285-5(2)) Lulu Pr., Inc.

Miller, Vern. Gypsy the Goat. Cotes Stanley, Marsha, illus. 2013. 36p. pap. 11.95 (978-1-61153-082-7(2)) Light Messages Publishing.

Moncure, Jane Belk. Nanny Goat's Boat: A Book of Rhyming. Girouard, Patrick, illus. 2013. (Magic Castle Readers Ser.). (ENG.). 32p. (J). (gr. -1-2). 25.64 (978-1-62323-567-3(7), 206301) Child's World, Inc., The.

Moore, Carol H. Marvin the Magnificent Nubian Goat. Harrell, Micheael, illus. 2006. (J). 20.00 (978-0-9792019-0-5(X)) iwishyouicecreamandcake.

Moore, Carol Hair. Marvin the Magnificent Nubian Goat. Harrell, Michael, illus. 2009. (I Wish You Ice Cream & Cake Ser.). 28p. (J). lib. bdg. 15.95 (978-1-935083-03-0(1)) CyPress Pubns.

—Marvin the Magnificent Nubian Goat. 2007. 28p. per. 17.49 (978-1-4257-6046-5(5)) Xlibris Corp.

Mortimer, Rachael. The Three Billy Goats Fluff. Pichon, Liz, illus. 2013. (ENG.). 32p. (J). (gr. -1-2). pap. 7.95 (978-1-58925-439-8(2)) Tiger Tales.

—Three Billy Goats Fluff. Pichon, Liz, illus. 2011. (ENG.). 36p. 15.95 (978-1-58925-101-4(6)) Tiger Tales.

Morton, Ken, illus. The Three Billy Goats Gruff: My First Reading Book. 2013. (ENG.). 24p. 5.99 (978-1-84322-832-5(7), Armadillo) Anness Publishing GBR. Dist: National Bk. Network.

Mustaine Hettinger, Cynthia. Doc the Pygmy Goat. Ramsey, Jayne, illus. 2003. (Electra's Acres Ser.). 32p. (J). per. 14.95 (978-0-9746330-0-8(3)) Anton Berkshire Publishing.

Nagy, Jennifer. Goats in Coats. Broughton, Ilona & Szigyarto, Cynthia, illus. 2009. 20p. pap. 12.99 (978-1-4389-6586-4(9)) AuthorHouse.

Nena L. Kircher & Julie A. Kircher. The Laid Back Legend of the Three Billy Goats Gruff. 2009. 24p. pap. 13.50 (978-1-4389-6650-2(4)) AuthorHouse.

Newberry, Peggy. Margie & the Goat. 2010. 24p. pap. 15.99 (978-1-4500-7475-9(8)) Xlibris Corp.

Nobleman, Marc Tyler. The Chupacabra Ate the Candelabra. Aranda, Ana, illus. 2017. (ENG.). 32p. (J). (gr. k-3). 17.99 (978-0-399-17443-8(5), Nancy Paulsen Books) Penguin Young Readers Group.

Nyeu, Tao. Bunny Days. Nyeu, Tao, illus. 2010. (ENG., Illus.). 48p. (J). (gr. -1-k). 16.99 (978-0-8037-3330-5(5), Dial Bks) Penguin Young Readers Group.

Once upon a Time Spanish Version-the Three Billy Goats Gruff. 2005. (J). (978-1-57022-564-2(8)) ECS Learning Systems, Inc.

Ottolenghi, Carol. The Three Billy Goats Gruff. 2009. (Keepsake Stories Ser.). (ENG.). 32p. (J). (gr. -1-3). pap. 3.99 (978-0-7696-5868-1(7), Brighter Child) Carson-Dellosa Publishing, LLC.

—The Three Billy Goats Gruff (Los Tres Chivitos) 2009. (Keepsake Stories Ser.). (ENG & SPA.). 32p. (gr. -1-2). pap. 3.99 (978-0-7696-5864-3(4), Brighter Child) Carson-Dellosa Publishing, LLC.

Page, Nick & Page, Claire. Read with Me Three Billy Goats Gruff: Sticker Activity Book. Saunders, Katie, illus. 2006. (Read with Me (Make Believe Ideas) Ser.). 12p. (J). (gr. k-2). pap. (978-1-84610-181-6(6)) Make Believe Ideas.

—Three Billy Goats Gruff. 2006. (Read with Me (Make Believe Ideas) Ser.). (Illus.). 32p. (J). (gr. k-2). (978-1-84610-165-6(4)) Make Believe Ideas.

Paltenghi, Madalena. Remus Goes to Town. Anderson, C. W., illus. 2011. 32p. 35.95 (978-1-258-10024-7(X)) Literary Licensing, LLC.

Pankhurst, Kate, illus. The Three Billy Goats Gruff. adapted ed. 2015. (My First Fairy Tales Ser.). (ENG.). 32p. (J). 7.99 (978-1-58925-459-6(7)) Tiger Tales.

Paschal Shija. The Proud Kid & the Stream. 2005. (Illus.). 14p. pap. (978-9987-686-97-1(4)) Mkuki na Nyoka Pubs. TZA. Dist: Michigan State Univ. Pr.

PC Treasures Staff, prod. The Three Billy Goats Gruff. 2007. (J). (978-1-60072-017-8(X)) PC Treasures, Inc.

Penguin Books Staff, ed. The Three Billy Goats Gruff. (Fairy Tale Fun Ser.). (J). 3.95 (978-0-7214-5430-6(5), Dutton Juvenile) Penguin Publishing Group.

Plato's Journey: Evaluation Guide. 2006. (J). (978-1-55942-421-9(4)) Witcher Productions.

Polacco, Patricia. G Is for Goat. Polacco, Patricia, illus. 2006. (ENG., Illus.). 32p. (J). (gr. -1-k). reprint ed. pap. 7.99 (978-0-14-240550-5(7), Puffin Books) Penguin Young Readers Group.

—Oh, Look! Polacco, Patricia, illus. 2004. (ENG., Illus.). 32p. (J). (gr. -1-3). 16.99 (978-0-399-24223-6(6), Philomel Bks.) Penguin Young Readers Group.

Rankin, Laura. My Turn! Rankin, Laura, illus. 2016. (ENG., Illus.). 32p. (J). 16.99 (978-1-59990-174-9(9), 9781599901749, Bloomsbury USA Childrens) Bloomsbury Publishing USA.

Rigo, L., illus. Little Lamb. 2012. (Mini Look at Me Bks.). (ENG.). 10p. (J). bds. 4.99 (978-0-7641-6511-5(9)) Barron's Educational Series, Inc.

Rix, Jamie. Bendro Bach. Williams, Dylan, tr. from ENG. Chapman, Lynne, illus. 2005. (WEL.). 36p. (978-1-902416-84-7(8)) Cymdeithas Lyfrau Ceredigion.

Robinson, Larry Jay. Stubborn Stanley. 2012. 68p. pap. 41.99 (978-1-4771-1385-1(1)) Xlibris Corp.

Robinson, Nikki Slade. Muddle & Mo. 2017. (ENG., Illus.). 32p. (J). (gr. -1-3). 14.99 (978-0-544-71612-4(4)) Houghton Mifflin Harcourt Publishing Co.

Rwakasisi, Rose. How Goats Lost Their Beautiful Tails. 2004. (Illus.). 19p. pap. (978-9970-02-436-0(1)) Fountain Pubs. Ltd. UGA. Dist: Michigan State Univ. Pr.

Sargent, Dave. Storky Stork: Be Trustworthy, 19 vols., Vol. 18. Lenoir, Jane, illus. 2003. (Feather Tales Ser.: 18). 42p. (J). pap. 10.95 (978-1-56763-754-0(X)) Ozark Publishing.

Sazaklis, John. Goat on a Boat, 1 vol. Bradley, Jessica, illus. 2013. (Comics Land Ser.). (ENG.). 32p. (gr. k-2). 7.95 (978-1-4342-6282-0(0)); lib. bdg. 25.32 (978-1-4342-4944-9(1)) Stone Arch Bks.

Schettler, Amanda. The Adventures of Mike & Fanny: A Story about A Dog & A Goat. 2011. 50p. 35.95 (978-1-258-08538-4(0)) Literary Licensing, LLC.

Seaberg, Richard Leonard. Elmoson the Christmas Goat. 2009. 20p. pap. 15.95 (978-1-4490-2321-8(5)) AuthorHouse.

Sharmat, Mitchell. Gregory, the Terrible Eater. Dewey, Ariane & Aruego, Jose, illus. 2009. (ENG.). 32p. (J). (gr. -1-3). pap. 6.99 (978-0-545-12931-2(1)) Scholastic, Inc.

Sharratt, Nick & Tucker, Stephen. The Three Billy Goats Gruff, 2 vols. Sharratt, Nick, illus. 2017. (Lift-The-Flap Fairy Tales Ser.). (ENG., Illus.). 24p. (J). (gr. -1-k). 10.99 **(978-1-5098-2978-1(4))** Pan Macmillan GBR. Dist: Independent Pubs. Group.

Shea, Bob. Unicorn Thinks He's Pretty Great. Shea, Bob, illus. 2013. (ENG., Illus.). 40p. (J). (gr. -1-k). 15.99 (978-1-4231-5952-0(7)) Hyperion Pr.

—What's Your Favorite Favorite? Shea, Bob, illus. 2017. (Ballet Cat Ser.). (ENG., Illus.). 56p. (J). (gr. 1-3). 9.99 (978-1-4847-7809-8(X)) Disney Pr.

Siegal, Aranka. Upon the Head of the Goat: A Childhood in Hungary, 1939-1944. 2003. (ENG.). 224p. (J). (gr. 5-8). pap. 8.99 (978-0-374-48079-0(6), 9780374480790) Square Fish.

Simpson, Albert. The Adventures of Billy, Ras, & Al. 2012. 24p. pap. 17.99 (978-1-4772-1641-5(3)) AuthorHouse.

Sims, Lesley. Goat in a Boat. 2015. (Phonics Readers (no Flaps) Ser.). (ENG.). 24p. (J). pap. 6.99 (978-0-7945-3408-0(2), Usborne) EDC Publishing.

Singer, Isaac Bashevis. Cuentos Judíos de la Aldea de Chelm.Tr. of Zlateh the Goat & Other Stories. (SPA.). 62p. (J). 7.96 (978-84-264-3404-3(5), LM2595) Editorial Lumen ESP. Dist: Lectorum Pubns., Inc.

Smithers, J. Megan, illus. Emma: An Interactive Storybook. 2nd ed. 2005. 60p. (J). (gr. k-4). pap. 9.00 (978-0-9713342-6-7(9)) B V Wespat.

Switzer, Vern. Hard Heads Make Soft Bottoms. Connally, Perry L., Sr., illus. 2007. 34p. (J). 15.95 (978-0-9753542-2-3(1)) Rural Farm Productions.

Taylor, Sean. Huck Runs Amuck! Reynolds, Peter, illus. 2011. (ENG.). 48p. (J). (gr. k-3). 16.99 (978-0-8037-3261-2(9), Dial Bks) Penguin Young Readers Group.

Three Billy Goats Gruff. 2005. (J). bds. 3.99 (978-1-933200-12-5(X)) Family Bks. at Home.

The Three Billy Goats Gruff. 2008. (Read & Learn Sticker Books Ser.). 48p. pap. (978-1-4075-3194-6(8)) Parragon, Inc.

Three Billy Goat's Gruff. 2004. (J). E-Book incl. cd-rom (978-1-84444-467-0(8)) Mantra Lingua.

Thronson, Lloyd. Gomer the Goat & His New Home. 2011. 30p. pap. 16.95 (978-1-4626-1590-2(2)) America Star Bks.

Timmons, Robbie. Twoey & the Goat. 2008. (ENG., Illus.). 192p. (J). (gr. 1-7). 15.95 (978-1-58726-517-4(6), Mitten Pr.) Ann Arbor Editions LLC.

Tulien, Sean. Super Billy Goats Gruff. Cano, Fernando, illus. 2015. (Far Out Fairy Tales Ser.). (ENG.). 40p. (gr. 3-4). lib. bdg. 25.32 (978-1-4342-9649-8(0)) Stone Arch Bks.

Van Patter, Bruce. Tucker Took It! 2010. (ENG., Illus.). 32p. (J). (gr. k-2). 16.95 (978-1-59078-698-7(X)) Boyds Mills Pr.

Waddell, Martin. Captain Small Pig, 1 vol. Varley, Susan, illus. 2010. (ENG.). 32p. (J). (gr. -1-3). 15.95 (978-1-56145-519-5(9)) Peachtree Pubs.

Ward, Joyce Claudine. Nanny the Goat. 2008. 22p. pap. 24.95 (978-1-4241-9139-0(4)) America Star Bks.

Weber, Elka. One Little Chicken. Kleven, Elisa, illus. 2011. (ENG.). 32p. (J). (gr. -1-2). 16.99 (978-1-58246-374-2(3), Tricycle Pr.) Random Hse. Children's Bks.

Westera, Marleen. Sheep & Goat. Forest-Flier, Nancy, tr. from DUT. Van Ommen, Sylvia, illus. 2006. (ENG.). 99p. (J). 16.95 (978-1-932425-81-9(0), Lemniscaat) Boyds Mills Pr.

Willis, Jeanne. Troll Stinks. Ross, Tony, illus. 2017. (Andersen Press Picture Bks.). (ENG.). 32p. (gr. -1-3). 35.99 **(978-1-5124-3964-9(9))** Lerner Publishing Group.

Wittenbach, Jennie. Little Stories for Little Folks. 2011. 36p. pap. 21.99 (978-1-4628-8818-4(6)) Xlibris Corp.

Young, Amy. A New Friend for Sparkle. 2017. (ENG., Illus.). 40p. (J). 16.99 (978-0-374-30553-6(6), 9780374305536, Farrar, Straus & Giroux (BYR)) Farrar, Straus & Giroux.

—A Unicorn Named Sparkle. Young, Amy, illus. 2016. (ENG., Illus.). 40p. (J). 16.99 (978-0-374-30185-9(9), 9780374301859, Farrar, Straus & Giroux (BYR)) Farrar, Straus & Giroux.

Zupsic, Kelly. Mrs. Sneeze & the Three Legged Goat. 2013. 28p. pap. 24.95 (978-1-62709-791-8(0)) America Star Bks.

Zyrro, Roggen. Il Goatino. Shields, Ruth, illus. 2004. 32p. (J). 16.95 (978-0-9762580-0-1(5)) Zyrro, Roggen.

GOBLINS

see Fairies

GOD

see also Christianity; Creation; Jesus Christ; Mythology; Religion; Theology

Abts, Stacey & Kleinman, Bertha A. I Have Two Little Hands. 2004. (Illus.). (J). 9.95 (978-1-59038-182-3(3)) Deseret Bk. Co.

Adams, Michelle Medlock. God Is Always with You. Siewert, Pauline, illus. 2014. (Peek-A-Boo Promises Ser.). 16p. (J). bds. 8.99 (978-0-8249-1907-8(6), Ideal Pubns.) Worthy Publishing.

—Why I Praise You, God. Chapman, Susan, illus. 2006. 20p. (J). (gr. -1). bds. 5.49 (978-0-7586-0912-0(4)) Concordia Publishing Hse.

Anderson, Debby. God Knows My Name. Anderson, Debby, illus. 2003. (Illus.). 32p. (J). 12.99 (978-1-58134-415-8(5)) Crossway.

Anderson, Linda A., et al. Big Big God: 13 Amazing Lessons Where Preschoolers Experience God, 28 vols. 2007. (ENG., Illus.). 112p. (J). (gr. -1 — 1). pap. 29.99 incl. audio compact disk (978-0-7644-3602-4(3)) Group Publishing, Inc.

Apologetics Press, creator. Creation Cards: Exploring God's Creation. 2007. (ENG., Illus.). (J). (gr. 4-7). 9.95 (978-0-932859-75-4(5)) Apologetics Pr., Inc.

Apologia Educational Ministries, et al. Who Is God? (and Can I Really Know Him?) Worldview Series Book 1. 2009. (Illus.). xiv, 252p. (J). 39.00 (978-1-935495-07-9(0)) Apologia Educational Ministries, Inc.

Arthur, Kay & Arndt, Janna. Fast-Forward to the Future: Daniel 7-12. 2008. (ENG., Illus.). 192p. (J). per. 11.99 (978-0-7369-2285-2(7)) Harvest Hse. Pubs.

Ashworth, Leon. Ancient Egypt. (Gods & Goddesses Ser.). (Illus.). 32p. (J). lib. bdg. 24.25 (978-1-58340-196-5(2)) Black Rabbit Bks.

—Gods & Goddesses of Ancient Greece. (Gods & Goddesses Ser.). (Illus.). 32p. (J). lib. bdg. 24.25 (978-1-58340-195-8(4)) Black Rabbit Bks.

—Gods & Goddesses of the Vikings & Northlands. (Gods & Goddesses Ser.). (Illus.). 32p. lib. bdg. 24.25 (978-1-58340-193-4(8)) Black Rabbit Bks.

Aymaz, Abdullah. No Room for Doubt: Selective Essays for Youth. 2011. (ENG.). 82p. (gr. 8-11). pap. 6.95 (978-1-59784-248-6(6)) Tughra Bks.

B&H Kids Editorial Staff. Jesus Loves Me, Sound Book. Conger, Holli, illus. 2015. (Little Words Matter(tm) Ser.). (ENG.). 12p. (J). (— 1). bds. 12.99 (978-1-4336-8675-7(9), B&H Kids) B&H Publishing Group.

—The Whole World in His Hands, Sound Book. Conger, Holli, illus. 2015. (Little Words Matter(tm) Ser.). (ENG.). 12p. (J). (— 1). bds. 12.99 (978-1-4336-8676-4(7), B&H Kids) B&H Publishing Group.

Bagley, Val Chadwick, illus. I Will Trust in Heavenly Father & Jesus. 2006. (J). (978-1-59811-056-2(X)) Covenant Communications.

Barrie, Ruthann. And I Love You, God. 2012. 28p. (J). pap. 16.99 (978-1-4497-7850-7(X), WestBow Pr.) Author Solutions, Inc.

Berg, Yehuda. 72 Names of God for Kids. 2005. (Illus.). 200p. (978-1-57189-347-5(4)) Klein, Richard A. scaneg Verlag.

—The 72 Names of God for Kids: A Treasury of Timeless Wisdom. 2006. (ENG., Illus.). 192p. (gr. 1-7). (978-1-57189-543-1(4)) Klein, Richard A. scaneg Verlag.

Beveridge, Amy. Let's Thank God for Freedom. 2006. 24p. (J). bds. 6.99 (978-0-7847-1505-5(X), 04384) Standard Publishing.

Bilinsky, Cornelia Mary. God Is with Me: Always & Everywhere. 2014. (ENG., Illus.). (J). (978-0-8198-3122-4(0)) Pauline Bks. & Media.

Blosser, Connie S. Destiny's Trouble: A True Story. 2013. 20p. pap. 24.95 (978-1-4626-9341-2(5)) America Star Bks.

Boynton, Jeannette. God Loves Variety. Boynton, Jeannette & Holdeen, Bonnie, illus. 2007. (J). per. 10.99 (978-1-59879-264-5(4)) Lifevest Publishing, Inc.

Braun, Eric. Cronus the Titan Tells All: Tricked by the Kids, 1 vol. Gilpin, Stephen, illus. 2014. (Other Side of the Myth Ser.). (ENG.). 32p. (gr. 2-3). 27.32 (978-1-4795-2184-5(1)) Picture Window Bks.

Burch, Deborah. God's Greatest Gift. Burch, Deborah, illus. l.t. ed. 2006. (ENG., Illus.). 32p. (J). lib. bdg. (978-0-9779445-3-8(0)) Zoe Life Publishing.

Bushnell, Larry. God's Diminishing Power: If We Don't Do It God's Way His Power Is Unavailable. 2012. 80p. (gr. -1). pap. 9.95 (978-1-4497-5256-9(X), WestBow Pr.) Author Solutions, Inc.

Butt, Kyle. God Made Plants. 2007. (ENG., Illus.). (J). 3.00 (978-0-932859-85-3(2)) Apologetics Pr., Inc.

Butt, Sheila K. Does God Love Michael's Two Daddies. Perkins, Ken, illus. 2007. (ENG.). 16p. (J). pap. 7.95 (978-0-932859-94-5(1)) Apologetics Pr., Inc.

Calcium Staff, contrib. by. The Gods & Goddesses of Greek Mythology, 1 vol. 2011. (Ancient Greek Mythology Ser.). (ENG., Illus.). 64p. (gr. 5-7). lib. bdg. 33.99 (978-0-7565-4479-9(3), CPB Grades 4-8) Compass Point Bks.

Campbell, Matt. God Made Snot. 2005. (Illus.). 64p. pap. (978-1-84427-068-2(8)) Scripture Union.

Campbell, Trenton, ed. Gods & Goddesses of Ancient China. 2014. (Gods & Goddesses of Mythology Ser.). 160p. (J). (gr. 9-12). 32.90 (978-1-62275-393-2(3)) Rosen Publishing Group, Inc., The.

Carnesecca, Michele. How Does the Holy Ghost Make Me Feel? Xanthos, Carol, illus. 2010. 44p. (978-1-60641-245-9(0)) Deseret Bk. Co.

Catch 22: The Book That Will Change the Way You See Life. 2004. 120p. (C). per. 9.99 (978-0-9759691-0-6(2)) Catch 22 Publishing Inc.

Chidvilasananda. Good Night, Sweet Dreams, I Love You! 2004. (Illus.). (J). (978-1-930939-01-1(9)) SYDA Foundation.

Chimento, Carmen C. Seven Paths to Glory: Simplified Theology for a Troubled World. 2004. (ENG.). 120p. per. 14.95 (978-0-9656847-1-2(7)) Spiritual Hse. Pr., The.

Christ at the Coffee Shop. 2004. lib. bdg. (978-0-9747425-0-2(3), 09747425) Tranquility Ranch Publishing.

Claybourne, Anna. Greek Myths. Sansom, Fiona, illus. 2009. (Myths from Many Lands Ser.). 48p. (YA). (gr. 2-6). pap. 12.85 (978-1-60754-225-4(0)); (gr. 4-7). 29.25 (978-1-60754-224-7(2)) Windmill Bks.

Cornella, Angels. Hablemos de Dios. 2003. (SPA.). (J). 11.98 (978-968-13-3508-3(2)) Editorial Diana, S.A. MEX. Dist: Giron Bks.

Cone, Molly. Hello, Hello, Are You There, God? Kaye, Rosalind Charney, illus. rev. ed. 2004. viii, 55p. (gr. k-3). pap. 13.95 (978-0-8074-0648-9(1), 102553) URJ Pr.

Connolly, Sean. Theocracy. 2012. (Systems of Government Ser.). 48p. (gr. 6-12). lib. bdg. 37.10 (978-1-59920-806-0(7)) Black Rabbit Bks.

Croy, Anita. Myths & Legends of Ancient Rome. 2015. (Illus.). 64p. (J). (978-0-7166-2635-0(7)) World Bk., Inc.

Daleski, Gil. Is God Sad? Kaufman, Shirley, tr. from HEB. Veinshtein, Debbie, illus. 2006. 40p. 14.95 (978-965-229-372-5(5)) Gefen Publishing Hse., Ltd ISR. Dist: Gefen Bks.

Dalmatian Press Staff, ed. God Loves Me. 2005. (Timeless Treasures Ser.). (ENG., Illus.). 30p. (J). bds. 7.99 (978-1-4037-0555-6(0), Spirit Pr.) Bendon, Inc.

Daning, Tom. Egyptian Mythology: Osiris & Isis. 2009. (Jr. Graphic Mythologies Ser.). (ENG.). 24p. (J). (gr. 2-3). 47.90 (978-1-61513-861-6(7), PowerKids Pr.) Rosen Publishing Group, Inc., The.

Davenport, Jeff. God Is Really, Really Real: 30 Easily Taught Bible Doctrines. Looney, Bill, illus. 2015. (ENG.). 96p. (J). 15.99 (978-0-89221-738-0(3)) New Leaf Pub. Group.

David, Juliet. God Helps Me, 1 vol. Byrne, Mike, illus. 2014. (ENG.). 10p. (J). bds. 7.99 (978-1-78128-112-3(2), Candle Bks.) Lion Hudson PLC GBR. Dist: Kregel Pubns.

—God Knows Me, 1 vol. Byrne, Mike, illus. 2014. (ENG.). 10p. (J). bds. 7.99 (978-1-78128-113-0(0), Candle Bks.) Lion Hudson PLC GBR. Dist: Kregel Pubns.

—God Loves Me, 1 vol. Byrne, Mike, illus. 2014. (ENG.). 10p. (J). bds. 7.99 (978-1-78128-114-7(9), Candle Bks.) Lion Hudson PLC GBR. Dist: Kregel Pubns.

—My Little Promise Bible, 1 vol. Barnard, Lucy, illus. 2016. (ENG.). 96p. (J). pap. 9.99 (978-1-78128-257-1(9), Candle Bks.) Lion Hudson PLC GBR. Dist: Kregel Pubns.

Davidson, Tish. Theocracy. Colton, Timothy J., ed. 2012. (Major Forms of World Government Ser.). 64p. (J). (gr. 5). 22.95 (978-1-4222-2143-3(1)) Mason Crest.

Davis, Mary J. My Answer Journal: What Kids Wonder about God & the Bible. 2004. (Journals Just for Kids Ser.). (Illus.). 136p. (J). (gr. 4-7). pap. 9.99 (978-1-885358-72-1(5), Legacy Pr.) Rainbow Pubs. & Legacy Pr.

Dayal, Mala. The Ramayana in Pictures. Joshi, Jagdish, illus. 2006. 64p. (J). (978-81-291-0896-8(8)) Rupa & Co.

Dear God 2001. 2004. (My First Prayers Ser.). 10p. (J). bds. 3.99 (978-1-85854-406-9(8)) Brimax Books Ltd. GBR. Dist: Byeway Bks.

Demarco, Stacey. Goddesses & Sirens. Manton, Jimmy, illus. 2013. 165p. (J). pap. (978-1-58270-381-7(7)) Beyond Words Publishing, Inc.

—Gods & Titans. Manton, Jimmy, illus. 2013. 160p. (J). (978-1-58270-380-0(9)) Beyond Words Publishing, Inc.

Diaz, Maritza. The Little God in Me. 2003. (Illus.). 32p. (J). 20.99 (978-1-4134-5549-6(2)) Xlibris Corp.

Dixon, Miranda. God Is Enormous! 2011. 24p. (gr. 1-2). 12.95 (978-1-4497-1273-0(8), WestBow Pr.) Author Solutions, Inc.

D'Ottavi, Francesca, illus. Isis & Osiris, 1 vol. 2012. (Egyptian Myths Ser.). (ENG.). 32p. (gr. 3-4). pap. 7.95 (978-1-4048-7240-0(X)); lib. bdg. 28.65 (978-1-4048-7148-9(9)) Picture Window Bks.

Douglas, Tasha K. God's Beautiful Daughter: Discover the Love of Your Heavenly Father, 1 vol. 2015. (Faithgirlz Ser.). (ENG.). 192p. (J). pap. 8.99 (978-0-310-74594-5(2)) Zonderkidz.

Dowley, Tim & Jefferson, Graham. Would You Like to Know God?, 1 vol. Reeves, Eira, illus. 2016. (ENG.). 28p. (J). pap. 2.99 (978-1-78128-275-5(7), Candle Bks.) Lion Hudson PLC GBR. Dist: Kregel Pubns.

Dunning, Lisa. Restless Spirits-Utah's Small Town Ghosts. 2010. 256p. (J). pap. 16.99 (978-1-59955-371-9(6), Cedar Fort, Inc.) Cedar Fort, Inc./CFI Distribution.

Dyan, Penelope. Beatitudes Are Attitudes. 2011. 34p. pap. 11.95 (978-1-935630-90-6(3)) Bellissima Publishing, LLC.

Edgren, David. The Kingdom Scroll. 2011. (J). pap. 11.99 (978-0-8163-2483-5(2)) Pacific Pr. Publishing Assn.

Elgin, Kathy. Egyptian Myths. Sansom, Fiona, illus. 2009. (Myths from Many Lands Ser.). 48p. (YA). (gr. 2-6). pap. 12.85 (978-1-60754-222-3(6)); (gr. 4-7). 29.25 (978-1-60754-221-6(8)) Windmill Bks.

—Roman Myths. Sansom, Fiona, illus. 2009. (Myths from Many Lands Ser.). 48p. (YA). (gr. 2-6). pap. 12.85 (978-1-60754-231-5(5)); (J). (gr. 4-7). 29.25 (978-1-60754-230-8(7)) Windmill Bks.

Elkins, Stephen. First Steps to God: Beginning Lessons of God's Love. Colton, Ellie, illus. 2006. (First Steps Ser.). 25p. (J). (gr. -1-k). 9.99 incl. audio compact disk (978-0-8054-2661-8(2)) B&H Publishing Group.

England, Don. God, Are You Really There? (YA). pap., stu. ed. 7.99 (978-0-89098-105-4(1)) Twentieth Century Christian Bks.

Ergün, Erol. The All-Merciful Master: The Beautiful Names of God. Egitim, Hasan, illus. 2009. 127p. (J). pap. (978-1-59784-223-5(0)) Tughra Bks.

Fawcett, Cheryl & Newman, Robert C. Kids' Questions about God & Jesus. Mazellan, Ron, illus. 2003. 71p. pap. (978-1-59402-081-0(7)) Regular Baptist Pr.

Ferry, Therese. Where Is God? Doran, David, illus. 2012. (ENG.). 26p. pap. 12.95 (978-1-85607-778-1(0)) Columba Pr. IRL. Dist: Dufour Editions, Inc.

Feyh, Janelle. Does God Have a Remote Control? Feyh, Alexa & Deghand, Tim, illus. l.t. ed. 2003. 66p. (J). per. 11.95 (978-1-932344-26-4(8)) Thornton Publishing, Inc.

Fontes, Justine & Fontes, Ron. Demeter & Persephone: Spring Held Hostage. Kurth, Steve & Schulz, Barbara, illus. 2008. (Graphic Myths & Legends Ser.). (ENG.). 48p. (gr. 4-8). per. 8.95 (978-0-8225-6570-3(6)) Lerner Publishing Group.

—Demeter & Persephone: Spring Held Hostage. Schulz, Barbara & Kurth, Steve, illus. 2007. (Graphic Myths & Legends Ser.). (ENG.). 48p. (J). (gr. 4-8). lib. bdg. 27.93 (978-0-8225-5966-5(8)) Lerner Publishing Group.

Forest, Christopher. Ancient Egyptian Gods & Goddesses, 1 vol. 2012. (Ancient Egyptian Civilization Ser.). (ENG.). 32p. (gr. 3-4). pap. 8.10 (978-1-4296-7970-1(0)); lib. bdg. 27.32 (978-1-4296-7628-1(0)) Capstone Press of Coughlan Cos. (Fact Finders).

Fritz, Greg. God Made You Special! Reed, Lisa, illus. 2015. (J). (978-0-8249-1947-4(5), Ideal Pubns.) Worthy Publishing.

Ganeri, Anita. Gods & Goddesses. 2012. (Illus.). 32p. (J). 70.50 (978-1-4488-5243-7(9)); pap. 11.75 (978-1-4488-5242-0(0)); lib. bdg. 26.50 (978-1-4488-5202-4(1)) Rosen Publishing Group, Inc., The. (PowerKids Pr.).

Geisen, Cynthia. What Is God Like? Just for Me Book. Fitzgerald, Anne, illus. 2012. 32p. (J). pap. 7.95 (978-0-87029-516-4(0)) Abbey Pr.

Gerstein, Mordicai. I Am Pan. 2016. (ENG., Illus.). 80p. (J). 18.99 (978-1-62672-035-0(5), 9781626720350) Roaring Brook Pr.

Gibson, Roxie C. Hey, God! Listen! Gibson, James C., illus. 2007. (ENG.). 64p. (J). (gr. -1-3). 7.99 (978-1-887654-59-3(3)) Premium Pr. America.

Gibson, Roxie Cawood. Hey God, Where Are You? Gibson, James C., illus. 2007. (ENG.). 64p. 7.99 (978-1-887654-63-0(1)) Premium Pr. America.

Glenn, Lauren J. Where Is God. 2005. (J). bds. 6.99 (978-0-9772459-0-1(X)) Glenn, Lauren.

Glory Praise & Honor. 7.50 (978-0-8054-5969-2(3)) B&H Publishing Group.

God Is Color. 2004. (J). spiral bd. 11.97 (978-0-9759551-0-9(1)) Creative Success Works.

God Made Everything Good. 3.50 (978-0-8054-5878-7(6)) B&H Publishing Group.

God Made Me. 3.50 (978-0-8054-5887-9(5)) B&H Publishing Group.

God Made the World (for Four-Year-Olds) 2004. (gr. -1-18). tchr. ed. 23.95 (978-0-8294-0818-8(5)) Loyola Pr.

God's Wonders. 3.50 (978-0-8054-5877-0(8)) B&H Publishing Group.

Gold, August. Does God Forgive Me? Waller, Diane Hardy, photos by. 2006. (ENG., Illus.). 32p. (J). pap. 8.99 (978-1-59473-142-6(X), 9781594731426, Skylight Paths Publishing) LongHill Partners, Inc.

Greiner, Ruth B. God, the Trinity, Worthy of Worship Vol. 43: New Testament Volume 43 Revelation Part 2. Henkel, Vernon & Hertzler, Frances H.., illus. 2013. 40p. (J). pap. (978-1-932381-65-8(1), 1043) Bible Visuals International, Inc.

Grimes, Nikki. At Break of Day. Collier, John & Morin, Paul, illus. 2004. 32p. (J). (gr. -1-3). 17.00 (978-0-8028-5104-8(5)) Eerdmans, William B. Publishing Co.

Gunderson, Jessica. Olympians vs. Titans: An Interactive Mythological Adventure. Arcabascio, Carolyn, illus. 2017. (You Choose: Ancient Greek Myths Ser.). (ENG.). 112p. (gr. 3-4). pap. 6.95 (978-1-5157-4825-0(1), You Choose Bks.) Capstone Press of Coughlan Cos.

Hale, Vincent, ed. Mesopotamian Gods & Goddesses, 1 vol., 1. 2014. (Gods & Goddesses of Mythology Ser.). (ENG.). 112p. (YA). (gr. 7-12). 32.90 *(978-1-62275-161-7(2))* Rosen Publishing Group, Inc., The.

Hall, Annalisa. The Holy Ghost Is Like a Blanket. Egbert, Corey, illus. 2013. (ENG.). 32p. (J). (gr. 3-7). 14.99 *(978-1-4621-1229-6(3))* Cedar Fort, Inc./CFI Distribution.

Hallinan, P. K. A Love Letter from God. Watson, Laura, illus. 2014. 24p. (J). 12.99 *(978-0-8249-5662-2(1),* Ideal Pubns.) Worthy Publishing.

Ham, Ken. The Answers Book for Kids, Volume 3: 22 Questions from Kids on God & the Bible. 2009. (Answers Book for Kids Ser.). (Illus.). 48p. (J). (gr. 4-7). 7.99 *(978-0-89051-525-9(5))* Master Bks.

Harder Tangvald, Christine. Thank You, God, for My Two Hands. Date not set. (J). bds. 5.99 *(978-1-55513-930-8(2))* Cook, David C.

Harrub, Brad. God Made Fish. 2007. (ENG., Illus.). (J). 3.00 *(978-0-932859-87-7(9))* Apologetics Pr., Inc.

Hartley, Bob. Childrens Adoration Prayer Book. Clonts, E. M. M., illus. 2012. 114p. pap. 24.95 *(978-0-615-58840-7(9))* Deeper Waters.

Hawkins, Tim. Awesome on the Inside. 2010. 46p. (YA). pap. *(978-0-9581843-3-5(X))* Good Bk. Co.

Haywood, John. Through the Ages: Gods, Beliefs & Ceremonies. 2008. (ENG., Illus.). 64p. (J). (gr. 4-7). pap. 12.99 *(978-1-84476-601-7(2))* Anness Publishing GBR. Dist: National Bk. Network.

Hess, Ingrid. Walk in Peace. 2009. (ENG.). 44p. (J). (gr. -1-k). pap. 13.99 *(978-0-8361-9469-2(1))* Herald Pr.

Hibbert, Clare. Terrible Tales of Ancient Greece, Vol. 1. 2014. (Monstrous Myths Ser.). 32p. (J). (gr. 4-6). 26.60 *(978-1-4824-0181-3(9))* Stevens, Gareth Publishing LLLP.

Hilton, Jennifer & McCurry, Kristen. Dios No Encuentra. Rimmington, Natasha, illus. 2016. (SPA.). (J). ***(978-1-5064-2091-2(5))*** Augsburg Fortress, Pubs.

I Can Follow Jesus. 2014. (Happy Day Ser.). (ENG., Illus.). 16p. (J). pap. 2.49 *(978-1-4143-9419-0(5))* Tyndale Hse. Pubs.

Innes, Brian. Ancient Roman Myths. 2010. (Myths from Around the World Ser.). 48p. (gr. 6-8). (YA). lib. bdg. 31.00 *(978-1-4339-3527-5(9));* (Illus.). (J). pap. 14.05 *(978-1-4339-3528-2(7))* Stevens, Gareth Publishing LLLP. (Gareth Stevens Secondary Library).

Joanna, Harris. He's My God!-(Book 2) Knowing God Through His Names - a Childrens' Devotional. Jen, Kallin, photos by. 2012. (Illus.). 48p. (J). 7.99 *(978-1-930547-78-0(1))* Deeper Roots Pubns. & Media.

Johari, Harish & Sperling, Vatsala. How Parvati Won the Heart of Shiva. Weltevrede, Pieter, illus. 2004. (Classic Indian Stories for Children Ser.). (ENG.). 32p. (J). (gr. -1-6). 15.95 *(978-1-59143-042-1(9),* Bear Cub Bks.) Bear & Co.

Johnson, Cathy Jo. What's in a Name? Learning the Special Names of God. 2012. 40p. pap. 16.99 *(978-1-4497-4908-8(9),* WestBow Pr.) Author Solutions, Inc.

Josef, Marion. We Thank God Col/Act Bk. 24p. pap. 1.25 *(978-0-8198-8303-2(4),* 332-411) Pauline Bks. & Media.

Kahrs, Evelyn. I Can Find God. 2013. 32p. pap. 16.99 *(978-1-4525-6385-5(3))* Balboa Pr.

Karas, G. Brian, illus. Young Zeus. 2010. (ENG.). 48p. (J). (gr. -1-3). 17.99 *(978-0-439-72806-5(1),* Scholastic Pr.) Scholastic, Inc.

Kraft, Tamera & Colkmire, Lance. Kid Konnection: Kids Entering the Presence of God, Vol. 5. 2003. (Illus.). 112p. ring bd. 69.99 *(978-0-87148-383-6(1))* Pathway Pr.

Kripke, Dorothy Karp. Let's Talk about God. Tripp, Christine, tr. Tripp, Christine, illus. 2003. (J). 9.95 *(978-1-881283-34-8(8))* Alef Design Group.

Kushner, Lawrence & Kushner, Karen. Because Nothing Looks Like God: A Guide for Jewish Educator & Parents. 2003. (SPA & ENG., Illus.). 22p. (gr. k-3). pap., tchr. ed. 10.99 *(978-1-58023-140-4(3),* Jewish Lights Publishing) LongHill Partners, Inc.

Learn As You Grow. God Loves You So Much... Reuben, Borgen & Jenny, Lindley, photos by. 2010. (ENG., Illus.). 24p. (J). 12.95 *(978-0-9824652-3-3(8))* Learn As You Grow, L.L.C.

Lemon, Willie Sells. Everything God Made Gives. 2010. 24p. 17.50 *(978-1-4490-7523-1(1))* AuthorHouse.

—Things Happen When You Disobey God. 2011. 24p. (gr. -1). pap. 17.50 *(978-1-4567-5120-3(4))* AuthorHouse.

Leonard, Scott A. Myths & Legends of Ancient Greece. 2015. (Illus.). 64p. (J). *(978-0-7166-2634-3(9))* World Bk., Inc.

Levey, Michael. The Book of the Holy Light. 2004. 204p. 17.95 *(978-1-59540-987-4(4),* Sunstar Publishing) 1st World Publishing, Inc.

Limke, Jeff. Isis & Osiris. 2008. pap. 52.95 *(978-0-8225-9455-0(2))* Lerner Publishing Group.

—Isis Y Osiris: Hasta el Fin Del Mundo; Isis & Osiris: to the Ends of the Earth. 2008. pap. 52.95 *(978-0-8225-9671-4(7))* Lerner Publishing Group.

Lindahl, Kay. How Does God Listen? Maloney, Cynthia, photos by. 2005. (ENG., Illus.). 32p. (J). pap. 8.99 *(978-1-59473-084-9(9),* 9781594730849, Skylight Paths Publishing) LongHill Partners, Inc.

Lloyd-Jones, Sally. Thoughts to Make Your Heart Sing, 1 vol. 2013. (ENG.). 224p. (J). 16.99 *(978-0-310-72993-8(9))* Zonderkidz.

Loh-Hagan, Virginia. Ares. 2017. (Gods & Goddesses of the Ancient World Ser.). (ENG., Illus.). 32p. (J). (gr. 4-8). 29.93 *(978-1-63472-134-9(9),* 209108, 45th Parallel Press) Cherry Lake Publishing.

—Zeus. 2017. (Gods & Goddesses of the Ancient World Ser.). (ENG., Illus.). 32p. (J). (gr. 4-8). 29.93 *(978-1-63472-131-8(4),* 209096, 45th Parallel Press) Cherry Lake Publishing.

The Lord's Lady Liberty (Children's Book) The Statue of Liberation Through Christ Helping America to Remember God. 2006. (J). pap. 7.00 *(978-0-9749019-8-5(9))* Understanding For Life Ministries, Inc.

Lucado, Max & Lucado, Jenna. Redefining Beautiful: What God Sees When God Sees You, 1 vol. 2009. (ENG.). 240p. (gr. 7-12). pap. 14.99 *(978-1-4003-1428-7(3))* Nelson, Thomas Inc.

Lupton, Hugh. Orpheus & Eurydice. Hénaff, Carole, illus. 2013. (Greek Myths Ser.: 3). (ENG.). 40p. (J). (gr. 3-6). pap. 8.99 *(978-1-84686-784-2(3))* Barefoot Bks., Inc.

Lyons, Eric. God Made Insects. 2007. (ENG., Illus.). (J). 3.00 *(978-0-932859-86-0(0))* Apologetics Pr., Inc.

MacKenzie, Carine. God Has Power. (Learn about God (Board Books) Ser.). (ENG., (J). 2015. Illus.). 14p. (gr. -1-k). bds. 3.99 *(978-1-85792-477-0(0),* bb5f91d8-383d-4407-96f9-1ac62981c2e6, Christian Focus) 2006. 16p. pap., act. bk. ed. 1.99 *(978-1-85792-634-7(X),* e590e91f-f37e-4203-bd49-31c0c16a320e) Christian Focus Pubns. GBR. Dist: Bookmasters Distribution.

—God Is Everywhere. 2015. (Learn about God (Board Books) Ser.). (ENG., Illus.). 14p. (J). (gr. -1-k). bds. 3.99 *(978-1-85792-480-0(0),* 007f4250-1020-4d2e-a607-2a067c0c8715, Christian Focus) Christian Focus Pubns. GBR. Dist: Bookmasters Distribution.

—God Is Faithful. 2015. (Learn about God (Board Books) Ser.). (ENG., Illus.). 14p. (J). (gr. -1-k). bds. 3.99 *(978-1-85792-481-7(9),* 9781857924817, Christian Focus) Christian Focus Pubns. GBR. Dist: Bookmasters Distribution.

—God Is Kind. 2015. (Learn about God (Board Books) Ser.). (ENG., Illus.). 14p. (J). (gr. -1-k). bds. 3.99 *(978-1-85792-476-3(2),* 5daee686-b202-4c2a-ad7e-9b555ebf60a8, Christian Focus) Christian Focus Pubns. GBR. Dist: Bookmasters Distribution.

—God Knows Everything. 2015. (Learn about God (Board Books) Ser.). (ENG., Illus.). 14p. (J). (gr. -1-k). bds. 3.99 *(978-1-85792-479-4(7),* 30d48f32-8452-4d71-b039-6984a8d3a099, Christian Focus) Christian Focus Pubns. GBR. Dist: Bookmasters Distribution.

—God Never Changes. 2015. (Learn about God (Board Books) Ser.). (ENG., Illus.). 14p. (J). (gr. -1-k). bds. 3.99 *(978-1-85792-478-7(9),* c860d3f1-ad73-4696-8b57-8f3806e2a455, Christian Focus) Christian Focus Pubns. GBR. Dist: Bookmasters Distribution.

MacKenzie, Catherine. What Is the Truth? 2013. (Little Lights Ser.). (ENG., Illus.). 24p. (J). 7.99 *(978-1-84550-560-8(3),* 281bfc81-447c-4f63-85f8-daa6919a36b7) Christian Focus Pubns. GBR. Dist: Bookmasters Distribution.

Marxhausen, Joanne. 3 In 1: A Picture of God. 2nd ed. 2004. (Illus.). 48p. (J). (gr. -1-4). 9.49 *(978-0-7586-0680-8(X))* Concordia Publishing Hse.

Mays, Blanche, ed. My Book about God's World. Magagna, Anna Marie, illus. 2011. 28p. pap. 35.95 *(978-1-258-10454-2(7))* Literary Licensing, LLC.

McKnight, Scot & McKnight Barringer, Laura. Sharing God's Love: The Jesus Creed for Children. Hill, David, illus. 2014. (ENG.). 32p. (J). pap. 15.99 *(978-1-61261-581-3(3))* Paraclete Pr., Inc.

Mcknight, Scot & McKnight Barringer, Laura. Sharing God's Love: the Jesus Creed for Children: Teacher Lesson & Activity Guide. 2014. (ENG., Illus.). 36p. (gr. 13). spiral bd. 19.95 *(978-1-61261-637-7(2))* Paraclete Pr., Inc.

McNeely, Tom, illus. Isis & the Seven Scorpions, 1 vol. 2012. (Egyptian Myths Ser.). (ENG.). 32p. (gr. 3-4). pap. 8.95 *(978-1-4048-7241-7(8));* lib. bdg. 28.65 *(978-1-4048-7150-2(0))* Picture Window Bks.

Meade, Starr. Mighty Acts of God: A Family Bible Story Book. O'Connor, Tim, illus. 2010. 288p. (J). 24.99 *(978-1-4335-0604-8(1))* Crossway.

Meadows, James L. God Speaks to Today's Teenagers. (YA). Vol. I. pap. 5.50 *(978-0-89098-375-1(5))* Vol. II. pap. 5.50 *(978-0-89098-376-8(3))* Twentieth Century Christian Bks.

Mehl, Ron, et al. Who Did It? Taylor, Jeannie St. John & St. John Taylor, Jeannie, illus. 2004. 32p. (J). (gr. k-4). 12.99 *(978-0-8254-3168-5(9))* Kregel Pubns.

Meschini, Leonardo, illus. The Prince & the Sphinx, 1 vol. 2012. (Egyptian Myths Ser.). (ENG.). 32p. (gr. 3-4). pap. 8.95 *(978-1-4048-7242-4(6));* lib. bdg. 28.65 *(978-1-4048-7149-6(7))* Picture Window Bks.

Michael, Sally. God's Names. Apps, Fred, illus. 2011. (J). pap. *(978-1-59638-219-0(8))* P & R Publishing.

—God's Providence. 2013. (ENG., Illus.). 120p. (J). (gr. -1-3). pap. 16.99 *(978-1-59638-714-0(9))* P & R Publishing.

Milbourne, Anna & Stowell, Louie. The Usborne Book of Greek Myths. Brocklehurst, Ruth, ed. Bursi, Simona et al, illus. 2014. (ENG.). 301p. (J). (gr. 4-7). pap. 22.99 *(978-0-7945-2130-1(4),* Usborne) EDC Publishing.

Miller, Dave. Birds, Bugs, & Bees. 2006. (ENG., Illus.). (J). 3.00 *(978-0-932859-90-7(9))* Apologetics Pr., Inc.

—Dogs, Frogs, & Hogs. 2006. (ENG., Illus.). (J). 3.00 *(978-0-932859-88-4(7))* Apologetics Pr., Inc.

Miller, Reagan. What Is a Theocracy? Crabtree Publishing Staff, ed. 2012. (Forms of Government Ser.: No. 4). (ENG.). 48p. (J). (gr. 5-8). pap. *(978-0-7787-5326-1(3))* Crabtree Publishing Co.

Morley, Jacqueline. World of Gods & Goddesses. Stewart, David, illus. 2013. (Mythology Ser.). (ENG.). 64p. (gr. 3-6). lib. bdg. 41.35 *(978-1-908973-92-4(7))* Book Hse. GBR. Dist: Black Rabbit Bks.

Mudge, Michael. Spiritual Warfare Basic Training. 2012. 44p. pap. 21.99 *(978-1-4772-8539-8(3))* AuthorHouse.

Napoli, Donna Jo. Treasury of Norse Mythology: Stories of Intrigue, Trickery, Love, & Revenge. Balit, Christina, illus. 2015. (ENG.). 192p. (J). (gr. 3-7). 24.99 *(978-1-4263-2098-9(1),* National Geographic Children's Bks.) National Geographic Society.

Naylor, Beth & Seifert, Sheila. Where Is God? 2007. (Discipleship Junction Ser.). (ENG., Illus.). 112p. (J). per. 19.99 *(978-0-7814-4444-6(6))* Cook, David C.

Nordenstrom, Michael, illus. & adapted by. Hina & the Sea of Stars. Nordenstrom, Michael, adapted by. 2003. 32p. 10.95 *(978-1-57306-167-4(0))* Bess Pr., Inc.

Notto, E. T. Light of God Bible Books: Bible Book 2. 2009. 64p. pap. 25.49 *(978-1-4389-7287-9(3))* AuthorHouse.

—Light of God Bible Books: Book 1 (Creation, God's Commandments, Faith) 2008. 52p. pap. 22.49 *(978-1-4389-1702-3(3))* AuthorHouse.

O'Connor, George. Apollo: The Brilliant One. 2016. (Olympians Ser.: 8). (ENG., Illus.). 80p. (J). pap. 10.99 *(978-1-62672-015-2(0),* 9781626720152, First Second Bks.) Roaring Brook Pr.

Oeltjenbruns, Joni. Where Is God. 2004. (Illus.). 16p. (J). 6.95 *(978-0-8198-8307-0(7),* 332-415) Pauline Bks. & Media.

Olsen, Debi W. My Very Own Book about God. 2004. 32p. (J). 10.95 *(978-1-931947-03-9(1))* Ink & Scribe.

O'Neal, Claire. Artemis. 2007. (Profiles in Greek & Roman Mythology Ser.). (Illus.). 48p. (YA). (gr. 4-7). lib. bdg. 29.95 *(978-1-58415-555-3(8))* Mitchell Lane Pubs., Inc.

Öze, Özkan. I Wonder about Allah, Bk. 1. Ayduz, Selma, tr. from TUR. 2014. (I Wonder about Islam Ser.). (ENG., Illus.). 128p. (J). (gr. 3). pap. 11.95 *(978-0-86037-592-0(7))* Kube Publishing Ltd. GBR. Dist: Consortium Bk. Sales & Distribution.

Peebles, Alice. Monsters of the Gods. Chivers, Nigel, illus. 2015. (Mythical Beasts Ser.). (ENG.). 32p. (J). (gr. 3-6). 26.65 *(978-1-4677-6342-4(X),* Lerner Pubns.) Lerner Publishing Group.

Pellegrino, Richard, illus. The Battle of the Olympians & the Titans, 1 vol. 2011. (Greek Myths Ser.). (ENG.). 32p. (gr. 4-5). lib. bdg. 28.65 *(978-1-4048-6667-6(1))* Picture Window Bks.

Pickett, Natalie R. S e M P Ly 4 Girlz. 2012. 100p. pap. 15.95 *(978-0-9833864-1-4(2))* Pickett Fennell Group, The.

Pollack-Brichto, Mira. The God Around Us: A Child's Garden of Prayer. Alko, Selina, illus. rev. ed. 2004. (ENG & HEB.). 32p. (J). (gr. -1-1). 13.95 *(978-0-8074-0701-1(1),* 101072) URJ Pr.

Raffa-Mulligan, Teena. Who Dresses God? ... for God's house Is this world we share & God Is in it Everywhere. Rooke, Veronica, illus. 2012. 32p. (J). pap. *(978-1-921883-28-6(6))* Pick-a-Woo Woo Pubs.

Redford, Marjorie & Rice, Courtney. God's Special Rule. Burroughs, Scott, illus. 2013. (Happy Day Ser.). (ENG.). 16p. (J). pap. 2.49 *(978-1-4143-9300-1(8))* Tyndale Hse. Pubs.

Reilly, Pamela. My Day at the Zoo. 2011. 24p. pap. 12.95 *(978-1-935268-72-7(4))* Halo Publishing International.

Reusser, Kayleen. Hades. 2009. (Profiles in Greek & Roman Mythology Ser.). 48p. (YA). (gr. 4-7). 29.95 *(978-1-58415-750-2(X))* Mitchell Lane Pubs., Inc.

—Hephaestus. 2010. (Profiles in Greek & Roman Mythology Ser.). 48p. (YA). (gr. 4-7). 29.95 *(978-1-58415-749-6(6))* Mitchell Lane Pubs., Inc.

—Hermes. 2009. (Profiles in Greek & Roman Mythology Ser.). (Illus.). 48p. (J). (gr. 4-7). 29.95 *(978-1-58415-748-9(8))* Mitchell Lane Pubs., Inc.

Rivers-Moore, Debbie. God Made the World, 1 vol. Haines, Emma, illus. 2017. 4p. 11.99 ***(978-0-8254-4520-0(5))*** Kregel Pubns.

Roytman, Arkady. Greek & Roman Gods Stained Glass Coloring Book. 2009. (Dover Stained Glass Coloring Book Ser.). (ENG., Illus.). 32p. (J). (gr. 2-5). pap. 6.99 *(978-0-486-46995-9(6))* Dover Pubns., Inc.

Rubow, Carol. God Loves You. 2010. (Illus.). 32p. (J). (gr. -1). 12.99 *(978-0-7586-1855-9(7))* Concordia Publishing Hse.

—God Loves You Mini Book. 2010. 32p. (J). (gr. -1). pap. 2.49 *(978-0-7586-1856-6(5))* Concordia Publishing Hse.

Sasso, Sandy Eisenberg. God's Paintbrush. Compton, Annette, illus. 2nd anniv. annot. ed. 2004. (GER & ENG.). 32p. (J). (gr. -1-2). 18.99 *(978-1-58023-195-4(0),* 9781580231954, Jewish Lights Publishing) LongHill Partners, Inc.

Sawyer, Judith L. This Is How I Pray. Sawyer, Judith L., illus. 2008. (Illus.). 24p. (J). pap. *(978-1-926585-11-6(9),* CCB Publishing) CCB Publishing.

Scherm, Deedra. Only One Me: A Sweet Little Rhyme to Help Your Light Shine. Dreyer, Laura, illus. 2008. (ENG.). 22p. (J). (gr. -1-3). 7.99 *(978-1-934789-02-5(X))* Lemon Vision Productions.

Shecter, Vicky Alvear. Anubis Speaks! A Guide to the Afterlife by the Egyptian God of the Dead. Revoy, Antoine, illus. 2013. (Secrets of the Ancient Gods Ser.). (ENG.). 128p. (J). (gr. 4-6). 16.95 *(978-1-59078-995-7(4))* Boyds Mills Pr.

—Hades Speaks! A Guide to the Underworld by the Greek God of the Dead. Larson, J. E., illus. 2014. (Secrets of the Ancient Gods Ser.). (ENG.). 128p. (J). (gr. 4-7). 16.95 *(978-1-62091-598-1(7))* Boyds Mills Pr.

—Thor Speaks! A Guide to the Viking Realms by the Nordic God of Thunder. Larson, J. E., illus. 2015. (Secrets of the Ancient Gods Ser.). (ENG.). 128p. (J). (gr. 3-7). 15.95 *(978-1-62091-599-8(5))* Boyds Mills Pr.

Shenton, Tim. The Life of Abraham: Faith, Courage, Children, God. 2003. (Daily Readings From Ser.). (Illus.). 76p. (J). (gr. -1-7). per. 7.99 *(978-1-903087-72-5(4))* DayOne Pubns. GBR. Dist: Send The Light Distribution LLC.

Simon, Mary Manz. My Picnic Basket: And How God Is Always Near. Fenimore, Kristina, illus. 2013. (ENG.). 14p. (J). (gr. -1-k). bds. 9.99 *(978-0-7847-3699-9(5),* B&H Kids) B&H Publishing Group.

Skinas, John. Pictures of God: A Child's Guide to Understanding Icons. 2009. (ENG.). 32p. pap. 12.95 *(978-1-888212-58-7(6))* Ancient Faith Publishing.

Smit, Nina. My First Book about God. 2013. (ENG.). 160p. pap. 9.95 *(978-1-4153-1295-7(8))* Struik Christian Media ZAF. Dist: Casemate Pubs. & Bk. Distributors, LLC.

Sperling, Vatsala. Hanuman's Journey to the Medicine Mountain. Johari, Sandeep, illus. 2006. (ENG.). 32p. (J). (gr. -1-6). 15.95 *(978-1-59143-063-6(1))* Inner Traditions International, Ltd.

Springer, Susan K. A Child Can Hear God's Voice. 2011. 24p. pap. 11.32 *(978-1-4567-4785-5(1))* AuthorHouse.

Stannard, Russell. The Curious History of God. Davies, Taffy, illus. 2003. (ENG.). 96p. (J). (gr. -1-3). pap. 7.95 *(978-1-932031-27-0(8))* Templeton Pr.

Stevens, Sherri. Where Is God? Freeman, Patricia, illus. 2005. 24p. (YA). 15.95 *(978-0-9769541-0-1(9),* 2005-1) Enlightened Bks.

Stewart, Henry. He Created Me. 2007. (Illus.). (J). 28.99 *(978-1-59879-345-1(4));* per. 20.99 *(978-1-59879-269-0(5))* Lifevest Publishing, Inc.

Stohs, Anita Reith. Hush, Little One: A Lullaby for God's Children. Kanzler, John, tr. Kanzler, John, illus. 2004. 32p. (J). 12.99 *(978-0-570-07144-0(5))* Concordia Publishing Hse.

Stortz, Diane. I Am: 40 Reasons to Trust God, 1 vol. 2016. (ENG., Illus.). 224p. (J). 16.99 *(978-0-529-12066-3(6))* Nelson, Thomas Inc.

Stortz, Diane. I Am Devotional: 100 Devotions about the Names of God, 1 vol. 2017. (ENG., Illus.). 224p. (J). 16.99 ***(978-0-7180-9673-1(8))*** Nelson, Thomas Inc.

Strobel, Lee. The Case for a Creator for Kids, 1 vol. rev. enl. ed. 2010. (Case for... Series for Kids Ser.). (ENG., Illus.). 128p. (J). pap. 7.99 *(978-0-310-71992-2(5))* Zonderkidz.

Taylor, Jane & Macleod, Una. God Made Me. Matthews, Derek, illus. 2015. (Board Books God Made Ser.). (ENG.). 16p. (J). bds. 3.99 *(978-1-85792-289-9(1),* 03f5af1b-96db-40aa-997a-68a2c4d74abd) Christian Focus Pubns. GBR. Dist: Bookmasters Distribution.

Taylor, Jane, et al. God Made the World. 2015. (Board Books God Made Ser.). (ENG., Illus.). 16p. (J). (gr. -1-k). bds. 3.99 *(978-1-85792-292-9(1),* 4833da61-2487-4961-8495-ce76e356ada2) Christian Focus Pubns. GBR. Dist: Bookmasters Distribution.

Toms, Kate. God Knows All about Me. 2008. 26p. (J). bds. 7.99 *(978-1-4003-1275-7(2))* Nelson, Thomas Inc.

Trammell, Fredi. Journey Through the Bible for Kids. 2009. (J). pap. *(978-1-61623-151-4(3))* Independent Pub.

Traywick-Jones, Andrea. God Loves Me! Thomas, James, illus. 2003. 24p. (J). *(978-1-55306-459-6(3),* Guardian Bks.) Essence Publishing.

Valeri, Jennifer. God from A-Z: A Child's Guide to Learning about God. 2009. 32p. pap. 15.00 *(978-1-60860-761-7(5),* Eloquent Bks.) Strategic Book Publishing & Rights Agency (SBPRA).

VanBuskirk, Luegenia. God Loves Me. 2003. 40p. (J). per. 12.95 *(978-1-56167-790-0(6))* American Literary Pr.

Vivian May Edwards. Creation's Praise: For little Ones. 2009. 20p. pap. 14.99 *(978-1-4389-5919-1(2))* AuthorHouse.

Walker, Joni. Tell Me What God Made. Walker, Joni, illus. 2007. (Illus.). 20p. (J). (gr. -1-3). bds. 6.49 *(978-0-7586-1247-2(8))* Concordia Publishing Hse.

Walsh, Brendan & Benchmark Education Co., LLC. Greek & Roman Gods & Goddesses. 2014. (Text Connections Ser.). (J). (gr. 3). *(978-1-4509-9666-2(3))* Benchmark Education Co.

Warnes, Tim, illus. Jesus Loves Me! 2008. (ENG.). 26p. (J). (gr. -1-k). bds. 7.99 *(978-1-4169-5367-8(1),* Little Simon) Little Simon.

Watson, Lori Ann. Beginnings. Bersani, Shennen, illus. 2009. 32p. (J). (gr. -1-1). 12.95 *(978-0-8198-1172-1(6))* Pauline Bks. & Media.

Wesleyan Publishing House, creator. Learning about God Student Activity Book: 52 Reproducible in-Class Activities & Family Devotionals. 2006. (Building Kids Faith Ser.). (Illus.). stu. ed., per., act. bk. ed. 15.99 *(978-0-89827-340-3(4))* Wesleyan Publishing Hse.

West, Edith. A World Just for Me. 2009. 32p. pap. 13.99 *(978-1-4389-7083-7(8))* AuthorHouse.

Wiens, Patti. A Child's ABCs of Praise Spieler, Leah, ed. LeTourneau, Anthony & Carlson, Josh, illus. 2004. 60p. (J). pap. 14.99 *(978-0-9761408-0-1(2))* Creative Marketing Concepts, Inc.

Wolfson, Ron. Be Like God: God's To-Do List for Kids. 2012. (ENG., Illus.). 144p. (J). pap. 15.99 *(978-1-58023-510-5(7),* 9781580235105, Jewish Lights Publishing) LongHill Partners, Inc.

Zona Biblica en el Desierto Preschool Kit Wrap. 2007. *(978-0-687-64773-6(8))* Abingdon Pr.

GOD—FICTION

Adams, Michelle Medlock. How Much Does God Love You? Keiser, Paige, illus. 2010. 22p. (J). (gr. -1-k). 6.99 *(978-0-8249-1848-4(7),* Ideal Pubns.) Worthy Publishing.

—Why I Love you, God. 2004. 20p. (J). bds. 5.49 *(978-0-570-07187-7(9))* Concordia Publishing Hse.

Albani, Rob. The Whole World Laughing at Once. 2009. 28p. pap. 12.49 *(978-1-4389-7947-2(9))* AuthorHouse.

Alderman, Rusty. Daddy S Little Princess. 2013. 18p. pap. 9.99 *(978-1-62697-788-4(7))* Salem Author Services.

Alexander, James W. Good - Better - Best: Classic Treatment of a Christian's Duty to the Poor. 2009. 224p. pap. 17.00 *(978-1-59925-143-1(4))* Solid Ground Christian Bks.

Arbogast, Christian Hunt. Heaven's Dentist. 2011. 15.00 *(978-1-936319-58-9(6))* Mascot Bks., Inc.

Arroyo, Kritzia. Angel Princess Star. 2008. 18p. 10.28 *(978-1-4303-2776-9(6))* Lulu Pr., Inc.

Backman, Tisha. Just As I Am. 2011. 16p. pap. 24.95 *(978-1-4560-4042-0(1))* America Star Bks.

Baldwin, Christy. Nine Things Nathan Noticed at Night. Barnes, Sarah, illus. 2005. 24p. (J). per. 13.00 *(978-0-9765072-1-5(8))* Tribute Bks.

Balestrino, Jerry. Pumpkin the Angel Cat: Pumpkins 1st Mission. 2009. 32p. pap. 13.99 *(978-1-4343-7105-8(0))* AuthorHouse.

Barnes, Denise Sullivan. Megan's Phone Call. 2012. 24p. pap. 17.99 *(978-1-4772-8437-7(0))* AuthorHouse.

Beeke, Joel R. & Kleyn, Diana. How God Used a Drought & an Umbrella. Anderson, Jeff, illus. 2006. (Building on the Rock Ser.). (ENG.). 176p. (J). pap. 8.99 *(978-1-85792-818-1(0),* 9781857928181, CF4Kids) Christian Focus Pubns. GBR. Dist: Bookmasters Distribution.

Bennett, Marian. God Made Kittens. Marlin, Kathryn, illus. 2015. (Faith That Sticks Bks.). (ENG.). 30p. (J). pap. 3.99 *(978-1-4964-0319-3(3))* Tyndale Hse. Pubs.

Bergren, Lisa T. God Gave Us Christmas. 2006. (God Gave Us Ser.). (ENG., Illus.). 40p. (J). (gr. -1-k). 10.99 *(978-1-4000-7175-3(5),* WaterBrook Pr.) Crown Publishing Group.

—God Gave Us Love. 2009. (ENG., Illus.). 40p. (gr. -1-2). 10.99 *(978-1-4000-7447-1(9),* WaterBrook Pr.) Crown Publishing Group.

—God Gave Us So Much: A Limited-Edition Three-Book Treasury. Bryant, Laura J., illus. 2010. (ENG.). 112p. 19.99 *(978-0-307-44629-9(8),* WaterBrook Pr.) Crown Publishing Group.

—How Big Is God? Bryant, Laura J., illus. 2008. (HarperBlessings Ser.). (ENG.). 32p. (J). (gr. -1-2). 10.99 *(978-0-06-113174-5(1))* HarperCollins Pubs.

Bertanzetti, Eileen Dunn. Poor Pio. 2008. (Illus.). 48p. (J). pap. 4.95 *(978-0-7599-0241-1(0))* Hard Shell Word Factory.

Blomenkamp Ed.D., Joel. The Storm: A Christian's Parable for Understanding Life's Hardships. 2013. 28p. pap. 13.95 *(978-1-4497-7796-8(1),* WestBow Pr.) Author Solutions, Inc.

Bond, Thomas A. The Mill Creek Kids. 2008. 124p. pap. 11.99 *(978-1-60647-947-6(4))* Salem Author Services.

Bostrom, Kathleen Long. Good Morning, God! Lyon, Tammie, illus. 2014. 20p. (J). bds. 6.99 *(978-0-8249-1939-9(4),* Ideal Pubns.) Worthy Publishing.

EFG

—Good Night, God! Lyon, Tammie, illus. 2014. 20p. (J). bds. 6.99 *(978-0-8249-1940-5(8),* Ideal Pubns.) Worthy Publishing.

Bradford, Bruce. An Angel Named Herald. 2011. 32p. pap. 12.77 *(978-1-4634-0407-9(7))* AuthorHouse.

Bridges, Moire. Hermanita y el Rey: Una Parabola. Bridges, Moire, illus. 2007. (Illus.). 28p. (J). (gr. -1-3). 13.99 *(978-1-59879-427-4(2))* Lifevest Publishing, Inc.

—Sissy & the King: A Parable. Bridges, Moire, illus. 2007. (Illus.). (J). (gr. -1-3). 32p. 19.99 *(978-1-59879-403-8(5));* 26p. 13.99 *(978-1-59879-425-0(6))* Lifevest Publishing, Inc.

Brouwer, Sigmund. Ambush. 2009. (Robot Wars Ser.: 3). (ENG.). 304p. (YA). pap. 7.99 *(978-1-4143-2311-4(5),* Tyndale Kids) Tyndale Hse. Pubs.

Cakes, Patty. God: When Will You Answer My Prayers. 2007. 56p. per. 17.95 *(978-1-59800-272-0(4))* Outskirts Pr., Inc.

Carnes, Daphane. Grace. 2009. 48p. (J). pap. 12.95 *(978-1-4327-3380-3(X))* Outskirts Pr., Inc.

Carney, Mary Lou. The Treasure Rock. 2009. 32p. 14.00 *(978-0-687-64537-4(9))* Abingdon Pr.

Carson Sr., Johnny. Little Dog. 2013. 28p. pap. 24.95 *(978-1-63000-014-1(0))* America Star Bks.

Castro, Edmund Lee. Crystal & Her Flying Adventure. 2010. 44p. 16.99 *(978-1-4490-6867-7(7))* AuthorHouse.

—Crystal & the Not-So-Scary Night. 2008. 36p. pap. 24.95 *(978-1-60672-236-7(0))* America Star Bks.

Cavalli, Frank. Before the Beginning Began. Riley, Kellee, illus. 2006. 56p. (J). (gr. -1-3). 19.95 *(978-0-9766662-0-2(0))* Star Dome Publishing, LLC.

Chiew, Suzanne. What a Wonderful World! McNaughton, Tina, illus. 2013. (ENG.). 32p. (J). (gr. -1-1). 16.95 *(978-1-58925-129-8(6))* Tiger Tales.

Coats, Vivian. In His Love. 2009. 32p. pap. 12.99 *(978-1-4389-4104-2(8))* AuthorHouse.

Cohen, Deborah. The Seventh Day. Hall, Melanie, illus. 2005. (ENG.). 24p. (J). (gr. -1-2). 16.95 *(978-0-929371-24-5(0));* per. 8.95 *(978-1-58013-125-4(5))* Lerner Publishing Group. (Kar-Ben Publishing).

Collins, Michael. Anu & the Blue. 2009. 166p. pap. 16.68 *(978-0-557-20316-1(3))* Lulu Pr., Inc.

Columbro, Judy. The Gift of Rainbows. Scottorosano, Deborah, illus. 2011. 24p. pap. 24.95 *(978-1-4626-0355-8(6))* PublishAmerica, Inc.

Dalmatian Press Staff. Thanks You, God: Board Book with Plush Toy. rev. ed. 2007. (ENG.). 7p. 12.99 *(978-1-4037-3074-9(1),* Spirit Pr.) Bendon, Inc.

Davies, Margaret Anne. God Made Me. 2008. 33p. pap. 24.95 *(978-1-60563-986-4(9))* America Star Bks.

Davis, Darlene. God Made Everything. 2008. 28p. pap. 24.95 *(978-1-60672-183-4(6))* PublishAmerica, Inc.

Dawson, Christopher B. Treasure in the Mirror. 2007. (Illus.). 32p. (J). *(978-0-9796456-1-7(1))* Unlock A Bk. Pubs., LLC.

DeLap, Mark. The Little Acorn, 1 vol. 2010. 40p. pap. 24.95 *(978-1-4489-9509-7(4))* PublishAmerica, Inc.

Derico, Laura Ring. All God's Bugs. Smith, Matt, illus. 2015. (Faith That Sticks Bks.). (ENG.). 30p. (J). pap. 3.99 *(978-1-4964-0317-9(7))* Tyndale Hse. Pubs.

Despain, Bree. The Shadow Prince. 2014. (ENG.). 496p. (J). (gr. 7). 18.99 *(978-1-60684-247-8(1),* Carolrhoda Lab™) Lerner Publishing Group.

Donohue, D. M. My Morning Prayer: A Gift from God. 2011. 20p. pap. 10.50 *(978-1-4634-3333-8(6))* AuthorHouse.

Dossantos, Laurie Staples. The Adventures of Stormy. 2009. 34p. pap. 10.50 *(978-1-60693-365-7(5),* Eloquent Bks.) Strategic Book Publishing & Rights Agency (SBPRA).

Du Bois, Crystal L. God Made My Butt Big. 2012. 24p. pap. 14.93 *(978-1-4669-0584-9(0))* Trafford Publishing.

Dubrule, Jackie. Little John, God, & the Circus. Swope, Brenda, illus. 2011. 32p. pap. 24.95 *(978-1-4560-0978-6(8))* America Star Bks.

Dyan, Penelope. Adam. 2011. 34p. pap. 11.96 *(978-1-935630-94-4(6))* Bellissima Publishing, LLC.

Dykes, Tami J. Being Too Small Is Big Enough. 2013. 42p. pap. 20.45 *(978-1-4497-8483-6(6),* WestBow Pr.) Author Solutions, Inc.

Espinoza, Carlota D. God Made a Very Big Big Bang! Espinoza, Gabbi & EspinoZa, Carlota D., illus. 2011. 32p. pap. 24.95 *(978-1-4560-9582-6(X))* America Star Bks.

Fairchild, Dianne. Are You There? Fairchild, Vincent, illus. 2007. 32p. (J). pap. 16.00 *(978-0-8059-7535-2(7))* Dorrance Publishing Co., Inc.

Fajnland, Leibel. Big Small or Just One Wall: A Book about Shuls. Rosenfeld, D. L., ed. Leff, Tova, illus. 2011. 36p. (J). 12.95 *(978-1-929628-59-9(5))* Hachai Publishing.

Falk, Elsa. Akio & the Moon Goddess. Kraynak, George, illus. 2011. 158p. 41.95 *(978-1-258-06311-5(5))* Literary Licensing, LLC.

Fisher, Catherine. The Oracle Betrayed. 2005. (Oracle Prophecies Ser.). (Illus.). 332p. (YA). (gr. 7-12). 14.65 *(978-0-7569-5269-3(7))* Perfection Learning Corp.

Fite, Ramona. A Boy & His God. Monick, Susie, illus. 2012. 36p. 22.50 *(978-1-937763-37-4(4))* Published by Westview, Inc.

Florence, Amy. A Big God Cares for a Little Me. 2008. 20p. pap. 24.95 *(978-1-60563-009-0(8))* America Star Bks.

Fortuna, Lorna. When God Spoke to Trees. 2006. 17.00 *(978-0-8059-9884-9(5))* Dorrance Publishing Co., Inc.

Foster, Ron, illus. I Like Rain. 2007. 28p. (J). (gr. 1-4). *(978-1-929039-39-5(5))* Ambassador Bks., Inc.

Fotheringham, Juanita. A Little Ranch on the Side. 2013. 38p. pap. 9.99 *(978-1-62697-215-5(X))* Salem Author Services.

Freed, Christina. Sophie's Cross. 2007. 48p. per. 16.95 *(978-1-4241-7677-9(8))* America Star Bks.

Freed, Crissy. The Child Within. 2008. 60p. pap. 12.99 *(978-1-4343-8478-2(0))* AuthorHouse.

Gateley, Edwina. God Goes on Vacation. Gateley, Edwina, illus. 2009. (Illus.). 32p. (Orig.). (J). pap. 9.95 *(978-0-8091-6747-0(6))* Paulist Pr.

Gateley, Edwina, illus. & text. God Goes to School. Gateley, Edwina, text. 2009. 32p. (J). pap. 9.95 *(978-0-8091-6748-7(4))* Paulist Pr.

Gendron, Elizabeth. In God's Playpen: For the Child in all of Us. 2011. 44p. 17.50 *(978-1-4269-6442-8(0))* Trafford Publishing.

Gibbons, Teresa Dominguez. Pancakes Every Morning. 2008. 24p. per. 24.95 *(978-1-60441-065-5(5))* America Star Bks.

Gibson, Angela S. The Colors of God. 2012. 34p. 34.99 *(978-1-62419-479-5(6));* (Illus.). pap. 24.99 *(978-1-62419-478-8(8))* Salem Author Services.

Gibson, Tonya. Hiking with Dad. 2008. 12p. pap. 24.95 *(978-1-60703-253-3(8))* America Star Bks.

Glowacki, Helen. God's Plan of Salvation. 2013. 152p. pap. 17.50 *(978-0-9893807-4-4(2))* Glowacki, Helen.

Godfrey, Jan. Who Made the Morning? Ayres, Honor, illus. 2008. (ENG.). 28p. (J). (gr. -1-3). 9.99 *(978-0-9798247-0-8(2))* New Day Publishing, Inc.

Gomez, Sally. Too Many Freckles! Mitchell, Hazel, illus. 2008. (ENG.). 32p. pap. *(978-1-934363-32-4(4))* Zoe Life Publishing.

Good, Linnea, et al. Adventures of the God Detectives. 2006. (ENG., Illus.). 96p. (J). (gr. 10-10). per. 6.95 *(978-1-55145-542-6(0))* Wood Lake Publishing, Inc. CAN. Dist: Westminster John Knox Pr.

Gray, Rev. Maxine A. Children's Lessons on Morality: Don't Use Your Friends. 2013. 24p. pap. 14.99 *(978-1-4669-8831-6(2))* Trafford Publishing.

Graziano-Strauss, Laura. The Happy Crabby Crying Happy Family's Blessing, 1 vol. 2009. 47p. pap. 24.95 *(978-1-60672-710-2(9))* America Star Bks.

Greathouse, Cindy. Wilbur Learns to Forgive, 1 vol. 2010. 18p. 24.95 *(978-1-4489-7374-3(0))* PublishAmerica, Inc.

Greene, Joshua M. Krishna & the Mystery of the Stolen Calves. Amendola, Dominique, illus. 2013. (ENG.). 24p. (gr. -1). 14.99 *(978-1-60887-173-5(8))* Mandala Publishing.

Greene, Rhonda Gowler. Only God Can Make a Kitten, 1 vol. Bryant, Laura J., illus. 2016. (ENG.). 28p. (J). bds. 9.99 *(978-0-310-75008-6(3))* Zonderkidz.

—Only God Can Make a Kitten, 1 vol. 2015. (ENG.). 32p. (J). 14.99 *(978-0-310-73170-2(4))* Zonderkidz.

Gustke, Carol Davis. An Angel's First Job. 2008. (Illus.). 24p. (J). lib. bdg. *(978-0-9801376-2-0(4));* per. *(978-0-9801376-3-7(2))* Dragonfly Publishing, Inc.

Hallinan, P. K. Thank You, God. 2008. (ENG., Illus.). 28p. (J). (gr. -1-k). bds. 7.95 *(978-0-8249-5457-4(2),* Ideal Pubns.) Worthy Publishing.

Hand, Reuben W. The Thirst for Life, 1 vol. 2010. 52p. pap. 16.95 *(978-1-4489-4897-0(5))* America Star Bks.

Hennesy, Carolyn. Pandora Gets Vain. 2008. (Mythic Misadventures Ser.). (ENG., Illus.). 288p. (YA). (gr. 3-6). 14.99 *(978-1-59990-197-8(8),* 9781599901978, Bloomsbury USA Childrens) Bloomsbury Publishing USA.

Herbstritt, Rj. God Loves You More Than Rainbows & Butterflies! Herbstritt, T. J., illus. 2011. 40p. pap. 24.95 *(978-1-4560-6735-9(4))* America Star Bks.

Hippie Bob. God's Cook Book What a Creation! A Hippie Bob Tale. 2009. 24p. pap. 14.99 *(978-1-4389-9834-3(1))* AuthorHouse.

Hocknell, Barbara. Gifts for God. 2007. (Illus.). 56p. per. *(978-1-84748-131-3(0))* Athena Pr.

Hodges, Lynn & Buchanan, Sue. I Love You This Much, 1 vol. Bendall-Brunello, John, illus. 2010. (ENG.). 36p. (J). pap. 6.99 *(978-0-310-72265-6(9))* Zonderkidz.

Hodges, Lynn, et al. I Love You This Much, 1 vol. Bendall-Brunello, John, illus. 2005. (Songs of Gods Love Ser.). (ENG.). 16p. (J). (gr. -1). bds. 6.99 *(978-0-310-70961-9(X))* Zonderkidz.

Holliday, S. L. My Identity Christ-Is: Stay in the Game. 2012. (ENG.). 166p. (J). pap. 12.95 *(978-1-4787-1827-7(7))* Outskirts Pr., Inc.

Holmes, Donna M. Jacob & Isabell, 1 vol. 2009. 18p. pap. 24.95 *(978-1-60813-826-5(7))* America Star Bks.

Holub, Joan & Williams, Suzanne. Aphrodite the Beauty. 2013. (Goddess Girls Ser.: 3). (ENG.). 176p. (J). (gr. 3-7). 17.99 *(978-1-4424-5751-5(1),* Aladdin) Simon & Schuster Children's Publishing.

—Persephone the Daring. 2013. (Goddess Girls Ser.: 11). (ENG., Illus.). 256p. (J). (gr. 3-7). 17.99 *(978-1-4424-8158-9(7));* pap. 7.99 *(978-1-4424-4939-8(X))* Simon & Schuster Children's Publishing. (Aladdin).

House, Catherine. Little Zebra. Whelan, Olwyn, illus. 2007. 39p. (J). 11.95 *(978-1-59325-094-2(0))* Word Among Us Pr.

Hub, Ulrich. Be at the Ark by Eight. Mühle, Jörg, illus. 2012. (ENG.). 68p. (J). 12.00 *(978-0-8028-5410-0(9),* Eerdmans Bks For Young Readers) Eerdmans, William B. Publishing Co.

Hudson, Wade. It's Church Going Time. 2008. (Illus.). 32p. (gr. -1-3). 16.95 *(978-1-60349-005-4(1),* Marimba Bks.) Hudson Publishing Group, The.

Huskins, Suzanne Hallier, illus. No Matter What! 2004. (J). *(978-1-887905-93-0(6))* Parkway Pubs., Inc.

Jador, Monisha Annabel. Before You Were Born. 2013. 20p. pap. 15.29 *(978-1-4669-9119-4(4))* Trafford Publishing.

Jennings, Arleen Naish. God Is in the Rain. 2012. 64p. (gr. 1-2). pap. 8.95 *(978-1-4759-3292-8(8))* iUniverse, Inc.

Jensen, Bonnie Rickner. God Loves Daddy & Me, 1 vol. 2017. (ENG., Illus.). 20p. (J). bds. 9.99 *(978-0-7180-9177-4(9))* Nelson, Thomas Inc.

Jewell, Laura. Ty Gets His Wings. 2012. (ENG.). (J). pap. 18.00 *(978-1-4675-4702-4(6))* Independent Pub.

Johnson, Susana M. Our Very Special Brother. 2010. 28p. pap. 15.99 *(978-1-4500-4394-6(1))* Xlibris Corp.

Johnson, William C. Little Tree. 2007. pap. 9.00 *(978-0-8059-8486-6(0))* Dorrance Publishing Co., Inc.

Jones Crabbe, Ann. T J & His Friend: It's Just a Baby Thing. 2009. 24p. pap. 13.99 *(978-1-4490-1185-7(3))* AuthorHouse.

Jones, Erik, illus. God Is in the Refrigerator. 2006. 38p. (J). 18.95 *(978-0-9771936-4-6(0))* InterWeave Corp.

Keaton, Skeet. The Adventures of Jd Losey. 2005. pap. 9.99 *(978-1-59781-353-2(2))* Salem Author Services.

Killingworth, Gerald. Lord of the Silver Hand. 2006. (ENG.). 188p. *(978-1-905886-01-2(2))* Troubador Publishing Ltd.

King, Kimberly. God Is in the Window. Jones, Erik, illus. 2007. 37p. (J). 18.95 *(978-0-9771936-6-0(7))* InterWeave Corp.

Knight, Jovannah. A Heavenly Message. 2011. 20p. pap. 16.95 *(978-1-61204-430-9(1),* Strategic Bk. Publishing) Strategic Book Publishing & Rights Agency (SBPRA).

Knipe, Sally J. The Angel with the Broken Wings. 2012. 28p. pap. 15.99 *(978-1-4691-4896-0(X))* Xlibris Corp.

Knowlton, Laurie Lazzaro. My Valentine for Jesus, 1 vol. Erdogan, Buket, illus. 2009. (ENG.). 10p. (J). bds. 4.99 *(978-0-310-71333-3(1))* Zonderkidz.

Krise, Carrie. Even Little Ones Are in God's Care. 2008. 16p. per. 24.95 *(978-1-4241-9902-0(6))* America Star Bks.

Labuda, Scott A. The Color of People. Franfou Studio, illus. 2011. (ENG.). 34p. (J). (gr. -1-3). 15.95 *(978-1-935268-94-9(5))* Halo Publishing International.

Lane, Sondra. Showin' Out to God's Glory. 2004. (Illus.). 28p. (J). 7.95 *(978-0-9743874-1-3(X))* Lane, Sondra Corp.

Lash, Jill. He Knows You. 2007. (J). 15.99 *(978-1-59955-089-3(X))* Cedar Fort, Inc./CFI Distribution.

Latimer, Brenda. I See God. 2008. (Illus.). 28p. 12.95 *(978-0-9797429-2-7(7))* Halo Publishing International.

Leathers, Rain. Purple Mountain. 2008. 36p. pap. 20.95 *(978-1-4327-2685-0(4))* Outskirts Pr., Inc.

Legall, D. Antoinette. A Gift for God. 2013. 16p. pap. 12.68 *(978-1-4669-7568-2(7))* Trafford Publishing.

Leslie, Emma. Gytha's Message: A Tale of Saxon England. Staniland, C., illus. 2007. 256p. 22.95 *(978-1-934671-11-5(8))* Salem Ridge Press LLC.

—The Martyr's Victory: A Story of Danish England. Stacey, W., illus. 2007. 300p. 24.95 *(978-1-934671-08-5(8));* per. 14.95 *(978-1-934671-09-2(6))* Salem Ridge Press LLC.

Lewis, Beverly. Holly's Heart. 2008. (ENG., (gr. 7-11). Vol. 2, Bks. 6-10. Illus.). 560p. pap. 13.99 *(978-0-7642-0459-3(9))* Vol. 3, Bks. 11-14. 448p. pap. 16.00 *(978-0-7642-0460-9(2))* Bethany Hse. Pubs.

—What Is God Like? Querin, Pamela, illus. 2008. (ENG.). 32p. (J). (gr. -1-3). 14.99 *(978-0-7642-0466-1(1))* Bethany Hse. Pubs.

Lile, Linda L. Nonnie, What's God? Julich, Jenniffer, illus. 2008. 16p. (J). 13.95 *(978-0-9817092-0-8(6))* A-Lu Publishing.

Lindquist, N. J. A Friend in Need. 2016. (Circle of Friends Ser.: Vol. 3). (ENG., Illus.). (YA). pap. ***(978-1-927692-06-6(7))*** That's Life! Communications.

Lodge, Ali, illus. The Leopard & the Sky God. 2007. (Usborne First Reading: Level 3 Ser.). 48p. (J). (gr. -1-3). 8.99 *(978-0-7945-1838-7(9),* Usborne) EDC Publishing.

Lopez, Denise M. If God Was a Superhero. 2013. 16p. pap. 7.95 *(978-1-4497-9707-2(5),* WestBow Pr.) Author Solutions, Inc.

Lucado, Max. One Hand, Two Hands, 1 vol. 2010. (ENG.). 32p. (gr. -1-3). 14.99 *(978-1-4003-1649-6(9))* Nelson, Thomas Inc.

Luna, Danielle. Precious & Loved. 2011. 20p. pap. 24.95 *(978-1-4626-0281-0(9))* America Star Bks.

Lyons, P. J. God Is Watching over You, 1 vol. Warnes, Tim, illus. 2016. (ENG.). 16p. (J). bds. 9.99 *(978-0-310-74881-6(X))* Zonderkidz.

Mackall, Dandi Daley. Cinnamon Lake Mysteries Set, 6 vols. (Cinnamon Lake Mysteries Ser.). (J). 33.74 *(978-0-7586-0006-6(2))* Concordia Publishing Hse.

—God Loves Me More Than That. 2008. (Dandilion Rhymes Ser.). (ENG., Illus.). 40p. (J). (gr. -1-2). 10.99 *(978-1-4000-7316-0(2),* WaterBrook Pr.) Crown Publishing Group.

Marcum, Lindsay A. God's Little Lydia Lu. 2010. 20p. pap. 10.95 *(978-1-4497-0700-2(9),* WestBow Pr.) Author Solutions, Inc.

Mattingly, Robin. Chicken Church. Swope, Brenda, illus. 2011. 28p. pap. 24.95 *(978-1-4560-0962-5(1))* America Star Bks.

McCollon, Donell. Tell Me about God Please. 2011. 48p. pap. 20.00 *(978-1-4490-6232-3(6))* AuthorHouse.

—When Fear Knocks at the Door. 2009. 28p. pap. 20.49 *(978-1-4490-0226-8(9))* AuthorHouse.

McCombs, Margi. Dios es Bueno Todo el Tiempo. Ivanov, Aleksey & Ivanov, Olga, illus. 2012. (SPA.). 20p. (J). (gr. -1-k). bds. 9.99 *(978-0-545-45618-0(5),* Scholastic en Espanol) Scholastic, Inc.

McCorkle, Brent & Parker, Amy. Firebird: He Lived for the Sunsine. Corley, Rob & Vollmer, Chuck, illus. 2014. (ENG.). 32p. (J). (gr. -1-3). 9.99 *(978-1-4336-8467-8(5),* B&H Kids) B&H Publishing Group.

McGillicuddy, Barbara. Adventures in the Kingdom of Mim: Buddie Saves the Day. 2006. (J). per. 13.95 *(978-0-9774513-7-1(2))* Changing Lives Publishing.

McMillin, Jack. Dodger the Dragon, 1 vol. Nevarez, Lisa, illus. 2009. pap. 24.95 *(978-1-60703-930-3(3))* PublishAmerica, Inc.

Mellen, Wynette. What Do You See? Rasmussen, Jennifer, illus. 2012. 42p. (J). pap. 9.95 *(978-0-9839957-4-6(5))* Freundship Pr., LLC.

Miller, Christopher & Miller, Allan. The Legend of Ten-Gallon Sam & the Perilous Mine, 2 bks., Bk.2. Miller, Christopher & Miller, Allan, illus. 2007. (Heroes of Promise Ser.). (ENG., Illus.). 32p. (J). (gr. -1-5). 12.99 *(978-1-59317-225-1(7))* Warner Pr., Inc.

Miller, Jay. Opal, Herby, & Squeaky. 2008. 44p. pap. 18.99 *(978-1-4389-1808-2(9))* AuthorHouse.

Mills, Samuel. The Demon Slayer. 2009. 192p. (YA). pap. 15.00 *(978-0-88010-701-3(4))* SteinerBooks, Inc.

Mishica, Clare. Samantha Stays Safe. Dubin, Jill, illus. 2012. 32p. (J). pap. 8.00 *(978-1-935014-40-9(4))* Hutchings, John Pubs.

Molengraf, Jonathan Eric. Take Me to Your Leader. 2012. 20p. pap. 24.95 *(978-1-4626-8208-9(1))* America Star Bks.

Monson, Lois. God Is for Every Day(r) - Horse Dreams: Teach-A-Child Companion Book with VCD, 2 vols., Vol. 2. JoySoul Corporation, illus. Monson, Lois, photos by. 2006. 24p. (J). spiral bd. 14.95 *(978-0-9727786-9-5(1))* JoySoul Corp.

—God Is for Every Day(r) - Horse Dreams: Teach-a-Child Companion Book/DVD Set. Monson, Lois, photos by. 2008. (Illus.). 28p. (J). ring bd. 14.95 *(978-0-9727786-8-8(3))* JoySoul Corp.

Moore, Katherine Roberts. Is God Behind the Big Blue Sky? Moore, Kristen L., illus. 2010. 34p. pap. 13.95 *(978-1-60911-705-4(0),* Eloquent Bks.) Strategic Book Publishing & Rights Agency (SBPRA).

Morel, John Henry. Odd Events Happen All Around Me. 2009. 96p. pap. 29.00 *(978-1-935436-28-7(7))* Rodaian Pr.

Moss, Maureen. God's Promise. Purnell, Gerald, illus. 2008. 30p. (J). (gr. -1-3). 15.95 *(978-0-9740190-7-9(0))* Illumination Arts Publishing Co., Inc.

Nesselrode, Sandra. Princess Kelsie & Her Special Gifts. 2008. 28p. pap. 19.95 *(978-1-4327-1708-7(1))* Outskirts Pr., Inc.

Neuls, Lillian. It's Okay to Talk to God. L'Eplattenier, Michelle, illus. 2008. 12p. pap. 24.95 *(978-1-60703-855-9(2))* America Star Bks.

Nolan, Allia Zobel. God's Light, Shining Bright. Bryant, Laura J., illus. 2006. 8p. (J). 12.99 *(978-0-8254-5527-8(8))* Kregel Pubns.

—God's Oak Tree. Chung, Chi, illus. 2007. 16p. (J). (gr. -1). 12.99 *(978-0-8254-5536-0(7))* Kregel Pubns.

—God's Rainbow. Chung, Chi, illus. 2007. 16p. (J). 12.99 *(978-0-8254-5537-7(5))* Kregel Pubns.

O'Donnell, Candy. Where Is God, Grandfather. Gillen, Rosemarie, illus. 2008. 28p. pap. 12.95 *(978-0-9814532-1-7(X))* Living Waters Publishing Co.

Otenbaker, Audrey Lee. God's Jewel. 2009. 48p. (J). pap. 17.95 *(978-1-4327-3340-7(0))* Outskirts Pr., Inc.

Overton, Lou Ann. Thank You, Moon. 2013. 24p. pap. 12.45 *(978-1-4908-0030-1(1),* WestBow Pr.) Author Solutions, Inc.

Parker, Amy. How High Is Hope? (padded Board Book) 2016. (Faith, Hope, Love Ser.). (ENG.). 24p. (J). (gr. -1-k). bds. 9.99 *(978-1-4336-9041-9(1),* B&H Kids) B&H Publishing Group.

—The Plans I Have for You, 1 vol. Newton, Vanessa & Brantley-Newton, Vanessa, illus. 2015. (ENG.). 32p. (J). 16.99 *(978-0-310-72410-0(4))* Zonderkidz.

Parr, Susan Sherwood. Christopher's Adventures: Chris Visits the Hospital, Vol. 2. Paraschiv, Doina, illus. 2nd alt. ed. 2013. (ENG.). 24p. (J). pap. 8.95 *(978-0-9827998-8-8(8),* KID-E Bks.) Word Prodns.

Peckham, Lori, ed. Guide's Greatest Animal Stories. 2006. 143p. (J). (gr. 5-9). per. 10.99 *(978-0-8280-1944-6(4))* Review & Herald Publishing Assn.

Pick, Alice. Jamey's Promise, 1 vol. 2009. 61p. pap. 19.95 *(978-1-61582-547-9(9))* America Star Bks.

Pilot Point Pranksters. 2008. 56p. pap. 6.99 *(978-0-8341-2343-4(6),* 083-412-3436) Beacon Hill Pr. of Kansas City.

Poer, Karla R. The Busy-Body Book of Fun-Atomy Tunes. 2008. (ENG.). 56p. pap. 21.99 *(978-1-4389-3296-5(0))* AuthorHouse.

Poland, Pitch & Poland, Inglan. Lost & Found. Rose, Drew, illus. 2013. 30p. (J). *(978-0-9853430-0-2(1))* Little P Pr. Co.

Poole, Susie. Always near Me. 2017. (ENG., Illus.). 24p. (J). (— 1). pap. 3.99 ***(978-1-4627-4515-9(6),*** B&H Kids) B&H Publishing Group.

Preik, Christel D. Sharing the Love. 2013. 36p. pap. 15.49 *(978-1-4669-9975-6(6))* Trafford Publishing.

Rafter, Dan. Atlas. 2010. (ENG., Illus.). 96p. pap. 9.99 *(978-1-61623-931-2(X))* Bluewater Productions, Inc.

Rainey, Barbara. What God Wants for Christmas. Walker, John, illus. 2011. (J). (gr. 4-7). pap. 29.99 incl. audio compact disk *(978-1-60200-428-3(5))* FamilyLife.

Reaves, Janice. It's Kool to Be Smart & to Have God. 2010. 44p. pap. 16.99 *(978-1-4490-7999-4(7))* AuthorHouse.

—Ser Inteligente y Tener a Dios en Tu Corazón Es Buena Ond. 2010. 44p. pap. 16.99 *(978-1-4490-8002-0(2))* AuthorHouse.

Richardson, Robert. Twin Hicks Noah's Ark. Hicks, Alan and Aaron, illus. 2008. 36p. pap. 16.95 *(978-1-4389-1809-9(7))* AuthorHouse.

Richey, Denise. The Handwriting on the Wall. 2012. 28p. pap. 19.99 *(978-1-4772-6606-9(2))* AuthorHouse.

Roberts, Paula Carol. Good Morning Billy. 2011. 32p. pap. 13.95 *(978-1-4497-1214-3(2),* WestBow Pr.) Author Solutions, Inc.

Roberts, Pauline. He Shined on Me. 2010. 20p. pap. 9.95 *(978-0-9841991-6-7(0))* Beckham Pubns. Group, Inc.

Rodgers, Phillip W. When Was God Born?, 1 vol. 2008. (Discovering God Ser.). 32p. (J). 12.99 *(978-0-8254-3608-6(7))* Kregel Pubns.

Rodriguez, Renae. Why You Are So Special. 2010. 16p. 9.99 *(978-1-4520-3540-6(7))* AuthorHouse.

Roesti, Delores. Mareena Maree Mulligan & the Flying Wheelchair: Book 2: The Busybodies. 2008. 102p. pap. 10.95 *(978-0-7414-4477-6(1))* Infinity Publishing.

Roots, Arleen. Except Ye Abide in the Ship. 2013. 32p. pap. 12.79 *(978-1-4251-6752-3(7))* Trafford Publishing.

Rosoff, Meg. There Is No Dog. (ENG.). 288p. (YA). (gr. 7). 2013. pap. 8.99 *(978-0-14-242384-4(X),* Speak) 2012. 17.99 *(978-0-399-25764-3(0),* G.P. Putnam's Sons Books for Young Readers) Penguin Young Readers Group.

—There Is No Dog. l.t. ed. 2012. (ENG.). 392p. (J). (gr. 7-12). 23.99 *(978-1-4104-4707-4(3))* Thorndike Pr.

Ross, Patrick. Joseph & Snowy Joe Blue, 1 vol. Burcham, David, illus. 2009. 25p. pap. 24.95 *(978-1-61582-314-7(X))* PublishAmerica, Inc.

Rupp, Dain Chistopher. The Greatest Saint Stories A-Z: (Book 1 of 2: A-M) 2008. 32p. per. 24.95 *(978-1-60441-067-9(1))* America Star Bks.

Rylant, Cynthia. God Got a Dog. Frazee, Marla, illus. 2013. (ENG.). 48p. (J). (gr. 5-5). 17.99 *(978-1-4424-6518-3(2),* Beach Lane Bks.) Beach Lane Bks.

—God Went to Beauty School. 2003. (ENG.). 64p. (J). 14.99 *(978-0-06-009433-1(8))* HarperCollins Pubs.

Salma, Hammad. I am Beautiful. 2007. (Illus.). 20p. (J). mass mkt. *(978-0-9787849-9-7(5))* Lucent Interpretations, LLC.

Sambrone, Erika Elizabeth. Heavenly Angel Bugs: God Answers Prayers. 2011. 56p. pap. 25.00 *(978-1-4634-6807-1(5))* AuthorHouse.

Sauro, Joan. Does God Ever Sleep? 2005. (ENG., Illus.). 32p. (J). (gr. -1-3). 8.99 *(978-1-59473-110-5(1),* 9781594731105, Skylight Paths Publishing) LongHill Partners, Inc.

Scaglione, Rebecca L. Jack: The trilogy ... the Truth. 2007. 204p. per. 14.95 *(978-0-595-47331-1(8))* iUniverse, Inc.

Schlessinger, Laura. Dr. Laura Schlessinger's Where's God? McFeeley, Daniel, illus. 2003. 40p. (J). (gr. -1-2). lib. bdg. 16.89 *(978-0-06-051910-0(X))* HarperCollins Pubs.

Schouest, Stacey. The Very 1st Christmas Tree. 2011. 44p. pap. 16.95 *(978-1-4497-2528-0(7),* WestBow Pr.) Author Solutions, Inc.

Scott, Janice B. Children's Stories from the Village Shepherd. 2008. 172p. pap. 15.95 *(978-0-7880-2618-8(6))* CSS Publishing.

Shemayne S. A Place Called There. 2011. 20p. pap. 10.95 *(978-1-4497-1611-0(3),* WestBow Pr.) Author Solutions, Inc.

Sherman, Paulette Kouffman. Shekhinah. Vine, Rachel Shana, illus. 2013. 26p. pap. 10.95 *(978-0-9852469-5-2(2))* Parachute Jump Publishing.

Signor Sr., S. Ernest. The Book of David: Volume One. 2013. 28p. pap. 13.99 *(978-1-4525-7316-8(6))* Balboa Pr.

Simmons, Glenn. My Father's Work. 2008. 19p. pap. 24.95 *(978-1-60672-196-4(8))* America Star Bks.
Simon, Mary Manz. God Made the Moon. Walkley, Lizzie, illus. 2016. (J). *(978-0-8249-1981-8(5),* Ideal Pubns.) Worthy Publishing.
—The Pumpkin Gospel (die-Cut) A Story of a New Start with God. Scudamore, Angelika, illus. 2016. (ENG.). 14p. (J). (gr. -1 — 1). bds. 12.99 *(978-1-4336-9163-8(9),* B&H Kids) B&H Publishing Group.
Smith, Blanche Z. A Gift from God. 2012. 20p. pap. 17.99 *(978-1-4685-8376-2(X))* AuthorHouse.
Smith, Jada. Touched by an Angel. 2009. 76p. pap. 13.95 *(978-1-4251-8552-7(5))* Trafford Publishing.
Smith, Jennifer Lynne. Things I Wonder. Perez, Angela J., ed. Gray, Angela M., illus. 2007. 36p. (J). 14.95 *(978-0-9778328-5-9(6))* His Work Christian Publishing.
Smith, Mary L. The Ramblings of Clyde Frog & Jasmine. Bermejo, Hilbert, illus. 2013. 30p. pap. 11.99 *(978-1-61286-156-2(3))* Avid Readers Publishing Group.
Snowballs & Coconuts. 2006. 56p. pap. 7.75 *(978-0-8341-2295-6(2),* 083-412-2952) Beacon Hill Pr. of Kansas City.
Stannard, Russell. www.Here-I-Am. Pugh, Jonathan, illus. 2011. (ENG.). 160p. (YA). (gr. 5-8). pap. 9.95 *(978-1-890151-85-0(8))* Templeton Pr.
Stephens, Dawn. The Little Pot. 2009. (Illus.). (J). (gr. -1-3). 17.95 *(978-1-933982-11-3(X),* bPlus Bks.) Bumble Bee Publishing.
Stockton, Lucille. God in a Child's World & King Catfish Roonie & His Neighbors. 2003. 48p. (J). per. *(978-1-932077-34-6(0))* Athena Pr.
Stone, Forrest. Loki & the Magic Hammer: A Norse Myth. 2006. (J). pap. *(978-1-4108-6178-8(3))* Benchmark Education Co.
Sullivan, Lori Lynn. Our Sunny Day Ride. 2011. 24p. (gr. 1-2). 10.95 *(978-1-4497-1467-3(6),* WestBow Pr.) Author Solutions, Inc.
Swann, Michelle. Angels Watching over Me. 2012. 48p. pap. 16.95 *(978-1-4626-9468-6(3))* America Star Bks.
Swartz, Nancy Sohn. How Did the Animals Help God? Hall, Melanie, illus. 2004. (ENG.). 24p. (J). bds. 8.99 *(978-1-59473-044-3(X),* 9781594730443, Skylight Paths Publishing) LongHill Partners, Inc.
Swinson, Joyce Ann. Noah's Boat. Clark, Casey, illus. 2007. 32p. per. 24.95 *(978-1-4241-9012-6(6))* America Star Bks.
Tamiel. I'm Special. 2012. 28p. pap. 16.09 *(978-1-4669-4049-9(2))* Trafford Publishing.
—Two Lives. 2013. 28p. pap. 16.09 *(978-1-4669-8591-9(7))* Trafford Publishing.
Tango Books. Book of Greek Gods Pop-Up Board Games. Maddison, Kevin, illus. 2007. (Pop-Up Board Games Ser.). (ENG.). 10p. (J). (gr. -1-2). 24.99 *(978-1-85707-689-9(3))* Tango Bks. GBR. Dist: Independent Pubs. Group.
Tanner, Sally Thompson. God Shoes. 2010. 20p. 16.95 *(978-1-4497-0309-7(7),* WestBow Pr.) Author Solutions, Inc.
Tewkesbury, Alexa. Benny's Barmy Bits. 2007. (Topz Secret Diaries). (ENG., Illus.). 128p. (J). *(978-1-85345-431-8(1))* Crusade for World Revival.
—Danny's Daring Days, 1 vol. 2009. (Topz Secret Diaries). (ENG., Illus.). 128p. pap. *(978-1-85345-502-5(4))* Crusade for World Revival.
The Thirsty Turtle. 2003. 32p. (J). per. 14.95 *(978-1-59094-049-5(0))* Jawbone Publishing Corp.
Tomlin, Chris & Barrett, Pat. Good Good Father, 1 vol. 2016. (ENG.). 32p. (J). 16.99 *(978-0-7180-8695-4(3))* Nelson, Thomas Inc.
Toms, Kate, et al. God Knows All about Me. 2009. (Kate Toms Ser.). (Illus.). 26p. (J). (gr. -1-k). bds. 7.99 *(978-1-84610-590-6(0))* Make Believe Ideas GBR. Dist: Nelson, Thomas Inc.
Trigueros, Nury. I Don't Like to Be Afraid. 2010. 24p. pap. 16.99 *(978-1-4490-7287-2(9))* AuthorHouse.
Trottot, Tammy. Little Judy Talks to God. 2012. 24p. pap. 24.95 *(978-1-4626-8899-9(3))* America Star Bks.
Tyler, M. Ramifications in Genesis 1-3. 2013. 186p. (gr. 10-12). 30.95 *(978-1-4497-9526-9(9));* pap. 13.95 *(978-1-4497-9524-5(2))* Author Solutions, Inc. (WestBow Pr.).
Veggietales. A Hoppy Easter: Finding God's Love for Me. 2015. (ENG.). 32p. (J). 6.99 *(978-1-61795-485-6(3))* Worthy Publishing.
Walker, Johnny. The Planet Blue: The Adventures of Harry Lee & Bingo. 2011. 24p. pap. 11.32 *(978-1-4567-4879-1(3))* AuthorHouse.
Wallace, Michael. You, Mommy & Me. 2006. 22p. spiral bd. 8.50 *(978-1-4116-9761-4(8))* Lulu Pr., Inc.
Ware, Richard. I'm Glad God Made Me... Me. McQuitty, LaVonia Corbin, illus. 2013. 32p. (J). 17.00 *(978-0-9884125-4-5(3))* Scribe's Closet Pubns., The.
Wargin, Kathy-jo. F Is for Fireflies: God's Summertime Alphabet, 1 vol. Bronson, Linda, illus. 2011. (ENG.). 40p. (J). (gr. -1-2). 15.99 *(978-0-310-71663-1(2))* Zonderkidz.
—P Is for Pumpkin: God's Harvest Alphabet, 1 vol. Pang, YaWen Ariel, illus. 2008. (ENG.). 40p. (J). (gr. -1-3). 15.99 *(978-0-310-71180-3(0))* Zonderkidz.
Warner, Jodi. Shia's Tail. 2012. 24p. pap. 10.99 *(978-1-4624-0182-6(1),* Inspiring Voices) Author Solutions, Inc.
Wick, Kimberly. Reaching for Heaven. 2009. 36p. pap. 16.99 *(978-1-4389-2268-3(X))* AuthorHouse.
Wilkinson, Simon. Noah's Ark Black & White Visual Development Book for Babies. 2008. 34p. pap. 17.95 *(978-1-4092-4702-9(3))* Lulu Pr., Inc.
Wilkinson, William L. Glorious Praise. Blackmon, Kim, illus. 2012. 32p. pap. 10.00 *(978-1-62050-019-4(1))* Angels of Agape.
Williams, Amy. Gertrude the Silly Puppy. 2011. 28p. pap. 24.95 *(978-1-4626-2603-8(3))* America Star Bks.
Wilson, W. Shane. Ryan of the Wildfire. 2009. 296p. pap. 19.75 *(978-0-557-14937-7(1))* Lulu Pr., Inc.
Wood, Douglas. Old Turtle: Questions of the Heart. Ruth, Greg, illus. 2017. (ENG.). 56p. (J). (gr. -1-3). 19.99 *(978-0-439-32111-2(5),* Scholastic Pr.) Scholastic, Inc.
Woupio, Isaac Jay. Making Faces. Woupio, Amy, illus. 2008. 20p. per. 24.95 *(978-1-4241-9865-8(8))* America Star Bks.
Wyneken, Cherise. Spaceship Lands in Africa, 1 vol. 2010. 50p. pap. 16.95 *(978-1-4489-5417-9(7))* America Star Bks.
Yerushalmi, Miriam. Let's Go Camping & Discover Our Nature. Perez, Esther Ido, illus. 2007. 28p. (J). (gr. 2-4). 16.50 *(978-0-911643-38-1(9))* Aura Printing, Inc.
Young, Lena. Karma: Reaping What We Sow. Tsai, Dora, illus. 2005. 26p. (J). pap. *(978-1-933554-00-6(2))* Primordia.
Young, Tonya. Here's to the Nights. 2011. 190p. pap. 19.99 *(978-1-4628-8707-1(4))* Xlibris Corp.
Zimmerman, Leora. God Loves Me. 2003. (Illus.). 28p. (gr. -1-5). 2.70 *(978-0-7399-2342-9(0),* 2786) Rod & Staff Pubs., Inc.
Zondervan Staff. Adam & Eve, God's First People, 1 vol. Jones, Dennis, illus. 2010. (I Can Read! / Dennis Jones Ser.). (ENG.). 32p. (J). (gr. -1-2). pap. 3.99 *(978-0-310-71883-3(X))* Zonderkidz.
Zondervan Staff & Poth, Karen. Junior Comes Clean, 1 vol. 2013. (I Can Read! / Big Idea Books / VeggieTales Ser.). (ENG.). 32p. (J). pap. 3.99 *(978-0-310-73208-2(5))* Zonderkidz.
—LarryBoy & the Mudslingers, 1 vol. 2013. (I Can Read! / Big Idea Books / VeggieTales Ser.). (ENG.). 32p. (J). pap. 3.99 *(978-0-310-73214-3(X))* Zonderkidz.

GODDARD, ROBERT HUTCHINGS, 1882-1945

Patchett, Kaye. Robert Goddard: Rocket Pioneer. 2003. (Giants of Science Ser.). (ENG., Illus.). 64p. (J). (gr. 3-7). lib. bdg. 28.35 *(978-1-56711-888-9(7),* Blackbirch Pr., Inc.) Cengage Gale.
Spilsbury, Louise. Robert Goddard & the Rocket, 01 vols., 1. 2016. (Inventions That Changed the World Ser.). (ENG.). 32p. (J). pap. 10.00 *(978-1-5081-4639-1(X),* PowerKids Pr.) Rosen Publishing Group, Inc., The.

GODS—FICTION

Adams, Michelle Medlock. Why I Thank You, God. Koeller, Carol, illus. 2006. 20p. (J). (gr. -1). bds. 5.49 *(978-0-7586-0911-3(6))* Concordia Publishing Hse.
Afterglow. 2014. (ENG., Illus.). 336p. (YA). (gr. 9). pap. 11.99 *(978-1-4424-5038-7(X),* Simon & Schuster Bks. For Young Readers) Simon & Schuster Bks. For Young Readers.
Alberti, Robert. Mitlanyal: The Gods of Stability, Vol. 1. 10th ed. 2004. (Illus.). 152p. (YA). pap. 19.95 *(978-0-9725880-2-7(7),* mit1) Zottola Publishing, Inc.
Alexander, Ron. And God Created Squirrels. 2007. 28p. per. 19.95 *(978-1-4327-1512-0(7))* Outskirts Pr., Inc.
Anderson, Debra. The Seed Sower, Walter's Special Garden. Lucas, Diane, illus. 2012. 24p. pap. 11.95 *(978-1-61244-097-2(5))* Halo Publishing International.
Armstrong, K. L. & Marr, M. A. Loki's Wolves. (Blackwell Pages Ser.: 1). (ENG.). (J). (gr. 3-7). 2014. 374p. pap. 8.99 *(978-0-316-20497-2(8));* 2013. (Illus.). 358p. 17.00 *(978-0-316-20496-5(X))* Little, Brown Bks. for Young Readers.
—Odin's Ravens. 2014. (Blackwell Pages Ser.: 2). (ENG., Illus.). 342p. (J). (gr. 3-7). 17.00 *(978-0-316-20498-9(6))* Little, Brown Bks. for Young Readers.
Beauvais, Gailanna. How Are We Blessed? Beauvais, Gailanna, illus. 2012. (Illus.). 40p. pap. 9.95 *(978-0-9884679-0-3(9))* Visual Velocity.
Berning, Terri J. Grace Alone Is Enough, 1 vol. Arling, Jackie L., illus. 2010. 34p. 24.95 *(978-1-4512-9045-5(4))* PublishAmerica, Inc.
Blake, Kendare. Antigoddess. (Goddess War Ser.: 1). (ENG.). (YA). (gr. 7-12). 2014. 352p. pap. 9.99 *(978-0-7653-3446-6(1),* 9780765334466) 2013. 336p. 17.99 *(978-0-7653-3443-5(7),* 9780765334435) Doherty, Tom Assocs., LLC. (Tor Teen).
—Mortal Gods. 2014. (Goddess War Ser.: 2). (ENG.). 352p. (YA). (gr. 7-12). 17.99 *(978-0-7653-3444-2(5),* 9780765334442, Tor Teen) Doherty, Tom Assocs., LLC.
Block, Francesca Lia. Psyche in a Dress. 2008. (ENG.). 128p. (YA). (gr. 9). pap. 8.99 *(978-0-06-076376-3(0),* HarperTeen) HarperCollins Pubs.
Brown, Abbie Farwell. In the Days of Giants. Smith, E. Boyd, illus. 2008. 204p. per. 9.95 *(978-1-59915-044-4(1))* Yesterday's Classics.
Burciaga, David. Say Cheese, God! Wisner, Luke, illus. l.t. ed. 2006. 24p. (J). (gr. -1-3). per. 11.99 *(978-1-59879-235-5(0))* Lifevest Publishing, Inc.
Cabot, Meg. Underworld. 2012. (Abandon Ser.). (ENG.). 336p. (J). (gr. 9). 17.99 *(978-0-545-28411-0(2))* Scholastic, Inc.
Carroll, Mona. Jacob's Storm, 1 vol. 2010. 22p. 24.95 *(978-1-4489-8069-7(0))* PublishAmerica, Inc.
Carter, Aimée. The Goddess Inheritance. 2013. (Goddess Test Ser.: 3). lib. bdg. 20.85 *(978-0-606-26948-3(7),* Turtleback) Turtleback Bks.
Chen, Wei Dong. The Expulsion of Sun Wu Kong. Peng, Chao, illus. 2013. (Monkey King Ser.: 7). 176p. (YA). (gr. 6-12). lib. bdg. 29.27 *(978-89-94208-75-6(5))* Lerner Publishing Group.
—Fight to the Death. Peng, Chao, illus. 2013. (Monkey King Ser.: 11). 176p. (YA). (gr. 6-12). lib. bdg. 29.27 *(978-89-94208-79-4(8))* Lerner Publishing Group.
—The Lost Children. Peng, Chao, illus. 2013. (Monkey King Ser.: 12). 176p. (YA). (gr. 6-12). lib. bdg. 29.27 *(978-89-94208-80-0(1))* Lerner Publishing Group.
—The Realm of the Infant King. Peng, Chao, illus. 2013. (Monkey King Ser.: 10). 176p. (YA). (gr. 6-12). lib. bdg. 29.27 *(978-89-94208-78-7(X))* Lerner Publishing Group.
—The Stolen Kingdom. Peng, Chao, illus. 2013. (Monkey King Ser.: 9). 176p. (YA). (gr. 6-12). lib. bdg. 29.27 *(978-89-94208-77-0(1))* Lerner Publishing Group.
—Treasures of the Mountain Kings. Peng, Chao, illus. 2013. (Monkey King Ser.: 8). 176p. (YA). (gr. 6-12). lib. bdg. 29.27 *(978-89-94208-76-3(3))* Lerner Publishing Group.
Church, Alfred J. Three Greek Children. 2008. (Illus.). 160p. pap. 9.95 *(978-1-59915-081-9(6))* Yesterday's Classics.
Coats, Lucy. Centaur School. 2016. (Beasts of Olympus Ser.: 5). lib. bdg. 17.20 *(978-0-606-38410-0(3))* Turtleback Bks.
—Centaur School #5. Bean, Brett, illus. 2016. (Beasts of Olympus Ser.: 5). (ENG.). 144p. (J). (gr. 2-4). 6.99 *(978-1-101-99505-1(X),* Grosset & Dunlap) Penguin Young Readers Group.
—Dragon Healer. Bean, Brett, illus. 2015. 136p. (J). ***(978-1-4806-8442-3(2),*** Grosset & Dunlap) Penguin Publishing Group.
—Dragon Healer. 2015. (Beasts of Olympus Ser.: 4). lib. bdg. 16.00 *(978-0-606-38409-4(X))* Turtleback Bks.
—Dragon Healer #4. Bean, Brett, illus. 2015. (Beasts of Olympus Ser.: 4). (ENG.). 144p. (J). (gr. 2-4). 5.99 *(978-0-448-46196-0(X),* Grosset & Dunlap) Penguin Young Readers Group.
—Hound of Hades #2. Bean, Brett, illus. 2015. (Beasts of Olympus Ser.: 2). (ENG.). 144p. (J). (gr. 2-4). 6.99 *(978-0-448-46194-6(3),* Grosset & Dunlap) Penguin Young Readers Group.
—Steeds of the Gods #3. Bean, Brett, illus. 2015. (Beasts of Olympus Ser.: 3). (ENG.). 144p. (J). (gr. 2-4). 6.99 *(978-0-448-46195-3(1),* Grosset & Dunlap) Penguin Young Readers Group.
Colloredo, Sabino. Apollo. Ferrari, Antongionata, illus. 2009. (Hotel Olympus Ser.). 128p. (J). (gr. 3-6). 31.95 *(978-1-60754-710-5(4))* Windmill Bks.
—Zeus. Ferrari, Antongionata, illus. 2009. (Hotel Olympus Ser.). 128p. (J). (gr. 3-6). 31.95 *(978-1-60754-707-5(4))* Windmill Bks.
Coville, Bruce. Thor's Wedding Day: By Thialfi, the Goat Boy. Cogswell, Matthew, illus. 2008. (ENG.). 144p. (J). (gr. 2-5). pap. 6.99 *(978-0-15-205872-2(9))* Houghton Mifflin Harcourt Publishing Co.
Cox, Tracey M. Angels Do That. Movshina, Marina, illus. 2012. 16p. pap. 9.95 *(978-1-61633-299-0(9))* Guardian Angel Publishing, Inc.
De Michel. What's an Egg Got to Do with It? A Dozen Adventures with God for Grades 4-6. 2007. 108p. pap. 19.95 *(978-1-4241-8994-6(2))* America Star Bks.
Denger, Monique. Who Colored the Rainbow, Mimi? 2010. 40p. pap. 16.99 *(978-1-4490-6166-1(4))* AuthorHouse.
Denis, Toni. How Do the Children Pray? Olds, Irene, illus. 2010. 16p. 10.99 *(978-1-4490-5164-8(2))* AuthorHouse.
Despain, Bree. The Eternity Key. 2015. (ENG.). 368p. (YA). (gr. 7). 18.99 *(978-1-60684-467-0(9));* (Into the Dark Ser.: 2). 18.99 *(978-1-5124-0179-0(X))* Lerner Publishing Group. (Carolrhoda Lab™).
DeSpain, Bree. The Immortal Throne. 2016. (Into the Dark Ser.: 3). (ENG.). 344p. (YA). (gr. 7-12). 18.99 *(978-1-5124-0583-5(3),* Carolrhoda Bks.) Lerner Publishing Group.
Despain, Bree. The Immortal Throne. 2016. (Into the Dark Ser.: 3). (ENG.). 344p. (YA). (gr. 7-12). 38.65 *(978-1-5124-0897-3(2),* Carolrhoda Lab™) Lerner Publishing Group.
—The Shadow Prince. 2015. (Into the Dark Ser.: Bk. 1). (ENG.). 496p. (gr. 7). pap. 9.99 *(978-1-60684-567-7(5),* Carolrhoda Lab™) Lerner Publishing Group.
Dong Chen, Wei. Expulsion of Sun Wu. Peng, Chao, illus. 2013. (Monkey King Ser.: 7). (ENG.). 176p. (YA). (gr. 6-12). pap. 9.99 *(978-89-94208-51-0(8))* Lerner Publishing Group.
—Fight to the Death. Peng, Chao, illus. 2013. (Monkey King Ser.: 11). (ENG.). 176p. (YA). (gr. 6-12). pap. 9.99 *(978-89-94208-56-5(9))* Lerner Publishing Group.
—Lost Children. Peng, Chao, illus. 2013. (Monkey King Ser.: 12). (ENG.). 176p. (YA). (gr. 6-12). pap. 9.99 *(978-89-94208-57-2(7))* Lerner Publishing Group.
—Realm of Infant King. Peng, Chao, illus. 2013. (Monkey King Ser.: 10). (ENG.). 176p. (YA). (gr. 6-12). pap. 9.99 *(978-89-94208-54-1(2))* Lerner Publishing Group.
—Stolen Kingdom. Peng, Chao, illus. 2013. (Monkey King Ser.: 9). (ENG.). 176p. (YA). (gr. 6-12). pap. 9.99 *(978-89-94208-53-4(4))* Lerner Publishing Group.
—Treasures of the Mountain Kings. Peng, Chao, illus. 2013. (Monkey King Ser.: 8). (ENG.). 176p. (YA). (gr. 6-12). pap. 9.99 *(978-89-94208-52-7(6))* Lerner Publishing Group.
Donovan, Michelle O. Joshua, Helmut, & Bethlehem. 2011. 56p. pap. 8.95 *(978-1-4620-5867-9(1))* iUniverse, Inc.
Eastridge, Jim. Gregory & the Moon. 2008. 12p. pap. 24.95 *(978-1-4241-9008-9(8))* America Star Bks.
Emerson, Darcie. One Sock. 2012. 24p. pap. 24.95 *(978-1-4626-7763-4(0))* America Star Bks.
Ergun, Erol. The All-Merciful Master. 2009. (Beautiful Names of God Ser.). (ENG.). 128p. (J). (gr. 4-7). 14.95 *(978-1-59784-202-0(8))* Tughra Bks.
Ergün, Erol. The Supreme Ruler. 2011. (ENG., Illus.). 192p. pap. 9.95 *(978-1-59784-259-4(1))* Tughra Bks.
Erich, James. Dreams of Fire & Gods: Gods [Library Edition]. 2014. 200p. pap. 14.99 *(978-1-62798-380-8(5),* Harmony Ink Pr.) Dreamspinner Pr.
Ertekin, Betul. Thank You God: This World I Love. 2011. (ENG.). 48p. pap. 4.95 *(978-1-59784-235-8(4))* Tughra Bks.
Farfan, Flores & Antonio, Jose. Axolotl: El Ajolote. Celestino, Cleofas Ramirez, illus. 2003. (SPA.). 40p. (J). *(978-968-411-569-9(5))* Ediciones Era.
Friesner, Esther M. & Friesner, Esther. Temping Fate. 2007. (ENG.). 288p. (YA). (gr. 7-18). 8.99 *(978-0-14-240848-3(4),* Speak) Penguin Young Readers Group.
Fujishima, Kosuke. Oh My Goddess! Fujishima, Kosuke, illus. (Oh My Goddess! Ser.). (ENG., Illus.). Vol. 25. 2007. 176p. pap. 10.95 *(978-1-59307-644-3(4))* Vol. 34. 2010. 144p. pap. 10.99 *(978-1-59582-448-6(0))* Dark Horse Comics.
—Oh My Goddess! Volume 36. 2010. (ENG., Illus.). 152p. pap. 10.99 *(978-1-59582-581-0(9))* Dark Horse Comics.
Gaiman, NEil. Odd & the Frost Giants. Riddell, Chris, illus. 2016. 128p. (J). (gr. 3-7). 19.99 *(978-0-06-256795-6(0))* HarperCollins Pubs.
—Odd & the Frost Giants. Helquist, Brett, illus. 128p. (J). 2009. (ENG.). (gr. 3-18). 14.99 *(978-0-06-167173-9(8))* 2008. lib. bdg. 15.89 *(978-0-06-167175-3(4))* HarperCollins Pubs.
Gorzelanczyk, Melissa. Arrows. 2016. (ENG.). 240p. (YA). (gr. 9). 17.99 *(978-0-553-51044-7(4),* Delacorte Pr.) Random Hse. Children's Bks.
Gratton, Tessa. The Apple Throne. 2015. (YA). *(978-0-307-97756-4(0))* Random Hse., Inc.
Greene, Joshua M. Kaliya, Serpent King. Wire, Patrick, illus. rev. ed. 2012. (ENG.). 24p. (gr. -1). 14.99 *(978-1-60887-148-3(7))* Mandala Publishing.
Hahn, Rebecca. The Shadow Behind the Stars. 2016. (ENG.). 256p. (YA). (gr. 7). pap. 10.99 *(978-1-4814-3572-7(8))* Simon & Schuster Children's Publishing.
Hall, Hannah C. God Bless My Boo Boo, 1 vol. Whitlow, Steve, illus. 2015. (God Bless Book Ser.). (ENG.). 20p. (J). bds. 9.99 *(978-0-7180-3051-3(6))* Nelson, Thomas Inc.
Harper, Donna. Hello God: Are You Here? 2013. 16p. pap. 15.99 *(978-1-4817-1253-8(5))* AuthorHouse.
Hennesy, Carolyn. Pandora Gets Angry. (Mythic Misadventures Ser.). (ENG.). (YA). (gr. 3-7). 2011. 320p. 14.99 *(978-1-59990-440-5(3),* 9781599904405) Vol. 5. 2012. 336p. pap. 7.99 *(978-1-59990-734-5(8),* 9781599907345) Bloomsbury Publishing USA. (Bloomsbury USA Childrens).
—Pandora Gets Frightened. 2014. (Mythic Misadventures Ser.). (ENG.). 320p. (YA). (gr. 3-6). pap. 7.99 *(978-1-61963-251-6(9),* 9781619632516, Bloomsbury USA Childrens) Bloomsbury Publishing USA.
—Pandora Gets Greedy. (Mythic Misadventures Ser.). (ENG., (YA). (gr. 3-6). 2013. Illus.). 320p. pap. 7.99 *(978-1-61963-010-9(9),* 9781619630109) 2012. 304p. 15.99 *(978-1-59990-441-2(1),* 9781599904412) Bloomsbury Publishing USA. (Bloomsbury USA Childrens).
—Pandora Gets Heart, No. 4. 2010. (Mythic Misadventures Ser.). (ENG.). 272p. (YA). (gr. 3-7). 14.99 *(978-1-59990-439-9(X),* 9781599904399, Bloomsbury USA Childrens) Bloomsbury Publishing USA.
—Pandora Gets Lazy. (Mythic Misadventures Ser.). (ENG.). (YA). (gr. 3-6). 2010. 304p. pap. 7.99 *(978-1-59990-481-8(0),* 9781599904818) 2009. 288p. 14.99 *(978-1-59990-198-5(6),* 9781599901985) Bloomsbury Publishing USA. (Bloomsbury USA Childrens).
—Pandora Gets Vain, Vol. 2. 2009. (Mythic Misadventures Ser.). (ENG.). 288p. (YA). (gr. 3-6). pap. 7.99 *(978-1-59990-329-3(6),* 9781599903293, Bloomsbury USA Childrens) Bloomsbury Publishing USA.
Hocutt, Rose (Webber). The Spoon Family. 2012. 44p. pap. 24.95 *(978-1-4560-0548-1(0))* America Star Bks.
Holub, Joan. Please Share, Aphrodite! Patricelli, Leslie, illus. 2015. (Mini Myths Ser.). (ENG.). 24p. (J). (gr. -1 — 1). bds. 6.95 *(978-1-4197-1678-2(6))* Abrams, Inc.
Holub, Joan & Suzanne Williams. Echo the Copycat. 2016. (Goddess Girls Ser.: 19). lib. bdg. 18.40 *(978-0-606-38269-4(0))* Turtleback Bks.
Holub, Joan & Williams, Suzanne. Aphrodite the Beauty. 2010. (Goddess Girls Ser.: 3). (ENG.). 176p. (J). (gr. 3-7). pap. 7.99 *(978-1-4169-8273-9(6),* Aladdin) Simon & Schuster Children's Publishing.
—Apollo & the Battle of the Birds. Phillips, Craig, illus. 2014. (Heroes in Training Ser.: 6). (ENG.). 128p. (J). (gr. 1-4). 16.99 *(978-1-4424-8846-5(8),* Simon & Schuster/Paula Wiseman Bks.) Simon & Schuster/Paula Wiseman Bks.
—Artemis the Brave. 2010. (Goddess Girls Ser.: 4). (ENG.). 240p. (J). (gr. 3-7). pap. 7.99 *(978-1-4169-8274-6(4),* Aladdin) Simon & Schuster Children's Publishing.
—Artemis the Loyal. 2013. (Goddess Girls Ser.: 7). (ENG., Illus.). 288p. (J). (gr. 3-7). 16.99 *(978-1-4424-8594-5(9),* Aladdin) Simon & Schuster Children's Publishing.
—Athena the Proud. 2014. (Goddess Girls Ser.: 13). (ENG., Illus.). 240p. (J). (gr. 3-7). 17.99 *(978-1-4424-8821-2(2),* Aladdin) Simon & Schuster Children's Publishing.
—Athena the Wise. (Goddess Girls Ser.: 5). (ENG., 256p. (J). (gr. 3-7). 2013. Illus.). 17.99 *(978-1-4424-7477-2(7))* 2011. pap. 7.99 *(978-1-4424-2097-7(9))* Simon & Schuster Children's Publishing. (Aladdin).
—Hestia the Invisible. 2015. (Goddess Girls Ser.: 18). lib. bdg. 18.40 *(978-0-606-37854-3(5))* Turtleback Bks.
—Medusa the Mean. (Goddess Girls Ser.: 8). (ENG., 256p. (J). (gr. 3-7). 2013. Illus.). 16.99 *(978-1-4424-8595-2(7))* 2012. pap. 7.99 *(978-1-4424-3379-3(5))* Simon & Schuster Children's Publishing. (Aladdin).
—Medusa the Mean. 2012. (Goddess Girls Ser.: 8). lib. bdg. 18.40 *(978-0-606-26348-1(9),* Turtleback) Turtleback Bks.
—Pheme the Gossip. 2013. (Goddess Girls Ser.: 10). (ENG.). 272p. (J). (gr. 3-7). pap. 7.99 *(978-1-4424-4937-4(3),* Aladdin) Simon & Schuster Children's Publishing.
—Pheme the Gossip. 2013. (Goddess Girls Ser.: 10). (ENG.). 272p. (J). (gr. 3-7). 16.99 *(978-1-4424-6138-3(1),* Simon & Schuster/Paula Wiseman Bks.) Simon & Schuster/Paula Wiseman Bks.
Hoover, P. J. Solstice. 2013. (ENG.). 384p. (YA). (gr. 8). 17.99 *(978-0-7653-3469-5(0),* Tor Teen) Doherty, Tom Assocs., LLC.
Houck, Colleen. Reawakened. 2015. (Reawakened Ser.: Bk. 1). (ENG.). 400p. (YA). (gr. 9-12). 17.99 *(978-0-385-37656-3(1),* Delacorte Pr.) Random Hse. Children's Bks.
—Recreated. (Reawakened Ser.: 2). (ENG.). 416p. (YA). (gr. 9). 2017. pap. 10.99 ***(978-0-385-37663-1(4),*** Ember) 2016. 17.99 *(978-0-385-37660-0(X),* Delacorte Pr.) Random Hse. Children's Bks.
—Reunited. 2017. (ENG.). 464p. (YA). (gr. 9). 17.99 ***(978-0-399-55568-8(4),*** Delacorte Pr.) Random Hse. Children's Bks.
Howard, Amalie. Alpha Goddess. 2014. (ENG.). 384p. (J). (gr. 6-12). 16.95 *(978-1-62636-208-6(4),* Sky Pony Pr.) Skyhorse Publishing Co., Inc.
Hu, Vicky. The Muses: Greek Mythology (Mitologia Griega) 2009. 44p. pap. 21.99 *(978-1-4415-3415-6(6))* Xlibris Corp.
Hyman, Trina Schart & Tchana, Katrin Hyman. Changing Woman & Her Sisters: Stories of Goddesses from Around the World. 2006. (ENG., Illus.). 80p. (J). (gr. 4-18). 18.95 *(978-0-8234-1999-9(1))* Holiday Hse., Inc.
Ireland, Justina. Promise of Shadows. 2014. (ENG., Illus.). 384p. (YA). (gr. 9). 17.99 *(978-1-4424-4464-5(9),* Simon & Schuster Bks. For Young Readers) Simon & Schuster Bks. For Young Readers.
James, Elizabeth. The Kids of Castle Grace. 2011. 48p. pap. 21.99 *(978-1-4535-8055-4(7));* pap. 21.99 *(978-1-4568-6212-1(X))* Xlibris Corp.
Jones, Allan Frewin. Blood Stone, Vol. 6. 6th ed. 2003. (ENG.). 176p. (J). mass mkt. *(978-0-330-37476-7(1),* Pan) Pan Macmillan.
Kahler, A. R. Echoes of Memory. 2017. (Ravenborn Ser.: 2). (ENG., Illus.). 336p. (YA). (gr. 9). 17.99 *(978-1-4814-3260-3(5),* Simon Pulse) Simon Pulse.
—Shades of Darkness. 2016. (Ravenborn Ser.: 1). (ENG., Illus.). 304p. (YA). (gr. 9). 17.99 *(978-1-4814-3257-3(5),* Simon Pulse) Simon Pulse.
Kato, Etsuo. The King Who Saved the Dove. Yasui, Koji, illus. 2014. (J). 8.95 *(978-1-935523-68-0(6))* World Tribune Pr.
King, Juaness. The Prodigal's Quest. 2012. 54p. 19.95 *(978-1-4626-9042-8(4))* America Star Bks.
Knight, Karsten. Afterglow. 2013. (ENG., Illus.). 336p. (YA). (gr. 9). 17.99 *(978-1-4424-5037-0(1),* Simon & Schuster Bks. For Young Readers) Simon & Schuster Bks. For Young Readers.
—Embers & Echoes. (ENG., (YA). (gr. 9). 2013. Illus.). 496p. pap. 9.99 *(978-1-4424-5035-6(5))* 2012. 480p. 16.99

(978-1-4424-5030-1(4)) Simon & Schuster Bks. For Young Readers. (Simon & Schuster Bks. For Young Readers).
—Wildefire. 2011. (ENG.). 400p. (YA). (gr. 9-18). 16.99 (978-1-4424-2117-2(7), Simon & Schuster Bks. For Young Readers) Simon & Schuster Bks. For Young Readers.
LaFevers, Robin. Dark Triumph. (His Fair Assassin Ser.: 2). (ENG.). 400p. (YA). (gr. 9). 2014. pap. 9.99 (978-0-544-22720-0(4), HMH Books For Young Readers) 2013. 17.99 (978-0-547-62838-7(2)) Houghton Mifflin Harcourt Publishing Co.
—Dark Triumph, 10 vols. 2013. (His Fair Assassin Ser.: 2). (YA). (978-1-4640-2397-2(2)) Recorded Bks., Inc.
—Grave Mercy. (His Fair Assassin Ser.: 1). (ENG., Illus.). (YA). (gr. 9). 2013. 576p. pap. 9.99 (978-0-544-02249-2(1)) 2012. 560p. 17.99 (978-0-547-62834-9(X)) Houghton Mifflin Harcourt Publishing Co.
—Grave Mercy, 10 vols. 2012. (His Fair Assassin Trilogy: Bk. 1). (YA). 132.75 (978-1-4640-2388-0(3)); 287.75 (978-1-4640-2386-6(7)); 130.75 (978-1-4640-2387-3(5)); 130.75 (978-1-4640-2390-3(5)) Recorded Bks., Inc.
—Mortal Heart. 2014. (His Fair Assassin Ser.: 3). (ENG.). 464p. (YA). (gr. 9). 17.99 (978-0-547-62840-0(4), HMH Books For Young Readers) Houghton Mifflin Harcourt Publishing Co.
Lake, A. J. The Circle of Stone. 2008. (Darkest Age Ser.). (ENG.). 304p. (YA). (gr. 4-7). 16.95 (978-1-59990-079-7(3), 9781599900797, Bloomsbury USA Childrens) Bloomsbury Publishing USA.
Lerangis, Peter. Seven Wonders Book 4: the Curse of the King. Norstrand, Torstein, illus. 2016. (Seven Wonders Ser.: 4). 320p. (J). (gr. 3-7). pap. 6.99 (978-0-06-207050-0(9)) HarperCollins Pubs.
Levine, Gail Carson. Ever. 2011. (ENG.). 288p. (J). (gr. 3-7). pap. 6.99 (978-0-06-122964-0(4)) HarperCollins Pubs.
Limke, Jeff. Isis y Osiris: Hasta el Fin del Mundo: Un Mito Egipcio. Witt, David, illus. 2007. (Mitos y leyendas en viñetas (Graphic Myths & Legends) Ser.). (SPA & ENG.). 48p. (J). (gr. 4-7). per. 8.95 (978-0-8225-7971-7(5), Ediciones Lerner) Lerner Publishing Group.
—Thor & Loki: In the Land of Giants - A Norse Myth. Randall, Ron, illus. 2007. (Graphic Myths & Legends Ser.). (ENG.). 48p. (gr. 4-8). per. 8.95 (978-0-8225-6481-2(5)) Lerner Publishing Group.
—Thor y Loki: en la Tierra de los Gigantes: Un Mito Escandinavo. Randall, Ron, illus. 2007. (Mitos y leyendas en viñetas (Graphic Myths & Legends) Ser.). (SPA.). 48p. (J). (gr. 4-7). per. 8.95 (978-0-8225-7969-4(3), Ediciones Lerner) Lerner Publishing Group.
Madkins, Doris J. God Made the Sun to Shine. 2004. (J). pap. 8.00 (978-0-8059-6625-1(0)) Dorrance Publishing Co., Inc.
Magee, Kanika. Where Is God at Midnight?? Thomas, Sonya, illus. 2003. (J). 10.00 net. (978-0-9748834-1-0(7)) Ebenezer A.M.E. Church.
Marmell, Ari. Covenant's End: A Widdershins Adventure. 2015. (ENG.). 271p. (YA). (gr. 7). 17.99 (978-1-61614-986-4(8), Pyr Bks.) Prometheus Bks., Pubs.
—Lost Covenant: A Widdershins Adventure. 2013. (ENG.). 279p. (YA). (gr. 7). 17.99 (978-1-61614-811-9(X), Pyr Bks.) Prometheus Bks., Pubs.
Massey, K. J. Everyday Things with Morgan. Bowser, Katya, illus. 2013. 24p. 19.99 (978-0-9910489-4-6(6)) NyreePr. Literary Group.
Maurer, Gretchen. Call Me Isis: Egyptian Goddess of Magic. 2014. (Treasury of Glorious Goddesses Ser.). (ENG.). 160p. (J). (gr. 3-8). 12.99 (978-1-937463-95-3(8)) Goosebottom Bks. LLC.
McMullan, Kate. Get Lost, Odysseus!, 1 vol. 2014. (Myth-O-Mania Ser.). (ENG., Illus.). 240p. (gr. 4-8). 25.32 (978-1-4342-6016-1(X)) Stone Arch Bks.
—Have a Hot Time, Hades!, 1 vol. Zilber, Denis, illus. 2011. (Myth-O-Mania Ser.: Bk. 1). (ENG.). 176p. (gr. 4-8). pap. 5.95 (978-1-4342-3437-7(1)); lib. bdg. 25.32 (978-1-4342-2136-0(9)) Stone Arch Bks. (Myth-O-Mania).
—Keep a Lid on It, Pandora!, 1 vol. Zilber, Denis, illus. (Myth-O-Mania Ser.: Bk. 6). (ENG.). 192p. (gr. 4-8). 2011. pap. 5.95 (978-1-4342-3439-1(8)) 2010. lib. bdg. 25.32 (978-1-4342-3195-6(X)) Stone Arch Bks. (Myth-O-Mania).
—Nice Shot, Cupid!, 1 vol. Zilber, Denis, illus. 2011. (Myth-O-Mania Ser.: Bk. 4). (ENG.). 208p. (gr. 4-8). pap. 5.95 (978-1-4342-3435-3(5)); lib. bdg. 25.32 (978-1-4342-1985-5(2)) Stone Arch Bks. (Myth-O-Mania).
—Phone Home, Persephone!, 1 vol. Zilber, Denis, illus. 2011. (Myth-O-Mania Ser.: Bk. 2). (ENG.). 176p. (gr. 4-8). pap. 5.95 (978-1-4342-3436-0(3)); lib. bdg. 25.32 (978-1-4342-2135-3(0)) Stone Arch Bks. (Myth-O-Mania).
—Say Cheese, Medusa!, 1 vol. Zilber, Denis, illus. 2011. (Myth-O-Mania Ser.: Bk. 3). (ENG.). 208p. (gr. 4-8). pap. 5.95 (978-1-4342-3442-1(8), Myth-O-Mania) Stone Arch Bks.
Meade, Saci & Nonino, Lila. ABCs for Little Yogis. Meade, Sarah, illus. 2014. (ENG.). 26p. (J). (gr. -1). 16.95 (978-1-60887-340-1(4)) Mandala Publishing.
Mebus, Scott. Gods of Manhattan, 1 vol. 2009. (ENG.). 368p. (J). (gr. 3-7). 8.99 (978-0-14-241307-4(0), Puffin Books) Penguin Young Readers Group.
—The Sorcerer's Secret, Bk. 3. 2011. (ENG.). 384p. (J). (gr. 5-18). 8.99 (978-0-14-241878-9(1), Puffin Books) Penguin Young Readers Group.
—Spirits in the Park. 2009. (Gods of Manhattan Ser.: No. 2). (J). (978-0-525-47963-5(5), Dutton Juvenile) Penguin Publishing Group.
—Spirits in the Park, Vol. 2. 2010. (ENG.). 400p. (J). (gr. 3-7). 8.99 (978-0-14-241645-7(2), Puffin Books) Penguin Young Readers Group.
Michaels, Fern, et al. Silver Bells. l.t. ed. 2008. (YA). 34.95 (978-1-59722-823-7(0)) Thorndike Pr.
Mills, Samuel. The Fire Bringer. 2009. 128p. (J). pap. 15.00 (978-0-88010-700-6(6)) SteinerBooks, Inc.
Morley, Farah, illus. The Spider & the Doves: The Story of the Hijra. 2012. (ENG.). 30p. (J). (gr. -1-2). 8.95 (978-0-86037-449-7(1)) Kube Publishing Ltd. GBR. Dist: Consortium Bk. Sales & Distribution.
Morris, Paula. The Eternal City. 2015. (ENG.). 304p. (J). (gr. 7). 17.99 (978-0-545-25133-4(8)) Scholastic, Inc.
Morris, Paula. The Eternal City. 2015. 291p. (YA). **(978-0-545-91986-9(X))** Scholastic, Inc.
Moyston, Connaelia. God's Faith Is Real. 2013. 44p. pap. 21.99 (978-1-4817-0155-6(X)) AuthorHouse.
Muten, Burleigh. Grandfather Mountain: Stories of Gods & Heroes from Many Cultures. Bailey, Sian, illus. 2004. (ENG.). 80p. (J). (gr. 3-6). 19.99 (978-1-84148-789-2(9)) Barefoot Bks., Inc.
Newton, Lesley. Ralphie's Christmas Story, 1 vol. 2010. 16p. pap. 24.95 (978-1-4489-2674-9(2)) PublishAmerica, Inc.
O'Connor, George. Athena Bk. 2: Grey-Eyed Goddess. O'Connor, George, illus. 2010. (Olympians Ser.: 2). (ENG., Illus.). 80p. (J). (gr. 4-9). 17.99 (978-1-59643-649-7(2), 9781596436497); pap. 10.99 (978-1-59643-432-5(5), 9781596434325) Roaring Brook Pr. (First Second Bks.).
—Zeus: King of the Gods. O'Connor, George, illus. 2010. (Olympians Ser.: 1). (ENG., Illus.). 80p. (J). (gr. 4-9). 18.99 (978-1-59643-625-1(5), 9781596436251); pap. 10.99 (978-1-59643-431-8(7), 9781596434318) Roaring Brook Pr. (First Second Bks.).
Padgett, Anthony. Divinityland. 2010. (Illus.). 20p. 21.50 (978-0-9561587-1-0(4)) Auditors of God, The GBR. Dist: Lulu Pr., Inc.
Pandey, Pooja. Little Monk's Ganesha. 2015. (ENG.). 100p. pap. 14.95 (978-81-8328-062-4(5)) SCB Distributors.
—Little Monk's Hanuman. 2015. (ENG., Illus.). 63p. 14.95 (978-81-8328-063-1(3)) SCB Distributors.
—Little Monk's Krishna. 2015. (ENG.). 100p. pap. 14.95 (978-81-8328-061-7(7)) SCB Distributors.
Paver, Michelle. The Burning Shadow. 2015. (Gods & Warriors Ser.: 2). (ENG.). 320p. (J). (gr. 5). 7.99 (978-0-14-242285-4(1), Puffin Books) Penguin Young Readers Group.
—Gods & Warriors. 2013. (Gods & Warriors Ser.: 1). (ENG.). 336p. (J). (gr. 5). pap. 8.99 (978-0-14-242284-7(3), Puffin Books) Penguin Young Readers Group.
—Warrior Bronze. 2017. (Gods & Warriors Ser.). (ENG.). 272p. (J). (gr. 3-7). 16.99 (978-0-8037-3884-3(6), Dial Bks) Penguin Young Readers Group.
Pelton, Lisa. Logos & Obedience: Listening to His Father's Voice. 2009. 32p. pap. 13.99 (978-1-4389-5177-5(9)) AuthorHouse.
Perritano, John. The Egyptian Prophecy, 1 vol. Laughead, Mike, illus. 2014. (Kid Squad Saves the World Ser.). (ENG.). 112p. (J). (gr. 8-12). 27.07 (978-1-62402-039-1(9)) Magic Wagon.
Pertzborn, Cindy. How Do We Get to Heaven? 2012. 36p. pap. 16.95 (978-1-4497-4585-1(7), WestBow Pr.) Author Solutions, Inc.
Petty, J. T. & Pope, Paul. The Fall of the House of West. Rubin, David, illus. 2015. 157p. (J). **(978-1-5182-0095-3(8)**, First Second Bks.) Roaring Brook Pr.
Quinn, Thalamus. Our Father God. 2012. 20p. pap. 14.95 (978-1-4634-3505-9(3)) AuthorHouse.
Rangel, Graciela. Anthony's Journey to God's Ark. 2007. 84p. pap. 8.95 (978-1-59526-907-2(X), Llumina Christian Bks.) Aeon Publishing Inc.
RH Disney. Moana Big Golden Book (Disney Moana) RH Disney, illus. 2016. (Big Golden Book Ser.). (ENG., Illus.). 48p. (J). (gr. -1-2). 9.99 (978-0-7364-3602-1(2), Golden/Disney) Random Hse. Children's Bks.
—Moana Junior Novelization. RH Disney, illus. 2016. (Junior Novel Ser.). (ENG., Illus.). 144p. (J). (gr. 2-5). 6.99 (978-0-7364-3600-7(6), RH/Disney) Random Hse. Children's Bks.
—Moana: the Deluxe Junior Novelization (Disney Moana) RH Disney, illus. 2016. (Deluxe Junior Novel Ser.). (ENG., Illus.). 144p. (J). (gr. 2-5). 9.99 (978-0-7364-3574-1(3), RH/Disney) Random Hse. Children's Bks.
—Quest for the Heart. RH Disney, illus. 2016. (Step into Reading Ser.). (ENG., Illus.). 32p. (J). (gr. -1-1). lib. bdg. 12.99 (978-0-7364-8226-4(1), RH/Disney) Random Hse. Children's Bks.
Rhodes, Jennifer. The Adventures of Kirby. Balogh, Jared, illus. 2012. 46p. 24.95 (978-1-4626-9473-0(X)) America Star Bks.
Riordan, Rick. The Hammer of Thor. 2016. (Magnus Chase & the Gods of Asgard Ser.: Bk. 2). (ENG.). 480p. (J). (gr. 5-9). 19.99 (978-1-4231-6092-2(4)) Hyperion Bks. for Children.
—The Heroes of Olympus, Book Five the Blood of Olympus. 2016. (Heroes of Olympus Ser.). (ENG.). 544p. (J). (gr. 5-9). pap. 9.99 (978-1-4231-4678-0(6)) Hyperion Bks. for Children.
—The Hidden Oracle. l.t. ed. 2016. (Trials of Apollo Ser.: 1). (ENG.). 488p. (J). 25.99 (978-1-4104-8945-6(0)) Cengage Gale.
—The Hidden Oracle. 2016. (Trials of Apollo Ser.: Bk. 1). (ENG.). 384p. (J). (gr. 5-9). 19.99 (978-1-4847-3274-8(X)) Hyperion Bks. for Children.
—The Hidden Oracle. 2017. (Trials of Apollo Ser.: 1). (J). lib. bdg. 20.85 **(978-0-606-40605-5(0))** Turtleback Bks.
—The Lightning Thief. (Percy Jackson & the Olympians Ser.: Bk. 1). (ENG.). (J). (gr. 5-9). 2005. 384p. 17.99 (978-0-7868-5629-9(7))Bk. 1. 2006. 416p. reprint ed. per. 7.99 (978-0-7868-3865-3(5)) Disney Publishing Worldwide.
—The Lightning Thief. 2008. (J). 54.99 (978-0-7393-7113-8(4)) Findaway World, LLC.
—The Lightning Thief. 2006. (Percy Jackson & the Olympians Ser.: Bk. 1). 377p. (J). (gr. 5-12). 15.65 (978-0-7569-6603-4(5)) Perfection Learning Corp.
—The Lightning Thief. rev. l.t. ed. 2006. (Percy Jackson & the Olympians Ser.: 1). (ENG.). 483p. (gr. 5-18). 22.95 (978-0-7862-8225-8(8)) Thorndike Pr.
—The Lightning Thief. 2006. (Percy Jackson & the Olympians Ser.: 1). (J). lib. bdg. 18.40 (978-1-4177-3247-0(4), Turtleback) Turtleback Bks.
—The Lost Hero. 2011. (Heroes of Olympus Ser.: Bk. 1). (ENG.). 576p. pap. 9.99 (978-1-4231-5537-9(8)) Disney Pr.
—The Lost Hero. 2010. (Heroes of Olympus Ser.). (ENG.). 576p. (YA). (gr. 5-9). pap. 12.00 (978-1-4231-4265-2(9)) Hyperion Bks. for Children.
—The Lost Hero. (Heroes of Olympus Ser.). (ENG.). (J). (gr. 5-9). 2012. 592p. pap. 9.99 (978-1-4231-1346-1(2)) 2010. 576p. 19.99 (978-1-4231-1339-3(X)) Hyperion Pr.
—The Lost Hero. l.t. ed. 2010. (Heroes of Olympus Ser.: Bk. 1). (ENG.). 708p. 23.99 (978-1-4104-3359-6(5)) Thorndike Pr.
—The Lost Hero. 2012. (Heroes of Olympus Ser.: 1). (J). lib. bdg. 20.85 (978-0-606-23615-7(5), Turtleback) Turtleback Bks.
—Percy Jackson's Greek Gods. Rocco, John, illus. (ENG.). (J). (gr. 3-7). 2016. 416p. pap. 12.99 (978-1-4847-1237-5(4)) 2014. 336p. 24.99 (978-1-4231-8364-8(9)) Hyperion Bks. for Children.
—Percy Jackson's Greek Gods. 2016. (Percy Jackson & the Olympians Ser.). 336p. (YA). lib. bdg. 24.50 (978-0-606-37400-2(0)) Turtleback Bks.
Riordan, Rick. The Trials of Apollo Book Two the Dark Prophecy (Special Limited Edition) Rocco, John, illus. 2017. (Trials of Apollo Ser.). (ENG.). 432p. (J). (gr. 5-9). 100.00 **(978-1-4847-4695-0(3))** Hyperion Bks. for Children.
Robinson, Bonita. The Little Seed That Could. 2011. 24p. pap. 24.95 (978-1-4626-4234-2(9)) America Star Bks.
Sarrasin, Alex. The Guardians of Neoegypti: Book One. 2007. 300p. per. 18.95 (978-0-595-45710-6(X)) iUniverse, Inc.
Schlessinger, Laura. Where's God? 2006. pap. (978-0-06-051911-7(8)) HarperCollins Canada, Ltd.
Schulz, Lori. Papa's Plan for Buddy Bee. 2012. 40p. pap. 13.95 (978-1-4497-3652-1(1), WestBow Pr.) Author Solutions, Inc.
Scott, Kieran. Only Everything. 2014. (True Love Ser.: 1). (ENG., Illus.). 352p. (YA). (gr. 7). pap. 9.99 (978-1-4424-7716-2(4), Simon & Schuster Bks. For Young Readers) Simon & Schuster Bks. For Young Readers.
—Something True. 2015. (True Love Ser.: 3). (ENG., Illus.). 288p. (YA). (gr. 7). pap. 9.99 (978-1-4424-7723-0(7)) Simon & Schuster Children's Publishing.
Shaughnessy, Adam. The Entirely True Story of the Unbelievable FIB. 2015. (Unbelievable FIB Ser.: 1). (ENG.). 272p. (J). (gr. 3-7). 16.95 (978-1-61620-498-3(2)) Algonquin Bks. of Chapel Hill.
—Over the Underworld. 2016. (Unbelievable FIB Ser.: 2). (ENG.). 304p. (J). (gr. 3-7). 16.95 (978-1-61620-499-0(0)) Algonquin Bks. of Chapel Hill.
Shaw, Rebecca. Elisha's Great Mission. 2010. 32p. pap. 11.95 (978-1-935268-43-7(0)) Halo Publishing International.
Shon, Henry Boothill: The Return of Nidagall, 1 vol. 2010. 52p. pap. 16.95 (978-1-4512-8700-4(3)) America Star Bks.
Simon, Mary Manz. God Made the Sun. Walkley, Lizzie, illus. 2016. (J). (978-0-8249-1980-1(7), Ideal Pubns.) Worthy Publishing.
Smith, Barbara Maxine. God Loves You & You Love Yourself -To God You Are Special. 2013. 38p. pap. 12.99 (978-0-578-11939-7(0)) Smith, Barbara Maxine.
Smith, Cheryl Jean. The Offering. 2006. (ENG.). 140p. per. 11.95 (978-0-7414-3181-3(5)) Infinity Publishing.
Strangway, Melissa. Finding Hope. 2012. 82p. pap. 11.65 (978-1-61933-676-6(6)) FastPrncil, Inc.
Sutherland, Tui T. Shadow Falling. 2007. (Avatars Ser.: Bk.2). 356p. (YA). (gr. 7-12). lib. bdg. 17.89 (978-0-06-085147-7(3), Eos) HarperCollins Pubs.
Taylor, Tijuana. The Adventures of Buddy Blue Bug & the Critters of the Gospel. 2012. 34p. pap. 19.99 (978-1-61996-655-0(7)) Salem Author Services.
Temple, Teri & Temple, Emily. Cupid: God of Love. Young, Eric, illus. 2015. (Roman Mythology Ser.). (ENG.). 32p. (J). (gr. 2-5). 29.93 (978-1-63143-715-1(1), 208558) Child's World, Inc., The.
Terrell, Brandon. Greek Mythology's Twelve Labors of Hercules, 1 vol. 2013. (Can You Survive? Ser.). (ENG.). 164p. (J). (gr. 4-6). pap. 8.95 (978-0-9883662-9-9(0)) Leadership Institute for Urban Education.
Verma, Jatinder. Prince of Fire PB. 2016. (ENG., Illus.). 64p. (J). (gr. 3-5). 9.99 (978-1-78285-307-7(3)) Barefoot Bks., Inc.
—The Story of Divaali. Mistry, Nilesh, illus. 2007. (ENG.). 40p. (J). (gr. -1-3). pap. 7.99 (978-1-84686-131-4(4)) Barefoot Bks., Inc.
Weston Woods Staff, creator. A Story-A Story. 2011. 29.95 (978-0-439-73521-6(1)); 18.95 (978-0-439-72891-1(6)) Weston Woods Studios, Inc.
—A Story-Astory. 2011. 38.75 (978-0-439-72892-8(4)) Weston Woods Studios, Inc.
White, Kiersten. The Chaos of Stars. (ENG.). (YA). (gr. 8). 2014. 304p. pap. 9.99 (978-0-06-213587-2(2)) 2013. 288p. 17.99 (978-0-06-213592-6(9)) HarperCollins Pubs. (HarperTeen).
Whitman, Emily. Radiant Darkness. 2009. 288p. (YA). (gr. 9-18). lib. bdg. 17.89 (978-0-06-178035-6(9)); (ENG.). 16.99 (978-0-06-172449-7(1)) HarperCollins Pubs. (Greenwillow Bks.).
Wilson-Timmons, Karen & Dubois, Marie Thérèse. Agha the Eight-Mile Monster. rev. ed. 2012. (ENG., Illus.). 32p. (J). (gr. -1). 16.99 (978-1-60887-124-7(X)) Mandala Publishing.
Wirth, Beverly. Flowers from Seeds: A Garden Parable. 2012. 40p. pap. 16.99 (978-1-4624-0101-7(5), Inspiring Voices) Author Solutions, Inc.
Xiong, Kim, illus. Kitchen God. 2008. 32p. (J). 18.95 (978-1-60603-001-1(9)) Better Chinese LLC.
Zondervan Staff. Story Preschool Curriculum: 31 Lessons, 1 vol. 2011. (Story Ser.). (ENG.). (J). cd-rom 34.99 (978-0-310-71920-5(8)) Zonderkidz.

GODZILLA (FICTITIOUS CHARACTER)—FICTION

Cerasini, Marc. Godzilla Saves America: A Monster Showdown In 3-D! Morgan, Tom & Mounts, Paul, illus. 2006. 20p. (J). (gr. k-4). reprint ed. 12.00 (978-1-4223-5409-4(1)) DIANE Publishing Co.

GOETHE, JOHANN WOLFGANG VON, 1749-1832—FICTION

Cohn, Diana. Mr Goethes Garden. Mirocha, Paul, illus. 2003. (ENG.). 32p. (J). 17.95 (978-0-88010-521-7(6)) SteinerBooks, Inc.

GOGH, VINCENT VAN, 1853-1890

Bailey, Jessica. Van Gogh, Vol. 7. 2015. (Great Artists Collection). (Illus.). 64p. (J). (gr. 7). lib. bdg. 23.95 (978-1-4222-3263-7(8)) Mason Crest.
Bassil, Andrea & van Gogh, Vincent. Vincent Van Gogh. 2004. (Lives of the Artists Ser.). (Illus.). 48p. (gr. 5-12). lib. bdg. 31.00 (978-0-8368-5602-6(3), Gareth Stevens Secondary Library) Stevens, Gareth Publishing LLLP.
—Vincent van Gogh. 2004. (Lives of the Artists Ser.). (Illus.). 48p. (gr. 5-12). pap. 14.05 (978-0-8368-5607-1(4), Gareth Stevens Secondary Library) Stevens, Gareth Publishing LLLP.
Bodden, Valerie. Vincent Van Gogh. 2016. (Illus.). 80p. (J). (978-1-60818-721-8(7), Creative Education) Creative Co., The.
Bowen, Richard. Vincent Van Gogh: Modern Artist. (Illus.). 32p. (J). 2013. (People of Importance Ser.: 21). (gr. 4-18). 19.95 (978-1-4222-2858-6(4)) 2004. (Great Names Ser.). (gr. 3-18). lib. bdg. 19.95 (978-1-59084-141-9(7)) Mason Crest.
Cernak, Linda. Vincent Van Gogh. Morrow, J. T., illus. 2014. (World's Greatest Artists Ser.). (ENG.). 24p. (J). (gr. 2-5). 28.50 (978-1-62687-355-1(0), 207195) Child's World, Inc., The.
Crispino, Enrica. Van Gogh. 2008. (Art Masters Ser.). 64p. (YA). (gr. 6-18). lib. bdg. 24.95 net. (978-1-934545-05-8(8)) Oliver Pr., Inc.
Fandel, Jennifer & Bodden, Valerie. Vincent Van Gogh. 2017. (Odysseys in Artistry Ser.). (ENG., Illus.). 80p. (J). (gr. 7-11). pap. 14.99 (978-1-62832-317-7(5), Creative Paperbacks) Creative Co., The.
Greenberg, Jan & Jordan, Sandra. Vincent Van Gogh: Portrait of an Artist. 2003. (ENG., Illus.). 144p. (J). (gr. 5). 6.99 (978-0-440-41917-4(4), Yearling) Random Hse. Children's Bks.
Howse, Jennifer. Vincent Van Gogh. 2016. (Illus.). 32p. (J). (978-1-4896-4627-9(2)) Weigl Pubs., Inc.
Klein, Adam G. Vincent Van Gogh, 1 vol. 2007. (Great Artists Set 2 Ser.). (ENG., Illus.). 32p. (gr. -1-3). 27.07 (978-1-59679-730-7(4), Checkerboard Library) ABDO Publishing Co.
Landau, Jennifer. Vincent Van Gogh: Master of Post-Impressionist Painting. 2015. (Britannica Beginner Bios Ser.). (ENG., Illus.). 32p. (J). 23.45 (978-1-62275-946-0(X), Britannica Educational Publishing) Rosen Publishing Group, Inc., The.
Martin, Carmen & Martín, Carme. Vincent Van Gogh. 2006. (SPA.). 64p. (J). (gr. 4-5). 7.60 (978-84-342-2682-1(0), PR33292) Parramon Ediciones S.A. ESP. Dist: Lectorum Pubns., Inc.
Nichols, Catherine. Vincent van Gogh. 2009. (Primary Source Library of Famous Artists Ser.). 32p. (gr. 3-4). 42.50 (978-1-60854-105-8(3), PowerKids Pr.) Rosen Publishing Group, Inc., The.
Roddam, George. The Life & Art of Vincent Van Gogh. Harasymowicz, Sawa, illus. 2016. (Lives of Great Artists Ser.). 00080p. (J). (gr. 8-8). 35.75 (978-1-4994-6583-9(1)) Rosen Publishing Group, Inc., The.
Sabbeth, Carol. Van Gogh & the Post-Impressionists for Kids: Their Lives & Ideas, 21 Activities. 2011. (For Kids Ser.). (ENG., Illus.). 144p. (J). (gr. 4-18). pap. 17.95 (978-1-56976-275-2(9)) Chicago Review Pr., Inc.
Soni, Jaymee & Schubert, Charles. A Kid at Art - Vincent Van Gogh. 2003. (J). pap. 14.99 (978-0-9743760-1-1(9)) Little Noggin LLC.
Spence, David. Vincent Van Gogh: Arte y Emocion. (Coleccion Grandes Artistas).Tr. of Vincent Van Gogh: Art & Emotion. (SPA.). (YA). (gr. 5-8). 12.76 (978-84-8211-136-0(1)) Celeste Ediciones, S.A. ESP. Dist: Lectorum Pubns., Inc.
Thomson, Ruth. Vincent Van Gogh, 01 vols., 1. 2016. (Inspiring Artists Ser.). (ENG.). 48p. (J). 30.25 (978-1-5081-7056-3(8), Rosen Young Adult) Rosen Publishing Group, Inc., The.
van Gogh, Vincent. Make a Masterpiece — Van Gogh's Starry Night. 2014. (Dover Little Activity Bks.). (ENG.). 4p. (J). (gr. k-3). pap. 1.99 (978-0-486-78950-7(0)) Dover Pubns., Inc.
—Vincent's Colors. 2005. (ENG., Illus.). 48p. (J). (gr. -1-17). 15.99 (978-0-8118-5099-5(4)) Chronicle Bks. LLC.
van Gogh, Vincent & Noble, Marty. Van Gogh Stained Glass Coloring Book. 2007. (Dover Stained Glass Coloring Book Ser.). (ENG., Illus.). 32p. (gr. 6-8). 6.99 (978-0-486-45671-3(4)) Dover Pubns., Inc.
Venezia, Mike. Vincent Van Gogh. Venezia, Mike, illus. rev. ed. 2014. (Getting to Know the World's Greatest Artists Ser.). (ENG., Illus.). 40p. (J). lib. bdg. 29.00 (978-0-531-21978-2(X)) Scholastic Library Publishing.
—Vincent Van Gogh (Revised Edition) 2014. (Getting to Know the World's Greatest Artists Ser.). (ENG.). 40p. (J). pap. 7.95 (978-0-531-22539-4(9)) Scholastic Library Publishing.
Whiting, Jim. Vincent Van Gogh. 2007. (Art Profiles for Kids Ser.). (Illus.). 48p. (YA). (gr. 4-7). lib. bdg. 29.95 (978-1-58415-564-5(7)) Mitchell Lane Pubs., Inc.
Wood, Alix. Vincent Van Gogh. 2013. (Artists Through the Ages Ser.). (ENG., Illus.). 32p. (gr. 3-6). 25.25 (978-1-61533-622-7(2)); pap. 10.00 (978-1-61533-631-9(1)) Windmill Bks.
Zaczek, Iain. Vincent Van Gogh. 2014. (Great Artists Ser.). 32p. (J). (gr. 3-6). pap. 63.00 (978-1-4824-1249-9(7)) Stevens, Gareth Publishing LLLP.

GOLD

see also Gold Mines and Mining; Jewelry; Money

Beck, Gail. Gold: Set Of 6. 2011. (Navigators Ser.). (J). pap. 48.00 net. (978-1-4108-6236-5(4)) Benchmark Education Co.
—Gold: Text Pairs. 2008. (BridgesNavigators Ser.). (J). (gr. 5). 94.00 (978-1-4108-8418-3(X)) Benchmark Education Co.
Belval, Brian. Gold. 2007. (Understanding the Elements of the Periodic Table Ser.). (ENG., Illus.). 48p. (YA). lib. bdg. 29.25 (978-1-4042-0708-0(2)) Rosen Publishing Group, Inc., The.
Edwards, Ron & Gladstone, James. Gold. 2004. (Rocks, Minerals, & Resources Ser.). (ENG., Illus.). 32p. (J). lib. bdg. (978-0-7787-1413-2(6)) Crabtree Publishing Co.
Haynes, Betsy. My Adventure Panning for Gold. 2007. 44p. (J). 8.99 (978-1-59092-444-0(4)) Blue Forge Pr.
Hulick, Kathryn. Gold. 2017. 64p. **(978-1-4222-3840-0(7))** Mason Crest.
Perritano, John. Gold & Silver, Vol. 12. 2015. (North American Natural Resources Ser.). (Illus.). 64p. (J). (gr. 7). 23.95 (978-1-4222-3382-5(0)) Mason Crest.
Petersen, Christine. Gold, 1 vol. 2013. (Earth's Treasures Ser.). (ENG.). 32p. (J). (gr. 3-6). lib. bdg. 27.07 (978-1-61783-871-2(3), Checkerboard Library) ABDO Publishing Co.
Ryan, Peter K. How the Gold Standard Works. 2011. (Real World Economics Ser.). (ENG.). 80p. (YA). lib. bdg. 33.25 (978-1-4488-1272-1(0)) Rosen Publishing Group, Inc., The.
Sargent, Brian. Gold: Greed & Glory Intermediate Book with Online Access. 2014. (ENG., Illus.). 28p. pap. 9.50 (978-1-107-65260-6(X)) Cambridge Univ. Pr.

Shea, Therese. Gold, Vol. 1. 2014. (Rare & Precious Metals Ser.). 24p. (J). (gr. 2-5). 22.60 *(978-1-4824-0503-3(2))* Stevens, Gareth Publishing LLLP.

Sterling, Kristin. Silver & Gold Everywhere. 2010. (Lightning Bolt Books — Colors Everywhere Ser.). (ENG., Illus.). 32p. (gr. k-2). pap. 7.95 *(978-0-7613-5662-2(2))*; lib. bdg. 26.60 *(978-0-7613-4593-0(0)*, Lerner Pubns.) Lerner Publishing Group.

GOLD—FICTION

Appleton, Victor. Tom Swift Omnibus #4: Tom Swift & His Electric Rifle, Tom Swift in the City of Gold, Tom Swift & His Air Glider. 2007. 304p. 24.95 *(978-1-60459-103-3(X))*; per. 12.99 *(978-1-60459-104-0(8))* Wilder Pubns., Corp.

Becket, Jim. Inca Gold: Choose Your Own Adventure #20. 2007. (Choose Your Own Adventure Ser.: 20). (Illus.). 144p. (J). per. 6.99 *(978-1-933390-20-8(4)*, CHCL20) Chooseco LLC.

Carothers, Nina. Gold Old Gets a Little Help from His Friends. Nilsen, Richard J., ed. Padovano, Chris, illus. 2013. 32p. pap. 12.97 *(978-1-937376-29-1(X))* All Star Pr.

Carson, Rae. Walk on Earth a Stranger. (Gold Seer Trilogy Ser.: 1). (YA). (gr. 8). 2016. 464p. pap. 9.99 *(978-0-06-224292-1(X))* 2015. (ENG.). 448p. 17.99 *(978-0-06-224291-4(1))* HarperCollins Pubs. (Greenwillow Bks.).

Crawford, K. Michael. The Mystery of Journeys Crowne-an Adventure Drawing Game. Crawford, K. Michael, illus. 2008. (Illus.). 52p. pap. 14.95 *(978-0-9817940-0-6(9))* Virtualbookworm.com Publishing, Inc.

Dixon, Franklin W. & Walker, Jeff. The Secret of the Soldier's Gold. 2003. (Hardy Boys Ser.: 182). (ENG., Illus.). 160p. (J). (gr. 3-7). pap. 5.99 *(978-0-689-85885-7(X)*, Aladdin) Simon & Schuster Children's Publishing.

Duk, Lor. The Firestorm Heart: A Dragon Friend Story. 2010. 236p. pap. 15.95 *(978-1-4401-9474-0(2))* iUniverse, Inc.

Geiger, Kay. Treasure. 2010. 36p. pap. 19.95 *(978-1-4457-6383-5(4))* Lulu Pr., Inc.

Gutman, Dan. Mr. Burke Is Berserk! Paillot, Jim, illus. 2012. (My Weirder School Ser.: 4). 112p. (J). (gr. 1-5). (ENG.). pap. 4.99 *(978-0-06-196922-5(2))*; lib. bdg. 15.89 *(978-0-06-196923-2(0))* HarperCollins Pubs.

—Mr. Burke Is Berserk! 2012. (My Weirder School Ser.: 4). (J). lib. bdg. 14.75 *(978-0-606-23571-6(X)*, Turtleback) Turtleback Bks.

Harvey, Paul E., Jr. The Adventures of Shamus the Leprechaun. 2009. 48p. pap. 15.50 *(978-1-60693-924-6(6)*, Strategic Bk. Publishing) Strategic Book Publishing & Rights Agency (SBPRA).

Hopkinson, Deborah. Sailing for Gold. Farnsworth, Bill, illus. 2005. 76p. (J). lib. bdg. 15.00 *(978-1-59054-915-5(5))* Fitzgerald Bks.

Howell, Troy. The Dragon of Cripple Creek. 2011. (ENG., Illus.). 400p. (J). (gr. 3-7). 16.95 *(978-0-8109-9713-4(4)*, Amulet Bks.) Abrams, Inc.

Hoyt, Charlene. Where the Leprechauns Hide. Fischer, Sandi, illus. 2007. (ENG.). 40p. per. 12.99 *(978-0-9792258-9-5(2))* Bezalel Bks.

Hunt, Elizabeth Singer. The Quest for Aztec Gold - Mexico, Bk. 10. 2009. (Secret Agent Jack Stalwart Ser.: 10). (ENG.). 128p. (J). (gr. 1-4). pap. 5.99 *(978-1-60286-079-7(3)*, Weinstein Bks.) Perseus Bks. Group.

The Hunt for Pirate Gold, 6 vols., Vol. 2. (Woodland Mysteriestm Ser.). 133p. (gr. 3-7). 42.50 *(978-0-7802-7934-6(4))* Wright Group/McGraw-Hill.

James, Dalton. The Sneakiest Pirates. 2008. 20p. pap. 10.95 *(978-1-4327-2477-1(0))* Outskirts Pr., Inc.

Johnson, Tim. Lost Dutchman in Cochise County? Incidents & Coincidences. 2003. (Illus.). 52p. 19.95 *(978-0-9742351-0-3(5))* MCM Prime, Inc.

Lorenzen, Margaret Brownell. Petunia Patch Pockets & the Golden Locket. Jocelyn, Sawyer & Liza, Behles, illus. 2005. 76p. (J). per. 12.50 *(978-0-9724922-7-0(5))* Authors & Artists Publishers of New York, Inc.

Martin, Brian. The Gold of Angel Island. McDonald, Kim, illus. 2007. 46p. (J). *(978-0-9798059-0-5(2))* Lunchbox Stories Inc.

McAfee, Joan K. The Road to el Dorado. 2003. (Illus.). 186p. (YA). pap. 12.95 *(978-0-89745-273-1(9))* Sunflower Univ. Pr.

Meister, Cari. Ora - El Monstruo Marino. Heck, Claudia M., tr. from ENG. Messner, Dennis, illus. 2012. (Los Amigos Monstruos/Monster Friends Ser.).Tr. of Ora - The Sea Monster. (MUL & SPA.). 32p. (gr. 2-3). lib. bdg. 22.65 *(978-1-4342-3784-2(2)*, Bilingual Stone Arch Readers) Stone Arch Bks.

—Ora - The Sea Monster. Messner, Dennis, illus. 2009. (Monster Friends Ser.). (ENG.). 32p. (gr. 2-3). pap. 6.25 *(978-1-4342-1746-2(9))* Stone Arch Bks.

—Ora the Sea Monster. Messner, Dennis, illus. 2009. (Monster Friends Ser.). (ENG.). 32p. (gr. 2-3). 22.65 *(978-1-4342-1631-1(4))* Stone Arch Bks.

O'Leary, John. ¡En Busca del Tesoro del Pirata! 2005. (SPA & ENG., Illus.). 14p. (J). (gr. -1-k). 15.95 *(978-84-7864-794-1(5))* Combel Editorial, S.A. ESP. Dist: Independent Pubs. Group.

Padma, T. V., et al. Growing Gold. 2007. (Story Cove Ser.). (ENG., Illus.). 32p. (J). (gr. -1-3). pap. 4.95 *(978-0-87483-860-2(6))* August Hse. Pubs., Inc.

Rasheed, Winona. Stories from Grandma's Garden. 2008. 41p. pap. 15.94 *(978-1-4357-5075-3(6))* Lulu Pr., Inc.

Sander, Sonia. Scooby-Doo & the International Express. 2009. (Illus.). 32p. (J). pap. *(978-0-545-16283-8(1))* Scholastic, Inc.

Santillo, LuAnn. Fred & Ed. Santillo, LuAnn, ed. 2003. (Half-Pint Kids Readers Ser.). (Illus.). 7p. (J). (gr. -1-1). pap. 1.00 *(978-1-59256-074-5(1))* Half-Pint Kids, Inc.

Shurtliff, Liesl. Rump: The True Story of Rumpelstiltskin. (ENG.). 272p. (J). (gr. 3-7). 2014. pap. 7.99 *(978-0-307-97796-0(X)*, Yearling) 2013. 16.99 *(978-0-307-97793-9(5)*, Knopf Bks. for Young Readers) 2013. lib. bdg. 19.99 *(978-0-307-97794-6(3)*, Knopf Bks. for Young Readers) Random Hse. Children's Bks.

Sommer, Carl. The Richest Poor Kid. Martinez, Jorge, illus. 2014. (J). pap. *(978-1-57537-965-4(1))* Advance Publishing, Inc.

—The Richest Poor Kid. Martinez, Jorge, illus. 2007. (Another Sommer-Time Story Ser.). (ENG.). 48p. (J). 23.95 incl. audio compact disk *(978-1-57537-724-7(1))*; (gr. -1-3). 9.95 *(978-1-57537-025-5(5))*; (gr. -1-3). 16.95 incl. audio compact disk *(978-1-57537-524-3(9))*; (gr. k-4). 16.95 *(978-1-57537-074-3(3))* Advance Publishing, Inc.

Thompson, Colin. The Last Alchemist. Thompson, Colin, illus. 2003. (Illus.). 30p. (J). (gr. k-3). reprint ed. 17.00 *(978-0-7567-6164-6(6))* DIANE Publishing Co.

Tousey, Sanford. Jack Finds Gold. 2011. 44p. 35.95 *(978-1-258-09840-7(7))* Literary Licensing, LLC.

GOLD FISH

see Goldfish

GOLD MINES AND MINING

Aretha, David. The Gold Rush to California's Riches. 2006. (Wild History of the American West Ser.). (Illus.). 128p. (J). (gr. 5-9). lib. bdg. 34.60 *(978-1-59845-012-5(3)*, MyReportLinks.com Bks.) Enslow Pubs., Inc.

Aronson, Marc. Trapped: How the World Rescued 33 Miners from 2,000 Feet below the Chilean Desert. 2012. (ENG., Illus.). 144p. (J). pap. 6.99 *(978-1-4424-4025-8(2)*, Atheneum Bks. for Young Readers) Simon & Schuster Children's Publishing.

Craats, Rennay. Gold Rush. 2003. (Real Life Stories Ser.). (Illus.). 24p. (J). lib. bdg. 24.45 *(978-1-59036-078-1(8))* Weigl Pubs., Inc.

Fradin, Dennis Brindell. The California Gold Rush. 2008. (Turning Points in U. S. History Ser.). 48p. (gr. 3-18). lib. bdg. 31.36 *(978-0-7614-3012-4(1)*, Benchmark Bks.) Marshall Cavendish Corp.

George, Lynn. What Do You Know about the Gold Rush? (20 Questions: History Ser.). 24p. (gr. 2-3). 2009. 42.50 *(978-1-60854-959-7(3)*, PowerKids Pr.) 2008. (J). lib. bdg. 22.60 *(978-1-4042-4188-6(4))* Rosen Publishing Group, Inc., The.

Grayson, Robert. California's Gold Rush, 1 vol. 2012. (Essential Events Set 8 Ser.). (ENG., Illus.). 112p. (J). (gr. 6-12). lib. bdg. 35.64 *(978-1-61783-096-9(8))* ABDO Publishing Co.

Holub, Joan. What Was the Gold Rush? Tomkinson, Tim, illus. 2013. (What Was? Ser.). (ENG.). 112p. (J). (gr. 3-7). pap. 5.99 *(978-0-448-46289-9(3)*, Penguin Workshop) Penguin Young Readers Group.

—What Was the Gold Rush? 2013. (What Was... ? Ser.). lib. bdg. 16.00 *(978-0-606-29972-5(6)*, Turtleback) Turtleback Bks.

Johnson, Robin. California Gold Rush! 2013. (ENG., Illus.). 48p. (J). *(978-0-7787-1170-4(6))*; pap. *(978-0-7787-1178-0(1))* Crabtree Publishing Co.

Kraft, Eric. Gold Rush! Set Of 6. 2011. (Navigators Ser.). (J). pap. 48.00 net. *(978-1-4108-0423-5(2))* Benchmark Education Co.

—Gold Rush! & ¡la fiebre del Oro! 6 English, 6 Spanish Adaptations. 2011. (ENG & SPA.). (J). 97.00 net. *(978-1-4108-5699-9(2))* Benchmark Education Co.

Levy, Janey. Life During the Gold Rush. 2013. (What You Didn't Know about History Ser.). (Illus.). 24p. (J). (gr. 2-5). pap. 8.15 *(978-1-4339-8430-3(X))*; lib. bdg. 22.60 *(978-1-4339-8429-7(6))* Stevens, Gareth Publishing LLLP.

Lusted, Marcia Amidon. The Chilean Miners' Rescue, 1 vol. 2011. (Essential Events Set 7 Ser.). (ENG., Illus.). 112p. (J). (gr. 6-12). lib. bdg. 35.64 *(978-1-61783-097-6(6))* ABDO Publishing Co.

Madison, Amelia & Shoup, Kate. Life As a Prospector in the California Gold Rush. 2016. (Life As... Ser.). (ENG., Illus.). 32p. (J). (gr. 3-3). 28.50 *(978-1-5026-1780-4(3))* Cavendish Square Publishing.

Mattern, Joanne. America's Gold Rush: John Sutter & the Discovery of Gold in California. 2004. (Great Moments in American History Ser.). (Illus.). 32p. (J). (gr. 4-7). lib. bdg. 22.50 *(978-0-8239-4365-4(8))* Rosen Publishing Group, Inc., The.

Micklos, John, Jr. The Gold Rush. 2016. (Primary Source History Ser.). (ENG., Illus.). 32p. (gr. 3-4). lib. bdg. 27.32 *(978-1-4914-8486-9(1)*, Fact Finders) Capstone Press of Coughlan Cos.

O'Donnell, Kerri. A Timeline of the California Gold Rush. 2009. (Real Life Readers Ser.). 32p. (gr. 4-5). pap. 10.00 *(978-1-4358-0161-5(X)*, Rosen Classroom); (gr. 4-4). 47.90 *(978-1-61511-366-8(5)*, PowerKids Pr.); (J). (gr. 3-4). lib. bdg. 25.25 *(978-1-4358-2989-3(1)*, PowerKids Pr.) Rosen Publishing Group, Inc., The.

Onsgard, Bethany. Life During the California Gold Rush, 1 vol. 2014. (Daily Life in US History Ser.). (ENG., Illus.). 48p. (J). (gr. 3-6). lib. bdg. 32.79 *(978-1-62403-624-8(4))* ABDO Publishing Co.

Raabe, Emily. The Gold Rush: California or Bust! (Westward Ho! Ser.). 24p. 2009. (gr. 2-3). 42.50 *(978-1-60854-762-3(0))* 2003. (Illus.). (J). lib. bdg. 22.60 *(978-0-8239-6494-9(9))* Rosen Publishing Group, Inc., The. (PowerKids Pr.).

Savage, Jeff. Rugged Gold Miners: True Tales of the Wild West. 2012. (True Tales of the Wild West Ser.). (Illus.). 48p. (J). (gr. 5-18). pap. 8.95 *(978-1-4644-0028-5(8))* Enslow Pubs., Inc.

Scott, Elaine. Buried Alive! How 33 Miners Survived 69 Days Deep under the Chilean Desert. 2012. (ENG., Illus.). 80p. (J). (gr. 5-7). 18.99 *(978-0-547-70778-5(9))* Houghton Mifflin Harcourt Publishing Co.

Staunton, Ted. Gold Rush. Geoffroi, Remie, illus. 2008. (Dreadful Truth Ser.). (ENG.). 104p. (YA). (gr. 3-8). *(978-0-88780-747-3(X))* Formac Publishing Co., Ltd.

Uschan, Michael V. The California Gold Rush. 2003. (Landmark Events in American History Ser.). (Illus.). 48p. (gr. 5-12). pap. 14.05 *(978-0-8368-5402-2(0))*; lib. bdg. 31.00 *(978-0-8368-5374-2(1))* Stevens, Gareth Publishing LLLP. (Gareth Stevens Secondary Library).

Vescia, Peter. The Pikes Peak Gold Rush, 01 vols., 1. 2016. (Spotlight on Colorado Ser.). (ENG.). 48p. (J). (gr. 4-5). pap. 11.75 *(978-1-4994-1456-1(0)*, PowerKids Pr.) Rosen Publishing Group, Inc., The.

GOLD MINES AND MINING—FICTION

Alger, Horatio. Joe's Luck. 2005. 28.95 *(978-1-4218-1455-1(2))*; 264p. pap. 13.95 *(978-1-4218-1555-8(9))* 1st World Publishing, Inc. (1st World Library - Literary Society).

—Joe's Luck: Or, Always Wide Awake. 2006. (ENG.). 172p. pap. 19.99 *(978-1-4264-6426-3(6))* 2006. (ENG.). 176p. pap. 19.99 *(978-1-4264-0883-0(8))* 2007. 186p. pap. 21.99 *(978-1-4264-6500-0(9))* 2006. (ENG.). 170p. pap. 21.99 *(978-1-4264-0864-9(1))* Creative Media Partners, LLC.

Arrigan, Mary & Quarto Generic Staff. Esty's Gold. 2010. (ENG.). 224p. (J). (gr. 6-9). pap. 8.95 *(978-1-84507-965-9(5)*, Frances Lincoln) Quarto Publishing Group UK GBR. Dist: Hachette Bk. Group.

Aviation Publications Staff & National Geographic Learning Staff. Hard Gold: The Colorado Gold Rush of 1859. 2010. (Rise & Shine Ser.). (ENG.). 240p. (C). (gr. 3-7). pap. 10.95 *(978-1-4231-0520-6(6))* National Geographic School Publishing, Inc.

Broach, Elise. Treasure on Superstition Mountain. Caparó, Antonio Javier, illus. 2013. (Superstition Mountain Mysteries Ser.: 2). (ENG.). 288p. (J). (gr. 3-7). 15.99 *(978-0-8050-7763-6(4)*, 9780805077636, Holt, Henry & Co. Bks. For Young Readers) Holt, Henry & Co.

Brown, Jeff. The Mount Rushmore Calamity. Pamintuan, Macky, illus. 2009. (Flat Stanley's Worldwide Adventures Ser.: 1). (ENG.). 96p. (J). (gr. 2-5). 15.99 *(978-0-06-142991-0(0))*; pap. 4.99 *(978-0-06-142990-3(2))* HarperCollins Pubs.

Carson, Rae. Walk on Earth a Stranger. 2015. (Gold Seer Trilogy Ser.: 1). (ENG.). 448p. (YA). (gr. 8). 17.99 *(978-0-06-224291-4(1)*, Greenwillow Bks.) HarperCollins Pubs.

Coren, Alan. Klondike Arthur. 2004. (Illus.). 64p. *(978-0-903895-93-4(5)*, Robson Bks. Ltd.) Pavilion Bks.

Golden, Christopher & Lebbon, Tim. The Wild. Ruth, Greg, illus. 2011. (Secret Journeys of Jack London Ser.: 1). (ENG.). 368p. (YA). (gr. 5-18). 15.99 *(978-0-06-186317-2(3)*, HarperTeen) HarperCollins Pubs.

Gunderson, J. Fire & Snow: A Tale of the Alaskan Gold Rush. Townsend, Shannon, illus. 2007. (Historical Fiction Ser.). (ENG.). 56p. (gr. 2-3). pap. 6.25 *(978-1-59889-405-9(6)*, Graphic Flash) Stone Arch Bks.

Henty, George Alfred. Captain Bayley's Heir: A Tale of the California Gold Fields. 2011. 314p. pap. 19.95 *(978-1-61179-115-0(4))* Fireship Pr.

Holt, Stephen & Lewis, Oscar. We Were There with the California Forty-Niners. Lufkin, Raymond, illus. 2011. 186p. 42.95 *(978-1-258-05988-0(6))* Literary Licensing, LLC.

Hope, Laura Lee. The Outdoor Girls in the Saddle: Or the Girl Miner of Gold Run. 2007. (ENG.). 138p. pap. 18.99 *(978-1-4264-9648-6(6))*; 150p. pap. 19.99 *(978-1-4264-6870-4(9))* Creative Media Partners, LLC.

Hopkins, Jackie Mims. The Gold Miner's Daughter: A Melodramatic Fairy Tale, 1 vol. Goodell, Jon, illus. 2006. (ENG.). 32p. (J). (gr. k-3). 15.95 *(978-1-56145-362-7(5))* Peachtree Pubs.

Isaacs, Anne. The Ghosts of Luckless Gulch. Santat, Dan, illus. 2008. (ENG.). 48p. (J). (gr. k-3). 18.99 *(978-1-4169-0201-0(5)*, Atheneum Bks. for Young Readers) Simon & Schuster Children's Publishing.

James, Will. Look-See with Uncle Bill. rev. ed. (Illus.). 190p. (J). (gr. 4). pap. *(978-0-87842-458-0(X)*, 814) Mountain Pr. Publishing Co., Inc.

Johnson, Tim. Lost Dutchman in Cochise County? Incidents & Coincidences. 2003. (Illus.). 52p. 19.95 *(978-0-9742351-0-3(5))* MCM Prime, Inc.

Johnston, Tony. Levi Strauss Gets a Bright Idea: A Fairly Fabricated Story of a Pair of Pants. Innerst, Stacy, illus. 2011. (ENG.). 32p. (J). (gr. -1-3). 16.99 *(978-0-15-206145-6(2))* Houghton Mifflin Harcourt Publishing Co.

Luxa, Sue. A Cabin in Cripple Creek. 2004. (Illus.). 99p. (J). pap. 8.95 *(978-1-932738-04-9(5)*, 1234249) Western Reflections Publishing Co.

Marsh, Carole. The Gosh Awful! Gold Rush Mystery. (Real Kids, Real Places Ser.). (Illus.). 146p. (J). 2009. lib. bdg. 18.99 *(978-0-635-07026-5(X)*, Marsh, Carole Mysteries) 2007. (gr. 2-8). 14.95 *(978-0-635-06390-8(5))* Gallopade International.

Melton, Marcia. Joe Henry's Journey. 2014. (Illus.). 169p. (J). pap. 12.00 *(978-1-937849-20-7(1))* Raven Publishing Inc. of Montana.

Murphy, Gold Rush Dog, 1 vol. 2014. (Dog Chronicles Ser.). (ENG., Illus.). 160p. (J). (gr. 2-5). 12.95 *(978-1-56145-769-4(8))* Peachtree Pubs.

Patron, Susan. Behind the Masks: The Diary of Angeline Reddy - Bodie, California 1880. 2012. (Dear America Ser.). (ENG.). 304p. (J). (gr. 3-7). 12.99 *(978-0-545-30437-5(7))* Scholastic, Inc.

Reichart, George. A Bag of Lucky Rice. Mitchell, Mark, illus. 2004. (ENG.). 160p. pap. 10.95 *(978-1-56792-278-3(3))* Godine, David R. Pub.

Roddy, Lee. The Mystery of the Black Hole Mine. 2008. (D. J. Dillon Adventure Ser.: No. 7). (J). 8.99 *(978-0-88062-271-4(7))* Mott Media.

Rose, Caroline Starr. Jasper & the Riddle of Riley's Mine. 2017. (ENG.). 288p. (J). (gr. 5). 16.99 *(978-0-399-16811-6(7)*, G.P. Putnam's Sons Books for Young Readers) Penguin Young Readers Group.

Schwartz, Joel. The Extraordinary Pupfish of Calaveras County. 2008. 216p. 25.95 *(978-1-4401-0892-1(7))* iUniverse, Inc.

Steiner, Barbara. Mystery at Chilkoot Pass. 2009. (Mysteries Through Time Ser.). 144 - 176p. (YA). (gr. 4-8). 31.95 *(978-1-60754-435-7(0))*; pap. 15.25 *(978-1-60754-434-0(2))* Windmill Bks.

Stites, Clara. Lixia of Gold Mountain: A Story of Early California. 2015. (ENG., Illus.). 100p. (J). pap. 8.95 *(978-1-56474-421-0(3)*, Fithian Pr) Daniel & Daniel, Pubs., Inc.

Teitelbaum, Michael. The Ghastly Ghost Town. 2015. (Cold Whispers Ser.). (ENG., Illus.). 32p. (J). (gr. 2-6). lib. bdg. 26.60 *(978-1-62724-811-2(0))* Bearport Publishing Co., Inc.

Trout, Richard. Devil's Breath Volcano, 1 vol. 2008. (MacGregor Family Adventure Ser.: 6). (ENG., Illus.). 208p. (YA). (gr. 6-10). 16.99 *(978-1-58980-558-3(5))* Pelican Publishing Co., Inc.

Turner, Ginger. Gold Mine! The California Gold Rush Story. 2004. (Illus.). 46p. (J). per. 15.95 *(978-0-9742502-2-9(8))* Gossamer Bks., LLC.

Turner, Ginger & Shimpi, Shekhar. Gold Mine! The California Gold Rush Story. 2004. (Illus.). 44p. (J). pap. 15.95 *(978-0-9742502-3-6(6))* Gossamer Bks., LLC.

Willingham, Ellie. Wildwood. Willingham, Ellie, illus. 2007. (ENG., Illus.). 136p. (J). (gr. -1-3). per. 10.00 *(978-0-9792371-0-2(6))* Keene Publishing.

Yamada, Debbie Leung. Striking It Rich: Treasures from Gold Mountain. Tang, You-shan, illus. l.t. ed. 2004. 128p. (J). (gr. 4-8). pap. 13.95 *(978-1-879965-21-8(6))* Polychrome Publishing Corp.

GOLD RUSH

see California—Gold Discoveries

GOLDFISH

Alderton, David. How to Look after Your Goldfish: A Practical Guide to Caring for Your Pet, in Step-By-Step Photographs. 2013. (ENG., Illus.). 20p. (J). (gr. -1-9). 8.99 *(978-1-84322-733-5(9)*, Armadillo) Anness Publishing GBR. Dist: National Bk. Network.

Barnes, Julia. Pet Goldfish. 2006. (Pet Pals Ser.). (Illus.). 32p. (gr. 2-6). lib. bdg. 26.00 *(978-0-8368-6778-7(5)*, Gareth Stevens Learning Library) Stevens, Gareth Publishing LLLP.

Carr, Aaron. Fish. 2011. (J). 27.13 *(978-1-61690-922-2(6))* Weigl Pubs., Inc.

—El Pez. 2012. (SPA.). (J). *(978-1-61913-183-5(8))* Weigl Pubs., Inc.

Cozier, Carl. Goldfish, Vol. 12. 2016. (Understanding & Caring for Your Pet Ser.: Vol. 12). (ENG., Illus.). 128p. (J). (gr. 5-8). 25.95 *(978-1-4222-3697-0(8))* Mason Crest.

Ganeri, Anita. Goldie's Guide to Caring for Your Goldfish, 1 vol. Peterson, Rick, illus. 2013. (Pets' Guides). (ENG.). 32p. (gr. 1-3). pap. 8.29 *(978-1-4329-7139-7(5))*; lib. bdg. 27.32 *(978-1-4329-7132-8(8))* Heinemann-Raintree. (Heinemann First Library).

Gibbs, Maddie. Goldfish. 2013. (PowerKids Readers: Fun Fish Ser.). (ENG.). 24p. (J). (gr. k-2). pap. 49.50 *(978-1-4777-0850-7(2))*; pap. 8.25 *(978-1-4777-0849-1(9))*; lib. bdg. 22.60 *(978-1-4777-0758-6(1))* Rosen Publishing Group, Inc., The. (PowerKids Pr.).

Gibbs, Maddie & Alamán, Eduardo. Goldfish: Los Carpines. 2013. (PowerKids Readers: Fun Fish / Peces Divertidos Ser.). (SPA & ENG.). 24p. (J). (gr. k-2). lib. bdg. 22.60 *(978-1-4777-1216-0(X)*, PowerKids Pr.) Rosen Publishing Group, Inc., The.

Goodbody, Slim & Burstein, John. Goldfish. McGinnis, Ben, illus. 2008. (Slim Goodbody's Inside Guide to Pets Ser.). 32p. (J). (gr. 2-6). lib. bdg. 26.00 *(978-0-8368-8956-7(8)*, Gareth Stevens Learning Library) Stevens, Gareth Publishing LLLP.

Hasenecz Calvert, Ellen. Nine Goldfish in David's Pond. 2009. 36p. pap. 17.99 *(978-1-4490-3020-9(3))* AuthorHouse.

Hutmacher, Kimberly M. I Want a Goldfish, 1 vol. 2012. (I Want a Pet Ser.). (ENG.). 24p. (gr. k-1). lib. bdg. 26.65 *(978-1-4296-7597-0(7)*, Pebble Plus) Capstone Press of Coughlan Cos.

Kawa, Katie. Colorful Goldfish. 2011. (Pet Corner Ser.). (Illus.). 24p. (gr. k-2). (J). pap. 8.15 *(978-1-4339-5599-0(7))*; (J). lib. bdg. 22.60 *(978-1-4339-5597-6(0))*; 69.20 *(978-1-4339-6882-2(7))* Stevens, Gareth Publishing LLLP.

—Colorful Goldfish: Peces Dorados Brillantes. 2011. (Pet Corner / RincóN de Las Mascotas Ser.). (SPA., Illus.). 24p. (J). (gr. k-3). lib. bdg. 22.60 *(978-1-4339-5601-0(2))* Stevens, Gareth Publishing LLLP.

MacAulay, Kelley & Kalman, Bobbie. Goldfish. Reiach, Margaret Amy & Crabtree, Marc, illus. Crabtree, Marc, photos by. 2004. (Pet Care Ser.). (ENG.). 32p. (J). pap. *(978-0-7787-1791-1(7))*; lib. bdg. *(978-0-7787-1759-1(3))* Crabtree Publishing Co.

MacAulay, Kelley, et al. Les Poissons Rouges. 2010. (Petit Monde Vivant Ser.). (FRE., Illus.). 32p. (J). pap. 9.95 *(978-2-89579-323-6(9))* Bayard Canada Livres CAN. Dist: Crabtree Publishing Co.

McCloskey, Kevin. Something's Fishy: TOON Level 1. 2017. (Giggle & Learn Ser.). (ENG., Illus.). 40p. (J). (gr. -1-3). 12.95 *(978-1-943145-15-7(6))* TOON Books / RAW Junior, LLC.

My Pet: KinderReaders Individual Title Six-Packs. (Kinderstarters Ser.). 8p. (gr. -1-1). 21.00 *(978-0-7635-8661-4(7))* Rigby Education.

Phillips, Jillian. What to Doodle? At the Aquarium. 2011. (Dover Doodle Bks.). (ENG., Illus.). 64p. (J). (gr. k-3). pap. 1.99 *(978-0-486-47819-7(X))* Dover Pubns., Inc.

Rober, Harold. I Love Goldfish. 2016. (Bumba Books (tm) — Pets Are the Best Ser.). (ENG., Illus.). 24p. (J). (gr. -1-1). lib. bdg. 25.32 *(978-1-5124-1415-8(8))* Lerner Publishing Group.

Smythe, Katie. Our Class Goldfish. 2015. (Rosen REAL Readers: STEM & STEAM Collection). (ENG.). 8p. pap. 5.46 *(978-1-4994-9678-9(8)*, Rosen Classroom) Rosen Publishing Group, Inc., The.

World Book, Inc Staff, contrib. by. Goldfish & Other Carp. 2007. (World Book's Animals of the World Ser.). (Illus.). 64p. (J). *(978-0-7166-1329-9(8))* World Bk., Inc.

GOLDING, WILLIAM, 1911-1993

Reiff, Raychel Haugrud. William Golding. 2009. (Writers & Their Works 4 Ser.). (Illus.). 144p. (gr. 7). 42.79 *(978-0-7614-4276-9(6))* Marshall Cavendish Corp.

GOLF

Bratton, Déboral B. & Bigly, Ashley D. Record-a-Sport Golf Organizer. Bratton, Deboral B. & Bigly, Ashley D., eds. Bigly, Ashley D., illus. 2003. (Illus.). (gr. 1-18). 18.95 *(978-1-931746-00-7(1))* Sport Your Stuff Corp.

Buckley, Jim. Golf. 2008. (21st Century Skills Innovation Library: Innovation in Sports Ser.). (ENG., Illus.). 32p. (gr. 4-8). lib. bdg. 28.50 *(978-1-60279-262-3(3)*, 200145) Cherry Lake Publishing.

Bussiere, Desireé. Golf by the Numbers, 1 vol. 2013. (Sports by the Numbers Ser.). (ENG.). 24p. (J). (gr. k-3). lib. bdg. 24.21 *(978-1-61783-843-9(8)*, SandCastle) ABDO Publishing Co.

Challen, Paul. Swing It Golf. 2010. (ENG., Illus.). 32p. (J). pap. *(978-0-7787-3179-5(0))*; lib. bdg. *(978-0-7787-3147-4(2))* Crabtree Publishing Co.

Chapleski, Gregory. Getting Started in Golf. 2006. (J). 4.95 *(978-0-9787759-1-9(0))* eDimples, Inc.

Chapleski, Gregory, creator. Moving Ahead in Golf. 2006. (J). 4.95 net. *(978-0-9787759-2-6(9))* eDimples, Inc.

Ferris, Julie Alfriend. Badges, Egg Salad, & Green Jackets: The Masters a to Z. 2012. (Illus.). (J). 14.95 *(978-1-62086-149-3(6))* Mascot Bks., Inc.

Gigliotti, Jim. Great Girl Golfers. 2016. 32p. (J). *(978-1-4896-4779-5(1))* Weigl Pubs., Inc.

GOLF Magazine: The Best Instruction Guide Ever. 2008. (Time Inc. Home Entertainment Library-Bound Titles Ser.).

E F G

144p. (YA). (gr. 5-12). lib. bdg. 39.93 *(978-0-8225-7278-7(8)*, Twenty-First Century Bks.) Lerner Publishing Group.

Gregory, C. Matt. To Announce at a Later Date. 2005. (Illus.). 20p. (J). 20.00 *(978-0-9766442-1-7(5))* Gregory, Charles Matthew.

Heidtke, John. Family Golf Adventures on Michigan Links. 2010. 242p. (J). pap. 12.95 *(978-1-60920-000-8(4))* Ajoyin Publishing, Inc.

Herzog, Brad. P Is for Putt: A Golf Alphabet. Langton, Bruce, illus. (Alphabet-Sports Ser.). (ENG.). 40p. 2009. (gr. k-6). pap. 7.95 *(978-1-58536-476-3(2))* 2005. (J). (gr. -1-5). 16.95 *(978-1-58536-252-3(2))* Sleeping Bear Pr.

—P Is for Putt: A Golf Alphabet. Langton, Bruce, illus. 2015. (Av2 Fiction Readalong 2016 Ser.). (ENG.). (J). (gr. 1-4). lib. bdg. 34.28 *(978-1-4896-3759-8(1)*, AV2 by Weigl) Weigl Pubs., Inc.

Howell, Brian. Golf, 1 vol. 2012. (ENG.). 64p. 32.79 *(978-1-61783-143-0(3)*, SportsZone) ABDO Publishing Co.

Hudson, Maryann. Girls' Golf, 1 vol. 2013. (Girls' SportsZone Ser.). (ENG., Illus.). 48p. (J). (gr. 3-6). lib. bdg. 32.79 *(978-1-61783-985-6(X)*, SportsZone) ABDO Publishing Co.

Jovenes Golfistas. (SPA.). (YA). (gr. 2-18). 20.76 *(978-84-272-4973-8(X))* Molino, Editorial ESP. Dist: Lectorum Pubns., Inc.

Kelly, Ann. Ready ... Set ... GOLF! An Essential Guide for Young Golfers. 2009. (Illus.). 86p. pap. *(978-0-9686289-1-1(5))* GAKELLY Publishing.

Leitch, Cecil. Golf for Girls. reprint ed. 150.00 *(978-0-7222-1908-9(3))* Library Reprints, Inc.

Loughran, Donna. A Day at Mini-Golf: What's the Length? 2013. (iMath Ser.). (Illus.). 24p. (J). (gr. k-2). pap. 11.94 *(978-1-60357-495-2(6))*; lib. bdg. 21.27 *(978-1-59953-556-2(4))* Norwood Hse. Pr.

MacMillan, Daniel. Golfing in Idaho & Montana. 3rd ed. 2010. (ENG.). 296p. per. 14.95 *(978-1-878591-60-9(6))* MAC Productions.

McClellan, Ray. Golf. 2010. (My First Sports Ser.). (ENG., Illus.). 24p. (J). (gr. 2-5). lib. bdg. 25.95 *(978-1-60014-461-5(6)*, Blastoff! Readers) Bellwether Media.

Parks, Peter. How to Improve at Golf. 2007. (How to Improve At... Ser.). (ENG., Illus.). 48p. (J). (gr. 3-7). pap. *(978-0-7787-3589-2(3))*; lib. bdg. *(978-0-7787-3567-0(2))* Crabtree Publishing Co.

Resch, Celeste. Alana's 12-Step Guide to Fun Golf: A How-to Book for Kids Who Want to Play Golf & Have Fun Doing It! 2003. (J). 7.99 *(978-0-9743851-0-5(7))* Star Write Creations.

Sotzek, Hannelore & Rouse, Bonna. Le Golf. 2011. (Sans Limites (No Limits!) Ser.: No. 20). (FRE., Illus.). 32p. (J). pap. 9.95 *(978-2-89579-368-7(9))* Bayard Canada Livres CAN. Dist: Crabtree Publishing Co.

Stanger, Rob. I Love Golf! I.t. ed. 2003. (Illus.). 20p. pap. 7.95 *(978-0-9725721-0-1(4))* Club Pro Products.

Uschan, Michael V. Golf. Greenhaven Press Editors, ed. 2014. (Science Behind Sports Ser.). (ENG., Illus.). 128p. (gr. 7-10). lib. bdg. 39.40 *(978-1-4205-1153-6(X)*, Lucent Bks.) Cengage Gale.

Webster, Christine. The Masters. 2012. (J). *(978-1-61913-617-5(1))*; pap. *(978-1-61913-619-9(8))* Weigl Pubs., Inc.

—Masters Golf Tournament. 2009. (Sporting Championships Ser.). 32p. (YA). (gr. 4-7). lib. bdg. 26.00 *(978-1-60596-640-3(1))* Weigl Pubs., Inc.

Wells, Don. For the Love of Golf. 2005. (For the Love of Sports Ser.). (Illus.). 24p. (J). (gr. 4-6). lib. bdg. 24.45 *(978-1-59036-296-9(9))* Weigl Pubs., Inc.

—Golf. 2005. (For the Love of Sports Ser.). (Illus.). 24p. (J). (gr. 3-7). per. 8.95 *(978-1-59036-300-3(0))* Weigl Pubs., Inc.

Wells, Donald. Golf. 2010. (In the Zone Ser.). (Illus.). 32p. (J). (gr. 3-5). pap. 11.95 *(978-1-60596-899-5(4))*; lib. bdg. 25.70 *(978-1-60596-898-8(6))* Weigl Pubs., Inc.

Williams, Doug. Tiger Woods Makes Masters History, 1 vol. 2014. (Greatest Events in Sports History Ser.). (ENG., Illus.). 48p. (J). (gr. 3-6). lib. bdg. 32.79 *(978-1-62403-598-2(1)*, SportsZone) ABDO Publishing Co.

Wright, David F., et al. Wright Balance Focus for Success Series - Relaxation: A Guide to Your Best Golf. 2005. (YA). per. 19.95 *(978-0-9767272-0-0(X))* Foundation Pr.

The Young Americans Golf Guide 2004. 2004. (YA). 422p. per. 24.95 *(978-0-9727998-1-2(8))*; cd-rom 19.95 *(978-0-9727998-2-9(6))* i wantz Publishing.

The Young Americans Golf Guide Record of Accomplishments 2004. 2004. 152p. (YA). per. 14.95 *(978-0-9727998-3-6(4))* i wantz Publishing.

Young, Jeff C. Michelle Wie. 2012. (Xtreme Athletes Ser.). (Illus.). 112p. (YA). (gr. 7-12). 28.95 *(978-1-59935-187-2(0))* Reynolds, Morgan Inc.

GOLF—BIOGRAPHY

Bates, Greg. Michelle Wie: Golf Superstar, 1 vol. 2016. (ENG., Illus.). 32p. (J). *(978-1-62403-843-3(3)*, 1391433, SportsZone) ABDO Publishing Co.

Brown, Jonatha A. & Raatma, Lucia. Tiger Woods. 2004. (People We Should Know Ser.). (Illus.). 24p. (gr. 1-4). pap. 8.15 *(978-0-8368-4320-0(7))*; lib. bdg. 22.00 *(978-0-8368-4313-2(4))* Stevens, Gareth Publishing LLLP. (Weekly Reader Leveled Readers).

Curtis, Walter J., Sr. History's Master Golfers: The Only Four-Time Champions of the U. S. Open & the Only Four-or-More Time Champions of the British Open. 2003. (Illus.). 272p. 24.95 *(978-0-9659419-2-1(2))* Cedar Creek Publishing Service.

Daniel, P. K. Best Golfers of All Time, 1 vol. 2014. (Sports' Best Ever Ser.). (ENG.). 64p. (gr. 3-6). lib. bdg. 32.79 *(978-1-62403-619-4(8)*, SportsZone) ABDO Publishing Co.

Dean, Cynthia A. Michelle Wie: She's Got the Power! 2005. (High Five Reading - Blue Ser.). (ENG., Illus.). 48p. (gr. 3-4). per. 9.00 *(978-0-7368-5746-8(X)*, High Five Reading (RBL)) Capstone Press of Coughlan Cos.

Doeden, Matt. Tiger Woods. 2005. (Sports Heroes & Legends Ser.). (ENG., Illus.). 112p. (gr. 5-12). lib. bdg. 30.60 *(978-0-8225-3082-4(1)* Lerner Publishing Group.

Dunn, Mary R. & David, Rose. Michelle Wie. 2016. (Women in Sports Ser.). (ENG., Illus.). 24p. (gr. k-1). lib. bdg. 26.65 *(978-1-4914-7976-6(0)*, Pebble Plus) Capstone Press of Coughlan Cos.

Feinstein, Stephen. Lee Sobre Tiger Woods/Read about Tiger Woods. 2006. (I Like Biographies! Bilingual Ser.). (ENG & SPA., Illus.). 24p. (J). (gr. 1-3). lib. bdg. 22.60 *(978-0-7660-2743-5(0)*, Enslow Elementary) Enslow Pubs., Inc.

—Read about Tiger Woods. 2005. (I Like Biographies! Ser.). (Illus.). 24p. (J). lib. bdg. 22.60 *(978-0-7660-2594-3(2)*, Enslow Elementary) Enslow Pubs., Inc.

Gigliotti, Jim. Great Girl Golfers. 2007. (Reading Rocks! Ser.). (ENG., Illus.). 32p. (J). (gr. 2-5). 28.50 *(978-1-59296-868-8(6)*, 200743) Child's World, Inc., The.

Glaser, Jason. Tiger Woods. (Sports Idols Ser.). 24p. (gr. 2-3). 2009. 42.50 *(978-1-60853-143-1(0)*, PowerKids Pr.) 2008. (Illus.). (J). lib. bdg. 22.60 *(978-1-4042-4179-4(5))* Rosen Publishing Group, Inc., The.

Goldsworthy, Steve. Golf. 2013. (J). *(978-1-62127-502-2(7))*; pap. *(978-1-62127-505-3(1))* Weigl Pubs., Inc.

Goodman, Michael E. Tiger Woods. 2003. (Ovations Ser.). (Illus.). 32p. (J). *(978-1-58341-246-6(8)*, Creative Education) Creative Co., The.

Hasday, Judy L. Tiger Woods. 2008. (Black Americans of Achievement Ser.). (Illus.). 95p. (YA). (gr. 7-12). 35.00 *(978-0-7910-9714-4(5))* Facts On File, Inc.

Horn, Geoffrey M. Michelle Wie. 2006. (Today's Superstars). (Illus.). 32p. (gr. 5-8). lib. bdg. 31.95 *(978-0-8368-6186-0(8))* Stevens, Gareth Publishing LLLP.

Logothetis, Paul. Rory McIlroy: Golf Champion, 1 vol. 2016. (ENG., Illus.). 32p. (J). *(978-1-62403-838-9(7)*, 1391425, SportsZone) ABDO Publishing Co.

Raatma, Lucia. Tiger Woods. 2007. (21st Century Skills Library: Life Skills Biographies Ser.). (ENG., Illus.). 48p. (gr. 4-8). lib. bdg. 31.36 *(978-1-60279-076-6(0)*, 200048) Cherry Lake Publishing.

Riddolls, Tom & Wearing, Judy. Tiger Woods. 2009. (Remarkable People Ser.). (Illus.). 24p. (J). (gr. 4-6). pap. 8.95 *(978-1-60596-623-6(1))*; lib. bdg. 24.45 *(978-1-60596-622-9(3))* Weigl Pubs., Inc.

Riner, Dax. Annika Sorenstam. 2007. (Sports Heroes & Legends Ser.). (YA). (gr. 7-12). lib. bdg. 30.60 *(978-0-8225-7160-5(9))* Twenty First Century Bks.

Roberts, Jeremy. Tiger Woods. 2008. pap. 52.95 *(978-0-8225-5238-3(8))* Lerner Publishing Group.

—Tiger Woods: Golf's Master. 2008. (USA TODAY Lifeline Biographies Ser.). (ENG.). 112p. (gr. 6-12). lib. bdg. 34.60 *(978-1-58013-569-6(2))* Lerner Publishing Group.

Savage, Jeff. Michelle Wie. 2007. (J). lib. bdg. 25.26 *(978-0-8225-7664-8(3)*, Lerner Pubns.) Lerner Publishing Group.

—Tiger Woods. (Amazing Athletes Ser.). 2007. (J). 23.93 *(978-0-8225-6889-6(6)*, Lerner Pubns.) 2005. (Illus.). 32p. (gr. 3-4). lib. bdg. 22.60 *(978-0-8225-1337-7(4))* rev. ed. 2007. (ENG., Illus.). 32p. (gr. 2-5). per. 7.95 *(978-0-8225-6890-2(X)*, First Avenue Editions) 2nd rev. ed. 2009. (ENG.). 32p. (gr. 2-5). pap. 7.95 *(978-0-7613-4923-5(5)*, First Avenue Editions) Lerner Publishing Group.

Sharp, Anne Wallace. Nancy Lopez. 2008. (Twentieth Century's Most Influencial Hispanics Ser.). (ENG., Illus.). 96-128p. (gr. 7-10). 34.80 *(978-1-4205-0060-8(0)*, Lucent Bks.) Cengage Gale.

Tieck, Sarah. Tiger Woods: Famous Golfer, 1 vol. 2008. (Big Buddy Biographies Ser.). (ENG.). 32p. (J). (gr. 2-5). 28.50 *(978-1-60453-127-5(4))* ABDO Publishing Co.

GOLF—FICTION

Arena, Felice & Kettle, Phil. Golf Legends. Gordon, Gus, illus. 2004. (J). pap. *(978-1-59336-367-3(2))* Mondo Publishing.

Barbour, Ralph Henry. The Half-Back. 2005. 27.95 *(978-1-4218-1494-0(3))*; 220p. pap. 12.95 *(978-1-4218-1594-7(X))* 1st World Publishing, Inc. (1st World Library - Literary Society).

—The Half-Back. 2007. 132p. per. *(978-1-4068-3665-3(6))* Echo Library.

Button, Mark. Finding Ti Ming & Tem Po: Legend of the Golf Gods. 2011. 208p. (gr. 12-15). 27.99 *(978-1-4685-0149-0(6))* AuthorHouse.

Captain Awesome Gets a Hole-In-One. 2014. (Captain Awesome Ser.: 12). (ENG., Illus.). 128p. (J). (gr. k-4). pap. 5.99 *(978-1-4814-1431-9(3)*, Little Simon) Little Simon.

Christopher, Matt. Fairway Phenom. 2005. (Sports Classics IV Ser.). 135p. (J). lib. bdg. 15.00 *(978-1-59054-756-4(X))* Fitzgerald Bks.

—Fairway Phenom. 2003. (ENG.). 144p. (J). (gr. 5-8). pap. 16.99 *(978-0-316-07551-0(5))* Little, Brown Bks. for Young Readers.

—Fairway Phenom. 2003. (Matt Christopher Sports Bio Bookshelf Ser.). 132p. (J). (gr. 4-7). 12.65 *(978-0-7569-1605-3(4))* Perfection Learning Corp.

Clover. Groundhogs & Golfers. 2011. 24p. pap. 11.50 *(978-1-4634-2909-6(6))* AuthorHouse.

Cochran, Randy. Critter Golf: The Adventures at Owl's Nest. 2013. (ENG.). 84p. (YA). pap. 8.95 *(978-1-4787-1263-3(5))* Outskirts Pr., Inc.

—Critter Golf II: Chaos at Owl's Nest. 2013. 148p. pap. 10.95 *(978-1-4787-0302-0(4))* Outskirts Pr., Inc.

Eugenio, Johnny. Lil' Jordan's 9 Holes of Fear. 2009. (Illus.). 32p. (J). (gr. -1). 16.95 *(978-1-60747-703-7(3))* Phoenix Bks., Inc.

—Lil Jordan's 9 Holes of Fear. 2009. 48p. (J). 11.95 *(978-1-60747-706-8(8))* Phoenix Bks., Inc.

Frashier, Giva. Bogey the Golf Bug. 2013. 36p. pap. 15.99 *(978-1-4808-0126-4(7))* Archway Publishing.

grunion. The Adventures of Poppy the Golf Ball. 2003. (J). pap. 9.00 *(978-0-8059-6441-7(X))* Dorrance Publishing Co., Inc.

Gutman, Dan. The Million Dollar Putt. 2007. 69p. (J). (gr. 3-7). 13.65 *(978-0-7569-8281-2(2))* Perfection Learning Corp.

Henkes, Kevin. Two under Par. Henkes, Kevin, illus. 2005. (ENG., Illus.). 128p. (J). (gr. 3-7). pap. 5.99 *(978-0-06-075695-6(0)*, Greenwillow Bks.) HarperCollins Pubs.

Henry, Chaz. St. Mulligan & the History of Golf. 2nd I.t. ed. 2003. (Illus.). 26p. (J). 21.95 *(978-0-9725355-1-9(9)*, 1) Newtonian Golf & Particle Physics, Inc.

Hillert, Margaret. Dear Dragon Gets a Hole-In-One. Pullan, Jack, illus. 2015. (BeginningtoRead Ser.). (ENG.). 32p. (J). (gr. k-2). pap. 11.94 *(978-1-60357-790-8(4))*; lib. bdg. 22.60 *(978-1-59953-705-4(2))* Norwood Hse. Pr.

Horowitz, Jeanine. My First Playing Lesson. I.t. ed. 2006. (Illus.). 32p. (J). lib. bdg. *(978-1-934190-04-3(7))* Ocean Front Bk. Publishing, Inc.

Howling, Eric. Drive, 1 vol. 2008. (Lorimer Sports Stories Ser.). (ENG.). 120p. (J). (gr. 4-8). 9.95 *(978-1-55277-009-2(5)*, 9781552770092); 16.95 *(978-1-55277-010-8(9)*, 9781552770108) Lorimer, James & Co., Ltd., Pubs. CAN. Dist: Casemate Pubs. & Bk. Distributors, LLC.

Jerome, Kate Boehm. Miniature Golf Madness. 2005. (Illus.). 32p. (J). 15.95 *(978-0-9769087-3-9(5))* Vertical Connect Pr.

Lawson, Jessica. Waiting for Augusta. 2016. (ENG., Illus.). 336p. (J). (gr. 3-7). 16.99 *(978-1-4814-4839-0(0)*, Simon & Schuster Bks. For Young Readers) Simon & Schuster Bks. For Young Readers.

Lawson-Williams, BerNadette. Blossom Bee's Golf Adventures. 2008. 76p. pap. 24.95 *(978-1-4327-0874-0(0))* Outskirts Pr., Inc.

London, Jonathan. Froggy's Day with Dad. Remkiewicz, Frank, illus. 2006. (Froggy Ser.). (ENG.). 32p. (J). (gr. -1-k). pap. 6.99 *(978-0-14-240634-2(1)*, Puffin Books) Penguin Young Readers Group.

LuckySports, illus. Adventures in SportsLand - the Golf Bully (with accompanying CD) The Golf Bully. LuckySports, . 2008. 32p. (J). pap. 19.95 *(978-0-935938-29-6(X))* Stogo, Malcolm Assocs.

Luper, Eric. Seth Baumgartner's Love Manifesto. 2010. (ENG.). 304p. (YA). (gr. 8-18). 16.99 *(978-0-06-182753-2(3))* HarperCollins Pubs.

Marsh, Carole. The Gargoyle Golf Course. 2006. 64p. (gr. 2-4). 14.95 *(978-0-635-06220-8(8))*; pap. 3.99 *(978-0-635-06214-7(3))* Gallopade International.

Mueller, Stephen R. Hermie & Bernie, 1 vol. 2009. 124p. pap. 19.95 *(978-1-4489-1813-3(8))* PublishAmerica, Inc.

Reichman, Justin. The Green. 2005. (Dream Ser.: Vol. 9). 150p. (gr. 3-8). pap. 9.95 *(978-0-9708992-9-3(7))* Scobre Pr. Corp.

Rey, H. A. & Rey, Margret. Plays Mini Golf. 2008. (Curious George Ser.). (ENG., Illus.). 24p. (J). (gr. -1-3). pap. 3.99 *(978-0-618-99986-6(8))* Houghton Mifflin Harcourt Publishing Co.

Routley, Becky. Moon Golf. 2009. (Illus.). 28p. pap. 12.49 *(978-1-4490-4713-9(0))* AuthorHouse.

Turner, Christina S. Chip Tees Off! 2008. (Illus.). 32p. (gr. -1-1). 16.95 *(978-0-9790347-1-8(X))* Mackenzie Smiles, LLC.

Villar Liebana, Luisa & Villar Liébana, Luisa. Misterio en el Campo de Golf. 2005. (Investigator Big Ears Ser.). (SPA., Illus.). 78p. (J). (gr. 2-3). 8.95 *(978-84-348-9424-2(6))* SM Ediciones ESP. Dist: Iaconi, Mariuccia Bk. Imports.

Wilson, Kris E. & Maurer, Toby. How Putter Learned His ABC's: An alphabet Book for Your Littlest Golfer. 2010. 17.00 *(978-0-578-05153-6(2))* Sandy Putter Pr.

GOOD AND EVIL

Dorling Kindersley Publishing Staff. Marvel Good vs Evil. 2016. (Ultimate Sticker Collections). (ENG.). 96p. (J). (gr. 1-4). pap. 12.99 *(978-1-4654-5159-0(5)*, DK Children) Dorling Kindersley Publishing, Inc.

Kahn, doc, Robert. Bobby & Mandee's Good Touch/Bad Touch: Children's Safety Book. Hardie, Chris, illus. 2011. (ENG.). 25p. pap. 6.95 *(978-1-935274-54-4(6))* Future Horizons, Inc.

Smith, L. J. & Clark, Aubrey. Unseen, 0 vols. 2013. (Vampire Diaries: the Salvation Ser.: 1). (ENG.). 306p. (YA). (gr. 7-9). pap. 9.99 *(978-1-4778-0967-9(8)*, 9781477809679, 47North) Amazon Publishing.

GOOD AND EVIL—FICTION

A. L. O. E. The Triumph over Midian. 2006. 344p. per. 23.99 *(978-1-4255-3466-0(X))* Michigan Publishing.

Abedi, C. J. Fae. 2013. (Fae Ser.: 1). (ENG.). 348p. pap. 16.99 *(978-1-62681-161-4(X))* Diversion Publishing Corp.

Adornetto, Alexandra. Halo. 2010. (Halo Trilogy Ser.: 1). (ENG.). 496p. (YA). (gr. 7-12). 16.99 *(978-0-312-65626-3(2))* Feiwel & Friends.

—Halo. 2011. (Halo Trilogy Ser.: 1). (ENG.). 512p. (YA). (gr. 7-12). pap. 10.99 *(978-0-312-67436-6(8)*, 9780312674366) Square Fish.

—HALO. 2010. (SPA.). 416p. (YA). pap. 22.95 *(978-84-9918-173-8(2))* Roca Editorial ESP. Dist: Spanish Pubs., LLC.

—Heaven. 2013. (Halo Trilogy Ser.: 3). (ENG.). 448p. (YA). (gr. 7-12). pap. 10.99 *(978-1-250-02941-6(4)*, 9781250029416) Square Fish.

Aikawa, Yu. Dark Edge, Vol. 3. 2005. (Dark Edge Ser.). (ENG., Illus.). 200p. (YA). pap. 9.95 *(978-1-59796-030-4(6))* DrMaster Pubns. Inc.

Alexander, James W. Good - Better - Best: Classic Treatment of a Christian's Duty to the Poor. 2009. 224p. pap. 17.00 *(978-1-59925-143-1(4))* Solid Ground Christian Bks.

Alexander, Lloyd. The High King. 2006. (Chronicles of Prydain: Bk. 5). (Illus.). 253p. (gr. 3-7). 17.00 *(978-0-7569-6816-8(X))* Perfection Learning Corp.

—The High King. Wyatt, David, illus. 5th rev. ed. 2006. (Chronicles of Prydain Ser.: 5). (ENG.). 272p. (J). (gr. 3-7). pap. 7.99 *(978-0-8050-8052-0(X)*, 9780805080520) Square Fish.

Alexander, Yvonne. Adventure in Autou. 2012. 230p. pap. 15.99 *(978-1-62230-262-8(1))* Salem Author Services.

Alpert, Mark. The Siege. 2016. (Six Ser.: 2). (ENG.). 288p. (J). (gr. 6-12). 17.99 *(978-1-4926-3170-5(1)*, 9781492631705) Sourcebooks, Inc.

Altbacker, E. J. The Last Emprex. 2013. (Shark Wars Ser.: 6). (ENG.). 272p. (J). (gr. 3-7). 12.99 *(978-1-59514-544-4(3)*, Razorbill) Penguin Young Readers Group.

Alvarez, Jennifer Lynn. Starfire. 2015. (Guardian Herd Ser.: 1). (J). lib. bdg. 17.20 *(978-0-606-36951-0(1))* Turtleback Bks.

Anderson, Al. Adventures with Bingo Borden. Agora Publications Staff, tr. Kurzyca, Krystyna Emilia, illus. 2010. 77p. (J). pap. 9.50 *(978-1-887250-46-7(8))* Agora Pubns., Inc.

Anderson, John David. Minion. 2014. (ENG.). 288p. (J). (gr. 3-7). 16.99 *(978-0-06-213311-3(X)*, Walden Pond Pr.) HarperCollins Pubs.

Anderson, Trey. Jesse & Midnight. 2007. 56p. per. 16.95 *(978-1-60474-062-2(0))* America Star Bks.

Angleberger, Tom. Star Wars - Return of the Jedi: Beware the Power of the Dark Side! McCaig, Iain, illus. 2015. (ENG.). 432p. (J). (gr. 3-7). 17.99 *(978-1-4847-0913-9(6)*, Disney Lucasfilm Press) Disney Publishing Worldwide.

Applegate, K. A., pseud. The Encounter. 2011. (Animorphs Ser.: 3). (ENG.). 176p. (J). (gr. 3-7). pap. 6.99 *(978-0-545-29153-8(4)*, Scholastic Paperbacks) Scholastic, Inc.

Argenta, Joan. The Wicked Princess Torment. 2009. (Illus.). 40p. pap. 16.99 *(978-1-4389-4345-9(8))* AuthorHouse.

Argyle, Amber. Winter Queen. 2013. 256p. 21.99 *(978-0-9857394-4-7(4))* Starling Publishing.

Auerbach, Annie, adapted by. Despicable Me 2: The Junior Novel. movie tie-in ed. 2013. (ENG.). 144p. (J). (gr. 3-7). pap. 6.99 *(978-0-316-23432-0(X))* Little, Brown Bks. for Young Readers.

Baccalario, Pierdomenico. Dragon of Seas. Janeczko, Leah D., tr. from ITA. 2013. (Century Ser.: 4). (ENG.). 320p. (J). (gr. 3-7). 7.99 *(978-0-375-85798-0(2)*, Yearling) Random Hse. Children's Bks.

—The Ring of Fire. Janeczko, Leah D., tr. from ITA. 2010. (Century Ser.). (ENG., Illus.). 320p. (J). (gr. 3-7). pap. 7.99 *(978-0-375-85795-9(8)*, Yearling) Random Hse. Children's Bks.

—Star of Stone. Janeczko, Leah D., tr. 2011. (Century Ser.). (ENG.). 320p. (J). (gr. 3-7). 7.99 *(978-0-375-85796-6(6)*, Yearling) Random Hse. Children's Bks.

Baldwin, Stephen. Spirit, No. 1. Simko, Joe, illus. 2006. (ENG.). 208p. (gr. 8-12). per. 9.99 *(978-0-8054-4357-8(6))* B&H Publishing Group.

—Spirit Warriors: Number Three. 2007. (Spirit Warriors Ser.). (Illus.). 208p. (YA). per. 9.99 *(978-0-8054-4356-1(8))* B&H Publishing Group.

Baldwin, Stephen & Rosato, Bruno. Spirit Warriors: Number Two. Simko, Joe & Tidwell, Jeral, illus. 2007. (Spirit Warriors Ser.). 208p. (YA). per. 9.99 *(978-0-8054-4355-4(X))* B&H Publishing Group.

Baltazar, Art & Aureliani, Franco. Young Justice. 2013. (Young Justice Ser.). (ENG.). 32p. (gr. 2-3). 90.40 *(978-1-4342-8834-9(X))*; 180.80 *(978-1-4342-8835-6(8))* Stone Arch Bks.

Banerjee, Anjali. The Silver Spell. Fiegenshuh, Emily, illus. 2005. (Knights of the Silver Dragon Ser.: Bk. 8). 174p. (J). *(978-1-4156-1645-1(0)*, Mirrorstone) Wizards of the Coast.

Banks, Rosie. Secret Kingdom #3: Cloud Island. 2014. (Secret Kingdom Ser.: 3). (ENG.). 128p. (J). (gr. 2-5). pap. 4.99 *(978-0-545-53555-7(7)*, Scholastic Paperbacks) Scholastic, Inc.

Barichella, Thomas. The Star Snatcher's Planet. 2013. (Little Prince Ser.: 5). (ENG., Illus.). 56p. (J). (gr. 4-8). pap. 7.95 *(978-1-4677-0737-4(6)*, Graphic Universe™) Lerner Publishing Group.

Barron, T. A. Ultimate Magic, 8 vols., Bk. 8. 2011. (Merlin Saga Ser.: 8). (ENG.). 256p. (J). (gr. 5-18). 8.99 *(978-0-14-241926-7(5)*, Puffin Books) Penguin Young Readers Group.

Batterson, Mark & Clark, Joel N. Jack Staples & the City of Shadows. 2015. (ENG.). 256p. (J). pap. 9.99 *(978-0-7814-1108-0(4))* Cook, David C.

Batterson, Mark, et al. Jack Staples & the Ring of Time. 2014. (ENG.). 240p. (J). pap. 9.99 *(978-0-7814-1107-3(6))* Cook, David C.

Beakman, Onk. The Mask of Power: Eruptor Meets the Nightmare King. Geremia, Daniela, illus. 2016. 157p. (J). ***(978-1-5182-2804-9(6)**, Grosset & Dunlap)* Penguin Publishing Group.

Beatty, Robert. Serafina & the Black Cloak. (Serafina Ser.). (ENG.). (J). (gr. 3-7). 2016. 320p. pap. 7.99 *(978-1-4847-1187-3(4))* 2015. 304p. 16.99 *(978-1-4847-0901-6(2))* Hyperion Bks. for Children.

—Serafina & the Black Cloak. 2016. (J). lib. bdg. 18.40 *(978-0-606-38336-3(0))* Turtleback Bks.

—Serafina & the Splintered Heart. 2017. (Serafina Ser.: bk.3). (ENG.). 368p. (J). (gr. 3-7). 16.99 ***(978-1-4847-7504-2(X))*** Hyperion Bks. for Children.

—Serafina & the Twisted Staff. (Serafina Ser.). (ENG.). (J). (gr. 3-7). 2017. 400p. pap. 7.99 ***(978-1-4847-7806-7(5))*** 2016. 384p. 16.99 *(978-1-4847-7503-5(1))* Hyperion Bks. for Children.

—Serafina & the Twisted Staff. 2017. (J). lib. bdg. 18.40 ***(978-0-606-39977-7(1))*** Turtleback Bks.

Becker-Doyle, Eve & Doyle, Evan Brain. Evan Brain's Christmas List & Other Shenanigans: Boy Warrior Fights Evil. Doyle, Evan Brain, illus. 2008. (ENG., Illus.). 64p. pap. 15.95 *(978-0-9794716-3-6(X))* BDA Publishing.

Beckham, David. Charlie Barker & the Secret of the Deep Dark Woods. 2006. 570p. pap. 33.20 *(978-1-4120-9264-7(7))* Trafford Publishing.

Beechen, Adam. Justice League Unlimited. 2013. (Justice League Unlimited Ser.). (ENG.). 32p. (gr. 2-3). 90.40 *(978-1-4342-3936-5(5))* Stone Arch Bks.

Beecroft, Simon. Stand Aside-Bounty Hunters! 2009. (Star Wars: the Clone Wars DK Readers Ser.). lib. bdg. 13.55 *(978-0-606-07065-2(6)*, Turtleback) Turtleback Bks.

Beeton, Abigail. A Pastor's Predicament. 2011. 42p. pap. 16.95 *(978-1-4560-6605-5(6))* America Star Bks.

Behruzi, Gulrukh. Mohan the Mynah, 1 vol. 2010. 26p. pap. 24.95 *(978-1-4489-6408-6(3))* PublishAmerica, Inc.

Beil, Michael D. Agents of the Glass: a New Recruit. 2016. (ENG.). 400p. (J). (gr. 4-7). 16.99 *(978-0-385-75321-0(7)*, Knopf Bks. for Young Readers) Random Hse. Children's Bks.

Beiler, Joyce. The Kingdom of Laughter. 2012. 30p. pap. 13.95 *(978-1-4497-6596-5(3)*, WestBow Pr.) Author Solutions, Inc.

Bell, Sophie. Lilac Attack! 2014. (Ultra Violets Ser.: 3). (ENG., Illus.). 304p. (J). (gr. 3-7). 12.99 *(978-1-59514-648-9(2)*, Razorbill) Penguin Young Readers Group.

—Power to the Purple! Battle, Christina, illus. 2013. (Ultra Violets Ser.: 2). (ENG.). 336p. (J). (gr. 3-7). 12.99 *(978-1-59514-647-2(4)*, Razorbill) Penguin Young Readers Group.

Benedetti, Hervé & Robin, Nicolas. The Planet of the Tortoise Driver. Elyum Studio Staff, illus. 2013. (Little Prince Ser.: 8). (ENG.). 56p. (J). (gr. 4-8). pap. 7.95 *(978-1-4677-0740-4(6)*, Graphic Universe™) Lerner Publishing Group.

Benz, Derek & Lewis, J. S. The Brimstone Key. 2011. (Grey Griffins: the Clockwork Chronicles Ser.: 1). (ENG.). 400p. (J). (gr. 3-7). pap. 22.99 *(978-0-316-04521-6(7))* Little, Brown Bks. for Young Readers.

—The Brimstone Key Bk. 1. 2010. (Grey Griffins: the Clockwork Chronicles Ser.: 1). (ENG., Illus.). 384p. (J). (gr. 3-7). 15.99 *(978-0-316-04522-3(5))* Little, Brown Bks. for Young Readers.

Bishop, Jennie. The Squire & the Scroll: A Tale of the Rewards of a Pure Heart. McDaniels, Preston, illus. 2009. (ENG.). 32p. (J). 15.99 (978-1-59317-382-1(2)) Warner Pr., Inc.

Bishop, Karen C. The Christmas Lantern. Donahue, Jim, illus. 2008. 32p. (J). (978-0-615-20131-3(8)) Three River Rambler.

Blabey, Aaron. The Bad Guys. 2016. (Bad Guys Ser.: 1). lib. bdg. 16.00 **(978-0-606-40039-8(7))** Turtleback Bks.

Black, Chuck. Lady Carliss & the Waters of Moorue. 2010. (Knights of Arrethtrae Ser.). (ENG.). 208p. (YA). (gr. 5-7). pap. 9.99 (978-1-60142-127-2(3), Multnomah Bks.) Crown Publishing Group.

—The Light of the Last, Bk. 3. 2016. (Wars of the Realm Ser.). (ENG.). 368p. (YA). (gr. 7). pap. 11.99 (978-1-60142-506-5(6), Multnomah Bks.) Crown Publishing Group.

—Rise of the Fallen: Wars of the Realm, Book 2. 2015. (Wars of the Realm Ser.). (ENG.). 320p. (YA). (gr. 7). pap. 11.99 (978-1-60142-504-1(X), Multnomah Bks.) Crown Publishing Group.

—Sir Dalton & the Shadow Heart. 2009. (Knights of Arrethtrae Ser.). (ENG., Illus.). 176p. (YA). (gr. 7-9). pap. 9.99 (978-1-60142-126-5(5), Multnomah Bks.) Crown Publishing Group.

—Sir Quinlan & the Swords of Valor. 2010. (Knights of Arrethtrae Ser.). (ENG., Illus.). 208p. (YA). (gr. 4-7). pap. 9.99 (978-1-60142-128-9(1), Multnomah) Doubleday Religious Publishing Group, The.

Black, Holly & Clare, Cassandra. The Bronze Key. 2016. (Magisterium Ser.: 3). (ENG., Illus.). 256p. (J). (gr. 3-7). 17.99 (978-0-545-52231-1(5), Scholastic Pr.) Scholastic, Inc.

Black, Jake. Batman Classic: Coin Toss. Tong, Andie, illus. 2016. 24p. (J). (gr. -1-3). pap. 3.99 (978-0-06-234491-5(9), HarperFestival) HarperCollins Pubs.

—Coin Toss. 2016. (Batman 8X8 Storybooks Ser.). (J). lib. bdg. 13.55 (978-0-606-38197-0(X)) Turtleback Bks.

Blackman, Haden & Caldwell, Ben. Star Wars: Clone Wars Adventures, 1 vol. 2012. (Star Wars Digests Ser.). (ENG., Illus.). 96p. (J). (gr. 4-7). 27.07 (978-1-59961-904-0(0)) Spotlight.

Blackman, Haden & The Fillbach Brothers. Star Wars: Clone Wars Adventures, 1 vol. 2012. (Star Wars Digests Ser.). (ENG., Illus.). 96p. (J). (gr. 4-7). 27.07 (978-1-59961-906-4(7)); 27.07 (978-1-59961-905-7(9)) Spotlight.

Blade, Adam. Deep Dive #4: Kraya the Blood Shark. 2013. (Deep Dive Ser.: 4). (ENG.). 128p. (J). (gr. 2-5). pap. 4.99 (978-0-545-42770-8(3), Scholastic Paperbacks) Scholastic, Inc.

Blaha-Black, Caroline. Anika & the Magic Top. 2008. 60p. pap. 11.95 (978-1-4357-1194-5(7)) Lulu Pr., Inc.

Blomfield, Alan. The Pendant of Epoch. 2008. 128p. (978-1-86950-714-5(2)) HarperCollins Pubs. Australia.

Blythe, Daniel. Shadow Breakers. 2013. (J). (978-0-545-47980-6(0)); (ENG.). 256p. (gr. 5-9). 16.99 (978-0-545-47979-0(7)) Scholastic, Inc. (Chicken Hse., The).

Boles Levy, Anne. The Temple of Doubt. 2015. (Temple of Doubt Ser.). (ENG., Illus.). 316p. (J). (gr. 6). 16.99 (978-1-63220-427-1(4), Sky Pony Pr.) Skyhorse Publishing Co., Inc.

—The Well of Prayers. 2016. (Temple of Doubt Ser.). (ENG., Illus.). 364p. (J). (gr. 6). 17.99 (978-1-63450-193-4(4), Sky Pony Pr.) Skyhorse Publishing Co., Inc.

Bowyer, Clifford B. The Darkness Within: The Imperium Saga: the Adventures of Kyria, 12 vols., Vol. 9. Brigman, June, illus. 2009. (Imperium Saga: 9). (ENG.). (J). 5.99 (978-0-9787782-4-8(3)) Silver Leaf Bks., LLC.

Bracken, Alexandra. Star Wars - A New Hope: The Princess, the Scoundrel, & the Farm Boy. McCaig, Iain, illus. 2015. (ENG.). 336p. (J). (gr. 3-7). 17.99 (978-1-4847-0912-2(8), 1384321, Disney Lucasfilm Press) Disney Publishing Worldwide.

Bramlett, Timothy A. Sharkey Explores the Unknown. 2007. pap. 14.95 (978-0-9796444-0-5(2)) Azuria Bks.

Bridges, Robin. The Katerina Trilogy, Vol. I: the Gathering Storm. 2012. (ENG.). 400p. (YA). (gr. 7). pap. 9.99 (978-0-385-74023-4(9), Ember) Random Hse. Children's Bks.

Briggs, Andy. Council of Evil. 2009. 1.00 (978-1-4074-4313-3(5)) Recorded Bks., Inc.

Brindley, John. The Rule of Claw. Benfold Haywood, Ian P., illus. 2009. (Exceptional Reading & Language Arts Titles for Intermediate Grades Ser.). (ENG.). 408p. (YA). (gr. 7-12). 18.95 (978-1-58013-608-2(7)) Lerner Publishing Group.

Britten, Adam. Captain Valiant & Me. Hamer, Arthur, illus. 2014. (Captain Valiant Ser.). (ENG.). 160p. (J). (gr. k-3). pap. 9.99 (978-1-84812-353-3(1)) Bonnier Publishing GBR. Dist: Independent Pubs. Group.

Broich, Erin. The Guardians of Light, Book: The Betrayer. 2007. 272p. 29.99 (978-1-4251-5733-3(5)) Trafford Publishing.

Burns, Jason M. Megamind: Bad, Blue, Brilliant. 2011. (ENG., Illus.). 52p. pap. 6.95 (978-1-936340-49-1(6), 9781936340491) Ape Entertainment.

Caballero, Erica. Mount Mole. 2006. pap. 10.00 (978-1-4257-2301-9(2)) Xlibris Corp.

Calonita, Jen. Flunked. 2015. (Fairy Tale Reform School Ser.: 1). (ENG.). 256p. (J). (gr. 5-8). 15.99 (978-1-4926-0156-2(X), 9781492601562, Sourcebooks Jabberwocky) Sourcebooks, Inc.

Cann, Kate. Consumed. (ENG.). 336p. (J). (gr. 9). 2012. pap. 9.99 (978-0-545-26387-0(5)) 2011. 16.99 (978-0-545-26388-7(3)) Scholastic, Inc.

—Possessed. (ENG.). 336p. (J). (gr. 9-9). 2011. pap. 9.99 (978-0-545-12813-1(7)) 2010. 16.99 (978-0-545-12812-4(9)) Scholastic, Inc.

Cappoccia, Héloïse. The Planet of the Overhearers. 2013. (Little Prince Ser.: 7). (ENG., Illus.). 56p. (J). (gr. 4-8). pap. 7.95 (978-1-4677-0739-8(2), Graphic Universe™) Lerner Publishing Group.

Cascone, Annette & Cascone, Gina. The Witching Game. 2012. (Deadtime Stories Ser.: 2). (ENG.). 192p. (J). (gr. 3-7). mass mkt. 5.99 (978-0-7653-6972-7(9), 9780765369727, Starscape) Doherty, Tom Assocs., LLC.

Cast, P. C. & Cast, Kristin. Hunted. (House of Night Novels Ser.: 5). (ENG.). 336p. (YA). (gr. 7-12). 2013. mass mkt. 9.99 (978-1-250-04696-3(3), 9781250046963, St. Martin's Paperbacks) 2010. pap. 10.99 (978-0-312-57799-5(0), 9780312577995, St. Martin's Griffin) St. Martin's Pr.

—Hunted. l.t. ed. 2010. (House of Night Ser.: Bk. 5). (ENG.). 548p. 23.95 (978-1-4104-1951-4(7)) Thorndike Pr.

—Redeemed: A House of Night Novel. 2014. (YA). (978-1-250-05952-9(6)); (House of Night Ser.: Vol. 12). (ENG.). 320p. (gr. 7-12). 18.99 (978-0-312-59444-2(5), 9780312594442, St. Martin's Griffin) St. Martin's Pr.

—Tempted. 2013. (House of Night Novels Ser.: 6). (ENG.). 352p. (YA). (gr. 7-12). mass mkt. 9.99 (978-1-250-04698-7(X), 9781250046987, St. Martin's Paperbacks) St. Martin's Pr.

Catmull, Katherine. The Radiant Road. 2016. (ENG.). 368p. (YA). (gr. 7). 17.99 (978-0-525-95347-0(7), Dutton Books for Young Readers) Penguin Young Readers Group.

Chainani, Soman. The Last Ever After. Bruno, Iacopo, illus. 2015. 655p. (J). (978-0-06-241756-5(8)) Harper & Row Ltd.

—The Last Ever After. (School for Good & Evil Ser.: 3). (J). (gr. 3-7). 2016. 704p. pap. 7.99 (978-0-06-210496-0(9)) 2015. 672p. pap. 9.99 (978-0-06-239625-9(0)) 2015. (ENG., Illus.). 672p. 17.99 (978-0-06-210495-3(0)) HarperCollins Pubs.

—The School for Good & Evil. (School for Good & Evil Ser.). (J). (gr. 3). 2016. 1760p. pap. 23.97 (978-0-06-245624-3(5)) 2015. (ENG.). 1334p. 53.97 (978-0-06-243497-5(7)) HarperCollins Pubs.

—The School for Good & Evil. Bruno, Iacopo, illus. (ENG.). (J). (gr. 3-7). 2014. (School for Good & Evil Ser.: 1). 544p. pap. 7.99 (978-0-06-210490-8(X)) 2013. (School for Good & Evil Trilogy: No. 1). 400p. 17.99 (978-0-06-210489-2(6)) HarperCollins Pubs.

—The School for Good & Evil. Bruno, Iacopo, illus. 2014. (School for Good & Evil Ser.: 1). 496p. (J). lib. bdg. 17.20 (978-0-606-36513-0(3)) Turtleback Bks.

—The School for Good & Evil #4: Quests for Glory. 2017. (School for Good & Evil Ser.: 4). 576p. (J). (gr. 3-7). 17.99 **(978-0-06-265847-0(6))** HarperCollins Pubs.

Chainani, Soman. A World Without Princes. 2014. (School for Good & Evil Trilogy: No. 2). 448p. (J). pap. (978-0-06-233135-9(3)) Harper & Row Ltd.

—A World Without Princes. Bruno, Iacopo, illus. 2014. (School for Good & Evil Trilogy: No. 2). (ENG.). 400p. (J). (978-0-06-234072-6(7)) Harper & Row Ltd.

—A World Without Princes. Bruno, Iacopo, illus. 2015. (School for Good & Evil Ser.: 2). (ENG.). 512p. (J). (gr. 3-7). pap. 7.99 (978-0-06-210493-9(4)) HarperCollins Pubs.

—A World Without Princes. 2014. (School for Good & Evil Trilogy: No. 2). (ENG., Illus.). 448p. (J). (gr. 3-7). 17.99 (978-0-06-210492-2(6)) HarperCollins Pubs.

—A World Without Princes. 2015. (School for Good & Evil Ser.: 2). (J). lib. bdg. 17.20 (978-0-606-36514-7(1)) Turtleback Bks.

Chandler, Elizabeth. The Deep End of Fear. 2008. (Dark Secrets Ser.: 4). (ENG.). 320p. (J). (gr. 7). pap. 13.99 (978-1-4169-7142-9(4), Simon Pulse) Simon Pulse.

Cheasebro, Margaret. The Healing Tree. 2015. (ENG.). 304p. (YA). 15.95 (978-1-937240-60-8(6)) Casa de Snapdragon LLC.

Chupeco, Rin. The Suffering. 2015. (ENG.). 320p. (YA). (gr. 8-12). 16.99 (978-1-4926-2983-2(9), 9781492629832) Sourcebooks, Inc.

Clayton, Emma. The Whisper. 2012. 309p. (978-0-545-43365-5(7), Chicken Hse., The) Scholastic, Inc.

Cochran, Molly. Legacy. (Legacy Ser.). (ENG.). (YA). (gr. 9). 2012. 448p. pap. 9.99 (978-1-4424-1740-3(4)) 2011. 432p. 17.99 (978-1-4424-1739-7(0)) Simon & Schuster/Paula Wiseman Bks. (Simon & Schuster/Paula Wiseman Bks.).

—Poison. (Legacy Ser.). (ENG., 368p. (YA). (gr. 9). 2014. Illus.). pap. 9.99 (978-1-4424-5051-6(7)) 2012. 17.99 (978-1-4424-5050-9(9)) Simon & Schuster/Paula Wiseman Bks. (Simon & Schuster/Paula Wiseman Bks.).

Cody, Matthew. The Dead Gentleman. 2012. (ENG.). 288p. (J). (gr. 5). 6.99 (978-0-375-84490-4(2), Yearling) Random Hse. Children's Bks.

Connolly, John. The Gates. 2009. (ENG.). 304p. 24.00 (978-1-4391-7263-6(3), Beyond Words/Atria Bks.) Atria Bks.

—The Gates. 2011. (Samuel Lord Ser.: 1). (ENG.). 320p. (J). (gr. 5-9). pap. 8.99 (978-1-4424-2933-8(X), Simon & Schuster Bks. For Young Readers) Simon & Schuster Bks. For Young Readers.

Coons, Timothy A. School of Chaos, 1 vol. 2010. 74p. pap. 19.95 (978-1-4512-9345-6(3)) America Star Bks.

Cooper, Susan. The Dark Is Rising. 2009. 10.36 (978-0-7848-3502-9(0), Everbind) Marco Bk. Co.

—The Dark Is Rising. 2007. (YA). 1.25 (978-1-4193-7923-9(2)) Recorded Bks., Inc.

Cordova, Sarah. Arch Angel, 1 vol. 2010. 220p. pap. 24.95 (978-1-4489-9778-7(X)) America Star Bks.

Cormier, Shawn P. NiDemon. 2005. (YA). per. 12.95 (978-0-9740151-1-8(3)) Pine View Pr.

Corwin, Susan Simon. The Cryptic Cat. Corwin, Stuart, illus. 2006. 99p. (YA). (978-0-9790632-0-6(5)) Lucky Duck Designs.

Courtauld, Sarah & Burniac, Lauren. The Perilous Princess Plot. 2015. (Buckle & Squash Ser.). (ENG., Illus.). 192p. (J). (gr. 2-5). 14.99 (978-1-250-05277-3(7), 9781250052773) Feiwel & Friends.

Cox, Greg. Riese: Kingdom Falling. 2013. (ENG., Illus.). 288p. (YA). (gr. 7). pap. 9.99 (978-1-4424-2970-3(4), Simon & Schuster Bks. For Young Readers) Simon & Schuster Bks. For Young Readers.

Curley, Marianne. Key. 2011. (Guardians of Time Ser.). (ENG.). 416p. (YA). (gr. 7). pap. 9.99 (978-1-59990-545-7(0), 9781599905457, Bloomsbury USA Childrens) Bloomsbury Publishing USA.

Curry, Kenneth. The Return of Gamalok: The Return of Gamalok. 2007. (Illus.). 83p. (J). per. 12.95 (978-0-9798364-2-8(5)) Curry Brothers Publishing Group.

Dahl, Michael. Alien Snow, 1 vol. Glass House Graphics Staff, illus. 2011. (Good vs Evil Ser.). (ENG.). 48p. (gr. 1-2). pap. 6.29 (978-1-4342-3444-5(4), Good vs Evil) Stone Arch Bks.

—Dungeon of Seven Dooms, 1 vol. 2011. (Good vs Evil Ser.). (ENG.). 48p. (gr. 1-2). lib. bdg. 23.99 (978-1-4342-2091-2(5), Good vs Evil) Stone Arch Bks.

Daniel, Tony. The Amber Arrow. 2017. (Wulf's Saga Ser.: 2). (ENG.). 416p. (J). (gr. 8-8). 18.99 **(978-1-4814-8253-0(X))** Baen Bks.

Davidson, Danica. Battle with the Wither: An Unofficial Overworld Adventure, Book Six. 2016. (Unofficial Overworld Adventure Ser.). (ENG.). 112p. (J). (gr. 1-7). pap. 7.99 (978-1-5107-1621-6(1), Sky Pony Pr.) Skyhorse Publishing Co., Inc.

Davies, Jocelyn. A Beautiful Dark. 2012. (ENG.). 416p. (YA). (gr. 8). pap. 9.99 (978-0-06-199066-3(3), HarperTeen) HarperCollins Pubs.

—A Fractured Light. 2013. (ENG.). 368p. (YA). (gr. 8). pap. 9.99 (978-0-06-199068-7(X), HarperTeen) HarperCollins Pubs.

—A Radiant Sky. 2014. (ENG.). 384p. (YA). (gr. 8). pap. 9.99 (978-0-06-199070-0(1), HarperTeen) HarperCollins Pubs.

DC Comics. Teen Titans Go! - Team Up! 2017. (Passport to Reading Level 2 Ser.). (ENG., Illus.). 192p. (J). (gr. -1-3). 9.99 **(978-0-316-54857-1(X))**; pap. 8.99 **(978-0-316-54847-2(2))** Little, Brown Bks. for Young Readers.

DC Super Friends. 2013. (DC Super Friends Ser.). (ENG.). 32p. (gr. 1-2). 180.80 (978-1-4342-4856-5(9)) Stone Arch Bks.

De la Cruz, Melissa. The Isle of the Lost. (Descendants Ser.). (ENG.). (J). 2017. 336p. (gr. 4-7). pap. 9.99 **(978-1-4847-2544-3(1))** 2015. 320p. (gr. 4-7). 17.99 (978-1-4847-2097-4(0))Set. 2017. 960p. (gr. 3-7). 47.99 **(978-1-368-01423-6(2))** Hyperion Bks. for Children.

Disney Book Group. Star Wars: The Original Trilogy Stories. 2015. (Storybook Collection). (ENG.). 304p. (J). (gr. -1-k). 16.99 (978-1-4847-0471-4(1), Disney Lucasfilm Press) Disney Publishing Worldwide.

Disney Book Group. Trapped in the Death Star! 2016. (Star Wars: World of Reading Ser.). (J). lib. bdg. 14.75 **(978-0-606-39174-0(6))** Turtleback Bks.

Disney Book Group & Rucka, Greg. Guardians of the Whills. 2017. (ENG.). 240p. (J). (gr. 5-9). 12.99 (978-1-4847-8081-7(7), Disney Lucasfilm Press) Disney Publishing Worldwide.

Disney Book Group Staff, et al. The Avengers. 2015. (Beginnings Ser.). (ENG.). 48p. (J). (gr. 1-3). 12.99 (978-1-4847-1382-2(6), Marvel Pr.) Disney Publishing Worldwide.

d'Lacey, Chris. Dark Fire. (Last Dragon Chronicles Ser.: 5). (ENG.). 576p. (J). (gr. 3-7). 2011. pap. 8.99 (978-0-545-10273-5(1)) 2010. 17.99 (978-0-545-10272-8(3), Orchard Bks.) Scholastic, Inc.

—Fire World. 2012. (Last Dragon Chronicles Ser.: 6). lib. bdg. 19.65 (978-0-606-23967-7(7), Turtleback) Turtleback Bks.

d'Lacey, Jay & d'Lacey, Chris. Rain & Fire. 2012. (Last Dragon Chronicles Ser.). (ENG.). 304p. (J). (gr. 3-7). 16.99 (978-0-545-41453-1(9), Orchard Bks.) Scholastic, Inc.

Donnelly, Jennifer. Dark Tide. 2015. (Waterfire Saga Ser.: Bk. 3). (ENG.). 400p. (YA). (gr. 7-12). 17.99 (978-1-4231-8201-6(4)) Hyperion Bks. for Children.

—Deep Blue. 2014. (Waterfire Saga Novel Ser.: Bk. 1). (ENG., Illus.). 352p. (YA). (gr. 7-12). 17.99 (978-1-4231-3316-2(1)) Disney Pr.

—Deep Blue. 2015. (Waterfire Saga Ser.: Bk. 1). (ENG.). 368p. (YA). (gr. 7-12). pap. 9.99 (978-1-4847-1310-5(9)) Hyperion Bks. for Children.

—Rogue Wave. 2015. (Waterfire Saga Novel Ser.: Bk. 2). (ENG.). 320p. (YA). (gr. 7-12). 17.99 (978-1-4231-8200-9(6)) Disney Pr.

—Rogue Wave. 2016. (Waterfire Saga Ser.: Bk. 2). (ENG.). 336p. (YA). (gr. 7-12). pap. 9.99 (978-1-4847-1301-3(X)) Hyperion Bks. for Children.

—Waterfire Saga, Book Four: Sea Spell. 2016. (Waterfire Saga Novel Ser.). (ENG.). 368p. (YA). (gr. 7-12). 17.99 (978-1-4847-1290-0(0)) Hyperion Bks. for Children.

—Waterfire Saga, Book Four Sea Spell. 2017. (Waterfire Saga Ser.). (ENG.). 368p. (YA). (gr. 7-12). pap. 9.99 **(978-1-4847-1303-7(6))** Hyperion Bks. for Children.

Donnelly, Jennifer. Waterfire Saga, Book Three Dark Tide. 2016. (Waterfire Saga Ser.). (ENG.). 416p. (YA). (gr. 7-12). pap. 9.99 (978-1-4847-1302-0(8)) Hyperion Bks. for Children.

Dorling Kindersley Publishing Staff. Attack of the Clones. 2013. (LEGO Star Wars DK Reader Ser.). lib. bdg. 13.55 (978-0-606-32111-2(X), Turtleback) Turtleback Bks.

—DK Adventures: Star Wars: Sith Wars: Star Wars: Sith Wars. 2013. (DK Adventures Ser.). (ENG., Illus.). 128p. (J). (gr. 3-7). 16.99 (978-1-4654-1814-2(8), DK Children) Dorling Kindersley Publishing, Inc.

—Secret Ninja Force. 2017. (DK Readers Ser.). (ENG.). 48p. (J). (gr. k-2). pap. 3.99 **(978-1-4654-6195-7(7)**, DK Children) Dorling Kindersley Publishing, Inc.

—Shark Attack! 2017. (DK Readers Ser.). (ENG.). 24p. (J). (-k). pap. 3.99 **(978-1-4654-6193-3(0)**, DK Children) Dorling Kindersley Publishing, Inc.

Dorling Kindersley Publishing Staff. Sith Wars. 2013. (DK Adventures Ser.). (ENG., Illus.). 128p. (J). (gr. 3-7). pap. 5.99 (978-1-4654-1725-1(7), DK Children) Dorling Kindersley Publishing, Inc.

Doyle, Malachy. Long Gray Norris. 2006. (Yellow Bananas Ser.). (ENG., Illus.). 48p. (J). (gr. -1-3). lib. bdg. (978-0-7787-0956-5(6)) Crabtree Publishing Co.

Edison, Richard E. Trouble on the Blue Planet. Santillan, Mariano, illus. 2012. 47p. (J). 4.99 (978-0-8280-2655-0(6)) Review & Herald Publishing Assn.

Egan, Catherine. Shade & Sorceress Bk. 1: The Last Days of Tian Di, 1 vol. 2012. (Last Days of Tian Di Ser.: 1). (ENG., Illus.). 352p. (J). (gr. 4-8). pap. 12.95 (978-1-55050-514-6(9)) Coteau Bks. CAN. Dist: Orca Bk. Pubs. USA.

Egan, Kate, adapted by. World's Apart. 2005. (W. I. T. C. H. Ser.: Bk. 14). 134p. (J). lib. bdg. 16.92 (978-1-4242-0788-6(6)) Fitzgerald Bks.

Elfgren, Sara B. & Strandberg, Mats. The Circle: The Engelsfors Trilogy — Book 1. 2013. (Engelsfors Trilogy Ser.: 1). (ENG.). 608p. (gr. 9-13). 18.99 (978-1-4683-0658-3(8), 460658) Overlook Pr., The.

—Fire: The Engelsfors Trilogy Book II. 2014. (Engelsfors Trilogy Ser.: 2). (ENG.). 704p. (gr. 9-13). 18.99 (978-1-4683-0672-9(3), 460672) Overlook Pr., The.

Ellsworth, Theo. Eyes of War. 2006. 385p. (YA). pap. 14.99 (978-0-9776114-0-9(X)) Hidden Talent Pr.

Elmer, Robert. Beyond Corista, 1 vol. 2009. (Shadowside Trilogy Ser.). (ENG.). 320p. (YA). (gr. 8-11). pap. 9.99 (978-0-310-71423-1(0)) Zondervan.

Fagan, Cary. Ten Lessons for Kaspar Snit. 2008. (ENG.). 192p. (J). (gr. 3-7). pap. 9.95 (978-0-88776-835-4(0), Tundra Bks.) Tundra Bks. CAN. Dist: Penguin Random Hse. LLC.

Farshtey, Greg. Danger in the Outlands. 2014. (LEGO Legends of Chima Chapter Bks.: 5). lib. bdg. 14.75 (978-0-606-35859-0(5)) Turtleback Bks.

Farshtey, Greg, et al. Night of the Nindroids. 2014. (Illus.). 63p. (J). (978-1-4844-1967-0(7)) Papercutz.

Ferguson, Alex. Tiggie: A Story of Good & Evil Written for Young People. 2011. 112p. 28.31 (978-1-4520-7799-4(1)); pap. 13.32 (978-1-4520-7798-7(3)) AuthorHouse.

Feuti, Norm. The King of Kazoo. 2016. (ENG.). 208p. (J). (gr. 2-5). 22.99 (978-0-545-77088-0(2), Graphix) Scholastic, Inc.

Fillbach, Brothers & The Fillbach Brothers. Star Wars: Clone Wars Adventures, 1 vol. 2012. (Star Wars Digests Ser.). (ENG., Illus.). (J). (gr. 4-7). 96p. 27.07 (978-1-59961-907-1(5)); 88p. 27.07 (978-1-59961-909-5(1)) Spotlight.

Fine, Sarah. Chaos, 0 vols. 2014. (Guards of the Shadowlands Ser.: 3). (ENG.). 368p. (J). (gr. 9-12). 17.99 (978-1-4778-4781-7(2), 9781477847817, Skyscape) Amazon Publishing.

—Fractured, 0 vols. 2013. (Guards of the Shadowlands Ser.: 2). (ENG.). 448p. (YA). (gr. 9-12). pap. 9.99 (978-1-4778-1691-2(7), 9781477816912, Amazon Children's Publishing) Amazon Publishing.

—Sanctum, 0 vols. 2014. (Guards of the Shadowlands Ser.: 1). (ENG., Illus.). 448p. (YA). (gr. 9-11). pap. 9.99 (978-1-4778-1033-0(1), 9781477810330, Skyscape) Amazon Publishing.

—Sanctum. 2012. 416p. pap. 17.99 (978-0-7614-6329-0(1)) Marshall Cavendish Corp.

Fisch, Sholly. DC Super Friends. 2013. (DC Super Friends Ser.). (ENG.). 32p. (gr. 1-2). 90.40 (978-1-4342-4855-8(0)) Stone Arch Bks.

Fisch, Sholly, et al. Through the Looking Glass! 2015. (All-New Batman: the Brave & the Bold Ser.). (ENG., Illus.). 32p. (gr. 2-3). lib. bdg. 22.60 (978-1-4342-9660-3(1)) Stone Arch Bks.

Fitzpatrick, Becca. The Complete Hush, Hush Saga: Hush, Hush; Crescendo; Silence; Finale. 2012. (Hush, Hush Saga Ser.: Bks. 1-4). (ENG.). 1744p. (YA). (gr. 9). 74.99 (978-1-4424-7372-0(X), Simon & Schuster Bks. For Young Readers) Simon & Schuster Bks. For Young Readers.

—Crescendo. 2011. (Hush, Hush Saga: Bk. 2). (SPA.). 408p. (YA). pap. 20.95 (978-84-666-4639-0(6)) Ediciones B ESP. Dist: Spanish Pubs., LLC.

—Crescendo. (Hush, Hush Saga Ser.: Bk. 2). (ENG.). (YA). (gr. 9). 2012. 464p. pap. 12.99 (978-1-4169-8944-8(7)) 2010. 432p. 18.99 (978-1-4169-8943-1(9)) Simon & Schuster Bks. For Young Readers. (Simon & Schuster Bks. For Young Readers).

—Finale. (Hush, Hush Saga Ser.). (ENG., (YA). (gr. 9). 2013. Illus.). 480p. pap. 12.99 (978-1-4424-2668-9(3)) 2012. 464p. 19.99 (978-1-4424-2667-2(5)) Simon & Schuster Bks. For Young Readers. (Simon & Schuster Bks. For Young Readers).

Flanagan, John A. The Tournament at Gorlan. 2016. (Ranger's Apprentice the Early Years Ser.: 1). lib. bdg. 19.65 (978-0-606-39332-4(3)) Turtleback Bks.

Fleming, Geronda. Among the Fairies. 2008. 149p. pap. 14.00 (978-0-615-16737-4(3)) Faye Bks.

Floreen, Tim. Tattoo Atlas. 2016. (ENG., Illus.). 384p. (YA). (gr. 9). 17.99 (978-1-4814-3280-1(X), Simon Pulse) Simon Pulse.

Flynn, Ian. Mega Man 3: Return of Dr. Wily. Bates, Ben, illus. 2012. (Mega Man Ser.: 3). (ENG.). 112p. (gr. 4-7). pap. 11.99 (978-1-936975-11-2(4), Archie Comics) Archie Comic Pubns., Inc.

—Mega Man 4: Spiritus Ex Machina. 2012. (Mega Man Ser.: 4). (ENG.). 112p. (gr. 4-7). pap. 11.99 (978-1-936975-27-3(0), Archie Comics) Archie Comic Pubns., Inc.

Foster, D. S. The Stone Heart. Lewis, Jesse, illus. 2012. (J). pap. 12.99 (978-1-937331-14-6(8)) ShadeTree Publishing, LLC.

French, Vivian. The Robe of Skulls: The First Tale from the Five Kingdoms. Collins, Ross, illus. 2009. (Tales from the Five Kingdoms Ser.: 1). (ENG.). 208p. (J). (gr. 3-7). pap. 5.99 (978-0-7636-4364-5(5)) Candlewick Pr.

Frost, Mark. Alliance: The Paladin Prophecy Book 2. 2015. (Paladin Prophecy Ser.: 2). (ENG.). 352p. (YA). (gr. 7). pap. 10.99 (978-0-375-87108-5(X), Ember) Random Hse. Children's Bks.

—The Paladin Prophecy, Bk. 1. 2014. (Paladin Prophecy Ser.). (ENG.). 528p. (YA). (gr. 7). pap. 10.99 (978-0-375-87106-1(3), Ember) Random Hse. Children's Bks.

—Rogue: The Paladin Prophecy Book 3. 2015. (Paladin Prophecy Ser.). (ENG.). 368p. (YA). (gr. 7). 17.99 (978-0-375-87047-7(4), Random Hse. Bks. for Young Readers) Random Hse. Children's Bks.

Funderburg, April. Soul Snatcher. 2009. 84p. pap. 19.95 (978-1-60749-765-3(4)) America Star Bks.

Gaiman, NEil & Reaves, Michael. Interworld. (InterWorld Trilogy Ser.: 1). (ENG.). (YA). (gr. 8). 2013. 304p. pap. 9.99 (978-0-06-212530-9(3), HarperTeen) 2008. 256p. pap. 9.99 (978-0-06-123898-7(8)) HarperCollins Pubs.

—Interworld. 2008. (Illus.). 181p. (J). (gr. 5-9). 60.00 (978-1-59606-173-6(1)) Subterranean Pr.

Gaiman, NEil, et al. Eternity's Wheel. (InterWorld Trilogy Ser.: 3). 288p. (YA). (gr. 8). 2016. pap. 9.99 (978-0-06-206800-2(8)) 2015. (ENG.). 17.99 (978-0-06-206799-9(0)) HarperCollins Pubs. (HarperTeen).

—The Silver Dream. (InterWorld Trilogy Ser.: 2). (ENG.). (YA). (gr. 8). 2015. 272p. pap. 9.99 (978-0-06-206797-5(4)) 2013. 256p. 18.99 (978-0-06-206796-8(6)) HarperCollins Pubs. (HarperTeen).

Garcia, Kami & Stohl, Margaret. Dangerous Deception. 2015. (ENG.). 352p. (YA). (gr. 7-17). 19.00 (978-0-316-37034-9(7)) Little Brown & Co.

Gee, Maurice. The Limping Man, 1 vol. 2011. (Salt Trilogy Ser.: 3). (ENG.). 208p. (YA). (gr. 7-12). lib. bdg. 18.00 (978-1-55469-216-3(4)) Orca Bk. Pubs. USA.

Gelford, Inga. Sophie Ma's Magical Glasses. 2012. 48p. pap. 18.00 (978-1-4670-8180-1(9)) AuthorHouse.

Gelsey, James, adapted by. Opposing Force. 2004. (Illus.). 92p. (J). *(978-1-4156-3935-1(3)*, Volo) Hyperion Bks. for Children.

Gibbons, Alan. Renegade. 2010. (ENG., Illus.). 336p. (YA). (gr. 7-17). 8.99 *(978-1-4440-0079-5(9)*, Orion Children's Bks.) Hachette Children's Group GBR. Dist: Hachette Bk. Group.

—Scared to Death. 2010. (ENG., Illus.). 352p. (J). (gr. 4-6). pap. 8.99 *(978-1-4440-0143-3(4)*, Orion Children's Bks.) Hachette Children's Group GBR. Dist: Hachette Bk. Group.

Gill, David Macinnis. Uncanny. 2017. 544p. (YA). (gr. 9). 17.99 ***(978-0-06-229016-8(9)***, Greenwillow Bks.) HarperCollins Pubs.

Gingeleski, Randolph J. The War of Lord Capani. 2008. 58p. pap. 16.95 *(978-1-60563-758-7(0))* America Star Bks.

Glanville, K. L. The Realm: The Awakening Begins, bk. 1. 2008. (ENG.). 314p. (YA). pap. 12.99 *(978-0-9821199-1-4(7))* Luminations Media Group, Inc.

Golden Books Staff. Star Wars: the Force Awakens (Star Wars) Golden Books Staff & Meurer, Caleb, illus. 2016. (Little Golden Book Ser.). (ENG.). 24p. (J). (-k). 4.99 *(978-0-7364-3491-1(7)*, Golden Bks.) Random Hse. Children's Bks.

Gonnard, Christel. The Planet of the Night Globes. 2013. (Little Prince Ser.: 6). (ENG., Illus.). 56p. (J). (gr. 4-8). pap. 7.95 *(978-1-4677-0738-1(4)*, Graphic Universe™) Lerner Publishing Group.

Grant, Donna. Hungrige Begierde. 2014.Tr. of The Hunger. (GER.). pap. 5.99 *(978-1-942017-15-8(4))* DL Grant, LLC.

Grant, Michael. The Call. (Magnificent 12 Ser.: 1). (ENG.). (J). (gr. 3-7). 2011. 272p. pap. 6.99 *(978-0-06-183367-0(3))* 2010. (Illus.). 256p. 16.99 *(978-0-06-183366-3(5))* HarperCollins Pubs. (Tegen, Katherine Bks).

—Fear. 2012. (Gone Ser.: 5). (ENG.). 528p. (YA). (gr. 9). 17.99 *(978-0-06-144915-4(6)*, Tegen, Katherine Bks) HarperCollins Pubs.

—Gone. (Gone Ser.: 1). 576p. 2014. (ENG.). (YA). (gr. 8). pap. 9.99 *(978-0-06-144878-2(8)*, Tegen, Katherine Bks) 2008. (Illus.). (J). (gr. 7-18). lib. bdg. 18.89 *(978-0-06-144877-5(X)*, HarperTeen) 2008. (ENG., Illus.). (YA). (gr. 8-18). 17.99 *(978-0-06-144876-8(1)*, Tegen, Katherine Bks) HarperCollins Pubs.

—Hunger. (Gone Ser.: 2). (ENG.). 608p. (YA). (gr. 8-18). 2014. pap. 9.99 *(978-0-06-144908-6(3))* 2009. (Illus.). 17.99 *(978-0-06-144906-2(7))* HarperCollins Pubs. (Tegen, Katherine Bks).

—The Key. (Magnificent 12 Ser.: 3). (ENG.). (J). (gr. 3-7). 2013. 304p. pap. 5.99 *(978-0-06-183371-7(1))* 2012. (Illus.). 288p. 16.99 *(978-0-06-183370-0(3))* HarperCollins Pubs. (Tegen, Katherine Bks).

—Lies. (Gone Ser.: 3). 464p. (YA). (gr. 8). 2014. (ENG.). pap. 9.99 *(978-0-06-144911-6(3))* 2010. lib. bdg. 18.89 *(978-0-06-144910-9(5))* 2010. (ENG.). 17.99 *(978-0-06-144909-3(1))* HarperCollins Pubs. (Tegen, Katherine Bks).

—Light. 2013. (Gone Ser.: 6). 432p. (YA). (gr. 9). (ENG.). 18.99 *(978-0-06-144918-5(0))*; lib. bdg. 19.89 *(978-0-06-144919-2(9))* HarperCollins Pubs. (Tegen, Katherine Bks).

—Messenger of Fear. 2014. (Messenger of Fear Ser.: 1). (ENG.). 272p. (YA). (gr. 9). 17.99 *(978-0-06-220740-1(7)*, Tegen, Katherine Bks) HarperCollins Pubs.

—Plague. (Gone Ser.: 4). (ENG.). (YA). (gr. 8). 2014. 528p. pap. 9.99 *(978-0-06-144914-7(8))* 2011. 512p. 17.99 *(978-0-06-144912-3(1))* HarperCollins Pubs. (Tegen, Katherine Bks).

—The Tattooed Heart. (Messenger of Fear Ser.: 2). (YA). (gr. 9). 2016. 416p. pap. 9.99 *(978-0-06-220744-9(X)*, Tegen, Katherine Bks) 2015. (ENG.). 400p. 17.99 *(978-0-06-220743-2(1))* HarperCollins Pubs.

—The Trap. (Magnificent 12 Ser.: 2). (ENG.). (J). (gr. 3-7). 2012. 320p. pap. 5.99 *(978-0-06-183369-4(X))* 2011. 304p. 16.99 *(978-0-06-183368-7(1))* HarperCollins Pubs. (Tegen, Katherine Bks).

Gray, Anne. Healer's Touch, 1 vol. 2009. (ENG.). 288p. (YA). (gr. 7-11). pap. *(978-1-894549-77-6(5)*, Sumach Pr.) Canadian Scholars.

Green, Sally. Half Bad. (ENG.). (YA). 2015. (Half Bad Trilogy Ser.: 1). 432p. (gr. 7). pap. 9.99 *(978-0-14-751146-1(1)*, Speak) 2014. (Half Bad Trilogy Ser.: 1). 416p. (gr. 7). 18.99 *(978-0-670-01678-5(0)*, Viking Books for Young Readers)Pack. 2015. pap. 89.91 *(978-0-14-751591-9(2)*, Speak) Penguin Young Readers Group.

Greenway, Glen. Ant Cook & the Giant Sangom. 2008. 144p. pap. 12.95 *(978-1-4327-1898-5(3))* Outskirts Pr., Inc.

Gunson, Jonathan. The Divine Calling. 2006. 289p. 24.30 *(978-1-4116-7790-6(0))* Lulu Pr., Inc.

Harper, Benjamin. Star Wars: the Power of the Dark Side. 2015. (ENG.). 32p. (J). (gr. 1-4). 17.99 *(978-0-7944-3532-5(7))* Reader's Digest Assn., Inc., The.

Henderson, Barbara. Down in Mr Brown's Garden. 2009. 40p. pap. 14.75 *(978-1-60860-703-7(8)*, Strategic Bk. Publishing) Strategic Book Publishing & Rights Agency (SBPRA).

Hendrickson, Kevis. The Legend of Witch Bane. 2008. 348p. per. 11.95 *(978-1-4327-1298-3(5))* Outskirts Pr., Inc.

Hervey, Cheston & Doane, Darren. Kill the Dragon, Get the Girl. 2017. (J). pap. ***(978-1-59128-188-7(1))*** Canon Pr.

Higgins, Wendy. Sweet Evil. 2012. (Sweet Evil Ser.: 1). (ENG.). 464p. (YA). (gr. 8). pap. 9.99 *(978-0-06-208561-0(1)*, HarperTeen) HarperCollins Pubs.

—Sweet Peril. 2013. (Sweet Evil Ser.: 2). (ENG.). 384p. (YA). (gr. 8). pap. 9.99 *(978-0-06-226594-4(6)*, HarperTeen) HarperCollins Pubs.

—Sweet Reckoning. 2014. (Sweet Evil Ser.: 3). (ENG.). 400p. (YA). (gr. 8). pap. 9.99 *(978-0-06-226597-5(0)*, HarperTeen) HarperCollins Pubs.

—Sweet Temptation. 2015. (Sweet Evil Ser.: 4). (ENG.). 512p. (YA). (gr. 8). pap. 9.99 *(978-0-06-238142-2(3)*, HarperTeen) HarperCollins Pubs.

Hill, Will. Darkest Night (Department 19, Book 5) 2016. (Department 19 Ser.: 5). (ENG.). 736p. (J). pap. 9.99 *(978-0-00-815427-1(9)*, HarperCollins Children's Bks.) HarperCollins Pubs. Ltd. GBR. Dist: HarperCollins Pubs.

Hoban, Russell. A Birthday for Frances. Hoban, Lillian, illus. 2012. (I Can Read Level 2 Ser.). (ENG.). 48p. (J). (gr. k-3). pap. 3.99 *(978-0-06-083797-6(7))* HarperCollins Pubs.

Holder, Nancy & Viguié, Debbie. Resurrection. 2009. (Wicked Ser.). (ENG.). 416p. (YA). (gr. 9-18). pap. 9.99 *(978-1-4169-7227-3(7)*, Simon Pulse) Simon Pulse.

Horowitz, Anthony. Oblivion. 2014. (Gatekeepers Ser.: 5). (ENG.). 592p. (J). (gr. 3-7). pap. 9.99 *(978-0-439-68005-9(0)*, Scholastic Paperbacks) Scholastic, Inc.

—Oblivion. 2014. (Gatekeepers Ser.: 5). lib. bdg. 20.85 *(978-0-606-36035-7(2))* Turtleback Bks.

—Return to Groosham Grange: The Unholy Grail. 2010. (ENG.). 224p. (J). (gr. 5-18). 7.99 *(978-0-14-241571-9(5)*, Puffin Books) Penguin Young Readers Group.

Hudson, Tara. Arise. (Hereafter Trilogy Ser.: 2). (ENG.). (YA). (gr. 8). 2013. 432p. pap. 9.99 *(978-0-06-202680-4(1))* 2012. 416p. 17.99 *(978-0-06-202679-8(8))* HarperCollins Pubs. (HarperTeen).

—Elegy. 2013. (Hereafter Trilogy Ser.: 3). (ENG.). 400p. (YA). (gr. 8). 17.99 *(978-0-06-202681-1(X)*, HarperTeen) HarperCollins Pubs.

—Hereafter. 2012. (Hereafter Trilogy Ser.: 1). (ENG.). 432p. (YA). (gr. 8). pap. 8.99 *(978-0-06-202678-1(X)*, HarperTeen) HarperCollins Pubs.

Huffstead, C. V. The Wielder of the Sengans: Including the Tomes of Ithren, 1 vol. 2010. 110p. pap. 19.95 *(978-1-4512-1446-8(4))* America Star Bks.

Hurley, Tonya. The Blessed. Watkins, Abbey, illus. 2012. (Blessed Ser.). (ENG.). 416p. (YA). (gr. 9). 17.99 *(978-1-4424-2951-2(8)*, Simon & Schuster Bks. For Young Readers) Simon & Schuster Bks. For Young Readers.

—Passionaries. (Blessed Ser.). (ENG., Illus.). 368p. (YA). (gr. 9). 2015. pap. 12.99 *(978-1-4424-2955-0(0))* 2014. 17.99 *(978-1-4424-2954-3(2))* Simon & Schuster Bks. For Young Readers. (Simon & Schuster Bks. For Young Readers).

—Precious Blood. Watkins, Abbey, illus. 2013. (Blessed Ser.). (ENG.). 432p. (YA). (gr. 9). pap. 9.99 *(978-1-4424-2952-9(6)*, Simon & Schuster Bks. For Young Readers) Simon & Schuster Bks. For Young Readers.

Irvin, William. The Adventures of Winston & Hazel: Episode 1: the Silver Medallion. 2006. 11.00 *(978-0-8059-8220-6(5))* Dorrance Publishing Co., Inc.

Irvine, Alex. Phase Three: MARVEL's Doctor Strange. 2017. (ENG.). 208p. (J). (gr. 3-7). 12.99 *(978-0-316-27159-2(4))* Little, Brown Bks. for Young Readers.

Jadestone, Justin. Mr Schemfumnickel: The Little Elf with the Real Bright Buttons! 2012. 32p. pap. 19.99 *(978-1-4634-1322-4(X))* AuthorHouse.

Jarvis, Robin. Dark Waters of Hagwood. 2013. (Hagwood Trilogy Ser.: 2). (ENG.). 318p. (J). (gr. 4-6). pap. 14.99 *(978-1-4532-9920-3(3)*, Open Road Media E-riginal) Open Road Integrated Media, Inc.

Jay, Stacey. Juliet Immortal. 2012. (ENG.). 324p. (YA). (gr. 9). pap. 9.99 *(978-0-385-74017-3(4)*, Ember) Random Hse. Children's Bks.

—Romeo Redeemed. 2013. (ENG.). 384p. (YA). (gr. 9). pap. 9.99 *(978-0-385-74019-7(0)*, Ember) Random Hse. Children's Bks.

Jenkins, Jerry B. & Fabry, Chris. The Author's Blood. 2008. (Wormling Ser.: 5). (ENG.). 368p. (J). (gr. 5-9). per. 7.99 *(978-1-4143-0159-4(6)*, Tyndale Kids) Tyndale Hse. Pubs.

—The Book of the King. 2007. (Wormling Ser.: 1). (ENG.). 288p. (J). (gr. 5-9). per. 7.99 *(978-1-4143-0155-6(3))* Tyndale Hse. Pubs.

—The Changeling. 2007. (Wormling Ser.: 3). (ENG.). 336p. (J). (gr. 5-9). per. 7.99 *(978-1-4143-0157-0(X))* Tyndale Hse. Pubs.

—El Libro del Rey. 2008. (Lombricero Ser.: 1).Tr. of Book of the King. (SPA.). 304p. (J). pap. 7.99 *(978-1-4143-2216-2(X)*, Tyndale Espanol) Tyndale Hse. Pubs.

—The Minions of Time. 2008. (Wormling Ser.: 4). (ENG.). 336p. (J). (gr. 5-9). per. 7.99 *(978-1-4143-0158-7(8))* Tyndale Hse. Pubs.

—Sword of the Wormling. 2007. (Wormling Ser.: 2). (ENG.). 336p. (J). (gr. 5-9). per. 7.99 *(978-1-4143-0156-3(1))* Tyndale Hse. Pubs.

Jenkins, Jerry B. & LaHaye, Tim. The Mark of the Beast: Witness Behind Bars. 2003. (Left Behind Ser.). 146p. (J). 13.65 *(978-0-7569-3532-0(6))* Perfection Learning Corp.

Jinks, Catherine. Evil Genius. 2007. 486p. (J). *(978-1-4287-3510-1(0))* Harcourt Trade Pubs.

—Evil Genius. 2008. (ENG., Illus.). 496p. (YA). (gr. 7). pap. 9.99 *(978-0-15-206185-2(1))* Houghton Mifflin Harcourt Publishing Co.

—Genius Squad. 2009. (ENG., Illus.). 448p. (J). (gr. 7). pap. 8.99 *(978-0-15-206650-5(0))* Houghton Mifflin Harcourt Publishing Co.

—The Genius Wars. 2011. (ENG.). 384p. (YA). (gr. 7). pap. 8.99 *(978-0-547-57727-2(3))* Houghton Mifflin Harcourt Publishing Co.

Jiya, Tapiwa. The Epic of Goz. 2008. 144p. pap. 11.99 *(978-1-4343-5730-4(9))* AuthorHouse.

John A. MacDonald. Pachung. 2010. 256p. 26.95 *(978-1-4502-1823-8(7))* iUniverse, Inc.

Johnson, Varian. The Return. 2016. (Spirit Animals: Fall of the Beasts Ser.: 3). (ENG.). 192p. (J). (gr. 3-7). 12.99 *(978-0-545-84207-5(7))* Scholastic, Inc.

Johnstone, Ian. The Bell Between Worlds (the Mirror Chronicles) 2016. (Mirror Chronicles Ser.). (ENG.). 512p. (J). pap. 9.99 *(978-0-00-815428-8(7)*, HarperCollins Children's Bks.) HarperCollins Pubs. Ltd. GBR. Dist: HarperCollins Pubs.

Jones, Gareth P. Ninja Meerkats (#6): Big City Bust-Up. Finlayson, Luke, illus. 2013. (Ninja Meerkats Ser.: 6). (ENG.). 128p. (J). (gr. 2-4). pap. 5.99 *(978-1-250-03403-8(5)*, 9781250034038) Square Fish.

Jordan, Jesse. This Is Not the End. 2016. (ENG.). 450p. (gr. 6). pap. 9.99 *(978-1-942546-30-6(0))* Nodin Pr.

Joyce, William. E. Aster Bunnymund & the Warrior Eggs at the Earth's Core!, Bk. 2. Joyce, William, illus. 2012. (Guardians Ser.: 2). (ENG., Illus.). 272p. (J). (gr. 2-6). 15.99 *(978-1-4424-3050-1(8)*, Atheneum Bks. for Young Readers) Simon & Schuster Children's Publishing.

—Ollie's Odyssey. Joyce, William, illus. 2017. (ENG., Illus.). 304p. (J). (gr. 2-6). pap. 9.99 *(978-1-4424-7356-0(8))* Simon & Schuster, Inc.

Joyce, William & Geringer, Laura. Nicholas St. North & the Battle of the Nightmare King, Bk. 1. Joyce, William, illus. 2011. (Guardians Ser.: 1). (ENG., Illus.). 240p. (J). (gr. 2-6). 15.99 *(978-1-4424-3048-8(6)*, Atheneum Bks. for Young Readers) Simon & Schuster Children's Publishing.

Juckes, Deborah Sioux. Meesha, Guardian of Grand Mountain: Book One of the Guardian Series. McCleary, Twila, illus. 2005. (YA). 18.95 *(978-0-9767748-1-5(X))* Red Earth Publishing.

Kagawa, Julie. The Iron Traitor. 2013. (Iron Fey Ser.: 6). lib. bdg. 20.85 *(978-0-606-35037-2(3)*, Turtleback) Turtleback Bks.

—The Lost Prince. 2012. (Iron Fey Ser.: 5). lib. bdg. 20.85 *(978-0-606-26946-9(0)*, Turtleback) Turtleback Bks.

Kazmierczak, Jean. National Chrome 2: The Good, the Bad & the Indifferent. 2008. 76p. pap. 16.95 *(978-1-60703-641-8(X))* PublishAmerica, Inc.

Keaton, Kelly. A Beautiful Evil. (ENG.). (YA). (gr. 9). 2013. 320p. pap. 11.99 *(978-1-4424-0928-6(2))* 2012. 304p. 17.99 *(978-1-4424-0927-9(4))* Simon Pulse. (Simon Pulse).

—The Wicked Within. (ENG., Illus.). 288p. (YA). (gr. 9). 2014. pap. 9.99 *(978-1-4424-9316-2(X))* 2013. 17.99 *(978-1-4424-9315-5(1))* Simon Pulse. (Simon Pulse).

Kelly, Joe. Supergirl, Volume 2: Breaking the Chain. 2016. (ENG.). 727p. 33.05 *(978-0-606-39223-5(8))* Turtleback Bks.

Kimberly, Anne. Dark Well of Decision. 2007. 136p. per. 7.99 *(978-0-9800356-5-0(1))* Highland Pr. Publishing.

King, Wesley. The Vindico. 2013. (ENG.). 320p. (YA). (gr. 7). pap. 8.99 *(978-0-14-242656-2(3)*, Speak) Penguin Young Readers Group.

Kirov, Erica. The Chalice of Immortality. 2011. (ENG.). 208p. (J). (gr. 4-7). pap. 7.99 *(978-1-4022-1503-2(7)*, Sourcebooks Jabberwocky) Sourcebooks, Inc.

—Magickeepers: The Eternal Hourglass. Fortune, Eric, illus. 2010. (ENG.). 256p. (J). (gr. 4-7). pap. 10.99 *(978-1-4022-3855-0(X)*, Sourcebooks Jabberwocky) Sourcebooks, Inc.

Kishimoto, Seishi. O-Parts Hunter, Vol. 3. Kishimoto, Seishi, illus. 2007. (O-Parts Hunter Ser.: 3). (ENG., Illus.). 200p. pap. 9.99 *(978-1-4215-0857-3(X))* Viz Media.

—O-Parts Hunter, Vol. 2. Kishimoto, Seishi, illus. 2007. (ENG., Illus.). 200p. pap. 9.99 *(978-1-4215-0856-6(7))* Viz Media.

Klodt, Louise. Door to Kandalaura: Book One of the Kandalaura Chronicles. 2015. (ENG.). 112p. pap. 9.99 *(978-1-62998-395-0(0)*, Creation Hse.) Charisma Media.

Knight, Aya. The Chronicles of Kale: Dawn of Retribution. 2012. 456p. 28.95 *(978-1-938083-13-6(X))*; pap. 15.95 *(978-1-938083-12-9(1))* Silver Knight Publishing, LLC.

Kohlhepp, Michael G. Within the Hearthstone Book 2: The Fountain of Balance. 2007. (ENG.). 184p. per. 24.95 *(978-1-4241-4446-4(9))* PublishAmerica, Inc.

Korman, Gordon. The Medusa Plot. 2011. (39 Clues: Cahills vs. Vespers Ser.: 1). (ENG., Illus.). 224p. (J). (gr. 3-7). 12.99 *(978-0-545-32409-0(2)*, Scholastic Pr.); 12.99 *(978-0-545-29839-1(3))* Scholastic, Inc.

Kotecki, Nathan. The Suburban Strange. 2012. (Suburban Strange Ser.). (ENG.). 368p. (YA). (gr. 9). 16.99 *(978-0-547-72996-1(0))* Houghton Mifflin Harcourt Publishing Co.

Kramer, Paul. Louie the Lobster Mobster. 2012. (ENG.). 48p. (J). (gr. 1-7). 15.95 *(978-0-9819745-2-1(X))* Aloha Wellness Pubs.

Kriszt, Ann Marie. Bestis Friends. 2008. 276p. pap. 27.95 *(978-1-60703-154-3(X))* PublishAmerica, Inc.

Krum, Atticus. The Taming. Donaera, Patrizia, illus. 2014. (ENG.). 227p. (J). pap. 12.99 *(978-0-9885349-1-9(6))* Huntly Hse.

Kunkel, Mike. Billy Batson & the Magic. Kunkel, Mike, illus. 2015. (Billy Batson & the Magic of Shazam! Ser.). (ENG., Illus.). 32p. (gr. 2-3). 226.00 *(978-1-4965-0290-2(6))* Stone Arch Bks.

—Billy Batson & the Magic of Shazam!, 1 vol. Kunkel, Mike, illus. 2014. (Billy Batson & the Magic of Shazam! Ser.). (ENG., Illus.). 32p. (gr. 2-3). 90.40 *(978-1-4342-9524-8(9))* Stone Arch Bks.

LaFevers, R. L. The Forging of the Blade. 2006. (ENG.). 144p. (J). (gr. 3-7). 5.99 *(978-0-14-240557-4(4)*, Puffin Books) Penguin Young Readers Group.

—Theodosia & the Serpents of Chaos. Tanaka, Yoko, illus. 2008. (ENG.). 352p. (J). (gr. 2-5). pap. 7.99 *(978-0-618-99976-7(0))* Houghton Mifflin Harcourt Publishing Co.

Lancett, Peter. The Bridge of Dark Tears. 2008. (Dark Man Ser.). (ENG., Illus.). 48p. pap. *(978-1-84167-746-0(9))* Ransom Publishing Ltd.

—The Bridge of Dark Tears, 1 vol. unabr. ed. 2011. (Dark Man Ser.). (ENG.). 47p. (YA). (gr. 9-12). 7.95 *(978-1-61651-294-1(6))* Saddleback Educational Publishing, Inc.

—Dark Candle. 2007. (Dark Man Ser.). (ENG.). 36p. pap. *(978-1-84167-603-6(9))* Ransom Publishing Ltd.

—The Dark Candle, 1 vol. unabr. ed. 2011. (Dark Man Ser.). (ENG.). 47p. (YA). (gr. 9-12). pap. 7.95 *(978-1-61651-026-8(9))* Saddleback Educational Publishing, Inc.

—The Dark Dreams, 1 vol. unabr. ed. 2010. (Dark Man Ser.). (ENG.). 34p. (YA). (gr. 9-12). pap. 7.95 *(978-1-61651-017-6(X))* Saddleback Educational Publishing, Inc.

—The Dark Fire of Doom (Blue Series), 1 vol. 2015. (Dark Man Ser.). (ENG.). 36p. (YA). (gr. 9-12). pap. 7.95 *(978-1-68021-123-8(4))* Saddleback Educational Publishing, Inc.

—The Dark Garden. 2008. (Dark Man Ser.). (ENG., Illus.). 48p. pap. *(978-1-84167-750-7(7))* Ransom Publishing Ltd.

—The Dark Garden, 1 vol. unabr. ed. 2011. (Dark Man Ser.). (ENG.). 47p. (YA). (gr. 9-12). 7.95 *(978-1-61651-298-9(9))* Saddleback Educational Publishing, Inc.

—The Dark Machine, 1 vol. unabr. ed. 2011. (Dark Man Ser.). (ENG.). 47p. (YA). (gr. 9-12). pap. 7.95 *(978-1-61651-027-5(7))* Saddleback Educational Publishing, Inc.

—The Dark Music. 2008. (Dark Man Ser.). (ENG., Illus.). 48p. pap. *(978-1-84167-749-1(3))* Ransom Publishing Ltd.

—The Dark Music, 1 vol. unabr. ed. 2011. (Dark Man Ser.). (ENG.). 47p. (YA). (gr. 9-12). 7.95 *(978-1-61651-297-2(0))* Saddleback Educational Publishing, Inc.

—The Dark Never Hides (Blue Series), 1 vol. 2015. (Dark Man Ser.). (ENG.). 36p. (YA). (gr. 9-12). pap. 7.95 *(978-1-68021-124-5(2))* Saddleback Educational Publishing, Inc.

—The Dark River. 2008. (Dark Man Ser.). (ENG., Illus.). 48p. pap. *(978-1-84167-745-3(0))* Ransom Publishing Ltd.

—The Dark River, 1 vol. unabr. ed. 2011. (Dark Man Ser.). (ENG.). 47p. (YA). (gr. 9-12). 7.95 *(978-1-61651-293-4(8))* Saddleback Educational Publishing, Inc.

—Dark Words. 2007. (Dark Man Ser.). (ENG.). 36p. pap. *(978-1-84167-602-9(0))* Ransom Publishing Ltd.

—The Dark Words, 1 vol. unabr. ed. 2011. (Dark Man Ser.). (ENG.). 47p. (YA). (gr. 9-12). pap. 7.95 *(978-1-61651-028-2(5))* Saddleback Educational Publishing, Inc.

—Day Is Dark. 2007. (Dark Man Ser.). (ENG.). 36p. pap. *(978-1-84167-606-7(3))* Ransom Publishing Ltd.

—The Day Is Dark, 1 vol. unabr. ed. 2011. (Dark Man Ser.). (ENG.). 47p. (YA). (gr. 9-12). pap. 7.95 *(978-1-61651-029-9(3))* Saddleback Educational Publishing, Inc.

—Dying for the Dark. 2007. (Dark Man Ser.). (ENG.). 36p. pap. *(978-1-84167-604-3(7))* Ransom Publishing Ltd.

—Dying for the Dark, 1 vol. unabr. ed. 2011. (Dark Man Ser.). (ENG.). 47p. (YA). (gr. 9-12). pap. 7.95 *(978-1-61651-030-5(7))* Saddleback Educational Publishing, Inc.

—The Face in the Dark Mirror (Blue Series), 1 vol. 2015. (Dark Man Ser.). (ENG.). 36p. (YA). (gr. 9-12). pap. 7.95 *(978-1-68021-127-6(7))* Saddleback Educational Publishing, Inc.

—Killer in the Dark. 2007. (Dark Man Ser.). (ENG.). 36p. pap. *(978-1-84167-605-0(5))* Ransom Publishing Ltd.

—Killer in the Dark, 1 vol. unabr. ed. 2011. (Dark Man Ser.). (ENG.). 47p. (YA). (gr. 9-12). pap. 7.95 *(978-1-61651-031-2(5))* Saddleback Educational Publishing, Inc.

—The Past Is Dark, 1 vol. unabr. ed. 2011. (Dark Man Ser.). (ENG.). 47p. (YA). (gr. 9-12). 7.95 *(978-1-61651-295-8(4))* Saddleback Educational Publishing, Inc.

—Playing the Dark Game. 2008. (Dark Man Ser.). (ENG., Illus.). 48p. pap. *(978-1-84167-748-4(5))* Ransom Publishing Ltd.

—Playing the Dark Game, 1 vol. unabr. ed. 2011. (Dark Man Ser.). (ENG.). 47p. (YA). (gr. 9-12). 7.95 *(978-1-61651-296-5(2))* Saddleback Educational Publishing, Inc.

Landers, Ace. Revenge of the Sith. White, David A., illus. 2015. (Lego Star Wars Ser.). (ENG.). 24p. (J). (gr. -1-3). pap. 3.99 *(978-0-545-78524-2(3))* Scholastic, Inc.

Langrish, Katherine. The Shadow Hunt. 2010. 322p. lib. bdg. *(978-0-06-111678-0(5))* HarperCollins Pubs.

Lasky, Kathryn. The Golden Tree. 2007. (Guardians of Ga'Hoole Ser.: 12). (Illus.). 192p. lib. bdg. 17.20 *(978-1-4177-8260-4(9)*, Turtleback) Turtleback Bks.

—The Journey. l.t. ed. 2007. (Guardians of Ga'Hoole Ser.: Bk. 2). (Illus.). 271p. (J). (gr. 3-7). 22.95 *(978-1-4104-0293-6(2))* Thorndike Pr.

—Shadow Wolf. 2010. (Wolves of the Beyond Ser.: 2). (ENG.). 272p. (J). (gr. 3-7). 17.99 *(978-0-545-09312-5(0)*, Scholastic Pr.) Scholastic, Inc.

—The Shattering. 2004. (Guardians of Ga'hoole Ser.: 5). (ENG., Illus.). 192p. (J). (gr. 3-7). 6.99 *(978-0-439-40561-4(0)*, Scholastic Paperbacks) Scholastic, Inc.

—The War of the Ember. 2008. (Guardians of Ga'hoole Ser.: 15). (ENG.). 256p. (J). (gr. 3-7). pap. 6.99 *(978-0-439-88809-7(3)*, Scholastic Paperbacks) Scholastic, Inc.

Lassiter, Rhiannon. Void: Hex; Shadows; Ghosts. 2011. (ENG.). 688p. (YA). (gr. 7). pap. 9.99 *(978-1-4424-2929-1(1)*, Simon Pulse) Simon Pulse.

Lavelle, Mary T. The Watcher. 2012. (Illus.). 44p. pap. 24.40 *(978-1-4772-5064-8(6))* AuthorHouse.

Leannah, Michael. Most People: (are Good People), 1 vol. Morris, Jennifer E., illus. 2017. (ENG.). 32p. (gr. -1-2). 16.95 *(978-0-88448-554-4(4)*, 884554) Tilbury Hse. Pubs.

Lee, Stan. The Dragon's Return. Tong, Andie, illus. 2017. (Zodiac Ser.). (ENG.). 448p. (J). (gr. 3-7). pap. 9.99 *(978-1-4847-5255-5(4))* Disney Pr.

—The Dragon's Return. 2017. (Zodiac Legacy Ser.: 2). (J). lib. bdg. 20.85 *(978-0-606-39500-7(8))* Turtleback Bks.

Lee, Stan & Moore, Stuart. The Dragon's Return. Tong, Andie, illus. 2016. (Zodiac Ser.: Bk. 2). (ENG.). 432p. (J). (gr. 3-7). 16.99 *(978-1-4847-1352-5(4))* Disney Pr.

Lemke, Donald. Diver Down, 1 vol. Glass House Graphics Staff, illus. 2011. (Good vs Evil Ser.). (ENG.). 48p. (gr. 1-2). pap. 6.29 *(978-1-4342-3446-9(0)*, Good vs Evil) Stone Arch Bks.

—Justice League Classic: Battle of the Power Ring. Spaziante, Patrick, illus. 2016. (I Can Read Level 2 Ser.). 32p. (J). (gr. -1-3). pap. 3.99 *(978-0-06-234494-6(3))* HarperCollins Pubs.

Lemke, Donald B. The Awakening, 1 vol. 2011. (Good vs Evil Ser.). (ENG.). 48p. (gr. 1-2). lib. bdg. 23.99 *(978-1-4342-2089-9(3)*, Good vs Evil) Stone Arch Bks.

—Diver Down, 1 vol. 2011. (Good vs Evil Ser.). (ENG.). 48p. (gr. 1-2). lib. bdg. 23.99 *(978-1-4342-2092-9(3)*, Good vs Evil) Stone Arch Bks.

Lenhard, Elizabeth. Different Path. 2004. (W. I. T. C. H. Ser.: Bk. 13). 158p. (J). lib. bdg. 16.92 *(978-1-4242-0791-6(6))* Fitzgerald Bks.

Lewis, Steven & Parker, Shelley. Return to Allapatria. 2006. 395p. (J). pap. *(978-0-9547092-9-7(2))* Accent Pr. Ltd.

Lindsay, Fitzroy A. My Daddy Came Home Long after the War. 2012. 28p. pap. 19.99 *(978-1-4685-6010-7(7))* AuthorHouse.

Lippmann, Wilfried. The Gift of Eye. 2008. 140p. (gr. 7-12). pap. 11.95 *(978-0-595-52251-4(3))* iUniverse, Inc.

Love, Emily. The Beginning of Freedom. 2010. 81p. pap. 9.00 *(978-0-557-56598-6(7))* Lulu Pr., Inc.

Lovegrove, James. The Lord of Fire (Five Lords of Pain Book 5) 2013. (Five Lords of Pain Ser.: 5). (ENG.). 96p. (YA). (gr. 8-12). pap. 7.95 *(978-1-78112-262-4(8))* Lerner Publishing Group.

—The Lord of Tears (Five Lords of Pain Book 3) 2013. (Five Lords of Pain Ser.: 3). (ENG.). 96p. (YA). (gr. 8-12). pap. 7.95 *(978-1-78112-256-3(3))* Lerner Publishing Group.

—The Lord of the Mountain (Five Lords of Pain Book 1) 2013. (Five Lords of Pain Ser.: 1). (ENG.). 96p. (YA). (gr. 8-12). pap. 7.95 *(978-1-78112-250-1(4))* Lerner Publishing Group.
—The Lord of the Typhoon (Five Lords of Pain Book 4) 2013. (Five Lords of Pain Ser.: 4). (ENG.). 96p. (YA). (gr. 8-12). pap. 7.95 *(978-1-78112-259-4(8))* Lerner Publishing Group.
Lovric, Michelle. The Undrowned Child. 2012. (ENG.). 464p. (J). (gr. 5). 7.99 *(978-0-375-86597-8(7)*, Yearling) Random Hse. Children's Bks.
Lyga, Barry. Archvillain. 2010. (Archvillain Ser.: 1). (ENG.). 192p. (J). (gr. 3-7). 16.99 *(978-0-545-19649-9(3)*, Scholastic Pr.) Scholastic, Inc.
MacCullough, Carolyn. Once a Witch. 2010. (ENG.). 320p. (YA). (gr. 7). pap. 8.99 *(978-0-547-41730-1(6))* Houghton Mifflin Harcourt Publishing Co.
Macdangereuse, T. T. The Untamed Scoundrel. 2014. (Epic Tales from Adventure Time Ser.). lib. bdg. 17.20 *(978-0-606-35718-0(1))* Turtleback Bks.
MacDonald, John A. Pachung. 2010. 256p. pap. 16.95 *(978-1-4502-1821-4(0))* iUniverse, Inc.
Maes, Nicholas. Transmigration. 2013. 296p. pap. *(978-1-4596-6404-3(3))* ReadHowYouWant.com, Ltd.
Malley, Gemma. The Returners. 2010. (Declaration Ser.). (ENG.). 256p. (YA). (gr. 7-18). 16.99 *(978-1-59990-443-6(8)*, 9781599904436, Bloomsbury USA Childrens) Bloomsbury Publishing USA.
Mangum, Lisa. The Forgotten Locket. (YA). 2012. pap. 8.99 *(978-1-60907-017-5(8))* 2011. (Hourglass Door Trilogy: Bk. 3). 416p. (gr. 3-18). 18.99 *(978-1-60908-049-5(1))* Deseret Bk. Co.
—The Hourglass Door. (Hourglass Door Trilogy: Bk. 1). (YA). 2010. 408p. mass mkt. 7.99 *(978-1-60641-679-2(0))* 2009. 432p. (gr. 9-18). 18.95 *(978-1-60641-093-6(8))* Shadow Mountain Publishing. (Shadow Mountain).
Marchetta, Melina. Quintana of Charyn: The Lumatere Chronicles. (Lumatere Chronicles Ser.). (ENG.). 528p. (YA). (gr. 9). 2014. pap. 10.99 *(978-0-7636-6930-0(X))* 2013. 18.99 *(978-0-7636-5835-9(9))* Candlewick Pr.
Marriott, Zoë. Darkness Hidden: the Name of the Blade, Book Two. 2015. (ENG.). 352p. (J). (gr. 7). 16.99 *(978-0-7636-6958-4(X))* Candlewick Pr.
—The Name of the Blade. 2014. (ENG.). 368p. (YA). (gr. 7). 16.99 *(978-0-7636-6957-7(1))* Candlewick Pr.
Marsham, Liz. Wonder Woman: Maze of Magic. 2017. (I Can Read! Level 2 Ser.). lib. bdg. 13.55 ***(978-0-606-40057-2(5))*** Turtleback Bks.
Marvel Book Group. The Avengers Storybook Collection. 2015. (Storybook Collection). (ENG.). 304p. (J). (gr. 1-3). 16.99 *(978-1-4847-0242-0(5)*, Marvel Pr.) Disney Publishing Worldwide.
Marz, Ron. Witchblade Redemption, Vol. 4. 2012. (ENG., Illus.). 160p. pap. 19.99 *(978-1-60706-424-4(3)*, 9781607064244) Image Comics.
Mason-Black, Jennifer. Devil & the Bluebird. 2016. (ENG.). 336p. (J). (gr. 8-17). 17.95 *(978-1-4197-2000-0(7)*, Amulet Bks.) Abrams, Inc.
Mason, Mike. The Blue Umbrella. 2009. (ENG.). 448p. (YA). pap. 10.99 *(978-1-4347-6526-0(1))* Cook, David C.
Maxwell, Robert W. The Weeb Book. Maxwell, Robert W., illus. 2009. (Illus.). 60p. pap. 20.00 *(978-1-59925-140-0(X))* Solid Ground Christian Bks.
Mayer, Kirsten. Despicable Me 2: Attack of the Evil Minions! Miller, Ed, illus. 2016. (ENG.). 32p. (J). (gr. -1-3). pap. 7.99 *(978-0-316-39294-5(4))* Little, Brown Bks. for Young Readers.
McClellan, Rachel. Fractured Truth. 2014. 16.99 *(978-1-4621-1392-7(3)*, Horizon Pubs.) Cedar Fort, Inc./CFI Distribution.
McCune, D. J. Fault Lines. 2016. (Death & Co Ser.: 3). (ENG.). 352p. (YA). (gr. 8). pap. 11.99 *(978-1-4714-0271-5(1))* Bonnier Publishing GBR. Dist: Independent Pubs. Group.
McGrath, Alister. Chosen Ones, 1 vol. 2010. (Aedyn Chronicles Ser.). (ENG.). 208p. (J). (gr. 4-7). 14.99 *(978-0-310-71812-3(0))* Zondervan.
McGrath, Milo & McGrath, Chris. South Pole Santa. 2007. 68p. pap. 12.50 *(978-1-84799-221-5(8))* Lulu Pr., Inc.
McLean, Matthew. The Invisible War: Book One of the Disciple Trilogy. 2007. 236p. 25.95 *(978-0-595-69953-7(7))*; per. 15.95 *(978-0-595-46152-3(2))* iUniverse, Inc.
Meadows, Daisy. Crystal the Snow Fairy. Ripper, Georgie, illus. 2006. (Weather Fairies Ser.: 1). (ENG.). 80p. (Orig.). (J). (gr. -1-3). mass mkt. 4.99 *(978-0-439-81387-7(5)*, Scholastic Paperbacks) Scholastic, Inc.
—Grace Woollyhop's Musical Mystery. 2016. (Magic Animal Friends Ser.: 12). lib. bdg. 14.75 *(978-0-606-38802-3(8))* Turtleback Bks.
—Grace Woollyhop's Musical Mystery (Magic Animal Friends #12) 2016. (Magic Animal Friends Ser.: 12). (ENG., Illus.). 112p. (J). (gr. 2-5). pap. 4.99 *(978-0-545-94079-5(6)*, Scholastic Paperbacks) Scholastic, Inc.
Melvin, Anita. What to do with Boogers. Melvin, Anita, illus. 2004. (Illus.). 14p. (J). per. 9.95 *(978-0-9760129-8-6(7))* The Publishing Place LLC.
Milford, Kate. The Broken Lands. Offermann, Andrea, illus. 2012. (ENG.). 464p. (YA). (gr. 7). 16.99 *(978-0-547-73966-3(4))* Houghton Mifflin Harcourt Publishing Co.
Miller, Christopher & Miller, Allan. The Legend of Gid the Kid & the Black Bean Bandits, 2 bks., Bk.1. Miller, Christopher & Miller, Allan, illus. 2007. (Heroes of Promise Ser.). (ENG., Illus.). 32p. (J). (gr. 1-5). 12.99 *(978-1-59317-202-2(8))* Warner Pr., Inc.
Milson, Matthew R. Young Arcan & the Garden of Loc. 2007. (Tales from Emberthel Ser.). 221p. (J). (gr. 3-7). per. 14.95 *(978-1-933770-03-1(1))* Avari Pr.
Molinari, Laurice E. Pillars of Fire, 1 vol. 2016. (Ether Novel Ser.). (ENG.). 368p. (J). pap. 8.99 *(978-0-310-73562-5(9))* Zonderkidz.
Molinari, Laurice Elehwany. Pillars of Fire, 1 vol. 2015. (Ether Novel Ser.). (ENG.). 368p. (J). 16.99 *(978-0-310-73556-4(4))* Zonderkidz.
Moore, Peter. V Is for Villain. 2014. (ENG.). 336p. (YA). (gr. 7-12). 17.99 *(978-1-4231-5749-6(4))* Hyperion Pr.
Moore, Stuart, et al. The Dragon's Return. 2016. *(978-1-4847-7415-1(9))* Disney Publishing Worldwide.
Morales, Rebecca Lynn. Walter Plume & the Dehydrated Imagination. 2016. (ENG.). viii, 150p. (J). pap. 11.99 *(978-1-4621-1780-2(5)*, Sweetwater Bks.) Cedar Fort, Inc./CFI Distribution.
Mull, Brandon. Keys to the Demon Prison. 2010. (Fablehaven Ser.: 5). (ENG., Illus.). 600p. (J). (gr. 3). 21.99 *(978-1-60641-238-1(8)*, Shadow Mountain) Shadow Mountain Publishing.
—Keys to the Demon Prison. Dorman, Brandon, illus. 2011. (Fablehaven Ser.: 5). (ENG.). 640p. (J). (gr. 3-8). pap. 8.99 *(978-1-4169-9029-1(1)*, Aladdin) Simon & Schuster Children's Publishing.
Mull, Brandon, et al. Tales of the Fallen Beasts. 2016. (Spirit Animals Ser.). (ENG.). 192p. (J). (gr. 3-7). 12.99 *(978-0-545-90129-1(4))* Scholastic, Inc.
Myers, Bill. Invisible Terror Collection, 1 vol., Vol. 2. 2011. (Forbidden Doors Ser.). (ENG.). 368p. (YA). pap. 12.99 *(978-0-310-72904-4(1))* Zondervan.
Narine, Vidya D. Kari. 2011. 66p. 24.99 *(978-1-4568-5348-8(1))*; pap. 15.99 *(978-1-4568-5347-1(3))* Xlibris Corp.
Neilsen, David. Dr. Fell & the Playground of Doom. (ENG.). (J). (gr. 3-7). 2017. 256p. 6.99 ***(978-1-101-93581-1(2)***, Yearling) 2016. (Illus.). 240p. 16.99 *(978-1-101-93578-1(2)*, Crown Books For Young Readers) Random Hse. Children's Bks.
Nelson, Peter. Herbert's Wormhole: AeroStar & the 3 1/2-Point Plan of Vengeance. Rao, Rohitash, illus. 2014. (Herbert's Wormhole Ser.: 3). (ENG.). 368p. (J). (gr. 3-7). pap. 6.99 *(978-0-06-201221-0(5))* HarperCollins Pubs.
Nettrour, Nelani. Angels in Training. l.t. ed. 2006. (Illus.). 114p. (J). pap. 12.95 *(978-1-932657-57-9(6))* Third Millennium Pubns.
Neubert, Oliver. Chantel's Quest for the Enchanted Medallion. 2009. (Cozy Classics Ser.). (ENG., Illus.). 224p. (J). (gr. 3-6). 16.95 *(978-1-897476-15-4(9))* Simply Read Bks. CAN. Dist: Ingram Publisher Services.
Nicholson, Simon. The Demon Curse. 2015. (Young Houdini Ser.: 2). (ENG.). 240p. (J). (gr. 5-8). 15.99 *(978-1-4926-0335-1(X)*, 9781492603351, Sourcebooks Jabberwocky) Sourcebooks, Inc.
Nix, Garth. Shade's Children. 2012. (ENG.). 368p. (YA). (gr. 8). pap. 9.99 *(978-0-06-207598-7(5))* HarperCollins Pubs.
Nix, Garth & Williams, Sean. The Missing. 2014. (Troubletwisters Ser.: 4). (ENG.). 320p. (J). (gr. 3-7). 17.99 *(978-0-545-25900-2(2)*, Scholastic Pr.) Scholastic, Inc.
Noël, Alyson. Echo. 2013. (Soul Seekers Ser.: 2). (ENG.). 352p. (YA). (gr. 7). mass mkt. 9.99 *(978-1-250-04689-5(0)*, 9781250046895, St. Martin's Paperbacks) St. Martin's Pr.
Nolan, Lea. Allure. 2013. (Hoodoo Apprentice Ser.: 2). (ENG.). 304p. (YA). (gr. 7-12). pap. 9.99 *(978-1-62266-022-3(6)*, 9781622660223) Entangled Publishing, LLC.
Northrop, Michael. Valley of Kings. 2015. (TombQuest Ser.: 3). (ENG.). 192p. (J). (gr. 3-7). 16.99 *(978-0-545-87104-4(2))*; 12.99 *(978-0-545-72340-4(X)*, Scholastic Pr.) Scholastic, Inc.
Nova, Jacy & Nova, Nick. City of the Lost Souls. 2008. (ENG., Illus.). 224p. (YA). (gr. 8-12). 9.99 *(978-0-7582-2528-3(8)*, K-Teen) Kensington Publishing Corp.
Nuri, Amanda. Emerald Butterfly. 2013. 284p. (J). 31.32 *(978-1-105-66481-6(3))* Lulu Pr., Inc.
Nykko. The Elsewhere Chronicles. 2009. (Elsewhere Chronicles Ser.). (ENG.). (J). (gr. 4-8). pap. 39.62 *(978-0-7613-5088-0(8))*;Pack, Set. pap. 237.69 *(978-0-7613-5090-3(X))* Lerner Publishing Group.
O'Brien, Fitz James. The Wondersmith. 2004. reprint ed. pap. 1.99 *(978-1-4192-8848-7(2))* Kessinger Publishing, LLC.
O'Guilin, Peadar. The Call. 2016. (ENG.). 320p. (YA). (gr. 9). 18.99 *(978-1-338-04561-1(X))* Scholastic, Inc.
Oladokun, Alexander. Acrux Manor: The Prodigal's Curse (Hardcover) 2013. 206p. 28.50 *(978-1-300-68651-4(0))* Lulu Pr., Inc.
Optic, Oliver, pseud. Northern Lands: Or, Young America in Russia & Prussia; A Story of Travel & Adventure / by William T. Adams (Oliver Optic). 2006. 384p. per. 26.99 *(978-1-4255-4074-6(0))* Michigan Publishing.
—Northern Lands; or, Young America in Russia & Prussia a Story of Travel & Adventure. 2006. 376p. per. 26.99 *(978-1-4255-3923-8(8))* Michigan Publishing.
—Sunny Shores; or, Young America in Italy & Austria a Story of Travel & Adventure by William T Adams. 2006. 428p. per. 26.99 *(978-1-4255-4627-4(7))* Michigan Publishing.
Osbourne, Ozzy, pseud & Zink, Michelle. Guardian of the Gate. 2011. (Prophecy of the Sisters Trilogy Ser.: 2). (ENG.). 368p. (YA). (gr. 7-17). pap. 8.99 *(978-0-316-02740-3(5))* Little, Brown Bks. for Young Readers.
Paige, Danielle. The Wicked Will Rise. (Dorothy Must Die Ser.: 2). (YA). (gr. 9). 2016. 320p. pap. 9.99 *(978-0-06-228071-8(6))* 2015. (ENG.). 304p. 17.99 *(978-0-06-228070-1(8))* HarperCollins Pubs.
—The Wicked Will Rise. 2016. (Dorothy Must Die Ser.: 2). (YA). lib. bdg. 20.85 *(978-0-606-38170-3(8))* Turtleback Bks.
Pashley, Hilton. Gabriel's Clock. 2014. (ENG.). 304p. (J). (gr. 5-7). 16.99 *(978-0-544-30176-4(5)*, HMH Books For Young Readers) Houghton Mifflin Harcourt Publishing Co.
Patterson, James. Watch the Skies. 2014. lthr. 79.00 *(978-1-62715-571-7(6))* Leatherbound Bestsellers.
—Watch the Skies. l.t. ed. 2009. (Daniel X Ser.: 2). (ENG.). 352p. pap. 21.99 *(978-0-316-04363-2(X))* Little Brown & Co.
—Watch the Skies. 2010. (Daniel X Ser.: 2). (J). lib. bdg. 18.45 *(978-0-606-10550-7(6)*, Turtleback) Turtleback Bks.
Patterson, James & Rust, Ned. Watch the Skies. 2010. (Daniel X Ser.: 2). (ENG.). 288p. (J). (gr. 3-7). pap. 8.00 *(978-0-316-11969-6(5)*, Jimmy Patterson) Little Brown & Co.
Paver, Michelle. Outcast. Taylor, Geoff, illus. (J). (gr. 5). 2009. (Chronicles of Ancient Darkness Ser.: 4). 352p. pap. 6.99 *(978-0-06-072836-6(1)*, Tegen, Katherine Bks) 2008. (Chronicles of Ancient Darkness: No. 4). 336p. 16.99 *(978-0-06-072834-2(5))* HarperCollins Pubs.
Peacock, Ann & Lewis, C. S. The Chronicles of Narnia. Barbera, Tony et al, illus. Barbera, Tony et al, photos by. 2005. (Chronicles of Narnia Ser.). 64p. (J). *(978-1-4156-3678-7(8))* HarperCollins Pubs.
Pearl, Michael & Bulanadi, Danny. Good & Evil Pt. 2: Abraham, Pt. 2. 2007. (ENG., Illus.). 12p. (J). pap. 2.99 *(978-0-9786372-5-5(9))* No Greater Joy Ministries, Inc.
Pearson, Ridley. Dark Passage. 2013. (Kingdom Keepers Ser.: Bk. 6). (ENG.). 448p. (YA). (gr. 5-9). 17.99 *(978-1-4231-6489-0(X))* Hyperion Pr.
—Dark Passage. 2014. (Kingdom Keepers Ser.: 6). (J). lib. bdg. 19.65 *(978-0-606-35254-3(6))* Turtleback Bks.
—Disney after Dark. 2005. (Kingdom Keepers Ser.: Bk. 1). 324p. *(978-1-4156-2836-2(X))* Disney Pr.
—Disney after Dark. Elwell, Tristan, illus. 2009. (Kingdom Keepers Ser.: Bk. 1). (ENG.). 336p. (J). (gr. 5-9). pap. 8.99 *(978-1-4231-2311-8(5))* Hyperion Pr.
—Disney at Dawn. Elwell, Tristan, illus. 2009. (Kingdom Keepers Ser.: Bk. 2). (ENG.). 384p. (J). (gr. 5-9). pap. 8.99 *(978-1-4231-0708-8(X))* Hyperion Pr.
—Disney in Shadow. Elwell, Tristan, illus. 2011. (Kingdom Keepers Ser.: Bk. 3). (ENG.). 576p. (J). (gr. 5-17). pap. 8.99 *(978-1-4231-3856-3(2))* Hyperion Pr.
—Disney Lands. 2015. (Kingdom Keepers: Bk. 1). (ENG., Illus.). 352p. (J). (gr. 4-7). 17.99 *(978-1-4231-8431-7(9))* Hyperion Bks. for Children.
—The Insider. 2015. (Kingdom Keepers Ser.). (ENG., Illus.). 626p. (J). (gr. 5-9). pap. 9.99 *(978-1-4231-6524-8(1))* Hyperion Bks. for Children.
—Kingdom Keepers Boxed Set. 2014. (Kingdom Keepers Ser.). (ENG., Illus.). 1296p. (J). (gr. 3-7). pap. 25.99 *(978-1-4847-0402-8(9))* Hyperion Bks. for Children.
—Kingdom Keepers the Return. 2017. (Kingdom Keepers Ser.). (ENG.). 480p. (J). (gr. 5-9). 17.99 *(978-1-4231-8433-1(5))* Hyperion Bks. for Children.
—Power Play. Elwell, Tristan, illus. 2011. (Kingdom Keepers Ser.: Bk. 4). (ENG.). 448p. (J). (gr. 5-9). 17.99 *(978-1-4231-3857-0(0))* Hyperion Pr.
—Power Play. 2012. (Kingdom Keepers Ser.: 4). (J). lib. bdg. 19.65 *(978-0-606-23613-3(9)*, Turtleback) Turtleback Bks.
—The Return: Legacy of Secrets. 2016. (Kingdom Keepers Ser.: Bk. 2). (ENG., Illus.). 394p. (J). (gr. 5-9). 17.99 *(978-1-4231-8432-4(7))* Hyperion Bks. for Children.
—Shell Game. 2013. (Kingdom Keepers Ser.: Bk. 5). (ENG.). 560p. (J). (gr. 5-9). pap. 8.99 *(978-1-4231-7195-9(0))* Hyperion Pr.
—Shell Game. 2013. (Kingdom Keepers Ser.: 5). (J). lib. bdg. 19.65 *(978-0-606-27067-0(1)*, Turtleback) Turtleback Bks.
—The Syndrome. 2015. (Kingdom Keepers Ser.). (ENG., Illus.). 300p. (J). (gr. 5-9). 12.99 *(978-1-4847-2408-8(9))* Hyperion Bks. for Children.
Perkins, T. J. On Forbidden Ground: Sequel to Mystery of the Attic. 2006. (Illus.). 112p. (YA). 10.99 *(978-0-9777538-7-1(5))* GumShoe Press.
Perrin. Rafi's Song & the Stones of Erebrus. 2006. 10.18 *(978-0-9738036-0-0(6))* Ankh Bks. CAN. Dist: Mountain Bk. Co.
Perry Sr., Audie. Heroic Kids of the Inner Dimension, 1 vol. 2010. 73p. pap. 19.95 *(978-1-4489-5037-9(6))* America Star Bks.
The Portal in the Park: By Cricket Casey, songs & audio book performed by Grandmaseter Melle Mel, features Lady Gaga, Included CD in Book. 2010. (Illus.). 132p. (J). mass mkt. 19.95 *(978-0-9786488-0-0(3))* SCOJO ENTERTAINMENT.
Poteat, Bruce S. Evil Deception. 2013. 192p. (gr. 10-12). 30.95 *(978-1-4497-9565-8(X))*; pap. 13.95 *(978-1-4497-9570-2(6))* Author Solutions, Inc. (WestBow Pr.).
Prineas, Sarah. Found. Caparo, Antonio Javier, illus. 2011. (Magic Thief Ser.: 3). (ENG.). 384p. (J). (gr. 5). pap. 7.99 *(978-0-06-137595-8(0))* HarperCollins Pubs.
—Heart of the Land. 2017. (Spirit Animals: Fall of the Beasts Ser.: 5). (ENG.). 192p. (J). (gr. 3-7). 12.99 ***(978-1-338-11665-6(7))*** Scholastic, Inc.
—Heart of the Land (Spirit Animals: Fall of the Beasts, Book 5) 2017. (Spirit Animals: Fall of the Beasts Ser.: 5). (ENG.). 192p. (J). (gr. 3-7). 16.99 ***(978-1-338-18981-0(6))*** Scholastic, Inc.
Purday, Paul. The Two Lands. 2006. 310p. (J). pap. *(978-1-905809-11-0(5))* Pneuma Springs Publishing.
Purdie, Kathryn. Crystal Blade. 2017. (Burning Glass Ser.: 2). 368p. (YA). (gr. 9). 17.99 *(978-0-06-241239-3(6)*, Tegen, Katherine Bks) HarperCollins Pubs.
Random House Staff & Webster, Christy. Robot Rampage! (Teenage Mutant Ninja Turtles) Random House Staff & Spaziante, Patrick, illus. 2013. (Step into Reading Ser.). (ENG.). 48p. (J). (gr. k-3). pap. 3.99 *(978-0-307-98212-4(2)*, Random Hse. Bks. for Young Readers) Random Hse. Children's Bks.
The Rebel Princess. 2014. pap. 12.99 *(978-1-4621-1430-6(X))* Cedar Fort, Inc./CFI Distribution.
Reh, Rusalka. Pizzicato: The Abduction of the Magic Violin, 0 vols. Wilson, David Henry, tr. from GER. 2011. (ENG.). 132p. (J). (gr. 4-6). pap. 9.95 *(978-1-61109-004-8(0)*, 9781611090048) Amazon Publishing.
—The Secret of the Water Knight, 0 vols. Derbyshire, Katy, tr. unabr. ed. 2011. (ENG.). 100p. (J). (gr. 4-7). pap. 9.95 *(978-1-61109-006-2(7)*, 9781611090062) Amazon Publishing.
Right, Emma. Keeper of Reign. 2013. 340p. pap. 17.99 *(978-1-939337-69-6(0))* Telemachus Pr., LLC.
Riley, Clifford. Operation Trinity. 2012. (39 Clues: the Cahill Files Ser.). (ENG.). 144p. (J). (gr. 3-7). 9.99 *(978-0-545-43143-9(3))* Scholastic, Inc.
—Spymasters. 2013. (39 Clues: the Cahill Files Ser.). (ENG., Illus.). 256p. (J). (gr. 3-7). 12.99 *(978-0-545-56468-7(9))* Scholastic, Inc.
Roberts, Jeyn. Dark Inside. (ENG.). (YA). (gr. 9). 2012. 352p. pap. 10.99 *(978-1-4424-2352-7(8))* 2011. 336p. 17.99 *(978-1-4424-2351-0(X))* Simon & Schuster Bks. For Young Readers. (Simon & Schuster Bks. For Young Readers).
—Rage Within. (ENG., 368p. (YA). (gr. 9). 2013. Illus.). pap. 9.99 *(978-1-4424-2355-8(2))* 2012. 17.99 *(978-1-4424-2354-1(4))* Simon & Schuster Bks. For Young Readers. (Simon & Schuster Bks. For Young Readers).
Rodda, Emily. City of the Rats. 2012. (Deltora Quest Ser.). (ENG.). 160p. (J). (gr. 3-7). pap. 5.99 *(978-0-545-46022-4(0))* Scholastic, Inc.
Rodkey, Geoff. Blue Sea Burning. 2015. (Chronicles of Egg Ser.: 3). (ENG.). 400p. (J). (gr. 5). 7.99 *(978-0-14-751443-1(6)*, Puffin Books) Penguin Young Readers Group.
—Deadweather & Sunrise. 2013. (Chronicles of Egg Ser.: 1). (ENG.). 320p. (J). (gr. 5). pap. 7.99 *(978-0-14-242662-3(8)*, Puffin Books) Penguin Young Readers Group.
Rosen, Lucy. Despicable Me 2: Meet the Minions. 2013. (Passport to Reading Level 2 Ser.). (J). lib. bdg. 13.55 *(978-0-606-31739-9(2)*, Turtleback) Turtleback Bks.
—Justice League: Meet the Justice League. Gordon, Eric A. & Gordon, Steven E., illus. 2013. (I Can Read Level 2 Ser.). (ENG.). 32p. (J). (gr. -1-3). pap. 3.99 *(978-0-06-221002-9(5))* HarperCollins Pubs.
Ross, K. N. Daughters of the Lost World. 2012. 132p. 29.99 *(978-1-4653-8397-6(2))*; pap. 19.99 *(978-1-4653-8396-9(4))* Xlibris Corp.
Sak., M. J. The Stone Summons. 2007. 141p. pap. 15.95 *(978-1-84799-791-3(0))* Lulu Pr., Inc.
Salane, Jeffrey. Justice. 2016. (Lawless Ser.: 2). (ENG.). 288p. (J). (gr. 3-7). pap. 6.99 *(978-0-545-45032-4(2)*, Scholastic Pr.) Scholastic, Inc.
—Lawless. (J). 2013. 277p. *(978-0-545-54882-3(9))*Bk. 1. 2015. (ENG.). 288p. (gr. 3-7). pap. 6.99 *(978-0-545-45030-0(6))* Scholastic, Inc. (Scholastic Pr.).
—Lawless: Book 1. 2013. (Lawless Ser.). (ENG.). 288p. (J). (gr. 5-9). 16.99 *(978-0-545-45029-4(2)*, Scholastic Pr.) Scholastic, Inc.
—Mayhem. 2016. (Lawless Ser.: 3). (ENG.). 304p. (J). (gr. 3-7). 17.99 *(978-0-545-45033-1(0)*, Scholastic Pr.) Scholastic, Inc.
Sanders, Stephanie S. Villain School: Good Curses Evil. 2011. (ENG.). 240p. (YA). (gr. 3-12). pap. 6.99 *(978-1-59990-848-9(4)*, 9781599908489, Bloomsbury USA Childrens) Bloomsbury Publishing USA.
—Villain School: Hero in Disguise. 2012. (ENG.). 240p. (YA). (gr. 5-8). 15.99 *(978-1-59990-907-3(3)*, 9781599909073, Bloomsbury USA Childrens) Bloomsbury Publishing USA.
Santan. Good & Evil: The Princess & Devil. 2011. (Illus.). 64p. pap. 25.80 *(978-1-4567-9683-9(6))* AuthorHouse.
Saunders, George P. The Last Elf. 2007. 180p. per. 13.95 *(978-0-595-40843-6(5))* iUniverse, Inc.
Sazaklis, John. Battle in Metropolis. 2013. (Justice League Classic 8X8 Ser.). lib. bdg. 13.55 *(978-0-606-31827-3(5)*, Turtleback) Turtleback Bks.
—Marvel Avengers Assemble: Rise of the Avengers: Freeze Frame 1. 2015. (ENG.). 80p. (J). (gr. k-5). pap. 6.99 *(978-0-7944-3271-3(9))* Studio Fun International.
—Optimus Prime Versus Predaking. 2013. (Transformers 8x8 Ser.). (J). lib. bdg. 13.55 *(978-0-606-32272-0(8)*, Turtleback) Turtleback Bks.
Schaefer, Elizabeth. The Force Awakens: Episode VII. White, Dave, illus. 2016. (LEGO Star Wars 8X8 Ser.). (ENG.). 24p. (J). (gr. -1-3). 13.55 *(978-0-606-39117-7(7))* Turtleback Bks.
Scholastic & Howard, Kate. Fright Knight!, Bk. 2. 2016. (LEGO NEXO Knights Ser.). (ENG.). 80p. (J). (gr. 2-5). pap. 4.99 *(978-0-545-92555-6(X))* Scholastic, Inc.
Scholastic Editors. Space Justice! 2015. (LEGO DC Super Heroes Ser.). lib. bdg. 13.55 *(978-0-606-37077-6(3))* Turtleback Bks.
Scholastic Editors & Fry, Jason. Darth Vader. 2017. (Backstories Ser.: Vol. 6). (ENG., Illus.). 128p. (J). (gr. 3-7). 16.00 *(978-0-606-39145-0(2))* Turtleback Bks.
Scholastic, Inc. Staff. Space Justice! 2015. (LEGO DC Super Heroes Ser.). (ENG., Illus.). 32p. (J). (gr. -1-3). pap. 3.99 *(978-0-545-82556-6(3))* Scholastic, Inc.
Schwab, Victoria. This Savage Song. (Monsters of Verity Ser.: 1). (YA). (gr. 9). 2017. 480p. pap. 9.99 *(978-0-06-238086-9(9))* 2016. (ENG.). 464p. 17.99 *(978-0-06-238085-2(0))* HarperCollins Pubs. (Greenwillow Bks.).
—This Savage Song. 2017. (Monsters of Verity Ser.: 1). lib. bdg. 20.85 ***(978-0-606-40071-8(0))*** Turtleback Bks.
Sealed with a Kick. 2015. (Kung Fu Panda TV Ser.). (ENG., Illus.). 32p. (J). (gr. k-2). pap. 3.99 *(978-1-4814-1748-8(7)*, Simon Spotlight) Simon Spotlight.
Seduction. 2014. (Legacy Ser.). (ENG., Illus.). 416p. (YA). (gr. 9). 17.99 *(978-1-4814-0023-7(1)*, Simon & Schuster/Paula Wiseman Bks.) Simon & Schuster/Paula Wiseman Bks.
Shaffer, Jeanne E. The Swimmer with a Rope in His Teeth: A Shadow Fable. Cruse, Howard, illus. 2004. (ENG.). 1p. pap. 15.98 *(978-1-59102-181-0(2)*, Pyr Bks.) Prometheus Bks., Pubs.
Sharpe, Gerald. Parade of Lights. Moya, Patricia, illus. 2007. (What Lies Beneath the Bed Ser.). 487p. (J). per. 11.00 *(978-1-933894-01-0(6))* IJN Publishing, Inc.
Sheryl the pearl productions, Sheryl Clayton. Teeny the Magic Genie. 2007. (Illus.). 170p. (J). per. 12.95 *(978-0-9795862-0-0(8))* STR8*UP Productions.
Shi, Charleston. The Quest of the Phoenix: Book 1, the Phoenix & the Yeti. 2009. 168p. pap. 14.95 *(978-1-60844-173-0(3))* Dog Ear Publishing, LLC.
—The Quest of the Phoenix: Book Two, Storm of the Kraken. 2010. 180p. pap. 14.95 *(978-1-60844-352-9(3))* Dog Ear Publishing, LLC.
Shirvington, Jessica. Emblaze. 2013. (Embrace Ser.: 3). (ENG.). 464p. (YA). (gr. 7-12). pap. 14.99 *(978-1-4022-7131-1(X))*; 16.99 *(978-1-4022-6846-5(7))* Sourcebooks, Inc.
—Embrace. 2012. (Embrace Ser.: 1). (ENG.). 400p. (YA). (gr. 7-12). pap. 9.99 *(978-1-4022-7125-0(5))* Sourcebooks, Inc.
—Empower. 2014. (Embrace Ser.: 5). (ENG.). 496p. (YA). (gr. 7-12). 16.99 *(978-1-4022-9460-0(3))* Sourcebooks, Inc.
—Endless. 2014. (Embrace Ser.: 4). (ENG.). 480p. (YA). (gr. 7-12). pap. 9.99 *(978-1-4022-8945-3(6))* Sourcebooks, Inc.
—Entice. 2013. (Embrace Ser.: 2). (ENG.). 464p. (YA). (gr. 7-12). pap. 10.99 *(978-1-4022-7128-1(X))* Sourcebooks, Inc.
Shon. Henry Boothill: The Return of Nidagall, 1 vol. 2010. 52p. pap. 16.95 *(978-1-4512-8700-4(3))* America Star Bks.
Sierra, JulieAnn. Legacy & the Dark Prince, 1 vol. 2009. 209p. pap. 24.95 *(978-1-61582-693-3(9))* America Star Bks.
Siglain, Michael. Breakout!, 1 vol. Marvel Illustrators, illus. 2012. (Avengers: Earth's Mightiest Heroes! Ser.). (ENG.). 24p. (J). (gr. -1-4). lib. bdg. 24.21 *(978-1-61479-001-3(9))* Spotlight.
—Captain America - The Winter Soldier: Rescue at Sea. 2014. (ENG.). 24p. (J). (gr. 3-7). pap. 4.99 *(978-1-4847-0537-7(8)*, Marvel Pr.) Disney Publishing Worldwide.
Simpson, N. J. Not So Random. 2011. 200p. pap. 13.67 *(978-0-557-83059-6(1))* Lulu Pr., Inc.
Smedman, Lisa. Sacrifice of the Widow. 2007. (Lady Penitent Ser.: Bk. 1). 311p. *(978-1-4287-1497-7(9))* Wizards of the Coast.
Smith, L. J. Dark Visions: The Strange Power - The Possessed - The Passion. 2009. (Dark Visions Ser.: Bks 1-3). (ENG.). 752p. (YA). (gr. 7). pap. 9.99 *(978-1-4169-8956-1(0)*, Simon Pulse) Simon Pulse.

—The Divide, Vol. 4. 2013. (Secret Circle Ser.: 4). (ENG.). 320p. (YA). (gr. 8). pap. 10.99 *(978-0-06-213041-9(2),* HarperTeen) HarperCollins Pubs.
Smith, Melinda. Soldiers for Battle. 2008. 192p. 24.50 *(978-1-60693-398-5(1),* Eloquent Bks.) Strategic Book Publishing & Rights Agency (SBPRA).
Smith, Ronald L. The Mesmerist. 2017. (ENG.). 272p. (J). (gr. 5-7). 16.99 *(978-0-544-44528-4(7),* Clarion Bks.) Houghton Mifflin Harcourt Trade & Reference Pubs.
Sniegoski, Thomas E. Aerie & Reckoning. 2010. (Fallen Ser.: 2). (ENG.). 576p. (YA). (gr. 11-18). pap. 9.99 *(978-1-4424-0863-0(4),* Simon Pulse) Simon Pulse.
—End of Days Vol. 3. 2011. (Fallen Ser.: 3). (ENG.). 384p. (YA). (gr. 9). pap. 9.99 *(978-1-4424-2349-7(8),* Simon Pulse) Simon Pulse.
—The Fallen 5: Armageddon. 2013. (Fallen Ser.: 5). (ENG., Illus.). 592p. (YA). (gr. 9). pap. 9.99 *(978-1-4424-6005-8(9),* Simon Pulse) Simon Pulse.
—The Fallen & Leviathan. 2010. (Fallen Ser.: 1). (ENG.). 544p. (YA). (gr. 11). pap. 11.99 *(978-1-4424-0862-3(6),* Simon Pulse) Simon Pulse.
—Forsaken. 2012. (Fallen Ser.: 4). (ENG.). 416p. (YA). (gr. 9). pap. 9.99 *(978-1-4424-4699-1(4),* Simon Pulse) Simon Pulse.
Sonoda, Hideki. Pokémon: Zoroark: Master of Illusions. 2011. (ENG.). 192p. (J). pap. 7.99 *(978-1-4215-4221-8(8))* Viz Media.
Spears, Jr. Derek's Dilemm. 2009. 148p. pap. 24.95 *(978-1-60836-387-2(2))* America Star Bks.
Star Wars Villains. 2011. (Illus.). (J). *(978-0-545-28664-0(6))* Scholastic, Inc.
Stein, Tammar. Kindred. 2012. (ENG.). 276p. (YA). (gr. 7). pap. 8.99 *(978-0-375-85349-4(9),* Ember) Random Hse. Children's Bks.
Stentiford, Tyler Michael. A Darker Secret. 2009. (ENG.). 128p. (YA). pap. 9.99 *(978-1-60138-315-0(0))* Atlantic Publishing Group, Inc.
Stevenson, Robert Louis. Dr Jekyll & Mr Hyde. Lubach, Vanessa, illus. 2014. (Classics of Science Fiction Ser.). (ENG.). 64p. pap. 6.95 *(978-1-906230-15-9(3))* Real Reads Ltd. GBR. Dist: Casemate Pubs. & Bk. Distributors, LLC.
—Dr. Jekyll & Mr. Hyde, 1 vol. 2010. (Illustrated Classics Ser.). (ENG., Illus.). 64p. (YA). (gr. 9-12). per. 9.95 *(978-1-56254-894-0(8))* Saddleback Educational Publishing, Inc.
—The Strange Case of Dr. Jekyll & Mr. Hyde. (Classics Illustrated Ser.). (Illus.). 52p. (YA). pap. 4.95 *(978-1-57209-008-8(1))* Classics International Entertainment, Inc.
—The Strange Case of Dr. Jekyll & Mr. Hyde. Andrews, Gary, illus. 2008. (Fast Track Classics Ser.). (ENG.). 48p. pap. 10.00 *(978-1-4190-5082-4(6))* Steck-Vaughn.
—The Strange Case of Dr. Jekyll & Mr. Hyde. McKowen, Scott, illus. 2011. (Sterling Unabridged Classics Ser.). (ENG.). 96p. (J). 9.95 *(978-1-4027-8402-6(3))* Sterling Publishing Co., Inc.
—The Strange Case of Dr. Jekyll & Mr. Hyde. Akib, Jamel, illus. 2006. (Classic Starts(tm) Ser.). (ENG.). 160p. (J). (gr. 2-4). 6.95 *(978-1-4027-2667-5(8),* 1252057) Sterling Publishing Co., Inc.
—Strange Case of Dr. Jekyll & Mr. Hyde. Kennedy, Cam, illus. 2008. (ENG.). 48p. (YA). (gr. 5). pap. 11.95 *(978-0-88776-882-8(2),* Tundra Bks.) Tundra Bks. CAN. Dist: Penguin Random Hse. LLC.
—The Strange Case of Dr. Jekyll & Mr Hyde (Quality Library Classics) 2008. (YA). pap. 14.95 *(978-1-57545-703-1(2))* RP Media.
Stevenson, Robert Louis & Venable, Alan. The Strange Case of Dr. Jekyll & Mr. Hyde. 2005. (Classic Literature Ser.). 108p. pap. 9.95 *(978-1-4105-0119-6(1));* pap., E-Book 69.00 incl. audio compact disk *(978-1-4105-0117-2(5))* Johnston, Don Inc.
Stiefvater, Maggie. Hunted, Bk. 2. 2014. (Spirit Animals Ser.: 2). (ENG., Illus.). 192p. (J). (gr. 3-7). 12.99 *(978-0-545-52244-1(7))* Scholastic, Inc.
Stilton, Geronimo & Heim, Julia. The Perilous Plants. Usai, Luca et al, illus. 2016. 117p. (J). ***(978-0-545-93092-5(8))*** Scholastic, Inc.
Stine, R. L. Darkest Dawn. 2005. (Fear Street Nights Ser.: No. 3). 182p. (YA). lib. bdg. 20.00 *(978-1-4242-0994-1(3))* Fitzgerald Bks.
—Darkest Dawn. 2012. (Fear Street Nights Ser.: 3). (ENG.). 192p. (YA). (gr. 7). pap. 9.99 *(978-1-4424-6058-4(X),* Simon Pulse) Simon Pulse.
—The Streets of Panic Park. 2009. (Goosebumps HorrorLand Ser.: No. 10). (Illus.). 136p. 16.00 *(978-1-60686-405-0(X))* Perfection Learning Corp.
Strickland, James R. Lincoln's Lost Papers. 2008. 131p. (J). pap. 11.95 *(978-0-7414-4601-5(4))* Infinity Publishing.
Sutherland, Tui T. Escaping Peril. 2017. (Wings of Fire Ser.: 8). lib. bdg. 17.20 ***(978-0-606-40142-5(3))*** Turtleback Bks.
Suzukaze, Ryo. Kuklo Unbound. Shibamoto, Thores, illus. 2015. (Attack on Titan Ser.). (ENG.). 298p. (J). (gr. 7). pap. 14.95 *(978-1-939130-87-7(5),* Vertical) Vertical, Inc.
Taneja, Sweta. Krishna - Defender of Dharma. Nagulakonda, Rajesh, illus. 2013. (Campfire Graphic Novels Ser.). (ENG.). 152p. (YA). (gr. 5-12). pap. 14.99 *(978-93-80741-12-3(X),* Campfire) Steerforth Pr.
Tarkoff, Sarah. Eye of the Beholder - Revelation. 2018. (Eye of the Beholder Ser.: 1). 304p. pap. 15.99 *(978-0-06-245638-0(5),* Harper Voyager) HarperCollins Pubs.
Taylor, G. P. The Shadowmancer Returns: The Curse of Salamander Street. 2007. (Shadowmancer; 04 Ser.). 240p. (J). *(978-1-4287-4670-1(6),* Putnam Juvenile) Penguin Publishing Group.
Teague, Victoria. Dragons, Demons, & Feathers. 2007. 48p. pap. 19.96 *(978-1-4357-0317-9(0))* Lulu Pr., Inc.
TenNapel, Doug. The Rise of Herk. 2016. (Nnewts Ser.: 2). (ENG.). 208p. (J). (gr. 3-7). 19.99 *(978-0-545-67652-6(5),* Graphix) Scholastic, Inc.
Terrell, Heather. Eternity. 2011. (Fallen Angel Ser.: 2). (ENG.). 304p. (YA). (gr. 8). pap. 8.99 *(978-0-06-196571-5(5),* HarperTeen) HarperCollins Pubs.
Terry, Teri. The Book of Lies. 2017. (ENG.). 384p. (YA). (gr. 7). 17.99 ***(978-0-544-90048-6(0),*** Clarion Bks.) Houghton Mifflin Harcourt Trade & Reference Pubs.
Thomas, Blair L. The Sabatini Prophecy. 2008. (ENG.). 496p. (YA). 8.99 *(978-0-9760237-4-6(1))* Axiom Hse.
Thomas, Rich. The Amazing Spider-Man: An Origin Story, 1 vol. Clark, Jeff, illus. 2012. (Marvel Origins Ser.). (ENG.). 48p. (J). (gr. -1-4). lib. bdg. 24.21 *(978-1-61479-007-5(8))* Spotlight.
—The Incredible Hulk: An Origin Story, 1 vol. Semeiks, Val, illus. 2012. (Marvel Origins Ser.). (ENG.). 48p. (J). (gr. -1-4). lib. bdg. 24.21 *(978-1-61479-009-9(4))* Spotlight.
—The Uncanny X-Men: An Origin Story, 1 vol. The Storybook Art Group, illus. 2012. (Marvel Origins Ser.). (ENG.). 48p. (J). (gr. -1-4). lib. bdg. 24.21 *(978-1-61479-012-9(4))* Spotlight.
Tiernan, Cate. Book of Shadows - The Coven - Blood Witch. 2010. (Sweep Ser.: 1). (ENG.). 592p. (YA). (gr. 7-18). 8.99 *(978-0-14-241717-1(3),* Speak) Penguin Young Readers Group.
—Sweep Vol. 3: The Calling - Changeling - Strife, 3 vols. 2011. (Sweep Ser.: 3). (ENG.). 576p. (YA). (gr. 7-18). 9.99 *(978-0-14-241965-7(9),* Speak) Penguin Young Readers Group.
Todorov, Boriana & Todorov, Vladimir. The Moon Rock. 2007. (ENG., Illus.). 110p. (J). (gr. 2-6). 19.95 *(978-1-894965-77-4(9))* Simply Read Bks. CAN. Dist: Ingram Publisher Services.
Toreeva, Natalia G. The Battle on the Kalinov-Bridge: A Russian Fairy Tale. 2012. 48p. pap. 18.50 *(978-1-61897-434-1(3),* Strategic Bk. Publishing) Strategic Book Publishing & Rights Agency (SBPRA).
Tucholke, April Genevieve. Between the Spark & the Burn. 2014. (ENG.). 336p. (YA). (gr. 7). 17.99 *(978-0-8037-4047-1(6),* Dial Bks) Penguin Young Readers Group.
Tucker, Peter. Pumpkin Bunch. 2009. 32p. 16.30 *(978-0-615-21675-1(7))* PT Publishing.
Turner, Katharine. Reptile Rampage. Gordon, Eric A. & Gordon, Steven E., illus. 2012. (I Can Read Level 2 Ser.). (ENG.). 32p. (J). (gr. -1-3). pap. 3.99 *(978-0-06-188521-1(5))* HarperCollins Pubs.
—Reptile Rampage. 2012. (Justice League Classic: I Can Read! Ser.). (J). lib. bdg. 13.55 *(978-0-606-23593-8(0),* Turtleback) Turtleback Bks.
Umezu, Kazuo. The Drifting Classroom. Roman, Annette, ed. Umezu, Kazuo, illus. 2007. (Drifting Classroom Ser.: 8). (ENG., Illus.). 192p. pap. 9.99 *(978-1-4215-0960-0(1))* Viz Media.
Universal. Mower Minions. Miller, Ed, illus. 2016. (ENG.). 24p. (J). (gr. -1-3). pap. 5.99 *(978-0-316-39297-6(9))* Little, Brown Bks. for Young Readers.
Universal & King, Trey. Best Boss Ever. 2017. (Passport to Reading Level 2 Ser.). (ENG., Illus.). 32p. (J). (gr. -1-3). pap. 4.99 ***(978-0-316-50761-5(X))*** Little, Brown Bks. for Young Readers.
Upton, Robert Jesten. Milo & the Dragon Cross: A Novel. 2017. (YA). pap. ***(978-1-63293-177-1(X))*** Sunstone Pr.
Valente, Catherynne M. The Girl Who Circumnavigated Fairyland in a Ship of Her Own Making. Juan, Ana, illus. 2011. (Fairyland Ser.: 1). (ENG.). 256p. (YA). (gr. 5-9). 16.99 *(978-0-312-64961-6(4),* 9780312649616) Feiwel & Friends.
—The Girl Who Circumnavigated Fairyland in a Ship of Her Own Making. 2012. (CHI & ENG., Illus.). 304p. (J). (gr. 5-8). pap. *(978-986-6026-24-9(8))* Muses Publishing Hse.
—The Girl Who Circumnavigated Fairyland in a Ship of Her Own Making. Juan, Ana, illus. 2012. (Fairyland Ser.: 1). (ENG.). 288p. (YA). (gr. 5-9). pap. 7.99 *(978-1-250-01019-3(5),* 9781250010193) Square Fish.
Valentino, Serena. Poor Unfortunate Soul: A Tale of the Sea Witch. Disney Storybook Art Team, illus. 2016. (Villains Ser.: 3). (ENG.). 208p. (J). (gr. 5-9). 17.99 *(978-1-4847-2405-7(4))* Disney Pr.
van Arsdale, Peternelle. The Beast Is an Animal. 2017. (ENG., Illus.). 352p. (YA). (gr. 9). 17.99 *(978-1-4814-8841-9(4),* McElderry, Margaret K. Bks.) McElderry, Margaret K. Bks.
Various, illus. 5-Minute Batman Stories. 2015. (ENG.). 192p. (J). (gr. -1-3). 12.99 *(978-0-06-235798-4(0),* HarperFestival) HarperCollins Pubs.
Velasquez, Crystal. The Circle of Lies. 2016. (Hunters of Chaos Ser.: 2). (ENG., Illus.). 240p. (J). (gr. 3-7). 16.99 *(978-1-4814-2455-4(6),* Aladdin) Simon & Schuster Children's Publishing.
—Hunters of Chaos. (Hunters of Chaos Ser.: 1). (ENG., Illus.). (J). (gr. 3-7). 2016. 288p. pap. 6.99 *(978-1-4814-2453-0(X))* 2015. 272p. 16.99 *(978-1-4814-2452-3(1))* Simon & Schuster Children's Publishing. (Aladdin).
Vivinetto, Gina. With Superman & Wonder Woman. Farley, Rick & Tripp, Kanila, illus. 2011. (ENG.). 24p. (J). (gr. -1-3). pap. 3.99 *(978-0-06-188531-0(2),* HarperFestival) HarperCollins Pubs.
Voltaire, Aurelio. Call of the Jersey Devil. 2013. (ENG.). 352p. pap. 7.95 *(978-1-939392-00-8(4),* Spence City) Spencer Hill Pr.
Wagner, Hilary. Lords of Trillium: Book III of the Nightshade Chronicles. Rayyan, Omar, illus. 2015. (Nightshade Chronicles Ser.: 3). (ENG.). 224p. (J). (gr. 4). pap. 7.95 *(978-0-8234-3306-3(4))* Holiday Hse., Inc.
—The White Assassin. 2012. (Nightshade Chronicles Ser.: 2). (ENG.). 304p. (J). (gr. 4). pap. 7.95 *(978-0-8234-2485-6(5))* Holiday Hse., Inc.
Waid, Mark. Incorruptible. Takara, Marcio, illus. 2012. (ENG.). 128p. Vol. 6. (Incorruptible Ser.: 6). (gr. 10). pap. 16.99 *(978-1-60886-084-5(1))* Vol. 7. (gr. 9). pap. 16.99 *(978-1-60886-085-2(X))* Boom! Studios.
Walden, Mark. Aftershock. 2014. (H. I. V. E. Ser.: 7). (ENG., Illus.). 304p. (J). (gr. 3-7). 17.99 *(978-1-4424-9467-1(0),* Simon & Schuster Bks. For Young Readers) Simon & Schuster Bks. For Young Readers.
—Deadlock. 2015. (H. I. V. E. Ser.: 8). (ENG., Illus.). 304p. (J). (gr. 3-7). 16.99 *(978-1-4424-9470-1(0),* Simon & Schuster Bks. For Young Readers) Simon & Schuster Bks. For Young Readers.
—Dreadnought. (H. I. V. E. Ser.: 4). (ENG.). (J). (gr. 3-7). 2012. 320p. pap. 8.99 *(978-1-4424-1368-9(9))* 2011. 304p. 16.99 *(978-1-4424-2186-8(X))* Simon & Schuster Bks. For Young Readers. (Simon & Schuster Bks. For Young Readers).
—Escape Velocity. (H. I. V. E. Ser.: 3). (ENG.). (J). (gr. 3-7). 2012. 368p. pap. 8.99 *(978-1-4424-1367-2(0))* 2011. 352p. 16.99 *(978-1-4424-2185-1(1))* Simon & Schuster Bks. For Young Readers. (Simon & Schuster Bks. For Young Readers).
—H. I. V. E. Higher Institute of Villainous Education. 2007. (H. I. V. E. Ser.: 1). (ENG., Illus.). 320p. (J). (gr. 3-7). 17.99 *(978-1-4169-3571-1(1),* Simon & Schuster Bks. For Young Readers) Simon & Schuster Bks. For Young Readers.
—The Higher Institute of Villainous Education. 2008. (H. I. V. E. Ser.: 1). (ENG.). 320p. (J). (gr. 3-7). pap. 8.99 *(978-1-4169-3572-8(X),* Simon & Schuster Bks. For Young Readers) Simon & Schuster Bks. For Young Readers.
—The Overlord Protocol. (H. I. V. E. Ser.: 2). (ENG.). 384p. (J). (gr. 3-7). 2009. pap. 7.99 *(978-1-4169-3574-2(6))* 2008. 18.99 *(978-1-4169-3573-5(8))* Simon & Schuster Bks. For Young Readers. (Simon & Schuster Bks. For Young Readers).
—Rogue. (H. I. V. E. Ser.: 5). (ENG.). (J). (gr. 3-7). 2012. 320p. pap. 8.99 *(978-1-4424-1369-6(7))* 2011. 304p. 16.99 *(978-1-4424-2187-5(8))* Simon & Schuster Bks. For Young Readers. (Simon & Schuster Bks. For Young Readers).
—Zero Hour. (H. I. V. E. Ser.: 6). (ENG.). 304p. (J). (gr. 3-7). 2013. pap. 7.99 *(978-1-4424-1373-3(5))* 2012. 18.99 *(978-1-4424-2188-2(6))* Simon & Schuster Bks. For Young Readers. (Simon & Schuster Bks. For Young Readers).
Walker, Rysa. Time's Divide, 0 vols. 2015. (Chronos Files Ser.: 3). (ENG.). 543p. (YA). (gr. 7-12). pap. 12.95 *(978-1-5039-4658-3(4),* 9781503946583, Skyscape) Amazon Publishing.
Waltz, Dan. Dragon Fly: A Gnome's Great Adventure. Waltz, Dan, illus. 2007. (Illus.). 360p. (YA). per. 12.49 *(978-0-9741774-7-2(4))* D. W. Publishing.
Wang, Sean, illus. Space Justice. 2015. 32p. (J). ***(978-0-545-82582-5(2))*** Scholastic, Inc.
Webber, Jerry. The Game: None. 2007. 52p. per. 9.95 *(978-1-4327-0911-2(9))* Outskirts Pr., Inc.
Webster, Christy. Robot Rampage! 2013. (Step into Reading Level 4 Ser.). lib. bdg. 13.55 *(978-0-606-26985-8(1),* Turtleback) Turtleback Bks.
West, Tracey, adapted by. Jack in! MegaMan! 2006. 59p. (J). *(978-0-439-76837-5(3))* Scholastic, Inc.
Weston, Paula. Shadows. 2013. (Rephaim Ser.). (ENG.). 400p. (YA). (gr. 9). 17.99 *(978-1-77049-547-0(9),* Tundra Bks.) Tundra Bks. CAN. Dist: Penguin Random Hse. LLC.
Weston Woods Staff, creator. Hansel & Gretel. 2011. 38.75 *(978-0-439-80425-7(6))* Weston Woods Studios, Inc.
Whelan, Daniel. The Box of Demons. 2016. (ENG.). 256p. (YA). (gr. 7). pap. 10.99 *(978-1-4472-7373-8(7))* Pan Macmillan GBR. Dist: Independent Pubs. Group.
White, Kiersten. And I Darken. (ENG.). (YA). (gr. 7). 2017. (And I Darken Ser.: 1). 512p. pap. 10.99 ***(978-0-553-52234-1(5),*** Ember) 2016. (Illus.). 496p. 18.99 *(978-0-553-52231-0(0),* Delacorte Pr.) 2016. (Illus.). 496p. lib. bdg. 21.99 *(978-0-553-52232-7(9),* Delacorte Pr.) Random Hse. Children's Bks.
—Now I Rise. 2017. (And I Darken Ser.: 2). (ENG.). 480p. (YA). (gr. 7). 18.99 ***(978-0-553-52235-8(3));*** lib. bdg. 21.99 ***(978-0-553-52236-5(1))*** Random Hse. Children's Bks. (Delacorte Pr.).
Wiebe, Joanna. The Wicked Awakening of Anne Merchant. 2015. (V Trilogy Ser.: Bk. 2). (ENG.). 320p. (gr. 7). pap. 12.95 *(978-1-940363-29-5(2))* BenBella Bks.
Wignall, K. J. Alchemy. Book Two of the Mercian Trilogy: Alchemy. 2012. (ENG.). 336p. (J). (gr. 7). 17.99 *(978-1-60684-265-2(X),* Carolrhoda Lab™) Lerner Publishing Group.
—Blood: Book One of the Mercian Trilogy. 2012. (ENG.). 272p. (J). (gr. 7). pap. 9.99 *(978-1-60684-387-1(7),* Carolrhoda Lab™) Lerner Publishing Group.
Wilde, Gloria. Lucifer: Good Angel Gone Bad. Bauer, John, illus. 2007. 36p. 14.95 *(978-1-57258-462-4(9),* 945-6323) TEACH Services, Inc.
Wills, Julia. Fleeced! an Aries Adventure. 2016. (Aries Adventure Ser.). (ENG.). 400p. (J). (gr. 4-7). pap. 10.99 *(978-1-84812-476-9(7))* Bonnier Publishing GBR. Dist: Independent Pubs. Group.
Windham, Ryder. Island of Lost Masks. 2015. lib. bdg. 16.00 *(978-0-606-37793-5(X))* Turtleback Bks.
—The Wrath of Darth Maul. 2012. 216p. (J). *(978-0-545-43367-9(3))* Scholastic, Inc.
Windsor, M. L. Jack Death. Ewald, Chris, illus. 2016. (ENG.). 165p. (J). (gr. 2-7). 12.99 *(978-1-939547-28-6(8))* Creston Bks.
Wood, Brian. The Cramp Twins: Lucien's Little. 2005. (Illus.). 112p. 13.95 *(978-1-904674-01-6(1))* Reynolds & Hearn GBR. Dist: Trafalgar Square Publishing.
Wrecks, Billy. Eye of the Dragon (Marvel: Iron Man) Spaziante, Patrick, illus. 2016. (Little Golden Book Ser.). (ENG.). 24p. (J). (-k). 4.99 *(978-0-307-97654-3(8),* Golden Bks.) Random Hse. Children's Bks.
—The Mighty Avengers (Marvel: the Avengers) Spaziante, Patrick, illus. 2016. (Little Golden Book Ser.). (ENG.). 24p. (J). (gr. k-k). 4.99 *(978-0-307-93109-2(9),* Golden Bks.) Random Hse. Children's Bks.
Yang, Gene Luen. Superman, Volume 1: Before Truth. 2016. lib. bdg. 29.40 *(978-0-606-39485-7(0))* Turtleback Bks.
Young, Lena. Karma: Reaping What We Sow. Tsai, Dora, illus. 2005. 26p. (J). pap. *(978-1-933554-00-6(2))* Primordia.
Zimmerman, Diana S. Kandide & the Secret of the Mists, Bk. 1. Gadd, Maxine, illus. 2008. (Calabiyau Chronicles Ser.). 289p. (J). (gr. 4-7). pap. 9.99 *(978-0-9794328-2-8(0))* Noesis Publishing.
Zink, Michelle. Circle of Fire. 2012. (Prophecy of the Sisters Trilogy Ser.: 3). (ENG.). 368p. (YA). (gr. 7-17). pap. 22.99 *(978-0-316-03446-3(0))* Little, Brown Bks. for Young Readers.
—Prophecy of the Sisters. 2010. (Prophecy of the Sisters Trilogy Ser.: 1). (ENG.). 368p. (YA). (gr. 7-17). pap. 8.99 *(978-0-316-02741-0(3))* Little, Brown Bks. for Young Readers.
—A Temptation of Angels. 2013. (ENG.). 448p. (YA). (gr. 7). pap. 9.99 *(978-0-14-242423-0(4),* Speak) Penguin Young Readers Group.

GOOD GROOMING

see Beauty, Personal

GOOFY (FICTITIOUS CHARACTER)—FICTION

Amano, Shiro. Chain of Memories, Vol. 2. 2nd rev. ed. 2007. (Kingdom Hearts Ser.). (Illus.). 232p. (gr. 4-7). pap. 9.99 *(978-1-59816-638-5(7),* Tokyopop Kids) TOKYOPOP, Inc.
Ambrosio, Stefano. Mouse Magic. Pastrovicchio, Lorenzo, illus. 2010. (ENG.). 112p. (J). 24.99 *(978-1-60886-550-5(9));* Vol. 1. pap. 9.99 *(978-1-60886-541-3(X))* Boom! Studios.
—Wizards of Mickey - Grand Tournament, Vol. 2. Pastrovicchio, Lorenzo & Magic Eye Studios, illus. 2010. (Wizards of Mickey Ser.). (ENG.). 128p. (J). (gr. 3-6). pap. 9.99 *(978-1-60886-564-2(9))* Boom! Studios.
Amerikaner, Susan. Goofy at Bat. 2013. (Mickey & Friends World of Reading Ser.). (J). lib. bdg. 13.55 *(978-0-606-27117-2(1),* Turtleback) Turtleback Bks.
Barks, Carl, et al. Walt Disney's Christmas Parade #5. 2008. (Illus.). 80p. pap. 9.50 *(978-1-60360-005-7(1))* Gemstone Publishing, Inc.
Castellan, Andrea. Mickey Mouse & the Orbiting Nightmare. 2011. (ENG., Illus.). 128p. (J). pap. *(978-1-60886-630-4(0))* Boom! Studios.
Disney Storybook Artists Staff, illus. Disney Mickey Mouse Clubhouse Movie Theater: Storybook & Movie Projector. 2012. (Movie Theater Ser.). (ENG.). 32p. (J). (gr. k-3). 19.99 *(978-0-7944-2587-6(9))* Reader's Digest Assn., Inc., The.
Mei, Michael. The Goofy Gourmet: Let's Cook Today! 2008. (J). pap. 12.95 *(978-0-9800752-1-2(1))* Big Company, LLC, The.
Ritchey, Kate. Goofy's Sledding Contest. 2013. (Mickey & Friends World of Reading Ser.). (J). lib. bdg. 13.55 *(978-0-606-32293-5(0),* Turtleback) Turtleback Bks.
Scollon, Bill. A Goofy Fairy Tale. 2014. (Mickey Mouse 8x8 Ser.). (J). lib. bdg. 14.75 *(978-0-606-35900-9(1))* Turtleback Bks.

GOOSE

see Geese

GOPHERS

Carr, Aaron. Gophers. 2014. (J). *(978-1-4896-2946-3(7))* Weigl Pubs., Inc.
McDonnell, Julia. Gophers. 2014. (Animals of Mass Destruction Ser.). 32p. (J). (gr. 2-5). 25.25 *(978-1-4824-1046-4(X))* Stevens, Gareth Publishing LLLP.

GORILLA

Applegate, Katherine. Ivan: the Remarkable True Story of the Shopping Mall Gorilla. Karas, G. Brian, illus. 2014. (ENG.). 40p. (J). (gr. -1-3). 17.99 *(978-0-544-25230-1(6),* Clarion Bks.) Houghton Mifflin Harcourt Publishing Co.
Barnes, Julia. The Secret Lives of Gorillas. 2007. (Secret Lives of Animals Ser.). (Illus.). 32p. (gr. 2-6). lib. bdg. 26.00 *(978-0-8368-7658-1(X),* Gareth Stevens Learning Library) Stevens, Gareth Publishing LLLP.
Books Are Fun 8 Title Animal Lives Set: Gorilla. 2006. (J). *(978-1-59566-307-8(X))* QEB Publishing Inc.
Brannon, Cecelia H. Baby Gorillas at the Zoo. 2016. (All about Baby Zoo Animals Ser.). (ENG.). 24p. (J). (gr. k-1). pap. 9.35 *(978-0-7660-7141-4(3));* (Illus.). 22.60 *(978-0-7660-7143-8(X))* Enslow Pubs., Inc.
Brewer, Stephen. Gorillas. 2010. (Amazing Animals Ser.). (ENG.). 48p. (J). (gr. 2-6). pap. 10.50 *(978-1-4339-4014-9(0));* lib. bdg. 28.00 *(978-1-4339-4013-2(2))* Stevens, Gareth Publishing LLLP. (Gareth Stevens Learning Library).
—Gorillas. 2007. (J). *(978-1-59939-123-6(6),* Reader's Digest Young Families, Inc.) Studio Fun International.
Chambers, Catherine E. Ape Adventures, Level 3. 2013. (DK Readers Ser.). (ENG.). 48p. (J). (gr. 2-4). pap. 3.99 *(978-1-4654-0239-4(X),* DK Children) Dorling Kindersley Publishing, Inc.
Clark, Willow. Gorillas: Gorilas: Life in the Troop: Vida en la Manada. 2011. (Animal Families / Familias de animales Ser.). (SPA & ENG., Illus.). 24p. lib. bdg. 22.60 *(978-1-4488-3127-2(X),* PowerKids Pr.) Rosen Publishing Group, Inc., The.
—Gorillas: Life in the Troop. 2011. (Animal Families Ser.). 24p. (J). (ENG.). pap. 8.25 *(978-1-4488-2614-8(4));* (Illus.). lib. bdg. 22.60 *(978-1-4488-2514-1(8))* Rosen Publishing Group, Inc., The. (PowerKids Pr.).
Claybourne, Anna. Gorilla. 2012. (Animals on the Edge Ser.). (ENG., Illus.). 48p. (gr. 3-8). pap. 12.00 *(978-1-4081-4959-1(1),* 9781408149591, Bloomsbury USA Childrens) Bloomsbury Publishing USA.
Costain, Meredith. Gorilla. Jackson-Carter, Stuart, illus. 2016. (Wild World Ser.). 00032p. (J). (gr. 1-2). pap. 10.00 *(978-1-4994-8209-6(4),* Windmill Bks.) Rosen Publishing Group, Inc., The.
Dakers, Diane. Dian Fossey: Animal Rights Activist & Protector of Mountain Gorillas. 2016. (ENG., Illus.). 112p. (J). lib. bdg. *(978-0-7787-2563-3(4))* Crabtree Publishing Co.
De Medeiros, Michael. Gorillas. 2006. (Amazing Animals Ser.). (Illus.). 24p. (J). (gr. 3-7). pap. 8.95 *(978-1-59036-396-6(5));* lib. bdg. 24.45 *(978-1-59036-390-4(6))* Weigl Pubs., Inc.
Dennard, Deborah. Gorillas. McGee, John F., illus. 2003. (Our Wild World Ser.). (ENG.). 48p. (J). (gr. 2-5). 10.95 *(978-1-55971-844-8(7));* pap. 7.95 *(978-1-55971-843-1(9))* Cooper Square Publishing Llc.
Diamond, Claudia C. Gorilla Families. 2009. (Reading Room Collection 2 Ser.). 24p. (gr. 3-4). 42.50 *(978-1-60851-965-1(1),* PowerKids Pr.) Rosen Publishing Group, Inc., The.
Doak, Robin S. Dian Fossey: Friend to Africa's Gorillas, 1 vol. 2014. (Women in Conservation Ser.). (ENG., Illus.). 48p. (gr. 3-6). 33.32 *(978-1-4846-0468-7(7));* pap. 8.99 *(978-1-4846-0473-1(3))* Heinemann-Raintree. (Heinemann InfoSearch).
Eszterhas, Suzi. Gorilla. 2012. (Eye on the Wild Ser.). (Illus.). 32p. (J). *(978-1-84780-202-6(8),* Frances Lincoln) Quarto Publishing Group UK.
Fleischer, Jayson & Lynch, Michelle. The Gorilla Family. Rupp, Kristina, illus. 2012. (2G Animals Ser.). (ENG.). 40p. (J). pap. 5.99 *(978-1-61406-203-5(X))* American Reading Co.
Franchino, Vicky. Gorillas. 2013. (Nature's Children Ser.). (ENG., Illus.). 48p. (J). pap. 6.95 *(978-0-531-24303-9(6));* lib. bdg. 28.00 *(978-0-531-20977-6(6))* Scholastic Library Publishing.
Francine, Gabriella & Vayanian, Solara. Let's Make a Difference: Protecting Mountain Gorillas. Velikan, Phil, illus. 2013. (Save Coins for Causes Ser.). (ENG.). 32p. (J). 15.00 *(978-1-938504-02-0(X))* BBM Bks.
Frost, Helen. Gorillas [Scholastic]. 2011. (Rain Forest Animals Ser.). 24p. pap. 0.50 *(978-1-4296-6315-1(4),* Pebble Bks.) Capstone Press of Coughlan Cos.

Gibbons, Gail. Gorillas. Gibbons, Gail, illus. (ENG., Illus.). 32p. (J). 2012. pap. 7.95 (978-0-8234-2433-7(2)) 2011. (gr. -1-3). 17.95 (978-0-8234-2236-4(4)) Holiday Hse., Inc.

Gish, Melissa. Gorillas. (Living Wild Ser.). 2011. (ENG., Illus.). 48p. (J). (gr. 4-7). pap. 12.00 (978-0-89812-552-8(9), Creative Paperbacks) 2010. 46p. (YA). (gr. 5-18). 23.95 (978-1-58341-969-4(1), Creative Education) Creative Co., The.

Goldish, Meish. Gorillas. 2007. (Smart Animals! Ser.). (Illus.). 32p. (YA). (gr. 2-5). lib. bdg. 25.27 (978-1-59716-369-9(4), 1265960) Bearport Publishing Co., Inc.

Green, Carl R. The Gorilla: A MyReportLinks. com Book. 2004. (Endangered & Threatened Animals Ser.). (Illus.). 48p. (J). lib. bdg. 26.60 (978-0-7660-5060-0(2), MyReportLinks.com Bks.) Enslow Pubs., Inc.

Hansen, Grace. Gorillas, 1 vol. 2015. (ENG., Illus.). 24p. (J). 21.70 (978-1-62970-894-2(1)) ABDO Publishing Co.

Hirsch, Rebecca E. Mountain Gorillas: Powerful Forest Mammals. 2015. (Comparing Animal Traits Ser.). (ENG., 32p. (gr. 2-4). Illus.). 39.99 (978-1-4677-8926-4(7), Lerner Digital); (J). pap. 8.99 (978-1-4677-6063-8(3), Lerner Pubns.); (J). lib. bdg. 26.65 (978-1-4677-5580-1(X), Lerner Pubns.) Lerner Publishing Group.

Imbriaco, Alison. The Mountain Gorilla: Help Save This Endangered Species! 2006. (Saving Endangered Species Ser.). (Illus.). 128p. (J). (gr. 4-7). lib. bdg. 34.60 (978-1-59845-035-4(2), MyReportLinks.com Bks.) Enslow Pubs., Inc.

Kalman, Bobbie. Les Gorilles de Montagne. 2009. (Petit Monde Vivant Ser.). (FRE., Illus.). 32p. (J). pap. 9.95 (978-2-89579-230-7(5)) Bayard Canada Livres CAN. Dist: Crabtree Publishing Co.

Kalman, Bobbie & Lundblad, Kristina. Endangered Mountain Gorillas. 2004. (Earth's Endangered Animals Ser.). (ENG., Illus.). 32p. (J). pap. (978-0-7787-1901-4(4)); lib. bdg. (978-0-7787-1855-0(7)) Crabtree Publishing Co.

Katirgis, Jane & Green, Carl R. Endangered Gorillas. 2015. (Wildlife at Risk Ser.). (ENG.). 48p. (J). (gr. 6-6). pap. 11.70 (978-0-7660-6896-4(X)); (Illus.). 27.93 (978-0-7660-6898-8(6)) Enslow Pubs., Inc.

Kushner, Jill Menkes. Who on Earth Is Dian Fossey? Defender of the Mountain Gorillas. 2009. (Scientists Saving the Earth Ser.). (Illus.). 112p. (J). (gr. 5-9). lib. bdg. 33.27 (978-1-59845-117-7(0)) Enslow Pubs., Inc.

Leaf, Christina. Baby Gorillas. 2015. (Super Cute! Ser.). (ENG., Illus.). 24p. (J). (gr. k-3). lib. bdg. 25.95 (978-1-62617-170-1(X), Blastoff! Readers) Bellwether Media.

Lewin, Betsy & Lewin, Ted, illus. Gorilla Walk Gorilla Walk, 1 vol. 2014. (Adventures Around the World Ser.). (ENG.). 48p. (J). pap. 11.95 (978-1-62014-182-3(5)) Lee & Low Bks., Inc.

Machajewski, Sarah. The Return of the Mountain Gorilla. 2017. (Bouncing Back from Extinction Ser.). 32p. (J). (gr. 9-10). 60.00 **(978-1-5081-5603-1(4)**, PowerKids Pr.) Rosen Publishing Group, Inc., The.

Macheske, Felicia. Brainy & Brawny: Gorilla. 2017. (Guess What Ser.). (ENG., Illus.). 24p. (J). (gr. k-2). lib. bdg. 28.50 (978-1-63472-173-8(X), 209264) Cherry Lake Publishing.

Macleod, Steve. Gorilla. 2011. (Illus.). 24p. (J). 27.13 (978-1-61690-757-0(6)); pap. 12.95 (978-1-61690-764-8(9)) Weigl Pubs., Inc.

—Soy el Gorila. 2012. (SPA.). (J). (978-1-61913-176-7(5)) Weigl Pubs., Inc.

Marsico, Katie. Gorillas. 2017. (True Book(tm) — The Most Endangered Ser.). (ENG.). 48p. (J). lib. bdg. 31.00 (978-0-531-22728-2(6), Children's Pr.) Scholastic Library Publishing.

McDowell, Pamela. Gorillas. 2014. (J). (978-1-4896-2878-7(9)) Weigl Pubs., Inc.

McLeese, Don. Gorillas. 2010. (ENG., Illus.). 24p. (gr. 3-6). pap. 8.95 (978-1-61590-514-0(6)) Rourke Educational Media.

McManus, Lori. Gorillas, 1 vol. 2012. (Living in the Wild: Primates Ser.). (ENG.). 48p. (gr. 3-6). pap. 8.99 (978-1-4329-5870-1(4)); lib. bdg. 33.32 (978-1-4329-5863-3(1)) Heinemann-Raintree. (Heinemann InfoSearch).

McNeil, Niki, et al. HOCPP 1147 King of the Apes: The Gorilla: the Gorilla. 2007. spiral bd. 22.00 (978-1-60308-147-4(X)) In the Hands of a Child.

Miller-Schroeder, Patricia. Gorillas. 2013. (Illus.). 48p. (978-1-61913-425-6(X)) Weigl Pubs., Inc.

—Gorillas with Code. 2012. (Animals on the Brink Ser.). (ENG., Illus.). 48p. (J). (gr. 5-9). pap. 14.95 (978-1-61913-426-3(8), AV2 by Weigl) Weigl Pubs., Inc.

Murray, Julie. Gorillas, 1 vol. 2003. (Animal Kingdom Ser.). (ENG.). 24p. (gr. k-4). 25.65 (978-1-57765-712-5(8), Buddy Bks.) ABDO Publishing Co.

Nichols, Michael & Carney, Elizabeth. Face to Face with Gorillas. 2009. (Face to Face with Animals Ser.). (ENG., Illus.). 32p. (J). (gr. 1-4). 16.95 (978-1-4263-0406-4(4)); lib. bdg. 25.90 (978-1-4263-0407-1(2)) National Geographic Society. (National Geographic Children's Bks.).

Nippert-Eng, Christena. What Is Baby Gorilla Doing? Dominski, John & Martinez, Miguel, illus. 2017. (ENG.). 22p. (J). bds. 7.99 (978-1-62779-479-4(4), 9781627794794, Holt, Henry & Co. Bks. For Young Readers) Holt, Henry & Co.

Nippert-Eng, Christena E. Gorillas up Close. 2016. (ENG., Illus.). 176p. (J). (gr. 3-7). 19.99 (978-1-62779-091-8(8), 9781627790918, Holt, Henry & Co. Bks. For Young Readers) Holt, Henry & Co.

Orme, Helen. Gorillas in Danger. 2006. (Wildlife Survival Ser.). (Illus.). 32p. (YA). (gr. 2-5). lib. bdg. 25.27 (978-1-59716-261-6(2)) Bearport Publishing Co., Inc.

Pohl, Kathleen. Gorillas. 2007. (Animals I See at the Zoo Ser.). 24p. (gr. k-3). pap. 8.15 (978-0-8368-8226-1(1)); (Illus.). lib. bdg. 22.00 (978-0-8368-8219-3(9)) Stevens, Gareth Publishing LLLP. (Weekly Reader Leveled Readers).

—Gorillas/Gorilas. 2007. (Animals I See at the Zoo/Animales que Veo en el Zoológico Ser.). (SPA & ENG., Illus.). 24p. (gr. k-3). lib. bdg. 22.00 (978-0-8368-8233-9(4), Weekly Reader Leveled Readers) Stevens, Gareth Publishing LLLP.

Portman, Michael. Gorillas in Danger. 2011. (Animals at Risk Ser.). 24p. (J). (gr. 2-5). pap. 8.15 (978-1-4339-5796-3(5)); lib. bdg. 22.60 (978-1-4339-5794-9(9)) Stevens, Gareth Publishing LLLP. (Gareth Stevens Learning Library).

Prebeg, Rick. Into the Jungle. Prebeg, Rick, photos by. 2005. (Illus.). (J). (978-1-933248-05-9(X)) World Quest Learning.

Redmond, Ian. Gorilas. Anderson, Peter & Brightling, Geoff, illus. 2003. (SPA.). 64p. 14.95 (978-84-372-2323-0(7)) Altea, Ediciones, S.A. - Grupo Santillana ESP. Dist: Santillana USA Publishing Co., Inc.

Riggs, Kate. Amazing Animals: Gorillas. 2012. (Amazing Animals Ser.). (ENG., Illus.). 24p. (J). (gr. 1-3). pap. 8.99 (978-0-89812-692-1(4), Creative Paperbacks) Creative Co., The.

—Gorillas. (J). 2014. (978-1-60818-454-5(4)) 2012. 25.65 (978-1-60818-107-0(3)) Creative Co., The. (Creative Education).

—Seedlings: Gorillas. 2015. (Seedlings Ser.). (ENG.). 24p. (J). (gr. -1-1). pap. 7.99 (978-1-62832-043-5(5), Creative Paperbacks) Creative Co., The.

Roe-Pimm, Nancy. Colo's Story. 2011. (ENG.). 80p. (gr. 4-8). 18.95 (978-0-9841554-4-6(9)); pap. 8.95 (978-0-9841554-5-3(7)) Columbus Zoo & Aquarium, The.

—The Heart of the Beast: Eight Great Gorilla Stories. 2007. (Exceptional Science Titles for Intermediate Grades Ser.). (Illus.). 112p. (J). (gr. 4-7). 18.95 (978-1-58196-054-9(9), Darby Creek) Lerner Publishing Group.

Royston, Angela. Save the Gorilla, 1. 2014. (Animal SOS! Ser.). (ENG., Illus.). 32p. (J). (gr. k-5). pap. 10.00 (978-1-4777-6037-6(7), Windmill Bks.) Rosen Publishing Group, Inc., The.

Sackett-Smith, Lucy. Gorillas: Beasts of the Wild. 2009. (Mighty Mammals Ser.). (Illus.). 24p. (YA). (gr. k-3). 22.60 (978-1-4042-8104-2(5)) Rosen Publishing Group, Inc., The.

Salzmann, Mary Elizabeth. Baby Gorillas, 1 vol. 2014. (Baby Animals Set 2 Ser.). (ENG.). 24p. (J). (gr. -1-3). 24.21 (978-1-62403-510-4(8)) ABDO Publishing Co.

Schindel, John. Busy Gorillas. Rouse, Andy, photos by. 2010. (Busy Book Ser.). (ENG., Illus.). 32p. (J). (— 1). bds. 6.99 (978-1-58246-352-0(2), Tricycle Pr.) Random Hse. Children's Bks.

Schuh, Mari. Gorillas. 2014. (Illus.). 24p. (J). lib. bdg. 25.65 (978-1-62031-109-7(7), Bullfrog Bks.) Jump! Inc.

Simon, Seymour. Gorillas. (ENG.). 32p. (J). 2009. 17.99 (978-0-06-089102-2(5)) 2008. (Illus.). pap. 6.99 (978-0-06-089101-5(7), Collins) HarperCollins Pubs.

Smith, Lucy. Gorillas: Beasts of the Wild. 2009. 24p. (YA). pap. 8.25 (978-1-4358-3278-7(7)) Rosen Publishing Group, Inc., The.

Sobol, Richard. Breakfast in the Rainforest: A Visit with Mountain Gorillas. Sobol, Richard, photos by. 2010. (Traveling Photographer Ser.). (ENG., Illus.). 48p. (J). (gr. 1-4). pap. 7.99 (978-0-7636-5134-3(6)) Candlewick Pr.

Somervill, Barbara A. Mountain Gorilla. 2007. (21st Century Skills Library: Road to Recovery Ser.). (ENG., Illus.). 32p. (gr. 4-8). lib. bdg. 28.50 (978-1-60279-033-9(7), 200086) Cherry Lake Publishing.

Stevens, Kathryn. Gorillas. 2015. (Animals of the Rain Forest Ser.). (ENG.). 24p. (J). (gr. 2-5). 27.07 (978-1-63143-704-5(6), 208518) Child's World, Inc., The.

Stone, Tanya Lee. Gorillas. 2003. (Wild Wild World Ser.). (Illus.). 24p. (J). 24.94 (978-1-56711-814-8(3), Blackbirch Pr., Inc.) Cengage Gale.

Thomson, Sarah L. Amazing Gorillas! Wildlife Conservation Society, photos by. 2006. (I Can Read Level 2 Ser.). (ENG., Illus.). 32p. (J). (gr. k-3). pap. 3.99 (978-0-06-054461-4(9)) HarperCollins Pubs.

Turnbull, Stephanie. Gorilla. 2013. (Big Beasts Ser.). (Illus.). 24p. (gr. k-3). 28.50 (978-1-59920-835-0(0)) Black Rabbit Bks.

Ward, Finn. Gorilas / Gorillas at the Zoo. 2015. (Animales Del Zoológico / Zoo Animals Ser.). (ENG & SPA.). 24p. (J). (gr. k-k). lib. bdg. 22.60 (978-1-4824-3231-2(5)) Stevens, Gareth Publishing LLLP.

—Gorillas at the Zoo. 2015. (Zoo Animals Ser.). (ENG., Illus.). 24p. (J). (gr. k-k). pap. 8.15 (978-1-4824-2597-0(1)) Stevens, Gareth Publishing LLLP.

Wexo, John Bonnett. Gorilas. Rountree, Monica, tr. 2003. (Zoobooks Ser.). Orig. Title: Gorillas. (SPA., Illus.). 24p. (J). (gr. k-6). lib. bdg. 15.95 (978-1-888153-78-1(4)) Wildlife Education, Ltd.

—Gorillas. rev. ed. 2003. (Illus.). 24p. (J). (gr. 1-7). 10.95 (978-1-932396-04-1(7), Zoo Bks.) Wildlife Education, Ltd.

World Book, Inc. Staff, contrib. by. Gorillas & Other Apes. 2005. (World Book's Animals of the World Ser.). (Illus.). 64p. (J). (978-0-7166-1263-6(1)) World Bk., Inc.

Zobel, Derek. Gorillas. 2011. (Animal Safari Ser.). (ENG., Illus.). 24p. (J). (gr. k-3). lib. bdg. 25.95 (978-1-60014-605-3(8), Blastoff! Readers) Bellwether Media.

GORILLA—FICTION

Anderson, Derek. Gladys Goes Out to Lunch. Anderson, Derek, illus. 2005.Tr. of Signed in American Sign Language. (ENG., Illus.). 40p. (J). (gr. -1-3). 17.99 (978-0-689-85688-4(1), Simon & Schuster Bks. For Young Readers) Simon & Schuster Bks. For Young Readers.

Antony, Steve. Betty Goes Bananas. 2014. (ENG., Illus.). 32p. (J). (-k). 16.99 (978-0-553-50761-4(3), Schwartz & Wade Bks.) Random Hse. Children's Bks.

Applegate, Katherine. The One & Only Ivan. Castelao, Patricia, illus. (Harper Classic Ser.). (J). (gr. 3-7). 2017. 336p. 16.99 (978-0-06-264194-6(8)) 2015. (ENG.). 352p. 24.99 (978-0-06-242524-9(2)) 2015. (ENG.). 272p. pap. 7.99 (978-0-06-199227-8(5)) 2012. (ENG.). 305p. 17.99 (978-0-06-199225-4(9)) HarperCollins Pubs.

—The One & Only Ivan. Castelao, Patricia, illus. 2015. (ENG.). (J). (gr. 3-7). lib. bdg. 18.60 **(978-1-62765-963-5(3))** Perfection Learning Corp.

—The One & Only Ivan. Castelao, Patricia, illus. 2015. (J). lib. bdg. 18.40 (978-0-606-35481-3(6)) Turtleback Bks.

Baena, Gloria. Invitacion a la Fiesta del Gran Gorila. Osorno, Laura, illus. 2003. (SPA.). 32p. (J). 8.95 (978-958-04-7072-4(3)) Norma S.A. COL. Dist: Distribuidora Norma, Inc.

Ballantyne, R. M. Gorilla Hunters A Tale of the Wilds of A. 2006. pap. 36.95 (978-1-4286-5952-0(8)) Kessinger Publishing, LLC.

Bollinger/Papp, illus. King Kong: Meet Kong & Ann. 2005. 32p. (J). lib. bdg. 13.85 (978-1-4242-0615-5(4)) Fitzgerald Bks.

Bornstein, Ruth. Little Gorilla Book & CD. 2014. (ENG., Illus.). 32p. (J). (— 1). audio compact disk 10.99 (978-0-544-22794-1(8), HMH Books For Young Readers) Houghton Mifflin Harcourt Publishing Co.

Bornstein, Ruth Lercher. Gorilita. 2004. (SPA & ENG., Illus.). 28p. (J). (gr. k — 1). bds. 4.95 (978-0-618-44214-0(6)) Houghton Mifflin Harcourt Publishing Co.

Bottner, Barbara. Priscilla Gorilla. Emberley, Michael, illus. 2017. (ENG.). 40p. (J). (gr. -1-2). 17.99 (978-1-4814-5897-9(3), Atheneum/Caitlyn Dlouhy Books) Simon & Schuster Children's Publishing.

Browne, Anthony. Gorilla. 30th anniv. ed. 2014. lib. bdg. 18.40 (978-0-606-35150-8(7)) Turtleback Bks.

—The Little Bear Book. Browne, Anthony, illus. 2014. (ENG., Illus.). 24p. (J). (gr. -1-2). 15.99 (978-0-7636-7007-8(3)) Candlewick Pr.

—Little Beauty. Browne, Anthony, illus. 2010. (ENG., Illus.). 32p. (J). (gr. -1-2). pap. 6.99 (978-0-7636-4967-8(8)) Candlewick Pr.

—Little Beauty. 2010. lib. bdg. 17.20 (978-0-606-14714-9(4), Turtleback) Turtleback Bks.

—One Gorilla. Browne, Anthony, illus. 2013. (ENG., Illus.). 32p. (J). (gr. -1-2). 17.99 (978-0-7636-6352-0(2)) Candlewick Pr.

Chachas, George & Wojtak, James. The Story of Doolittle: An Exceptional Young Gorilla. De Soto, Ben, illus. 2011. 32p. (J). pap. 9.95 (978-0-9793144-0-7(2)) Dragonetti.

Chinnien, Kim. Tim Tim: The White Gorilla. 2012. 48p. pap. 21.99 (978-1-4691-9049-5(4)) Xlibris Corp.

Clarke, Jane. Who Woke the Baby? Fuge, Charles, illus. 2016. (ENG.). (J). (gr. -1-2). 12.99 (978-0-7636-8662-8(X), Nosy Crow) Candlewick Pr.

Cordell, Matthew. Dream. Cordell, Matthew, illus. 2017. (Wish Ser.). (ENG., Illus.). 48p. (J). (gr. -1-k). 16.99 (978-1-4847-7340-6(3)) Hyperion Bks. for Children.

Derubertis, Barbara. Gertie Gorilla's Glorious Gift. 2010. pap. 45.32 (978-0-7613-6509-9(5)) Kane Press, Inc.

deRubertis, Barbara. Gertie Gorilla's Glorious Gift. Alley, R. W., illus. 2010. (Animal Antics A to Z Ser.). 32p. (J). (gr. -1-3). pap. 7.95 (978-1-57565-311-2(7)); lib. bdg. 22.60 (978-1-57565-318-1(4)) Kane Press, Inc.

deRubertis, Barbara & DeRubertis, Barbara. Gertie Gorilla's Glorious Gift. Alley, R. W., illus. 2012. (Animal Antics A to Z Ser.). 32p. (J). (gr. 2 — 1). cd-rom 7.95 (978-1-57565-400-3(8)) Kane Press, Inc.

Durango, Julia. Go-Go Gorillas. Taylor, Eleanor, illus. 2010. (ENG.). 32p. (J). (gr. -1-1). 15.99 (978-1-4169-3779-1(X), Simon & Schuster Bks. For Young Readers) Simon & Schuster Bks. For Young Readers.

Everyday Signs of Zoo Animals. 2007. (J). bds. (978-0-9791059-1-3(9)) Dakitab, Inc.

Fairgray, Richard & Jones, Terry. Gorillas in Our Midst. 2015. (ENG., Illus.). 32p. (J). (gr. -1-k). 16.99 (978-1-63220-607-7(2), Sky Pony Pr.) Skyhorse Publishing Co., Inc.

Faulconer, Maria. A Mom for Umande. Hartung, Susan Kathleen, illus. 2014. (ENG.). 32p. (J). (gr. -1-3). 16.99 (978-0-8037-3762-4(9), Dial Bks) Penguin Young Readers Group.

Fisch, Sholly. Monkey Business, 1 vol. McKenny, Stewart & Moy, Phil, illus. 2013. (DC Super Friends Ser.). (ENG.). 32p. (gr. 1-2). 22.60 (978-1-4342-4700-1(7)) Stone Arch Bks.

Fonte, Mary Roessler & Hoppe, Jessica. Big Green Gorilla. Verhoosky, Michele, illus. 2013. 34p. 17.99 (978-1-937260-92-7(5)) Sleepytown Pr.

Francois, Saragine. The White Gorilla & the Three Chimpanzees a Day from the Zoo. 2011. 28p. pap. 14.99 (978-1-4520-3190-3(8)) AuthorHouse.

Graves, Keith. Second Banana. 2015. (ENG., Illus.). 32p. (J). (gr. 2-5). 17.99 (978-1-59643-883-5(5), 9781596438835) Roaring Brook Pr.

Grey, Chelsea Gillian. Jeshi the Gorilla. 2005. (Meet Africa's Animals Ser.). (ENG., Illus.). 36p. (J). (gr. 2-2). pap. 6.95 (978-1-59249-416-3(1), S6504) Soundprints.

—Jeshi the Gorilla. Leeper, Christopher, ed. 2005. (Meet Africa's Animals Ser.). (ENG., Illus.). 36p. (J). (gr. 2-2). 14.95 (978-1-59249-415-6(3), H6504) Soundprints.

—Jeshi the Gorilla. Leeper, Christopher J., illus. 2005. (Meet Africa's Animals Ser.). (ENG.). 32p. (J). (gr. -1-2). 2.95 (978-1-59249-418-7(8), S6554) Soundprints.

Huxman, K. D. Grizzelda Gorilla. l.t. ed. 2007. (Illus.). 24p. (J). 24.99 (978-0-9794660-2-1(4)); per. 12.99 (978-0-9794660-3-8(2)) Dragonfly Publishing, Inc.

Kin, Pamphil. The Gorilla Princess. 2012. (ENG.). pap. (978-1-4675-2345-5(3)) Independent Pub.

Kruse, Donald W. Fleas, Please. Crank, Donny, illus. 2012. 48p. pap. 12.95 (978-1-59663-858-7(3), Castle Keep Pr.) Rock, James A. & Co. Pubs.

—Gorilla Soup! 2012. 48p. pap. 12.95 (978-1-59663-862-4(1), Castle Keep Pr.) Rock, James A. & Co. Pubs.

LeLeu, Lisa. Percilla the Gorilla Gift Set: Puppet Book Gift Set with 2 Books. 2004. (J). bds. 19.99 (978-0-9710537-3-1(1)) LeLeu, Lisa Studios! Inc.

Lewis, Gill. Gorilla Dawn. Meyer, Susan, illus. 2017. (J). pap. **(978-1-4814-8658-3(6))**; (ENG.). 432p. (gr. 4-9). 16.99 (978-1-4814-8657-6(8), Atheneum/Caitlyn Dlouhy Books) Simon & Schuster Children's Publishing.

Lewis, J. Patrick. That's What Friends Are For. Denise, Christopher, illus. 2012. (I Am A Reader! Ser.). (ENG.). 40p. (gr. k-3). pap. 3.99 (978-1-58536-687-3(0)) Sleeping Bear Pr.

—Tugg & Teeny. Denise, Christopher, illus. 2011. (I am a Reader Ser.). (ENG.). 40p. (J). (gr. k-2). pap. 3.99 (978-1-58536-685-9(4));Bk. 1. lib. bdg. 9.95 (978-1-58536-514-2(9)) Sleeping Bear Pr.

—Tugg & Teeny: That's What Friends Are For. Denise, Christopher, illus. 2012. (I Am A Reader! Ser.). (ENG.). 40p. (gr. k-3). lib. bdg. 9.95 (978-1-58536-516-6(5)) Sleeping Bear Pr.

—Tugg & Teeny - Jungle Suprises, Bk. 2. Denise, Christopher, illus. 2011. (I am a Reader Ser.). (ENG.). 40p. (J). (gr. k-2). lib. bdg. 9.95 (978-1-58536-515-9(7)) Sleeping Bear Pr.

—Tugg & Tweeny - Jungle Surprises, Bk. 2. Denise, Christopher, illus. 2011. (I am a Reader Ser.). (ENG.). 40p. (J). (gr. k-2). pap. 3.99 (978-1-58536-686-6(2)) Sleeping Bear Pr.

Lively, Deborah Dreher. Vanishing Treasure of the Virungas. 2008. 88p. pap. 11.50 (978-1-934925-54-6(3), Strategic Bk. Publishing) Strategic Book Publishing & Rights Agency (SBPRA).

Lunablau, Jani. Little Snowflake. 2006. (ENG., Illus.). 32p. (J). (gr. -1-k). (978-1-59692-139-9(0)) MacAdam/Cage Publishing, Inc.

Mack, Jeff. Look! Mack, Jeff, illus. 2015. (ENG., Illus.). 32p. (J). (gr. -1-k). 16.99 (978-0-399-16205-3(4), Philomel Bks.) Penguin Young Readers Group.

—Playtime? Mack, Jeff, illus. 2016. (ENG., Illus.). 32p. (J). (-k). 16.99 (978-0-399-17598-5(9), Philomel Bks.) Penguin Young Readers Group.

Maggs, William Alan. The Jungle Adventures of Henry Littlejohn. 2012. 96p. pap. 11.52 (978-1-4669-1252-6(9)) Trafford Publishing.

Marchus, Linda. The Gorilla Who Wanted to Dance. Marchus, Linda, illus. 2003. (Illus.). 32p. (J). lib. bdg. 15.95 (978-0-9723122-1-9(8)) Wee Read Publishing.

Mayer, Jeffrey J. Si Javais Gorille. (FRE.). (J). pap. (978-2-07-050613-2(4)) Gallimard, Editions FRA. Dist: Distribooks, Inc.

McGowan, Steve. The Adventures of Keke & the Golden Coconut. 2012. 48p. pap. 21.92 (978-1-4251-4407-4(1)) Trafford Publishing.

McMahon, P. J. The Mystery of the Swimming Gorilla. Manders, John, illus. 2004. (Freaky Joe Club Ser.: 1). (ENG.). 112p. (J). (gr. 2-5). pap. 6.99 (978-0-689-86260-1(1), Aladdin) Simon & Schuster Children's Publishing.

Miles, Brenda & Sweet, Susan D. King Calm: Mindful Gorilla in the City. Langdo, Bryan, illus. 2016. (J). (978-1-4338-2272-8(5), Magination Pr.) American Psychological Assn.

Monks, Lydia. Go, Go, Gorilla! 2017. (ENG., Illus.). 32p. (J). (gr. -1-k). pap. 9.99 (978-1-4052-7815-7(3)) Egmont Bks., Ltd. GBR. Dist: Independent Pubs. Group.

Norman, Kim. Still a Gorilla! Geran, Chad, illus. 2016. (ENG.). 32p. (J). (gr. -1-k). 16.99 (978-0-545-75791-1(6)) Scholastic, Inc.

OHora, Zachariah. No Fits, Nilson! OHora, Zachariah, illus. 2013. (ENG., Illus.). 32p. (J). (gr. -1-k). 16.99 (978-0-8037-3852-2(8), Dial Bks) Penguin Young Readers Group.

Osborne, Mary Pope, et al. Buenos Días, Gorilas. Murdocca, Sal, illus. 2014. 26. (SPA.). 88p. (J). (gr. 2-4). pap. 5.99 (978-1-933032-93-1(6)) Lectorum Pubns., Inc.

Paulsen, Aimee. Mambo & the Runaway Gorill. 2011. (Illus.). 40p. pap. 21.99 (978-1-4628-5878-1(3)) Xlibris Corp.

Pepper, Lily. Bananas. 2012. (Illus.). 20p. pap. 19.82 (978-1-4772-1964-5(1)) AuthorHouse.

Philip, Simon. I Don't Know What to Call My Cat. Bailey, Ella, illus. 2017. (ENG.). 32p. (J). (gr. -1-3). 16.99 (978-0-544-97143-1(4), HMH Books For Young Readers) Houghton Mifflin Harcourt Publishing Co.

Punniyamurthi, Kavitha. Lucy's Purple Pullover. Punniyamurthi, Kavitha, illus. 2010. (Illus.). 16p. pap. 9.95 (978-1-61633-075-0(9)) Guardian Angel Publishing, Inc.

Robinson, Michelle. Ding Dong! Gorilla!, 1 vol. Lord, Leonie, illus. 2013. (ENG.). 32p. (J). (gr. -1-3). 15.95 (978-1-56145-730-4(2)) Peachtree Pubs.

Sattler, Jennifer. Frankie the Blankie. 2016. (ENG., Illus.). 32p. (J). 16.99 (978-1-61963-675-0(1), 9781619636750, Bloomsbury USA Childrens) Bloomsbury Publishing USA.

Seven, John. Gorilla Gardener: How to Help Nature Take over the World. Christy, Jana, illus. 2017. (Wee Rebel Ser.). (ENG.). 44p. (J). (gr. -1). 16.95 (978-1-945665-00-4(9)) Manic D Pr.

Shulman, Mark. Gorilla Garage, 0 vols. Nguyen, Vincent, illus. 2013. (ENG.). 42p. (J). (gr. -1-3). pap. 9.99 (978-1-4778-1663-9(1), 9781477816639, Amazon Children's Publishing) Amazon Publishing.

Smalley, Roger. Gorilla Guardian. Shaw, Charles, illus. 2005. (J). (978-1-933248-14-1(9)) World Quest Learning.

Smith, Lane. It's a Book. Smith, Lane, illus. 2010. (ENG., Illus.). 32p. (J). (gr. 1-5). 15.99 (978-1-59643-606-0(9), 9781596436060) Roaring Brook Pr.

—It's a Little Book. 2011. (ENG., Illus.). 24p. (J). (— 1). bds. 7.99 (978-1-59643-758-6(8), 9781596437586) Roaring Brook Pr.

Stephens, Sarah. Midway Monkey Madness, 1 vol. Baltazar, Art, illus. 2011. (DC Super-Pets Ser.). (ENG.). 56p. (gr. 2-2). pap. 4.95 (978-1-4048-6619-5(1)); lib. bdg. 23.99 (978-1-4048-6305-7(2)) Picture Window Bks. (DC Super-Pets).

Strathie, Chae. Gorilla Loves Vanilla. O'Byrne, Nicola, illus. 2016. (ENG.). 32p. (J). (gr. -1-k). 11.99 (978-0-7641-6853-6(3)) Barron's Educational Series, Inc.

Sutton, Laurie S. Going Ape. Gordon, Eric A. & Gordon, Steven E., illus. 2012. (I Can Read Level 2 Ser.). (ENG.). 32p. (J). (gr. -1-3). pap. 3.99 (978-0-06-188522-8(3)) HarperCollins Pubs.

—Going Ape. 2012. (Justice League Classic: I Can Read! Ser.). (J). lib. bdg. 13.55 (978-0-606-26260-6(1), Turtleback) Turtleback Bks.

Tomlinson, Jill. The Gorilla Who Wanted to Grow Up. Howard, Paul, illus. 2014. (ENG.). 112p. (J). (gr. -1-2). pap. 9.99 (978-1-4052-7195-0(7)) Egmont Bks., Ltd. GBR. Dist: Independent Pubs. Group.

Wallace, Jim. Search for the Mountain Gorillas. Nugent, Suzanne & Donploypetch, Jintanan, illus. 2008. (Choose Your Own Adventure Ser.: No. 25). 125p. (J). (gr. 4-7). pap. 6.99 (978-1-933390-25-3(5)) Chooseco LLC.

Walton, Rick. Girl & Gorilla. Berger, Joe, illus. 2016. 32p. (J). (gr. -1-3). 17.99 (978-0-06-227891-3(6)) HarperCollins Pubs.

Wegelius, Jakob. The Murderer's Ape. 2017. (ENG.). 624p. (YA). (gr. 7). 17.99 (978-1-101-93175-2(2), Delacorte Pr.) Random Hse. Children's Bks.

Wegelius, Jakob & Graves, Peter. The Murderer's Ape. 2017. (YA). lib. bdg. (978-1-101-93176-9(0), Delacorte Pr) Random House Publishing Group.

Wensink, Patrick. Go Go Gorillas: A Romping Bedtime Tale. Wragg, Nate, illus. 2017. 32p. (J). (gr. -1-3). 17.99 **(978-0-06-238118-7(0))** HarperCollins Pubs.

GOVERNMENT, LOCAL

see Local Government

GOVERNMENT, MUNICIPAL

see Municipal Government

GOVERNMENT, RESISTANCE TO

see also Anarchism

Altman, Linda Jacobs. Escape-Teens on the Run: Primary Sources from the Holocaust. 2010. (True Stories of Teens in the Holocaust Ser.). (Illus.). 128p. (YA). (gr. 9-12). 33.27 (978-0-7660-3270-5(1)) Enslow Pubs., Inc.

Byers, Ann. Courageous Teen Resisters: Primary Sources from the Holocaust. 2010. (True Stories of Teens in the Holocaust Ser.). (Illus.). 128p. (YA). (gr. 9-12). 33.27 (978-0-7660-3269-9(8)) Enslow Pubs., Inc.

Hoose, Phillip. The Boys Who Challenged Hitler: Knud Pedersen & the Churchill Club. 2015. (ENG., Illus.). 208p. (YA). (gr. 7-12). 19.99 (978-0-374-30022-7(4), 9780374300227, Farrar, Straus & Giroux (BYR)) Farrar, Straus & Giroux.

Schmermund, Elizabeth. Civil Disobedience. 2017. (J). pap. **(978-1-5345-0063-1(4))** Greenhaven Publishing LLC.

GOVERNMENT EMPLOYEES

see Civil Service

GOVERNMENT SERVICE

see Civil Service

GOVERNORS

Alter, Judy. Miriam Ma Ferguson: First Woman Governor of Texas. Messersmith, Patrick, illus. 2006. (Stars of Texas Ser.: 3). (ENG.). 72p. (gr. 4-7). 17.95 (978-1-933337-01-2(X)) State Hse. Pr.

Aretha, David. Mitt Romney. 2012. (Illus.). 112p. (J). (978-1-59935-344-9(X)) Reynolds, Morgan Inc.

Baicker, Karen. Conquistador: Francisco Pizarro Ravages the Inca Empire. 2011. (J). pap. (978-0-545-32940-8(X)) Scholastic, Inc.

Bailey, Tom. Jean Baptiste le Moyne, Sieur de Bienville: Father of Mobile. 2012. (Illus.). 112p. (J). (978-1-59421-082-2(9), Blackbirch Pr., Inc.) Seacoast Publishing, Inc.

Benge, Janet & Benge, Geoff. William Bradford: Plymouth's Rock. 2016. (ENG., Illus.). 200p. (J). pap. 9.99 (978-1-62486-092-8(3)) Emerald Bks.

Bodden, Valerie. Samuel Houston: Army Leader & Historic Politician, 1 vol. 2010. (Military Heroes Ser.). (ENG.). 112p. (J). (gr. 6-12). lib. bdg. 35.64 (978-1-60453-962-2(3)) ABDO Publishing Co.

Bodie, Idella. Light-Horse Harry. 2004. (Illus.). 86p. (J). pap. 6.95 (978-0-87844-172-3(7)) Sandlapper Publishing Co., Inc.

Boelts, Maribeth. Being the Governor. 2016. (Spring Forward Ser.). (J). (gr. 2). (978-1-4900-9458-8(X)) Benchmark Education Co.

Caravantes, Peggy. American in Texas: The Story of Sam Houston. 2004. (Notable Americans Ser.). (Illus.). 144p. (YA). (gr. 6-12). 23.95 (978-1-931798-19-8(2)) Reynolds, Morgan Inc.

Cody, Matt W. Peter Stuyvesant. 2010. (Leaders of the Colonial Era Ser.). 120p. (gr. 5-8). 35.00 (978-1-60413-740-8(1), Chelsea Hse.) Facts On File, Inc.

Cohen, Sheila & Terman Cohen, Sheila. Gaylord Nelson: Champion for Our Earth. 2010. (Badger Biographies Ser.). (ENG., Illus.). 120p. (J). pap. 12.95 (978-0-87020-443-2(2)) Wisconsin Historical Society.

De Capua, Sarah. Being a Governor. 2004. (True Bks.). (ENG.). 48p. 25.00 (978-0-516-22797-9(1), Watts, Franklin) Scholastic Library Publishing.

Donohue, Moira Rose. L. Douglas Wilder. 2012. (Illus.). 32p. (J). (978-1-935884-63-7(8)); pap. (978-1-935884-69-9(7)) State Standards Publishing, LLC.

Dubé, Jean-Claude. The Chevalier de Montmagny: First Governor of New France. Rapley, Elizabeth, tr. from FRE. 2005. (French America Ser.). (ENG., Illus.). 430p. 65.00 (978-0-7766-3028-1(8)) Univ. of Ottawa Pr./Presses de l'Universite d'Ottawa CAN. Dist: Two Rivers Distribution.

Duncan, E. E. Ralph Carr: Defender of Japanese Americans. 2011. (ENG & SPA., Illus.). 66p. (J). pap. 8.95 (978-0-86541-116-6(6)) Filter Pr., LLC.

Ebon Research Systems Staff. Dare to Be Vol. 4: Luis Munoz Marion. l.t. ed. 2003.Tr. of Atrevete Ser... Un Heroe Luis Munoz Marin. (ENG & SPA., Illus.). 14p. (J). 3.99 (978-0-9648313-7-7(6)) Ebon Research Systems Publishing, LLC.

Finley, Toiya Kristen. Russell Simmons. 2007. (Sharing the American Dream Ser.). 64p. (YA). (gr. 7-18). pap. 9.95 (978-1-4222-0762-8(5)) Mason Crest.

Goldsworthy, Steve. Sarah Palin. 2010. (Remarkable People Ser.). (Illus.). 24p. (J). (gr. 4-6). pap. 11.95 (978-1-61690-167-7(5)); lib. bdg. 25.70 (978-1-61690-166-0(7)) Weigl Pubs., Inc.

Gorman, Jacqueline Laks. Gobernador (Governor) 2009. (Conoce tu gobierno (Know Your Government) Ser.). (SPA., Illus.). 24p. (J). (gr. 2-4). lib. bdg. 22.00 (978-1-4339-0098-3(X), Weekly Reader Leveled Readers) Stevens, Gareth Publishing LLLP.

—Governor. 2009. (Know Your Government Ser.). 24p. (gr. 2-4). (J). lib. bdg. 22.00 (978-1-4339-0091-4(2)); pap. 8.15 (978-1-4339-0119-5(6)) Stevens, Gareth Publishing LLLP. (Weekly Reader Leveled Readers).

Greenberg, Keith Elliot. Jesse Ventura. 2003. (Biography Ser.). (Illus.). 112p. (YA). (gr. 6-12). pap. 7.95 (978-0-8225-9680-6(6), Carolrhoda Bks.) Lerner Publishing Group.

Higgins, Melissa. Mitt Romney. 2013. (Presidents of the U. S. A. Ser.). (ENG.). 48p. (gr. 3-6). 32.79 (978-1-62323-401-0(8), 206178) Child's World, Inc., The.

Jakubiak, David J. What Does a Governor Do? 2010. (How Our Government Works Ser.). 24p. (J). (gr. 3-6). lib. bdg., E-Book 42.50 (978-1-4488-0022-3(6)) Rosen Publishing Group, Inc., The.

Klein, Adria F. Arnold Schwarzenegger. 2009. pap. 13.25 (978-1-60559-054-7(1)) Hameray Publishing Group, Inc.

Knudsen, Anders. Antoine de la Mothe Cadillac: French Settlements at Detroit & Louisiana. 2006. (In the Footsteps of Explorers Ser.). (ENG., Illus.). 32p. (J). (gr. 3-9). lib. bdg. (978-0-7787-2429-2(8)); (gr. 4-7). pap. (978-0-7787-2465-0(4)) Crabtree Publishing Co.

Kovach, John. Bob Ehrlich: His Historical Campaign for Governor & How a Young Girl Made a Difference. 2003. (Illus.). 52p. (J). pap. 9.95 (978-0-7414-1497-7(X)) Infinity Publishing.

Krizner, L. J. Peter Stuyvesant: New Amsterdam, & the Origins of New York. 2009. (Library of American Lives & Times Ser.). 112p. (gr. 5-5). 69.20 (978-1-60853-498-2(7)) Rosen Publishing Group, Inc., The.

Laks Gorman, Jacqueline. Gobernador (Governor) 2009. (Conoce tu gobierno (Know Your Government) Ser.). (SPA., Illus.). 24p. (J). (gr. 2-4). pap. 8.15 (978-1-4339-0126-3(9), Weekly Reader Leveled Readers) Stevens, Gareth Publishing LLLP.

Lee, Sally. Arnold Schwarzenegger: From Superstar to Governor. 2006. (People to Know Today Ser.). (Illus.). 128p. (J). (gr. 6-12). lib. bdg. 33.27 (978-0-7660-2625-4(6)) Enslow Pubs., Inc.

Mahoney, Emily Jankowski. Becoming a State Governor. 2016. (Who's Your Candidate? Choosing Government Leaders Ser.). (ENG., Illus.). 32p. (J). (gr. 3-4). pap. 10.50 (978-1-4824-4047-8(4)) Stevens, Gareth Publishing LLLP.

Maloof, Torrey. James Oglethorpe: Not for Self, but for Others. 2016. (Primary Source Readers Ser.). (Illus.). 32p. (gr. 2-2). 8.99 (978-1-4938-2555-4(0)) Teacher Created Materials, Inc.

Manning, Jack. The State Governor, 1 vol. 2014. (Our Government Ser.). (ENG.). 24p. (gr. 1-2). lib. bdg. 25.32 (978-1-4914-0335-8(7)) Capstone Press of Coughlan Cos.

Mattern, Joanne. Sam Houston: A Fearless Statesman, 1 vol. 2012. (Primary Source Readers Ser.). (ENG.). 32p. (J). (gr. 3-3). pap. 8.99 (978-1-4333-5049-8(1)) Teacher Created Materials, Inc.

Miller, Barbara Kiely. Sam Houston. 2007. (Great Americans Ser.). 24p. (gr. 1-4). pap. 8.15 (978-0-8368-8323-7(3)); lib. bdg. 22.00 (978-0-8368-8316-9(0)); (SPA., Illus.). lib. bdg. 22.00 (978-0-8368-8329-9(2)) Stevens, Gareth Publishing LLLP. (Weekly Reader Leveled Readers).

Nagelhout, Ryan. Standing in a Governor's Shoes. 2015. (My Government Ser.). (ENG., Illus.). 32p. (J). (gr. 4-4). pap. 10.58 (978-1-5026-0475-0(2)) Cavendish Square Publishing.

Peppas, Lynn. Why Sam Houston Matters to Texas. 2014. (Illus.). 32p. (J). lib. bdg. 26.25 (978-1-4777-0912-2(6)) Rosen Publishing Group, Inc., The.

Petrillo, Lisa. Sarah Palin. 2009. (Political Profiles Ser.). 100p. (YA). (gr. 6-9). 28.95 (978-1-59935-133-9(1)) Reynolds, Morgan Inc.

Rice, Liz. Bill Richardson. (Sharing the American Dream Ser.). 64p. (YA). (gr. 7-12). 2009. 22.95 (978-1-4222-0589-1(4)) 2007. pap. 9.95 (978-1-4222-0761-1(7)) Mason Crest.

Sanford, William R. & Green, Carl R. Sam Houston: Courageous Texas Hero. 2012. (Courageous Heroes of the American West Ser.). (Illus.). 48p. (J). pap. 8.95 (978-1-4644-0092-6(X)); (gr. 5-18). lib. bdg. 22.60 (978-0-7660-4009-0(7)) Enslow Pubs., Inc.

Sexton, Colleen A. Arnold Schwarzenegger. 2005. (A&E Biography Ser.). (Illus.). 112p. (J). (gr. 6-12). 29.27 (978-0-8225-1634-7(9)); (ENG & SPA., pap. 7.95 (978-0-8225-5328-1(7)) Lerner Publishing Group.

Solberg, Jessica L. First Dog: Unleashed in the Montana Capitol. Rath, Robert, illus. 2007. (J). 11.95 (978-1-56037-419-0(5)) Farcountry Pr.

Sonneborn, Liz. Pizarro: Conqueror of the Mighty Incas. 2010. (Great Explorers of the World Ser.). (Illus.). 112p. (J). (gr. 7-12). 33.27 (978-1-59845-128-3(6)) Enslow Pubs., Inc.

Stotts, Stuart. Lucius Fairchild: Civil War Hero. 2011. (Badger Biographies Ser.). (ENG., Illus.). 112p. (J). pap. 12.95 (978-0-87020-460-9(2)) Wisconsin Historical Society.

Stumpff, April D. & Messersmith, Patrick. Ann Richards: A Woman's Place Is in the Dome. 2006. (Stars of Texas Ser.: 6). (ENG., Illus.). 80p. (gr. 4-7). 14.95 (978-1-933337-12-8(5)) State Hse. Pr.

Turner, Carolyn. Sam Houston. 2010. pap. 9.95 (978-1-61690-066-3(0)); 24p. (J). (gr. 2-4). lib. bdg. 25.70 (978-1-61690-065-6(2)) Weigl Pubs., Inc.

Wagner, Heather Lehr. William Bradford. 2010. (Leaders of the Colonial Era Ser.). 120p. (gr. 5-8). 35.00 (978-1-60413-743-9(6), Chelsea Hse.) Facts On File, Inc.

Watson, Marilyn Myrick. Raul Castro: Arizona's First Hispanic Governor. 2007. (J). (978-0-9790826-6-5(8)); (978-0-9790826-5-8(X)) Acacia Publishing, Inc.

—Rose Mofford: State Greats Arizona. 2007. (Acacia Biographies Ser.). (Illus.). 28p. (J). (gr. 3-7). lib. bdg. 16.95 (978-0-9788283-5-6(6)); (gr. 4-7). per. 6.95 (978-0-9790826-1-0(7)) Acacia Publishing, Inc.

Weintraub, Aileen. Henry Morgan: 17th-Century Buccaneer. 2009. (Library of Pirates Ser.). 24p. (gr. 3-3). 42.50 (978-1-60853-812-6(5), PowerKids Pr.) Rosen Publishing Group, Inc., The.

Wheeler, Jill C. Abigail Adams, 1 vol. 2010. (First Ladies Set 2 Ser.). (ENG., Illus.). 32p. (YA). (gr. 1-4). 27.07 (978-1-60453-629-4(2)) ABDO Publishing Co.

Whitehurst, Susan. William Bradford & Plymouth: A Colony Grows. 2009. (Library of the Pilgrims Ser.). 24p. (gr. 3-4). 42.50 (978-1-60853-916-1(4), PowerKids Pr.) Rosen Publishing Group, Inc., The.

Whiting, Jim. Peter Stuyvesant. 2007. (Profiles in American History Ser.). (Illus.). 48p. (J). (gr. 3-7). lib. bdg. 29.95 (978-1-58415-526-3(4)) Mitchell Lane Pubs., Inc.

Woodward, Mac. Sam Houston: For Texas & the Union. 2009. (Library of American Lives & Times Ser.). 112p. (gr. 5-5). 69.20 (978-1-60853-504-0(5)) Rosen Publishing Group, Inc., The.

Yeager, Alice. George C. Wallace: Alabama Political Power. 2003. (Alabama Roots Biography Ser.). (Illus.). 104p. (J). pap. (978-1-59421-003-7(9)) Seacoast Publishing, Inc.

—Lurleen B. Wallace: Alabama's First Woman Governor. 2003. (Alabama Roots Biography Ser.). (ENG., Illus.). 104p. (J). pap. 7.95 (978-1-59421-002-0(0)) Seacoast Publishing, Inc.

Yomtov, Nel. Sarah Palin: Political Rebel, 1 vol. D'Ottavi, Francesca, illus. 2011. (American Graphic Ser.). (ENG.). 32p. (gr. 3-4). pap. 8.10 (978-1-4296-7341-9(9)); pap. 47.70 (978-1-4296-7342-6(7)) Capstone Press of Coughlan Cos. (Graphic Library).

Yomtov, Nelson. Sarah Palin: Political Rebel, 1 vol. D'Ottavi, Francesca, illus. 2011. (American Graphic Ser.). (ENG.). 32p. (gr. 3-4). lib. bdg. 30.65 (978-1-4296-6018-1(X), Graphic Library) Capstone Press of Coughlan Cos.

Young, Jeff C. Arnold Schwarzenegger. 2007. (Political Profiles Ser.). (Illus.). 112p. (YA). (gr. 5-9). 27.95 (978-1-59935-050-9(5)) Reynolds, Morgan Inc.

GOYA, FRANCISCO, 1746-1828

McNeese, Tim. Francisco Goya. 2008. (Great Hispanic Heritage Ser.). (Illus.). 151p. (gr. 6-12). lib. bdg. 35.00 (978-0-7910-9664-2(5), Chelsea Hse.) Facts On File, Inc.

Rockett, Paul. Francisco Goya, 01 vols., 1. 2016. (Inspiring Artists Ser.). (ENG.). 48p. (J). 30.25 (978-1-5081-7058-7(4), Rosen Young Adult) Rosen Publishing Group, Inc., The.

Venezia, Mike. Francisco Goya. 2016. (Getting to Know the World's Greatest Artists Ser.). (ENG.). 40p. (J). pap. 7.95 (978-0-531-22106-8(7), Children's Pr.) Scholastic Library Publishing.

—Francisco Goya (Revised Edition) 2016. (Getting to Know the World's Greatest Artists Ser.). (ENG.). 40p. (J). lib. bdg. 29.00 (978-0-531-21667-5(5), Children's Pr.) Scholastic Library Publishing.

Wood, Alix. Francisco Goya. 2013. (Artists Through the Ages Ser.). (ENG., Illus.). 32p. (J). (gr. 3-6). pap. 10.00 (978-1-61533-635-7(4)); lib. bdg. 25.25 (978-1-61533-624-1(9)) Windmill Bks.

GRAAL

see Grail

GRAHAM, BILLY, 1918-

Martin, William C. Prophet with Honor: The Billy Graham Story, 1 vol. 2013. (ZonderKidz Biography Ser.). (ENG., Illus.). 144p. (J). pap. 6.99 (978-0-310-71935-9(6)) Zonderkidz.

GRAHAM, MARTHA, 1894-1991

Kessel, Kristin. Martha Graham. (Library of American Choreographers Ser.). 48p. (gr. 5-8). 2009. 53.00 (978-1-60853-460-9(X), Rosen Reference) 2006. (ENG., Illus.). pap. 11.75 (978-1-4042-0644-1(2)) Rosen Publishing Group, Inc., The.

GRAIL

see also Arthur, King

Church, J. R. Guardians of the Grail: And the Men Who Plan to Rule the World. Griffin, Ralph G. & Stearman, G. G., eds. 2003. (Illus.). 318p. (Orig.). (gr. 12). pap. 11.95 (978-0-941241-02-1(5)) Prophecy Pubns.

McIntosh, Kenneth. The Grail, the Shroud, & Other Religious Relics: Secrets & Ancient Mysteries. 2007. (Religion & Modern Culture Ser.). (Illus.). 112p. (YA). (gr. 3-7). lib. bdg. 22.95 (978-1-59084-978-1(7), 1248067) Mason Crest.

GRAIL—FICTION

Crompton, Anne Eliot. Percival's Angel. 2011. (ENG.). 240p. (YA). (gr. 8-12). pap. 7.99 (978-1-4022-3784-3(7)) Sourcebooks, Inc.

Spradlin, Michael. Orphan of Destiny: Book 3, 3 vols. 2011. (Youngest Templar Ser.: 3). (ENG.). 272p. (J). (gr. 5-18). 7.99 (978-0-14-241959-5(1), Puffin Books) Penguin Young Readers Group.

Spradlin, Michael P. Keeper of the Grail, Bk. 1. 2009. (Youngest Templar Ser.: 1). (ENG.). 272p. (J). (gr. 5-6). 7.99 (978-0-14-241461-3(1), Puffin Books) Penguin Young Readers Group.

—Trail of Fate, 2 vols., Bk. 2. 2010. (Youngest Templar Ser.: 2). (ENG.). 256p. (J). (gr. 5-7). 7.99 (978-0-14-241707-2(6), Puffin Books) Penguin Young Readers Group.

Upton, Robert Jesten. Milo & the Dragon Cross: A Novel. 2017. (YA). pap. **(978-1-63293-177-1(X))** Sunstone Pr.

Wilson, John. Grail. 2010. (Heretic's Secret Ser.: Bk. II). (ENG., Illus.). 304p. (YA). (gr. 7-18). pap. (978-1-55470-306-7(9)) Me to We.

GRAIN

Aboff, Marcie. The Great Grains Group, 1 vol. Poling, Kyle, illus. 2011. (First Graphics: Myplate & Healthy Eating Ser.). (ENG.). 24p. (gr. 1-2). lib. bdg. 23.99 (978-1-4296-6088-4(0)); pap. 35.70 (978-1-4296-7167-5(X)) Capstone Press of Coughlan Cos.

Adams, Julia. Grains. 2011. (Good Food Ser.). (ENG.). 24p. (J). lib. bdg. 22.60 (978-1-4488-3273-6(X), PowerKids Pr.) Rosen Publishing Group, Inc., The.

Alexander, Carol. Grains. (Rookie Read-About Health Ser.). (ENG., Illus.). 32p. (J). (gr. k-2). 2006. per. 5.95 (978-0-516-24649-9(6)) 2005. lib. bdg. 20.50 (978-0-516-23646-9(6)) Scholastic Library Publishing. (Children's Pr.).

Benduhn, Tea. Bread & Cereal. 2007. (Find Out about Food Ser.). 24p. (gr. k-3). pap. 8.15 (978-0-8368-8257-5(1)); (Illus.). lib. bdg. 22.00 (978-0-8368-8250-6(4)) Stevens, Gareth Publishing LLLP. (Weekly Reader Leveled Readers).

—Bread & Cereal/Pan y Cereales. 2007. (Find Out about Food/ Conoce la comida Ser.). (SPA & ENG., Illus.). 24p. (gr. k-3). pap. 8.15 (978-0-8368-8461-6(2)); lib. bdg. 22.00 (978-0-8368-8454-8(X)) Stevens, Gareth Publishing LLLP. (Weekly Reader Leveled Readers).

Bodden, Valerie. Grains. 2015. (J). (978-1-60818-510-8(9), Creative Education) Creative Co., The.

—Healthy Plates: Grains. 2015. (Healthy Plates Ser.). (ENG.). 24p. (J). (gr. 1-3). pap. 9.99 (978-1-62832-110-4(5), Creative Paperbacks) Creative Co., The.

Borgert-Spaniol, Megan. Grains Group. 2012. (Eating Right with Myplate Ser.). (ENG., Illus.). 24p. (J). (gr. k-3). lib. bdg. 25.95 (978-1-60014-756-2(9), Blastoff! Readers) Bellwether Media.

Burstein, John. Glorious Grains. 2009. (Slim Goodbody's Nutrition Edition Ser.). (ENG., Illus.). 24p. (J). (gr. k-3). pap. (978-0-7787-5058-1(2)); lib. bdg. (978-0-7787-5043-7(4)) Crabtree Publishing Co.

Cleary, Brian P. & Nelson, Jennifer K. Macaroni & Rice & Bread by the Slice: What Is in the Grains Group? Goneau, Martin, illus. 2010. (Food Is CATegorical Ser.). (ENG.). 32p. (gr. k-3). lib. bdg. 25.26 (978-1-58013-587-0(0)) Lerner Publishing Group.

Dickmann, Nancy. Grains. 2012. (Healthy Eating with Myplate Ser.). (ENG.). 24p. (gr. -1-1). pap. 6.29 (978-1-4329-6982-0(X)); lib. bdg. 22.65 (978-1-4329-6975-2(7)) Heinemann-Raintree. (Acorn).

Dilkes, D. H. Bread & Grains. 2011. (All about Good Foods We Eat Ser.). (Illus.). 24p. (J). (gr. -1-18). pap. 7.95 (978-1-59845-252-5(5), Enslow Elementary); (gr. k-3). lib. bdg. 22.60 (978-0-7660-3923-0(4)) Enslow Pubs., Inc.

Edwards, Nicola. Cereals. 2007. (See How Plants Grow Ser.). (Illus.). 24p. (J). (gr. 3-7). lib. bdg. 22.60 (978-1-4042-3702-5(X)) Rosen Publishing Group, Inc., The.

Green, Emily K. Grains. 2006. (Blastoff! Readers Ser.). (ENG., Illus.). 24p. (J). (gr. k-3). lib. bdg. 24.95 (978-1-60014-003-7(3), Blastoff! Readers) Bellwether Media.

—Grains. 2011. (Blastoff! Readers Ser.). (Illus.). 24p. (J). pap. 5.95 (978-0-531-25851-4(3), Children's Pr.) Scholastic Library Publishing.

Hewitt, Sally. Grains & Cereals. 2008. (Good for Me Ser.). (Illus.). 24p. (J). (gr. -1-3). lib. bdg. 22.60 (978-1-4042-4270-8(8), PowerKids Pr.) Rosen Publishing Group, Inc., The.

Hoffmann, Sara. Kinds of Grains. 2012. (First Step Nonfiction - Kinds of Plants Ser.). (ENG., Illus.). 8p. (gr. -1-1). pap. 4.95 (978-1-4677-0498-4(9), Lerner Pubns.) Lerner Publishing Group.

Kalz, Jill. Grains. 2003. 24p. (J). lib. bdg. 21.35 (978-1-58340-301-3(9)) Black Rabbit Bks.

Lassieur, Allison. Grains. 2015. (Illus.). 32p. (J). lib. bdg. 28.50 (978-1-60753-497-6(5)) Amicus Publishing.

Marsico, Katie. Your Healthy Plate - Grains. 2012. (21st Century Basic Skills Library: Your Healthy Plate Ser.). (ENG.). 24p. (J). (gr. k-3). lib. bdg. 22.79 (978-1-61080-348-9(5), 201294) Cherry Lake Publishing.

—Your Healthy Plate: Grains. 2012. (21st Century Basic Skills Library: Your Healthy Plate Ser.). (ENG.). 24p. (J). (gr. k-3). pap. 12.79 (978-1-61080-401-1(5), 201336) Cherry Lake Publishing.

Mayo, Gretchen Will. Cereal. 2004. (Where Does Our Food Come From? Ser.). (Illus.). 24p. (gr. 1-4). lib. bdg. 21.00 (978-0-8368-4065-0(8), Weekly Reader Leveled Readers) Stevens, Gareth Publishing LLLP.

Nelson, Robin. Grains. 2003. (First Step Nonfiction - Food Groups Ser.). (ENG., Illus.). 24p. (gr. k-2). lib. bdg. 23.93 (978-0-8225-4628-3(0)) Lerner Publishing Group.

—Los Cereales. Castañer, Mercedes & Fitzpatrick, Julia, trs. 2003. (Mi Primer Paso Al Mundo Real - Los Grupos de Alimentos (First Step Nonfiction - Food Groups) Ser.).Tr. of Grains. (SPA., Illus.). 24p. (gr. k-2). lib. bdg. 23.93 (978-0-8225-5063-1(6)) Lerner Publishing Group.

Nugent, Samantha. Whole Grains. 2015. (Let's Learn about Food Ser.). (ENG.). (J). lib. bdg. 27.13 (978-1-4896-4007-9(X), AV2 by Weigl) Weigl Pubs., Inc.

Reinke, Beth Bence. The Grains Group. 2013. (Healthy Eating with Myplate Ser.). (ENG.). 24p. (J). (gr. 1-4). 28.50 (978-1-62323-604-5(5), 206406) Child's World, Inc., The.

Rondeau, Amanda. Grains Are Good, 1 vol. 2003. (What Should I Eat? Ser.). (ENG., Illus.). 24p. (J). (gr. k-3). lib. bdg. 24.21 (978-1-57765-833-7(7), SandCastle) ABDO Publishing Co.

Sayre, April Pulley. Let's Go Nuts! Seeds We Eat. Sayre, April Pulley, illus. 2013. (ENG., Illus.). 32p. (J). (gr. -1-3). 16.99 (978-1-4424-6728-6(2), Beach Lane Bks.) Beach Lane Bks.

Schuh, Mari. Grains on Myplate, 1 vol. 2012. (What's on Myplate? Ser.). (ENG., 24p. (gr. k-1). (Illus.). pap. 7.29 (978-1-4296-9416-2(5)); pap. 41.70 (978-1-4296-9417-9(3)) Capstone Press of Coughlan Cos. (Pebble Plus).

Schuh, Mari C. Grains on Myplate, 1 vol. 2012. (What's on Myplate? Ser.). (ENG., Illus.). 24p. (gr. k-1). lib. bdg. 26.65 (978-1-4296-8742-3(8), Pebble Plus) Capstone Press of Coughlan Cos.

Shores, Erika L. How Food Gets from Farms to Store Shelves. 2016. (Here to There Ser.). (ENG.). 24p. (gr. k-1). lib. bdg. 26.65 (978-1-4914-8428-9(4), Pebble Plus) Capstone Press of Coughlan Cos.

Snyder, Inez. Welcome Books: Grains to Bread: How Things Are Made. 2005. (How Things Are Made Ser.). (ENG., Illus.). 24p. (J). (gr. -1-2). pap. 4.95 (978-0-516-25527-9(4), Children's Pr.) Scholastic Library Publishing.

Somervill, Barbara A. Producing Grains, 1 vol. 2012. (Technology of Farming Ser.). (ENG.). 48p. (gr. 4-6). lib. bdg. 33.32 (978-1-4329-6409-2(7), Heinemann InfoSearch) Heinemann-Raintree.

Squire, Ann O. Grains & Cereal. 2017. (True Book(tm), a — Farm to Table Ser.). (ENG., Illus.). 48p. (J). lib. bdg. 31.00 (978-0-531-22932-3(7), Children's Pr.) Scholastic Library Publishing.

—Grains & Cereals. 2017. (True Book(tm) — Farm to Table Ser.). (ENG., Illus.). 48p. (J). pap. 7.95 (978-0-531-23551-5(3), Children's Pr.) Scholastic Library Publishing.

Staniford, Linda. Where Do Grains Come From? 2016. (From Farm to Fork: Where Does My Food Come From? Ser.). (ENG.). 24p. (gr. k-2). lib. bdg. 23.99 (978-1-4846-3349-6(0)) Capstone Press of Coughlan Cos.

Tuminelly, Nancy. Let's Cook with Cereal! Delicious & Fun Cereal Dishes Kids Can Make, 1 vol. 2012. (Super Simple Recipes Ser.). (ENG.). 32p. (J). (gr. k-4). lib. bdg. 27.07 (978-1-61783-419-6(X), Super SandCastle) ABDO Publishing Co.

Waters, Rosa. My Daily Diet: Grains. Prock, Lisa Albers, ed. 2014. (On My Plate Ser.: 6). 48p. (J). (gr. 5-18). 20.95 (978-1-4222-3098-5(8)) Mason Crest.

Yadav, S. S. Chickpea Breeding & Management. Chen, W. et al, eds. 2007. (ENG., Illus.). 638p. 250.00 (978-1-84593-213-8(7)) CABI GBR. Dist: Stylus Publishing, LLC.

GRAMMAR

see also Language and Languages

also names of languages with the subdivision Grammar, e.g. English Language—Grammar

Brocket, Jane. Stickiest, Fluffiest, Crunchiest: Super Superlatives. Brocket, Jane, photos by. 2015. (ENG., Illus.). 32p. (gr. -1-2). (J). 26.60 (978-1-4677-9241-7(1)); 26.65 (978-1-4677-9268-4(3)) Lerner Publishing Group. (Millbrook Pr.).

Escoffier, Michaël. Take Away the A. Di Giacomo, Kris, illus. 2014. (ENG.). 56p. (J). (gr. -1-3). 17.95 (978-1-59270-156-8(6)) Enchanted Lion Bks., LLC.

Latin Grammar Student Workbook. 2003. stu. ed., ring bd., wbk. ed. (978-1-931680-42-4(6)) Teaching Point, Inc.

Lyons, Shelly. If You Were an Exclamation Point, 1 vol. Gray, Sara, illus. 2009. (Word Fun Ser.). (ENG.). 24p. (gr. 2-4). lib. bdg. 27.99 (978-1-4048-5326-3(X)) Picture Window Bks.

McDougal-Littell Publishing Staff, creator. Grammar, Usage, & Mechanics Book: Teaching, More Practice, Application. 2006. (Illus.). 219p. (gr. 7-18). per. (978-0-618-15376-3(4), 2-04131) Holt McDougal.

—Grammar, Usage, & Mechanics Book Grade 8: Teaching More Practice Application. 2006. (Illus.). 222p. (J). (gr. 4-7). per. (978-0-618-15382-4(9), 2-04137) Holt McDougal.

Park, Linda Sue & Durango, Julia. Yum! Yuck! A Foldout Book of People Sounds. Rama, Sue, illus. 2005. (ENG.). 36p. (J). (gr. -1-3). 9.95 *(978-1-57091-659-5(4))* Charlesbridge Publishing, Inc.

Sterling-Orth, Angela. Sound Reading: Literature Lists for Phonology & Articulation. 2005. (Illus.). (J). pap. 10.95 *(978-1-932054-28-6(6))* Super Duper Pubns.

Turrell, Linda. Mastering Prepositions, Conjunctions, Phrases & Clauses Student Activities Book: Mastering Language Arts Series. Matthews, Douglas L., ed. 2003. (Illus.). stu. ed., wbk. ed. *(978-1-931680-65-3(5)*, Expert Systems for Teachers) Teaching Point, Inc.

Voyages in English: Writing & Grammar. 2004. (gr. 4-18). *(978-0-8294-1305-2(7))*; (gr. 5-18). *(978-0-8294-1307-6(3))*; (gr. 5-18). tchr. ed. *(978-0-8294-0989-5(0))*; (gr. 5-18). tchr. ed., wbk. ed. *(978-0-8294-1323-6(5))*; (gr. 5-18). stu. ed. *(978-0-8294-0990-1(4))*; (gr. 5-18). stu. ed., wbk. ed. *(978-0-8294-1322-9(7))*; (gr. 6-18). *(978-0-8294-1310-6(3))*; (gr. 6-18). tchr. ed. *(978-0-8294-0991-8(2))*; (gr. 6-18). tchr. ed., wbk. ed. *(978-0-8294-1325-0(1))*; (gr. 6-18). stu. ed. *(978-0-8294-0992-5(0))*; (gr. 6-18). stu. ed., wbk. ed. *(978-0-8294-1324-3(3))*; (gr. 7-18). *(978-0-8294-1313-7(8))*; (gr. 7-18). tchr. ed. *(978-0-8294-0993-2(9))*; (gr. 7-18). tchr. ed., wbk. ed. *(978-0-8294-1328-1(6))*; (gr. 7-18). stu. ed. *(978-0-8294-0994-9(7))*; (gr. 7-18). stu. ed., wbk. ed. *(978-0-8294-1327-4(8))*; (gr. 8-18). *(978-0-8294-1315-1(4))*; (gr. 8-18). tchr. ed. *(978-0-8294-0995-6(5))*; (gr. 8-18). tchr. ed., wbk. ed. *(978-0-8294-1330-4(8))*; (gr. 8-18). stu. ed. *(978-0-8294-0996-3(3))*; (gr. 8-18). stu. ed., wbk. ed. *(978-0-8294-1329-8(4))* Loyola Pr.

GRAMMAR SCHOOLS

see Education, Elementary; Public Schools

GRAMOPHONE

see Phonograph

GRAND CANAL (CHINA)

Bodden, Valerie. Grand Canyon. 2010. (Big Outdoors Ser.). 24p. (J). (gr. k-3). 16.95 *(978-1-58341-815-4(6))* Creative Co., The.

GRAND CANYON (ARIZ.)

Adams, Colleen. Exploring the Grand Canyon. 2009. (Reading Room Collection 2 Ser.). 24p. (gr. 3-4). 42.50 *(978-1-60851-963-7(5)*, PowerKids Pr.) Rosen Publishing Group, Inc., The.

Augustin, Byron & Kubena, Jake. The Grand Canyon. 2009. (Nature's Wonders 2 Ser.). 96p. (gr. 6). 35.64 *(978-0-7614-3935-6(8))* Marshall Cavendish Corp.

Barlowe, Dot. Grand Canyon Plants & Animals. 2010. (Dover Nature Coloring Book Ser.). (ENG., Illus.). 32p. (gr. 3-8). pap. 3.99 *(978-0-486-47294-2(9))* Dover Pubns., Inc.

Bauer, Marion Dane. The Grand Canyon. Wallace, John, illus. 2006. (Wonders of America Ser.). (ENG.). 32p. (J). (gr. -1-1). pap. 3.99 *(978-0-689-86946-4(0)*, Simon Spotlight) Simon Spotlight.

—Wonders of America Ready-To-Read Value Pack: The Grand Canyon; Niagara Falls; the Rocky Mountains; Mount Rushmore; the Statue of Liberty; Yellowstone. Wallace, John, illus. 2014. (Wonders of America Ser.). (ENG.). 192p. (J). (gr. -1-1). pap. 15.96 *(978-1-4814-2724-1(5)*, Simon Spotlight) Simon Spotlight.

Buchheit, Mike. Going to Grand Canyon National Park. 2012. 48p. (J). 14.95 *(978-1-56037-515-9(9))* Farcountry Pr.

Chin, Jason. Grand Canyon. 2017. (ENG., Illus.). 56p. (J). 19.99 *(978-1-59643-950-4(5)*, 9781596439504) Roaring Brook Pr.

Dorling Kindersley Publishing Staff & Green, Jen. Grand Canyon: And Other Wonders of the World. 2016. (DK Readers Ser.). (ENG., Illus.). 96p. (J). (gr. 3-7). pap. 3.99 *(978-1-4654-4412-7(2)*, DK Children) Dorling Kindersley Publishing, Inc.

Fitzpatrick, Anne, tr. Grand Canyon. 2004. (Natural Wonders of the World Ser.). (Illus.). 32p. (J). lib. bdg. *(978-1-58341-323-4(5)*, Creative Education) Creative Co., The.

Frisch, Nate. Grand Canyon National Park. 2013. (Illus.). 48p. (J). 35.65 *(978-1-60818-196-4(0)*, Creative Education) Creative Co., The.

Gamble, Adam & Jasper, Mark. Good Night Grand Canyon. Kelly, Cooper, illus. 2016. (Good Night Our World Ser.). (ENG.). 20p. (J). (— 1). bds. 9.95 *(978-1-60219-503-5(X))* Good Night Bks.

Gilbert, Sara. Grand Canyon. 2016. (Illus.). 22p. (J). *(978-1-60818-632-7(6)*, Creative Education) Creative Co., The.

Gonzales, Doreen. Grand Canyon National Park: Adventure, Explore, Discover. 2009. (America's National Parks Ser.). (Illus.). 128p. (J). (gr. 5-9). lib. bdg. 34.60 *(978-1-59845-100-9(6))* Enslow Pubs., Inc.

Gregory, Josh. Grand Canyon National Park. 2017. (True Book — National Parks Ser.). (ENG.). 48p. (J). lib. bdg. 31.00 ***(978-0-531-23393-1(6)***, Children's Pr.) Scholastic Library Publishing.

Herrington, Lisa M. Grand Canyon. 2017. (Rookie National Parks Ser.). (ENG.). 32p. (J). lib. bdg. 25.00 ***(978-0-531-23332-0(4)***, Children's Pr.) Scholastic Library Publishing.

Lerner Classroom & Zuehlke, Jeffrey. The Grand Canyon. 2010. (Lightning Bolt Books (tm) — Famous Places Ser.). (ENG.). 32p. (gr. k-2). pap. 7.95 *(978-0-7613-5573-1(1))* Lerner Publishing Group.

Lomberg, Michelle. The Grand Canyon. 2004. (Natural Wonders of the U. S. A. Ser.). (Illus.). 32p. (J). (gr. 4-7). per. 9.95 *(978-1-59036-161-0(X))* Weigl Pubs., Inc.

—The Grand Canyon: The Largest Canyon in the United States. 2004. (Natural Wonders of the U. S. A. Ser.). (Illus.). 32p. (J). (gr. 3-7). lib. bdg. 26.00 *(978-1-59036-038-5(9))* Weigl Pubs., Inc.

Mis, Melody S. Exploring Canyons. 2009. (Geography Zone: Landforms Ser.). (Illus.). 24p. (J). (gr. 2-4). pap. 8.25 *(978-1-4358-3114-8(4))*; 24p. (gr. 2-3). 42.50 *(978-1-61512-692-7(9))*; (J). lib. bdg. 22.60 *(978-1-4358-2716-5(3))* Rosen Publishing Group, Inc., The. (PowerKids Pr.).

Murray, Julie. Grand Canyon, 1 vol. 2005. (All Aboard America Ser.). (ENG., Illus.). 24p. (J). (gr. 1-4). 25.65 *(978-1-59197-505-2(0))* ABDO Publishing Co.

O'connor, Jim. Where Is the Grand Canyon? 2015. (Where Is... ? Ser.). lib. bdg. 16.00 *(978-0-606-36588-8(5))* Turtleback Bks.

O'Connor, Jim & dePaola, Tomie. Where Is the Grand Canyon? Groff, David & Colón, Daniel, illus. 2015. (Where Is? Ser.). (ENG.). 112p. (J). (gr. 3-7). 5.99 *(978-0-448-48357-3(2)*, Grosset & Dunlap) Penguin Young Readers Group.

Rome, Lori April. The Adventures of Salt & Soap at Grand Canyon. Bauerle, Tanja, illus. 2009. (ENG.). 32p. (gr. 2-4). pap. 9.95 *(978-1-934656-04-4(6))* Grand Canyon Assn.

Wade, Linda R. & Hamilton, John. Grand Canyon National Park, 1 vol. 2005. (National Parks Ser.). (ENG., Illus.). 32p. (YA). (gr. 4-7). 27.07 *(978-1-59197-426-0(7))* ABDO Publishing Co.

Weintraub, Aileen. The Grand Canyon: The Widest Canyon. 2009. (Great Record Breakers in Nature Ser.). 24p. (gr. 3-4). 42.50 *(978-1-61513-183-9(3)*, PowerKids Pr.) Rosen Publishing Group, Inc., The.

Zuehlke, Jeffrey. The Grand Canyon. 2010. (Lightning Bolt Books (tm) — Famous Places Ser.). (ENG.). 32p. (gr. k-2). lib. bdg. 26.60 *(978-0-7613-4261-8(3)*, Lerner Pubns.) Lerner Publishing Group.

GRAND CANYON (ARIZ.)—FICTION

Allred, Sylvester & Iverson, Diane. Rascal, the Tassel-Eared Squirrel. 2007. (ENG., Illus.). 64p. pap. 9.95 *(978-0-938216-44-5(9))* Grand Canyon Assn.

Brezenoff, Steve. The Grand Canyon Burros That Broke, 1 vol. Calo, Marcos, illus. 2012. (Field Trip Mysteries Ser.). (ENG.). 88p. (gr. 2-3). pap. 6.10 *(978-1-4342-4198-6(X))*; lib. bdg. 25.32 *(978-1-4342-3788-0(5))* Stone Arch Bks.

Brown, Craig. Mule Train Mail. Brown, Craig, illus. 2009. (ENG., Illus.). 36p. (J). (gr. -1-3). pap. 7.95 *(978-1-58089-188-2(8))* Charlesbridge Publishing, Inc.

Carson, James. The Saddle Boys in the Grand Canyon: Or the Hermit of the Cave. 2007. (ENG.). 136p. pap. 18.99 *(978-1-4346-4441-1(3))*; 148p. pap. 19.99 *(978-1-4346-4442-8(1))* Creative Media Partners, LLC.

Chandler, Mitzi. I See Something Grand. 2003. (Illus.). 32p. (J). (gr. -1-1). pap. 8.95 *(978-0-938216-50-6(3))* Grand Canyon Assn.

Edman Lamote, Lisa. A Day Out for Opus. Wilson, Alisha, illus. 2006. (Bookmann Family Presents Ser.). 32p. (J). (gr. k-3). 15.99 *(978-1-933673-03-5(6)*, BookMann Pr.) Mann Publishing Group.

Friedman, Laurie. On the Road with Mallory. Kalis, Jennifer, illus. 2016. (Mallory Ser.: 25). (ENG.). 160p. (gr. 2-5). (J). 15.95 *(978-1-4677-5029-5(8))*; 31.99 *(978-1-4677-9567-8(4))* Lerner Publishing Group. (Darby Creek).

Gabriel, Thora. Chessie Bligh & the Scroll of Andelthor. 2006. 284p. (J). 27.95 *(978-0-595-83579-9(1))* iUniverse, Inc.

Gutman, Dan. The Return of the Homework Machine. (ENG.). (J). (gr. 3-7). 2011. 192p. pap. 7.99 *(978-1-4169-5459-0(7))* 2009. 176p. 15.99 *(978-1-4169-5416-3(3))* Simon & Schuster Bks. For Young Readers. (Simon & Schuster Bks. For Young Readers).

Hansel, Karen & Ham, Ken. Charlie & Trike Grand Canyon Adventure. 2010. (Illus.). 24p. (J). spiral bd. 15.99 *(978-0-89051-569-3(7))* Master Bks.

Hautman, Pete. Hole in the Sky. 2007. (ENG.). 224p. (YA). (gr. 7). pap. 11.95 *(978-1-4169-6822-1(9)*, Simon Pulse) Simon Pulse.

Henry, Marguerite. Brighty of the Grand Canyon. 2015. (ENG., Illus.). 256p. (J). (gr. 3-7). 19.99 *(978-1-4814-1582-8(4)*, Aladdin) Simon & Schuster Children's Publishing.

Hobbs, Will. Downriver. 2012. (ENG., Illus.). 208p. (J). (gr. 5-9). pap. 7.99 *(978-1-4424-4547-5(5)*, Atheneum Bks. for Young Readers) Simon & Schuster Children's Publishing.

Iverson, Diane. Rascal, the Tassel Eared Squirrel. 2007. 64p. pap. 9.95 *(978-0-932821-64-5(2))* Grand Canyon Assn.

Jenkins, Jerry B. & Fabry, Chris. Canyon Echoes. 2005. (Red Rock Mysteries Ser.: 8). (ENG.). 234p. (YA). pap. 6.99 *(978-1-4143-0147-1(2)*, Tyndale Kids) Tyndale Hse. Pubs.

Lowell, Susan. The Great Grand Canyon Time Train. Shroades, John / W., illus. 2011. 32p. (J). 15.95 *(978-1-933855-63-9(0))* Rio Nuevo Pubs.

Marsh, Carole. The Ghost of the Grand Canyon. 2009. (Real Kids, Real Places Ser.). (Illus.). 146p. (J). lib. bdg. 18.99 *(978-0-635-07003-6(0)*, Marsh, Carole Mysteries) Gallopade International.

Nesbit, Troy. Mystery at Rustlers Fort. 2014. (Wilderness Mystery Ser.). (ENG., Illus.). 282p. (J). (gr. 3-7). pap. 12.95 *(978-1-58979-867-0(8))* Taylor Trade Publishing.

Patchin, Frank Gee. The Pony Rider Boys in the Grand Canyon: The Mystery of Bright Angel Gulch. 2007. (ENG.). 158p. pap. 19.99 *(978-1-4264-7084-4(3))*; 176p. pap. 21.99 *(978-1-4264-7160-5(2))* Creative Media Partners, LLC.

Perlman, Rhea. Canyon Catastrophe. Santat, Dan, illus. 2006. (Otto Undercover Ser.). 128p. (J). (gr. 4-7). 14.99 *(978-0-06-075498-3(2))* HarperCollins Pubs.

Ratnayake, Kumari/Keiko. Monsieur Bagel's War. Ratnayake, Kumari/Keiko, illus. 2007. (Illus.). 25p. (J). spiral bd. 15.00 net. *(978-0-9797015-1-1(1))* Augustana College Geology Dept. Pr.

Rogers, Christopher M., illus. Homer the Helicopter Grand Canyon Adventures. 2007. 72p. (J). 18.95 *(978-0-9786352-3-7(X))* Buscher, Julie W.

Scanlon, Liz Garton. In the Canyon. Wolff, Ashley, illus. 2015. (ENG.). 40p. (J). (gr. -1-3). 17.99 *(978-1-4814-0348-1(6)*, Beach Lane Bks.) Beach Lane Bks.

GRAND CENTRAL TERMINAL (NEW YORK, N.Y.)

Stanley, Ed. Grand Central Terminal: Gateway to New York City. 2003. (Illus.). 48p. (J). 16.95 *(978-1-59034-491-0(X))*; pap. *(978-1-59034-492-7(8))* Mondo Publishing.

GRAND CENTRAL TERMINAL (NEW YORK, N.Y.)—FICTION

Allende, Isabel. Forest of the Pygmies. 2009. (City of the Beasts Ser.: Bk. 3).Tr. of Bosque de los Pigmeos. (ENG.). 320p. pap. 14.99 *(978-0-06-182510-1(7)*, Harper Perennial) HarperCollins Pubs.

GRAND OPERA

see Opera

GRANDPARENTS

Ajmera, Maya, et al. Our Grandparents: A Global Album. 2010. (ENG.). 32p. (J). (gr. -1-3). 16.95 *(978-1-57091-458-4(3))*; (Illus.). pap. 7.95 *(978-1-57091-459-1(1))* Charlesbridge Publishing, Inc.

At My Grandfather's, 6 Pcks. (gr. -1-2). 27.00 *(978-0-7635-9435-0(0))* Rigby Education.

Auld, Mary. Mis Abuelos. Carrillo, Consuelo & Coffey, Colleen, trs. from ENG. 2004. (Conoce la Familia Ser.). (SPA., Illus.). 24p. (gr. k-3). lib. bdg. 22.00 *(978-0-8368-3934-0(X)*, Gareth Stevens Learning Library) Stevens, Gareth Publishing LLLP.

—My Grandparents. 2004. (Meet the Family Ser.). (Illus.). 24p. (gr. k-3). lib. bdg. 22.00 *(978-0-8368-3926-5(9)*, Gareth Stevens Learning Library) Stevens, Gareth Publishing LLLP.

Baniti, Nailah. Papa's Bella Ros. 2012. 26p. pap. 9.99 *(978-0-9853574-0-5(1))* Mountan Creek Pubns.

Beeby, Betty. Great Granny's Sturdy Stable Picnic Tables. 2004. (Illus.). 32p. (J). *(978-0-9674525-2-4(X))* Pearl Pr.

Berry, Joy. I Love Grandmas & Grandpas. Regan, Dana, illus. 2010. (Teach Me About Ser.). (ENG.). 40p. (J). (gr. k — 1). pap. 5.99 *(978-1-60577-003-1(5))* Berry, Joy Enterprises.

Burns, Marie. The Quest for Gold. 2012. 64p. pap. 15.99 *(978-1-4691-4632-4(0))* Xlibris Corp.

Cameron, Merilee Ann. The Violet-Covered Teacup. 2013. (ENG.). 28p. (J). 14.95 *(978-1-4525-7810-1(9)*, Balboa Pr.) Author Solutions, Inc.

Carter-Reed, Lorye. Grandpa Isn't Coming Anymore: A Child's Look at Death. 2010. 24p. 12.99 *(978-1-4520-6271-6(4))* AuthorHouse.

Catt, Thessaly. My Grandparents. 2010. (My Family Ser.). (ENG.). 24p. (J). pap. 8.25 *(978-1-4488-1486-2(3))*; lib. bdg. 22.60 *(978-1-4488-1460-2(X))* Rosen Publishing Group, Inc., The. (PowerKids Pr.).

—My Grandparents: MIS Abuelos. 2010. (My Family / Mi Familia Ser.). (SPA & ENG.). 24p. lib. bdg. 22.60 *(978-1-4488-0716-1(6))* Rosen Publishing Group, Inc., The.

Coll-Seck, Jayden. I Live with My Grandma & Grandpa, 01 vols., 1. 2016. (Rosen REAL Readers: Social Studies Nonfiction / Fiction: Family, Community, & the World Ser.). (ENG.). 8p. (J). pap. 5.46 *(978-1-5081-1638-7(5)*, Rosen Classroom) Rosen Publishing Group, Inc., The.

Delisle, Carolynne E. Nonna & Grandp. 2012. 16p. pap. 15.99 *(978-1-4772-6841-4(3))* AuthorHouse.

Dicker, Katie. My Grandparents. 2017. (Popcorn: Families Ser.). (ENG., Illus.). 24p. (J). (gr. k-2). pap. 10.99 *(978-0-7502-8881-1(7)*, Wayland) Hachette Children's Group GBR. Dist: Hachette Bk. Group.

English, Carolyn B. Grandpa & the Orange Bowl. 2010. 32p. pap. 12.99 *(978-1-4490-4741-2(6))* AuthorHouse.

Eystad, Janet Lynn. What I Got into Last Summer. 2012. 28p. 24.95 *(978-1-4626-5316-4(2))* America Star Bks.

Fuerst, Jeffrey B. Visiting Grandma: Lap Book. 2009. (My First Reader's Theater Set B Ser.). (J). 28.00 *(978-1-60634-991-5(0))* Benchmark Education Co.

Gachot, Lynn. June-Ah-Vee's Blessing. 2010. 24p. 14.50 *(978-1-4520-7747-5(9))* AuthorHouse.

Gamble, Adam & Jasper, Mark. Good Night Grandma. Kelly, Cooper, illus. 2016. (ENG.). 20p. (J). (— 1). bds. 9.95 *(978-1-60219-409-0(2))* Good Night Bks.

Gizicki-Lipson, Coryn & Gizicki, Carlie. An Angel in the Sky. Gizicki-Lipson, Coryn, illus. 2003. (ENG., Illus.). 32p. (J). 14.95 *(978-0-9740438-0-7(X))* In the Sky Publishing.

Gologan, Trena. Grandparents are Special. 2009. 35p. pap. 17.15 *(978-1-4357-3971-0(X))* Lulu Pr., Inc.

Grandma Fudgie. A Day at the Beach. 2011. 24p. pap. 14.99 *(978-1-4567-5548-5(X))* AuthorHouse.

—A Walk to the Park. 2011. 24p. pap. 12.99 *(978-1-4634-2695-8(X))* AuthorHouse.

Gribble, John. The Grandpas' Book: For the Grandpa Who's Best at Everything. Woodroffe, David, illus. 2010. (Best at Everything Ser.). (ENG.). 144p. (J). (gr. 3-7). 9.99 *(978-0-545-13396-8(3)*, Scholastic Nonfiction) Scholastic, Inc.

Grove, Craig J. Frog Water. 2013. 24p. *(978-1-4602-2634-6(8))*; pap. *(978-1-4602-2635-3(6))* FriesenPress.

Hall, Petisamaria G. Why Grandmas Go to Heaven. 2009. 24p. pap. 11.49 *(978-1-4490-4962-1(1))* AuthorHouse.

Hamilton, Alice. Loving Hands of Grandma: A True Story. 2012. 24p. pap. 24.95 *(978-1-4626-7432-9(1))* PublishAmerica, Inc.

Harrison, Lorraine. I Learn from My Grandma. 2016. (Things I Learn Ser.). (Illus.). 24p. (J). (gr. 1-1). pap. 8.25 *(978-1-4994-2367-9(5)*, PowerKids Pr.) Rosen Publishing Group, Inc., The.

Holtzman, Claudia Ann. Why Are They Called... Grandparents! 2012. 36p. pap. 24.95 *(978-1-4626-8404-5(1))* America Star Bks.

Hord, Janice. The Walking Stick Adventure. 2007. 52p. per. 19.95 *(978-1-934335-05-5(3))* WordWright.biz, Inc.

Horrocks, Anita. Silas' Seven Grandparents, 1 vol. Flook, Helen, illus. 2010. (ENG.). 32p. (J). (gr. -1-3). 19.95 *(978-1-55143-561-9(6))* Orca Bk. Pubs. USA.

Jenner, Caryn. My Grandparents. 2017. (Family World Ser.). (ENG., Illus.). 24p. (J). (gr. 1-3). pap. 9.99 *(978-1-4451-5221-9(5)*, Franklin Watts) Hachette Children's Group GBR. Dist: Hachette Bk. Group.

Kilmer, Jim. Adventures with Grandp. 2012. 48p. pap. 18.50 *(978-1-4685-6629-1(6))* AuthorHouse.

Knoke, Paul. The Storm on Godfather Mountain: A True Story. 2010. 24p. pap. 14.99 *(978-1-4490-5773-2(X))* AuthorHouse.

Konrad, Marla Stewart. Grand. 2010. (Early Reader Ser.). (ENG., Illus.). 24p. (J). (gr. -1-2). 12.95 *(978-0-88776-997-9(7)*, Tundra Bks.) Tundra Bks. CAN. Dist: Penguin Random Hse. LLC.

Kramer, Nash. Where Did My Grandparents Come From? 2014. (Little Books of Answers: Level C Ser.). (Illus.). 16p. (gr. k-2). pap. 7.95 *(978-1-927136-21-8(0))* Three Crows Media NZL. Dist: RiverStream Publishing.

Lovelace, Eloise. Your Ema Loves You. 2011. 24p. pap. 12.99 *(978-1-4567-4378-9(3))* AuthorHouse.

Marcet, Jane. Mary's Grammar. 2011. 336p. pap. 13.95 *(978-1-59915-390-2(4))* Yesterday's Classics.

Masterson, Josephine. My Grandfather's Workshop. 2015. (Rosen REAL Readers: STEM & STEAM Collection). (ENG.). 8p. pap. 5.46 *(978-1-4994-9708-3(3)*, Rosen Classroom) Rosen Publishing Group, Inc., The.

McBain, Madelaine (Maddie). A Day with Non. 2012. 24p. pap. 17.99 *(978-1-4772-2387-1(8))* AuthorHouse.

McConnell, Lynn. Grandma's Tree. 2009. 24p. pap. 11.49 *(978-1-4389-8069-0(8))* AuthorHouse.

McCune, Susan. My Grandma Lives in Our House, 01 vols., 1. 2016. (Rosen REAL Readers: Social Studies Nonfiction / Fiction: Family, Community, & the World Ser.). (ENG.). 8p. (J). pap. 5.46 *(978-1-5081-1650-9(4)*, Rosen Classroom) Rosen Publishing Group, Inc., The.

McDermott, Mary. The Special Women We Call Grandmom, 1 vol. Braun, Lisa, illus. 2010. 20p. pap. 24.95 *(978-1-4489-9749-7(6))* PublishAmerica, Inc.

Miller, Vivian. Grandma's Mercedes. 2010. 36p. pap. 15.49 *(978-1-4520-1710-5(7))* AuthorHouse.

Monn, Margaret A. Cause I Live Here. Monn, Margaret A., illus. 2011. (Illus.). 32p. pap. 24.95 *(978-1-4560-7311-4(7))* PublishAmerica, Inc.

Morris, Ann. Grandma Hekmat Remembers: An Arab-American Family Story. Linenthal, Peter, photos by. 2003. (What Was It Like, Grandma? Ser.). (ENG., Illus.). 32p. (gr. 2-5). lib. bdg. 22.60 *(978-0-7613-2864-3(5)*, Millbrook Pr.) Lerner Publishing Group.

—Grandma Hekmat Remembers: An Egyptian - American Family Story. Linenthal, Peter, photos by. 2003. (Illus.). 32p. (J). (gr. 5-18). pap. 7.95 *(978-0-7613-1944-3(1)*, Millbrook Pr.) Lerner Publishing Group.

My Granddad Is Great. 2008. (My Great Relatives... Ser.). 32p. *(978-1-4075-0942-6(X))* Parragon, Inc.

My Grandma Is Great. 2008. (My Great Relatives... Ser.). 32p. *(978-1-4075-0859-7(8))* Parragon, Inc.

Nachbar, Patricia Depoyster. Love Doesn't Die. 2013. 16p. pap. 12.70 *(978-1-4669-6292-7(5))* Trafford Publishing.

North, Merry. My Grandma & Me: A Picture, Play & Tote Book. 2004. 10p. (J). (gr. -1-18). bds. 5.99 *(978-1-57151-724-1(3))* Playhouse Publishing.

Parr, Todd. The Grandma Book. 2011. (ENG., Illus.). 24p. (gr. -1-1). pap. 7.00 *(978-0-316-07041-6(6))* Little, Brown Bks. for Young Readers.

—The Grandpa Book. 2011. (ENG., Illus.). 24p. (gr. -1-1). pap. 8.00 *(978-0-316-07043-0(2))* Little, Brown Bks. for Young Readers.

Poole, H. W. Multigenerational Families, Vol. 12. 2016. (Families Today Ser.). (Illus.). 48p. (J). (gr. 5). 20.95 *(978-1-4222-3621-5(8))* Mason Crest.

Raatma, Lucia. Grandfathers Are Part of a Family. 2017. (Our Families Ser.). (ENG.). 24p. (gr. k-1). lib. bdg. 21.99 ***(978-1-5157-7458-7(9)***, Pebble Bks.) Capstone Press of Coughlan Cos.

—Grandmothers Are Part of a Family. 2017. (Our Families Ser.). (ENG.). 24p. (gr. k-1). lib. bdg. 21.99 ***(978-1-5157-7454-9(6)***, Pebble Bks.) Capstone Press of Coughlan Cos.

Reeves, Barbara. Grandpa's Crooked Smile: A Story of Stroke Survival. Sinclair, Peter, illus. 2007. (J). *(978-1-4276-2013-2(X))* Aardvark Global Publishing.

Richards, Keith. Gus & Me: The Story of My Granddad & My First Guitar. Richards, Theodora, illus. 2014. (ENG.). 32p. (J). (gr. -1-1). 18.00 *(978-0-316-32065-8(X))* Little, Brown Bks. for Young Readers.

Rissman, Rebecca. Grandparents, 1 vol. 2011. (Families Ser.). (ENG.). 24p. (gr. -1-1). 22.65 *(978-1-4329-4658-6(7))*; pap. 6.29 *(978-1-4329-4666-1(8))* Heinemann-Raintree. (Acorn).

Russell, Carol & Russell, Tally. I Like Rocks! Russell, Fletch, photos by. 2011. (Illus.). 32p. pap. 12.95 *(978-1-4634-3271-3(2))* AuthorHouse.

Rykken, Cheryl. My Shaky Grandma. 2008. 32p. pap. 11.50 *(978-1-4357-3496-8(3))* Lulu Pr., Inc.

Sanschagrin, Joceline. At Grandma & Grandpa's. Brignaud, Pierre & Depratto, Marcel, illus. 2008. (Big Dipper Ser.). (ENG.). 24p. (J). (gr. -1-k). pap. 3.99 *(978-2-89450-656-1(2))* Caillouet, Gerry.

Schaefer, Lola M. Grandfathers. Saunders-Smith, Gail, ed. rev. ed. 2008. (Families Ser.). (ENG., Illus.). 24p. (gr. k-1). 21.99 *(978-1-4296-1225-8(8))*; per. 6.29 *(978-1-4296-1754-3(3))* Capstone Press of Coughlan Cos. (Pebble Bks.).

—Grandmothers. Saunders-Smith, Gail, ed. rev. ed. 2008. (Families Ser.). (ENG., Illus.). 24p. (gr. k-1). 21.99 *(978-1-4296-1226-5(6))*; per. 6.29 *(978-1-4296-1755-0(1))* Capstone Press of Coughlan Cos. (Pebble Bks.).

Sermons, Faye. My Granma Lives at the Airport. 2012. 20p. pap. 12.00 *(978-1-4490-1893-1(9))* AuthorHouse.

Simons, Rae. Grandparents Raising Kids. 2010. (Changing Face of Modern Families Ser.). (Illus.). 64p. (YA). (gr. 6-18). lib. bdg. 22.95 *(978-1-4222-1496-1(6))* Mason Crest.

Sundermann, Dan & Sundermann, Sally. Childhood Memories: Grandma & Grandpa's Earliest Recollections. 2008. 48p. pap. 9.95 *(978-0-595-52763-2(9))* iUniverse, Inc.

Swainston, Jeani. Grandma Stuff: ... it's what love Is made Of. 2006. (J). *(978-0-9791384-0-9(X))* Rock Cliff Media.

Symons, Anna Jane. Nanna & Me. 2012. 24p. pap. 28.03 *(978-1-4797-3630-0(9))* Xlibris Corp.

Taylor, B. J. Ella Mae & the Great Depression. 2013. 40p. pap. 19.57 *(978-1-4907-1016-7(7))* Trafford Publishing.

Thomas, Gina. Mr Taxi Man Meets Irene. 2009. 48p. pap. 19.99 *(978-1-4490-3495-5(0))* AuthorHouse.

Tingle, Tim. Saltypie: A Choctaw Journey from Darkness into Light. Clarkson, Karen, illus. 2010. (ENG.). 40p. (J). (gr. 2-6). 17.95 *(978-1-933693-67-5(3))* Cinco Puntos Pr.

Tweedy, Bonnie. Grandma Bonnie's Cats: In Love Again. 2011. 28p. pap. 12.98 *(978-1-4520-1150-9(8))* AuthorHouse.

VanTassell - Luto, Ceneca. The Other White House. 2011. 28p. (gr. -1). pap. 14.95 *(978-1-4567-4052-8(0))* AuthorHouse.

Verderosa, Laura. At Grandma's House. 2010. (Sight Word Readers Ser.). (J). 3.49 *(978-1-60719-607-5(7))* Newmark Learning LLC.

Voight, Joseph. My Grandma Has Alzheimer's Too. 2008. 26p. (J). (gr. 2-7). pap. 12.95 *(978-1-933255-44-6(7))* DNA Pr.

Weber, Rebecca. My Grandma. 2011. (Early Connections Ser.). (J). *(978-1-61672-330-9(0))* Benchmark Education Co.

Yazzie, Serphine G. Beauty Beside Me: Stories of My Grandmother's Skirts. 2011. (ENG & NAV., Illus.). 32p. (J). (gr. -1-3). 21.95 *(978-1-893354-07-4(5))* Salina Bookshelf Inc.

GRANDPARENTS—FICTION

Abbott, D. K. Mrs. Potter's Cat. McKenzie, Josie, illus. 2007. 28p. per. 24.95 *(978-1-4241-8345-6(6))* America Star Bks.

Abbott, Simon. Little Mouse Visits Grandma: Mouse on Ribbon, Flaps, Acetates. Abbott, Simon, illus. 2006. (ENG.,

Illus.). 16p. (J). (gr. -1-k). 15.99 *(978-1-85707-668-4(0))* Tango Bks. GBR. Dist: Independent Pubs. Group.

Abbruzzi, Danielle. Penelope's Piggies. Sampson, Kathleen, illus. 2012. 42p. 24.95 *(978-1-4626-6264-7(1))* America Star Bks.

Abedí, Isabel. Farewell, Grandpa Elephant: What Happens When a Loved One Dies? Cordes, Miriam, illus. 2012. (ENG.). 28p. (J). (gr. -1-k). 16.95 *(978-1-61608-655-8(6),* 608655, Sky Pony Pr.) Skyhorse Publishing Co., Inc.

Aboff, Marcie. Grandpa's Lost Pin. Tolton, Laura, illus. 2016. (Spring Forward Ser.). (J). (gr. 1). *(978-1-4900-9373-4(7))* Benchmark Education Co.

Abraham, Michelle Shapiro. Where Is Grandpa Dennis? Fried, Janice, illus. 2009. (J). *(978-0-8074-1083-7(7))* URJ Pr.

Abrahams, Peter. Into the Dark. 2009. (Echo Falls Mystery Ser.: 3). (ENG.). 352p. (J). (gr. 5-18). pap. 6.99 *(978-0-06-073710-8(7))* HarperCollins Pubs.

Abreu, Raquel, illus. Little Ruth Reddingford (and the Wolf) An Old Tale retold by Hank Wesselman, PH. D. 2004. 32p. (J). per. 15.95 *(978-0-9740190-0-0(3))* Illumination Arts Publishing Co., Inc.

Acampora, Paul. How to Avoid Extinction. 2016. (ENG.). 208p. (J). (gr. 3-7). 16.99 *(978-0-545-89906-2(0),* Scholastic Pr.) Scholastic, Inc.

Acheson, Alison. Grandpa's Music: A Story about Alzheimer's. Farnsworth, Bill, illus. 2009. (ENG.). 32p. (J). (gr. 3-3). 16.99 *(978-0-8075-3052-8(2))* Whitman, Albert & Co.

Ackerman, Karen. Song & Dance Man. Gammell, Stephen, illus. 2015. 32p. pap. 8.00 *(978-1-61003-554-5(2))* Center for the Collaborative Classroom.

—Song & Dance Man. Gammell, Stephen, illus. 2003. (ENG.). 32p. (J). (gr. -1-2). 15.95 *(978-0-394-89330-3(1),* Knopf Bks. for Young Readers) Random Hse. Children's Bks.

Acosta, Margarita. Summer at Grandma's. 2013. 36p. pap. 14.95 *(978-1-60594-983-3(3),* Llumina Pr.) Aeon Publishing Inc.

Adams-Cantrell;, Renee. Peanut Bunny & the Christmas Lights. Daley-Prado, M. J., illus. 2009. 48p. pap. 24.95 *(978-1-60610-432-3(2))* America Star Bks.

Adams, Julie. Kern's Adventures: The Fishing Trip. 2009. 40p. pap. 16.99 *(978-1-4389-8458-2(8))* AuthorHouse.

Adams, Misty Pedersen. Grandma Goes Home, 1 vol. 2010. 48p. pap. 16.95 *(978-1-4512-9673-0(8))* America Star Bks.

Adams, Sandi. Watch What You Wish: Kajsa Conquers Her World. 2009. 36p. pap. 15.49 *(978-1-4490-3513-6(2))* AuthorHouse.

Adams, Sheila Murphy. Beads, Bands, & a Brass Ring. 2011. 28p. pap. 14.95 *(978-1-4567-1550-2(X))* AuthorHouse.

Addasi, Maha. Time to Pray. Albitar, Nuha, tr. Gannon, Ned, illus. 2010. (ENG & ARA.). 32p. (J). (gr. 2-4). 17.95 *(978-1-59078-611-6(4))* Boyds Mills Pr.

Addy, Sharon. In Grandpa's Woods. Akins, Tamlyn, illus. 2004. (J). *(978-1-931599-42-9(4),* Trails Bks.) Bower Hse.

Adler, David A. Bones & the Birthday Mystery, No. 5. Newman, Barbara Johansen, illus. 2009. (Bones Ser.: 5). (ENG.). 32p. (J). (gr. 1-3). mass mkt. 3.99 *(978-0-14-241432-3(8),* Penguin Young Readers) Penguin Young Readers Group.

—Bones & the Dinosaur Mystery, No. 4. Newman, Barbara Johansen, illus. 2009. (Bones Ser.: 4). (ENG.). 32p. (J). (gr. 1-3). mass mkt. 3.99 *(978-0-14-241341-8(0),* Penguin Young Readers) Penguin Young Readers Group.

—Bones & the Roller Coaster Mystery, 7 vols. Newman, Barbara Johansen, illus. 2010. (Bones Ser.: 7). (ENG.). 32p. (J). (gr. 1-3). mass mkt. 3.99 *(978-0-14-241687-7(8),* Penguin Young Readers) Penguin Young Readers Group.

—A Little at a Time. Tong, Paul, illus. 2010. (ENG.). 32p. (J). (gr. -1-3). 16.95 *(978-0-8234-1739-1(5))* Holiday Hse., Inc.

—Young Cam Jansen & the Knock, Knock Mystery. Natti, Susanna, illus. (Young Cam Jansen Ser.: 20). (ENG.). 32p. (J). (gr. 1-3). 2015. pap. 3.99 *(978-0-14-242225-0(8))* 2014. 14.99 *(978-0-670-01261-9(0))* Penguin Young Readers Group. (Penguin Young Readers).

The Adventures of Molly. 2004. pap. 13.95 *(978-1-59526-180-9(X))* Aeon Publishing Inc.

Ahmad, M. I. Aldebaram. 2009. 95p. pap. 13.00 *(978-0-557-08323-7(0))* Lulu Pr., Inc.

Airgood, Ellen. Prairie Evers. (ENG.). 224p. (J). (gr. 3-7). 2014. pap. 7.99 *(978-0-14-242668-5(7),* Puffin Books) 2012. 15.99 *(978-0-399-25691-2(1),* Nancy Paulsen Books) Penguin Young Readers Group.

Alarid, Carilyn & Markel, Marilyn. Old Grandfather Teaches a Lesson: Mimbres Children Learn Respect. Alarid, Carilyn & Markel, Marilyn, illus. 2004. (Illus.). 116p. (J). pap. 16.95 *(978-0-86534-418-1(3))* Sunstone Pr.

Albo, Pablo. The Glutton. 2007. (ENG., Illus.). 48p. (J). 18.95 *(978-84-96788-91-6(1))* OQO, Editora ESP. Dist: Baker & Taylor Bks.

Alcántara, Ricardo. Mauro Ojos Brillantes. 9th ed. 2003. (SPA., Illus.). 48p. *(978-84-236-2865-0(5),* ED6279) Edebé ESP. Dist: Lectorum Pubns., Inc.

Ale, Leandra. Spoiled by Grandp. 2008. 28p. pap. 14.51 *(978-1-4389-0461-0(4))* AuthorHouse.

Allen, Crystal. The Laura Line. 2013. (ENG.). 336p. (J). (gr. 3-7). 16.99 *(978-0-06-199274-2(7))* HarperCollins Pubs.

Allen, Debbie. Winker & the Kitten. 2009. 28p. pap. 13.99 *(978-1-4389-8266-3(6))* AuthorHouse.

Allende, Isabel. A Cidade das Feras. 2006.Tr. of Ciudad de las Bestias. (POR.). 280p. (YA). pap. 26.95 *(978-85-286-0977-6(4))* Bertrand Brasil Editora SA BRA. Dist: Distribooks, Inc.

—City of the Beasts. 2009. (P. S. Ser.: Bk. 1). (ENG.). 448p. pap. 14.99 *(978-0-06-182511-8(5),* Harper Perennial) 2005. 464p. (J). (gr. 7-17). pap. 7.99 *(978-0-06-077645-9(5),* Rayo) HarperCollins Pubs.

—City of the Beasts. Peden, Margaret Sayers, tr. from SPA. 2004. (City of the Beasts Ser.: Bk. 1). (ENG.). 432p. (J). (gr. 5-18). reprint ed. pap. 7.99 *(978-0-06-053503-2(2),* Rayo) HarperCollins Pubs.

—Forest of the Pygmies. Peden, Margaret Sayers, tr. from SPA. (City of the Beasts Ser.: Bk. 3).Tr. of Bosque de los Pigmeos. 304p. (J). (gr. 5-12). 2006. (ENG.). pap. 10.99 *(978-0-06-076198-1(9))* 2005. 19.99 *(978-0-06-076196-7(2))* HarperCollins Pubs. (Rayo).

—Forest of the Pygmies. l.t. ed. 2005. (City of the Beasts Ser.: Bk. 3).Tr. of Bosque de los Pigmeos. 304p. (J). (gr. 5-18). pap. 19.99 *(978-0-06-076200-1(4),* Rayo) HarperCollins Pubs.

—Kingdom of the Golden Dragon. 2009. (City of the Beasts Ser.: Bk. 2).Tr. of Reino del Dragón de Oro. (ENG.). 480p. pap. 14.99 *(978-0-06-182512-5(3),* Harper Perennial) HarperCollins Pubs.

Almond, David. Kit's Wilderness. unabr. ed. 2004. 240p. (J). (gr. 7-18). pap. 36.00 incl. audio *(978-0-8072-8216-8(2),* Listening Library) Random Hse. Audio Publishing Group.

Alten, Steve. Sharkman. 2014. (ENG.). 272p. 22.95 *(978-1-63076-019-9(6))* Taylor Trade Publishing.

Altés, Marta. My Grandpa. 2013. (ENG., Illus.). 32p. (J). (gr. k-2). 16.95 *(978-1-4197-0588-5(1),* Abrams Bks. for Young Readers) Abrams, Inc.

Amateau, Gigi. Claiming Georgia Tate. (ENG.). 208p. (YA). (gr. 9-12). 2007. per. 7.99 *(978-0-7636-3311-0(9))* 2005. 15.99 *(978-0-7636-2339-5(3))* Candlewick Pr.

And Then it was Sugar, 6 vols. (Multicultural Programs Ser.). 16p. (gr. 1-6). 31.95 *(978-0-7802-8324-4(4))* Wright Group/McGraw-Hill.

Andersen, Jill. My Grandma's Green Thumb. 2016. (Rosen REAL Readers: STEM & STEAM Collection). 8p. (gr. 1-k). pap. 5.46 *(978-1-5081-2601-0(1),* Rosen Classroom) Rosen Publishing Group, Inc., The.

Anderson, Cathysue. Through Grandmother's Window. 2013. 32p. pap. 13.99 *(978-1-4624-0579-4(7),* Inspiring Voices) Author Solutions, Inc.

Anderson, Jennifer. Honey Creek Royalty. 2013. 246p. pap. 12.99 *(978-1-62237-148-8(8))* Turquoise Morning Pr.

Anderson, Jodi Lynn. Loser/Queen. Lee, Brittney, illus. 2010. (ENG.). 272p. (YA). (gr. 7-18). pap. 9.99 *(978-1-4169-9646-0(X),* Simon & Schuster Bks. For Young Readers) Simon & Schuster Bks. For Young Readers.

Anderson, Joyce E. Walking with Grandm. 2009. 36p. pap. 16.99 *(978-1-4389-4642-9(2))* AuthorHouse.

Anderson, Laurie Halse. End of the Race, 12 vols. 2012. (Vet Volunteers Ser.: 12). (ENG.). 160p. (J). (gr. 3-7). 6.99 *(978-0-14-241228-2(7),* Puffin Books) Penguin Young Readers Group.

—Fever 1793. 2014. (ENG.). 272p. (J). 12.24 *(978-1-63245-124-8(7))* Lectorum Pubns., Inc.

—Helping Hands. 2013. (Vet Volunteers Ser.: 15). (ENG.). 144p. (J). (gr. 3-7). pap. 6.99 *(978-0-14-241677-8(0),* Puffin Books) Penguin Young Readers Group.

Anderson, P. G. Grandma's Day. Sandford, Barbara, illus. 2013. 32p. 16.00 *(978-1-61170-133-3(3))* Robertson Publishing.

Anderson, Renae. Upon the Heads of the Children. 2009. 236p. 25.75 *(978-1-60860-483-8(7),* Strategic Bk. Publishing) Strategic Book Publishing & Rights Agency (SBPRA).

Andreae, Giles. Heaven Is Having You. Cabban, Vanessa, illus. 2007. (Padded Board Bks.). 18p. (J). (gr. -1-1). bds. 7.95 *(978-1-58925-820-4(7))* Tiger Tales.

—I Love My Grandma. Dodd, Emma, illus. 2016. (ENG.). 32p. (J). (gr. -1-k). 16.99 *(978-1-4847-3407-0(6))* Disney Pr.

Angelastro, Yvonne. The Four Lost Chicks. 2013. 28p. pap. 16.99 *(978-1-4808-0292-6(1))* Archway Publishing.

Angstrom, Gwen R. Silent, Snowy Night in Sunriver, Book 2: The Eemlets & Grandma Eema Stories. 2007. 76p. per. 19.95 *(978-1-4241-9000-3(2))* America Star Bks.

Anholt, Laurence & Coplestone, Jim. Seven for a Secret. 2006. (ENG., Illus.). 32p. (J). pap. *(978-1-84507-590-3(0),* Frances Lincoln) Quarto Publishing Group UK.

Ann, Cameron. The Most Beautiful Place in the World. 2014. (ENG.). 64p. (J). (gr. k-3). 10.24 *(978-1-63245-260-3(X))* Lectorum Pubns., Inc.

Anna, Jennifer. Grandma's Button Box. 2006. (Trutle's Back Bks.). (Illus.). 50p. (Orig.). (J). (gr. k-4). pap. 14.99 *(978-1-886383-36-4(7))* Blue Forge Pr.

Ansley, Frank & Wheeler, Lisa. Who's Afraid of Granny Wolf? Ansley, Frank, tr. 2004. (Fitch & Chip Ser.: 3). (ENG., Illus.). 48p. (J). (gr. 1-3). 16.99 *(978-0-689-84952-7(4),* Simon Spotlight) Simon Spotlight.

Ant., Mary. The Shiniest Treasure: The Journey with Grammy & Grampa! 2012. 100p. pap. 37.00 *(978-1-105-89261-5(1))* Lulu Pr., Inc.

—The Shiniest Treasure: The Journey with Grammy & Grampa! Part 2. 2012. 38p. pap. 15.10 *(978-1-300-24962-7(5))* Lulu Pr., Inc.

Antesberger, Barbara. My Grandma's Hands Are Special, 1 vol. 2009. 19p. pap. 24.95 *(978-1-61582-730-5(7))* America Star Bks.

Antonios, Joseph. Portal:Earth. 2010. 126p. pap. 12.99 *(978-0-557-40539-8(4))* Lulu Pr., Inc.

Appel, Cindy. The Best Christmas Gift. Collier, Kevin Scott, illus. 2005. (J). E-Book 6.00 incl. cd-rom *(978-1-933090-19-1(7))* Guardian Angel Publishing, Inc.

Applegate, Katherine. The Buffalo Storm. Ormerod, Jan, illus. 2014. (ENG.). 32p. (J). (gr. -1-3). pap. 7.99 *(978-0-544-33921-7(5),* HMH Books For Young Readers) Houghton Mifflin Harcourt Publishing Co.

Argueta, Jorge. La Gallinita en la Ciudad: The Little Hen in the City. Castro, Mima, illus. 2006. (Bilingual Bks). 32p. (gr. 3-5). 15.95 *(978-1-59820-093-5(3),* Alfaguara) Santillana USA Publishing Co., Inc.

Argueta, Jorge & Perez, Lucia Angela. Hablando Con Madre Tierra, 1 vol. 2006.Tr. of Talking with Mother Earth. (ENG & SPA., Illus.). 36p. (J). (gr. k-3). 17.95 *(978-0-88899-626-8(8))* Groundwood Bks. CAN. Dist: Publishers Group West (PGW).

Armistead, John & Gregory, Fran. The $66 Summer: A Novel of the Segregated South. 2nd ed. 2006. (Milkweed Prize for Children's Literature Ser.). (ENG., Illus.). 240p. (J). (gr. 3-8). reprint ed. per. 8.00 *(978-1-57131-663-9(9))* Milkweed Editions.

Armstrong, Jeannette C. Dancing with the Cranes. Hall, Ron, illus. 2nd rev. ed. 2009. (ENG.). 24p. pap. 10.95 *(978-1-894778-70-1(7))* Theytus Bks., Ltd. CAN. Dist: Univ. of Toronto Pr.

Arnold, Janet. The Special Number. 2011. 28p. pap. 15.99 *(978-1-4568-8982-1(6))* Xlibris Corp.

Arnold, Tedd. There Was an Old Lady Who Swallowed Fly Guy. Arnold, Tedd, illus. 2007. (Fly Guy Ser.: 4). (ENG., Illus.). 32p. (J). (gr. -1-3). 6.99 *(978-0-439-63906-4(9))* Scholastic, Inc.

Arrington, Linda. Ugly Trees. Arrington, Linda, photos by. 2012. (Illus.). 24p. pap. 24.95 *(978-1-4626-8925-5(6))* America Star Bks.

Arthur, Peggy Ann. Come & Look in Grandma's Garden. 2012. 26p. 24.95 *(978-1-4560-3988-2(1))* America Star Bks.

Asay, Colleen. What Happened to Grandpa's Hair? 2005. (J). per. 11.95 *(978-0-9767658-0-6(2))* Calico Connection, Inc., The.

Ash. The Thrush's Song. 2011. 20p. pap. 24.95 *(978-1-4626-3720-1(5))* America Star Bks.

Avingaq, Susan & Vsetula, Maren. Fishing with Grandma, 1 vol. Chua, Charlene, illus. 2016. (ENG.). 32p. (J). (gr. k-2). pap. 10.95 *(978-1-77227-084-6(9))* Inhabit Media Inc. CAN. Dist: Independent Pubs. Group.

Aylesworth, Jim. Goldilocks & the Three Bears. McClintock, Barbara, illus. 2003. (ENG.). 32p. (J). (gr. -1-3). 17.99 *(978-0-439-39545-8(3),* Scholastic Pr.) Scholastic, Inc.

Azam, Shamim. Sabrina & Her Quest. 2011. 108p. (gr. -1). pap. 12.19 *(978-1-4670-0044-4(2))* AuthorHouse.

Babbitt, Natalie. Elsie Times Eight. Babbitt, Natalie, illus. 2005. (Illus.). 26p. (J). (gr. k-4). reprint ed. 16.00 *(978-0-7567-9640-2(7))* DIANE Publishing Co.

—The Eyes of the Amaryllis. 2007. (ENG.). 144p. (J). (gr. 5-8). per. 7.99 *(978-0-312-37008-4(3),* 9780312370084) Square Fish.

Babcock, Nona Burroughs. Little Wolf's Adventure: A Medicine Dream & Warrior Ghosts. 2008. 212p. 24.95 *(978-0-595-49087-5(5));* pap. 14.95 *(978-0-595-46072-4(0))* iUniverse, Inc.

Baca, Ana. Tía's Tamales. Chilton, Noel, illus. 2012. (ENG & SPA.). 32p. (J). pap. 16.95 *(978-0-8263-5027-5(5))* Univ. of New Mexico Pr.

Baccelia, Kim. Goddesses Can Wait. 2015. (YA). *(978-1-61271-297-0(5))* Zumaya Pubns. LLC.

Bader, Arlys Elaine. The Adventures of Garth & Cloey. 2008. 40p. pap. 16.99 *(978-1-4389-2472-4(0))* AuthorHouse.

Badoe, Adwoa. Nana's Cold Days, 1 vol. Junaid, Bushra, illus. 2009. (ENG.). 24p. (J). (gr. k-k). pap. 6.95 *(978-0-88899-937-5(2))* Groundwood Bks. CAN. Dist: Publishers Group West (PGW).

Bagnoli, Christine. Miguel's Family Picnic. 2006. (Neighborhood Readers Ser.). (ENG.). 16p. (gr. 1-3). pap. 6.50 *(978-1-4042-7006-0(X),* Rosen Classroom) Rosen Publishing Group, Inc., The.

Bailey, Ethel M. T. Lily Pond Village, 1 vol. 2009. 57p. pap. 16.95 *(978-1-60703-379-0(8))* America Star Bks.

Bailey, Jennifer P. I Call Mine Mimi. What Do You Call Your Grandmother?, 1 vol. 2010. 24p. pap. 24.95 *(978-1-4489-7141-1(1))* PublishAmerica, Inc.

Bailey, Linda. When Addie Was Scared. 2004. (Illus.). (J). (gr. k-3). spiral bd. *(978-0-616-01535-3(6));* spiral bd. *(978-0-616-01537-7(2))* Canadian National Institute for the Blind/Institut National Canadien pour les Aveugles.

Bair, Sheila. Rock, Brock, & the Savings Shock. Gott, Barry, illus. (ENG.). 32p. (J). 2017. (gr. -1-3). pap. 7.99 ***(978-0-8075-7095-1(8))*** 2006. (gr. 1-3). 16.99 *(978-0-8075-7094-4(X))* Whitman, Albert & Co.

Baker, Deirdre. Becca at Sea, 1 vol. (ENG.). 168p. (J). (gr. 3-7). 2009. pap. 8.95 *(978-0-88899-738-8(8))* 2007. 16.95 *(978-0-88899-737-1(X))* Groundwood Bks. CAN. Dist: Publishers Group West (PGW).

Baker, Mary. Amy's Apple Butter Granny. 2009. 48p. pap. 16.95 *(978-1-61582-032-0(9))* America Star Bks.

Baker, Matthew. If You Find This. 2015. (ENG.). 368p. (J). (gr. 3-7). 17.00 *(978-0-316-24008-6(7))* Little, Brown Bks. for Young Readers.

Balasubramanian, Lalitha. The Twins at the Ancient Villa, 1 vol. 2009. 48p. pap. 16.95 *(978-1-61582-601-8(7))* America Star Bks.

Ballard, George Anne & Bolton, Georgia Helen. The Trouble with Cats. Aguilar, Arelys, illus. 2012. 24p. pap. 12.00 *(978-0-9855312-1-8(5))* Bolton Publishing LLC.

Balliett, Blue. The Danger Box. 2012. (ENG.). 320p. (J). (gr. 3-7). pap. 7.99 *(978-0-439-85210-4(2),* Scholastic Paperbacks) Scholastic, Inc.

Ballou, Kathy. The Tracks Out Back. l.t. ed. 2005. (Illus.). 24p. (J). per. 10.00 *(978-1-932338-50-8(0))* Lifevest Publishing, Inc.

Bancroft, Greg. Betsy's Day at the Game. Blackmore, Katherine, illus. 2013. (ENG.). 40p. (gr. k-5). pap. 13.95 *(978-1-938063-01-5(5),* Mighty Media Kids) Mighty Media Pr.

Bandy, Michael S. & Stein, Eric. Granddaddy's Turn. Ransome, James, illus. 2015. (ENG.). 32p. (J). (gr. 1-4). 16.99 *(978-0-7636-6593-7(2))* Candlewick Pr.

Banerjee, Anjali. Looking for Bapu. 2008. (ENG.). 176p. (J). (gr. 3-7). 6.50 *(978-0-553-49425-9(2),* Yearling) Random Hse. Children's Bks.

Barbo, Maria S. & Preller, James. The Case of the Four-Leaf Clover. Smith, Jamie, illus. 2008. 104p. (J). pap. *(978-0-545-03837-9(5))* Scholastic, Inc.

Barnes, Kenneth Edward. In Search of A Golden Sparrow. 2011. 124p. (gr. 2-4). 21.23 *(978-1-4634-0878-7(1));* pap. 12.01 *(978-1-4634-0879-4(X))* AuthorHouse.

Barnes, Peter W. Little Miss Patriot. Barnes, Cheryl Shaw, illus. 2007. 32p. (J). lib. bdg. 17.95 *(978-1-893622-20-3(7),* VSP Bks.) Vacation Spot Publishing.

Barnwell, Ysaye M. No Mirrors in My Nana's House. Saint James, Synthia, illus. 2005. (ENG.). 32p. (J). (gr. -1-3). reprint ed. 10.99 *(978-0-15-205243-0(7))* Houghton Mifflin Harcourt Publishing Co.

Barrett, John F. The Stories of Jake. 2008. 64p. pap. 31.99 *(978-1-4363-2010-8(0))* Xlibris Corp.

Barrett, Judi. Cloudy with a Chance of Meatballs. Barrett, Ron, illus. 2011. (Classic Board Bks.). (ENG.). 34p. (J). (gr. -1-k). bds. 7.99 *(978-1-4424-3023-5(0),* Little Simon) Little Simon.

—Pickles to Pittsburgh: Cloudy with a Chance of Meatballs 2. Barrett, Ronald, illus. (Classic Board Bks.). (ENG.). (J). (gr. -1-k). 2013. 34p. bds. 7.99 *(978-1-4424-6493-3(3))* 2012. 32p. pap. 9.99 *(978-1-4424-4459-1(2))* Little Simon. (Little Simon).

—Pickles to Pittsburgh: The Sequel to Cloudy with a Chance of Meatballs. Barrett, Ron, illus. 2004. 26p. (gr. -1-3). 17.00 *(978-0-7569-4215-1(2))* Perfection Learning Corp.

Barrett, Judi & Barret. Nublado con Probabilidades de Albóndigas. 2012.Tr. of Cloudy with a Chance of Meatballs. (SPA.). 36p. (gr. 1-3). 24.99 *(978-84-8470-447-8(5))* Corimbo, Editorial S.L. ESP. Dist: Lectorum Pubns., Inc.

Bartek, Mary. Funerals & Fly Fishing. 2009. (ENG.). 160p. (J). (gr. 3-7). pap. 16.99 *(978-0-312-56124-6(5),* 9780312561246) Square Fish.

Base, Graeme, et al. Dinosaurs in Your Backyard: The Coolest, Scariest Creatures Ever Found in the USA! 2009. (ENG., Illus.). 32p. (J). (gr. 1-4). 16.95 *(978-0-8109-7099-1(6),* Abrams Bks. for Young Readers) Abrams, Inc.

Baskin, Nora Raleigh. The Truth about My Bat Mitzvah. 2009. (Mix Ser.). (ENG.). 144p. (J). (gr. 4-8). pap. 7.99 *(978-1-4169-7469-7(5),* Aladdin) Simon & Schuster Children's Publishing.

Basore, Polly M. Santa's Stray in A Piano for Christmas. Williams, Carlene H., illus. 2005. 32p. (J). per. *(978-0-9771749-1-1(3))* AngelBooks.

Bassett, Alisa Cuthbertson. Threads of Time. 2013. 24p. pap. 24.95 *(978-1-63000-063-9(9))* America Star Bks.

Bastianich, Lidia Matticchio. Nonna Tell Me a Story: Lidia's Christmas Kitchen. Logan, Laura, illus. 2010. (ENG.). 56p. (J). (gr. -1-3). 15.95 *(978-0-7624-3692-7(1))* Running Pr. Bk. Pubs.

Bateman, Teresa. April Foolishness. Westcott, Nadine Bernard, illus. 2004. (ENG.). 32p. (J). (gr. k-3). 6.99 *(978-0-8075-0405-5(X))* Whitman, Albert & Co.

Bates, Janet. Seaside Dream, 1 vol. Davis, Lambert, illus. 2016. (ENG.). 32p. (J). pap. 9.95 *(978-1-62014-256-1(2))* Lee & Low Bks., Inc.

Bates, Janet Costa. Seaside Dream. Davis, Lambert, illus. 2013. (ENG.). 32p. (J). (gr. k-5). 17.95 *(978-1-60060-347-1(5))* Lee & Low Bks., Inc.

Bauer, Joan. Stand Tall. 2005. (ENG.). 192p. (YA). (gr. 7-5). pap. 8.99 *(978-0-14-240427-0(6),* Speak) Penguin Young Readers Group.

—Sticks. 2005. (ENG., Illus.). 192p. (YA). (gr. 7-5). pap. 7.99 *(978-0-14-240428-7(4),* Speak) Penguin Young Readers Group.

Bauer, Jutta. Grandpa's Angel. Bauer, Jutta, illus. 2005. (ENG., Illus.). 48p. (J). (gr. k-12). 12.99 *(978-0-7636-2743-0(7))* Candlewick Pr.

Bauer, Marion Dane. The Blue Ghost. Wang, Suling, illus. 2006. (Stepping Stone Book Ser.). (ENG.). 96p. (J). (gr. 1-4). 3.99 *(978-0-375-83339-7(0),* Random Hse. Bks. for Young Readers) Random Hse. Children's Bks.

—Grandmother's Song. Rossi, Pamela, illus. 2007. (ENG.). 32p. (J). (gr. -1-3). 10.99 *(978-1-4169-6849-8(0),* Simon & Schuster/Paula Wiseman Bks.) Simon & Schuster/Paula Wiseman Bks.

Baum, L. Frank. Mary Louise in the Country. 2011. 188p. pap. 14.95 *(978-1-4638-0069-7(X))* Rodgers, Alan Bks.

Baum, L. Frank & van Dyne, Edith. Mary Louise in the Country. 2011. 188p. 26.95 *(978-1-4638-9605-8(0))* Rodgers, Alan Bks.

Beall, Kirsten. Jake & the Big Cake Mistake. Desmond, Hillary, illus. 2011. 36p. pap. 24.95 *(978-1-4626-4524-4(0))* America Star Bks.

Beamish, Diane. Grandma's Magic Button Necklace. 2006. 25p. 12.16 *(978-1-4116-5487-7(0))* Lulu Pr., Inc.

Beard, Darleen Bailey & Maione, Heather Harms. Annie Glover Is Not a Tree Lover. Maione, Heather Harms, illus. 2009. (ENG., Illus.). 128p. (J). (gr. 2-5). 15.99 *(978-0-374-30351-8(7),* 9780374303518, Farrar, Straus & Giroux (BYR)) Farrar, Straus & Giroux.

Beasley, Cassie. Circus Mirandus. 2016. (SPA.). 25.99 *(978-84-246-5686-7(5))* La Galera, S.A. Editorial ESP. Dist: Lectorum Pubns., Inc.

—Circus Mirandus. (ENG., Illus.). 304p. (J). (gr. 4-7). 2016. pap. 8.99 *(978-0-14-751554-4(8),* Puffin Books) 2015. 17.99 *(978-0-525-42843-5(7),* Dial Bks) Penguin Young Readers Group.

—Circus Mirandus. 2016. (ENG.). 304p. (J). (gr. 3-7). 19.65 *(978-0-606-39311-9(0))* Turtleback Bks.

Beaty, Andrea. Dorko the Magnificent. (ENG.). (J). (gr. 3-7). 2014. 240p. pap. 7.95 *(978-1-4197-1019-3(2))* 2013. (Illus.). 224p. 17.95 *(978-1-4197-0638-7(1))* Abrams, Inc. (Amulet Bks.).

Beck, Glenn, et al. The Christmas Sweater. Dorman, Brandon, illus. 2009. (ENG.). 40p. (J). (gr. -1-2). 17.99 *(978-1-4169-9543-2(9),* Aladdin) Simon & Schuster Children's Publishing.

—The Snow Angel. Dorman, Brandon, illus. 2011. (ENG.). 40p. (J). (gr. -1-2). 7.99 *(978-1-4424-4448-5(7),* Simon & Schuster/Paula Wiseman Bks.) Simon & Schuster/Paula Wiseman Bks.

Bedell, Lorraine Frances. The Christmas Cat Story, 1 vol. 2010. 48p. pap. 16.95 *(978-1-4512-0249-6(0))* America Star Bks.

Bee, Ersila. The Everywhere Armchair. 2010. 26p. pap. 9.99 *(978-1-60911-110-6(9),* Eloquent Bks.) Strategic Book Publishing & Rights Agency (SBPRA).

Beheler, Rhonda. They Chose Me: A Story of Grandparent Adoption. 2008. 32p. per. 24.95 *(978-1-4241-8616-7(1))* America Star Bks.

Bell, Juliet. Kepler's Dream. 2013. (ENG.). 256p. (J). (gr. 5). pap. 6.99 *(978-0-14-242648-7(2),* Puffin Books) Penguin Young Readers Group.

Bell, Lindzi. Sherlock Times Three, 1 vol. 2009. 62p. pap. 19.95 *(978-1-61582-028-3(0))* America Star Bks.

Bell, Ossie S. When Grandma Is Not Grandma: Alzheimer's Steals Family's Treasures. 2006. 51p. pap. 16.95 *(978-1-4241-2920-1(6))* PublishAmerica, Inc.

Bencastro, Mario. A Promise to Keep. Giersbach-Rascon, Susan, tr. from SPA. 2005. 134p. (J). (gr. 3-7). pap. 9.95 *(978-1-55885-457-4(6),* Piñata Books) Arte Publico Pr.

—Viaje a la Tierra del Abuelo. 2004. (SPA.). 144p. pap. 9.95 *(978-1-55885-404-8(5),* Piñata Books) Arte Publico Pr.

Benedict, Norma. Grammy Hits the Road. 2009. 40p. pap. 16.99 *(978-1-4490-0905-2(0))* AuthorHouse.

Benjamin, Floella. My Two Grannies. Chamberlain, Margaret, illus. 2009. (ENG.). 32p. (J). (gr. k-3). pap. 7.95 *(978-1-84780-034-3(3),* Frances Lincoln Children's Bks.) Quarto Publishing Group UK GBR. Dist: Hachette Bk. Group.

Benn, Jente. My Grandma Was There. 2009. 40p. pap. 16.99 *(978-1-4389-7084-4(6))* AuthorHouse.

Bennett, Gretchen. Gina's Great Day. 2011. 28p. pap. 24.95 *(978-1-4626-0938-3(4))* America Star Bks.

Bennett, Kelly. Your Daddy Was Just Like You. Walker, David, illus. 2010. (ENG.). 32p. (J). (gr. -1-k). 16.99 *(978-0-399-25258-7(4),* G.P. Putnam's Sons Books for Young Readers) Penguin Young Readers Group.

Bennett, Marcia. Backpack Cat. Bennett, Michele & Dunlap, Joan, illus. 2004. 124p. 19.95 *(978-1-932196-50-4(1))* WordWright.biz, Inc.
—Backpack Cat. 2004. 124p. pap. 12.95 *(978-1-932196-37-5(4))* WordWright.biz, Inc.
Bennett, W. J., Jr. Sydney & Garrett's Great Arkansas Adventury. 2005. (J). pap. *(978-0-9794044-6-7(0))* Archeological Assessments, Inc.
Benson, Judith. The Noise in Grandma's Attic. 2005. (Illus.). 48p. (J). 4.95 *(978-1-895836-55-4(7))* River Bks. CAN. Dist: Fitzhenry & Whiteside, Ltd.
Bentley, Nancy Kaye. Mema's back Yard. 2010. 39p. pap. 17.95 *(978-0-557-68242-3(8))* Lulu Pr., Inc.
Bentley, Sue. Party Dreams, 5 vols. Farley, Andrew & Swan, Angela, illus. 2010. (Magic Puppy Ser.: 5). (ENG.). 128p. (J). (gr. 1-3). pap. 5.99 *(978-0-448-45064-3(X)*, Grosset & Dunlap) Penguin Young Readers Group.
Benton, Jim. Live Each Day to the Dumbest. 2015. (Dear Dumb Diary: Year Two Ser.: 6). lib. bdg. 16.00 *(978-0-606-37074-5(9))* Turtleback Bks.
Bercowetz, Cynthia. Grandpa Herman's Petting Zoo. 2007. (Illus.). 48p. (J). per. 14.95 *(978-0-9708430-9-8(7))* Uitti, Daniel.
Bernal, Estela. Can You See Me Now? 2014. (ENG.). (YA). pap. 10.95 *(978-1-55885-783-4(4)*, Piñata Books) Arte Publico Pr.
Bernstein, Susan H. N. E. Pominonous Epstein & Change. Lt. ed. 2003. (E. Pominonous Epstein Ser.: No. 3). (Illus.). 20p. (Orig.). (J). (gr. k-3). pap. 8.95 *(978-0-9706596-2-0(8))* Bernstein, Susan.
Besson, Luc. Arthur & the Forbidden City. Sowchek, Ellen, tr. 2006. (ENG., Illus.). 192p. (J). (gr. 3-7). pap., pap. 5.99 *(978-0-06-059628-6(7)*, Harper Trophy) HarperCollins Pubs.
—Arthur & the Forbidden City. 2005. (ENG., Illus.). 192p. (J). 15.99 *(978-0-06-059626-2(0))* HarperCollins Pubs.
Best, Cari. Three Cheers for Catherine the Great! Potter, Giselle, illus. 2003. (Catherine the Great Ser.). (ENG.). 32p. (J). (gr. -1-3). pap. 8.99 *(978-0-374-47551-2(2)*, 9780374475512) Square Fish.
Betances, Brendan. Granny's Garden. 2006. (Neighborhood Readers Ser.). (ENG., Illus.). 12p. (gr. 1-3). pap. 5.90 *(978-1-4042-7022-0(1)*, Rosen Classroom) Rosen Publishing Group, Inc., The.
Bethune, Helen. Way Back When, 1 vol. 2013. (Fiction Readers Ser.). (ENG., Illus.). 28p. (J). (gr. 2-2). pap. 6.99 *(978-1-4333-5570-7(1))* Shell Educational Publishing.
Bevan, Lizzie. Never Far When in My Heart. 2013. (ENG., Illus.). 31p. (J). pap. 15.95 *(978-1-4787-1027-1(6))* Outskirts Pr., Inc.
Bevis, Brittany. Two Foals, a Dash of Sprinkles & a Cherry on Top! Talley, Pam, illus. 2011. 32p. (J). 18.47 *(978-0-9824766-7-3(1))*; pap. 18.47 *(978-0-9824766-8-0(X))* Caballo Pr. of Ann Arbor. (Caballito Children's Bks.).
Bevis, Mary. Bird on My Hand (hardcover) Making Friends with Chickadees, 1 vol. Powell, Consie, illus. 2014. (ENG.). 32p. (J). (gr. 1-2). 17.95 *(978-0-9883508-9-2(0))* Raven Productions, Inc.
—Bird on My Hand (softcover) Making Friends with Chickadees. Powell, Consie, illus. 2014. (ENG.). 32p. (J). (gr. 1-2). pap. 9.95 *(978-0-9883508-8-5(2))* Raven Productions, Inc.
Bice, Charles. What Lies Beneath. 2009. 208p. pap. 16.50 *(978-0-578-03340-2(2))* Wimabi Pr.
The Big Rain. 2003. (Illus.). 32p. (J). mass mkt. *(978-0-9740599-2-1(7)*, 3) Omnibus Publishing.
Birch, Manuel James. Dudley the Angel & His Buddy Gabby the Elf. 2009. 40p. pap. 18.49 *(978-1-4490-1704-0(5))* AuthorHouse.
Birdseye, Tom. A Tough Nut to Crack. 2006. (ENG.). 128p. (J). (gr. 3-7). 16.95 *(978-0-8234-1967-8(3))* Holiday Hse., Inc.
Birtha, Becky. Grandmama's Pride. Bootman, Colin, illus. 2016. (ENG.). 32p. (J). (gr. -1-3). pap. 6.99 *(978-0-8075-3022-1(0))* Whitman, Albert & Co.
Bischoff, Marlene A. Charming Chirp. 2013. 26p. pap. 13.95 *(978-1-4796-0132-5(2))* TEACH Services, Inc.
Bishop, Carol. The Chronicles of Rusty. 2013. 68p. pap. *(978-3-7103-0628-0(0))* united p.c. Verlag.
Bishop, Mary Harelkin & Coteau Books Staff. Tunnels of Tyranny: A Fourth Moose Jaw Adventure, 1 vol. 2005. (Moose Jaw Adventure Ser.). (ENG.). 248p. (J). (gr. 4-7). pap. 7.95 *(978-1-55050-316-6(2))* Coteau Bks. CAN. Dist: Orca Bk. Pubs. USA.
Bissonette, Aimee M. North Woods Girl. McGehee, Claudia, illus. 2015. (ENG.). 32p. (J). 16.95 *(978-0-87351-966-3(3))* Minnesota Historical Society Pr.
Bjornson, Nancy. Llamas, Ponies & Pyrite. 2007. (J). *(978-1-930596-82-5(0))* Amherst Pr.
Black, Shonda. Where Has Grandma Gone? 2013. 20p. pap. 24.95 *(978-1-63004-618-7(3))* America Star Bks.
Black, Sonia W. Jumping the Broom. Van Wright, Cornelius & Hu, Ying-Hwa, illus. 2004. 32p. (J). lib. bdg. 15.00 *(978-1-4242-0234-8(5))* Fitzgerald Bks.
Blackburn, Sheila M. Stewie Scraps & the Giant Joggers. 2008. 76p. pap. *(978-1-903853-86-3(9))* Brilliant Pubns.
—Stewie Scraps & the Trolley Cart. 2008. 72p. pap. *(978-1-903853-88-7(5))* Brilliant Pubns.
Blackmon, Rodney Allan. A Kitten Named Buddy: Buddy Stays Clean. 2013. 20p. pap. 24.95 *(978-1-62709-675-1(2))* America Star Bks.
Blackstone, Stella. My Granny Went to Market: A Round-the-World Counting Rhyme. Corr, Christopher, illus. 2005. (ENG.). 24p. (J). 16.99 *(978-1-84148-792-2(9))* Barefoot Bks., Inc.
Blackstone, Stella & Corr, Christopher. My Granny Went to Market: A Round-the-World Counting Rhyme. 2006. (ENG., Illus.). 24p. (J). (gr. -1-2). 6.99 *(978-1-905236-62-6(X))* Barefoot Bks., Inc.
Blair, Marcia L. Nana's Birthday Bubbles. 2012. 24p. pap. 24.95 *(978-1-4626-7880-8(7))* America Star Bks.
Blair, Marion E. Just Beyond a Finger's Reach. 2013. (ENG.). 54p. (YA). pap. 21.95 *(978-1-4787-1396-8(8))* Outskirts Pr., Inc.
Blake, Edna L. & Boatwright, Edith. Grandma & her Amazing Colt, Dripper! Allen, Kathy, illus. 2005. 50p. (J). 12.00 *(978-0-9668906-3-1(9))* Blake, Edna.
Blanchard, Daniel. Granddaddy's Secrets: Feeling Good. 2012. 114p. 19.95 *(978-1-4626-6150-3(5))* PublishAmerica, Inc.
Block, Francesca Lia. Teen Spirit. 2014. (ENG.). 240p. (YA). (gr. 9). 17.99 *(978-0-06-200809-1(9)*, HarperTeen) HarperCollins Pubs.
Blomenkamp Ed.D., Joel. The Storm: A Children's Parable for Understanding Life's Hardships. 2013. 28p. pap. 13.95 *(978-1-4497-7796-8(1)*, WestBow Pr.) Author Solutions, Inc.
Blumstein, Amy Beth. Jamie & Tallulah. 2009. 16p. pap. 12.00 *(978-1-4389-3997-1(3))* AuthorHouse.
Bobbie, Gramma. The Bright Stars. 2009. 20p. pap. 11.49 *(978-1-4490-3474-0(8))* AuthorHouse.
Bobeck, Jade. Paxton's Adventures: A Day on Grandpa's Farm. 2012. 24p. pap. 15.99 *(978-1-4797-4415-2(8))* Xlibris Corp.
Bobic, Marilyn Kay. My Nana My Special Friend. 2006. (J). per. 15.95 *(978-0-9748426-9-1(9)*, Accent Pubns.) Ajoyin Publishing, Inc.
Boelts, Maribeth. Those Shoes. Jones, Noah Z., illus. 2009. (ENG.). 40p. (J). (gr. k-3). pap. 6.99 *(978-0-7636-4284-6(3))* Candlewick Pr.
—Those Shoes. Jones, Noah, illus. 2007. (J). *(978-1-4287-6554-2(9))* Candlewick Pr.
—Those Shoes. 2014. 17.00 *(978-1-63419-735-9(6))* Perfection Learning Corp.
Bohrer, Maria. Sofia's Stoop Story: 18th Street, Brooklyn: 18th Street, Brooklyn. Fancher, Lou & Johnson, Steve, illus. 2014. 32p. (J). 17.95 *(978-0-9885295-2-6(1))* Blue Marlin Pubns.
Bolden, Tonya. Finding Family. (ENG., Illus.). 192p. (YA). (gr. 3-12). 2012. pap. 7.99 *(978-1-59990-830-4(1)*, 9781599908304) 2010. 15.99 *(978-1-59990-318-7(0)*, 9781599903187) Bloomsbury Publishing USA. (Bloomsbury USA Childrens).
Bollen, Christina. An Angel in My Garden, 1 vol. Matyuschenko, Tanya, illus. 2009. 47p. pap. 24.95 *(978-1-60813-661-2(2))* America Star Bks.
Booker, Catina M. Granny & Me. 2012. (ENG.). 14p. (J). pap. 13.95 *(978-1-4327-9283-1(0))* Outskirts Pr., Inc.
Bootman, Colin. Fish for the Grand Lady. Bootman, Colin, illus. 2006. (ENG., Illus.). 32p. (J). (gr. -1-3). 16.95 *(978-0-8234-1898-5(7))* Holiday Hse., Inc.
Bortnick, Lori. A Straw Hat So Big. Santos, Carriel Ann, illus. 2013. 52p. pap. 11.95 *(978-0-9851492-6-0(4))* Flying Turtle Publishing.
Bosak, Susan V. A Little Something. McGaw, Laurie, illus. 2008. 32p. (J). *(978-1-896232-06-5(X)*, TCP Pr.) Communication Project, The.
—Something to Remember Me By. 2015. 32p. pap. 8.00 *(978-1-61003-553-8(4))* Center for the Collaborative Classroom.
—Something to Remember Me By: A Story about Love & Legacies. McGaw, Laurie, illus. 2003. 32p. (gr. 1-6). *(978-1-896232-01-0(9)*, TCP Pr.) Communication Project, The.
Boston, Lucy M. The Children of Green Knowe Collection. 2013. (ENG., Illus.). 368p. (J). 12.95 *(978-0-571-30347-2(1))* Faber & Faber, Inc.
Boucher, Paul. A Stickeee & Gooweee Week of Fun. 2012. 16p. pap. 15.99 *(978-1-4772-7289-3(5))* AuthorHouse.
Bourgeois, Paulette. Oma's Quilt. 2004. (Illus.). (J). (gr. k-3). spiral bd. *(978-0-616-11099-7(5))*; spiral bd. *(978-0-616-11100-0(2))* Canadian National Institute for the Blind/Institut National Canadien pour les Aveugles.
—Postal Workers. LaFave, Kim, illus. 2005. 32p. (J). lib. bdg. 15.38 *(978-1-4242-1192-0(1))* Fitzgerald Bks.
Bourgeois, Paulette & Paulette, Bourgeois. El Principe y el Mendigo. Jorisch, Stéphane, illus. 2003.Tr. of Oma's Quilt. (SPA.). 32p. (J). (gr. k-2). 14.99 *(978-84-241-8644-9(3))* Everest Editora ESP. Dist: Lectorum Pubns., Inc.
Bow, Patricia. The Ruby Kingdom. 2007. (Passage to Mythrin Ser.: 1). (ENG.). 256p. (YA). (gr. 7). pap. 12.99 *(978-1-55002-667-2(4)*, Boardwalk Bks.) Dundurn CAN. Dist: Ingram Publisher Services.
Bowen, Anne. When You Visit Grandma & Grandpa. Bogacki, Tomasz, tr. Bogacki, Tomasz, illus. 2004. (Carolrhoda Picture Books Ser.). 32p. (J). (gr. -1-3). 15.95 *(978-1-57505-610-4(0))* Lerner Publishing Group.
Bowen, Anne M. I Loved You Before You Were Born. Shed, Greg, illus. 2004. (ENG.). 32p. (J). (gr. -1-3). reprint ed. pap. 6.99 *(978-0-06-443631-1(4))* HarperCollins Pubs.
Bowen, Cynthia Wiesner. Tamika & Grandpa Jake. 2007. 32p. per. 14.95 *(978-1-4327-0642-5(X))* Outskirts Pr., Inc.
Bowlby, Linda S. Is That So. Helms, Dana, illus. 2008. 29p. (J). pap. 9.95 *(978-0-9779993-5-4(1))* Red Earth Publishing.
Bowman, Andy. The Quilt. Travis, Stephanie, illus. 25p. (J). (gr. 1-6). pap. 6.95 *(978-1-931650-04-5(7))*; lib. bdg. 14.95 *(978-1-931650-05-2(5))* Coastal Publishing Carolina, Inc.
Bowman, Silas. The Daudyhouse. Horst, Melisa, illus. 2012. 51p. (J). *(978-0-7399-2450-1(8))* Rod & Staff Pubs., Inc.
Boyd, Lizi. I Love Grandma. Boyd, Lizi, illus. 2009. (Super Sturdy Picture Bks.). (ENG., Illus.). 24p. (J). (gr. -1-k). 8.99 *(978-0-7636-3728-6(9))* Candlewick Pr.
—I Love Grandpa. Boyd, Lizi, illus. 2009. (Super Sturdy Picture Bks.). (ENG., Illus.). 24p. (J). (gr. -1-k). 8.99 *(978-0-7636-3727-9(0))* Candlewick Pr.
Bozarth, Jan. Zally's Book. Burden, Andrea, illus. 2010. (Fairy Godmother Academy Ser.: No. 3). (ENG.). 208p. (J). (gr. 3-7). pap. 6.99 *(978-0-375-85185-8(2)*, Yearling) Random Hse. Children's Bks.
Bradley, Judy. The Naughty Grandmother. Mitchell, Hazle, illus. 2012. (J). *(978-0-615-57032-7(1))* Bradley, Judy & Assocs., LLC.
Bradman, Tony. Red Riding Hood Takes Charge, 1 vol. Warburton, Sarah, illus. 2009. (After Happily Ever After Ser.). (ENG.). 56p. (gr. 2-3). 25.32 *(978-1-4342-1308-2(0)*, After Happily Ever After) Stone Arch Bks.
Bradman, Tony & Chatterton, Martin. The Surprise Party. 2005. (Red Bananas Ser.). (ENG., Illus.). 48p. (J). (gr. 1-3). *(978-0-7787-1084-4(X))* Crabtree Publishing Co.
Braithwaite, Pamela. Missing Jessic. 2012. 44p. pap. *(978-1-105-74130-2(3))* Lulu.com.
Brammer, Ethriam Cash. The Rowdy, Rowdy Ranch / Alla en el Rancho Grande. Cruz, D. Nina, illus. 2003. (ENG & SPA.). 32p. (J). 16.95 *(978-1-55885-409-3(6)*, Piñata Books) Arte Publico Pr.
Bredsdorff, Bodil. The Crow-Girl: The Children of Crow Cove. Ingwersen, Faith, tr. from DAN. 2007. (Illus.). 155p. (gr. 3-7). 18.00 *(978-0-7569-8186-0(7))* Perfection Learning Corp.
—The Crow-Girl: The Children of Crow Cove. Ingwersen, Faith, tr. 2006. (Children of Crow Cove Ser.: 1). (ENG., Illus.). 160p. (J). (gr. 3-7). reprint ed. pap. 8.99 *(978-0-374-40003-3(2)*, 9780374400033, Farrar, Straus & Giroux (BYR)) Farrar, Straus & Giroux.
Brekke, Nancy Rose. But Grandma Didn't Mind. 2005. (Illus.). 28p. (J). (gr. 1-2). 9.95 *(978-0-9766264-0-4(3))* Raven Productions, Inc.
—But That's OK with Grandpa. 2005. (Illus.). 28p. (J). (gr. 1-2). 9.95 *(978-0-9766264-1-1(1))* Raven Productions, Inc.
Brennan, Martin. I Saw It in the Garden. Monroe, Michael Glenn, illus. 2006. 32p. (J). (gr. -1-3). 17.95 *(978-1-58726-296-8(7)*, Mitten Pr.) Ann Arbor Editions LLC.
Brett, Jan. On Noah's Ark. Brett, Jan, illus. (ENG., Illus.). (J). (gr. -1 — 1). 2009. 34p. bds. 7.99 *(978-0-399-25220-4(7))* 2003. 32p. 17.99 *(978-0-399-24028-7(4))* Penguin Young Readers Group. (G.P. Putnam's Sons Books for Young Readers).
Briggs, Raymond. The Puddleman. Briggs, Raymond, illus. 2006. (ENG., Illus.). 32p. (J). (gr. k-2). pap. 16.95 *(978-0-09-945642-1(7)*, Red Fox) Random House Children's Books GBR. Dist: Independent Pubs. Group.
Bright, Belle. Crash, Bang, Boom, Zing. Bright, Michael, illus. 2009. 12p. pap. 24.95 *(978-1-60749-383-9(7))* America Star Bks.
Brimhall Snow, Virginia. Summer Walk, 1 vol. 2016. (ENG., Illus.). 32p. (J). 16.99 *(978-1-4236-4215-2(5))* Gibbs Smith, Publisher.
Bringing the Sea Back Home: Individual Title Six-Packs. (Literatura 2000 Ser.). (gr. 2-3). 33.00 *(978-0-7635-0218-8(9))* Rigby Education.
Brockway, Stephanie. Mystic Phyles: Beasts. Masiello, Ralph, illus. 2011. (ENG.). 144p. (J). (gr. 4-7). 15.95 *(978-1-57091-718-9(3))* Charlesbridge Publishing, Inc.
Brodeur, Tom. Regina Silsby's Phantom Militia. 2005. (Illus.). 267p. (J). (gr. 3-7). 7.49 *(978-1-59166-385-0(7))* BJU Pr.
Brodine, Linda. Gramma Please Tell Us a Story. 2012. (ENG.). (J). pap. 12.99 *(978-1-4675-1215-2(X))* Independent Pub.
Bronson, Wilfrid S. Pinto's Journey. 2007. (ENG.). 64p. (J). per. 14.95 *(978-0-86534-557-7(0))* Sunstone Pr.
Brookover, Brian D. Neddy & Little Roy Go to Town. 2013. 40p. pap. 20.99 *(978-1-4817-1185-2(7))* AuthorHouse.
Brooks, G. Alan & Grandchildren. The Adventures of Zumba & Rumb: Book One - the Separation. 2012. 164p. 29.99 *(978-1-4691-9820-0(7))* Xlibris Corp.
Brosgol, Vera. Leave Me Alone! Brosgol, Vera, illus. 2016. (ENG., Illus.). 40p. (J). 17.99 *(978-1-62672-441-9(5)*, 9781626724419) Roaring Brook Pr.
Brothers Grimm. Little Red Riding Hood. Cowley, Joy, ed. Choi, Min-ho, illus. 2015. (World Classics Ser.). (ENG.). 32p. (J). (gr. k-4). pap. 7.99 *(978-1-925186-62-8(8))* Lerner Publishing Group.
Brouwer, Sigmund. Devil's Pass, 1 vol. 2012. (Seven (the Series) Ser.). (ENG., Illus.). 256p. (J). (gr. 5-10). pap. 9.95 *(978-1-55469-938-4(X))* Orca Bk. Pubs. USA.
—Tin Soldier, 1 vol. 2014. (Seven Sequels Ser.). (ENG., Illus.). 272p. (J). (gr. 5-10). pap. 10.95 *(978-1-4598-0546-0(1))* Orca Bk. Pubs. USA.
Brown, Irene Bennett. Before the Lark. 2011. (ENG.). 208p. (J). (gr. 4-7). pap. 18.95 *(978-0-89672-727-4(0))* Texas Tech Univ. Pr.
Brown, Monica. Butterflies on Carmen Street/Mariposas en la Calle Carmen. Ward, April, illus. 2007. (SPA & ENG.). 32p. (J). (gr. -1-2). 16.95 *(978-1-55885-484-0(3)*, Piñata Books) Arte Publico Pr.
—Marisol McDonald & the Clash Bash/Marisol Mcdonald y la Fiesta Sin Igual. Palacios, Sara, illus. 2013. (Marisol Mcdonald Ser.). (ENG & SPA.). 40p. (J). 18.95 *(978-0-89239-273-5(8))* Lee & Low Bks., Inc.
Brown, Pat. A Penny for Your Thoughts. 2011. 36p. pap. *(978-1-4269-6340-7(8))* Trafford Publishing (UK) Ltd.
Brown, Paul. Still Another Time , Times Remembered. 2011. 128p. pap. 38.28 *(978-1-4670-2548-5(8))* AuthorHouse.
Brown Sr., David F. Tabby Goes to School: The First in the Tabatha Adventures Series, 1 vol. Brown Jr., David F., illus. 2009. 20p. pap. 24.95 *(978-1-60836-181-6(0))* America Star Bks.
Brown, Timothy E. W. Grandma's Spirit. 2011. (Illus.). 44p. pap. 20.36 *(978-1-4567-7874-3(9))* AuthorHouse.
Brown-Wood, Janay & Burris, Priscilla. Grandma's Tiny House. 2017. (ENG., Illus.). 32p. (J). (-k). lib. bdg. 16.99 *(978-1-58089-712-9(6))* Charlesbridge Publishing, Inc.
Broyles, Anne. Arturo & the Navidad Birds, 1 vol. Lewis, K. E., illus. 2013. (ENG & SPA.). 32p. (J). (gr. k-3). 16.99 *(978-1-4556-1801-9(2))* Pelican Publishing Co., Inc.
Broyles, Beverly Ashley, illus. Grandmother's Alligator/Burukenge Wa Nyanya Activity Guide. 2005. (ENG & SWA.). (J). 12.95 *(978-0-9703632-7-5(3))* Wakefield Connection, The.
Brumbach, Andrew. The Eye of Midnight. 2016. (ENG.). 256p. (J). (gr. 4-7). 16.99 *(978-0-385-74461-4(7))*; lib. bdg. 19.99 *(978-0-375-99176-9(X))* Random Hse. Children's Bks. (Delacorte Bks. for Young Readers).
Bruton, Georgia. Escape. 2012. 210p. pap. 11.95 *(978-1-936083-10-5(5))* Silver Knight Publishing, LLC.
Bryan, Alexandra Faer. Green Kitty. 2010. 88p. pap. 27.49 *(978-1-4520-1736-5(0))* AuthorHouse.
Bryan, Ashley. Can't Scare Me! Bryan, Ashley, illus. 2013. (ENG., Illus.). 40p. (J). (gr. -1-3). 16.99 *(978-1-4424-7657-8(5)*, Atheneum Bks. for Young Readers) Simon & Schuster Children's Publishing.
Bryant, Annie. Katani's Jamaican Holiday. 2008. (Beacon Street Girls Ser.: No. 4). (ENG., Illus.). 192p. (J). (gr. 4-8). pap. 6.99 *(978-1-4169-6443-8(6)*, Aladdin) Simon & Schuster Children's Publishing.
Buckallew, Rodney. One Full Cycle. 2011. 28p. pap. 15.99 *(978-1-4535-8588-7(5))* Xlibris Corp.
Buckley, Colleen. Grandma Kathy Has Cancer. Sponaugle, Kim, illus. 2007. 24p. per. 11.50 *(978-1-59858-422-6(7))* Dog Ear Publishing, LLC.
Buckley, Michael. The Fairy-Tale Detectives. Ferguson, Peter, illus. 2005. (ENG.). 288p. (J). (gr. 3-7). 16.95 *(978-0-8109-5925-5(9)*, Abrams Bks. for Young Readers) Abrams, Inc.
—The Fairy-Tale Detectives. (Sisters Grimm Ser.: 1). (J). 2008. 81.45 *(978-1-4361-0398-5(3))* 2007. 214.75 *(978-1-4193-6197-5(X))* 2007. 1.25 *(978-1-4193-6193-7(7))* 2006. 71.75 *(978-1-4193-6198-2(8))* 2006. 86.75 *(978-1-4193-8749-4(9))* 2006. 74.75 *(978-1-4193-6196-8(1))* 2006. 89.75 *(978-1-4193-8747-0(2))* Recorded Bks., Inc.
—The Fairy-Tale Detectives: And the Unusual Suspects. Ferguson, Peter, illus. 2012. 580p. (J). *(978-1-4351-4487-3(2)*, Amulet Bks.) Abrams, Inc.
—Magic & Other Misdemeanors. Ferguson, Peter, illus. 2008. (Sisters Grimm Ser.). (ENG.). 304p. (J). (gr. 3-7). pap. 7.95 *(978-0-8109-7263-6(8)*, Amulet Bks.) Abrams, Inc.
—The Problem Child. Ferguson, Peter, illus. 2006. (Sisters Grimm Ser.). (ENG.). 320p. (J). (gr. 3-7). 16.95 *(978-0-8109-4914-0(8)*, Amulet Bks.) Abrams, Inc.
—The Sisters Grimm: The Fairy-Tale Detectives. Ferguson, Peter, illus. 10th anniv. ed. 2017. (Sisters Grimm Ser.). (ENG.). 288p. (J). (gr. 3-7). pap. 8.95 *(978-1-4197-2005-5(8)*, Amulet Bks.) Abrams, Inc.
—The Sisters Grimm: The Problem Child. Ferguson, Peter, illus. 10th ed. 2017. (Sisters Grimm Ser.). (ENG.). 288p. (J). (gr. 3-7). pap. 8.95 *(978-1-4197-2004-8(X)*, Amulet Bks.) Abrams, Inc.
—The Sisters Grimm: The Unusual Suspects. Ferguson, Peter, illus. 10th ed. 2017. (Sisters Grimm Ser.). (ENG.). 288p. (J). (gr. 3-7). pap. 8.95 *(978-1-4197-2008-6(2)*, Amulet Bks.) Abrams, Inc.
—The Unusual Suspects. 2006. (Sisters Grimm Ser.: Bk. 2). 1.00 *(978-1-4237-8623-8(8))* Recorded Bks., Inc.
—The Unusual Suspects. 2007. (Sisters Grimm Ser.: 2). (J). lib. bdg. 18.40 *(978-1-4178-0732-1(6)*, Turtleback) Turtleback Bks.
—A Very Grimm Guide. Ferguson, Peter, illus. 2012. (Sisters Grimm Ser.). (ENG.). 128p. (J). (gr. 3-7). 16.95 *(978-1-4197-0201-3(7)*, Amulet Bks.) Abrams, Inc.
Buckner, Andrew. Grand Poppa's Favorite Chair: No One Is As Special As You. Welker, Matthew S., illus. 2011. 48p. pap. 24.95 *(978-1-4560-8294-9(9))* America Star Bks.
Buffie, Margaret. Who Is Frances Rain? 20th ed. 2007. (ENG.). 184p. (J). (gr. 7-9). 7.95 *(978-1-55453-209-4(4))* Kids Can Pr., Ltd. CAN. Dist: Hachette Bk. Group.
Buhlig Meister, Victoria. Tell Me a Story, Please, Mi-Mi! 2009. 36p. pap. 16.99 *(978-1-4389-2430-4(5))* AuthorHouse.
Bullock, Cecile Boyd. Grands Visit the Stars: A Trip to the Planetarium. 2013. 36p. pap. 18.41 *(978-1-4669-8856-9(8))* Trafford Publishing.
Bullock, Rob. Noah Ramsbottom & the Cave Elves. 2009. 48p. pap. 12.25 *(978-1-60860-335-0(0)*, Strategic Bk. Publishing) Strategic Book Publishing & Rights Agency (SBPRA).
Bunting, Eve. So Far from the Sea. Soentpiet, Chris K., illus. 2009. (ENG.). 32p. (J). (gr. 5-7). pap. 7.99 *(978-0-547-23752-7(9))* Houghton Mifflin Harcourt Publishing Co.
—Wash Day. Sneed, Brad, illus. 2014. (ENG.). 32p. (J). (gr. -1-3). 16.95 *(978-0-8234-2868-7(0))* Holiday Hse., Inc.
Burgess, Lisa Maria. Juma on Safari. Gugu, Abdul M., illus. 2013. 32p. 19.95 *(978-1-939604-07-1(9))*; pap. 9.99 *(978-1-939604-03-3(6))* Barranca Pr.
Burgess, Thornton W. Mother West Wind 'Where' Stories. 2009. 108p. 22.95 *(978-1-60664-597-0(8))*; 104p. pap. 9.95 *(978-1-60664-326-6(6))* Rodgers, Alan Bks.
Burlington, Marie. Helpful Hannah. 2004. (Pandas Ser.: 29). (ENG., Illus.). 64p. (J). pap. 9.95 *(978-0-86278-837-7(4))* O'Brien Pr., Ltd., The IRL. Dist: Dufour Editions, Inc.
Burnett, Frances Hodgson. Little Lord Fauntleroy. 2004. (Aladdin Classics Ser.). (ENG.). 288p. (J). (gr. 3-7). pap. 6.99 *(978-0-689-86994-5(0)*, Simon & Schuster/Paula Wiseman Bks.) Simon & Schuster/Paula Wiseman Bks.
—Little Lord Fauntleroy. Howell, Troy, illus. 2008. (Classic Starts(tm) Ser.). (ENG.). 160p. (J). (gr. 2-4). 5.95 *(978-1-4027-4578-2(8))* Sterling Publishing Co., Inc.
Burningham, John. Granpa. Burningham, John, illus. 2003. (ENG., Illus.). 32p. (J). (gr. -1-2). pap. 14.99 *(978-0-09-943408-5(3)*, Red Fox) Random House Children's Books GBR. Dist: Independent Pubs. Group.
Burns, Catherine Lloyd. The Half-True Lies of Cricket Cohen. 2017. (ENG.). 256p. (J). 16.99 *(978-0-374-30041-8(0)*, 9780374300418, Farrar, Straus & Giroux (BYR)) Farrar, Straus & Giroux.
Burrell, Carol klio. Summertime Blues. Neel, Julien, illus. 2012. (Lou! Ser.: 2). (ENG.). 48p. (J). (gr. 6-9). lib. bdg. 27.93 *(978-0-7613-8777-0(3)*, Graphic Universe™) Lerner Publishing Group.
Burrowes, Adjoa J. Grandma's Purple Flowers. 2004. (J). (gr. k-3). spiral bd. *(978-0-616-08496-0(X))*; spiral bd. *(978-0-616-07252-3(X))* Canadian National Institute for the Blind/Institut National Canadien pour les Aveugles.
Burrus, Denise. Heavenly Balloons. 2011. 12p. pap. 12.50 *(978-1-4567-1458-1(9))* AuthorHouse.
Burt, Vickie. Alvin the Proud Prankster. Thompson, Jessica, illus. 2011. 24p. pap. 13.99 *(978-1-937129-10-1(1))* Faithful Life Pubs.
Burton, Sharon Ann. Grammy Loves Me. 2012. 26p. pap. 24.95 *(978-1-4575-1267-4(X))* Dog Ear Publishing, LLC.
—When I Grow Up. 2013. 28p. (J). 24.95 *(978-1-4575-1802-7(3))* Dog Ear Publishing, LLC.
Bush, Leanne. Sarah's Happy Harvest Time, 1 vol. Briggs, Charlotte, illus. 2009. 32p. pap. 24.95 *(978-1-60813-818-0(6))* America Star Bks.
—A Very Special Christmas with Grandm. 2008. 18p. pap. 24.95 *(978-1-4241-9777-4(5))* America Star Bks.
Bushweller, Ellie. The Tree with A Hundred Hands. 2008. 40p. 18.50 *(978-0-615-24478-5(5))* Bushweller, Ellie.
Butler, Matthew. Billy Goes Hunting: A boy's journey to discover the values & traditions of Hunting. 2007. (Illus.). 28p. (J). pap. 9.95 *(978-0-9800643-0-8(9))* Antlers & Fins LLC.
Butterworth, MyLinda. The Monster Run. Day, Linda S., ed. Mercer, Matthew, illus. Lt. ed. 2004. 32p. (J). (gr. -1-3). 14.95 *(978-1-890905-23-1(2)*, Writers Collective, The) Day to Day Enterprises.
Byars, Betsy. A Blossom Promise. Haley, Amanda, illus. 4th ed. 2008. (Blossom Family Book Ser.: Bk. 4). (ENG.). 192p. (J). (gr. 4-7). pap. 6.95 *(978-0-8234-2147-3(3))* Holiday Hse., Inc.

—A Blossom Promise. (Blossom Family Ser.: Bk. 4). 145p. (J). (gr. 4-6). pap. 4.50 *(978-0-8072-1444-2(2),* Listening Library) Random Hse. Audio Publishing Group.

—La Casa de las Alas.Tr. of House of Wings. (SPA., Illus.). (YA). (gr. 5-8). pap. *(978-84-406-0861-1(6),* EB3416) Ediciones B ESP. Dist: Lectorum Pubns., Inc.

Byers, Marcella. Mitsy & Marty Mouse Visit Grandpa. Grant, Cheryl, illus. 2014. (ENG.). 32p. (gr. -1-2). pap. 8.95 *(978-1-61448-740-1(5),* 9781614487401) Morgan James Publishing.

Byrne, Gayle. Sometimes It's Grandmas & Grandpas: Not Mommies & Daddies. Haverfield, Mary, illus. 2009. (ENG.). 32p. (J). (gr. -1-3). 15.95 *(978-0-7892-1028-9(2),* Abbeville Kids) Abbeville Pr., Inc.

C. Larene Hall. Martha's Freedom Train. 2009. 100p. pap. 10.49 *(978-1-4389-7977-9(0))* AuthorHouse.

Cabot, Meg. The New Girl. 2008. (Allie Finkle's Rules for Girls Ser.: 2). (ENG.). 240p. (J). (gr. 3-7). 15.99 *(978-0-545-04049-5(3),* Scholastic Pr.) Scholastic, Inc.

Caglaroglu, Nurefsan. My Sweet Grandparents. 2011. (ENG.). 120p. 14.95 *(978-1-59784-230-3(3))* Tughra Bks.

Caird, Frankie Telfer. The Secret of Ellis Meadow. 2013. 160p. pap. 12.95 *(978-1-60911-616-3(X),* Strategic Bk. Publishing) Strategic Book Publishing & Rights Agency (SBPRA).

Cali, Davide. Piano, Piano. Rivers, Randi, tr. from FRE. Heliot, Eric, illus. 2007. 28p. (J). (gr. 4-7). 15.95 *(978-1-58089-191-2(8))* Charlesbridge Publishing, Inc.

Callahan, Sean. The Bear Hug. 2015. (Illus.). 24p. (J). *(978-1-4896-3852-6(0))* Weigl Pubs., Inc.

—The Leprechaun Who Lost His Rainbow, 1 vol. Cote, Nancy, illus. 2010. (ENG.). 32p. (J). (gr. 1-3). pap. 6.99 *(978-0-8075-4455-6(8))* Whitman, Albert & Co.

Callen, Sharon. Grandpa & Me, 1 vol. rev. ed. 2013. (Fiction Readers Ser.). (ENG., Illus.). 12p. (J). (gr. 1-1). pap. 12.96 *(978-1-4807-1132-7(2));* pap. 4.99 *(978-1-4333-5453-3(5))* Shell Educational Publishing.

Cameron, Ann. El Lugar Mas Bonito del Mundo. Alonso, Juan Ramon, illus. 2003. (SPA.). 70p. (gr. 3-5). pap. 8.95 *(978-968-19-0402-9(8))* Santillana USA Publishing Co., Inc.

Campbell, Michelle M. Granpa's Workshop: How Granpa Shows His Love. 2010. 24p. 12.95 *(978-1-4490-8520-9(2))* AuthorHouse.

Campbell, Nicola I. Grandpa's Girls, 1 vol. LaFave, Kim, illus. 2011. (ENG & SAL.). 32p. (J). (gr. -1-2). 16.95 *(978-1-55498-084-0(4))* Groundwood Bks. CAN. Dist: Publishers Group West (PGW).

Candlewick Press, Candlewick. Peppa Pig & the Treasure Hunt. 2015. (Peppa Pig Ser.). (ENG.). 32p. (J). (-k). 12.99 *(978-0-7636-7703-9(5),* Candlewick Entertainment) Candlewick Pr.

Cantor, Jillian. Searching for Sky. 2014. (ENG.). 288p. (YA). (gr. 7-12). 17.99 *(978-1-61963-351-3(5),* 9781619633513, Bloomsbury USA Childrens) Bloomsbury Publishing USA.

Caplin, Daniel. Grandfather Turtle. 2003. pap. 14.95 *(978-0-9726781-0-0(7))* Evening Sun Pr.

Cappuccetto Rosso. pap. 14.95 *(978-88-04-44204-2(2))* Mondadori ITA. Dist: Distribooks, Inc.

Caprio-Scalera, Jill. Gramma's 'Jammas. Caprio-Scalera, Jill & Edrington, Greg Q., illus. 2013. 28p. pap. 12.50 *(978-1-60976-464-7(1),* Strategic Bk. Publishing) Strategic Book Publishing & Rights Agency (SBPRA).

Caraballo, Samuel. Mis abuelos y yo / My Grandparents & I. Brammer, Ethriam Cash, tr. Cruz, D. Nina, illus. (ENG & SPA.). 32p. 16.95 *(978-1-55885-407-9(X),* Piñata Books) Arte Publico Pr.

Caraballo, Samuel & Torrecilla, Pablo. Estrellita en la Ciudad Grande. Caraballo, Samuel & Torrecilla, Pablo, illus. 2008. (SPA & ENG., Illus.). 32p. (J). (gr. -1-4). 16.95 *(978-1-55885-498-7(3),* Piñata Books) Arte Publico Pr.

Carlow, Emma & Bradman, Tony. Flora the Fairy. Carlow, Emma, illus. 2005. (Green Bananas Ser.). (ENG., Illus.). 48p. (J). lib. bdg. *(978-0-7787-1022-6(X))* Crabtree Publishing Co.

Carlson, J. Kelley. Freeing Golden Eagle. 2007. 140p. 19.95 *(978-1-4327-0315-8(3));* per. 10.95 *(978-1-4327-0302-8(1))* Outskirts Pr., Inc.

Carlson, Melody. Mixed Bags, 1 vol. 2014. (Carter House Girls Ser.). (ENG.). 224p. (YA). pap. 9.99 *(978-0-310-74756-7(2))* Zondervan.

—Stealing Bradford, 1 vol. 2014. (Carter House Girls Ser.). (ENG.). 224p. (YA). pap. 9.99 *(978-0-310-74654-6(X))* Zondervan.

—Viva Vermont!, 1 vol. 2014. (Carter House Girls Ser.). (ENG.). 224p. (YA). pap. 9.99 *(978-0-310-74714-7(7))* Zondervan.

Carolan, Debra. Puppets No Strings Attached. 2012. 58p. (-18). pap. 16.95 *(978-1-4626-8906-4(X))* America Star Bks.

Carolyn, Larsen. Grandmas 8 Special Stories for Little Boys. 2003. *(978-1-892354-87-7(X))* Educational Publishing Concepts, Inc.

Carpenter, Angie. Digewi Deer: The Tale of a Blind Deer. Berner Coble, Lynn, ed. 2013. 82p. (J). pap. 8.99 *(978-0-9846724-3-1(5))* Paws and Claws Publishing, LLC.

Carpenter, Ray. The Adventures of Benny Bell. 2004. 252p. 26.45 *(978-1-4140-8467-1(6))* AuthorHouse.

Carr, Pat. Border Ransom. 2006. (Chaparral Bks.). (ENG., Illus.). 178p. (J). (gr. 3-7). per. 11.95 *(978-0-87565-332-7(4))* Texas Christian Univ. Pr.

Carr, Sharleen. Watch for Fallen Rock. 2007. 68p. per. 19.95 *(978-1-4241-6704-3(3))* America Star Bks.

Carson, John E. & Carson, Marlene R. Ramblin' Rose: The Porcelain Mines in Russia. 2007. (Ramblin' Rose Ser.). 191p. (J). (gr. 8-12). per. 8.99 *(978-0-9776043-7-1(3))* Beast Stew.

Carter, Rachel. Find Me Where the Water Ends. 2014. (ENG.). 352p. (YA). (gr. 9). 17.99 *(978-0-06-208111-7(X),* HarperTeen) HarperCollins Pubs.

—So Close to You. 2013. (ENG.). 336p. (YA). (gr. 9). pap. 9.99 *(978-0-06-208106-3(3),* HarperTeen) HarperCollins Pubs.

—This Strange & Familiar Place. 2013. (ENG.). 272p. (YA). (gr. 9). 17.99 *(978-0-06-208108-7(X),* HarperTeen) HarperCollins Pubs.

Caruso, Carla. El Secreto de la Abuela Maria. 2003. (ENG & SPA., Illus.). 24p. pap. 6.95 *(978-85-7416-187-7(X))* Callis Editora Ltda BRA. Dist: Independent Pubs. Group.

Caseley, Judith. In Style with Grandma Antoinette. 2005. (ENG., Illus.). 32p. (J). (gr. -1-3). 15.95 *(978-0-9749303-4-2(3))* Tanglewood Pr.

Casey, Carin Jayne. Granny Babysits: The Mischievous Five. 2012. 62p. 31.95 *(978-1-4582-0474-5(X),* Abbott Pr.) Author Solutions, Inc.

Cassidy, Colette. DIVCO, the Little Milk Truck. 2007. (Illus.). 28p. (J). pap. 7.99 *(978-0-615-17346-7(2))* Redcay Publishing.

Castañeda, Omar S. Abuela's Weave. Sanchez, Enrique O., illus. 2013. (ENG.). 75p. (J). (gr. 1-4). pap. 9.95 *(978-1-880000-20-5(2))* Lee & Low Bks., Inc.

—El Tapiz de Abuela. 2004.Tr. of Abuela's Weave. (SPA., Illus.). (J). (gr. k-3). spiral bd. *(978-0-616-03088-2(6))* Canadian National Institute for the Blind/Institut National Canadien pour les Aveugles.

Castellucci, Cecil. Grandma's Gloves. Denos, Julia, illus. 2010. (ENG.). 32p. (J). (gr. k-3). 15.99 *(978-0-7636-3168-0(X))* Candlewick Pr.

Castillo, Lauren. Nana in the City. 2014. (ENG., Illus.). 40p. (J). (gr. -1-3). 16.99 *(978-0-544-10443-3(9))* Houghton Mifflin Harcourt Publishing Co.

Castleberry, Stephen B., Sr. & Castleberry, Susie. The History Mystery. 2005. (Farm Mystery Ser.). per. 8.50 *(978-1-891907-16-6(6))* Castleberry Farms Pr.

Catalanotto, Peter & Schembri, Pamela. The Veterans Day Visitor. Catalanotto, Peter, illus. 2008. (Second Grade Friends Ser.). (ENG., Illus.). 64p. (J). (gr. 2-5). 16.99 *(978-0-8050-7840-4(1),* 9780805078404, Holt, Henry & Co. Bks. For Young Readers) Holt, Henry & Co.

Catchpool, Michael. Grandpa's Boat. Williams, Sophy, illus. 2008. (ENG.). 32p. (J). (gr. k-k). 21.95 *(978-1-84270-690-9(X))* Andersen Pr. GBR. Dist: Independent Pubs. Group.

Catherine, Maria. Me & Grandma. Campion, Pascal, illus. 2015. (Time Together Ser.). (ENG.). 32p. (gr. -1-2). 8.95 *(978-1-4795-5795-0(1),* Fiction Picture Bks.) Picture Window Bks.

—Me & Grandpa. Campion, Pascal, illus. 2015. (Time Together Ser.). (ENG.). 32p. (gr. -1-2). 8.95 *(978-1-4795-5796-7(X),* Fiction Picture Bks.) Picture Window Bks.

Cauvin, Raoul. Cedric Vol. 4: Hot & Cold. Laudec, illus. 2013. (Cedric Ser.: 4). (ENG.). 48p. pap. 11.95 *(978-1-84918-158-7(6))* CineBook GBR. Dist: National Bk. Network.

Caygill, Ronald. Scrope Hall. 2009. 48p. pap. 11.49 *(978-1-4490-5078-8(6))* AuthorHouse.

Cazet, Denys. Grandpa Spanielson's Chicken Pox Stories No. 1: The Octopus. Cazet, Denys, illus. 2005. (I Can Read Bks.). (Illus.). 48p. (J). (gr. -1-3). lib. bdg. 16.89 *(978-0-06-051089-3(7))* HarperCollins Pubs.

—The Octopus. Cazet, Denys, illus. 2008. (Grandpa Spanielson's Chicken Pox Stories Ser.). (Illus.). (J). (gr. -1-3). pap. 16.95 incl. audio *(978-1-4301-0455-1(4));*Set. pap. 29.95 incl. audio *(978-1-4301-0457-5(0));*Set. pap. 31.95 incl. audio compact disk *(978-1-4301-0460-5(0))* Live Oak Media.

—The Shrunken Head. 2007. (I Can Read Bks.: No. 3). (Illus.). 48p. (J). (gr. -1-3). lib. bdg. 16.89 *(978-0-06-073014-7(5))* HarperCollins Pubs.

—A Snout for Chocolate. 2006. (I Can Read Bks.). (Illus.). (J). (gr. -1-3). (ENG.). 48p. 15.99 *(978-0-06-051093-0(5));* 47p. lib. bdg. 16.89 *(978-0-06-051094-7(3))* HarperCollins Pubs.

—A Snout for Chocolate. Cazet, Denys, illus. 2008. (Grandpa Spanielson's Chicken Pox Stories Ser.). (Illus.). (J). (gr. -1-3). pap. 16.95 incl. audio *(978-1-4301-0463-6(5));*Set. pap. 31.95 incl. audio compact disk *(978-1-4301-0468-1(6));*Set. pap. 29.95 incl. audio *(978-1-4301-0465-0(1))* Live Oak Media.

—A Snout for Chocolate. 2007. (I Can Read Bks.). (Illus.). 48p. (gr. -1-3). 15.00 *(978-0-7569-8056-6(9))* Perfection Learning Corp.

Cervantes, Angela. Allie, First at Last. 2016. (ENG.). 208p. (J). (gr. 3-7). 16.99 *(978-0-545-81223-8(2),* Scholastic Pr.) Scholastic, Inc.

Cervantes, Jennifer. Tortilla Sun. 2014. (ENG.). 224p. (J). (gr. 3-7). pap. 6.99 *(978-1-4521-3150-4(3))* Chronicle Bks. LLC.

Cervantes, Jennifer & Chronicle Books Staff. Tortilla Sun. 2010. (ENG.). 224p. (J). (gr. 4-7). 16.99 *(978-0-8118-7015-3(4))* Chronicle Bks. LLC.

Chall, Marsha Wilson. A Secret Keeps. 2012. (Carolrhoda Picture Bks.). (ENG., Illus.). 32p. (J). (gr. k-3). lib. bdg. 16.95 *(978-0-7613-5593-9(6))* Lerner Publishing Group.

Chamberlin, Kate. Charles & David. Wroth, Dean, illus. 2010. 32p. (J). pap. 9.95 *(978-0-944727-37-9(9));* lib. bdg. 15.95 *(978-0-944727-36-2(0))* Jason & Nordic Pubs. (Turtle Bks.).

Chambers, Aidan. Postcards from No Man's Land. (ENG.). 320p. (YA). (gr. 9-18). 2007. 10.00 *(978-0-14-240788-2(7))* 2004. reprint ed. 8.99 *(978-0-14-240145-3(5))* Penguin Young Readers Group. (Speak).

Chandler, Mitzi. I See Something Grand. 2003. (Illus.). 32p. (J). (gr. -1-1). pap. 8.95 *(978-0-938216-50-6(3))* Grand Canyon Assn.

Chapman, Jane. Me Too, Grandma! Chapman, Jane, illus. 2017. (ENG., Illus.). 32p. (J). (gr. -1-2). 16.99 ***(978-1-68010-042-6(4))*** Tiger Tales.

Chappell, Aimee. Good Bye Grandpa. 2013. 28p. pap. 9.21 *(978-1-4669-9463-8(0))* Trafford Publishing.

Charley, Grace. The Trouble with Benny Bubble. 2007. (Illus.). 72p. per. 9.76 *(978-1-4251-0147-3(X))* Trafford Publishing.

Chatterton, Martin & Bradman, Tony. The Surprise Party. Chatterton, Martin, illus. 2005. (Red Bananas Ser.). (ENG., Illus.). 48p. (J). lib. bdg. *(978-0-7787-1068-4(8))* Crabtree Publishing Co.

Cheaney, J. B. & Cheaney, Janie. The Middle of Somewhere. 2008. (ENG.). 224p. (J). (gr. 3-7). 7.99 *(978-0-440-42165-8(9),* Yearling) Random Hse. Children's Bks.

Cheng, Andrea. Goldfish & Chrysanthemums. Chang, Michelle, illus. 2003. (ENG.). 32p. (J). 16.95 *(978-1-58430-057-1(4));* pap. 8.95 *(978-1-60060-889-6(2))* Lee & Low Bks., Inc.

Cheng, Andrea, et al. Grandfather Counts. Zhang, Ange, illus. 2003. (Avenues Ser.). (ENG.). 32p. (C). pap. 11.95 *(978-1-58430-158-5(9))* National Geographic School Publishing, Inc.

Cherry, Alison. The Classy Crooks Club. 2016. (ENG., Illus.). 336p. (J). (gr. 3-7). 16.99 *(978-1-4814-4637-2(1),* Aladdin) Simon & Schuster Children's Publishing.

Cheryl A. Page; Illustrations By Kimberl. Grammie, What's That? 2012. 32p. 24.95 *(978-1-4626-5875-6(X))* America Star Bks.

Chichester Clark, Emma. Mimi's Book of Counting. Chichester Clark, Emma, illus. 2004. (Illus.). 24p. (J). 9.95 *(978-1-57091-573-4(3))* Charlesbridge Publishing, Inc.

Childress, Story. The Old Codger, 1 vol. 2009. 23p. pap. 19.95 *(978-1-4489-2511-7(8))* PublishAmerica, Inc.

Choudhry, Fahima. The Snow Surprise. 2011. 24p. pap. 15.99 *(978-1-4653-4628-5(7))* Xlibris Corp.

Chris, Crowe. Mississippi Trial 1955. 2014. (ENG.). 240p. (YA). (gr. 7-12). 10.24 *(978-1-63245-211-5(1))* Lectorum Pubns., Inc.

Christie, Ed. The Sweet Smell of Rotten Eggs: Volume Two, the Dude Ranch Rangers. 2009. 108p. pap. 10.95 *(978-1-4401-3764-8(1))* iUniverse, Inc.

Churchill, Ginger. Wild Rose's Weaving. Wong, Nicole, illus. 2011. (ENG.). 32p. (J). (gr. -1-3). 15.95 *(978-1-933718-56-9(0))* Tanglewood Pr.

Ciocca, Donna. Tavern Tales. 2005. 136p. per. 14.95 *(978-0-9747361-3-6(9))* Oak Manor Publishing, Inc.

Citra, Becky. Sam's Ride, 1 vol. Meissner, Amy, illus. 2009. (Orca Echoes Ser.). (ENG.). 64p. (J). (gr. 2-3). pap. 6.95 *(978-1-55469-160-9(5))* Orca Bk. Pubs. USA.

Clark, Clara Gillow. Hattie on Her Way. Thompson, John, illus. 2005. (ENG.). 208p. (J). (gr. 5-18). 15.99 *(978-0-7636-2286-2(9))* Candlewick Pr.

—Secrets of Greymoor. 2009. (ENG., Illus.). 176p. (J). (gr. 5). 15.99 *(978-0-7636-3249-6(X))* Candlewick Pr.

Clark, Eleanor. Eleanor Jo: The Farmer's Daughter. 2007. (Eleanor Ser.: Bk. 5). (Illus.). 193p. 14.99 *(978-0-9788726-1-8(4))* HonorNet.

—Melanie Ann: A Legacy of Love. 2007. (Eleanor Ser.: Bk. 6). (Illus.). 181p. 14.99 *(978-0-9788726-2-5(2))* HonorNet.

—Sarah Jane: Liberty's Torch. 2007. (Eleanor Ser.: Bk. 4). 188p. 14.99 *(978-0-9753036-9-6(4))* HonorNet.

Clark, Isabelle. The Enchanted Forest of Hope. 2009. 44p. pap. 18.50 *(978-1-4389-7781-2(6))* AuthorHouse.

Clark, Katie. Grandma Drove the Garbage Truck. Huntington, Amy, illus. 2006. (ENG.). 32p. (J). (gr. -1-17). 15.95 *(978-0-89272-698-1(9))* Down East Bks.

—Grandma Drove the Lobsterboat, 1 vol. Huntington, Amy, illus. 2012. (ENG.). 32p. (J). (gr. -1-1). 16.95 *(978-1-60893-004-3(1))* Down East Bks.

Clark, M. H. Grandma Is a Superhero. 2013. (Story Lines Ser.). (ENG.). 32p. (J). (gr. -1-3). 9.95 *(978-1-935414-94-0(1))* Casemate Pubs. & Bk. Distributors, LLC.

Clark, Margaret. Love Charms. 2008. (ENG.). 192p. (J). (gr. 7). pap. 12.95 *(978-1-74166-264-1(8))* Random Hse. Australia AUS. Dist: Independent Pubs. Group.

Clarke, Judith. One Whole & Perfect Day. (ENG.). 2013. 248p. (YA). (gr. 9-12). pap. 9.95 *(978-1-62091-025-2(X))* 2007. 250p. (J). (gr. 8-13). 16.95 *(978-1-932425-95-6(0),* Front Street) Boyds Mills Pr.

Clausman, Rachel. Miriam, Come Sit. 2011. 24p. pap. 11.32 *(978-1-4634-4812-7(0))* AuthorHouse.

Clements, Andrew. Because Your Grandparents Love You. Alley, R. W., illus. 2015. (ENG.). 32p. (J). (gr. -1-3). 16.99 *(978-0-544-14854-3(1))* Houghton Mifflin Harcourt Publishing Co.

—Things Hoped For. 2008. (ENG.). 176p. (J). (gr. 5-18). 7.99 *(978-0-14-241073-8(X),* Puffin Books) Penguin Young Readers Group.

—Things Hoped For. 2008. 167p. (gr. 5-9). 17.00 *(978-0-7569-8933-0(7))* Perfection Learning Corp.

Cline, Penny. The Extremely Strange Story of Ermintrude Bold. 2016. (ENG., Illus.). 36p. (J). pap. ***(978-0-9546827-3-6(4))*** Fig Tree Press Brighton.

Coates, Charmian. Secret Staircase. 2011. (Illus.). 88p. pap. 27.76 *(978-1-4567-8715-8(2))* AuthorHouse.

Coates, Paul. Tim & the Iceberg, 1 vol. Haywood, Ian Benfold, illus. 2011. (ENG.). 32p. (J). (gr. k-3). 16.95 *(978-1-59572-205-8(X));* pap. 6.95 *(978-1-59572-206-5(8))* Star Bright Bks., Inc.

Cobb, Amy. Shredding with the Geeks, 1 vol. Cattish, Anna, illus. 2015. (ENG.). 112p. (J). *(978-1-62402-076-6(3))* Magic Wagon.

Cochard, Nadège. Grandma & Grandpa Visit Connor. Fanny, illus. 2009. (My First Stories Ser.). 24p. (J). (gr. -1-3). 22.60 *(978-1-60754-357-2(5))* Windmill Bks.

Cochard, Nadège. Grandma & Grandpa Visit Connor. Fanny, illus. 2009. (My First Stories Ser.). 24p. (J). (gr. -1-3). pap. 8.15 *(978-1-60754-356-5(7))* Windmill Bks.

Cocks, Nancy & Marton, Jirina. Fergie Goes to Grandma's. 2003. (Illus.). 16p. pap. *(978-2-89507-312-3(0))* Novalis Publishing.

Cohen, Deborah Bodin. Papa Jethro. Dippold, Jane, illus. 2007. (Jewish Identity Ser.). (ENG.). 32p. (J). (gr. -1-1). 9.95 *(978-1-58013-250-3(2));* per. 7.95 *(978-1-58013-252-7(9))* Lerner Publishing Group. (Kar-Ben Publishing).

Cola, Arthur. Papa & the Gingerbread Man. 2006. 14.95 *(978-0-9789423-0-4(2))* Cola, Arthur.

Colburn, Cherie Foster. Our Shadow Garden. 2010. (ENG., Illus.). 32p. (J). 19.95 *(978-1-933979-69-4(0),* 2a670c16-6bf1-4046-9b18-a6f621294483) Bright Sky Pr.

Cole, Babette. The Trouble with Gran. 2005. (ENG., Illus.). 32p. (J). pap. 3.99 *(978-1-4052-1123-9(7))* Egmont Bks., Ltd. GBR. Dist: Trafalgar Square Publishing.

Cole, Barbara H. Wash Day, 1 vol. Himler, Ronald, illus. 2004. (ENG.). 32p. (J). 15.95 *(978-1-932065-36-7(9),* 7187849112) Star Bright Bks., Inc.

Coll-Seck, Jayden. Grandma's Room, 01 vols., 1. 2016. (Rosen REAL Readers: Social Studies Nonfiction / Fiction: Family, Community, & the World Ser.). (ENG.). 8p. (J). pap. 5.46 *(978-1-5081-1418-5(8),* Rosen Classroom) Rosen Publishing Group, Inc., The.

Collard, Sneed B., III. Dog Sense, 1 vol. (ENG.). 192p. (J). (gr. 3-7). 2008. pap. 7.95 *(978-1-56145-460-0(5))* 2005. 14.95 *(978-1-56145-351-1(X))* Peachtree Pubs.

A Collection of Stories Inspired by My Grandchildren. 2005. (YA). per. *(978-1-59872-111-9(9))* Instant Pub.

Collier, Kevin Scott & Collier, Kristen. Dreamchaser. 2008. 64p. pap. 6.95 *(978-1-933090-93-1(6))* Guardian Angel Publishing, Inc.

Collins, Rachel. Sidney Swallow Sings. 2010. 32p. pap. 15.95 *(978-0-557-44696-4(1))* Lulu Pr., Inc.

Collins, Wendy Jane. The Adventure Door: Book 1 'How it all began' & Book 2 'Return to Courtney Bay' 2010. 112p. pap. 10.99 *(978-1-4520-4228-2(4))* AuthorHouse.

Comperchio, Shheila. The Club House & the Gang. 2011. 114p. pap. 9.95 *(978-0-9837803-0-4(7))* Fiction Publishing, Inc.

Compestine, Ying Chang. Crouching Tiger. Nascimbene, Yan, illus. 2011. (ENG.). 40p. (J). (gr. 1-4). 16.99 *(978-0-7636-4642-4(3))* Candlewick Pr.

Condon, Bill. Riley & the Fantastic Plan. Hopgood, Andrew, illus. 2015. (Legends in Their Own Lunchbox Ser.). (ENG.). 56p. (gr. 2-3). pap. 7.99 *(978-1-4966-0252-7(8),* Legends in Their Own Lunchbox) Capstone Classroom.

Cone, Stephanie M. Grandma's Moving In! Sample, Matthew & Sample, Matthew, illus. 2013. (Learning to Care Ser.). (ENG.). (J). 18.00 *(978-1-937460-68-6(1))* Vision Forum, Inc., The.

Conly, Jane Leslie. Impetuous R., Secret Agent. Leick, Bonnie, illus. 2008. (ENG.). 240p. (gr. 3-7). 16.99 *(978-1-4231-0418-6(8))* Hyperion Pr.

Connelly, Peggy. My Quirky, Oddball, Eccentric, Unpredictable Grandma. 2006. (ENG.). 112p. per. 19.95 *(978-1-4241-4486-0(8))* PublishAmerica, Inc.

Connelly, Valerie. Goosh Gosh from the Lilac Kitchen & Other Childhood Stories. 2013. (Illus.). 42p. pap. 14.95 *(978-1-935993-49-0(6))* Nightengale Pr.

Contreras, Kathleen. Braids - Trencitas. Lindmark, Margaret, illus. 2009. (ENG & SPA.). 32p. (J). (gr. -1-3). 14.99 *(978-1-933032-27-6(8))* Lectorum Pubns., Inc.

Contreras, Kathleen & Lindmark, Margaret. Sweet Memories/Dulces Recuerdos. Lindmark, Margaret, illus. 2014. (SPA & ENG., Illus.). 32p. (J). (gr. 2-4). pap. 14.99 *(978-1-933032-91-7(X))* Lectorum Pubns., Inc.

Cook, Jeremy. Illusion of Time, 1 vol. 2010. 118p. pap. 19.95 *(978-1-4489-6235-8(8))* America Star Bks.

—The Illusion Stick. 2008. 115p. pap. 19.95 *(978-1-60474-705-8(6))* America Star Bks.

Cook, Kajsa. Discoveries in the Shriver Family Attic: How a Woman & Her Children Dealt with the Battle of Gettysburg. 2009. (Illus.). 122p. (J). (gr. 4-8). pap. 8.95 *(978-1-57249-398-8(4),* White Mane Kids) White Mane Publishing Co., Inc.

Cooke, Trish. Full, Full, Full of Love. Howard, Paul, illus. 2008. (ENG.). 32p. (J). (gr. -1-k). pap. 3.99 *(978-0-7636-3883-2(8))* Candlewick Pr.

Cooke, Trish. Look Back! Binch, Caroline, illus. (ENG.). 32p. (J). 2017. pap. 8.95 ***(978-1-56656-099-3(3))*** 2014. 17.95 *(978-1-56656-980-4(X))* Interlink Publishing Group, Inc. (Crocodile Bks.).

Coomber, Suzanne. The Run Away Persimmon. 2009. 20p. pap. 12.49 *(978-1-4490-0911-3(5))* AuthorHouse.

Coon, Dianne. Nerual's Adventures & the Greatness of Agnes. 2010. 68p. pap. 11.49 *(978-1-4520-2321-2(2))* AuthorHouse.

Cooney, Caroline B. Hit the Road. rev. l.t. ed. 2007. (Thorndike Literacy Bridge Ser.). 259p. (YA). (gr. 7-12). 23.95 *(978-0-7862-9429-9(9))* Thorndike Pr.

Cooper, Floyd. Max & the Tag-Along Moon. Cooper, Floyd, illus. (ENG., Illus.). 32p. (J). (gr. -1-2). 2015. pap. 8.99 *(978-0-14-751546-9(7),* Puffin Books) 2013. 16.99 *(978-0-399-23342-5(3),* Philomel Bks.) Penguin Young Readers Group.

Cooper, Wendy. My First Ride with Isaiah. Elizabeth Mobley, illus. 2006. 18p. (J). 11.95 *(978-0-9772964-8-4(2))* Kingdom Publishing Group, Inc.

Cope, Clifford D. Caleb: The mouse Engineer. 2009. 24p. pap. 12.99 *(978-1-4389-9877-0(5))* AuthorHouse.

Corderoy, Tracey. Hubble Bubble, Granny Trouble. Berger, Joe, illus. 2012. (ENG.). 32p. (J). (gr. -1-2). 14.99 *(978-0-7636-5904-2(5),* Nosy Crow) Candlewick Pr.

—I Want My Mommy! Edgson, Alison, illus. 2014. (ENG.). 32p. (J). (gr. -1-3). mass mkt. 3.99 *(978-1-58925-453-4(8))* Tiger Tales.

—Whizz! Pop! Granny, Stop! Berger, Joe, illus. 2013. (ENG.). 32p. (J). (gr. -1-2). 14.99 *(978-0-7636-6551-7(7),* Nosy Crow) Candlewick Pr.

Córdova, Amy. Abuelita's Heart. Córdova, Amy, illus. 2008. (ENG., Illus.). 32p. (J). (gr. -1-3). 13.99 *(978-1-4169-7576-2(4),* Simon & Schuster/Paula Wiseman Bks.) Simon & Schuster/Paula Wiseman Bks.

Coriell, Shelley. Welcome, Caller, This Is Chloe. 2013. (ENG.). 320p. (YA). (gr. 7-17). pap. 7.95 *(978-1-4197-0545-8(8),* Amulet Bks.) Abrams, Inc.

Corlett, Mary Lee. Belle's Wild Ride: The Artful Adventure of a Butterfly & a Cabbie. Cayless, Sophie, illus. 2015. (ENG.). 32p. (J). (gr. 3-7). 17.95 *(978-1-907804-51-9(X))* Giles, D. Ltd. GBR. Dist: Consortium Bk. Sales & Distribution.

Cornette, Sylvia. The House Across the Lake. 2007. 132p. per. 24.95 *(978-1-4241-8247-3(6))* America Star Bks.

Cornwell, Autumn. Carpe Diem. 2009. (ENG.). 368p. (YA). (gr. 7-12). pap. 12.99 *(978-0-312-56129-1(6),* 9780312561291) Square Fish.

Costain, Meredith. Stella, Circus Star. McGowan, Shane, illus. 2015. (Legends in Their Own Lunchbox Ser.). (ENG.). 56p. (gr. 2-3). pap. 7.99 *(978-1-4966-0255-8(2),* Legends in Their Own Lunchbox) Capstone Classroom.

Costales, Amy. Abuelita Full of Life: Abuelita llena de Vida. Avilés, Martha, illus. 2007. (ENG, SPA & MUL.). 32p. (J). (gr. -1-3). 14.95 *(978-0-87358-914-7(9))* Cooper Square Publishing Llc.

—Abuelo Vivia Solo/Grandpa Used to Live Alone. Gama, Esperanza, illus. 2010. (ENG.). 32p. (J). (gr. -1-3). 16.95 *(978-1-55885-531-1(9))* Arte Publico Pr.

Cottrell, Laura. Introducing: Honey Gem Sheasby, 1 vol. 2010. 48p. pap. 16.95 *(978-1-4489-7874-8(2))* America Star Bks.

Couloumbis, Audrey. Jake. 2011. (ENG.). 176p. (J). (gr. 3-7). pap. 6.99 *(978-0-375-85631-0(5),* Yearling) Random Hse. Children's Bks.

Coulton, Mia. At Grandma Ruth's House. Coulton, Mia, photos by. 2008. (ENG., Illus.). pap. 5.35 *(978-1-933624-32-7(9))* Maryruth Bks., Inc.

Court, Georgia. Traitor of Bled. 2005. 108p. pap. 19.95 *(978-1-4137-9595-0(1))* PublishAmerica, Inc.

Cousins Camp. 2010. 32p. pap. 12.99 *(978-1-4490-8387-8(0))* AuthorHouse.

Covey, Sean. Goob & His Grandpa. Curtis, Stacy, illus. 2013. (7 Habits of Happy Kids Ser.: 7). (ENG.). 32p. (J). (gr. -1-1). 7.99 *(978-1-4424-7653-0(2)*, Simon & Schuster Bks. For Young Readers) Simon & Schuster Bks. For Young Readers.

Coville, Bruce. I Lost My Grandfather's Brain. unabr. ed. 2004. (I Was a Sixth Grade Alien Ser.: Vol. 3). 160p. (J). (gr. 3-6). pap. 29.00 incl. audio *(978-0-8072-8385-1(1)*, YA180SP, Listening Library) Random Hse. Audio Publishing Group.

Coville, Katherine. Ivy. 2017. (ENG.). 144p. (J). (gr. 2-5). lib. bdg. 19.99 *(978-0-553-53976-9(0)*, Knopf Bks. for Young Readers) Random Hse. Children's Bks.

Covington, Jean. Nanny Planted Love. (J). 2006. per. 11.99 *(978-1-933732-12-1(1))* 2005. lib. bdg. 19.95 *(978-0-9754728-9-7(5))* Big Ransom Studio.

—Nanny Planted Love: Color Book. 2006. (J). per. 6.99 *(978-1-933732-13-8(X))* Big Ransom Studio.

Cowley, Joy. Dan & the Parrot. 2009. pap. 8.25 *(978-1-60559-217-6(X))* Hameray Publishing Group, Inc.

—Meanies in the House Big Book. 2010. 48.25 *(978-1-60559-251-0(X))* Hameray Publishing Group, Inc.

Crabb, James Anthony. The Dinosaur & Dragon Juice Café. 2008. (Illus.). 32p. pap. 17.95 *(978-0-9556105-8-5(3))* Picnic Publishing Ltd. GBR. Dist: Trans-Atlantic Pubns., Inc.

Craddock, Sonia. Runaway Gran, 1 vol. 2006. (Lorimer Streetlights Ser.). (ENG.). 168p. (J). (gr. 2-5). 7.95 *(978-1-55028-953-4(5)*, 9781550289534) Lorimer, James & Co., Ltd., Pubs. CAN. Dist: Casemate Pubs. & Bk. Distributors, LLC.

Cramer, Gayle Shaw. The Secret of the Dragonfly: A Story of Hope & Promise. Jones, Jan, illus. 2006. (YA). pap. 19.95 *(978-0-9729346-7-1(7))* Ambrosia Press LLC.

Crear, Williadean. Anika & Her New Body. 2011. 28p. pap. 21.99 *(978-1-4568-9480-1(3))* Xlibris Corp.

Creech, Sharon. Granny Torrelli Makes Soup. Raschka, Chris, illus. 2012. (ENG.). 160p. (J). (gr. 3-7). reprint ed. pap. 6.99 *(978-0-06-440960-5(0))* HarperCollins Pubs.

—Granny Torrelli Makes Soup. Raschka, Chris, illus. 2004. (Joanna Cotler Bks.). 141p. (gr. 3-7). 17.00 *(978-0-7569-4604-3(2))* Perfection Learning Corp.

—Heartbeat. 2012. (ENG.). 208p. (J). (gr. 3-7). pap. 6.99 *(978-0-06-054024-1(9))* HarperCollins Pubs.

—Walk Two Moons. (Walk Two Moons Ser.: 1). (J). (gr. 3-7). 2011. 288p. pap. 7.99 *(978-0-06-440517-1(6))* 2003. 304p. pap. 7.99 *(978-0-06-056013-3(4)*, HarperTeen) HarperCollins Pubs.

—Walk Two Moons. 280p. (J). (gr. 4-6). pap. 4.95 *(978-0-8072-1509-8(0)*, Listening Library) Random Hse. Audio Publishing Group.

—Walk Two Moons. (J). 2011. (gr. 5-8). lib. bdg. 18.40 *(978-0-613-00204-2(0))* 2003. (gr. 7-12). 18.40 *(978-0-613-81971-8(3))* Turtleback Bks. (Turtleback).

—The Wanderer. Diaz, David, illus. 2011. (ENG.). 304p. (J). (gr. 3-7). pap. 6.99 *(978-0-06-441032-8(3))* HarperCollins Pubs.

Creevy, Anne. Lets Go Birding, You & Me. 2006. (J). pap. *(978-0-9785108-0-0(1))* ABC Bks.

Crespo, Ana. JP & the Stinky Monster: Feeling Jealous. Sirotich, Erica, illus. 2016. (My Emotions & Me Ser.). (ENG.). 32p. (J). (gr. -1-3). 16.99 *(978-0-8075-3979-8(1))* Whitman, Albert & Co.

Crispian. Mystery on the Tambo River. 2011. 120p. (gr. 4-6). 20.95 *(978-1-4502-6506-5(5))*; pap. 10.95 *(978-1-4502-6504-1(9))* iUniverse, Inc.

Cronin, B. B. The Lost House. 2016. (ENG., Illus.). 40p. (J). (gr. -1-2). 18.99 *(978-1-101-99921-9(7)*, Viking Books for Young Readers) Penguin Young Readers Group.

Croom, Terry, illus. Grandma's Here. 2013. 20p. (J). pap. 9.99 *(978-0-9888650-2-0(5))* Soar Publishing, LLC.

Cross, Laurie. Down to the Folks: A Visit with Grandpa & Grandma. 2011. 32p. pap. *(978-1-4269-7105-1(2))* Trafford Publishing (UK) Ltd.

Croteau, Marie-Danielle. Fred & the Mysterious Letter. St-Aubin, Bruno, illus. 2005. 61p. (J). lib. bdg. 12.00 *(978-1-4242-1199-9(9))* Fitzgerald Bks.

Crouch, Katie. The Magnolia League. 2012. (Magnolia League Ser.: 1). (ENG.). 384p. (YA). (gr. 10-17). pap. 8.99 *(978-0-316-07848-1(4)*, Poppy) Little, Brown Bks. for Young Readers.

—The White Glove War. 2013. (Magnolia League Ser.: 2). (ENG.). 320p. (YA). (gr. 10-17). pap. 9.00 *(978-0-316-18749-7(6)*, Poppy) Little, Brown Bks. for Young Readers.

Crow, Marilee. Does Heaven Get Mail? Snider, K. C., illus. 2008. 24p. pap. 10.95 *(978-1-935137-12-2(3))* Guardian Angel Publishing, Inc.

Crowe, Chris. Mississippi Trial 1955. 2003. (ENG.). 240p. (YA). (gr. 7-18). 5.99 *(978-0-14-250192-4(1)*, Speak) Penguin Young Readers Group.

—The Mississippi Trial 1955. 2003. (gr. 7-12). lib. bdg. 16.00 *(978-0-613-86522-7(7)*, Turtleback) Turtleback Bks.

Crowley-Ranelli, D. Holiday Island: Santa in a Bathing Suit? 2009. 56p. pap. 9.95 *(978-1-60860-268-1(0)*, Eloquent Bks.) Strategic Book Publishing & Rights Agency (SBPRA).

Crownberry, Ethan. Johnny Jetpack. 2013. 52p. 17.95 *(978-0-9898533-1-6(4))* Jetpack Publishing.

—Johnny Jetpack. 2012. 84p. pap. 8.95 *(978-1-300-00783-8(4))* Lulu Pr., Inc.

Crum, Shutta. My Mountain Song. 2007. (Illus.). 32p. (J). 16.00 *(978-1-4223-6590-8(5))* DIANE Publishing Co.

Crutcher, Anquisha Janea. To Grandma's House I Go. 2012. 16p. pap. 15.99 *(978-1-4772-0536-5(5))* AuthorHouse.

Crystal, Billy. Grandpa's Little One. Porfirio, Guy, illus. 2006. 40p. (J). (gr. -1-k). lib. bdg. 17.89 *(978-0-06-078174-3(2))* HarperCollins Pubs.

—I Already Know I Love You. Sayles, Elizabeth, illus. (J). 2008. (ENG.). 32p. (gr. -1-3). bds. 7.99 *(978-0-06-145057-0(X)*, HarperFestival) 2007. (ENG.). 40p. (gr. -1-3). pap. 6.99 *(978-0-06-059393-3(8))* 2004. (ENG.). 40p. 16.99 *(978-0-06-059391-9(1))* 2004. 40p. lib. bdg. 17.89 *(978-0-06-059392-6(X))* HarperCollins Pubs.

Cuff, Ed. D. City of Thieves. 2013. 114p. pap. 7.99 *(978-1-61798-076-3(5))* Wild Child Publishing.

Culverwell, C. Ellen. The Horse Lady. 2009. (J). pap. *(978-0-88092-723-9(2))*; lib. bdg. *(978-0-88092-722-2(4))* Royal Fireworks Publishing Co.

Cummings, Alicia. The Adventures of Jayda. 2010. 44p. pap. 16.99 *(978-1-4520-2564-3(9))* AuthorHouse.

Cummings, Priscilla. Autumn Journey, 1 vol. Ben-Ami, Doron, illus. 2009. (ENG.). 120p. (J). pap. 12.95 *(978-0-87033-606-5(1)*, 9780870336065, Cornell Maritime Pr./Tidewater Pubs.) Schiffer Publishing, Ltd.

Currim, Nazli. Grandma Lives with Us. Tung, Kadhima Ren, illus. 2010. 46p. (J). 16.95 *(978-0-9814629-5-0(2))* Acacia Publishing, Inc.

Curry, Kenneth. The Legend of the Dancing Trees: An African American Folk Tale. 2007. 111p. (J). per. 14.95 *(978-0-9798364-0-4(9))* Curry Brothers Publishing Group.

Curry, Kenneth, et al. The Legend of the Dancing Trees Teachers Resource: The Legend of the Dancing Trees. 2007.Tr. of Teachers Resource. per. 19.95 *(978-0-9798364-1-1(7))* Curry Brothers Publishing Group.

Curtis, Jessica Lynn. Papa's New Home. Harmon, Steve, illus. 2012. (ENG.). 40p. (J). *(978-0-931674-64-8(6)*, Waldman House Pr.) TRISTAN Publishing, Inc.

Custard, Stefanie. The Story of Baby Moose Joe. 2008. (Illus.). 32p. pap. 20.99 *(978-1-4343-9138-4(8))* AuthorHouse.

D. Good Morning World. 2013. 46p. pap. 21.99 *(978-1-4575-2154-6(7))* Dog Ear Publishing, LLC.

Dade, Barbara A. Story Time with Grandm. 2008. 88p. pap. 41.99 *(978-1-4363-5325-0(4))* Xlibris Corp.

Dahl, Roald. George's Marvelous Medicine. Blake, Quentin, illus. 2007. (ENG.). 112p. (J). (gr. 3-7). 7.99 *(978-0-14-241035-6(7)*, Puffin Books) Penguin Young Readers Group.

—George's Marvelous Medicine. Blake, Quentin, illus. 2008. 88p. (gr. 4-7). 18.00 *(978-0-7569-8777-0(6))* Perfection Learning Corp.

—George's Marvelous Medicine. 2007. lib. bdg. 18.40 *(978-1-4177-8619-0(1)*, Turtleback) Turtleback Bks.

—The Witches. Blake, Quentin, illus. 30th ed. 2013. (ENG.). 240p. (J). (gr. 3-6). 21.99 *(978-0-374-38459-3(2)*, 9780374384593, Farrar, Straus & Giroux (BYR)) Farrar, Straus & Giroux.

—The Witches. Blake, Quentin, illus. 2007. (ENG.). 224p. (J). (gr. 3-7). 7.99 *(978-0-14-241011-0(X)*, Puffin Books) Penguin Young Readers Group.

—The Witches. Blake, Quentin, illus. 2007. 206p. (gr. 4-7). 17.00 *(978-0-7569-8229-4(4))* Perfection Learning Corp.

Dahlstrom, S. J. Texas Grit: the Adventures of Wilder Good #2. 2014. (Adventures of Wilder Good Ser.). (ENG.). 141p. (J). (gr. 3). pap. 7.95 *(978-1-58988-094-8(3))* Dry, Paul Bks., Inc.

Dajani, Suad Farsakh. Grandma's Stories: A Collection of Six Children's Stories. 2013. 40p. 25.99 *(978-1-4808-0051-9(1))*; pap. 16.99 *(978-1-4808-0049-6(X))* Archway Publishing.

Dale, Jay. Gran & Me, 1 vol. Dybing, Michelle, illus. 2012. (Wonder Words Ser.). (ENG.). 32p. (gr. k-2). pap. 5.99 *(978-1-4296-8898-7(X)*, Engage Literacy) Capstone Press of Coughlan Cos.

—Who Is under There?, 1 vol. Webb, Philip, illus. 2012. (Wonder Words Ser.). (ENG.). 32p. (gr. k-2). pap. 5.99 *(978-1-4296-8924-3(2)*, Engage Literacy) Capstone Press of Coughlan Cos.

Daley, Debbie. The Harp of Elvyth. 2013. 292p. pap. *(978-1-78299-840-2(3))* FeedARead.com.

Daley-Prado, M. J. Baby Duck Gets A New Grandma. 2008. 40p. pap. 17.95 *(978-1-4357-1312-3(5))* Lulu Pr., Inc.

—Grandma,What Is Cancer? 2007. 20p. 13.95 *(978-1-4357-0204-2(2))* Lulu Pr., Inc.

Dalhaimer Bartkowski, Anna. Maggie Visits Grandpa: A Coloring Adventure. Dalhaimer Bartkowski, Anna, illus. 2007. (Illus.). 32p. pap. 8.99 *(978-0-9790720-1-7(8))* Infinite Adventure.

Dalton, Kippy. Grandma's Visit. 2016. (Spring Forward Ser.). (J). (gr. 1). *(978-1-4900-3713-4(6))* Benchmark Education Co.

Dalton, Linda J. The Mystery of the Broomstick Horse. 2012. 116p. 29.99 *(978-1-4797-4781-8(5))*; pap. 19.99 *(978-1-4797-4780-1(7))* Xlibris Corp.

Dana Kittendorf. Trail of Dreams. 2009. 136p. 21.95 *(978-1-4401-7787-3(2))*; pap. 11.95 *(978-1-4401-7785-9(6))* iUniverse, Inc.

Danczyk, Kenneth. Grandpas Farm. 2008. 35p. pap. 16.00 *(978-1-4357-4021-1(1))* Lulu Pr., Inc.

Daniels, Darla. Carrie Goes Camping. 2011. 24p. pap. 16.95 *(978-1-4626-0642-9(3))* America Star Bks.

Danowski, Jeff. Grandma's Necklace. 2012. 286p. 27.95 *(978-1-62709-147-3(5))* America Star Bks.

Das, Christina. Swinging under the Stars. l.t. ed. 2005. (Illus.). 32p. (J). 15.95 *(978-0-9763082-1-8(5)*, A JuneOne Production) JuneOne Publishing Hub.

Dauvillier, Loic & Salsedo, Greg. Hidden. Lizano, Marc, illus. 2014. (ENG.). 80p. (J). (gr. 1-6). 16.99 *(978-1-59643-873-6(8)*, 9781596438736, First Second Bks.) Roaring Brook Pr.

Davenport, Kelly. Do Hotdogs Grow on Trees? 2010. 32p. pap. 17.99 *(978-1-4520-6636-3(1))* AuthorHouse.

Davidson, Jean. My Grandma Rides a Harley: She's Cool! Bauknecht, Julie, illus. 2007. (J). *(978-1-930596-79-5(0))* Amherst Pr.

Davies, Benji. Grandad's Island. Davies, Benji, illus. 2016. (ENG., Illus.). 32p. (J). (gr. -1-3). 16.99 *(978-0-7636-9005-2(8))* Candlewick Pr.

Davies, Jacqueline. The Bell Bandit. (Lemonade War Ser.). (ENG., Illus.). 192p. (J). (gr. 2-5). 2013. pap. 7.99 *(978-0-544-02274-4(2))* 2012. 16.99 *(978-0-547-56737-2(5))* Houghton Mifflin Harcourt Publishing Co.

—The Bell Bandit. 2013. (Lemonade War Ser.: 3). lib. bdg. 18.40 *(978-0-606-31669-9(8)*, Turtleback) Turtleback Bks.

Davies, Nicola. White Owl, Barn Owl: Read & Wonder. Foreman, Michael, illus. 2009. (Read & Wonder Ser.). (ENG.). 32p. (J). (gr. -1-3). pap. 6.99 *(978-0-7636-4143-6(X))* Candlewick Pr.

Davis, Anita. Grandma, It's Beautiful. 2012. 16p. pap. 7.99 *(978-1-4624-0155-0(4)*, Inspiring Voices) Author Solutions, Inc.

Davis, Catherine. Abby & Alex Feel Their Hearts' Little. 2006. 57p. pap. 16.95 *(978-1-4241-4586-7(4))* PublishAmerica, Inc.

Davis, Jacky. Ladybug Girl's Day Out with Grandpa. Soman, David, illus. 2017. (Ladybug Girl Ser.). (ENG.). 40p. (J). (-k). 17.99 *(978-0-8037-4032-7(8)*, Dial Bks) Penguin Young Readers Group.

Davis, Jacky & Soman, David. Ladybug Girl Feels Happy. Soman, David, illus. 2012. (Ladybug Girl Ser.). (ENG., Illus.). 12p. (J). (gr. -1 — 1). bds. 5.99 *(978-0-8037-3890-4(0)*, Dial Bks) Penguin Young Readers Group.

Davis, Rachel. My Life at Mapleleaf Cabin. 2nd ed. 2004. (YA). per. 10.00 *(978-0-9741176-8-3(4))* Wu Li Turtle Corp.

Dawn, Nyrae, et al. Out of Play. 2013. (Entangled Teen Ser.). (ENG.). 320p. (YA). pap. 9.99 *(978-1-62266-010-0(2)*, 9781622660100) Entangled Publishing, LLC.

Day, Jan. The World's Greatest Explorer, 1 vol. Mason, Janeen, illus. 2009. (ENG.). 32p. (J). (gr. k-3). 16.99 *(978-1-58980-603-0(4))* Pelican Publishing Co., Inc.

De Anda, Diane. The Patchwork Garden. Ventura, Gabriela Baeza, tr. Kemarskaya, Oksana, illus. 2013.Tr. of Pedacitos de Huerto. (ENG & SPA.). 32p. (J). 16.95 *(978-1-55885-763-6(X)*, Piñata Books) Arte Publico Pr.

De Blumenthal, Verra X. K. Folk Tales from the Russian. 2008. 88p. pap. 8.95 *(978-1-60664-152-1(2))* Aegypan.

De la Peña, Matt. Last Stop on Market Street. Robinson, Christian, illus. 2015. (ENG.). 32p. (J). 16.99 *(978-0-399-25774-2(8)*, G.P. Putnam's Sons Books for Young Readers) Penguin Publishing Group.

Deak, Mike. The Magical Land of Kallamazoo. 2011. 52p. pap. 22.28 *(978-1-4520-4915-1(7))* AuthorHouse.

Dear Abuelita, 6, Pack. (Greetings Ser.: Vol. 2). (gr. 3-5). 31.00 *(978-0-7635-1765-6(8))* Rigby Education.

DeCarmelo, Marie. A Little Christmas Story. 2008. 40p. pap. 18.95 *(978-0-557-02844-3(2))* Lulu Pr., Inc.

DeFelice, Cynthia. Wild Life. 2011. (ENG.). 192p. (J). (gr. 3-7). 17.99 *(978-0-374-38001-4(5)*, 9780374380014, Farrar, Straus & Giroux (BYR)) Farrar, Straus & Giroux.

—Wild Life. 2013. (ENG.). 208p. (J). (gr. 3-7). pap. 7.99 *(978-1-250-03407-6(8)*, 9781250034076) Square Fish.

Defillippo, Steve. Growing up Nicely! Grammy Helps Adam Grow up & Develop Social Skills & Moral Values. 2012. 24p. (-18). pap. 15.99 *(978-1-4797-0957-1(3))* Xlibris Corp.

Del Greco, Marjorie. Special Time with Grandm: The Snow Fort. 2011. 24p. pap. 11.32 *(978-1-4634-3620-9(3))* AuthorHouse.

Delgado, Linda D. The Visitors. 2006. 169p. (J). per. *(978-0-9767861-1-5(7))* Muslim Writers Publishing.

Delisle, Annette Gonzalez. Nettey Loves Shoeboxes. Leyva, Juan Camilo, illus. 2011. 28p. pap. 9.99 *(978-1-61170-015-2(9))* Robertson Publishing.

Dellinger, Hampton. Thanks for Nothing: How Willie & Abe Saved Thanksgiving. 2008. 24p. 12.99 *(978-0-615-24971-1(X))* Dellinger, Hampton.

delMazo, Deborah. No Cookies for Christmas: The Story of Grandma's Missing Package. Horsfall, Jacqueline, ed. Balvanz, Gwynessa, illus. 2010. 32p. (J). pap. 9.95 *(978-0-615-32691-7(9))* Zoombird Bks.

Delp, Randy. The Ugly Bug & the Beautiful Butterfly. 2011. 76p. pap. *(978-1-4269-5354-5(2))* Trafford Publishing (UK) Ltd.

Demas, Corinne. Everything I Was. (Carolrhoda YA Ser.). (ENG.). 216p. (YA). (gr. 6-10). 2012. pap. 9.95 *(978-0-7613-9011-4(1))* 2011. 17.95 *(978-0-7613-7303-2(9))* Lerner Publishing Group. (Carolrhoda Lab™).

Demers, David & Demers, Lee Ann. My Grandpa Loves Trains: A Picture Storybook for Preschoolers. Demers, David, photos by. l.t. ed. 2005. (Illus.). 76p. (J). 27.95 *(978-0-922993-36-9(X))* Marquette Bks., LLC.

—My Grandpa Loves Trains: A Storybook for Preschoolers. Demers, David, photos by. l.t. ed. 2005. (Illus.). 76p. (J). per. 19.95 *(978-0-922993-23-9(8))* Marquette Bks., LLC.

Demetris, Jean. Grandma's Box of Memories: Helping Grandma to Remember. Demetris, Alex, illus. 2014. (ENG.). 32p. 17.95 *(978-1-84905-993-0(4)*, 2767) Kingsley, Jessica Pubs. GBR. Dist: Macmillan Distribution Ltd.

Dempsey, Kristy. Me with You. Denise, Christopher, illus. 2013. (ENG.). 28p. (J). (gr. -1-k). bds. 7.99 *(978-0-399-16262-6(3)*, Philomel Bks.) Penguin Young Readers Group.

DeMuth, Robert R. Grandpa's Treasures. 2006. (ENG., Illus.). 22p. (J). (gr. 2-4). pap. *(978-1-933255-20-0(X))* DNA Pr.

Denise, Anika. Baking Day at Grandma's. Denise, Christopher, illus. 2014. (ENG.). 32p. (J). (gr. -1-k). 16.99 *(978-0-399-24244-1(9)*, Philomel Bks.) Penguin Young Readers Group.

Denman, K. L. Rebel's Tag, 1 vol. 2007. (Orca Currents Ser.). (ENG.). (J). (gr. 5-9). 128p. pap. 9.95 *(978-1-55143-740-8(6))*; 112p. lib. bdg. 14.95 *(978-1-55143-742-2(2))* Orca Bk. Pubs. USA.

DePalma, Mary Newell. The Perfect Gift. 2010. (J). pap. *(978-0-545-15403-1(0)*, Levine, Arthur A. Bks.) Scholastic, Inc.

dePaola, Tomie. Nana Upstairs & Nana Downstairs. unabr. ed. 2006. (J). (gr. k-3). pap. 17.95 incl. audio *(978-0-8045-6943-9(6))*; pap. 19.95 incl. audio compact disk *(978-0-8045-4157-2(4))* Spoken Arts, Inc.

—Now One Foot, Now the Other. dePaola, Tomie, illus. (ENG., Illus.). 48p. (J). (gr. k-3). 2006. pap. 7.99 *(978-0-14-240104-0(8)*, Puffin Books) 2005. reprint ed. 16.99 *(978-0-399-24259-5(7)*, G.P. Putnam's Sons Books for Young Readers) Penguin Young Readers Group.

—Now One Foot, Now the Other. unabr. ed. 2006. (J). (gr. k-3). 27.95 incl. audio *(978-0-8045-6947-7(9))*; 29.95 incl. audio compact disk *(978-0-8045-4161-9(2))* Spoken Arts, Inc.

Derby, Sally. No Mush Today, 1 vol. Tadgell, Nicole, illus. 2008. (ENG.). 32p. (J). (gr. -1-3). 17.95 *(978-1-60060-238-2(X))* Lee & Low Bks., Inc.

—Sunday Shopping, 1 vol. Strickland, Shadra, illus. 2015. (ENG.). 32p. (J). 17.95 *(978-1-60060-438-6(2)*, 9781600000000) Lee & Low Bks., Inc.

Deriso, C. H. Elisabeth & the Unwanted Advice. 2016. (Babysitter Chronicles Ser.). (ENG., Illus.). 160p. (gr. 4-7). lib. bdg. 26.65 *(978-1-4965-2757-8(7))* Stone Arch Bks.

Deriso, Christine Hurley. Elisabeth & the Unwanted Advice. 2016. (Babysitter Chronicles Ser.). (ENG., Illus.). 160p. (gr. 4-7). pap. 6.95 *(978-1-4914-8864-5(6))* Stone Arch Bks.

Derubertis, Barbara. Izzy Impala's Imaginary Illnesses. 2010. pap. 45.32 *(978-0-7613-6511-2(7))* Kane Press, Inc.

deRubertis, Barbara. Izzy Impala's Imaginary Illnesses. Alley, R. W., illus. 2010. (Animal Antics A to Z Ser.). 32p. (J). (gr. -1-3). pap. 7.95 *(978-1-57565-313-6(3))*; lib. bdg. 22.60 *(978-1-57565-320-4(6))* Kane Press, Inc.

deRubertis, Barbara & DeRubertis, Barbara. Izzy Impala's Imaginary Illnesses. Alley, R. W., illus. 2012. (Animal Antics A to Z Ser.). 32p. (J). (gr. 2 — 1). cd-rom 7.95 *(978-1-57565-402-7(4))* Kane Press, Inc.

Desio, Delores. The Legend of Ruby O'Grady: Grandma Was A Hippie. 2011. 122p. pap. 19.95 *(978-1-4560-7039-7(8))* America Star Bks.

Devlin, Ivy. Low Red Moon. 2010. (ENG., Illus.). 256p. (YA). (gr. 7-18). 16.99 *(978-1-59990-510-5(8)*, 9781599905105, Bloomsbury USA Childrens) Bloomsbury Publishing USA.

Devlin, Wende. Cranberry Thanksgiving. Devlin, Harry, illus. 2012. (ENG.). 32p. (J). (gr. -1-3). 18.95 *(978-1-930900-63-9(5))* Purple Hse. Pr.

Dewdney, Anna & Wells, Rosemary. Llama Llama Gram & Grandpa. 2015. (Llama Llama Ser.). (ENG., Illus.). 40p. (J). (-k). bds. 17.99 *(978-0-670-01396-8(X)*, Viking Books for Young Readers) Penguin Young Readers Group.

Dickson, Diane. Daisy & the Dust Angel. 2010. 35p. pap. 20.50 *(978-1-4452-1375-0(3))* Lulu Pr., Inc.

Dillon, Elizabeth. Forgetful Lucy Goes to the Ranch. 2012. 62p. pap. 19.50 *(978-1-60911-688-0(7)*, Strategic Bk. Publishing) Strategic Book Publishing & Rights Agency (SBPRA).

Dilz. My Grandma Could Do Anything in Hawaii. 2006. (J). 7.95 *(978-0-9758704-2-6(4))* Ric Design LLC.

Dilz, Ric. My Grandma Could Do Anything! 2008. (J). 14.95 *(978-0-9758704-3-3(2))* Ric Design LLC.

—My Grandma Could Do Anything in Hawaii! 2008. (Illus.). 32p. (J). 14.95 *(978-0-9758704-5-7(9))* Ric Design LLC.

—My Grandma Could Do Anything in the Great Outdoors! 2008. (Illus.). 32p. (J). 14.95 *(978-0-9758704-6-4(7))* Ric Design LLC.

Dionne, Erin. Moxie & the Art of Rule Breaking: A 14-Day Mystery. (ENG.). (J). (gr. 5). 2014. 288p. pap. 6.99 *(978-0-14-242614-2(8)*, Puffin Books) 2013. 256p. 16.99 *(978-0-8037-3871-3(4)*, Dial Bks) Penguin Young Readers Group.

Disney Book Group Staff & Richards, Kitty. The Lost Tiara. Disney Storybook Art Team & Studio Iboix Staff, illus. 2012. (Jewel Story Ser.). (ENG.). 96p. (J). (gr. 1-3). pap. 4.99 *(978-1-4231-5197-5(6))* Disney Pr.

Dittmar, Gordie Cheney. A Message for Natalie. 2010. 20p. pap. 18.49 *(978-1-4520-5980-8(2))* AuthorHouse.

Dodson, Bert. Helping Santa: My First Christmas Adventure with Grandma. Dodson, Bert, illus. 2011. (ENG., Illus.). 32p. (J). (gr. 1-3). 17.95 *(978-1-59373-093-2(4))* Bunker Hill Publishing, Inc.

Dodson, Bert, illus. Super Grandpa. 2nd rev. ed. 2005. 32p. (J). (gr. -1 — 1). 18.95 *(978-1-889910-33-8(3))* Tortuga Pr.

Doherty, Glen. The Magic Sucker or How Love Really Works. 2012. 24p. pap. 12.99 *(978-1-4797-0978-6(6))* Xlibris Corp.

Dolan, Penny. Plip & Plop. Smith, Lisa, illus. 2004. (Read-It! Readers Ser.). (J). lib. bdg. 18.60 *(978-1-4048-0551-4(6))* Picture Window Bks.

Dolson, Carol Bland. Hattie & the Higgledy-Piggledy Hedge. Rabon, Elaine Hearn, illus. 2012. (ENG.). 32p. (J). 18.95 *(978-0-9827614-4-1(9)*, 9780982761441) Moose Hill Bks., Inc.

Domanska, Mary Ann. Emic Rizzle, Tinkerer. 2016. (J). pap. **(978-1-59021-777-1(2))** Lethe Pr.

Donaldson, Babette. Emma Lea's Magic Teapot. Van Dijk, Jerianne, illus. 2007. 32p. (J). lib. bdg. 16.95 *(978-0-9792612-1-3(X))* Blue Gate Bks.

Donoghue, Emma. The Lotterys Plus One. Hadilaksono, Caroline, illus. 2017. (ENG.). 320p. (J). (gr. 3-7). 17.99 *(978-0-545-92581-5(9))* Scholastic, Inc.

Dorros, Arthur. Abuelo. Colón, Raúl, illus. 2014. (ENG.). 32p. (J). (gr. -1-3). 17.99 *(978-0-06-168627-6(1))* HarperCollins Pubs.

Dos Santos, Lisa. Grandpa's Bridge. 2004. (Illus.). 32p. (J). *(978-0-9708571-1-8(X))* Mango Tree Pr.

DOT. My Grandkids Need to Go Home!, 1 vol. 2010. 20p. pap. 24.95 *(978-1-4489-9254-6(0))* PublishAmerica, Inc.

Douglass, E. The Squirrel Friends Adventures: The Monster & the Great Storm. 2013. 100p. 19.95 *(978-1-4759-6640-4(7))*; pap. 9.95 *(978-1-4759-6638-1(5))* iUniverse, Inc.

Dowell, F. M. C. The Little Palace. 2004. (YA). per. 14.95 *(978-1-932205-48-0(9))* Word Association Pubs.

Dowell, Frances O'Roark. Chicken Boy. Krause, George, photos by. 2007. (ENG., Illus.). 224p. (J). (gr. 5-9). pap. 6.99 *(978-1-4169-3482-0(0)*, Atheneum Bks. for Young Readers) Simon & Schuster Children's Publishing.

—Chicken Boy. 2005. (ENG., Illus.). 208p. (J). (gr. 5-9). 17.99 *(978-0-689-85816-1(7)*, Atheneum Bks. for Young Readers) Simon & Schuster Children's Publishing.

Dower, Laura. Maggie's Magic Chocolate Moon. Lazuli, Lilly, illus. 2016. (Dessert Diaries). (ENG.). 160p. (gr. 4-5). pap. 5.95 *(978-1-4965-4141-3(3))*; lib. bdg. 26.65 *(978-1-4965-3121-6(3))* Stone Arch Bks.

Dowler, Pattie. Suzie Squirrel & the Disappearing Pies. 2012. 24p. pap. 24.95 *(978-1-4626-7636-1(7))* America Star Bks.

Dowling, Iris Gray. A Pony for My Birthday. Bouthyette, Valerie, illus. 2012. 36p. pap. 10.99 *(978-1-937129-50-7(0))* Faithful Life Pubs.

Downham, Jenny. Unbecoming. (ENG.). 384p. (J). (gr. 9-9). 2017. pap. 9.99 **(978-1-338-16072-7(9))** 2016. 17.99 *(978-0-545-90717-0(9))* Scholastic, Inc.

Doyle, Malachy, et al. Owain A'r Mynydd. 2005. (WEL., Illus.). 32p. pap. *(978-0-86381-738-0(6))* Gwasg Carreg Gwalch.

Doyle, Patrick H. T. Edgar Font's Hunt for a House to Haunt: Adventure One: the Castle Tower Lighthouse. 2006. (Illus.). 213p. (J). (gr. -1). per. 6.99 *(978-0-9786132-0-4(1))* Armadillo Bks.

—Edgar Font's Hunt for a House to Haunt: Adventure Three: the Flint Island Treehouse. 2008. (Illus.). 300p. (J). per. 7.99 *(978-0-9786132-2-8(8))* Armadillo Bks.

—Edgar Font's Hunt for a House to Haunt: Adventure Two: the Fakersville Power Station. Doyle, Patrick H. T., illus. 2007. (Edgar Font's Hunt for a House to Haunt Ser.). (Illus.). 303p. (J). (gr. 4-7). per. 7.99 *(978-0-9786132-1-1(X))* Armadillo Bks.

Doyle, Roddy. A Greyhound of a Girl. 2013. (ENG.). 224p. (YA). (gr. 3-7). pap. 7.95 *(978-1-4197-0798-8(1)*, Amulet Bks.) Abrams, Inc.

Dream Catchers - Evaluation Guide: Evaluation Guide. 2006. (J). *(978-1-55942-403-5(6))* Witcher Productions.

Drew, Joyce. Grandma's Adventures with Benjamin. Drew, Benjamin, illus. 2013. 16p. pap. 24.95 *(978-1-63004-098-7(3))* America Star Bks.

EFG

Driggs, Howard R. When Grandfather Was a Boy. Hales, J. Rulon, illus. 2011. 88p. 38.95 *(978-1-258-07716-7(7))* Literary Licensing, LLC.

Drinnon, Sheila. Cuddles. 2008. 24p. pap. 24.95 *(978-1-60474-857-4(5))* America Star Bks.

Duble, Kathleen Benner. Bravo Zulu, Samantha!, 1 vol. 2007. (ENG.). 144p. (J). (gr. 3-7). 14.95 *(978-1-56145-401-3(X))* Peachtree Pubs.

Dude, Rosanna Eubank. Natalia's Favorite Color. Eubank, Patricia Reeder, illus. 2008. (ENG.). 32p. (J). (gr. -1-3). 12.99 *(978-0-8249-5523-6(4),* Ideal Pubns.) Worthy Publishing.

Duder, Tessa. Carpet of Dreams. Wilson, Mark, illus. 2008. 32p. pap. *(978-0-207-19991-2(4))* HarperCollins Pubs. Australia.

Dudgeon, Pat & Dudgeon, Laura. Lilli & Her Shadow. 2010. (Waarda Series for Young Readers Ser.). (ENG.). 48p. (J). (gr. 2-4). pap. 7.00 *(978-1-921361-97-5(2))* Fremantle Pr. AUS. Dist: Independent Pubs. Group.

Duncan, Brenda. Reese - the Dog Who Almost Ruined Christmas. 2012. 24p. pap. 17.99 *(978-1-4772-6105-7(2))* AuthorHouse.

Dunham, Wendy. My Name Is River. 2015. (ENG.). 144p. (J). (gr. 2-7). pap. 7.99 *(978-0-7369-6461-6(4))* Harvest Hse. Pubs.

Dunn, Carrie. Gracie Goes to Grandma's, 1 vol. 2010. 36p. pap. 24.95 *(978-1-4489-5483-4(5))* PublishAmerica, Inc.

Durben, Toni. Grandpa Isn't Grandpa Anymore. Mulholland, Bailey, illus. 2006. (J). lib. bdg. *(978-1-933556-33-8(1))* Publishers' Graphics, L.L.C.

Durrant, Geraldine. Pirate Gran. Forshall, Rose, illus. 2009. 32p. (J). 19.95 *(978-0-948065-96-5(6))* National Maritime Museum GBR. Dist: Independent Pubs. Group.

Duvall, John. The Great Spruce. Gibbon, Rebecca, illus. 2016. (ENG.). 40p. (J). (gr. k-3). 17.99 *(978-0-399-16084-4(1),* G.P. Putnam's Sons Books for Young Readers) Penguin Young Readers Group.

Dyan, Penelope. Grandma's Suitcase — -Where a Kid Can Always Find a Surprise! Dyan, Penelope, illus. 2008. (Illus.). 44p. pap. 11.95 *(978-1-935118-36-7(6))* Bellissima Publishing, LLC.

—Great Grandma Is Getting Old. Dyan, Penelope, illus. 2010. (Illus.). 42p. pap. 11.95 *(978-1-935118-97-8(8))* Bellissima Publishing, LLC.

Dyer, K. C. A Walk Through a Window. 2009. (ENG.). 240p. (J). (gr. 5-7). pap. 12.50 *(978-0-385-66637-4(3),* Doubleday Canada) Penguin Random House Canada Young Readers CAN. Dist: Penguin Random Hse. LLC.

Eagar, Lindsay. Hour of the Bees. (ENG.). 368p. (J). (gr. 5-9). 2017. pap. 8.99 ***(978-0-7636-9120-2(8))*** 2016. 16.99 *(978-0-7636-7922-4(4))* Candlewick Pr.

Eagle Feathers, 6 vols. (Multicultural Programs Ser.). 16p. (gr. 1-6). 31.95 *(978-0-7802-8327-5(9))* Wright Group/McGraw-Hill.

East, Bob. Tommy Cat & the Haunted Well, 1 vol. 2009. 42p. pap. 24.95 *(978-1-60703-754-5(8))* America Star Bks.

Ebel, Sherry. Cassie's Magic Doors. 2008. 28p. pap. 15.99 *(978-1-4363-2970-5(1))* Xlibris Corp.

Eberhart, Nancy. The Adventures of Granny: Granny Goes to the Zoo. Pyers, Kelsey, illus. 2007. (J). 24p. per. 10.99 *(978-1-59879-372-7(1));* (gr. -1-3). 13.99 *(978-1-59879-373-4(X))* Lifevest Publishing, Inc.

Edge, A. M. Frankie Feinstein & the Fenworld Thief-Takers. 2013. 156p. (J). pap. *(978-1-78299-419-0(X))* FeedARead.com.

Edman Lamote, Lisa. A Day Out for Opus. Wilson, Alisha, illus. 2006. (Bookmann Family Presents Ser.). 32p. (J). (gr. k-3). 15.99 *(978-1-933673-03-5(6),* BookMann Pr.) Mann Publishing Group.

—Don't Judge a Book by Its Cover. Wilson, Alisha, illus. 2006. (Bookmann Family Presents Ser.). 32p. (J). (gr. k-3). 15.99 *(978-1-933673-01-1(X),* BookMann Pr.) Mann Publishing Group.

Edward, Judy. Calvin Can - Be Happy. Edward, Aaron, illus. 2012. 32p. pap. *(978-1-4602-0097-1(7))* FriesenPress.

Edwards, Jeannell. A New House for Jennie. 2011. 20p. pap. 16.95 *(978-1-4512-2485-6(0))* America Star Bks.

Edwards, Michelle. Zero Grandparents. 2005. (Jackson Friends Bks.). (Illus.). 59p. (gr. 1-4). 15.95 *(978-0-7569-5774-2(5))* Perfection Learning Corp.

Eenie Meanie Me & the Very Sad Day. 2005. (J). *(978-0-9772878-0-2(7))* Bishop, Susan Lynn.

Eggers, Jeanette S. Grandmas Don't Rollerskate. 2008. 24p. pap. 12.99 *(978-1-4389-1434-3(2))* AuthorHouse.

—Grandmas Don't Tilt-A-Whirl(r). 2009. 44p. pap. 18.49 *(978-1-4490-0546-7(2))* AuthorHouse.

Eggleton, Jill. Granny Groggin: Big Book Only. (Sails Literacy Ser.). 24p. (gr. 3-18). 27.00 *(978-0-7578-6981-5(5))* Rigby Education.

Ehrenberg, Pamela. Ethan, Suspended. 2009. (ENG.). 272p. (J). (gr. 6-9). pap. 8.50 *(978-0-8028-5317-2(X))* 2007. 266p. (YA). (gr. 7-18). 16.00 *(978-0-8028-5324-0(2),* Eerdmans Bks For Young Readers) Eerdmans, William B. Publishing Co.

Eisner, Fern. Saba's Room. 2009. 28p. pap. 15.99 *(978-1-4415-1843-9(6))* Xlibris Corp.

Ellsworth, Mark R. Grawnma Becky's Bread. 2005. (J). pap. 8.00 *(978-0-8059-6631-2(5))* Dorrance Publishing Co., Inc.

Elster, Jean Alicia. I'll Do the Right Thing. Tadgell, Nicole, illus. 2010. (ENG.). 32p. (J). pap. 11.99 *(978-0-8170-1658-6(9))* Judson Pr.

Enderle, Dotti. Book 14: Plop!, 1 vol. 2014. (Ghost Detectors Set 3 Ser.). (ENG., Illus.). 80p. (J). (gr. 2-5). lib. bdg. 27.07 *(978-1-62402-002-5(X),* Calico Chapter Bks) Magic Wagon.

Enderle, Dotti & Sansum, Vicki. Grandpa for Sale. Gentry, T. Kyle, illus. 2007. (ENG.). 32p. (J). (gr. k-3). 17.95 *(978-0-9729225-8-6(X))* Flashlight Pr.

England, Kathryn. Grandfather's Wrinkles. McFarland, Richard, illus. 2007. (ENG.). 32p. (J). (gr. k-3). 15.95 *(978-0-9729225-9-3(8))* Flashlight Pr.

Erickson, Mary Ellen. Snowstorm. 2005. (J). *(978-0-9765453-3-0(0))* Dr. Mary's Bks.

—What Happened to the Deer? Peanut Butter Club Mysteries. 2007. 182p. (J). 23.95 *(978-0-595-68396-3(7));* per. 13.95 *(978-0-595-42799-4(5))* iUniverse, Inc.

—Who Jinxed the CG Ranch? 2009. 196p. 24.95 *(978-1-4401-4218-5(1));* pap. 14.95 *(978-1-4401-4216-1(5))* iUniverse, Inc.

Errico, Jessica / C. Grandpa's Magical Accordion. Star, Brenda, illus. 2007. 28p. (J). pap. 17.95 incl. cd-rom *(978-0-9800577-0-6(1))* Three Part Harmony LLC.

Ervin, Randy. Maycroft From 232nd. 2010. 150p. (YA). pap. 10.00 *(978-0-578-05732-3(8))* Ervin, Randy.

Escalante, Travis. The Story of Rocks & Balloons. 2013. 28p. 16.99 *(978-0-9897168-5-7(6))* Mindstir Media.

Esdaille-Richardson, Eudora. Malcolm & the Money Tree. Williams, Christopher, illus. 2014. 31p. (J). pap. *(978-1-934370-49-0(5))* Editorial Campana.

Evans, Connie. Sasha & Babushka: A Story of Russia. Schpitalnik, Vladimir, illus. (Make Friends Around the World Ser.). (ENG.). 32p. (J). (gr. k-3). 8.95 *(978-1-59249-446-0(3),* SC8007) Soundprints.

Evans, Cordelia. Olivia & Grandma's Visit. Johnson, Shane L., illus. 2013. (Olivia TV Tie-In Ser.). (ENG.). 24p. (J). (gr. -1-2). pap. 3.99 *(978-1-4424-4586-4(6),* Simon Spotlight) Simon Spotlight.

Evans, Cornelia & Shpitalnik, Vladimir. Sasha & Babushka: A Story of Russia. 2005. (Make Friends Around the World Ser.). (ENG., Illus.). 32p. (J). (gr. k-3). 19.95 *(978-1-59249-445-3(5),* BC8007) Soundprints.

Everett-Camplin, Helen. Grandad's Magic Gadgets. 2009. (ENG.). 64p. pap. 12.00 *(978-84-8323-522-5(6))* Cambridge Univ. Pr.

Facey, Paulet. Annie & the Washpan of Ripe Bananas. 2012. 24p. pap. 15.99 *(978-1-4797-2659-2(1))* Xlibris Corp.

Faircloth, M. L. Shawn's Book about Grandfathers. 2013. 26p. pap. 11.95 *(978-1-61863-461-0(5))* Bookstand Publishing.

Fairgray, Richard & Jones, Terry, illus. My Grandpa Is a Dinosaur. 2016. (ENG.). 32p. (J). (gr. -1-k). 16.99 *(978-1-63450-632-8(4),* Sky Pony Pr.) Skyhorse Publishing Co., Inc.

Falla, Lynne. World of the Weeples: Sophie & the Weeples. 2012. 24p. pap. 15.99 *(978-1-4771-2078-1(5))* Xlibris Corp.

Fallon, Kevin A. Rest in Peas: What Does that Mean? 2005. per. 12.95 *(978-1-59196-943-3(3))* Instant Pub.

Farnsley, Kathleen. This Little Piggy Named Pony. 2008. 24p. pap. 12.99 *(978-1-4389-2659-9(6))* AuthorHouse.

Farrell, Lynne. Bennie's Forever Gift. 2012. 40p. pap. 15.95 *(978-1-4497-6133-2(X),* WestBow Pr.) Author Solutions, Inc.

Farren, Rick. Eliza's Wish. 2007. 154p. (J). per. 14.95 *(978-0-9794863-8-8(6))* Summerland Publishing.

—Grandpa & the Pirate. 2003. (J). per. 9.95 *(978-0-9728716-4-8(0))* Journey Pubns., LLC.

—Grandpa & the Pirate. 2007. 49p. (J). per. 9.95 *(978-0-9794863-6-4(X))* Summerland Publishing.

—The Secret of the Lighthouse. 2007. 127p. (J). (gr. 1-7). per. 12.95 *(978-0-9794863-7-1(8))* Summerland Publishing.

Feiffer, Kate. Signed by Zelda. (ENG.). 240p. (J). (gr. 3-7). 2013. pap. 6.99 *(978-1-4424-3332-8(9))* 2012. (Illus.). 16.99 *(978-1-4424-3331-1(0))* Simon & Schuster/Paula Wiseman Bks. (Simon & Schuster/Paula Wiseman Bks.).

Fellure, Kathy Boyd. Mr Snowman Ate Our Picnic Lunch. 2011. 36p. pap. 16.95 *(978-0-557-79684-7(9))* Lulu Pr., Inc.

Ferguson, Dwayne. Mess at Loch Ness. 2004. (Kid Caramel). 72p. (J). pap. 4.50 *(978-0-940975-74-3(2),* Sankofa Bks.) Just Us Bks., Inc.

Ferrier, Charlotte. Little Red Riding Hood. 2016. (Fairytale Cottages Ser.). (ENG.). 12p. (J). (gr. -1-k). bds. 8.99 *(978-0-7641-6818-5(5))* Barron's Educational Series, Inc.

Fiford, Tanya. How to Bake Grandm. 2009. (Illus.). 16p. pap. 8.49 *(978-1-4389-6352-5(1))* AuthorHouse.

Filipi, Carmen. The Marvelous Fountain: And other stories my grandma told Me. Long, Dave, illus. 2007.Tr. of Fuente Maravillosa y otros cuentos que me conto mi Abuela. (ENG & SPA.). 55p. (J). per. 14.95 *(978-0-9797814-0-7(X))* Hispanic Institute of Social Issues.

Fine, Arnold & Spielman, Howard. Too Many Toys. (J). 9.99 *(978-0-89906-422-2(1),* TOYH) Mesorah Pubns., Ltd.

Finley, Lou. How to Do Nothin' 2010. 24p. 12.99 *(978-1-4520-8438-1(6))* AuthorHouse.

Finley, Martha. Christmas with Grandma Elsie. 2006. 28.95 *(978-1-4218-2988-3(6));* pap. 13.95 *(978-1-4218-3088-9(4))* 1st World Publishing, Inc.

—Christmas with Grandma Elsie. l.t. ed. 2007. (ENG.). 216p. pap. 22.99 *(978-1-4346-2529-8(X))* Creative Media Partners, LLC.

—Elsie at Home, Vol. 22. 320p. (gr. 4-7). pap. 5.95 *(978-1-58182-175-8(1),* Cumberland Hse.) Sourcebooks, Inc.

Fischer, Kelly. The Most Beautiful Color of All. Duckworth, Michelle, illus. 2011. (ENG.). 36p. (J). 19.50 *(978-1-58385-281-1(6))* ktf-writers-studio.

Fischer, P. J. Grandma & Her Chocolate Labrador. 2014. (ENG.). 36p. (J). (gr. k-2). 14.99 *(978-0-9905721-8-3(8))* Minted Prose, LLC.

Fisher, Phyllis Mae Richardson. Twiglet the Little Christmas Tree. Fisher, Phyllis Mae Richardson & Fisher, Douglas W., illus. 2003. (J). 30.00 *(978-0-9745615-1-6(7),* Twiglet The Little Christmas Tree); 186p. 12.00 *(978-0-9745615-4-7(1))* PJs Corner.

Fisher, Rick. Unknown Heroes. 2007. (ENG., Illus.). 32p. (J). per. 14.95 *(978-1-59800-899-9(4))* Outskirts Pr., Inc.

Fisher, Terri. The Adventures of Grandma Terri: Grandma Terri's Hospital Visit. 2012. 24p. pap. 13.95 *(978-1-4685-4647-7(3))* AuthorHouse.

Fishman, Linda Charles. The Little Girl Who Loves Colors: Book Four of Grandma's Girls. 2012. 24p. pap. 17.99 *(978-1-4772-9277-8(2))* AuthorHouse.

—The Little Girl Who Loves Make Believe: Book 2 of Grandma's Girls. 2012. 24p. pap. 17.99 *(978-1-4685-4467-1(5))* AuthorHouse.

—The Little Girl Who Loves Music: Book Three of Grandma's Girls. 2012. 24p. pap. 17.99 *(978-1-4772-6156-9(7))* AuthorHouse.

Fite, Ramona. A Boy & His God. Monick, Susie, illus. 2012. 36p. 22.50 *(978-1-937763-37-4(4))* Published by Westview, Inc.

Fitzgerald, Sarah Moore. Back to Blackbrick. 2013. (ENG., Illus.). 208p. (J). (gr. 5-9). 15.99 *(978-1-4424-8155-8(2),* McElderry, Margaret K. Bks.) McElderry, Margaret K. Bks.

Fitzl, Richelle Kristi, illus. Grandma's Garden. 2004. (J). *(978-0-9741657-1-4(9))* Galaxia Publishing Group, LLC.

Fiz. George & the Treasure Box Mysteries. 2012. (Illus.). 105p. pap. 8.49 *(978-1-78035-223-7(9),* Fastprint Publishing) Upfront Publishing Ltd. GBR. Dist: Printondemand-worldwide.com.

Flamburis, Georgia M. How Kahi's Kitten Got Its Name. 2012. 34p. pap. 9.99 *(978-0-615-47908-8(1))* Flamburis, Georgia.

Flatley, Paula Chorman. Olivia's Tree, 1 vol. Palmer, Kimmy, illus. 2010. 16p. pap. 24.95 *(978-1-4489-5870-2(9))* America Star Bks.

Flaxman, Andrew. Little Red Riding Hood: The Classic Grimm's Fairy Tale. Delisa, Patricia, illus. 2006. 32p. (J). (gr. -1-3). 14.95 *(978-0-88010-571-2(2),* Bell Pond Bks.) SteinerBooks, Inc.

Fleischman, Paul. The Matchbox Diary. Ibatoulline, Bagram, illus. (ENG.). 40p. (J). (gr. 1-4). 2016. 7.99 *(978-0-7636-7638-4(1))* 2013. 16.99 *(978-0-7636-4601-1(6))* Candlewick Pr.

Fleming, Theresa. Going Home with Jesus, 1 vol. Fleming, Yvonne B., illus. 2009. 22p. pap. 24.95 *(978-1-60813-703-9(1))* America Star Bks.

Flood, Pansie Hart. Sometimey Friend. Marshall, Felicia, illus. 2005. 124p. (J). (gr. 3-7). 15.95 *(978-1-57505-866-5(9))* Lerner Publishing Group.

Flor Ada, Alma. Celebrate Hanukkah with Bubbe's Tales. Hayes, Joe & Franco, Sharon, trs. Epelbaum, Mariano, illus. 2007. (Cuentos para Celebrar / Stories to Celebrate Ser.). 30p. (gr. k-6). per. 11.95 *(978-1-59820-134-5(4))* Santillana USA Publishing Co., Inc.

—I Love Saturdays y Domingos. Savadier, Elivia, illus. 2004. (ENG.). 32p. (J). (gr. -1-3). reprint ed. 7.99 *(978-0-689-87409-3(X),* Atheneum Bks. for Young Readers) Simon & Schuster Children's Publishing.

Flor Ada, Alma & Zubizarreta, Gabriel M. Con Cariño, Amalia. (SPA., Illus.). (J). (gr. 3-7). 2013. 160p. pap. 6.99 *(978-1-4424-2406-7(0))* 2012. 144p. 15.99 *(978-1-4424-2405-0(2),* Atheneum Bks. for Young Readers) Simon & Schuster Children's Publishing.

—Love, Amalia. (ENG., Illus.). (J). (gr. 3-7). 2013. 160p. pap. 6.99 *(978-1-4424-2403-6(6))* 2012. 144p. 15.99 *(978-1-4424-2402-9(8))* Simon & Schuster Children's Publishing. (Atheneum Bks. for Young Readers).

Flowers, J. J. Juan Pablo & the Butterflies. 2017. (ENG., Illus.). 224p. (YA). (gr. 9-12). 17.99 *(978-1-5072-0214-2(8),* Simon Pulse) Simon Pulse.

Fogelin, Adrian. Sister Spider Knows All, 1 vol. 2007. (ENG.). 224p. (J). (gr. 3-7). pap. 6.95 *(978-1-56145-386-3(2))* Peachtree Pubs.

—Summer on the Moon, 1 vol. (ENG.). 256p. (J). 2014. (gr. 3-6). pap. 7.95 *(978-1-56145-785-4(X))* 2012. 15.95 *(978-1-56145-626-0(8))* Peachtree Pubs.

Fontenot, Martha Leonard. Grandma Liza's Rainbow Cake. 2009. 28p. pap. 13.99 *(978-1-4490-0772-0(4))* AuthorHouse.

Forte, Lauren. Olivia Makes Memories. 2015. (Olivia 8x8 Ser.). lib. bdg. 13.55 *(978-0-606-37868-0(5))* Turtleback Bks.

Forward, Toby. The Wolf's Story: What Really Happened to Little Red Riding Hood. Cohen, Izhar, illus. 2005. (ENG.). 32p. (J). (gr. -1-3). 17.99 *(978-0-7636-2785-0(2))* Candlewick Pr.

Fotheringham, Juanita. A Little Ranch on the Side. 2013. 38p. pap. 9.99 *(978-1-62697-215-5(X))* Salem Author Services.

Francis, Lee DeCora. Kunu's Basket: A Story of Indian Island, 1 vol. Drucker, Susan, illus. 2012. (ENG.). 32p. (J). 16.95 *(978-0-88448-330-4(4))* Tilbury Hse. Pubs.

Franco, Betsy. Going to Grandma's Farm. 2004. (Rookie Reader Español Ser.). (ENG., Illus.). 24p. (J). (gr. k-2). pap. 4.95 *(978-0-516-27787-5(1),* Children's Pr.) Scholastic Library Publishing.

Francois, Rose Darlie. The Sixteen Eggs & the Frying Pan Clock. 2009. 41p. pap. 18.00 *(978-0-557-07155-5(0))* Lulu Pr., Inc.

Franjelica. Two Little Memory Collectors. 2011. 28p. pap. 24.95 *(978-1-4560-0908-3(7))* America Star Bks.

Frazier, Angie. The Mastermind Plot. 2012. (ENG.). 240p. (J). (gr. 3-7). 16.99 *(978-0-545-20864-2(5),* Scholastic Pr.) Scholastic, Inc.

Frazier, Laurence. Cranky the Rooster. 2011. 24p. pap. 12.79 *(978-1-4567-6258-2(3))* AuthorHouse.

Frazier, Sundee T. Brendan Buckley's Universe & Everything in It. 2008. (ENG.). 208p. (J). (gr. 3-7). 6.99 *(978-0-440-42206-8(X),* Yearling) Random Hse. Children's Bks.

—The Other Half of My Heart. 2011. (ENG.). 304p. (J). (gr. 3-7). 7.99 *(978-0-440-24006-8(9),* Yearling) Random Hse. Children's Bks.

Frederick, Heather Vogel. Once upon a Toad. 2012. (ENG., Illus.). 272p. (J). (gr. 5-9). 16.99 *(978-1-4169-8478-8(X),* Simon & Schuster Bks. For Young Readers) Simon & Schuster Bks. For Young Readers.

Fredericks, Anthony D. The Tsunami Quilt: Grandfather's Story. Yee, Tammy, illus. rev. ed. 2007. (Tales of Young Americans Ser.). (ENG.). 32p. (J). (gr. -1-3). 17.95 *(978-1-58536-313-1(8))* Sleeping Bear Pr.

Freedman, Claire. Good Night, Sleep Tight! Tyger, Rory, illus. 2007. 32p. (J). (gr. -1-1). pap. 6.95 *(978-1-58925-405-3(8))* Tiger Tales.

—My Grandparents Love Me. Abbot, Judi, illus. 2016. (ENG.). 32p. (J). (gr. -1-3). 17.99 *(978-1-4814-7937-0(7),* Simon & Schuster/Paula Wiseman Bks.) Simon & Schuster/Paula Wiseman Bks.

French, Simon. Where in the World, 1 vol. 208p. (J). (gr. 3-7). 2008. (ENG.). pap. 7.95 *(978-1-56145-443-3(5))* 2003. 14.95 *(978-1-56145-292-7(0),* Q34443) Peachtree Pubs.

French, Vivian. I Love You, Grandpa. Kubick, Dana, illus. 2006. (ENG.). 32p. (J). (gr. -1-2). 5.99 *(978-0-7636-2748-5(8))* Candlewick Pr.

—Yucky Worms. Ahlberg, Jessica, illus. 2012. (Read & Wonder Ser.). (ENG.). 32p. (J). (gr. -1-3). pap. 6.99 *(978-0-7636-5817-5(0))* Candlewick Pr.

—Yucky Worms. 2012. (Read & Wonder Ser.). lib. bdg. 17.20 *(978-0-606-23803-8(4),* Turtleback) Turtleback Bks.

Friedman, Becky. Tiger Family Trip. 2017. (Daniel Tiger's Neighborhood 8X8 Ser.). lib. bdg. 13.55 ***(978-0-606-39755-1(8))*** Turtleback Bks.

Friedman, Laurie. A Twist of Fate. Shaloshvili, Natasha, illus. (Mostly Miserable Life of April Sinclair Ser.: Vol. 7). (ENG.). 168p. (gr. 5-9). 2017. (J). pap. 5.95 ***(978-1-5124-5866-4(X))*** 2016. 17.95 *(978-1-4677-8590-7(3))* 2016. 35.99 *(978-1-5124-0899-7(9))* Lerner Publishing Group. (Darby Creek).

Frost, Robert Temple. Long Trip Home: Stand up Paddleboard Fantasy. 2013. 82p. pap. 10.95 *(978-1-62212-924-9(5),* Strategic Bk. Publishing) Strategic Book Publishing & Rights Agency (SBPRA).

Frueh, Pamela. Who Loves Pugs? 2007. 24p. 10.95 *(978-1-4303-2286-3(1))* Lulu Pr., Inc.

Fry, Stella. Grandpa's Garden. Jago & Moxley, Sheila, illus. 2012. (ENG.). 40p. (J). 16.99 *(978-1-84686-053-9(9))* Barefoot Bks., Inc.

—Grandpa's Garden. 2012. lib. bdg. 19.65 *(978-0-606-23824-3(7),* Turtleback) Turtleback Bks.

Fry, Stella & Moxley, Sheila. Grandpa's Garden. Moxley, Sheila, illus. 2012. (ENG., Illus.). 40p. (J). (gr. -1-2). pap. 8.99 *(978-1-84686-809-2(2))* Barefoot Bks., Inc.

Fuller, Susan. Grandma's Wisdom: Secure in His Love, Faith & Joy. 2004. 32p. (J). per. 14.95 *(978-1-58930-106-1(4))* Selah Publishing Group, LLC.

Funke, Julie Ann & Foekel, Alessandra. Conner's Cubbyhole. 2004. 20p. pap. 24.95 *(978-1-4137-3192-7(9))* PublishAmerica, Inc.

Fyfe, Connie. Grandma's Christmas Candy. 2011. 24p. pap. 12.79 *(978-1-4567-5437-2(8))* AuthorHouse.

Gail, Ginnie. The Great Pigeon Race. Griffin, Don, illus. 2008. 28p. per. 24.95 *(978-1-4241-9457-5(1))* America Star Bks.

Gales, Rick. Granny Puckerlips: Keepin' It Real with Kindness & Respect. 2013. 108p. (gr. 9-12). pap. 11.95 *(978-1-4908-0437-8(4),* WestBow Pr.) Author Solutions, Inc.

Galindo, Claudia & Pluecker, John. Do You Know the Cucuy? Conoces Al Cucuy? Coombs, Jonathan, illus. 2008. (SPA & ENG.). 32p. (J). (gr. -1-2). 16.95 *(978-1-55885-492-5(4),* Piñata Books) Arte Publico Pr.

Galindo, Mary Sue. Icy Watermelon/Sandia Fria. Rodriguez Howard, Pauline & Howard, Pauline Rodriguez, illus. 2008. (J). (gr. -1-2). pap. 7.95 *(978-1-55885-307-2(3),* Piñata Books) Arte Publico Pr.

Gansie, Sherry. Oops, a Curious Horse Big Book. Light, Carol, illus. 2003. 56p. (J). *(978-0-9745803-6-4(8))* Little Big Tomes.

—Oops, a Curious Horse Little Book. Light, Carol, illus. 2003. 52p. (J). *(978-0-9745803-7-1(6))* Little Big Tomes.

—Oops, a Curious Horse Story Book Reader. Light, Carol, illus. 2003. 58p. (J). *(978-0-9745803-5-7(X))* Little Big Tomes.

Gantos, Jack. What Would Joey Do? 2004. (Joey Pigza Ser.). 229p. (J). (gr. 5-9). 13.65 *(978-0-7569-2597-0(5))* Perfection Learning Corp.

—What Would Joey Do? 2004. (Joey Pigza Ser.: Bk. 3). 240p. (J). (gr. 5-9). pap. 36.00 incl. audio *(978-1-4000-9020-4(2),* Listening Library) Random Hse. Audio Publishing Group.

—What Would Joey Do? 2014. (Joey Pigza Ser.: 3). (ENG.). 256p. (J). (gr. 5-9). pap. 7.99 *(978-1-250-06169-0(5),* 9781250061690) Square Fish.

Ganz, Yaffa. Four in One: Four Favorites. Klineman, Harvey, illus. 2008. 24.99 *(978-1-59826-183-7(5))* Feldheim Pubs.

Garay, Erin. Angel Birthdays. Abbott, Kristin, illus. 2013. (ENG.). 32p. (J). (gr. 2-3). 16.95 *(978-1-938301-94-0(3))* Familius LLC.

Garcia, Cristina. I Wanna Be Your Shoebox. 2009. (ENG.). 208p. (J). (gr. 3-7). pap. 6.99 *(978-1-4169-7904-3(2),* Simon & Schuster Bks. For Young Readers) Simon & Schuster Bks. For Young Readers.

Garcia, Nasario. Grandma Lale's Tamales: A Christmas Story. Aragon, Dolores, illus. 2014. (SPA & ENG.). 58p. (J). *(978-1-936744-26-8(0),* Rio Grande Bks.) LPD Pr.

—Grandpa Lolo & Trampa: A Story of Surprise & Mystery = Abuelito Lolo y Trampa: Un Cuento de Sorpresa y Misterio. Montoya, Jeremy, illus. 2014. (SPA & ENG.). (J). 9.99 *(978-1-936744-30-5(9))* LPD Pr.

—Grandpa Lolo's Navajo Saddle Blanket: La Tilma de Abuelito Lolo. Moeller, Richard, illus. Moeller, Richard, photos by. 2012. (J). *(978-0-8263-5078-7(X));* (SPA.). 72p. pap. *(978-0-8263-5079-4(8));* 61p. pap. *(978-0-8263-5080-0(1))* Univ. of New Mexico Pr.

Garis, Howard R. The Curlytops on Star Island. 2009. 120p. 22.95 *(978-1-60664-611-3(7));* pap. 10.95 *(978-1-60664-343-3(6))* Rodgers, Alan Bks.

Garis, Howard Roger. Johnnie & Billie Bushytail. 2004. reprint ed. pap. 1.99 *(978-1-4192-2786-8(6));* pap. 15.95 *(978-1-4191-2786-1(1))* Kessinger Publishing, LLC.

Garland, Michael. Grandpa's Tractor. Garland, Michael, illus. 2011. (ENG., Illus.). 32p. (J). (gr. k-1). 16.95 *(978-1-59078-762-5(5))* Boyds Mills Pr.

Garsee, Linmarie. Annabelle's Vacation with Grandma Hayley: A Mountain Quiltfest Adventure. 2012. 50p. pap. 21.99 *(978-1-4772-7737-9(4))* AuthorHouse.

Garver, Sonya. The Peanut Butter Jelly Gang & Grandpa's Gift. 2013. 20p. pap. 12.45 *(978-1-4908-1093-5(5),* WestBow Pr.) Author Solutions, Inc.

Garza, Xavier. Juan & the Chupacabras/Juan y el Chupacabras. Ward, April, illus. 2006. (ENG & SPA.). 32p. (J). (gr. -1-2). 16.95 *(978-1-55885-454-3(1),* Piñata Books) Arte Publico Pr.

Gates, Josephine Scribner. Nannette goes to visit her Grandmother. 2007. (J). lib. bdg. 59.00 *(978-1-60304-021-1(8))* Dollworks.

Gatty, Alfred. The Fairy Godmothers & Other Tales. 2007. 120p. per. *(978-1-4065-2815-2(3))* Dodo Pr.

—The Fairy Godmothers & Other Tales. 2007. 104p. (gr. 4-7). per. *(978-1-4068-0918-3(7))* Echo Library.

—The Fairy Godmothers & Other Tales. 2004. reprint ed. pap. 15.95 *(978-1-4191-6178-0(4));* pap. 1.99 *(978-1-4192-6178-7(9))* Kessinger Publishing, LLC.

Gausselin, Richard J. How the Grandmas & Grandpas Saved Christmas. 2012. 24p. pap. 17.99 *(978-1-4772-4771-6(8))* AuthorHouse.

Gebhart, Ryan. There Will Be Bears. (ENG.). 224p. (J). (gr. 5). 2016. pap. 8.99 *(978-0-7636-8765-6(0))* 2014. 16.99 *(978-0-7636-6521-0(5))* Candlewick Pr.

George & His Best Friend. 2003. (Illus.). 32p. (J). 6.99 *(978-0-9744520-0-5(9))* Glitter Creek, Inc.

George, Jean Craighead. Charlie's Raven. George, Jean Craighead, illus. 2006. (ENG., Illus.). 208p. (J). (gr. 5-18). reprint ed. 6.99 *(978-0-14-240547-5(7),* Puffin Books) Penguin Young Readers Group.

—Dear Katie, the Volcano Is a Girl. 32p. (J). pap. *(978-0-7868-1178-6(1))* Hyperion Bks. for Children.

—My Side of the Mountain. l.t. ed. 2005. (ENG.). 211p. pap. 10.95 *(978-0-7862-7359-1(3)*, Large Print Pr.) Thorndike Pr.

—A Special Gift for Grammy. Johnson, Steve & Fancher, Lou, illus. 2013. (ENG.). 32p. (J). (gr. -1-3). 17.99 *(978-0-06-053176-8(2))* HarperCollins Pubs.

Gerdner, Linda & Langford, Sarah. Grandfather's Story Cloth. Loughridge, Stuart, illus. 2008. (Grandfather's Story Cloth Ser.). 32p. (J). (gr. 2-4). 16.95 *(978-1-885008-34-3(1)*, Shen's Bks.) Lee & Low Bks., Inc.

Gershator, Phillis. Sambalena Show-Off. 2011. (ENG.). 32p. (J). (gr. -1-3). pap. 16.99 *(978-1-4424-3410-3(4)*, Simon & Schuster Bks. For Young Readers) Simon & Schuster Bks. For Young Readers.

Gewirtz, Adina Rishe. Zebra Forest. (ENG.). 208p. (J). (gr. 4-7). 2014. Illus.). pap. 7.99 *(978-0-7636-7166-2(5))* 2013. 15.99 *(978-0-7636-6041-3(8))* Candlewick Pr.

Gibeau, Claire Janvier. The Circus in Grandpa's Day. 2009. 16p. pap. 8.49 *(978-1-4490-3382-8(2))* AuthorHouse.

Gibson, Angela S. The Colors of God. 2012. 34p. 34.99 *(978-1-62419-479-5(6))*; (Illus.). pap. 24.99 *(978-1-62419-478-8(8))* Salem Author Services.

Giddens, Martha Anne. The Unluckiest Kid in the Universe. 2006. 56p. pap. 9.95 *(978-1-4120-7935-8(7))* Trafford Publishing.

Giff, Patricia Reilly. Eleven. 2009. (ENG.). 176p. (J). (gr. 3-7). 7.99 *(978-0-440-23802-7(1)*, Yearling) Random Hse. Children's Bks.

Gil, Lydia. Letters from Heaven. 2014.Tr. of Cartas Del Cielo. (ENG & SPA.). 128p. (J). pap. 9.95 *(978-1-55885-798-8(2)*, Piñata Books) Arte Publico Pr.

Gilbert, Julie. Into the Storm: A Mermaid's Journey. Fagan, Kirbi, illus. 2017. (Dark Waters Ser.). (ENG.). 160p. (gr. 2-4). pap. 6.95 *(978-1-4965-4175-8(8))*; lib. bdg. 26.65 *(978-1-4965-4171-0(5))* Stone Arch Bks.

—The Sighting: A Mermaid's Journey. Fagan, Kirbi, illus. 2017. (Dark Waters Ser.). (ENG.). 160p. (gr. 2-4). lib. bdg. 26.65 *(978-1-4965-4170-3(7))* Stone Arch Bks.

Gill, David Macinnis. Soul Enchilada. (ENG.). (YA). (gr. 9). 2010. 384p. pap. 8.99 *(978-0-06-167303-0(X))* 2009. 368p. 16.99 *(978-0-06-167301-6(3))* HarperCollins Pubs. (Greenwillow Bks.).

Gill, Janie S. When Grandma Comes to Visit. Date not set. 5.95 *(978-0-89868-351-6(3))* ARO Publishing Co.

Gill, Mehmaz S. The Yellow Butterfly. Ward, Lindsay, illus. 2010. (ENG.). 24p. (J). (gr. k-2). 17.95 *(978-1-933979-71-7(2)*, 45f00f36-ed1a-4633-929a-2bb04d2073f4) Bright Sky Pr.

Gill, Patricia. Pabi, Beega & the Mongoose Monster. 2009. 28p. pap. 14.99 *(978-1-4490-2566-3(8))* AuthorHouse.

Gilmore, Dorina Lazo. A Stone in the Soup. Hires, Josh, illus. 2006. 39p. per. 15.00 *(978-0-938911-29-6(5))* Individualized Education Systems/Poppy Lane Publishing.

Gilmore, Rachna. Grandpa's Clock, 1 vol. Meissner, Amy, illus. 2006. (ENG.). 32p. (J). (gr. -1-3). 17.95 *(978-1-55143-333-2(8))* Orca Bk. Pubs. USA.

—When-I-Was-a-Little-Girl, 1 vol. Benoit, Renne, illus. 2007. (ENG.). 24p. (J). (gr. -1-2). 14.95 *(978-1-897187-12-8(2))* Second Story Pr. CAN. Dist: Orca Bk. Pubs. USA.

Giulieri, Anne. Grandpa's Farm, 1 vol. Bailey, Martin, illus. 2012. (Engage Literacy Blue Ser.). (ENG.). 32p. (gr. k-2). pap. 5.99 *(978-1-4296-8988-5(9)*, Engage Literacy) Capstone Press of Coughlan Cos.

Glass, Graeme. A Bee's Kiss. Trone, Jo, illus. 2012. 60p. pap. 21.50 *(978-1-61897-383-2(5)*, Strategic Bk. Publishing) Strategic Book Publishing & Rights Agency (SBPRA).

Gleitzman, Morris. Now. 2012. (Once Ser.: 3). (ENG.). 192p. (YA). (gr. 7). 16.99 *(978-0-8050-9378-0(8)*, 9780805093780, Holt, Henry & Co. Bks. For Young Readers) Holt, Henry & Co.

—Now. 2013. (Once Ser.: 3). (ENG.). 192p. (YA). (gr. 7). pap. 9.99 *(978-1-250-03417-5(5)*, 9781250034175) Square Fish.

Goddard, D. L. Agondray: The Guardian of the Clouds. 2012. (Illus.). 100p. pap. 10.67 *(978-1-4678-8516-4(9))* AuthorHouse.

Godell, Rick. My Grandpa Tom & Me, 1 vol. Neighbor, Douglas, illus. 2009. 29p. pap. 24.95 *(978-1-61546-026-7(8))* America Star Bks.

Gogolewski, Kathe, illus. Tato. 2008. (J). *(978-0-9800064-2-1(2))* Red Engine Pr.

Gogonya, Carol. The African Mermaid & Other Stories. 2011. 40p. pap. 32.70 *(978-1-4568-5416-4(X))* Xlibris Corp.

Gold, Carolyn J. Dragonfly Secret. 2014. (ENG., Illus.). 144p. (J). (gr. 3-7). pap. 13.99 *(978-1-4814-3755-4(0)*, Atheneum Bks. for Young Readers) Simon & Schuster Children's Publishing.

Gold-Vukson, Marji. Grandpa & Me on Tu B'Shevat. Evans, Leslie, illus. 2004. (ENG.). 32p. (J). (gr. -1-3). pap. 6.95 *(978-1-58013-122-3(0)*, Kar-Ben Publishing) Lerner Publishing Group.

Golden Books Staff & Carbone, Courtney. Grandma's House (Dora the Explorer) Goddard, Brenda & Haskett, Dan, illus. 2013. (Little Golden Book Ser.). (ENG.). 24p. (J). (-k). 3.99 *(978-0-307-98105-9(3)*, Golden Bks.) Random Hse. Children's Bks.

Goldrush, Jds. The Adventures of Chris & Tom's Grandp: Great Grand Pappy's Treasure Map & the Bat Gold Cave. 2011. 50p. pap. 15.99 *(978-1-4628-9660-8(X))* Xlibris Corp.

Gollahon, Carleen Anderson. Sophie & the Mysterious Ring. 2012. 62p. (gr. 4-18). pap. 8.99 *(978-1-4624-0379-0(4)*, Inspiring Voices) Author Solutions, Inc.

Goode, Diane. Thanksgiving Is Here! Goode, Diane, illus. 2005. (ENG., Illus.). 32p. (J). (gr. -1-3). pap. 6.99 *(978-0-06-051590-4(2))* HarperCollins Pubs.

Gooden, Sean Lawrence. The Mother of the Green Bear, 1 vol. 2009. (ENG.). 191p. pap. 24.95 *(978-1-60749-815-5(4))* America Star Bks.

Goodhart, Pippa. Slow Magic. Kelly, John, illus. (Flying Foxes Ser.). (J). 2015. (ENG.). 32p. *(978-0-7787-1535-1(3))* 2003. 48p. *(978-0-7787-1489-7(6))* Crabtree Publishing Co.

Goodhart, Pippa & Goodheart, Pippa. Slow Magic. Kelly, John, illus. 2003. (Flying Foxes Ser.). (ENG.). 48p. (J). *(978-0-7787-1528-3(0))*; lib. bdg. *(978-0-7787-1482-8(9))* Crabtree Publishing Co.

Gordon, Marie Elaina. My Grand-Mom Told Me... Book 1. 2006. 48p. pap. 16.95 *(978-1-4241-2655-2(X))* America Star Bks.

—My Grand-Mom Told Me-down by the Sea. 2008. 108p. pap. 19.95 *(978-1-4241-9095-9(9))* America Star Bks.

Gordon, Mike, illus. Little Red Riding Hood. 2007. (Picture Book Classics Ser.). 24p. (J). (gr. 1-4). 9.99 *(978-0-7945-1787-8(0)*, Usborne) EDC Publishing.

Gorgas, Paula Blais. The Perfect Purple Present. 2007. (Illus.). (J). 20p. per. 11.99 *(978-0-9797574-4-0(4))*; 24p. 24.99 *(978-0-9794660-4-5(0))*; 24p. per. 12.99 *(978-0-9794660-5-2(9))* Dragonfly Publishing, Inc.

Gormley, Greg. Grandad's Busy Day. 2007. (Fantastic Phones Ser.). (ENG., Illus.). 12p. (J). (gr. k-k). bds. 9.99 *(978-0-7475-8377-6(3))* Bloomsbury Publishing Plc GBR. Dist: Independent Pubs. Group.

—Grandma Goes to Tea. 2007. (Fantastic Phones Ser.). (ENG., Illus.). 12p. (J). (gr. k-k). bds. 9.99 *(978-0-7475-8379-0(X))* Bloomsbury Publishing Plc GBR. Dist: Independent Pubs. Group.

Gosselin, Kim. Smoking Stinks!! Buttner, Thom, illus. 2nd ed. 2009. (Substance Free Kids Ser.). 30p. (J). (gr. -1-3). pap. 16.95 *(978-1-891383-20-5(3))* JayJo Bks., LLC.

Gould, Susan Lynn. A Gift from Grandma. Verkruysse, Toni, illus. 2013. 56p. pap. 20.50 *(978-1-61897-230-9(8)*, Strategic Bk. Publishing) Strategic Book Publishing & Rights Agency (SBPRA).

Gower, Catherine & Zhihong, He. Long-Long's New Year. 2005. (ENG., Illus.). 32p. (J). (gr. k-3). 16.95 *(978-0-8048-3666-1(3))* Tuttle Publishing.

Grabo, Carl. The Cat in Grandfather's House. 2008. 120p. 23.95 *(978-1-60664-842-1(X))*; pap. 10.95 *(978-1-60664-087-6(9))* Aegypan.

Graham, J. Lee. In the Nick of Time. 2008. 108p. pap. 10.95 *(978-0-595-52621-5(7))* iUniverse, Inc.

Graham-Morgan, Ivet. Grandma's Garden. 2009. 24p. pap. 12.99 *(978-1-4389-2733-6(9))* AuthorHouse.

Gramp's Magic Gift. 2011. 98p. 24.99 *(978-1-4628-2980-4(5))*; pap. 15.99 *(978-1-4628-2979-8(1))* Xlibris Corp.

Grandad's Dinosaur: Level M, 6 vols. 128p. (gr. 2-3). 49.95 *(978-0-7699-0984-4(1))* Shortland Pubns. (U. S. A.) Inc.

Grandfather's Dream. (Lexile Levels Ser.). 9.09 *(978-1-56334-707-8(5))* CENGAGE Learning.

Grandma Carol's Plant: Individual Title Six-Packs. (gr. k-1). 23.00 *(978-0-7635-9039-0(8))* Rigby Education.

Grandma is a Runner. (J). 26.20 *(978-0-8136-8449-9(8))*; (gr. -1-3). 59.50 *(978-0-8136-8020-0(4))* Modern Curriculum Pr.

Grandma Is Now A Butterfly. 2005. (Illus.). 24p. (J). 8.00 *(978-0-9767077-0-7(5))* Carson, Tracy.

Grandma Janet Mary. Grandma's Treasure Chest. Pennington, Craig, illus. l.t. ed. 2005. (Grandma Janet Mary Ser.). 50p. (J). 16.95 *(978-0-9742732-3-5(6))* My Grandma & Me Pubs.

—Grandpa's Fishin' Friend. Pennington, Craig, illus. 2nd ed. 2007. (Grandma Janet Mary Ser.). 28p. (J). 16.95 *(978-0-9742732-7-3(9))* My Grandma & Me Pubs.

Grandma Jenny's Trip: Six-Pack. (Greetings Ser.: Vol. 3). (gr. 3-5). 31.00 *(978-0-7635-1778-6(X))* Rigby Education.

Grandma Moves In: Six-Pack. (Greetings Ser.: Vol. 2). (gr. 2-3). 31.00 *(978-0-7635-9429-9(6))* Rigby Education.

Grandma Net's Stories for the Flannelboard. 2005. (Illus.). 130p. (J). 7.50 net. *(978-0-9771210-0-7(3))* Graham Bay, Jeanette.

Grandma Pearl: A Story about Inner Beauty. 2008. (Illus.). 32p. (J). 17.95 *(978-0-9799021-1-6(8))* Aspire Publishing.

Grandma's Attic. 2008. (Max & Ruby Ser.). 7p. (J). (gr. -1-k). 9.99 *(978-0-448-44895-4(5)*, Grosset & Dunlap) Penguin Publishing Group.

Grandma's Memories, 6 Pack. (Literatura 2000 Ser.). (gr. 1-2). 28.00 *(978-0-7635-0134-1(4))* Rigby Education.

Grandma's Pictures: Individual Title Six-Packs. (gr. k-1). 23.00 *(978-0-7635-8842-7(3))* Rigby Education.

Grandma's Pie: Individual Title Six-Packs. (Story Steps Ser.). (gr. k-2). 32.00 *(978-0-7635-9816-7(X))* Rigby Education.

Grandmother & I: Individual Title Six-Packs. (gr. -1-2). 23.00 *(978-0-7635-8791-8(5))* Rigby Education.

Grandmother Sparrow: Copyright TXu1-280-697. 2007. (J). *(978-0-9792641-0-8(3))* Shelle, Carole Creative Arts.

Grandpa & Grandma & the Mischievous Kids. 2004. (J). per. 15.99 *(978-0-9759122-0-1(8))* Golden Eagle Publishing Hse., Inc.

Grandpa & I: Individual Title Six-Packs. (gr. -1-2). 23.00 *(978-0-7635-8792-5(3))* Rigby Education.

Grandpa & Little Guy. 2004. (J). 15.95 *(978-0-9764012-0-9(7))* Rockmill Publishing Co.

Grandpa's Birthday: Individual Title Six-Packs. (Literatura 2000 Ser.). (gr. 2-3). 33.00 *(978-0-7635-0199-0(9))* Rigby Education.

Grandpa's House. (J). 26.20 *(978-0-8136-8407-9(2))*; 26.20 *(978-0-8136-8408-6(0))*; (gr. -1-4). 59.50 *(978-0-8136-7936-5(2))* Modern Curriculum Pr.

Granny's Favorite Tales. 2006. (Illus.). 156p. (J). per. 39.95 *(978-1-60002-098-8(4)*, 3915) Mountain Valley Publishing, LLC.

Grant, Myrna. Ivan & the Hidden Bible. 2006. (Flamingo Fiction 9-13s Ser.). (ENG., Illus.). 144p. (J). (gr. 4-7). per. 6.99 *(978-1-84550-133-4(0)*, 9394aef3-942b-4824-b0b8-0ae3449d32e0) Christian Focus Pubns. GBR. Dist: Bookmasters Distribution.

Grasso, Mary Ann. The Tale of a Tooth or Two or Three. 2011. 24p. pap. *(978-1-4269-7956-9(8))* Trafford Publishing (UK) Ltd.

Gravatt, Andrea R. The Lavender Ribbon. 2009. 32p. pap. 12.99 *(978-1-4490-4135-9(3))* AuthorHouse.

Green, D. L. Sparkling Jewel. Wallis, Emily, illus. 2015. (Silver Pony Ranch Ser.: 1). (ENG.). 96p. (J). (gr. 1-3). pap. 4.99 *(978-0-545-79765-8(9))* Scholastic, Inc.

—Sweet Buttercup. Wallis, Emily, illus. 2016. (Silver Pony Ranch Ser.: 2). (ENG.). 96p. (J). (gr. 1-3). 15.99 *(978-0-545-79770-2(5))* Scholastic, Inc.

—Zeke Meeks vs the No-Fun Fund-Raiser, 1 vol. Alves, Josh, illus. 2013. (Zeke Meeks Ser.). (ENG.). 128p. (gr. 2-2). lib. bdg. 22.65 *(978-1-4048-7640-8(5)*, Zeke Meeks) Picture Window Bks.

Green, Holly G. Don't Slam the Door. Scott, Sarah Chamberlin, illus. 2005. (ENG.). 39p. (J). (gr. 2-7). 19.95 *(978-0-9744803-7-4(1))* PublishingWorks.

Greene, Jacqueline. Nathan's Hanukkah Bargain, 1 vol. Hierstein, Judith, illus. 2008. (ENG.). 32p. (J). (gr. 1-3). 16.99 *(978-1-58980-454-8(6))* Pelican Publishing Co., Inc.

Greene, Kimberly. Fame Game & Me. 2011. (My Sister's a Pop Star Ser.). 320p. (J). pap. 5.99 *(978-0-7945-2900-0(3)*, Usborne) EDC Publishing.

Greene, Stephanie. Falling into Place. 2006. (ENG.). 128p. (J). (gr. 5-7). pap. 8.95 *(978-0-618-68928-6(1))* Houghton Mifflin Harcourt Publishing Co.

Greenfield, Eloise. William & the Good Old Days. Date not set. (Illus.). 32p. (J). (gr. k-3). pap. 4.99 *(978-0-06-443453-9(2))* HarperCollins Pubs.

Greer, Hannah. The Lighthouse Summer Greer, Tica, illus. 2009. 156p. pap. 24.95 *(978-1-60813-493-9(8))* America Star Bks.

Greer, Tom. Honey Visits Grandpa Smith. 2008. (Adventures of Honey Ser.). (Illus.). (J). pap. 9.95 *(978-0-9789227-2-6(7))* Weeping Willow Publishing.

Gregory, Dee. The Accidental Daughter: A Children's Story about Hope. 2008. 96p. pap. 10.49 *(978-1-4389-3338-2(X))* AuthorHouse.

Gregory, Nan. Wild Girl & Gran. 2004. (Illus.). (J). (gr. k-3). spiral bd. *(978-0-616-11112-3(6))* Canadian National Institute for the Blind/Institut National Canadien pour les Aveugles.

Griffin, Marcia. Debbie's Letter to God. Davies, Michelle, illus. 2005. (J). pap. 8.00 *(978-0-8059-6409-7(6))* Dorrance Publishing Co., Inc.

Griffin, Ramona Rorie. The Gift That Grandma Gave: Including Bloom's Leveled Questions Study Guide. Tunstel Jr., Robert L., illus. 2011. 44p. pap. 24.95 *(978-1-4560-1034-8(4))* America Star Bks.

Griffith, Diane. Granny's Magic Garden. 2010. 66p. pap. 19.95 *(978-1-60693-925-3(4)*, Eloquent Bks.) Strategic Book Publishing & Rights Agency (SBPRA).

Griffiths, Georgina. Granny Carstairs: The Wrinkled Fairy. 2010. (Illus.). 64p. pap. 23.49 *(978-1-4490-7479-1(0))* AuthorHouse.

Grillo, Trine. I'm Not Afraid of That. 2011. (Illus.). 44p. (J). pap. 18.99 *(978-1-59092-761-8(3))* Blue Forge Pr.

Grimm Brothers Staff. Little Red Riding Hood. Cowley, Joy, ed. Choi, Min-ho, illus. 2015. (World Classics Ser.). (ENG.). 32p. (J). (gr. k-4). 26.65 *(978-1-925186-68-0(7))* Lerner Publishing Group.

Grimm, Jeanette. Living with Grandma & Grandpa. 2010. 24p. pap. 15.99 *(978-1-4535-5573-6(0))* Xlibris Corp.

Grimm, Wilhelm K. & Grimm, Jacob. Little Red Cap. Zwerger, Lisbeth, illus. 37p. (J). (gr. k-2). pap. 5.95 *(978-0-8072-1285-1(7)*, Listening Library) Random Hse. Audio Publishing Group.

Griner, Sophia Maria. Hooray for Saturday! 2013. 24p. pap. *(978-1-4602-1806-8(X))* FriesenPress.

Grisham, John. La Casa Dipinta. pap. 21.95 *(978-88-04-50528-0(1))* Mondadori ITA. Dist: Distribooks, Inc.

Groethe, Kd. The Virtual Adventures of Megan & Timmy. 2012. 230p. (gr. 4-6). 27.99 *(978-1-4685-5050-4(0))*; pap. 16.95 *(978-1-4685-5049-8(7))* AuthorHouse.

Grover, Lorie Ann. On Pointe. 2008. (ENG.). 320p. (J). (gr. 3-7). pap. 14.99 *(978-1-4169-7826-8(7)*, McElderry, Margaret K. Bks.) McElderry, Margaret K. Bks.

Guarneri, Lauren. Do You Know Who I Am Now? 2011. 36p. pap. 16.86 *(978-1-4670-2618-5(2))* AuthorHouse.

Guerra, Juan J. The Little Doctor / el Doctorcito. Castillo, Victoria, illus. 2017. (ENG & SPA.). 32p. (J). (gr. k-3). 17.95 *(978-1-55885-846-6(6)*, Piñata Books) Arte Publico Pr.

Guest, Elissa Haden. Iris & Walter & Baby Rose. Davenier, Christine, illus. 2012. (Iris & Walter — Green Light Reader Ser.). lib. bdg. 13.55 *(978-0-606-26612-3(7)*, Turtleback) Turtleback Bks.

—Iris & Walter & the Substitute Teacher. Davenier, Christine, illus. 2006. (Iris & Walter Ser.). 44p. (gr. 1-4). 15.95 *(978-0-7569-7122-9(5))* Perfection Learning Corp.

Guevara, Melva Vizcarrondo. My Grandma, My Hero. 2007. 58p. pap. 10.00 *(978-0-8059-7296-2(X))* Dorrance Publishing Co., Inc.

Guibert, Emmanuel. A Beautiful Cow. 2014. (Ariol Ser.: 4). (J). lib. bdg. 24.50 *(978-0-606-35103-4(5)*, Turtleback) Turtleback Bks.

Guiffre, William. Gramma's Glasses. Pippin, Barbara, illus. 2008. 32p. (J). (gr. -1-3). pap. 9.95 *(978-1-931650-35-9(7))* Bks. for Children Publishing.

Gunlock, Sheila. Groovy Granny & the Character Bees. 2012. 24p. (-18). pap. 10.95 *(978-1-4497-6910-9(1)*, WestBow Pr.) Author Solutions, Inc.

Gurtler, Janet. If I Tell. 2011. (ENG.). 256p. (YA). (gr. 7-12). pap. 12.99 *(978-1-4022-6103-9(9))* Sourcebooks, Inc.

Gutierrez-Green, Sandra. The Colors in My Garden. 2005. 36p. per. 19.25 *(978-1-4208-4266-1(8))* AuthorHouse.

Gutknecht, Allison. Pizza Is the Best Breakfast: And Other Lessons I've Learned. Lewis, Stevie, illus. 2015. (ENG.). 176p. (J). (gr. 2-5). pap. 6.99 *(978-1-4814-2961-0(2)*, Aladdin) Simon & Schuster Children's Publishing.

Guzman, Lila & Guzman, Rick. Lorenzo's Secret Mission. 2005. 153p. (gr. 4-7). 19.95 *(978-0-7569-5599-1(8))* Perfection Learning Corp.

Haas, Jessie. Birthday Pony. Apple, Margot, illus. 2004. 80p. (J). (gr. 2-18). 15.99 *(978-0-06-057359-1(7))* HarperCollins Pubs.

Haave, Meghan. Christopher's Night at Grandma & Grandpa's. 2012. 32p. (J). 9.95 *(978-1-59530-458-2(4))* Hallmark Card, Inc.

Haddix, Margaret Peterson. The House on the Gulf. (ENG., Illus.). 208p. (J). (gr. 3-7). 2006. pap. 7.99 *(978-1-4169-1406-8(4))* 2004. 17.99 *(978-0-689-85422-4(6))* Simon & Schuster Bks. For Young Readers. (Simon & Schuster Bks. For Young Readers).

Hadley, Caroline. Woodside; or, Look, Listen & Learn. 2007. (ENG., Illus.). 80p. per. *(978-1-4065-1557-2(4))* Dodo Pr.

Hagman, Harvey Dixon. Majesty from Assateague, 1 vol. Aiken, David, illus. 2009. (ENG.). 80p. (J). pap. 8.95 *(978-0-87033-552-5(9)*, 9780870335525, Cornell Maritime Pr./Tidewater Pubs.) Schiffer Publishing, Ltd.

Hahn, Betty Brandt. Grandma's House. 2004. 28p. pap. 9.98 *(978-1-4116-1077-4(6))* Lulu Pr., Inc.

Hahnke. Through the Eyes of a Raptor. 2007. 424p. per. 19.95 *(978-0-595-42609-6(3))* iUniverse, Inc.

Haislip, Phyllis Hall. Anybody's Hero: The Battle of Old Men & Young Boys. 2004. (Illus.). 220p. (J). pap. 8.95 *(978-1-57249-343-8(7)*, White Mane Kids) White Mane Publishing Co., Inc.

Haley, Olivia. Jellybeans. 2008. 52p. pap. 20.50 *(978-1-4259-7781-8(2))* AuthorHouse.

Hall, Dorothy. The Story of Little Granny Munklestump. 2012. 44p. pap. 32.70 *(978-1-4691-4754-3(8))* Xlibris Corp.

Hall, J. Darroll. The Lollipop Club. 2011. (ENG.). 290p. pap. 4.99 *(978-0-615-56231-5(0))* Fantasy Island Bk. Publishing.

Hall, Kirsten. Grandma's House. Calderas, Gloria, illus. 2004. (My First Reader Ser.). (ENG.). 32p. (J). (gr. k-1). pap. 3.95 *(978-0-516-25502-6(9)*, Children's Pr.) Scholastic Library Publishing.

Hall, Nancy R. My Grandparents Live in an RV Hall, Nancy R., illus. l.t. ed. 2005. (Illus.). 32p. (J). 16.95 *(978-0-9761759-0-2(8))* Jasnans Publishing Co.

Halley, Jane E. The Unidentified Flight-Less Object. 2008. 52p. pap. 22.49 *(978-1-4343-6491-3(7))* AuthorHouse.

Halley, Marilyn. Apple-Green Eyes. 2005. pap. 8.00 *(978-0-8059-6681-7(1))* Dorrance Publishing Co., Inc.

Hallinan, P. K. Christmas at Grandma's House. 2006. (ENG., Illus.). 32p. (J). (gr. -1-3). 8.95 *(978-0-8249-5535-9(8)*, 1262731, Ideal Pubns.) Worthy Publishing.

—Grandma Loves You. 2008. (ENG., Illus.). 26p. (J). (gr. -1-k). bds. 7.99 *(978-0-8249-6728-4(3)*, Ideal Pubns.) Worthy Publishing.

—Grandma Loves You! Kirkland, Katherine, illus. 2014. 22p. (J). bds. 8.99 *(978-0-8249-1931-3(9)*, Ideal Pubns.) Worthy Publishing.

—Grandpa Loves You! Kirkland, Katherine, illus. 2014. 22p. (J). bds. 8.99 *(978-0-8249-1932-0(7)*, Ideal Pubns.) Worthy Publishing.

—We're Very Good Friends, My Grandma & I. 24p. (J). 7.95 *(978-0-8249-5379-9(7))*; 5.95 *(978-0-8249-5380-5(0))* Worthy Publishing. (Ideal Pubns.).

—We're Very Good Friends, My Grandpa & I. 24p. (J). 7.95 *(978-0-8249-5377-5(0))*; (ENG.). pap. 5.95 *(978-0-8249-5378-2(9))* Worthy Publishing. (Ideal Pubns.).

Hallwood, Cheri L. The Curious Polka-Dot Present. Rose, Patricia M., illus. 2007. (ENG.). 32p. (J). 16.99 *(978-0-9774422-1-8(7))* Forever Young Pubs.

Hamanaka, Sheila. Grandparents Song. Hamanaka, Sheila, illus. 2003. (Illus.). 32p. (J). 15.99 *(978-0-688-17852-9(9))* HarperCollins Pubs.

Hamilton, Pamela Greenhalgh. Snow Day. 2011. 34p. (J). pap. 18.95 *(978-1-4327-5743-4(1))* Outskirts Pr., Inc.

Hamlett, Martha. Bats in the Air, Bats in My Hair. 2008. 32p. pap. 13.99 *(978-1-4389-2358-1(9))* AuthorHouse.

Hansen, Jeff. Alibriana Visits the Branch Office. 2009. 36p. pap. 16.99 *(978-1-4389-4534-7(5))* AuthorHouse.

Hanson, Warren. Grandpa Has a Great Big Face. Elliott, Mark, illus. 2006. 32p. (J). (gr. -1-3). 17.89 *(978-0-06-078776-9(7)*, Geringer, Laura Book) HarperCollins Pubs.

Harazin, S. A. Painless. 2015. (ENG.). 304p. (YA). (gr. 8-12). 16.99 *(978-0-8075-6288-8(2))* Whitman, Albert & Co.

Harker, Jillian. I Love You, Grandma. (I Love... Ser.). pap. *(978-1-4054-6660-8(X))* Parragon, Inc.

Harkness, Peter. The Ishcabibble Encounter. 2017. (ENG.). 372p. pap. 14.95 ***(978-1-78629-642-9(X)***, 8012016d-15d9-4521-a8f2-9f7782b725e0) Austin, Stan AUS. Dist: Bookmasters Distribution.

Harlow, Joan Hiatt. Shadows on the Sea. (ENG., Illus.). (J). (gr. 3-7). 2005. 272p. pap. 7.99 *(978-0-689-84927-5(3))* 2003. 256p. 17.99 *(978-0-689-84926-8(5))* McElderry, Margaret K. Bks. (McElderry, Margaret K. Bks.).

Harper, John. Time Lapse: Collapse. 2011. 184p. 24.99 *(978-1-4490-7045-8(0))*; pap. 17.99 *(978-1-4490-7044-1(2))* AuthorHouse.

Harrington, Claudia. My Grandparents, 1 vol. Persico, Zoe, illus. 2016. (ENG.). 32p. (J). *(978-1-62402-105-3(0))* Magic Wagon.

Harris, Andy. Tick-Tock Grandad's Sweetshop Skills for Life. 2009. 20p. pap. 9.99 *(978-1-60693-933-8(5)*, Eloquent Bks.) Strategic Book Publishing & Rights Agency (SBPRA).

Harris, Angela Brent -. Sweet Jamaican Summertime at Grandma's. 2011. 28p. pap. 21.99 *(978-1-4628-7271-8(9))* Xlibris Corp.

Harris, Donna. Ruff Life. 2011. 240p. pap. 17.99 *(978-1-4567-5081-7(X))* AuthorHouse.

Harris, Dorothy Joan. Un Perro Muy Diferente. Rioja, Alberto Jimenez, tr. from ENG. LaFave, Kim, illus. 2006. (SPA.). 28p. (J). (gr. 5-6). pap. 7.99 *(978-1-933032-04-7(9))* Lectorum Pubns., Inc.

Harris, Patrice. Grandma Asks: Were You Good at School Today? Harrison, Nicholas, illus. 2013. 26p. pap. 10.00 *(978-0-9892358-5-3(8))* CLF Publishing.

Harris, Patricia. Do You Wonder Why? 2017. (Jungle Fun Ser.). 24p. (gr. 4-6). pap. 8.25 ***(978-1-5383-2132-4(7)***, PowerKids Pr.) Rosen Publishing Group, Inc., The.

Harshbarger, D. The Treasures of Dawn. 2011. 44p. pap. 19.99 *(978-1-4634-1585-3(0))* AuthorHouse.

Hartgraves, Richard. Little Cedar. 2006. 130p. pap. 24.95 *(978-1-4241-4603-1(8))* PublishAmerica, Inc.

Hartley, Grandpa. Further Jolly Bedtime Tales for Big & Little People. 2010. 88p. pap. 30.99 *(978-1-4490-8267-3(X))* AuthorHouse.

Härtling, Peter. La Abuela. Mizsenko, Ingrid, illus. 2003. (SPA.). 103p. (J). (gr. 5-8). pap. 9.95 *(978-968-19-0730-3(2))* Santillana USA Publishing Co., Inc.

—El Viejo John. Habinger, Renate, illus. 2003.Tr. of Old John. (SPA.). 144p. (YA). (gr. 5-8). 12.95 *(978-84-204-4816-9(8))* Ediciones Alfaguara ESP. Dist: Santillana USA Publishing Co., Inc.

—El viejo John. Habinger, Renate, illus. (SPA.). 144p. (J). (gr. 5-8). pap. 9.95 *(978-968-19-0720-4(5))* Santillana USA Publishing Co., Inc.

Hartman, Colleen Kelley. My Grandma Calls Me Lovey. Hammons, Mark, illus. 2011. pap. 19.95 *(978-1-934333-26-6(3))* Eagle Bk. Bindery.

Hartnett, Sonya. Sadie & Ratz. James, Ann, illus. 2013. (ENG.). 64p. (J). (gr. k-3). pap. 5.99 *(978-0-7636-6461-9(8))* Candlewick Pr.

—What the Birds See. 2007. (ENG., Illus.). 208p. (YA). (gr. 9). pap. 7.99 *(978-0-7636-3680-7(0))* Candlewick Pr.

Hartt-Snowbell, Sarah. Vivian Untangled. 2006. (ENG., Illus.). 136p. (J). per. 8.95 *(978-1-894917-25-4(1)*, Napoleon & Co.) Dundurn CAN. Dist: Ingram Publisher Services.

Hartt-Sussman, Heather. Nana's Getting Married. Graham, Georgia, illus. 2010. (ENG.). 32p. (J). (gr. -1-1). 17.95

EFG

(978-0-88776-911-5(X), Tundra Bks.) Tundra Bks. CAN. Dist: Penguin Random Hse. LLC.

—Nana's Summer Surprise. Graham, Georgia, illus. 2013. (ENG.). 32p. (J). (gr. -1-1). 17.95 (978-1-77049-324-7(7), Tundra Bks.) Tundra Bks. CAN. Dist: Penguin Random Hse. LLC.

Hatch, Bee. Grandma Talks to Me. Lt. ed. 2005. (Illus.). 46p. (J). per. 12.99 (978-1-59879-022-1(6)) Lifevest Publishing, Inc.

Hauber, Jennifer. Just Like Om. 2008. 20p. pap. 12.49 (978-1-4389-0992-9(6)) AuthorHouse.

Haugaard, Kay. The Day the Dragon Danced. Barritt, Carolyn Reed, illus. 2004. (Day the Dragon Danced Ser.). 32p. (J). (gr. -1-3). 16.95 (978-1-885008-30-5(9), Shen's Bks.) Lee & Low Bks., Inc.

Hauser, Michele. The Crystal Palace: Rescue of the Baby Fairy Prince. 2009. (Illus.). 84p. pap. 9.95 (978-1-4327-1157-3(1)) Outskirts Pr., Inc.

Hawkesworth, Asha. Grandma's Roses. Kathie, Gabriel, illus. 2006. (J). per. (978-0-9738442-9-0(9)) Avatar Pubns., Inc. CAN. Dist: .

Haworth-Attard, Barbara. My Life from Air-Bras to Zits. 2009. (ENG.). 288p. (YA). (gr. 7-10). pap. 9.95 (978-0-7387-1483-7(6), Flux) North Star Editions.

Hawxhurst, Joan C. Bubbe & Gram: My Two Grandmothers. Bynum-Nwulu, Jane, illus. 2003. 32p. (J). (gr. -1-2). 12.95 (978-0-9651284-2-1(3)) Dovetail Publishing.

Hay, Angela. Grace S Incredible! Unforgettable! Summer! 2012. 38p. pap. 19.99 (978-1-62419-562-4(8)) Salem Author Services.

Hayden, Gwendolen Lampshire. Mary Martha's Really Truly Stories: Book 1. 2nd ed. 2013. 130p. pap. 11.95 (978-1-4796-0099-1(7)) TEACH Services, Inc.

—Mary Martha's Really Truly Stories: Book 2. 2nd ed. 2013. (Illus.). 136p. pap. 11.95 (978-1-4796-0102-8(0)) TEACH Services, Inc.

—Mary Martha's Really Truly Stories: Book 4. 2nd ed. 2013. 130p. pap. 11.95 (978-1-4796-0108-0(X)) TEACH Services, Inc.

—Mary Martha's Really Truly Stories: Book 5. 2nd ed. 2013. 130p. pap. 11.95 (978-1-4796-0111-0(X)) TEACH Services, Inc.

—Mary Martha's Really Truly Stories: Book 6. 2nd ed. 2013. 130p. pap. 11.95 (978-1-4796-0114-1(4)) TEACH Services, Inc.

—Mary Martha's Really Truly Stories: Book 7. 2nd ed. 2013. 130p. pap. 11.95 (978-1-4796-0117-2(9)) TEACH Services, Inc.

—Mary Martha's Really Truly Stories: Book 8. 2nd ed. 2013. 130p. pap. 11.95 (978-1-4796-0120-2(9)) TEACH Services, Inc.

Hayes, Daniel. Flyers. 2013. (ENG.). 208p. (YA). (gr. 7). pap. 10.99 (978-1-4424-8881-6(6), Simon & Schuster Bks. For Young Readers) Simon & Schuster Bks. For Young Readers.

Hayes, Joe. The Recycled Hambone. Castro L., Antonio, illus. 2016. (ENG.). 32p. (J). (gr. -1-2). 16.95 (978-1-941026-54-0(0)) Cinco Puntos Pr.

—Recycled Hambone. Castro L., Antonio, illus. 2016. (ENG.). 32p. (J). (gr. -1-2). pap. 7.95 (978-1-941026-55-7(9)) Cinco Puntos Pr.

Hayes, Linda. Grandma's First Computer. 2008. 34p. pap. 17.95 (978-0-557-01609-9(6)) Lulu Pr., Inc.

Hayes, Mabel Ditch. Would Grandma Still Love Me? 2013. 32p. pap. 14.62 (978-1-4251-8891-7(5)) Trafford Publishing.

Hayes, Rosemary. Loose Connections. 2012. 208p. (J). pap. (978-1-84780-293-4(1), Frances Lincoln) Quarto Publishing Group UK.

Heacock, David & Giles, Inga. Child of Oz. 2010. (J). pap. (978-0-88092-479-5(9)) Royal Fireworks Publishing Co.

Hearne, Betsy. Seven Brave Women. Andersen, Bethanne, illus. 2006. (gr. -1-3). 17.00 (978-0-7569-6669-0(8)) Perfection Learning Corp.

Heasley, Gwendolyn. Where I Belong. 2011. (Where I Belong Ser.: 1). (ENG.). 304p. (YA). (gr. 8-18). pap. 9.99 (978-0-06-197884-5(1), HarperTeen) HarperCollins Pubs.

Heck, C. S. Memory-Kisses. 2007. 104p. per. 9.95 (978-0-595-41514-4(8)) iUniverse, Inc.

Hedderwick, Mairi. Katie Morag & the Two Grandmothers. Hedderwick, Mairi, illus. 2010. (Katie Morag Ser.: 2). (ENG., Illus.). 32p. (J). (gr. k-2). pap. 12.99 (978-1-84941-086-1(0), Red Fox) Random House Children's Books GBR. Dist: Independent Pubs. Group.

—Walk with Grannie. 2003. (Illus.). 32p. (J). 19.99 (978-0-340-86642-9(X)) Hodder & Stoughton GBR. Dist: Trafalgar Square Publishing.

—A Walk with Grannie. Date not set. (ENG., Illus.). 32p. pap. (978-0-340-87353-3(1), Hodder Children's Books) Hachette Children's Group.

Hege, Evelyn. A Letter for Titus. 2004. (Illus.). 24p. (gr. -1-5). 2.70 (978-0-7399-2345-0(5), 2791) Rod & Staff Pubs., Inc.

Heible, Beverly. A River Row: Andrew & Luke Fishing with Grandpa. 2012. 24p. 24.95 (978-1-4626-6648-5(5)) America Star Bks.

Heine, Teresa & Heine, Theresa. Elephant Dance: Memories of India. Moxley, Sheila, illus. 2004. (ENG.). 40p. (J). 16.99 (978-1-84148-917-9(4)) Barefoot Bks., Inc.

Heller, Linda. The Castle on Hester Street. Kulikov, Boris, illus. 25th ed. 2007. (ENG.). 40p. (J). (gr. -1-3). 18.99 (978-0-689-87434-5(0), Simon & Schuster Bks. For Young Readers) Simon & Schuster Bks. For Young Readers.

Helowicz, Cathy. On Grandpop's Lap. 1. 2004. (Illus.). 32p. (J). 18.95 (978-0-9752684-0-7(6)) Bodkin Pointe Pr.

Hemingway, Edith M. Road to Tater Hill. 2011. (ENG.). 224p. (J). (gr. 3-7). 7.99 (978-0-375-84544-4(5), Yearling) Random Hse. Children's Bks.

Hemphill, Helen. Long Gone Daddy. (ENG.). 176p. 2014. (YA). (gr. 6). pap. 8.95 (978-1-62091-737-4(8)) 2006. (J). (gr. 8-12). 16.95 (978-1-932425-38-3(1), Lemniscaat) Boyds Mills Pr.

Henderson, Kathy. And the Good Brown Earth. Henderson, Kathy, illus. 2008. (ENG., Illus.). 40p. (J). (gr. -1-2). per. 6.99 (978-0-7636-3841-2(2)) Candlewick Pr.

Henkes, Kevin. Olive's Ocean. (ENG.). 224p. (J). (gr. 3-7). 2003. 16.99 (978-0-06-053543-8(1), 53396925) 2005. reprint ed. pap. 6.99 (978-0-06-053545-2(8)) HarperCollins Pubs. (Greenwillow Bks.).

—Sun & Spoon. 2007. (ENG.). 144p. (J). (gr. 3-7). pap. 8.99 (978-0-06-128875-3(6), Greenwillow Bks.) HarperCollins Pubs.

Henry, Nancy. Where's Papa? 2008. 24p. per. 24.95 (978-1-60474-000-4(0)) America Star Bks.

Hensdill, Norma Mae. I'm Granny's Little Mess, Just Look at the Rest. 2009. 36p. pap. 17.99 (978-1-4389-5054-9(3)) AuthorHouse.

Hensel, Rita. Humble Stew in Going Country. 2008. 41p. pap. 24.95 (978-1-60563-219-3(8)) America Star Bks.

Henson, Heather. Grumpy Grandpa. MacDonald, Ross, illus. 2009. (ENG.). 40p. (J). (gr. -1-3). 16.99 (978-1-4169-0811-1(0), Atheneum Bks. for Young Readers) Simon & Schuster Children's Publishing.

Hermes, Patricia. Emma Dilemma & the New Nanny, 0 vols. Carter, Abby, illus. 2010. (Emma Dilemma Ser.: 1). (ENG.). 114p. (J). (gr. 3-6). pap. 6.99 (978-0-7614-5619-3(8), 9780761456193, Amazon Children's Publishing) Amazon Publishing.

—Emma Dilemma, the Nanny, & the Best Horse Ever, 0 vols. Carter, Abby, illus. 2013. (Emma Dilemma Ser.: 6). (ENG.). 144p. (J). (gr. 3-6). pap. 9.99 (978-1-4778-1633-2(X), 9781477816332, Amazon Children's Publishing) Amazon Publishing.

—Emma Dilemma, the Nanny, & the Secret Ferret, 0 vols. Carter, Abby, illus. 2010. (Emma Dilemma Ser.: 5). (ENG.). 112p. (J). (gr. 3-6). 15.99 (978-0-7614-5650-6(3), 9780761456506, Amazon Children's Publishing) Amazon Publishing.

Herrick, Steven. Do-Wrong Ron. Magerl, Caroline, illus. 2005. (ENG.). 132p. (J). (gr. 1-5). pap. 11.99 (978-1-86508-661-3(4)) Allen & Unwin AUS. Dist: Independent Pubs. Group.

Hest, Amy. When Charley Met Grampa. Oxenbury, Helen, illus. 2013. (ENG.). 40p. (J). (gr. -1-2). 15.99 (978-0-7636-5314-9(4)) Candlewick Pr.

—When Jessie Came Across the Sea. 2003. 17.20 (978-0-613-69484-1(8), Turtleback) Turtleback Bks.

Hetherington, Sally. Where's Pa? Hetherington, Jan, illus. 2013. 28p. pap. 15.97 (978-1-62516-299-1(5), Strategic Bk. Publishing) Strategic Book Publishing & Rights Agency (SBPRA).

Hewat, Jo-Anne. Where's Grandma Daddy? 2012. 28p. pap. 32.70 (978-1-4691-6932-3(0)) Xlibris Corp.

Higdon, Patrick A. Grandpa & My Report. 1 vol. 2009. 48p. pap. 16.95 (978-1-61582-752-7(8)) PublishAmerica, Inc.

High, Gracia. I am not going to sleep Now. 2004. 21p. pap. 24.95 (978-1-4137-3000-5(0)) PublishAmerica, Inc.

High, Linda. Lap Talks with Granny at Easter. 2003. (J). pap. 9.95 (978-0-9661186-9-8(3)) Bks. for Children of the World.

Hill, Eric. Spot Loves His Grandma. Hill, Eric, illus. 2008. (Spot Ser.). (ENG., Illus.). 12p. (J). (gr. -1 — 1). bds. 5.99 (978-0-399-24728-6(9), Warne) Penguin Young Readers Group.

Hines, Jerry E. Silly & Stinky Stories My Grandpa Tells. 2011. (ENG., Illus.). 144p. (J). (gr. 4-7). pap. 8.00 (978-0-9831839-1-4(0)) Amber Skye Publishing LLC.

Hinks, Roy H. Cybo Soccer & Heavens Above. 2011. 116p. pap. 13.32 (978-1-4567-7327-4(5)) AuthorHouse.

Hinman, Bobbie. The Belly Button Fairy. Adams, Mark Wayne, illus. 2009. (ENG.). 32p. (J). (gr. -1-1). 16.95 (978-0-9786791-3-2(X)) Best Fairy Bks.

Hinton, Paul Richard. Rammy. 1 vol. 2009. 177p. pap. 24.95 (978-1-4489-2641-1(6)) America Star Bks.

Hippely, Hilary Horder. A Song for Lena. Baker, Leslie, illus. 2011. (ENG.). 40p. (J). (gr. -1-3). 19.99 (978-1-4424-2946-8(1), Simon & Schuster Bks. For Young Readers) Simon & Schuster Bks. For Young Readers.

Hirahara, Naomi. 1001 Cranes. 2009. (ENG.). 240p. (J). (gr. 3-7). 7.99 (978-0-440-42234-1(5), Yearling) Random Hse. Children's Bks.

Hobbs, Ellen Youngs. Oh ! Hannah. 2012. 24p. pap. 19.99 (978-1-4685-9895-7(3)) AuthorHouse.

Hogan, Jamie. Seven Days of Daisy. 1 vol. Hogan, Jamie, illus. 2011. (ENG., Illus.). 32p. (J). (gr. -1-3). 14.95 (978-0-89272-919-7(8)) Down East Bks.

Hogan, Janice M. As Big as the Sky. 2008. 32p. per. 24.95 (978-1-4241-9181-9(5)) America Star Bks.

Holczer, Tracy. The Secret Hum of a Daisy. 2014. (ENG.). 320p. (J). (gr. 5). 16.99 (978-0-399-16393-7(X), G.P. Putnam's Sons Books for Young Readers) Penguin Young Readers Group.

Holden, Pam. Hunting for Treasure, 6 pack. Whimp, Pauline, illus. 2009. (Red Rocket Readers Ser.). (ENG.). 16p. (gr. 2-2). pap. (978-1-877363-65-8(0), Red Rocket Readers) Flying Start Bks.

—Surprise from the Sky, 6 pack. Whimp, Pauline, illus. 2009. (Red Rocket Readers Ser.). (ENG.). 16p. (gr. 2-1). pap. (978-1-877363-68-9(5)) Flying Start Bks.

Hollyer, Belinda. River Song. 2008. (ENG.). 198p. (J). (gr. 3-7). 16.95 (978-0-8234-2149-7(X)) Holiday Hse., Inc.

Holm, Jennifer L. The Fourteenth Goldfish. 2015. (CHI.). 264p. (J). pap. (978-986-320-783-2(7)) Commonwealth Publishing Co., Ltd.

—The Fourteenth Goldfish. (ENG.). (J). (gr. 3-7). 2016. 240p. 7.99 (978-0-375-87114-6(4), Yearling) 2014. 208p. 16.99 (978-0-375-87064-4(4), Random Hse. Bks. for Young Readers) 2014. 208p. lib. bdg. 19.99 (978-0-375-97064-1(9), Random Hse. Bks. for Young Readers) Random Hse. Children's Bks.

—The Fourteenth Goldfish. 2016. lib. bdg. 18.40 (978-0-606-38465-0(0)) Turtleback Bks.

—Sunny Side Up. Holm, Matthew, illus. 2015. (ENG.). 224p. (J). (gr. 3-7). 23.99 (978-0-545-74165-1(3)); pap. 12.99 (978-0-545-74166-8(1)) Scholastic, Inc. (Graphix).

Holmes, Oliver Wendell, Sr. Grandmother's Story of Bunker Hill Battle. 2009. 45p. pap. 14.80 (978-0-557-05927-0(5)) Lulu Pr., Inc.

Holt, Kimberly Willis. Blooming at the Texas Sunrise Motel. Rosenberry, Vera, illus. 2017. (ENG.). 336p. (J). 16.99 (978-1-62779-324-7(0), 9781627793247, Holt, Henry & Co. Bks. For Young Readers) Holt, Henry & Co.

—Dancing in Cadillac Light. 2003. (ENG.). 176p. (J). (gr. 5-9). 5.99 (978-0-698-11970-3(3), Puffin Books) Penguin Young Readers Group.

—Dancing in Cadillac Light. 2004. 176p. (J). (gr. 4-7). pap. 36.00 incl. audio (978-0-8072-2095-5(7), Listening Library) Random Hse. Audio Publishing Group.

—My Louisiana Sky. 208p. (YA). (gr. 5-18). 4.99 (978-0-8072-8291-5(X), Listening Library) Random Hse. Audio Publishing Group.

—My Louisiana Sky. 2011. (ENG.). 224p. (J). (gr. 4-7). pap. 7.99 (978-0-312-66095-6(2), 9780312660956) Square Fish.

—Piper Reed, Rodeo Star. Davenier, Christine, illus. 2012. (Piper Reed Ser.: 5). (ENG.). 176p. (J). (gr. 3-6). pap. 6.99 (978-1-250-00409-3(8), 9781250004093) Square Fish.

Holubitsky, Katherine. The Big Snapper. 1 vol. 2006. (Orca Young Readers Ser.). (ENG., Illus.). 144p. (J). (gr. 3-5). per. 6.95 (978-1-55143-563-3(2)) Orca Bk. Pubs. USA.

Hong, Chen Jian. La Leyenda De la Cometa. (SPA.). 32p. (978-84-95150-29-5(8)); (978-84-95150-39-4(5)) Corimbo, Editorial S.L.

Hood-Caddy, Karen. Howl. 2011. (Wild Place Adventure Ser.: 1). (ENG.). 256p. (J). (gr. 6-8). pap. 9.99 (978-1-926607-25-2(2)) Dundurn CAN. Dist: Ingram Publisher Services.

Hooray for Midsommar! 6 Small Books. (Greetings Ser.: Vol. 1). 24p. (gr. 2-3). 31.00 (978-0-7635-9410-7(5)) Rigby Education.

Hooray for Midsommar! Big Book. (Greetings Ser.: Vol. 1). 24p. (gr. 2-3). 31.00 (978-0-7635-5694-5(7)) Rigby Education.

Hope, Laura Lee. Bunny Brown & His Sister Sue on Grandpa's Farm. 2007. 192p. 26.95 (978-1-4218-3283-8(6)); per. 11.95 (978-1-4218-3383-5(2)) 1st World Publishing, Inc. (1st World Library - Literary Society).

—Bunny Brown & His Sister Sue on Grandpa's Farm. 2007. (ENG.). 144p. pap. 18.99 (978-1-4346-3268-5(7)); 156p. pap. 21.99 (978-1-4346-3269-2(5)) Creative Media Partners, LLC.

—Six Little Bunkers at Grandma Bell's. 2005. 26.95 (978-1-4218-1066-9(2)); 188p. pap. 11.95 (978-1-4218-1166-6(9)) 1st World Publishing, Inc. (1st World Library - Literary Society).

—Six Little Bunkers at Grandpa Ford's. 2007. 188p. 25.96 (978-1-4218-3889-2(3), 1st World Library - Literary Society) 1st World Publishing, Inc.

—Six Little Bunkers at Grandpa Ford's. 2007. (ENG.). 138p. pap. 18.99 (978-1-4346-1214-4(7)); 156p. pap. 21.99 (978-1-4346-1285-4(6)) Creative Media Partners, LLC.

Hope, Lee Laura. Six Little Bunkers at Aunt Jo's. 2007. (ENG.). 144p. pap. 18.99 (978-1-4346-3234-0(2)); 156p. pap. 21.99 (978-1-4346-3235-7(0)) Creative Media Partners, LLC.

—Six Little Bunkers at Aunt Jo's. 2007. 164p. 95.99 (978-1-4280-7622-8(0)); per. 89.99 (978-1-4280-7620-4(4)) IndyPublish.com.

—Six Little Bunkers at Cowboy Jack's. 2007. (ENG.). 138p. pap. 18.99 (978-1-4346-3242-5(3)); 156p. pap. 21.99 (978-1-4346-3243-2(1)) Creative Media Partners, LLC.

Hopkins, Nicolia. What was Grandma Doing? Wiggins, Margaret W., illus. 2007. (J). per. 9.99 (978-0-9768579-8-3(7)) eVision, LLC.

Horning, Sandra. The Giant Hug. Gorbachev, Valeri, illus. 2008. (ENG.). 40p. (J). (gr. -1-2). pap. 7.99 (978-0-553-11262-7(7), Dragonfly Bks.) Random Hse. Children's Bks.

Horse, Harry. The Last Castaways. Horse, Harry, illus. 2009. (ENG., Illus.). 128p. (J). (gr. 1-5). 12.95 (978-1-56145-439-6(7)) Peachtree Pubs.

—The Last Cowboys. Horse, Harry, illus. 2008. (ENG., Illus.). 128p. (J). (gr. 1-5). 12.95 (978-1-56145-451-8(6), Peachtree Junior) Peachtree Pubs.

—The Last Gold Diggers: Being as It Were, an Account of a Small Dog's Adventures, down Under. Horse, Harry, illus. 2008. (ENG., Illus.). 128p. (J). (gr. 1-5). 12.95 (978-1-56145-435-8(4)) Peachtree Pubs.

—The Last Polar Bears. Horse, Harry, illus. 2007. (ENG., Illus.). 128p. (J). (gr. 1-5). 12.95 (978-1-56145-379-5(X), Peachtree Junior) Peachtree Pubs.

Horvath, Polly. Northward to the Moon. 2012. (ENG.). 256p. (J). (gr. 5-8). 7.99 (978-0-307-92980-8(9), Yearling) Random Hse. Children's Bks.

Hosford, Kate. Infinity & Me. Swiatkowska, Gabi, illus. 2012. (Carolrhoda Picture Bks.). (ENG.). 32p. (J). (gr. k-4). lib. bdg. 16.95 (978-0-7613-6726-0(8)) Lerner Publishing Group.

Howard, Ryan & Howard, Krystle. The Best Bat. Madrid, Erwin, illus. 2015. (Little Rhino Ser.: 2). (ENG.). 112p. (J). (gr. 2-5). 16.99 (978-0-545-67494-2(8)); pap. 4.99 (978-0-545-67493-5(X)) Scholastic, Inc. (Scholastic Paperbacks).

—My New Team. Madrid, Erwin, illus. 2015. (Little Rhino Ser.: 1). (ENG.). 112p. (J). (gr. 2-5). pap. 4.99 (978-0-545-67490-4(5), Scholastic Paperbacks) Scholastic, Inc.

Howard, Vera. My Gran: Country Stories for Young Children. 2004. 88p. pap. (978-1-84401-331-9(6)) Athena Pr.

Howe, James. Addie on the Inside. (Misfits Ser.). (ENG., Illus.). (J). (gr. 5-9). 2012. 240p. pap. 8.99 (978-1-4169-1385-6(8)) 2011. 224p. 16.99 (978-1-4169-1384-9(X)) Simon & Schuster Children's Publishing. (Atheneum Bks. for Young Readers).

Howell, Julie. The Pepper Tree, How the Seeds Were Planted! LaGrange, Tiffany, illus. 2007. 28p. per. 12.95 (978-1-934246-51-1(4)) Peppertree Pr., The.

Howell, Julie Ann. The Pepper Tree, How the Seeds Were Planted! LaGrange, Tiffany, illus. 2008. 28p. pap. 12.95 (978-0-9820479-0-3(8)) Peppertree Pr., The.

Hubery, Julia. When Grandma Saved Christmas. Pedler, Caroline, illus. 2014. (ENG.). 32p. (J). (gr. -1-3). 16.99 (978-1-58925-164-9(4)) Tiger Tales.

Hudicourt, Caroline. A Mango for Grandpa. Sainsilus, Ismer, illus. 2007. 32p. (J). (ARA & ENG.). pap. 14.95 (978-1-60195-085-7(3)); (POL.). pap. 14.95 (978-1-60195-093-2(4)) International Step by Step Assn.

Hudson-Monger, Nadine. Brooke-Lynn's Trip to the Botanical Gardens with Grandm. 2012. 24p. pap. 15.99 (978-1-4691-8418-0(4)) Xlibris Corp.

Hudson, Wade. It's Church Going Time. 2008. (Illus.). 32p. (gr. -1-3). 16.95 (978-1-60349-005-4(1), Marimba Bks.) Hudson Publishing Group, The.

Hughes, Dean. Missing in Action. 2010. (ENG.). 240p. (J). (gr. 5-9). 16.99 (978-1-4169-1502-7(8), Atheneum Bks. for Young Readers) Simon & Schuster Children's Publishing.

Hull, Claire. Isn;T That Silly. 2012. 82p. pap. 15.95 (978-0-9846558-7-8(5)) Taylor and Seale Publishing, LLC.

Hull, Maureen. The View from a Kite, 1 vol. 2007. (ENG., Illus.). 320p. (YA). (gr. 8-12). pap. 15.95 (978-1-55109-591-2(2), Vagrant Pr.) Nimbus Publishing, Ltd. CAN. Dist: Orca Bk. Pubs. USA.

Hulst, W. G. van de & Hulst, Willem G. van de, illus. The Woods Beyond the Wall. 2017. (J). (978-1-928136-08-8(7)) Inheritance Pubns.

Hultquist, A. A Day with Parkinson's. Lew-Vriethoff, Joanne, illus. 2016. (ENG.). 32p. (J). (gr. -1-3). 16.99 (978-0-8075-5581-1(9)) Whitman, Albert & Co.

Humphrey, Anna. Ruby Goldberg's Bright Idea. Newton, Vanessa Brantley, illus. 2013. (ENG.). 144p. (J). (gr. 3-7). 15.99 (978-1-4424-8027-8(0), Simon & Schuster Bks. For Young Readers) Simon & Schuster Bks. For Young Readers.

Hunter, Mollie. The Mermaid Summer. 2003. 118p. (J). (978-1-4131-4688-2(0), Harper Trophy) HarperCollins Pubs.

Hunter, Sara Hoagland. The Unbreakable Code. Miner, Julia, illus. 2007. (ENG.). 32p. (J). (gr. 1-3). per. 7.95 (978-0-873358-917-8(3)) Cooper Square Publishing Llc.

Hurst, Carol Otis. Terrible Storm. 2007. (Illus.). 32p. (J). (gr. k-3). lib. bdg. 17.89 (978-0-06-009002-9(2)) HarperCollins Pubs.

Huskins, T. A. I Am a Whosoever. 2006. 62p. pap. 16.95 (978-1-4241-0308-9(8)) PublishAmerica, Inc.

Hysen, Sylvia. A Very Dairy Christmas. 2005. 290p. 24.95 (978-0-9763365-6-3(1)) 1st Impression Publishing.

I Love My Grandma. (Early Intervention Levels Ser.). 23.10 (978-0-7362-0020-2(7)) CENGAGE Learning.

I Love You, Grandpa. (I Love... Ser.). 32p. 4.99 (978-1-4054-8627-9(9)) Parragon, Inc.

I Remember Mama. 2004. (J). per. 5.99 (978-0-9760112-0-0(4)) Smith, Tyjauna.

Ingersoll, Donna. Rock-A-Bye, Little Child of Mine. 2013. 28p. pap. 24.95 (978-1-4626-9508-9(6)) America Star Bks.

Inzana, Ryan. Ichiro. 2012. (ENG., Illus.). 288p. (YA). (gr. 7). 24.99 (978-0-547-25269-8(2)) Houghton Mifflin Harcourt Publishing Co.

Isadora, Rachel. Happy Belly, Happy Smile. Isadora, Rachel, illus. 2009. (ENG., Illus.). 32p. (J). (gr. -1-3). 16.00 (978-0-15-206546-1(6)) Houghton Mifflin Harcourt Publishing Co.

—What a Family! A Fresh Look at Family Trees. 2006. (Illus.). (J). (978-1-4156-5634-1(7), Putnam Juvenile) Penguin Publishing Group.

Ismail, Yasmeen. Imagine That! 2017. (ENG., Illus.). 32p. (J). 16.99 (978-1-68119-362-5(0), 9781681193625, Bloomsbury USA Childrens) Bloomsbury Publishing USA.

It's a Zoo! Individual Title, 6 Packs. (gr. -1-2). 27.00 (978-0-7635-9454-1(7)) Rigby Education.

Itterman, Bert. Growing up with Grandpa. 2006. (Illus.). 112p. pap. (978-1-57579-330-6(X)) Pine Hill Pr.

Jackson, Nellie O. The Worst Day of My Life. 2008. 24p. pap. 24.95 (978-1-60474-524-5(X)) America Star Bks.

Jackson, Richard. In Plain Sight. Pinkney, Jerry, illus. 2016. (ENG.). 40p. (J). 17.99 (978-1-62672-255-2(2), 9781626722552) Roaring Brook Pr.

Jacobs, Sherry. Grampa's Teeth. 2012. (ENG.). 42p. (J). pap. 16.95 (978-1-4327-8104-0(9)) Outskirts Pr., Inc.

Jacobson, Jennifer Richard. Andy Shane & the Pumpkin Trick. Carter, Abby, illus. 2007. (Andy Shane Ser.: 2). (ENG.). 64p. (J). (gr. k-3). per. 4.99 (978-0-7636-3306-6(2)) Candlewick Pr.

—Andy Shane & the Pumpkin Trick. Carter, Abby, illus. 2008. (Andy Shane Ser.). (J). (gr. -1-3). 25.95 incl. audio (978-1-4301-0313-4(2)); pap. 16.95 incl. audio (978-1-4301-0312-7(4)) Live Oak Media.

Jacoby, Sue. The Sneakies in Las Vegas: A Coby Jay Adventure. 2012. 128p. (gr. 4-6). 22.60 (978-1-4669-6672-7(6)); pap. 12.60 (978-1-4669-6670-3(X)) Trafford Publishing.

James, Helen Foster. Grandma Loves You! Brown, Petra, illus. 2013. (ENG.). 32p. (J). (gr. -1 — 1). 14.99 (978-1-58536-836-5(9), 202884) Sleeping Bear Pr.

—Grandpa Loves You! Brown, Petra, illus. 2016. (ENG.). 32p. (J). (gr. -1-1). 15.99 (978-1-58536-940-9(3), 204032) Sleeping Bear Pr.

James, Katy. My Favorite Summer Vacations. 2013. 12p. pap. 12.68 (978-1-4669-9690-8(0)) Trafford Publishing.

January, Rick. Come Out to the Garden. January, Stella, illus. 2012. (ENG.). 30p. (J). (gr. k-3). pap. 12.95 (978-1-937084-66-0(3)) Boutique of Quality Books Publishing Co., Inc.

January, Rick & January, Stella. Come Out to the Garden. 2012. (ENG., Illus.). 30p. (J). 24.95 (978-1-937084-40-0(X), BQB Publishing) Boutique of Quality Books Publishing Co., Inc.

Janvier Gibeau, Claire. Here Comes Grandpa Now. 2009. 16p. pap. 8.49 (978-1-4490-3829-8(8)) AuthorHouse.

Jaques-Plester, Carol. Grandma Goes to Heaven. 2007. pap. 17.00 (978-0-8059-8887-1(4)) Dorrance Publishing Co., Inc.

Jardine, Alan. Sloop John B: A Pirate's Tale. Pickering, Jimmy, illus. 2005. (ENG.). 32p. (J). (gr. 4-7). 17.95 (978-1-59687-181-6(4)) IBks., Inc.

—Sloop John B: A Pirate's Tale. Pickering, Jimmy, illus. 2005. 32p. 17.95 (978-0-689-03596-8(9), Milk & Cookies) ibooks, Inc.

Jarman, Julia. Little Bad Riding Hood. 2014. (ENG., Illus.). 32p. (J). (978-0-7787-0442-3(4)); pap. (978-0-7787-0450-8(5)) Crabtree Publishing Co.

—Lovely Old Lion. Varley, Susan, illus. 2015. (ENG.). 32p. (J). (gr. -1-3). 17.99 (978-1-4677-9310-0(8)) Andersen Pr. GBR. Dist: Lerner Publishing Group.

Jaskwhich, Cynthia Sheperd. Mema Says Good-Bye. Mazibuko, Luthando, illus. 2010. (J). (978-0-87743-710-9(6)) Baha'i Publishing Trust, U.S.

Jean. Jean's Story. 2009. 40p. pap. 18.49 (978-1-4389-4531-6(0)) AuthorHouse.

Jeanne Taylor Thomas Illustrator: Pr. Austin & Harlow's First Adventure. Hardy, Pris, illus. 2011. 28p. pap. 24.95 (978-1-4560-8383-0(X)) America Star Bks.

Jeffers, Susan. Jingle Bells. Jeffers, Susan, illus. 2017. (Illus.). 40p. (J). (gr. -1-3). 17.99 ***(978-0-06-236020-5(5))*** HarperCollins Pubs.

Jeffs, Dixie. The Little Pink Dress. 2012. 24p. 24.95 *(978-1-4626-5853-4(9))* America Star Bks.

Jennings, Patrick. The Ears of Corn: An Ike & Mem Story. Alter, Anna, illus. 2003. (ENG.). 56p. (J). (gr. k-3). tchr. ed. 15.95 *(978-0-8234-1770-4(0))* Holiday Hse., Inc.

Jennings, Terry Catasús. Vivian & the Legend of the Hoodoos. Saroff, Phyllis, illus. 2017. (ENG & SPA.). 32p. (J). (gr. k-3). 17.95 *(978-1-62855-957-6(8))* Arbordale Publishing.

—Viviana y la Leyenda de Los Hoodoos. Saroff, Phyllis, illus. 2017. (SPA.). 32p. (J). (gr. k-3). pap. 9.95 *(978-1-62855-959-0(4))* Arbordale Publishing.

Jensen, Derrick. Mischief in the Forest: A Yarn Yarn. McMillan, Stephanie, illus. 2010. (Flashpoint Press Ser.). (ENG.). 40p. (J). (gr. -1-k). pap. 14.95 *(978-1-60486-081-8(2))* PM Pr.

Jepson, Gill. Out of Time: The Secret of the Swan. 2011. (ENG.). 144p. pap. *(978-1-84876-612-9(2))* Troubador Publishing Ltd.

Jimenez, Joe. Bloodline. 2016. (ENG.). 128p. (YA). (gr. 8-12). pap. 11.95 *(978-1-55885-828-2(8))*, Piñata Books) Arte Publico Pr.

Joe, Saqamaw Mi'sel. Muinjij Becomes a Man. McQuane, Antonia, illus. 2012. (ENG.). 64p. pap. *(978-1-55081-167-4(3))* Breakwater Bks., Ltd.

Johnson, Angela. Just Like Josh Gibson. Peck, Beth, illus. 2007. (J). 14.65 *(978-0-7569-8088-7(7))* Perfection Learning Corp.

—Just Like Josh Gibson. Peck, Beth, illus. 2007. (ENG.). 32p. (J). (gr. k-2). reprint ed. 7.99 *(978-1-4169-2728-0(X)*, Simon & Schuster Bks. For Young Readers) Simon & Schuster Bks. For Young Readers.

Johnson, Jann A. Wisdom Weaver/Bina'nitin Bidziilgo Atl'ohi. Manavi, Lorraine Begay, tr. from ENG. Taylor, Linda, illus. 2006. (ENG.). 32p. (J). (gr. -1-3). 17.95 *(978-1-893354-82-1(2))* Salina Bookshelf Inc.

Johnson, Marion. Caillou: The Carrot Patch. Sevigny, Eric, illus. 2017. (Read with Caillou Ser.). (ENG.). 32p. (J). (gr. -1-k). 3.99 *(978-2-89718-367-7(5))* Caillouet, Gerry.

Johnson, Michael E. Barley & Betsy: Journey #1 A cat & dog's great adventure to the Mall. Atchley, Kendra, illus. 2011. 36p. pap. 24.95 *(978-1-4560-4077-2(4))* America Star Bks.

Johnson, Sandi. Baseball Billy. Johnson, Britt, ed. Nadaskay, Lori, illus. I.t. ed. 2003. 12p. (J). (gr. k-5). spiral bd. 5.99 *(978-1-929063-30-7(X)*, 320) Moons & Stars Publishing For Children.

Johnson, Temeka & Phillips, Quency. Decisions, Decisions, Decisions. 2010. 32p. 19.99 *(978-1-4520-5758-3(3))* AuthorHouse.

Johnson, Terry David. As I Sat on My Grandpa's Knee. 2009. 32p. pap. 16.50 *(978-1-60860-202-5(8)*, Eloquent Bks.) Strategic Book Publishing & Rights Agency (SBPRA).

Johnson, Young, et al. Princess Hope & the Hidden Treasure, 1 vol. Aranda, Omar, illus. 2012. (I Can Read! / Princess Parables Ser.). (ENG.). 32p. (J). pap. 3.99 *(978-0-310-73250-1(6))* Zonderkidz.

Johnston, Annie Fell. The Little Colonel. 2006. (Illus.). pap. *(978-1-4065-1132-1(3))* Dodo Pr.

—The Little Colonel. 2005. reprint ed. pap. 21.95 *(978-0-7661-9402-1(7))* Kessinger Publishing, LLC.

Johnston, Shawn. A Tale from the Forest of Fairshaw: The Big Fish Story. 2012. 24p. 24.95 *(978-1-4626-6830-4(5))* America Star Bks.

Johnston, Tony. My Abuelita. Morales, Yuyi, illus. 2009. (ENG.). 32p. (J). (gr. -1-3). 17.99 *(978-0-15-216330-3(1))* Houghton Mifflin Harcourt Publishing Co.

Jones, Callie Carol Rodgers. Sweet Potato Pie. 2012. 20p. pap. 17.99 *(978-1-4685-6114-2(6))* AuthorHouse.

Jones, Carl. Rudy the Rangifer & Why Her Nose Turned Orange. 2007. 64p. pap. 14.99 *(978-0-9748266-3-9(4))* Grampa Jones's Publishing Co.

Jones, Carroll. Grandma Battles the Mouse. Giovannini, Jody, illus. 2007. 52p. pap. 16.95 *(978-0-9774260-1-0(7))* Omdee Omnimedia, Inc.

Jones, Margaret. Nat. 2004. (ENG., Illus.). 112p. pap. 13.95 *(978-1-84323-327-5(4))* Beekman Bks., Inc.

Jones, Meinir Pierce & Jones, Jac. Taid Ar Binnau. 2005. (WEL., Illus.). 16p. pap. 4.99 *(978-1-84323-381-7(9))* Gomer Pr. GBR. Dist: Gomer Pr.

Jones, Patrick. Doing Right. 2015. (J). 27.99 *(978-1-4677-7691-2(2))*; (ENG.). 104p. (gr. 6-12). lib. bdg. 27.99 *(978-1-4677-5803-1(5))* Lerner Publishing Group.

Jones, Susan & Jones, Susan. Until We Meet Again. 2007. (ENG., Illus.). 64p. 24.95 *(978-0-9778209-4-8(7))* Soulo Communications.

Jones, Vickie E. The Many Worlds of Sachsawan. 2012. 62p. 19.95 *(978-1-4626-5957-9(8))* America Star Bks.

Jones, Wendy Lou. Last Knight of Golden Downs. 2013. 176p. pap. 9.95 *(978-0-9777110-4-8(8))* Royal Knight Inc.

Jonsberg, Barry. Ironbark. 2010. (ENG.). 210p. (YA). (gr. 8-18). 13.99 *(978-1-74114-955-5(X))* Allen & Unwin AUS. Dist: Independent Pubs. Group.

Jordison, P. B. Voices in the Attic. 2007. 36p. per. 12.95 *(978-1-4327-0135-2(5))* Outskirts Pr., Inc.

Judson, Clara Ingram. Mary Jane - Her Visit. White, Frances, illus. 2008. 220p. 22.95 *(978-1-934671-15-3(0))*; per. 12.95 *(978-1-934671-16-0(9))* Salem Ridge Press LLC.

Jules, Jacqueline. Abuela's Birthday. Smith, Kim, illus. 2015. (Sofia Martinez Ser.). (ENG.). 32p. (gr. k-2). lib. bdg. 21.32 *(978-1-4795-5775-2(7)*, Sofia Martinez) Picture Window Bks.

—Abuela's Special Letters. Smith, Kim, illus. 2017. (Sofia Martinez Ser.). (ENG.). 32p. (gr. k-2). lib. bdg. 21.32 *(978-1-5158-0728-5(2)*, Sofia Martinez) Picture Window Bks.

—The Secret Recipe. Smith, Kim, illus. 2016. (Sofia Martinez Ser.). (ENG.). 32p. (gr. k-2). lib. bdg. 21.32 *(978-1-4795-8717-9(6)*, Sofia Martinez) Picture Window Bks.

Just Like Grandpa: Individual Title Six-Packs. (Literatura 2000 Ser.). (gr. 1-2). 28.00 *(978-0-7635-0093-1(3))* Rigby Education.

Just Like My Grandpa. (Early Intervention Levels Ser.). 23.10 *(978-0-7362-0033-2(9))* CENGAGE Learning.

Juster, Norton. The Hello, Goodbye Window. Raschka, Chris, illus. 2005. (ENG.). 32p. (J). (gr. -1-17). 18.99 *(978-0-7868-0914-1(0)*, di Capua, Michael Bks.) Hyperion Bks. for Children.

Kaderli, Janet. Patchwork Trail. Arnold, Patricia, illus. 2005. 59p. (J). 9.95 *(978-0-9754796-2-9(8))* GASLight Publishing.

Kadohata, Cynthia. The Thing about Luck. Kuo, Julia, illus. (ENG.). (J). (gr. 5-9). 2014. 304p. pap. 8.99 *(978-1-4424-7465-9(3)*, Atheneum Bks. for Young Readers) 2013. 288p. 16.99 *(978-1-4169-1882-0(5))* Simon & Schuster Children's Publishing.

—The Thing about Luck. 2014. lib. bdg. 18.40 *(978-0-606-35798-2(X))* Turtleback Bks.

Kadono, Eiko. Grandpa's Soup. Ichikawa, Santomi, illus. 2009. (ENG.). 40p. (J). (gr. -1-3). pap. 9.00 *(978-0-8028-5347-9(1)*, Eerdmans Bks For Young Readers) Eerdmans, William B. Publishing Co.

Kakkar, Renu. Granny's Return from Heaven as an Incredible Car. 2011. (Illus.). 180p. (gr. 4-6). pap. 14.49 *(978-1-4490-9859-9(2))* AuthorHouse.

Kakugawa, Frances. Wordsworth Dances the Waltz. DeSica, Melissa, illus. 2007. 32p. (J). 10.95 *(978-0-9790647-3-9(2))* Watermark Publishing, LLC.

Kanu, Rosslyn. The Little Girl Called Princess: Princess Where Are You? 2012. 32p. pap. 19.99 *(978-1-4685-2375-1(9))* AuthorHouse.

Karandeev, Oleg. Dmitri II: The Kind Storyteller Book Two of Five. Ciesinska, Izabela, illus. 2007. 76p. (YA). per. 15.95 *(978-0-9793944-3-0(0))* Digi-Tali Media.

Kasza, Keiko. Los Secretos de Abuelo Sapo. (SPA., Illus.). (J). (gr. 1-3). *(978-958-04-3624-9(X)*, NR7688) Norma S.A.

Katcher, Brian. Deacon Locke Went to Prom. 2017. 400p. (YA). (gr. 8). 17.99 *(978-0-06-242252-1(9)*, Tegen, Katherine Bks) HarperCollins Pubs.

Kaufman, Seufert. Wee Wilhelmina & Her Magic Marbles. 2012. (ENG.). pap. *(978-1-4675-4364-4(0))* Independent Pub.

Kaupp, Rosemarie. The Amberella Tales: Amberella in the City. 2012. 120p. (gr. 4-6). 22.33 *(978-1-4669-0594-8(8))*; pap. 12.33 *(978-1-4669-0595-5(6))* Trafford Publishing.

Kaur, K. S. The Horncastles & the Magnopeus Medicine. Kaur, Bal, illus. 2012. 154p. pap. *(978-1-78148-023-6(0))* Grosvenor Hse. Publishing Ltd.

Kearns, Zannah & Quarto Generic Staff. No Use Crying. 2012. (ENG.). 320p. (J). (gr. 7-9). pap. 8.99 *(978-1-84780-214-9(1)*, Frances Lincoln) Quarto Publishing Group UK GBR. Dist: Hachette Bk. Group.

Keegan, Anne. A Cat for Claire. 2008. 28p. pap. 15.00 *(978-1-4389-2737-4(1))* AuthorHouse.

Keene, Carolyn. The Stolen Bones. 29th ed. 2008. (Nancy Drew (All New) Girl Detective Ser.: 29). (ENG.). 160p. (J). (gr. 3-7). pap. 5.99 *(978-1-4169-3614-5(9)*, Aladdin) Simon & Schuster Children's Publishing.

Kellenbarger, Sandy Hurst. Magic Gnomes. 2012. 24p. (gr. 2-4). pap. 14.93 *(978-1-4669-6526-3(6))* Trafford Publishing.

—Magic Gnomes Treasure Hunt. 2013. 28p. pap. 16.09 *(978-1-4669-8892-7(4))* Trafford Publishing.

Kelly, Jacqueline. La Evolución de Calpurnia Tate. 2010.Tr. of Evolution of Calpurnia Tate. (SPA.). 272p. (YA). pap. 20.95 *(978-84-9918-103-5(1))* Roca Editorial ESP. Dist: Spanish Pubs., LLC.

—La Evolucion de Calpurnia Tate, Vol. 2. 2011.Tr. of Evolution of Calpurnia Tate. (SPA.). 272p. pap. 12.95 *(978-84-92833-15-3(7))* Roca Editorial ESP. Dist: Spanish Pubs., LLC.

—The Evolution of Calpurnia Tate. 2009. (Calpurnia Tate Ser.: 1). (ENG.). 352p. (J). (gr. 4-7). 17.99 *(978-0-8050-8841-0(5)*, 9780805088410, Holt, Henry & Co. Bks. For Young Readers) Holt, Henry & Co.

—The Evolution of Calpurnia Tate. 2010. 340p. 18.00 *(978-1-60686-849-2(7))* Perfection Learning Corp.

—The Evolution of Calpurnia Tate. 2011. (Calpurnia Tate Ser.: 1). (ENG.). 368p. (J). (gr. 4-7). pap. 7.99 *(978-0-312-65930-1(X)*, 9780312659301) Square Fish.

—The Evolution of Calpurnia Tate. 2011. (Calpurnia Tate Ser.: 1). (J). lib. bdg. 18.40 *(978-0-606-20974-8(3)*, Turtleback) Turtleback Bks.

Kelly, Matthew. Why Am I Here? A Story about Becoming The-Best-Version-of-Yourself! Mitchell, Hazel, illus. 2009. 60p. (J). 17.99 *(978-0-9841318-0-8(9))* Beacon Publishing.

Ken Lindstrom To Ken Lindstrom. Ollie & Grampa Go to the Zoo: How the Polar Bear Got to the Zoo. Jones., Amber, illus. 2011. 28p. pap. 12.49 *(978-1-4520-1529-3(5))* AuthorHouse.

Kennedy, Pamela. Granny's Cozy Quilt of Memories: Remembering Grandmother's Love Through Her Lasting Gift. Wummer, Amy, illus. 2006. (ENG.). 32p. (J). (gr. k-3). 8.95 *(978-0-8249-5538-0(2)*, Ideal Pubns.) Worthy Publishing.

Kephart, Beth. House of Dance. 2010. (ENG.). 272p. (J). (gr. 8). pap. 10.99 *(978-0-06-142930-9(9))* 2008. 263p. (YA). (gr. 7-18). lib. bdg. 17.89 *(978-0-06-142929-3(5))* HarperCollins Pubs. (HarperTeen).

Kerr, Judith. Twinkles, Arthur & Puss. Kerr, Judith, illus. 2008. (ENG., Illus.). 40p. (J). (gr. k-2). pap. 9.95 *(978-0-00-725447-7(4))* HarperCollins Pubs. Ltd. GBR. Dist: Independent Pubs. Group.

Kessler, Liz. North of Nowhere. 2015. (ENG.). 272p. (J). (gr. 4-7). pap. 7.99 *(978-0-7636-7672-8(1))* Candlewick Pr.

Key, Janet Rhyme. Rosa in Bloom. 2013. 86p. (J). pap. 13.95 *(978-1-4817-1956-8(4))* AuthorHouse.

Khzouz, Medlaine. Suzie Time. 2011. 24p. pap. 15.99 *(978-1-4568-7454-4(3))* Xlibris Corp.

Kiely, Brendan. The Last True Love Story. 2016. (ENG., Illus.). 288p. (YA). (gr. 9). 17.99 *(978-1-4814-2988-7(4)*, McElderry, Margaret K. Bks.) McElderry, Margaret K. Bks.

—Last True Love Story. 2017. (ENG., Illus.). 288p. (YA). (gr. 9). pap. 11.99 *(978-1-4814-2989-4(2)*, McElderry, Margaret K. Bks.) McElderry, Margaret K. Bks.

Kimmel, Smith Robert. The War with Grandpa. 2014. (Yearling Ser.). (ENG.). 160p. (J). (gr. 3-7). 11.24 *(978-1-63245-333-4(9))* Lectorum Pubns., Inc.

Kimmelman, Leslie. The Shabbat Puppy, 0 vols. Zollars, Jaime, illus. 2012. (Shofar Ser.: 0). (ENG.). 32p. (J). (gr. -1-3). 17.99 *(978-0-7614-6145-6(0)*, 9780761461456, Amazon Children's Publishing) Amazon Publishing.

Kimpton, Paul & Kimpton, Ann Kaczkowski. Starting Early: A Boy & His Bugle in America During WWII. 2011. (Adventures with Music Ser.: 1). (ENG., Illus.). 204p. (J). (gr. 4-7). pap. 8.95 *(978-1-57999-805-9(4))* G I A Pubns., Inc.

Kindt, Matt. Poppy! & the Lost Lagoon. 2016. (ENG., Illus.). 144p. (J). (gr. 3-7). 14.99 *(978-1-61655-943-4(8))* Dark Horse Comics.

King, A. S. Everybody Sees the Ants. 2011. (ENG.). 288p. (YA). (gr. 10-17). 18.00 *(978-0-316-12928-2(3))* Little Brown & Co.

—Everybody Sees the Ants. 2012. (ENG.). 320p. (YA). (gr. 10-17). pap. 10.00 *(978-0-316-12927-5(5))* Little, Brown Bks. for Young Readers.

King, Emily. Mrs. Twiggenbotham Goes to Town. 2003. (Twiggenbotham Adventure Ser.). (Illus.). 32p. (J). 12.99 *(978-0-8254-3064-0(X))* Kregel Pubns.

Kingsbury, Karen & Smith, Alex. Go Ahead & Dream. Banning, Greg, illus. 2013. (ENG.). 32p. (J). (gr. -1-3). 17.99 *(978-0-06-168625-2(5))* HarperCollins Pubs.

Kirk, Bill. My Grandma's Kitchen Rules. Movshina, Marina, illus. 2009. 24p. pap. 10.95 *(978-1-935137-88-7(3))* Guardian Angel Publishing, Inc.

Kirk, Janice. The Christmas Redwood. Kirk, Janice, illus. 2007. (Illus.). 56p. per. 18.95 *(978-1-60290-147-6(3))* OakTara Publishing Group LLC.

Kirkup, Mary. The Tales of Granny Grunt. 2008. 32p. pap. 12.99 *(978-1-4389-1040-6(1))* AuthorHouse.

Kitz, Judith. Grandma Wants You To. 2009. 16p. pap. 8.49 *(978-1-4389-5136-2(1))* AuthorHouse.

Kleczka, John A. Flick the Butterfly: Flick & Mom Go to Grandma's. 2008. 48p. per. 24.95 *(978-1-60441-290-1(9))* America Star Bks.

Klein, Adria F. Max Come Al Aire Libre, 1 vol. Robledo, Sol, tr. from ENG. Gallagher-Cole, Mernie, illus. 2007. (Read-It! Readers en Español: la Vida de Max Ser.). (SPA.). 24p. (gr. -1-3). lib. bdg. 21.32 *(978-1-4048-3795-9(7)*, Easy Readers) Picture Window Bks.

—Max Goes to the Farm, 1 vol. Gallagher-Cole, Mernie, illus. 2007. (Read-It! Readers: the Life of Max Ser.). (ENG.). 24p. (gr. -1-2). lib. bdg. 21.32 *(978-1-4048-3678-5(0)*, Easy Readers) Picture Window Bks.

Klimpton, Diana. Amy Wild, Animal Talker - the Secret Necklace 1. 2013. pap. 4.99 *(978-0-7945-3144-7(X)*, Usborne) EDC Publishing.

Kline, Suzy. Horrible Harry & the Holidaze. Remkiewicz, Frank, illus. 2004. (Horrible Harry Ser.). (ENG.). 80p. (J). (gr. 2-4). 4.99 *(978-0-14-240205-4(2)*, Puffin Books) Penguin Young Readers Group.

—Horrible Harry & the Secret Treasure. Wummer, Amy, illus. (Horrible Harry Ser.). (ENG.). 80p. (J). (gr. 2-4). 2012. 4.99 *(978-0-14-242021-8(2)*, Puffin Books) 2011. 14.99 *(978-0-670-01181-0(9)*, Viking Books for Young Readers) Penguin Young Readers Group.

Klinkerman, Anthonette. Battle of the Grandmas. 2012. (ENG.). 34p. (J). pap. 13.95 *(978-1-4787-1930-4(3))* Outskirts Pr., Inc.

Klise, Kate. Grammy Lamby & the Secret Handshake. Klise, Kate & Klise, M. Sarah, illus. 2012. (ENG.). 32p. (J). (gr. -1-3). 17.99 *(978-0-8050-9313-1(3)*, 9780805093131, Holt, Henry & Co. Bks. For Young Readers) Holt, Henry & Co.

Knight, Chris. The Statue. 2013. 52p. pap. *(978-1-78299-440-4(8))* FeedARead.com.

Knight, Mary. Saving Wonder. 2016. (ENG.). 288p. (J). (gr. 3-7). 16.99 *(978-0-545-82893-2(7)*, Scholastic Pr.) Scholastic, Inc.

Knight, Richard. Winter Shadow. Johnson, Richard, illus. 2011. (ENG.). 80p. (J). (gr. 1-5). pap. 9.99 *(978-1-84686-624-1(3))* Barefoot Bks., Inc.

Knight, Richard John & Walker, Richard. Winter Shadow. Johnson, Richard, illus. 2009. (ENG.). 80p. (J). (gr. 3-9). pap. 16.99 *(978-1-84686-116-1(0))* Barefoot Bks., Inc.

Kohlhepp, Michael G. Within the Hearthstone Book 2: The Fountain of Balance. 2007. (ENG.). 184p. per. 24.95 *(978-1-4241-4446-4(9))* PublishAmerica, Inc.

Koncerak, Veronica. The Bubble That Never Popped. 2010. 24p. 11.49 *(978-1-4520-3935-0(6))* AuthorHouse.

Koraido, Beth S. On the Farm with Grandma Gert. 2008. 53p. pap. 16.95 *(978-1-60474-400-2(6))* America Star Bks.

—Summers with Grampa Gus. 2008. 63p. pap. 19.95 *(978-1-60703-384-4(4))* America Star Bks.

Korman, Gordon. Schooled. 2008. (ENG.). 224p. (J). (gr. 3-7). pap. 6.99 *(978-1-4231-0516-9(8))* Hyperion Bks. for Children.

—Schooled. 2010. 17.00 *(978-1-60686-894-2(2))* Perfection Learning Corp.

—Schooled. (J). 2012. 1.25 *(978-1-4281-7185-5(1))* 2008. 70.75 *(978-1-4361-1568-1(X))* 2008. 69.75 *(978-1-4281-7190-9(8))* 2007. 92.75 *(978-1-4281-7192-3(4))* 2007. 90.75 *(978-1-4281-7194-7(0))* 2007. 71.75 *(978-1-4281-7188-6(6))* 2007. 147.75 *(978-1-4281-7189-3(4))* Recorded Bks., Inc.

—Schooled. 2008. (J). lib. bdg. 17.20 *(978-1-4178-2839-5(0)*, Turtleback) Turtleback Bks.

Korngold, Jamie. Sadie & Ori & the Blue Blanket. Fortenberry, Julie, illus. 2015. (ENG.). 32p. (J). (gr. -1-2). 17.99 *(978-1-4677-1191-3(8)*, Kar-Ben Publishing) Lerner Publishing Group.

Kotchman, Susan C. With Love, from Grandma. 2011. 44p. pap. 18.46 *(978-1-4567-4458-8(5))* AuthorHouse.

Koutsky, Jan Dale. My Grandma, My Pen Pal. Koutsky, Jan Dale, illus. 2003. (ENG., Illus.). 32p. (J). (gr. k-2). 15.95 *(978-1-56397-118-1(6))* Boyds Mills Pr.

Kovalski, Maryann. Jenny & Joanna Album. 2005. *(978-1-55041-941-2(2))* Fitzhenry & Whiteside, Ltd.

Kramer, Stacy & Thomas, Valerie. Karma Bites. 2010. (ENG.). 348p. (J). (gr. 5-7). pap. 18.99 *(978-0-547-36301-1(X))* Houghton Mifflin Harcourt Publishing Co.

Krebs, Laurie & Cis, Valeria. The Beeman. Cis, Valeria, illus. 2008. (ENG., Illus.). 40p. (J). (gr. -1-3). 16.99 *(978-1-84686-146-8(2))* Barefoot Bks., Inc.

Kreuger, Jim & Averdonz, N. R. My Double-Edged Life, 1 vol. Padilla, Ariel, illus. 2007. (Z Graphic Novels / Tomo Ser.). (ENG.). 160p. (J). (gr. 3-7). pap. 6.99 *(978-0-310-71301-2(3))* Zondervan.

Krinsky, Ed. Pip, Veronica & the Harmonica. Evans, Casey, illus. 2013. 32p. pap. 13.00 *(978-1-62516-945-7(0)*, Strategic Bk. Publishing) Strategic Book Publishing & Rights Agency (SBPRA).

Kropf, Latifa Berry. It's Hanukkah Time! Cohen, Tod, photos by. 2004. (ENG., Illus.). 24p. (J). (gr. -1-1). 12.95 *(978-1-58013-120-9(4)*, Kar-Ben Publishing) Lerner Publishing Group.

Kropik, Linda Kristine. Christopher the Choo Choo Train. Haezer, Jane, illus. 2011. 24p. pap. 11.50 *(978-1-60911-522-7(8)*, Strategic Bk. Publishing) Strategic Book Publishing & Rights Agency (SBPRA).

Krouskop, Adrienne. The Bakers Moon. 2013. 24p. pap. 10.50 *(978-1-938743-92-4(X))* Reimann Bks.

Kuipers, Jennifer L. Lynn's Magic Trunk: An Adventure in King Arthur's Court. 2007. 76p. per. 19.95 *(978-1-4241-9860-3(7))* America Star Bks.

Kurtz, Carmen. Veva y el Mar.Tr. of Veva & the Sea. (SPA.). 144p. (J). (gr. 3-5). *(978-84-279-3129-9(8))* Noguer y Caralt Editores, S. A. ESP. Dist: Lectorum Pubns., Inc.

Labrecque, Candida. A Riverside Walk with Grandma. Labrecque, Candida & Labrecque, Candida, illus. I.t. ed. 2006. (Illus.). 23p. (J). per. 11.95 *(978-1-59879-137-2(0))* Lifevest Publishing, Inc.

LaFleur, Suzanne. Love, Aubrey. 2011. (ENG.). 272p. (J). (gr. 3-7). pap. 7.99 *(978-0-375-85159-9(3)*, Yearling) Random Hse. Children's Bks.

Lai, Thanhhà. Listen, Slowly. (J). (gr. 3-7). 2016. 288p. pap. 6.99 *(978-0-06-222919-9(2))* 2015. (ENG.). 272p. 16.99 *(978-0-06-222918-2(4))* 2015. (ENG.). 288p. E-Book *(978-0-06-222920-5(6))* HarperCollins Pubs.

Lainez, René Colato. Playing Lotería Mexicana: El Juego de la Lotería Mexicana. Arena, Jillayne, illus. 2005. (ENG, SPA & MUL.). 32p. (J). (gr. -1-3). 15.95 *(978-0-87358-881-2(9))* Cooper Square Publishing Llc.

Lairamore, Dawn. Ivy's Ever After. 2010. (ENG.). 192p. (J). (gr. 3-7). 16.95 *(978-0-8234-2261-6(5))* Holiday Hse., Inc.

Lake, Julie. Galveston's Summer of the Storm. 2003. (Chaparral Bks.). (ENG.). 158p. pap. 17.95 *(978-0-87565-272-6(7))* Texas Christian Univ. Pr.

Lam, Fiona Tinwei. Rainbow Rocket. 2013. (ENG., Illus.). 32p. 19.95 *(978-0-88982-282-5(4))* Oolichan Bks. CAN. Dist: Univ. of Toronto Pr.

Lamb, Steven. Eliot. 2007. 56p. per. 16.95 *(978-1-4241-9042-3(8))* America Star Bks.

Laminack, Lester. Saturdays & Teacakes. 2009. 0032p. 19.95 *(978-1-56145-313-9(7))* Peachtree Pubs.

Laminack, Lester L. Saturdays & Teacakes, 1 vol. Soentpiet, Chris K., illus. (ENG.). 32p. (J). 2009. 19.95 *(978-1-56145-513-3(X))* 2004. 16.95 *(978-1-56145-303-0(X))* Peachtree Pubs.

Lampkin, Laveta M. Where Is Grandmother? Nicely, Darthy, illus. 2011. 36p. pap. 24.95 *(978-1-4626-1579-7(1))* America Star Bks.

The Land Beyond Forever. 2006. 25.00 *(978-0-9785570-0-3(X))* Three Sisters Publishing Hse., Ltd.

Landis, Mary. David & Susan at the Little Green House. 2005. (Illus.). 170p. 8.20 *(978-0-7399-2352-8(8)*, 2185.3) Rod & Staff Pubs., Inc.

Lane, Jessica E. The Secret of the Swans. 2009. 52p. pap. 31.99 *(978-1-4415-5517-5(X))* Xlibris Corp.

Lane, Kathleen, et al. Nana Cracks the Case! Home, Sarah, illus. 2009. (ENG.). 112p. (J). (gr. -1-7). 14.99 *(978-0-8118-6258-5(5))* Chronicle Bks. LLC.

Langcaon, Jeff, illus. My Grandpa's Battleship Missouri Tour. 2007. (J). 14.95 *(978-1-56647-831-1(6))* Mutual Publishing LLC.

Lange, Jessica. It's about a Little Bird. 2013. (ENG., Illus.). 40p. (J). (-3). 16.99 *(978-1-4022-8526-4(4)*, 9781402285264, Sourcebooks Jabberwocky) Sourcebooks, Inc.

Langston, W. R. Why I Like My Grandma's House. 2011. 92p. pap. 15.99 *(978-1-4568-9615-7(6))* Xlibris Corp.

Lanqcaon, Jeff. Grandpa's Magic Banyan Tree. 2005. 32p. (J). 12.95 *(978-1-56647-740-6(9))* Mutual Publishing LLC.

Lapin Feeblebunny. The Gang That Couldn't Think Straight. 2005. 83p. pap. 10.00 *(978-1-4134-9979-7(1))* Xlibris Corp.

Larsen, Jen. Future Perfect. 2015. (ENG.). 320p. (YA). (gr. 8-12). 17.99 *(978-0-06-232123-7(4)*, HarperTeen) HarperCollins Pubs.

Larson, Deborah Jo. One Frozen Lake. Johnson, Steve & Fancher, Lou, illus. 2012. (ENG.). 32p. (J). 16.95 *(978-0-87351-866-6(7))* Minnesota Historical Society Pr.

Lasaracina, Barbara. Mermaid Tears: A Magical Sea Tale. Peer, Nancy, illus. 2010. 28p. pap. 11.99 *(978-1-60844-451-9(1))* Dog Ear Publishing, LLC.

Lasswell, Barbara. Different Ways, 1 vol. 2009. 29p. pap. 24.95 *(978-1-60749-328-0(4))* America Star Bks.

Latimer, Alex. Stay! a Top Dog Story, 1 vol. Latimer, Alex, illus. 2015. (ENG., Illus.). 32p. (J). (gr. -1-3). 16.95 *(978-1-56145-884-4(8))* Peachtree Pubs.

Latimer, Miriam. Emily's Tiger. 2008. (ENG., Illus.). 32p. (J). (gr. -1-3). 16.99 *(978-1-84686-138-3(1))* Barefoot Bks., Inc.

Latimor, Miriam. Emily's Tiger. Latimor, Miriam, illus. 2011. (ENG., Illus.). 32p. (J). (gr. -1-2). 7.99 *(978-1-84686-594-7(8))* Barefoot Bks., Inc.

Laura Lee Hope. Six Little Bunkers at Grandma Bell's. I.t. ed. 2007. (ENG.). 162p. pap. 21.99 *(978-1-4264-8193-2(4))* Creative Media Partners, LLC.

—Six Little Bunkers at Grandpa Ford's. 2007. 188p. per. 11.95 *(978-1-4218-3989-9(X)*, 1st World Library - Literary Society) 1st World Publishing, Inc.

Law, Ingrid. Switch. 2015. (ENG.). 368p. (J). (gr. 3-7). 16.99 *(978-0-8037-3862-1(5)*, Dial Bks) Penguin Young Readers Group.

Lawrence, Antoinette & Lewis, Terry. My Dad, My Granddad, & Me. 2013. (ENG.). 32p. (J). pap. 12.95 *(978-1-4787-0013-5(0))* Outskirts Pr., Inc.

Layton, Roxanne A. Tommy's Happy Place. 2012. 28p. 24.95 *(978-1-4626-6551-8(9))* America Star Bks.

Leavitt, Martine. Keturah & Lord Death. (ENG.). (YA). 2012. 224p. (gr. 9-12). pap. 9.95 *(978-1-59078-949-0(0))* 2006. 216p. (gr. 7-7). 16.95 *(978-1-932425-29-1(2)*, Front Street) Boyds Mills Pr.

Lee, HaeDa. Ida's Present. Kim, IhHyeon, illus. 2014. (MySELF Bookshelf Ser.). (ENG.). 32p. (J). (gr. k-2). lib. bdg. 25.27 *(978-1-59953-659-0(5))* Norwood Hse. Pr.

Lee, Ingrid. Maybe Later, 1 vol. Grimard, Gabrielle, illus. 2008. (Orca Echoes Ser.). (ENG.). 64p. (J). (gr. 2-3). pap. 6.95 *(978-1-55143-764-4(3))* Orca Bk. Pubs. USA.

Leibovici, Danielle. With You Always. Gabrielov, Julia, illus. I.t. ed. 2012. (ENG.). 62p. pap. 14.95 *(978-1-4565-2627-6(8))* CreateSpace Independent Publishing Platform.

EFG

Leonard, Nellie M. Grand Daddy Whiskers, M. D. 2004. reprint ed. pap. 1.99 *(978-1-4192-2227-6(9))*; pap. 15.95 *(978-1-4191-2227-9(4))* Kessinger Publishing, LLC.

Leone, Elaine H. Grandy Goose Rhymes. 2013. (ENG.). 116p. pap. 10.99 *(978-1-4675-6477-9(X))* Independent Pub.

Leopold, Nikia Speliakos Clark. Adam's Crayons. Nemett, Barry & Nemett, Laini, illus. 2011. (J). *(978-0-9817519-1-7(1))* Galileo Pr.

Leopold-Strauss, Linda. A Different Kind of Passover. Tugeau, Jeremy, illus. 2017. (ENG.). 32p. (gr. -1-3). 17.99 *(978-1-5124-0097-7(1)*, Kar-Ben Publishing) Lerner Publishing Group.

Leray, Merrill. The House of Lady Chase. 2009. 70p. pap. 15.99 *(978-1-4415-4381-3(3))* Xlibris Corp.

Leslie, Sherrie L. An Apple A Day: The Adventures of Grannie Annie & Pickles #1. 2011. 52p. (gr. 2-4). pap. 8.95 *(978-1-4620-4606-5(1))* iUniverse, Inc.

Levine, Arthur A. & Kath, Katie. What a Beautiful Morning. 2016. (ENG., Illus.). 40p. (J). (gr. -1-17). 16.95 *(978-0-7624-5906-3(9)*, Running Pr. Kids) Running Pr. Bk. Pubs.

Levine, Gail Carson. Betsy Red Hoodie. Nash, Scott, illus. 2010. (ENG.). 40p. (J). (gr. -1-3). 16.99 *(978-0-06-146870-4(3))* HarperCollins Pubs.

Levy, Janice. I Remember Abuelito: A Day of the Dead Story. Arisa, Miguel, tr. Lopez, Loretta, illus. 2007.Tr. of Yo Recuerdo a Abuelito - Un Cuento del Dia de los Muertos. (SPA & ENG.). 32p. (J). (gr. -1-3). 6.99 *(978-0-8075-3517-2(6))* Whitman, Albert & Co.

Levy, Janice & Arisa, Miguel. I Remember Abuelito: A Day of the Dead Story. Lopez, Loretta, illus. 2012.Tr. of Yo Recuerdo a Abuelito - Un Cuento del Dia de los Muertos. (SPA & ENG.). (J). *(978-1-61913-114-9(5))* Weigl Pubs., Inc.

Lewis, Axel. Rain Forest Rampage, 1 vol. 2014. (Robot Racers Ser.). (ENG.). 160p. (gr. 2-4). 26.65 *(978-1-4342-6571-5(4))* Stone Arch Bks.

Lewis, Jill & Blue Bananas. Coconut Jack. Waters, Erica-Jane, illus. 2009. (Blue Bananas Ser.). (ENG.). 48p. (J). (gr. k-2). pap. 5.99 *(978-1-4052-4132-8(2))* Egmont Bks., Ltd. GBR. Dist: Independent Pubs. Group.

Lewis, Siân. Josh in the Jungle. Roberts, Gill, illus. 2005. (ENG.). 32p. pap. 12.95 *(978-1-84323-462-3(9))* Beekman Bks., Inc.

Light, Carol, illus. Oops, a Curious Horse Story Telling Board. 2003. (J). *(978-0-9745803-4-0(1))* Little Big Tomes.

Lile, Linda L. Nonnie, What's God? Julich, Jennifer, illus. 2008. 16p. (J). 13.95 *(978-0-9817092-0-8(6))* A-Lu Publishing.

Lin, Grace. When the Sea Turned to Silver. (ENG.). (J). (gr. 3-7). 2017. 400p. pap. 9.99 ***(978-0-316-12594-9(6))*** 2016. (Illus.). 384p. 18.99 *(978-0-316-12592-5(X))* Little, Brown Bks. for Young Readers.

—When the Sea Turned to Silver. 2017. (J). lib. bdg. 20.85 ***(978-0-606-40629-1(8))*** Turtleback Bks.

Lindbergh, Reeve. My Little Grandmother Often Forgets. Brown, Kathryn, illus. 2007. (ENG.). 32p. (J). (gr. -1-1). 16.99 *(978-0-7636-1989-3(2))* Candlewick Pr.

Lindo, Elvira. Manolito Four-Eyes, 0 vols. Emilio, Urberuaga & Urberuaga, Emilio, illus. 2010. (Manolito Four-Eyes Ser.: 1). (ENG.). 155p. (J). (gr. 3-7). pap. 9.99 *(978-0-7614-5729-9(1)*, 9780761457299, Amazon Children's Publishing) Amazon Publishing.

—Manolito Gafotas, 0 vols. Urberuaga, Emilio, illus. 2010. (SPA & ENG.). 192p. (J). (gr. 3-7). pap. 9.99 *(978-0-7614-5730-5(5)*, 9780761457305, Amazon Children's Publishing) Amazon Publishing.

Lindstrom, Ken. Grandpa, Is There Really a Santa Claus? 2008. 20p. pap. 10.99 *(978-1-4389-2127-3(6))* AuthorHouse.

Ling, Nancy Tupper. Double Happiness. Chau, Alina, illus. 2015. (ENG.). 48p. (J). (gr. k-3). 16.99 *(978-1-4521-2918-1(5))* Chronicle Bks. LLC.

Lipp, Frederick J. Bread Song. Gaillard, Jason, tr. Gaillard, Jason, illus. 2004. (J). 15.95 *(978-1-59336-000-9(2))*; pap. *(978-1-59336-001-6(0))* Mondo Publishing.

Little Red Riding Hood: 6 Small Books. (gr. k-2). 23.00 *(978-0-7635-8510-5(6))* Rigby Education.

Little Red Riding Hood: Individual Title Six-Packs. (Story Steps Ser.). (gr. k-2). 32.00 *(978-0-7635-9841-9(0))* Rigby Education.

Little, Robert. Grandma's Biscuits. Richmond, Jamea, illus. 2004. 32p. (J). (gr. -1-7). 15.95 *(978-0-9701863-5-5(5))* Relde Publishing.

Littman, Sarah Darer. Confessions of a Closet Catholic. 2006. (ENG.). 208p. (J). (gr. 5-18). reprint ed. 7.99 *(978-0-14-240597-0(3)*, Puffin Books) Penguin Young Readers Group.

Litzenberg, Corinne M. Grandpa's Basement, 1 vol. 2007. (ENG., Illus.). 32p. (J). 14.95 *(978-0-7643-2720-9(8)*, 9780764327209) Schiffer Publishing, Ltd.

Liu, Sylvia. A Morning with Gong Gong. Forshay, Christina, illus. 2016. (ENG.). 32p. (J). (gr. -1-3). 17.95 *(978-1-62014-192-2(2))* Lee & Low Bks., Inc.

Lloyd-Jones, Sally. The Ultimate Guide to Grandmas & Grandpas! Emberley, Michael, illus. 2008. (ENG.). 32p. (J). (gr. -1-3). 14.99 *(978-0-06-075687-1(X))* HarperCollins Pubs.

Loccisano, Rina. Baby Dario Eats His First Carrot. Baker, David, illus. 2012. 48p. pap. 24.95 *(978-1-4560-6100-5(3))* America Star Bks.

Lombardi, Mary. Grandpa's Chair. l.t. ed. 2005. (Illus.). 17p. (J). per. 9.99 *(978-1-59879-016-0(1))* Lifevest Publishing, Inc.

Londner, Renee. Stones for Grandpa. Avilés Junco, Martha, illus. 2013. 24p. (J). (gr. k-3). lib. bdg. 17.95 *(978-0-7613-7495-4(7)*, Kar-Ben Publishing) Lerner Publishing Group.

—Stones for Grandpa. Aviles, Martha, illus. 2013. (ENG.). 24p. (J). (gr. k-3). pap. 7.95 *(978-0-7613-7496-1(5)*, Kar-Ben Publishing) Lerner Publishing Group.

London, Jonathan. Froggy Goes to Grandma's. 2017. (Froggy Ser.). (ENG., Illus.). 32p. (J). (-k). 16.99 *(978-1-101-99964-6(0)*, Viking Books for Young Readers) Penguin Young Readers Group.

Long, Kathy. Christopher SAT Straight up in Bed. Cantor, Patricia, illus. 2013. (ENG.). 40p. (J). 16.00 *(978-0-8028-5359-2(5)*, Eerdmans Bks For Young Readers) Eerdmans, William B. Publishing Co.

Longoria, Eugene R., Jr. Junior y la Llorona en la Montana de Nieve. 2006. (SPA., Illus.). 40p. (J). 12.00 *(978-0-9796818-0-6(4))* Longoria, Eugene R.

Longstreet, Olivia. Edgar's Moon. 2011. 24p. pap. 15.99 *(978-1-4568-6524-5(2))* Xlibris Corp.

Look, Lenore. Alvin Ho: Allergic to Dead Bodies, Funerals, & Other Fatal Circumstances. Pham, LeUyen, illus. 2012. (Alvin Ho Ser.). (ENG.). 208p. (J). (gr. 1-4). 6.99 *(978-0-307-97695-6(5)*, Yearling) Random Hse. Children's Bks.

Looper, Grace W. Great-Grandpa's Hidden Treasure. 2006. (YA). pap. *(978-1-933523-18-7(2))* Bella Rosa Bks.

Loper, Kathleen. Angelina Katrina: Bugs in My Backyard. Waltz, Dan, illus. l.t. ed. 2004. 24p. (J). 17.95 *(978-0-9741774-4-1(X))* D. W. Publishing.

Lopez, Lois. Grandpape. 2003. 27p. pap. 9.00 *(978-0-8059-6247-5(6))* Dorrance Publishing Co., Inc.

Lord, Cynthia. A Handful of Stars. (ENG.). 192p. (J). (gr. 3-7). 2017. pap. 6.99 ***(978-0-545-70028-3(0))*** 2015. 16.99 *(978-0-545-70027-6(2))* Scholastic, Inc. (Scholastic Pr.).

Lord, Janet. Here Comes Grandma! Paschkis, Julie, illus. rev. ed. 2005. (ENG.). 32p. (J). (gr. -1-k). 16.99 *(978-0-8050-7666-0(2)*, 9780805076660, Holt, Henry & Co. Bks. For Young Readers) Holt, Henry & Co.

Lore, Erin, illus. Timmy the Dragon. l.t. ed. 2007. 32p. (J). 8.95 *(978-0-9741562-7-9(2))* Yarrow Pr.

Lorenz, Jinye, Sr. Grandfather, the Tiger & Ryong. Lorenz, Virginia O., Sr., ed. Lorenz, Jinye, Sr., illus. ltd. ed. 2005. (Illus.). 65p. (J). spiral bd. 14.95 *(978-1-888350-10-4(5))* Lighted Lamp Pr.

Lorenz, Jinye. Ryong's Story: Extended Version of Grandfather, the Tiger & Ryong. Lorenz, Virginia O., ed. 2006. (Illus.). 135p. (YA). per. 14.95 *(978-1-888350-11-1(3))* Lighted Lamp Pr.

Lorimer, Janet. Ruby's Terrible Secret, 1 vol. unabr. ed. 2010. (Q Reads Ser.). (ENG.). 32p. (YA). (gr. 9-12). pap. 6.95 *(978-1-61651-218-7(0))* Saddleback Educational Publishing, Inc.

Love, Maryann Cusimano. You Are My Wish. Ichikawa, Satomi, illus. 2010. (ENG.). 32p. (J). (gr. -1-k). 16.99 *(978-0-399-24752-1(1)*, Philomel Bks.) Penguin Young Readers Group.

Lovelace, Eloise. I Was a Boy Just Like You. 2011. 36p. pap. 15.14 *(978-1-4634-4378-8(1))* AuthorHouse.

Lovell, Patty. Have Fun, Molly Lou Melon. Lovell, Patty & Catrow, David, illus. 2012. (ENG.). 32p. (J). (gr. k-3). 16.99 *(978-0-399-25406-2(4)*, G.P. Putnam's Sons Books for Young Readers) Penguin Young Readers Group.

Lovett, Tracy M. Buck's Rodeo. Lovett, Tracy M., illus. 2012. (Illus.). 470p. pap. 16.50 *(978-0-9819736-6-1(3))* Inclement Pr.

Loving, Winifred "Oyoko". My Grandma Loves to Play. 2013. 28p. pap. 16.99 *(978-1-4669-7405-0(2))* Trafford Publishing.

Low, William. Chinatown. 2014. 32p. pap. 9.00 *(978-1-61003-224-7(1))* Center for the Collaborative Classroom.

Lowery, Linda. Truth & Salsa, 1 vol. (ENG.). 176p. (J). 2009. pap. 7.95 *(978-1-56145-498-3(2))* 2006. (gr. 3-7). 15.95 *(978-1-56145-366-5(8))* Peachtree Pubs.

Loye, David. Grandfather's Garden: Bedtime Stories for Little & Big Folk. 2008. (J). pap. 18.95 *(978-0-9795257-7-3(2))* Benjamin Franklin Pr.

Lozano, Neal. Can God See Me in the Dark? Hatke, Ben, illus. 2007. (ENG.). 32p. (J). 16.95 *(978-1-883551-45-2(5)*, Maple Corners Press) Attic Studio Publishing Hse.

Lucas, Ian & Medoza, Chris. The Million Year Meal. Cruz, Cheryl, illus. 2012. 32p. (J). 19.95 *(978-1-60131-099-6(4))* Big Tent Bks.

Luciani, Brigitte. The Carnival. Tharlet, Eve, illus. 2014. (ENG.). 32p. (J). pap. 6.95 *(978-1-4677-4204-7(X))*; lib. bdg. 25.26 *(978-1-4677-4203-0(1)*, Graphic Universe™) Lerner Publishing Group.

Luenn, Nancy. A Gift for Abuelita/Un Regalo para Abuelita: Celebrating the Day of the Dead/En Celebration del Dia de los Muertos. Chapman, Robert, illus. 2004.Tr. of Un Regalo para Abuelita: En Celebration del Dia de los Muertos. (ENG, SPA & MUL.). 32p. (J). (gr. k-3). 15.95 *(978-0-87358-688-7(3))* Cooper Square Publishing Llc.

Lundy, Charlotte. Thank You, Jesus. Waldrep, Evelyn L., ed. Claremont, Heather, illus. 2003. 32p. (gr. k-3). 15.95 *(978-0-9670280-1-9(9))* Bay Light Publishing.

Lunsford, Gary. Georgia Is on My Mind: A Tale of a Guardian Angel. 2010. 374p. 30.50 *(978-1-60911-164-9(8)*, Eloquent Bks.) Strategic Book Publishing & Rights Agency (SBPRA).

Lunsford, Judy. Sally & the Buccaneers. 2009. 77p. pap. 12.98 *(978-0-557-10064-4(X))* Lulu Pr., Inc.

Lynch, Chris. Freewill. 2014. (ENG., Illus.). 160p. (YA). (gr. 7). 17.99 *(978-1-4424-8270-8(2)*, Simon & Schuster Bks. For Young Readers) Simon & Schuster Bks. For Young Readers.

—Kill Switch. (ENG., (YA). (gr. 7). 2013. Illus.). 192p. pap. 9.99 *(978-1-4424-5442-2(3))* 2012. 176p. 16.99 *(978-1-4169-2702-0(6))* Simon & Schuster Bks. For Young Readers. (Simon & Schuster Bks. For Young Readers).

Lynn, Sarah. Tip-Tap Pop, 0 vols. Docampo, Valeria, illus. 2010. (ENG.). 32p. (J). (gr. -1-4). 17.99 *(978-0-7614-5712-1(7)*, 9780761457121, Amazon Children's Publishing) Amazon Publishing.

Lyons, Kelly Starling. Tea Cakes for Tosh. Lewis, E. B., illus. 2012. (ENG.). 32p. (J). (gr. k-3). 16.99 *(978-0-399-25213-6(4)*, G.P. Putnam's Sons Books for Young Readers) Penguin Young Readers Group.

MacCaughrean, Geraldine, et al. El Reloj de Mi Abuela. Lambert, Stephen, illus. 2003. (SPA.). 32p. (J). (gr. k-2). 14.99 *(978-84-241-8643-2(5))* Everest Editora ESP. Dist: Lectorum Pubns., Inc.

MacDonald, Annie. Bubbles for Poppo. 2011. 32p. pap. 19.95 *(978-1-4520-1720-4(4))* AuthorHouse.

—Poppo's Very Best Trick. 2010. 32p. pap. 17.95 *(978-1-4520-1808-9(1))* AuthorHouse.

—What's up with Poppo? 2009. 36p. pap. 19.95 *(978-1-4343-4621-6(8))* AuthorHouse.

MacDonald, George. Princess & Curdie. 2006. 136p. per. 10.95 *(978-1-59818-617-8(5))* Aegypan.

MacDonald, Margaret Read. The Squeaky Door. DePalma, Mary Newell, illus. 2006. (ENG.). 40p. (J). (gr. -1-1). 16.99 *(978-0-06-028373-5(4))* HarperCollins Pubs.

MacDonald, Tom. Secret of the Tree: Marcus Speer's Ecosentinel. Stieber, Joel, illus. 2009. 300p. pap. 18.95 *(978-0-595-52402-0(8))* iUniverse, Inc.

Mace, Aubrey. My Fairy Grandmother. 2009. 270p. pap. 16.99 *(978-1-59955-217-0(5))* Cedar Fort, Inc./CFI Distribution.

MacHado, Ana Maria. De carta en Carta. Basulto, Rita, illus. 2004. (SPA.). 44p. (gr. 3-5). pap. 7.95 *(978-968-19-1483-7(X))* Santillana USA Publishing Co., Inc.

Mackall, Dandi Daley. The Story of the Easter Robin, 1 vol. Vojtech, Anna, illus. 2010. (ENG.). 32p. (J). (gr. -1-2). 15.99 *(978-0-310-71331-9(5))* Zonderkidz.

Mackintosh, David. The Frank Show. 2012. (ENG., Illus.). 32p. (J). (gr. k-2). 16.95 *(978-1-4197-0393-5(5)*, Abrams Bks. for Young Readers) Abrams, Inc.

MacLachlan, Marie. Granny Grotbag's Bedtime Stories. 2010. 20p. pap. 8.49 *(978-1-4490-1519-0(0))* AuthorHouse.

MacLachlan, Patricia. Grandfather's Dance. (Sarah, Plain & Tall Ser.: 5). (J). 2007. (ENG.). 96p. (gr. 1-5). pap. 5.99 *(978-0-06-134003-1(0))* 2006. 84p. (gr. 3-5). lib. bdg. 15.89 *(978-0-06-027561-7(8)*, Cotler, Joanna Books) HarperCollins Pubs.

—Kindred Souls. (J). (gr. 1-5). 2013. (ENG.). 144p. pap. 5.99 *(978-0-06-052299-5(2))* 2012. (ENG.). 128p. 16.99 *(978-0-06-052297-1(6))* 2012. 128p. lib. bdg. 17.89 *(978-0-06-052298-8(4))* HarperCollins Pubs. (Tegen, Katherine Bks).

—The True Gift. Floca, Brian, illus. 2013. (ENG.). 112p. (J). (gr. 2-6). pap. 6.99 *(978-1-4424-8858-8(1)*, Atheneum Bks. for Young Readers) Simon & Schuster Children's Publishing.

—The True Gift: A Christmas Story. Floca, Brian, illus. 2009. (ENG.). 96p. (J). (gr. 2-6). 14.99 *(978-1-4169-9081-9(X)*, Atheneum Bks. for Young Readers) Simon & Schuster Children's Publishing.

—The Truth of Me. (J). (gr. 1-5). 2015. (ENG.). 144p. pap. 5.99 *(978-0-06-199861-4(3))* 2013. (ENG.). 128p. 16.99 *(978-0-06-199859-1(1))* 2013. 128p. lib. bdg. 17.89 *(978-0-06-199860-7(5))* HarperCollins Pubs. (Tegen, Katherine Bks).

MacLelland, Edith Bennett. Grandma Tell Me a Story. 2011. 264p. 24.59 *(978-1-4634-1386-6(6))*; pap. 14.03 *(978-1-4634-1384-2(X))* AuthorHouse.

Macomber, Debbie & Carney, Mary Lou. The Truly Terribly Horrible Sweater... That Grandma Knit. Nguyen, Vincent, illus. 2009. (ENG.). 32p. (J). (gr. -1-2). 16.99 *(978-0-06-165093-2(5))* HarperCollins Pubs.

Madden, Gloria. Grandmothers Bedtime Stories. 2008. 68p. (gr. -1-7). pap. 10.49 *(978-1-4343-9201-5(5))* AuthorHouse.

Maddox, Jake. El Lanzador Bajo Presión. Heck, Claudia M., tr. from ENG. Tiffany, Sean, illus. 2012. (Jake Maddox en Español Ser.). (SPA.). 72p. (gr. 2-3). 25.32 *(978-1-4342-3815-3(6))* Stone Arch Bks.

—Soccer Shake-Up. Aburto, Jesus, illus. 2015. (Jake Maddox Sports Stories Ser.). (ENG.). 72p. (gr. 2-3). lib. bdg. 25.32 *(978-1-4965-0495-1(X))* Stone Arch Bks.

Madormo, John V. The Homemade Stuffing Caper, Bk. 1. 2013. (Charlie Collier, Snoop for Hire Ser.: 1). (ENG.). 272p. (J). (gr. 5). pap. 7.99 *(978-0-14-242380-6(7)*, Puffin Books) Penguin Young Readers Group.

Magness, Vicki. Stephen: A Strong Man to Run a Race. 2012. 40p. pap. 21.99 *(978-1-4771-2562-5(0))* Xlibris Corp.

Magnuson, James. Emma's First Agate, 1 vol. LeMay, Meagan, illus. 2014. (ENG.). 32p. (J). (gr. 1-2). pap. 7.95 *(978-1-59193-443-1(5))* Adventure Pubns.

Magrane, Mijares. Grandma Garcia: La Abuela Garcia - An Intimate Journey into the Past. 2004. (SPA & ENG., Illus.). 96p. pap. 13.95 *(978-0-9741167-0-9(X))* Magrane, Etna International.

Maki-Griffis, Linda R. In the Berry Patch. 2012. (ENG.). (YA). pap. *(978-1-4675-3814-5(0))* Independent Pub.

Maliszewski, Julia. Grandmas Got the Goodies. 2013. 28p. pap. 14.93 *(978-1-4669-8718-0(9))* Trafford Publishing.

Malkin, Arlene Swinson. Adventures with Grandma & Grandpa: The Secret of the Old Trunk. 2006. 48p. pap. 16.95 *(978-1-4241-1621-8(X))* PublishAmerica, Inc.

Malone, Peter & Prokofiev, Sergei. Sergei Prokofiev's Peter & the Wolf: With a Fully-Orchestrated & Narrated CD. Malone, Peter, illus. 2004. (ENG., Illus.). 40p. (J). (gr. -1-2). 19.99 *(978-0-375-82430-2(8)*, Knopf Bks. for Young Readers) Random Hse. Children's Bks.

Malot, Hector & Crewe-Jones, Florence. Nobody's Girl: Companion Story to Nobody's Boy. Gooch, Thelma, illus. 2006. 220p. (J). pap. *(978-1-894666-76-3(3))* Inheritance Pubns.

Malpass, Suzanne M. A Lab's Tale. Morgan, Trish, illus. 2012. 38p. (J). 12.95 *(978-1-937406-68-4(7))* Mascot Bks., Inc.

Mama Doo. Zachary & the Magic Pumpkin Seeds, 1 vol. 2007. (ENG.). 35p. 24.95 *(978-1-4241-8579-5(3))* America Star Bks.

Mamburay, Yankuba & Mamburay, Khadijah. A Day at Grandma's Farm. 2011. 20p. pap. 24.95 *(978-1-4560-6707-6(9))* America Star Bks.

Mancusi, Mari. Scorched. (Scorched Ser.: 1). (ENG.). (YA). (gr. 6-12). 2014. 368p. pap. 9.99 *(978-1-4022-9227-9(9))* 2013. 352p. 16.99 *(978-1-4022-8458-8(6)*, 9781402284588) Sourcebooks, Inc.

Mandelkorn, Carole. Grandma, Will You Clap! Phillips, Laverne, illus. 2013. 16p. pap. 10.95 *(978-1-61493-196-6(8))* Peppertree Pr., The.

Mangskau, Monica. My Grandpa the Super Hero. 2010. 16p. 9.49 *(978-1-4343-8088-3(2))* AuthorHouse.

Mangum, Kay Lynn. A Love Like Lilly. 2006. 336p. (YA). pap. 15.95 *(978-1-59038-580-7(2))* Deseret Bk. Co.

Manushkid, Fran. Grandma Beatrice Brings Spring to Minsk. 2005. 32p. (J). *(978-0-7868-2147-1(7))* Hyperion Bks. for Children.

Manushkin, Fran. A Nervous Night, 1 vol. Lyon, Tammie, illus. 2010. (Katie Woo Ser.). (ENG.). 32p. (gr. k-2). pap. 5.95 *(978-1-4048-6060-5(6))*; lib. bdg. 21.32 *(978-1-4048-5725-4(7))* Picture Window Bks.

Manzano, Sonia. The Revolution of Evelyn Serrano. (ENG.). 224p. (J). 2014. (gr. 9). pap. 9.99 *(978-0-545-32506-6(4))* 2012. (gr. 7-9). 17.99 *(978-0-545-32505-9(6)*, Scholastic Pr.) Scholastic, Inc.

Marie, Tina. Raccoon Round-Up at the Diamond R Ranch. 2012. 32p. pap. 24.95 *(978-1-4626-7599-9(9))* America Star Bks.

Markel, Michelle. Dream Town. Reese, Rick, illus. 2006. (J). 15.95 *(978-1-59714-022-5(8))* Heyday.

Markette, Paul Scott. I'm with Poppy!! Lee, Joe, illus. 2010. 24p. pap. 12.99 *(978-1-4520-6276-1(5))* AuthorHouse.

Markle, Sandra. The Fledglings. 2003. (ENG.). 144p. (YA). (gr. 4-6). pap. 9.95 *(978-1-56397-696-4(X))* Boyds Mills Pr.

Marks, Alan, illus. The Story of Heidi. 2007. (Picture Book Classics Ser.). 24p. (J). (gr. -1-3). 9.99 *(978-0-7945-1716-8(1)*, Usborne) EDC Publishing.

Marlar, Debra L. Morgan's Sleepover at Grandma's. 2010. 36p. 16.99 *(978-1-4520-6496-3(2))* AuthorHouse.

Marr, Melissa. Challenge. Xian Nu Studio Staff, illus. 2010. (Wicked Lovely: Desert Tales Ser.: 2). (ENG.). 176p. (YA). (gr. 8-18). pap. 9.99 *(978-0-06-149349-2(X))* HarperCollins Pubs.

Marsh, Barry. Good Harbor Bay. 2009. (J). 14.95 *(978-0-9767268-1-4(5))* Crofton Creek Pr.

Marsh, Carole. The Gosh Awful! Gold Rush Mystery. 2007. (Real Kids, Real Places Ser.). (Illus.). 146p. (J). (gr. 2-8). per. 5.95 *(978-0-635-06334-2(4))* Gallopade International.

—The Mystery of the Ancient Pyramid: Cairo, Egypt. 2006. (Around the World in 80 Mysteries Ser.). (Illus.). 128p. (J). (gr. 4-7). 14.95 *(978-0-635-03473-1(5))* Gallopade International.

—The Mystery on the Great Barrier Reef. 2006. (Around the World in 80 Mysteries Ser.). (Illus.). 132p. (J). (gr. 3-5). per. 5.95 *(978-0-635-06206-2(2))* Gallopade International.

—The Mystery on the Great Barrier Reef: Sydney, Australia. 2006. (Around the World in 80 Mysteries Ser.). (Illus.). 132p. (J). (gr. 3-5). 14.95 *(978-0-635-06210-9(0))* Gallopade International.

—The Mystery on the Great Wall of China. 2006. (Around the World in 80 Mysteries Ser.). (Illus.). 132p. (J). (gr. 3-5). per. 7.99 *(978-0-635-06205-5(4))* Gallopade International.

—The Mystery on the Great Wall of China: Beijing, China. 2006. (Around the World in 80 Mysteries Ser.). (Illus.). 132p. (J). (gr. 3-5). 14.95 *(978-0-635-06209-3(7))* Gallopade International.

Marshall, Joseph. In the Footsteps of Crazy Horse. Yellowhawk, James Mark, illus. 2015. (ENG.). 176p. (J). (gr. 5-9). 16.95 *(978-1-4197-0785-8(X)*, Amulet Bks.) Abrams, Inc.

Marshall, Kenneth L. The Adventures of Maya & Grandpa. 2004. 60p. (J). pap. 9.95 *(978-0-7414-2016-9(3))*Bk. II. 2005. 65p. pap. 9.95 *(978-0-7414-2238-5(7))* Infinity Publishing.

Marshall, Linda Elovitz. Grandma Rose's Magic. Jatkowska, Ag, illus. 2012. (Shabbat Ser.). (ENG.). 32p. (J). (gr. -1-2). pap. 7.95 *(978-0-7613-5216-7(3)*, Kar-Ben Publishing) Lerner Publishing Group.

—Grandma Rose's Magic/By Linda Elovitz Marshall; Illustrated by Ag Jatkowska. Jatkowska, Ag, illus. 2012. (Shabbat Ser.). (ENG.). 32p. (J). (gr. -1-2). lib. bdg. 17.95 *(978-0-7613-5215-0(5)*, Kar-Ben Publishing) Lerner Publishing Group.

—Talia & the Haman-Tushies. Assirelli, Francesca, illus. 2017. (ENG.). 24p. (J). (gr. -1-2). 17.99 *(978-1-5124-0825-6(5)*, Kar-Ben Publishing) Lerner Publishing Group.

—Talia & the Very YUM Kippur. Assirelli, Francesca, illus. 2015. (ENG.). 24p. (J). (gr. -1-2). 17.99 *(978-1-4677-5236-7(3)*, Kar-Ben Publishing) Lerner Publishing Group.

—Talia & the Very Yum Kippur. Assirelli, Francesca, illus. 2015. (ENG.). 24p. (J). (gr. -1-2). pap. 7.99 *(978-1-4677-5240-4(1)*, Kar-Ben Publishing) Lerner Publishing Group.

Martin, Ann M. Needle & Thread. Andreasen, Dan, illus. 2007. 205p. (J). pap. *(978-0-545-03660-3(7))* Scholastic, Inc.

—Ten Rules for Living with My Sister. 2011. (ENG.). 240p. (J). (gr. 4-7). 16.99 *(978-0-312-36766-4(X)*, 9780312367664) Feiwel & Friends.

—Ten Rules for Living with My Sister. 2012. (ENG.). 256p. (J). (gr. 4-7). pap. 7.99 *(978-1-250-01021-6(7)*, 9781250010216) Square Fish.

Martin, J. Marshall. The Bird. 2008. 88p. pap. 12.50 *(978-0-9801224-1-1(4))* Boys Read Bks.

Martinez, Claudia Guadalupe. The Smell of Old Lady Perfume. 2008. (ENG., Illus.). 248p. (J). (gr. 4-9). 15.95 *(978-1-933693-18-7(5))* Cinco Puntos Pr.

Martínez, Claudia Guadalupe. Smell of Old Lady Perfume. 2011. (ENG., Illus.). 256p. (J). (gr. 4-10). pap. 7.95 *(978-1-933693-88-0(6))* Cinco Puntos Pr.

Martínez, Rafael. El Deseo de Aurelio. Martinez, Enrique, illus. 2006. (la Orilla del Viento Ser.). (SPA.). 48p. (J). (gr. 8-10). pap. *(978-968-16-7988-0(1))* Fondo de Cultura Economica.

Martins, E. V. Cookie Nana's Story Book: Featuring " Grumpy Granddad " 2009. (Illus.). 40p. pap. 16.99 *(978-1-4389-2325-3(2))* AuthorHouse.

Martone, Ginny. The White Stallion. 2006. (ENG.). 60p. per. 16.95 *(978-1-4241-4332-0(2))* PublishAmerica, Inc.

Masilela, Johnny. We Shall Not Weep. 2010. (ENG.). 132p. pap. *(978-0-7957-0147-4(0))* NB Pubs. Ltd.

Mason, Bonita. T-Bear the Most Special Bear. Hendricks, Sandy, illus. 2008. 26p. (J). 19.95 *(978-0-9798718-0-1(8))* Encore Pubns.

Mason, Charlene. Landon's Backyard Adventures. 2012. 24p. pap. 24.95 *(978-1-4626-7470-1(4))* America Star Bks.

Mason, Margaret H. These Hands. Cooper, Floyd, illus. 2011. (ENG.). 32p. (J). (gr. -1-3). 16.99 *(978-0-547-21566-2(5))* Houghton Mifflin Harcourt Publishing Co.

Mason, Mimi Canda. Lola's Cane. 2009. 48p. pap. 19.95 *(978-1-4389-1464-0(4))* AuthorHouse.

Masters, S. Ian's Visit with Gamma ... at the Beach. 2011. 40p. pap. 18.46 *(978-1-4567-4846-3(7))* AuthorHouse.

Masterson, Josephine. Grandma Makes Potato Pancakes. 2015. (Rosen REAL Readers: STEM & STEAM Collection). (ENG.). 8p. pap. 5.46 *(978-1-4994-9539-3(0)*, Rosen Classroom) Rosen Publishing Group, Inc., The.

Mastnak, Rosemary. Dancing with Grandma. Mastnak, Rosemary, illus. 2016. (ENG., Illus.). 32p. (J). (gr. -1-k). pap. 9.99 *(978-1-76012-618-6(7))* Little Hare Bks. AUS. Dist: Independent Pubs. Group.

Mateos, Pilar. El Cuento Interrumpido. (SPA.). 128p. (YA). (gr. 5-8). *(978-84-279-3149-7(2)*, NG0388) Noguer y Caralt Editores, S. A. ESP. Dist: Lectorum Pubns., Inc.

Matheron, Annaliese. Ninja Nan & Her Merry Men. 2013. 180p. pap. *(978-1-909411-22-7(1))* Mauve Square Publishing.

—Ninja Nan & Sidekick Grandad. 2011. (Illus.). 80p. pap. 8.95 *(978-1-4478-3079-5(2))* Lulu Pr., Inc.
—Ninja Nan & Sidekick Grandad. 2013. 124p. pap. *(978-1-909411-20-3(5))* Mauve Square Publishing.
—Ninja Nan Strikes Again. 2013. 132p. pap. *(978-1-909411-21-0(3))* Mauve Square Publishing.
Mathieson, Karen. Thirteen Times Three: Book One of the Rosemary Ridge Trilogy. 2013. 164p. (J). pap. 7.99 *(978-1-940350-02-8(6))* Portable COO, The.
Mathis, Sharon Bell. The Hundred Penny Box. Dillon, Diane & Dillon, Leo, illus. 2006. (ENG.). 48p. (J). (gr. 1-4). pap. 7.99 *(978-0-14-240702-8(X),* Puffin Books) Penguin Young Readers Group.
—The Hundred Penny Box. Dillon, Leo & Dillon, Diane, illus. 2006. 47p. (gr. 1-4). 18.00 *(978-0-7569-6786-4(4))* Perfection Learning Corp.
Matthews, Elli. The Everyday Easter Dress. Matthews, John, illus. 2011. 24p. pap. 24.95 *(978-1-4560-9411-9(4))* America Star Bks.
Mattingly Jr., Joseph C. Logan's Big Surprise. 2013. 28p. pap. 24.95 *(978-1-62709-717-8(1))* America Star Bks.
Maurer, Jayne. Grandpa Goes to Horse Camp. 2012. 40p. 16.95 *(978-1-62709-874-8(7));* pap. 16.95 *(978-1-62709-141-1(6))* America Star Bks.
Mawhinney, Art, illus. Olivia the Magnificent: A Lift-the-Flap Story. 2009. (Olivia TV Tie-In Ser.). (ENG.). 16p. (J). (gr. -1-2). pap. 6.99 *(978-1-4169-8297-5(3),* Simon Spotlight) Simon Spotlight.
Maya Z And Nadajia R. Hall. The New-Fangled Adventures of Alexia & Z: The Case of Grams' Missing Teeth. 2009. 36p. pap. 15.95 *(978-1-4389-4508-8(6))* AuthorHouse.
Mayer, Mercer. Grandma, Grandpa, & Me. 2007. (Little Critter Ser.). (Illus.). 22p. (J). (gr. -1-3). lib. bdg. 13.55 *(978-1-4177-8161-4(0),* Turtleback) Turtleback Bks.
—Just Grandma, Grandpa, & Me. 2016. (Pictureback(R) Ser.). (ENG., Illus.). 48p. (J). (gr. -1-2). 5.99 *(978-0-553-53986-8(8),* Random Hse. Bks. for Young Readers) Random Hse. Children's Bks.
—Just Grandma, Grandpa, & Me. 2016. (Little Critter Ser.). lib. bdg. 16.00 *(978-0-606-38482-7(0))* Turtleback Bks.
Mayer, Mercer & Mayer, Gina. Just Fishing with Grandma. Mayer, Mercer, illus. 2015. (Little Critter Ser.). (ENG., Illus.). 24p. (J). (gr. -1-3). pap. 3.99 *(978-0-06-147808-6(3),* HarperFestival) HarperCollins Pubs.
—Just Fishing with Grandma. 2015. (Little Critter Ser.). (J). lib. bdg. 13.55 *(978-0-606-36492-8(7))* Turtleback Bks.
Mayer, Pamela. Chicken Soup, Chicken Soup. Melmon, Deborah, illus. 2016. (ENG.). 32p. (J). (gr. -1-3). 17.99 *(978-1-4677-8934-9(8),* Kar-Ben Publishing) Lerner Publishing Group.
Mayfield, Sue. The Four Franks. 2005. (Blue Go Bananas Ser.). (ENG., Illus.). 48p. (J). (gr. 1-2). lib. bdg. *(978-0-7787-2629-6(0))* Crabtree Publishing Co.
Mazeroski, Kelly. Maz, You're Up! Lauso, Judith, illus. 2010. 24p. (J). pap. 12.95 *(978-0-936340-18-0(5))* Historical Society of Western Pennsylvania.
Mazur, Gabrielle. Boppy & Me. Collins, Linda, illus. 2013. 38p. pap. 14.97 *(978-1-4507-3897-2(4))* Bush Publishing Inc.
—Boppy & Me. Collins, Linda, illus. 2013. 38p. pap. 12.95 *(978-1-4507-3906-1(7))* Bush Publishing Inc.
McAllister, Margaret. Emily & the Lamb. Vince, Dawn, illus. 2005. (ENG.). 24p. (J). lib. bdg. 23.65 *(978-1-59646-756-9(8))* Dingles & Co.
—15 Things Not to Do with a Grandma. Sterling, Holly, illus. 2016. (15 Things Not to Do Ser.). (ENG.). 32p. (J). (gr. -1-2). 17.99 *(978-1-84780-854-7(9),* Frances Lincoln Children's Bks.) Quarto Publishing Group UK GBR. Dist: Hachette Bk. Group.
McClintock, Norah. Close to the Heel, 1 vol. 2012. (Seven (the Series) Ser.). (ENG., Illus.). 272p. (J). (gr. 5-10). pap. 9.95 *(978-1-55469-950-6(9))* Orca Bk. Pubs. USA.
—From the Dead, 1 vol. 2014. (Seven Sequels Ser.). (ENG., Illus.). 288p. (J). (gr. 5-10). pap. 10.95 *(978-1-4598-0537-8(2))* Orca Bk. Pubs. USA.
—Watch Me, 1 vol. 2008. (Orca Currents Ser.). (ENG.). (J). (gr. 5-9). 112p. 16.95 *(978-1-55469-040-4(4));* 128p. pap. 9.95 *(978-1-55469-039-8(0))* Orca Bk. Pubs. USA.
McConduit, Denise Walter. D. J. & the Debutante Ball, 1 vol. Henriquez, Emile F., illus. 2004. (D. J. Ser.). (ENG.). 32p. (J). (gr. k-3). 16.99 *(978-1-58980-173-8(3))* Pelican Publishing Co., Inc.
McCooke, Valerie J. Grandfather's Chest. 2012. 40p. pap. 32.70 *(978-1-4771-0543-6(3))* Xlibris Corp.
McCully, Emily Arnold. First Snow. McCully, Emily Arnold, illus. 2003. (ENG., Illus.). 32p. (J). (gr. -1-3). 17.99 *(978-0-06-623852-4(8))* HarperCollins Pubs.
McCune, Susan. A Grandmother's Story, 01 vols., 1. 2016. (Rosen REAL Readers: Social Studies Nonfiction / Fiction: Family, Community, & the World Ser.). (ENG.). 8p. (J). pap. 5.46 *(978-1-5081-1522-9(2),* Rosen Classroom) Rosen Publishing Group, Inc., The.
McCutcheon, John. Christmas in the Trenches, 1 vol. Sorensen, Henri, illus. 2006. (ENG.). 32p. (J). (gr. 1-5). 18.95 *(978-1-56145-374-0(9))* Peachtree Pubs.
McDaniel, Paula. Grandpa's Woods. Austin, Tereasa, illus. 2008. 44p. pap. 24.95 *(978-1-60474-465-1(0))* America Star Bks.
McDonald, Kirsten. The Perfect Piñatas. 2016. (Carlos & Carmen Set 3 Ser.). (ENG.). (gr. -1-3). lib. bdg. 27.07 ***(978-1-62402-183-1(2))*** ABDO Publishing Co.
McDonald, Megan. Judy Moody & the Bucket List. Reynolds, Peter H., illus. 2017. (Judy Moody Ser.: 13). (ENG.). 176p. (J). (gr. 1-4). pap. 5.99 ***(978-0-7636-9759-4(1))*** Candlewick Pr.
McDonnell, Margot. Torn to Pieces. 2010. (ENG.). 272p. (YA). (gr. 7). pap. 8.99 *(978-0-385-73557-5(X),* Delacorte Bks. for Young Readers) Random Hse. Children's Bks.
Mcduffee, William. Story Time with Grandpa Bill Collection. 2006. 50p. pap. 16.95 *(978-1-4241-4001-5(3))* America Star Bks.
McElroy, Jean. Let's Go, Baby! Vase, Catherine, illus. 2010. (ENG.). 12p. (J). (gr. -1 — 1). 4.99 *(978-1-4424-0901-9(0),* Little Simon) Little Simon.
McGann, Oisín. Mad Grandad & the Flying Saucer. 2017. (ENG., Illus.). 64p. (J). 10.00 ***(978-1-84717-870-1(7))*** O'Brien Pr., Ltd., The IRL. Dist: Dufour Editions, Inc.
—Mad Grandad & the Kleptoes. 2005. (Flyers Ser.). (ENG., Illus.). 64p. (J). pap. 9.95 *(978-0-86278-938-1(9))* O'Brien Pr., Ltd., The IRL. Dist: Dufour Editions, Inc.
—Mad Grandad & the Mutant River. 2005. (Flyers Ser.: 14). (ENG., Illus.). 64p. (J). pap. 9.95 *(978-0-86278-939-8(7))* O'Brien Pr., Ltd., The IRL. Dist: Dufour Editions, Inc.
—Mad Grandad & the Robot Garden. 2017. (ENG., Illus.). 64p. (J). 10.00 ***(978-1-84717-869-5(3))*** O'Brien Pr., Ltd., The IRL. Dist: Dufour Editions, Inc.
McGann, Oisín. Mad Grandad's Wicked Pictures. 2007. (ENG., Illus.). 64p. (J). pap. 9.95 *(978-1-84717-063-7(3))* O'Brien Pr., Ltd., The IRL. Dist: Dufour Editions, Inc.
Mcgee, Ken. Forever. 2013. 224p. pap. 15.49 *(978-1-62509-504-6(X))* Salem Author Services.
McGovern, DeeDee Jean. The Heartland of Home: Tight Quarters in the City. 2008. 58p. pap. 16.95 *(978-1-60610-058-5(0))* America Star Bks.
Mcintosh, Sharon. Grandma S Donut Hat. 2013. 22p. pap. 9.99 *(978-1-62697-407-4(1))* Salem Author Services.
McJarrow, Shandy. The Adventures of Papilio the Butterfly. 2009. 112p. 20.95 *(978-1-4401-3850-8(8));* pap. 10.95 *(978-1-4401-3840-9(0))* iUniverse, Inc.
McKay, Hilary. The Exiles at Home. 2007. (ENG.). 208p. (J). (gr. 3-7). pap. 12.95 *(978-1-4169-6729-3(X),* McElderry, Margaret K. Bks.) McElderry, Margaret K. Bks.
—The Exiles in Love. 2007. (ENG.). 176p. (J). (gr. 3-7). pap. 9.95 *(978-1-4169-6797-2(4),* McElderry, Margaret K. Bks.) McElderry, Margaret K. Bks.
—Lulu & the Cat in the Bag. Lamont, Priscilla, illus. (Lulu Ser.: 3). (ENG.). 112p. (J). (gr. 1-5). 2014. pap. 4.99 *(978-0-8075-4805-9(7))* 2013. 13.99 *(978-0-8075-4804-2(9))* Whitman, Albert & Co.
McKay, Sindy. We Both Read-My Car Trip. Johnson, Meredith, illus. 2005. (We Both Read Ser.). 48p. (J). (gr. -1-2). lib. bdg. 7.99 *(978-1-891327-63-6(1));* per. 4.99 *(978-1-891327-64-3(X))* Treasure Bay, Inc.
McKee, David. Elmer & Grandpa Eldo. McKee, David, illus. 2016. (ENG., Illus.). 32p. (J). (gr. -1-3). 17.99 *(978-1-5124-0569-9(8))* Lerner Publishing Group.
McKenna, Sharon Michelle, illus. Good Morning, Sunshine: A Grandpa Story. 2006. 32p. (J). (gr. -1-3). 15.95 *(978-1-60108-003-5(4))* Red Cygnet Pr.
McKinlay, Meg. Bella & the Wandering House. 2016. (ENG.). 80p. (J). (gr. k-2). 11.99 *(978-1-925162-30-1(3))* Fremantle Pr. AUS. Dist: Independent Pubs. Group.
McKoin, Cathy Taylor. Little Pup Finds a Home! 2009. 28p. pap. 15.99 *(978-1-4415-3407-1(5))* Xlibris Corp.
McLaughlin, Dawn L. Two Tickets to Heaven, Please! 2009. 48p. pap. 16.25 *(978-1-60693-061-8(3),* Eloquent Bks.) Strategic Book Publishing & Rights Agency (SBPRA).
McMillan, Kathleen. A Very Blueberry Christmas - a Show-And-Tell Book. 2013. 32p. pap. *(978-1-4602-1319-3(X))* FriesenPress.
McMullen, Nigel. Let's Dance, Grandma! McMullen, Nigel, illus. 2014. (ENG., Illus.). 32p. (J). (gr. -1-3). 16.99 *(978-0-06-050747-3(0))* HarperCollins Pubs.
McMullin, Perry. The Boy Who Could Fly. 2009. 44p. pap. 18.95 *(978-1-4490-0904-5(2))* AuthorHouse.
McNair, Barbara. Tea Parties with Grandm. Hogan, Eric, illus. 2009. 48p. pap. 24.95 *(978-1-60749-617-5(8))* America Star Bks.
McNatt, Martha. Grandmother's Face in the Mirror. 2003. (YA). per. 14.00 *(978-0-9741294-0-2(2))* Main St Publishing, Inc.
McQueen, Amelia. A Penny for Your Thoughts. 2010. 56p. pap. 23.99 *(978-1-4490-8046-4(4))* AuthorHouse.
McQuestion, Karen. Celia & the Fairies, 0 vols. unabr. ed. 2010. (ENG.). 142p. (gr. 4-6). pap. 7.95 *(978-1-935597-28-5(0),* 9781935597285, Two Lions) Amazon Publishing.
McVoy, Terra Elan. Drive Me Crazy. 2015. (ENG.). 288p. (J). (gr. 3-7). 16.99 *(978-0-06-232243-2(5),* Tegen, Katherine Bks) HarperCollins Pubs.
Means-Dallas, Anastasia. Fourth Street. 2012. 24p. pap. 17.99 *(978-1-4772-0900-4(X))* AuthorHouse.
Meddaugh, Susan. Martha Says It with Flowers. 2010. (Martha Speaks Ser.). (ENG., Illus.). 32p. (J). (gr. -1-3). 12.99 *(978-0-547-21058-2(2))* Houghton Mifflin Harcourt Publishing Co.
Medlyn, Lynda Lee & Staudenmier, Kelley Anne. The Best Belcher. Parish, Shannon, illus. 2008. (ENG.). 32p. (J). (gr. k-2). lib. bdg. *(978-0-9793738-0-8(8))* Window Box Pr. LLC.
Meierhenry, Mark V. & Volk, David. The Mystery of the Maize. Two Bulls, Marty Grant, illus. 2010. (J). *(978-0-9822749-1-0(2),* South Dakota State Historical Society Pr.) South Dakota State Historical Society Pr.
Meister, Cari. Airplane Adventure, 1 vol. Janovitz, Marilyn, illus. 2010. (My First Graphic Novel Ser.). (ENG.). 32p. (gr. k-2). pap. 6.25 *(978-1-4342-2286-2(1),* My First Graphic Novel) Stone Arch Bks.
Mellor, Colleen Kelly. Grandpa & the Truck Book 2. Irwin, Dana M., illus. 2012. 34p. pap. 9.99 *(978-0-9856770-2-2(3))* truckerkidzPr.
—Grandpa & the Truck Book One. Irwin, Dana, illus. 2012. 34p. pap. 9.99 *(978-0-9856770-0-8(7))* truckerkidzPr.
Melvin, Alice, illus. Grandma's House. 2015. (ENG.). 32p. (J). (gr. -1-3). 19.95 *(978-1-84976-222-9(8))* Tate Publishing, Ltd. GBR. Dist: Abrams, Inc.
Menchin, Scott. Grandma in Blue with Red Hat. Bliss, Harry, illus. 2015. (ENG.). 32p. (J). (gr. -1-3). 16.95 *(978-1-4197-1484-9(8),* Abrams Bks. for Young Readers) Abrams, Inc.
Mendes, Valerie. Lost & Found. 2004. (ENG.). 256p. (J). per. 8.99 *(978-0-689-86049-2(8))* Simon & Schuster, Ltd. GBR. Dist: Simon & Schuster, Inc.
Menges, Thais D. Granny & the Tractor. King, Joseph, illus. 2012. 36p. pap. 10.95 *(978-1-60920-047-3(0))* Ajoyin Publishing, Inc.
Mervyn, Catherine Antolino. Call Me Nona. 2013. 32p. pap. *(978-1-4602-1570-8(2))* FriesenPress.
Meshon, Aaron. Delivery! Meshon, Aaron, illus. 2017. (ENG., Illus.). 48p. (J). (gr. -1-3). 17.99 *(978-1-4814-4175-9(2))* Simon & Schuster Children's Publishing.
—Take Me Out to the Yakyu. Meshon, Aaron, illus. 2013. (ENG., Illus.). 40p. (J). (gr. -1-3). 16.99 *(978-1-4424-4177-4(1),* Atheneum Bks. for Young Readers) Simon & Schuster Children's Publishing.
Messner, Kate. The Brilliant Fall of Gianna Z. (ENG.). 224p. 2017. (J). pap. 8.99 ***(978-1-68119-547-6(X),*** 9781681195476) 2010. (YA). (gr. 3-6). pap. 8.99 *(978-0-8027-2173-0(7),* 9780802721730) Bloomsbury Publishing USA. (Bloomsbury USA Childrens).
—The Brilliant Fall of Gianna Z. 2017. (J). lib. bdg. 19.65 ***(978-0-606-40595-9(X))*** Turtleback Bks.
Messner, Kate. Marty McGuire Digs Worms! Floca, Brian, illus. 2012. (ENG.). 176p. (J). (gr. -1-3). pap. 5.99 *(978-0-545-14247-2(4),* Scholastic Pr.) Scholastic, Inc.
Mestas, Nolan & the Magic Bridge. 2009. 28p. pap. 13.99 *(978-1-4490-0812-3(7))* AuthorHouse.
Metivier, Gary. Cody & Grandpa's Christmas Tradition, 1 vol. Van Wagoner, Traci, illus. 2016. (ENG.). 32p. (J). (gr. k-3). 16.99 *(978-1-4556-2170-5(6))* Pelican Publishing Co., Inc.
—Saluting Grandpa: Celebrating Veterans & Honor Flight, 1 vol. Rath, Robert, illus. 2012. (ENG.). 32p. (J). (gr. k-3). 16.99 *(978-1-4556-1748-7(2))* Pelican Publishing Co., Inc.
Meyer, Carolyn. Jubilee Journey. 2007. 271p. (J). (gr. 5-9). 14.60 *(978-0-7569-6682-9(5))* Perfection Learning Corp.
Meyer, Megan. Flicker Finds His Flame. 2011. 28p. pap. 24.95 *(978-1-4626-3750-8(7))* America Star Bks.
Michaels, Joanna. Call Me Charly. Specht, Jessica, illus. 2012. 92p. pap. 10.95 *(978-1-61493-102-7(X))* Peppertree Pr., The.
Michie, Brandon J. Caleb the Porcupine: Animal Lessons. 2011. 16p. pap. 10.75 *(978-1-4634-3015-3(9))* AuthorHouse.
Miller, Daniel, et al. A Miller Cousin Mystery. 2010. 120p. pap. 49.00 *(978-0-557-57235-9(5));* pap. 17.80 *(978-0-557-57118-5(9))* Lulu Pr., Inc.
Miller, Debra Warren. Grandpa Popsicle. 2013. 28p. pap. 13.99 *(978-1-4624-0205-2(4),* Inspiring Voices) Author Solutions, Inc.
Miller, J. P. No Greater Love: The History of the African American Nurse, 1 vol. 2009. (ENG.). 159p. pap. 19.95 *(978-1-60836-135-9(7))* PublishAmerica, Inc.
Miller, Jay. Bingo the Banjo Picking Bear. 2007. 40p. (YA). per. 14.95 *(978-1-4327-0739-2(6))* Outskirts Pr., Inc.
Miller, Judith J. Just Too Little. Panse, Sonal, illus. 2013. 16p. pap. 9.95 *(978-1-61633-413-0(4))* Guardian Angel Publishing, Inc.
Miller, Mike. The Woodland Girls: Quest for the Rings. 2011. 120p. pap. 12.95 *(978-1-4502-8934-4(7))* iUniverse, Inc.
Mills-Darlow, Beryl C. My Beach Granny. 2012. 36p. pap. 14.50 *(978-1-61897-681-9(8),* Strategic Bk. Publishing) Strategic Book Publishing & Rights Agency (SBPRA).
Mills, Susan & Shara, Diana. Frankie & Her Little Pals - Save the Watermelons. 2007. 32p. (J). *(978-0-9790690-3-1(3))* Lucky Red Pr., LLC.
Mills, Timothy. The Mystery Kids: the Phantom Camper. 2010. 88p. pap. 14.95 *(978-0-557-55089-0(0))* Lulu Pr., Inc.
Mills, Wynette. The Backyard Explorer: The Nana & Me Series. 2010. 36p. pap. 15.49 *(978-1-4520-2483-7(9))* AuthorHouse.
Minarik, Else Holmelund. Little Bear & the Marco Polo. Doubleday, Dorothy, illus. 2010. (I Can Read Level 1 Ser.). (ENG.). 32p. (J). (gr. k-3). 16.99 *(978-0-06-085485-0(5));* pap. 3.99 *(978-0-06-085487-4(1))* HarperCollins Pubs.
Miranda, Edward. The Truth about Dragons & Dinosaurs. Cassetta, Andrea, illus. 2007. 32p. per. 10.95 *(978-1-934246-22-1(0))* Peppertree Pr., The.
Mitchard, Jacquelyn & Lewis, Michael S. Eagle Eyes. 2009. (ENG.). 128p. (gr. 4-7). pap. 9.99 *(978-0-9790072-2-4(4))* MAHVL Publishing.
Mitchell, Margaree King. When Grandmama Sings. Ransome, James E., illus. 2012. (ENG.). 40p. (J). (gr. k-4). 16.99 *(978-0-688-17563-4(5),* Amistad) HarperCollins Pubs.
Mochizuki, Chiemi. The Promise. Randle, Walt R., ed. Mochizuki, Chiemi, illus. 2003. (Illus.). 38p. (J). (gr. 3-6). 16.99 *(978-0-9720691-0-6(0))* Berkeley Major Publishing.
Molesworth & Molesworth, Mary Louisa S. Grandmother Dear. 2008. 128p. pap. 10.95 *(978-1-60664-225-2(1))* Aegypan.
—Us. 2008. 116p. per. 9.95 *(978-1-60312-539-0(6))* Aegypan.
Molesworth, Mary Louisa S. & Molesworth. Grandmother Dear. 2008. 128p. 23.95 *(978-1-60664-726-4(1))* Rodgers, Alan Bks.
Moloney, James. Black Taxi. 2005. 272p. (J). (gr. 7-18). 15.99 *(978-0-06-055937-3(3))* HarperCollins Pubs.
—Black Taxi. 2003. 288p. *(978-0-207-19989-9(2))* HarperCollins Pubs. Australia.
Monk, Isabell. Blackberry Stew. Porter, Janice Lee, illus. 2005. 32p. (J). (gr. -1 — 1). lib. bdg. 15.95 *(978-1-57505-605-0(4))* Lerner Publishing Group.
Monks, Barbara. Thank You Weasel Abbs! 2011. (Illus.). 72p. pap. 24.83 *(978-1-4567-7816-3(1))* AuthorHouse.
Montes, Gerardo David. My Grandmother's Tortillas. 2012. 21.95 *(978-0-7414-7056-0(X));* pap. 11.95 *(978-0-7414-7055-3(1))* Infinity Publishing.
Montgomery, Corey. Ask Grandma Pearl. 2011. 28p. pap. 15.99 *(978-1-4628-9498-7(4))* Xlibris Corp.
Montgomery, L. M. Jane of Lantern Hill. 2014. (ENG.). 272p. (YA). (gr. 5-12). pap. 11.99 *(978-1-4022-8930-9(8))* Sourcebooks, Inc.
Montgomery, R. A. Your Grandparents Are Zombies! 2010. (Illus.). 64p. (J). pap. 7.99 *(978-1-933390-90-1(5))* Chooseco LLC.
Moon, Catherine R. & Everette, Maureen C. The Adventures of NanaCat & Her Children: Someone New. Richardson, Kara, illus. 2004. 32p. (J). per. 6.95 *(978-0-930507-02-2(9))* GRAND Media, LLC.
Moore, Helen H. Nobody Else's Grannie. 2011. 28p. 12.95 *(978-1-4567-3047-5(9))* AuthorHouse.
Moore, Margaret & Moore, John Travers. The Three Tripps. Funk, Clotilde Embree, illus. 2011. 158p. 41.95 *(978-1-258-08478-3(3))* Literary Licensing, LLC.
Moore, Nancy Delano. Kiernan's Jam. Peck, Bill, illus. 2006. (J). 10.00 *(978-0-9785775-0-6(7))* Moore, Hullihen.
Moore, Shawn. Sam & the Tale of the Dragon Prints. Baker, David, illus. 2011. 28p. pap. 24.95 *(978-1-4560-7724-2(4))* America Star Bks.
Moorthy, Anita. Monkey's Drum. Sarkar, Soumitro, illus. 2003. (ENG.). 24p. pap. 3.99 *(978-81-86211-15-1(2))* Penguin Publishing Group.
Mora, Pat & Ventura, Gabriela Baeza. The Remembering Day / el Día de Los Muertos. Casilla, Robert, illus. 2015. (SPA & ENG.). 32p. (J). (gr. k-3). 17.95 *(978-1-55885-805-3(9),* Piñata Books) Arte Publico Pr.
Morel, John Henry. Little Button Annie. 2009. 48p. pap. 14.99 *(978-1-935436-94-2(5))* Rodaian Pr.
Moreton, Clara. Frank & Fanny: A Rural Story. 2007. (ENG.). 66p. per. 16.99 *(978-1-4346-2717-9(9));* per. 18.99 *(978-1-4346-2723-0(3))* Creative Media Partners, LLC.
Morpurgo, Michael. Colly's Barn. Andrew, Ian, illus. 2nd ed. 2016. (Reading Ladder Ser.). (ENG.). 48p. (J). (gr. k-2). 7.99 *(978-1-4052-8253-6(3))* Egmont Bks., Ltd. GBR. Dist: Independent Pubs. Group.
—Farm Boy. Foreman, Michael, illus. 2007. (ENG.). 76p. (J). (gr. 4-7). pap. 15.99 *(978-1-84365-090-4(8))* Pavilion Bks. GBR. Dist: Independent Pubs. Group.
—Half a Man. O'Callaghan, Gemma, illus. 2015. (ENG.). 64p. (J). (gr. 5). 16.99 *(978-0-7636-7747-3(7))* Candlewick Pr.
—Snakes & Ladders. Wilson, Anne, illus. 2006. (Yellow Bananas Ser.). (ENG.). 48p. (J). (gr. -1-3). lib. bdg. *(978-0-7787-0952-7(3))* Crabtree Publishing Co.
Morris, Chad. Cragbridge Hall, Book 2: The Avatar Battle. 2014. (Cragbridge Hall Ser.: 2). (ENG., Illus.). 360p. (J). (gr. 3-9). 17.99 *(978-1-60907-809-6(8),* Shadow Mountain) Shadow Mountain Publishing.
—Cragbridge Hall, Book 3: The Impossible Race. 2015. (Cragbridge Hall Ser.: 3). (ENG., Illus.). 432p. (J). (gr. 3-9). 18.99 *(978-1-60907-979-6(5),* Shadow Mountain) Shadow Mountain Publishing.
Morris, Jennifer E. Please Write Back! Morris, Jennifer E., illus. 2010. (Scholastic Reader Level 1 Ser.). (ENG., Illus.). 32p. (J). (gr. -1-3). pap. 3.99 *(978-0-545-11506-3(X),* Cartwheel Bks.) Scholastic, Inc.
—Please Write Back! 2010. (Scholastic Reader Level 1 Ser.). lib. bdg. 13.55 *(978-0-606-06822-2(8),* Turtleback) Turtleback Bks.
Morris, Sandra. Willow & Her Grandm. 2011. 32p. pap. 21.99 *(978-1-4628-8900-6(X))* Xlibris Corp.
Morrison, Toni & Morrison, Slade. Peeny Butter Fudge. Cepeda, Joe, illus. 2009. (ENG.). 32p. (J). (gr. -1-3). 17.99 *(978-1-4169-8332-3(5),* Simon & Schuster/Paula Wiseman Bks.) Simon & Schuster/Paula Wiseman Bks.
Morrissey, Dean & Krensky, Stephen. The Monster Trap. Morrissey, Dean, illus. 2004. (Illus.). 40p. (J). lib. bdg. 17.89 *(978-0-06-052499-9(5))* HarperCollins Pubs.
Morro, Scott. Danni's Gift. 2008. pap. 24.95 *(978-1-4241-7540-6(2))* America Star Bks.
Mortimer, Rachael. Red Riding Hood & the Sweet Little Wolf. Pichon, Liz, illus. 2013. (ENG.). 32p. 12.95 *(978-1-58925-117-5(2))* Tiger Tales.
Mortmain, Beatrice. I Help at Grandpa's House. Aguilera, Aurora, illus. 2017. (Ways I Help Ser.). 24p. (J). (gr. 4-6). pap. 8.25 ***(978-1-5081-5677-2(8),*** PowerKids Pr.) Rosen Publishing Group, Inc., The.
Moser, Lisa. Kisses on the Wind. Brown, Kathryn, illus. 2009. (ENG.). 32p. (J). (gr. -1-2). 16.99 *(978-0-7636-3110-9(8))* Candlewick Pr.
Moses, Sheila P. The Legend of Buddy Bush. 2004. (ENG., Illus.). 224p. (YA). (gr. 7). 19.99 *(978-0-689-85839-0(6),* McElderry, Margaret K. Bks.) McElderry, Margaret K. Bks.
—The Legend of Buddy Bush, 3 vols. unabr. ed. 2005. (YA). (gr. 3-7). 54.75 *(978-1-4193-3575-4(8),* 42043) Recorded Bks., Inc.
Mosher, Jennifer. Who Caught the Yawn? & Where Did the Sneeze Go? Sharp, Todd, illus. 2013. 38p. pap. *(978-0-9874832-3-2(4))* MoshPit Publishing.
Mosher, Richard. Zazoo. 2004. (ENG.). 272p. (YA). (gr. 7-18). reprint ed. pap. 15.95 *(978-0-618-43904-1(8))* Houghton Mifflin Harcourt Publishing Co.
Most, Bernard. Catch Me If You Can! (¡A Que No Me Alcanzas!) Flor Ada, Alma & Campoy, F. Isabel, trs. from ENG. 2007. (Green Light Readers Level 2 Ser.). (SPA & ENG., Illus.). 28p. (J). (gr. -1-3). pap. 3.95 *(978-0-15-205967-5(9))* Houghton Mifflin Harcourt Publishing Co.
Moster, Jamey S. Fly, Fly Away. 2009. 28p. pap. 13.99 *(978-1-4490-0140-7(8))* AuthorHouse.
Moundlic, Charlotte. The Bathing Costume. Tallec, Olivier & Sorman, Joy, illus. 2013. (ENG.). 40p. (J). (gr. k-3). 15.95 *(978-1-59270-141-4(8))* Enchanted Lion Bks., LLC.
Mr. Blacky & His Palace. l.t. ed. 2006. (Illus.). 27p. (J). per. 13.99 *(978-1-59879-267-6(9))* Lifevest Publishing, Inc.
Mudrovich, Jane. Exorcising the Googie. 2012. 154p. pap. 14.97 *(978-1-61897-939-1(6),* Strategic Bk. Publishing) Strategic Book Publishing & Rights Agency (SBPRA).
Mueller, Janet. A Star from Grandma. Mueller, Janet, illus. 2004. (Illus.). (J). pap. 8.96 *(978-0-9746932-3-1(5))* Stella Bks, Inc.
Mull, Brandon. Fablehaven. 2006. (ENG., Illus.). 351p. (J). lib. bdg. 20.00 *(978-1-4242-4831-5(0))* Fitzgerald Bks.
—Fablehaven. 2009. (SPA.). 306p. (YA). (gr. 5-8). 24.95 *(978-84-9918-033-5(7))* Roca Editorial ESP. Dist: Spanish Pubs., LLC.
—Fablehaven. 2006. (Fablehaven Ser.: 1). (ENG., Illus.). 368p. (J). (gr. 3-7). 19.99 *(978-1-59038-581-4(0),* Shadow Mountain) Shadow Mountain Publishing.
—Fablehaven. Dorman, Brandon, illus. 2007. (Fablehaven Ser.: 1). (ENG.). 384p. (J). (gr. 3-8). pap. 8.99 *(978-1-4169-4720-2(5),* Aladdin) Simon & Schuster Children's Publishing.
—Fablehaven. 2007. (Fablehaven Ser.: 01). lib. bdg. 18.40 *(978-1-4177-9328-0(7),* Turtleback) Turtleback Bks.
—Fablehaven: Las Llaves de la Prision de los Demonios. 2012. (SPA.). 466p. (YA). 24.95 *(978-84-9918-438-8(3))* Roca Editorial ESP. Dist: Spanish Pubs., LLC.
—Fablehaven Vol. 5: The Complete Series Boxed Set. 2010. (Fablehaven Ser.: Bks. 1-3). 99.99 *(978-1-60641-832-1(7),* Shadow Mountain) Shadow Mountain Publishing.
—Fablehaven Collection Set. Dorman, Brandon, illus. 2011. (Fablehaven Ser.). (ENG.). 2512p. (J). (gr. 3-8). pap. 42.99 *(978-1-4424-2977-2(1),* Aladdin) Simon & Schuster Children's Publishing.
—Grip of the Shadow Plague. Dorman, Brandon, illus. 2008. (Fablehaven Ser.: 3). (ENG.). 480p. (J). (gr. 3-7). 19.99 *(978-1-59038-898-3(4),* Shadow Mountain) Shadow Mountain Publishing.
—Keys to the Demon Prison. Dorman, Brandon, illus. 2011. (Fablehaven Ser.: 5). (ENG.). 640p. (J). (gr. 3-8). pap. 8.99 *(978-1-4169-9029-1(1),* Aladdin) Simon & Schuster Children's Publishing.

—Rise of the Evening Star. Dorman, Brandon, illus. 2007. (Fablehaven Ser.: 2). (ENG.). 456p. (J). (gr. 3-7). 19.99 (978-1-59038-742-9(2), Shadow Mountain) Shadow Mountain Publishing.

—Rise of the Evening Star. Dorman, Brandon, illus. 2008. (Fablehaven Ser.: 2). (ENG.). 480p. (J). (gr. 3-8). pap. 7.99 (978-1-4169-5770-6(7), Aladdin) Simon & Schuster Children's Publishing.

Mun-Ensor, Michelle. The Faithful Christmas. 2011. 28p. pap. 24.95 (978-1-4560-7077-9(0)) America Star Bks.

Munro, Ken. Grandfather's Secret: Sammy & Brian Mystery Series #16. 2004. (Sammy & Brian Mystery Ser.: 16). (J). pap. 6.95 (978-1-932864-04-5(0)) Masthof Pr.

Murdock, Catherine Gilbert. Heaven Is Paved with Oreos. (ENG.). 208p. (J). (gr. 5-7). 2015. pap. 6.99 (978-0-544-43932-0(5), HMH Books For Young Readers) 2013. 16.99 (978-0-547-62538-6(3)) Houghton Mifflin Harcourt Publishing Co.

Murphy, Sally. Pearl Verses the World. Potter, Heather, illus. 2011. (ENG.). 80p. (J). (gr. 3-7). 14.99 (978-0-7636-4821-3(3)) Candlewick Pr.

Murray, Scott. Granny's Christmas Blunder. 2012. 28p. pap. 18.00 (978-1-4772-0990-5(5)) AuthorHouse.

Murrow, Marjorie. The Surprise in Grandma's Eyes. 2009. (Illus.). 16p. pap. 10.98 (978-1-4389-8104-8(X)) AuthorHouse.

My Grandma Is Great. (My Great Relatives... Ser.). 32p. (J). (978-1-84250-575-5(0), Bright Sparks) Parragon, Inc.

My Grandpa Is Great. (Great Relatives Ser.). (Illus.). 32p. (J). (978-1-84250-576-2(9), Bright Sparks) Parragon, Inc.

My Great Grandma Clara. 2006. (J). pap. 12.95 (978-0-9677047-8-4(2)) Marble Hse. Editions.

Myers, Tim J. The Christmas Stick: A Children's Story. Yilmaz, Necdet, illus. 2014. (ENG.). 32p. (J). pap. 13.99 (978-1-61261-571-4(6)) Paraclete Pr., Inc.

Myers, Walter Dean. It Ain't All for Nothin' 2003. 226p. (gr. 7-12). 17.00 (978-0-7569-1460-8(4)) Perfection Learning Corp.

Myott, Lanita. RJ Saves the Day. 2003. 19p. 11.16 (978-1-4116-0354-7(0)) Lulu Pr., Inc.

Myracle, Lauren. Bliss. 2008. (ENG.). 464p. (YA). (gr. 9-17). 16.95 (978-0-8109-7071-7(6), Amulet Bks.) Abrams, Inc.

The Mystery of October Island. 2003. (Illus.). 50p. (J). per. 12.95 (978-0-9754823-0-8(0)) Pumpkin Patch Publishing.

The Mystery of the Tiny Key. 2008. 32p. pap. 4.99 (978-0-8341-2351-9(7), 083-412-3517) Beacon Hill Pr. of Kansas City.

Nadin, Joanna. Paradise. 2012. (ENG., Illus.). 272p. (YA). (gr. 9). 16.99 (978-0-7636-5713-0(1)) Candlewick Pr.

Naegele, K. Z. The Chatty Hat. 2011. 36p. pap. 24.95 (978-1-4626-3652-5(7)) America Star Bks.

Namioka, Lensey. April & the Dragon Lady. 2007. (ENG., Illus.). 224p. (YA). (gr. 7-12). pap. 13.95 (978-0-15-205669-8(6)) Houghton Mifflin Harcourt Publishing Co.

Nanji, Shenaaz. An Alien in My House, 1 vol. McLeod, Chum, illus. 2003. (ENG.). 24p. (J). (gr. -1-3). 15.95 (978-1-896764-77-1(0)) Second Story Pr. CAN. Dist: Orca Bk. Pubs. USA.

Nannestad, Katrina. When Mischief Came to Town. 2016. (ENG.). 192p. (J). (gr. 5-7). 16.99 (978-0-544-53432-2(8), HMH Books For Young Readers) Houghton Mifflin Harcourt Publishing Co.

Nanny & I Meet Odie. 2006. (J). lib. bdg. 18.99 (978-0-9724394-1-1(2)) Sylables.

National Geographic Learning Staff. The Secret under the Tree. Life, Kay, illus. 2010. (Rise & Shine Ser.: 7). (ENG.). 32p. (C). (gr. 1-3). pap. 13.95 (978-0-8075-0643-1(5)) National Geographic School Publishing, Inc.

Nelson, Nancy. Grandma's Drip Castles. 2011. (J). 16.99 (978-0-9703041-7-9(X)) Stellar Publishing.

Nelson, S. D. The Star People: A Lakota Story. 2003. (ENG., Illus.). 36p. (J). (gr. -1-3). 18.95 (978-0-8109-4584-5(3)) Abrams, Inc.

Nelson, Vaunda Micheaux. Don't Call Me Grandma. Zunon, Elizabeth, illus. 2016. (ENG.). 32p. (gr. k-3). (J). lib. bdg. 19.99 (978-1-4677-4208-5(2)); (J). 30.65 (978-1-4677-9559-3(3)); 35.99 (978-1-5124-0661-0(9)) Lerner Publishing Group. (Carolrhoda Bks.).

Newbery, Linda. A Dog Called Whatnot. 2006. (Red Bananas Ser.). (ENG., Illus.). 48p. (J). (gr. -1-3). (978-0-7787-1094-3(7)) Crabtree Publishing Co.

Newcomb, Victoria. Gathering Grace. 2008. 250p. (YA). pap. 15.95 (978-1-59275-009-2(5)) Hanford Mead Pubs., Inc.

Newman, Lesléa. My Name Is Aviva. Jatkowska, Ag, illus. 2015. (ENG.). 32p. (J). (gr. -1-2). pap. 7.99 (978-1-4677-2656-6(7)); lib. bdg. 17.99 (978-1-4677-2654-2(0)) Lerner Publishing Group. (Kar-Ben Publishing).

Newman, Nanette. What Will You Be, Grandma? Chichester Clark, Emma, illus. 2012. (ENG.). 32p. (J). (gr. -1-2). 15.99 (978-0-7636-6099-4(X), Templar) Candlewick Pr.

Newman, Nanette & Cook, Beryl. My Granny. (Illus.). 32p. (YA). 2004. (978-1-84365-058-4(4)) 2003. (978-1-84365-059-1(2)) Pavilion Bks. (Pavilion Children's Books).

Newman, Patrice Tomasetti. Beautiful Colors. 2013. 24p. pap. 24.95 (978-1-63000-660-0(2)) America Star Bks.

Newsome, Tandy. Mr. Miyataki's Marvelous Machine. Robinson, Don, illus. 2004. 28p. (J). (gr. -1-3). 12.95 (978-0-931548-68-0(3)) Island Heritage Publishing.

Newton, Renae. Having Fun with Granny. 2010. 16p. 9.00 (978-1-4520-0000-8(X)) AuthorHouse.

Nicholson, Doris. A Day with Grandma. 2006. 9.00 (978-0-8059-9914-3(0)) Dorrance Publishing Co., Inc.

Nigh, Linda. Emily's Christmas Tree. 2011. 24p. pap. 24.95 (978-1-4560-6822-6(9)) America Star Bks.

Nimmo, Jenny. Chestnut Soldier. 2009. (Magician Trilogy Ser.). (ENG.). 208p. (J). (gr. 3-7). 5.99 (978-0-545-07127-7(5), Scholastic Paperbacks) Scholastic, Inc.

Nislick, June Levitt. Zayda Was a Cowboy. 2005. (ENG.). 88p. pap. 11.95 (978-0-8276-0817-7(9)) Jewish Pubn. Society.

Nitz, Kristin Wolden. Suspect, 1 vol. 2010. (ENG.). 224p. (YA). (gr. 7-11). 16.95 (978-1-56145-543-0(1)) Peachtree Pubs.

Nix, Garth & Williams, Sean. The Magic, Bk. 1. 2012. (Troubletwisters Ser.: 1). (ENG.). 304p. (J). (gr. 3-7). pap. 7.99 (978-0-545-25903-3(7), Scholastic Paperbacks) Scholastic, Inc.

—The Monster. (Troubletwisters Ser.: 2). (ENG.). 304p. (J). (gr. 3-7). 2013. pap. 6.99 (978-0-545-25904-0(5), Scholastic Paperbacks) 2012. 16.99 (978-0-545-25898-2(7), Scholastic Pr.) Scholastic, Inc.

—Troubletwisters, Bk. 1. 2011. (Troubletwisters Ser.: 1). (ENG.). 304p. (J). (gr. 3-7). 16.99 (978-0-545-25897-5(9), Scholastic Pr.) Scholastic, Inc.

Noel, Pamela. Same Ol' Moon: The little things of life & Love. 2010. 191p. pap. 13.95 (978-1-4327-6132-5(3)) Outskirts Pr., Inc.

Noensie, Pamela & Lamore, Garretta. Tari: the Little Balinese Dancer. 2013. (ENG., Illus.). 32p. (J). (gr. k-3). 14.95 (978-0-8048-4387-4(2)) Tuttle Publishing.

Nolan, Han. A Face in Every Window. 2008. (ENG., Illus.). 276p. (YA). (gr. 7). pap. 15.95 (978-0-15-206418-1(4)) Houghton Mifflin Harcourt Publishing Co.

—When We Were Saints. 2005. (ENG.). 312p. (YA). (gr. 7-12). pap. 15.95 (978-0-15-205322-2(0)) Houghton Mifflin Harcourt Publishing Co.

Noland, Monica. My Nana Looks Like a Telephone, 1 vol. 2007. (ENG.). 22p. 24.95 (978-1-4241-8532-0(7)) America Star Bks.

Noonan, Loretta. My Gramma Doesn't Knit. 2010. 24p. 12.99 (978-1-4520-5661-6(7)) AuthorHouse.

Nora, David, Jr. Happy Balloon to You. 2005. 9.00 (978-0-8059-9870-2(5)) Dorrance Publishing Co., Inc.

Norfolk, Bobby & Norfolk, Sherry. Anansi & the Pot of Beans. Hoffmire, Baird, illus. 2006. (Story Cove Ser.). (ENG.). 32p. (J). (gr. -1-3). 4.95 (978-0-87483-811-4(8)) August Hse. Pubs., Inc.

Norman, Kim. This Old Van. Conahan, Carolyn Digby, illus. 2015. (ENG.). 30p. (J). (gr. -1-2). 14.95 (978-1-4549-1063-3(1)) Sterling Publishing Co., Inc.

North, Laura. Cinderella's Big Foot. 2014. (ENG., Illus.). 32p. (J). (978-0-7787-0440-9(8)); pap. (978-0-7787-0448-5(3)) Crabtree Publishing Co.

Northrop, Nancy. Momma - Where Has Grandpa Gone? 2012. 28p. pap. 13.99 (978-1-4624-0157-4(0), Inspiring Voices) Author Solutions, Inc.

Nosy Crow Staff. Big Bug Log. Braun, Sebastien, illus. 2017. (ENG.). 18p. (J). (gr. -1-2). bds. 9.99 (978-0-7636-9322-0(7), Nosy Crow) Candlewick Pr.

—Little Red Riding Hood: a Nosy Crow Fairy Tale. Bryan, Ed, illus. 2017. (ENG.). 32p. (J). (gr. -1-2). 9.99 (978-0-7636-9331-2(6), Nosy Crow) Candlewick Pr.

Nuchols, Galand A. Dragon Hatchling. 2007. 144p. per. 11.95 (978-0-595-46346-6(0)) iUniverse, Inc.

Nydam, Anne. The Bad Advice of Grandma Hasenfuss. 2010. 112p. pap. 14.00 (978-0-557-26037-9(X)) Lulu Pr., Inc.

Oberon, Daphne. The Ghost Tree: Tonantzin's Blessing. 2009. 50p. pap. 23.95 (978-1-4327-3153-3(X)) Outskirts Pr., Inc.

O'Brien, Anne Sibley. A Path of Stars. O'Brien, Anne Sibley, illus. 2012. (ENG., Illus.). 40p. (J). (gr. k-3). 15.95 (978-1-57091-735-6(3)) Charlesbridge Publishing, Inc.

O'Connor, Barbara. The Small Adventure of Popeye & Elvis. 2011. (ENG.). 176p. (J). (gr. 3-7). pap. 7.99 (978-0-312-65932-5(6), 9780312659325) Square Fish.

O'Connor, Jane. Bonjour, Butterfly. Glasser, Robin Preiss, illus. 2008. (Fancy Nancy Ser.). (ENG.). 32p. (J). (gr. -1-2). 17.99 (978-0-06-123588-7(1)) HarperCollins Pubs.

—Fancy Nancy: My Family History. Glasser, Robin Preiss et al, illus. 2010. (I Can Read Level 1 Ser.). (ENG.). 32p. (J). (gr. -1-3). 16.99 (978-0-06-188270-8(4)) HarperCollins Pubs.

—My Family History. Glasser, Robin Preiss et al, illus. 2010. (I Can Read Level 1 Ser.). (ENG.). 32p. (J). (gr. -1-3). pap. 3.99 (978-0-06-188271-5(2)) HarperCollins Pubs.

O'Connor, Peggy. The Little Boy Who Was Born Purple, 1 vol. 2010. 20p. 24.95 (978-1-4489-4994-6(7)) PublishAmerica, Inc.

Odegaard, Sarah. Don Hummer Visits Nana Jane. 2009. 32p. pap. 12.99 (978-1-4389-6816-2(7)) AuthorHouse.

Odom, Rebecca. Grandpa & the Raccoon. Tebbit, Jake, illus. 2009. 36p. pap. 24.95 (978-1-60749-912-1(6)) America Star Bks.

O'Donnell, Candy. Where Is God, Grandfather. Gillen, Rosemarie, illus. 2008. 28p. pap. 12.95 (978-0-9814532-1-7(X)) Living Waters Publishing Co.

Oelschlager, Van. My Grampy Can't Walk. 2006. (ENG., Illus.). 40p. (J). (gr. -1-3). 17.95 (978-1-59624-015-5(6)) Cleveland Clinic Pr.

Oelschlager, Vanita. My Grampy Can't Walk. Hegan, Robin & Blackwood, Kristin, illus. 2008. (ENG.). 36p. (J). (gr. -1-3). 9.95 (978-0-9800162-0-8(7)) VanitaBooks.

Ofanansky, Allison. The Patchwork Torah. Oriol, Elsa, illus. 2014. (Sukkot & Simchat Torah Ser.). (ENG.). 32p. (J). (gr. -1-5). 17.95 (978-1-4677-0426-7(1)); 7.95 (978-1-4677-0427-4(X)) Lerner Publishing Group. (Kar-Ben Publishing).

Ogilvie, Yolanda. Nana: A Portrait of Inspiration. 2013. 28p. pap. 8.99 (978-1-62697-503-3(5)) Salem Author Services.

Okibedi, Agnes Ada-Nwaneri. Happy Times with Grandm. 2011. 40p. pap. 18.49 (978-1-4567-3449-7(0)) AuthorHouse.

Olds, Laurie. Cars on Vacation. 2009. 24p. pap. 12.25 (978-1-4490-1633-3(2)) AuthorHouse.

Oleson, Susan. Sammy Tails: Finding a Home, 1. 2006. (Illus.). 28p. (J). pap. (978-0-9779251-0-0(2)) Oleson, Susan.

Olsen, Sylvia. Yetsa's Sweater, 1 vol. Larson, Joan, illus. 2007. (ENG.). 40p. (J). (gr. -1-5). 19.95 (978-1-55039-155-8(0)) Sono Nis Pr. CAN. Dist: Orca Bk. Pubs. USA.

Olson, John J. Wild Child & Annie. 2010. 44p. pap. 26.49 (978-0-557-32534-4(X)) Lulu Pr., Inc.

Olson, Nancy. Thanksgiving at Grandma's. Marino, Michael F., illus. 2009. 24p. pap. 10.95 (978-1-4251-8909-9(1)) Trafford Publishing.

Olson, Steve. My Grandpa & Me: The Grandpa Steve Series. 2008. 32p. pap. 14.49 (978-1-4389-1148-9(3)) AuthorHouse.

O'Malley Cerra, Kerry. Just a Drop of Water. 2014. (ENG.). 320p. (J). (gr. 2-7). 14.95 (978-1-62914-613-3(7), Sky Pony Pr.) Skyhorse Publishing Co., Inc.

O'Neil, Paula. Valley of the Moon. 2011. pap. 10.95 (978-0-7414-6333-3(4)) Infinity Publishing.

Onyefulu, Ifeoma. Grandma Comes to Stay. Onyefulu, Ifeoma, photos by. 2010. (First Experiences Ser.). (ENG., Illus.). 32p. (J). (gr. -1-2). 17.99 (978-1-84507-865-2(9), Frances Lincoln) Quarto Publishing Group UK GBR. Dist: Hachette Bk. Group.

Oplinger, Jon & Cooke, Elizabeth. The Wicked Small People of Whiskey Bridge. 2011. 156p. (gr. 4-6). 22.95 (978-1-4620-4948-6(6)); pap. 12.95 (978-1-4620-4947-9(8)) iUniverse, Inc.

Ørbeck-Nilssen, Constance. I'm Right Here. Düzakin, Akin, illus. 2015. (ENG.). 28p. (J). 16.00 (978-0-8028-5455-1(9), Eerdmans Bks For Young Readers) Eerdmans, William B. Publishing Co.

Orlando, Martha Jane. A Trip, a Tryst & a Terror. 2012. 134p. pap. 10.95 (978-1-939289-03-2(3), Little Creek Bks.) Jan-Carol Publishing, INC.

Orloff, Karen Kaufman. I Wanna Go Home. Catrow, David, illus. 2014. (ENG.). 32p. (J). (gr. k-3). 16.99 (978-0-399-25407-9(2), G.P. Putnam's Sons Books for Young Readers) Penguin Young Readers Group.

Orr, Fran E. When Mommy Was a Soldier, 1 vol. 2008. (ENG.). 26p. 24.95 (978-1-4241-9576-3(4)) America Star Bks.

Orr, Wendy. Abandoned! - A Lion Called Kiki. Castelao, Patricia, illus. 2012. (Rainbow Street Shelter Ser.: 4). (ENG.). 128p. (J). (gr. 2-5). 15.99 (978-0-8050-9501-2(2), 9780805095012, Holt, Henry & Co. Bks. For Young Readers) Holt, Henry & Co.

—Ark in the Park. pap. 6.95 (978-0-8050-6818-4(X), Holt, Henry & Co. Bks. For Young Readers) Holt, Henry & Co.

Ortega, Cristina. The Eyes of the Weaver: Los Ojos Del Tejedor. Garcia, Patricio E., illus. 2006. (ENG.). 64p. (J). 19.95 (978-0-8263-3990-4(5)) Univ. of New Mexico Pr.

Osborne, Robin. The Boy who Loved to Shim-sham Shimmy. 2004. (Illus.). 40p. (J). lib. bdg. 14.95 (978-0-9762852-0-5(7)) Wooden Shoe Pr.

Ostermann, Ruby. Willie Tucker & His Gramma: The Life of a Dog. l.t. ed. 2012. (Illus.). 30p. (J). pap. 16.95 (978-1-937912-93-2(0)) Cordon Pubns.

Ostrove, Karen. Rise & Shine: A Challah-Day Tale. Scott, Kimberley, illus. 2013. (Shabbat Ser.). (ENG.). 24p. (J). (gr. -1-3). 7.95 (978-0-7613-7500-5(7)); lib. bdg. 17.95 (978-0-7613-7499-2(X)) Lerner Publishing Group. (Kar-Ben Publishing).

Oxenbury, Helen. En Casa de los Abuelos (At Grandparents' House) (SPA.). 24p. (J). 7.50 (978-84-261-2066-3(0)) Juventud, Editorial ESP. Dist: AIMS International Bks., Inc.

Pace, Betty. Donald's Dump Truck. 2007. 36p. per. 12.95 (978-1-4327-0029-4(4)) Outskirts Pr., Inc.

Packer, Evelyn. The Adventures of Jarv & Trudie: Angel. 2010. 24p. 11.49 (978-1-4520-3848-3(1)) AuthorHouse.

Padian, Maria. Brett McCarthy: Work in Progress. 2009. (ENG.). 288p. (YA). (gr. 7). pap. 8.99 (978-0-440-24055-6(7), Knopf Bks. for Young Readers) Random Hse. Children's Bks.

Pagel, Beth. What's Wrong with Grandma? 2008. 32p. pap. 11.96 (978-0-557-00302-0(4)) Lulu Pr., Inc.

Pak, Jiyeon. My Grandpa's Chair. 2017. (ENG.). 32p. (J). (gr. -1-2). 17.99 (978-1-5247-0075-1(4)); lib. bdg. 20.99 (978-1-5247-0076-8(2)) Random Hse. Children's Bks. (Knopf Bks. for Young Readers).

Palazzolo, Gail M. Mommy, How Can We Catch the Moon? 2008. 15p. pap. 24.95 (978-1-60672-864-2(4)) America Star Bks.

Palmer, Robin. Little Miss Red. 2010. (ENG.). 320p. (YA). (gr. 7-18). 9.99 (978-0-14-241123-0(X), Speak) Penguin Young Readers Group.

Pan, Hui-Mei. ¿Qué hay en la bolsa de Abuelita? Pan, Hui-Mei, illus. 2004.Tr. of What's in Grandma's Grocery Bag? (SPA., Illus.). 16p. (J). bds. 6.25 (978-1-932065-05-3(9)) Star Bright Bks., Inc.

Panagopoulos, Janie Lynn. Mark of the Bear Claw. 2004. (J). 15.95 (978-0-938682-78-3(4)) River Road Pubns., Inc.

Parenteau, Shirley. Ship of Dolls. 2014. (ENG.). 272p. (J). (gr. 3-7). 16.99 (978-0-7636-7003-0(0)) Candlewick Pr.

Parish, Herman. Amelia Bedelia's First Apple Pie. Avril, Lynne, illus. 2012. (Amelia Bedelia Ser.). (ENG.). 32p. (J). (gr. -1-3). pap. 6.99 (978-0-06-196411-4(5), Greenwillow Bks.) HarperCollins Pubs.

Park, Barbara. The Graduation of Jake Moon. unabr. ed. 2004. 115p. (J). (gr. 4-7). pap. 29.00 incl. audio (978-0-8072-8722-4(9), Listening Library) Random Hse. Audio Publishing Group.

Parker, Amy. Thank You, God, for Grandma, 1 vol. 2017. (ENG., Illus.). 20p. (J). bds. 9.99 (978-0-7180-8925-2(1)) Nelson, Thomas Inc.

—Thank You, God, for Grandpa, 1 vol. 2017. (ENG., Illus.). 20p. (J). bds. 9.99 (978-0-7180-8929-0(4)) Nelson, Thomas Inc.

Parker, Beth. Tom Turtle Visits Grandma's Farm. 2011. 28p. pap. 24.95 (978-1-4560-1000-3(X)) America Star Bks.

Parker, Emma. Granny Odd Legs. 2010. (Illus.). pap. (978-1-877547-86-7(7)) First Edition Ltd.

Parker, Emma Rae. Papa's Book of Mormon Christmas. 2015. (Illus.). (J). 14.99 (978-1-4621-1741-3(4)) Cedar Fort, Inc./CFI Distribution.

Parr, Todd. The Grandma Book. 2006. (ENG., Illus.). 24p. (J). (gr. -1-1). 11.99 (978-0-316-05802-5(5), Tingley, Megan Bks.) Little, Brown Bks. for Young Readers.

Parrish, Edith. Sarah the Purple Goose Gets Lost. Odom, Kelly, illus. 2011. 34p. 23.95 (978-1-60844-930-9(0)) Dog Ear Publishing, LLC.

Pascuzzo, Margaret I. Anton Loses a Friend. Bicking, Judith, illus. 2009. 20p. pap. 12.00 (978-1-4269-0650-3(1)) Trafford Publishing.

Paterson, Katherine. The Same Stuff As Stars. 2015. (ENG.). 256p. (J). (gr. 5-7). pap. 7.99 (978-0-544-54030-9(1), HMH Books For Young Readers) Houghton Mifflin Harcourt Publishing Co.

—The Same Stuff as Stars. 2004. 270p. (gr. 3-7). 17.00 (978-0-7569-2801-8(X)) Perfection Learning Corp.

Patricia Diane Craine, Ma-Lmft. Our Miracle Our Earth. 2009. 56p. pap. 24.49 (978-1-4389-5918-4(4)) AuthorHouse.

Patrick, Cat & Young, Suzanne. Just Like Fate. (ENG., Illus.). (YA). (gr. 9). 2014. 336p. pap. 9.99 (978-1-4424-7272-3(3)) 2013. 304p. 16.99 (978-1-4424-7271-6(5)) Simon Pulse. (Simon Pulse).

Patrick, Denise Lewis. MaDear's Old Green House. Sadler, Sonia Lynn, illus. 2004. 32p. (J). (gr. k-3). 16.95 (978-0-940975-55-2(6), Sankofa Bks.) Just Us Bks., Inc.

Patron, Kristine Mary. An Artist? That's Me! 2013. 20p. (J). pap. 6.95 (978-1-4327-8377-8(7)) Outskirts Pr., Inc.

Patterson, James. Public School Superhero. 2015. (ENG., Illus.). 304p. (J). (gr. 3-7). 13.99 (978-0-316-32214-0(8), Jimmy Patterson) Little Brown & Co.

Patterson, James & Tebbetts, Chris. Public School Superhero. Thomas, Cory, illus. 2016. (ENG.). 304p. (J). (gr. 3-7). pap. 7.99 (978-0-316-26598-0(5), Jimmy Patterson) Little Brown & Co.

Patterson, James, et al. Public School Superhero. 2015. (978-0-316-34231-5(9)) Little, Brown Bks. for Young Readers.

Patton, Jim & Dee. Grandmother's Heart. 2007. 194p. pap. 13.99 (978-1-4116-3377-3(6)) Lulu Pr., Inc.

Pauline Roberts & Donnie Obina. Promises! Promises! Who Can I Trust. 2013. 28p. pap. 16.09 (978-1-4669-7959-8(3)) Trafford Publishing.

Paulsen, Gary. Molly Mcginty Has a Really Good Day. 2006. (Illus.). 105p. (J). (gr. 3-7). 13.15 (978-0-7569-6621-8(3)) Perfection Learning Corp.

—The Quilt. 2005. 83p. (gr. 3-7). 16.00 (978-0-7569-4781-1(2)) Perfection Learning Corp.

—The Quilt. 2005. (ENG., Illus.). 96p. (J). (gr. 3-7). 6.99 (978-0-440-22936-0(7), Yearling) Random Hse. Children's Bks.

Pavanello, Roberto. King Tut's Grandmother, 1 vol. Zeni, Marco, tr. from ITA. Pisapia, Blasco & Brughera, Pamela, illus. 2012. (Echo & the Bat Pack Ser.). (ENG.). 128p. (gr. 2-3). 9.95 (978-1-4342-4245-7(5)); lib. bdg. 25.32 (978-1-4342-3823-8(7), Echo & the Bat Pack) Stone Arch Bks.

P.A.W. My Summer Road Trip. 2012. 28p. pap. 15.99 (978-1-4691-5077-2(8)) Xlibris Corp.

Payne, C. C. Lula Bell on Geekdom, Freakdom, & the Challenges of Bad Hair, 0 vols. 2012. (ENG.). 276p. (J). (gr. 3-7). 16.99 (978-0-7614-6225-5(2), 9780761462255, Amazon Children's Publishing) Amazon Publishing.

Payne, Sandy. Find Your Magic. Goodpaster, Nancy, illus. 2013. 50p. pap. 12.95 (978-1-937508-16-6(1)) Bearhead Publishing, LLC.

PC Treasures Staff, prod. Little Red Riding Hood. 2007. (J). (978-1-60072-031-4(5)) PC Treasures, Inc.

Peacock, Shane. Double You, 1 vol. 2014. (Seven Sequels Ser.). (ENG., Illus.). 272p. (J). (gr. 5-10). pap. 10.95 (978-1-4598-0534-7(8)) Orca Bk. Pubs. USA.

Pearce, Margaret. A Belinda Robinson Novel Book 3: Belinda & the Missing Will. 2013. 80p. pap. (978-1-922233-23-3(4)) Writers Exchange E-Publishing.

Pearson, Elizabeth. My Grandma Says. 2009. 36p. pap. 13.95 (978-1-60693-979-6(3), Strategic Bk. Publishing) Strategic Book Publishing & Rights Agency (SBPRA).

Pechero-Loewen, Mariella. I Want to Know How You Found Me. 2004. 39p. pap. 24.95 (978-1-4137-2955-9(X)) PublishAmerica, Inc.

Peck, James E. Meet Mr. Chair Bear. 2008. 52p. pap. 16.95 (978-1-4241-7959-6(9)) America Star Bks.

Peck, Richard. A Long Way from Chicago. 2004. (Puffin Modern Classics Ser.). (ENG.). 160p. (J). (gr. 5-7). pap. 7.99 (978-0-14-240110-1(2), Puffin Books) Penguin Young Readers Group.

—A Year down Yonder. unabr. ed. 2004. (Middle Grade Cassette Librariestm Ser.). 144p. (J). (gr. 5-9). pap. 29.00 incl. audio (978-0-8072-0991-2(0), S YA 256 SP, Listening Library) Random Hse. Audio Publishing Group.

Peck, Robert Newton. Bro. 2004. (ENG.). 160p. (J). (gr. 7-18). 16.99 (978-0-06-052974-1(1)) HarperCollins Pubs.

Peek, Renee W. Grandma's Miracles. 2013. 26p. pap. 12.95 (978-1-4575-1954-3(2)) Dog Ear Publishing, LLC.

Peet, Mal. Tamar: A Novel of Espionage, Passion, & Betrayal. (ENG., Illus.). 432p. (YA). (gr. 9). 2008. pap. 8.99 (978-0-7636-4063-7(8)) 2007. 17.99 (978-0-7636-3488-9(3)) Candlewick Pr.

Penson, Mary. Billy Bardin & the Witness Tree. 2004. (Chaparral Bks.). (ENG.). 146p. (J). pap. 11.95 (978-0-87565-283-2(2)) Texas Christian Univ. Pr.

Pepper, Lily. In the Garden at Granddad's. 2012. (Illus.). 24p. pap. 19.82 (978-1-4772-2642-1(7)) AuthorHouse.

Perdomo, Willie. Abuela. Date not set. (J). 16.95 (978-0-8050-7302-7(7), Holt, Henry & Co. Bks. For Young Readers) Holt, Henry & Co.

Pérez, Amada Irma. Nana's Big Surprise. Gonzalez, Maya Christina, illus. 2013.Tr. of Nana, ¡Qué Sorpresa! (ENG & SPA.). 32p. (J). pap. 9.95 (978-0-89239-307-7(6), Children's Book Press) Lee & Low Bks., Inc.

Perez, Amada Irma & Children's Book Press Staff. Nana, Que Sorpresa! Gonzalez, Maya Christina, illus. 2007.Tr. of Nana's Big Surprise. (ENG & SPA.). 32p. (J). (gr. k-2). lib. bdg. 16.95 (978-0-89239-190-5(1)) Lee & Low Bks., Inc.

Perkyns, Dorothy. Last Days in Africville. 2005. (Illus.). 144p. (YA). pap., tchr. ed. (978-0-88878-446-9(5), Sandcastle Bks.) Dundurn.

—Last Days in Africville. 2006. (ENG.). 120p. (J). (gr. 4-7). pap. 10.99 (978-1-55002-630-6(5), Dundurn Pr.) Dundurn CAN. Dist: Ingram Publisher Services.

Perl, Erica S. Aces Wild. (ENG.). 224p. (J). (gr. 3-7). 2015. 7.99 (978-0-307-93173-3(0), Yearling) 2013. 15.99 (978-0-307-93172-6(2), Knopf Bks. for Young Readers) Random Hse. Children's Bks.

—When Life Gives You O. J. 2013. (ENG.). 224p. (J). (gr. 3-7). 6.99 (978-0-375-85902-1(0), Yearling) Random Hse. Children's Bks.

Peschke, Marci. Fishing Queen. Mourning, Tuesday, illus. 2017. (Kylie Jean Ser.). (ENG.). 112p. (gr. 2-3). lib. bdg. 22.65 (978-1-4795-9900-4(X), Kylie Jean) Picture Window Bks.

Peterson, Lois. The Wrong Bus, 1 vol. Meissner, Amy, illus. 2012. (Orca Echoes Ser.). (ENG.). 64p. (J). (gr. 2-3). pap. 6.95 (978-1-55469-869-1(3)) Orca Bk. Pubs. USA.

Peterson, Will. The Gathering. 2010. (Triskellion Ser.: 3). (ENG., Illus.). 384p. (YA). (gr. 9-18). 16.99 (978-0-7636-4847-3(7)) Candlewick Pr.

Petretti, Silvia I. Rachel's Easter Vacation in Mexico. James, Elizabeth, ed. 2011. (Illus.). 50p. (J). pap. 14.99 (978-1-931671-37-8(0)) FM Publishing Co.

Petrovic, Svetlana. Brown Bear, White Bear. Hardy, Vincent, illus. 2009. 28p. (J). (gr. -1-3). 17.00 (978-0-8028-5353-0(6),

Eerdmans Bks For Young Readers) Eerdmans, William B. Publishing Co.

Phillips, illus. Bubbie's Baby. Phillips, . 2006. 28p. (J). 14.99 *(978-0-9774552-0-1(3))* Danza Pubns.

Phillips, Merrill. Tell Me Again Grampa. 2013. 172p. pap. 13.96 *(978-1-4669-9676-2(5))* Trafford Publishing.

Pinson, Isabel. Bubbe's Belated Bat Mitzvah. Cis, Valeria, illus. 2014. (ENG.). 32p. (J). (gr. -1-3). 7.95 *(978-1-4677-1950-6(1))*; lib. bdg. 17.95 *(978-1-4677-1949-0(8))* Lerner Publishing Group. (Kar-Ben Publishing).

Pippin-Mathur, Courtney, illus. Maya Was Grumpy. 2013. (J). *(978-0-545-62077-2(5))* Flashlight Pr.

Pirnot, Karen Hutchins. Keeper of the Lullabies, a Book for Grandmothers Who Cherish the World of Children. Pirnot, Karen Hutchins, illus. 2007. (Illus.). 36p. per. 12.95 *(978-1-934246-90-0(5))* Peppertree Pr., The.

Pittar, Gill. Milly, Molly & Grandpa Friday. 2004. 28p. *(978-1-86972-029-2(6))* Milly Molly Bks.

—Milly, Molly & Grandpa Friday (book W/dolls) 2006. 28p. pap. *(978-1-86972-107-7(1))* Milly Molly Bks.

Plourde, Lynn. Bella's Fall Coat. Gal, Susan, illus. 2016. (ENG.). 40p. (J). (gr. -1-k). 17.99 *(978-1-4847-2697-6(9))* Disney Pr.

The Poet's Basket. 2006. (J). 10.00 *(978-0-9769827-0-8(6))* Wren Song Pr.

Polacco, Ernest L. When Lightning Comes in a Jar. Polacco, Patricia, illus. 2007. (ENG.). 40p. (J). (gr. k-3). 6.99 *(978-0-14-240350-1(4)*, Puffin Books) Penguin Young Readers Group.

Polacco, Patricia. Bun Bun Button. Polacco, Patricia, illus. 2011. (ENG., Illus.). 36p. (J). (gr. -1-k). 17.99 *(978-0-399-25472-7(2)*, G.P. Putnam's Sons Books for Young Readers) Penguin Young Readers Group.

—Chicken Sunday. 2015. 32p. pap. 8.00 *(978-1-61003-527-9(5))* Center for the Collaborative Classroom.

—Someone for Mr. Sussman. Polacco, Patricia, illus. 2008. (ENG., Illus.). 40p. (J). (gr. 1-3). 17.99 *(978-0-399-25075-0(1)*, Philomel Bks.) Penguin Young Readers Group.

—Thunder Cake. 2015. 32p. pap. 8.00 *(978-1-61003-536-1(4))* Center for the Collaborative Classroom.

—When Lightning Comes in a Jar. 2007. (Illus.). (gr. -1-3). 17.00 *(978-0-7569-8196-9(4))* Perfection Learning Corp.

Polinski, Jo. Minnesota Moon. Webber, Carol, illus. 2007. 20p. per. 12.95 *(978-1-933482-60-6(5))* White Turtle Bks.

Polk, Douglas. The Legend of Garie Pond. 2008. 60p. pap. 16.95 *(978-1-60703-985-3(0))* America Star Bks.

Pont, Beattie. Grandma, Tell Me More: Fishing with Grandpa. 2013. 80p. (gr. 2-4). pap. 19.95 *(978-1-4817-2073-1(2))* AuthorHouse.

Popper, Carol. David, Mormor, Homo & the Yak: An Alphabet Mystery. 2008. 24p. pap. 24.95 *(978-1-4241-8772-0(9))* America Star Bks.

Porada, Henry. The Inner Light. Michaels, Lisa J., illus. 2013. 32p. pap. 12.99 *(978-1-937260-98-9(4))* Sleepytown Pr.

Porpora, Donnamarie. Grampa's Wings. 2013. 32p. pap. *(978-1-4602-1366-7(1))* FriesenPress.

Porrata, Mayra. The Day Kyle Met Nuf. Rice, Kaleb & Deasey, Kevin, illus. 2013. 28p. pap. 12.95 *(978-0-9825480-2-8(8))* Sunny Day Publishing, LLC.

Porter, Cullen. Grandpa Grumpy Pants. 2006. (ENG., Illus.). 32p. (J). 19.95 *(978-1-932278-05-7(2))* Mayhaven Publishing, Inc.

Powell, Jim S. The Mystery of the Totem Trees: A Plumroy Pack Adventure. 2009. 124p. pap. 10.95 *(978-1-4401-3921-5(0))* iUniverse, Inc.

Poydar, Nancy. Busy Bea. Poydar, Nancy, illus. 2013. (ENG., Illus.). 32p. (J). (gr. -1-2). 16.99 *(978-1-4814-2161-4(1)*, McElderry, Margaret K. Bks.) McElderry, Margaret K. Bks.

Pressler, Mirjam. Let Sleeping Dogs Lie. Macki, Erik J., tr. from GER. 2007. (ENG.). 208p. (J). (gr. 9-12). 16.95 *(978-1-932425-84-0(5)*, Front Street) Boyds Mills Pr.

Price, M. J. Momot. Grandma & Grandpa Are Retiring. 2013. 32p. pap. 24.95 *(978-1-63000-966-3(0))* America Star Bks.

Price, Mara & Ventura, Gabriela Baeza. Grandma's Chocolate/El Chocolate de Abuelita. Fields, Lisa, illus. 2010. (SPA.). 32p. (J). (gr. -1-3). 16.95 *(978-1-55885-587-8(4)*, Piñata Books) Arte Publico Pr.

Price, Marilyn. Grandma's Cookies. 2011. 32p. pap. 12.95 *(978-1-934527-28-3(9))* Torah Aura Productions.

Project Blastoff. 2015. (Astrotwins Ser.). (ENG., Illus.). 224p. (J). (gr. 3-7). 17.99 *(978-1-4814-1545-3(X)*, Simon & Schuster/Paula Wiseman Bks.) Simon & Schuster/Paula Wiseman Bks.

Prokofiev, Sergei. Peter & the Wolf. Raschka, Chris, illus. 2008. (ENG.). 40p. (J). (gr. -1-2). 19.99 *(978-0-689-85652-5(0)*, Atheneum/Richard Jackson Bks.) Simon & Schuster Children's Publishing.

PS, I Love You, Gramps: Individual Title, 6 packs. (Action Packs Ser.). 120p. (gr. 3-5). 44.00 *(978-0-7635-8389-7(8))* Rigby Education.

Publications International Ltd. Staff, ed. Grandma Loves You: Stories to Share. 2010. (J). bds. 7.98 *(978-1-60553-433-6(1))* Phoenix International Publications, Inc.

—Record A Story: My Grandma Is Special. 2011. 20p. (J). bds. 19.99 *(978-1-4508-1352-5(6))* Phoenix International Publications, Inc.

—Record a Story: My Grandpa Is Special. 2011. 20p. (J). bds. 25.98 *(978-1-4508-1381-5(X))* Phoenix International Publications, Inc.

Puckett, Annie Marie. Pedro Learns about Salvation. 2006. 56p. per. 9.95 *(978-1-57258-453-2(X)*, 945-6314) TEACH Services, Inc.

Puentes, Christina. On the Way to Granny's House. 2005. 28p. per. 17.32 *(978-1-4134-3612-9(9))* Xlibris Corp.

Purmell, Ann. Christmas Tree Farm. Weber, Jill, illus. 2006. (ENG.). 32p. (J). (gr. -1-3). 16.95 *(978-0-8234-1886-2(3))* Holiday Hse., Inc.

Quarles, Pamela. Jake & Josh Go Camping. Denison, Susan, illus. 2007. 40p. per. 14.00 *(978-1-59858-407-3(3))* Dog Ear Publishing, LLC.

Quetel, Julie. The Adventures of Shayne & His Flying Grandma. 2011. 60p. (gr. -1). pap. 10.49 *(978-1-4490-5553-0(2))* AuthorHouse.

Quinn, Timothy. Marvelous Miriam's Magnificent Hawaiian Adventure. 2011. 56p. pap. 16.95 *(978-1-4560-9630-4(3))* America Star Bks.

Rabe, Tish. I Love You, Grandma! Hitch, David, illus. 2016. (J). ***(978-1-5182-1618-3(8)***, Golden Bks.) Random Hse. Children's Bks.

Rabley, Stephen. The Twins & the Time Machine/Les Jumeaux et la Machine du Temps. Bougard, Marie-Therese, tr. Eudes-Pascal, Elisabeth, illus. 2008. (Let's Read! Bks.). (ENG & FRE.). 32p. (J). (gr. 3-7). pap. 5.99 *(978-0-7641-4048-8(5))* Barron's Educational Series, Inc.

Rader, Jared. Sandy's Dream. Meyers, Sarah, illus. 2007. 16p. (J). (gr. -1-3). 10.99 *(978-1-59879-398-7(5))* Lifevest Publishing, Inc.

Rahaman, Vashanti. Divali Rose. Akib, Jamel, illus. 2008. (ENG.). 32p. (J). (gr. 2-4). 16.95 *(978-1-59078-524-9(X))* Boyds Mills Pr.

Rankine-Van Wassenhoven, Jacqueline. Sundays at Grandmother's House. 2008. 32p. pap. 18.50 *(978-0-557-01709-6(2))* Lulu Pr., Inc.

—Who Stole Grandpa's Teeth? 2008. 20p. 10.94 *(978-1-4357-0522-7(X))* Lulu Pr., Inc.

Ransom, Candice. Finding Day's Bottom. 2006. 176p. (J). (gr. 3-7). lib. bdg. 15.95 *(978-1-57505-933-4(9))*, Carolrhoda Bks.) Lerner Publishing Group.

Rath, Tom & Reckmeyer, Mary. How Full Is Your Bucket? For Kids. Manning, Maurie J., illus. 2009. (ENG.). 32p. (J). (gr. -1-4). 17.95 *(978-1-59562-027-9(3))* Gallup Pr.

Raven, Margot Theis. Circle Unbroken. Lewis, E. B., illus. 2007. (ENG.). 48p. (J). (gr. -1-3). per. 8.99 *(978-0-312-37603-1(0)*, 9780312376031) Square Fish.

Ray, Sandra. Grandma & Me Oh What Do We See When We Go to the Zoo? Bailey, Sidney, illus. 2011. 32p. 14.99 *(978-1-4520-8133-5(6))* AuthorHouse.

Raye, Varuna. Frederick & the Scaries. 2009. 32p. pap. 15.50 *(978-0-557-11104-6(8))* Lulu Pr., Inc.

Reagan, Jean. How to Babysit a Grandma, 2 vols. (ENG.). 32p. (J). (gr. k-3). 2016. 33.98 *(978-1-5247-1435-2(6))* 2014. (Illus.). 16.99 *(978-0-385-75384-5(5))* Random Hse. Children's Bks. (Knopf Bks. for Young Readers).

—How to Babysit a Grandpa. Wildish, Lee, illus. 2012. (ENG.). 32p. (J). (gr. k-3). 16.99 *(978-0-375-86713-2(9)*, Knopf Bks. for Young Readers) Knopf, Alfred A. Inc.

Redmond, Diane. Peter & the Wolf: Band 09/Gold. Bendall-Brunello, John, illus. 2007. (Collins Big Cat Ser.). (ENG.). 24p. (J). (gr. 1-2). pap. 7.99 *(978-0-00-718674-7(6))* HarperCollins Pubs. Ltd. GBR. Dist: Independent Pubs. Group.

Reece, P. J. Roxy, 1 vol. 2010. (ENG., Illus.). 192p. (YA). (gr. 9-12). pap. 12.95 *(978-1-896580-01-2(7))* Tradewind Bks. CAN. Dist: Orca Bk. Pubs. USA.

Reed, Jennifer. The Falling Flowers. Cole, Dick, illus. 2005. (Falling Flowers Ser.). 32p. (J). (gr. -1-3). 16.95 *(978-1-885008-28-2(7)*, Shen's Bks.) Lee & Low Bks., Inc.

Reed, Joel B. Grandpa's New Kitty. Reed, Joel B., illus. 2008. (Illus.). 28p. pap. 12.95 *(978-1-933482-65-1(6))* White Turtle Bks.

Rees, Gwyneth. Fairy Dreams Vol. 1: A Magical Journey to Fairyland. 3rd unabr. ed. 2005. (Fairy Dust Ser.: 3). (ENG., Illus.). 224p. (J). (gr. 2-4). pap. 8.99 *(978-0-330-43476-8(4))* Pan Macmillan GBR. Dist: Independent Pubs. Group.

Refrrolo, C. T. Grandchild of Mine: You & I. 2006. (J). 12.00 *(978-0-8059-6845-3(8))* Dorrance Publishing Co., Inc.

Reid-Tulloch, Joseth. Manu's Special Day. 2012. 16p. pap. 14.99 *(978-1-4520-9150-1(1))* AuthorHouse.

Reimiller, Diane L. A Duck Named Quackers, 1 vol. Jastrzebski, Brandy, illus. 2009. 12p. pap. 24.95 *(978-1-60836-771-9(1))* America Star Bks.

Reisenauer, Cynthia Mauro. Emerita. Reisenauer, Cynthia Mauro, illus. 2007. (Illus.). 48p. (J). 18.95 *(978-0-9726487-5-2(5))* Puddle Jump Pr., Ltd.

Reiss, Mike. City of Hamburgers. Feinberg, Xeth, illus. 2008. 32p. (J). 14.95 *(978-1-59299-346-8(X))* Inkwater Pr.

Renaud, Anne. How the Sea Came to Marissa. Durland, Maud, illus. 2006. 32p. (J). *(978-1-58270-129-5(6))* Beyond Words Publishing, Inc.

Renier, Aaron. The Unsinkable Walker Bean. Renier, Aaron, illus. 2010. (Unsinkable Walker Bean Ser.: 1). (ENG., Illus.). 208p. (J). (gr. 4-9). pap. 15.99 *(978-1-59643-453-0(8)*, 9781596434530, First Second Bks.) Roaring Brook Pr.

Resau, Laura. What the Moon Saw. 2008. (ENG.). 272p. (J). (gr. 3-7). pap. 7.99 *(978-0-440-23957-4(5)*, Yearling) Random Hse. Children's Bks.

Reuterstrand, Siri. Ellis Is Scared of the Dark. Wik, Jenny, illus. 2012. (ENG.). 24p. (J). (gr. -1-k). 12.95 *(978-1-61608-667-1(X)*, 608667, Sky Pony Pr.) Skyhorse Publishing Co., Inc.

Revell, Mike. Stonebird. 2016. (ENG.). 288p. (J). (gr. 5-9). pap. 9.99 *(978-1-68144-514-4(X))* Quercus NA.

Reynolds, Cynthia Furlong. Across the Reach. 2007. 269p. (J). (gr. 3-7). 16.95 *(978-1-58726-518-1(4)*, Mitten Pr.) Ann Arbor Editions LLC.

—Grammie's Secret Cupboard. Dodson, Bert, illus. 2007. 32p. (J). (gr. -1-3). 17.95 *(978-1-58726-310-1(6)*, Mitten Pr.) Ann Arbor Editions LLC.

Reynolds, Gardiner John. Stone Fox. 30th rev. ed. 2014. (Trophy Bk Ser.). (ENG.). 96p. (J). (gr. 7-12). 10.24 *(978-1-63245-175-0(1))* Lectorum Pubns., Inc.

Reynolds, Jason. As Brave As You. (ENG.). 432p. (J). (gr. 5). 2017. pap. 7.99 *(978-1-4814-1591-0(3)*, Atheneum Bks. for Young Readers) 2016. (Illus.). 16.99 *(978-1-4814-1590-3(5)*, Atheneum/Caitlyn Dlouhy Books) Simon & Schuster Children's Publishing.

Reynolds, Jean. Gwen & the Talking Napkin. 2007. (Grandma Ser.: 4). (J). per. 7.99 *(978-1-59872-897-2(0))* Instant Pub.

Rhodes, Jewell Parker. Bayou Magic. 2015. (ENG., Illus.). 256p. (J). (gr. 3-7). 17.99 *(978-0-316-22484-0(7))* Little Brown & Co.

—Bayou Magic. 2016. (ENG.). 272p. (J). (gr. 3-7). pap. 7.99 *(978-0-316-22485-7(5))* Little, Brown Bks. for Young Readers.

Ricchi, Brenda. The Grandchildren's Bible Journeys - the Creation Story. 2010. 35p. pap. 17.00 *(978-0-557-14903-2(7))* Lulu Pr., Inc.

Ricci, Christine. I Love My Abuela! Miller, Victoria, illus. 2009. (Dora the Explorer Ser.: 28). (ENG.). 24p. (J). pap. 3.99 *(978-1-4169-6866-5(0)*, Simon Spotlight/Nickelodeon) Simon Spotlight/Nickelodeon.

Rice, Dona Herwick & Sugarman, Dorothy. World War II: Battle of Normandy, 1 vol. 2009. (Building Fluency Through Reader's Theater Ser.). (ENG., Illus.). 32p. (J). (gr. 3-5). pap. 7.99 *(978-1-4333-0553-5(4))* Teacher Created Materials, Inc.

Richards, Josie Aleardi. Grandma's Just Not Herself. Rowland, Lauri, illus. 2010. 36p. pap. 13.95 *(978-1-60911-236-3(9)*, Eloquent Bks.) Strategic Book Publishing & Rights Agency (SBPRA).

Richardson, Bernard. Freddy Weller's Holiday. 2011. 50p. 24.99 *(978-1-4628-9548-9(4))*; pap. 15.99 *(978-1-4628-9547-2(6))* Xlibris Corp.

Richardson, Faith. The Peacock's Stone. 2003. 192p. (J). 21.95 *(978-0-9744989-0-4(4))*; (Illus.). pap. 12.95 *(978-0-9744989-1-1(2))* Fox Song Bks.

Richardson, Lilith. TORO Special Edition Paperback. 2010. 63p. pap. 24.00 *(978-0-578-04792-8(6))* Richardson, Lilith.

Richardson, Mike. The Return of the Gremlins. 2009. (Illus.). 88p. pap. 12.95 *(978-1-59582-170-6(8))* Dark Horse Comics.

Richmond, Marianne. Grandma Loves Me! 2nd ed. 2015. (Marianne Richmond Ser.: 0). (ENG., Illus.). 24p. (J). (-2). bds. 7.99 *(978-1-4926-2295-6(8)*, Sourcebooks Jabberwocky) Sourcebooks, Inc.

—Grandpa Loves Me! (Marianne Richmond Ser.: 0). (ENG., Illus.). 24p. (J). 2009. (gr. -1-2). bds. 7.95 *(978-1-934082-45-4(7)*, 9781934082454, Marianne Richmond Studios, Inc.) 2nd ed. 2015. (-2). bds. 7.99 *(978-1-4926-2298-7(2)*, Sourcebooks Jabberwocky) Sourcebooks, Inc.

Richter, Bernd & Richter, Susan. Gandma & Grandpa Cruise Alaska Inside Passage. 2008. (Illus.). 52p. (J). pap. 9.95 *(978-1-931353-35-9(2))* Saddle Pal Creations, Inc.

—Grandma & Grandpa Ride Alaska Train. 2008. (Illus.). 48p. (J). pap. 9.95 *(978-1-931353-34-2(4))* Saddle Pal Creations, Inc.

—Grandma & Grandpa Visit Denali. Drashner, Diane, illus. 2008. 48p. (J). pap. 9.95 *(978-1-931353-33-5(6))* Saddle Pal Creations, Inc.

—When Grandma & Grandpa Cruised Through Alaska. 2008. (ENG., Illus.). 18p. (J). bds. 8.95 *(978-1-931353-39-7(5))* Saddle Pal Creations, Inc.

—When Grandma & Grandpa Rode the Alaska Train. 2008. (ENG., Illus.). 16p. (J). bds. 8.95 *(978-1-931353-40-3(9))* Saddle Pal Creations, Inc.

Riddle, Jamie. Beach Bum Babies & Sand Sisters Stormy. 2006. 48p. pap. 16.95 *(978-1-4241-3600-1(8))* PublishAmerica, Inc.

RIGBY. My Grandmother's Hands: First Grade Big Books. 2003. (Rigby on Our Way to English Ser.). (ENG.). 16p. (gr. 1-1). pap. 50.70 *(978-0-7578-1503-4(0))* Rigby Education.

Riggs, Ransom. Miss Peregrine's Home for Peculiar Children. (ENG., Illus.). (YA). (gr. 9). 2013. 368p. pap. 10.99 *(978-1-59474-603-1(6))* 2011. (Miss Peregrine's Peculiar Children Ser.: 1). 352p. 18.99 *(978-1-59474-476-1(9))* 2016. (Miss Peregrine's Peculiar Children Ser.: 1). 392p. pap. 11.99 *(978-1-59474-902-5(7))* Quirk Bks.

—Miss Peregrine's Home for Peculiar Children. l.t. ed. 2012. (ENG.). 484p. (J). (gr. 8-12). 23.99 *(978-1-4104-5023-4(6))* Thorndike Pr.

—Miss Peregrine's Home for Peculiar Children. 2013. (Miss Peregrine's Peculiar Children Ser.: 1). lib. bdg. 22.10 *(978-0-606-32081-8(4)*, Turtleback) Turtleback Bks.

Riggs, Ransom, et al. Miss Peregrine's Home for Peculiar Children. 2011. pap. *(978-1-59474-574-4(9))* Quirk Bks.

Riley, Elliot. Miguel's Family. Bassani, Srimalie, illus. 2017. (All Kinds of Families Ser.). (ENG.). (J). (gr. k-1). 28.51 ***(978-1-68342-147-4(7))*** Rourke Educational Media.

—Owen's Family. Bassani, Srimalie, illus. 2017. (All Kinds of Families Ser.). (ENG.). (J). (gr. k-1). 28.51 ***(978-1-68342-148-1(5))*** Rourke Educational Media.

Riley, Penelope A. Duckie Dan the Traveling Man. 2009. 44p. pap. 16.99 *(978-1-4490-4634-7(7))* AuthorHouse.

Rippy, Patricia J. Here Comes the Tornado. 2012. 20p. pap. 17.99 *(978-1-4772-4905-5(2))* AuthorHouse.

Ritchie, Janet. Remember That I Love You. 2008. (ENG.). 40p. 18.99 *(978-1-4389-3155-5(7))* AuthorHouse.

Rivard, Émilie & Quinn, Sarah. Really & Truly. Delisle, Anne-Claire & Owlkids Books Inc. Staff, illus. 2012. (ENG.). 24p. (J). (gr. -1-3). 15.95 *(978-1-926973-40-1(2))* Owlkids Bks. Inc. CAN. Dist: Publishers Group West (PGW).

Rivera-Ashford, Roni Capin. My Tata's Remedies - Los Remedios de Mi Tata. Castro L., Antonio, illus. 2015. (ENG & SPA.). 40p. (J). (gr. 1-6). pap. 8.95 *(978-1-935955-89-4(6))* Cinco Puntos Pr.

Robbins, Eliza & National Geographic Learning Staff. Nana's New Room. 2010. (Rise & Shine Ser.). (ENG.). 12p. (C). (gr. -1-3). pap. 9.95 *(978-1-4042-6734-3(4))* National Geographic School Publishing, Inc.

Roberts, Carmen. Inseparable: The Tale of the Amulet. 2009. 120p. 21.49 *(978-1-4490-3394-1(6))*; pap. 10.99 *(978-1-4490-3396-5(2))* AuthorHouse.

Roberts, Laura Peyton. Green. 2011. (ENG.). 272p. (J). (gr. 3-7). 7.99 *(978-0-440-42235-8(3)*, Yearling) Random Hse. Children's Bks.

Roberts, Willo Davis. Rebel. 2005. 153p. (J). (gr. 3-7). 13.65 *(978-0-7569-5076-7(7))* Perfection Learning Corp.

—Rebel. 2012. (ENG., Illus.). 160p. (J). (gr. 3-7). pap. 8.99 *(978-0-689-85081-3(6)*, Aladdin) Simon & Schuster Children's Publishing.

—To Grandmother's House We Go. 2012. (ENG., Illus.). 192p. (J). (gr. 3-7). pap. 9.99 *(978-0-689-71838-0(1)*, Simon & Schuster/Paula Wiseman Bks.) Simon & Schuster/Paula Wiseman Bks.

Robertson, Jean. Grandpa Comes to First Grade. Dufalla, Anita, illus. 2011. (ENG.). 24p. (gr. k-1). pap. 8.95 *(978-1-61236-004-1(1))* Rourke Educational Media.

Robinson, Brenda. A Monster Came to Our House. 2013. 40p. pap. 16.46 *(978-1-4669-9569-7(6))* Trafford Publishing.

Robinson, Kathleen Marie. The Magic Doorknob, 1 vol. 2009. 56p. pap. 16.95 *(978-1-60813-362-8(1))* America Star Bks.

Robinson, Linda M. Dear Grandchild, When You Come for a Visit. Larkins, Mona, illus. 2005. 37p. (J). (gr. -1-4). 15.99 *(978-0-9740841-4-5(X))* K&B Products.

Robinson, Sharon. Under the Same Sun. Ford, A. G., illus. 2014. (ENG.). 40p. (J). (gr. -1-3). 17.99 *(978-0-545-16672-0(1)*, Scholastic Pr.) Scholastic, Inc.

Robyck, Michael. Where Is Lauren's Cat, Chaulky? 2011. 28p. pap. 15.99 *(978-1-4568-8797-1(1))* Xlibris Corp.

Rochester, B. The Joey Jenkins Mysteries: Something Is Missing at Redding Lake. 2005. 67p. pap. 16.95 *(978-1-4241-0065-1(8))* PublishAmerica, Inc.

Rocini, Mary L. Getting Ready. 2011. 28p. pap. 15.99 *(978-1-4628-7774-4(5))* Xlibris Corp.

Rodda, Emily. The Charm Bracelet. Vitale, Raoul, illus. 2003. (Fairy Realm Ser.). 128p. (J). (gr. 2-5). 8.99 *(978-0-06-009583-3(0))* HarperCollins Pubs.

—The Charm Bracelet Bk. 1. Vitale, Raoul, illus. 2009. (Fairy Realm Ser.: No. 1). (ENG.). 128p. (J). (gr. 2-5). pap. 4.99 *(978-0-06-009585-7(7))* HarperCollins Pubs.

Roddy, Lee. Ghost of the Moaning Mansion. 2008. (D. J. Dillon Adventure Ser.: No. 8). (J). 7.99 *(978-0-88062-272-1(5))* Mott Media.

Roddy-Worsham, Clara. Bear Baby Goes Fishing. 2013. 24p. 24.95 *(978-1-63004-070-3(3))* America Star Bks.

Rodriguez, Angelica. Mia y Primos/Mia & Cousins: Yo grito,corro y grito / I scream, run & Scream. 2009. 24p. pap. 12.49 *(978-1-4389-7095-0(1))* AuthorHouse.

Rogers, Elizabeth E. A Can of Magic Smiles. 2008. 32p. pap. 24.95 *(978-1-4241-8671-6(4))* America Star Bks.

Rollins, Janice. Bunny's Dream. 2009. 56p. pap. 23.99 *(978-1-4389-9146-7(0))* AuthorHouse.

Romano, Jennifer. Saturday Morning. 2010. 44p. pap. 16.99 *(978-1-4520-0165-4(0))* AuthorHouse.

Romig, Hilary. Mrs Crumbs' Trunk. 2009. 24p. pap. 12.99 *(978-1-4490-0466-8(0))* AuthorHouse.

Root, Phyllis. Rattletrap Car Big Book. Barton, Jill, illus. 2009. (ENG.). 40p. (J). (gr. -1-3). pap. 24.99 *(978-0-7636-4139-9(1))* Candlewick Pr.

Rose, Naomi C. Tashi & the Tibetan Flower Cure. 2016. (ENG.). 40p. (J). (gr. 1-6). pap. 10.95 ***(978-1-62014-318-6(6))*** Lee & Low Bks., Inc.

Rose, Simon. The Emerald Curse, 1 vol. Nugent, Cynthia, illus. 384th ed. 2006. (ENG.). 96p. (J). (gr. 3-6). per. 7.95 *(978-1-896580-90-6(4))* Tradewind Bks. CAN. Dist: Orca Bk. Pubs. USA.

Rosebrough, Ellen. Dora's Chilly Day. 2013. (Dora the Explorer 8X8 Ser.). lib. bdg. 13.55 *(978-0-606-32215-7(9)*, Turtleback) Turtleback Bks.

Rosenbaum, Andria Warmflash. A Grandma Like Yours. Bjornson, Barb, illus. 2006. (ENG.). 32p. (J). (gr. -1-1). per. 6.95 *(978-1-58013-168-1(9)*, Kar-Ben Publishing) Lerner Publishing Group.

—A Grandma Like Yours: A Grandpa Like Yours. Björnson, Barbara, illus. 2006. 32p. (J). 16.95 *(978-1-58013-167-4(0)*, Kar-Ben Publishing) Lerner Publishing Group.

Rosenberg, Amye. A Surprise in the Mail! Salanitro, Robert, illus. 2009. (Discovery Ser.). (ENG.). 12p. (J). 7.99 *(978-1-60436-018-9(6))* Educational Publishing LLC.

Rosenbluth, Roz. Getting to Know Ruben Plotnick. Manning, Maurie J., illus. 2005. (ENG.). 32p. (J). (gr. k-2). 15.95 *(978-0-9729225-5-5(5))* Flashlight Pr.

Rosenthal, Betsy R. It's Not Worth Making a Tzimmes Over! Rivers, Ruth, illus. 2006. 32p. (J). (gr. k-3). lib. bdg. 16.99 *(978-0-8075-3677-3(6))* Whitman, Albert & Co.

Ross, Mandy. Dominic Grows Sweetcorn. Bartlett, Alison, illus. 2014. (ENG.). 32p. (J). (gr. 1-5). 17.99 *(978-1-84780-327-6(X)*, Frances Lincoln) Quarto Publishing Group UK GBR. Dist: Hachette Bk. Group.

Ross, Margaret Clark. Jumpy the Frog Learns the Meaning of Love, 1 vol. McNeely, William, illus. 2010. 20p. pap. 24.95 *(978-1-4489-8370-4(3))* PublishAmerica, Inc.

Rosseau, Paul. Lucifer, Mon Grand-Père, Tome 1. Guénette, Geneviève, illus. 2004. (Mon Roman Ser.). (FRE.). 160p. (J). (gr. 2). pap. *(978-2-89021-650-1(0))* Diffusion du livre Mirabel (DLM).

Rosseter, Patrick W. Grampa Pat's Little Animal Tales. 2008. 88p. pap. 10.99 *(978-1-60647-466-2(9))* Salem Author Services.

Rossi, Joyce. The Gullywasher: El Chaparron Torrencial. 2004. (ENG, SPA & MUL., Illus.). 32p. (J). (gr. k-3). pap. 7.95 *(978-0-87358-728-0(6))* Cooper Square Publishing Llc.

Rostoker-Gruber, Karen. Maddie the Mitzvah Clown. 2016. (J). *(978-1-68115-523-4(0))* Behrman Hse., Inc.

Round, Suzanne. The Dragonfire Crystal. 2011. 154p. pap. *(978-0-7552-1359-7(9))* Authors OnLine, Ltd.

Rowley, Deborah Pace. Easter Walk: A Treasure Hunt for the Real Meaning of Easter. Burr, Dan, illus. 2010. (J). *(978-1-60641-055-4(5))* Deseret Bk. Co.

Roy, Kasi. Elizabeth Dreams: And the Christmas House Clock. 2011. 96p. pap. 12.10 *(978-1-4520-1864-5(2))* AuthorHouse.

Rozman, Jennifer Blue. With You Forever. 2011. 24p. pap. 11.95 *(978-1-4520-9941-5(3))* AuthorHouse.

Ruelle, Karen Gray. Easy As Apple Pie: A Harry & Emily Adventure. 2003. (Holiday House Readers Ser.). (ENG., Illus.). 32p. (J). (gr. k-3). 4.95 *(978-0-8234-1800-8(6))* Holiday Hse., Inc.

Rule, Rebecca. The Iciest, Diciest, Scariest Sled Ride Ever!, 1 vol. Thermes, Jennifer, illus. 2012. (ENG.). 36p. (J). 17.95 *(978-1-934031-88-9(7)*, 7e0b5554-6142-497e-ae8f-c0cb24d9743a) Islandport Pr., Inc.

Ruley, Garrett. Hollin. 2011. 226p. pap. 15.00 *(978-0-557-55873-5(5))* Lulu Pr., Inc.

Russo, Marisabina. I Will Come Back for You. 2014. (ENG.). 40p. (J). (gr. k-4). 7.99 *(978-0-385-39149-8(8)*, Dragonfly Bks.) Random Hse. Children's Bks.

Ryan, Pam Muñoz. Becoming Naomi Leon. 2005. (ENG.). 272p. (J). (gr. 3-7). reprint ed. per. 7.99 *(978-0-439-26997-1(0)*, Scholastic Paperbacks) Scholastic, Inc.

—Mice & Beans. Cepeda, Joe, illus. 2005. (gr. -1-3). lib. bdg. 17.00 *(978-0-7569-5089-7(9))* Perfection Learning Corp.

Ryan, Pam Muñoz & McInerney, Kathleen. Paint the Wind. 2009. (ENG.). 352p. (J). (gr. 3-7). pap. 7.99 *(978-0-545-10176-9(X)*, Scholastic Paperbacks) Scholastic, Inc.

Rylant, Cynthia. Annie & Snowball & the Grandmother Night. Stevenson, Suçie, illus. (Annie & Snowball Ser.: 12). (ENG.). 40p. (J). (gr. k-2). 2013. pap. 3.99 *(978-1-4169-7204-4(8))*

2012. 16.99 (978-1-4169-7203-7(X)) Simon Spotlight. (Simon Spotlight).

—Annie & Snowball & the Grandmother Night. 2013. (Annie & Snowball Ready-To-Read Ser.). lib. bdg. 13.55 (978-0-606-35183-6(3)) Turtleback Bks.

Sacre, Antonio. La Noche Buena: A Christmas Story. Dominguez, Angela, illus. 2010. (ENG.). 32p. (J). (gr. k-2). 17.95 (978-0-8109-8967-2(0), Abrams Bks. for Young Readers) Abrams, Inc.

Sáenz, Benjamin Alire. A Gift from Papa Diego: Un Regalo de Papa Diego. Garcia, Geronimo, illus. 2008. (Little Diego Book Ser.). (ENG & SPA.). 40p. (J). pap. 10.95 (978-0-938317-33-3(4)) Cinco Puntos Pr.

Saito, Ryusuke & Takidaira, Jiro. The Tree of Courage. Laughlin, Sako, tr. 2008. (Illus.). 32p. (J). 14.95 incl. audio compact disk (978-1-74126-442-5(1)) R.I.C. Pubns. AUS. Dist: SCB Distributors.

Salisbury, Linda G. No Sisters Sisters Club: A Bailey Fish Adventure. Grotke, Christopher A., illus. 2005. 188p. (J). per. 8.95 (978-1-881539-40-7(7)) Tabby Hse. Bks.

—Trouble in Contrary Woods: A Bailey Fish Adventure. Tomatore, Carol, illus. 2009. (J). 8.85 (978-1-881539-46-9(6)) Tabby Hse. Bks.

—The Wild Women of Lake Anna: A Bailey Fish Adventure. 2005. (Illus.). 159p. (J). (978-1-881539-37-7(7)) Tabby Hse. Bks.

Salter, Sydney. Swoon at Your Own Risk. 2010. (ENG., Illus.). 360p. (YA). (gr. 7-18). pap. 15.95 (978-0-15-206649-9(7)) Houghton Mifflin Harcourt Publishing Co.

Saltzberg, Barney. Tea with Grandpa. Saltzberg, Barney, illus. 2014. (ENG., Illus.). 40p. (J). (gr. -1-2). 15.99 (978-1-59643-894-1(0), 9781596438941) Roaring Brook Pr.

Salway, Ruth. Through Rose Coloured Glasses. 2006. (Illus.). 252p. per. (978-1-905529-58-2(9)) Grosvenor Hse. Publishing Ltd.

Sams, Carl R. & Stoick, Jean. Tea with Lady Sapphire. 2011. 48p. 19.95 (978-0-9827625-1-6(8)) Sams, II, Carl R. Photography, Inc.

Samuel, Kyrie. Kyrie Loves Grandma Soooo Much. 2012. 28p. pap. 24.95 (978-1-4626-8429-8(7)) America Star Bks.

Sanchez, Juanita L. Pancho the Green Parrot Lays an Egg, 1 vol. Ramirez, Samuel, illus. 2009. 24p. pap. 24.95 (978-1-61546-150-9(7)) America Star Bks.

Sandemose, Iben. Gracie & Grandma. Sandemose, Iben, illus. 2008. (Gracie & Grandma Ser.). (Illus.). 36p. (J). (gr. -1-1). 14.95 (978-0-9790347-3-2(6)) Mackenzie Smiles, LLC.

—Underwater. Vetleseter, Tonje, tr. from NOR. 2008. (Gracie & Grandma Ser.). (Illus.). 32p. (J). (gr. -1-1). 14.95 (978-0-9790347-4-9(4)) Mackenzie Smiles, LLC.

Sanders, Addie Meyer. I Don't Want to Go. l.t. ed. 2012. 43p. (J). pap. (978-1-4596-3449-7(7)) ReadHowYouWant.com, Ltd.

Sanders, E. T. Ninja Grandm. 2012. 24p. pap. 28.03 (978-1-4691-9063-1(X)) Xlibris Corp.

Sanderson, Brandon. Alcatraz Versus the Evil Librarians. Lazo, Hayley, illus. 2016. (Alcatraz Versus the Evil Librarians Ser.: 1). (ENG.). 320p. (J). 16.99 (978-0-7653-7894-1(9), 9780765378941, Starscape) Doherty, Tom Assocs., LLC.

—The Scrivener's Bones. 2016. (Alcatraz Versus the Evil Librarians Ser.: 2). (ENG.). 368p. (J). 16.99 (978-0-7653-7896-5(5), 9780765378965, Starscape) Doherty, Tom Assocs., LLC.

Sandi A. Why, Pops? 2011. 24p. pap. 11.99 (978-1-4670-4047-1(9)) AuthorHouse.

Sands, Monty. King of Nine Mile Canyon. 2008. 124p. 11.99 (978-0-615-25788-4(7)) Sands, Monty.

Sapre, Reshme. The Unfortunate Tale of Kachuva the Tortoise: As Told by Chukwa Sulcata. Robinson, Jayme, illus. 2012. (ENG.). 40p. 16.95 (978-0-9829362-0-7(6)) Hathi Chiti Bks. for Kids.

Sarfatti, Esther, tr. Caperucita Roja. Rovira, Francesc, illus. 2006. (Bilingual Tales Ser.). (SPA & ENG.). 24p. (J). (gr. -1-3). pap. 3.99 (978-0-439-77375-1(X), Scholastic en Espanol) Scholastic, Inc.

Sava, Scott Christian. My Grandparents Are Secret Agents. 2008. (Illus.). 112p. (J). 12.95 (978-0-9789168-6-2(7)) Blue Dream Studios.

Savage, Melissa. Lemons. 2017. (ENG.). 320p. (J). (gr. 3-7). lib. bdg. 19.99 **(978-1-5247-0013-3(4)**, Crown Books For Young Readers) Random Hse. Children's Bks.

Savageau, Cheryl & Hynes, Robert. Muskrat Will Be Swimming, 1 vol. 2006. (ENG., Illus.). 32p. (J). (gr. 3-7). 7.95 (978-0-88448-280-2(4), 884280) Tilbury Hse. Pubs.

Say, Allen. Grandfather's Journey. Say, Allen, illus. 2008. (ENG., Illus.). 32p. (J). (gr. -1-3). 7.99 (978-0-547-07680-5(0)) Houghton Mifflin Harcourt Publishing Co.

—Grandfather's Journey. 2008. (ENG.). 32p. (J). (gr. -1-3). pap. 7.99 (978-0-547-14178-7(5), Sandpiper) Houghton Mifflin Harcourt Trade & Reference Pubs.

—Grandfather's Journey. 2011. (J). (gr. k-5). 18.95 (978-0-545-12708-0(4)); 29.95 (978-0-545-10696-2(6)) Weston Woods Studios, Inc.

Sayre, Jill K. The Fairies of Turtle Creek. 2013. 322p. 22.17 (978-0-9885066-4-0(5)); pap. 15.70 (978-0-9885066-6-4(1)) Infinity Oak Bks.

Scacco, Linda. Always My Grandpa: A Story for Children about Alzheimer's Disease. Wong, Nicole, illus. 2005. 48p. (J). (gr. -1-3). 14.95 (978-1-59147-311-4(X)); per. 9.95 (978-1-59147-312-1(8)) American Psychological Assn. (Magination Pr.).

Scanlon, Cara. Where Did Grandma Go? Mattes-Ruggiero, Lynn, illus. 2008. (J). (978-1-930596-85-6(5)) Amherst Pr.

—Where Did Grandpa Go? Mattes-Ruggiero, Lynn, illus. 2008. (J). (978-1-930596-86-3(3)) Amherst Pr.

Scattergood, Augusta. Making Friends with Billy Wong. 2016. (ENG.). 224p. (J). (gr. 3-7). 16.99 (978-0-545-92425-2(1), Scholastic Pr.) Scholastic, Inc.

Scelsa, Greg. Granny's Coming 'Round the Mountain'. Faulkner, Stacey, ed. Leary, Catherine, illus. 2006. (J). pap. 2.99 (978-1-59198-350-7(9)) Creative Teaching Pr., Inc.

Schachner, Judy. The Grannyman. 2003. (ENG., Illus.). 32p. (J). (gr. -1-2). 6.99 (978-0-14-250062-0(3), Puffin Books) Penguin Young Readers Group.

Schaefer, Laura. The Secret Ingredient. Rim, Sujean, illus. (ENG.). 240p. (J). (gr. 4-8). 2012. pap. 6.99 (978-1-4424-1960-5(1)) 2011. 15.99 (978-1-4424-1959-9(8)) Simon & Schuster/Paula Wiseman Bks. (Simon & Schuster/Paula Wiseman Bks.).

—The Teashop Girls. Rim, Sujean, illus. 2009. (ENG.). 272p. (J). (gr. 4-9). pap. 6.99 (978-1-4169-6794-1(X), Simon & Schuster/Paula Wiseman Bks.) Simon & Schuster/Paula Wiseman Bks.

Schaumberg, Rose Mary & Schaumberg, Emily Rose. I'll Miss My Grandma, Wouldn't You? 2008. (Illus.). 40p. pap. 16.99 (978-1-4389-1335-3(4)) AuthorHouse.

Scheie, Jesse. Kisses to Heaven, 1 vol. Scheie, Jesse, illus. 2009. (Illus.). 16p. pap. 24.95 (978-1-61582-707-7(2)) America Star Bks.

Schindler, Holly. The Junction of Sunshine & Lucky. 2014. (ENG.). 240p. (J). (gr. 3-7). 16.99 (978-0-8037-3725-9(4), Dial Bks) Penguin Young Readers Group.

Schlesinger, Gretchen. Send Me the Soap #1: The Emerald Isle Adventure. Pietla, David, illus. 2006. (J). 11.95 (978-0-9778536-0-1(8)) Eco-thumb Publishing Co.

—Send Me the Soap #1: The Emerald Isle Adventure (lib. Bdg.) Pietla, David, illus. 2006. (J). lib. bdg. (978-0-9778536-1-8(6)) Eco-thumb Publishing Co.

Schlessinger, Laura. Dr. Laura Schlessinger's Where's God? McFeeley, Daniel, illus. 2003. 40p. (J). (gr. -1-2). lib. bdg. 16.89 (978-0-06-051910-0(X)) HarperCollins Pubs.

—Where's God? 2006. pap. (978-0-06-051911-7(8)) HarperCollins Canada, Ltd.

Schoen, Robin. Grandmother's Guest: The Blue Lady of Wilton. Hoar, Gail, illus. 2013. 32p. 16.95 (978-0-615-89154-5(3)) Hobby Horse Publishing, LLC.

Scholastic, Inc. Staff & Black, Sonia. Jumping the Broom. Hu, Ying-Hwa & Van Wright, Cornelius, illus. 2004. (Just for You Ser.). (ENG.). 32p. pap. 3.99 (978-0-439-56878-4(1), Teaching Resources) Scholastic, Inc.

Scholastic, Inc. Staff & Boyd, Dee. Only the Stars. Rich, Anna, illus. 2004. (Just for You Ser.). (ENG.). 32p. pap. 3.99 (978-0-439-56862-3(5), Teaching Resources) Scholastic, Inc.

Schossow, Peter. Where Is Grandma? Schossow, Peter, illus. 2017. (ENG., Illus.). 64p. (J). (gr. k-5). 17.99 **(978-1-77657-154-3(1))** Gecko Pr. NZL. Dist: Lerner Publishing Group.

Schotter, Roni. All about Grandmas. Nadeau, Janice, illus. 2012. (ENG.). 32p. (J). (gr. -1-k). 16.99 (978-0-8037-3714-3(9), Dial Bks) Penguin Young Readers Group.

Schroeder, Lisa. My Secret Guide to Paris. 2015. (ENG.). 224p. (J). (gr. 3-7). 16.99 (978-0-545-70808-1(7), Scholastic Pr.) Scholastic, Inc.

Schulz, Heidi. Hook's Revenge. 2015. (Hook's Revenge Ser.: 1). (J). lib. bdg. 18.40 (978-0-606-37398-2(5)) Turtleback Bks.

Schumacher, Julie. The Book of One Hundred Truths. 2008. (Yearling Bks.). (ENG.). 192p. (J). (gr. 3-7). 6.99 (978-0-440-42085-9(7), Yearling) Random Hse. Children's Bks.

Schwartz, Amy. Oma & Bobo. 2013. (ENG., Illus.). 32p. (J). (gr. -1-3). 16.99 (978-1-4814-2149-2(2), Atheneum Bks. for Young Readers) Simon & Schuster Children's Publishing.

Schwartz, David M. Superabuelo. Guzman, Martin Luis, tr. Dodson, Bert, illus. 2005. (SPA.). (J). 32p. (gr. -1-4). pap. 18.95 incl. audio compact disk (978-1-889910-37-6(6)); pap. 6.95 (978-1-889910-38-3(4)) Tortuga Pr.

Schwartz, Howard. Gathering Sparks. Swarner, Kristina, illus. 2010. (ENG.). 32p. (J). (gr. -1-3). 16.99 (978-1-59643-280-2(2), 9781596432802) Roaring Brook Pr.

Schwartz, Joanne. Our Corner Grocery Store. Beingessner, Laura, illus. 2009. (ENG.). 32p. (J). (gr. -1-2). 19.95 (978-0-88776-868-2(7), Tundra Bks.) Tundra Bks. CAN. Dist: Penguin Random Hse. LLC.

Scott, Gwen. Blackberry Junction. Baker, David, illus. 2011. 28p. pap. 24.95 (978-1-4560-0951-9(6)) America Star Bks.

Scott, Luke. Through a Crystal Doorknob. 2012. 88p. 24.95 (978-1-4626-9420-4(9)) America Star Bks.

Scott, Marilyn. A Lightening Bug's Message of Love. 2009. pap. (978-1-61658-333-0(9)) Independent Pub.

Scraper, Katherine. Garden Lunch. 2006. (Early Explorers Ser.). (J). pap. (978-1-4108-6027-9(2)) Benchmark Education Co.

Scrimger, Richard. The Wolf & Me, 1 vol. 2014. (Seven Sequels Ser.). (ENG., Illus.). 256p. (J). (gr. 5-10). pap. 10.95 (978-1-4598-0531-6(3)) Orca Bk. Pubs. USA.

Sealey, Edmund J. Toast. 2009. 76p. pap. (978-1-84923-790-1(5)) YouWriteOn.

Secret Soup: Individual Title Six-Packs. (Literatura 2000 Ser.). (gr. 1-2). 28.00 (978-0-7635-0111-2(5)) Rigby Education.

Sellen, Sandi. The Splendiddly Fazztabulous Grandmas. Maltman Dinwoodie, Heather, illus. 2013. 32p. pap. (978-1-77069-893-2(0)) Word Alive Pr.

Seltzer, Eric. Granny Doodle Day. Seltzer, Eric, illus. 2006. (Doodle Dog Ser.). (ENG., Illus.). 32p. (J). (gr. -1-1). pap. 3.99 (978-0-689-85911-3(2), Simon & Schuster/Paula Wiseman Bks.) Simon & Schuster/Paula Wiseman Bks.

Sendak, Philip. In Grandpa's House. Sendak, Maurice, illus. 2003. (Sendak Reissues Ser.). (ENG.). 48p. (J). reprint ed. 16.95 (978-0-06-028787-0(X)) HarperCollins Pubs.

Senkungu, Dinah. How the Tortoise Got His Scars. 2011. 40p. pap. 18.66 (978-1-4567-1811-4(8)) AuthorHouse.

Seredy, Kate. Philomena. Seredy, Kate, illus. 2008. (Illus.). 93p. (J). pap. 11.95 (978-1-932350-19-7(5)) Bethlehem Bks.

Sesame Street Staff & Studio Mouse Staff. Learning Fun. 2008. (ENG.). 60p. (J). 4.99 (978-1-59069-671-2(9)) Studio Mouse LLC.

Seuling, Barbara. Robert Takes a Stand. Brewer, Paul, illus. 2004. (Robert Bks.). (ENG.). 120p. (J). 15.95 (978-0-8126-2712-1(1)) Cricket Bks.

S.E.W. The Year at Widows' Creek: The Beginning. 2009. 44p. pap. 17.49 (978-1-4389-5546-9(4)) AuthorHouse.

Shahan, Sherry. Death Mountain, 1 vol. (ENG.). 176p. (YA). (gr. 5-9). 2007. pap. 7.95 (978-1-56145-428-0(1)) 2005. 15.95 (978-1-56145-353-5(6)) Peachtree Pubs.

Shamane, Aunty. Grandma of the Gardens. 2011. 20p. pap. 11.50 (978-1-4634-3119-8(8)) AuthorHouse.

Shankman, Ed. My Grandma Lives in Florida. O'Neill, Dave, illus. 2013. (Shankman & O'Neill Ser.). (ENG.). 32p. (J). (gr. -1-3). 14.95 (978-1-933212-35-7(7), Commonwealth Editions) Applewood Bks.

Shanks, Melanie. The Squints. 2007. 116p. per. 10.95 (978-0-595-44849-4(6)) iUniverse, Inc.

Shapiro, Jody Fickes. Up, up, up! It's Apple-Picking Time. Harvill, Kitty, illus. 2008. (ENG.). 32p. (J). (gr. -1-3). pap. 6.95 (978-0-8234-2166-4(X)) Holiday Hse., Inc.

Sharp, J. L. Persephia. 2009. 73p. pap. 19.95 (978-1-60813-836-4(4)) America Star Bks.

Shasha, Mark. Night of the Moonjellies: 15th Anniversary Edition. 2007. (Illus.). 32p. (J). (gr. -1-2). 12.95 (978-1-930900-34-9(1)) Purple Hse. Pr.

Shaw-Burns, Carol. Grandma's House: Jacob's Adventure. 2012. 24p. pap. 17.99 (978-1-4685-5318-5(6)) AuthorHouse.

Shawver, Margaret. What's Wrong with Grandma? A Family's Experience with Alzheimer's. Bagby, Jeffrey K., illus. 2003. (ENG.). 62p. (J). (gr. -1-3). pap. 16.99 (978-1-59102-174-2(X)) Prometheus Bks., Pubs.

Shea, Bob. What's Your Favorite Favorite? Shea, Bob, illus. 2017. (Ballet Cat Ser.). (ENG., Illus.). 56p. (J). (gr. 1-3). 9.99 (978-1-4847-7809-8(X)) Disney Pr.

Sheckels, Astrid, illus. Nic & Nellie, 1 vol. 2013. (ENG.). 32p. (J). (gr. 1-4). 17.95 (978-1-934031-52-0(6), 9781934031520) Islandport Pr., Inc.

Shelton, Angela. Tilda Pinkerton's Magical Hats. 2013. 196p. 19.95 (978-0-9859443-8-4(2)) Quiet Owl Bks.

—Tilda Pinkerton's Magical Hats. Murray, James, illus. 2013. 196p. pap. 11.99 (978-0-9859443-7-7(4)) Quiet Owl Bks.

Shelton, Jayne C. In Grandma's Arms. Katz, Karen, illus. 2008. (ENG.). 24p. (J). (gr. -1-k). bds. 6.99 (978-0-545-06868-0(1)) Scholastic, Inc.

Sherman, Linda. Art Fair for Grandma. 2007. (Illus.). 28p. (J). per. 10.00 (978-0-615-16017-7(4)) Sherman, Linda.

Sheth, Kashmira. Monsoon Afternoon, 1 vol. Jaeggi, Yoshiko, illus. 2008. (ENG.). 32p. (J). (gr. k-3). 16.95 (978-1-56145-455-6(9), Peachtree Junior) Peachtree Pubs.

—My Dadima Wears a Sari, 1 vol. Jaeggi, Yoshiko, illus. 2007. (ENG.). 32p. (J). (gr. k-3). 16.95 (978-1-56145-392-4(7)) Peachtree Pubs.

Shimalla, Jen. Heaven Cent. 2013. 24p. pap. 10.95 (978-1-4525-8042-5(1), Balboa Pr.) Author Solutions, Inc.

Shireman, Abbie. The Fish Tank. 2012. 20p. pap. 17.99 (978-1-4772-8173-4(8)) AuthorHouse.

Shpitalnik, Vladimir & Evans, Connie. Sasha & Babushka: A Story of Russia. 2005. (Make Friends Around the World Ser.). (ENG., Illus.). 32p. (J). (gr. k-3). pap. 6.95 (978-1-59249-444-6(7), S8007) Soundprints.

Shpitalnik, Vladimir & Evans, Cornelia. Sasha & Babushka: A Story of Russia. 2005. (Make Friends Around the World Ser.). (ENG., Illus.). 32p. (J). (gr. k-3). 15.95 (978-1-59249-443-9(9), B8007) Soundprints.

Shriver, Maria. What's Happening to Grandpa? Speidel, Sandra, illus. 2004. (ENG.). 48p. (J). (gr. -1-3). 18.99 (978-0-316-00101-4(5)) Little, Brown Bks. for Young Readers.

—What's Heaven? 2004. (Illus.). (J). (gr. k-3). spiral bd. (978-0-616-03056-1(8)) Canadian National Institute for the Blind/Institut National Canadien pour les Aveugles.

Shrode, Donna. Fun with Nan: A Trip to the Zoo. 2012. 28p. pap. 19.99 (978-1-4685-4598-2(1)) AuthorHouse.

—Fun with Nana: Let's Play. 2011. 28p. (gr. -1). pap. 12.03 (978-1-4567-4600-1(6)) AuthorHouse.

Shukla, Umesh. Love You Back Grandma. Balogh, Andras, illus. 2018. 32p. (J). 15.95 (978-0-9963756-5-8(1)) All About Kids Publishing.

Shulimson, Sarene. Lights Out Shabbat. Ebbeler, Jeff, illus. 2012. (Shabbat Ser.). (ENG.). 32p. (J). (gr. -1-2). pap. 7.95 (978-0-7613-7565-4(1), Kar-Ben Publishing) Lerner Publishing Group.

—Lights Out Shabbat. Ebbeler, Jeffrey, illus. 2012. (Shabbat Ser.). (ENG.). 32p. (J). (gr. -1-2). lib. bdg. 17.95 (978-0-7613-7564-7(3), Kar-Ben Publishing) Lerner Publishing Group.

Shulman, Goldie. Way Too Much Challah Dough. 2006. (ENG., Illus.). 30p. (J). 12.95 (978-1-929628-23-0(4)) Hachai Publishing.

Shurtliff, Liesl. Red: the True Story of Red Riding Hood. (ENG.). 256p. (J). (gr. 3-7). 2017. 7.99 (978-0-385-75586-3(4), Yearling) 2016. 16.99 (978-0-385-75583-2(X), Knopf Bks. for Young Readers) Random Hse. Children's Bks.

Shusterman, Neal. Chasing Forgiveness. 2015. (ENG., Illus.). 240p. (YA). (gr. 7). pap. 9.99 (978-1-4814-2991-7(4)) Simon & Schuster Children's Publishing.

—Red Rider's Hood. 2006. (Dark Fusion Ser.: 3). (ENG.). 192p. (YA). (gr. 7-18). 6.99 (978-0-14-240678-6(3), Speak) Penguin Young Readers Group.

Siciari, Theresa. The Pond Behind Grandmother's House. 2007. 32p. per. 24.95 (978-1-4137-8597-5(2)) America Star Bks.

Sidney, Margaret. The Adventures of Joel Pepper. 2008. 192p. 26.95 (978-1-60664-740-0(7)) Rodgers, Alan Bks.

Silver, Gail. Anh's Anger. Kromer, Christiane, illus. 2011. (J). (978-1-935209-65-2(5), Plum Blossom Bks.) Parallax Pr.

—Anh's Anger. Krömer, Christiane, illus. 2009. (ENG.). 40p. (J). (gr. -1-3). 16.95 (978-1-888375-94-7(9), Plum Blossom Bks.) Parallax Pr.

Silvera, Elvia. Candida. Peli, Peli, illus. 2005. (SPA.). (J). (gr. 2-3). pap. 7.95 (978-980-257-281-6(0)) Ekare, Ediciones VEN. Dist: Iaconi, Mariuccia Bk. Imports.

Silverman, Toby. The Garbage Grandma. Strapec, Amy, illus. 2005. 23p. (J). 9.50 (978-0-9793475-0-4(5)) Silverman, Toby.

Silverthorne, Judith. The Secret of Sentinel Rock. 2007. (From Many Peoples Ser.). (Illus.). 159p. (J). (gr. 3-5). per. (978-1-55050-386-9(3)) Coteau Bks.

Simard, Danielle. Little Word Catcher, 1 vol. Côté, Geneviève & Second Story Press Staff, illus. 2008. (ENG.). 32p. (J). (gr. 1-3). 14.95 (978-1-897187-44-9(0)) Second Story Pr. CAN. Dist: Orca Bk. Pubs. USA.

Simmons, Andrew & Averdonz, N. R. I Was an Eighth-Grade Ninja, 1 vol. Padilla, Ariel, illus. 2007. (Z Graphic Novels / Tomo Ser.). (ENG.). 160p. (J). (gr. 3-7). pap. 6.99 (978-0-310-71300-5(5)) Zondervan.

Simmons, Martha. Grandma Perkido & Sidney. 2007. (Illus.). 24p. (J). 14.95 (978-0-9777041-4-9(9)) Third Dimension Publishing.

Simon, Nadine. Flickers of True Destiny. 2010. 58p. pap. 11.95 (978-1-60860-948-2(0), Eloquent Bks.) Strategic Book Publishing & Rights Agency (SBPRA).

Simonson, Lona Marie. Grandma Lucy Feeds the Birds, 1 vol. Herges, Connie, illus. 2009. 44p. pap. 24.95 (978-1-60836-732-0(0)) America Star Bks.

Sims, Janice. Grandma's Basket. Storr, Nicola, illus. 2010. 28p. pap. (978-1-904408-68-0(0)) Bank House Bks.

Singlehurst, Naomi. Grandpa, What's That Sound in the Middle of the Night? Ellen Koski, Rachel, ed. Jamieson, Victoria, illus. 2008. (ENG.). 32p. (J). (gr. k-2). 14.95 (978-1-930650-24-4(8)) mTrellis Publishing, Inc.

Singletary, Nicole. My Grandmamma's X-Ray. 2011. 24p. pap. 12.99 (978-1-4567-5535-5(8)) AuthorHouse.

Singleton, Linda Joy. Dead Girl in Love. 2009. (Dead Girl Ser.: 3). (ENG.). 288p. (YA). pap. 9.95 (978-0-7387-1407-3(0), B06XZ9TSKM, Flux) North Star Editions.

—Don't Die, Dragonfly. Karre, Andrew, ed. 2004. (Seer Ser.: 1). (ENG.). 288p. (YA). pap. 9.95 (978-0-7387-0526-2(8)) Llewellyn Pubns.

—Fatal Charm. 2007. (Seer Ser.: 5). (ENG.). 384p. (YA). (gr. 7-12). per. 9.95 (978-0-7387-1153-9(5), Flux) North Star Editions.

—Last Dance. 2005. (Seer Ser.: 2). (ENG.). 264p. (YA). pap. 9.95 (978-0-7387-0638-2(8), Flux) Llewellyn Pubns.

Sinke, Grandma Janet Mary. I Wanna Go to Grandma's House. Pennington, Craig, illus. 2003. (Grandma Janet Mary Ser.). 50p. (J). (978-0-9742732-0-4(1)) My Grandma & Me Pubs.

Sinke, Janet Mary. I Wanna Go to Grandma's House & Grandma's Treasure Chest, 2, Set. Pennington, Craig, illus. 2006. 80p. (J). (978-0-9742732-6-6(0)) My Grandma & Me Pubs.

Sioux Rose. Cassandra's Tale: Invitation to the Circle. 2010. 200p. pap. 16.95 (978-1-4401-9510-5(2)) iUniverse, Inc.

Sipp, Leora Janson. Emma & Sara Learn about Harvest Time. 2008. 40p. pap. 14.95 (978-1-934925-01-0(2), Eloquent Bks.) Strategic Book Publishing & Rights Agency (SBPRA).

Sis, Peter. Ice Cream Summer. 2015. (ENG., Illus.). 40p. (J). (gr. k-3). 17.99 (978-0-545-73161-4(5), Scholastic Pr.) Scholastic, Inc.

Skocz, Anita Joyce. Kite Tale. 2011. 40p. pap. 16.95 (978-1-4525-3889-1(1)) Get Published.

Skovron, Jon. Struts & Frets. 2009. (ENG.). 304p. (YA). (gr. 7-11). 16.95 (978-0-8109-4174-8(0), Amulet Bks.) Abrams, Inc.

Skyberg, Andrea, creator. Snickeyfritz. 2009. (ENG., Illus.). 48p. (J). 17.99 (978-0-615-25177-6(3)) Wooden Nickel Pr.

Smith, B. M. My Very Own Picnic Basket: An Evan & Cassie Adventure. 2012. 28p. pap. 24.95 (978-1-4626-7551-7(4)) America Star Bks.

Smith, Clete Barrett. Alien on a Rampage. 2013. (Intergalactic Bed & Breakfast Ser.). (ENG.). 320p. (J). (gr. 3-7). pap. 6.99 (978-1-4231-5525-6(4)) Hyperion Pr.

Smith, Danna. Arctic White. White, Lee, illus. 2016. (ENG.). 32p. (J). (gr. -1-3). 17.99 (978-1-62779-104-5(3), 9781627791045, Holt, Henry & Co. Bks. For Young Readers) Holt, Henry & Co.

—Dos en el Zoológico: Un Libro para Contar. Petrone, Valeria, illus. 2011.Tr. of Two at the Zoo - A Counting Book. (ENG & SPA.). 30p. (J). (gr. k — 1). bds. 4.99 (978-0-547-58137-8(8)) Houghton Mifflin Harcourt Publishing Co.

Smith-Eubanks, Jennifer. Balloons for Grandpa, 1 vol. Schneider, Robin, illus. 2010. 20p. pap. 24.95 (978-1-4489-5282-3(4)) PublishAmerica, Inc.

Smith, Greg Leitich. Chronal Engine. Henry, Blake, illus. 2013. (ENG.). 192p. (J). (gr. 5-7). pap. 6.99 (978-0-544-02277-5(7)) Houghton Mifflin Harcourt Publishing Co.

Smith-Henderson, Susie. The Adventures of Snorro & the Keepers from Sleep. 2009. 32p. pap. 14.18 (978-0-557-08682-5(5)) Lulu Pr., Inc.

Smith, Kathy Jo. Come Play with Me. 2009. 26p. (J). pap. 17.95 (978-1-4327-3464-0(4)) Outskirts Pr., Inc.

Smith, Lane. Grandpa Green. Smith, Lane, illus. 2011. (ENG., Illus.). 32p. (J). (gr. k-4). 16.99 (978-1-59643-607-7(7), 9781596436077) Roaring Brook Pr.

Smith, Lauren E. Ashley Enright & the Darnell Diamonds, 1 vol. 2009. 90p. pap. 19.95 (978-1-60836-332-2(5)) America Star Bks.

Smith, Robert Kimmel. The War with Grandpa. 128p. (J). (gr. 4-6). pap. 4.99 (978-0-8072-1407-7(8), Listening Library) Random Hse. Audio Publishing Group.

Smith, Rosemary. Three Wishes for Maddy. 2012. 48p. pap. 10.00 (978-1-61204-798-0(X), Strategic Bk. Publishing) Strategic Book Publishing & Rights Agency (SBPRA).

Smith, Sarah. The Butterfly House. 2014. (ENG., Illus.). 32p. (gr. -1-3). 19.95 (978-1-84976-205-2(8)) Tate Publishing, Ltd. GBR. Dist: Abrams, Inc.

Smith, Suzanne C. Ande-Lu & Grampa, Too. 2009. 32p. pap. 14.99 (978-1-4389-2292-8(2)) AuthorHouse.

Smith, Walter. Grandad's Ashes. 2007. (ENG., Illus.). 32p. (gr. -1-3). 15.95 (978-1-84310-517-6(9), 4937) Kingsley, Jessica Pubs. GBR. Dist: Macmillan Distribution Ltd.

Smith, William. Frankie & Earnie Meet, 1 vol. 2009. pap. 24.95 (978-1-60749-333-4(0)) America Star Bks.

Sneve, Virginia Driving Hawk & Sneve, Virginia. Lana's Lakota Moons. 2007. (ENG., Illus.). 127p. (gr. 3-7). pap. 14.95 (978-0-8032-6028-3(8), Bison Bks.) Univ. of Nebraska Pr.

Snow, Carol. Switch. 2009. (ENG.). 240p. (YA). (gr. 8). pap. 8.99 (978-0-06-145210-9(6), HarperTeen) HarperCollins Pubs.

Snow, Susie. The Old Cookie Jar. Motz, Mike, illus. 2012. 34p. pap. 19.99 (978-1-61996-595-9(X)) Salem Author Services.

Snyder, Jennifer. Grandad's Book. Bruner, Tammy, illus. 2005. (J). 8.99 (978-1-4183-0079-1(9)) Christ Inspired, Inc.

Snyder, Karen. Mona Lisa's Makeover. LaGrange, Tiffany, illus. 2010. 24p. pap. 12.95 (978-1-936343-15-7(0)) Peppertree Pr., The.

—Safari Smooches. LaGrange, Tiffany, illus. 2011. 24p. pap. 12.95 (978-1-936343-95-9(9)) Peppertree Pr., The.

Snyder, Marilyn. A Second Chance for Tina. Shiffman, Lena, illus. 2003. (Hello Reader! Ser.). (J). (978-0-439-44154-4(4)) Scholastic, Inc.

Soetoro-Ng, Maya. Ladder to the Moon. Morales, Yuyi, illus. (ENG.). 48p. (J). (gr. -1-3). 2017. 7.99

(978-0-7636-9343-5(X)) 2011. 16.99 *(978-0-7636-4570-0(2))* Candlewick Pr.

—Ladder to the Moon with CD. Morales, Yuyi, illus. 2012. (ENG.). 48p. (J). (gr. -1-3). 19.99 *(978-0-7636-6006-2(X))* Candlewick Pr.

Solomon, Sharon. A Walk With Grandpa/Un Paseo con el Abuelo. Del Risco, Eida, tr. Barcita, Pamela, illus. 2009. (ENG & SPA.). 32p. (J). (gr. -1-3). 16.95 *(978-1-932748-91-8(1),* Raven Tree Pr.,Csi) Continental Sales, Inc.

Solomon, Sharon K. A Walk with Grandpa. Barcita, Pamela, illus. (ENG.). 32p. (J). 2010. (gr. 4-7). pap. 7.95 *(978-1-934960-12-7(8))* 2009. (gr. -1-3). 16.95 *(978-1-934960-11-0(X))* Continental Sales, Inc. (Raven Tree Pr.,Csi).

Soni, Parwinder Singh, illus. Little Red Riding Hood. 2010. (J). *(978-1-60617-132-5(1))* Teaching Strategies, LLC.

Sonnenblick, Jordan. Curveball: The Year I Lost My Grip. 304p. 2014. (ENG.). (J). (gr. 7). pap. 9.99 *(978-0-545-32070-2(4),* Scholastic Paperbacks) 2012. pap. 17.99 *(978-0-545-39311-9(6))* Scholastic, Inc.

Soper, Stuart A. Milky Saves Christmas. 2011. (Illus.). 290p. pap. 16.00 *(978-1-60976-193-6(6),* Strategic Bk. Publishing) Strategic Book Publishing & Rights Agency (SBPRA).

Spangler, Lois. The Fort on Fourth Street, 1 vol. Wald, Christina, illus. 2013. (ENG.). 32p. (J). (gr. 1-4). 17.95 *(978-1-60718-620-5(9));* pap. 9.95 *(978-1-60718-632-8(2))* Arbordale Publishing.

Speakman, David. The Adventures of Sierra Rae: The Forgotten Map, 1 vol. 2009. 59p. pap. 16.95 *(978-1-4489-2657-2(2))* PublishAmerica, Inc.

Spindler, Brenda Lee. The Night Granny Came. 2011. 24p. pap. 15.99 *(978-1-4628-6425-6(2))* Xlibris Corp.

Spinelli, Eileen. Something to Tell the Grandcows. Slavin, Bill, illus. 2004. 32p. (J). 16.00 *(978-0-8028-5236-6(X));* (gr. -1-3). 8.00 *(978-0-8028-5304-2(8),* Eerdmans Bks For Young Readers) Eerdmans, William B. Publishing Co.

Spinelli, Jerry. Eggs. 2008. (ENG., Illus.). 240p. (J). (gr. 3-7). pap. 8.99 *(978-0-316-16647-8(2))* Little, Brown Bks. for Young Readers.

Spinner, Stephanie. It's a Miracle! A Hanukkah Storybook. McElmurry, Jill, illus. 2007. (ENG.). 48p. (J). (gr. -1-3). 6.99 *(978-1-4169-5001-1(X),* Aladdin) Simon & Schuster Children's Publishing.

Spitz, Mary Y. Mint's Christmas Message. Pierce, Joanne Y., illus. 2003. 32p. 14.95 *(978-0-9724570-0-2(3))* Mother Moose Pr.

Springer, Audrey. Rusty's Gift. Richards, Kris, illus. 2012. 28p. 24.95 *(978-1-4626-6589-1(6))* America Star Bks.

Spruill, Beverle. The Dream Box. 2009. 24p. pap. 13.50 *(978-1-4490-3783-3(6))* AuthorHouse.

Spyri, Johanna. Heidi. 2014. (ENG.). 345p. 17.50 *(978-1-78270-044-9(7))* Award Pubns. Ltd. GBR. Dist: Parkwest Pubns., Inc.

—Heidi. Marks, Alan, illus. 2006. 63p. (J). (gr. 2). 8.99 *(978-0-7945-1237-8(2),* Usborne) EDC Publishing.

—Heidi. 2003. pap. *(978-1-84637-585-9(1))* Echo Library.

—Heidi. 2013. (ENG., Illus.). 336p. (J). (gr. 2-7). 14.95 *(978-1-62087-686-2(8),* 620686, Sky Pony Pr.) Skyhorse Publishing Co., Inc.

—Heidi. Akib, Jamel, illus. 2007. (Classic Starts(tm) Ser.). (ENG.). 160p. (J). (gr. 2-4). 6.95 *(978-1-4027-3691-9(6))* Sterling Publishing Co., Inc.

—Heidi: With a Discussion of Optimism. Clift, Eva, illus. 2003. (Values in Action Illustrated Classics Ser.). 190p. (J). *(978-1-59203-030-9(0))* Learning Challenge, Inc.

Spyri, Johanna & Blaisdell, Robert. Heidi: Adapted for Young Readers. Kliros, Thea, illus. 2011. (Dover Children's Thrift Classics Ser.). (ENG.). 80p. (J). (gr. 3-8). pap. 3.00 *(978-0-486-40166-9(9))* Dover Pubns., Inc.

Spyri, Johanna & Lacey, Mike. Heidi, 1 vol. 2012. (Calico Illustrated Classics Ser.: No. 4). (ENG., Illus.). 112p. (J). (gr. 3-6). 27.07 *(978-1-61641-613-3(0))* Magic Wagon.

Spyri, Johanna & Stork, Elisabeth P. Heidi. Kirk, Maria L., illus. 2014. (J). 13.32 *(978-1-4677-5846-8(9),* First Avenue Editions) Lerner Publishing Group.

St. Antoine, Sarah. Three Bird Summer. 2014. (ENG.). 256p. (J). (gr. 5). 16.99 *(978-0-7636-6564-7(9))* Candlewick Pr.

St. John, Lauren. The Last Leopard. 2010. (ENG.). 224p. (J). (gr. 3-7). 6.99 *(978-0-14-241515-3(4),* Puffin Books) Penguin Young Readers Group.

St John, Patricia. Other Kitten. 2007. (Illus.). 96p. pap. *(978-1-84427-290-7(7))* Scripture Union.

Stahl, Hilda. Big Trouble for Roxie. 2003. (Best Friends Ser.: No. 2). 160p. (YA). (gr. 4-7). pap. 4.99 *(978-0-89107-658-2(1))* Crossway.

Staley, S. Little Tommie. 2008. 24p. pap. 24.95 *(978-1-60474-784-3(6))* America Star Bks.

Standiford, Natalie. Confessions of the Sullivan Sisters. (ENG.). 320p. (J). 2012. (gr. 9). pap. 9.99 *(978-0-545-10711-2(3),* Scholastic Paperbacks) 2010. (gr. 8-18). 17.99 *(978-0-545-10710-5(5),* Scholastic Pr.) Scholastic, Inc.

Stang, Debra L. Visiting Grandma. 2003. 136p. (YA). pap. 12.95 *(978-1-59113-322-3(X))* Booklocker.com, Inc.

Staunton, Ted. Coda, 1 vol. 2014. (Seven Sequels Ser.). (ENG., Illus.). 224p. (J). (gr. 5-10). pap. 10.95 *(978-1-4598-0549-1(6))* Orca Bk. Pubs. USA.

Steele, Giselle V. Nicholas & the Magical Wind. 2005. 32p. 23.95 *(978-1-58275-093-4(9))* Stuart & Weitz Publishing Group.

Steers, Amanda . M. Old's Cool. 2011. 24p. pap. 28.03 *(978-1-4628-6253-3(6))* Xlibris Corp.

Stein, David Ezra. Love, Mouserella. Stein, David Ezra, illus. 2011. (ENG., Illus.). 32p. (J). (gr. -1-k). 15.99 *(978-0-399-25410-9(2),* Nancy Paulsen Books) Penguin Young Readers Group.

Steiner, Barbara. The Cry of the Loon: A Samantha Mystery. Tibbles, Jean-Paul, illus. (ENG.). 192p. (gr. 4-18). 2009. (YA). pap. 6.95 *(978-1-59369-480-7(6))* 2006. 10.95 *(978-1-59369-479-1(2))* American Girl Publishing, Inc.

Steinkellner, Elisabeth. My New Granny. Roher, Michael, illus. 2012. (ENG.). 32p. (J). (gr. -1-3). 16.95 *(978-1-62087-223-9(4),* 620223, Sky Pony Pr.) Skyhorse Publishing Co., Inc.

Steinmann, Donna. Hello, Grand Mamoon! Guion, Tamara, illus. 2005. 32p. (J). 16.95 *(978-0-9663286-4-6(7))* EarthTime Pubns.

Stephens, Helen. Betsy Visits Her Grandparents. 2015. (Betsy First Experiences Ser.). (ENG., Illus.). 32p. (J). (gr. -1-k). 10.99 *(978-1-4052-6825-7(5))* Egmont Bks., Ltd. GBR. Dist: Independent Pubs. Group.

Sterer, Gideon. Skyfishing. Bernatene, Poly, illus. 2017. (ENG.). 40p. (J). (gr. -1-3). 17.95 *(978-1-4197-1911-0(4),* Abrams Bks. for Young Readers) Abrams, Inc.

Stevenson, Sarah Jamila. The Truth Against the World. 2014. (ENG.). 360p. (YA). pap. 9.99 *(978-0-7387-4058-4(6),* Flux) North Star Editions.

Stewart, Kiera. Fetching. 2012. (ENG.). 304p. (YA). (gr. 5-9). pap. 7.99 *(978-1-4231-4245-4(4))* Hyperion Pr.

Stine, R. L. Scarecrow Walks at Midnight. 2010. (Classic Goosebumps Ser.: 16). (ENG.). 160p. (J). (gr. 3-7). 6.99 *(978-0-545-17801-3(0),* Scholastic Paperbacks) Scholastic, Inc.

Stinson, Aimee & Somson, Kathy. The Bearless City, 1 vol. 2009. 22p. pap. 24.95 *(978-1-60749-406-5(X))* America Star Bks.

Stone, Jeff. Five Ancestors Out of the Ashes: Phoenix. 2013. (Five Ancestors Out of the Ashes Ser.: 1). (ENG.). 304p. (J). (gr. 4-7). 6.99 *(978-0-375-87097-2(0),* Yearling) Random Hse. Children's Bks.

—Five Ancestors Out of the Ashes #1: Phoenix. 2012. (Five Ancestors Out of the Ashes Ser.). (ENG.). 288p. (J). (gr. 4-7). 16.99 *(978-0-375-87018-7(0),* Random Hse. Bks. for Young Readers) Random Hse. Children's Bks.

Stone, Phoebe. The Boy on Cinnamon Street. 2012. 234p. (J). *(978-0-545-43368-6(1),* Levine, Arthur A. Bks.) Scholastic, Inc.

Stout, Shawn K. Penelope Crumb. 2013. (Penelope Crumb Ser.: 1). (ENG.). 240p. (J). (gr. 2-5). pap. 5.99 *(978-0-14-242478-0(1),* Puffin Books) Penguin Young Readers Group.

Strange, David. Why Grandpa Rides a Harley. 2005. 16.95 *(978-0-9772771-0-0(0))* Cherry Tree Pr. LLC.

Studer, Diana. The Tabby's Gift. 2009. 24p. pap. 12.55 *(978-1-4389-5582-7(0))* AuthorHouse.

Stuve-Bodeen, Stephanie. Babu's Song. Boyd, Aaron, illus. 2003. (ENG.). 32p. (J). 16.95 *(978-1-58430-058-8(2));* (gr. -1-3). pap. 9.95 *(978-1-60060-275-7(4))* Lee & Low Bks., Inc.

Suchecki, Carol. My Dream with Grandp. 2011. 44p. pap. 21.99 *(978-1-4568-3643-6(9))* Xlibris Corp.

Sullivan, Jacqueline Levering. Annie's War. 2007. (Illus.). 183p. (J). (gr. 3-7). 15.00 *(978-0-8028-5325-7(0),* Eerdmans Bks For Young Readers) Eerdmans, William B. Publishing Co.

Sullivan, Jean. The Blakely Field Stories. 2005. 58p. pap. 16.95 *(978-1-4137-8611-8(1))* PublishAmerica, Inc.

Sullivan, Sarah. All That's Missing. 2013. (ENG.). 368p. (J). (gr. 3-7). 16.99 *(978-0-7636-6102-1(3))* Candlewick Pr.

Sunnex, Hayley. Grandma's Hugs. 2012. 24p. pap. 28.03 *(978-1-4771-4764-1(0))* Xlibris Corp.

Sutton, Kay. Nan & Grandad's Book of Short Stories. 2009. (Illus.). 52p. pap. 20.49 *(978-1-4490-0575-7(6))* AuthorHouse.

Suzhen, Fang. Grandma Lives in a Perfume Village. Danowski, Sonja, illus. 2015. (ENG.). 48p. (J). 19.95 *(978-0-7358-4216-8(7))* North-South Bks., Inc.

Svoboda, Linda Sue. Loving Times with Grandma. 2013. 24p. pap. 24.95 *(978-1-63004-270-7(6))* America Star Bks.

Swanson, Stan. The Misadventures of Hobart Hucklebuck. 2007. (J). 16.95 *(978-0-9787925-3-4(X));* per. 9.95 *(978-0-9787925-2-7(1))* Stony Meadow Publishing.

Swarabi, Fatma Abdulla & El Amin, Khalid Hamid. Marim & Her Grandmother. 2010. 28p. pap. 13.99 *(978-1-4490-8156-0(8))* AuthorHouse.

Swerts, An. Get Well Soon, Grandpa. Bakker, Jenny, illus. 2013. (ENG.). 32p. (J). (gr. k-2). 15.95 *(978-1-60537-155-9(6))* Cobblestone Publishing Co.

Sylvester, Sr. Talking Memories. Morrison, Nancy, illus. 2011. 36p. pap. 24.95 *(978-1-4489-4967-0(X))* America Star Bks.

Szymanski, Lois K. Grandfather's Secret, 1 vol. 2010. (ENG., Illus.). 64p. (J). pap. 12.99 *(978-0-7643-3535-8(9),* 9780764335358) Schiffer Publishing, Ltd.

Tague, James E. The Krankel Family. 2008. 32p. pap. 21.99 *(978-1-4363-7170-4(8))* Xlibris Corp.

Tak, Bibi Dumon. Mikis & the Donkey. Hopman, Philip, illus. 2014. (ENG.). 89p. (J). 13.00 *(978-0-8028-5430-8(3),* Eerdmans Bks For Young Readers) Eerdmans, William B. Publishing Co.

Talarico Msn, Karen M. My Hands. 2008. 36p. pap. 15.75 *(978-1-4389-3521-8(8))* AuthorHouse.

Tarpley, Todd. My Grandma's a Ninja. Chatzikonstantinou, Danny, illus. 2015. (ENG.). 40p. (J). 17.95 *(978-0-7358-4199-4(3))* North-South Bks., Inc.

Tate, Nancy. Grandmother Ellie's Attic. 2010. 232p. pap. 32.50 *(978-1-60976-033-5(6),* Eloquent Bks.) Strategic Book Publishing & Rights Agency (SBPRA).

Tate, Nikki. Trouble on Tarragon Island, 1 vol. 2005. (Tarragon Island Ser.). (ENG.). 208p. (J). (gr. 3-7). per. 8.95 *(978-1-55039-154-1(2))* Sono Nis Pr. CAN. Dist: Orca Bk. Pubs. USA.

Tavares, Matt. Oliver's Game. Tavares, Matt, illus. (Tavares Baseball Bks.). (ENG., Illus.). 32p. (J). (gr. 1-4). 2009. pap. 6.99 *(978-0-7636-4137-5(5))* 2004. 15.99 *(978-0-7636-1852-0(7))* Candlewick Pr.

Taylor, Christine. Red Riding Hood & the Toad. 2009. (Illus.). 44p. (gr. -1 — 1). 18.49 *(978-1-4389-3483-9(1))* AuthorHouse.

Taylor, Phillip J. Brian, His Granddad & the Cup of Ages. 2012. 310p. pap. *(978-1-78003-422-5(9))* Pen Pr. Pubs., Ltd.

Tazewell, Lora A. Jelly Bread & Water Juice. 2009. 48p. pap. 17.49 *(978-1-4389-1973-7(5))* AuthorHouse.

Teel, Julie. The Biggest Bear in the World: As Told by Grandpa Kingsford. 2009. 36p. pap. 16.99 *(978-1-4389-7983-0(5))* AuthorHouse.

Terborg-Hershman, Donna M. Why Sheep Don't Shrink. 2008. 28p. pap. 12.49 *(978-1-4389-3720-5(2))* AuthorHouse.

Terrell, Brandon. Pluck & Perfection. Max, Iman, illus. 2016. (Time Machine Magazine Ser.). (ENG.). 128p. (gr. 3-4). lib. bdg. 22.65 *(978-1-4965-2595-6(7))* Capstone Press of Coughlan Cos.

Testa, Maria. Becoming Joe Dimaggio. Hunt, Scott, illus. 2005. (ENG.). 64p. (J). (gr. 5-9). reprint ed. pap. 6.99 *(978-0-7636-2444-6(6))* Candlewick Pr.

Tetzlaff, Wendy Jo. A Girl Named Frannie. 2008. 28p. pap. 24.95 *(978-1-60703-055-3(1))* America Star Bks.

Tharlet, Eve. Happy Birthday, Davy Tuff Book. 2011. (ENG., Illus.). 28p. (J). (gr. -1-3). 6.95 *(978-0-7358-4026-3(1))* North-South Bks., Inc.

Thebeau, Anthony W. On the Way to Grandpa's, 1 vol. 2009. 15p. pap. 24.95 *(978-1-60749-430-0(2))* America Star Bks.

Thelen, Bob. Adventures with Grandpa: The Fishing Trip. 2010. 28p. pap. 12.99 *(978-1-4520-2255-0(0))* AuthorHouse.

Theroux, Phyllis. Serefina under the Circumstances. Priceman, Marjorie, illus. 2004. 30p. (J). (gr. k-4). reprint ed. *(978-0-7567-7756-2(9))* DIANE Publishing Co.

Things Don't Change Much: Individual Title Six-Packs. (gr. k-1). 23.00 *(978-0-7635-9055-0(X))* Rigby Education.

Thoene, Rachel. The Vase of Many Colors. 2007. 60p. per. 18.95 *(978-1-60290-003-5(5))* OakTara Publishing Group LLC.

Thomas, Debbie. Dead Hairy. MacDonald, Stella, illus. 2011. (ENG.). 256p. (J). pap. 14.95 *(978-1-85635-678-7(7))* Mercier Pr., Ltd., The IRL. Dist: Dufour Editions, Inc.

Thomas, Maria Jose & Thomas, María José. !Bravo, Rosina! Muñoz, Claudio, illus. 2005. (SPA.). 48p. (J). (gr. -1-5). 10.40 *(978-980-257-242-7(X),* EK33833) Ekare, Ediciones VEN. Dist: Lectorum Pubns., Inc.

Thompson, Gareth. Sunshine to the Sunless. 2008. (ENG.). 256p. (YA). (gr. 7). pap. 11.99 *(978-1-86230-467-3(X))* Transworld Publishers Ltd. GBR. Dist: Independent Pubs. Group.

Thompson, Holly. The Wakame Gatherers. Wilds, Kazumi, illus. 2007. (Wakame Gatherers Ser.). 32p. (J). (gr. -1-3). 16.95 *(978-1-885008-33-6(3),* Shen's Bks.) Lee & Low Bks., Inc.

Thompson, Susan A. Katie the Christian Caterpillar: The Loss of a Loved One. 2012. 20p. pap. 10.99 *(978-1-4624-0223-6(2),* Inspiring Voices) Author Solutions, Inc.

Thong, Roseanne Greenfield. Noodle Magic. So, Meilo, illus. 2014. (ENG.). 32p. (J). (gr. -1-3). 17.99 *(978-0-545-52167-3(X))* Scholastic, Inc.

—The Wishing Tree. McLennan, Connie, illus. 2004. (Wishing Tree Ser.). 32p. (J). (gr. -1-3). 16.95 *(978-1-885008-26-8(0),* Shen's Bks.) Lee & Low Bks., Inc.

Thorson, Robert & Thorson, Kristine. Stone Wall Secrets. Moore, Gustav, illus. 2010. 40p. (J). (gr. 3-7). 16.95 *(978-0-88448-195-9(6))* Tilbury Hse. Pubs.

Thumser, Judith. Grady & Gus Go to Grandmas. 2008. 20p. pap. 12.49 *(978-1-4343-8869-8(7))* AuthorHouse.

Time, Nicholas O. Going, Going, Gone. 2016. (In Due Time Ser.: 1). (ENG., Illus.). 160p. (J). (gr. 3-7). pap. 6.99 *(978-1-4814-6729-2(8),* Simon Spotlight) Simon Spotlight.

—Going, Going, Gone. 2016. (In Due Time Ser.: 1). lib. bdg. 17.20 *(978-0-606-38985-3(7))* Turtleback Bks.

Tinsley, Helen. Me & My Grandma: A Story for Children about AIDS. 2012.Tr. of 32. (Illus.). 34p. (J). pap. 14.95 *(978-1-937622-21-3(5),* Nefu Bks.) Africana Homestead Legacy Pubs., Inc.

Tirgari, Simin. Color of the Heart. 2011. 84p. pap. 8.95 *(978-1-4620-4966-0(4))* iUniverse, Inc.

Tobias, Tobi. Wishes for You. Sorensen, Henri, illus. 40p. (J). (gr. -1-2). 2005. pap. 6.99 *(978-0-06-443730-1(2))* 2003. 16.99 *(978-0-688-10838-0(5))* HarperCollins Pubs.

Todorov, Boriana & Todorov, Vladimir. The Moon Rock. 2007. (ENG., Illus.). 110p. (J). (gr. 2-6). 19.95 *(978-1-894965-77-4(9))* Simply Read Bks. CAN. Dist: Ingram Publisher Services.

Toft, Di. The Twilight Circus. 2011. (Wolven Ser.: 2). (ENG.). 384p. (J). (gr. 3-7). 17.99 *(978-0-545-29492-8(4),* Chicken Hse., The) Scholastic, Inc.

—Wolven, Bk. 1. 2011. (Wolven Ser.: 1). (ENG.). 352p. (J). (gr. 3-7). pap. 7.99 *(978-0-545-17110-6(5),* Chicken Hse., The) Scholastic, Inc.

Torres, Jennifer. Finding the Music, 1 vol. Alarcão, Renato, illus. 2015.Tr. of En Pos de la Música. (ENG & SPA.). 40p. (J). 18.95 *(978-0-89239-291-9(6))* Lee & Low Bks., Inc.

Tran, Truong. Going Home, Coming Home. Phong, Ann, illus. 2003.Tr. of Ve Nha Tham Que Hu'o'Ng. (ENG & VIE.). 32p. (J). 16.95 *(978-0-89239-179-0(0))* Lee & Low Bks., Inc.

Treanor, H. T. The Sun Stone. Tarnowski, Mark, illus. 2012. 16p. pap. 10.00 *(978-1-60976-125-7(1),* Strategic Bk. Publishing) Strategic Book Publishing & Rights Agency (SBPRA).

Trine, Greg. Dinos Are Forever. Dormer, Frank W., illus. (Adventures of Jo Schmo Ser.: 1). (ENG.). 112p. (J). (gr. 1-4). 2014. pap. 5.99 *(978-0-544-00325-5(X),* HMH Books For Young Readers) 2012. 12.99 *(978-0-547-76341-5(7))* Houghton Mifflin Harcourt Publishing Co.

Trip to Freedom: Six-Pack. (Greetings Ser.: Vol. 3). (gr. 3-5). 31.00 *(978-0-7635-1777-9(1))* Rigby Education.

Trooboff, Rhoda. Ben, the Bells & the Peacocks. Bucher, Cecile, illus. 2006. (ENG.). 36p. (J). per. 15.00 *(978-0-9773536-0-6(5))* Univ. of Toledo Pr.

—A Book for Elie. Radjou, Anna Nazaretz, illus. 2008. (ENG.). 31p. pap. 15.00 *(978-0-9773536-1-3(3))* Univ. of Toledo Pr.

Trotter, Deborah W. A Summer's Trade/Shiigo Na'iini' Toddy, Irving, illus. 2007. (ENG & NAV.). 32p. (J). (gr. -1-3). 17.95 *(978-1-893354-71-5(7))* Salina Bookshelf Inc.

Truax, Lois. Grandmothers Are Magic. 2010. 28p. pap. 5.95 *(978-1-935355-01-4(5))* New Shelves Bks.

Tulloch, S. A. The Night Prayers. 2008. 40p. 18.95 *(978-1-4357-0962-1(4))* Lulu Pr., Inc.

Tunks, Karyn. Jubilee!, 1 vol. Buckner, Julie, illus. 2012. (ENG.). 32p. (J). (gr. k-3). 16.99 *(978-1-58980-880-5(0))* Pelican Publishing Co., Inc.

Tunnell, Michael O. Mailing May. Rand, Ted, illus. 2015. 32p. pap. 7.00 *(978-1-61003-610-8(7))* Center for the Collaborative Classroom.

Turnbull, Elizabeth J. Janjak & Freda Go to the Iron Market. Turnbull, Wally R., tr. Jones, Mark, illus. 2013. 36p. pap. 12.95 *(978-1-61153-062-9(8))* Light Messages Publishing.

Turner, Corey W. Little Benjamin & the Red Fire Ants. 2009. 24p. pap. 14.99 *(978-1-4389-1747-4(3))* AuthorHouse.

Turner, Rosebud Alford. Through Talen's Eyes: A Visit to Grandma's House. 2012. 26p. (-18). pap. 10.99 *(978-0-9885180-0-1(7))* Mindstir Media.

Tweedy, Bonnie. Grandma Bonnie's Cats: A Happy Place. 2009. 28p. pap. 12.98 *(978-1-4343-8793-6(3))* AuthorHouse.

Twin Sister Produtions & Shepherd, Jodie. Sesame Street Big Red Riding Hood. 2010. (J). (gr. k-2). 14.99 *(978-1-59922-635-4(9))* Twin Sisters IP, LLC.

Twin Sister Produtions Staff & Shepherd, Jodie. Sesame Street Big Red Riding Hood. 2010. (J). (gr. k-2). 14.99 *(978-1-59922-526-5(3))* Twin Sisters IP, LLC.

Ueda, Rinko. Tail of the Moon, Vol. 4. Ueda, Rinko, illus. 2007. (ENG., Illus.). 200p. (gr. 11). pap. 8.99 *(978-1-4215-0816-0(8))* Viz Media.

Unobagha, Uzo. Grandma, How Do You Say I Love You? Krassa, Victoria, illus. 2007. 28p. (J). 16.95 *(978-0-9773180-0-1(1))* Adonoke Inc.

Urbanek Reese, Dorothy. When Mice Sing — the Story of Mei & Yu. 2008. 138p. pap. 13.95 *(978-1-4357-6104-9(9))* Lulu Pr., Inc.

Usher, Sam. Snow. Usher, Sam, illus. 2015. (ENG., Illus.). 40p. (J). (gr. -1-2). 16.99 *(978-0-7636-7958-3(5),* Templar) Candlewick Pr.

V., Patti. My Na Na Stories. 2005. 18.00 *(978-0-8059-9806-1(3))* Dorrance Publishing Co., Inc.

Vakker, Hans Alric. The Riddle of the Jade Collar: A Twelve Cousins Book. 2013. 292p. 26.95 *(978-1-4759-7522-2(8));* pap. 16.95 *(978-1-4759-7521-5(X))* iUniverse, Inc.

Valentin, Karen. Allie's World: Abuela & Abuelo Move: Abuela & Abuelo Move. 2009. 32p. 6.95 *(978-1-60349-021-4(3),* Marimba Bks.) Hudson Publishing Group, The.

Van Den Abeele, Veronique. Still My Grandma. Dubois, Claude K., illus. 2007. (ENG.). 28p. (J). (gr. -1-5). 16.00 *(978-0-8028-5323-3(4),* Eerdmans Bks For Young Readers) Eerdmans, William B. Publishing Co.

Van Draanen, Wendelin. Sammy Keyes & the Hotel Thief. 2008. (Sammy Keyes Ser.: Bk. 1). (J). 54.99 *(978-1-60640-642-7(6))* Findaway World, LLC.

Van Dyne, Edith. Mary Louise. 2007. (ENG.). 148p. pap. 18.99 *(978-1-4264-1952-2(X))* Creative Media Partners, LLC.

Van Laan, Nancy. Forget Me Not. Graegin, Stephanie, illus. 2014. (ENG.). 40p. (J). (gr. -1-3). 16.99 *(978-0-449-81543-4(9),* Schwartz & Wade Bks.) Random Hse. Children's Bks.

Vanderlaan, Karen. Special Friends. 2008. 28p. pap. 24.95 *(978-1-60813-353-6(2))* America Star Bks.

Velasquez, Eric. Grandma's Gift. Velasquez, Eric, illus. 2013. (ENG., Illus.). 32p. (J). (gr. k-1). pap. 9.99 *(978-0-8027-3536-2(3),* 9780802735362, Bloomsbury USA Childrens) Bloomsbury Publishing USA.

—Grandma's Records. 2014. 32p. pap. 9.00 *(978-1-61003-346-6(9))* Center for the Collaborative Classroom.

—Grandma's Records. 2004. (Illus.). 32p. (J). (gr. k-3). 17.85 *(978-0-8027-8761-3(4));* 16.95 *(978-0-8027-8760-6(6))* Walker & Co.

Velasquez, Eric & National Geographic Learning Staff. Grandma's Records. Velasquez, Eric, illus. 2004. (ENG., Illus.). 32p. (J). (gr. k-3). pap. 9.99 *(978-0-8027-7660-0(4),* 9780802776600, Bloomsbury USA Childrens) Bloomsbury Publishing USA.

Velásquez, Gloria. Rudy's Memory Walk. 2009. (Roosevelt High School Ser.). 140p. (YA). (gr. 6-18). pap. 9.95 *(978-1-55885-593-9(9))* Arte Publico Pr.

Velez, Edia L. Jessica's Summer Vacation - Las Vacaciones de Verano de Jéssic. 2011. 44p. pap. 18.49 *(978-1-4490-2301-0(0))* AuthorHouse.

Venkatraman, Padma. Climbing the Stairs. 2010. (ENG., Illus.). 272p. (YA). (gr. 7-18). 9.99 *(978-0-14-241490-3(5),* Speak) Penguin Young Readers Group.

Viano, Hannah. Arrow to Alaska: A Pacific Northwest Adventure. 2015. (ENG., Illus.). 32p. (J). (gr. k-4). 16.99 *(978-1-57061-949-6(2),* Little Bigfoot) Sasquatch Bks.

Vicente, Alidis. The Case of the Three Kings / el Caso de Los Reyes Magos: The Flaca Files / Los Expedientes de Flaca. 2016. (Flaca Files / Los Expedientes de Flaca Ser.). (MUL, ENG & SPA., Illus.). 96p. (J). (gr. 3-6). pap. 9.95 *(978-1-55885-822-0(9),* Piñata Books) Arte Publico Pr.

Viguie, Debbie & Holder, Nancy. Unleashed. 2012. (Wolf Spring Chronicles Ser.). (ENG.). 400p. (YA). (gr. 7). pap. 9.99 *(978-0-385-74099-9(9),* Ember) Random Hse. Children's Bks.

Vincent, Harris T. & Brewer, Mary. When Grandmother Was A Little Girl. 2010. 40p. 23.99 *(978-1-4520-7728-4(2))* AuthorHouse.

Vision, David & Vision, Mutiya Sahar. Missing You. Alcantara, Ignacio, illus. 2009. 32p. 17.00 *(978-0-9659538-6-3(6))* Von Curtis Publishing.

Vitaliev, Vitali. Granny Yaga. 2014. 200p. 18.99 *(978-1-78308-164-6(3),* Thames River Pr.) Anthem Pr. GBR. Dist: Books International, Inc.

Vogl, Nancy & Strange, David. Grandma Loves Her Harley Too. Gibson, Nichoel, illus. 2006. (J). per. 16.95 *(978-0-9772771-1-7(9))* Cherry Tree Pr. LLC.

Von Meck. My Name Is Vaselinetjie. 2011. 256p. pap. *(978-0-624-04658-5(3))* NB Pubs. Ltd.

Vrabel, Beth. A Blind Guide to Normal. 2016. (ENG.). 272p. (J). (gr. 2-7). 16.99 *(978-1-5107-0228-8(8),* Sky Pony Pr.) Skyhorse Publishing Co., Inc.

Wagner, Elaine J. & Wagner, Elaine. Meshom & the Little One. Hamelin, Marie-Micheline et al, illus. 2006. (Meshom & the Little One Ser.). (ENG.). 58p. pap. 12.95 *(978-1-894778-35-0(9))* Theytus Bks., Ltd. CAN. Dist: Univ. of Toronto Pr.

Wagner, Sally R. The Grandmother Who Climbed to the Top of the World. 9p. (J). (gr. 1-5). pap. 3.95 *(978-1-880589-40-3(0))* Sky Carrier Pr.

Walford, N. E. The Island Hunters Bk. 1. 2011. (ENG.). 130p. pap. 14.99 *(978-1-4196-6072-6(1))* CreateSpace Independent Publishing Platform.

Walker-Cox, Krysten. Amber's Metal Singlet. 2009. 48p. pap. 12.13 *(978-1-60860-316-9(4),* Eloquent Bks.) Strategic Book Publishing & Rights Agency (SBPRA).

Walker, Crystal. Maceys Magic Tree. 2009. 28p. pap. 12.49 *(978-1-4490-4916-4(8))* AuthorHouse.

Walker, Nan. Check It Out! Sims, Blanche, illus. 2006. (Social Studies Connects). 32p. (J). (gr. -1-3). pap. 5.95 *(978-1-57565-166-8(1))* Kane Press, Inc.

Walker, Russell D. Michelle & the Magic Timepiece. 2006. 108p. pap. 19.95 *(978-1-4241-3143-3(X))* PublishAmerica, Inc.

Walker, Rysa. Time's Edge, 0 vols. 2014. (Chronos Files Ser.: 2). (ENG.). 450p. (J). (gr. 7-12). pap. 9.99 *(978-1-4778-2582-2(7)*, 9781477825822, Skyscape) Amazon Publishing.

Wallace, Bill. Beauty. 2007. (ENG.). 192p. (J). (gr. 3-7). pap. 6.99 *(978-1-4169-4942-8(9)*, Simon & Schuster/Paula Wiseman Bks.) Simon & Schuster/Paula Wiseman Bks.

—Pick of the Litter. 2005. (ENG.). 160p. (J). (gr. 4-7). 16.95 *(978-0-8234-1921-0(5))* Holiday Hse., Inc.

—Pick of the Litter. 2006. (ENG.). 176p. (J). (gr. 3-7). pap. 5.99 *(978-1-4169-2511-8(2)*, Aladdin) Simon & Schuster Children's Publishing.

Wallace, Nancy Elizabeth. Seeds! Seeds! Seeds!, 0 vols. Wallace, Nancy Elizabeth, illus. 2007. (ENG., Illus.). 40p. (J). (gr. -1-3). 7.99 *(978-0-7614-5366-6(0)*, 9780761453666, Amazon Children's Publishing) Amazon Publishing.

Walley, Diane D. Codger & Baggs. 2004. 78p. (J). per. 9.95 *(978-0-9748591-3-2(3)*, MSP) Main St Publishing, Inc.

Walliams, David. Grandpa's Great Escape. Ross, Tony, illus. 2017. 464p. (J). (gr. 3-7). 16.99 *(978-0-06-256089-6(1))* HarperCollins Pubs.

Walter, Jon. Close to the Wind. 2015. (ENG.). 304p. (J). (gr. 5-9). 17.99 *(978-0-545-81662-5(9))* Scholastic, Inc.

Walter, Mildred Pitts. Justin & the Best Biscuits in the World. Stock, Catherine, illus. 2010. (ENG.). 144p. (J). (gr. 3-7). pap. 5.99 *(978-0-06-195891-5(3)*, Amistad) HarperCollins Pubs.

—Justin & the Best Biscuits in the World. 2011. 8.32 *(978-0-7848-3586-9(1)*, Everbind) Marco Bk. Co.

Walters, Eric. Between Heaven & Earth, 1 vol. 2012. (Seven (the Series) Ser.). (ENG., Illus.). 264p. (J). (gr. 5-10). pap. 9.95 *(978-1-55469-941-4(X))* Orca Bk. Pubs. USA.

—The Matatu, 1 vol. Campbell, Eva, illus. 2012. (ENG.). 32p. (J). (gr. -1-3). 19.95 *(978-1-55469-301-6(2))* Orca Bk. Pubs. USA.

—Sleeper, 1 vol. 2014. (Seven Sequels Ser.). (ENG., Illus.). 240p. (J). (gr. 5-10). pap. 10.95 *(978-1-4598-0543-9(7))* Orca Bk. Pubs. USA.

Walz, C. E. Mary's Treasure Box. Merz, Bruno, illus. 2015. (ENG.). 32p. (J). (gr. -1-3). 12.99 *(978-1-4336-8394-7(6)*, B&H Kids) B&H Publishing Group.

Wangerin, Walter, Jr. I Am My Grandpa's Enkelin. Tate, Don, illus. 2008. 30p. (J). (gr. 3-7). 18.95 *(978-1-55725-468-9(0))* Paraclete Pr., Inc.

Ward, Kris A. Tony's Day in the Park. 2008. 42p. pap. 24.95 *(978-1-60813-351-2(6))* America Star Bks.

Ward, Pat Mays. Big Mama's Storm Cellar. 2010. 24p. 14.99 *(978-1-4490-8236-9(X))* AuthorHouse.

Ward, Rachel. The Chaos. 2011. (Numbers Ser.: 2). (ENG.). 352p. (J). (gr. 9-9). 17.99 *(978-0-545-24269-1(X)*, Chicken Hse., The) Scholastic, Inc.

Warner, Tucker. The Breakthrough & Funeral of a Grandfather, 1 vol. 2009. 48p. pap. 16.95 *(978-1-4489-6684-4(1))* PublishAmerica, Inc.

Waterbury, Matthew. The Little Pig. Muro, Jenny, illus. 2013. 16p. pap. 24.95 *(978-1-4512-2919-6(4))* America Star Bks.

Waters, Rachel. Wanamea: A Choctaw Princess. 2007. 88p. per. 10.00 *(978-1-4257-5976-6(9))* Xlibris Corp.

Waters, Zack C. Blood Moon Rider. 2006. (Florida Historical Fiction for Youth Ser.). (ENG.). 126p. (J). (gr. 4-9). 13.95 *(978-1-56164-350-9(5))* Pineapple Pr., Inc.

Watkins, Constance L. Happy Was His Name. 2011. 24p. (gr. 1-2). pap. 11.75 *(978-1-4634-0421-5(2))* AuthorHouse.

Watson, M. C. V. Fairy Tales & Pixie Trails: From the Series. 2012. 48p. pap. 21.99 *(978-1-4771-5249-2(0))* Xlibris Corp.

Watson, Renée. What Momma Left Me. (ENG.). 240p. (YA). 2012. pap. 7.99 *(978-1-59990-704-8(6)*, 9781599907048) 2010. (gr. 5-8). 16.99 *(978-1-59990-446-7(2)*, 9781599904467) Bloomsbury Publishing USA. (Bloomsbury USA Childrens).

Weatherbee, Tabatha. Shasta, 1 vol. 2009. 216p. pap. 24.95 *(978-1-60703-586-2(3))* PublishAmerica, Inc.

Weber, Lori. Strange Beauty, 1 vol. 2006. (Lorimer SideStreets Ser.). (ENG.). 144p. (YA). (gr. 9-12). 16.95 *(978-1-55028-944-2(6)*, 9781550289442); 9.95 *(978-1-55028-941-1(1)*, 9781550289411) Lorimer, James & Co., Ltd., Pubs. CAN. Dist: Casemate Pubs. & Bk. Distributors, LLC.

Wedding, Linda. The Blue-Eyed, Tri-Colored American Paint: A Lesson in Trust for Baby. 2008. 44p. pap. 24.95 *(978-1-4241-9925-9(5))* America Star Bks.

Wehrman, Tom. Grandpa's a Martian. Dunnier, Tina, illus. 2013. 28p. pap. 8.99 *(978-1-938768-27-9(2))* Gypsy Pubns.

Weingart, Sharlene. Grandpa's Proud Loud. 2011. 28p. pap. 15.99 *(978-1-4568-9221-0(5))* Xlibris Corp.

Weiss, Ellen. The Taming of Lola: A Shrew Story. Smath, Jerry, illus. 2010. (ENG.). 32p. (J). (gr. k-2). 15.95 *(978-0-8109-4066-6(3)*, Abrams Bks. for Young Readers) Abrams, Inc.

Weiss, Rebecca J. Grandpa & Me Love Hotdogs! 2012. 36p. pap. 20.99 *(978-1-4772-8714-9(0))* AuthorHouse.

Welch, Ginger. The Dream Reader. 2012. 76p. 19.95 *(978-1-4626-7276-9(0))*; pap. 19.95 *(978-1-4626-8291-1(X))* America Star Bks.

Welchlin, Jewell. Babysitting Grandmama. 2013. (ENG.). 24p. (J). pap. 12.95 *(978-1-4787-2554-1(0))* Outskirts Pr., Inc.

Wells, Rosemary. Bunny Mail. Wells, Rosemary, illus. 2004. (Max & Ruby Ser.). (ENG., Illus.). 32p. (J). (gr. -1-k). 15.99 *(978-0-670-03630-1(7)*, Viking Books for Young Readers) Penguin Young Readers Group.

—Following Grandfather. Denise, Christopher, illus. 2012. (ENG.). 64p. (J). (gr. 1-4). 14.99 *(978-0-7636-5069-8(2))* Candlewick Pr.

—Max & Ruby's Treasure Hunt. 2012. (Max & Ruby Ser.). (ENG.). 32p. (J). (gr. -1-k). 17.99 *(978-0-670-06317-8(7)*, Viking Books for Young Readers) Penguin Young Readers Group.

—Ruby's Rainbow. 2012. (Max Ruby Ser.). lib. bdg. 13.55 *(978-0-606-26091-6(9)*, Turtleback) Turtleback Bks.

West, L. J. Mr. Blacky & His Palace. l.t. ed. 2006. (Illus.). 31p. (J). 19.99 *(978-1-59879-268-3(7))* Lifevest Publishing, Inc.

West, Lily June Wolford. A Trip to the Cellar. West, June & Wright, Shannon, illus. 2007. (J). (gr. -1-3). 16.99 *(978-1-59879-347-5(0))* Lifevest Publishing, Inc.

West, Stephen Earl. My Grandfather's Farm. Eller, Jerod R., illus. 2011. 20p. pap. 24.95 *(978-1-4560-6628-4(5))* America Star Bks.

Westergard, Tim. The Jesus Box, 1 vol. 2009. 16p. pap. 24.95 *(978-1-60749-694-6(1))* America Star Bks.

Westerman, Robert. Alohalani Kalikimaka Auntie: Sheet Music & Lyrics. Westerman, Robert, . 2006. (Illus.). 12p. (J). 6.95 *(978-0-9761992-1-2(1))* Gold Boy Music & Pubn.

Westheimer, Ruth K. Leopold. 2015. (ENG., Illus.). 34p. (J). 23.99 *(978-1-63026-918-0(2))* Turner Publishing Co.

Weston Woods Staff, creator. Grandfather's Journey. 2011. 38.75 *(978-0-545-12710-3(6))* Weston Woods Studios, Inc.

—Little Bear's Visit. 2011. 38.75 *(978-0-439-72743-3(X))*; 29.95 *(978-0-439-73484-4(3))*; 18.95 *(978-0-439-72741-9(3))* Weston Woods Studios, Inc.

—Red Riding Hood. 2011. 38.75 *(978-0-439-72883-6(5))*; 18.95 *(978-0-439-72882-9(7))*; 29.95 *(978-0-439-73518-6(1))* Weston Woods Studios, Inc.

—Three Cheers for Catherine the Great. 2011. 18.95 *(978-0-439-80506-3(6))* Weston Woods Studios, Inc.

—Three Cheers for Catherine the Great! 2011. 38.75 *(978-0-439-78620-1(7))* Weston Woods Studios, Inc.

Wetterer, Charles M. When Grandad Babysat. 2012. 24p. pap. 14.93 *(978-1-4669-5627-8(5))* Trafford Publishing.

Weyn, Suzanne. The Diamond Secret. 2009. (Once upon a Time Ser.). (ENG.). 240p. (YA). (gr. 7-18). mass mkt. 7.99 *(978-1-4169-7530-4(6)*, Simon Pulse) Simon Pulse.

What's in the Suitcase, Grandma? My Solar-Powered History, Book 3. 2013. (Illus.). 116p. pap. 12.99 *(978-1-937848-08-8(6))* Do Life Right, Inc.

Wheeler, Lance. Kula & the Old Ukulele. 2007. 32p. 12.95 *(978-1-56647-844-1(8))* Mutual Publishing LLC.

Wheeler, Lisa. Who's Afraid of Granny Wolf? Ansley, Frank, illus. 2006. (Fitch & Chip Ser.: 3). (ENG.). 48p. (J). (gr. 1-3). pap. 3.99 *(978-0-689-84957-2(5)*, Simon Spotlight) Simon Spotlight.

When I'm Older, 6 Packs. (Literatura 2000 Ser.). (gr. 1-2). 28.00 *(978-0-7635-0154-9(0))* Rigby Education.

Where Is Nancy?, 6 Pack. (Literatura 2000 Ser.). (gr. k-1). 28.00 *(978-0-7635-0079-5(8))* Rigby Education.

Whilldin, Sunny. Alex P. Maxwell's Rainy Day Adventure. 2009. 38p. pap. 25.40 *(978-0-557-13284-3(3))* Lulu Pr., Inc.

Whipple, Natalie. House of Ivy & Sorrow. 2014. (ENG.). 368p. (YA). (gr. 8). pap. 9.99 *(978-0-06-212018-2(2)*, HarperTeen) HarperCollins Pubs.

Whitby, Rozene. Luke & Nana, 1 vol. Fowler, Elizabeth, illus. 2010. 16p. 24.95 *(978-1-4489-3826-1(0))* PublishAmerica, Inc.

White, Aaron D. Creek Babies. 2013. 44p. pap. 16.95 *(978-1-63000-671-6(8))* America Star Bks.

White, Howard. The Airplane Ride. Guzek, Greta, illus. unabr. ed. 2006. (ENG.). 32p. (J). bds. 16.95 *(978-0-88971-224-9(7))* Harbour Publishing Co., Ltd. CAN. Dist: Midpoint Trade Bks., Inc.

White, Jan. Mystery of Mingus Mountain. 2012. (ENG., Illus.). 138p. (YA). (gr. 7-13). pap. 9.99 *(978-0-89824-370-3(X))* Royal Fireworks Publishing Co.

White, Kathy. Little Green Riding Hood. 2006. (J). pap. *(978-1-4108-6182-5(1))* Benchmark Education Co.

White, Matthew & Sanderson, Ana. Little Red Riding Hood & the Wolf: A Howling Hilarious Musical, 1 vol. Balton, Janice, ed. Eccles, Jane, illus. 2005. (and C Black Musicals Ser.). (ENG.). 56p. (J). (gr. 2-6). pap. 42.95 incl. cd-rom ***(978-0-7136-6958-9(6))*** HarperCollins Pubs. Ltd. GBR. Dist: Independent Pubs. Group.

White, Pamela. Magic Number 5. 2012. 12p. pap. 15.99 *(978-1-4772-9222-8(5))* AuthorHouse.

White, Prentice L. Christmas at Mimi's. 2012. 24p. (-18). pap. 14.00 *(978-1-4772-4856-0(0))* AuthorHouse.

Whybrow, Ian. Hello! Is This Grandma? Allwright, Deborah, illus. 2008. (Tiger Tales Ser.). 32p. (J). (gr. -1-2). 15.95 *(978-1-58925-072-7(9))* Tiger Tales.

Whyte, Elana. My Gift: A Book about a Child Who Sees Spirit. 2013. 32p. pap. 13.95 *(978-1-4525-8724-0(8)*, Balboa Pr.) Author Solutions, Inc.

Wiedeman, Connie. Grandma, Do Angels Have Wings?, 1 vol. Gaston, Sierra, illus. 2010. 40p. 24.95 *(978-1-4512-1054-5(X))* PublishAmerica, Inc.

Wiggins, Leah Holder. My Neighbor Is Gone. Wiggins, Margaret W., illus. 2006. 28p. (J). per. 17.99 *(978-0-9768579-5-2(2))* eVision, LLC.

Wilcox, Brian & David, Lawrence. Full Moon. Wilcox, Brian, illus. 2004. (Illus.). 30p. (J). (gr. k-4). reprint ed. 16.00 *(978-0-7567-7762-3(3))* DIANE Publishing Co.

Wild, Margaret. Piglet & Granny. King, Stephen Michael, illus. 2009. (ENG.). 32p. (J). (gr. -1-k). 15.95 *(978-0-8109-4063-5(9)*, Abrams Bks. for Young Readers) Abrams, Inc.

Wilder, Vickie. The Umbrella. 2013. 24p. pap. 11.97 *(978-1-62212-534-0(7)*, Strategic Bk. Publishing) Strategic Book Publishing & Rights Agency (SBPRA).

Wiles, Deborah. Love, Ruby Lavender. 2005. (ENG., Illus.). 240p. (J). (gr. 2-5). reprint ed. pap. 7.99 *(978-0-15-205478-6(2))* Houghton Mifflin Harcourt Publishing Co.

—Love, Ruby Lavender. 2004. 216p. (J). (gr. 3-7). pap. 36.00 incl. audio *(978-0-8072-2096-2(5)*, Listening Library) Random Hse. Audio Publishing Group.

Wilhelm, Kj. Grandma Coocoonutts Goes to Boston. 2009. 28p. pap. 15.99 *(978-1-4363-9933-3(5))* Xlibris Corp.

Wilkins, Verna. Twinkle, Twinkle, Little Star. Kubler, Annie, illus. 2003. (Classic Books with Holes 8x8 Ser.). (ENG.). 16p. (J). (gr. -1-3). pap. *(978-0-85953-133-7(3))* Child's Play International Ltd.

Willard, Claudette. Chloe & Banana Island. 2008. 40p. pap. 16.99 *(978-1-4343-8756-1(9))* AuthorHouse.

Willems, Mo. Knuffle Bunny Free: An Unexpected Diversion. Willems, Mo, illus. 2010. (Illus.). 52p. (J). (gr. -1-3). (ENG.). 17.99 *(978-0-06-192957-1(3))*; lib. bdg. 18.89 *(978-0-06-192958-8(1))* HarperCollins Pubs.

—Knuffle Bunny Free: An Unexpected Diversion. 2012. *(978-0-545-44810-9(7))* Scholastic, Inc.

Williams-Garcia, Rita. Clayton Byrd Goes Underground. Morrison, Frank, illus. 2017. 176p. (J). (gr. 3-7). 16.99 *(978-0-06-221591-8(4))*; (ENG.). E-Book *(978-0-06-221594-9(9))* HarperCollins Pubs. (Amistad).

—Gone Crazy in Alabama. (J). (gr. 3-7). 2016. 320p. pap. 6.99 *(978-0-06-221589-5(2)*, Amistad) 2015. (ENG., Illus.). 304p. 16.99 *(978-0-06-221587-1(6))* HarperCollins Pubs.

Williams, Katina T. Jeremiah Pie. 2011. 36p. pap. 24.95 *(978-1-4626-2332-7(8))* America Star Bks.

Williams, Laura E. The Best Winds. Neilan, Eujin Kim, illus. 2006. (ENG.). 32p. (J). (gr. -1-2). 16.95 *(978-1-59078-274-3(7))* Boyds Mills Pr.

Williams, Marian. Bigdaddy: A Grand-daughter's Love Story. 2007. 32p. 16.00 *(978-1-4303-1426-4(5))* Lulu Pr., Inc.

Williams, Nate & Snow, Virginia Brimhall. Spring Walk, 1 vol. 2015. (ENG., Illus.). 32p. (J). (gr. 2-3). 16.99 *(978-1-4236-3879-7(4))* Gibbs Smith, Publisher.

Williams, Rozanne Lanczak. Grandma's Lists. Briles, Patty, illus. 2006. (Learn to Write Ser.). 8p. (J). (gr. k-2). pap. 3.49 *(978-1-59198-284-5(7)*, 6178) Creative Teaching Pr., Inc.

—Grandma's Lists. Maio, Barbara & Faulkner, Stacey, eds. Briles, Patty, illus. 2006. (J). per. 6.99 *(978-1-59198-335-4(5))* Creative Teaching Pr., Inc.

Williams, Versey. My Grandma's Dog. l.t. ed. 2004. (Illus.). 50p. 19.00 *(978-0-9763357-0-2(0))* Christian Bible Studies.

Williamson, Sharon. Grandma Says, Don't Climb the Peach Tree. 2011. 18p. pap. 16.95 *(978-1-4560-8794-4(0))* America Star Bks.

Wilson, Angela. Grandma's Traditions. Basta, Stormie, illus. 2012. 24p. pap. 24.95 *(978-1-4626-9410-5(1))* America Star Bks.

Wilson, John. Broken Arrow, 1 vol. 2014. (Seven Sequels Ser.). (ENG., Illus.). 240p. (J). (gr. 5-10). pap. 10.95 *(978-1-4598-0540-8(2))* Orca Bk. Pubs. USA.

—Lost Cause, 1 vol. 2012. (Seven (the Series) Ser.). (ENG., Illus.). 224p. (J). (gr. 5-10). pap. 9.95 *(978-1-55469-944-5(4))* Orca Bk. Pubs. USA.

Wilson, Rebekah. Grandmother's Hope Chest: Lucie's Snowflakes. l.t. ed. 2004. (Illus.). 80p. (J). 15.00 *(978-1-59565-003-0(2))* Hope Chest Legacy, Inc.

—Grandmother's Hope Chest: The Running Rooster. l.t. ed. 2004. (Illus.). 52p. (J). 15.00 *(978-1-59565-002-3(4))* Hope Chest Legacy, Inc.

Winget, Dianna Dorisi. A Million Ways Home. 2014. (ENG.). 272p. (J). (gr. 3-7). 16.99 *(978-0-545-66706-7(2)*, Scholastic Pr.) Scholastic, Inc.

Winningham, Barbara. The Turtle Pit. 2013. 36p. 24.95 *(978-1-62709-875-5(5))*; pap. 24.95 *(978-1-62709-493-1(8))* America Star Bks.

Winthrop, Elizabeth & Winthrop. Dancing Granny, 1 vol. Murdocca, Sal, illus. 2003. (ENG.). 32p. (J). 16.95 *(978-0-7614-5141-9(2))* Marshall Cavendish Corp.

Wisnewski, Andrea. Little Red Riding Hood. 2006. (ENG., Illus.). 32p. (J). (gr. 3-7). 18.95 *(978-1-56792-303-2(8))* Godine, David R. Pub.

Wissinger, Tamera Will. Gone Camping: A Novel in Verse. Cordell, Matthew, illus. 2017. (ENG.). 112p. (J). (gr. 1-4). 15.99 *(978-0-544-63873-0(5)*, HMH Books For Young Readers) Houghton Mifflin Harcourt Publishing Co.

Witmer, Edith. Helping Grandfather. Reinford, Luanne & Horst, Melissa, illus. 2016. 91p. (J). ***(978-0-7399-2537-9(7))*** Rod & Staff Pubs., Inc.

Wolf, Claudia. Grandma & Me. Wolf, Claudia, illus. 2006. (Illus.). 24p. (J). per. 2.99 *(978-1-59958-024-1(1))* Journey Stone Creations, LLC.

Wolford, Merle & Harvey, Karen. Pau Pua & the Watering Hole. 2013. 40p. pap. *(978-1-4602-1383-4(1))* FriesenPress.

Wong, Janet S. Homegrown House. Lewis, E. B., illus. 2009. (ENG.). 40p. (J). (gr. -1-3). 16.99 *(978-0-689-84718-9(1)*, McElderry, Margaret K. Bks.) McElderry, Margaret K. Bks.

Wood, Cary D. Davis & Pop Go Hiking. Turner, Cecilia, illus. 2014. (ENG.). 32p. (gr. -1-4). pap. 14.95 *(978-1-63047-068-5(6))* Morgan James Publishing.

Wood, David. The Little House on Buchanan Street. 2007. 24p. per. 12.95 *(978-1-934246-64-1(6))* Peppertree Pr., The.

Wood, Douglas. Grandad's Prayers of the Earth. Lynch, P. J., illus. 2009. 32p. pap. 6.99 *(978-0-7636-1865-0(9))*; (ENG.). (J). (gr. 1-4). pap. 7.99 *(978-0-7636-4675-2(X))* Candlewick Pr.

—Grandad's Prayers of the Earth. Lynch, P. J., illus. 2004. 28p. (J). (gr. k-4). reprint ed. 17.00 *(978-0-7567-7101-0(3))* DIANE Publishing Co.

—What Grandmas Can't Do. Cushman, Doug, illus. (ENG.). 32p. (J). (gr. -1-3). 2008. 6.99 *(978-1-4169-5483-5(X))* 2005. 17.99 *(978-0-689-84647-2(9))* Simon & Schuster Bks. For Young Readers. (Simon & Schuster Bks. For Young Readers).

—When a Grandpa Says I Love You. Bell, Jennifer A., illus. 2014. (ENG.). 32p. (J). (gr. -1-3). 16.99 *(978-0-689-81512-6(3)*, Simon & Schuster Bks. For Young Readers) Simon & Schuster Bks. For Young Readers.

Woodruff, Liza, illus. What Time Is It? 2005. (My First Reader Ser.). (ENG.). 32p. (J). (gr. k-4). per. 3.95 *(978-0-516-25279-7(8)*, Children's Pr.) Scholastic Library Publishing.

Woodruff, Liza & Demar, Regier. What Time Is It? Woodruff, Liza, illus. 2005. (My First Reader Ser.). (ENG., Illus.). 32p. (J). (gr. k-1). 18.50 *(978-0-516-25180-6(5)*, Children's Pr.) Scholastic Library Publishing.

Woodson, Jacqueline. Coming on Home Soon. Lewis, Earl & Lewis, E. B., illus. 2004. (ENG.). 32p. (J). (gr. k-3). 17.99 *(978-0-399-23748-5(8)*, G.P. Putnam's Sons Books for Young Readers) Penguin Young Readers Group.

Worcester, Daryl D. Traves Travislot's Going South for the Winter. 2011. 46p. pap. 16.95 *(978-1-4626-1091-4(9))* America Star Bks.

Workman, Joan. Scavenger Hunt: The Twokay Kids at the Mall. 2004. 42p. per. 12.95 *(978-1-932344-14-1(4))* Thornton Publishing, Inc.

Worstine, Waneta Cotner. Grandma's Yarn. 2012. 38p. pap. 16.95 *(978-1-4497-6661-0(7)*, WestBow Pr.) Author Solutions, Inc.

Worth, Sharon. Jacob's Garden, 1 vol. 2009. 132p. pap. 19.95 *(978-1-60813-963-7(8))* America Star Bks.

Wright, Mary H. Grandma Spoils Me. Megenhardt, Bill, illus. l.t. ed. 2005. 32p. (J). lib. bdg. 16.95 *(978-0-9645493-4-0(4))* Bluebonnets, Boots & Bks. Pr.

Wright, Susan. Grandma's Haunted House. 2007. 64p. per. 16.95 *(978-1-4241-0466-6(1))* PublishAmerica, Inc.

Wurge, B. B. Billy & the Birdfrogs. 2008. (ENG.). 178p. (J). (gr. 3-8). pap. 9.95 *(978-0-9815148-2-6(0))* Leapfrog Pr.

Wyatt, Winnie Dowden. Travis' Ladder. 2011. 64p. pap. 12.99 *(978-1-4567-2894-6(6))* AuthorHouse.

Xiong, Kim, illus. Paper Horse. 2008. (ENG & CHI.). 37p. (J). 18.95 *(978-1-60603-003-5(5))* Better Chinese LLC.

Yamada, Debbie Leung. Striking It Rich: Treasures from Gold Mountain. Tang, You-shan, illus. l.t. ed. 2004. 128p. (J). (gr. 4-8). pap. 13.95 *(978-1-879965-21-8(6))* Polychrome Publishing Corp.

Yates, Alexander. The Winter Place. 2015. (ENG., Illus.). 448p. (YA). (gr. 9). 17.99 *(978-1-4814-1981-9(1))* Simon & Schuster Children's Publishing.

Yayo. The Tales of Pop & Grace: Pop's Lucky Token. 2013. 94p. (gr. 2-4). pap. 10.67 *(978-1-4817-8033-9(6))* AuthorHouse.

—The Tales of Pop & Grace: The Burglar. 2013. 94p. (gr. 2-4). pap. 10.67 *(978-1-4817-8108-4(1))* AuthorHouse.

Yazzie, Seraphine G. Beauty Beside Me: Stories of My Grandmother's Skirts. Ruffenach, Jessie Eve, ed. Whitethorne, Baje, Sr., illus. 2011. (NAV & ENG.). 32p. (J). (gr. -1-3). 17.95 *(978-1-893354-77-7(6))* Salina Bookshelf Inc.

Yep, Laurence. Child of the Owl. (Golden Mountain Chronicles). (J). pap., stu. ed. *(978-0-13-053125-4(1))* Prentice Hall (Schl. Div.).

—The Magic Paintbrush. Wang, Suling, illus. 2003. (ENG.). 96p. (J). (gr. 3-7). pap. 6.99 *(978-0-06-440852-3(3))* HarperCollins Pubs.

—The Magic Paintbrush. Wang, Suling, illus. 2003. 89p. (J). (gr. 3-7). 12.65 *(978-0-7569-1444-8(2))* Perfection Learning Corp.

Yisrael, A'mon. Mr. Jerry's Nap. 2005. (Illus.). 9p. (J). 8.99 *(978-0-9772424-0-5(4))* Yisrael, Sean Publishing Co.

Ylvisaker, Anne. Button Down. (ENG.). 192p. (J). (gr. 3-7). 2013. pap. 6.99 *(978-0-7636-6463-3(4))* 2012. (Illus.). 15.99 *(978-0-7636-5396-5(9))* Candlewick Pr.

Young, Beryl. Follow the Elephant. 2010. (ENG., Illus.). 248p. pap. 10.95 *(978-1-55380-098-9(2))* Ronsdale Pr. CAN. Dist: SPD-Small Pr. Distribution.

Young, Helen Ann. Hello to Hellie's World. Young, Tim Blair, illus. 2013. 46p. pap. *(978-1-908353-00-9(7))* Young Editions.

Young, Judy. Promise. 2016. (ENG.). 368p. (J). (gr. 4-6). pap. 8.99 *(978-1-58536-915-7(2)*, 204079) Sleeping Bear Pr.

Young, Pershail Catherine. Rusty & Mr. Earlie. 2010. 28p. pap. 12.49 *(978-1-4520-4514-6(3))* AuthorHouse.

Yuricich, Jillian Grace, illus. What did Grandma See? 2006. (J). lib. bdg. 15.99 *(978-0-9774696-0-4(3))* Gilboy Publishing.

Zabini, Eleni & Livanios, Eleni. Best Grandma in the World! Lütje, Susanne, illus. 2015. (ENG.). 16p. (J). bds. 7.95 *(978-0-7358-4225-0(6))* North-South Bks., Inc.

—Best Grandpa in the World! Lütje, Susanne, illus. 2015. (ENG.). 16p. (J). bds. 7.95 *(978-0-7358-4237-3(X))* North-South Bks., Inc.

Zadunajsky, Donna M. Tayla Takes a Trip. Bicking, Judith, illus. 2013. (ENG.). 40p. pap. 9.99 *(978-1-938037-36-8(7))* Zadunajsky, Donna M.

Zafrilla, Marta. Grandpa Monty's Muddles. 2012. (ENG., Illus.). 32p. (J). (gr. 2-4). *(978-84-15241-17-1(8))* D P & G Military Pubs.

Zajac, Kristen. Chasing the Spirit of Service. Tucker, Julie, illus. 2013. 24p. 19.95 *(978-1-61633-393-5(6))* Guardian Angel Publishing, Inc.

Zepeda, Gwendolyn & Ventura, Gabriela Baeza. Sunflowers/Girasoles. Gambino, Alisha Ann Guadalupe, illus. 2009. (SPA & ENG.). 32p. (J). (gr. -1-2). 16.95 *(978-1-55885-267-9(0)*, Piñata Books) Arte Publico Pr.

Zepeda, Monique. Las Piñatas. Graullera, Fabiola, illus.Tr. of Pinatas. (SPA.). 26p. (J). (gr. 3-5). pap. 6.95 *(978-968-19-0612-2(8))* Santillana USA Publishing Co., Inc.

Zera, Annette & Szekeres, Vivienne. Grandma Gets a Fright. 2013. (Illus.). 20p. pap. 9.50 *(978-1-78035-634-1(X)*, Fastprint Publishing) Upfront Publishing Ltd. GBR. Dist: Printondemand-worldwide.com.

—Grandma Gets a Visitor. 2013. (Illus.). 20p. pap. 9.50 *(978-1-78035-633-4(1)*, Fastprint Publishing) Upfront Publishing Ltd. GBR. Dist: Printondemand-worldwide.com.

Zermeno, Mariana. Nuevo Peinado para Abuelitas. 2003. (SPA., Illus.). 24p. (J). (gr. k-5). pap. 7.95 *(978-968-19-0678-8(0))* Aguilar, Altea, Taurus, Alfaguara, S.A. de C.V MEX. Dist: Santillana USA Publishing Co., Inc.

Zia, F. Hot, Hot Roti for Dada-Ji. Min, Ken, illus. 2011. (ENG.). 32p. (J). (gr. k-5). 17.95 *(978-1-60060-443-0(9))* Lee & Low Bks., Inc.

Zia, F. & Min, Ken. Hot Hot Roti for Dada-Ji. 2016. (ENG.). 32p. (J). (gr. k-3). pap. 9.95 ***(978-1-62014-352-0(6))*** Lee & Low Bks., Inc.

Zirlin, Sande H. Visits to Gradma's House. 2006. 18.00 *(978-0-8059-9920-4(5))* Dorrance Publishing Co., Inc.

GRANT, JULIA (DENT), 1826-1902

Larkin, Tanya. What Was Cooking in Julia Grant's White House? 2009. (Cooking Throughout American History Ser.). 24p. (gr. 3-3). 42.50 *(978-1-61511-952-3(3)*, PowerKids Pr.) Rosen Publishing Group, Inc., The.

GRANT, ULYSSES S. (ULYSSES SIMPSON), 1822-1885

Adler, Susan Bivin. Ulysses S. Grant. 2006. (History Maker Bios Ser.). (Illus.). 48p. (J). (gr. 3-7). lib. bdg. 26.60 *(978-0-8225-2438-0(4)*, Lerner Pubns.) Lerner Publishing Group.

Archer, Jules. A House Divided: The Lives of Ulysses S. Grant & Robert E. Lee. rev. ed. 2015. (Jules Archer History for Young Readers Ser.). (ENG., Illus.). 176p. (J). (gr. 6). 16.99 *(978-1-63220-604-6(8)*, Sky Pony Pr.) Skyhorse Publishing Co., Inc.

Aronson, Billy. Ulysses S. Grant. 2007. (Presidents & Their Times Ser.). (Illus.). 96p. (J). (gr. 3-7). lib. bdg. 34.21 *(978-0-7614-2430-7(X)*, Benchmark Bks.) Marshall Cavendish Corp.

Ashby, Ruth. Lee vs. Grant, Great Battles of the Civil War. 2016. (Civil War Chronicles Ser.: Vol. 4). (ENG., Illus.). (J). (gr. 5-6). 23.95 ***(978-1-59687-514-2(3)***, ipicturebooks) ibooks, Inc.

Benoit, Peter. The Surrender at Appomattox. 2011. (Cornerstones of Freedom, Third Ser.). 64p. (J). (ENG.). pap. 8.95 *(978-0-531-26566-6(8))*; lib. bdg. 30.00

(978-0-531-25041-9(5)) Scholastic Library Publishing. (Children's Pr.).

Chorlian, Meg & Hale, Sarah Elder, eds. Ulysses S. Grant: Confident Leader & Hero. 2005. (ENG., Illus.). 48p. (J). (gr. 3-9). 17.95 *(978-0-8126-7906-9(7))* Cobblestone Publishing Co.

Conklin, Wendy. Ulysses S. Grant, 1 vol. 2005. (Primary Source Readers Ser.). (ENG.). 24p. (J). (gr. 4-4). pap. 8.99 *(978-0-7439-8920-6(1))* Shell Educational Publishing.

Crompton, Samuel Willard. Ulysses S. Grant. 2009. (Leaders of the Civil War Era Ser.). (Illus.). 119p. (J). (gr. 6-12). 35.00 *(978-1-60413-301-1(5)*, Chelsea Hse.) Facts On File, Inc.

Dunn, Joeming & Espinosa De Santayana, Rodrigo De. Ulysses S. Grant: 18th U. S. President, 1 vol. 2011. (Presidents of the United States Bio-Graphics Ser.). (ENG., Illus.). 32p. (YA). (gr. 3-6). 28.50 *(978-1-61641-646-1(7))* Magic Wagon.

Gaines, Ann Graham. Ulysses S. Grant. 2008. (Presidents of the U. S. A. Ser.). (ENG., Illus.). 48p. (J). (gr. 3-6). 32.79 *(978-1-60253-047-8(5)*, 206686) Child's World, Inc., The.

Havelin, Kate. Ulysses S. Grant. 2004. (Presidential Leaders Ser.). (Illus.). 112p. (J). 29.27 *(978-0-8225-0814-4(1)*, Lerner Pubns.) Lerner Publishing Group.

Kantor, MacKinlay. Lee & Grant at Appomattox. 2015. (ENG.). 144p. pap. 9.95 *(978-0-9904604-0-4(1))* Flying Point Pr.

—Lee & Grant at Appomattox. (Great Leaders & Events Ser.). (ENG.). 208p. (J). (gr. 4-8). 2017. lib. bdg. 35.99 ***(978-1-942875-25-3(8))*** 2016. (Illus.). pap. 12.99 *(978-0-7603-5226-7(7))* Quarto Publishing Group USA. (Voyageur Pr.).

Larkin, Tanya. What Was Cooking in Julia Grant's White House? 2009. (Cooking Throughout American History Ser.). 24p. (gr. 3-3). 42.50 *(978-1-61511-952-3(3)*, PowerKids Pr.) Rosen Publishing Group, Inc., The.

Patrick, Bethanne Kelly. Ulysses S. Grant. 2004. (Childhoods of the Presidents Ser.). (Illus.). 48p. (J). (gr. 4-18). lib. bdg. 17.95 *(978-1-59084-276-8(6))* Mason Crest.

Ransom, Candice. Willie McLean & the Civil War Surrender. Reeves, Jeni, illus. 2004. (On My Own History Ser.). (ENG.). 48p. (gr. 2-4). 25.26 *(978-1-57505-588-6(0))*; pap. 6.95 *(978-1-57505-698-2(4))* Lerner Publishing Group.

Rice, Earle, Jr. Ulysses S. Grant: Defender of the Union. 2005. (Civil War Leaders Ser.). (Illus.). 176p. (gr. 6-12). 28.95 *(978-1-931798-48-8(6))* Reynolds, Morgan Inc.

Rumsch, BreAnn. Ulysses S. Grant, 1 vol. 2009. (United States Presidents Ser.). (ENG., Illus.). 40p. (YA). (gr. 3-6). 27.07 *(978-1-60453-453-5(2))* ABDO Publishing Co.

Sapp, Richard. Ulysses S. Grant & the Road to Appomattox. 2006. (In the Footsteps of American Heroes Ser.). (Illus.). 64p. (gr. 5-12). pap. 14.05 *(978-0-8368-6436-6(0))*; lib. bdg. 34.00 *(978-0-8368-6431-1(X))* Stevens, Gareth Publishing LLLP. (Gareth Stevens Secondary Library).

Stark, Ken. Marching to Appomattox: The Footrace That Ended the Civil War. Stark, Ken & Stark, illus. 2009. (ENG.). 48p. (J). (gr. 4-7). 17.99 *(978-0-399-24212-0(0)*, G.P. Putnam's Sons Books for Young Readers) Penguin Young Readers Group.

Stine, Megan. Who Was Ulysses S. Grant? Harrison, Nancy & Geyer, Mark Edward, illus. 2014. (Who Was? Ser.). (ENG.). 112p. (J). (gr. 3-7). 5.99 *(978-0-448-47894-4(3)*, Grosset & Dunlap) Penguin Young Readers Group.

—Who Was Ulysses S. Grant? 2014. (Who Was... ? Ser.). lib. bdg. 16.00 *(978-0-606-35694-7(0))* Turtleback Bks.

Tecco, Betsy Dru. How to Draw the Life & Times of Ulysses S. Grant. (Kid's Guide to Drawing the Presidents of the United States of America Ser.). 2009. 32p. (gr. 4-4). 50.50 *(978-1-61511-162-6(X)*, PowerKids Pr.) 2006. (YA). (gr. 2-5). 26.50 *(978-1-4042-2995-2(7))* Rosen Publishing Group, Inc., The.

Vansant, Wayne. Grant vs. Lee: The Graphic History of the Civil War's Greatest Rivals During the Last Year of the War. Vansant, Wayne, illus. 2015. (Graphic Histories Ser.). (ENG., Illus.). 104p. (J). (gr. 8-12). 34.65 *(978-1-939581-78-5(8))* Quarto Publishing Group USA.

—Grant vs. Lee: The Graphic History of the Civil War's Greatest Rivals During the Last Year of the War. 2013. (Zenith Graphic Histories Ser.). (ENG., Illus.). 104p. pap. 19.99 *(978-0-7603-4531-3(7)*, 0760345317, Zenith Pr.) Quarto Publishing Group USA.

Venezia, Mike. Ulysses S. Grant. Venezia, Mike, illus. 2005. (Getting to Know the U. S. Presidents Ser.). (ENG., Illus.). 32p. (J). (gr. 3-7). lib. bdg. 28.00 *(978-0-516-22623-1(1)*, Children's Pr.) Scholastic Library Publishing.

Wilhelm, Jeffrey. Ulysses S. Grant: From Failure to Hero. 2017. (ENG.). 32p. pap. 5.99 ***(978-1-63437-839-0(3))*** American Reading Co.

GRANT, ULYSSES S. (ULYSSES SIMPSON), 1822-1885—FICTION

Altsheler, Joseph A. The Tree of Appomattox: A Story of the Civil War's Close. 2006. (Civil War Ser.: Vol. 8). 324p. (J). reprint ed. 29.95 *(978-1-4218-2338-6(1))*; pap. 14.95 *(978-1-4218-2438-3(8))* 1st World Publishing, Inc. (1st World Library - Literary Society).

—The Tree of Appomattox: A Story of the Civil War's Close. l.t. ed. (Civil War Ser.: Vol. 8). (J). reprint ed. 2007. (ENG.). 298p. pap. 23.99 *(978-1-4346-1261-8(9))* 2008. 300p. 25.99 *(978-0-554-35782-9(8))* 2008. 300p. 28.99 *(978-0-554-26479-0(X))* 2007. (ENG.). 266p. pap. 21.99 *(978-1-4346-1190-1(6))* Creative Media Partners, LLC.

—The Tree of Appomattox: A Story of the Civil War's Close. 2006. (Civil War Ser.: Vol. 8). (J). reprint ed. pap. *(978-1-4065-0828-4(4))* Dodo Pr.

—The Tree of Appomattox: A Story of the Civil War's Close. 2007. (Civil War Ser.: Vol. 8). 192p. (J). reprint ed. per. *(978-1-4068-1693-8(0))* Echo Library.

—The Tree of Appomattox: A Story of the Civil War's Close. 2010. (Civil War Ser.: Vol. 8). (Illus.). 174p. (J). (gr. 4-7). reprint ed. pap. 19.99 *(978-1-153-72402-9(2))* General Bks. LLC.

—The Tree of Appomattox: A Story of the Civil War's Close. Wrenn, Charles L., illus. (Civil War Ser.: Vol. 8). 332p. (J). (gr. 4-7). reprint ed. 2011. 45.95 *(978-1-169-88135-8(1))* 2010. 36.76 *(978-1-163-21361-2(6))* 2010. pap. 24.76 *(978-1-162-78752-7(X))* Kessinger Publishing, LLC.

—The Tree of Appomattox: A Story of the Civil War's Close. 2005. (Civil War Ser.: Vol. 8). (J). reprint ed. pap. 30.95 *(978-1-4179-2071-6(8))* Kessinger Publishing, LLC.

—The Tree of Appomattox: A Story of the Civil War's Close. Wrenn, Charles L., illus. 2005. (Civil War Ser.: Vol. 8). 332p. (J). reprint ed. 45.95 *(978-1-4326-1333-4(2))* Kessinger Publishing, LLC.

—The Tree of Appomattox: A Story of the Civil War's Close. 2011. (Civil War Ser.: Vol. 8). 294p. (J). (gr. 4-7). reprint ed. pap. *(978-3-8424-8485-6(2))* Tredition GmbH.

GRAPHIC ARTS

see also Drawing; Painting; Printing; Prints

The Animaniacs in a Hip-Hopera Christmas. (Illus.). 32p. (J). (gr. -1-18). pap. 5.89 incl. audio *(978-1-56826-788-3(6)*, KR5) Rhino Entertainment Co, A Warner Music Group Co.

Beech, Terry. Design, Graphics & Visual Communication for New Zealand Years 9 & 10. 2013. (ENG.). pap., stu. ed. *(978-1-107-61205-1(5))* Cambridge Univ. Pr.

Bow, James. Maker Projects for Kids Who Love Graphic Design. 2016. (ENG., Illus.). 32p. (J). *(978-0-7787-2250-2(3))* Crabtree Publishing Co.

Cooties! 2004. (YA). cd-rom *(978-0-9762083-8-9(5))* GoKnow Learning.

Crabtree Publishing, compiled by. Graphic America Set. 2008. (Graphic America Ser.). (ENG., Illus.). 32p. (J). (gr. 4-7). *(978-0-7787-4184-8(2))*; pap. *(978-0-7787-4211-1(3))* Crabtree Publishing Co.

Creative Team at Walter Foster Publishing Staff. Learn to Draw Angry Birds: Learn to Draw All of Your Favorite Angry Birds & Those Bad Piggies! 2012. (Licensed Learn to Draw Ser.). (ENG., Illus.). 64p. (J). (gr. 1-3). pap. 9.95 *(978-1-60058-306-3(7)*, 1600583067) Quarto Publishing Group USA.

Dombek, Jeff. Caveman Art Teacher. Dombek, Jeff, illus. 2004. (Illus.). 28p. (J). pap. 4.95 *(978-0-9752597-0-2(9))* Corn Tassel Pr.

Elder, Jeremy. Manga Mazes. 2009. (Dover Children's Activity Bks.). (ENG., Illus.). 48p. (J). (gr. -1-5). pap. 4.99 *(978-0-486-47329-1(5))* Dover Pubns., Inc.

Greek, Joe. A Career in Computer Graphics & Design, 1 vol. 2015. (ENG., Illus.). 80p. (J). 34.25 *(978-1-4777-7888-3(8)*, Rosen Young Adult) Rosen Publishing Group, Inc., The.

Hart, Christopher. ¡Dibuja Manga! Nivel Básico. Miralles, Charles, tr. 2005. (SPA., Illus.). 64p. pap. 17.95 *(978-1-59497-092-4(0))* Public Square Bks.

Kidd, Chip. Go: A Kidd's Guide to Graphic Design. 2013. (ENG., Illus.). 160p. (gr. 5-12). 17.95 *(978-0-7611-7219-2(X)*, 17219) Workman Publishing Co., Inc.

Page, Phil. Hodder Graphics: Heroes. 2007. (Illus.). 64p. pap. 21.95 *(978-0-340-92749-6(6)*, Hodder Education) Hodder Education Group GBR. Dist: Trans-Atlantic Pubns., Inc.

Page, Phil & Blackmore, Ruth Benton. Hodder Graphics: A Kestrel for a Knave. 2007. (Illus.). 64p. pap. 21.95 *(978-0-340-92748-9(8)*, Hodder Education) Hodder Education Group GBR. Dist: Trans-Atlantic Pubns., Inc.

Pease, Pamela. Design Dossier. 2010. (Design Dossiers Ser.). (ENG., Illus.). 96p. (J). (gr. 4). 24.00 *(978-0-9777905-2-4(5))* Paintbox Pr.

Sato, Koichi. Infinite Coloring Dazzling Designs. 2009. (Dover Design Coloring Bks.). (ENG., Illus.). 96p. (gr. 3-5). pap. 8.99 incl. cd-rom *(978-0-486-46950-8(6))* Dover Pubns., Inc.

Special Effects, 6 vols. 2005. (QEB Learn Art Ser.). (Illus.). 32p. (J). per. 8.95 *(978-1-59566-126-5(3))* QEB Publishing Inc.

Torres, Daniel. El arte de Daniel Torres. 2005. (SPA., Illus.). 80p. 14.95 *(978-1-59497-051-1(3))* Public Square Bks.

Williams, Cheryl & Williams, Sheila. People of Colour Illustrations: Klip-Klik Art, 2 disc. (J). pap. 39.95 incl. cd-rom *(978-1-889926-98-8(1))* TwinAtaa Studio.

GRAPHIC METHODS

see also Statistics—Graphic Methods

Adams, Colleen. The Everglades: Analyzing Graphs, Tables, & Charts. (PowerMath Ser.). 32p. 2009. (ENG.). (gr. 5-6). pap. 10.00 *(978-1-4042-5127-4(8))* 2009. (gr. 4-5). 47.90 *(978-1-60851-420-5(X))* 2005. (Illus.). (J). (gr. 3-6). lib. bdg. 25.25 *(978-1-4042-2933-4(7))* Rosen Publishing Group, Inc., The. (PowerKids Pr.).

Alaina, Maria. Graphs, 1 vol. (Wonder Readers Next Steps: Math Ser.). (ENG.). (gr. -1-1). 2013. 20p. lib. bdg. 22.65 *(978-1-4765-0033-1(9))* 2011. 32p. pap. 5.99 *(978-1-4296-8056-1(3))* 2011. 16p. pap. 35.94 *(978-1-4296-8092-9(X))* Capstone Press of Coughlan Cos. (Wonder Readers).

Arias, Lisa. Groovy Graphing: Quadrant One & Beyond. 2014. (ENG.). 32p. (gr. 3-6). 32.79 *(978-1-62717-720-7(5))* Rourke Educational Media.

Bader, Bonnie. Family Reunion. Cole, Mernie Gallagher, illus. 2003. (Penguin Young Readers, Level 3 Ser.). (ENG.). 48p. (J). (gr. 1-3). mass mkt. 3.99 *(978-0-448-42896-3(2)*, Penguin Young Readers) Penguin Young Readers Group.

Becker, Helaine. Lines, Bars & Circles: How William Playfair Invented Graphs. Tremblay, Marie-Ève, illus. 2017. (ENG.). 36p. (J). (gr. 1-4). 17.95 *(978-1-77138-570-1(7))* Kids Can Pr., Ltd. CAN. Dist: Hachette Bk. Group.

Bellavia, Rebecca. Planting Sunflowers: Represent & Interpret Data. 2014. (Math Masters: Measurement & Data Ser.). 24p. (J). (gr. 2-3). 23.60 *(978-1-4777-6408-4(9))*; (ENG.). pap. 8.25 *(978-1-4777-4825-1(3))* Rosen Publishing Group, Inc., The. (Rosen Classroom).

Block, Marta Segal. Graphing Global Politics, 1 vol. 2010. (Real World Data Ser.). (ENG., Illus.). 32p. (gr. 3-5). lib. bdg. 29.99 *(978-1-4329-2624-3(1)*, NA-h) Heinemann-Raintree.

Bodach, Vijaya Khisty. Gráficas Circulares. 2012. (Hacer Gráficas/Making Graphs Ser.).Tr. of Pie Graphs. (MUL & SPA.). 32p. (gr. 1-2). pap. 8.10 *(978-1-4296-8539-9(5))*; pap. 47.70 *(978-1-4296-8540-5(9))* Capstone Press of Coughlan Cos. (A+ Bilingue/Bilingual).

—Gráficas de Barras. 2012. (Hacer Gráficas/Making Graphs Ser.).Tr. of Bar Graphs. (MUL.). 32p. (gr. 1-2). pap. 47.70 *(978-1-4296-8543-6(3))*; pap. 8.10 *(978-1-4296-8542-9(5))* Capstone Press of Coughlan Cos. (A+ Bilingue/Bilingual).

—Hacer Gráficas. 2012. (Hacer Gráficas/Making Graphs Ser.).Tr. of Making Graphs. (MUL.). 32p. (gr. 1-2). pap. 24.30 *(978-1-4296-8548-1(4))*; pap. 190.80 *(978-1-4296-8549-8(2))* Capstone Press of Coughlan Cos. (A+ Bilingue/Bilingual).

—Pictografías. 2010. (Hacer Gráficas/Making Graphs Ser.). (MUL, SPA & ENG.). 32p. (gr. 1-2). lib. bdg. 27.32 *(978-1-4296-6101-0(1)*, A+ Bilingue/Bilingual) Capstone Press of Coughlan Cos.

Boothroyd, Jennifer. Graphing. 2007. (First Step Nonfiction - Early Math Ser.). (ENG.). 8p. (gr. -1-1). pap. 4.95 *(978-0-8225-6830-8(6))* Lerner Publishing Group.

Boswell, Kelly. Graphs, Graphs, Graphs!, 1 vol. 2013. (Displaying Information Ser.). (ENG.). 32p. (gr. 1-2). 27.32 *(978-1-4765-0259-5(5))*; pap. 8.95 *(978-1-4765-3336-0(9))* Capstone Press of Coughlan Cos. (Aplus Bks.).

Bradshaw, Cody. Cultures in My Class: Represent & Interpret Data. 2014. (Rosen Common Core Math Readers Ser.). (ENG., Illus.). 24p. (J). (gr. 2-3). pap. 8.25 *(978-1-4777-4831-2(8)*, Rosen Classroom) Rosen Publishing Group, Inc., The.

Burton, Margie, et al. Reading a Graph. 2011. (Early Connections Ser.). (J). *(978-1-61672-306-4(8))* Benchmark Education Co.

Cefrey, Holly. Exploring Australia: Using Charts, Graphs, & Tables. 2009. (PowerMath Ser.). (ENG., Illus.). 24p. (gr. 3-4). pap. 8.25 *(978-0-8239-8883-9(X)*, PowerKids Pr.) Rosen Publishing Group, Inc., The.

Cocca, Lisa Colozza. Bar Graphs. 2013. (Explorer Junior Library: Math Explorer Junior Ser.). (ENG.). 24p. (gr. 1-4). 28.50 *(978-1-61080-911-5(4)*, 202623); pap. 12.79 *(978-1-61080-936-8(X)*, 202625) Cherry Lake Publishing.

—Pictographs. 2013. (J). *(978-1-61080-988-7(2))* Cherry Lake Publishing.

Collins, Kathleen. On the Trail with Lewis & Clark: Learning to Use Line Graphs. (Math for the REAL World Ser.). 16p. (gr. 2-3). 2009. pap. 7.05 *(978-0-8239-8853-2(8)*, Rosen Classroom) 2004. (ENG.). 37.95 *(978-0-8239-7639-3(4))* Rosen Publishing Group, Inc., The.

Dee, Nora. Making Circle Graphs. 2014. (Graph It! Ser.). 24p. (J). (gr. 1-3). 22.60 *(978-1-4824-0829-4(5))* Stevens, Gareth Publishing LLLP.

Dowdy, Penny. Graphing. 2008. (My Path to Math Ser.). (ENG., Illus.). 24p. (J). (gr. k-3). pap. *(978-0-7787-4357-6(8))*; lib. bdg. *(978-0-7787-4339-2(X))* Crabtree Publishing Co.

Edgar, Sherra G. Bar Graphs. 2013. (21st Century Basic Skills Library: Let's Make Graphs Ser.). (ENG., Illus.). 24p. (J). (gr. k-3). 22.79 *(978-1-62431-390-5(6)*, 202680); pap. 12.79 *(978-1-62431-466-7(X)*, 202682) Cherry Lake Publishing.

—Graphing Story Problems. 2013. (21st Century Basic Skills Library: Let's Make Graphs Ser.). (ENG., Illus.). 24p. (J). (gr. k-3). 22.79 *(978-1-62431-391-2(4)*, 202684); pap. 12.79 *(978-1-62431-467-4(8)*, 202686) Cherry Lake Publishing.

—Line Graphs. 2013. (21st Century Basic Skills Library: Let's Make Graphs Ser.). (ENG., Illus.). 24p. (J). (gr. k-3). 22.79 *(978-1-62431-392-9(2)*, 202688); pap. 12.79 *(978-1-62431-468-1(6)*, 202690) Cherry Lake Publishing.

—Pie Graphs. 2013. (21st Century Basic Skills Library: Let's Make Graphs Ser.). (ENG., Illus.). 24p. (J). (gr. k-3). 22.79 *(978-1-62431-394-3(9)*, 202696); pap. 12.79 *(978-1-62431-470-4(8)*, 202698) Cherry Lake Publishing.

Edson, Ann & Insel, Eunice. Reading Maps, Globes, Charts, Graphs. (J). (gr. 4-6). stu. ed., instr.'s gde. ed. 39.00 incl. audio *(978-0-89525-175-6(2)*, AKC 356) Educational Activities, Inc.

Estigarribia, Diana. Learning about the Effects of Natural Events with Graphic Organizers. (Graphic Organizers in Science Ser.). 24p. 2009. (gr. 3-4). 42.50 *(978-1-61513-050-4(0))* 2006. (ENG., Illus.). (gr. 4-6). pap. 8.25 *(978-1-4042-5038-3(7))* 2005. (Illus.). (J). (gr. -1-3). lib. bdg. 22.60 *(978-1-4042-2804-7(7))* Rosen Publishing Group, Inc., The. (PowerKids Pr.).

Flatt, Lizann. Line Graphs. 2016. (Get Graphing! Building Data Literacy Skills Ser.). (ENG., Illus.). 24p. (J). (gr. k-3). *(978-0-7787-2625-8(8))* Crabtree Publishing Co.

Freudenthal. Graph Equations. 3rd ed. 2003. (Math in Context Ser.). (Illus.). 8.33 *(978-0-03-071659-1(4))* Holt McDougal.

Graham, Noel & Blundell, Graham. Graph Pack. (Illus.). 22p. (J). (gr. k-3). 10.00 *(978-1-871098-29-7(7))* Claire Pubns. GBR. Dist: Parkwest Pubns., Inc.

Graham, Roland & National Geographic Learning Staff. Let's Vote! Learning to Use Simple Bar Graphs. 2010. (Rise & Shine Ser.). (ENG.). 12p. (C). (gr. 1-2). pap. 9.95 *(978-0-8239-8864-8(3))* National Geographic School Publishing, Inc.

Guzman, Sienna. Visiting Death Valley: Represent & Interpret Data. 2014. (Rosen Common Core Math Readers Ser.). (ENG.). 24p. (J). (gr. 3-4). pap. 8.25 *(978-1-4777-4909-8(8)*, Rosen Classroom) Rosen Publishing Group, Inc., The.

Hacer Gráficas. 2010. (Hacer Gráficas/Making Graphs Ser.).Tr. of Making Graphs. (MUL.). 32p. (gr. 1-2). lib. bdg. 81.96 *(978-1-4296-6104-1(6)*, A+ Bilingue/Bilingual) Capstone Press of Coughlan Cos.

Harasymiw, Therese. Graph It! 2014. (Graph It! Ser.). 24p. (J). (gr. 1-3). 135.60 *(978-1-4824-1039-6(7))* Stevens, Gareth Publishing LLLP.

Heos, Bridget. Making Graphs. Longhi, Katya, illus. 2015. (Math World Ser.). 24p. (J). lib. bdg. 27.10 *(978-1-60753-463-1(0))* Amicus Publishing.

Hixson, Bryce. Great Graphs in Ten Days. Hixson, Bryce, illus. 2003. (Illus.). (J). 6.95 *(978-1-931801-18-8(5))* Loose In The Lab.

Johnson, Rebecca L. Decoding Data. 2007. (Reading Expeditions Ser.). (ENG., Illus.). 24p. (J). pap. 14.95 *(978-0-7922-4588-9(1))* CENGAGE Learning.

Oxlade, Chris. Animal Infographics, 1 vol. 2014. (Infographics Ser.). (ENG.). 32p. (gr. 1-3). lib. bdg. 29.99 *(978-1-4109-6216-4(4)*, Read Me!) Heinemann-Raintree.

—Environment Infographics, 1 vol. 2014. (Infographics Ser.). (ENG.). 32p. (gr. 1-3). lib. bdg. 29.99 *(978-1-4109-6217-1(2)*, Read Me!) Heinemann-Raintree.

—Infographics, 1 vol. 2014. (Infographics Ser.). (ENG.). 32p. (gr. 1-3). lib. bdg. 119.96 *(978-1-4109-6220-1(2)*, Read Me!) Heinemann-Raintree.

—Population Infographics, 1 vol. 2014. (Infographics Ser.). (ENG.). 32p. (gr. 1-3). lib. bdg. 29.99 *(978-1-4109-6218-8(0)*, Read Me!) Heinemann-Raintree.

—Weather Infographics, 1 vol. 2014. (Infographics Ser.). (ENG.). 32p. (gr. 1-3). lib. bdg. 29.99 *(978-1-4109-6219-5(9)*, Read Me!) Heinemann-Raintree.

Perritano, John. Football Numbers: Graphing Data. 2013. (iMath Ser.). 32p. (J). (gr. 3-4). lib. bdg. 22.60 *(978-1-59953-566-1(1))* Norwood Hse. Pr.

—Football Numbers: Graphing Numbers. 2013. (iMath Ser.). (Illus.). 32p. (J). (gr. 3-4). pap. 11.94 *(978-1-60357-505-8(7))* Norwood Hse. Pr.

Piddock, Claire. Line, Bar, & Circle Graphs. 2010. (ENG., Illus.). 24p. (J). *(978-0-7787-5247-9(X))*; pap. *(978-0-7787-5294-3(1))* Crabtree Publishing Co.

Pistoia, Sara. Graphs. 2013. (Simply Math Ser.). (ENG.). 24p. (J). (gr. -1-2). 27.07 *(978-1-62323-530-7(8)*, 206336) Child's World, Inc., The.

QEB Let's Start! Computing National Book Stores Edition: Making Charts. 2006. (J). per. *(978-1-59566-297-2(9))* QEB Publishing Inc.

Robinson, C. L. MATH1on1 Graphing Foundation. 2006. (YA). per. 9.99 *(978-0-9786767-7-3(7))* Robinson, Consuelo.

Roy, Gregory & Roy, Jennifer Rozines. Graphing in the Desert. 2006. (Math All Around Ser.). (Illus.). 32p. (gr. 2-7). lib. bdg. 29.93 *(978-0-7614-2262-4(5)*, Benchmark Bks.) Marshall Cavendish Corp.

Roy, Jennifer Rozines & Roy, Gregory. Graphing in the Desert. 2007. (Math All Around Ser.). (Illus.). 31p. (J). (gr. 3-7). pap. 6.99 *(978-0-7614-3382-8(1)*, Benchmark Bks.) Marshall Cavendish Corp.

Shah, Keiran. Making Pictographs. 2014. (Graph It! Ser.). 24p. (J). (gr. 1-3). 22.60 *(978-1-4824-0839-3(2))* Stevens, Gareth Publishing LLLP.

Shea, Mary Molly. Making Line Graphs. 2014. (Graph It! Ser.). 24p. (J). (gr. 1-3). 22.60 *(978-1-4824-0834-8(1))* Stevens, Gareth Publishing LLLP.

Sikkens, Crystal. Picture Graphs. 2016. (Get Graphing! Building Data Literacy Skills Ser.). (ENG., Illus.). 24p. (J). (gr. k-3). *(978-0-7787-2632-6(0))* Crabtree Publishing Co.

Somervill, Barbara A. Graphing Natural Disasters, 1 vol. 2010. (Real World Data Ser.). (ENG., Illus.). 32p. (gr. 3-5). pap. 8.95 *(978-1-4329-2631-1(4))*; lib. bdg. 29.99 *(978-1-4329-2622-9(5))* Heinemann-Raintree. (NA-h).

Steck-Vaughn Staff. Math Level J-M: Graphing the Rain Forest. 2003. (Steck-Vaughn Shutterbug Bks.). (ENG., Illus.). 16p. (gr. 2-3). pap. 41.55 *(978-0-7398-7700-5(3))* Houghton Mifflin Harcourt Publishing Co.

Sundance/Newbridge LLC Staff. Charts & Graphs. 2004. (Reading PowerWorks Ser.). (gr. 1-3). 37.50 *(978-0-7608-8987-9(2))*; pap. 6.10 *(978-0-7608-8988-6(0))* Sundance/Newbridge Educational Publishing.

Taylor-Butler, Christine. Understanding Charts & Graphs. 2012. (True Book Ser.). (ENG.). 48p. (J). pap. 6.95 *(978-0-531-26240-5(5))* Scholastic Library Publishing.

—Understanding Diagrams. 2012. (True Book(tm), a — Information Literacy Ser.). (ENG.). 48p. (J). lib. bdg. 31.00 *(978-0-531-26008-1(9))*; pap. 6.95 *(978-0-531-26239-9(1))* Scholastic Library Publishing.

Vaughan, Susan. Let's Eat Lunch: Learning about Picture Graphs. 2009. (Math for the Real World: Early Emergent Ser.). (ENG., Illus.). 8p. (gr. k-1). pap. 5.15 *(978-0-8239-8885-3(6))* Rosen Publishing Group, Inc., The.

Visto, Joy. Where Does a Graph Go? 2015. (Illus.). 48p. (J). *(978-1-60818-575-7(3)*, Creative Education) Creative Co., The.

Webb, Barbara L. Graph It! 2012. (ENG., Illus.). 24p. (gr. -1-1). pap. 8.95 *(978-1-61810-203-4(6))* Rourke Educational Media.

Weingarten, Ethan. Graphs with Giraffes. 2013. (Animal Math Ser.). 24p. (J). (gr. 1-3). 22.60 *(978-1-4339-9313-8(9))*; pap. 48.90 *(978-1-4339-9315-2(5))* Stevens, Gareth Publishing LLLP.

Weingarten, Ethan & Weingarten, E. T. Graphs with Giraffes. 2013. 24p. (J). (gr. 1-3). pap. 8.15 *(978-1-4339-9314-5(7))* Stevens, Gareth Publishing LLLP.

Williams, Jane & Cohen. Graphing Across the Curriculum. 2nd ed. 2003. (Illus.). 32p. (J). pap. 10.95 *(978-0-590-53551-9(X))* Scholastic, Inc.

Wilson, Natashya. The Census & America's People: Analyzing Data Using Line Graphs & Tables. (PowerMath Ser.). (ENG.). 32p. (gr. 4-5). 2009. Illus.). pap. 10.00 *(978-0-8239-8903-4(8)*, PowerKids Pr.) 2004. 47.50 *(978-0-8239-7647-8(5))* Rosen Publishing Group, Inc., The.

Wingard-Nelson, Rebecca. Data, Graphing, & Statistics. 2004. (Math Success Ser.). (Illus.). 64p. (J). lib. bdg. 23.94 *(978-0-7660-2567-7(5))* Enslow Pubs., Inc.

Wirkner, Linda. Learning about the Settlement of the Americas with Graphic Organizers. 2006. (Graphic Organizers in Science & Social Studies Ser.). (ENG.). 24p. (gr. 4-6). pap. 8.25 *(978-1-4042-5057-4(3)*, Rosen Classroom) Rosen Publishing Group, Inc., The.

Wolny, Philip. Creating Electronic Graphic Organizers. 2010. (Digital & Information Literacy Ser.). (ENG.). 48p. (YA). pap. 11.75 *(978-1-4488-0596-9(1))*; lib. bdg. 29.25 *(978-1-4358-9428-0(6))* Rosen Publishing Group, Inc., The. (Rosen Reference).

Youssef, Jagger. Making Bar Graphs. 2014. (Graph It! Ser.). 24p. (J). (gr. 1-3). 22.60 *(978-1-4824-0779-2(5))* Stevens, Gareth Publishing LLLP.

Zuravicky, Orli. The Amazon & the Sahara: Using Double Line Graphs & Double Bar Graphs. (PowerMath Ser.). 32p. 2009. (ENG., Illus.). (gr. 4-5). pap. 10.00 *(978-0-8239-8868-6(6))* 2009. (gr. 4-5). 47.90 *(978-1-60851-401-4(3))* 2004. (Illus.). (J). lib. bdg. 23.95 *(978-0-8239-8981-2(X))* Rosen Publishing Group, Inc., The. (PowerKids Pr.).

GRAPHS

see Graphic Methods

GRASSES

Arnold, Quinn M. Grasslands. 2017. (Seedlings Ser.). (ENG., Illus.). 24p. (J). (gr. k-2). pap. 7.99 *(978-1-62832-349-8(3)*, Creative Paperbacks) Creative Co., The.

Bow, James. Grasslands Inside Out. 2014. (ENG.). 32p. (J). (978-0-7787-0633-5(8)) Crabtree Publishing Co.

Brexel, Bernadette. Grass Is Green. 2015. (Rosen REAL Readers: STEM & STEAM Collection). (ENG.). 8p. pap. 5.46 *(978-1-4994-9656-7(7)*, Rosen Classroom) Rosen Publishing Group, Inc., The.

Giant Grass: Individual Title Six-Packs. (Story Steps Ser.). (gr. k-2). 32.00 *(978-0-7635-9840-2(2))* Rigby Education.

Levy, Janey. Discovering the Tropical Savanna. 2009. (World Habitats Ser.). 32p. (gr. 4-5). 47.90 *(978-1-60854-837-8(6)*, PowerKids Pr.) Rosen Publishing Group, Inc., The.

Mattern, Joanne. How Grass Grows. 2006. (How Plants Grow Ser.). (Illus.). 24p. (gr. k-2). pap. 8.15 *(978-0-8368-6338-3(0))*; lib. bdg. 22.00 *(978-0-8368-6331-4(3))* Stevens, Gareth Publishing LLLP. (Weekly Reader Leveled Readers).

EFG

—How Grass Grows (Como Crece La Hierba) 2006. (How Plants Grow/ Como crecen las plantas Ser.). (ENG & SPA., Illus.). 24p. (gr. k-3). pap. 8.15 *(978-0-8368-6469-4(7),* Weekly Reader Leveled Readers) Stevens, Gareth Publishing LLLP.

—How Grass Grows (Cómo crece la Hierba) 2006. (How Plants Grow/ Como crecen las plantas Ser.). (ENG & SPA., Illus.). 24p. (gr. k-3). lib. bdg. 22.00 *(978-0-8368-6462-5(X),* Weekly Reader Leveled Readers) Stevens, Gareth Publishing LLLP.

Murray, Aaron R. Counting in the Grasslands 1-2-3. 2012. (All about Counting in the Biomes Ser.). (Illus.). 24p. (J). (gr. -1-1). 22.60 *(978-0-7660-4054-0(2))* Enslow Pubs., Inc.

Rajczak, Kristen. Watch Grass Grow. 2011. (Watch Plants Grow! Ser.). 24p. (gr. k-2). 69.20 *(978-1-4339-6156-4(3))* Stevens, Gareth Publishing LLLP.

—Watch Grass Grow / ¡Mira cómo crece el Césped! 2011. (Watch Plants Grow! / ¡Mira cómo crecen las plantas! Ser.). (ENG & SPA., Illus.). 24p. (J). (gr. -1-2). 22.60 *(978-1-4339-4831-2(1))* Stevens, Gareth Publishing LLLP.

Rice, William B. African Grasslands, 1 vol. 2nd rev. ed. 2014. (TIME for KIDS(r) Nonfiction Readers Ser.). (ENG., Illus.). 32p. (J). (gr. 3-3). pap. 25.96 *(978-1-4807-1079-5(2))* Shell Educational Publishing.

Silverman, Buffy. Grasslands, 1 vol. 2012. (Habitat Survival Ser.). (ENG.). 32p. (gr. 2-4). pap. 8.29 *(978-1-4109-4605-8(3))*; lib. bdg. 30.65 *(978-1-4109-4596-9(0))* Heinemann-Raintree. (Raintree Perspectives).

World Book, Inc Staff, contrib. by. Mountains, Deserts, & Grasslands. 2008. 64p. (J). *(978-0-7166-1403-6(0))* World Bk., Inc.

GRASSHOPPERS

see Locusts

GRASSLAND ECOLOGY

Allaby, Michael. Grasslands. Garratt, Richard, illus. 2006. (Biomes of the Earth Ser.). 288p. (gr. 6-12). 39.50 *(978-0-8160-5323-0(5))* Facts On File, Inc.

Allgor, Marie. Endangered Grassland Animals. 2012. (Save Earth's Animals! Ser.). (ENG., Illus.). 24p. (J). (gr. k-5). pap. 8.25 *(978-1-4488-7498-9(X))*; lib. bdg. 22.60 *(978-1-4488-7425-5(4))* Rosen Publishing Group, Inc., The. (PowerKids Pr.).

Anderson, Sheila. Plains. 2008. (First Step Nonfiction - Landforms Ser.). (Illus.). 23p. (J). (gr. -1-3). lib. bdg. 18.60 *(978-0-8225-8593-0(6),* Lerner Pubns.) Lerner Publishing Group.

Arnold, Quinn M. Grasslands. 2016. (Illus.). 24p. (J). *(978-1-60818-796-6(9),* Creative Education) Creative Co., The.

Boothroyd, Jennifer. Let's Visit the Grassland. 2016. (Lightning Bolt Books (tm) — Biome Explorers Ser.). (ENG., Illus.). 32p. (J). (gr. 1-3). 26.65 *(978-1-5124-1192-8(2))* Lerner Publishing Group.

Bow, James. Grasslands Inside Out. 2014. (ENG.). 32p. (J). *(978-0-7787-0633-5(8))* Crabtree Publishing Co.

Butterfield, Moira. Who Eats Who in Grasslands? 2006. (Food Chains in Action Ser.). (Illus.). 32p. (J). lib. bdg. 28.50 *(978-1-58340-964-0(5))* Black Rabbit Bks.

Cefrey, Holly. Grasslands. 2003. (Biomes Ser.). (Illus.). 24p. (J). lib. bdg. 22.60 *(978-0-8239-6457-4(4),* PowerKids Pr.) Rosen Publishing Group, Inc., The.

Dunphy, Madeleine. Here Is the African Savanna. Leonard, Tom, illus. 2006. (Web of Life Ser.). (ENG.). 32p. (J). (gr. -1-3). 16.95 *(978-0-9773795-3-8(1))*; pap. 9.95 *(978-0-9773795-2-1(3))* Web of Life Children's Bks.

Endres, Hollie. Prairies. 2007. (Learning about the Earth Ser.). (ENG., Illus.). 24p. (J). (gr. k-3). lib. bdg. 25.95 *(978-1-60014-114-0(5))* Bellwether Media.

Erlic, Lily. Grasslands. (Illus.). 32p. (J). 2017. ***(978-1-5105-0872-9(4))*** 2016. *(978-1-5105-0870-5(8))* SmartBook Media, Inc.

—Grasslands. (J). 2012. 13.95 *(978-1-61913-235-1(4))* 2012. 28.55 *(978-1-61913-072-2(6))* 2005. (Illus.). 32p. (gr. 4-6). lib. bdg. 26.00 *(978-1-59036-346-1(9))* Weigl Pubs., Inc.

Eszterhas, Suzi. Eye on the Wild: Lion. 2012. (Eye on the Wild Ser.: 3). (Illus.). 32p. (J). *(978-1-84780-310-8(5),* Frances Lincoln) Quarto Publishing Group UK.

Finton, Nancy. Ecosystems. 2007. (Nonfiction Reading & Writing Workshops Ser.). (ENG., Illus.). 32p. (J). pap. 17.95 *(978-0-7922-4578-0(4))* CENGAGE Learning.

Fleisher, Paul. Grassland Food Webs. 2008. pap. 52.95 *(978-0-8225-9350-8(5))* 2007. (ENG., Illus.). 48p. (gr. 2-5). lib. bdg. 26.60 *(978-0-8225-6730-1(X),* Lerner Pubns.) Lerner Publishing Group.

—Grassland Food Webs in Action. 2013. (Searchlight Books What Is a Food Web Ser.). (ENG., Illus.). 40p. (gr. 3-5). pap. 8.95 *(978-1-4677-1554-6(9))*; lib. bdg. 27.93 *(978-1-4677-1293-4(0),* Lerner Pubns.) Lerner Publishing Group.

Freedman, Jeri. Grasslands: Sweeping Savannahs. 2009. (Biomes of the World Ser.). (YA). (gr. 5-9). lib. bdg. 29.25 *(978-1-4358-5003-3(3))* Rosen Publishing Group, Inc., The.

—Grasslands: Sweeping Savannas. 2009. (Biomes of the World Ser.). 48p. (gr. 5-8). (ENG., Illus.). (J). pap. 11.75 *(978-1-4358-5429-1(2))*; 53.00 *(978-1-61511-605-8(2),* Rosen Reference) Rosen Publishing Group, Inc., The.

Gaarder-Juntti, Oona. What Lives in the Prairie?, 1 vol. 2008. (Animal Habitats Ser.). (ENG., Illus.). 24p. (J). (gr. k-3). 25.65 *(978-1-60453-176-3(2))* ABDO Publishing Co.

Gagne, Tammy. Grassland Ecosystems. 2018. (ENG.). 32p. (gr. 3-6). ***(978-1-63235-457-0(8),*** 12-Story Library) Pr. Room Editions LLC.

Gardner, Robert. Grasslands Experiments: 11 Science Experiments in One Hour or Less. 2014. (Last Minute Science Projects with Biomes Ser.). (Illus.). 48p. (gr. 5-12). (J). 25.27 *(978-0-7660-5927-6(8))*; (YA). pap. 8.95 *(978-0-7660-5928-3(6),* Enslow Elementary) Enslow Pubs., Inc.

Gilkerson, Patricia. My Adventure in a Meadow. 2006. 44p. (J). 8.99 (978-1-59092-274-3(3)) Blue Forge Pr.

Gray, Leon. Grasslands. 2015. (Amazing Biomes Ser.). (Illus.). 32p. (gr. 3-6). 31.35 *(978-1-78121-242-4(2))* Brown Bear Bks.

Hoare, Ben. Temperate Grasslands, 1 vol. 2nd ed. 2010. (Biomes Atlases Ser.). (ENG.). 64p. (gr. 6-9). 34.65 *(978-1-4329-4181-9(X))* Heinemann-Raintree.

Hollar, Sherman. Investigating Earth's Desert, Grassland, & Rainforest Biomes. 2011. (J). lib. bdg. 31.70 *(978-1-61530-502-5(5))* Rosen Publishing Group, Inc., The.

Johansson, Philip. The Grasslands: Discover This Wide Open Biome. 2015. (Discover the World's Biomes Ser.). 48p. (J). (gr. 3-4). 25.27 *(978-0-7660-6405-8(0))*; pap. 8.95 *(978-0-7660-6406-5(9))* Enslow Pubs., Inc. (Enslow Elementary).

—The Wide Open Grasslands: A Web of Life. 2004. (World of Biomes Ser.). (Illus.). 48p. (J). lib. bdg. 25.27 *(978-0-7660-2201-0(3))* Enslow Pubs., Inc.

Kalman, Bobbie. Baby Animals in Grassland Habitats. 2011. (Habitats of Baby Animals Ser.). (ENG.). 24p. (J). (gr. k-3). *(978-0-7787-7727-4(8))*; pap. *(978-0-7787-7740-3(5))* Crabtree Publishing Co.

Kalman, Bobbie & Dyer, Hadley. Savanna Food Chains. 2006. (Food Chains Ser.). (ENG., Illus.). 32p. (J). (gr. -1-3). pap. *(978-0-7787-1998-4(7))*; lib. bdg. *(978-0-7787-1952-6(9))* Crabtree Publishing Co.

Kalman, Bobbie & Sjonger, Rebecca. A Savanna Habitat. 2006. (Introducing Habitats Ser.). (ENG., Illus.). 32p. (J). (gr. 3-7). pap. *(978-0-7787-2980-8(X))* Crabtree Publishing Co.

Kavanagh, James. My First Grasslands Nature. Leung, Raymond, illus. 2011. (Nature Activity Book Ser.). (ENG.). 32p. (J). (gr. 2-4). act. bk. ed. 6.95 *(978-1-58355-589-7(7))* Western National Parks Assn.

King, Zelda. Examining Meadow Habitats. 2009. (Graphic Organizers: Habitats Ser.). (J). lib. bdg. 22.60 *(978-1-4358-2722-6(8),* PowerKids Pr.) Rosen Publishing Group, Inc., The.

LaPlante, Walter. There Are Grasslands in My Backyard! 2016. (Backyard Biomes Ser.). 00024p. (J). pap. 8.15 *(978-1-4824-5551-9(X))* Stevens, Gareth Publishing LLLP.

Levy, Janey. Discovering the Tropical Savanna. 2007. (World Habitats Ser.). (Illus.). 32p. (YA). (gr. 3-6). lib. bdg. 25.25 *(978-1-4042-3783-4(6))* Rosen Publishing Group, Inc., The.

MacAulay, Kelley & Kalman, Bobbie. A Grassland Habitat. 2006. (Introducing Habitats Ser.). (ENG., Illus.). 32p. (J). (gr. -1-3). pap. *(978-0-7787-2987-7(7))*; lib. bdg. *(978-0-7787-2959-4(1))* Crabtree Publishing Co.

—Un Habitat de Pastizal. 2007. (Introduction a Los Habitats Ser.). (SPA., Illus.). 32p. (J). (gr. 3-7). lib. bdg. *(978-0-7787-8334-3(0))*; (gr. k-3). pap. *(978-0-7787-8358-9(8))* Crabtree Publishing Co.

Mataya, Marybeth. Grassland Food Chains, 1 vol. Adams, Hazel, illus. 2010. (Fascinating Food Chains Ser.). (ENG.). 32p. 28.50 *(978-1-60270-795-5(2),* Looking Glass Library-Nonfiction) Magic Wagon.

McKissack, Fredrick L. & McKissack, Lisa Beringer. Counting in the Grasslands. 2008. (Counting in the Biomes Ser.). (Illus.). 32p. (J). (gr. 1-3). lib. bdg. 23.94 *(978-0-7660-2991-0(3),* Enslow Elementary) Enslow Pubs., Inc.

McNeil, Niki, et al. Grassland Habitats. 2007. (In the Hands of a Child: Custom Designed Project Pack Ser.). (Illus.). 108p. spiral bd. 24.50 *(978-1-60308-093-4(7))* In the Hands of a Child.

Morgan, Ben. Tropical Grasslands, 1 vol. 2nd ed. 2010. (Biomes Atlases Ser.). (ENG.). 64p. (gr. 6-9). 34.65 *(978-1-4329-4182-6(8))* Heinemann-Raintree.

Morrison, Cathy, illus. The Prairie That Nature Built, 1 vol. 2014. (ENG.). 32p. (J). (gr. k-4). pap. 8.95 *(978-1-58469-492-2(0))* Dawn Pubns.

Pascoe, Elaine. The Ecosystem of a Grassy Field. (Library of Small Ecosystems Ser.). 24p. 2009. (gr. 3-4). 47.90 *(978-1-60853-853-9(2))* 2003. (Illus.). (J). lib. bdg. 25.25 *(978-0-8239-6305-8(5))* Rosen Publishing Group, Inc., The. (PowerKids Pr.).

—The Ecosystem of a Milkweed Patch. 2003. (Library of Small Ecosystems Ser.). (Illus.). 24p. (J). lib. bdg. 25.25 *(978-0-8239-6309-6(8))* Rosen Publishing Group, Inc., The.

Pattison, Darcy. Prairie Storms, 1 vol. Rietz, Kathleen, illus. 2011. (ENG.). 32p. (J). (gr. -1-4). 16.95 *(978-1-60718-129-3(0))*; pap. 8.95 *(978-1-60718-139-2(8))* Arbordale Publishing.

Penny, Malcolm. Grasslands. (Illus.). 64p. (YA). (gr. 4-18). lib. bdg. 29.95 *(978-1-59389-127-5(X))* Chrysalis Education.

Pyers, Greg. Biodiversity of Grasslands. 2011. (Biodiversity 2 Ser.). 32p. (gr. 4). 28.50 *(978-1-60870-529-0(3))* Marshall Cavendish Corp.

Rice, William B. African Grasslands, 1 vol. 2nd rev. ed. 2012. (Nonfiction Readers Ser.). (ENG.). 32p. (J). (gr. 3-3). pap. 8.99 *(978-1-4333-3670-6(7))* Teacher Created Materials, Inc.

Riggs, Kate. Food for Life: Prairies. 2015. (Food for Life Ser.). (ENG.). 24p. (J). (gr. 1-3). pap. 9.99 *(978-1-62832-104-3(0),* Creative Paperbacks) Creative Co., The.

Roth, Susan L. & Trumbore, Cindy. Prairie Dog Song. Roth, Susan L., illus. 2016. (ENG., Illus.). 40p. (J). (gr. 1-7). 18.95 *(978-1-62014-245-5(7))* Lee & Low Bks., Inc.

Roumanis, Alexis. Grasslands. 2014. (Illus.). 24p. (J). *(978-1-4896-3006-3(6))* Weigl Pubs., Inc.

Royston, Angela. Grassland Food Chains, 1 vol. 2014. (Food Chains & Webs Ser.). (ENG., Illus.). 32p. (gr. 1-3). 27.32 *(978-1-4846-0522-6(5),* Heinemann First Library) Heinemann-Raintree.

Sill, Cathryn P. About Habitats-Grasslands, 1 vol. Sill, John, illus. 2011. (About Habitats Ser.). (ENG.). 48p. (J). (gr. -1-3). 16.95 *(978-1-56145-559-1(8))* Peachtree Pubs.

Silverman, Buffy. Grassland Food Chains, 1 vol. 2010. (Protecting Food Chains Ser.). (ENG.). 48p. (gr. 3-6). 33.32 *(978-1-4329-3857-4(6))*; pap. 9.95 *(978-1-4329-3864-2(9))* Heinemann-Raintree. (Heinemann InfoSearch).

Slade, Suzanne. What If There Were No Bees? A Book about the Grassland Ecosystem, 1 vol. Schwartz, Carol, illus. 2010. (Food Chain Reactions Ser.). (ENG.). 24p. (gr. 2-4). pap. 9.95 *(978-1-4048-6394-1(X))* Picture Window Bks.

Stone, Lynn M. Grasslands. 2003. (Rourke Discovery Library). (Illus.). 24p. (J). 20.64 *(978-1-58952-685-3(6))* Rourke *Educational* Media.

Warhol, Tom. Chaparral & Scrub. 2006. (Earth's Biomes Ser.). (Illus.). 80p. (gr. 6-7). lib. bdg. 34.21 *(978-0-7614-2195-5(5),* Benchmark Bks.) Marshall Cavendish Corp.

—Grassland. 2006. (Earth's Biomes Ser.). (Illus.). 80p. (J). (gr. 3-7). lib. bdg. 32.79 *(978-0-7614-2196-2(3),* Benchmark Bks.) Marshall Cavendish Corp.

Waxman, Laura Hamilton. Life in a Grassland. 2016. (Biomes Alive! Ser.). (ENG., Illus.). 24p. (J). (gr. k-3). lib. bdg. 25.95 *(978-1-62617-318-7(4),* Blastoff! Readers) Bellwether Media.

Weldon-Owe. Grassland Safari. 2003. (Rigby InfoQuest Ser.). (ENG.). 24p. (gr. 4-4). pap. 9.50 *(978-0-7578-5709-6(4))* Rigby Education.

World Book, Inc Staff, contrib. by. Grasslands. 2012. (J). *(978-0-7166-0446-4(9))* World Bk., Inc.

GRAVES

see Cemeteries; Funeral Rites and Ceremonies; Mounds and Mound Builders

GRAVEYARDS

see Cemeteries

GRAVITATION

Biskup, Agnieszka. The Gripping Truth about Forces & Motion. Lum, Bernice, illus. 2012. (LOL Physical Science Ser.). (ENG.). 32p. (gr. 3-4). pap. 47.70 *(978-1-4296-9299-1(5),* Fact Finders) Capstone Press of Coughlan Cos.

Blobaum, Cindy. Explore Gravity! With 25 Great Projects. Stone, Bryan, illus. 2013. (Explore Your World Ser.). (ENG.). 96p. (J). (gr. k-4). pap. 13.95 *(978-1-61930-207-5(1))* Open City Bks.

Boothroyd, Jennifer. What Holds Us to Earth? A Look at Gravity. 2010. (Lightning Bolt Books (tm) — Exploring Physical Science Ser.). (ENG.). 32p. (gr. k-2). pap. 7.95 *(978-0-7613-6058-2(1))*; lib. bdg. 26.60 *(978-0-7613-5430-7(1))* Lerner Publishing Group.

—What Holds Us to the Earth? 2010. pap. 45.32 *(978-0-7613-6934-9(1))* Lerner Publishing Group.

Branley, Franklyn M. Gravity Is a Mystery. 2nd rev. ed. Date not set. 40p. (J). (gr. k-4). lib. bdg. 16.89 *(978-0-06-028533-3(8))* HarperCollins Pubs.

—Gravity Is a Mystery. Miller, Edward, illus. 2007. (Let's-Read-and-Find-Out Science Ser.). 33p. (gr. k-4). 16.00 *(978-0-7569-8103-7(4))* Perfection Learning Corp.

—Gravity Is a Mystery. Miller, Edward, illus. 2nd rev. ed. 2007. (Let's-Read-And-Find-Out Science 2 Ser.). (ENG.). 40p. (J). (gr. k-4). pap. 5.99 *(978-0-06-445201-4(8))* HarperCollins Pubs.

Branley, Franklyn Mansfield. Gravity Is a Mystery. Miller, Edward, illus. 2nd rev. ed. 2007. (Let's-Read-and-Find-Out Science Ser.). (ENG.). 40p. (J). (gr. k-4). 15.99 *(978-0-06-028532-6(X))* HarperCollins Pubs.

Castle, Patricia. Gravity. 2009. (Real Life Readers Ser.). 16p. (gr. 2-3). pap. 7.05 *(978-1-4358-0111-0(3),* Rosen Classroom) Rosen Publishing Group, Inc., The.

Chin, Jason. Gravity. Chin, Jason, illus. 2014. (ENG., Illus.). 32p. (J). (gr. k-3). 16.99 *(978-1-59643-717-3(0),* 9781596437173) Roaring Brook Pr.

Claybourne, Anna. Gut-Wrenching Gravity & Other Fatal Forces. 2013. (ENG., Illus.). 32p. (J). *(978-0-7787-0950-3(7))*; pap. *(978-0-7787-0957-2(4))* Crabtree Publishing Co.

Cobb, Vicki. I Fall Down. Gorton, Julia, illus. 2004. (Science Play Ser.). (ENG.). 40p. (J). (gr. -1-3). 17.99 *(978-0-688-17842-0(1))* HarperCollins Pubs.

Conrad, David. La Gravedad a Nuestro Alrededor. 2011. (Ciencia Física/Physical Science Ser.).Tr. of Gravity All Around. (MUL & SPA.). 24p. (gr. k-1). lib. bdg. 26.65 *(978-1-4296-6906-1(3))* Capstone Press of Coughlan Cos.

Czarnecki, Kevin R. Gravity. 2016. (Great Discoveries in Science Ser.). 128p. (J). (gr. 9-9). 45.64 *(978-1-5026-1957-0(1))* Cavendish Square Publishing.

Figorito, Marcus. Friction & Gravity: Snowboarding Science. 2009. (Real Life Readers Ser.). (ENG., Illus.). 32p. (J). (gr. 5-6). pap. 10.00 *(978-1-4358-0185-1(7))*; 32p. (gr. 5-5). 47.90 *(978-1-60853-053-3(1))*; (J). (gr. 4-6). lib. bdg. 25.25 *(978-1-4358-2995-4(6))* Rosen Publishing Group, Inc., The. (PowerKids Pr.).

Frisch-Schmoll, Joy. Gravity. (J). 2015. pap. *(978-1-62832-261-3(6),* Creative Paperbacks) 2008. (Illus.). 24p. (gr. -1). lib. bdg. 34.25 *(978-1-58341-576-4(9),* Creative Education) Creative Co., The.

Geiger, Beth & National Geographic Learning (Firm) Staff. Earth's Changing Land. 2007. (Avenues Ser.). (ENG., Illus.). 36p. (J). pap. 18.95 *(978-0-7922-5427-0(9))* CENGAGE Learning.

Gravity. 2010. (Science Foundations Ser.). (Illus.). 144p. (gr. 6-12). 35.00 *(978-1-60413-296-0(5),* Chelsea Hse.) Facts On File, Inc.

Hansen, Amy S. How Do We Stay on Earth? A Gravity Mystery, 1 vol. Scott, Korey, illus. 2011. (First Graphics: Science Mysteries Ser.). (ENG.). 24p. (gr. 1-2). pap. 6.29 *(978-1-4296-7174-3(2))*; pap. 35.70 *(978-1-4296-7178-1(5))* Capstone Press of Coughlan Cos.

Hantula, Richard. Electricity & Forces. 2006. (Real World Science Ser.). (Illus.). 32p. (gr. 2-6). lib. bdg. 26.00 *(978-0-8368-6305-5(4),* Gareth Stevens Learning Library) Stevens, Gareth Publishing LLLP.

Herweck, Don. Gravity, 1 vol. 2015. (Science Readers: Content & Literacy Ser.). (ENG., Illus.). 32p. (gr. 3-3). pap. 8.99 *(978-1-4807-4644-2(4))* Teacher Created Materials, Inc.

Higgins, Nadia. Marvelous Motion, 1 vol. Ricci, Andres Martinez, illus. 2008. (Science Rocks Ser.). (ENG.). 32p. (gr. -1-4). 28.50 *(978-1-60270-278-3(0),* 1287326, Looking Glass Library- Nonfiction) Magic Wagon.

—Marvelous Motion CD+Book. Martinez Ricci, Andres, illus. 2010. (Science Rocks! Set 2 CD+Book Ser.). 32p. lib. bdg. 54.14 incl. cd-rom *(978-1-60270-993-5(9))* ABDO Publishing Co.

—Marvelous Motion Site CD+Book. Martinez Ricci, Andres, illus. 2010. (Science Rocks! Set 2 Site CD+Book Ser.). 32p. lib. bdg. 84.14 incl. cd-rom *(978-1-61641-010-0(8))* ABDO Publishing Co.

Hiton, Lisa. Gravity, Orbiting Objects, & Planetary Motion. 2016. (Space Systems Ser.). 112p. (J). 42.79 *(978-1-5026-2287-7(4))* Cavendish Square Publishing.

Holl, Kristi. Discovering the Nature of Gravity, 1 vol. 2015. (ENG.). 112p. (YA). 35.60 (978-1-4777-8057-2(2), Rosen Young Adult) Rosen Publishing Group, Inc., The.

Honders, Christine. What Is Gravity? 2014. (Let's Find Out! Ser.). 32p. (J). (gr. 3-6). 23.45 *(978-1-62275-512-7(X))* Windmill Bks.

Hopwood, James. Cool Gravity Activities: Fun Science Projects about Balance, 1 vol. 2008. (Cool Science Ser.). (ENG.). 32p. (YA). (gr. 2-5). 28.50 *(978-1-59928-908-3(3))* ABDO Publishing Co.

Hunter, Nick. Gravity. 2017. (Great Scientific Theories Ser.). (ENG.). 32p. (gr. 4-6). lib. bdg. 30.65 ***(978-1-4109-8729-7(9),*** Raintree Perspectives) Heinemann-Raintree.

Jedicke, Peter. Gravity, & How It Works. 2007. (Scientific American Ser.). (Illus.). 64p. (YA). (gr. 5-9). lib. bdg. 30.00 *(978-0-7910-9051-0(5))* Facts On File, Inc.

Jerome, Kate Boehm. Forces That Move. 2007. (Language, Literacy, & Vocabulary - Reading Expeditions Ser.). (ENG., Illus.). 36p. (J). pap. 18.95 *(978-0-7922-5437-9(6))* CENGAGE Learning.

Kenney, Karen Latchana. Forces & Motion Investigations. 2017. (Key Questions in Physical Science Ser.). (ENG.). 32p. (J). (gr. 3-6). 27.99 ***(978-1-5124-4008-9(6))*** Lerner Publishing Group.

Kenney, Karen Latchana. The Science of Roller Coasters: Understanding Energy, 1 vol. 2016. (Science in Action Ser.). (ENG., Illus.). 32p. (J). (gr. 3-6). 27.07 *(978-1-62403-964-5(2))* ABDO Publishing Co.

Kleiner, Mariela. Meet Einstein. Garofoli, Viviana, illus. 2011. 28p. (J). (gr. -1-1). lib. bdg. *(978-0-615-31579-9(8))* Meet Bks., LLC.

Korb, Rena. Groovy Gravity, 1 vol. Reibeling, Brandon, illus. 2007. (Science Rocks Ser.). (ENG.). 32p. (gr. -1-4). 28.50 *(978-1-60270-039-0(7),* Looking Glass Library- Nonfiction) Magic Wagon.

Kukla, Lauren. Mass at Work, 1 vol. 2016. (ENG., Illus.). 24p. (J). *(978-1-68078-143-4(X))* ABDO Publishing Co.

Kuskowski, Alex. Science Experiments with Gravity & Motion, 1 vol. 2013. (More Super Simple Science Ser.). (ENG.). 32p. (gr. k-4). lib. bdg. 27.07 *(978-1-61783-850-7(0),* Super SandCastle) ABDO Publishing Co.

Lilly, Melinda. Gravity. Thompson, Scott M., illus. 2003. (Read & Do Science Ser.). 24p. (J). 22.79 *(978-1-58952-642-6(2))* Rourke Educational Media.

Lin, Yoming S. Isaac Newton & Gravity. 2012. (Eureka! Ser.). (Illus.). 24p. (YA). (gr. 3-6). lib. bdg. 22.60 *(978-1-4488-5032-7(0))* Rosen Publishing Group, Inc., The.

Lindeen, Carol K. A Look at Gravity, 6 vols., Set E. 2004. (Phonics Readers Books 37-72 Ser.). (ENG.). 16p. (gr. k-1). pap. 35.70 *(978-0-7368-4072-9(9),* Phonics Readers) Capstone Press of Coughlan Cos.

Lyons, Suzanne. Gravity: Set Of 6. 2010. (Early Connections Ser.). (J). pap. 39.00 net. *(978-1-4108-1547-7(1))* Benchmark Education Co.

—Pete Discovers Gravity. 2011. (Early Connections Ser.). (J). *(978-1-61672-668-3(7))* Benchmark Education Co.

Manolis, Kay. Gravity. 2008. (First Science Ser.). (ENG., Illus.). 24p. (J). (gr. 2-5). lib. bdg. 25.95 *(978-1-60014-226-0(5))* Bellwether Media.

Marshall Cavendish Benchmark, prod. Heavy/Light. 2nd rev. ed. 2011. (Bookworms 2nd Edition: Opposites Ser.). 16p. (gr. k-1). 21.36 *(978-1-60870-408-8(4))* Marshall Cavendish Corp.

Merrill, Amy French. Everyday Physical Science Experiments with Gravity. 2009. (Science Surprises Ser.). 24p. (gr. 3-3). 42.50 *(978-1-60853-060-1(4),* PowerKids Pr.) Rosen Publishing Group, Inc., The.

Moore, Rob. Why Do Balls Bounce? 2010. (Solving Science Mysteries Ser.). 24p. (ENG.). (J). pap. 8.25 *(978-1-61531-910-7(7),* PowerKids Pr.); (Illus.). (J). 49.50 *(978-1-61531-911-4(5),* 1307162, PowerKids Pr.); (Illus.). (YA). (gr. 3-6). lib. bdg. 22.60 *(978-1-61531-889-6(5))* Rosen Publishing Group, Inc., The.

Mullins, Matt. Gravity. 2011. (True Bk Ser.). (ENG., Illus.). 48p. (J). pap. 6.95 *(978-0-531-26584-0(6),* Children's Pr.) Scholastic Library Publishing.

Murray, Julie. Gravity, 1 vol. 2006. (First Science - 12 Titles Ser.). (ENG., Illus.). 24p. (gr. k-4). 25.65 *(978-1-59679-824-3(6),* Buddy Bks.) ABDO Publishing Co.

Nelson, Robin. La Gravedad. Translations.com Staff, tr. from ENG. 2007. (Mi Primer Paso Al Mundo Real - Fuerzas y Movimiento (First Step Nonfiction - Forces & Motion) Ser.). (SPA., Illus.). 24p. (gr. k-2). lib. bdg. 23.93 *(978-0-8225-7807-9(7),* Ediciones Lerner) Lerner Publishing Group.

—La Gravedad; Gravity. 2008. pap. 34.95 *(978-0-8225-9897-8(3))* Lerner Publishing Group.

—Gravity. 2004. (First Step Nonfiction Ser.). (Illus.). 24p. (gr. k-2). (J). lib. bdg. 18.60 *(978-0-8225-5133-1(0))*; (ENG., pap. 6.95 *(978-0-8225-5297-0(3))* Lerner Publishing Group.

Newton, Joan. Gravity in Action: Roller Coasters! 2009. (Real Life Readers Ser.). 24p. (gr. 3-4). pap. 8.25 *(978-1-4358-0008-3(7),* Rosen Classroom); (J). (gr. 2-5). lib. bdg. 22.60 *(978-1-4358-2976-3(X),* PowerKids Pr.) Rosen Publishing Group, Inc., The.

Novelli, Luca. Newton & the Antigravity Formula. 2017. (Flashes of Genius Ser.). (ENG., Illus.). 112p. (J). (gr. 2). pap. 9.99 ***(978-1-61373-861-0(7))*** Chicago Review Pr., Inc.

Petersen, Kristen. Understanding Forces of Nature: Gravity, Electricity, & Magnetism. 2015. (J). lib. bdg. *(978-1-62713-437-8(9))*; (ENG.). 48p. (gr. 7-7). 31.36 *(978-1-5026-0142-1(7))* Cavendish Square Publishing.

Prasad, Kamal S. Why Can't I Jump Very High? A Book about Gravity. Simonnet, Aurore, illus. 2004. 32p. (J). lib. bdg. 14.95 *(978-0-9740861-5-6(0))* Science Square Publishing.

Rooney, Anne. You Wouldn't Want to Live Without Gravity! Bergin, Mark, illus. 2016. (You Wouldn't Want to Live Without... Ser.). (ENG.). 32p. (J). lib. bdg. 29.00 *(978-0-531-21487-9(7),* Watts, Franklin) Scholastic Library Publishing.

Scientific American Staff. Beyond Extreme Physics. 2009. (Scientific American Cutting-Edge Science Ser.). 160p. (gr. 9-9). 63.90 *(978-1-60853-073-1(6))* Rosen Publishing Group, Inc., The.

ShackletonCaroline. UP IN THE AIR: OUR FIGHT AGAINST GRAVITY INTERMEDIATE BOOK WITH ONLINE ACCESS. 2014. (ENG.). 28p. (J). pap. 9.50 (978-1-107-63470-1(9)) Cambridge Univ. Pr.

Silverman, Buffy. Gravity! Do You Feel It? 2011. (ENG., Illus.). 24p. (gr. 2-3). pap. 8.95 *(978-1-61741-956-0(7))* Rourke Educational Media.

Sohn, Emily & Brennan, Joseph. Balance & Motion: Toying with Gravity. 2011. (IScience Readers Ser.). 24p. (J). (gr. k-2). lib. bdg. 21.27 *(978-1-59953-405-3(3))* Norwood Hse. Pr.

Sonneborn, Liz. Forces in Nature: Understanding Gravitational, Electrical, & Magnetic Force. 2009. (Planet Earth Ser.). 48p. (gr. 5-8). pap. 8.25 *(978-1-4358-5160-3(9),* Rosen Classroom) Rosen Publishing Group, Inc., The.

Sullivan, Laura L. What Is Gravity? 2016. (Unseen Science Ser.). (ENG., Illus.). 32p. (J). (gr. 3-3). pap. 10.58 *(978-1-5026-0906-9(1))* Cavendish Square Publishing.

Sundance/Newbridge LLC Staff. Gravity. 2007. (Early Science Ser.). (gr. k-3). 18.95 *(978-1-4007-6468-6(8))*; pap. 6.10 *(978-1-4007-6464-8(5))* Sundance/Newbridge Educational Publishing.

Trumbauer, Lisa. What Is Gravity? 2004. (Rookie Read-About Science Ser.). (ENG.). (J). 32p. (gr. 1-2). pap. 4.95 *(978-0-516-25844-7(3),* Children's Pr.); (Illus.). 31p. 20.50 *(978-0-516-23448-9(X),* Watts, Franklin) Scholastic Library Publishing.

Walker, Sally M. & Feldmann, Roseann. Put Pulleys to the Test. 2011. (Searchlight Books (tm) — How Do Simple Machines Work? Ser.). (ENG., Illus.). 40p. (gr. 3-5). lib. bdg. 27.93 *(978-0-7613-5322-5(4))* Lerner Publishing Group.

Weakland, Mark. Whoosh! Wile E. Coyote Experiments with Flight & Gravity. Brown, Alan, illus. 2017. (Wile E. Coyote, Physical Science Genius Ser.). (ENG.). 32p. (gr. 3-5). lib. bdg. 30.65 *(978-1-5157-3732-2(2))* Capstone Press of Coughlan Cos.

Whiting, Jim. Gravity. 2012. (Mysteries of the Universe Ser.). (Illus.). 48p. (J). (gr. 5-12). 23.95 *(978-1-60818-189-6(8),* Creative Education) Creative Co., The.

—Mysteries of the Universe: Gravity. 2013. (Mysteries of the Universe Ser.). (ENG., Illus.). 48p. (J). (gr. 4-7). pap. 12.00 *(978-0-89812-914-4(1),* Creative Paperbacks) Creative Co., The.

Woodford, Chris. Gravity: Investigating the Force, Mass, & Attraction of Physical Bodies. 2012. (Scientific Pathways Ser.). (ENG., Illus.). 48p. (J). (gr. 5-8). lib. bdg. 27.95 *(978-1-4488-7201-5(4),* Rosen Reference) Rosen Publishing Group, Inc., The.

World Book, Inc Staff, contrib. by. Gravity. 2011. (J). *(978-0-7166-1424-1(3))* World Bk., Inc.

GRAVITATION—FICTION

Beauregard, Lynda. The Missing Cuckoo Clock: A Mystery about Gravity. Helmer, Der-Shing, illus. 2013. (Summer Camp Science Mysteries Ser.: 5). (ENG.). 48p. (gr. 3-6). pap. 6.95 *(978-1-4677-0733-6(3),* Graphic Universe™) Lerner Publishing Group.

Disney Book Group Staff, et al. Gravity Falls - Dipper's & Mabel's Guide to the Unknown & Nonstop Fun! Ramirez, Stephanie, illus. 2014. (Guide to Life Ser.). (ENG.). 160p. (J). (gr. 3-7). 12.99 *(978-1-4847-1080-7(0))* Disney Pr.

Lyons, Suzanne. Pete Discovers Gravity: Set Of 6. 2011. (Early Connections Ser.). (J). pap. 39.00 net. *(978-1-4108-1559-0(5))* Benchmark Education Co.

GRAVITY

see Gravitation

GREAT BRITAIN

Atkinson, Tim. Discover the United Kingdom. 2012. (Discover Countries Ser.). (Illus.). 32p. (YA). (gr. 4-7). lib. bdg. 26.50 *(978-1-4488-5265-9(X))* Rosen Publishing Group, Inc., The.

Blomquist, Christopher. A Primary Source Guide to the United Kingdom. 2009. (Countries of the World). 24p. (gr. 2-3). 42.50 *(978-1-61512-047-5(5),* PowerKids Pr.) Rosen Publishing Group, Inc., The.

—A Prmiary Source Guide to the United Kingdom. 2005. (Countries of the World). (Illus.). 24p. (J). (gr. k-5). lib. bdg. 22.60 *(978-1-4042-2760-6(1),* PowerKids Pr.) Rosen Publishing Group, Inc., The.

Burgan, Michael. United Kingdom in Our World. 2011. (Countries in Our World Ser.). 32p. (YA). (gr. 4-7). lib. bdg. 28.50 *(978-1-59920-435-2(5))* Black Rabbit Bks.

Campbell, Kumari. United Kingdom in Pictures. 2nd rev. expurg. ed. 2004. (Visual Geography Series, Second Ser.). (ENG., Illus.). 80p. (gr. 5-12). 31.93 *(978-0-8225-1995-9(X))* Lerner Publishing Group.

Collins Maps Staff. United Kingdom: Wall Map. 2014. (ENG.). 448p. (J). (gr. -1). pap. 12.99 ***(978-0-00-753612-2(7))*** HarperCollins Pubs. Ltd. GBR. Dist: Independent Pubs. Group.

Collinson, Clare. British Trees & Flowers. 2017. (Nature in Your Neighbourhood Ser.). (ENG., Illus.). 32p. (J). (gr. 2-4). 17.99 *(978-1-4451-3641-7(4),* Franklin Watts) Hachette Children's Group GBR. Dist: Hachette Bk. Group.

Copeland, Tim. Investigating Romans. (Illus.). 32p. (J). pap. 8.95 *(978-0-7078-0330-2(6))* National Trust, Aylesbury GBR. Dist: Trafalgar Square Publishing.

Donaldson, Madeline. United Kingdom. 2010. pap. 51.02 *(978-0-7613-6977-6(5))* Lerner Publishing Group.

Everett-Camplin, Helen. Two Worlds Level 4 Intermediate. 2010. (ENG.). 96p. pap. 16.50 *(978-84-8323-566-9(8))* Cambridge Univ. Pr.

Farm Holiday England, Scotland, Wales, Ireland. 2004. 16.95 *(978-1-58843-361-9(7))* Hunter Publishing, Inc.

Fiscus, James W. The Suez Crisis. 2004. (War & Conflict in the Middle East Ser.). (Illus.). 64p. (gr. 7-12). lib. bdg. 31.95 *(978-0-8239-4550-4(2))* Rosen Publishing Group, Inc., The.

Gray, Leon. Horrible Jobs of the Industrial Revolution, Vol. 1. 2014. (History's Most Horrible Jobs Ser.). (ENG.). 48p. (J). (gr. 5-6). 31.95 *(978-1-4824-0343-5(9))* Stevens, Gareth Publishing LLLP.

HarperCollins UK Staff & Collins Easy Learning Staff. Grammar & Punctuation Practice. 2012. (Collins Easy Learning Age 7-11 Ser.). (ENG.). 96p. (J). pap. 6.99 *(978-0-00-746735-8(4))* HarperCollins Pubs. Ltd. GBR. Dist: Independent Pubs. Group.

Hawthorne, Kate & Sheppard, Daniela. The Young Person's Guide to the Internet: The Essential Website Reference Book for Young People, Parents & Teachers. 2nd ed. 2005. (ENG., Illus.). 224p. (C). (gr. 3-7). per. 38.95 *(978-0-415-34505-7(7))* Routledge.

Lynch, Annabelle. Northern Ireland. 2016. (Let's Visit Ser.). (ENG., Illus.). 24p. (J). (gr. 1-3). pap. 10.99 *(978-1-4451-3709-4(7),* Franklin Watts) Hachette Children's Group GBR. Dist: Hachette Bk. Group.

Marsh, Carole. United Kingdom: The Country of Ships, Sealing Wax, Cabbages & Kings! 2009. (It's Your World Ser.). 48p. (J). (gr. 2-9). pap. 7.99 *(978-0-635-06811-8(7))* Gallopade International.

Munson, Victoria. British Insects. 2016. (Nature Detective Ser.). (ENG., Illus.). 64p. (J). (gr. 2-4). pap. 9.99 *(978-0-7502-9321-1(7),* Wayland) Hachette Children's Group GBR. Dist: Hachette Bk. Group.

—British Seashore. 2016. (Nature Detective Ser.). (ENG., Illus.). 64p. (J). (gr. 2-4). pap. 9.99 *(978-0-7502-9323-5(3),* Wayland) Hachette Children's Group GBR. Dist: Hachette Bk. Group.

Oliver, Clare. Great Britain. 2003. (Country Files Ser.). (Illus.). 32p. (J). lib. bdg. 24.25 *(978-1-58340-204-7(7))* Black Rabbit Bks.

—Great Britain. 2009. (J). 28.50 *(978-1-59771-116-6(0))* Sea-To-Sea Pubns.

Orr, Tamra. Meet Our New Student from Great Britain. 2008. (Meet Our New Student Ser.). (Illus.). 48p. (J). (gr. 4-7). lib. bdg. 29.95 *(978-1-58415-648-2(1))* Mitchell Lane Pubs., Inc.

Popper, Garry. James & Jemma in Great Britain. Johnson, Andi, illus. 2004. 36p. (gr. -1-7). 4.00 *(978-1-84161-054-2(2))* Ravette Publishing, Ltd. GBR. Dist: Parkwest Pubns., Inc.

Powell, Jillian. Looking at Great Britain. 2007. (Looking at Countries Ser.). 32p. (gr. 1-5). pap. 10.50 *(978-0-8368-8177-6(X))*; (Illus.). lib. bdg. 26.00 *(978-0-8368-8170-7(2))* Stevens, Gareth Publishing LLLP. (Gareth Stevens Learning Library).

Scoffham, Stephen & Collins Maps Staff. UK in Maps. 2014. (Collins Primary Atlases Ser.). (ENG., Illus.). 24p. (J). (gr. 5-10). pap. 12.99 *(978-0-00-752476-1(5))* HarperCollins Pubs. Ltd. GBR. Dist: Independent Pubs. Group.

Superstars! Superstars! One Direction. 2012. (ENG.). 128p. (J). (gr. 3-17). pap. 9.99 *(978-1-60320-970-0(0))* Time Inc. Bks.

Tecco, Betsy Dru. How to Draw the United Kingdom's Sights & Symbols. 2009. (Kid's Guide to Drawing the Countries of the World Ser.). 48p. (gr. 4-4). 53.00 *(978-1-61511-129-9(8),* PowerKids Pr.) Rosen Publishing Group, Inc., The.

Tieck, Sarah. United Kingdom, 1 vol. 2013. (Explore the Countries Ser.). (ENG.). 40p. (J). (gr. 2-5). lib. bdg. 29.93 *(978-1-61783-819-4(5),* Big Buddy Bks.) ABDO Publishing Co.

The United Kingdom: Northern Ireland, Scotland, & Wales. 2013. (Britannica Guide to Countries of the European Union Ser.). 208p. (YA). (gr. 9-12). 106.00 *(978-1-62275-057-3(8))* Rosen Publishing Group, Inc., The.

Wallenfeldt, Jeff. The United Kingdom: Northern Ireland, Scotland, & Wales. Wallenfeldt, Jeff, ed. 2013. 208p. (YA). (gr. 9-12). 53.00 *(978-1-62275-055-9(1))* Rosen Publishing Group, Inc., The.

Watts, Duncan. US/UK Government & Politics, Vol. 2003. (Understandings MUP Ser.). (ENG.). 352p. pap., instr.'s gde. ed. 23.95 *(978-0-7190-6721-1(9))* Manchester Univ. Pr. GBR. Dist: Oxford Univ. Pr., Inc.

Woolf, Alex. Focus on the United Kingdom. 2006. (World in Focus (Milwaukee, Wis.) Ser.). (Illus.). 64p. (gr. 5-12). pap. 14.05 *(978-0-8368-6731-2(9))*; lib. bdg. 34.00 *(978-0-8368-6724-4(6))* Stevens, Gareth Publishing LLLP. (Gareth Stevens Secondary Library).

GREAT BRITAIN—ANTIQUITIES

Capek, Michael. Stonehenge, 1 vol. 2014. (Digging up the Past Ser.). (ENG., Illus.). 112p. (YA). (gr. 6-12). lib. bdg. 35.64 *(978-1-62403-237-0(0),* Essential Library) ABDO Publishing Co.

Crewe-Read, Caroline. Stone Circles. 2006. (ENG., Illus.). 84p. (C). pap. 16.00 *(978-1-85074-928-8(0))* Historic England Publishing GBR. Dist: Casemate Academic.

Green, Jen. The Celts & the Iron Age. 2016. (Discover Through Craft Ser.). (ENG., Illus.). 32p. (J). (gr. 2-4). pap. 12.99 *(978-1-4451-3749-0(6),* Franklin Watts) Hachette Children's Group GBR. Dist: Hachette Bk. Group.

—The Stone Age & Bronze Age. 2016. (Discover Through Craft Ser.). (ENG., Illus.). 32p. (J). (gr. 1-3). pap. 12.99 *(978-1-4451-3746-9(1),* Franklin Watts) Hachette Children's Group GBR. Dist: Hachette Bk. Group.

Henzel, Cynthia Kennedy. Stonehenge, 1 vol. 2011. (Troubled Treasures: World Heritage Sites Ser.). (ENG., Illus.). 32p. (YA). (gr. 3-6). 27.07 *(978-1-61613-567-6(0))* ABDO Publishing Co.

Hunter, Nick. Did King Arthur Really Exist? 2016. (Top Secret! Ser.). (ENG., Illus.). 48p. (gr. 4-6). lib. bdg. 33.32 *(978-1-4109-8160-8(6))* Heinemann-Raintree.

Lace, William W. King Arthur. 2008. (Mysterious & Unknown Ser.). (Illus.). 104p. (YA). (gr. 3-7). lib. bdg. *(978-1-60152-033-3(6))* ReferencePoint Pr., Inc.

McDaniel, Sean. Stonehenge. 2011. (Unexplained Ser.). (ENG., Illus.). 24p. (J). (gr. 3-7). lib. bdg. 25.95 *(978-1-60014-645-9(7),* Torque Bks.) Bellwether Media.

Owings, Lisa. Stonehenge. 2015. (Unexplained Mysteries Ser.). (ENG., Illus.). 24p. (J). (gr. 3-7). lib. bdg. 25.95 *(978-1-62617-204-3(8),* Epic Bks.) Bellwether Media.

Parker-Pearson, Mike & Aronson, Marc. If Stones Could Speak: Unlocking the Secrets of Stonehenge. 2010. (ENG., Illus.). 64p. (J). (gr. 5-8). 17.95 *(978-1-4263-0599-3(0))*; 26.90 *(978-1-4263-0600-6(8))* National Geographic Society. (National Geographic Children's Bks.).

Raum, Elizabeth. Stonehenge. 2015. (Ancient Wonders Ser.). (Illus.). 32p. (J). 28.50 *(978-1-60753-469-3(X))* Amicus Publishing.

Wolfson, Evelyn. Mythology of King Arthur & His Knights. 2014. (Mythology, Myths, & Legends Ser.). (Illus.). 96p. (J). (gr. 6-12). 27.94 *(978-0-7660-6182-8(5))* Enslow Pubs., Inc.

World Book, Inc Staff, contrib. by. The Legend of King Arthur. 2014. (J). *(978-0-7166-2664-0(0))* World Bk., Inc.

GREAT BRITAIN—BIOGRAPHY

Aldridge, Rebecca. Stella Mccartney. 2011. (Famous Fashion Designers Ser.). (Illus.). 112p. (gr. 6-12). 35.00 *(978-1-60413-982-2(X),* Chelsea Hse.) Facts On File, Inc.

Aller, Susan Bivin. Florence Nightingale. Butler, Tad, illus. 2007. (History Maker Biographies Ser.). (ENG.). 48p. (gr. 3-6). lib. bdg. 27.93 *(978-0-8225-7609-9(0),* Lerner Pubns.) Lerner Publishing Group.

Allport, Alan. Gordon Brown. 2009. (Modern World Leaders Ser.). (Illus.). 144p. (YA). (gr. 7-12). 30.00 *(978-1-60413-080-5(6))* Facts On File, Inc.

Anderson, Dale. Leaders of the American Revolution. 2005. (World Almanac Library of the American Revolution Ser.). 48p. (gr. 5-12). pap. 14.05 *(978-0-8368-5940-9(5))*; lib. bdg. 31.00 *(978-0-8368-5931-7(6))* Stevens, Gareth Publishing LLLP. (Gareth Stevens Secondary Library).

Anderson, Jennifer Joline. John Lennon: Legendary Musician & Beatle, 1 vol. 2010. (Lives Cut Short Set 1 Ser.). (ENG.). 112p. (J). (gr. 6-12). lib. bdg. 35.64 *(978-1-60453-790-1(6))* ABDO Publishing Co.

Anderson, Kirsten. Who Is Elton John? Qiu, Joseph J. M.   & Harrison, Nancy, illus. 2016. (Who Was? Ser.). (ENG.). 112p. (J). (gr. 3-7). pap. 5.99 *(978-0-448-48846-2(9),* Grosset & Dunlap) Penguin Young Readers Group.

—Who Is Elton John? 2016. (Who Is... ? Ser.). lib. bdg. 16.00 *(978-0-606-38396-7(4))* Turtleback Bks.

Anderson, Margaret J. Charles Darwin: Genius of a Revolutionary Theory. 2015. (Genius Scientists & Their Genius Ideas Ser.). 96p. (J). (gr. 5-12). 27.94 *(978-0-7660-6545-1(6))*; pap. 10.95 *(978-0-7660-6546-8(4))* Enslow Pubs., Inc.

—Isaac Newton: Greatest Genius of Science. 2015. (Genius Scientists & Their Genius Ideas Ser.). 96p. (J). (gr. 5-12). 27.94 *(978-0-7660-6570-3(7))*; pap. 10.95 *(978-0-7660-6571-0(5))* Enslow Pubs., Inc.

Anderson, Margaret Jean. Isaac Newton: The Greatest Scientist of All Time. 2008. (Great Minds of Science Ser.). (Illus.). 128p. (J). (gr. 3-7). lib. bdg. 33.27 *(978-0-7660-2793-0(7))* Enslow Pubs., Inc.

Anderson, Zachary. John Cabot: Searching for a Westward Passage to Asia. 2015. (Incredible Explorers Ser.). (ENG., Illus.). 64p. (J). (gr. 7-7). 34.21 *(978-1-5026-0173-5(7))* Cavendish Square Publishing.

Anita Roddick. 2010. (Women of Achievement Ser.). (Illus.). 120p. (gr. 6-12). 35.00 *(978-1-60413-688-3(X),* Chelsea Hse.) Facts On File, Inc.

Apps, Roy. Jamie Vardy. 2017. (EDGE: Sporting Heroes Ser.). (ENG., Illus.). 48p. (J). (gr. 2-7). 12.99 ***(978-1-4451-5322-3(X),*** Franklin Watts) Hachette Children's Group GBR. Dist: Hachette Bk. Group.

—Louis Smith. King, Chris, illus. 2017. (EDGE - Dream to Win Ser.). (ENG.). 48p. (J). (gr. 2-4). pap. 9.99 *(978-1-4451-4092-6(6),* Franklin Watts) Hachette Children's Group GBR. Dist: Hachette Bk. Group.

—Nicola Adams. King, Chris, illus. 2017. (EDGE - Dream to Win Ser.). (ENG.). 48p. (J). (gr. 2-4). pap. 9.99 *(978-1-4451-4136-7(1),* Franklin Watts) Hachette Children's Group GBR. Dist: Hachette Bk. Group.

Aretha, David. Amy Winehouse: RandB, Jazz, & Soul Musician, 1 vol. 2012. (Lives Cut Short Set 2 Ser.). (ENG.). 112p. (J). (gr. 6-12). 35.64 *(978-1-61783-483-7(1))* ABDO Publishing Co.

Ashby, Ruth. Young Charles Darwin & the Voyage of the Beagle, 1 vol. Duranceau, Suzanne, illus. 2009. (ENG.). 128p. (J). (gr. 2-5). 12.95 *(978-1-56145-478-5(8),* Peachtree Junior) Peachtree Pubs.

Aykroyd, Clarissa. Savage Satire: The Story of Jonathan Swift. 2006. (World Writers Ser.). (Illus.). 160p. (J). (gr. 3-7). lib. bdg. 27.95 *(978-1-59935-027-1(0))* Reynolds, Morgan Inc.

Azzarelli, Ally. Adele! Singing Sensation. 2013. (Sizzling Celebrities Ser.). 48p. (J). lib. bdg. 25.27 *(978-0-7660-4172-1(7))* Enslow Pubs., Inc.

Baden-Powell, Robert. My Adventures as a Spy. 2014. (ENG., Illus.). 128p. pap. 13.95 *(978-1-4456-3610-8(7))* Amberley Publishing GBR. Dist: Independent Pubs. Group.

Bailey, Ellen. One Dream, One Direction. 2012. (ENG.). 64p. (J). (gr. 3-7). pap. 9.99 *(978-1-4424-7308-9(8),* Aladdin) Simon & Schuster Children's Publishing.

Barnham, Kay. Emmeline Pankhurst. 2017. (History VIPs Ser.). (ENG., Illus.). 32p. (J). (gr. 4-6). 17.99 *(978-0-7502-8850-7(7),* Wayland) Hachette Children's Group GBR. Dist: Hachette Bk. Group.

—Emmeline Pankhurst - Votes for Women! Brilliant Biographies of the Dead Famous. 2017. (History VIPs Ser.). (ENG., Illus.). 32p. (J). (gr. 4-6). pap. 12.99 *(978-0-7502-9940-4(1),* Wayland) Hachette Children's Group GBR. Dist: Hachette Bk. Group.

—Mary Anning. 2017. (History VIPs Ser.). (ENG., Illus.). 32p. (J). (gr. 4-6). pap. 11.99 *(978-0-7502-9914-5(2),* Wayland) Hachette Children's Group GBR. Dist: Hachette Bk. Group.

Baxter, Roberta. Skeptical Chemist: The Story of Robert Boyle. 2006. (Profiles in Science Ser.). (Illus.). 128p. (gr. 6-12). lib. bdg. 27.95 *(978-1-59935-025-7(4))* Reynolds, Morgan Inc.

Beauregarde, Constance & Antal, Lara. Princess Diana: Royal Activist & Fashion Icon. 2016. (Leading Women Ser.). (Illus.). 128p. (J). (gr. 7-7). 39.93 *(978-1-5026-1987-7(3))* Cavendish Square Publishing.

Behnke, Alison. Death of a Dreamer: The Assassination of John Lennon. 2012. (Single Titles Ser.). (ENG.). 96p. (gr. 6-12). lib. bdg. 33.26 *(978-0-8225-9036-1(0),* Twenty-First Century Bks.) Lerner Publishing Group.

Belmonte, Kevin. A Journey Through the Life of William Wilberforce: The Abolitionist Who Changed the Face of a Nation. 2007. (Illus.). 122p. *(978-0-89221-671-0(9))* New Leaf Pub. Group.

Benge, Janet & Benge, Geoff. Christian Heroes - Then & Now - John Wesley: The World, His Parish. 2007. (Christian Heroes Ser.). (ENG.). 192p. (YA). (gr. 3-7). pap. 9.99 *(978-1-57658-382-1(1))* YWAM Publishing.

—Paul Brand: Helping Hands. 2011. (ENG.). (YA). pap. 9.99 *(978-1-57658-536-8(0))* YWAM Publishing.

—William Wilberforce: Take up the Fight. 2015. (ENG.). 201p. (YA). pap. 9.99 *(978-1-62486-057-7(5))* Emerald Bks.

Bertozzi, Nick. Shackleton: Antarctic Odyssey. Bertozzi, Nick, illus. 2014. (ENG., Illus.). 128p. (YA). (gr. 7-12). pap. 16.99 *(978-1-59643-451-6(1),* First Second Bks.) Roaring Brook Pr.

Bingham, Derick. Michael Faraday: Spiritual Dynamo. 2010. (Trailblazers Ser.). (ENG.). 176p. (J). pap. 8.99 *(978-1-84550-156-3(X),* 6da8f6db-c74f-4245-818d-6fca339103d3) Christian Focus Pubns. GBR. Dist: Bookmasters Distribution.

Bingham, Hettie. Adele: The Golden Voice. 2016. (ENG., Illus.). 32p. (J). (gr. 4-6). pap. 11.99 *(978-0-7502-8965-8(1),* Wayland) Hachette Children's Group GBR. Dist: Hachette Bk. Group.

—Banksy: Art Breaks the Rules. 2017. (ENG., Illus.). 48p. (J). (gr. 4-6). 14.99 ***(978-0-7502-9976-3(2),*** Wayland) Hachette Children's Group GBR. Dist: Hachette Bk. Group.

—Brian Cox. 2016. (Real-Life Stories Ser.). (ENG., Illus.). 32p. (J). (gr. 4-6). pap. 11.99 *(978-0-7502-8954-2(6),* Wayland) Hachette Children's Group GBR. Dist: Hachette Bk. Group.

—Gary Barlow. 2016. (Real-Life Stories Ser.). (ENG., Illus.). 32p. (J). (gr. 4-6). pap. 11.99 *(978-0-7502-8955-9(4),* Wayland) Hachette Children's Group GBR. Dist: Hachette Bk. Group.

Bodden, Valerie. One Direction. 2015. (J). *(978-1-60818-497-2(8),* Creative Education) Creative Co., The.

—Programming Pioneer ADA Lovelace. 2016. (STEM Trailblazer Bios Ser.). (ENG.). 32p. (J). (gr. 2-5). 26.65 *(978-1-5124-0784-6(4))* Lerner Publishing Group.

—To the South Pole. 2012. (Great Expeditions Ser.). (ENG.). 48p. (J). (gr. 4-7). pap. 12.00 *(978-0-89812-667-9(3),* Creative Paperbacks) Creative Co., The.

Bortz, Fred. Charles Darwin & the Theory of Evolution by Natural Selection. 2013. (Revolutionary Discoveries of Scientific Pioneers Ser.). (Illus.). 80p. (J). (gr. 7-12). 33.25 *(978-1-4777-1802-5(8))* Rosen Publishing Group, Inc., The.

Bowe, Brian J. Judas Priest: Metal Gods. 2009. (Rebels of Rock Ser.). (Illus.). 112p. (J). (gr. 5-18). pap. 10.95 *(978-0-7660-3621-5(9))* Enslow Pubs., Inc.

Bowen, Richard. Captain James Cook: British Explorer. 2013. (People of Importance Ser.: 21). (Illus.). 32p. (J). (gr. 4-18). 19.95 *(978-1-4222-2843-2(6))* Mason Crest.

Brasch, Nicolas. Ernest Shackleton's Antarctic Expedition. 2013. (Discovery Education: Sensational True Stories Ser.). (ENG., Illus.). 32p. (J). (gr. 3-6). pap. 10.00 *(978-1-4777-0111-9(7))*; lib. bdg. 25.25 *(978-1-4777-0063-1(3))* Rosen Publishing Group, Inc., The. (PowerKids Pr.).

Bridy, Dan & Solomon, Sharon K. Christopher Newport: Jamestown Explorer, 1 vol. 2013. (ENG., Illus.). 32p. (J). (gr. k-3). 16.99 *(978-1-4556-1752-4(0))* Pelican Publishing Co., Inc.

Briscoe, Diana. Jane Goodall: Finding Hope in the Wilds of Africa. 2004. (High Five Reading - Purple Ser.). (ENG., Illus.). 64p. (gr. 3-4). per. 9.00 *(978-0-7368-3851-1(1),* High Five Reading (RBL)) Capstone Press of Coughlan Cos.

Brooks, Philip. King George III: America's Enemy. 2009. (Wicked History Ser.). (ENG., Illus.). 128p. (J). (gr. 6-12). 31.00 *(978-0-531-21803-7(1),* Watts, Franklin) Scholastic Library Publishing.

Brooks, Riley & Hodgin, Molly. One Direction: Straight to the Top! 2012. (ENG., Illus.). 48p. (J). (gr. -1-3). pap. 4.99 *(978-0-545-49988-0(7))* Scholastic, Inc.

Browning, Oscar. True Stories from English History from T. 2006. pap. 33.95 *(978-1-4254-9960-0(0))* Kessinger Publishing, LLC.

Bryant, Jen. The Right Word: Roget & His Thesaurus. Sweet, Melissa, illus. 2014. (ENG.). 42p. (J). 17.50 *(978-0-8028-5385-1(4),* Eerdmans Bks For Young Readers) Eerdmans, William B. Publishing Co.

Buckley, James, Jr. Who Was Ernest Shackleton? Hergenrother, Max, illus. 2013. (Who Was? Ser.). (ENG.). 112p. (J). (gr. 3-7). 5.99 *(978-0-448-47931-6(1),* Grosset & Dunlap) Penguin Young Readers Group.

Burgan, Michael. Who Is Richard Branson? Hammond, Ted, illus. 2015. 105p. (J). *(978-1-4844-6180-8(0),* Grosset & Dunlap) Penguin Young Readers Group.

Burgan, Michael & dePaola, Tomie. Who Is Richard Branson? Hammond, Ted, illus. 2015. (Who Was? Ser.). (ENG.). 112p. (J). (gr. 3-7). 5.99 *(978-0-448-48315-3(7),* Grosset & Dunlap) Penguin Young Readers Group.

Burlingame, Jeff. John Lennon: "Imagine" 2010. (American Rebels Ser.). 160p. (YA). (gr. 7-12). 35.94 *(978-0-7660-3675-8(8))* Enslow Pubs., Inc.

Buster Books Staff. I Love Niall. 2013. (I Love One Direction Ser.). (ENG., Illus.). 96p. (J). (gr. 3-7). pap. 8.99 *(978-1-78055-216-3(5))* O'Mara, Michael Bks., Ltd. GBR. Dist: Independent Pubs. Group.

Carr, Simonetta. John Owen. Abraxas, Matt, illus. 2010. (ENG.). 62p. (J). 18.00 *(978-1-60178-088-1(5))* Reformation Heritage Bks.

Collins Big Cat Staff. Fossil Hunter, Bd. 17. 2017. (ENG., Illus.). 56p. (J). pap. 8.95 ***(978-0-00-820893-6(X))*** HarperCollins Pubs. Ltd. GBR. Dist: Independent Pubs. Group.

Colson, Mary. Charles Darwin & Alfred Russel Wallace. 2014. (Dynamic Duos of Science Ser.). 48p. (YA). (gr. 5-8). pap. 84.30 *(978-1-4824-1280-2(2))* Stevens, Gareth Publishing LLLP.

Connors, Kathleen. The Life of Florence Nightingale, Vol. 1. 2014. (Famous Lives Ser.). (ENG.). 24p. (J). (gr. 1-2). 22.60 *(978-1-4824-0405-0(2))* Stevens, Gareth Publishing LLLP.

Cook, Diane. Charles Darwin: British Naturalist. 2013. (People of Importance Ser.: 21). (Illus.). 32p. (J). (gr. 4-18). 19.95 *(978-1-4222-2844-9(4))* Mason Crest.

Cooke, Tim. Explore with Henry Hudson. 2014. (ENG., Illus.). 32p. (J). *(978-0-7787-1246-6(X))*; pap. *(978-0-7787-1258-9(3))* Crabtree Publishing Co.

Cornell, Kari. Theoretical Physicist Stephen Hawking. 2016. (STEM Trailblazer Bios Ser.). (ENG., Illus.). 32p. (J). (gr. 2-5). 26.65 *(978-1-4677-9528-9(3),* Lerner Pubns.) Lerner Publishing Group.

Corporate Contibutor Staff & Roberts, Steve. King George Iii: England's Struggle to Keep America. 2012. (ENG.). 48p. (J). *(978-0-7787-0800-1(4))* Crabtree Publishing Co.

Dahl, Roald. Boy & Going Solo. Blake, Quentin, illus. 2010. (ENG.). 400p. (J). (gr. 3-7). 10.99 *(978-0-14-241741-6(6),* Puffin Books) Penguin Young Readers Group.

Dakers, Diane. The Beatles: Leading the British Invasion. 2013. (ENG., Illus.). 112p. (J). pap. *(978-0-7787-1045-5(9))* Crabtree Publishing Co.

Dalrymple, Lisa. Explore with James Cook. 2015. (Travel with the Great Explorers Ser.). (ENG., Illus.). 32p. (J). (gr. 3-6). *(978-0-7787-1701-0(1))* Crabtree Publishing Co.

Davis, Rebecca. George Mueller: A Father to the Fatherless. 2004. (Illus.). 135p. (J). pap. 7.49 *(978-1-59166-255-6(9))* BJU Pr.

Doak, Robin S. Jane Goodall: Chimpanzee Protector, 1 vol. 2014. (Women in Conservation Ser.). (ENG., Illus.). 48p. (gr. 3-6). 33.32 *(978-1-4846-0469-4(5))*; pap. 8.99 *(978-1-4846-0474-8(1))* Heinemann-Raintree. (Heinemann InfoSearch).

—Kate Middleton. 2015. (True Book(tm), A— Biographies Ser.). (ENG., Illus.). 48p. (J). lib. bdg. 31.00 *(978-0-531-21596-8(2),* Children's Pr.) Scholastic Library Publishing.

E
F
G

—Kate Middleton: Dutchess of Cambridge. 2015. (True Book(tm) — Biographies Ser.). (ENG., Illus.). 48p. (J). pap. 6.95 *(978-0-531-21758-0(2)*, Children's Pr.) Scholastic Library Publishing.

Doeden, Matt. Adele: Soul Music's Magical Voice. 2013. (USA TODAY Lifeline Biographies Ser.). (ENG., Illus.). 112p. (gr. 6-12). lib. bdg. 34.60 *(978-1-4677-0808-1(9))* Lerner Publishing Group.

—Prince William & Kate: A Royal Romance. 2011. (Gateway Biographies Ser.). pap. 51.02 *(978-0-7613-8357-4(3))*; (ENG.). 48p. (gr. 4-8). pap. 8.95 *(978-0-7613-8030-6(2))* Lerner Publishing Group.

Donohue, Moira Rose. Christopher Newport. 2013. (Illus.). 24p. (J). *(978-1-938813-05-4(7))*; pap. *(978-1-938813-09-2(X))* State Standards Publishing, LLC.

Dougherty, Terri. Daniel Radcliffe. 2009. (People in the News Ser.). (ENG.). 128p. (gr. 7-12). 39.40 *(978-1-4205-0156-8(9))* Cengage Gale.

Dredge, Kath. Living 4 God: Learning from the Lives of William Tyndale, John Newton, David Brainerd, Eric Liddell. 2007. (Illus.). 80p. 7.00 *(978-1-84625-034-7(X))* DayOne Pubns. GBR. Dist: Send The Light Distribution LLC.

Eason, Sarah. Alex Ferguson: A Football Legend! 2017. (Real-Life Stories Ser.). (ENG., Illus.). 32p. (J). (gr. 4-6). pap. 11.99 *(978-0-7502-9475-1(2)*, Wayland) Hachette Children's Group GBR. Dist: Hachette Bk. Group.

Edison, Erin. Florence Nightingale, 1 vol. 2014. (Great Women in History Ser.). (ENG.). 24p. (gr. k-1). lib. bdg. 21.99 *(978-1-4765-4214-0(7)*, Pebble Bks.) Capstone Press of Coughlan Cos.

—Jane Goodall. 2013. (Great Women in History Ser.). (ENG.). 24p. (gr. k-1). pap. 35.70 *(978-1-4765-0145-1(9))*; pap. 6.29 *(978-1-4765-0144-4(0))*; lib. bdg. 21.99 *(978-1-4765-0143-7(2))* Capstone Press of Coughlan Cos. (Pebble Bks.).

Edward, Herman. Pink Floyd. 2008. (Pop Rock Ser.). (Illus.). 64p. (YA). (gr. 3-7). lib. bdg. 22.95 *(978-1-4222-0214-2(3))* Mason Crest.

Edwards, Andrew & Thornton, Fleur. Wilberforce: an Activity Book: 24 Ready to Use Lesson Plans. 2007. (Illus.). 32p. (J). (gr. 3-7). pap. 6.99 *(978-0-89221-672-7(7))* New Leaf Pub. Group.

Edwards, Roberta. Who Is Jane Goodall? Marchesi, Stephen et al, illus. 2012. (Who Was? Ser.). (ENG.). 112p. (J). (gr. 3-7). 5.99 *(978-0-448-46192-2(7)*, Grosset & Dunlap) Penguin Young Readers Group.

Feinstein, Stephen. Captain Cook: Great Explorer of the Pacific. 2010. (Great Explorers of the World Ser.). (Illus.). 112p. (J). (gr. 7-12). 33.27 *(978-1-59845-102-3(2))* Enslow Pubs., Inc.

Fenton, Corinne. My Friend Tertius. Swan, Owen, illus. 2017. (ENG.). 32p. (J). (gr. k-3). 19.99 ***(978-1-76011-382-7(4))*** Allen & Unwin AUS. Dist: Independent Pubs. Group.

Ferran, Alexandri, et al. Agatha Christie. 2010. (Me Llamo... Ser.). (SPA., Illus.). 63p. (J). pap. *(978-84-342-3460-4(2))* Parramon Ediciones S.A.

Foreman, Michael. War Boy: A Wartime Childhood. 2006. (ENG., Illus.). 96p. (J). (gr. 4-7). pap. 16.99 *(978-1-84365-087-4(8))* Pavilion Bks. GBR. Dist: Independent Pubs. Group.

Foy, Debbie. Simon Cowell: Global Music Mogul. 2011. (Famous Lives Ser.). (Illus.). 32p. (YA). (gr. 3-6). lib. bdg. 26.50 *(978-1-4488-3290-3(X))* Rosen Publishing Group, Inc., The.

Gagne, Tammy. Ed Sheeran. 2017. lib. bdg. 25.70 ***(978-1-68020-129-1(8))*** Mitchell Lane Pubs., Inc.

Galioto, Annette. Gordon Ramsay. 2012. (J). *(978-1-61900-022-3(9))*; pap. *(978-1-61900-023-0(7))* Eldorado Ink.

Gallagher, James. The Beatles. 2008. (Pop Rock Ser.). (Illus.). 64p. (YA). (gr. 4-7). lib. bdg. 22.95 *(978-1-4222-0186-2(4))* Mason Crest.

Ganeri, Anita. Kings & Queens: The History of the British Monarchy. 2011. (Haynes Pocket Manual Ser.). (ENG., Illus.). 128p. (J). (gr. 3-17). pap. 7.95 *(978-1-84425-960-1(9)*, 1844259609) Haynes Publishing PLC GBR. Dist: Hachette Bk. Group.

Garnett, Emmeline. Florence Nightingale's Nuns. 2009. (Saints for Youth: Ser.). 150p. pap. 9.95 *(978-1-58617-297-8(2))* Ignatius Pr.

Gianopoulos, Andrea & Barnett III, Charles. Isaac Newton & the Laws of Motion [Scholastic]. Miller, Phil, illus. 2010. (Inventions & Discovery Ser.). 32p. pap. 0.45 *(978-1-4296-5969-7(6)*, Capstone Interactive Library) Capstone Digital.

Gibbons, Alan. Charles Darwin. 2008. (Illus.). 64p. (J). *(978-0-7534-1729-4(4)*, Kingfisher) Roaring Brook Pr.

Gifford, Clive. Amir Khan: Champion Boxer. 2017. (Inspirational Lives Ser.). (ENG., Illus.). 32p. (J). (gr. 4-6). pap. 12.99 ***(978-1-5263-0126-0(1)***, Wayland) Hachette Children's Group GBR. Dist: Hachette Bk. Group.

Glaser, Jason. David Beckham. 2009. (Sports Idols Ser.). 24p. (gr. 2-3). 42.50 *(978-1-60853-141-7(4)*, PowerKids Pr.) Rosen Publishing Group, Inc., The.

Goldsworthy, Steve. Richard Branson. 2011. (J). (gr. 4-6). pap. 12.95 *(978-1-61690-676-4(6)*, AV2 by Weigl); (Illus.). 24p. (YA). (gr. 3-6). 27.13 *(978-1-61690-671-9(5))* Weigl Pubs., Inc.

Goodridge, Catherine. Jane Goodall & Jane Goodall (Spanish) 6 English, 6 Spanish Adaptations. 2011. (ENG & SPA.). (J). 79.00 net. *(978-1-4108-5658-6(5))* Benchmark Education Co.

Gould, Jane H. Henry Hudson. 2013. (Jr. Graphic Famous Explorers Ser.). (ENG., Illus.). 24p. (J). (gr. 3-6). pap. 10.60 *(978-1-4777-0127-0(3))*; lib. bdg. 25.25 *(978-1-4777-0071-6(4))* Rosen Publishing Group, Inc., The. (PowerKids Pr.).

Gow, Mary. Robert Hooke: Creative Genius, Scientist, Inventor. 2006. (Great Minds of Science Ser.). (Illus.). 128p. (J). (gr. 6-10). lib. bdg. 31.93 *(978-0-7660-2547-9(0))* Enslow Pubs., Inc.

Graham, Ian. You Wouldn't Want to Be Sir Isaac Newton! A Lonely Life You'd Rather Not Lead. Antram, David, illus. 2013. (You Wouldn't Want to... Ser.). (ENG.). 32p. (J). 29.00 *(978-0-531-25943-6(9))*; pap. 9.95 *(978-0-531-23040-4(6))* Scholastic Library Publishing. (Watts, Franklin).

—You Wouldn't Want to Be Sir Isaac Newton! A Lonely Life You'd Rather Not Lead. 2013. (You Wouldn't Want To... Ser.). lib. bdg. 20.80 *(978-0-606-31632-3(9)*, Turtleback) Turtleback Bks.

Granfield, Linda. Out of Slavery: The Journey to Amazing Grace. Wilson, Janet, illus. 2009. (ENG.). 40p. (J). (gr. k-12). 15.95 *(978-0-88776-915-3(2)*, Tundra Bks.) Tundra Bks. CAN. Dist: Penguin Random Hse. LLC.

Gray, Nick & Scandiffio, Laura. Escape from Tibet: A True Story. 2014. (ENG., Illus.). 164p. (YA). (gr. 6-12). pap. 12.95 *(978-1-55451-662-9(5)*, 9781554516629) Annick Pr., Ltd. CAN. Dist: Publishers Group West (PGW).

Greenhaven Press Staff, ed. Prince Harry. 2012. (People in the News Ser.). (ENG., Illus.). 128p. (J). (gr. 7-10). lib. bdg. 33.95 *(978-1-4205-0760-7(5)*, Lucent Bks.) Cengage Gale.

Gregory, Peter. Queen. 2008. (Pop Rock Ser.). (Illus.). 64p. (YA). (gr. 4-7). lib. bdg. 22.95 *(978-1-4222-0193-0(7))* Mason Crest.

Guidi, Victoria. Who on Earth Is Jane Goodall? Champion for the Chimpanzees. 2009. (Scientists Saving the Earth Ser.). (Illus.). 112p. (J). (gr. 5-9). lib. bdg. 33.27 *(978-1-59845-119-1(7))* Enslow Pubs., Inc.

Guillain, Charlotte. Beatrix Potter, 1 vol. 2012. (Author Biographies Ser.). (ENG., Illus.). 24p. (gr. 1-2). pap. 6.79 *(978-1-4329-5966-1(2)*, Heinemann Read & Learn) Heinemann-Raintree.

Hamilton, Sue. Bartholomew Roberts, 1 vol. 2007. (Pirates Ser.). (ENG., Illus.). 32p. (gr. 4-8). 27.07 *(978-1-59928-757-7(9)*, Abdo & Daughters) ABDO Publishing Co.

Hamilton, Sue L. Captain Kidd, 1 vol. 2007. (Pirates! Ser.). (ENG., Illus.). 32p. (gr. 4-8). 27.07 *(978-1-59928-759-1(5)*, Abdo & Daughters) ABDO Publishing Co.

Hand, Carol. Jane Goodall. 2014. (Great Science Writers Ser.). (Illus.). 112p. (J). (gr. 7-12). 35.60 *(978-1-4777-7685-8(0))* Rosen Publishing Group, Inc., The.

Hanson-Harding, Alexandra. Charles Darwin, Naturalist. 2017. (J). pap. ***(978-1-68048-800-5(7))*** Rosen Publishing Group, Inc., The.

Harrison, Paul. Boudicca: Rebelled Against the Romans. 2017. (History VIPs Ser.). (ENG., Illus.). 32p. (J). (gr. 4-6). pap. 12.99 *(978-0-7502-9917-6(7)*, Wayland) Hachette Children's Group GBR. Dist: Hachette Bk. Group.

Harrison, Paul. King John - The King Who Signed Magna Carta: Brilliant Biographies of the Dead Famous. 2017. (History VIPs Ser.). (ENG., Illus.). 32p. (J). (gr. 4-6). pap. 12.99 ***(978-0-7502-9913-8(4)***, Wayland) Hachette Children's Group GBR. Dist: Hachette Bk. Group.

Heiligman, Deborah. Charles & Emma: The Darwins' Leap of Faith. 2011. (ENG., Illus.). 296p. (YA). (gr. 8-12). pap. 10.99 *(978-0-312-66104-5(5)*, 9780312661045) Square Fish.

Helms, Neil. J. R. R. Tolkien. 2004. (Great Writers Ser.). (Illus.). 128p. (YA). (gr. 9-13). 31.95 *(978-0-7910-7847-1(7)*, Chelsea Hse.) Facts On File, Inc.

Higgins, Nadia. Emma Watson: From Wizards to Wallflowers. 2014. (Pop Culture Bios Ser.). (ENG., Illus.). 32p. (gr. 3-6). lib. bdg. 26.60 *(978-1-4677-1442-6(9)*, Lerner Pubns.) Lerner Publishing Group.

—Nicholas Hoult: Beast of the Silver Screen. 2014. (Pop Culture Bios Ser.). (ENG., Illus.). 32p. (gr. 3-6). lib. bdg. 26.60 *(978-1-4677-1444-0(5)*, Lerner Pubns.) Lerner Publishing Group.

Hilliam, David. William Shakespeare: England's Greatest Playwright & Poet. 2009. (Rulers, Scholars, & Artists of the Renaissance Ser.). 112p. (gr. 5-8). 66.50 *(978-1-60852-945-2(2)*, Rosen Reference) Rosen Publishing Group, Inc., The.

Hollander, Barbara Gottfried. Elizabeth I: Queen of England. 2017. (Women Who Changed History Ser.). 48p. (gr. 10-12). lib. bdg. 26.85 ***(978-1-68048-643-8(8)***, Britannica Educational Publishing) Rosen Publishing Group, Inc., The.

Hoogenboom, Lynn. Sir Francis Drake. 2009. (Primary Source Library of Famous Explorers Ser.). 24p. (gr. 4-4). 42.50 *(978-1-60854-131-7(2)*, PowerKids Pr.) Rosen Publishing Group, Inc., The.

Houle, Michelle M. Modern British Poetry: "The World Is Never the Same" 2010. (Poetry Rocks! Ser.). (Illus.). 160p. (YA). (gr. 9-12). 35.94 *(978-0-7660-3278-1(7))* Enslow Pubs., Inc.

Howell, Izzi. Edith Cavell. 2016. (Fact Cat: History Ser.). (ENG., Illus.). 24p. (J). (gr. k-2). 14.99 *(978-0-7502-9772-1(7)*, Wayland) Hachette Children's Group GBR. Dist: Hachette Bk. Group.

—Emily Davison. 2016. (Fact Cat: History Ser.). (ENG., Illus.). 24p. (J). (gr. k-2). 14.99 *(978-0-7502-9770-7(0)*, Wayland) Hachette Children's Group GBR. Dist: Hachette Bk. Group.

Hunter, Nick. Catherine, Duchess of Cambridge, 1 vol. 2014. (Extraordinary Women Ser.). (ENG.). 48p. (gr. 6-6). lib. bdg. 32.65 *(978-1-4109-5942-3(2))* Heinemann-Raintree.

Indovino, Shaina C. Simon Cowell: From the Mailroom to Idol Fame. 2012. (Extraordinary Success with a High School Diploma or Less Ser.). 64p. (J). (gr. 7-8). 22.95 *(978-1-4222-2296-6(9))* Mason Crest.

Indovino, Shaina Carmel. Simon Cowell: From the Mailroom to Idol Fame. 2012. pap. *(978-1-4222-2307-9(8))* Mason Crest.

Jankowski, Connie. Jane Goodall: Animal Scientist & Friend, 1 vol. 2007. (Science Readers Ser.). (SPA & ENG.). 32p. (J). (gr. 3-3). pap. 8.99 *(978-0-7439-0594-7(6))* Shell Educational Publishing.

Jay, Ruth Johnson. Mary Slessor: Missionary to Calabar. 2006. (Illus.). 143p. (J). *(978-1-56265-077-3(7))* Accelarated Christian Education, Inc.

Jeffrey, Laura S. Pink Floyd: The Rock Band. 2009. (Rebels of Rock Ser.). (Illus.). 112p. (J). (gr. 7-12). lib. bdg. 33.27 *(978-0-7660-3030-5(X))* Enslow Pubs., Inc.

Johnson, Robin. Robert Pattinson. 2010. (Superstars! Ser.). (ENG., Illus.). 32p. (J). pap. *(978-0-7787-7260-6(8))*; (gr. 3-6). lib. bdg. *(978-0-7787-7251-4(9))* Crabtree Publishing Co.

Kaiser, Lisbeth. Emmeline Pankhurst. Sanfelippo, Ana, illus. 2017. (Little People, Big Dreams Ser.). (ENG.). 32p. (J). (gr. k-3). 14.99 ***(978-1-78603-020-7(9)***, Frances Lincoln Children's Bks.) Quarto Publishing Group UK GBR. Dist: Hachette Bk. Group.

Kallen, Stuart A. The Beatles. 2011. (Innovators Ser.). (ENG., Illus.). 48p. (gr. 4-8). lib. bdg. 34.60 *(978-0-7377-5868-9(6))* Cengage Gale.

Kjelle, Marylou. John Dalton & the Atomic Theory. 2004. (Uncharted, Unexplored, & Unexplained Ser.). (Illus.). 48p. (J). (gr. 4-8). lib. bdg. 29.95 *(978-1-58415-308-5(3))* Mitchell Lane Pubs., Inc.

Kostyal, K. M. Trial by Ice: A Photobiography of Sir Ernest Shackleton. 2006. (Illus.). 64p. pap. 7.99 *(978-0-15-356619-6(1))* Houghton Mifflin Harcourt School Pubs.

Kraft Rector, Rebecca. Alan Turing, 01 vols., 1. 2016. (Tech Pioneers Ser.). (ENG.). 112p. (J). 35.60 *(978-1-4994-6280-7(8)*, Rosen Young Adult) Rosen Publishing Group, Inc., The.

Krasner, Barbara. Sir Francis Drake. 2016. (Spotlight on Explorers & Colonization Ser.). 00048p. (J). (gr. 6-6). pap. 11.75 *(978-1-5081-7218-5(8))* Rosen Publishing Group, Inc., The.

Krull, Kathleen. Charles Darwin. Kulikov, Boris, illus. 2010. (Giants of Science Ser.). (ENG.). 144p. (J). (gr. 3-7). 15.99 *(978-0-670-06335-2(5)*, Viking Books for Young Readers) Penguin Young Readers Group.

—Isaac Newton. Kulikov, Boris, illus. 2008. (Giants of Science Ser.). (ENG.). 128p. (J). (gr. 3-7). 7.99 *(978-0-14-240820-9(4)*, Puffin Books) Penguin Young Readers Group.

Krumenauer, Heidi. Harry Styles of One Direction: Harry Styles. 2014. (ENG.). 32p. (J). 25.70 *(978-1-62469-008-2(4))* Purple Toad Publishing, Inc.

Labrecque, Ellen & dePaola, Tomie. Who Was Winston Churchill? Hoare, Jerry & Harrison, Nancy, illus. 2015. (Who Was? Ser.). (ENG.). 112p. (J). (gr. 3-7). 5.99 *(978-0-448-48300-9(9)*, Grosset & Dunlap) Penguin Young Readers Group.

Labrecque, Ellen & Harrison, Nancy. Who Was Princess Diana? Hoare, Jerry, illus. 2017. (Who Was? Ser.). (ENG.). 112p. (J). (gr. 3-7). 5.99 *(978-0-448-48855-4(8)*, Grosset & Dunlap) Penguin Young Readers Group.

Lace, William W. Captain James Cook. 2009. (Great Explorers Ser.). (Illus.). 112p. (gr. 6-12). 30.00 *(978-1-60413-416-2(X)*, Chelsea Hse.) Facts On File, Inc.

—Sir Francis Drake. 2009. (Great Explorers Ser.). (Illus.). 112p. (gr. 6-12). 30.00 *(978-1-60413-417-9(8)*, Chelsea Hse.) Facts On File, Inc.

Lajiness, Katie. Kate Middleton, 1 vol. 2016. (Big Buddy Pop Biographies Ser.). (ENG., Illus.). 32p. (J). (gr. 2-5). 28.50 *(978-1-68078-055-0(7))* ABDO Publishing Co.

—One Direction, 1 vol. 2016. (Big Buddy Pop Biographies Ser.). (ENG., Illus.). 32p. (J). (gr. 2-5). lib. bdg. 28.50 *(978-1-68078-056-7(5)*, Big Buddy Bks.) ABDO Publishing Co.

Langston-George, Rebecca. Fearless Spies & Daring Deeds of World War II. 2017. (Spies! Ser.). (ENG., Illus.). 64p. (gr. 5-6). lib. bdg. 33.99 *(978-0-7565-5500-9(0)*, CPB Grades 4-8) Compass Point Bks.

Lasky, Kathryn. One Beetle Too Many: The Extraordinary Adventures of Charles Darwin. Trueman, Matthew, illus. 2014. (Candlewick Biographies Ser.). (ENG.). 48p. (J). (gr. 2-5). 14.99 *(978-0-7636-6842-6(7))* Candlewick Pr.

Lee, T. S. The Stephen Hawking Story: The First Stephen Hawking Comic Biography. 2010. 179p. (J). pap. 14.95 *(978-0-9819542-9-5(4))* DASANBOOKS.

Leonard, Dion. Finding Gobi: The True Story of One Little Dog's Big Journey. 2017. (ENG.). 208p. (J). pap. 14.99 ***(978-0-7180-7531-6(5))*** Nelson, Thomas Inc.

Levete, Sarah. David Walliams: A Cosmic Genius. 2016. (ENG., Illus.). 32p. (J). (gr. 4-6). pap. 11.99 *(978-0-7502-9051-7(X)*, Wayland) Hachette Children's Group GBR. Dist: Hachette Bk. Group.

—Stella McCartney: Queen of the Catwalk! 2016. (Real-Life Stories Ser.). (ENG., Illus.). 32p. (J). (gr. 4-6). pap. 11.99 *(978-0-7502-9054-8(4)*, Wayland) Hachette Children's Group GBR. Dist: Hachette Bk. Group.

Lew, Kristi. ADA Lovelace: Mathematician & First Programmer. 2017. (J). ***(978-1-5383-0022-0(2))*** Rosen Publishing Group, Inc., The.

Linde, Barbara M. Daniel Radcliffe. 2010. (Today's Superstars Ser.). (ENG.). 48p. (J). (gr. 5-8). pap. 14.05 *(978-1-4339-3990-7(8))*; lib. bdg. 31.95 *(978-1-4339-3989-1(4))* Stevens, Gareth Publishing LLLP.

Lindeen, Mary. Jane Goodall: Friend of the Apes, 1 vol. Soud, illus. 2008. (Beginner Biographies Ser.). (ENG.). 32p. (gr. -1-3). 28.50 *(978-1-60270-249-3(7)*, Looking Glass Library-Nonfiction) Magic Wagon.

Lusted, Marcia Amidon. One Direction: Breakout Boy Band. 2012. (Pop Culture Bios Ser.). (ENG., Illus.). 32p. (gr. 3-6). pap. 7.95 *(978-1-4677-0879-1(8))*; lib. bdg. 26.60 *(978-1-4677-0877-7(1))* Lerner Publishing Group.

Maloney, Jim. I Love Liam. Maloney, Jim, illus. 2013. (I Love One Direction Ser.). (ENG., Illus.). 96p. (J). (gr. 3-7). pap. 7.99 *(978-1-78055-217-0(3))* O'Mara, Michael Bks., Ltd. GBR. Dist: Independent Pubs. Group.

Maloney, Jim & Buster Books Staff. I Love Harry. Maloney, Jim, illus. 2013. (I Love One Direction Ser.). (ENG., Illus.). 96p. (J). (gr. 3-7). pap. 7.99 *(978-1-78055-213-2(0))* O'Mara, Michael Bks., Ltd. GBR. Dist: Independent Pubs. Group.

Markel, Michelle. Balderdash!: John Newbery & the Boisterous Birth of Children's Books. Carpenter, Nancy, illus. 2017. (ENG.). 44p. (J). 17.99 *(978-0-8118-7922-4(4))* Chronicle Bks. LLC.

Mattern, Joanne. One Direction. 2012. (Illus.). 32p. (gr. 4-8). lib. bdg. 25.70 *(978-1-61228-407-1(8))* Mitchell Lane Pubs., Inc.

—Orlando Bloom. 2008. (Pop Culture Ser.). (Illus.). 64p. (YA). (gr. 3-7). lib. bdg. 22.95 *(978-1-4222-0198-5(8))* Mason Crest.

Matthews, C. M., et al. A Pageant of Kings & Queens. Brooke, Iris, illus. 2011. (ENG.). 98p. pap. 20.99 *(978-0-521-23596-9(0))* Cambridge Univ. Pr.

McDowell, Pamela. Adele. 2013. (J). *(978-1-62127-389-9(X))* Weigl Pubs., Inc.

McNeese, Tim. John Smith. 2010. (Leaders of the Colonial Era Ser.). 128p. (gr. 5-8). 35.00 *(978-1-60413-742-2(8)*, Chelsea Hse.) Facts On File, Inc.

McPherson, Stephanie Sammartino. Tim Berners-Lee: Inventor of the World Wide Web. 2009. (USA TODAY Lifeline Biographies Ser.). (ENG., Illus.). 112p. (J). (gr. 6-12). lib. bdg. 34.60 *(978-0-8225-7273-2(7))* Lerner Publishing Group.

Meltzer, Brad. I Am Jane Goodall. Eliopoulos, Christopher, illus. 2016. (Ordinary People Change the World Ser.). (ENG.). 40p. (J). (gr. k-3). 14.99 *(978-0-525-42849-7(6)*, Dial Bks) Penguin Young Readers Group.

Meyer, Susan. Isaac Newton. 2017. (Leaders of the Scientific Revolution Ser.). 112p. (J). (gr. 12-13). 37.10 ***(978-1-5081-7470-7(9)***, Rosen Young Adult) Rosen Publishing Group, Inc., The.

Miklowitz, Gloria D. Jane Goodall. 2004. (ENG., Illus.). 28p. (J). (gr. 2-5). pap. 7.33 *(978-0-7685-1218-2(2)*, Dominie Elementary) Pearson Schl.

Miller, Calvin Craig. David Beckham. 2008. (Xtreme Athletes Ser.). (Illus.). 100p. (J). (gr. 5-13). lib. bdg. 27.95 *(978-1-59935-082-0(3))* Reynolds, Morgan Inc.

Miller, Kat. I Love Daniel Radcliffe. 2010. (Fan Club Ser.). (ENG.). 24p. (J). (gr. 3-6). lib. bdg. 22.60 *(978-1-61533-054-6(2))*; (Illus.). pap. 8.15 *(978-1-61533-055-3(0))* Windmill Bks.

—I Love Robert Pattinson. 2010. (Fan Club Ser.). (ENG.). 24p. (gr. 3-6). lib. bdg. 22.60 *(978-1-61533-057-7(7))*; (Illus.). (J). pap. 8.15 *(978-1-61533-058-4(5))* Windmill Bks.

Moore, Cathy. Ellen Craft's Escape from Slavery. Braught, Mark, illus. 2010. (History Speaks: Picture Books Plus Reader's Theater Ser.). (ENG.). 48p. (gr. 2-4). pap. 9.95 *(978-0-7613-6672-0(5))*; lib. bdg. 27.93 *(978-0-7613-5875-6(7)*, Millbrook Pr.) Lerner Publishing Group.

Morreale, Marie. Ed Sheeran. 2014. (ENG.). 48p. (J). pap. 7.95 *(978-0-531-21274-5(2))* Scholastic Library Publishing.

—One Direction. 2014. (ENG.). 48p. (J). pap. 7.95 *(978-0-531-21271-4(8))*; lib. bdg. 29.00 *(978-0-531-21196-0(7))* Scholastic Library Publishing.

Nelson, Maria. Robert Pattinson. 2011. (Rising Stars Ser.). 32p. (J). (gr. 3-6). pap. 10.50 *(978-1-4339-5900-4(3))*; lib. bdg. 25.25 *(978-1-4339-5898-4(8))* Stevens, Gareth Publishing LLLP.

Newland, Sonya. David Attenborough: Naturalist Visionary. 2016. (Inspirational Lives Ser.). (ENG., Illus.). 32p. (J). (gr. 4-6). 17.99 *(978-0-7502-8569-8(9)*, Wayland) Hachette Children's Group GBR. Dist: Hachette Bk. Group.

—Stephen Hawking: Pioneering Scientist. 2016. (Inspirational Lives Ser.). (ENG., Illus.). 32p. (J). (gr. 4-6). pap. 11.99 *(978-0-7502-9209-2(1)*, Wayland) Hachette Children's Group GBR. Dist: Hachette Bk. Group.

Nick, Charles. Sir Francis Drake: Slave Trader & Pirate. 2010. (ENG., Illus.). 128p. (C). (gr. 6-12). pap. 9.95 *(978-0-531-20740-6(4))* National Geographic School Publishing, Inc.

—Sir Francis Drake: Slave Trader & Pirate. 2009. (Wicked History Ser.). (ENG., Illus.). 128p. (J). (gr. 6-12). 31.00 *(978-0-531-21800-6(7)*, Watts, Franklin) Scholastic Library Publishing.

Norwich, Grace. Daniel Radcliffe: No Ordinary Wizard. 2008. (ENG.). 128p. (J). (gr. 4-9). pap. 5.99 *(978-1-4169-6771-2(0)*, Simon Spotlight) Simon Spotlight.

Obregon, Jose M. David Beckham. Benson, Megan, tr. 2008. (World Soccer Stars / Estrellas Del Fútbol Mundial Ser.). (SPA., Illus.). 24p. (J). (gr. 2-5). lib. bdg. 22.60 *(978-1-4042-7665-9(3))* Rosen Publishing Group, Inc., The.

Obregon, Jose Maria. David Beckham. 2009. (World Soccer Stars / Estrellas del fútbol mundial Ser.). (ENG & SPA.). 24p. (gr. 2-2). 42.50 *(978-1-60854-841-5(4)*, Editorial Buenas Letras) Rosen Publishing Group, Inc., The.

O'Brien, Cynthia. Explore with John Franklin. 2015. (Travel with the Great Explorers Ser.). (ENG., Illus.). 32p. (J). (gr. 3-6). *(978-0-7787-1703-4(8))* Crabtree Publishing Co.

O'Donnell, Kerri. Sir Isaac Newton: Using the Laws of Motion to Solve Problems. 2009. (PowerMath: Advanced Proficiency Plus Ser.). 32p. (gr. 5-5). 47.90 *(978-1-60851-366-6(1)*, PowerKids Pr.) Rosen Publishing Group, Inc., The.

Oldfield, Tom & Oldfield, Matt. Gareth Bale: The Boy Who Became a Galáctico. 2016. (ENG.). 160p. (J). (gr. 4-7). pap. 8.99 *(978-1-78418-645-6(7))* Blake, John Publishing, Ltd. GBR. Dist: Independent Pubs. Group.

—Raheem Sterling: Red Lightning. 2016. (ENG.). 160p. (J). (gr. 4-7). pap. 8.99 *(978-1-78418-646-3(5))* Blake, John Publishing, Ltd. GBR. Dist: Independent Pubs. Group.

—Steven Gerrard. 2017. (ENG.). 160p. (J). (gr. 4-7). pap. 9.99 ***(978-1-78606-219-2(4))*** Blake, John Publishing, Ltd. GBR. Dist: Independent Pubs. Group.

Oldfield, Tom & Oldfield, Matt. Wayne Rooney: Captain of England. 2016. (ENG.). 160p. (J). (gr. 4-7). pap. 8.99 *(978-1-78418-647-0(3))* Blake, John Publishing, Ltd. GBR. Dist: Independent Pubs. Group.

Ollhoff, Jim. Captain Cook. 2013. (Great Explorers Ser.). 32p. (gr. 5-9). lib. bdg. 27.07 *(978-1-61783-965-8(5)*, Abdo & Daughters) ABDO Publishing Co.

Olson, Steven P. Sir Walter Raleigh: Explorer for the Court of Queen Elizabeth. 2003. (Library of Explorers & Exploration Ser.). (Illus.). 112p. (gr. 5-8). lib. bdg. 34.60 *(978-0-8239-3631-1(7)*, Rosen Reference) Rosen Publishing Group, Inc., The.

Orr, Tamra. Robert Pattison. 2010. (Blue Banner Biography Ser.). (Illus.). 32p. (YA). (gr. 4-7). lib. bdg. 25.70 *(978-1-58415-905-6(7))* Mitchell Lane Pubs., Inc.

Orr, Tamra B. Orlando Bloom. 2006. (Blue Banner Biography Ser.). (Illus.). 32p. (YA). (gr. 4-7). lib. bdg. 25.70 *(978-1-58415-515-7(9))* Mitchell Lane Pubs., Inc.

Otfinoski, Steven. Patriots & Redcoats: Stories of American Revolutionary War Leaders. 2015. (Revolutionary War Ser.). (ENG.). 48p. (gr. 3-4). pap. 8.95 *(978-1-4914-2158-1(4))* Capstone Press of Coughlan Cos.

Owings, Lisa. Adele: Grammy-Winning Singer & Songwriter, 1 vol. 2013. (Contemporary Lives Set 2 Ser.). (ENG.). 112p. (J). (gr. 6-12). lib. bdg. 35.64 *(978-1-61783-616-9(8)*, Essential Library) ABDO Publishing Co.

—Diana: The People's Princess, 1 vol. 2012. (Lives Cut Short Set 2 Ser.). (ENG.). 112p. (J). (gr. 6-12). lib. bdg. 35.64 *(978-1-61783-545-2(5)*, Essential Library) ABDO Publishing Co.

Paprocki, Sherry Beck. Diana, Princess of Wales. 2nd rev. ed. 2009. (Women of Achievement Ser.). (Illus.). 144p. (gr. 6-12). 35.00 *(978-1-60413-463-6(1)*, Chelsea Hse.) Facts On File, Inc.

Pendleton, Ken. David Beckham. 2007. (Sports Heroes & Legends Ser.). (Illus.). 106p. (YA). (gr. 7-12). lib. bdg. 30.60 *(978-0-8225-7161-2(7))* Twenty First Century Bks.

Pendleton, Ken & Savage, Jeff. David Beckham. 2008. (Sports Heroes & Legends Ser.). (ENG.). (gr. 5-12). pap. 56.72 *(978-1-57505-993-8(2))* Lerner Publishing Group.

Penguin Young Readers. The Tale of Beatrix Potter. 2016. (Penguin Young Readers, Level 4 Ser.). (ENG.). 48p. (J). (gr. 1-3). pap. 3.99 *(978-0-241-24937-6(6)*, Penguin Young Readers) Penguin Young Readers Group.

Peppas, Lynn. One Direction. 2013. (ENG., Illus.). 32p. (J). *(978-0-7787-1049-3(1))*; pap. *(978-0-7787-1053-0(X))* Crabtree Publishing Co.

Perrin, Pat & Coleman, Wim. The Mystery of the Murdered Playwright. 2004. (Cover-To-Cover Books). (Illus.). 56p. pap. 9.00 *(978-0-7891-6001-0(3))*; (gr. 4-7). lib. bdg. 17.95 *(978-0-7569-1353-3(5))* Perfection Learning Corp.

Petrie, Kristin. Sir Walter Raleigh, 1 vol. 2007. (Explorers Set 2 Ser.). (ENG., Illus.). 32p. (gr. 4-7). 27.07 *(978-1-59679-748-2(7)*, Checkerboard Library) ABDO Publishing Co.

Pollack, Pamela D. & Belviso, Meg. Who Was Alfred Hitchcock? 2014. (Who Was... ? Ser.). lib. bdg. 14.75 *(978-0-606-36176-7(6))* Turtleback Bks.

Porterfield, Jason. Tim Berners-Lee, 01 vols., 1. 2016. (Tech Pioneers Ser.). (ENG.). 112p. (J). 35.60 *(978-1-4994-6290-6(5)*, Rosen Young Adult) Rosen Publishing Group, Inc., The.

Pratt, Mary K. Elizabeth I: English Renaissance Queen, 1 vol. 2011. (Essential Lives Set 7 Ser.). (ENG., Illus.). 112p. (J). (gr. 6-12). lib. bdg. 35.64 *(978-1-61783-003-7(8))* ABDO Publishing Co.

Price, Sean Stewart & Price, Sean. Henry VIII: Royal Beheader. 2009. (Wicked History Ser.). (ENG.). 128p. (J). (gr. 6-12). pap. 5.95 *(978-0-531-22173-0(3)*, Children's Pr.) Scholastic Library Publishing.

Radford, James & Wooders, Dave. Adventures on the Queen Mary: ... tales of a Teenage Crew Member! 2015. (ENG., Illus.). 274p. pap. 25.00 *(978-0-692-54554-6(9))* Perfect Page, The.

Rappaport, Doreen. John's Secret Dreams: The Life of John Lennon. Collier, Bryan, illus. 2016. (Big Words Ser.). (ENG.). 48p. (J). (gr. 1-3). pap. 8.99 *(978-1-4847-4962-3(6))* Hyperion Bks. for Children.

Rawson, Katherine. Daniel Radcliffe. (J). 2010. pap. 9.40 *(978-1-4358-3404-0(6))* 2009. (Illus.). 24p. lib. bdg. 22.60 *(978-1-4042-8135-6(5))* Rosen Publishing Group, Inc., The. (PowerKids Pr.).

Redgrave, Roy. The Adventures of Colonel Daffodil: Balkan Beginnings, Memorable Travels & Forgotten Conflicts. 2007. (Illus.). 202p. (J). 45.00 *(978-1-84415-525-5(0))* Pen & Sword Bks. Ltd. GBR. Dist: Casemate Pubs. & Bk. Distributors, LLC.

Reed, Avery & dePaola, Tomie. Who Were the Brothers Grimm? O'brien, John, illus. 2015. (Who Was? Ser.). (ENG.). 112p. (J). (gr. 3-7). 5.99 *(978-0-448-48314-6(9)*, Grosset & Dunlap) Penguin Young Readers Group.

Reef, Catherine. The Brontë Sisters: The Brief Lives of Charlotte, Emily, & Anne. 2012. (ENG., Illus.). 240p. (J). (gr. 5-7). 18.99 *(978-0-547-57966-5(7))* Houghton Mifflin Harcourt Publishing Co.

Rengel, Marian. John Cabot: The Ongoing Search for a Westward Passage to Asia. 2003. (Library of Explorers & Exploration Ser.). (Illus.). 112p. (J). (gr. 5-8). lib. bdg. 34.60 *(978-0-8239-3626-7(0)*, Rosen Reference) Rosen Publishing Group, Inc., The.

Ribke, Simone T. William & Kate: The Prince & Princess. 2016. (Rookie Biographies(tm) Ser.). (ENG., Illus.). 32p. (J). lib. bdg. 25.00 *(978-0-531-22548-6(8)*, Children's Pr.) Scholastic Library Publishing.

Rice, William. Jane Goodall. 2017. (TIME for Kids en Español - Level 3 Ser.). (SPA.). 32p. (gr. 3-3). lib. bdg. 31.99 ***(978-1-5157-5191-5(0))*** Time for Kids Inc AUS. Dist: Capstone Pub.

Richter, Sandy. The Life of Florence Nightingale. 2009. (Real Life Readers Ser.). 16p. (gr. 2-3). pap. 7.05 *(978-1-4358-0225-4(X)*, Rosen Classroom) Rosen Publishing Group, Inc., The.

Riddle, John. Robert F. Scott: British Explorer of the South Pole. 2013. (People of Importance Ser.: 21). (Illus.). 32p. (J). (gr. 4-18). 19.95 *(978-1-4222-2855-5(X))* Mason Crest.

Ridley, Sarah. Charles Darwin. 2017. (Super Scientists Ser.). (ENG., Illus.). 24p. (J). (gr. 1-3). pap. 9.99 ***(978-1-4451-5355-1(6)***, Franklin Watts) Hachette Children's Group GBR. Dist: Hachette Bk. Group.

—David Attenborough. 2017. (Super Scientists Ser.). (ENG., Illus.). 24p. (J). (gr. 1-3). pap. 9.99 ***(978-1-4451-5357-5(2)***, Franklin Watts) Hachette Children's Group GBR. Dist: Hachette Bk. Group.

Robbins, Trina & Capstone Press Staff. Florence Nightingale: Lady with the Lamp, 1 vol. Timmons, Anne, illus. 2007. (Graphic Biographies Ser.). (ENG.). 32p. (gr. 3-4). 30.65 *(978-0-7368-6850-1(X)*, Graphic Library) Capstone Press of Coughlan Cos.

Roberts, Steven. John Cabot. 2013. (Jr. Graphic Famous Explorers Ser.). (ENG., Illus.). 24p. (J). (gr. 3-6). pap. 10.60 *(978-1-4777-0129-4(X))*; lib. bdg. 25.25 *(978-1-4777-0072-3(2))* Rosen Publishing Group, Inc., The. (PowerKids Pr.).

Robinson, Tom. David Beckham: Soccer's Superstar. 2008. (People to Know Today Ser.). (Illus.). 112p. (J). (gr. 3-7). lib. bdg. 33.27 *(978-0-7660-3110-4(1))* Enslow Pubs., Inc.

Roselius, J. Chris. David Beckham: Gifted & Giving Soccer Star. 2010. (Sports Stars Who Give Back Ser.). (Illus.). 128p. (J). (gr. 5-9). lib. bdg. 33.27 *(978-0-7660-3587-4(5))* Enslow Pubs., Inc.

Rosen, Michael. Fantastic Mr. Dahl. Blake, Quentin, illus. 2012. (ENG.). 176p. (J). (gr. 3-7). pap. 6.99 *(978-0-14-132213-1(6)*, Puffin Books) Penguin Young Readers Group.

Rosenberg, Aaron. Thomas Hobbes: An English Philosopher in the Age of Reason. 2005. (Philosophers of the Enlightenment Ser.). (Illus.). 112p. (J). (gr. 3-7). lib. bdg. 34.60 *(978-1-4042-0419-5(9))* Rosen Publishing Group, Inc., The.

Ross, Stewart. Will's Dream. Shields, Susan, illus. 28p. pap. 9.99 *(978-0-7502-2965-4(9))* Hodder & Stoughton GBR. Dist: Trafalgar Square Publishing.

Roth, B. A. David Beckham: Born to Play. 2007. (All Aboard Reading Station Stop 3 Collection). (Illus.). 48p. (gr. 1-3). 14.00 *(978-0-7569-8918-7(3))* Perfection Learning Corp.

Rowell, Rebecca. Randolph Caldecott: Renowned British Illustrator, 1 vol. 2009. (Publishing Pioneers Ser.). (ENG., Illus.). 112p. (J). (gr. 6-12). lib. bdg. 35.64 *(978-1-60453-760-4(4)*, Essential Library) ABDO Publishing Co.

Roza, Greg. David Beckham: Soccer Superstar. 2006. (Tony Stead Nonfiction Independent Reading Collection). (ENG.). 24p. (gr. 3-6). pap. 8.85 *(978-1-4042-5539-5(7))* Rosen Publishing Group, Inc., The.

Salamoff, Paul. The Cast of Doctor Who. 2012. (ENG., Illus.). 40p. pap. 7.99 *(978-1-4507-8451-1(8))* Bluewater Productions, Inc.

Salazar, Sam. One Direction. 2013. (Rising Stars Ser.). 32p. (J). (gr. 3-6). 25.25 *(978-1-4339-8985-8(9))*; pap. 10.50 *(978-1-4339-8986-5(7))*; pap. 63.00 *(978-1-4339-8987-2(5))* Stevens, Gareth Publishing LLLP.

Salzmann, Mary Elizabeth. Michael Faraday, 1 vol. 2016. (ENG., Illus.). 24p. (J). *(978-1-68078-156-4(1))* ABDO Publishing Co.

Sapet, Kerrily. Eleanor of Aquitaine: Medieval Queen. 2006. (European Queens Ser.). (Illus.). 192p. (J). (gr. 6-12). lib. bdg. 26.95 *(978-1-931798-90-7(7))* Reynolds, Morgan Inc.

Saucerman, Linda. Ozzy Osbourne & Kelly Osbourne. 2009. (Famous Families Ser.). 48p. (gr. 5-5). 53.00 *(978-1-61512-509-8(4))* Rosen Publishing Group, Inc., The.

Savage, Jeff. David Beckham. (Amazing Athletes Ser.). (Illus.). 32p. 2008. (J). (gr. -1). per. 6.95 *(978-0-8225-8975-4(3)*, First Avenue Editions) 2008. (YA). (gr. 2-5). lib. bdg. 23.93 *(978-0-8225-8834-4(X))* 2013. (ENG., (gr. 2-5). pap. 7.95 *(978-1-4677-1160-9(8))* 2013. (ENG., (gr. 2-5). lib. bdg. 25.26 *(978-1-4677-1159-3(4))* Lerner Publishing Group.

Schanzer, Rosalyn & Darwin, Charles. What Darwin Saw: The Journey That Changed the World. 2009. (ENG., Illus.). 48p. (J). (gr. 5). lib. bdg. 26.90 *(978-1-4263-0397-5(1))*; 17.95 *(978-1-4263-0396-8(3))* National Geographic Society. (National Geographic Children's Bks.).

Schrey, Sophie & Buster Books Staff. I Love Louis. Schrey, Sophie, illus. 2013. (I Love One Direction Ser.). (ENG., Illus.). 96p. (J). (gr. 3-7). pap. 7.99 *(978-1-78055-215-6(7))* O'Mara, Michael Bks., Ltd. GBR. Dist: Independent Pubs. Group.

Schuman, Michael A. Led Zeppelin: Legendary Rock Band. 2009. (Rebels of Rock Ser.). (Illus.). 112p. (J). (gr. 7-12). lib. bdg. 33.27 *(978-0-7660-3026-8(1))* Enslow Pubs., Inc.

—Robert Pattinson: Shining Star. 2011. (Hot Celebrity Biographies Ser.). (Illus.). 48p. (J). (gr. 5-18). pap. 8.95 *(978-1-59845-284-6(3))* Enslow Pubs., Inc.

Schwartz, Heather. Little Mix: Singers with X-Tra Success. 2014. (Pop Culture Bios Ser.). (Illus.). 32p. (J). (gr. 3-6). lib. bdg. 26.60 *(978-1-4677-3668-8(6)*, Lerner Pubns.) Lerner Publishing Group.

Schwartz, Heather E. Adele: Soulful Singer. 2015. (Pop Culture Bios Ser.). (ENG., Illus.). 32p. (J). (gr. 3-6). pap. 7.95 *(978-1-4677-6101-7(X)*, Lerner Pubns.) Lerner Publishing Group.

—Code-Breaker & Mathematician Alan Turing. 2017. (J). ***(978-1-5124-9980-3(3))*** Lerner Publishing Group.

Schwartz, Heather E. The Wanted: British Boy Band Sensation. 2013. (Pop Culture Bios Ser.). (ENG., Illus.). 32p. (gr. 3-6). pap. 7.95 *(978-1-4677-1548-5(4))*; lib. bdg. 26.60 *(978-1-4677-1307-8(4)*, Lerner Pubns.) Lerner Publishing Group.

Sheehan, Robert. Francis Drake: Patriot or Pirate? 2013. (Discovery Education: Sensational True Stories Ser.). (ENG., Illus.). 32p. (J). (gr. 3-6). pap. 10.00 *(978-1-4777-0105-8(2))*; lib. bdg. 25.25 *(978-1-4777-0060-0(9))* Rosen Publishing Group, Inc., The. (PowerKids Pr.).

Sherman, Josepha. Henry Hudson: Exploring the Northwest Passage. 2015. (Incredible Explorers Ser.). (ENG., Illus.). 64p. (J). (gr. 7-7). 34.21 *(978-1-5026-0127-8(3))* Cavendish Square Publishing.

Silvey, Anita & National Geographic Kids Staff. Untamed: The Wild Life of Jane Goodall. 2015. (ENG., Illus.). 96p. (J). (gr. 3-7). 18.99 *(978-1-4263-1518-3(X)*, National Geographic Children's Bks.) National Geographic Society.

Sir Francis Drake. 2013. 56p. 15.95 *(978-0-9897533-0-2(1))* Croce, Pat & Co.

Stanley, Diane. Ada Lovelace. Hartland, Jessie, illus. 2016. (ENG.). 40p. (J). (gr. -1-3). 17.99 *(978-1-4814-5249-6(5)*, Simon & Schuster Bks. For Young Readers) Simon & Schuster Bks. For Young Readers.

Stanley, Diane & Vennema, Peter. Bard of Avon. Stanley, Diane, illus. 2015. (ENG., Illus.). 48p. (J). (gr. 1-5). pap. 7.99 *(978-0-06-241925-5(0))* HarperCollins Pubs.

Steele, Philip. Isaac Newton: Mi Mejor Amigo Es la Verdad. 2007. (SPA., Illus.). 416p. (J). (gr. 4-8). pap. 14.99 *(978-970-58-0222-5(X))* Altea, Ediciones, S.A. - Grupo Santillana ESP. Dist: Two Rivers Distribution.

Stefoff, Rebecca. Captain Kidd. 2015. (J). lib. bdg. *(978-1-62713-529-0(4))*; (ENG.). 48p. (gr. 3-3). 31.36 *(978-1-5026-0205-3(9))* Cavendish Square Publishing.

Sterling, Kristin. Jane Goodall: A Life of Loyalty. 2008. (Pull Ahead Bks.). (Illus.). 32p. (J). (gr. -1-3). lib. bdg. 22.60 *(978-0-8225-8727-9(0)*, Lerner Pubns.) Lerner Publishing Group.

Streissguth, Tom. Richard the Lionheart: Crusader King of England. 2007. (Rulers of the Middle Ages Ser.). (Illus.). 160p. (YA). (gr. 6-12). lib. bdg. 35.94 *(978-0-7660-2714-5(7))* Enslow Pubs., Inc.

Sullivan, Anne Marie. Sir Isaac Newton: Famous English Scientist. 2013. (People of Importance Ser.: 21). (Illus.). 32p. (J). (gr. 4-18). 19.95 *(978-1-4222-2856-2(8))* Mason Crest.

Sullivan, Laura L. Sir Henry Morgan. 2015. (J). lib. bdg. *(978-1-62713-308-1(9))* Cavendish Square Publishing.

Summers, Portia. Kate Middleton: Duchess of Cambridge. 2017. (Junior Biographies Ser.). 24p. (J). (gr. 3-4). pap. 9.35 ***(978-0-7660-8781-1(6))***; lib. bdg. 22.60 ***(978-0-7660-8672-2(0))*** Enslow Pubs., Inc.

Superstars! Editors. Superstars! One Direction: Inside Their World. Superstars! Editors, ed. 2012. (ENG., Illus.). 128p. (J). (gr. 3-17). pap. 14.95 *(978-1-60320-950-2(6)*, Liberty St.) Time Inc. Bks.

Tieck, Sarah. Adele: Singing Sensation, 1 vol. 2013. (Big Buddy Biographies Set 9 Ser.). (ENG.). 32p. (J). (gr. 2-5). lib. bdg. 28.50 *(978-1-61783-747-0(4)*, Big Buddy Bks.) ABDO Publishing Co.

—David Beckham: Soccer Superstar, 1 vol. 2008. (Big Buddy Biographies Ser.). (ENG.). 32p. (J). (gr. 2-5). 28.50 *(978-1-60453-116-9(9))* ABDO Publishing Co.

—Kate Middleton: Real-Life Princess, 1 vol. 2011. (Big Buddy Biographies Set 7 Ser.). (ENG., Illus.). 32p. (J). (gr. 2-5). 28.50 *(978-1-61783-020-4(8))* ABDO Publishing Co.

—One Direction: Popular Boy Band, 1 vol. 2013. (Big Buddy Biographies Set 9 Ser.). (ENG.). 32p. (J). (gr. 2-5). lib. bdg. 28.50 *(978-1-61783-752-4(0)*, Big Buddy Bks.) ABDO Publishing Co.

—Prince William: Real-Life Prince, 1 vol. 2011. (Big Buddy Biographies Set 7 Ser.). (ENG., Illus.). 32p. (J). (gr. 2-5). 28.50 *(978-1-61783-022-8(4))* ABDO Publishing Co.

Toth, Henrietta. Henry Hudson. 2016. (Spotlight on Explorers & Colonization Ser.). 00048p. (J). (gr. 6-6). pap. 11.75 *(978-1-5081-7222-2(6))* Rosen Publishing Group, Inc., The.

Tougas, Joe. The Beatles: Defining Rock 'n' Roll. 2015. (Legends of Rock Ser.). (ENG.). 32p. (gr. 3-4). lib. bdg. 27.99 *(978-1-4914-1816-1(8))* Capstone Press of Coughlan Cos.

Trachtenberg, Martha P. Bono: Rock Star Activist. 2008. (People to Know Today Ser.). (Illus.). 128p. (J). (gr. 6-18). lib. bdg. 33.27 *(978-0-7660-2695-7(7))* Enslow Pubs., Inc.

Tracy, Kathleen. Emma Watson. 2010. (Robbie Reader Ser.). (Illus.). 32p. (YA). (gr. 2-5). lib. bdg. 25.70 *(978-1-58415-901-8(4))* Mitchell Lane Pubs., Inc.

—Prince William of Wales. 2011. (Blue Banner Biography Ser.). (YA). (gr. 4-7). 25.70 *(978-1-61228-191-9(5))* Mitchell Lane Pubs., Inc.

Trussell-Cullen, Alan. Princess Diana. 2009. pap. 13.25 *(978-1-60559-068-4(1))* Hameray Publishing Group, Inc.

Tucker, Margaret E. Biography of Richard Bullard: From Shoe Cobbler in England to Minister for Jesus Christ in America. 2003. pap. 6.75 *(978-0-9672363-3-9(9))* Heritage Publishing.

Ungs, Tim. Paul McCartney & Stella McCartney. 2004. (Famous Families Ser.). (Illus.). 48p. (J). lib. bdg. 29.25 *(978-1-4042-0263-4(3))* Rosen Publishing Group, Inc., The.

—Paul Mccartney & Stella Mccartney. 2009. (Famous Families Ser.). 48p. (gr. 5-5). 53.00 *(978-1-61512-510-4(8))* Rosen Publishing Group, Inc., The.

Uschan, Michael V. David Beckham. 2008. (People in the News Ser.). (ENG., Illus.). 128p. (gr. 3-7). lib. bdg. 39.40 *(978-1-4205-0054-7(6)*, Lucent Bks.) Cengage Gale.

Venezia, Mike. The Beatles (Revised Edition) Venezia, Mike, illus. 2017. (Getting to Know the World's Greatest Composers Ser.). (ENG., Illus.). 40p. (J). pap. 7.95 *(978-0-531-22243-0(8)*, Children's Pr.) Scholastic Library Publishing.

—Jane Goodall: Researcher Who Champions Chimps. 2010. (Getting to Know the World's Greatest Inventors & Scientists Ser.). 32p. (J). (gr. 3-4). pap. 6.95 *(978-0-531-22352-9(3)*, Children's Pr.) Scholastic Library Publishing.

—Jane Goodall: Researcher Who Champions Chimps. Venezia, Mike, illus. 2010. (Getting to Know the World's Greatest Inventors & Scientists Ser.). (ENG., Illus.). 32p. (J). (gr. 3-4). 28.00 *(978-0-531-23731-1(1))* Scholastic Library Publishing.

—Stephen Hawking: Cosmologist Who Gets a Big Bang Out of the Universe. Venezia, Mike, illus. 2009. (Getting to Know the World's Greatest Inventors & Scientists Ser.). (ENG., Illus.). 32p. (J). (gr. 3-4). pap. 6.95 *(978-0-531-21337-7(4)*, Children's Pr.) Scholastic Library Publishing.

Wallace, Susan Helen & Jablonski, Patricia E. Saint Thomas More: Courage, Conscience, & the King. Lachuk, Dani, illus. 2014. (ENG.). 144p. (J). pap. 8.95 *(978-0-8198-9021-4(9))* Pauline Bks. & Media.

Ward, Nancy. Sir Walter Raleigh: Founding the Virginia Colony. 2006. (In the Footsteps of Explorers Ser.). (ENG., Illus.). 32p. (J). (gr. 4-7). lib. bdg. *(978-0-7787-2424-7(7)*, 1253445) Crabtree Publishing Co.

Watson, Galadriel. David Beckham. 2007. (Remarkable People Ser.). (Illus.). 24p. (J). (gr. 3-7). pap. 8.95 *(978-1-59036-642-4(5))* Weigl Pubs., Inc.

Watson, Galadriel Findlay. David Beckham. 2007. (Remarkable People Ser.). (Illus.). 24p. (J). (gr. 3-7). lib. bdg. 24.45 *(978-1-59036-641-7(7))* Weigl Pubs., Inc.

Watson, Stephanie. Daniel Radcliffe: Film & Stage Star. 2009. (Hot Celebrity Biographies Ser.). (Illus.). 48p. (J). (gr. 5-9). lib. bdg. 25.27 *(978-0-7660-3209-5(4))* Enslow Pubs., Inc.

—Jamie Oliver. Greenhaven Press Editors, ed. 2013. (People in the News Ser.). (ENG., Illus.). 128p. (gr. 7-10). lib. bdg. 39.40 *(978-1-4205-0886-4(5)*, Lucent Bks.) Cengage Gale.

Waxman, Laura Hamilton. Jane Goodall. Butler, Tad, illus. 2007. (History Maker Biographies Ser.). (ENG.). 48p. (J). (gr. 3-6). lib. bdg. 27.93 *(978-0-8225-7610-5(4)*, Lerner Pubns.) Lerner Publishing Group.

Weaver, Anne H. The Voyage of the Beetle: A Journey Around the World with Charles Darwin & the Search for the Solution to the Mystery of Mysteries, as Narrated by Rosie, an Articulate Beetle. Lawrence, George, illus. 2007. (ENG.). 80p. (J). (gr. 5-8). 19.95 *(978-0-8263-4304-8(X))* Univ. of New Mexico Pr.

Welty, Tara. Jane Goodall. 2011. (Conservation Heroes Ser.). (Illus.). 128p. (gr. 6-12). 35.00 *(978-1-60413-952-5(8)*, Chelsea Hse.) Facts On File, Inc.

Wentzel, Jim. The Beatles. 2009. (Rock & Roll Hall of Famers Ser.). 112p. (gr. 5-8). 63.90 *(978-1-60852-477-8(9)*, Rosen Reference) Rosen Publishing Group, Inc., The.

White, Danny. One Direction: La Historia. 2nd ed. 2013. (Corazon Joven Ser.). (SPA., Illus.). 254p. (YA). pap. *(978-84-15579-15-1(2))* Akcent, Vydavatelstvi, Drahomir Rybnicek.

White, Katherine. Elton John. 2009. (Rock & Roll Hall of Famers Ser.). 112p. (gr. 5-8). 63.90 *(978-1-60852-473-0(6)*, Rosen Reference) Rosen Publishing Group, Inc., The.

White-Thomson, Stephen. Elizabeth I. 2017. (Popcorn: People in History Ser.). (ENG., Illus.). 24p. (J). (gr. k-2). pap. 10.99 *(978-0-7502-8412-7(9)*, Wayland) Hachette Children's Group GBR. Dist: Hachette Bk. Group.

—Guy Fawkes. 2017. (Popcorn: People in History Ser.). (ENG., Illus.). 24p. (J). (gr. 4-6). pap. 10.99 *(978-0-7502-8372-4(6)*, Wayland) Hachette Children's Group GBR. Dist: Hachette Bk. Group.

—Henry VIII. 2017. (Popcorn: People in History Ser.). (ENG., Illus.). 24p. (J). (gr. k-2). pap. 10.99 *(978-0-7502-8413-4(7)*, Wayland) Hachette Children's Group GBR. Dist: Hachette Bk. Group.

Whiting, Jim. David Beckham. 2012. (Role Model Athletes Ser.). 64p. (J). (gr. 7). 22.95 *(978-1-4222-2708-4(1))* Mason Crest.

Williams, Mel. Robert Pattinson: Fated for Fame. 2009. (ENG.). 48p. (YA). pap. 9.99 *(978-1-4169-8997-4(8)*, Simon Pulse) Simon Pulse.

Wilson, J. H. Bright Sunset. 2006. (ENG., Illus.). 144p. (J). per. 7.99 *(978-1-84550-114-3(4)*, b61e23be-8f6b-4f53-b2ba-20d49c6ad50e) Christian Focus Pubns. GBR. Dist: Bookmasters Distribution.

Winter, Jeanette. The Watcher: Jane Goodall's Life with the Chimps. Winter, Jeanette, illus. 2011. (ENG., Illus.). 48p. (J). (gr. -1-3). 17.99 *(978-0-375-86774-3(0)*, Schwartz & Wade Bks.) Random Hse. Children's Bks.

Yasuda, Anita. Robert Pattinson. 2010. (Remarkable People Ser.). (Illus.). 24p. (J). (gr. 4-6). pap. 11.95 *(978-1-61690-155-4(1))*; lib. bdg. 25.70 *(978-1-61690-154-7(3))* Weigl Pubs., Inc.

Young, Serinity. Richard Francis Burton: Explorer, Scholar, Spy. 2006. (Great Explorations Ser.). (Illus.). 80p. (gr. 6-7). lib. bdg. 22.95 *(978-0-7614-2222-8(6)*, Benchmark Bks.) Marshall Cavendish Corp.

Yount, Lisa. Rosalind Franklin. 2011. (Trailblazers in Science & Technology Ser.). 152p. (gr. 6-12). 35.00 *(978-1-60413-660-9(X)*, Chelsea Hse.) Facts On File, Inc.

—William Harvey: Discoverer of How Blood Circulates. 2008. (Great Minds of Science Ser.). (Illus.). 128p. (J). (gr. 4-10). lib. bdg. 33.27 *(978-0-7660-3010-7(5))* Enslow Pubs., Inc.

—William Harvey: Genius Discoverer of Blood Circulation. 2015. (Genius Scientists & Their Genius Ideas Ser.). 96p. (J). (gr. 5-12). 27.94 *(978-0-7660-6585-7(5))*; pap. 10.95 *(978-0-7660-6586-4(3))* Enslow Pubs., Inc.

Yuan, Margaret Speaker. Beatrix Potter. 2005. (Who Wrote That? Ser.). (Illus.). 120p. (gr. 6-12). lib. bdg. 35.00 *(978-0-7910-8655-1(0)*, Chelsea Hse.) Facts On File, Inc.

Zeiger, Jennifer. Queen Elizabeth II. 2015. (ENG., Illus.). 48p. (J). lib. bdg. *(978-0-531-21599-9(7)*, Orchard Bks.) Scholastic, Inc.

GREAT BRITAIN—CIVILIZATION

Banting, Erinn. England: The Culture. 2012. (ENG.). 32p. (J). pap. *(978-0-7787-9831-6(3))*; *(978-0-7787-9828-6(3))* Crabtree Publishing Co.

Jeffrey, Gary. The Dark Ages & the Vikings. 2014. (ENG., Illus.). 48p. (J). *(978-0-7787-0401-0(7))* Crabtree Publishing Co.

Lacey, Saskia. The History of Victorian Innovations: Equivalent Fractions (Grade 3) 2017. (Mathematics Readers Ser.). (Illus.). 32p. (gr. 3-3). 8.99 ***(978-1-4807-5803-2(5))*** Teacher Created Materials, Inc.

Maloof, Torrey. Stepping into William Shakespeare's World (Grade 7) 2017. (TIME for KIDS(r) Nonfiction Readers Ser.). (Illus.). 48p. (J). (gr. 7-7). pap. 9.99 ***(978-1-4938-3618-5(8))*** Teacher Created Materials, Inc.

Peal, Robert. Modern Britain - The Age of Reform. 2017. (Knowing History Ser.). (ENG.). 16p. (J). (gr. 5-9). 3.99 ***(978-0-00-819542-7(0))*** HarperCollins Pubs. Ltd. GBR. Dist: Independent Pubs. Group.

Richert, Scott P. King Lear. 2010. (Shakespeare Explained 3 Ser.). (Illus.). 112p. (J). (gr. 7-18). 42.79 *(978-1-60870-016-5(X))* Marshall Cavendish GBR. Dist: Marshall Cavendish Corp.

Roberts, Russell. Elizabethan England. 2009. (How'd They Do That? Ser.). (Illus.). 64p. (J). (gr. 4-8). lib. bdg. 33.95 *(978-1-58415-823-3(9))* Mitchell Lane Pubs., Inc.

Sobran, Joseph. Twelfth Night. 2009. (Shakespeare Explained 2 Ser.). 112p. (gr. 7). 42.79 *(978-0-7614-3425-2(9))* Marshall Cavendish Corp.

Tatlock, Ann. Medieval England. 2014. (ENG.). 48p. (J). lib. bdg. 29.95 *(978-1-62469-000-6(9))* Purple Toad Publishing, Inc.

Wood, Alix. Uncovering the Culture of Ancient Britain, 01 vols., 1. 2016. (Archaeology & Ancient Cultures Ser.). (ENG.). 32p. (J). pap. 10.00 *(978-1-5081-4647-6(0)*, PowerKids Pr.) Rosen Publishing Group, Inc., The.

Wukovits, John F. Victorian Era. Greenhaven Press Editors, ed. 2013. (World History Ser.). (ENG., Illus.). 128p. (gr. 7-10). lib. bdg. 39.90 *(978-1-4205-0933-5(0)*, Lucent Bks.) Cengage Gale.

GREAT BRITAIN—COLONIES

Colonialism. 2010. (Key Concepts in American History Ser.). (Illus.). 128p. (gr. 6-12). 45.00 *(978-1-60413-217-5(5)*, Chelsea Hse.) Facts On File, Inc.

Davies, Gill. The British Colonies. Aronson, Marc, ed. 2005. (National Geographic Timelines Ser.). (Illus.). 64p. (J). lib. bdg. 27.90 *(978-0-7922-7980-8(8))* CENGAGE Learning.

—The Thirteen Colonies 1584 - 1776. Aronson, Marc, ed. 2005. (National Geographic Timelines Ser.). (Illus.). 64p. (J). 17.95 *(978-0-7922-7978-5(6))* CENGAGE Learning.

Huey, Lois Miner. American Archaeology Uncovers the Earliest English Colonies. 2009. (American Archaeology Ser.). 64p. (gr. 5-6). 31.36 *(978-0-7614-4264-6(2))* Marshall Cavendish Corp.

Marshall, H. E. Our Empire Story. Skelton, J. R., illus. 2012. 402p. *(978-1-78139-188-4(2))* Benediction Classics.

Muhall, Jill K. & Alarcon, Jill. Causes of the Revolution, 1 vol. 2004. (Primary Source Readers Ser.). (ENG., Illus.). 24p. (J). (gr. 5-5). pap. 8.99 *(978-0-7439-8785-1(3))* Shell Educational Publishing.

Nardo, Don. The Age of Colonialism. 2006. (World History Ser.). (ENG., Illus.). 104p. (YA). (gr. 7-10). lib. bdg. 33.45 *(978-1-59018-833-0(0)*, Lucent Bks.) Cengage Gale.

Nelson, Sheila. Britain's Canada, 1613-1770. 2007. (How Canada Became Canada Ser.). (Illus.). 87p. (YA). (gr. 3-7). lib. bdg. 21.95 *(978-1-4222-0003-2(5))* Mason Crest.

—A Nation Is Born: World War I & Independence, 1910-1929. 2007. (How Canada Became Canada Ser.). (Illus.). 87p. (YA). (gr. 3-7). lib. bdg. 21.95 *(978-1-4222-0006-3(X)*, 1247972) Mason Crest.

Parker, Lewis K. English Colonies in the Americas. (European Colonies in the Americas Ser.). 24p. 2009. (gr. 2-2). 42.50 *(978-1-61512-317-9(2))* 2003. (Illus.). (J). lib. bdg. 22.60 *(978-0-8239-6475-8(2))* Rosen Publishing Group, Inc., The. (PowerKids Pr.).

EFG

Peal, Robert. Modern Britain - The British Empire. 2017. (Knowing History Ser.). (ENG.). 16p. (J). (gr. 6-9). 3.99 ***(978-0-00-819538-0(2))*** HarperCollins Pubs. Ltd. GBR. Dist: Independent Pubs. Group.

Riley, Michael, et al. Impact of Empire. 2005. (Illus.). 64p. pap., tchr. ed. 62.50 *(978-0-7195-8562-3(7)*, Hodder Education) Hodder Education Group GBR. Dist: Trans-Atlantic Pubns., Inc.

—Impact of Empire: A World Study of The British Empire - 1585 to The Present. 2004. (Illus.). 128p. pap. 29.50 *(978-0-7195-8561-6(9)*, Hodder Education) Hodder Education Group GBR. Dist: Trans-Atlantic Pubns., Inc.

Roxburgh, Ellis. The British Empire. 2015. (Great Empires Ser.). (ENG., Illus.). 48p. (J). (gr. 7-7). 31.36 *(978-1-5026-0634-1(8))* Cavendish Square Publishing.

Slavicek, Louise Chipley. The Boer War. 2011. (Milestones in Modern World History Ser.). (Illus.). 128p. (C). (gr. 9). 35.00 *(978-1-60413-458-2(5)*, Chelsea Hse.) Facts On File, Inc.

GREAT BRITAIN—ECONOMIC CONDITIONS

Allport, Alan. The British Industrial Revolution. 2011. (Milestones in Modern World History Ser.). (Illus.). 128p. (C). (gr. 9). 35.00 *(978-1-60413-498-8(4)*, Chelsea Hse.) Facts On File, Inc.

Connolly, Sean & Claybourne, Anna. Insurance. 2011. (On the Edge Ser.). 32p. (YA). (gr. 3-6). 28.50 *(978-1-59920-519-9(X))* Black Rabbit Bks.

Nardo, Don. The Industrial Revolution in Britain. 2009. (Lucent Library of Historical Eras). (ENG., Illus.). 128p. (YA). (gr. 7-10). lib. bdg. 34.80 *(978-1-4205-0152-0(6)*, LML02109-246064, Lucent Bks.) Cengage Gale.

Senker, Cath. ASOS. 2016. (Big Business Ser.). (ENG., Illus.). 32p. (J). (gr. 4-6). pap. 11.99 *(978-0-7502-8953-5(8)*, Wayland) Hachette Children's Group GBR. Dist: Hachette Bk. Group.

GREAT BRITAIN—FICTION

Albert, Melissa & Gray, Lucinda. The Gilded Cage. 2016. (ENG.). 256p. (YA). (gr. 7). 17.99 *(978-1-62779-181-6(7)*, 9781627791816, Holt, Henry & Co. Bks. For Young Readers) Holt, Henry & Co.

Angus, Sam. Soldier Dog. 2014. (ENG.). 272p. (J). (gr. 4-7). pap. 7.99 *(978-1-250-04417-4(0)*, 9781250044174) Square Fish.

Antony, Steve. The Queen's Handbag. 2017. (ENG.). 32p. (J). (gr. -1-k). 17.99 ***(978-1-338-03293-2(3)***, Scholastic Pr.) Scholastic, Inc.

Archer, Catharine. Doug the Pug: A Fine Working Dog. 2016. (Illus.). 64p. pap. *(978-1-910455-15-9(6))* Intersentia Ltd.

Archer, E. Geek Fantasy Novel. 2011. (ENG.). 320p. (J). (gr. 7-7). 17.99 *(978-0-545-16040-7(5)*, Scholastic Pr.) Scholastic, Inc.

Ashe, Susan. Cuda of the Celts. 2005. (Yellow Go Bananas Ser.). (ENG., Illus.). 48p. (J). (gr. 3-4). *(978-0-7787-2742-2(4))* Crabtree Publishing Co.

Austen, Jane. Pride & Prejudice. Miralles, Joseph, illus. 2005. (Great Illustrated Classics Ser.). 236p. (gr. 3-8). 21.35 *(978-1-59679-249-4(3))* Spotlight.

Bagnold, Enid. National Velvet. 2013. (ENG.). 320p. (J). (gr. 3-12). pap. 7.99 *(978-0-486-49297-1(4))* Dover Pubns., Inc.

Baldwin, Kathleen. A School for Unusual Girls: A Stranje House Novel. 2016. (Stranje House Ser.: 1). (ENG.). 352p. (YA). pap. 9.99 *(978-0-7653-7601-5(6)*, 9780765376015, Tor Teen) Doherty, Tom Assocs., LLC.

Beckham, David. Charlie Barker & the Secret of the Deep Dark Woods. 2006. 570p. pap. 33.20 *(978-1-4120-9264-7(7))* Trafford Publishing.

Beddor, Frank. The Looking Glass Wars, 1 vol. 2007. (Looking Glass Wars Ser.: 1). (ENG., Illus.). 400p. (YA). (gr. 7-18). 9.99 *(978-0-14-240941-1(3)*, Speak) Penguin Young Readers Group.

Bee, Harry. Printer Street's War. 2008. (ENG.). 140p. pap. 10.99 *(978-1-4196-5700-9(3))* CreateSpace Independent Publishing Platform.

Berry, Julie. The Scandalous Sisterhood of Prickwillow Place. 2014. (ENG.). 368p. (J). (gr. 5-9). 15.99 *(978-1-59643-956-6(4)*, 9781596439566) Roaring Brook Pr.

Bethell, Zillah. A Whisper of Horses. 2017. (ENG.). 352p. (J). 16.99 *(978-1-250-09394-3(5)*, 9781250093943) Feiwel & Friends.

Bird, Helen. Fighting Back. 2005. (Shades Ser.). 64p. (J). pap. *(978-0-237-52845-4(2))* Evans Brothers, Ltd.

Blackwood, Gary. Shakespeare's Spy. 2005. 281p. (gr. 5-9). 17.00 *(978-0-7569-5216-7(6))* Perfection Learning Corp.

Blum, Paul. Dawn of the Zombies. 2007. (Extraordinary Files Ser.). (ENG., Illus.). 48p. (J). (gr. 4-7). pap. 10.99 *(978-1-84680-250-8(4))* Evans Brothers, Ltd. GBR. Dist: Independent Pubs. Group.

—Day of Judgement. 2007. (Extraordinary Files Ser.). (ENG., Illus.). 48p. (J). (gr. 4-7). pap. 11.99 *(978-1-84680-251-5(2))* Evans Brothers, Ltd. GBR. Dist: Independent Pubs. Group.

—Gene Machine. 2007. (Extraordinary Files Ser.). (ENG., Illus.). 48p. (J). (gr. 4-7). pap. 10.99 *(978-1-84680-252-2(0))* Evans Brothers, Ltd. GBR. Dist: Independent Pubs. Group.

—Killer Robot. 2007. (Extraordinary Files Ser.). (ENG., Illus.). 48p. (J). (gr. 4-7). pap. 10.99 *(978-1-84680-178-5(8))* Evans Brothers, Ltd. GBR. Dist: Independent Pubs. Group.

—Secrets & Lies. 2007. (Extraordinary Files Ser.). (ENG., Illus.). 48p. (J). (gr. 4-7). pap. 10.99 *(978-1-84680-249-2(0))* Evans Brothers, Ltd. GBR. Dist: Independent Pubs. Group.

—Sleep Walker. 2007. (Extraordinary Files Ser.). (ENG., Illus.). 48p. (J). (gr. 4-7). pap. 10.99 *(978-1-84680-174-7(5))* Evans Brothers, Ltd. GBR. Dist: Independent Pubs. Group.

Borden, Louise. The Little Ships: The Heroic Rescue at Dunkirk in World War II. Foreman, Michael, illus. 2003. (ENG.). 32p. (J). (gr. 4-7). 7.99 *(978-0-689-85396-8(3)*, McElderry, Margaret K. Bks.) McElderry, Margaret K. Bks.

Bradbury, Jennifer. Wrapped. 2011. (ENG., Illus.). 320p. (YA). (gr. 7-18). 16.99 *(978-1-4169-9007-9(0)*, Atheneum Bks. for Young Readers) Simon & Schuster Children's Publishing.

Brand, Christianna. Nurse Matilda Goes to Hospital. Ardizzone, Edward, illus. (ENG.). 128p. *(978-0-7475-7678-5(5))* Bloomsbury Publishing Plc GBR. Dist: Macmillan.

Brigham, Anthea. Henrietta, World War II Hen: This Is a True Story. Brigham, Anthea, illus. 2008. (ENG., Illus.). 28p. (J). 7.00 *(978-0-9740778-2-6(8))* Whale's Jaw Publishing.

Brighton, Catherine. The Fossil Girl: Mary Anning's Dinosaur Discovery. 2007. (ENG., Illus.). 32p. (J). (gr. k-3). pap. 9.99 *(978-1-84507-732-7(6)*, Frances Lincoln) Quarto Publishing Group UK GBR. Dist: Hachette Bk. Group.

Brouwer, Sigmund. Wings of an Angel. 2004. (Winds of Light Ser.). 214p. (YA). pap. 5.99 *(978-1-55305-032-2(0))* Cygnet Publishing Group, Inc./Coolreading.com CAN. Dist: Orca Bk. Pubs. USA.

Buckland, Augustus Robert. The Empire Annual for Girls: With Illustrations. 2007. 370p. pap. 25.99 *(978-1-4264-9397-3(5))*; 412p. pap. 28.99 *(978-1-4264-9778-0(4))* Creative Media Partners, LLC.

Bullock, Robert John. Jacob's War. 2013. 246p. pap. 13.97 *(978-1-62212-582-1(7)*, Strategic Bk. Publishing) Strategic Book Publishing & Rights Agency (SBPRA).

Burchett, Jan & Vogler, Sara. Deadly Storm & Fatal Voyage. 2017. (Spy Master Ser.). (ENG.). 400p. (J). (gr. 4-6). 7.99 ***(978-1-4440-1074-9(3)***, Orion Children's Bks.) Hachette Children's Group GBR. Dist: Hachette Bk. Group.

Burgis, Stephanie. Stolen Magic. (Kat, Incorrigible Ser.: 3). (ENG., Illus.). 400p. (YA). (gr. 5-8). 2014. pap. 7.99 *(978-1-4169-9452-7(1))* 2013. 17.99 *(978-1-4169-9451-0(3)*, Atheneum Bks. for Young Readers) Simon & Schuster Children's Publishing.

Butler, Dave. The Kidnap Plot (the Extraordinary Journeys of Clockwork Charlie) 2017. (Extraordinary Journeys of Clockwork Charlie Ser.). (ENG.). 336p. (J). (gr. 3-7). 7.99 ***(978-0-553-51298-4(6)***, Yearling) Random Hse. Children's Bks.

Cameron, Sharon. The Dark Unwinding. 2013. (ENG.). 336p. (J). (gr. 7). pap. 9.99 *(978-0-545-32787-9(3)*, Scholastic Paperbacks) Scholastic, Inc.

Carriger, Gail. Manners & Mutiny. 2015. (Finishing School Ser.: 4). (ENG., Illus.). 336p. (YA). (gr. 7-17). 18.00 *(978-0-316-19028-2(4))* Little, Brown Bks. for Young Readers.

Cassidy, Cathy. Dizzy. 2005. (ENG.). 272p. (J). (gr. 3-7). 6.99 *(978-0-14-240474-4(8)*, Puffin Books) Penguin Young Readers Group.

Chadda, Sarwat. The Savage Fortress. 2012. (ENG.). 304p. (J). (gr. 4-7). 16.99 *(978-0-545-38516-9(4)*, Levine, Arthur A. Bks.) Scholastic, Inc.

Collingwood, Harry. The Rover's Secret. 2011. 274p. 29.95 *(978-1-4638-9505-1(4))* Rodgers, Alan Bks.

Condie, Catherine. Whirl of the Wheel. 2010. 107p. pap. 12.95 *(978-1-4452-8648-8(3))* Lulu Pr., Inc.

Cooper, Mark A. Fledgling: Jason Steed. 2010. (ENG.). 240p. (J). (gr. 3-7). pap. 10.99 *(978-1-4022-3999-1(8)*, Sourcebooks Jabberwocky) Sourcebooks, Inc.

Cornwell, Nicki. Armel's Revenge. Pal, Erika, illus. 2012. (ENG.). 96p. (J). (gr. 3-6). pap. 8.99 *(978-1-84780-224-8(9)*, Frances Lincoln) Quarto Publishing Group UK GBR. Dist: Hachette Bk. Group.

De Angeli, Marguerite. The Door in the Wall. unabr. ed. 2004. 121p. (J). (gr. 4-7). pap. 29.00 incl. audio *(978-0-8072-8691-3(5)*, YA237SP, Listening Library) Random Hse. Audio Publishing Group.

Dennis, Peter, illus. The Adventures of King Arthur. 2003. (Usborne Young Reading: Series Two Ser.). 64p. (J). (gr. k-7). 8.99 *(978-0-7945-1871-4(0)*, Usborne) EDC Publishing.

Diamand, Emily. Raiders' Ransom. 2009. (Raiders' Ransom Ser.: 1). (ENG.). 368p. (J). (gr. 3-7). 17.99 *(978-0-545-14297-7(0))* Scholastic, Inc.

Dickens, Charles. A Christmas Carol & the Remembrance of Mugby. 2012. (Classics Illustrated Deluxe Graphic Nove Ser.). (ENG., Illus.). 96p. (J). (gr. 2-8). pap. 11.99 *(978-1-59707-345-5(8)*, 9781597073455) Papercutz.

Edge, Christopher. Twelve Minutes to Midnight. 2014. (Penelope Tredwell Mysteries Ser.: Book 1). (ENG.). 256p. (J). (gr. 3-7). 16.99 *(978-0-8075-8133-9(X))* Whitman, Albert & Co.

Ewing, Juliana Horatia. Six to Sixteen. 2007. (ENG.). 190p. pap. 19.99 *(978-1-4264-9664-6(8))*; 206p. pap. 22.99 *(978-1-4264-9206-8(5))* Creative Media Partners, LLC.

Farb, Carolyn. Lucas Comes to America. 2011. 34p. (J). 14.99 *(978-1-4567-4541-7(7))* AuthorHouse.

Fidler, Kathleen. Flash the Sheepdog. 3rd rev. ed. (ENG., Illus.). 176p. 12.00 *(978-0-86315-581-9(2))* Floris Bks. GBR. Dist: SteinerBooks, Inc.

Fisher, Linda C. A Will of Her Own. 2006. (YA). pap. *(978-0-88092-641-6(4))*; lib. bdg. *(978-0-88092-640-9(6))* Royal Fireworks Publishing Co.

Fitzgerald, John D. Me & My Little Brain. Mayer, Mercer, illus. 2004. (Great Brain Ser.). 137p. (gr. 3-7). 16.00 *(978-0-7569-2541-3(X))* Perfection Learning Corp.

Gallagher, Brian. Stormclouds: New Friends. Old Differences. 2014. (ENG.). 224p. (J). 13.95 *(978-1-84717-579-3(1))* O'Brien Pr., Ltd., The IRL. Dist: Dufour Editions, Inc.

Gaughen, A. C. Lady Thief. 2015. (Scarlet Ser.: No. 2). (ENG.). 336p. (YA). (gr. 7). pap. 9.99 *(978-0-8027-3788-5(9)*, 9780802737885, Bloomsbury USA Childrens) Bloomsbury Publishing USA.

—Lion Heart: A Scarlet Novel. 2016. (Scarlet Ser.). (ENG.). 352p. (YA). pap. 9.99 *(978-1-61963-928-7(9)*, 9781619639287, Bloomsbury USA Childrens) Bloomsbury Publishing USA.

Hall, Tim. Shadow of the Wolf. 2016. (ENG.). 480p. (J). (gr. 9). pap. 9.99 *(978-1-338-03250-5(X))* Scholastic, Inc.

Hayes, Malcolm. The Dreamcatchers. 2006. 282p. pap. 20.14 *(978-1-4120-8320-1(6))* Trafford Publishing.

Higgy, M. J. Creator's Dream. 2012. (Illus.). 16p. pap. 18.30 *(978-1-4772-3862-2(X))* AuthorHouse.

Huggins-Cooper, Lynn & Hayward, Ian Benfold. One Boy's War. 2014. (ENG., Illus.). 32p. (J). (gr. 2-6). pap. 8.99 *(978-1-84780-126-5(9)*, Frances Lincoln) Quarto Publishing Group UK GBR. Dist: Hachette Bk. Group.

Jones, Ursula. Star Turn. 2012. (Inside Pocket Single Titles Ser.). (ENG.). 32p. (gr. 5-12). pap. *(978-1-908458-16-2(X))* Inside Pocket Publishing, Ltd.

Lasky, Kathryn. Hawksmaid: The Untold Story of Robin Hood & Maid Marian. 2011. (ENG.). 320p. (J). (gr. 5). pap. 6.99 *(978-0-06-000072-1(4))* HarperCollins Pubs.

Lockwood, Vicki. The Magnificent Lizzie Brown & the Ghost Ship. Hans, Stephanie, illus. 2015. (Magnificent Lizzie Brown Ser.). (ENG.). 200p. (gr. 5-9). lib. bdg. 26.65 *(978-1-4342-9806-5(X))* Stone Arch Bks.

Macauley, Jo. Inferno, 1 vol. 2014. (Secrets & Spies Ser.). (ENG.). 224p. (gr. 4-7). 26.65 *(978-1-4342-9595-8(8))* Stone Arch Bks.

—Treason. 2014. (J). pap. *(978-1-4342-7944-6(8))* Stone Arch Bks.

MacColl, Michaela. Always Emily. 2014. (ENG.). 282p. (YA). (gr. 7-17). 16.99 *(978-1-4521-1174-2(X))* Chronicle Bks. LLC.

MacDonald, Tom. Secret of the Tree: Marcus Speer's Ecosentinel. Stieber, Joel, illus. 2009. 300p. pap. 18.95 *(978-0-595-52402-0(8))* iUniverse, Inc.

Magorian, Michelle. Just Henry. 2015. (ENG.). 720p. (J). (gr. 5-7). pap. 12.99 *(978-1-4052-7695-5(9))* Egmont Bks., Ltd. GBR. Dist: Independent Pubs. Group.

Manning, Sarra. Guitar Girl. 2005. 217p. (gr. 9-12). 17.00 *(978-0-7569-5702-5(8))* Perfection Learning Corp.

Martin, Caroline Jane. The Flow. 2013. (ENG.). 276p. pap. *(978-0-9928101-0-8(8))* Lovell Pr.

McDine, Donna M. Powder Monkey. Snider, Kc, illus. 2013. 24p. 19.95 *(978-1-61633-384-3(7))*; pap. 10.95 *(978-1-61633-385-0(5))* Guardian Angel Publishing, Inc.

McFadden, Deanna. Robin Hood. Calo, Marcos, illus. 2013. (Silver Penny Stories Ser.). (ENG.). 48p. (J). (gr. -1-1). 4.95 *(978-1-4027-8339-5(6))* Sterling Publishing Co., Inc.

Meyer, L. A. Viva Jacquelina! Being an Account of the Further Adventures of Jacky Faber, over the Hills & Far Away. 2012. (Bloody Jack Adventures Ser.: 10). (ENG.). 368p. (YA). (gr. 9). 16.99 *(978-0-547-76350-7(6))* Houghton Mifflin Harcourt Publishing Co.

Molesworth & Molesworth, Mary Louisa S. The Rectory Children. 2008. 124p. 23.95 *(978-0-60664-728-8(8))*; pap. 10.95 *(978-0-60664-227-6(8))* Rodgers, Alan Bks.

Nesbit, E. The Phoenix & the Carpet. l.t. ed. 2005. 352p. pap. *(978-1-84637-204-9(6))* Echo Library.

—Wouldbegoods. 2006. pap. *(978-1-4068-3508-3(0))* Echo Library.

Newbery, Linda. Polly's March. 2009. (Historical House Ser.). 192p. (YA). (gr. 5-18). pap. 5.99 *(978-0-7945-2336-7(6)*, Usborne) EDC Publishing.

Norfolk, Bobby & Norfolk, Sherry. Billy Brown & the Belly Button Beastie. Hoffmire, Baird, illus. 2007. (Buried Treasure Ser.). (ENG.). 32p. (J). (gr. -1-3). 16.95 *(978-0-87483-831-2(2))* August Hse. Pubs., Inc.

Orme, David & Orme, Helen. Up for It? 2008. (Backstreet Ser.). (ENG., Illus.). 36p. pap. *(978-1-84167-769-9(8))* Ransom Publishing Ltd.

Orme, Helen. New Boy. 2008. (Backstreet Ser.). (ENG., Illus.). 36p. pap. *(978-1-84167-770-5(1))* Ransom Publishing Ltd.

—Rats! 2008. (Backstreet Ser.). (ENG., Illus.). 36p. pap. *(978-1-84167-772-9(8))* Ransom Publishing Ltd.

—Won't Talk, Can't Talk. 2008. (Backstreet Ser.). (Illus.). 36p. pap. *(978-1-84167-777-4(9))* Ransom Publishing Ltd.

Oulton, Harry. Heather's Piglets. 2017. (Pig Called Heather Ser.: 3). (ENG., Illus.). 240p. (J). (gr. 4-7). pap. 8.99 ***(978-1-84812-479-0(1))*** Bonnier Publishing GBR. Dist: Independent Pubs. Group.

—The Return of a Pig Called Heather. 2017. (Pig Called Heather Ser.: 2). (ENG., Illus.). 192p. (J). (gr. 4-7). pap. 8.99 ***(978-1-84812-473-8(2))*** Bonnier Publishing GBR. Dist: Independent Pubs. Group.

Paschkis, Julie, illus. The Great Smelly, Slobbery, Small-Tooth Dog: A Folktale from Great Britain. 2007. (ENG.). 32p. (J). (gr. -1-3). 16.95 *(978-0-87483-808-4(8))* August Hse. Pubs., Inc.

Phillips, Dee. Tail Gunner. 2014. (Yesterday's Voices Ser.). (YA). lib. bdg. 19.60 *(978-0-606-35579-7(0))* Turtleback Bks.

Quinn, K. A. S. The Queen Alone. 2015. (Chronicles of the Tempus Ser.). (ENG.). 328p. (J). (gr. 4-7). pap. 10.99 *(978-1-84887-056-7(6))* Atlantic Bks., Ltd. GBR. Dist: Independent Pubs. Group.

Radwan, Hassan. Rashid & the Missing Body. 2010. (ENG., Illus.). 80p. (J). (gr. 2-6). pap. 5.95 *(978-0-86037-395-7(9))* Kube Publishing Ltd. GBR. Dist: Consortium Bk. Sales & Distribution.

Rayner, Shoo. Boar Wars. 2016. (Roman Brit Ser.). (ENG., Illus.). 64p. (J). (gr. k-2). pap. 7.99 *(978-1-4083-3455-3(0)*, Orchard Bks.) Hachette Children's Group GBR. Dist: Hachette Bk. Group.

Robin, Ink & Rivard, Joanna. A Real Prince Is Hard to Find: A Modern Fairy Tale. 2013. (ENG., Illus.). 32p. (J). (gr. -1-3). 17.89 *(978-1-61963-216-5(0)*, 9781619632165); 16.99 *(978-1-61963-215-8(2)*, 9781619632158) Bloomsbury Publishing USA. (Bloomsbury USA Childrens).

Rohmer, Sax, pseud. The Sins of Severac Bablon. 2008. 200p. per. 14.95 *(978-1-60312-545-1(0))* Aegypan.

Rosen, Michael. You're Thinking about Tomatoes. 2005. (Illus.). 150p. (J). (gr. 3-7). per. 5.95 *(978-1-903015-44-5(8))* Barn Owl Bks, London GBR. Dist: Independent Pubs. Group.

Rylance, Maureen. The Spur on the Plate. 2005. 102p. (YA). pap. 12.15 *(978-1-4120-5459-1(1))* Trafford Publishing.

Schrefer, Eliot. Geek Fantasy Novel. 2016. (ENG.). 320p. (J). (gr. 7). pap. 9.99 *(978-0-545-16041-4(3))* Scholastic, Inc.

Scott, Walter, ed. Ivanhoe. 2nd ed. 2003. (Historias de Siempre Ser.). (SPA., Illus.). 92p. (J). (gr. 5-8). pap. 12.95 *(978-84-204-5721-5(3))* Santillana USA Publishing Co., Inc.

Shevah, Emma. Dara Palmer's Major Drama. 2016. (ENG.). 288p. (J). (gr. 3-7). 16.99 *(978-1-4926-3138-5(8)*, 9781492631385, Sourcebooks Jabberwocky) Sourcebooks, Inc.

Springer, Nancy. Wild Boy. 2005. (Tales of Rowan Hood Ser.). 115p. (J). (gr. 3). 13.65 *(978-0-7569-5490-1(8))* Perfection Learning Corp.

Stier, Catherine. Welcome to America, Champ. Ettlinger, Doris, illus. 2013. (Tales of the World Ser.). (ENG.). 32p. (J). (gr. 1-4). 17.95 *(978-1-58536-606-4(4)*, 202360) Sleeping Bear Pr.

Stone, Phoebe. Romeo Blue. 2013. (ENG.). 352p. (J). (gr. 3-7). 16.99 *(978-0-545-44360-9(1)*, Levine, Arthur A. Bks.) Scholastic, Inc.

Sutcliff, Rosemary. The Eagle of the Ninth. Hodges, C. Walter, illus. 2015. (ENG.). 304p. (J). *(978-1-85715-520-4(3))* Knopf, Alfred A. Inc.

Sutcliffe, William. Bad Influence. Anderson, Laura Ellen & Busby, Ailie, illus. 2015. (ENG.). 224p. (YA). (gr. 9). pap. 15.99 *(978-1-4088-3653-8(X)*, 9781408836538, Bloomsbury USA Childrens) Bloomsbury Publishing USA.

Talburt, Tony. The History on the Page: Adventures in Black British History. 2012. 182p. pap. *(978-1-909039-23-0(3))* Legend Pr.

Turk, Judy Vanslyke, et al. Laughing Thief. 2007. (Clifton Ser.: 2). (ENG., Illus.). 48p. (J). (gr. 4-7). per. 9.99 *(978-1-905460-07-6(4))* CineBook GBR. Dist: National Bk. Network.

—My Dear Wilkinson. 2007. (Clifton Ser.: 1). (ENG., Illus.). 48p. (J). (gr. 4-7). per. 11.95 *(978-1-905460-06-9(6))* CineBook GBR. Dist: National Bk. Network.

Twain, Mark, pseud. A Connecticut Yankee in King Arthur's Court. 2008. (Bring the Classics to Life Ser.). (ENG., Illus.). 72p. (gr. 3-12). pap., act. bk. ed. 10.95 *(978-1-55576-357-2(X)*, EDCTR-309B) EDCON Publishing Group.

Umansky, Kaye. Solomon Snow & the Stolen Jewel. Nash, Scott, illus. 2007. (ENG.). 256p. (J). (gr. 2-5). 12.99 *(978-0-7636-2793-5(3))* Candlewick Pr.

Uncle Markie. Piglette & Bobo in the United Kingdom. 2003. (YA). ring bd. 9.95 *(978-1-933129-14-3(X))* Studio 403.

Van Hamme, Jean. The Strange Encounter, Vol. 5. 2009. (Blake & Mortimer Ser.: 5). (ENG., Illus.). 66p. pap. 15.95 *(978-1-905460-75-5(9))* CineBook GBR. Dist: National Bk. Network.

Vehlmann, Fabien. Green Manor Pt. 1: Assassins & Gentleman. Bodart, Denis, illus. 2008. (Expresso Collection). (ENG.). 56p. pap. 13.95 *(978-1-905460-53-3(8))* CineBook GBR. Dist: National Bk. Network.

Webb, Holly. Return to the Secret Garden. 2016. (ENG.). 224p. (J). (gr. 3-7). 16.99 *(978-1-4926-3909-1(5)*, 9781492639091) Sourcebooks, Inc.

Webster, Wendy. Magicus Perfecticum. 2009. (Illus.). 60p. pap. 11.49 *(978-1-4490-0765-2(1))* AuthorHouse.

Wilson, John. And in the Morning. 2010. (ENG.). 200p. (YA). (gr. 7-18). pap. *(978-1-55470-264-0(X))* Me to We.

Wishinsky, Frieda & Griffiths, Dean. Far from Home. Franson, Leanne & Owlkids Books Inc. Staff, illus. 2008. (Canadian Flyer Adventures Ser.: 11). (ENG.). 96p. (J). (gr. 1-4). pap. 7.95 *(978-1-897349-43-4(2)*, Maple Tree Pr.) Owlkids Bks. Inc. CAN. Dist: Publishers Group West (PGW).

Wolcott, P. A. The Fox, the Badger, & the Bunny: A Dales Tale. Wolcott, K. Hannah, ed. Schweitzer, Patty, illus. 2009. 20p. pap. 24.95 *(978-1-60749-525-3(2))* America Star Bks.

Wood, Maryrose & Duchess of Northumberland Staff. The Poison Diaries. 2010. (Poison Diaries: 1). (ENG.). 288p. (YA). (gr. 8-18). 16.99 *(978-0-06-180236-2(0))* HarperCollins Pubs.

Woodruff, Elvira. Fearless. 2011. (ENG.). 240p. (J). (gr. 3-7). pap. 6.99 *(978-0-439-67704-2(1)*, Scholastic Pr.) Scholastic, Inc.

GREAT BRITAIN—HISTORY

Abbott, Jacob. History of King Richard the First of England. 2003. 336p. 99.00 *(978-0-7950-3593-7(4))* New Library Press LLC.

—History of King Richard the Second of England. 2003. 347p. 99.00 *(978-0-7950-3594-4(2))* New Library Press LLC.

—History of William the Conqueror. 2003. 291p. 89.00 *(978-0-7950-4508-0(5))* New Library Press LLC.

—King Alfred of England, Makers of Histor. 2006. pap. *(978-1-4065-0359-3(2))* Dodo Pr.

Abrams, Dennis. The Treaty of Nanking. 2011. (Milestones in Modern World History Ser.). (Illus.). 120p. (C). (gr. 9). 35.00 *(978-1-60413-495-7(X)*, Chelsea Hse.) Facts On File, Inc.

Anderson, Dale. Soldiers & Sailors in the American Revolution. 2005. (World Almanac Library of the American Revolution Ser.). 48p. (gr. 5-12). pap. 14.05 *(978-0-8368-5938-6(3))*; lib. bdg. 31.00 *(978-0-8368-5929-4(4))* Stevens, Gareth Publishing LLLP. (Gareth Stevens Secondary Library).

Anglo-Saxons. 2016. (Ladybird Histories Ser.). (ENG., Illus.). 64p. (J). (gr. 2-4). pap. 9.99 *(978-0-7232-9442-9(9))* Penguin Bks., Ltd. GBR. Dist: Independent Pubs. Group.

Ashworth, Leon. Guy Fawkes. (Illus.). 32p. *(978-0-7451-5288-2(0))* Cherrytree Bks.

Awfully Ancient. 2015. (Awfully Ancient Ser.). (ENG.). 32p. (J). (gr. 5-5). pap., pap., pap. 378.00 *(978-1-4824-3438-5(5))* Stevens, Gareth Publishing LLLP.

Azzarelli, Ally. Adele! Singing Sensation. 2013. (Sizzling Celebrities Ser.). 48p. (J). (gr. 4-9). pap. 8.95 *(978-1-4644-0283-8(3))* Enslow Pubs., Inc.

Bailey, Jacqui. Queen Elizabeth II's Britain: A Celebration of British History under Its Longest Reigning Monarch. 2017. (ENG., Illus.). 48p. (J). (gr. 4-6). pap. 11.99 *(978-1-4451-4222-7(8)*, Franklin Watts) Hachette Children's Group GBR. Dist: Hachette Bk. Group.

Baker, Gayle. Cambria: A HarborTown History. 2003. (Illus.). 96p. per. 8.95 *(978-0-9710984-2-8(5))* HarborTown Histories.

Banting, Erinn. England - The Land. 2012. (ENG.). 32p. (J). pap. *(978-0-7787-9832-3(1))* Crabtree Publishing Co.

Baxter, Roberta. The Magna Carta: Cornerstone of the Constitution, 1 vol. 2012. (Documenting U. S. History Ser.). (ENG.). 48p. (gr. 3-6). pap. 9.95 *(978-1-4329-6765-9(7))*; lib. bdg. 32.65 *(978-1-4329-6756-7(8))* Heinemann-Raintree. (NA-h).

Bean, Rachel. United Kingdom. 2007. (Countries of the World Ser.). (ENG., Illus.). 64p. (J). (gr. 5-9). lib. bdg. 27.90 *(978-1-4263-0126-1(X)*, National Geographic Children's Bks.) National Geographic Society.

Beller, Susan Provost. Yankee Doodle & the Redcoats: Soldiering in the Revolutionary War. Day, Larry, illus. 2003. (Single Titles Ser.). (ENG.). 96p. (gr. 5-8). lib. bdg. 26.60 *(978-0-7613-2612-0(X)*, Twenty-First Century Bks.) Lerner Publishing Group.

Bingham, Jane. Anglo-Saxons. 2017. (Explore! Ser.). (ENG., Illus.). 32p. (J). (gr. 4-6). pap. 12.99 *(978-0-7502-9734-9(4)*, Wayland) Hachette Children's Group GBR. Dist: Hachette Bk. Group.

—Victorians. 2017. (Explore! Ser.). (ENG., Illus.). 32p. (J). (gr. 4-6). pap. 11.99 *(978-0-7502-8879-8(5)*, Wayland) Hachette Children's Group GBR. Dist: Hachette Bk. Group.

Blashfield, Jean F. England. 2012. (Enchantment of the World, Second Ser.). (ENG., Illus.). 144p. (J). (gr. 5-8). lib. bdg. 40.00 *(978-0-531-27542-9(6)*, Children's Pr.) Scholastic Library Publishing.

Bober, Natalie S. Countdown to Independence. 2007. (ENG.). 368p. (YA). (gr. 7). pap. 19.95 *(978-1-4169-6392-9(8)*, Atheneum Bks. for Young Readers) Simon & Schuster Children's Publishing.

Brimson, Samuel. United Kingdom-Zimbabwe, 8 vols. 2003. (Nations of the World Ser.: Vol. 8). (Illus.). 64p. (gr. 5-12). lib.

bdg. 31.00 (978-0-8368-5492-3(6), Gareth Stevens Secondary Library) Stevens, Gareth Publishing LLLP.
Brocklehurst, Ruth. Roman Britain: Internet-Linked. Chisholm, Jane, ed. Gaudenzi, Giacinto, illus. 2006. (Usborne History of Britain Ser.). 48p. (J). (gr. 4-7). per. 8.99 (978-0-7945-1232-3(1), Usborne) EDC Publishing.
Brooks, Philip. King George III: America's Enemy. 2009. (Wicked History Ser.). (ENG.). 128p. (J). (gr. 6-12). pap. 5.95 (978-0-531-20739-0(0), Watts, Franklin) Scholastic Library Publishing.
Brooks, Riley. One Direction: Superstardom! 2013. (ENG., Illus.). 48p. (J). (gr. 3-7). pap. 4.99 (978-0-545-59131-7(7)) Scholastic, Inc.
Browning, Oscar. True Stories from English History from T. 2006. pap. 33.95 (978-1-4254-9960-0(0)) Kessinger Publishing, LLC.
Burgan, Michael. Weapons, Gear, & Uniforms of the American Revolution, 1 vol. 2012. (Equipped for Battle Ser.). (ENG.). 32p. (gr. 3-4). lib. bdg. 27.99 (978-1-4296-7647-2(7), Edge Bks.) Capstone Press of Coughlan Cos.
Butterfield, Moira. Art & Culture. 2017. (Discover the Anglo-Saxons Ser.). (ENG., Illus.). 32p. (J). (gr. 4-6). pap. 11.99 (978-1-4451-3343-0(1), Franklin Watts) Hachette Children's Group GBR. Dist: Hachette Bk. Group.
—Iron Age. 2017. (Britain in the Past Ser.). (ENG., Illus.). 32p. (J). (gr. 2-5). pap. 12.99 **(978-1-4451-4065-0(9)**, Franklin Watts) Hachette Children's Group GBR. Dist: Hachette Bk. Group.
—Kings & Warriors. 2016. (Discover the Anglo-Saxons Ser.). (ENG., Illus.). 32p. (J). (gr. 4-6). pap. 11.99 (978-1-4451-3327-0(X), Franklin Watts) Hachette Children's Group GBR. Dist: Hachette Bk. Group.
—Religion & Saints. 2016. (Discover the Anglo-Saxons Ser.). (ENG., Illus.). 32p. (J). (gr. 4-6). pap. 11.99 (978-1-4451-3339-3(3), Franklin Watts) Hachette Children's Group GBR. Dist: Hachette Bk. Group.
—The Romans. 2017. (Britain in the Past Ser.). (ENG., Illus.). 32p. (J). (gr. 4-6). pap. 12.99 **(978-1-4451-4056-8(X)**, Franklin Watts) Hachette Children's Group GBR. Dist: Hachette Bk. Group.
—Vikings. 2017. (Britain in the Past Ser.). (ENG., Illus.). 32p. (J). (gr. 2-5). pap. 12.99 **(978-1-4451-4068-1(3)**, Franklin Watts) Hachette Children's Group GBR. Dist: Hachette Bk. Group.
Capt, E. Raymond. Isle of Iona. 2003. 160p. per. 11.95 (978-0-934666-58-9(X)) Artisan Pubs.
Catel, Patrick. Soldiers of the Revolutionary War, 1 vol. 2011. (Why We Fought: the Revolutionary War Ser.). (ENG.). 48p. (gr. 3-6). pap. 9.95 (978-1-4329-3903-8(3), Heinemann InfoSearch) Heinemann-Raintree.
Cawood, Ian. Britain in the Twentieth Century. 2003. (Spotlight History Ser.). (ENG., Illus.). 496p. (C). 43.95 (978-0-415-25457-1(4)); (gr. 8-12). 140.00 (978-0-415-25456-4(6), 0415254566) Routledge.
Chibi, Andrew A. The English Reformation: The Effect on a Nation. 2003. (Studymates Ser.). (Illus.). 98p. pap. (978-1-84285-024-4(5)) GLMP Ltd.
Children's Encyclopedia of British History. rev. ed. 2013. (Illus.). 240p. (978-0-7534-1189-6(X)) Callender Pr.
Clare, John D. Medieval Britain, 1066-1500. 2003. (Illus.). 96p. pap. 29.50 (978-0-340-86903-1(8), Hodder Education) Hodder Education Group GBR. Dist: Trans-Atlantic Pubns., Inc.
Clark, Veronica, et al. Class Assemblies 1, 1 vol. 2010. (and C Black Assembly Packs Ser.). (ENG., Illus.). 64p. (J). pap. 32.95 incl. audio compact disk **(978-1-4081-2456-7(4))** HarperCollins Pubs. Ltd. GBR. Dist: Independent Pubs. Group.
—Class Assemblies 2, 1 vol. 2010. (and C Black Assembly Packs Ser.). (ENG., Illus.). 64p. (J). pap. 32.95 incl. audio compact disk **(978-1-4081-2457-4(2))** HarperCollins Pubs. Ltd. GBR. Dist: Independent Pubs. Group.
—Class Assemblies 3, 1 vol. 2010. (and C Black Assembly Packs Ser.). (ENG., Illus.). 64p. (J). pap. 32.95 incl. audio compact disk **(978-1-4081-2458-1(0))** HarperCollins Pubs. Ltd. GBR. Dist: Independent Pubs. Group.
Connolly, Sean. Insurance. 2010. (World Economy Explained Ser.). (Illus.). 48p. (YA). (gr. 7-12). 35.65 (978-1-60753-078-7(3)) Amicus Publishing.
Corporate Contibutor Staff & Roberts, Steve. King George Iii: England's Struggle to Keep America. 2012. (ENG.). 48p. (J). (978-0-7787-0800-1(4)) Crabtree Publishing Co.
Costain, Meredith. You Wouldn't Want to Be an 18th-Century British Convict! A Trip to Australia You'd Rather Not Take. Antram, David, illus. 2006. (You Wouldn't Want to Ser.). (ENG.). 32p. (J). (gr. 2-5). pap. 9.95 (978-0-531-16998-8(7), Watts, Franklin) Scholastic Library Publishing.
Crompton, Samuel Willard. Thomas More: And His Struggles of Conscience. 2005. (Makers of the Middle Ages & Renaissance Ser.). (Illus.). 152p. (J). (gr. 5-8). lib. bdg. 32.95 (978-0-7910-8636-0(4), Chelsea Hse.) Facts On File, Inc.
Damon, Duane C. Life in Victorian England. 2005. (Way People Live Ser.). (ENG., Illus.). 112p. (YA). (gr. 7-10). 30.85 (978-1-56006-391-9(2), 1251192, Lucent Bks.) Cengage Gale.
Davis, Kenneth C. Don't Know Much about the Kings & Queens of England. Date not set. 48p. (J). (gr. 1-4). pap. 5.99 (978-0-06-446229-7(3)) HarperCollins Pubs.
Demi. Florence Nightingale. Demi, illus. 2014. (ENG., Illus.). 40p. (J). (gr. -1-3). 17.99 (978-0-8050-9729-0(5), 9780805097290, Holt, Henry & Co. Bks. For Young Readers) Holt, Henry & Co.
Dickens, Charles. A Child 's History of England. 2013. 384p. pap. (978-3-95564-232-7(1)) Ehv-history in Europäischer Hochschulverlag GmbH & Co. KG.
—A Child's History of England. 2010. 384p. pap. (978-3-86741-285-8(5)) CT Salzwasser-Verlag GmbH & Co. KG.
—A Child's History of England, 2 vols. 2013. 425p. reprint ed. lthr. 69.00 (978-0-7426-2323-1(8)) Classic Bks.
—A Child's History of England. 2012. 416p. pap. 34.75 (978-1-248-89394-4(8)) 2011. 362p. pap. 32.75 (978-1-179-36354-7(X)) 2011. 296p. pap. 28.75 (978-1-178-70477-8(7)) 2010. 536p. pap. 40.75 (978-1-143-97379-6(8)) 2010. (ENG.). 340p. pap. 31.75 (978-1-143-97367-3(4)) 2010. (ENG.). 234p. pap. 25.75 (978-1-176-54196-2(X)) 2010. 886p. pap. 59.75 (978-1-176-68457-7(4)) 2010. (ENG.). 300p. pap. 29.75 (978-1-176-54436-9(5)) 2010. (ENG.). 374p. pap. 32.75 (978-1-176-53927-3(2)) 2010. (ENG.). 234p. pap. 25.75 (978-1-176-53706-4(7)) 2010. (ENG.). 346p. pap. 32.75 (978-1-176-40721-3(X)) 2010. (ENG.). 444p. pap. 36.75 (978-1-174-83244-4(4)) 2010. 240p. pap. 26.75 (978-1-149-32218-5(7)) 2010. 418p. pap. 34.75 (978-1-149-25989-4(2)) 2010. 436p. 41.99 (978-1-140-20643-9(5)) 2010. 366p. 38.99 (978-1-140-05732-1(4)) 2010. 366p. pap. 32.75 (978-1-140-05733-8(2)) 2010. 364p. pap. 32.75 (978-1-146-82515-3(3)) 2010. 334p. pap. 31.75 (978-1-146-80885-9(2)) 2010. 298p. pap. 28.75 (978-1-148-09605-6(1)) 2010. 320p. pap. 30.75 (978-1-146-75130-8(3)) 2010. 336p. pap. 31.75 (978-1-147-12818-5(9)) 2010. 342p. pap. 31.75 (978-1-147-06784-2(8)) 2010. 604p. pap. 45.75 (978-1-145-54528-1(9)) 2010. 320p. pap. 30.75 (978-1-143-36005-3(2)) 2010. 322p. pap. 30.75 (978-1-143-85220-6(6)) 2010. 294p. pap. 28.75 (978-1-145-57785-5(7)) 2010. 518p. pap. 39.75 (978-1-142-10014-8(6)) 2010. 536p. pap. 40.75 (978-1-143-02304-0(8)) 2010. 374p. pap. 32.75 (978-1-141-99746-6(0)) 2009. 290p. 30.99 (978-1-110-72709-4(7)) 2009. 290p. pap. 27.75 (978-1-110-72706-3(2)) 2009. (ENG.). 289p. pap. 23.99 (978-1-110-72705-6(4), BiblioLife) 2009. (ENG.). 289p. pap. 21.99 (978-1-110-72703-2(8), BiblioLife) 2009. 292p. 24.99 (978-1-103-21192-0(7)) 2009. 292p. pap. 18.99 (978-1-103-21189-0(7)) 2008. 328p. 25.99 (978-0-559-19433-7(1)) 2008. 328p. pap. 30.75 (978-0-559-19432-0(3)) 2008. 170p. 27.99 (978-0-554-80658-7(4)) 2008. 211p. 24.99 (978-0-554-80664-8(9)) 2008. 166p. pap. 24.75 (978-0-554-80661-7(4)) 2008. 275p. pap. 25.75 (978-0-554-80659-4(2)) Creative Media Partners, LLC.
—A Child's History of England. 2009. pap. 8.99 (978-1-4209-3375-8(2)) Digireads.com Publishing.
—A Child's History of England. Townsend, F. H., illus. 2007. (ENG.). 420p. per. (978-1-4065-5448-9(0)) Dodo Pr.
—A Child's History of England. 2009. 328p. pap. 17.95 (978-1-4341-0248-5(3)) Editorium, The.
—A Child's History of England. 2012. 70p. pap. 19.99 (978-1-231-83367-4(X)) 2010. 268p. pap. 23.74 (978-1-153-74750-9(2)) 2010. (Illus.). 264p. pap. 14.26 (978-1-154-15512-9(9)) 2010. 120p. pap. 34.79 (978-1-151-96568-4(5)) 2010. 78p. pap. 23.84 (978-1-151-96565-3(0)) 2009. 144p. pap. 19.99 (978-1-151-67688-7(8)) 2009. 306p. pap. 23.37 (978-1-150-73859-3(6)) 2009. 324p. pap. 34.79 (978-0-217-15737-7(8)) 2009. 148p. pap. 19.99 (978-0-217-14864-1(6)) General Bks. LLC.
—A Child's History of England. 2008. (ENG., Illus.). 448p. (J). pap. 20.00 (978-1-84831-024-7(2)) Icon Bks., Ltd. GBR. Dist: Publishers Group Canada.
—A Child's History of England. 2010. 342p. 37.56 (978-1-169-32503-6(3)) 2010. 366p. 37.56 (978-1-164-37822-8(8)) 2010. 366p. pap. 25.56 (978-1-164-09984-0(1)) 2010. 342p. pap. 25.56 (978-1-162-64785-2(X)) 2010. 342p. 46.95 (978-1-161-41650-3(1)) 2008. 364p. 46.95 (978-1-4365-8955-0(X)) 2007. (ENG.). 364p. per. 31.95 (978-0-548-79292-6(5)) 2004. reprint ed. pap. 31.95 (978-1-4191-0042-0(4)) 2004. reprint ed. pap. 1.99 (978-1-4192-0042-7(9)) Kessinger Publishing, LLC.
—A Child's History of England. 2011. 384p. pap. (978-3-86403-008-6(0)) Outlook Verlagsgesellschaft mbH.
—A Child's History of England. 2008. 500p. pap. (978-1-4437-0150-1(5)) Read Bks.
—A Child's History of England. 2007. (ENG.). 404p. per. 17.45 (978-1-60424-113-6(6)); 616p. per. 24.45 (978-1-59462-818-4(1)) Standard Pubns., Inc. (Book Jungle).
—A Child's History of England. 2011. 432p. pap. (978-3-8424-3846-0(X)) Tredition GmbH.
—A Child's History of England: England from the Ancient Times, to the Reign of Henry the Fifth. 2010. 292p. pap. 28.75 (978-1-141-83850-9(8)) Creative Media Partners, LLC.
—A Child's History of England: England from the Ancient Times, to the Reign of Henry the Fifth - Primary Source Edition. 2013. 292p. pap. 28.75 (978-1-293-29544-1(2)) Creative Media Partners, LLC.
—A Child's History of England: England from the Reign of Henry the Sixth to the Revolution Of 1688. 2010. 312p. pap. 29.75 (978-1-145-42884-3(3)) Creative Media Partners, LLC.
—A Child's History of England: With Original Engravings. 2011. 528p. pap. 40.75 (978-1-179-90761-1(2)) Creative Media Partners, LLC.
—A Child's History of England: With Original Engravings - Primary Source Edition. 2013. 528p. pap. 40.75 (978-1-294-05410-8(4)) Creative Media Partners, LLC.
—A Child's History of England V1: England from the Ancient Times to the Reign of Henry the Fifth (1854) 288p. 2010. 35.16 (978-1-164-75172-4(7)) 2010. pap. 23.16 (978-1-164-51930-0(1)) 2008. 43.95 (978-1-4369-5285-9(9)) 2008. pap. 28.95 (978-1-4367-2041-0(9)) Kessinger Publishing, LLC.
Dickens, Charles & Mahony, J. A Child's History of England. 2010. (ENG.). 512p. pap. 39.75 (978-1-171-69650-6(7)) Creative Media Partners, LLC.
Dickens, Charles, et al. A Child's History of England. 2010. (ENG.). 364p. pap. 32.75 (978-1-177-62677-4(2)) Creative Media Partners, LLC.
Dillon, Patrick. The Story of Britain from the Norman Conquest to the European Union. Lynch, P. J., illus. 2011. (ENG.). 352p. (J). (gr. 5-18). 21.99 (978-0-7636-5122-0(2)) Candlewick Pr.
Donaldson, Madeline. United Kingdom. 2010. (Country Explorers Ser.). (ENG.). 48p. (gr. 2-4). pap. 9.95 (978-0-7613-6037-7(9)); lib. bdg. 29.27 (978-0-7613-5315-7(1)) Lerner Publishing Group.
Dyan, Penelope. The Kingdom of York, a Kid's Guide to York, Uk. Weigand, John D., photos by. 2011. (Illus.). 34p. pap. 11.95 (978-1-61477-004-6(2)) Bellissima Publishing, LLC.
—Over Dover — -A Kid's Guide to Dover, Uk. Weigand, John D., photos by. 2011. (Illus.). 38p. pap. 11.95 (978-1-61477-005-3(0)) Bellissima Publishing, LLC.
—Rockin' the Rock, a Kid's Guide to the Rock of Gibraltar. Weigand, John D., photos by. 2012. (Illus.). 34p. pap. 11.95 (978-1-61477-037-4(9)) Bellissima Publishing, LLC.
Evers, Charlotte & Welbourne, Dave. Britain, 1783-1851: From Disaster to Triumph? 2003. (Illus.). 272p. (YA). pap. 54.00 (978-0-7195-7482-5(X), Hodder Education) Hodder Education Group GBR. Dist: Trans-Atlantic Pubns., Inc.
Ferguson, Amanda. SAS: British Special Air Service. 2003. (Inside Special Operations Ser.). (Illus.). 64p. (YA). (gr. 5-8). lib. bdg. 31.95 (978-0-8239-3810-0(7), Rosen Reference) Rosen Publishing Group, Inc., The.
Finn, Allan. England. 2017. (Countries We Come From Ser.). (ENG., Illus.). 32p. (J). (gr. -1-3). 19.95 (978-1-68402-054-6(9)) Bearport Publishing Co., Inc.
Foster, Jo. The Great Exhibition Mission Vol. 3, Vol. 3. Anderson, Scoular, illus. unabr. ed. 2011. (History Spies Ser.). (ENG.). 160p. (J). (gr. 4-7). pap. 7.99 (978-0-330-44901-4(X)) Macmillan Pubs., Ltd. GBR. Dist: Independent Pubs. Group.
Fowler, Will. Counterterrorism in West Africa: The Most Dangerous SAS Assault. 2011. (Most Daring Raids in History Ser.). (Illus.). 64p. (YA). (gr. 7-12). lib. bdg. 31.95 (978-1-4488-1871-6(0)) Rosen Publishing Group, Inc., The.
Fremont-Barnes, Gregory. Rescue at the Iranian Embassy: The Most Daring SAS Raid. 2011. (Most Daring Raids in History Ser.). (Illus.). 64p. (YA). (gr. 7-12). lib. bdg. 31.95 (978-1-4488-1869-3(9)) Rosen Publishing Group, Inc., The.
Fuller, Barbara & Nevins, Debbie. Great Britain. 2015. (Cultures of the World (r) Ser.). (ENG., Illus.). 144p. (J). (gr. 5-5). 47.07 (978-1-5026-0334-0(9)) Cavendish Square Publishing.
Gail, Margaret. Moggie Grows up, 1939-1945. 2006. (ENG., Illus.). 74p. pap. (978-0-7552-0227-0(9)) Authors OnLine, Ltd.
Ganeri, Anita. England. Isik, Semur, illus. 2015. (Country Guides, with Benjamin Blog & His Inquisitive Dog Ser.). (ENG.). 32p. (gr. 1-3). 29.99 (978-1-4109-6848-7(0), Read Me!) Heinemann-Raintree.
—King Arthur's Tale. 2011. (ENG.). 24p. (J). pap. (978-0-7787-7872-1(X)); (gr. 3-6). (978-0-7787-7850-9(9)) Crabtree Publishing Co.
Goodman, Michael E. Spies Around the World: the SIS & Other British Spies. 2014. (Spies Around the World Ser.). (ENG., Illus.). 48p. (J). (gr. 4-7). pap. 12.00 (978-0-89812-972-4(9), Creative Paperbacks) Creative Co., The.
Gorman, Jacqueline & Guy, John. British Kings & Queens: 1,000 Years of Intrigue, Struggle, Passion & Power. 2009. (ENG.). 128p. (J). (gr. 4-7). pap. 12.95 (978-1-84696-987-4(5), TickTock Books) Octopus Publishing Group GBR. Dist: Independent Pubs. Group.
Gray, Leon. Solving the Mysteries of Stonehenge. 2008. (Digging into History Ser.). 32p. (gr. 4-18). lib. bdg. 29.93 (978-0-7614-3110-7(1), Benchmark Bks.) Marshall Cavendish Corp.
Guillain, Charlotte. Spreading the Word. 2015. (Collins Big Cat Ser.). (ENG.). 32p. (J). (gr. 2-2). pap. 7.95 (978-0-00-759127-5(6)) HarperCollins Pubs. Ltd. GBR. Dist: Independent Pubs. Group.
Harman, Alice. Northern Ireland. 2016. (Fact Cat: United Kingdom Ser.). (ENG., Illus.). 24p. (J). (gr. k-2). pap. 9.99 (978-0-7502-8942-9(2), Wayland) Hachette Children's Group GBR. Dist: Hachette Bk. Group.
HarperCollins UK Staff. Real Heroes Vol. 2: Courage under Fire. 2011. (ENG., Illus.). 192p. 19.95 (978-0-00-737903-3(X)) HarperCollins Pubs. Ltd. GBR. Dist: Independent Pubs. Group.
Harrison, Paul. King John - The King Who Signed Magna Carta: Brilliant Biographies of the Dead Famous. 2017. (History VIPs Ser.). (ENG., Illus.). 32p. (J). (gr. 4-6). pap. 12.99 **(978-0-7502-9913-8(4)**, Wayland) Hachette Children's Group GBR. Dist: Hachette Bk. Group.
Heinrichs, Ann. Luxembourg. 2005. (Enchantment of the World Ser.). (ENG., Illus.). 48p. (YA). (gr. 5-9). 39.00 (978-0-516-23681-0(4)) Scholastic Library Publishing.
Hepplewhite, Peter. Thomas Crapper, Corsets, & Cruel Britannia: A Grim History of the Vexing Victorians! 2015. (Awfully Ancient Ser.). (ENG., Illus.). 32p. (J). (gr. 5-5). pap. 10.50 (978-1-4824-3133-9(5)) Stevens, Gareth Publishing LLLP.
—Victorian Wokers Turned Dog Poo into Gold! The Fact or Fiction Behind Victorians. 2017. (Truth or Busted Ser.). (ENG., Illus.). 96p. (J). (gr. 4-7). pap. 7.99 (978-0-7502-9744-8(1), Wayland) Hachette Children's Group GBR. Dist: Hachette Bk. Group.
Herold, Vickey. Discover the Renaissance in England. 2006. (J). pap. (978-1-4108-6466-6(9)) Benchmark Education Co.
—The Renaissance in England. 2006. (J). pap. (978-1-4108-6463-5(4)) Benchmark Education Co.
Hicks, Peter. Documenting Women's Suffrage. 2010. (Documenting History Ser.). (Illus.). 48p. (J). pap. 11.75 (978-1-4358-9675-8(0), Rosen Reference); (YA). (gr. 5-9). lib. bdg. 29.25 (978-1-4358-9672-7(6)) Rosen Publishing Group, Inc., The.
Hilliam, Paul. William the Conqueror: First Norman King of England. 2009. (Leaders of the Middle Ages Ser.). 112p. (gr. 5-8). 66.50 (978-1-61513-903-3(6), Rosen Reference) Rosen Publishing Group, Inc., The.
Hinds, Kathryn. The Church. 2007. (Life in Elizabethan England Ser.). (Illus.). 80p. (J). (gr. 3-7). lib. bdg. 32.79 (978-0-7614-2545-8(4), Benchmark Bks.) Marshall Cavendish Corp.
—The City. 2007. (Life in Elizabethan England Ser.). 80p. (J). (gr. 4-7). lib. bdg. 32.79 (978-0-7614-2544-1(6), Benchmark Bks.) Marshall Cavendish Corp.
—The Countryside. 2007. (Life in Elizabethan England Ser.). (Illus.). 80p. (J). (gr. 4-7). lib. bdg. 32.79 (978-0-7614-2543-4(8), Benchmark Bks.) Marshall Cavendish Corp.
HOCPP 1101 the Norman Conquest. 2006. spiral bd. 23.50 (978-1-60308-101-6(1)) In the Hands of a Child.
Hollander, Barbara Gottfried. Elizabeth I: Queen of England. 2017. (Women Who Changed History Ser.). 48p. (gr. 10-12). lib. bdg. 26.85 **(978-1-68048-643-8(8)**, Britannica Educational Publishing) Rosen Publishing Group, Inc., The.
Howell, Izzi. Vikings. 2017. (Fact Cat: History: Early Britons Ser.). (ENG., Illus.). 24p. (J). (gr. k-2). 16.99 (978-0-7502-9581-9(3), Wayland) Hachette Children's Group GBR. Dist: Hachette Bk. Group.
Howse, Jennifer. The British Museum. 2014. (J). (978-1-4896-1186-4(X)) Weigl Pubs., Inc.
John, Judith. The Untold History of Henry VIII & the Tudors. 2016. (History Exposed Ser.). (ENG.). 224p. (YA). (gr. 9-9). 55.00 (978-1-5026-1904-4(0)) Cavendish Square Publishing.
Johnson, Robert. British History 1870-1918: The Emergence of a Nation. 2003. (Studymates Ser.). (ENG., Illus.). 156p. (C). pap. 27.50 (978-1-84285-026-8(1)) GLMP Ltd. GBR. Dist: Chicago Distribution Ctr.
Kelley, True. Where Is Stonehenge? Hinderliter, John & Groff, David, illus. 2016. (Where Is? Ser.). (ENG.). 112p. (J). (gr. 3-7). pap. 5.99 (978-0-448-48693-2(8), Grosset & Dunlap) Penguin Young Readers Group.
Kemper, Bitsy. United Kingdom. 2015. (One World, Many Countries Ser.). (ENG.). 32p. (J). (gr. 1-4). 28.50 (978-1-63407-059-1(3), 208895) Child's World, Inc., The.
Kennedy, Mike & Stewart, Mark. Soccer in the British Isles. 2011. (Smart about Soccer Ser.). 24p. (J). (gr. k-3). lib. bdg. 22.60 (978-1-59953-442-8(8)) Norwood Hse. Pr.
Lace, William W. Elizabethan England. 2005. (World History Ser.). (ENG., Illus.). 112p. (J). (gr. 4-7). lib. bdg. 33.45 (978-1-59018-655-8(9), Lucent Bks.) Cengage Gale.
Ladybird Books Staff & Du Garde Peach, L. King John & Magna Carta: A Ladybird Adventure from History Book. 2016. (Adventure from History Ser.). (ENG., Illus.). 56p. (J). (gr. 3-7). 9.99 (978-0-7232-9402-3(X)) Penguin Bks., Ltd. GBR. Dist: Independent Pubs. Group.
Lassieur, Allison. Life as a Viking: An Interactive History Adventure. 2010. (You Choose: Warriors Ser.). (ENG., Illus.). 112p. (gr. 3-4). pap. 6.95 (978-1-4296-5639-9(5), You Choose Bks.) Capstone Press of Coughlan Cos.
Lonely Planet Publications Staff. Not for Parents Great Britain: Every Thing You Wanted to Know, 1 vol. 2012. (Lonely Planet Kids Ser.). (ENG., Illus.). 96p. (J). pap. 14.99 (978-1-74321-421-3(9), 4352) Lonely Planet Pubns.
Losure, Mary. The Fairy Ring: Or Elsie & Frances Fool the World. 2012. (ENG., Illus.). 192p. (J). (gr. 5). 16.99 (978-0-7636-5670-6(4)) Candlewick Pr.
Lynch, Annabelle. England. 2016. (Let's Visit Ser.). (ENG., Illus.). 24p. (J). (gr. k-2). pap. 10.99 (978-1-4451-3700-1(3), Franklin Watts) Hachette Children's Group GBR. Dist: Hachette Bk. Group.
—Living in Northern Ireland. 2017. (Living in the UK Ser.). (ENG., Illus.). 24p. (J). (gr. k-2). pap. 11.99 (978-1-4451-4820-5(X), Franklin Watts) Hachette Children's Group GBR. Dist: Hachette Bk. Group.
—Northern Ireland. 2016. (Let's Visit Ser.). (ENG., Illus.). 24p. (J). (gr. k-2). 16.99 (978-1-4451-3707-0(0), Franklin Watts) Hachette Children's Group GBR. Dist: Hachette Bk. Group.
—Wales. 2016. (Let's Visit Ser.). (ENG., Illus.). 24p. (J). (gr. k-2). 16.99 (978-1-4451-3704-9(6), Franklin Watts) Hachette Children's Group GBR. Dist: Hachette Bk. Group.
MacDonald, Fiona & Macdonald, Fiona. You Wouldn't Want to Be a Victorian Servant! A Thankless Job You'd Rather Not Have. Antram, David, illus. 2006. (You Wouldn't Want to Ser.). (ENG.). 32p. (J). (gr. 2-5). 29.00 (978-0-531-14972-0(2)) Scholastic Library Publishing.
Malam, John. Be a Victorian Mill Worker! A Grueling Job You'd Rather Not Have. Antram, David, illus. 2007. (You Wouldn't Want to...: History of the World Ser.). (ENG.). 32p. (J). (gr. 2-5). 29.00 (978-0-531-18747-0(0)); pap. 9.95 (978-0-531-13928-8(X)) Scholastic Library Publishing. (Watts, Franklin).
—Burial Places: Discover Stone, Bronze & Iron Age Britain. 2017. (Prehistoric Adventures Ser.). (ENG., Illus.). 32p. (J). (gr. 2-4). 17.99 (978-0-7502-9594-9(5), Wayland) Hachette Children's Group GBR. Dist: Hachette Bk. Group.
Manning, Mick & Granström, Brita. The Story of Britain. 2017. (ENG., Illus.). 80p. (J). (gr. 2-4). pap. 10.99 (978-1-4451-2788-0(1), Franklin Watts) Hachette Children's Group GBR. Dist: Hachette Bk. Group.
Marcus, Leonard S. Randolph Caldecott: The Man Who Could Not Stop Drawing. Caldecott, Randolph, illus. 2013. (ENG.). 64p. (YA). (gr. 5-9). 24.99 (978-0-374-31025-7(4), 9780374310257, Farrar, Straus & Giroux (BYR)) Farrar, Straus & Giroux.
Marshall, H. E. Our Island Story. 2008. 304p. pap. 9.99 (978-1-60459-492-8(6)) Wilder Pubns., Corp.
—Our Island Story: A History of Britain for Boys & Girls, from the Romans to Queen Victoria. adapted ed. 2005. (Illus.). 494p. (978-1-902984-74-2(9), Galore Park) Hodder Education Group.
—Our Island Story (Yesterday's Classics) Forrest, A. S., illus. l.t. ed. 2006. 676p. (J). per. 19.95 (978-1-59915-009-3(3)) Yesterday's Classics.
Marshall, Henrietta. Our Island Story Unabridged. 2005. (Illus.). 560p. (YA). pap. 24.95 (978-1-903386-52-1(7)) Civitas:Institute for the Study of Civil Society GBR. Dist: Coronet Bks.
Martin, Claudia & Howell, Izzi. Remembrance Day. 2016. (ENG., Illus.). 32p. (J). (gr. 1-3). 17.99 (978-1-4451-4847-2(1), Franklin Watts) Hachette Children's Group GBR. Dist: Hachette Bk. Group.
Maurer, Gretchen. Mary Tudor: "Bloody Mary" Malone, Peter, illus. 2011. (Thinking Girl's Treasury of Dastardly Dames Ser.). (ENG.). 32p. (J). (gr. 3-8). 18.95 (978-0-9834256-2-5(0)) Goosebottom Bks. LLC.
McCaughrean, Geraldine. Ghosts, Rogues & Highwaymen: 20 Stories from British History. Brassey, Richard, illus. 2003. 128p. (J). pap. 9.99 (978-1-85881-894-8(X), Orion) Orion Publishing Group, Ltd. GBR. Dist: Trafalgar Square Publishing.
—Rebels & Royals: 20 Stories from British History. Brassey, Richard, illus. 2003. (Britannia Ser.). 128p. (J). pap. 9.99 (978-1-85881-852-8(4), Orion) Orion Publishing Group, Ltd. GBR. Dist: Trafalgar Square Publishing.
McCollum, Sean, et al. Eyewitness to Titanic. 2015. (ENG., Illus.). 160p. (gr. 3-4). pap. 9.95 (978-1-62370-131-4(7)) Capstone Young Readers of Coughlan Cos.

McCormack, Shaun. Inside Britain's MI6: Military Intelligence 6. (Inside the World's Most Famous Intelligence Agencies Ser.). 64p. 2009. (gr. 5-5). 58.50 *(978-1-61513-568-4(5))* 2005. (Illus.). (YA). (gr. 7-12). lib. bdg. 31.95 *(978-0-8239-3812-4(3))* Rosen Publishing Group, Inc., The.

McNeil, Niki, et al. HOCPP 1092 Romans in Britain. 2006. spiral bd. 19.50 *(978-1-60308-092-7(9))* In the Hands of a Child.

Medina, Nico. Where Is the Great Barrier Reef? Hinderliter, John, illus. 2016. (Where Is? Ser.). (ENG.). 112p. (J). (gr. 3-7). lib. bdg. 15.99 *(978-0-399-54239-8(6))*, Grosset & Dunlap) Penguin Young Readers Group.

Mercer, Abbie. Happy 4th of July. 2007. (Holiday Fun Ser.). (Illus.). 24p. (J). (gr. -1-3). lib. bdg. 22.60 *(978-1-4042-3810-7(7))* Rosen Publishing Group, Inc., The.

Morley, Jacqueline. You Wouldn't Want to Be a Shakespearean Actor! Some Roles You Might Not Want to Play. Antram, David, illus. 2010. (You Wouldn't Want to Ser.). (ENG.). 32p. (J). (gr. 3-18). pap. 9.95 *(978-0-531-22826-5(6))* Scholastic Library Publishing.

Morriss, Roger. Captain Cook & His Exploration of the Pacific. 2010. (History of Exploration Ser.). 48p. 32.80 *(978-1-84898-303-8(4))* Black Rabbit Bks.

Mullenbach, Cheryl. Torpedoed! A World War II Story of a Sinking Passenger Ship & Two Children's Survival at Sea. 2017. (ENG.). 176p. (J). (gr. 5). 17.99 ***(978-1-61373-824-5(2))*** Chicago Review Pr., Inc.

Nardo, Don. The Age of Colonialism. 2006. (World History Ser.). (ENG., Illus.). 104p. (YA). (gr. 7-10). lib. bdg. 33.45 *(978-1-59018-833-0(0))*, Lucent Bks.) Cengage Gale.

Nelson, Sheila. A Nation Is Born: World War I & Independence, 1910-1929. 2007. (How Canada Became Canada Ser.). (Illus.). 87p. (YA). (gr. 3-7). lib. bdg. 21.95 *(978-1-4222-0006-3(X)*, 1247972) Mason Crest.

Newland, Sonya. Celts. 2017. (Explore! Ser.). (ENG., Illus.). 32p. (J). (gr. 4-6). pap. 12.99 ***(978-0-7502-9735-6(2))***, Wayland) Hachette Children's Group GBR. Dist: Hachette Bk. Group.

—Stone, Bronze & Iron Ages. 2017. (Explore! Ser.). (ENG., Illus.). 32p. (J). (gr. 4-6). pap. 12.99 ***(978-0-7502-9736-3(0))***, Wayland) Hachette Children's Group GBR. Dist: Hachette Bk. Group.

North, Peter & McKay, Susan. England. 2010. (Welcome to My Country Ser.). 48p. (gr. 3-5). 28.50 *(978-1-60870-152-0(2))* Marshall Cavendish Corp.

Oliver, Martin. Off with Their Heads! Pinder, Andrew, illus. 2017. (Buster Reference Ser.). (ENG.). 128p. (J). (gr. 3-7). pap. 8.99 ***(978-1-78055-465-5(6))*** O'Mara, Michael Bks., Ltd. GBR. Dist: Independent Pubs. Group.

Oliver, Martin. Off with Their Heads! All the Cool Bits in British History. Pinder, Andrew, illus. (ENG.). 128p. (J). (gr. 4-7). 2014. pap. 8.99 *(978-1-78055-134-0(7))* 2010. 11.99 *(978-1-906082-72-7(3))* O'Mara, Michael Bks., Ltd. GBR. Dist: Independent Pubs. Group.

Olson, Steven P. Sir Walter Raleigh: Explorer for the Court of Queen Elizabeth. 2009. (Library of Explorers & Exploration Ser.). 112p. (gr. 5-8). 66.50 *(978-1-60853-612-2(2))*, Rosen Reference) Rosen Publishing Group, Inc., The.

One Direction Staff. One Direction: A Year with One Direction. 2013. 64p. (J). (gr. 3-7). pap. 10.99 *(978-0-06-222317-3(8))*, HarperFestival) HarperCollins Pubs.

Paprocki, Greg, illus. M Is for Monocle - Victorian Alphabet. 1 vol. 2016. (ENG.). 32p. (J). bds. 9.99 *(978-1-4236-4284-8(8))* Gibbs Smith, Publisher.

Parker, Lewis K. English Colonies in the Americas. 2009. (European Colonies in the Americas Ser.). 24p. (gr. 2-2). 42.50 *(978-1-61512-317-9(2))*, PowerKids Pr.) Rosen Publishing Group, Inc., The.

Parsons, Martin. Rationing World War II. 2017. (History Detective Investigates Ser.). (ENG., Illus.). 32p. (J). (gr. 4-6). pap. 11.99 *(978-0-7502-9631-1(3))*, Wayland) Hachette Children's Group GBR. Dist: Hachette Bk. Group.

—Women in World War II. 2017. (History Detective Investigates Ser.). (ENG., Illus.). 32p. (J). (gr. 4-6). pap. 11.99 *(978-0-7502-9638-0(0))*, Wayland) Hachette Children's Group GBR. Dist: Hachette Bk. Group.

Peal, Robert. Early Modern Britain, 1509-1760. 2016. (Knowing History Ser.). (ENG.). 80p. (J). (gr. 6-9). pap. 12.99 ***(978-0-00-819524-3(2))*** HarperCollins Pubs. Ltd. GBR. Dist: Independent Pubs. Group.

—Georgian Britain. 2016. (Knowing History Ser.). (ENG.). 16p. (J). (gr. 6-9). 3.99 ***(978-0-00-819537-3(4))*** HarperCollins Pubs. Ltd. GBR. Dist: Independent Pubs. Group.

—KS3 History Modern Britain (1760-1900) 2017. (Knowing History Ser.). (ENG.). 80p. (J). (gr. 5-9). pap. 12.99 ***(978-0-00-819525-0(0))*** HarperCollins Pubs. Ltd. GBR. Dist: Independent Pubs. Group.

—Medieval Britain (400-1485) 2016. (Knowing History Ser.). (ENG.). 80p. (J). (gr. 6-9). pap. 12.99 ***(978-0-00-819523-6(4))*** HarperCollins Pubs. Ltd. GBR. Dist: Independent Pubs. Group.

—Modern Britain - The Victorian empire. 2017. (Knowing History Ser.). (ENG.). 16p. (J). (gr. 6-9). 3.95 *(978-0-00-819543-4(9))* HarperCollins Pubs. Ltd. GBR. Dist: Independent Pubs. Group.

Peal, Robert. Norman England. 2016. (Knowing History Ser.). (ENG.). 16p. (J). (gr. 6-9). 3.99 ***(978-0-00-819527-4(7))*** HarperCollins Pubs. Ltd. GBR. Dist: Independent Pubs. Group.

Phillips, Charles. Kings & Queens of Britain's Modern Age: From Hanover to Windsor - 1714-Today. 2009. (ENG., Illus.). 96p. pap. 14.99 *(978-1-84476-520-1(2))* Anness Publishing GBR. Dist: National Bk. Network.

Pollard, Michael. Great Rivers of Britain: The Clyde, Mersey, Severn, Tees, Thames, Trent. (Illus.). 45p. *(978-0-237-51829-5(5))* Evans Brothers, Ltd.

—Rivers of Britain & Ireland: The Avon, Yorkshire Ouse, Tyne, Wye, Forth, Liffey, Lagan. (Illus.). 46p. (J). *(978-0-237-51805-9(8))* Evans Brothers, Ltd.

Powell, Jillian. Descubramos Gran Bretaña. 2007. (Descubramos países del mundo (Spanish- Looking at Countries) Ser.). (SPA.). 32p. (gr. 1-5). pap. 10.50 *(978-0-8368-8191-2(5))*; (Illus.). lib. bdg. 26.00 *(978-0-8368-8184-4(2))* Stevens, Gareth Publishing LLLP. (Gareth Stevens Learning Library).

Price, Sean Stewart & Price, Sean. Henry VIII: Royal Beheader. 2009. (Wicked History Ser.). (ENG.). 128p. (J). (gr. 6-12). pap. 5.95 *(978-0-531-22173-0(3))*, Children's Pr.) Scholastic Library Publishing.

Rasheed, Leila. Collins Big Cat - Sister Queens: The Lives & Reigns of Mary & Elizabeth: Band 15/Emerald. 2015. (Collins Big Cat Ser.). (ENG., Illus.). 48p. (J). (gr. 3-4). pap. 9.95 *(978-0-00-812785-5(9))* HarperCollins Pubs. Ltd. GBR. Dist: Independent Pubs. Group.

Raum, Elizabeth. At Battle in the Revolutionary War: An Interactive Battlefield Adventure. 2015. (You Choose: Battlefields Ser.). (ENG., Illus.). 112p. (gr. 3-4). pap. 6.95 *(978-1-4914-2392-9(7))*, You Choose Bks.) Capstone Press of Coughlan Cos.

Reynoldson, Fiona. The Home Front. (Illus.). 48p. (J). pap. *(978-0-7502-2696-7(X))*, Wayland) Hachette Children's Group.

Riley, Gail Blasser. Tower of London: England's Ghostly Castle. 2006. (Castles, Palaces, & Tombs Ser.). (Illus.). 32p. (YA). (gr. 2-5). lib. bdg. 25.27 *(978-1-59716-249-4(3))* Bearport Publishing Co., Inc.

Ross, Stewart. Henry VIII: Guilty or Innocent? 2011. (Timewarp Trials Ser.). (ENG., Illus.). 48p. (J). (gr. 5). pap. 7.99 *(978-0-237-54248-1(X))* Evans Brothers, Ltd. GBR. Dist: Independent Pubs. Group.

—The Home Front in World War II. (Illus.). 32p. 22.99 *(978-0-7502-4184-7(5))* Hodder & Stoughton GBR. Dist: Trafalgar Square Publishing.

—Sink the Armada! Sir Francis Drake & the Spanish Armada of 1588. Shields, Susan, illus. 62p. (J). pap. *(978-0-237-51959-9(3))* Evans Brothers, Ltd.

—Will's Dream. Shields, Susan, illus. 28p. pap. 9.99 *(978-0-7502-2965-4(9))* Hodder & Stoughton GBR. Dist: Trafalgar Square Publishing.

Roxburgh, Ellis. Elizabeth I of England vs. Mary, Queen of Scots: Battle for the Throne. 2016. (History's Greatest Rivals Ser.). (ENG., Illus.). 48p. (J). (gr. 6-8). pap. 14.05 *(978-1-4824-4227-4(2))* Stevens, Gareth Publishing LLLP.

Sasek, Miroslav. This Is Britain. 2008. (ENG., Illus.). 62p. (J). (gr. 2-12). 17.95 *(978-0-7893-1753-7(2))* Universe Publishing.

Scott, Patricia, et al. Music Express Early Years Foundation Stage: Complete Music Scheme for Early Years Foundation Stage, 3 vols. 2nd ed. 2012. (Music Express Ser.). (ENG., Illus.). 88p. pap. 55.00 incl. audio compact disk ***(978-1-4081-8707-4(8))*** HarperCollins Pubs. Ltd. GBR. Dist: Independent Pubs. Group.

Senior, Kathryn. You Wouldn't Want to Be Sick in the 16th Century! (Revised Edition) 2014. (You Wouldn't Want to... Ser.). (ENG.). 32p. (J). lib. bdg. 29.00 *(978-0-531-21176-2(2))*, Watts, Franklin) Scholastic Library Publishing.

Simons, Rae & Indovino, Shaina Carmel. United Kingdom. 2012. (J). pap. *(978-1-4222-2292-8(6))* Mason Crest.

—United Kingdom. Bruton, John, ed. 2012. (Major European Union Nations Ser.). 64p. (J). (gr. 7). 22.95 *(978-1-4222-2261-4(6))* Mason Crest.

Smith, Neil. Robin Hood. 1 vol. 2015. (ENG., Illus.). 80p. (J). 35.60 *(978-1-4777-8139-5(0))*, Rosen Young Adult) Rosen Publishing Group, Inc., The.

Stephens, Chris S. A Wartime Scrapbook, Pack. 2004. (ENG., Illus.). 48p. pap. 42.95 *(978-1-84323-329-9(0))* Beekman Bks., Inc.

Streissguth, Tom. Richard the Lionheart: Crusader King of England. 2007. (Rulers of the Middle Ages Ser.). (Illus.). 160p. (YA). (gr. 6-12). lib. bdg. 35.94 *(978-0-7660-2714-5(7))* Enslow Pubs., Inc.

Strum, Richard M. Causes of the American Revolution. 2005. (Road to War Ser.). (Illus.). 64p. (J). pap. 12.95 *(978-1-59556-005-6(X))*; (gr. 4-18). lib. bdg. 22.95 *(978-1-59556-001-8(7))* OTTN Publishing.

Summers, Kimberly Dillon. United Kingdom. 1 vol. 2011. (Countries of the World Set 1 Ser.). (ENG., Illus.). 144p. (J). (gr. 6-12). lib. bdg. 37.07 *(978-1-61783-119-5(0))* ABDO Publishing Co.

Sutcliff, Rosemary. The Eagle of the Ninth. Hodges, C. Walter, illus. 2015. (Everyman's Library Children's Classics Ser.). (ENG.). 256p. 20.00 *(978-1-101-90769-6(X))*, Everyman's Library) Knopf Doubleday Publishing Group.

Thorold, David, et al. Roman Invaders & Settlers. 2013. (Step up History Ser.). (ENG., Illus.). 32p. (J). pap. 12.99 *(978-0-237-54378-5(8))* Evans Brothers, Ltd. GBR. Dist: Independent Pubs. Group.

Throp, Claire. England. 1 vol. 2011. (Countries Around the World Ser.). (ENG.). 48p. (gr. 3-6). pap. 9.95 *(978-1-4329-5226-6(9))*, NA-h) Heinemann-Raintree.

Wayland Publishers & Newland, Sonya. Celts. 2016. (ENG., Illus.). 32p. (J). (gr. 4-6). 17.99 *(978-0-7502-9550-5(3))*, Wayland) Hachette Children's Group GBR. Dist: Hachette Bk. Group.

West, David. Richard the Lionheart: The Life of a King & Crusader. 2009. (Graphic Nonfiction Biographies Ser.). (Illus.). 48p. (YA). (gr. 4-5). 58.50 *(978-1-61513-025-2(X))*, Rosen Reference) Rosen Publishing Group, Inc., The.

West, David & Gaff, Jackie. Richard the Lionheart: The Life of a King & Crusader. 2005. (Graphic Nonfiction Biographies Ser.). (ENG., Illus.). 48p. (YA). (gr. 4-7). lib. bdg. 31.95 *(978-1-4042-0241-2(2))* Rosen Publishing Group, Inc., The.

Weston Woods Staff, creator. Can't You Make Them Behave, King George? 2004. 29.95 *(978-1-55592-378-5(X))*; (J). 38.75 *(978-1-55592-379-2(8))*; (J). 18.95 *(978-1-55592-377-8(1))* Weston Woods Studios, Inc.

Whistler, Charles W. Wulfric the Weapon Thane. 2006. (ENG.). 222p. pap. 20.99 *(978-1-4264-7331-9(1))*; 250p. pap. 22.99 *(978-1-4264-7404-0(0))* Creative Media Partners, LLC.

White-Thomson, Stephen. Guy Fawkes. 2017. (Popcorn: People in History Ser.). (ENG., Illus.). 24p. (J). (gr. 4-6). pap. 10.99 *(978-0-7502-8372-4(6))*, Wayland) Hachette Children's Group GBR. Dist: Hachette Bk. Group.

—Henry VIII. 2017. (Popcorn: People in History Ser.). (ENG., Illus.). 24p. (J). (gr. k-2). pap. 10.99 *(978-0-7502-8413-4(7))*, Wayland) Hachette Children's Group GBR. Dist: Hachette Bk. Group.

Whittock, Martyn J. Medieval Britain, 1066-1500. 2003. (ENG., Illus.). 96p. pap. 29.50 *(978-0-340-86904-8(6))*, Hodder Education) Hodder Education Group GBR. Dist: Trans-Atlantic Pubns., Inc.

William the Conqueror: a Ladybird Adventure from History Book. 2016. (Ladybird Histories Ser.). (ENG., Illus.). 56p. (J). (gr. k-3). 10.99 ***(978-0-241-24947-5(3))*** Penguin Bks., Ltd. GBR. Dist: Independent Pubs. Group.

Wilson, Todd. Investigating Childhood in Tudor England. (Illus.). 32p. (J). pap. 8.95 *(978-0-7078-0335-7(7))* National Trust, Aylesbury GBR. Dist: Trafalgar Square Publishing.

Wiseman, Blaine. United Kingdom. 2016. (Illus.). 32p. (J). *(978-1-4896-4613-2(2))* Weigl Pubs., Inc.

Wood, Alix. Uncovering the Culture of Ancient Britain. 01 vols., 1. 2016. (Archaeology & Ancient Cultures Ser.). (ENG.). 32p. (J). pap. 10.00 *(978-1-5081-4647-6(0))*, PowerKids Pr.) Rosen Publishing Group, Inc., The.

Wukovits, John F. Victorian Era. Greenhaven Press Editors, ed. 2013. (World History Ser.). (ENG., Illus.). 128p. (gr. 7-10). lib. bdg. 39.90 *(978-1-4205-0933-5(0))*, Lucent Bks.) Cengage Gale.

Yonge, Charlotte M. Young Folks' History of England. 2004. reprint ed. pap. 1.99 *(978-1-4192-9531-7(4))*; pap. 19.95 *(978-1-4191-9531-0(X))* Kessinger Publishing, LLC.

5,000 Miles to Freedom: Ellen & William Craft's Flight from Slavery. Lt. ed. 2013. 202p. pap. *(978-1-4596-6713-6(1))* ReadHowYouWant.com, Ltd.

GREAT BRITAIN—HISTORY—BIOGRAPHY

Brooks, Philip. King George III: America's Enemy. 2009. (Wicked History Ser.). (ENG.). 128p. (J). (gr. 6-12). pap. 5.95 *(978-0-531-20739-0(0))*, Watts, Franklin) Scholastic Library Publishing.

Buchanan, Jane. Mary Tudor: Courageous Queen or Bloody Mary? 2008. (Wicked History Ser.). (ENG.). 128p. (J). (gr. 6-18). pap. 5.95 *(978-0-531-20502-0(9))*, Watts, Franklin) Scholastic Library Publishing.

Burnett, Allan. Bonnie Prince Charlie & All That. Anderson, Scoular, illus. 2006. (ENG.). 103p. pap. *(978-1-84158-496-6(7))* Birlinn, Ltd.

Crabtree Staff & Roberts, Steve. King George III: England's Struggle to Keep America. 2012. (ENG., Illus.). 48p. (J). pap. *(978-0-7787-0811-7(X))* Crabtree Publishing Co.

Hilliam, David. Eleanor of Aquitaine: The Richest Queen in Medieval Europe. (Leaders of the Middle Ages Ser.). 112p. 2009. (gr. 5-8). 66.50 *(978-1-61513-897-5(8))*, Rosen Reference) 2004. (Illus.). (J). lib. bdg. 34.60 *(978-1-4042-0162-0(9))* Rosen Publishing Group, Inc., The.

Koestler-Grack, Rachel A. Eleanor of Aquitaine: Heroine of the Middle Ages. 2005. (Makers of the Middle Ages & Renaissance Ser.). (Illus.). 168p. (gr. 5-8). lib. bdg. 32.95 *(978-0-7910-8633-9(X))*, Chelsea Hse.) Facts On File, Inc.

Malam, John. Queen Elizabeth II: Her Story. 2017. (ENG., Illus.). 24p. (J). (gr. 4-6). pap. 9.99 *(978-0-7502-9878-0(2))*, Wayland) Hachette Children's Group GBR. Dist: Hachette Bk. Group.

GREAT BRITAIN—HISTORY—FICTION

All My Noble Dreams & Then What Happens. 2013. (ENG.). 272p. (J). (gr. 4-7). 15.99 *(978-1-4424-4976-3(4))*, Simon & Schuster/Paula Wiseman Bks.) Simon & Schuster/Paula Wiseman Bks.

Almond, David. The Fire-Eaters. 2010. (ENG.). 224p. (J). (gr. 3-7). mass mkt. 7.99 *(978-0-375-85751-5(6))*, Laurel Leaf) Random Hse. Children's Bks.

Anderson, Jodi Lynn. Midnight at the Electric. 2017. 272p. (YA). (gr. 9). 17.99 *(978-0-06-239354-8(5))*, HarperTeen) HarperCollins Pubs.

Angleberger, Tom. Horton Halfpott: Or, the Fiendish Mystery of Smugwick Manor - Or, the Loosening of M'Lady Luggertuck's Corset. (ENG., Illus.). (J). (gr. 3-7). 2012. 240p. pap. 7.99 *(978-1-4197-0169-6(X))* 2011. 224p. 16.95 *(978-0-8109-9715-8(0))* Abrams, Inc. (Amulet Bks.).

Anstey, Cindy & Anstey, Cynthia. Love, Lies & Spies. 2016. (ENG.). 368p. (YA). pap. 10.99 *(978-1-250-08403-3(2))*, 9781250084033) Feiwel & Friends.

Ashe, Susan. Cuda of the Celts. Lawrie, Robin, illus. 2005. (Yellow Go Bananas Ser.). (ENG.). 48p. (J). (gr. 3-4). lib. bdg. *(978-0-7787-2720-0(3))* Crabtree Publishing Co.

Avi. Crispin: La Cruz de Plomo. 2004.Tr. of Crispin: The Cross of Lead. (SPA., Illus.). (YA). pap. 7.99 *(978-84-348-9601-7(X))* SM Ediciones ESP. Dist: Lectorum Pubns., Inc.

—Crispin: The Cross of Lead. 2004. (Crispin Ser.). (ENG.). 320p. (J). (gr. 3-7). reprint ed. pap. 7.99 *(978-0-7868-1658-3(9))* Hyperion Pr.

—The End of Time, No. 3. 2010. (ENG.). 240p. (J). (gr. 5-18). 16.99 *(978-0-06-174080-0(2))* HarperCollins Pubs.

Aviation Book Company Staff. Crispin: The Cross of Lead. 2004. (J). (gr. 3-6). 18.40 *(978-0-613-74965-7(0))*, Turtleback) Turtleback Bks.

Bailey, Kristin. Legacy of the Clockwork Key. 2014. (Secret Order Ser.: 1). (ENG., Illus.). 432p. (YA). (gr. 9). pap. 9.99 *(978-1-4424-4027-2(9))*, Simon Pulse) Simon Pulse.

Baratz-Logsted, Lauren. The Twin's Daughter. 2010. (ENG.). 400p. (YA). (gr. 9-12). 16.99 *(978-1-59990-513-6(2))*, 9781599905136, Bloomsbury USA Childrens) Bloomsbury Publishing USA.

Barraclough, Lindsey. Long Lankin. (ENG.). 464p. (YA). (gr. 7). 2014. pap. 9.99 *(978-0-7636-6937-9(7))* 2012. (Illus.). 16.99 *(978-0-7636-5808-3(1))* Candlewick Pr.

Barratt, Mark. The Wild Man. 2010. (ENG.). 352p. (YA). (gr. 6-18). pap. 9.00 *(978-0-8028-5377-6(3))*, Eerdmans Bks For Young Readers) Eerdmans, William B. Publishing Co.

Blackwood, Gary. Around the World in 100 Days. 2011. (ENG.). 368p. (J). (gr. 5-18). 7.99 *(978-0-14-241963-2(X))*, Puffin Books) Penguin Young Readers Group.

Blackwood, Gary L. Shakespeare's Spy. 2005. (ENG.). 288p. (J). (gr. 3-7). 6.99 *(978-0-14-240311-2(3))*, Puffin Books) Penguin Young Readers Group.

Boecker, Virginia. The King Slayer. 2016. (Witch Hunter Ser.: 2). (ENG.). 368p. (YA). (gr. 10-17). 17.99 *(978-0-316-32723-7(9))* Little, Brown Bks. for Young Readers.

Bond, Douglas. Hand of Vengeance. 2012. (J). pap. *(978-1-59638-215-2(5))* P & R Publishing.

—Hostage Lands. 2006. 234p. (YA). (gr. 7). per. 9.99 *(978-1-59638-027-1(6))* P & R Publishing.

Bradley, Kimberly Brubaker. The War That Saved My Life. (ENG.). (J). (gr. 4-7). 2016. 336p. 8.99 *(978-0-14-751048-1(1))*, Puffin Books) 2015. 320p. 17.99 *(978-0-8037-4081-5(6))*, Dial Bks) Penguin Young Readers Group.

—The War That Saved My Life. 2016. (J). lib. bdg. 19.65 *(978-0-606-38843-6(5))* Turtleback Bks.

Broach, Elise. Shakespeare's Secret. 2007. (Illus.). 258p. (gr. 4-9). 17.00 *(978-0-7569-8204-1(9))* Perfection Learning Corp.

—Shakespeare's Secret. 2007. (ENG.). 272p. (YA). (gr. 5-10). per. 7.99 *(978-0-312-37132-6(2))*, 9780312371326) Square Fish.

—Shakespeare's Secret. Lt. ed. 2006. (Thorndike Literacy Bridge Ser.). (Illus.). 263p. (J). (gr. 5-10). 22.95 *(978-0-7862-8735-2(7))* Thorndike Pr.

Brontë, Charlotte. Jane Eyre. 2006. (Reader's Workshop Ser.). (ENG.). 120p. (C). pap. 19.95 *(978-0-7362-3137-4(4))* CENGAGE Learning.

Bross, Lee. Tangled Webs. 2016. (Tangled Webs Ser.). (ENG., Illus.). 400p. (YA). (gr. 9-17). pap. 9.99 *(978-1-4231-9467-5(5))* Hyperion Bks. for Children.

Buckey, Sarah Masters. Clue in the Castle Tower: A Samantha Mystery. Ross, Peg, ed. Giovine, Sergio, illus. 2011. (ENG.). 184p. (YA). (gr. 4-18). pap. 6.95 *(978-1-59369-752-5(X))* American Girl Publishing, Inc.

Buckley-Archer, Linda. The Time Quake. 2009. (Gideon Trilogy Ser.: 3). (ENG.). 464p. (J). (gr. 5-9). 17.99 *(978-1-4169-1529-4(X))*, Simon & Schuster Bks. For Young Readers) Simon & Schuster Bks. For Young Readers.

—The Time Travelers. 2012. (Gideon Trilogy Ser.: 1). (ENG.). 416p. (J). (gr. 5-9). 17.99 *(978-1-4424-6551-0(4))*, Simon & Schuster Bks. For Young Readers) Simon & Schuster Bks. For Young Readers.

Burgess, Melvin. Nicholas Dane. 2013. (ENG.). 432p. (YA). (gr. 9-13). pap. 9.99 *(978-0-312-55146-9(0))*, 9780312551469) Square Fish.

Burgis, Stephanie. Renegade Magic. 2012. (Kat, Incorrigible Ser.: 2). (ENG., Illus.). 336p. (J). (gr. 5-9). 16.99 *(978-1-4169-9449-7(1))*, Atheneum Bks. for Young Readers) Simon & Schuster Children's Publishing.

Burgis, Stephanie & Ward, Barnaby. Kat, Incorrigible. 2011. (Kat, Incorrigible Ser.: 1). (ENG., Illus.). 304p. (J). (gr. 5-9). 16.99 *(978-1-4169-9447-3(5))*, Atheneum Bks. for Young Readers) Simon & Schuster Children's Publishing.

Burnett, Frances Hodgson. The Secret Garden. Moore, Inga, illus. 2008. (ENG.). 272p. (J). (gr. 1-4). 22.99 *(978-0-7636-3161-1(2))* Candlewick Pr.

—The Secret Garden. Lawrie, Robin, illus. 2008. (Puffin Classics Ser.). (ENG.). 368p. (J). (gr. 3-7). 5.99 *(978-0-14-132106-6(7))*, Puffin Books) Penguin Young Readers Group.

—The Secret Garden. 1 vol. Simon, Ute, illus. 2011. (Calico Illustrated Classics Ser.: No. 3). (ENG.). 112p. (J). (gr. 3-6). 27.07 *(978-1-61641-108-4(2))* Magic Wagon.

Burnett, Frances Hodgson & Naxos of America Staff. The Secret Garden. 3rd ed. 2008. (Hear It Read It Classics Ser.: 0). (ENG., Illus.). 144p. (J). (gr. 2-4). 9.95 *(978-1-4022-1244-4(5))*, Sourcebooks Jabberwocky) Sourcebooks, Inc.

Cain, Cate. The Jade Boy. 2013. (Jade Boy Ser.). (ENG.). 448p. (J). (gr. 4-7). pap. 11.99 *(978-1-84877-229-8(7))* Bonnier Publishing GBR. Dist: Independent Pubs. Group.

—The Moon Child. 2016. (Jade Boy Ser.: 2). (ENG.). 432p. (J). (gr. 4-7). pap. 11.99 *(978-1-78370-058-5(0))* Bonnier Publishing GBR. Dist: Independent Pubs. Group.

Cameron, Eileen. Rupert's Parchment: Story of Magna Carta. Ettlinger, Doris, illus. 2015. (ENG.). (J). (gr. -1-3). 17.95 *(978-1-62086-984-0(5))* Mascot Bks., Inc.

Cameron, Sharon. The Dark Unwinding. 2012. (ENG.). 336p. (J). (gr. 7). 17.99 *(978-0-545-32786-2(5))*, Scholastic Pr.) Scholastic, Inc.

Carey, Janet Lee. Dragonswood. 2013. (ENG.). 416p. (YA). (gr. 7). pap. 9.99 *(978-0-14-242432-2(3))*, Firebird) Penguin Young Readers Group.

Carpenter, Ann. The Slumber Girls & the Mystical Dollhouse. 2006. (J). per. 8.99 *(978-0-9771030-0-3(5))* Kidz By Dezign Pr., Inc.

Carriger, Gail. Manners & Mutiny. 2016. (Finishing School Ser.: 4). (ENG., Illus.). 352p. (YA). (gr. 7-17). pap. 10.99 *(978-0-316-19029-9(2))* Little, Brown Bks. for Young Readers.

The Case of the Vanishing Emerald. 2015. (Mysteries of Maisie Hitchins Ser.: 2). (ENG., Illus.). 176p. (J). (gr. 2-5). 14.99 *(978-0-544-33927-9(4))*, HMH Books For Young Readers) Houghton Mifflin Harcourt Publishing Co.

Castor, H. M. VIII. 2014. (ENG., Illus.). 432p. (YA). (gr. 7). pap. 9.99 *(978-1-4424-7419-2(X))*, Simon & Schuster Bks. For Young Readers) Simon & Schuster Bks. For Young Readers.

Cavendish, Grace. The Grace Mysteries: Assassin & Betrayal. 2011. (Grace Mysteries Ser.). (ENG.). 384p. (J). (gr. 3-7). pap. 6.99 *(978-0-385-74005-0(0))*, Delacorte Bks. for Young Readers) Random Hse. Children's Bks.

The Cheshire Cheese Cat. 1 vol. 2014. (ENG., Illus.). 234p. (J). (gr. 3-6). pap. 8.95 *(978-1-56145-810-3(4))* Peachtree Pubs.

Clement-Davies, David. The Telling Pool. Huebsch, Rand, illus. 2007. (ENG.). 382p. (YA). (gr. 7-17). per. 8.95 *(978-0-8109-9257-3(4))* Abrams, Inc.

—The Telling Pool. 2005. (ENG., Illus.). 376p. (J). (gr. 7-17). 19.95 *(978-0-8109-5758-9(2))*, Abrams Bks. for Young Readers) Abrams, Inc.

Cluess, Jessica. A Poison Dark & Drowning (Kingdom on Fire, Book Two) 2017. (Kingdom on Fire Ser.: 2). (ENG.). 432p. (YA). (gr. 7). 17.99 ***(978-0-553-53594-5(3))***, Random Hse. Bks. for Young Readers) Random Hse. Children's Bks.

Cody, Matthew. Will in Scarlet. 2014. (ENG., Illus.). 272p. (J). (gr. 5). pap. 6.99 *(978-0-375-87292-1(2))*, Yearling) Random Hse. Children's Bks.

Colfer, Eoin. The Forever Man. 2016. (Warp Ser.). (ENG.). 368p. (YA). (gr. 7-12). pap. 9.99 *(978-1-4847-2616-7(2))* Hyperion Bks. for Children.

Connolly, Kara. No Good Deed. 2017. (ENG.). 352p. (YA). (gr. 9). 17.99 ***(978-0-385-74393-8(9))***; lib. bdg. 20.99 ***(978-0-375-99140-0(9))*** Random Hse. Children's Bks. (Delacorte Pr.).

Cooper, Michelle. The FitzOsbornes at War. 2013. (Montmaray Journals). (ENG.). 560p. (YA). (gr. 7). pap. 10.99 *(978-0-307-93058-3(0))*, Ember) Random Hse. Children's Bks.

—The FitzOsbornes in Exile. 2012. (Montmaray Journals). (ENG.). 464p. (YA). (gr. 7). pap. 10.99

(978-0-375-85155-1(0), Ember) Random Hse. Children's Bks.

Crake, A. Alfgar the Dane. 2007. 216p. per. 14.95 *(978-1-60312-219-1(2))*; 26.95 *(978-1-60312-797-4(6))* Aegypan.

Crake, Augustine David. Alfgar the Dane or the Second Chronicle of Aescendune. 2006. (ENG.). 224p. pap. 20.99 *(978-1-4264-6907-7(1))*; 254p. pap. 23.99 *(978-1-4264-6989-3(6))* Creative Media Partners, LLC.

Crossley-Holland, Kevin. At the Crossing-Places. 2004. (Arthur Trilogy). (Illus.). 394p. (YA). (gr. 7-12). 15.65 *(978-0-7569-3182-7(7))* Perfection Learning Corp.

—Crossing to Paradise. 2008. (J). pap. *(978-0-545-05868-1(6)*, Levine, Arthur A. Bks.) Scholastic, Inc.

Curry, Jane Louise. The Black Canary. 2005. (ENG., Illus.). 288p. (J). (gr. 5-9). 18.99 *(978-0-689-86478-0(7)*, McElderry, Margaret K. Bks.) McElderry, Margaret K. Bks.

Cushman, Karen. Alchemy & Meggy Swann. 2011. (ENG.). 176p. (J). (gr. 5-7). pap. 7.99 *(978-0-547-57712-8(5))* Houghton Mifflin Harcourt Publishing Co.

—Will Sparrow's Road. 2014. (ENG.). 224p. (J). (gr. 5-7). pap. 6.99 *(978-0-544-33632-2(1)*, HMH Books For Young Readers) Houghton Mifflin Harcourt Publishing Co.

Dahme, Joanne, et al. The Plague. 2009. (ENG., Illus.). 272p. (YA). (gr. 7-17). 16.95 *(978-0-7624-3344-5(2))* Running Pr. Bk. Pubs.

Davis, Lydia & Ollivant, Alfred. Alfred Ollivant's Bob, Son of Battle: The Last Gray Dog of Kenmuir. Kirmse, Marguerite, illus. 2014. (ENG.). 320p. (J). (gr. 3-7). 17.95 *(978-1-59017-729-7(0)*, NYR Children's Collection) New York Review of Bks., Inc., The.

Dickens, Charles. Great Expectations. Freeberg, Eric, illus. 2010. (Classic Starts(tm) Ser.). (ENG.). 160p. (J). (gr. 2-4). 6.95 *(978-1-4027-6645-9(9))* Sterling Publishing Co., Inc.

—Oliver Twist & Other Classic Tales. Thorne, Jenny, illus. 2015. (ENG.). 80p. (J). (gr. -1-12). pap. 9.99 *(978-1-86147-408-7(3)*, Armadillo) Anness Publishing GBR. Dist: National Bk. Network.

Doherty, Berlie. Treason. 2012. (ENG.). 352p. (J). (gr. 4-7). pap. 12.99 *(978-1-84939-121-4(1))* Andersen Pr. GBR. Dist: Independent Pubs. Group.

Doyle, Arthur Conan. #09 Sherlock Holmes & the Adventure of the Six Napoleons. Rohrbach, Sophie & Morrow, Jt, illus. 2011. (On the Case with Holmes & Watson Set II Ser.). pap. 39.62 *(978-0-7613-7611-8(9)*, Graphic Universe™) Lerner Publishing Group.

Doyle, Marissa. Betraying Season. 2010. (ENG.). 336p. (YA). (gr. 9-13). pap. 19.99 *(978-0-312-62916-8(8)*, 9780312629168) Square Fish.

—Courtship & Curses. 2013. (ENG.). 368p. (YA). (gr. 9-13). pap. 10.99 *(978-1-250-02744-3(6))* Square Fish.

Duble, Kathleen Benner. Quest. 2008. (ENG.). 256p. (J). (gr. 5-9). 17.99 *(978-1-4169-3386-1(7)*, McElderry, Margaret K. Bks.) McElderry, Margaret K. Bks.

Dunkle, Clare B. The Hollow Kingdom. 2006. (Hollow Kingdom Trilogy Ser.: 1). (ENG.). 240p. (J). (gr. 6-9). reprint ed. pap. 10.99 *(978-0-8050-8108-4(9)*, 9780805081084, Holt, Henry & Co. Bks. For Young Readers) Holt, Henry & Co.

—The House of Dead Maids. Arrasmith, Patrick, illus. 2011. (ENG.). 176p. (YA). (gr. 7-12). pap. 16.99 *(978-0-312-55155-1(X)*, 9780312551551) Square Fish.

Edge, Christopher. Shadows of the Silver Screen. 2014. (Penelope Tredwell Mysteries Ser.: 2). (ENG.). 256p. (J). (gr. 3-7). 16.99 *(978-0-8075-7319-8(1))* Whitman, Albert & Co.

Erskine, Kathryn. The Badger Knight. 2014. (Illus.). (J). 325p. *(978-0-545-66293-2(1))*; (ENG.). 352p. (gr. 3-7). 17.99 *(978-0-545-46442-0(0))* Scholastic, Inc. (Scholastic Pr.).

Farenhorst, Christine. A Cup of Cold Water: The Compassion of Nurse Edith Cavell. 2007. 222p. (J). (gr. 3-7). per. 11.99 *(978-1-59638-026-4(8))* P & R Publishing.

Finn, Mary. Belladonna. 2011. (ENG., Illus.). 384p. (YA). (gr. 7-18). 16.99 *(978-0-7636-5106-0(0))* Candlewick Pr.

Fisher, Catherine. Circle of Stones. 2014. (ENG.). 304p. (YA). (gr. 7). 17.99 *(978-0-8037-3819-5(6)*, Dial Bks) Penguin Young Readers Group.

—Darkwater. 2012. (ENG.). 240p. (YA). (gr. 7). 16.99 *(978-0-8037-3818-8(8)*, Dial Bks) Penguin Young Readers Group.

Fisher, Linda C. Runaway Will. 2010. (J). pap. *(978-0-88092-720-8(8))* Royal Fireworks Publishing Co.

Flavin, Teresa. The Crimson Shard. (ENG.). (J). (gr. 4-7). 2015. 288p. pap. 6.99 *(978-0-7636-7172-3(X))* 2012. (Illus.). 256p. 15.99 *(978-0-7636-6093-2(0))* Candlewick Pr. (Templar).

Fletcher, J. S. Scarhaven Keep. 2011. (YA). *(978-1-60682-173-2(3))* BJU Pr.

Fortescue, W. J. The Drummer's Coat. 2007. 120p. 94.99 *(978-1-4280-7656-3(5))*; per. 88.99 *(978-1-4280-7658-7(1))* IndyPublish.com.

Gallivan, Susan. The Return of Mr Jeffries. 2009. 88p. pap. 10.49 *(978-1-4389-4183-7(8))* AuthorHouse.

Gashler, Stephen. The Bent Sword. 2010. (YA). pap. 15.99 *(978-1-59955-401-3(1))* Cedar Fort, Inc./CFI Distribution.

Gaughen, A. C. Lion Heart. 2015. (Scarlet Trilogy: No. 3). (ENG.). 352p. (YA). 17.99 *(978-0-8027-3616-1(5)*, 9780802736161, Bloomsbury USA Childrens) Bloomsbury Publishing USA.

Gayton, Sam. Lilliput. 1 vol. Ratterree, Alice, illus. 256p. (J). (gr. 3-6). 2017. (ENG.). pap. 8.95 ***(978-1-68263-006-8(4))*** 2016. (SPA & ENG.). 16.95 *(978-1-56145-806-6(6))* Peachtree Pubs.

Gier, Kerstin. Ruby Red. Bell, Anthea, tr. from GER. 2011. (Ruby Red Trilogy Ser.: 1). (ENG.). 336p. (YA). (gr. 7-12). 18.99 *(978-0-8050-9252-3(8)*, 9780805092523, Holt, Henry & Co. Bks. For Young Readers) Holt, Henry & Co.

—Ruby Red. Bell, Anthea, tr. 2012. (Ruby Red Trilogy Ser.: 1). (ENG.). 352p. (YA). (gr. 7-12). pap. 10.99 *(978-0-312-55151-3(7)*, 9780312551513) Square Fish.

—Sapphire Blue. Bell, Anthea, tr. from GER. 2012. (Ruby Red Trilogy Ser.: 2). (ENG.). 368p. (YA). (gr. 7). 18.99 *(978-0-8050-9266-0(8)*, 9780805092660, Holt, Henry & Co. Bks. For Young Readers) Holt, Henry & Co.

—Sapphire Blue. Bell, Anthea, tr. 2013. (Ruby Red Trilogy Ser.: 2). (ENG.). 384p. (YA). (gr. 7). pap. 10.99 *(978-1-250-03416-8(7)*, 9781250034168) Square Fish.

Goodman, Alison. The Dark Days Pact. 2017. (Lady Helen Novel Ser.: 2). (ENG.). 496p. (YA). (gr. 9). 18.99 *(978-0-670-78548-3(2)*, Viking Books for Young Readers) Penguin Young Readers Group.

Gosling, Sharon. The Diamond Thief. 2014. (Diamond Thief Ser.). (ENG.). 336p. (gr. 9-12). 16.95 *(978-1-63079-002-8(8))* Switch Pr.

—The Ruby Airship. 2015. (Diamond Thief Ser.). (ENG.). 496p. (gr. 9-12). 16.95 *(978-1-63079-004-2(4))* Switch Pr.

Grahame, Abby. Wentworth Hall. (ENG.). 288p. (YA). (gr. 7). 2013. pap. 9.99 *(978-1-4424-5197-1(1))* 2012. 16.99 *(978-1-4424-5196-4(3))* Simon & Schuster Bks. For Young Readers. (Simon & Schuster Bks. For Young Readers).

Guibord, Maurissa. Warped. 2012. (ENG.). 348p. (YA). (gr. 7). pap. 9.99 *(978-0-385-73892-7(7)*, Ember) Random Hse. Children's Bks.

Hahn, Mary Downing. The Ghost of Crutchfield Hall. (ENG.). 160p. (J). (gr. 5-7). 2011. pap. 6.99 *(978-0-547-57715-9(X))* 2010. 17.00 *(978-0-547-38560-0(9))* Houghton Mifflin Harcourt Publishing Co.

Hall, Tim K. Shadow of the Wolf. 2015. (ENG.). 480p. (J). (gr. 9). 18.99 *(978-0-545-81664-9(5))* Scholastic, Inc.

Hamley, Dennis. Divided Loyalties. 2010. (J). *(978-0-7636-3418-6(2))* Candlewick Pr.

Hardinge, Frances. Cuckoo Song. (ENG.). (YA). (gr. 7-12). 2016. 432p. pap. 9.95 *(978-1-4197-1939-4(4))* 2015. 416p. 17.95 *(978-1-4197-1480-1(5))* Abrams, Inc. (Amulet Bks.).

—The Lie Tree. 2016. (ENG.). 384p. (YA). (gr. 8-17). 17.95 *(978-1-4197-1895-3(9)*, Amulet Bks.) Abrams, Inc.

Harvey, Alyxandra. Whisper the Dead. 2014. (Lovegrove Legacy Ser.: Bk. 2). (ENG.). 408p. (YA). (gr. 7). 17.99 *(978-0-8027-3750-2(1)*, 9780802737502, Bloomsbury USA Childrens) Bloomsbury Publishing USA.

Harvey, Damian & Remphry, Martin. Robin & the Monk. 2009. (Hopscotch Adventures Ser.). (Illus.). 31p. (J). (gr. 1). lib. bdg. 25.65 *(978-1-59771-179-1(9))* Sea-To-Sea Pubns.

Hayner, Linda K. Ellanor's Exchange. 2005. 195p. (YA). 8.99 *(978-1-59166-462-8(4))* BJU Pr.

Hearn, Julie. Hazel. 2009. (ENG.). 400p. (YA). (gr. 7-18). 17.99 *(978-1-4169-2504-0(X)*, Atheneum Bks. for Young Readers) Simon & Schuster Children's Publishing.

—Hazel: A Novel. 2010. (ENG.). 416p. (YA). (gr. 7). pap. 8.99 *(978-1-4169-2505-7(8)*, Atheneum Bks. for Young Readers) Simon & Schuster Children's Publishing.

—Ivy. 2009. (ENG.). 384p. (YA). (gr. 7). pap. 9.99 *(978-1-4169-2507-1(4)*, Atheneum Bks. for Young Readers) Simon & Schuster Children's Publishing.

—The Minister's Daughter. 2006. (ENG.). 272p. (YA). (gr. 7-12). pap. 7.99 *(978-0-689-87691-2(2)*, Atheneum Bks. for Young Readers) Simon & Schuster Children's Publishing.

Henty, George Alfred. Beric the Briton: A Story of the Roman Invasion. 2012. 258p. pap. 14.95 *(978-1-61895-050-5(9))* Bibliotech Pr.

—Under Drake's Flag: A Tale of the Spanish Main. 2007. (ENG.). 290p. pap. 21.99 *(978-1-4346-3056-8(0))*; 322p. pap. 24.99 *(978-1-4346-3070-4(6))* Creative Media Partners, LLC.

—Under Drake's Flag: A Tale of the Spanish Main. 2011. 316p. pap. 19.95 *(978-1-61179-182-2(0))* Fireship Pr.

—When London Burned: A Story of Restoration Times & the Great Fire. l.t. ed. 2005. 724p. pap. *(978-1-84637-212-4(7))* Echo Library.

Hopkinson, Deborah. The Great Trouble: A Mystery of London, the Blue Death, & a Boy Called Eel. 2013. (ENG.). 256p. (J). (gr. 5). 16.99 *(978-0-375-84818-6(5)*, Knopf Bks. for Young Readers) Random Hse. Children's Bks.

Hughes, Shirley. The Christmas Eve Ghost. Hughes, Shirley, illus. 2010. (ENG., Illus.). 32p. (J). (gr. -1-3). 15.99 *(978-0-7636-4472-7(2))* Candlewick Pr.

—Daisy Saves the Day. Hughes, Shirley, illus. 2015. (ENG., Illus.). 32p. (J). (gr. k-4). 16.99 *(978-0-7636-7323-9(4))* Candlewick Pr.

Hulme-Cross, Benjamin. The Knight's Enemies. Rinaldi, Angelo, illus. 2015. (ENG.). 160p. (J). *(978-0-7787-1765-2(8))* Crabtree Publishing Co.

Jinks, Catherine. The Last Bogler. 2016. (How to Catch a Bogle Ser.: 3). (ENG., Illus.). 336p. (J). (gr. 5-7). 16.99 *(978-0-544-08696-8(1)*, HMH Books For Young Readers) Houghton Mifflin Harcourt Publishing Co.

Jocelyn, Marthe. What We Hide. (ENG.). 288p. (YA). (gr. 9). 2015. pap. 9.99 *(978-0-375-85544-3(0)*, Ember) 2014. 16.99 *(978-0-385-73847-7(1)*, Lamb, Wendy Bks.) Random Hse. Children's Bks.

Jones, Janey Louise. The Secrets of Sophia Musgrove No. 1: Dancing & Deception. 2011. (ENG.). 250p. (J). (gr. 4-7). pap. 8.99 *(978-0-552-55822-8(2))* Transworld Publishers Ltd. GBR. Dist: Independent Pubs. Group.

Jones, Rob Lloyd. The Story of Robin Hood. Marks, Alan, illus. 2010. (Picture Book Classics Ser.). 24p. (J). 9.99 *(978-0-7945-2859-1(7)*, Usborne) EDC Publishing.

Klein, Lisa. Cate of the Lost Colony. 2012. (ENG.). 336p. (YA). (gr. 9-12). pap. 9.99 *(978-1-59990-739-0(9)*, 9781599907390, Bloomsbury USA Childrens) Bloomsbury Publishing USA.

LaFevers, R. L. Theodosia & the Eyes of Horus. Tanaka, Yoko, illus. 2011. (ENG.). 384p. (J). (gr. 2-5). pap. 7.99 *(978-0-547-55011-4(1))* Houghton Mifflin Harcourt Publishing Co.

—Theodosia & the Serpents of Chaos. Tanaka, Yoko, illus. 2008. (ENG.). 352p. (J). (gr. 2-5). pap. 7.99 *(978-0-618-99976-7(0))* Houghton Mifflin Harcourt Publishing Co.

Lamprey, L. Masters of the Guild. l.t. ed. 2006. 168p. pap. 21.99 *(978-1-4264-2076-4(5))* Creative Media Partners, LLC.

Lane, Andrew. Black Ice. 2013. (Sherlock Holmes: the Legend Begins Ser.: 3). (ENG.). 288p. (YA). (gr. 7-12). 17.99 *(978-0-374-38769-3(9)*, 9780374387693, Farrar, Straus & Giroux (BYR)) Farrar, Straus & Giroux.

—Black Ice. 2013. (Sherlock Holmes: the Legend Begins Ser.: 3). (ENG.). 304p. (YA). (gr. 7-12). pap. 11.99 *(978-1-250-03654-4(2)*, 9781250036544) Square Fish.

—Fire Storm. 2013. (Sherlock Holmes: the Legend Begins Ser.: 4). (ENG.). 352p. (YA). (gr. 7-12). 17.99 *(978-0-374-32311-0(9)*, 9780374323110, Farrar, Straus & Giroux (BYR)) Farrar, Straus & Giroux.

—Fire Storm. 2014. (Sherlock Holmes: the Legend Begins Ser.: 4). (ENG.). 368p. (YA). (gr. 7-12). pap. 12.99 *(978-1-250-05072-4(3)*, 9781250050724) Square Fish.

—Rebel Fire. 2012. (Sherlock Holmes: the Legend Begins Ser.: 2). (ENG.). 352p. (YA). (gr. 7-12). 16.99 *(978-0-374-38768-6(0)*, 9780374387686, Farrar, Straus & Giroux (BYR)) Farrar, Straus & Giroux.

Larwood, Kieran. Freaks. 2013. (J). (ENG.). 256p. (gr. 5-9). 16.99 *(978-0-545-47424-5(8))*; *(978-0-545-47425-2(6))* Scholastic, Inc. (Chicken Hse., The).

Laurie, Victoria. The Curse of Deadman's Forest. 2011. (ENG.). 432p. (J). (gr. 3-7). 8.99 *(978-0-440-42259-4(0)*, Yearling) Random Hse. Children's Bks.

—Oracles of Delphi Keep. 2010. (Oracles of Delphi Keep Ser.). (ENG.). 576p. (J). (gr. 3-7). 7.99 *(978-0-440-42258-7(2)*, Yearling) Random Hse. Children's Bks.

Lawlor, Laurie. The Two Loves of Will Shakespeare. 2006. (ENG.). 256p. (YA). (gr. 12). 16.95 *(978-0-8234-1901-2(0))* Holiday Hse., Inc.

Lawson, Jessica. Nooks & Crannies. Andrewson, Natalie, illus. 2015. (ENG.). 336p. (J). (gr. 3-7). 16.99 *(978-1-4814-1921-5(8)*, Simon & Schuster Bks. For Young Readers) Simon & Schuster Bks. For Young Readers.

Lee, Y. S. The Body at the Tower. 2010. (Agency Ser.: 2). (ENG., Illus.). 352p. (YA). (gr. 7-18). 16.99 *(978-0-7636-4968-5(6))* Candlewick Pr.

—The Traitor in the Tunnel. 2012. (Agency Ser.: 3). (ENG., Illus.). 384p. (YA). (gr. 7). 16.99 *(978-0-7636-5316-3(0))* Candlewick Pr.

Leslie, Emma. For Merrie England: A Tale of the Weavers of Norfolk. Taylor, R., illus. 2010. 168p. 20.95 *(978-1-934671-38-2(X))*; pap. 10.95 *(978-1-934671-39-9(8))* Salem Ridge Press LLC.

Lloyd, Michael. The Pirate Children. 2017. (ENG.). 334p. (J). pap. 15.95 ***(978-1-78693-666-0(6)***, c1ba7e42-0295-4a40-bb92-9690da2fc058) Austin, Stan AUS. Dist: Bookmasters Distribution.

Longshore, Katherine. Gilt. 2012. (ENG.). 416p. (YA). (gr. 7-18). 17.99 *(978-0-670-01399-9(4)*, Viking Books for Young Readers) Penguin Young Readers Group.

Macauley, Jo. New World. 1 vol. 2014. (Secrets & Spies Ser.). (ENG.). 224p. (gr. 4-7). 26.65 *(978-1-4342-9596-5(6))* Stone Arch Bks.

—Plague. 2014. 221p. (J). *(978-1-4342-7945-3(6)*, Capstone Bks.) Capstone Press of Coughlan Cos.

—Plague, 1 vol. 2014. (Secrets & Spies Ser.). (ENG.). 224p. (gr. 4-7). pap. 8.95 *(978-1-62370-053-9(1))* Capstone Young Readers of Coughlan Cos.

MacColl, Michaela. Secrets in the Snow: A Novel of Intrigue & Romance. 2016. (ENG., Illus.). 288p. (YA). (gr. 7-12). 16.99 *(978-1-4521-3358-4(1))* Chronicle Bks. LLC.

MacDonald, Bailey. Wicked Will: A Mystery of Young William Shakespeare. 2009. (ENG.). 208p. (J). (gr. 4-7). 16.99 *(978-1-4169-8660-7(X)*, Simon & Schuster/Paula Wiseman Bks.) Simon & Schuster/Paula Wiseman Bks.

MacLean, Sarah. The Season. 2009. 345p. (J). *(978-0-545-24214-1(2))* Scholastic, Inc.

Maid of Deception. 2014. (Maids of Honor Ser.). (ENG., Illus.). 416p. (YA). (gr. 7). 17.99 *(978-1-4424-4141-5(0)*, Simon & Schuster Bks. For Young Readers) Simon & Schuster Bks. For Young Readers.

Malkus, Alida Sims. The Story of Good Queen Bess. Meadowcroft, Enid Lamonte, ed. Gorsline, Douglas W., illus. 2011. 192p. 42.95 *(978-1-258-09564-2(5))* Literary Licensing, LLC.

Marryat, Captian & Marryat, Frederick. The Children of the New Forest. 2014. (ENG., Illus.). 266p. (J). (gr. 4-7). pap. 14.99 *(978-1-84391-487-7(5))* Hesperus Pr. GBR. Dist: Independent Pubs. Group.

McGowan, Jennifer. Maid of Secrets. (Maids of Honor Ser.). (ENG.). (YA). (gr. 7). 2014. 432p. pap. 9.99 *(978-1-4424-4139-2(9))* 2013. 416p. 17.99 *(978-1-4424-4138-5(0))* Simon & Schuster Bks. For Young Readers. (Simon & Schuster Bks. For Young Readers).

—Maid of Wonder. 2015. (Maids of Honor Ser.). (ENG., Illus.). 336p. (YA). (gr. 7). 17.99 *(978-1-4814-1826-3(2))* Simon & Schuster Children's Publishing.

McKay, Hilary. Wishing for Tomorrow: The Sequel to a Little Princess. Maland, Nick, illus. 2010. (ENG.). 288p. (J). (gr. 3-7). 16.99 *(978-1-4424-0169-3(9)*, McElderry, Margaret K. Bks.) McElderry, Margaret K. Bks.

Meyer, Carolyn. Loving Will Shakespeare. 2008. (ENG., Illus.). 272p. (YA). (gr. 7-12). pap. 6.95 *(978-0-15-206221-7(1))* Houghton Mifflin Harcourt Publishing Co.

—Patience, Princess Catherine: A Young Royals Book. 2009. (Young Royals Ser.: 4). (ENG., Illus.). 208p. (YA). (gr. 7-12). pap. 13.95 *(978-0-15-205447-2(2))* Houghton Mifflin Harcourt Publishing Co.

—Victoria Rebels. 2014. (ENG., Illus.). 272p. (YA). (gr. 7). pap. 9.99 *(978-1-4169-8730-7(4)*, Simon & Schuster/Paula Wiseman Bks.) Simon & Schuster/Paula Wiseman Bks.

Mooser, Stephen. Young Marian's Adventures in Sherwood Forest. Lansky, Bruce, ed. 2013. (Girls to the Rescue Ser.: 9). (ENG.). 144p. (J). (gr. 3-7). pap. 5.99 *(978-1-4424-9201-1(5))* Meadowbrook Pr.

Moran, Katy. Bloodline. 2009. (ENG., Illus.). 320p. (YA). (gr. 7). 16.99 *(978-0-7636-4083-5(2))* Candlewick Pr.

Morgan, Angie. Sedric & the Hairy Troll Invasion. 2015. (ENG., Illus.). 192p. (J). (gr. 2-6). pap. 10.99 *(978-1-4052-7512-5(X))* Egmont Bks., Ltd. GBR. Dist: Independent Pubs. Group.

Morpurgo, Michael. Private Peaceful. 2006. 18.00 *(978-0-7569-6630-0(2))* Perfection Learning Corp.

—Private Peaceful. 2006. (YA). 1.25 *(978-1-4193-2976-0(6))* Recorded Bks., Inc.

—Private Peaceful. 2006. (After Words Ser.). (ENG., Illus.). 224p. (J). (gr. 7-12). per. 7.99 *(978-0-439-63653-7(1)*, Scholastic Paperbacks) Scholastic, Inc.

Morris, Gerald. The Adventures of Sir Gawain the True. Renier, Aaron, illus. 2013. (Knights' Tales Ser.: 3). (ENG.). 128p. (J). (gr. 1-4). pap. 5.99 *(978-0-544-02264-5(5))* Houghton Mifflin Harcourt Publishing Co.

Nesbit, E. The House of Arden. 2006. 184p. (gr. 3-7). per. 14.95 *(978-1-59818-967-4(0))*; 26.95 *(978-1-59818-181-4(5))* Aegypan.

—The House of Arden. 2006. (New York Review Children's Collection). (ENG.). 260p. (J). (gr. 4-7). 17.95 *(978-1-59017-202-5(7)*, NYR Children's Collection) New York Review of Bks., Inc., The.

Odom, Mel. The Mystery Unravels. 2013. (Hunter's League Ser.: 2). (ENG.). 256p. (YA). (gr. 7). pap. 16.99 *(978-1-4814-0154-8(8)*, Simon Pulse) Simon Pulse.

Orczy, Emmuska. The Nest of the Sparrowhawk. 2008. 236p. pap. 15.95 *(978-1-60664-232-0(4))* Rodgers, Alan Bks.

—The Old Man in the Corner. 2008. 188p. pap. 13.95 *(978-1-60664-231-3(6))* Rodgers, Alan Bks.

Ortiz, Michael J. Swan Town: The Secret Journal of Susanna Shakespeare. 2006. (Illus.). 197p. (J). (gr. 5-9). 15.99 *(978-0-06-058126-8(3))* HarperCollins Pubs.

Osborne, Mary Pope. A Ghost Tale for Christmas Time. Murdocca, Sal, illus. (Magic Tree House Merlin Mission Ser.: No. 16). (ENG.). (J). (gr. 2-5). 2012. 144p. pap. 5.99 *(978-0-375-85653-2(6))* 2010. 128p. 12.99 *(978-0-375-85652-5(8))* Random Hse. Children's Bks. (Random Hse. Bks. for Young Readers).

Osborne, Mary Pope, et al. Miedo Escénico en una Noche de Verano. Murdocca, Sal, illus. 2014. 25. (SPA.). 86p. (J). (gr. 2-4). pap. 5.99 *(978-1-933032-92-4(8))* Lectorum Pubns., Inc.

Peck, Richard. The Mouse with the Question Mark Tail. Murphy, Kelly, illus. 2013. (ENG.). 240p. (J). (gr. 3-7). 16.99 *(978-0-8037-3838-6(2)*, Dial Bks) Penguin Young Readers Group.

Peyton, K. M. Minna's Quest IR. 2013. (Roman Pony Trilogy Ser.). 186p. (J). pap. 5.99 *(978-0-7945-3143-0(1)*, Usborne) EDC Publishing.

—No Turning Back IR. 2013. pap. 5.99 *(978-0-7945-3148-5(2)*, Usborne) EDC Publishing.

Picard, Barbara Leonie. Ransom for a Knight. 2008. (Nautilus Ser.). (ENG.). 314p. (J). (gr. 6). pap. 14.95 *(978-1-58988-043-6(9))* Dry, Paul Bks., Inc.

Pierce, Nicola. Behind the Walls. 2015. (ENG., Illus.). 368p. (J). pap. 13.00 *(978-1-84717-646-2(1))* O'Brien Pr., Ltd., The IRL. Dist: Dufour Editions, Inc.

Priestley, Chris. The Dead of Winter. 2012. (ENG., Illus.). 224p. (YA). (gr. 7-12). 16.99 *(978-1-59990-745-1(3)*, 9781599907451, Bloomsbury USA Childrens) Bloomsbury Publishing USA.

Prince & the Pauper App Clas. 2003. (J). pap. 2.75 *(978-0-590-43283-2(4))* Scholastic, Inc.

Pullman, Philip. Sally y la Sombra del Norte. 2003.Tr. of Shadow in the North. (SPA., Illus.). 352p. (YA). 14.95 *(978-84-95618-43-6(5)*, Umbriel) Ediciones Urano S. A. ESP. Dist: Spanish Pubs., LLC.

—Two Crafty Criminals! And How They Were Captured by the Daring Detectives of the New Cut Gang. 2013. (ENG.). 288p. (J). (gr. 3-7). 7.99 *(978-0-307-93035-4(1)*, Yearling) Random Hse. Children's Bks.

Pyle, Ernie Howard. Men of Iron. 2005. 272p. 28.95 *(978-1-4218-0617-4(7)*, 1st World Library - Literary Society) 1st World Publishing, Inc.

—Men of Iron. 2007. (ENG.). 198p. pap. 19.99 *(978-1-4346-1014-0(4))*; 218p. pap. 22.99 *(978-1-4346-1113-0(2))* Creative Media Partners, LLC.

Pyle, Howard. Men of Iron. unabr. ed. 2003. (Dover Children's Classics Ser.). (ENG.). 192p. (J). (gr. 3-8). pap. 10.95 *(978-0-486-42841-3(9))* Dover Pubns., Inc.

Rabin, Staton. Black Powder. 2005. (ENG.). 256p. (YA). (gr. 7-9). 16.95 *(978-0-689-86876-4(6)*, McElderry, Margaret K. Bks.) McElderry, Margaret K. Bks.

Rasheed, Leila. Diamonds & Deceit. 2014. (At Somerton Ser.). (ENG.). 432p. (YA). (gr. 7-12). 17.99 *(978-1-4231-7118-8(7))* Hyperion Bks. for Children.

Rattle, Alison. The Beloved. 2016. (ENG.). 304p. (YA). (gr. 11). pap. 12.99 *(978-1-4714-0379-8(3))* Bonnier Publishing GBR. Dist: Independent Pubs. Group.

Rautenberg, Karen Rita. Lady Lucy's Gallant Knight. 2007. (ENG.). 156p. (J). (gr. 4-7). per. *(978-1-933255-22-4(6))* DNA Pr.

Rayner, Shoo. Fighting Forum. 2016. (First Look At Ser.). (ENG., Illus.). 64p. (J). (gr. k-2). pap. 7.99 *(978-1-4083-3460-7(7)*, Orchard Bks.) Hachette Children's Group GBR. Dist: Hachette Bk. Group.

—Grizzly Gladiator. 2015. (Roman Brit Ser.: 1). (ENG., Illus.). 64p. (J). (gr. k-2). pap. 8.99 *(978-1-4083-3452-2(6))* Hodder & Stoughton GBR. Dist: Hachette Bk. Group.

—Stinkius Maximus. 2016. (Roman Brit Ser.). (ENG., Illus.). 64p. (J). (gr. k-2). pap. 7.99 *(978-1-4083-3448-5(8)*, Orchard Bks.) Hachette Children's Group GBR. Dist: Hachette Bk. Group.

Rees, Celia. The Fool's Girl. 2010. (ENG.). 304p. (YA). (gr. 7-18). 16.99 *(978-1-59990-486-3(1)*, 9781599904863, Bloomsbury USA Childrens) Bloomsbury Publishing USA.

Richards, Justin. Rewind Assassin. 2007. (Time Runners Ser.: 2). (ENG.). 208p. (J). (gr. 4-7). pap. 8.99 *(978-1-4169-2643-6(7))* Simon & Schuster, Ltd. GBR. Dist: Simon & Schuster, Inc.

Rinaldi, Ann. Mutiny's Daughter. 2005. 218p. (J). (gr. 3-7). 13.65 *(978-0-7569-5602-8(1))* Perfection Learning Corp.

—Nine Days a Queen: The Short Life & Reign of Lady Jane Grey. 2006. (ENG.). 240p. (J). (gr. 8-12). pap. 8.99 *(978-0-06-054925-1(4)*, HarperTeen) HarperCollins Pubs.

Russell, Christopher. Hunted. 2007. (J). (gr. 5-9). 254p. 15.99 *(978-0-06-084119-5(2))*; 272p. lib. bdg. 16.89 *(978-0-06-084120-1(6)*, Greenwillow Bks.) HarperCollins Pubs.

Saunders, Kate. Beswitched. 2012. (ENG.). 272p. (J). (gr. 4-7). 7.99 *(978-0-375-87329-4(5)*, Yearling) Random Hse. Children's Bks.

Saunders, Kate & Nesbit, E. Five Children on the Western Front. 2016. (J). *(978-0-553-49785-4(5)*, Delacorte Pr) Random House Publishing Group.

Scheier, Leah. Secret Letters. 2013. (ENG., Illus.). 320p. (J). (gr. 5-17). pap. 8.99 *(978-1-4231-2758-1(7))* Hyperion Pr.

Scott, Walter, ed. Ivanhoe. (SPA., Illus.). 176p. (YA). 14.95 *(978-84-7281-096-9(8)*, AF1096) Auriga, Ediciones S.A. ESP. Dist: Continental Bk. Co., Inc.

Sewell, Anna. Black Beauty: The Autobiography of a Horse. 2016. 193p. (J). pap. *(978-1-5124-0214-8(1)*, First Avenue Editions) Lerner Publishing Group.

Shanker, Tarun & Zekas, Kelly. These Vicious Masks. 2016. (These Vicious Masks Ser.). (ENG.). 320p. (YA). pap. 9.99 *(978-1-250-07389-1(8)*, 9781250073891) Feiwel & Friends.

Shinn, Sharon. The Safe-Keeper's Secret. 2005. (ENG.). 240p. (YA). (gr. 7-7). 7.99 *(978-0-14-240357-0(1)*, Firebird) Penguin Young Readers Group.

Slade, Arthur G. The Dark Deeps. 2011. (Hunchback Assignments Ser.: Vol. 2). (ENG.). 320p. (YA). (gr. 7). pap. 9.99 *(978-0-375-85404-0(5)*, Ember) Random Hse. Children's Bks.
—Empire of Ruins. 2012. (Hunchback Assignments Ser.). (ENG.). 300p. (YA). (gr. 7). pap. 8.99 *(978-0-375-85405-7(3)*, Ember) Random Hse. Children's Bks.
Sleiman, Dina L. Chivalrous. 2015. (Valiant Hearts Ser.: 2). (ENG.). 368p. (YA). pap. 16.00 *(978-0-7642-1313-7(X))* Bethany Hse. Pubs.
—Courageous. 2016. (Valiant Hearts Ser.: 3). (ENG.). 368p. (YA). pap. 13.99 *(978-0-7642-1314-4(8))* Bethany Hse. Pubs.
—Dauntless. 2015. (Valiant Hearts Ser.: 1). (ENG.). 368p. (YA). pap. 13.99 *(978-0-7642-1312-0(1))* Bethany Hse. Pubs.
Small Acts of Amazing Courage. 2013. (ENG., Illus.). 240p. (J). (gr. 4-7). pap. 6.99 *(978-1-4424-9495-4(6)*, Simon & Schuster/Paula Wiseman Bks.) Simon & Schuster/Paula Wiseman Bks.
Smith, Daniel. My Friend the Enemy. 2014. (ENG.). 288p. (J). (gr. 3-7). 17.99 *(978-0-545-66542-1(6)*, Chicken Hse., The) Scholastic, Inc.
Smith, Ronald L. The Mesmerist. 2017. (ENG.). 272p. (J). (gr. 5-7). 16.99 *(978-0-544-44528-4(7)*, Clarion Bks.) Houghton Mifflin Harcourt Trade & Reference Pubs.
Spinner, Stephanie. Damosel: In Which the Lady of the Lake Renders a Frank & Often Startling Account of Her Wondrous Life & Times. 2010. (ENG.). 208p. (YA). (gr. 7). pap. 8.99 *(978-0-553-49511-9(9)*, Knopf Bks. for Young Readers) Random Hse. Children's Bks.
Stevermer, Caroline. Magic below Stairs. 2011. (ENG.). 208p. (J). (gr. 3-7). 6.99 *(978-0-14-241871-0(4)*, Puffin Books) Penguin Young Readers Group.
Stewart, Paul & Riddell, Chris. Barnaby Grimes: Curse of the Night Wolf. 2012. (Barnaby Grimes Ser.). (ENG.). 224p. (J). (gr. 3-7). 6.99 *(978-0-385-73697-8(5)*, Yearling) Random Hse. Children's Bks.
—Barnaby Grimes: Legion of the Dead. 2012. (Barnaby Grimes Ser.). (ENG.). 240p. (J). (gr. 4-7). 6.99 *(978-0-385-73699-2(1)*, Yearling) Random Hse. Children's Bks.
—Barnaby Grimes: Phantom of Blood Alley. 2013. (Barnaby Grimes Ser.). (ENG.). 208p. (J). (gr. 3-7). 6.99 *(978-0-385-73700-5(9)*, Yearling) Random Hse. Children's Bks.
Stone, Phoebe. The Romeo & Juliet Code. 2012. (ENG.). 320p. (J). (gr. 3-7). pap. 7.99 *(978-0-545-21827-6(6)*, Levine, Arthur A. Bks.) Scholastic, Inc.
—Romeo Blue. 2015. (ENG.). 352p. (J). (gr. 3-7). pap. 7.99 *(978-0-545-44361-6(X)*, Levine, Arthur A. Bks.) Scholastic, Inc.
Stone, Reuben. Guardians of the Cambrian Lode: An Ancient People - A Timeless Quest. 2005. 254p. (YA). (gr. 8-12). per. 7.99 *(978-0-9550034-0-0(7))* Bethania Bks. GBR. Dist: Send The Light Distribution LLC.
Strang, Herbert. With Marlborough to Malplaquet. 2006. pap. *(978-1-4068-3126-9(3))* Echo Library.
Stratford, Jordan. The Case of the Girl in Grey (the Wollstonecraft Detective Agency, Book 2) Murphy, Kelly, illus. 2016. (Wollstonecraft Detective Agency Ser.). (ENG.). 224p. (J). (gr. 3-7). 16.99 *(978-0-385-75444-6(2)*, Knopf Bks. for Young Readers) Random Hse. Children's Bks.
Streatfeild, Noel. Party Shoes. 2008. (Oxford Children's Classics Ser.). (ENG., Illus.). 320p. (YA). 9.95 *(978-0-19-272010-8(4))* Oxford Univ. Pr., Inc.
Sullivan, Laura L. Ladies in Waiting. 2013. (ENG.). 336p. (YA). (gr. 9). pap. 18.99 *(978-0-544-02220-1(3))* Houghton Mifflin Harcourt Publishing Co.
—Love by the Morning Star. 2014. (ENG.). 320p. (YA). (gr. 7-12). 17.99 *(978-0-547-68951-7(9)*, HMH Books For Young Readers) Houghton Mifflin Harcourt Publishing Co.
Sutcliff, Rosemary. Dawn Wind. 2010. (ENG.). 312p. pap. 12.95 *(978-1-59078-672-7(6)*, Front Street) Boyds Mills Pr.
—The Eagle. movie tie-in ed. 2011. (Roman Britain Trilogy Ser.: 1). (ENG.). 240p. (YA). (gr. 5). pap. 9.99 *(978-0-312-56434-6(1)*, 9780312564346) Square Fish.
—The Lantern Bearers. 2010. (Roman Britain Trilogy Ser.: 3). (ENG.). 240p. (YA). (gr. 7). pap. 10.99 *(978-0-312-64430-7(2)*, 9780312644307) Square Fish.
—The Silver Branch. 2010. (Roman Britain Trilogy Ser.: 2). (ENG.). 208p. (YA). (gr. 6). pap. 9.99 *(978-0-312-64431-4(0)*, 9780312644314) Square Fish.
Tappan, Eva March. In the Days of Queen Victori. 2009. 160p. pap. 9.95 *(978-1-60459-620-5(1))* Wilder Pubns., Corp.
Taylor, Janet B. Into the Dim. 2016. (ENG.). 432p. (YA). (gr. 9). 17.99 *(978-0-544-60200-7(5)*, HMH Books For Young Readers) Houghton Mifflin Harcourt Publishing Co.
Thompson, Ricki. City of Cannibals. 2010. (ENG.). 269p. (YA). (gr. 9-12). 18.95 *(978-1-59078-623-9(8)*, Front Street) Boyds Mills Pr.
Travers, P. L. I Go by Sea, I Go by Land. Hermes, Gertrude, illus. 2016. (Vmc Ser.). (ENG.). 208p. (J). (gr. 4-17). 11.99 *(978-0-349-00574-4(5)*, Virago Press) Little, Brown Book Group Ltd. GBR. Dist: Hachette Bk. Group.
Trevayne, Emma. The Accidental Afterlife of Thomas Marsden. 2016. (ENG.). 272p. (J). (gr. 3-7). pap. 7.99 *(978-1-4424-9884-6(6)*, Simon & Schuster Bks. For Young Readers) Simon & Schuster Bks. For Young Readers.
Tripp, Ben. The Accidental Highwayman: Being the Tale of Kit Bristol, His Horse Midnight, a Mysterious Princess, & Sundry Magical Persons Besides. 2014. (ENG., Illus.). 304p. (YA). (gr. 6). 17.99 *(978-0-7653-3549-4(2)*, Tor Teen) Doherty, Tom Assocs., LLC.
Twain, Mark, pseud. The Prince & the Pauper. 2008. (Bring the Classics to Life Ser.). (Illus.). 72p. (gr. 2-12). pap., act. bk. ed. 10.95 *(978-1-55576-096-0(1)*, EDCTR-206B) EDCON Publishing Group.
—The Prince & the Pauper. 2003. (Modern Library Classics Ser.). (ENG., Illus.). 240p. pap. 11.00 *(978-0-375-76112-6(8)*, Modern Library) Random House Publishing Group.
—The Prince & the Pauper. Akib, Jamel, illus. 2007. (Classic Starts(tm) Ser.). (ENG.). 160p. (J). (gr. 2-4). 6.95 *(978-1-4027-3687-2(8))* Sterling Publishing Co., Inc.
Twain, Mark, pseud, et al. The Prince & the Pauper. Kliros, Thea, illus. abr. ed. 2011. (Dover Children's Thrift Classics Ser.). (ENG.). 112p. (J). (gr. 3-8). reprint ed. pap. 4.00 *(978-0-486-29383-7(1))* Dover Pubns., Inc.
Updale, Eleanor. Johnny Swanson. 2012. (ENG.). 384p. (J). (gr. 3-7). 8.99 *(978-0-385-75228-2(8)*, Yearling) Random Hse. Children's Bks.
—Thief, Liar, Gentleman? 2005. (Montmorency Ser.). 232p. (J). (gr. 4-7). 14.65 *(978-0-7569-6316-3(8))* Perfection Learning Corp.
Uttley, Alison & Singh, Mahendra. A Traveller in Time. Bray, Phyllis, illus. 2011. (ENG.). 336p. (J). (gr. 4-7). 17.95 *(978-1-59017-388-6(0)*, NYR Children's Collection) New York Review of Bks., Inc., The.
Vipont, Elfrida. The Lark in the Morn. Freeman, T. R., illus. 2007. 196p. (YA). pap. 12.95 *(978-1-932350-22-7(5))* Bethlehem Bks.
—The Lark on the Wing. Freeman, T. R., illus. 2008. 233p. (J). pap. 12.95 *(978-1-932350-11-1(X))* Bethlehem Bks.
Wallace, Karen. Wendy. 2005. 307p. (gr. 7-12). 17.00 *(978-0-7569-5658-5(7))* Perfection Learning Corp.
Wallace, Karen & Chapman, Neil. Arthur the King. 2009. (Hopscotch Adventures Ser.). (Illus.). 31p. (J). (gr. 1). lib. bdg. 25.65 *(978-1-59771-173-9(X))* Sea-To-Sea Pubns.
—The Round Table. 2009. (Hopscotch Adventures Ser.). (Illus.). 31p. (J). (gr. 1). lib. bdg. 25.65 *(978-1-59771-175-3(6))* Sea-To-Sea Pubns.
—Sir Lancelot & the Ice Castle. 2009. (Hopscotch Adventures Ser.). (Illus.). 31p. (J). (gr. 1). lib. bdg. 25.65 *(978-1-59771-174-6(8))* Sea-To-Sea Pubns.
Walsh, Pat. The Crowfield Curse. (ENG.). (J). (gr. 3-7). 2012. 352p. pap. 7.99 *(978-0-545-23103-9(5))* 2010. 336p. 16.99 *(978-0-545-22922-7(7))* Scholastic, Inc. (Chicken Hse., The).
Webb, Holly. The Case of the Feathered Mask. Lindsay, Marion, illus. 2016. (Mysteries of Maisie Hitchins Ser.: 4). (ENG.). 176p. (J). (gr. 2-5). 15.99 *(978-0-544-61993-7(5)*, HMH Books For Young Readers) Houghton Mifflin Harcourt Publishing Co.
—The Case of the Phantom Cat. Lindsay, Marion, illus. (Mysteries of Maisie Hitchins Ser.: 3). (ENG.). 176p. (J). (gr. 2-5). 2016. pap. 5.99 *(978-0-544-81084-6(8))* 2015. 15.99 *(978-0-544-58243-9(8))* Houghton Mifflin Harcourt Publishing Co. (HMH Books For Young Readers).
—The Case of the Secret Tunnel. Lindsay, Marion, illus. 2016. (Mysteries of Maisie Hitchins Ser.: 5). (ENG.). 176p. (J). (gr. 2-5). 15.99 *(978-0-544-81554-4(8)*, HMH Books For Young Readers) Houghton Mifflin Harcourt Publishing Co.
Webb, Holly & Lindsay, Marion. The Case of the Stolen Sixpence. Lindsay, Marion, illus. 2014. (Mysteries of Maisie Hitchins Ser.: 1). (ENG., Illus.). 176p. (J). (gr. 2-5). 14.99 *(978-0-544-33928-6(2)*, HMH Books For Young Readers) Houghton Mifflin Harcourt Publishing Co.
Wein, Elizabeth. Code Name Verity. (ENG.). (YA). (gr. 9-17). 2013. 368p. pap. 9.99 *(978-1-4231-5288-0(3))* 2012. 352p. 16.99 *(978-1-4231-5219-4(0))* Hyperion Pr.
—Code Name Verity. 2013. (YA). lib. bdg. 20.85 *(978-0-606-31760-3(0)*, Turtleback) Turtleback Bks.
Wells, Helen. Cherry Ames, Companion Nurse. 2007. (Cherry Ames Nurse Stories Ser.). 224p. (J). (gr. 3-7). 14.95 *(978-0-8261-0431-1(2))* Springer Publishing Co., Inc.
Westall, Robert. The Machine Gunners. 2010. (KOR., Illus.). 287p. (J). pap. *(978-89-522-1325-9(4))* Salrim Pubn.
Whelan, Gloria. All My Noble Dreams & Then What Happens. 2014. (ENG., Illus.). 272p. (J). (gr. 4-7). pap. 6.99 *(978-1-4424-5157-5(2)*, Simon & Schuster/Paula Wiseman Bks.) Simon & Schuster/Paula Wiseman Bks.
—Listening for Lions. 2006. (ENG.). 208p. (J). (gr. 5-9). pap. 6.99 *(978-0-06-058176-3(X))* HarperCollins Pubs.
—Listening for Lions. 2007. 194p. (gr. 5-9). 16.00 *(978-0-7569-7800-6(9))* Perfection Learning Corp.
—Small Acts of Amazing Courage. 2011. (ENG.). 224p. (J). (gr. 4-7). 15.99 *(978-1-4424-0931-6(2)*, Simon & Schuster/Paula Wiseman Bks.) Simon & Schuster/Paula Wiseman Bks.
Whistler, Charles W. King Alfred's Vikings, a Story of the First English Fleet. 2012. 202p. *(978-1-78139-109-9(2))* Benediction Classics.
Whitby, Adele. Kate's Story 1914. 2014. (Secrets of the Manor Ser.: 2). (ENG., Illus.). 160p. (J). (gr. 3-7). 16.99 *(978-1-4814-0635-2(3)*, Simon Spotlight) Simon Spotlight.
Whitman, Emily. Wildwing. 2010. (ENG.). 368p. (YA). (gr. 8-18). 16.99 *(978-0-06-172452-7(1)*, Greenwillow Bks.) HarperCollins Pubs.
Winter, Jonah. The Fabulous Feud of Gilbert & Sullivan. Egielski, Richard, illus. 2009. (J). pap. *(978-0-439-93051-2(0)*, Levine, Arthur A. Bks.) Scholastic, Inc.
Wood, James Playsted. The Queen's Most Honorable Pirate. Fisher, Leonard Everett, illus. 2011. 192p. 42.95 *(978-1-258-09722-6(2))* Literary Licensing, LLC.
Worsley, Lucy. Maid of the King's Court. 2017. (ENG.). 368p. (J). (gr. 7). 16.99 *(978-0-7636-8806-6(1))* Candlewick Pr.
Zettel, Sarah. Palace of Spies. 2013. (Palace of Spies Ser.: 1). (ENG.). 368p. (YA). (gr. 7). 16.99 *(978-0-544-07411-8(4))* Houghton Mifflin Harcourt Publishing Co.

GREAT BRITAIN—HISTORY, NAVAL

Crompton, Samuel Willard. Francis Drake & the Oceans of the World. Goetzmann, William H., ed. 2005. (Explorers of New Worlds Ser.). (Illus.). 160p. (J). (gr. 5-8). lib. bdg. 30.00 *(978-0-7910-8615-5(1))* Facts On File, Inc.
Hoogenboom, Lynn. Sir Francis Drake: A Primary Source Biography. 2006. (Primary Source Library of Famous Explorers Ser.). (Illus.). 24p. (YA). (gr. 2-5). lib. bdg. 22.60 *(978-1-4042-3035-4(1))* Rosen Publishing Group, Inc., The.
Malam, John. You Wouldn't Want to Sail in the Spanish Armada! An Invasion You'd Rather Not Launch. Antram, David, illus. 2006. (You Wouldn't Want to Ser.). (ENG.). 32p. (J). (gr. 2-5). 29.00 *(978-0-531-14974-4(9))* Scholastic Library Publishing.
Micklos, John. How the Revolutionary War Was Won. 2008. (Revolutionary War Library). (Illus.). 48p. (J). (gr. 3-4). lib. bdg. 25.27 *(978-0-7660-3016-9(4)*, Enslow Elementary) Enslow Pubs., Inc.
—Why We Won the American Revolution — Through Primary Sources. 2013. (American Revolution Through Primary Sources Ser.). 48p. (J). (gr. 4-18). 25.27 *(978-0-7660-4134-9(4))* Enslow Pubs., Inc.
—Why We Won the American Revolution—Through Primary Sources. 2013. (American Revolution Through Primary Sources Ser.). 48p. (J). (gr. 4-10). pap. 8.95 *(978-1-4644-0192-3(6))* Enslow Pubs., Inc.
Nick, Charles. Sir Francis Drake: Slave Trader & Pirate. 2010. (ENG., Illus.). 128p. (C). (gr. 6-12). pap. 9.95 *(978-0-531-20740-6(4))* National Geographic School Publishing, Inc.
—Sir Francis Drake: Slave Trader & Pirate. 2009. (Wicked History Ser.). (ENG., Illus.). 128p. (J). (gr. 6-12). 31.00 *(978-0-531-21800-6(7)*, Watts, Franklin) Scholastic Library Publishing.
Schneppler, Bill. British Royal Marines: Amphibious Division of the United Kingdom's Royal Navy. 2009. (Inside Special Operations Ser.). 64p. (gr. 6-6). 58.50 *(978-1-61513-550-9(2)*, Rosen Reference) Rosen Publishing Group, Inc., The.

GREAT BRITAIN—HISTORY, NAVAL—FICTION

Collingwood, Harry. The Log of a Privateersman. 2008. 216p. 26.95 *(978-1-60664-899-5(3))*; pap. 15.95 *(978-1-60664-018-0(6))* Aegypan.
Cooper, Susan. Victory. (ENG., Illus.). (J). 2013. 224p. (gr. 5-9). 17.99 *(978-1-4424-8079-7(3))* 2013. 224p. (gr. 5-9). pap. 6.99 *(978-1-4424-8080-3(7))* 2006. 208p. (gr. 4-7). 16.95 *(978-1-4169-1477-8(3))* McElderry, Margaret K. Bks. (McElderry, Margaret K. Bks.).
Golding, Julia. Cat among the Pigeons. 2010. (Cat Royal Adventure Ser.: 2). (ENG.). 400p. (J). (gr. 5-9). pap. 22.99 *(978-0-312-60215-4(4)*, 9780312602154) Square Fish.

GREAT BRITAIN—HISTORY—TO 1066

see also Celts

Abbott, Jacob. King Alfred of England. 2006. pap. *(978-1-4068-0240-5(9))* Echo Library.
Butterfield, Moira. Everyday Life. 2016. (ENG., Illus.). 32p. (J). (gr. 2-4). 17.99 *(978-1-4451-4815-1(3)*, Franklin Watts) Hachette Children's Group GBR. Dist: Hachette Bk. Group.
—The Romans. 2016. (Britain in the Past Ser.). (ENG., Illus.). 32p. (J). (gr. 2-5). 17.99 *(978-1-4451-4054-4(3)*, Franklin Watts) Hachette Children's Group GBR. Dist: Hachette Bk. Group.
—Vikings. 2016. (Britain in the Past Ser.). (ENG., Illus.). 32p. (J). (gr. 2-5). 17.99 *(978-1-4451-4066-7(7)*, Franklin Watts) Hachette Children's Group GBR. Dist: Hachette Bk. Group.
—Warriors & Weapons. 2016. (ENG., Illus.). 32p. (J). (gr. 2-4). 17.99 *(978-1-4451-4816-8(1)*, Franklin Watts) Hachette Children's Group GBR. Dist: Hachette Bk. Group.
Clements, Jonathan, et al. Early Kings of England. 2016. (ENG., Illus.). 48p. (J). (gr. 3-4). pap. 9.95 *(978-0-00-816386-0(3))* HarperCollins Pubs. Ltd. GBR. Dist: Independent Pubs. Group.
Harrison, Paul. Boudicca: Rebelled Against the Romans. 2017. (History VIPs Ser.). (ENG., Illus.). 32p. (J). (gr. 4-6). pap. 12.99 *(978-0-7502-9917-6(7)*, Wayland) Hachette Children's Group GBR. Dist: Hachette Bk. Group.
Howell, Izzi. Anglo Saxons. 2016. (Fact Cat: History: Early Britons Ser.). (ENG., Illus.). 24p. (J). (gr. k-2). pap. 9.99 *(978-0-7502-9939-8(8)*, Wayland) Hachette Children's Group GBR. Dist: Hachette Bk. Group.
—Roman Britain. 2016. (Fact Cat: History: Early Britons Ser.). (ENG., Illus.). 24p. (J). (gr. k-2). pap. 9.99 *(978-0-7502-9936-7(3)*, Wayland) Hachette Children's Group GBR. Dist: Hachette Bk. Group.
—Vikings. 2016. (Fact Cat: History: Early Britons Ser.). (ENG., Illus.). 24p. (J). (gr. k-2). pap. 9.99 *(978-0-7502-9935-0(5)*, Wayland) Hachette Children's Group GBR. Dist: Hachette Bk. Group.
Hunter, Nick. Did King Arthur Really Exist? 2016. (Top Secret! Ser.). (ENG., Illus.). 48p. (gr. 4-6). lib. bdg. 33.32 *(978-1-4109-8160-8(6))* Heinemann-Raintree.
Jeffrey, Gary. The Dark Ages & the Vikings. 2014. (ENG., Illus.). 48p. (J). *(978-0-7787-0401-0(7))* Crabtree Publishing Co.
Lace, William W. King Arthur. 2008. (Mysterious & Unknown Ser.). (Illus.). 104p. (YA). (gr. 3-7). lib. bdg. *(978-1-60152-033-3(6))* ReferencePoint Pr., Inc.
Mersey, Daniel. King Arthur, 1 vol. 2015. (ENG., Illus.). 80p. (J). 35.60 *(978-1-4777-8135-7(8)*, Rosen Young Adult) Rosen Publishing Group, Inc., The.
Murtagh, Ciaran & Collins UK Staff. Roman Life in Britain. 2016. (ENG.). 32p. (J). (gr. 2-3). pap. 8.95 *(978-0-00-816377-8(4))* HarperCollins Pubs. Ltd. GBR. Dist: Independent Pubs. Group.
Roberts, Jeremy. King Arthur. 2005. (How History Is Invented Ser.). (Illus.). 112p. (J). (gr. 6-12). lib. bdg. 23.93 *(978-0-8225-4891-1(7))* Lerner Publishing Group.
Wolfson, Evelyn. Mythology of King Arthur & His Knights. 2014. (Mythology, Myths, & Legends Ser.). (Illus.). 96p. (J). (gr. 6-12). 27.94 *(978-0-7660-6182-8(5))* Enslow Pubs., Inc.
World Book, Inc Staff, contrib. by. The Legend of King Arthur. 2014. (J). *(978-0-7166-2664-0(0))* World Bk., Inc.

GREAT BRITAIN—HISTORY—TO 1066—FICTION

Duey, Kathleen. Arthur. Gould, Robert, photos by. 2006. (Time Soldiers Ser.). (ENG., Illus.). 96p. (gr. -1-4). 24.21 *(978-1-59961-224-9(0))* Spotlight.
Lake, A. J. The Coming of Dragons: The Darkest Age. 2007. (Darkest Age Ser.). (ENG., Illus.). 256p. (YA). (gr. 4-7). per. 7.99 *(978-1-58234-902-2(9)*, 9781582349022, Bloomsbury USA Childrens) Bloomsbury Publishing USA.
Morris, Gerald. The Adventures of Sir Givret the Short. Renier, Aaron, illus. 2009. (Knights' Tales Ser.: 2). (ENG.). 112p. (J). (gr. 1-4). pap. 8.95 *(978-0-547-24818-9(0))* Houghton Mifflin Harcourt Publishing Co.
—The Lioness & Her Knight. 2008. (Squire's Tales Ser.: 7). (ENG.). 352p. (J). (gr. 5-7). pap. 7.99 *(978-0-547-01485-2(6))* Houghton Mifflin Harcourt Publishing Co.
Reeve, Philip. Here Lies Arthur. 2010. lib. bdg. 19.65 *(978-0-606-10557-6(3)*, Turtleback) Turtleback Bks.
Sutcliff, Rosemary. The Eagle of the Ninth. 2010. (Roman Britain Trilogy Ser.: 1). (ENG.). 240p. (YA). (gr. 7). pap. 9.99 *(978-0-312-64429-1(9)*, 9780312644291) Square Fish.
Vande Velde, Vivian & Bash, Barbara. The Book of Mordred. 2007. (ENG.). 352p. (YA). (gr. 7-12). pap. 8.99 *(978-0-618-80916-5(3))* Houghton Mifflin Harcourt Publishing Co.

GREAT BRITAIN—HISTORY—MEDIEVAL PERIOD, 1066-1485

Banham, Dale & Luff, Ian. History, Year 9. 2009. (Illus.). 240p. pap., stu. ed. 39.50 *(978-0-340-90739-9(8))* Hodder Education Group GBR. Dist: Trans-Atlantic Pubns., Inc.
Dorling Kindersley Publishing Staff. Castles & Knights. 2014. (Eye Wonder Ser.). (ENG.). 56p. (J). (gr. k-4). 10.99 *(978-1-4654-1562-2(9)*, DK Children) Dorling Kindersley Publishing, Inc.
Jeffrey, Gary. Rebellion & Revolt. 2014. (ENG., Illus.). 48p. (J). *(978-0-7787-0399-0(1))* Crabtree Publishing Co.
Mattern, Joanne. Medieval Times: England in the Middle Ages, 1 vol. 2012. (Primary Source Readers Ser.). (ENG.). 32p. (J). (gr. 5-5). pap. 8.99 *(978-1-4333-5005-4(X))* Teacher Created Materials, Inc.
Tatlock, Ann. Medieval England. 2014. (ENG.). 48p. (J). lib. bdg. 29.95 *(978-1-62469-000-6(9))* Purple Toad Publishing, Inc.

GREAT BRITAIN—HISTORY—NORMAN PERIOD, 1066-1154

Hamilton, Janice. The Norman Conquest of England. 2007. (Pivotal Moments in History Ser.). (ENG., Illus.). 160p. (J). (gr. 9-12). lib. bdg. 38.60 *(978-0-8225-5902-3(1))* Lerner Publishing Group.
Harkins, Susan Sales & Harkins, William H. The Life & Times of William the Conqueror. 2008. (Biography from Ancient Civilizations Ser.). (Illus.). 48p. (J). (gr. 4-8). lib. bdg. 29.95 *(978-1-58415-700-7(3))* Mitchell Lane Pubs., Inc.
Howell, Izzi. Normans. 2017. (Explore! Ser.). (ENG., Illus.). 32p. (J). (gr. 4-6). 16.99 *(978-1-5263-0061-4(3)*, Wayland) Hachette Children's Group GBR. Dist: Hachette Bk. Group.
Jeffrey, Gary. The Dark Ages & the Vikings. 2014. (ENG., Illus.). 48p. (J). *(978-0-7787-0401-0(7))* Crabtree Publishing Co.
McGowen, Tom. William the Conqueror: Last Invader of England. 2007. (Rulers of the Middle Ages Ser.). (Illus.). 160p. (YA). (gr. 6-12). lib. bdg. 35.94 *(978-0-7660-2713-8(9))* Enslow Pubs., Inc.

GREAT BRITAIN—HISTORY—NORMAN PERIOD, 1066-1154—FICTION

Henty, George Alfred. Wulf the Saxon. 2007. 322p. pap. 23.99 *(978-1-4264-2278-2(4))* Creative Media Partners, LLC.
—Wulf the Saxon: A Story of the Norman Conquest. Peacock, Ralph, illus. 2010. (Dover Children's Classics Ser.). (ENG.). 352p. (YA). (gr. 3-8). pap. 8.95 *(978-0-486-47595-0(6))* Dover Pubns., Inc.
Sutcliff, Rosemary. Knight's Fee. 2008. (ENG.). 240p. (J). pap. 10.95 *(978-1-59078-640-6(8)*, Front Street) Boyds Mills Pr.

GREAT BRITAIN—HISTORY—PLANTAGENETS, 1154-1399

Harkins, Susan Sales & Harkins, William H. The Life & Times of Richard the Lionheart. 2008. (Biography from Ancient Civilizations Ser.). (Illus.). 48p. (J). (gr. 4-8). lib. bdg. 29.95 *(978-1-58415-699-4(6))* Mitchell Lane Pubs., Inc.
Hilliam, David. Thomas Becket: English Saint & Martyr. 2009. (Leaders of the Middle Ages Ser.). 112p. (gr. 5-8). 66.50 *(978-1-61513-902-6(8)*, Rosen Reference) Rosen Publishing Group, Inc., The.
Plain, Nancy. Eleanor of Aquitaine & the High Middle Ages. 2005. (Rulers & Their Times Ser.). (Illus.). 80p. (gr. 6-7). lib. bdg. 23.95 *(978-0-7614-1834-4(2)*, Benchmark Bks.) Marshall Cavendish Corp.
Rice, Earle. The Life & Times of Eleanor of Aquitaine. 2009. (Biography of Ancient Civilizations Ser.). 48p. (J). (gr. 4-8). 29.95 *(978-1-58415-743-4(7))* Mitchell Lane Pubs., Inc.
Sapet, Kerrily. Eleanor of Aquitaine: Medieval Queen. 2006. (European Queens Ser.). (Illus.). 192p. (J). (gr. 6-12). lib. bdg. 26.95 *(978-1-931798-90-7(7))* Reynolds, Morgan Inc.

GREAT BRITAIN—HISTORY—PLANTAGENETS, 1154-1399—FICTION

Clement-Davies, David. The Telling Pool. 2006. 1.00 *(978-1-4237-6417-5(X))* Recorded Bks., Inc.
Dickerson, Melanie. The Silent Songbird, 1 vol. 2016. (ENG.). 304p. (YA). 14.99 *(978-0-7180-2631-8(4))* Nelson, Thomas Inc.
Harris, Mark W., et al. Ivanhoe. Scott, Walter, ed. (Classics Illustrated Ser.). (Illus.). 52p. (YA). pap. 4.95 *(978-1-57209-023-1(5))* Classics International Entertainment, Inc.
Henty, George Alfred. St. George for England. 2007. (ENG.). 260p. pap. 21.99 *(978-1-4346-4677-4(7))*; 292p. pap. 23.99 *(978-1-4346-4678-1(5))* Creative Media Partners, LLC.
Scott, Walter, ed. Ivanhoe. 2008. (Bring the Classics to Life Ser.). (Illus.). 72p. (gr. 5-12). pap., act. bk. ed. 10.95 *(978-1-55576-099-1(6)*, EDN506B) EDCON Publishing Group.
Walsh, Pat. The Crowfield Demon. (J). 2013. 360p. *(978-0-545-37350-0(6))* 2012. (ENG.). 368p. (gr. 3-7). 16.99 *(978-0-545-31769-6(X)*, Chicken Hse., The) Scholastic, Inc.

GREAT BRITAIN—HISTORY—LANCASTER AND YORK, 1399-1485—FICTION

Haddix, Margaret Peterson. Sent. (Missing Ser.: 2). (YA). 2011. 82.75 *(978-1-4407-2678-1(7))* 2009. 1.25 *(978-1-4407-2679-8(5))* 2009. 218.75 *(978-1-4407-2670-5(1))* 2009. 98.75 *(978-1-4407-2675-0(2))* Recorded Bks., Inc.
—Sent. (Missing Ser.: 2). (ENG.). (J). (gr. 3-7). 2010. 336p. pap. 7.99 *(978-1-4169-5423-1(6))* 2009. 320p. 16.99 *(978-1-4169-5422-4(8))* Simon & Schuster Bks. For Young Readers. (Simon & Schuster Bks. For Young Readers).
—Sent. abr. ed. 2009. *(978-1-4424-0767-1(0))* Simon & Schuster Children's Publishing.
—Sent. l.t. ed. 2010. (Missing Ser.: Bk. 2). (ENG.). 346p. 23.99 *(978-1-4104-3245-2(9))* Thorndike Pr.
—Sent. 2010. (Missing Ser.: 2). lib. bdg. 18.40 *(978-0-606-14699-9(7)*, Turtleback) Turtleback Bks.
McAllister, Margaret. High Crag Linn. 2008. (ENG.). 224p. (YA). (gr. 7-18). pap. 8.95 *(978-0-7459-6062-3(6))* Lion Hudson PLC GBR. Dist: Independent Pubs. Group.
Rose, Simon. The Sorcerer's Letterbox, 1 vol. 2004. (ENG., Illus.). 114p. (J). (gr. 4-6). per. 7.95 *(978-1-896580-52-4(1))* Tradewind Bks. CAN. Dist: Orca Bk. Pubs. USA.

GREAT BRITAIN—HISTORY—WARS OF THE ROSES, 1455-1485—FICTION

Stevenson, Robert Louis. The Black Arrow. l.t. ed. 2005. 448p. pap. *(978-1-84637-164-6(3))* Echo Library.

GREAT BRITAIN—HISTORY—TUDORS, 1485-1603

Adams, Simon. Elizabeth I: The Outcast Who Became England's Queen. (National Geographic World History Biographies Ser.). (ENG., Illus.). 64p. (J). (gr. 3-7). 2008. pap. 7.99 *(978-1-4263-0172-8(3))* 2005. 17.95 *(978-0-7922-3649-8(1))* 2005. lib. bdg. 27.90 *(978-0-7922-3654-2(8))* National Geographic Society. (National Geographic Children's Bks.).

Anderson, Scoular. How to Be a Tudor in 20 Easy Stages. Anderson, Scoular, illus. 2007. (Collins Big Cat Ser.). (ENG., Illus.). 128p. (J). (gr. 3-4). pap. 8.99 *(978-0-00-723090-7(7))* HarperCollins Pubs. Ltd. GBR. Dist: Independent Pubs. Group.

Barnham, Kay. Built a 14-Seat Lavatory! Fact or Fiction Behind the Tudors. 2017. (Truth or Busted Ser.). (ENG., Illus.). 96p. (J). (gr. 4-6). pap. 7.99 *(978-0-7502-9743-1(3),* Wayland) Hachette Children's Group GBR. Dist: Hachette Bk. Group.

Bingham, Jane. Tudors. 2017. (Explore! Ser.). (ENG., Illus.). 32p. (J). (gr. 4-6). pap. 11.99 *(978-0-7502-8880-4(9),* Wayland) Hachette Children's Group GBR. Dist: Hachette Bk. Group.

Buchanan, Jane. Mary Tudor: Courageous Queen or Bloody Mary? 2008. (Wicked History Ser.). (ENG.). 128p. (J). (gr. 6-18). pap. 5.95 *(978-0-531-20502-0(9),* Watts, Franklin) Scholastic Library Publishing.

Courtauld, Sarah. The Queen's Pirate - Francis Drake. Dutrait, Vincent, illus. 2008. (Usborne Young Reading: Series Three Ser.). 64p. (J). 8.99 *(978-0-7945-2048-9(0),* Usborne) EDC Publishing.

Crompton, Samuel Willard. Queen Elizabeth: And England's Golden Age. 2005. (Makers of the Middle Ages & Renaissance Ser.). (Illus.). 160p. (J). (gr. 5-8). lib. bdg. 32.95 *(978-0-7910-8632-2(1),* Chelsea Hse.) Facts On File, Inc.

Guy, John. Elizabeth: The Forgotten Years. 2004. (Illus.). 32p. (J). (gr. 4-7). pap. 5.95 *(978-1-86007-029-7(9),* TickTock Books) Octopus Publishing Group GBR. Dist: Independent Pubs. Group.

—Tudor & Stuart Life. 2004. (Illus.). 32p. (J). (gr. 4-7). pap. 6.95 *(978-1-86007-003-7(5),* TickTock Books) Octopus Publishing Group GBR. Dist: Independent Pubs. Group.

Harman, Alice. Tudors. 2017. (Popcorn: History Corner Ser.). (ENG.). 24p. (J). (gr. k-2). pap. 10.99 *(978-0-7502-9526-0(0),* Wayland) Hachette Children's Group GBR. Dist: Hachette Bk. Group.

Hepplewhite, Peter. Royals, Rebels, & Horrible Headchoppers: A Bloodthirsty History of the Terrifying Tudors! 2015. (Awfully Ancient Ser.). (ENG., Illus.). 32p. (J). (gr. 5-5). pap. 10.50 *(978-1-4824-3129-2(7))* Stevens, Gareth Publishing LLLP.

Hilliam, Paul. Elizabeth I: Queen of England's Golden Age. (Rulers, Scholars, & Artists of the Renaissance Ser.). 112p. 2009. (gr. 5-8). 66.50 *(978-1-60852-940-7(1),* Rosen Reference) 2004. (Illus.). (YA). lib. bdg. 34.60 *(978-1-4042-0313-6(3))* Rosen Publishing Group, Inc., The.

Hinds, Kathryn. Elizabeth & Her Court. 2007. (Life in Elizabethan England Ser.). (Illus.). 80p. (J). (gr. 4-7). lib. bdg. 34.21 *(978-0-7614-2542-7(X),* Benchmark Bks.) Marshall Cavendish Corp.

Hollihan, Kerrie Logan. Elizabeth I, the People's Queen: Her Life & Times, 21 Activities. 2011. (For Kids Ser.). (ENG., Illus.). 144p. (J). (gr. 4-18). pap. 16.95 *(978-1-56976-349-0(6))* Chicago Review Pr., Inc.

Hoogenboom, Lynn. Sir Francis Drake. 2009. (Primary Source Library of Famous Explorers Ser.). 24p. (gr. 4-4). 42.50 *(978-1-60854-131-7(2),* PowerKids Pr.) Rosen Publishing Group, Inc., The.

Krasner, Barbara. Sir Francis Drake. 2016. (Spotlight on Explorers & Colonization Ser.). 00048p. (J). (gr. 6-6). pap. 11.75 *(978-1-5081-7218-5(8))* Rosen Publishing Group, Inc., The.

Marcovitz, Hal. Life in the Time of Shakespeare. 2015. (ENG., Illus.). 96p. (J). lib. bdg. *(978-1-60152-778-3(0))* ReferencePoint Pr., Inc.

Morris, Heather. The Tudors: How It Started, Key Events, Famous People. 2016. (ENG., Illus.). 48p. (J). (gr. 4-6). pap. 9.99 *(978-0-7502-9275-7(X),* Wayland) Hachette Children's Group GBR. Dist: Hachette Bk. Group.

Nick, Charles. Sir Francis Drake: Slave Trader & Pirate. 2010. (ENG., Illus.). 128p. (C). (gr. 6-12). pap. 9.95 *(978-0-531-20740-6(4))* National Geographic School Publishing, Inc.

—Sir Francis Drake: Slave Trader & Pirate. 2009. (Wicked History Ser.). (ENG., Illus.). 128p. (J). (gr. 6-12). 31.00 *(978-0-531-21800-6(7),* Watts, Franklin) Scholastic Library Publishing.

Powell, Jillian. Tudor Times. 2017. (Craft Box Ser.). (ENG., Illus.). 32p. (J). (gr. 4-6). pap. 11.99 *(978-0-7502-8405-9(6),* Wayland) Hachette Children's Group GBR. Dist: Hachette Bk. Group.

Purkiss, Sue. The Life & Times of William Shakespeare: Band 18/Pearl. 2017. (ENG., Illus.). 80p. (J). pap. 9.99 ***(978-0-00-820898-1(0))*** HarperCollins Pubs. Ltd. GBR. Dist: Independent Pubs. Group.

Roberts, Russell. Elizabethan England. 2009. (How'd They Do That? Ser.). (Illus.). 64p. (J). (gr. 4-8). lib. bdg. 33.95 *(978-1-58415-823-3(9))* Mitchell Lane Pubs., Inc.

Sapet, Kerrily. Elizabeth I of England. 2005. (Illus.). 176p. (J). (gr. 4-7). lib. bdg. 26.95 *(978-1-931798-70-9(2))* Reynolds, Morgan Inc.

Shone, Rob. Elizabeth I: The Life of England's Renaissance Queen. 2009. (Graphic Nonfiction Biographies Ser.). (Illus.). 48p. (YA). (gr. 4-5). 58.50 *(978-1-61513-016-0(0),* Rosen Reference) Rosen Publishing Group, Inc., The.

Shone, Rob & Ganeri, Anita. Elizabeth I: The Life of England's Renaissance Queen. 2005. (Graphic Nonfiction Biographies Ser.). (Illus.). 48p. (YA). (gr. 4-7). lib. bdg. 31.95 *(978-1-4042-0246-7(3))* Rosen Publishing Group, Inc., The.

Steele, Philip. Hail! Tudors. 2010. (ENG., Illus.). 32p. (J). *(978-0-7787-6626-1(8))*; pap. *(978-0-7787-6633-9(0))* Crabtree Publishing Co.

Williams, Marcia. The Tudors: Kings, Queens, Scribes, & Ferrets! Williams, Marcia, illus. 2016. (ENG., Illus.). 48p. (J). (gr. 3-7). 17.99 *(978-0-7636-8122-7(9))* Candlewick Pr.

Woolf, Alex. Meet the Tudors. 2014. (Encounters with the Past Ser.). 32p. (J). (gr. 3-6). 26.60 *(978-1-4824-0897-3(X))* Stevens, Gareth Publishing LLLP.

GREAT BRITAIN—HISTORY—TUDORS, 1485-1603—FICTION

Armstrong, Alan. Raleigh's Page. Jessell, Tim, illus. 2009. (ENG.). 336p. (J). (gr. 3-7). 7.99 *(978-0-375-83320-5(X),* Yearling) Random Hse. Children's Bks.

Avi. The Player King. 2017. (J). pap. ***(978-1-4814-3769-1(0))*** Simon & Schuster Children's Publishing.

Castor, H. M. VIII. 2013. (ENG., Illus.). 432p. (YA). (gr. 7). 17.99 *(978-1-4424-7418-5(1),* Simon & Schuster Bks. For Young Readers) Simon & Schuster Bks. For Young Readers.

Dyer, K. C. Shades of Red: An Eagle Glen Trilogy Book. 2005. (Eagle Glen Trilogy Ser.: 3). (ENG.). 272p. (YA). (gr. 7). pap. 12.99 *(978-1-55002-545-3(7))* Dundurn CAN. Dist: Ingram Publisher Services.

Hand, Cynthia, et al. My Lady Jane. 512p. (YA). (gr. 8). 2017. pap. 9.99 *(978-0-06-239176-6(3))* 2016. 17.99 *(978-0-06-239174-2(7))* HarperCollins Pubs. (HarperTeen).

Hannah, Martha. The Ghost of Hampton Court. Dowell, Larry, illus. 2006. 32p. (J). 17.95 *(978-0-9779808-0-2(4))* CicadaSun.

Longshore, Katherine. Gilt. 2013. (ENG.). 432p. (YA). (gr. 7). pap. 9.99 *(978-0-14-242619-7(9),* Speak) Penguin Young Readers Group.

O'Brien, Johnny. Day of Deliverance. Hardcastle, Nick, illus. 2010. (Jack Christie Adventure Ser.: 2). (ENG.). 192p. (J). (gr. 4-7). 15.99 *(978-0-7636-5075-9(7),* Templar) Candlewick Pr.

Thomas, Jane Resh. The Counterfeit Princess. 2005. 197p. (J). *(978-0-618-93780-6(3),* Clarion Bks.) Houghton Mifflin Harcourt Trade & Reference Pubs.

GREAT BRITAIN—HISTORY—17TH CENTURY

see Great Britain—History—Stuarts, 1603-1714

GREAT BRITAIN—HISTORY—STUARTS, 1603-1714

Burling, Alexis. Robert Boyle. 2017. (Leaders of the Scientific Revolution Ser.). 112p. (gr. 12-13). 37.10 ***(978-1-5081-7476-9(8),*** Rosen Young Adult) Rosen Publishing Group, Inc., The.

Guy, John. Tudor & Stuart Life. 2004. (Illus.). 32p. (J). (gr. 4-7). pap. 6.95 *(978-1-86007-003-7(5),* TickTock Books) Octopus Publishing Group GBR. Dist: Independent Pubs. Group.

Howell, Izzi. Samuel Pepys. 2016. (Fact Cat: History Ser.). (ENG., Illus.). 24p. (J). (gr. k-2). 14.99 *(978-1-5263-0097-3(4),* Wayland) Hachette Children's Group GBR. Dist: Hachette Bk. Group.

Malam, John. Gunpowder Plot. 2007. (Dates with History Ser.). (ENG., Illus.). 48p. (J). pap. 9.99 *(978-1-84234-536-8(2))* Evans Brothers, Ltd. GBR. Dist: Independent Pubs. Group.

GREAT BRITAIN—HISTORY—STUARTS, 1603-1714—FICTION

Greenfield, Amy Butler. Chantress Alchemy. 2015. (Chantress Ser.). (ENG., Illus.). 368p. (YA). (gr. 7). pap. 10.99 *(978-1-4424-5708-9(2),* McElderry, Margaret K. Bks.) McElderry, Margaret K. Bks.

Hooper, Mary. Newes from the Dead. 2010. (ENG., Illus.). 272p. (YA). (gr. 9-13). pap. 16.99 *(978-0-312-60864-4(0),* 9780312608644) Square Fish.

Marryat. The Children of the New Forest, Level 2. Bassett, Jennifer, ed. 3rd ed. 2008. (ENG., Illus.). 64p. pap. 10.00 *(978-0-19-479054-3(1))* Oxford Univ. Pr., Inc.

GREAT BRITAIN—HISTORY—PURITAN REVOLUTION, 1642-1660

Ashworth, Leon. Oliver Cromwell. (Illus.). 32p. *(978-0-7451-5287-5(2))*; pap. *(978-0-7540-9010-6(8))* Cherrytree Bks.

Farman, John. Roundhead & Cavaliers. 2003. (ENG., Illus.). 64p. (J). pap. 3.99 *(978-0-330-37646-4(2),* Macmillan Children's Bks.) Pan Macmillan GBR. Dist: Trafalgar Square Publishing.

GREAT BRITAIN—HISTORY—PURITAN REVOLUTION, 1642-1660—FICTION

Frederick Marryat. The Children of the New Forest. 2007. 412p. per. 17.95 *(978-1-4218-4823-5(6))*; 33.95 *(978-1-4218-4726-9(4))* 1st World Publishing, Inc. (1st World Library - Literary Society).

Henty, George Alfred. Friends Though Divided: A Tale of the Civil War. 2004. reprint ed. pap. 26.95 *(978-1-4191-2099-2(9))*; pap. 1.99 *(978-1-4192-2099-9(3))* Kessinger Publishing, LLC.

Marryat, Captian. The Children of the New Forest. 2008. 332p. (gr. 8-12). 29.99 *(978-0-554-29238-0(6))*; 28.99 *(978-0-554-38541-9(4))* Creative Media Partners, LLC.

—The Children of the New Forest. 2007. 312p. per. *(978-1-4065-5647-6(5))* Dodo Pr.

—The Children of the New Forest. 2006. 216p. pap. *(978-1-84637-527-9(4))*; pap. *(978-1-84702-355-1(X))* Echo Library.

—The Children of the New Forest. 2004. reprint ed. pap. 1.99 *(978-1-4192-5655-4(6))*; pap. 28.95 *(978-1-4191-5655-7(1))* Kessinger Publishing, LLC.

—The Children of the New Forest. 2008. 292p. pap. 16.95 *(978-1-60597-491-0(9),* Book Jungle) Standard Pubns., Inc.

Marryat, Frederick. Children of the New Forest (Yesterday's Classics) 2007. (J). pap. 12.95 *(978-1-59915-050-5(6))* Yesterday's Classics.

GREAT BRITAIN—HISTORY—18TH CENTURY—FICTION

Everett-Green, Evelyn. Tom Tufton's Travels. 2007. 196p. per. *(978-1-4065-3395-8(5))* Dodo Pr.

Holmes, Victoria. Rider in the Dark: An Epic Horse Story. 2004. (Illus.). 320p. (J). (gr. 5-18). (ENG.). 15.99 *(978-0-06-052025-0(6))*; lib. bdg. 16.89 *(978-0-06-052026-7(4))* HarperCollins Pubs.

Thompson, Kate. Highway Robbery. Dress, Robert & Duddle, Johnny, illus. 2009. (ENG.). 128p. (J). (gr. 5-18). 15.99 *(978-0-06-173034-4(3),* Greenwillow Bks.) HarperCollins Pubs.

GREAT BRITAIN—HISTORY—1714-1837

Brooks, Philip. King George III: America's Enemy. 2009. (Wicked History Ser.). (ENG., Illus.). 128p. (J). (gr. 6-12). 31.00 *(978-0-531-21803-7(1),* Watts, Franklin) Scholastic Library Publishing.

Clare, John D. Britain, 1750-1900. 2003. (Illus.). 96p. pap. 29.50 *(978-0-340-86909-3(7))*; pap. 29.50 *(978-0-340-86910-9(0))* Hodder Education Group GBR. (Hodder Education). Dist: Trans-Atlantic Pubns., Inc.

Marsh, Carole. King George III. 2004. 12p. (gr. k-4). 2.95 *(978-0-635-02364-3(4))* Gallopade International.

Schanzer, Rosalyn. George vs. George: The American Revolution as Seen from Both Sides. 2007. (ENG., Illus.). 64p. (J). (gr. 4-7). per. 6.95 *(978-1-4263-0042-4(5),* National Geographic Children's Bks.) National Geographic Society.

—George vs. George: The Revolutionary War as Seen by Both Sides. 2004. (ENG., Illus.). 64p. (J). (gr. 4-7). 25.90 *(978-0-7922-6999-1(3),* National Geographic Children's Bks.) National Geographic Society.

GREAT BRITAIN—HISTORY—1714-1837—FICTION

Bross, Lee. Tangled Webs. 2015. (Tangled Webs Ser.). (ENG., Illus.). 304p. (YA). (gr. 9-17). 17.99 *(978-1-4231-8423-2(8))* Hyperion Bks. for Children.

Buckley-Archer, Linda. The Time Quake. 2010. (Gideon Trilogy Ser.: 3). (ENG.). 464p. (J). (gr. 5-9). pap. 9.99 *(978-1-4169-1530-0(3),* Simon & Schuster Bks. For Young Readers) Simon & Schuster Bks. For Young Readers.

—The Time Thief. 2008. (Gideon Trilogy Ser.: 2). (ENG.). 512p. (J). (gr. 5-9). pap. 9.99 *(978-1-4169-1528-7(1),* Simon & Schuster Bks. For Young Readers) Simon & Schuster Bks. For Young Readers.

Burgis, Stephanie. Kat, Incorrigible. 2012. (Kat, Incorrigible Ser.: 1). (ENG., Illus.). 320p. (J). (gr. 5-9). pap. 7.99 *(978-1-4169-9448-0(3),* Atheneum Bks. for Young Readers) Simon & Schuster Children's Publishing.

Gray, Lucinda. The Gilded Cage. 2017. (ENG., Illus.). 256p. (YA). pap. 9.99 *(978-1-62779-182-3(5),* 9781627791823) Square Fish.

Kindl, Patrice & Wells, Rosemary. A School for Brides. 2015. (ENG.). 272p. (J). (gr. 7). bds. 17.99 *(978-0-670-78608-4(X),* Viking Books for Young Readers) Penguin Young Readers Group.

Olds, Barbara Anne. Haven House. Amatrula, Michele, illus. 2007. (ENG.). 141p. (J). pap. 8.95 *(978-0-9744446-0-4(X))* All About Kids Publishing.

Rees, Celia. Sovay. 2010. (ENG.). 432p. (YA). (gr. 7). pap. 9.99 *(978-1-59990-483-2(7),* 9781599904832, Bloomsbury USA Childrens) Bloomsbury Publishing USA.

—Sovay. 2009. 1.00 *(978-1-4074-4516-8(2))* Recorded Bks., Inc.

GREAT BRITAIN—HISTORY—19TH CENTURY

see also South African War, 1899-1902

Allport, Alan. The British Industrial Revolution. 2011. (Milestones in Modern World History Ser.). (Illus.). 128p. (C). (gr. 9). 35.00 *(978-1-60413-498-8(4),* Chelsea Hse.) Facts On File, Inc.

Bailey, Gerry & Foster, Karen. Queen Victoria's Diamond. Noyes, Leighton & Radford, Karen, illus. 2008. (Stories of Great People Ser.). (ENG.). 40p. (J). (gr. 3-6). lib. bdg. *(978-0-7787-3697-4(0))*; pap. *(978-0-7787-3719-3(5))* Crabtree Publishing Co.

Benchmark Education Co., LLC. The Industrial Revolution. 2014. (PRIME Ser.). (J). (gr. 6-8). pap. *(978-1-4509-9495-8(4))* Benchmark Education Co.

Clare, John D. Britain, 1750-1900. 2003. (Illus.). 96p. pap. 29.50 *(978-0-340-86909-3(7))*; pap. 29.50 *(978-0-340-86910-9(0))* Hodder Education Group GBR. (Hodder Education). Dist: Trans-Atlantic Pubns., Inc.

Cooke, Tim. The Victorians. 2015. (At Home With... Ser.). (Illus.). 32p. (gr. 5-9). lib. bdg. 31.35 *(978-1-78121-087-1(X))* Windmill Bks. Ltd. GBR. Dist: Black Rabbit Bks.

Gale Research Staff. Industrial Revolution: Biographies. 2003. (Industrial Revolution Reference Library). (ENG., Illus.). 240p. (J). (gr. 6-10). 106.00 *(978-0-7876-6514-2(2),* GML00502-182382, UXL) Cengage Gale.

—Industrial Revolution: Primary Sources. 2003. (Industrial Revolution Reference Library). (ENG., Illus.). 240p. (J). (gr. 6-10). 106.00 *(978-0-7876-6515-9(0),* GML00502-182383, UXL) Cengage Gale.

Gigliotti, Jim. Who Was Queen Victoria? Harrison, Nancy & Hergenrother, Max, illus. 2014. (Who Was? Ser.). (ENG.). 112p. (J). (gr. 3-7). 5.99 *(978-0-448-48182-1(0),* Grosset & Dunlap) Penguin Young Readers Group.

—Who Was Queen Victoria? 2014. (Who Was... ? Ser.). lib. bdg. 16.00 *(978-0-606-35697-8(5))* Turtleback Bks.

Guy, John. Victorian Life. 2004. (Illus.). 32p. (J). (gr. 4-7). pap. 5.95 *(978-1-86007-005-1(1),* TickTock Books) Octopus Publishing Group GBR. Dist: Independent Pubs. Group.

Lacey, Saskia. The History of Victorian Innovations: Equivalent Fractions (Grade 3) 2017. (Mathematics Readers Ser.). (Illus.). 32p. (gr. 3-3). 8.99 ***(978-1-4807-5803-2(5))*** Teacher Created Materials, Inc.

Lee, Stephen J. Gladstone & Disraeli. 2005. (Questions & Analysis in History Ser.). (ENG., Illus.). 208p. (C). 110.00 *(978-0-415-32356-7(8),* RU27027); per. 30.95 *(978-0-415-32357-4(6))* Routledge.

Malam, John. You Wouldn't Want to Be a 19th-Century Coal Miner in England! A Dangerous Job You'd Rather Not Have. Antram, David, illus. 2006. (You Wouldn't Want to Ser.). (ENG.). 32p. (J). (gr. 2-5). 29.00 *(978-0-531-14971-3(4))* Scholastic Library Publishing.

Nardo, Don. The Industrial Revolution in Britain. 2009. (Lucent Library of Historical Eras). (ENG., Illus.). 128p. (YA). (gr. 7-10). lib. bdg. 34.80 *(978-1-4205-0152-0(6),* LML02109-246064, Lucent Bks.) Cengage Gale.

Peal, Robert. KS3 History the Industrial Revolution. 2017. (Knowing History Ser.). (ENG.). 16p. (J). (gr. 6-9). 3.99 *(978-0-00-819541-0(2))* HarperCollins Pubs. Ltd. GBR. Dist: Independent Pubs. Group.

Pierce, Alan. Industrial Revolution, 1 vol. 2005. (American Moments Ser.). (ENG., Illus.). 48p. (gr. 4-8). 27.07 *(978-1-59197-933-3(1),* Abdo & Daughters) ABDO Publishing Co.

Schomp, Virginia. The Church. 2010. (Life in Victorian England Ser.). 80p. (gr. 6). 34.21 *(978-1-60870-031-8(3))* Marshall Cavendish GBR. Dist: Marshall Cavendish Corp.

—The Countryside. 2010. (Life in Victorian England Ser.). 80p. (gr. 6). 34.21 *(978-1-60870-030-1(5))* Marshall Cavendish GBR. Dist: Marshall Cavendish Corp.

Swisher, Clarice. Women of Victorian England. 2004. (Women in History Ser.). (ENG., Illus.). 112p. (YA). (gr. 7-12). lib. bdg. 33.45 *(978-1-59018-571-1(4),* Lucent Bks.) Cengage Gale.

Victorians. 2014. (Ladybird Histories Ser.). (ENG., Illus.). 64p. (J). (gr. 2-4). pap. 13.99 ***(978-0-7232-7729-3(X))*** Penguin Bks., Ltd. GBR. Dist: Independent Pubs. Group.

GREAT BRITAIN—HISTORY—19TH CENTURY—FICTION

Avi. The Traitors' Gate. Raude, Karina, illus. 2007. (ENG.). 368p. (J). (gr. 5-8). 17.99 *(978-0-689-85335-7(1),* Atheneum/Richard Jackson Bks.) Simon & Schuster Children's Publishing.

Baratz-Logsted, Lauren. The Education of Bet. 2011. (ENG.). 192p. (YA). (gr. 7). pap. 11.99 *(978-0-547-55024-4(3))* Houghton Mifflin Harcourt Publishing Co.

Burnett, Frances Hodgson. Little Lord Fauntleroy. (J). 21.95 *(978-0-8488-0792-4(8))* Amereon Ltd.

—Little Lord Fauntleroy. 2005. 104p. per. 4.95 *(978-1-4209-2556-2(3))* Digireads.com Publishing.

—Little Lord Fauntleroy. 2006. 164p. (YA). 18.95 *(978-1-934169-22-3(6))*; pap. 6.95 *(978-1-934169-23-0(4))* Norilana Bks.

—Little Lord Fauntleroy. 2005. (Twelve-Point Ser.). lib. bdg. 24.00 *(978-1-58287-319-0(4))* North Bks.

—Little Lord Fauntleroy. Howell, Troy, illus. 2008. (Classic Starts(tm) Ser.). (ENG.). 160p. (J). (gr. 2-4). 5.95 *(978-1-4027-4578-2(8))* Sterling Publishing Co., Inc.

—Little Lord Fauntleroy. Birch, Reginald, illus. 2004. reprint ed. pap. 27.95 *(978-1-4179-4302-9(5))* Kessinger Publishing, LLC.

—Little Lord Fauntleroy. 2004. reprint ed. pap. 1.99 *(978-1-4192-3078-3(6))* Kessinger Publishing, LLC.

—Little Lord Fauntleroy. l.t. ed. 2005. (Large Print Ser.). lib. bdg. 25.00 *(978-1-58287-813-3(7))* North Bks.

—Sara Crewe. l.t. ed. 2006. 92p. pap. *(978-1-84637-263-6(1))* Echo Library.

Carriger, Gail. Curtsies & Conspiracies. (Finishing School Ser.: 2). (ENG.). (YA). (gr. 7-17). 2014. 336p. pap. 10.00 *(978-0-316-19020-6(9))* 2013. 320p. 18.00 *(978-0-316-19011-4(X))* Little, Brown Bks. for Young Readers.

—Etiquette & Espionage. 2013. (Finishing School Ser.: 1). (ENG.). 320p. (YA). (gr. 7-17). 18.99 *(978-0-316-19008-4(X))* Little Brown & Co.

—Etiquette & Espionage. 2013. (Finishing School Ser.: 1). (ENG.). 336p. (YA). (gr. 7-17). pap. 10.99 *(978-0-316-19010-7(1))* Little, Brown Bks. for Young Readers.

—Waistcoats & Weaponry. 2014. (Finishing School Ser.: 3). (ENG.). 304p. (YA). (gr. 7-17). 18.00 *(978-0-316-19027-5(6))* Little Brown & Co.

—Waistcoats & Weaponry. 2015. (Finishing School Ser.: 3). (ENG.). 320p. (YA). (gr. 7-17). pap. 10.00 *(978-0-316-19025-1(X))* Little, Brown Bks. for Young Readers.

Clare, Cassandra. Clockwork Angel. (Infernal Devices Ser.: Bk. 1). (ENG., Illus.). (YA). (gr. 9). 2015. 544p. pap. 13.99 *(978-1-4814-5602-9(4))* 2010. 496p. 24.99 *(978-1-4169-7586-1(1))* McElderry, Margaret K. Bks. (McElderry, Margaret K. Bks.).

—Clockwork Angel. 2012. (Infernal Devices Ser.: 1). (ENG.). 240p. (gr. 8-17). pap. 13.00 *(978-0-316-20098-1(0),* Yen Pr.) Orbit.

—Clockwork Angel. 2015. (Infernal Devices Ser.: Bk. 1). 544p. (YA). lib. bdg. 25.75 *(978-0-606-37737-9(9))* 2012. (Infernal Devices Graphic Novel Ser.: 1). lib. bdg. 24.55 *(978-0-606-32257-7(4),* Turtleback) Turtleback Bks.

—Clockwork Prince. (Infernal Devices Ser.: Bk. 2). (YA). 2015. (ENG., Illus.). 560p. (gr. 9). pap. 13.99 *(978-1-4814-5601-2(6))* 2011. (ENG., Illus.). 528p. (gr. 9-18). 24.99 *(978-1-4169-7588-5(8))* 2011. 502p. *(978-1-4424-5174-2(2))* McElderry, Margaret K. Bks. (McElderry, Margaret K. Bks.).

—Clockwork Prince. 2013. (Infernal Devices Ser.: 2). (ENG., Illus.). 256p. (gr. 8-17). pap. 13.00 *(978-0-316-20096-7(4),* Yen Pr.) Orbit.

—Clockwork Prince. 2015. (Infernal Devices Ser.: Bk. 2). 560p. (YA). lib. bdg. 25.75 *(978-0-606-37895-6(2))* 2013. (Infernal Devices Graphic Novel Ser.: 2). lib. bdg. 24.55 *(978-0-606-32258-4(2),* Turtleback) Turtleback Bks.

—Clockwork Princess. 2013. (Infernal Devices Ser.: 3). (ENG., Illus.). 592p. (YA). (gr. 9). 24.99 *(978-1-4169-7590-8(X),* McElderry, Margaret K. Bks.) McElderry, Margaret K. Bks.

—The Infernal Devices: Clockwork Angel; Clockwork Prince; Clockwork Princess. 2013. (Infernal Devices Ser.: Bks. 1-3). (ENG.). 1520p. (YA). (gr. 9). 74.99 *(978-1-4424-8372-9(5),* McElderry, Margaret K. Bks.) McElderry, Margaret K. Bks.

Collingwood, Harry. The Log of a Privateersman. 2008. 216p. 26.95 *(978-1-60664-899-5(3))*; pap. 15.95 *(978-1-60664-018-0(6))* Aegypan.

Cooper, Susan. Victory. 2013. (ENG., Illus.). 224p. (J). (gr. 5-9). 17.99 *(978-1-4424-8079-7(3))*; pap. 6.99 *(978-1-4424-8080-3(7))* McElderry, Margaret K. Bks. (McElderry, Margaret K. Bks.).

Deedy, Carmen Agra & Wright, Randall. The Cheshire Cheese Cat: A Dickens of a Tale, 1 vol. Moser, Barry, illus. 2011. (ENG.). 256p. (J). 16.95 *(978-1-56145-595-9(4))* Peachtree Pubs.

Dickens, Charles. A Christmas Carol. 2009. (Foundation Classics Ser.). 56p. (J). (gr. 5-9). lib. bdg. 27.95 *(978-1-60754-850-8(X))* Windmill Bks.

—David Copperfield, 1 vol. McWilliam, Howard, illus. 2011. (Calico Illustrated Classics Ser.). (ENG.). 112p. (YA). (gr. 3-6). 27.07 *(978-1-60270-745-0(6))* Magic Wagon.

—Oliver Twist. 2009. (Foundation Classics Ser.). (Illus.). 56p. (J). (gr. 5-9). lib. bdg. 27.95 *(978-1-60754-542-2(X))* Windmill Bks.

—Oliver Twist, 1 vol. McWilliam, Howard, illus. 2011. (Calico Illustrated Classics Ser.: No. 3). (ENG.). 112p. (J). (gr. 3-6). 27.07 *(978-1-61641-106-0(6))* Magic Wagon.

Dickens, Charles & Wright, Brett. Scrooge #worstgiftever. 2016. (OMG Classics Ser.). (ENG., Illus.). 112p. (YA). (gr. 9). 9.99 *(978-0-399-55064-5(X),* Random Hse. Bks. for Young Readers) Random Hse. Children's Bks.

Dowswell, Paul. Prison Ship: Adventures of a Youn Sailor. 2006. 306p. 16.95 *(978-1-58237-674-5(3))* Let's Think-kids Foundation, Inc.

Eagland, Jane. The World Within: A Novel of Emily Bronte. 2015. (ENG.). 336p. (J). (gr. 7). 18.99 *(978-0-545-49295-9(5))* Scholastic, Inc.

East, Cathy. Anna Sewell's Black Beauty. Wald, Christina, illus. 2009. (Penguin Young Readers, Level 4 Ser.: No. 3). (ENG.). 48p. (J). (gr. 3-4). pap. 3.99 (978-0-448-45190-9(5), Penguin Young Readers) Penguin Young Readers Group.

Foxlee, Karen. A Most Magical Girl. (ENG.). 304p. (J). (gr. 3-7). 2017. 7.99 **(978-0-553-51288-5(9)**, Yearling) 2016. 16.99 (978-0-553-51285-4(4), Knopf Bks. for Young Readers) 2016. lib. bdg. 19.99 (978-0-553-51286-1(2), Knopf Bks. for Young Readers) Random Hse. Children's Bks.

Heneghan, Judith. The Magician's Apprentice. 2008. (Illus.). 168p. (J). (gr. 3-7). 16.95 (978-0-8234-2150-3(3)) Holiday Hse., Inc.

Hooper, Mary. Velvet. 2012. (ENG.). 336p. (YA). (gr. 7-12). 16.99 (978-1-59990-912-7(X), 9781599909127, Bloomsbury USA Childrens) Bloomsbury Publishing USA.

Hopkinson, Deborah. A Boy Called Dickens. Hendrix, John, illus. 2012. (ENG.). 40p. (J). (gr. -1-3). 17.99 (978-0-375-86732-3(5), Schwartz & Wade Bks.) Random Hse. Children's Bks.

Lane, Andrew. Death Cloud. 2012. (ENG.). (YA). (gr. 7-12). 64.99 (978-1-4272-2800-0(0)) Findaway World, LLC.

—Death Cloud. 2011. (Sherlock Holmes: the Legend Begins Ser.: 1). (ENG.). 336p. (YA). (gr. 7-12). pap. 10.99 (978-0-312-56371-4(X), 9780312563714) Square Fish.

—Death Cloud. l.t. ed. 2011. (Young Sherlock Holmes Ser.). 367p. 23.99 (978-1-4104-3971-0(2)) Thorndike Pr.

—Death Cloud. 2011. (Sherlock Holmes: the Legend Begins Ser.: 1). (YA). lib. bdg. 22.10 (978-0-606-23781-9(X), Turtleback) Turtleback Bks.

Le Feuvre, Amy. Harebell's Friend. 2004. (Golden Inheritance Ser.: Vol. 8). (Illus.). 140p. (J). pap. (978-0-921100-84-3(1)) Inheritance Pubns.

Lee, Y. S. The Agency: A Spy in the House. 2016. (Agency Ser.). (ENG.). 352p. (YA). (gr. 7). pap. 7.99 (978-0-7636-8748-9(0)) Candlewick Pr.

Lockwood, Vicki. The Magnificent Lizzie Brown, 1 vol. 2014. (Magnificent Lizzie Brown Ser.). (ENG.). 200p. (gr. 5-9). 53.30 (978-1-4342-9515-6(X)) Stone Arch Bks.

—The Magnificent Lizzie Brown & the Mysterious Phantom, 1 vol. 2014. (Magnificent Lizzie Brown Ser.). (ENG., Illus.). 200p. (gr. 5-9). 10.95 (978-1-62370-069-0(8)); lib. bdg. 26.65 (978-1-4342-7940-8(5)) Stone Arch Bks.

—The Magnificent Lizzie Brown & the Mysterious Phantom, 1 vol. Hans, Stephanie, illus. 2014. (ENG.). 200p. (J). pap. (978-1-4342-7942-2(1)) Stone Arch Bks.

MacColl, Michaela. Always Emily. 2015. (ENG.). 304p. (YA). (gr. 7-12). pap. 9.99 (978-1-4521-4130-5(4)) Chronicle Bks. LLC.

—Prisoners in the Palace: How Princess Victoria Became Queen with the Help of Her Maid, a Reporter, & a Scoundrel. 2013. (ENG.). 368p. (J). (gr. 8-17). pap. 9.99 (978-1-4521-1958-8(9)) Chronicle Bks. LLC.

MacColl, Michaela & Chronicle Books Staff. A Novel of Intrigue & Romance. 2010. (ENG., Illus.). 368p. (YA). (gr. 7-17). 16.99 (978-0-8118-7300-0(5)) Chronicle Bks. LLC.

Mack, Tracy & Citrin, Michael. The Fall of the Amazing Zalindas. 2006. (Illus.). 259p. (J). (978-1-4287-0951-5(7), Orchard Bks.) Scholastic, Inc.

—Fall of the Amazing Zalindas. 2009. (Sherlock Holmes & the Baker St. Irregulars Ser.: 1). (ENG.). 272p. (J). (gr. 3-7). 6.99 (978-0-545-06939-7(4), Scholastic Paperbacks) Scholastic, Inc.

Maniscalco, Kerri. Stalking Jack the Ripper. (ENG., Illus.). (YA). (gr. 10-17). 2017. 352p. pap. 10.99 **(978-0-316-27351-0(1))** 2016. 336p. 18.99 (978-0-316-27349-7(X)) 2016. 464p. 20.99 (978-0-316-46428-4(7)) Little Brown & Co. (Jimmy Patterson).

Nesbit, E. Story of the Treasure Seekers. 2006. pap. (978-1-4068-3507-6(2)) Echo Library.

—The Story of the Treasure Seekers: Being the Adventures of the Bastable Children in Search of a Fortune. 2007. (ENG.). 150p. pap. 18.99 (978-1-4346-5163-1(0)); 170p. pap. 21.99 (978-1-4346-5164-8(9)) Creative Media Partners, LLC.

—The Story of the Treasure Seekers: Being the Adventures of the Bastable Children in Search of A Fortune. l.t. ed. 2005. 288p. pap. (978-1-84637-207-0(0)) Echo Library.

Pullman, Philip. The Ruby in the Smoke. 2009. 9.84 (978-0-7848-2919-6(5), Everbind) Marco Bk. Co.

—The Ruby in the Smoke. (Sally Lockhart Ser.: Bk. 1). (YA). 2008. (ENG.). 256p. (gr. 7). pap. 9.99 (978-0-375-84516-1(X), Ember) 2003. (Illus.). pap. 9.95 (978-0-375-82545-3(2), Knopf Bks. for Young Readers) Random Hse. Children's Bks.

—Two Crafty Criminals! And How They Were Captured by the Daring Detectives of the New Cut Gang. 2012. (ENG., Illus.). 288p. (J). (gr. 3-7). 16.99 (978-0-375-87029-3(6), Knopf Bks. for Young Readers) Random Hse. Children's Bks.

Schlitz, Laura Amy. Splendors & Glooms. (ENG.). 400p. (J). 2014. (gr. 5-9). pap. 8.99 (978-0-7636-6926-3(1)) 2012. (Illus.). (gr. 4-7). 17.99 (978-0-7636-5380-4(2)) Candlewick Pr.

—Splendors & Glooms. 2014. (ENG.). (J). (gr. 4-7). lib. bdg. 18.60 **(978-1-62765-443-2(7))** Perfection Learning Corp.

—Splendors & Glooms. 2014. lib. bdg. 18.40 (978-0-606-35170-6(1)) Turtleback Bks.

Springer, Nancy. The Case of the Cryptic Crinoline. 2011. (Enola Holmes Mystery Ser.: 5). (ENG.). 176p. (J). (gr. 5-7). 6.99 (978-0-14-241690-7(8), Puffin Books) Penguin Young Readers Group.

—The Case of the Peculiar Pink Fan: An Enola Holmes Mystery. 2010. (Enola Holmes Mystery Ser.: 4). (ENG.). 192p. (J). (gr. 5-7). 6.99 (978-0-14-241517-7(0), Puffin Books) Penguin Young Readers Group.

Stratford, Jordan. The Case of the Missing Moonstone. Murphy, Kelly, illus. 2015. (Wollstonecraft Detective Agency Ser.). (ENG.). 240p. (J). (gr. 3-7). 16.99 (978-0-385-75440-8(X), Knopf Bks. for Young Readers) Random Hse. Children's Bks.

Stretton, Hesba. Cassy. Hymper, W. & Stacey, W. S., illus. 2006. (Golden Inheritance Ser.: Vol. 9). 117p. (J). pap. (978-0-921100-94-2(9)) Inheritance Pubns.

—Lost Gip. 2003. (Golden Inheritance Ser.: Vol. 7). (Illus.). 121p. (J). (978-0-921100-93-5(0)) Inheritance Pubns.

Voigt, Cynthia. The Book of Lost Things. Bruno, Iacopo, illus. 2013. (Mister Max Ser.: Bk. 1). (ENG.). 400p. (J). (gr. 3-7). 16.99 (978-0-307-97681-9(5), Knopf Bks. for Young Readers) Random Hse. Children's Bks.

Wheeler, E. B. The Haunting of Springett Hall. 2015. (ENG.). 256p. (YA). (gr. 7-13). pap. 16.99 (978-1-4621-1672-0(8), Sweetwater Bks.) Cedar Fort, Inc./CFI Distribution.

GREAT BRITAIN—HISTORY—20TH CENTURY

Barber, Nicola. Who Broke the Wartime Codes?, 1 vol. 2014. (Primary Source Detectives Ser.). (ENG., Illus.). 64p. (gr. 7-8). lib. bdg. 35.99 (978-1-4329-9606-2(1)) Heinemann-Raintree.

Nixon, James. The 1980s. 2016. (My Family Remembers Ser.). (ENG., Illus.). 32p. (J). (gr. 2-17). pap. 11.99 (978-1-4451-4356-9(9), Franklin Watts) Hachette Children's Group GBR. Dist: Hachette Bk. Group.

—The 1990s. 2016. (My Family Remembers Ser.). (ENG., Illus.). 32p. (J). (gr. 2-17). pap. 11.99 (978-1-4451-4357-6(7), Franklin Watts) Hachette Children's Group GBR. Dist: Hachette Bk. Group.

—The 2000s. 2016. (My Family Remembers Ser.). (ENG., Illus.). 32p. (J). (gr. 2-17). pap. 11.99 (978-1-4451-4358-3(5), Franklin Watts) Hachette Children's Group GBR. Dist: Hachette Bk. Group.

Ridley, Sarah. Family. 2017. (Tell Me What You Remember Ser.). (ENG., Illus.). 24p. (J). (gr. k-2). 17.99 (978-1-4451-3985-2(5), Franklin Watts) Hachette Children's Group GBR. Dist: Hachette Bk. Group.

—Remembering the Fallen of the First World War. 2016. (ENG., Illus.). 48p. (J). (gr. 6-11). 18.99 (978-1-4451-4250-0(3), Franklin Watts) Hachette Children's Group GBR. Dist: Hachette Bk. Group.

—Sport. 2016. (ENG., Illus.). 24p. (J). (gr. k-2). 17.99 (978-1-4451-4007-0(1), Franklin Watts) Hachette Children's Group GBR. Dist: Hachette Bk. Group.

Schomp, Virginia. The City. 2010. (Life in Victorian England Ser.). (Illus.). 80p. (gr. 6). 34.21 (978-1-60870-029-5(1)) Marshall Cavendish Corp.

Selbert, Kathryn. War Dogs. Selbert, Kathryn, illus. 2016. (ENG., Illus.). 48p. (J). (gr. 2-5). pap. 7.95 (978-1-58089-415-9(1)) Charlesbridge Publishing, Inc.

Stephens, Chris S. A Wartime Scrapbook. 2004. (ENG., Illus.). 32p. pap. 14.95 (978-1-84323-285-8(5)) Beekman Bks., Inc.

Trussell-Cullen, Alan. Winston Churchill. 2009. pap. 13.25 (978-1-60559-072-1(X)) Hameray Publishing Group, Inc.

Walker, Kathryn. The 1950s. 2017. (My Family Remembers Ser.). (ENG., Illus.). 32p. (J). (gr. 2-17). pap. 11.99 (978-1-4451-4353-8(4), Franklin Watts) Hachette Children's Group GBR. Dist: Hachette Bk. Group.

—The 1960s. 2017. (My Family Remembers Ser.). (ENG., Illus.). 32p. (J). (gr. 2-6). pap. 11.99 (978-1-4451-4354-5(2), Franklin Watts) Hachette Children's Group GBR. Dist: Hachette Bk. Group.

—The 1970s. 2017. (My Family Remembers Ser.). (ENG., Illus.). 32p. (J). (gr. 2-17). pap. 11.99 (978-1-4451-4355-2(0), Franklin Watts) Hachette Children's Group GBR. Dist: Hachette Bk. Group.

Woolf, Alex. A Photographic View of Holidays. 2016. (Past in Pictures Ser.). (ENG., Illus.). 32p. (J). (gr. 4-6). pap. 11.99 (978-0-7502-8353-3(X), Wayland) Hachette Children's Group GBR. Dist: Hachette Bk. Group.

GREAT BRITAIN—KINGS AND RULERS

Abbott, Jacob. History of William the Conqueror. 2003. 291p. 89.00 (978-0-7950-4508-0(5)) New Library Press LLC.

Adams, Simon. Monarchs. 2017. (History Detective Investigates Ser.). (ENG., Illus.). 32p. (J). (gr. 4-6). pap. 11.99 (978-0-7502-9425-6(6), Wayland) Hachette Children's Group GBR. Dist: Hachette Bk. Group.

Ashworth, Leon. King Henry VIII. (Illus.). 32p. (978-0-7451-5289-9(9)); pap. (978-0-7540-9012-0(4)) Cherrytree Bks.

Barnes-Murphy, Rowan. Kings & Queens of Britain. 2003. (Illus.). 40p. (YA). (978-1-84365-027-0(4), Pavilion Children's Books) Pavilion Bks.

Brooks, Philip. King George III: America's Enemy. 2009. (Wicked History Ser.). (ENG.). 128p. (J). (gr. 6-12). pap. 5.95 (978-0-531-20739-0(0)); (Illus.). 31.00 (978-0-531-21803-7(1)) Scholastic Library Publishing. (Watts, Franklin).

Browning, Oscar. True Stories from English History from T. 2006. pap. 33.95 (978-1-4254-9960-0(0)) Kessinger Publishing, LLC.

Burnett, Allan. Bonnie Prince Charlie & All That. Anderson, Scoular, illus. 2006. (ENG.). 103p. pap. (978-1-84158-496-6(7)) Birlinn, Ltd.

—Robert the Bruce. Anderson, Scoular, illus. 2006. (ENG.). 105p. pap. (978-1-84158-497-3(5)) Birlinn, Ltd.

Butterfield, Moira. Kings & Warriors. 2016. (Discover the Anglo-Saxons Ser.). (ENG., Illus.). 32p. (J). (gr. 4-6). pap. 11.99 (978-1-4451-3327-0(X), Franklin Watts) Hachette Children's Group GBR. Dist: Hachette Bk. Group.

Clark, Connie & Weiss, Jim. Who in the World Was the Unready King? The Story of Ethelred. unabr. ed. 2008. (ENG.). 1p. 12.95 (978-1-933339-28-3(4), 333928) Well-Trained Mind Pr.

Clements, Jonathan, et al. Early Kings of England. 2016. (ENG., Illus.). 48p. (J). (gr. 3-4). pap. 9.95 (978-0-00-816386-0(3)) HarperCollins Pubs. Ltd. GBR. Dist: Independent Pubs. Group.

Collins Publishers Staff & Bodleian Library Staff. The Chapter of Kings. 2005. (Illus.). 40p. 9.99 (978-1-85124-320-4(8)) Bodleian Library GBR. Dist: Chicago Distribution Ctr.

Corporate Contibutor Staff & Roberts, Steve. King George Iii: England's Struggle to Keep America. 2012. (ENG.). 48p. (J). (978-0-7787-0800-1(4)) Crabtree Publishing Co.

Crabtree Staff & Roberts, Steve. King George III: England's Struggle to Keep America. 2012. (ENG., Illus.). 48p. (J). pap. (978-0-7787-0811-7(X)) Crabtree Publishing Co.

Gigliotti, Jim. Who Was Queen Victoria? Harrison, Nancy & Hergenrother, Max, illus. 2014. (Who Was? Ser.). (ENG.). 112p. (J). (gr. 3-7). 5.99 (978-0-448-48182-1(0), Grosset & Dunlap) Penguin Young Readers Group.

—Who Was Queen Victoria? 2014. (Who Was...? Ser.). lib. bdg. 16.00 (978-0-606-35697-8(5)) Turtleback Bks.

Graves, Michael A. R. Henry VIII. 2003. (Profiles in Power Ser.). (ENG.). 232p. (C). pap. 27.80 (978-0-582-38110-0(X)) Longman Publishing.

Green, John. Kings & Queens of England. 2005. (Dover History Coloring Book Ser.). (ENG., Illus.). 32p. (J). (gr. 3-8). 3.99 (978-0-486-44666-0(2)) Dover Pubns., Inc.

Gregory, Joy. Buckingham Palace. 2015. 24p. (J). (978-1-4896-3392-7(8)) Weigl Pubs., Inc.

Harkins, Susan Sales & Harkins, William H. The Life & Times of Richard the Lionheart. 2008. (Biography from Ancient Civilizations Ser.). (Illus.). 48p. (J). (gr. 4-8). lib. bdg. 29.95 (978-1-58415-699-4(6)) Mitchell Lane Pubs., Inc.

—The Life & Times of William the Conqueror. 2008. (Biography from Ancient Civilizations Ser.). (Illus.). 48p. (J). (gr. 4-8). lib. bdg. 29.95 (978-1-58415-700-7(3)) Mitchell Lane Pubs., Inc.

Harrison, Paul. King John: The King Who Signed Magna Carta - Brilliant Biographies of the Dead Famous. 2016. (History VIPs Ser.). (ENG., Illus.). 32p. (J). (gr. 4-6). 17.99 (978-0-7502-8851-4(5), Wayland) Hachette Children's Group GBR. Dist: Hachette Bk. Group.

Harrison, Paul. King John - The King Who Signed Magna Carta: Brilliant Biographies of the Dead Famous. 2017. (History VIPs Ser.). (ENG., Illus.). 32p. (J). (gr. 4-6). pap. 12.99 **(978-0-7502-9913-8(4)**, Wayland) Hachette Children's Group GBR. Dist: Hachette Bk. Group.

Hilliam, Paul. William the Conqueror: First Norman King of England. (Leaders of the Middle Ages Ser.). 112p. 2009. (gr. 5-8). 66.50 (978-1-61513-903-6(5), Rosen Reference) 2004. (Illus.). (J). lib. bdg. 34.60 (978-1-4042-0166-8(1)) Rosen Publishing Group, Inc., The.

King, Andrew A. The British Monarchy. 2012. (World History Ser.). (ENG., Illus.). 128p. (gr. 7-10). lib. bdg. 39.90 (978-1-4205-0790-4(7), Lucent Bks.) Cengage Gale.

Malam, John. Queen Elizabeth II: Her Story. 2017. (ENG., Illus.). 24p. (J). (gr. 4-6). pap. 9.99 (978-0-7502-9878-0(2), Wayland) Hachette Children's Group GBR. Dist: Hachette Bk. Group.

Matthews, C. M., et al. A Pageant of Kings & Queens. Brooke, Iris, illus. 2011. (ENG.). 98p. pap. 20.99 (978-0-521-23596-9(0)) Cambridge Univ. Pr.

McGowen, Tom. William the Conqueror: Last Invader of England. 2007. (Rulers of the Middle Ages Ser.). (Illus.). 160p. (YA). (gr. 6-12). lib. bdg. 35.94 (978-0-7660-2713-8(9)) Enslow Pubs., Inc.

Price, Sean Stewart & Price, Sean. Henry VIII: Royal Beheader. 2009. (Wicked History Ser.). (ENG.). 128p. (J). (gr. 6-12). pap. 5.95 (978-0-531-22173-0(3), Children's Pr.) Scholastic Library Publishing.

Ralph Lewis, Brenda. The Untold History of the Kings & Queens of England. 2016. (History Exposed Ser.). (ENG.). 224p. (YA). (gr. 9-9). 55.00 (978-1-5026-1906-8(7)) Cavendish Square Publishing.

—The Untold History of the Kings & Queens of Europe. 2016. (History Exposed Ser.). (ENG.). 224p. (YA). (gr. 9-9). 55.00 (978-1-5026-1908-2(3)) Cavendish Square Publishing.

Roxburgh, Ellis. Elizabeth I of England vs. Mary, Queen of Scots: Battle for the Throne. 2016. (History's Greatest Rivals Ser.). (ENG., Illus.). 48p. (J). (gr. 6-8). pap. 14.05 (978-1-4824-4227-4(2)) Stevens, Gareth Publishing LLLP.

Schanzer, Rosalyn. George vs. George: The American Revolution as Seen from Both Sides. 2007. (ENG., Illus.). 64p. (J). (gr. 4-7). per. 6.95 (978-1-4263-0042-4(5), National Geographic Children's Bks.) National Geographic Society.

—George vs. George: The Revolutionary War as Seen by Both Sides. 2004. (ENG., Illus.). 64p. (J). (gr. 4-7). 25.90 (978-0-7922-6999-1(3), National Geographic Children's Bks.) National Geographic Society.

Steele, Philip. Hail! Tudors. 2010. (ENG., Illus.). 32p. (J). (978-0-7787-6626-1(8)); pap. (978-0-7787-6633-9(0)) Crabtree Publishing Co.

Streissguth, Tom. Richard the Lionheart: Crusader King of England. 2007. (Rulers of the Middle Ages Ser.). (Illus.). 160p. (YA). (gr. 6-12). lib. bdg. 35.94 (978-0-7660-2714-5(7)) Enslow Pubs., Inc.

West, David. Richard the Lionheart: The Life of a King & Crusader. 2009. (Graphic Nonfiction Biographies Ser.). (Illus.). 48p. (YA). (gr. 4-5). 58.50 (978-1-61513-025-2(X), Rosen Reference) Rosen Publishing Group, Inc., The.

West, David & Gaff, Jackie. Richard the Lionheart: The Life of a King & Crusader. 2005. (Graphic Nonfiction Biographies Ser.). (ENG., Illus.). 48p. (YA). (gr. 4-7). lib. bdg. 31.95 (978-1-4042-0241-2(2)) Rosen Publishing Group, Inc., The.

Weston Woods Staff, creator. Can't You Make Them Behave, King George? 2004. 29.95 (978-1-55592-378-5(X)); (J). 18.95 (978-1-55592-377-8(1)); (J). 38.75 (978-1-55592-379-2(8)) Weston Woods Studios, Inc.

GREAT BRITAIN—POLITICS AND GOVERNMENT

Allport, Alan. Gordon Brown. 2009. (Modern World Leaders Ser.). (Illus.). 144p. (YA). (gr. 7-12). 30.00 (978-1-60413-080-5(6)) Facts On File, Inc.

Alvarez, Pilar. New Jobs, New Opportunities: British Immigrants Arrive in America (1830s-1890s), 01 vols., 1. 2016. (Spotlight on Immigration & Migration Ser.). (ENG., Illus.). 24p. (J). pap. 10.00 (978-1-5081-4090-0(1), PowerKids Pr.) Rosen Publishing Group, Inc., The.

Belmonte, Kevin. Travel with William Wilberforce: The Friend of Humanity. 2006. (Travel With... Ser.). (Illus.). 128p. per. 15.00 (978-1-84625-027-9(7)) DayOne Pubns. GBR. Dist: Send The Light Distribution LLC.

Benge, Janet & Benge, Geoff. William Wilberforce: Take up the Fight. 2015. (ENG.). 201p. (YA). pap. 9.99 (978-1-62486-057-5(5)) Emerald Bks.

Benjamin, Floella. Coming to England. 2016. (ENG., Illus.). 144p. (J). (gr. 4-6). 14.99 **(978-1-5098-3548-5(2))** Pan Macmillan GBR. Dist: Independent Pubs. Group.

Collins, Thomas M. Tony Blair. 2005. (Biography Ser.). (Illus.). 112p. (J). (gr. 6-18). pap. 7.95 (978-0-8225-9622-6(9)); 29.27 (978-0-8225-2373-4(6), Lerner Pubns.) Lerner Publishing Group.

Fiscus, James. The Suez Crisis. 2009. (War & Conflict in the Middle East Ser.). 64p. (gr. 5-5). 58.50 (978-1-60854-741-8(8)) Rosen Publishing Group, Inc., The.

Gifford, Clive. The Empire Windrush. 2014. (Collins Big Cat Progress Ser.). (ENG., Illus.). 32p. (J). (gr. 3-4). pap. 7.99 (978-0-00-751926-2(5)) HarperCollins Pubs. Ltd. GBR. Dist: Independent Pubs. Group.

Goodwin, Jane. The Victorians. 2016. (ENG., Illus.). 48p. (J). (gr. 4-6). pap. 9.99 (978-0-7502-9274-0(1), Wayland) Hachette Children's Group GBR. Dist: Hachette Bk. Group.

Howell, Izzi. Samuel Pepys. 2016. (Fact Cat: History Ser.). (ENG., Illus.). 24p. (J). (gr. k-2). 14.99 (978-1-5263-0097-3(4), Wayland) Hachette Children's Group GBR. Dist: Hachette Bk. Group.

Jedson, Lee. The Treaty of Paris 1783: A Primary Source Examination of the Treaty That Recognized American Independence. 2009. (Primary Sources of American Treaties Ser.). 64p. (gr. 5-8). 58.50 (978-1-60851-517-2(6)) Rosen Publishing Group, Inc., The.

Kesselring, Mari. How to Analyze the Works of Winston Churchill, 1 vol. 2013. (Essential Critiques Set 4 Ser.). (ENG.). 112p. (J). (gr. 6-12). lib. bdg. 35.64 (978-1-61783-649-7(4), Essential Library) ABDO Publishing Co.

Levy, Janey. The Magna Carta. 2013. 32p. (J). (gr. 4-6). 26.60 (978-1-4339-9001-4(6)); pap. 10.50 (978-1-4339-9002-1(4)) Stevens, Gareth Publishing LLLP.

The Magna Carta. 2013. (Documents That Shaped America Ser.). 32p. (J). (gr. 4-6). pap. 63.00 (978-1-4339-9003-8(2)) Stevens, Gareth Publishing LLLP.

Marciniak, Kristin. The Revolutionary War: Why They Fought. 2015. (What Were They Fighting For? Ser.). (ENG., Illus.). 64p. (gr. 5-9). lib. bdg. 34.65 (978-0-7565-5169-8(2)) Compass Point Bks.

Morris, Heather. The Tudors: How It Started, Key Events, Famous People. 2016. (ENG., Illus.). 48p. (J). (gr. 4-6). pap. 9.99 (978-0-7502-9275-7(X), Wayland) Hachette Children's Group GBR. Dist: Hachette Bk. Group.

Murray, Laura K. Spies in the SIS. 2016. (Illus.). 24p. (J). (978-1-60818-619-8(9), Creative Education) Creative Co., The.

Peal, Robert. Modern Britain - The Age of Reform. 2017. (Knowing History Ser.). (ENG.). 16p. (J). (gr. 5-9). 3.99 **(978-0-00-819542-7(0))** HarperCollins Pubs. Ltd. GBR. Dist: Independent Pubs. Group.

Schomp, Virginia. Victoria & Her Court. 2010. (Life in Victorian England Ser.). 80p. (gr. 6). 34.21 (978-1-60870-028-8(3)) Marshall Cavendish Corp.

Thornton, Jeremy. New Industries, New Jobs: British Immigrants Come to America(1830s-1890s) 2009. (Primary Sources of Immigration & Migration in America Ser.). 24p. (gr. 3-4). 42.50 (978-1-60851-782-4(9), PowerKids Pr.) Rosen Publishing Group, Inc., The.

Vander Hook, Sue. Winston Churchill: British Prime Minister & Statesman, 1 vol. 2009. (Essential Lives Set 3 Ser.). (ENG., Illus.). 112p. (J). (gr. 6-12). lib. bdg. 35.64 (978-1-60453-523-5(7)) ABDO Publishing Co.

Walker, Ida. William Blackstone & Commentaries upon the Laws of England. 2016. (J). lib. bdg. (978-1-68048-552-3(0)) Rosen Publishing Group, Inc., The.

GREAT BRITAIN—POLITICS AND GOVERNMENT—FICTION

Chandler, Paul. Mouse of Commons - Mouse of Lords. 2006. 186p. pap. 14.99 (978-1-4116-8447-8(8)) Lulu Pr., Inc.

GREAT BRITAIN—ROYAL AIR FORCE

Ferguson, Amanda. SAS: British Special Air Service. 2009. (Inside Special Operations Ser.). 64p. (gr. 6-6). 58.50 (978-1-61513-557-8(X), Rosen Reference) Rosen Publishing Group, Inc., The.

Graham, Ian. You Wouldn't Want to Be a World War II Pilot! Air Battles You Might Not Survive. Antram, David, illus. 2009. (You Wouldn't Want to Ser.). (ENG.). 32p. (J). 29.00 (978-0-531-21326-1(9)); (gr. 3-18). pap. 9.95 (978-0-531-20517-4(7)) Scholastic Library Publishing.

GREAT BRITAIN—SOCIAL LIFE AND CUSTOMS

Bailey, Jacqui. Queen Elizabeth II's Britain: A Celebration of British History under Its Longest Reigning Monarch. 2017. (ENG., Illus.). 48p. (J). (gr. 4-6). pap. 11.99 (978-1-4451-4222-7(8), Franklin Watts) Hachette Children's Group GBR. Dist: Hachette Bk. Group.

Bailey Publishing Staff & Elgin, Kathy. Elizabethan England. 2009. (Costume Source Bks). (Illus.). 64p. (gr. 6-12). 35.00 (978-1-60413-379-0(1), Chelsea Hse.) Facts On File, Inc.

Banting, Erinn. England: The Culture. 2012. (ENG.). 32p. (J). pap. (978-0-7787-9831-6(3)); (978-0-7787-9828-6(3)) Crabtree Publishing Co.

—England: The People. 2012. (ENG.). 32p. (J). (978-0-7787-9830-9(5)) Crabtree Publishing Co.

—England - The People. 2012. (ENG.). 32p. (J). pap. (978-0-7787-9833-0(X)) Crabtree Publishing Co.

Butterfield, Moira. Iron Age. 2017. (Britain in the Past Ser.). (ENG., Illus.). 32p. (J). (gr. 2-5). pap. 12.99 **(978-1-4451-4065-0(9)**, Franklin Watts) Hachette Children's Group GBR. Dist: Hachette Bk. Group.

Cooke, Tim. The Victorians. 2015. (At Home With... Ser.). (Illus.). 32p. (gr. 5-9). lib. bdg. 31.35 (978-1-78121-087-1(X)) Windmill Bks. Ltd. GBR. Dist: Black Rabbit Bks.

Enderlein, Cheryl L. Christmas in England, 1 vol. 2013. (Christmas Around the World Ser.). (ENG.). 24p. (gr. 1-2). lib. bdg. 25.32 (978-1-62065-141-4(6)) Capstone Press of Coughlan Cos.

Gardner, Faye, et al. Shopping in the 1940s. 2011. (When I Was Young Ser.). (ENG., Illus.). 32p. (J). pap. 10.99 (978-0-237-54389-1(3)) Evans Brothers, Ltd. GBR. Dist: Independent Pubs. Group.

—A Wartime Childhood. 2011. (When I Was Young Ser.). (ENG., Illus.). 32p. (J). pap. 10.99 (978-0-237-54384-6(2)) Evans Brothers, Ltd. GBR. Dist: Independent Pubs. Group.

Garratt, Richard. United Kingdom, Vol. 12. 2015. (Major Nations in a Global World: Tradition, Culture, & Daily Life Ser.). (Illus.). 64p. (J). (gr. 7). 23.95 (978-1-4222-3351-1(0)) Mason Crest.

Goodwin, Jane. The Victorians. 2016. (ENG., Illus.). 48p. (J). (gr. 4-6). pap. 9.99 (978-0-7502-9274-0(1), Wayland) Hachette Children's Group GBR. Dist: Hachette Bk. Group.

Harman, Alice. Tudors. 2017. (Popcorn: History Corner Ser.). (ENG.). 24p. (J). (gr. k-2). pap. 10.99 (978-0-7502-9526-0(0), Wayland) Hachette Children's Group GBR. Dist: Hachette Bk. Group.

Hepplewhite, Peter. Royals, Rebels, & Horrible Headchoppers: A Bloodthirsty History of the Terrifying Tudors! 2015. (Awfully Ancient Ser.). (ENG., Illus.). 32p. (J). (gr. 5-9). pap. 10.50 (978-1-4824-3129-2(7)) Stevens, Gareth Publishing LLLP.

Hunter, Rebecca & Walker, Kathryn. Growing up in the Forties. 2003. (Illus.). 32p. pap. (978-0-7502-3434-4(2), Wayland) Hachette Children's Group.

—Growing up in the Thirties. 2003. (Illus.). 32p. pap. *(978-0-7502-3433-7(4),* Wayland) Hachette Children's Group.

Kalman, Bobbie. A Visual Dictionary of Victorian Life. 2010. (Crabtree Visual Dictionaries Ser.). (ENG., Illus.). 32p. (J). (gr. 1-7). pap. *(978-0-7787-3527-4(3))* Crabtree Publishing Co.

Lacey, Saskia. The History of Victorian Innovations: Equivalent Fractions (Grade 3) 2017. (Mathematics Readers Ser.). (Illus.). 32p. (gr. 3-3). 8.99 ***(978-1-4807-5803-2(5))*** Teacher Created Materials, Inc.

MacDonald, Fiona & Macdonald, Fiona. You Wouldn't Want to Be a Victorian Servant! A Thankless Job You'd Rather Not Have. Antram, David, illus. 2006. (You Wouldn't Want to Ser.). (ENG.). 32p. (J). (gr. 2-5). 29.00 *(978-0-531-14972-0(2))* Scholastic Library Publishing.

Malam, John. You Wouldn't Want to Be a 19th-Century Coal Miner in England! A Dangerous Job You'd Rather Not Have. Antram, David, illus. 2006. (You Wouldn't Want to Ser.). (ENG.). 32p. (J). (gr. 2-5). 29.00 *(978-0-531-14971-3(4))* Scholastic Library Publishing.

Marcovitz, Hal. Life in the Time of Shakespeare. 2015. (ENG., Illus.). 96p. (J). lib. bdg. *(978-1-60152-778-3(0))* ReferencePoint Pr., Inc.

Morris, Heather. The Tudors: How It Started, Key Events, Famous People. 2016. (ENG., Illus.). 48p. (J). (gr. 4-6). pap. 9.99 *(978-0-7502-9275-7(X),* Wayland) Hachette Children's Group GBR. Dist: Hachette Bk. Group.

Nixon, James. The 1980s. 2016. (My Family Remembers Ser.). (ENG., Illus.). 32p. (J). (gr. 2-17). pap. 11.99 *(978-1-4451-4356-9(9),* Franklin Watts) Hachette Children's Group GBR. Dist: Hachette Bk. Group.

—The 1990s. 2016. (My Family Remembers Ser.). (ENG., Illus.). 32p. (J). (gr. 2-17). pap. 11.99 *(978-1-4451-4357-6(7),* Franklin Watts) Hachette Children's Group GBR. Dist: Hachette Bk. Group.

—The 2000s. 2016. (My Family Remembers Ser.). (ENG., Illus.). 32p. (J). (gr. 2-17). pap. 11.99 *(978-1-4451-4358-3(5),* Franklin Watts) Hachette Children's Group GBR. Dist: Hachette Bk. Group.

Peal, Robert. Georgian Britain. 2016. (Knowing History Ser.). (ENG.). 16p. (J). (gr. 6-9). 3.99 ***(978-0-00-819537-3(4))*** HarperCollins Pubs. Ltd. GBR. Dist: Independent Pubs. Group.

Peppas, Lynn. Cultural Traditions in the United Kingdom. 2014. (ENG., Illus.). 32p. (J). *(978-0-7787-0301-3(0))* Crabtree Publishing Co.

Richardson, Nigel. Finding Out about Life in Britain in the 1960's. (Finding Out about Ser.). (Illus.). 48p. (J). (gr. 7-12). *(978-0-7134-4816-0(4))* Trafalgar Square Publishing.

Ridley, Sarah. Food. 2017. (Tell Me What You Remember Ser.). (ENG., Illus.). 24p. (J). (gr. k-2). 17.99 *(978-1-4451-3986-9(3),* Franklin Watts) Hachette Children's Group GBR. Dist: Hachette Bk. Group.

Roberts, Russell. Elizabethan England. 2009. (How'd They Do That? Ser.). (Illus.). 64p. (J). (gr. 4-8). lib. bdg. 33.95 *(978-1-58415-823-3(9))* Mitchell Lane Pubs., Inc.

Sexton, Colleen & Simmons, Walter. England. 2010. (Exploring Countries Ser.). (ENG., Illus.). 32p. (J). (gr. 3-7). lib. bdg. 26.95 *(978-1-60014-479-0(9),* Blastoff! Readers) Bellwether Media.

Steele, Philip. Hail! Tudors. 2010. (ENG., Illus.). 32p. (J). *(978-0-7787-6626-1(8));* pap. *(978-0-7787-6633-9(0))* Crabtree Publishing Co.

Stott, Colin. Victorian Transport. (Illus.). 32p. pap. *(978-0-7502-3752-9(X),* Wayland) Hachette Children's Group.

Walker, Kathryn. The 1950s. 2017. (My Family Remembers Ser.). (ENG., Illus.). 32p. (J). (gr. 2-17). pap. 11.99 *(978-1-4451-4353-8(4),* Franklin Watts) Hachette Children's Group GBR. Dist: Hachette Bk. Group.

—The 1960s. 2017. (My Family Remembers Ser.). (ENG., Illus.). 32p. (J). (gr. 2-6). pap. 11.99 *(978-1-4451-4354-5(2),* Franklin Watts) Hachette Children's Group GBR. Dist: Hachette Bk. Group.

—The 1970s. 2017. (My Family Remembers Ser.). (ENG., Illus.). 32p. (J). (gr. 2-17). pap. 11.99 *(978-1-4451-4355-2(0),* Franklin Watts) Hachette Children's Group GBR. Dist: Hachette Bk. Group.

Whyte, Harlinah. England. 2010. (Festivals of the World Ser.). 32p. (gr. 3). 28.50 *(978-1-60870-098-1(4))* Marshall Cavendish GBR. Dist: Marshall Cavendish Corp.

Woolf, Alex. Meet the Tudors. 2014. (Encounters with the Past Ser.). 32p. (J). (gr. 3-6). 26.60 *(978-1-4824-0897-3(X))* Stevens, Gareth Publishing LLLP.

Wukovits, John F. Victorian Era. Greenhaven Press Editors, ed. 2013. (World History Ser.). (ENG., Illus.). 128p. (gr. 7-10). lib. bdg. 39.90 *(978-1-4205-0933-5(0),* Lucent Bks.) Cengage Gale.

GREAT LAKES (NORTH AMERICA)

see also Michigan, Lake

Anderson, Zachary. Samuel de Champlain: Exploring the Great Lakes. 2015. (Incredible Explorers Ser.). (ENG., Illus.). 64p. (J). (gr. 7-7). 34.21 *(978-1-5026-0138-4(9))* Cavendish Square Publishing.

Blocksma, Mary. What's on the Beach? A Great Lakes Treasure Hunt. 2012. (ENG., Illus.). 48p. (gr. 3-8). pap. 12.50 *(978-0-9708575-2-1(7))* Beaver Island Arts.

—What's on the Beach? A Great Lakes Treasure Hunt. Blocksma, Mary, illus. 2003. (Great Lakes Treasure Hunts Ser.: No. 1). (Illus.). 48p. (J). pap. 9.95 *(978-0-9708575-1-4(9))* Beaver Island Arts.

Exploring the Great Lakes. 2014. (Exploring the Great Lakes Ser.). 32p. (J). (gr. 3-6). 159.60 *(978-1-4824-1171-3(7))* Stevens, Gareth Publishing LLLP.

Jankowski, Emily. History of the Great Lakes. 2014. (Exploring the Great Lakes Ser.). 32p. (J). (gr. 3-6). pap. 63.00 *(978-1-4824-1191-1(1))* Stevens, Gareth Publishing LLLP.

Kummer, Patricia K. The Great Lakes. 2008. (Nature's Wonders Ser.). 96p. (gr. 6-18). lib. bdg. 35.64 *(978-0-7614-2853-4(4),* Benchmark Bks.) Marshall Cavendish Corp.

Laplante, Walter. Conserving the Great Lakes. 2014. (Exploring the Great Lakes Ser.). 32p. (J). (gr. 3-6). pap. 63.00 *(978-1-4824-1190-4(3))* Stevens, Gareth Publishing LLLP.

—Plants & Animals of the Great Lakes. 2014. (Exploring the Great Lakes Ser.). 32p. (J). (gr. 3-6). pap. 63.00 *(978-1-4824-1193-5(8))* Stevens, Gareth Publishing LLLP.

—Waterways of the Great Lakes. 2014. (Exploring the Great Lakes Ser.). 32p. (J). (gr. 3-6). pap. 63.00 *(978-1-4824-1195-9(4))* Stevens, Gareth Publishing LLLP.

Piehl, Janet. The Great Lakes. 2010. (Lightning Bolt Books (tm) — Famous Places Ser.). (ENG.). 32p. (gr. k-2). lib. bdg. 26.60 *(978-0-7613-4456-8(X),* Lerner Pubns.) Lerner Publishing Group.

Rajczak, Michael. Visiting the Great Lakes. 2014. (Exploring the Great Lakes Ser.). 32p. (J). (gr. 3-6). pap. 63.00 *(978-1-4824-1194-2(6))* Stevens, Gareth Publishing LLLP.

Roza, Greg. The Great Lakes. 2009. (Real Life Readers Ser.). 16p. (gr. 2-3). pap. 7.05 *(978-1-4358-0113-4(X),* Rosen Classroom) Rosen Publishing Group, Inc., The.

Thompson, Linda. Grandes Lagos. 2005. (Expansion de America II Ser.). (SPA., Illus.). 48p. (J). (gr. 4-8). pap. 8.95 *(978-1-59515-705-8(0))* Rourke Educational Media.

Valzania, Kimberly. Great Lakes. 2004. (Rookie Read-About Geography Ser.). (ENG.). 32p. (J). (gr. 1-2). pap. 5.95 *(978-0-516-24648-2(8),* Children's Pr.) Scholastic Library Publishing.

Westfield, Patricia & Soper, Nan. Exploring the Great Lakes: A Logbook of Adventures. 2003. (Illus.). 64p. (J). spiral bd. 27.95 incl. cd-rom *(978-0-938682-73-8(3))* River Road Pubns., Inc.

World Book, Inc Staff, contrib. by. Fabled Waters. 2017. (J). ***(978-0-7166-3369-3(8))*** World Bk., Inc.

GREAT LAKES (NORTH AMERICA)—FICTION

Brennan-Nelson, Denise & Hartung, Susan Kathleen. Tallulah: Mermaid of the Great Lakes. 2015. (ENG., Illus.). 40p. (J). (gr. 1-4). 16.99 *(978-1-58536-909-6(8),* 203812) Sleeping Bear Pr.

Brezenoff, Steven. The Case of the Portrait Vandal. Weber, Lisa K., illus. 2015. (Museum Mysteries Ser.). (ENG.). 128p. (gr. 2-3). lib. bdg. 26.65 *(978-1-4342-9685-6(7))* Stone Arch Bks.

Marsh, Carole. The Mystery on the Great Lakes. 2010. (Real Kids, Real Places Ser.). (Illus.). 158p. (J). 18.99 *(978-0-635-07449-2(4),* Marsh, Carole Mysteries) Gallopade International.

Maurer, Tracy Nelson. Storm Codes. Rodriguez, Christina, illus. 2007. 40p. (J). pap. 8.95 *(978-0-89317-064-6(X),* WW-064X); (gr. 1-7). lib. bdg. 17.95 *(978-0-89317-063-9(1),* WW-0631) Finney Co., Inc. (Windward Publishing).

Rand, Johnathan. Michigan Chillers #11 Great Lakes Ghost Ship. 2005. (Michigan Chillers: No. 11). 208p. (J). pap. 5.99 *(978-1-893699-84-7(6))* AudioCraft Publishing, Inc.

Winfield, Arthur M. The Rover Boys on the Great Lakes. 2007. 244p. 26.95 *(978-1-4218-4137-3(1));* per. 11.95 *(978-1-4218-4235-6(1))* 1st World Publishing, Inc. (1st World Library - Literary Society).

Yaroslavskaya, Lyudmila. The Great Lakes Legends & Fairy Tales. 2006. (ENG & RUS., Illus.). (J). per. *(978-0-9791248-0-8(8))* Yaroslavskaya, Lyudmila.

GREAT LAKES (NORTH AMERICA)—HISTORY

Bekkering, Annalise. The Great Lakes. 2008. (Natural Wonders Ser.). (Illus.). 32p. (J). (gr. 5-6). pap. 8.95 *(978-1-59036-945-6(9));* lib. bdg. 26.00 *(978-1-59036-944-9(0))* Weigl Pubs., Inc.

Exploring the Great Lakes. 2014. (Exploring the Great Lakes Ser.). 32p. (J). (gr. 3-6). pap. 63.00 *(978-1-4824-1565-0(8))* Stevens, Gareth Publishing LLLP.

Green, Cathy, et al. Great Ships on the Great Lakes: A Maritime History. 2013. (ENG., Illus.). 144p. (J). pap. 18.95 *(978-0-87020-582-8(X))* Wisconsin Historical Society.

—Great Ships on the Great Lakes Teacher's Guide: A Maritime History. 2013. (ENG., Illus.). cd-rom 49.95 *(978-0-87020-583-5(8))* Wisconsin Historical Society.

Kavanagh, James. Great Lakes Wildlife Nature Activity Book. Leung, Raymond, illus. 2nd ed. 2011. (Nature Activity Book Ser.). (ENG.). 32p. (J). (gr. 4-7). 6.95 *(978-1-58355-580-4(3))* Western National Parks Assn.

Lerner Classroom Staff & Piehl, Janet. The Great Lakes. 2010. (Lightning Bolt Books (tm) — Famous Places Ser.). (ENG., Illus.). 32p. (gr. k-2). pap. 7.95 *(978-0-7613-5577-9(4))* Lerner Publishing Group.

Nagelhout, Ryan. People of the Great Lakes. 2014. (Exploring the Great Lakes Ser.). 32p. (J). (gr. 3-6). pap. 63.00 *(978-1-4824-1192-8(X))* Stevens, Gareth Publishing LLLP.

Newman, Mark. Sooper Yooper: Environmental Defender. Heckman, Mark, illus. 2010. 48p. (J). 17.95 *(978-1-933272-26-9(0))* Thunder Bay Pr.

St. Antoine, Sara & Milkweed Editions Staff. The Great Lakes: A Literary Field Guide. 2005. (Stories from Where We Live Ser.). (ENG., Illus.). 264p. (J). pap., instr.'s gde. ed. 10.95 *(978-1-57131-654-7(X))* Milkweed Editions.

GREAT PLAINS

Brown, Don. The Great American Dust Bowl. 2017. (ENG., Illus.). 80p. (YA). (gr. 7). pap. 9.99 ***(978-1-328-74087-8(0),*** HMH Books For Young Readers) Houghton Mifflin Harcourt Publishing Co.

—The Great American Dust Bowl. Brown, Don, illus. 2013. (ENG., Illus.). 80p. (YA). (gr. 7). 18.99 *(978-0-547-81550-3(6))* Houghton Mifflin Harcourt Publishing Co.

Cimarusti, Marie Torres & George, Jean Craighead. The Buffalo Are Back. Peterson, Stephanie & Minor, Wendell, illus. 2010. (ENG.). 32p. (J). (gr. k-3). 16.99 *(978-0-525-42215-0(3),* Dutton Books for Young Readers) Penguin Young Readers Group.

Connell, Kate. Hoping for Rain: The Dust Bowl Adventures of Patty & Earl Buckler. 2004. (I Am American Ser.). (ENG., Illus.). 40p. (J). (gr. 3-7). pap. 6.99 *(978-0-7922-6903-8(9),* National Geographic Children's Bks.) National Geographic Society.

Connell, Kate & National Geographic Learning Staff. Dust Bowl Days. 2007. (Reading Expeditions Ser.). (ENG., Illus.). 40p. (J). pap. 19.95 *(978-0-7922-4557-5(1))* CENGAGE Learning.

Coombs, Karen Mueller. Children of the Dust Days. 2005. (Picture the American Past Ser.). (Illus.). 48p. (gr. 2-5). lib. bdg. 22.60 *(978-1-57505-360-8(8))* Lerner Publishing Group.

Costain, Meredith. Native Americans of the Great Plains. 2013. (Discovery Education: Ancient Civilizations Ser.). (ENG., Illus.). 32p. (J). (gr. 3-6). pap. 10.00 *(978-1-4777-0089-1(7));* lib. bdg. 25.25 *(978-1-4777-0052-5(8))* Rosen Publishing Group, Inc., The. (PowerKids Pr.).

Curry, Jane Louise. Hold up the Sky: And Other Native American Tales from Texas & The. Watts, James, illus. 2010. (ENG.). 176p. (J). (gr. 3-7). pap. 9.99 *(978-1-4424-2155-4(X),* McElderry, Margaret K. Bks.) McElderry, Margaret K. Bks.

Fitzgerald, Michael Oren, ed. Children of the Tipi: Life in the Buffalo Days. 2013. (ENG., Illus.). 40p. (J). (gr. -1-3). 15.95 *(978-1-937786-09-0(9),* Wisdom Tales) World Wisdom, Inc.

Garland, Sherry. Voices of the Dust Bowl, 1 vol. Hierstein, Judith, illus. 2012. (Voices of History Ser.). (ENG.). 40p. (J). (gr. 3-3). 17.99 *(978-1-58980-964-2(5))* Pelican Publishing Co., Inc.

Johnson, Michael. Native Tribes of the Plains & Prairie. 2004. (Native Tribes of North America Ser.). (Illus.). 64p. (gr. 5-12). lib. bdg. 34.00 *(978-0-8368-5613-2(9),* Gareth Stevens Secondary Library) Stevens, Gareth Publishing LLLP.

Kalman, Bobbie. Nations of the Plains. 2003. (Native Nations of North America Ser.). (ENG., Illus.). 32p. (J). (gr. 5). pap. *(978-0-7787-0460-7(2));* lib. bdg. *(978-0-7787-0368-6(1))* Crabtree Publishing Co.

Langston-George, Rebecca. A Primary Source History of the Dust Bowl. 2015. (Primary Source History Ser.). (ENG., Illus.). 32p. (gr. 3-4). lib. bdg. 27.32 *(978-1-4914-1840-6(0))* Capstone Press of Coughlan Cos.

Levey, Richard H. & Franck, Daniel H. Dust Bowl! The 1930s Black Blizzards. 2016. (X-Treme Disasters That Changed America Ser.). (ENG.). 32p. (J). (gr. 2-7). pap. 8.95 *(978-1-944998-75-2(6))* Bearport Publishing Co., Inc.

Marrin, Albert. Years of Dust: The Story of the Dust Bowl. 2009. (ENG., Illus.). 128p. (J). (gr. 5-18). 22.99 *(978-0-525-42077-4(0),* Dutton Books for Young Readers) Penguin Young Readers Group.

National Geographic, et al. Living on the Plains. 2014. (Ladders Social Studies). (ENG.). 24p. 8.95 *(978-1-285-34796-7(X))* National Geographic School Publishing, Inc.

O'Hara, Megan. Plains Communities Past & Present, 1 vol. 2014. (Who Lived Here? Ser.). (ENG.). 24p. (gr. 1-2). lib. bdg. 25.32 *(978-1-4765-4061-0(6),* First Facts) Capstone Press of Coughlan Cos.

Ransom, Candice. The Day of the Black Blizzard. Harden, Laurie, illus. (On My Own History Ser.). 48p. (J). 2016. (ENG.). (gr. 2-4). pap. 6.95 *(978-1-5124-1152-2(3))* 2011. pap. 6.95 *(978-0-7613-3938-0(8))* Lerner Publishing Group. (First Avenue Editions).

Rea, Amy C. Perspectives on the Dust Bowl. 2018. (ENG.). 32p. (gr. 3-6). ***(978-1-63235-399-3(7),*** 12-Story Library) Pr. Room Editions LLC.

Reis, Ronald A. The Dust Bowl. 2008. (Great Historic Disasters Ser.). (Illus.). 128p. (gr. 5-8). lib. bdg. 35.00 *(978-0-7910-9737-3(4),* Chelsea Hse.) Facts On File, Inc.

Rickard, Kris A. & Bial, Raymond. The People & Culture of the Blackfeet. 2016. (First Peoples of North America Ser.). 128p. (J). 45.64 *(978-1-5026-2247-1(5))* Cavendish Square Publishing.

Rigby. When Day Turned to Night. 2014. (Rigby Literacy Ser.). (ENG.). 32p. (gr. 4-4). pap. 11.10 *(978-0-7578-2002-1(6))* Rigby Education.

Rucker, Jeffrey A. The Story of Sitting Bull. 2003. (Rosen Real Readers Big Bookstm Ser.). (ENG.). 24p. (gr. 3-4). 43.95 *(978-0-8239-8731-3(0))* Rosen Publishing Group, Inc., The.

Sandler, Martin W. The Dust Bowl Through the Lens: How Photography Revealed & Helped Remedy a National Disaster. 2009. (Through the Lens Ser.). (ENG., Illus.). 96p. (J). (gr. 5-9). 22.99 *(978-0-8027-9547-2(1),* 9780802795472, Bloomsbury USA Childrens) Bloomsbury Publishing USA.

Vander Hook, Sue. The Dust Bowl, 1 vol. 2009. (Essential Events Set 3 Ser.). (ENG., Illus.). 112p. (J). (gr. 6-12). lib. bdg. 35.64 *(978-1-60453-512-9(1))* ABDO Publishing Co.

Zuchora-Walske, Christine. The Dust Bowl: A History Perspectives Book. 2013. (Perspectives Library). (ENG., Illus.). 32p. (J). (gr. 4-8). 28.50 *(978-1-62431-417-9(1),* 202788); pap. 14.21 *(978-1-62431-493-3(7),* 202790) Cherry Lake Publishing.

GREAT SMOKY MOUNTAINS (N.C. AND TENN.)

Frisch, Nate. Great Smoky Mountains National Park. 2013. (Illus.). 48p. (J). 35.65 *(978-1-60818-197-1(9),* Creative Education) Creative Co., The.

—Preserving America: Great Smoky Mountains National Park. 2014. (Preserving America Ser.). (ENG., Illus.). 48p. (J). (gr. 4-7). pap. 12.00 *(978-0-89812-880-2(3),* Creative Paperbacks) Creative Co., The.

Gilbert, Sara. Great Smoky Mountains. 2016. (Illus.). 22p. (J). *(978-1-60818-633-4(4),* Creative Education) Creative Co., The.

Graham, Amy. Great Smoky Mountains National Park: Adventure, Explore, Discover. 2008. (America's National Parks Ser.). (Illus.). 128p. (J). (gr. 5-9). lib. bdg. 34.60 *(978-1-59845-093-4(X))* Enslow Pubs., Inc.

Gregory, Josh. Great Smoky Mountains National Park. 2017. (True Book — National Parks Ser.). (ENG.). 48p. (J). lib. bdg. 31.00 ***(978-0-531-23392-4(8),*** Children's Pr.) Scholastic Library Publishing.

Hamilton, John. Great Smoky Mountains National Park, 1 vol. 2005. (National Parks Ser.). (ENG., Illus.). 32p. (gr. 3-8). 27.07 *(978-1-59197-943-2(9),* Abdo & Daughters) ABDO Publishing Co.

Herrington, Lisa M. The Great Smoky Mountains. 2017. (Rookie National Parks Ser.). (ENG.). 32p. (J). lib. bdg. 25.00 ***(978-0-531-23333-7(2),*** Children's Pr.) Scholastic Library Publishing.

Horstman, Lisa. Smoky Mountain Wee Ones. Kemp, Steve, ed. Horstman, Lisa, illus. 2003. (Illus.). 16p. (J). bds. 6.99 *(978-0-937207-41-3(1))* Great Smoky Mountains Assn.

Ogintz, Eileen. The Kid's Guide to the Great Smoky Mountains. 2016. (ENG., Illus.). 128p. pap. 12.95 *(978-1-4930-2432-2(9))* Globe Pequot Pr., The.

GREAT SMOKY MOUNTAINS (N.C. AND TENN.)—FICTION

Holmes, Kathryn. The Distance Between Lost & Found. 2015. (ENG.). 304p. (YA). (gr. 8). 17.99 *(978-0-06-231726-1(1))* HarperCollins Pubs.

O'Connor, Barbara. Greetings from Nowhere. 2008. (ENG.). 208p. (J). (gr. 5-8). 17.99 *(978-0-374-39937-5(9),* 9780374399375, Farrar, Straus & Giroux (BYR)) Farrar, Straus & Giroux.

Webb, Ryan. Buddy: Dog of the Smoky Mountains. 2013. (Illus.). 34p. (J). pap. 12.00 *(978-0-9847836-3-2(6))* Celtic Cat Publishing.

GRECO, 1541?-1614

Mis, Melody S. El Greco. (Meet the Artist Ser.). 24p. (gr. 2-3). 2009. 42.50 *(978-1-61514-630-7(X),* PowerKids Pr.) 2007. (Illus.). (YA). lib. bdg. 22.60 *(978-1-4042-3844-2(1))* Rosen Publishing Group, Inc., The.

Venezia, Mike. El Greco. Venezia, Mike, illus. rev. ed. 2016. (Getting to Know the World's Greatest Artists Ser.). (ENG., Illus.). 40p. (J). pap. 7.95 *(978-0-531-22088-7(5),* Children's Pr.) Scholastic Library Publishing.

GREECE

Adare, Sierra. Greece - The Land. 3rd rev. ed. 2007. (Lands, Peoples & Cultures Ser.). (ENG., Illus.). 32p. (J). (gr. 3-7). lib. bdg. *(978-0-7787-9308-3(7))* Crabtree Publishing Co.

—Greece the Land. 3rd rev. ed. 2007. (Lands, Peoples & Cultures Ser.). (ENG., Illus.). 32p. (J). (gr. 3-7). pap. *(978-0-7787-9676-3(0))* Crabtree Publishing Co.

Baikie, James. Peeps at Many Lands: Ancient Greece (Yesterday's Classics) Fulleylove, John & Baikie, Constance N., illus. 2008. 128p. pap. 8.95 *(978-1-59915-289-9(4))* Yesterday's Classics.

Bartell, Jim. Greece. 2011. (Exploring Countries Ser.). (ENG., Illus.). 32p. (J). (gr. 3-7). lib. bdg. 26.95 *(978-1-60014-574-2(4),* Blastoff! Readers) Bellwether Media.

Brooks, Susie. Greece. 2006. (Our Lives, Our World Ser.). (J). *(978-1-59389-287-6(X))* Chrysalis Education.

—Let's Visit Greece. 2009. (Around the World Ser.). (Illus.). 32p. (J). (ENG.). pap. 10.00 *(978-1-4358-8610-0(0),* 1300367); (gr. 2-5). lib. bdg. 25.25 *(978-1-4358-3028-8(8),* 1300367) Rosen Publishing Group, Inc., The. (PowerKids Pr.).

Donaldson, Madeline. Greece. 2009. pap. 52.95 *(978-0-7613-4728-6(3))* Lerner Publishing Group.

Fuller, Barbara. Greece. 2013. (Cultures of the World 4 Ser.). 144p. (J). (gr. 6-9). pap. 23.51 *(978-1-62712-160-6(9))* Cavendish Square Publishing.

Gow, Mary. The Great Thinker: Aristotle & the Foundations of Science. 2010. (Great Minds of Ancient Science & Math Ser.). 128p. (J). (gr. 4-7). 33.27 *(978-0-7660-3121-0(7))* Enslow Pubs., Inc.

Green, Jen. Greece. 2009. (Countries of the World Ser.). (ENG., Illus.). 64p. (J). (gr. 5). 27.90 *(978-1-4263-0470-5(6),* National Geographic Children's Bks.) National Geographic Society.

Kaplan, Leslie C. A Primary Source Guide to Greece. 2009. (Countries of the World). 24p. (gr. 2-3). 42.50 *(978-1-61512-032-1(7),* PowerKids Pr.) Rosen Publishing Group, Inc., The.

—A Prmiary Source Guide to Greece. 2005. (Countries of the World). (Illus.). 24p. (J). (gr. k-5). lib. bdg. 22.60 *(978-1-4042-2753-8(9),* PowerKids Pr.) Rosen Publishing Group, Inc., The.

Kohen Winter & Fuller, Barbara. Greece. 3rd ed. 2013. 144p. (J). (gr. 6-9). 47.07 *(978-1-60870-869-7(1))* Cavendish Square Publishing.

Marsh, Carole. Greece: A Volcanic Land of Ancient Olympic Origins! 2009. (It's Your World Ser.). 48p. (J). (gr. 2-9). pap. 7.99 *(978-0-635-06818-7(4))* Gallopade International.

Ohlin, Nancy. Ancient Greece. Larkum, Adam, illus. 2016. (Blast Back! Ser.). (ENG.). 112p. (J). (gr. 2-5). pap. 5.99 *(978-1-4998-0118-7(1))* Little Bee Books Inc.

Pavlovic, Zoran. Greece. Gritzner, Charles F., ed. 2006. (Modern World Nations Ser.). (Illus.). 104p. (gr. 6-12). lib. bdg. 35.00 *(978-0-7910-8797-8(2))* Facts On File, Inc.

Sasek, Miroslav. This Is Greece. 2009. (ENG., Illus.). 64p. (J). (gr. 2-12). 17.95 *(978-0-7893-1855-8(5))* Universe Publishing.

Whiting, Jim. The Volcanic Eruption on Santorini, 1650 BCE. 2007. (Natural Disasters Ser.). (Illus.). 32p. (J). (gr. 1-4). lib. bdg. 25.70 *(978-1-58415-568-3(X))* Mitchell Lane Pubs., Inc.

GREECE—ANTIQUITIES

Briers, Audrey. True Stories about Greek Coins. (Illus.). 48p. pap. 6.95 *(978-0-907849-56-8(3))* Ashmolean Museum GBR. Dist: Weatherhill, Inc.

Edwards, Roberta. Where Is the Parthenon? 2016. (Where Is... ? Ser.). lib. bdg. 16.00 *(978-0-606-38412-4(X))* Turtleback Bks.

Evans, Arthur. The Palace of Minos 4 Volume Set in 7 Pieces: A Comparative Account of the Successive Stages of the Early Cretan Civilization As Illustrated by the Discoveries at Knossos. 2013. (Cambridge Library Collection - Archaeology Ser.). (ENG.). 3734p. pap., pap., pap. 417.00 *(978-1-108-06107-0(9))* Cambridge Univ. Pr.

Malam, John. Ancient Greece. 2004. (Picturing the Past Ser.). (Illus.). 32p. (J). 15.95 *(978-1-59270-022-6(5))* Enchanted Lion Bks., LLC.

—Ancient Greece Inside Out. 2017. (Ancient Worlds Inside Out Ser.). (ENG.). 32p. (J). ***(978-0-7787-2876-4(5));*** (Illus.). pap. ***(978-0-7787-2890-0(0))*** Crabtree Publishing Co.

Malam, John. The Greeks. 2011. (Dig It: History from Objects Ser.). (Illus.). 32p. (YA). (gr. 2-5). lib. bdg. 26.50 *(978-1-4488-3284-2(5))* Rosen Publishing Group, Inc., The.

von Däniken, Erich. Alien Contact in Ancient Greece, 01 vols., 1. 2016. (Ancient Secrets & Alien Gods Ser.). (ENG.). 224p. (YA). 38.25 *(978-1-5081-7103-4(3),* Rosen Young Adult) Rosen Publishing Group, Inc., The.

Woods, Michael & Woods, Mary B. Seven Wonders of Ancient Greece. 2008. (Seven Wonders Ser.). (ENG., Illus.). 80p. (J). (gr. 5-8). lib. bdg. 33.26 *(978-0-8225-7574-0(4))* Lerner Publishing Group.

GREECE—BIOGRAPHY

Adams, Simon. World History Biographies: Alexander: The Boy Soldier Who Conquered the World. 2013. (National Geographic World History Biographies Ser.). (ENG., Illus.). 64p. (J). (gr. 3-7). pap. 7.99 *(978-1-4263-1449-0(3),* National Geographic Children's Bks.) National Geographic Society.

Anderson, Margaret J. & Stephenson, Karen F. Aristotle: Genius Philosopher & Scientist. 2015. (Genius Scientists & Their Genius Ideas Ser.). 96p. (J). (gr. 5-12). 27.94 *(978-0-7660-6535-2(9));* pap. 10.95 *(978-0-7660-6536-9(7))* Enslow Pubs., Inc.

E F G

Bankston, John. Alexander the Great. 2013. (ENG.). 48p. (J). (gr. 3-6). lib. bdg. 29.95 *(978-1-61228-431-6(0))* Mitchell Lane Pubs., Inc.

Behnke, Alison. The Conquests of Alexander the Great. 2007. (Pivotal Moments in History Ser.). (ENG., Illus.). 160p. (gr. 9-12). lib. bdg. 38.60 *(978-0-8225-5920-7(X))* Lerner Publishing Group.

Bendick, Jeanne. Archimedes & the Door of Science: Immortals of Science. 2011. 154p. (gr. 5-8). 41.95 *(978-1-258-01488-9(2))* Literary Licensing, LLC.

—Herodotus & the Road to History. Bendick, Jeanne, illus. 2009. (Illus.). (J). pap. 13.95 *(978-1-932350-20-3(9))* Bethlehem Bks.

Bowen, Richard. Socrates: Greek Philosopher. 2013. (People of Importance Ser.: 21). (Illus.). 32p. (J). (gr. 4-18). 19.95 *(978-1-4222-2857-9(6))* Mason Crest.

Bridges, Shirin Yim & Yim Bridges, Shirin. Artemisia of Caria. Nguyen, Albert, illus. 2010. (Thinking Girl's Treasury of Real Princesses Ser.). (ENG.). 24p. (J). (gr. 3-8). 18.95 *(978-0-9845098-1-2(X))* Goosebottom Bks. LLC.

Campbell, Josette & Hayhurst, Chris. Euclid: The Father of Geometry. 2015. (Greatest Greek Philosophers Ser.). (ENG., Illus.). 112p. (J). (gr. 7-8). 35.60 *(978-1-4994-6128-2(3)*, Rosen Young Adult) Rosen Publishing Group, Inc., The.

Coakley, Louis C. & Karamanides, Dimitra. Pythagoras: Mathematician & Mystic. 2015. (Greatest Greek Philosophers Ser.). (ENG., Illus.). 112p. (J). (gr. 7-8). 35.60 *(978-1-4994-6132-9(1)*, Rosen Young Adult) Rosen Publishing Group, Inc., The.

Demi Staff & Marshall Cavendish Corporation Staff. Alexander the Great, 0 vols. 2010. (ENG., Illus.). 64p. (J). (gr. 3-7). 19.99 *(978-0-7614-5700-8(3)*, 9780761457008, Amazon Children's Publishing) Amazon Publishing.

Dhillon, Natasha C. & Lim, Jun. Socrates: The Father of Ethics & Inquiry. 2015. (Greatest Greek Philosophers Ser.). (ENG.). 112p. (J). (gr. 7-8). 35.60 *(978-1-4994-6134-3(8)*, Rosen Young Adult) Rosen Publishing Group, Inc., The.

Gow, Mary. Archimedes: Genius Mathematician. 2015. (Genius Scientists & Their Genius Ideas Ser.). 96p. (J). (gr. 5-12). 27.94 *(978-0-7660-6530-7(8))*; pap. 10.95 *(978-0-7660-6531-4(6))* Enslow Pubs., Inc.

—The Greatest Doctor of Ancient Times: Hippocrates & His Oath. 2009. (Great Minds of Ancient Science & Math Ser.). (Illus.). 128p. (J). (gr. 4-7). lib. bdg. 33.27 *(978-0-7660-3118-0(7))* Enslow Pubs., Inc.

—Measuring the Earth: Eratosthenes & His Celestial Geometry. 2009. (Great Minds of Ancient Science & Math Ser.). (Illus.). 128p. (J). (gr. 4-7). lib. bdg. 33.27 *(978-0-7660-3120-3(9))* Enslow Pubs., Inc.

Haaren, John. Famous Men of Greece. 2008. 112p. pap. 12.95 *(978-1-60459-523-9(X))* Wilder Pubns., Corp.

Haaren, John H. & Poland, A. Famous Men of Greece (Yesterday's Classics) 2006. (Illus.). 252p. (J). per. 11.95 *(978-1-59915-045-1(X))* Yesterday's Classics.

Harkins, Susan Sales & Harkins, William H. The Life & Times of Pythagoras. 2007. (Biography from Ancient Civilizations Ser.). (Illus.). 48p. (J). (gr. 4-8). lib. bdg. 29.95 *(978-1-58415-545-4(0))* Mitchell Lane Pubs., Inc.

Harlan Rowe Junior High. Everyday Heroes; Biographies & Memoirs from the Athens Area School District Eighth Grade Oral History Project. 2008. 172p. pap. 15.95 *(978-0-9800429-7-9(6))* Pen & Publish Inc.

Hasan, Heather. Archimedes: The Father of Mathematics. 2009. (Library of Greek Philosophers Ser.). 112p. (gr. 6-6). 66.50 *(978-1-60853-657-3(2)*, Rosen Reference) Rosen Publishing Group, Inc., The.

Hightower, Paul. The Father of Geometry: Euclid & His 3-D World. 2010. (Great Minds of Ancient Science & Math Ser.). 112p. (J). 33.27 *(978-0-7660-3409-9(7))* Enslow Pubs., Inc.

—The Greatest Mathematician: Archimedes & His Eureka! Moment. 2009. (Great Minds of Ancient Science & Math Ser.). (Illus.). 128p. (J). (gr. 4-7). lib. bdg. 33.27 *(978-0-7660-3408-2(9))* Enslow Pubs., Inc.

Isle, Mick. Aristotle: Pioneering Philosopher & Founder of the Lyceum. 2009. (Library of Greek Philosophers Ser.). 112p. (gr. 6-6). 66.50 *(978-1-60853-658-0(0)*, Rosen Reference) Rosen Publishing Group, Inc., The.

Jones, Viola & Hasan, Heather. Archimedes: Innovative Mathematician, Engineer, & Inventor. 2015. (Greatest Greek Philosophers Ser.). (ENG., Illus.). 112p. (J). (gr. 7-8). 35.60 *(978-1-4994-6124-4(0)*, Rosen Young Adult) Rosen Publishing Group, Inc., The.

Keating, Susan. Archimedes: Ancient Greek Mathematician. 2013. (People of Importance Ser.: 21). (Illus.). 32p. (J). (gr. 4-18). 19.95 *(978-1-4222-2841-8(X))* Mason Crest.

Nardo, Don. Alexander the Great: Conqueror of the Known World. 2009. (World Leaders Ser.). (Illus.). 100p. (J). 28.95 *(978-1-59935-126-1(9))* Reynolds, Morgan Inc.

Roscoe, Kelly & Isle, Mick. Aristotle: The Father of Logic. 2015. (Greatest Greek Philosophers Ser.). (ENG.). 112p. (J). (gr. 7-8). 35.60 *(978-1-4994-6126-8(7)*, Rosen Young Adult) Rosen Publishing Group, Inc., The.

Santillian, Beatriz & Aird, Hamish. Pericles: Athenian Statesman & Patron of the Arts. 2017. (Leaders of the Ancient World Ser.). 112p. (J). (gr. 12-11). 37.10 ***(978-1-5081-7487-5(3)***, Rosen Young Adult) Rosen Publishing Group, Inc., The.

Santillian, Beatriz & Randall, Bernard. Solon: Athenian Statesman & Poet. 2017. (Leaders of the Ancient World Ser.). 112p. (J). (gr. 12-11). 37.10 ***(978-1-5081-7493-6(8)***, Rosen Young Adult) Rosen Publishing Group, Inc., The.

Shecter, Vicky Alvear. Alexander the Great Rocks the World. Naughton, Terry, illus. 2006. 128p. (J). (gr. 5-7). lib. bdg. 18.95 *(978-1-58196-045-7(X)*, Darby Creek) Lerner Publishing Group.

Shone, Rob. Alexander the Great: The Life of a King & Conqueror. 2009. (Graphic Nonfiction Biographies Ser.). (ENG.). 48p. (YA). (gr. 4-5). 58.50 *(978-1-61513-012-2(8)*, Rosen Reference) Rosen Publishing Group, Inc., The.

Turner, Tracey. Hard As Nails in Ancient Greece. Lenman, Jamie, illus. 2015. (ENG.). 64p. (J). *(978-0-7787-1512-2(4))* Crabtree Publishing Co.

Waterfield, Robin H., et al. Who Was Alexander the Great? Thomson, Andrew, illus. 2016. (Who Was? Ser.). (ENG.). 112p. (J). (gr. 3-7). lib. bdg. 15.99 *(978-0-399-54235-0(3)*, Grosset & Dunlap) Penguin Young Readers Group.

White, John S. The Boys' & Girls' Plutarch. 2004. reprint ed. pap. 1.99 *(978-1-4192-5511-3(8))*; pap. 28.95 *(978-1-4191-5511-6(3))* Kessinger Publishing, LLC.

Whiting, Jim. The Life & Times of Thucydides. 2008. (Biography from Ancient Civilizations Ser.). (Illus.). 48p. (J). (gr. 4-8). lib. bdg. 29.95 *(978-1-58415-698-7(8))* Mitchell Lane Pubs., Inc.

Wilhelm, Doug. Alexander the Great: Master of the Ancient World. 2009. (Wicked History Ser.). (ENG.). 128p. (J). (gr. 5-9). 31.00 *(978-0-531-21275-2(0))* Scholastic Library Publishing.

GREECE—CIVILIZATION

Adare, Sierra. Greece: The Culture. 3rd rev. ed. 2007. (Lands, Peoples & Cultures Ser.). (ENG., Illus.). 32p. (J). (gr. 3-7). lib. bdg. *(978-0-7787-9310-6(9))* Crabtree Publishing Co.

—Greece - The Culture. 3rd rev. ed. 2007. (Lands, Peoples & Cultures Ser.). (ENG., Illus.). 32p. (J). (gr. 3-7). pap. *(978-0-7787-9678-7(7))* Crabtree Publishing Co.

Ancient Greeks. 2016. (Ladybird Histories Ser.). (ENG., Illus.). 64p. (J). (gr. 2-4). pap. 9.99 *(978-0-7232-9443-6(7))* Penguin Bks., Ltd. GBR. Dist: Independent Pubs. Group.

Anderson, Michael. Ancient Greece. 2011. (J). lib. bdg. 31.70 *(978-1-61530-513-1(0))* Rosen Publishing Group, Inc., The.

Anderson, Zachary. Ancient Greece: From Tyranny to Democracy. 2015. (Exploring the Ancient & Medieval Worlds Ser.). (ENG., Illus.). 160p. (J). (gr. 8-8). 45.64 *(978-1-5026-0570-2(8))* Cavendish Square Publishing.

Apel, Melanie Ann. Art & Religion in Ancient Greece. 2004. (Primary Sources of Ancient Civilizations Ser.). (ENG., Illus.). 24p. (gr. 4-8). pap. 8.25 *(978-0-8239-8938-6(0)*, PowerKids Pr.) Rosen Publishing Group, Inc., The.

—Land & Resources of Ancient Greece. 2004. (Primary Sources of Ancient Civilizations Ser.). (ENG., Illus.). 24p. (gr. 4-8). pap. 8.25 *(978-0-8239-8937-9(2)*, PowerKids Pr.) Rosen Publishing Group, Inc., The.

Bailey, Diane. Ancient Greece, 1 vol. 2014. (Ancient Civilizations Ser.). (ENG., Illus.). 112p. (J). (gr. 6-12). lib. bdg. 35.64 *(978-1-62403-538-8(8)*, Essential Library) ABDO Publishing Co.

Benduhn, Tea. Ancient Greece. 2007. (Life Long Ago Ser.). (Illus.). 24p. (gr. 1-4). pap. 8.15 *(978-0-8368-7787-8(X))*; lib. bdg. 22.00 *(978-0-8368-7782-3(9))* Stevens, Gareth Publishing LLLP. (Weekly Reader Leveled Readers).

Bennett, Doraine. Greece & Our American Heritage. 2009. (J). *(978-1-935077-71-8(6))*; pap. *(978-1-935077-72-5(4))* State Standards Publishing, LLC.

Benoit, Peter. Ancient Greece. 2012. (Ancient World Ser.). (ENG., Illus.). 112p. (J). pap. 9.95 *(978-0-531-25978-8(1))*; lib. bdg. 34.00 *(978-0-531-25178-2(0))* Scholastic Library Publishing.

Bensinger, Henry. Ancient Greek Culture. 2013. (Spotlight on Ancient Civilizations: Greece Ser.). (ENG.). 24p. (J). (gr. 3-4). 23.60 *(978-1-4777-0769-2(7))*; (Illus.). pap. 10.00 *(978-1-4777-0871-2(5))* Rosen Publishing Group, Inc., The. (PowerKids Pr.).

—Ancient Greek Geography. 2013. (Spotlight on Ancient Civilizations: Greece Ser.). (ENG., Illus.). 24p. (J). (gr. 3-4). pap. 10.00 *(978-1-4777-0879-8(0))*; lib. bdg. 23.60 *(978-1-4777-0773-9(5))* Rosen Publishing Group, Inc., The. (PowerKids Pr.).

—Ancient Greek Government. 2013. (Spotlight on Ancient Civilizations: Greece Ser.). (ENG., Illus.). 24p. (J). (gr. 3-4). pap. 10.00 *(978-1-4777-0873-6(1))*; lib. bdg. 23.60 *(978-1-4777-0770-8(0))* Rosen Publishing Group, Inc., The. (PowerKids Pr.).

—Ancient Greek Technology. 2013. (Spotlight on Ancient Civilizations: Greece Ser.). (ENG.). 24p. (J). (gr. 3-4). 23.60 *(978-1-4777-0774-6(3)*, PowerKids Pr.) Rosen Publishing Group, Inc., The.

Bodden, Valerie. Ancient Civilization: Greece. 2015. (Ancient Civilization Ser.). (ENG.). 48p. (J). (gr. 5-8). pap. 12.00 *(978-0-89812-980-9(X)*, Creative Paperbacks) Creative Co., The.

—Greece. 2014. (J). *(978-1-60818-393-7(9)*, Creative Education) Creative Co., The.

Broida, Marian. Projects about Ancient Greece. 2006. (Hands-On History Ser.). (Illus.). 48p. (gr. 3-7). lib. bdg. 21.95 *(978-0-7614-2259-4(5)*, Benchmark Bks.) Marshall Cavendish Corp.

Burrell, Carol M. Scavella. Did Greek Soldiers Really Hide Inside the Trojan Horse? And Other Questions about the Ancient World. 2010. (Is That a Fact? Ser.). (ENG.). 40p. (gr. 4-6). lib. bdg. 26.60 *(978-0-7613-4912-9(X))* Lerner Publishing Group.

Calcium Staff, contrib. by. The Epics of Greek Mythology, 1 vol. 2011. (Ancient Greek Mythology Ser.). (ENG.). 64p. (gr. 5-7). lib. bdg. 33.99 *(978-0-7565-4482-9(3)*, CPB Grades 4-8) Compass Point Bks.

Caper, William. Ancient Greece: An Interactive History Adventure. 2010. (You Choose: Historical Eras Ser.). (ENG.). 112p. (gr. 3-4). pap. 41.70 *(978-1-4296-5100-4(8)*, You Choose Bks.) Capstone Press of Coughlan Cos.

Catel, Patrick. What Did the Ancient Greeks Do for Me?, 1 vol. 2010. (Linking the Past & Present Ser.). (ENG.). 32p. (gr. 3-6). pap. 8.29 *(978-1-4329-3753-9(7)*, Heinemann InfoSearch) Heinemann-Raintree.

Cline, Eric H. & Rubalcaba, Jill. Digging for Troy: From Homer to Hisarlik. Brannen, Sarah S., illus. 2011. (ENG.). 80p. (J). (gr. 4-7). 17.95 *(978-1-58089-326-8(0))*; pap. 9.95 *(978-1-58089-327-5(9))* Charlesbridge Publishing, Inc.

Cohn, Jessica. The Ancient Greeks. 2012. (Crafts from the Past Ser.). (Illus.). 48p. (J). (gr. 4-6). pap. 14.05 *(978-1-4339-7706-0(0))*; lib. bdg. 31.95 *(978-1-4339-7705-3(2))* Stevens, Gareth Publishing LLLP.

Conklin, Wendy. You Are There! Ancient Greece 432 BC. 2016. (TIME for KIDS(r) Nonfiction Readers Ser.). 32p. (J). (gr. 6-6). 8.99 *(978-1-4938-3600-0(5))* Teacher Created Materials, Inc.

Conklin, Wendy. You Are There! Ancient Greece 432 BC. 2016. (Time for Kids Nonfiction Readers Ser.). (ENG.). (J). (gr. 5-8). lib. bdg. 19.65 ***(978-0-606-39536-6(9))*** Turtleback Bks.

Cottrell, George. Ancient Greece. 2017. (Unlocking Ancient Civilizations Ser.). (J). (gr. 4-5). pap. 63.00 ***(978-1-5345-2030-1(9))***; 32p. pap. 10.50 ***(978-1-5345-2029-5(5))***; 32p. lib. bdg. 27.25 ***(978-1-5345-2031-8(7))*** Greenhaven Publishing LLC. (KidHaven Publishing).

Covert, Kim. Ancient Greece: Birthplace of Democracy, 1 vol. 2011. (Great Civilizations Ser.). (ENG.). 32p. (gr. 3-4). pap. 8.10 *(978-1-4296-7237-5(4))*; pap. 47.70 *(978-1-4296-7238-2(2))*; lib. bdg. 27.32 *(978-1-4296-6831-6(8))* Capstone Press of Coughlan Cos. (Fact Finders).

Cricket Books Staff & Cobblestone Publishing Staff. If I Were a Kid in Ancient Greece: Children of the Ancient World. Sheldon, Ken, ed. 2007. (If I Were a Kid In... Ser.). (ENG., Illus.). 32p. (J). (gr. 1-5). 17.95 *(978-0-8126-7929-8(6))* Cricket Bks.

DiPrimio, Pete. Ancient Sparta. 2012. (Explore Ancient Worlds Ser.). (J). (gr. 3-6). lib. bdg. 29.95 *(978-1-61228-276-3(8))* Mitchell Lane Pubs., Inc.

Doeden, Matt. Tools & Treasures of Ancient Greece. 2014. (Searchlight Books: What Can We Learn from Early Civilizations? Ser.). (ENG., Illus.). 40p. (gr. 3-5). lib. bdg. 27.93 *(978-1-4677-1430-3(5)*, Lerner Pubns.) Lerner Publishing Group.

Editors of Kingfisher. Glorious Greeks. 2017. (It's All About... Ser.). (ENG.). 32p. pap. 5.99 *(978-0-7534-7283-5(X)*, 9780753472835, Kingfisher) Roaring Brook Pr.

England, Victoria. Top 10 Worst Things about Ancient Greece. Antram, David, illus. 2012. (Top 10 Worst Ser.). (ENG.). 32p. (J). (gr. 3-6). pap. 10.50 *(978-1-4339-6692-7(1))*; lib. bdg. 26.60 *(978-1-4339-6691-0(3))* Stevens, Gareth Publishing LLLP. (Gareth Stevens Learning Library).

Gogerly, Liz. Greeks. 2009. (Flashback History Ser.). (Illus.). 48p. (J). pap. 11.75 *(978-1-4358-5496-3(9)*, PowerKids Pr.); (YA). (gr. 3-6). 29.25 *(978-1-4358-5495-6(0))* Rosen Publishing Group, Inc., The.

Green, Jen. Hail! Ancient Greeks. 2010. (ENG.). 32p. (J). *(978-0-7787-6623-0(3))*; pap. *(978-0-7787-6630-8(6))* Crabtree Publishing Co.

Greenberg, Imogen. The Ancient Greeks. Greenberg, Isabel, illus. 2017. (Discover... Ser.). (ENG.). 32p. (J). (gr. 3-6). 14.99 ***(978-1-84780-951-3(0)***, Frances Lincoln Children's Bks.) Quarto Publishing Group UK GBR. Dist: Hachette Bk. Group.

Los Griegos: El Nacimiento de la Democracia y de la Cultura Occidental. (Coleccion Bravo). (SPA., Illus.). (YA). (gr. 5-8). pap. 11.16 *(978-84-7131-908-1(X)*, EDI30264) Editex, Editorial S.A. ESP. Dist: Lectorum Pubns., Inc.

Hawes, Alison. Go Greek! (ENG.). 32p. (J). (gr. 3-5). 2011. *(978-0-7787-9894-1(1))* 2010. (Crabtree Connections Ser.: No. 2). pap. *(978-0-7787-9915-3(8))* Crabtree Publishing Co.

Hewitt, Sally. The Greeks. 2007. (Starting History/Watts Ser.). (Illus.). 30p. (J). (gr. 4-7). lib. bdg. 28.50 *(978-1-59920-045-3(7))* Black Rabbit Bks.

History Pockets: Ancient Greece, Grades 4-6. 2003. (History Pockets Ser.). (ENG., Illus.). 96p. (J). (gr. 4-6). pap., suppl. ed. 14.99 *(978-1-55799-903-0(1)*, EMC 3705) Evan-Moor Educational Pubs.

Holm, Kirsten C. Everyday Life in Ancient Greece. 2012. (Jr. Graphic Ancient Civilizations Ser.). (ENG.). 24p. (J). (gr. 3-6). pap. 10.60 *(978-1-4488-6387-7(2))*; lib. bdg. 25.25 *(978-1-4488-6214-6(0))* Rosen Publishing Group, Inc., The. (PowerKids Pr.).

Hull, Robert. Ancient Greece. 2010. (Exploring the Ancient World Ser.). (Illus.). 64p. (YA). (gr. 6-8). lib. bdg. 34.60 *(978-1-4339-4159-7(7)*, Gareth Stevens Secondary Library) Stevens, Gareth Publishing LLLP.

Hunt, Norman Bancroft. Living in Ancient Greece. 2008. (Living in the Ancient World Ser.). 96p. (YA). (gr. 7-12). 35.00 *(978-0-8160-6339-0(7))* Facts On File, Inc.

Hurdman, Charlotte, et al. Find Out about Ancient Egypt, Rome & Greece: Exploring the Great Classical Civilizations, with 60 Step-By-Step Projects & 1500 Exciting Images. 2013. (ENG., Illus.). 256p. (J). (gr. 3-7). 17.99 *(978-1-84322-804-2(1)*, Armadillo) Anness Publishing GBR. Dist: National Bk. Network.

Hynson, Colin. In Ancient Greece. 2006. (Ancient Civilizations Ser.). (Illus.). 48p. (gr. 5-12). lib. bdg. 31.00 *(978-0-8368-6190-7(6)*, Gareth Stevens Secondary Library) Stevens, Gareth Publishing LLLP.

Jovinelly, Joann. The Crafts & Culture of the Ancient Greeks. 2009. (Crafts of the Ancient World Ser.). 48p. (gr. 5-8). 58.50 *(978-1-61512-063-5(7)*, Rosen Reference) Rosen Publishing Group, Inc., The.

Kemp, Ellwood W. Streams of History: Ancient Greece (Yesterday's Classics) 2008. 80p. per. 7.95 *(978-1-59915-255-4(X))* Yesterday's Classics.

Kerns, Ann. Troy. 2008. (Unearthing Ancient Worlds Ser.). (ENG.). 80p. (gr. 5-8). lib. bdg. 30.60 *(978-0-8225-7582-5(5))* Lerner Publishing Group.

Kerrigan, Michael. Greeks. 2010. (Ancients in Their Own Words Ser.). 64p. (gr. 5). 32.79 *(978-1-60870-065-3(8))* Marshall Cavendish GBR. Dist: Marshall Cavendish Corp.

Kovacs, Vic. The Culture of Sparta. 2016. (Ancient Cultures & Civilizations Ser.). 32p. (gr. 5-5). 26.25 *(978-1-4994-2260-3(1)*, PowerKids Pr.) Rosen Publishing Group, Inc., The.

Krieg, Katherine. What We Get from Greek Mythology. 2015. (21st Century Skills Library: Mythology & Culture Ser.). (ENG., Illus.). 32p. (J). (gr. 3-6). 29.93 *(978-1-63188-913-4(3)*, 205976) Cherry Lake Publishing.

Kuhtz, Cleo & Martell, Hazel. Ancient Greek Civilization. D'Ottavi, Francesca, illus. 2009. (Ancient Civilizations & Their Myths & Legends Ser.). (YA). (gr. 5-9). lib. bdg. 29.25 *(978-1-4042-8033-5(2))* Rosen Publishing Group, Inc., The.

Landau, Elaine. Exploring Ancient Greece with Elaine Landau. 2005. (Exploring Ancient Civilizations with Elaine Landau Ser.). (Illus.). 48p. (J). (gr. 4-7). lib. bdg. 25.27 *(978-0-7660-2342-0(7)*, Enslow Elementary) Enslow Pubs., Inc.

Leavitt, Amie Jane. Ancient Athens. 2012. (Explore Ancient Worlds Ser.). 48p. (J). (gr. 3-6). lib. bdg. 29.95 *(978-1-61228-275-6(X))* Mitchell Lane Pubs., Inc.

Levine, Michelle. The Greeks: Life in Ancient Greece. Hiti, Samuel, illus. 2009. (Life in Ancient Civilizations Ser.). (ENG.). 48p. (gr. 3-6). lib. bdg. 29.27 *(978-0-8225-8680-7(0)*, Lerner Pubns.) Lerner Publishing Group.

Macdonald, Fiona. Ancient Greece. 2013. (Illus.). 48p. (J). *(978-1-4351-5082-9(1))* Barnes & Noble, Inc.

MacDonald, Fiona. I Wonder Why Greeks Built Temples: And Other Questions about Ancient Greece. 2012. (I Wonder Why Ser.). (ENG., Illus.). 32p. (J). (gr. k-3). pap. 6.99 *(978-0-7534-6705-3(4)*, 9780753467053, Kingfisher) Roaring Brook Pr.

Malam, John. Ancient Greece. 2004. (Picturing the Past Ser.). (Illus.). 32p. (J). 15.95 *(978-1-59270-022-6(5))* Enchanted Lion Bks., LLC.

—Ancient Greece Inside Out. 2017. (Ancient Worlds Inside Out Ser.). (ENG.). 32p. (J). ***(978-0-7787-2876-4(5))***; (Illus.). pap. ***(978-0-7787-2890-0(0))*** Crabtree Publishing Co.

—The Greeks. 2011. (Dig It: History from Objects Ser.). (Illus.). 32p. (YA). (gr. 2-5). lib. bdg. 26.50 *(978-1-4488-3284-2(5))* Rosen Publishing Group, Inc., The.

—How the Ancient Greeks Lived. 2010. (Life in Ancient Times Ser.). (ENG.). 32p. (J). (gr. 3-6). lib. bdg. 26.60 *(978-1-4339-4091-0(4)*, Gareth Stevens Learning Library) Stevens, Gareth Publishing LLLP.

Marcovitz, Hal. Ancient Greece. 2012. (Illus.). 96p. (YA). lib. bdg. *(978-1-60152-284-9(3))* ReferencePoint Pr., Inc.

Maynard, Charles W. The Technology of Ancient Greece. (Technology of the Ancient World Ser.). 48p. 2009. (gr. 6-6). 61.20 *(978-1-60854-240-6(8)*, Rosen Reference) 2005. (Illus.). (J). (gr. 5-8). lib. bdg. 29.25 *(978-1-4042-0555-0(1))* Rosen Publishing Group, Inc., The.

Meyer, Susan. The Totally Gross History of Ancient Greece, 01 vols., 1. 2016. (Totally Gross History Ser.). (ENG.). 48p. (J). pap. 11.75 *(978-1-4994-3748-5(X)*, Rosen Central) Rosen Publishing Group, Inc., The.

Miles, Liz. Meet the Ancient Greeks. 2014. (Encounters with the Past Ser.). 32p. (J). (gr. 3-6). 26.60 *(978-1-4824-0882-9(1))* Stevens, Gareth Publishing LLLP.

Morris, Ting. Arts & Crafts of Ancient Greece. Young, Emma, illus. 2006. (Arts & Crafts of Ser.). 32p. (J). lib. bdg. 28.50 *(978-1-58340-912-1(2)*, 1262692) Black Rabbit Bks.

Naden, Corinne J. & Blue, Rose. Ancient Greeks & the Parthenon. 2003. (J). *(978-1-58417-314-4(9))*; pap. *(978-1-58417-315-1(7))* Lake Street Pubs.

Nardo, Don. Ancient Greece, 1 vol. 2012. (Exploring the Ancient World Ser.). (ENG., Illus.). 48p. (gr. 5-6). pap. 9.10 *(978-0-7565-4582-6(X))* Compass Point Bks.

—Cause & Effect: Ancient Greece. 2017. (ENG.). 80p. (J). (gr. 5-12). 39.93 ***(978-1-68282-152-7(8))*** ReferencePoint Pr., Inc.

Nardo, Don. Life in Ancient Greece. 2015. (ENG., Illus.). 96p. (YA). lib. bdg. *(978-1-60152-804-9(3))* ReferencePoint Pr., Inc.

Newman, Sandra. Ancient Greece. (True Book Ser.). (ENG., 48p. (J). 2010. Illus.). pap. 6.95 *(978-0-531-24107-3(6))* 2009. (gr. 2-5). 29.00 *(978-0-531-25226-0(4))* Scholastic Library Publishing.

O'Connell, Kim A. Ancient Greece: A MyReportLinks. com Book. 2004. (Civilizations of the Ancient World Ser.). (Illus.). 48p. (J). lib. bdg. 25.26 *(978-0-7660-5250-5(8)*, MyReportLinks.com Bks.) Enslow Pubs., Inc.

—Discover Ancient Greece. 2014. (Discover Ancient Civilizations Ser.). 104p. (J). pap. 10.95 *(978-1-4644-0335-4(X))*; (Illus.). (gr. 5-18). 33.27 *(978-0-7660-4196-7(4))* Enslow Pubs., Inc.

The Origins of Greek Civilization (NCHS) (J). spiral bd., tchr.'s planning gde. ed. 13.50 *(978-0-382-40948-6(5))* Cobblestone Publishing Co.

Park, Louise. Ancient Greece. 2013. (Discovery Education: Ancient Civilizations Ser.). (ENG., Illus.). 32p. (J). (gr. 3-6). pap. 10.00 *(978-1-4777-0083-9(8))*; lib. bdg. 25.25 *(978-1-4777-0049-5(8))* Rosen Publishing Group, Inc., The. (PowerKids Pr.).

Pearson, Anne. DK Eyewitness Books: Ancient Greece: Ancient Greece. 2014. (DK Eyewitness Bks.). (ENG.). 72p. (J). (gr. 3-7). pap. 9.99 *(978-1-4654-2049-7(5)*, DK Children) Dorling Kindersley Publishing, Inc.

Peppas, Lynn. Life in Ancient Greece. 2004. (Peoples of the Ancient World Ser.). (ENG., Illus.). 32p. (J). pap. *(978-0-7787-2065-2(9))* Crabtree Publishing Co.

Phipps, Liza & Thompson, Avril. History Showtime: Ancient Greeks. 2016. (History Showtime Ser.). (ENG., Illus.). 32p. (J). (gr. 2-4). pap. 11.99 *(978-1-4451-1489-7(5)*, Franklin Watts) Hachette Children's Group GBR. Dist: Hachette Bk. Group.

Platt, Richard. The Greeks. Lawrence, David, illus. 2011. (How They Made Things Work! Ser.). 32p. (J). (gr. 2-5). lib. bdg. 28.50 *(978-1-59771-288-0(4))* Sea-To-Sea Pubns.

Powell, Jillian. The Greeks. 2010. (Gruesome Truth about Ser.). (ENG.). 32p. (J). (gr. 4-6). lib. bdg. 22.60 *(978-1-61533-218-2(9))* Windmill Bks.

Randolph, Joanne, ed. Living & Working in Ancient Greece. 2017. (Back in Time Ser.). 48p. (gr. 5-6). pap. 11.70 ***(978-0-7660-8969-3(X))*** Enslow Pubs., Inc.

Reece, Katherine E. The Greeks: Leaders in Democracy. 2005. (Ancient Civilizations Ser.). (Illus.). 48p. (J). (gr. 4-8). lib. bdg. *(978-1-59515-506-1(6)*, 1244351) Rourke Educational Media.

Ridley, Sarah. Life in Ancient Greece. 2015. (Everyday History Ser.). (Illus.). 32p. (J). 31.35 *(978-1-59920-950-0(0))* Black Rabbit Bks.

Riggs, Sandy. Three Ancient Communities: Text Pairs. 2008. (Bridges/Navigators Ser.). (J). (gr. 3). 89.00 *(978-1-4108-8374-2(4))* Benchmark Education Co.

Roberts, Russell. Ancient Greece. 2009. (How'd They Do That? Ser.). (Illus.). 64p. (J). (gr. 4-8). lib. bdg. 33.95 *(978-1-58415-819-6(0))* Mitchell Lane Pubs., Inc.

Robinson, Tony. Romans & Greeks. 2016. (Weird World of Wonders Ser.). (ENG., Illus.). 320p. (J). (gr. 4-6). pap. 12.99 *(978-1-5098-0539-6(7))* Pan Macmillan GBR. Dist: Independent Pubs. Group.

Ross, Stewart. Rich & Poor in Ancient Greece. 2005. (Rich & Poor in Ser.). (Illus.). 32p. (YA). (gr. 4-7). lib. bdg. 27.10 *(978-1-58340-721-9(9))* Black Rabbit Bks.

Royston, Angela. Ancient Greek Adventure. 2010. (ENG., Illus.). 32p. (J). (gr. 3-5). *(978-0-7787-9900-9(X))*; pap. *(978-0-7787-9921-4(2))* Crabtree Publishing Co.

Rustad, Martha E. H. Great Leaders & Thinkers of Ancient Greece, 1 vol. 2014. (Ancient Greece Ser.). (ENG.). 24p. (gr. 1-2). 25.32 *(978-1-4914-0275-7(X))* Capstone Press of Coughlan Cos.

Samuels, Charlie. Technology in Ancient Greece. 2013. (Technology in the Ancient World Ser.). 48p. (J). (gr. 4-6). pap. 84.30 *(978-1-4339-9634-4(0))*; pap. 14.05

(978-1-4339-9633-7(2)); (ENG., Illus.). lib. bdg. 31.95 (978-1-4339-9632-0(4)) Stevens, Gareth Publishing LLLP.
Schlitz, Laura Amy. The Hero Schliemann: The Dreamer Who Dug up Troy. Byrd, Robert, illus. 2006. (ENG.). 80p. (J). (gr. 4-7). lib. bdg. 17.99 (978-0-7636-2283-1(4)) Candlewick Pr.
Shoup, Kate. The Technology of Ancient Greece. 2016. (Ancient Innovations Ser.). 64p. (J). 34.21 (978-1-5026-2231-0(9)) Cavendish Square Publishing.
Snedden, Robert. Ancient Greece. 2009. (Technology in Times Past Ser.). 32.80 (978-1-59920-296-9(4)) Black Rabbit Bks.
Spotlight on Ancient Civilizations: Greece. 2013. (Spotlight on Ancient Civilizations: Greece Ser.). 24p. (J). (gr. 3-4). (ENG.). 141.60 (978-1-4777-1143-9(0)); (ENG.). pap. 60.00 (978-1-4777-2687-7(X)); pap. 297.00 (978-1-4777-2688-4(8)) Rosen Publishing Group, Inc., The. (PowerKids Pr.).
Stafford, Emma. Exploring the Life, Myth, & Art of Ancient Greece. 2011. (Civilizations of the World Ser.). (YA). (gr. 7-12). lib. bdg. 42.60 (978-1-4488-4830-0(X)) Rosen Publishing Group, Inc., The.
Steele, Philip & Powell, Anton. History News: the Greek News. 2009. (History News Ser.). (ENG., Illus.). 32p. (J). (gr. 4-7). pap. 7.99 (978-0-7636-4197-9(9)) Candlewick Pr.
Tames, Richard. Ancient Greece. 2009. (Passport to the Past Ser.). (Illus.). 61p. (J). (gr. 4-7). lib. bdg. 31.95 (978-1-4358-5175-7(7)) Rosen Publishing Group, Inc., The.
—Hands-On History! Ancient Greece: Step into the World of the Classical Greeks, with 15 Step-by-Step Projects & 350 Exciting Pictures. 2013. (ENG., Illus.). 64p. 12.99 (978-1-84322-964-3(1)) Anness Publishing GBR. Dist: National Bk. Network.
—Step Into: Ancient Greece. 2008. (ENG., Illus.). 64p. (J). (gr. 4-7). pap. 12.99 (978-1-84476-510-2(5)) Anness Publishing GBR. Dist: National Bk. Network.
Tracy, Kathleen. The Life & Times of Homer. 2004. (Biography from Ancient Civilizations Ser.). (Illus.). 48p. (J). (gr. 4-8). lib. bdg. 29.95 (978-1-58415-260-6(5)) Mitchell Lane Pubs., Inc.
Tsakiridis, Dimitra. Art & Culture of Ancient Greece. 2010. (Ancient Art & Cultures Ser.). 40p. (YA). (gr. 5-8). lib. bdg., E-Book 53.00 (978-1-61532-964-9(1)) Rosen Publishing Group, Inc., The.
Tsakiridis, Dimitra & Bardi, Matilde. Art & Culture of Ancient Greece. 2010. (Ancient Art & Cultures Ser.). (Illus.). 40p. (J). pap. 11.75 (978-1-61532-883-3(1)); (YA). (gr. 5-8). lib. bdg. 26.50 (978-1-4358-3590-0(5)) Rosen Publishing Group, Inc., The. (Rosen Reference).
Van Vleet, Carmella. Explore Ancient Greece! 25 Great Projects, Activities, Experiments. Shedd, Blair & Kim, Alex, illus. 2008. (Explore Your World Ser.). (ENG.). 96p. (J). (gr. k-4). pap. 12.95 (978-1-934670-11-8(1)) Octavio Publishing.
Villing, Alexandra. The Ancient Greeks: Their Lives & Their World. 2010. (ENG., Illus.). 80p. (gr. 7-18). 17.95 (978-0-89236-985-0(X)) Oxford Univ. Pr., Inc.
Waldron, Melanie. Geography Matters in Ancient Greece. 2015. (Geography Matters in Ancient Civilizations Ser.). (ENG., Illus.). 48p. (gr. 3-6). 33.32 (978-1-4846-0963-7(8), Heinemann InfoSearch) Heinemann-Raintree.
West, David. The Ancient Greeks. 2016. (Discovering Ancient Civilizations Ser.). 32p. (gr. 3-3). pap. 10.50 (978-1-4824-5063-7(1)) Stevens, Gareth Publishing LLLP.
Wheatley, A. Greeks. rev. ed. 2004. (Illustrated World History Ser.). (Illus.). 96p. (J). pap. 12.99 (978-0-7945-0428-1(0)) EDC Publishing.
Williams, Jean Kinney. Empire of Ancient Greece, Revised Edition. 2nd rev. ed. 2009. (Great Empires of the Past Ser.). (Illus.). 160p. (gr. 6-12). 35.00 (978-1-60413-165-9(9), Chelsea Hse.) Facts On File, Inc.
Wood, Alix. Uncovering the Culture of Ancient Greece, 01 vols., 1. 2016. (Archaeology & Ancient Cultures Ser.). (ENG.). 32p. (J). pap. 10.00 (978-1-5081-4655-1(1), PowerKids Pr.) Rosen Publishing Group, Inc., The.
World Book, Inc Staff, contrib. by. Ancient Greeks. 2009. (J). (978-0-7166-2130-0(4)) World Bk., Inc.
Yasuda, Anita. Exploring Ancient Greece. 2018. (ENG.). 32p. (gr. 3-6). **(978-1-63235-463-1(2)**, 12-Story Library) Pr. Room Editions LLC.
Yasuda, Anita. Greeks. 2016. (Illus.). 32p. (J). (978-1-5105-1100-2(8)) SmartBook Media, Inc.
You Choose: Historical Eras [Capstone Sole Source]. 2010. (You Choose: Historical Eras Ser.). 112p. 122.60 (978-1-4296-5893-5(2), You Choose Bks.) Capstone Press of Coughlan Cos.
You Choose: Historical Eras Set. 2010. (You Choose: Historical Eras Ser.). (ENG.). 112p. (gr. 3-4). pap. 166.80 (978-1-4296-5120-2(2), You Choose Bks.) Capstone Press of Coughlan Cos.
Zannos, Susan. The Life & Times of Archimedes. 2004. (Biography from Ancient Civilizations Ser.). (Illus.). 48p. (J). (gr. 4-8). lib. bdg. 29.95 (978-1-58415-242-2(7)) Mitchell Lane Pubs., Inc.

GREECE—FICTION

Berry, Erick. The Winged Girl of Knossos. 2017. (ENG., Illus.). 220p. (J). (gr. 3-7). pap. 11.95 (978-1-58988-120-4(6)) Dry, Paul Bks., Inc.
Block, Francesca Lia. Psyche in a Dress. 2008. (ENG.). 128p. (YA). (gr. 9). pap. 8.99 (978-0-06-076376-3(0), HarperTeen) HarperCollins Pubs.
Blyton, Enid. The Ship of Adventure. Cobb, Rebecca, illus. unabr. ed. 2014. (Adventure Ser.: 6). (ENG.). 288p. (J). (gr. 4-7). pap. 9.99 (978-1-4472-6280-0(8)) Pan Macmillan GBR. Dist: Independent Pubs. Group.
Bowman, Patrick. Arrow Through the Axes. 2014. (ENG.). 200p. pap. 11.95 (978-1-55380-323-2(X)) Ronsdale Pr. CAN. Dist: SPD-Small Pr. Distribution.
Brown, Elizabeth. Aristotle: the Firefly's Message. Schuna, Ramona, illus. 2007. (ENG.). 40p. per. 19.95 (978-1-59800-557-8(X)) Outskirts Pr., Inc.
Carter, Caela. My Best Friend, Maybe. 2014. (ENG.). 352p. (YA). (gr. 9). 17.99 (978-1-59990-970-7(7), 9781599909707, Bloomsbury USA Childrens) Bloomsbury Publishing USA.
Childs, Tera Lynn. Goddess Boot Camp. 2010. (ENG.). 272p. (YA). (gr. 7-18). pap. 7.99 (978-0-14-241665-5(7), Speak) Penguin Young Readers Group.
Childs, Tera Lynn & Childs, Tera. Oh. My. Gods. 2009. (ENG.). 288p. (YA). (gr. 7-18). 7.99 (978-0-14-241420-0(4), Speak) Penguin Young Readers Group.
Church, Alfred J. Three Greek Children. 2008. (Illus.). 160p. pap. 9.95 (978-1-59915-081-9(6)) Yesterday's Classics.
Church, Anna. Hug-A-Bug Travels to Greece. Taylor, Nicole, illus. 2012. 44p. pap. 12.00 (978-0-9831449-5-3(8)) Mighty Lion Ventures.
Citra, Becky. Jeremy & the Enchanted Theater, 1 vol. Milne, Jessica, illus. 2004. (Orca Echoes Ser.). (ENG.). 64p. (J). (gr. 2-3). pap. 6.95 (978-1-55143-322-6(2)) Orca Bk. Pubs. USA.
—Jeremy & the Fantastic Flying Machine, 1 vol. Milne, Jessica, illus. 2008. (Orca Echoes Ser.). (ENG.). 64p. (J). (gr. 2-3). pap. 6.95 (978-1-55143-950-1(6)) Orca Bk. Pubs. USA.
Coats, Lucy. Atticus the Storyteller's 100 Greek Myths. Lewis, Anthony, tr. Lewis, Anthony, illus. 2003. (ENG.). 264p. (gr. 2-4). pap. 17.99 (978-1-84255-279-7(1), Orion Children's Bks.) Hachette Children's Group GBR. Dist: Hachette Bk. Group.
Colloredo, Sabino. Zeus. Ferrari, Antongionata, illus. 2009. (Hotel Olympus Ser.). 128p. (J). (gr. 3-6). 31.95 (978-1-60754-707-5(4)) Windmill Bks.
Colum, Padraic & Pogány, Willy. The Adventures of Odysseus & the Tale of Troy. 2008. 280p. per. 27.95 (978-0-548-81877-0(0)) Kessinger Publishing, LLC.
Cook, Jennifer. Ariadne: The Maiden & the Minotaur. 2005. 206p. (Orig.). (J). (gr. -1-7). per. (978-0-7344-0637-8(1), Lothian Children's Bks.) Hachette Australia.
Couloumbis, Audrey & Couloumbis, Akila. War Games. 2011. (ENG.). 240p. (J). (gr. 3-7). pap. 6.99 (978-0-375-85629-7(3), Yearling) Random Hse. Children's Bks.
Coville, Bruce. William Shakespeare's a Midsummer Night's Dream. Nolan, Dennis, illus. 2003. (ENG.). 48p. (J). (gr. k-3). pap. 7.99 (978-0-14-250168-9(9), Puffin Books) Penguin Young Readers Group.
Cross, Gillian. The Odyssey. Packer, Neil, illus. 2012. (ENG.). 178p. (J). (gr. 3-7). 19.99 (978-0-7636-4791-9(8)) Candlewick Pr.
Dashner, James. The Iron Empire. 2014. (Infinity Ring Ser.: 7). (ENG., Illus.). 192p. (J). (gr. 3-7). 12.99 (978-0-545-38702-6(7)) Scholastic, Inc.
—The Iron Empire (Infinity Ring, Book 7) 2016. (Infinity Ring Ser.: 7). (ENG.). 192p. (J). (gr. 3-7). pap. 6.99 (978-0-545-90124-6(3), Scholastic Pr.) Scholastic, Inc.
Deary, Terry. The Fire Thief. 2005. (Fire Thief Trilogy: Bk. 1). 253p. (J). (978-1-4156-3464-6(5), Kingfisher) Roaring Brook Pr.
DeHoratius, Ed. The Journey of Odysseus. Delandro Hardison, Brian, illus. 2009. (Follow Your Fates Ser.). 116p. (J). pap. 12.00 (978-0-86516-710-0(9)) Bolchazy-Carducci Pubs.
—Wrath of Achilles. 2009. 62p. pap. 12.00 (978-0-86516-708-7(7)) Bolchazy-Carducci Pubs.
Delaney, Joseph. Clash of the Demons. Arrasmith, Patrick, illus. (Last Apprentice Ser.: 6). (YA). (gr. 8). 2009. 416p. lib. bdg. 18.89 (978-0-06-134463-3(X)) 2009. (ENG.). 416p. 17.99 (978-0-06-134462-6(1))Bk. 6. 2010. (ENG.). 432p. pap. 9.99 (978-0-06-134464-0(8)) HarperCollins Pubs. (Greenwillow Bks.).
Dogiakis, Helen. Captain Terry the Pirate Cow's Adventure to Greece. 2012. 24p. pap. 17.99 (978-1-4685-9403-4(6)) AuthorHouse.
Dostis, Isaac & Haddad Ikonomopoulos, Marcia. Ten Gold Medals: Glory or Freedom. 2005. (Illus.). ii, 72p. (J). (978-0-8197-0770-3(8)) Bloch Publishing Co.
Eboch, M. M. Monster Island. 2015. (ENG.). 96p. (gr. 3-6). 31.36 (978-1-63430-394-1(6)) Rourke Educational Media.
Foster, Hal & Murphy, John Cullen. Queen of the Amazons, Vol. 47. 2003. (Prince Valiant Ser.: Vol. 47). (ENG., Illus.). 48p. pap. 16.95 (978-1-56097-527-4(X)) Fantagraphics Bks.
Gabrielson, Ernest & Gabrielson, Brian. Home in Ithaca: A novel of Ancient Greece & Troy. 2004. 120p. (YA). pap. 10.95 (978-0-595-30889-7(9)) iUniverse, Inc.
Galloway, Priscilla. Aleta y la Reina: Una Historia de la Antigua Grecia.Tr. of Aleta & the Queen: A Tale of Ancient Greece. (SPA.). (YA). (gr. 5-8). pap. (978-968-6582-27-7(4)) Samara, Ediciones, S. A. de C. V.
Geras, Adèle. Ithaka. 2007. (ENG., Illus.). 368p. (YA). (gr. 9-12). pap. 8.99 (978-0-15-206104-3(5)) Houghton Mifflin Harcourt Publishing Co.
Green, John. Sparta! Warriors of the Ancient World. 2013. (Dover History Coloring Book Ser.). (ENG.). 32p. (gr. 3-12). pap. 3.99 (978-0-486-49813-3(1)) Dover Pubns., Inc.
Helfand, Lewis. 400 BC: The Story of the Ten Thousand. Singh, Lalit Kumar, illus. 2011. (Campfire Graphic Novels Ser.). (ENG.). 72p. (YA). (gr. 5-12). pap. 9.99 (978-93-80028-61-3(X), Campfire) Steerforth Pr.
Hemyng, Bracebridge. Jack Harkaway & His Son's Escape from the Brigand's of Greece. 2007. (ENG.). 342p. pap. 23.99 (978-1-4264-2290-4(3)); 386p. pap. 26.99 (978-1-4264-2325-3(X)) Creative Media Partners, LLC.
—Jack Harkaway & His Son's Escape from the Brigands of Greece. 2004. reprint ed. pap. 1.99 (978-1-4192-2705-9(X)); pap. 37.95 (978-1-4191-2705-2(5)) Kessinger Publishing, LLC.
Hennesy, Carolyn. Pandora Gets Greedy. (Mythic Misadventures Ser.). (ENG., (YA). (gr. 3-6). 2013. Illus.). 320p. pap. 7.99 (978-1-61963-010-9(9), 9781619630109) 2012. 304p. 15.99 (978-1-59990-441-2(1), 9781599904412) Bloomsbury Publishing USA. (Bloomsbury USA Childrens).
—Pandora Gets Jealous. 2009. (Mythic Misadventures Ser.). (ENG., Illus.). 288p. (YA). (gr. 3-6). pap. 7.99 (978-1-59990-291-3(5), 9781599902913, Bloomsbury USA Childrens) Bloomsbury Publishing USA.
—Pandora Gets Lazy. 2010. (Mythic Misadventures Ser.). (ENG.). 304p. (YA). (gr. 3-6). pap. 7.99 (978-1-59990-481-8(0), 9781599904818, Bloomsbury USA Childrens) Bloomsbury Publishing USA.
—Pandora Gets Vain. 2008. (Mythic Misadventures Ser.). (ENG., Illus.). 288p. (YA). (gr. 3-6). 14.99 (978-1-59990-197-8(8), 9781599901978, Bloomsbury USA Childrens) Bloomsbury Publishing USA.
Holub, Joan & Williams, Suzanne. Pheme the Gossip. 2013. (Goddess Girls Ser.: 10). lib. bdg. 18.40 (978-0-606-27040-3(X), Turtleback) Turtleback Bks.
Hulme-Cross, Benjamin. The Spartan's March. 2016. (Warrior Heroes Ser.). (ENG., Illus.). 176p. (J). (gr. 6-9). (978-0-7787-2865-8(X)) Crabtree Publishing Co.
Ioannides, Mara W. Cohen. A Shout in the Sunshine. 2007. (ENG.). 120p. (gr. 5). per. 14.95 (978-0-8276-0838-2(1)) Jewish Pubn. Society.
Johnson, Vargie. Alexander the Great the All-Powerful: What Made Them Famous? 2006. 156p. (J). per. 15.00 (978-1-931195-93-5(5)) KiwE Publishing, Ltd.
Jones, Allan Frewin. Blood Stone, Vol. 6. 6th ed. 2003. (ENG.). 176p. (J). mass mkt. (978-0-330-37476-7(1), Pan) Pan Macmillan.
Jones, Vernon. Aesop's Fables. Rackham, Arthur, illus. 2007. 160p. (J). pap. 5.00 (978-0-9788914-4-2(9)) Kahley, Glenn.
Lang, Andrew, ed. The Lilac Fairy Book. 2011. 238p. 26.95 (978-1-4638-9786-4(3)); pap. 16.95 (978-1-4638-0112-0(2)) Rodgers, Alan Bks.
Lawrence, Caroline. The Fugitive from Corinth. 2006. (ENG., Illus.). 240p. (gr. 7-9). pap. 10.99 (978-1-84255-515-6(4), Orion Children's Bks.) Hachette Children's Group GBR. Dist: Hachette Bk. Group.
Lindsay, Maud. Mother Stories. Ives, Sarah Noble, illus. 2008. 160p. pap. 9.95 (978-1-59915-167-0(7)) Yesterday's Classics.
Maroudas, N. G. The Adventures of Athena & Odysseus. 2011. (ENG.). 276p. pap. (978-1-84876-593-1(2)) Troubador Publishing Ltd.
Marsh, Carole. The Curse of the Ancient Acropolis: Athens, Greece. 2008. (Carole Marsh Mysteries Ser.). 133p. (J). (gr. 3-5). per. 7.99 (978-0-635-06470-7(7), Marsh, Carole Bks.) Gallopade International.
Mcfaul, Jason & Macdonald, Eric. What A Trip. 2007. pap. 77.53 (978-0-7575-4014-1(7)) Kendall Hunt Publishing Co.
McLaren, Clemence. Aphrodite's Blessing. 2008. (ENG.). 208p. (YA). (gr. 7). pap. 10.99 (978-1-4169-7860-2(7), Simon Pulse) Simon Pulse.
—Waiting for Odysseus. 2004. (ENG., Illus.). 160p. (YA). (gr. 7). mass mkt. 6.99 (978-0-689-86705-7(0), Simon Pulse) Simon Pulse.
McLeese, Don. Spartans. 2009. (ENG., Illus.). 32p. (gr. 4-8). pap. 9.95 (978-1-60694-545-2(9)) Rourke Educational Media.
Mihalko, Ross, et al. Ant & the Grasshopper (Musical) 2012. (J). 8.95 (978-0-573-70112-2(1)) French, Samuel Inc.
Mills, Samuel. The Fire Bringer. 2009. 128p. (J). pap. 15.00 (978-0-88010-700-6(6)) SteinerBooks, Inc.
Mogford, Thomas. Sleeping Dogs: A Spike Sanguinetti Novel. 2015. (Spike Sanguinetti Novel Ser.). (ENG.). 256p. 26.00 (978-1-63286-088-0(0), 9781632860880) Bloomsbury Publishing USA.
Nick Barry. Revenge of Poseidon's Trident: An Ethan Sparks Adventure. 2010. 176p. 23.95 (978-1-4502-1090-4(2)); pap. 13.95 (978-1-4502-1088-1(0)) iUniverse, Inc.
Noël, Alyson. Forever Summer. 2011. (ENG.). 464p. (YA). (gr. 8-12). pap. 9.99 (978-0-312-60439-4(4), 9780312604394, St. Martin's Griffin) St. Martin's Pr.
O'Hearn, Kate. The End of Olympus. 2016. (Pegasus Ser.: 6). (ENG., Illus.). 432p. (J). (gr. 3-7). 17.99 (978-1-4814-4717-1(3), Simon & Schuster/Paula Wiseman Bks.) Simon & Schuster/Paula Wiseman Bks.
—Olympus at War. 2013. (Pegasus Ser.: 2). (ENG.). 400p. (J). (gr. 3-7). 16.99 (978-1-4424-4412-6(6), Simon & Schuster/Paula Wiseman Bks.) Simon & Schuster/Paula Wiseman Bks.
Olesen, Demetria Vassiliou. Lambyro. Forcada, Adiela & Giron, Elizabeth, illus. 2011. (ENG.). 32p. (J). 19.00 (978-0-615-47664-3(3)) Elissian Publishing Co.
O'Malley, Kevin. Mount Olympus Basketball. 2004. (Illus.). 32p. (J). (gr. 2-6). 16.85 (978-0-8027-8845-0(9)) Walker & Co.
Osborne, Mary Pope. Hour of the Olympics. unabr. ed. 2004. (Magic Tree House Ser.: No. 16). 70p. (J). (gr. k-3). pap. 17.00 incl. audio (978-0-8072-0785-7(3), LFTR 244 SP, Listening Library) Random Hse. Audio Publishing Group.
Plante, Raymond. Le Monde de Xéros. Delezenne, Christine, illus. 2004. (Roman Jeunesse Ser.). (FRE.). 96p. (J). (gr. 4-7). pap. (978-2-89021-615-0(2)) Diffusion du livre Mirabel (DLM).
Plato's Journey: Evaluation Guide. 2006. (J). (978-1-55942-421-9(4)) Witcher Productions.
Platt, Richard. Roman Diary: The Journal of Iliona, a Young Slave. Parkins, David, illus. 2014. (ENG.). 128p. (J). (gr. 4-7). pap. 6.99 (978-0-7636-7053-5(7)) Candlewick Pr.
Price, Jennifer L. Half Moon: Phases of the Moon: Book 2, 1 vol. 2009. 252p. pap. 27.95 (978-1-4489-2193-5(7)) PublishAmerica, Inc.
Reece, P. J. Roxy, 1 vol. 2010. (ENG., Illus.). 192p. (YA). (gr. 9-12). pap. 12.95 (978-1-896580-01-2(7)) Tradewind Bks. CAN. Dist: Orca Bk. Pubs. USA.
Richards, Jean. The First Olympic Games: A Gruesome Greek Myth with a Happy Ending. Thacker, Kat, illus. 2004. 32p. pap. 10.95 (978-0-7613-2443-0(7), Millbrook Pr.) Lerner Publishing Group.
Russon, Penni. Breathe. 2007. (ENG., Illus.). 368p. (YA). (gr. 9-18). 16.99 (978-0-06-079393-7(7)) HarperCollins Pubs.
Sanderson, Jeannette. The Odyssey: A Greek Myth. 2006. (J). pap. (978-1-4108-6177-1(5)) Benchmark Education Co.
Scieszka, Jon. It's All Greek to Me. Smith, Lane, illus. 2006. (Time Warp Trio Ser.: No. 8). 71p. (gr. 4-7). 15.00 (978-0-7569-6780-2(5)) Perfection Learning Corp.
Scott, Kieran. Only Everything. 2014. (True Love Ser.: 1). (ENG., Illus.). 352p. (YA). (gr. 7). pap. 9.99 (978-1-4424-7716-2(4), Simon & Schuster Bks. For Young Readers) Simon & Schuster Bks. For Young Readers.
Shanower, Eric. Betrayal, Pt. 1, Vol. 3. 2007. (ENG., Illus.). 176p. (YA). (gr. 10-18). 27.99 (978-1-58240-845-3(9), 9781582408453) Image Comics.
Simon, Francesca. Helping Hercules. Ross, Tony, illus. 2013. (ENG.). 128p. (J). (gr. 3-6). pap. 7.99 (978-1-84255-153-0(1), Orion Children's Bks.) Hachette Children's Group GBR. Dist: Hachette Bk. Group.
Spinner, Stephanie. Quicksilver. 2006. (ENG.). 240p. (YA). (gr. 7-11). per. 6.99 (978-0-440-23845-4(5), Laurel Leaf) Random Hse. Children's Bks.
Spyri, Johanna. Erick & Sally. 2006. pap. (978-1-4068-0692-2(7)) Echo Library.
Stevenson, William. Ricky's Dream Trip to Ancient Greece. 2012. 36p. pap. 14.00 (978-1-936517-77-0(9)) Micro Publishing Media, Inc.
Tak, Bibi Dumon. Mikis & the Donkey. Hopman, Philip, illus. 2014. (ENG.). 89p. (J). 13.00 (978-0-8028-5430-8(3), Eerdmans Bks For Young Readers) Eerdmans, William B. Publishing Co.
Torbert, Wayne E. Twelve for Thebes, a Tale of Ancient Greece. Torbert, Wayne E., illus. 2009. (Illus.). 82p. pap. 8.95 (978-1-936051-73-1(7)) Peppertree Pr., The.
Trest, Candace D. Zack & Tripp & the Indian Village. 2007. 64p. per. 9.99 (978-1-60477-526-6(2)) Salem Author Services.
Warner, Rex. Men & Gods: Myths & Legends of the Ancient Greeks. Gorey, Edward, illus. 2008. (New York Review Books Classics). (ENG.). 288p. 17.95 (978-1-59017-263-6(9), NYRB Classics) New York Review of Bks., Inc., The.
Whitman, Emily. Radiant Darkness. 2009. 288p. (YA). (gr. 9-18). lib. bdg. 17.89 (978-0-06-178035-6(9)); (ENG.). 16.99 (978-0-06-172499-7(1)) HarperCollins Pubs. (Greenwillow Bks.).
Wilding, Val. Dodging the Donkey Doo. Broad, Michael, illus. 2008. (Toby Tucker Ser.). (ENG.). 144p. (J). (gr. 2-4). pap. 7.95 (978-1-4052-2547-2(5)) Egmont Bks., Ltd. GBR. Dist: Independent Pubs. Group.
Yomtov, Nel, et al. Jason & the Golden Fleece, 1 vol. Sandoval, Gerardo, illus. 2009. (Mythology Ser.). (ENG.). 72p. (gr. 2-3). pap. 7.15 (978-1-4342-1385-3(4)); lib. bdg. 27.99 (978-1-4342-1172-9(X)) Stone Arch Bks. (Graphic Revolve).
—Theseus & the Minotaur, 1 vol. Smith, Tod G., illus. (Mythology Ser.). (ENG.). 72p. (gr. 2-3). 2010. pap. 7.15 (978-1-4342-1387-7(0)) 2009. lib. bdg. 27.99 (978-1-4342-1171-2(1)) Stone Arch Bks. (Graphic Revolve).

GREECE—HISTORY

Abbott, Jacob. Alexander the Great. 2009. 212p. pap. 10.95 (978-1-59915-132-8(4)) Yesterday's Classics.
Ackroyd, Peter. Ancient Greece. 2006. (Voyages through Time Ser.). 144p. (J). pap. 9.99 (978-0-7566-2167-4(4)) Dorling Kindersley Publishing, Inc.
Adams, Simon. World History Biographies: Alexander: The Boy Soldier Who Conquered the World. 2013. (National Geographic World History Biographies Ser.). (ENG., Illus.). 64p. (J). (gr. 3-7). pap. 7.99 (978-1-4263-1449-0(3), National Geographic Children's Bks.) National Geographic Society.
Ancient Greece DBA. 2003. spiral bd. 16.95 (978-1-56004-152-8(8)) Social Studies Schl. Service.
Ancient Greeks. 2016. (Ladybird Histories Ser.). (ENG., Illus.). 64p. (J). (gr. 2-4). pap. 9.99 (978-0-7232-9443-6(7)) Penguin Bks., Ltd. GBR. Dist: Independent Pubs. Group.
Apel, Melanie Ann. Economy & Industry in Ancient Greece. 2004. (Primary Sources of Ancient Civilizations Ser.). (ENG., Illus.). 24p. (gr. 4-8). pap. 8.25 (978-0-8239-8942-3(9), PowerKids Pr.) Rosen Publishing Group, Inc., The.
—Politics & Government in Ancient Greece. 2004. (Primary Sources of Ancient Civilizations Ser.). (ENG., Illus.). 24p. (gr. 4-8). pap. 8.25 (978-0-8239-8939-3(9), PowerKids Pr.) Rosen Publishing Group, Inc., The.
Bankston, John. Alexander the Great. 2013. (ENG.). 48p. (J). (gr. 3-6). lib. bdg. 29.95 (978-1-61228-431-6(0)) Mitchell Lane Pubs., Inc.
—The Life & Times of Alexander the Great. 2004. (Biography of Ancient Civilizations Ser.). (Illus.). 48p. (J). lib. bdg. (978-1-58415-235-4(4)) Mitchell Lane Pubs., Inc.
Bartell, Jim. Greece. 2011. (Illus.). 32p. (J). (978-0-531-20953-0(9)) Bellwether Media.
Behnke, Alison. The Conquests of Alexander the Great. 2007. (Pivotal Moments in History Ser.). (ENG., Illus.). 160p. (gr. 9-12). lib. bdg. 38.60 (978-0-8225-5920-7(X)) Lerner Publishing Group.
Benchmark Education Company. Greece Long Ago (Teacher Guide) 2005. (978-1-4108-4675-4(X)) Benchmark Education Co.
Bendick, Jeanne. Herodotus & the Road to History. Bendick, Jeanne, illus. 2009. (Illus.). (J). pap. 13.95 (978-1-932350-20-3(9)) Bethlehem Bks.
Benduhn, Tea. La Antigua Grecia. 2007. (vida en el pasado (Life Long Ago) Ser.). (SPA., Illus.). 24p. (gr. 1-4). pap. 8.15 (978-0-8368-8038-0(2)); lib. bdg. 22.00 (978-0-8368-8033-5(1)) Stevens, Gareth Publishing LLLP. (Weekly Reader Leveled Readers).
Bensinger, Henry. The Ancient Greek Economy. 2013. (Spotlight on Ancient Civilizations: Greece Ser.). (ENG.). 24p. (J). (gr. 3-4). 23.60 (978-1-4777-0771-5(9)); (Illus.). pap. 10.00 (978-1-4777-0875-0(8)) Rosen Publishing Group, Inc., The. (PowerKids Pr.).
Bingham, Jane. Classical Myth: A Treasury of Greek & Roman Legends, Art, & History. 2007. (Myth Ser.). (Illus.). 96p. (J). (gr. 4-7). pap. 7.99 (978-0-7858-2350-6(6)) Book Sales, Inc.
—Classical Myth: A Treasury of Greek & Roman Legends, Art, & History. 2007. (ENG., Illus.). 96p. (C). (gr. 6-18). lib. bdg. 140.00 (978-0-7656-8104-1(8), Y181755) Routledge.
Bordessa, Kris & Martin, W. Eric. Tools of the Ancient Greeks: A Kid's Guide to the History & Science of Life in Ancient Greece. 2006. (Build It Yourself Ser.). (ENG., Illus.). 128p. (J). (gr. 3-7). pap. 16.95 (978-0-9749344-6-4(1)) Nomad Trails Pr.
Brannon, Barbara. Discover Ancient Greece. 2005. (J). pap. (978-1-4108-5163-5(X)) Benchmark Education Co.
Bridges, Shirin Yim & Yim Bridges, Shirin. Artemisia of Caria. Nguyen, Albert, illus. 2010. (Thinking Girl's Treasury of Real Princesses Ser.). (ENG.). 24p. (J). (gr. 3-8). 18.95 (978-0-9845098-1-2(X)) Goosebottom Bks. LLC.
Burns, Kylie. Sparta! 2013. (ENG.). 48p. (J). (978-0-7787-1099-8(8)); pap. (978-0-7787-1105-6(6)) Crabtree Publishing Co.
Callery, Sean. The Dark History of Ancient Greece. 2010. (Dark Histories Ser.). 64p. (gr. 5). 32.79 (978-1-60870-083-7(6)) Marshall Cavendish Corp.
Caper, William. Ancient Greece: Set Of 6. 2011. (Navigators Ser.). (J). pap. 50.00 net. (978-1-4108-5114-7(1)) Benchmark Education Co.
—Ancient Greece: Text Pairs. 2008. (Bridges/Navigators Ser.). (J). (gr. 6). 81.00 (978-1-4108-8428-2(7)) Benchmark Education Co.
Cline, Diane Harris. The Greeks: An Illustrated History. 2016. (ENG., Illus.). 224p. 30.00 (978-1-4262-1670-1(X), National Geographic) National Geographic Society.
Colum, Padraic. The Story of the Golden Fleece. Pogány, Willy, illus. unabr. ed. 2005. (Dover Children's Classics Ser.).

(ENG.). 256p. (J). (gr. 3-5). per. 5.95 (978-0-486-44366-9(3)) Dover Pubns., Inc.

Conklin, Wendy. You Are There! Ancient Greece 432 BC. 2016. (TIME for KIDS(r) Nonfiction Readers Ser.). 32p. (J). (gr. 6-6). 8.99 (978-1-4938-3600-0(5)) Teacher Created Materials, Inc.

Conklin, Wendy. You Are There! Ancient Greece 432 BC. 2016. (Time for Kids Nonfiction Readers Ser.). (ENG.). (J). (gr. 5-8). lib. bdg. 19.65 (978-0-606-39536-6(9)) Turtleback Bks.

Cooke, Tim. The Ancient Greeks. 2015. (At Home With... Ser.). (Illus.). 32p. (gr. 5-9). lib. bdg. 31.35 (978-1-78121-084-0(5), Brown Bear Bks.) Windmill Bks. Ltd. GBR. Dist: Black Rabbit Bks.

Corr, Kendra & Coletti, Sharon. The Ancient Greeks: I Think: It's Elementary! 2013. pap. 29.95 (978-1-938275-05-0(5)) InspirEd Educators.

Covert, Kim. Ancient Greece: Birthplace of Democracy, 1 vol. 2011. (Great Civilizations Ser.). (ENG.). 32p. (gr. 3-4). pap. 8.10 (978-1-4296-7237-5(4)); pap. 47.70 (978-1-4296-7238-2(2)); lib. bdg. 27.32 (978-1-4296-6831-6(8)) Capstone Press of Coughlan Cos. (Fact Finders).

Crompton, Samuel Willard. Alexander the Great. 2003. (Ancient World Leaders Ser.). (Illus.). 112p. (J). (gr. 6-12). 30.00 (978-0-7910-7219-6(3), Chelsea Hse.) Facts On File, Inc.

Demi Staff & Marshall Cavendish Corporation Staff. Alexander the Great, 0 vols. 2010. (ENG., Illus.). 64p. (J). (gr. 3-7). 19.99 (978-0-7614-5700-8(3), 9780761457008, Amazon Children's Publishing) Amazon Publishing.

Dickmann, Nancy. Ancient Greece. 2016. (History Hunters Ser.). (ENG.). 32p. (gr. 3-4). lib. bdg. 27.99 (978-1-5157-2535-0(9), Edge Bks.) Capstone Press of Coughlan Cos.

Dinzeo, Paul. Spartans. 2012. (History's Greatest Warriors Ser.). (ENG., Illus.). 24p. (J). (gr. 3-7). lib. bdg. 25.95 (978-1-60014-749-4(6), Torque Bks.) Bellwether Media.

DiPrimio, Pete. Ancient Sparta. 2012. (Explore Ancient Worlds Ser.). (J). (gr. 3-6). lib. bdg. 29.95 (978-1-61228-276-3(8)) Mitchell Lane Pubs., Inc.

Donaldson, Madeline. Greece. 2009. (Country Explorers Ser.). (J). (gr. 2-5). 27.93 (978-1-58013-600-6(1)) Lerner Publishing Group.

Etingoff, Kim & Indovino, Shaina C. Greece. 2012. (Major European Union Nations Ser.). 64p. (J). (gr. 7). 22.95 (978-1-4222-2244-7(6)) Mason Crest.

Etingoff, Kim & Indovino, Shaina Carmel. Greece. 2012. (J). pap. (978-1-4222-2275-1(6)) Mason Crest.

Ford, Michael. You Wouldn't Want to Be a Greek Athlete! (Revised Edition) 2014. (You Wouldn't Want to... Ser.). (ENG.). 32p. (J). lib. bdg. 29.00 (978-0-531-21175-5(4), Watts, Franklin) Scholastic Library Publishing.

Fullman, Joe. Ancient Greeks. 2009. (Hands-On History Ser.). (ENG.). 32p. (J). (gr. k-3). lib. bdg. 17.99 (978-1-59566-152-4(2)) QEB Publishing Inc.

—Ancient Greeks. 2011. (ENG., Illus.). 32p. (J). pap. 10.95 (978-1-926853-93-2(8)) Saunders Bk. Co. CAN. Dist: RiverStream Publishing.

Gagne, Tammy. The Evolution of Government & Politics in Greece. 2014. (gr. 4-8). 29.95 (978-1-61228-584-9(8)) Mitchell Lane Pubs., Inc.

Ganeri, Anita. Alexander the Great: The Life of a King & Conqueror. 2005. (Graphic Nonfiction Biographies Ser.). (ENG., Illus.). 48p. (J). (gr. 4-7). lib. bdg. 31.95 (978-1-4042-0238-2(2), 1241094) Rosen Publishing Group, Inc., The.

George, Joshua. Ancient Greeks Sticker Book: Create Spectacular Greek Sticker Scenes! Myer, Ed, illus. 2017. (Sticker History Ser.). (ENG.). 38p. (J). (gr. 2-6). pap. 8.99 (978-1-78445-867-6(8)) Top That! Publishing PLC GBR. Dist: Independent Pubs. Group.

The Golden Age of Greece (NCHS) (YA). (gr. 6-9). spiral bd., tchr.'s planning gde. ed. 15.00 (978-0-382-40950-9(7)) Cobblestone Publishing Co.

Gow, Mary. The Great Philosopher: Plato & His Pursuit of Knowledge. 2010. (Great Minds of Ancient Science & Math Ser.). 128p. (J). (gr. 4-7). 33.27 (978-0-7660-3119-7(5)) Enslow Pubs., Inc.

Green, Jen. Hail! Ancient Greeks. 2010. (ENG.). 32p. (J). (978-0-7787-6623-0(3)); pap. (978-0-7787-6630-8(6)) Crabtree Publishing Co.

Greenberg, Imogen. The Ancient Greeks. Greenberg, Isabel, illus. 2017. (Discover... Ser.). (ENG.). 32p. (J). (gr. 3-6). 14.99 **(978-1-84780-951-3(0)**, Frances Lincoln Children's Bks.) Quarto Publishing Group UK GBR. Dist: Hachette Bk. Group.

Haaren, John. Famous Men of Greece. 2008. 112p. pap. 12.95 (978-1-60459-523-9(X)) Wilder Pubns., Corp.

Hardwick, Susan. Greece: World-Wise Kids Guides. 2004. 96p. (978-1-59258-092-7(0)) Hylas Publishing.

Heinrichs, Ann. Greece. 2012. (ENG.). 144p. (J). (gr. 5-9). lib. bdg. 40.00 (978-0-531-27543-6(4)) Scholastic Library Publishing.

Hirsch, E. D., Jr., ed. Ancient Greece. 2003. (J). stu. ed. 49.95 (978-0-7690-2952-8(3)) Pearson Learning.

Hull, Robert. Ancient Greece. 2010. (Exploring the Ancient World Ser.). (Illus.). 64p. (YA). (gr. 6-8). lib. bdg. 34.60 (978-1-4339-4159-7(7), Gareth Stevens Secondary Library) Stevens, Gareth Publishing LLLP.

—Trade & Warfare. 2007. (World of Ancient Greece Ser.). (Illus.). 32p. (YA). (gr. 3-6). lib. bdg. 27.10 (978-1-59771-062-6(8)) Sea-To-Sea Pubns.

Hunter, Nick. Alexander the Great, 1 vol. 2013. (Hero Journals). (ENG.). 48p. (gr. 4-6). 33.32 (978-1-4109-5357-5(2), NA-r) Heinemann-Raintree.

Hunter, Nick & Faure, Florence. Alexander the Great, 1 vol. 2013. (Hero Journals). (ENG.). 48p. (gr. 4-6). pap. 9.95 (978-1-4109-5364-3(5), NA-r) Heinemann-Raintree.

Hurdman, Charlotte, et al. Find Out about Ancient Egypt, Rome & Greece: Exploring the Great Classical Civilizations, with 60 Step-By-Step Projects & 1500 Exciting Images. 2013. (ENG., Illus.). 256p. (J). (gr. 3-7). 17.99 (978-1-84322-804-2(1), Armadillo) Anness Publishing GBR. Dist: National Bk. Network.

Hynson, Colin. How People Lived in Ancient Greece. 2009. (How People Lived Ser.). (Illus.). 32p. (gr. 4-8). pap. 10.60 (978-1-4358-2621-2(3), Rosen Classroom) Rosen Publishing Group, Inc., The.

Kemp, Ellwood W. Streams of History: Ancient Greece (Yesterday's Classics) 2008. 80p. per. 7.95 (978-1-59915-255-4(X)) Yesterday's Classics.

Lacey, Saskia. Hidden by Time. 2015. (Building Fluency Through Reader's Theater Ser.). (ENG., Illus.). 32p. (J). (gr. 4-4). pap. 7.99 (978-1-4938-1292-9(0)) Teacher Created Materials, Inc.

Leonard, Scott A. Myths & Legends of Ancient Greece. 2015. (Illus.). 64p. (J). (978-0-7166-2634-3(9)) World Bk., Inc.

Leoni, Cristiana. In Pericles' Athens with Socrates. Cappon, Manuela, illus. 2008. (Come See My City Ser.). 48p. (gr. 4-8). lib. bdg. 28.50 (978-0-7614-4326-1(6), Benchmark Bks.) Marshall Cavendish Corp.

Lusted, Marcia Amidon. Greece, 1 vol. 2013. (Countries of the World Set 2 Ser.). (ENG.). 144p. (J). (gr. 6-12). lib. bdg. 37.07 (978-1-61783-629-9(X), Essential Library) ABDO Publishing Co.

Macdonald, Fiona. You Wouldn't Want to Be a Slave in Ancient Greece! A Life You'd Rather Not Have. Antram, David, illus. rev. ed. 2013. (ENG.). (J). 32p. 29.00 (978-0-531-27102-5(1)); 40p. pap. 9.95 (978-0-531-23853-0(9)) Scholastic Library Publishing. (Watts, Franklin).

Manning, Mick & Granström, Brita. Greek Hero. Manning, Mick & Granström, Brita, illus. 2015. (Fly on the Wall Ser.). (ENG., Illus.). 40p. (J). (gr. k-3). pap. 9.99 (978-1-84780-622-2(8), Frances Lincoln) Quarto Publishing Group UK GBR. Dist: Hachette Bk. Group.

Marsico, Katie. Alexander the Great: Ancient King & Conqueror, 1 vol. 2009. (Essential Lives Set 3 Ser.). (ENG., Illus.). 112p. (J). (gr. 6-12). lib. bdg. 35.64 (978-1-60453-520-4(2)) ABDO Publishing Co.

Mason, Paul. Sports Heroes of Ancient Greece. 2010. (ENG.). 32p. (J). (gr. 3-5). (978-0-7787-9911-5(5)); pap. (978-0-7787-9932-0(8)) Crabtree Publishing Co.

Matthews, Rupert. Spartans. 2015. (History's Fearless Fighters Ser.). (ENG., Illus.). 48p. (J). (gr. 5-6). pap. 14.05 (978-1-4824-3181-0(5)) Stevens, Gareth Publishing LLLP.

McGee, Marni. Ancient Greece: Archaeology Unlocks the Secrets of Greece's Past. 2006. (National Geographic Investigates Ser.). (ENG., Illus.). 64p. (J). (gr. 4-7). lib. bdg. 27.90 (978-0-7922-7872-6(0), National Geographic Children's Bks.) National Geographic Society.

—National Geographic Investigates: Ancient Greece: Archaeology Unlocks the Secrets of Ancient Greece. 2006. (National Geographic Investigates Ser.). (ENG., Illus.). 64p. (J). (gr. 3-7). 17.95 (978-0-7922-7826-9(7), National Geographic Children's Bks.) National Geographic Society.

McGinnis, Maura. Greece: A Primary Source Cultural Guide. 2009. (Primary Sources of World Cultures Ser.). 128p. (gr. 4-5). 79.90 (978-1-60851-922-4(8)) Rosen Publishing Group, Inc., The.

McGowen, Tom. Alexander the Great: Conqueror of the Ancient World. 2006. (Rulers of the Ancient World Ser.). (Illus.). 160p. (YA). (gr. 6-12). lib. bdg. 29.27 (978-0-7660-2560-8(8)) Enslow Pubs., Inc.

McLeese, Don. Spartans. 2009. 32p. pap. 7.99 (978-0-8249-1446-2(5), Ideal Pubns.) Worthy Publishing.

Mika, Christina & Benchmark Education Co., LLC. My Trip to Greece. 2014. (Text Connections Ser.). (J). (gr. 3). (978-1-4509-9667-9(1)) Benchmark Education Co.

Miles, Lisa, et al. The Usborne Encyclopedia of Ancient Greece: Internet Linked. rev. ed. 2007. (History Encyclopedias Ser.). (Illus.). 144p. (J). pap. 16.99 (978-0-7945-1800-4(1), Usborne) EDC Publishing.

Mole, Gavin. Sing It & Say - Ancient Greece. (Illus.). 156p. (J). 10.95 incl. audio (978-1-85909-389-4(2), Warner Bros. Pubns.) Alfred Publishing Co., Inc.

Morley, Jacqueline. Ancient Greek Athlete. 2005. (How to Be Ser.). (ENG., Illus.). 32p. (J). (gr. 3-7). 21.90 (978-0-7922-7495-7(4), National Geographic Children's Bks.) National Geographic Society.

Morris, Neil. Everyday Life in Ancient Greece. 2008. (Uncovering History Ser.). (ENG., Illus.). 48p. (J). (gr. 2-7). 19.95 (978-88-89272-56-5(2)) McRae Bks. Srl ITA. Dist: Independent Pubs. Group.

Murray, Julie. Greece, 1 vol. 2014. (Explore the Countries Set 2 Ser.). (ENG.). 40p. (gr. 7-11). lib. bdg. 29.93 (978-1-62403-342-1(3), Big Buddy Bks.) ABDO Publishing Co.

Murrell, Deborah Jane & Dennis, Peter. Greek Warrior. 2012. (Illus.). 32p. (gr. 3-5). pap. 8.95 (978-1-926853-53-6(9)) Saunders Bk. Co. CAN. Dist: RiverStream Publishing.

Nardo, Don. Alexander the Great: Conqueror of the Known World. 2009. (World Leaders Ser.). (Illus.). 100p. (J). 28.95 (978-1-59935-126-1(9)) Reynolds, Morgan Inc.

—Pericles: Great Leader of Ancient Athens. 2006. (Rulers of the Ancient World Ser.). (Illus.). 160p. (YA). (gr. 6-12). lib. bdg. 29.27 (978-0-7660-2561-5(6)) Enslow Pubs., Inc.

O'Connell, Kim A. Discover Ancient Greece. 2014. (Discover Ancient Civilizations Ser.). 104p. (J). pap. 10.95 (978-1-4644-0335-4(X)) Enslow Pubs., Inc.

O'Neal, Claire. Mount Olympus. 2014. (ENG.). 48p. (J). 29.95 (978-1-62469-009-9(2)) Purple Toad Publishing, Inc.

Osborne, Mary Pope & Boyce, Natalie Pope. Ancient Greece & the Olympics: A Nonfiction Companion to Hour of the Olympics. Murdocca, Sal, tr. Murdocca, Sal, illus. 2004. (Magic Tree House - Fact Tracker Ser.: 10). (ENG.). 128p. (J). (gr. 2-5). pap. 6.99 (978-0-375-82378-7(6), Random Hse. Bks. for Young Readers) Random Hse. Children's Bks.

Otfinoski, Steven. Spartans, 1 vol. 2013. (ENG.). 48p. (J). (Great Warriors Ser.). (gr. 3-6). lib. bdg. 32.79 (978-1-61783-728-9(8)); (Great Warriors EBook Ser.:). (Illus.). pap. 15.64 (978-1-61783-778-4(4), Core Library) ABDO Publishing Co.

Park, Louise & Love, Timothy. The Spartan Hoplites. 2009. (Ancient & Medieval People Ser.). 32p. (gr. 5). 28.50 (978-0-7614-4449-7(1)) Marshall Cavendish GBR. Dist: Marshall Cavendish Corp.

Peach, Susan & Millard, Anne. Greeks. Jackson, Ian, illus. 2004. (Illustrated World History Ser.). 96p. (J). (gr. 6). lib. bdg. 20.95 (978-1-58086-631-6(X), Usborne) EDC Publishing.

Pearson, Anne. La Antigua Grecia. (Coleccion Biblioteca Visual).Tr. of Ancient Greece. (SPA., Illus.). 64p. (YA). (gr. 5-8). (978-84-372-3771-8(8)) Altea, Ediciones, S.A. - Grupo Santillana.

Powell, Anton. Ancient Greece. 3rd rev. ed. 2007. (Cultural Atlas for Young People Ser.). (Illus.). 96p. (YA). (gr. 5-9). 35.00 (978-0-8160-6821-0(6)) Facts On File, Inc.

Rajczak, Kristen. 20 Fun Facts about Women in Ancient Greece & Rome. 2015. (Fun Fact File: Women in History Ser.). (ENG., Illus.). 32p. (J). (gr. 2-3). 25.25 (978-1-4824-2818-6(0)) Stevens, Gareth Publishing LLLP.

Rice, Rob S. Ancient Greek Warfare. 2009. (Ancient Warfare Ser.). (Illus.). 32p. (J). (gr. 5-8). lib. bdg. 26.00 (978-1-4339-1972-5(9), Gareth Stevens Learning Library) Stevens, Gareth Publishing LLLP.

Robinson, Joanna J. Greece. 2015. (One World, Many Countries Ser.). (ENG.). 32p. (J). (gr. 1-4). 28.50 (978-1-63407-045-4(3), 208882) Child's World, Inc., The.

Robinson, Tony. Romans & Greeks. 2016. (Weird World of Wonders Ser.). (ENG., Illus.). 320p. (J). (gr. 4-6). pap. 12.99 (978-1-5098-0539-6(7)) Pan Macmillan GBR. Dist: Independent Pubs. Group.

Royston, Angela. Ancient Greek Adventure. 2010. (ENG., Illus.). 32p. (J). (gr. 3-5). (978-0-7787-9900-9(X)); pap. (978-0-7787-9921-4(2)) Crabtree Publishing Co.

Ryall, Michael. Greece Long Ago. 2005. (J). pap. (978-1-4108-4627-3(X)) Benchmark Education Co.

Sanderson, Caroline. Pick Your Brains about Greece. Williams, Caspar, illus. 2005. (Pick Your Brains Ser.). 128p. pap. 9.95 (978-1-86011-220-1(X)) Cadogan Guides GBR. Dist: Globe Pequot Pr., The.

Santillian, Beatriz & Morris, Ian Macgregor. Leonidas I: Warrior King of Sparta. 2017. (Leaders of the Ancient World Ser.). 112p. (J). (gr. 12-11). 37.10 **(978-1-5081-7520-9(9)**, Rosen Young Adult) Rosen Publishing Group, Inc., The.

Santillian, Beatriz & Randall, Bernard. Alexander the Great: Macedonian King & Conqueror. 2017. (Leaders of the Ancient World Ser.). 112p. (J). (gr. 12-11). 37.10 **(978-1-5081-7482-0(2)**, Rosen Young Adult) Rosen Publishing Group, Inc., The.

Schomp, Virginia. The Ancient Greeks. 2007. (Myths of the World Ser.). (Illus.). 96p. (gr. 6-7). lib. bdg. 34.21 (978-0-7614-2547-2(0), Benchmark Bks.) Marshall Cavendish Corp.

Schreiber, Sophia. Greek Thought. Miller, Zachary N., ed. 2007. (Ancient Greek Mystery Ser.). (J). pap. 4.95 (978-1-58659-217-2(3)) Artesian Pr.

Shaw, Charles D. Stories of the Ancient Greeks. Harker, George A., illus. 2008. 332p. pap. 13.95 (978-1-59915-269-1(X)) Yesterday's Classics.

Shecter, Vicky Alvear. Alexander the Great Rocks the World. Naughton, Terry, illus. 2006. 128p. (J). (gr. 5-7). lib. bdg. 18.95 (978-1-58196-045-7(X), Darby Creek) Lerner Publishing Group.

Shone, Rob. Alexander the Great: The Life of a King & Conqueror. 2009. (Graphic Nonfiction Biographies Ser.). (ENG.). 48p. (YA). (gr. 4-5). 58.50 (978-1-61513-012-2(8), Rosen Reference) Rosen Publishing Group, Inc., The.

Shoup, Kate. The Technology of Ancient Greece. 2016. (Ancient Innovations Ser.). 64p. (J). 34.21 (978-1-5026-2231-0(9)) Cavendish Square Publishing.

Sirota, Lyn A. The Acropolis Museum. 2014. (J). (978-1-4896-3248-7(4)) Weigl Pubs., Inc.

Smith-Llera, Danielle, et al. Ancient Greece, 1 vol. 2014. (Ancient Greece Ser.). (ENG.). 24p. (gr. 1-2). 101.28 (978-1-4914-0276-4(8), First Facts) Capstone Press of Coughlan Cos.

Smith, Miranda & Steele, Philip. Ancient Worlds: A Thrilling Adventure Through the Ancient Worlds. 2016. (Navigators Ser.). (ENG., Illus.). 80p. (J). 15.99 (978-0-7534-7239-2(2), 9780753472392, Kingfisher) Roaring Brook Pr.

Spilsbury, Richard. Discover Greece. 2012. (Discover Countries Ser.). (ENG., Illus.). 32p. (J). (gr. 3-5). pap. 10.60 (978-1-4488-7048-6(8)); lib. bdg. 26.50 (978-1-4488-6622-9(7)) Rosen Publishing Group, Inc., The. (PowerKids Pr.).

Steele, Philip. Navigators: Ancient Greece. 2013. (Navigators Ser.). (ENG., Illus.). 48p. (J). (gr. 4-7). pap. 8.99 (978-0-7534-6955-2(3), 9780753469552, Kingfisher) Roaring Brook Pr.

Sylvester, Diane. Ancient Greece. VanBlaricum, Pam, ed. Hillam, Corbin & Ciccarelli, Gary, illus. 2006. (Museum Ser.). 64p. pap. 13.99 (978-0-88160-387-3(2), LW441, Learning Works, The) Creative Teaching Pr., Inc.

Tames, Richard. Step Into: Ancient Greece. 2008. (ENG., Illus.). 64p. (J). (gr. 4-7). pap. 12.99 (978-1-84476-510-2(5)) Anness Publishing GBR. Dist: National Bk. Network.

Thucydides. Thucydides, Bk. 4. Cress, J. H. E. & Wordsworth, J. C., eds. 2010. (Cambridge Elementary Classics: Greek Ser.). (ENG.). 114p. pap. 19.99 (978-0-521-14117-8(6)) Cambridge Univ. Pr.

Tsakiridis, Dimitra. Art & Culture of Ancient Greece. 2010. (Ancient Art & Cultures Ser.). 40p. (YA). (gr. 5-8). lib. bdg., E-Book 53.00 (978-1-61532-964-9(1)) Rosen Publishing Group, Inc., The.

Tsakiridis, Dimitra & Bardi, Matilde. Art & Culture of Ancient Greece. 2010. (Ancient Art & Cultures Ser.). (Illus.). 40p. (J). pap. 11.75 (978-1-61532-883-3(1)); (YA). (gr. 5-8). lib. bdg. 26.50 (978-1-4358-3590-0(5)) Rosen Publishing Group, Inc., The. (Rosen Reference).

Turner, Tracey. Hard As Nails in Ancient Greece. Lenman, Jamie, illus. 2015. (ENG.). 64p. (J). (978-0-7787-1512-2(4)) Crabtree Publishing Co.

Villing, Alexandra. The Ancient Greeks: Their Lives & Their World. 2010. (ENG., Illus.). 80p. (gr. 7-18). 17.95 (978-0-89236-985-0(X)) Oxford Univ. Pr., Inc.

Waldron, Melanie. Geography Matters in Ancient Greece. 2015. (Geography Matters in Ancient Civilizations Ser.). (ENG., Illus.). 48p. (gr. 3-6). 33.32 (978-1-4846-0963-7(8), Heinemann InfoSearch) Heinemann-Raintree.

Waterfield, Robin H., et al. Who Was Alexander the Great? Thomson, Andrew, illus. 2016. (Who Was? Ser.). (ENG.). 112p. (J). (gr. 3-7). lib. bdg. 15.99 (978-0-399-54235-0(3), Grosset & Dunlap) Penguin Young Readers Group.

Wheatley, A. Greeks. rev. ed. 2004. (Illustrated World History Ser.). (Illus.). 96p. (J). pap. 12.99 (978-0-7945-0428-1(0)) EDC Publishing.

Whiting, Jim. The Life & Times of Herodotus. 2006. (Biography from Ancient Civilizations Ser.). (Illus.). 48p. (J). (gr. 3-7). lib. bdg. 29.95 (978-1-58415-509-6(4)) Mitchell Lane Pubs., Inc.

—The Life & Times of Pericles. 2005. (Biography from Ancient Civilizations Ser.). (Illus.). 48p. (J). (gr. -1-7). lib. bdg. 29.95 (978-1-58415-339-9(3)) Mitchell Lane Pubs., Inc.

—The Life & Times of Thucydides. 2008. (Biography from Ancient Civilizations Ser.). (Illus.). 48p. (J). (gr. 4-8). lib. bdg. 29.95 (978-1-58415-698-7(8)) Mitchell Lane Pubs., Inc.

Wilhelm, Doug. Alexander the Great. rev. ed. 2015. (Wicked History Ser.). (ENG., Illus.). 144p. (J). lib. bdg. 33.00 (978-0-531-22124-2(5), Children's Pr.) Scholastic Library Publishing.

—Alexander the Great: Master of the Ancient World. 2010. (Wicked History Ser.). (ENG.). 128p. (J). (gr. 6-12). pap. 5.95 (978-0-531-22821-0(5), Watts, Franklin) Scholastic Library Publishing.

Williams, Jean Kinney. Empire of Ancient Greece, Revised Edition. 2nd rev. ed. 2009. (Great Empires of the Past Ser.). (Illus.). 160p. (gr. 6-12). 35.00 (978-1-60413-165-9(9), Chelsea Hse.) Facts On File, Inc.

Wood, Alix. Uncovering the Culture of Ancient Greece, 01 vols., 1. 2016. (Archaeology & Ancient Cultures Ser.). (ENG.). 32p. (J). pap. 10.00 (978-1-5081-4655-1(1), PowerKids Pr.) Rosen Publishing Group, Inc., The.

Woods, Michael & Woods, Mary B. Seven Wonders of Ancient Greece. 2008. (Seven Wonders Ser.). (ENG., Illus.). 80p. (J). (gr. 5-8). lib. bdg. 33.26 (978-0-8225-7574-0(4)) Lerner Publishing Group.

Zamosky, Lisa. Greece, 1 vol. 2007. (Primary Source Readers Ser.). (ENG.). 32p. (J). (gr. 5-5). pap. 8.99 (978-0-7439-0434-6(6)) Shell Educational Publishing.

GREECE—SOCIAL LIFE AND CUSTOMS

Adare, Sierra. Greece - The People. 3rd rev. ed. 2007. (Lands, Peoples & Cultures Ser.). (ENG., Illus.). 32p. (J). (gr. 3-7). pap. (978-0-7787-9677-0(9)) Crabtree Publishing Co.

—Greece -The People. 3rd rev. ed. 2007. (Lands, Peoples & Cultures Ser.). (ENG., Illus.). 32p. (J). (gr. 3-7). lib. bdg. (978-0-7787-9309-0(5)) Crabtree Publishing Co.

Apel, Melanie Ann. Home Life in Ancient Greece. 2004. (Primary Sources of Ancient Civilizations Ser.). (ENG., Illus.). 24p. (gr. 4-8). pap. 8.25 (978-0-8239-8940-9(2), PowerKids Pr.) Rosen Publishing Group, Inc., The.

Bailey, Diane. Ancient Greece, 1 vol. 2014. (Ancient Civilizations Ser.). (ENG., Illus.). 112p. (J). (gr. 6-12). lib. bdg. 35.64 (978-1-62403-538-8(8), Essential Library) ABDO Publishing Co.

Bedford, Kate. Greeks. 2011. (Children in History Ser.). 32p. (YA). (gr. 4-7). lib. bdg. 28.50 (978-1-59771-270-5(1)) Sea-To-Sea Pubns.

Benduhn, Tea. Ancient Greece. 2007. (Life Long Ago Ser.). (Illus.). 24p. (gr. 1-4). pap. 8.15 (978-0-8368-7787-8(X)); lib. bdg. 22.00 (978-0-8368-7782-3(9)) Stevens, Gareth Publishing LLLP. (Weekly Reader Leveled Readers).

Bensinger, Henry. Ancient Greek Daily Life. 2013. (Spotlight on Ancient Civilizations: Greece Ser.). (ENG., Illus.). 24p. (J). (gr. 3-4). pap. 10.00 (978-1-4777-0877-4(4)); lib. bdg. 23.60 (978-1-4777-0772-2(7)) Rosen Publishing Group, Inc., The. (PowerKids Pr.).

Buckley, James. My Teenage Life in Greece. 2017. (Custom & Cultures of the World Ser.). (ENG.). (YA). (gr. 7-12). 23.95 **(978-1-4222-3904-9(7))** Mason Crest.

Cricket Books Staff & Cobblestone Publishing Staff. If I Were a Kid in Ancient Greece: Children of the Ancient World. Sheldon, Ken, ed. 2007. (If I Were a Kid In... Ser.). (ENG., Illus.). 32p. (J). (gr. 1-5). 17.95 (978-0-8126-7929-8(6)) Cricket Bks.

Hynson, Colin. How People Lived in Ancient Greece. 2008. (How People Lived Ser.). (Illus.). 30p. (J). lib. bdg. 26.50 (978-1-4042-4431-3(X)) Rosen Publishing Group, Inc., The.

Kerrigan, Juliet. Ancient Greeks & Why They Matter to Us, Bd. 16. 2017. (ENG., Illus.). 56p. (J). pap. 8.99 **(978-0-00-820892-9(1))** HarperCollins Pubs. Ltd. GBR. Dist: Independent Pubs. Group.

Leavitt, Amie Jane. Ancient Athens. 2012. (Explore Ancient Worlds Ser.). 48p. (J). (gr. 3-6). lib. bdg. 29.95 (978-1-61228-275-6(X)) Mitchell Lane Pubs., Inc.

Manning, Mick & Granström, Brita. Greek Hero. Manning, Mick & Granström, Brita, illus. 2015. (Fly on the Wall Ser.). (ENG., Illus.). 40p. (J). (gr. k-3). pap. 9.99 (978-1-84780-622-2(8), Frances Lincoln) Quarto Publishing Group UK GBR. Dist: Hachette Bk. Group.

Morley, Jacqueline. How to Be an Ancient Greek Athlete. Antram, David, illus. 2008. (How to Be Ser.). (ENG.). 32p. (J). (gr. 3-7). pap. 5.95 (978-1-4263-0278-7(9), National Geographic Children's Bks.) National Geographic Society.

Nardo, Don. Daily Life in Ancient Greece. 2015. (Daily Life in Ancient Civilizations Ser.). (ENG., Illus.). 48p. (gr. 3-6). pap. 8.99 (978-1-4846-0835-7(6), Heinemann InfoSearch) Heinemann-Raintree.

—Life in Ancient Greece. 2015. (ENG., Illus.). 96p. (YA). lib. bdg. (978-1-60152-804-9(3)) ReferencePoint Pr., Inc.

Orr, Tamra. The Food of Greece. 2011. (Flavors of the World Ser.). (Illus.). 64p. (J). (gr. 4). 31.36 (978-1-60870-235-0(9)) Marshall Cavendish GBR. Dist: Marshall Cavendish Corp.

Peppas, Lynn. Cultural Traditions in Greece. 2012. (ENG.). 32p. (J). (978-0-7787-7518-8(6)); (Illus.). pap. (978-0-7787-7523-2(2)) Crabtree Publishing Co.

Royston, Angela. Ancient Greek Adventure. 2010. (ENG., Illus.). 32p. (J). (gr. 3-5). (978-0-7787-9900-9(X)); pap. (978-0-7787-9921-4(2)) Crabtree Publishing Co.

Sanderson, Caroline. Pick Your Brains about Greece. Williams, Caspar, illus. 2005. (Pick Your Brains Ser.). 128p. pap. 9.95 (978-1-86011-220-1(X)) Cadogan Guides GBR. Dist: Globe Pequot Pr., The.

Senker, Cath. Everyday Life in Ancient Greece. 2003. (Uncovering History Ser.). 46p. (J). lib. bdg. 28.50 (978-1-58340-248-1(9)) Black Rabbit Bks.

Simons, Lisa M. Bolt. Daily Life in Ancient Greece, 1 vol. 2014. (Ancient Greece Ser.). (ENG.). 24p. (gr. 1-2). 25.32 (978-1-4914-0272-6(5)) Capstone Press of Coughlan Cos.

Steele, Philip. Navigators: Ancient Greece. 2013. (Navigators Ser.). (ENG., Illus.). 48p. (J). (gr. 4-7). pap. 8.99 (978-0-7534-6955-2(3), 9780753469552, Kingfisher) Roaring Brook Pr.

Tames, Richard. Step Into: Ancient Greece. 2008. (ENG., Illus.). 64p. (J). (gr. 4-7). pap. 12.99 *(978-1-84476-510-2(5))* Anness Publishing GBR. Dist: National Bk. Network.
Tsakiridis, Dimitra. Art & Culture of Ancient Greece. 2010. (Ancient Art & Cultures Ser.). 40p. (YA). (gr. 5-8). lib. bdg., E-Book 53.00 *(978-1-61532-964-9(1))* Rosen Publishing Group, Inc., The.
Tsakiridis, Dimitra & Bardi, Matilde. Art & Culture of Ancient Greece. 2010. (Ancient Art & Cultures Ser.). (Illus.). 40p. (J). pap. 11.75 *(978-1-61532-883-3(1))*; (YA). (gr. 5-8). lib. bdg. 26.50 *(978-1-4358-3590-0(5))* Rosen Publishing Group, Inc., The. (Rosen Reference).
Van Vleet, Carmella. Explore Ancient Greece! 25 Great Projects, Activities, Experiments. Shedd, Blair & Kim, Alex, illus. 2008. (Explore Your World Ser.). (ENG.). 96p. (J). (gr. k-4). pap. 12.95 *(978-1-934670-11-8(1))* Octavio Publishing.
Villing, Alexandra. The Ancient Greeks: Their Lives & Their World. 2010. (ENG., Illus.). 80p. (gr. 7-18). 17.95 *(978-0-89236-985-0(X))* Oxford Univ. Pr., Inc.
Villios, Lynne W. Cooking the Greek Way. 2003. (Easy Menu Ethnic Cookbooks). (Illus.). 72p. pap. 7.95 *(978-0-8225-0533-4(9))* Lerner Publishing Group.

GREED

Berry, Joy Wilt. A Book about Being Greedy. 2005. (Illus.). (J). *(978-0-7172-8598-3(7))* Scholastic, Inc.
Leigh, Susan K. God, I Need to Talk to You about Greed. Clark, Bill, illus. 2005. 16p. (J). pap. 1.19 *(978-0-7586-0795-9(4))* Concordia Publishing Hse.

GREED—FICTION

Barrett, Ron. Cats Get Famous. Barrett, Ron, illus. 2015. (ENG., Illus.). 32p. (J). (gr. -1-3). 17.99 *(978-1-4424-9453-4(0))*, Simon & Schuster Bks. For Young Readers) Simon & Schuster Bks. For Young Readers.
Basye, Dale E. Rapacia. Dob, Bob, illus. 2010. (Heck Ser.). (ENG.). 384p. (J). (gr. 3-7). pap. 6.99 *(978-0-375-84078-4(8))*, Yearling) Random Hse. Children's Bks.
Black, Chuck. Sir Bentley & Holbrook Court. 2009. (Knights of Arrethtrae Ser.). (ENG., Illus.). 208p. (YA). (gr. 5-7). pap. 9.99 *(978-1-60142-125-8(7))*, Multnomah Bks.) Crown Publishing Group.
Brothers Grimm & Isadora, Rachel. The Fisherman & His Wife. Isadora, Rachel, illus. 2008. (ENG., Illus.). 32p. (J). (gr. -1-3). 16.99 *(978-0-399-24771-2(8))*, G.P. Putnam's Sons Books for Young Readers) Penguin Young Readers Group.
Buckley, Richard. The Greedy Python. Carle, Eric, illus. 2012. (World of Eric Carle Ser.). (ENG.). 24p. (J). (gr. -1-1). 16.99 *(978-1-4424-4577-2(7))*; pap. 3.99 *(978-1-4424-4576-5(9))* Simon Spotlight. (Simon Spotlight).
—The Greedy Python. 2012. (Eric Carle Ready-To-Read Ser.). lib. bdg. 13.55 *(978-0-606-26357-3(8))*, Turtleback) Turtleback Bks.
—The Greedy Python: Lap Edition. Carle, Eric, illus. 2013. (World of Eric Carle Ser.). (ENG.). 24p. (J). (gr. -1-k). bds. 12.99 *(978-1-4424-8991-2(X))*, Little Simon) Little Simon.
Byrd, Michael. The Adventures of Banter & Jafar: Spoiled Rotten, 1 vol. Bai, Jenny, illus. 2009. 36p. pap. 24.95 *(978-1-60836-131-1(4))* America Star Bks.
Carberry, Marie. This Is My House!, 1 vol. 2010. 20p. pap. 24.95 *(978-1-61546-991-8(5))* America Star Bks.
Carr, Elias. Ava y el Picnic Raquitico. Garton, Michael, illus. 2016. (SPA.). (J). **(978-1-5064-2095-0(8))** Augsburg Fortress, Pubs.
Cox, Judy. One Is a Feast for Mouse: A Thanksgiving Tale. Ebbeler, Jeffrey, illus. 2009. (ENG.). 32p. (J). (gr. -1-3). pap. 7.99 *(978-0-8234-2231-9(3))* Holiday Hse., Inc.
Cox, Phil Roxbee. Don't Be Greedy, Graham. Tyler, Jenny, ed. McCafferty, Jan, illus. 2006. (Cautionary Tales Ser.). 24p. (J). (gr. -1). lib. bdg. 15.99 *(978-1-58086-972-0(6))*; pap. 7.99 *(978-0-7945-1361-0(1))* EDC Publishing. (Usborne).
Daemicke, Songju Ma. Un Case con Sentido Común. Bersani, Shennen, illus. 2016. (SPA.). 32p. (J). (gr. k-3). pap. 9.95 *(978-1-62855-854-8(7))* Arbordale Publishing.
—A Case of Sense, 1 vol. Bersani, Shennen, illus. 2016. (ENG & SPA.). 32p. (J). (gr. k-3). 17.95 *(978-1-62855-852-4(0))* Arbordale Publishing.
Dahl, Michael. Ooze Is It? Sinkovec, Igor, illus. 2015. (Igor's Lab of Fear Ser.). (ENG.). 40p. (gr. 1-3). lib. bdg. 23.99 *(978-1-4965-0457-9(7))* Stone Arch Bks.
Donnelly, Jennifer. Humble Pie. Gammell, Stephen, illus. 2007. (ENG.). 32p. (J). (gr. -1-2). 13.99 *(978-1-4169-6751-4(6))*, Aladdin) Simon & Schuster Children's Publishing.
Downing, Johnette. The Fifolet, 1 vol. Lindsley, Jennifer, illus. 2015. (ENG.). 32p. (J). (gr. k-3). 16.99 *(978-1-4556-2036-4(X))* Pelican Publishing Co., Inc.
—Why the Oyster Has the Pearl, 1 vol. Hill, Bethanne, illus. 2011. (ENG.). 32p. (J). (gr. k-3). 16.99 *(978-1-4556-1460-8(2))* Pelican Publishing Co., Inc.
Ducote, Billie Seaon. The Adventures of Artie Eco Part One: The Problem with Greed, 2 vols, Vol. 1. Ducote, Billie Seaon, illus. 2007. (ENG., Illus.). 26p. (J). 18.95 *(978-0-9787597-5-9(3))* PureLight Pubns.
—The Adventures of Artie Eco Part Two: The Problem with Greed Artie Eco Goes to Dirtyville, 2 vols., Vol. 2. Ducote, Billie Seaon, illus. 2007. (Illus.). 26p. (J). act. bk. ed. 18.95 *(978-0-9787597-1-1(0))* PureLight Pubns.
Fotso, Serge. The Hungry Little Cat. Woods, Michele, illus. 2011. 32p. pap. 24.95 *(978-1-4626-1805-7(7))* America Star Bks.
Holden, Pam. Greedy Gus the Pirate, 6 pack. Whimp, Pauline, illus. 2009. (Red Rocket Readers Ser.). (ENG.). 16p. (gr. 2-2). pap. *(978-1-877363-74-0(X))* Flying Start Bks.
Howell, Troy. The Dragon of Cripple Creek. 2011. (ENG., Illus.). 400p. (J). (gr. 3-7). 16.95 *(978-0-8109-9713-4(4))*, Amulet Bks.) Abrams, Inc.
Howells, William Dean. Christmas Every Day. (J). lib. bdg. 16.95 *(978-0-8488-1866-1(0))* Amereon Ltd.
Kaiser, Lori. Gigi the Greedy Giraffe. Kaiser, Lori, illus. 2012. (Illus.). 28p. pap. *(978-0-9836651-8-2(4))* Roxby Media Ltd.
Kaplan, Michael B. Betty Bunny Wants Everything. Jorisch, Stéphane, illus. 2012. (Betty Bunny Ser.). (ENG.). 32p. (J). (gr. -1-k). 17.99 *(978-0-8037-3408-1(5))*, Dial Bks) Penguin Young Readers Group.
Kasbarian, Lucine. The Greedy Sparrow: An Armenian Tale, 0 vols. Zaikina, Maria, illus. 2011. (ENG.). 32p. (J). (gr. -1-3). 17.99 *(978-0-7614-5821-0(2))*, 9780761458210, Amazon Children's Publishing) Amazon Publishing.
Kumiega, Michelle. The Greedy Bunny. 2008. 28p. pap. 24.95 *(978-1-60672-966-3(7))* America Star Bks.
Lawrence, D. H. The Rocking-Horse Winner. 2010. (Illus.). 40p. (J). 19.95 *(978-1-58341-924-3(1))*, Creative Education) Creative Co., The.
Lester, Helen. All for Me & None for All. Munsinger, Lynn, illus. 2012. (ENG.). 32p. (J). (gr. -1-3). 16.99 *(978-0-547-68834-3(2))* Houghton Mifflin Harcourt Publishing Co.
Major, Roberta Olsen. The 24-Karat King. 2008. (Royal Pains Ser.: 7). (ENG.). (YA). pap. 11.95 *(978-1-59705-671-7(5))* Wings ePress, Inc.
Mayo, Frank, illus. King Midas & the Golden Touch: A Tale about Greed. 2006. (J). 6.99 *(978-1-59939-022-2(1))* Cornerstone Pr.
Mello, Roger. You Can't Be Too Careful! Hahn, Daniel, tr. from POR. Mello, Roger, illus. 2017. (ENG., Illus.). 36p. (J). (gr. k-3). 18.00 *(978-0-914671-64-0(2))*, Elsewhere Editions) Steerforth Pr.
Nuttall, Lesley. Ollie the Ogre. 2012. (Illus.). 16p. pap. 18.30 *(978-1-4678-8908-7(3))* AuthorHouse.
Orford, Margie. The Magic Fish. Littlewort, Lizza, illus. 2012. (Best Loved Tales for Africa Ser.). (ENG.). 32p. (J). (gr. k-2). pap. 9.95 *(978-1-77009-822-0(4))* Jacana Media ZAF. Dist: Independent Pubs. Group.
Parker, Emma. Cecil the Caterpillar. 2010. (Illus.). pap. *(978-1-877547-95-9(6))* First Edition Ltd.
Reiss, Mike & Reiss, Mike. The Boy Who Wouldn't Share. Catrow, David, illus. 2008. (ENG.). 32p. (J). (gr. 1-3). 16.99 *(978-0-06-059132-8(3))* HarperCollins Pubs.
Schmidt, Gary D. Straw into Gold. 2009. (ENG.). 176p. (J). (gr. 2-5). pap. 7.99 *(978-0-547-23776-3(6))* Houghton Mifflin Harcourt Publishing Co.
Steve, Smallman. Very Greedy Bee. Jack, Tickle, illus. 2010. (ENG.). 32p. (J). pap. 7.95 *(978-1-58925-422-0(8))* Tiger Tales.
Stevens, Janet & Crummel, Susan Stevens. The Great Fuzz Frenzy. (ENG., Illus.). 56p. (J). (gr. -1-3). 2017. pap. 7.99 *(978-0-544-94391-9(0))*, HMH Books For Young Readers) 2005. 17.99 *(978-0-15-204626-2(7))* Houghton Mifflin Harcourt Publishing Co.
—The Great Fuzz Frenzy. unabr. ed. 2006. (J). (gr. k-3). 27.99 incl. audio *(978-0-8045-6940-8(1))*, SAC6941) Spoken Arts, Inc.
—The Great Fuzz Frenzy. 2017. (ENG.). (J). (gr. -1-3). lib. bdg. 18.40 **(978-0-606-39816-9(3))** Turtleback Bks.
Tegen, Katherine Brown. The Story of the Jack O'Lantern. Dorman, Brandon, illus. 2010. (ENG.). 32p. (J). (gr. -1-3). 12.99 *(978-0-06-143088-6(9))* HarperCollins Pubs.
Travers, Georgia. The Wily Woodchucks. Gag, Flavia, illus. 2009. (Fesler-Lampert Minnesota Heritage Ser.). (ENG.). 32p. 14.95 *(978-0-8166-6548-8(6))* Univ. of Minnesota Pr.
Weigl Publishers, creator. The Goose & the Golden Egg: What Happens When You Are Greedy? 2013. (AV2 Animated Storytime Ser.: Vol. 14). (ENG., Illus.). 32p. (J). (gr. -1-3). lib. bdg. 29.99 *(978-1-62127-918-1(9))*, AV2 by Weigl) Weigl Pubs., Inc.
Witte, Anna. El Loro Tico Tango. Witte, Anna, illus. 2005. (SPA., Illus.). 24p. (J). pap. 6.99 *(978-1-84148-971-1(9))* Barefoot Bks., Inc.
—The Parrot Tico Tango. 2005. (ENG., Illus.). 24p. (J). (gr. -1-3). 6.99 *(978-1-905236-11-4(5))* Barefoot Bks., Inc.
—The Parrot Tico Tango. Witte, Anna, illus. 2005. (Illus.). 24p. (J). (gr. k-3). 15.99 *(978-1-84148-243-9(9))* Barefoot Bks., Inc.
Witte, Anna & Amador, Brian. The Parrot Tico Tango. Witte, Anna, illus. 2011. (ENG., Illus.). 24p. (J). (gr. -1-2). 9.99 *(978-1-84686-669-2(3))* Barefoot Bks., Inc.

GREEK ANTIQUITIES

see Classical Antiquities

GREEK ART

see Art, Greek

GREEK CIVILIZATION

see Greece—Civilization

GREEK LANGUAGE, MODERN—CONVERSATION AND PHRASE BOOKS

Papaloizos, Theodore. Level Two - the Kids of the Neighborhood. 2006. (J). pap. *(978-0-932416-99-5(3))* Papaloizos Pubns., Inc.
Perrin, Christopher. Greek for Children, Primer A. 2010. (ENG.). 280p. (J). (gr. 3-17). pap. 24.95 *(978-1-60051-023-6(X))* Classical Academic Pr.

GREEK LANGUAGE, MODERN—GRAMMAR

Kudela, Katy R. My First Book of Greek Words. Translations.com Staff, tr. (Bilingual Picture Dictionaries Ser.). (MUL.). 32p. (gr. 1-2). 2011. pap. 47.70 *(978-1-4296-6172-0(0))* 2010. lib. bdg. 27.32 *(978-1-4296-5966-6(1))* Capstone Press of Coughlan Cos. (Aplus Bks.).

GREEK LITERATURE

Church, Alfred J. Stories of the East from Herodotus. 2009. (Illus.). 230p. pap. 10.95 *(978-1-59915-386-5(6))* Yesterday's Classics.
Kerrigan, Michael. Greeks. 2010. (Ancients in Their Own Words Ser.). 64p. (gr. 5). 32.79 *(978-1-60870-065-3(8))* Marshall Cavendish GBR. Dist: Marshall Cavendish Corp.
Kudela, Katy R. My First Book of Greek Words, 1 vol. Translations.com Staff, tr. 2011. (Bilingual Picture Dictionaries Ser.). (ENG, GRE & MUL., Illus.). 32p. (gr. 1-2). pap. 8.10 *(978-1-4296-6171-3(2))*, Aplus Bks.) Capstone Press of Coughlan Cos.

GREEK LITERATURE—HISTORY AND CRITICISM

Thucydides. Thucydides, Bk. 4. Cress, J. H. E. & Wordsworth, J. C., eds. 2010. (Cambridge Elementary Classics: Greek Ser.). (ENG.). 114p. pap. 19.99 *(978-0-521-14117-8(6))* Cambridge Univ. Pr.

GREEK MYTHOLOGY

see Mythology, Classical

GREEK PHILOSOPHY

see Philosophy, Ancient

GREEKS—FICTION

Aesop. Aesop's Fables. Winter, Milo, illus. 2008. (J). *(978-1-934941-08-9(5))* Red & Black Pubs.
Angelini, Josephine. Dreamless. 2012. (Starcrossed Trilogy Ser.: 2). (ENG.). 496p. (YA). (gr. 8). 17.99 *(978-0-06-201201-2(0))*, HarperTeen) HarperCollins Pubs.
—Goddess. 2013. (Starcrossed Trilogy Ser.: 3). (ENG.). 432p. (YA). (gr. 8). 17.99 *(978-0-06-201203-6(7))*, HarperTeen) HarperCollins Pubs.
Ashley, Bernard. Aftershock. 2011. (ENG.). 144p. (J). (gr. 4-7). pap. 8.95 *(978-1-84780-055-8(6))*, Frances Lincoln Children's Bks.) Quarto Publishing Group UK GBR. Dist: Hachette Bk. Group.
Block, Francesca Lia. Roses & Bones: Myths, Tales, & Secrets. 2010. (ENG.). 400p. (YA). (gr. 9). pap. 8.99 *(978-0-06-201954-7(6))*, HarperTeen) HarperCollins Pubs.
Childs, Tera Lynn. Sweet Legacy. 2013. (Sweet Venom Ser.: 3). (ENG.). 384p. (YA). (gr. 8). 17.99 *(978-0-06-200185-6(X))*, Tegen, Katherine Bks) HarperCollins Pubs.
—Sweet Shadows. 2013. (Sweet Venom Ser.: 2). (ENG.). 352p. (YA). (gr. 8). pap. 9.99 *(978-0-06-200184-9(1))*, Tegen, Katherine Bks) HarperCollins Pubs.
Colloredo, Sabino. Athena. Ferrari, Antongionata, illus. 2009. (Hotel Olympus Ser.). 128p. (J). (gr. 3-6). 31.95 *(978-1-60754-709-9(0))* Windmill Bks.
Colum, Padraic. The Adventures of Odysseus & Tales of Troy. 2005. pap. *(978-1-4065-0125-4(5))* Dodo Pr.
Crawford, Philip & Crawford, Philip Charles. The Fruit of All Evil. Schoening, Dan, illus. 2014. (Wonder Woman Ser.). (ENG.). 56p. (gr. 2-3). pap. 4.95 *(978-1-4342-2766-9(9))*, DC Super Heroes) Stone Arch Bks.
DiTocco, Robyn & DiTocco, Tony. The Hero Perseus: A Mad Myth Mystery. 2004. 220p. (gr. 3-12). 19.95 *(978-0-9723429-0-2(7))*; pap. 11.95 *(978-0-9723429-1-9(5))* Brainstorm Pubns., Inc.
Evslin, Bernard. The Trojan War. 2012. (ENG.). 192p. (gr. 3-6). pap. 13.99 *(978-1-4532-7413-2(8))*, Open Road Young Readers) Open Road Integrated Media, Inc.
Garfield, Leon & Blishen, Edward. God Beneath the Sea. Keeping, Charles, illus. 2015. (ENG.). 224p. (J). (gr. 4-6). 19.99 *(978-0-85753-311-1(8))* Transworld Publishers Ltd. GBR. Dist: Independent Pubs. Group.
The Goddess Girls: Pandora the Curious; Pheme the Gossip; Persephone the Daring; Cassandra the Lucky. 2014. (Goddess Girls Ser.). (ENG., Illus.). 1040p. (J). (gr. 3-7). pap. 29.99 *(978-1-4814-2730-2(X))*, Aladdin) Simon & Schuster Children's Publishing.
Hardy, Ralph. Argos: The Story of Odysseus As Told by His Loyal Dog. 2016. 400p. (J). (gr. 3-7). 16.99 *(978-0-06-239678-5(1))* HarperCollins Pubs.
Hashway, Kelly. Stalked by Death. 2013. (Touch of Death Ser.: 2). (ENG.). 320p. (YA). (gr. 10-12). pap. 9.95 *(978-1-937053-51-2(2))* Spencer Hill Pr.
Hennesy, Carolyn. Pandora Gets Angry, Vol. 5. 2012. (Mythic Misadventures Ser.). (ENG.). 336p. (YA). (gr. 3-12). pap. 7.99 *(978-1-59990-734-5(8))*, 9781599907345, Bloomsbury USA Childrens) Bloomsbury Publishing USA.
—Pandora Gets Frightened. 2013. (Mythic Misadventures Ser.). (ENG.). 320p. (YA). (gr. 3-6). 16.99 *(978-1-59990-442-9(X))*, 9781599904429, Bloomsbury USA Childrens) Bloomsbury Publishing USA.
—Pandora Gets Heart, No. 4. 2010. (Mythic Misadventures Ser.). (ENG.). 272p. (YA). (gr. 3-7). 14.99 *(978-1-59990-439-9(X))*, 9781599904399, Bloomsbury USA Childrens) Bloomsbury Publishing USA.
Holub, Joan. Be Careful, Icarus! Patricelli, Leslie, illus. 2015. (Mini Myths Ser.). (ENG.). 24p. (J). (gr. -1 — 1). bds. 6.95 *(978-1-4197-1677-5(8))* Abrams, Inc.
—Brush Your Hair, Medusa! Patricelli, Leslie, illus. 2015. (Mini Myths Ser.). (ENG.). 24p. (J). (gr. -1 — 1). bds. 6.95 *(978-1-4197-0953-1(4))* Abrams, Inc.
—Make a Wish, Midas! Patricelli, Leslie, illus. 2015. (Mini Myths Ser.). (ENG.). 24p. (J). (gr. -1 — 1). bds. 6.95 *(978-1-4197-0952-4(6))* Abrams, Inc.
—Please Share, Aphrodite! Patricelli, Leslie, illus. 2015. (Mini Myths Ser.). (ENG.). 24p. (J). (gr. -1 — 1). bds. 6.95 *(978-1-4197-1678-2(6))* Abrams, Inc.
Holub, Joan & Williams, Suzanne. Aphrodite the Beauty. 2013. (Goddess Girls Ser.: 3). (ENG.). 176p. (J). (gr. 3-7). 17.99 *(978-1-4424-5751-5(1))*, Aladdin) Simon & Schuster Children's Publishing.
—Ares & the Spear of Fear. Phillips, Craig, illus. 2014. (Heroes in Training Ser.: 7). (ENG.). 112p. (J). (gr. 1-4). pap. 5.99 *(978-1-4424-8848-9(4))*, Aladdin) Simon & Schuster Children's Publishing.
—Artemis the Brave. (Goddess Girls Ser.: 4). (ENG.). 240p. (J). (gr. 3-7). 2013. 17.99 *(978-1-4424-6139-0(X))* 2010. pap. 7.99 *(978-1-4169-8274-6(4))* Simon & Schuster Children's Publishing. (Aladdin).
—Athena the Brain. 2010. (Goddess Girls Ser.: 1). (ENG.). 176p. (J). (gr. 3-7). pap. 7.99 *(978-1-4169-8271-5(X))*, Aladdin) Simon & Schuster Children's Publishing.
—Athena the Proud. 2014. (Goddess Girls Ser.: 13). (ENG., Illus.). 240p. (J). (gr. 3-7). pap. 7.99 *(978-1-4424-8820-5(4))*, Aladdin) Simon & Schuster Children's Publishing.
—Crius & the Fright of Night. Phillips, Craig, illus. 2015. (Heroes in Training Ser.: 9). (ENG.). 96p. (J). (gr. 1-4). pap. 5.99 *(978-1-4814-3506-2(X))*, Aladdin) Simon & Schuster Children's Publishing.
—The Girls' Games. 2012. (Goddess Girls Ser.). lib. bdg. 18.40 *(978-0-606-26349-8(7))*, Turtleback) Turtleback Bks.
—Goddess Girls Set, Bks. 1-4: Athena the Brave - Persephone the Phony; Aphrodite the Beauty; Artemis the Brave. 2012. (Goddess Girls Ser.). (ENG., Illus.). 752p. (J). (gr. 3-7). pap. 31.99 *(978-1-4424-8210-4(9))*, Aladdin) Simon & Schuster Children's Publishing.
—Hades & the Helm of Darkness. 2013. (Heroes in Training Ser.: 3). lib. bdg. 16.00 *(978-0-606-27041-0(8))*, Turtleback) Turtleback Bks.
—Persephone the Phony. 2010. (Goddess Girls Ser.: 2). (ENG., Illus.). 160p. (J). (gr. 3-7). pap. 7.99 *(978-1-4169-8272-2(8))*, Aladdin) Simon & Schuster Children's Publishing.
Howard, Annabelle. Three Greek Myths: Pandora, Icarus & Midas. 2005. (J). pap. *(978-1-4108-4226-8(6))* Benchmark Education Co.
Landmann, Bimba. The Fate of Achilles. 2011. (ENG., Illus.). 32p. (J). 19.95 *(978-1-60606-085-8(6))*, J. Paul Getty Museum) Getty Pubns.
Maddox, Jake & McMullan, Kate. Stop That Bull, Theseus!, 1 vol. Zilber, Denis, illus. 2010. (Myth-O-Mania Ser.: Bk. 5). (ENG.). 192p. (gr. 4-8). 25.32 *(978-1-4342-3034-8(1))*, Myth-O-Mania) Stone Arch Bks.
Matthews, Rodney, illus. Greek & Norse Legends. 2004. (Myths & Legends Ser.). 112p. (J). (gr. 6). lib. bdg. 20.95 *(978-1-58086-603-3(4))* EDC Publishing.
McLaren, Clemence. Inside the Walls of Troy. 2004. (ENG., Illus.). 208p. (YA). (gr. 7-12). mass mkt. 7.99 *(978-0-689-87397-3(2))*, Simon Pulse) Simon Pulse.
McMullan, Kate. Hit the Road, Helen! 2013. (Myth-O-Mania Ser.: Bk. 9). (ENG.). 240p. (gr. 4-8). 10.95 *(978-1-4342-6219-6(7))*; lib. bdg. 25.32 *(978-1-4342-4990-6(5))* Stone Arch Bks.
—Myth-O-Mania. 2013. (Myth-O-Mania Ser.). (ENG.). (gr. 4-8). 227.88 *(978-1-4342-6061-1(5))*, Myth-O-Mania) Stone Arch Bks.
—Say Cheese, Medusa!, 1 vol. Zilber, Denis, illus. 2011. (Myth-O-Mania Ser.: Bk. 3). (ENG.). 208p. (gr. 4-8). pap. 5.95 *(978-1-4342-3442-1(8))*; lib. bdg. 25.32 *(978-1-4342-2998-4(X))* Stone Arch Bks. (Myth-O-Mania).
—Stop That Bull, Theseus!, 1 vol. Zilber, Denis, illus. 2011. (Myth-O-Mania Ser.: Bk. 5). (ENG.). 192p. (gr. 4-8). pap. 5.95 *(978-1-4342-3438-4(X))*, Myth-O-Mania) Stone Arch Bks.
The New Olympians. 2014. (Pegasus Ser.: 3). (ENG., Illus.). 448p. (J). (gr. 3-7). pap. 8.99 *(978-1-4424-4416-4(9))*, Simon & Schuster/Paula Wiseman Bks.) Simon & Schuster/Paula Wiseman Bks.
Noto, Nick & Noto, Larissa. The Adventures of Pyrgos: Volume 1. 2011. 36p. pap. 16.39 *(978-1-4634-5250-6(0))* AuthorHouse.
O'Hearn, Kate. The Flame of Olympus. 2013. (Pegasus Ser.: 1). (ENG.). 416p. (J). (gr. 3-7). pap. 7.99 *(978-1-4424-4410-2(X))*, Simon & Schuster/Paula Wiseman Bks.) Simon & Schuster/Paula Wiseman Bks.
—Rise of the Titans. 2015. (Pegasus Ser.: 5). (ENG., Illus.). 448p. (J). (gr. 3-7). 17.99 *(978-1-4814-4714-0(9))*, Simon & Schuster/Paula Wiseman Bks.) Simon & Schuster/Paula Wiseman Bks.
The Origins of Olympus. 2014. (Pegasus Ser.: 4). (ENG., Illus.). 432p. (J). (gr. 3-7). 18.99 *(978-1-4424-9715-3(7))*, Simon & Schuster/Paula Wiseman Bks.) Simon & Schuster/Paula Wiseman Bks.
Osterbach, Batya Kirshenbaum. Pini the Pitcher: A Story for Hanukkah. Eisby, Lizzy, illus. 2005. 32p. (J). (gr. 1-4). 16.95 *(978-1-932687-50-7(5))*, Devora Publishing) Simcha Media Group.
Riordan, Rick. The Blood of Olympus. 2014. (Heroes of Olympus Ser.: Bk. 5). (ENG.). 528p. (J). (gr. 5-9). 19.99 *(978-1-4231-4673-5(5))* Hyperion Bks. for Children.
—The Mark of Athena. 2014. (Heroes of Olympus Ser.: 3). (J). lib. bdg. 20.85 *(978-0-606-35255-0(4))* Turtleback Bks.
Tomlinson, Theresa. Voyage of the Snake Lady. 2007. 385p. (YA). (gr. 7-12). lib. bdg. 18.89 *(978-0-06-084740-1(9))*, Eos) HarperCollins Pubs.
Ursu, Anne. The Immortal Fire. Swaab, Neil, illus. 2010. (Cronus Chronicles Ser.: 3). (ENG.). 528p. (J). (gr. 3-7). pap. 7.99 *(978-1-4169-0592-9(8))*, Atheneum Bks. for Young Readers) Simon & Schuster Children's Publishing.
Yardley Hastings Primary School. Tim & Holly's Olympic Adventure. 2012. 74p. pap. *(978-1-909039-52-0(7))* Legend Pr.

GREEKS—UNITED STATES

Frank, Sarah. Greeks in America. 2006. (J). lib. bdg. 27.93 *(978-0-8225-2686-5(7))*, Lerner Pubns.) Lerner Publishing Group.

GREEN TURTLE

Becker, John E. Green Sea Turtles. 2003. (Returning Wildlife Ser.). (Illus.). 48p. (J). 26.20 *(978-0-7377-1831-7(5))*, Greenhaven Pr., Inc.) Cengage Gale.
Blomquist, Christopher. Green Sea Turtles. (Library of Turtles & Tortoises Ser.). 24p. 2009. (gr. 3-3). 42.50 *(978-1-60853-947-5(4))* 2004. (Illus.). (J). lib. bdg. 22.60 *(978-0-8239-6738-4(7))* Rosen Publishing Group, Inc., The. (PowerKids Pr.).
Fletcher, Marty & Scherer, Glenn. The Green Sea Turtle: Help Save This Endangered Species! 2006. (Saving Endangered Species Ser.). (Illus.). 128p. (J). (gr. 4-10). lib. bdg. 34.60 *(978-1-59845-033-0(6))*, MyReportLinks.com Bks.) Enslow Pubs., Inc.
Gareth Stevens Publishing Staff, contrib. by. Turtles. 2004. (All about Wild Animals Ser.). (Illus.). 32p. (gr. k-4). lib. bdg. 26.00 *(978-0-8368-4123-7(9))*, Gareth Stevens Learning Library) Stevens, Gareth Publishing LLLP.
Hirsch, Rebecca. Green Sea Turtle Migration. 2012. (Animal Migrations Ser.). (ENG., Illus.). 32p. (J). (gr. 2-5). lib. bdg. 29.93 *(978-1-60973-621-7(4))*, 201198) Child's World, Inc., The.
Hirsch, Rebecca E. Green Sea Turtles: A Nesting Journey. 2016. (Illus.). 32p. (J). *(978-1-4896-4517-3(9))* Weigl Pubs., Inc.
Jackson, Tom. Green Sea Turtle. 2013. (Science Slam: the Deep End-Animal Life Underwater Ser.). 24p. (J). (gr. -1-3). lib. bdg. 23.93 *(978-1-61772-920-1(5))* Bearport Publishing Co., Inc.
Shofner, Melissa Raé. The Return of the Green Sea Turtle. 2017. (Bouncing Back from Extinction Ser.). 32p. (J). (gr. 9-10). 26.25 **(978-1-5081-5617-8(4))**, PowerKids Pr.) Rosen Publishing Group, Inc., The.

GREEN BAY PACKERS (FOOTBALL TEAM)

Burgess, Zack. Meet the Green Bay Packers. 2016. (Big Picture Sports Ser.).Tr. of cb. (ENG., Illus.). 24p. (J). (gr. k-3). lib. bdg. 22.60 *(978-1-59953-740-5(0))* Norwood Hse. Pr.
Epstein, Brad M. Green Bay Packers 101. 2010. (ENG., Illus.). 24p. (J). bds. *(978-1-60730-111-0(3))*, 101 Bk.) Michaelson Entertainment.
Frisch, Aaron. Green Bay Packers. (Super Bowl Champions Ser.). (J). 2011. (gr. 1-3). 24.25 *(978-1-60818-018-9(2))* 2005. (Illus.). 24p. (gr. 5-9). lib. bdg. 16.95 *(978-1-58341-384-5(7))* Creative Co., The.
—Green Bay Packers. 2014. (Illus.). 24p. (J). *(978-1-60818-376-0(9))*, Creative Education) Creative Co., The.
Gilbert, Sara. NFL Today: Green Bay Packers. 2013. (NFL Today Ser.). (ENG., Illus.). 48p. (J). (gr. 4-7). pap. 12.00

E
F
G

(978-0-89812-856-7(0), Creative Paperbacks) Creative Co., The.

—The Story of the Green Bay Packers. 2013. (Illus.). 47p. (J). 35.65 (978-1-60818-303-6(3), Creative Education) Creative Co., The.

Hoblin, Paul. Aaron Rodgers: Super Bowl MVP, 1 vol. 2012. (Playmakers Ser.). (ENG.). 32p. (J). (gr. 3-6). 27.07 (978-1-61783-295-6(2)) ABDO Publishing Co.

Holmes, Parker. Packers vs. Bears. 2014. (J). (978-1-4777-2791-1(4), PowerKids Pr.) Rosen Publishing Group, Inc., The.

Howell, Brian. Green Bay Packers. 2015. (Insider's Guide to Pro Football Ser.). (ENG.). 32p. (J). (gr. k-3). 28.50 (978-1-63407-009-6(7), 208844) Child's World, Inc., The.

LeBoutillier, Nate. The Story of the Green Bay Packers. 2009. (NFL Today Ser.). 48p. (YA). (gr. 5-9). 22.95 (978-1-58341-756-0(7)) Creative Co., The.

MacRae, Sloan. The Green Bay Packers. 2011. (America's Greatest Teams Ser.). (Illus.). 24p. (J). pap. 8.25 (978-1-4488-2747-3(7)); lib. bdg. 22.60 (978-1-4488-2579-0(2)) Rosen Publishing Group, Inc., The. (PowerKids Pr.).

Morey, Allan. The Green Bay Packers Story. 2016. (NFL Teams Ser.). (ENG., Illus.). 32p. (J). (gr. 3-7). lib. bdg. 26.95 (978-1-62617-366-8(4), Torque Bks.) Bellwether Media.

Publications International Ltd. Staff. Yesterday & Today Nfl Greenbay Packers. 2009. 160p. 9.95 (978-1-4127-6116-1(6)) Publications International, Ltd.

Reischel, Rob. Green Bay Packers, 1 vol. 2010. (Inside the NFL Ser.). (ENG.). 48p. (YA). (gr. 3-6). lib. bdg. 32.79 (978-1-61714-012-9(0)) ABDO Publishing Co.

Sandler, Michael. Aaron Rodgers & the Green Bay Packers: Super Bowl XLV. 2011. (Super Bowl Superstars Ser.). 24p. (YA). (gr. k-3). lib. bdg. 22.61 (978-1-61772-309-4(6)) Bearport Publishing Co., Inc.

—Brett Favre. 2009. (Football Heroes Making a Difference Ser.). (Illus.). 24p. (YA). (gr. 2-5). lib. bdg. 22.61 (978-1-59716-771-0(1)) Bearport Publishing Co., Inc.

Savage, Jeff. Brett Favre. 2010. pap. 39.62 (978-0-7613-6965-3(1)) Lerner Publishing Group.

Wyner, Zach. Green Bay Packers. (Illus.). 32p. (J). 2015. pap. (978-1-4896-0827-7(3)) 2014. (ENG., (gr. 4-7). lib. bdg. 28.55 (978-1-4896-0826-0(5), AV2 by Weigl) Weigl Pubs., Inc.

Zappa, Marcia. Green Bay Packers, 1 vol. 2014. (NFL's Greatest Teams Ser.). (ENG.). 32p. (gr. 7-11). lib. bdg. 28.50 (978-1-62403-361-2(X), Big Buddy Bks.) ABDO Publishing Co.

GREENBACKS

see Paper Money

GREENE, NATHANAEL, 1742-1786

Mierka, Gregg A. Nathanael Greene: The General Who Saved the Revolution. 2006. (J). pap. (978-1-59556-017-9(3)); (Illus.). 88p. (gr. 5-11). lib. bdg. 23.95 (978-1-59556-012-4(2)) OTTN Publishing.

GREENHOUSES

Faust, Daniel R. Global Warming: Greenhouse Gases & the Ozone Layer. 2008. (Jr. Graphic Environmental Dangers Ser.). (ENG.). 24p. (J). 47.90 (978-1-61532-096-7(2), PowerKids Pr.) Rosen Publishing Group, Inc., The.

Sawyer, Ava. Humans & Earth's Atmosphere: What's in the Air? 2017. (Humans & Our Planet Ser.). (ENG.). 32p. (gr. 3-4). lib. bdg. 27.32 **(978-1-5157-7199-9(7)**, Fact Finders) Capstone Press of Coughlan Cos.

GREENLAND

Blashfield, Jean F. Greenland. 2005. (Enchantment of the World Ser.). (ENG., Illus.). 144p. (YA). (gr. 5-9). 39.00 (978-0-516-23678-0(4)) Scholastic Library Publishing.

King, David C. Greenland. 2008. (Cultures of the World Ser.). 144p. (gr. 6-18). lib. bdg. 42.79 (978-0-7614-3118-3(7), Benchmark Bks.) Marshall Cavendish Corp.

Mattern, Joanne. Greenland: World's Largest Island. 2009. (Nature's Greatest Hits Ser.). 24p. (gr. 2-2). 42.50 (978-1-61514-840-0(X), PowerKids Pr.) Rosen Publishing Group, Inc., The.

—Groenlandia. 2004. (Maravillas Naturales (Natures Greatest Hits) Ser.). (SPA.). 24p. (J). (gr. 3-6). lib. bdg. 22.60 (978-0-8239-6876-3(6), Editorial Buenas Letras) Rosen Publishing Group, Inc., The.

—Groenlandia: La isla más grande del mundo (Greenland: World's Largest Island) 2009. (Maravillas naturales (Natures Greatest Hits) Ser.). (SPA.). 24p. (gr. 2-2). 42.50 (978-1-61514-363-4(7), Editorial Buenas Letras) Rosen Publishing Group, Inc., The.

Rice, Earle. The Life & Times of Erik the Red. 2008. (Biography from Ancient Civilizations Ser.). (Illus.). 48p. (J). (gr. 4-8). lib. bdg. 29.95 (978-1-58415-701-4(1)) Mitchell Lane Pubs., Inc.

GREENLAND—FICTION

Casey, Dawn. Little Bear: A Folktale from Greenland. Corner, Chris, illus. 2014. (Collins Big Cat Progress Ser.). (ENG.). 32p. (J). (gr. 3-4). pap. 7.99 (978-0-00-751925-5(7)) HarperCollins Pubs. Ltd. GBR. Dist: Independent Pubs. Group.

Davis, Mike. Land of the Lost Mammoths: A Science Adventure. 2003. (Illus.). 174p. (J). 15.95 (978-0-9747078-0-8(5)) Perceval Pr.

Hamel, Mike. Rylan the Renegade, 6. 2007. (Matterhorn the Brave Ser.: 6). (ENG.). 192p. (J). (gr. 8-7). per. 9.99 (978-0-89957-838-5(1)) AMG Pubs.

Lund, Celia. Square Sails & Dragons. 2006. 284p. per. 19.95 (978-1-4120-5758-5(2)) Trafford Publishing.

Riel, Jörn & Chodzin, Sherab. The Raiders Vol. 2: The Inuk Quartet. Cann, Helen, illus. 2013. (ENG.). 128p. (J). (gr. 4-6). pap. 9.99 (978-1-84686-744-6(4)) Barefoot Bks., Inc.

Stead, Rebecca. First Light. 2008. (ENG.). 336p. (J). (gr. 3-7). 7.99 (978-0-440-42222-8(1), Yearling) Random Hse. Children's Bks.

GREETING CARDS

AG Publishers Editors. Sparkle Card Kit: Everything You Need to Create More than 20 Glittery Greetings! 2003. (American Girl Library). (Illus.). 64p. (J). 19.95 (978-1-58485-707-5(2)) American Girl Publishing, Inc.

Blanchette, Peg & Thibault, Terri. Make Your Own Cool Cards: 40 Awesome Notes & Invitations! 2004. (ENG., Illus.). 64p. (J). 8.95 (978-1-885593-96-2(1), Ideal Pubns.) Worthy Publishing.

Calabazza, Della & Monckeberg, Paulina. Ludovico & Ooops 2006. 2005. (Pascualina Family of Products Ser.). (ENG., Illus.). 240p. (J). (gr. 3-7). spiral bd. 11.99 (978-956-8222-23-9(5)) Pascualina Producciones S.A.

Chan, Mari. Super Fun Kids. 2003. 4.99 (978-1-56971-922-0(5)) Dark Horse Comics.

CICO Kidz, compiled by. My First Card-Making Book: 35 Easy-To-make Cards for Every Occasion for Children Aged 7+ 2017. (ENG., Illus.). 112p. (J). (gr. 7-11). pap. 14.95 (978-1-78249-445-4(6), CICO Books) Ryland Peters & Small GBR. Dist: WIPRO.

Henry, Sally. Card Making. 2009. (Make Your Own Art Ser.). (Illus.). 32p. (ENG.). (gr. 2-6). pap. 11.75 (978-1-4358-2639-7(6)); (J). (gr. 3-6). lib. bdg. 26.50 (978-1-4358-2506-2(3)) Rosen Publishing Group, Inc., The. (PowerKids Pr.).

Humphrey, Paul. How to Make a Card. Fairclough, Chris, photos by. 2007. (Crafty Kids Ser.). (Illus.). 24p. (J). (gr. -1-3). lib. bdg. 24.25 (978-1-59771-100-5(4)) Sea-To-Sea Pubns.

LaFosse, Michael. Making Origami Cards Step by Step. 2004. (Kid's Guide to Origami Ser.). (Illus.). 24p. (J). lib. bdg. 25.25 (978-0-8239-6701-8(8), PowerKids Pr.) Rosen Publishing Group, Inc., The.

LaFosse, Michael G. Making Origami Cards Step by Step. 2009. (Kid's Guide to Origami Ser.). 24p. (gr. 3-4). 47.90 (978-1-61511-183-1(2), PowerKids Pr.) Rosen Publishing Group, Inc., The.

Lovell, Katie, illus. Christmas Stencil Cards. 2007. (Christmas Stencil Cards Ser.). 16p. (J). 9.99 (978-0-7945-1896-7(6), Usborne) EDC Publishing.

Monckeberg, Paulina. Pascualina 2006. 2005. (Pascualina Family of Products Ser.). (ENG., Illus.). 272p. (J). spiral bd. 16.99 (978-956-8222-28-4(6)) Pascualina Producciones S.A.

—Rosamunda Della Calabazza 2006 Agenda & Stationary 2006: The Youngest & Most Dangerous Sister of Pascualina. 2005. (Pascualina Family of Products Ser.). (ENG., Illus.). 228p. (J). spiral bd. 11.99 (978-956-8222-21-5(9)) Pascualina Producciones S.A.

Sneesby, Frederick. A Believer's Christmas. 2008. 92p. pap. 15.25 (978-1-4389-0031-5(7)) AuthorHouse.

Storey, Rita. Make Your Own Creative Cards. 2010. (Do It Yourself Projects! Ser.). (Illus.). 24p. (J). (gr. 4-6). lib. bdg. 25.25 (978-1-61532-591-7(3), PowerKids Pr.) Rosen Publishing Group, Inc., The.

Turnbull, Stephanie. Cards & Gifts: Style Secrets for Girls. 2013. (Girl Talk Ser.). 32p. (gr. 4-7). lib. bdg. 31.35 (978-1-59920-944-9(6)) Black Rabbit Bks.

—Cards & Gifts: Style Secrets for Girls. 2014. (Girl Talk Ser.). (ENG., Illus.). 32p. (J). (gr. 4-8). pap. 9.95 (978-1-77092-201-3(6)) Saunders Bk. Co. CAN. Dist: RiverStream Publishing.

Watt, Fiona. Christmas decorations & Cards. 2005. 34p. (J). pap. 8.95 (978-0-7945-0795-4(6), Usborne) EDC Publishing.

—Making Cards. Figg, Non Et Al, illus. 2007. 64p. (J). pap. 14.99 (978-0-7945-1356-6(5), Usborne) EDC Publishing.

Wild, Anne S. Wildlife Pop-Ups: A Collection of 3-D Greetings Cards on Wildlife Themes to Cut Out & Make. 2004. (Illus.). 36p. (J). 12.00 (978-1-899618-48-4(1)) Tarquin Pubns. GBR. Dist: Parkwest Pubns., Inc.

GREETING CARDS—FICTION

Su, Lucy. Make Cards. Su, Lucy, illus. 2003. (Kitten & Baby Kitten Ser.). (Illus.). 32p. (YA). (978-1-85602-446-4(6), Pavilion Children's Books) Pavilion Bks.

GRENFELL, WILFRED THOMASON, SIR, 1865-1940

Benge, Janet & Benge, Geoff. Christian Heroes - Then & Now - Wilfred Grenfell: Fisher of Men. 2003. (Christian Heroes Ser.). (ENG.). 190p. (YA). pap. 9.99 (978-1-57658-292-3(2)) YWAM Publishing.

GRIEF

Ahern, Dianne. Today Someone I Love Passed Away. Shurtliff, William, illus. 2008. (J). (978-0-9679437-4-9(4)) Aunt Dee's Attic, Inc.

Bender, Janet M. Getting Yourself Together When Your Family Comes Apart: Coping with Family Changes. 2004. (Illus.). 50p. per. 19.95 (978-1-931636-28-5(1)) National Ctr. For Youth Issues.

Bow, James. Dealing with Loss. 2015. (ENG., Illus.). 48p. (J). (978-0-7787-2201-4(5)) Crabtree Publishing Co.

Britain, Lory. My Grandma Died: Child's Story about Death & Loss. Deach, Carol, illus. 2003. (ENG.). 32p. (J). (gr. -1-3). pap. 7.95 (978-1-884734-26-7(X)) Parenting Pr., Inc.

Carpenter, Holly & Chouinard, Karen. Healing Together: An Alphabet Book. 2012. 56p. pap. 20.95 (978-1-4497-3442-8(1), WestBow Pr.) Author Solutions, Inc.

Chenault, Jean Elkins. What Star? 2009. 28p. pap. 15.99 (978-1-4415-2441-6(X)) Xlibris Corp.

Chepokas, Rebecca & Stanchfield, Ronald M. Good-bye, Mitch: Sorrow, Grief, Inspiration 2004. per. 14.95 (978-0-9743717-4-0(2)) Amber Woods Publishing.

Coping: Set 1. 2017. (Coping Ser.). 112p. (gr. 12-12). 222.60 **(978-1-4994-6631-7(5)**, Rosen Young Adult) Rosen Publishing Group, Inc., The.

Coping with the Loss of a Loved One: An Inspiring New Book about Appreciating Human Life & Death. 2003. 60p. per. 10.00 net. (978-0-9620180-3-9(1)) Black, Clinton L.

Crosetto, Alice & Garcha, Rajinder. Death, Loss, & Grief in Literature for Youth: A Selective Annotated Bibliography for K-12. 2012. (Literature for Youth Ser.). (ENG.). 266p. (gr. 17). 95.00 (978-0-8108-8560-8(3)) Scarecrow Pr., Inc.

Dennison, Amy, et al, as told by. Our Dad Died: The True Story of Three Kids Whose Lives Changed. 2004. (Illus.). 112p. (J). pap. 9.95 (978-1-57542-135-3(6)) Free Spirit Publishing, Inc.

Edwards, Dianna. Meet Patou. 2006. (J). pap. 29.95 (978-0-9767756-0-7(3)) Patou Bks., LLC.

—My Journal & Drawings. 2004. (J). spiral bd. (978-0-9767756-4-5(6)) Patou Bks., LLC.

—Why Can't Everything Just Stay the Same? Book Three. 2004. (J). (978-0-9767756-3-8(8)) Patou Bks., LLC.

Faulkner, Rhiannon. Talking about Grief, with Brian & the Faulkner Fairies. 2010. (ENG., Illus.). 24p. (J). pap. (978-0-9565388-1-9(9)) Say It with Angels Ltd.

Gainer, Shannon. When I Die, Will You Cry? 2012. 28p. 24.95 (978-1-4626-6029-2(0)) America Star Bks.

Giddens, Sandra. Coping with Grieving & Loss. 2009. (Coping Ser.). 192p. (gr. 7-12). 63.90 (978-1-61511-999-8(X)) Rosen Publishing Group, Inc., The.

Giddens, Sandra & Giddens, Owen. Coping with Grieving & Loss. 2003. (Coping Ser.). 124p. (YA). (gr. 7-12). lib. bdg. 34.60 (978-0-8239-3758-5(5)) Rosen Publishing Group, Inc., The.

Gootman, Marilyn E. When a Friend Dies: A Book for Teens about Grieving & Healing. 2005. (ENG., Illus.). 128p. (YA). (gr. 6-18). pap. 9.99 (978-1-57542-170-4(4)) Free Spirit Publishing, Inc.

Grebin, Margaret. Baseball Forever! A Boy's Book on Grief, Loss, & Healing. 2004. (J). per. 10.95 (978-1-59094-076-1(8)) Jawbone Publishing Corp.

Hampton-Johnson, Rasheeda. Mommy Where Is Daddy? 2013. 16p. pap. 15.99 (978-1-4817-1437-2(6)) AuthorHouse.

Jackson, Deb. Creamy Goes to Heaven. 2013. 48p. pap. 17.45 (978-1-4497-8762-2(2), WestBow Pr.) Author Solutions, Inc.

Jackson, Denise. Mom Lovd Me A Blizzard: A Young Boy's Journey Through Grief. 2010. 36p. (J). pap. 27.00 (978-0-9842171-2-0(6)) Masterpiece Creations Graphics & Publishing.

Kane, Darlene. Missing Hannah: Based on a True Story of Sudden Infant Death. 2006. 60p. pap. 26.49 (978-1-4259-0136-3(0)) AuthorHouse.

Larabie, Gayle. Is My Dad Still My Dad? 2005. (Illus.). 32p. (J). (978-1-55306-873-0(4)) Essence Publishing.

Liss-Levinson, Nechama & Baskette, Molly Phinney. Remembering My Grandparent: A Kid's Own Grief Workbook in the Christian Tradition. 2006. (ENG., Illus.). 48p. (gr. 2-8). wbk. ed. 30.99 (978-1-59473-212-6(4), 9781594732126, Skylight Paths Publishing) LongHill Partners, Inc.

Loewen, Nancy. Saying Good-Bye to Uncle Joe: What to Expect When Someone You Love Dies, 1 vol. Lyles, Christopher, illus. 2011. (Life's Challenges Ser.). (ENG.). 24p. (gr. 2-3). lib. bdg. 25.99 (978-1-4048-6677-5(9)) Picture Window Bks.

Moore Niver, Heather. When Elephants Cry. 2017. (Animal Emotions Ser.). 32p. (J). (gr. 3-3). pap. 10.52 **(978-0-7660-8860-3(X))** Enslow Pubs., Inc.

Mundy, Linus. Being Sad When Someone Dies: A Book about Grief... Just for Me! Fitzgerald, Anne, illus. 2012. 32p. (J). pap. 7.95 (978-0-87029-501-0(2)) Abbey Pr.

Nachbar, Patricia Depoyster. Love Doesn't Die. 2013. 16p. pap. 12.70 (978-1-4669-6292-7(5)) Trafford Publishing.

Naik, Anita. Coping with Loss: The Life Changes Handbook. 2009. (Really Useful Handbooks Ser.). (ENG.). 48p. (J). (gr. 5-11). pap. (978-0-7787-4404-7(3)) Crabtree Publishing Co.

Naik, Anita & Cronin, Ali. Coping with Loss: The Life Changes Handbook. 2009. (Really Useful Handbooks Ser.). (ENG.). 48p. (J). (gr. 5-11). lib. bdg. (978-0-7787-4391-0(8)) Crabtree Publishing Co.

Peacock, Carol Antoinette. Death & Dying. (Life Balance Ser.). (ENG., Illus.). 80p. (J). 2005. (gr. 5-8). pap. 6.95 (978-0-531-16728-1(3)) 2004. 20.50 (978-0-531-12370-6(7)) Scholastic Library Publishing. (Watts, Franklin).

Philips, Tracy A. Did Someone You Love Die? 2015. (Got Issues? Ser.). (ENG.). 128p. (J). (gr. 7-7). 37.27 (978-0-7660-6985-5(0)) Enslow Pubs., Inc.

Phillips, Tracy A. Losing Someone You Love: Dealing with Death & Dying. 2009. (Issues in Focus Today Ser.). (Illus.). 104p. (J). (gr. 6-12). lib. bdg. 33.27 (978-0-7660-3067-1(9)) Enslow Pubs., Inc.

Roberts, Jillian. What Happens When a Loved One Dies? Our First Talk about Death, 1 vol. Revell, Cindy, illus. 2016. (Just Enough Ser.). (ENG.). 32p. (J). (gr. k-1). 19.95 (978-1-4598-0945-1(9)) Orca Bk. Pubs. USA.

Ruiz, Ruth Ann. Coping with the Death of a Brother or Sister. 2009. (Coping Ser.). 192p. (gr. 7-12). 63.90 (978-1-61512-015-4(7)) Rosen Publishing Group, Inc., The.

Ruiz, Ruth Anne. Coping with the Death of a Brother or Sister. 2005. (Coping Ser.). (Illus.). 192p. (YA). (gr. 7-12). lib. bdg. 34.60 (978-0-8239-2851-4(9)) Rosen Publishing Group, Inc., The.

Sabin, Ellen. The Healing Book: Facing the Death-and Celebrating the Life-of Someone You Love. 2006. (Illus.). 63p. (J). (gr. 1-8). 17.95 (978-0-9759868-3-7(X)) Watering Can.

Sanna, Ellyn. Those Who Remain: What It Means to Be a Survivor. (Survivors Ser.). (Illus.). 128p. (J). 2010. (gr. 7-12). 24.95 (978-1-4222-0457-3(X)) 2009. pap. 24.95 (978-1-4222-1470-1(2)) Mason Crest.

Schleifer, Jay. Todo lo que necesitas saber sobre Cuando alguien a quien conoces ha mureto (Everything You Need to Know When Someone You Know Has Been Killed) 2009. (Todo lo que necesitas (the Need to Know Library) Ser.). (SPA.). 64p. (gr. 6-6). 58.50 (978-1-60854-406-6(0), Editorial Buenas Letras) Rosen Publishing Group, Inc., The.

Schuler, Kimberly B. I Will Remember You: My Catholic Guide Through Grief. 2011. 144p. (J). (gr. 2-6). pap. 10.95 (978-0-8198-3704-2(0)) Pauline Bks. & Media.

Sherry. Always & Forever: Angel's Ladybugs. 2009. 16p. pap. 10.95 (978-1-4389-0137-4(2)) AuthorHouse.

Smith, B. Good Night Jonathan - Good Morning Laura. 2008. 300p. pap. (978-1-84747-425-4(X)) Chipmunkapublishing.

Stone, Penny. How to Help Someone Who Is Grieving. 2005. (New Line of Grief Guides). 9.95 (978-1-891400-38-4(X)) Sourcebooks, Inc.

Sunderland, Margot & Hancock, Nicky. Helping Children with Loss: A Guidebook. Armstrong, Nicky, tr. 2007. (Helping Children with Feelings Ser.). (ENG., Illus.). 88p. (C). pap. 34.95 (978-0-86388-467-2(9), Y329808, Routledge) Taylor & Francis Group GBR. Dist: Taylor & Francis Group.

Tsioumanis, Marina. Mum & Dad Are Separating: A Practical Resource for Separating Families & Family Therapy Professionals, 2 vols. 2017. (ENG., Illus.). 176p. (C). pap. 51.95 **(978-0-86388-669-0(8)**, Y329910) Routledge.

Weaver, Susan B. Forever Friend: Activities for Kids Who Have Lost a Pet. 2011. (ENG., Illus.). 80p. (J). pap. 13.95 (978-0-9829490-4-7(9)) Rainbow Reach.

—Love & Memories: Activities for Kids Who Have Lost a Loved One. 2011. (ENG., Illus.). 80p. (J). pap. 13.95 (978-0-9829490-1-6(4)) Rainbow Reach.

Wheeler, Jenny Lee. Weird Is Normal When Teenagers Grieve. 2010. 110p. pap. 9.95 (978-0-9816219-8-2(8)) Quality of Life Publishing Co.

Wheeler, Karla. Heart-Shaped Pickles: Gentle Grief Support for Kids & Grownups. Wheeler, Jenny Lee, illus. l.t. ed. 2003. (ENG.). 36p. (J). 4.95 (978-0-9675532-2-1(9)) Quality of Life Publishing Co.

Witkin, Kim. Butterfly Blessings. 2012. 44p. pap. 17.45 (978-1-4525-5751-9(9)) Balboa Pr.

Zucker, Bonnie. Something Very Sad Happened: A Toddler's Guide to Understanding Death. Fleming, Kim, illus. 2016. 32p. (J). 14.95 (978-1-4338-2266-7(0), Magination Pr.) American Psychological Assn.

GRIEF—FICTION

Alegre, Mari. Destiny. 2011. 174p. 29.99 (978-1-4568-2040-4(0)); pap. 19.99 (978-1-4568-2039-8(7)) Xlibris Corp.

Alexander, Jill S. The Sweetheart of Prosper County. 2010. (ENG.). 240p. (YA). (gr. 7-12). pap. 18.99 (978-0-312-54857-5(5), 9780312548575) Square Fish.

Alexander, Sarah. The Art of Not Breathing. (ENG.). 288p. (YA). (gr. 9). 2017. pap. 9.99 (978-0-544-93687-4(6)) 2016. 17.99 (978-0-544-63388-9(1)) Houghton Mifflin Harcourt Publishing Co. (HMH Books For Young Readers).

Alsaid, Adi. Let's Get Lost. 2015. (ENG.). 384p. (YA). pap. 9.99 (978-0-373-21149-4(X), Harlequin Teen) Harlequin Enterprises, Ltd. CAN. Dist: HarperCollins Pubs.

Appelt, Kathi & Mcghee, Alison. Maybe a Fox. 2016. (ENG., Illus.). 272p. (J). (gr. 5-9). 17.99 (978-1-4424-8242-5(7), Atheneum/Caitlyn Dlouhy Books) Simon & Schuster Children's Publishing.

Arcos, Carrie. There Will Come a Time. 2014. (ENG., Illus.). 320p. (YA). (gr. 9). 17.99 (978-1-4424-9585-2(5), Simon Pulse) Simon Pulse.

Arenella, Betsy Bottino. Isabelle's Dream: A Story & Activity Book for a Child's Grief Journey. Henderson, Dana, illus. 2007. 64p. (gr. -1-3). per. 7.95 (978-0-9675532-9-0(6)) Quality of Life Publishing Co.

Arnold, Elana K. The Question of Miracles. 2016. (ENG.). 256p. (J). (gr. 5-7). pap. 6.99 (978-0-544-66852-2(9), HMH Books For Young Readers) Houghton Mifflin Harcourt Publishing Co.

Ashes to Ashes. 2014. (ENG., Illus.). 400p. (YA). (gr. 9). 18.99 (978-1-4424-4081-4(3), Simon & Schuster Bks. For Young Readers) Simon & Schuster Bks. For Young Readers.

Auseon, Andrew. Freak Magnet. 2010. (ENG.). 304p. (YA). (gr. 9-18). 16.99 (978-0-06-113926-0(2), HarperTeen) HarperCollins Pubs.

Austen, Catherine. Walking Backward, 1 vol. 2009. (ENG., Illus.). 176p. (J). (gr. 4-7). pap. 9.95 (978-1-55469-147-0(8)) Orca Bk. Pubs. USA.

Avasthi, Swati. Chasing Shadows. Phillips, Craig, illus. 2015. (ENG.). 336p. (YA). (gr. 9). pap. 10.99 (978-0-375-86343-1(5), Ember) Random Hse. Children's Bks.

Avery, Tom. My Brother's Shadow. 2014. (ENG.). 176p. (J). (gr. 4-7). 16.99 (978-0-385-38487-2(4), Schwartz & Wade Bks.) Random Hse. Children's Bks.

Bacho, Peter. Leaving Yesler. 2010. 285p. (YA). pap. 16.00 (978-1-929355-57-0(2)) Pleasure Boat Studio: A Literary Pr.

Bagley, Jessixa. Boats for Papa. 2015. (ENG., Illus.). 40p. (J). (gr. -1-2). 17.99 (978-1-62672-039-8(8), 9781626720398) Roaring Brook Pr.

Bahr, Mary. If Nathan Were Here. Jerome, Karen A., illus. 2004. 32p. (J). (gr. 1-7). 16.00 (978-0-8028-5187-1(8)) Eerdmans, William B. Publishing Co.

Baker, Chandler. This Is Not the End. 2017. (ENG.). 384p. (YA). (gr. 9-17). 17.99 **(978-1-4847-5024-7(1))** Hyperion Bks. for Children.

Ballard, Elizabeth Silance. Kate's Fan. Napier, Louise S., illus. 2008. 48p. (J). pap. 18.95 (978-0-9706823-3-8(6)) Righter Publishing Co., Inc.

Banting, Celia. I only said I couldn't Cope. 2006. (Illus.). 240p. (YA). per. 14.99 (978-0-9786648-2-4(5)) Wighita Pr.

Barnaby, Hannah. Some of the Parts. 2016. (ENG.). 304p. (YA). (gr. 7). 17.99 (978-0-553-53963-9(9), Knopf Bks. for Young Readers) Random Hse. Children's Bks.

Barnes, David-Matthew. Mesmerized. 2010. (ENG.). 264p. (J). (gr. 7). pap. 13.95 (978-1-60282-191-0(7)) Bold Strokes Bks.

Bateman, Rachel. Someone Else's Summer. 2017. (ENG.). 320p. (YA). (gr. 8-17). 17.99 (978-0-7624-6219-3(1), Running Pr.) Running Pr. Bk. Pubs.

Bauer, A. C. E. Gil Marsh. 2013. (ENG.). 192p. (YA). (gr. 7). pap. 7.99 (978-0-375-87374-4(0), Ember) Random Hse. Children's Bks.

Beaty, Andrea. Secrets of the Cicada Summer. 2008. (ENG.). 176p. (J). (gr. 3-7). 16.95 (978-0-8109-9472-0(0), Amulet Bks.) Abrams, Inc.

Belasco, Sonia. Speak of Me As I Am. 2017. (ENG.). 272p. (YA). (gr. 7). 17.99 (978-0-399-54676-1(6), Philomel Bks.) Penguin Young Readers Group.

Bell, Hilari. Trickster's Girl: The Raven Duet Book #1. 2011. (Raven Duet Ser.). (ENG.). 288p. (YA). (gr. 7). pap. 15.99 (978-0-547-57724-1(9)) Houghton Mifflin Harcourt Publishing Co.

Benjamin, Ali. The Thing about Jellyfish. (ENG.). 352p. (J). (gr. 5-17). 2017. pap. 8.99 (978-0-316-38084-3(9)) 2015. 17.99 (978-0-316-38086-7(5)) Little, Brown Bks. for Young Readers.

—The Thing about Jellyfish. 2017. (J). lib. bdg. 19.65 **(978-0-606-40218-7(7))** Turtleback Bks.

Berni, K. S. Angels of Children: Sarafina Teaches the Importance of Prayer. 2012. 40p. pap. 20.99 (978-1-4772-7708-9(0)) AuthorHouse.

Bevan, Lizzie. Never Far When in My Heart. 2013. (ENG., Illus.). 31p. (J). pap. 15.95 (978-1-4787-1027-1(6)) Outskirts Pr., Inc.

Binns, B. A. & McKenzie, C. Lee. The Princess of Las Pulgas. 2010. 334p. (YA). (gr. 8-18). 16.95 (978-1-934813-44-7(3)) Westside Bks.

Bishop, Jenn. The Distance to Home. (ENG.). 240p. (J). (gr. 3-7). 2017. 6.99 **(978-1-101-93874-4(9)**, Yearling) 2016. 16.99 (978-1-101-93871-3(4), Knopf Bks. for Young Readers) Random Hse. Children's Bks.

Blackman, Malorie. Knife Edge. 2007. (ENG., Illus.). 368p. (YA). (gr. 9-12). 16.99 *(978-1-4169-0018-4(7),* Simon & Schuster Bks. For Young Readers) Simon & Schuster Bks. For Young Readers.

Blackstone, Matt. Sorry You're Lost. 2014. (ENG.). 320p. (J). (gr. 5-9). 15.99 *(978-0-374-38065-6(1),* 9780374380656, Farrar, Straus & Giroux (BYR)) Farrar, Straus & Giroux.

Blumenthal, Deborah. The Blue House Dog, 1 vol. Gustavson, Adam, illus. 2010. (ENG.). 32p. (J). (gr. -1-3). 15.95 *(978-1-56145-537-9(7),* Peachtree Junior) Peachtree Pubs.

Borden, Louise & Borden, Louise W. Across the Blue Pacific: A World War II Story. Parker, Robert Andrew, illus. 2006. (ENG.). 48p. (J). (gr. -1-3). 17.00 *(978-0-618-33922-8(1))* Houghton Mifflin Harcourt Publishing Co.

Borden, Louise W. Across the Blue Pacific: A World War II Story. Parker, Robert Andrew, illus. 2015. (ENG.). 48p. (J). (gr. -1-3). 7.99 *(978-0-544-55552-5(X),* HMH Books For Young Readers) Houghton Mifflin Harcourt Publishing Co.

Boyce, Frank Cottrell. Millions. 2005. 247p. (gr. 3-7). 19.00 *(978-0-7569-5439-0(8))* Perfection Learning Corp.

Bozarth, Jan. Kerka's Book. Burden, Andrea, illus. 2010. (Fairy Godmother Academy Ser.: No. 2). (ENG.). 224p. (J). (gr. 3-7). pap. 6.99 *(978-0-375-85183-4(6),* Yearling) Random Hse. Children's Bks.

Brahmachari, Sita. Mira in the Present Tense. (ENG.). 288p. (J). (gr. 3-7). 2015. pap. 9.99 *(978-0-8075-5151-6(1))* 2013. 16.99 *(978-0-8075-5149-3(X))* Whitman, Albert & Co.

Braithwaite, Pamela. Missing Jessic. 2012. 44p. pap. *(978-1-105-74130-2(3))* Lulu.com.

Bryant, Jen. Pieces of Georgia. 2007. (ENG., Illus.). 176p. (J). (gr. 5-9). per. 6.99 *(978-0-440-42055-2(5),* Yearling) Random Hse. Children's Bks.

Burak, Kathryn. Emily's Dress & Other Missing Things. 2012. (ENG.). 240p. (YA). (gr. 8-12). 17.99 *(978-1-59643-736-4(7))* Roaring Brook Pr.

Buxbaum, Julie. Tell Me Three Things. (ENG.). (YA). (gr. 7). 2017. 352p. pap. 9.99 ***(978-0-553-53567-9(6),*** Ember) 2016. 336p. 17.99 *(978-0-553-53564-8(1),* Delacorte Pr.) 2016. 336p. lib. bdg. 20.99 *(978-0-553-53565-5(X),* Delacorte Pr.) Random Hse. Children's Bks.

Buxbaum, Julie. What to Say Next. 2017. (ENG.). 304p. (YA). (gr. 7). 18.99 *(978-0-553-53568-6(4),* Delacorte Pr.) Random Hse. Children's Bks.

Caletti, Deb. Essential Maps for the Lost. 2016. (ENG., Illus.). 336p. (YA). (gr. 9). 17.99 *(978-1-4814-1516-3(6),* Simon Pulse) Simon Pulse.

—Essential Maps for the Lost. 2017. lib. bdg. 22.10 ***(978-0-606-39750-6(7))*** Turtleback Bks.

Caletti, Deb. The Last Forever. 2014. (ENG., Illus.). 336p. (YA). (gr. 7-7). 17.99 *(978-1-4424-5000-4(2),* Simon Pulse) Simon Pulse.

Call, Brian D., tr. & illus. Sarah's Cloud. Call, Brian D., illus. 2003. (J). 15.95 *(978-1-57008-955-8(8))* Deseret Bk. Co.

Candelario, Margo. Looking to the Clouds for Daddy. Craft, Jerry, illus. 2009. (J). *(978-0-9820221-7-7(4))* Hunter, Karen Media.

Carestio, Michael A. Black Jack Jetty: A Boy's Journey Through Grief. 2010. (Illus.). 64p. (J). (gr. 3-8). 14.95 *(978-1-4338-0784-8(X));* pap. 9.95 *(978-1-4338-0786-2(6))* American Psychological Assn. (Magination Pr.).

Carpenter, Angie. Digewi Deer: The Tale of a Blind Deer. Berner Coble, Lynn, ed. 2013. 82p. (J). pap. 8.99 *(978-0-9846724-3-1(5))* Paws and Claws Publishing, LLC.

Carter, M. Scott. Stealing Kevin's Heart: A Novel, 1 vol. 2012. (ENG.). 244p. (YA). pap. 12.99 *(978-1-937054-06-9(3))* Roadrunner Pr.

Cashore, Kristin. Jane, Unlimited. 2017. (ENG.). 464p. (YA). (gr. 9). 18.99 ***(978-0-8037-4149-2(9),*** Kathy Dawson Books) Penguin Young Readers Group.

Castle, Jennifer. The Beginning of After. 2013. (ENG.). 448p. (YA). (gr. 8). pap. 9.99 *(978-0-06-198580-5(5),* HarperTeen) HarperCollins Pubs.

Chalifour, Francis. Le Fils du Pendu. 2006. (FRE.). 168p. (J). (gr. 7). per. 7.95 *(978-0-88776-795-1(8),* Livres Toundra) Tundra Bks. CAN. Dist: Penguin Random Hse. LLC.

Chan, Crystal. Bird. (ENG.). (J). (gr. 3-7). 2015. 320p. pap. 8.99 *(978-1-4424-5091-2(6))* 2014. (Illus.). 304p. 16.99 *(978-1-4424-5089-9(4),* Atheneum Bks. for Young Readers) Simon & Schuster Children's Publishing.

Chandler, Elizabeth. The Back Door of Midnight. 2010. (Dark Secrets Ser.: Vol. 5). (ENG.). 320p. (YA). (gr. 7-18). pap. 9.99 *(978-1-4424-0626-1(7),* Simon Pulse) Simon Pulse.

Charara, Hayan & Brown, Monica. The Three Lucys, 1 vol. Kahn, Sara & Palacios, Sara, illus. 2016. (ENG.). 40p. (J). 18.95 *(978-1-60060-998-5(8))* Lee & Low Bks., Inc.

Clark, Melissa. Bear Witness: A Novel. 2015. (ENG.). 118p. pap. 13.00 *(978-1-940716-75-6(6))* SparkPr. (a Bks.parks Imprint).

Clark, Sandra. Goldie Is Upside Down. 2005. (Illus.). 54p. (J). per. *(978-0-9755145-3-5(9),* Gibson Bks.) Glory Days Group Publishing.

Cochrane, Mick. The Girl Who Threw Butterflies. 2010. (ENG.). 192p. (J). (gr. 3-7). 6.99 *(978-0-375-84610-6(7),* Yearling) Random Hse. Children's Bks.

Coker, Rachel. Interrupted: A Life Beyond Words, 1 vol. 2013. (ENG.). 256p. (YA). pap. 9.99 *(978-0-310-72810-8(X))* Zondervan.

Condie, Ally. Summerlost. (ENG.). 272p. (J). (gr. 5). 2017. 8.99 *(978-0-399-18721-6(9),* Puffin Books) 2016. 17.99 *(978-0-399-18719-3(7),* Dutton Books for Young Readers) Penguin Young Readers Group.

—Summerlost. 2017. lib. bdg. 19.65 ***(978-0-606-40105-0(9))*** Turtleback Bks.

Cook, Julia. I Just Want to Do It My Way! De Weerd, Kelsey, illus. 2013. (ENG.). 32p. (J). 16.95 *(978-1-934490-44-0(X))* Boys Town Pr.

Cooney, Caroline B. If the Witness Lied. 2010. (ENG.). 224p. (YA). (gr. 7). pap. 8.99 *(978-0-385-73449-3(2),* Ember) Random Hse. Children's Bks.

Couloumbis, Audrey. Getting near to Baby. unabr. ed. 2004. 211p. (J). (gr. 5-9). pap. 36.00 incl. audio *(978-0-8072-8876-4(4),* LYA 287 SP, Listening Library) Random Hse. Audio Publishing Group.

Coutts, Alexandra. Young Widows Club. 2015. (ENG.). 304p. (YA). (gr. 7). 17.99 *(978-0-374-30126-2(3),* 9780374301262, Farrar, Straus & Giroux (BYR)) Farrar, Straus & Giroux.

Covey, Sean. Goob & His Grandpa. Curtis, Stacy, illus. 2013. (7 Habits of Happy Kids Ser.: 7). (ENG.). 32p. (J). (gr. -1-1). 7.99 *(978-1-4424-7653-0(2),* Simon & Schuster Bks. For Young Readers) Simon & Schuster Bks. For Young Readers.

Crenshaw, Mills. The Christmas of 45. 2010. 176p. pap. 11.99 *(978-1-59955-455-6(0))* Cedar Fort, Inc./CFI Distribution.

Crowley, James. The Magic Hour. 2003. (Illus.). 280p. (J). pap. 17.95 *(978-1-55517-713-3(1),* 77131) Cedar Fort, Inc./CFI Distribution.

—Monsterland. 2017. (ENG.). 384p. (J). (gr. 5). 16.99 *(978-0-399-17589-3(X),* G.P. Putnam's Sons Books for Young Readers) Penguin Young Readers Group.

Cullen, Lynn. Diary of Nelly Vandorn. Date not set. 128p. (gr. 3-18). mass mkt. 4.99 *(978-0-06-440926-1(0))* HarperCollins Pubs.

Culverwell, C. Ellen. The Horse Lady. 2009. (J). pap. *(978-0-88092-723-9(2));* lib. bdg. *(978-0-88092-722-2(4))* Royal Fireworks Publishing Co.

Currie, Colleen & Currie, David. Loving Baby Louie: Hope in the Midst of Grief. Streeter, Talena, illus. 2015. (ENG.). 54p. (J). 24.95 *(978-1-941447-44-4(9))* Emmaus Road Publishing.

Damaged. 2014. (ENG., Illus.). 384p. (YA). (gr. 8). 17.99 *(978-1-4424-5699-0(X),* Simon Pulse) Simon Pulse.

Danticat, Edwidge. Untwine: A Novel. 2015. (ENG.). 320p. (J). (gr. 7). 16.99 *(978-0-545-42303-8(1),* Scholastic Pr.) Scholastic, Inc.

Davis, Katie. The Curse of Addy Mcmahon. 2008. (ENG., Illus.). 288p. (J). (gr. 5-9). 16.99 *(978-0-06-128711-4(3),* Greenwillow Bks.) HarperCollins Pubs.

—The Curse of Addy McMahon. 2008. (Illus.). 288p. (J). (gr. 5-9). lib. bdg. 17.89 *(978-0-06-128712-1(1),* Greenwillow Bks.) HarperCollins Pubs.

Davis, Lisa Selin. Lost Stars. 2016. (ENG.). 288p. (YA). (gr. 9). 17.99 *(978-0-544-78506-9(1),* HMH Books For Young Readers) Houghton Mifflin Harcourt Publishing Co.

Dawley, Linda. Wee Mac. 2014. (ENG.). 146p. (J). pap. *(978-0-9941011-8-1(X),* The Little Red Hen Community Pr.) CCB Publishing.

Dawson, Joy. Maggie, the Color-Blind Cow: A loving heart—that didn't see Color. 2006. (ENG., Illus.). 36p. (J). per. 12.95 *(978-1-59800-892-0(7))* Outskirts Pr., Inc.

DeBiase, Johanna. Mama & the Hungry Hole. 2015. 154p. *(978-1-877655-85-2(6))* Wordcraft of Oregon, LLC.

DeFelice, Cynthia. Wild Life. 2011. (ENG.). 192p. (J). (gr. 3-7). 17.99 *(978-0-374-38001-4(5),* 9780374380014, Farrar, Straus & Giroux (BYR)) Farrar, Straus & Giroux.

—Wild Life. 2013. (ENG.). 208p. (J). (gr. 3-7). pap. 7.99 *(978-1-250-03407-6(8),* 9781250034076) Square Fish.

Delacre, Lulu. Alicia Afterimage. 2008. (ENG.). 144p. (YA). (gr. 7-18). 19.95 *(978-1-60060-242-9(8))* Lee & Low Bks., Inc.

Delaney, Mark. Pepperland, 1 vol. (ENG.). (YA). (gr. 7-18). 2007. 224p. pap. 7.95 *(978-1-56145-402-0(8))* 2004. 160p. 14.95 *(978-1-56145-317-7(X))* Peachtree Pubs.

Delany, Shannon & Redgrave, Saoirse. Secrets & Shadows: A 13 to Life Novel. 2011. (13 to Life Ser.: 2). (ENG.). 320p. (YA). (gr. 7-18). pap. 9.99 *(978-0-312-60915-3(9),* 9780312609153, St. Martin's Griffin) St. Martin's Pr.

Dellaira, Ava. Love Letters to the Dead. 2014. (ENG.). 336p. (YA). (gr. 7). 17.99 *(978-0-374-34667-6(4),* 9780374346676, Farrar, Straus & Giroux (BYR)) Farrar, Straus & Giroux.

Demas, Corinne. Saying Goodbye to Lulu. Hoyt, Ard, illus. 2009. (ENG.). 32p. (J). (gr. -1-3). pap. 7.99 *(978-0-316-04749-4(X))* Little, Brown Bks. for Young Readers.

Deriso, Christine Hurley. Tragedy Girl. 2016. (ENG.). 240p. (YA). pap. 11.99 *(978-0-7387-4703-3(3),* Flux) North Star Editions.

Dessen, Sarah. The Truth about Forever. 2006. (ENG.). 400p. (YA). (gr. 7-18). reprint ed. 10.99 *(978-0-14-240625-0(2),* Speak) Penguin Young Readers Group.

—The Truth about Forever. 2007. 374p. (gr. 7-12). 20.00 *(978-0-7569-8275-1(8))* Perfection Learning Corp.

—The Truth about Forever. (YA). 2006. 1.25 *(978-1-4193-2647-9(3))* 2005. 127.75 *(978-1-4193-3880-9(3))* 2005. 107.75 *(978-1-4193-2650-9(3))* Recorded Bks., Inc.

DeStefano, Lauren. The Girl with the Ghost Machine. 2017. (ENG.). 224p. (J). 16.99 *(978-1-68119-444-8(9),* 9781681194448, Bloomsbury USA Childrens) Bloomsbury Publishing USA.

Donnelly, Jennifer. Revolution. 2011. (ENG.). 512p. (YA). (gr. 9). pap. 9.99 *(978-0-385-73764-7(5),* Ember) Random Hse. Children's Bks.

Dooley, Sarah. Ashes to Asheville. 2017. (ENG.). 256p. (J). (gr. 5). 16.99 *(978-0-399-16504-7(5),* G.P. Putnam's Sons Books for Young Readers) Penguin Young Readers Group.

Dower, Laura. Maggie's Magic Chocolate Moon. Lazuli, Lilly, illus. 2016. (Dessert Diaries). (ENG.). 160p. (gr. 4-5). pap. 5.95 *(978-1-4965-4141-3(3));* lib. bdg. 26.65 *(978-1-4965-3121-6(3))* Stone Arch Bks.

Doyle, Roddy. Her Mother's Face. Blackwood, Freya, illus. 2008. (J). pap. *(978-0-439-81502-4(9),* Levine, Arthur A. Bks.) Scholastic, Inc.

Dunbar, Helene. What Remains. 2015. (ENG.). 264p. (YA). pap. 9.99 *(978-0-7387-4430-8(1),* Flux) North Star Editions.

Easton, Kelly. Aftershock. 2007. (ENG.). 176p. (YA). (gr. 7-12). pap. 6.99 *(978-1-4169-0053-5(5),* McElderry, Margaret K. Bks.) McElderry, Margaret K. Bks.

Edge, Christopher. The Many Worlds of Albie Bright. 2017. (ENG.). 176p. (J). (gr. 4-7). 16.99 ***(978-1-5247-1357-7(0));*** lib. bdg. 19.99 ***(978-1-5247-1359-1(7))*** Random Hse. Children's Bks. (Delacorte Bks. for Young Readers).

Eenie Meanie Me & the Very Sad Day. 2005. (J). *(978-0-9772878-0-2(7))* Bishop, Susan Lynn.

Elmer, Robert. Candy Bombers, 1 vol. 2006. (Wall Ser.: Bk. 1). (ENG.). 160p. (J). pap. 6.99 *(978-0-310-70943-5(1))* Zonderkidz.

Engelman, Stephanie. A Single Bead. 2016. 199p. (YA). pap. *(978-0-8198-9054-2(5))* Pauline Bks. & Media.

Ephron, Delia. Frannie in Pieces. Beckerman, Chad, illus. 2007. 374p. (YA). (gr. 7-12). lib. bdg. 17.89 *(978-0-06-074717-6(X),* HarperTeen) HarperCollins Pubs.

Erskine, Kathryn. Seeing Red. 2013. (YA). *(978-0-545-57645-1(8));* (ENG.). 352p. (J). (gr. 5-9). 16.99 *(978-0-545-46440-6(4))* Scholastic, Inc. (Scholastic Pr.).

Fallenstein, J. Graffiti. 2017. (Midnight Ser.). (ENG.). 88p. (YA). (gr. 6-12). 26.65 *(978-1-5124-2767-7(5));* 12.99 ***(978-1-5124-3489-7(2),*** Darby Creek); 39.99 ***(978-1-5124-3488-0(4),*** Darby Creek); 39.99 ***(978-1-5124-2787-5(X),*** Darby Creek) Lerner Publishing Group.

Farrant, Natasha. After Iris. 2013. (ENG.). 272p. (J). (gr. 5). 16.99 *(978-0-8037-3982-6(6),* Dial Bks) Penguin Young Readers Group.

Federle, Tim. The Great American Whatever. (ENG.). (YA). (gr. 9). 2017. 304p. pap. 10.99 *(978-1-4814-0410-5(5))* 2016. (Illus.). 288p. E-Book *(978-1-4814-0411-2(3))* 2016. (Illus.). 288p. 17.99 *(978-1-4814-0409-9(1))* Simon & Schuster Bks. For Young Readers. (Simon & Schuster Bks. For Young Readers).

Firestone, Carrie. The Loose Ends List. (ENG.). (YA). (gr. 9-17). 2017. 368p. pap. 9.99 *(978-0-316-38283-0(3))* 2016. 352p. 17.99 *(978-0-316-38282-3(5))* Little, Brown Bks. for Young Readers.

Forman, Gayle. I Was Here. l.t. ed. 2015. (ENG.). 420p. 24.99 *(978-1-4104-8255-6(3))* Cengage Gale.

—I Was Here. 2015. (ENG.). 288p. (J). (gr. 9). 18.99 *(978-0-451-47147-5(4),* Viking Books for Young Readers) Penguin Publishing Group.

—I Was Here. 2016. (ENG.). 304p. (YA). (gr. 9). pap. 10.99 *(978-0-14-751403-5(7),* Speak) Penguin Young Readers Group.

—I Was Here. 2016. lib. bdg. 22.10 *(978-0-606-38404-9(9))* Turtleback Bks.

Foxlee, Karen. The Anatomy of Wings. 2010. (ENG.). 384p. (Orig.). (YA). (gr. 9). pap. 9.99 *(978-0-375-84761-5(8),* Knopf Bks. for Young Readers) Random Hse. Children's Bks.

France, Emily. Signs of You. (ENG.). 240p. (YA). (gr. 9). 2017. pap. 10.99 *(978-1-61695-815-2(4))* 2016. 18.99 *(978-1-61695-657-8(7))* Soho Pr., Inc. (Soho Teen).

Frank, E. R. Wrecked. (ENG., (YA). 2015. Illus.). 336p. (gr. 9). pap. 10.99 *(978-1-4814-5137-6(5))* 2007. 256p. (gr. 7-12). pap. 9.99 *(978-0-689-87384-3(0))* Simon & Schuster Children's Publishing. (Atheneum Bks. for Young Readers).

Freitas, Donna. The Survival Kit. 2011. (ENG.). 368p. (YA). (gr. 7-12). 17.99 *(978-0-374-39917-7(4),* Farrar, Straus & Giroux (BYR)) Farrar, Straus & Giroux.

Friend, Natasha. Perfect. 2004. (ENG.). 232p. (J). pap. 7.95 *(978-1-57131-651-6(5))* Milkweed Editions.

Furniss, Clare. The Year of the Rat. 2015. (ENG.). 304p. (YA). (gr. 7). pap. 10.99 *(978-1-4814-2100-3(X),* McElderry, Margaret K. Bks.) McElderry, Margaret K. Bks.

Galante, Cecilia. Stealing Our Way Home. 2017. (ENG.). 304p. (J). (gr. 3-7). 17.99 ***(978-1-338-04296-2(3),*** Scholastic Pr.) Scholastic, Inc.

Garcia, Kami. The Lovely Reckless. 2016. (ENG.). 384p. (YA). 18.99 *(978-1-250-07919-0(5),* 9781250079190) Imprint IND. Dist: Macmillan.

Geithner, Carole. If Only. 2012. (ENG.). 336p. (J). (gr. 5-9). 16.99 *(978-0-545-23499-3(9),* Scholastic Pr.) Scholastic, Inc.

Gil, Lydia. Letters from Heaven. 2014.Tr. of Cartas Del Cielo. (ENG & SPA.). 128p. (J). pap. 9.95 *(978-1-55885-798-8(2),* Piñata Books) Arte Publico Pr.

Gingras, Charlotte. Pieces of Me. Ouriou, Susan, tr. from FRE. 2009. (ENG.). 144p. (J). (gr. 7-9). 17.95 *(978-1-55453-242-1(6))* Kids Can Pr., Ltd. CAN. Dist: Hachette Bk. Group.

Glines, Abbi. Until Friday Night. 2015. (Field Party Ser.: Bk. 1). (ENG.). 336p. (YA). pap. *(978-1-4711-2502-7(5),* Simon Pulse) Simon Pulse.

Gogolewski, Kathe, illus. Tato. 2008. (J). *(978-0-9800064-2-1(2))* Red Engine Pr.

Going, K. L. The Garden of Eve. 2009. (ENG., Illus.). 240p. (J). (gr. 2-5). pap. 14.95 *(978-0-15-206614-7(4))* Houghton Mifflin Harcourt Publishing Co.

Gormally, Eleanor. The Little Flower Bulb: Helping Children Bereaved by Suicide. Loki & Splink, illus. 2011. (ENG.). 32p. (J). (gr. -1-3). pap. 21.95 *(978-1-84730-260-1(2))* Veritas Pubns. IRL. Dist: Dufour Editions, Inc.

Grace & the Guiltless. 2014. (Wanted Ser.). (ENG.). 272p. 16.95 *(978-1-63079-001-1(X))* Switch Pr.

Graff, Lisa. Umbrella Summer. 2011. (ENG.). 240p. (J). (gr. 3-7). pap. 6.99 *(978-0-06-143189-0(3))* HarperCollins Pubs.

Gray, Kristin L. Vilonia Beebe Takes Charge. 2017. (ENG., Illus.). 208p. (J). (gr. 3-7). 16.99 *(978-1-4814-5842-9(6),* Simon & Schuster/Paula Wiseman Bks.) Simon & Schuster/Paula Wiseman Bks.

Gregory, Nan. Wild Girl & Gran. 2004. (Illus.). (J). (gr. k-3). spiral bd. *(978-0-616-11112-3(6))* Canadian National Institute for the Blind/Institut National Canadien pour les Aveugles.

Haber, Melissa Glenn. Dear Anjali. 2010. (ENG.). 288p. (J). (gr. 4-8). 16.99 *(978-1-4169-9599-9(4),* Simon & Schuster/Paula Wiseman Bks.) Simon & Schuster/Paula Wiseman Bks.

—Your Best Friend, Meredith. 2011. (ENG.). 288p. (J). (gr. 4-8). pap. 6.99 *(978-1-4169-9600-2(1),* Aladdin) Simon & Schuster Children's Publishing.

Haddix, Margaret Peterson. Claim to Fame. (ENG.). 272p. (YA). (gr. 7). 2010. pap. 9.99 *(978-1-4169-3918-4(0))* 2009. 16.99 *(978-1-4169-3917-7(2))* Simon & Schuster Bks. For Young Readers. (Simon & Schuster Bks. For Young Readers).

Hahn, Mary Downing. Mister Death's Blue-Eyed Girls. (ENG.). 336p. (YA). (gr. 7). 2012. 16.99 *(978-0-547-76062-9(0))* 2013. pap. 8.99 *(978-0-544-02224-9(6))* Houghton Mifflin Harcourt Publishing Co.

Hainsworth, Emily. Take the Fall. 2016. 368p. (YA). (gr. 9). 17.99 *(978-0-06-209422-3(X))* HarperCollins Pubs.

—Through to You. 2012. (ENG.). 272p. (YA). (gr. 8). 17.99 *(978-0-06-209419-3(X))* HarperCollins Pubs.

Hale, Marian. The Goodbye Season. 2009. (ENG.). 288p. (YA). (gr. 7-12). 16.99 *(978-0-8050-8855-7(5),* 9780805088557, Holt, Henry & Co. Bks. For Young Readers) Holt, Henry & Co.

Hand, Cynthia. The Last Time We Say Goodbye. 400p. (YA). (gr. 8). 2016. pap. 9.99 *(978-0-06-231848-0(9))* 2015. (ENG.). 17.99 *(978-0-06-231847-3(0))* HarperCollins Pubs. (HarperTeen).

—The Last Time We Say Goodbye. 2016. (YA). lib. bdg. 20.85 *(978-0-606-38130-7(9))* Turtleback Bks.

Hapgood, Harriet Reuter & Peppermint Frog Limited. The Square Root of Summer. 2016. (ENG.). 304p. (YA). 17.99 *(978-1-62672-373-3(7),* 9781626723733) Roaring Brook Pr.

Harrington, Janine. Soul Sister. 2012. 244p. pap. *(978-1-78176-139-7(6))* FeedARead.com.

Harrington, Karen. Mayday. 2016. (ENG.). 352p. (J). (gr. 3-7). 16.99 *(978-0-316-29801-8(8))* Little, Brown Bks. for Young Readers.

Harris, Mary. Freckles from Heaven. Harris, Brandy, illus. 2007. 28p. per. 24.95 *(978-1-4241-8647-1(1))* America Star Bks.

Hautala, Beth. Waiting for Unicorns. 2015. (ENG.). 256p. (J). (gr. 5). 16.99 *(978-0-525-42631-8(0),* Philomel Bks.) Penguin Young Readers Group.

Hayes, Nicole. The Whole of My World. l.t. ed. 2013. 618p. pap. *(978-1-4596-6746-4(8))* ReadHowYouWant.com, Ltd.

Hays, Tommy. What I Came to Tell You. 2014. (ENG., Illus.). 304p. (J). (gr. 5). pap. 8.99 *(978-1-60684-545-5(4),* Carolrhoda Bks.) Lerner Publishing Group.

Heckman, Ashley. The Last Three Words. 2013. 104p. pap. *(978-1-77130-651-5(3))* Evernight Publishing.

Heffernan, John. Hotaka: Through My Eyes - Natural Disaster Zones. White, Lyn, ed. 2017. (Through My Eyes Ser.). (ENG.). 224p. (J). (gr. 6-9). pap. 12.99 ***(978-1-76011-376-6(X))*** Allen & Unwin AUS. Dist: Independent Pubs. Group.

Hemery, Kathleen Maresh. Sunflower Promise. Bordelois, Augusto, illus. 2005. (J). *(978-1-56123-188-1(6))* Centering Corp.

Hemingway, Edith M. Road to Tater Hill. 2011. (ENG.). 224p. (J). (gr. 3-7). 7.99 *(978-0-375-84544-4(5),* Yearling) Random Hse. Children's Bks.

Henkes, Kevin. Bird Lake Moon. (ENG.). 192p. (J). (gr. 3-7). 2010. pap. 5.99 *(978-0-06-147079-0(1))* 2008. 17.99 *(978-0-06-147076-9(7))* HarperCollins Pubs. (Greenwillow Bks.).

—Sun & Spoon. 2007. (ENG.). 144p. (J). (gr. 3-7). pap. 8.99 *(978-0-06-128875-3(6),* Greenwillow Bks.) HarperCollins Pubs.

Henson, Heather. The Whole Sky. 2017. (ENG., Illus.). 256p. (J). (gr. 5-7). 16.99 ***(978-1-4424-1405-1(7),*** Atheneum/Caitlyn Dlouhy Books) Simon & Schuster Children's Publishing.

Hernandez, David. No More Us for You. 2009. (YA). 281p. lib. bdg. 17.89 *(978-0-06-117334-9(7));* (ENG.). 288p. (gr. 9-18). 16.99 *(978-0-06-117333-2(9))* HarperCollins Pubs. (HarperTeen).

Hershey, Mary. My Big Sister Is So Bossy She Says You Can't Read This Book. 2006. (ENG., Illus.). 176p. (J). (gr. 3-7). per. 6.99 *(978-0-553-48797-8(3),* Yearling) Random Hse. Children's Bks.

Heyne, Kara. The Locket's Secret. 2013. (ENG.). 162p. (J). pap. 8.95 *(978-0-8198-7484-9(1))* Pauline Bks. & Media.

Hickman, Rachel. One Silver Summer. 2016. (ENG.). 272p. (J). (gr. 9). 17.99 *(978-0-545-80892-7(8),* Scholastic Pr.) Scholastic, Inc.

Hicks-Alessi, Nicole. Raccoon Hollow: Marky's Troubles. 2011. 40p. pap. 16.95 *(978-1-4560-6541-6(6))* America Star Bks.

Hicks, Betty. Out of Order. 2007. (ENG.). 176p. (J). (gr. 3-7). pap. 14.99 *(978-0-312-37355-9(4),* 9780312373559) Square Fish.

Hoang, Melanie Rowland. The Gift. 2011. 32p. pap. 13.95 *(978-1-4525-3524-1(8))* Get Published.

Hoban, Julia. Willow. 2010. (ENG.). 336p. (YA). (gr. 9-18). 8.99 *(978-0-14-241666-2(5),* Speak) Penguin Young Readers Group.

Hoffman, Alice. Green Heart. 2012. (ENG.). 272p. (J). (gr. 7-7). pap. 10.99 *(978-0-545-14196-3(6),* Scholastic Paperbacks) Scholastic, Inc.

—Green Heart. 2012. lib. bdg. 22.10 *(978-0-606-23954-7(5),* Turtleback) Turtleback Bks.

Holt, Kimberly Willis. Blooming at the Texas Sunrise Motel. Rosenberry, Vera, illus. 2017. (ENG.). 336p. (J). 16.99 *(978-1-62779-324-7(0),* 9781627793247, Holt, Henry & Co. Bks. For Young Readers) Holt, Henry & Co.

—Keeper of the Night. 2011. (ENG.). 336p. (YA). (gr. 7-12). pap. 14.99 *(978-0-312-66103-8(7),* 9780312661038) Square Fish.

Hopkins, Ellen. Rumble. 2016. (ENG., Illus.). 576p. (YA). (gr. 9). pap. 12.99 *(978-1-4424-8285-2(0),* McElderry, Margaret K. Bks.) McElderry, Margaret K. Bks.

—Smoke. (ENG., Illus.). (YA). (gr. 9). 2015. 576p. pap. 12.99 *(978-1-4169-8329-3(5))* 2013. 560p. 19.99 *(978-1-4169-8328-6(7))* McElderry, Margaret K. Bks. (McElderry, Margaret K. Bks.).

Howland, Leila. Nantucket Blue. 2014. (Nantucket Blue Ser.). (ENG.). 320p. (YA). (gr. 9-17). pap. 8.99 *(978-1-4231-6139-4(4))* Hyperion Bks. for Children.

Hurwin, Davida Wills. A Time for Dancing. 2009. (ENG.). 272p. (YA). (gr. 7-17). pap. 10.00 *(978-0-316-03634-4(X))* Little Brown & Co.

Hutchings, Harriet Anne. Amanda & the Angel. Cragg, Marcelyn Martin, illus. 2010. 24p. pap. 9.95 *(978-1-936051-81-6(8))* Peppertree Pr., The.

Hutchinson, Shaun David. The Five Stages of Andrew Brawley. Larsen, Christine, illus. 2015. (ENG.). 304p. (YA). (gr. 7). 17.99 *(978-1-4814-0310-8(9),* Simon Pulse) Simon Pulse.

—We Are the Ants. 2016. (ENG., Illus.). 464p. (YA). (gr. 9). 17.99 *(978-1-4814-4963-2(X),* Simon Pulse) Simon Pulse.

Israel, Julie. Juniper Lemon's Happiness Index. 2017. (ENG.). 352p. (YA). (gr. 7). 17.99 ***(978-0-7352-2817-7(5),*** Kathy Dawson Books) Penguin Young Readers Group.

Jacobs, Evan. Varsity 170, 1 vol., Bk. 10. 2015. (Gravel Road Ser.). (ENG.). (YA). (gr. 9-12). pap. 9.95 *(978-1-62250-889-1(0))* Saddleback Educational Publishing, Inc.

Jaden, Denise. Losing Faith. 2010. (ENG.). 400p. (YA). (gr. 9-18). pap. 9.99 *(978-1-4169-9609-5(5),* Simon Pulse) Simon Pulse.

James, Henry. Alexandra's Accident: A Little Girl Comes to Grief While Out with Her Pa. 2012. 24p. pap. 28.03 *(978-1-4797-5649-0(0))* Xlibris Corp.

Jaques-Plester, Carol. Grandma Goes to Heaven. 2007. pap. 17.00 *(978-0-8059-8887-1(4))* Dorrance Publishing Co., Inc.

Jayne, Hannah. The Dare. 2014. (ENG.). 288p. (YA). (gr. 7-12). pap. 9.99 *(978-1-4022-9457-0(3),* 9781402294570) Sourcebooks, Inc.

Jennings, Richard W. Scribble. 2004. (ENG.). 160p. (YA). (gr. 5-9). tchr. ed. 15.00 *(978-0-618-43367-4(8))* Houghton Mifflin Harcourt Publishing Co.

EFG

Johnson, Angela. Looking for Red. 2003. (ENG., Illus.). 128p. (YA). (gr. 7). pap. 6.99 (978-0-689-86388-2(8), Simon Pulse) Simon Pulse.

Johnson, Maureen. The Key to the Golden Firebird. 2004. (ENG.). 304p. (J). (gr. 7-18). 15.99 (978-0-06-054138-5(5)) HarperCollins Pubs.

—13 Little Blue Envelopes. (13 Little Blue Envelopes Ser.: 1). (ENG., Illus.). (YA). (gr. 8-18). 2005. 336p. 17.99 (978-0-06-054141-5(5)) 2010. 368p. reprint ed. pap. 9.99 (978-0-06-054143-9(1)) HarperCollins Pubs. (HarperTeen).

—13 Little Blue Envelopes. 2007. 317p. 20.00 (978-0-7569-7830-3(0)) Perfection Learning Corp.

Jones, Carrie. Need. 2009. (Need Ser.). (ENG.). 336p. (YA). (gr. 7). pap. 9.99 (978-1-59990-453-5(5), 9781599904535, Bloomsbury USA Childrens) Bloomsbury Publishing USA.

Jones, Patrick. On Guard. 2016. (Bounce Ser.). (ENG.). 104p. (YA). (gr. 6-12). lib. bdg. 26.65 (978-1-5124-1123-2(X), Darby Creek) Lerner Publishing Group.

Jones, Traci L. Silhouetted by the Blue. 2011. (ENG.). 208p. (J). (gr. 5-9). 16.99 (978-0-374-36914-9(3), 9780374369149, Farrar, Straus & Giroux (BYR)) Farrar, Straus & Giroux.

Joseph, Beverly L. Don't Forget about Me. Swope, Brenda, illus. 2011. 28p. pap. 24.95 (978-1-4560-0972-4(9)) America Star Bks.

Kade, Stacey. For This Life Only. 2016. (ENG., Illus.). 320p. (YA). (gr. 9). 17.99 (978-1-4814-3248-1(6), Simon & Schuster Bks. For Young Readers) Simon & Schuster Bks. For Young Readers.

Kadono, Eiko. Grandpa's Soup. Ichikawa, Santomi, illus. 2009. (ENG.). 40p. (J). (gr. -1-3). pap. 9.00 (978-0-8028-5347-9(1), Eerdmans Bks For Young Readers) Eerdmans, William B. Publishing Co.

Kain, Jamie. The Good Sister. 2015. (ENG.). 304p. (YA). (gr. 9-12). pap. 9.99 (978-1-250-04774-8(9), 9781250047748, St. Martin's Griffin) St. Martin's Pr.

Kaulen, Diane Bouman. In the Wake of Suicide: A Child's Journey. McAdoo, Grami & McAdoo, O'Pa, illus. 2008. (J). (gr. 3-5). 14.95 (978-0-9764026-5-7(3)) Longhorn Creek Pr.

Kear, Nicole C. The Fix-It Friends: Wish You Were Here. Dockray, Tracy, illus. 2017. (Fix-It Friends Ser.: 4). (ENG.). 160p. (J). pap. 5.99 (**978-1-250-08670-9(1)**, 9781250086709) Imprint IND. Dist: Macmillan.

Kearney, Meg. The Girl in the Mirror. 2012. (ENG.). 176p. (YA). (gr. 9-17). pap. 15.00 (978-0-89255-385-3(5), 255385) Persea Bks., Inc.

Keckler, Ben. Incredibly Lonely, That's Me. Davis, Dick, illus. 2007. (Express Yourself Ser.). 42p. (J). (gr. 3-7). 17.95 (978-0-9769093-2-3(4)) Eagle Creek Pubns., LLC.

Kelly, Keith. Peace Comes to Ajani. Kelly, Keith, illus. 2009. (Illus.). 56p. (J). pap. 9.95 (978-0-932112-59-0(5)) Carolina Wren Pr.

Kelly, Tom. Finn's Going. 2007. 278p. (YA). (gr. 8-12). 16.99 (978-0-06-121453-0(1), Greenwillow Bks.) HarperCollins Pubs.

Kemmerer, Brigid. Letters to the Lost. 2017. (ENG.). 400p. (YA). 17.99 (978-1-68119-008-2(7), 9781681190082, Bloomsbury USA Childrens) Bloomsbury Publishing USA.

Kendall, Christine. Riding Chance. 2016. (ENG.). 224p. (J). (gr. 5-9). 16.99 (978-0-545-92404-7(9), Scholastic Pr.) Scholastic, Inc.

Kenneally, Miranda. Breathe, Annie, Breathe. (Hundred Oaks Ser.: Bk. 5). (ENG.). (YA). (gr. 8-12). 2015. 336p. pap. 9.99 (978-1-4926-0866-0(1), 9781492608660) 2014. 320p. 16.99 (978-1-4022-8479-3(9), 9781402284793) Sourcebooks, Inc.

Kennedy, Pamela. Granny's Cozy Quilt of Memories: Remembering Grandmother's Love Through Her Lasting Gift. Wummer, Amy, illus. 2006. (ENG.). 32p. (J). (gr. k-3). 8.95 (978-0-8249-5538-0(2), Ideal Pubns.) Worthy Publishing.

Kephart, Beth. Nothing but Ghosts. 2009. (ENG.). 288p. (J). (gr. 8-18). 17.99 (978-0-06-166796-1(X), HarperTeen) HarperCollins Pubs.

Keyser, Amber J. The Way Back from Broken. 2015. (ENG.). 216p. (YA). (gr. 6-12). 18.99 (978-1-4677-8817-5(1), Carolrhoda Lab™); 18.99 (978-1-4677-7590-8(8)) Lerner Publishing Group.

Kim, Cecil. Friendship Quilt. Jeong, HaJin, illus. rev. ed. 2014. (MySELF Bookshelf Ser.). (ENG.). 32p. (J). (gr. k-2). pap. 11.94 (978-1-60357-659-8(2)); lib. bdg. 25.27 (978-1-59953-650-7(1)) Norwood Hse. Pr.

King, Eva. Dear Sweetie, I'm Okay: Helping Children Understand Death. 2012. 36p. pap. 13.95 (978-1-4497-6192-9(5), WestBow Pr.) Author Solutions, Inc.

Kiplinger Pandy, Lori, illus. Flying Hugs & Kisses. l.t. ed. 2006. 32p. (J). 15.95 (978-1-59879-119-8(2)) Lifevest Publishing, Inc.

Kirby, Jessi. In Honor. (ENG., (YA). (gr. 9). 2013. Illus.). 256p. pap. 9.99 (978-1-4424-1698-7(X)) 2012. 240p. 16.99 (978-1-4424-1697-0(1)) Simon & Schuster Bks. For Young Readers. (Simon & Schuster Bks. For Young Readers).

—Things We Know by Heart. 304p. (YA). (gr. 9). 2016. pap. 9.99 (978-0-06-229944-4(1)) 2015. (ENG.). 17.99 (978-0-06-229943-7(3)) HarperCollins Pubs. (HarperTeen).

Kittle, Katrina. Reasons to Be Happy. 2011. (ENG.). 288p. (J). (gr. 6-8). pap. 10.99 (978-1-4022-6020-9(2), Sourcebooks Jabberwocky) Sourcebooks, Inc.

Klauss, Lucas. Everything You Need to Survive the Apocalypse. 2012. (ENG.). 416p. (gr. 9). (J). pap. 9.99 (978-1-4424-2389-3(7)); (YA). 16.99 (978-1-4424-2388-6(9)) Simon Pulse. (Simon Pulse).

Klise, Kate. Grounded. 2013. (ENG.). 224p. (J). (gr. 4-8). pap. 8.99 (978-0-312-55591-7(1), 9780312555917) Square Fish.

Knowles, Jo. See You at Harry's. 2012. (ENG., Illus.). 310p. (J). (gr. 5). 16.99 (978-0-7636-5407-8(8)) Candlewick Pr.

Koertge, Ronald. Strays. 2007. (ENG.). 176p. (YA). (gr. 9-12). 16.99 (978-0-7636-2705-8(4)) Candlewick Pr.

Kroll, Jeri. Mickey's Little Book of Letters. 2005. 160p. pap. (978-0-7344-0686-6(X), Lothian Children's Bks.) Hachette Australia.

Kuhlman, Evan. The Last Invisible Boy. Coovert, J. P., illus. (ENG.). 240p. (J). (gr. 5-9). 2010. pap. 6.99 (978-1-4169-6089-8(9)) 2008. 16.99 (978-1-4169-5797-3(9)) Simon & Schuster Children's Publishing. (Atheneum Bks. for Young Readers).

Kuipers, Alice. Lost for Words. 2010. 224p. (YA). (gr. 8-18). 16.99 (978-0-06-142922-4(8), HarperTeen) HarperCollins Pubs.

Kyi, Tanya Lloyd. Anywhere but Here. 2013. (ENG., Illus.). 320p. (YA). (gr. 9). 17.99 (978-1-4424-8070-4(X)); pap. 9.99 (978-1-4424-8069-8(6)) Simon Pulse. (Simon Pulse).

LaCour, Nina. Hold Still. 2010. (ENG.). 272p. (YA). (gr. 7-18). 10.99 (978-0-14-241694-5(0), Speak) Penguin Young Readers Group.

—We Are Okay. 2017. (ENG.). 240p. (YA). (gr. 9). 17.99 (978-0-525-42589-2(6), Dutton Books for Young Readers) Penguin Young Readers Group.

LaFleur, Suzanne. Love, Aubrey. 2011. (ENG.). 272p. (J). (gr. 3-7). pap. 7.99 (978-0-375-85159-9(3), Yearling) Random Hse. Children's Bks.

Laird, Elizabeth. Red Sky in the Morning. 2012. (ENG.). 192p. (gr. 3-10). pap. 12.95 (978-1-60846-153-0(X)) Haymarket Bks.

Lane, Dakota. Gothic Lolita: A Mystical Thriller. Lane, Dakota, illus. 2008. (ENG., Illus.). 208p. (YA). (gr. 7-18). 17.99 (978-1-4169-1396-2(3), Atheneum Bks. for Young Readers) Simon & Schuster Children's Publishing.

Larsen, Elisabeth Helland. Life & I: A Story about Death. Schneider, Marine, illus. 2016. (ENG.). 48p. (J). (gr. -1-3). 19.95 (**978-3-89955-771-8(9)**) Die Gestalten Verlag DEU. Dist: Penguin Random Hse. LLC.

Lasky, Kathryn. More Than Magic. 2016. (ENG.). 224p. (J). (gr. 3-7). 16.99 (978-0-553-49891-2(6), Lamb, Wendy Bks.) Random Hse. Children's Bks.

Lawson, Jessica. Waiting for Augusta. 2016. (ENG., Illus.). 336p. (J). (gr. 3-7). 16.99 (978-1-4814-4839-0(0), Simon & Schuster Bks. For Young Readers) Simon & Schuster Bks. For Young Readers.

Lean, Sarah. A Dog Called Homeless. 2012. (ENG.). 208p. (J). (gr. 3-7). 16.99 (978-0-06-212220-9(7), Tegen, Katherine Bks) HarperCollins Pubs.

Leibovici, Danielle. With You Always. Gabrielov, Julia, illus. l.t. ed. 2012. (ENG.). 62p. pap. 14.95 (978-1-4565-2627-6(8)) CreateSpace Independent Publishing Platform.

Lettich, Sheldon, et al. Max: Best Friend, Hero, Marine. 2015. (ENG.). 256p. (J). (gr. 3-7). pap. 6.99 (978-0-06-242039-8(9)) HarperCollins Pubs.

Levis, Caron. Ida, Always. Santoso, Charles, illus. 2016. (ENG.). 40p. (J). (gr. -1-3). 17.99 (978-1-4814-2640-4(0)) Simon & Schuster Children's Publishing.

Levithan, David. Marly's Ghost. Selznick, Brian, illus. 2007. (ENG.). 208p. (YA). (gr. 7-18). 7.99 (978-0-14-240912-1(X), Speak) Penguin Young Readers Group.

Levy, Michelle. Not after Everything. 2015. (ENG.). 336p. (YA). (gr. 9-12). 17.99 (978-0-8037-4158-4(8), Dial Bks) Penguin Publishing Group.

Lewis, Stewart. You Have Seven Messages. 2012. (ENG.). 304p. (YA). (gr. 7). pap. 9.99 (978-0-385-74029-6(8), Ember) Random Hse. Children's Bks.

Lindstrom, Eric. A Tragic Kind of Wonderful. 2017. (ENG.). 288p. (YA). (gr. 10-17). 17.99 (978-0-316-26006-0(1), Poppy) Little, Brown Bks. for Young Readers.

Luck, Gail. Bumduggle Davis Beats the Boobrats or the Inauguration of the Motherless Club. 2011. 146p. pap. 12.50 (978-1-61204-727-0(0), Strategic Bk. Publishing) Strategic Book Publishing & Rights Agency (SBPRA).

Lupica, Mike. The Only Game. 2015. (Home Team Ser.). (ENG., Illus.). 320p. (J). (gr. 3-7). 16.99 (978-1-4814-0995-7(6), Simon & Schuster Bks. For Young Readers) Simon & Schuster Bks. For Young Readers.

—The Only Game. 2016. (Home Team Ser.). lib. bdg. 18.40 (978-0-606-38252-6(6)) Turtleback Bks.

Lynch, Chris. Pieces. 2013. (ENG., (YA). (gr. 7). Illus.). 192p. pap. 9.99 (978-1-4424-5441-5(5)); 176p. 16.99 (978-1-4169-2703-7(4)) Simon & Schuster Bks. For Young Readers. (Simon & Schuster Bks. For Young Readers).

MacDonald, Annie. Poppo's Memory Book: A Child's Guide to Remember & S. M. I. L. E. after Loss. 2011. 64p. pap. 14.95 (978-1-4670-7273-1(7)) AuthorHouse.

Magnin, Joyce. Jelly Bean Summer. 2017. (ENG.). 272p. (J). (gr. 3-7). 16.99 (978-1-4926-4672-3(5), Sourcebooks Jabberwocky) Sourcebooks, Inc.

Magoon, Kekla. 37 Things I Love (in No Particular Order) 2012. (ENG.). 224p. (YA). (gr. 9-13). 16.99 (978-0-8050-9465-7(2), Holt, Henry & Co. Bks. For Young Readers) Holt, Henry & Co.

—37 Things I Love (in No Particular Order) 2013. (ENG.). 240p. (YA). (gr. 9-13). pap. 14.99 (978-1-250-03430-4(2), 9781250034304) Square Fish.

Maier, Inger M. Ben's Flying Flowers. Bogade, Maria, illus. 2012. (J). 14.95 (978-1-4338-1133-3(2)); pap. 9.95 (978-1-4338-1132-6(4)) American Psychological Assn. (Magination Pr.).

Mangum, Kay Lynn. A Love Like Lilly. 2006. 336p. (YA). pap. 15.95 (978-1-59038-580-7(2)) Deseret Bk. Co.

—When the Bough Breaks. 2007. 352p. (YA). pap. 15.95 (978-1-59038-748-1(1)) Deseret Bk. Co.

Manushkin, Fran. Goodbye to Goldie, 1 vol. Lyon, Tammie, illus. 2009. (Katie Woo Ser.). (ENG.). 32p. (gr. k-2). 21.32 (978-1-4048-5495-6(9)) Picture Window Bks.

Manushkin, Fran & Lyon, Tammie. Adiós a Goldie. Lyon, Tammie, illus. 2012. (Katie Woo en Español Ser.). (SPA., Illus.). 32p. (gr. k-2). pap. 6.95 (978-1-4048-7676-7(6)); lib. bdg. 21.32 (978-1-4048-7524-1(7)) Picture Window Bks.

Marchetta, Melina. The Piper's Son. 2012. (ENG.). 336p. (YA). (gr. 9). pap. 7.99 (978-0-7636-6062-8(0)) Candlewick Pr.

Marino, Nan. Neil Armstrong Is My Uncle & Other Lies Muscle Man McGinty Told Me. 2012. (ENG.). 176p. (J). (gr. 3-7). pap. 6.99 (978-0-312-66548-7(2), 9780312665487) Square Fish.

Martin, Ann M. Everything for a Dog. 2011. (ENG.). 240p. (J). (gr. 4-7). pap. 7.99 (978-0-312-67484-7(6), 9780312674847) Square Fish.

Maschari, Jennifer. The Remarkable Journey of Charlie Price. 2016. 304p. (J). (gr. 3-7). 16.99 (978-0-06-238010-4(9)) HarperCollins Pubs.

Mason, Bonita. T-Bear the Most Special Bear. Hendricks, Sandy, illus. 2008. 26p. (J). 19.95 (978-0-9798718-0-1(8)) Encore Pubns.

Matson, Morgan. Amy & Roger's Epic Detour. (ENG.). (YA). (gr. 7). 2011. 384p. pap. 10.99 (978-1-4169-9066-6(6)) 2010. 352p. 19.99 (978-1-4169-9065-9(8)) Simon & Schuster Bks. For Young Readers. (Simon & Schuster Bks. For Young Readers).

Mayhew, Julie. Red Ink. 2016. (ENG.). 320p. (YA). (gr. 9). 16.99 (978-0-7636-7731-2(0)) Candlewick Pr.

McCarthy, Cori. You Were Here. 2016. (ENG., Illus.). 400p. (YA). (gr. 8-12). 17.99 (978-1-4926-1704-4(0), 9781492617044) Sourcebooks, Inc.

McDaniel, Lurlene. The End of Forever. 2013. (ENG.). 320p. (YA). (gr. 7). pap. 8.99 (978-0-385-74380-8(7), Ember) Random Hse. Children's Bks.

—Keep Me in Your Heart: Three Novels. 2010. (ENG.). 624p. (YA). (gr. 7). pap. 10.99 (978-0-385-73982-5(6), Ember) Random Hse. Children's Bks.

—Letting Go of Lisa. 2007. (ENG.). 192p. (YA). (gr. 7-12). mass mkt. 6.99 (978-0-440-23868-3(4), Laurel Leaf) Random Hse. Children's Bks.

—Losing Gabriel: a Love Story. 2017. (ENG.). 336p. (YA). (gr. 7). pap. 9.99 (**978-0-385-74422-5(6)**, Ember) Random Hse. Children's Bks.

McDaniel, Lurlene. Raina's Story. 2006. (Angels in Pink Ser.). (ENG.). 208p. (YA). (gr. 7-12). mass mkt. 6.99 (978-0-440-23866-9(8), Laurel Leaf) Random Hse. Children's Bks.

McDonald, Joyce. Swallowing Stones. 2012. (ENG.). 256p. (YA). (gr. 7). pap. 9.99 (978-0-307-97609-3(2), Ember) Random Hse. Children's Bks.

Mcghee, Alison. All Rivers Flow to the Sea. 2005. (ENG.). 176p. (YA). (gr. 9-12). 15.99 (978-0-7636-2591-7(4)) Candlewick Pr.

—Firefly Hollow. Denise, Christopher, illus. 2015. (ENG.). 304p. (J). (gr. 3-7). 16.99 (978-1-4424-2336-7(6), Atheneum Bks. for Young Readers) Simon & Schuster Children's Publishing.

McInnes, Nicole. Brianna on the Brink. 2013. (ENG.). 176p. (YA). (gr. 10). 16.95 (978-0-8234-2741-3(2)) Holiday Hse., Inc.

McKenzie, C. Lee. The Princess of Las Pulgas. 2010. (ENG.). (YA). (978-1-934813-46-1(X)) Westside Bks.

McNamara, Amy. Lovely, Dark & Deep. (ENG.). 352p. (YA). (gr. 9). 2013. pap. 10.99 (978-1-4424-3437-0(6)) 2012. 16.99 (978-1-4424-3435-6(X)) Simon & Schuster Bks. For Young Readers. (Simon & Schuster Bks. For Young Readers).

McNish, Cliff. Breathe: A Ghost Story. (Exceptional Reading & Language Arts Titles for Intermediate Grades Ser.). (ENG.). 264p. (J). (gr. 4-8). 2009. pap. 6.95 (978-0-7613-4962-4(6), First Avenue Editions) 2006. lib. bdg. 15.95 (978-0-8225-6443-0(2), Carolrhoda Bks.) Lerner Publishing Group.

Mear, Shirley A. Feathers from Heaven. 2013. 24p. (J). pap. (978-1-78148-567-5(4)) Grosvenor Hse. Publishing Ltd.

Messer, Celeste M. Three Miracles. 2004. (Adventures of Andi O'Malley Ser.). (Illus.). 82-92p. (J). (gr. 4-7). 4.95 (978-0-9702171-4-1(5)) AshleyAlan Enterprises.

Mettler-Eells, Kimberly. Does God Have an Airplane? A Candid Journey of Bereavement Through the Eyes of a Child. 2010. 60p. pap. 23.99 (978-1-4259-1642-8(2)) AuthorHouse.

Michaelis, Antonia. The Secret Room. 2012. (ENG., Illus.). 208p. (J). (gr. 2-7). 14.95 (978-1-61608-960-3(1), 608960, Sky Pony Pr.) Skyhorse Publishing Co., Inc.

Miracles, Max & Brigitte, Smadja. Los Milagros de Max. Rubio, Gabriela, illus. (SPA.). 84p. (J). (978-84-392-8700-1(3)) Gaviota Ediciones ESP. Dist: Lectorum Pubns., Inc.

Mitchard, Jacquelyn. All We Know of Heaven. 2008. (ENG.). 320p. (YA). (gr. 8-18). 16.99 (978-0-06-134578-4(4), HarperTeen) HarperCollins Pubs.

Moir, Louise. Rafi's Red Racing Car: Explaining Suicide & Grief to Young Children. 2016. (ENG., Illus.). 40p. 17.95 (978-1-78592-200-8(9), 8893) Kingsley, Jessica Pubs. GBR. Dist: Macmillan Distribution Ltd.

Molina, Silvia & Silvia, Molina. Le Comieron la Lengua los Ratones. Rodriguez, Mari, illus. 2005. (Montana Encantada Ser.). (SPA.). 96p. (YA). (gr. 3-5). pap. 9.50 (978-84-241-8557-2(9)) Everest Editora ESP. Dist: Lectorum Pubns., Inc.

Monroe Donovan, Jane. Winter's Gift. Monroe Donovan, Jane, illus. 2004. (Holiday Ser.). (ENG., Illus.). 32p. (J). 16.95 (978-1-58536-231-8(X)) Sleeping Bear Pr.

Montoya, Louis R. Camilla. 2007. (J). pap. 8.00 (978-0-8059-7424-9(5)) Dorrance Publishing Co., Inc.

Moore, Nicholas & Murton, Gareth. Princess Lydia & the wailing Monster. 2008. 32p. pap. 18.95 (978-1-4092-4993-1(X)) Lulu Pr., Inc.

Moore, Suzi. Lexiland. 2013. (ENG.). 288p. (J). pap. 6.99 (978-0-85707-508-6(X), Simon & Schuster Children's) Simon & Schuster, Ltd. GBR. Dist: Simon & Schuster, Inc.

Moranville, Sharelle Byars. 27 Magic Words. 2016. (ENG.). 208p. (J). (gr. 3-7). 16.95 (978-0-8234-3657-6(8)) Holiday Hse., Inc.

Morris, Paula. Dark Souls. 2011. (ENG.). 304p. (J). (gr. 7-7). 17.99 (978-0-545-25132-7(X)) Scholastic, Inc.

Moses, Shelia P. Joseph's Grace. 2011. (ENG.). 160p. (YA). (gr. 7-18). 16.99 (978-1-4169-3942-9(3), McElderry, Margaret K. Bks.) McElderry, Margaret K. Bks.

Moskowitz, Hannah. Zombie Tag. 2011. (ENG.). 240p. (J). (gr. 4-7). 15.99 (978-1-59643-720-3(0), 9781596437203) Roaring Brook Pr.

Moundlic, Charlotte. The Scar. Tallec, Olivier, illus. 2011. (ENG.). 32p. (J). (gr. k-4). 14.99 (978-0-7636-5341-5(1)) Candlewick Pr.

Murphy, Barbara & Murphy, Barbara Beasley. Life! How I Love You! Baca, Elena, illus. 2004. (ENG.). 136p. (J). 9.95 (978-0-89013-468-9(5)) Museum of New Mexico Pr.

Myers, Edward. Ice. 2005. 222p. (J). per. 12.95 net. (978-0-9674477-9-7(8)) Montemayor Pr.

Nadin, Joanna. Wonderland. 2011. (ENG., Illus.). 224p. (YA). (gr. 9-18). 16.99 (978-0-7636-4846-6(9)) Candlewick Pr.

Naidoo, Vahini. Fall to Pieces, 0 vols. 2012. (ENG.). 324p. (YA). (gr. 8-12). 16.99 (978-0-7614-6217-0(1), 9780761462170, Amazon Children's Publishing) Amazon Publishing.

Nannestad, Katrina. When Mischief Came to Town. 2016. (ENG.). 192p. (J). (gr. 5-7). 16.99 (978-0-544-53432-2(8), HMH Books For Young Readers) Houghton Mifflin Harcourt Publishing Co.

Neil Wallace, Sandra. Muckers. 2013. (ENG.). 288p. (YA). (gr. 7). 16.99 (978-0-375-86754-5(6), Knopf Bks. for Young Readers) Random Hse. Children's Bks.

Nelson, Jandy. I'll Give You the Sun. 2015. (CHI.). 384p. (YA). (gr. 9). pap. (978-986-359-180-1(7)) Ecus Publishing Hse.

—I'll Give You the Sun. 2014. (ENG.). 384p. (YA). (gr. 9). 17.99 (978-0-8037-3496-8(4), Dial Bks) Penguin Publishing Group.

—I'll Give You the Sun. 2015. (ENG.). 400p. (YA). (gr. 9-12). pap. 10.99 (978-0-14-242576-3(1), Speak) Penguin Young Readers Group.

—I'll Give You the Sun. 2015. (ENG.). 400p. (YA). (gr. 9). 21.30 (978-1-68065-512-4(4)) Perfection Learning Corp.

—I'll Give You the Sun. 2015. lib. bdg. 22.10 (978-0-606-37572-6(4)) Turtleback Bks.

—The Sky Is Everywhere. (ENG.). (YA). (gr. 9-18). 2011. 320p. 9.99 (978-0-14-241780-5(7), Speak) 2010. 288p. 17.99 (978-0-8037-3495-1(6), Dial Bks) Penguin Young Readers Group.

—The Sky Is Everywhere. 2011. (ENG., Illus.). 275p. (gr. 9-12). 19.00 (978-1-61383-223-3(0)) Perfection Learning Corp.

Ness, Patrick. A Monster Calls: Inspired by an Idea from Siobhan Dowd. (ENG.). 240p. (YA). (gr. 7). 2016. pap. 9.99 (978-0-7636-9215-5(8)) 2015. pap. 12.00 (978-0-7636-8081-7(8)) Candlewick Pr.

—A Monster Calls: Inspired by an Idea from Siobhan Dowd. Kay, Jim, illus. (ENG.). 224p. (YA). (gr. 7). 2013. pap. 12.00 (978-0-7636-6065-9(5)) 2011. 16.99 (978-0-7636-5559-4(7)) Candlewick Pr.

—A Monster Calls: Inspired by an Idea from Siobhan Dowd. 2011. (Playaway Children Ser.). (YA). (gr. 7-12). 54.99 (978-1-4558-4499-9(3)) Findaway World, LLC.

—A Monster Calls: Inspired by an Idea from Siobhan Dowd. 2013. lib. bdg. 23.30 (978-0-606-31603-3(5), Turtleback) Turtleback Bks.

Newcomb, Victoria. Gathering Grace. 2008. 250p. (YA). pap. 15.95 (978-1-59275-009-2(5)) Hanford Mead Pubs., Inc.

Newman, John. Mimi. 2011. (ENG., Illus.). 192p. (J). (gr. 3-7). 15.99 (978-0-7636-5415-3(9)) Candlewick Pr.

Newman, Lesléa. The Best Cat in the World. Himler, Ronald, illus. 2004. 32p. (J). (gr. 1-4). 16.00 (978-0-8028-5252-6(1)) Eerdmans, William B. Publishing Co.

Newton, Chelle. The Butterfly Princess. Padovano, Chris, illus. 2012. 44p. pap. 11.99 (978-1-61286-129-6(6)) Avid Readers Publishing Group.

Nicholls, Sally. Season of Secrets. 2011. (J). 225p. pap. (978-0-545-21826-9(8)); (ENG.). 240p. (gr. 3-7). 16.99 (978-0-545-21825-2(X)) Scholastic, Inc. (Levine, Arthur A. Bks.).

Novak, Ali. My Life with the Walter Boys. 2014. (ENG.). 368p. (YA). (gr. 7-12). pap. 10.99 (978-1-4022-9786-1(6), 9781402297861) Sourcebooks, Inc.

Nuzum, K. A. The Leanin' Dog. (ENG.). 256p. (J). (gr. 3-7). 2010. pap. 6.99 (978-0-06-113936-9(X)) 2008. 15.99 (978-0-06-113934-5(3)) HarperCollins Pubs.

O'Brien, Anne Sibley. A Path of Stars. O'Brien, Anne Sibley, illus. 2012. (ENG., Illus.). 40p. (J). (gr. k-3). 15.95 (978-1-57091-735-6(3)) Charlesbridge Publishing, Inc.

Ockler, Sarah. Twenty Boy Summer. 2010. (ENG.). 320p. (YA). (gr. 7-17). pap. 10.99 (978-0-316-05158-3(6)) Little, Brown Bks. for Young Readers.

O'Connell, Janet. When They Died, Where Did They Go? 2013. 24p. pap. 12.45 (978-1-4497-9618-1(4), WestBow Pr.) Author Solutions, Inc.

Oechsle, Michael. The Lost Cipher. 2017. (ENG.). 272p. (J). (gr. 3-7). pap. 9.99 (**978-0-8075-8065-3(1)**) Whitman, Albert & Co.

Olsen, Sylvia & Martin, Ron. Which Way Should I Go?, 1 vol. Charko, Kasia, illus. 2008. (ENG.). 40p. (J). (gr. 1-5). 19.95 (978-1-55039-161-9(5)) Sono Nis Pr. CAN. Dist: Orca Bk. Pubs. USA.

O'Neill, Gemma. Oh Dear, Geoffrey! O'Neill, Gemma, illus. 2014. (ENG., Illus.). 32p. (J). (gr. -1-2). 15.99 (978-0-7636-6659-0(9), Templar) Candlewick Pr.

Otoshi, Kathryn. Two. 2014. (ENG., Illus.). 40p. (J). (gr. -1). 18.95 (978-0-9723946-6-6(4)) KO Kids Bks.

Parr, Todd. The Goodbye Book. Parr, Todd, illus. 2015. (ENG., Illus.). 32p. (J). (gr. -1-1). 17.00 (978-0-316-40497-6(7)) Little Brown & Co.

Paterson, Katherine. Bridge to Terabithia. Diamond, Donna, illus. l.t. ed. 2007. (Literacy Bridge Middle Reader Ser.). 187p. (J). (gr. 4-7). 23.95 (978-0-7862-9620-0(8)) Thorndike Pr.

Paterson, Katherine. Bridge to Terabithia: a Harper Classic. Diamond, Donna, illus. 2017. (Harper Classic Ser.). 192p. (J). (gr. 3-7). 16.99 (**978-0-06-265874-6(3)**) HarperCollins Pubs.

Patterson, James. The Worst Years of My Life. 2014. lthr. 79.00 (978-1-62715-524-3(4)) Leatherbound Bestsellers.

—The Worst Years of My Life. 2012. 18.00 (978-1-61383-331-5(8)) Perfection Learning Corp.

Patterson, James & Tebbetts, Chris. The Worst Years of My Life. Park, Laura, illus. (Middle School Ser.: Bk. 1). (ENG.). (J). (gr. 3-7). 2014. 320p. 13.99 (978-0-316-32202-7(4), Jimmy Patterson) 2013. pap. 0.01 (978-0-316-25251-5(4)) 2012. 336p. pap. 8.00 (978-0-316-10169-1(9), Jimmy Patterson) Little Brown & Co.

—The Worst Years of My Life. Park, Laura, illus. 2012. (Middle School Ser.: 1). (J). lib. bdg. 18.45 (978-0-606-26164-7(8), Turtleback) Turtleback Bks.

Patterson, Valerie O. The Other Side of Blue. 2011. (ENG.). 240p. (YA). (gr. 7). pap. 13.99 (978-0-547-55215-6(7)) Houghton Mifflin Harcourt Publishing Co.

Pavlicin, Karen. Perch, Mrs. Sackets, & Crow's Nest. 2007. (J). (ENG.). 160p. 16.95 (978-1-934617-00-7(8)); pap. (978-1-934617-01-4(6)) Elva Resa Publishing, LLC. (Alma Little).

—Summer of Courage. 2014. (ENG.). 160p. (J). pap. 12.95 (978-1-934617-24-3(5), Alma Little) Elva Resa Publishing, LLC.

Penn, Audrey. Chester Raccoon & the Acorn Full of Memories. Gibson, Barbara L., illus. 2009. (Kissing Hand Ser.). (ENG.). 32p. (J). (gr. -1-3). 16.95 (978-1-933718-29-3(3)) Tanglewood Pr.

Pérez, Amada Irma. Nana's Big Surprise. Gonzalez, Maya Christina, illus. 2013.Tr. of Nana, ¡Qué Sorpresa! (ENG & SPA.). 32p. (J). pap. 9.95 (978-0-89239-307-7(6), Children's Book Press) Lee & Low Bks., Inc.

Perez, Amada Irma & Children's Book Press Staff. Nana, Que Sorpresa! Gonzalez, Maya Christina, illus. 2007.Tr. of Nana's

Big Surprise. (ENG & SPA.). 32p. (J). (gr. k-2). lib. bdg. 16.95 *(978-0-89239-190-5(1))* Lee & Low Bks., Inc.

Perkins, C. Gale. A Pumpkin for God. 2009. 28p. pap. 14.95 *(978-1-4389-4336-7(9))* AuthorHouse.

Peters, Julie Anne. Lies My Girlfriend Told Me. 2017. (ENG.). 256p. (YA). (gr. 10-17). pap. 9.99 ***(978-0-316-23495-5(8))*** Little, Brown Bks. for Young Readers.

Philbrick, Rodman & Philbrick, W. R. The Young Man & the Sea. 2005. 192p. (gr. 4-7). 17.00 *(978-0-7569-4899-3(1))* Perfection Learning Corp.

Phillips, Niki. The Far Side of the Rainbow. 2013. (ENG., Illus.). 96p. pap. *(978-1-78306-120-4(0))* Troubador Publishing Ltd.

Pincus, Donna & Kaplow, Julie. Samantha Jane's Missing Smile: A Story about Coping with the Loss of a Parent. Speigel, Beth, illus. 2007. 32p. (J). (gr. -1-3). 14.95 *(978-1-59147-808-9(1))*; per. 9.95 *(978-1-59147-809-6(X))* American Psychological Assn. (Magination Pr.).

Pinkney, Andrea Davis. Bird in a Box. Qualls, Sean, illus. 2012. (J). lib. bdg. 18.45 *(978-0-606-26157-9(5),* Turtleback) Turtleback Bks.

Pitcher, Annabel. Ketchup Clouds. 2013. (ENG.). 272p. (YA). (gr. 7-17). 18.00 *(978-0-316-24676-7(X))* Little Brown & Co.

—My Sister Lives on the Mantelpiece. (ENG.). (YA). (gr. 7-17). 2013. 240p. pap. 10.00 *(978-0-316-17689-7(3))* 2012. 224p. 18.00 *(978-0-316-17690-3(7))* Little, Brown Bks. for Young Readers.

—Yours Truly. 2014. (ENG., Illus.). 288p. (YA). (gr. 7-17). pap. 9.99 *(978-0-316-24678-1(6))* Little, Brown Bks. for Young Readers.

Plum, Amy. Die for Me. (Die for Me Ser.: 1). (ENG.). (YA). (gr. 9). 2012. 368p. pap. 8.99 *(978-0-06-200402-4(6))* 2011. 352p. 17.99 *(978-0-06-200401-7(8))* HarperCollins Pubs. (HarperTeen).

Polisner, Gae. The Pull of Gravity. 2013. (ENG.). 224p. (YA). (gr. 7). pap. 10.99 *(978-1-250-01933-2(8),* 9781250019332) Square Fish.

Porada, Henry. The Inner Light. Michaels, Lisa J., illus. 2013. 32p. pap. 12.99 *(978-1-937260-98-9(4))* Sleepytown Pr.

Porter, Tracey. Lark. 2011. (ENG.). 192p. (YA). (gr. 8-18). 15.99 *(978-0-06-112287-3(4),* HarperTeen) HarperCollins Pubs.

Potter, Ellen. Slob. 2009. (ENG.). 208p. (J). (gr. 3-7). 16.99 *(978-0-399-24705-7(X),* Philomel Bks.) Penguin Young Readers Group.

Price, Reynolds. A Perfect Friend. 2013. (ENG.). (J). pap. 4.99 *(978-0-689-83148-5(X),* Simon & Schuster/Paula Wiseman Bks.) Simon & Schuster/Paula Wiseman Bks.

Prinz, Yvonne. All You Get Is Me. 2010. (ENG.). 288p. (YA). (gr. 9-18). 16.99 *(978-0-06-171580-8(8))* HarperCollins Pubs.

Proimos, James. 12 Things to Do Before You Crash & Burn. 2011. (ENG.). 128p. (YA). (gr. 9-13). 14.99 *(978-1-59643-595-7(X))* Roaring Brook Pr.

Prose, Francine. Bullyville. 2007. 260p. (YA). (gr. 7-12). 16.99 *(978-0-06-057497-0(6))*; lib. bdg. 17.89 *(978-0-06-057498-7(4))* HarperCollins Pubs. (HarperTeen).

—Bullyville. 2011. 10.36 *(978-0-7848-3625-5(6),* Everbind) Marco Bk. Co.

Rabb, Margo. Cures for Heartbreak. 2016. 256p. (YA). (gr. 9). pap. 9.99 *(978-0-06-247156-7(2))* HarperCollins Pubs.

Rabbett, Martin. Forever Buster: What a Name! What a Dog, We Exclaim! Burns, Donna, illus. 2007. (J). 13.95 *(978-0-9794649-0-4(0))* Hula Moon Pr.

Rabin, Staton. Black Powder. 2005. (ENG.). 256p. (YA). (gr. 7-9). 16.95 *(978-0-689-86876-4(6),* McElderry, Margaret K. Bks.) McElderry, Margaret K. Bks.

Ransom, Candice. Finding Day's Bottom. 2006. 176p. (J). (gr. 3-7). lib. bdg. 15.95 *(978-1-57505-933-4(9),* Carolrhoda Bks.) Lerner Publishing Group.

Rapp, Adam. Punkzilla. 2009. (ENG., Illus.). 256p. (YA). (gr. 9). 16.99 *(978-0-7636-3031-7(4))* Candlewick Pr.

Ratchford, Marjorie. A Party in the Sky, 1 vol. 2009. 24p. pap. 24.95 *(978-1-60813-296-6(X))* America Star Bks.

Ray, Delia. Ghost Girl: A Blue Ridge Mountain Story. 2016. (ENG.). 272p. (J). (gr. 5-7). pap. 6.99 *(978-0-544-70633-0(1),* HMH Books For Young Readers) Houghton Mifflin Harcourt Publishing Co.

Reagan, Jean & Pollema-Cahill, Phyllis. Always My Brother, 1 vol. 2009. (ENG., Illus.). 32p. (gr. 2-6). 16.95 *(978-0-88448-313-7(4),* 884313) Tilbury Hse. Pubs.

Reisfeld, Randi & Gilmour, H. B. What the Dog Said. 2012. (ENG.). 256p. (YA). (gr. 4-14). 16.99 *(978-1-59990-702-4(X),* 9781599907024, Bloomsbury USA Childrens) Bloomsbury Publishing USA.

Revell, Mike. Stormwalker. 2016. (ENG.). 304p. (J). (gr. 5-9). 16.99 *(978-1-68144-493-2(3))* Quercus NA.

Reynolds, Jason. The Boy in the Black Suit. 2015. (ENG., Illus.). 272p. (YA). (gr. 7). 17.99 *(978-1-4424-5950-2(6))* Simon & Schuster Children's Publishing.

—The Boy in the Black Suit. 2016. (ENG.). (J). lib. bdg. 22.10 *(978-0-606-38272-4(0))* Turtleback Bks.

Rheaume, Sherry D. Lulu the Prairie Dog. 2011. 16p. pap. 24.95 *(978-1-4626-3987-8(9))* America Star Bks.

Ringtved, Glenn. Cry, Heart, but Never Break. Moulthrop, Robert, tr. from DAN. Pardi, Charlotte, illus. 2016. (ENG.). 32p. (J). (gr. -1-3). 16.95 *(978-1-59270-187-2(6))* Enchanted Lion Bks., LLC.

Ripton, Kyle. The Mourning Tree. 2012. 74p. pap. 9.97 *(978-1-300-31829-3(5))* Lulu Pr., Inc.

Rivers, Karen. Before We Go Extinct: A Novel. 2016. (ENG.). 256p. (YA). 17.99 *(978-0-374-30240-5(5),* 9780374302405, Farrar, Straus & Giroux (BYR)) Farrar, Straus & Giroux.

Rivett, Rachel. Are You Sad, Little Bear? A Book about Learning to Say Goodbye. Macnaughton, Tina, illus. 2013. (ENG.). 32p. (J). (-k). 9.99 *(978-0-7459-6430-0(3))* Lion Hudson PLC GBR. Dist: Independent Pubs. Group.

Roberts, Willo Davis. Blood on His Hands. 2014. (ENG., Illus.). 192p. (YA). (gr. 7). pap. 13.99 *(978-1-4814-4461-3(1),* Simon Pulse) Simon Pulse.

—The One Left Behind. 2007. (ENG., Illus.). 144p. (J). (gr. 3-7). pap. 7.99 *(978-0-689-85083-7(2),* Aladdin) Simon & Schuster Children's Publishing.

Rose, Sandra. Doggone Grief. 2008. 20p. pap. 24.95 *(978-1-60474-623-5(8))* America Star Bks.

Rovere, Amy. And Still They Bloom: A Family's Journey of Loss & Healing. Spector, Joel, illus. 2012. (ENG.). 48p. (J). (gr. 4-7). 14.95 *(978-1-60443-036-3(2))* American Cancer Society, Inc.

Rubright, Lynn. Mama's Window. Smith, Duane, illus. 2005. 89p. (J). 16.95 *(978-1-57480-160-6(0))* Lee & Low Bks., Inc.

Rumble. 2014. (ENG., Illus.). 560p. (YA). (gr. 9). 19.99 *(978-1-4424-8284-5(2),* McElderry, Margaret K. Bks.) McElderry, Margaret K. Bks.

Rupp, Rebecca. After Eli. 2015. (ENG.). 256p. (J). (gr. 4-7). pap. 8.99 *(978-0-7636-7674-2(8))* Candlewick Pr.

Ryan, Amy Kathleen. Zen & Xander Undone. 2011. (ENG.). 228p. (YA). (gr. 9). pap. 13.99 *(978-0-547-55030-5(8))* Houghton Mifflin Harcourt Publishing Co.

Ryan, Darlene. Five Minutes More, 1 vol. 2009. (ENG.). 224p. (YA). (gr. 7-12). pap. 12.95 *(978-1-55469-006-0(4))* Orca Bk. Pubs. USA.

Rylant, Cynthia. Missing May. unabr. ed. 2004. 89p. (J). (gr. 5-9). pap. 29.00 incl. audio *(978-0-8072-8701-9(6),* YA240SP, Listening Library) Random Hse. Audio Publishing Group.

—Missing May. 2004. (ENG.). 112p. (J). (gr. 3-7). pap. 5.99 *(978-0-439-61383-5(3),* Scholastic Paperbacks) Scholastic, Inc.

Sample, Jewel. Flying Hugs & Kisses Activity Book. Kiplinger Pandy, Lori, illus. 2007. 68p. (J). (gr. -1-3). per. 13.99 *(978-1-59879-377-2(2))* Lifevest Publishing, Inc.

Sanchez, Jenny Torres. Because of the Sun. 2017. (ENG.). 272p. (YA). (gr. 7). 17.99 *(978-0-399-55145-1(X),* Delacorte Pr.) Random Hse. Children's Bks.

Sandell, Lisa Ann. A Map of the Known World. (ENG.). 288p. (J). (gr. 7-7). 2011. pap. 8.99 *(978-0-545-06971-7(8))* 2009. 16.99 *(978-0-545-06970-0(X))* Scholastic, Inc. (Scholastic Pr.).

Sappenfield, Heather. Life at the Speed of Us. 2016. (ENG.). 384p. (YA). pap. 11.99 *(978-0-7387-4730-9(0),* Flux) North Star Editions.

Schaumberg, Rose Mary & Schaumberg, Emily Rose. I'll Miss My Grandma, Wouldn't You? 2008. (Illus.). 40p. pap. 16.99 *(978-1-4389-1335-3(4))* AuthorHouse.

Schnitt, Deborah. Petey's Angel. 2012. 25.95 *(978-0-7414-7845-0(5))*; pap. 18.95 *(978-0-7414-7844-3(7))* Infinity Publishing.

Schröder, Monika. Be Light Like a Bird. 2016. (ENG.). 240p. (gr. 3-7). lib. bdg. 14.95 *(978-1-62370-749-1(8))* Capstone Young Readers of Coughlan Cos.

—Be Light Like a Bird. 2016. (Middle-Grade Novels Ser.). (ENG.). 240p. (gr. 4-7). 26.65 *(978-1-4965-3301-2(1))* Stone Arch Bks.

Schroeder, Lisa. Chasing Brooklyn. (ENG.). 432p. (YA). (gr. 9). 2011. pap. 11.99 *(978-1-4169-9174-8(3))* 2010. 15.99 *(978-1-4169-9168-7(9))* Simon Pulse. (Simon Pulse).

—My Secret Guide to Paris. 2016. (ENG.). 224p. (J). (gr. 3-7). pap. 6.99 *(978-0-545-70810-4(9))* Scholastic, Inc.

Schwiebert, Pat. We Were Gonna Have a Baby, but We Had an Angel Instead. Bills, Taylor, illus. 2004. 24p. pap. 7.95 *(978-0-9724241-1-0(3),* 717) Grief Watch.

Scott, Mindi. Freefall. 2010. (ENG.). 336p. (YA). (gr. 9-18). pap. 8.99 *(978-1-4424-0278-2(4),* Simon Pulse) Simon Pulse.

Sedell, Kirsten J. Remembering Sarah: A Child's Story. 2007. (J). *(978-0-9800838-0-4(X))* Sedell, Kirsten.

Sedgwick, Chantele. Love, Lucas. 2015. (ENG.). 280p. (J). (gr. 6). 16.99 *(978-1-63220-417-2(7),* Sky Pony Pr.) Skyhorse Publishing Co., Inc.

Seyderhelm, Amanda. Isaac & the Red Jumper. Scott, Ann, illus. 2013. 26p. pap. *(978-0-9572146-1-3(8))* HARK Pubns.

Seyvos, Florence. Pockety: The Tortoise Who Lived As She Pleased. Provata-Carlone, Mika, tr. from FRE. Ponti, Claude, illus. 2014. (ENG.). 64p. (J). (gr. 2-4). pap. 9.99 *(978-1-78269-025-2(5),* Pushkin Press) Steerforth Pr.

Shaw, Susan. One of the Survivors. (ENG.). 208p. (J). (gr. 5-9). 2011. pap. 6.99 *(978-1-4169-6389-9(8))* 2009. 15.99 *(978-1-4169-6129-1(1))* McElderry, Margaret K. Bks. (McElderry, Margaret K. Bks.).

Shaw, Tucker. Oh Yeah, Audrey! 2014. (ENG., Illus.). 256p. (YA). (gr. 8-17). 16.95 *(978-1-4197-1223-4(3),* Amulet Bks.) Abrams, Inc.

Shearer, Alex. A Message to the Sea. 2016. (ENG.). 224p. (J). (gr. 4-7). pap. 8.99 *(978-1-84812-569-8(0))* Bonnier Publishing GBR. Dist: Independent Pubs. Group.

Sheinmel, Courtney. Positively. 2010. (ENG.). 240p. (J). (gr. 4-9). pap. 6.99 *(978-1-4424-0622-3(4),* Simon & Schuster Bks. For Young Readers) Simon & Schuster Bks. For Young Readers.

Silberberg, Alan. Milo: Sticky Notes & Brain Freeze. Silberberg, Alan, illus. (ENG., Illus.). 288p. (J). (gr. 4-8). 2011. pap. 7.99 *(978-1-4169-9431-2(9))* 2010. 15.99 *(978-1-4169-9430-5(0))* Simon & Schuster Children's Publishing. (Aladdin).

Silvera, Adam. History Is All You Left Me. 2017. (ENG.). 304p. (YA). (gr. 9). 18.99 *(978-1-61695-692-9(5),* Soho Teen) Soho Pr., Inc.

Sinclair, Mehded Maryam. When Wings Expand. 2013. (ENG., Illus.). 150p. (J). (gr. 5-9). pap. 9.95 *(978-0-86037-499-2(8))* Kube Publishing Ltd. GBR. Dist: Consortium Bk. Sales & Distribution.

Sirowy, Alexandra. The Telling. 2016. (ENG., Illus.). 400p. (YA). (gr. 7). 17.99 *(978-1-4814-1889-8(0),* Simon & Schuster Bks. For Young Readers) Simon & Schuster Bks. For Young Readers.

Small Acts of Amazing Courage. 2013. (ENG., Illus.). 240p. (J). (gr. 4-7). pap. 6.99 *(978-1-4424-9495-4(6),* Simon & Schuster/Paula Wiseman Bks.) Simon & Schuster/Paula Wiseman Bks.

Smith-Ready, Jeri. This Side of Salvation. 2014. (ENG., Illus.). 384p. (YA). (gr. 9). 17.99 *(978-1-4424-3948-1(3),* Simon Pulse) Simon Pulse.

Smith, Tamara Ellis. Another Kind of Hurricane. 2015. (ENG.). 336p. (J). (gr. 4-7). 16.99 *(978-0-553-51193-2(9))*; 19.99 *(978-0-553-51194-9(7))* Random Hse. Children's Bks. (Schwartz & Wade Bks.).

Sones, Sonya. One of Those Hideous Books Where the Mother Dies. (ENG.). (YA). (gr. 7). 2013. Illus.). 288p. pap. 9.99 *(978-1-4424-9383-4(6))* 2005. 272p. reprint ed. pap. 7.99 *(978-1-4169-0788-6(2))* Simon & Schuster Bks. For Young Readers. (Simon & Schuster Bks. For Young Readers).

Spergel, Heather. Cloud City: A Child's Journey Through Bereavement. Stylou, Georgia, illus. 2013. (ENG.). 40p. (J). 15.95 *(978-1-938501-45-6(4))* Turn the Page Publishing.

Spinelli, Jerry. Eggs. 2008. (ENG., Illus.). 240p. (J). (gr. 3-7). pap. 8.99 *(978-0-316-16647-8(2))* Little, Brown Bks. for Young Readers.

—The Warden's Daughter. 2017. (ENG.). 352p. (J). (gr. 4-7). 16.99 *(978-0-375-83199-7(1))*; lib. bdg. 19.99 *(978-0-375-93199-4(6))* Random Hse. Children's Bks. (Knopf Bks. for Young Readers).

Springer, Nancy. Blood Trail. 2006. (ENG.). 164p. (YA). (gr. 8-12). pap. 6.95 *(978-0-8234-2063-6(9))* Holiday Hse., Inc.

—Possessing Jessie. 2010. (ENG.). 128p. (YA). (gr. 7-18). pap. 16.95 *(978-0-8234-2259-3(3))* Holiday Hse., Inc.

St. Anthony, Jane. Isabelle Day Refuses to Die of a Broken Heart. 2015. (ENG.). 152p. (J). 14.95 *(978-0-8166-9799-1(X))* Univ. of Minnesota Pr.

Stahler, David, Jr. Gathering of Shades. 2006. (ENG.). 256p. pap. *(978-0-06-052296-4(8))* HarperCollins Canada, Ltd.

—A Gathering of Shades. 2005. (ENG.). 304p. (J). 15.99 *(978-0-06-052294-0(1),* HarperTeen) HarperCollins Pubs.

Stanley, George E. Night Fires. 2009. (ENG.). 192p. (J). (gr. 3-7). 15.99 *(978-1-4169-7559-5(4),* Simon & Schuster/Paula Wiseman Bks.) Simon & Schuster/Paula Wiseman Bks.

Stanley, George Edward. Night Fires. 2011. (ENG.). 192p. (J). (gr. 3-7). pap. 6.99 *(978-1-4169-1250-7(9),* Simon & Schuster/Paula Wiseman Bks.) Simon & Schuster/Paula Wiseman Bks.

Stoddard, Laura. The Dreamosphere. 2014. pap. 14.99 *(978-1-4621-1444-3(X))* Cedar Fort, Inc./CFI Distribution.

Strasnick, Lauren. Nothing Like You. 2010. (ENG.). 240p. (YA). (gr. 9). pap. 8.99 *(978-1-4169-8265-4(5),* Simon Pulse) Simon Pulse.

Summers, Courtney. Fall for Anything. 2010. (ENG.). 240p. (YA). (gr. 7-18). pap. 15.99 *(978-0-312-65673-7(4),* 9780312656737, St. Martin's Griffin) St. Martin's Pr.

Sundberg, Ingrid. All We Left Behind. 2015. (ENG.). 432p. (YA). (gr. 9). 17.99 *(978-1-4814-3742-4(9),* Simon Pulse) Simon Pulse.

Supplee, Suzanne. When Irish Guys Are Smiling. 2008. (S. A. S. S. Ser.). (ENG.). 224p. (YA). (gr. 7-18). 6.99 *(978-0-14-241016-5(0),* Speak) Penguin Young Readers Group.

Tate, Nikki. Fallout, 1 vol. 2011. (Orca Soundings Ser.). (ENG.). 168p. (YA). (gr. 8-12). pap. 9.95 *(978-1-55469-272-9(5))* Orca Bk. Pubs. USA.

Taylor, L. D. Motive Games. 2012. (ENG.). 192p. pap. *(978-1-921632-25-9(9))* Wombat Bks.

Teckentrup, Britta. The Memory Tree. Teckentrup, Britta, illus. 2014. (ENG., Illus.). 32p. (J). (gr. -1-k). pap. 9.99 *(978-1-4083-2634-3(5))* Hodder & Stoughton GBR. Dist: Hachette Bk. Group.

Thompson, Michelle. Taming the Wind. 2010. 176p. pap. 12.99 *(978-1-59955-379-5(1))* Cedar Fort, Inc./CFI Distribution.

Thong, Roseanne Greenfield. The Wishing Tree. McLennan, Connie, illus. 2004. (Wishing Tree Ser.). 32p. (J). (gr. -1-3). 16.95 *(978-1-885008-26-8(0),* Shen's Bks.) Lee & Low Bks., Inc.

Tinsley, Helen. Me & My Grandma: A Story for Children about AIDS. 2012.Tr. of 32. (Illus.). 34p. (J). pap. 14.95 *(978-1-937622-21-3(5),* Nefu Bks.) Africana Homestead Legacy Pubs., Inc.

Treichel, Eliot. A Series of Small Maneuvers. 2015. (ENG.). 300p. (YA). pap. 14.95 *(978-1-932010-79-4(3))* Ooligan Pr.

Trueman, Terry. No Right Turn. 2009. (ENG.). 176p. (YA). (gr. 9). pap. 8.99 *(978-0-06-057493-2(3),* HarperTeen) HarperCollins Pubs.

Ulch, Virginia. Love You, Teddy - a Tail of Loss & Hope. Burkert, Howard, photos by. 2007. (Illus.). 32p. per. 18.95 *(978-1-59858-354-0(9))* Dog Ear Publishing, LLC.

Valentine, Jenny. Broken Soup. 2009. (YA). 216p. 17.89 *(978-0-06-085072-2(8))*; 224p. (gr. 9-18). 16.99 *(978-0-06-085071-5(X))* HarperCollins Pubs. (HarperTeen).

Verday, Jessica. The Haunted. (ENG.). (YA). (gr. 9). 2011. 496p. pap. 11.99 *(978-1-4169-7896-1(8))* 2010. 480p. 17.99 *(978-1-4169-7895-4(X))* Simon Pulse. (Simon Pulse).

—The Hollow. (ENG.). (YA). (gr. 7). 2010. 528p. pap. 11.99 *(978-1-4169-7894-7(1))*No. 1. 2009. 544p. 17.99 *(978-1-4169-7893-0(3))* Simon Pulse. (Simon Pulse).

Vigilante, Danette. The Trouble with Half a Moon. 2015. (ENG.). 208p. (J). (gr. 5). 7.99 *(978-0-14-751550-6(5),* Puffin Books) Penguin Young Readers Group.

Walker, Dan. Secondhand Summer. 2016. (ENG.). 184p. (YA). 23.99 *(978-1-943328-79-6(X),* Alaska Northwest Bks.) Graphic Arts Ctr. Publishing Co.

Wallace, Bill. No Dogs Allowed! 2004. (ENG.). 214p. (J). (gr. 4-6). tchr. ed. 16.95 *(978-0-8234-1818-3(9))* Holiday Hse., Inc.

Walton, K. M. Ultimatum. 2017. (ENG.). 320p. (YA). (gr. 7-12). 17.99 *(978-1-4926-3507-9(3),* 9781492635079) Sourcebooks, Inc.

Warwillow, Lucas D. Marick's Cross, 1 vol. 2010. 48p. pap. 16.95 *(978-1-61546-563-7(4))* America Star Bks.

Watson, Renée. What Momma Left Me. (ENG.). 240p. (YA). 2012. pap. 7.99 *(978-1-59990-704-8(6),* 9781599907048) 2010. (gr. 5-8). 16.99 *(978-1-59990-446-7(2),* 9781599904467) Bloomsbury Publishing USA. (Bloomsbury USA Childrens).

Welch, Sheila Kelly. The Shadowed Unicorn. 2011. 192p. (gr. -1). pap. 12.95 *(978-1-4502-6991-9(5))* iUniverse, Inc.

Welsh, Phoebe. Wonder What Do First Day Heaven. 2006. 70p. pap. 16.95 *(978-0-9769618-1-9(4))* Less is More Publishing, LLC.

Weston, Carol. Speed of Life. 2017. (ENG.). 352p. (J). (gr. 6-8). 16.99 ***(978-1-4926-5449-0(3),*** Sourcebooks Jabberwocky) Sourcebooks, Inc.

Weston, Paula. Shadows. 2013. (Rephaim Ser.). (ENG.). 400p. (YA). (gr. 9). 17.99 *(978-1-77049-547-0(9),* Tundra Bks.) Tundra Bks. CAN. Dist: Penguin Random Hse. LLC.

Whelan, Gloria. Small Acts of Amazing Courage. 2011. (ENG.). 224p. (J). (gr. 4-7). 15.99 *(978-1-4424-0931-6(2),* Simon & Schuster/Paula Wiseman Bks.) Simon & Schuster/Paula Wiseman Bks.

When Aunt Mattie Got Her Wings. 2014. (ENG., Illus.). 32p. (J). (gr. -1-3). 17.99 *(978-1-4814-1044-1(X),* Beach Lane Bks.) Beach Lane Bks.

Wiles, Deborah. Each Little Bird That Sings. 2006. (ENG., Illus.). 288p. (J). (gr. 2-5). reprint ed. pap. 7.99 *(978-0-15-205657-5(2))* Houghton Mifflin Harcourt Publishing Co.

Williams, Carol Lynch. Waiting. (ENG.). 352p. (YA). (gr. 9). 2013. pap. 9.99 *(978-1-4424-4354-9(5))* 2012. 16.99 *(978-1-4424-4353-2(7))* Simon & Schuster/Paula Wiseman Bks. (Simon & Schuster/Paula Wiseman Bks.).

Williams-Garcia, Rita. Clayton Byrd Goes Underground. Morrison, Frank, illus. 2017. 176p. (J). (gr. 3-7). 16.99 *(978-0-06-221591-8(4))*; (ENG.). E-Book *(978-0-06-221594-9(9))* HarperCollins Pubs. (Amistad).

Williams, Maiya. The Golden Hour. 2006. (ENG.). 288p. (J). (gr. 5-10). per. 5.95 *(978-0-8109-9216-0(7))* Abrams, Inc.

Willie's Reflection: A Story of Grief, Hope & Healing. 2008. (Illus.). 32p. (J). 15.95 *(978-0-9799021-0-9(X))* Aspire Publishing.

Willis, Cynthia Chapman. Dog Gone. 2009. (ENG.). 240p. (J). (gr. 3-7). pap. 17.99 *(978-0-312-56113-0(X),* 9780312561130) Square Fish.

Wilson, Wayne L. Kate, the Ghost Dog: Coping with the Death of a Pet. Soud, illus. 2009. 48p. (J). (gr. 3-8). 14.95 *(978-1-4338-0554-7(5))*; pap. 9.95 *(978-1-4338-0555-4(3))* American Psychological Assn. (Magination Pr.).

Wittlinger, Ellen. Blind Faith. 2007. (ENG.). 304p. (YA). (gr. 7-12). pap. 9.99 *(978-1-4169-4906-0(2),* Simon & Schuster Bks. For Young Readers) Simon & Schuster Bks. For Young Readers.

Wolitzer, Meg. Belzhar. 2015. lib. bdg. 22.10 *(978-0-606-37573-3(2))* Turtleback Bks.

Wood, Debra. Just A Little Child. Blake, Joshua Aaron, illus. l.t. ed. 2006. 33p. (J). per. 12.95 *(978-1-59879-087-0(0))* Lifevest Publishing, Inc.

Wood, Fiona. Wildlife. 2016. (ENG.). 416p. (YA). (gr. 10-17). pap. 9.99 *(978-0-316-24208-0(X),* Poppy) Little, Brown Bks. for Young Readers.

Woodson, Jacqueline. Behind You. 2010. (ENG.). 176p. (YA). (gr. 7-18). 7.99 *(978-0-14-241554-2(5),* Puffin Books) Penguin Young Readers Group.

—Beneath a Meth Moon: An Elegy. (ENG.). (YA). (gr. 7). 2013. 240p. pap. 8.99 *(978-0-14-242392-9(0),* Speak) 2012. 144p. 16.99 *(978-0-399-25250-1(9),* Nancy Paulsen Books) Penguin Young Readers Group.

—Beneath a Meth Moon: An Elegy. 2013. lib. bdg. 19.65 *(978-0-606-30566-2(1),* Turtleback) Turtleback Bks.

—If You Come Softly & Behind You. 2010. (ENG.). 352p. (YA). (gr. 7-18). 8.99 *(978-0-14-241918-2(4),* Puffin Books) Penguin Young Readers Group.

Young, Suzanne. The Epidemic. 2016. (Program Ser.: 4). (ENG., Illus.). 384p. (YA). (gr. 9). 17.99 *(978-1-4814-4470-5(0),* Simon Pulse) Simon Pulse.

—Hotel for the Lost. 2016. (ENG., Illus.). 304p. (YA). (gr. 9). pap. 10.99 *(978-1-4814-2301-4(0),* Simon Pulse) Simon Pulse.

—The Remedy. 2015. (Program Ser.: 3). (ENG., Illus.). 416p. (YA). (gr. 9). 17.99 *(978-1-4814-3765-3(8),* Simon Pulse) Simon Pulse.

Yovanoff, Brenna. Paper Valentine. 2013. (ENG.). 320p. (YA). (gr. 7). 17.99 *(978-1-59514-599-4(0),* Razorbill) Penguin Young Readers Group.

Zarr, Sara. How to Save a Life. 2012. (ENG.). 368p. (YA). (gr. 7-17). pap. 10.99 *(978-0-316-03605-4(6))* Little, Brown Bks. for Young Readers.

Zaugg, Sandra L. Secret of the Yellow Van: A Book about Dealing with Loss. 2008. (J). pap. 8.99 *(978-0-8163-2246-6(5))* Pacific Pr. Publishing Assn.

Zentner, Jeff. Goodbye Days. 2017. (ENG.). 416p. (YA). (gr. 9). 17.99 *(978-0-553-52406-2(2),* Crown Books For Young Readers) Random Hse. Children's Bks.

Zink, Michelle. A Walk in the Sun. 2016. 336p. (YA). (gr. 8). 17.99 *(978-0-06-243446-3(2),* HarperTeen) HarperCollins Pubs.

Zorn, Claire. Protected. 2017. (ENG.). 288p. (YA). (gr. 6-12). 17.99 ***(978-1-4926-5213-7(X))*** Sourcebooks, Inc.

GRIFFEY, KEN, JR., 1969-

Mills, Elizabeth. Ken Griffey Sr. & Ken Griffey Jr: Baseball Heroes. l.t. ed. 2012. 96p. (J). pap. *(978-1-4596-3355-1(5))* ReadHowYouWant.com, Ltd.

Mills, J. Elizabeth. Ken Griffey Sr. & Ken Griffey Jr: Baseball Heroes. 2010. (Sports Families Ser.). (ENG., Illus.). 48p. (J). pap. 11.75 *(978-1-4358-8514-1(7),* Rosen Reference) Rosen Publishing Group, Inc., The.

Rolfe, John. Ken Griffey, Jr: Superstar Centerfielder. 2009. (Sports Illustrated for Kids Bks). 176p. (gr. 7-12). 63.90 *(978-1-60853-149-3(X))* Rosen Publishing Group, Inc., The.

Rolfe, John, et al. Ken Griffey, Jr: Superstar Centerfielder. 2005. (Sports Illustrated for Kids Books Ser.). (Illus.). 176p. (YA). (gr. 7-12). lib. bdg. 33.25 *(978-0-8239-3687-8(2))* Rosen Publishing Group, Inc., The.

Stone, Larry. Ken Griffey, Jr. The Home Run Kid. Rains, Rob, ed. 2003. (Superstar Ser.). (Illus.). 96p. (J). (gr. 4-7). pap. 4.95 *(978-1-58261-041-2(X))* Sports Publishing, LLC.

GRIFFINS

Juettner, Bonnie. Griffins. 2008. (Monsters Ser.). (ENG., Illus.). 48p. (gr. 4-7). lib. bdg. 35.20 *(978-0-7377-4043-1(4),* LML02109-240010) Cengage Gale.

Marsico, Katie. Beastly Monsters: From Dragons to Griffins. 2017. (Monster Mania Ser.). (ENG.). 32p. (J). (gr. 2-5). 12.99 ***(978-1-5124-3818-5(9),*** Lerner Pubns.); 39.99 ***(978-1-5124-3819-2(7),*** Lerner Pubns.); 39.99 ***(978-1-5124-2814-8(0),*** Lerner Pubns.); (Illus.). 26.65 *(978-1-5124-2592-5(3))* Lerner Publishing Group.

Sautter, A. J. A Field Guide to Griffins, Unicorns, & Other Mythical Beasts, 1 vol. Juta, Jason, illus. 2014. (Fantasy Field Guides). (ENG.). 32p. (gr. 3-4). lib. bdg. 27.99 *(978-1-4914-0690-8(9))* Capstone Press of Coughlan Cos.

GRIFFINS—FICTION

Coville, Bruce. Diary of a Runaway Griffin. Douglas, Allen, illus. 2016. (Enchanted Files Ser.: 2). (ENG.). 272p. (J). (gr. 3-7). 16.99 *(978-0-385-39255-6(9),* Random Hse. Bks. for Young Readers) Random Hse. Children's Bks.

—Hatched. Kidby, Paul, illus. 2017. (Enchanted Files Ser.: 2). (ENG.). 288p. (J). (gr. 3-7). pap. 6.99 *(978-0-385-39258-7(3),* Yearling) Random Hse. Children's Bks.

Nitz, Kristin Wolden. Saving the Griffin, 1 vol. Jaeggi, Yoshiko, illus. 2007. (ENG.). 192p. (J). (gr. 3-7). 14.95 *(978-1-56145-380-1(3))* Peachtree Pubs.

EFG

Pickford, Susan T. It's up to You, Griffin!, 1 vol. Ramsey, Marcy Dunn, illus. 2009. (ENG.). 32p. (J). (gr. -1-3). 10.95 *(978-0-87033-446-7(8)*, 9780870334467, Cornell Maritime Pr./Tidewater Pubs.) Schiffer Publishing, Ltd.

Rodda, Emily. The Flower Fairies. Vitale, Raoul, illus. 2003. (Fairy Realm Ser.). 128p. (J). 8.99 *(978-0-06-009586-4(5))* HarperCollins Pubs.

Stockton, Frank Richard & Stockton. The Griffin & the Minor Canon. Sendak, Maurice, illus. 2005. (Sendak Reissues Ser.). (ENG.). 56p. (J). 15.95 *(978-0-06-029731-2(X))* HarperCollins Pubs.

Sutherland, Tui T. & Sutherland, Kari H. The Menagerie. 2013. (Menagerie Ser.: 1). (ENG., Illus.). 288p. (J). (gr. 3-7). 16.99 *(978-0-06-078064-7(9))* HarperCollins Pubs.

GRIMKE, ANGELINA EMILY, 1805-1879

Dudley Gold, Susan. The Women's Rights Movement & Abolitionism. 2015. (Primary Sources of the Abolitionist Movement Ser.). (ENG., Illus.). 64p. (J). (gr. 6-6). lib. bdg. 34.21 *(978-1-5026-0536-8(8))* Cavendish Square Publishing.

GRIMKE, SARAH MOORE, 1792-1873

Dudley Gold, Susan. The Women's Rights Movement & Abolitionism. 2015. (Primary Sources of the Abolitionist Movement Ser.). (ENG., Illus.). 64p. (J). (gr. 6-6). lib. bdg. 34.21 *(978-1-5026-0536-8(8))* Cavendish Square Publishing.

GRINCH (FICTITIOUS CHARACTER)—FICTION

Rabe, Tish. Cooking with the Grinch (Dr. Seuss) Brannon, Tom, illus. 2017. (Step into Reading Ser.). (ENG.). 32p. (J). (gr. -1-1). pap. 4.99 ***(978-1-5247-1462-8(3))***; lib. bdg. 12.99 ***(978-1-5247-1463-5(1))*** Random Hse. Children's Bks. (Random Hse. Bks. for Young Readers).

Seuss, Dr. Comment le Grinch a Volé Noël! 2013. (FRE & ENG., Illus.). 64p. (J). (gr. -1-3). 12.95 *(978-1-61243-244-1(1))* Ulysses Pr.

—How the Grinch Stole Christmas! Seuss, Dr., illus. 50th ed. 2007. (ENG., Illus.). 64p. pap. *(978-0-00-725860-4(7)*, HarperCollins) HarperCollins Pubs. Ltd.

—How the Grinch Stole Christmas! Jonaitis, Alice, ed. Seuss, Dr., illus. deluxe ed. 2014. (Classic Seuss Ser.). (ENG., Illus.). 64p. (J). (gr. k-4). 25.99 *(978-0-679-89153-6(6)*, Random Hse. Bks. for Young Readers) Random Hse. Children's Bks.

—How the Grinch Stole Christmas! Book & Grinch. 2015. (Classic Seuss Ser.). (ENG.). 64p. (J). (gr. k-4). 26.99 *(978-0-553-52445-1(3)*, Random Hse. Bks. for Young Readers) Random Hse. Children's Bks.

Washington, LaVonne & Washington, LaShawn. How the Grinch Hare Became a Christian. 2005. 37p. 11.95 *(978-1-4116-2322-4(3))* Lulu Pr., Inc.

GRISSOM, VIRGIL I., 1926-1967

Greenberger, Robert. Gus Grissom. 2004. (Library of Astronaut Biographies Ser.). (Illus.). 112p. (gr. 5-8). lib. bdg. 34.60 *(978-0-8239-4458-3(1)*, Rosen Reference) Rosen Publishing Group, Inc., The.

—Gus Grissom: The Tragedy of Apollo 1. 2009. (Library of Astronaut Biographies Ser.). 112p. (gr. 5-8). 63.90 *(978-1-60853-521-7(5)*, Rosen Reference) Rosen Publishing Group, Inc., The.

GROCERIES

Meachen Rau, Dana. Un Tendero. 2007. (En el Trabajo Ser.). (SPA., Illus.). 24p. (gr. k-1). lib. bdg. 15.95 *(978-0-7614-2784-1(8)*, Benchmark Bks.) Marshall Cavendish Corp.

Minden, Cecilia. Grocery Shopping by the Numbers. 2007. (21st Century Skills Library: Real World Math Ser.). (ENG., Illus.). 32p. (gr. 4-8). lib. bdg. 28.50 *(978-1-60279-006-3(X)*, 200065) Cherry Lake Publishing.

GROCERY TRADE

see also Supermarkets

Adamson, Heather. The Grocery Store. 2010. (My Community Ser.). 24p. (J). 25.65 *(978-1-60753-027-5(9))* Amicus Publishing.

Colby, Jennifer. Grocery Store. 2016. (21st Century Junior Library: Explore a Workplace Ser.). (ENG., Illus.). 24p. (J). (gr. 2-5). 27.07 *(978-1-63471-073-2(8)*, 208371) Cherry Lake Publishing.

Endres, Hollie J. The Letter Nn Set: At the Grocery Store, 6 vols. 2004. (Letter Bks.). (ENG.). 8p. (gr. k-1). pap. 29.70 *(978-0-7368-4113-9(X)*, Letter Bks.) Capstone Press of Coughlan Cos.

Gillis, Jennifer Blizin. Time to Open! 2006. (Reader's Clubhouse Level 2 Reader Ser.). (ENG., Illus.). 24p. (J). (gr. 1-4). pap. 3.99 *(978-0-7641-3301-5(2))* Barron's Educational Series, Inc.

Jovin, Michelle. Your World: Shopping Secrets: Multiplication (Grade 3) 2017. (Mathematics Readers Ser.). (Illus.). 32p. (J). (gr. 3-3). pap. 8.99 ***(978-1-4807-5796-7(9))*** Teacher Created Materials, Inc.

Linde, Barbara M. A Shopping Trip: Learning to Add Dollars & Cents up to $10.00 Without Regrouping. 2009. (Math for the REAL World Ser.). 16p. (gr. 2-3). pap. 7.05 *(978-0-8239-8900-3(3)*, Rosen Classroom) Rosen Publishing Group, Inc., The.

Marsico, Katie. Working at a Grocery Store. 2008. (21st Century Junior Library: Careers Ser.). (ENG., Illus.). 24p. (gr. 2-5). lib. bdg. 25.64 *(978-1-60279-265-4(8)*, 200170) Cherry Lake Publishing.

Null Petersen, Christine. Mercados Alrededor Del Mundo. 2017. (TIME for Kids en Español - Level 3 Ser.). (SPA.). 32p. (gr. 3-3). lib. bdg. 31.99 ***(978-1-5157-5164-9(3))*** Time for Kids Inc AUS. Dist: Capstone Pub.

Reeves, Diane Lindsey. Get a Job at the Grocery Store. 2016. (Bright Futures Press: Get a Job Ser.). (ENG., Illus.). 32p. (J). (gr. 4-6). 29.93 *(978-1-63471-906-3(9)*, 208945) Cherry Lake Publishing.

Sarver, Amy. Science at the Grocery. 2007. (Reading Expeditions Ser.). (ENG., Illus.). 24p. (J). pap. 14.95 *(978-0-7922-4567-4(9))* CENGAGE Learning.

GROMIT (FICTITIOUS CHARACTER)—FICTION

see Wallace and Gromit (Fictitious Characters)—Fiction

GROOMING, PERSONAL

see Beauty, Personal

GROOMING FOR WOMEN

see Beauty, Personal

GROTTOES

see Caves

GROUND-EFFECT MACHINES

see also Helicopters

Bullard, Lisa. Hovercraft. 2007. (Pull Ahead Bks.). (Illus.). 32p. (J). pap. 6.95 *(978-0-8225-6427-0(0)*, First Avenue Editions); (ENG., lib. bdg. 22.60 *(978-0-8225-6421-8(1)*, Lerner Pubns.) Lerner Publishing Group.

Gabrielson, Curt. Kinetic Contraptions: Build a Hovercraft, Airboat, & More with a Hobby Motor. 2010. (ENG., Illus.). 192p. (J). (gr. 7-18). pap. 16.95 *(978-1-55652-957-3(0))* Chicago Review Pr., Inc.

Hanson, Anders. Let's Go by Hovercraft, 1 vol. 2008. (Let's Go Ser.). (ENG., Illus.). 24p. (J). (gr. k-3). lib. bdg. 24.21 *(978-1-59928-900-7(8)*, SandCastle) ABDO Publishing Co.

Holzweiss, Kristina & Barth, Amy. I Can Make Fantastic Flyers. 2017. (Rookie Star — MakerSpace Projects Ser.). (ENG.). 32p. (J). lib. bdg. 25.00 ***(978-0-531-23412-9(6)***, Children's Pr.) Scholastic Library Publishing.

Mayo, Margaret. Mini Tab: Dig Dig Digging. Ayliffe, Alex, illus. 2017. (ENG.). 14p. (J). bds. 6.99 *(978-1-62779-714-6(9)*, 9781627797146, Holt, Henry & Co. Bks. For Young Readers) Holt, Henry & Co.

Scheff, Matt. Hovercraft, 1 vol. 2014. (Speed Machines Ser.). (ENG., Illus.). 32p. (gr. 3-6). lib. bdg. 27.07 *(978-1-62403-610-1(4)*, SportsZone) ABDO Publishing Co.

Tieck, Sarah. Hovercraft, 1 vol. 2011. (Amazing Vehicles Set 2 Ser.). (ENG., Illus.). 32p. (J). (gr. 2-5). 28.50 *(978-1-61714-696-5(6))* ABDO Publishing Co.

GROUND PROXIMITY MACHINES

see Ground-Effect Machines

GROUNDHOG

see Woodchuck

GROUP LIVING

see Collective Settlements

GROUSE

Harris, Tim. Grouse. 2008. (Nature's Children Ser.). (Illus.). 52p. (J). *(978-0-7172-6236-6(7))* Grolier, Ltd.

London, Jonathan. Gone Again Ptarmigan. Van Zyle, Jon, illus. 2013. 32p. (J). pap. 12.95 *(978-1-60223-204-4(0))* Univ. of Alaska Pr.

GROUSE—FICTION

Beckhorn, Susan Williams. Moose Eggs: Or, Why Moose Has Flat Antlers. Stevens, Helen, illus. 2007. (ENG.). 32p. (J). (gr. -1-3). 15.95 *(978-0-89272-689-9(X))* Down East Bks.

Rosen, Michael J. The Forever Flowers. Danowski, Sonja, illus. 2014. (ENG.). 32p. (J). (gr. 1-3). 18.99 *(978-1-56846-273-8(5)*, Creative Editions) Creative Co., The.

GROWTH

see also Children—Growth; Growth (Plants)

Arégui, Matthias & Ramstein, Anne-Margot. Before After. Arégui, Matthias & Ramstein, Anne-Margot, illus. 2014. (ENG., Illus.). 176p. (J). (gr. -1-3). 19.99 *(978-0-7636-7621-6(7))* Candlewick Pr.

Bailey, Jacqui. What Happens When You Are Born & Grow? 2009. 32p. (gr. k-5). pap. 10.60 *(978-1-4358-2615-1(9)*, Rosen Classroom) Rosen Publishing Group, Inc., The.

Captain, Tamira. When Do You Grow? Thorne, Sean, illus. 2003. (J). pap. 6.95 *(978-0-9742288-0-8(X))* Stories From Four Publishing Co.

Clark, M. H. I Am... 2011. (Growth Chart Bks.). (Illus.). (gr. -1-5). bds. 8.95 *(978-1-935414-06-3(2))* Compendium, Inc., Publishing & Communications.

—I Can... 2011. (Growth Chart Bks.). (Illus.). (gr. -1-5). bds. 8.95 *(978-1-932319-81-1(6))* Compendium, Inc., Publishing & Communications.

Claybourne, Anna. Make It Grow!, 1 vol. Scott, Kimberly & Dean, Venetia, illus. 2014. (Whiz Kid Science Ser.). (ENG.). 32p. (gr. 2-4). 29.99 *(978-1-4109-6748-0(4)*, Read Me!) Heinemann-Raintree.

Corbett, Pie. Growing Up. 2005. (Sing & Play Ser.). (Illus.). 24p. (J). (gr. -1-3). lib. bdg. 22.80 *(978-1-59389-208-1(X))* Chrysalis Education.

Dickmann, Nancy. ¡Mira Cómo Crece!, 11 vols., Set. Incl. Vida de la Abeja. pap. 6.29 *(978-1-4329-5282-2(X))*; Vida de la Manzana. (Illus.). pap. 6.29 *(978-1-4329-5286-0(2))*; Vida de la Mariposa. (Illus.). pap. 6.29 *(978-1-4329-5283-9(8))*; Vida de la Rana. pap. 6.29 *(978-1-4329-5285-3(4))*; Vida de la Tortuga. pap. 6.29 *(978-1-4329-5292-1(7))*; Vida del Frijol. (Illus.). pap. 6.29 *(978-1-4329-5287-7(0))*; Vida del Girasol. pap. 6.29 *(978-1-4329-5289-1(7))*; Vida del Perro. pap. 6.29 *(978-1-4329-5290-7(0))*; Vida del Pingüino. (Illus.). pap. 6.29 *(978-1-4329-5291-4(9))*; Vida del Pollo. (Illus.). pap. 6.29 *(978-1-4329-5284-6(6))*; Vida del Roble. pap. 6.29 *(978-1-4329-5288-4(9))*; (gr. -1-1). (¡Mira Cómo Crece! Ser.). (SPA.). 24p. 2011. Set pap. 69.19 *(978-1-4329-5293-8(5))*; Set lib. bdg. 203.85 *(978-1-4329-5281-5(1))* Heinemann-Raintree. (Bellota).

Driscoll, Laura. Apples: And How They Grow. Smith, Tammy, illus. 2003. (Penguin Young Readers, Level 2 Ser.). (ENG.). 32p. (J). (gr. 1-2). mass mkt. 3.99 *(978-0-448-43275-5(7)*, Penguin Young Readers) Penguin Young Readers Group.

Favor, Lesli J. Everything You Need to Know about Growth Spurts & Delayed Growth. 2005. (Need to Know Library). (Illus.). 64p. (YA). (gr. 4-6). lib. bdg. 31.95 *(978-0-8239-3549-9(3))* Rosen Publishing Group, Inc., The.

Favor, Leslie. Everything You Need to Know about Growth Spurts & Delayed Growth. 2009. (Need to Know Library). 64p. (gr. 5-5). 58.50 *(978-1-60854-071-6(5))* Rosen Publishing Group, Inc., The.

Fiscus, James. Coping with Growth Spurts & Delayed Growth. 2005. (Coping Ser.). (Illus.). 192p. (YA). (gr. 7-12). lib. bdg. 34.60 *(978-0-8239-3508-6(6))* Rosen Publishing Group, Inc., The.

Fiscus, Jim. Coping with Growth Spurts & Delayed Growth. 2009. (Coping Ser.). 192p. (gr. 7-12). 63.90 *(978-1-61512-000-0(9))* Rosen Publishing Group, Inc., The.

Gaff, Jackie. Looking at Growing Up: How Do People Change? 2008. (Looking at Science: How Things Change Ser.). (Illus.). 32p. (J). (gr. 3-7). lib. bdg. 23.94 *(978-0-7660-3090-9(3)*, Enslow Elementary) Enslow Pubs., Inc.

Glover, David & Glover, Penny. Growing. 2005. (Humans & Animals Ser.). (Illus.). 30p. (J). (gr. 2-4). lib. bdg. 27.10 *(978-1-58340-690-8(5))* Black Rabbit Bks.

Growing: Individual Title Six-Packs. (Story Steps Ser.). (gr. k-2). 29.00 *(978-0-7635-9582-1(9))*; (gr. 1-2). 22.00 *(978-0-7578-5422-4(2))* Rigby Education.

HarrisNic. GROWING UP: FROM BABY TO ADULT HIGH BEGINNING BOOK WITH ONLINE ACCESS. 2014. (ENG.). 24p. (J). pap. 9.50 *(978-1-107-68744-8(6))* Cambridge Univ. Pr.

How Does It Grow?, 6 Packs. (gr. k-1). 23.00 *(978-0-7635-9037-6(1))* Rigby Education.

Kalman, Bobbie. Crezco y Cambio. 2010. (SPA, ENG & MUL.). 16p. (J). pap. *(978-0-7787-8267-4(0))* Crabtree Publishing Co.

—How & Why Do Animals Change As They Grow? 2014. (ENG., Illus.). 24p. (J). *(978-0-7787-0545-1(5))* Crabtree Publishing Co.

—I Am Growing & Changing / Crezco y Cambio. 2010. (SPA, ENG & MUL.). 16p. (J). lib. bdg. *(978-0-7787-8274-2(3))* Crabtree Publishing Co.

—Los Seres Vivos Necesitan Agua. 2008.Tr. of Animals Grow & Change. (SPA.). 24p. (J). pap. *(978-0-7787-8691-7(9))* Crabtree Publishing Co.

Llewellyn, Claire. Asi Nace una Mariposa. Giraldo, Maria Cristina, tr. Mendez, Simon, illus. 2003. (Colección Así Nace... / Starting Life Collection Ser.). (SPA.). 24p. (gr. k-6). pap. 14.95 *(978-1-59437-788-4(X))* Santillana USA Publishing Co., Inc.

—How Animals Grow. 2006. (I Know That, Growth & Change Set Ser.). (Illus.). 24p. (J). lib. bdg. 22.80 *(978-1-59771-022-0(9))* Sea-To-Sea Pubns.

Madaras, Lynda, et al. "What's Happening to My Body?" Book for Boys. 3rd rev. ed. 2007. (What's Happening to My Body? Ser.). (ENG., Illus.). 256p. (gr. 5-7). pap. 15.99 *(978-1-55704-765-6(0)*, William Morrow Paperbacks) HarperCollins Pubs.

—"What's Happening to My Body?" Book for Girls. 3rd rev. ed. 2007. (What's Happening to My Body? Ser.). (ENG., Illus.). 288p. (gr. 7-9). pap. 14.99 *(978-1-55704-764-9(2)*, William Morrow Paperbacks) HarperCollins Pubs.

—The "What's Happening to My Body?" Book for Boys. 3rd rev. ed. 2007. (What's Happening to My Body? Ser.). (ENG., Illus.). 256p. (gr. 7-9). 24.99 *(978-1-55704-769-4(3)*, Morrow, William & Co.) HarperCollins Pubs.

Merritt, Robin. The Life Cycle of a Human. 2011. (Life Cycles Ser.). (ENG., Illus.). 32p. (J). (gr. k-3). lib. bdg. 29.93 *(978-1-60973-147-2(6)*, 201174) Child's World, Inc., The.

National Science Teachers Association Staff, contrib. by. Toward High School Biology, Student Edition: Understanding Growth in Living Things. 2017. pap. 19.95 ***(978-1-68140-443-1(5))*** National Science Teachers Assn.

Owen, Ruth. What Happens When I Grow? 2013. (My Body: Inside & Out! Ser.). 24p. (J). (gr. -1-3). lib. bdg. 23.93 *(978-1-909673-32-8(3))* Ruby Tuesday Books Limited GBR. Dist: Bearport Publishing Co., Inc.

Oxlade, Chris. Growth, 1 vol. 2012. (Science Behind Ser.). (ENG., Illus.). 32p. (gr. 3-3). pap. 8.29 *(978-1-4109-4501-3(4))*; lib. bdg. 30.65 *(978-1-4109-4490-0(5))* Heinemann-Raintree. (Raintree Perspectives).

Peak, Lizabeth. Growth Disorders. 2007. (Diseases & Disorders Ser.). (ENG.). 128p. (gr. 7-12). 39.90 *(978-1-59018-673-2(7))* Cengage Gale.

Randolph, Joanne, ed. Growth & Aging. 2017. (Amazing Human Body Ser.). 48p. (J). (gr. 6-6). pap. 11.70 ***(978-0-7660-8981-5(9))*** Enslow Pubs., Inc.

Rice, Dona. Growing Up, 1 vol. rev. ed. 2014. (Science Readers: Content & Literacy Ser.). (ENG., Illus.). 24p. (gr. k-k). pap. 22.96 *(978-1-4938-1134-2(7))*; pap. 8.99 *(978-1-4807-4524-7(3))* Teacher Created Materials, Inc.

—Growth & Change, 1 vol. rev. ed. 2014. (Science Readers: Content & Literacy Ser.). (ENG., Illus.). 24p. (gr. 1-1). pap. 22.96 *(978-1-4938-1149-6(5))*; pap. 8.99 *(978-1-4807-4562-9(6))* Teacher Created Materials, Inc.

Rockwell, Anne F. Growing Like Me. Keller, Holly, illus. 2010. (Rise & Shine Ser.). (ENG.). 24p. (C). (gr. -1-3). 25.95 *(978-0-15-202202-0(3))* National Geographic School Publishing, Inc.

Salzmann, Ann. Kids Do Grown Up. 2012. (ENG.). pap. *(978-1-4675-4026-1(9))* Independent Pub.

Savage, Candace. Get Growing! Clement, Gary, illus. (J). pap. 6.95 *(978-1-55054-203-5(6))* Da Capo Pr., Inc.

Sévigny, Eric, illus. Caillou, Old Shoes, New Shoes. 2016. (Read with Caillou Ser.). (ENG.). 32p. (J). (gr. -1-k). 3.99 *(978-2-89718-341-7(1))* Caillouet, Gerry.

Silverstein, Alvin, et al. Growth & Development. 2007. (Science Concepts, Second Ser.). (Illus.). 112p. (YA). (gr. 5-9). lib. bdg. 31.93 *(978-0-8225-6057-9(7))* Lerner Publishing Group.

Spilsbury, Richard, et al. Your Body for Life. 2013. (Your Body for Life Ser.). (ENG.). 64p. (gr. 7-8). pap. 59.94 *(978-1-4329-7095-6(X))* Heinemann-Raintree.

Walden, Libby. Things That Grow. Stadtlander, Becca, illus. 2017. (360 Degrees Ser.). (ENG.). 76p. (gr. 3-12). 12.99 ***(978-1-944530-05-1(3)***, 360 Degrees) Tiger Tales.

Weber, Rebecca. The Cycle of Your Life, 1 vol. 2010. (Health & Your Body Ser.). (ENG.). 24p. (gr. k-1). lib. bdg. 26.65 *(978-1-4296-6610-7(2)*, Pebble Plus) Capstone Press of Coughlan Cos.

GROWTH—FICTION

Angelou, Maya. Cedric of Jamaica. Rockwell, Lizzy, illus. 2005. (Random House Pictureback Book Ser.). (J). *(978-0-375-83269-7(6))* Random Hse., Inc.

Bacon, Daskam Josephine. While Caroline Was Growing. 2007. 188p. 95.99 *(978-1-4280-7721-8(9))*; per. 89.99 *(978-1-4280-7710-2(3))* IndyPublish.com.

Badescu, Ramona & Bedrick, Claudia Z. Pomelo Begins to Grow. Chaud, Benjamin, illus. 2011. (Pomelo the Garden Elephant Ser.). (ENG.). 48p. (J). (gr. -1-2). 16.95 *(978-1-59270-111-7(6))* Enchanted Lion Bks., LLC.

Baer, Julie. Love Me Later. 2005. (Illus.). 28p. (J). (gr. -1-3). 16.99 *(978-1-932188-03-5(7))* Bollix Bks.

Baer, Julie, illus. & text. I Only Like What I Like. Baer, Julie, text. 2003. 32p. (J). 15.99 *(978-1-932188-00-4(2))* Bollix Bks.

Barber, Tiki & Barber, Ronde. Goal Line. (Barber Game Time Bks.). (ENG., Illus.). 176p. (J). (gr. 3-7). 2013. pap. 6.99 *(978-1-4169-9096-3(8))* 2011. 15.99 *(978-1-4169-9095-6(X))* Simon & Schuster/Paula Wiseman Bks. (Simon & Schuster/Paula Wiseman Bks.).

Becker Holstein, Barbara. Secrets: Diary of a Gutsy Teen. 2015. (ENG.). 144p. (J). (gr. 2-7). 12.95 *(978-1-62914-626-3(9)*, Sky Pony Pr.) Skyhorse Publishing Co., Inc.

—The Truth: Diary of a Gutsy Tween. 2014. (ENG.). 176p. (J). (gr. 2-7). 12.95 *(978-1-62873-611-3(9)*, Sky Pony Pr.) Skyhorse Publishing Co., Inc.

Bergstein, Rita M. Your Own Big Bed. Hartung, Susan Kathleen, illus. 2008. (ENG.). 36p. (J). (gr. -1-k). 15.99 *(978-0-670-06079-5(8)*, Viking Books for Young Readers) Penguin Young Readers Group.

Best, Cari. Sally Jean, the Bicycle Queen. Davenier, Christine, illus. 2006. (ENG.). 32p. (J). (gr. -1-3). 17.99 *(978-0-374-36386-4(2)*, 9780374363864, Farrar, Straus & Giroux (BYR)) Farrar, Straus & Giroux.

Bluthenthal, Diana Cain, illus. I'm a Kid. You're a Baby. 2020. (J). *(978-0-689-85470-5(6))* Simon & Schuster Children's Publishing.

Brimner, Larry Dane. Baby Bear. Date not set. (ENG.). 40p. (J). (gr. -1-3). pap. 5.99 *(978-0-06-443703-5(5))* HarperCollins Pubs.

Brody, Jessica. Addie Bell's Shortcut to Growing Up. 2017. (ENG.). 368p. (J). (gr. 5). 16.99 *(978-0-399-55510-7(2)*, Delacorte Bks. for Young Readers) Random Hse. Children's Bks.

Bronstein, Christine. Stewie BOOM! Boss of the Big Boy Bed: Boss of the Big Boy Bed. Young, Karen L., illus. 2015. (Stewie BOOM! Ser.). (ENG.). 60p. (gr. -1-2). 17.99 *(978-0-9904652-9-4(2))*; pap. 11.99 *(978-0-9963074-0-6(0))* Nothing But The Truth, LLC.

Burfoot, Ella, illus. Bear & Me. 2013. (J). *(978-1-4351-4753-9(7))* Barnes & Noble, Inc.

Capucilli, Alyssa Satin. This Bear's Birthday. Hussey, Lorna, illus. 2017. (ENG.). 32p. (J). 16.99 *(978-1-62779-701-6(7)*, 9781627797016, Holt, Henry & Co. Bks. For Young Readers) Holt, Henry & Co.

Carlson, Nancy. It's Going to Be Perfect! Carlson, Nancy, illus. 2012. (Nancy Carlson Picture Bks). (Illus.). 32p. (J). (gr. k-2). (ENG.). 9.95 *(978-0-7613-8944-6(X))*; 56.72 *(978-0-7613-9299-6(8))* Lerner Publishing Group. (Carolrhoda Bks.).

Carter, Candace. Sid's Surprise. Kim, Joung Un, illus. 2005. (Green Light Readers Level 1 Ser.). (ENG.). 32p. (J). (gr. -1-3). pap. 3.95 *(978-0-15-205182-2(1))* Houghton Mifflin Harcourt Publishing Co.

—Sid's Surprise. Kim, Joung Un, illus. 2005. (Green Light Readers Level 1 Ser.). (gr. -1-3). 13.95 *(978-0-7569-5242-6(5))* Perfection Learning Corp.

Chering, Don. The Acorn That Doubted. 2008. 32p. pap. 14.49 *(978-1-4389-0493-1(2))* AuthorHouse.

Child, Lauren. I Want to Be Much More Bigger Like You. 2008. (Charlie & Lola Ser.). (ENG.). 24p. (J). (gr. -1-k). mass mkt. 3.99 *(978-0-448-44867-1(X)*, Grosset & Dunlap) Penguin Young Readers Group.

Clarke, Jane. Only Tadpoles Have Tails. Gray, Jane, illus. 2003. (Flying Foxes Ser.). (ENG.). 48p. (J). lib. bdg. *(978-0-7787-1484-2(5))* Crabtree Publishing Co.

Clay Iii, J. Percy. Sampson's Pumpkin Playhouse. 2012. 30p. 24.95 *(978-1-4626-7226-4(4))* America Star Bks.

Cohn, Arlen. Firsts. Vasconcellos, Daniel, illus. gif. ed. 2004. (ENG.). 28p. (J). bds. 9.99 *(978-1-57939-168-3(0))* Andrews McMeel Publishing.

Conway, Jill Ker, et al. El Flamingo Felipe. Millis, Lokken, illus. 2009. (SPA & ENG.). 32p. (J). (gr. -1-3). pap. 9.95 *(978-1-55591-714-2(3))* Fulcrum Publishing.

Curtis, Jamie Lee. It's Hard to Be Five: Learning How to Work My Control Panel. Cornell, Laura, illus. 40p. (J). (gr. -1-3). 2007. (ENG.). 16.99 *(978-0-06-008095-2(7))* 2004. lib. bdg. 17.89 *(978-0-06-008096-9(5)*, Cotler, Joanna Books) HarperCollins Pubs.

—My Brave Year of Firsts: Tries, Sighs, & High Fives. Cornell, Laura, illus. 2012. (ENG.). 40p. (J). (gr. -1-3). 16.99 *(978-0-06-144155-4(4))* HarperCollins Pubs.

—When I Was Little: A Four-Year-Old's Memoir of Her Youth. braille ed. 2004. (Illus.). (J). (gr. k-3). spiral bd. *(978-0-616-01625-1(5))*; spiral bd. *(978-0-616-01626-8(3))* Canadian National Institute for the Blind/Institut National Canadien pour les Aveugles.

Dahl, Michael. Bye-Bye Bottles, Zebra. Vidal, Oriol, illus. 2015. (Hello Genius Ser.). (ENG.). 20p. (gr. 1-2). bds. 7.99 *(978-1-4795-5792-9(7))* Picture Window Bks.

—No More Pacifier, Duck. Vidal, Oriol, illus. 2015. (Hello Genius Ser.). (ENG.). 20p. (gr. 1-2). bds. 7.99 *(978-1-4795-5793-6(5))* Picture Window Bks.

—Thumbs up, Brown Bear. Vidal, Oriol, illus. 2015. (Hello Genius Ser.). (ENG.). 20p. (gr. 1-2). bds. 7.99 *(978-1-4795-5794-3(3))* Picture Window Bks.

Davies, Gill. A Special Wish: A Story of Confidence. O'Neill, Rachael, illus. 2009. (Let's Grow Together Ser.). 32p. (J). (gr. -1-2). pap. 10.55 *(978-1-60754-769-3(4))*; lib. bdg. 22.60 *(978-1-60754-760-0(0))* Windmill Bks.

Diesen, Deborah. Bloom. Lundquist, Mary, illus. 2017. (ENG.). 32p. (J). 16.99 *(978-0-374-30250-4(2)*, 9780374302504, Farrar, Straus & Giroux (BYR)) Farrar, Straus & Giroux.

Fitzpatrick, Marie-Louise. There. Fitzpatrick, Marie-Louise, illus. 2009. (ENG., Illus.). 32p. (J). (gr. -1-2). 18.99 *(978-1-59643-087-7(7)*, 9781596430877) Roaring Brook Pr.

Fraley, Patty. One Day I Will Grow Up. 2012. 16p. pap. 15.99 *(978-1-4772-5460-8(9))* AuthorHouse.

Frazier, Daniele. The Tiny Brown Seed. Frazier, Craig, illus. 2003. 24p. (J). (gr. -1-1). 14.95 *(978-1-932026-11-5(8))* Graphis, U.S., Inc.

Friedman, Laurie B. Birthday Rules. Murfin, Teresa, illus. 2015. (J). (gr. k-3). (ENG.). 32p. lib. bdg. 16.99 *(978-0-7613-6071-1(9))*; 17.32 *(978-1-4677-6177-2(X))* Lerner Publishing Group. (Carolrhoda Bks.).

Fruchter, Jason, illus. Big Enough to Help. 2015. (Daniel Tiger's Neighborhood Ser.). (ENG.). 24p. (J). (gr. -1-1). pap. 5.99 *(978-1-4814-2942-9(6)*, Simon Spotlight) Simon Spotlight.

Gellman, Ellie B. Netta & Her Plant. Ugliano, Natascia, illus. 2014. (Tu B'Shevat Ser.). (ENG.). 32p. (J). (gr. -1-2). 17.95 *(978-1-4677-0422-9(9)*, Kar-Ben Publishing) Lerner Publishing Group.

Giggle & grow with Plush. 2007. bds. 15.95 *(978-1-58117-644-5(9)*, Intervisual/Piggy Toes) Bendon, Inc.

Gomi, Taro. My Friends. 2014. 40p. pap. 7.00 *(978-1-61003-331-2(0))* Center for the Collaborative Classroom.

—My Friends/Mis Amigos. 2006. (ENG & SPA., Illus.). 40p. (J). (gr. -1-7). pap. 6.99 *(978-0-8118-5204-3(0))* Chronicle Bks. LLC.

Goodhart, Pippa. Hoppy Birthday, Jo-Jo! Birkett, Georgie, illus. 2005. (Green Bananas Ser.). (ENG.). 48p. (J). lib. bdg. *(978-0-7787-1025-7(4))* Crabtree Publishing Co.

Hood, Susan. Leaps & Bounce. Cordell, Matthew, illus. 2016. (ENG.). 32p. (J). (gr. -1-k). 16.99 *(978-1-4231-5234-7(4))* Disney Pr.

—Rooting for You. Cordell, Matthew, illus. 2014. (ENG.). 32p. (J). (gr. -1-k). 16.99 *(978-1-4231-5230-9(1))* Disney Pr.

Horning, Sandra. The Biggest Pumpkin, 1 vol. Stone-Barker, Holly, illus. 2014. 32p. (J). 16.99 *(978-1-4556-1925-2(6))* Pelican Publishing Co., Inc.

Howard, Arthur. When I Was Five. 2014. 40p. pap. 7.00 *(978-1-61003-185-1(7))* Center for the Collaborative Classroom.

Hughes, Jenny. Audrey's Tree House. Bentley, Jonathan, illus. 2015. (J). pap. *(978-0-545-81405-8(7))*; (ENG.). 32p. (gr. -1-k). 17.99 *(978-0-545-81327-3(1))* Scholastic, Inc. (Scholastic Pr.).

Jones, Patrick. Pass It Forward. 2016. (Bounce Ser.). (ENG.). 104p. (YA). (gr. 6-12). lib. bdg. 26.65 *(978-1-5124-1125-6(6),* Darby Creek) Lerner Publishing Group.

Karas, G. Brian. As an Oak Tree Grows. Karas, G. Brian, illus. 2014. (ENG., Illus.). 32p. (J). (gr. k-3). 17.99 *(978-0-399-25233-4(9),* Nancy Paulsen Books) Penguin Young Readers Group.

Katz, Karen. Now I'm Big! Katz, Karen, illus. 2013. (ENG., Illus.). 32p. (J). (gr. -1-k). 15.99 *(978-1-4169-3547-6(9),* McElderry, Margaret K. Bks.) McElderry, Margaret K. Bks.

Keller, Holly. Farfallina & Marcel. Keller, Holly, illus. 2005. (ENG., Illus.). 32p. (J). (gr. -1-4). reprint ed. pap. 6.99 *(978-0-06-443872-8(4),* Greenwillow Bks.) HarperCollins Pubs.

—Farfallina & Marcel. Keller, Holly, illus. 2005. (Illus.). (gr. -1-3). 17.00 *(978-0-7569-5785-8(0))* Perfection Learning Corp.

Kimble, Maggie T. Peep Learns to Sing. 2004. 21p. pap. 24.95 *(978-1-4137-2005-1(6))* PublishAmerica, Inc.

Kingsbury, Karen. Whatever You Grow up to Be, 1 vol. Docampo, Valeria, illus. rev. ed. 2014. (ENG.). 32p. (J). 15.99 *(978-0-310-71646-4(2))* Zonderkidz.

Kittinger, Jo S. Cuando Sea Grande. Lucas, Margeaux, illus. 2005. (Rookie Reader Español Ser.). (SPA & ESP.). 23p. (J). (gr. k-2). per. 4.95 *(978-0-516-24692-5(5),* Children's Pr.) Scholastic Library Publishing.

Krensky, Stephen. I Know a Lot! Gillingham, Sara, illus. 2013. (Empowerment Ser.). (ENG.). 12p. (J). (gr. -1 — 1). bds. 6.95 *(978-1-4197-0938-8(0),* Abrams Appleseed) Abrams, Inc.

Kroll, Virginia. On the Way to Kindergarten. Schlossberg, Elizabeth, illus. 2008. (ENG.). 32p. (J). (gr. -1-k). pap. 6.99 *(978-0-14-241144-5(2),* Puffin Books) Penguin Young Readers Group.

Krulik, Nancy. Katie Kazoo, Switcheroo: A Collection of Katie. John and Wendy, illus. 2008. (Katie Kazoo, Switcheroo Ser.: Bks. 1-4). (ENG.). 320p. (J). (gr. 2-4). 10.99 *(978-0-448-44910-4(2),* Grosset & Dunlap) Penguin Young Readers Group.

Laden, Nina. Grow Up! 2003. (ENG., Illus.). 26p. (J). (gr. -1-7). bds. 6.99 *(978-0-8118-3761-3(0))* Chronicle Bks. LLC.

—Once upon a Memory. Liwksa, Renata, illus. 2013. (ENG.). 40p. (J). (gr. -1-3). 17.00 *(978-0-316-20816-1(7))* Little, Brown Bks. for Young Readers.

Lewis-Brown, Alscess. Mosquito Get in Trouble Too. Hatfield, Cynthia, illus. 2009. (J). *(978-1-934370-09-4(6))* Editorial Campana.

L'Heureux, Christine. Baby Caillou, I'm Growing! Brignaud, Pierre, illus. 2013. (Baby Caillou Ser.). (ENG.). 10p. (J). (gr. -1-k). bds. *(978-2-89718-041-6(2))* Filmer Ltd.

Lucado, Max. The Oak Inside the Acorn, 1 vol. Angelini, George, illus. 2006. (ENG.). 48p. 16.99 *(978-1-4003-0601-5(9))* Nelson, Thomas Inc.

MacKay, Elly. If You Hold a Seed. MacKay, Elly, illus. 2013. (ENG., Illus.). 32p. (J). (gr. -1-17). 16.95 *(978-0-7624-4721-3(4),* Running Pr. Kids) Running Pr. Bk. Pubs.

Mayer, Mercer. Just a Little Too Little. 2012. (Little Critter Ser.). (Illus.). (J). lib. bdg. 13.55 *(978-0-606-23567-9(1),* Turtleback) Turtleback Bks.

—Just Big Enough. Mayer, Mercer, illus. 2013. (Little Critter Ser.). (ENG., Illus.). 24p. (J). (gr. -1-2). pap. 3.99 *(978-0-06-147805-5(9),* HarperFestival) HarperCollins Pubs.

—Just Big Enough. 2013. (Little Critter Ser.). (J). lib. bdg. 13.55 *(978-0-606-31809-9(7),* Turtleback) Turtleback Bks.

—When I Grow Up. 2003. (Look-Look Ser.). (ENG., Illus.). 24p. (J). (gr. -1-k). pap. 3.99 *(978-0-375-82632-0(7),* Random Hse. Bks. for Young Readers) Random Hse. Children's Bks.

—When I Grow Up. 2003. (Little Critter Ser.). (gr. -1-2). lib. bdg. 13.55 *(978-0-613-82737-9(6),* Turtleback) Turtleback Bks.

Mcghee, Alison. Bye-Bye, Crib. MacDonald, Ross, illus. 2008. (ENG.). 32p. (J). (gr. -1-1). 16.99 *(978-1-4169-1621-5(0),* Simon & Schuster/Paula Wiseman Bks.) Simon & Schuster/Paula Wiseman Bks.

—Only a Witch Can Fly. Yoo, Taeeun, illus. movie tie-in ed. 2009. (ENG.). 32p. (J). (gr. -1-3). 16.99 *(978-0-312-37503-4(4),* 9780312375034) Feiwel & Friends.

Mockford, Caroline. What's This? A Seed's Story. Mockford, Caroline, illus. 2007. (ENG., Illus.). 32p. (J). (gr. -1-2). pap. 7.99 *(978-1-84686-071-3(7))* Barefoot Bks., Inc.

Moynihan, Dan. Hiding Dinosaurs. 2015. (I Like to Read(r) Ser.). (ENG., Illus.). 24p. (J). (gr. -1-3). 14.95 *(978-0-8234-3196-0(7))* Holiday Hse., Inc.

Newman, Jeff. Hand Book. Newman, Jeff, illus. 2011. (ENG., Illus.). 40p. (J). (gr. -1-3). 15.99 *(978-1-4169-5013-4(3),* Simon & Schuster Bks. For Young Readers) Simon & Schuster Bks. For Young Readers.

Oppel, Kenneth. Silverwing. braille ed. 2003. (Silverwing Saga: Bk. 1). (J). (gr. 2). spiral bd. *(978-0-616-15274-4(4))* Canadian National Institute for the Blind/Institut National Canadien pour les Aveugles.

—Silverwing. 2007. (Silverwing Trilogy Ser.). (ENG.). 224p. (J). (gr. 3-7). per. 7.99 *(978-1-4169-4998-5(4),* Simon & Schuster Bks. For Young Readers) Simon & Schuster Bks. For Young Readers.

Ostermann, Riley. So Big. 2009. 24p. pap. 12.00 *(978-1-60693-970-3(X),* Eloquent Bks.) Strategic Book Publishing & Rights Agency (SBPRA).

Parker, Emma. Lulu & the Seed. 2010. (Illus.). pap. *(978-1-877547-82-9(4))* First Edition Ltd.

Petty, Dev. I Don't Want to Be a Frog. Boldt, Mike, illus. 2016. (ENG.). 32p. (J). (gr. -1-2). 16.99 *(978-1-101-93920-8(6),* Doubleday Bks. for Young Readers) Random Hse. Children's Bks.

Piggy Toes Press, creator. Giggle & Grow Baby's Body! 2007. (ENG., Illus.). 14p. (gr. -1-k). bds. 7.99 *(978-1-58117-586-8(8),* Intervisual/Piggy Toes) Bendon, Inc.

Pignataro, Anna. Our Love Grows. 2016. (ENG.). 24p. (J). (-4). 16.99 *(978-1-4926-3418-8(2),* 9781492634188, Sourcebooks Jabberwocky) Sourcebooks, Inc.

Pinkham, Mark Amaru. Love Me Later. 2005. 202p. 14.95 *(978-1-932188-02-8(9))* Adventures Unlimited Pr.

Pitino, Donna Marie. Too-Tall Tina. Woodruff, Liza, illus. 2005. (Math Matters Ser.). (ENG.). 32p. (J). (gr. -1-3). pap. 5.95 *(978-1-57565-150-7(5))* Kane Press, Inc.

Pittar, Gill. Milly, Molly & Jimmy's Seeds. 2004. (Illus.). 28p. *(978-1-86972-000-1(8))* Milly Molly Bks.

Rand, Ann. I Know a Lot of Things. Rand, Paul, illus. 2009. (ENG.). 40p. (J). (gr. -1-1). 16.99 *(978-0-8118-6615-6(7))* Chronicle Bks. LLC.

Reil-Berry, Stacie. Stop! Growing. 2012. 24p. 24.95 *(978-1-4626-4706-4(5))* America Star Bks.

Renee, Sherry. Bye Bye Bed-Dy: Andrew Gets a Big Boy Bed. 2012. 20p. pap. 17.99 *(978-1-4685-7498-2(1))* AuthorHouse.

Restrepo, Bettina. Moose & Magpie, 1 vol. Rogers, Sherry, illus. 2009. (ENG.). 32p. (J). (gr. -1-3). pap. 8.95 *(978-1-60718-042-5(1))* Arbordale Publishing.

Restrepo, Bettina & Rogers, Sherry. Moose & Magpie, 1 vol. 2009. (ENG., Illus.). 32p. (J). (gr. -1-3). 16.95 *(978-1-934359-97-6(1))* Arbordale Publishing.

Rey, H. A. Curious George Plants a Seed. 2007. (Curious George Ser.). (ENG., Illus.). 24p. (J). (gr. -1-3). 4.99 *(978-0-618-77710-5(5))* Houghton Mifflin Harcourt Publishing Co.

—Tadpole Trouble. 2007. (Curious George Ser.). (ENG., Illus.). 24p. (J). (gr. -1-3). 4.99 *(978-0-618-77712-9(1))* Houghton Mifflin Harcourt Publishing Co.

Rhode, Paul. Presents for Phoebe: Growing Independent. Margolis, Al, illus. 2011. 24p. (YA). pap. 9.95 *(978-1-935706-05-2(5))* Wiggles Pr.

Richmond, Marianne. If I Could Keep You Little. (ENG.). (J). 2012. 24p. bds. 8.99 *(978-1-4022-7237-0(5))* 2010. (Marianne Richmond Ser.: 0). 32p. 9.95 *(978-1-934082-92-8(9))* Sourcebooks, Inc. (Sourcebooks Jabberwocky).

—If I Could Keep You Little... 2010. (Marianne Richmond Ser.). (ENG.). 32p. (J). (gr. -1-2). 16.99 *(978-1-4022-5559-5(4),* Sourcebooks Jabberwocky) Sourcebooks, Inc.

—Si Pudiera Conservarte Pequeño... 2014. (SPA & ENG., Illus.). 24p. (J). bds. 6.99 *(978-1-4926-0369-6(4),* Sourcebooks Jabberwocky) Sourcebooks, Inc.

Robinson, Sharon. The Littlest Pumpkin. 2012. 24p. 24.95 *(978-1-4626-5963-0(2))* America Star Bks.

Rodhe, Paul & Wallas Reidy, Sarah. The Little Plum Tree. Margolis, Al & Young, Bill, illus. 2010. 24p. (J). pap. 9.95 *(978-1-935706-06-9(3))* Wiggles Pr.

Rovetch, L. Bob. TLC Grow with Me! McLeod, Chum, illus. 2005. (J). *(978-1-58987-114-4(6))* Kindermusik International.

Rowen, Amy & Rowen, Tyla Marie. Waggin' Tails. 2003. 182p. 23.95 *(978-0-595-65740-7(0))*; pap. 13.95 *(978-0-595-28171-8(0))* iUniverse, Inc.

Schafer, Milton. I'm Big! Lew-Vriethoff, Joanne, illus. 2006. (J). *(978-1-4156-8150-3(3),* Dial) Penguin Publishing Group.

Schubert, Jan. The Sun Seed. Schubert, Jan, illus. 2007. (Illus.). 28p. (J). (gr. -1-k). lib. bdg. *(978-0-88010-585-9(2),* Bell Pond Bks.) SteinerBooks, Inc.

Schultz, Agnes Szenozicska. The Little Tree. 2007. 32p. (J). 14.00 *(978-0-8059-7211-5(0))* Dorrance Publishing Co., Inc.

Simon, Coco. Alexis: The Icing on the Cupcake. 2014. (Cupcake Diaries: 20). lib. bdg. 17.20 *(978-0-606-35786-9(6))* Turtleback Bks.

—Alexis the Icing on the Cupcake. 2014. (Cupcake Diaries: 20). (ENG., Illus.). 160p. (J). (gr. 3-7). pap. 6.99 *(978-1-4814-0468-6(7),* Simon Spotlight) Simon Spotlight.

Spinelli, Eileen. A Big Boy Now. Lloyd, Megan, illus. 2012. (ENG.). 32p. (J). (gr. -1-3). 16.99 *(978-0-06-008673-2(4))* HarperCollins Pubs.

Spinelli, Jerry. Hokey Pokey. 2013. (J). 282p. pap. *(978-0-375-83201-7(7))*; (ENG.). 304p. (gr. 5). 15.99 *(978-0-375-83198-0(3))*; (ENG.). 304p. (gr. 5). lib. bdg. 18.99 *(978-0-375-93198-7(8))* Random Hse. Children's Bks. (Knopf Bks. for Young Readers).

Stein, David Ezra. Pouch! Stein, David Ezra, illus. 2010. (Rise & Shine Ser.). (ENG., Illus.). 32p. (C). (gr. -1-k). 25.95 *(978-0-399-25051-4(4))* National Geographic School Publishing, Inc.

—Pouch! Stein, David Ezra, illus. 2012. (ENG., Illus.). 32p. (J). (gr. -1 — 1). bds. 7.99 *(978-0-399-25738-4(1),* Nancy Paulsen Books) Penguin Young Readers Group.

Stinson, Kathy. Parfois Grand, Parfoit Petit. Homel, David, tr. from ENG. Lewis, Robin Baird, illus. 2006. (FRE.). 23p. (J). (gr. -1-2). reprint ed. pap. 5.00 *(978-1-4223-5663-0(9))* DIANE Publishing Co.

Stott, Ann. I'll Be There. Phelan, Matt, illus. 2011. (ENG.). 32p. (J). (gr. -1-2). 14.99 *(978-0-7636-4711-7(X))* Candlewick Pr.

Sudduth, Brent H. Buster. Spengler, Kenneth J., illus. 2003. 32p. (J). 15.95 *(978-1-59034-478-1(2))* Mondo Publishing.

Thermes, Jennifer. Sam Bennett's New Shoes. 2006. (Illus.). (J). 15.95 *(978-1-57505-822-1(7),* Carolrhoda Bks.) Lerner Publishing Group.

Torrey, Richard. Almost. Torrey, Richard, illus. 2009. (ENG., Illus.). 40p. (J). (gr. -1-3). 17.99 *(978-0-06-156166-5(5))* HarperCollins Pubs.

van Genechten, Guido. Kangaroo Christine. van Genechten, Guido, illus. 2005. (Illus.). 24p. (J). (gr. 3-7). pap. 6.95 *(978-1-58925-396-4(5))* Tiger Tales.

van Lieshout, Maria. Bye-Bye Binky: I'm a Big Kid Now. 2016. (Big Kid Power Ser.). (ENG., Illus.). 24p. (J). (gr. -1 — 1). 9.99 *(978-1-4521-3536-6(3))* Chronicle Bks. LLC.

Waring, Geoff. Oscar & the Frog: A Book about Growing. Waring, Geoff, illus. 2007. (Start with Science Ser.). (ENG., Illus.). 32p. (J). (gr. -1-3). 11.99 *(978-0-7636-3558-9(8))* Candlewick Pr.

Willems, Mo & Keller, Laurie. We Are Growing! Willems, Mo & Keller, Laurie, illus. 2016. (Elephant & Piggie Like Reading! Ser.). (ENG., Illus.). 64p. (J). (gr. 1-3). 9.99 *(978-1-4847-2635-8(9))* Hyperion Bks. for Children.

Williamson, Stafford. Puppyfish. 2005. 48p. (J). pap. 18.49 *(978-1-4116-3836-5(0))* Lulu Pr., Inc.

Wunderli, Stephen. Little Boo. Zeltner, Tim, illus. 2014. (ENG.). 32p. (J). (gr. -1-2). 16.99 *(978-0-8050-9708-5(2),* 9780805097085, Holt, Henry & Co. Bks. For Young Readers) Holt, Henry & Co.

Zepeda, Gwendolyn & Ventura, Gabriela Baeza. Growing up with Tamales: Los Tamales de Ana. Ward, April, illus. 2008. (SPA & ENG.). 32p. (J). (gr. -1-2). 16.95 *(978-1-55885-493-2(2),* Piñata Books) Arte Publico Pr.

Zoss, Lori. A Bed for Fred. 2013. 24p. 15.95 *(978-1-936449-52-1(8))* Roberts & Ross Publishing.

GROWTH (PLANTS)

Anderson, Michael. A Closer Look at Plant Reproduction, Growth, & Ecology. 2011. (J). lib. bdg. 31.70 *(978-1-61530-530-8(0))* Rosen Publishing Group, Inc., The.

Beullens, Nathalie, ed. Our Wonderful World (Cantonese-Chinese) Set. 2016. (Our Wonderful World (Cantonese-Chinese) Ser.). (ENG.). 8p. pap. 56.10 *(978-1-5081-1265-5(7),* Rosen Classroom) Rosen Publishing Group, Inc., The.

Bodach, Vijaya Khisty. How Does It Grow? 2008. (Discovering & Exploring Science Ser.). (Illus.). 16p. (J). (gr. -1-3). lib. bdg. 12.95 *(978-0-7569-8432-8(7))* Perfection Learning Corp.

Brynie, Faith Hickman. What Helps Plants Grow? The Nitrogen Cycle Case. 2003. (J). pap. *(978-1-58417-156-0(1))* Lake Street Pubs.

Cardenas, Ernesto A. Learn about Plants. 2009. pap. 4.95 *(978-1-60698-068-2(8))* Milo Educational Bks. & Resources.

Edwards, Nicola. Flowers. 2007. (See How Plants Grow Ser.). (Illus.). 24p. (J). (gr. 4-7). lib. bdg. 22.60 *(978-1-4042-3699-8(6))* Rosen Publishing Group, Inc., The.

Edwards, Tanille & Edwards, Latoya. Jordan & Justine's Weekend Adventures Tm: Plantas Partes 1 y 2 Spanish Language Version. 2007. 32p. (J). (gr. -1-3). pap. 12.95 *(978-0-9787302-5-3(9))* Fire Flies Entertainment, LLC.

Flynn, Claire E. Why Plants Need Light. 2009. (Real Life Readers Ser.). 12p. (gr. 1-2). pap. 5.90 *(978-1-4042-7919-3(9),* Rosen Classroom) Rosen Publishing Group, Inc., The.

Granger, Ronald. Know Your Leaves. 2013. (InfoMax Readers Ser.). (ENG.). 24p. (J). (gr. 2-3). pap. 8.25 *(978-1-4777-2422-4(2))*; pap. 49.50 *(978-1-4777-2425-5(7))* Rosen Publishing Group, Inc., The. (Rosen Classroom).

Growing a Plant: a Journal: Individual Title Six-Packs. (Discovery World Ser.). 16p. (gr. 1-2). 28.00 *(978-0-7635-8462-7(2))* Rigby Education.

Helbrough, Emma. How Flowers Grow. Silver, Maggie & Mayer, Uwe, illus. 2007. (Beginners Nature Ser.). 32p. (J). (gr. -1-3). 4.99 *(978-0-7945-1340-5(9),* Usborne) EDC Publishing.

Higgins, Nadia. Experiment with What a Plant Needs to Grow. 2015. (Lightning Bolt Books (tm) — Plant Experiments Ser.). (ENG., Illus.). 32p. (gr. k-2). pap. 8.99 *(978-1-4677-6077-5(3))*; lib. bdg. 26.65 *(978-1-4677-5730-0(6))* Lerner Publishing Group. (Lerner Pubns.).

Hirsch, Rebecca E. Plants Can't Sit Still. Posada, Mia, illus. 2016. (ENG.). 32p. (gr. k-4). (J). 19.99 *(978-1-4677-8031-5(6))*; 38.65 *(978-1-5124-1109-6(4))* Lerner Publishing Group. (Millbrook Pr.).

Hoffman, Mary Ann. Plant Experiments: What Affects Plant Growth? 2009. (Real Life Readers Ser.). 24p. (gr. 3-4). pap. 8.25 *(978-1-4358-0131-8(8),* Rosen Classroom); 24p. (gr. 3-3). 42.50 *(978-1-61511-217-3(0),* PowerKids Pr.); (J). lib. bdg. 22.60 *(978-1-4358-2971-8(9),* PowerKids Pr.) Rosen Publishing Group, Inc., The.

Hopkins, William G., ed. Plant Development. 2006. (Green World Ser.). (Illus.). 151p. (gr. 6-12). lib. bdg. 37.50 *(978-0-7910-8562-2(7))* Facts On File, Inc.

Hotchkins, Dewayne. All about Hydroponics. 2016. (Rosen REAL Readers: STEM & STEAM Collection). 12p. (gr. 1-k). pap. 6.33 *(978-1-5081-2458-0(2),* Rosen Classroom) Rosen Publishing Group, Inc., The.

Jeffries, Katherine. Plants Grow: Lap Book. 2009. (My First Reader's Theater Set B Ser.). (J). 28.00 *(978-1-60634-985-4(6))* Benchmark Education Co.

Kravetz, Jonathan. Learning about Plant Growth with Graphic Organizers. 2006. (Graphic Organizers in Science Ser.: Vol. 3). (Illus.). 24p. (YA). (gr. 3-6). lib. bdg. 22.60 *(978-1-4042-3413-0(6))* Rosen Publishing Group, Inc., The.

Lawrence, Ellen. Cooking with Sunshine: How Plants Make Food. 2012. (Science Slam: Plant-Ology Ser.). 24p. (J). (gr. -1-3). lib. bdg. 23.93 *(978-1-61772-586-9(2))* Bearport Publishing Co., Inc.

Leigh, A. It Grows in Spring: Learning the GR Sound. 2009. (PowerPhonics Ser.). 24p. (gr. 1-1). 39.90 *(978-1-60851-453-3(6),* PowerKids Pr.) Rosen Publishing Group, Inc., The.

Lilly, Melinda. Make It Grow. Thompson, Scott M., illus. 2003. (Rourke Discovery Library). 24p. (J). 22.79 *(978-1-58952-637-2(6))* Rourke Educational Media.

Llewellyn, Claire. How Plants Grow. 2006. (I Know That, Growth & Change Set Ser.). (Illus.). 24p. (J). lib. bdg. 24.25 *(978-1-59771-021-3(0))* Sea-To-Sea Pubns.

Lowery, Lawrence F. How Does a Plant Grow? Smith, Phil, illus. (J). 2013. pap. 11.95 *(978-1-936959-60-0(7))* 2012. (ENG.). 32p. pap. 11.95 *(978-1-936959-47-1(X))* National Science Teachers Assn.

Lundgren, Julie K. ¿Cómo Crecen Las Plantas? / How Do Plants Grow? 2011. (SPA & ENG.). 24p. (gr. k-1). pap. 8.95 *(978-1-61236-898-6(0))* Rourke Educational Media.

—How Do Plants Grow? 2011. (ENG., Illus.). 24p. (gr. k-1). pap. 8.95 *(978-1-61741-923-2(0))* Rourke Educational Media.

MacDonald, Margaret. How Do Plants Grow? 2011. (Learn-Abouts Ser.). (Illus.). 16p. (J). pap. 9.95 *(978-1-59920-635-6(8))* Palgrave Macmillan.

Mattern, Joanne. How Peas Grow(Cómo Crecen los Guisantes) 2006. (How Plants Grow/ Como crecen las plantas Ser.). (ENG & SPA., Illus.). 24p. (gr. k-3). lib. bdg. 22.00 *(978-0-8368-6463-2(8),* Weekly Reader Leveled Readers) Stevens, Gareth Publishing LLLP.

Morgan, Emily R. Next Time You See a Maple Seed. 2014. (Next Time You See Ser.). (ENG.). 32p. (J). (gr. k-5). 12.95 *(978-1-938946-35-6(9))* National Science Teachers Assn.

Nadeau, Isaac. Plant Development & Growth. (Life Science Library). 24p. (gr. 3-4). 2009. 42.50 *(978-1-60854-008-2(1),* PowerKids Pr.) 2006. (Illus.). (YA). 22.60 *(978-1-4042-2820-7(9))* Rosen Publishing Group, Inc., The.

Pressberg, Dava. How Leaves Work. 2013. (Rosen Readers Ser.). (ENG.). 24p. (J). (gr. 2-3). pap. 49.50 *(978-1-4777-2273-2(4))*; pap. 8.25 *(978-1-4777-2272-5(6))* Rosen Publishing Group, Inc., The. (Rosen Classroom).

Prokos, Anna. Seed Power: Discovering How Plants Grow. Clegg, Dave, illus. 2017. (Imagine That! Ser.). (ENG.). 32p. (J). (gr. 2-4). lib. bdg. 26.65 *(978-1-63440-151-7(4))*; 39.99 ***(978-1-63440-163-0(8))*** Red Chair Pr.

Rattini, Kristin Baird. Seed to Plant. 2014. (Readers Ser.). (ENG., Illus.). 32p. (J). (gr. -1-1). pap. 3.99 *(978-1-4263-1470-4(1),* National Geographic Children's Bks.) National Geographic Society.

René, Ellen. Investigating How Flowers Grow. 2009. (Science Detectives Ser.). 24p. (gr. 2-3). 42.50 *(978-1-60853-012-0(4),* PowerKids Pr.); (Illus.). (J). lib. bdg. 22.60 *(978-1-4042-4484-9(0))* Rosen Publishing Group, Inc., The.

Rice, Dona. Good Work. 2015. (TIME for KIDS(r) Nonfiction Readers Ser.). (ENG., Illus.). 12p. (gr. k-k). 4.99 *(978-1-4938-2139-6(3))* Teacher Created Materials, Inc.

Rice, Dona Herweck. Buen Trabajo. 2016. (TIME for KIDS(r) Nonfiction Readers Ser.). (SPA.). 12p. (J). (gr. k-k). 4.99 *(978-1-4938-3020-6(1))* Teacher Created Materials, Inc.

—Cómo Crecen las Plantas, 1 vol. 2nd rev. ed. 2011. (Nonfiction Readers Ser.). (SPA.). 12p. (J). (gr. 1-1). pap. 4.99 *(978-1-4333-4416-9(5))* Teacher Created Materials, Inc.

—How Plants Grow, 1 vol. 2nd rev. ed. 2011. (Nonfiction Readers Ser.). (ENG.). 12p. (J). (gr. 1-1). pap. 4.99 *(978-1-4333-3577-8(8))* Teacher Created Materials, Inc.

Rigby Education Staff. Discovery World Org Growing Plant. (Discovery World Ser.). (Illus.). 12p. (gr. 1-2). 27.00 *(978-0-7635-2701-3(7))* Rigby Education.

Senker, Cath. Plant Reproduction: How Do You Grow a Giant Pumpkin?, 1 vol. 2014. (Show Me Science Ser.). (ENG.). 32p. (gr. 3-5). lib. bdg. 30.65 *(978-1-4329-8749-7(6),* Raintree Perspectives) Heinemann-Raintree.

Shea, Therese. Watch Peas Grow. 2011. (Watch Plants Grow! Ser.). (Illus.). 24p. (J). (gr. k-2). pap. 8.15 *(978-1-4339-4834-3(6))*; lib. bdg. 22.60 *(978-1-4339-4833-6(8))* Stevens, Gareth Publishing LLLP.

Spilsbury, Louise & Spilsbury, Richard. Plant Growth. 2016. (Life of Plants Ser.). (ENG.). 48p. (gr. 3-5). pap. 7.99 *(978-1-4846-3694-7(5),* NA-h) Heinemann-Raintree.

Stewart, David. How a Seed Grows into a Sunflower. Franklin, Carolyn, illus. 2008. (Amaze Ser.). (ENG.). 32p. (J). (gr. k-3). 27.00 *(978-0-531-20442-9(1),* Children's Pr.) Scholastic Library Publishing.

Stewart, Melissa. How Do Plants Grow? 2006. (Tell Me Why, Tell Me How Ser.). (Illus.). 32p. (gr. 3-7). lib. bdg. 29.93 *(978-0-7614-2111-5(4),* Benchmark Bks.) Marshall Cavendish Corp.

Time for Kids Magazine Staff, ed. Plants! 2006. (Time for Kids Science Scoops Ser.). (Illus.). 32p. (gr. 1-3). 14.00 *(978-0-7569-6982-0(4))* Perfection Learning Corp.

Top That Publishing Staff, ed. Make it Grow. 2004. (Fun Kits Ser.). (Illus.). 48p. (J). *(978-1-84510-132-9(4))* Top That! Publishing PLC.

Wade, Mary Dodson. Plants Grow! 2009. (I Like Plants! Ser.). (Illus.). 24p. (J). (gr. k-3). lib. bdg. 22.60 *(978-0-7660-3152-4(7))* Enslow Pubs., Inc.

GRUBER, FRANZ XAVIER, 1787-1863

Jackson, Mary Helene. Weaver of Song: The Birth of Silent Night. Winstead, Leo, illus. l.t. ed. 2009. 40p. (J). 16.95 *(978-0-9825713-0-9(5))* Clifton Carriage House Pr.

GUADALCANAL, BATTLE OF, SOLOMON ISLANDS, 1942-1943

Hama, Larry. The Battle of Guadalcanal: Land & Sea Warfare in the South Pacific. (Graphic Battles of World War II Ser.). (ENG., Illus.). 48p. 2008. (gr. 3-8). pap. 14.05 *(978-1-4042-7426-6(X))* 2007. (YA). (gr. 4-7). lib. bdg. 31.95 *(978-1-4042-0784-4(8))* Rosen Publishing Group, Inc., The.

GUADALUPE, OUR LADY OF

Bernier-Grand, Carmen T. Our Lady of Guadalupe, 0 vols. Engel, Tonya, illus. 2012. (ENG.). 32p. (J). (gr. 3-7). 17.99 *(978-0-7614-6135-7(3),* 9780761461357, Amazon Children's Publishing) Amazon Publishing.

Cordova, Amy & Gollogly, Gene. Talking Eagle & the Lady of Roses: The Story of Juan Diego & Our Lady of Guadalupe. Cordova, Amy, illus. 2010. (Illus.). 40p. (J). (gr. k-7). 17.95 *(978-0-88010-719-8(7))* SteinerBooks, Inc.

Serrano, Francisco. Our Lady of Guadalupe, 1 vol. Davalos, Felipe, illus. 2nd ed. 2011. (ENG.). 12p. (gr. -1). 22.95 *(978-1-55498-074-1(7))* Groundwood Bks. CAN. Dist: Publishers Group West (PGW).

GUAM—FICTION

Arvidson, Douglas. Brothers of the Fire Star. Scarborough, Rob, illus. 2012. 207p. (YA). pap. 15.95 *(978-1-890109-91-2(6),* Cross Time) Crossquarter Publishing Group.

Holt, Kimberly Willis. Keeper of the Night. 2011. (ENG.). 336p. (YA). (gr. 7-12). pap. 14.99 *(978-0-312-66103-8(7),* 9780312661038) Square Fish.

GUATEMALA

Aboff, Marcie. Guatemala ABCs: A Book about the People & Places of Guatemala, 1 vol. Trover, Zachary, illus. 2006. (Country ABCs Ser.). (ENG.). 32p. (gr. k-5). 27.99 *(978-1-4048-1570-4(8))* Picture Window Bks.

Amado, Elisa. Un Barrilete: Para el Dia de los Muertos. Hairs, Joya, photos by. 2012. (SPA & ENG., Illus.). 32p. (J). (gr. k-4). pap. 9.95 *(978-1-55498-112-0(3))* Groundwood Bks. CAN. Dist: Publishers Group West (PGW).

Croy, Anita. Guatemala. 2009. (Countries of the World Ser.). (ENG., Illus.). 64p. (J). (gr. 5). 27.90 *(978-1-4263-0471-2(4),*

National Geographic Children's Bks.) National Geographic Society.

Dendinger, Roger. Guatemala. 2003. (Modern World Nations Ser.). (Illus.). 150p. (gr. 6-12). 35.00 (978-0-7910-7477-0(3), Chelsea Hse.) Facts On File, Inc.

Hudak, Heather C. A Refugee's Journey from Guatemala. 2017. 32p. (J). **(978-0-7787-3673-8(3))** Crabtree Publishing Co.

Knudsen, Shannon. Guatemala. 2011. (Country Explorers Ser.). 48p. pap. 51.02 (978-0-7613-7624-8(0)); (ENG.). (gr. 2-4). 29.27 (978-0-7613-6412-2(9)); (ENG.). (gr. 2-4). pap. 9.95 (978-0-7613-7081-9(1)) Lerner Publishing Group.

Markel, Rita J. Guatemala in Pictures. 2nd rev. expurg. ed. 2004. (Visual Geography Series, Second Ser.). (ENG., Illus.). 80p. (gr. 5-12). 31.93 (978-0-8225-1998-0(4)) Lerner Publishing Group.

Morrison, Marion. Guatemala. 2005. (Enchantment of the World Ser.: Vol. 2). (ENG., Illus.). 144p. (YA). (gr. 5-9). 39.00 (978-0-516-23674-2(1)) Scholastic Library Publishing.

Robinson, Anthony, et al. Street Children. Robinson, Anthony, photos by. 2016. (ENG., Illus.). 40p. (J). (gr. 4-7). pap. 10.99 (978-1-84780-598-0(1), Frances Lincoln) Quarto Publishing Group UK GBR. Dist: Littlehampton Bk Services, Ltd.

Robinson, Joanna J. Guatemala. 2015. (One World, Many Countries Ser.). (ENG.). 32p. (J). (gr. 1-4). 28.50 (978-1-63407-046-1(1), 208883) Child's World, Inc., The.

Rudolph, Jessica. Guatemala. 2015. (Countries We Come From Ser.). (ENG., Illus.). 32p. (J). (gr. k-3). lib. bdg. 26.60 (978-1-62724-856-3(0)) Bearport Publishing Co., Inc.

Schuetz, Kari. Guatemala. 2011. (Exploring Countries Ser.). (ENG., Illus.). 32p. (J). (gr. 3-7). lib. bdg. 26.95 (978-1-60014-618-3(X), Blastoff! Readers) Bellwether Media.

Sheehan, Sean & Koh, Magdalene. Guatemala. 2nd rev. ed. 2008. (Cultures of the World Ser.). 144p. (gr. 6-18). lib. bdg. 42.79 (978-0-7614-3412-2(7), Benchmark Bks.) Marshall Cavendish Corp.

Shields, Charles J. Guatemala. 2010. (Central America Today Ser.). 63p. (YA). (gr. 7-18). pap. 9.95 (978-1-4222-0715-4(3)); (Illus.). (gr. 9-12). 21.95 (978-1-4222-0648-5(3)) Mason Crest.

—Guatemala, Vol. 8. Henderson, James D., ed. 2015. (Discovering Central America: History, Politics, & Culture Ser.). (Illus.). 64p. (J). (gr. 7). lib. bdg. 22.95 (978-1-4222-3289-7(1)) Mason Crest.

Slade, Suzanne, et al. The Soda Bottle School: A True Story about Recycling, Teamwork, & One Crazy Idea. 2014. (ENG., Illus.). 32p. (gr. 1-7). 16.95 (978-0-88448-371-7(1), 884371) Tilbury Hse. Pubs.

Torres, John Albert. The Guatemalan Genocide of the Maya People. 2017. (J). **(978-1-5081-7736-4(8))** Rosen Publishing Group, Inc., The.

GUATEMALA—FICTION

Ann, Cameron. The Most Beautiful Place in the World. 2014. (ENG.). 64p. (J). (gr. k-3). 10.24 (978-1-63245-260-3(X)) Lectorum Pubns., Inc.

Barefoot Books Staff & Amador Family Staff. The Wheels on the Bus. Williamson, Melanie, illus. 2014. 24p. (J). (gr. -1-2). 9.99 (978-1-84686-788-0(6)) Barefoot Bks., Inc.

Bogunya, Angels. El Maiz Amargo. 2004. (SPA.). 144p. (J). (978-84-263-5237-8(5)) Vives, Luis Editorial (Edelvives) ESP. Dist: Lectorum Pubns., Inc.

Brasch, Nicolas. Escape from Pacaya, 1 vol. 2013. (Fiction Readers Ser.). (ENG., Illus.). 24p. (J). (gr. 2-2). pap. 6.99 (978-1-4333-5529-5(9)) Shell Educational Publishing.

Brown, Skila. Caminar. (ENG.). 208p. (J). (gr. 5-9). 2016. pap. 7.99 (978-0-7636-9094-6(5)) 2014. 15.99 (978-0-7636-6516-6(9)) Candlewick Pr.

—Caminar. 2016. (ENG.). 208p. (J). (gr. 5-9). 18.40 (978-0-606-39096-5(0)) Turtleback Bks.

Cameron, Ann. Colibri. 2005. (Readers Circle Ser.). (ENG.). 256p. (YA). (gr. 7). mass mkt. 5.99 (978-0-440-42052-1(0), Laurel Leaf) Random Hse. Children's Bks.

—El Lugar Mas Bonito del Mundo. Alonso, Juan Ramon, illus. 2003. (SPA.). 70p. (gr. 3-5). pap. 8.95 (978-968-19-0402-9(8)) Santillana USA Publishing Co., Inc.

Carling, Amelia Lau, et al. Mama & Papa Have a Store. 2003. (Avenues Ser.). (ENG., Illus.). 32p. (C). (gr. -1-3). pap. 23.95 (978-0-8037-2044-2(0)) National Geographic School Publishing, Inc.

Gardner, Graham. The Santa Beacon. LeBlanc, Nancy, illus. 2012. 40p. (J). 19.95 (978-0-9859358-0-1(4), Belle Isle Bks.) Brandylane Pubs., Inc.

Guillain, Adam. Bella Balistica & the Izta Warriors. 2012. (Bella Balistica Ser.). (ENG., Illus.). 170p. (J). (gr. 4-7). pap. 9.95 (978-1-84059-771-4(2)) Milet Publishing.

Marshall, Linda Elovitz. Rainbow Weaver/Tejedora del Arcoíris. Chavarri, Elisa, illus. 2016. (ENG & SPA.). 40p. (J). (gr. 1-4). 18.95 (978-0-89239-374-9(2)) Lee & Low Bks., Inc.

Mikaelsen, Ben. Red Midnight. 2003. (ENG.). 224p. (J). (gr. 5-18). pap. 6.99 (978-0-380-80561-7(8), Rayo) HarperCollins Pubs.

—Red Midnight. 2003. 212p. (gr. 5-9). 17.00 (978-0-7569-1550-6(3)) Perfection Learning Corp.

—Tree Girl. 2005. (ENG.). 240p. (YA). (gr. 8). pap. 9.99 (978-0-06-009006-7(5), HarperTeen) HarperCollins Pubs.

Newman, Lesléa. Felicia's Favorite Story. Romo, Adriana, illus. 2003. 24p. (J). pap. 9.95 (978-0-9674468-5-1(6)) Two Lives Publishing.

Resau, Laura. Red Glass. 2009. (ENG.). 304p. (YA). (gr. 7). pap. 8.99 (978-0-440-24025-9(5), Delacorte Bks. for Young Readers) Random Hse. Children's Bks.

Shaw, Nancy. Elena's Story. 2012. (Tales of the World Ser.). (ENG., Illus.). 32p. (J). (gr. 1-5). 16.95 (978-1-58536-528-9(9)) Sleeping Bear Pr.

Sporn, Jessica. Old Enough to do Good in the World. 2010. 21p. 12.95 (978-0-557-34196-2(5)) Lulu Pr., Inc.

GUERRILLA WARFARE

see also World War, 1939-1945—Underground Movements

Bruce, Julia. Siege! Can You Capture a Castle? Dennis, Peter, illus. 2009. (Step into History Ser.). 32p. (J). (gr. 2-5). lib. bdg. 23.94 (978-0-7660-3475-4(5)) Enslow Pubs., Inc.

Derkins, Susie. The Irish Republican Army. 2009. (Inside the World's Most Infamous Terrorist Organizations Ser.). 64p. (gr. 5-5). 58.50 (978-1-61513-579-0(0)) Rosen Publishing Group, Inc., The.

GUEVARA, ERNESTO, 1928-1967

Bodden, Valerie. Che Guevara: Political Activist & Revolutionary, 1 vol. 2011. (Essential Lives Set 6 Ser.). (ENG., Illus.). 112p. (J). (gr. 6-12). lib. bdg. 35.64 (978-1-61714-780-7(X), Essential Library) ABDO Publishing Co.

Crompton, Samuel. Che Guevara: The Making of a Revolutionary. 2009. (Life Portraits Ser.). (Illus.). 112p. (J). (gr. 7-12). lib. bdg. 36.00 (978-1-4339-0053-2(X)) Stevens, Gareth Publishing LLLP.

Ernesto Che Guevara. 2010. (Great Hispanic Heritage Ser.). (Illus.). 128p. (gr. 6-12). 35.00 (978-1-60413-732-3(0), Chelsea Hse.) Facts On File, Inc.

Kallen, Stuart A. Che Guevara: You Win or You Die. 2012. (Single Titles Ser.). (ENG., Illus.). 88p. (gr. 6-12). lib. bdg. 33.27 (978-0-8225-9035-4(2)) Lerner Publishing Group.

Marabini, Sergio. Che Guevara. 2007. (Protagonistas Ser.). (SPA.). 96p. (YA). (978-987-1129-07-2(6)) Grupo Visor E.A.S.A.

Miller, Calvin Craig. Che Guevara: In Search of Revolution. 2006. (World Leaders Ser.). (Illus.). 192p. (J). (gr. 6-12). lib. bdg. 26.95 (978-1-931798-93-8(1)) Reynolds, Morgan Inc.

Smith-Llera, Danielle. Che Guevara's Face: How a Cuban Photographer's Image Became a Cultural Icon. 2016. (Captured World History Ser.). (ENG., Illus.). 64p. (gr. 5-7). lib. bdg. 34.65 (978-0-7565-5440-8(3), CPB Grades 4-8) Compass Point Bks.

GUIDANCE

see Counseling; Educational Counseling; Vocational Guidance

GUIDE DOGS

Bozzo, Linda & Library Association Staff. Guide Dog Heroes. 2010. (Amazing Working Dogs with American Humane Ser.). (Illus.). 48p. (J). (gr. 2-5). 25.27 (978-0-7660-3198-2(5)) Enslow Pubs., Inc.

Carolina Canines for Service & Nowak, Pat. A Job for Arabella. Baumgardner, Mary Alice, illus. 2007. 56p. (J). per. (978-0-9800070-0-8(3)) Carolina Canines for Service Inc.

Fretland VanVoorst, Jenny. Seeing-Eye Dogs. 2013. (We Work! Animals with Jobs Ser.). 24p. (J). (gr. -1-3). lib. bdg. 21.32 (978-1-61772-894-5(2)) Bearport Publishing Co., Inc.

Green, Sara. Guide Dogs. 2013. (Dogs to the Rescue! Ser.). (ENG., Illus.). 24p. (J). (gr. 3-8). lib. bdg. 25.95 (978-1-60014-955-9(3), Pilot Bks.) Bellwether Media.

Hall, Becky. Morris & Buddy: The Story of the First Seeing Eye Dog, 1 vol. Ettinger, Doris, illus. 2007. (ENG.). 40p. (J). (gr. 2-3). 16.99 (978-0-8075-5284-1(4)) Whitman, Albert & Co.

Kovatch, Sarah. Special Helpers. 2005. (Illus.). 16p. (J). (978-0-7367-2854-6(6)) Zaner-Bloser, Inc.

Laughlin, Kara L. Guide Dogs. 2014. (Service Dogs Ser.). (ENG.). 24p. (J). (gr. 1-4). 27.07 (978-1-62687-309-4(7), 207150) Child's World, Inc., The.

LeTourneau, Anthony Alex, illus. Hanni & Beth: Safe & Sound. 2007. (J). (gr. k-3). 17.95 (978-0-9792918-0-7(1)) Blue Marlin Pubns.

McDaniel, Melissa. Guide Dogs. 2005. (Dog Heroes Ser.). (Illus.). 32p. (J). lib. bdg. 25.27 (978-1-59716-013-1(X)) Bearport Publishing Co., Inc.

Miller, Marie-Therese. Helping Dogs. 2007. (Dog Tales: True Stories about Amazing Dogs Ser.). (Illus.). 80p. (gr. 4-6). lib. bdg. 28.00 (978-0-7910-9035-0(3), Chelsea Hse.) Facts On File, Inc.

Mueller, Pamela Bauer. Aloha Crossing. 2008. (Aloha Set Ser.: 2). (ENG., Illus.). 176p. (J). (gr. 3-7). pap. 8.99 (978-0-9685097-9-1(7)) Pinata Publishing CAN. Dist: Midpoint Trade Bks., Inc.

Raum, Elizabeth. Guide Dogs. 2013. (Animals with Jobs Ser.). (ENG.). 32p. (gr. 1-4). 28.50 (978-1-60753-382-5(0)) Amicus Publishing.

Richter, Abigail. Guide Dogs. 2008. (Rosen Real Readers: Upper Emergent Ser.). (ENG., Illus.). 12p. (gr. 1-2). pap. 5.90 (978-0-8239-8196-0(7)) Rosen Publishing Group, Inc., The.

Rudolph, Jessica. Guide Dogs. 2014. (Bow Wow! Dog Helpers Ser.). 24p. (J). (gr. -1-3). lib. bdg. 23.93 (978-1-62724-118-2(3)) Bearport Publishing Co., Inc.

Tovey, John & Clark, Veronica. A Puppy Called Dez. 2015. (ENG., Illus.). 208p. (J). (gr. k-2). pap. 9.99 (978-1-78418-423-0(3)) Blake, John Publishing, Ltd. GBR. Dist: Independent Pubs. Group.

GUIDE DOGS—FICTION

Aardvark, E. Gartner Jake. 2005. Orig. Title: Jake, the Gardener. (DAN.). 18.95 (978-0-9766859-6-8(5)) Macaronic Pr.

—Giacco il Giardiniere. 2005. Orig. Title: Jake, the Gardener. (ITA.). 18.95 (978-0-9766859-3-7(0)) Macaronic Pr.

—Jakke, den Traedgaardaren. 2005. (SWE.). 18.95 (978-0-9766859-7-5(3)) Macaronic Pr.

Aardvark, E. S. Jakke Puutarhurina. 2005. (FIN.). 18.95 (978-0-9766859-8-2(1)) Macaronic Pr.

—Joao o Jardineiro. 2005. (POR.). 18.95 (978-0-9766859-5-1(7)) Macaronic Pr.

Aardvark, Esperanza. Jaap de Tuinman. Zimmer, Dirk, illus. 2006. (DUT.). 14.95 (978-0-9766859-9-9(X)) Macaronic Pr.

Anderson, Laurie Halse. Teacher's Pet. 2009. (Vet Volunteers Ser.: 7). (ENG.). 160p. (J). (gr. 3-7). 6.99 (978-0-14-241252-7(X), Puffin Books) Penguin Young Readers Group.

Corriveau, Art. How I, Nicky Flynn, Finally Got a Life (And a Dog) 2010. (ENG.). 272p. (YA). (gr. 3-7). 16.95 (978-0-8109-8298-7(6), Amulet Bks.) Abrams, Inc.

Ingle, Annie & Klimo, Kate. Dog Diaries #2: Buddy. Jessell, Tim, illus. 2013. (Dog Diaries). (ENG.). 160p. (J). (gr. 2-5). pap. 7.99 (978-0-307-97904-9(0), Random Hse. Bks. for Young Readers) Random Hse. Children's Bks.

Mueller, Pamela Bauer. Hello, Goodbye, I Love You: The Story of Aloha, a Guide Dog for the Blind. 2003. (Aloha Set Ser.: 1). (ENG., Illus.). 160p. (gr. 3-7). per. 8.99 (978-0-9685097-3-9(8)) Pinata Publishing CAN. Dist: Midpoint Trade Bks., Inc.

Payne, Danyelle. McKayla, a Working Dog. 2008. 19p. pap. 24.95 (978-1-60563-854-6(4)) America Star Bks.

GUIDE POSTS

see Signs and Signboards

GUIDED MISSILES

Byers, Ann. American Star Wars Program. 2004. (Library of Weapons of Mass Destruction Ser.). (Illus.). 64p. (J). lib. bdg. 31.95 (978-1-4042-0287-0(0)) Rosen Publishing Group, Inc., The.

Gordon, Nick. Bomb Squad Technician. 2012. (Dangerous Jobs Ser.). (ENG., Illus.). 24p. (J). (gr. 3-7). lib. bdg. 25.95 (978-1-60014-777-7(1), Torque Bks.) Bellwether Media.

In the Air: Missiles. 2013. (Military Experience: in the Air Ser.). (ENG., Illus.). 64p. (YA). (gr. 3-7). 27.45 (978-1-59935-386-9(5)) Reynolds, Morgan Inc.

Nardo, Don. In the Water: Torpedoes, Missiles, & Dive-Bombs. 2014. (ENG.). (J). 27.45 (978-1-59935-460-6(8)) Reynolds, Morgan Inc.

Perritano, John. Bomb Squad Technician, Vol. 12. 2015. (On a Mission Ser.). (Illus.). 48p. (J). (gr. 5). 20.95 (978-1-4222-3392-4(8)) Mason Crest.

Rice, Earle. Missiles: Self-Guided Explosives. 2016. (Military Engineering in Action Ser.). (Illus.). 48p. (J). (gr. 6-5). pap. 11.70 (978-0-7660-7521-4(4)) Enslow Pubs., Inc.

White, Steve D. Modern Bombs. 2006. (High-Tech Military Weapons Ser.). (ENG., Illus.). 48p. (J). (gr. 4-7). lib. bdg. 24.50 (978-0-531-12093-4(7), Children's Pr.) Scholastic Library Publishing.

Wood, Alix. Guided Missiles, 01 vols., 1. 2016. (Today's High-Tech Weapons Ser.). (ENG.). 32p. (J). pap. 10.00 (978-1-5081-4691-9(8), PowerKids Pr.) Rosen Publishing Group, Inc., The.

GUILDS

see also Labor Unions

Jovinelly, Joann. The Crafts & Culture of a Medieval Guild. 2009. (Crafts & Cultures of the Middle Ages Ser.). 48p. (gr. 5-5). 58.50 (978-1-61512-055-0(6), Rosen Reference) Rosen Publishing Group, Inc., The.

Jovinelly, Joann & Netelkos, Jason. The Crafts & Culture of a Medieval Guild. 2006. (Crafts & Cultures of the Middle Ages Ser.). (Illus.). 48p. (J). (gr. 3-7). lib. bdg. 29.25 (978-1-4042-0757-8(0)) Rosen Publishing Group, Inc., The.

GUILDS—FICTION

Calhoun, Dia. After the River the Sun. Slater, Kate, illus. 2013. (ENG.). 368p. (J). (gr. 4-7). 16.99 (978-1-4424-3985-6(8)) Simon & Schuster Children's Publishing.

Hardinge, Frances. Fly by Night. 2008. 512p. (J). (gr. 5-9). per. 7.99 (978-0-06-087630-2(1)) HarperCollins Pubs.

Lamprey, L. Masters of the Guild. l.t. ed. 2006. 168p. pap. 21.99 (978-1-4264-2076-4(5)) Creative Media Partners, LLC.

GUINEA PIGS

Alderton, David. How to Look after Your Guinea Pig: A Practical Guide to Caring for Your Pet, in Step-By-Step Photographs. 2013. (ENG., Illus.). 20p. 8.99 (978-1-84322-768-7(1)) Anness Publishing GBR. Dist: National Bk. Network.

Baker, Brynn. Pet Guinea Pigs up Close. 2015. (Pets up Close Ser.). (ENG.). 24p. (gr. k-1). 26.65 (978-1-4914-2110-9(X), Pebble Plus) Capstone Press of Coughlan Cos.

Barnes, Julia. Pet Guinea Pigs. 2006. (Pet Pals Ser.). (Illus.). 32p. (gr. 2-6). lib. bdg. 26.00 (978-0-8368-6779-4(3), Gareth Stevens Learning Library) Stevens, Gareth Publishing LLLP.

Bearce, Stephanie. Care for a Pet Guinea Pig. 2009. (How to Convince Your Parents You Can ... Ser.). 32p. (J). (gr. 1-4). 25.70 (978-1-58415-797-7(6)) Mitchell Lane Pubs., Inc.

Beck, Angela. Guinea Pigs: Keeping & Caring for Your Pet. 2013. (Keeping & Caring for Your Pet Ser.). 72p. (J). lib. bdg. 29.27 (978-0-7660-4184-4(0)) Enslow Pubs., Inc.

Biniok, Janice. Guinea Pigs. (J). 2009. (Illus.). 112p. 14.95 (978-1-932904-37-6(9)) 2008. (978-1-932904-29-1(8)) Eldorado Ink.

Bodden, Valerie. Guinea Pigs. 2009. (My First Look at: Pets Ser.). (J). (gr. 1-5). 24.25 (978-1-58341-723-2(0), Creative Education) Creative Co., The.

Bozzo, Linda. Mi Primera Mascota Pequeña. 2008. (My First Pet Bilingual Library from the American Humane Association Ser.).Tr. of My First Guinea Pig & Other Small Pets. (ENG & SPA., Illus.). 32p. (J). (gr. 1-3). lib. bdg. 23.94 (978-0-7660-3037-4(7)) Enslow Pubs., Inc.

—My First Guinea Pig & Other Small Pets. 2007. (My First Pet Library from the American Humane Association Ser.). (Illus.). 32p. (J). (gr. 1-2). lib. bdg. 23.94 (978-0-7660-2752-7(X), Enslow Elementary) Enslow Pubs., Inc.

Carr, Aaron. Guinea Pig. 2014. (Illus.). 24p. (J). (978-1-62127-294-6(X)) Weigl Pubs., Inc.

Carraway, Rose. Great Guinea Pigs. 2012. (Pet Corner Ser.). (ENG.). 24p. (J). (gr. k-2). pap. 8.15 (978-1-4339-6291-2(8)); lib. bdg. 22.60 (978-1-4339-6289-9(6)) Stevens, Gareth Publishing LLLP.

Coppendale, Jean. Guinea Pig. 2004. (QEB Animal Lives Ser.). (Illus.). 32p. (J). lib. bdg. 18.95 (978-1-59566-052-7(6)) QEB Publishing Inc.

Dunn, Mary R. Capybaras, 1 vol. 2012. (South American Animals Ser.). (ENG., Illus.). 24p. (gr. k-1). lib. bdg. 26.65 (978-1-4296-8681-5(2), Pebble Plus) Capstone Press of Coughlan Cos.

Foran, Jill. Caring for Your Guinea Pig. 2004. (Caring for Your Pet Ser.). (Illus.). 32p. (J). per. 9.95 (978-1-59036-151-2(2)); lib. bdg. 26.00 (978-1-59036-116-0(4)) Weigl Pubs., Inc.

—Guinea Pig. 2009. (My Pet Ser.). (Illus.). 32p. (J). (gr. 3-5). pap. 9.95 (978-1-60596-091-3(8)); lib. bdg. 26.00 (978-1-60596-090-6(X)) Weigl Pubs., Inc.

Foran, Jill & Gillespie, Katie. Guinea Pig. 2015. (J). (978-1-4896-2962-3(9)) Weigl Pubs., Inc.

Goodbody, Slim & Burstein, John. Guinea Pigs. McGinnis, Ben, illus. 2008. (Slim Goodbody's Inside Guide to Pets Ser.). 32p. (J). (gr. 2-6). lib. bdg. 26.00 (978-0-8368-8957-4(6), Gareth Stevens Learning Library) Stevens, Gareth Publishing LLLP.

Guinea Pigs. 2014. (ENG.). 48p. (J). lib. bdg. 28.00 (978-0-531-20663-8(7)) Scholastic Library Publishing.

Heos, Bridget. Do You Really Want a Guinea Pig? Longhi, Katya, illus. 2015. (Do You Really Want a Pet? Ser.). (ENG.). 24p. (J). (gr. 1-3). 19.95 (978-1-60753-749-6(4)) Amicus Publishing.

Howell, Laura. Guinea Pigs. Fox, Christyan, illus. Burton, James, photos by. 2005. (Usborne First Pets Ser.). 32p. (J). (gr. k-4). pap. 5.95 (978-0-7945-1115-9(5), Usborne) EDC Publishing.

Jacobs, Pat. Guinea Pig Pals. 2017. 32p. (J). **(978-0-7787-3552-6(4))** Crabtree Publishing Co.

Johnson, Jinny. Guinea Pig. 2014. (My New Pet Ser.). 24p. (gr. k-3). lib. bdg. 28.50 (978-1-62588-029-1(4)) Black Rabbit Bks.

—Guinea Pig. 2014. (My New Pet Ser.). (ENG., Illus.). 24p. (J). (gr. -1-3). pap. 8.95 (978-1-77092-206-8(7)) Saunders Bk. Co. CAN. Dist: RiverStream Publishing.

—Guinea Pigs. 2009. (Get to Know Your Pet Ser.). (J). 28.50 (978-1-59920-211-2(5)) Black Rabbit Bks.

—Guinea Pigs. 2009. (Get to Know Your Pet Ser.). (Illus.). 32p. (J). (gr. 4-7). pap. (978-1-897563-30-4(2)) Saunders Bk. Co.

Kalman, Bobbie & MacAulay, Kelley. Los Cobayos. Crabtree, Marc, photos by. 2006. (Cuidado de las Mascotas Ser.). (SPA., Illus.). 32p. (J). (gr. 3-7). pap. (978-0-7787-8479-1(7)); lib. bdg. (978-0-7787-8457-9(6)) Crabtree Publishing Co.

—Les Cochons D'Inde. 2011. (FRE., Illus.). 32p. (J). pap. 9.95 (978-2-89579-391-5(3)) Bayard Canada CAN. Dist: Crabtree Publishing Co.

—Guinea Pigs. Crabtree, Marc, illus. Crabtree, Marc, photos by. 2003. (Pet Care Ser.). (ENG.). 32p. (J). lib. bdg. (978-0-7787-1755-3(0)) Crabtree Publishing Co.

Knutson, Barbara. Love & Roast Chicken: A Trickster Tale from the Andes Mountains. Knutson, Barbara, illus. 2004. (Carolrhoda Picture Books Ser.). (ENG., Illus.). 40p. (J). (gr. k-3). 17.95 (978-1-57505-657-9(7)) Lerner Publishing Group.

Macken, JoAnn Early. Guinea Pigs. 2003. (Weekly Reader Early Learning Library). (Illus.). 24p. (gr. k-3). pap. 8.15 (978-0-8368-3845-9(9), Weekly Reader Leveled Readers) Stevens, Gareth Publishing LLLP.

McBride, Anne. Guinea Pigs, Vol. 12. 2016. (Understanding & Caring for Your Pet Ser.: Vol. 12). (ENG., Illus.). 128p. (J). (gr. 5-8). 25.95 (978-1-4222-3698-7(6)) Mason Crest.

Meister, Cari. Guinea Pigs. 2014. (Illus.). 24p. (J). lib. bdg. 25.65 (978-1-62031-127-1(5), Bullfrog Bks.) Jump! Inc.

Nelson, Robin. Pigs. 2009. pap. 34.95 (978-0-7613-4094-2(7)) Lerner Publishing Group.

Petrylak, Ashley. Guinea Pigs. 2009. (Great Pets 3 Ser.). 48p. (gr. 3). 29.93 (978-0-7614-4148-9(4)) Marshall Cavendish Corp.

Randolph, Joanne. Guinea Pigs. (Classroom Pets Ser.). 24p. 2009. (gr. 2-3). 42.50 (978-1-61511-857-1(8)) 2007. (Illus.). (J). (gr. 3-7). lib. bdg. 22.60 (978-1-4042-3676-9(7)) Rosen Publishing Group, Inc., The. (PowerKids Pr.).

Rayner, Matthew. Guinea Pig. Sawyer, Darren, photos by. 2007. (I Am Your Pet Ser.). (Illus.). 32p. (gr. k-4). lib. bdg. 26.00 (978-0-8368-8385-5(3), Gareth Stevens Learning Library) Stevens, Gareth Publishing LLLP.

Rober, Harold. I Love Guinea Pigs. 2016. (Bumba Books (tm) — Pets Are the Best Ser.). (ENG., Illus.). 24p. (J). (gr. -1-1). lib. bdg. 25.32 (978-1-5124-1416-5(6)) Lerner Publishing Group.

Royer, Anne. Little Guinea Pigs. 2006. (Born to Be Wild Ser.). (Illus.). 24p. (gr. k-3). lib. bdg. 23.00 (978-0-8368-6166-2(3), Gareth Stevens Learning Library) Stevens, Gareth Publishing LLLP.

Ryan, Evelyn. Guinea Pigs Are Not Pigs! 2014. (Confusing Creature Names Ser.). 24p. (J). (gr. 1-3). 22.60 (978-1-4824-0946-8(1)) Stevens, Gareth Publishing LLLP.

Salzmann, Mary Elizabeth. Goofy Guinea Pigs, 1 vol. Craig, Diane, ed. 2007. (Perfect Pets Ser.). (ENG., Illus.). 24p. (J). (gr. k-3). lib. bdg. 24.21 (978-1-59928-749-2(8), SandCastle) ABDO Publishing Co.

Silkies & Other Guinea Pigs. 2007. (World Book's Animals of the World Ser.). (Illus.). 64p. (J). (978-0-7166-1334-3(4)) World Bk., Inc.

Thomas, Isabel. Gordon's Guide to Caring for Your Guinea Pigs, 1 vol. Peterson, Rick, illus. 2014. (Pets' Guides). (ENG.). 32p. (gr. 1-3). pap. 8.29 (978-1-4846-0268-3(4)); 27.32 (978-1-4846-0261-4(7)) Heinemann-Raintree. (Heinemann First Library).

GUINEA PIGS—FICTION

Aguayo, Sal. The Tiny Detective. 2008. 48p. pap. 16.95 (978-1-60703-859-7(5)) America Star Bks.

Amy's Very Merry Christmas. 2014. (Critter Club Ser.: 9). (ENG., Illus.). 128p. (J). (gr. k-4). pap. 5.99 (978-1-4424-9531-9(6), Little Simon) Little Simon.

Anderson, Julie. Erik the Red Sees Green: A Story about Color Blindness. Lopez, David, illus. 2013. (ENG.). 32p. (J). (gr. -1-3). 16.99 (978-0-8075-2141-0(8)) Whitman, Albert & Co.

Bateson, Catherine. Being Bee. (ENG.). 136p. (J). 2008. (gr. 3-7). pap. 7.95 (978-0-8234-2208-1(9)) 2007. (Illus.). (gr. 4-7). 16.95 (978-0-8234-2104-6(X)) Holiday Hse., Inc.

Berenzy, Alix. Sammy: The Classroom Guinea Pig. Berenzy, Alix, illus. 2008. (ENG., Illus.). 32p. (J). (gr. k-3). pap. 8.99 (978-0-312-37964-3(1), 9780312379643) Square Fish.

Blabey, Aaron. The Bad Guys. Blabey, Aaron, illus. 2017. (Bad Guys Ser.: bk.3). (ENG., Illus.). 144p. (J). (gr. 2-5). pap. 5.99 **(978-1-338-08749-9(5)**, Scholastic Paperbacks) Scholastic, Inc.

Black, Wills W. Touch the Moon & Other Adventures of the Fliff Family. 2010. (J). pap. 14.95 (978-0-7414-5885-8(3)) Infinity Publishing.

Blumenthal, Deborah. Charlie Hits It Big. Brunkus, Denise, illus. 2008. 32p. (J). (gr. -1). lib. bdg. 17.89 (978-0-06-056354-7(0)) HarperCollins Pubs.

Bryant, Ann. Stinky! Elkerton, Andy, illus. 2014. (ENG.). 32p. (J). (978-0-7787-1289-3(3)) Crabtree Publishing Co.

Bryson, Brenda. The Adventures of Roo & Winston - Crop Circles. 2009. 64p. pap. 12.43 (978-0-557-17564-2(X)) Lulu Pr., Inc.

Cochrane, Gillian. A Week at Aunty Betty's. 2004. 44p. (J). per. 11.41 (978-1-4116-0957-0(3)) Lulu Pr., Inc.

Dempsey, Sheena. Bruno & Titch. Dempsey, Sheena, illus. 2014. (ENG., Illus.). 32p. (J). (gr. -1-2). 16.99 (978-0-7636-7316-1(1)) Candlewick Pr.

Duke, Kate. Ready for Pumpkins. 2012. (ENG., Illus.). 40p. (J). (gr. k-3). 16.99 (978-0-375-87068-2(7), Knopf Bks. for Young Readers) Random Hse. Children's Bks.

Duling, Astrid. The Guinea Pigs Twiggy & Molly. 2012. 134p. pap. (978-3-8423-1287-6(3)) Books on Demand GmbH.

Frederick, Heather Vogel. For Your Paws Only. Comport, Sally Wern, illus. 2005. (Spy Mice Ser.). (ENG.). 272p. (J). (gr. 4-6). 9.95 (978-1-4169-0573-8(1)) Simon & Schuster Children's Publishing.

Freysinger, Karen. Adventures of Countess Pigula Her Royal Imagination. Freysinger, Karen, illus. 2006. (Illus.). (J). 15.95 (978-0-9786729-0-4(9)) Aha! Elora Danan Productions.

freysinger, karen. Adventures of Countess Pigula up, up & Away. freysinger, karen, illus. 2009. (Illus.). 32p. (J). 16.99 (978-0-9786729-1-1(7)) Aha! Elora Danan Productions.
Garis, Howard Roger. Bed Time Stories. 2007. 148p. per. (978-1-4065-2769-8(6)); 132p. per. (978-1-4065-2762-9(9)); 152p. per. (978-1-4065-2761-2(0)); 140p. per. (978-1-4065-2760-5(2)) Dodo Pr.
Graves, Annie. Guinea Pig Killer. McElhinney, Glenn, illus. 2015. (Nightmare Club Ser.: 4). (ENG.). 64p. (J). (gr. 2-5). pap. 6.99 (978-1-4677-6044-7(7)); lib. bdg. 25.32 (978-1-4677-4351-8(8)) Lerner Publishing Group.
Gray, Jennifer, et al. Guinea Pigs Online: Viking Victory. 2014. (Guinea Pigs Online Ser.: 3). (ENG., Illus.). 160p. (J). (gr. 1-4). 12.99 (978-1-62365-347-7(9), Quercus) Quercus NA.
Green, D. L. Zeke Meeks vs the Pain-In-the-Neck Pets, 1 vol. Alves, Josh, illus. 2014. (Zeke Meeks Ser.). (ENG.). 128p. (gr. 2-2). 22.65 (978-1-4795-2166-1(3), Zeke Meeks) Picture Window Bks.
Guinea Pig, Pet Shop Private Eye, 3 vols., Set. 2010. (J). (gr. 2-5). lib. bdg. 55.86 (978-0-7613-4597-8(3), Graphic Universe™) Lerner Publishing Group.
Hay, Sam. Gasp of the Ghoulish Guinea Pig. 2016. (Undead Pets Ser.: 7). lib. bdg. 16.00 (978-0-606-38406-3(5)) Turtleback Bks.
—Gasp of the Ghoulish Guinea Pig #7. Cooper, Simon, illus. 2016. (Undead Pets Ser.: 7). (ENG.). 112p. (J). (gr. 1-3). 5.99 (978-0-448-49003-8(X), Grosset & Dunlap) Penguin Young Readers Group.
Herrick, Steven. Do-Wrong Ron. Magerl, Caroline, illus. 2005. (ENG.). 132p. (J). (gr. 1-5). pap. 11.99 (978-1-86508-661-3(4)) Allen & Unwin AUS. Dist: Independent Pubs. Group.
Hudson, Iris. Mac & the Messmaker. Smath, Jerry, illus. 2005. (Social Studies Connects). 32p. (J). (gr. k-2). pap. 5.95 (978-1-57565-158-3(0)) Kane Press, Inc.
Jennings, Patrick. Guinea Dog. (Guinea Dog Ser.). (ENG.). 192p. (gr. 3-7). 2011. (J). 6.99 (978-1-60684-153-2(X)) 2010. 15.99 (978-1-60684-053-5(3)) Lerner Publishing Group. (Darby Creek).
—Guinea Dog 2. 2013. (Guinea Dog Ser.). (ENG.). 176p. (J). (gr. 3-7). 15.99 (978-1-60684-452-6(0), Darby Creek) Lerner Publishing Group.
Jitchotvisut, Donna M. Mittens for Christmas. 2009. 376p. 31.95 (978-1-4401-0372-8(0)); pap. 21.95 (978-1-4401-0370-4(4)) iUniverse, Inc.
Kelly, Katy. Here's the Thing about Me. Rex, Adam, illus. 2006. (Lucy Rose Ser.). (ENG.). 160p. (J). (gr. 3-7). reprint ed. per. 6.99 (978-0-440-42026-2(1), Yearling) Random Hse. Children's Bks.
King, Sarah. The Great Adventures of Piggy the Peruvian Guinea Pig. 2016. (ENG., Illus.). 36p. (J). pap. 10.95 (978-1-63047-568-0(8)) Morgan James Publishing.
Koniver, Laura. Jake, A Guinea Pig Finds Adventure. 2010. 40p. pap. 17.99 (978-0-557-64364-6(3)) Lulu Pr., Inc.
Kroll, Steven. Patches Lost & Found, 0 vols. Gott, Barry, illus. 2005. (ENG.). 32p. (J). (gr. k-4). pap. 5.95 (978-0-7614-5217-1(6), 9780761452171, Amazon Children's Publishing) Amazon Publishing.
Lord, Cynthia. Jelly Bean. McGuire, Erin, illus. 2014. (Shelter Pet Squad Ser.: 1). (ENG.). 128p. (J). (gr. 1-3). 16.99 (978-0-545-63596-7(9)); (gr. 2-5). pap. 5.99 (978-0-545-63597-4(7)) Scholastic, Inc. (Scholastic Pr.).
—Jelly Bean. 2014. (Shelter Pet Squad Ser.: 1). lib. bdg. 16.00 (978-0-606-36063-0(8)) Turtleback Bks.
Maddock, Lisa. The Bridezilla Who Stole Christmas: A Teddy & Pip Story. 2009. 108p. pap. 9.95 (978-1-60844-258-4(6)) Dog Ear Publishing, LLC.
—A Tale of Two Guinea Pigs. 2009. 184p. pap. 11.95 (978-1-59858-960-3(1)) Dog Ear Publishing, LLC.
Magnin, Joyce. Jelly Bean Summer. 2017. (ENG.). 272p. (J). (gr. 3-7). 16.99 (978-1-4926-4672-3(5), Sourcebooks Jabberwocky) Sourcebooks, Inc.
Manushkin, Fran. Katie & the Class Pet, 1 vol. Lyon, Tammie, illus. 2011. (Katie Woo Ser.). (ENG.). 32p. (gr. k-2). pap. 5.95 (978-1-4048-6856-4(9)); lib. bdg. 21.32 (978-1-4048-6520-4(9)) Picture Window Bks.
Maude Spelman, Cornelia & Spelman, Cornelia Maude. When I Feel Worried. Parkinson, Kathy, illus. 2014. (Way I Feel Bks.). (ENG.). 24p. (J). (gr. -1-3). pap. 6.99 (978-0-8075-8895-6(4)) Whitman, Albert & Co.
McDonald, Megan. Stink & the Great Guinea Pig Express, Bk. 4. Reynolds, Peter H., illus. 2013. (Stink Ser.: 4). (ENG.). (J). (gr. 1-4). 128p. 12.99 (978-0-7636-6391-9(3)); 144p. pap. 4.99 (978-0-7636-6421-3(9)) Candlewick Pr.
—Stink & the Great Guinea Pig Express. Reynolds, Peter H., illus. 2010. (Stink Ser.: No. 4). 128p. (J). (gr. k-4). 24.21 (978-1-59961-683-4(1)) Spotlight.
—Stink & the Great Guinea Pig Express. 2013. (Stink Ser.: 4). lib. bdg. 14.75 (978-0-606-31590-6(X), Turtleback) Turtleback Bks.
McGinty, Alice B. Eliza's Kindergarten Pet, 0 vols. Speir, Nancy, illus. 2010. (ENG.). 32p. (J). (gr. k-3). 15.99 (978-0-7614-5702-2(X), 9780761457022, Amazon Children's Publishing) Amazon Publishing.
McMullan, Kate. Fluffy's Happy Halloween. Smith, Mavis, illus. 2004. (Fluffy, the Classroom Guinea Pig Ser.). 40p. (J). lib. bdg. 15.00 (978-1-59054-464-8(1)) Fitzgerald Bks.
Meade, Holly. John Willy & Freddy Mcgee, 0 vols. unabr. ed. 2003. (ENG., Illus.). 32p. (J). (gr. -1-k). pap. 9.99 (978-0-7614-5143-3(9), 9780761451433, Amazon Children's Publishing) Amazon Publishing.
Meadows, Daisy. Pet Fairies to the Rescue! 2013. (Rainbow Magic — Scholastic Reader Ser.). lib. bdg. 13.55 (978-0-606-31510-4(1), Turtleback) Turtleback Bks.
—Rosie Gigglepip's Lucky Escape. 2016. (Magic Animal Friends Ser.: 8). (ENG., Illus.). 112p. (J). (gr. 2-5). pap. 4.99 (978-0-545-90747-7(0), Scholastic Paperbacks) Scholastic, Inc.
Mitchell, Sara. Carlos & Diego: A Tale from Peru. Vasquez, Natalia, illus. 2016. 24p. (J). pap. (978-1-927244-57-9(9)) Flying Start Bks.
—Carlos & Diego (Big Book Edition) A Tale from Peru. Vasquez, Natalia, illus. 2016. 24p. (J). pap. (978-1-927244-67-8(6)) Flying Start Bks.
Orr, Wendy. Wanted! - A Guinea Pig Called Henry. Castelao, Patricia, illus. 2012. (Rainbow Street Shelter Ser.: 3). (ENG.). 128p. (J). (gr. 2-5). 15.99 (978-0-8050-8933-2(0), 9780805089332, Holt, Henry & Co. Bks. For Young Readers) Holt, Henry & Co.
Pankhurst, Kate. Mariella Mystery Investigates the Ghostly Guinea Pig. 2014. (Mariella Mysteries Ser.). (ENG., Illus.). 176p. (J). (gr. 2-6). pap. 5.99 (978-1-4380-0460-0(5)) Barron's Educational Series, Inc.
Popova, Natalya. The Guinea Pig Story. 2008. 54p. pap. 24.50 (978-1-4092-1336-9(6)) Lulu Pr., Inc.
Rabei, Carolina. Crunch! Rabei, Carolina, illus. 2016. (Child's Play Library). (ENG., Illus.). 36p. (J). (978-1-84643-733-5(4)) Child's Play International Ltd.
Rylant, Cynthia. Little Whistle. Bowers, Tim, illus. 2007. (Little Whistle Ser.). 32p. (gr. -1-3). 24.21 (978-1-59961-253-9(4)) Spotlight.
—Little Whistle's Dinner Party. Bowers, Tim, illus. 2007. (Little Whistle Ser.). 32p. (gr. -1-3). 24.21 (978-1-59961-255-3(0)) Spotlight.
—Little Whistle's Medicine. Bowers, Tim, illus. 2007. (Little Whistle Ser.). 32p. (gr. -1-2). 24.21 (978-1-59961-256-0(9)) Spotlight.
Sattler, Jennifer. My Friend Moe. 2017. (ENG., Illus.). 22p. (J). (gr. -1 — 1). bds. 7.99 **(978-0-7641-6897-0(5))** Barron's Educational Series, Inc.
Sebring, Ruthie. Charlie, Itty's Guinea Pig, 1 vol. 2010. 30p. 24.95 (978-1-4489-4391-3(4)) PublishAmerica, Inc.
Shava, Ryder. Grace & the Guinea Pig, 01 vols., 1. 2016. (Rosen REAL Readers: STEM & STEAM Collection). (ENG.). 12p. (J). pap. 6.33 (978-1-5081-1545-8(1), Rosen Classroom) Rosen Publishing Group, Inc., The.
Shipton, Paul. The Guinea Pigs. Dunton, Trevor, illus. 2006. (Collins Big Cat Ser.). (ENG.). 48p. (J). (gr. -1-k). pap. 5.99 (978-0-00-718648-8(7)) HarperCollins Pubs. Ltd. GBR. Dist: Independent Pubs. Group.
Spaeth, Heidi. Cici Finds a Home. 2009. 32p. pap. 16.99 (978-1-4490-3708-6(9)) AuthorHouse.
Spelman, Cornelia Maude. When I Feel Worried. Parkinson, Kathy, illus. 2013. (Way I Feel Bks.). (ENG.). 24p. (J). (gr. -1-3). 15.99 (978-0-8075-8893-2(8)) Whitman, Albert & Co.
Surplice, Holly. Guinea Pig Party. Surplice, Holly, illus. 2015. (ENG., Illus.). 24p. (J). (— 1). bds. 7.99 (978-0-7636-7604-9(7), Nosy Crow) Candlewick Pr.
Taylor, Thomas. The Pets You Get. Reynolds, Adrian, illus. 2013. 32p. (gr. -1-3). 16.95 (978-1-4677-1143-2(8)) Andersen Pr. GBR. Dist: Lerner Publishing Group.
Venable, Colleen A. F. And Then There Were Gnomes. Yue, Stephanie, illus. 2010. (Guinea Pig, Pet Shop Private Eye Ser.: 2). (ENG.). 48p. (J). (gr. 2-5). pap. 6.95 (978-0-7613-5480-2(8)); lib. bdg. 27.93 (978-0-7613-4599-2(X)) Lerner Publishing Group.
—The Ferret's a Foot, 3 vols. Yue, Stephanie, illus. 2011. (Guinea Pig, Pet Shop Private Eye Ser.: 3). (ENG.). 48p. (J). (gr. 2-5). 27.93 (978-0-7613-5223-5(6)); pap. 6.95 (978-0-7613-5629-5(0)) Lerner Publishing Group.
—Fish You Were Here, No. 4. Yue, Stephanie, illus. 2011. (Guinea Pig, Pet Shop Private Eye Ser.: 4). (ENG.). 48p. (J). (gr. 2-5). pap. 6.95 (978-0-7613-5630-1(4)); lib. bdg. 27.93 (978-0-7613-5224-2(4)) Lerner Publishing Group.
—Going, Going, Dragon! 2013. 48p. pap. 14.95 (978-1-4677-0973-6(5)) Lerner Publishing Group.
—Going, Going, Dragon! Yue, Stephanie, illus. 2013. (Guinea Pig, Pet Shop Private Eye Ser.: 6). (ENG.). 48p. (J). (gr. 2-5). pap. 6.95 (978-1-4677-0726-8(0)); lib. bdg. 27.93 (978-0-7613-6009-4(3)) Lerner Publishing Group.
—Going, Going, Dragon! Yue, Stephanie, illus. 2013. (Guinea Pig, Pet Shop Private Eye Ser.: 6). (ENG.). 46p. lib. bdg. 17.15 (978-0-606-33994-0(9), Turtleback) Turtleback Bks.
—Hamster & Cheese. Yue, Stephanie, illus. 2010. (Guinea Pig, Pet Shop Private Eye Ser.: 1). (ENG.). 48p. (J). (gr. 2-5). pap. 6.95 (978-0-7613-5479-6(4)); lib. bdg. 27.93 (978-0-7613-4598-5(1)) Lerner Publishing Group.
—Raining Cats & Detectives. Yue, Stephanie, illus. 2012. (Guinea Pig, Pet Shop Private Eye Ser.: 5). (ENG.). 48p. (J). (gr. 2-5). lib. bdg. 27.93 (978-0-7613-6008-7(5)) Lerner Publishing Group.
—Raining Cats & Detectives. Yue, Stephanie, illus. 2012. (Guinea Pig, Pet Shop Private Eye Ser.: 5). lib. bdg. 17.15 (978-0-606-26631-4(3), Turtleback) Turtleback Bks.
Walker-Jones, Alexandra & Herrera, Hanna. The Adventures of Hobnob & Raisin - Paris Airport. 2013. 32p. 9.99 (978-0-9830470-0-1(6)) O.L.D. Inc.
Wells, Rosemary. Felix Stands Tall. Wells, Rosemary, illus. (Felix & Fiona Ser.). (ENG., Illus.). 32p. (J). (gr. k-3). 2017. 4.99 (978-0-7636-9418-0(5)) 2015. 14.99 (978-0-7636-6111-3(2)) Candlewick Pr.
—Felix Stands Tall. Wells, Rosemary, illus. 2017. (Felix & Fiona Ser.). (ENG., Illus.). (J). (gr. k-3). lib. bdg. 14.75 **(978-0-606-39838-1(4))** Turtleback Bks.
Whiteside, Andy. Valentino Finds a Home, 1 vol. Hnatov, Catherine, illus. 2012. (ENG.). (J). 32p. 15.95 (978-1-59572-284-3(X)); 24p. pap. 5.95 (978-1-59572-286-7(6)) Star Bright Bks., Inc.

GUITAR

America Staff. America - Guitar Anthology. 2005. (Guitar Anthology Ser.). (ENG.). 72p. (gr. 7-18). pap. 21.99 (978-0-7692-6757-9(2), 0769267572) Alfred Publishing Co., Inc.
Amoroso, Cynthia & Noyed, Robert B. Guitars. 2010. (Music Makers Ser.). (ENG., Illus.). 24p. (J). (gr. -1-2). 27.07 (978-1-60253-354-7(7), 200505) Child's World, Inc., The.
Aranjo, Karl W. Guitar Tab: Blank Manuscript Papaer for Guitar Teachers, Students & Songwriters. 2003. (YA). spiral bd. 6.00 (978-0-9770667-2-8(X)) Aranjo, Karl.
Blaxland, Wendy. Guitars. 2009. (How Are They Made? 2 Ser.). 32p. (gr. 4). lib. bdg. 18.56 (978-0-7614-4754-2(7)) Marshall Cavendish GBR. Dist: Marshall Cavendish Corp.
Blues Guitar Legends (German Version) 2004. (GER.). (YA). cd-rom (978-1-891155-19-2(9)) EMedia Corp.
Bryan, Colgan & Stang, Aaron, eds. Dream Theater: Awake. 2007. (ENG.). 160p. pap. 26.99 (978-0-89724-608-8(X), 089724608X) Alfred Publishing Co., Inc.
Carroll, Quincy. Play Guitar, Vol. 12. 2005. (Illus.). 72p. per. 19.95 incl. DVD (978-0-9760487-2-5(8)) iPlayMusic, Inc.
Carter, James. The Story of the Electric Guitar. 2016. (ENG.). 56p. (J). (gr. 5-6). pap. 9.95 (978-0-00-816401-0(0)) HarperCollins Pubs. Ltd. GBR. Dist: Independent Pubs. Group.
Casey, Bert. Acoustic Guitar Book 2 Deluxe Edition: Book/DVD/CD, vol. 2. l.t. ed. 2003. (Watch & Learn Ser.: 2). (ENG., Illus.). 80p. pap. 15.95 incl. audio compact disk (978-1-893907-43-0(0), 256-535) Watch & Learn, Inc.
Ciravolo, Tish. Everything a Girl Needs to Know Abut Playing Guitar! 2003. (Girl's Guitar Method Ser.: Bk 2). (ENG.). 40p. pap. 15.99 (978-0-7390-3175-9(9), 21971) Alfred Publishing Co., Inc.
Claybourne, Anna. The Science of a Guitar: The Science of Sound. 2009. (Science of... Ser.). (Illus.). 32p. (YA). (gr. 3-6). lib. bdg. 26.00 (978-1-4339-0042-6(4)) Stevens, Gareth Publishing LLLP.
Clayton, Stuart. Xtreme Bass. 2005. (Illus.). 80p. audio compact disk 11.95 (978-1-84492-022-8(4)) Sanctuary Publishing, Ltd. GBR. Dist: Leonard, Hal Corp.
Easy Guitar For Kids. 2007. 34.95 (978-1-59773-231-4(1), 1597732311) Homespun Video.
The Fundamental Guitar Method Book 1: An Introduction to the Guitar & the Fundamentals of Music. 2003. (YA). spiral bd. (978-0-9771357-0-7(5)) Sound Craft Designs.
The Fundamental Guitar Method Book 2: The Science of Harmony. 2004. (YA). spiral bd. (978-0-9771357-1-4(3)) Sound Craft Designs.
Green, Andrew. Jazz Guitar Structures: Boosting Your Solo Power. 2013. (ENG.). 136p. pap. 24.99 (978-0-9700576-0-0(1)) Mel Bay Pubns., Inc.
Green, Dan & Clark, Tom. How to Improve at Playing Guitar. 2010. (ENG.). 48p. (J). pap. (978-0-7787-3600-4(8)); lib. bdg. (978-0-7787-3578-6(8)) Crabtree Publishing Co.
Griggs, John R. Learning to Play Guitar. 2004. Orig. Title: American Guitar Method. (YA). 7.95 (978-0-9753385-0-6(1)) Griggs Music Co.
Hale, Connie. Elementary Guitar. Holl, Brent, ed. 2012. (Illus.). 44p. (J). spiral bd. 24.95 (978-0-9832648-4-2(8)) Beatin' Path Pubns., LLC.
Hargett, Paul R. Me & My Bass Guitar: The Life & Music of Victor Lemonte Wooten. unabr. ed. 2004. (Illus.). 336p. per. 18.50 (978-0-9754636-0-4(8)) Amberock Pubns.
Jackson, Jake. Chords for Kids Made Easy: Comprehensive Sound Links. 2016. (Music Made Easy Ser.). (ENG., Illus.). 256p. pap. 15.99 (978-1-78361-219-2(3), 9781783612192) Flame Tree Publishing GBR. Dist: Bookmasters Distribution.
Jamie, Humphries. Xtreme Electric Guitar. 2005. (Illus.). 80p. audio compact disk 11.95 (978-1-84492-016-7(X)) Sanctuary Publishing, Ltd. GBR. Dist: Leonard, Hal Corp.
Lacey, Minna. Guitar for Beginners. 2011. (Music Ser.). 64p. (J). pap. 16.99 (978-0-7945-2131-8(2), Usborne) EDC Publishing.
Landau, Elaine. Is the Guitar for You? 2010. (Ready to Make Music Ser.). (ENG., Illus.). 40p. (gr. 4-6). lib. bdg. 27.93 (978-0-7613-5424-6(7), Lerner Pubns.) Lerner Publishing Group.
Laufer, Peter. Hecho en Mexico. Reyes, Victor, tr. Roth, Susan L., illus. 2008. (SPA.). 32p. (J). (gr. 3-7). 16.95 (978-1-4263-0364-7(5), National Geographic Children's Bks.) National Geographic Society.
Manus, Ron & Harnsberger, L. C. Alfred's Kid's Ukulele Course Notespeller 1 & 2: Music Reading Activities That Make Learning Even Easier! 2012. (Kid's Ukulele Course Ser.). (ENG.). 40p. pap. 8.99 (978-0-7390-9382-5(7)) Alfred Publishing Co., Inc.
—Guitar for Kids! Book & CD. 2008. (ENG.). 24p. pap. 9.95 (978-0-7390-5361-4(2)) Alfred Publishing Co., Inc.
Marks, Anthony. Easy Guitar Tunes Internet Referenced. Abel, Simone, illus. 2004. 32p. (J). pap. 8.95 (978-0-7945-0775-6(1), Usborne) EDC Publishing.
McCabe, Larry. Easiest Country Guitar for Children: In Standard Notation & Tablature, 1 vol. 2007. (Easiest Tunes for Children Ser.). (ENG., Illus.). 32p. pap. 14.95 (978-0-7866-7563-0(2)) Mel Bay Pubns., Inc.
—Easiest Fingerpicking Guitar for Children: In Standard Notation & Tablature, 1 vol. 2007. (Easiest Tunes for Children Ser.). (ENG., Illus.). 32p. 14.95 (978-0-7866-7562-3(4)) Mel Bay Pubns., Inc.
McCarthy, John. Childrens Guitar Method: The Road to Stardom Begins Here! Gorenburg, Steve, ed. 2007. (ENG.). 48p. pap. 17.99 (978-0-9796229-1-5(3), 0979622913) Russell, Fred Publishing.
Parker, Ben. My First Guitar - Learn to Play: Kids. 2013. 32p. pap. (978-1-908707-13-0(5)) Kyle Craig Publishing.
Publications International Ltd. Staff, ed. Hello Kitty(r); Hello Kitty's Guitar. 2014. 12p. (J). bds. 17.98 (978-1-4508-7603-2(X), 145087603X) Phoenix International Publications, Inc.
Quick Star Guitar: Symbols, Shapes & Patterns. 2003. (978-0-9746011-0-6(1)) Karma Valley Music.
Riggs, Kate. Making Music: Guitar. 2014. (Making Music Ser.). (ENG.). 24p. (J). (gr. 1-3). pap. 7.99 (978-0-89812-947-2(8), Creative Paperbacks) Creative Co., The.
Salzmann, Mary Elizabeth. What in the World Is a Guitar?, 1 vol. 2012. (ENG.). 24p. 25.65 (978-1-61783-206-2(5), Super SandCastle) ABDO Publishing Co.
Scharfglass, Matt. Starting Guitar: The Number One Method for Young Guitarists. 2005. (ENG., Illus.). 48p. (gr. -1-7). pap. 9.95 incl. audio compact disk (978-0-7119-6750-2(4), 0711967504, Amsco Music) Music Sales Corp.
Shava, Ryder. My Grandfather Plays the Guitar, 01 vols., 1. 2016. (Rosen REAL Readers: Social Studies Nonfiction / Fiction: Family, Community, & the World Ser.). (ENG.). 8p. (J). pap. 5.46 (978-1-5081-1692-9(X), Rosen Classroom) Rosen Publishing Group, Inc., The.
Smith, Douglas W. Classical Guitar for Young Children, Ages 5-12: For Development of Technique, Musicianship, & Memory, Rote Book 1. 2003. (J). 24.95 (978-0-9729879-0-5(8)) Musictech College Pr.
Sommerville, L. & Pells, T. Guitar. 2008. 64p. pap. 10.99 (978-0-7945-2425-8(7)); (J). pap. 10.99 (978-0-7945-1534-8(7), Usborne) EDC Publishing.
Tomaselli, Anthony. Play Guitar 1. 2003. cd-rom (978-0-9714299-5-6(2)) I Save A Tree.
Turner, Gary. Guitar Method for Young Beginners, Book 1. Stewart, James, illus. 2006. (Young Beginner Giant Coloring Bks.). 36p. pap. incl. audio compact disk (978-1-86469-096-5(8)) LearnToPlayMusic.com Pty Ltd.
Wesson, Seb. Guitar. 2010. (Master This! Ser.). (ENG.). 32p. (J). lib. bdg. 25.25 (978-1-61532-599-3(9), PowerKids Pr.) Rosen Publishing Group, Inc., The.
Witmer, Scott. Guitars & Bass, 1 vol. 2009. (Rock Band Ser.). (ENG., Illus.). 32p. (YA). (gr. 4-7). 27.07 (978-1-60453-691-1(8)) ABDO Publishing Co.

GUITAR—FICTION

Amato, Mary. Guitar Notes. (ENG., Illus.). 304p. (J). (gr. 7). 2014. pap. 8.99 (978-1-60684-503-5(9)) 2012. 16.99 (978-1-60684-124-2(6)) Lerner Publishing Group. (Carolrhoda Lab™).
Auch, M. J. Guitar Boy. 2012. (ENG.). 288p. (J). (gr. 5-9). pap. 14.99 (978-0-312-64124-5(9), 9780312641245) Square Fish.
Brammer, Ethriam Cash. My Tata's Guitar / la guitarra de mi Tata. Lechon, Daniel, illus. (ENG & SPA.). 32p. (J). 16.95 (978-1-55885-369-0(3), Piñata Books) Arte Publico Pr.
Burian, Natalka. Welcome to the Slipstream. 2017. (ENG., Illus.). 272p. (YA). (gr. 9-12). 17.99 (978-1-5072-0075-9(7), Simon Pulse) Simon Pulse.
Capetta, Amy Rose. Entangled. (ENG.). (YA). (gr. 9). 2014. 352p. pap. 9.99 (978-0-544-33624-7(0), HMH Books For Young Readers) 2013. 336p. 17.99 (978-0-544-08744-6(5)) Houghton Mifflin Harcourt Publishing Co.
Cline, Thornton. The Amazing Incredible Shrinking Guitar. 2016. (ENG.). 48p. pap. 9.99 (978-1-57424-329-1(2), 1574243292) Centerstream Publishing.
Delaney, Mark. Pepperland, 1 vol. (ENG.). (YA). (gr. 7-18). 2007. 224p. pap. 7.95 (978-1-56145-402-0(8)) 2004. 160p. 14.95 (978-1-56145-317-7(X)) Peachtree Pubs.
Dumas Lachtman, Ofelia. Looking for la Unica. 2004. (ENG & SPA., Illus.). 190p. (J). pap. 9.95 (978-1-55885-412-3(6), Piñata Books) Arte Publico Pr.
Kelly, Erin Entrada. Blackbird Fly. Peterschmidt, Betsy, illus. 2015. (ENG.). 304p. (J). (gr. 3-7). 16.99 (978-0-06-223861-0(2), Greenwillow Bks.) HarperCollins Pubs.
Loever, Charmaine. David's Big Break. Bohman, Natasha, illus. 2008. 52p. pap. 22.99 (978-1-4389-3173-9(5)) AuthorHouse.
Meadown, Daisy. Ellie the Guitar Fairy #2. 2010. (ENG.). 80p. (J). lib. bdg. 15.39 (978-1-4242-4730-1(6)) Fitzgerald Bks.
Meadows, Daisy. Ellie the Guitar Fairy. 2010. (Rainbow Magic — the Music Fairies Ser.: 02). lib. bdg. 14.75 (978-0-606-07089-8(3), Turtleback) Turtleback Bks.
Musselwhite, Harry. Martin - The Guitar. 2012. (ENG.). 32p. 19.99 incl. audio compact disk (978-1-57424-280-5(6), 1574242806) Centerstream Publishing.
Sonnenblick, Jordan. Are You Experienced? 2015. (ENG.). 304p. (YA). (gr. 7). pap. 9.99 (978-1-250-06304-5(3), 9781250063045) Square Fish.
—Notes from the Midnight Driver. 2009. 265p. 18.00 (978-1-60686-516-3(1)) Perfection Learning Corp.
—Notes from the Midnight Driver. 2007. (ENG.). 288p. (J). (gr. 7-12). pap. 9.99 (978-0-439-75781-2(9), Scholastic Paperbacks) Scholastic, Inc.
Torres, Jennifer. Finding the Music, 1 vol. Alarcão, Renato, illus. 2015.Tr. of En Pos de la Música. (ENG & SPA.). 40p. (J). 18.95 (978-0-89239-291-9(6)) Lee & Low Bks., Inc.
Valenzuela, Roger. Paulie Pick Finds Studioland. Valenzuela, Raquel, tr. from ENG. Valenzuela, Roger, illus. 2003.Tr. of Paulie Pick encuentra Estudiolandia. (SPA., Illus.). 32p. 20.00 (978-0-944551-69-1(6)) Bk. Pubs. of El Paso.

GULF STATES

Here are entered works on the states of the United States that border on the Gulf of Mexico.

Chiang, Mona. Oil Spill: Disaster in the Gulf. 2010. (Illus.). 32p. (J). pap. (978-0-545-31128-1(4)) Scholastic, Inc.
Freed, Kira. Surviving Hurricane Katrina. 2015. (Surviving Disaster Ser.). (ENG., Illus.). 48p. (J). (gr. 5-6). 30.25 (978-1-4994-3665-5(3), Rosen Central) Rosen Publishing Group, Inc., The.
Hoena, Blake. Hurricane Katrina: An Interactive Modern History Adventure, 1 vol. 2014. (You Choose: Modern History Ser.). (ENG.). 112p. (gr. 3-4). 31.99 (978-1-4765-4189-1(2), You Choose Bks.) Capstone Press of Coughlan Cos.

GULLS

Harper, Kathryn. Seagull Red Band. Villalba, Ana, illus. 2016. (Cambridge Reading Adventures Ser.). (ENG.). 16p. pap. 6.56 (978-1-316-50310-2(0)) Cambridge Univ. Pr.
Jackson, Tom. Gulls. 2008. (Nature's Children Ser.). (Illus.). 52p. (J). (978-0-7172-6256-4(1)) Grolier, Ltd.
Metz, Lorijo. Discovering Seagulls. 2012. (Along the Shore Ser.). (Illus.). 24p. (J). (gr. k-3). lib. bdg. 22.60 (978-1-4488-4995-6(0)) Rosen Publishing Group, Inc., The.
Thomas, Isabel. Seagull: City Safari, 1 vol. 2014. (City Safari Ser.). (ENG., Illus.). 24p. (gr. 1-1). lib. bdg. 23.32 (978-1-4329-8810-4(7), Heinemann Read & Learn) Heinemann-Raintree.

GULLS—FICTION

Birch, Vanessa Giancamilli. Seagull by the Shore: The Story of a Herring Gull. Langford, Alton, illus. 2011. (Smithsonian Oceanic Collection Ser.). (ENG.). 31p. (J). (gr. -1-3). pap. 4.95 (978-1-60727-540-4(6)) Soundprints.
—Seagull by the Shore: The Story of a Herring Gull. 2011. (ENG.). 32p. (J). 8.95 (978-1-60727-160-4(5)) Soundprints.
Bond, Michael. Paddington at the Beach. Alley, R. W., illus. 2015. (Paddington Ser.). 32p. (J). (gr. -1-3). 17.99 (978-0-06-231720-9(2)) HarperCollins Pubs.
Burton, Gina. The Adventures of Bill the Seagull. 2009. (Illus.). 52p. pap. (978-1-84748-636-3(3)) Athena Pr.
Clark, Katherine. Seagull Sam. Huntington, Amy, illus. 2007. (ENG.). 32p. (J). (gr. -1-3). 15.95 (978-0-89272-715-5(2)) Down East Bks.
Cosgrove, Stephen. Pickles & the P-Flock Bullies. James, Robin, illus. 2014. (ENG.). 32p. (J). (gr. k-3). 16.99 (978-1-57061-887-1(9), Little Bigfoot) Sasquatch Bks.
Kay, L. M. Frederick's Birthday Surprise. 2009. 36p. pap. 24.95 (978-1-60836-944-7(7)) America Star Bks.
Montecalvo, Jane. Sammy C-Gull: Second Adventure. 2012. 28p. pap. 16.09 (978-1-4669-5511-0(2)) Trafford Publishing.
Murphy, Julie. Gilly's Treasure. Fontano, Jay, illus. 2016. (ENG.). 14.99 (978-1-4621-1845-8(3), Sweetwater Bks.) Cedar Fort, Inc./CFI Distribution.
Sargent, Dave & Sargent, David, Jr. Sandy Sea Gull: Making Friends, 20 vols., Vol. 16. Lenoir, Jane, illus. 2nd ed. 2003. (Feather Tales Ser.: 16). 42p. (J). lib. bdg. 20.95 (978-1-56763-749-6(3)) Ozark Publishing.

Seymour, Marysue. Where Will We Fly. Spadaccini, Cheryl, illus. 2013. 20p. pap. 9.95 (978-1-61633-417-8(7)) Guardian Angel Publishing, Inc.

Smith, Claude Clayton. The Gull That Lost the Sea. Cathcart, Sharyn, illus. 2008. (ENG.). 34p. pap. 5.95 (978-0-9667359-7-0(8), BeanPole Bks.) Harren Communications, LLC.

Trussell-Cullen, Alan. The Seagull & the Fish. Teo, Ali, illus. 2010. (ENG.). 16p. (gr. k-2). pap. 7.95 (978-1-61181-039-4(6), Kaeden Bks.) Kaeden Corp.

—The Seagull & the Fish (6 Packs) Teo, Ali, illus. 2010. (ENG.). 16p. (gr. k-2). pap. (978-1-61181-040-0(X), Kaeden Bks.) Kaeden Corp.

GUMBY (FICTITIOUS CHARACTER)—FICTION

Running Press Staff. Gumby & Pokey, Kit. 2007. (Miniature Editions Ser.). (ENG., Illus.). 32p. pap. 8.95 (978-0-7624-2183-1(5)) Running Pr. Bk. Pubs.

GUN CONTROL

Here are entered general and non-legal works on the control of guns. Works on the legal aspects of gun control are entered under Firearms—Law and Legislation.

Apel, Lorelei. Dealing with Weapons at School & at Home. (Conflict Resolution Library). 24p. 2009. (gr. 2-3). 42.50 (978-1-60853-411-1(1)) 2004. (Illus.). (J). 22.60 (978-0-8239-6932-6(0)) Rosen Publishing Group, Inc., The. (PowerKids Pr.).

Bjorklund, Ruth. Gun Control. 2012. (J). 32.79 (978-0-7614-4974-4(4)) Marshall Cavendish Corp.

—Gun Control. 2014. (Illus.). 80p. (J). (978-1-62712-416-4(0)) Musa Publishing.

Croft, Jennifer. Everything You Need to Know about Guns in Your Home. 2005. (Need to Know Library). (Illus.). 64p. (YA). (gr. 7-12). lib. bdg. 31.95 (978-0-8239-3162-0(5), NTGUHO) Rosen Publishing Group, Inc., The.

Cunningham, Anne C. Critical Perspectives on Gun Control. 2016. (Analyzing the Issues Ser.). 208p. (YA). lib. bdg. 47.93 (978-0-7660-8125-3(7)) Enslow Pubs., Inc.

Doeden, Matt. Gun Control: Preventing Violence or Crushing Constitutional Rights? 2011. (USA TODAY's Debate: Voices & Perspectives Ser.). (ENG., Illus.). 128p. (gr. 9-12). lib. bdg. 35.93 (978-0-7613-6433-7(1), Twenty-First Century Bks.) Lerner Publishing Group.

Ferguson, John E., et al. Gun Control. 2nd rev. ed. 2011. (Point/Counterpoint Ser.). 120p. (C). (gr. 9). 35.00 (978-1-60413-905-1(6), Chelsea Hse.) Facts On File, Inc.

Furgang, Adam. Everything You Need to Know about Gun Violence. 2017. (Need to Know Library). 64p. (J). (gr. 12-11). pap. 12.95 **(978-1-5081-7402-8(4)**, Rosen Young Adult) Rosen Publishing Group, Inc., The.

Gerdes, Louise. Guns & Crime. 2008. (At Issue Ser.). (ENG., Illus.). 91p. (gr. 10-12). pap. 22.50 (978-0-7377-3919-0(3), Greenhaven Pr., Inc.); 80-128p. (YA). (gr. 9-12). pap. 31.80 (978-0-7377-3918-3(5)) Cengage Gale.

Gonzales, Doreen. A Look at the Second Amendment: To Keep & Bear Arms. 2007. (Constitution of the United States Ser.). (Illus.). 128p. (J). (gr. 5). lib. bdg. 34.60 (978-1-59845-061-3(1), MyReportLinks.com Bks.) Enslow Pubs., Inc.

Greenhaven Press Editors & MacKay, Jennifer, eds. Gun Control. 2013. (Hot Topics Ser.). (ENG., Illus.). 128p. (gr. 7-10). lib. bdg. 33.95 (978-1-4205-0815-4(6), Lucent Bks.) Cengage Gale.

Heing, Bridey. Investigating Mass Shootings in the United States. 2017. (Terrorism in the 21st Century: Causes & Effects Ser.). 64p. (gr. 12-11). lib. bdg. 34.45 **(978-1-5081-7462-2(8)**, Rosen Young Adult) Rosen Publishing Group, Inc., The.

Kevin, Brian. Gun Rights & Responsibilities, 1 vol. 2012. (Gun Education & Safety Ser.). (ENG.). 32p. 27.07 (978-1-61783-315-1(0), Checkerboard Library) ABDO Publishing Co.

Lankford, Ronnie D. Gun Violence. 2010. (Social Issues Firsthand Ser.). (Illus.). 192p. (J). 33.75 (978-0-7377-4797-3(8), Greenhaven Pr., Inc.) Cengage Gale.

Magoon, Kekla. Gun Control, 1 vol. 2007. (Essential Viewpoints Set 1 Ser.). (ENG., Illus.). 112p. (J). (gr. 6-12). lib. bdg. 35.64 (978-1-59928-860-4(5)) ABDO Publishing Co.

Merino, No'l, ed. Gun Control. 2012. (Introducing Issues with Opposing Viewpoints Ser.). (ENG., Illus.). 144p. (gr. 7-10). lib. bdg. 36.95 (978-0-7377-6278-5(0), Greenhaven Pr., Inc.) Cengage Gale.

Murray, Hallie. The Right to Bear Arms: The Second Amendment. 2017. (Bill of Rights Ser.). 48p. (J). (gr. 5-6). pap. 11.70 **(978-0-7660-8729-3(8))**; lib. bdg. 27.93 **(978-0-7660-8551-0(1))** Enslow Pubs., Inc.

Nakaya, Andrea C. Thinking Critically Mass Shootings. 2015. (Illus.). 80p. (J). lib. bdg. 28.95 (978-1-60152-822-3(1)) ReferencePoint Pr., Inc.

Otfinoski, Steven. Gun Control. 2014. (Cornerstones of Freedom Ser.: 3). (ENG.). 64p. (J). lib. bdg. 30.00 (978-0-531-21331-5(5)) Scholastic Library Publishing.

Rosenthal, Beth & Des Chenes, Elizabeth, eds. Gun Control. 2006. (Introducing Issues with Opposing Viewpoints Ser.). (ENG., Illus.). 112p. (YA). (gr. 8-12). lib. bdg. 36.95 (978-0-7377-3597-0(X), Greenhaven Pr., Inc.) Cengage Gale.

Scherer, Lauri S. Gun Violence. Friedman, Lauri S., ed. 2012. (Issues That Concern You Ser.). (ENG., Illus.). 144p. (gr. 7-10). lib. bdg. 42.00 (978-0-7377-6295-2(0)) Cengage Gale.

Streissguth, Tom. District of Columbia V. Heller: The Right to Bear Arms Case. 2010. (Landmark Supreme Court Cases, Gold Edition Ser.). (Illus.). 112p. (J). (gr. 7-12). 33.27 (978-0-7660-3430-3(5)) Enslow Pubs., Inc.

Wolny, Philip. Gun Rights: Interpreting the Constitution. 2014. (Understanding the United States Constitution Ser.). (Illus.). 112p. (J). (gr. 7-12). 35.60 (978-1-4777-7516-5(1)) Rosen Publishing Group, Inc., The.

Ziff, John. Gun Laws. 2014. (J). (978-1-61900-055-1(5)); 33.95 (978-1-61900-049-0(0)) Eldorado Ink.

GUNNING

see Hunting; Shooting

GUNPOWDER PLOT, 1605

Ashworth, Leon. Guy Fawkes. (Illus.). 32p. (978-0-7451-5288-2(0)) Cherrytree Bks.

Bradman, Tom & Bradman, Tony. Mr Fawkes, the King & the Gunpowder Plot. 2016. (ENG., Illus.). 32p. (J). (gr. 1-3). 11.99 (978-0-7502-9666-3(6), Wayland) Hachette Children's Group GBR. Dist: Hachette Bk. Group.

Howell, Izzi. Guy Fawkes & the Gunpowder Plot. 2016. (Why Do We Remember? Ser.). (ENG., Illus.). 32p. (J). (gr. 1-3). 17.99 (978-1-4451-4850-2(1), Franklin Watts) Hachette Children's Group GBR. Dist: Hachette Bk. Group.

Malam, John. Gunpowder Plot. 2007. (Dates with History Ser.). (ENG., Illus.). 48p. (J). pap. 9.99 (978-1-84234-536-8(2)) Evans Brothers, Ltd. GBR. Dist: Independent Pubs. Group.

White-Thomson, Stephen. Guy Fawkes. 2017. (Popcorn: People in History Ser.). (ENG., Illus.). 24p. (J). (gr. 4-6). pap. 10.99 (978-0-7502-8372-4(6), Wayland) Hachette Children's Group GBR. Dist: Hachette Bk. Group.

GUNS

see Firearms; Ordnance; Rifles

GUTENBERG, JOHANN, 1397?-1468

Beckham, Robert. Who in the World Was the Secretive Printer? The Story of Johannes Gutenberg (Audio CD) unabr. ed. 2008. (ENG.). 1p. audio compact disk 12.95 (978-1-933339-27-6(6), 333927) Well-Trained Mind Pr.

Beckham, Robert & Mickle, Jed. Who in the World Was the Secretive Printer? The Story of Johannes Gutenberg. 2005. (Who in the World Ser.: 0). (ENG., Illus.). 40p. (gr. 2-18). pap. 9.50 (978-0-9728603-6-9(3), 86036) Well-Trained Mind Pr.

Childress, Diana. Johannes Gutenberg & the Printing Press. 2008. (Pivotal Moments in History Ser.). (ENG., Illus.). 160p. (gr. 9-12). lib. bdg. 38.60 (978-0-8225-7520-7(5)) Lerner Publishing Group.

Feinstein, Stephen. Johannes Gutenberg: The Printer Who Gave Words to the World. 2008. (Inventors Who Changed the World Ser.). (Illus.). 128p. (J). (gr. 3-7). lib. bdg. 34.60 (978-1-59845-077-4(8), MyReportLinks.com Bks.) Enslow Pubs., Inc.

Krensky, Stephen. Breaking into Print: Before & after the Invention of the Printing Press. Christensen, Bonnie, illus. 2003. 30p. (J). (gr. 3-8). reprint ed. 18.00 (978-0-7567-6843-0(8)) DIANE Publishing Co.

Olson, Kay Melchisedech. Johann Gutenberg & the Printing Press, 1 vol. Smith, Tod G., illus. 2006. (Inventions & Discovery Ser.). (ENG.). 32p. (gr. 3-4). pap. 8.10 (978-0-7368-9644-3(9), Graphic Library) Capstone Press of Coughlan Cos.

Rumford, James. From the Good Mountain: How Gutenberg Changed the World. Rumford, James, illus. 2012. (ENG., Illus.). 36p. (J). (gr. -1-3). 17.99 (978-1-59643-542-1(9), 9781596435421) Roaring Brook Pr.

Spilsbury, Louise. Johannes Gutenberg & the Printing Press, 01 vols., 1. 2016. (Inventions That Changed the World Ser.). (ENG.). 32p. (J). pap. 10.00 (978-1-5081-4631-5(4), PowerKids Pr.) Rosen Publishing Group, Inc., The.

Vander Hook, Sue. Johannes Gutenberg: Printing Press Innovator, 1 vol. 2009. (Publishing Pioneers Ser.). (ENG., Illus.). 112p. (J). (gr. 6-12). lib. bdg. 35.64 (978-1-60453-762-8(0), Essential Library) ABDO Publishing Co.

GUTHRIE, WOODY, 1912-1967

Coombs, Karen Mueller. Woody Guthrie: America's Folksinger. 2003. (Illus.). 120p. (J). pap. 8.95 (978-0-8225-3750-2(8)) Lerner Publishing Group.

Golio, Gary. When Bob Met Woody: The Story of the Young Bob Dylan. Burckhardt, Marc, illus. 2011. (ENG.). 40p. (J). (gr. 3-7). 17.99 (978-0-316-11299-4(2)) Little, Brown Bks. for Young Readers.

Neimark, Anne. There Ain't Nobody That Can Sing Like Me: The Life of Woody Guthrie. 2017. (ENG., Illus.). 128p. (J). (gr. 5-9). pap. 13.99 **(978-1-5344-0950-7(5)**, Atheneum Bks. for Young Readers) Simon & Schuster Children's Publishing.

GUYANA

Jermyn, Leslie & Wong, Winnie. Guyana. 2nd rev. ed. 2010. (Cultures of the World 20 Ser.). 144p. (gr. 6). 42.79 (978-1-60870-023-3(2)) Marshall Cavendish Corp.

Morrison, Marion. Guyana. 2003. (Enchantment of the World Ser.). (ENG., Illus.). 144p. (YA). (gr. 5-9). 39.00 (978-0-516-22377-3(1)) Scholastic Library Publishing.

Sirvaitis, Karen. Guyana in Pictures. 2009. (Visual Geography Series, Second Ser.). (ENG.). 80p. (gr. 5-12). 31.93 (978-1-57505-963-1(0), Twenty-First Century Bks.) Lerner Publishing Group.

Temple, Bob. Guyana. (South America Today Ser.). 64p. (gr. 4-7). 2009. (Illus.). (J). 21.95 (978-1-4222-0637-9(8)) 2007. (YA). pap. 9.95 (978-1-4222-0704-8(8)) Mason Crest.

—Guyana, Vol. 13. Henderson, James D., ed. 2015. (Discovering South America: History, Politics, & Culture Ser.). (Illus.). 64p. (J). (gr. 7). lib. bdg. 22.95 (978-1-4222-3300-9(6)) Mason Crest.

GYMNASTICS

see also Physical Education and Training

American Girl Editors. Girls Love Gymnastics. Yoshizumi, Carol, illus. 2007. 64p. (J). (gr. 4-7). pap. 8.95 (978-1-59369-283-4(8)) American Girl Publishing, Inc.

Borth, Teddy. Gimnasia: Grandes Momentos, Records y Datos. 2017. (SPA., Illus.). 24p. **(978-1-68080-836-0(2)**, Abdo Kids) ABDO Publishing Co.

Borth, Teddy. Gymnastics: Great Moments, Records, & Facts, 1 vol. 2014. (Great Sports Ser.). (ENG., Illus.). 24p. (J). (gr. 2-4). lib. bdg. 28.50 (978-1-62970-690-0(6)) ABDO Publishing Co.

Bragg, Linda Wallenberg. Gymnastics. King, Andy, photos by. 2005. (Play-by-Play Ser.). (Illus.). 80p. (gr. 4-8). pap., lib. bdg. 23.93 (978-0-8225-9877-0(9)) Lerner Publishing Group.

Bussiere, Desireé. Gymnastics by the Numbers, 1 vol. 2013. (Sports by the Numbers Ser.). (ENG.). 24p. (J). (gr. k-3). lib. bdg. 24.21 (978-1-61783-844-6(6), SandCastle) ABDO Publishing Co.

Canetti, Yanitzia. Acrobacias: Ellos lo hace bien, ¡nosotros También! 2010. (SPA.). 24p. (J). pap. 5.99 (978-1-59835-158-3(3), BrickHouse Education) Cambridge BrickHouse, Inc.

—What They Do... We Can, Too! Gymnastics: Gymnastics. 2010. 24p. (J). pap. 5.99 (978-1-59835-163-7(X), BrickHouse Education) Cambridge BrickHouse, Inc.

Capucilli, Alyssa Satin. My First Gymnastics Class. Hanifin, Laura, photos by. 2016. (My First Ser.). (ENG., Illus.). 32p. (J). (gr. -1-k). pap. 3.99 (978-1-4814-6187-0(7), Simon Spotlight) Simon Spotlight.

—My First Gymnastics Class: A Book with Foldout Pages. Hanifin, Laura, photos by. 2012. (My First Ser.). (ENG., Illus.). 14p. (J). (gr. -1-k). 9.99 (978-1-4424-2749-5(3), Little Simon) Little Simon.

Carmichael, L. E. The Science Behind Gymnastics. 2016. (Illus.). 32p. (J). (978-1-4747-1142-5(1)) Capstone Press of Coughlan Cos.

Challen, Paul. Flip It Gymnastics. 2010. (ENG., Illus.). 32p. (J). pap. (978-0-7787-3176-4(6)); lib. bdg. (978-0-7787-3144-3(8)) Crabtree Publishing Co.

Conklin, Wendy. No Way! Amazing Acrobatics. 2017. (TIME for KIDS(r) Nonfiction Readers Ser.). (Illus.). 48p. (J). (gr. 7-7). pap. 9.99 (978-1-4938-3611-6(0)) Teacher Created Materials, Inc.

—No Way! Amazing Acrobatics. 2017. (Time for Kids Nonfiction Readers Ser.). lib. bdg. 20.85 **(978-0-606-40290-3(X))** Turtleback Bks.

Crossingham, John. La Gymnastique. Kalman, Bobbie, photos by. 2011. (FRE., Illus.). 32p. (J). pap. 9.95 (978-2-89579-414-1(6)) Bayard Canada CAN. Dist: Crabtree Publishing Co.

Douglas, Gabrielle & Burford, Michelle. Grace, Gold & Glory: My Leap of Faith, 1 vol. 2013. (ENG.). 224p. pap. 16.99 (978-0-310-74067-4(3)) 2012. (ENG.). 224p. 24.99 (978-0-310-74061-2(4)) 2012. (978-0-310-74200-5(5)) Zondervan.

—Raising the Bar, 1 vol. 2013. (ENG.). 144p. (J). 19.99 (978-0-310-74070-4(3)) Zondervan.

Feeney, Rik. Cheerleading Conditioning for Back Hands. 2007. (Illus.). 96p. per. 17.95 (978-0-9637991-8-0(5)) Richardson Publishing, Inc.

Flynn, Brendan. Gymnastics Time! 2016. (Bumba Books (tm) — Sports Time! Ser.). (ENG., Illus.). 24p. (J). (gr. -1-1). 25.32 (978-1-5124-1436-3(0)) Lerner Publishing Group.

—¡Hora de Gimnasia! 2017. (Bumba Books (tm) en Español — ¡Hora de Deportes! (Sports Time!) Ser.). (SPA., Illus.). 24p. (J). (gr. -1-1). 25.32 (978-1-5124-2873-5(6)) Lerner Publishing Group.

Gerstein, Mordicai. The Man Who Walked Between the Towers. 2007. (J). 18.40 (978-1-4177-7491-3(6), Turtleback) Turtleback Bks.

Gifford, Clive. Gymnastics. 2011. (ENG., Illus.). 32p. (J). pap. 10.95 (978-1-77092-038-5(2)) Saunders Bk. Co. CAN. Dist: RiverStream Publishing.

Gray, Karlin. Nadia: The Girl Who Couldn't Sit Still. Davenier, Christine, illus. 2016. (ENG.). 40p. (J). (gr. 1-4). 17.99 (978-0-544-31960-8(5), HMH Books For Young Readers) Houghton Mifflin Harcourt Publishing Co.

Grips-Gymnastik: Gedaechtnis und Denkvermoegen Fix Trainiert. (Pocket-Quizspiel Ser.). (Illus.). 56p. bds. (978-3-411-09401-1(X)) Bibliographisches Institut & F. A. Brockhaus AG DEU. Dist: i. b. d., Ltd.

Heneghan, Judith. Gymnastics. 2016. (ENG., Illus.). 32p. (J). (gr. 4-6). pap. 11.99 (978-0-7502-9459-1(0), Wayland) Hachette Children's Group GBR. Dist: Hachette Bk. Group.

Hernandez, Laurie. I Got This: To Gold & Beyond. 240p. (J). (gr. 3-7). 2018. (ENG.). pap. 8.99 **(978-0-06-267732-7(2))** 2017. 17.99 **(978-0-06-267731-0(4))** HarperCollins Pubs.

Hoena, Blake. Gymnastics. 2015. (J). lib. bdg. 25.65 (978-1-62031-179-0(8), Bullfrog Bks.) Jump! Inc.

Hofstetter, Adam B. Olympic Gymnastics. (Great Moments in Olympic History Ser.). 48p. 2009. (gr. 5-6). 53.00 (978-1-61513-160-0(4)) 2007. (Illus.). (J). (gr. 3-7). lib. bdg. 29.25 (978-1-4042-0968-8(9)) Rosen Publishing Group, Inc., The. (Rosen Reference).

Joven, C. C. Gymnastics Jump. Shems, Ed, illus. 2017. (Sports Illustrated Kids Starting Line Readers Ser.). (ENG.). 32p. (gr. -1-1). lib. bdg. 22.65 (978-1-4965-4250-2(9)) Capstone Press of Coughlan Cos.

Kawa, Katie. The Science of Gymnastics. 2015. (Sports Science Ser.). (ENG.). 32p. (J). (gr. 4-5). pap. 10.00 (978-1-4994-1068-6(9), PowerKids Pr.) Rosen Publishing Group, Inc., The.

Labrecque, Ellen. Jumping Gymnastics. 2008. (Reading Rocks! Ser.). (ENG., Illus.). 32p. (J). (gr. 2-5). 28.50 (978-1-60253-099-7(8), 200760) Child's World, Inc., The.

Laughlin, Kara L. Gymnastics. 2016. (Beginning Sports Ser.). (ENG.). 24p. (J). (gr. k-3). 27.07 (978-1-5038-0776-1(2), 210604) Child's World, Inc., The.

Lawrence, Blythe. Girls' Gymnastics, 1 vol. 2013. (Girls' SportsZone Ser.). (ENG., Illus.). 48p. (J). (gr. 3-6). lib. bdg. 32.79 (978-1-61783-986-3(8), SportsZone) ABDO Publishing Co.

—Great Moments in Olympic Gymnastics, 1 vol. 2014. (Great Moments in Olympic Sports Ser.). (ENG.). 64p. (gr. 10-14). lib. bdg. 32.79 (978-1-62403-394-0(6), SportsZone) ABDO Publishing Co.

LeBoutillier, Nate. Gymnastics. 2012. (J). 35.65 (978-1-60818-210-7(X), Creative Education) Creative Co., The.

Lindner, Heidi, ed. Animals, Animals, Animals. 2004. (Let's Move Ser.). (Illus.). 96p. pap. 12.95 (978-1-84126-065-5(7)) Meyer & Meyer Sport, Ltd. GBR. Dist: Lewis International, Inc.

—Great Games for Small Children, Vol. 1. 2004. (Let's Move Ser.). (Illus.). 96p. pap. 12.95 (978-1-84126-064-8(9)) Meyer & Meyer Sport, Ltd. GBR. Dist: Lewis International, Inc.

—Off We Go Outside! 2004. (Let's Move Ser.). (Illus.). 96p. pap. 12.95 (978-1-84126-066-2(5)) Meyer & Meyer Sport, Ltd. GBR. Dist: Lewis International, Inc.

Macken, JoAnn Early. Gymnastics. 2005. (After-School Fun Ser.). (Illus.). 24p. (gr. k-3). lib. bdg. 21.00 (978-0-8368-4513-6(7), Weekly Reader Leveled Readers) Stevens, Gareth Publishing LLLP.

Mara, Wil. Gymnastics. 2012. (Rookie Read-about Ser.). (ENG., Illus.). 32p. (J). pap. 5.95 (978-0-531-20928-8(8)); (gr. -1-1). lib. bdg. 23.00 (978-0-531-20859-5(1)) Scholastic Library Publishing. (Children's Pr.).

Mason, Crest. Gymnastics, Vol. 13. 2016. (Inside the World of Sports Ser.: Vol. 13). (ENG., Illus.). 80p. (J). (gr. 7-12). 24.95 (978-1-4222-3462-4(2)) Mason Crest.

Maurer, Tracy Nelson. First Source to Gymnastics: Rules, Equipment, & Key Routine Tips. 2017. (First Sports Source Ser.). (ENG.). 24p. (gr. 1-2). lib. bdg. 25.32 **(978-1-5157-6945-3(3)**, First Facts) Capstone Press of Coughlan Cos.

—Uneven Bars: Tips, Rules, & Legendary Stars. 2016. (Gymnastics Ser.). (ENG., Illus.). 32p. (gr. 3-4). lib. bdg. 27.99 (978-1-5157-2219-9(8), Snap Bks.) Capstone Press of Coughlan Cos.

—Uneven Bars: Tips, Rules & Legendary Start. 2016. (Gymnastics Ser.). (ENG., Illus.). 32p. (gr. 3-4). E-Book 27.99 (978-1-5157-2225-0(2), Snap Bks.) Capstone Press of Coughlan Cos.

—Vaulting: Tips, Rules, & Legendary Stars. 2016. (Gymnastics Ser.). (ENG., Illus.). 32p. (gr. 3-4). lib. bdg. 27.99 (978-1-5157-2221-2(X), Snap Bks.) Capstone Press of Coughlan Cos.

McAneney, Caitie. Simone Biles: Greatest Gymnast of All Time. 2017. (Breakout Biographies Ser.). 32p. (J). (gr. 9-10). 26.25 **(978-1-5081-6072-4(4))**; pap. 10.00 **(978-1-5081-6070-0(8))** Rosen Publishing Group, Inc., The. (PowerKids Pr.).

McIntosh, J. S. Gymnastics. 2010. (Getting the Edge Ser.). 96p. (YA). lib. bdg. 24.95 (978-1-4222-1734-4(5)) Mason Crest.

Meyer, Kathy. Gymnastics. 2012. (On the Team Ser.). (ENG., Illus.). 24p. (J). (gr. 2-5). pap. 8.15 (978-1-4339-6446-6(5)); lib. bdg. 22.60 (978-1-4339-6444-2(9)) Stevens, Gareth Publishing LLLP. (Gareth Stevens Learning Library).

Moceanu, Dominique & Thompson, Alicia. Go-For-Gold Gymnasts Bind-up [#1: Winning Team + #2: Balancing Act]. 2016. (Go-For-Gold Gymnasts Ser.). (ENG., Illus.). 496p. (J). (gr. 5-9). pap. 8.99 (978-1-4847-7178-5(8)) Hyperion Bks. for Children.

Morey, Allan. Gymnastics. 2015. (Summer Olympic Sports Ser.). (ENG., Illus.). 32p. (J). (gr. 2-4). 19.95 (978-1-60753-808-0(3)) Amicus Publishing.

Mullarkey, Lisa. Cheerleading Stunts & Tumbling. 2010. (Ready, Set, Cheer! Ser.). (Illus.). 48p. (J). pap. 8.95 (978-1-59845-200-6(2)) Enslow Pubs., Inc.

Mullarkey, Lisa & Library. Cheerleading Stunts & Tumbling. 2010. (Ready, Set, Cheer! Ser.). (Illus.). 48p. (J). lib. bdg. 25.27 (978-0-7660-3537-9(9)) Enslow Pubs., Inc.

Nagelhout, Ryan. I Love Gymnastics. 2014. (My Favorite Sports Ser.). (Illus.). 24p. (J). (gr. k-2). 22.60 (978-1-4824-0728-0(0)) Stevens, Gareth Publishing LLLP.

—Me Encanta la Gimnasia / I Love Gymnastics. 2014. (My Favorite Sports Ser.). (SPA.). 24p. (J). (gr. k-2). 22.60 (978-1-4824-0852-2(X)) Stevens, Gareth Publishing LLLP.

Nixon, James. Gymnastics. 2017. (First Sport Ser.). (ENG., Illus.). 24p. (J). (gr. k-2). pap. 9.99 (978-1-4451-4922-6(2), Franklin Watts) Hachette Children's Group GBR. Dist: Hachette Bk. Group.

Page, Jason. Gymnastics Events. 2008. (Olympic Sports Ser.). (ENG., Illus.). 32p. (J). (gr. 3-7). pap. (978-0-7787-4032-2(3)); lib. bdg. (978-0-7787-4015-5(3)) Crabtree Publishing Co.

Pakizer, Debi & Sears, Mary A. Vaulting: The Art of Gymnastics on Horseback. Anderson, Julia & Barnette, Jackie, eds. Sears, Mary A., illus. (Illus.). 24p. (Orig.). (J). (gr. k-6). pap. 5.00 (978-0-9639785-6-1(X)) Sears, M.A.

Savage, Jeff. Top 25 Gymnastics Skills, Tips, & Tricks. 2011. (Top 25 Sports Skills, Tips, & Tricks Ser.). (Illus.). 48p. (J). (gr. 2-5). lib. bdg. 25.27 (978-0-7660-3868-4(8)); (gr. 4-18). pap. 8.95 (978-1-59845-358-4(0)) Enslow Pubs., Inc.

Schlegel, Elfi & Dunn, Claire Ross. Thr Gymnastics Book: The Young Performer's Guide to Gymnastics. 2nd rev. ed. 2012. (ENG., Illus.). 144p. (J). (gr. 2-6). pap. 19.95 (978-1-77085-133-7(X), 9781770851337) Firefly Bks., Ltd.

Schuh, Mari C. Gymnastics. 2017. (Spot Sports Ser.). (ENG.). 16p. (gr. k-3). 17.95 **(978-1-68151-087-3(1))** Amicus Publishing.

Schwartz, Heather E. Balance Beam: Tips, Rules, & Legendary Stars. 2016. (Gymnastics Ser.). (ENG., Illus.). 32p. (gr. 3-4). lib. bdg. 27.99 (978-1-5157-2222-9(8), Snap Bks.) Capstone Press of Coughlan Cos.

—Floor Exercise: Tips, Rules, & Legendary Stars. 2016. (Gymnastics Ser.). (ENG., Illus.). 32p. (gr. 3-4). lib. bdg. 27.99 (978-1-5157-2218-2(X), Snap Bks.) Capstone Press of Coughlan Cos.

Schwartz, Heather E. & Maurer, Tracy Nelson. Gymnastics. 2016. (Gymnastics Ser.). (ENG.). 32p. (gr. 3-4). 111.96 (978-1-5157-2345-5(3), Snap Bks.) Capstone Press of Coughlan Cos.

Simkins, Kate & Dorling Kindersley Publishing Staff. I Want to Be a Gymnast, Level 2. 2006. (DK Readers Ser.). (ENG., Illus.). 32p. (J). (gr. 1-3). pap. 3.99 (978-0-7566-2011-0(2), DK Children) Dorling Kindersley Publishing, Inc.

Smith, Nikkolas, illus. The Golden Girls of Rio. 2016. (ENG.). 32p. (J). (gr. -1-3). 16.99 (978-1-5107-2247-7(5), Sky Pony Pr.) Skyhorse Publishing Co., Inc.

Sports Illustrated for Kids Books. 2005. (Illus.). 176p. (gr. 7-12). lib. bdg. 388.65 (978-0-8239-3925-1(1)) Rosen Publishing Group, Inc., The.

Stanley, Glen F. & Wesley, Ann. Gymnastics: Girls Rocking It, 01 vols., 1. 2016. (Title IX Rocks! Ser.). (ENG., Illus.). 64p. (J). 32.95 (978-1-5081-7037-2(1), Rosen Young Adult) Rosen Publishing Group, Inc., The.

Tieck, Sarah. Gabby Douglas: Historic Olympic Champion, 1 vol. 2013. (Big Buddy Biographies Set 9 Ser.). (ENG., Illus.). 32p. (J). (gr. 2-5). lib. bdg. 28.50 (978-1-61783-748-7(2), Big Buddy Bks.) ABDO Publishing Co.

Tometich, Annabelle. I Know Gymnastics. 2013. (21st Century Basic Skills Library: I Know Sports Ser.). (ENG., Illus.). 24p. (J). (gr. k-3). 22.79 (978-1-62431-400-1(7), 202720); pap. 12.79 (978-1-62431-476-6(7), 202722) Cherry Lake Publishing.

Tweddle, Beth. Becoming an Olympic Gymnast. 2012. (Collins Big Cat Ser.). (ENG., Illus.). 80p. (J). (gr. 5). pap. 9.99 (978-0-00-742837-3(5)) HarperCollins Pubs. Ltd. GBR. Dist: Independent Pubs. Group.

Veitch, Catherine. Gimnasia, 1 vol. 2010. (Deporte y Mi Cuerpo Ser.).Tr. of Gymnastics. (SPA.). 24p. (gr. k-2). 23.32 (978-1-4329-4343-1(X)); pap. 6.79 (978-1-4329-4349-3(9)) Heinemann-Raintree.

—Gymnastics, 1 vol. 2009. (Sports & My Body Ser.). (ENG.). 24p. (gr. k-2). 22.65 (978-1-4329-3454-5(6), Heinemann Read & Learn) Heinemann-Raintree.

Wendorff, Anne. Gymnastics. 2009. (My First Sports Ser.). (ENG., Illus.). 24p. (J). (gr. 2-5). lib. bdg. 25.95

(978-1-60014-327-4(X), Blastoff! Readers) Bellwether Media.

Weston Woods Staff, creator. Man Who Walked Between the Towers. 2011. 38.75 (978-0-545-14931-0(2)); 18.95 (978-0-545-14930-3(4)) Weston Woods Studios, Inc.

—The Man Who Walked Between the Towers. 2011. 29.95 (978-0-439-76703-3(2)) Weston Woods Studios, Inc.

Wood, Alix. You Can Be a Gymnast, Vol. 1. 2014. (Let's Get Moving! Ser.). (ENG.). 32p. (J). (gr. 3-4). 26.60 (978-1-4824-0275-9(0)) Stevens, Gareth Publishing LLLP.

Worsley, Arlene. For the Love of Gymnastics. 2006. (For the Love of Sports Ser.). (Illus.). 24p. (J). (gr. 3-7). lib. bdg. 24.45 (978-1-59036-386-7(8)); per. 8.95 (978-1-59036-387-4(6)) Weigl Pubs., Inc.

—Gymnastics. 2010. (In the Zone Ser.). (Illus.). 32p. (J). (gr. 3-5). pap. 11.95 (978-1-60596-902-2(8)); lib. bdg. 25.70 (978-1-60596-901-5(X)) Weigl Pubs., Inc.

GYMNASTICS—FICTION

Berg, R. J. Jenny Martin & the Unexpected Gift. 2004. (Illus.). 139p. (YA). per. 9.95 (978-0-9666104-2-0(3)) Ziert, Paul Assocs., Inc.

Burnett, Eric. Gymnastics Jenny Stands on Her Own. 2003. 108p. pap. 9.95 (978-0-595-27919-7(8)) iUniverse, Inc.

Carter, Caela. Tumbling. 2016. (ENG.). 432p. (YA). (gr. 7). 17.99 (978-0-451-47300-4(0), Viking Books for Young Readers) Penguin Young Readers Group.

Christopher, Matt. Dive Right In. 2005. (Sports Classics IV Ser.). 133p. (J). lib. bdg. 15.00 (978-1-59054-753-3(5)) Fitzgerald Bks.

Crow, Marilee. Cartwheel Annie. Snider, K. C., illus. 2009. 24p. pap. 10.95 (978-1-935137-71-9(9)) Guardian Angel Publishing, Inc.

Depken, Kristen L. I Can Be a Gymnast. 2014. (Barbie Step into Reading Level 1 Ser.). lib. bdg. 13.55 (978-0-606-35993-1(1)) Turtleback Bks.

—I Can Be a Gymnast (Barbie) 2014. (Step into Reading Ser.). (ENG., Illus.). 32p. (J). (gr. -1-1). lib. bdg. 12.99 (978-0-375-97347-5(8), Random Hse. Bks. for Young Readers) Random Hse. Children's Bks.

deRubertis, Barbara. Alexander Anteater's Amazing Act. Alley, R. W., illus. 2010. (Animal Antics A to Z Ser.). 32p. (J). (ENG.). (gr. -1-3). pap. 7.95 (978-1-57565-300-6(1)); (gr. k-1). lib. bdg. 22.60 (978-1-57565-304-4(4)) Kane Press, Inc.

deRubertis, Barbara & DeRubertis, Barbara. Alexander Anteater's Amazing Act. Alley, R. W., illus. 2012. (Animal Antics A to Z Ser.). 32p. (J). (gr. 2 — 1). cd-rom 7.95 (978-1-57565-394-5(X)) Kane Press, Inc.

Freitas, Donna. Gold Medal Summer. (ENG.). 240p. (J). 2014. (gr. 5-9). pap. 6.99 (978-0-545-32789-3(X)) 2012. (gr. 4-7). 16.99 (978-0-545-32788-6(1)) Scholastic, Inc. (Levine, Arthur A. Bks.).

Gunderson, Jessica. Don't Break the Balance Beam!, 1 vol. Santillan, Jorge H., illus. 2010. (Sports Illustrated Kids Victory School Superstars Ser.). (ENG.). 56p. (gr. 1-3). 26.65 (978-1-4342-2057-8(5)); pap. 5.95 (978-1-4342-2807-9(X)) Stone Arch Bks.

—I Broke into Gymnastics Camp, 1 vol. Santillan, Jorge H., illus. 2012. (Sports Illustrated Kids Victory School Superstars Ser.). (ENG.). 56p. (gr. 1-3). pap. 5.95 (978-1-4342-3869-6(5)); lib. bdg. 26.65 (978-1-4342-2245-9(4)) Stone Arch Bks.

Gurevich, Margaret. Gina's Balance. 2016. (What's Your Dream? Ser.). (ENG., Illus.). 96p. (gr. 3-4). lib. bdg. 25.32 (978-1-4965-3443-9(3)) Capstone Press of Coughlan Cos.

Hooks, Gwendolyn. The Lucky Charm: A Pet Club Story, 1 vol. Byrne, Mike, illus. 2011. (Pet Club Ser.). (ENG.). 32p. (gr. 1-2). pap. 6.25 (978-1-4342-3052-2(X)) Stone Arch Bks.

Isadora, Rachel. Jake at Gymnastics. Isadora, Rachel, illus. 2014. (ENG., Illus.). 32p. (J). (gr. -1-k). 14.99 (978-0-399-16048-6(5), Nancy Paulsen Books) Penguin Young Readers Group.

Jakubowski, Michele. Sleepover. 2017. (Ashley Small & Ashlee Tall Ser.). (ENG., Illus.). 64p. (gr. 1-3). pap. 4.95 (978-1-5158-0015-6(6)) Capstone Press of Coughlan Cos.

—Sleepover. 2016. (Ashley Small & Ashlee Tall Ser.). (ENG., Illus.). 64p. (gr. 1-3). lib. bdg. 20.65 (978-1-5158-0011-8(3)) Picture Window Bks.

Janovitz, Marilyn. I Will Try. Janovitz, Marilyn, illus. (I Like to Read(r) Ser.). (ENG., Illus.). 24p. (J). 2013. pap. 6.99 (978-0-8234-2756-7(0)) 2012. 14.95 (978-0-8234-2399-6(9)) Holiday Hse., Inc.

Johnson, Shawn. The Flip Side. 2016. (ENG., Illus.). 320p. (YA). (gr. 7). 17.99 (978-1-4814-6021-7(8), Simon & Schuster Bks. For Young Readers) Simon & Schuster Bks. For Young Readers.

Kilby, Tracie. Gymnastics Gina. 2010. 32p. pap. 16.00 (978-1-4520-6277-8(3)) AuthorHouse.

Lewis, Beverly. Girls Only! 2008. (Girls Only (Go!) Ser.: Vols. 5-8). (ENG.). (J). (gr. 4-7). 510p. pap. 20.00 (978-0-7642-0462-3(9)); Vols. 1-4. 512p. pap. 16.00 (978-0-7642-0461-6(0)) Bethany Hse. Pubs.

Maddox, Jake. Back on the Beam, 1 vol. Mourning, Tuesday, illus. 2009. (Jake Maddox Girl Sports Stories Ser.). (ENG.). 72p. (gr. 2-3). 25.32 (978-1-4342-1211-5(4)) Stone Arch Bks.

—Gymnastics Jitters, 1 vol. Wood, Katie, illus. 2012. (Jake Maddox Girl Sports Stories Ser.). (ENG.). 72p. (gr. 2-3). pap. 5.95 (978-1-4342-3908-2(X)); lib. bdg. 25.32 (978-1-4342-3293-9(X)) Stone Arch Bks.

—Victory Vault, 1 vol. Pulsar Studios Staff, illus. 2011. (Jake Maddox Girl Sports Stories Ser.). (ENG.). 72p. (gr. 2-3). 25.32 (978-1-4342-2498-9(8)) Stone Arch Bks.

Manushkin, Fran. Cartwheel Katie. Lyon, Tammie, illus. 2015. (Katie Woo Ser.). (ENG.). 32p. (gr. k-2). 21.32 (978-1-4795-5894-0(X)) Picture Window Bks.

Meadows, Daisy. Gemma the Gymnastics Fairy. 2010. (Sports Fairies Ser.: 7). (ENG.). 80p. (J). (gr. 2-5). 4.99 (978-0-545-20258-9(2), Scholastic Paperbacks) Scholastic, Inc.

Meister, Cari. Lily's Lucky Leotard, 1 vol. Ho, Jannie, illus. 2009. (My First Graphic Novel Ser.). (ENG.). 32p. (gr. k-2). pap. 6.25 (978-1-4342-1411-9(7)); lib. bdg. 24.65 (978-1-4342-1296-2(3)) Stone Arch Bks. (My First Graphic Novel).

Moceanu, Dominique & Thompson, Alicia. Reaching High. 2012. (Go-For-Gold Gymnasts Ser.). (ENG.). 224p. (J). (gr. 5-9). pap. 5.99 (978-1-4231-3657-6(8)) Hyperion Pr.

Peschke, Marci. Gymnastics Queen. Mourning, Tuesday, illus. 2016. (Kylie Jean Ser.). (ENG.). 112p. (gr. 2-3). lib. bdg. 22.65 (978-1-5158-0052-1(0)) Picture Window Bks.

Roy, Ron. August Acrobat. Gurney, John Steven, illus. 2012. (Calendar Mysteries Ser.: 8). (ENG.). 80p. (J). (gr. 1-4). 4.99 (978-0-375-86886-3(0)); lib. bdg. 12.99 (978-0-375-96886-0(5)) Random Hse. Children's Bks. (Random Hse. Bks. for Young Readers).

Sateren, Shelley Swanson. Max & Zoe at the Doctor, 1 vol. Sullivan, Mary, illus. 2011. (Max & Zoe Ser.). (ENG.). 32p. (gr. k-2). lib. bdg. 21.32 (978-1-4048-6212-8(9), Max & Zoe) Picture Window Bks.

Schraff, Anne. Going for Gold. 2008. 124p. lib. bdg. 13.95 (978-0-7569-8403-8(3)) Perfection Learning Corp.

Shearwater, Cate. Somersaults & Dreams - Going for Gold. 2016. (Somersaults & Dreams Ser.). (ENG., Illus.). 288p. (J). (gr. 4-7). pap. 10.99 (978-1-4052-6902-5(2)) Egmont Bks., Ltd. GBR. Dist: Independent Pubs. Group.

Simmons, Cari & Alexander, Heather. Bending over Backwards. 2015. (Picture Perfect Ser.: 1). (ENG.). 224p. (J). (gr. 3-7). pap. 6.99 (978-0-06-231022-4(4)) HarperCollins Pubs.

Weston Woods Staff, creator. The Gym Teacher from the Black Lagoon. 2011. 38.75 (978-0-545-19711-3(2)) Weston Woods Studios, Inc.

Wilson, J. M. & Zolkowski, Cathy A. Blue: Adventures of a Gymnast. 2004. 150p. (YA). per. 11.95 (978-0-9667037-5-7(8)) Verona (Bk.) Publishing, Inc.

Zaglada, Vladimir. Gymmy the Owl & His Friends: Tales in Rhyme about the Animal Kingdom's Natural Gymnasts. 2012. 52p. pap. 24.99 (978-1-4685-6011-4(5)) AuthorHouse.

GYROSCOPE

Hixon, Rena. Mindstorms: Level 4. 2016. (21st Century Skills Innovation Library: Unofficial Guides). (ENG., Illus.). 32p. (J). (gr. 4-8). 29.93 (978-1-63470-527-1(0), 207839) Cherry Lake Publishing.

H

HABITATIONS, HUMAN

see Architecture, Domestic; Houses; Housing

HABITATIONS OF WILD ANIMALS

see Animals—Habitations

HABITS OF ANIMALS

see Animals—Habits and Behavior

HAIKU

Bodden, Valerie. Poetry Basics: Haiku. 2011. (Poetry Basics Ser.). (ENG.). 32p. (J). (gr. 4-7). pap. 9.99 (978-0-89812-736-2(X), Creative Paperbacks) Creative Co., The.

Caswell, Deanna. Boo! Haiku. Shea, Bob, illus. 2016. (ENG.). 24p. (J). (gr. -1-k). 12.95 (978-1-4197-2118-2(6), Abrams Appleseed) Abrams, Inc.

Donegan, Patricia. Haiku: Learn to Express Yourself by Writing Poetry in the Japanese Tradition. 2003. (Asian Arts & Crafts for Creative Kids Ser.). (ENG., Illus.). 64p. (J). (gr. 2-6). 15.95 (978-0-8048-3501-5(2)) Tuttle Publishing.

Han, John J. Little Guy Haiku: Life with Bailey, a Maltese. Han, Joy, illus. 2009. 48p. pap. 24.95 (978-1-61546-044-1(6)) America Star Bks.

Harvey, Sarah N. & Buffam, Leslie. Great Lakes & Rugged Ground: Imagining Ontario, 1 vol. Charko, Kasia, illus. 2010. (ENG.). 32p. (J). (gr. -1-7). 19.95 (978-1-55469-105-0(2)) Orca Bk. Pubs. USA.

Macken, JoAnn Early. Read, Recite, & Write Haiku. 2015. (ENG., Illus.). 32p. (J). (978-0-7787-1964-9(2)) Crabtree Publishing Co.

Muth, Jon J. Hi, Koo! A Year of Seasons. 2014. (ENG., Illus.). 32p. (J). (gr. -1-3). 17.99 (978-0-545-16668-3(3), Scholastic Pr.) Scholastic, Inc.

Prelutsky, Jack. If Not for the Cat. Rand, Ted, illus. 2004. (ENG.). 40p. (J). (gr. -1-3). 17.99 (978-0-06-059677-4(5), Greenwillow Bks.) HarperCollins Pubs.

Snyder, Betsy E. I Haiku You. 2012. (ENG., Illus.). 32p. (J). (gr. -1-3). 9.99 (978-0-375-86750-7(3), Random Hse. Bks. for Young Readers) Random Hse. Children's Bks.

Spivak, Dawnine. Grass Sandals: The Travels of Basho. Demi, illus. 2009. (ENG.). 40p. (J). (gr. 4-6). 13.99 (978-1-4424-0936-1(3), Atheneum Bks. for Young Readers) Simon & Schuster Children's Publishing.

Vatcher-Martin M.A., Cheryl. Haiku for You: With Some One Room School House History. 2009. 92p. pap. 33.00 (978-1-4389-4582-8(5)) AuthorHouse.

HAIL

Appleby, Alex. It's Hailing! 2013. (What's the Weather? Ser.). 24p. (J). (gr. k-2). pap. 8.15 (978-1-4339-9393-0(7)); pap. 48.90 (978-1-4339-9394-7(5)); (ENG., Illus.). lib. bdg. 22.60 (978-1-4339-9392-3(9)) Stevens, Gareth Publishing LLLP.

—It's Hailing! / Est Granizando! 2013. (What's the Weather? / Qu Tiempo Hace? Ser.). (SPA & ENG., Illus.). 24p. (J). (gr. k-2). 22.60 (978-1-4339-9462-3(3)) Stevens, Gareth Publishing LLLP.

Ghigna, Charles. Hail to Spring! Watson, Laura, illus. 2015. (Springtime Weather Wonders Ser.). (ENG.). (gr. -1-2). 20p. bds. 7.99 (978-1-4795-6041-7(3)); 24p. lib. bdg. 21.99 (978-1-4795-6029-5(4)) Picture Window Bks.

Higgins, Nadia. It's Hailing!, 1 vol. Ward, Damian, illus. 2010. (Weather Watchers Ser.). (ENG.). 32p. (J). (gr. k-3). 28.50 (978-1-60270-732-0(4)) Magic Wagon.

Honders, Christine. When Hail Hits. 2015. (Eye on the Sky Ser.). (ENG., Illus.). 32p. (J). (gr. 3-4). pap. 10.50 (978-1-4824-2884-1(9)) Stevens, Gareth Publishing LLLP.

Jensen, Belinda. Raindrops on a Roller Coaster: Hail. Kurilla, Renee, illus. 2016. (Bel the Weather Girl Ser.). (ENG.). 24p. (J). (gr. -1-3). 25.32 (978-1-4677-7958-6(X), Millbrook Pr.) Lerner Publishing Group.

Mezzanotte, Jim. Granizadas. 2007. (Tormentas (Storms) Ser.). (ENG & SPA., Illus.). 24p. (gr. 1-4). pap. 8.15 (978-0-8368-8077-9(3)); lib. bdg. 22.00 (978-0-8368-8070-0(6)) Stevens, Gareth Publishing LLLP. (Weekly Reader Leveled Readers).

—Granizadas (Hailstorms) 2009. (Tiempo extremo Ser.). (SPA.). 24p. (J). (gr. k-3). pap. 8.15 (978-1-4339-2367-8(X)); lib. bdg. 22.00 (978-1-4339-2353-1(X)) Stevens, Gareth Publishing LLLP. (Weekly Reader Leveled Readers).

—Hailstorms. 2007. (Storms Ser.). (Illus.). 24p. (gr. 1-4). pap. 8.15 (978-0-8368-7919-3(8)); lib. bdg. 22.00 (978-0-8368-7912-4(0)) Stevens, Gareth Publishing LLLP. (Weekly Reader Leveled Readers).

Piattner, Josh & Craig, Diane. Hail or Freezing Rain?, 1 vol. 2016. (This or That? Weather Ser.). (ENG., Illus.). 24p. (J). (gr. k-4). 25.65 (978-1-62403-954-6(5)) ABDO Publishing Co.

Rain, Snow, & Hail: Individual Title Six-Packs. (Discovery World Ser.). 16p. (gr. 1-2). 28.00 (978-0-7635-8466-5(5)) Rigby Education.

HAIR

Andrus, Aubre. Spray, Smooth, & Shampoo: DIY Crafts & Recipes for Healthy Hair. 2017. (DIY Day Spa Ser.). (ENG., Illus.). 48p. (gr. 4-5). lib. bdg. 31.32 (978-1-5157-3444-4(7)) Capstone Press of Coughlan Cos.

Badt, Karin Luisa. Hair There & Everywhere. 2006. (Illus.). 32p. (J). (gr. k-4). reprint ed. 17.00 (978-0-7567-9930-4(9)) DIANE Publishing Co.

Beaumont, Holly. Why Do Monkeys & Other Mammals Have Fur? 2015. (Animal Body Coverings Ser.). (ENG., Illus.). 24p. (gr. 1-3). pap. 6.99 (978-1-4846-2539-2(0), Heinemann Read & Learn) Heinemann-Raintree.

Behnke, Alison. Barbers. 2005. (Pull Ahead Books: Community Helpers Ser.). (ENG., Illus.). 32p. (gr. k-3). lib. bdg. 22.60 (978-0-8225-2799-2(5)) Lerner Publishing Group.

Birch, Ann. Head Lice up Close 6 Pack. 2004. pap. 40.50 (978-1-4109-1154-4(3)) Harcourt Schl. Pubs.

Bozzo, Linda. Amazing Animal Skin. (Creature Features Ser.). 24p. 2009. (gr. 2-3). 42.50 (978-1-61512-067-3(X)) 2008. (Illus.). (J). (gr. 3-7). lib. bdg. 22.60 (978-1-4042-4168-8(X)) Rosen Publishing Group, Inc., The. (PowerKids Pr.).

Canavan, Thomas. Is Your Hair Stronger Than Steel? Questions about Hair, Skin, & Teeth. 2016. (Human Body FAQ Ser.). 00032p. (J). (gr. 3-3). pap. 10.00 (978-1-4994-3168-1(6), PowerKids Pr.) Rosen Publishing Group, Inc., The.

Canetti, Yanitzia. La Adaptación, ¡qué Sensación! 2010. (SPA.). (J). (978-1-59835-176-7(1)) Cambridge BrickHouse, Inc.

—Amazing Adaptations! 2010. (J). (978-1-59835-200-9(8)) Cambridge BrickHouse, Inc.

Derkazarian, Susan. You Have Head Lice! 2005. (Rookie Read-About Health Ser.). (ENG., Illus.). 32p. (J). (gr. k-2). 20.50 (978-0-516-25879-9(6), Children's Pr.) Scholastic Library Publishing.

Dickmann, Nancy. What You Need to Know about Head Lice. 2016. (Focus on Health Ser.). (ENG., Illus.). 32p. (gr. 3-4). lib. bdg. 27.32 (978-1-4914-8242-1(7)) Capstone Press of Coughlan Cos.

Ehrmann, Johanna. The Life of a Colonial Wigmaker. 2013. (Jr. Graphic Colonial America Ser.). (ENG., Illus.). 24p. (J). (gr. 3-6). pap. 10.60 (978-1-4777-1431-7(6)); lib. bdg. 25.25 (978-1-4777-1307-5(7)) Rosen Publishing Group, Inc., The. (PowerKids Pr.).

Friendship & Hair Braiding. 2003. 32p. 12.98 (978-1-4054-1639-9(4)) Parragon, Inc.

Giblin. Curl It, Braid It, Shave It. Date not set. (J). mass mkt. 4.99 (978-0-06-446210-5(2)) HarperCollins Pubs.

Halvorson, Karin. Inside the Skin, Hair, & Nails, 1 vol. 2016. (Super Simple Body Set 2 Ser.). (ENG., Illus.). 32p. (J). (gr. k-4). 27.07 (978-1-62403-942-3(1)) ABDO Publishing Co.

Harrison, Emma. From Head to Toe: The Girls' Life Guide to Taking Care of You. Montagna, Frank, illus. 2004. 124p. (J). (978-0-439-44983-0(9)) Scholastic, Inc.

Horstschaefer, Felicitas. Paper Style: Hairdos. 2014. (ENG., Illus.). 15p. (J). (gr. 3-7). 16.99 (978-1-4521-2031-7(5)) Chronicle Bks. LLC.

Hunt, Sara R. & Kenney, Karen Latchana. Hair Care Tips & Tricks. Heschke, Elena, illus. 2015. (ENG.). 32p. (J). (gr. 4-8). lib. bdg. 26.65 (978-1-4677-5218-3(5), Lerner Pubns.) Lerner Publishing Group.

Johnson, Elizabeth. Hair: Do It Yourself! 2012. (Illus.). (978-1-77069-378-4(5)) Word Alive Pr.

Kenney, Karen Latchana. Hair Care Tips & Tricks. Heschke, Elena, illus. 2015. (Style Secrets Ser.). (ENG.). 32p. (gr. 4-8). 26.65 (978-1-4677-8653-9(5), Lerner Pubns.) Lerner Publishing Group.

Klingel, Cynthia & Noyed, Robert B. Hair. 2010. (Let's Read about Our Bodies Ser.). 24p. (gr. k-3). (J). lib. bdg. 22.00 (978-1-4339-3362-2(4)); (Illus.). pap. 8.15 (978-1-4339-3363-9(2)) Stevens, Gareth Publishing LLLP.

—Hair / el Cabello. 2010. (Let's Read about Our Bodies / Hablemos del cuerpo humano Ser.). (SPA., Illus.). 24p. (gr. k-3). pap. 8.15 (978-1-4339-3739-2(5)) Stevens, Gareth Publishing LLLP.

—Hair/el Cabello. 2010. (Let's Read about Our Bodies / Hablemos del cuerpo humano Ser.). (SPA., Illus.). 24p. (J). (gr. k-3). lib. bdg. 22.00 (978-1-4339-3738-5(7)) Stevens, Gareth Publishing LLLP.

Levy, Janey. Alopecia Areata. (Genetic Diseases & Disorders Ser.). 64p. 2009. (gr. 6-6). 58.50 (978-1-61512-662-0(7)) 2006. (Illus.). (YA). (gr. 5-9). lib. bdg. 31.95 (978-1-4042-0693-9(0)) Rosen Publishing Group, Inc., The.

The Life of a Colonial Wigmaker. 2013. (Jr. Graphic Colonial America Ser.). 24p. (J). (gr. 3-6). pap. 63.60 (978-1-4777-1432-4(4), PowerKids Pr.) Rosen Publishing Group, Inc., The.

Llewellyn, Claire. Your Hair. 2008. (Look after Yourself Ser.). (Illus.). 30p. (J). (gr. 1-4). lib. bdg. 28.50 (978-1-59771-097-8(0)) Sea-To-Sea Pubns.

Markle, Sandra. What If You Had Animal Hair? McWilliam, Howard, illus. 2014. (ENG.). 32p. (J). (gr. 1-3). pap. 3.99 (978-0-545-63085-6(1), Scholastic Paperbacks) Scholastic, Inc.

Meyers, Barbara & Mays, Lydia. The Long & the Short of It: A Tale about Hair. Bersani, Shennen, illus. 2011. (ENG.). 32p. (J). (gr. 2-4). 14.95 (978-1-60443-017-2(6)) American Cancer Society, Inc.

Neuman, Maria & Dorling Kindersley Publishing Staff. Fabulous Hair. Coppola, Angela, photos by. 2006. (ENG., Illus.). 96p. (J). (gr. 3-7). pap. 9.99 (978-0-7566-1589-5(5), DK Children) Dorling Kindersley Publishing, Inc.

Patricelli, Leslie. Hair. Patricelli, Leslie, illus. 2017. (Leslie Patricelli Board Bks.). (ENG., Illus.). 26p. (J). (— 1). bds. 6.99 (978-0-7636-7931-6(3)) Candlewick Pr.

Petty, Kate. Hair. 2006. (World Show-And-Tell Ser.). (ENG., Illus.). 32p. (J). (gr. -1-1). pap. 8.95 (978-1-58728-532-5(0)) Cooper Square Publishing Llc.

Rabe, Tish. Hooray for Hair! Brannon, Tom, illus. 2013. (Step into Reading Ser.). (ENG.). 48p. (J). (gr. k-3). pap. 3.99 (978-0-375-87048-4(2), Random Hse. Bks. for Young Readers) Random Hse. Children's Bks.

Rainis, Kenneth G. Hair, Clothing, & Tire Track Evidence: Crime-Solving Science Experiments. 2006. (Forensic Science Projects Ser.). (Illus.). 128p. (J). (gr. 5-18). lib. bdg. 33.27 (978-0-7660-2729-9(5)) Enslow Pubs., Inc.

Rau, Dana Meachen. Braiding Hair. 2012. (How-To Library). (ENG.). 32p. (gr. 3-6). 28.50 (978-1-61080-471-4(6), 202081); pap. 14.21 (978-1-61080-645-9(X), 202255) Cherry Lake Publishing.

Rice, Dona. Always Growing. 2015. (TIME for KIDS(r) Nonfiction Readers Ser.). (ENG., Illus.). 12p. (gr. k-k). 4.99 (978-1-4938-2058-0(3)) Teacher Created Materials, Inc.

Rice, Dona Herweck. Siempre Crece. 2016. (TIME for KIDS(r) Nonfiction Readers Ser.). (SPA., Illus.). 12p. (J). (gr. k-k). 4.99 (978-1-4938-2967-5(X)) Teacher Created Materials, Inc.

Royston, Angela. Head Lice. 2009. (How's Your Health? Ser.). (J). (gr. 1-4). 28.50 (978-1-59920-218-1(2)) Black Rabbit Bks.

Silverman, Buffy. Hair Traits: Color, Texture, & More. 2012. (Lightning Bolt Books (tm) — What Traits Are in Your Genes? Ser.). (Illus.). 32p. (gr. k-2). (SPA & ENG.). pap. 7.95 (978-1-58013-956-4(6)); (ENG., lib. bdg. 26.60 (978-0-7613-8941-5(5), Lerner Pubns.) Lerner Publishing Group.

Souza, D. M. Look What Whiskers Can Do. 2006. (Look What Animals Can Do Ser.). (ENG., Illus.). 48p. (gr. 2-4). lib. bdg. 25.26 (978-0-7613-9459-4(1), Lerner Pubns.) Lerner Publishing Group.

Stewart, Melissa. Here We Grow: The Secrets of Hair & Nails. 2010. (Gross & Goofy Body 2 Ser.). 48p. (gr. 3). 29.93 (978-0-7614-4172-4(7)) Marshall Cavendish Corp.

Turnbull, Stephanie. Beauty Blitz. 2016. (Sleepover Secrets Ser.). 24p. (gr. 2-6). 28.50 (978-1-62588-376-6(5), Smart Apple Media) Black Rabbit Bks.

Vogel, Elizabeth. El Cuidado de Tu Cabello. 2004. (Limpieza y Salud Todo el Dia Ser.). (SPA & ENG., Illus.). 24p. (J). (gr. -1-2). lib. bdg. 18.75 (978-0-8239-6610-3(0)) Rosen Publishing Group, Inc., The.

—¡el cuidado de tu cabello! (Taking Care of My Hair) 2009. (Limpieza y salud todo el día (Clean & Healthy All Day Long) Ser.). (SPA.). 24p. (gr. 1-1). 37.50 (978-1-61514-295-8(9), Editorial Buenas Letras) Rosen Publishing Group, Inc., The.

—Taking Care of My Hair. 2009. (Clean & Healthy All Day Long Ser.). 24p. (gr. 1-1). 37.50 (978-1-61511-867-0(5), PowerKids Pr.) Rosen Publishing Group, Inc., The.

—Taking Care of My Hair: El Cuidado de Tu Cabello. 2004. (Limpieza y Salud Todo el Dia Ser.). (SPA & ENG., Illus.). 24p. (J). lib. bdg. 18.75 (978-0-8239-6611-0(9), Editorial Buenas Letras) Rosen Publishing Group, Inc., The.

—Taking Care of My Hair / ¡el cuidado de tu Cabello! 2009. (Clean & Healthy All Day Long / Limpieza y salud todo el día Ser.). (ENG & SPA.). 24p. (gr. 1-1). 37.50 (978-1-61511-872-4(1), Editorial Buenas Letras) Rosen Publishing Group, Inc., The.

Young, Thomas. How Do Hair & Nails Grow?, Vol. 1. 2014. (My Body Does Strange Stuff! Ser.). 24p. (J). (gr. 1-2). (ENG.). pap. 8.15 (978-1-4824-0250-6(5)); 22.60 (978-1-4824-0247-6(5)) Stevens, Gareth Publishing LLLP.

HAIR—FICTION

Abassi, Ines. My Beautiful Hair. Kala, Sabah, illus. 2016. (Stories & Fables from Around the World Ser.). (ENG.). 24p. (J). (gr. 2-1). lib. bdg. 24.60 (978-1-4777-5695-9(7), Windmill Bks.) Rosen Publishing Group, Inc., The.

Addie's Bad Day. 2003. 22.95 (978-0-673-75904-7(0)) Celebration Pr.

Alberto, Daisy. A Horse & a Hero. Random House Disney Staff, illus. 2011. (Step into Reading Ser.). (ENG.). 32p. (J). (gr. k-3). pap. 3.99 (978-0-7364-2746-3(5), RH/Disney) Random Hse. Children's Bks.

Anderson, Erin. Repulsive. 2008. 16p. pap. 24.95 (978-1-4241-9429-2(6)) America Star Bks.

Anderson, Laurie Halse. The Hair of Zoe Fleefenbacher Goes to School. Hoyt, Ard, illus. 2009. (ENG.). 32p. (J). (gr. 1-5). 17.99 (978-0-689-85809-3(4), Simon & Schuster Bks. For Young Readers) Simon & Schuster Bks. For Young Readers.

Anholt, Laurence. Hairy Harold. Ross, Tony, illus. 2015. (Seriously Scary Ser.: 8). (ENG.). 48p. (J). (gr. k-2). pap. 8.99 (978-1-4083-3752-3(5)) Hodder & Stoughton GBR. Dist: Hachette Bk. Group.

—Picasso & the Girl with a Ponytail. 2007. (Anholt's Artists Books for Children Ser.). (ENG., Illus.). 32p. (J). (gr. -1-3). pap. 8.99 (978-0-7641-3853-9(7)) Barron's Educational Series, Inc.

Asay, Colleen. What Happened to Grandpa's Hair? 2005. (J). per. 11.95 (978-0-9767658-0-6(2)) Calico Connection, Inc., The.

Azore, Barbara. Wanda & the Wild Hair. Graham, Georgia, illus. 2005. (ENG.). 32p. (J). (gr. -1-2). 15.95 (978-0-88776-717-3(6), Tundra Bks.) Tundra Bks. CAN. Dist: Penguin Random Hse. LLC.

B. Robert Clark. The Man with Big Hair. 2009. 32p. pap. 14.49 (978-1-4389-7636-5(4)) AuthorHouse.

Balukoff, Constance. Mooky's Bad Hair Day . 2004. 21p. pap. 24.95 (978-1-4137-1480-7(3)) PublishAmerica, Inc.

Barnes, Derrick. Crown: An Ode to the Fresh Cut. James, Gordon C., illus. 2017. (Denene Millner Bks.). (ENG.). 32p. (J). (gr. -1-3). 17.95 **(978-1-57284-224-3(5))** Agate Publishing, Inc.

Beall, Linda R. We , Four Paws & Me at Yellowstone National Park. 2012. 40p. pap. 24.95 (978-1-4626-8305-5(3)) America Star Bks.

Bennett, Cindy C. Rapunzel Untangled. 2013. (ENG.). 294p. (gr. 7). 16.99 (978-1-4621-1156-5(4), Sweetwater Bks.) Cedar Fort, Inc./CFI Distribution.

Benton, Jim. What I Don't Know Might Hurt Me. 2013. (Dear Dumb Diary: Year Two Ser.: 4). lib. bdg. 16.00 (978-0-606-32009-2(1), Turtleback) Turtleback Bks.

Bernheimer, Kate. The Girl Who Wouldn't Brush Her Hair. Parker, Jake, illus. 2013. (ENG.). 40p. (J). (gr. -1-3). 17.99 (978-0-375-86878-8(X), Schwartz & Wade Bks.) Random Hse. Children's Bks.

Bernreuter, Bob J. The Gift. 2006. (Illus.). 25p. (J). (978-1-4120-7546-6(7)) Trafford Publishing.

Beserra, Donna. Twirly Shirley In Hurricane Shirley. 2005. 22p. (J). 8.00 (978-0-9729484-4-9(9)) Seventh Street Pr.

Biever, Rick. The Tall Tale of a Barber Named Bill. 2008. 28p. pap. 16.95 (978-1-4327-2594-5(7)) Outskirts Pr., Inc.

Bradman, Tony. Rapunzel Lets Her Hair Down, 1 vol. Warburton, Sarah, illus. (After Happily Ever After Ser.). (ENG.). 56p. (gr. 2-3). 2014. pap. 5.05 (978-1-4342-7965-1(0)) 2009. lib. bdg. 25.32 (978-1-4342-1307-5(2)) Stone Arch Bks. (After Happily Ever After).

Braids for Naya, 6, Pack. (gr. -1-2). 27.00 (978-0-7635-9439-8(3)) Rigby Education.

Brisson, Pat. Melissa Parkington's Beautiful, Beautiful Hair. Bloom, Suzanne, illus. 2006. (ENG.). 32p. (J). (gr. 1-3). 16.95 (978-1-59078-409-9(X)) Boyds Mills Pr.

Butler, Mark. Jonathan's Raspberry Beard. 2011. 20p. (gr. 1-2). pap. 11.99 (978-1-4567-6884-3(0)) AuthorHouse.

Bynum, Betty. I'm a Pretty Little Black Girl! 2013. 32p. pap. 14.95 (978-0-615-78551-6(4)) Workhouse Road Productions.

Callen, Sharon. Maddy's Mad Hair Day, 1 vol. rev. ed. 2013. (Fiction Readers Ser.). (ENG., Illus.). 12p. (J). (gr. 1-1). pap. 12.96 (978-1-4807-1129-7(2)); pap. 4.99 (978-1-4333-5450-2(0)) Shell Educational Publishing.

Cardin, Jodi. Bernice's Bad Hair Days. Chin, Todd, illus. 2009. 56p. (J). pap. (978-1-60800-004-3(4)) LifeReloaded Specialty Publishing LLC.

Censullo, Chris. The Boy with the Big Blue Hair. 2013. 30p. (J). 16.99 (978-0-9797868-7-7(8), OddInt Media) Greenwood Hill Pr.

Cisneros, Sandra. Hairs. 2004. Orig. Title: Pelitos. (SPA., Illus.). (J). (gr. k-3). spiral bd. (978-0-616-01616-9(6)) Canadian National Institute for the Blind/Institut National Canadien pour les Aveugles.

Claverie, Jean & Chapouton, Anne Marie. Julian. 2003. (SPA., Illus.). 28p. (978-84-85334-71-1(X)) Lóguez Ediciones ESP. Dist: Lectorum Pubns., Inc.

Contreras, Kathleen. Braids - Trencitas. Lindmark, Margaret, illus. 2009. (ENG & SPA.). 32p. (J). (gr. -1-3). 14.99 (978-1-933032-27-6(8)) Lectorum Pubns., Inc.

Cottrell, Kim. Izaboo, Izaboo, What Are We to Do. 2009. 36p. pap. 15.49 (978-1-4389-5210-9(4)) AuthorHouse.

Croissant-Madden, Gayle. My Wild, Wild Hair! Croissant-Madden, Gayle, illus. 2006. (Illus.). (J). 10.00 (978-0-9786478-0-3(7)) airjam.com.

Dale, Jay. Off You Go!, 1 vol. Zamazing, Cherie, illus. 2012. (Wonder Words Ser.). (ENG.). 32p. (gr. k-2). pap. 5.99 (978-1-4296-8910-6(2), Engage Literacy) Capstone Press of Coughlan Cos.

Daugherty, Deborah Kay. Hair in the Way. 2013. 40p. pap. 15.99 (978-1-4908-0130-8(8), WestBow Pr.) Author Solutions, Inc.

Davi. El Senor Simplon. 2003. (SPA.). (978-968-494-088-8(2), CI30723) Centro de Informacion y Desarrollo de la Comunicacion y la Literatura MEX. Dist: Lectorum Pubns., Inc.

Davis, Jack E. & Palatini, Margie. Bedhead. 2003. (ENG., Illus.). 40p. (J). (gr. -1-3). 7.99 (978-0-689-86002-7(1), Simon & Schuster Bks. For Young Readers) Simon & Schuster Bks. For Young Readers.

Dinbergs, Holly Smith. Hair Scare. Stewart, Chantal, illus. 2005. (Girlz Rock! Ser.). (J). pap. (978-1-59336-702-2(3)) Mondo Publishing.

Doolan, Catherine. Drochla Gruaige. Kelly, Maeve, illus. 2004. (Sraith Sos Ser.: 09). (IRI, ENG & GLE.). 64p. (J). pap. 9.95 (978-0-86278-866-7(8)) O'Brien Pr., Ltd., The IRL. Dist: Dufour Editions, Inc.

Doyle, Malachy. Hair Scare. Allen, Jonathan, illus. 2005. (ENG.). 24p. (J). lib. bdg. 23.65 (978-1-59646-724-8(X)) Dingles & Co.

Dyan, Penelope. Jordan's Hair — the Big Dilemm. Dyan, Penelope, illus. 2008. (Illus.). 44p. pap. 11.95 (978-1-935118-34-3(X)) Bellissima Publishing, LLC.

Elin Hirschman, Jessica & Bright, Bonnie. The Tangle Tower. Bright, Bonnie, illus. 2006. (Illus.). 32p. (J). (gr. k-2). 14.95 (978-0-9701155-6-0(3)) Cookie Bear Pr., Inc.

Eubank, Patricia Reeder. The Princess & the Snarls. Eubank, Patricia Reeder, illus. 2006. (ENG., Illus.). 32p. (J). (gr. k-3). 16.95 (978-0-8249-5536-6(6), Ideal Pubns.) Worthy Publishing.

Fenwick, Margaret. Stella's Hair. 2009. 36p. pap. 14.75 (978-1-60693-857-7(6), Eloquent Bks.) Strategic Book Publishing & Rights Agency (SBPRA).

Figueras, Nuria. Las Trenzas del Abuelo. Olmos, Roger, illus. 2003. (Libros para Soñar Ser.). (SPA.). 32p. (978-84-8464-180-3(5)) Kalandraka Editora, S.L. ESP. Dist: Lectorum Pubns., Inc.

Fitzgerald, F. Scott. Bernice Bobs Her Hair & Other Stories. Date not set. (Nelson Readers Ser.). (Illus.). 86p. (J). pap. (978-0-17-557051-5(5)) Addison-Wesley Longman, Inc.

Ford, Juwanda G. Shop Talk. Hoston, Jim, illus. 2004. 32p. (J). lib. bdg. 15.00 (978-1-4242-0236-2(1)) Fitzgerald Bks.

Francis-Harris, Annabel. The Other Side of the Forest. 2006. pap. 19.95 (978-1-59526-458-9(2)) Aeon Publishing Inc.

Froemming, Kaylee. My Mama's Hair Is Everywhere: It just won't go Away!! 2008. 12p. pap. 8.49 (978-1-4389-0385-9(5)) AuthorHouse.

Gaiman, NEil. Crazy Hair. McKean, Dave, illus. (ENG.). 40p. (J). (gr. -1-3). 2015. pap. 6.99 (978-0-06-057910-4(2)) 2009. 18.99 (978-0-06-057908-1(0)) HarperCollins Pubs.

—Crazy Hair. 2015. (J). lib. bdg. 17.20 (978-0-606-36478-2(1)) Turtleback Bks.

Gantt-Smith, Michelle. Little Feet Goes to the Barbershop. 2013. 48p. pap. 12.00 (978-0-9847885-1-4(4)) Gantt Smith Publishing Hse.

Garis, Howard R. The Curlytops & Their Playmates. 2009. 120p. 22.95 (978-1-60664-610-6(9)); pap. 10.95 (978-1-60664-342-6(8)) Rodgers, Alan Bks.

—Curlytops at Uncle Frank's Ranch. 2009. 120p. pap. 10.95 (978-1-60664-408-9(4)) Rodgers, Alan Bks.

—The Curlytops on Star Island. 2009. 120p. 22.95 (978-1-60664-611-3(7)); pap. 10.95 (978-1-60664-343-3(6)) Rodgers, Alan Bks.

Glatzer, Jenna. Hattie, Get a Haircut! Kendall, Monica, illus. 2005. (ENG.). 32p. (J). (gr. -1-3). lib. bdg. 19.95 (978-0-9724853-0-2(9)) Keene Publishing.

Goldberg, Mara J. Issavich's Unruly Nest. 2009. 20p. pap. 12.49 (978-1-4343-7992-4(2)) AuthorHouse.

Gray, Diane. The Bears with Unruly Hairs. 2011. 28p. pap. 15.99 (978-1-4568-8129-0(9)) Xlibris Corp.

Griffin, Michele. It's Haircut Time! How one little boy overcame his fear of haircut Day. 2012. (ENG., Illus.). 32p. pap. 9.95 (978-1-935567-33-2(0)) Sensory Resources.

Gurule, Jennifer. Look at Aunt Clare's Hair. Gurule, Jennifer, illus. 2005. (Daddy's Collection). (Illus.). (J). pap. 11.50 (978-1-59134-033-1(0)) Maval Publishing, Inc.

Hager, Janet. Truly Julie. 2012. 26p. 14.95 (978-1-4626-6121-3(1)) America Star Bks.

Haircuts for Bella & Rosie. 2004. (Bella & Rosie Set 2 Ser.). (J). 7.67 (978-1-932570-18-2(7)) Pioneer Valley Bks.

Hale, Shannon & Hale, Dean. Rapunzel's Revenge. Hale, Nathan, illus. 2008. (ENG.). 144p. (YA). (gr. 5-8). pap. 16.99 (978-1-59990-288-3(5), 9781599902883, Bloomsbury USA Childrens) Bloomsbury Publishing USA.

Hardy, S. F. The Empress' New Hair. 2012. 40p. pap. 10.00 (978-0-9849360-9-0(2)) G Publishing LLC.

Hawkins-Rodgers, Donzella. No Bulley Destroy's Chloe's Hairdo. Hewins, Shirley, illus. 2003. 32p. (J). (gr. 3-18). lib. bdg. 16.95 (978-1-884242-56-4(1)) Multicultural Pubns.

Hay, Sam. Knit-Knotters. Tran, Turine, illus. 2016. (Stella & the Night Sprites Ser.: 1). (ENG.). 96p. (J). (gr. 1-3). pap. 4.99 (978-0-545-81998-5(9)) Scholastic, Inc.

Herbach, Geoff. Hair-Pocalypse. Gilpin, Stephen, illus. 2017. (Fiction Picture Bks.). (ENG.). 32p. (gr. 1-3). lib. bdg. 23.32 (978-1-5158-1411-5(4), Fiction Picture Bks.) Picture Window Bks.

Hietpas, Polly. Rosie Cat's Bad Fur Day. 2009. 20p. pap. 10.49 (978-1-4490-0777-5(5)) AuthorHouse.

Higgins, Ryan. Wilfred. Higgins, Ryan, illus. 2013. (ENG., Illus.). 40p. (J). (gr. -1-k). 16.99 (978-0-8037-3732-7(7), Dial Bks) Penguin Young Readers Group.

Hilton, Perez. The Boy with Pink Hair. Hill, Jenn, illus. 2011. (ENG.). 32p. (J). (gr. -1-k). 17.99 (978-0-451-23420-9(0), Celebra Young Readers) Penguin Publishing Group.

Hinman, Bobbie. The Knot Fairy. Bridgeman, Kristi, illus. 2010. (ENG.). 32p. (J). (gr. -1-1). 16.95 (978-0-9786791-0-1(5)) Best Fairy Bks.

Holub, Joan & Williams, Suzanne. Rapunzel Cuts Loose. 2014. (Grimmtastic Girls Ser.: 4). (ENG.). 192p. (J). (gr. 3-7). pap. 5.99 (978-0-545-51986-1(1), Scholastic Paperbacks) Scholastic, Inc.

—Rapunzel Cuts Loose. 2014. (Grimmtastic Girls Ser.: 4). lib. bdg. 16.00 (978-0-606-36064-7(6)) Turtleback Bks.

Hooks, Bell. Happy to Be Nappy (Board Book) Happy to Be Nappy. Raschka, Chris, illus. 2017. (ENG.). 32p. (J). (gr. -1 — 1). bds. 7.99 (978-1-4847-8841-7(9), Jump at the Sun) Hyperion Bks. for Children.

Hosford, Kate. Big Bouffant. Clifton-Brown, Holly, illus. 2011. (ENG.). 32p. (J). (gr. k-2). 16.95 (978-0-7613-5409-3(3), Carolrhoda Bks.) Lerner Publishing Group.

Hyatt, Patricia Rusch. The Quite Contrary Man: A True American Tale. Brown, Kathryn, illus. 2011. (ENG.). 32p. (J). (gr. 1-4). 16.95 (978-0-8109-4065-9(5), Abrams Bks. for Young Readers) Abrams, Inc.

Impey, Martin, illus. Rapunzel. 2006. (First Fairy Tales Ser.). 31p. (J). (gr. -1-3). lib. bdg. 28.50 (978-1-59771-076-3(8)) Sea-To-Sea Pubns.

Jensen, Lisa. If My Hair Were Like Spagetti. Jensen, Lisa, illus. Date not set. (Illus.). (J). (gr. -1-3). mass mkt. 15.95 (978-0-9666973-0-8(8)) Jensen, Lissa.

Johnson, Vincent L. Of Corn Silk & Black Braids. Crockett, Linda, illus. 2005. 32p. (J). (gr. k-3). 17.95 (978-0-9657033-2-1(0)) Marzetta Bks.

Kann, Victoria. Crazy Hair Day. 2014. (Pinkalicious Ser.). (J). lib. bdg. 13.55 (978-0-606-36265-8(7)) Turtleback Bks.

Kearney, Rena. Mimi Fairy's Purple Hair. 2009. 32p. pap. 15.99 (978-1-4490-1554-1(9)) AuthorHouse.

Klein, Zoë. The Goblins of Knottingham: A History of Challah. Bogert, Beth, illus. 2017. (J). (978-1-68115-526-5(5)) Behrman Hse., Inc.

Koren, Edward. Very Hairy Harry. Koren, Edward, illus. 2003. (Illus.). (978-0-06-057744-5(4)); (J). (978-0-06-056868-9(2)) HarperCollins Pubs.

—Very Hairy Harry. 2003. (Illus.). 40p. (J). (gr. -1-3). 15.99 (978-0-06-050907-1(4), Cotler, Joanna Books) HarperCollins Pubs.

Krosoczka, Jarrett J. Baghead. Krosoczka, Jarrett J., illus. 2004. (ENG., Illus.). 40p. (J). (gr. -1-2). reprint ed. pap. 7.99 (978-0-553-11172-9(8), Dragonfly Bks.) Random Hse. Children's Bks.

Krulik, Nancy. Hair Today, Gone Tomorrow!, 34 vols., No. 34. John and Wendy Staff, illus. 2010. (Katie Kazoo, Switcheroo Ser.: 34). (ENG.). 80p. (J). (gr. 2-4). pap. 3.99 (978-0-448-45231-9(6), Grosset & Dunlap) Penguin Young Readers Group.

Lacamara, Laura. Dalia's Wondrous Hair / el Maravilloso Cabello de Dalia. Baeza Ventura, Gabriela, tr. from SPA. Lacamara, Laura, illus. 2014. (ENG & SPA., Illus.). (J). 17.95 (978-1-55885-789-6(3), Piñata Books) Arte Publico Pr.

Lee, Katie Bertoch. Ma Ma's Hair Is Everywhere. 2008. 28p. pap. 24.95 (978-1-60563-435-7(2)) America Star Bks.

Madrigal, Antonio Hernandez. Erandi's Braids. dePaola, Tomie, illus. 2015. 32p. pap. 7.00 (978-1-61003-530-9(5)) Center for the Collaborative Classroom.

Mahalik, Cathy. The Longest Hair Ever. 2011. 40p. 18.41 (978-1-4269-4396-6(2)) Trafford Publishing.

Marek, Catherine. Luke's 1st Haircut. Mitchell, Hazel, illus. 2007. (ENG.). 32p. (J). (gr. -1-3). per. (978-0-9748251-5-1(8)) Zoe Life Publishing.

—Sara's 1st Haircut Mitchell, Hazel, illus. l.t. ed. 2007. (ENG.). 32p. (J). (gr. -1-3). per. (978-0-9748251-3-7(1)) Zoe Life Publishing.

Marsh, Carole. The Case of the Hunchback Hairdresser. 2006. (Criss Cross Applesauce Ser.). (Illus.). 54p. (J). (gr. 4-7). 14.95 (978-0-635-06202-4(X)) Gallopade International.

Mathison, Anne. I Love My Hair. Flowerpot Press, ed. 2012. (Illus.). 20p. (J). (978-1-77093-110-7(4)) Flowerpot Children's Pr. Inc.

McAllen, Bob. Dirtiest Hair in the World. McClure, Tom, illus. 2008. (ENG.). 44p. (J). (gr. k-3). lib. bdg. 17.99 (978-1-934277-24-9(X)) Mam Green Publishing, Inc.

McElligott, Matthew. Even Monsters Need Haircuts. McElligott, Matthew, illus. 2012. (ENG., Illus.). 40p. (J). (gr. k-8). pap. 8.99 (978-0-8027-2801-2(4), 9780802728012, Bloomsbury USA Childrens) Bloomsbury Publishing USA.

McGann, Oisín. The Evil Hairdo. 2006. (Forbidden Files Ser.). (ENG., Illus.). 80p. (J). pap. 10.95 (978-0-86278-940-4(0)) O'Brien Pr., Ltd., The IRL. Dist: Dufour Editions, Inc.

Miller, Lorna. Jumper the Pony: Thomas Learns a Lesson. 2008. 32p. per. 24.95 (978-1-4241-9578-7(0)) America Star Bks.

Moorthy, Anita. Monkey's Drum. Sarkar, Soumitro, illus. 2003. (ENG.). 24p. pap. 3.99 (978-81-86211-15-1(2)) Penguin Publishing Group.

Morrison, Danette W. & Johnson, Dana A. My Eyebrows Are Hiding. 2009. 48p. pap. 12.99 (978-1-4343-4029-0(5)) AuthorHouse.

Mullarkey, Lisa. Hair's Looking at You: Book 12, 1 vol. Harris, Phyllis, illus. 2012. (Katharine the Almost Great Ser.). (ENG.). 80p. (J). (gr. 1-4). 27.07 (978-1-61641-833-5(8)) Magic Wagon.

Munsch, Robert. Stephanie's Ponytail. Martchenko, Michael, illus. 16th ed. 2007. (Annikin Ser.). (ENG.). 24p. (J). (gr. -1-2). 1.99 (978-1-55451-114-3(3), 9781554511143) Annick Pr., Ltd. CAN. Dist: Publishers Group West (PGW).

—Stephanie's Ponytail. 2006. (J). 15.10 (978-0-7569-7162-5(4)) Perfection Learning Corp.

Newman, Patrice Tomasetti. Where Oh Where? It's in My Hair! 2012. 26p. 24.95 (978-1-4626-6284-5(6)) America Star Bks.

O'Connor, Jane. Hair Dos & Hair Don'ts. Glasser, Robin Preiss, illus. 2011. (I Can Read Level 1 Ser.). (ENG.). 32p. (J). (gr. -1-3). pap. 3.99 (978-0-06-200179-5(5)) HarperCollins Pubs.

—Hair DOS & Hair Don'ts. Glasser, Robin Preiss, illus. 2011. (I Can Read Level 1 Ser.). (ENG.). 32p. (J). (gr. -1-3). 16.99 (978-0-06-200180-1(9)) HarperCollins Pubs.

Palatini, Margie. Bedhead. 2003. lib. bdg. 18.40 (978-0-613-66481-3(7), Turtleback) Turtleback Bks.

Park, Barbara. Junie B. Jones Is a Beauty Shop Guy. unabr. ed. 2004. (Junie B. Jones Ser.: No. 11). 67p. (J). (gr. k-3). pap. 17.00 incl. audio (978-0-8072-0532-7(X), Listening Library) Random Hse. Audio Publishing Group.

Pliszka, Jodi. Bella & Gizmo's Adventures — the Hairless Sphynx Cats. 2005. (Illus.). 30p. (J). per. 18.95 (978-1-933449-27-2(6)) Nightengale Pr.

Pliszka, Jodi A. Bella & Gizmo's Adventures: The Hairless Sphynx Cats. 2005. (Illus.). 30p. (J). per. 18.95 (978-1-933449-03-6(9)) Nightengale Pr.

Powell, Amy. Absolutely the Best. 2007. (J). per. 12.00 (978-0-9773608-6-4(5)) Shiny Red Ball Publishing.

Ramanathan, Priya. The Mustache Man. Gupta, Garima, illus. 2013. (ENG.). 32p. (J). (gr. -1). pap. 9.95 (978-81-8190-186-6(X)) Karadi Tales Co. Pvt, Ltd. IND. Dist: Consortium Bk. Sales & Distribution.

Rippin, Sally. The Beautiful Haircut. Fukuoka, Aki, illus. 2014. (ENG.). 48p. (J). pap. 4.99 (978-1-61067-100-2(7)) Kane Miller.

Roache, Marjorie D. My Hair Is Too Big! 2011. 28p. pap. 15.99 (978-1-4634-0716-2(5)) AuthorHouse.

Rose, Gerald. Horrible Melena. (SPA.). (J). 8.95 (978-958-04-7343-5(9)) Norma S.A. COL. Dist: Distribuidora Norma, Inc.

Saltzberg, Barney. Crazy Hair Day. Saltzberg, Barney, illus. 2008. (ENG., Illus.). 32p. (J). (gr. k-3). pap. 6.99 (978-0-7636-2464-4(0)) Candlewick Pr.

—Crazy Hair Day. Saltzberg, Barney, illus. 2011. (Illus.). (J). (gr. k-3). 29.95 (978-0-545-13450-7(1)) Weston Woods Studios, Inc.

—Crazy Hair Day, 5 bks., Set. 2011. (J). (gr. k-3). 38.75 (978-0-545-15157-3(0)) Weston Woods Studios, Inc.

—Crazy Hair Day Big Book. Saltzberg, Barney, illus. 2008. (ENG., Illus.). 32p. (J). (gr. k-3). pap. 24.99 (978-0-7636-3969-3(9)) Candlewick Pr.

Santa Gets A Haircut. 2005. (J). 5.95 (978-0-9769321-3-0(X)) Steingart, Nathan Publishing.

Scholastic, Inc. Staff & Ford, Juwanda G. Shop Talk. Hoston, Jim, illus. 2004. (Just for You Ser.). (ENG.). 32p. (gr. k-3). pap. 3.99 (978-0-439-56873-9(0), Teaching Resources) Scholastic, Inc.

Scott-Dixon, Valerie. My Fuzzy Wuzzy Hair. 2012. 32p. pap. 24.95 (978-1-4626-6426-9(1)) America Star Bks.

Shannon, David. Bugs in My Hair! Shannon, David, illus. 2013. (ENG., Illus.). 32p. (J). (gr. -1-3). 17.99 (978-0-545-14313-4(6), Blue Sky Pr., The) Scholastic, Inc.

Shaw, Nancy Jo. Give Her a Pixie. Sikorskaia, Margarita, illus. 2016. (ENG.). (J). (978-1-59298-723-8(0)) Beaver's Pond Pr., Inc.

Sheinmel, Courtney & Bell, Jennifer A. Stella Batts: Hair Today, Gone Tomorrow. 2012. (Stella Batts Ser.). (ENG., Illus.). (J). (gr. 1-3). 152p. pap. 5.99 (978-1-58536-191-5(7), 202269); 160p. lib. bdg. 9.99 (978-1-58536-189-2(5), 202268) Sleeping Bear Pr.

Sitner, Nechama. What Did Pinny Do? An Upsherin Story. Leff, Tova, illus. 2013. 36p. (J). 12.95 (978-1-929628-72-8(2)) Hachai Publishing.

Skidmore, Marlene. Wesley's Swoo-Foo. 2008. 28p. pap. 9.99 (978-0-9821408-5-7(1)) Faithful Life Pubs.

Spruill, Edward L. & Spruill, Sonya. Jordan's Hair. Peringer, Stephen Mercer, illus. 2005. 16p. (J). (gr. -1-3). 8.00 (978-0-8170-1484-1(5)) Judson Pr.

Sullivan, Kevin & Goldman, Leslie. Anne's Red Hair. 2010. (Anne of Green Gables Picture Bks.). (ENG.). 32p. (J). (gr. k-2). pap. 4.95 (978-0-9736803-3-1(4)) Davenport Pr. CAN. Dist: Independent Pubs. Group.

Susko, Mark D. Sally Sassafras, the Girl with Monster Hair. 2011. 50p. pap. 16.95 (978-1-4560-5521-9(6)) America Star Bks.

Tarpley, Natasha Anastasia. Bippity Bop Barbershop. Lewis, E. B., illus. 2009. (ENG.). 32p. (gr. -1-3). pap. 7.99 (978-0-316-03382-4(0)) Little, Brown Bks. for Young Readers.

—I Love My Hair! Lewis, E. B., illus. 2014. 32p. pap. 7.00 (978-1-61003-348-0(5)) Center for the Collaborative Classroom.

—I Love My Hair! Lewis, E. B., illus. 2003. (ENG.). 22p. (J). (gr. -1 — 1). bds. 6.99 (978-0-316-52558-9(8)) Little, Brown Bks. for Young Readers.

—I Love My Haircut! Lewis, E. B., illus. 2017. (ENG.). 22p. (J). (gr. -1 — 1). bds. 6.99 (978-0-316-27606-1(5)) Little, Brown Bks. for Young Readers.

Thomas, Debbie. Dead Hairy. MacDonald, Stella, illus. 2011. (ENG.). 256p. (J). pap. 14.95 (978-1-85635-678-7(7)) Mercier Pr., Ltd., The IRL. Dist: Dufour Editions, Inc.

Tyree, Omar R. 12 Brown Boys. 2008. 196p. (J). (gr. 3-7). pap. 9.95 (978-1-933491-12-7(4)) Just Us Bks., Inc.

Vandygrift, Wendy. Lilly Lamoo & the Stray Gray Hair: A Book about Bad Hair, Bullies & Being Your Best. 2011. 24p. (J). 16.95 (978-1-4327-7109-6(4)) Outskirts Pr., Inc.

Victoria, Lisa, illus. Clara's Gift from the Heart. 2006. (J). 17.95 (978-0-9674602-9-1(8)) Blue Marlin Pubns.

Villnave, Erica. Sophie's Lovely Locks, 0 vols. Villnave, Erica, illus. 2011. (ENG., Illus.). 32p. (J). (gr. k-3). 16.99 (978-0-7614-5820-3(4), 9780761458203, Amazon Children's Publishing) Amazon Publishing.

Waters-Porter, Amber Rae. Rachael's Auntie Is Bald-Headed. 2010. (ENG.). 16p. pap. 9.49 (978-1-4490-7755-6(2)) AuthorHouse.

Webb Quest, Sara. Aydil Vice & Her Disgustin' Hair Knots. 2008. 72p. pap. 7.00 (978-1-4357-5150-7(7)) Lulu Pr., Inc.

Weston Woods Staff, creator. Crazy Hair Day. 2011. 18.95 (978-0-545-15156-6(2)) Weston Woods Studios, Inc.

Wilkerson, L. Kobie, 3rd, reader. Fred & Mary. 2008. (Illus.). 32p. (J). 24.95 incl. DVD, audio compact disk (978-0-9796679-0-9(9)) Love II Learn Bks.

Williams-Garcia, Rita. Catching the Wild Waiyuuzee. Reed, Mike, illus. 2007. (ENG.). 32p. (J). (gr. -1-1). 12.99 (978-1-4169-6141-3(0), Simon & Schuster/Paula Wiseman Bks.) Simon & Schuster/Paula Wiseman Bks.

Williams, Vivienne. Mummy's Gorgeous Hair. Neogi, Joyeeta, illus. 2013. 26p. pap. (978-0-9576680-9-6(0)) Williams, Vivienne.

Wimberly, Nikisha. Hair Like That. Drewes, Dan, illus. 2010. 24p. 13.00 (978-1-4520-0177-7(4)) AuthorHouse.

Wood, Maryrose. Why I Let My Hair Grow Out. 2007. (ENG.). 224p. (YA). (gr. 9). 11.00 (978-0-425-21380-3(3), Berkley) Penguin Publishing Group.

Wuehr, Tina L. Neela Potts Has Lots of Knots. Brown, Mari, illus. 2008. 30p. (J). (gr. -1-3). (978-0-9739962-3-4(4)) Wuehr, Tina.

HAITI

Bartell, Jim. Haiti. 2011. (Exploring Countries Ser.). (ENG., Illus.). 32p. (J). (gr. 3-7). lib. bdg. 26.95 (978-1-60014-575-9(2), Blastoff! Readers) Bellwether Media.

Benoit, Peter. The Haitian Earthquake of 2010. 2011. (True Bk Ser.). (ENG., Illus.). 48p. (J). pap. 6.95 (978-0-531-26625-0(7)); (gr. 3-5). lib. bdg. 29.00 (978-0-531-25420-2(8)) Scholastic Library Publishing. (Children's Pr.).

Blashfield, Jean F. & Blashfield, Jean. Haiti. 2007. (Enchantment of the World Ser.). (ENG., Illus.). 144p. (YA). (gr. 5-9). 39.00 (978-0-516-25949-9(0)) Scholastic Library Publishing.

Blashfield, Jean F., et al. Countries Around the World. 2011. (Countries Around the World Ser.). (ENG., Illus.). 48p. (gr. 3-6). pap. 238.80 (978-1-4329-5244-0(7), NA-h) Heinemann-Raintree.

Callaway, Julie. My Haiti, My Homeland. 2004. (Illus.). 32p. (J). 12.50 (978-1-58432-181-1(4)) Educa Vision Inc.

Devillers, Carole. L' Histoire des Grottes D'Haiti: Racontée Par la Petite Goutte D'eau. 2014.Tr. of Story of the Caves of Haiti, Told by the Little Water Drop. (FRE & ENG., Illus.). 61p. (J). pap. 17.50 (978-1-62632-220-2(1)) Educa Vision Inc.

Freeburg, Jessica. Collapse & Chaos: The Story of the 2010 Earthquake in Haiti. 2017. (Tangled History Ser.). (ENG., Illus.). 112p. (gr. 3-4). lib. bdg. 31.99 (978-1-5157-3606-6(7)) Capstone Press of Coughlan Cos.

Gaines, Jena. Haitian Immigration. 2003. (Changing Face of North America Ser.). (Illus.). 112p. (J). lib. bdg. (978-1-59084-691-9(5)) Mason Crest.

Gritzner, Charles F. Haiti. 2nd rev. ed. 2011. (Modern World Nations Ser.). (Illus.). 118p. (gr. 6-12). 35.00 (978-1-60413-940-2(4), Chelsea Hse.) Facts On File, Inc.

Latimer, Kiki. Heal of the Hand. Griffeth, Bunny, illus. 2012. 44p. (J). pap. 19.50 (978-1-58432-851-3(7)) Educa Vision Inc.

Lies, Anne. The Earthquake in Haiti, 1 vol. 2010. (Essential Events Set 5 Ser.). (ENG., Illus.). 112p. (J). (gr. 6-12). lib. bdg. 35.64 (978-1-61613-682-6(0)) ABDO Publishing Co.

Mara, Wil. Haiti. 2006. (Discovering Cultures Ser.). (Illus.). 48p. (J). (gr. 3-7). lib. bdg. 28.50 (978-0-7614-1987-7(X), Benchmark Bks.) Marshall Cavendish Corp.

Markovics, Joyce L. Haiti. 2016. (Countries We Come From Ser.). (ENG., Illus.). 32p. (J). (gr. -1-3). lib. bdg. 19.95 (978-1-943553-36-5(X)) Bearport Publishing Co., Inc.

Nevins, Debbie. Haiti. 2016. (ENG., Illus.). 144p. (J). lib. bdg. (978-1-5026-0802-4(2)) Cavendish Square Publishing.

Ngcheong-Lum, Roseline & Jermyn, Leslie. Haiti. 2nd rev. ed. 2005. (Cultures of the World Ser.). (Illus.). 144p. (gr. 6-10). lib. bdg. 42.79 (978-0-7614-1968-6(3), Benchmark Bks.) Marshall Cavendish Corp.

Parkes, Elle. Let's Explore Haiti. 2017. (Bumba Books (tm) — Let's Explore Countries Ser.). (ENG.). 24p. (J). (gr. -1-1). lib. bdg. 25.32 (978-1-5124-3365-4(9)) Lerner Publishing Group.

Raum, Elizabeth. Haiti, 1 vol. 2011. (Countries Around the World Ser.). (ENG.). 48p. (gr. 3-6). pap. 9.95 (978-1-4329-5230-3(7)); 33.32 (978-1-4329-5205-1(6)) Heinemann-Raintree. (NA-h).

Roumain, Maryse Noel. Anacaona, Ayiti's Taino Queen/Anacaona, la Reine Taino D'Ayiti. 2012. 36p. pap. 18.41 (978-1-4669-5199-0(0)) Trafford Publishing.

Temple, Bob. Haiti. 2010. (Caribbean Today Ser.). (Illus.). 64p. (YA). (gr. 9-12). 21.95 (978-1-4222-0625-6(4)) Mason Crest.

—Haiti, Vol. 11. Henderson, James D., ed. 2015. (Discovering the Caribbean: History, Politics, & Culture Ser.). (Illus.). 64p. (J). (gr. 7). lib. bdg. 22.95 (978-1-4222-3312-2(X)) Mason Crest.

Torres, John A. Meet Our New Student from Haiti. 2008. (Meet Our New Student Ser.). (Illus.). 48p. (YA). (gr. 2-5). lib. bdg. 29.95 *(978-1-58415-653-6(8))* Mitchell Lane Pubs., Inc.
Torres, John Albert. Threat to Haiti. 2008. (On the Verge of Extinction Ser.). (Illus.). 32p. (YA). (gr. 2-5). lib. bdg. 25.70 *(978-1-58415-686-4(4))* Mitchell Lane Pubs., Inc.
Victor, Archimede J. In the Name of Liberty: A History of Haiti (Pre-1492-1806). 1000. 2004. (Illus.). 300p. (YA). per. 30.00 net. *(978-0-9720954-1-9(1))* Linive Kreyol Publishing.
Vilsaint, Fequiere. Writing about the History of Haiti. Date not set. 36p. (J). (gr. 3-6). wbk. ed. 5.50 *(978-1-881839-58-3(3))* Educa Vision Inc.
Wiseman, Blaine. Haiti. 2016. (J). ***(978-1-4896-6079-4(8))*** Weigl Pubs., Inc.
Worth, Richard. Toussaint L'Ouverture: Fighting for Haitian Independence. 2017. (Rebels with a Cause Ser.). 128p. (J). (gr. 8-8). lib. bdg. 37.27 ***(978-0-7660-8521-3(X))*** Enslow Pubs., Inc.
Yomtov, Nelson. Haiti. 2011. (Enchantment of the World Ser.). (ENG., Illus.). 144p. (J). (gr. 5-9). lib. bdg. 40.00 *(978-0-531-25353-3(8))* Scholastic Library Publishing.

HAITI—FICTION

Ali, Amani Elcheikh. Under the Rubble. 2011. 56p. 24.99 *(978-1-4568-4267-3(6))*; pap. 15.99 *(978-1-4568-4266-6(8))* Xlibris Corp.
Burg, Ann E. Serafina's Promise. (ENG.). 304p. (J). (gr. 3-7). 2015. pap. 7.99 *(978-0-545-53567-0(0))* 2013. 16.99 *(978-0-545-53564-9(5))* Scholastic, Inc. (Scholastic Pr.).
Condé, Maryse. Reves Amers. pap. 17.95 *(978-2-7470-0350-6(7))* Bayard Editions FRA. Dist: Distribooks, Inc.
Corbett, Robyn. Kokoye Kiko Yo: Kiko's Coconuts. 2013. (ENG.). 44p. (J). pap. 18.95 *(978-1-4787-1533-7(2))* Outskirts Pr., Inc.
Danticat, Edwidge. Behind the Mountains. 2004. (First Person Fiction Ser.). (ENG.). 192p. (J). (gr. 7-10). pap. 6.99 *(978-0-439-37300-5(X))*, Orchard Bks.) Scholastic, Inc.
Dauphin, Lili. I Will Fly Again: The Restavek. 2007. 284p. 29.95 *(978-0-9748329-9-9(5))*; per. 18.95 *(978-0-9748329-8-2(7))* MiraQuest.
Elvgren, Jennifer. Josias, Hold the Book. Tadgell, Nicole, illus. 2011. (ENG.). 32p. (J). (gr. 2-4). pap. 10.95 *(978-1-59078-856-1(7))* Boyds Mills Pr.
English, James. Galia's Dad Is in a Wheelchair. 2017. (ENG., Illus.). 20p. (gr. 1). pap. 6.95 ***(978-0-87565-649-6(8))*** Texas Christian Univ. Pr.
Green, Dawn A. Marianne Wellman's School for Girls. 2011. 236p. pap. 24.95 *(978-1-4626-0715-0(2))* America Star Bks.
Heurtelou, Maude. Sandra: Cinderalla in Haiti. 2004. (CRP & ENG., Illus.). 24p. (J). 8.50 *(978-1-58432-176-7(8))* Educa Vision Inc.
Lake, Nick. In Darkness. (ENG.). (YA). (gr. 9). 2014. 368p. pap. 10.99 *(978-1-61963-122-9(9))*, 9781619631229) 2012. 352p. 17.99 *(978-1-59990-743-7(7))*, 9781599907437) Bloomsbury Publishing USA. (Bloomsbury USA Childrens).
Landowne, Youme. Selavi, That Is Life: A Haitian Story of Hope. Landowne, Youme, illus. 2004. (ENG., Illus.). 40p. (J). (gr. k-2). 17.95 *(978-0-938317-84-5(9))* Cinco Puntos Pr.
StJohn, Amanda. Bouki Cuts Wood: A Haitian Folktale. Revell, Cindy, illus. 2011. (Folktales from Around the World Ser.). (ENG.). 24p. (J). (gr. k-3). 28.50 *(978-1-60973-135-9(2))*, 201140) Child's World, Inc., The.
Temple, Frances. Taste of Salt: A Story of Modern Haiti. 2004. (Trophy Bk.). (ENG.). 192p. (YA). (gr. 8-18). pap. 6.99 *(978-0-06-447136-7(5))*, HarperTeen) HarperCollins Pubs.
Trombley, Stacey. Pushing the Boundaries. 2017. (ENG., Illus.). (YA). pap. 15.99 ***(978-1-68281-386-7(X))*** Entangled Publishing, LLC.
Turnbull, Elizabeth. Bonnwit Kabrit. Vaganos, Erin, illus. 2013. 36p. 17.95 *(978-1-61153-073-5(3))* Light Messages Publishing.
Turnbull, Elizabeth J. Janjak & Freda Go to the Iron Market. Turnbull, Wally R., tr. Jones, Mark, illus. 2013. 36p. pap. 12.95 *(978-1-61153-062-9(8))* Light Messages Publishing.
Wagner, Laura Rose. Hold Tight, Don't Let Go. 2015. (ENG.). 272p. (YA). (gr. 9-17). 17.95 *(978-1-4197-1204-3(7))*, Amulet Bks.) Abrams, Inc.
Williams, Karen Lynn. Circles of Hope. Saport, Linda, illus. 2005. (ENG.). 32p. (J). 16.00 *(978-0-8028-5276-2(9))* Eerdmans, William B. Publishing Co.

HALE, NATHAN, 1755-1776

Cefrey, Holly. One Life to Lose for My Country: The Arrest & Execution of Nathan Hale. (Great Moments in American History Ser.). 32p. 2009. (gr. 3-3). 47.90 *(978-1-61513-135-8(3))* 2004. (Illus.). (gr. 4-8). lib. bdg. 22.50 *(978-0-8239-4371-5(2))*, Rosen Reference) Rosen Publishing Group, Inc., The.
DeVillier, Christy. Nathan Hale, 1 vol. 2004. (First Biographies Set Iv Ser.). (ENG., Illus.). 32p. (gr. k-4). 27.07 *(978-1-59197-513-7(1))*, Buddy Bks.) ABDO Publishing Co.
Koestler-Grack, Rachel A. Nathan Hale: Courageous Spy. 2005. (Leaders of the American Revolution Ser.). (Illus.). 100p. (gr. 5-8). lib. bdg. 30.00 *(978-0-7910-8623-0(2))* Facts On File, Inc.
Liberston, Jody. Nathan Hale: Heroe de la guerra de Independencia. 2004. (Grandes personajes en la historia de los Estados Unidos Ser.). (SPA.). 32p. (gr. 3-6). pap. 10.00 *(978-0-8239-4235-0(X))*, Rosen Classroom) Rosen Publishing Group, Inc., The.
Libertson, Jody. Nathan Hale: Hero of the American Revolution. (Primary Sources of Famous People in American History Ser.). 32p. 2009. (gr. 2-3). 47.90 *(978-1-60851-709-1(8))* 2004. (ENG., Illus.). (gr. 4-8). pap. 10.00 *(978-0-8239-4189-6(2))* Rosen Publishing Group, Inc., The.
—Nathan Hale: Héroe revolucionario / Hero of the American Revolution. 2009. (Famous People in American History/Grandes personajes en la historia de los Estados Unidos Ser.). (ENG & SPA.). 32p. (gr. 2-3). 47.90 *(978-1-61512-552-4(3))*, Editorial Buenas Letras) Rosen Publishing Group, Inc., The.
—Nathan Hale: Héroe revolucionario (Nathan Hale: Hero of the American Revolution) 2009. (Grandes personajes en la historia de los Estados Unidos (Famous People in American History) Ser.). (SPA.). 32p. (gr. 2-3). 47.90 *(978-1-61512-805-1(0))*, Editorial Buenas Letras) Rosen Publishing Group, Inc., The.
Olson, Nathan. Nathan Hale: Revolutionary Spy. Martin, Cynthia & Schoonover, Brent, illus. 2005. (Graphic Biographies Ser.). (ENG.). 32p. (gr. 3-4). 30.65 *(978-0-7368-4968-5(8))*, Graphic Library) Capstone Press of Coughlan Cos.
Olson, Nathan & Glaser, Jason. Nathan Hale: Revolutionary Spy, 1 vol. Martin, Cynthia & Schoonover, Brent, illus. 2006. (Graphic Biographies Ser.). (ENG.). 32p. (gr. 3-4). per. 8.10 *(978-0-7368-6199-1(8))*, Graphic Library) Capstone Press of Coughlan Cos.
Tracy, Kathleen. Nathan Hale. 2006. (Profiles in American History Ser.). (Illus.). 48p. (J). (gr. 3-7). lib. bdg. 29.95 *(978-1-58415-447-1(0))* Mitchell Lane Pubs., Inc.

HALE, SARAH JOSEPHA BUELL, 1788-1879

Allegra, Mike. Sarah Gives Thanks: How Thanksgiving Became a National Holiday. Gardner, David, illus. 2012. (ENG.). 32p. (J). (gr. 1-3). 16.99 *(978-0-8075-7239-9(X))* Whitman, Albert & Co.
Anderson, Laurie Halse. Thank You, Sarah: The Woman Who Saved Thanksgiving. Faulkner, Matt, illus. 2005. (ENG.). 40p. (J). (gr. k-3). 7.99 *(978-0-689-85143-8(X))*, Simon & Schuster Bks. For Young Readers) Simon & Schuster Bks. For Young Readers.
Dubois, Muriel L. To My Countrywomen: The Life of Sarah Josepha Hale. 2006. 16.00 *(978-0-9723410-1-1(3))* Apprentice Shop Bks., LLC.

HALLOWEEN

Aloian, Molly. Halloween. 2009. (Celebrations in My World Ser.). (ENG., Illus.). 32p. (J). (gr. 1-3). pap. *(978-0-7787-4310-1(1))* Crabtree Publishing Co.
Appleby, Alex. Happy Halloween!, Vol. 1. 2014. (Happy Holidays! Ser.). (ENG., Illus.). 24p. (J). (gr. k-k). 22.60 *(978-1-4339-9939-0(0))* Stevens, Gareth Publishing LLLP.
Barbaresi, Nina. Glow-in-the-Dark Halloween Stickers. 2006. (Dover Little Activity Books Stickers Ser.). (ENG., Illus.). 2p. (J). (gr. 1-4). 1.99 *(978-0-486-44922-7(X))* Dover Pubns., Inc.
Beylon, Cathy. Halloween Stained Glass Coloring Book. 2007. (Holiday Stained Glass Coloring Book Ser.). (ENG., Illus.). 32p. (J). (gr. -1-2). 6.99 *(978-0-486-45677-5(3))* Dover Pubns., Inc.
Bickico Enterprises, concept. BabyKids: Halloween Book. 2005. 16p. (J). pap. 2.95 *(978-0-9746508-6-9(2))* Bickico Enterprises, Inc.
Bloomsbury USA. My Halloween Activity & Sticker Book. 2016. (ENG., Illus.). 112p. (J). pap. 12.99 *(978-1-61963-996-6(3))*, 9781619639966, Bloomsbury Activity Bks.) Bloomsbury Publishing USA.
Bodden, Valerie. Halloween. 2005. (My First Look at Holidays Ser.). (Illus.). 24p. (J). (gr. k-3). lib. bdg. 15.95 *(978-1-58341-368-5(5))*, Creative Education) Creative Co., The.
Bond, Felicia. The Halloween Play. Bond, Felicia, illus. 2003. Orig. Title: The Halloween Performance. (Illus.). 32p. (J). (gr. -1-18). 6.99 *(978-0-06-054443-0(0))* HarperCollins Pubs.
Brennan-Nelson, Denise. J Is for Jack-O'-Lantern: A Halloween Alphabet. Wu, Donald, illus. 2009. (Holiday Ser.). (ENG.). 40p. (J). (gr. -1-3). 14.95 *(978-1-58536-443-5(6))* Sleeping Bear Pr.
—Little Halloween. Urban, Helle, illus. 2013. (Little Ser.). (ENG.). 20p. (J). (gr. -1-k). 8.99 *(978-1-58536-885-3(7))*, 202891) Sleeping Bear Pr.
Brown, Louann Mattes & Nemeth, Jason D. How to Create Spectacular Halloween Costumes, 1 vol. 2010. (Halloween Extreme Ser.). (ENG.). 32p. (gr. 3-4). lib. bdg. 27.99 *(978-1-4296-5422-7(8))*, Edge Bks.) Capstone Press of Coughlan Cos.
Bullard, Lisa. Hailey's Halloween. Conger, Holli, illus. 2012. (Cloverleaf Books (tm) — Fall & Winter Holidays Ser.). (ENG.). 24p. (gr. k-2). 6.95 *(978-0-7613-8586-8(X))*; lib. bdg. 23.93 *(978-0-7613-5083-5(7))* Lerner Publishing Group. (Millbrook Pr.).
Butterfield, Moira & Golding, Elizabeth. A Moonlight Book: Halloween Hide-And-Seek. Gray, Dean, illus. 2015. (ENG.). 12p. (J). (gr. -1-17). 10.95 *(978-0-7624-5846-2(1))*, Running Pr. Kids) Running Pr. Bk. Pubs.
Christensen, Jo-Anne. Haunted Halloween Stories Vol. 1: A Collection of Ghost Stories, 1 vol. Kubish, Shelagh, ed. rev. ed. 2003. (Ghost Stories Ser.). (ENG., Illus.). 208p. (gr. 4). pap. 12.95 *(978-1-894877-34-3(9))*, 1894877349, Ghost Hse. Bks.) Lone Pine Publishing USA.
Coffelt, Soraya Diase. It's Not about You Mr. Pumpkin: A Love Letter about the True Meaning of Halloween. 2015. (Love Letters Book Ser.). (ENG., Illus.). 32p. (J). pap. 8.99 *(978-1-63047-639-7(0))* Morgan James Publishing.
Daning, Tom. Fun-To-Make Crafts for Halloween. 2005. (Illus.). 63p. (J). *(978-0-329-43124-2(2))* Boyds Mills Pr.
Disney Book Group. Disney Baby My First Halloween. Disney Storybook Art Team, illus. 2017. (ENG.). 12p. (J). (gr. -1 — 1). bds. 8.99 ***(978-1-4847-9936-9(4))*** Disney Pr.
Dolby, Karen. Spooks' Surprise. Marks, Alan, illus. 2003. (Young Puzzle Adventures Ser.). 32p. (J). (gr. 1-18). lib. bdg. 12.95 *(978-1-58086-492-3(9))* EDC Publishing.
Dorling Kindersley Publishing Staff. Baby Touch & Feel: Halloween. 2017. (Baby Touch & Feel Ser.). (ENG., Illus.). 14p. (J). (— 1). bds. 5.99 ***(978-1-4654-6235-0(X))***, DK Children) Dorling Kindersley Publishing, Inc.
—Ultimate Sticker Book Halloween. 2017. (Ultimate Sticker Bks.). (ENG.). 32p. (J). (gr. k-2). pap. 6.99 ***(978-1-4654-6406-4(9))***, DK Children) Dorling Kindersley Publishing, Inc.
Dorling Kindersley Publishing Staff & Pearson, Nicole. My First Halloween Board Book. 2012. (My First Bks.). (ENG.). 36p. (J). (gr. -1-k). bds. 5.99 *(978-0-7566-9856-0(1))*, DK Children) Dorling Kindersley Publishing, Inc.
Douglas, Bettye. Safari Oklahoma Presents: The Magic of Christmas Around the World. Douglas, Bettye, ed. Douglas, Punchye, illus. (Multicultural). 16p. (J). (gr. k-6). 5.00 *(978-0-9703183-4-3(0))* Douglas, Bettye Forum, Inc., The.
Douglas, Punchye, illus. Safari Oklahoma Presents Operation Safe 2000: Halloween Coloring Book. (Safari Oklahoma Presents). 16p. (J). (gr. k-6). 5.00 *(978-0-9703183-2-9(4))* Douglas, Bettye Forum, Inc., The.
Dover Publications Inc. Staff, ed. Boxed/Decorate for Halloween Fun Kit. 2008. (Dover Fun Kits Ser.). (ENG.). 12p. (J). (gr. 1). pap. 16.95 *(978-0-486-46792-4(9))* Dover Pubns., Inc.
Esbaum, Jill. Seed, Sprout, Pumpkin, Pie. 2009. (Picture the Seasons Ser.). (ENG., Illus.). 16p. (J). (gr. -1-3). pap. 5.95 *(978-1-4263-0582-5(6))*, National Geographic Children's Bks.) National Geographic Society.
Felix, Rebecca. We Celebrate Halloween in Fall. 2013. (J). *(978-1-61080-978-8(5))*; (ENG.). 24p. 22.79 *(978-1-61080-903-0(3))*, 202591); (ENG.). 24p. pap. 12.79 *(978-1-61080-928-3(9))*, 202593) Cherry Lake Publishing.
Freedman, Claire. Monstersaurus. Cort, Ben, illus. 2013. (J). *(978-1-4351-4952-6(1))* Barnes & Noble, Inc.
Friedman, Pamela. Activités d'Halloween. Bauer, Larry, illus. (FRE.). 16p. pap. *(978-0-439-00533-3(7))* Scholastic Canada, Ltd.
Gibbons, Gail. Halloween Is... 2003. (ENG., Illus.). 32p. (J). (gr. k-3). pap. 7.99 *(978-0-8234-1797-1(2))* Holiday Hse., Inc.
Gillespie, Katie. Halloween. 2015. (Let's Celebrate American Holidays Ser.). (ENG.). (J). lib. bdg. 27.13 *(978-1-4896-3621-8(8))*, AV2 by Weigl) Weigl Pubs., Inc.
Gleisner, Jenna Lee. It's Halloween! 2017. (Welcome, Fall! Ser.). (ENG.). 24p. (J). (gr. -1-2). lib. bdg. 27.07 *(978-1-5038-1661-9(3))*, 211499) Child's World, Inc., The.
Goeller, Dorothy. Halloween. 2010. (All about Holidays Ser.). (Illus.). 24p. (J). 22.60 *(978-0-7660-3807-3(6))*; pap. 7.95 *(978-1-59845-176-4(6))* Enslow Pubs., Inc. (Enslow Elementary).
Golden Books. Halloweenie Genies! (Shimmer & Shine) Aikins, David, illus. 2016. (Color Plus Cardstock & Stickers Ser.). (ENG.). 32p. (J). (gr. -1-2). pap. 5.99 *(978-1-101-93702-0(5))*, Golden Bks.) Random Hse. Children's Bks.
Goldsworthy, Kaite. Halloween. 2011. (J). (gr. 3-5). pap. 12.95 *(978-1-61690-687-0(1))*, AV2 by Weigl); (Illus.). 24p. (YA). (gr. 2-5). 27.13 *(978-1-61690-681-8(2))* Weigl Pubs., Inc.
Grack, Rachel. Halloween. 2017. (Celebrating Holidays! Ser.). (ENG.). 24p. (J). (gr. k-3). lib. bdg. 25.95 ***(978-1-62617-621-8(3))***, Blastoff! Readers) Bellwether Media.
Greene, Carol. The Story of Halloween. Bronson, Linda, illus. 2004. 40p. (J). 15.99 *(978-0-06-027946-2(X))*; lib. bdg. 16.89 *(978-0-06-029560-8(0))* HarperCollins Pubs.
Halloween Extreme, 4 vols., Set. Incl. How to Build Hair-Raising Haunted Houses. Peterson, Megan Cooley. lib. bdg. 27.99 *(978-1-4296-5421-0(X))*; How to Carve Freakishly Cool Pumpkins. Schuette, Sarah L. lib. bdg. 27.99 *(978-1-4296-5420-3(1))*; How to Create Spectacular Halloween Costumes. Brown, Louann Mattes & Nemeth, Jason D. lib. bdg. 27.99 *(978-1-4296-5422-7(8))*; How to Make Frightening Halloween Decorations. Ipcizade, Catherine. lib. bdg. 27.99 *(978-1-4296-5423-4(6))*; (gr. 3-4). (Halloween Extreme Ser.). (ENG.). 32p. 2010. Set lib. bdg. 111.96 *(978-1-4296-5424-1(4))*, Edge Bks.) Capstone Press of Coughlan Cos.
Halloween Hunt. 64p. (YA). (gr. 6-12). pap. *(978-0-8224-2334-8(0))* Globe Fearon Educational Publishing.
Harte, May. Halloween. 2009. (My Library of Holidays Ser.). 24p. (gr. 1-1). 37.50 *(978-1-61514-694-9(6))*, PowerKids Pr.) Rosen Publishing Group, Inc., The.
—Halloween. Gonzalez, Tomas, tr. from ENG. 2004. (My Library of Holidays). (SPA & ENG., Illus.). 24p. (J). (gr. 1-2). lib. bdg. 16.00 *(978-1-4042-7529-4(0))*, 1219514, PowerKids Pr.) Rosen Publishing Group, Inc., The.
Heiligman, Deborah & U. S. National Geographic Society Staff. Celebrate Halloween: With Pumpkins, Costumes, & Candy. 2009. (Holidays Around the World Ser.). (ENG., Illus.). 32p. (J). (gr. 1-4). 6.95 *(978-1-4263-0477-4(3))*, National Geographic Children's Bks.) National Geographic Society.
Higgs, Liz Curtis. The Pumpkin Patch Parable. (Parable Ser.). 2005. 32p. (J). pap. 3.99 *(978-1-4003-0668-8(X))* 2006. (ENG., Illus.). 36p. (gr. -1-2). 7.99 *(978-1-4003-0846-0(1))* Nelson, Thomas Inc.
Highlights for Children Editorial Staff, creator. Halloween Fun. 2016. (Highlights(tm) Carry-And-Play Board Bks.). (ENG.). 24p. (J). (gr. -1-k). bds. 8.99 *(978-1-62979-710-6(3))*, Highlights) Boyds Mills Pr.
Hinkler Studios Staff., ed. Baby's First Halloween. 2011. (Baby's First Ser.). 12p. (J). bds. 5.99 *(978-1-74184-700-0(1))* Hinkler Bks. Pty. Ltd. AUS. Dist: Ideals Pubns.
Hopkins, Lee Bennett. Halloween Howls: Holiday Poetry. Schuett, Stacey, illus. 2005. (I Can Read Bks.). 32p. (J). (gr. k-3). lib. bdg. 16.89 *(978-0-06-008061-7(2))* HarperCollins Pubs.
Hubbell, Patricia & Hubbell. Boo! Halloween Poems & Limericks, 1 vol. Spackman, Jeff, illus. 2005. (ENG.). 32p. (YA). pap. 5.95 *(978-0-7614-5151-8(X))* Marshall Cavendish Corp.
Ipcizade, Catherine. How to Make Frightening Halloween Decorations, 1 vol. 2010. (Halloween Extreme Ser.). (ENG.). 32p. (gr. 3-4). lib. bdg. 27.99 *(978-1-4296-5423-4(6))*, Edge Bks.) Capstone Press of Coughlan Cos.
Johnson, J. Angelique. Making a Jack-O'-Lantern, Step by Step. 2011. (Step-By-Step Stories Ser.). (ENG.). 32p. (gr. 1-2). lib. bdg. 27.32 *(978-1-4296-6023-5(6))*, Aplus Bks.) Capstone Press of Coughlan Cos.
Jones, Theodore. Halloween's Spooky History. 2016. (History of Our Holidays Ser.). (ENG., Illus.). 24p. (J). (gr. 1-2). pap. 8.15 *(978-1-4824-3890-1(9))* Stevens, Gareth Publishing LLLP.
Keogh, Josie. Halloween. 2013. (PowerKids Readers: Happy Holidays! Ser.). (ENG., Illus.). 24p. (J). (gr. k-2). pap. 8.25 *(978-1-4488-9702-5(5))*; lib. bdg. 22.60 *(978-1-4488-9623-3(1))* Rosen Publishing Group, Inc., The. (PowerKids Pr.).
—Halloween. Alamán, Eduardo, tr. from SPA. 2013. (PowerKids Readers: Happy Holidays! / ¡Felices Fiestas! Ser.). (ENG & SPA., Illus.). 24p. (J). (gr. k-2). lib. bdg. 22.60 *(978-1-4488-9966-1(4))*, PowerKids Pr.) Rosen Publishing Group, Inc., The.
Kessel, Joyce K. Halloween. Carlson, Nancy, illus. 2007. (Yo Solo - Festividades (on My Own - Holidays) Ser.). (SPA.). (gr. 2-4). pap. 39.62 *(978-0-8225-9676-9(8))* Lerner Publishing Group.
—Halloween. Translations.com Staff, tr. from ENG. Carlson, Nancy, illus. 2007. (Yo Solo - Festividades (on My Own - Holidays) Ser.). (SPA.). 48p. (gr. 2-4). lib. bdg. 25.26 *(978-0-8225-7790-4(9))*; per. 6.95 *(978-0-8225-7793-5(3))* Lerner Publishing Group.
Kubish, Shelagh & Craig, Lee, eds. Pumpkin Carving, 1 vol., Vol. 1. rev. ed. 2003. (Ghost Stories Ser.). (ENG., Illus.). 48p. (gr. 4). pap. 7.95 *(978-1-894877-26-8(8))*, 1894877268, Ghost Hse. Bks.) Lone Pine Publishing USA.
Lee, Sally. A Short History of Halloween. 2015. (Holiday Histories Ser.). (ENG.). 24p. (gr. k-1). lib. bdg. 26.65 *(978-1-4914-6096-2(2))* Capstone Press of Coughlan Cos.
Levy, Barbara Soloff. How to Draw Halloween Pictures. 2010. (Dover How to Draw Ser.). (ENG., Illus.). 64p. (J). (gr. k-5). pap. 4.99 *(978-0-486-47671-1(5))* Dover Pubns., Inc.
Lewis, Anne Margaret. What Am I? Halloween. Mills, Tom, illus. 2011. (ENG.). 24p. (J). (gr. -1 — 1). bds. 9.99 *(978-0-8075-8959-5(4))* Whitman, Albert & Co.
Lindeen, Mary. Halloween! 2015. (BeginningtoRead Ser.). (ENG., Illus.). 32p. (J). (gr. k-2). lib. bdg. 22.60 *(978-1-59953-689-7(7))* Norwood Hse. Pr.
—Halloween. 2015. (BeginningtoRead Ser.). (ENG.). 32p. (J). (gr. k-2). pap. 11.94 *(978-1-60357-749-6(1))* Norwood Hse. Pr.
Limós, Anna. Haunted House Adventure Crafts. 2010. (Fun Adventure Crafts Ser.). (Illus.). 32p. (J). pap. 7.95 *(978-0-7660-3731-1(2))*, Enslow Elementary) Enslow Pubs., Inc.
Machell, Dawn, illus. Super Sticker Activity: Tricks & Treats. 2016. (Super Sticker Activity Ser.). (ENG.). 32p. (J). (gr. -1). 5.99 *(978-1-62686-705-5(4))*, Silver Dolphin Bks.) Readerlink Distribution Services, LLC.
Margaret, Amy. Halloween. 2009. (Library of Holidays Ser.). 24p. (gr. 2-3). 42.50 *(978-1-60853-712-9(9))*, PowerKids Pr.) Rosen Publishing Group, Inc., The.
Marsh, Laura. Halloween. 2012. (Readers Ser.). (ENG., Illus.). 32p. (J). (gr. -1-1). pap. 3.99 *(978-1-4263-1034-8(X))*, National Geographic Children's Bks.) National Geographic Society.
—National Geographic Readers: Halloween. 2012. (Readers Ser.). (ENG., Illus.). 32p. (J). (gr. -1-1). lib. bdg. 13.90 *(978-1-4263-1035-5(8))*, National Geographic Children's Bks.) National Geographic Society.
Mass, Wendy. Celebrate Halloween. 2006. (Celebrate Holidays Ser.). (Illus.). 104p. (J). (gr. 3-7). lib. bdg. 33.27 *(978-0-7660-2491-5(1))* Enslow Pubs., Inc.
Matters, Print & Montillo, Roseanne. Halloween & Commemorations of the Dead. 2009. (Holidays & Celebration Ser.). (Illus.). 104p. (gr. 5-8). 40.00 *(978-1-60413-097-3(0))*, Chelsea Hse.) Facts On File, Inc.
Mazurkiewicz, Jessica. HalloweenScapes. 2011. (Dover Holiday Coloring Book Ser.). (ENG.). 32p. (J). (gr. 2-5). pap. 3.99 *(978-0-486-48179-1(4))* Dover Pubns., Inc.
—3-D Coloring Book — Happy Halloween. 2011. (Dover 3-D Coloring Book Ser.). (ENG., Illus.). 32p. (J). (gr. 2-6). pap. 5.99 *(978-0-486-48411-2(4))* Dover Pubns., Inc.
McCabe, Dennis, illus. Haunted Halloween: Color & Create with Spooky Stickers. 2004. 10p. (J). (gr. -1-18). bds. 4.99 *(978-1-57151-730-2(8))* Playhouse Publishing.
McGee, Randel. Paper Crafts for Halloween. (Paper Craft Fun for Holidays Ser.). (Illus.). 48p. (J). (gr. 3-4). 2012. pap. 8.95 *(978-1-4644-0325-5(2))* 2009. lib. bdg. 25.27 *(978-0-7660-2947-7(6))* Enslow Pubs., Inc. (Enslow Elementary).
Mead, Brian. The Spooky Halloween Cut & Color Activity Book. 2003. 48p. (J). (gr. -1-3). pap. 3.99 *(978-0-9717509-1-3(2))* Mead, Brian Publishing.
Mercer, Abbie. Happy Halloween. (Holiday Fun Ser.). 24p. (gr. 2-3). 2009. 42.50 *(978-1-61513-375-8(5))*, PowerKids Pr.) 2007. (Illus.). (J). lib. bdg. 22.60 *(978-1-4042-3806-0(9))* Rosen Publishing Group, Inc., The.
Morey, Allan. Halloween. Mulryan, Doreen, illus. 2017. (Holidays in Rhythm & Rhyme Ser.). (ENG.). 24p. (gr. 1-3). 33.99 ***(978-1-68410-031-6(3))*** Cantata Learning.
Murphy, Angela. The Tricks & Treats of Halloween! Wake, Rich, illus. 2014. (History of Fun Stuff Ser.). (ENG.). 48p. (J). (gr. 1-3). pap. 3.99 *(978-1-4814-0978-0(6))*, Simon Spotlight) Simon Spotlight.
Murray, Julie. Halloween, 1 vol. 2003. (Holidays Ser.). (ENG.). 24p. (gr. k-4). 25.65 *(978-1-57765-952-5(X))*, Buddy Bks.) ABDO Publishing Co.
My Spooky Halloween Activity & Sticker Book. 2014. (Sticker Activity Bks.). (ENG.). 32p. (J). (gr. -1-1). pap. 4.99 *(978-1-61963-332-2(9))*, 9781619633322, Bloomsbury USA Childrens) Bloomsbury Publishing USA.
Nudelman, Edwar, ed. A Halloween Reader. 2004. (Illus.). 12p. 8.95 *(978-1-58980-260-5(8))* Pelican Publishing Co., Inc.
O'Connell, Jennifer Barrett. It's Halloween Night! Morris, Jennifer E., illus. 2012. (ENG.). 32p. (J). (gr. -1-k). pap. 6.99 *(978-0-545-40283-5(2))*, Cartwheel Bks.) Scholastic, Inc.
O'Connor, Rachel. Halloween / Halloween. 2009. (My Library of Holidays / Mi biblioteca de celebraciones Ser.). (ENG & SPA.). 24p. (gr. 1-1). 37.50 *(978-1-61514-700-7(4))*, Editorial Buenas Letras) Rosen Publishing Group, Inc., The.
Owen, Ruth. The Halloween Gross-Out Guide, 1 vol., 1. 2014. (DIY for Boys Ser.). (ENG.). 32p. (J). (gr. 3-6). 27.50 *(978-1-4777-6290-5(6))*, PowerKids Pr.) Rosen Publishing Group, Inc., The.
—Halloween Origami. 2012. (Holiday Origami Ser.). (ENG., Illus.). 32p. (J). (gr. 3-6). 26.50 *(978-1-4488-7862-8(4))*; pap. 11.75 *(978-1-4488-7921-2(3))* Rosen Publishing Group, Inc., The. (PowerKids Pr.).
—More Halloween Origami, 1 vol. 2015. (Holiday Origami Ser.). (ENG.). 32p. (J). 27.50 *(978-1-4777-5702-4(3))*, PowerKids Pr.) Rosen Publishing Group, Inc., The.
Pearson, Maria, illus. Spooky Stencil Cards. 2008. (Stencil Cards Ser.). 16p. (J). 9.99 *(978-0-7945-2415-9(X))*, Usborne) EDC Publishing.
Peterson, Megan Cooley & Rustad, Martha E. H. Black Cats, 1 vol. 2013. (Halloween Fun Ser.). (ENG.). 24p. (gr. k-1). lib. bdg. 26.65 *(978-1-4765-2181-7(6))*, Pebble Plus) Capstone Press of Coughlan Cos.
—Celebrate Halloween, 1 vol. 2013. (Halloween Fun Ser.). (ENG.). 24p. (gr. k-1). lib. bdg. 26.65 *(978-1-4765-2183-1(2))*, Pebble Plus) Capstone Press of Coughlan Cos.
—Halloween Fun. 2013. (Halloween Fun Ser.). (ENG.). 24p. (gr. k-1). lib. bdg. 106.60 *(978-1-4765-3702-3(X))*, Pebble Plus) Capstone Press of Coughlan Cos.
—Jack-O'-Lanterns, 1 vol. 2013. (Halloween Fun Ser.). (ENG.). 24p. (gr. k-1). 26.65 *(978-1-4765-2180-0(8))*, Pebble Plus) Capstone Press of Coughlan Cos.

H
I

—Trick-Or-Treat Safety, 1 vol. 2013. (Halloween Fun Ser.). (ENG.). 24p. (gr. k-1). 26.65 *(978-1-4765-2182-4(4)*, Pebble Plus) Capstone Press of Coughlan Cos.

Peterson, Megan Cooley, et al. How to Build Hair-Raising Haunted Houses, 1 vol. 2010. (Halloween Extreme Ser.). (ENG.). 32p. (gr. 3-4). lib. bdg. 27.99 *(978-1-4296-5421-0(X)*, Edge Bks.) Capstone Press of Coughlan Cos.

Pettiford, Rebecca. Halloween. 2015.Tr. of Halloween. (Illus.). 24p. (J). (SPA.). lib. bdg. *(978-1-62031-243-8(3))*; lib. bdg. *(978-1-62031-185-1(2))* Jump! Inc. (Bullfrog Bks.).

Platt, Richard. Halloween. Watson, Richard, illus. 2017. (Flip Flap Journeys Ser.). (ENG.). 14p. (J). (gr. k-2). 12.99 ***(978-1-4052-7659-7(2))*** Egmont Bks., Ltd. GBR. Dist: Independent Pubs. Group.

Ponto, Joanna & Robinson, Fay. Halloween. 2016. (Story of Our Holidays Ser.). (Illus.). 32p. (J). (gr. 3-3). pap. 10.52 *(978-0-7660-7650-1(4))* Enslow Pubs., Inc.

Priddy, Roger. Funny Faces Halloween Jack. 2012. (Funny Faces Ser.). (ENG., Illus.). 10p. (J). (gr. -1-1). bds. 8.99 *(978-0-312-51554-6(5)*, 9780312515546, Priddy Bks.) St. Martin's Pr.

—Funny Faces Haunted House. 2012. (Funny Faces Ser.). (ENG., Illus.). 10p. (J). (gr. -1-1). bds. 8.99 *(978-0-312-51557-7(X)*, 9780312515577, Priddy Bks.) St. Martin's Pr.

—Slide & Find Spooky. 2011. (ENG., Illus.). 8p. (J). (— 1). bds. 8.99 *(978-0-312-51095-4(0)*, 9780312510954, Priddy Bks.) St. Martin's Pr.

—Sticker Friends: Halloween. 2016. (ENG., Illus.). 24p. (J). pap. 4.99 *(978-0-312-52020-5(4)*, 9780312520205, Priddy Bks.) St. Martin's Pr.

—Vampire Pets. 2014. (Funny Faces Ser.). (ENG.). 10p. (J). (gr. -1-1). bds. 8.99 *(978-0-312-51721-2(1)*, 9780312517212, Priddy Bks.) St. Martin's Pr.

Rabe, Tish. Halloween Fun for Everyone! (Dr. Seuss/Cat in the Hat) Brannon, Tom, illus. 2016. (ENG.). 12p. (J). (— 1). bds. 9.99 *(978-1-101-93495-1(6)*, Random Hse. Bks. for Young Readers) Random Hse. Children's Bks.

Radtke, Becky J. Halloween Color by Number. 2017. (Dover Children's Activity Bks.). (ENG.). 32p. (J). (gr. -1-2). pap. 3.99 *(978-0-486-81216-8(2))* Dover Pubns., Inc.

Rau, Dana Meachen. Creating Halloween Crafts. Petelinsek, Kathleen, illus. 2013. (How-To Library). (ENG.). 32p. (J). (gr. 3-6). pap. 14.21 *(978-1-62431-281-6(0)*, 202918) Cherry Lake Publishing.

Robinson, Fay. Fun Halloween Crafts. 2015. (Kid Fun Holiday Crafts! Ser.). 32p. (J). (gr. 3-4). 23.94 *(978-0-7660-6235-1(X))*; pap. 7.95 *(978-0-7660-6236-8(8)*, Enslow Elementary) Enslow Pubs., Inc.

—Halloween: Disfraces y Golosinas en la Vispera de Todos los Santos. 2005. (Días Festivos Ser.). (SPA., Illus.). 48p. (J). (gr. 3-4). lib. bdg. 25.27 *(978-0-7660-2614-8(0)*, Enslow Elementary) Enslow Pubs., Inc.

—Halloween Crafts. 2004. (Fun Holiday Crafts Kids Can Do! Ser.). (Illus.). 32p. (J). lib. bdg. 23.94 *(978-0-7660-2236-2(6))* Enslow Pubs., Inc.

Ross, Dave. The Not-so-Scary Monster Handbook: Halloween. Ross, Dave, illus. 2003. (Illus.). (J). 135.44 *(978-0-06-055492-7(4))* HarperCollins Pubs.

Ross, Kathy. All New Crafts for Halloween. Leonard, Barbara, illus. 2003. (All New Holiday Crafts for Kids Ser.). 48p. lib. bdg. 23.90 *(978-0-7613-2554-3(9)*, Millbrook Pr.) Lerner Publishing Group.

—All New Crafts for Halloween. Leonard, Barbara & Holm, Sharon, illus. 2003. (All New Holiday Crafts for Kids Ser.). (ENG.). 48p. (gr. k-3). pap. 7.95 *(978-0-7613-1577-3(2)*, Millbrook Pr.) Lerner Publishing Group.

Rowlands, Caroline. The Halloween Tattoo Book: With 24 Spooky Play Tattoos to Wear & Share! 2013. (ENG.). 48p. (J). (gr. 1-5). pap. 6.99 *(978-1-4380-0325-2(0))* Barron's Educational Series, Inc.

Roytman, Arkady. Build-a-Window Halloween Stained Glass Coloring Book. 2011. (Build Window Stained Glass Coloring Book Ser.). (ENG., Illus.). 32p. (J). (gr. 3-5). pap. 6.99 *(978-0-486-48391-7(6))* Dover Pubns., Inc.

Savage, Christine Lyseng & Poulin, Rosa. Halloween Recipes & Crafts, 1 vol., Vol. 1. Eder, Tamara, photos by. rev. ed. 2003. (Ghost Stories Ser.). (ENG., Illus.). 160p. (gr. 4). pap. 9.95 *(978-1-894877-10-7(1)*, 1894877101, Ghost Hse. Bks.) Lone Pine Publishing USA.

Schaefer, Lola M. Boo Who? A Foldout Halloween Adventure. Frost, Michael, photos by. 2009. (ENG., Illus.). 12p. (J). (gr. -1-k). bds. 7.99 *(978-1-4169-5911-3(4)*, Little Simon) Little Simon.

Schuette, Sarah L. A Halloween Cookbook: Simple Recipes for Kids, 1 vol. 2012. (First Cookbooks Ser.). (ENG., Illus.). 24p. (gr. 1-2). lib. bdg. 25.32 *(978-1-4296-7619-9(1)*, First Facts) Capstone Press of Coughlan Cos.

—Halloween Hunt: A Spot-It Challenge, 1 vol. 2010. (Spot It Ser.). (ENG.). 32p. (gr. 1-2). lib. bdg. 27.32 *(978-1-4296-4460-0(5)*, Aplus Bks.) Capstone Press of Coughlan Cos.

—How to Carve Freakishly Cool Pumpkins, 1 vol. 2010. (Halloween Extreme Ser.). (ENG.). 32p. (gr. 3-4). lib. bdg. 27.99 *(978-1-4296-5420-3(1)*, Edge Bks.) Capstone Press of Coughlan Cos.

Sebra, Richard. It's Halloween! 2016. (Bumba Books (tm) — It's a Holiday! Ser.). (ENG., Illus.). 24p. (J). (gr. -1-1). lib. bdg. 25.32 *(978-1-5124-1430-1(1))* Lerner Publishing Group.

Semple, Veronique & Semple, J. J. Halloween Ooga-Ooga Ooum. Semple, J. J., ed. Turner, Suzette, illus. 2011. (ENG.). 38p. (J). 9.95 *(978-0-9795331-5-0(5)*, Zardoz Pr.) Life Force Bks.

Sévigny, Eric, illus. Caillou: Happy Halloween. 2nd ed. 2012. (ENG.). 24p. (J). (gr. -1-1). pap. 4.99 *(978-2-89450-932-6(4))* Caillouet, Gerry.

Smith, Mary Lou. Celebrate Halloween. 2015. (Our Holidays Ser.). (ENG., Illus.). 24p. (J). (gr. 1-1). pap. 8.22 *(978-1-5026-0415-6(9))* Cavendish Square Publishing.

Stevens, Kathryn. Halloween Jack-O'-Lanterns. 2015. (Our Holiday Symbols Ser.). (ENG.). 24p. (J). (gr. 1-4). 25.64 *(978-1-63143-745-8(3)*, 208554) Child's World, Inc., The.

Stortz, Diane. Let's Shine Jesus' Light on Halloween. 2014. (Happy Day Ser.). (ENG.). (J). pap. 2.49 *(978-1-4143-9420-6(9)*, Happy Day) Tyndale Hse. Pubs.

Stowell, Louie. Spooky Sticker Dressing. 2012. (Sticker Dressing Ser.). 34p. (J). pap. 8.99 *(978-0-7945-3259-8(4)*, Usborne) EDC Publishing.

Tallarico, Tony J., Jr. Frightfully Fun Halloween Activity Book. 2009. (Dover Children's Activity Bks.). (ENG., Illus.). 48p. (J). (gr. -1-8). pap. 4.99 *(978-0-486-47131-0(4))* Dover Pubns., Inc.

Thomas Nelson. Maze Activity Books Halloween. 2016. (ENG.). 38p. (J). (gr. -1-7). pap. *(978-1-78598-399-3(7))* Make Believe Ideas.

Tiger Tales, ed. & compiled by. Halloween Surprise. Tiger Tales, compiled by. 2014. (My First Lift & Learn Ser.). (ENG.). 10p. (J). (gr. -1 — 1). bds. 7.99 *(978-1-58925-571-5(2))* Tiger Tales.

Toufexis, George. Halloween Super Sticker Book. 2011. (Dover Sticker Bks.). (ENG., Illus.). 1p. (J). (gr. 1-5). 7.99 *(978-0-486-48380-1(0))* Dover Pubns., Inc.

Trueit, Trudi Strain. Halloween. 2010. (Benchmark Rebus: Holiday Fun Ser.). 24p. (gr. k-1). 15.95 *(978-0-7614-4886-0(1))* Marshall Cavendish Corp.

Twin Sisters(r) Staff. Five Trick or Treaters. 2009. 16p. 4.99 *(978-1-59922-417-6(8))* Twin Sisters IP, LLC.

—Kids' Halloween Party. 2009. 16p. 4.99 *(978-1-59922-419-0(4))*; 64p. 9.99 *(978-1-59922-424-4(0))*; 6.99 *(978-1-59922-350-6(3))*; 9.99 *(978-1-59922-335-3(X))* Twin Sisters IP, LLC.

U. S. National Geographic Society Staff. Halloween Book of Fun! 2011. (ENG., Illus.). 80p. (J). (gr. 1-4). pap. 6.99 *(978-1-4263-0848-2(5)*, National Geographic Children's Bks.) National Geographic Society.

Vega, Ali. Witches' Brew & Other Horrifying Party Foods. 2017. (Little Kitchen of Horrors Ser.). (ENG.). 32p. (J). (gr. 2-5). 12.99 ***(978-1-5124-3777-5(8)***, Lerner Pubns.); 39.99 ***(978-1-5124-2808-7(6)***, Lerner Pubns.); 39.99 ***(978-1-5124-3776-8(X)***, Lerner Pubns.); (Illus.). 26.65 *(978-1-5124-2576-5(1))* Lerner Publishing Group.

Venturi-Pickett, Stacy. The Halloween. (Illus.). 24p. (J). pap., act. bk. ed. 4.95 *(978-0-8249-5303-4(7)*, Ideal Pubns.) Worthy Publishing.

Vidrine, Beverly Barras. Halloween Alphabet, 1 vol. Lyne, Alison Davis, illus. 2004. (ENG.). 32p. (J). (gr. k-1). pap. 8.95 *(978-1-58980-242-1(X))* Pelican Publishing Co., Inc.

Walker, Sylvia. Halloween ABC Coloring Book. 2011. (Dover Holiday Coloring Book Ser.). (ENG.). 32p. (J). (gr. -1-3). pap. 3.99 *(978-0-486-48175-3(1))* Dover Pubns., Inc.

Watt, F. Halloween Activities. 2004. (Illus.). 32p. (J). pap., act. bk. ed. 6.95 *(978-0-7945-0337-6(3))* EDC Publishing.

Watt, Fiona. Spooky Sticker Book. 2008. (Sticker Bks). (Illus.). 32p. (J). pap. 8.99 *(978-0-7945-2342-8(0)*, Usborne) EDC Publishing.

Williams, Colleen Madonna Flood. My Adventure on Halloween. 2006. 44p. (J). 8.99 *(978-1-59092-549-2(1))* Blue Forge Pr.

Yoon, Salina. One Halloween Night: A Spooky Seek-and-Count Book. 2011. (ENG., Illus.). 14p. (J). bds. 6.95 *(978-1-4027-8413-2(9))* Sterling Publishing Co., Inc.

Zocchi, Judy. On Halloween Night. Wallis, Rebecca, illus. 2005. (Holiday Happenings Ser.). (J). 32p. pap. 10.95 *(978-1-59646-220-5(5))*; (ENG.). 32p. lib. bdg. 21.65 *(978-1-891997-77-8(7))*; per. 10.95 *(978-1-59646-221-2(3))* Dingles & Co.

—On Halloween Night/la noche de Halloween. Wallis, Rebecca, illus. 2005. (Holiday Happenings Ser.).Tr. of noche de Halloween. 32p. (J). pap. 10.95 *(978-1-59646-222-9(1))*; (ENG & SPA.). per. 10.95 *(978-1-59646-223-6(X))* Dingles & Co.

—On Halloween Night/la Noche de Halloween. Wallis, Rebecca, illus. 2005. (Holiday Happenings Ser.). (ENG & SPA.). 32p. (J). lib. bdg. 21.65 *(978-1-891997-76-1(9))* Dingles & Co.

HALLOWEEN—FICTION

Aaron, Taylor. Pumpkin Goblin Makes Friends. 2008. 36p. (J). 16.95 *(978-1-934572-00-9(4))* Emerald Bk. Co.

Abramsen, Ruth M. Akeelah's Spider. 2008. 36p. per. 13.95 *(978-1-59800-440-3(9))* Outskirts Pr., Inc.

Accord Publishing Staff & Stone, Kate. One Spooky Night: A Halloween Adventure. 2011. (ENG.). 36p. (J). pap. 11.99 *(978-1-4494-0330-0(1))* Andrews McMeel Publishing.

Adams, Adrienne. A Woggle of Witches. Adams, Adrienne, illus. 2017. (ENG., Illus.). 32p. (J). (gr. -1-3). 13.99 ***(978-1-5344-1246-0(8)***, Aladdin) Simon & Schuster Children's Publishing.

Adams, Michelle Medlock. What Is Halloween? Wummer, Amy, illus. 2007. (ENG.). 26p. (J). (gr. -1-3). bds. 6.99 *(978-0-8249-6712-3(7)*, Ideal Pubns.) Worthy Publishing.

Albee, Sarah. Halloween ABC. Woolf, Julia, illus. 2009. (Little Golden Book Ser.). (ENG.). 24p. (J). (gr. -1-k). 4.99 *(978-0-375-84823-0(1)*, Golden Bks.) Random Hse. Children's Bks.

Alleyne, Pat. The Night They Came Out to Play, 1 vol. 2010. 48p. pap. 16.95 *(978-1-4489-4533-7(X))* America Star Bks.

Anderson, Connie Kingrey. Toadies. 2013. (Creepers Mysteries Ser.: Bk. 2). (ENG.). 142p. (J). pap. 7.99 *(978-1-935793-03-8(9))* Movies for the Ear, LLC.

Anderson, Lonzo. Halloween Party. 2017. (ENG.). 32p. (J). (gr. -1-3). 13.99 ***(978-1-5344-1243-9(3)***, Atheneum Bks. for Young Readers) Simon & Schuster Children's Publishing.

Andrews, Julie & Hamilton, Emma Walton. A Spooky, Sparkly Halloween. 2016. (Very Fairy Princess Ser.). (J). lib. bdg. 16.00 *(978-0-606-38317-2(4))* Turtleback Bks.

Andrews, Julie & Walton Hamilton, Emma. The Very Fairy Princess: A Spooky, Sparkly Halloween. 2016. (ENG., Illus.). 32p. (J). (gr. -1-3). pap. 5.99 *(978-0-316-28326-7(6))* Little, Brown Bks. for Young Readers.

—The Very Fairy Princess: a Spooky, Sparkly Halloween. Davenier, Christine, illus. 2015. (ENG.). 32p. (J). (gr. -1-3). 18.00 *(978-0-316-28304-5(5))* Little, Brown Bks. for Young Readers.

Anthony, David & David, Charles. Heroes A2Z #2: (Heroes a to Z): Bowling over Halloween: Bowling over Halloween. Blakeslee, Lys, illus. 2007. (Heroes A2Z Ser.). 128p. (J). pap. 4.99 *(978-0-9728461-9-6(0))* Sigil Publishing.

Arena, Felice & Kettle, Phil. Halloween Gotcha! Gordon, Gus, illus. 2004. (J). pap. *(978-1-59336-373-4(7))* Mondo Publishing.

Arnett, Dee. Gifted. 2008. 240p. pap. 18.95 *(978-1-4092-0442-8(1))* Lulu Pr., Inc.

Arthur, Jenny. Little Witch. Arthur, Jenny, illus. 2012. (Spooky Sounds Ser.). (ENG., Illus.). 10p. (J). (gr. k — 1). 7.99 *(978-0-230-74487-5(7))* Macmillan Pubs., Ltd. GBR. Dist: Independent Pubs. Group.

Arthur, Sherry. Magical Hallows Eve. 2009. 44p. pap. 24.00 *(978-0-557-07264-4(6))* Lulu Pr., Inc.

Asch, Frank. Popcorn. 2015. lib. bdg. 17.20 *(978-0-606-36289-4(4))* Turtleback Bks.

Atwood, Karen. Halloween Coloring Book. 2011. (ENG.). 26p. pap. 5.38 *(978-1-4679-1124-5(0))* CreateSpace Independent Publishing Platform.

Auch, Mary Jane. Poultrygeist. Jane, Mary & Auch, Herm, illus. 2004. (ENG.). 32p. (J). (gr. k-3). reprint ed. 6.95 *(978-0-8234-1876-3(6))* Holiday Hse., Inc.

Averill, Esther. Jenny's Moonlight Adventure. 32p. (J). pap. 12.95 *(978-0-553-15145-9(2))* Random House Publishing Group.

—Jenny's Moonlight Adventure: A Jenny's Cat Club Book. Averill, Esther, illus. 2005. (New York Review Children's Collection). (ENG., Illus.). 32p. (J). (gr. -1-2). 14.00 *(978-1-59017-160-8(8)*, NYR Children's Collection) New York Review of Bks., Inc., The.

Awdry, W. A Ghost on the Track (Thomas & Friends) 2015. (Step into Reading Ser.). (ENG., Illus.). 24p. (J). (gr. -1-1). 4.99 *(978-0-553-52168-9(3)*, Random Hse. Bks. for Young Readers) Random Hse. Children's Bks.

—Thomas' Halloween Delivery (Thomas & Friends) Durk, Jim, illus. 2011. (Glow-In-the-Dark Sticker Book Ser.). (ENG.). 48p. (J). (gr. -1-2). pap. 3.99 *(978-0-375-87229-7(9)*, Golden Bks.) Random Hse. Children's Bks.

Awdry, Wilbert V. Halloween in Anopha. Courtney, Richard, illus. 2008. (Thomas in Town Ser.). (ENG.). 32p. (J). (gr. -1-2). 5.99 *(978-0-375-84413-3(9)*, Random Hse. Bks. for Young Readers) Random Hse. Children's Bks.

AZ Books Staff & Evans, Olivia. Haunted Castle. Shumovich, Nadezhda, ed. 2012. (Terribly Funny Monsters Ser.). (ENG., Illus.). 10p. (J). bds. 15.95 *(978-1-61889-134-1(0))* AZ Bks. LLC.

Ballarini, Joe. A Babysitter's Guide to Monster Hunting #1. To, Vivienne, illus. 2017. (Babysitter's Guide to Monsters Ser.: 1). 352p. (J). (gr. 3-7). 13.99 *(978-0-06-243783-9(6)*, Tegen, Katherine Bks) HarperCollins Pubs.

Banks, Steven. The Big Halloween Scare. Martinez, Heather, illus. 2003. (SpongeBob SquarePants Ser.: Vol. 1). (ENG.). 32p. (J). (gr. k-2). pap. 3.99 *(978-0-689-84196-5(5)*, Simon Spotlight/Nickelodeon) Simon Spotlight/Nickelodeon.

Beall, Pamela Conn & Nipp, Susan Hagen. Who's There on Halloween? Reasoner, Charles, illus. 2003. 18p. (J). bds. 4.99 *(978-0-8431-0495-0(3)*, Price Stern Sloan) Penguin Publishing Group.

—Who's There on Halloween? Reasoner, Charles, illus. 2003. (ENG.). 18p. (J). (gr. -1-k). bds. 5.99 *(978-0-8431-0510-0(0)*, Price Stern Sloan) Penguin Young Readers Group.

Beraducci, Deborah. Tyler's Halloween Horror, 1 vol. Eyre, Jane, illus. 2009. 22p. pap. 24.95 *(978-1-4489-2133-1(3))* America Star Bks.

Berenstain, Stan & Berenstain, Jan. The Berenstain Bears Happy Halloween! 2013. (First Time Books(R) Ser.). (ENG., Illus.). 96p. (J). (gr. -1-2). 9.99 *(978-0-385-37191-9(8)*, Random Hse. Bks. for Young Readers) Random Hse. Children's Bks.

Berenstain, Stan, et al. The Berenstain Bears & the Haunted House. 2010. (Berenstain Bears Ser.). (ENG., Illus.). 16p. (J). (gr. -1-1). pap. 6.99 *(978-0-06-057426-0(7)*, HarperFestival) HarperCollins Pubs.

Berger, Samantha. Boo-La-La Witch Spa. Roxas, Isabel, illus. 2015. (ENG.). 32p. (J). (gr. -1-k). 16.99 *(978-0-8037-3886-7(2)*, Dial Bks) Penguin Young Readers Group.

Berry, Ron. It Was a Dark Dark Night. Sharp, Chris, illus. 2012. 14p. (J). bds. 12.99 *(978-0-8249-1602-2(6)*, Ideal Pubns.) Worthy Publishing.

Biedrzycki, David. Me & My Dragon: Scared of Halloween. Biedrzycki, David, illus. 2013. (ENG., Illus.). 32p. (J). (gr. -1-3). pap. 7.95 *(978-1-58089-659-7(6))* Charlesbridge Publishing, Inc.

Billings, Tirrea. The Monster in the Basement. 2010. 12p. pap. 10.99 *(978-1-4490-2817-6(9))* AuthorHouse.

Blackburn, Winfrey P. Putney-a little pumpkin with BIG Ideas. 2007. 48p. (J). 14.95 *(978-0-9790025-5-7(9))* Acclaim Pr., Inc.

Blissman, Rodger J. Spookster the Halloween Cat. 2004. 85p. (J). (gr. 3-7). pap. 5.99 *(978-0-9745895-0-3(0))* Oxfordshire Publishing Co.

Blueraven, Solaris. Mr. Sun & the Halloween Ball. 2010. 20p. 13.99 *(978-1-4520-0431-0(5))* AuthorHouse.

Bohannon, C. S. Spatula Boy: And the Secret of the Mysterious Old House. 2007. 52p. per. 16.95 *(978-1-4241-6956-6(9))* America Star Bks.

Bollinger, Peter. Algernon Graeves Is Scary Enough. Bollinger, Peter, illus. 2005. (Illus.). 32p. (J). (gr. -1-3). lib. bdg. 15.89 *(978-0-06-052269-8(0)*, Geringer, Laura Book) HarperCollins Pubs.

Bond, Felicia. The Halloween Play. Bond, Felicia, illus. 2008. Orig. Title: The Halloween Performance. (ENG., Illus.). 32p. (J). (gr. -1-1). pap. 7.99 *(978-0-06-135796-1(0))* HarperCollins Pubs.

Borraga, Charles R. The Old Parson's House. 2008. 24p. pap. 11.49 *(978-1-4389-0698-0(6))* AuthorHouse.

Bowen, Deangelo. The Halloween Surprise. 2012. 16p. pap. 15.99 *(978-1-4685-7962-8(2))* AuthorHouse.

Bowman, Andy. Pokey's Garden. Travis, Stephanie, illus. 26p. (J). (gr. k-5). pap. 6.95 *(978-1-931650-08-3(X))*; lib. bdg. 14.95 *(978-1-931650-09-0(8))* Coastal Publishing Carolina, Inc.

Boynton, Sandra. Eek! Halloween! 2016. (ENG., Illus.). 24p. (J). bds. 6.95 *(978-0-7611-9300-5(6))* Workman Publishing Co., Inc.

Bradbury, Ray. The Halloween Tree. (J). 20.95 *(978-0-8488-0432-9(5))* Amereon Ltd.

—The Halloween Tree. Eller, Jon, ed. Bradbury, Ray & Mugnaini, Joe, illus. 2005. 494p. (J). (gr. 4-12). per. 75.00 *(978-1-887368-80-3(9))* Gauntlet, Inc.

—The Halloween Tree. Mugnaini, Joseph, illus. 2007. (ENG.). 160p. (J). (gr. 3-7). reprint ed. 15.99 *(978-0-394-82409-3(1)*, Knopf Bks. for Young Readers) Random Hse. Children's Bks.

Branning, Debe. The Adventures of Chickolet Pigolet: The Bribe of Frankenbeans. Knold, Nijlon, illus. 2008. 48p. pap. 7.95 *(978-1-935137-40-5(9))* Guardian Angel Publishing, Inc.

Brenda Jenkins. Trick or Treat Every Night. 2012. 24p. 24.95 *(978-1-4626-6055-1(X))* America Star Bks.

Brendler, Carol. Not Very Scary. Pizzoli, Greg, illus. 2014. (ENG.). 40p. (J). (gr. -1-1). 12.99 *(978-0-374-35547-0(9)*, 9780374355470, Farrar, Straus & Giroux (BYR)) Farrar, Straus & Giroux.

Brenner, Tom. And Then Comes Halloween. Meade, Holly, illus. (ENG.). 32p. (J). (gr. -1-3). 2011. pap. 6.99 *(978-0-7636-5299-9(7))* 2009. 16.99 *(978-0-7636-3659-3(2))* Candlewick Pr.

Bridwell, Norman. Clifford's First Halloween. Bridwell, Norman, illus. 2010. (Clifford Ser.). (ENG., Illus.). 20p. (J). (gr. k — 1). bds. 6.99 *(978-0-545-21774-3(1)*, Cartwheel Bks.) Scholastic, Inc.

—Clifford's Halloween. Bridwell, Norman, illus. 2011. (Clifford 8x8 Ser.). (ENG., Illus.). 32p. (J). (gr. -1-k). pap. 3.99 *(978-0-545-21595-4(1)*, Cartwheel Bks.) Scholastic, Inc.

Bridwell, Norman. Halloween. Bridwell, Norman, illus. 2017. (Clifford Ser.). (ENG., Illus.). 48p. (J). (gr. -1-k). 8.99 ***(978-1-338-18831-8(3))*** Scholastic, Inc.

Bridwell, Norman & Scholastic, Inc. Staff. The Big Red Dog. 2010. (Clifford Ser.). (ENG.). (J). (gr. -1-3). pap. 12.99 incl. audio compact disk *(978-0-545-25415-1(9))* Scholastic, Inc.

Brimner, Larry Dane. Trick or Treat, Old Armadillo. Catalano, Dominic, illus. 2010. (ENG.). 32p. (J). (gr. k-2). 16.95 *(978-1-59078-758-8(7))* Boyds Mills Pr.

Brokamp, Elizabeth. The Picky Little Witch, 1 vol. Riti, Marsha, illus. 2011. (ENG.). 32p. (J). (gr. k-3). 16.99 *(978-1-58980-882-9(7))* Pelican Publishing Co., Inc.

Brown, Lisa. Vampire Boy's Good Night. Brown, Lisa, illus. 2010. (ENG., Illus.). 32p. (J). (gr. -1-2). 16.99 *(978-0-06-114011-2(2))* HarperCollins Pubs.

Brown, Margaret Wise. The Little Scarecrow Boy. Diaz, David, illus. 2005. (ENG.). 40p. (J). (gr. -1-2). reprint ed. pap. 6.99 *(978-0-06-077891-0(1))* HarperCollins Pubs.

Brown, Margaret Wise & Brown. The Fierce Yellow Pumpkin. Egielski, Richard, illus. 2003. (ENG.). 32p. (J). (gr. -1-1). 16.99 *(978-0-06-024479-8(8))* HarperCollins Pubs.

Brown, Monica. Lola Levine & the Halloween Scream. 2017. (Lola Levine Ser.: 6). (ENG., Illus.). 96p. (J). (gr. 1-5). 15.99 ***(978-0-316-50642-7(7))***; pap. 5.99 ***(978-0-316-50643-4(5))*** Little, Brown Bks. for Young Readers.

—Lola Levine & the Halloween Scream. 2017. (Lola Levine Ser.: 6). (J). lib. bdg. 16.00 ***(978-0-606-40223-1(3))*** Turtleback Bks.

Bruel, Nick. Bad Kitty Scaredy-Cat. 2016. (Bad Kitty Ser.). (ENG., Illus.). 32p. (J). 16.99 *(978-1-59643-978-8(5)*, 9781596439788) Roaring Brook Pr.

Brugger, Ruth L. Count Candy Corn. 2013. 32p. pap. 13.99 *(978-1-4808-0190-5(9))* Archway Publishing.

Bullard, Lisa. Trick-or-Treat on Milton Street. Oeltjenbruns, Joni, illus. (Carolrhoda Picture Books Ser.). 32p. (J). 2004. (ENG.). (gr. k-4). pap. 6.95 *(978-1-57505-793-4(X))* 2003. (gr. -1-3). 15.95 *(978-1-57505-158-1(3)*, Carolrhoda Bks.) Lerner Publishing Group.

Bunting, Eve. The Bones of Fred McFee. Cyrus, Kurt, illus. 2005. (ENG.). 32p. (J). (gr. -1-3). pap. 7.99 *(978-0-15-205423-6(5))* Houghton Mifflin Harcourt Publishing Co.

—In the Haunted House. Meddaugh, Susan, illus. 2013. (ENG.). 16p. (J). (gr. -1-3). 6.99 *(978-0-544-06670-0(7))* Houghton Mifflin Harcourt Publishing Co.

—Scary, Scary Halloween, 1 vol. Brett, Jan, illus. 2013. (ENG.). 40p. (J). (gr. -1-3). audio compact disk 10.99 *(978-0-544-11114-1(1))* Houghton Mifflin Harcourt Publishing Co.

Burkhart, Jessica. Masquerade. 2012. (Canterwood Crest Ser.: 16). lib. bdg. 18.40 *(978-0-606-26887-5(1)*, Turtleback) Turtleback Bks.

Burton, Tim & Disney Book Group Staff. Nightmare Before Christmas. Burton, Tim, illus. 20th anniv. ed. 2013. (ENG., Illus.). 40p. (J). (gr. 1-3). 17.99 *(978-1-4231-7869-9(6))* Disney Pr.

Butler, Leah & Peters, Trudy. Owen's Choice: The Night of the Halloween Vandals. Armstrong, Neal, illus. 2005. 64p. (J). (gr. 1-5). 18.95 *(978-0-9771666-0-2(0))* Spencer's Mill Pr.

Byrne, Marlene F. Ghost in the Graveyard. Graber, Jesse, illus. 2010. 57p. (J). pap. 9.99 *(978-0-9777135-4-7(7))* Celtic Marketing Inc.

Capucilli, Alyssa Satin. Biscuit's Pet & Play Halloween. Andreasen, Dan & Schories, Pat, illus. 2007. (Biscuit Ser.). (ENG.). 12p. (J). (gr. -1-1). bds. 7.99 *(978-0-06-112833-2(3)*, HarperFestival) HarperCollins Pubs.

—Katy Duck's Happy Halloween. Cole, Henry, illus. 2014. (Katy Duck Ser.). (ENG.). 24p. (J). (gr. -1-1). pap. 3.99 *(978-1-4424-9806-8(4)*, Simon Spotlight) Simon Spotlight.

Carlson, Nancy. Harriet's Halloween Candy. (Harriet Bks.). (Illus.). 32p. (gr. k-2). anniv. rev. ed. 2003. (ENG.). (J). per. 6.95 *(978-0-87614-926-3(3)*, Carolrhoda Bks.) 20th anniv. ed. 2005. 15.95 *(978-0-87614-913-3(1))* Lerner Publishing Group.

—Harriet's Halloween Candy. Carlson, Nancy, illus. unabr. ed. (Illus.). (J). pap., tchr. ed. 31.95 incl. audio *(978-0-941078-52-8(3))*; 24.95 incl. audio *(978-0-941078-53-5(1))*; pap. 15.95 incl. audio *(978-0-941078-51-1(5))* Live Oak Media.

Cartee, Mary. Go Forth My Angels. 2011. 82p. pap. 19.95 *(978-1-4626-4058-4(3))* America Star Bks.

Carter, David A. Halloween Bugs, Vol. 16. Carter, David A., illus. 2003. (David Carter's Bugs Ser.). (ENG., Illus.). 14p. (J). (gr. -1-3). 12.99 *(978-0-689-85916-8(3)*, Little Simon) Little Simon.

Cat's Pyjamas. Haunted House: A Touch & Feel Spooky Tour. 2013. (ENG.). 22p. (J). (gr. -1-1). 12.99 *(978-0-7641-6641-9(7))* Barron's Educational Series, Inc.

Cazet, Denys. Minnie & Moo: The Night of the Living Bed. Cazet, Denys, illus. 2003. (I Can Read Bks.). (Illus.). 48p. (J). (gr. k-3). lib. bdg. 16.89 *(978-0-06-000504-7(1))* HarperCollins Pubs.

—Minnie & Moo - The Night of the Living Bed. Cazet, Denys, illus. 2004. (I Can Read Level 3 Ser.). (ENG., Illus.). 48p. (J). (gr. k-3). pap. 3.99 *(978-0-06-000505-4(X))* HarperCollins Pubs.

—The Night of the Living Bed. Cazet, Denys, illus. unabr. ed. 2005. (Minnie & Moo Ser.). (Illus.). (J). (gr. k-4). 25.95 incl. audio *(978-1-59519-389-6(8))*;Set. pap. 29.95 incl. audio *(978-1-59519-390-2(1))*;Set. pap. 31.95 incl. audio compact disk *(978-1-59519-394-0(4))* Live Oak Media.

—The Perfect Pumpkin Pie. Cazet, Denys, illus. 2005. (ENG., Illus.). 32p. (J). (gr. -1-1). 17.99 *(978-0-689-86467-4(1),* Atheneum/Richard Jackson Bks.) Simon & Schuster Children's Publishing.

Cecil, Lauren. Lalaloopsy: Halloween Surprise. Fruchter, Jason, illus. 2012. (Lalaloopsy Ser.). (ENG.). 24p. (J). (gr. -1-3). pap. 3.99 *(978-0-545-43388-4(6))* Scholastic, Inc.

Chalmers, Jason. Fall Nightmares. 2011. 166p. pap. 24.95 *(978-1-4560-8988-7(9))* America Star Bks.

Charlie Bumpers vs. the Squeaking Skull, 1 vol. 2014. (Charlie Bumpers Ser.). (ENG., Illus.). (J). (gr. 2-4). 10p. 16.95 *(978-1-56145-809-7(0))*; 160p. 13.95 *(978-1-56145-808-0(2))* Peachtree Pubs.

Christelow, Eileen. Five Little Monkeys Trick-Or-Treat. 2013. (Five Little Monkeys Story Ser.). (ENG., Illus.). 40p. (J). (gr. -1-3). 16.99 *(978-0-547-85893-7(0))* Houghton Mifflin Harcourt Publishing Co.

Christian, Cheryl. Witches, 1 vol. Williams, Wish, illus. 2011. (ENG.). 32p. (J). pap. 5.95 *(978-1-59572-283-6(1))* Star Bright Bks., Inc.

Christianson, Leslie Rose. Malinda Matters: Malinda's Halloween Adventure. 2010. 32p. 12.99 *(978-1-4490-5186-0(3))* AuthorHouse.

Christopher, Matt. Day of the Dragon, No. 2. 2004. (ENG., Illus.). 64p. (J). (gr. 1-4). pap. 13.99 *(978-0-316-73753-1(4))* Little, Brown Bks. for Young Readers.

Church, Caroline Jayne. Here Comes Halloween! Church, Caroline Jayne, illus. 2009. (ENG., Illus.). 8p. (J). (gr. k — 1). bds. 7.99 *(978-0-545-11815-6(8),* Cartwheel Bks.) Scholastic, Inc.

Cinebook. Halloween. Jeffrey, Erica, tr. from FRE. 2007. (Melusine Ser.: 2). (ENG., Illus.). 48p. (J). (gr. 4-7). pap. 11.95 *(978-1-905460-34-2(1))* CineBook GBR. Dist: National Bk. Network.

Clarke, Jane. Creaky Castle. Fox, Christyan, illus. 2013. *(978-1-4351-4951-9(3))* Barnes & Noble, Inc.

Classic Goosebumps & Stine, R. L. The Haunted Mask. 2008. (Classic Goosebumps Ser.: 4). (ENG.). 144p. (J). (gr. 3-7). 6.99 *(978-0-545-03521-7(X),* Scholastic Paperbacks) Scholastic, Inc.

Clough, Lisa. Petal & Poppy & the Spooky Halloween! Briant, Ed, illus. 2014. (Green Light Readers Level 2 Ser.). (ENG.). 32p. (J). (gr. -1-3). 12.99 *(978-0-544-33602-5(X),* HMH Books For Young Readers) Houghton Mifflin Harcourt Publishing Co.

Cocca-Leffler, Maryann. It's Halloween Night. Cocca-Leffler, Maryann, illus. 2009. (Sneak a Peek Ser.). (ENG., Illus.). 16p. (J). (gr. -1-3). pap. 6.99 *(978-0-06-125674-5(9),* HarperFestival) HarperCollins Pubs.

Cofer, Amadeus. Mystery of the Golden Pearls: A Halloween Adventure in Clarkesville, 1. l.t. ed. 2004. (Illus.). 36p. (J). 14.00 *(978-1-932957-02-0(2))* Legacy Pubs.

Colandro, Lucille. There Was an Old Lady Who Swallowed a Bat! Lee, Jared D., illus. 2009. (ENG.). (J). (gr. -1-3). 9.99 *(978-0-545-16353-8(6))* Scholastic, Inc.

Collins, Carleen. Everyone Loves Chocolate. 2009. 60p. pap. 23.99 *(978-1-4490-3049-0(1))* AuthorHouse.

Compagnucci, Veronica M. Emily Finds Her Voice. 2013. 40p. pap. 24.95 *(978-1-63004-288-2(9))* America Star Bks.

Condenzio, Mary. Oliver. 2013. 20p. pap. 24.95 *(978-1-62709-305-7(2))* America Star Bks.

Connolly, John. The Gates. 2009. (ENG.). 304p. 24.00 *(978-1-4391-7263-6(3),* Beyond Words/Atria Bks.) Atria Bks.

Conrad, Liz, illus. Skeleton Shake. 2008. (ENG.). 12p. (J). 6.95 *(978-1-58117-798-5(4),* Intervisual/Piggy Toes) Bendon, Inc.

Cooper, Bernice Soroka. The Little Elf-Frog. 2012. 24p. pap. 17.99 *(978-1-4772-9525-0(9))* AuthorHouse.

Cooper, Helen Wendy. The Vegetarian Vampire. 2012. (Illus.). 53p. pap. 8.50 *(978-1-78035-365-4(0),* Fastprint Publishing) Upfront Publishing Ltd. GBR. Dist: Printondemand-worldwide.com.

Cooper, Ilene. Lucy's Tricks & Treats. Merrell, David, illus. 2012. (Lucy Ser.). (ENG.). 112p. (J). (gr. 1-4). 4.99 *(978-0-375-86997-6(2),* Random Hse. Bks. for Young Readers) Random Hse. Children's Bks.

Copeland, Mindy. Halloween Spanish for Young Children. 2005. 12p. 13.52 *(978-1-4116-4872-2(2))* Lulu Pr., Inc.

Corderoy, Tracey. The Super-Spooky Fright Night! Hubble Bubble. Berger, Joe, illus. 2017. (ENG.). 128p. (J). (gr. 1-4). 14.99 *(978-0-7636-9502-6(5),* Nosy Crow) Candlewick Pr.

Corey, Shana. Monster Parade. Terry, Will, illus. 2009. (Step into Reading Ser.). (ENG.). 24p. (J). (gr. -1-1). 3.99 *(978-0-375-85638-9(2),* Random Hse. Bks. for Young Readers) Random Hse. Children's Bks.

Cotler, Steve. Cheesie Mack Is Sort of Freaked Out. Holgate, Douglas, illus. 2014. (Cheesie Mack Ser.). (ENG.). 256p. (J). (gr. 3-7). 15.99 *(978-0-385-36988-6(3),* Random Hse. Bks. for Young Readers) Random Hse. Children's Bks.

Cottrell-Bentley, Lisa M. Wright on Time: Iowa. Bauerle, Tanja, illus. 2013. 164p. pap. 12.99 *(978-1-937848-06-4(X))* Do Life Right, Inc.

Couteaud, Cheryl. A Monster for Halloween. Couteaud, Cheryl, illus. 2009. (Illus.). 24p. pap. 10.96 *(978-1-4251-8563-3(0))* Trafford Publishing.

Coven, Wanda. Heidi Heckelbeck in Disguise. Burris, Priscilla, illus. 2012. (Heidi Heckelbeck Ser.: 4). (ENG.). 128p. (J). (gr. k-2). 16.99 *(978-1-4424-4169-9(0))*; pap. 5.99 *(978-1-4424-4168-2(2))* Little Simon. (Little Simon).

—Heidi Heckelbeck in Disguise. 2012. (Heidi Heckelbeck Ser.: 4). lib. bdg. 16.00 *(978-0-606-26329-0(2),* Turtleback) Turtleback Bks.

Coville, Bruce. The Monster's Ring. Coville, Katherine, illus. 2008. (Magic Shop Book Ser.: 1). (ENG.). 128p. (J). (gr. 5-7). pap. 6.99 *(978-0-15-206442-6(7))* Houghton Mifflin Harcourt Publishing Co.

Cox, Judy. Haunted House, Haunted Mouse. Ebbeler, Jeffrey, illus. (ENG.). 32p. (J). (gr. -1-2). 2012. pap. 7.99 *(978-0-8234-2544-0(4))* 2011. 16.95 *(978-0-8234-2315-6(8))* Holiday Hse., Inc.

Craddock, Erik. Stone Rabbit #6: Night of the Living Dust Bunnies. Craddock, Erik, illus. 2011. (Stone Rabbit Ser.: 6). (ENG., Illus.). 96p. (J). (gr. 3-7). pap. 6.99 *(978-0-375-86724-8(4),* Random Hse. Bks. for Young Readers) Random Hse. Children's Bks.

Crawford, Shannon Joseph. Halloween War. 2011. 88p. pap. 19.95 *(978-1-61546-348-0(8))* America Star Bks.

Crimi, Carolyn. Boris & Bella. Grimly, Gris, illus. 2006. (ENG.). 32p. (J). (gr. -1-3). reprint ed. pap. 7.99 *(978-0-15-205900-2(8))* Houghton Mifflin Harcourt Publishing Co.

Cronin, Doreen. Click, Clack, Boo! A Tricky Treat. Lewin, Betsy, illus. 2013. (ENG.). 40p. (J). (gr. -1-2). 17.99 *(978-1-4424-6553-4(0))* Simon & Schuster Children's Publishing.

Crownberry, Ethan. The Willies. 2013. 52p. 17.95 *(978-0-9898533-2-3(2))* Jetpack Publishing.

—The Willies. 2012. 80p. pap. 8.95 *(978-1-300-00798-2(2))* Lulu Pr., Inc.

—The Willies. 2012. 80p. pap. 10.95 *(978-0-557-96056-9(8))* Lulu.com GBR. Dist: Lulu Pr., Inc.

Cuyler, Margery. Skeleton Hiccups. Schindler, S. D., illus. 2005. (ENG.). 32p. (J). (gr. -1-3). reprint ed. 7.99 *(978-1-4169-0276-8(7),* McElderry, Margaret K. Bks.) McElderry, Margaret K. Bks.

Czajak, Paul. Monster Needs a Costume. Grieb, Wendy, illus. (Monster & Me Ser.). (ENG.). 32p. (J). (-k). 2014. 6.99 *(978-1-938063-38-1(4))* 2013. 16.95 *(978-1-938063-09-1(0))* Mighty Media Pr. (Mighty Media Kids).

Dahl, Michael. Halloween. Ho, Jannie, illus. 2015. (Baby Face Ser.). (ENG.). 10p. (gr. -1 — 1). bds. 7.99 *(978-1-62370-293-9(3))* Capstone Young Readers of Coughlan Cos.

Danescary, Pollygeist. Have a Claw-Some Howloween: A Creepy-Cool Activity Book. 2015. (ENG., Illus.). 32p. (J). (gr. 3-7). pap. 7.99 *(978-0-316-33742-7(0))* Little, Brown Bks. for Young Readers.

Danziger, Paula. Orange You Glad It's Halloween, Amber Brown?, 4 bks., Set. Ross, Tony, illus. 2007. (Amber Brown Ser.). (J). (gr. 1-3). pap. 29.95 incl. audio *(978-1-4301-0080-5(X))* Live Oak Media.

—Orange You Glad It's Halloween, Amber Brown? Ross, Tony, illus. 2007. (Is for Amber Ser.). (ENG.). 48p. (J). (gr. 1-3). 3.99 *(978-0-14-240809-4(3),* Penguin Young Readers) Penguin Young Readers Group.

—Orange You Glad It's Halloween, Amber Brown? Ross, Tony, illus. 2007. (Amber Brown Ser.). 48p. (J). (gr. k-3). 11.65 *(978-0-7569-8154-9(9))* Perfection Learning Corp.

Davies, Donna. Night of the Candy Creepers. Peters, Rob, illus. 2013. 32p. pap. 9.95 *(978-0-9853082-1-6(4))* All Hallows Eve Pr.

Davis, Chip, concept. Mannheim Steamroller Halloween - the World Between Davis, Chip, . 2004. (Illus.). 216p. (YA). per. 19.95 *(978-0-9754149-0-3(9))* Mannheim Steamroller L.L.C.

Davis, Jacky & Soman, David. Ladybug Girl & the Dress-Up Dilemma. Soman, David, illus. 2014. (Ladybug Girl Ser.). (ENG., Illus.). 40p. (J). (gr. -1-k). 17.99 *(978-0-8037-3584-2(7),* Dial Bks) Penguin Publishing Group.

Davis, Jim & Evanier, Mark. Catzilla. Ellipsanime Staff & Dargaud Media, illus. 2011. (Garfield Graphic Novels Ser.). (ENG.). 32p. (J). (gr. 1-6). 7.99 *(978-1-59707-278-6(8),* 9781597072786) Papercutz.

Davis, Nancy. Halloween Faces. Davis, Nancy, illus. 2010. (ENG., Illus.). 18p. (J). (gr. k — 1). bds. 6.99 *(978-0-545-16586-0(5),* Cartwheel Bks.) Scholastic, Inc.

Day, Alexandra. Carl's Halloween. Day, Alexandra, illus. 2015. (Carl Ser.). (ENG., Illus.). 32p. (J). (gr. -1-2). 14.99 *(978-0-374-31082-0(3),* 9780374310820, Farrar, Straus & Giroux (BYR)) Farrar, Straus & Giroux.

Day, Nancy Raines. On a Windy Night. Bates, George, illus. 2010. (ENG.). 40p. (J). (gr. k-2). 16.95 *(978-0-8109-3900-4(2),* Abrams Bks. for Young Readers) Abrams, Inc.

de Las Casas, Dianne. The House That Witchy Built, 1 vol. Stone-Barker, Holly, illus. 2011. (ENG.). 32p. (J). (gr. k-k). 16.99 *(978-1-58980-965-9(3))* Pelican Publishing Co., Inc.

Dean, James. Five Little Pumpkins. Dean, James, illus. 2015. (Pete the Cat Ser.). (ENG., Illus.). 32p. (J). (gr. -1-3). 9.99 *(978-0-06-230418-6(6))* HarperCollins Pubs.

deGroat, Diane. Trick or Treat, Smell My Feet. deGroat, Diane, illus. 2008. (Illus.). (J). (gr. -1-7). pap. 16.95 incl. audio *(978-1-4301-0425-4(2))* Live Oak Media.

—Trick or Treat, Smell My Feet, 4 bks., Set. 2008. (J). (gr. -1-2). pap. 39.95 incl. audio compact disk *(978-1-4301-0428-5(7))*; pap. 37.95 incl. audio *(978-1-4301-0426-1(0))* Live Oak Media.

Dellinger, Hampton. Thanks for Nothing: How Willie & Abe Saved Thanksgiving. 2008. 24p. 12.99 *(978-0-615-24971-1(X))* Dellinger, Hampton.

dePaola, Tomie. My First Halloween. 2008. (ENG.). 14p. (J). (gr. -1-k). bds. 5.99 *(978-0-448-44858-9(0),* Grosset & Dunlap) Penguin Young Readers Group.

Depken, Kristen & Depken, Kristen L. One, Two... Boo! Gévry, Claudine, illus. 2009. (ENG.). 12p. (J). (gr. -1 — 1). bds. 3.99 *(978-0-375-84418-8(X),* Golden Bks.) Random Hse. Children's Bks.

Depken, Kristen L. Sweets & Treats (Disney Princess) RH Disney Staff et al, illus. 2016. (Pictureback(R) Ser.). (ENG.). 16p. (J). (-k). 4.99 *(978-0-7364-3353-2(8),* RH/Disney) Random Hse. Children's Bks.

DePrisco, Dorothea. Peek-A-Boooo Who? A Lift-the-Flap & Sound Book. Hedgecock, Lucie, illus. 2009. 12p. 8.95 *(978-1-58117-952-1(9),* Intervisual/Piggy Toes) Bendon, Inc.

Devlin, Wende. Cranberry Halloween. Devlin, Harry, illus. 2013. (Cranberryport Ser.). (ENG.). (J). (gr. -1-3). 18.95 *(978-1-930900-69-1(4))* Purple Hse. Pr.

Dewdney, Anna. Llama Llama Trick or Treat. Dewdney, Anna, illus. 2014. (Llama Llama Ser.). (ENG., Illus.). 14p. (J). (— 1). bds. 5.99 *(978-0-451-46978-6(X),* Viking Books for Young Readers) Penguin Publishing Group.

DiCamillo, Kate. Mercy Watson: Princess in Disguise. Van Dusen, Chris, illus. 2010. (Mercy Watson Ser.: 4). (ENG.). 80p. (J). (gr. 1-4). pap. 5.99 *(978-0-7636-4951-7(1))* Candlewick Pr.

DiCamillo, Kate & Van Dusen, Chris. Mercy Watson: Princess in Disguise. Van Dusen, Chris, illus. 2007. (Mercy Watson Ser.: 4). (ENG., Illus.). 80p. (J). (gr. 1-4). 14.99 *(978-0-7636-3014-0(4))* Candlewick Pr.

Dickinson, Rebecca. Over in the Hollow. Britt, Stephanie, illus. 2009. (ENG.). 36p. (J). (gr. -1-2). 15.99 *(978-0-8118-5035-3(8))* Chronicle Bks. LLC.

Disney Book Group. Mickey Mouse Clubhouse Mickey's Halloween. Disney Storybook Art Team, illus. 2015. (ENG.). 10p. (J). (gr. -1-k). bds. 8.99 *(978-1-4847-2096-7(2))* Disney Pr.

Disney Book Group Staff. Haunted Clubhouse. 2010. (ENG., Illus.). 12p. (J). (gr. -1-k). bds. 6.99 *(978-1-4231-2832-8(X))* Disney Pr.

—Mickey & Friends Mickey's Spooky Night: Purchase Includes Digital App! Disney Storybook Artists Staff & Disney Storybook Art Team, illus. 2014. (ENG.). 24p. (J). (gr. 1-3). bds. 10.99 *(978-1-4847-0841-5(5))* Disney Pr.

—5-Minute Spooky Stories. Disney Storybook Artists Staff & Disney Storybook Art Team, illus. 2014. (5-Minute Stories Ser.). (ENG.). 192p. (J). (gr. -1-k). 12.99 *(978-1-4231-8915-2(9))* Disney Pr.

Disney Book Group Staff & Higginson, Sheila Sweeny. Minnie: Minnie's Costume Contest. Disney Storybook Artists Staff, illus. 2014. (ENG.). 12p. (J). (gr. -1-k). bds. 7.99 *(978-1-4231-9427-9(6))* Disney Pr.

Disney Book Group Staff, et al. Doc Mcstuffins Boo to You! Disney Storybook Artists Staff, illus. 2014. (ENG.). 12p. (J). (gr. -1-k). bds. 7.99 *(978-1-4231-8388-4(6))* Disney Pr.

Disney Storybook Art Team, illus. Whisker Haven Tales - Halloween in Whisker Haven. 2016. (Read-Along Storybook & CD Ser.). (ENG.). 32p. (J). (gr. -1-k). pap. 6.99 *(978-1-4847-4707-0(0))* Disney Pr.

Diviny, Sean. Halloween Motel. Rocco, Joe, illus. Date not set. 32p. (J). (gr. -1-3). 5.25 hd 5.99 *(978-0-06-443651-9(9))* HarperCollins Pubs.

Dolphin Halloween & Elsie's Scrapbook. l.t. ed. 2004. (Illus.). 32p. (J). mass mkt. 4.99 *(978-0-9760868-0-2(8))* Pluegl Bks.

Donaldson, Julia. Room on the Broom Board Book. Sheffler, Axel, illus. 2012. (ENG.). 24p. (J). (— 1). bds. 6.99 *(978-0-8037-3841-6(2),* Dial Bks) Penguin Young Readers Group.

Donbavand, Tommy. Skull of the Skeleton, Bk. 5. Cartoon Saloon Staff, illus. 2010. (Scream Street Ser.: 5). (ENG.). 128p. (J). (gr. 3-7). pap. 5.99 *(978-0-7636-4635-6(0))* Candlewick Pr.

—Skull of the Skeleton: Book 5, 1 vol. Cartoon Saloon, illus. 2012. (ENG.). 120p. (J). 24.21 *(978-1-59961-996-5(2),* Chapter Bks.) Spotlight.

Donnell, Frances. Goblins Will Be Seen: When It's Time for Halloween. Hebert, Catherine, ed. Merchant, Donna, illus. 2005. 38p. (J). 16.95 *(978-0-9770893-0-7(4))* 2 Donn Bks.

Donovan, Dan. Holiday Tails! 2011. 48p. pap. 19.26 *(978-1-4520-9628-5(7))* AuthorHouse.

Doyen, Denise. The Pomegranate Witch. Wheeler, Eliza, illus. 2017. (ENG.). 40p. (J). (gr. k-3). 16.99 ***(978-1-4521-4589-1(X))*** Chronicle Bks. LLC.

—The Pomegranate Witch. Moser, Barry, illus. 2013. (J). *(978-0-375-87057-6(1))*; lib. bdg. *(978-0-375-97057-3(6))* Random Hse., Inc.

Dudley, Sean. Who's Afraid of the Pumpkin Man??? 2009. 47p. pap. 10.01 *(978-0-557-12616-3(9))* Lulu Pr., Inc.

Dunagan, Jennifer. Santana's Harrowing Halloween. Hines, Marcel, illus. 2012. 26p. pap. 12.95 *(978-1-60911-977-5(0),* Strategic Bk. Publishing) Strategic Book Publishing & Rights Agency (SBPRA).

Duncan, Billy. A Haunting Good Time, 1 vol. 2009. 48p. pap. 16.95 *(978-1-60836-120-5(9))* America Star Bks.

Dunrea, Olivier. Ollie's Halloween. 2013. (Gossie & Friends Ser.). (ENG., Illus.). 30p. (J). (gr. -1 — 1). bds. 6.99 *(978-0-544-05720-3(1))* Houghton Mifflin Harcourt Publishing Co.

—Ollie's Halloween (reader) 2016. (Gossie & Friends Ser.). (ENG., Illus.). 32p. (J). (gr. -1-3). 12.99 *(978-0-544-64052-8(7),* HMH Books For Young Readers) Houghton Mifflin Harcourt Publishing Co.

Durgan, Lori Origer. The Little Scrub Lady. 2012. 28p. pap. 15.99 *(978-1-4797-4259-2(7))* Xlibris Corp.

Duval, Kathy. The Three Bears' Halloween. Meisel, Paul, illus. 2007. (ENG.). 32p. (J). (gr. -1-3). 16.95 *(978-0-8234-2032-2(9))* Holiday Hse., Inc.

Edwards, Jean E. Adventure Tales: For Kids Who Want to Become Better Readers. 2012. 102p. 24.99 *(978-1-4771-4118-2(9))* Xlibris Corp.

Ella & the Halloween Mystery. 2016. (Illus.). 24p. (J). ***(978-1-5182-3174-2(8))*** Baker & Taylor, CATS.

Emerson, Carl. Monster Boy & the Halloween Parade, 1 vol. Levin, Lon, illus. 2010. (Monster Boy Set 2 Ser.). (ENG.). 32p. (J). (gr. k-3). 28.50 *(978-1-60270-777-1(4))* ABDO Publishing Co.

Enderle, Dotti & McWilliam, Howard. Ghost Detectors Book 7: Pop!, 1 vol. 2012. (Ghost Detectors Ser.). (ENG., Illus.). 80p. (J). (gr. 2-5). 27.07 *(978-1-61641-623-2(8))* Magic Wagon.

Engelbreit, Mary. Queen of Halloween. Engelbreit, Mary, illus. 2008. (Illus.). 32p. (J). (gr. -1-3). lib. bdg. 17.89 *(978-0-06-008191-1(0))*; (ENG.). 16.99 *(978-0-06-008190-4(2))* HarperCollins Pubs.

Engleman, Dennis. Holloween Town. 2004. 37p. (J). (gr. 1-4). pap. 16.95 *(978-1-928653-18-9(9))* Regina Orthodox Pr.

Eone, illus. Peppa's Halloween Party. 2016. (Peppa Pig Ser.). (ENG.). 24p. (J). (gr. -1-k). 4.99 *(978-0-545-92543-3(6))* Scholastic, Inc.

Erickson, John R. The Case of the Halloween Ghost. Holmes, Gerald L., illus. 2011. (Hank the Cowdog Ser.). (ENG.). 123p. (J). (gr. 3-6). pap. 5.99 *(978-1-59188-109-4(9))* Maverick Bks., Inc.

Eubank, Patricia Reeder. ABCs of Halloween. Eubank, Patricia Reeder, illus. 2013. (Illus.). 32p. (J). pap. 4.99 *(978-0-8249-5658-5(3),* Ideal Pubns.) Worthy Publishing.

—Halloween 123s. Eubank, Patricia Reeder, illus. 2011. (Illus.). 22p. (J). bds. 6.99 *(978-0-8249-1868-2(1),* Ideal Pubns.) Worthy Publishing.

Eubank, Patti Reeder. ABCs of Halloween. 2003. (ENG., Illus.). 30p. (J). (gr. -1-k). 8.95 *(978-0-8249-5467-3(X),* Ideal Pubns.) Worthy Publishing.

Evans, Cambria. Bone Soup. 2016. (ENG., Illus.). 32p. (J). (gr. 2-5). 7.99 *(978-0-544-66836-2(7),* HMH Books For Young Readers) Houghton Mifflin Harcourt Publishing Co.

Farley, Robin. Time to Trick or Treat! Ivanov, Olga & Ivanov, Aleksey, illus. 2012. (Mia Ser.). (ENG.). 24p. (J). (gr. -1-3). pap. 4.99 *(978-0-06-210011-5(4),* HarperFestival) HarperCollins Pubs.

Feder, Joel A. Kokomo's Halloween Adventure. 2012. 32p. pap. 15.99 *(978-1-4685-7331-2(4))* AuthorHouse.

Feehan-Vilería, Elaine. The Legend of Old Mr. Clarke. 2004. 58p. per. 17.95 *(978-1-4116-1523-6(9))* Lulu Pr., Inc.

Fernandez, Alberto. A Halloween Story: A frightfully delightful tale by a 5-year-old, for other little monsters Everywhere. de la Fuente, Pilar, illus. 2007.Tr. of Historia de Halloween. 48p. (J). *(978-0-9796465-0-8(2))* Maroma Bks.

—A Halloween Story: A frightfully-delightful tale, by a 5-year-old, for other little monsters, Everywhere. de la Fuente, Pilar, illus. 2007. (J). pap. 9.95 *(978-0-9796465-2-2(9))* Maroma Bks.

Fisch, Sholly. Nothing to Fear, 1 vol. McKenny, Stewart & Moy, Phil, illus. 2013. (DC Super Friends Ser.). (ENG.). 32p. (gr. 1-2). lib. bdg. 22.60 *(978-1-4342-4703-2(1))* Stone Arch Bks.

Fisher-Price. Fisher-Price Little People: Halloween Is Here! 2016. (ENG.). 10p. (J). (gr. -1-k). bds. 9.99 *(978-0-7944-3756-5(7),* Reader's Digest Children's Bks.) Studio Fun International.

—Fisher-Price Little People: Trick or Treat! 2016. (ENG.). 12p. (J). (gr. -1-k). bds. 5.99 *(978-0-7944-3757-2(5),* Reader's Digest Children's Bks.) Studio Fun International.

Fleming, Denise. Pumpkin Eye. 2009. (J). (gr. k-2). 27.95 incl. audio *(978-0-8045-6979-8(7))* Spoken Arts, Inc.

—Pumpkin Eye. Fleming, Denise, illus. rev. ed. 2005. (ENG., Illus.). 32p. (J). (gr. -1-k). reprint ed. pap. 7.99 *(978-0-8050-7635-6(2),* 9780805076356) Square Fish.

Fliess, Sue. Goblin Hood. Thibodeau, Piper, illus. 2016. (ENG.). 32p. (J). (gr. -1-k). pap. 3.99 *(978-0-448-48933-9(3),* Grosset & Dunlap) Penguin Young Readers Group.

Flor Ada, Alma. Celebrate Halloween & the Day of the Dead with Cristina & Her Blue Bunny. Martinez, Ivanova, illus. 2006. (Cuentos para Celebrar / Stories to Celebrate Ser.). 30p. (gr. k-6). per. 11.95 *(978-1-59820-132-1(8))* Santillana USA Publishing Co., Inc.

Franklin, Linda. Into the Pumpkin, 1 vol. 2012. (ENG., Illus.). 48p. (J). 16.99 *(978-0-7643-4183-0(9),* 9780764341830) Schiffer Publishing, Ltd.

Fraser, Mary Ann. Heebie-Jeebie Jamboree. 2011. (ENG.). 32p. (J). (gr. -1-2). 15.95 *(978-1-59078-857-8(5))* Boyds Mills Pr.

Freeman, Don. Halloween Is Here, Corduroy! McCue, Lisa & Kong, Emilie, illus. 2007. (Corduroy Ser.). (ENG.). 16p. (J). (gr. -1-k). pap. 5.99 *(978-0-448-44563-2(8),* Grosset & Dunlap) Penguin Young Readers Group.

Freeman, Martha. Who Stole Halloween? 2005. (Chickadee Court Mystery Ser.). (ENG.). 224p. (J). (gr. 3-7). 16.95 *(978-0-8234-1962-3(2))* Holiday Hse., Inc.

Freese, Thomas & Riddell, Fran. Halloween Sleepwalker, 1 vol. 2013. (ENG., Illus.). 64p. (J). 16.99 *(978-0-7643-4399-5(8),* 9780764343995) Schiffer Publishing, Ltd.

Friedman, Laurie. Mallory Makes a Difference. Kalis, Jennifer, illus. 2017. (Mallory Ser.: 28). (ENG.). 152p. (gr. 2-5). 15.95 ***(978-1-4677-5032-5(8))*** Lerner Publishing Group.

Fry, Sonali. I'm a Little Vampire. Rescek, Sanja, illus. 2014. (ENG.). 16p. (J). (gr. -1 — 1). bds. 5.99 *(978-1-4814-0504-1(7),* Little Simon) Little Simon.

—The Itsy Bitsy Pumpkin. Rescek, Sanja, illus. 2014. (Itsy Bitsy Ser.). (ENG.). 16p. (J). (gr. -1 — 1). bds. 5.99 *(978-1-4814-0505-8(5),* Little Simon) Little Simon.

Galbraith, Kathryn O. Boo, Bunny! Mack, Jeff, illus. 2008. (ENG.). 40p. (J). (gr. -1-2). 16.00 *(978-0-15-216246-7(1))* Houghton Mifflin Harcourt Publishing Co.

—Boo, Bunny! Board Book. Mack, Jeff, illus. 2012. (ENG.). 32p. (J). (gr. -1 — 1). bds. 5.99 *(978-0-547-81850-4(5))* Houghton Mifflin Harcourt Publishing Co.

Gallagher, Diana G. Haunted Love, 1 vol. (Claudia & Monica: Freshman Girls Ser.). (ENG.). 144p. (gr. 3-6). 2013. 9.95 *(978-1-4342-6286-8(3))* 2012. lib. bdg. 26.65 *(978-1-4342-3277-9(8))* Stone Arch Bks. (Claudia & Monica: Freshman Girls).

Gallion, Sue Lowell. Pug & Pig Trick-or-Treat. Wan, Joyce, illus. 2017. (Pug & Pig Ser.). (ENG.). 40p. (J). (gr. -1-3). 17.99 ***(978-1-4814-4977-9(X),*** Beach Lane Bks.) Beach Lane Bks.

Garofoli, Viviana, illus. Halloween Hugs: A HUGS Book. 2014. (Hugs Book Ser.: 6). (ENG.). 10p. (J). (gr. -1-k). bds. 9.99 *(978-0-7944-3240-9(9))* Reader's Digest Assn., Inc., The.

Garton, Sam. Otter Loves Halloween! Garton, Sam, illus. 2015. (ENG., Illus.). 32p. (J). (gr. -1-3). 9.99 *(978-0-06-236666-5(1),* Balzer & Bray) HarperCollins Pubs.

Gehl, Laura. I'm Not Trick-Or-Treating. Wan, Joyce, illus. 2016. (Peep & Egg Ser.). (ENG.). 40p. (J). 16.99 *(978-0-374-30122-4(0),* 9780374301224, Farrar, Straus & Giroux (BYR)) Farrar, Straus & Giroux.

Gelsey, James & Duendes Del Sur Staff. Scooby-Doo & the Vampire's Revenge, 1 vol. 2011. (Scooby-Doo Mysteries Ser.). (ENG., Illus.). 64p. (J). (gr. 3-6). 24.21 *(978-1-59961-894-4(X))* Spotlight.

George, Ben W. Wanda the Witch's Broom: How an Old School Witch Learns New Tricks. 2011. 24p. pap. 12.99 *(978-1-4634-4380-1(3))* AuthorHouse.

Gerber, Carole. 10 Busy Brooms. Fleming, Michael, illus. 2016. (ENG.). 32p. (J). (gr. -1-2). 12.99 *(978-0-553-53341-5(X),* Doubleday Bks. for Young Readers) Random Hse. Children's Bks.

Gilbert, Jeff. Trick or Shriek. 2006. 72p. pap. 5.97 *(978-0-9646781-1-8(X))* Hairball Pr.

Giles, Mike, illus. Halloween Is Fun! 2009. (Yo Gabba Gabba! Ser.). (ENG.). 16p. (J). (gr. -1-1). pap. 6.99 *(978-1-4169-7824-4(0),* Simon Spotlight) Simon Spotlight.

Glass, Calliope. Disney Tails Figaro's Halloween Surprise. Disney Storybook Art Team, illus. 2015. (Disney Tails Ser.). (ENG.). 10p. (J). (gr. -1 — 1). bds. 6.99 *(978-1-4847-1372-3(9),* 1392357) Disney Pr.

Glassman, Miriam. Halloweena. Roberts, Victoria, illus. 2015. (ENG.). 40p. (J). (gr. -1-3). 13.99 *(978-1-4814-7996-7(2),* Atheneum Bks. for Young Readers) Simon & Schuster Children's Publishing.

Glori, Debi. Witch Baby & Me after Dark, No. 3. 2010. (ENG., Illus.). 304p. (J). (gr. 2-4). pap. 11.99 *(978-0-552-55678-1(5))* Transworld Publishers Ltd. GBR. Dist: Independent Pubs. Group.

Golden Books. Howl for Halloween! (PAW Patrol) Golden Books & Lovett, Nate, illus. 2016. (Big Golden Book Ser.). (ENG.). 32p. (J). (gr. -1-2). 9.99 *(978-0-399-55873-3(X)*, Golden Bks.) Random Hse. Children's Bks.
Golden Books Staff. We Love Halloween! Fruchter, Jason, illus. 2010. (Glow-In-the-Dark Sticker Book Ser.). (ENG.). 48p. (J). (gr. -1-2). pap. 3.99 *(978-0-375-86513-8(6)*, Golden Bks.) Random Hse. Children's Bks.
Goldstein, Bobby. The Story of the Pink Gorilla Monster. 2012. 40p. pap. 17.99 *(978-1-4490-6377-1(2))* AuthorHouse.
Gownley, Jim. Amelia in Loosely in Disguise & Frightened: #3, 1 vol. Gownley, Jim, illus. 2011. (Amelia Rules! Ser.). (ENG., Illus.). 36p. 24.21 *(978-1-59961-789-3(7))* Spotlight.
Grabill, Rebecca. Halloween Good Night. Økstad, Ella, illus. 2017. (ENG.). 32p. (J). (gr. -1-3). 17.99 *(978-1-4814-5061-4(1))* Simon & Schuster Children's Publishing.
Grambling, Lois G. T. Rex Trick-or-Treats. Davis, Jack E., illus. 32p. (J). 2008. (ENG.). (gr. -1-3). pap. 6.99 *(978-0-06-050254-6(1))* 2005. 12.99 *(978-0-06-050252-2(5))* HarperCollins Pubs. (Tegen, Katherine Bks).
Granata, Nancy. The Perfect Porch for Witch Watching. 2008. 52p. pap. 22.49 *(978-1-4389-0107-7(0))* AuthorHouse.
Graves, Keith. The Monsterator. 2014. (ENG., Illus.). 40p. (J). (gr. 2-5). 17.99 *(978-1-59643-855-2(X)*, 9781596438552) Roaring Brook Pr.
Gray, C. M. Zombiefied!: Apocalypse. 2017. (Zombiefied Ser.: 04). 192p. pap. 5.99 *(978-0-7333-3424-5(5))* ABC Bks. AUS. Dist: HarperCollins Pubs.
Graziani, Maria. A Black Cat on Halloween: Un Gato Negro en Dia de Brujas. Elejalde, Eliana, illus. l.t. ed. 2004. (SPA.). 23p. (J). 7.00 *(978-0-9762361-1-5(7))* Ed. Acespanish S.A.C.- Lima, Peru.
Green, D. L. Zeke Meeks vs the Horrendous Halloween, 1 vol. Alves, Josh, illus. 2013. (Zeke Meeks Ser.). (ENG.). 128p. (gr. 2-2). lib. bdg. 22.65 *(978-1-4048-7638-5(3)*, Zeke Meeks) Picture Window Bks.
Greene, Stephanie. Princess Posey & the Monster Stew, 4 vols. Sisson, Stéphanie Roth, illus. 2012. (Princess Posey, First Grader Ser.: 4). (ENG.). 96p. (J). (gr. k-3). pap. 5.99 *(978-0-14-242105-5(7)*, Puffin Books) Penguin Young Readers Group.
Gritton, Steve. The Kandy Witch. 2007. (Illus.). (J). 18.95 *(978-0-9795361-0-6(3))* Bad Frog Art/SMG Bks.
Grogan, John. Trick or Treat, Marley! Cowdrey, Richard, illus. (Marley Ser.). (ENG.). 40p. (J). (gr. -1-3). 2013. 9.99 *(978-0-06-211368-9(2))* 2011. 17.99 *(978-0-06-185755-3(6))* HarperCollins Pubs.
Grosset & Dunlap & Adler, Eve. Ella & the Halloween Mystery. 2016. (Ella the Elephant Ser.). (ENG., Illus.). 24p. (J). (gr. -1-k). pap. 3.99 *(978-1-101-99591-4(2)*, Grosset & Dunlap) Penguin Young Readers Group.
Gruber, Michael. The Legend of the Brog. Gruber, Michael & Graves, Linda, illus. 2005. (J). per. 9.95 *(978-0-9770413-0-5(1))* Gruber Enterprises.
Guardo, Attilio. Halloween at Clear Creek. 2005. 208p. pap. 24.95 *(978-1-4137-8325-4(2))* America Star Bks.
Gunnufson, Charlotte. Halloween Hustle, 0 vols. Atteberry, Kevan, illus. 2013. (ENG.). 32p. (J). (gr. -1-2). 16.99 *(978-1-4778-1723-0(9)*, 9781477817230, Amazon Children's Publishing) Amazon Publishing.
Gutman, Dan. Deck the Halls, We're off the Walls! 2013. (My Weird School Ser.). (J). lib. bdg. 16.00 *(978-0-606-32165-5(9)*, Turtleback) Turtleback Bks.
—It's Halloween, I'm Turning Green! Paillot, Jim, illus. 2013. (My Weird School Special Ser.). 144p. (J). (gr. 1-5). (ENG.). pap. 5.99 *(978-0-06-220679-4(6))*; lib. bdg. 16.89 *(978-0-06-220680-0(X))* HarperCollins Pubs.
—It's Halloween, I'm Turning Green! 2013. (My Weird School Ser.). (J). lib. bdg. 16.00 *(978-0-606-32560-8(3)*, Turtleback) Turtleback Bks.
—Mrs. Patty Is Batty! Paillot, Jim, illus. 2006. (My Weird School Ser.: 13). (ENG.). 112p. (J). (gr. 1-5). pap. 4.99 *(978-0-06-085380-8(8))* HarperCollins Pubs.
Hall, Kirsten. I'm a Princess. DeRosa, Dee, illus. 2004. (My First Reader Ser.). (ENG.). 32p. (J). (gr. k-1). pap. 3.95 *(978-0-516-24630-7(5)*, Children's Pr.) Scholastic Library Publishing.
Hallinan, P. K. Today Is Halloween! (J). (gr. -1-k). 5.95 *(978-0-8249-5306-5(1)*, Ideal Pubns.) Worthy Publishing.
—Today Is Halloween! Hallinan, P. K., illus. 2008. (ENG., Illus.). 26p. (J). (gr. -1-k). bds. 6.99 *(978-0-8249-1805-7(3)*, Ideal Pubns.) Worthy Publishing.
The Halloween Caper. 2007. (Spaceboy Chapter Ser.). (J). 7.67 *(978-1-932570-63-2(2))* Pioneer Valley Bks.
Hamilton, Sharon. Shine On. 2008. 259p. pap. 22.99 *(978-1-59879-466-3(3)*, Lifevest) Lifevest Publishing, Inc.
Hapka, Cathy, pseud, et al. Pooh's Halloween Pumpkin. Disney Storybook Artists Staff, illus. 2013. (ENG.). 10p. (J). (gr. -1-k). bds. 5.99 *(978-1-4231-6767-9(8))* Disney Pr.
Hargreaves, Adam & Hargreaves, Roger. Mr. Tickle & the Scary Halloween. 2014. (Mr. Men & Little Miss Ser.). (ENG.). 32p. (J). (gr. -1-2). 3.99 *(978-0-8431-8063-3(3)*, Price Stern Sloan) Penguin Young Readers Group.
Harley, Bill. Charlie Bumpers vs. the Squeaking Skull, 1 vol. Gustavson, Adam, illus. 2015. (Charlie Bumpers Ser.). (ENG.). 176p. (J). (gr. 2-4). pap. 6.95 *(978-1-56145-888-2(0))* Peachtree Pubs.
HarperCollins Publishers Ltd. Staff, et al. An I Can Read Halloween Treat. Set. Zimmer, Dirk, illus. 2004. (I Can Read Bks.). (J). (gr. k-3). pap. 11.99 *(978-0-06-054237-5(3)*, Harper Trophy) HarperCollins Pubs.
The Haunted Halloween, 6 vols. (Woodland Mysteriestm Ser.). 133p. (gr. 3-7). 42.50 *(978-0-7802-7924-7(7))* Wright Group/McGraw-Hill.
Hayden, Jeanne. Last Minute Wilma & Her Toad Soup. 2009. 24p. pap. 14.95 *(978-1-4327-3857-0(7))* Outskirts Pr., Inc.
Hegarty, Patricia. Five Black Cats. Woolf, Julia, illus. 2013. (ENG.). 22p. (J). (gr. -1). bds. 8.95 *(978-1-58925-611-8(5))* Tiger Tales.
—Five Little Ghosts. Woolf, Julia, illus. 2014. (ENG.). 22p. (J). (gr. -1-k). bds. 8.99 *(978-1-58925-587-6(9))* Tiger Tales.
The Hell House Experience. 2008. (ENG.). 70p. 14.99 *(978-0-9817520-8-2(X))* Torch Legacy Pubns.
Hendrix, Heather. What Should I Be for Halloween?, 1 vol. 2010. 16p. pap. 24.95 *(978-1-4489-8139-7(5))* PublishAmerica, Inc.
Henkes, Kevin. Julius's Candy Corn. Henkes, Kevin, illus. 2003. (ENG., Illus.). 24p. (J). (gr. -1-k). bds. 6.99 *(978-0-06-053789-0(2)*, Greenwillow Bks.) HarperCollins Pubs.
Herman, R. A. Littlest Pumpkin. Ogden, Betina, illus. 2006. (ENG.). (J). (gr. -1-3). 18.95 *(978-0-439-89837-9(4))* Scholastic, Inc.
Hesse, Laura. The Great Pumpkin Ride. 2004. ix, 133p. (J). *(978-0-9734013-1-8(1))* Running L. Productions.
Highlights for Children Editorial Staff, creator. Halloween Tales. 2016. (Highlights(tm) Hidden Pictures(r) Silly Sticker Stories Ser.). (ENG.). 48p. (J). (gr. k-4). pap. 5.99 *(978-1-62979-712-0(X)*, Highlights) Boyds Mills Pr.
Hill, Eric. Spot's Halloween. Hill, Eric, illus. 2003. (Spot Ser.). (ENG., Illus.). 14p. (J). (gr. -1 — 1). bds. 5.99 *(978-0-399-24185-7(X)*, Warne) Penguin Young Readers Group.
Hillert, Margaret. Es Halloween, Querido Dragón. Pullan, Jack, illus. 2017. (BeginningtoRead Ser.).Tr. of It's Halloween, Dear Dragon. (ENG & SPA.). 32p. (J). (-2). 22.60 ***(978-1-59953-836-5(9))*** Norwood Hse. Pr.
—It's Halloween, Dear Dragon. Pullan, Jack, illus. 2016. (BeginningtoRead Ser.). (ENG.). 32p. (J). (-2). lib. bdg. 22.60 *(978-1-59953-773-3(7))*; (gr. -1-2). pap. 11.94 *(978-1-60357-886-8(2))* Norwood Hse. Pr.
—The Witch Who Went for a Walk. Gallagher-Cole, Mernie, illus. 2016. (BeginningtoRead Ser.). (ENG.). 32p. (J). (gr. -1-2). pap. 11.94 *(978-1-60357-951-3(6))*; (gr. 1-2). 22.60 *(978-1-59953-810-5(5))* Norwood Hse. Pr.
Hills, Tad. Find a Pumpkin. Hills, Tad, illus. 2009. (Duck & Goose Ser.). (ENG., Illus.). 22p. (J). (gr. k — 1). bds. 7.99 *(978-0-375-85813-0(X)*, Schwartz & Wade Bks.) Random Hse. Children's Bks.
Hills, Tad & Hills, Tad. Duck & Goose, Honk! Quack! Boo! 2017. (Duck & Goose Ser.). (ENG., Illus.). 40p. (J). (gr. -1-2). 16.99 ***(978-1-5247-0175-8(0))***; lib. bdg. 19.99 ***(978-1-5247-0176-5(9))*** Random Hse. Children's Bks. (Schwartz & Wade Bks.).
Hirsch, Jennifer & Sisson, Stéphanie Roth. The Bitty Twins' Halloween. 2006. (Illus.). (J). *(978-1-59369-187-5(4))* American Girl Publishing, Inc.
Hirschmann, Kris & Langdo, Bryan, illus. We're Going on a Ghost Hunt. 2011. (J). *(978-0-545-34173-8(6))* Scholastic, Inc.
Hoberman, Mary Ann & Emberley, Michael. You Read to Me, I'll Read to You No. 2: Very Short Scary Tales to Read Together. Emberley, Michael, illus. 2009. (ENG., Illus.). 32p. (J). (gr. -1-3). pap. 7.99 *(978-0-316-04351-9(6))* Little Brown & Co.
Hoena, Blake. Halloween Scream. Regan, Dana, illus. 2014. (Jess & Jaylen Ser.). (ENG.). 48p. (J). (gr. 1-4). 27.07 *(978-1-63143-438-9(1)*, 208262) Child's World, Inc., The.
Hoena, Blake A. Eek & Ack vs the Wolfman, 1 vol. Harpster, Steve, illus. 2009. (Eek & Ack Ser.). (ENG.). 40p. (gr. 1-3). lib. bdg. 23.99 *(978-1-4342-1189-7(4)*, Graphic Sparks) Stone Arch Bks.
Hoff, Syd. Danny & the Dinosaur: Happy Halloween. Hoff, Syd, illus. 2016. (Illus.). 24p. (J). (gr. -1-3). pap. 6.99 *(978-0-06-241043-6(1)*, HarperFestival) HarperCollins Pubs.
Hoffman, Mary. Dracula's Daughter. 2006. (Yellow Bananas Ser.). (ENG., Illus.). 48p. (J). (gr. -1-3). *(978-0-7787-1000-4(9))*; lib. bdg. *(978-0-7787-0954-1(X))* Crabtree Publishing Co.
Holm, Jennifer L. & Holm, Matthew. Monster Mash. Holm, Jennifer L. & Holm, Matthew, illus. 2008. (Babymouse Ser.: 9). (ENG., Illus.). 96p. (J). (gr. 2-5). pap. 6.99 *(978-0-375-84387-7(6))*; lib. bdg. 12.99 *(978-0-375-93789-7(7))* Random Hse. Children's Bks. (Random Hse. Bks. for Young Readers).
Holt, Kimberly Willis. Piper Reed, Campfire Girl. Davenier, Christine, illus. 2010. (Piper Reed Ser.: 4). (ENG.). 160p. (J). (gr. 3-6). 15.99 *(978-0-8050-9006-2(1)*, 9780805090062, Holt, Henry & Co. Bks. For Young Readers) Holt, Henry & Co.
—Piper Reed, Campfire Girl. Davenier, Christine, illus. 2011. (Piper Reed Ser.: 4). (ENG.). 176p. (J). (gr. 3-6). pap. 6.99 *(978-0-312-67482-3(1)*, 9780312674823) Square Fish.
Holub, Joan. Scaredy-Pants! A Halloween Story. Terry, Will, illus. 2007. (Ant Hill Ser.). (ENG.). 24p. (J). (gr. -1-k). pap. 3.99 *(978-1-4169-0956-9(7)*, Simon Spotlight/Nickelodeon) Simon Spotlight/Nickelodeon.
—Vampoodle. Bowers, Tim, illus. 2017. (Step into Reading Ser.). (ENG.). 32p. (J). (gr. -1-1). pap. 3.99 *(978-1-101-93666-5(5)*, Random Hse. Bks. for Young Readers) Random Hse. Children's Bks.
Hood, Susan. Just Say Boo! Henry, Jed, illus. 2012. (ENG.). 32p. (J). (gr. -1-3). 12.99 *(978-0-06-201029-2(8))* HarperCollins Pubs.
Hooley, Rachelle B. & Butler, Mackay M. The Halloween Chase. Jarman, Brandy S., illus. 2012. 36p. 24.95 *(978-1-4626-7160-1(8))* America Star Bks.
Horowitz, Dave. The Ugly Pumpkin. Horowitz, Dave, illus. 2008. (ENG., Illus.). 40p. (J). (gr. -1-k). pap. 6.99 *(978-0-14-241145-2(0)*, Puffin Books) Penguin Young Readers Group.
Houdek, Andi. J P S Halloween Parade. Collier, Kevin, illus. 2012. 20p. pap. 9.95 *(978-1-61633-263-1(8))* Guardian Angel Publishing, Inc.
Howe, James. Scared Silly. Mack, Jeff, illus. 2006. (Bunnicula & Friends Ser.). 42p. (gr. 1-3). 14.00 *(978-0-7569-7225-7(6))* Perfection Learning Corp.
—Scared Silly. Mack, Jeff, illus. 2005. (Bunnicula & Friends Ser.: 3). (ENG.). 48p. (J). (gr. 1-3). 16.99 *(978-0-689-85726-3(8)*, Atheneum Bks. for Young Readers) Simon & Schuster Children's Publishing.
—Scared Silly. Mack, Jeff, illus. 2006. (Bunnicula & Friends Ser.: 3). (ENG.). 48p. (J). (gr. 1-3). pap. 3.99 *(978-0-689-85751-5(9)*, Simon Spotlight) Simon Spotlight.
Hughes, Vi. The Graveyard Hounds, 1 vol. Liest, Christina, illus. 2009. (ENG.). 168p. (J). (gr. 3-5). pap. 12.95 *(978-1-896580-49-4(1))* Tradewind Bks. CAN. Dist: Orca Bk. Pubs. USA.
Hulme, Joy N. Eerie Feary Feeling: A Hairy Scary Pop-up Book. Ely, Paul & Dudley, Dick, illus. 2006. 12p. (J). (gr. k-4). reprint ed. 14.00 *(978-1-4223-5171-0(8))* DIANE Publishing Co.
Hutchings, Paul. Halloween Tails. 2012. 24p. pap. 24.95 *(978-1-4626-7106-9(3))* America Star Bks.
J. Katyn. Boo & the Halloween Grin. 2011. 36p. pap. *(978-1-4269-7197-6(4))* Trafford Publishing (UK) Ltd.
Jacobson, Jennifer Richard. Andy Shane & the Pumpkin Trick. Carter, Abby, illus. 2007. (Andy Shane Ser.: 2). (ENG.). 64p. (J). (gr. k-3). per. 4.99 *(978-0-7636-3306-6(2))* Candlewick Pr.
—Andy Shane & the Pumpkin Trick. Carter, Abby, illus. 2008. (Andy Shane Ser.). (J). (gr. -1-3). 25.95 incl. audio *(978-1-4301-0313-4(2))*; pap. 16.95 incl. audio *(978-1-4301-0312-7(4))* Live Oak Media.
Jaeger, Elizabeth. It's Halloween, Little Pumpkin! Boyer, Robin, illus. 2014. 16p. (J). bds. 12.99 *(978-0-8249-1942-9(4)*, Ideal Pubns.) Worthy Publishing.
Jakubowski, Michele. Sidney & Sydney. 2013. (Sidney & Sydney Ser.). (ENG.). 128p. (gr. 1-3). 50.64 *(978-1-4795-1696-4(1))* Picture Window Bks.
—Third Grade Mix-Up. Montalto, Luisa, illus. (Sidney & Sydney Ser.). (ENG.). 128p. (gr. 1-3). 2015. pap. 7.15 *(978-1-4795-6754-6(X))* 2013. 8.95 *(978-1-4048-8104-4(2))* 2013. lib. bdg. 25.32 *(978-1-4048-8001-6(1))* Picture Window Bks.
James, Eric. A Halloween Scare at My House. Le Ray, Marina, illus. 2014. (ENG.). 32p. (J). (-5). 9.99 *(978-1-4926-0612-3(X)*, 9781492606123, Sourcebooks Jabberwocky) Sourcebooks, Inc.
—A Halloween Scare in Alabama. Le Ray, Marina, illus. 2015. (ENG.). 32p. (J). (-5). 9.99 *(978-1-4926-2359-5(8)*, 9781492623595, Sourcebooks Jabberwocky) Sourcebooks, Inc.
—A Halloween Scare in Alaska. Le Ray, Marina, illus. 2015. (ENG.). 32p. (J). (-5). 9.99 *(978-1-4926-2360-1(1)*, 9781492623601, Sourcebooks Jabberwocky) Sourcebooks, Inc.
—A Halloween Scare in Albuquerque. Le Ray, Marina, illus. 2015. (ENG.). 32p. (J). (-5). 9.99 *(978-1-4926-2361-8(X)*, 9781492623618, Sourcebooks Jabberwocky) Sourcebooks, Inc.
—A Halloween Scare in Arizona. Le Ray, Marina, illus. 2015. (ENG.). 32p. (J). (-5). 9.99 *(978-1-4926-2362-5(8)*, 9781492623625, Sourcebooks Jabberwocky) Sourcebooks, Inc.
—A Halloween Scare in Arkansas. Le Ray, Marina, illus. 2015. (ENG.). 32p. (J). (-5). 9.99 *(978-1-4926-2363-2(6)*, 9781492623632, Sourcebooks Jabberwocky) Sourcebooks, Inc.
—A Halloween Scare in Bentonville. Le Ray, Marina, illus. 2015. (ENG.). 32p. (J). (-5). 9.99 *(978-1-4926-2364-9(4)*, 9781492623649, Sourcebooks Jabberwocky) Sourcebooks, Inc.
—A Halloween Scare in Boise. Le Ray, Marina, illus. 2015. (ENG.). 32p. (J). (-5). 9.99 *(978-1-4926-2365-6(2)*, 9781492623656, Sourcebooks Jabberwocky) Sourcebooks, Inc.
—A Halloween Scare in Boston. Le Ray, Marina, illus. 2015. (ENG.). 32p. (J). (-5). 9.99 *(978-1-4926-2366-3(0)*, 9781492623663, Sourcebooks Jabberwocky) Sourcebooks, Inc.
—A Halloween Scare in Calgary. Le Ray, Marina, illus. 2015. (ENG.). 32p. (J). (-5). 11.99 *(978-1-4926-2367-0(9)*, 9781492623670, Sourcebooks Jabberwocky) Sourcebooks, Inc.
—A Halloween Scare in California. Le Ray, Marina, illus. 2014. (ENG.). 32p. (J). (-5). 9.99 *(978-1-4926-0570-6(0)*, 9781492605706, Sourcebooks Jabberwocky) Sourcebooks, Inc.
—A Halloween Scare in Canada. Le Ray, Marina, illus. 2014. (ENG.). 32p. (J). (-5). 9.99 *(978-1-4926-0573-7(5)*, 9781492605737, Sourcebooks Jabberwocky) Sourcebooks, Inc.
—A Halloween Scare in Charleston. Le Ray, Marina, illus. 2015. (ENG.). 32p. (J). (-5). 9.99 *(978-1-4926-2368-7(7)*, 9781492623687, Sourcebooks Jabberwocky) Sourcebooks, Inc.
—A Halloween Scare in Chicago. Le Ray, Marina, illus. 2014. (ENG.). 32p. (J). (-5). 9.99 *(978-1-4926-0579-9(4)*, 9781492605799, Sourcebooks Jabberwocky) Sourcebooks, Inc.
—A Halloween Scare in Cincinnati. Le Ray, Marina, illus. 2015. (ENG.). 32p. (J). (-5). 9.99 *(978-1-4926-2369-4(5)*, 9781492623694, Sourcebooks Jabberwocky) Sourcebooks, Inc.
—A Halloween Scare in Colorado. Le Ray, Marina, illus. 2014. (ENG.). 32p. (J). (-5). 9.99 *(978-1-4926-0582-9(4)*, 9781492605829, Sourcebooks Jabberwocky) Sourcebooks, Inc.
—A Halloween Scare in Connecticut. Le Ray, Marina, illus. 2015. (ENG.). 32p. (J). (-5). 9.99 *(978-1-4926-2370-0(9)*, 9781492623700, Sourcebooks Jabberwocky) Sourcebooks, Inc.
—A Halloween Scare in Edmonton. Le Ray, Marina, illus. 2015. (ENG.). 32p. (J). (-5). 11.99 *(978-1-4926-2372-4(5)*, 9781492623724, Sourcebooks Jabberwocky) Sourcebooks, Inc.
—A Halloween Scare in Florida. Le Ray, Marina, illus. 2014. (ENG.). 32p. (J). (-5). 9.99 *(978-1-4926-0585-0(9)*, 9781492605850, Sourcebooks Jabberwocky) Sourcebooks, Inc.
—A Halloween Scare in Georgia. Le Ray, Marina, illus. 2014. (ENG.). 32p. (J). (-5). 9.99 *(978-1-4926-0588-1(3)*, 9781492605881, Sourcebooks Jabberwocky) Sourcebooks, Inc.
—A Halloween Scare in Hawaii. Le Ray, Marina, illus. 2015. (ENG.). 32p. (J). (-5). 9.99 *(978-1-4926-2373-1(3)*, 9781492623731, Sourcebooks Jabberwocky) Sourcebooks, Inc.
—A Halloween Scare in Idaho. Le Ray, Marina, illus. 2015. (ENG.). 32p. (J). (-5). 9.99 *(978-1-4926-2374-8(1)*, 9781492623748, Sourcebooks Jabberwocky) Sourcebooks, Inc.
—A Halloween Scare in Illinois. Le Ray, Marina, illus. 2015. (ENG.). 32p. (J). (-5). 9.99 *(978-1-4926-2375-5(X)*, 9781492623755, Sourcebooks Jabberwocky) Sourcebooks, Inc.
—A Halloween Scare in Indiana. Le Ray, Marina, illus. 2014. (ENG.). 32p. (J). (-5). 9.99 *(978-1-4926-0591-1(3)*, 9781492605911, Sourcebooks Jabberwocky) Sourcebooks, Inc.
—A Halloween Scare in Iowa. Le Ray, Marina, illus. 2014. (ENG.). 32p. (J). (-5). 9.99 *(978-1-4926-0594-2(8)*, 9781492605942, Sourcebooks Jabberwocky) Sourcebooks, Inc.
—A Halloween Scare in Kansas. Le Ray, Marina, illus. 2015. (ENG.). 32p. (J). (-5). 9.99 *(978-1-4926-2376-2(8)*, 9781492623762, Sourcebooks Jabberwocky) Sourcebooks, Inc.
—A Halloween Scare in Kansas City. Le Ray, Marina, illus. 2015. (ENG.). 32p. (J). (-5). 9.99 *(978-1-4926-2377-9(6)*, 9781492623779, Sourcebooks Jabberwocky) Sourcebooks, Inc.
—A Halloween Scare in Kentucky. Le Ray, Marina, illus. 2014. (ENG.). 32p. (J). (-5). 9.99 *(978-1-4926-0597-3(2)*, 9781492605973, Sourcebooks Jabberwocky) Sourcebooks, Inc.
—A Halloween Scare in Las Vegas. Le Ray, Marina, illus. 2015. (ENG.). 32p. (J). (-5). 9.99 *(978-1-4926-2378-6(4)*, 9781492623786, Sourcebooks Jabberwocky) Sourcebooks, Inc.
—A Halloween Scare in Los Angeles. Le Ray, Marina, illus. 2015. (ENG.). 32p. (J). (-5). 9.99 *(978-1-4926-2379-3(2)*, 9781492623793, Sourcebooks Jabberwocky) Sourcebooks, Inc.
—A Halloween Scare in Louisiana. Le Ray, Marina, illus. 2014. (ENG.). 32p. (J). (-5). 9.99 *(978-1-4926-0600-0(6)*, 9781492606000, Sourcebooks Jabberwocky) Sourcebooks, Inc.
—A Halloween Scare in Maine. Le Ray, Marina, illus. 2015. (ENG.). 32p. (J). (-5). 9.99 *(978-1-4926-2380-9(6)*, 9781492623809, Sourcebooks Jabberwocky) Sourcebooks, Inc.
—A Halloween Scare in Maryland. Le Ray, Marina, illus. 2014. (ENG.). 32p. (J). (-5). 9.99 *(978-1-4926-0603-1(0)*, 9781492606031, Sourcebooks Jabberwocky) Sourcebooks, Inc.
—A Halloween Scare in Massachusetts. Le Ray, Marina, illus. 2015. (ENG.). 32p. (J). (-5). 9.99 *(978-1-4926-2381-6(4)*, 9781492623816, Sourcebooks Jabberwocky) Sourcebooks, Inc.
—A Halloween Scare in Michigan. Le Ray, Marina, illus. 2014. (ENG.). 32p. (J). (-5). 9.99 *(978-1-4926-0606-2(5)*, 9781492606062, Sourcebooks Jabberwocky) Sourcebooks, Inc.
—A Halloween Scare in Minnesota. Le Ray, Marina, illus. 2014. (ENG.). 32p. (J). (-5). 9.99 *(978-1-4926-0609-3(X)*, 9781492606093, Sourcebooks Jabberwocky) Sourcebooks, Inc.
—A Halloween Scare in Mississippi. Le Ray, Marina, illus. 2015. (ENG.). 32p. (J). (-5). 9.99 *(978-1-4926-2382-3(2)*, 9781492623823, Sourcebooks Jabberwocky) Sourcebooks, Inc.
—A Halloween Scare in Missouri. Le Ray, Marina, illus. 2015. (ENG.). 32p. (J). (-5). 9.99 *(978-1-4926-2383-0(0)*, 9781492623830, Sourcebooks Jabberwocky) Sourcebooks, Inc.
—A Halloween Scare in Montana. Le Ray, Marina, illus. 2015. (ENG.). 32p. (J). (-5). 9.99 *(978-1-4926-2384-7(9)*, 9781492623847, Sourcebooks Jabberwocky) Sourcebooks, Inc.
—A Halloween Scare in Nebraska. Le Ray, Marina, illus. 2015. (ENG.). 32p. (J). (-5). 9.99 *(978-1-4926-2385-4(7)*, 9781492623854, Sourcebooks Jabberwocky) Sourcebooks, Inc.
—A Halloween Scare in Nevada. Le Ray, Marina, illus. 2015. (ENG.). 32p. (J). (-5). 9.99 *(978-1-4926-2386-1(5)*, 9781492623861, Sourcebooks Jabberwocky) Sourcebooks, Inc.
—A Halloween Scare in New England. Le Ray, Marina, illus. 2014. (ENG.). 32p. (J). (-5). 9.99 *(978-1-4926-0615-4(4)*, 9781492606154, Sourcebooks Jabberwocky) Sourcebooks, Inc.
—A Halloween Scare in New Hampshire. Le Ray, Marina, illus. 2015. (ENG.). 32p. (J). (-5). 9.99 *(978-1-4926-2387-8(3)*, 9781492623878, Sourcebooks Jabberwocky) Sourcebooks, Inc.
—A Halloween Scare in New Jersey. Le Ray, Marina, illus. 2014. (ENG.). 32p. (J). (-5). 9.99 *(978-1-4926-0618-5(9)*, 9781492606185, Sourcebooks Jabberwocky) Sourcebooks, Inc.
—A Halloween Scare in New Mexico. Le Ray, Marina, illus. 2015. (ENG.). 32p. (J). (-5). 9.99 *(978-1-4926-2388-5(1)*, 9781492623885, Sourcebooks Jabberwocky) Sourcebooks, Inc.
—A Halloween Scare in New York. Le Ray, Marina, illus. 2014. (ENG.). 32p. (J). (-5). 9.99 *(978-1-4926-0621-5(9)*, 9781492606215, Sourcebooks Jabberwocky) Sourcebooks, Inc.
—A Halloween Scare in New York City. Le Ray, Marina, illus. 2015. (ENG.). 32p. (J). (-5). 9.99 *(978-1-4926-2389-2(X)*, 9781492623892, Sourcebooks Jabberwocky) Sourcebooks, Inc.
—A Halloween Scare in North Carolina. Le Ray, Marina, illus. 2015. (ENG.). 32p. (J). (-5). 9.99 *(978-1-4926-2855-2(7)*, 9781492628552, Sourcebooks Jabberwocky) Sourcebooks, Inc.
—A Halloween Scare in North Dakota. Le Ray, Marina, illus. 2015. (ENG.). 32p. (J). (-5). 9.99 *(978-1-4926-2390-8(3)*, 9781492623908, Sourcebooks Jabberwocky) Sourcebooks, Inc.
—A Halloween Scare in Ohio. Le Ray, Marina, illus. 2014. (ENG.). 32p. (J). (-5). 9.99 *(978-1-4926-0624-6(3)*, 9781492606246, Sourcebooks Jabberwocky) Sourcebooks, Inc.
—A Halloween Scare in Oklahoma. Le Ray, Marina, illus. 2015. (ENG.). 32p. (J). (-5). 9.99 *(978-1-4926-2391-5(1)*, 9781492623915, Sourcebooks Jabberwocky) Sourcebooks, Inc.
—A Halloween Scare in Omaha. Le Ray, Marina, illus. 2015. (ENG.). 32p. (J). (-5). 9.99 *(978-1-4926-2392-2(X)*, 9781492623922, Sourcebooks Jabberwocky) Sourcebooks, Inc.
—A Halloween Scare in Oregon. Le Ray, Marina, illus. 2015. (ENG.). 32p. (J). (-5). 9.99 *(978-1-4926-2393-9(8)*,

9781492623939, Sourcebooks Jabberwocky) Sourcebooks, Inc.

—A Halloween Scare in Ottawa. Le Ray, Marina, illus. 2015. (ENG.). 32p. (J). (-5). 11.99 *(978-1-4926-2394-6(6)*, 9781492623946, Sourcebooks Jabberwocky) Sourcebooks, Inc.

—A Halloween Scare in Pennsylvania. Le Ray, Marina, illus. 2014. (ENG.). 32p. (J). (-5). 9.99 *(978-1-4926-0627-7(8)*, 9781492606277, Sourcebooks Jabberwocky) Sourcebooks, Inc.

—A Halloween Scare in Philadelphia. Le Ray, Marina, illus. 2015. (ENG.). 32p. (J). (-5). 9.99 *(978-1-4926-2395-3(4)*, 9781492623953, Sourcebooks Jabberwocky) Sourcebooks, Inc.

—A Halloween Scare in Pittsburgh. Le Ray, Marina, illus. 2015. (ENG.). 32p. (J). (-5). 9.99 *(978-1-4926-2396-0(2)*, 9781492623960, Sourcebooks Jabberwocky) Sourcebooks, Inc.

—A Halloween Scare in Rhode Island. Le Ray, Marina, illus. 2015. (ENG.). 32p. (J). (-5). 9.99 *(978-1-4926-2398-4(9)*, 9781492623984, Sourcebooks Jabberwocky) Sourcebooks, Inc.

—A Halloween Scare in San Francisco. Le Ray, Marina, illus. 2015. (ENG.). 32p. (J). (-5). 9.99 *(978-1-4926-2399-1(7)*, 9781492623991, Sourcebooks Jabberwocky) Sourcebooks, Inc.

—A Halloween Scare in South Carolina. Le Ray, Marina, illus. 2015. (ENG.). 32p. (J). (-5). 9.99 *(978-1-4926-2860-6(3)*, 9781492628606, Sourcebooks Jabberwocky) Sourcebooks, Inc.

—A Halloween Scare in South Dakota. Le Ray, Marina, illus. 2015. (ENG.). 32p. (J). (-5). 9.99 *(978-1-4926-2400-4(4)*, 9781492624004, Sourcebooks Jabberwocky) Sourcebooks, Inc.

—A Halloween Scare in St. Louis. Le Ray, Marina, illus. 2015. (ENG.). 32p. (J). (-5). 9.99 *(978-1-4926-2401-1(2)*, 9781492624011, Sourcebooks Jabberwocky) Sourcebooks, Inc.

—A Halloween Scare in Tampa Bay. Le Ray, Marina, illus. 2015. (ENG.). 32p. (J). (-5). 9.99 *(978-1-4926-2402-8(0)*, 9781492624028, Sourcebooks Jabberwocky) Sourcebooks, Inc.

—A Halloween Scare in Tennessee. Le Ray, Marina, illus. 2014. (ENG.). 32p. (J). (-5). 9.99 *(978-1-4926-0630-7(8)*, 9781492606307, Sourcebooks Jabberwocky) Sourcebooks, Inc.

—A Halloween Scare in Texas. Le Ray, Marina, illus. 2014. (ENG.). 32p. (J). (-5). 9.99 *(978-1-4926-0633-8(2)*, 9781492606338, Sourcebooks Jabberwocky) Sourcebooks, Inc.

—A Halloween Scare in the Carolinas. Le Ray, Marina, illus. 2014. (ENG.). 32p. (J). (-5). 9.99 *(978-1-4926-0576-8(X)*, 9781492605768, Sourcebooks Jabberwocky) Sourcebooks, Inc.

—A Halloween Scare in Toronto. Le Ray, Marina, illus. 2015. (ENG.). 32p. (J). (-5). 11.99 *(978-1-4926-2403-5(9)*, 9781492624035, Sourcebooks Jabberwocky) Sourcebooks, Inc.

—A Halloween Scare in Tulsa. Le Ray, Marina, illus. 2015. (ENG.). 32p. (J). (-5). 9.99 *(978-1-4926-2404-2(7)*, 9781492624042, Sourcebooks Jabberwocky) Sourcebooks, Inc.

—A Halloween Scare in Vancouver. Le Ray, Marina, illus. 2015. (ENG.). 32p. (J). (-5). 11.99 *(978-1-4926-2406-6(3)*, 9781492624066, Sourcebooks Jabberwocky) Sourcebooks, Inc.

—A Halloween Scare in Vermont. Le Ray, Marina, illus. 2015. (ENG.). 32p. (J). (-5). 9.99 *(978-1-4926-2407-3(1)*, 9781492624073, Sourcebooks Jabberwocky) Sourcebooks, Inc.

—A Halloween Scare in Virginia. Le Ray, Marina, illus. 2014. (ENG.). 32p. (J). (-5). 9.99 *(978-1-4926-0636-9(7)*, 9781492606369, Sourcebooks Jabberwocky) Sourcebooks, Inc.

—A Halloween Scare in Washington. Le Ray, Marina, illus. 2014. (ENG.). 32p. (J). (-5). 9.99 *(978-1-4926-0639-0(1)*, 9781492606390, Sourcebooks Jabberwocky) Sourcebooks, Inc.

—A Halloween Scare in Washington, DC. Le Ray, Marina, illus. 2015. (ENG.). 32p. (J). (-5). 9.99 *(978-1-4926-2408-0(X)*, 9781492624080, Sourcebooks Jabberwocky) Sourcebooks, Inc.

—A Halloween Scare in West Virginia. Le Ray, Marina, illus. 2015. (ENG.). 32p. (J). (-5). 9.99 *(978-1-4926-2409-7(8)*, 9781492624097, Sourcebooks Jabberwocky) Sourcebooks, Inc.

—A Halloween Scare in Wisconsin. Le Ray, Marina, illus. 2014. (ENG.). 32p. (J). (-5). 9.99 *(978-1-4926-0642-0(1)*, 9781492606420, Sourcebooks Jabberwocky) Sourcebooks, Inc.

—A Halloween Scare in Wyoming. Le Ray, Marina, illus. 2015. (ENG.). 32p. (J). (-5). 9.99 *(978-1-4926-2410-3(1)*, 9781492624103, Sourcebooks Jabberwocky) Sourcebooks, Inc.

Jane, Pamela. Little Goblins Ten. Jane, Pamela & Manning, Jane, illus. 2011. (ENG.). 32p. (J). (gr. -1-3). 16.99 *(978-0-06-176798-2(0))* HarperCollins Pubs.

—Monster Mischief. Rosenberry, Vera, illus. 2014. (ENG.). 32p. (J). (gr. -1-2). 16.99 *(978-1-4814-2535-3(8)*, Atheneum Bks. for Young Readers) Simon & Schuster Children's Publishing.

Jenkins, Emily. Dangerous Pumpkins. Bliss, Harry, illus. 2012. (Invisible Inkling Ser.: 2). (ENG.). 160p. (J). (gr. 1-5). 14.99 *(978-0-06-180223-2(9))* HarperCollins Pubs.

Jenkins, Jerry B. & Fabry, Chris. Hollywood Holdup. 2006. (Red Rock Mysteries Ser.: 12). (ENG.). 224p. (YA). (gr. 8-12). per. 6.99 *(978-1-4143-0151-8(0)*, Tyndale Kids) Tyndale Hse. Pubs.

Jessell, Tim, illus. The Boxcar Children, Set. 2013. (Boxcar Children Mysteries Ser.). (ENG.). 538p. (J). (gr. 1-5). 45.00 *(978-0-8075-0864-0(0))* Whitman, Albert & Co.

Johnson, Jay, illus. Ten Little Pumpkins. 2012. (J). *(978-0-545-46862-6(0))* Scholastic, Inc.

Johnson, Kathleen Jeffrie. A Fast & Brutal Wing. unabr. ed. 2005. (YA). 46.70 incl. audio *(978-1-4193-3247-0(3)*, 42029) Recorded Bks., Inc.

Johnson, Lisa. All Hallows' Eve: The Story of the Halloween Fairy. Johnson, Tucker, illus. l.t. ed. 2005. 32p. (J). 12.95 *(978-0-9773096-0-3(6))* Positive Spin Pr.

Johnson, Sandi, et al. Haunted Doghouse II: Halloween Night, 3 vols., bk. 2. Durant, Sybrina, ed. Stargeon, Bobbi, illus. l.t. ed. 2014. (ENG.). 36p. (J). (gr. k-5). pap. 12.99 *(978-1-929063-27-7(X)*, 351) Moons & Stars Publishing For Children.

Jones, Jen. Willow's Boy-Crazy Birthday. Franco, Paula, illus. 2014. (Sleepover Girls Ser.). (ENG.). 128p. (gr. 3-5). lib. bdg. 22.65 *(978-1-4342-9757-0(8))* Stone Arch Bks.

Jones, Kim P. Maggie & the Halloween Bandit. 2007. 124p. per. 19.95 *(978-1-60441-158-4(9))* America Star Bks.

Jordan, Apple. A Fairy-Tale Fall. Legramandi, Francesco, illus. 2010. (Step into Reading Ser.). (ENG.). 32p. (J). (gr. k-3). pap. 3.99 *(978-0-7364-2674-9(4)*, RH/Disney) Random Hse. Children's Bks.

—A Fairy-Tale Fall. 2010. (Disney Princess Step into Reading Ser.). lib. bdg. 13.55 *(978-0-606-14879-5(5)*, Turtleback) Turtleback Bks.

Jougla, Frederic. Tricked on Halloween: Rina & Jax's Stories. Jougla, Karina, illus. l.t. ed. 2004. 36p. (J). bds. 14.99 *(978-0-9754287-0-2(5))* Imagery Pr.

Kann, Victoria. Pink or Treat! Kann, Victoria, illus. 2013. (Pinkalicious Ser.). (ENG., Illus.). 24p. (J). (gr. -1-3). pap. 4.99 *(978-0-06-218770-3(8)*, HarperFestival) HarperCollins Pubs.

—Pink or Treat! 2013. (Pinkalicious Ser.). (J). lib. bdg. 14.75 *(978-0-606-31824-2(0)*, Turtleback) Turtleback Bks.

Karr, Lily. My Pumpkin. Marts, Doreen Mulryan, illus. 2014. (ENG.). 12p. (J). (gr. -1 — 1). bds. 4.99 *(978-0-545-49332-1(3)*, Cartwheel Bks.) Scholastic, Inc.

—Spooky Boo: A Halloween Adventure. Poling, Kyle, illus. 2011. (ENG.). 12p. (J). (gr. -1 — 1). bds. 6.99 *(978-0-545-29867-4(9)*, Cartwheel Bks.) Scholastic, Inc.

Keene, Carolyn. The Halloween Hoax. Pamintuan, Macky, illus. 9th ed. 2007. (Nancy Drew & the Clue Crew Ser.: 9). (ENG.). 96p. (J). (gr. 1-4). pap. 4.99 *(978-1-4169-3664-0(5)*, Aladdin) Simon & Schuster Children's Publishing.

Kelman, Marcy & Disney Book Group Staff. Trick or Treasure? Disney Storybook Artists Staff, illus. 2013. (ENG.). 24p. (J). (gr. -1-k). pap. 5.99 *(978-1-4231-7140-9(3))* Disney Pr.

Kessel, Joyce K. Halloween. Carlson, Nancy, illus. rev. ed. 2003. (On My Own Holidays Ser.). (ENG.). 48p. (gr. 2-4). lib. bdg. 25.26 *(978-0-87614-933-1(6))* Lerner Publishing Group.

Kimmelman, Leslie. Trick ARRR Treat: A Pirate Halloween. Monlongo, Jorge, illus. 2017. (ENG.). 32p. (J). (gr. -1-k). pap. 7.99 ***(978-0-8075-8066-0(X))*** Whitman, Albert & Co.

Kimmelman, Leslie. Trick Arrr Treat: A Pirate Halloween. Monlongo, Jorge, illus. 2015. (ENG.). 32p. (J). (gr. -1-3). 16.99 *(978-0-8075-8061-5(9))* Whitman, Albert & Co.

King, Carole & King, E. Gregory. The Hollow Weens. 2012. 26p. 16.95 *(978-1-4575-1224-7(6))*; pap. 11.95 *(978-1-4575-1448-7(6))* Dog Ear Publishing, LLC.

King, Trey. Halloween Rescue! Wang, Sean, illus. 2013. (Lego City Ser.). (ENG.). 24p. (J). (gr. -1-3). 4.99 *(978-0-545-51572-6(6))* Scholastic, Inc.

Kinney, Jeff. Double Down. 2016. (Diary of a Wimpy Kid Ser.: Bk. 11). (ENG., Illus.). 224p. (J). (gr. 3-7). 13.95 *(978-1-4197-2344-5(8))*; E-Book 12.56 *(978-1-61312-992-0(0))* Abrams, Inc. (Amulet Bks.).

—Double Down. 2016. (Diary of a Wimpy Kid Ser.: 11). (J). lib. bdg. 25.70 *(978-0-606-38998-3(9))* Turtleback Bks.

Kirby, Stan. Captain Awesome vs. the Spooky, Scary House. O'Connor, George, illus. 2013. (Captain Awesome Ser.: 8). (ENG.). 128p. (J). (gr. k-2). 16.99 *(978-1-4424-7255-6(3))*; pap. 5.99 *(978-1-4424-7254-9(5))* Little Simon. (Little Simon).

—Captain Awesome vs. the Spooky, Scary House. 2013. (Captain Awesome Ser.: 8). lib. bdg. 16.00 *(978-0-606-32048-1(2)*, Turtleback) Turtleback Bks.

Kirk & Rossiter, Sofia. The Story of the Great Pumpkin Man. 2012. 44p. pap. 21.99 *(978-1-4691-7989-6(X))* Xlibris Corp.

Klein, Abby. Halloween Parade. McKinley, John, illus. 2009. (Ready, Freddy! Reader List: No. 3). 32p. (J). *(978-0-545-14174-1(5))* Scholastic, Inc.

Kleinberg, Naomi. Elmo's Monster Mash. Moroney, Christopher, illus. 2010. (ENG.). 12p. (J). (gr. k — 1). 4.99 *(978-0-375-85804-8(0)*, Random Hse. Bks. for Young Readers) Random Hse. Children's Bks.

Kline, C. A. The Fright Night Series. 2010. 88p. pap. 11.00 *(978-1-4490-3795-6(X))* AuthorHouse.

Kline, C. A. & Lauder, M. F. Halloween Night. 2012. 24p. pap. 17.99 *(978-1-4772-7417-0(0))* AuthorHouse.

Klise, Kate. Over My Dead Body. Klise, M. Sarah, illus. (43 Old Cemetery Road Ser.: 2). (ENG.). 128p. (J). (gr. 2-5). 2011. pap. 6.99 *(978-0-547-57713-5(3))* 2009. 15.99 *(978-0-15-205734-3(X))* Houghton Mifflin Harcourt Publishing Co.

Knight, Chris. Skaggy the Scarecrow: A Halloween Story. 2010. (Illus.). 40p. pap. 18.49 *(978-1-4520-2473-8(1))* AuthorHouse.

Kole MacLean, Christine. Mary Margaret Running Scared. 2010. 152p. pap. 14.98 *(978-0-557-24676-2(8))* Lulu Pr., Inc.

Kontis, Alethea. AlphaOops! H Is for Halloween. Kolar, Bob, illus. 2010. (ENG.). 40p. (J). (gr. -1-3). 15.99 *(978-0-7636-3966-2(4))* Candlewick Pr.

—Alphaoops! H Is for Halloween. Kolar, Bob, illus. 2011. (ENG.). 40p. (J). (gr. -1-3). 7.99 *(978-0-7636-5686-7(0))* Candlewick Pr.

Kraus, Robert. Daddy Long Ears' Halloween. 2014. (ENG., Illus.). 32p. (J). (gr. -1-3). 13.99 *(978-1-4814-3108-8(0)*, Simon & Schuster/Paula Wiseman Bks.) Simon & Schuster/Paula Wiseman Bks.

Krieb & Kreib. We're off to Find the Witch's House. Alley, R. W., illus. 2007. (ENG.). 32p. (J). (gr. -1-2). 6.99 *(978-0-14-240854-4(9)*, Puffin Books) Penguin Young Readers Group.

Kroll, Steven. The Biggest Pumpkin Ever. Bassett, Jeni, illus. 2007. (ENG.). 32p. (J). (gr. -1-k). pap. 4.99 *(978-0-439-92946-2(6))* Scholastic, Inc.

—The Biggest Pumpkin Surprise Ever. Bassett, Jeni, illus. 2012. (ENG.). 10p. (J). (gr. -1-k). bds. 6.99 *(978-0-545-40285-9(9)*, Cartwheel Bks.) Scholastic, Inc.

Krosoczka, Jarrett J. Annie Was Warned. 2013. (ENG., Illus.). 32p. (J). (gr. -1-2). 7.99 *(978-0-385-75341-8(1)*, Dragonfly Bks.) Random Hse. Children's Bks.

—Annie Was Warned. 2013. lib. bdg. 18.40 *(978-0-606-32188-4(8)*, Turtleback) Turtleback Bks.

Krulik, Nancy. Burp or Treat... Smell My Feet! 2014. (George Brown, Class Clown Ser.: No. 3). lib. bdg. 16.00 *(978-0-606-35704-3(1))* Turtleback Bks.

Krull, Kathleen. How to Trick or Treat in Outer Space. Brewer, Paul, illus. 2004. (ENG.). 32p. (J). (gr. k-3). tchr. ed. 16.95 *(978-0-8234-1844-2(8))* Holiday Hse., Inc.

Kwiat, Ernie, illus. Sesame Street Boo! Guess Who, Elmo! 2015. (Guess Who! Book Ser.). (ENG.). 10p. (J). (gr. -1-k). bds. 10.99 *(978-0-7944-3475-5(4))* Reader's Digest Assn., Inc., The.

Labatt, Mary. Sam's First Halloween. Sarrazin, Marisol, illus. 2003. (Kids Can Read Ser.). (ENG.). 32p. (J). (gr. k-1). pap. 4.99 *(978-1-55337-356-8(1))* Kids Can Pr., Ltd. CAN. Dist: Hachette Bk. Group.

LaFleur, John & Dubin, Shawn. The Misadventures of Dreary & Naughty, 1 vol. 2013. (ENG., Illus.). 64p. (J). 14.99 *(978-0-7643-4494-7(3)*, 9780764344947) Schiffer Publishing, Ltd.

Lakin, Patricia. Max & Mo's Halloween Surprise. Floca, Brian, illus. 2008. (Max & Mo Ser.). (ENG.). 32p. (J). (gr. -1-1). pap. 3.99 *(978-1-4169-2539-2(2)*, Simon Spotlight) Simon Spotlight.

Lamonica, Lisa. On Halloween, I Love You As Big As the Moon. 2009. 20p. pap. 24.95 *(978-1-61546-884-3(6))* America Star Bks.

Landry, Leo. Trick or Treat. 2012. (ENG., Illus.). 32p. (J). (gr. -1-3). 12.99 *(978-0-547-24969-8(1))* Houghton Mifflin Harcourt Publishing Co.

Laterra, Joann. Halloween Crossing. 2004. 127p. (YA). pap. 14.95 *(978-0-7414-2101-2(1))* Infinity Publishing.

Lazo, Jeanne Rae. If Looks Could Kill. 2005. 160p. (J). lib. bdg. 14.95 *(978-0-9713756-4-2(X))* Stargazer Publishing Co.

Lee, Vanessa Rose. The Haunted House of Riddles. Gillen, Rosemarie, illus. 2011. 28p. pap. 7.99 *(978-1-61286-053-4(2))* Avid Readers Publishing Group.

Leighton, Noreen. Mr Tilly & the Halloween Mystery. Wilson, Lorna, illus. 2013. 42p. pap. *(978-0-9573315-6-3(8))* Tatterdemalion Blue.

Lester, Helen. Tacky & the Haunted Igloo. Munsinger, Lynn, illus. 2015. (Tacky the Penguin Ser.). (ENG.). 32p. (J). 16.99 *(978-0-544-33994-1(0)*, HMH Books For Young Readers) Houghton Mifflin Harcourt Publishing Co.

Lewis, Anne Margaret. The Runaway Pumpkin. Zenz, Aaron, illus. 2015. (ENG.). 40p. (J). (gr. -1-k). 15.99 *(978-1-63450-214-6(0)*, Sky Pony Pr.) Skyhorse Publishing Co., Inc.

Lindner, Brooke. Diego's Halloween Party. Mawhinney, Art, illus. 2008. (Go, Diego, Go! Ser.). (ENG.). 16p. (J). (gr. -1-k). bds. 5.99 *(978-1-4169-5497-2(X)*, Simon Spotlight/Nickelodeon) Simon Spotlight/Nickelodeon.

Lindsay, Courtney B. ABC Scream, It's Halloween! 2010. 48p. 17.99 *(978-1-4520-3889-6(9))* AuthorHouse.

Litter Bug's Halloween. 2006. (J). 8.95 *(978-0-9788536-4-8(4))* G Publishing LLC.

Litton, Jonathan. Boo! My Little World. Galloway, Fhiona, illus. 2015. (My Little World Ser.). (ENG.). 16p. (J). bds. 7.99 *(978-1-68010-501-8(9))* Tiger Tales.

—Mouse in the Haunted House. Anderson, Nicola, illus. 2015. (Planet Pop-Up Ser.). (ENG.). 12p. (J). (gr. -1). 12.95 *(978-1-62686-485-6(3)*, Silver Dolphin Bks.) Readerlink Distribution Services, LLC.

London, Jonathan. Froggy's Halloween. Remkiewicz, Frank, illus. 2010. lib. bdg. 16.10 *(978-0-7569-8999-6(X))* Penguin Publishing Group.

Long, Ethan. Fright Club. 2015. (ENG., Illus.). 32p. (J). (gr. -1-2). 16.99 *(978-1-61963-337-7(X)*, 9781619633377, Bloomsbury USA Childrens) Bloomsbury Publishing USA.

Lord, Cynthia. Hot Rod Hamster & the Haunted Halloween Party. Anderson, Derek & Paprocki, Greg, illus. 2015. (Scholastic Reader, Level 2 Ser.). (ENG.). 32p. (J). (gr. k-2). pap. 3.99 *(978-0-545-81528-4(2)*, Scholastic Pr.) Scholastic, Inc.

—Hot Rod Hamster & the Haunted Halloween Party! Anderson, Derek, illus. 2015. (ENG.). 32p. (J). (gr. -1-3). 16.99 *(978-0-545-81529-1(0)*, Scholastic Pr.) Scholastic, Inc.

Lorini, Andrea. Spooky Castle. 2014. (ENG.). 8p. (J). (gr. -1-k). bds. 6.99 *(978-0-7641-6734-8(0))* Barron's Educational Series, Inc.

—A Spooky Halloween. Rigo, Laura, illus. 2016. (ENG.). 8p. (J). (gr. -1-k). bds. 6.99 *(978-0-7641-6852-9(5))* Barron's Educational Series, Inc.

—Trick or Treat. 2015. (ENG., Illus.). 8p. (J). (gr. -1-k). bds. 6.99 *(978-0-7641-6783-6(9))* Barron's Educational Series, Inc.

MacLean, Heather. The Mousecat & the Moonicorns on Halloween Night. 2013. 40p. pap. 16.95 *(978-1-4525-7617-6(3)*, Balboa Pr.) Author Solutions, Inc.

MacLennan, Cathy. Spooky Spooky Spooky! (ENG., Illus.). (J). 2012. 26p. (gr. k — 1). bds. 6.95 *(978-1-907967-15-3(X))* 2009. 32p. (gr. -1-1). 16.95 *(978-1-906250-67-6(7))* Boxer Bks., Ltd. GBR. Dist: Sterling Publishing Co., Inc.

Magsamen, Sandra. I Love You, Little Pumpkin. 2017. (ENG.). 10p. (J). (gr. -1 — 1). 7.99 ***(978-1-338-11085-2(3)***, Cartwheel Bks.) Scholastic, Inc.

Magsamen, Sandra. Itsy-Bitsy I Love You! Magsamen, Sandra, illus. 2016. (Heart-Felt Bks.). (ENG., Illus.). 10p. (J). (— 1). 7.99 *(978-0-545-46841-1(8)*, Cartwheel Bks.) Scholastic, Inc.

Mama Doo. Zachary & the Magic Pumpkin Seeds, 1 vol. 2007. (ENG.). 35p. 24.95 *(978-1-4241-8579-5(3))* America Star Bks.

Man-Kong, Mary. A Boo-Tiful Halloween! Riley, Kellee, illus. 2013. (Pictureback(R) Ser.). (ENG.). 16p. (J). (gr. -1-2). 4.99 *(978-0-449-81860-2(8)*, Random Hse. Bks. for Young Readers) Random Hse. Children's Bks.

—A Spook-Tacular Halloween! (Barbie) 2015. (Big Coloring Book Ser.). (ENG., Illus.). 48p. (J). (gr. -1-2). pap. 6.99 *(978-0-553-52340-9(6)*, Golden Bks.) Random Hse. Children's Bks.

—The Spooky Smells of Halloween. Garofoli, Viviana, illus. 2005. (Scented Storybook Ser.). (ENG.). 32p. (J). (gr. -1-2). 8.99 *(978-0-375-83285-7(8)*, Golden Bks.) Random Hse. Children's Bks.

—The Sweetest Halloween (Barbie) Golden Books Staff & Duarte, Pamela, illus. 2012. (Glow-In-the-Dark Sticker Book Ser.). (ENG.). 48p. (J). (gr. -1-2). pap. 3.99 *(978-0-307-93115-3(3)*, Golden Bks.) Random Hse. Children's Bks.

Mangan, Anne. Emu's Halloween. Cornish, David, illus. 2017. 32p. 9.99 *(978-0-7322-9890-6(3))* HarperCollins Pubs. Australia AUS. Dist: HarperCollins Pubs.

Mantle, Ben, illus. Trick or Treat: 12 Board Books, 12 vols. 2011. (J). *(978-1-4508-1914-5(1))* Phoenix International Publications, Inc.

—Trick or Treat: 12 Board Books, 12 vols. 2011. (J). *(978-1-4508-2462-0(5))*; *(978-1-4508-2457-6(9))*; *(978-1-4508-2460-6(9))*; *(978-1-4508-2459-0(5))*; *(978-1-4508-2458-3(7))*; *(978-1-4508-2465-1(X))*; *(978-1-4508-2461-3(7))*; *(978-1-4508-2466-8(8))*; *(978-1-4508-2467-5(6))*; *(978-1-4508-2463-7(3))*; *(978-1-4508-2464-4(1))*; *(978-1-4508-2468-2(4))* Publications International, Ltd.

Manushkin, Fran. Boo, Katie Woo!, 1 vol. Lyon, Tammie, illus. 2010. (Katie Woo Ser.). (ENG.). 32p. (gr. k-2). lib. bdg. 21.32 *(978-1-4048-5987-6(X))*; pap. 5.95 *(978-1-4048-6366-8(4))* Picture Window Bks.

Marsoli, Lisa Ann & Disney Book Group Staff. The Halloween Ball. Disney Storybook Art Team, illus. 2013. (ENG.). 24p. (J). (gr. -1-k). pap. 5.99 *(978-1-4231-7144-7(6))* Disney Pr.

Martin, Bill, Jr. & Sampson, Michael. Trick or Treat? Meisel, Paul, illus. 2005. (ENG.). 32p. (J). (gr. -1-3). reprint ed. 7.99 *(978-1-4169-0262-1(7)*, Aladdin) Simon & Schuster Children's Publishing.

Martinez, Roland L. The Evil Leaf. 2009. 232p. 24.99 *(978-1-4490-0916-8(6))*; pap. 14.90 *(978-1-4490-0917-5(4))* AuthorHouse.

Marvel Book Group. Ultimate Spider-Man - Spider-Man vs Dracula. 2014. (ENG.). 24p. (J). (gr. 3-7). pap. 5.99 *(978-1-4847-1110-1(6)*, Marvel Pr.) Disney Publishing Worldwide.

Marvel Book Group Staff. Ultimate Spider-Man Halloween. 2014. (Marvel 8x8s Ser.). (J). lib. bdg. 16.00 *(978-0-606-35286-4(4))* Turtleback Bks.

Mathias, Irene. The Short Straw. Uhren, Anja, illus. 2017. (ENG.). 30p. (J). (gr. -1-4). 14.99 ***(978-1-941429-77-8(7))*** Handersen Publishing.

Matthews, Elli. Surprising Katie on Halloween. Written by Elli Matthews; Illustrated by, illus. 2011. 24p. pap. 24.95 *(978-1-4560-7486-9(5))* America Star Bks.

Mayer, Mercer. Happy Halloween, Little Critter! Mayer, Mercer, illus. 2004. (Little Critter Ser.). (ENG., Illus.). 16p. (J). (gr. -1-1). pap. 6.99 *(978-0-06-053971-9(2)*, HarperFestival) HarperCollins Pubs.

—Just a Little Too Little. Mayer, Mercer, illus. 2012. (Little Critter Ser.). (ENG., Illus.). 24p. (J). (gr. -1-3). pap. 3.99 *(978-0-06-147802-4(4)*, HarperFestival) HarperCollins Pubs.

—Little Critter: We Are Moving. Mayer, Mercer, illus. 2012. (Little Critter Ser.). (ENG., Illus.). 24p. (J). (gr. -1-2). pap. 3.99 *(978-0-06-147803-1(2)*, HarperFestival) HarperCollins Pubs.

—Phonics Fun. Mayer, Mercer, illus. 2012. (My First I Can Read Ser.). (ENG., Illus.). 144p. (J). (gr. -1-k). pap. 12.99 *(978-0-06-147825-3(3))* HarperCollins Pubs.

McChiller, BBH. Monster Moon: Curse of Zala Manor. 2009. 192p. (J). (gr. 3-6). 15.95 *(978-1-933277-10-3(6))* Stargazer Publishing Co.

McClellan, Sara, ed. After Halloween. Davis, Daniel M., illus. 2007. 64p. (J). per. 20.00 *(978-0-9774173-4-6(4))* Steam Crow Pr.

McCormick, Scott. Trick or Feet! Lazzell, R. H., illus. 2015. (Mr. Pants Ser.: 3). (ENG.). 128p. (J). (gr. k-3). 12.99 *(978-0-525-42811-4(9)*, Dial Bks) Penguin Young Readers Group.

McCourt, Lisa. Happy Halloween, Stinky Face. Moore, Cyd, illus. (ENG.). 32p. (J). 2016. (gr. -1-k). 3.99 *(978-1-338-02920-8(7))* 2011. (gr. k — 1). bds. 6.99 *(978-0-545-28542-1(9)*, Cartwheel Bks.) Scholastic, Inc.

McDonald, Jill, illus. Ghoulish Gang. 2008. (ENG.). 12p. (J). 9.95 *(978-1-58117-782-4(8)*, Intervisual/Piggy Toes) Bendon, Inc.

McDonald, Kirsten. The Costume Contest. 2016. (Carlos & Carmen Set 3 Ser.). (ENG.). (gr. -1-3). lib. bdg. 27.07 ***(978-1-62402-182-4(4))*** ABDO Publishing Co.

McDonald, Megan. Ant & Honey Bee: A Pair of Friends at Halloween. Karas, G. Brian, illus. 2013. (Candlewick Sparks Ser.). (ENG.). 48p. (J). (gr. k-4). pap. 3.99 *(978-0-7636-6864-8(8))* Candlewick Pr.

McGee, Warner, illus. Monster Halloween Party. 2007. (Backyardigans Ser.). (ENG.). 14p. (J). (gr. -1-k). bds. 6.99 *(978-1-4169-3435-6(9)*, Simon Spotlight/Nickelodeon) Simon Spotlight/Nickelodeon.

McGeorge Endres. Boomer's Halloween. (J). 14.95 *(978-0-8118-4229-7(0))* Chronicle Bks. LLC.

Mcghee, Alison. The Sweetest Witch Around. Bliss, Harry, illus. 2014. (ENG.). 32p. (J). (gr. -1-3). 15.99 *(978-1-4424-7833-6(0)*, Simon & Schuster/Paula Wiseman Bks.) Simon & Schuster/Paula Wiseman Bks.

—A Very Brave Witch. Bliss, Harry, illus. 2007. (J). (gr. -1-3). 24.95 incl. audio *(978-0-545-04268-0(2))* Scholastic, Inc.

—A Very Brave Witch. Bliss, Harry, illus. (ENG.). 32p. (J). (gr. -1-3). 2011. 7.99 *(978-0-689-86731-6(X))* 2009. 9.99 *(978-1-4169-8670-6(7))* 2006. 17.99 *(978-0-689-86730-9(1))* Simon & Schuster/Paula Wiseman Bks. (Simon & Schuster/Paula Wiseman Bks.).

—A Very Brave Witch. 2011. (J). (gr. -1-3). 29.95 *(978-0-545-04267-3(4))* Weston Woods Studios, Inc.

McGrath, Barbara Barbieri. Halloween Colors. Tagel, Peggy, illus. 2016. (First Celebrations Ser.). (ENG.). 12p. (J). (— 1). bds. 6.95 *(978-1-58089-533-0(6))* Charlesbridge Publishing, Inc.

—The M & M's(r) Brand Halloween Treat Book. 2004. (Illus.). 14p. (J). (gr. -1-3). bds. 6.95 *(978-1-57091-420-1(6))* Charlesbridge Publishing, Inc.

McGuirk, Leslie. Tucker's Spooky Halloween. McGuirk, Leslie, illus. 2011. (Candlewick Storybook Animations Ser.). (ENG., Illus.). 32p. (J). (gr. k-k). 8.99 *(978-0-7636-5113-8(3))* Candlewick Pr.

—Tucker's Spooky Halloween. 2009. 32p. 14.99 *(978-0-7636-4468-0(4))* Candlewick Pr.

—Tucker's Spooky Halloween. McGuirk, Leslie, illus. (Candlewick Storybook Animations Ser.). (ENG., Illus.). (J).

2009. 32p. (gr. k-k). 14.99 (978-0-7636-4469-7(2)) 2007. 28p. (gr. -1-k). bds. 7.99 (978-0-7636-3181-9(7)) Candlewick Pr.

McHugh, Sean & McHugh Parker, Katie. Broomsticks the Halloween Spirit. 2012. 70p. pap. 9.95 (978-1-935290-24-7(X)) Diversion Pr.

McMullan, Kate. Fluffy's Happy Halloween. Smith, Mavis, illus. 2004. (Fluffy, the Classroom Guinea Pig Ser.). 40p. (J). lib. bdg. 15.00 (978-1-59054-464-8(1)) Fitzgerald Bks.

McNamara, Margaret. Halloween Fun. Gordon, Mike, illus. 2008. (Robin Hill School Ser.). (ENG.). 32p. (J). (gr. -1-1). pap. 3.99 (978-1-4169-3496-7(0), Simon Spotlight) Simon Spotlight.

—Snow Day. Gordon, Mike, illus. 2007. (Robin Hill School Ser.). (ENG.). 32p. (J). (gr. -1-1). pap. 3.99 (978-1-4169-3493-6(6), Simon Spotlight) Simon Spotlight.

McRoberts, Eddison. Sneaking Treats: A Halloween Hunt. Gadra, Jessica, illus. 2012. 48p. 19.95 (978-1-62137-136-6(0)) Virtualbookworm.com Publishing, Inc.

Mead, David & Berry, Ron. Can You Make the Monster Giggle? A Halloween Self-Scare Book! Sharp, Chris, illus. 2011. 16p. (J). 10.99 (978-0-8249-1526-1(7), Ideal Pubns.) Worthy Publishing.

—Who's at the Door? 2010. (Illus.). 12p. (J). (gr. -1-1). 10.99 (978-0-8249-1431-8(7), Ideal Pubns.) Worthy Publishing.

Meadows, Daisy. A Fairyland Costume Ball. 2012. (Scholastic Reader Level 2 Ser.). (ENG., Illus.). 32p. (J). (gr. 2-5). pap. 3.99 (978-0-545-43389-1(4), Scholastic Paperbacks) Scholastic, Inc.

—A Fairyland Costume Ball. 2012. (Rainbow Magic — Scholastic Reader Ser.). lib. bdg. 13.55 (978-0-606-26235-4(0), Turtleback) Turtleback Bks.

—Trixie the Halloween Fairy. 2009. (Rainbow Magic Ser.). (ENG., Illus.). 176p. (J). (gr. 2-5). 6.99 (978-0-545-10613-9(3), Scholastic Paperbacks) Scholastic, Inc.

Meddaugh, Susan. The Witches' Supermarket. 2014. (Martha Speaks Ser.). (ENG., Illus.). 32p. (J). (gr. -1-3). pap. 4.99 (978-0-544-32358-2(0), HMH Books For Young Readers) Houghton Mifflin Harcourt Publishing Co.

Mesker, Erma Medrano. Bullies on the Prowl on a Hallow's Eve. 2011. 56p. (gr. 4-6). pap. 27.98 (978-1-4567-5622-2(2)) AuthorHouse.

Metzger, Steve. Skeleton Meets the Mummy. Zenz, Aaron, illus. 2011. (ENG.). 32p. (J). (gr. -1-3). pap. 6.99 (978-0-545-23032-2(2), Cartwheel Bks.) Scholastic, Inc.

Metzger, Steve & Hohnstadt, Cedric. Big Shark's Halloween Mystery. 2007. (Illus.). (J). pap. (978-0-545-00237-0(0)) Scholastic, Inc.

Miceli, Mary Anne. Boston North Shore's ... Salem's Golden Broomstick. 2013. 44p. pap. 20.00 (978-0-9888654-0-2(8)) Miceli, Mary Anne.

Middle, Myra. Rabi's Halloween Adventure. 2012. 28p. pap. 21.99 (978-1-4691-5380-3(7)) Xlibris Corp.

Miller, Jayna. Too Much Trick or Treat. Thatch, Nancy, ed. Miller, Jayna, illus. 2005. (Illus.). 29p. (J). per. 19.95 (978-0-933849-83-9(4)) landmark Hse., Ltd.

Montes, Marisa. Los Gatos Black on Halloween. Morales, Yuyi, illus. rev. ed. 2006. (ENG.). 32p. (J). (gr. -1-3). 18.99 (978-0-8050-7429-1(5), 9780805074291, Holt, Henry & Co. Bks. For Young Readers) Holt, Henry & Co.

—Los Gatos Black on Halloween. 2011. (SPA.). (J). (gr. -1-3). 29.95 (978-0-545-19701-4(5)) Weston Woods Studios, Inc.

—Los Gatos Black on Halloween. 2016. (ENG & SPA.). (J). lib. bdg. 18.40 (978-0-606-39564-9(4)) Turtleback Bks.

Montijo, Rhode. The Halloween Kid. Montijo, Rhode, illus. 2010. (ENG., Illus.). 40p. (J). (gr. -1-3). 14.99 (978-1-4169-3575-9(4), Simon & Schuster Bks. For Young Readers) Simon & Schuster Bks. For Young Readers.

Moore, Brenna L. Under the Halloween Moon. 2012. (ENG.). 24p. (J). pap. 11.95 (978-1-4327-9184-1(2)) Outskirts Pr., Inc.

Morgan, Dennis W. & Morgan, Dennis W. Pumpkin Head Harvey. 2013. (Illus.). 40p. pap. 14.99 (978-0-9892295-1-7(3)) Dreamstreet Studios, Inc. (A Div. of DSMV Industries, Inc.).

Morgan, Emily. Lucy & the Halloween Miracle. Prince, Andrea, illus. 2013. 24p. 16.99 (978-0-9910324-8-8(9)) Mindstir Media.

Morris, Paris. My Twins First Halloween. 2008. (J). pap. 12.95 (978-0-9760095-9-7(5)) New Year Publishing.

Mortimer, Anne. Pumpkin Cat. Mortimer, Anne, illus. 2011. (ENG., Illus.). 24p. (J). (gr. -1-2). 14.99 (978-0-06-187485-7(X), Tegen, Katherine Bks) HarperCollins Pubs.

Moulton, Mark. Miss Fiona's Stupendous Pumpkin Pies. Good, Karen Hillard, illus. 2011. 32p. (J). pap. 7.99 (978-0-8249-5635-6(4), Ideal Pubns.) Worthy Publishing.

Moulton, Mark Kimball. Miss Fiona's Stupendous Pumpkin Pies. Crouch, Karen Hillard, illus. 2008. (ENG.). 28p. (J). 14.95 (978-0-8249-5489-5(0), Ideal Pubns.) Worthy Publishing.

—Twisted Sistahs. 2003. (Illus.). 32p. (J). (gr. 3-6). 18.00 (978-0-7412-1600-7(0)) Lang Graphics, Ltd.

Mullarkey, Lisa. Can't Keep Trackula of Jackula, 1 vol. Harris, Phyllis, illus. 2009. (Katharine the Almost Great Ser.: No. 1). (ENG.). 80p. (J). (gr. 1-4). 27.07 (978-1-60270-584-5(4)) Magic Wagon.

Muncaster, Harriet. Happy Halloween, Witch's Cat! Muncaster, Harriet, illus. 2015. (ENG., Illus.). 32p. (J). (gr. -1-3). 15.99 (978-0-06-222916-8(8)) HarperCollins Pubs.

Murray, Marjorie Dennis. Halloween Night. Dorman, Brandon, illus. (ENG.). 40p. (J). (gr. k-4). 2013. pap. 6.99 (978-0-06-185773-7(4)) 2010. 9.99 (978-0-06-201293-7(2)) HarperCollins Pubs. (Greenwillow Bks.).

Muth, Jon J. Zen Ghosts. 2010. (ENG.). 40p. (J). (gr. -1-3). 17.99 (978-0-439-63430-4(X), Scholastic Pr.) Scholastic, Inc.

Naughton, Colin Charles. Not So Spooky Book Series: Book One. 2012. 28p. pap. 24.95 (978-1-4626-7856-3(4)) America Star Bks.

Neitzel, Shirley. Who Will I Be? A Halloween Rebus Story. Parker, Nancy Winslow, illus. 2005. 32p. (J). lib. bdg. 13.89 (978-0-06-056068-3(1)) HarperCollins Pubs.

Neubecker, Robert. Too Many Monsters! A Halloween Counting Book. Neubecker, Robert, illus. 2010. (ENG., Illus.). 26p. (J). (gr. -1-k). bds. 7.99 (978-1-4424-0172-3(9), Little Simon) Little Simon.

Nicholas, J. B. The Waving Girl, 1 vol. Waites, Joan C., illus. 2004. (ENG.). 32p. (J). (gr. k-3). pap. 8.99 (978-1-58980-185-1(7)) Pelican Publishing Co., Inc.

Nickelodeon Dora the Explorer Staff. Say Boo! 2013. (Guess Who! Book Ser.: 1). (ENG.). 10p. (J). (gr. -1-1). bds. 10.99 (978-0-7944-2857-0(6)) Reader's Digest Assn., Inc., The.

Night, P. J. Home, Sweet Haunt. 2013. (You're Invited to a Creepover Ser.: 15). (ENG., Illus.). 160p. (J). (gr. 3-7). pap. 6.99 (978-1-4424-7240-2(5), Simon Spotlight) Simon Spotlight.

—Home, Sweet Haunt. 2013. (Creepover Ser.: 15). lib. bdg. 16.00 (978-0-606-32047-4(4), Turtleback) Turtleback Bks.

—No Trick-Or-Treating!, 1 vol. 2013. (You're Invited to a Creepover Ser.). (ENG.). 192p. (J). (gr. 3-6). lib. bdg. 24.21 (978-1-61479-061-7(2), Essential Library) ABDO Publishing Co.

—No Trick-Or-Treating! 2012. (Creepover Ser.: 9). lib. bdg. 17.20 (978-0-606-26337-5(3), Turtleback) Turtleback Bks.

—No Trick-or-Treating! Superscary Superspecial. 2012. (You're Invited to a Creepover Ser.: 9). (ENG.). 208p. (J). (gr. 3-7). pap. 6.99 (978-1-4424-5053-0(3), Simon Spotlight) Simon Spotlight.

Nosy Crow Staff. Bizzy Bear: Spooky House. Davies, Benji, illus. 2017. (Bizzy Bear Ser.). (ENG.). 8p. (J). (— 1). bds. 6.99 **(978-0-7636-9327-5(8)**, Nosy Crow) Candlewick Pr.

Nosy Crow Staff. Wickle Woo Has a Halloween Party. Ho, Jannie, illus. 2014. (ENG.). 8p. (J). (— 1). bds. 7.99 (978-0-7636-7400-7(1), Nosy Crow) Candlewick Pr.

Novak, Matt. No Zombies Allowed. Novak, Matt, illus. 2014. (ENG., Illus.). 32p. (J). (gr. -1-1). 16.99 (978-1-4814-2540-7(4), Atheneum Bks. for Young Readers) Simon & Schuster Children's Publishing.

O'Brien, Sarah. Whack-a-Zombie: You Can't Keep a Good Zombie Down! 2008. (Miniature Editions Ser.). (ENG.). 32p. pap. 6.95 (978-0-7624-3424-4(4), Running Pr.) Running Pr. Bk. Pubs.

O'Connell, Jennifer Barrett. It's Halloween Night! 2012. lib. bdg. 17.20 (978-0-606-26206-4(7), Turtleback) Turtleback Bks.

O'Connor, Jane. Fancy Nancy: Candy Bonanza. Glasser, Robin Preiss, illus. 2015. (Fancy Nancy Ser.). (ENG.). 24p. (J). (gr. -1-3). pap. 4.99 (978-0-06-226958-4(5), HarperFestival) HarperCollins Pubs.

—Halloween... or Bust! Glasser, Robin Preiss & Bracken, Carolyn, illus. 2009. (Fancy Nancy Ser.). (ENG.). 24p. (J). (gr. -1-3). pap. 4.99 (978-0-06-123595-5(4), HarperFestival) HarperCollins Pubs.

—Haunted Mansion: A Reusable Sticker Book for Halloween. Glasser, Robin Preiss, illus. 2011. (Fancy Nancy Ser.). (ENG.). 12p. (J). (gr. -1-2). pap. 6.99 (978-0-06-170388-1(5), HarperFestival) HarperCollins Pubs.

Oliver, Ilanit. Ten Flying Brooms. Poling, Kyle, illus. 2015. (J). (ENG.). 24p. (gr. -1-k). 3.99 (978-0-545-81336-5(0)); (978-1-4844-5738-2(2)) Scholastic, Inc. (Cartwheel Bks.).

Oliver, Lin, et al. There's a Zombie in My Bathtub #5. Garrett, Scott, illus. 2015. (Here's Hank Ser.: 5). (ENG.). 128p. (J). (gr. 1-3). bds. 5.99 (978-0-448-48512-6(5), Grosset & Dunlap) Penguin Young Readers Group.

Olsen, Mary-Kate & Olsen, Ashley. Dare to Scare. 2005. (ENG., Illus.). 112p. (978-0-00-715887-4(4)) HarperCollins Pubs. Australia.

—Hocus Pocus. 2006. (ENG.). 112p. (978-0-00-718093-6(4)) HarperCollins Pubs. Australia.

O'Reilly, Sean. The King of Halloween Castle, 1 vol. 2010. (Mighty Mighty Monsters Ser.). (ENG., Illus.). 48p. (gr. 2-3). lib. bdg. 23.99 (978-1-4342-2150-6(4)) Stone Arch Bks.

O'Ryan, Ray. A Haunted Halloween. Kraft, Jason, illus. 2015. (Galaxy Zack Ser.: 11). (ENG.). 128p. (J). (gr. k-4). 16.99 (978-1-4814-3491-1(8), Little Simon) Little Simon.

Osborne, Mary Pope. Haunted Castle on Hallows Eve. Murdocca, Sal, illus. 2010. (Magic Tree House Merlin Mission Ser.: 2). (ENG.). 144p. (J). (gr. 2-5). pap. 5.99 (978-0-375-86090-4(8), Random Hse. Bks. for Young Readers) Random Hse. Children's Bks.

—Haunted Castle on Hallows Eve. 2010. (Magic Tree House Merlin Missions Ser.: 2). lib. bdg. 16.00 (978-0-606-13992-2(3), Turtleback) Turtleback Bks.

Owens, Donna. NIBBLES:VOLUME 3, Nibbles enjoys the Holidays. 2008. 38p. pap. 14.95 (978-1-4357-4715-9(1)) Lulu Pr., Inc.

Palacios, Tomas. Guardians of the Galaxy Hallo-Scream Spook-Tacular!!! 2016. (J). lib. bdg. 16.00 (978-0-606-38338-7(7)) Turtleback Bks.

Palacios, Tomas & Hosten, Colin. Guardians of the Galaxy Hallo-Scream Spook-tacular!!! 2016. (ENG.). 24p. (J). (gr. 1-3). pap. 5.99 (978-1-4847-3214-4(6), Marvel Pr.) Disney Publishing Worldwide.

Pammer, Victoria. Katelyn & the Crooked Tooth. 2011. 28p. pap. 24.95 (978-1-4560-0996-0(6)) America Star Bks.

Papp, Robert, illus. Spooktacular Special. 2013. (Boxcar Children Mysteries Ser.). (ENG.). 400p. (J). (gr. 1-5). 9.99 (978-0-8075-7605-2(0)) Whitman, Albert & Co.

Paprocki, Greg. Halloween Alphabet, 1 vol. 2017. (ENG.). 32p. (J). bds. 9.99 **(978-1-4236-4780-5(7))** Gibbs Smith, Publisher.

Parish, Herman. Happy Haunting, Amelia Bedelia. Sweat, Lynn, illus. (I Can Read Level 2 Ser.). 64p. (J). (gr. k-3). 2006. (ENG.). pap. 3.99 (978-0-06-051895-0(2)) 2004. (ENG.). 16.99 (978-0-06-051893-6(6)) 2004. lib. bdg. 16.89 (978-0-06-051894-3(4)) HarperCollins Pubs. (Greenwillow Bks.).

Park, Barbara. Boo... & I Mean It! Brunkus, Denise, illus. 2005. (Junie B. Jones Ser.: Bk. 7). 86p. (gr. 1-4). 15.00 (978-0-7569-4783-5(9)) Perfection Learning Corp.

—Boo... & I Mean It! Brunkus, Denise, illus. 2004. (Junie B. Jones Ser.: No. 7). (ENG.). 96p. (J). (gr. 1-4). lib. bdg. 13.99 (978-0-375-92806-2(5), Random Hse. Bks. for Young Readers) Random Hse. Children's Bks.

—Junie B., First Grader - Boo...and I Mean It! Brunkus, Denise, illus. 2005. (Junie B. Jones Ser.: No. 7). (ENG.). 96p. (J). (gr. 1-4). 4.99 (978-0-375-82807-2(9), Random Hse. Bks. for Young Readers) Random Hse. Children's Bks.

Parrish, Emma, illus. Halloween Doodles: Spooky Designs to Complete & Create. 2009. (ENG.). 64p. (J). (gr. 1-17). pap. 7.95 (978-0-7624-3760-3(X)) Running Pr. Bk. Pubs.

Pasillo, Susan. The Perfect Pumpkin. 2006. (J). lib. bdg. 20.95 (978-1-933732-14-5(8)) Big Ransom Studio.

Passen, Lisa. The Attack of the 50-Foot Teacher. 2005. (Illus.). 28p. (J). (gr. k-4). reprint ed. 16.00 (978-0-7567-9665-5(2)) DIANE Publishing Co.

Patricelli, Leslie. Boo! Patricelli, Leslie, illus. 2015. (Leslie Patricelli Board Bks.). (ENG., Illus.). 26p. (J). (— 1). bds. 6.99 (978-0-7636-6320-9(4)) Candlewick Pr.

—Boo! / ¡Bu! Patricelli, Leslie, illus. 2017. (Leslie Patricelli Board Bks.). (ENG & SPA., Illus.). 26p. (J). (— 1). bds. 6.99 (978-0-7636-9314-5(6)) Candlewick Pr.

Patrick, Wellman. Mr. Duz Trick or Treat. Sam, Kagan, illus. 2007. 24p. (J). 5.95 (978-0-9796226-4-9(6)) MrDuz.com.

Pavlovsky, Marsha. I Am Not Scared of Halloween. 2004. 24p. pap. 24.95 (978-1-4137-2368-7(3)) PublishAmerica, Inc.

Pendleton, Sherry. 'Twas the Night Before Halloween. 2003. (J). per. 13.95 (978-1-932303-35-3(9), Llumina Pr.) Aeon Publishing Inc.

Pilkey, Dav. Dragon's Halloween. 2007. (Dragon's Tales Ser.: Bk. 5). (Illus.). 48p. (gr. -1-3). 16.00 (978-0-7569-7861-7(0)) Perfection Learning Corp.

—Dragon's Halloween. Pilkey, Dav, illus. 2003. (Dragon's Tales Ser.: Bk. 5). (ENG., Illus.). 48p. (J). (gr. -1-3). pap. 5.99 (978-0-439-54847-2(0), Orchard Bks.) Scholastic, Inc.

—The Hallo-Wiener. Pilkey, Dav, illus. 2014. (ENG., Illus.). 32p. (J). (gr. -1-k). bds. 6.99 (978-0-545-66136-2(6)) Scholastic, Inc.

Pitchford, Dean. Captain Nobody. 2010. (ENG.). 208p. (J). (gr. 3-7). 6.99 (978-0-14-241667-9(3), Puffin Books) Penguin Young Readers Group.

Polacco, Patricia. Picnic at Mudsock Meadow. 2009. (ENG.). 32p. (J). (gr. k-3). pap. 7.99 (978-0-14-241392-0(5), Puffin Books) Penguin Young Readers Group.

Pottie, Marjolein & Auzary-Luton, Sylvie. Going Batty! Special Glow-in-the-Dark Surprise Pictures. Auzary-Luton, Sylvie, illus. 2005. (Illus.). 32p. (J). 15.95 (978-0-689-04635-3(9), Milk & Cookies) ibooks, Inc.

Powell-Tuck, Maudie. Pumpkin Party! Guile, Gill, illus. 2015. (ENG.). 22p. (J). (gr. -1-2). bds. 8.99 (978-1-58925-206-6(3)) Tiger Tales.

Poydar, Nancy. The Perfectly Horrible Halloween. Poydar, Nancy, illus. 2005. (ENG., Illus.). 32p. (J). (gr. k-3). pap. 6.95 (978-0-8234-1769-8(7)) Holiday Hse., Inc.

Preller, James. Jigsaw Jones: the Case of the Mummy Mystery. 2017. (Jigsaw Jones Mysteries Ser.). (ENG., Illus.). 96p. (J). pap. 4.99 (978-1-250-11082-4(3), 9781250110824) Feiwel & Friends.

Priddy, Roger. Halloween. 2015. (Chunky 3 Pack Ser.). (ENG.). 12p. (J). (gr. -1 — 1). bds. 4.99 (978-0-312-51851-6(X), 9780312518516, Priddy Bks.) St. Martin's Pr.

—Lift-The-Flap Tab: Spooky House. 2015. (Lift-The-Flap Tab Bks.). (ENG., Illus.). 16p. (J). (gr. -1 — 1). bds. 8.99 (978-0-312-51868-4(4), 9780312518684, Priddy Bks.) St. Martin's Pr.

—Mix & Match: Halloween. 2016. (Mix & Match Ser.). (ENG., Illus.). 14p. (J). bds. 5.99 (978-0-312-52021-2(2), 9780312520212, Priddy Bks.) St. Martin's Pr.

—Spooky Bus. 2013. (Shaped Board Bks.). (ENG., Illus.). 6p. (J). (gr. -1-k). bds. 6.99 (978-0-312-51618-5(5), 9780312516185, Priddy Bks.) St. Martin's Pr.

Principe, Tami. The Green Rabbit: Rabbits Aren't Supposed to Be Green! 2012. 32p. pap. 10.95 (978-1-4626-7509-8(3)) America Star Bks.

Prochovnic, Dawn Babb. One Trick for One Treat: Sign Language for Numbers, 1 vol. Bauer, Stephanie, illus. 2012. (ENG.). 32p. 28.50 (978-1-61641-838-0(9), Looking Glass Library) Magic Wagon.

Public Domain Staff. Five Little Pumpkins. Yaccarino, Dan, illus. 2003. (ENG.). 16p. (J). (gr. -1-k). pap. 6.99 (978-0-694-01177-3(0), HarperFestival) HarperCollins Pubs.

Publications International Ltd. Staff, ed. My Friends Tigger & Pooh. 2008. (J). bds. 5.98 (978-1-4127-8483-2(2)) Publications International, Ltd.

Quin-Harkin, Janet. Friday Night Fright. 2014. (Tgif Ser.: 2). (ENG., Illus.). 128p. (J). (gr. 3-7). pap. 13.99 (978-1-4814-2880-4(2), Simon & Schuster/Paula Wiseman Bks.) Simon & Schuster/Paula Wiseman Bks.

Rabe, Tish. Trick-or-Treat!/Aye-Aye! Ruiz, Aristides & Mathieu, Joe, illus. 2012. (Pictureback(R) Ser.). (ENG.). 32p. (J). (gr. -1-2). pap. 4.99 (978-0-307-93056-9(4), Random Hse. Bks. for Young Readers) Random Hse. Children's Bks.

Rains, Deborah Jane. A Spooky Happy Halloween with Cuddles & Snuggles. 2011. 20p. pap. 24.95 (978-1-4489-4423-1(6)) America Star Bks.

Random House. Halloween Heroes! (Paw Patrol) Random House, illus. 2017. (ENG., Illus.). 22p. (J). (— 1). bds. 6.99 **(978-1-5247-6622-1(4)**, Random Hse. Bks. for Young Readers) Random Hse. Children's Bks.

—Happy Troll-O-ween! Random House, illus. 2017. (Pictureback(R) Ser.). (ENG., Illus.). 16p. (J). (gr. -1-2). pap. 4.99 **(978-1-5247-6958-1(4)**, Random Hse. Bks. for Young Readers) Random Hse. Children's Bks.

Random House. Haunted House Party! (Bubble Guppies) MJ Illustrations, illus. 2015. (Hologramatic Sticker Book Ser.). (ENG.). 64p. (J). (gr. -1-2). pap. 4.99 (978-0-385-38407-0(6), Golden Bks.) Random Hse. Children's Bks.

Random House Disney Staff. Sweet & Spooky Halloween. Marrucchi, Elisa, illus. 2007. (Pictureback(R) Ser.). (ENG.). 24p. (J). (gr. -1-2). pap. 3.99 (978-0-7364-2453-0(9), RH/Disney) Random Hse. Children's Bks.

Reasoner, Charles. Charles Reasoner Halloween Books. 2015. (Charles Reasoner Halloween Bks.). (ENG.). 12p. (gr. -1 — 1). bds. 23.96 (978-1-4795-8505-2(X)) Picture Window Bks.

—Halloween Ghost, 1 vol. 2014. (Charles Reasoner Halloween Bks.). (ENG.). 12p. (gr. -1 — 1). bds. 5.99 (978-1-4795-5971-8(7)) Picture Window Bks.

—Pumpkin Shapes. 2015. (Charles Reasoner Halloween Bks.). (ENG., Illus.). 12p. (gr. -1 — 1). bds. 5.99 (978-1-4795-8499-4(1)) Picture Window Bks.

Reasoner, Charles & Wood, Steven. Little Monster. 2015. (Charles Reasoner Halloween Bks.). (ENG., Illus.). 12p. (gr. -1 — 1). bds. 5.99 (978-1-4795-8502-1(5)) Picture Window Bks.

—Owl's Halloween. 2015. (Charles Reasoner Halloween Bks.). (ENG., Illus.). 12p. (gr. -1 — 1). bds. 5.99 (978-1-4795-8500-7(9)) Picture Window Bks.

—Scaredy Cat. 2015. (Charles Reasoner Halloween Bks.). (ENG., Illus.). 12p. (gr. -1 — 1). bds. 5.99 (978-1-4795-8501-4(7)) Picture Window Bks.

Rees, Celia. A Is for Apparition. (Haunts Ser.: Vol. 2). 122p. (J). pap. (978-0-340-71488-1(3)) Hodder & Stoughton.

Reid, Carol. Spook-Ee Wook-Ee Halloween. 2012. 24p. pap. 17.99 (978-1-4772-5845-3(0)) AuthorHouse.

Reisner, Molly. Halloween Hoedown! 2013. (Dora the Explorer 8X8 Ser.). lib. bdg. 13.55 (978-0-606-32217-1(5), Turtleback) Turtleback Bks.

—Halloween Hoedown! (Dora the Explorer) Aikins, David, illus. 2013. (Pictureback(R) Ser.). (ENG.). 24p. (J). (gr. -1-2). 3.99 (978-0-449-81762-9(8), Random Hse. Bks. for Young Readers) Random Hse. Children's Bks.

Revenson, Jody. Candy Bonanza. 2015. (Fancy Nancy Picture Bks.). (J). lib. bdg. 14.75 (978-0-606-36965-7(1)) Turtleback Bks.

Rey, H. A. Curious George Haunted Halloween. 2014. (Curious George Ser.). (ENG., Illus.). 24p. (J). (gr. -1-3). pap. 3.99 (978-0-544-32079-6(4), HMH Books For Young Readers) Houghton Mifflin Harcourt Publishing Co.

—Curious George Haunted Halloween (CGTV Reader) 2014. (Curious George Ser.). (ENG., Illus.). 24p. (J). (gr. -1-3). 12.99 (978-0-544-32077-2(8), HMH Books For Young Readers) Houghton Mifflin Harcourt Publishing Co.

—Happy Halloween. 2008. (Curious George Ser.). (ENG., Illus.). 14p. (J). (gr. -1 — 1). bds. 7.99 (978-0-618-91952-9(X)) Houghton Mifflin Harcourt Publishing Co.

—Hooray for Halloween, Curious George. 2016. (Curious George Ser.). (ENG., Illus.). 24p. (J). (gr. -1-3). 9.99 (978-0-544-69956-4(4), HMH Books For Young Readers) Houghton Mifflin Harcourt Publishing Co.

—Jorge el Curioso Va a una Fiesta de Disfraces/Curious George Goes to a Costume Party (Bilingual) 2012. (Curious George Ser.). (ENG & SPA., Illus.). 24p. (J). (gr. -1-3). pap. 3.99 (978-0-547-86575-1(9)) Houghton Mifflin Harcourt Publishing Co.

RH Disney. The Frozen Monster (Disney Frozen) RH Disney, illus. 2017. (Pictureback(R) Ser.). (ENG., Illus.). 24p. (J). (gr. -1-2). pap. 4.99 **(978-0-7364-3729-5(0)**, RH/Disney) Random Hse. Children's Bks.

—A Paw-Some Costume Party! (Disney Palace Pets Whisker Haven Tales) RH Disney, illus. 2017. (Little Golden Book Ser.). (ENG., Illus.). 24p. (J). (-k). 4.99 **(978-0-7364-3723-3(1)**, Golden/Disney) Random Hse. Children's Bks.

Riley, Kellee, illus. Happy Halloween, Kai-lan! A Lift-the-Flap Story. 2010. (Ni Hao, Kai-Lan Ser.). (ENG.). 16p. (J). pap. 6.99 (978-1-4424-0178-5(8), Simon Spotlight/Nickelodeon) Simon Spotlight/Nickelodeon.

Rim, Sujean. Birdie's Happiest Halloween. 2016. (ENG., Illus.). 40p. (J). (gr. -1-3). 16.99 (978-0-316-40746-5(1)) Little Brown & Co.

Ritchie, Joseph R. Baby Looney Tunes Visit a Haunted House. Halverson, Lydia, illus. 2005. (Baby Looney Tunes Ser.). 14p. (J). (gr. -1-3). bds. 9.95 (978-0-8249-6609-6(0), Ideal Pubns.) Worthy Publishing.

—Peek-a-Boo! Halverson, Lydia, illus. 2004. (ENG.). 14p. (J). bds. 7.95 (978-0-8249-6550-1(7), Ideal Pubns.) Worthy Publishing.

Roberts, Bethany. Halloween Mice! Cushman, Doug, illus. 2011. (ENG.). 28p. (J). (gr. k — 1). bds. 5.99 (978-0-547-57573-5(4)) Houghton Mifflin Harcourt Publishing Co.

Roberts, Chris. A Mcspooky Halloween. 2006. (J). pap. 9.00 (978-0-8059-7196-5(3)) Dorrance Publishing Co., Inc.

Robinson, Barbara. The Best Halloween Ever. 2006. (ENG.). 144p. (J). (gr. 3-18). pap. 5.99 (978-0-06-076601-6(8)) HarperCollins Pubs.

—The Best Halloween Ever. 2006. (Illus.). 117p. (J). (gr. 3-7). 13.65 (978-0-7569-6985-1(9)) Perfection Learning Corp.

Rocklin, Joanne. This Book Is Haunted. Adinolfi, JoAnn, illus. 2004. (I Can Read Bks.). 48p. (gr. k-3). 14.00 (978-0-7569-3081-3(2)) Perfection Learning Corp.

Rockwell, Anne. Apples & Pumpkins. Rockwell, Lizzy, illus. 2014. (Classic Board Bks.). (ENG.). 28p. (J). (gr. -1-k). bds. 7.99 (978-1-4424-9977-5(X), Little Simon) Little Simon.

Rockwell, Anne F. Apples & Pumpkins. Rockwell, Lizzy, illus. (ENG.). 24p. (J). (gr. -1-3). 2012. 5.99 (978-1-4424-7656-1(7)) 2011. 14.99 (978-1-4424-0350-5(0)) Simon & Schuster Children's Publishing. (Aladdin).

Rogers, Michelle Elizabeth. The Adventures of Brutus & Baby: A Haunted Halloween. Collier, Kevin Scott, illus. 2010. 50p. pap. 16.50 (978-1-60860-592-7(2), Eloquent Bks.) Strategic Book Publishing & Rights Agency (SBPRA).

Rohmann, Eric. Bone Dog. Rohmann, Eric, illus. 2011. (ENG., Illus.). 32p. (J). (gr. -1-3). 16.99 (978-1-59643-150-8(4), 9781596431508) Roaring Brook Pr.

Root, Phyllis. Who Said Boo? A Lift-the-Flap Book. Larrañaga, Ana Martín, illus. 2005. (ENG.). 14p. (J). (gr. -1-k). bds. 5.99 (978-0-689-85408-8(0), Little Simon) Little Simon.

Rounds, Melissa M. The Skeleton by the Bay. 2009. 23p. (J). pap. 14.95 (978-1-4327-2351-4(0)) Outskirts Pr., Inc.

Rowntree, G. M. Wizards Spell Magic in the Legends of Mere Leander. 2010. 291p. pap. 32.50 (978-1-4452-6812-5(4)) Lulu Pr., Inc.

—Wizards Spell Magic in the Legends of Mere Leander - US Trade Size. 2010. 291p. pap. 24.95 (978-1-4452-9266-3(1)) Lulu Pr., Inc.

Roy, Ron. October Ogre. Gurney, John Steven, illus. 2013. (Calendar Mysteries Ser.: 10). (ENG.). 80p. (J). (gr. 1-4). 4.99 (978-0-375-86888-7(7)); lib. bdg. 12.99 (978-0-375-96888-4(1)) Random Hse. Children's Bks. (Random Hse. Bks. for Young Readers).

—October Ogre. 2013. (Calendar Mysteries Ser.: 10). lib. bdg. 14.75 (978-0-606-32232-4(9), Turtleback) Turtleback Bks.

—Sleepy Hollow Sleepover. Gurney, John Steven, illus. 4th ed. 2010. (to Z Mysteries Ser.: 4). (ENG.). 144p. (J). (gr. 1-4). pap. 5.99 (978-0-375-86669-2(8), Random Hse. Bks. for Young Readers) Random Hse. Children's Bks.

—Sleepy Hollow Sleepover. 4th ed. 2010. (to Z Mysteries Ser.: 30). lib. bdg. 16.00 (978-0-606-14007-2(7), Turtleback) Turtleback Bks.

Ruelle, Karen Gray. Spookier Than a Ghost. (Holiday House Readers Ser.). (ENG., Illus.). 32p. (J). (gr. k-3). pap. 4.95 *(978-0-8234-1801-5(4))* Holiday Hse., Inc.

Russell, Rachel Renée. Tales from a Not-So-Popular Party Girl. Russell, Rachel Renée, illus. 2010. (Dork Diaries: 2). (ENG., Illus.). 288p. (J). (gr. 4-8). 13.99 *(978-1-4169-8008-7(3)*, Aladdin) Simon & Schuster Children's Publishing.

—Tales from a Not-So-Popular Party Girl. 2010. (Dork Diaries: 2). lib. bdg. 25.75 *(978-0-606-32420-5(8)*, Turtleback) Turtleback Bks.

Russell, Rachel Renée, et al. Tales from a Not-So-Popular Party Girl. 2010. (ENG.). pap. *(978-1-4424-4042-5(2)*, Aladdin Paperbacks) Simon & Schuster Children's Publishing.

Ryan, Pam Muñoz. Tony Baloney Yo Ho Ho, Halloween! Fotheringham, Edwin, illus. 2016. (Tony Baloney Ser.). (ENG.). 40p. (J). (gr. k-2). 6.99 *(978-0-545-90885-6(X)*, Scholastic Pr.) Scholastic, Inc.

—Yo Ho Ho, Halloween! Fotheringham, Ed, illus. 2015. 39p. (J). pap. *(978-0-545-91590-8(2))* Scholastic, Inc.

Rylant, Cynthia. Herbert's First Halloween. Henry, Steven, illus. 2017. (ENG.). 36p. (J). (gr. -1 — 1). 15.99 *(978-1-4521-2533-6(3))* Chronicle Bks. LLC.

—Moonlight: The Halloween Cat. Sweet, Melissa, illus. (ENG.). 32p. (J). (gr. -1-3). 2009. pap. 6.99 *(978-0-06-443814-8(7))* 2003. 17.99 *(978-0-06-029711-4(5))* HarperCollins Pubs.

Salzmann, Mary Elizabeth. Robin Hoods, 1 vol. Haberstroh, Anne, illus. 2007. (Critter Chronicles Ser.). (ENG.). 24p. (J). (gr. k-3). lib. bdg. 24.21 *(978-1-59928-466-8(9)*, SandCastle) ABDO Publishing Co.

Sander, Sonia. Witching Hour. 2009. (Scooby Reader 25 Ser.). (ENG., Illus.). 32p. (J). (gr. -1-3). pap. 3.99 *(978-0-545-16106-0(1))* Scholastic, Inc.

Sanrio. Hello Kitty, Hello Halloween! 2014. (ENG., Illus.). 24p. (J). (gr. k-2). 6.95 *(978-1-4197-1375-0(2)*, Abrams Bks. for Young Readers) Abrams, Inc.

—Trick or Treat: Hello Kitty & Me. 2014. (ENG.). 32p. (J). (-2). 9.99 *(978-1-4022-9665-9(7)*, 9781402296659) Sourcebooks, Inc.

Santomero, Angela C. Happy Halloween, Daniel Tiger! Style Guide Staff & Fruchter, Jason, illus. 2014. (Daniel Tiger's Neighborhood Ser.). (ENG.). 14p. (J). (gr. -1-2). bds. 6.99 *(978-1-4814-0429-7(6)*, Simon Spotlight) Simon Spotlight.

Savage, Stephen. Ten Orange Pumpkins: A Counting Book. 2013. (ENG., Illus.). 48p. (J). (gr. -1-k). 16.99 *(978-0-8037-3938-3(9)*, Dial Bks) Penguin Young Readers Group.

Schaefer, Lola M. Happy Halloween, Mittens. Hartung, Susan Kathleen, illus. 2010. (My First I Can Read Ser.). (ENG.). 32p. (J). (gr. -1-3). 16.99 *(978-0-06-170222-8(6))*; pap. 3.99 *(978-0-06-170221-1(8))* HarperCollins Pubs.

Schaefer, Peggy. A Haunted Halloween Activity Book. Arif, Tasneem & Reed, Lisa, illus. 2014. 16p. (J). 4.99 *(978-0-8249-5666-0(4)*, Ideal Pubns.) Worthy Publishing.

—Trick or Treat! Halverson, Lydia, illus. 2009. (ENG.). 16p. (J). (gr. -1-k). bds. 12.99 *(978-0-8249-1828-6(2)*, Ideal Pubns.) Worthy Publishing.

Schertle, Alice. Little Blue Truck's Halloween. McElmurry, Jill, illus. 2016. (Little Blue Truck Ser.). (ENG.). 16p. (J). (— 1). bds. 12.99 *(978-0-544-77253-3(9)*, HMH Books For Young Readers) Houghton Mifflin Harcourt Publishing Co.

Schnitzlein, Danny. Trick or Treat on Monster Street, 1 vol. Faulkner, Matt, illus. 2008. (ENG.). 32p. (J). (gr. k-3). 16.95 *(978-1-56145-465-5(6))* Peachtree Pubs.

Scholastic Editors. Peppa's Halloween Party. 2016. (Peppa Pig 8X8 Ser.). lib. bdg. 14.75 *(978-0-606-38827-6(3))* Turtleback Bks.

Schulman, Janet. 10 Trick-or-Treaters: A Halloween Counting Book. Davick, Linda, illus. (ENG.). (J). (gr. -1-2). 2009. 26p. bds. 6.99 *(978-0-375-85347-0(2)*, Knopf Bks. for Young Readers) 2008. 32p. pap. 7.99 *(978-0-385-73614-5(2)*, Dragonfly Bks.) Random Hse. Children's Bks.

Schulz, Charles. It's the Great Pumpkin, Charlie Brown, 1 vol. 2013. (Peanuts Picture Bks.). (ENG.). 48p. (J). (gr. -1-4). lib. bdg. 24.21 *(978-1-61479-032-7(9))* ABDO Publishing Co.

—You Got a Rock, Charlie Brown! Pope, Robert, illus. 2015. (Peanuts Ser.). (ENG.). 32p. (J). (gr. k-2). pap. 3.99 *(978-1-4814-3602-1(3)*, Simon Spotlight) Simon Spotlight.

Schulz, Charles & Schulz, Charles M. It's the Great Pumpkin, Charlie Brown: with Sound & Music. 2012. (ENG., Illus.). 48p. (J). (gr. -1-3). 19.95 *(978-0-7624-4606-3(4)*, Running Pr. Kids) Running Pr. Bk. Pubs.

Schulz, Charles M. It's the Great Pumpkin, Charlie Brown. 2004. (Miniature Editions Ser.). (ENG., Illus.). 128p. (gr. -1-17). 5.95 *(978-0-7624-2033-9(2))* Running Pr. Bk. Pubs.

Scotton, Rob. Scaredy-Cat, Splat! Scotton, Rob, illus. (Splat the Cat Ser.). (Illus.). 40p. (J). (gr. -1-3). 2015. (ENG.). 9.99 *(978-0-06-236897-3(4))* 2010. (ENG.). 16.99 *(978-0-06-117760-6(1))* 2010. lib. bdg. 17.89 *(978-0-06-117761-3(X))* HarperCollins Pubs.

—Splat the Cat: What Was That? Scotton, Rob, illus. deluxe ed. 2013. (Splat the Cat Ser.). (ENG., Illus.). 16p. (J). (gr. k-3). pap. 6.99 *(978-0-06-197863-0(9)*, HarperFestival) HarperCollins Pubs.

Seagle, Steven T. Frankie Stein. 2010. (ENG., Illus.). 48p. 14.99 *(978-1-60706-191-5(0)*, 9781607061915) Image Comics.

Seal, Kerry. Five Silly Pumpkins: A Pop-up Halloween Book. Smith, Jane, illus. 2009. 10p. (J). 5.95 *(978-1-58117-908-8(1)*, Intervisual/Piggy Toes) Bendon, Inc.

Seeger, Laura Vaccaro. Dog & Bear: Tricks & Treats. Seeger, Laura Vaccaro, illus. 2014. (Dog & Bear Ser.). (ENG., Illus.). 32p. (J). (gr. -1-3). 14.99 *(978-1-59643-632-9(8)*, 9781596436329) Roaring Brook Pr.

Serafin, Jordan. Bella: The Crooked Hat Witch. Rubino, Alisa A., illus. 2004. (J). *(978-0-932991-57-7(2))* Place In The Woods, The.

Sesame Workshop. Happy Halloween! 2014. (Sesame Street Scribbles Elmo Ser.: 0). (ENG., Illus.). 32p. (J). (-3). 10.99 *(978-1-4022-9750-2(5)*, 9781402297502, Sourcebooks Jabberwocky) Sourcebooks, Inc.

Sharp, Euan. Diggedy Dozer in Ned at Night. 2009. 32p. pap. 13.90 *(978-0-557-04447-4(2))* Lulu Pr., Inc.

Sharratt, Nick. What's in the Witch's Kitchen? Sharratt, Nick, illus. 2011. (ENG., Illus.). 20p. (J). (gr. -1-2). 12.99 *(978-0-7636-5224-1(5))* Candlewick Pr.

Shaw, Gina. Oh My! Ginny Fry! Barton, Patrice, illus. 2010. 48p. (J). *(978-0-545-24384-1(X))* Scholastic, Inc.

Shepherd, Jodie. Olivia & the Haunted Hotel. Spaziante, Patrick, illus. 2010. (Olivia TV Tie-In Ser.). (ENG.). 24p. (J). (gr. -1-2). pap. 4.99 *(978-1-4424-0182-2(6)*, Simon Spotlight) Simon Spotlight.

—Olivia & the Haunted Hotel. 2010. (Olivia 8x8 Ser.). lib. bdg. 14.75 *(978-0-606-26573-7(2)*, Turtleback) Turtleback Bks.

Silberstein, James. The Night Crystal Mcgoober Had Seven Heads. 2004. 132p. 21.95 *(978-0-595-66716-1(3))* iUniverse, Inc.

Sill, Cathryn. About Mollusks: A Guide for Children, 1 vol. Sill, John, illus. 2008. (About... Ser.). (ENG.). 40p. (J). (gr. k-3). pap. 7.95 *(978-1-56145-406-8(0))* Peachtree Pubs.

Silva, Amanda. The Day That Jack Became a Jack O'Lantern. 2013. 20p. pap. 24.95 *(978-1-62709-387-3(7))* PublishAmerica, Inc.

Silverhardt, Lauryn. SpongeBob SpookyPants. Style Guide Staff, illus. 2004. (SpongeBob SquarePants Ser.). (ENG.). 16p. (J). bds. 5.99 *(978-0-689-87320-1(4)*, Simon Spotlight/Nickelodeon) Simon Spotlight/Nickelodeon.

Slegers, Liesbet. Happy Halloween! Slegers, Liesbet, illus. 2011. (ENG., Illus.). 32p. (J). (gr. -1-k). 15.95 *(978-1-60537-101-6(7))* Cobblestone Publishing Co.

Smart Kids Publishing. The Scary Sounds of Halloween. 2005. (Illus.). 20p. (J). (gr. -1-3). bds. 10.95 *(978-0-8249-6623-2(6)*, Ideal Pubns.) Worthy Publishing.

Smith, Audrey. The Halloween Misfits. 2004. 23p. (J). pap. 9.95 incl. audio compact disk *(978-0-9722673-4-2(4))* Audrey Productions.

Smith, Jessica Gillis. Charlotte's Halloween. 2012. 28p. pap. 19.99 *(978-1-4772-0522-8(5))* AuthorHouse.

Snider, Brandon T. Transformers Rescue Bots: Ghost in the Machine. 2017. (ENG., Illus.). 24p. (J). (gr. -1-3). pap. 4.99 ***(978-0-316-31880-8(9))*** Little, Brown Bks. for Young Readers.

Sobel, Gerrie. Jacob & His Magical Flying Bears, a Halloween Story. Torres, Dottie, illus. 2009. 32p. pap. 12.95 *(978-1-936051-42-7(7))* Peppertree Pr., The.

Soderberg, Erin. The Quirks & the Freaky Field Trip. Jack, Colin, illus. 2015. (Quirks Ser.). (ENG.). 208p. (YA). (gr. 3-6). 13.99 *(978-1-61963-668-2(9)*, 9781619636682, Bloomsbury USA Childrens) Bloomsbury Publishing USA.

Soman, David & Davis, Jacky. Happy Halloween, Ladybug Girl! Soman, David, illus. 2014. (Ladybug Girl Ser.). (ENG., Illus.). 16p. (J). (gr. -1-k). 6.99 *(978-0-448-47860-9(9)*, Grosset & Dunlap) Penguin Young Readers Group.

Speirs, John. Best Halloween Hunt Ever. Speirs, John, illus. 2008. (ENG., Illus.). 32p. (J). (gr. -1-3). pap. 4.99 *(978-0-545-06867-3(3)*, Cartwheel Bks.) Scholastic, Inc.

Spohn, Kate. Turtle & Snake's Spooky Halloween. Spohn, Kate, illus. 2003. (Easy-to-Read Ser.). (Illus.). 32p. (J). (gr. -1-3). 11.65 *(978-0-7569-1949-8(5))* Perfection Learning Corp.

Spurr, Elizabeth. Halloween Sky Ride. Long, Ethan, illus. (ENG.). 32p. (J). 2006. 6.95 *(978-0-8234-2041-4(8))* 2005. (gr. -1-3). 16.95 *(978-0-8234-1870-1(7))* Holiday Hse., Inc.

—Happy Sparkling Halloween. Madden, Colleen, illus. 2010. (Sparkling Stories Ser.). (ENG.). 14p. (J). (gr. k-k). bds. 5.95 *(978-1-4027-7138-5(X))* Sterling Publishing Co., Inc.

Staake, Bob. This Is Not a Pumpkin. Staake, Bob, illus. 2007. (ENG., Illus.). 32p. (J). (gr. -1 — 1). bds. 6.99 *(978-1-4169-3353-3(0)*, Little Simon) Little Simon.

Stauffacher, Sue. Animal Rescue Team: Hide & Seek. Lamont, Priscilla, illus. 2011. (Animal Rescue Team Ser.). (ENG.). 160p. (J). (gr. 3-7). 5.99 *(978-0-375-85133-9(X)*, Yearling) Random Hse. Children's Bks.

Steer, Dugald A. Snappy Little Halloween. Matthews, Derek, illus. 2004. 20p. (J). (gr. k-4). reprint ed. 13.00 *(978-0-7567-7403-5(9))* DIANE Publishing Co.

Stein, Garth. Enzo's Very Scary Halloween. Alley, R. W., illus. 2016. 40p. (J). (gr. -1-3). 17.99 *(978-0-06-238061-6(3))* HarperCollins Pubs.

Stephens, Sarah Hines. Lights Out. 2006. (Zoey 101 Ser.). 110p. (J). *(978-1-4287-0831-0(6))* Scholastic, Inc.

—Night of the Scaredy Crows, 1 vol. Baltazar, Art, illus. 2012. (DC Super-Pets Ser.). (ENG.). 56p. (gr. 2-2). pap. 4.95 *(978-1-4048-7663-7(4))*; lib. bdg. 23.99 *(978-1-4048-6492-4(X))* Picture Window Bks. (DC Super-Pets).

Stiberth, Elizabeth. Halloween Mystery. 2008. 32p. pap. 14.49 *(978-1-4389-1112-0(2))* AuthorHouse.

Stilton, Geronimo. It's Halloween, You 'Fraidy Mouse! Wolf, Matt, illus. 2004. 113p. (J). lib. bdg. 10.00 *(978-1-4242-0280-5(9))* Fitzgerald Bks.

—It's Halloween, You 'Fraidy Mouse! Wolf, Matt, illus. 2004. (Geronimo Stilton Ser.: 11). (ENG.). 128p. (J). (gr. 2-5). pap. 7.99 *(978-0-439-55973-7(1)*, Scholastic Paperbacks) Scholastic, Inc.

—The Peculiar Pumpkin Thief. 2010. (Geronimo Stilton Ser.: 42). (ENG.). 128p. (J). (gr. 2-5). 7.99 *(978-0-545-10372-5(X)*, Scholastic Paperbacks) Scholastic, Inc.

Stine, R. L. Goosebumps Wanted: the Haunted Mask. 2013. (Goosebumps: Wanted Ser.). (ENG.). 240p. (J). (gr. 3-7). pap. 6.99 *(978-0-545-41797-6(X)*, Scholastic Paperbacks) Scholastic, Inc.

—The Haunter. 2016. (Goosebumps Most Wanted Ser.). lib. bdg. 18.40 *(978-0-606-38784-2(6))* Turtleback Bks.

—The Scream of the Haunted Mask. 2008. (Goosebumps Horrorland Ser.: 4). (ENG.). 160p. (J). (gr. 3-7). pap. 6.99 *(978-0-439-91872-5(3)*, Scholastic Paperbacks) Scholastic, Inc.

—Trick or Trap. 2015. (Goosebumps Most Wanted Special Edition Ser.: 3). (ENG.). 192p. (J). (gr. 3-7). pap. 7.99 *(978-0-545-62778-8(8)*, Scholastic Paperbacks) Scholastic, Inc.

—Wanted: The Haunted Mask. 2012. (Goosebumps Ser.). (ENG.). 240p. (J). (gr. 3-7). 15.99 *(978-0-545-41793-8(7)*, Scholastic Paperbacks) Scholastic, Inc.

—Weirdo Halloween. 2010. (Goosebumps HorrorLand Ser.: No. 16). 240p. (J). pap. *(978-1-4071-1637-2(1))* Scholastic, Inc.

—Zombie Halloween. 2014. (Goosebumps Most Wanted Special Edition Ser.: 1). (ENG.). 192p. (J). (gr. 3-7). pap. 7.99 *(978-0-545-62776-4(1)*, Scholastic Paperbacks) Scholastic, Inc.

—Zombie Halloween. 2014. (Goosebumps Most Wanted Ser.). lib. bdg. 18.40 *(978-0-606-35855-2(2))* Turtleback Bks.

Stone Arch Books. Halloween & Thanksgiving, 1 vol. Nguyen, Dustin, illus. 2014. (Batman: Li'l Gotham Ser.). (ENG.). 32p. (gr. 2-3). 22.60 *(978-1-4342-9208-7(8))* Stone Arch Bks.

Stutson, Caroline. By the Light of the Halloween Moon, 0 vols. Hawkes, Kevin, illus. 2012. (ENG.). 32p. (J). (gr. k-4). pap. 7.99 *(978-0-7614-6244-6(9)*, 9780761462446, Amazon Children's Publishing) Amazon Publishing.

Super Why Staff. The Ghost Who Was Afraid of Halloween. 2009. 32p. pap. 3.99 *(978-0-448-45179-4(4)*, Grosset & Dunlap) Penguin Publishing Group.

Sutton, Benn. Hedgehug's Halloween. Pinto, Dan, illus. 2013. (ENG.). 40p. (J). (gr. -1-3). 9.99 *(978-0-06-196104-5(3))* HarperCollins Pubs.

Swindells, Robert. Trick or Treat. 2012. (Stoke Books Titles Ser.). (ENG.). 64p. (YA). (gr. 8-12). pap. 6.95 *(978-1-78112-118-4(4))*; lib. bdg. 22.60 *(978-1-78112-119-1(2))* Lerner Publishing Group.

Swindle, Stephanie. Pumpkin Pants. 2009. 32p. pap. 13.95 *(978-1-60860-461-6(6)*, Strategic Bk. Publishing) Strategic Book Publishing & Rights Agency (SBPRA).

Swiney, Wendy D. Harvey's First Halloween. 2010. (Illus.). 28p. pap. 12.99 *(978-1-4520-0540-9(0))* AuthorHouse.

Tagg, Christine. Who Will You Meet on Scary Street? Nine Pop-up Nightmares! Fuge, Charles, illus. 2004. 20p. (J). reprint ed. 15.00 *(978-0-7567-8003-6(9))* DIANE Publishing Co.

Tegen, Katherine. Dracula & Frankenstein Are Friends. Cushman, Doug, illus. 2003. 32p. (J). (gr. -1-3). 15.99 *(978-0-06-000115-5(1))* HarperCollins Pubs.

Tegen, Katherine Brown. The Story of the Jack O'Lantern. Dorman, Brandon, illus. 2010. (ENG.). 32p. (J). (gr. -1-3). 12.99 *(978-0-06-143088-6(9))* HarperCollins Pubs.

Teitelbaum, Michael. Halloween Howlers: Frightfully Funny Knock-Knock Jokes. Ho, Jannie, illus. 2011. (ENG.). 16p. (J). (gr. k-3). pap. 6.99 *(978-0-06-180891-3(1)*, HarperFestival) HarperCollins Pubs.

Testa, Maggie. Happy Halloween, Brobee! 2013. (Yo Gabba Gabba! Ser.). (ENG., Illus.). 12p. (J). (gr. -1-k). bds. 5.99 *(978-1-4424-7407-9(6)*, Simon Spotlight) Simon Spotlight.

—OLIVIA Loves Halloween. Osterhold, Jared, illus. 2014. (Olivia TV Tie-In Ser.). (ENG.). 24p. (J). (gr. -1-1). pap. 3.99 *(978-1-4814-0462-4(8)*, Simon Spotlight) Simon Spotlight.

Thaler, Mike. Church Harvest Mess-Tivall, 1 vol. Lee, Jared, illus. 2010. (Tales from the Back Pew Ser.). (ENG.). 32p. (J). pap. 3.99 *(978-0-310-71595-5(4))* Zonderkidz.

Thomas, Deborah Kadiar. Cemetery Jamboree, 1 vol. Thomas, Deborah Kadiar, illus. 2016. (ENG., Illus.). 32p. (J). (gr. k-5). pap. 9.95 *(978-1-4556-2239-9(7))* Pelican Publishing Co., Inc.

Thompson, Jill. The Revenge of Jimmy. 2006. (Illus.). 48p. pap. 9.95 *(978-1-57989-071-1(7))* Sirius Entertainment, Inc.

—Scary Godmother. 2010. (ENG., Illus.). 192p. (J). (gr. 5-7). 24.99 *(978-1-59582-589-6(4))* Dark Horse Comics.

—Scary Godmother. 2005. (Illus.). 48p. pap. 9.95 *(978-1-57989-070-4(9))* Sirius Entertainment, Inc.

Thompson, Jill, creator. Scary Godmother: The Mystery Date. 2004. (Illus.). 48p. pap. 9.95 *(978-1-57989-072-8(5))* Sirius Entertainment, Inc.

Thompson, Lauren. Mouse's First Halloween. Erdogan, Buket, illus. 2003. (Classic Board Bks.). (ENG.). 34p. (J). (gr. -1 — 1). bds., bds. 7.99 *(978-0-689-85584-9(2)*, Little Simon) Little Simon.

Tiger Tales Staff & Mantle, Ben. Five Little Pumpkins. Tiger Tales Staff, ed. 2010. (ENG., Illus.). 24p. (J). (gr. -1-k). bds. 8.95 *(978-1-58925-856-3(8))* Tiger Tales.

Tomos, Angharad. Mali Melpen. 6th ed. 2005. (WEL., Illus.). 48p. pap. *(978-0-86243-104-4(2))* Y Lolfa.

Town, Vicky. The Runaway Pumpkin Pie Man, 1 vol. Baird, Roberta, illus. 2015. (ENG.). 32p. (J). (gr. k-3). 16.99 *(978-1-4556-2025-8(4))* Pelican Publishing Co., Inc.

Trapani, Iza. Haunted Party. Trapani, Iza, illus. 2010. (ENG., Illus.). 28p. (J). (gr. -1-2). pap. 7.95 *(978-1-58089-247-6(7))* Charlesbridge Publishing, Inc.

Tremblay, Patrick. Poor, Poor Jack. 2010. 40p. pap. 26.00 *(978-0-557-25375-3(6))* Lulu Pr., Inc.

Van Draanen, Wendelin. Sammy Keyes & the Night of Skulls. 2012. (Sammy Keyes Ser.: 14). (ENG.). 336p. (J). (gr. 5-7). 8.99 *(978-0-375-85457-6(6)*, Yearling) Random Hse. Children's Bks.

Vande Velde, Vivian. All Hallows' Eve: 13 Stories. 2010. (ENG., Illus.). 240p. (YA). (gr. 7). pap. 8.99 *(978-0-15-206473-0(7))* Houghton Mifflin Harcourt Publishing Co.

Vanholme, Virginie. Malevolence & Mandrake. 2nd ed. 2009. (Scared to Death Ser.: 2). (ENG., Illus.). 48p. (gr. 3-17). pap. 11.95 *(978-1-905460-77-9(5))* CineBook GBR. Dist: National Bk. Network.

Vant, Jeanie. The Witch's Cat. Vant, Tim, illus. 2010. 24p. pap. 11.50 *(978-1-60976-051-9(4)*, Eloquent Bks.) Strategic Book Publishing & Rights Agency (SBPRA).

Vasilovich, Guy. The 13 Nights of Halloween. Vasilovich, Guy, illus. 2011. (ENG., Illus.). 40p. (J). (gr. -1-3). 16.99 *(978-0-06-180445-8(2))* HarperCollins Pubs.

Vatcher-Martin M.A., Cheryl A. The Cornstalks Are Whispering. 2009. 20p. pap. 17.99 *(978-1-4490-1206-9(X))* AuthorHouse.

Vernon, Ursula. No Such Thing as Ghosts. 5th ed. 2011. (Dragonbreath Ser.: 5). (ENG.). 208p. (J). (gr. 3-7). 12.99 *(978-0-8037-3527-9(8)*, Dial Bks) Penguin Young Readers Group.

Viguié, Debbie. The Fall of Candy Corn, 1 vol. 2008. (Sweet Seasons Novel Ser.). (ENG.). 224p. (YA). (gr. 8-11). pap. 9.99 *(978-0-310-71559-7(8))* Zondervan.

Vischer, Phil. God Is Bigger Than the Boogie Man. Pulley, Kelly & Reed, Lisa, illus. 2014. (VeggieTales Book Ser.). 16p. (J). bds. 12.99 *(978-0-8249-1943-6(2)*, Ideal Pubns.) Worthy Publishing.

Walker, Sally M. Druscilla's Halloween. White, Lee, illus. 2009. (Carolrhoda Picture Bks.). (ENG.). 32p. (J). (gr. k-3). 16.95 *(978-0-8225-8941-9(9))* Lerner Publishing Group.

Wallace, Adam. How to Catch a Monster. Elkerton, Andy, illus. 2017. (ENG.). 40p. (J). (-3). 10.99 ***(978-1-4926-4894-9(9)***, Sourcebooks Jabberwocky) Sourcebooks, Inc.

Wallace, Rich. Wicked Cruel. 2015. (ENG.). 208p. (J). (gr. 5). pap. 6.99 *(978-0-375-86514-5(4)*, Yearling) Random Hse. Children's Bks.

Walton, Rick. What Do We Do with the Baby? Miglio, Paige, illus. 2008. 32p. (J). (gr. -1-k). lib. bdg. 17.89 *(978-0-06-008420-2(0))* HarperCollins Pubs.

Warner, Gertrude Chandler, creator. Hidden in the Haunted School. 2016. (Boxcar Children Mysteries Ser.: 144). (ENG.). 128p. (J). (gr. 1-5). 15.99 *(978-0-8075-0718-6(0))* Whitman, Albert & Co.

Watt, Mélanie. Scaredy Squirrel Prepares for Halloween. Watt, Mélanie, illus. 2013. (ENG., Illus.). 64p. (J). (gr. -1-3). 17.95 *(978-1-894786-87-4(4))* Kids Can Pr., Ltd. CAN. Dist: Hachette Bk. Group.

Wayne, Richard, ed. Poppin's Pumpkin Patch Parade. Carlson, Patrick, illus. 2016. (ENG.). 32p. (J). pap. 12.98 *(978-0-9801692-1-8(6))* Gemstone Literary.

Weck, Peter. Lima Bear's Halloween. DiSalvo, Len, illus. 2012. (Lima Bear Stories Ser.). 40p. (J). 15.95 *(978-1-933872-16-2(0))* Lima Bear Pr LLC, The.

Welling, Peter J. Darlene Halloween & the Great Chicago Fire, 1 vol. Welling, Peter J., illus. 2007. (ENG., Illus.). 32p. (J). (gr. k-3). 16.99 *(978-1-58980-479-1(1))* Pelican Publishing Co., Inc.

Wells, Rosemary. Max's Halloween. Wells, Rosemary, illus. 2004. (Max & Ruby Ser.). (ENG., Illus.). 16p. (J). (gr. -1 — 1). bds. 6.99 *(978-0-670-05899-0(8)*, Viking Books for Young Readers) Penguin Young Readers Group.

Whalen, Erin T. Charlie Gets Spooked, 3 vols. 2004. (Illus.). 32p. (J). (gr. k-3). 16.95 *(978-1-929265-04-6(2))*; pap. 8.95 *(978-1-929265-05-3(0))* Lily & Co. Publishing.

Wheeler, Lisa. When Pigs Fly. Ansley, Frank, illus. 2005. (Fitch & Chip Ser.: 2). (ENG.). 48p. (J). (gr. 1-3). pap. 3.99 *(978-0-689-84956-5(7)*, Simon Spotlight) Simon Spotlight.

White, George. Halloween at the Zoo: A Pop-up Trick of Treat Experience. 2007. (Illus.). 16p. (J). 16.99 *(978-0-9795441-0-1(6))* Jumping Jack Pr.

Wilkinson, James H. Yang the Dragon Tells His Story, Halloween Train. Blake, Carol, illus. 2013. 32p. pap. 15.99 *(978-0-9886360-0-2(X))* Kids At Heart Publishing, LLC.

Willson, Sarah. Dora's Halloween Adventure. Savitsky, Steven, illus. 2003. (Dora the Explorer Ser.). (ENG.). 14p. (J). bds. 5.99 *(978-0-689-85844-4(2)*, Simon Spotlight/Nickelodeon) Simon Spotlight/Nickelodeon.

Wilson, Karma. Trick or Treat, Calico! Erdogan, Buket, illus. 2014. (J). *(978-1-4351-5610-4(2)*, Little Simon) Little Simon.

Winkler, Henry & Oliver, Lin. My Dog's a Scaredy-Cat, 10 vols. Watson, Jesse Joshua, illus. 2006. (Hank Zipzer Ser.: 10). (ENG.). 160p. (J). (gr. 3-7). pap. 5.99 *(978-0-448-43878-8(X)*, Grosset & Dunlap) Penguin Young Readers Group.

Wojciechowski, Susan. The Best Halloween of All. Meddaugh, Susan, illus. 2012. (ENG.). 24p. (J). (gr. -1-3). pap. 3.99 *(978-0-7636-6008-6(6))* Candlewick Pr.

Wolf, Jackie. My Sparkle Pumpkin. 2003. (Picture Me Ser.). (Illus.). 10p. (J). (gr. -1-18). bds. 6.99 *(978-1-57151-721-0(9))* Playhouse Publishing.

—Picture Me Peek-a-Boo! 2004. (Picture Me Ser.). (Illus.). 10p. (J). (gr. -1-18). bds. 4.99 *(978-1-57151-570-4(4))* Playhouse Publishing.

Woods, Jeanne & Lugo, Patricia. Bonita Bones & the Halloween Surprise. 2012. 24p. pap. 17.99 *(978-1-4772-4103-5(5))* AuthorHouse.

Wunderli, Stephen. Little Boo. Zeltner, Tim, illus. 2014. (ENG.). 32p. (J). (gr. -1-2). 16.99 *(978-0-8050-9708-5(2)*, 9780805097085, Holt, Henry & Co. Bks. For Young Readers) Holt, Henry & Co.

Yee, Wong Herbert. A Perfect Halloween. 2011. (Mouse & Mole Story Ser.). (ENG., Illus.). 48p. (J). (gr. 1-4). 14.99 *(978-0-547-55152-4(5))* Houghton Mifflin Harcourt Publishing Co.

Yoon, Salina. Five Trick-or-Treaters. 2010. 10p. bds. 5.95 *(978-1-60747-745-7(9)*, Pickwick Pr.) Phoenix Bks., Inc.

—Jack & Jill: A Halloween Nursery Rhyme. Yoon, Salina, illus. 2012. (ENG., Illus.). 18p. (J). (gr. -1 — 1). bds. 5.99 *(978-1-4424-1410-5(3)*, Little Simon) Little Simon.

—Where's Boo? 2013. (ENG., Illus.). 18p. (J). (— 1). bds. 6.99 *(978-0-307-97808-0(7)*, Random Hse. Bks. for Young Readers) Random Hse. Children's Bks.

Young, Jessica. Super Spooktacular. Secheret, Jessica, illus. 2017. (Finley Flowers Ser.). (ENG.). 128p. (gr. 2-3). lib. bdg. 25.32 ***(978-1-4795-9807-6(0)***, Finley Flowers) Picture Window Bks.

Ziefert, Harriet. Ding-Dong, Trick or Treat! Demarest, Chris L., illus. 2004. 22p. (J). (gr. -1-3). reprint ed. pap. 12.00 *(978-0-7567-8258-0(9))* DIANE Publishing Co.

—Two Little Witches: A Halloween Counting Story. Taback, Simms, illus. 2007. (ENG.). 32p. (J). (gr. k-k). pap. 3.99 *(978-0-7636-3309-7(7))* Candlewick Pr.

Zolotow, Charlotte. A Tiger Called Thomas. 2017. (J). *(978-1-4926-0171-5(3))* Sourcebooks, Inc.

Zuravicky, Orli. Dear Diary: Monster House. 2006. (Illus.). 32p. (J). lib. bdg. 15.00 *(978-1-4242-1561-4(7))* Fitzgerald Bks.

HALLUCINOGENIC DRUGS

Cefrey, Holly. Hallucinogens & Your Neurons: The Incredibly Disgusting Story. (Incredibly Disgusting Drugs Ser.). 48p. 2009. (gr. 5-8). 53.00 *(978-1-61513-499-1(9))* 2005. (Illus.). (J). (gr. k-3). lib. bdg. 29.25 *(978-1-4042-0633-5(7))* Rosen Publishing Group, Inc., The. (Rosen Reference).

Eldridge, Alison & Eldridge, Stephen. Investigate Club Drugs. 2014. (Investigate Drugs Ser.). (Illus.). 112p. (J). (gr. 5-12). lib. bdg. 33.27 *(978-0-7660-4221-6(9))* Enslow Pubs., Inc.

Lockwood, Brad. Ketamine: Dangerous Hallucinogen. 2009. (Drug Abuse & Society Ser.). 64p. (gr. 6-6). 58.50 *(978-1-61512-223-3(0))* Rosen Publishing Group, Inc., The.

MacKay, Jenny. The Dangers of Hallucinogens. 2016. (ENG.). 80p. (YA). (gr. 5-12). *(978-1-68282-016-2(5))* ReferencePoint Pr., Inc.

McCage, Crystal D. Hallucinogens: Drugs. 2007. (Compact Research Ser.). (Illus.). 104p. (YA). (gr. 7-12). lib. bdg. 25.95 *(978-1-60152-014-2(X))* ReferencePoint Pr., Inc.

Mehling, Randi. Hallucinogens. 2003. (Drugs Ser.). (Illus.). 128p. (C). (gr. 9-13). 30.00 *(978-0-7910-7261-5(4)*, Chelsea Hse.) Facts On File, Inc.

Nelson, Sheila. Hallucinogens: Unreal Visions. Henningfield, Jack E., ed. 2012. (Illicit & Misused Drugs Ser.). 128p. (J). (gr. 7). 24.95 *(978-1-4222-2432-8(5))*; pap. 14.95 *(978-1-4222-2451-9(1))* Mason Crest.

H
I

—Hallucinogens: Unreal Visions. 2009. (Illicit & Misused Drugs Ser.). (Illus.). 128p. (YA). (gr. 7-18). lib. bdg. 24.95 *(978-1-4222-0155-8(4))* Mason Crest.

Perritano, John. Hallucinogens: Ecstasy, LSD, & Ketamine, Vol. 13. Becker, Sara, ed. 2016. (Drug Addiction & Recovery Ser.). (Illus.). 64p. (J). (gr. 7). 23.95 *(978-1-4222-3604-8(8))* Mason Crest.

Poolos, Christine. The Truth about Pcp. 2013. (Drugs & Consequences Ser.). (Illus.). 64p. (J). (gr. 7-12). 31.95 *(978-1-4777-1899-5(0))* Rosen Publishing Group, Inc., The.

Santella, Thomas & Triggle, David J. Hallucinogens. 2012. (Understanding Drugs Ser.). 104p. (C). (gr. 9-12). 34.95 *(978-1-60413-539-8(5))* Facts On File, Inc.

HAMER, FANNIE LOU, 1918-1977

Fiorelli, June Estep. Fannie Lou Hamer: A Voice for Freedom. 2004. (Avisson Young Adult Ser.). (Illus.). 117p. (J). pap. 19.95 *(978-1-888105-62-9(3))* Avisson Pr., Inc.

HAMILTON, ALEXANDER, 1757-1804

Brockenbrough, Martha. Alexander Hamilton, Revolutionary. 2017. (ENG.). 384p. (YA). 19.99 ***(978-1-250-12319-0(4)***, 9781250123190) Feiwel & Friends.

Brown, Don. Aaron & Alexander: The Most Famous Duel in American History. 2015. (ENG., Illus.). 32p. (J). (gr. k-4). 17.99 *(978-1-59643-998-6(X)*, 9781596439986) Roaring Brook Pr.

Collier, James Lincoln. The Alexander Hamilton. 2003. (You Never Knew Ser.). (ENG., Illus.). 80p. (J). 25.50 *(978-0-516-24345-0(4)*, Children's Pr.) Scholastic Library Publishing.

Davies, Monika. The Schuyler Sisters (Alexander Hamilton). 2017. (Primary Source Readers Focus On Ser.). (Illus.). 32p. (J). (gr. 4-8). pap. 8.99 ***(978-1-4258-6352-4(3))*** Teacher Created Materials, Inc.

—True Life: Alexander Hamilton. 2016. (TIME for KIDS(r) Nonfiction Readers Ser.). (Illus.). 48p. (J). (gr. 8-8). pap. 9.99 ***(978-1-4938-3633-8(1))*** Teacher Created Materials, Inc.

DeCarolis, Lisa. Alexander Hamilton: Federalist & Founding Father. (Library of American Lives & Times Ser.). 112p. 2009. (gr. 5-5). 69.20 *(978-1-60853-470-8(7))* 2005. (Illus.). (J). (gr. 4-8). lib. bdg. 34.60 *(978-0-8239-5735-4(7))* Rosen Publishing Group, Inc., The.

DeGraw, Aleine. Alexander Hamilton: American Statesman. (Primary Sources of Famous People in American History Ser.). 32p. 2009. (gr. 2-3). 47.90 *(978-1-60851-646-9(6))* 2004. (ENG., Illus.). (gr. 4-8). pap. 10.00 *(978-0-8239-4173-5(6))* Rosen Publishing Group, Inc., The.

—Alexander Hamilton: American Statesman / Estadista Estadounidense. 2009. (Famous People in American History/Grandes personajes en la historia de los Estados Unidos Ser.). (SPA.). 32p. (gr. 2-3). 47.90 *(978-1-61512-536-4(1)*, Editorial Buenas Letras) Rosen Publishing Group, Inc., The.

—Alexander Hamilton: Estadista Estadounidense. 2004. (Grandes Personajes en la Historia de Los Estados Unidos Ser.). (SPA., Illus.). 32p. (gr. 5-8). pap. 10.00 *(978-0-8239-4219-0(8))* Rosen Publishing Group, Inc., The.

—Alexander Hamilton: Estadista estadounidense (Alexander Hamilton: American Statesman) 2009. (Grandes personajes en la historia de los Estados Unidos (Famous People in American History) Ser.). 32p. (gr. 2-3). 47.90 *(978-1-61512-788-7(7)*, Editorial Buenas Letras) Rosen Publishing Group, Inc., The.

Fritz, Jean. Alexander Hamilton: The Outsider. 2012. (ENG.). 144p. (J). (gr. 3-7). 8.99 *(978-0-14-241986-1(9)*, Puffin Books) Penguin Young Readers Group.

Gould, Jane H. Alexander Hamilton. 2012. (Jr. Graphic Founding Fathers Ser.). (ENG., Illus.). 24p. (J). (gr. 3-6). pap. 10.60 *(978-1-4488-7989-2(2))*; lib. bdg. 25.25 *(978-1-4488-7895-6(0))* Rosen Publishing Group, Inc., The. (PowerKids Pr.).

Greeley, August. Pistols & Politics: Alexander Hamilton Duels Aaron Burr. 2004. (Primary Sources of Famous People in American History Ser.). (ENG.). 32p. (gr. 4-8). pap. 10.00 *(978-0-8239-4327-2(5)*, Rosen Classroom) Rosen Publishing Group, Inc., The.

—Pistols & Politics: Alexander Hamilton's Great Duel. 2009. (Great Moments in American History Ser.). 32p. (gr. 3-3). 47.90 *(978-1-61513-149-5(3))* Rosen Publishing Group, Inc., The.

Herweck Rice, Dona. Alexander Hamilton's New York City (Alexander Hamilton) 2017. (Primary Source Readers Focus On Ser.). (Illus.). 32p. (J). (gr. 4-8). pap. 8.99 ***(978-1-4258-6351-7(5))*** Teacher Created Materials, Inc.

Keller, Susanna. Alexander Hamilton: America's First Treasury Secretary. 2017. (J). pap. ***(978-1-68048-808-1(2))***; lib. bdg. ***(978-1-68048-809-8(0))*** Rosen Publishing Group, Inc., The. (Britannica Educational Publishing).

Kelley, K. C. Alexander Hamilton: American Hero. 2017. (Rookie Biographies(tm) Ser.). (ENG., Illus.). 32p. (J). lib. bdg. 25.00 *(978-0-531-22290-4(X))* Scholastic Library Publishing.

Kent, Zachary. Alexander Hamilton: Creating a Nation. 2004. (America's Founding Fathers Ser.). (Illus.). 128p. (J). lib. bdg. 26.60 *(978-0-7660-2181-5(5))* Enslow Pubs., Inc.

Kulling, Monica. Alexander Hamilton. 2017. (Step into Reading Level 3 Ser.). lib. bdg. 13.55 ***(978-0-606-39848-0(1))*** Turtleback Bks.

Kulling, Monica. Alexander Hamilton: From Orphan to Founding Father. 2017. (Step into Reading Ser.). (ENG., Illus.). 48p. (J). (gr. k-3). pap. 3.99 *(978-1-5247-1698-1(7)*, Random Hse. Bks. for Young Readers) Random Hse. Children's Bks.

McLeese, Don. Alexander Hamilton. 2004. (Heroes of the American Revolution Ser.). (Illus.). 32p. (gr. 2-5). lib. bdg. *(978-1-59515-219-0(9))* Rourke Educational Media.

McNeese, Tim. Alexander Hamilton: Framer of the Constitution. 2005. (Leaders of the American Revolution Ser.). (Illus.). 100p. (gr. 5-8). lib. bdg. 30.00 *(978-0-7910-8616-2(X))* Facts On File, Inc.

Miller, Chuck. Alexander Hamilton. 2003. (America's Founders Ser.). (J). pap. *(978-1-58417-081-5(6))*; lib. bdg. *(978-1-58417-018-1(2))* Lake Street Pubs.

Newton, Michael E. Alexander Hamilton: The Formative Years. 2015. (ENG., Illus.). 774p. 40.00 *(978-0-9826040-3-8(3))* Eleftheria Publishing.

Perrin, Pat. The Mystery of the Deadly Duel. 2004. (Illus.). 64p. pap. 9.00 *(978-0-7891-5996-0(1))* Perfection Learning Corp.

Pollack, Pam & Belviso, Meg. Who Was Alexander Hamilton? Putra, Dede, illus. 2017. (Who Was? Ser.). (ENG.). 112p. (J). (gr. 3-7). 5.99 ***(978-0-399-54427-9(5))***; lib. bdg. 15.99 ***(978-0-399-54429-3(1))*** Penguin Young Readers Group. (Penguin Workshop).

Randolph, Ryan. Alexander Hamilton's Economic Plan: Solving Problems in America's New Economy. 2009. (Life in the New American Nation Ser.). 32p. (gr. 4-4). 47.90 *(978-1-61514-276-7(2))* Rosen Publishing Group, Inc., The.

Roberts, Russell. The Life & Times of Alexander Hamilton. 2006. (Profiles in American History Ser.). (Illus.). 48p. (J). (gr. 3-7). lib. bdg. 29.95 *(978-1-58415-436-5(5))* Mitchell Lane Pubs., Inc.

Rosenberg, Pam. Alexander Hamilton: Soldier & Statesman. 2004. (Our People Ser.). (ENG., Illus.). 32p. (J). (gr. 3-6). 29.93 *(978-1-59296-172-6(X)*, 200626) Child's World, Inc., The.

Ryckman, Tatiana. Alexander Hamilton: The First Secretary of Treasury & an Author of the Federalist Papers. 2016. (Great American Thinkers Ser.). (Illus.). 128p. (J). (gr. 9-9). 45.64 *(978-1-5026-1934-1(2))* Cavendish Square Publishing.

Seeley, M. H. 20 Fun Facts about Alexander Hamilton. 2017. (Fun Fact File: Founding Fathers Ser.). 32p. (gr. 2-3). pap. 10.50 ***(978-1-5382-0288-3(3))*** Stevens, Gareth Publishing LLLP.

Shea, Therese M. Alexander Hamilton: Founding Father & Treasury Secretary. 2017. (J). pap. ***(978-0-7660-9045-3(0))*** Enslow Pubs., Inc.

Slepian, Curtis. Hamilton vs. Jefferson (Alexander Hamilton) 2017. (Primary Source Readers Focus On Ser.). (Illus.). 32p. (J). (gr. 4-8). pap. 8.99 ***(978-1-4258-6354-8(X))*** Teacher Created Materials, Inc.

St. George, Judith. The Duel: The Parallel Lives of Alexander Hamilton & Aaron Burr. 2016. lib. bdg. 20.85 *(978-0-606-38853-5(2))* Turtleback Bks.

Whitelaw, Nancy. More Perfect Union: The Story of Alexander Hamilton. 2nd rev. exp. ed. 2004. (Notable Americans Ser.). (Illus.). 128p. (YA). (gr. 6-12). 23.95 *(978-1-931798-03-7(6))* Reynolds, Morgan Inc.

HAMSTERS

Alderton, David. How to Look after Your Hamster: A Practical Guide to Caring for Your Pet, in Step-By-Step Photographs. 2014. (ENG., Illus.). 20p. (J). (gr. -1-3). 8.99 *(978-1-84322-833-2(5)*, Armadillo) Anness Publishing GBR. Dist: National Bk. Network.

Bader, Bonnie. Ham-Ham-Hamsters. 2016. (Penguin Young Readers, Level 2 Ser.). (ENG., Illus.). 32p. (J). (gr. 1-2). 14.99 *(978-0-399-54166-7(7)*, Penguin Young Readers) Penguin Young Readers Group.

Birney, Betty G. Humphrey's Book of Fun Fun Fun. 2013. (Humphrey Ser.). (ENG.). 240p. (J). (gr. 3-7). pap. 6.99 *(978-0-14-750951-2(3)*, Puffin Books) Penguin Young Readers Group.

—Humphrey's World of Pets. 2013. (Humphrey Ser.). (ENG.). 224p. (J). (gr. 3-7). 10.99 *(978-0-14-750953-6(X)*, Puffin Books) Penguin Young Readers Group.

Bodden, Valerie. Hamsters. (My First Look At Ser.). 24p. (J). 2011. (ENG.). (gr. 1-17). pap. 7.99 *(978-1-926722-41-2(8)*, Creative Paperbacks) 2006. (Illus.). (gr. -1-3). lib. bdg. 15.95 *(978-1-58341-459-0(2)*, Creative Education) Creative Co., The.

Carr, Aaron. Hamster. 2011. (J). *(978-1-61690-569-9(7))* Weigl Pubs., Inc.

—El Hamster. 2012. (SPA.). (J). *(978-1-61913-184-2(6))* Weigl Pubs., Inc.

Colson, Mary. The Truth about Hamsters: What Hamsters Do When You're Not Looking. 2017. (Pets Undercover! Ser.). (ENG., Illus.). 32p. (gr. 2-4). lib. bdg. 29.99 *(978-1-4109-8607-8(1)*, Read Me!) Heinemann-Raintree.

Coppendale, Jean. Gerbils & Hamsters. 2004. (QEB You & Your Pet Ser.). (Illus.). 32p. (J). lib. bdg. 18.95 *(978-1-59566-055-8(0))* QEB Publishing Inc.

Ellis, Carol. Hamsters & Gerbils. 2008. (Great Pets Ser.). 48p. (gr. 3-18). lib. bdg. 29.93 *(978-0-7614-2999-9(9)*, Benchmark Bks.) Marshall Cavendish Corp.

Foran, Jill. Caring for Your Hamster. Marshall, Diana & Nault, Jennifer, eds. 2003. (Caring for Your Pet Ser.). (Illus.). 32p. (J). pap. 9.95 *(978-1-59036-066-8(4))* Weigl Pubs., Inc.

—Hamster. 2008. (My Pet Ser.). (Illus.). 32p. (J). (gr. 3-5). pap. 9.95 *(978-1-59036-907-4(6))*; lib. bdg. 26.00 *(978-1-59036-906-7(8))* Weigl Pubs., Inc.

Gardeski, Christina Mia. Hamsters: Questions & Answers. 2016. (Pet Questions & Answers Ser.). (ENG., Illus.). 24p. (gr. k-1). pap. 6.95 *(978-1-5157-0359-4(2))*; lib. bdg. 26.65 *(978-1-5157-0352-5(5))* Capstone Press of Coughlan Cos. (Pebble Plus).

Graubart, Norman D. Mi Hmster / My Hamster, 1 vol., 1. Green, Christina, ed. 2014. (¡Las Mascotas Son Geniales! / Pets Are Awesome! Ser.). (SPA & BYN.). 24p. (J). (gr. k-2). 23.60 *(978-1-4777-3313-4(2)*, PowerKids Pr.) Rosen Publishing Group, Inc., The.

—My Hamster, 1 vol., 1. 2014. (Pets Are Awesome! Ser.). (ENG.). 24p. (J). (gr. k-2). 23.60 *(978-1-4777-2868-0(6)*, PowerKids Pr.) Rosen Publishing Group, Inc., The.

Hamster. 2003. 38.95 *(978-0-8136-4200-0(0))* Modern Curriculum Pr.

Hamsters. 2007. (Illus.). (J). cd-rom 9.99 *(978-0-9795190-3-1(9))* Color & Learn.

Heneghan, Judith. Love Your Hamster. 2013. (Your Perfect Pet Ser.). (ENG., Illus.). 32p. (gr. k-5). 25.25 *(978-1-4777-0186-7(9))*; pap. 10.00 *(978-1-4777-0200-0(8))* Windmill Bks.

Hibbert, Clare. Hamster. 2004. (Illus.). 32p. (J). lib. bdg. 27.10 *(978-1-58340-433-1(3))* Black Rabbit Bks.

Hutmacher, Kimberly M. I Want a Hamster, 1 vol. 2012. (I Want a Pet Ser.). (ENG.). 24p. (gr. k-1). lib. bdg. 26.65 *(978-1-4296-7598-7(5)*, Pebble Plus) Capstone Press of Coughlan Cos.

Jacobs, Pat. Hamster Pals. 2017. 32p. (J). ***(978-0-7787-3560-1(5))*** Crabtree Publishing Co.

Johnson, Jinny. Hamster & Gerbil. 2014. (My New Pet Ser.). 24p. (gr. k-3). lib. bdg. 28.50 *(978-1-62588-030-7(8))* Black Rabbit Bks.

—Hamster & Gerbil. 2014. (My New Pet Ser.). (ENG., Illus.). 24p. (J). (gr. -1-3). pap. 8.95 *(978-1-77092-207-5(5))* Saunders Bk. Co. CAN. Dist: RiverStream Publishing.

Kawa, Katie. Furry Hamsters. 2011. (Pet Corner Ser.). (Illus.). 24p. (gr. k-2). (J). pap. 8.15 *(978-1-4339-5605-8(5))*; (J). lib. bdg. 22.60 *(978-1-4339-5603-4(9))*; 69.20 *(978-1-4339-6883-9(5))* Stevens, Gareth Publishing LLLP.

—Furry Hamsters: Hámsteres Peludos. 2011. (Pet Corner / RincóN de Las Mascotas Ser.). (SPA., Illus.). 24p. (J). (gr. k-3). lib. bdg. 22.60 *(978-1-4339-5607-2(1))* Stevens, Gareth Publishing LLLP.

Landau, Elaine. Your Pet Hamster. rev. ed. 2007. (True Bks.). (ENG., Illus.). 48p. (J). (gr. 3-5). pap. 6.95 *(978-0-531-15467-0(X)*, Children's Pr.) Scholastic Library Publishing.

McBride, Anne. Hamsters, Vol. 12. 2016. (Understanding & Caring for Your Pet Ser.). (Illus.). 128p. (J). (gr. 5). 25.95 *(978-1-4222-3699-4(4))* Mason Crest.

McCarville, Mary Michele. Merry Hairy. 2008. 25p. 14.00 *(978-0-615-25486-9(1))* Michele, Mary.

Meister, Cari. Hamsters. 2014. (Illus.). 24p. (J). lib. bdg. 25.65 *(978-1-62031-124-0(0)*, Bullfrog Bks.) Jump! Inc.

Meredith, Susan. Hamsters. rev. ed. 2004. (First Pets Ser.). 32p. (J). (gr. 1-18). pap. 5.95 *(978-0-7945-0796-1(4)*, Usborne) EDC Publishing.

Meredith, Susan, et al. Hamsters. Fox, Christyan, illus. 2004. 30p. (J). *(978-0-439-78698-0(3))* Scholastic, Inc.

Morgan, Sally. Gerbils & Hamsters. 2012. (Pets Plus Ser.). (Illus.). 32p. (gr. 3-6). lib. bdg. 31.35 *(978-1-59920-701-8(X))* Black Rabbit Bks.

Murray, Julie. Hamsters, 1 vol. (ENG., 24p. 2015. Illus.). (J). 27.07 *(978-1-62970-902-4(6))* 2003. 25.65 *(978-1-57765-725-5(X)*, Buddy Bks.) ABDO Publishing Co.

Nelson, Robin. Pet Hamster. 2003. (First Step Nonfiction). (Illus.). 24p. (J). (gr. k-2). lib. bdg. 18.60 *(978-0-8225-1269-1(6))* Lerner Publishing Group.

Rayner, Matthew & BVetMed MRCVS Staff. Hamster. Greenaway, Frank & Burton, Jane, photos by. 2004. (I Am Your Pet Ser.). (Illus.). 32p. (gr. k-4). lib. bdg. 26.00 *(978-0-8368-4104-6(2)*, Gareth Stevens Learning Library) Stevens, Gareth Publishing LLLP.

Reeg, Cynthia. Hamster Holidays: Noun & Adjective Adventures. Grady, Kit, illus. 2009. 24p. pap. 10.95 *(978-1-935137-62-7(X))* Guardian Angel Publishing, Inc.

Rober, Harold. I Love Hamsters. 2016. (Bumba Books (tm) — Pets Are the Best Ser.). (ENG.). 24p. (J). (gr. -1-1). lib. bdg. 25.32 *(978-1-5124-1417-2(4))* Lerner Publishing Group.

Sjonger, Rebecca & Kalman, Bobbie. Hamsters. Crabtree, Marc, illus. Crabtree, Marc, photos by. 2003. (Pet Care Ser.). (ENG.). 32p. (J). lib. bdg. *(978-0-7787-1753-9(4))* Crabtree Publishing Co.

—Los Hamsters. Crabtree, Marc, photos by. 2006. (Cuidado de las Mascotas Ser.). (ENG & SPA., Illus.). 32p. (J). (gr. 3-7). lib. bdg. *(978-0-7787-8456-2(8))* Crabtree Publishing Co.

—Los Hámsters. Crabtree, Marc, photos by. 2006. (Cuidado de las Mascotas Ser.). (SPA & ENG., Illus.). 32p. (J). (gr. 3-7). pap. *(978-0-7787-8478-4(9))* Crabtree Publishing Co.

Sjonger, Rebecca, et al. Les Hamsters. 2010. (Petit Monde Vivant Ser.). (FRE., Illus.). 32p. (J). pap. 9.95 *(978-2-89579-324-3(7))* Bayard Canada Livres CAN. Dist: Crabtree Publishing Co.

Smalley, Carol Parenzan. Care for a Pet Hamster. 2009. (How to Convince Your Parents You Can ... Ser.). 32p. (J). (gr. 1-4). 25.70 *(978-1-58415-804-2(2))* Mitchell Lane Pubs., Inc.

Starosta, Paul. Face-to-Face with the Hamster. 2004. (Illus.). 25p. (J). 9.95 *(978-1-57091-456-0(7))* Charlesbridge Publishing, Inc.

Stevens, Kathryn. Hamsters. 2015. (Pet Care Ser.). (ENG.). 24p. (J). (gr. -1-2). 25.64 *(978-1-63143-728-1(3)*, 208546) Child's World, Inc., The.

Stoltman, Joan. My First Hamster. 2017. (Let's Get a Pet! Ser.). 24p. (gr. 1-2). pap. 8.15 ***(978-1-4824-6457-3(8))*** Stevens, Gareth Publishing LLLP.

Sullivant, Holly. Hamsters. 2009. (Illus.). 112p. (J). 14.95 *(978-1-932904-38-3(7))* Eldorado Ink.

Sullivant, Holly J. Hamsters. 2008. (J). *(978-1-932904-30-7(1))* Eldorado Ink.

Thomas, Isabel. Hip Hamster Projects. 2015. (Pet Projects Ser.). (ENG., Illus.). 32p. (gr. 3-5). 27.99 *(978-1-4109-8067-0(7)*, Snap Bks.) Capstone Press of Coughlan Cos.

Wood, Selina. Hamster. 2008. (Owning a Pet Ser.). (Illus.). 32p. (J). (gr. 2-5). lib. bdg. 24.25 *(978-1-59771-054-1(7))* Sea-To-Sea Pubns.

World Book, Inc Staff, contrib. by. Hamsters & Other Pet Rodents. 2009. (J). *(978-0-7166-1370-1(0))* World Bk., Inc.

Zobel, Derek. Caring for Your Hamster. 2010. (Pet Care Library). (ENG., Illus.). 24p. (J). (gr. 2-5). lib. bdg. 25.95 *(978-1-60014-468-4(3)*, Blastoff! Readers) Bellwether Media.

HAMSTERS—FICTION

All Aboard! Softi's Adventures. 2003. (J). mass mkt. *(978-1-932233-36-0(9))* Aurora Libris Corp.

Anderson, Amanda. The Story of Larry the Hamster. 2008. 24p. pap. 24.95 *(978-1-60703-125-3(6))* America Star Bks.

Andrews, Julie & Hamilton, Emma Walton. The Very Fairy Princess: Teacher's Pet. Davenier, Christine, illus. 2013. (Passport to Reading Level 1 Ser.). (ENG.). 32p. (J). (gr. -1-3). 4.99 *(978-0-316-21959-4(2))* Little Brown & Co.

Barkley, Callie. Marion & the Secret Letter. 2017. (Critter Club Ser.: 16). lib. bdg. 16.00 ***(978-0-606-39739-1(6))*** Turtleback Bks.

Bee, William. Stanley the Farmer, 1 vol. Bee, William, illus. 2015. (Stanley Ser.). (ENG., Illus.). 32p. (J). (gr. 1-2). 14.95 *(978-1-56145-803-5(1))* Peachtree Pubs.

—Stanley the Mailman, 1 vol. Bee, William, illus. 2016. (Stanley Ser.). (ENG., Illus.). 32p. (J). (gr. -1-2). 14.95 *(978-1-56145-867-7(8))* Peachtree Pubs.

—Stanley's Colors, 1 vol. Bee, William, illus. 2016. (Stanley Ser.). (ENG., Illus.). 20p. (J). (gr. -1-k). bds. 6.95 *(978-1-56145-948-3(8)*, Freestone) Peachtree Pubs.

—Stanley's Diner, 1 vol. Bee, William, illus. 2015. (Stanley Ser.). (ENG., Illus.). 32p. (J). (gr. -1-2). 14.95 *(978-1-56145-802-8(3))* Peachtree Pubs.

—Stanley's Numbers, 1 vol. Bee, William, illus. 2017. (Stanley Ser.). (ENG., Illus.). 20p. (J). (gr. -1 — 1). bds. 6.95 ***(978-1-56145-976-6(3))*** Peachtree Pubs.

—Stanley's Opposites, 1 vol. Bee, William, illus. 2017. (Stanley Ser.). (ENG., Illus.). 20p. (J). (gr. -1 — 1). bds. 6.95 ***(978-1-56145-977-3(1))*** Peachtree Pubs.

Bee, William. Stanley's Shapes, 1 vol. Bee, William, illus. 2016. (Stanley Ser.). (ENG., Illus.). 20p. (J). (gr. -1-k). bds. 6.95 *(978-1-56145-949-0(6)*, Freestone) Peachtree Pubs.

Bee, William, illus. Stanley the Mailman. 2016. (J). pap. ***(978-1-56145-946-9(1)***, Peachtree Junior) Peachtree Pubs.

Birney, Betty G. Adventure According to Humphrey. 2009. (Humphrey Ser.: 5). (ENG.). 128p. (J). (gr. 3-7). 15.99 *(978-0-399-24731-6(9)*, G.P. Putnam's Sons Books for Young Readers) Penguin Young Readers Group.

—Friendship According to Humphrey. (Humphrey Ser.: 2). (ENG.). (J). (gr. 3-7). 2006. 176p. 5.99 *(978-0-14-240633-5(3)*, Puffin Books) 2005. 160p. 15.99 *(978-0-399-24264-9(3)*, G.P. Putnam's Sons Books for Young Readers) Penguin Young Readers Group.

—Friendship According to Humphrey. 2007. (Humphrey Ser.). 150p. (gr. 4-7). 16.00 *(978-0-7569-8277-5(4))* Perfection Learning Corp.

—Humphrey's Creepy-Crawly Camping Adventure. Burris, Priscilla, illus. 2015. (Humphrey's Tiny Tales Ser.: 3). (ENG.). 96p. (J). (gr. k-3). 4.99 *(978-0-14-751459-2(2)*, Puffin Books); 14.99 *(978-0-399-17227-4(0)*, G.P. Putnam's Sons Books for Young Readers) Penguin Young Readers Group.

—Humphrey's Mixed-Up Magic Trick. Burris, Priscilla, illus. 2016. (Humphrey's Tiny Tales Ser.: 5). (ENG.). 96p. (J). (gr. k-3). 4.99 *(978-0-14-751461-5(4)*, Puffin Books) Penguin Young Readers Group.

—Humphrey's Playful Puppy Problem. Burris, Priscilla, illus. 2014. (Humphrey's Tiny Tales Ser.: 2). (ENG.). 96p. (J). (gr. k-3). pap. 4.99 *(978-0-14-751484-4(3)*, Puffin Books) Penguin Young Readers Group.

—Humphrey's Really Wheely Racing Day. Burris, Priscilla, illus. 2014. (Humphrey's Tiny Tales Ser.: 1). (ENG.). 96p. (J). (gr. k-3). pap. 4.99 *(978-0-14-751485-1(1)*, Puffin Books) Penguin Young Readers Group.

—Humphrey's School Fair Surprise. Burris, Priscilla, illus. 2016. (Humphrey's Tiny Tales Ser.: 4). (ENG.). 112p. (J). (gr. k-3). 14.99 *(978-0-399-17229-8(7)*, G.P. Putnam's Sons Books for Young Readers) Penguin Young Readers Group.

—Humphrey's Treasure Hunt Trouble. Burris, Priscilla, illus. 2017. (Humphrey's Tiny Tales Ser.: 6). (ENG.). 96p. (J). (gr. k-3). 4.99 ***(978-0-14-751462-2(2)***, Puffin Books); 14.99 ***(978-0-399-17231-1(9)***, G.P. Putnam's Sons Books for Young Readers) Penguin Young Readers Group.

—Imagination According to Humphrey. 2015. (Humphrey Ser.: 11). (ENG.). 128p. (J). (gr. 2-4). 15.99 *(978-0-399-25797-1(7)*, G.P. Putnam's Sons Books for Young Readers) Penguin Young Readers Group.

—Mysteries According to Humphrey. 2013. (Humphrey Ser.: 8). (ENG.). 176p. (J). (gr. 3-7). pap. 5.99 *(978-0-14-242669-2(5)*, Puffin Books) Penguin Young Readers Group.

—Mysteries According to Humphrey. 2013. (According to Humphrey Ser.: 8). lib. bdg. 16.00 *(978-0-606-31699-6(X)*, Turtleback) Turtleback Bks.

—School Days According to Humphrey. (Humphrey Ser.: 7). (ENG.). (J). (gr. 3-7). 2012. 176p. pap. 5.99 *(978-0-14-242106-2(5)*, Puffin Books) 2011. 160p. 15.99 *(978-0-399-25413-0(7)*, G.P. Putnam's Sons Books for Young Readers) Penguin Young Readers Group.

—School Days According to Humphrey. 2012. (According to Humphrey Ser.: 7). lib. bdg. 16.00 *(978-0-606-26085-5(4)*, Turtleback) Turtleback Bks.

—Secrets According to Humphrey. 2015. (Humphrey Ser.: 10). (ENG.). 160p. (J). (gr. 3-7). 5.99 *(978-0-14-751431-8(2)*, Puffin Books) Penguin Young Readers Group.

—Summer According to Humphrey. (Humphrey Ser.: 6). (ENG.). (J). (gr. 3-7). 2011. 192p. 5.99 *(978-0-14-241818-5(8)*, Puffin Books) 2010. 176p. 14.99 *(978-0-399-24732-3(7)*, G.P. Putnam's Sons Books for Young Readers) Penguin Young Readers Group.

—Surprises According to Humphrey. (Humphrey Ser.: 4). (ENG.). (J). (gr. 3-7). 2009. 160p. 5.99 *(978-0-14-241296-1(1)*, Puffin Books) 2008. 144p. 15.99 *(978-0-399-24730-9(0)*, G.P. Putnam's Sons Books for Young Readers) Penguin Young Readers Group.

—Surprises According to Humphrey. 2009. (According to Humphrey Ser.: 4). lib. bdg. 16.00 *(978-0-606-00906-5(X)*, Turtleback) Turtleback Bks.

—Trouble According to Humphrey. (Humphrey Ser.: 3). (ENG.). (J). (gr. 3-7). 2008. 192p. 5.99 *(978-0-14-241089-9(6)*, Puffin Books) 2007. 176p. 15.99 *(978-0-399-24505-3(7)*, G.P. Putnam's Sons Books for Young Readers) Penguin Young Readers Group.

—Winter According to Humphrey. 2013. (Humphrey Ser.: 9). (ENG.). 176p. (J). (gr. 3-7). pap. 5.99 *(978-0-14-242759-0(4)*, Puffin Books) Penguin Young Readers Group.

—Winter According to Humphrey. 2013. (According to Humphrey Ser.: 9). lib. bdg. 16.00 *(978-0-606-32138-9(1)*, Turtleback) Turtleback Bks.

—The World According to Humphrey. (Humphrey Ser.: 1). (ENG.). (J). (gr. 3-7). 2005. 144p. pap. 5.99 *(978-0-14-240352-5(0)*, Puffin Books) 2004. 160p. 15.99 *(978-0-399-24198-7(1)*, G.P. Putnam's Sons Books for Young Readers) Penguin Young Readers Group.

—The World According to Humphrey. 2005. (According to Humphrey Ser.: 1). lib. bdg. 16.00 *(978-1-4176-7532-6(2)*, Turtleback) Turtleback Bks.

Blackford, Andy. George & the Dragonfly. Mason, Sue, illus. 2014. (ReadZone Picture Bks.). (ENG.). 32p. (J). (gr. k-3). pap. 8.99 *(978-1-78322-423-4(1))* ReadZone Bks. GBR. Dist: Independent Pubs. Group.

—George & the Dragonfly. Mason, Sue, illus. 2011. (ENG.). 32p. (J). (gr. -1-k). pap. *(978-1-84089-624-4(8))* Zero to Ten, Ltd.

The Busy Hamster. 2003. (J). per. *(978-1-57657-889-6(5))* Paradise Pr., Inc.

Calmenson, Stephanie. Oopsy, Teacher! Yoshikawa, Sachiko, illus. 2012. (Carolrhoda Picture Bks.). (ENG.). 32p. (J). (gr. -1-2). lib. bdg. 16.95 *(978-0-7613-5894-7(3))* Lerner Publishing Group.

Calvani, Mayra. Humberto, the Bookworm Hamster. Grady, Kit, illus. 2009. 20p. pap. 10.95 *(978-1-935137-92-4(1))* Guardian Angel Publishing, Inc.

Clarke, Jane. Pumpkin the Hamster. 2017. (Dr. KittyCat Ser.: 6). (ENG.). 96p. (J). (gr. 2-5). pap. 4.99

(978-0-545-94193-8(8), Scholastic Paperbacks) Scholastic, Inc.

Clymer, Susan. There's a Rabbit in My Backpack. 2007. 100p. pap. 8.50 (978-1-4303-2959-6(9)) Lulu Pr., Inc.

Coe, Victoria J. Fenway & Hattie. 2016. (Fenway & Hattie Ser.). (ENG.). 176p. (J). (gr. 3-7). 15.99 (978-0-399-17274-8(2), G.P. Putnam's Sons Books for Young Readers) Penguin Young Readers Group.

Davies, Katie. The Great Hamster Massacre. Shaw, Hannah, illus. 2011. (Great Critter Capers Ser.). (ENG.). 208p. (J). (gr. 3-7). 12.99 (978-1-4424-2062-5(6), Beach Lane Bks.) Beach Lane Bks.

Deacon, Alexis. A Place to Call Home. Schwarz, Viviane, illus. 2011. (ENG.). 40p. (J). (gr. -1-2). 16.99 (978-0-7636-5360-6(8)) Candlewick Pr.

Delittle, Cathy. Hamster Cheeks. Milicevic, Adam, illus. 2007. 32p. (J). 14.95 (978-1-892633-14-9(0)) Delittle Storyteller Co.

Desbordes, Astrid & Martin, Pauline. Daydreams of a Solitary Hamster. 2010. (ENG., Illus.). 56p. (J). (gr. 1-2). 17.95 (978-1-59270-093-6(4)) Enchanted Lion Bks., LLC.

Dick, Beth-Ann. Henry the Hart Room Hamster. 2011. 28p. pap. 15.99 (978-1-4568-6140-7(9)) Xlibris Corp.

Disney Book Group. World of Reading: Doc Mcstuffins Take Your Pet to the Vet: Level 1. Disney Storybook Art Team, illus. 2015. (World of Reading Ser.). (ENG.). 32p. (J). (gr. -1-k). pap. 3.99 (978-1-4847-1966-4(2)) Disney Pr.

Disney Book Group Staff & Miller, Sara. Doc Mcstuffins: Take Your Pet to the Vet. 2015. (World of Reading Ser.). (J). lib. bdg. 13.55 (978-0-606-37535-1(X)) Turtleback Bks.

Donald, Margaret. Tipsy: The Hurricane Hero. 2007. (ENG.). 26p. (J). (gr. k-2). (978-81-8386-050-5(8)) India Research Pr. IND. Dist: Independent Pubs. Group.

Duckers, John. The Amazing Adventures of the Silly Six. 2013. (Illus.). 188p. pap. (978-1-78148-626-9(3)) Grosvenor Hse. Publishing Ltd.

Frederick, Heather Vogel. For Your Paws Only. Comport, Sally Wern, illus. 2005. (Spy Mice Ser.). (ENG.). 272p. (J). (gr. 4-6). 9.95 (978-1-4169-0573-8(1)) Simon & Schuster Children's Publishing.

Freytag, Lorna. My Humongous Hamster Goes to School. Freytag, Lorna, illus. 2015. (My Humongous Hamster Ser.). (ENG., Illus.). 32p. (J). (gr. -1-3). 16.99 (978-1-62779-140-3(X), 9781627791403, Holt, Henry & Co. Bks. For Young Readers) Holt, Henry & Co.

Froeb, Lori C. I Am Nibbles, Level 2. Lyon, Tammie, illus. 2015. (Rescue Readers Ser.: 3). (ENG.). 32p. (J). (gr. 1-3). pap. 3.99 (978-0-7944-3455-7(X), Reader's Digest Children's Bks.) Studio Fun International.

Gallagher, Diana G. A No-Sneeze Pet, 1 vol. Juarez, Adriana & Puglisi, Adriana, illus. 2013. (Pet Friends Forever Ser.). (ENG.). 88p. (gr. 1-3). pap. 5.95 (978-1-4795-1862-3(X)); lib. bdg. 25.32 (978-1-4048-7499-2(2)) Picture Window Bks.

Gaston County Museum of Art & History, ed. The Secret Adventures of Hamster Sam: Attack of the Evil Boll Weevils! 2008. (Illus.). 32p. (J). 15.95 (978-0-9798445-0-8(9)) DM Creative.

Gent, Ron. A Tale of Two Hamsters. 2008. 52p. pap. 12.99 (978-1-4343-2319-4(6)) AuthorHouse.

Good, Jackie. Houdini the Hamster's Great Escape. 2012. 24p. 24.95 (978-1-4626-6269-2(2)) America Star Bks.

Gowar, Mick. Leo's New Pet. Morgan, Richard, illus. 2008. (Tadpoles Ser.). (ENG.). 24p. (J). (gr. -1-3). pap. (978-0-7787-3886-2(8)); lib. bdg. (978-0-7787-3855-8(8)) Crabtree Publishing Co.

Griffin, N. Smashie Mcperter & the Mystery of Room 11. Hindley, Kate, illus. 2015. (ENG.). 256p. (J). (gr. 2-5). 15.99 (978-0-7636-6145-8(7)) Candlewick Pr.

Guinea Pig, Pet Shop Private Eye, 3 vols., Set. 2010. (J). (gr. 2-5). lib. bdg. 55.86 (978-0-7613-4597-8(3), Graphic Universe™) Lerner Publishing Group.

Hannan, Peter. Petlandia. Hannan, Peter, illus. 2015. (ENG., Illus.). 144p. (J). (gr. 2-5). 8.99 (978-0-545-16211-1(4), Scholastic Pr.) Scholastic, Inc.

Hay, Sam. Return of the Hungry Hamster. Cooper, Simon, illus. 2014. (Undead Pets Ser.: 1). (ENG.). 112p. (J). (gr. 1-3). 5.99 (978-0-448-47795-4(5), Grosset & Dunlap) Penguin Young Readers Group.

Hiebert, Elfrieda H. & Juel, Connie. My Hamster, Van. (Little Book Practice Reader Ser.). (J). (978-0-8136-0790-0(6)) Modern Curriculum Pr.

Jane, Rebecca. Hamster Heroes to the Rescue: The Mystery of the Shadow in the Yard & Retirement. 2012. 84p. 19.95 (978-1-4626-6862-5(3)) America Star Bks.

Jensen, Joel, et al. Tiny Hamster Is a Giant Monster. 2015. (ENG., Illus.). 32p. (J). (gr. -1-3). 17.99 (978-1-4814-5110-9(3), Simon & Schuster Bks. For Young Readers) Simon & Schuster Bks. For Young Readers.

Johnson, Sandi. Harold the Hopping Hamster. Johnson, Britt, ed. Sturgeon, Bobbi, illus. l.t. ed. 2003. (ENG.). 34p. (J). (gr. k-5). pap. 12.99 (978-1-929063-91-8(1), 322) Moons & Stars Publishing For Children.

Jonell, Lynne. Hamster Magic. Dorman, Brandon, illus. 2012. (Magical Mix-Ups Ser.: 1). (ENG.). 112p. (J). (gr. 1-4). pap. 4.99 (978-0-375-86616-6(7), Random Hse. Bks. for Young Readers) Random Hse. Children's Bks.

Kawai, Ritsuko. Hamtaro. Kawai, Ritsuko, illus. 2003. (ENG., Illus.). 16p. (J). pap. 7.95 (978-1-56931-815-7(8)) Viz Media.

—Hamtaro Gets Lost & Other Stories. Kawai, Ritsuko, illus. 2003. (Adventures of Hamtaro Ser.: Vol. 2). (ENG., Illus.). 92p. (J). (gr. 1-3). 9.95 (978-1-56931-817-1(4)) Viz Media.

—Hamtaro, Vol. 3. Kawai, Ritsuko, illus. 2003. (ENG., Illus.). 16p. (J). pap. 7.95 (978-1-56931-816-4(6)) Viz Media.

—Let's Play! Vol. 4: A Playground for Ham-Ham. Kawai, Ritsuko, illus. 2003. (Hamtaro Ser.). (ENG., Illus.). 16p. (J). (gr. 1-3). pap. 7.95 (978-1-56931-821-8(2)) Viz Media.

Kelley, Marty. Sammy's Great Escape. Kelley, Marty, illus. 2017. (Molly Mac Ser.). (ENG., Illus.). 56p. (gr. k-2). lib. bdg. 22.65 (978-1-5158-0835-0(1)) Picture Window Bks.

Kenah, Katharine. The Best Seat in Second Grade. Carter, Abby, illus. 2006. (I Can Read Level 2 Ser.). (ENG.). 48p. (J). (gr. k-3). pap. 3.99 (978-0-06-000736-2(2)) HarperCollins Pubs.

—The Best Seat in Second Grade. Carter, Abby, illus. 2006. (I Can Read Bks.). 48p. (J). (gr. -1-3). 11.65 (978-0-7569-6979-0(4)) Perfection Learning Corp.

Kimmel, Eric A. & Korelitz, Jean Hanff. The Great Texas Hamster Drive, 0 vols. Whatley, Bruce, illus. 2007. (ENG.). 40p. (J). (gr. k-3). 16.99 (978-0-7614-5357-4(1), 9780761453574, Amazon Children's Publishing) Amazon Publishing.

Kirby, Stan. Captain Awesome to the Rescue! O'Connor, George, illus. 2012. (Captain Awesome Ser.: 1). (ENG.). 128p. (J). (gr. k-2). 16.99 (978-1-4424-4090-6(2)); pap. 5.99 (978-1-4424-3561-2(5)) Little Simon. (Little Simon).

—Captain Awesome to the Rescue! 2012. (Captain Awesome Ser.: 1). lib. bdg. 16.00 (978-0-606-26322-1(5), Turtleback) Turtleback Bks.

Klein, Abby. Stop That Hamster! McKinley, John, illus. 2008. (Ready, Freddy! Ser.: Bk. 12). 95p. (gr. -1-3). 16.00 (978-0-7569-8300-0(2)) Perfection Learning Corp.

Lakin, Patricia. Max & Mo Go Apple Picking. Floca, Brian, illus. 2007. (Max & Mo Ser.). (ENG.). 32p. (J). (gr. -1-1). pap. 3.99 (978-1-4169-2535-4(X), Simon Spotlight) Simon Spotlight.

—Max & Mo Make a Snowman. Floca, Brian, illus. 2007. (Max & Mo Ser.). (ENG.). 32p. (J). (gr. -1-1). pap. 3.99 (978-1-4169-2537-8(6), Simon Spotlight) Simon Spotlight.

—Max & Mo's First Day at School. Floca, Brian, illus. 2007. (Max & Mo Ser.). (ENG.). 32p. (J). (gr. -1-1). pap. 3.99 (978-1-4169-2533-0(3), Simon Spotlight) Simon Spotlight.

Löhlein, Susanne. Hamster Monster. Löhlein, Henning, illus. 2014. (ENG.). 32p. (J). 17.95 (978-0-7358-4178-9(0)) North-South Bks., Inc.

Lord, Cynthia. Happy Birthday Hamster. Anderson, Derek, illus. 2011. (ENG.). 40p. (J). (gr. -1-k). 18.99 (978-0-545-25522-6(8), Scholastic Pr.) Scholastic, Inc.

—Hot Rod Hamster. Anderson, Derek, illus. 2010. (ENG.). 40p. (J). (gr. -1-k). 18.99 (978-0-545-03530-9(9), Scholastic Pr.) Scholastic, Inc.

—Hot Rod Hamster & the Awesome ATV Adventure! Anderson, Derek, illus. 2015. (ENG.). 32p. (J). 16.99 (978-0-545-76734-7(2)); pap. 3.99 (978-0-545-62680-4(3)) Scholastic, Inc. (Scholastic Pr.).

—Hot Rod Hamster & the Haunted Halloween Party. Anderson, Derek & Paprocki, Greg, illus. 2015. (Scholastic Reader, Level 2 Ser.). (ENG.). 32p. (J). (gr. k-2). pap. 3.99 (978-0-545-81528-4(2), Scholastic Pr.) Scholastic, Inc.

—Hot Rod Hamster & the Haunted Halloween Party! Anderson, Derek, illus. 2015. (ENG.). 32p. (J). (gr. -1-3). 16.99 (978-0-545-81529-1(0), Scholastic Pr.) Scholastic, Inc.

—Hot Rod Hamster & the Wacky Whatever Race! Anderson, Derek, illus. 2014. (ENG.). 32p. (J). (gr. -1-3). pap. 3.99 (978-0-545-62678-1(1), Scholastic Pr.) Scholastic, Inc.

—Hot Rod Hamster Meets His Match! Anderson, Derek, illus. 2016. (Scholastic Reader, Level 2 Ser.). (ENG.). 32p. (J). (gr. -1-2). pap. 3.99 (978-0-545-82591-7(1), Scholastic Pr.) Scholastic, Inc.

—Monster Truck Mania! Anderson, Derek, illus. 2014. (ENG.). 40p. (J). (gr. -1-k). 16.99 (978-0-545-46261-7(4), Scholastic Pr.) Scholastic, Inc.

Mango's Quest: The story of a home lost & Found. 2008. 4.95 (978-0-9724425-8-9(8), White Tiger Pr.) Homes for the Homeless Institute, Inc.

Masterson, Josephine. Henry's Hamster Goes to School. 2015. (Rosen REAL Readers: STEM & STEAM Collection). (ENG.). 8p. pap. 5.46 (978-1-4994-9595-9(1), Rosen Classroom) Rosen Publishing Group, Inc., The.

McCreely, Havelock. My Zombie Hamster. 2014. (ENG.). 200p. (J). (gr. 3-7). 15.99 (978-1-60684-491-5(1), Carolrhoda Bks.) Lerner Publishing Group.

McMahon, P. J. Case of the Psychic Hamster. Manders, John, illus. 2005. 153p. (J). lib. bdg. 15.38 (978-1-4242-0404-5(6)) Fitzgerald Bks.

McNamara, Margaret. Groundhog Day. Gordon, Mike, illus. 2005. (Robin Hill School Ser.). 32p. (J). (gr. -1-3). 11.65 (978-0-7569-7146-5(2)) Perfection Learning Corp.

—Groundhog Day. Gordon, Mike, illus. 2006. (Robin Hill School Ser.). (ENG.). 32p. (J). (gr. -1-1). pap. 3.99 (978-1-4169-0507-3(3), Simon Spotlight) Simon Spotlight.

McNeely Schultz, Geri. Kristie's Excellent Adventures: A Visit to the Fridge. Bertolami, Vince, illus. 2013. (ENG.). 40p. (J). pap. 9.99 (978-1-935766-88-9(0)) Windy City Pubs.

Miller, Michael John. Harry Hamster Adventures. 2012. 24p. pap. 15.99 (978-1-4691-6861-6(8)) Xlibris Corp.

Milway, Alex. Pigsticks & Harold & the Incredible Journey. Milway, Alex, illus. 2014. (ENG., Illus.). 84p. (J). (gr. k-4). 12.99 (978-0-7636-6615-6(7)) Candlewick Pr.

—Pigsticks & Harold & the Tuptown Thief. Milway, Alex, illus. 2015. (ENG., Illus.). 80p. (J). (gr. k-4). 12.99 (978-0-7636-7809-8(0)) Candlewick Pr.

Norac, Carl. La Isla de los Mimos. 2003.Tr. of I Love to Cuddle. (SPA., Illus.). 32p. (J). (978-84-95150-66-0(2), COR3070) Corimbo, Editorial S.L.

O'Donnell, Tom. Hamstersaurus Rex. Miller, Tim, illus. 2016. (Hamstersaurus Rex Ser.: 1). 272p. (J). (gr. 3-7). 12.99 (978-0-06-237754-8(X)) HarperCollins Pubs.

Perl, Erica S. Ferocious Fluffity: A Mighty Bite-Y Class Pet. Cole, Henry, illus. 2016. (ENG.). 32p. (J). (gr. k-2). 16.95 (978-1-4197-2182-3(8), Abrams Bks. for Young Readers) Abrams, Inc.

Pressberg, Dava. Harold the Hamster. 2017. (Pet Tales! Ser.). 24p. (J). (gr. 4-6). 23.60 **(978-1-5081-5734-2(0)**, PowerKids Pr.) Rosen Publishing Group, Inc., The.

Reich, Kass. Hooray for Hamsters! A Two-Book Set, 2 vols. 2015. (ENG.). 48p. (J). (gr. -1-k). bds. 15.95 (978-1-4598-1100-3(3)) Orca Bk. Pubs. USA.

Reiche, Dietlof & Brownjohn, John. Freddy in Peril: Book Two in the Golden Hamster Saga. Cepeda, Joe, illus. 2004. 202p. (J). pap. (978-0-439-64984-1(6)) Scholastic, Inc.

Richter, Debra A. Hamster on the Run. LiveLearn, Robert, illus. 2011. 24p. pap. 24.95 (978-1-4626-3897-0(X)) America Star Bks.

—Hamster on the Run, Let's Play in the Snow. LiveLearn, Robert, illus. 2012. 28p. pap. 24.95 (978-1-4626-5064-4(3)) America Star Bks.

Riley, Ford & Nee, Chris. Take Your Pet to the Vet. 2015. (Illus.). 32p. (J). (978-1-4844-6746-6(9)) Disney Publishing Worldwide.

Rone, Trenton. Once upon a Hamster 2003. (YA). spiral bd. 14.95 (978-0-9744437-3-7(5)) Imagination Workshop, The.

Root, Andrew. Hamsters Don't Fight Fires! Olien, Jessica, illus. 2017. 40p. (J). (gr. -1-3). 17.99 **(978-0-06-245294-8(0))** HarperCollins Pubs.

Rovetch, L. Bob. Hot Dog & Bob: And the Dangerously Dizzy Attack of the Hypno Hamsters. Whamond, Dave, illus. 2007. (Hot Dog & Bob Ser.: HOTD). (ENG.). 96p. (J). (gr. 1-5). per. 4.95 (978-0-8118-5602-7(X)) Chronicle Bks. LLC.

Sadar, Albin. Hamster Holmes: A Mystery Comes Knocking. Fabbretti, Valerio, illus. 2015. (Hamster Holmes Ser.: 1). (ENG.). 32p. (J). (gr. k-2). 16.99 (978-1-4814-2037-2(2), Simon Spotlight) Simon Spotlight.

—Hamster Holmes, Combing for Clues. Fabbretti, Valerio, illus. 2015. (Hamster Holmes Ser.: 2). (ENG.). 32p. (J). (gr. k-2). pap. 3.99 (978-1-4814-2039-6(9), Simon Spotlight) Simon Spotlight.

—Hamster Holmes, on the Right Track. Fabbretti, Valerio, illus. 2016. (Hamster Holmes Ser.). (ENG.). 32p. (J). (gr. k-2). pap. 3.99 (978-1-4814-2042-6(9), Simon Spotlight) Simon Spotlight.

—Hamster Holmes, on the Right Track. 2016. (Simon & Schuster Ready-To-Read Level 2 Ser.). lib. bdg. 13.55 (978-0-606-38245-8(3)) Turtleback Bks.

—A Mystery Comes Knocking. Fabbretti, Valerio, illus. 2015. (Hamster Holmes Ser.: 1). (ENG.). 32p. (J). (gr. k-2). pap. 3.99 (978-1-4814-2036-5(4), Simon Spotlight) Simon Spotlight.

Scillian, Devin. Memoirs of a Hamster. Bowers, Tim, illus. 2013. (ENG.). 32p. (J). (gr. -1-2). 15.99 (978-1-58536-831-0(8), 202365) Sleeping Bear Pr.

Stanek, Gerald. Sarah 'n' Dippity. Stanek, Joyce Huntington, illus. 2004. (ENG.). 28p. (J). 14.95 (978-0-9747417-0-3(1)) Shiver Hill Bks.

Stanley the Builder, 1 vol. 2014. (Stanley Ser.). (ENG., Illus.). 32p. (J). (gr. -1-2). 14.95 (978-1-56145-801-1(5)) Peachtree Pubs.

Stanley's Garage, 1 vol. 2014. (Stanley Ser.). (ENG., Illus.). 32p. (J). (gr. -1-2). 14.95 (978-1-56145-804-2(X)) Peachtree Pubs.

Stine, R. L. Little Shop of Hamsters. 2010. 160p. (J). (Goosebumps Horrorland Ser.: 14). (ENG.). (gr. 3-7). 6.99 (978-0-545-16195-4(9), Scholastic Paperbacks); pap. 2.99 (978-1-4071-1635-8(5)) Scholastic, Inc.

—Little Shop of Hamsters. 2010. (Goosebumps HorrorLand Ser.: 14). lib. bdg. 17.20 (978-0-606-10559-0(X), Turtleback) Turtleback Bks.

Tashjian, Janet. Einstein the Class Hamster. Tashjian, Jake, illus. 2013. (Einstein the Class Hamster Ser.: 1). (ENG.). 160p. (J). (gr. 2-5). 12.99 (978-0-8050-9610-1(8), 9780805096101, Holt, Henry & Co. Bks. For Young Readers) Holt, Henry & Co.

—Einstein the Class Hamster & the Very Real Game Show. Tashjian, Jake, illus. 2014. (Einstein the Class Hamster Ser.: 2). (ENG.). 176p. (J). (gr. 2-5). 12.99 (978-1-62779-026-0(8), 9781627790260, Holt, Henry & Co. Bks. For Young Readers) Holt, Henry & Co.

—Einstein the Class Hamster Saves the Library. Tashjian, Jake, illus. 2015. (Einstein the Class Hamster Ser.: 3). (ENG.). 192p. (J). (gr. 2-5). 13.99 (978-1-62779-061-1(6), 9781627790611, Holt, Henry & Co. Bks. For Young Readers) Holt, Henry & Co.

Thomas Nelson. Playdate Pals Hamster Learns to Help. 2016. (ENG.). 24p. (J). (gr. -1-7). pap. (978-1-78598-478-5(0)) Make Believe Ideas.

Tracy, Kathleen. The Hamster in Our Class. 2011. (Randy's Corner Ser.). (Illus.). 32p. (J). (gr. -1-2). lib. bdg. 25.70 (978-1-58415-980-3(4)) Mitchell Lane Pubs., Inc.

Van Allsburg, Chris. The Misadventures of Sweetie Pie. 2014. (ENG., Illus.). 32p. (J). (gr. -1-3). 18.99 (978-0-547-31582-9(1), HMH Books For Young Readers) Houghton Mifflin Harcourt Publishing Co.

Venable, Colleen A. F. And Then There Were Gnomes. Yue, Stephanie, illus. 2010. (Guinea Pig, Pet Shop Private Eye Ser.: 2). (ENG.). 48p. (J). (gr. 2-5). pap. 6.95 (978-0-7613-5480-2(8)); lib. bdg. 27.93 (978-0-7613-4599-2(X)) Lerner Publishing Group.

—The Ferret's a Foot, 3 vols. Yue, Stephanie, illus. 2011. (Guinea Pig, Pet Shop Private Eye Ser.: 3). (ENG.). 48p. (J). (gr. 2-5). 27.93 (978-0-7613-5223-5(6)); pap. 6.95 (978-0-7613-5629-5(0)) Lerner Publishing Group.

—Fish You Were Here, No. 4. Yue, Stephanie, illus. 2011. (Guinea Pig, Pet Shop Private Eye Ser.: 4). (ENG.). 48p. (J). (gr. 2-5). pap. 6.95 (978-0-7613-5630-1(4)); lib. bdg. 27.93 (978-0-7613-5224-2(4)) Lerner Publishing Group.

—Going, Going, Dragon! 2013. 48p. pap. 14.95 (978-1-4677-0973-6(5)) Lerner Publishing Group.

—Going, Going, Dragon! Yue, Stephanie, illus. 2013. (Guinea Pig, Pet Shop Private Eye Ser.: 6). (ENG.). 48p. (J). (gr. 2-5). pap. 6.95 (978-1-4677-0726-8(0)); lib. bdg. 27.93 (978-0-7613-6009-4(3)) Lerner Publishing Group.

—Going, Going, Dragon! Yue, Stephanie, illus. 2013. (Guinea Pig, Pet Shop Private Eye Ser.: 6). (ENG.). 46p. lib. bdg. 17.15 (978-0-606-33994-0(9), Turtleback) Turtleback Bks.

—Hamster & Cheese. Yue, Stephanie, illus. 2010. (Guinea Pig, Pet Shop Private Eye Ser.: 1). (ENG.). 48p. (J). (gr. 2-5). pap. 6.95 (978-0-7613-5479-6(4)); lib. bdg. 27.93 (978-0-7613-4598-5(1)) Lerner Publishing Group.

—Raining Cats & Detectives. Yue, Stephanie, illus. 2012. (Guinea Pig, Pet Shop Private Eye Ser.: 5). (ENG.). 48p. (J). (gr. 2-5). lib. bdg. 27.93 (978-0-7613-6008-7(5)) Lerner Publishing Group.

Vernon, Ursula. Harriet the Invincible. 2015. (Hamster Princess Ser.: 1). (ENG., Illus.). 208p. (J). (gr. 3-7). 12.99 (978-0-8037-3983-3(4), Dial Bks) Penguin Young Readers Group.

—Of Mice & Magic. 2016. (Hamster Princess Ser.: 2). (ENG., Illus.). 240p. (J). (gr. 3-7). 12.99 (978-0-8037-3984-0(2), Dial Bks) Penguin Young Readers Group.

—Ratpunzel. 2016. (Hamster Princess Ser.: 3). (ENG., Illus.). 240p. (J). (gr. 3-7). 12.99 (978-0-8037-3985-7(0), Dial Bks) Penguin Young Readers Group.

Wallace, Carol. One Nosy Pup. Björkman, Steve, illus. 2004. (ENG.). 40p. (J). 15.95 (978-0-8234-1917-3(7)) Holiday Hse., Inc.

Watt, Fiona. That's Not My Hamster. 2012. (Touchy-Feely Board Bks). 10p. (J). bds. 8.99 (978-0-7945-3277-2(2), Usborne) EDC Publishing.

Weiss, Ellen. I Don't Want to Go to School! A Fold-Out Surprise Book. Bennett, Andy, illus. 2006. (PBS Kids Ser.). 12p. (J). 6.95 (978-1-57791-313-9(2)) Brighter Minds Children's Publishing.

Welford, Ross. Time Traveling with a Hamster. 2016. (ENG.). 432p. (J). (gr. 3-7). 16.99 (978-0-399-55149-9(2), Schwartz & Wade Bks.) Random Hse. Children's Bks.

HANCOCK, JOHN, 1737-1793

Fritz, Jean. Will You Sign Here, John Hancock? Hyman, Trina Schart, illus. 2005. (J). (gr. 2-7). 29.95 (978-0-439-76750-7(4), WHCD480) Weston Woods Studios, Inc.

Kjelle, Marylou Morano. John Hancock. 2006. (Profiles in American History Ser.). (Illus.). 48p. (J). (gr. 3-7). lib. bdg. 29.95 (978-1-58415-443-3(8)) Mitchell Lane Pubs., Inc.

Ransom, Candice. John Hancock. 2005. (History Maker Bios Ser.). (Illus.). 48p. (J). (gr. 3-4). 26.60 (978-0-8225-1547-0(4), Lerner Pubns.) Lerner Publishing Group.

Sisson, Kathryn Cleven. John Hancock: Independent Boy. Underdown, Harold D., ed. Morrison, Cathy, illus. 2005. (Young Patriots Ser.: 9). (ENG.). 120p. (J). (gr. 4-7). 15.95 (978-1-882859-45-0(6)); pap. 9.95 (978-1-882859-46-7(4)) Patria Pr., Inc.

HAND

Agassi, Martine. Hands Are Not for Hitting. Heinlen, Marieka, illus. rev. ed. 2009. (Best Behavior Ser.). (ENG.). 40p. (J). (gr. -1-2). pap. 11.95 (978-1-57542-308-1(1)) Free Spirit Publishing, Inc.

Agassi, Martine & Verdick, Elizabeth. Las Manos No Son para Pegar. Heinlen, Marieka, illus. 2009. (Best Behavior Ser.).Tr. of Hands Are Not for Hitting. (SPA & ENG.). 40p. (J). (gr. -1-2). pap. 11.95 (978-1-57542-310-4(3)) Free Spirit Publishing, Inc.

Agassi, Martine, et al. Las Manos No Son para Pegar. Heinlen, Marieka, illus. 2009. (Best Behavior Ser.).Tr. of Hands Are Not for Hitting. (SPA, ENG & MUL.). 24p. (J). (gr. -1 — 1). bds. 7.95 (978-1-57542-309-8(X)) Free Spirit Publishing, Inc.

Andrus, Aubre. Lotions, Potions, & Polish: DIY Crafts & Recipes for Hands, Nails, & Feet. 2017. (DIY Day Spa Ser.). (ENG., Illus.). 48p. (gr. 4-5). lib. bdg. 31.32 (978-1-5157-3445-1(5)) Capstone Press of Coughlan Cos.

Bokhari, Raana. Allah Gave Me Two Hands & Feet. Clarke, Asiya, illus. 2015. (ENG.). 32p. (J). 8.95 (978-0-86037-348-3(7)) Kube Publishing Ltd. GBR. Dist: Consortium Bk. Sales & Distribution.

Brown, Janet Allison. Left Hand, Right Hand: A Hands-on Book about Left & Right. Endersby, Frank, illus. 2006. (ENG.). 16p. (J). (gr. -1-1). bds. 5.99 (978-0-7641-5924-4(0)) Barron's Educational Series, Inc.

Enslow, Brian. My Hands & Feet. 2010. (All about My Body Ser.). (Illus.). 24p. (J). 22.60 (978-0-7660-3816-5(5)); pap. 7.95 (978-1-59845-173-3(1)) Enslow Pubs., Inc. (Enslow Elementary).

Fernandez, A. & Fernandez, Q. Hooray for My Hands. (Hooray for My Senses Ser.). (Illus.). (J). 19.27 (978-1-58952-377-7(6)) Rourke Educational Media.

Hands: Big Book: Level B. 8p. 20.95 (978-0-322-00360-6(1)) Wright Group/McGraw-Hill.

Hengel, Katherine. Hands Are for Holding: The Sense of Touch, 1 vol. 2012. (All about Your Senses Ser.). (ENG.). 24p. (J). (gr. k-3). lib. bdg. 24.21 (978-1-61783-198-0(0), SandCastle) ABDO Publishing Co.

Holden, Pam. My Hands, 6 pack. Hawley, Kelvin, illus. 2009. (Red Rocket Readers Ser.). (ENG.). 16p. (gr. -1-1). pap. (978-1-877363-25-2(1), Red Rocket Readers) Flying Start Bks.

Hunt, Connie. Hooray for Hands! Melmon, Deborah, illus. 2008. (J). (978-1-58728-700-8(5), Two-Can Publishing) T&N Children's Publishing.

Klingel, Cynthia & Noyed, Robert B. Hands. 2010. (Let's Read about Our Bodies Ser.). (Illus.). 24p. (gr. k-3). pap. 8.15 (978-1-4339-3366-0(7)); (J). lib. bdg. 22.00 (978-1-4339-3365-3(9)) Stevens, Gareth Publishing LLLP.

—Hands / Las Manos. 2010. (Let's Read about Our Bodies / Hablemos del cuerpo humano Ser.). (SPA., Illus.). 24p. (gr. k-3). pap. 8.15 (978-1-4339-3742-2(5)) Stevens, Gareth Publishing LLLP.

—Hands/Las Manos. 2010. (Let's Read about Our Bodies / Hablemos del cuerpo humano Ser.). (SPA., Illus.). 24p. (J). (gr. k-3). lib. bdg. 22.00 (978-1-4339-3741-5(7)) Stevens, Gareth Publishing LLLP.

Minden, Cecilia. Time to Wash Up. 2010. (21st Century Basic Skills Library: Keep It Clean Ser.). (ENG.). 24p. (gr. k-3). lib. bdg. 22.79 (978-1-60279-855-7(9), 200576) Cherry Lake Publishing.

Prasadam, Smriti & Mitchell, Melanie. Peepo Paw Printes. 2008. (ENG., Illus.). 14p. (J). bds. 13.95 (978-0-7475-9535-9(6)) Bloomsbury Publishing Plc GBR. Dist: Independent Pubs. Group.

Rice, Dona. Marvelous Me: My Hands. 2015. (TIME for KIDS(r) Nonfiction Readers Ser.). (ENG., Illus.). 12p. (gr. k-k). 4.99 (978-1-4938-2148-8(2)) Teacher Created Materials, Inc.

—Soy Maravilloso. 2016. (Nonfiction Readers Ser.). (SPA.). 12p. (J). (gr. k-k). pap. 4.99 (978-1-4938-3029-9(5)) Teacher Created Materials, Inc.

Rounce, Rebekah Barlow. Happy Hands. 2009. 24p. pap. 15.99 (978-1-4415-1922-1(X)) Xlibris Corp.

Stewart, Melissa. Give Me a Hand: The Secrets of Hands, Feet, Arms, & Legs. Hamlin, Janet, illus. 2010. (Gross & Goofy Body 2 Ser.). 48p. (gr. 3). lib. bdg. 29.93 (978-0-7614-4158-8(1)) Marshall Cavendish Corp.

Tekiela, Stan. Paws & Claws, 1 vol. 2013. (Adventure Boardbook Ser.). (ENG.). 22p. (J). (gr. -1-k). bds. 6.95 (978-1-59193-425-7(7)) Adventure Pubns.

HANDBALL

Ventura, Marne. The Perfect Pair! Purses, Handbags, & Wallets for All Occasions. 2016. (Accessorize Yourself! Ser.). (ENG., Illus.). 48p. (gr. 4-5). lib. bdg. 34.65 (978-1-4914-8230-8(3)) Capstone Press of Coughlan Cos.

HANDEL, GEORGE FRIDERIC, 1685-1759

Anderson, M. T. Handel, Who Knew What He Liked. Hawkes, Kevin, illus. 2013. (Candlewick Biographies Ser.). (ENG.). 48p. (J). (gr. 3-7). 14.99 (978-0-7636-6599-9(1)); pap. 4.99 (978-0-7636-6600-2(9)) Candlewick Pr.

Getzinger, Donna & Felsenfeld, Daniel. George Frideric Handel & Music for Voices. 2004. (Classical Composers Ser.). (Illus.). 144p. (YA). (gr. 6-12). lib. bdg. 26.95 (978-1-931798-23-5(0)) Reynolds, Morgan Inc.

Lee, Lavina. Handel's World. 2009. (Music Throughout History Ser.). 64p. (gr. 5-6). 58.50 (978-1-61514-684-0(9), Rosen Reference) Rosen Publishing Group, Inc., The.

Wheeler, Opal. Handel: at the Court of Kings. Greenwalt, Mary, illus. 2006. 166p. per. 13.95 (978-1-933573-03-8(1), 4481) Zeezok Publishing, LLC.

HANDICAPPED

see People with Disabilities

HANDICRAFT

see also Basket Making; Beadwork; Bookbinding; Decoration and Ornament; Design, Decorative; Enamel and Enameling; Glass Painting and Staining; Hobbies; Jewelry; Leatherwork; Metal-Work; Modeling; Needlework; Puppet Making; Stencil Work; Weaving

ABDO Publishing Company Staff. Cool Fiber Art. 2014. (Cool Fiber Art Ser.: 6). (ENG.). 32p. (gr. 8-12). lib. bdg. 171.00 (978-1-62403-305-6(9), Checkerboard Library) ABDO Publishing Co.

—Super Simple Nature Crafts. 2014. (Super Simple Nature Crafts Ser.: 6). (ENG.). 32p. (gr. k-4). lib. bdg. 162.42 (978-1-62403-077-2(7), Super SandCastle) ABDO Publishing Co.

ABDO Publishing Company Staff, ed. Cool Stuff, 1 vol. 2012. (Cool Stuff Ser.: 6). (ENG., Illus.). 32p. 171.00 (978-1-61714-979-5(9), Checkerboard Library) ABDO Publishing Co.

Abell, Tracy. Build a Compost Tumbler. Stewart, Roger, illus. 2016. (Earth-Friendly Projects Ser.). (ENG.). 24p. (J). (gr. 2-5). 28.50 (978-1-5038-0785-3(1), 210621) Child's World, Inc., The.

AG Publishers Editors. Sparkle Card Kit: Everything You Need to Create More than 20 Glittery Greetings! 2003. (American Girl Library). (Illus.). 64p. (J). 19.95 (978-1-58485-707-5(2)) American Girl Publishing, Inc.

American Girl Editors. Scrapbook Studio: Everything You Need to Make a Fresh & Funky Scrapbook — In a Flash! 2008. (American Girl Library). (Illus.). 32p. (gr. 3-7). spiral bd. 17.95 (978-1-58485-731-0(5), American Girl) American Girl Publishing, Inc.

Anderson, Maxine. Amazing Leonardo Da Vinci Inventions: You Can Build Yourself. 2006. (Build It Yourself Ser.). (ENG., Illus.). 128p. (J). (gr. 3-7). pap. 15.95 (978-0-9749344-2-6(9)) Northern Trails Pr.

—Great Civil War Projects: You Can Build Yourself. 2nd ed. 2012. (Build It Yourself Ser.). (ENG.). 128p. (J). (gr. 3-7). 21.95 (978-1-936749-46-1(7)); pap. 15.95 (978-1-936749-45-4(9)) Open City Bks.

—Proyectos Impresionantes de la Guerra Civil: Que Puedes Construir Tú Mismo. 2012. (Construyelo Tu Mismo Ser.). (SPA & ENG.). 128p. (J). (gr. 3-7). pap. 15.95 (978-1-936749-47-8(5)) Open City Bks.

Andrews-Goebel, Nancy. La Vasija Que Juan Fabrico. Cortes, Eunice, tr. Diaz, David, illus. 2004. (SPA.). (J). 16.95 (978-1-58430-229-2(1)) Lee & Low Bks., Inc.

Andrus, Aubre. Bathe, Buff, & Beautify: DIY Crafts & Recipes for Natural Body Care. 2017. (DIY Day Spa Ser.). (ENG.). 48p. (gr. 4-5). lib. bdg. 31.32 (978-1-5157-3446-8(3)) Capstone Press of Coughlan Cos.

—Botanical Beauty: 80 Essential Recipes for Natural Spa Products. 2017. (ENG., Illus.). 160p. (gr. 9-12). pap. 14.95 (978-1-63079-075-2(3)) Switch Pr.

—Gloss, Floss, & Wash: DIY Crafts & Recipes for a Fresh Face & Teeth. 2017. (DIY Day Spa Ser.). (ENG., Illus.). 48p. (gr. 4-5). lib. bdg. 31.32 (978-1-5157-3447-5(1)) Capstone Press of Coughlan Cos.

—Lotions, Potions, & Polish: DIY Crafts & Recipes for Hands, Nails, & Feet. 2017. (DIY Day Spa Ser.). (ENG., Illus.). 48p. (gr. 4-5). lib. bdg. 31.32 (978-1-5157-3445-1(5)) Capstone Press of Coughlan Cos.

—Spray, Smooth, & Shampoo: DIY Crafts & Recipes for Healthy Hair. 2017. (DIY Day Spa Ser.). (ENG., Illus.). 48p. (gr. 4-5). lib. bdg. 31.32 (978-1-5157-3444-4(7)) Capstone Press of Coughlan Cos.

Anholt, Laurence. Anholt's Artists Activity Book. 2012. (ENG.). 48p. (J). (gr. -1-3). pap. 11.99 (978-1-4380-0114-2(2)) Barron's Educational Series, Inc.

Anness Publishing Staff, et al. The Great Big Book of Things to Make & Do: Cooking, Painting, Crafts, Science, Gardening, Magic, Music & Having a Party - Simple & Fun Step-by-Step Projects for Young Children. 2013. (ENG., Illus.). 256p. (J). (gr. -1-12). pap. 18.99 (978-1-84038-552-6(9), Hermes House) Anness Publishing GBR. Dist: National Bk. Network.

Apache Helicopter. 2004. (Press-Out & Build Ser.). (Illus.). 24p. (J). per. (978-1-84229-723-0(6)) Top That! Publishing PLC.

Arts & Crafts. Date not set. (Get Crafty Ser.). (Illus.). 48p. (J). pap. 4.98 (978-0-7525-8408-9(1)) Parragon, Inc.

Ashman, Iain. Wizard's Castle. 2004. (Cut-Out Models Ser.). (Illus.). 32p. (J). (gr. 4-18). pap. 9.95 (978-0-7945-0016-0(1), Usborne) EDC Publishing.

Atlantic, Leonard. We Do Crafts! 2017. (Ways to Play Ser.). 24p. (J). (gr. k-k). pap. 8.15 **(978-1-4824-6341-5(5))** Stevens, Gareth Publishing LLLP.

Austin, John. Labcraft Wizards: Magical Projects & Experiments. 2016. (ENG., Illus.). 256p. (J). (gr. 4). pap. 16.99 (978-1-61373-621-0(5)) Chicago Review Pr., Inc.

Barbara, Diane & Donnier, Christine. Mom & Me: A Special Book for You & Your Mom to Fill in Together & Share with Each Other. 2004. (ENG., Illus.). 48p. (J). (gr. -1-3). 16.95 (978-0-8109-4820-4(6)) Abrams, Inc.

Baxter, Nicola & Birkinshaw, Marie. A Treasury for Little Ones: Hours of Fun for Babies & Toddlers - Stories & Rhymes, Puzzles to Solve, & Things to Make & Do. Endersby, Frank, illus. 2014. (ENG.). 80p. (J). (gr. -1-6). 14.99 (978-1-86147-368-4(0), Armadillo) Anness Publishing GBR. Dist: National Bk. Network.

Beak, Nick Huckleberry. How to Bend Balloons. 2013. (ENG., Illus.). 64p. (J). (gr. 3-7). 9.99 (978-1-84322-864-6(5), Armadillo) Anness Publishing GBR. Dist: National Bk. Network.

Beard, Daniel. The American Boy's Handy Book: Turn-of-the-Century Classic of Crafts & Activities. unabr. ed. 2003. (Dover Children's Activity Bks.). (ENG., Illus.). 464p. (J). pap. 12.95 (978-0-486-43138-3(X)) Dover Pubns., Inc.

Beard, Lina & Beard, Adelia B. The American Girl's Handy Book: Turn-of-the-Century Classic of Crafts & Activities. 2008. (Dover Children's Activity Bks.). (ENG., Illus.). 496p. (J). (gr. 6-8). pap. 12.99 (978-0-486-46772-6(4)) Dover Pubns., Inc.

Beaton, Clare. Make Your Own Noah's Ark. Beaton, Clare, illus. 2007. (Illus.). (J). (gr. k-3). 9.95 (978-0-8198-4862-8(X)) Pauline Bks. & Media.

—My Book of Things to Make & Do. 2007. (ENG., Illus.). 96p. (J). (gr. 1-4). pap. 15.99 (978-1-902915-95-1(X)) B Small Publishing GBR. Dist: Independent Pubs. Group.

Beaty, Andrea. Rosie Revere's Big Project Book for Bold Engineers. Roberts, David, illus. 2017. (ENG.). 96p. (J). (gr. k-2). pap. 14.95 (978-1-4197-1910-3(6), Abrams Bks. for Young Readers) Abrams, Inc.

Bell-Rehwoldt, Sheri. The Kids' Guide to Duct Tape Projects, 1 vol. 2011. (Kids' Guides). (ENG.). 32p. (gr. 3-4). 27.99 (978-1-4296-6010-5(4), Edge Bks.) Capstone Press of Coughlan Cos.

Bell-Rehwoldt, Sheri & Ventura, Marne. My First Guide to Duct Tape Projects. 2017. (My First Guides). (ENG., Illus.). 24p. (gr. 1-2). lib. bdg. 25.32 (978-1-5157-3593-9(1)) Capstone Press of Coughlan Cos.

Bell, Samantha S. Build a Flytrap. Stewart, Roger, illus. 2016. (Earth-Friendly Projects Ser.). (ENG.). 24p. (J). (gr. 2-5). 28.50 (978-1-5038-0786-0(X), 210622) Child's World, Inc., The.

—Build a Solar Cooker. Stewart, Roger, illus. 2016. (Earth-Friendly Projects Ser.). (ENG.). 24p. (J). (gr. 2-5). 28.50 (978-1-5038-0788-4(6), 210625) Child's World, Inc., The.

Beller, Dyan. Creative Bible Crafts: Reproducible Activities. 2004. (Illus.). 64p. (J). pap. 9.95 (978-0-937282-42-7(1), RB36236); (gr. -1-k). pap. 9.95 (978-0-937282-43-4(X), RB36237); (gr. 1-2). pap. 9.95 (978-0-937282-44-1(8), RB36238); (gr. 3-4). pap. 9.95 (978-0-937282-45-8(6), RB36240); (gr. 5-6). pap. 9.95 (978-1-885358-15-8(6), B36240) Rainbow Pubs. & Legacy Pr.

Berne, Emma Carlson. Jewelry Tips & Tricks. Heschke, Elena, illus. 2015. (ENG.). 32p. (gr. 4-8). (J). lib. bdg. 26.65 (978-1-4677-5220-6(7)); 26.65 (978-1-4677-8654-6(3)) Lerner Publishing Group. (Lerner Pubns.).

Bernhardt, Carolyn. Duct Tape Animals. 2017. (Create with Duct Tape Ser.). (ENG.). 32p. (J). (gr. 2-5). 12.99 **(978-1-5124-3846-8(4)**, Lerner Pubns.); 39.99 **(978-1-5124-3845-1(6)**, Lerner Pubns.); 39.99 **(978-1-5124-2765-3(9)**, Lerner Pubns.); (Illus.). 26.65 (978-1-5124-2668-7(7)) Lerner Publishing Group.

—Duct Tape Costumes. 2017. (Create with Duct Tape Ser.). (ENG.). 32p. (J). (gr. 2-5). 12.99 **(978-1-5124-3849-9(9)**, Lerner Pubns.); 39.99 **(978-1-5124-2764-6(0)**, Lerner Pubns.); 39.99 **(978-1-5124-3848-2(0)**, Lerner Pubns.); (Illus.). 26.65 (978-1-5124-2667-0(9)) Lerner Publishing Group.

—Duct Tape Fashion. 2017. (Create with Duct Tape Ser.). (ENG.). 32p. (J). (gr. 2-5). 12.99 **(978-1-5124-3852-9(9)**, Lerner Pubns.); 39.99 **(978-1-5124-2766-0(7)**, Lerner Pubns.); 39.99 **(978-1-5124-3851-2(0)**, Lerner Pubns.); (Illus.). 26.65 (978-1-5124-2669-4(5)) Lerner Publishing Group.

The Best of Bridal Ideas. 2003. 11.99 (978-0-930184-00-1(9)) Clapper Publishing Co.

The Best of Clay Pots II. 2003. 11.99 (978-0-930184-03-2(3)) Clapper Publishing Co.

Better Homes and Gardens Books Staff, contrib. by. Big Book of Kids' Crafts: 301 Projects for Kids 4 to 12. 2004. (Illus.). 304p. (J). (978-0-696-22540-6(9)) Meredith Bks.

Biddle, Steve & Biddle, Megumi. Paper Capers — a First Book of Paper-Folding Fun: Includes 24 Sheets of Origami Paper. 2014. (ENG.). 64p. (J). (gr. 4-4). pap. 9.99 (978-0-486-49164-6(1)) Dover Pubns., Inc.

Blake, Susannah. Crafts for Revamping Your Room. 2013. (Eco Chic Ser.). 32p. (J). lib. bdg. 23.94 (978-0-7660-4315-2(0)); (gr. 4-12). pap. 7.95 (978-1-4644-0575-4(1)) Enslow Pubs., Inc.

—Crafts for Styling Your Wardrobe. 2013. (Eco Chic Ser.). 32p. (J). lib. bdg. 23.94 (978-0-7660-4316-9(9)) Enslow Pubs., Inc.

Blanchette, Peg & Thibault, Terri. Make Your Own Cool Cards: 40 Awesome Notes & Invitations! 2004. (ENG., Illus.). 64p. (J). 8.95 (978-1-885593-96-2(1), Ideal Pubns.) Worthy Publishing.

Bledsoe, Karen E. Chinese New Year Crafts. 2005. (Fun Holiday Crafts Kids Can Do! Ser.). (Illus.). 32p. (J). lib. bdg. 23.94 (978-0-7660-2347-5(8), Enslow Elementary) Enslow Pubs., Inc.

—Fun Chinese New Year Crafts. 2015. (Kid Fun Holiday Crafts! Ser.). 32p. (J). (gr. 3-4). 23.94 (978-0-7660-6240-5(6)); pap. 7.95 (978-0-7660-6241-2(4), Enslow Elementary) Enslow Pubs., Inc.

—Hanukkah Crafts. 2004. (Fun Holiday Crafts Kids Can Do! Ser.). (Illus.). 32p. (J). lib. bdg. 23.94 (978-0-7660-2238-6(2)) Enslow Pubs., Inc.

Boase, Petra. Brilliant Badges to Make Yourself: 25 Amazing Step-By-Step Badge-Making Projects. 2014. (ENG., Illus.). 64p. (J). (gr. 2-10). 9.99 (978-1-84322-828-8(9), Armadillo) Anness Publishing GBR. Dist: National Bk. Network.

—Christmas Crafts for Kids: 50 Step-By-Step Decorations & Gift Ideas for Festive Fun. 2013. (ENG., Illus.). 96p. (J). (gr. k-5). 13.99 (978-1-84322-945-2(5), Armadillo) Anness Publishing GBR. Dist: National Bk. Network.

Bolte, Mari. Colorful Creations You Can Make & Share, 1 vol. Franco, Paula, illus. 2014. (Sleepover Girls Crafts Ser.). (ENG.). 32p. (gr. 3-4). 27.99 (978-1-4914-1734-8(X), Snap Bks.) Capstone Press of Coughlan Cos.

—Eco Gifts: Upcycled Gifts You Can Make. 2015. (Make It, Gift It Ser.). (ENG., Illus.). 32p. (gr. 3-4). lib. bdg. 27.99 (978-1-4914-5202-8(1), Snap Bks.) Capstone Press of Coughlan Cos.

—Fab Fashions You Can Make & Share, 1 vol. Franco, Paula, illus. 2014. (Sleepover Girls Crafts Ser.). (ENG.). 32p. (gr. 3-4). lib. bdg. 27.99 (978-1-4914-1735-5(8), Snap Bks.) Capstone Press of Coughlan Cos.

—From Me to You: Handmade Gifts for Your VIPs. 2015. (Make It, Gift It Ser.). (ENG., Illus.). 32p. (gr. 3-4). lib. bdg. 27.99 (978-1-4914-5201-1(3), Snap Bks.) Capstone Press of Coughlan Cos.

—Homemade Holiday: Gifts for Every Occasion. 2015. (Make It, Gift It Ser.). (ENG., Illus.). 32p. (gr. 3-4). lib. bdg. 27.99 (978-1-4914-5199-1(8), Snap Bks.) Capstone Press of Coughlan Cos.

—Make It, Gift It. 2015. (Make It, Gift It Ser.). (ENG.). 32p. (gr. 3-4). 111.96 (978-1-4914-6959-0(5), Snap Bks.) Capstone Press of Coughlan Cos.

—Make It, Gift It: Handmade Gifts for Every Occasion. 2015. (Craft It Yourself Ser.). (ENG., Illus.). 144p. (gr. 3-4). pap. 14.95 (978-1-62370-319-6(0)) Capstone Press of Coughlan Cos.

—Sleepover Girls Crafts, 4 vols. 2015. (Sleepover Girls Crafts Ser.). (ENG.). 32p. (gr. 3-4). 111.96 (978-1-4914-6960-6(9)) Capstone Press of Coughlan Cos.

—Sleepover Girls Crafts: Colorful Creations You Can Make & Share, 1 vol. Franco, Paula, illus. 2014. (Sleepover Girls Crafts Ser.). (ENG.). 64p. (gr. 3-4). pap. 9.95 (978-1-62370-198-7(8)) Capstone Press of Coughlan Cos.

—Sleepover Girls Crafts: Fab Fashions You Can Make & Share, 1 vol. Franco, Paula, illus. 2014. (Sleepover Girls Crafts Ser.). (ENG.). 64p. (gr. 3-4). pap. 9.95 (978-1-62370-199-4(6)) Capstone Press of Coughlan Cos.

—Sleepover Girls Crafts: Spa Projects You Can Make & Share, 1 vol. Franco, Paula, illus. 2014. (Sleepover Girls Crafts Ser.). (ENG.). 64p. (gr. 3-4). pap. 9.95 (978-1-62370-200-7(3)) Capstone Press of Coughlan Cos.

—Spa Projects You Can Make & Share, 1 vol. Franco, Paula, illus. 2014. (Sleepover Girls Crafts Ser.). (ENG.). 32p. (gr. 3-4). lib. bdg. 27.99 (978-1-4914-1736-2(6), Snap Bks.) Capstone Press of Coughlan Cos.

—Super Science Projects: You Can Make & Share. 2015. (Sleepover Girls Crafts Ser.). (ENG., Illus.). 64p. (gr. 3-4). pap. 9.95 (978-1-62370-422-3(7)) Capstone Press of Coughlan Cos.

—Super Science Projects You Can Make & Share. 2015. (Sleepover Girls Crafts Ser.). (ENG.). 32p. (gr. 3-4). lib. bdg. 27.99 (978-1-62065-177-3(7), Snap Bks.) Capstone Press of Coughlan Cos.

—Unique Accessories: You Can Make & Share. 2015. (Sleepover Girls Crafts Ser.). (ENG.). 64p. (gr. 3-4). pap. 9.95 (978-1-62370-421-6(9)) Capstone Press of Coughlan Cos.

—Unique Accessories You Can Make & Share. 2015. (Sleepover Girls Crafts Ser.). (ENG.). 32p. (gr. 3-4). lib. bdg. 27.99 (978-1-62065-176-6(9), Snap Bks.) Capstone Press of Coughlan Cos.

Bolte, Mari, et al. Lazy Crafternoon. 2016. (Lazy Crafternoon Ser.). (ENG.). 32p. (gr. 3-4). 111.96 (978-1-5157-1443-9(8), Snap Bks.) Capstone Press of Coughlan Cos.

Bone, Emily. Cowboy Things to Make & Do. Harrison, Erica, illus. 2008. (Activity Bks). 34p. (J). (gr. 1). pap. 6.99 (978-0-7945-2077-9(4), Usborne) EDC Publishing.

Bone, Emily & Pratt, Leonie. Recycling Things to Make & Do. 2010. (Activity Book Ser.). 32p. (J). pap. 6.99 (978-0-7945-2675-7(6), Usborne) EDC Publishing.

Boniface, William. Yummy Bunny Easter Treats! Poling, Kyle, illus. 2013. (ENG.). 12p. (J). (gr. -1-1). 9.99 (978-1-4424-5724-9(4), Little Simon) Little Simon.

Boone, Mary. Busting Boredom with Art Projects. 2017. (Boredom Busters Ser.). (ENG., Illus.). 32p. (gr. 3-4). lib. bdg. 27.99 (978-1-5157-4704-8(2)) Capstone Press of Coughlan Cos.

Bosch, Sammy. Super Simple Backyard Critter Crafts: Fun & Easy Animal Crafts. 2016. (ENG., Illus.). 32p. (J). (978-1-68078-160-1(X)) ABDO Publishing Co.

—Super Simple Wetland Critter Crafts: Fun & Easy Animal Crafts. 2016. (ENG., Illus.). 32p. (J). (978-1-68078-164-9(2)) ABDO Publishing Co.

—Super Simple Zoo Critter Crafts: Fun & Easy Animal Crafts. 2016. (ENG., Illus.). 32p. (J). (978-1-68078-165-6(0)) ABDO Publishing Co.

Boursin, Didier. Easy Origami. 2005. (ENG., Illus.). 64p. (J). (gr. 2-8). pap. 9.95 (978-1-55297-939-6(3), 9781552979396) Firefly Bks., Ltd.

Boxes of Fun: Individual Title Six-Packs. (Story Steps Ser.). (gr. k-2). 29.00 (978-0-7635-9594-4(2)) Rigby Education.

Boyds Mills Press Staff. Look What You Can Make with Egg Cartons. Ochester, Betsy, ed. Schneider, Hank & Filipski, J. W., photos by. 2013. (Look What You Can Make Ser.). (ENG., Illus.). 48p. (J). (gr. k-7). pap. 6.95 (978-1-56397-906-4(3)) Boyds Mills Pr.

—Look What You Can Make with Tubes: Creative Crafts from Everyday Objects. Richmond, Margie Hayes, ed. Schneider, Hank, photos by. 2013. (Look What You Can Make Ser.). (ENG., Illus.). 48p. (J). (gr. k-9). pap., stu. ed. 6.95 (978-1-56397-677-3(3)) Boyds Mills Pr.

Braden, Linda. Mason Jar Crafts for Kids: More Than 25 Cool, Crafty Projects to Make for Your Friends, Your Family, & Yourself! 2015. (ENG., Illus.). 160p. (J). (gr. 1). pap. 14.99 (978-1-63220-413-4(4), Sky Pony Pr.) Skyhorse Publishing Co., Inc.

Brennan, Lara. The Adventurous Girl's Handbook - For Ages 9 to 99. Brennan, Stephen & Brennan, Lara, eds. 2nd ed. 2011. (ENG., Illus.). 208p. (J). (gr. 2-5). pap. 12.95 (978-1-61608-164-5(3), 608164) Skyhorse Publishing Co., Inc.

Britannica's Practical Guide to the Arts. 2016. (Britannica's Practical Guide to the Arts Ser.). 128p. (gr. 10-10). 181.25 (978-1-68048-585-1(7), Britannica Educational Publishing) Rosen Publishing Group, Inc., The.

Brothers Grimm & Sweeney, Monica. Loom Magic Charms! 25 Cool Designs That Will Rock Your Rainbow. 2014. (ENG., Illus.). 128p. (J). (gr. k). 12.95 (978-1-63220-259-8(X), Sky Pony Pr.) Skyhorse Publishing Co., Inc.

Brown, Robin C. The Crafts of Florida's First People. 2003. (ENG., Illus.). 63p. (J). pap. 9.95 (978-1-56164-282-3(7)) Pineapple Pr., Inc.

Brown, Tessa. Costume Crafts. 2010. (Creative Crafts for Kids Ser.). 32p. (J). (gr. 2-5). lib. bdg. 28.00 (978-1-4339-3555-8(4)); (Illus.). pap. 10.50 (978-1-4339-3556-5(2)) Stevens, Gareth Publishing LLLP. (Gareth Stevens Learning Library).

Bruder, Mikyla. Button Girl: 25 Pretty Projects from Belts to Barrettes. Nobles, Scott, photos by. 2005. (ENG., Illus.). 64p. (J). (gr. 4-17). 12.95 (978-0-8118-4553-3(2)) Chronicle Bks. LLC.

Bullivant, Cecil. Every Boys Book of Hobbies. 2006. 544p. per. (978-1-4067-9704-6(9), Hesperides Pr.) Read Bks.

Capstone Press. Green Crafts. 2010. (Green Crafts Ser.). (ENG.). 32p. lib. bdg. 159.90 (978-1-4296-5940-6(8), Snap Bks.) Capstone Press of Coughlan Cos.

—Paper Airplanes. 2010. (Paper Airplanes Ser.). (ENG.). 32p. lib. bdg. 106.60 (978-1-4296-5918-5(1), Edge Bks.) Capstone Press of Coughlan Cos.

Carlile, Candy. Crafts with Rhymes - Growing up God's Way. (Illus.). 64p. (J). (gr. k-5). pap. 9.95 (978-0-937282-12-0(X)) Rainbow Pubs. & Legacy Pr.

—Crafts with Rhymes - Learning from God's Word. (Illus.). 64p. (J). (gr. k-5). pap. 9.95 (978-0-937282-61-8(8)) Rainbow Pubs. & Legacy Pr.

—Crafts with Rhymes - Living in God's World. (Illus.). 64p. (J). (gr. k-5). pap. 9.95 (978-0-937282-60-1(X)) Rainbow Pubs. & Legacy Pr.

Carole Marsh. Patriotic Projects. 2004. (Patriotic Favorites Ser.). 32p. pap. 5.95 (978-0-635-02386-5(5)) Gallopade International.

Carreiro, Jen. Felt Flowers: 7 Fabulous Flowers to Make & Share. 2015. (ENG., Illus.). 32p. 9.95 (978-1-63186-349-3(5), 9781631863493) Taunton Pr., Inc.

Casagranda, Brigitte. Salt Dough Fun. 2005. (I Made It Myself! Ser.). (Illus.). 24p. (gr. k-3). lib. bdg. 23.00 (978-0-8368-5967-6(7), Gareth Stevens Learning Library) Stevens, Gareth Publishing LLLP.

Ceceri, Kathy. The Silk Road: Explore the World's Most Famous Trade Route with 20 Projects. Ceceri, Kathy, illus. 2011. (Build It Yourself Ser.). (ENG., Illus.). 128p. (J). (gr. 3-7). 21.95 (978-1-934670-65-1(0)); pap. 15.95 (978-1-934670-62-0(6)) Open City Bks.

Challen, Paul. The Culture & Crafts of Egypt. 2015. (Cultural Crafts Ser.). (ENG., Illus.). 32p. (J). (gr. 4-6). pap. 11.75 (978-1-4994-1120-1(0), 1391363, PowerKids Pr.) Rosen Publishing Group, Inc., The.

—The Culture & Crafts of Italy. 2015. (Cultural Crafts Ser.). (ENG., Illus.). 32p. (J). (gr. 4-6). pap. 11.75 (978-1-4994-1123-2(5), 1391365, PowerKids Pr.) Rosen Publishing Group, Inc., The.

Chapman, Gillian. Bible Make & Do, Vol. 4. 32p. (J). 7.99 (978-0-7586-0582-5(X)) Concordia Publishing Hse.

Chapman, Gillian & Robson, Pam. Making Art with Fabric. 2007. (Everyday Art Ser.). (Illus.). 32p. (YA). (gr. 4-7). lib. bdg. 26.50 (978-1-4042-3722-3(4)) Rosen Publishing Group, Inc., The.

—Making Art with Rocks & Shells. 2007. (Everyday Art Ser.). (Illus.). 32p. (YA). (gr. 4-7). lib. bdg. 26.50 (978-1-4042-3727-8(5)) Rosen Publishing Group, Inc., The.

Check, Laura. Almost-Instant Scrapbooks. Day, Betsy, tr. Day, Betsy, illus. 2004. (Quick Starts for Kids! Ser.). 64p. (J). pap. 8.95 (978-1-885593-90-0(2), Ideal Pubns.) Worthy Publishing.

Chorba, April. Mini Pom-Pom Pets: Make Your Own Fuzzy Friends. 2014. (ENG.). 64p. (J). (gr. 3). 19.99 (978-0-545-70319-2(0)) Klutz.

—Pom-Pom Puppies: Make Your Own Adorable Dogs. 2013. (ENG.). 56p. (J). (gr. 3). 19.99 (978-0-545-56164-8(7)) Klutz.

Chorba, April & Kane, Barbara. Potholders & Other Loopy Projects. 2013. (ENG.). 40p. (J). (gr. 2-5). 19.99 (978-0-545-44943-4(X)) Klutz.

Christian, Judy, et al. Scribble, Dribble, & Glue: Bible Art Projects for Kids. 2007. (Illus.). 64p. pap. 10.99 (978-0-7586-1308-0(3)) Concordia Publishing Hse.

CICO Kidz Staff, compiled by. Let's Get Crafty with Cardboard & Paint: 25 Creative & Fun Projects for Kids Aged 2 & Up. 2016. (ENG., Illus.). 80p. (J). (gr. 2-7). pap. 12.95 (978-1-78249-383-9(2), 1782493832, CICO Books) Ryland Peters & Small GBR. Dist: WIPRO.

—Let's Get Crafty with Fabric & Felt: 25 Creative & Fun Projects for Kids Age 2 & Up. 2016. (ENG.). 80p. (J). (gr. 2-7). pap. 12.95 (978-1-78249-336-5(0), 1782493360, CICO Books) Ryland Peters & Small GBR. Dist: WIPRO.

—Let's Get Crafty with Salt Dough: 25 Creative & Fun Projects for Kids Aged 2 & Up. 2016. (ENG., Illus.). 80p. (J). (gr. 2-7). pap. 12.95 (978-1-78249-384-6(0), 1782493840, CICO Books) Ryland Peters & Small GBR. Dist: WIPRO.

Cohn, Jessica. The Ancient Egyptians. 2012. (Crafts from the Past Ser.). (Illus.). 48p. (J). (gr. 4-6). 31.95 (978-1-4339-7701-5(X)); pap. 14.05 (978-1-4339-7702-2(8)) Stevens, Gareth Publishing LLLP.

—The Ancient Indians. 2012. (Crafts from the Past Ser.). (Illus.). 48p. (J). (gr. 4-6). 31.95 (978-1-4339-7718-3(4)); pap. 14.05 (978-1-4339-7719-0(2)) Stevens, Gareth Publishing LLLP. (Gareth Stevens Learning Library).

Coleman, Miriam. The Culture & Crafts of India. 2015. (Cultural Crafts Ser.). (ENG., Illus.). 32p. (J). (gr. 4-6). pap. 11.75 (978-1-4994-1121-8(9), PowerKids Pr.) Rosen Publishing Group, Inc., The.

—The Culture & Crafts of Japan. 2015. (Cultural Crafts Ser.). (ENG., Illus.). 32p. (J). (gr. 4-6). pap. 11.75 (978-1-4994-1125-6(1), PowerKids Pr.) Rosen Publishing Group, Inc., The.

—The Culture & Crafts of Mexico. 2015. (Cultural Crafts Ser.). (ENG., Illus.). 32p. (J). (gr. 4-6). pap. 11.75 (978-1-4994-1126-3(X), PowerKids Pr.) Rosen Publishing Group, Inc., The.

Cook Communications Ministries, creator. Bible Crafts for All Seasons. 2005. (Godprints Bible Funstuff Ser.). (Illus.). 112p. pap., per. 19.99 (978-0-7814-4205-3(2), 0781442052) Cook, David C.

Cool Crafts for Kids. 2016. (Cool Crafts for Kids Ser.). 00032p. (J). (gr. 3-3). 171.00 (978-1-4994-8131-0(4), Windmill Bks.) Rosen Publishing Group, Inc., The.

Coon, Cyndi, illus. Art That Pops! How to Make Wacky 3-D Creations That Jump, Spin, & Spring! 2006. 48p. (J). pap. (978-0-439-81337-2(9)) Scholastic, Inc.

Cooper, Stephanie, et al. The Children's Year: Seasonal Crafts & Clothes. 2006. (Festivals (Hawthorn Press) Ser.). (ENG., Illus.). 192p. (978-1-903458-59-4(5)) Hawthorn Pr.

Corwin, Judith Hoffman. Native American Crafts of the Northeast & Southeast. Corwin, Judith Hoffman, illus. 2003. (Native American Crafts Ser.). (ENG., Illus.). 48p. (J). (gr. 3-6). pap. 7.95 (978-0-531-15593-6(5), Watts, Franklin) Scholastic Library Publishing.

Cousins, Lucy. Create with Maisy: A Maisy First Arts-and-Crafts Book. Cousins, Lucy, illus. 2012. (Maisy Ser.). (ENG., Illus.). 48p. (J). (gr. -1-3). 16.99 (978-0-7636-6122-9(8)) Candlewick Pr.

Craft Box. 2017. (Craft Box Ser.). 32p. (gr. 8-8). 110.00 ***(978-1-4994-3407-1(3))***; pap. 47.00 ***(978-1-4994-3409-5(X))*** Rosen Publishing Group, Inc., The. (PowerKids Pr.).

Crafts. (Butterfly Bks.). (ARA., Illus.). 15p. (J). 11.95 *(978-0-86685-616-4(1)*, LDL6161) International Bk. Ctr., Inc.

Crafts for Baby. 2008. (Gift Ser.). 96p. *(978-1-4075-2077-3(6))* Parragon, Inc.

Creative Bracelets. 2004. (Formula Fun Ser.). (Illus.). 48p. (J). *(978-1-84229-877-0(1))* Top That! Publishing PLC.

Creative Crafts for Kids. 2006. 48p. pap. 3.99 *(978-0-7666-2273-9(8))* Modern Publishing.

Creepy Glowing Magic: Glow-In-the-dark Thrills & Chills! 2013. (Craft Box Kids Ser.). (ENG., Illus.). 48p. (J). *(978-1-77132-000-9(1))* SpiceBox Products Ltd.

Crexells, Cristina, et al. Plants & Seeds. 2003. (Let's Create! Ser.). (Illus.). 32p. (gr. 1-4). lib. bdg. 26.00 *(978-0-8368-3748-3(7)*, Gareth Stevens Learning Library) Stevens, Gareth Publishing LLLP.

Cryan, Mary Beth. Make Your Own Glasses: Tear Them, Share Them, Color & Wear Them! 2015. (ENG.). 64p. (J). (gr. 1-4). pap. 7.99 *(978-0-486-79408-2(3))* Dover Pubns., Inc.

Cultural Crafts. 2015. (Cultural Crafts Ser.). (ENG.). 32p. (J). (gr. 4-6). pap., pap., pap. 423.00 *(978-1-4994-1282-6(7)*, PowerKids Pr.) Rosen Publishing Group, Inc., The.

Cuxart, Bernadette. Art Painting on Everyday Items. 2015. (Art Painting Ser.). (ENG., Illus.). 36p. (J). (gr. k-3). pap. 6.99 *(978-1-4380-0651-2(9))* Barron's Educational Series, Inc.

—Art Painting with Different Tools. 2015. (Art Painting Ser.). (ENG.). 36p. (J). (gr. k-3). pap. 6.99 *(978-1-4380-0653-6(5))* Barron's Educational Series, Inc.

—Art Painting with Everyday Materials. 2015. (Art Painting Ser.). (ENG., Illus.). 36p. (J). (gr. k-3). pap. 6.99 *(978-1-4380-0654-3(3))* Barron's Educational Series, Inc.

—Art Stamping Using Everyday Objects. 2015. (Art Painting Ser.). (ENG., Illus.). 36p. (J). (gr. k-3). pap. 6.99 *(978-1-4380-0652-9(7))* Barron's Educational Series, Inc.

—Fantasy Characters: Easy-To-Follow Clay-Making Projects in Simple Steps. 2013. (Modeling Clay Bks.). (ENG.). 36p. (J). (gr. k-4). pap. 6.99 *(978-1-4380-0357-3(9))* Barron's Educational Series, Inc.

Dailey, Dan & Dailey, Allison, illus. Glassigator. 2007. 33p. (J). *(978-0-935172-29-4(7))* Hudson Hills Pr. LLC.

Dakota, Heather. Tote-Ally You: Design Your Own Purse. 2005. (Illus.). 47p. *(978-0-439-73671-8(4))* Scholastic, Inc.

Dale, Jay. Make a Monkey, 1 vol. Kreinberg, Sylvia, photos by. 2012. (Engage Literacy Red Ser.). (ENG., Illus.). 32p. (gr. k-2). pap. 5.99 *(978-1-4296-8946-5(3)*, Engage Literacy) Capstone Press of Coughlan Cos.

Dalkin, Monika & Hollis, Mignonne. The Other Rope Book. 30p. (J). (gr. 2-6). 10.95 *(978-0-9644524-0-4(5))* Jolly Geranium, Inc.

Dall, Mary Doerfler. Little Hands Create! Art & Activities for Kids Ages 3 to 6. Rakitin, Sarah, illus. (J). 2008. (ENG.). 20p. pap. 12.95 *(978-0-8249-8664-3(4))* 2004. pap. 12.95 *(978-1-885593-65-8(1))* Worthy Publishing. (Ideal Pubns.).

Danescary, Pollygeist. Monster High - Happy Howlidays! 2014. (ENG., Illus.). 32p. (J). (gr. 1-4). pap. 7.99 *(978-0-316-27709-9(6))* Little, Brown Bks. for Young Readers.

Daning, Tom. Fun-To-Make Crafts for Halloween. 2005. (Illus.). 63p. (J). *(978-0-329-43124-2(2))* Boyds Mills Pr.

Danks, Fiona, et al. Nature's Playground: Activities, Crafts, & Games to Encourage Children to Get Outdoors. 2007. (ENG., Illus.). 192p. (J). (gr. 2-4). pap. 19.95 *(978-1-55652-723-4(3))* Chicago Review Pr., Inc.

Dann, Penny. My Big Rainy Day Activity Book. Smee, Nicola, illus. 2004. 96p. (J). act. bk. ed. 7.99 *(978-1-85854-554-7(4))* Brimax Books Ltd. GBR. Dist: Byeway Bks.

David C. Cook Publishing Company Staff, creator. Memory Maker Bible Crafts. 2008. (Bible Fun Stuff for 2nd-3rd Grades Ser.). (Illus.). 112p. (J). (gr. 2-3). pap. 19.99 *(978-1-4347-6859-9(7))* Cook, David C.

—Stick'em up Bible Crafts. 2008. (Bible Fun Stuff for Preschool Ser.). (Illus.). 112p. (J). (gr. -1-k). pap. 19.99 *(978-1-4347-6864-3(3))* Cook, David C.

—Through-the-Bible Crafts. 2008. (Bible Fun Stuff for K-1 Ser.). (Illus.). 112p. (J). (gr. k-1). pap. 19.99 *(978-1-4347-6862-9(7))* Cook, David C.

D'Cruz, Anna-Marie. Make Your Own Purses & Bags. 2009. (Do It Yourself Projects! Ser.). 24p. (J). (gr. 3-4). lib. bdg. 25.25 *(978-1-4358-2856-8(9)*, PowerKids Pr.) Rosen Publishing Group, Inc., The.

DeCristoforo, Jennifer. Lucky Bamboo Book of Crafts: Over 100 Projects & Ideas Celebrating Chinese Culture, vols. 2, vol. 101. DeCristoforo, Jennifer, illus. 2013. (ENG & CHI., Illus.). 136p. 26.99 *(978-0-9884648-0-3(2))* Lucky Bamboo Crafts.

Dennis, Yvonne Wakim & Hirschfelder, Arlene. A Kid's Guide to Native American History: More Than 50 Activities. 2009. (Kid's Guide Ser.). (ENG.). 256p. (J). (gr. 2-4). pap. 16.95 *(978-1-55652-802-6(7))* Chicago Review Pr., Inc.

dePaola, Tomie. Charlie Needs a Cloak. 2015. 32p. pap. 7.00 *(978-1-61003-601-6(8))* Center for the Collaborative Classroom.

Dickerson, Jennifer. Mini Flower Loom Crafts: 18 Super Simple Projects. 2015. (ENG., Illus.). 32p. 9.95 *(978-1-63186-483-4(1)*, 9781631864834) Taunton Pr., Inc.

Dickinson, Gill. Creative Crafts for Kids. 2013. (ENG.). 256p. pap. 14.99 *(978-0-600-62710-4(1)*, Hamlyn) Octopus Publishing Group GBR. Dist: Hachette Bk. Group.

Dickinson, Gill & Lowe, Jason. Crafts for Kids: Birthdays - Easter - Halloween - Christmas - Mother's Day - Thanksgiving - And More... 2008. (ENG., Illus.). 128p. (gr. -1-17). pap. 12.95 *(978-0-600-61506-4(5)*, Hamlyn) Octopus Publishing Group GBR. Dist: Hachette Bk. Group.

Dixon, Louisa. What Did I Do Today? 42p. (J). (gr. k-3). pap. 12.95 *(978-0-9635811-0-5(4))* Rosemont, Ltd.

Dixon, Louisa & Boshers, Martha. What Did I Do Today? For Young Writers. 42p. (J). (gr. 3-7). pap. 12.95 *(978-0-9635811-1-2(2))* Rosemont, Ltd.

Dog 'n' Bone Books Staff & CICO Kidz Staff, compiled by. My First Christmas Craft Book: 35 Fun Festive Projects for Children Aged 7+ 2016. (ENG., Illus.). 128p. (J). (gr. 7-11). pap. 14.95 *(978-1-78249-381-5(6)*, 1782493816, CICO Books) Ryland Peters & Small GBR. Dist: WIPRO.

Doney, Meryl. Paper Crafts. 2004. (Crafts from Many Cultures Ser.). (Illus.). 32p. (gr. 2-5). lib. bdg. 26.00 *(978-0-8368-4046-9(1)*, Gareth Stevens Learning Library) Stevens, Gareth Publishing LLLP.

Don't Throw It Away... Craft It! 2017. (Don't Throw It Away... Craft It! Ser.). 32p. (gr. 8-8). 171.00 ***(978-1-4994-8269-0(8))***; pap. 70.50 ***(978-1-4994-8405-2(4))*** Rosen Publishing Group, Inc., The. (Windmill Bks.).

Dorling Kindersley Publishing Staff. The Big Book of Crafts & Activities. 2013. (ENG., Illus.). 128p. (J). (gr. 2-5). 16.99 *(978-1-4654-0256-1(X)*, DK Children) Dorling Kindersley Publishing, Inc.

—My Art Book. 2011. (ENG., Illus.). 80p. (J). (gr. 2-5). 15.99 *(978-0-7566-7582-0(0)*, DK Children) Dorling Kindersley Publishing, Inc.

Dorsey, Colleen. Epic Rubber Band Crafts: Totally Cool Gadget Gear, Never Before Seen Bracelets, Awesome Action Figures, & More! 2014. (ENG., Illus.). 48p. pap. 7.99 *(978-1-57421-914-2(6)*, 9781574219142, Design Originals) Fox Chapel Publishing Co., Inc.

—Totally Awesome Rubber Band Jewelry: Make Bracelets, Rings, Belts & More with Rainbow Loom(r), Cra-Z-Loom & FunLoom. 2013. lib. bdg. 18.40 *(978-0-606-35178-2(7))* Turtleback Bks.

Dover Publications Inc. Staff, ed. Boxed/Decorate for Halloween Fun Kit. 2008. (Dover Fun Kits Ser.). (ENG.). 12p. (J). (gr. 1). pap. 16.95 *(978-0-486-46792-4(9))* Dover Pubns., Inc.

Downs, Dorothy. Patchwork: Seminole & Miccosukee Art & Activities. 2005. (ENG., Illus.). 55p. (J). (gr. 3-7). per. 12.95 *(978-1-56164-332-5(7))* Pineapple Pr., Inc.

Durrie, Karen. Artes. 2012. (SPA.). (J). *(978-1-61913-212-2(5))* Weigl Pubs., Inc.

Dybvik, Tina. Trendy Jewelry for the Crafty Fashionista, 1 vol. 2011. (Fashion Craft Studio Ser.). (ENG.). 32p. (gr. 3-4). lib. bdg. 27.99 *(978-1-4296-6549-0(1)*, Snap Bks.) Capstone Press of Coughlan Cos.

Eastman, Linda Sue. Leathercraft. 2008. (ENG., Illus.). 120p. (gr. 4-7). pap. 14.95 *(978-1-56523-370-6(0)*, 3706) Fox Chapel Publishing Co., Inc.

Easy-To-Make Pom-Pom Animals: 12 Adorable Little Animal Projects. 2013. (Craft Box Kids Ser.). (ENG., Illus.). 48p. (J). *(978-1-77132-023-8(0))* SpiceBox Products Ltd.

Easy-To-Make Sock Puppets: Lots of Crazy, Quirky Puppets to Make! 2013. (Craft Box Kids Ser.). (ENG., Illus.). 48p. (J). *(978-1-77132-024-5(9))* SpiceBox Products Ltd.

Eder, Enelle. Create & Take Bible Crafts: Exploring Nature. 2004. (Create & Take Bible Crafts). 96p. (J). (gr. k-6). pap. 11.95 *(978-1-58411-005-7(8))* Rainbow Pubs. & Legacy Pr.

—Create & Take Bible Crafts: Old Testament Heroes. 2004. 96p. (J). (gr. k-6). pap. 11.95 *(978-1-58411-006-4(6))* Rainbow Pubs. & Legacy Pr.

—Create & Take Bible Crafts: Special Days. 2004. 96p. (J). (gr. k-6). pap. 11.95 *(978-1-58411-008-8(2))* Rainbow Pubs. & Legacy Pr.

Edwards, Diane. Norwegian Rosemaling for Young People. 2003. (Illus.). 40p. 10.95 *(978-0-9674583-4-2(X)*, 1) Rosemaling & Crafts.

Ejaz, Khadija. Recipe & Craft Guide to India. 2010. (World Crafts & Recipes Ser.). (Illus.). 48p. (J). (gr. 4-8). lib. bdg. 29.95 *(978-1-58415-938-4(3))* Mitchell Lane Pubs., Inc.

Elliot, Marion. Recycled Craft Projects for Kids: 50 Fantastic Things to Make from Junk, Shown. 2014. (ENG., Illus.). 96p. (J). (gr. 2-7). 13.99 *(978-0-84322-891-2(2)*, Armadillo) Anness Publishing GBR. Dist: National Bk. Network.

Elton, Richard & Elton, Candice. Every Kid Needs a Rubber Band Launcher. 2007. (J). *(978-1-4236-0268-2(4))* Gibbs Smith, Publisher.

Enz, Tammy. Awesome Craft Stick Science. 2016. (Recycled Science Ser.). (ENG., Illus.). 32p. (gr. 3-4). lib. bdg. 27.99 *(978-1-5157-0861-2(6))* Capstone Press of Coughlan Cos.

—Build Your Own Periscope, Flashlight, & Other Useful Stuff. 2011. (Build It Yourself Ser.). (ENG.). 32p. (gr. 3-4). pap. 47.70 *(978-1-4296-6431-8(2)*, Edge Bks.) Capstone Press of Coughlan Cos.

—Cool Plastic Bottle & Milk Jug Science. 2016. (Recycled Science Ser.). (ENG., Illus.). 32p. (gr. 3-4). lib. bdg. 27.99 *(978-1-5157-0862-9(4))* Capstone Press of Coughlan Cos.

Enz, Tammy & Wheeler-Toppen, Jodi. Whizzy Science with Recyclables: Bring Out Your Science Genius with Soda Bottles, Potato Chip Bags & More Unexpected Stuff. 2016. (Recycled Science Ser.). (ENG.). 112p. (gr. 3-4). pap. 9.95 *(978-1-62370-697-5(1))* Capstone Press of Coughlan Cos.

Erlbach, Arlene & Erlbach, Herb. Fun Mother's Day Crafts. 2015. (Kid Fun Holiday Crafts! Ser.). 32p. (J). (gr. 3-4). 23.94 *(978-0-7660-6245-0(7))* Enslow Pubs., Inc.

Erlbach, Arlene & Erlbach, Herbert. Fun Mother's Day Crafts. 2015. (Kid Fun Holiday Crafts! Ser.). 32p. (J). (gr. 3-4). pap. 7.95 *(978-0-7660-6246-7(5)*, Enslow Elementary) Enslow Pubs., Inc.

—Fun Thanksgiving Day Crafts. 2015. (Kid Fun Holiday Crafts! Ser.). 32p. (J). (gr. 3-4). pap. 7.95 *(978-0-7660-6251-1(1)*, Enslow Elementary) Enslow Pubs., Inc.

—Mother's Day Crafts. 2005. (Fun Holiday Crafts Kids Can Do! Ser.). (Illus.). 32p. (J). lib. bdg. 23.94 *(978-0-7660-2348-2(6)*, Enslow Elementary) Enslow Pubs., Inc.

—Thanksgiving Day Crafts. Ponte, June, illus. 2005. (Fun Holiday Crafts Kids Can Do! Ser.). 32p. (J). lib. bdg. 23.94 *(978-0-7660-2345-1(1)*, Enslow Elementary) Enslow Pubs., Inc.

—Valentine's Day Crafts. 2004. (Fun Holiday Crafts Kids Can Do! Ser.). (Illus.). 32p. (J). lib. bdg. 23.94 *(978-0-7660-2237-9(4))* Enslow Pubs., Inc.

Fab Fingers. 2004. (Formula Fun Ser.). (Illus.). 48p. (J). *(978-1-84229-581-6(0))* Top That! Publishing PLC.

Falligant, Erin, ed. Clutter Control: Tips & Crafts to Organize Your Bedroom, Backpack, Locker, Life. McGuinness, Tracy, illus. 2008. (ENG.). 64p. (J). (gr. 3-7). pap. 8.95 *(978-1-59369-341-1(9))* American Girl Publishing, Inc.

Farm Fun Crafts for Kids. 16.99 *(978-0-8307-2990-6(9)*, Gospel Light) Gospel Light Pubns.

Farrell, Mia. Exploring African-American Culture Through Crafts. 2015. (Multicultural Crafts Ser.). (ENG., Illus.). 32p. (J). (gr. 3-4). pap. 10.52 *(978-0-7660-6769-1(6)*, 1392089) Enslow Pubs., Inc.

—Exploring Asian Cultures Through Crafts. 2015. (Multicultural Crafts Ser.). (ENG., Illus.). 32p. (J). (gr. 3-4). pap. 10.52 *(978-0-7660-6773-8(4)*, 1392090) Enslow Pubs., Inc.

—Exploring Latino Cultures Through Crafts. 2015. (Multicultural Crafts Ser.). (ENG., Illus.). 32p. (J). (gr. 3-4). pap. 10.52 *(978-0-7660-6777-6(7)*, 1392091) Enslow Pubs., Inc.

—Exploring Middle Eastern Cultures Through Crafts. 2015. (Multicultural Crafts Ser.). (ENG., Illus.). 32p. (J). (gr. 3-4). pap. 10.52 *(978-0-7660-6781-3(5)*, 1392092) Enslow Pubs., Inc.

—Exploring Native American Cultures Through Crafts. 2015. (Multicultural Crafts Ser.). (ENG., Illus.). 32p. (J). (gr. 3-4). pap. 10.52 *(978-0-7660-6785-1(8))* Enslow Pubs., Inc.

Felix, Rebecca. Cool Crayons, Chalks, & Paints: Crafting Creative Toys & Amazing Games, 1 vol. 2016. (Cool Toys & Games Ser.). (ENG., Illus.). 32p. (J). (gr. 3-6). lib. bdg. 28.50 *(978-1-68078-048-2(4)*, Checkerboard Library) ABDO Publishing Co.

—Cool Doughs, Putties, Slimes, & Goops: Crafting Creative Toys & Amazing Games, 1 vol. 2016. (Cool Toys & Games Ser.). (ENG., Illus.). 32p. (J). (gr. 3-6). lib. bdg. 28.50 *(978-1-68078-049-9(2)*, Checkerboard Library) ABDO Publishing Co.

—Cool Springy, Slinky, & Stretchy Projects: Crafting Creative Toys & Amazing Games, 1 vol. 2016. (Cool Toys & Games Ser.). (ENG., Illus.). 32p. (J). (gr. 3-6). lib. bdg. 28.50 *(978-1-68078-050-5(6)*, Checkerboard Library) ABDO Publishing Co.

—Mini Decorating. 2017. (Mini Makers Ser.). (ENG.). 32p. (J). (gr. 2-5). 12.99 ***(978-1-5124-3834-5(0)***, Lerner Pubns.); 39.99 ***(978-1-5124-3833-8(2)***, Lerner Pubns.); 39.99 ***(978-1-5124-2810-0(8)***, Lerner Pubns.); (Illus.). 26.65 *(978-1-5124-2632-8(6))* Lerner Publishing Group.

—Mini Holiday Crafts. 2017. (Mini Makers Ser.). (ENG.). 32p. (J). (gr. 2-5). 12.99 ***(978-1-5124-3837-6(5)***, Lerner Pubns.); 39.99 ***(978-1-5124-2811-7(6)***, Lerner Pubns.); 39.99 ***(978-1-5124-3836-9(7)***, Lerner Pubns.); (Illus.). 26.65 *(978-1-5124-2633-5(4))* Lerner Publishing Group.

—Mini Science Fun. 2017. (Mini Makers Ser.). (ENG.). 32p. (J). (gr. 2-5). 12.99 ***(978-1-5124-3840-6(5)***, Lerner Pubns.); 39.99 ***(978-1-5124-3839-0(1)***, Lerner Pubns.); 39.99 ***(978-1-5124-2812-4(4)***, Lerner Pubns.); (Illus.). 26.65 *(978-1-5124-2634-2(2))* Lerner Publishing Group.

—Mini Wearables. 2017. (Mini Makers Ser.). (ENG.). 32p. (J). (gr. 2-5). 12.99 ***(978-1-5124-3843-7(X)***, Lerner Pubns.); 39.99 ***(978-1-5124-3842-0(1)***, Lerner Pubns.); 39.99 ***(978-1-5124-2813-1(2)***, Lerner Pubns.); (Illus.). 26.65 *(978-1-5124-2635-9(0))* Lerner Publishing Group.

Fernandez, Caroline. More Boredom Busters: Over 50 Awesome Activities for Children Aged 7 Years + 2015. (ENG., Illus.). 128p. (J). (gr. 7-11). pap. 14.95 *(978-1-78249-199-6(6)*, CICO Books) Ryland Peters & Small GBR. Dist: WIPRO.

Fields, Stella. Accessory Projects for a Lazy Crafternoon. 2016. (Lazy Crafternoon Ser.). (ENG.). 32p. (gr. 3-4). lib. bdg. 27.99 *(978-1-5157-1436-1(5)*, Snap Bks.) Capstone Press of Coughlan Cos.

—Back-To-School Projects for a Lazy Crafternoon. 2016. (Lazy Crafternoon Ser.). (ENG.). 32p. (gr. 3-4). lib. bdg. 27.99 *(978-1-5157-1438-5(1)*, Snap Bks.) Capstone Press of Coughlan Cos.

—Decorating Projects for a Lazy Crafternoon. 2016. (Lazy Crafternoon Ser.). (ENG.). 32p. (gr. 3-4). lib. bdg. 27.99 *(978-1-5157-1435-4(7)*, Snap Bks.) Capstone Press of Coughlan Cos.

—Lazy Crafternoon. 2016. (Craft It Yourself Ser.). (ENG.). 128p. (gr. 3-4). pap. 14.95 *(978-1-62370-751-4(X))* Capstone Young Readers of Coughlan Cos.

—Party Planning for a Lazy Crafternoon. 2016. (Lazy Crafternoon Ser.). (ENG.). 32p. (gr. 3-4). lib. bdg. 27.99 *(978-1-5157-1437-8(3)*, Snap Bks.) Capstone Press of Coughlan Cos.

Fittes, Francine. Craft Lacing Madness. 2006. (ENG., Illus.). 48p. (J). (gr. 4-7). pap. 6.99 *(978-0-7153-2480-6(2))* David & Charles Pubs. GBR. Dist: F&W Media, Inc.

Fitzsimons, Cecilia. 50 Nature Projects for Kids: Fun-Packed Outdoor & Indoor Things to Do & Make. 2013. (ENG., Illus.). 96p. (J). (gr. 2-9). 13.99 *(978-1-84322-852-3(1)*, Armadillo) Anness Publishing GBR. Dist: National Bk. Network.

Flanders, Aaron. Balloon Animals. 2003. 128p. pap. 8.95 *(978-0-07-143742-4(8))* McGraw-Hill Cos., The.

—Balloon Cartoons & Other Favorites. 2003. 128p. pap. 8.95 *(978-0-07-143744-8(4))* McGraw-Hill Cos., The.

—Balloon Hats & Accessories. 2003. 128p. pap. 8.95 *(978-0-07-143745-5(2))* McGraw-Hill Cos., The.

Flower, Miri. The Pencil Book: Loads of Things You Can Make or Do with a Pencil. 2014. (ENG., Illus.). 128p. pap. 15.99 *(978-0-7112-3584-7(8)*, Frances Lincoln) Quarto Publishing Group UK GBR. Dist: Littlehampton Bk Services, Ltd.

Fontichiaro, Kristin. Organizing a MakerFest. 2017. (21st Century Skills Innovation Library: Makers As Innovators Junior Ser.). (ENG., Illus.). 24p. (J). (gr. 2-5). lib. bdg. 28.50 *(978-1-63472-190-5(X)*, 209332) Cherry Lake Publishing.

Formaro, Amanda. Button Mania: Buttons, Bottlecaps, & Beyond! 2015. (ENG., Illus.). 72p. (J). (gr. k-6). pap. 8.99 *(978-0-7944-3339-0(1)*, Reader's Digest Children's Bks.) Studio Fun International.

—Paper Fun Mania. 2015. (Mania Ser.: 4). (ENG., Illus.). 72p. (J). (gr. k-6). pap. 8.99 *(978-0-7944-3338-3(3)*, Reader's Digest Children's Bks.) Studio Fun International.

Forte, Imogene. Arts & Crafts. 2004. (Fun Things to Make & Do Ser.). (Illus.). 80p. (J). per. 9.95 *(978-0-86530-613-4(3))* Incentive Pubns., Inc.

Foster, Juliana. The Girls' Book: How to Be the Best at Everything. Wingate, Philippa, ed. Enright, Amanda, illus. 2007. (Best at Everything Ser.). (ENG.). 128p. (J). (gr. 3-7). 9.99 *(978-0-545-01629-2(0)*, Scholastic Pr.) Scholastic, Inc.

French, Cathy. Make an Animal Mobile & Haz un móvil de Animales: 6 English, 6 Spanish Adaptations. 2011. (SPA & ENG.). (J). 75.00 net. *(978-1-4108-5619-7(4))* Benchmark Education Co.

Freshman, Wendy & Jansson, Kristin. Making History: Have a Blast with 15 Crafts. 2014. (ENG., Illus.). 216p. (J). (gr. 2-6). pap. 17.95 *(978-0-87351-919-9(1))* Minnesota Historical Society Pr.

Friday, Megan. Green Crafts: Become an Earth-Friendly Craft Star, Step by Easy Step! 2012. (Craft Star Ser.). (Illus.). 64p. (gr. 2-4). 32.80 *(978-1-936309-38-2(6))* Quarto Publishing Group USA.

—Pet Crafts: Everything You Need to Become Your Pet's Craft Star! 2012. (Craft Star Ser.). 64p. (gr. 2-4). 32.80 *(978-1-936309-41-2(6))* Quarto Publishing Group USA.

From the Editors of Faithgirlz!, From the. 101 Ways to Have Fun: Things You Can Do with Friends, Anytime!, 1 vol. 2016. (Faithgirlz Ser.). (ENG., Illus.). 128p. (J). pap. 14.99 *(978-0-310-74613-3(2))* Zonderkidz.

From Trash to Treasure. 2013. (From Trash to Treasure Ser.). 32p. (J). (gr. 3-6). 159.00 *(978-1-4777-1539-0(8))*; pap. 70.50 *(978-1-4777-2703-4(5))*; pap. 423.00 *(978-1-4777-2704-1(3))* Rosen Publishing Group, Inc., The. (PowerKids Pr.).

Fun Fabrics. 2013. (From Trash to Treasure Ser.). 32p. (J). (gr. 3-6). pap. 70.50 *(978-1-4777-1363-1(8)*, PowerKids Pr.) Rosen Publishing Group, Inc., The.

Fun for Little Hands Series, 7 bks., Set. 2003. (Illus.). (J). 21.33 *(978-0-929371-92-4(5)*, Kar-Ben Publishing) Lerner Publishing Group.

Fun Projects for Kids. Date not set. (Get Crafty Ser.). (Illus.). 48p. (J). pap. 4.98 *(978-0-7525-8409-6(X))* Parragon, Inc.

Fun Things to Make & Do: Individual Title Six-Packs. (Discovery World Ser.). 16p. (gr. 1-2). 28.00 *(978-0-7635-8458-0(4))* Rigby Education.

Furgang, Adam. 10 Great Makerspace Projects Using Art. 2017. (Using Makerspaces for School Projects Ser.). 64p. (gr. 11-11). 34.45 ***(978-1-4994-3842-0(7)***, Rosen Central) Rosen Publishing Group, Inc., The.

Gabriel, Faith K. Nifty Thrifty Animal Crafts. Ponte, June, illus. 2007. (Nifty Thrifty Crafts for Kids Ser.). 32p. (J). (gr. 3-4). lib. bdg. 23.94 *(978-0-7660-2779-4(1)*, Enslow Elementary) Enslow Pubs., Inc.

Galvin, Jennifer. My Catholic Lent & Easter. 2003. 32p. act. bk. ed. 8.95 *(978-0-8091-6706-7(9)*, 6706-9) Paulist Pr.

Garner, Lynne. African Crafts: Fun Things to Make & Do from West Africa. 2008. (ENG., Illus.). 48p. (J). (gr. 4-7). 12.95 *(978-1-55652-748-7(9))* Chicago Review Pr., Inc.

Garza, Carmen Lomas, illus. Making Magic Windows. 2014. (ENG & SPA.). 32p. (J). (gr. 4-7). pap. 11.95 *(978-0-89239-159-2(6))* Lee & Low Bks., Inc.

Gibbons, Gail. From Sheep to Sweater. Date not set. (J). *(978-0-8234-1885-5(5))* Holiday Hse., Inc.

Gibson, R. Recortar y Pegar. 2004.Tr. of I Can Cut & Stick. (SPA., Illus.). 32p. (J). lib. bdg. 12.95 *(978-1-58086-361-2(2))* EDC Publishing.

—What Shall I Make? 2004. (What Shall I Do Today? Ser.). 32p. (J). pap. 7.95 *(978-0-7945-0376-5(4))* EDC Publishing.

Gibson, R. & Watt, F. Summer Activities. 2004. (Illus.). 32p. (J). pap., act. bk. ed. 6.95 *(978-0-7945-0398-7(5))* EDC Publishing.

Gibson, Ray. Big Book of Things to Do: Combined Volume. Stitt, Sue, illus. 2004. (What Shall I Do Today? Ser.). 192p. (J). pap. 18.95 *(978-0-7945-0442-7(6)*, Usborne) EDC Publishing.

—Ideas para Navidad. 2004.Tr. of Christmas Activities. (ENG & SPA., Illus.). 34p. (J). (gr. -1-3). pap. 8.95 *(978-0-7460-3899-4(2))* EDC Publishing.

Gilpin, R. Fairy Things to Make & Do. 2004. (Illus.). 32p. (J). pap., act. bk. ed. 6.95 *(978-0-7945-0576-9(7))* EDC Publishing.

Gilpin, Rebecca. Animal Things to Make & Do. 2009. (Activity Bks). 32p. (J). pap. 6.99 *(978-0-7945-2349-7(8)*, Usborne) EDC Publishing.

—Monster Things to Make & Do. Harrison, Erica et al, illus. Allman, Howard, photos by. 2006. (Usborne Activities Ser.). 32p. (J). (gr. -1-3). pap. 6.99 *(978-0-7945-1354-2(9)*, Usborne) EDC Publishing.

—Travel Activity Book. 2013. (Doodle Bks). 96p. (J). pap. 12.99 *(978-0-7945-3287-1(X)*, Usborne) EDC Publishing.

—Valentine Things to Make & Do. 2006. (Usborne Activities Ser.). (Illus.). 31p. (J). *(978-0-439-78705-5(X))* Scholastic, Inc.

Gilpin, Rebecca & Brocklehurst, Ruth. Wizard, Pirate & Princess Things to Make & Do. Harrison, Erica, illus. 2006. 96p. (J). (gr. 1-4). 14.99 *(978-0-7945-1415-0(4)*, Usborne) EDC Publishing.

Girls Art & Craft Assortment. 2013. (None Ser.). (ENG.). pap. 49.99 *(978-1-62370-159-8(7))* Capstone Young Readers of Coughlan Cos.

Giulieri, Anne. Make a Secret Playhouse, 1 vol. Meldrum, Ned, photos by. 2012. (Engage Literacy Green Ser.). (ENG., Illus.). 32p. (gr. k-2). pap. 5.99 *(978-1-4296-9001-0(1)*, Engage Literacy) Capstone Press of Coughlan Cos.

Glassman, Michael & Ely, Lisa. Kinder Gardens: Games & Adventures, 1 vol. 2011. (ENG., Illus.). 64p. (J). pap. 12.99 *(978-0-7643-3811-3(0)*, 9780764338113, Schiffer Publishing Ltd) Schiffer Publishing, Ltd.

Glenn, Joshua & Larsen, Elizabeth Foy. UNBORED Adventure. Leone, Tony et al, illus. 2015. (ENG.). 176p. pap. 16.00 *(978-1-63286-096-5(1)*, 9781632860965) Bloomsbury Publishing USA.

Glitter It Up! 2013. (Kits for Kids Ser.). (ENG., Illus.). 64p. (J). (gr. 3-7). *(978-1-894722-67-4(1))* SpiceBox Products Ltd.

Gnojewski, Carol. African-American Crafts Kids Can Do! 2006. (Multicultural Crafts Kids Can Do! Ser.). (Illus.). 32p. (J). (gr. 3-4). lib. bdg. 23.94 *(978-0-7660-2457-1(1)*, Enslow Elementary) Enslow Pubs., Inc.

—American Indian Crafts Kids Can Do! 2006. (Multicultural Crafts Kids Can Do! Ser.). (Illus.). 32p. (J). (gr. 3-4). lib. bdg. 23.94 *(978-0-7660-2458-8(X)*, Enslow Elementary) Enslow Pubs., Inc.

—Cinco de Mayo Crafts. 2005. (Fun Holiday Crafts Kids Can Do! Ser.). (Illus.). 32p. (J). lib. bdg. 23.94 *(978-0-7660-2344-4(3)*, Enslow Elementary) Enslow Pubs., Inc.

—Earth Day Crafts. 2005. (Fun Holiday Crafts Kids Can Do! Ser.). (Illus.). 32p. (J). lib. bdg. 23.94 *(978-0-7660-2346-8(X)*, Enslow Elementary) Enslow Pubs., Inc.

—Fun St. Patrick's Day Crafts. 2015. (Kid Fun Holiday Crafts! Ser.). 32p. (J). (gr. 3-4). 23.94 *(978-0-7660-6230-6(9))*; pap. 7.95 *(978-0-7660-6231-3(7)*, Enslow Elementary) Enslow Pubs., Inc.

H
I

—Kwanzaa Crafts. 2004. (Fun Holiday Crafts Kids Can Do! Ser.). (Illus.). 32p. (J). lib. bdg. 23.94 *(978-0-7660-2203-4(X))* Enslow Pubs., Inc.

—St. Patrick's Day Crafts. 2004. (Fun Holiday Crafts Kids Can Do! Ser.). (Illus.). 32p. (J). lib. bdg. 23.94 *(978-0-7660-2256-0(0))* Enslow Pubs., Inc.

Golosi, Rosanne. Best Friends Forever! Martini, Angela, illus. 2005. 64p. (J). *(978-0-439-80072-3(2))* Scholastic, Inc.

Good, Keith. Shape It! Magnificent Projects for Molding Materials. 2008. (Design It! Ser.). (ENG.). 32p. (gr. 4-6). pap. 6.95 *(978-0-8225-9927-2(9))* Lerner Publishing Group.

Goodings, Christina. Christmas - Fun Things to Make & Do. 2017. (ENG.). 104p. (J). (gr. k-2). spiral bd. 9.99 ***(978-0-7459-7616-7(6))*** Lion Hudson PLC GBR. Dist: Independent Pubs. Group.

—Whizzy Bizzy Christmas Fun Book. 2004. (ENG., Illus.). 32p. (J). (gr. k-4). pap. 5.50 *(978-0-7459-4888-1(X))* Lion Hudson PLC GBR. Dist: Independent Pubs. Group.

—25 Crafts for a Rainy Day. Meredith, Samantha, illus. 2016. (ENG.). 32p. (J). (gr. k-2). pap. 9.99 *(978-0-7459-7672-3(7))* Lion Hudson PLC GBR. Dist: Independent Pubs. Group.

Gors, Steven E. The Secret Files of Professor L. Otto Funn: Or, Stop Being a Slug, Open This Book, & Make Your Brain Happy. Carrington, Matt, illus. 2013. 159p. (J). pap. *(978-0-7166-1324-4(7))* World Bk., Inc.

Gould, Roberta. The Kid's Book of Incredibly Fun Crafts. Martin Jourdenais, Norma Jean, illus. 2004. (Williamson's Kids Can! Ser.). 128p. (J). pap. 14.95 *(978-1-885593-85-6(6),* Ideal Pubns.) Worthy Publishing.

—The Kids' Multicultural Craft Book: 35 Crafts from Around the World. Jourdenais, Norma Jean, illus. 2004. (Williamson Multicultural Kids Can! Book Ser.). (ENG.). 128p. (J). pap. 14.29 *(978-1-885593-91-7(0),* Ideal Pubns.) Worthy Publishing.

Green Crafts. 2010. (Green Crafts Ser.). 32p. (ENG.). (gr. 3-4). lib. bdg. 167.94 *(978-1-4296-5460-9(0))*; (ENG.). (gr. 3-4). lib. bdg. 55.98 *(978-1-4296-5459-3(7))*; (ENG.). (gr. 3-4). lib. bdg. 111.96 *(978-1-4296-4768-7(X))*; (ENG.). (gr. 3-4). lib. bdg. 55.98 *(978-1-4296-4769-4(8))*; lib. bdg. 106.60 *(978-1-4296-5862-1(2))*; (ENG.). (gr. 3-4). lib. bdg. 55.98 *(978-1-4296-4426-6(5))* Capstone Press of Coughlan Cos. (Snap Bks.).

Green, Gail. The Kids' Guide to Projects for Your Pet, 1 vol. 2012. (Kids' Guides). (ENG.). 32p. (gr. 3-4). lib. bdg. 27.99 *(978-1-4296-7662-5(0),* Edge Bks.) Capstone Press of Coughlan Cos.

Green, Jen. The Celts & the Iron Age. 2016. (Discover Through Craft Ser.). (ENG., Illus.). 32p. (J). (gr. 2-4). pap. 12.99 *(978-1-4451-3749-0(6),* Franklin Watts) Hachette Children's Group GBR. Dist: Hachette Bk. Group.

—Projects with Plants. 2014. (Make & Learn Ser.). (Illus.). 32p. (J). (gr. 3-6). 27.50 *(978-1-4777-7161-7(1),* PowerKids Pr.) Rosen Publishing Group, Inc., The.

—Projects with the Seaside. 2014. (Make & Learn Ser.). (Illus.). 32p. (J). (gr. 3-6). lib. bdg. 27.50 *(978-1-4777-7173-0(5),* PowerKids Pr.) Rosen Publishing Group, Inc., The.

—The Stone Age & Bronze Age. 2016. (Discover Through Craft Ser.). (ENG., Illus.). 32p. (J). (gr. 1-3). pap. 12.99 *(978-1-4451-3746-9(1),* Franklin Watts) Hachette Children's Group GBR. Dist: Hachette Bk. Group.

Grossman, Mahesh. The Silly Rubber Band Handbook: The Ultimate Guide to Collecting & Trading Shaped Bandz. 2010. (Customs & Etiquette Pocket Guides Ser.). 60p. (J). pap. 3.99 *(978-1-933174-90-7(0))* 10 Finger Pr.

Gulati, Annette. Build a Neighborhood Library. Stewart, Roger, illus. 2016. (Earth-Friendly Projects Ser.). (ENG.). 24p. (J). (gr. 2-5). 28.50 *(978-1-5038-0790-7(8),* 210623) Child's World, Inc., The.

—Thanksgiving Crafts. Gallagher-Cole, Mernie, illus. 2016. (Holiday Crafts Ser.). (ENG.). 24p. (J). (gr. k-3). 28.50 *(978-1-5038-0821-8(1),* 210657) Child's World, Inc., The.

Haab, Rachel. Hadas. Esteve, Laura, tr. Esparza, Bob, photos by. 2005. (SPA., Illus.). 38p. (J). spiral bd. 20.95 *(978-987-1078-27-1(7))* Klutz Latino MEX. Dist: Independent Pubs. Group.

Haab, Sherri. Clay So Cute! 21 Polymer Clay Projects for Cool Charms, Itty-Bitty Animals, & Tiny Treasures. 2009. (ENG.). 112p. pap. 14.95 *(978-0-8230-9899-6(0),* Potter Craft) Potter/TenSpeed/Harmony.

—Creative Kids Complete Photo Guide to Braiding & Knotting. 2016. (Creative Kids Ser.). (ENG., Illus.). 144p. pap. 19.99 *(978-1-58923-937-1(7),* Creative Publishing International) Quarto Publishing Group USA.

—Unas Divertidas. 2005. (SPA., Illus.). 59p. (J). (gr. 4-7). 23.95 *(978-968-5528-12-2(8))* Klutz Latino MEX. Dist: Independent Pubs. Group.

Halls, Kelly Milner. Look What You Can Make with Craft Sticks. Halls, Kelly Milner, ed. Schneider, Hank & Filipski, J. W., photos by. 2013. (Look What You Can Make Ser.). (ENG., Illus.). 48p. (J). (gr. k-7). pap. 6.95 *(978-1-56397-997-2(7))* Boyds Mills Pr.

Halstead, Rachel & Reid, Struan. Everyday Life in the Ancient World: Learn about Houses, Homes & What the Romans, Celts, Egyptians & Other Peoples of the Past Used to Eat. 2009. (ENG., Illus.). 64p. (J). (gr. 4-7). pap. 7.99 *(978-1-84476-711-3(6))* Anness Publishing GBR. Dist: National Bk. Network.

—120 Great History Projects: Bring the Past into the Present with Hours of Creative Activity. 2016. (ENG.). 256p. (J). (gr. -1-12). pap. 14.99 *(978-1-84309-368-8(5),* Armadillo) Anness Publishing GBR. Dist: National Bk. Network.

Hammonds, Heather. Modellieren MIT Knete. 2005. (GER., Illus.). 64p. (J). *(978-3-937495-94-1(0))* Mud Puddle, Inc.

Handmade Holiday Crafts. 2016. (Handmade Holiday Crafts Ser.). 00032p. (J). lib. bdg. 159.60 ***(978-1-4824-6194-7(3))*** Stevens, Gareth Publishing LLLP.

Hannah, Sue. Crafty Concoctions: 101 Craft Supply Recipes. 2003. (Illus.). xi, 140p. (J). 7.95 *(978-0-88166-462-1(6))* Meadowbrook Pr.

Hanson, Anders & Mann, Elissa. Cool Paper Folding: Creative Activities That Make Math & Science Fun for Kids!, 1 vol. 2013. (Cool Art with Math & Science Ser.). (ENG.). 32p. (J). (gr. 3-6). lib. bdg. 28.50 *(978-1-61783-823-1(3),* Checkerboard Library) ABDO Publishing Co.

—Cool String Art: Creative Activities That Make Math & Science Fun for Kids!, 1 vol. 2013. (Cool Art with Math & Science Ser.). (ENG.). 32p. (J). (gr. 3-6). lib. bdg. 28.50 *(978-1-61783-824-8(1),* Checkerboard Library) ABDO Publishing Co.

Harbo, Christopher. Origami Paperpalooza. 2015. (Origami Paperpalooza Ser.). (ENG.). 32p. (gr. 3-4). lib. bdg. 111.96 *(978-1-4914-2548-0(2),* Edge Bks.) Capstone Press of Coughlan Cos.

Harbo, Christopher L. Origami Explosion: Scorpions, Whales, Boxes, & More! 2015. (Origami Paperpalooza Ser.). (ENG.). 32p. (gr. 3-4). lib. bdg. 27.99 *(978-1-4914-2023-2(5))* Capstone Press of Coughlan Cos.

—Origami Folding Frenzy: Boats, Fish, Cranes, & More! 2015. (Origami Paperpalooza Ser.). (ENG.). 32p. (gr. 3-4). lib. bdg. 27.99 *(978-1-4914-2021-8(9))* Capstone Press of Coughlan Cos.

—Origami Palooza: Dragons, Turtles, Birds, & More! 2015. (Origami Paperpalooza Ser.). (ENG.). 32p. (gr. 3-4). lib. bdg. 27.99 *(978-1-4914-2024-9(3))* Capstone Press of Coughlan Cos.

—Origami Paperpalooza! 2015. (ENG., Illus.). 144p. (gr. 3-4). pap. 14.95 *(978-1-62370-227-4(5))* Capstone Press of Coughlan Cos.

—Origami Papertainment: Samurai, Owls, Ninja Stars, & More! 2015. (Origami Paperpalooza Ser.). (ENG.). 32p. (gr. 3-4). lib. bdg. 27.99 *(978-1-4914-2022-5(7))* Capstone Press of Coughlan Cos.

Hardy, Emma. My First Craft Book. Akass, Susan, ed. 2011. (ENG., Illus.). 128p. (J). (gr. 7-7). pap. 14.95 *(978-1-907563-34-8(2),* CICO Books) Ryland Peters & Small GBR. Dist: WIPRO.

Harrington, Jamie. The Unofficial Guide to Crafting the World of Harry Potter: 30 Magical Crafts for Muggles, Witches, & Wizards Alike. 2016. (ENG., Illus.). 192p. pap. 17.99 *(978-1-4405-9504-2(6))* Adams Media Corp.

Hartman, Sarah. Asian-American Crafts Kids Can Do! 2006. (Multicultural Crafts Kids Can Do! Ser.). (Illus.). 32p. (J). (gr. 3-4). lib. bdg. 23.94 *(978-0-7660-2455-7(5),* Enslow Elementary) Enslow Pubs., Inc.

—Middle Eastern Crafts Kids Can Do! Ponte, June, illus. 2006. (Multicultural Crafts Kids Can Do! Ser.). 32p. (J). (gr. 3-4). lib. bdg. 23.94 *(978-0-7660-2456-4(3),* Enslow Elementary) Enslow Pubs., Inc.

Hauser, Jill Frankel. Little Hands Celebrate America! Learning about the U.S.A Through Crafts & Activities. 2004. (Williamson's Little Hands Book Ser.). (ENG., Illus.). 128p. (J). 14.29 *(978-1-885593-93-1(7),* Ideal Pubns.) Worthy Publishing.

Hayn, Carter. Bo's Seed Pot. 2015. (Rosen REAL Readers: STEM & STEAM Collection). (ENG.). 12p. (gr. 1-2). pap. 6.33 *(978-1-4994-9855-4(1),* Rosen Classroom) Rosen Publishing Group, Inc., The.

Heller, D. M. Let's Make a Dump Truck with Everyday Materials. 2009. (Let's Do Arts & Crafts Ser.). 24p. (gr. 2-2). 42.50 *(978-1-61514-197-5(9),* PowerKids Pr.) Rosen Publishing Group, Inc., The.

—Let's Make a Fish with Everyday Materials. 2009. (Let's Do Arts & Crafts Ser.). 24p. (gr. 2-2). 42.50 *(978-1-61514-198-2(7),* PowerKids Pr.) Rosen Publishing Group, Inc., The.

—Let's Make a Lion with Everyday Materials. (Let's Do Arts & Crafts Ser.). 24p. 2009. (gr. 2-2). 42.50 *(978-1-61514-199-9(5),* PowerKids Pr.) 2006. (Illus.). (J). 22.60 *(978-1-4042-3060-6(2))* Rosen Publishing Group, Inc., The.

—Let's Make a Monkey with Everyday Materials. 2009. (Let's Do Arts & Crafts Ser.). 24p. (gr. 2-2). 42.50 *(978-1-61514-200-2(2),* PowerKids Pr.) Rosen Publishing Group, Inc., The.

—Let's Make an Owl with Everyday Materials. (Let's Do Arts & Crafts Ser.). 24p. 2009. (gr. 2-2). 42.50 *(978-1-61514-201-9(0),* PowerKids Pr.) 2006. (Illus.). (J). lib. bdg. 22.60 *(978-1-4042-3063-7(7))* Rosen Publishing Group, Inc., The.

Henley, Karyn. Arts & Crafts, Volume 1: Bible Story Activities for ages 2 To 5, Vol. 1. 2004. (J). per. 19.99 *(978-1-933803-00-5(2))* Child Sensitive Communication, LLC.

—Arts & Crafts, Volume 2: Bible Story Activities for ages 2 To 5, Vol. 2. 2004. (J). per. 19.99 *(978-1-933803-01-2(0),* AC2) Child Sensitive Communication, LLC.

Henry, Sally & Cook, Trevor. Cool Stuff to Do: Jam-Packed with Brilliant Things to Make & Do! 2012. (ENG.). 128p. (J). pap. 9.95 *(978-1-84858-084-8(3))* Arcturus Publishing GBR. Dist: Bookmasters Distribution.

—Making Masks. 2010. (Make Your Own Art Ser.). (Illus.). 32p. (J). pap. 11.75 *(978-1-4488-1613-2(0))*; (gr. 3-6). 26.50 *(978-1-4488-1583-8(5))* Rosen Publishing Group, Inc., The. (PowerKids Pr.).

Henry, Sandi. Making Amazing Art! 40 Activities Using the 7 Elements of Art Design. Cole, Sarah, illus. (ENG.). 128p. (J). (gr. 3-7). 2008. pap. 12.99 *(978-0-8249-6795-6(X))* 2007. 16.99 *(978-0-8249-6794-9(1))* Worthy Publishing. (Ideal Pubns.).

Higham, Cindy. Snowflakes for All Seasons: 72 Fold & Cut Paper Snowflakes, 1 vol. 2004. Orig. Title: Snowflakes Made Easy & Fun. (ENG., Illus.). 80p. pap. 9.99 *(978-1-58685-528-4(X))* Gibbs Smith, Publisher.

Highlights for Children Editorial Staff. Look What You Can Make with Plastic Containers. Schneider, Hank & Filipski, J. W., photos by. 2013. (Look What You Can Make Ser.). (ENG., Illus.). 48p. (J). (gr. k). pap. 6.95 *(978-1-62091-533-2(2))* Boyds Mills Pr.

Highlights for Children Editorial Staff & Boyds Mills Press Staff. Look What You Can Make with Paper Plates: Creative Crafts from Everyday Objects. Richmond, Margie Hayes, ed. Schneider, Hank, photos by. 2013. (Look What You Can Make Ser.). (ENG., Illus.). 48p. (J). (gr. k-7). pap., stu. ed. 6.95 *(978-1-56397-643-8(9))* Boyds Mills Pr.

Ho, Jannie. Stuck on Fun! Play with Patterns, Sticker Tape, & More! 2016. (Kids Craft Kit Ser.). (ENG., Illus.). 40p. (J). (gr. k-3). 14.95 *(978-1-63322-140-6(7),* Walter Foster Jr) Quarto Publishing Group USA.

Hoffman, Joan. Preschool Practice. 2007. (ENG.). 32p. (J). pap. 3.99 *(978-1-60159-116-6(0))* School Zone Publishing Co.

Holland, Gini. Holiday Crafts. 2013. (From Trash to Treasure Ser.). 32p. (J). (gr. 3-6). 26.50 *(978-1-4777-1286-3(0))*; pap. 11.75 *(978-1-4777-1366-2(2))* Rosen Publishing Group, Inc., The. (PowerKids Pr.).

Hollein, Nina & Hollein, Max. Cut-Out Fun with Matisse. 2014. (ENG., Illus.). 40p. (J). (gr. 3-7). pap. 9.95 *(978-3-7913-7192-4(4))* Prestel Verlag GmbH & Co KG. DEU. Dist: Penguin Random Hse. LLC.

Hollow, Michele C. Nifty Thrifty Math Crafts. Ponte, June, illus. 2007. (Nifty Thrifty Crafts for Kids Ser.). 32p. (J). (gr. 3-4). lib. bdg. 23.94 *(978-0-7660-2781-7(3),* 1264782, Enslow Elementary) Enslow Pubs., Inc.

—Nifty Thrifty Sports Crafts. Ponte, June, illus. 2007. (Nifty Thrifty Crafts for Kids Ser.). 32p. (J). (gr. 3-4). lib. bdg. 23.94 *(978-0-7660-2782-4(1),* Enslow Elementary) Enslow Pubs., Inc.

Holzweiss, Kristina. Amazing MakerSpace DIY Fliers. 2017. (True Book — MakerSpace Projects Ser.). (ENG.). 48p. (J). lib. bdg. 31.00 ***(978-0-531-23846-2(6),*** Children's Pr.) Scholastic Library Publishing.

—Amazing Makerspace DIY Movers. 2017. (True Book — MakerSpace Projects Ser.). (ENG.). 48p. (J). lib. bdg. 31.00 ***(978-0-531-23847-9(4),*** Children's Pr.) Scholastic Library Publishing.

Holzweiss, Kristina & Barth, Amy. I Can Make Exciting Electronics. 2017. (Rookie Star — MakerSpace Projects Ser.). (ENG.). 32p. (J). pap. 5.95 ***(978-0-531-23880-6(6))***; lib. bdg. 25.00 ***(978-0-531-23411-2(8))*** Scholastic Library Publishing. (Children's Pr.).

—I Can Make Fantastic Flyers. 2017. (Rookie Star — MakerSpace Projects Ser.). (ENG.). 32p. (J). lib. bdg. 25.00 ***(978-0-531-23412-9(6),*** Children's Pr.) Scholastic Library Publishing.

—I Can Make Marvelous Movers. 2017. (Rookie Star — MakerSpace Projects Ser.). (ENG.). 32p. (J). lib. bdg. 25.00 ***(978-0-531-23413-6(4),*** Children's Pr.) Scholastic Library Publishing.

Holzweiss, Kristina A. Fliers. 2017. (True Book — MakerSpace Projects Ser.). (ENG.). 48p. (J). pap. 7.95 ***(978-0-531-24097-7(5),*** Children's Pr.) Scholastic Library Publishing.

Hopping, Lucy. My First Pompom Book: 35 Fantastic & Fun Projects for Children Aged 7+ 2017. (ENG., Illus.). 128p. (J). (gr. 7-11). pap. 14.95 *(978-1-78249-444-7(8),* CICO Books) Ryland Peters & Small GBR. Dist: WIPRO.

Hord, Colleen. How to Make a Kite. 2015. (ENG.). 24p. (gr. k-3). 28.50 *(978-1-63430-355-2(5))* Rourke Educational Media.

How-To Library (Set), 26 vols. 2014. (How-To Library). (ENG.). 32p. (J). (gr. 3-6). pap. 369.46 *(978-1-63137-796-9(5),* 205348) Cherry Lake Publishing.

How to Make a Sun Hat. (gr. -1-2). 23.00 *(978-0-7635-9011-6(8))* Rigby Education.

Huff, Abby. Draw Your Own Animal Zendoodles. Scudamore, Angelika et al, illus. 2017. (Draw Your Own Zendoodles Ser.). (ENG.). 48p. (gr. 4-5). lib. bdg. 31.32 *(978-1-5157-4840-3(5))* Capstone Press of Coughlan Cos.

—Draw Your Own Fairy Tale Zendoodles. Preston, Lizzie et al, illus. 2017. (Draw Your Own Zendoodles Ser.). (ENG.). 48p. (gr. 4-5). lib. bdg. 31.32 *(978-1-5157-4842-7(1))* Capstone Press of Coughlan Cos.

—Draw Your Own Lettering & Decorative Zendoodles. Grover, James et al, illus. 2017. (Draw Your Own Zendoodles Ser.). (ENG.). 48p. (gr. 4-5). lib. bdg. 31.32 *(978-1-5157-4841-0(3))* Capstone Press of Coughlan Cos.

Humphrey, Paul. How to Make a Present. Fairclough, Chris, photos by. 2007. (Crafty Kids Ser.). (Illus.). 24p. (J). (gr. -1-3). lib. bdg. 24.25 *(978-1-59771-103-6(9))* Sea-To-Sea Pubns.

Hurdman, Charlotte. Hands-on History! Stone Age. 2013. (ENG., Illus.). 64p. (J). (gr. k-3). 12.99 *(978-1-84322-974-2(9),* Armadillo) Anness Publishing GBR. Dist: National Bk. Network.

Hutnick, Theresa & Phillips, Karen. Insectos Insolitos. Fox, Peter, photos by. 2005. (SPA., Illus.). 38p. (J). spiral bd. 17.95 *(978-987-1078-43-1(9))* Klutz Latino MEX. Dist: Independent Pubs. Group.

I Love Crafts. 2016. (I Love Crafts Ser.). 32p. (gr. 3-3). 165.00 *(978-1-5081-5037-4(0))*; pap. 70.50 *(978-1-4994-2448-5(5))* Rosen Publishing Group, Inc., The. (PowerKids Pr.).

Icanberry, Mark. LooLeDo. 96p. Bk. 1. 2010. (Illus.). 12.95 *(978-1-893327-12-2(4))*Bk. 2. 2011. 14.95 *(978-1-893327-11-5(6))*Bk. 3. 2011. 14.95 *(978-1-893327-10-8(8))* Look, Learn & Do Pubns.

Ikids Staff. Made with Love for Mom. Kalis, Jennifer, illus. 2008. (ENG.). 24p. (J). (gr. 1-17). 7.99 *(978-1-58476-660-5(3),* IKIDS) Innovative Kids.

I'm an Artist: Individual Title Six-Packs. (Literatura 2000 Ser.). (gr. 2-3). 33.00 *(978-0-7635-0202-7(2))* Rigby Education.

Imamori, Mitsuhiko. Everybody Kirigami! 2014. (ENG., Illus.). 88p. pap. 18.95 *(978-1-939130-17-4(4),* Vertical) Kodansha America, Inc.

Instructables.com Staff. The Ultimate Unofficial Rainbow Loom Handbook: Step-by-Step Instructions to Stitching, Weaving, & Looping Colorful Bracelets, Rings, Charms, & More. 2015. (ENG., Illus.). 192p. (gr. k). pap. 14.95 *(978-1-63450-049-4(0),* Sky Pony Pr.) Skyhorse Publishing Co., Inc.

Irvine, Joan & Hendry, Linda. Outside the Box! Creative Activities for Ecology-Minded Kids. Hendry, Linda, illus. 2009. (Dover Children's Activity Bks.). (ENG., Illus.). 96p. (J). (gr. 2-5). pap. 8.99 *(978-0-486-47000-9(8))* Dover Pubns., Inc.

Issa, Joanna. I Can Make a Bunch of Flowers, 1 vol. 2014. (What Can I Make Today? Ser.). (ENG., Illus.). 24p. (gr. k-2). 22.65 *(978-1-4846-0460-1(1),* Heinemann Read & Learn) Heinemann-Raintree.

—I Can Make a Mask, 1 vol. 2014. (What Can I Make Today? Ser.). (ENG., Illus.). 24p. (gr. k-2). 22.65 *(978-1-4846-0461-8(X),* Heinemann Read & Learn) Heinemann-Raintree.

—I Can Make a Truck, 1 vol. 2014. (What Can I Make Today? Ser.). (ENG., Illus.). 24p. (gr. k-2). 22.65 *(978-1-4846-0462-5(8),* Heinemann Read & Learn) Heinemann-Raintree.

—What Can I Make Today?, 1 vol. 2014. (What Can I Make Today? Ser.). (ENG.). 24p. (gr. k-2). 67.95 *(978-1-4846-0463-2(6),* Heinemann Read & Learn) Heinemann-Raintree.

J., Mary & Davis, Wayne R. Spur of the Moment Preschool. 2005. (Godprints Bible Funstuff Ser.). 112p. pap., pap. 16.99 *(978-0-7814-4230-5(3),* 0781442303) Cook, David C.

Jacobs, Daniel. Patterns. 2005. (Yellow Umbrella Fluent Level Ser.). (ENG., Illus.). 16p. (gr. k-1). pap. 35.70 *(978-0-7368-5317-0(0),* Yellow Umbrella Bks.) Capstone Press of Coughlan Cos.

Jalali, Yassaman. Celebrating Norouz (Persian New Year) Zamanian, Marjan, illus. 2003. 28p. (J). (gr. -1-6). pap. 12.99 *(978-0-9728020-0-0(2))* Saman Publishing.

Jeffus, Sharon, as told by. Artsy Animals: In the Ocean. 2006. (Illus.). 55p. (J). 19.95 *(978-0-9715970-6-8(5))* Visual Manna.

Jennings, Terry. Wood. 2006. (Illus.). 32p. (YA). (gr. 1-18). lib. bdg. 27.10 *(978-1-932333-00-8(2))* Chrysalis Education.

Jewelry. 2013. (From Trash to Treasure Ser.). 32p. (J). (gr. 3-6). pap. 70.50 *(978-1-4777-1361-7(1),* PowerKids Pr.) Rosen Publishing Group, Inc., The.

Jocelyn, Marthe. Sneaky Art: Crafty Surprises to Hide in Plain Sight. Jocelyn, Marthe, illus. 2013. (ENG., Illus.). 64p. (J). (gr. 3-7). 12.99 *(978-0-7636-5648-5(8))* Candlewick Pr.

Johnson, Anne Akers. Juegos con una Cuerda. 2004. Orig. Title: Cat's Cradle: A Book of String Figures. (SPA., Illus.). 36p. (J). spiral bd. 11.95 *(978-968-5528-14-6(4))* Klutz Latino MEX. Dist: Independent Pubs. Group.

—Make Your Own Washi Tape Stickers. 2014. (ENG.). 44p. (J). (gr. 3). 16.99 *(978-0-545-64776-2(2))* Klutz.

—Trenzas Locas. 2005. (SPA., Illus.). 32p. (J). spiral bd. 17.95 *(978-968-5528-06-1(3))* Klutz Latino MEX. Dist: Independent Pubs. Group.

Johnson, Anne Akers, ed. Bead Loom Bracelets. 2008. (ENG., Illus.). 60p. (J). (gr. 7). 24.95 *(978-1-59174-504-4(7))* Klutz.

Johnson, Susan & Johnson, Wil. Making Collages. 2003. (Illus.). 32p. (J). pap. 6.00 *(978-1-59034-183-4(X))* Mondo Publishing.

Jones, Jen. Planning Perfect Parties: The Girls' Guide to Fun, Fresh, Unforgettable Events. 2014. (Craft It Yourself Ser.). (ENG.). 128p. (gr. 3-4). pap. 14.95 *(978-1-62370-063-8(9))* Capstone Young Readers of Coughlan Cos.

Jones, Jen & Sirrine, Carol. Re-Craft: Unique Projects That Look Great (And Save the Planet) 2011. (Craft It Yourself Ser.). (ENG.). 112p. (gr. 3-4). pap. 12.95 *(978-1-4296-6637-4(4))* Capstone Young Readers of Coughlan Cos.

Jovinelly, Joann. The Crafts & Culture of a Medieval Cathedral. 2009. (Crafts & Cultures of the Middle Ages Ser.). 48p. (gr. 5-5). 58.50 *(978-1-61512-054-3(8),* Rosen Reference) Rosen Publishing Group, Inc., The.

—The Crafts & Culture of a Medieval Guild. 2009. (Crafts & Cultures of the Middle Ages Ser.). 48p. (gr. 5-5). 58.50 *(978-1-61512-055-0(6),* Rosen Reference) Rosen Publishing Group, Inc., The.

—The Crafts & Culture of a Medieval Manor. 2009. (Crafts & Cultures of the Middle Ages Ser.). 48p. (gr. 5-5). 58.50 *(978-1-61512-053-6(X),* Rosen Reference) Rosen Publishing Group, Inc., The.

—The Crafts & Culture of a Medieval Monastery. 2009. (Crafts & Cultures of the Middle Ages Ser.). 48p. (gr. 5-5). 58.50 *(978-1-61512-056-7(4),* Rosen Reference) Rosen Publishing Group, Inc., The.

—The Crafts & Culture of the Ancient Greeks. 2009. (Crafts of the Ancient World Ser.). 48p. (gr. 5-8). 58.50 *(978-1-61512-063-5(7),* Rosen Reference) Rosen Publishing Group, Inc., The.

—The Crafts & Culture of the Aztecs. 2009. (Crafts of the Ancient World Ser.). 48p. (gr. 5-8). 58.50 *(978-1-61512-064-2(5),* Rosen Reference) Rosen Publishing Group, Inc., The.

—The Crafts & Culture of the Romans. 2009. (Crafts of the Ancient World Ser.). 48p. (gr. 5-8). 58.50 *(978-1-61512-065-9(3),* Rosen Reference) Rosen Publishing Group, Inc., The.

Jovinelly, Joann & Netelkos, Jason. The Crafts & Culture of a Medieval Cathedral. 2006. (Crafts & Cultures of the Middle Ages Ser.). (Illus.). 48p. (J). (gr. 3-7). lib. bdg. 29.25 *(978-1-4042-0758-5(9))* Rosen Publishing Group, Inc., The.

—The Crafts & Culture of a Medieval Guild. 2006. (Crafts & Cultures of the Middle Ages Ser.). (Illus.). 48p. (J). (gr. 3-7). lib. bdg. 29.25 *(978-1-4042-0757-8(0))* Rosen Publishing Group, Inc., The.

—The Crafts & Culture of a Medieval Manor. 2006. (Crafts & Cultures of the Middle Ages Ser.). (Illus.). 48p. (J). (gr. 3-7). lib. bdg. 29.25 *(978-1-4042-0756-1(2))* Rosen Publishing Group, Inc., The.

—The Crafts & Culture of a Medieval Monastery. 2006. (Crafts & Cultures of the Middle Ages Ser.). (Illus.). 48p. (J). (gr. 4-8). lib. bdg. 29.25 *(978-1-4042-0759-2(7))* Rosen Publishing Group, Inc., The.

Kachidurian, Debbie, et al. Accessorize Yourself! 77 Projects to Personalize Your Look. 2016. (Craft It Yourself Ser.). (ENG., Illus.). 144p. (gr. 3-4). pap. 14.95 *(978-1-62370-645-6(9))* Capstone Young Readers of Coughlan Cos.

—Bring on the Bling! Bracelets, Anklets, & Rings for All Occasions. 2016. (Accessorize Yourself! Ser.). (ENG., Illus.). 48p. (gr. 4-5). lib. bdg. 34.65 *(978-1-4914-8231-5(1))* Capstone Press of Coughlan Cos.

Kachidurian, Debbie Prestine, et al. Bring on the Bling! Bracelets, Anklets, & Rings for All Occasions. 2017. (Illus.). 47p. (J). pap. *(978-1-4914-8621-4(X))* Capstone Press of Coughlan Cos.

Kaehler, Lorie King. Chalk on the Wild Side. 2016. (DIY Ser.). (ENG., Illus.). 128p. (J). (gr. 3-8). 34.65 *(978-1-942875-11-6(8),* Walter Foster Jr) Quarto Publishing Group USA.

Kavin, Kim & Hetland, Beth. Native Americans: Discover the History & Cultures of the First Americans with 15 Projects. 2013. (Build It Yourself Ser.). (ENG., Illus.). 128p. (J). (gr. 3-7). 21.95 *(978-1-61930-175-7(X))*; pap. 16.95 *(978-1-61930-170-2(9))* Open City Bks.

Kaye, Teri, ed. Christmas Crafts on a Budget: Over 100 Project Ideas. 2005. 19.99 *(978-0-9759638-2-1(1))* Gizmo Enterprises, Inc.

Kemarskaya, Oksana. Planet Earth Projects. 2011. (Dover Children's Activity Bks.). (ENG., Illus.). 64p. (J). (gr. 3-5). pap. 6.99 *(978-0-486-47923-1(4))* Dover Pubns., Inc.

Kenney, Karen Latchana. Super Simple Art to Wear: Fun & Easy-to-Make Crafts for Kids, 1 vol. 2009. (Super Simple Crafts Ser.). (ENG., Illus.). 32p. (gr. k-4). 27.07

(978-1-60453-622-5(5), Super SandCastle) ABDO Publishing Co.
—Super Simple Crafts, 6 vols., Set. Incl. Super Simple Art to Wear: Fun & Easy-to-Make Crafts for Kids. 27.07 (978-1-60453-622-5(5)); Super Simple Clay Projects: Fun & Easy-to-Make Crafts for Kids. 27.07 (978-1-60453-623-2(3)); Super Simple Glass Jar Art: Fun & Easy-to-Make Crafts for Kids. 27.07 (978-1-60453-624-9(1)); Super Simple Jewelry: Fun & Easy-to-Make Crafts for Kids. 27.07 (978-1-60453-625-6(X)); Super Simple Magnets: Fun & Easy-to-Make Crafts for Kids. 27.07 (978-1-60453-626-3(8)); Super Simple Masks: Fun & Easy-to-Make Crafts for Kids. 27.07 (978-1-60453-627-0(6)); (gr. k-4). (Super Simple Crafts Ser.). (Illus.). 32p. 2009. 162.42 (978-1-60453-621-8(7), Super SandCastle) ABDO Publishing Co.
—Super Simple Glass Jar Art: Fun & Easy-to-Make Crafts for Kids, 1 vol. 2009. (Super Simple Crafts Ser.). (ENG., Illus.). 32p. (gr. k-4). 27.07 (978-1-60453-624-9(1), Super SandCastle) ABDO Publishing Co.
—Super Simple Magnets: Fun & Easy-to-Make Crafts for Kids, 1 vol. 2009. (Super Simple Crafts Ser.). (ENG., Illus.). 32p. (gr. k-4). 27.07 (978-1-60453-626-3(8), Super SandCastle) ABDO Publishing Co.
Kerr, Sophie. A Kid's Guide to Sewing: 16 Projects You'll Love to Make & Use. 2013. (ENG., Illus.). 144p. (J). (gr. 6-9). pap. 21.95 (978-1-60705-751-2(4), FunStitch Studio) C & T Publishing.
Kimberl, Karen. A Tea Party for All Seasons. 2012. 56p. pap. 21.95 (978-1-4685-4210-3(9)) AuthorHouse.
King, David C. Projects about the Ancient Aztecs. 2006. (Hands-On History Ser.). (Illus.). 48p. (gr. 3-7). lib. bdg. 21.95 (978-0-7614-2256-3(0), Benchmark Bks.) Marshall Cavendish Corp.
Kingloff, Amanda. Project Kid - Crafts That Go! 60 Imaginative Projects That Fly, Sail, Race, & Dive. 2016. (ENG., Illus.). 272p. (J). pap. 19.95 (978-1-57965-683-6(8)) Artisan.
Kinmont, Ritchie. Every Kid Needs Things That Fly, 1 vol. Casey, Robert, photos by. 2005. (ENG., Illus.). 136p. (J). pap. 14.95 (978-1-58685-509-3(3), 1241179) Gibbs Smith, Publisher.
Klutz Boondoggle 24-pack. (J). (978-1-878257-78-9(1)) Klutz.
Klutz Editors. Arte en Ventanas. 2004. (SPA., Illus.). 62p. (J). spiral bd. 23.95 (978-968-5528-16-0(0)) Klutz Latino MEX. Dist: Independent Pubs. Group.
—Charm Bracelet Studio. 2015. (ENG.). 56p. (J). (gr. 3-7). 24.99 (978-0-545-85848-9(8)) Klutz.
—Design & Dye with No-Heat Batik. 2015. (ENG.). 48p. (J). (gr. 3-7). 21.99 (978-0-545-85843-4(7)) Klutz.
—Design Your Own Charm Watch. 2005. (ENG., Illus.). 26p. (YA). 21.95 (978-1-57054-212-1(0)) Klutz.
—Doodlewire. 2010. (ENG.). 40p. (J). (gr. 3). 14.99 (978-1-59174-843-4(7)) Klutz.
—Make Glitter Clay Charms. 2015. (ENG.). 48p. (J). (gr. 3-7). 21.99 (978-0-545-85846-5(1)) Klutz.
—Personalized Friendship Bracelets. 2015. (ENG.). 58p. (J). (gr. 5-9). 16.99 (978-0-545-85856-4(9)) Klutz.
—Pop Collage: Make Your Stuff Stand Out! 2015. (ENG.). 56p. (J). (gr. 3-7). 21.99 (978-0-545-85863-2(1)) Klutz.
Klutz Editors, contrib. by. The Cootie Catcher Book. 2009. (ENG.). 70p. (J). (gr. 1). 14.95 (978-1-59174-680-5(9)) Klutz.
—SlingChute. (ENG.). (J). 14.95 (978-1-57054-581-8(2)) Klutz.
—Window Art Deluxe Refill Set. (ENG.). (J). 19.95 (978-1-57054-798-0(X)) Klutz.
Klutz Editors, ed. Glossy Bands: Stretchy Bracelets to Share with Your Friends. 2010. (ENG.). 40p. (J). (gr. 3-18). 19.95 (978-1-59174-730-7(9)) Klutz.
—Why I Love My Dad. 2009. (ENG.). 10p. (J). (gr. 1). 12.95 (978-1-59174-656-0(6)) Klutz.
Klutz Editors & Scholastic Book Editors. Pom-Pom Kitties. 2017. (ENG.). 56p. (J). (gr. 3-7). 19.99 (978-1-338-10643-5(0)) Klutz.
Klutz Slappies Leopard Dash Animal Bracelet. (J). 4.95 (978-1-57054-616-7(9)) Klutz.
Klutz Slappies Lion Ruff Animal Bracelet. (J). 4.95 (978-1-57054-627-3(4)) Klutz.
Klutz Slappies Spotted Dog Pepper Anim Bracelet. (J). 4.95 (978-1-57054-629-7(0)) Klutz.
Knighton, Kate. 50 Easter Things to Make & Do. 2009. (50 Easter Things to Make & Do Ser.). 104p. (J). (gr. 1). spiral bd. 9.99 (978-0-7945-2206-3(8), Usborne) EDC Publishing.
Knox, Joy, compiled by. Croppin' Dictum: Big, Strong Titles. 2004. (YA). spiral bd. (978-0-9754972-1-0(9)) JoyRox, LLC.
—Croppin' Dictum: Travel & Holiday. 2004. (YA). spiral bd. (978-0-9754972-2-7(7)) JoyRox, LLC.
Kohl, MaryAnn F. & Zaborowski, Barbara. Action ART: Hands-On Active Art Adventures. 2015. (Bright Ideas for Learning (TM) Ser.: 9). (ENG., Illus.). 144p. (J). (gr. -1-7). pap. 21.95 (978-0-935607-34-5(X)) Chicago Review Pr., Inc.
Kollmar, Elizabeth M. Hooked on Rubber Band Jewelry: 12 Off-the-Loom Designs for Bracelets, Necklaces, & Other Accessories. 2014. (ENG., Illus.). 52p. pap. 9.99 (978-1-57421-915-9(4), 9781574219159, Design Originals) Fox Chapel Publishing Co., Inc.
Kopp, Megan. Maker Projects for Kids Who Love Designing Spaces. 2016. (Be a Maker! Ser.). (ENG.). 32p. (J). (gr. 5-8). (978-0-7787-2574-9(X)) Crabtree Publishing Co.
Krenz, Nancy & Byrnes, Patricia. Arts & Crafts Projects of the American Southwest. 2016. (Illus.). 150p. (YA). pap. (978-1-63293-113-9(3), Blackbirch Pr., Inc.) Sunstone Pr.
Kubish, Shelagh & Craig, Lee, eds. Pumpkin Carving, 1 vol., Vol. 1. rev. ed. 2003. (Ghost Stories Ser.). (ENG., Illus.). 48p. (gr. 4). pap. 7.95 (978-1-894877-26-8(8), 1894877268, Ghost Hse. Bks.) Lone Pine Publishing USA.
kumon publishing, ed. My Book of Pasting. 2005. (ENG., Illus.). 80p. (J). per. 7.95 (978-1-933241-02-9(0)) Kumon Publishing North America, Inc.
Kumon Publishing, ed. My First Book of Cutting. 2004. (Illus.). 80p. (J). per. 7.95 (978-4-7743-0708-4(4)) Kumon Publishing North America, Inc.
Kumon Publishing North America, creator. My Book of Easy Crafts. 2005. (Illus.). 80p. per. 7.95 (978-1-933241-03-6(9)) Kumon Publishing North America, Inc.
Kuskowski, Alex. Cool Outdoor Arts & Crafts: Great Things to Do in the Great Outdoors, 1 vol. 2016. (ENG.). 32p. (978-1-62403-697-2(X)) ABDO Publishing Co.
—Cool Refashioned Hardware: Fun & Easy Fashion Projects, 1 vol. 2016. (ENG.). 32p. (J). (978-1-62403-700-9(3)) ABDO Publishing Co.
—Cool Refashioned Jeans: Fun & Easy Fashion Projects, 1 vol. 2016. (ENG.). 32p. (J). (978-1-62403-701-6(1)) ABDO Publishing Co.
—Cool Refashioned Odds & Ends: Fun & Easy Fashion Projects, 1 vol. 2016. (ENG.). 32p. (J). (978-1-62403-702-3(X)) ABDO Publishing Co.
—Cool Refashioned Scarves & Ties: Fun & Easy Fashion Projects, 1 vol. 2016. (ENG.). 32p. (J). (978-1-62403-703-0(8)) ABDO Publishing Co.
—Cool Refashioned Sweaters: Fun & Easy Fashion Projects, 1 vol. 2016. (ENG.). 32p. (J). (978-1-62403-704-7(6)) ABDO Publishing Co.
—Cool Refashioned T-Shirts: Fun & Easy Fashion Projects, 1 vol. 2016. (ENG.). 32p. (J). (978-1-62403-705-4(4)) ABDO Publishing Co.
—Super Simple African Art: Fun & Easy Art from Around the World, 1 vol. 2012. (ENG.). 32p. 27.07 (978-1-61783-210-9(3), Super SandCastle) ABDO Publishing Co.
—Super Simple American Art: Fun & Easy Art from Around the World, 1 vol. 2012. (ENG.). 32p. 27.07 (978-1-61783-211-6(1), Super SandCastle) ABDO Publishing Co.
—Super Simple Australian Art: Fun & Easy Art from Around the World, 1 vol. 2014. (Super Simple Cultural Art Set 2 Ser.). (ENG.). 32p. (gr. 5-10). lib. bdg. 27.07 (978-1-62403-278-3(8), Super SandCastle) ABDO Publishing Co.
—Super Simple Chinese Art: Fun & Easy Art from Around the World, 1 vol. 2012. (ENG.). 32p. 27.07 (978-1-61783-212-3(X), Super SandCastle) ABDO Publishing Co.
—Super Simple European Art: Fun & Easy Art from Around the World, 1 vol. 2014. (Super Simple Cultural Art Set 2 Ser.). (ENG.). 32p. (gr. 5-10). lib. bdg. 27.07 (978-1-62403-279-0(6), Super SandCastle) ABDO Publishing Co.
—Super Simple Farm Critter Crafts: Fun & Easy Animal Crafts. 2016. (ENG., Illus.). 32p. (J). (978-1-68078-161-8(8)) ABDO Publishing Co.
—Super Simple Forest Critter Crafts: Fun & Easy Animal Crafts. 2016. (ENG., Illus.). 32p. (J). (978-1-68078-162-5(6)) ABDO Publishing Co.
—Super Simple Indian Art: Fun & Easy Art from Around the World, 1 vol. 2014. (Super Simple Cultural Art Set 2 Ser.). (ENG.). 32p. (gr. 5-10). lib. bdg. 27.07 (978-1-62403-280-6(X), Super SandCastle) ABDO Publishing Co.
—Super Simple Japanese Art: Fun & Easy Art from Around the World, 1 vol. 2014. (Super Simple Cultural Art Set 2 Ser.). (ENG.). 32p. (gr. 5-10). lib. bdg. 27.07 (978-1-62403-281-3(8), Super SandCastle) ABDO Publishing Co.
—Super Simple Mediterranean Art: Fun & Easy Art from Around the World, 1 vol. 2014. (Super Simple Cultural Art Set 2 Ser.). (ENG.). 32p. (gr. 5-10). lib. bdg. 27.07 (978-1-62403-282-0(6), Super SandCastle) ABDO Publishing Co.
—Super Simple Mexican Art: Fun & Easy Art from Around the World, 1 vol. 2012. (ENG.). 32p. 27.07 (978-1-61783-213-0(8), Super SandCastle) ABDO Publishing Co.
—Super Simple Native American Art: Fun & Easy Art from Around the World, 1 vol. 2012. (ENG.). 32p. 27.07 (978-1-61783-214-7(6), Super SandCastle) ABDO Publishing Co.
—Super Simple Pet Critter Crafts: Fun & Easy Animal Crafts. 2016. (ENG., Illus.). 32p. (J). (978-1-68078-163-2(4)) ABDO Publishing Co.
—Super Simple Scandinavian Art: Fun & Easy Art from Around the World, 1 vol. 2014. (Super Simple Cultural Art Set 2 Ser.). (ENG.). 32p. (gr. 5-10). lib. bdg. 27.07 (978-1-62403-283-7(4), Super SandCastle) ABDO Publishing Co.
—Super Simple South & Central American Art: Fun & Easy Art from Around the World, 1 vol. 2012. (ENG.). 32p. 27.07 (978-1-61783-215-4(4), Super SandCastle) ABDO Publishing Co.
Kyle, Carolyn. Let There Be Light. 2004. (Illus.). 40p. (YA). 19.95 (978-1-932327-10-6(X), 2032710X) CKE Pubns.
Lacey, Minna, ed. 50 Fairy Things to Make & Do. 2009. (Fairies Ser.). 104p. (J). (gr. 1). spiral bd. 9.99 (978-0-7945-2392-3(7), Usborne) EDC Publishing.
LaFosse, Michael. Making Origami Cards Step by Step. 2004. (Kid's Guide to Origami Ser.). (Illus.). 24p. (J). lib. bdg. 25.25 (978-0-8239-6701-8(8), PowerKids Pr.) Rosen Publishing Group, Inc., The.
LaFosse, Michael G. Making Origami Cards Step by Step. 2009. (Kid's Guide to Origami Ser.). 24p. (gr. 3-4). 47.90 (978-1-61511-183-1(2), PowerKids Pr.) Rosen Publishing Group, Inc., The.
—Making Origami Masks Step by Step. 2009. (Kid's Guide to Origami Ser.). 24p. (gr. 3-4). 47.90 (978-1-61511-188-6(3), PowerKids Pr.) Rosen Publishing Group, Inc., The.
—Making Origami Puzzles Step by Step. 2009. (Kid's Guide to Origami Ser.). 24p. (gr. 3-4). 47.90 (978-1-61511-194-7(8), PowerKids Pr.) Rosen Publishing Group, Inc., The.
—Making Origami Science Experiments Step by Step. 2009. (Kid's Guide to Origami Ser.). 24p. (gr. 3-4). 47.90 (978-1-61511-195-4(6), PowerKids Pr.) Rosen Publishing Group, Inc., The.
Lane, Nickel. Book Making for Everyone. 2004. 33p. (J). pap. 9.77 (978-1-4116-1729-2(0)) Lulu Pr., Inc.
LaRoche, Amelia. Recipe & Craft Guide to France. 2010. (World Crafts & Recipes Ser.). (Illus.). 48p. (J). (gr. 4-8). lib. bdg. 29.95 (978-1-58415-936-0(7)) Mitchell Lane Pubs., Inc.
Larsen, Elizabeth Foy & Glenn, Joshua. Unbored: The Essential Field Guide to Serious Fun. Leone, Tony et al, illus. 2012. (ENG.). 352p. 28.00 (978-1-60819-641-8(0), 9781608196418) Bloomsbury Publishing USA.
Laughlin, Kara L. Beautiful Bags for the Crafty Fashionista, 1 vol. 2011. (Fashion Craft Studio Ser.). (ENG.). 32p. (gr. 3-4). lib. bdg. 27.99 (978-1-4296-6550-6(5), Snap Bks.) Capstone Press of Coughlan Cos.
—Fun Things to Do with Egg Cartons, 1 vol. 2014. (10 Things to Do Ser.). (ENG.). 32p. (gr. 1-2). 27.32 (978-1-4765-9896-3(7)) Capstone Press of Coughlan Cos.
—Fun Things to Do with Paper Cups & Plates, 1 vol. 2014. (10 Things to Do Ser.). (ENG.). 32p. (gr. 1-2). 27.32 (978-1-4765-9897-0(5)) Capstone Press of Coughlan Cos.
—Sparkle & Shine! Trendy Earrings, Necklaces, & Hair Accessories for All Occasions. 2016. (Accessorize Yourself! Ser.). (ENG., Illus.). 48p. (gr. 4-5). lib. bdg. 34.65 (978-1-4914-8228-5(1)) Capstone Press of Coughlan Cos.
Laughlin, Kara L., et al. Accessorize Yourself! 2016. (Accessorize Yourself! Ser.). (ENG.). 48p. (gr. 4-5). lib. bdg. 138.60 (978-1-4914-8696-2(1)) Capstone Press of Coughlan Cos.
Laz, Ashley Ann. Totally Washi! More Than 45 Super Cute Washi Tape Crafts for Kids. 2014. (ENG., Illus.). 160p. pap. 15.99 (978-1-4405-7941-7(5)) Adams Media Corp.
Lecreux, Michele & Gallais, Celia. The Girl's Book of Adventure: The Little Guidebook for Smart & Resourceful Girls. Millet, Esao & Millet, Jocelyn, illus. 2013. (ENG.). 128p. (J). (gr. 3-7). 14.99 (978-0-7641-6610-5(7)) Barron's Educational Series, Inc.
Lee, Jacqueline. Twirled Paper. 2nd ed. 2012. (ENG.). 56p. (J). (gr. 3-7). 19.99 (978-0-545-45991-4(5)) Klutz.
Leedy, Loreen. Look at My Book! How Kids Can Write & Illustrate Terrific Books. 2005. (ENG., Illus.). 32p. (J). 8.99 (978-0-8234-1959-3(2)) Holiday Hse., Inc.
—Look at My Book! How Kids Can Write & Illustrate Terrific Books. Leedy, Loreen, tr. 2005. (ENG., Illus.). 32p. (J). (gr. -1-3). tchr. ed. 17.95 (978-0-8234-1590-8(2)) Holiday Hse., Inc.
Leisure Arts, creator. Cool Stuff Teach Me to Quilt. 2005. (ENG.). 52p. pap. 10.95 (978-1-57486-635-3(4)) Leisure Arts, Inc.
—Rubber Band Loom Crafts. 2013. (ENG., Illus.). 24p. pap. 6.99 (978-1-4647-1549-5(1)) Leisure Arts, Inc.
—Rubber Band Loom Fun! 2013. (ENG., Illus.). 48p. (J). (gr. 4-7). pap. 9.99 (978-1-4647-1578-5(5)) Leisure Arts, Inc.
Let's Do Arts & Crafts. (Illus.). (J). (gr. k-1). 103.50 (978-1-4042-3290-7(7), Powerstart Pr.) Rosen Publishing Group, Inc., The.
Let's Make a Dump Truck with Everyday Materials. 2006. (Let's Do Arts & Crafts Ser.). (Illus.). 24p. (J). (gr. -1-3). lib. bdg. 22.60 (978-1-4042-3059-0(9)) Rosen Publishing Group, Inc., The.
Let's Make a Fish with Everyday Materials. 2006. (Let's Do Arts & Crafts Ser.). (Illus.). 24p. (J). (gr. -1-3). lib. bdg. 22.60 (978-1-4042-3062-0(9)) Rosen Publishing Group, Inc., The.
Let's Make a Monkey with Everyday Materials. 2006. (Let's Do Arts & Crafts Ser.). (Illus.). 24p. (J). (gr. 3-7). lib. bdg. 22.60 (978-1-4042-3061-3(0)) Rosen Publishing Group, Inc., The.
Levete, Sarah. Maker Projects for Kids Who Love Exploring the Outdoors. 2016. (Be a Maker! Ser.). (ENG., Illus.). 32p. (J). (gr. 5-8). (978-0-7787-2576-3(6)) Crabtree Publishing Co.
—Maker Projects for Kids Who Love Woodworking. 2016. (Be a Maker! Ser.). (ENG., Illus.). 32p. (J). (gr. 5-8). (978-0-7787-2579-4(0)) Crabtree Publishing Co.
Lewis, Eric. Garbage Flowers: Green & Groovy Crafts. 2012. (Green & Groovy Ser.: 4). (ENG.). 48p. (J). (gr. 6). 16.99 (978-1-935703-16-7(1)) Downtown Bookworks.
Lewis, Sue. Month-by-Month Crafts. 2005. (Illus.). 112p. (J). (gr. 3-7). per. 15.99 (978-1-59198-130-5(1), 2495) Creative Teaching Pr., Inc.
Liddle, Charlotte. Pimp Your Pumps: 35 Easy Ways to Transform Your Shoes. 2014. (ENG., Illus.). 128p. (J). (gr. 7-11). pap. 14.95 (978-1-78249-106-4(6), CICO Books) Ryland Peters & Small GBR. Dist: WIPRO.
Lim, Annalees. Christmas Crafts, 01 vols., 1. 2016. (10-Minute Crafts Ser.). (ENG., Illus.). 24p. (J). pap. 10.60 (978-1-5081-9077-6(1), Windmill Bks.) Rosen Publishing Group, Inc., The.
—Creepy-Crawly Crafts, 01 vols., 1. 2016. (Creating Creature Crafts Ser.). (ENG., Illus.). 24p. (J). pap. 10.60 (978-1-5081-9101-8(8), 1397689, Windmill Bks.) Rosen Publishing Group, Inc., The.
—Easter Crafts, 01 vols., 1. 2016. (10-Minute Crafts Ser.). (ENG., Illus.). 24p. (J). pap. 10.60 (978-1-5081-9085-1(2), 1397685, Windmill Bks.) Rosen Publishing Group, Inc., The.
—Fun with Nature. 2013. (Clever Crafts Ser.). (ENG., Illus.). 24p. (gr. k-3). 25.25 (978-1-4777-0181-2(8)); pap. 10.60 (978-1-4777-0190-4(7)) Windmill Bks.
—Fun with Paint. 2013. (Clever Crafts Ser.). (ENG., Illus.). 24p. (gr. k-3). 25.25 (978-1-4777-0182-9(6)); pap. 10.60 (978-1-4777-0192-8(3)) Windmill Bks.
—Halloween Crafts, 01 vols., 1. 2016. (10-Minute Crafts Ser.). (ENG., Illus.). 24p. (J). pap. 10.60 (978-1-5081-9089-9(5), 1397687, Windmill Bks.) Rosen Publishing Group, Inc., The.
—Jewelry Crafts, Vol. 1. 2014. (Craft Attack! Ser.). (ENG.). 32p. (J). (gr. 3-3). 26.60 (978-1-4824-0199-8(1)) Stevens, Gareth Publishing LLLP.
—Mother's & Father's Day Crafts, 01 vols., 1. 2016. (10-Minute Crafts Ser.). (ENG., Illus.). 24p. (J). pap. 10.60 (978-1-5081-9093-6(3), 1397686, Windmill Bks.) Rosen Publishing Group, Inc., The.
—Pet Crafts, 01 vols., 1. 2016. (Creating Creature Crafts Ser.). (ENG., Illus.). 24p. (J). pap. 10.60 (978-1-5081-9109-4(3), 1397691, Windmill Bks.) Rosen Publishing Group, Inc., The.
—Recycling Crafts, Vol. 1. 2014. (Craft Attack! Ser.). (ENG.). 32p. (J). (gr. 3-3). 26.60 (978-1-4824-0218-6(1)) Stevens, Gareth Publishing LLLP.
—Sea Animal Crafts, 01 vols., 1. 2016. (Creating Creature Crafts Ser.). (ENG., Illus.). 24p. (J). pap. 10.60 (978-1-5081-9113-1(1), 1397692, Windmill Bks.) Rosen Publishing Group, Inc., The.
—Textile Crafts, Vol. 1. 2014. (Craft Attack! Ser.). 32p. (J). (gr. 3-3). (ENG.). 26.60 (978-1-4824-0224-7(6)); pap. 10.50 (978-1-4824-3301-2(X)) Stevens, Gareth Publishing LLLP.
—Wild Animal Crafts, 01 vols., 1. 2016. (Creating Creature Crafts Ser.). (ENG., Illus.). 24p. (J). pap. 10.60 (978-1-5081-9117-9(4), Windmill Bks.) Rosen Publishing Group, Inc., The.
—10-Minute Seasonal Crafts for Summer. 2014. (10-Minute Seasonal Crafts Ser.). (Illus.). 24p. (J). (gr. k-3). lib. bdg. 26.25 (978-1-4777-9210-0(4)) Windmill Bks.
Lincoln, Margarette. The Pirate's Handbook: How to Become a Rogue of the High Seas. (Illus.). (J). pap. 15.99 (978-0-590-24558-6(9)) Scholastic, Inc.
Lingo, Susan L. Collect-n-Make Crafts for Kids. Stoker, Bruce, ed. Carter, Paula Becker, illus. 2006. 112p. (YA). (gr. 1-7). 15.99 (978-0-7847-1198-9(4), 02432) Standard Publishing.
Little Kid Crafts for All Seasons: Kid Tested Crafts That Parents Love Too! 2003. (Illus.). per. 29.95 (978-0-9741210-4-8(5)) Christine, Yates.
Littlefield, Cindy A. Crafts Across America. Caputo, Jim, illus. 2008. (ENG.). 128p. (J). 16.99 (978-0-8249-6809-0(3)); pap. 12.99 (978-0-8249-6810-6(7)) Worthy Publishing. (Ideal Pubns.).
Llimós, Anna. Earth-Friendly Christmas Crafts in 5 Easy Steps. 2013. (Earth-Friendly Crafts in 5 Easy Steps Ser.). 32p. (J). (gr. 3-4). pap. 7.95 (978-1-4644-0307-1(4), Enslow Elementary) Enslow Pubs., Inc.
—Earth-Friendly Crafts from Recycled Stuff in 5 Easy Steps. 2013. (Earth-Friendly Crafts in 5 Easy Steps Ser.). 32p. (J). (gr. 3-4). pap. 7.95 (978-1-4644-0311-8(2), Enslow Elementary) Enslow Pubs., Inc.
—Earth-Friendly Papier-Mâché Crafts in 5 Easy Steps. 2013. (Earth-Friendly Crafts in 5 Easy Steps Ser.). 32p. (J). (gr. 3-4). pap. 7.95 (978-1-4644-0315-6(5), Enslow Elementary) Enslow Pubs., Inc.
—Earth-Friendly Wood Crafts in 5 Easy Steps. 2013. (Earth-Friendly Crafts in 5 Easy Steps Ser.). 32p. (J). (gr. 3-4). pap. 7.95 (978-1-4644-0317-0(1), Enslow Elementary) Enslow Pubs., Inc.
—Easy Cardboard Crafts in 5 Steps. 2010. (Easy Crafts in 5 Steps Ser.). (Illus.). 32p. (J). pap. 7.95 (978-0-7660-3758-8(4), Enslow Elementary) Enslow Pubs., Inc.
—Easy Clay Crafts in 5 Steps. 2010. (Easy Crafts in 5 Steps Ser.). (Illus.). 32p. (J). pap. 7.95 (978-0-7660-3759-5(2), Enslow Elementary) Enslow Pubs., Inc.
—Easy Cloth Crafts in 5 Steps. 2010. (Easy Crafts in 5 Steps Ser.). (Illus.). 32p. (J). pap. 7.95 (978-0-7660-3760-1(6), Enslow Elementary) Enslow Pubs., Inc.
—Easy Earth-Friendly Crafts in 5 Steps. 2008. (Easy Crafts in 5 Steps Ser.). (Illus.). 32p. (J). (gr. 3-7). lib. bdg. 23.94 (978-0-7660-3086-2(5), Enslow Elementary) Enslow Pubs., Inc.
—Easy Earth-Friendly Crafts in 5 Steps. 2010. (Easy Crafts in 5 Steps Ser.). (Illus.). 32p. (J). pap. 7.95 (978-0-7660-3761-8(4), Enslow Elementary) Enslow Pubs., Inc.
—Fairy Tale Adventure Crafts. 2010. (Fun Adventure Crafts Ser.). (Illus.). 32p. (J). pap. 7.95 (978-0-7660-3737-3(1), Enslow Elementary) Enslow Pubs., Inc.
—Haunted House Adventure Crafts. 2010. (Fun Adventure Crafts Ser.). (Illus.). 32p. (J). pap. 7.95 (978-0-7660-3731-1(2), Enslow Elementary) Enslow Pubs., Inc.
—Medieval Castle Adventure Crafts. 2010. (Fun Adventure Crafts Ser.). (Illus.). 32p. (J). pap. 7.95 (978-0-7660-3735-9(5), Enslow Elementary) Enslow Pubs., Inc.
—Pirate Ship Adventure Crafts. 2010. (Fun Adventure Crafts Ser.). (Illus.). 32p. (J). pap. 7.95 (978-0-7660-3729-8(0), Enslow Elementary) Enslow Pubs., Inc.
—Space Adventure Crafts. 2010. (Fun Adventure Crafts Ser.). (Illus.). 32p. (J). pap. 7.95 (978-0-7660-3733-5(9), Enslow Elementary) Enslow Pubs., Inc.
Llimós, Anna & Library Association Staff. Fairy Tale Adventure Crafts. 2010. (Fun Adventure Crafts Ser.). (Illus.). 32p. (J). 23.94 (978-0-7660-3736-6(3), Enslow Elementary) Enslow Pubs., Inc.
—Medieval Castle Adventure Crafts. 2010. (Fun Adventure Crafts Ser.). (Illus.). 32p. (J). 23.94 (978-0-7660-3734-2(7), Enslow Elementary) Enslow Pubs., Inc.
—Pirate Ship Adventure Crafts. 2010. (Fun Adventure Crafts Ser.). (Illus.). 32p. (J). 23.94 (978-0-7660-3728-1(2), Enslow Elementary) Enslow Pubs., Inc.
—Space Adventure Crafts. 2010. (Fun Adventure Crafts Ser.). (Illus.). 32p. (J). 23.94 (978-0-7660-3732-8(0), Enslow Elementary) Enslow Pubs., Inc.
Llimós Plomer, Anna. Earth-Friendly Christmas Crafts in 5 Easy Steps. 2013. (Earth-Friendly Crafts in 5 Easy Steps Ser.). (Illus.). 32p. (J). lib. bdg. 23.94 (978-0-7660-4188-2(3)) Enslow Pubs., Inc.
—Earth-Friendly Crafts from Recycled Stuff in 5 Easy Steps. 2013. (Earth-Friendly Crafts in 5 Easy Steps Ser.). (Illus.). 32p. (J). lib. bdg. 23.94 (978-0-7660-4190-5(5)) Enslow Pubs., Inc.
—Earth-Friendly Wood Crafts in 5 Easy Steps. 2013. (Earth-Friendly Crafts in 5 Easy Steps Ser.). (Illus.). 32p. (J). lib. bdg. 23.94 (978-0-7660-4193-6(X)) Enslow Pubs., Inc.
—Haunted House Adventure Crafts. 2010. (Fun Adventure Crafts Ser.). (Illus.). 32p. (J). 23.94 (978-0-7660-3730-4(4), Enslow Elementary) Enslow Pubs., Inc.
Llimos Plomer, Anna. Paper. 2003. (Let's Create! Ser.). (Illus.). 32p. (gr. 1-4). lib. bdg. 26.00 (978-0-8368-3747-6(9), Gareth Stevens Learning Library) Stevens, Gareth Publishing LLLP.
Llimos Plomer, Anna & Parramon's Editorial Team Staff. Clay. 2003. (Let's Create! Ser.). (Illus.). 32p. (gr. 1-4). lib. bdg. 26.00 (978-0-8368-3746-9(0), Gareth Stevens Learning Library) Stevens, Gareth Publishing LLLP.
—Wood & Cork. 2003. (Let's Create! Ser.). (Illus.). 32p. (gr. 1-4). lib. bdg. 26.00 (978-0-8368-3749-0(5), Gareth Stevens Learning Library) Stevens, Gareth Publishing LLLP.
Locke, Sue. Back-To-School Crafts. 2010. (Creative Crafts for Kids Ser.). (Illus.). 32p. (J). (gr. 2-5). pap. 10.50 (978-1-4339-3544-2(9), Gareth Stevens Learning Library) Stevens, Gareth Publishing LLLP.
—Back-to-School Crafts. 2010. (Creative Crafts for Kids Ser.). 32p. (J). (gr. 2-5). lib. bdg. 28.00 (978-1-4339-3542-8(2), Gareth Stevens Learning Library) Stevens, Gareth Publishing LLLP.
Loh-Hagan, Virginia. Craft Fair. 2017. (D. I. Y. Make It Happen Ser.). (ENG.). 32p. (J). (gr. 4-8). 29.93 (978-1-63472-143-1(8), 209144, 45th Parallel Press) Cherry Lake Publishing.
Look What I Found at Grandma's! 2004. (J). 11.99 (978-0-930184-10-0(6)) Clapper Publishing Co.

H
I

Look What You Can Make! Individual Title Six-Packs. (Story Steps Ser.). (gr. k-2). 29.00 *(978-0-7635-9600-2(0))* Rigby Education.

Make a Rainbow, 6 Pk. (Story Steps Ser.). (gr. k-2). 23.00 *(978-0-7635-9812-9(7))* Rigby Education.

Make It Work Geography, 4 vol. set. 2003. (gr. 4-8). 59.00 *(978-0-7166-5124-6(6))* World Bk., Inc.

Makosz, Rory. Latino Arts & Their Influence on the United States: Songs, Dreams, & Dances. 2007. (Hispanic Heritage Ser.). (Illus.). 112p. (J). (gr. 4-7). lib. bdg. 22.95 *(978-1-59084-938-5(8),* 1234500) Mason Crest.

Malaspina, Ann. St. Patrick's Day Crafts. Gallagher-Cole, Mernie, illus. 2016. (Holiday Crafts Ser.). (ENG.). 24p. (J). (gr. k-3). 28.50 *(978-1-5038-0818-8(1),* 210654) Child's World, Inc., The.

Mannino, Stephanie. Cool Careers Without College for People Who Love Crafts. (Cool Careers Without College Ser.). 144p. 2009. (gr. 6-6). 66.50 *(978-1-61511-962-2(0))* 2004. (Illus.). (YA). (gr. 7-12). lib. bdg. 35.95 *(978-0-8239-3785-1(2))* Rosen Publishing Group, Inc., The.

Marsh, Carole. Wyoming People Projects: 30 Cool, Activities, Crafts, Experiments & More for Kids to Do to Learn about Your State! 2003. (Wyoming Experience Ser.). 32p. (gr. k-5). pap. 5.95 *(978-0-635-02019-2(X),* Marsh, Carole Bks.) Gallopade International.

Martha Stewart Living Magazine Staff. Martha Stewart's Favorite Crafts for Kids: 175 Projects for Kids of All Ages to Create, Build, Design, Explore, & Share. 2013. (ENG., Illus.). 352p. pap. 24.99 *(978-0-307-95474-9(9),* Potter Craft) Potter/TenSpeed/Harmony.

Martin, Laura C. Recycled Crafts Box: Sock Puppets, Cardboard Castles, Bottle Bugs & 37 More Earth-Friendly Projects & Activities You Can Create. 2004. (ENG., Illus.). 96p. (J). (gr. 3-8). pap. 10.95 *(978-1-58017-522-7(8),* 67522) Storey Publishing, LLC.

Martin, Laura C. & Cain, David. Nature's Art Box: From T-Shirts to Twig Baskets, 65 Cool Projects for Crafty Kids to Make with Natural Materials You Can Find Anywhere. Cain, David, illus. 2003. (ENG., Illus.). 192p. (J). (gr. 3-8). pap. 16.95 *(978-1-58017-490-9(6),* 67490) Storey Publishing, LLC.

Martineau, Susan. Astonishing Art. Ursell, Martin, illus. 2011. (Awesome Activities Ser.). (ENG.). 24p. (J). (gr. 3-6). pap. 10.60 *(978-1-61533-406-3(8));* lib. bdg. 25.25 *(978-1-61533-369-1(X))* Windmill Bks.

Marxhausen, Kim. Paper Paint & Print. 2004. 80p. (gr. -1-3). 10.99 *(978-0-7586-0054-7(2))* Concordia Publishing Hse.

Mathiowetz, Claire. Valentine's Day Crafts. Gallagher-Cole, Mernie, illus. 2016. (Holiday Crafts Ser.). (ENG.). 24p. (J). (gr. k-3). 28.50 *(978-1-5038-0822-5(X),* 210658) Child's World, Inc., The.

Matter, Joanne. Recipe & Craft Guide to China. 2010. (World Crafts & Recipes Ser.). (Illus.). 48p. (J). (gr. 4-8). lib. bdg. *(978-1-58415-937-7(5))* Mitchell Lane Pubs., Inc.

Maurer, Tracy Nelson. Fabulous Fashion Crafts. 2009. (Illus.). 32p. (J). pap. 8.95 *(978-1-60694-503-2(3))* Rourke Educational Media.

—Rock Your Room with Crafts. 2009. (Illus.). 32p. (J). pap. 8.95 *(978-1-60694-507-0(6))* Rourke Educational Media.

Mazurkiewicz, Jessica. How to Create Mehndi Designs. 2014. (ENG., Illus.). 48p. (J). (gr. 6). pap. 5.99 *(978-0-486-49465-4(9))* Dover Pubns., Inc.

McCann, John & Brothers Grimm. Loom Magic! 25 Awesome, Never-Before-Seen Designs for an Amazing Rainbow of Projects. 2013. (ENG., Illus.). 128p. (gr. k). 12.95 *(978-1-62914-334-7(0),* 914334) Skyhorse Publishing Co., Inc.

McCann, John, et al. Loom Magic Xtreme! 25 Spectacular, Never-Before-Seen Designs for Rainbows of Fun. 2014. (ENG., Illus.). 128p. (gr. k). 12.95 *(978-1-62914-342-2(1),* Sky Pony Pr.) Skyhorse Publishing Co., Inc.

Mccormick, Anita Louise. 10 Great Makerspace Projects Using Language Arts. 2017. (Using Makerspaces for School Projects Ser.). 64p. (J). (gr. 11-11). 34.45 ***(978-1-4994-3844-4(3),*** Rosen Central) Rosen Publishing Group, Inc., The.

McGee, Randel. Fun & Festive Fall Crafts: Leaf Rubbings, Dancing Scarecrows, & Pinecone Turkeys. 2014. (Fun & Festive Crafts for the Seasons Ser.). (Illus.). 48p. (J). (gr. 3-4). lib. bdg. 25.27 *(978-0-7660-4320-6(7),* Enslow Elementary) Enslow Pubs., Inc.

—Fun & Festive Spring Crafts: Flower Puppets, Bunny Masks, & Mother's Day Pop-Up Cards. 2014. (Fun & Festive Crafts for the Seasons Ser.). (Illus.). 48p. (J). (gr. 3-4). lib. bdg. 25.27 *(978-0-7660-4318-3(5),* Enslow Elementary) Enslow Pubs., Inc.

—Fun & Festive Summer Crafts: Tie-Dyed Shirts, Bug Cages, & Sand Castles. 2014. (Fun & Festive Crafts for the Seasons Ser.). (Illus.). 48p. (J). (gr. 3-4). lib. bdg. 25.27 *(978-0-7660-4319-0(3),* Enslow Elementary) Enslow Pubs., Inc.

—Fun & Festive Winter Crafts: Snow Globes, Groundhog Puppets, & Fairy Masks. 2014. (Fun & Festive Crafts for the Seasons Ser.). (Illus.). 48p. (J). (gr. 3-4). lib. bdg. 25.27 *(978-0-7660-4317-6(7),* Enslow Elementary) Enslow Pubs., Inc.

—Paper Crafts for Christmas. 2012. (Paper Craft Fun for Holidays Ser.). (Illus.). 48p. (J). (gr. 3-4). pap. 8.95 *(978-1-4644-0321-7(X),* Enslow Elementary) Enslow Pubs., Inc.

McGraw, Sally. Build a Rain Barrel. Stewart, Roger, illus. 2016. (Earth-Friendly Projects Ser.). (ENG.). 24p. (J). (gr. 2-5). 28.50 *(978-1-5038-0787-7(8),* 210624) Child's World, Inc., The.

McNeill, Suzanne, et al. Wire Art for Kids. 2013. (ENG., Illus.). 32p. pap. 9.99 *(978-1-57421-435-2(7),* 9781574214352, Design Originals) Fox Chapel Publishing Co., Inc.

McNutt, Nan. The Spindle Whorl. Fernandes, Roger & Point, Susan, illus. 2nd ed. 2011. (Native American Art Activity Book Ser.). (ENG.). 56p. (J). (gr. 3-5). pap. 9.95 *(978-0-88240-762-3(7),* West Winds Pr.) Graphic Arts Ctr. Publishing Co.

McOmber, Rachel B., ed. McOmber Phonics Storybooks: You Can Make It. rev. ed. (Illus.). (J). *(978-0-944991-51-0(3))* Swift Learning Resources.

Mead, Brian. The Spooky Halloween Cut & Color Activity Book. 2003. 48p. (J). (gr. -1-3). pap. 3.99 *(978-0-9717509-1-3(2))* Mead, Brian Publishing.

Medina, Conni. Haz Papel Picado, 1 vol. 2nd rev. ed. 2012. (Nonfiction Readers Ser.).Tr. of Make Papel Picado. (SPA.). 20p. (J). (gr. 1-1). pap. 4.99 *(978-1-4333-4425-1(4))* Teacher Created Materials, Inc.

—Haz un Dragón del Año Nuevo Chino, 1 vol. 2nd rev. ed. 2012. (Nonfiction Readers Ser.). (SPA.). 20p. (J). (gr. 1-1). pap. 4.99 *(978-1-4333-4426-8(2))* Teacher Created Materials, Inc.

—Haz un Muñequito de Jengibre, 1 vol. 2nd rev. ed. 2012. (Nonfiction Readers Ser.). (SPA.). 20p. (J). (gr. 1-1). pap. 4.99 *(978-1-4333-4427-5(0))* Teacher Created Materials, Inc.

—Make a Chinese New Year Dragon, 1 vol. 2nd rev. ed. 2011. (Nonfiction Readers Ser.). (ENG.). 20p. (J). (gr. 1-1). pap. 4.99 *(978-1-4333-3593-8(X))* Teacher Created Materials, Inc.

—Make a Gingerbread Man, 1 vol. 2nd rev. ed. 2011. (Nonfiction Readers Ser.). (ENG.). 20p. (J). (gr. 1-1). pap. 4.99 *(978-1-4333-3594-5(8))* Teacher Created Materials, Inc.

—Make Papel Picado, 1 vol. 2nd rev. ed. 2014. (TIME for KIDS(r) Nonfiction Readers Ser.). (ENG., Illus.). 20p. (J). (gr. 1-1). pap. 19.96 *(978-1-4807-1025-2(3))* Shell Educational Publishing.

—Make Papel Picado, 1 vol. 2nd rev. ed. 2011. (Nonfiction Readers Ser.). (ENG.). 20p. (J). (gr. 1-1). pap. 4.99 *(978-1-4333-3592-1(1))* Teacher Created Materials, Inc.

Medina, Sarah. Having Fun with Paint. 2007. (Fun Art Projects Ser.). (Illus.). 24p. (J). (gr. -1-3). lib. bdg. 25.25 *(978-1-4042-3718-6(6),* PowerKids Pr.) Rosen Publishing Group, Inc., The.

—Having Fun with Printing. 2007. (Fun Art Projects Ser.). (Illus.). 24p. (J). (gr. -1-3). lib. bdg. 25.25 *(978-1-4042-3719-3(4),* PowerKids Pr.) Rosen Publishing Group, Inc., The.

—Having Fun with Sculpture. 2007. (Fun Art Projects Ser.). (Illus.). 24p. (J). (gr. -1-3). lib. bdg. 25.25 *(978-1-4042-3720-9(8),* PowerKids Pr.) Rosen Publishing Group, Inc., The.

—Having Fun with Textiles. 2007. (Fun Art Projects Ser.). (Illus.). 24p. (J). (gr. -1-3). lib. bdg. 25.25 *(978-1-4042-3717-9(8),* PowerKids Pr.) Rosen Publishing Group, Inc., The.

Mehtani, Henu. Handprint Animals. 2017. (Illus.). 32p. (J). ***(978-0-7787-3108-5(1))*** Crabtree Publishing Co.

—Handprint Garden. 2017. (Illus.). 32p. (J). ***(978-0-7787-3110-8(3))*** Crabtree Publishing Co.

—Handprint People. 2017. (Illus.). 32p. (J). ***(978-0-7787-3111-5(1))*** Crabtree Publishing Co.

Meinking, Mary. Start Your Crafting Business. 2017. (Build Your Business Ser.). (ENG.). 32p. (gr. 3-4). lib. bdg. 27.99 ***(978-1-5157-6690-2(X))*** Capstone Press of Coughlan Cos.

Meinking, Mary & Peschke, Marci. Kylie Jean Pirate Craft Queen, 1 vol. Mourning, Tuesday, illus. 2014. (Kylie Jean Craft Queen Ser.). (ENG.). 32p. (gr. 2-3). lib. bdg. 26.65 *(978-1-4795-2192-0(2))* Picture Window Bks.

—Kylie Jean Rodeo Craft Queen, 1 vol. Mourning, Tuesday, illus. 2014. (Kylie Jean Craft Queen Ser.). (ENG.). 32p. (gr. 2-3). lib. bdg. 26.65 *(978-1-4795-2190-6(6))* Picture Window Bks.

Mercer, Abbie. Happy New Year. (Holiday Fun Ser.). 24p. 2009. (gr. 2-3). 42.50 *(978-1-61513-376-5(3),* PowerKids Pr.) 2007. (Illus.). (J). (gr. 3-7). lib. bdg. 22.60 *(978-1-4042-3808-4(5))* Rosen Publishing Group, Inc., The.

—Happy Valentine's Day. 2007. (Holiday Fun Ser.: Vol. 4). (Illus.). 24p. (J). (gr. 3-7). lib. bdg. 22.60 *(978-1-4042-3809-1(3))* Rosen Publishing Group, Inc., The.

Merrill, Yvonne Y. America Vol. 2: Art Activities about Colonial America, African-Americans, & Southeast Indians. 2006. (Hands-on Ser.). (ENG., Illus.). 71p. (J). (gr. k-9). pap. 20.00 *(978-0-9778797-0-0(4))* KK.

Michaels, Alexandra. The Kids' Multicultural Art Book: Art & Craft Experiences from Around the World. 2008. (ENG., Illus.). 160p. (gr. 1-2). pap. 14.29 *(978-0-8249-6808-3(5),* Ideal Pubns.) Worthy Publishing.

Miller, Brandon Marie. Benjamin Franklin, American Genius: His Life & Ideas with 21 Activities. 2009. (For Kids Ser.). (ENG., Illus.). 144p. (J). (gr. 4-7). pap. 16.95 *(978-1-55652-757-9(8))* Chicago Review Pr., Inc.

Miller, Heather. Nifty Thrifty Art Crafts. Ponte, June, illus. 2007. (Nifty Thrifty Crafts for Kids Ser.). 32p. (J). (gr. 3-7). lib. bdg. 23.94 *(978-0-7660-2780-0(5),* Enslow Elementary) Enslow Pubs., Inc.

Miller, Jocelyn. My Carry-Along Easter: Activity Book with Stickers. Hughes, Cathy, illus. 2014. (ENG.). 32p. (J). (gr. k-2). pap. 9.99 *(978-0-7459-6290-0(4))* Lion Hudson PLC GBR. Dist: Independent Pubs. Group.

—My Carry-Along Noah: Activity Book with Stickers. Hughes, Cathy, illus. 2014. (ENG.). 32p. (J). (gr. k-2). pap. 9.99 *(978-0-7459-6939-8(9))* Lion Hudson PLC GBR. Dist: Independent Pubs. Group.

Miller, Reagan. Mother's Day & Other Family Days. 2010. (Celebrations in My World Ser.). (ENG.). 32p. (J). (gr. k-3). pap. *(978-0-7787-4937-0(1));* lib. bdg. *(978-0-7787-4930-1(4))* Crabtree Publishing Co.

Milligan, Lynda & Smith, Nancy. The Best of Sewing Machine Fun for Kids: Ready, Set, Sew - 37 Projects & Activities. 2nd ed. 2016. (ENG., Illus.). 128p. (J). (gr. 4-9). pap. 16.95 *(978-1-61745-263-5(7),* FunStitch Studio) C & T Publishing.

Minnesota Historical Society & Mille Lacs Indian Museum. Ojibwe Shoulder Bag Kit. 2013. (ENG., Illus.). 24p. (J). (gr. 1-6). 18.95 *(978-0-87351-825-3(X))* Minnesota Historical Society Pr.

Mitchell, Mari Rutz. Creating Clever Castles & Cars (from Boxes & Other Stuff) Kids Ages 3-8 Make Their Own Pretend Play Spaces. Kline, Michael, illus. 2006. (Williamson Little Hands Book Ser.). (ENG.). 128p. (J). (gr. -1-3). 14.95 *(978-0-8249-6783-3(6),* 1256115); (gr. 3-7). pap. 12.95 *(978-0-8249-6782-6(8),* 1256115) Worthy Publishing. (Ideal Pubns.).

Mitchem, James. The Big Book of Things to Make. 2013. (ENG.). 128p. (J). (gr. 2-5). 16.99 *(978-1-4654-0255-4(1),* DK Children) Dorling Kindersley Publishing, Inc.

Modelos. (One Hundred One Things to Do Ser.).Tr. of Models. (SPA.). (J). (gr. 3-5). pap. 4.76 *(978-950-724-206-9(6))* Lumen ARG. Dist: Lectorum Pubns., Inc.

Mofford, Juliet. Recipe & Craft Guide to Japan. 2010. (World Crafts & Recipes Ser.). (Illus.). 48p. (J). (gr. 4-8). lib. bdg. 29.95 *(978-1-58415-933-9(2))* Mitchell Lane Pubs., Inc.

—Recipe & Craft Guide to the Caribbean. 2010. (World Crafts & Recipes Ser.). (Illus.). 48p. (J). (gr. 4-8). lib. bdg. 29.95 *(978-1-58415-935-3(9))* Mitchell Lane Pubs., Inc.

Mommy & Me Craft. 2014. (ENG.). 80p. (J). (gr. k-4). 15.99 *(978-1-4654-1657-5(9),* DK Children) Dorling Kindersley Publishing, Inc.

Monaghan, Kimberly. Organic Crafts: 75 Earth-Friendly Art Activities. 2007. (ENG., Illus.). 160p. (J). (gr. -1-4). pap. 16.95 *(978-1-55652-640-4(7))* Chicago Review Pr., Inc.

Monster Stickers. 2004. (Art Rom Create Your Own... Ser.). (Illus.). 24p. (J). pap. incl. audio compact disk *(978-1-84229-734-6(1))* Top That! Publishing PLC.

Montroll, John. Batman Origami: Amazing Folding Projects for the Dark Knight. Ku, Min Sung, illus. 2015. (DC Origami Ser.). (ENG.). 48p. (gr. 4-5). lib. bdg. 27.99 *(978-1-4914-1786-7(2))* Capstone Press of Coughlan Cos.

—DC Origami. Ku, Min Sung, illus. 2015. (DC Origami Ser.). (ENG.). 48p. (gr. 4-5). 111.96 *(978-1-4914-1790-4(0),* DC Super Heroes) Stone Arch Bks.

—DC Super Heroes Origami: 46 Folding Projects for Batman, Superman, Wonder Woman, & More! Ku, Min Sung, illus. 2015. (DC Super Heroes Ser.). (ENG.). 448p. (gr. 4-5). pap. 14.95 *(978-1-62370-217-5(8))* Capstone Young Readers of Coughlan Cos.

—Justice League Origami: Amazing Folding Projects for the JLA. Ku, Min Sung, illus. 2015. (DC Origami Ser.). (ENG.). 48p. (gr. 4-5). lib. bdg. 27.99 *(978-1-4914-1789-8(7))* Capstone Press of Coughlan Cos.

—Superman Origami: Amazing Folding Projects for the Man of Steel. Ku, Min Sung, illus. 2015. (DC Origami Ser.). (ENG.). 48p. (gr. 4-5). lib. bdg. 27.99 *(978-1-4914-1787-4(0))* Capstone Press of Coughlan Cos.

—Wonder Woman Origami: Amazing Folding Projects for the Warrior Princess. Ku, Min Sung, illus. 2015. (DC Origami Ser.). (ENG.). 48p. (gr. 4-5). lib. bdg. 27.99 *(978-1-4914-1788-1(9))* Capstone Press of Coughlan Cos.

Mooney, Carla. Amazing Africa Projects. Sterns, Megan, illus. 2010. (Build It Yourself Ser.). (ENG.). 128p. (J). (gr. 3-7). pap. 15.95 *(978-1-934670-41-5(3))* Octavio Publishing.

—George Washington: 25 Great Projects You Can Build Yourself. Carbaugh, Samuel, illus. 2010. (Build It Yourself Ser.). (ENG.). 128p. (J). (gr. 3-7). 21.95 *(978-1-934670-64-4(2))* Open City Bks.

Mooney, Carla & Stearns, Megan. Amazing Africa Projects. 2010. (Build It Yourself Ser.). (ENG., Illus.). 128p. (J). (gr. 3-7). 21.95 *(978-1-934670-42-2(1))* Octavio Publishing.

Moran, Erin. Colorful Spring. Pickett, Danny, illus. 2005. 32p. (J). mass mkt. 15.95 *(978-0-9763778-0-1(2))* Seal Rock Publishing, LLC.

Morgan, Richela Fabian. Tape It & Wear It: 60 Duct-Tape Activities to Make & Wear. 2014. (Tape It and... Duct Tape Ser.). (ENG.). 128p. pap. 14.99 *(978-1-4380-0519-5(9))* Barron's Educational Series, Inc.

Morgan, Sally. How We Use Plants for Making Everyday Things. 2009. (How We Use Plants Ser.). 32p. (gr. 2-5). pap. 10.60 *(978-1-4358-2614-4(0),* Rosen Classroom) Rosen Publishing Group, Inc., The.

—How We Use Plants to Make Everyday Things. 2008. (How We Use Plants Ser.). (Illus.). 32p. lib. bdg. 26.50 *(978-1-4042-4424-5(7),* PowerKids Pr.) Rosen Publishing Group, Inc., The.

—Old Clothes. 2007. (Dealing with Waste/Watts Ser.). (Illus.). 30p. (J). (gr. 4-7). lib. bdg. 28.50 *(978-1-59920-011-8(2))* Black Rabbit Bks.

Mornu, Nathalie & Lark Crafts Staff, eds. Craft Camp. 2015. (ENG., Illus.). 144p. (J). (gr. 1-6). pap. 19.95 *(978-1-4547-0900-8(6))* Lark Bks.

Morris, Ting. Arts & Crafts of Ancient China. Young, Emma, illus. 2006. (Arts & Crafts of Ser.). 32p. (J). lib. bdg. 27.10 *(978-1-58340-914-5(9),* 1262690) Black Rabbit Bks.

—Arts & Crafts of Ancient Greece. Young, Emma, illus. 2006. (Arts & Crafts of Ser.). 32p. (J). lib. bdg. 28.50 *(978-1-58340-912-1(2),* 1262692) Black Rabbit Bks.

—Arts & Crafts of Ancient Rome. Young, Emma, illus. 2006. (Arts & Crafts of Ser.). 32p. (J). lib. bdg. 28.50 *(978-1-58340-913-8(0),* 1262693) Black Rabbit Bks.

—Arts & Crafts of the Aztecs & Maya. Young, Emma, illus. 2006. (Arts & Crafts of the Ancient World Ser.). 32p. (J). lib. bdg. 28.50 *(978-1-58340-915-2(7),* 1262694) Black Rabbit Bks.

—Arts & Crafts of the Native Americans. Young, Emma, illus. 2006. (Arts & Crafts of the Ancient World Ser.). 32p. (J). lib. bdg. 28.50 *(978-1-58340-916-9(5))* Black Rabbit Bks.

Morris, Ting & Morris, Neil. Animals. Levy, Ruth, illus. 2006. (Sticky Fingers Ser.). 32p. (J). lib. bdg. 28.50 *(978-1-59771-025-1(3))* Sea-To-Sea Pubns.

—Dinosaurs. Levy, Ruth & Cowne, Joanne, illus. 2006. (Sticky Fingers Ser.). 32p. (J). lib. bdg. 28.50 *(978-1-59771-029-9(6))* Sea-To-Sea Pubns.

—Rainforest. Hulse, Gillian, illus. 2006. (Sticky Fingers Ser.). 32p. (J). lib. bdg. 28.50 *(978-1-59771-028-2(8))* Sea-To-Sea Pubns.

—Space. Turvey, Raymond, illus. 2006. (Sticky Fingers Ser.). 32p. (J). lib. bdg. 27.10 *(978-1-59771-032-9(6))* Sea-To-Sea Pubns.

Muehlenhardt, Amy Bailey. Thanksgiving Crafts, 1 vol. Takvorian, Nadine, illus. 2010. (Thanksgiving Ser.). (ENG.). 24p. (gr. 1-2). lib. bdg. 27.32 *(978-1-4048-6282-1(X))* Picture Window Bks.

Mulanax, Carol. How to Make a Towel Monkey & other Cruise Ship Favorites. 2006. spiral bd. 14.95 *(978-0-9787477-0-1(4))* Tiny Tortoise Publishing, LLC.

Mulcahy, Lisa, et al. Bye Bye Boredom! The Girl's Life Big Book of Fun. 2003. (Illus.). 124p. (J). *(978-0-439-44976-2(6))* Scholastic, Inc.

Multicultural Crafts. 2015. (Multicultural Crafts Ser.). (ENG.). 32p. (J). (gr. 3-4). 126.35 *(978-0-7660-6678-6(9));* pap., pap., pap. 315.60 *(978-0-7660-6679-3(7));* pap., pap., pap. 52.60 *(978-0-7660-7054-7(9))* Enslow Pubs., Inc.

Murray, Patricia. Make It & Pray It: The Rosary Kit for Young People, 10 pack. Murray, Patricia, illus. 2005. (Illus.). 63p. (J). (gr. -1-7). 58.75 *(978-0-88489-870-2(9))* St. Mary's Pr. of MN.

Mystery Crafts for Kids. 2004. pap. 14.99 *(978-0-570-05270-8(X))* Concordia Publishing Hse.

Neuburger, Emily K. Show Me a Story: 40 Craft Projects & Activities to Spark Children's Storytelling. 2012. (ENG.). 144p. 26.95 *(978-1-61212-148-2(9),* 622148); (Illus.). (J). pap. 16.95 *(978-1-60342-988-7(3),* 62988) Storey Publishing, LLC.

Newman, Lesléa. Here Is the World: A Year of Jewish Holidays. Gal, Susan, illus. 2014. (ENG.). 48p. (J). (gr. k-2). 18.95 *(978-1-4197-1185-5(7),* Abrams Bks. for Young Readers) Abrams, Inc.

Nichols, Kaitlyn. Make Clay Charms. 2013. (ENG.). 56p. (J). (gr. 3). 21.99 *(978-0-545-49856-2(2))* Klutz.

Nicoll, Allison. Sew It! Make 17 Projects with Yummy Precut Fabric - Jelly Rolls, Layer Cakes, Charm Packs & Fat Quarters. 2014. (ENG., Illus.). 128p. (J). (gr. 1). pap. 19.95 *(978-1-60705-874-8(X),* FunStitch Studio) C & T Publishing.

Niven, Felicia Lowenstein. Nifty Thrifty Music Crafts. Ponte, June, illus. 2007. (Nifty Thrifty Crafts for Kids Ser.). 32p. (J). (gr. 3-4). lib. bdg. 23.94 *(978-0-7660-2784-8(8),* 1264783, Enslow Elementary) Enslow Pubs., Inc.

Norton, Frances Maree. The Victorian Tea Spirit: A Girl's Guide to Her Secret Self, 1. 100th ed. 2003. (Illus.). 230p. (YA). per. 19.95 *(978-0-9632938-1-7(8))* Norton, Frances M.

Nunn, Daniel. Buttons & Beads, 1 vol. 2011. (From Trash to Treasures Ser.). (ENG.). 24p. (gr. k-2). 23.32 *(978-1-4329-5152-8(1),* Heinemann Read & Learn) Heinemann-Raintree.

—Jars & Pots, 1 vol. 2011. (From Trash to Treasures Ser.). (ENG.). 24p. (gr. k-2). 23.32 *(978-1-4329-5154-2(8),* Heinemann Read & Learn) Heinemann-Raintree.

—Plastic, 1 vol. 2011. (From Trash to Treasures Ser.). (ENG.). 24p. (gr. k-2). 23.32 *(978-1-4329-5148-1(3),* Heinemann Read & Learn) Heinemann-Raintree.

Ocean Friends. (Dough Craft Ser.). 9p. bds. *(978-1-4054-9444-1(1))* Parragon, Inc.

Orr, Anne. Tatting with Anne Orr. 2017. (Dover Needlework Ser.). (ENG., Illus.). 32p. pap. 9.95 *(978-0-486-25982-6(X))* Dover Pubns., Inc.

Owen, Ruth. Fun Fabrics. 2013. (From Trash to Treasure Ser.). 32p. (J). (gr. 3-6). 26.50 *(978-1-4777-1284-9(4));* pap. 11.75 *(978-1-4777-1362-4(X))* Rosen Publishing Group, Inc., The. (PowerKids Pr.).

—Gifts. 2013. (From Trash to Treasure Ser.). 32p. (J). (gr. 3-6). 26.50 *(978-1-4777-1287-0(9));* pap. 11.75 *(978-1-4777-1368-6(9));* pap. 70.50 *(978-1-4777-1369-3(7))* Rosen Publishing Group, Inc., The. (PowerKids Pr.).

—The Halloween Gross-Out Guide, 1 vol., 1. 2014. (DIY for Boys Ser.). (ENG.). 32p. (J). (gr. 3-6). 27.50 *(978-1-4777-6290-5(6),* PowerKids Pr.) Rosen Publishing Group, Inc., The.

—Handmade Easter Crafts. 2016. (Handmade Holiday Crafts Ser.). 00032p. (J). pap. 10.50 ***(978-1-4824-6083-4(1))*** Stevens, Gareth Publishing LLLP.

—Handmade Halloween Crafts. 2016. (Handmade Holiday Crafts Ser.). 00032p. (J). pap. 10.50 ***(978-1-4824-6085-8(8))*** Stevens, Gareth Publishing LLLP.

—Handmade St. Patrick's Day Crafts. 2016. (Handmade Holiday Crafts Ser.). 00032p. (J). pap. 10.50 ***(978-1-4824-6087-2(4))*** Stevens, Gareth Publishing LLLP.

—Handmade Thanksgiving Crafts. 2016. (Handmade Holiday Crafts Ser.). 00032p. (J). pap. 10.50 ***(978-1-4824-6089-6(0))*** Stevens, Gareth Publishing LLLP.

—Handmade Valentine's Day Crafts. 2016. (Handmade Holiday Crafts Ser.). 00032p. (J). pap. 10.50 ***(978-1-4824-6091-9(2))*** Stevens, Gareth Publishing LLLP.

—Holiday Crafts. 2013. (From Trash to Treasure Ser.). 32p. (J). (gr. 3-6). pap. 70.50 *(978-1-4777-1367-9(0),* PowerKids Pr.) Rosen Publishing Group, Inc., The.

—Jewelry. 2013. 32p. (J). (gr. 3-6). 26.50 *(978-1-4777-1283-2(6));* pap. 11.75 *(978-1-4777-1360-0(3))* Rosen Publishing Group, Inc., The. (PowerKids Pr.).

—Nature Crafts. 2013. (From Trash to Treasure Ser.). 32p. (J). (gr. 3-6). 26.50 *(978-1-4777-1285-6(2));* pap. 70.50 *(978-1-4777-1365-5(4));* pap. 11.75 *(978-1-4777-1364-8(6))* Rosen Publishing Group, Inc., The. (PowerKids Pr.).

—Science & Craft Projects with Insects, Spiders, & Other Minibeasts. 2013. (Get Crafty Outdoors Ser.). (ENG., Illus.). 32p. (J). (gr. k-3). 26.50 *(978-1-4777-0245-1(8));* pap. 11.75 *(978-1-4777-0253-6(9))* Rosen Publishing Group, Inc., The. (PowerKids Pr.).

—Science & Craft Projects with Plants & Seeds. 2013. (Get Crafty Outdoors Ser.). (ENG., Illus.). 32p. (J). (gr. k-3). 26.50 *(978-1-4777-0247-5(4));* pap. 11.75 *(978-1-4777-0257-4(1))* Rosen Publishing Group, Inc., The. (PowerKids Pr.).

—Science & Craft Projects with Rocks & Soil. 2013. (Get Crafty Outdoors Ser.). (ENG., Illus.). 32p. (J). (gr. k-3). 26.50 *(978-1-4777-0246-8(6));* pap. 11.75 *(978-1-4777-0255-0(5))* Rosen Publishing Group, Inc., The. (PowerKids Pr.).

—Science & Craft Projects with Trees & Leaves. 2013. (Get Crafty Outdoors Ser.). (ENG., Illus.). 32p. (J). (gr. k-3). 26.50 *(978-1-4777-0248-2(2));* pap. 11.75 *(978-1-4777-0259-8(8))* Rosen Publishing Group, Inc., The. (PowerKids Pr.).

—Science & Craft Projects with Weather. 2013. (Get Crafty Outdoors Ser.). (ENG., Illus.). 32p. (J). (gr. k-3). 26.50 *(978-1-4777-0244-4(X));* pap. 11.75 *(978-1-4777-0251-2(2))* Rosen Publishing Group, Inc., The. (PowerKids Pr.).

—Science & Craft Projects with Wildlife. 2013. (Get Crafty Outdoors Ser.). (ENG., Illus.). 32p. (J). (gr. k-3). 26.50 *(978-1-4777-0243-7(1),* PowerKids Pr.) Rosen Publishing Group, Inc., The.

Oxlade, Chris, et al. The Science & History Project Book: 300 Step-By-Step Fun Science Experiments & History Craft Projects for Home Learning & School Study. 2013. (ENG., Illus.). 512p. (J). (gr. 2-7). pap. 17.99 *(978-1-84322-745-8(2),* Armadillo) Anness Publishing GBR. Dist: National Bk. Network.

Painter, Lucy. The Outrageously Big Activity, Play & Project Book: Cookery, Painting, Crafts, Science, & Much More. 2014. (ENG., Illus.). 512p. (J). (gr. k-6). pap. 18.99 *(978-1-84309-192-9(5))* Anness Publishing GBR. Dist: National Bk. Network.

—The Really Big Book of Amazing Things to Make & Do: With 2000 Step-By-Step Photos! 2017. (ENG., Illus.). 256p. (J). (gr. -1-12). pap. 11.99 ***(978-1-78214-226-3(6),*** Armadillo) Anness Publishing GBR. Dist: National Bk. Network.

Painter, Lucy. 100 Fantastic Things to Make, Do & Play: Simple, Fun Projects That Use Easy Everyday Materials - Cooking, Growing, Science, Music, Painting, Crafts & Party Games! 2014. (ENG., Illus.). 256p. (J). (gr. -1 — 1). pap. 16.99 *(978-1-84322-941-4(2),* Armadillo) Anness Publishing GBR. Dist: National Bk. Network.

Panchyk, Richard & Ketchum, William C., Jr. American Folk Art for Kids: With 21 Activities. 2004. (For Kids Ser.). (ENG., Illus.). 128p. (J). (gr. 4). pap. 16.95 *(978-1-55652-499-8(4))* Chicago Review Pr., Inc.

Panik, Alison Saeger. Angel Cake's Cupcake Book. 2004. (Strawberry Shortcake Crafts Club Ser.). (Illus.). 39p. (J). *(978-0-439-70311-6(5))* Scholastic, Inc.

Paper Airplanes, 1 vol. 2010. (Paper Airplanes Ser.). (ENG.). 32p. (gr. 3-4). lib. bdg. 111.96 *(978-1-4296-4745-8(0),* Edge Bks.) Capstone Press of Coughlan Cos.

Parain, Nathalie. My Cut-Out Pictures. 2015. (ENG., Illus.). 24p. (gr. k-2). pap. 19.95 *(978-1-84976-258-8(9))* Tate Publishing, Ltd. GBR. Dist: Abrams, Inc.

Paris, David. Fantastic Kids: Young Artists (Level 4) 2017. (Exploring Reading Ser.). (Illus.). 32p. (gr. 4-4). 9.99 ***(978-1-4258-4982-5(2))*** Teacher Created Materials, Inc.

Parramon's Editorial Team Staff. Papier-Mâché. Parramon's Editorial Team Staff, photos by. 2004. (Let's Create! Ser.). (Illus.). 32p. (gr. 1-4). lib. bdg. 26.00 *(978-0-8368-4017-9(8),* Gareth Stevens Learning Library) Stevens, Gareth Publishing LLLP.

—Recyclables. Parramon's Editorial Team Staff, photos by. 2004. (Let's Create! Ser.). (Illus.). 32p. (gr. 1-4). lib. bdg. 26.00 *(978-0-8368-4018-6(6),* Gareth Stevens Learning Library) Stevens, Gareth Publishing LLLP.

—Stones & "Stuff" Parramon's Editorial Team Staff, photos by. 2004. (Let's Create! Ser.). (Illus.). 32p. (gr. 1-4). lib. bdg. 26.00 *(978-0-8368-4019-3(4),* Gareth Stevens Learning Library) Stevens, Gareth Publishing LLLP.

Parramon's Editorial Team Staff & Parramon's Editorial Team. Metal. Parramon's Editorial Team Staff, photos by. 2004. (Let's Create! Ser.). (Illus.). 32p. (gr. 1-4). lib. bdg. 26.00 *(978-0-8368-4016-2(X),* Gareth Stevens Learning Library) Stevens, Gareth Publishing LLLP.

Payne-Krzyzanowski, Anna, et al. 52 More Crafts: For the Church Year. Kyle, Margaret, illus. 2008. (ENG.). 64p. pap. 16.95 *(978-1-55145-570-9(6))* Wood Lake Publishing, Inc. CAN. Dist: Westminster John Knox Pr.

Petelinsek, Kathleen. Crafting with Duct Tape: Even More Projects. Petelinsek, Kathleen, illus. 2015. (How-To Library). (ENG., Illus.). 32p. (J). (gr. 3-6). 29.93 *(978-1-63362-374-3(2),* 206916) Cherry Lake Publishing.

—Crafting with Tissue Paper. Petelinsek, Kathleen, illus. 2014. (How-To Library). (ENG., Illus.). 32p. (J). (gr. 3-6). 28.50 *(978-1-63137-779-2(5),* 205359) Cherry Lake Publishing.

—Learning to Sew. Petelinsek, Kathleen, illus. 2014. (How-To Library). (ENG., Illus.). 32p. (J). (gr. 3-6). 28.50 *(978-1-63137-780-8(9),* 205363) Cherry Lake Publishing.

—Making Clay Bead Crafts. Petelinsek, Kathleen, illus. 2014. (How-To Library). (ENG., Illus.). 32p. (J). (gr. 3-6). 28.50 *(978-1-63137-777-8(9),* 205351) Cherry Lake Publishing.

—Making Jewelry with Rubber Bands. Petelinsek, Kathleen, illus. 2014. (How-To Library). (ENG., Illus.). 32p. (J). (gr. 3-6). 28.50 *(978-1-63137-781-5(7),* 205367) Cherry Lake Publishing.

—Making Sock Puppets. Petelinsek, Kathleen, illus. 2014. (How-To Library). (ENG., Illus.). 32p. (J). (gr. 3-6). 28.50 *(978-1-63137-782-2(5),* 205371) Cherry Lake Publishing.

—Modeling Clay Creations. Petelinsek, Kathleen, illus. 2014. (How-To Library). (ENG., Illus.). 32p. (J). (gr. 3-6). 28.50 *(978-1-63137-783-9(3),* 205375) Cherry Lake Publishing.

—Pipe Cleaner Crafts. Petelinsek, Kathleen, illus. 2014. (How-To Library). (ENG., Illus.). 32p. (J). (gr. 3-6). lib. bdg. 28.50 *(978-1-63137-784-6(1),* 205379) Cherry Lake Publishing.

Peter Pig & his Food. 2004. (Play Pals Ser.). (Illus.). 12p. (J). bds. *(978-1-84229-646-2(9))* Top That! Publishing PLC.

Peterson, Megan Cooley & Rustad, Martha E. H. Kid Style: Boss Backpacks for You!, 1 vol. 2014. (Make It Mine Ser.). (ENG.). 24p. (gr. k-1). lib. bdg. 26.65 *(978-1-4765-3969-0(3),* Pebble Plus) Capstone Press of Coughlan Cos.

—Kid Style: Cool Clothes for You!, 1 vol. 2014. (Make It Mine Ser.). (ENG.). 24p. (gr. k-1). lib. bdg. 26.65 *(978-1-4765-3971-3(5),* Pebble Plus) Capstone Press of Coughlan Cos.

—Kid Style: Rockin' Bedrooms for You!, 1 vol. 2014. (Make It Mine Ser.). (ENG.). 24p. (gr. k-1). lib. bdg. 26.65 *(978-1-4765-3970-6(7),* Pebble Plus) Capstone Press of Coughlan Cos.

—Kid Style: Sweet Shoes for You!, 1 vol. 2014. (Make It Mine Ser.). (ENG.). 24p. (gr. k-1). lib. bdg. 26.65 *(978-1-4765-3968-3(5),* Pebble Plus) Capstone Press of Coughlan Cos.

—Make It Mine, 1 vol. 2014. (Make It Mine Ser.). (ENG.). 24p. (gr. k-1). lib. bdg. 106.60 *(978-1-4765-7927-6(X),* Pebble Plus) Capstone Press of Coughlan Cos.

Pfeffer, Wendy. The Longest Day: Celebrating the Summer Solstice. Bleck, Linda, illus. 2015. (ENG.). 40p. (J). (gr. 2-4). pap. 8.99 *(978-0-14-751556-8(4),* Puffin Books) Penguin Young Readers Group.

Philips, Karen, ed. My [Not-So] Perfect Life: A Fill-in-the-Blanks Journal. 2009. (ENG.). 40p. (J). (gr. 3). 16.95 *(978-1-59174-671-3(X))* Klutz.

Phillips, Jennifer. Picture Perfect! Glam Scarves, Belts, Hats, & Other Fashion Accessories for All Occassions. 2016. (Accessorize Yourself! Ser.). (ENG., Illus.). 48p. (gr. 4-5). lib. bdg. 34.65 *(978-1-4914-8229-2(X))* Capstone Press of Coughlan Cos.

Phillips, Karen. Write in White Doodle Journal: My Brilliant Scribbles. 2012. (ENG.). 76p. (J). (gr. 3-7). 16.99 *(978-0-545-39626-4(3))* Klutz.

Phillips, Karen, ed. My All-Time Top 5: Make the Lists of Your Life. 2008. (ENG., Illus.). 60p. (J). (gr. 3-18). 16.95 *(978-1-59174-516-7(0))* Klutz.

Phillips, Karen & Klutz Editors. Straw Shooter Jets: Make Your Own Mini Air Force. 2014. (ENG.). 60p. (J). (gr. 3). 16.99 *(978-0-545-64779-3(7))* Klutz.

Piece of Cake, 6 Packs. (gr. k-1). 23.00 *(978-0-7635-9051-2(7))* Rigby Education.

Pincock, Amy. Quiet Book Patterns. 2013. 14.99 *(978-1-4621-1245-6(5),* Horizon Pubs.) Cedar Fort, Inc./CFI Distribution.

Pitcher, Amy B. The Big Book of Bible Lessons for Crafty Kids. 2015. (Big Bks.). (ENG., Illus.). 224p. (J). (gr. 1-6). pap. 29.99 *(978-0-8307-4400-8(2))* Gospel Light Pubns.

Planes That Fly. 2008. (Build it now Ser.). 16p. pap. *(978-1-4075-2248-7(5))* Parragon, Inc.

Polydoros, Lori & Benchmark Education Co., LLC. Storytelling on Fabrics: Quilts, Tapestries, Story Cloths, & More. 2014. (Text Connections Ser.). (J). (gr. 3). *(978-1-4509-9646-4(9))* Benchmark Education Co.

Pomaska, Anna. Sun, Moon & Stars Armband Tattoos. 2003. (Dover Tattoos Ser.). (ENG., Illus.). 2p. (J). (gr. -1-5). pap. 1.50 *(978-0-486-42642-6(4))* Dover Pubns., Inc.

Ponte, June. Fun & Simple Great Lakes State Crafts: Michigan, Ohio, Indiana, Illinois, Wisconsin, & Minnesota. 2009. (Fun & Simple State Crafts Ser.). (Illus.). 48p. (J). (gr. 2-5). lib. bdg. 25.27 *(978-0-7660-2983-5(2))* Enslow Pubs., Inc.

—Fun & Simple Mid-Atlantic State Crafts. 2008. (Fun & Simple State Crafts Ser.). (Illus.). 48p. (J). (gr. 2-5). lib. bdg. 25.27 *(978-0-7660-2933-0(6))* Enslow Pubs., Inc.

—Fun & Simple Midwestern State Crafts: North Dakota, South Dakota, Nebraska, Iowa, Missouri, & Kansas. 2009. (Fun & Simple State Crafts Ser.). (Illus.). 48p. (J). (gr. 2-5). lib. bdg. 25.27 *(978-0-7660-2984-2(0))* Enslow Pubs., Inc.

—Fun & Simple New England State Crafts: Maine, New Hampshire, Vermont, Massachusetts, Rhode Island, & Connecticut. 2008. (Fun & Simple State Crafts Ser.). (Illus.). 48p. (J). (gr. 2-5). lib. bdg. 25.27 *(978-0-7660-2934-7(4))* Enslow Pubs., Inc.

—Fun & Simple Pacific West State Crafts: California, Oregon, Washington, Alaska, & Hawaii. 2009. (Fun & Simple State Crafts Ser.). (Illus.). 48p. (J). (gr. 2-5). lib. bdg. 25.27 *(978-0-7660-2987-3(5))* Enslow Pubs., Inc.

—Fun & Simple Southeastern State Crafts: West Virginia, Virginia, North Carolina, South Carolina, Georgia, & Florida. 2008. (Fun & Simple State Crafts Ser.). (Illus.). 48p. (J). (gr. 2-5). lib. bdg. 25.27 *(978-0-7660-2935-4(2))* Enslow Pubs., Inc.

—Fun & Simple Southern State Crafts: Kentucky, Tennessee, Alabama, Mississippi, Louisiana, & Arkansas. 2008. (Fun & Simple State Crafts Ser.). (Illus.). 48p. (J). (gr. 2-5). lib. bdg. 25.27 *(978-0-7660-2936-1(0))* Enslow Pubs., Inc.

—Fun & Simple Southwestern State Crafts: Colorado, Oklahoma, Texas, New Mexico, & Arizona. 2009. (Fun & Simple State Crafts Ser.). (Illus.). 48p. (J). (gr. 2-5). lib. bdg. 25.27 *(978-0-7660-2986-6(7))* Enslow Pubs., Inc.

—Fun & Simple Western State Crafts: Montana, Wyoming, Idaho, Utah, & Nevada. 2009. (Fun & Simple State Crafts Ser.). (Illus.). 48p. (J). (gr. 2-5). lib. bdg. 25.27 *(978-0-7660-2985-9(9))* Enslow Pubs., Inc.

Popular Mechanics Press Editors. The Boy Mechanic. 2006. (Dover Children's Activity Bks.). (ENG., Illus.). 144p. (gr. 6-12). per. 8.95 *(978-0-486-45227-2(1))* Dover Pubns., Inc.

Powell, Jillian. Projects with Rainforests. 2014. (Make & Learn Ser.). (Illus.). 32p. (J). (gr. 3-6). 27.50 *(978-1-4777-7165-5(4),* PowerKids Pr.) Rosen Publishing Group, Inc., The.

—Projects with Weather & Seasons. 2014. (Make & Learn Ser.). (Illus.). 32p. (J). (gr. 3-6). lib. bdg. 27.50 *(978-1-4777-7181-5(6),* PowerKids Pr.) Rosen Publishing Group, Inc., The.

—Tudor Times. 2017. (Craft Box Ser.). (ENG., Illus.). 32p. (J). (gr. 4-6). pap. 11.99 *(978-0-7502-8405-9(6),* Wayland) Hachette Children's Group GBR. Dist: Hachette Bk. Group.

Pratt, Leonie. Knights & Castles Things to Make & Do. Thompson, Josephine Et Al, illus. 2006. 32p. (J). pap. 6.99 *(978-0-7945-1355-9(7),* Usborne) EDC Publishing.

—Sparkly Things to Make & Do. 2005. (Illus.). 32p. (J). pap. 6.95 *(978-0-7945-0834-0(0),* Usborne) EDC Publishing.

Press, Judy. Big Fun Christmas Crafts & Activities: Over 200 Quick & Easy Activities for Holiday Fun! Cole, Sarah, illus. 2006. (ENG.). 128p. (J). (gr. -1-3). 16.95 *(978-0-8249-6787-1(9));* pap. 12.95 *(978-0-8249-6786-4(0))* Worthy Publishing. (Ideal Pubns.).

—The Little Hands Art Book: Exploring Arts & Crafts with 2-6 Year Olds. Braren, Loretta Trezzo, illus. 2008. (ENG.). 160p. (J). (gr. -1-1). 16.99 *(978-0-8249-6819-9(0));* per. 12.99 *(978-0-8249-6820-5(4))* Worthy Publishing. (Ideal Pubns.).

—Little Hands Sea Life Art & Activities: Creative Learning Experiences for 3-7-Year Olds. 2004. (Williamson's Little Hands Book Ser.). (Illus.). 128p. (J). pap. 12.95 *(978-1-885593-94-8(5),* Ideal Pubns.) Worthy Publishing.

Press, Judy & Trezzo-Braren, Loretta. Big Fun Craft Book: Creative Fun for 2 to 6 Year Olds. Trezzo-Braren, Loretta, illus. 2008. (ENG., Illus.). (J). (gr. -1-1). 160p. 16.99 *(978-0-8249-6826-7(3));* 142p. pap. 12.99 *(978-0-8249-6827-4(1))* Worthy Publishing. (Ideal Pubns.).

Price, Pam. Cool Rubber Stamp Art, 1 vol. 2005. (Cool Crafts Ser.). (ENG.). 32p. (gr. k-6). 28.50 *(978-1-59197-743-8(6),* Checkerboard Library) ABDO Publishing Co.

Priddy, Roger. Builders Tool Kit. 2009. (Let's Pretend Ser.). (ENG.). 10p. (J). (gr. -1 — 1). 14.95 *(978-0-312-50490-8(X),* Priddy Bks.) St. Martin's Pr.

—My Press-Out Tea Set, Set. 2009. (Let's Pretend Ser.). (ENG.). 10p. (J). (gr. -1 — 1). 14.95 *(978-0-312-50491-5(8),* Priddy Bks.) St. Martin's Pr.

Priddy, Roger & Powell, Sarah. The Cardboard Box Book. Sido, Barbi, illus. 2014. (ENG.). 48p. (J). (gr. k-3). 12.99 *(978-0-312-51738-0(6),* 9780312517380, Priddy Bks.) St. Martin's Pr.

Prime, D. Hacen un Album de Recortes. (Serie Sara y Pablo - Sarah & Paul Ser.: No. 4).Tr. of Make a Scrapbook. (SPA.). (J). 2.99 *(978-0-7899-0498-0(5),* 498898) Editorial Unilit.

Publishing, Arcturus. The Really Cool Craft Book. 2015. (ENG.). 128p. (J). pap. 12.95 *(978-1-78404-509-8(8),* 9781784045098) Arcturus Publishing GBR. Dist: Bookmasters Distribution.

Pugliano-Martin, Carol. Making Crafts from Around the World: Set Of 6. 2011. (Navigators Ser.). (J). pap. 44.00 net. *(978-1-4108-0410-5(0))* Benchmark Education Co.

—Making Crafts from Around the World & Artesanías del Mundo: 6 English, 6 Spanish Adaptations. 2011. (ENG & SPA.). (J). 89.00 net. *(978-1-4108-5674-6(7))* Benchmark Education Co.

Pyper, Brittanie. Adorkable Bubble Bath Crafts: 50 Easy, Geeky Clean Crafts to Make Kids' Bath Time Awesome. 2017. (ENG., Illus.). 192p. pap. 19.99 *(978-1-62414-375-5(X),* 9781624143755) Page Street Publishing Co.

Quan, Adalucia. The Magic of Clay. 2003. (Illus.). 29p. (J). 18.95 *(978-0-9742956-0-2(4))* Cholita Prints & Pub. Co.

Quasha, Jennifer. The Birth & Growth of a Nation: Hands-on Projects about Symbols of American Liberty. 2009. (Great Social Studies Projects Ser.). 24p. (gr. 3-3). 42.50 *(978-1-61513-212-6(0),* PowerKids Pr.) Rosen Publishing Group, Inc., The.

—Covered Wagons: Hands-on Projects about America's Westward Expansion. 2009. (Great Social Studies Projects Ser.). 24p. (gr. 3-3). 42.50 *(978-1-61513-208-9(2),* PowerKids Pr.) Rosen Publishing Group, Inc., The.

—Gold Rush: Hands-on Projects about Mining the Riches of California. 2009. (Great Social Studies Projects Ser.). 24p. (gr. 3-3). 42.50 *(978-1-61513-209-6(0),* PowerKids Pr.) Rosen Publishing Group, Inc., The.

Quick to Create Snowmen, Vol. I. 2003. 11.99 *(978-0-930184-04-9(1))* Clapper Publishing Co.

Quick to Create Snowmen 2, Vol. II. 2003. 11.99 *(978-0-930184-05-6(X))* Clapper Publishing Co.

Quinn, Amy. Sewing Circuits. 2017. (21st Century Skills Innovation Library: Makers As Innovators Junior Ser.). (ENG., Illus.). 24p. (J). (gr. 2-5). lib. bdg. 28.50 *(978-1-63472-191-2(8),* 209336) Cherry Lake Publishing.

Rainbow Publishers Staff. Bible Crafts: Reproducible Activity Book. 2004. (Illus.). 64p. (J). (gr. -1-k). pap. 9.95 *(978-0-937282-26-7(X),* RB36212); (gr. 1-2). pap. 9.95 *(978-0-937282-27-4(8),* RB36213); (gr. 3-4). pap. 9.95 *(978-0-937282-28-1(6),* RB36214); (gr. 5-6). pap. 9.95 *(978-0-937282-29-8(4),* RB36215) Rainbow Pubs. & Legacy Pr.

Rainy Day Projects. Date not set. (Get Crafty Ser.). (Illus.). 48p. (J). pap. 4.98 *(978-0-7525-8410-2(3))* Parragon, Inc.

Rau, Dana Meachen. Crafting with Duct Tape. Petelinsek, Kathleen, illus. 2013. (How-To Library). (ENG.). 32p. (J). (gr. 3-6). 28.50 *(978-1-62431-147-5(4),* 202908); pap. 14.21 *(978-1-62431-279-3(9),* 202910) Cherry Lake Publishing.

—Crafting with Papier-Mâché. 2015. (How-To Library). (ENG., Illus.). 32p. (J). (gr. 3-6). lib. bdg. 29.93 *(978-1-63362-367-5(X),* 206888) Cherry Lake Publishing.

—Crafting with Recyclables. Petelinsek, Kathleen, illus. 2013. (How-To Library). (ENG.). 32p. (J). (gr. 3-6). 28.50 *(978-1-62431-146-8(6),* 202904); pap. 14.21 *(978-1-62431-278-6(0),* 202906) Cherry Lake Publishing.

—Crafting with Recyclables: Even More Projects. Petelinsek, Kathleen, illus. 2016. (How-To Library). (ENG.). 32p. (J). (gr. 3-6). lib. bdg. 29.93 *(978-1-63471-419-8(9),* 208455) Cherry Lake Publishing.

—Creating Crafts from Nature. 2015. (How-To Library). (ENG., Illus.). 32p. (J). (gr. 3-6). lib. bdg. 29.93 *(978-1-63362-368-2(8),* 206892) Cherry Lake Publishing.

—Creating Halloween Crafts. Petelinsek, Kathleen, illus. 2013. (How-To Library). (ENG.). 32p. (J). (gr. 3-6). 28.50 *(978-1-62431-149-9(0),* 202916); pap. 14.21 *(978-1-62431-281-6(0),* 202918) Cherry Lake Publishing.

—Creating Party Favors. 2015. (How-To Library). (ENG., Illus.). 32p. (J). (gr. 3-6). lib. bdg. 29.93 *(978-1-63362-369-9(6),* 206896) Cherry Lake Publishing.

—Creating Thanksgiving Crafts. Petelinsek, Kathleen, illus. 2013. (How-To Library). (ENG.). 32p. (J). (gr. 3-6). 28.50 *(978-1-62431-148-2(2),* 202912); pap. 14.21 *(978-1-62431-280-9(2),* 202914) Cherry Lake Publishing.

—Creating Winter Crafts. Petelinsek, Kathleen, illus. 2013. (How-To Library). (ENG.). 32p. (J). (gr. 3-6). 28.50 *(978-1-62431-150-5(4),* 202920); pap. 14.21 *(978-1-62431-282-3(9),* 202922) Cherry Lake Publishing.

—Having Fun with Felting. Petelinsek, Kathleen, illus. 2015. (How-To Library). (ENG.). 32p. (J). (gr. 3-6). pap. 14.21 *(978-1-63362-398-9(X),* 206901) Cherry Lake Publishing.

—Having Fun with Hair Feathering. Petelinsek, Kathleen, illus. 2015. (How-To Library). (ENG.). 32p. (J). (gr. 3-6). 29.93 *(978-1-63362-371-2(8),* 206904) Cherry Lake Publishing.

—Learning to Make Prints. 2015. (How-To Library). (ENG., Illus.). 32p. (J). (gr. 3-6). lib. bdg. 29.93 *(978-1-63362-373-6(4),* 206912) Cherry Lake Publishing.

—Making Knot Projects. Petelinsek, Kathleen, illus. 2016. (How-To Library). (ENG.). 32p. (J). (gr. 3-6). 29.93 *(978-1-63471-420-4(2),* 208459) Cherry Lake Publishing.

Reid, Struan. Hands-on History Projects: Art & Craft. 2008. (ENG., Illus.). 64p. (J). (gr. 4-7). pap. 7.99 *(978-1-84476-618-5(7))* Anness Publishing GBR. Dist: National Bk. Network.

Reusser, Kayleen. Recipe & Craft Guide to Indonesia. 2010. (World Crafts & Recipes Ser.). (Illus.). 48p. (J). (gr. 4-8). lib. bdg. 29.95 *(978-1-58415-934-6(0))* Mitchell Lane Pubs., Inc.

Reynolds, Toby. Papercraft. 2014. (Mini Artist Ser.). 24p. (J). (gr. k-3). lib. bdg. 26.25 *(978-1-4777-9123-3(X))* Windmill Bks.

—Printing. 2014. (Mini Artist Ser.). 24p. (J). (gr. k-3). lib. bdg. 26.25 *(978-1-4777-9127-1(2))* Windmill Bks.

Rhatigan, Joe, et al. Craft It! 50 Fun Stamp, Paper & Polymer Clay Projects. 2005. (Illus.). 176p. (J). *(978-0-7607-9514-9(2))* Barnes & Noble, Inc.

Rhodes, Judith & Hodgson, Julie, eds. Games for the Early Years: 26 Games to Make & Play. 2005. (Illus.). 88p. pap. *(978-1-903853-55-9(9))* Brilliant Pubns.

Ribble, Karen. Beginning Hair Braiding Taught. 2005. (Illus.). 22p. 7.00 *(978-0-9725170-6-5(5))* Braided Image.

Riechmann, Annie & Smith, Dawn Suzette. Whatever the Weather: Science Experiments & Art Activities for No Matter What the Day Brings. 2016. (ENG., Illus.). 216p. pap. 19.95 *(978-1-61180-231-3(8),* Roost Books) Shambhala Pubns., Inc.

Rigby Education Staff. Discovery World Org Fun Things. (Discovery World Ser.). (Illus.). 12p. (gr. 1-2). 27.00 *(978-0-7635-2700-6(9))* Rigby Education.

Rigg, Annie & Woram, Catherine. Fun Christmas Crafts to Make & Bake: Over 60 Festive Projects to Make with Your Kids. 2012. (ENG., Illus.). 160p. *(978-1-84975-273-2(7))* Ryland Peters & Small.

Riley, Karen. Landfill Lunch Box. (Illus.). 32p. (J). pap. 11.95 *(978-0-9708135-0-3(3))* S.C.R.A.P. Gallery.

Riley, Margaret. Awesome Foam Craft: Quick & Easy Kids' Projects. 2012. (ENG., Illus.). 32p. pap. 9.99 *(978-1-57421-352-2(0),* 9781574213522, Design Originals) Fox Chapel Publishing Co., Inc.

—Crafty Parties for Kids: Creative Ideas, Invitations, Games, Favors, & More. 2013. (ENG., Illus.). 32p. pap. 9.99 *(978-1-57421-353-9(9),* 9781574213539, Design Originals) Fox Chapel Publishing Co., Inc.

Robins, Deri. Mixed Media. 2006. (Art Smart Ser.). (ENG., Illus.). 32p. (J). (gr. 2-5). pap. 9.95 *(978-1-58728-545-5(2))* Cooper Square Publishing Llc.

Robinson, Fay. Christmas Crafts. 2004. (Fun Holiday Crafts Kids Can Do! Ser.). (Illus.). 32p. (J). lib. bdg. 23.94 *(978-0-7660-2257-7(9))* Enslow Pubs., Inc.

—Father's Day Crafts. 2005. (Fun Holiday Crafts Kids Can Do! Ser.). (Illus.). 32p. (J). lib. bdg. 23.94 *(978-0-7660-2343-7(5),* Enslow Elementary) Enslow Pubs., Inc.

—Fun Halloween Crafts. 2015. (Kid Fun Holiday Crafts! Ser.). 32p. (J). (gr. 3-4). 23.94 *(978-0-7660-6235-1(X));* pap. 7.95 *(978-0-7660-6236-8(8),* Enslow Elementary) Enslow Pubs., Inc.

—Halloween Crafts. 2004. (Fun Holiday Crafts Kids Can Do! Ser.). (Illus.). 32p. (J). lib. bdg. 23.94 *(978-0-7660-2236-2(6))* Enslow Pubs., Inc.

—Hispanic-American Crafts Kids Can Do! 2006. (Multicultural Crafts Kids Can Do! Ser.). (Illus.). 32p. (J). (gr. 4-7). lib. bdg. 23.94 *(978-0-7660-2459-5(8),* Enslow Elementary) Enslow Pubs., Inc.

Rock Your Locker. 2015. (ENG.). 44p. (J). pap. *(978-1-78393-705-9(X))* Make Believe Ideas.

Rockwell, Eve, illus. Make Your Own Christmas Cards. 2012. (Christmas Ser.). (ENG.). 8p. pap. 8.95 *(978-1-59583-452-2(4))* Laughing Elephant.

Ros, Jordina & Estadella, Pere. Fun Crafts with 2D & 3D Figures. 2006. (Arts & Crafts Fun Ser.). (Illus.). 48p. (J). (gr. 3-4). lib. bdg. 25.27 *(978-0-7660-2652-0(3),* Enslow Elementary) Enslow Pubs., Inc.

—Fun Crafts with Colors. 2006. (Arts & Crafts Fun Ser.). (Illus.). 48p. (J). (gr. 3-7). lib. bdg. 25.27 *(978-0-7660-2655-1(8),* Enslow Elementary) Enslow Pubs., Inc.

—Fun Crafts with Dots & Lines. 2006. (Arts & Crafts Fun Ser.). (Illus.). 48p. (J). (gr. 3-7). lib. bdg. 25.27 *(978-0-7660-2656-8(6),* Enslow Elementary) Enslow Pubs., Inc.

—Fun Crafts with Shapes. 2006. (Arts & Crafts Fun Ser.). (Illus.). 48p. (J). (gr. 3-7). lib. bdg. 25.27 *(978-0-7660-2657-5(4),* Enslow Elementary) Enslow Pubs., Inc.

—Fun Crafts with Sizes & Spaces. 2006. (Arts & Crafts Fun Ser.). (Illus.). 48p. (J). (gr. 3-4). lib. bdg. 25.27 *(978-0-7660-2653-7(1),* Enslow Elementary) Enslow Pubs., Inc.

—Fun Crafts with Textures. 2006. (Arts & Crafts Fun Ser.). (Illus.). 48p. (J). (gr. 3-4). lib. bdg. 25.27 *(978-0-7660-2654-4(X),* Enslow Elementary) Enslow Pubs., Inc.

Roslund, Samantha & Rodgers, Emily Puckett. Makerspaces. 2013. (21st Century Skills Innovation Library: Makers As Innovators Ser.). (ENG.). 32p. (J). (gr. 4-8). pap. 14.21 *(978-1-62431-273-1(X),* 202886); (Illus.). 28.50 *(978-1-62431-141-3(5),* 202884) Cherry Lake Publishing.

Ross, Kathy. All-Girl Crafts. Garvin, Elaine, illus. 2005. (Girl Crafts Ser.). (ENG.). 48p. (gr. 2-5). lib. bdg. 26.60 *(978-0-7613-2776-9(2),* Millbrook Pr.); per. 7.95 *(978-0-7613-2391-4(0),* First Avenue Editions) Lerner Publishing Group.

—All New Crafts for Earth Day. Holm, Sharon Lane, illus. 2006. (All New Holiday Crafts for Kids Ser.). (ENG.). 48p. (gr. k-3). lib. bdg. 25.26 *(978-0-7613-3400-2(9),* Millbrook Pr.); per. 7.95 *(978-0-8225-5976-4(5),* First Avenue Editions) Lerner Publishing Group.

—All New Crafts for Easter. Holm, Sharon Lane, tr. Holm, Sharon Lane, illus. 2005. (All New Holiday Crafts for Kids Ser.). (ENG.). 48p. (gr. k-3). pap. 7.95 *(978-0-7613-2392-1(9));* lib. bdg. 25.26 *(978-0-7613-2921-3(8))* Lerner Publishing Group. (Millbrook Pr.).

—All New Crafts for Halloween. Leonard, Barbara, illus. 2003. (All New Holiday Crafts for Kids Ser.). 48p. lib. bdg. 23.90 *(978-0-7613-2554-3(9),* Millbrook Pr.) Lerner Publishing Group.

—All New Crafts for Halloween. Leonard, Barbara & Holm, Sharon, illus. 2003. (All New Holiday Crafts for Kids Ser.). (ENG.). 48p. (gr. k-3). pap. 7.95 *(978-0-7613-1577-3(2),* Millbrook Pr.) Lerner Publishing Group.

—All New Crafts for Kwanzaa. Holm, Sharon Lane, illus. 2006. (All New Holiday Crafts for Kids Ser.). 48p. (J). (gr. -1-3). per. 7.95 *(978-0-8225-3435-8(5),* First Avenue Editions) Lerner Publishing Group.

—All New Crafts for Mother's Day & Father's Day. Holm, Sharon Lane, illus. 2007. (All New Holiday Crafts for Kids Ser.). (ENG.). 48p. (gr. k-3). per. 7.95 *(978-0-8225-6368-6(1),* First Avenue Editions) Lerner Publishing Group.

—All New Crafts for Thanksgiving. Holm, Sharon Lane, illus. 2005. 48p. (gr. k-2). (J). per. 7.95 *(978-0-7613-2394-5(5),* First Avenue Editions); (ENG.). lib. bdg. 25.26 *(978-0-7613-2922-0(6),* Millbrook Pr.) Lerner Publishing Group.

—All New Holiday Crafts for Mother's & Father's Day. Holm, Sharon Lane, illus. 2007. (All New Holiday Crafts for Kids Ser.). (ENG.). 48p. (gr. k-3). lib. bdg. 25.26 *(978-0-8225-6367-9(3),* Millbrook Pr.) Lerner Publishing Group.

—Beautiful Beads. Bosch, Nicole in den, illus. 2009. (Girl Crafts Ser.). (ENG.). 48p. (gr. 2-5). 26.60 *(978-0-8225-9214-3(2),* Millbrook Pr.) Lerner Publishing Group.

—Bedroom Makeover Crafts. Bosch, Nicole in den, illus. 2008. (Girl Crafts Ser.). (ENG.). 48p. (gr. 2-5). 26.60 *(978-0-8225-7593-1(0),* Millbrook Pr.); pap. 7.95 *(978-1-58013-823-9(3),* First Avenue Editions) Lerner Publishing Group.

—Community Workers. Barger, Jan, illus. 2005. (Crafts for Kids Who Are Learning about Ser.). (ENG.). 48p. (gr. k-3). lib. bdg., tchr. ed. 26.60 *(978-0-7613-2743-1(6))* Lerner Publishing Group.

—Crafts for Kids Who Are Learning about Dinosaurs. Barger, Jan, illus. 2008. (Crafts for Kids Who Are Learning about Ser.). (ENG.). 48p. (gr. k-3). lib. bdg. 26.60 *(978-0-8225-6809-4(8))* Lerner Publishing Group.

—Crafts for Kids Who Are Learning about Farm Animals. Barger, Jan, illus. 2007. (Crafts for Kids Who Are Learning

H
I

about Ser.). (ENG.). 48p. (gr. k-3). lib. bdg. 26.60 *(978-0-8225-6366-2(5))* Lerner Publishing Group.

—Crafts for Kids Who Are Learning about Insects. Barger, Jan, illus. 2008. (Crafts for Kids Who Are Learning about Ser.). (ENG.). 48p. (gr. k-3). 26.60 *(978-0-8225-7591-7(4))* Lerner Publishing Group.

—Crafts for Kids Who Are Learning about Transportation. Barger, Jan, illus. 2006. (Crafts for Kids Who Are Learning about Ser.). 48p. (J). (gr. 3-6). lib. bdg. 25.26 *(978-0-7613-9464-8(8))* Lerner Publishing Group.

—Crafts to Make in the Fall. Enright, Vicky, illus. 2003. (Crafts for All Seasons Ser.). (ENG.). 64p. (J). (gr. k-3). pap. 9.95 *(978-0-7613-0335-0(9),* First Avenue Editions) Lerner Publishing Group.

—Crafts to Make in the Summer. Enright, Vicky, illus. 2003. (Crafts for All Seasons Ser.: 3). (ENG.). 64p. (gr. k-3). pap. 9.95 *(978-0-7613-0334-3(0),* First Avenue Editions) Lerner Publishing Group.

—Creative Kitchen Crafts. In Den Bosch, Nicole, illus. 2010. (Girl Crafts Ser.). (ENG.). 48p. (gr. 2-5). pap. 7.95 *(978-1-58013-886-4(1),* First Avenue Editions) Lerner Publishing Group.

—Creative Kitchen Crafts. Bosch, Nicole in den, illus. 2010. (Girl Crafts Ser.). (ENG.). 48p. (gr. 2-5). lib. bdg. 26.60 *(978-0-8225-9217-4(7),* Millbrook Pr.) Lerner Publishing Group.

—Earth-Friendly Crafts: Clever Ways to Reuse Everyday Items. Malépart, Céline, illus. (ENG.). 48p. (gr. 2-5). 2011. pap. 7.95 *(978-0-7613-7409-1(4))* 2009. 26.60 *(978-0-8225-9099-6(9))* Lerner Publishing Group. (Millbrook Pr.).

—Fairy World Crafts. Bosch, Nicole in den, illus. 2008. (Girl Crafts Ser.). (ENG.). 48p. (gr. 2-5). lib. bdg. 26.60 *(978-0-8225-7509-2(4),* Millbrook Pr.) Lerner Publishing Group.

—Fairy World Crafts. In Den Bosch, Nicole, illus. 2008. (Girl Crafts Ser.). (ENG.). 48p. (gr. 2-5). per. 7.95 *(978-0-8225-9024-8(7),* First Avenue Editions) Lerner Publishing Group.

—Girlfriends' Get-Together Craft Book. Bosch, Nicole in den, illus. 2007. (Girl Crafts Ser.). (ENG.). 48p. (gr. 2-5). pap. 7.95 *(978-0-7613-9465-5(6),* First Avenue Editions) Lerner Publishing Group.

—Girlfriends' Get-Together Craft Book. In Den Bosch, Nicole, illus. 2007. (Girl Crafts Ser.). (ENG.). 48p. (gr. 2-5). lib. bdg. 26.60 *(978-0-7613-3408-8(4),* Millbrook Pr.) Lerner Publishing Group.

—Jazzy Jewelry, Pretty Purses, & More! Bosch, Nicole in den, illus. 2009. (Girl Crafts Ser.). (ENG.). 48p. (gr. 2-5). 26.60 *(978-0-8225-9212-9(6))*; pap. 7.95 *(978-1-58013-883-3(7),* Millbrook Pr.) Lerner Publishing Group.

—Kathy Ross Crafts Colors. Barger, Jan, illus. 2003. (Crafts from Kathy Ross Ser.). 48p. (J). lib. bdg. 23.93 *(978-0-7613-2651-9(0),* Millbrook Pr.) Lerner Publishing Group.

—Kathy Ross Crafts Numbers. Barger, Jan, illus. 2003. 48p. (J). lib. bdg. 23.90 *(978-0-7613-2105-7(5),* Millbrook Pr.) Lerner Publishing Group.

—Look What You Can Make with Plastic Bottles & Tubs: Over 80 Pictured Crafts & Dozens of Other Ideas. Schneider, Hank, photos by. 2003. (ENG., Illus.). 48p. (YA). (gr. -1-7). pap. 5.95 *(978-1-56397-567-7(X))* Boyds Mills Pr.

—Look What You Can Make with Recycled Paper. Schneider, Hank & Filipski, J. W., photos by. 2013. (Look What You Can Make Ser.). (ENG., Illus.). 48p. (J). (gr. k). pap. 6.95 *(978-1-62091-534-9(0))* Boyds Mills Pr.

—More of the Best Holiday Crafts Ever! Holm, Sharon Lane, illus. 2005. 160p. (J). (gr. k-4). bds. 19.95 *(978-0-7613-2345-7(7))* Lerner Publishing Group.

—One-of-a-Kind Stamps & Crafts. Bosch, Nicole, illus. 2010. (Girl Crafts Ser.). (ENG.). 48p. (gr. 2-5). pap. 7.95 *(978-1-58013-885-7(3))* Lerner Publishing Group.

—One-of-a-Kind Stamps & Crafts. Bosch, Nicole in den, illus. 2010. (Girl Crafts Ser.). (ENG.). 48p. (gr. 2-5). lib. bdg. 26.60 *(978-0-8225-9216-7(9),* Millbrook Pr.) Lerner Publishing Group.

—Step-By-Step Crafts for Spring. Emery, Jennifer, illus. 2007. 48p. (J). *(978-1-59078-359-7(X))*; pap. *(978-1-59078-476-1(6))* Boyds Mills Pr.

—Things to Make for Your Doll. Garvin, Elaine, illus. (Girl Crafts Ser.). 48p. 2005. (ENG.). (gr. 2-5). lib. bdg. 26.60 *(978-0-7613-2861-2(0),* Millbrook Pr.) 2003. (J). (gr. k-2). pap. 7.95 *(978-0-7613-1781-4(3),* First Avenue Editions) Lerner Publishing Group.

Rowe, Brooke. Building a Lava Lamp. Bane, Jeff, illus. 2016. (My Early Library: My Science Fun Ser.). (ENG.). 24p. (J). (gr. k-1). 28.50 *(978-1-63471-026-8(6),* 208184) Cherry Lake Publishing.

Ryall, Jeanette. Food Art. 2012. (Awesome Art Ser.). (ENG., Illus.). 32p. (J). (gr. 3-6). 26.50 *(978-1-4488-8086-7(6))*; pap. 11.75 *(978-1-4488-8139-0(0))* Windmill Bks.

—Junk Art. 2012. (Awesome Art Ser.). (ENG., Illus.). 32p. (J). (gr. 3-6). 26.50 *(978-1-4488-8087-4(4))*; pap. 11.75 *(978-1-4488-8140-6(4))* Windmill Bks.

Ryland Peters and Small Staff, creator. Now I am a Pirate. 2008. (ENG., Illus.). 48p. *(978-1-84597-743-6(2))* Ryland Peters & Small.

—Now I Am a Princess. 2008. (ENG., Illus.). 48p. *(978-1-84597-741-2(6))* Ryland Peters & Small.

Sadler, Judy Ann. Beads.Tr. of Perles. (FRE., Illus.). (J). pap. 7.99 *(978-0-590-24194-6(X))* Scholastic, Inc.

—The New Jumbo Book of Easy Crafts. Price, Caroline, illus. 2009. (Jumbo Bks.). (ENG.). 176p. (J). (gr. -1-2). pap. 18.95 *(978-1-55453-239-1(6))* Kids Can Pr., Ltd. CAN. Dist: Hachette Bk. Group.

Sanchez, Courtney. DIY Box Creations: Fun & Creative Projects to Make Out of Really Big Boxes! 2016. (ENG.). 80p. (J). (gr. 3-7). pap. 9.95 *(978-1-63322-139-0(3),* Walter Foster Jr) Quarto Publishing Group USA.

Santa Maria, Christa, des. Zoo Animal Crafts, 01 vols., 1. 2016. (Creating Creature Crafts Ser.). (ENG., Illus.). 24p. (J). pap. 10.60 *(978-1-5081-9121-6(2),* 1397694, Windmill Bks.) Rosen Publishing Group, Inc., The.

Savage, Christine Lyseng & Poulin, Rosa. Halloween Recipes & Crafts, 1 vol., Vol. 1. Eder, Tamara, photos by. rev. ed. 2003. (Ghost Stories Ser.). (ENG., Illus.). 160p. (gr. 4). pap. 9.95 *(978-1-894877-10-7(1),* 1894877101, Ghost Hse. Bks.) Lone Pine Publishing USA.

Schader, Kim, et al. Loom Band It: 60 Rubberband Projects for the Budding Loomineer. 2014. (ENG.). 128p. pap. 14.99 *(978-1-4380-0520-1(2))* Barron's Educational Series, Inc.

Schecter, Deborah. Nursery Rhymes: Adorable Art Projects with Easy Directions & Rebus Support That Build Beginning Reading Skills. 2009. (Follow-the-Directions Ser.). (ENG.). 80p. (gr. -1-1). pap. 12.99 *(978-0-545-10219-3(7),* Teaching Resources) Scholastic, Inc.

Scheunemann, Pam. Cool Clay Projects, 1 vol. 2005. (Cool Crafts Ser.). (ENG., Illus.). 32p. (gr. k-6). 28.50 *(978-1-59197-740-7(1),* Checkerboard Library) ABDO Publishing Co.

—Cool Fabric Projects: Creative Ways to Upcycle Your Trash into Treasure, 1 vol. 2012. (Cool Trash to Treasure Ser.). (ENG.). 32p. (J). (gr. 3-6). lib. bdg. 27.07 *(978-1-61783-432-5(7),* Checkerboard Library) ABDO Publishing Co.

—Cool Odds & Ends Projects: Creative Ways to Upcycle Your Trash into Treasure, 1 vol. 2012. (Cool Trash to Treasure Ser.). (ENG.). 32p. (J). (gr. 3-6). 27.07 *(978-1-61783-435-6(1),* Checkerboard Library) ABDO Publishing Co.

—Cool Plastic Projects: Creative Ways to Upcycle Your Trash into Treasure, 1 vol. 2012. (Cool Trash to Treasure Ser.). (ENG.). 32p. (J). (gr. 3-6). 27.07 *(978-1-61783-437-0(8),* Checkerboard Library) ABDO Publishing Co.

—Cool Stuff for Family & Friends: Creative Projects for Kids, 1 vol. 2012. (Cool Stuff Ser.). (ENG., Illus.). 32p. (J). (gr. 3-6). 28.50 *(978-1-61714-981-8(0))* ABDO Publishing Co.

—Cool Stuff for Your Room: Creative Projects for Kids, 1 vol. 2012. (Cool Stuff Ser.). (ENG., Illus.). 32p. (J). (gr. 3-6). 28.50 *(978-1-61714-985-6(3))* ABDO Publishing Co.

—Trash to Treasure: A Kid's Upcycling Guide to Crafts. 2013. (ENG., Illus.). 144p. (gr. 3). pap. 15.95 *(978-1-938063-18-3(X),* Mighty Media Junior Readers) Mighty Media Pr.

Scholastic, Inc. Staff & Chorba, April. Pom-Pom Monster Salon. 2011. (ENG.). 44p. (J). (gr. 9). 16.99 *(978-0-545-34624-5(X))* Klutz.

Scholastic, Inc. Staff & Klutz Editors. Harry Potter Paper Flyers. 2017. (ENG.). 62p. (J). (gr. 3-7). 19.99 *(978-1-338-10639-8(2))* Klutz.

Schulz, Charles. The Peanuts Guide to the Seasons: A Jumbo Activity Book. Bennett, Elizabeth, illus. 2003. (Peanuts Club with Charlie Brown & Friends Ser.). 144p. (J). *(978-0-439-46826-8(4))* Scholastic, Inc.

Schulz, Charles & Bennett, Elizabeth. The Peanuts Guide to Sports: A Jumbo Activity Book. 2003. (Peanuts Club with Charlie Brown & Friends Ser.). (Illus.). 144p. (J). *(978-0-439-46824-4(8))* Scholastic, Inc.

Schuman, Jo Miles. Art from Many Hands: Multicultural Art Projects. rev. ed. 2003. (ENG., Illus.). 304p. pap. 29.95 *(978-0-87192-593-0(1))* Davis Pubns., Inc.

Schwake, Susan. Susan Schwake's Kids Art: Art Camp. Schwake, Rainer, photos by. 2015. (ENG., Illus.). 144p. (J). pap. 16.95 *(978-0-9912935-6-8(8))* Two Little Birds Bks.

Schwarz, Renée. Funky Junk: Cool Stuff to Make with Hardware. Schwarz, Renée, illus. 2003. (Kids Can Do It Ser.). (ENG., Illus.). 40p. (J). (gr. 3-7). 5.95 *(978-1-55337-388-9(X))* Kids Can Pr., Ltd. CAN. Dist: Hachette Bk. Group.

Schwarz, Renee. Wind Chimes & Whirligigs. Schwarz, Renee, illus. 2007. (Kids Can Do It Ser.). (ENG., Illus.). 40p. (J). (gr. 3-18). 12.95 *(978-1-55337-868-6(7))*; pap. 6.95 *(978-1-55337-870-9(9))* Kids Can Pr., Ltd. CAN. Dist: Hachette Bk. Group.

Scott, Colin. Children's Secret Diary. 2013. (ENG.). 50p. 12.55 *(978-1-63022-414-1(6),* Speedy Publishing Books (General)) Speedy Publishing LLC.

Scott, Steph & Akers, Katie. Let's Go Outside: Imaginative Outdoor Games & Projects for Kids. 2015. (ENG., Illus.). 144p. (J). (gr. -1-2). 12.95 *(978-1-84994-276-8(5),* Batsford) Pavilion Bks. GBR. Dist: Sterling Publishing Co., Inc.

Scouting Crafts. 2004. (J). 11.99 *(978-0-930184-08-7(4))* Clapper Publishing Co.

Senisi, Ellen B. Berry Smudges & Leaf Prints: Finding & Making Colors from Nature. Senisi, Ellen B., photos by. 2005. (Illus.). 40p. (J). (gr. 4-8). reprint ed. 17.00 *(978-0-7567-9707-2(1))* DIANE Publishing Co.

Sherman, Michael. Suction Cup Critters: Make Your Own Window Grabbers. 2005. (ENG., Illus.). 20p. (J). (gr. 1-18). 14.95 *(978-1-57054-267-1(8))* Klutz.

Shirley, Rebekah Joy. I Want to Be a Fairy. 2011. (Let's Play Dress up Ser.). (ENG., Illus.). 24p. (J). (gr. k-3). lib. bdg. 25.25 *(978-1-61533-358-5(4))* Windmill Bks.

—I Want to Be a Knight. 2011. (Let's Play Dress up Ser.). (ENG., Illus.). 24p. (J). (gr. k-3). pap. 10.60 *(978-1-61533-392-9(4))*; lib. bdg. 25.25 *(978-1-61533-354-7(1))* Windmill Bks.

—I Want to Be a Pirate. 2011. (Let's Play Dress up Ser.). (ENG., Illus.). 24p. (J). (gr. k-3). pap. 10.60 *(978-1-61533-393-6(2))*; lib. bdg. 25.25 *(978-1-61533-355-4(X))* Windmill Bks.

—I Want to Be a Princess. 2011. (Let's Play Dress up Ser.). (ENG., Illus.). 24p. (J). (gr. k-3). pap. 10.60 *(978-1-61533-394-3(0))*; lib. bdg. 25.25 *(978-1-61533-356-1(8))* Windmill Bks.

—I Want to Be a Robot. 2011. (Let's Play Dress up Ser.). (ENG., Illus.). 24p. (J). (gr. k-3). pap. 10.60 *(978-1-61533-395-0(9))*; lib. bdg. 25.25 *(978-1-61533-357-8(6))* Windmill Bks.

—I Want to Be an Astronaut. 2011. (Let's Play Dress up Ser.). (ENG., Illus.). 24p. (J). (gr. k-3). pap. 10.60 *(978-1-61533-397-4(5))*; lib. bdg. 25.25 *(978-1-61533-359-2(2))* Windmill Bks.

Siomades, Lorianne, ed. Look What You Can Make with Boxes: Creative Crafts from Everyday Objects. Schneider, Hank, photos by. 2013. (Look What You Can Make Ser.). (ENG., Illus.). 48p. (J). (gr. k-7). pap. 6.95 *(978-1-56397-704-6(4))* Boyds Mills Pr.

Sirrine, Carol. Cool Crafts with Old CDs: Green Projects for Resourceful Kids. 2010. (Green Crafts Ser.). (ENG.). 32p. (gr. 3-4). lib. bdg. 27.99 *(978-1-4296-4007-7(3),* Snap Bks.) Capstone Press of Coughlan Cos.

—Cool Crafts with Old Jeans: Green Projects for Resourceful Kids. 2010. (Green Crafts Ser.). (ENG.). 32p. (gr. 3-4). lib. bdg. 27.99 *(978-1-4296-4006-0(5),* Snap Bks.) Capstone Press of Coughlan Cos.

Sjonger, Rebecca. Maker Projects for Kids Who Love Paper Engineering. 2016. (Be a Maker! Ser.). (ENG., Illus.). 32p. (J). (gr. 5-8). *(978-0-7787-2577-0(4))* Crabtree Publishing Co.

Skiles, Janet. Crafts Around the House. 2013. (Dover Children's Activity Bks.). (ENG., Illus.). 64p. (J). (gr. -1-2). pap. 5.99 *(978-0-486-49759-4(3))* Dover Pubns., Inc.

Skillicorn, Helen. Friendship Crafts. 2010. (Creative Crafts for Kids Ser.). 32p. (J). (gr. 2-5). lib. bdg. 28.00 *(978-1-4339-3558-9(9))*; (Illus.). pap. 10.50 *(978-1-4339-3559-6(7))* Stevens, Gareth Publishing LLLP. (Gareth Stevens Learning Library).

—Spooky Crafts. 2010. (Creative Crafts for Kids Ser.). 32p. (J). (gr. 2-5). lib. bdg. 28.00 *(978-1-4339-3564-0(3))*; (Illus.). pap. 10.50 *(978-1-4339-3565-7(1))* Stevens, Gareth Publishing LLLP. (Gareth Stevens Learning Library).

Smith, A. G. Cut & Assemble an Early American Seaport, Vol. 181. 2017. (ENG.). 48p. (J). (gr. 2-8). pap. 12.95 *(978-0-486-24754-0(6))* Dover Pubns., Inc.

—Cut & Assemble an Old-Fashioned Train. 2010. (Dover Children's Activity Bks.). (ENG.). 40p. (J). (gr. 6-12). 11.95 *(978-0-486-25324-4(4))* Dover Pubns., Inc.

Smith, Bruce. Poppies in Bloom, 6 vols. 2013. (ENG.). 17.50 *(978-1-4236-3377-8(6))* Gibbs Smith, Publisher.

Smith, Tana. DIY Bedroom Decor: 50 Awesome Ideas for Your Room. 2015. (ENG., Illus.). 192p. pap. 16.99 *(978-1-4405-8802-0(3))* Adams Media Corp.

Smith, Thomasina. Crafty Fun with Clay! 25 Brilliant Ideas, from Pretty Pots to Scary Monsters. 2015. (ENG., Illus.). 64p. (J). (gr. 3-7). 9.99 *(978-1-86147-417-9(2),* Armadillo) Anness Publishing GBR. Dist: National Bk. Network.

Snedeker, Gus. Quilts, Rag Dolls, & Rocking Chairs: Folk Arts & Crafts. 2013. (Illus.). 48p. (J). pap. *(978-1-4222-2501-1(1))* Mason Crest.

—Quilts, Rag Dolls, & Rocking Chairs: Folk Arts & Crafts. Jabbour, Alan, ed. 2012. (North American Folklore for Youth Ser.). (Illus.). 48p. (J). (gr. 4). 19.95 *(978-1-4222-2490-8(2))* Mason Crest.

Sokol, Dawn DeVries. The Doodle Circle: A Fill-In Journal for BFFs to Share. 2013. (ENG.). 160p. (J). (gr. 3-7). pap. 12.95 *(978-1-61769-053-2(8),* Amulet Bks.) Abrams, Inc.

Song, Sok. Origami Chic: A Guide to Foldable Fashion. Song, Sok, illus. 2016. (ENG., Illus.). 240p. (gr. 3-3). pap. 14.95 *(978-1-62370-771-2(4))* Capstone Young Readers of Coughlan Cos.

Speechley, Greta. Arts & Crafts for Myths & Tales. 2010. (Creative Crafts for Kids Ser.). 32p. (J). (gr. 2-5). lib. bdg. 28.00 *(978-1-4339-3567-1(8))*; (Illus.). pap. 10.50 *(978-1-4339-3568-8(6))* Stevens, Gareth Publishing LLLP. (Gareth Stevens Learning Library).

—Backyard Crafts. 2010. (Creative Crafts for Kids Ser.). (Illus.). 32p. (J). (gr. 2-5). pap. 10.50 *(978-1-4339-3547-3(3),* Gareth Stevens Learning Library) Stevens, Gareth Publishing LLLP.

—Birthday Crafts. 2010. (Creative Crafts for Kids Ser.). 32p. (J). (gr. 2-5). lib. bdg. 28.00 *(978-1-4339-3552-7(X))*; (Illus.). pap. 10.50 *(978-1-4339-3553-4(8))* Stevens, Gareth Publishing LLLP. (Gareth Stevens Learning Library).

—Valentine Crafts. 2010. (Creative Crafts for Kids Ser.). 32p. (J). (gr. 2-5). lib. bdg. 28.00 *(978-1-4339-3600-5(3))*; (Illus.). pap. 10.50 *(978-1-4339-3598-5(8))* Stevens, Gareth Publishing LLLP. (Gareth Stevens Learning Library).

—World Crafts. 2010. (Creative Crafts for Kids Ser.). 32p. (J). (gr. 2-5). lib. bdg. 28.00 *(978-1-4339-3561-9(9))*; (Illus.). pap. 10.50 *(978-1-4339-3562-6(7))* Stevens, Gareth Publishing LLLP. (Gareth Stevens Learning Library).

Spilsbury, Louise. Projects with Recycling & Reusing. 2014. (Make & Learn Ser.). 32p. (J). (gr. 3-6). lib. bdg. 27.50 *(978-1-4777-7169-3(7),* PowerKids Pr.) Rosen Publishing Group, Inc., The.

—Projects with Space. 2014. (Make & Learn Ser.). (Illus.). 32p. (J). (gr. 3-6). lib. bdg. 27.50 *(978-1-4777-7177-8(8),* PowerKids Pr.) Rosen Publishing Group, Inc., The.

Spilsbury, Louise & Childs, Rob. Tapestries & Textiles. 2016. (ENG., Illus.). 32p. (J). (gr. 4-6). pap. 11.99 *(978-0-7502-9441-6(8),* Wayland) Hachette Children's Group GBR. Dist: Hachette Bk. Group.

Spohn, Rebecca. Ready, Set, Create! A Kid's Guide to Crafting. 2012. (ENG., Illus.). 92p. pap. 19.95 *(978-1-59647-425-3(4))* Good Year Bks.

Spooky Stickers. 2004. (Art Rom Create Your Own... Ser.). (Illus.). 24p. (J). pap. incl. audio compact disk *(978-1-84229-738-4(4))* Top That! Publishing PLC.

Statue of Liberty. 2008. (Build it now Ser.). 16p. pap. *(978-1-4075-2249-4(3))* Parragon, Inc.

Steele, Philip. Hands-On History! Viking World: Learn about the Legendary Norse Raiders, with 15 Step-By-step Projects & More Than 350 Exciting Pictures. 2013. (ENG., Illus.). 64p. (J). (gr. 3-7). 12.99 *(978-1-84322-694-9(4))* Anness Publishing GBR. Dist: National Bk. Network.

Steele-Saccio, Eva. Ribbon Bangles: Make 5 Beautiful Wrapped Bracelets. 2011. (ENG.). 50p. (J). (gr. 3-7). 19.99 *(978-0-545-34625-2(8))* Klutz.

Steele-Saccio, Eva & Klutz Editors. Twisted Critters: The Pipe Cleaner Book. 2011. (ENG.). 60p. (J). 16.99 *(978-0-545-34623-8(1))* Klutz.

Steele-Staccio, Eva. String Art: Turn String & Pins into Works of Art. Klutz Editors, ed. 2014. (ENG.). 60p. (J). (gr. 5). 19.99 *(978-0-545-70321-5(2))* Klutz.

Stein, David & Klutz Editors. How to Make Monstrous, Huge, Unbelievably Big Bubbles, 6, Pack. 2005. (ENG.). (J). 101.70 *(978-1-57054-258-9(9))* Klutz.

Stephens, Cassie. Clay Lab for Kids: 52 Projects to Make, Model, & Mold with Air-Dry, Polymer, & Homemade Clay. 2017. (Lab Ser.). (ENG., Illus.). 144p. (J). (gr. -1-5). pap. 24.99 *(978-1-63159-270-6(X),* Quarry Bks.) Quarto Publishing Group USA.

Sterling Children's, Sterling. Curious Jane. 2017. (ENG., Illus.). 128p. (J). (gr. 1-6). pap. 16.95 *(978-1-4549-2235-3(4))* Sterling Publishing Co., Inc.

Stern, Sam & Stern, Susan. Get Cooking. Campbell, Lorne, photos by. 2009. (ENG., Illus.). 144p. (J). (gr. 5-18). pap. 17.99 *(978-0-7636-3926-6(5))* Candlewick Pr.

Stevenson, Robert Louis. Artfolds - Sun: Treasure Island & Other Adventures. 2015. (ArtFolds Classic Editions Ser.: 5). (ENG.). 480p. (gr. 3). 20.00 *(978-0-7944-3335-2(9))* Reader's Digest Assn., Inc., The.

Stewart, Martha. Martha Stewart's Favorite Crafts for Kids. 2013. lib. bdg. 39.15 *(978-0-606-32096-2(2),* Turtleback) Turtleback Bks.

Stiles, David. Forts for Kids. 2011. (ENG., Illus.). 96p. pap. 16.95 *(978-0-7627-6453-2(8),* Lyons Pr.) Globe Pequot Pr., The.

Stillinger, Doug. Aviones de Papel. 2005. (SPA., Illus.). 56p. (J). spiral bd. 19.95 *(978-987-1078-44-8(7))* Klutz Latino MEX. Dist: Independent Pubs. Group.

—Baterías en Accion. 2005. (SPA., Illus.). 62p. (J). spiral bd. 23.95 *(978-987-1078-28-8(5))* Klutz Latino MEX. Dist: Independent Pubs. Group.

Stohs, Anita Reith. Praise God with Paper Cups: 45 Easy Bible Crafts; Grades 1-5. Koehler, Ed, illus. 2005. (CPH Teaching Resource Ser.). 64p. pap. 10.99 *(978-0-7586-0842-0(X))* Concordia Publishing Hse.

Storey, Rita. Animals. 2013. (Have Fun with Arts & Crafts Ser.). 32p. (gr. 4-7). 31.35 *(978-1-59920-896-1(2))* Black Rabbit Bks.

—Dinosaurs. 2013. (Have Fun with Arts & Crafts Ser.). 32p. (gr. 4-7). 31.35 *(978-1-59920-897-8(0))* Black Rabbit Bks.

—Fairies. 2013. (Have Fun with Arts & Crafts Ser.). 48p. (gr. 2-5). 28.50 *(978-1-59920-898-5(9))* Black Rabbit Bks.

—Knights & Castles. 2013. (Have Fun with Arts & Crafts Ser.). 32p. (gr. 4-7). 31.35 *(978-1-59920-899-2(7))* Black Rabbit Bks.

—Masks. Rhodes, Harry, illus. Rhodes, Harry, photos by. 2014. (J). lib. bdg. 26.60 *(978-1-4677-4195-8(7),* Lerner Pubns.) Lerner Publishing Group.

—Pirates. 2013. (Have Fun with Arts & Crafts Ser.). 32p. (gr. 4-7). 31.35 *(978-1-59920-900-5(4))* Black Rabbit Bks.

—Tractors & Trucks. 2013. (Have Fun with Arts & Crafts Ser.). (Illus.). 32p. (gr. 4-7). lib. bdg. 31.35 *(978-1-59920-901-2(2))* Black Rabbit Bks.

Strand, Jessica. Holiday Crafting & Baking with Kids: Gifts, Sweets, & Treats for the Whole Family! Herring, Aimée, photos by. 2011. (ENG., Illus.). 128p. (gr. 13-17). pap. 19.95 *(978-1-4521-0109-5(4))* Chronicle Bks. LLC.

Strand, Jessica & Massman-Johnson, Tammy. Kids in the Holiday Kitchen. 2008. (J). *(978-0-8118-6135-9(X))* Chronicle Bks. LLC.

Strand, Jessica, et al. Kids in the Holiday Kitchen. 2008. (ENG., Illus.). 96p. (gr. 8-17). pap. 16.95 *(978-0-8118-6139-7(2))* Chronicle Bks. LLC.

Sturgill, Ruthy. Christmas Tree Advent Calendar: A Country Quilted & Appliquéd Project. 2006. 96p. pap. 24.95 *(978-1-59800-539-4(1))* Outskirts Pr., Inc.

Super Skeleton. 2008. (Build it now Ser.). 16p. pap. *(978-1-4075-2246-3(9))* Parragon, Inc.

Swanson, Maggie. Easy Christmas Crafts: 12 Holiday Cut & Make Decorations. 2014. (ENG., Illus.). 24p. (J). (gr. 1-5). pap. 9.99 *(978-0-486-78336-9(7))* Dover Pubns., Inc.

—Easy Easter Tabletop Crafts. 2014. (ENG., Illus.). 24p. (J). (gr. 1-5). pap. 9.99 *(978-0-486-49631-3(7))* Dover Pubns., Inc.

Tai, Elise See & Cole, Linda. The Creative Card Making Pack: Blank Cards, Decoupage, Stencils, Stickers. 2015. (ENG.). 48p. (J). (gr. 2-6). 12.99 *(978-0-7641-6792-8(8))* Barron's Educational Series, Inc.

Taylor, Terry. Clay Play! 2014. (ENG., Illus.). 80p. (J). (gr. 3-6). pap. 12.99 *(978-0-486-77984-3(X))* Dover Pubns., Inc.

—Clay Play! JEWELRY. 2016. (ENG., Illus.). 80p. (J). (gr. 3-6). pap. 12.99 *(978-0-486-79944-5(1))* Dover Pubns., Inc.

Temko, Florence. Cut & Color My Fun Furniture. 2006. (Dover Children's Activity Bks.). (ENG., Illus.). 32p. (J). (gr. 1-5). pap. 3.95 *(978-0-486-45293-7(X))* Dover Pubns., Inc.

—Traditional Crafts from China. Gooch, Randall, illus. 2005. (Culture Crafts Ser.). 64p. (gr. 3-8). 23.93 *(978-0-8225-2939-2(4))* Lerner Publishing Group.

—Traditional Crafts from Japan. Gooch, Randall, illus. 2005. (Culture Crafts Ser.). 64p. (gr. 3-8). 23.93 *(978-0-8225-2938-5(6))* Lerner Publishing Group.

—Traditional Crafts from the Caribbean. 2005. (Culture Crafts Ser.). (Illus.). 64p. (gr. 3-8). 23.93 *(978-0-8225-2937-8(8))* Lerner Publishing Group.

Terzian, Alexandria M. The Kids Multicultural Art Book. Terzian, Alexandria M., illus. 2007. (ENG., Illus.). 160p. (gr. 1-2). 16.99 *(978-0-8249-6807-6(7),* Ideal Pubns.) Worthy Publishing.

Things to Make & Do. (Get Crafty Ser.). (J). Date not set. 48p. pap. 4.98 *(978-0-7525-8411-9(1))* 64p. 5.98 *(978-1-4054-0412-9(4))* 2003. (Illus.). 64p. 12.98 *(978-1-4054-1220-9(8))* Parragon, Inc.

Thoenig, Donald. Double Image Magic Artwork & Cards: Christmas. 2003. pap. 16.95 *(978-0-9729546-0-0(0))* SMC Pubns., LLC.

Thomas, Danita & Thomas, John E. Kid Concoctions of Biblical Proportions. 2007. (Kid Concoctions Ser.). (Illus.). 78p. (J). per. 14.99 *(978-0-8054-4447-6(5))* B&H Publishing Group.

—The Ultimate Book of Holiday Kid Concoctions: More Than 50 Wacky, Wild, & Crazy Concoctions for All Occasions. 2006. (Ultimate Book of Kid Concoctions Ser.). (Illus.). 80p. (J). (gr. 4-7). per. 14.99 *(978-0-8054-4445-2(9))* B&H Publishing Group.

—The Ultimate Book of Kid Concoctions. 2006. (Illus.). 80p. (J). (gr. 4-7). per. 14.99 *(978-0-8054-4443-8(2))* B&H Publishing Group.

Thomas, Isabel. Cool Cat Projects. 2015. (Pet Projects Ser.). (ENG., Illus.). 32p. (gr. 3-5). 27.99 *(978-1-4109-8064-9(2),* Snap Bks.) Capstone Press of Coughlan Cos.

—Designer Dog Projects. 2015. (Pet Projects Ser.). (ENG., Illus.). 32p. (gr. 3-5). 27.99 *(978-1-4109-8066-3(9),* Snap Bks.) Capstone Press of Coughlan Cos.

—Handy Horse Projects. 2015. (Pet Projects Ser.). (ENG., Illus.). 32p. (gr. 3-5). 27.99 *(978-1-4109-8065-6(0),* Snap Bks.) Capstone Press of Coughlan Cos.

—Hip Hamster Projects. 2015. (Pet Projects Ser.). (ENG., Illus.). 32p. (gr. 3-5). 27.99 *(978-1-4109-8067-0(7),* Snap Bks.) Capstone Press of Coughlan Cos.

Thomas, John E. & Thomas, Danita. Kid Concoctions & Contraptions. 2006. (Illus.). 80p. (J). (gr. 4-7). per. 14.99 *(978-0-8054-4446-9(7))* B&H Publishing Group.

—The Ultimate Book of Kid Concoctions 2. 2006. (Illus.). 80p. (J). (gr. 4-7). per. 14.99 *(978-0-8054-4444-5(0))* B&H Publishing Group.

Thomas Nelson. Art Books Weave Art. 2016. (ENG.). 80p. (J). (gr. 1-7). bds. *(978-1-78598-255-2(9))* Make Believe Ideas.

—Emily's Room: Butterfly Garden. 2015. (ENG.). (J). *(978-1-78393-883-4(8))* Make Believe Ideas.

Thompson, Sharon & Booth, Vanessa. Christian Crafts for Gift-Giving. Seltzer, Erin, ed. 2004. (Christian Education Resource Ser.). (Illus.). 64p. (J). per. 9.99 *(978-1-59441-008-6(9)*, CD-204002) Carson-Dellosa Publishing, LLC.

Thomson, Ruth. The Art Creativity Book. 2012. (Creativity Bks.). (ENG.). 80p. (J). (gr. 1-6). pap. 12.99 *(978-1-4380-0126-5(6))* Barron's Educational Series, Inc.

—What Are Textiles? 2005. (Art's Alive! Ser.). (Illus.). 30p. (J). (gr. 3-7). lib. bdg. 27.10 *(978-1-932889-90-1(6))* Sea-To-Sea Pubns.

Tiede, Karen. Carve Smart. 2004. 189p. (YA). pap. 19.95 *(978-0-7414-2093-0(7))* Infinity Publishing.

Tierney, Tom. Soap Opera Divas Paper Dolls. 2007. (Dover Celebrity Paper Dolls Ser.). (ENG., Illus.). 32p. (gr. 7-8). pap. 6.95 *(978-0-486-46222-6(6))* Dover Pubns., Inc.

Tin Treasures: Six-Pack. (Greetings Ser.: Vol. 3). 24p. (gr. 2-3). 31.00 *(978-0-7635-9419-0(9))* Rigby Education.

Tofts, Hannah. Collage. 2004. (Crafty Ideas Ser.). (SPA., Illus.). 32p. (J). (gr. 2-5). pap. 5.95 *(978-1-58728-121-1(X)*, Two-Can Publishing) T&N Children's Publishing.

Top That Publishing Editors, ed. Fiendish Faces. Dahl, Roald, illus. 2005. 24p. (J). pap. *(978-1-905359-53-0(5))* Top That! Publishing PLC.

—Stupendous Stampers. Dahl, Roald, illus. 2005. 24p. (J). pap. *(978-1-905359-50-9(0))* Top That! Publishing PLC.

Torres, Laura. Formas Fantasticas. 2004. (SPA., Illus.). 40p. (J). spiral bd. 17.95 *(978-968-5528-04-7(7))* Klutz Latino MEX. Dist: Independent Pubs. Group.

—Rock Your Party. 2012. (Illus.). 32p. (gr. 3-5). pap. 8.95 *(978-1-926853-86-4(5))* Saunders Bk. Co. CAN. Dist: RiverStream Publishing.

—Rock Your Room. 2012. (Illus.). 32p. (gr. 3-5). pap. 8.95 *(978-1-926853-87-1(3))* Saunders Bk. Co. CAN. Dist: RiverStream Publishing.

—Rock Your School Stuff. 2012. (Illus.). 32p. (gr. 3-5). pap. 8.95 *(978-1-926853-88-8(1))* Saunders Bk. Co. CAN. Dist: RiverStream Publishing.

Truett, Trudi Strain. Birthday Crafts. Gallagher-Cole, Memie, illus. 2016. (Holiday Crafts Ser.). (ENG.). 24p. (J). (gr. k-3). 28.50 *(978-1-5038-0815-7(7)*, 210651) Child's World, Inc., The.

—Mother's Day Crafts. Gallagher-Cole, Memie, illus. 2016. (Holiday Crafts Ser.). (ENG.). 24p. (J). (gr. k-3). 28.50 *(978-1-5038-0819-5(X)*, 210655) Child's World, Inc., The.

Trulock, Alison. Build Your Own Snow Globe. 2003. (Miniature Editions Ser.). (ENG., Illus.). 32p. pap. 9.95 *(978-0-7624-1620-2(3))* Running Pr. Bk. Pubs.

Trusty, Brad & Trusty, Cindy. The Kids' Guide to Balloon Twisting. 1 vol. 2010. (Kids' Guides). (ENG.). 32p. (gr. 3-4). lib. bdg. 27.99 *(978-1-4296-5444-9(9)*, Edge Bks.) Capstone Press of Coughlan Cos.

Turck, Mary C. Mexico & Central America: A Fiesta of Cultures, Crafts, & Activities for Ages 8-12. 2004. (ENG., Illus.). 160p. (J). (gr. 4-7). pap. 16.95 *(978-1-55652-525-4(7))* Chicago Review Pr., Inc.

Turnbull, Stephanie. Accessories: Style Secrets for Girls. 2013. (Girl Talk Ser.). 32p. (gr. 4-7). 31.35 *(978-1-59920-943-2(8))* Black Rabbit Bks.

—Accessories: Style Secrets for Girls. 2014. (Girl Talk Ser.). (ENG., Illus.). 32p. (J). (gr. 4-8). pap. 9.95 *(978-1-77092-200-6(8))* Saunders Bk. Co. CAN. Dist: RiverStream Publishing.

—Bedroom Makeovers. 2016. (Sleepover Secrets Ser.). 24p. (gr. 2-6). 28.50 *(978-1-62588-377-3(3)*, Smart Apple Media) Black Rabbit Bks.

—Cards & Gifts: Style Secrets for Girls. 2013. (Girl Talk Ser.). 32p. (gr. 4-7). lib. bdg. 31.35 *(978-1-59920-944-9(6))* Black Rabbit Bks.

—Cards & Gifts: Style Secrets for Girls. 2014. (Girl Talk Ser.). (ENG., Illus.). 32p. (J). (gr. 4-8). pap. 9.95 *(978-1-77092-201-3(6))* Saunders Bk. Co. CAN. Dist: RiverStream Publishing.

—Cool Crafts. 2016. (Sleepover Secrets Ser.). 24p. (gr. 2-6). 28.50 *(978-1-62588-378-0(1)*, Smart Apple Media) Black Rabbit Bks.

—Cool Stuff to Sew. 2014. (Cool Stuff Ser.). 32p. (gr. 2-5). 31.35 *(978-1-62588-191-5(6))* Black Rabbit Bks.

—Craft Skills. 2012. (Super Skills Ser.). (Illus.). 32p. (gr. 3-6). lib. bdg. 31.35 *(978-1-59920-796-4(6))* Black Rabbit Bks.

—A Craft Star. 2016. (How to Be... Ser.). 24p. (gr. 2-6). 28.50 *(978-1-62588-368-1(4)*, Smart Apple Media) Black Rabbit Bks.

—Diaries & Keepsakes: Style Secrets for Girls. 2013. (Girl Talk Ser.). 32p. (gr. 4-7). 31.35 *(978-1-59920-945-6(4))* Black Rabbit Bks.

—Diaries & Keepsakes: Style Secrets for Girls. 2014. (Girl Talk Ser.). (ENG., Illus.). 32p. (J). (gr. 4-8). pap. 9.95 *(978-1-77092-202-0(4))* Saunders Bk. Co. CAN. Dist: RiverStream Publishing.

—Fun & Games. 2016. (Sleepover Secrets Ser.). 24p. (gr. 2-6). 28.50 *(978-1-62588-380-3(3)*, Smart Apple Media) Black Rabbit Bks.

—Fun with Friends: Style Secrets for Girls. 2013. (Girl Talk Ser.). 32p. (gr. 4-7). 31.35 *(978-1-59920-946-3(2))* Black Rabbit Bks.

—Fun with Friends: Style Secrets for Girls. 2014. (Girl Talk Ser.). (ENG., Illus.). 32p. (J). (gr. 4-8). pap. 9.95 *(978-1-77092-203-7(2))* Saunders Bk. Co. CAN. Dist: RiverStream Publishing.

—Wardrobe Makeovers. 2016. (Sleepover Secrets Ser.). 24p. (gr. 2-6). 28.50 *(978-1-62588-381-0(1)*, Smart Apple Media) Black Rabbit Bks.

Turnbull, Stephaniel & Turnbull, Stephanie. Cool Stuff to Make with Paper. 2014. (Cool Stuff Ser.). 32p. (gr. 2-5). 31.35 *(978-1-62588-189-2(4))* Black Rabbit Bks.

Twin Sisters(r), et al. Easy-To-Make Christmas Crafts for Kids. 2016. (I'm Learning the Bible Activity Book Ser.). (ENG.). 32p. (J). pap. 4.99 *(978-1-63409-803-8(X))* Barbour Publishing, Inc.

Usborne Books, creator. The Usborne Big Book of Christmas Things to Make & Do. 2013. (ENG., Illus.). 128p. pap. 14.99 *(978-0-7945-2950-5(X)*, Usborne) EDC Publishing.

—50 Fairy Things to Make & Do. 2006. (Activity Cards Ser.). 50p. (J). 9.99 *(978-0-7945-1318-4(2)*, Usborne) EDC Publishing.

Using Makerspaces for School Projects. 2017. (Using Makerspaces for School Projects Ser.). 64p. (gr. 11-11). 172.25 ***(978-1-4777-8986-5(3)***, Rosen Central) Rosen Publishing Group, Inc., The.

Van Vleet, Carmella. Great Ancient Egypt Projects. 2006. (Build It Yourself Ser.). (ENG., Illus.). 128p. (J). (gr. 3-7). pap. 15.95 *(978-0-9771294-5-4(4))* Northern Trails Pr.

—Seven Wonders of the World: Discover Amazing Monuments to Civilization with 20 Projects. Rizvi, Farah, illus. 2011. (Build It Yourself Ser.). (ENG.). 128p. (J). (gr. 3-7). 21.95 *(978-1-934670-82-8(0))*; pap. 15.95 *(978-1-936313-73-0(1))* Open City Bks.

Veigele, William J. Sea Bag of Memories: Images, Poems, Thoughts, & Crafts of the small Ship Sailors of World War II. 2003. 320p. (YA). (gr. 10-18). 39.95 *(978-0-9645867-4-1(6))* Astral Publishing Co.

Ventura, Marne. Amazing Recycled Projects You Can Create. 2015. (Imagine It, Build It Ser.). (ENG., Illus.). 32p. (gr. 3-4). lib. bdg. 27.99 *(978-1-4914-4292-0(1))* Capstone Press of Coughlan Cos.

—Awesome Paper Projects You Can Create. 2015. (Imagine It, Build It Ser.). (ENG., Illus.). 32p. (gr. 3-4). lib. bdg. 27.99 *(978-1-4914-4293-7(X))* Capstone Press of Coughlan Cos.

—Big Book of Building: Duct Tape, Paper, Cardboard, & Recycled Projects to Blast Away Boredom. 2015. (Imagine It, Build It Ser.). (ENG., Illus.). 144p. (gr. 3-4). pap. 14.95 *(978-1-4914-4371-2(5))* Capstone Press of Coughlan Cos.

—Cool Cardboard Projects You Can Create. 2015. (Imagine It, Build It Ser.). (ENG., Illus.). 32p. (gr. 3-4). lib. bdg. 27.99 *(978-1-4914-4291-3(3))* Capstone Press of Coughlan Cos.

—Fun Things to Do with Cardboard Tubes, 1 vol. 2014. (10 Things to Do Ser.). (ENG.). 32p. (gr. 1-2). 27.32 *(978-1-4765-9895-6(9))* Capstone Press of Coughlan Cos.

—Fun Things to Do with Milk Jugs, 1 vol. 2014. (10 Things to Do Ser.). (ENG.). 32p. (gr. 1-2). 27.32 *(978-1-4765-9894-9(0))* Capstone Press of Coughlan Cos.

—Imagine It, Build It. 2015. (Imagine It, Build It Ser.). (ENG.). 32p. (gr. 3-4). 111.96 *(978-1-4914-6663-6(4)*, Edge Bks.) Capstone Press of Coughlan Cos.

—Incredible Duct Tape Projects You Can Create. 2015. (Imagine It, Build It Ser.). (ENG., Illus.). 32p. (gr. 3-4). lib. bdg. 27.99 *(978-1-4914-4290-6(5))* Capstone Press of Coughlan Cos.

—The Perfect Pair! Purses, Handbags, & Wallets for All Occasions. 2016. (Accessorize Yourself! Ser.). (ENG., Illus.). 48p. (gr. 4-5). lib. bdg. 34.65 *(978-1-4914-8230-8(3))* Capstone Press of Coughlan Cos.

Ventura, Marne & Peschke, Marci. Kylie Jean Party Craft Queen, 1 vol. Mourning, Tuesday, illus. 2014. (Kylie Jean Craft Queen Ser.). (ENG.). 32p. (gr. 2-3). lib. bdg. 26.65 *(978-1-4795-2191-3(4))* Picture Window Bks.

—Kylie Jean Summer Camp Craft Queen, 1 vol. Mourning, Tuesday, illus. 2014. (Kylie Jean Craft Queen Ser.). (ENG.). 32p. (gr. 2-3). lib. bdg. 26.65 *(978-1-4795-2193-7(0))* Picture Window Bks.

Ventura, Marne, et al. Kylie Jean Craft Queen, 1 vol. Mourning, Tuesday, illus. 2014. (Kylie Jean Craft Queen Ser.). (ENG.). 112p. (gr. 2-3). pap. 9.95 *(978-1-4795-2971-1(0))* Picture Window Bks.

Vodicka-Paredes, Lenka & Curte, Asia. Forest Fairy Crafts: Enchanting Fairies & Felt Friends from Simple Supplies. 2013. (ENG., Illus.). 144p. (J). (gr. k-3). pap. 19.95 *(978-1-60705-690-4(9))* C & T Publishing.

Wagner, Lisa. Cool Painted Stuff, 1 vol. 2005. (Cool Crafts Ser.). (ENG., Illus.). 32p. (gr. k-6). 28.50 *(978-1-59197-742-1(8)*, Checkerboard Library) ABDO Publishing Co.

Waley, Safiya & Woodcock, Victoria. Making Stuff for Kids. Smith, Raven, photos by. 2007. (ENG., Illus.). 160p. pap. 24.95 *(978-1-906155-00-1(3))* Black Dog Publishing Ltd. GBR. Dist: Two Rivers Distribution.

Wallace, Mary & Owlkids Books Inc. Staff. I Can Make That! Fantastic Crafts for Kids, 0 vols. 2nd rev. ed. 2014. (ENG., Illus.). 152p. (J). (gr. -1-3). 18.95 *(978-1-926973-97-5(6)*, Owlkids) Owlkids Bks. Inc. CAN. Dist: Publishers Group West (PGW).

Walters, Cloe. Get Quilting with Angela & Cloe: 14 Projects for Kids to Sew. 2015. (ENG., Illus.). 128p. pap. 24.95 *(978-1-60705-955-4(X))* C & T Publishing.

Walton, Sally. I Can Do Crafts: Creative Things for Young Children to Make, Shown Step by Step. 2015. (ENG., Illus.). 48p. (J). (gr. -1-4). 7.99 *(978-1-86147-365-3(6)*, Armadillo) Anness Publishing GBR. Dist: National Bk. Network.

Walton, Sally & Painter, Lucy. 100 Fantastic Things to Make, Do & Play: Simple, Fun Projects That Use Easy Everyday Materials. 2008. (ENG., Illus.). 256p. (J). (gr. -1-2). pap. 24.99 *(978-1-84476-473-0(7))* Anness Publishing GBR. Dist: National Bk. Network.

Walton, Sally, et al. Fun Projects & Amazing Things to Make, Do, Play & Give: Two Fantastic Books in a Box - the Ultimate Rainy-Day Collection with 220 Exciting Step-By-Step Projects Shown in over 3000 Photographs, 2 vols. 2013. (ENG., Illus.). 265p. 25.00 *(978-1-84322-960-5(9))* Anness Publishing GBR. Dist: National Bk. Network.

Walton, Stewart & Walton, Sally. Stamp Decorating: A Step-by-Step Guidebook & Inspirational Sourcebook, with over 80 Projects & Techniques. (Illus.). 256p. (J). pap. *(978-0-681-64292-8(0))* Anness Publishing.

Warne, Frederick & Barker, Cicely Mary. Flower Fairies Art Activity Book. 2007. (Flower Fairies Ser.). (ENG., Illus.). 72p. (J). (gr. -1-2). pap., act. bk. ed. 9.99 *(978-0-7232-5915-2(1)*, Warne) Penguin Young Readers Group.

Warwick, Ellen. Stuff for Your Space. Lum, Bernice, tr. Lum, Bernice, illus. 2004. (Kids Can Do It Ser.). (ENG.). 40p. (J). (gr. 3-7). 6.95 *(978-1-55337-399-5(5))* Kids Can Pr., Ltd. CAN. Dist: Hachette Bk. Group.

Warwick, Ellen & Di Salle, Rachel. Junk Drawer Jewelry. Kurisu, Jane, illus. 2006. (Kids Can Do It Ser.). (ENG.). 40p. (J). (gr. 3-7). 6.95 *(978-1-55337-966-9(7))* Kids Can Pr., Ltd. CAN. Dist: Hachette Bk. Group.

Watt, Fiona. Animal Fun. 2008. (Preschool Activities Ser.). 23p. (J). spiral bd. 12.99 *(978-0-7945-2049-6(9)*, Usborne) EDC Publishing.

—Dinosaur Fun. Lovell, Katie, illus. 2009. (Preschool Activities Ser.). 24p. (J). (gr. -1). spiral bd. 12.99 *(978-0-7945-2133-2(9)*, Usborne) EDC Publishing.

—Easter Fun. 2009. (Preschool Activities Ser.). (Illus.). 24p. (J). (gr. -1). spiral bd. 12.99 *(978-0-7945-2482-1(6)*, Usborne) EDC Publishing.

—Fairy Things to Stitch & Sew. Fearn, Katrina & Hussain, Nelupa, illus. 2006. (Usborne Activities Ser.). 32p. (J). (gr. 1-4). pap. 6.99 *(978-0-7945-1235-4(6)*, Usborne) EDC Publishing.

—Spooky Things to Make & Do. 2012. (Activity Bks). 34p. (J). pap. 6.99 *(978-0-7945-1863-9(X)*, Usborne) EDC Publishing.

—365 Things to Make & Do. Harrison, Erica, illus. 2008. (Usborne Activities Ser.). 127p. (J). (gr. 1). 24.99 *(978-0-7945-1954-4(7)*, Usborne) EDC Publishing.

Watt, Fiona & Gilpin, Rebecca. Big Bk of Fairy Things to Make & Do. 2006. 96p. (J). pap. 14.99 *(978-0-7945-1437-2(5)*, Usborne) EDC Publishing.

—The Usborne Big Book of Christmas Things to Make & Do. Fearn, Katrina, illus. 2005. 99p. (J). *(978-0-439-81506-2(1))* Scholastic, Inc.

Watt, Fiona, et al. The Usborne Big Book of Vacation Things to Make & Do. Baggott, Stella, illus. 2006. 96p. (J). (gr. 1-4). pap. 14.99 *(978-0-7945-1317-7(4)*, Usborne) EDC Publishing.

Weatherill, Sue & Weatherill, Stephen. Romans. 2005. (ENG., Illus.). 24p. (J). (gr. 1-4). pap., act. bk. ed. 7.99 *(978-1-902915-34-0(8))* B Small Publishing GBR. Dist: Independent Pubs. Group.

What a Great Idea!, 6 Packs. (gr. k-1). 23.00 *(978-0-7635-9072-7(X))* Rigby Education.

Wheeler-Toppen, Jodi. Amazing Cardboard Tube Science. 2016. (Recycled Science Ser.). (ENG., Illus.). 32p. (gr. 3-4). lib. bdg. 27.99 *(978-1-5157-0860-5(8))* Capstone Press of Coughlan Cos.

Wilbur, Helen L. F Is for Friendship: A Quilt Alphabet. van Frankenhuyzen, Gijsbert, illus. 2011. (Sleeping Bear Alphabets Ser.). (ENG.). 32p. (J). (gr. 1-4). lib. bdg. 16.95 *(978-1-58536-532-6(7)*, 202215) Sleeping Bear Pr.

Willems, Mo. We Are in an ART-Ivity Book! Willems, Mo, illus. 2017. (Elephant & Piggie Book Ser.). (ENG., Illus.). 144p. (J). (gr. -1-3). pap. 14.99 ***(978-1-4847-9816-4(3))*** Hyperion Bks. for Children.

Williams, Jack S. Craftsmen & Craftswomen. 2004. (People of the California Missions Ser.). (Illus.). 64p. (YA). (gr. 3-6). lib. bdg. 26.50 *(978-0-8239-6280-8(6))* Rosen Publishing Group, Inc., The.

—Craftsmen & Craftswomen of the California Mission Frontier. 2009. (People of the California Missions Ser.). 64p. (gr. 4-4). 58.50 *(978-1-60851-156-3(1)*, PowerKids Pr.) Rosen Publishing Group, Inc., The.

Williams, Nancy Noel. Don't Lose It, Reuse It. 2010. *(978-1-60617-134-9(8))* Teaching Strategies, LLC.

Williams, Pam. Starting a Makerspace. 2017. (21st Century Skills Innovation Library: Makers As Innovators Junior Ser.). (ENG., Illus.). 24p. (J). (gr. 2-5). lib. bdg. 28.50 *(978-1-63472-192-9(6)*, 209340) Cherry Lake Publishing.

Wirtzfeld, Beverly. Bear's Designs Unlimited, Vol. I. 60p. (J). (gr. 4-10). ring bd. 4.95 *(978-0-9638473-0-0(9))* Bear's Designs Unlimited.

Wolf, Laurie Goldrich. Crafty Princess: Green & Groovy. 2012. (Green & Groovy Ser.: 5). (ENG.). 64p. (J). (gr. k). 18.99 *(978-1-935703-42-6(0))* Downtown Bookworks.

—The Lonely Sock Club: One Sock, Tons of Cool Projects! 2011. (Green & Groovy Ser.: 1). (ENG.). 64p. (J). (gr. 3). 16.99 *(978-1-935703-06-8(4))* Downtown Bookworks.

Wolf, Laurie Goldrich & Abrams, Pam. Fairy Crafts: Green & Groovy. 2011. (Green & Groovy Ser.: 2). (ENG.). 64p. (J). (gr. 1). 16.99 *(978-1-935703-33-4(1))* Downtown Bookworks.

Woods, Karen. Creative Textiles Projects for Children. 2011. (ENG., Illus.). 128p. pap. 25.95 *(978-0-7136-8541-1(7)*, 9780713685411, A&C Black Visual Arts) Bloomsbury Publishing Plc GBR. Dist: Macmillan.

Woram, Catherine. Christmas Crafting with Kids. Wreford, Polly, photos by. 2011. (ENG., Illus.). 128p. pap. *(978-1-84975-141-4(2))* Ryland Peters & Small.

—Christmas Crafting with Kids: 35 Projects for the Festive Season. 2008. (ENG., Illus.). 128p. (J). *(978-1-84597-700-9(9))* Ryland Peters & Small.

—Crafting with Kids: Creative Fun for Children Aged 3-10. Davies, Vanessa, photos by. 2006. (ENG., Illus.). 128p. (J). (gr. 3-7). pap. *(978-1-84597-252-3(X))* Ryland Peters & Small.

—What Shall We Do Today? 60 creative crafting projects for Kids. 2009. (ENG., Illus.). 160p. (J). (gr. 3-12). pap. 19.95 *(978-1-84597-887-7(0))* Ryland Peters & Small GBR. Dist: Simon & Schuster, Inc.

Woram, Catherine & Youngs, Clare. Rainy Day Book of Things to Make & Do. 2012. (ENG., Illus.). 160p. pap. *(978-1-84975-272-5(9))* Ryland Peters & Small.

World Book, Inc Staff, contrib. by. Fun with Cultural Crafts & Performing Arts. 2011. (J). *(978-0-7166-0227-9(X))* World Bk., Inc.

World Crafts & Recipes, 6 vols., Set. Incl. Recipe & Craft Guide to China. Matter, Joanne. lib. bdg. 29.95 *(978-1-58415-937-7(5))*; Recipe & Craft Guide to France. LaRoche, Amelia. lib. bdg. 29.95 *(978-1-58415-936-0(7))*; Recipe & Craft Guide to India. Ejaz, Khadija. lib. bdg. 29.95 *(978-1-58415-938-4(3))*; Recipe & Craft Guide to Indonesia. Reusser, Kayleen. lib. bdg. 29.95 *(978-1-58415-934-6(0))*; Recipe & Craft Guide to Japan. Mofford, Juliet. lib. bdg. 29.95 *(978-1-58415-933-9(2))*; Recipe & Craft Guide to the Caribbean. Mofford, Juliet. lib. bdg. 29.95 *(978-1-58415-935-3(9))*; 48p. (J). (gr. 4-8). (Illus.). 2010. Set lib. bdg. 203.70 *(978-1-58415-939-1(1))* Mitchell Lane Pubs., Inc.

Wright, Shannon. Children's Secret Diary: Kid's Diary. 2013. (ENG.). 50p. 11.78 *(978-1-62884-684-3(4)*, Baby Professor (Education Kids)) Speedy Publishing LLC.

Wrigley, Annabel. We Love to Sew: 28 Pretty Things to Make. 2013. (ENG., Illus.). 176p. pap. 22.95 *(978-1-60705-632-4(1))* C & T Publishing.

—We Love to Sew — Bedrooms: 23 Projects, Cool Stuff for Your Space. 2014. (ENG., Illus.). 176p. (J). (gr. 2-8). pap. 21.95 *(978-1-60705-824-3(3)*, FunStitch Studio) C & T Publishing.

Yanish, Brian. ScrapKins: Junk Re-Thunk: Amazing Creations You Can Build from Junk. Yanish, Brian, illus. 2016. (ENG., Illus.). 80p. (J). pap. 12.99 *(978-1-62779-133-5(7)*, 9781627791335, Holt, Henry & Co. Bks. For Young Readers) Holt, Henry & Co.

Yasuda, Anita. Easter Crafts. Gallagher-Cole, Memie, illus. 2016. (Holiday Crafts Ser.). (ENG.). 24p. (J). (gr. k-3). 28.50 *(978-1-5038-0817-1(3)*, 210653) Child's World, Inc., The.

—Halloween Crafts. Gallagher-Cole, Memie, illus. 2016. (Holiday Crafts Ser.). (ENG.). 24p. (J). (gr. k-3). 28.50 *(978-1-5038-0820-1(3)*, 210656) Child's World, Inc., The.

Yates, Jane. Duct Tape Creations. 2016. (Cool Crafts for Kids Ser.). 00032p. (J). (gr. 3-3). pap. 11.75 *(978-1-4994-8229-4(9)*, Windmill Bks.) Rosen Publishing Group, Inc., The.

—Fun with Felt. 2016. (Cool Crafts for Kids Ser.). 00032p. (J). (gr. 3-3). pap. 11.75 *(978-1-4994-8232-4(9)*, Windmill Bks.) Rosen Publishing Group, Inc., The.

—Pipe Cleaner Projects. 2016. (Cool Crafts for Kids Ser.). 00032p. (J). (gr. 3-3). pap. 11.75 *(978-1-4994-8237-9(X)*, Windmill Bks.) Rosen Publishing Group, Inc., The.

Youngs, Clare & Young, Clare. Explorar y Crear. 2012. (SPA.). 128p. (gr. 13-13). pap. 20.99 *(978-84-261-3887-3(X))* Juventud, Editorial ESP. Dist: Lectorum Pubns., Inc.

Zondervan Staff. Redo Your Room: 50 Bedroom DIYs You Can Do in a Weekend, 1 vol. Faithgirlz! and Girls' Life Magazine Editors, ed. 2015. (Faithgirlz Ser.). (ENG.). 128p. (J). pap. 14.99 *(978-0-310-74632-4(9))* Zonderkidz.

25 Crafts for Christmas. 2015. (ENG., Illus.). 32p. (J). (gr. -1-2). pap. 9.99 *(978-0-7459-6387-7(0))* Lion Hudson PLC GBR. Dist: Independent Pubs. Group.

HANDWRITING

see Writing

HANGING

see Capital Punishment

HANNIBAL, 247 B.C.-183 B.C.

Abbott, Jacob. Hannibal. 2009. (J). pap. 12.00 *(978-1-59128-059-0(1))* Canon Pr.

—Hannibal. 2005. reprint ed. pap. 28.95 *(978-0-7661-9515-8(5))* Kessinger Publishing, LLC.

Brooks, Philip. Hannibal. rev. ed. 2015. (Wicked History Ser.). (ENG., Illus.). 144p. (J). lib. bdg. 33.00 *(978-0-531-22122-8(9)*, Children's Pr.) Scholastic Library Publishing.

—Hannibal: Rome's Worst Nightmare. (Wicked History Ser.). (ENG.). 128p. (J). 2009. pap. 5.95 *(978-0-531-22174-7(1)*, Children's Pr.) 2008. (Illus.). 31.00 *(978-0-531-18553-7(2)*, Watts, Franklin) Scholastic Library Publishing.

Mills, Clifford W. Hannibal. 2008. (Ancient World Leaders Ser.). (Illus.). 120p. (gr. 6-12). lib. bdg. 30.00 *(978-0-7910-9580-5(0)*, Chelsea Hse.) Facts On File, Inc.

Newsome, Joel. Hannibal. 2017. (J). ***(978-1-5026-2869-5(4))*** Cavendish Square Publishing.

Price, Sean. Hannibal of Carthage, 1 vol. 2013. (Hero Journals). (ENG., Illus.). 48p. (gr. 4-6). 33.32 *(978-1-4109-5359-9(9))*; pap. 9.95 *(978-1-4109-5366-7(1))* Heinemann-Raintree. (NA-r).

Warrick, Karen Clemens. Hannibal: Great General of the Ancient World. 2006. (Rulers of the Ancient World Ser.). (Illus.). 160p. (J). (gr. 6-12). lib. bdg. 27.93 *(978-0-7660-2564-6(0))* Enslow Pubs., Inc.

HANNIBAL, 247 B.C.-183 B.C.—FICTION

Henty, George Alfred. The Young Carthaginian: A Tale of the Times of Hannibal. 2004. reprint ed. pap. 27.95 *(978-1-4191-8911-1(5))*; pap. 1.99 *(978-1-4192-8911-8(X))*; pap. 27.95 *(978-1-4191-8911-1(5))* Kessinger Publishing, LLC.

—The Young Carthaginian: A Tale of the Times of Hannibal. 2004. pap. 8.95 *(978-1-57646-874-6(7))* Quiet Vision Publishing.

HANUKKAH

Accord Publishing Staff & Ohrt, Kate. Hanukkah: A Mini AniMotion Book. 2010. (ENG.). 12p. (J). (gr. -1). 9.99 *(978-0-7407-9799-6(9))* Andrews McMeel Publishing.

Adler, David A. The Kids' Catalog of Hanukkah. 2004. (Kids' Catalog Ser.). (ENG., Illus.). 160p. pap. 19.95 *(978-0-8276-0805-4(5))* Jewish Pubn. Society.

—The Story of Hanukkah. Weber, Jill, illus. 2012. (ENG.). 32p. (J). (gr. -1-2). pap. 6.99 *(978-0-8234-2547-1(9))* Holiday Hse., Inc.

Aloian, Molly. Hanukkah. 2008. (ENG., Illus.). 32p. (J). lib. bdg. *(978-0-7787-4283-8(0))*; pap. *(978-0-7787-4301-9(2))* Crabtree Publishing Co.

Amstutz, Lisa J. Hanukkah. 2017. (Holidays Around the World Ser.). (ENG., Illus.). 24p. (J). (gr. k-1). lib. bdg. 21.99 *(978-1-5157-4854-0(5)*, Pebble Bks.) Capstone Press of Coughlan Cos.

Balsley, Tilda. Eight Is Great. Takahashi, Hideko, illus. 2012. (Hanukkah Ser.). (ENG.). 12p. (J). (gr. -1 — 1). bds. 5.95 *(978-0-7613-6623-2(7)*, Kar-Ben Publishing) Lerner Publishing Group.

—Maccabee! The Story of Hanukkah. Harrington, David, illus. 2010. (Hanukkah Ser.). (ENG.). 32p. (J). (gr. -1-2). pap. 7.95 *(978-0-7613-4508-4(6))*; lib. bdg. 7.95 *(978-0-7613-4507-7(8))* Lerner Publishing Group. (Kar-Ben Publishing).

Bledsoe, Karen E. Hanukkah Crafts. 2004. (Fun Holiday Crafts Kids Can Do! Ser.). (Illus.). 32p. (J). lib. bdg. 23.94 *(978-0-7660-2238-6(2))* Enslow Pubs., Inc.

Bodden, Valerie. Hanukkah. 2005. (My First Look at Holidays Ser.). (Illus.). 24p. (J). (gr. k-3). lib. bdg. 15.95 *(978-1-58341-369-2(3)*, Creative Education) Creative Co., The.

Bullard, Lisa. Caleb's Hanukkah. Basaluzzo, Constanza, illus. 2012. (Cloverleaf Books (tm) — Fall & Winter Holidays Ser.). (ENG.). 24p. (gr. k-2). (J). lib. bdg. 23.93 *(978-0-7613-5077-4(2))*; 6.95 *(978-0-7613-8587-5(8))* Lerner Publishing Group. (Millbrook Pr.).

Chanukah Treats: For Kids, by Kids. 2009. (Illus.). 16p. (J). spiral bd. *(978-0-9772560-2-0(2))* Rite Lite Limited.

Dice, Elizabeth A. & Matters, Print. Christmas & Hanukkah. 2009. (Holidays & Celebration Ser.). (Illus.). 120p. (gr. 5-8).

H
I

40.00 *(978-1-60413-092-8(X)*, Chelsea Hse.) Facts On File, Inc.

Dickmann, Nancy. Hanukkah, 1 vol. 2010. (Holidays & Festivals Ser.). (ENG., Illus.). 24p. (gr. -1-1). pap. 6.29 *(978-1-4329-4071-3(6)*, Acorn) Heinemann-Raintree.

—Janucá, 1 vol. 2011. (Fiestas Ser.). 24p. (gr. -1-1). (SPA & ENG.). 22.65 *(978-1-4329-5382-9(6))*; (ENG & SPA.). pap. 6.29 *(978-1-4329-5401-7(6))* Heinemann-Raintree. (Bellota).

Dorling Kindersley Publishing Staff, ed. Hanukkah. 2004. (Ultimate Sticker Bks.). (ENG.). 16p. (J). (gr. k-3). pap. 6.99 *(978-0-7566-0546-9(6)*, DK Children) Dorling Kindersley Publishing, Inc.

Felix, Rebecca. We Celebrate Hanukkah in Winter. 2014. (21st Century Basic Skills Library: Let's Look at Winter Ser.). (ENG.). 24p. (J). (gr. k-3). 22.79 *(978-1-63137-610-8(1)*, 205223) Cherry Lake Publishing.

Fishman, Cathy Goldberg. Hanukkah. Young, Mary O'Keefe, illus. (On My Own Holidays Ser.). 48p. (gr. 2-4). 2004. (J). lib. bdg. 25.26 *(978-1-57505-195-6(8))* 2003. (ENG.). pap. 6.95 *(978-1-57505-583-1(X))* Lerner Publishing Group.

—On Hanukkah. Hall, Melanie W., illus. 2005. 27p. (J). (gr. k-4). reprint ed. 16.00 *(978-0-7567-9289-3(4))* DIANE Publishing Co.

Foran, Jill. Hanukkah. 2003. (Celebrating Cultures Ser.). (Illus.). 24p. (J). lib. bdg. 24.45 *(978-1-59036-092-7(3))* Weigl Pubs., Inc.

Grack, Rachel. Hanukkah. 2017. (Hanukkah Ser.). 24p. (J). (gr. k-3). pap. 6.99 ***(978-1-61891-274-9(7))***; (ENG., Illus.). lib. bdg. 25.95 *(978-1-62617-595-2(0))* Bellwether Media. (Blastoff! Readers).

Groner, Judye & Wikler, Madeline. Maccabee Meals: Food & Fun for Hanukkah. Roma, Ursula, illus. 2012. (Hanukkah Ser.). (ENG.). 64p. (J). (gr. 2-5). pap. 8.95 *(978-0-7613-5144-3(2)*, Kar-Ben Publishing) Lerner Publishing Group.

Hall, Margaret. Hanukkah. 2010. (Little World Holidays & Celebrations Ser.). (Illus.). 24p. (J). (gr. k-2). 22.79 *(978-1-61590-242-2(2))* Rourke Educational Media.

Heiligman, Deborah. Celebrate Hanukkah: With Light, Latkes, & Dreidels. 2006. (Holidays Around the World Ser.). (ENG., Illus.). 32p. (J). (gr. 1-4). 15.95 *(978-0-7922-5924-4(6))*; lib. bdg. 23.90 *(978-0-7922-5925-1(4))* National Geographic Society. (National Geographic Children's Bks.).

—Holidays Around the World: Celebrate Hanukkah: With Lights, Latkes, & Dreidels. 2016. (Holidays Around the World Ser.). (ENG., Illus.). 32p. (J). (gr. 1-4). pap. 7.99 *(978-1-4263-2476-5(6)*, National Geographic Children's Bks.) National Geographic Society.

Heiligman, Deborah & National Geographic Kids Staff. Celebrate Hanukkah: With Light, Latkes, & Dreidels. 2008. (Holidays Around the World Ser.). (ENG., Illus.). 32p. (J). (gr. 1-4). 6.95 *(978-1-4263-0293-0(2)*, National Geographic Children's Bks.) National Geographic Society.

Heller, Daryl. Hannukah. (My Library of Holidays Ser.). 24p. 2009. (gr. 1-1). 37.50 *(978-1-61514-695-6(4))* 2004. (Illus.). (J). lib. bdg. 18.75 *(978-1-4042-2525-1(0))* Rosen Publishing Group, Inc., The. (PowerKids Pr.).

—Hanukkah / Jánuca. 2009. (My Library of Holidays / Mi biblioteca de celebraciones Ser.). (ENG & SPA.). 24p. (gr. 1-1). 37.50 *(978-1-61514-701-4(2)*, Editorial Buenas Letras) Rosen Publishing Group, Inc., The.

—Hanukkah/Januca. 2004. (My Library of Holidays). (SPA & ENG., Illus.). 24p. (J). (gr. k-1). lib. bdg. 16.00 *(978-1-4042-7525-6(8)*, PowerKids Pr.) Rosen Publishing Group, Inc., The.

Heller, Esther Susan. Menorah under the Sea. Ginsburg, David, photos by. 2009. (Hanukkah Ser.). (Illus.). 32p. (J). (gr. k-2). 17.95 *(978-0-8225-7386-9(5)*, Kar-Ben Publishing) Lerner Publishing Group.

—Menorah under the Sea. 2009. (Hanukkah Ser.). (ENG.). 32p. (J). (gr. k-3). pap. 7.95 *(978-0-8225-7390-6(3)*, Kar-Ben Publishing) Lerner Publishing Group.

Herrington, Lisa M. Hanukkah. 2013. (Rookie Read-About(tm) Holidays Ser.). (ENG.). 32p. (J). 25.00 *(978-0-531-27201-5(X))*; pap. 5.95 *(978-0-531-27351-7(2))* Scholastic Library Publishing.

Kaiser, Cecily. On the First Night of Chanukah. Schatell, Brian, illus. 2007. (ENG.). 24p. (J). (gr. -1-3). pap. 3.99 *(978-0-439-75802-4(5)*, Cartwheel Bks.) Scholastic, Inc.

Keogh, Josie. Hanukkah. 2013. (PowerKids Readers: Happy Holidays! Ser.). (ENG., Illus.). 24p. (J). (gr. k-2). pap. 8.25 *(978-1-4488-9708-7(4))*; lib. bdg. 22.60 *(978-1-4488-9626-4(6))* Rosen Publishing Group, Inc., The. (PowerKids Pr.).

—Hanukkah: Janucá. Alamán, Eduardo, tr. from SPA. 2013. (PowerKids Readers: Happy Holidays! / !Felices Fiestas! Ser.). (ENG & SPA., Illus.). 24p. (gr. k-2). lib. bdg. 22.60 *(978-1-4488-9969-2(9)*, PowerKids Pr.) Rosen Publishing Group, Inc., The.

Kropf, Latifa Berry. It's Hanukkah Time! Cohen, Tod, photos by. 2011. (Hanukkah Ser.). (ENG., Illus.). 24p. (J). (gr. -1-1). pap. 8.95 *(978-0-7613-8306-2(9)*, Kar-Ben Publishing) Lerner Publishing Group.

Lawrence, Elizabeth. Celebrating Hanukkah. 2015. (Our Holidays Ser.). (ENG., Illus.). 24p. (J). (gr. 1-1). pap. 8.22 *(978-1-5026-0409-5(4))* Cavendish Square Publishing.

Lehman-Wilzig, Tami. Hanukkah Around the World. Wehrman, Vicki, illus. 2009. (Hanukkah Ser.). 48p. (J). (gr. k-2). 16.95 *(978-0-8225-8761-3(0))*; (ENG.). (gr. 3-5). pap. 7.95 *(978-0-8225-8762-0(9))* Lerner Publishing Group. (Kar-Ben Publishing).

Leon, Sarah & Eisikowitz, Michal. The Story of Chanukah. Katz, Tova, illus. 2008. 63p. (J). *(978-1-4226-0875-3(1))* Mesorah Pubns., Ltd.

Levin, Freddie. Chanukah Coloring Book. 2011. (Dover Holiday Coloring Book Ser.). (ENG., Illus.). 32p. (J). (gr. -1-2). pap. 3.99 *(978-0-486-48286-6(3))* Dover Pubns., Inc.

Lynette, Rachel. Let's Throw a Hanukkah Party! 2011. (Holiday Parties Ser.). (J). 22.60 *(978-1-4488-2572-1(5))*; 49.50 *(978-1-4488-2734-3(5))*; pap. 8.25 *(978-1-4488-2733-6(7))* Rosen Publishing Group, Inc., The. (PowerKids Pr.).

Marsh, Carole. Hanukkah: Activities, Crafts, Recipes & More! 2003. 32p. (J). (gr. 1-6). pap. 6.95 *(978-0-635-02174-8(9))* Gallopade International.

Martin, David. Hanukkah Lights. Sweet, Melissa, illus. 2015. (ENG.). 26p. (J). (gr. -1-2). 5.99 *(978-0-7636-7972-9(0))* Candlewick Pr.

Martin, David Lozell. Hanukkah Lights. Sweet, Melissa, illus. 2009. (ENG.). 26p. (J). (gr. -1 — 1). bds. 5.99 *(978-0-7636-3029-4(2))* Candlewick Pr.

Morey, Allan. Hanukkah. Séguin-Magee, Luke, illus. 2017. (Holidays in Rhythm & Rhyme Ser.). (ENG.). 24p. (gr. 1-3). 33.99 ***(978-1-68410-033-0(X))*** Cantata Learning.

Murray, Julie. Hanukkah, 1 vol. 2003. (Holidays Ser.). (ENG.). 24p. (gr. k-4). 25.65 *(978-1-57765-953-2(8)*, Buddy Bks.) ABDO Publishing Co.

Newman, Lesléa. Hanukkah Delight! Husband, Amy, illus. 2016. (ENG.). 12p. (gr. -1 — 1). bds. 5.99 *(978-1-4677-9353-7(1))*; 23.99 *(978-1-5124-0937-6(5))* Lerner Publishing Group. (Kar-Ben Publishing).

Ofanansky, Allison. Harvest of Light. Alpern, Eliyahu, photos by. 2011. (Hanukkah Ser.). (ENG., Illus.). 32p. (J). (gr. -1-5). pap. 8.95 *(978-0-7613-8305-5(0)*, Kar-Ben Publishing) Lerner Publishing Group.

Owen, Ruth. Christmas & Hanukkah Origami. 2012. (Holiday Origami Ser.). (ENG., Illus.). 32p. (J). (gr. 3-6). 26.50 *(978-1-4488-7860-4(8))*; pap. 11.75 *(978-1-4488-7919-9(1))* Rosen Publishing Group, Inc., The. (PowerKids Pr.).

—More Hanukkah Origami, 1 vol. 2015. (Holiday Origami Ser.). (ENG., Illus.). 32p. (J). 27.50 *(978-1-4777-5714-7(7)*, 1384076, PowerKids Pr.) Rosen Publishing Group, Inc., The.

Owens, L. L. Hanukkah, 1 vol. Conger, Holli, illus. 2009. (Cultural Holidays Ser.). (ENG.). 32p. (gr. -1-4). 28.50 *(978-1-60270-603-3(4)*, Looking Glass Library- Nonfiction) Magic Wagon.

Pettiford, Rebecca. Hanukkah. 2014. (Illus.). 24p. (J). lib. bdg. 25.65 *(978-1-62031-130-1(5)*, Bullfrog Bks.) Jump! Inc.

Ponto, Joanna & Erlbach, Arlene. Hanukkah. 2016. (Story of Our Holidays Ser.). (Illus.). 32p. (J). (gr. 3-3). pap. 10.52 *(978-0-7660-7625-9(3))* Enslow Pubs., Inc.

Priddy, Roger. Bright Baby Touch & Feel Hanukkah. 2011. (Bright Baby Touch & Feel Ser.). (ENG., Illus.). 12p. (J). (gr. -1 — 1). bds. 4.95 *(978-0-312-51338-2(0)*, 9780312513382, Priddy Bks.) St. Martin's Pr.

Randall, Ronne. Hanukkah Sweets & Treats. 2012. (Holiday Cooking for Kids! Ser.). (ENG., Illus.). 32p. (J). (gr. 3-6). 26.50 *(978-1-4488-8083-6(1))*; pap. 11.75 *(978-1-4488-8130-7(7))* Windmill Bks.

Rivers-Moore, Debbie. The Story of Hanukkah. 2014. (Create & Celebrate! Ser.). (ENG.). 48p. (J). (gr. -1-2). pap. 6.99 *(978-1-4380-0544-7(X))* Barron's Educational Series, Inc.

Rouss, Sylvia. Touch of Chanukah: A Touch & Feel Book. Becker, Boruch, illus. 2011. (J). bds. 9.95 *(978-0-8266-0013-4(1))* Kehot Pubn. Society.

Rouss, Sylvia A. & Tumdorf, Genene Levy. Sammy Spider's First Taste of Hanukkah. Kahn, Katherine Janus, illus. 2015. (ENG.). 32p. (J). (gr. -1-3). pap. 7.99 *(978-1-4677-5243-5(6)*, Kar-Ben Publishing) Lerner Publishing Group.

—Sammy Spider's First Taste of Hanukkah: A Cookbook. Kahn, Katherine Janus, illus. 2015. (ENG.). 32p. (J). (gr. -1-3). 6.99 *(978-1-4677-8842-7(2))*; 16.99 *(978-1-4677-5237-4(1))* Lerner Publishing Group. (Kar-Ben Publishing).

Rubin, Ellen. Hanakkah Puzzle Book. 2005. (Illus.). 4p. (J). bds. 12.95 *(978-1-930143-87-6(7)*, Devora Publishing) Simcha Media Group.

Schram, Peninnah. The Chanukah Blessing. Allon, Jeffrey, illus. 2004. (J). (gr. -1-3). 13.95 *(978-0-8074-0733-2(X)*, 101973) URJ Pr.

Sebra, Richard. It's Hanukkah! 2016. (Bumba Books (tm) — It's a Holiday! Ser.). (ENG.). 24p. (J). (gr. -1-1). 25.32 *(978-1-5124-1427-1(1))* Lerner Publishing Group.

Silberg, Francis Barry. The Story of Chanukah. Levy, Pamela R., illus. 2017. 24p. (J). ***(978-0-8249-1665-7(4))*** Worthy Publishing.

Trueit, Trudi Strain. Hanukkah. 2010. (Benchmark Rebus Ser.). 24p. (gr. k-1). 15.95 *(978-0-7614-4884-6(5))* Marshall Cavendish Corp.

Webster, Christine. How to Draw Hanukkah Symbols. 2009. (Kid's Guide to Drawing Ser.). 24p. (gr. 3-3). 47.90 *(978-1-61511-033-9(X)*, PowerKids Pr.) Rosen Publishing Group, Inc., The.

Zocchi, Judy. On Hanukkah. Wallis, Rebecca, illus. 2005. (Holiday Happenings Ser.). 32p. (J). pap. 10.95 *(978-1-59646-196-3(9))*; lib. bdg. 21.65 *(978-1-891997-45-7(9))*; per. 10.95 *(978-1-59646-197-0(7))* Dingles & Co.

—On Hanukkah/la Hanukkah. Wallis, Rebecca, illus. 2005. (Holiday Happenings Ser.).Tr. of Hanukkah. (ENG & SPA.). 32p. (J). pap. 10.95 *(978-1-59646-198-7(5))*; lib. bdg. 21.65 *(978-1-891997-46-4(7))*; per. 10.95 *(978-1-59646-199-4(3))* Dingles & Co.

HANUKKAH—FICTION

Adler, David A. Hanukkah Cookies with Sprinkles. Ebbeler, Jeffrey, illus. 2015. (J). *(978-0-87441-918-4(2))*; *(978-1-68115-500-5(1))* Behrman Hse., Inc.

—Story of Hanukkah. Weber, Jill, illus. 2011. (ENG.). 32p. (J). (gr. -1-2). 14.95 *(978-0-8234-2295-1(X))* Holiday Hse., Inc.

Alko, Selina. Daddy Christmas & Hanukkah Mama. 2012. (ENG., Illus.). 32p. (J). (gr. k-3). 16.99 *(978-0-375-86093-5(2)*, Knopf Bks. for Young Readers) Random Hse. Children's Bks.

Balsley, Tilda. ABC Hanukkah Hunt. Poole, Helen, illus. 2013. 32p. 17.95 *(978-1-4677-1637-6(5))*; (ENG.). (J). (gr. -1-2). 7.95 *(978-1-4677-0421-2(0)*, Kar-Ben Publishing); (ENG.). (J). (gr. -1-2). lib. bdg. 17.95 *(978-1-4677-0420-5(2)*, Kar-Ben Publishing) Lerner Publishing Group.

Balsley, Tilda & Fischer, Ellen. The Count's Hanukkah Countdown. Leigh, Tom, illus. 2012. (Hanukkah Ser.). 24p. (J). (gr. -1-1). (SPA & ENG.). 6.95 *(978-0-7613-7557-9(0))*; (ENG.). lib. bdg. 16.95 *(978-0-7613-7556-2(2))* Lerner Publishing Group. (Kar-Ben Publishing).

Barash, Chris. Is It Hanukkah Yet? Psacharopulo, Alessandra, illus. 2015. (ENG.). 32p. (J). (gr. -1-3). 16.99 *(978-0-8075-3384-0(X))* Whitman, Albert & Co.

Baroff, Raina. The Chanukah Puppet Show. 2008. 20p. per. 24.95 *(978-1-4241-8612-9(9))* America Star Bks.

Benderly, Beryl Lieff. Jason's Miracle: A Hanukkah Story. 2004. 114p. (J). (gr. 4-8). reprint ed. *(978-0-7567-7792-0(5))* DIANE Publishing Co.

Berlin, Bill & Berlin, Susan Isakoff. The Kvetch Who Stole Hanukkah, 1 vol. Welling, Peter J., illus. 2010. (ENG.). 32p. (J). (gr. k-3). 16.99 *(978-1-58980-798-3(7))* Pelican Publishing Co., Inc.

Bloom, Daniel Halevi. Bubbie & Zadie Come to My House: A Story for Hanukkah. Lankevich, George J., ed. Meilichson, Alex, illus. 2006. (ENG.). 32p. (J). (gr. -1-3). 16.95 *(978-0-7570-0298-4(6))* Square One Pubs.

Bunting, Eve. One Candle. Popp, K. Wendy, illus. 2004. (ENG.). 40p. (J). (gr. -1-3). pap. 6.99 *(978-0-06-008560-5(6))* HarperCollins Pubs.

Burstein, Chaya M. Hanukkah Cat. Henn, Judy Hanks, illus. 2003. 32p. (J). (gr. -1-3). pap. 6.95 *(978-1-58013-029-5(1)*, Kar-Ben Publishing) Lerner Publishing Group.

Capucilli, Alyssa Satin. Biscuit's Hanukkah. Schories, Pat & Young, Mary O'Keefe, illus. 2005. (Biscuit Ser.). (ENG.). 16p. (J). (gr. -1-3). bds. 4.99 *(978-0-06-009469-0(9)*, HarperFestival) HarperCollins Pubs.

Cleary, Brian P. Eight Wild Nights: A Family Hanukkah. Udovic, David, illus. 2006. 24p. (J). (gr. -1-3). lib. bdg. 16.95 *(978-1-58013-152-0(2)*, Kar-Ben Publishing) Lerner Publishing Group.

—Eight Wild Nights: A Family Hanukkah Tale. Udovic, David, illus. 2006. (ENG.). 24p. (J). (gr. k-3). 8.95 *(978-1-58013-229-9(4)*, Kar-Ben Publishing) Lerner Publishing Group.

Cohen, Deborah Bodin. Engineer Ari & the Hanukkah Mishap. Kober, Shahar, illus. 2011. (Hanukkah Ser.). (ENG.). 32p. (J). (gr. k-3). pap. 7.95 *(978-0-7613-5146-7(9))*; lib. bdg. 17.95 *(978-0-7613-5145-0(0))* Lerner Publishing Group. (Kar-Ben Publishing).

Conway, Diana Cohen. Northern Lights: A Hanukkah Story. Haas, Shelly O., illus. 2004. (J). 16.95 *(978-0-929371-79-5(8)*, Kar-Ben Publishing) Lerner Publishing Group.

Cookie Jar Entertainment Inc Staff. It's a Happy Holiday! 2007. 32p. (J). mass mkt. 4.99 *(978-1-60095-271-5(2)*, Doodlebops) Cookie Jar.

Da Costa, Deborah. Hanukkah Moon. Mosz, Gosia, illus. 2007. (Hanukkah Ser.). 32p. (J). (gr. -1-3). 17.95 *(978-1-58013-244-2(8)*, Kar-Ben Publishing) Lerner Publishing Group.

—Hanukkah Moon. Mosz, Gosia, illus. 2007. (Hanukkah Ser.). (ENG.). 32p. (J). (gr. 1-4). 10.95 *(978-1-58013-245-9(6)*, Kar-Ben Publishing) Lerner Publishing Group.

dePaola, Tomie. My First Chanukah. dePaola, Tomie, illus. 2008. (ENG., Illus.). 14p. (J). (gr. -1-k). bds. 6.99 *(978-0-448-44859-6(9)*, Grosset & Dunlap) Penguin Young Readers Group.

DiOrio, Ariel, illus. The Mystery of the Missing Menorahs: A Hanukkah Humdinger! 2007. 52p. (J). pap. 9.95 *(978-0-9659546-4-8(1))* Oak Leaf Systems.

Dresner, Hal. The Amazing Menorah of Mazeltown. Shapiro, Neil, illus. 2009. (ENG.). 32p. (J). (gr. -1-3). 16.95 *(978-1-933176-28-4(8))* Red Rock Pr., Inc.

Fischer, Ellen. Latke, the Lucky Dog. Beeke, Tiphanie, illus. 2014. 24p. (J). (gr. -1-2). 17.95 *(978-0-7613-9038-1(3)*, Kar-Ben Publishing) Lerner Publishing Group.

Fisman, Karen. Nonna's Hanukkah Surprise. Avilés, Martha, illus. 2015. (ENG.). 32p. (J). (gr. -1-3). 17.99 *(978-1-4677-3476-9(4)*, Kar-Ben Publishing) Lerner Publishing Group.

Flor Ada, Alma. Celebrate Hanukkah with Bubbe's Tales. Hayes, Joe & Franco, Sharon, trs. Epelbaum, Mariano, illus. 2007. (Cuentos para Celebrar / Stories to Celebrate Ser.). 30p. (gr. k-6). per. 11.95 *(978-1-59820-134-5(4))* Santillana USA Publishing Co., Inc.

Freeman, Don. Happy Hanukkah, Corduroy. McCue, Lisa, illus. 2009. (Corduroy Ser.). (ENG.). 16p. (J). (gr. -1 — 1). bds. 6.99 *(978-0-670-01127-8(4)*, Viking Books for Young Readers) Penguin Young Readers Group.

Gellman, Ellie. Jeremy's Dreidel. Mola, Maria, illus. 2012. (Hanukkah Ser.). 32p. (J). (gr. k-3). (ENG.). lib. bdg. 17.95 *(978-0-7613-7507-4(4))*; (SPA & ENG.). 7.95 *(978-0-7613-7508-1(2))* Lerner Publishing Group. (Kar-Ben Publishing).

Goldin, Barbara Diamond. The Best Hanukkah Ever, 0 vols. 2013. (ENG.). 34p. (J). (gr. k-3). pap. 9.99 *(978-1-4778-1055-2(2)*, 9781477810552, Amazon Children's Publishing) Amazon Publishing.

Goldman, Dara. Boris & Stella & the Perfect Gift. 2013. (ENG.). (J). *(978-1-58536-859-4(8))* Sleeping Bear Pr.

Greene, Jacqueline. Nathan's Hanukkah Bargain, 1 vol. Hierstein, Judith, illus. 2008. (ENG.). 32p. (J). (gr. 1-3). 16.99 *(978-1-58980-454-8(6))* Pelican Publishing Co., Inc.

Hillert, Margaret. Happy Hanukkah, Dear Dragon. Schimmell, David, illus. 2008. (BeginningtoRead Ser.). 32p. (J). (-2). (ENG.). pap. 11.94 ***(978-1-68404-011-7(6))***; lib. bdg. 22.60 *(978-1-59953-159-5(3))* Norwood Hse. Pr.

Ho, Jannie, illus. Light the Menorah. 2009. (ENG.). 12p. (J). (gr. -1-k). 7.99 *(978-0-8431-8954-4(1)*, Price Stern Sloan) Penguin Young Readers Group.

Howland, Naomi. Latkes, Latkes, Good to Eat: A Chanukah Story. 2004. (ENG., Illus.). 32p. (J). (gr. -1-3). pap. 6.99 *(978-0-618-49295-4(X))* Houghton Mifflin Harcourt Publishing Co.

Hyde, Heidi Smith. Emanuel & the Hanukkah Rescue. Akib, Jamel, illus. 2012. (Hanukkah Ser.). (SPA & ENG.). 32p. (J). (gr. k-3). 7.95 *(978-0-7613-6627-0(X)*, Kar-Ben Publishing) Lerner Publishing Group.

—Emanuel & the Whale Oil Lamp. Akib, Jamel, illus. 2012. (Hanukkah Ser.). (ENG.). 32p. (J). (gr. -1-1). lib. bdg. 17.95 *(978-0-7613-6625-6(3)*, Kar-Ben Publishing) Lerner Publishing Group.

Hyman, Trina Schart, illus. Hershel & the Hanukkah Goblins. 25th anniv. ed. 2014. (ENG.). 32p. (J). (gr. -1-3). 17.95 *(978-0-8234-3164-9(9))* Holiday Hse., Inc.

Izzy, Joel Ben. Dreidels on the Brain. 2016. (ENG.). 320p. (J). (gr. 5-9). 17.99 *(978-0-8037-4097-6(2)*, Dial Bks) Penguin Young Readers Group.

Jules, Jacqueline. Happy Hanukkah Lights. Shapiro, Michelle, illus. 2010. (Hanukkah Ser.). (ENG.). 12p. (J). (gr. -1 — 1). 5.95 *(978-0-7613-5120-7(5)*, Kar-Ben Publishing) Lerner Publishing Group.

—The Ziz & the Hanukkah Miracle. Kahn, Katherine Janus, illus. 2006. (ENG.). 32p. (J). (gr. -1-2). per. 9.95 *(978-1-58013-164-3(6)*, Kar-Ben Publishing) Lerner Publishing Group.

Jules, Jacqueline & Hechtkopf, Jacqueline. The Ziz & the Hanukkah Miracle. Kahn, Katherine Janus, illus. 2006. (ENG.). 32p. (J). (gr. -1-2). lib. bdg. 17.95 *(978-1-58013-160-5(3)*, Kar-Ben Publishing) Lerner Publishing Group.

Katz, Karen. Where Is Baby's Dreidel? Katz, Karen, illus. 2007. (ENG., Illus.). 14p. (J). (gr. -1 — 1). bds. 7.99 *(978-1-4169-3623-7(8)*, Little Simon) Little Simon.

Kimmel, Eric A. The Chanukkah Guest. Carmi, Giora, illus. (ENG.). 32p. (J). (gr. k-3). tchr. ed. 17.95 *(978-0-8234-0788-0(8))* Holiday Hse., Inc.

—The Golem's Latkes, 0 vols. Jasinski, Aaron, illus. 2011. (ENG.). 40p. (J). (gr. k-3). 17.99 *(978-0-7614-5904-0(9)*, 9780761459040, Amazon Children's Publishing) Amazon Publishing.

—Hanukkah Bear. Wohnoutka, Mike, illus. (ENG.). 32p. (J). (gr. -1-3). 2014. 6.99 *(978-0-8234-3169-4(X))* 2013. 17.95 *(978-0-8234-2855-7(9))* Holiday Hse., Inc.

Kimmel, Eric A. & Trueman, Matthew. Simon & the Bear: A Hanukkah Tale. 2014. (ENG., Illus.). 40p. (J). (gr. -1-k). 16.99 *(978-1-4231-4355-0(8))* Hyperion Bks. for Children.

Kleinberg, Naomi. Elmo's Little Dreidel (Sesame Street) Moroney, Christopher, illus. 2011. (ENG.). 12p. (J). (gr. k — 1). bds. 5.99 *(978-0-375-87396-6(1)*, Random Hse. Bks. for Young Readers) Random Hse. Children's Bks.

Kober, Shahar, illus. Dreidel, Dreidel, Dreidel. 2014. (ENG.). 12p. (J). (gr. -1 — 1). bds. 4.99 *(978-0-545-53364-5(3)*, Cartwheel Bks.) Scholastic, Inc.

Koffsky, Ann D. Judah Maccabee Goes to the Doctor. Shipman, Talitha, illus. 2017. (J). ***(978-1-68115-522-7(2))*** Behrman Hse., Inc.

Kollin, Dani. My Very Own Dreidel: A Pop-up Hanakkah Celebration! Howard, Juliet, illus. 2007. (ENG.). 12p. 10.95 *(978-1-58117-592-9(2)*, Intervisual/Piggy Toes) Bendon, Inc.

Korngold, Jamie. Sadie's Almost Marvelous Menorah. Fortenberry, Julie, illus. 2013. 24p. 17.95 *(978-1-4677-0051-1(7))*; (ENG.). (J). (gr. -1-1). 7.95 *(978-0-7613-6495-5(1)*, Kar-Ben Publishing) Lerner Publishing Group.

Korngold, Jamie S. Sadie's Almost Marvelous Menorah. Fortenberry, Julie, illus. 2013. (Hanukkah Ser.). 24p. (J). (gr. -1-1). lib. bdg. 17.95 *(978-0-7613-6493-1(5)*, Kar-Ben Publishing) Lerner Publishing Group.

Kroll, Steven. The Hanukkah Mice, 0 vols. Shapiro, Michelle, illus. 2012. (ENG.). 42p. (J). (gr. -1-3). pap. 7.99 *(978-0-7614-5988-0(X)*, 9780761459880, Amazon Children's Publishing) Amazon Publishing.

Kropf, Latifa Berry. It's Hanukkah Time! Cohen, Tod, photos by. 2004. (ENG., Illus.). 24p. (J). (gr. -1-1). 12.95 *(978-1-58013-120-9(4)*, Kar-Ben Publishing) Lerner Publishing Group.

Lehman-Wilzig, Tami & Katzman, Nicole. Nathan Blows Out the Hanukkah Candles. Tugeau, Jeremy, illus. 2011. (Hanukkah Ser.). (ENG.). 32p. (J). (gr. k-3). pap. 7.95 *(978-0-7613-6658-4(X)*, Kar-Ben Publishing) Lerner Publishing Group.

Levine, Abby. This Is the Dreidel. Billin-Frye, Paige, illus. 2012. (J). 34.28 *(978-1-61913-134-7(X))* Weigl Pubs., Inc.

Levine, Anna. Jodie's Hanukkah Dig. Topaz, Ksenia, illus. 2008. (Hanukkah Ser.). (ENG.). 32p. (J). (gr. k-3). 17.95 *(978-0-8225-7391-3(1))*; pap. 7.95 *(978-0-8225-7402-6(0))* Lerner Publishing Group. (Kar-Ben Publishing).

Londner, Renee. The Missing Letters: A Dreidel Story. Bodnaruk, Iryna, illus. 2017. (ENG.). 32p. (gr. -1-3). 17.99 *(978-1-4677-8933-2(X)*, Kar-Ben Publishing) Lerner Publishing Group.

McCarthy, Rebecca. Hanukkah Mad Libs. 2012. (Mad Libs Ser.). (ENG.). 48p. (J). (gr. 3-7). 4.99 *(978-0-8431-7245-4(2)*, Mad Libs) Penguin Young Readers Group.

Meachen Rau, Dana. Holiday Time. 2004. (Compass Point Early Reader Ser.). (J). 18.60 *(978-0-7565-0571-4(2))* Compass Point Bks.

Miller-Stehr, Felicia. Are You Chanukah or Christmas? 2008. 32p. pap. 17.99 *(978-1-4343-9517-7(0))* AuthorHouse.

Mott, Chuck. The Hannukah Moose. 2009. 48p. pap. 19.99 *(978-1-4490-4974-4(5))* AuthorHouse.

Naliboff, Jane. The Only One Club. Hopkins, Jeff, illus. 2013. (ENG.). 32p. (J). (gr. k-2). 6.95 *(978-1-936261-30-7(8))* Flashlight Pr.

Newman, Tracy. Hanukkah Is Coming! Garofoli, Viviana, illus. 2015. (ENG.). 12p. (J). (gr. -1 — 1). pap. 5.99 *(978-1-4677-5241-1(X)*, Kar-Ben Publishing) Lerner Publishing Group.

Ofanansky, Allison. Harvest of Light. Alpern, Eliyahu, photos by. 2008. (Hanukkah Ser.). (ENG., Illus.). 32p. (J). (gr. -1-5). 15.95 (978-0-8225-7389-0(X), Kar-Ben Publishing) Lerner Publishing Group.

Osterbach, Batya. Pini the Pitcher: A Story for Hanukkah. Elsby, Lizzy, illus. 2005. 32p. (J). (gr. 1-4). per. 9.95 *(978-1-932687-51-4(3)*, Devora Publishing) Simcha Media Group.

Peltz, Jason. Who Is Hanukah Heshie? 2013. 12p. pap. 5.99 *(978-1-4566-2001-1(0))* eBookit.com.

Penn, Audrey. The Miracle Jar: A Hanukkah Story. Lyon, Lea, illus. 2009. (ENG.). 32p. (J). (gr. -1-3). pap. 8.95 *(978-1-933718-26-2(9))* Tanglewood Pr.

Pinkwater, Daniel M. Beautiful Yetta's Hanukkah Kitten. Pinkwater, Jill, illus. 2014. (ENG.). 32p. (J). (gr. -1-2). 17.99 *(978-0-312-62134-6(5)*, 9780312621346) Feiwel & Friends.

Randall, Ronne. The Hanukkah Mice. Kneep, Maggie, illus. 2010. (ENG.). 18p. (J). (gr. -1-1). 9.99 *(978-0-8118-7663-6(2))* Chronicle Bks. LLC.

Rauchwerger, Diane Levin. Dinosaur on Hanukkah. Wolff, Jason, illus. 2005. (ENG.). 24p. (J). (gr. -1-1). 15.95 *(978-1-58013-145-2(X))*; per. 7.95 *(978-1-58013-143-8(3))* Lerner Publishing Group. (Kar-Ben Publishing).

Rosen, Michael J. Chanukah Lights. Sabuda, Robert, illus. 2011. (ENG.). 16p. (J). (gr. k-4). 34.99 *(978-0-7636-5533-4(3))* Candlewick Pr.

—Chanukah Lights Everywhere. 2010. (ENG.). 22p. (J). pap. 6.00 *(978-1-4379-7172-9(5))* DIANE Publishing Co.

—Chanukah Lights Everywhere. Iwai, Melissa, illus. 2006. (ENG.). 32p. (J). (gr. -1-3). pap. 7.99 *(978-0-15-205675-9(0))* Houghton Mifflin Harcourt Publishing Co.

Rosenberg, Amye. Melly's Menorah. 2012. (Illus.). 24p. (J). *(978-0-87441-884-2(4))* Behrman Hse., Inc.

Rosenberg, Faigy & Weiss, Esti. Hot! Hot! Hot! David, Racheli, illus. 2013. 32p. 10.95 (978-1-60091-268-9(0)) Israel Bookshop Pubns.

Rostoker-Gruber, Karen & Isaacs, Ronald H. Farmer Kobi's Hanukkah Match. Decker, C. B., illus. 2015. (J). (978-1-68115-501-2(X)); pap. (978-0-87441-924-5(7)) Behrman Hse., Inc.

Rouss, Sylvia A. The Littlest Maccabee: An Original Story. Cohen, Greg A., illus. 2006. (J). (978-1-932687-76-7(9), Pitspopany Pr.) Simcha Media Group.

—A Sammy Spider Hanukkah Colors. Kahn, Katherine, illus. 2017. (ENG.). 12p. (gr. -1 — 1). bds. 5.99 (978-1-4677-5238-1(X), Kar-Ben Publishing) Lerner Publishing Group.

Salem, Iosi, illus. The Mr. Mentch Coloring Book. 2008. (J). (gr. -1-3). 6.95 (978-1-934440-37-7(X), Pitspopany Pr.) Simcha Media Group.

Schnur, Susan & Schnur-Fishman, Anna. Potatoes at Turtle Rock. Steele-Morgan, Alexandra, illus. 2016. (ENG.). 32p. (J). (gr. k-3). 17.99 (978-1-4677-9321-6(3), Kar-Ben Publishing) Lerner Publishing Group.

Scholastic, Inc. Staff & Karr, Lily. A Chanukah Present for Me! McDonald, Jill, illus. 2009. (ENG.). 7p. (J). (gr. k — 1). bds. 6.99 (978-0-545-14874-0(X), Cartwheel Bks.) Scholastic, Inc.

Schotter, Roni. Hanukkah! Hafner, Marylin, illus. 2014. (ENG.). 32p. (J). (gr. -1-3). pap. 7.99 (978-0-316-37028-8(2)) Little, Brown Bks. for Young Readers.

Schuman, Burt E. Chanukah on the Prairie. Kaye, Rosalind Charney, illus. 2004. (gr. k-3). 13.95 (978-0-8074-0814-8(X), 381780) URJ Pr.

Shostak, Myra. Rainbow Candles: A Hanukkah Counting Book. Springer, Sally, illus. 2003. 12p. (J). (gr. -1-18). 4.95 (978-1-58013-031-8(3), Kar-Ben Publishing) Lerner Publishing Group.

Silverman, Erica. The Hanukkah Hop! D'Amico, Steven, illus. 2011. (ENG.). 32p. (J). (gr. -1-3). 12.99 (978-1-4424-0604-9(6), Simon & Schuster Bks. For Young Readers) Simon & Schuster Bks. For Young Readers.

Simon, Tanya & Simon, Richard. Oskar & the Eight Blessings. Siegel, Mark, illus. 2015. (ENG.). 40p. (J). (gr. -1-3). 17.99 (978-1-59643-949-8(1), 9781596439498) Roaring Brook Pr.

Simpson, Martha Seif. The Dreidel That Wouldn't Spin: A Toyshop Tale of Hanukkah. Bernhard, Durga Yael, illus. 2014. (ENG.). 32p. (J). (gr. -1-2). 16.95 (978-1-937786-28-1(5), Wisdom Tales) World Wisdom, Inc.

Singer, Isaac Bashevis. The Parakeet Named Dreidel. Berkson, Suzanne Raphael, illus. 2015. (J). pap. (978-0-374-30096-8(8)); (ENG.). 32p. 17.99 (978-0-374-30094-4(1), 9780374300944, Farrar, Straus & Giroux (BYR)) Farrar, Straus & Giroux.

Spinner, Stephanie. It's a Miracle! A Hanukkah Storybook. McElmurry, Jill, illus. 2007. (ENG.). 48p. (J). (gr. -1-3). 6.99 (978-1-4169-5001-1(X), Aladdin) Simon & Schuster Children's Publishing.

Spurr, Elizabeth. Happy Sparkling Hanukkah. Madden, Colleen, illus. 2011. (J). (978-1-4027-9660-9(9)) Sterling Publishing Co., Inc.

Stein, Joel Edward. A Hanukkah with Mazel. Vavouri, Elisa, illus. 2016. (ENG.). 32p. (gr. -1-2). 17.99 (978-1-4677-8171-8(1), Kar-Ben Publishing) Lerner Publishing Group.

Stern, Ariella. Chanukah Guess Who? A Lift the Flap Book. Argoff, Patti, illus. 2012. (ENG.). 32p. (J). 9.95 (978-1-929628-68-1(4)) Hachai Publishing.

Sutton, Jane. Esther's Hanukkah Disaster. Rowland, Andrew, illus. 2013. (Hanukkah Ser.). 32p. (J). (gr. -1-3). lib. bdg. 17.95 (978-0-7613-9043-5(X), Kar-Ben Publishing) Lerner Publishing Group.

—Esther's Hanukkah Disaster. Rowland, Andy, illus. 2013. 32p. 17.95 (978-1-4677-1638-3(3)); (ENG.). (J). (gr. -1-3). 7.95 (978-0-7613-9044-2(8), Kar-Ben Publishing) Lerner Publishing Group.

Van Syckle, A. & Schwartz, Josh. The OC: 'twas the Night Before Chrismukkah. 2005. 206p. (YA): (978-1-4156-3915-3(9)) Scholastic, Inc.

Wing, Natasha. The Night Before Hanukkah. Wummer, Amy, illus. 2014. (Night Before Ser.). (ENG.). 32p. (J). (gr. -1-k). 4.99 (978-0-448-48140-1(5), Grosset & Dunlap) Penguin Young Readers Group.

—The Night Before Hanukkah. 2014. (Night Before Ser.). lib. bdg. 13.55 (978-0-606-36160-6(X)) Turtleback Bks.

Wohl, Lauren L. The Eighth Menorah. Hughes, Laura, illus. 2013. (ENG.). 32p. (J). (gr. -1-3). 16.99 (978-0-8075-1892-2(1)) Whitman, Albert & Co.

Wolfe, Greg. Shmelf the Hanukkah Elf. McWilliam, Howard, illus. 2016. (ENG.). 32p. (J). 16.99 (978-1-61963-521-0(6), 9781619635210, Bloomsbury USA Childrens) Bloomsbury Publishing USA.

Yolen, Jane. How Do Dinosaurs Say Happy Chanukah? Teague, Mark, illus. 2012. (How Do Dinosaurs... ? Ser.). (ENG.). 40p. (J). (— 1). 16.99 (978-0-545-41677-1(9), Blue Sky Pr., The) Scholastic, Inc.

Yoon, Salina. My Chanukah Playbook. Yoon, Salina, illus. 2009. (ENG., Illus.). 10p. (J). (gr. -1-k). 10.99 (978-1-4169-8957-8(9), Little Simon) Little Simon.

Yorinks, Arthur. The Flying Latke. 2004. (Illus.). (J). (gr. k-3). spiral bd. (978-0-616-03066-0(5)) Canadian National Institute for the Blind/Institut National Canadien pour les Aveugles.

Zortman, Bruce. Eight Little Candles Plus: A Hanukkah Tale. 2011. (Illus.). 38p. pap. 14.50 (978-1-60976-905-5(8), Eloquent Bks.) Strategic Book Publishing & Rights Agency (SBPRA).

HAPPINESS

Adriana. Things to Be Happy About. 2008. pap. 17.00 (978-0-8059-7987-9(5)) Dorrance Publishing Co., Inc.

Atkinson, Tina Louise. Shape Up. 2012. 20p. pap. 13.77 (978-1-4669-3293-7(7)) Trafford Publishing.

B&H Kids Editorial Staff. If You're Happy & You Know It, Sound Book. Conger, Holli, illus. 2016. (Little Words Matter(tm) Ser.). (ENG.). 12p. (J). (gr. -1 — 1). bds. 12.99 (978-1-4336-8678-8(3), B&H Kids) B&H Publishing Group.

Baby Genius Publishing Staff. The Wheels on the Bus. 2009. (ENG.). 16p. (J). (-k). bds. 6.99 (978-1-4169-7644-8(2)) Meadowbrook Pr.

Bingham, Jane. Everybody Feels Happy. 2008. (Everybody Feels (Crabtree) Ser.). (ENG., Illus.). 24p. (J). (gr. 3-7). pap. (978-0-7787-4065-0(X)) Crabtree Publishing Co.

Bingham, Jane & Turner, Helen. Happy. 2006. (QEB Everybody Feels Ser.). (Illus.). 24p. (J). lib. bdg. 17.95 (978-1-59566-213-2(8)) QEB Publishing Inc.

Carlson, Nancy. Think Happy! Carlson, Nancy, illus. (Nancy Carlson Picture Bks). (Illus.). 32p. (J). (gr. k-3). 2012. (ENG.). 9.95 (978-0-7613-9175-3(4)) 2012. 56.72 (978-0-7613-9312-2(9)) 2009. (ENG., 16.95 (978-0-8225-8940-2(0)) Lerner Publishing Group. (Carolrhoda Bks.).

Clark, Rosalyn. Feeling Happy. 2017. (Bumba Books (tm) — Feelings Matter Ser.). (ENG.). (J). (gr. -1-1). pap. 6.99 **(978-1-5124-5545-8(8))**; (Illus.). lib. bdg. 25.32 **(978-1-5124-3368-5(3))** Lerner Publishing Group.

Dyer, Wayne W. Incredible You! 10 Ways to Let Your Greatness Shine Through. Siegel, Melanie, illus. 2005. (ENG.). 32p. (gr. -1-3). 15.99 (978-1-4019-0782-2(2)) Hay Hse., Inc.

Franzen, Lenore. Happiness. 2004. (My Feelings Ser.). (Illus.). 24p. (J). lib. bdg. 15.95 (978-1-58341-320-3(0), Creative Education) Creative Co., The.

Hagen, E. Happiness. 2012. 32p. pap. 17.25 (978-1-4669-6450-1(2)) Trafford Publishing.

Hill, Z. B. Happiness. Croft, Cindy, ed. 2014. (Causes & Effects of Emotions Ser.: 13). 64p. (J). (gr. 7-18). 23.95 (978-1-4222-3074-9(0)) Mason Crest.

Johansen, Heidi. What I Look Like When I Am Happy. 2004. (Let's Look at Feelings / un Vistazo a Los Sentimientos Ser.).Tr. of What I Look Like When I am Happy. (ENG & SPA., Illus.). 24p. (gr. -1-1). lib. bdg. 22.60 (978-1-4042-7506-5(1), Editorial Buenas Letras) Rosen Publishing Group, Inc., The.

—What I Look Like When I Am Happy: N. 2009. (Let's Look at Feelings Ser.). 24p. (gr. k-1). 42.50 (978-1-61514-240-8(1), PowerKids Pr.) Rosen Publishing Group, Inc., The.

—What I Look Like When I am Happy / Cómo me veo cuando estoy Contento. 2009. (Let's Look at Feelings / un vistazo a los sentimientos Ser.). (ENG & SPA.). 24p. (gr. k-1). 42.50 (978-1-61514-244-6(4), Editorial Buenas Letras) Rosen Publishing Group, Inc., The.

Knudsen, Sherilyn. The Smart Way to Be. Bodily, Michael, illus. 2005. 32p. (J). per. 9.95 (978-0-9768451-0-2(5)) HPN Publishing.

Lazear, Jonathon. Come On, Get Happy. 2004. (ENG., Illus.). 384p. (978-0-00-717532-1(9), HarperElement) HarperCollins Pubs. Ltd.

Leonard, Marcia. I Feel Happy. Bartholomew, illus. 2003. 24p. (J). bds. 2.95 (978-0-8249-6523-5(X), Ideal Pubns.) Worthy Publishing.

Mandino, Og. Og Mandino's Great Trilogy: The Greatest Salesman in the World, the Greatest Secret in the World & the Greatest Miracle in the World. 2008. 420p. (J). (978-0-8119-0428-5(8)) Lifetime Bks.

Marcotte, Arline Seibert. Obeying Rules Brings Happiness. 2010. 16p. 9.49 (978-1-4520-1076-2(5)) AuthorHouse.

McCloud, Carol. Baby's Bucket Book. Zimmer, Glenn, illus. 2014. (ENG.). 16p. (J). (— 1). bds. 7.95 (978-0-9960999-2-9(1)) Bucket Fillers, Inc.

—Have You Filled a Bucket Today? A Guide to Daily Happiness for Kids. Messing, David, illus. 10th ed. 2015. (ENG.). 32p. (J). (gr. -1-4). pap. 9.95 (978-0-9960999-3-6(X)) Bucket Fillers, Inc.

—Have You Filled a Bucket Today? A Guide to Daily Happiness for Kids. Messing, David, illus. 2006. (ENG.). 32p. (J). (gr. -1-3). pap. 9.95 (978-0-9785075-1-0(7), Ferne Pr.) Nelson Publishing & Marketing.

McCloud, Carol & Martin, Katherine. Fill a Bucket: A Guide to Daily Happiness for Young Children. David, Messing, illus. 2009. (ENG.). 26p. (J). (-2). 9.95 (978-1-933916-43-9(5)) Bucket Fillers, Inc.

Meister, Cari. Everyone Feels Happy Sometimes, 1 vol. Ward, Damian, illus. 2010. (Everyone Has Feelings Ser.). (ENG.). 24p. (gr. k-2). lib. bdg. 25.99 (978-1-4048-5754-4(0)) Picture Window Bks.

Miller, Connie Colwell. Happy Is... 2011. (Know Your Emotions Ser.). (ENG.). 24p. (gr. 1-2). pap. 47.70 (978-1-4296-7058-6(4)); lib. bdg. 27.32 (978-1-4296-6042-6(2)) Capstone Press of Coughlan Cos. (Aplus Bks.).

—Happy Is ... 2011. (Know Your Emotions Ser.). (ENG.). 24p. (gr. 1-2). pap. 8.10 (978-1-4296-7051-7(7), Aplus Bks.) Capstone Press of Coughlan Cos.

—Happy Is... (Felicidad Es...) Strictly Spanish LLC. Staff, tr. 2013. (Reconoce Tus Emociones/Know Your Emotions Ser.). (ENG, SPA & MUL.). 24p. (gr. 1-2). lib. bdg. 27.32 (978-1-62065-155-1(6)) Capstone Press of Coughlan Cos.

Murphy, Patricia J. Staying Happy. (Pull Ahead Books: Health Ser.). (ENG., Illus.). 32p. (gr. k-3). 2006. pap. 7.95 (978-0-8225-2774-9(X)) 2005. lib. bdg. 22.60 (978-0-8225-2796-1(0)) Lerner Publishing Group.

Nagia, Jyoti. Smile: It's a Curved Line That Sets Everything Straight & Fine! 2012. 24p. pap. 17.99 (978-1-4685-6078-7(6)) AuthorHouse.

Rebman, Nick. Who Is Happy? A Book about Emotions. 2016. (Concept Fun Ser.). (ENG.). 16p. (J). (gr. -1-2). 25.64 (978-1-5038-0767-9(3), 210615) Child's World, Inc., The.

Sheehan, Monica. Be Happy! Sheehan, Monica, illus. 2014. (ENG., Illus.). 68p. (J). (gr. -1-3). 14.99 (978-1-4424-9857-0(9), Little Simon) Little Simon.

Thomas, Isabel. Dealing with Feeling Happy, 1 vol. 2013. (Dealing with Feeling... Ser.). (ENG.). 24p. (gr. 1-2). pap. 6.79 (978-1-4329-7114-4(X), Heinemann Read & Learn) Heinemann-Raintree.

—Dealing with Feeling... Happy. 2013. (Dealing with Feeling... Ser.). (ENG.). 24p. (gr. 1-2). lib. bdg. 23.32 (978-1-4329-7105-2(0), Heinemann Read & Learn) Heinemann-Raintree.

Thompson, Chad. If You're Happy & You Know It, 1 vol. 2012. (Early Childhood Themes Ser.). (ENG.). 16p. (J). (gr. -1-2). pap. 19.99 (978-1-4333-3483-2(6)) Teacher Created Materials, Inc.

Warhola, James & Scholastic, Inc. Staff. If You're Happy & You Know It. Geist, Ken, ed. Warhola, James, illus. 2007. (ENG., Illus.). 32p. (J). (gr. -1-k). 16.99 (978-0-439-72766-2(9), Orchard Bks.) Scholastic, Inc.

Waters, Rosa. Emotional Self-Awareness. 2014. (J). (978-1-4222-3067-1(8)) Mason Crest.

Williams, Pharrell. Happy! (ENG., Illus.). (J). (gr. -1 — 1). 2016. 30p. bds. 6.99 (978-0-399-54812-3(2)) 2015. 32p. 19.99 (978-0-399-17643-2(8)) Penguin Young Readers Group. (G.P. Putnam's Sons Books for Young Readers).

HARALD III HARDRADI, KING OF NORWAY, 1015-1066—FICTION

Golding, Julia. The Silver Sea, 0 vols. 2013. (ENG.). 352p. (YA). (gr. 7-11). pap. 9.99 (978-1-4778-1598-4(8), 9781477815984, Amazon Children's Publishing) Amazon Publishing.

HARBORS

see also Pilots and Pilotage

Goldish, Meish. Marine Firefighters. 2014. (Fire Fight! the Bravest Ser.). 32p. (J). (gr. 2-7). lib. bdg. 26.60 (978-1-62724-098-7(5)) Bearport Publishing Co., Inc.

Harbor. 2007. (Busy Books Large Ser.). 5p. (978-1-4054-9498-4(0)) Parragon, Inc.

El Puerto (The Harbour) (Coleccion Aqui Se Trabaja). (SPA., Illus.). (J). 10.95 (978-84-207-3625-9(2), ANY764) Grupo Anaya, S.A. ESP. Dist: Continental Bk. Co., Inc.

Sciarrino, Stephanie. Multiplication at the Marina: Multiply Within 100. 2014. (Rosen Common Core Math Readers Ser.). (Illus.). 24p. (J). (gr. 3-4). (ENG.). pap. 8.25 (978-1-4777-4950-0(0)); lib. bdg. 23.60 (978-1-4777-6451-0(8)) Rosen Publishing Group, Inc., The. (PowerKids Pr.).

Smith, A. G. Cut & Assemble an Early American Seaport, Vol. 181. 2017. (ENG.). 48p. (J). (gr. 2-8). pap. 12.95 (978-0-486-24754-0(6)) Dover Pubns., Inc.

HARBORS—FICTION

Branson, Eve. Sarky Puddleboat. Lowe, Wes, illus. 2011. 44p. (J). 14.99 (978-1-4520-9754-1(2)) AuthorHouse.

Cortez, Jess S. My Trip to the Harbor. Cortez, Jess S., illus. 2005. (Illus.). 16p. (J). (978-0-9776291-0-7(4)) Jesus Estanislado.

Gunderson, J. Ropes of Revolution: The Boston Tea Party, 1 vol. Schoonover, Brent, illus. 2008. (Historical Fiction Ser.). (ENG.). 56p. (gr. 2-3). pap. 6.25 (978-1-4342-0492-9(8), Graphic Flash) Stone Arch Bks.

Italia, John. The Birds of the Harbor. Caravela, Elena, illus. 2006. (ENG.). 32p. (J). (gr. -1-3). 15.95 (978-0-9726614-7-8(6)) Shenanigan Bks.

Snell, Roy J. Lost in the Air. 2011. 112p. pap. 9.95 (978-1-60664-429-4(7)) Rodgers, Alan Bks.

Teckentrup, Britta, illus. Busy Bunny Days: In the Town, on the Farm & at the Port. 2014. (ENG.). 56p. (J). (gr. -1-3). 17.99 (978-1-4521-1700-3(4)) Chronicle Bks. LLC.

HARDING, WARREN G. (WARREN GAMALIEL), 1865-1923

Elston, Heidi M. D. Warren G. Harding, 1 vol. 2009. (United States Presidents Ser.). (ENG., Illus.). 40p. (YA). (gr. 3-6). 27.07 (978-1-60453-454-2(0)) ABDO Publishing Co.

Landau, Elaine. Warren G. Harding. 2005. (Presidential Leaders Ser.). (Illus.). 120p. (J). 29.27 (978-0-8225-0850-2(8), Lerner Pubns.) Lerner Publishing Group.

Parker, Lewis. How to Draw the Life & Times of Warren G. Harding. 2009. (Kid's Guide to Drawing the Presidents of the United States of America Ser.). 32p. (gr. 4-4). 50.50 (978-1-61511-163-3(8), PowerKids Pr.) Rosen Publishing Group, Inc., The.

Parker, Lewis K. How to Draw the Life & Times of Warren G. Harding. 2007. (Kid's Guide to Drawing the Presidents of the United States of America Ser.). (Illus.). 32p. (J). (gr. 2-5). 26.50 (978-1-4042-3005-7(X)) Rosen Publishing Group, Inc., The.

Schultz, Randy. Warren G. Harding: A MyReportLinks. Com Book. 2003. (Presidents Ser.). (Illus.). 48p. (J). (gr. 4-10). lib. bdg. 25.26 (978-0-7660-5103-4(X), MyReportLinks.com Bks.) Enslow Pubs., Inc.

Venezia, Mike. Warren G. Harding: Twenty-Ninth President, 1921-1923. Venezia, Mike, illus. 2006. (Getting to Know the U. S. Presidents Ser.). (ENG., Illus.). 32p. (J). (gr. 3-7). lib. bdg. 28.00 (978-0-516-22633-0(9)) Scholastic Library Publishing.

HARDY BOYS (FICTITIOUS CHARACTERS)—FICTION

ABDO Publishing Company Staff. Hardy Boys - 3 Titles. 2005. (Hardy Boys Ser.). (ENG., Illus.). 88p. (gr. 3-8). 72.63 (978-1-59961-060-3(4)) Spotlight.

The Battle of Bayport. 2014. (Hardy Boys Adventures Ser.: 6). (ENG., Illus.). 160p. (J). (gr. 3-7). 16.99 (978-1-4814-0007-7(X)); pap. 6.99 (978-1-4814-0006-0(1)) Simon & Schuster Children's Publishing. (Aladdin).

BookSource Staff, compiled by. Balloon Blow-Up. 2013. (Hardy Boys: Secret Files Ser.: 13). lib. bdg. 16.00 (978-0-606-32328-4(7), Turtleback) Turtleback Bks.

—Robot Rumble. 2013. (Hardy Boys: Secret Files Ser.: 11). lib. bdg. 16.00 (978-0-606-27027-4(2), Turtleback) Turtleback Bks.

—Sports Sabotage. 2012. (Hardy Boys: Secret Files Ser.: 8). lib. bdg. 16.00 (978-0-606-23673-7(2), Turtleback) Turtleback Bks.

Burroughs, Scott, illus. Fossil Frenzy. 2014. (Hardy Boys: the Secret Files Ser.: 14). (ENG.). 96p. (J). (gr. 1-4). pap. 5.99 (978-1-4424-9043-7(8), Aladdin) Simon & Schuster Children's Publishing.

—The Great Coaster Caper. 2012. (Hardy Boys: the Secret Files Ser.: 9). (ENG.). 112p. (J). (gr. 1-4). pap. 4.99 (978-1-4424-1669-7(6), Aladdin) Simon & Schuster Children's Publishing.

—The Hardy Boys Secret Files Collection: Trouble at the Arcade - The Missing Mitt - Mystery Map - Hopping Mad - A Monster of a Mystery. 2014. (Hardy Boys: the Secret Files Ser.). (ENG.). 496p. (J). (gr. 1-4). pap. 29.99 (978-1-4814-1473-9(9), Aladdin) Simon & Schuster Children's Publishing.

—Robot Rumble. 2013. (Hardy Boys: the Secret Files Ser.: 11). (ENG.). 96p. (J). (gr. 1-4). pap. 5.99 (978-1-4424-5367-8(2), Aladdin) Simon & Schuster Children's Publishing.

—Sports Sabotage. 2012. (Hardy Boys: the Secret Files Ser.: 8). (ENG.). 112p. (J). (gr. 1-4). pap. 5.99 (978-1-4424-2316-9(1), Aladdin) Simon & Schuster Children's Publishing.

The Case of the Myface Kidnapper (W. T.) 2012. (Hardy Boys (All New) Undercover Brothers Ser.: 40). (ENG.). 160p. (J). pap. 5.99 (978-1-4424-2235-3(1), Simon & Schuster/Paula Wiseman Bks.) Simon & Schuster/Paula Wiseman Bks.

The Children of the Lost, Bk. 1. 2010. (Hardy Boys (All New) Undercover Brothers Ser.: 34). (ENG.). 192p. (J). (gr. 3-7). pap. 5.99 (978-1-4424-0262-1(8), Aladdin) Simon & Schuster Children's Publishing.

Conway, Gerry. Break-Up! 2011. (Hardy Boys the New Case Files Ser.). (ENG., Illus.). 64p. (J). (gr. 3-7). pap. 6.99 (978-1-59707-242-7(7), 9781597072427) Papercutz.

—Break-Up! Henrique, Paulo, illus. 2011. (Hardy Boys the New Case Files Ser.: 2). (ENG.). 64p. (J). (gr. 3-7). 10.99 (978-1-59707-243-4(5), 9781597072434) Papercutz.

—Crawling with Zombies. 2010. (Hardy Boys the New Case Files Ser.). (ENG., Illus.). 64p. (J). (gr. 3-7). pap. 6.99 (978-1-59707-219-9(2), 9781597072199) Papercutz.

—Nancy Drew: Together with the Hardy Boys. 2011. (Nancy Drew the New Case Files Ser.). (ENG., Illus.). 64p. (J). (gr. 3-7). pap. 7.99 (978-1-59707-262-5(1), 9781597072625) Papercutz.

Dixon, Franklin W. Bayport Buccaneers. 16th ed. 2007. (Hardy Boys (All New) Undercover Brothers Ser.: 16). (ENG., Illus.). 176p. (J). (gr. 3-7). pap. 5.99 (978-1-4169-3403-5(0), Aladdin) Simon & Schuster Children's Publishing.

—Blown Away. 10th ed. 2006. (Hardy Boys (All New) Undercover Brothers Ser.: 10). (ENG., Illus.). 160p. (J). (gr. 3-7). pap. 5.99 (978-1-4169-1173-9(1), Aladdin) Simon & Schuster Children's Publishing.

—Burned. 2005. 154p. (J). lib. bdg. 16.92 (978-1-4242-0391-8(0)) Fitzgerald Bks.

—Camping Chaos. 2014. (Hardy Boys: Secret Files Ser.: 16). lib. bdg. 16.00 (978-0-606-36100-2(6)) Turtleback Bks.

—The Dangerous Transmission. 2005. (Hardy Boys II Ser.: No. 184). 147p. (J). lib. bdg. 15.00 (978-1-59054-850-9(7)) Fitzgerald Bks.

—Death & Diamonds. 15th ed. 2007. (Hardy Boys (All New) Undercover Brothers Ser.: 15). (ENG., Illus.). 176p. (J). (gr. 3-7). pap. 5.99 (978-1-4169-3402-8(2), Aladdin) Simon & Schuster Children's Publishing.

—Deception on the Set. 2015. (Hardy Boys Adventures Ser.: 8). (ENG., Illus.). 128p. (J). (gr. 3-7). pap. 6.99 (978-1-4814-1406-7(2), Aladdin) Simon & Schuster Children's Publishing.

—Double Jeopardy. 2005. (Hardy Boys II Ser.: No. 181). 150p. (J). lib. bdg. 15.00 (978-1-59054-838-7(8)) Fitzgerald Bks.

—Double Jeopardy. 2003. (Hardy Boys Ser.: 181). (ENG.). 160p. (J). (gr. 3-7). pap. 5.99 (978-0-689-85780-5(2), Aladdin) Simon & Schuster Children's Publishing.

—Extreme Danger. 2005. (Hardy Boys (All New) Undercover Brothers Ser.: 1). (ENG.). 176p. (J). (gr. 3-7). pap. 5.99 (978-1-4169-0002-3(0), Aladdin) Simon & Schuster Children's Publishing.

—Farming Fear. 2005. (Hardy Boys II Ser.: No. 188). 154p. (J). lib. bdg. 15.00 (978-1-59054-839-4(6)) Fitzgerald Bks.

—Feeding Frenzy. 20th ed. 2008. (Hardy Boys (All New) Undercover Brothers Ser.: 20). (ENG., Illus.). 160p. (J). (gr. 3-7). pap. 7.99 (978-1-4169-5499-6(6), Aladdin) Simon & Schuster Children's Publishing.

—Fossil Frenzy. 2014. (Hardy Boys: Secret Files Ser.: 14). lib. bdg. 16.00 (978-0-606-35434-9(4)) Turtleback Bks.

—Foul Play. 19th ed. 2007. (Hardy Boys (All New) Undercover Brothers Ser.: 19). (ENG., Illus.). 192p. (J). (gr. 3-7). pap. 5.99 (978-1-4169-4977-0(1), Aladdin) Simon & Schuster Children's Publishing.

—Hardy Boys Collector's Boxed Set. 2010. (Hardy Boys Ser.). (ENG., Illus.). 1250p. (gr. 3). 75.00 (978-1-55709-153-6(6)) Applewood Bks.

—Haunted. 2008. (Hardy Boys Undercover Brothers: Super Mystery Ser.). (ENG., Illus.). 192p. (J). (gr. 3-7). pap. 5.99 (978-1-4169-6169-7(0), Aladdin) Simon & Schuster Children's Publishing.

—Hazed. 14th ed. 2007. (Hardy Boys (All New) Undercover Brothers Ser.: 14). (ENG., Illus.). 160p. (J). (gr. 3-7). pap. 6.99 (978-1-4169-1803-5(5), Aladdin) Simon & Schuster Children's Publishing.

—The Hidden Harbor Mystery, No. 14. Gretter, J. Clemens, illus. 2003. (Hardy Boys Ser.). (ENG.). 228p. (J). (gr. 4-7). 14.95 (978-1-55709-272-4(9)) Applewood Bks.

—House Arrest. 23rd ed. 2008. (Hardy Boys (All New) Undercover Brothers Ser.: 23). (ENG., Illus.). 176p. (J). (gr. 3-7). pap. 5.99 (978-1-4169-6171-0(2), Aladdin) Simon & Schuster Children's Publishing.

—In Plane Sight. 2005. (Hardy Boys I Ser.: No. 176). 148p. (J). lib. bdg. 15.00 (978-1-59054-842-4(6)) Fitzgerald Bks.

—Kickoff to Danger. 2005. (Hardy Boys I Ser.: No. 170). 149p. (J). lib. bdg. 15.00 (978-1-59054-843-1(4)) Fitzgerald Bks.

—Kidnapped at the Casino. 2007. (Hardy Boys Undercover Brothers: Super Mystery Ser.: 2). (ENG., Illus.). 240p. (J). (gr. 3-7). pap. 5.99 (978-1-4169-3923-8(7), Aladdin) Simon & Schuster Children's Publishing.

—Line of Fire. (Illus.). (J). mass mkt. 2.95 (978-0-671-70492-6(3), Simon Pulse) Simon Pulse.

—Martial Law. 9th ed. 2006. (Hardy Boys (All New) Undercover Brothers Ser.: 9). (ENG., Illus.). 160p. (J). (gr. 3-7). pap. 5.99 (978-1-4169-0398-7(4), Aladdin) Simon & Schuster Children's Publishing.

—The Missing Playbook. David, Matt, illus. 2016. (Hardy Boys Clue Book Ser.: 2). (ENG.). 96p. (J). (gr. 1-4). 16.99 (978-1-4814-5178-9(2), Aladdin) Simon & Schuster Children's Publishing.

—Motocross Madness. 2005. (Hardy Boys II Ser.: No. 190). 154p. (J). lib. bdg. 15.00 (978-1-59054-844-8(2)) Fitzgerald Bks.

—Murder at the Mall. 17th ed. 2007. (Hardy Boys (All New) Undercover Brothers Ser.: 17). (ENG., Illus.). 176p. (J). (gr. 3-7). pap. 5.99 (978-1-4169-3930-6(X), Aladdin) Simon & Schuster Children's Publishing.

—Murder House, Bk. 3. 24th ed. 2008. (Hardy Boys (All New) Undercover Brothers Ser.: 24). (ENG.). 160p. (J). (gr. 3-7). pap. 6.99 (978-1-4169-6409-4(6), Aladdin) Simon & Schuster Children's Publishing.

—The Mystery of the Black Rhino. 2005. (Hardy Boys I Ser.: No. 178). 151p. (J). lib. bdg. 15.00 (978-1-59054-851-6(5)) Fitzgerald Bks.

—No Way Out. 2005. (Hardy Boys II Ser.: No. 187). 149p. (J). lib. bdg. 15.00 (978-1-59054-845-5(0)) Fitzgerald Bks.

—One False Step. 2005. (Hardy Boys II Ser.: No. 189). 150p. (J). lib. bdg. 15.00 *(978-1-59054-846-2(9))* Fitzgerald Bks.
—Passport to Danger. 2005. (Hardy Boys I Ser.: No. 179). 147p. (J). lib. bdg. 15.00 *(978-1-59054-847-9(7))* Fitzgerald Bks.
—Pushed. 18th ed. 2007. (Hardy Boys (All New) Undercover Brothers Ser.: 18). (ENG., Illus.). 160p. (J). (gr. 3-7). pap. 5.99 *(978-1-4169-4802-5(3),* Aladdin) Simon & Schuster Children's Publishing.
—The Race Is On. Burroughs, Scott, illus. 2015. (Hardy Boys: the Secret Files Ser.: 19). (ENG.). 96p. (J). (gr. 1-4). pap. 5.99 *(978-1-4814-2271-0(5),* Aladdin) Simon & Schuster Children's Publishing.
—Running on Fumes. 2005. 150p. (J). lib. bdg. 16.92 *(978-1-4242-0384-0(8))* Fitzgerald Bks.
—The Secret of the Soldier's Gold. 2005. (Hardy Boys II Ser.: No. 182). 147p. (J). lib. bdg. 15.00 *(978-1-59054-852-3(3))* Fitzgerald Bks.
—Ship of Secrets. 2014. (Hardy Boys: Secret Files Ser.: 15). lib. bdg. 14.75 *(978-0-606-35781-4(5))* Turtleback Bks.
—The Sinister Sign Post, No. 15. 2004. (Hardy Boys Ser.). (ENG.). 228p. (J). (gr. 4-7). 17.95 *(978-1-55709-273-1(7))* Applewood Bks.
—Skin & Bones. 2005. (Hardy Boys I Ser.: No. 164). 148p. (J). lib. bdg. 15.00 *(978-1-59054-848-6(5))* Fitzgerald Bks.
—Speed Times Five. 2005. (Hardy Boys I Ser.: No. 173). 150p. (J). lib. bdg. 15.00 *(978-1-59054-849-3(3))* Fitzgerald Bks.
—Thrill Ride. 2005. 154p. (J). lib. bdg. 16.92 *(978-1-4242-0386-4(4))* Fitzgerald Bks.
—Top Ten Ways to Die. 2006. 169p. (J). lib. bdg. 16.92 *(978-1-4242-0390-1(2))* Fitzgerald Bks.
—Top Ten Ways to Die. 8th ed. 2006. (Hardy Boys (All New) Undercover Brothers Ser.: 8). (ENG., Illus.). 160p. (J). (gr. 3-7). pap. 5.99 *(978-1-4169-0846-3(3),* Aladdin) Simon & Schuster Children's Publishing.
—Training for Trouble. 2005. (Hardy Boys I Ser.: No. 161). 147p. (J). lib. bdg. 15.00 *(978-1-59054-853-0(1))* Fitzgerald Bks.
—Trick-or-Trouble. 2005. (Hardy Boys I Ser.: No. 175). 154p. (J). lib. bdg. 15.00 *(978-1-59054-854-7(X))* Fitzgerald Bks.
—Trouble in Paradise. 12th ed. 2006. (Hardy Boys (All New) Undercover Brothers Ser.: 12). (ENG., Illus.). 176p. (J). (gr. 3-7). pap. 5.99 *(978-1-4169-1178-4(2),* Aladdin) Simon & Schuster Children's Publishing.
—Trouble in Warp Space. 2005. (Hardy Boys I Ser.: No. 172). 154p. (J). lib. bdg. 15.00 *(978-1-59054-855-4(8))* Fitzgerald Bks.
—The Video Game Bandit. David, Matt, illus. 2016. (Hardy Boys Clue Book Ser.: 1). (ENG.). 96p. (J). (gr. 1-4). 16.99 *(978-1-4814-5053-9(0),* Aladdin) Simon & Schuster Children's Publishing.
—Wanted. 2006. (Hardy Boys Undercover Brothers: Super Mystery Ser.: 1). (ENG., Illus.). 192p. (J). (gr. 3-7). pap. 5.99 *(978-1-4169-1258-3(4),* Aladdin) Simon & Schuster Children's Publishing.
—Warehouse Rumble. 2005. (Hardy Boys II Ser.: No. 183). 152p. (J). lib. bdg. 15.00 *(978-1-59054-858-5(2))* Fitzgerald Bks.
—Water-Ski Wipeout. David, Matt, illus. 2016. (Hardy Boys Clue Book Ser.: 3). (ENG.). 96p. (J). (gr. 1-4). pap. 5.99 *(978-1-4814-5055-3(7),* Aladdin) Simon & Schuster Children's Publishing.
—Wreck & Roll. 2005. (Hardy Boys II Ser.: No. 185). 153p. (J). lib. bdg. 15.00 *(978-1-59054-859-2(0))* Fitzgerald Bks.
Dixon, Franklin W. & Frost, Michael. Double Trouble. 25th ed. 2008. (Hardy Boys (All New) Undercover Brothers Ser.: 25). (ENG.). 176p. (J). (gr. 3-7). pap. 5.99 *(978-1-4169-6765-1(6),* Aladdin) Simon & Schuster Children's Publishing.
Dixon, Franklin W. & Keele, Kevin. A con Artist in Paris. 2017. (Hardy Boys Adventures Ser.: 15). (ENG.). 128p. (J). (gr. 3-7). 17.99 ***(978-1-4814-9007-8(9))***; pap. 6.99 ***(978-1-4814-9006-1(0))*** Simon & Schuster Children's Publishing. (Aladdin).
Dixon, Franklin W. & Keene, Carolyn. Bonfire Masquerade. 2011. (Nancy Drew/Hardy Boys Ser.: 5). (ENG.). 176p. (J). (gr. 3-7). pap. 6.99 *(978-1-4424-0328-4(4),* Aladdin) Simon & Schuster Children's Publishing.
Dixon, Franklin W. & Walker, Jeff. The Mystery of the Black Rhino. 178th ed. 2003. (Hardy Boys Ser.: 178). (ENG., Illus.). 160p. (J). (gr. 3-7). pap. 6.99 *(978-0-689-85598-6(2),* Aladdin) Simon & Schuster Children's Publishing.
—Passport to Danger, Vol. 179. 179th ed. 2003. (Hardy Boys Ser.: 179). (ENG., Illus.). 160p. (J). (gr. 3-7). pap. 5.99 *(978-0-689-85779-9(9),* Aladdin) Simon & Schuster Children's Publishing.
Extreme Danger. 2007. 15.00 *(978-0-7569-7603-3(0))* Perfection Learning Corp.
Forever Lost. 2011. (Hardy Boys (All New) Undercover Brothers Ser.: 36). (ENG.). 160p. (J). (gr. 3-7). pap. 6.99 *(978-1-4424-0264-5(4),* Aladdin) Simon & Schuster Children's Publishing.
Frost, Michael, photos by. Private Killer, Bk. 2. 2010. (Hardy Boys (All New) Undercover Brothers Ser.: 32). (ENG., Illus.). 160p. (J). (gr. 3-7). pap. 5.99 *(978-1-4169-8697-3(9),* Aladdin) Simon & Schuster Children's Publishing.
Keene, Carolyn. Stage Fright. 2012. (Nancy Drew/Hardy Boys Ser.: 6). (ENG.). 176p. (J). (gr. 3-7). pap. 6.99 *(978-1-4424-5681-5(7),* Aladdin) Simon & Schuster Children's Publishing.
Keene, Carolyn & Dixon, Franklin W. Danger Overseas. 2008. (Nancy Drew/Hardy Boys Ser.: 2). (ENG., Illus.). 224p. (J). (gr. 3-7). pap. 5.99 *(978-1-4169-5777-5(4),* Aladdin) Simon & Schuster Children's Publishing.
—Terror on Tour. 2007. (Nancy Drew/Hardy Boys Ser.: 1). (ENG., Illus.). 224p. (J). (gr. 3-7). pap. 5.99 *(978-1-4169-2726-6(3),* Aladdin) Simon & Schuster Children's Publishing.
Killer Connections. 2010. (Hardy Boys (All New) Undercover Brothers Ser.: 33). (ENG.). 176p. (J). (gr. 3-7). pap. 6.99 *(978-1-4169-8696-6(0),* Aladdin) Simon & Schuster Children's Publishing.
Lobdell, Scott. Haley Danelle's Top Eight! 2008. (Hardy Boys Graphic Novels Ser.: 14). (ENG., Illus.). 96p. (J). (gr. 3-7). pap. 7.95 *(978-1-59707-113-0(7),* 9781597071130) Papercutz.
—Identity Theft. Rendon, Daniel, illus. 2005. (Hardy Boys Undercover Brothers Ser.). 88p. (gr. 3-8). 24.21 *(978-1-59961-062-7(0))* Spotlight.
—Live Free, Die Hardy!, No. 15. 2008. (Hardy Boys Graphic Novels Ser.: 15). (ENG., Illus.). 96p. (J). (gr. 3-7). pap. 7.95 *(978-1-59707-123-9(4),* 9781597071239) Papercutz.
—Mad House. Rendon, Daniel, illus. 2005. (Hardy Boys Undercover Brothers Ser.). 88p. (gr. 3-7). 24.21 *(978-1-59961-063-4(9))* Spotlight.
—The Ocean of Osyria. Rendon, Daniel, illus. 2005. (Hardy Boys Undercover Brothers Ser.). 88p. (gr. 3-7). 24.21 *(978-1-59961-061-0(2))* Spotlight.
—The Opposite Numbers. Rendon, Daniel et al, illus. 2006. 111p. (J). *(978-1-4156-9815-0(5))* Papercutz.
Lost Brother: Book Two in the Lost Mystery Trilogy. 2010. (Hardy Boys (All New) Undercover Brothers Ser.: 35). (ENG.). 160p. (J). (gr. 3-7). pap. 5.99 *(978-1-4424-0256-0(3),* Aladdin) Simon & Schuster Children's Publishing.
Movie Mayhem. 2012. (Hardy Boys (All New) Undercover Brothers Ser.: 39). (ENG.). 176p. (J). (gr. 3-7). pap. 5.99 *(978-1-4424-0260-7(1),* Aladdin) Simon & Schuster Children's Publishing.
Movie Menace. 2011. (Hardy Boys (All New) Undercover Brothers Ser.: 37). (ENG.). 176p. (J). (gr. 3-7). pap. 5.99 *(978-1-4424-0258-4(X),* Aladdin) Simon & Schuster Children's Publishing.
Mystery of the Phantom Heist. 2013. (Hardy Boys Adventures Ser.: 2). (ENG.). 160p. (J). (gr. 3-7). 15.99 *(978-1-4424-6586-2(7))*; pap. 6.99 *(978-1-4424-2237-7(8))* Simon & Schuster Children's Publishing. (Aladdin).
Peril at Granite Peak. 2014. (Hardy Boys Adventures Ser.: 5). (ENG., Illus.). 160p. (J). (gr. 3-7). pap. 6.99 *(978-1-4424-9395-7(X),* Aladdin) Simon & Schuster Children's Publishing.
Secret of the Red Arrow. 2013. (Hardy Boys Adventures Ser.: 1). (ENG.). 176p. (J). (gr. 3-7). 15.99 *(978-1-4424-6585-5(9))*; pap. 6.99 *(978-1-4424-4615-1(3))* Simon & Schuster Children's Publishing. (Aladdin).
The Vanishing Game. 2013. (Hardy Boys Adventures Ser.: 3). (ENG.). 144p. (J). (gr. 3-7). 15.99 *(978-1-4424-7344-7(4))*; (Illus.). pap. 6.99 *(978-1-4424-5981-6(6))* Simon & Schuster Children's Publishing. (Aladdin).
X-Plosion. 2009. (Hardy Boys (All New) Undercover Brothers Ser.: 29). (ENG.). 160p. (J). (gr. 3-7). pap. 6.99 *(978-1-4169-7870-1(4),* Aladdin) Simon & Schuster Children's Publishing.

HARES

see Rabbits

HARLEM (NEW YORK, N.Y.)

Arora, Sabina G., ed. The Great Migration & the Harlem Renaissance. 2015. (African American Experience: from Slavery to the Presidency Ser.). (ENG.). 80p. (YA). (gr. 7-8). 65.80 *(978-1-68048-046-7(4),* Britannica Educational Publishing) Rosen Publishing Group, Inc., The.
Lassieur, Allison. Harlem Renaissance: An Interactive History Adventure. 2013. (You Choose: History Ser.). (ENG.). 112p. (gr. 3-4). pap. 6.95 *(978-1-4765-3609-5(0))*; 31.99 *(978-1-4765-0256-4(0))* Capstone Press of Coughlan Cos. (You Choose Bks.).
Lewis, J. Patrick. Harlem Hellfighters. Kelley, Gary, illus. 2014. (ENG.). 32p. (J). (gr. 4-7). 19.99 *(978-1-56846-246-2(8),* Creative Editions) Creative Co., The.

HARLEM (NEW YORK, N.Y.)—FICTION

Blumenthal, Scott & Hodus, Brett. Hoop City. 2005. (Dream Ser.). 145p. (gr. 3-8). pap. 9.95 *(978-0-9708992-1-7(1))* Scobre Pr. Corp.
Bootman, Colin, illus. The Steel Pan Man of Harlem. 2009. (Carolrhoda Picture Bks.). 32p. (J). (gr. 1-3). 16.95 *(978-0-8225-9026-2(3))* Lerner Publishing Group.
Carlon, Mick. Riding on Duke's Train. 2011. (LeapKids Ser.). (ENG.). 160p. (J). (gr. k-7). pap. 9.95 *(978-1-935248-06-4(5))* Leapfrog Pr.
Coleman, Evelyn. Mystery of the Dark Tower. 2009. (Mysteries Through Time Ser.). 160p. (YA). (gr. 4-8). 31.95 *(978-1-60754-188-2(2))*; pap. 15.25 *(978-1-60754-189-9(0))* Windmill Bks.
Collier, Bryan. Uptown. unabr. ed. 2007. (J). (gr. k-3). 28.95 incl. audio compact disk *(978-1-4301-0054-6(0))* Live Oak Media.
—Uptown, 4 bks., Set. Collier, Bryan, illus. 2007. (Illus.). (J). (gr. k-3). pap. 39.95 incl. audio compact disk *(978-1-4301-0055-3(9))* Live Oak Media.
—Uptown, 4 bks., Set. unabr. ed. 2007. (J). (gr. k-3). pap. 37.95 incl. audio *(978-1-4301-0052-2(4))* Live Oak Media.
Collier, Bryan & National Geographic Learning Staff. Uptown. Collier, Bryan, illus. rev. ed. 2004. (ENG., Illus.). 32p. (J). (gr. -1-3). pap. 8.99 *(978-0-8050-7399-7(X),* 9780805073997) Square Fish.
Dean, Myers Walter. Scorpions. 2014. (Trophy Bk Ser.). (ENG.). 240p. (J). (gr. 7-12). 13.24 *(978-1-63245-216-0(2))* Lectorum Pubns., Inc.
Eulberg, Elizabeth. The Great Shelby Holmes: Girl Detective. 2016. (ENG., Illus.). 256p. (J). 16.99 *(978-1-68119-051-8(6),* 9781681190518, Bloomsbury USA Childrens) Bloomsbury Publishing USA.
Godin, Thelma Lynne. Hula-Hoopin' Queen. Brantley-Newton, Vanessa, illus. 2014. (ENG.). 40p. (J). 18.95 *(978-1-60060-846-9(9))* Lee & Low Bks., Inc.
Goldberg, Whoopi. Dancing Diva. Roos, Maryn, illus. 2012. (ENG.). 160p. (J). (gr. 1-5). pap. 4.99 *(978-0-7868-5265-9(8),* Jump at the Sun) Hyperion Bks. for Children.
Goldberg, Whoopi & Underwood, Deborah. Plum Fantastic Bk. 1. Cato, Nancy & Roos, Maryn, illus. 2008. (ENG.). 160p. (J). (gr. 1-17). pap. 4.99 *(978-0-7868-5260-4(7),* Jump at the Sun) Hyperion Bks. for Children.
Guy, Rosa. The Friends. 2006. (Reader's Workshop Ser.). (ENG.). 224p. (C). pap. 19.95 *(978-0-7362-3152-7(8))* CENGAGE Learning.
Harvey, Jeanne Walker. My Hands Sing the Blues: Romare Bearden's Childhood Journey, 0 vols. Zunon, Elizabeth, illus. 2011. (ENG.). 40p. (J). (gr. k-3). 17.99 *(978-0-7614-5810-4(7),* 9780761458104, Amazon Children's Publishing) Amazon Publishing.
Hijuelos, Óscar & Óscar, Hijuelos. Dark Dude. Roja, Alberto Jimenez, tr. 2010. (SPA.). 430p. (YA). (gr. 9-18). 19.99 *(978-84-441-4316-3(2))* Everest Editora ESP. Dist: Lectorum Pubns., Inc.
Levine, Gail Carson. Dave at Night. 2006. (ENG.). 304p. (J). (gr. 3-7). reprint ed. pap. 7.99 *(978-0-06-440747-2(0))* HarperCollins Pubs.
—Dave at Night. 2004. 281p. (gr. 3-7). 17.00 *(978-0-7569-4101-7(6))* Perfection Learning Corp.
—Dave at Night. unabr. ed. 2004. 278p. (J). (gr. 4-7). pap. 38.00 incl. audio *(978-0-8072-8379-0(7),* YA174SP, Listening Library) Random Hse. Audio Publishing Group.
McKissack, Patricia C. A Song for Harlem. 2008. (Scraps of Time Ser.). (ENG.). 128p. (J). (gr. 3-7). 6.99 *(978-0-14-241238-1(4),* Puffin Books) Penguin Young Readers Group.
Myers, Walter Dean. All the Right Stuff. 2012. 224p. (YA). (gr. 8). (ENG.). 17.99 *(978-0-06-196087-1(X))*; lib. bdg. 18.89 *(978-0-06-196088-8(8))* HarperCollins Pubs. (Amistad).
—The Beast. 2005. 17.00 *(978-0-7569-5107-8(0))* Perfection Learning Corp.
—The Cruisers. (ENG.). 144p. (J). (gr. 5-9). 2015. (News Crew Ser.). pap. 6.99 *(978-0-545-82874-1(0))* 2011. (Cruisers Ser.: 1). pap. 5.99 *(978-0-439-91633-2(X))* 2010. (Cruisers Ser.: 1). 15.99 *(978-0-439-91626-4(7))* Scholastic, Inc. (Scholastic Pr.).
—Darius & Twig. 2013. 208p. (YA). (gr. 8). (ENG.). 17.99 *(978-0-06-172823-5(3))*; lib. bdg. 18.89 *(978-0-06-172824-2(1))* HarperCollins Pubs. (Amistad).
—Dope Sick. 2010. (ENG.). 208p. (YA). (gr. 9). pap. 9.99 *(978-0-06-121479-0(5),* Amistad) HarperCollins Pubs.
—The Dream Bearer. 2003. (ENG.). 192p. (J). (gr. 5-18). 15.99 *(978-0-06-029521-9(X))*; 15.99 *(978-0-06-029521-9(X))* HarperCollins Pubs. (Amistad).
—The Dream Bearer. 2004. 16.00 *(978-0-7569-3242-8(4))* Perfection Learning Corp.
—Los Escorpiones.Tr. of Scorpions. (SPA.). (YA). (gr. 5-8). pap. *(978-958-04-4381-0(5),* NR8278); 258p. (gr. 7-9). 9.95 *(978-958-04-1505-3(6),* 10266247) Norma S.A. COL. Dist: Lectorum Pubns., Inc., Distribuidora Norma, Inc.
—Game. (ENG.). (YA). (gr. 8). 2009. 240p. pap. 9.99 *(978-0-06-058296-8(0))* 2008. 224p. 17.99 *(978-0-06-058294-4(4))* HarperCollins Pubs. (HarperTeen).
—Handbook for Boys. 2003. (Amistad Ser.). (ENG.). 224p. (YA). (gr. 5-18). pap. 8.99 *(978-0-06-440930-8(9),* Amistad) HarperCollins Pubs.
—Handbook for Boys. 2003. 19.00 *(978-0-7569-1459-2(0))* Perfection Learning Corp.
—Harlem Summer. 2015. (YA). 1.25 *(978-1-4906-2986-5(6))* Recorded Bks., Inc.
—Looking Like Me. Myers, Christopher, illus. 2009. (ENG.). 32p. (J). (gr. k-4). 18.99 *(978-1-60684-001-6(0),* Carolrhoda Bks.) Lerner Publishing Group.
—The Mouse Rap. 3rd ed. (J). pap. 3.95 *(978-0-13-800087-5(5))* Prentice Hall (Schl. Div.).
—Oh, Snap! 2013. (Cruisers Ser.: Bk. 4). (ENG.). 128p. (J). (gr. 5-9). 17.99 *(978-0-439-91629-5(1),* Scholastic Pr.) Scholastic, Inc.
—Scorpions. 2013. (Trophy Bk.). (ENG.). 240p. (YA). (gr. 8-18). pap. 8.99 *(978-0-06-447066-7(0))*; 25th anniv. ed. pap. 9.99 *(978-0-06-440623-9(7))* HarperCollins Pubs. (Amistad).
—Scorpions. 2013. 216p. (YA). (gr. 7-12). lib. bdg. 19.65 *(978-0-8335-4233-5(8),* Turtleback) Turtleback Bks.
—A Star Is Born. (J). 2015. (News Crew Ser.). (ENG.). 176p. (gr. 5-9). pap. 6.99 *(978-0-545-82876-5(7),* Scholastic Pr.) 2012. (Cruisers Ser.: Bk. 3). *(978-0-439-91631-8(3))* 2012. (Cruisers Ser.: Bk. 3). (ENG.). 176p. (gr. 5-9). 17.99 *(978-0-439-91628-8(3))* Scholastic, Inc.
—Street Love. (ENG.). 2007. 160p. (YA). (gr. 8-18). pap. 9.99 *(978-0-06-440732-8(2))* 2006. 144p. (J). (gr. 7-18). 15.99 *(978-0-06-028079-6(4))* HarperCollins Pubs. (Amistad).
—Street Love. 2007. 19.00 *(978-0-7569-8102-0(6))* Perfection Learning Corp.
—Sunrise over Fallujah. 2008. (ENG., Illus.). 304p. (J). (gr. 7-18). 17.99 *(978-0-439-91624-0(0),* Scholastic Pr.) Scholastic, Inc.
—What They Found: Love on 145th Street. 2011. 10.54 *(978-0-7848-3386-5(9))*; 10.54 *(978-0-7848-3499-2(7))* Marco Bk. Co. (Everbind).
—What They Found: Love on 145th Street. 2009. (ENG.). 256p. (YA). (gr. 9). pap. 8.99 *(978-0-375-84545-1(3),* Lamb, Wendy Bks.) Random Hse. Children's Bks.
Nelson, Vaunda Micheaux. No Crystal Stair: A Documentary Novel of the Life & Work of Lewis Michaux, Harlem Bookseller. Christie, R. Gregory, illus. 2012. (Carolrhoda YA Ser.). (ENG.). 192p. (YA). (gr. 7-12). 17.95 *(978-0-7613-6169-5(3),* Carolrhoda Lab™) Lerner Publishing Group.
Ramsey, R. M. The Browser Bunch: The Browser Files Presents... the Big Lie. 2006. (J). pap. 8.00 *(978-0-8059-7172-9(6))* Dorrance Publishing Co., Inc.
Ringgold, Faith. Harlem Renaissance. Ringgold, Faith, illus. 2015. (ENG., Illus.). 40p. (J). (gr. -1-3). 17.99 *(978-0-06-057911-1(0),* Amistad) HarperCollins Pubs.
—Tar Beach. 2014. 32p. pap. 7.00 *(978-1-61003-377-0(9))* Center for the Collaborative Classroom.
Rosa, Guy. The Friends. 2014. (ENG.). 192p. (YA). 10.75 *(978-1-63245-201-6(4))* Lectorum Pubns., Inc.
Tate, Eleanora E. Celeste's Harlem Renaissance. 2009. (ENG.). 304p. (J). (gr. 3-7). pap. 7.99 *(978-0-316-11362-5(X))* Little, Brown Bks. for Young Readers.
Taylor, Debbie & Morrison, Frank. Sweet Music in Harlem, 1 vol. 2004. (ENG., Illus.). 32p. (J). 17.95 *(978-1-58430-165-3(1))* Lee & Low Bks., Inc.
Taylor, Debbie A. Sweet Music in Harlem. Morrison, Frank, illus. 2014. 32p. pap. 9.00 *(978-1-61003-220-9(9))* Center for the Collaborative Classroom.
Volponi, Paul. Rucker Park Setup. 2008. (ENG.). 160p. (YA). (gr. 7-18). 6.99 *(978-0-14-241207-7(4),* Speak) Penguin Young Readers Group.
Weatherford, Carole Boston. Sugar Hill: Harlem's Historic Neighborhood. Christie, R. Gregory, illus. 2014. (ENG.). 32p. (J). (gr. k-3). 16.99 *(978-0-8075-7650-2(6))* Whitman, Albert & Co.
Weisleder, Stanley. Wings of the Panther. 2010. (ENG.). 224p. pap. 15.00 *(978-0-936783-38-3(9))* Merril Pr.
Wright, Richard. Rite of Passage. 2014. (Trophy Bk Ser.). (ENG.). 160p. (J). (gr. 8-12). 13.24 *(978-1-63245-325-9(8))* Lectorum Pubns., Inc.

HARLEM (NEW YORK, N.Y.)—SOCIAL CONDITIONS

Arora, Sabina G. The Great Migration & the Harlem Renaissance. 2015. (African American Experience: from Slavery to the Presidency Ser.). (ENG., Illus.). 80p. (J). (gr. 7-8). 32.90 *(978-1-68048-045-0(6),* Britannica Educational Publishing) Rosen Publishing Group, Inc., The.
Kallen, Stuart A. A Travel Guide to Harlem Renaissance. 2003. (Travel Guide To Ser.). (ENG.). (J). 30.85 *(978-1-59018-358-8(4),* Lucent Bks.) Cengage Gale.
Worth, Richard. The Harlem Renaissance: An Explosion of African-American Culture. 2008. (America's Living History Ser.). (Illus.). 128p. (J). (gr. 5-9). lib. bdg. 33.27 *(978-0-7660-2907-1(7))* Enslow Pubs., Inc.

HARMONICA

Donovan, Sandy. Hawk & Drool: Gross Stuff in Your Mouth. Slack, Michael H., illus. 2009. (Gross Body Science Ser.). (ENG.). 48p. (gr. 3-5). lib. bdg. 29.27 *(978-0-8225-8966-2(4))* Lerner Publishing Group.
Maxwell, Stuart "Son". Starting Blues Harmonica: The Number One Method for Young Blues Harp Players. 2006. (ENG., Illus.). 32p. pap. 9.95 incl. audio compact disk *(978-0-8256-3442-0(3),* 0825634423, Amsco Music) Music Sales Corp.
Souza, D. M. Look What Mouths Can Do. 2007. (Look What Animals Can Do Ser.). (Illus.). 48p. (J). pap. 7.95 *(978-0-8225-6669-4(9),* Lerner Pubns.) Lerner Publishing Group.
Stieg, Megan & Myers, Lawrence Eddie. How to Be a Harmonica Hero. 2009. (Illus.). 48p. (J). *(978-0-545-13209-1(6))* Scholastic, Inc.

HARMONICA—FICTION

England, Linda. The Old Cotton Blues. Flavin, Teresa, illus. 2011. (ENG.). 32p. (J). (gr. -1-2). 14.99 *(978-1-4424-2945-1(3),* McElderry, Margaret K. Bks.) McElderry, Margaret K. Bks.
Guest, Elissa Haden. Iris & Walter: Lost & Found. Davenier, Christine, illus. 2014. (Green Light Readers Level 3 Ser.). (ENG.). 44p. (J). (gr. 1-4). pap. 3.99 *(978-0-544-22789-7(1),* HMH Books For Young Readers) Houghton Mifflin Harcourt Publishing Co.
Robertson, J. Jean. Charlie's Harmonica. Snape, Jenny, illus. 2012. (ENG.). 24p. (gr. 1-2). pap. 8.95 *(978-1-61810-312-3(1))* Rourke Educational Media.
Ryan, Pam Muñoz. Echo. 2015. (ENG., Illus.). 512p. (J). (gr. 5-9). 19.99 *(978-0-439-87402-1(5),* Scholastic Pr.) Scholastic, Inc.

HAROLD (FICTITIOUS CHARACTER: JOHNSON)—FICTION

Crockett, Johns. Harold et le crayon Rose. pap. 13.95 *(978-2-266-09592-1(7))* Presses Pocket FRA. Dist: Distribooks, Inc.
Johnson, Crockett. Harold & the Purple Crayon. Johnson, Crockett, illus. 50th anniv. ed. 2015. (ENG., Illus.). 64p. (J). (gr. -1-3). pap. 6.99 *(978-0-06-443022-7(7))*; 16.99 *(978-0-06-022935-1(7))* HarperCollins Pubs.
—Harold's ABC Board Book. Johnson, Crockett, illus. 2015. (ENG., Illus.). 34p. (J). (gr. -1 — 1). bds. 7.99 *(978-0-06-242731-1(8),* HarperFestival) HarperCollins Pubs.
Johnson, Crockett, illus. Harold et le Crayon Violet: The French Edition of Harold & the Purple Crayon. 2013. (FRE & ENG.). 64p. (J). (gr. -1-3). 10.00 *(978-1-61243-164-2(X))* Ulysses Pr.
Weston Woods Staff, creator. Harold & the Purple Crayon. 2011. 29.95 *(978-0-439-73474-5(6))*; 18.95 *(978-0-439-72691-7(3))*; 38.75 *(978-0-439-72693-1(X))* Weston Woods Studios, Inc.
—Harold's Fairy Tale. 2011. 18.95 *(978-0-439-72704-4(9))*; 38.75 *(978-0-439-72706-8(5))* Weston Woods Studios, Inc.

HARRIET THE SPY (FICTITIOUS CHARACTER)—FICTION

Fitzhugh, Louise. Harriet the Spy. 298p. (J). (gr. 3-5). pap. 5.95 *(978-0-8072-1535-7(X),* Listening Library) Random Hse. Audio Publishing Group.

HARRISON, BENJAMIN, 1833-1901

Adelson, Bruce. Benjamin Harrison. 2006. (Presidential Leaders Ser.). (Illus.). 112p. (J). (gr. 3-7). lib. bdg. 29.27 *(978-0-8225-1497-8(4),* Lerner Pubns.) Lerner Publishing Group.
Gunderson, Megan M. Benjamin Harrison, 1 vol. 2009. (United States Presidents Ser.). (ENG., Illus.). 40p. (YA). (gr. 3-6). 27.07 *(978-1-60453-455-9(9))* ABDO Publishing Co.
Mis, Melody S. How to Draw the Life & Times of Benjamin Harrison. (Kid's Guide to Drawing the Presidents of the United States of America Ser.). 32p. 2009. (gr. 4-4). 50.50 *(978-1-61511-133-6(6),* PowerKids Pr.) 2007. (Illus.). (YA). (gr. 2-5). 26.50 *(978-1-4042-3000-2(9))* Rosen Publishing Group, Inc., The.
Venezia, Mike. Benjamin Harrison. Venezia, Mike, illus. 2006. (Getting to Know the U. S. Presidents Ser.). (ENG., Illus.). 32p. (J). (gr. 3-7). lib. bdg. 28.00 *(978-0-516-22628-6(2),* Children's Pr.) Scholastic Library Publishing.

HARRISON, WILLIAM HENRY, 1773-1841

Barton Billman, Hilary. How to Draw the Life & Times of William Henry Harrison. 2009. (Kid's Guide to Drawing the Presidents of the United States of America Ser.). 32p. (gr. 4-4). 50.50 *(978-1-61511-164-0(6),* PowerKids Pr.) Rosen Publishing Group, Inc., The.
Billman, Hilary Barton. How to Draw the Life & Times of William Henry Harrison. 2006. (Kid's Guide to Drawing the Presidents of the United States of America Ser.). (Illus.). 32p. (YA). (gr. 2-5). 26.50 *(978-1-4042-2986-0(8))* Rosen Publishing Group, Inc., The.
Elston, Heidi M. D. William H. Harrison, 1 vol. 2009. (United States Presidents Ser.). (ENG., Illus.). 40p. (YA). (gr. 3-6). 27.07 *(978-1-60453-456-6(7))* ABDO Publishing Co.
Gaines, Ann Graham. William Henry Harrison. 2008. (Presidents of the U. S. A. Ser.). (ENG., Illus.). 48p. (J). (gr. 3-6). 32.79 *(978-1-60253-038-6(6),* 200677) Child's World, Inc., The.
Greene, Meg. William H. Harrison. 2007. (Presidential Leaders Ser.). (Illus.). 112p. (J). (gr. 3-7). lib. bdg. 29.27

(978-0-8225-1511-1(3), Twenty-First Century Bks.) Lerner Publishing Group.

Lillard, David. William Henry Harrison: A MyReportLinks. Com Book. 2003. (Presidents Ser.). (Illus.). 48p. (J). lib. bdg. 25.26 (978-0-7660-5150-8(1), MyReportLinks.com Bks.) Enslow Pubs., Inc.

Peckham, Howard Henry. William Henry Harrison, Young Tippecanoe: Childhood of Famous Americans Series. Laune, Paul, illus. 2011. 190p. 42.95 (978-1-258-07766-2(3)) Literary Licensing, LLC.

Venezia, Mike. William Henry Harrison. Venezia, Mike, illus. 2005. (Getting to Know the U. S. Presidents Ser.). (ENG., Illus.). 32p. (J). (gr. 3-4). 28.00 (978-0-516-22614-9(2), Children's Pr.) Scholastic Library Publishing.

—William Henry Harrison: Ninth President 1841. Venezia, Mike, illus. 2005. (Getting to Know the U. S. Presidents Ser.). (ENG., Illus.). 32p. (J). (gr. 3-4). per. 7.95 (978-0-516-27483-6(X), Children's Pr.) Scholastic Library Publishing.

HARVEY, WILLIAM, 1578-1657

Elford, Jole Shack. William Harvey & the Mechanics of the Heart. 2005. (Illus.). 141p. (YA). (gr. 6-10). reprint ed. 28.00 (978-0-7567-9712-6(8)) DIANE Publishing Co.

Yount, Lisa. William Harvey: Discoverer of How Blood Circulates. 2008. (Great Minds of Science Ser.). (Illus.). 128p. (J). (gr. 4-10). lib. bdg. 33.27 (978-0-7660-3010-7(5)) Enslow Pubs., Inc.

—William Harvey: Genius Discoverer of Blood Circulation. 2015. (Genius Scientists & Their Genius Ideas Ser.). 96p. (J). (gr. 5-12). 27.94 (978-0-7660-6585-7(5)); pap. 10.95 (978-0-7660-6586-4(3)) Enslow Pubs., Inc.

HASIDISM

Lumer, Marc, illus. When Miracles Happened- Wondrous Stories of Tzaddikim. 2009. 22p. (J). (978-1-56871-484-4(X)) Targum Pr., Inc.

HASIDISM—FICTION

Wiseman, Eva. The World Outside. 2014. (ENG., Illus.). 236p. (YA). (gr. 7). 19.99 (978-0-88776-981-8(0), Tundra Bks.) Tundra Bks. CAN. Dist: Penguin Random Hse. LLC.

HASTINGS, BATTLE OF, ENGLAND, 1066

Baker, Chris & Ladybird Books Staff. The Battle of Hastings. 2016. (Ladybird Histories Ser.). (ENG., Illus.). 48p. (J). (gr. 1-3). pap. 14.99 (978-0-241-24822-5(1)) Penguin Bks., Ltd. GBR. Dist: Independent Pubs. Group.

Howell, Izzi & Martin, Claudia. The Battle of Hastings. 2016. (ENG., Illus.). 32p. (J). (gr. 1-3). 17.99 (978-1-4451-4844-1(7), Franklin Watts) Hachette Children's Group GBR. Dist: Hachette Bk. Group.

Roberts, Russell. Battle of Hastings. 2011. (Technologies & Strategies in Battle Ser.). (Illus.). 48p. (J). (gr. 4-7). lib. bdg. 29.95 (978-1-61228-075-2(7)) Mitchell Lane Pubs., Inc.

HATS

Cooper, Sharon Katz. Whose Hat Is This? A Look at Hats Workers Wear - Hard, Tall, & Shiny, 1 vol. Muehlenhardt, Amy Bailey, illus. 2006. (Whose Is It?: Community Workers Ser.). (ENG.). 24p. (gr. -1-2). lib. bdg. 26.65 (978-1-4048-1600-8(3)) Picture Window Bks.

Corbett, Sara. Hats off to Hats! 2006. (Illus.). 32p. (J). (gr. k-4). reprint ed. 17.00 (978-0-7567-9929-8(5)) DIANE Publishing Co.

Hats: Big Book: Level B. 8p. 20.95 (978-0-322-00359-0(8)) Wright Group/McGraw-Hill.

Hats: Level B. 8p. 24.95 (978-0-7802-8919-2(6)) Wright Group/McGraw-Hill.

Hats: Level G, 6 vols. (Wonder Worldtm Ser.). 16p. 29.95 (978-0-7802-4579-2(2)) Wright Group/McGraw-Hill.

Seto, Alex. Whose Hat? 2006. (Illus.). 14p. bds. (978-0-9734496-5-5(9)) ADVAN Pr., Inc.

HATS—FICTION

Adams, Pam. Mrs. Honey's Hat. 2007. (Early Reading Ser.). (ENG., Illus.). 32p. (J). (gr. 2-2). pap. (978-1-84643-126-5(3)) Child's Play International Ltd.

Adler, David A. Bones & the Football Mystery. 2013. (Bones Ser.: 9). (ENG.). 32p. (J). (gr. 1-3). pap. 3.99 (978-0-448-47942-2(7), Penguin Young Readers) Penguin Young Readers Group.

—Bones & the Football Mystery. 2013. (Bones Penguin Young Readers Ser.: 9). lib. bdg. 13.55 (978-0-606-32450-2(X), Turtleback) Turtleback Bks.

Anin, Ravi & Benchmark Education Co., LLC Staff. Pete Mule's Hat. 2015. (BuildUp Ser.). (J). (gr. 1). (978-1-4900-0729-8(6)) Benchmark Education Co.

Antony, Steve. The Queen's Hat. 2015. (ENG., Illus.). 32p. (J). (gr. -1-k). 16.99 (978-0-545-83556-5(9), Scholastic Pr.) Scholastic, Inc.

Armstrong, Tiffani. Zach & the Incredible Traveling Hat. 2010. 28p. pap. 13.00 (978-1-4490-8129-4(0)) AuthorHouse.

Ashburn, Boni. I Had a Favorite Hat. Ng, Robyn, illus. 2015. (ENG.). 32p. (J). (gr. -1-3). 16.95 (978-1-4197-1462-7(7), Abrams Bks. for Young Readers) Abrams, Inc.

Bandsuh, Jim. Helmet Hank. 2007. (Illus.). (J). per. 15.99 (978-1-933156-19-4(8), Visikid Bks.) GSVQ Publishing.

Beaty, Andrea. Happy Birthday, Madame Chapeau. Roberts, David, illus. 2014. (ENG.). 32p. (J). (gr. k-2). 16.95 (978-1-4197-1219-7(5), Abrams Bks. for Young Readers) Abrams, Inc.

Beaumont, Karen. Hats off to You! Pham, LeUyen, illus. 2017. (ENG.). 40p. (J). (gr. -1-3). 16.99 (978-0-545-47423-8(X), Scholastic Pr.) Scholastic, Inc.

Bianchi, John, illus. Bear Gets a Hat. 2012. (Bird, Bunny, & Bear Ser.). (ENG.). 12p. (J). pap. 5.99 (978-1-61406-305-6(2)) American Reading Co.

Boyd, Cathy. The Little Snowman's New Hat. 2011. 28p. pap. 24.95 (978-1-4560-2751-3(4)) PublishAmerica, Inc.

Butler, M. Christina. One Snowy Rescue. Macnaughton, Tina, illus. 2015. (ENG.). 32p. (J). (gr. -1-3). 16.99 (978-1-58925-196-0(2)) Tiger Tales.

Casad, Mary Brooke. Bluebonnet at the State Fair of Texas, 1 vol. Binder, Pat, illus. 2010. (ENG.). 40p. (J). (gr. k-3). pap. 8.95 (978-1-58980-830-0(4)) Pelican Publishing Co., Inc.

Catipon, Atreyu. The Wizard's Magic Hat. 2012. 26p. 16.00 (978-1-61863-390-3(2)) Bookstand Publishing.

Chaconas, Dori. Virginnie's Hat. Meade, Holly, illus. 2007. (ENG.). 32p. (J). (gr. -1-1). 16.99 (978-0-7636-2397-5(0)) Candlewick Pr.

Chand, Dianne. Hats! 2012. 28p. pap. 32.70 (978-1-4797-0647-1(7)) Xlibris Corp.

Charlesworth, Liza. Seven Magic Hats. Lewis, Stephen, illus. 2005. (Number Tales Ser.). (ENG.). 16p. (J). (gr. -1-1). pap. 2.99 (978-0-439-69018-8(8)) Scholastic, Inc.

Cinar, Lisa. The Day It All Blew Away. 2007. (ENG., Illus.). 52p. (J). (gr. -1-3). 16.95 (978-1-894965-71-2(X)) Simply Read Bks. CAN. Dist: Ingram Publisher Services.

Claus, Nancy. Santa's Hat. Ferchaud, Steve, illus. 2006. (J). (978-0-9746747-6-6(1)) Cypress Bay Publishing.

Cowley, Joy. Dan's Lost Hat. 2009. pap. 8.25 (978-1-60559-219-0(6)) Hameray Publishing Group, Inc.

D'Amico, Carmela & D'Amico, Steven. Ella the Elegant Elephant. 2004. (Illus.). (J). (ENG.). 56p. (gr. -1-3). 17.99 (978-0-439-62792-4(3)); (978-0-439-62793-1(1)) Scholastic, Inc. (Levine, Arthur A. Bks.).

David, Kate. Murphy & the Magical Hat. 2012. (ENG.). 26p. (J). 18.95 (978-1-4327-8582-6(6)) Outskirts Pr., Inc.

Davis, Bonita. Jasmine & the Missing Hat. 2011. 24p. pap. 16.99 (978-1-4634-4298-9(X)) AuthorHouse.

Deak, Gloria. The Kissing Skunks. Nathan, Cheryl, illus. 2006. 40p. (J). (gr. -1). 16.95 (978-1-932065-46-6(6)) Star Bright Bks., Inc.

Delibero, Bob. Petrucchio. 2012. 234p. 24.95 (978-1-4626-6155-8(6)) America Star Bks.

deRubertis, Barbara. Corky Cub's Crazy Caps. Alley, R. W., illus. 2010. (Animal Antics A to Z Ser.). 32p. (J). lib. bdg. 22.60 (978-1-57565-306-8(0)); (ENG.). (gr. -1-3). pap. 7.95 (978-1-57565-302-0(8)) Kane Press, Inc.

deRubertis, Barbara & DeRubertis, Barbara. Corky Cub's Crazy Caps. Alley, R. W., illus. 2012. (Animal Antics A to Z Ser.). 32p. (J). (gr. 2 — 1). cd-rom 7.95 (978-1-57565-396-9(6)) Kane Press, Inc.

Donaldson, Julia. Rosie's Hat. Currey, Anna, illus. 2015. (ENG.). 32p. (J). (-k). pap. 9.99 (978-1-4472-6612-9(9)) Pan Macmillan GBR. Dist: Independent Pubs. Group.

Dowling, Iris Gray. A Change of Hats. Bouthyette, Valerie, illus. 2012. 28p. pap. 14.99 (978-1-937129-36-1(5)) Faithful Life Pubs.

Dubin, Lawrence. Santa's Big Red Hat. 2012. (ENG.). (J). pap. 20.00 (978-1-4675-3866-4(3)) Independent Pub.

Dunrea, Olivier. Peedie. 2008. (Gossie & Friends Ser.). (ENG., Illus.). 32p. (J). (gr. -1 — 1). bds. 6.95 (978-0-618-75506-6(3)) Houghton Mifflin Harcourt Publishing Co.

Eissler, Trevor. That 17th Hat. de Vries, Marloes, illus. 2012. 32p. (J). 20.00 (978-0-9835558-1-0(8)) June Bks., LLC.

Engelbreit, Mary. Queen of Easter. Engelbreit, Mary, illus. 2009. (Ann Estelle Stories Ser.). (ENG., Illus.). 32p. (J). (gr. -1-3). pap. 6.99 (978-0-06-008186-7(4)) HarperCollins Pubs.

Erhard, Lorie. Mama's Many Hats. Kalis, Jennifer, illus. 2014. (ENG.). 32p. (J). 18.99 (978-0-9914701-4-3(1)) Bumble Bee Bks.

Esphyr, Slobodkina & Slobodkina. Caps for Sale: A Tale of a Peddler, Some Monkeys & Their Monkey Business. 2014. (Reading Rainbow Bks). (ENG.). 48p. (J). 11.24 (978-1-63245-155-2(7)) Lectorum Pubns., Inc.

Farber, Erica. Richard Scarry's Readers (Level 1): Get That Hat! Scarry, Huck, illus. 2015. (Richard Scarry's Great Big Schoolhouse Ser.). (ENG.). 24p. (J). (gr. -1-k). pap. 3.95 (978-1-4027-9919-8(5)) Sterling Publishing Co., Inc.

The Flat Hat: KinderReaders Individual Title Six-Packs. (Kinderstarters Ser.). 8p. (gr. -1-1). 21.00 (978-0-7635-8662-1(5)) Rigby Education.

Fox, Mem. The Magic Hat. Tusa, Tricia, illus. 2006. (ENG.). 32p. (J). (gr. -1-3). reprint ed. pap. 7.99 (978-0-15-205715-2(3)) Houghton Mifflin Harcourt Publishing Co.

Frederick, John. The Flying Hat. 2010. (Illus.). 24p. 12.99 (978-1-4520-1901-7(0)) AuthorHouse.

Freeman, Tor. Olive & the Embarrassing Gift. Freeman, Tor, illus. 2014. (ENG., Illus.). 32p. (J). (gr. -1-3). 15.99 (978-0-7636-7406-9(0), Templar) Candlewick Pr.

Fuller, T. Nat. A Good Day for a Hat. Hodgson, Rob, illus. 2017. (ENG.). 32p. (J). (gr. -1-k). 15.95 (978-1-4197-2300-1(6), Abrams Appleseed) Abrams, Inc.

Golden Books Staff. Oh, the Things Spring Brings! Ruiz, Aristides, illus. 2013. (Color Plus Stencil Ser.). (ENG.). 64p. (J). (-k). pap. 5.99 (978-0-307-98123-3(1), Golden Bks.) Random Hse. Children's Bks.

Gorbachev, Valeri. Whose Hat Is It? 2004. 30p. (J). lib. bdg. 13.85 (978-1-4242-0713-8(4)) Fitzgerald Bks.

—Whose Hat Is It? Gorbachev, Valeri, illus. (My First I Can Read Ser.). (Illus.). 32p. (J). (gr. -1 — 1). 2005. (ENG.). pap. 3.99 (978-0-06-053436-3(2)) 2004. (ENG., 14.99 (978-0-06-053434-9(6)) 2004. lib. bdg. 15.89 (978-0-06-053435-6(4)) HarperCollins Pubs.

Graves, Jonathan. Isabella Propeller & the Magic Beanie. Haley, Gail E., illus. 2011. (J). 15.95 (978-1-933251-74-5(3)) Parkway Pubs., Inc.

Graves, Sue. Harry's Hat. Worsley, Belinda, illus. 2008. (Reading Corner Ser.). (ENG.). 24p. (J). (gr. k-2). pap. 6.99 (978-0-7496-7692-6(2), Franklin Watts) Hachette Children's Group GBR. Dist: Hachette Bk. Group.

H. P. Lawrence. The Adventures of Wilfred & Henri: The Staff of Knowledge. 2009. 88p. pap. 10.49 (978-1-4389-6374-7(2)) AuthorHouse.

Hamilton, Tim. But! Hamilton, Tim, illus. 2014. (ENG., Illus.). 32p. (J). (gr. -1-2). 16.95 (978-0-8234-3046-8(4)) Holiday Hse., Inc.

Hanson, Warren. Kiki's Hats: Our Gifts Live on & On. Hanson, Warren, illus. 2007. (ENG., Illus.). 36p. (J). (gr. -1-3). 16.95 (978-0-931674-94-5(8), Waldman House Pr.) TRISTAN Publishing, Inc.

Hassett, Ann. The Finest Christmas Tree. Hassett, John, illus. 2010. (ENG.). 32p. (J). (gr. -1-3). pap. 6.99 (978-0-547-40623-7(1)) Houghton Mifflin Harcourt Publishing Co.

The Hat. (Little Book Practice Reader). (J). (978-0-8136-5339-6(8)) Modern Curriculum Pr.

Hats. Date not set. 5.95 (978-0-89868-349-3(1)) ARO Publishing Co.

Hats: Individual Title Six-Packs. (Sails Literacy Ser.). 16p. (gr. k-18). 27.00 (978-0-7635-4443-0(4)) Rigby Education.

Hofmeister, Alan, et al. The Hat. (Reading for All Learners Ser.). (Illus.). (J). pap. (978-1-56861-105-1(6)) Swift Learning Resources.

—Mat in the Hat. (Reading for All Learners Ser.). (Illus.). (J). pap. (978-1-56861-106-8(4)) Swift Learning Resources.

Hoppe, Paul. Hat. Hoppe, Paul, illus. 2009. (ENG., Illus.). 32p. (J). (gr. -1-1). 14.99 (978-1-59990-247-0(8), 9781599902470, Bloomsbury USA Childrens) Bloomsbury Publishing USA.

Houghton, Jackolyn. Detective Billy Pears & the Missing Hat. 2008. 36p. pap. 24.95 (978-1-60474-543-6(6)) America Star Bks.

Howard, Elizabeth Fitzgerald. Aunt Flossie's Hats (and Crab Cakes Later) Ransome, James, illus. 2015. 32p. pap. 8.00 (978-1-61003-491-3(0)) Center for the Collaborative Classroom.

Hume, Maureen. The Pizza Gang: Facing the Witch. 2009. 80p. pap. 9.95 (978-1-60860-337-4(7), Eloquent Bks.) Strategic Book Publishing & Rights Agency (SBPRA).

James, Carol. The Lady Who Loved Hats, 1 vol. 2009. 44p. pap. 24.95 (978-1-60813-777-0(5)) America Star Bks.

Johnson, D. B. Magritte's Marvelous Hat. Johnson, D. B., illus. 2012. (ENG., Illus.). 32p. (J). (gr. -1-3). 17.99 (978-0-547-55864-6(3)) Houghton Mifflin Harcourt Publishing Co.

Judge, Lita. Red Hat. Judge, Lita, illus. 2013. (ENG., Illus.). 40p. (J). (gr. -1-k). 16.99 (978-1-4424-4232-0(8), Atheneum Bks. for Young Readers) Simon & Schuster Children's Publishing.

Kann, Victoria. Pinkalicious & the Pink Hat Parade. Kann, Victoria, illus. 2012. (Pinkalicious Ser.). (ENG., Illus.). 24p. (J). (gr. -1-2). pap. 6.99 (978-0-06-198960-5(6), HarperFestival) HarperCollins Pubs.

Kasza, Keiko & McPike, Elizabeth. Finders Keepers. Kasza, Keiko, illus. 2015. (ENG., Illus.). 32p. (J). (gr. -1-k). bds. 16.99 (978-0-399-16898-7(2), G.P. Putnam's Sons Books for Young Readers) Penguin Young Readers Group.

Keats, Ezra Jack. Jennie's Hat. Keats, Ezra Jack, illus. 2003. (ENG., Illus.). 40p. (J). (gr. -1-2). 6.99 (978-0-14-250035-4(6), Puffin Books) Penguin Young Readers Group.

—Jennie's Hat. 2003. (gr. k-3). 17.20 (978-0-613-61710-9(X), Turtleback) Turtleback Bks.

Keller, Holly. The Hat. 2005. (Green Light Readers Level 1 Ser.). (ENG., Illus.). 24p. (J). (gr. -1-3). pap. 3.95 (978-0-15-205178-5(3)) Houghton Mifflin Harcourt Publishing Co.

—The Hat. Keller, Holly, illus. 2005. (Green Light Readers Level 1 Ser.). (Illus.). (gr. -1-1). 13.95 (978-0-7569-5241-9(7)) Perfection Learning Corp.

Kemnitz, Dianna. A New Hat for Jack. 2012. 38p. 24.95 (978-1-4626-6816-8(X)) 2011. 40p. pap. 24.95 (978-1-4626-2215-3(1)) America Star Bks.

Kim, Cecil & Kim, Joo-Kyung, illus. A Happy Hat. 2014. (J). (978-1-4338-1337-5(8), Magination Pr.) American Psychological Assn.

Kirk, Ruth Lynn. Charlie Ate My Hat! 2004. 32p. pap. 7.99 (978-0-9675410-2-0(6)) Shamrock Pr.

Kitamura, Satoshi. Millie's Marvellous Hat. 2009. (Andersen Press Picture Bks). (ENG., Illus.). 32p. (J). (gr. -1-3). 16.95 (978-0-7613-5153-5(1)) Lerner Publishing Group.

Klassen, Jon. I Want My Hat Back. Klassen, Jon, illus. 2011. (ENG., Illus.). 40p. (J). (gr. -1-3). 16.99 (978-0-7636-5598-3(8)) Candlewick Pr.

—I Want My Hat Back. 2012. (CHI.). 40p. (J). (gr. k-3). (978-7-5332-6789-6(3)) Mingtian Chubanshe.

—This Is Not My Hat. Klassen, Jon, illus. 2012. (ENG., Illus.). 40p. (J). (gr. -1-3). 16.99 (978-0-7636-5599-0(6)) Candlewick Pr.

—We Found a Hat. Klassen, Jon, illus. 2016. (ENG., Illus.). 56p. (J). (gr. -1-3). 17.99 (978-0-7636-5600-3(3)) Candlewick Pr.

Klise, Kate. Shall I Knit You a Hat? A Christmas Yarn. Klise, M. Sarah, illus. 2007. (ENG.). 32p. (J). (gr. -1-2). per. 8.99 (978-0-312-37139-5(X), 9780312371395) Square Fish.

Ladd, Debbie. Nurse Robin's Hats. Nakasone, Shaun, illus. 2006. 52p. (J). 16.95 (978-0-9727615-3-6(5)) Deb on Air Bks.

Langdo, Bryan. Tornado Slim & the Magic Cowboy Hat, 0 vols. 2011. (ENG.). 32p. (J). (gr. k-4). 17.99 (978-0-7614-5962-0(6), 9780761459620, Amazon Children's Publishing) Amazon Publishing.

Langford, Jane. An Old Red Hat. Axworthy, Anni, illus. 2004. (ENG.). 24p. (J). lib. bdg. 23.65 (978-1-59646-676-0(6)) Dingles & Co.

LeBaron, Cecilia. The Cap. 2007. (Illus.). 16p. (J). 5.95 (978-0-9798869-2-8(9)) Crush Publishing.

—The Map. 2007. (Illus.). 16p. (J). 5.95 (978-0-9798869-1-1(0)) Crush Publishing.

Lemke, Donald. Book-O-Hats. Lentz, Bob, illus. 2015. (Wearable Bks.). (ENG.). 12p. (gr. -1-1). bds. 7.99 (978-1-62370-184-0(8), Wear-A-Book) Capstone Young Readers of Coughlan Cos.

Lichtenheld, Tom. Bridget's Beret. Lichtenheld, Tom, illus. 2010. (ENG., Illus.). 40p. (J). (gr. -1-2). 16.99 (978-0-8050-8775-8(3), 9780805087758, Holt, Henry & Co. Bks. For Young Readers) Holt, Henry & Co.

Lipson, Amy Kron & Laddy, Lee. Penelope Pratt's Hats: A Young Girl's Dilemma Turns Rhyme to Reason. 2012. (ENG.). 44p. (J). pap. 20.95 (978-1-4327-8173-6(1)) Outskirts Pr., Inc.

Lockhart, Kendra. Favorite Hat. 2010. (Illus.). 24p. (J). pap. 14.95 (978-0-9843883-3-2(8), Green Lady Pr., The) RealityIsBooks.com, Inc.

Macnaughton, Tina. One Snowy Rescue. 2015. (ENG.). pap. (978-0-545-92909-7(1)) Scholastic, Inc.

McCann, Jesse Leon. The Cat in the Hat. 2003. (Illus.). 24p. (J). (gr. k-k). 0.33 (978-0-375-82780-8(3), Golden Bks.) Random Hse. Children's Bks.

McClatchy, Lisa & Thompson, Kay. Eloise's New Bonnet. Lyon, Tammie Speer & Lyon, Tammie, illus. 2007. (Eloise Ser.). (ENG.). 32p. (J). (gr. -1-1). pap. 3.99 (978-0-689-87452-9(9), Simon Spotlight) Simon Spotlight.

McCollum, Kimberly. Gloves in a Hat. 2011. 16p. (gr. -1). pap. 8.32 (978-1-4567-3430-5(X)) AuthorHouse.

McDoogle, Farrah. A Mystery in Gabba Land. Scanlon, Michael, illus. 2010. (Yo Gabba Gabba! Ser.). (ENG.). 24p. (J). (gr. -1-k). pap. 3.99 (978-1-4424-0652-0(6), Simon Spotlight) Simon Spotlight.

McMurtrie, Kevin. The Prince That Always Wore His Top Hat. 2013. 40p. pap. 16.26 (978-1-4669-9602-1(1)) Trafford Publishing.

McNally, Jeanne. The Girl Who Wore Many Hats. 2010. 40p. pap. 16.99 (978-1-4490-5735-0(7)) AuthorHouse.

Melling, David. Dont Worry Douglas. Melling, David, illus. 2011. (ENG., Illus.). 32p. 12.95 (978-1-58925-106-9(7)) Tiger Tales.

Mercier, Deborah. The Captain's Hat. Mills, Faythe, illus. 2007. 32p. (J). 17.99 (978-0-9799410-0-9(8)) Minnewaska Pr.

Miller, Margaret. What's on My Head? Miller, Margaret, photos by. 2009. (Look Baby! Bks.). (ENG., Illus.). 14p. (J). (gr. -1 — 1). bds. 4.99 (978-1-4169-8995-0(1), Little Simon) Little Simon.

Miskimen, Cora. Mrs. Hunny Bunny's New Spring Hat. 2008. 32p. pap. 24.95 (978-1-4241-8939-7(X)) America Star Bks.

Mom Likes Hats. 2003. (Mom & Dad Ser.). (J). 7.33 (978-1-58453-253-8(X)) Pioneer Valley Bks.

Moncure, Jane Belk. Away Went the Farmer's Hat: A Book about an Adventure. Regan, Dana, illus. 2013. (Magic Castle Readers Ser.). (ENG.). 32p. (J). (gr. -1-2). 25.64 (978-1-62323-572-7(3), 206309) Child's World, Inc., The.

Mortensen, Lyn. Effie May & Her Outrageous Hats. Mortensen, Lyn, illus. 2006. (Illus.). (J). per. (978-0-9767570-1-6(X)) Whitegate Bks.

Nash, Margaret. Hetty's New Hat. Impey, Martin, illus. 2005. (Reading Corner Ser.). 24p. (J). (gr. k-3). lib. bdg. 22.80 (978-1-59771-007-7(5)) Sea-To-Sea Pubns.

O'Donnell, Kerri. Whose Hat Is That? 2006. (Neighborhood Readers Ser.). (ENG.). 8p. (gr. -1-3). pap. 5.15 (978-1-4042-5647-7(4), Rosen Classroom) Rosen Publishing Group, Inc., The.

Olive, Gloria D. My Hat! My Hat! Where Is My Hat? Barge III, John, illus. 2011. 28p. pap. 24.95 (978-1-4626-0730-3(6)) America Star Bks.

Olsen, Jan Z. Mat Man Hats. Delaney, Molly, illus. 2008. (ENG.). 36p. stu. ed. 13.75 (978-1-891627-93-4(7)) Handwriting Without Tears.

Opheim, Sandra. Whose Hat Is That? Horton, Lori, illus. 2004. (J). 5.95 (978-0-9758958-0-1(X)) Better Than One Publishing.

Parker, Emma. Splat & the Hat. 2010. (Illus.). pap. (978-1-877561-04-7(5)) First Edition Ltd.

Pepin, Brenda. Cordelia Rae Is Crazy for Hats. 2012. 32p. pap. 14.51 (978-1-4669-1518-3(8)) Trafford Publishing.

Pittar, Gill. Milly, Molly & the Sunhat (book W/dolls) 2006. 28p. pap. (978-1-86972-102-2(0)) Milly Molly Bks.

Plass, Beverly. Where Is Matt's Cap? Pierce, Linda, illus. 2006. (ENG.). 12p. (gr. k-2). pap. 7.95 (978-1-57874-295-0(1), Kaeden Bks.) Kaeden Corp.

—Where Is Matt's Cap? (6 Pack) Pierce, Linda, illus. 2006. (ENG.). 12p. (gr. k-2). pap. (978-1-57874-296-7(X), Kaeden Bks.) Kaeden Corp.

Pope, Brennan & Pope, Janet. The Adventures of William Walkingstick. 2007. 132p. (gr. 2-2). per. 11.95 (978-0-595-45786-1(X)); Vol. 1. 21.95 (978-0-595-69866-0(2)) iUniverse, Inc.

Powell, Richard. Whose Hat Is That? Martín Larrañaga, Ana, illus. 2004. (Ana's Mini Movers Ser.). 12p. (J). 5.95 (978-1-58925-740-5(5)) Tiger Tales.

Prahin, Andrew. Brimsby's Hats. Prahin, Andrew, illus. 2013. (ENG., Illus.). 40p. (J). (gr. -1-3). 15.99 (978-1-4424-8147-3(1), Simon & Schuster Bks. For Young Readers) Simon & Schuster Bks. For Young Readers.

Pratt, Pierre. Leon Sans Son Chapeau. 2004. (J). (gr. k-3). spiral bd. (978-0-616-03076-9(2)) Canadian National Institute for the Blind/Institut National Canadien pour les Aveugles.

Price, Roger & Stern, Leonard, creators. Adventure Time Mad Libs. 2012. (Adventure Time Ser.). (ENG.). 48p. (J). (gr. 3-7). 4.99 (978-0-8431-7221-8(5), Mad Libs) Penguin Young Readers Group.

Publications International Ltd. Staff, ed. Little Lift & Listen Sound Mickey Mouse Clubhouse. 2007. (J). 10.98 (978-1-4127-8457-3(3)) Phoenix International Publications, Inc.

Rabe, Tish. I Love the Nightlife! Ruiz, Aristides & Mathieu, Joe, illus. 2010. (Pictureback Ser.). (ENG.). 16p. (J). (gr. -1-2). pap. 3.99 (978-0-375-86354-7(0), Random Hse. Bks. for Young Readers) Random Hse. Children's Bks.

—Trick-or-Treat!/Aye-Aye! Ruiz, Aristides & Mathieu, Joe, illus. 2012. (Pictureback(R) Ser.). (ENG.). 32p. (J). (gr. -1-2). pap. 4.99 (978-0-307-93056-9(4), Random Hse. Bks. for Young Readers) Random Hse. Children's Bks.

Racaniello, P. Marcella & the Magic Hat. 2012. 20p. pap. 9.99 (978-1-105-02672-0(8)) Lulu Pr., Inc.

RH Disney. The Royal Derby (Disney Palace Pets: Whisker Haven Tales) RH Disney, illus. 2016. (Pictureback Ser.). (ENG., Illus.). 24p. (J). (gr. -1-2). 4.99 (978-0-7364-3496-6(8), Random Hse. Bks. for Young Readers) Random Hse. Children's Bks.

Riemer, Bernice. The Old Straw Hat. 2006. (ENG., Illus.). 40p. (J). per. 15.95 (978-1-59800-844-9(7)) Outskirts Pr., Inc.

Rigby Education Staff. Animal Advertisements. (Sails Literacy Ser.). (Illus.). 16p. (gr. 2-3). 27.00 (978-0-7635-9944-7(1), 699441C99) Rigby Education.

Rohmer, Harriet. Uncle Nacho's Hat: El Sombrero Del to Nacho. Flor Ada, Alma & Zubizarreta, Rosalma, trs. Reisberg, Mira, illus. 2013. (ENG & SPA.). 32p. (J). (gr. k-18). pap. 9.95 (978-0-89239-112-7(X)) Lee & Low Bks., Inc.

Sadler, Marilyn & Comstock, Eric. Charlie Piechart & the Case of the Missing Hat. Comstock, Eric, illus. 2016. (Charlie Piechart Ser.). (Illus.). 40p. (J). (gr. -1-3). 17.99 (978-0-06-237056-3(1), Tegen, Katherine Bks) HarperCollins Pubs.

Sands, Maria. Sanjee & Her Delightful Hats. 2008. 20p. pap. 24.95 (978-1-60563-700-6(9)) America Star Bks.

Sanrio. Easter Bonnet Surprise. 2013. (ENG., Illus.). 24p. (J). (gr. k-2). pap. 6.99 (978-1-4197-0910-4(0), Abrams Bks. for Young Readers) Abrams, Inc.

Sansone, V. K. Heavenly Hannah's Little Black Hat. 2009. 32p. pap. 14.98 (978-0-557-07065-7(1)) Lulu Pr., Inc.

Santa's Hat. 2003. (J). per. (978-1-57657-927-5(1)) Paradise Pr., Inc.

Sasso, Sandy Eisenberg. Butterflies under Our Hats. Rothenberg, Joani Keller, illus. 2006. (ENG.). 32p. (gr. -1-3). 16.95 (978-1-55725-474-0(5)) Paraclete Pr., Inc.

Savage, Stephen. Where's Walrus? Savage, Stephen, illus. 2011. (ENG., Illus.). 32p. (J). (gr. -1-k). 16.99 *(978-0-439-70049-8(3)*, Scholastic Pr.) Scholastic, Inc.

Savoie, Jacques & Zekina, Daniela. Un Chapeau Qui Tournait Autour de la Terre. 2003. (Illus.). 24p. (J). pap. *(978-2-89021-295-4(5))* Diffusion du livre Mirabel (DLM).

Scarry, Richard. Richard Scarry's Mr. Frumble's Big, Flat Hat. 2014. (Richard Scarry's Lift the Flaps Bks.). (ENG.). 10p. (J). (gr. -1 — 1). 7.99 *(978-0-7641-6674-7(3))* Barron's Educational Series, Inc.

Seuss, Dr. The Cat in the Hat. (Beginner Books(R) Ser.). (ENG.). (J). 2012. 72p. (gr. k-3). 17.99 *(978-0-449-81086-6(0))* 2005. (Illus.). 64p. (gr. -1-2). 9.95 *(978-0-375-83492-9(3))* Random Hse. Children's Bks. (Random Hse. Bks. for Young Readers).

—The Cat in the Hat Book & Hat. 2012. (Beginner Books Ser.). (ENG.). 72p. (J). (gr. k-3). 24.99 *(978-0-307-93044-6(0)*, Random Hse. Bks. for Young Readers) Random Hse. Children's Bks.

—The Cat in the Hat Cloth Book. 2015. (Bright & Early Cloth Book Ser.). (ENG., Illus.). 8p. (J). (— 1). 14.99 *(978-0-385-39268-6(0)*, Random Hse. Bks. for Young Readers) Random Hse. Children's Bks.

Shelton, Angela. Tilda Pinkerton's Magical Hats. 2013. 196p. 19.95 *(978-0-9859443-8-4(2))* Quiet Owl Bks.

—Tilda Pinkerton's Magical Hats. Murray, James, illus. 2013. 196p. pap. 11.99 *(978-0-9859443-7-7(4))* Quiet Owl Bks.

Slobodkina, Esphyr. Caps for Sale. Slobodkina, Esphyr, illus. 75th ed. 2015. (Reading Rainbow Bks.). (ENG., Illus.). 32p. (J). (gr. -1-3). bds. 8.99 *(978-0-06-147453-8(3)*, HarperFestival) HarperCollins Pubs.

—Caps for Sale: A Tale of a Peddler, Some Monkeys & Their Monkey Business. Slobodkina, Esphyr, illus. 2008. (Young Scott Bks.). (Illus.). 48p. (J). (gr. -1-3). lib. bdg. 17.89 *(978-0-06-025778-1(4))* HarperCollins Pubs.

—Circus Caps for Sale. Slobodkina, Esphyr, illus. 2004. (Illus.). 40p. (J). (gr. -1-2). reprint ed. 17.00 *(978-0-7567-8345-7(3))* DIANE Publishing Co.

Slobodkina, Esphyr & Slobodkina. Caps for Sale: A Tale of a Peddler, Some Monkeys & Their Monkey Business. Slobodkina, Esphyr, illus. 2015. (Young Scott Bks.). (ENG., Illus.). 48p. (J). (gr. -1-3). 17.99 *(978-0-201-09147-2(X))*; 75th ed. pap. 7.99 *(978-0-06-443143-9(6))* HarperCollins Pubs.

—Circus Caps for Sale. Slobodkina, Esphyr, illus. 2004. (ENG., Illus.). 48p. (J). (gr. -1-3). reprint ed. pap. 7.99 *(978-0-06-443793-6(0))* HarperCollins Pubs.

Slobodkina, Esphyr & Slobodkina, E. Caps for Sale. 2015. (J). (gr. k-3). 17.20 *(978-0-8085-2604-9(9)*, Turtleback) Turtleback Bks.

Smith, N. L. Elle's Silly Hats. 2010. 12p. 10.99 *(978-1-4490-5169-3(3))* AuthorHouse.

El Sombrero de Juan: Harry's Hat. 2005. (Take-Home Bks.). (SPA.). (YA). (gr. -1-3). 15.75 *(978-0-8215-1203-6(X))* Sadlier, William H. Inc.

El Sombrero de Juan/Harry's Hat. 2005. (Libros en Espanol Para Ninos Ser.). (SPA.). (YA). (gr. -1-1). 11.97 *(978-0-8215-0993-7(4))* Sadlier, William H. Inc.

Son, John. Finding My Hat. 2005. (First Person Fiction Ser.). (ENG.). 192p. (J). (gr. 7). reprint ed. pap. 6.99 *(978-0-439-43539-0(0)*, Scholastic Paperbacks) Scholastic, Inc.

Spanyol, Jessica. Clive & His Hats. Spanyol, Jessica, illus. 2016. (All about Clive Ser.). (ENG., Illus.). 14p. (J). bds. *(978-1-84643-885-1(3))* Child's Play International Ltd.

Staton, Debbie. Twiggle. Patzelt, Kasie, illus. l.t. ed. 2007. 26p. (J). (gr. -1-3). per. 12.99 *(978-1-59879-199-0(0))* Lifevest Publishing, Inc.

Steinkraus, Kyla. Nobody's Watching. Dufalla, Anita, illus. 2012. (ENG.). 24p. (gr. 2-3). pap. 8.95 *(978-1-61810-328-4(8))* Rourke Educational Media.

Strauss, Kevin. Pecos Bill Invents the Ten-Gallon Hat, 1 vol. Harrington, David, illus. 2012. (ENG.). 32p. (J). (gr. k-3). 16.99 *(978-1-4556-1502-5(1))* Pelican Publishing Co., Inc.

Tait, Barbara. Timothy Toot.... Finds A Hat. Margolis, Al, illus. 2011. 32p. (J). 24.95 *(978-1-58909-917-3(6))* Bookstand Publishing.

Thompson, Bruce R. If I Made a Hat. 2012. 28p. pap. 10.95 *(978-1-4575-1206-3(8))* Dog Ear Publishing, LLC.

Thorp, Gloria J. & Ruotsala, Charity Aili. Anna's Hats: Anna has a hat for every Adventure. 2009. 40p. pap. 19.49 *(978-1-4389-8967-9(9))* AuthorHouse.

Tillworth, Mary. Dora in Magic Land (Dora & Friends) Haskett, Dan & Goddard, Brenda, illus. 2016. (Little Golden Book Ser.). (ENG.). 24p. (J). (gr. -1-2). 4.99 *(978-0-553-53840-3(3)*, Golden Bks.) Random Hse. Children's Bks.

Tompert, Ann. Harry's Hats. Elizalde, Marcelo, illus. 2004. (Rookie Readers Ser.). 31p. (J). 19.50 *(978-0-516-23613-1(X)*, Children's Pr.) Scholastic Library Publishing.

Tracey, Andrée. Storyland: Poppy & Her Magic Hat: A Story Coloring Book. 2015. (Dover Coloring Bks.). (ENG., Illus.). 32p. (J). (gr. k-5). pap. 3.99 *(978-0-486-79403-7(2))* Dover Pubns., Inc.

Ungerer, Tomi. El Sombrero.Tr. of Hat. (SPA.). 40p. (J). (gr. 2-3). 8.50 *(978-84-204-3026-3(9))* Ediciones Alfaguara ESP. Dist: Lectorum Pubns., Inc.

van Genechten, Guido. Can't We Share? 2012. (Little Snowman Stan Ser.). (ENG.). 30p. (J). (gr. -1-k). 16.95 *(978-1-60537-121-4(1))* Cobblestone Publishing Co.

Ward, Jennifer. The Sunhat. Sisson, Stéphanie Roth, illus. 2013. (ENG.). (J). 15.95 *(978-1-933855-78-3(9)*, Rio Nuevo Pubs.) Rio Nuevo Pubs.

We Like Hats. 2004. (Bella & Rosie Set 2 Ser.). (J). 7.67 *(978-1-932570-16-8(0))* Pioneer Valley Bks.

Weeks, Sarah. Who's under That Hat? A Lift-the-Flap Pop-up Adventure. Carter, David A., illus. 2006. 14p. (J). (gr. -1-2). 14.00 *(978-1-4223-5440-7(7))* DIANE Publishing Co.

Weston Woods Staff, creator. *Caps for Sale*. 2011. 38.75 *(978-0-439-72925-3(4))*; 18.95 *(978-0-439-72924-6(6))* Weston Woods Studios, Inc.

Widgen, Susan. A Caring Deed for Becky. Novak, Steven, illus. 2012. 36p. pap. 8.99 *(978-1-60820-579-0(7))* MLR Pr., LLC.

Won, Brian. Hooray for Hat! 2014. (ENG., Illus.). 40p. (J). (gr. -1-3). 16.99 *(978-0-544-15903-7(9)*, HMH Books For Young Readers) Houghton Mifflin Harcourt Publishing Co.

—Hooray for Hat! (Board Book) 2016. (ENG., Illus.). 32p. (J). (— 1). bds. 7.99 *(978-0-544-78988-3(1)*, HMH Books For Young Readers) Houghton Mifflin Harcourt Publishing Co.

Wood, A. J. The Christmas Hat. Kneen, Maggie, illus. 2004. (ENG.). 24p. (J). *(978-1-55168-267-9(2))* Fenn, H. B. & Co., Ltd.

Worth, Bonnie. Oh, the Places on Earth! A Cat in the Hat's Learning Library Collection, 4 vols. 2012. (ENG., Illus.). 48p. (J). (gr. k-3). 39.96 *(978-0-307-93139-9(0)*, Random Hse. Bks. for Young Readers) Random Hse. Children's Bks.

Yoxen, Jackie. Hannah's Sunday Hats. Francis, Lauren, illus. l.t. ed. 2006. 32p. (J). 19.95 *(978-1-59879-184-6(2))* Lifevest Publishing, Inc.

HATSHEPSUT, QUEEN OF EGYPT

Baum, Margaux & Thomas, Susanna. Hatshepsut. 2016. (Leaders of the Ancient World Ser.). 00112p. (J). (gr. 6-6). 37.10 *(978-1-5081-7250-5(1))* Rosen Publishing Group, Inc., The.

Galford, Ellen. Hatshepsut: The Princess Who Became King. (National Geographic World History Biographies Ser.). (ENG., Illus.). 64p. (J). (gr. 3-7). 2007. pap. 7.99 *(978-1-4263-0133-9(2))* 2005. lib. bdg. 27.90 *(978-0-7922-3646-7(7))* National Geographic Society. (National Geographic Children's Bks.).

Galford, Ellen & National Geographic Learning Staff. Hatshepsut: The Princess Who Became King. 2005. (National Geographic World History Biographies Ser.). (ENG., Illus.). 64p. (J). (gr. 3-7). 17.95 *(978-0-7922-3645-0(9)*, National Geographic Children's Bks.) National Geographic Society.

Jordan, Shirley J. Hatshepsut: First Female Pharaoh, 1 vol. 2007. (Primary Source Readers Ser.). (ENG.). 32p. (J). (gr. 4-4). pap. 8.99 *(978-0-7439-0429-2(X))* Shell Educational Publishing.

HAUNTED HOUSES

see also Ghosts

Axelrod-Contrada, Joan. Haunted Houses Around the World. 2017. (It's Haunted! Ser.). (ENG., Illus.). 32p. (gr. 3-4). lib. bdg. 27.99 *(978-1-5157-3860-2(4)*, Snap Bks.) Capstone Press of Coughlan Cos.

Bingham, Jane. Ghosts & Haunted Houses, 1 vol. King, Chris, illus. 2013. (Solving Mysteries with Science Ser.). (ENG.). 48p. (gr. 3-6). pap. 9.95 *(978-1-4109-5506-7(0))* Heinemann-Raintree.

—Ghosts & Haunted Houses, 1 vol. 2013. (Solving Mysteries with Science Ser.). (ENG.). 48p. (gr. 3-6). 29.99 *(978-1-4109-5500-5(1))* Heinemann-Raintree.

Bodden, Valerie. Haunted Houses. 2017. (J). *(978-1-60818-808-6(6)*, Creative Education) Creative Co., The.

Brucken, Kelli M. Haunted Houses. 2006. (Mysterious Encounters Ser.). (ENG., Illus.). 48p. (gr. 4-8). lib. bdg. 33.60 *(978-0-7377-3475-1(2)*, Greenhaven Pr., Inc.) Cengage Gale.

Brzycki, M. L. & Krueger, S. L. It Came from the Freezer ... or Was it the Drapes? l.t. ed. 2004. (Illus.). 110p. (YA). per. 13.00 *(978-0-9747581-0-7(8))* StrangeDays Publishing.

Camisa, Kathryn. Spooky Hotels. 2017. (Tiptoe into Scary Places Ser.). (ENG., Illus.). 24p. (J). (gr. k-3). 18.95 ***(978-1-68402-046-1(8))*** Bearport Publishing Co., Inc.

Cantor, Rachel Anne. Haunted Amusement Parks. 2017. (Tiptoe into Scary Places Ser.). (ENG., Illus.). 24p. (J). (gr. k-3). 18.95 ***(978-1-68402-050-8(6))*** Bearport Publishing Co., Inc.

Chandler, Matt, et al. You Choose: Haunted Places. 2016. (You Choose: Haunted Places Ser.). (ENG.). 112p. (gr. 3-4). 127.96 *(978-1-5157-2589-3(8)*, You Choose Bks.) Capstone Press of Coughlan Cos.

Cooley Peterson, Megan. Haunted Hotels Around the World. 2017. (It's Haunted! Ser.). (ENG., Illus.). 32p. (gr. 3-4). lib. bdg. 27.99 *(978-1-5157-3858-9(2)*, Snap Bks.) Capstone Press of Coughlan Cos.

Cooley Peterson, Megan, et al. It's Haunted! 2017. (It's Haunted! Ser.). (ENG.). 32p. (gr. 3-4). 111.96 *(978-1-5157-3879-4(5)*, Snap Bks.) Capstone Press of Coughlan Cos.

DeMolay, Jack. Amitiville: La casa encantada (Ghosts in Amityville:the Haunted House) 2009. (Historietas Juveniles: Misterios (Jr. Graphic Mysteries) Ser.). (SPA.). 24p. (gr. 2-3). 47.90 *(978-1-61513-344-4(5)*, Editorial Buenas Letras) Rosen Publishing Group, Inc., The.

—Amityville: La Casa Encantada. Obregón, José María, tr. from ENG. 2008. (Historietas Juveniles: Misterios (Jr. Graphic Mysteries) Ser.). (SPA., Illus.). 24p. (J). (gr. 2-5). lib. bdg. 25.25 *(978-1-4358-2537-6(3))* Rosen Publishing Group, Inc., The.

—Ghosts in Amityville: The Haunted House. (Jr. Graphic Mysteries Ser.). (ENG.). 24p. 2009. (J). (gr. 2-3). 47.90 *(978-1-61513-843-2(9)*, PowerKids Pr.) 2007. (Illus.). (J). (gr. 2-5). lib. bdg. 25.25 *(978-1-4042-3402-4(0))* 2007. (Illus.). (gr. 3-8). pap. 10.60 *(978-1-4042-2155-0(7)*, PowerKids Pr.) Rosen Publishing Group, Inc., The.

Doeden, Matt. Edinburgh Castle: A Chilling Interactive Adventure. 2017. (You Choose: Haunted Places Ser.). (ENG., Illus.). 112p. (gr. 3-4). lib. bdg. 31.99 *(978-1-5157-3648-6(2)*, You Choose Bks.) Capstone Press of Coughlan Cos.

—Gettysburg Battlefield: A Chilling Interactive Adventure. 2017. (You Choose: Haunted Places Ser.). (ENG., Illus.). 112p. (gr. 3-4). lib. bdg. 31.99 *(978-1-5157-3649-3(0)*, You Choose Bks.) Capstone Press of Coughlan Cos.

—The Haunted Sanatorium: A Chilling Interactive Adventure. 2017. (You Choose: Haunted Places Ser.). (ENG., Illus.). 112p. (gr. 3-4). lib. bdg. 31.99 *(978-1-5157-3651-6(2)*, You Choose Bks.) Capstone Press of Coughlan Cos.

—The Winchester Mystery House: A Chilling Interactive Adventure. 2016. (You Choose: Haunted Places Ser.). (ENG., Illus.). 112p. (gr. 3-4). lib. bdg. 31.99 *(978-1-5157-2577-0(4)*, You Choose Bks.) Capstone Press of Coughlan Cos.

—You Choose: Haunted Places. 2017. (You Choose: Haunted Places Ser.). (ENG.). 112p. (gr. 3-4). 255.92 *(978-1-5157-3652-3(0)*, You Choose Bks.) Capstone Press of Coughlan Cos.

Everett, Lawrence. Ghosts & Legends of Southeastern Ohio & Beyond: Tales of Legends, Hauntings & the Unexplained, 2. 2003. 124p. (YA). pap. 11.95 *(978-0-7414-1760-2(X))* Infinity Publishing.

Gordon, Nick. Edinburgh Castle. 2013. (Scariest Places on Earth Ser.). (ENG., Illus.). 24p. (J). (gr. 3-7). lib. bdg. 25.95 *(978-1-60014-948-1(0)*, Torque Bks.) Bellwether Media.

Hamilton, John. Haunted Places, 1 vol. 2007. (World of Horror Ser.). (ENG., Illus.). 32p. (gr. 4-8). 27.07 *(978-1-59928-768-3(4)*, Abdo & Daughters) ABDO Publishing Co.

Higgins, Nadia. Haunted Houses. 2014. (Unexplained Mysteries Ser.). (ENG., Illus.). 24p. (J). (gr. 3-7). lib. bdg. 25.95 *(978-1-62617-105-3(X)*, Epic Bks.) Bellwether Media.

Kallen, Stuart A. Haunted Houses. 2007. (Mysterious & Unknown Ser.). (Illus.). 96p. (YA). (gr. 7-12). lib. bdg. 25.95 *(978-1-60152-026-5(3))* ReferencePoint Pr., Inc.

Kallio, Jamie. Haunted Houses. 2015. (Unsolved Mysteries Ser.). (ENG.). 24p. (J). (gr. 1-4). 28.50 *(978-1-63407-074-4(7)*, 208907) Child's World, Inc., The.

Klepeis, Alicia Z. Haunted Cemeteries Around the World. 2017. (It's Haunted! Ser.). (ENG., Illus.). 32p. (gr. 3-4). lib. bdg. 27.99 *(978-1-5157-3861-9(2)*, Snap Bks.) Capstone Press of Coughlan Cos.

Klise, Kate. Dying to Meet You. Klise, M. Sarah, illus. 2009. (43 Old Cemetery Road Ser.: 1). (ENG.). 160p. (J). (gr. 2-5). 16.99 *(978-0-15-205727-5(7))* Houghton Mifflin Harcourt Publishing Co.

Krohn, Katherine. Mystery of Haunted Houses. 2013. (Unexplained Mysteries Ser.). (ENG.). 24p. (gr. 1-2). 25.32 *(978-1-4765-3097-0(1)*, First Facts) Capstone Press of Coughlan Cos.

—The Unsolved Mystery of Haunted Houses. 2013. (Unexplained Mysteries Ser.). (ENG.). 24p. (gr. 1-2). pap. 7.95 *(978-1-4765-3442-8(X)*, First Facts) Capstone Press of Coughlan Cos.

Lake, G. G. Take Your Pick of Haunted Places. 2017. (Take Your (Equally Horrible) Pick! Ser.). (ENG., Illus.). 32p. (gr. 1-2). lib. bdg. 26.65 *(978-1-5157-4471-9(X)*, Blazers) Capstone Press of Coughlan Cos.

Lassieur, Allison. Stanley Hotel: A Chilling Interactive Adventure. 2017. (You Choose: Haunted Places Ser.). (ENG., Illus.). 112p. (gr. 3-4). lib. bdg. 31.99 *(978-1-5157-3650-9(4)*, You Choose Bks.) Capstone Press of Coughlan Cos.

MacKay, Jenny. Do Haunted Houses Exist? 2015. (ENG., Illus.). 80p. (J). lib. bdg. *(978-1-60152-858-2(2))* ReferencePoint Pr., Inc.

Markovics, Joyce L. Ghostly Towns. 2017. (Tiptoe into Scary Places Ser.). (ENG., Illus.). 24p. (J). (gr. k-3). 18.95 *(978-1-68402-051-5(4))* Bearport Publishing Co., Inc.

McCollum, Sean. Handbook to Ghosts, Poltergeists, & Haunted Houses. 2016. (Paranormal Handbooks Ser.). (ENG., Illus.). 32p. (gr. 3-4). lib. bdg. 27.99 *(978-1-5157-1308-1(3)*, Edge Bks.) Capstone Press of Coughlan Cos.

McCullum, Kenya. 12 Notorious Ghosts. 2017. (Scary & Spooky Ser.). (ENG.). 32p. (J). (gr. 3-6). 21.95 *(978-1-63235-294-1(X))* Pr. Room Editions LLC.

Morey, Allan. 12 Spooky Haunted Places. 2017. (Scary & Spooky Ser.). (ENG., Illus.). 32p. (J). (gr. 3-6). 21.95 *(978-1-63235-296-5(6))* Pr. Room Editions LLC.

Nagle, Jeanne. Haunted Houses, 01 vols., 1. 2016. (Role-Playing for Fun & Profit Ser.). (ENG.). 48p. (J). pap. 11.75 *(978-1-4994-3716-4(1)*, Rosen Central) Rosen Publishing Group, Inc., The.

Oester, Dave. My Adventure in a Haunted House. 2006. 44p. (J). 8.99 *(978-1-59092-418-1(5))* Blue Forge Pr.

Omoth, Tyler. Handbook to Stonehenge, the Bermuda Triangle, & Other Mysterious Locations. 2016. (Paranormal Handbooks Ser.). (ENG., Illus.). 32p. (gr. 3-4). lib. bdg. 27.99 *(978-1-5157-1310-4(5)*, Edge Bks.) Capstone Press of Coughlan Cos.

Perritano, John. Amityville. 2014. (Jr. Graphic Ghost Stories Ser.). 24p. (J). (gr. 3-6). lib. bdg. 26.25 *(978-1-4777-7121-1(2)*, PowerKids Pr.) Rosen Publishing Group, Inc., The.

Polydoros, Lori. Top 10 Haunted Places, 1 vol. 2012. (Top 10 Unexplained Ser.). (ENG., Illus.). 32p. (gr. 1-2). lib. bdg. 26.65 *(978-1-4296-8435-4(6)*, Blazers) Capstone Press of Coughlan Cos.

Priddy, Roger. Pop-Up Surprise Haunted House. 2012. (ENG., Illus.). 10p. (J). (gr. -1-1). 7.99 *(978-0-312-51471-6(9)*, 9780312514716, Priddy Bks.) St. Martin's Pr.

Rajczak, Michael. Haunted! The White House. 2013. (History's Most Haunted Ser.). (Illus.). 32p. (J). (gr. 3-6). pap. 10.50 *(978-1-4339-9269-8(8))*; lib. bdg. 26.60 *(978-1-4339-9268-1(X))* Stevens, Gareth Publishing LLLP.

Red Bird Press Staff. Secret Spex Haunted House. 2004. (Secret Picture Search Ser.). 18p. (J). pap. 5.95 *(978-1-902626-67-3(2))* Red Bird Publishing GBR. Dist: Weatherhill, Inc.

Rudolph, Jessica. Creaky Castles. 2017. (Tiptoe into Scary Places Ser.). (ENG., Illus.). 24p. (J). (gr. k-3). 18.95 ***(978-1-68402-047-8(6))*** Bearport Publishing Co., Inc.

Rudolph, Jessica. Ghost Houses. 2017. (Tiptoe into Scary Places Ser.). (ENG., Illus.). 24p. (J). (gr. k-3). 18.95 *(978-1-68402-045-4(X))* Bearport Publishing Co., Inc.

Smith, Barbara. Horribly Haunted Houses, 1 vol., Vol. 1. rev. ed. 2004. (Haunted Kids Ser.). (ENG., Illus.). 144p. (J). (gr. 4-6). pap. 6.95 *(978-1-894877-54-1(3)*, 1894877543, Ghost Hse. Bks.) Lone Pine Publishing USA.

Stone, Adam. Haunted Houses. 2010. (Unexplained Ser.). (ENG., Illus.). 24p. (J). (gr. 3-7). lib. bdg. 25.95 *(978-1-60014-501-8(9)*, Torque Bks.) Bellwether Media.

Thay, Edrick. Haunted Houses, 1 vol., Vol. 1. French, Diana, ed. rev. ed. 2003. (Ghost Stories Ser.). (ENG., Illus.). 256p. (gr. 4). pap. 12.95 *(978-1-894877-30-5(6)*, 1894877306, Ghost Hse. Bks.) Lone Pine Publishing USA.

Ventura, Marne & Omoth, Tyler. Kids Can Cook! 2017. (Kids Can Cook! Ser.). (ENG.). 32p. (gr. 3-4). 111.96 *(978-1-5157-3628-2(0)*, Edge Bks.) Capstone Press of Coughlan Cos.

Walsh, Liza Gardner. Ghost Hunter's Handbook. 2016. (ENG., Illus.). 96p. (J). (gr. 1-6). 15.95 *(978-1-60893-570-3(1))* Down East Bks.

Williams, Dinah. Dark Mansions. (Scary Places Ser.). 32p. (J). (gr. 4-8). 2016. (ENG.). pap. 8.95 *(978-1-944998-71-4(3))* 2012. lib. bdg. 25.27 *(978-1-61772-457-2(2))* Bearport Publishing Co., Inc.

—Haunted Houses. 2008. (Scary Places Ser.). (Illus.). 32p. (YA). (gr. 4-7). lib. bdg. 25.27 *(978-1-59716-573-0(5))* Bearport Publishing Co., Inc.

Wlodarski, Robert James & Nathan-Wlodarski, Anne. The Haunted Whaley House, Old Town, San Diego, California: A History & Guide to the Most Haunted House in America. 2nd ed. 2004. (Illus.). xxii, 196p. (J). *(978-0-9649088-7-1(5))* G-Host Publishing.

Wood, Alix. Haunted Houses. 2016. (World's Scariest Places Ser.). 00032p. (J). pap. 10.50 ***(978-1-4824-5912-8(4))*** Stevens, Gareth Publishing LLLP.

HAWAII

Adams, Colleen. Hawaii: The Aloha State. (Reading Room Collection 2 Ser.). 24p. 2009. (gr. 3-4). 42.50 *(978-1-60851-967-5(8)*, PowerKids Pr.) 2003. (Illus.). (J). lib. bdg. 22.60 *(978-0-8239-3714-3(5))* Rosen Publishing Group, Inc., The.

BeachHouse Publishing. 1-2-3 Waikiki Trolley. Moen Cabanting, Ruth, illus. 2005. (ENG.). 20p. (J). (gr. -1-1). bds. 8.95 *(978-1-933067-06-3(3))* Beachhouse Publishing, LLC.

Bellamy, Fannie Lillian Miles. Fanning Island. 2006. (Illus.). 40p. (J). pap. 14.95 *(978-1-59663-509-8(6)*, Castle Keep Pr.) Rock, James A. & Co. Pubs.

Bradley, Barbara. Hawaiian Kids Cook & Color Book. pap. 5.95 *(978-0-930492-43-4(9))* Hawaiian Service, Inc.

Burnham, Brad. Kazumura Cave: The World's Longest Lava Tube. (Famous Caves of the World Ser.). 24p. 2009. (gr. 3-4). 42.50 *(978-1-61512-497-8(7))* 2003. (Illus.). (J). lib. bdg. 22.60 *(978-0-8239-6261-7(X))* Rosen Publishing Group, Inc., The. (PowerKids Pr.).

Cachola, Jean Iwata, et al. O Kamehameha III: Kauikeaouli. 2004. (HAW & ENG., Illus.). xiv, 120p. (J). pap. *(978-0-87336-047-0(8))* Kamehameha Publishing.

Carolan. B Is for Beach: An Alphabet Book. 2007. 64p. 18.95 incl. audio compact disk *(978-0-9715333-8-7(5))* Banana Patch Pr.

Doak, Robin S. Hawaii: The Aloha State. 2003. (World Almanac Library of the States). (Illus.). 48p. (gr. 4-9). pap. 14.05 *(978-0-8368-5320-9(2))*; lib. bdg. 31.00 *(978-0-8368-5149-6(8))* Stevens, Gareth Publishing LLLP. (Gareth Stevens Learning Library).

Feher, Joseph & Kane, Herb K., illus. Hawai'i. 2010. (ENG.). 72p. pap. *(978-1-59700-839-6(7))* Island Heritage Publishing.

Foran, Jill. Hawai'i. 2011. (Guide to American States Ser.). (Illus.). 48p. (YA). (gr. 3-6). 29.99 *(978-1-61690-783-9(5))* Weigl Pubs., Inc.

Furgang, Kathy. Kilauea: Hawaii's Most Active Volcano. 2009. (Volcanoes of the World Ser.). 24p. (gr. 3-3). 42.50 *(978-1-60854-729-6(9)*, PowerKids Pr.) Rosen Publishing Group, Inc., The.

Gaines, Ann Graham. Hawaii. 2006. (It's My State! Ser.). (Illus.). 80p. (J). (gr. 4-7). lib. bdg. 29.93 *(978-0-7614-1926-6(8)*, Benchmark Bks.) Marshall Cavendish Corp.

Gill, Shelley. Hawai'i. Goto, Scott, illus. 2006. (ENG.). 32p. (J). (gr. 2-5). lib. bdg. 16.95 *(978-0-88106-296-0(0))* Charlesbridge Publishing, Inc.

Goldberg, Jake & Hart, Joyce. Hawai'i. 2nd rev. ed. 2006. (Celebrate the States Ser.). (Illus.). 144p. (gr. 6-7). lib. bdg. 42.79 *(978-0-7614-2349-2(4)*, Benchmark Bks.) Marshall Cavendish Corp.

Goldsberry, U'ilani. A Is for Aloha: A Hawaii Alphabet. Yee, Tammy, illus. 2005. (Discover America State by State Ser.). (ENG.). 40p. (J). (gr. k-5). 17.95 *(978-1-58536-146-5(1))* Sleeping Bear Pr.

Hirschi, Ron. Swimming with Humuhumu: A Young Snorkeler's First Guide to Hawaiian Sea Life. Yee, Tammy, illus. 32p. (J). 14.99 *(978-0-931548-67-3(5)*, 25098-000) Island Heritage Publishing.

—Winter Is for Whales: A Book of Hawaiian Seasons. Green, Yuko, illus. 2007. (ENG.). 36p. (J). (gr. -1-3). *(978-1-59700-504-3(5))* Island Heritage Publishing.

Johnston, Joyce. Hawaii. 2012. (J). lib. bdg. 25.26 *(978-0-7613-4529-9(9)*, Lerner Pubns.) Lerner Publishing Group.

Kent, Deborah. Hawai'i. 2014. (America the Beautiful Ser.: 3). (ENG.). 144p. (J). lib. bdg. 40.00 *(978-0-531-24882-9(8))* Scholastic Library Publishing.

—Hawaii's Road to Statehood. 2004. (Cornerstones of Freedom Ser.). (ENG., Illus.). 48p. (YA). (gr. 4-7). 26.00 *(978-0-516-24241-5(5))* Scholastic Library Publishing.

Lopes, Marilyn/Jansen. Amaryllis of Hawaii Big Coloring Book: Drawings of Hawaii to Color. 2007. (ENG & HAW., Illus.). (YA). pap. 5.00 *(978-0-9761070-5-7(8))* Jansen, Marilyn.

—Amaryllis of Hawaii Pocket Coloring Book: Drawings of Hawaii to Color. 2007. (ENG & HAW., Illus.). (J). pap. 3.00 *(978-0-9761070-7-1(4))* Jansen, Marilyn.

Lowe, Ruby Hasegawa, et al. O Kamehameha IV: Alexander Liholiho. 2004. (HAW & ENG., Illus.). x, 115p. (J). pap. *(978-0-87336-054-8(0))* Kamehameha Publishing.

Markrich, Mike & Bourke, Bob. Hanauma Bay. Kanae, Billy, illus. (J). pap. 5.95 *(978-0-9643421-0-1(3))* Ecology Comics.

Marsh, Carole. Hawaii Current Events Projects: 30 Cool, Activities, Crafts, Experiments & More for Kids to Do to Learn about Your State! 2003. (Hawaii Experience Ser.). 32p. (gr. k-5). pap. 5.95 *(978-0-635-02030-7(0)*, Marsh, Carole Bks.) Gallopade International.

—Hawaii Geography Projects: 30 Cool, Activities, Crafts, Experiments & More for Kids to Do to Learn about Your State! 2003. (Hawaii Experience Ser.). 32p. (gr. k-5). pap. 5.95 *(978-0-635-01830-4(6)*, Marsh, Carole Bks.) Gallopade International.

—Hawaii Government Projects: 30 Cool, Activities, Crafts, Experiments & More for Kids to Do to Learn about Your State! 2003. (Hawaii Experience Ser.). 32p. (gr. k-5). pap. 5.95 *(978-0-635-01930-1(2)*, Marsh, Carole Bks.) Gallopade International.

—Hawaii People Projects: 30 Cool, Activities, Crafts, Experiments & More for Kids to Do to Learn about Your State! 2003. (Hawaii Experience Ser.). 32p. (gr. k-5). pap. 5.95 *(978-0-635-01980-6(9)*, Marsh, Carole Bks.) Gallopade International.

—Hawaii Symbols & Facts Projects: 30 Cool, Activities, Crafts, Experiments & More for Kids to Do to Learn about Your

State! 2003. (Hawaii Experience Ser.). 32p. (gr. k-5). pap. 5.95 *(978-0-635-01880-9(2),* Marsh, Carole Bks.) Gallopade International.

Mattern, Joanne. Hawai'i. 2017. (True Book — My United States Ser.). (ENG.). 48p. (J). pap. 7.95 ***(978-0-531-23285-9(9),*** Children's Pr.) Scholastic Library Publishing.

Mattern, Joanne. Mauna Loa. 2004. (Maravillas Naturales (Natures Greatest Hits) Ser.). (SPA.). 24p. (J). (gr. 3-6). lib. bdg. 22.60 *(978-0-8239-6877-0(4),* Editorial Buenas Letras) Rosen Publishing Group, Inc., The.

Mattox-Primacio, M. Nalani. Mahalo e ke Akua. 2007. (J). lib. bdg. *(978-0-9773495-5-5(1))* Na Kamalei Koolauloa Early Education Program.

Murray, Julie. Hawaii, 1 vol. 2006. (United States Ser.). (ENG., Illus.). 32p. (gr. 2-4). 27.07 *(978-1-59197-670-7(7),* Buddy Bks.) ABDO Publishing Co.

Neri, P. J. Hawaii. 2003. (From Sea to Shining Sea Ser.: 2). (ENG., Illus.). 80p. (J). (gr. 3-5). 30.50 *(978-0-516-22383-4(6),* Children's Pr.) Scholastic Library Publishing.

Noland, Karen L. Friends of the Menehune. (J). 9.95 *(978-0-9643674-0-1(8))* Kaukini Ranch Pr.

Obregón, José María. Hawaii. 2009. (Bilingual Library of the United States of America Ser.). (ENG & SPA.). 32p. (gr. 2-2). 47.90 *(978-1-60853-356-5(5),* Editorial Buenas Letras) Rosen Publishing Group, Inc., The.

Ollhoff, Jim. Hawaii, 1 vol. 2009. (United States Ser.). (ENG., Illus.). 48p. (YA). (gr. 2-5). 27.07 *(978-1-60453-646-1(2))* ABDO Publishing Co.

Petechuk, David. Non-Continental: Alaska, Hawaii, Vol. 19. 2015. (Let's Explore the States Ser.). (Illus.). 64p. (J). (gr. 5). 23.95 *(978-1-4222-3328-3(6))* Mason Crest.

Quasha, Jennifer. How to Draw Hawaii's Sights & Symbols. 2009. (Kid's Guide to Drawing America Ser.). 32p. (gr. k-k). 50.50 *(978-1-61511-058-2(5),* PowerKids Pr.) Rosen Publishing Group, Inc., The.

Riley, Cooper. Absolutely Awesome Island Animals. 2009. 24p. pap. 9.95 *(978-0-9740582-4-5(6))* Tiki Tales.

Rozier, Dana. Natural Hawai'i: An Inquisitive Kid's Guide. 2011. (ENG., Illus.). 112p. (J). (gr. 4-7). pap. 12.95 *(978-0-9670750-1-3(7))* Dot Dot Bks.

Shofner, Shawndra. Hawaii. 2008. (This Land Called America Ser.). 32p. (YA). (gr. 3-6). 22.95 *(978-1-58341-636-5(6))* Creative Co., The.

Swanson, Angie. Hawaii. 2016. (States Ser.). (ENG., Illus.). 32p. (gr. 3-4). lib. bdg. 27.32 *(978-1-5157-0397-6(5))* Next Page Pr., The.

Taylor-Butler, Christine. Hawaii. 2007. (Rookie Read-About Geography Ser.). (ENG., Illus.). 32p. (J). (gr. 1-2). 20.50 *(978-0-531-12571-7(8),* Children's Pr.) Scholastic Library Publishing.

Thomas, William David. Hawaii. 2006. (Portraits of the States Ser.). 32p. (gr. 2-6). pap. 10.50 *(978-0-8368-4716-1(4),* Gareth Stevens Learning Library) Stevens, Gareth Publishing LLLP.

—Hawaii. 2006. (Portraits of the States Ser.). (Illus.). 32p. (gr. 2-6). lib. bdg. 26.00 *(978-0-8368-4699-7(0),* Gareth Stevens Learning Library) Stevens, Gareth Publishing LLLP.

Voyagers. 2005. 160p. 29.95 *(978-0-943357-04-1(7))* Kawainui Pr.

Webster, Christine. Mauna Loa: The Largest Volcano in the United States. 2004. (Natural Wonders of the U. S. A. Ser.). (Illus.). 32p. (J). (gr. 3-6). per. 9.95 *(978-1-59036-162-7(8))* Weigl Pubs., Inc.

HAWAII—FICTION

Alessi, Patty. Rrreggie T Rex's Vacation on Maui, 1 vol. 2009. (ENG.). 90p. pap. 19.95 *(978-1-60836-639-2(1))* America Star Bks.

Aloha Potter! Evaluation Guide: Evaluation Guide. 2006. (J). *(978-1-55942-397-7(8))* Witcher Productions.

Armitage, Kimo. The Healers. 2016. (ENG.). 208p. pap. 16.99 *(978-0-8248-5645-8(7),* 4598) Univ. of Hawaii Pr.

Aslan, Austin. The Islands at the End of the World. (ENG., Illus.). 384p. (YA). (gr. 7). 2015. pap. 9.99 *(978-0-385-74403-4(X),* Ember) 2014. lib. bdg. 20.99 *(978-0-375-99145-5(X),* Lamb, Wendy Bks.) Random Hse. Children's Bks.

Bates, Robert L. Lopaka's Legends of Hawaii. 2008. 28p. pap. 19.95 *(978-1-4327-3655-2(8))* Outskirts Pr., Inc.

BeachHouse Publishing. If You Were a Dinosaur in Hawaii. Braffet, Holly, illus. 2010. 22p. (J). (gr. -1-1). bds. 7.95 *(978-1-933067-39-1(X))* Beachhouse Publishing, LLC.

Beamer, Winona Desha & Beamer-Trapp, Kaliko. Pua Polu: The Pretty Blue Hawaiian Flower. Loebel-Fried, Caren Keala, illus. 2005. (HAW & ENG.). 36p. (J). audio compact disk 14.95 *(978-1-58178-041-3(9))* Bishop Museum Pr.

Beamer, Winona Desha, et al. Naupaka: By Nona Beamer: Illustrations by Caren Loebel-Fried: Hawaiian Translation by Kaliko Beamer-Trapp: Music by Keola Beamer. Loebel-Fried, Caren, illus. 2008. (J). 14.95 *(978-1-58178-089-5(3))* Bishop Museum Pr.

Beirne-Keawe, Danielle Ululani. Makalii Sleeps. 2006.Tr. of Moe O Makalii. (ENG & HAW.). (J). lib. bdg. 12.95 *(978-0-9773495-0-0(0),* Ho'ulu Hou Project: Stories Told by Us) Na Kamalei Koolauloa Early Education Program.

Berardy, Lloyd, 1st. A Tropical Bear in Hawaii Goes Underwater. 2006. (J). 12.95 *(978-1-4276-0212-1(3))* Aardvark Global Publishing.

Blake-Brekke, Carri. Billy Bully Bug: Learns a Lesson in Hawaii. Melton, Jodi, illus. 2003. (Mrs. B's Story Time... With a Twist! Ser.). 20p. (J). pap. 11.95 incl. audio compact disk *(978-0-9720549-2-8(8))* Mom's Pride Enterprises.

Boyden, Linda. Boy & Poi Poi Puppy. Boyden, Linda, illus. 2013. (ENG., Illus.). 50p. (J). (gr. -1-2). 17.95 *(978-1-940834-00-9(7))* Rising Phoenix Pr.

Braffet, Mary. Malie & the Huli Hula Chicken. Braffet, Holly, illus. 2010. 32p. (J). 12.95 *(978-1-56647-925-7(8))* Mutual Publishing LLC.

Bridgman, C. A. Santa's Hawaiian Vacation. (J). 14.95 *(978-0-681-32827-3(4))* Booklines Hawaii, Ltd.

Brown, Lenoard. The Adventure of Paul & Page in Hawaii (the Big Island) (Identical Twins) l.t. ed. 2011. (ENG.). 50p. pap. 12.50 *(978-1-4635-6162-8(8))* CreateSpace Independent Publishing Platform.

Bryant, Annie. Ready! Set! Hawaii! 2009. (Beacon Street Girls Ser.: No. 7). (ENG.). 304p. (J). (gr. 4-8). pap. 8.99 *(978-1-4169-6436-0(3),* Aladdin) Simon & Schuster Children's Publishing.

Buckingham-Smith, Celestia. College Life in Paradise: Hawaiian Style, 1 vol. 2010. 260p. pap. 27.95 *(978-1-4489-6689-9(2))* America Star Bks.

Bundschuh, Rick. Clash, 1 vol. 2014. (Faithgirlz / Soul Surfer Ser.). (ENG.). 128p. (J). pap. 7.99 *(978-0-310-74582-2(9))* Zonderkidz.

Bustard, Anne. Anywhere but Paradise. 2015. (ENG.). 288p. (gr. 5). 16.99 *(978-1-60684-585-1(3));* (J). 16.99 *(978-1-5124-0110-3(2))* Lerner Publishing Group. (Carolrhoda Bks.).

Carolan. Goodnight Hawaiian Moon. 2006. 32p. 17.95 *(978-0-9715333-2-5(6))* Banana Patch Pr.

Carolan, Joanna F. Old Makana Had a Taro Farm. Carolan, Joanna F., illus. 2008. (Illus.). 48p. 17.95 *(978-0-9715333-9-4(3))* Banana Patch Pr.

Carson, John & Carson, Marlene. Ramblin' Rose: The Chinese Fortune Cookie. 2008. 291p. pap. 8.99 *(978-0-9800034-1-3(5))* BBM Bks.

Chananie, Gloria. Fearful Frannie & Her Fateful Trip to Maui. 2003. 57p. 16.95 *(978-1-4137-0162-3(0))* America Star Bks.

Ching, Tokie. Boy's Day in Hawaii. Arai, Setsuo, illus. 2008. 32p. (J). 12.95 *(978-1-56647-852-6(9))* Mutual Publishing LLC.

—Girl's Day in Hawaii with Yuki Chan. 2006. 40p. (J). 14.95 *(978-1-56647-820-5(0))* Mutual Publishing LLC.

Correa, Shan. Gaff, 1 vol. 2010. (ENG.). 224p. (J). (gr. 3-7). 15.95 *(978-1-56145-526-3(1),* Peachtree Junior) Peachtree Pubs.

Culbertson, Jan E. The Legend of the Lost Tiki. 2006. 95p. (YA). pap. 13.95 *(978-1-58909-315-7(1))* Bookstand Publishing.

David, Jamie. Johann Sebastian Humpbach. David, Jamie, illus. 2009. (Illus.). 167p. pap. 14.95 *(978-0-615-31840-0(1))* Chai Yo Maui Pr.

De Laurentiis, Giada, et al. Hawaii! #6. Gambatesa, Francesca, illus. 2015. (Recipe for Adventure Ser.: 6). (ENG.). 160p. (J). (gr. 2-4). bds. 6.99 *(978-0-448-48391-7(2),* Grosset & Dunlap) Penguin Young Readers Group.

Diamond, Charlotte. Slippery Fish in Hawaii. Aardema, John, illus. 2013. (ENG.). 16p. (J). (gr. -1-1). bds. 7.95 *(978-1-933067-57-5(8))* Beachhouse Publishing, LLC.

Dilz. My Grandma Could Do Anything in Hawaii. 2006. (J). 7.95 *(978-0-9758704-2-6(4))* Ric Design LLC.

Dilz, Ric. My Grandma Could Do Anything in Hawaii! 2008. (Illus.). 32p. (J). 14.95 *(978-0-9758704-5-7(9))* Ric Design LLC.

Disney Book Group. Puppy Dog Pals Hawaii Pug-O. Disney Storybook Art Team & Premise Entertainment Staff, illus. 2017. (ENG.). 24p. (J). (gr. -1-k). pap. 5.99 ***(978-1-368-00419-0(9))*** Disney Pr.

Disney Storybook Artists Staff, ed. Disney Lilo & Stitch Drawing Book & Kit. 2008. 32p. pap. 10.95 *(978-1-60058-103-8(X))* Quarto Publishing Group USA.

Donivee, Martin. Snow White & the Seven Menehune. 2004. (Illus.). 44p. 9.95 *(978-1-57306-235-0(9))* Bess Pr., Inc.

Duckett, Brenda. The Giggling Purple Dragon. 2006. 84p. pap. 9.99 *(978-1-4116-3826-6(3))* Lulu Pr., Inc.

Dyan, Penelope. Animal Rescue, Book 2, Hanauma Bay, Hawaii. Weigand, John D., photos by. 2008. (Illus.). 56p. pap. 15.95 *(978-1-935118-43-5(9))* Bellissima Publishing, LLC.

Ebie, Mora. Going to the Zoo in Hawaii. 2006. (Illus.). 28p. (J). 10.95 *(978-1-56647-790-1(5))* Mutual Publishing LLC.

—Little Mouse's Hawaiian Christmas Present. Braffet, Holly, illus. 2011. 28p. (J). *(978-1-56647-956-1(8))* Mutual Publishing LLC.

Ellis, Greg & BeachHouse Publishing. Baby's First 1-2-3 in Hawaii. 2008. (ENG.). 20p. (J). (gr. -1-1). bds. 7.95 *(978-1-933067-24-7(1))* Beachhouse Publishing, LLC.

Eyre, David. Breaking the Blood. Kalahele, Imaikalani, illus. 2008. 40p. 14.95 *(978-0-87336-162-0(8))* Kamehameha Publishing.

—White Rainbow Black Curse. 2007. 31p. 14.95 *(978-0-87336-117-0(2))* Kamehameha Publishing.

Eyre, David & Kalahele, Imaikalani. Floating Islands. 2009. 35p. 14.95 *(978-0-87336-216-0(0))* Kamehameha Publishing.

Farley, Terri. Phantom Stallion - Wild Horse Island Bk. 2: The Shining Stallion. 2007. (Phantom Stallion: Wild Horse Island Ser.: 2). (ENG., Illus.). 224p. (J). (gr. 5-9). pap. 4.99 *(978-0-06-081543-1(4))* HarperCollins Pubs.

Foston, Desirae. The Hawaiian Hiatus of Herkimer Street. Foston, Desirae, illus. 2013. (Illus.). 24p. 24.00 *(978-1-940021-00-3(6))* Bliss Group.

Fried, Caren Loebel. Legend of the Gourd. 2010. (HAW & ENG.). 36p. (J). 16.95 *(978-1-58178-103-8(2))* Bishop Museum Pr.

Frost, Robert Temple. Long Trip Home: Stand up Paddleboard Fantasy. 2013. 82p. pap. 10.95 *(978-1-62212-924-9(5),* Strategic Bk. Publishing) Strategic Book Publishing & Rights Agency (SBPRA).

Furuya, Michael, illus. Keoni's Special Gift. 2009. (J). *(978-1-56647-915-8(0))* Mutual Publishing LLC.

Gamble, Adam. Good Night Hawaii. Veno, Joe, illus. 2007. (Good Night Our World Ser.). (ENG.). 20p. (J). (gr. k — 1). bds. 9.95 *(978-1-60219-007-8(0))* Good Night Bks.

Garcia, Jeffrey. Santa Claus & the Molokai Mules. 2009. 32p. 17.95 *(978-0-9840942-0-2(2))* Garcia, Jeffrey.

George, Jean Craighead. Dear Katie, the Volcano Is a Girl. 32p. (J). pap. *(978-0-7868-1178-6(1))* Hyperion Bks. for Children.

Germain, Kerry. Kimo's Summer Vacation. Montes, Keoni, illus. 2003. 52p. (J). 12.95 *(978-0-9705889-4-4(1))* Island Paradise Publishing.

—Kimo's Surfing Lesson. Moore, Nicolette, illus. 2007. 48p. pap. 12.95 *(978-0-9705889-3-7(3))* Island Paradise Publishing.

Gillespie, Jane. G Is for Gecko: An Alphabet Adventure in Hawai'i. Robinson, Don, illus. 2013. (ENG.). 26p. (J). (gr. -1-1). 12.95 *(978-1-933067-51-3(9))* Beachhouse Publishing, LLC.

Gladwell, Michael. Slappers Maui Vacation. 2008. 32p. pap. 6.95 *(978-0-615-21549-5(1))* Hawaii Fine Art Studio.

Gleasner, Diana C. Popoki, the Hawaiian Cat: An Amazing Adventure with the Whale. Winton, Andrea Evans, illus. 2004. (J). *(978-0-9651185-7-6(6))* Gleasner, Bill & Diana Inc.

Golembe, Carla. The Story of Hula. 2004. (Illus.). 32p. (J). 16.95 incl. audio compact disk *(978-1-57306-185-8(9))* Bess Pr., Inc.

Goodwin, Brian. Pineapple Soap. 2007. 130p. pap. 9.50 *(978-0-615-16104-4(9))* Goodwin, Brian.

Griffiths, Gary Wayne. Hawaiian Ponies: A Mystery in Paradise, 1 vol. 2010. 48p. pap. 16.95 *(978-1-4489-4793-5(6))* America Star Bks.

Gunn, Robin Jones. Whispers. 2004. (Glenbrooke Ser.: Bk. 2). (ENG.). 288p. pap. 14.99 *(978-1-59052-192-2(7),* Multnomah) Doubleday Religious Publishing Group, The.

Gutman, Dan. The Million Dollar Putt. 2007. 69p. (J). (gr. 3-7). 13.65 *(978-0-7569-8281-2(2))* Perfection Learning Corp.

Hamilton, Elizabeth L. Date with Responsibility. 2004. (Character-in-Action Ser.: No. 2). (Illus.). 384p. (YA). per. 19.95 *(978-0-9713749-0-4(2),* Character-in-Action) Quiet Impact, Inc.

Hampton, Francesca. Children's Voyage the Long Journey Home. 2010. 222p. pap. 13.96 *(978-0-557-23497-4(2))* Lulu Pr., Inc.

Hawaii Winter Baseball. Major Mynah & Da Menehune Crew. 2007. (Illus.). 18p. (J). pap. 4.99 *(978-0-9796769-5-6(9))* Watermark Publishing, LLC.

Henderson, Brandon. The Legend of the Kukui Nut. 2008. 32p. (J). 15.99 *(978-1-59955-119-7(5))* Cedar Fort, Inc./CFI Distribution.

Higginson, Sheila Sweeny. Leilani's Luau. Disney Storybook Artists Staff, illus. 2014. (ENG.). 32p. (J). (gr. -1-k). pap. 4.99 *(978-1-4231-9417-0(9))* Disney Pr.

Honda, Liana. Kou Lima. Kukahiko, Puni, illus. 2010. 22p. 8.00 *(978-0-87336-236-8(5))* Kamehameha Publishing.

—Kou Wawae. Kukahiko, Puni, illus. 2010. 22p. 8.00 *(978-0-87336-237-5(3))* Kamehameha Publishing.

Hopkins, Jane. Diving for Colors in Hawaii: A Color Identification Book for Keiki. Bosgra, Johann, illus. 2003. (ENG.). 18p. (J). (gr. -1-1). bds. 7.95 *(978-0-9729905-1-6(8))* Beachhouse Publishing, LLC.

—Diving for Numbers in Hawaii. Bosgra, Johann, illus. 2003. (ENG.). 20p. (J). (gr. -1-k). bds. 7.95 *(978-0-9729905-0-9(X))* Beachhouse Publishing, LLC.

Ide, Laurie Shimizu. Okazu at the Zoo. Kanekuni, Daniel, illus. 2006. (J). *(978-1-56647-776-5(X))* Mutual Publishing LLC.

Ikuwa, Robert Lono. The Face of Her King. 2007.Tr. of Ke Alo o Kona Moi. (ENG & HAW.). (J). lib. bdg. *(978-0-9773495-3-1(5))* Na Kamalei Koolauloa Early Education Program.

Isom, Michelle. Human Dogs. 2012. 28p. (-18). pap. 16.09 *(978-1-4669-5842-5(1))* Trafford Publishing.

Jacobs, Lily. The Littlest Bunny in Hawaii: An Easter Adventure. 2015. (ENG.). 32p. (J). (-3). 9.99 *(978-1-4926-1075-5(5),* Sourcebooks Jabberwocky) Sourcebooks, Inc.

James, Eric. A Halloween Scare in Hawaii. Le Ray, Marina, illus. 2015. (ENG.). 32p. (J). (-5). 9.99 *(978-1-4926-2373-1(3),* 9781492623731, Sourcebooks Jabberwocky) Sourcebooks, Inc.

—Santa's Sleigh Is on Its Way to Hawaii: A Christmas Adventure. Dunn, Robert, illus. 2016. (ENG.). 32p. (J). (-2). 12.99 *(978-1-4926-4328-9(9),* 9781492643289, Sourcebooks Jabberwocky) Sourcebooks, Inc.

Jarek, Janice. Mya & the Mermaid. 2012. 28p. 24.95 *(978-1-4626-3277-0(7))* America Star Bks.

Jensen, Kathryn. Splash! 2012. 194p. 29.95 *(978-1-4489-6574-8(8))* America Star Bks.

Johnson, Kristin F. Wall of Water. 2017. (Day of Disaster Ser.). (ENG.). 112p. (gr. 6-12). (J). 26.65 *(978-1-5124-2778-3(0));* (YA). 12.99 ***(978-1-5124-3516-0(3),*** Darby Creek); (YA). 39.99 ***(978-1-5124-2786-8(1),*** Darby Creek); (YA). 39.99 ***(978-1-5124-3515-3(5),*** Darby Creek) Lerner Publishing Group.

Johnson, R. Kikuo. The Shark King. Loeffler, Trade & Johnson, R. Kikuo, illus. 2012. (ENG.). 40p. (J). (gr. -1-3). 12.95 *(978-1-935179-16-0(0))* TOON Books / RAW Junior, LLC.

Jones, Patrick. Combat Zone. 2015. (ENG.). 96p. (YA). (gr. 6-12). pap. 7.99 *(978-1-4677-8094-0(4))* Lerner Publishing Group.

Kammerer, Heitiare. Pa'a Pono. 2008. (ENG & HAW.). (J). lib. bdg. *(978-0-9773495-7-9(8))* Na Kamalei Koolauloa Early Education Program.

Kawaiae, Kekaulelenaeole A. Kohala Kuamoo. Kawaiae, Aaron A, illus. 2010. 32p. 16.00 *(978-0-87336-232-0(2))* Kamehameha Publishing.

Keoni the Good Menehune. 2005. (Illus.). 28p. (J). (gr. 1-2). 12.95 *(978-0-9764474-0-5(1))* Kaimanu Prodns., Ltd.

Kita, Suzanne. Three Whales: Who Won the Heart of the World. Sundram, Steve, illus. 2010. (ENG.). 40p. (J). (gr. 3). *(978-1-59700-761-0(7))* Island Heritage Publishing.

Kredensor, Diane. Ollie & Moon: Aloha! 2013. (Step into Reading Ser.). (ENG., Illus.). 48p. (J). (gr. 1-4). 3.99 *(978-0-307-97950-6(4),* Random Hse. Bks. for Young Readers) Random Hse. Children's Bks.

Krulik, Nancy. Catch That Wave. Braun, Sebastien, illus. 2013. (Magic Bone Ser.: 2). (ENG.). 128p. (J). (gr. 1-3). pap. 5.99 *(978-0-448-46444-2(6),* Grosset & Dunlap) Penguin Young Readers Group.

—Catch That Wave. 2013. (Magic Bone Ser.: 2). lib. bdg. 14.75 *(978-0-606-31681-1(7),* Turtleback) Turtleback Bks.

Lê, Christine & Lê, Michel, illus. The Hawai'i Snowman. 2008. (J). 14.95 *(978-1-56647-879-3(0))* Mutual Publishing LLC.

Leota, Kealaulaokamamo. Zhaka. 2008. (ENG & HAW., Illus.). (J). lib. bdg. *(978-0-9773495-9-3(4))* Na Kamalei Koolauloa Early Education Program.

Linmark, R. Zamora. Rolling the R's. 20th ed. 2016. (ENG.). 180p. (YA). pap. 16.95 *(978-1-885030-51-1(7))* Muae Publishing, Inc.

London, Jack. House of Pride & Other Tales of Hawaii. 2006. 116p. per. 9.95 *(978-1-59818-974-2(3))* Aegypan.

London, Jonathan. Froggy Goes to Hawaii. Remkiewicz, Frank, illus. 2012. (Froggy Ser.). (ENG.). 32p. (J). (gr. -1-k). pap. 6.99 *(978-0-14-242119-2(7),* Puffin Books) Penguin Young Readers Group.

—Froggy Goes to Hawaii. 2012. (Froggy Ser.). lib. bdg. 17.20 *(978-0-606-26083-1(8),* Turtleback) Turtleback Bks.

Lovins, Jennifer O. Opihi Baby. 2008. 32p. pap. 14.95 *(978-1-57306-285-5(5))* Bess Pr., Inc.

Maness, Branda Edwards. Animal Tales of Hawaii. 2011. 28p. pap. 12.15 *(978-1-4634-3484-7(7))* AuthorHouse.

Marsh, Carole. The Mystery in Hawaii. Friedlander, Randolyn, illus. 2010. (Real Kids, Real Places Ser.). 32p. pap. 7.99 *(978-0-635-07447-8(8),* Marsh, Carole Mysteries) Gallopade International.

—The Mystery in Hawaii: The 50th State. 2010. (Real Kids, Real Places Ser.). (Illus.). 157p. (J). 18.99 *(978-0-635-07446-1(X),* Marsh, Carole Mysteries) Gallopade International.

Masters, Elaine. The Royal Waker-Upper. Leung, Andrew, illus. 2003. (ENG.). 39p. (J). *(978-0-89610-992-6(5))* Island Heritage Publishing.

Matsuura, Richard & Matsuura, Ruth. Ali'i Kai. Chao, Linus, illus. (J). 7.95 *(978-1-887916-05-9(9))* Orchid Isle Publishing Co.

—Hawaiian Christmas Story. Chao, Linus, illus. (J). 8.95 *(978-1-887916-01-1(6))* Orchid Isle Publishing Co.

McDermott, Gerald. Pig-Boy: A Trickster Tale from Hawai'i. 2009. (ENG., Illus.). 32p. (J). (gr. -1-3). 17.99 *(978-0-15-216590-1(8))* Houghton Mifflin Harcourt Publishing Co.

McLaren, Clemence. Dance for the Aina. 2003. 160p. 9.95 *(978-1-57306-151-3(4))* Bess Pr., Inc.

Meckel, Jamie & BeachHouse Publishing. Down at the Beach. 2011. (ENG.). 16p. (J). (gr. -1-1). bds. 7.95 *(978-1-933067-41-4(1))* Beachhouse Publishing, LLC.

Meyers, Tim. Let's Call Him Lau-Wiliwili-Humuhumu-Nukunuku-Nukunuku-Apua'a-Oi'oi. 2005. (Illus.). 24p. (J). 16.95 incl. audio compact disk *(978-1-57306-252-7(9))* Bess Pr., Inc.

Michaels, Robbie. A Star Is Born. 2016. (ENG., Illus.). (J). 24.99 ***(978-1-63477-930-2(4))*** 2012. 200p. pap. 14.99 *(978-1-61372-730-0(5))* Dreamspinner Pr. (Harmony Ink Pr.).

Morgan, Melissa J. Sunrise. 2009. (Summer Confidential Ser.: 1). (ENG.). 240p. (J). (gr. 5-6). pap. 7.99 *(978-0-448-44988-3(9),* Grosset & Dunlap) Penguin Young Readers Group.

—Twilight. 2009. (Summer Confidential Ser.: 3). (ENG.). 240p. (J). (gr. 5-18). pap. 7.99 *(978-0-448-44990-6(0),* Grosset & Dunlap) Penguin Young Readers Group.

Mun-Ensor, Michelle. Aloh. 2011. 32p. pap. 24.95 *(978-1-4560-9848-3(9))* America Star Bks.

Murakami, Jon & BeachHouse Publishing. Geckos Surf. 2007. (ENG.). 16p. (J). (gr. -1-5). bds. 7.95 *(978-1-933067-22-3(5))* Beachhouse Publishing, LLC.

—Geckos up Geckos Down. 2010. (ENG.). 20p. (J). (gr. -1-1). bds. 7.95 *(978-1-933067-31-5(4))* Beachhouse Publishing, LLC.

Murakami, Jon & Yeh, Phil. The Winged Tiger & the Dragons of Hawaii. 2005. 48p. pap. 11.95 *(978-0-9755635-0-2(5))* Eastwind Studios.

Novesky, Amy & Morales, Yuyi. Georgia in Hawaii: When Georgia O'Keeffe Painted What She Pleased. Morales, Yuyi, illus. 2012. (ENG., Illus.). 40p. (J). (gr. 1-4). 17.99 *(978-0-15-205420-5(0))* Houghton Mifflin Harcourt Publishing Co.

Ogata, Michael, illus. New Friend for Nai'a. 2009. (J). *(978-1-56647-912-7(6))* Mutual Publishing LLC.

Omoto, Gail. Kai the 'Opihi Gets the Point. Omoto, Garrett, illus. 2006. 32p. (J). 16.95 *(978-1-933835-05-1(2))* Partners in Development Foundation.

O'Neill, Elizabeth. Alfred Visits Hawaii. 2009. 24p. (J). pap. 12.00 *(978-0-9822288-5-2(6))* Global Business Information Strategies, Inc.

Osborne, Mary Pope. High Tide in Hawaii. Murdocca, Sal, illus. 2003. (Magic Tree House (R) Ser.: 28). (ENG.). 96p. (J). (gr. 1-4). pap. 5.99 *(978-0-375-80616-2(4),* Random Hse. Bks. for Young Readers) Random Hse. Children's Bks.

—High Tide in Hawaii. 2003. (Magic Tree House Ser.: 28). (gr. k-3). lib. bdg. 16.00 *(978-0-613-62386-5(X),* Turtleback) Turtleback Bks.

Park, Alexander. The Thunderbolts & the Circle of Power. 2012. 316p. pap. 25.86 *(978-1-60746-939-1(1))* FastPrncil, Inc.

Park, Barbara. Aloha-Ha-Ha! Brunkus, Denise, illus. (Junie B. Jones Ser.: 26). (ENG.). 128p. (J). (gr. 1-4). 2007. per. 4.99 *(978-0-375-83404-2(4))* 2006. lib. bdg. 13.95 *(978-0-375-93403-2(0))* Random Hse. Children's Bks. (Random Hse. Bks. for Young Readers).

—Junie B., First Grader - Aloha-Ha-Ha! Brunkus, Denise, illus. 2007. (Junie B. Jones Ser.). 119p. (gr. 1-4). 15.00 *(978-0-7569-8085-6(2))* Perfection Learning Corp.

—Junie B. First Grader - Aloha-Ha-Ha! 2007. (Junie B. Jones Ser.: 26). lib. bdg. 14.75 *(978-1-4177-8157-7(2),* Turtleback) Turtleback Bks.

Patel, Sonia. Rani Patel in Full Effect. 2016. (ENG.). 224p. (J). (gr. 6). 16.95 *(978-1-941026-49-6(4))* Cinco Puntos Pr.

Patterson, James. Max. 2009. (Maximum Ride Ser.: 5). (ENG.). (YA). (gr. 5-17). 352p. pap. 9.99 *(978-0-316-00290-5(9),* Jimmy Patterson); 416p. 23.99 *(978-0-316-03759-4(1))* Little Brown & Co.

—Saving the World: And Other Extreme Sports. 3rd rev. ed. 2008. (Maximum Ride Ser.: 3). (ENG.). 432p. (YA). (gr. 5-17). pap. 10.00 *(978-0-316-15427-7(X),* Jimmy Patterson) Little Brown & Co.

—Saving the World & Other Extreme Sports. l.t. ed. 2007. (Maximum Ride Ser.: No. 3). 489p. (J). (gr. 3-7). 23.95 *(978-0-7862-9887-7(1))* Thorndike Pr.

Peacock-Williams, Carol A. & Williams, Christy Jo. Benny the Beetle, 1 vol. Peacock, Bessie Merle, illus. 2010. 28p. 24.95 *(978-1-4489-8373-5(8))* PublishAmerica, Inc.

Quinn, Timothy. Marvelous Miriam's Magnificent Hawaiian Adventure. 2011. 56p. pap. 16.95 *(978-1-4560-9630-4(3))* America Star Bks.

Richardson, Faith. Angel Walker. 2003. Orig. Title: The Sea, the Song & the Trumpetfish. (Illus.). 172p. (J). 19.95 *(978-0-9744989-2-8(0));* pap. 12.95 *(978-0-9744989-3-5(9))* Fox Song Bks.

Riley, Judi. When I Am Quiet on Maui. 40p. 2008. 15.95 *(978-0-9740582-3-8(8))* 2005. 12.95 *(978-0-9740582-1-4(1))* Tiki Tales.

—When I Am Quiet on Oahu. 2006. 40p. (gr. 1-2). 12.95 *(978-0-9740582-2-1(X))* Tiki Tales.

H
I

Robison, Dan, Jr. Kimo's Escape: The Story of a Hawaiian Boy Who Learns to Believe in Himself. 2005. 100p. (J). per. 19.95 (978-0-922993-28-4(9)) Marquette Bks., LLC.
Roddy, Lee. The Legend of Fire. 2006. (Ladd Family Adventure Ser.: Vol. 2). (Illus.). 133p. (J). (gr. 3-7). per. 7.99 (978-0-88062-251-6(2)) Mott Media.
—Panic in the Wild Waters. 2007. (Ladd Family Adventure Ser.: Vol. 12). (Illus.). 136p. (J). (gr. 3-7). per. 7.99 (978-0-88062-261-5(X)) Mott Media.
—Peril at Pirate's Point. 2006. (Ladd Family Adventure Ser.: Vol. 7). (Illus.). 153p. (J). (gr. 4-7). per. 7.99 (978-0-88062-256-1(3)) Mott Media.
—Terror at Forbidden Falls. 2006. (Ladd Family Adventure Ser.: Vol. 8). (Illus.). 157p. (J). (gr. 3-7). per. 7.99 (978-0-88062-257-8(1)) Mott Media.
Rooks, Elizabeth. Where Does Santa Go on Vacation after Christmas? 2012. 24p. pap. 17.99 (978-1-4772-6535-2(X)) AuthorHouse.
Salisbury, Graham. Calvin Coconut: Rocket Ride. Rogers, Jacqueline, illus. 2013. (Calvin Coconut Ser.). (ENG.). 160p. (J). (gr. 2-5). pap. 6.99 (978-0-375-86508-4(X), Yearling) Random Hse. Children's Bks.
—Calvin Coconut: Dog Heaven. Rogers, Jacqueline, illus. 2011. (Calvin Coconut Ser.). (ENG.). 160p. (J). (gr. 3-7). 6.99 (978-0-375-84602-1(6), Yearling) Random Hse. Children's Bks.
—Calvin Coconut: Man Trip. Rogers, Jacqueline, illus. 2013. (Calvin Coconut Ser.). (ENG.). 144p. (J). (gr. 2-5). pap. 6.99 (978-0-375-86507-7(1), Yearling) Random Hse. Children's Bks.
—Calvin Coconut: Zoo Breath. Rogers, Jacqueline, illus. 2011. (Calvin Coconut Ser.). (ENG.). 160p. (J). (gr. 3-7). 6.99 (978-0-375-84603-8(4), Yearling) Random Hse. Children's Bks.
—Extra Famous. Rogers, Jacqueline, illus. 2014. (Calvin Coconut Ser.). (ENG.). 176p. (J). (gr. 2-5). pap. 6.99 (978-0-307-93075-0(0), Yearling) Random Hse. Children's Bks.
—Hero of Hawaii. Rogers, Jacqueline, illus. 2012. (Calvin Coconut Ser.). (ENG.). 160p. (J). (gr. 2-5). pap. 6.99 (978-0-375-86505-3(5), Yearling) Random Hse. Children's Bks.
—House of the Red Fish. 2014. (ENG.). 318p. (YA). (gr. 7). pap. 9.99 (978-0-385-38657-9(5), Ember) Random Hse. Children's Bks.
—Kung Fooey. Rogers, Jacqueline, illus. 2012. (Calvin Coconut Ser.). (ENG.). 144p. (J). (gr. 2-5). 6.99 (978-0-375-86506-0(3), Yearling) Random Hse. Children's Bks.
—Lord of the Deep. braille ed. 2003. (J). (gr. 2). spiral bd. (978-0-616-15872-2(6)) Canadian National Institute for the Blind/Institut National Canadien pour les Aveugles.
—Lord of the Deep. 2003. (ENG.). 192p. (YA). (gr. 7). mass mkt. 6.99 (978-0-440-22911-7(1), Laurel Leaf) Random Hse. Children's Bks.
—Lord of the Deep: A Novel. 2006. 182p. (J). (gr. 6-10). reprint ed. 16.00 (978-1-4223-5841-2(0)) DIANE Publishing Co.
—Trouble Magnet. Rogers, Jacqueline, illus. 2010. (Calvin Coconut Ser.). (ENG.). 160p. (J). (gr. 3-7). pap. 6.99 (978-0-375-84600-7(X), Yearling) Random Hse. Children's Bks.
—Under the Blood Red Sun. 246p. (YA). 22.00 (978-0-8446-7322-6(6)) Smith, Peter Pub., Inc.
—Under the Blood-Red Sun. 2014. (ENG.). 272p. (YA). (gr. 7-7). pap. 9.99 (978-0-385-38655-5(9), Ember) Random Hse. Children's Bks.
—The Zippy Fix. Rogers, Jacqueline, illus. 2010. (Calvin Coconut Ser.). (ENG.). 176p. (J). (gr. 3-7). pap. 6.99 (978-0-375-84601-4(8), Yearling) Random Hse. Children's Bks.
Salter-Mathieson, Nigel C. S. Little Chief Mischief: From Tales of the Menehune. Gruen, Chuck, illus. 2011. 44p. pap. 35.95 (978-1-258-10135-0(1)) Literary Licensing, LLC.
Seashore Touch & See Hi? 2004. (J). 11.95 (978-0-89610-999-5(2)) Island Heritage Publishing.
Shapiro, Jane. Daddy, What Is Love? Robinson, Don, illus. 2008. (ENG.). 28p. (J). (gr. -1-3). (978-1-59700-244-8(5)) Island Heritage Publishing.
Sheldon, Kaylene Kauwila. A Day with Makana. 2007.Tr. of I Kekahi la me Makana. (ENG & HAW.). (J). lib. bdg. (978-0-9773495-2-4(7)) Na Kamalei Koolauloa Early Education Program.
Silvano, Wendi. Love Is All Around Hawaii. Czernichowska, Joanna, illus. 2016. (ENG.). 32p. (J). (-6). 12.99 (978-1-4926-2920-7(0), Sourcebooks Jabberwocky) Sourcebooks, Inc.
Smallman, Steve. Santa Is Coming to Hawaii. Dunn, Robert, illus. 2013. (ENG.). 32p. (J). (-3). 9.99 (978-1-4022-9009-1(8), Sourcebooks Jabberwocky) Sourcebooks, Inc.
—Santa Is Coming to Honolulu. Dunn, Robert, illus. 2015. (ENG.). 32p. (J). (-3). 9.99 (978-1-4926-2653-4(8), Sourcebooks Jabberwocky) Sourcebooks, Inc.
Sorenson, Margo. Aloha for Carol Ann. Burris, Priscilla, illus. 2011. 32p. (J). (gr. -1-3). pap. 8.95 (978-1-60349-027-6(2), Marimba Bks.) Hudson Publishing Group, The.
Stamper, Judith. Voyage to the Volcano. Speirs, John, illus. 2003. (Magic School Bus Science Chapter Bks.). 87p. (gr. 3-6). 15.00 (978-0-7569-1581-0(3)) Perfection Learning Corp.
Steele, Margaret. Wuz Da Nite Befo: A Pidgin Christmas Story in Hawaii. Chang, Roy, illus. 2005. 24p. 10.95 (978-1-56647-750-5(6)) Mutual Publishing LLC.
Stravinskas, Janice. Pam the Dog: A Hawaiian Adventure. 2009. 32p. pap. 13.00 (978-1-60860-692-4(9), Eloquent Bks.) Strategic Book Publishing & Rights Agency (SBPRA).
Stuefloten, Helen. There's A Giant in the Garden. Janguay, Patricia, illus. l.t. ed. 2006. 35p. (J). per. 11.99 (978-1-59879-161-7(3)) Lifevest Publishing, Inc.
Suzuki, Genevieve A. The Original Poi Cats on Oahu. 2005. 40p. 13.95 (978-1-56647-718-5(2)) Mutual Publishing LLC.
Tackett, Mike. Holoholo I Hawaii. 2007. 24p. (J). pap. 5.95 (978-1-56647-791-8(3)) Mutual Publishing LLC.
Takayama, Sandi. The Musubi Baby. Hall, Pat, illus. 2007. 32p. (J). (gr. -1-3). 10.95 (978-1-57306-272-5(3)) Bess Pr., Inc.
Talley, Linda. Aloha Potter! - hardcover Book. Chase, Andra, illus. 2004. 30p. (J). (978-1-55942-200-0(9)) Witcher Productions.
Terrell, Brandon & Majado, Caio. Tunnel Vision, Vol. 6. Ito, Leonardo, illus. 2012. (Tony Hawk's 900 Revolution Ser.). (ENG.). 128p. (gr. 3-4). pap. 7.19 (978-1-4342-3888-7(1)); lib. bdg. 26.65 (978-1-4342-3312-7(X)) Stone Arch Bks. (Tony Hawk's 900 Revolution).
Terrell, Brandon, et al. Riptide Pride, 1 vol. 2011. (Sports Illustrated Kids Graphic Novels Ser.). (ENG., Illus.). 56p. (gr. 2-3). pap. 7.19 (978-1-4342-3399-8(5)); lib. bdg. 26.65 (978-1-4342-2238-1(1)) Stone Arch Bks.
Tokyopop Staff, creator. Contents under Pressure, Vol. 3. 2005. (Lilo & Stitch Ser.). (Illus.). 89p. (gr. 3-7). pap. 14.99 (978-1-59532-069-8(5), Tokyopop Kids) TOKYOPOP, Inc.
Tribolet, Leslie L. Danny's Tale: Adventures of an Arabian Horse in his Own Words. 2010. (Illus.). 112p. 24.95 (978-1-4490-6065-7(X)); pap. 14.95 (978-1-4490-6064-0(1)) AuthorHouse.
Troupe, Thomas Kingsley. Volcano: a Fiery Tale of Survival. Fagan, Kirbi, illus. 2016. (Survive! Ser.). (ENG.). 56p. (gr. 4-6). lib. bdg. 25.32 (978-1-4965-2555-0(8)) Stone Arch Bks.
Tutu Nene - Hawaiian Mother Goose Rhymes. 2004. (J). audio compact disk 14.99 (978-0-931548-60-4(8)) Island Heritage Publishing.
Wasson, Dawn K. T. Kuu Tutu. 2008. (ENG & HAW., Illus.). (J). lib. bdg. (978-0-9773495-8-6(6)) Na Kamalei Koolauloa Early Education Program.
Wasson, Dawn Kahalaomapuana Tautafa. Kilia & Wahiopua the Reefs of Hauula. 2006.Tr. of Kilia a me Wahiopua Na Papa o Hauula. (ENG & HAW.). (J). lib. bdg. 12.95 (978-0-9773495-1-7(9), Ho'ulu Hou Project: Stories Told by Us) Na Kamalei Koolauloa Early Education Program.
Westerman, Rob. The Legend of Kalikimaka: Alohalani, Kalikimaka Auntie. Tahleh, Eleykaa, illus. 2003. 32p. (J). 12.95 (978-0-9761992-0-5(3)) Gold Boy Music & Pubn.
Westerman, Robert. Alohalani Kalikimaka Auntie: Sheet Music & Lyrics. Westerman, Robert, . 2006. (Illus.). 12p. (J). 6.95 (978-0-9761992-1-2(1)) Gold Boy Music & Pubn.
Wheeler, Lance. Kula & the Old Ukulele. 2007. 32p. 12.95 (978-1-56647-844-1(8)) Mutual Publishing LLC.
Wing, Carol. Lio the Carousel Horse. Moen, Ruth, illus. 2010. (ENG.). 32p. (J). (gr. -1-2). 14.95 (978-1-933067-37-7(3)) Beachhouse Publishing, LLC.
Winkler, Henry & Oliver, Lin. Summer School! What Genius Thought That Up? 2006. (Hank Zipzer Ser.: No. 8). (Illus.). 157p. (J). (gr. 3-9). lib. bdg. 24.21 (978-1-59961-107-5(4)) Spotlight.
Yeh, Julie. Poppie's Adventures: Serpents in Paradise. Hsu, Jack, illus. 2003. 48p. (J). per. (978-0-9742386-0-9(0)) Way Out Comics.

HAWAII—HISTORY

Carolan, Joanna & Carolan, Terry. A President from Hawaii. Zunon, Elizabeth, illus. 2012. (ENG.). 24p. (J). (gr. 2-5). 15.99 (978-0-7636-5230-2(X)); pap. 7.99 (978-0-7636-6282-0(8)) Candlewick Pr.
Collins, Erica. Aloha Activity Book. Collins, Erica, illus. 2009. (Illus.). 24p. pap. 4.98 (978-1-933735-59-7(7)) Pacifica Island Art, Inc.
Coste, Marion. Hawaii's Animals Do the Most Amazing Things! Ekmanis, Rena, illus. 2014. 47p. (J). (978-0-8248-3962-8(5)) Univ. of Hawaii Pr.
Dennis, Yvonne Wakim & Hirschfelder, Arlene. A Kid's Guide to Native American History: More Than 50 Activities. 2009. (Kid's Guide Ser.). (ENG.). 256p. (J). (gr. 2-4). pap. 16.95 (978-1-55652-802-6(7)) Chicago Review Pr., Inc.
Durrie, Karen. Hawaii. 2012. (J). (978-1-61913-320-4(2)); (978-1-61913-319-8(9)) Weigl Pubs., Inc.
Dyan, Penelope. Hangin' Loose! a Kid's Guide to Oahu, Hawaii. Weigand, John D., photos by. 2009. (Illus.). 44p. pap. 11.95 (978-1-935118-78-7(1)) Bellissima Publishing, LLC.
—Kona Forevermore — A Kid's Guide to Kona Hawaii. Weigand, John D., photos by. 2013. (Illus.). 36p. pap. 11.95 (978-1-61477-116-6(2)) Bellissima Publishing, LLC.
—The Road to Hilo! a Kid's Guide to Hilo, Hawaii. Weigand, John D., illus. 2013. 34p. pap. 11.95 (978-1-61477-117-3(0)) Bellissima Publishing, LLC.
—See You 2-Maui — -A Kid's Guide to Maui, Hawaii. Weigand, John D., photos by. 2012. (Illus.). 34p. pap. 11.95 (978-1-61477-038-1(7)) Bellissima Publishing, LLC.
—Yesterday's Rain — - a Kid's Guide to Kauai, Hawaii. Weigand, John D., photos by. 2013. (Illus.). 34p. pap. 11.95 (978-1-61477-100-5(6)) Bellissima Publishing, LLC.
Foran, Jill. Hawai'i: The Aloha State. 2016. (J). (978-1-4896-4848-8(8)) Weigl Pubs., Inc.
Hayashi, Leslie Ann. Celebrating Holidays in Hawaii. Bishop, Kathleen Wong, illus. 2010. (ENG.). 36p. (J). 14.95 (978-1-56647-914-1(2)) Mutual Publishing LLC.
Holm, Barbara. A Visit to Hawaii. Ingram, Anne, illus. 2005. 32p. (J). pap. 5.95 (978-0-9772200-0-7(1)) Visit to Hawaii, A.
Howse, Jennifer. Alaska & Hawaii. 2016. (Illus.). 48p. (J). (978-1-5105-1134-7(2)) SmartBook Media, Inc.
Jerome, Kate B. Lucky to Live in Hawaii. 2017. (Arcadia Kids Ser.). (ENG., Illus.). 32p. (J). 16.99 **(978-0-7385-2800-7(5))** Arcadia Publishing.
Kavanagh, James. Hawaii Trees & Wildflowers: A Folding Pocket Guide to Familiar Species. Leung, Raymond, illus. 2010. (Pocket Naturalist Guide Ser.). (ENG.). 1p. 6.95 (978-1-58355-509-5(9)) Western National Parks Assn.
Lusted, Marcia Amidon. Hawaii: The Aloha State. 2010. (Our Amazing States Ser.). (ENG.). 24p. (J). pap. 8.25 (978-1-4488-0766-6(2)); lib. bdg. 22.60 (978-1-4488-0665-2(8)) Rosen Publishing Group, Inc., The. (PowerKids Pr.).
Marsh, Carole. Exploring Hawaii Through Project-Based Learning. 2016. (Hawaii Experience Ser.). (ENG.). (J). pap. 9.99 (978-0-635-12335-0(5)) Gallopade International.
—Hawaii History Projects: 30 Cool, Activities, Crafts, Experiments & More for Kids to Do to Learn about Your State! 2003. (Hawaii Experience Ser.). 32p. (gr. k-5). pap. 5.95 (978-0-635-01780-2(6), Marsh, Carole Bks.) Gallopade International.
—I'm Reading about Hawaii. 2014. (Hawaii Experience Ser.). (ENG., Illus.). (J). pap., pap. 8.99 (978-0-635-11286-6(8)) Gallopade International.
Mattern, Joanne. Hawaii: Past & Present. 2010. (United States: Past & Present Ser.). (ENG.). 48p. (YA). pap. 11.75 (978-1-4358-9506-5(1)); lib. bdg. 29.25 (978-1-4358-9479-2(0)) Rosen Publishing Group, Inc., The. (Rosen Reference).
—Mauna Loa: El volcan en actividad más grande del mundo (Mauna Loa: World's Largest Active Volcano) 2009. (Maravillas naturales (Natures Greatest Hits) Ser.). (SPA.). 24p. (gr. 2-2). 42.50 (978-1-61514-364-1(5), Editorial Buenas Letras) Rosen Publishing Group, Inc., The.
—Mauna Loa: World's Largest Active Volcano. 2009. (Nature's Greatest Hits Ser.). 24p. (gr. 2-2). 42.50 (978-1-61514-841-7(8), PowerKids Pr.) Rosen Publishing Group, Inc., The.
McDonnell, Peter. The Last Princess. 2005. (Illus.). 16p. (978-0-7367-2910-9(0)) Zaner-Bloser, Inc.
Meinking, Mary. What's Great about Hawaii? 2015. (ENG., Illus.). 32p. (J). (gr. 2-5). 26.65 (978-1-4677-3887-3(5)) Lerner Publishing Group.
Miller, Debbie S. Flight of the Golden Plover: The Amazing Migration Between Hawaii & Alaska. Van Zyle, Daniel, illus. 2011. (ENG.). 32p. pap. 11.95 (978-1-60223-151-1(6)) Univ. of Alaska Pr.
Obregon, Jose Maria. Hawaii/Hawai. 2005. (Bilingual Library of the United States of America Ser.: Set 1). (ENG & SPA., Illus.). 32p. (J). (gr. 3-6). lib. bdg. 25.25 (978-1-4042-3076-7(9)) Rosen Publishing Group, Inc., The.
Otfinoski, Steven, et al. Hawaii. 2015. (It's My State! (r) Ser.). (ENG., Illus.). 80p. (J). (gr. 4-4). 34.21 (978-1-62713-157-5(4)) Cavendish Square Publishing.
Rayson, Ann. Hawai'i: The Pacific State. 2012. (Illus.). vi, 228p. (J). (978-1-57306-452-1(1)) Bess Pr., Inc.
—Modern History of Hawai'i. 2004. (Illus.). 304p. lib. bdg. (978-1-57306-209-1(X)) Bess Pr., Inc.
Salzmann, Mary Elizabeth. The Great Lei Race: A Story about Hawaii, 1 vol. Doucet, Bob, illus. 2010. (Fact & Fable: State Stories Set 2 Ser.). (ENG.). 24p. (J). (gr. -1-2). 25.65 (978-1-60453-923-3(2)) ABDO Publishing Co.
Sherman, Josepha. Queen Lydia Liliuokalani, Last Ruler of Hawaii. 2004. (On My Own Biography Ser.). (J). lib. bdg. 22.60 (978-1-57505-650-0(X), Carolrhoda Bks.) Lerner Publishing Group.
Wade, Mary Dodson. Deadly Waves: Tsunamis. 2012. (Disasters — People in Peril Ser.). (Illus.). 48p. (J). (gr. 5-18). 25.27 (978-0-7660-4018-2(6)) Enslow Pubs., Inc.
Walker, Harvey Jeanne. Honey Girl: The Hawaiian Monk Seal. Bersani, Shennen, illus. 2017. (ENG.). 32p. (J). (gr. k-3). 17.95 (978-1-62855-921-7(7)) Arbordale Publishing.
Webster, Christine. Mauna Loa. 2013. (J). (978-1-62127-474-2(8)); pap. (978-1-62127-480-3(2)) Weigl Pubs., Inc.
Whitman, Nancy C. Counting Petals: Using Flowers of Hawaii. Chong, Luther, photos by. 2009. (Illus.). 31p. (J). (978-1-4363-8562-6(8)) Xlibris Corp.

HAWAII—HISTORY—FICTION

Crowl, Janice. Kili & the Singing Snails. Orme, Harinani, illus. 2011. (J). 16.95 (978-1-58178-104-5(0)) Bishop Museum Pr.
Eyre, David. Lumpy Poi & Twisting Eels. Kalahele, Imaikalani, illus. 2007. 32p. 14.95 (978-0-87336-154-5(7)) Kamehameha Publishing.
Frederick, Heather Vogel. The Education of Patience Goodspeed. 2006. (ENG., Illus.). 320p. (J). (gr. 3-7). reprint ed. pap. 6.99 (978-1-4169-1394-8(7), Simon & Schuster Bks. For Young Readers) Simon & Schuster Bks. For Young Readers.
Fredericks, Anthony D. The Tsunami Quilt: Grandfather's Story. Yee, Tammy, illus. rev. ed. 2007. (Tales of Young Americans Ser.). (ENG.). 32p. (J). (gr. -1-3). 17.95 (978-1-58536-313-1(8)) Sleeping Bear Pr.
Greenway, Beth. A True Princess of Hawai'i. Yee, Tammy, illus. 2017. (ENG & SPA.). 32p. (J). (gr. k-3). 17.95 (978-1-62855-948-4(9)) Arbordale Publishing.
—Una Verdadera Princesa de Hawái. Yee, Tammy, illus. 2017. (SPA.). 32p. (J). (gr. k-3). pap. 9.95 (978-1-62855-950-7(0)) Arbordale Publishing.
Hood, Ann. Queen Liliuokalani: Royal Prisoner. Altmann, Scott & Zilber, Denis, illus. 2013. (Treasure Chest Ser.: 6). (ENG.). 176p. (J). (gr. 3-7). 15.99 (978-0-448-45739-0(3)); pap. 6.99 (978-0-448-45729-1(6)) Penguin Young Readers Group. (Grosset & Dunlap).
Mazer, Harry. A Boy at War: A Novel of Pearl Harbor. 2004. (Illus.). 104p. (gr. 5-9). 16.00 (978-0-7569-4088-1(5)) Perfection Learning Corp.
Osborne, Mary Pope, et al. Maremoto en Hawái. Murdocca, Sal, illus. 2014. 28. (SPA.). 88p. (J). (gr. 2-4). pap. 5.99 (978-1-933032-95-5(2)) Lectorum Pubns., Inc.
Pellegrino, Victor. Uncle Kawaiolas Dream. 2010. 32p. 18.95 (978-0-945045-08-3(5)) Maui Arthoughts Co.
Robison, Dan. Death Chant: Kimo's Battle with the Shamanic Forces. 2006. 194p. (J). pap. (978-0-922993-52-9(1)) Marquette Bks., LLC.
—Kimo's Legacy: The Battle to Unite Hawaii. 2007. 220p. (J). per. 22.95 (978-0-922993-78-9(5)) Marquette Bks., LLC.
Salisbury, Graham. House of the Red Fish. 2008. (Readers Circle Ser.). (ENG.). 320p. (YA). (gr. 7-9). mass mkt. 6.50 (978-0-440-23838-6(2), Laurel Leaf) Random Hse. Children's Bks.
—Night of the Howling Dogs. 2009. (ENG.). 208p. (YA). (gr. 7-7). mass mkt. 6.99 (978-0-440-23839-3(0), Laurel Leaf) Random Hse. Children's Bks.

HAWAIIAN LANGUAGE

Au, May Parker. Princess Huilua & Kamapuaa. 2007.Tr. of Ke Kamalii Wahine o Huilua a me Kamapuaa. (ENG & HAW.). (J). lib. bdg. (978-0-9773495-4-8(3)) Na Kamalei Koolauloa Early Education Program.
Carolan. This Is My Piko. Carolan, Joanna, illus. 2009. 58p. 17.95 incl. audio compact disk (978-0-9715333-0-1(X)) Banana Patch Pr.
Hawaiian Kids Coloring Book. No. 1. pap. 4.95 (978-0-930492-41-0(2))No. 2. pap. 4.95 (978-0-930492-42-7(0)) Hawaiian Service, Inc.
Murray, Patricia Lei. Let's Learn the Hawaiian Alphabet. Carter, Sharon, illus. 2005. 24p. (J). 14.95 (978-1-59700-102-1(3)) Island Heritage Publishing.
Nogelmeier, Puakea, ed. Keiki's First Word Book. 2008. 32p. 14.95 (978-1-57306-275-6(8)) Bess Pr., Inc.
Omoto, Garrett, illus. Tutu Books Preschool Library, 3 bks. 2006. (ENG & HAW.). 48p. (YA). 29.95 (978-1-933835-04-4(4)) Partners in Development Foundation.
Phillips, Lori. Satawalese Alphabet. 2006. (Island Alphabet Books). (Illus.). 58p. (J). (gr. -1-k). 4.95 (978-1-57306-261-9(8)) Bess Pr., Inc.
Wallace, William K. Kuleana. 2006. (ENG & HAW.). (J). lib. bdg. 12.95 (978-0-9760892-9-2(7), Ho'ulu Hou Project: Stories Told by Us) Na Kamalei Koolauloa Early Education Program.

HAWKING

see Falconry

HAWKS

Bates, Matthew. Hawks, 01 vols., 1. 2016. (Raptors! Ser.). (ENG., Illus.). 24p. (J). pap. 8.25 (978-1-5081-4248-5(3), PowerKids Pr.) Rosen Publishing Group, Inc., The.
Borgert-Spaniol, Megan. Red-Tailed Hawks. 2015. (North American Animals Ser.). (ENG., Illus.). 24p. (J). (gr. k-3). lib. bdg. 25.95 (978-1-62617-194-7(7), Blastoff! Readers) Bellwether Media.
Gish, Melissa. Hawks. 2014. 46p. (978-1-60818-418-7(8), Creative Education) Creative Co., The.
—Living Wild: Hawks. 2015. (Living Wild Ser.). (ENG., Illus.). 48p. (J). (gr. 5-8). pap. 12.00 (978-1-62832-004-6(4), Creative Paperbacks) Creative Co., The.
Harris, Tim. Hawks. 2008. (Nature's Children Ser.). (Illus.). 52p. (J). (978-0-7172-6237-3(5)) Grolier, Ltd.
Haywood, Karen. Hawks & Falcons. 2010. (Endangered! 2 Ser.). 48p. (gr. 3). lib. bdg. 29.93 (978-0-7614-4051-2(8)) Marshall Cavendish Corp.
Hill, Melissa. Red-Tailed Hawks. 2015. (Birds of Prey Ser.). (ENG.). 24p. (gr. k-1). pap. 6.95 (978-1-4914-2311-0(0), Pebble Plus) Capstone Press of Coughlan Cos.
Lundgren, Julie. Hawks. 2009. (Illus.). 24p. (J). pap. 7.95 (978-1-60694-775-3(3)) Rourke Educational Media.
Marsico, Katie. How Do We Live Together? Hawks. 2010. (Community Connections: How Do We Live Together? Ser.). (ENG.). 24p. (gr. 2-5). lib. bdg. 25.64 (978-1-60279-624-9(6), 200327) Cherry Lake Publishing.
McCarthy, Cecilia Pinto. Hawks, 1 vol. 2012. (Birds Ser.). (ENG.). 24p. (gr. 1-2). lib. bdg. 25.32 (978-1-4296-8607-5(3)) Capstone Press of Coughlan Cos.
McCarthy, Meghan. City Hawk: The Story of Pale Male. McCarthy, Meghan, illus. 2007. (ENG., Illus.). 40p. (J). (gr. -1-3). 17.99 (978-1-4169-3359-5(X), Simon & Schuster/Paula Wiseman Bks.) Simon & Schuster/Paula Wiseman Bks.
Patterson, Stacey. Fidget's Folly. Gorbatov, Vadim, illus. 2012. 36p. (J). 18.00 (978-0-87842-594-5(2)) Mountain Pr. Publishing Co., Inc.
Riggs, Kate. Amazing Animals: Hawks. 2015. (Amazing Animals Ser.). (ENG.). 24p. (J). (gr. 1-3). pap. 8.99 (978-1-62832-090-9(7), Creative Paperbacks) Creative Co., The.
—Hawks. 2015. (J). (978-1-60818-490-3(0), Creative Education) Creative Co., The.
Schuetz, Kari. Hawks. 2014. (Backyard Wildlife Ser.). (ENG., Illus.). 24p. (J). (gr. k-3). lib. bdg. 25.95 (978-1-62617-058-2(4), Blastoff! Readers) Bellwether Media.
Vail, Grace. Hunting with Hawks, Vol. 1. 2014. (Animal Attack! Ser.). 32p. (J). (gr. 2-5). 22.60 (978-1-4824-0486-9(9)) Stevens, Gareth Publishing LLLP.
Warhol, Tom. Hawks. 2005. (Animalways Ser.). (Illus.). 104p. (gr. 6-7). lib. bdg. 24.95 (978-0-7614-1744-6(3), Benchmark Bks.) Marshall Cavendish Corp.
Wechsler, Doug. Red- Tailed Hawks. 2009. (Really Wild Life of Animals Ser.). 24p. (gr. 3-4). 42.50 (978-1-60854-209-3(2), PowerKids Pr.) Rosen Publishing Group, Inc., The.

HAWKS—FICTION

Baltazar, Art. Starro & the Space Dolphins, 1 vol. Baltazar, Art, illus. 2012. (DC Super-Pets Ser.). (ENG., Illus.). 56p. (gr. 2-2). pap. 4.95 (978-1-4048-7217-2(5)); lib. bdg. 23.99 (978-1-4048-6487-0(3)) Picture Window Bks. (DC Super-Pets).
Barton, Chris. That's Not Bunny! Jack, Colin, illus. 2016. (ENG.). 32p. (J). (gr. -1-k). 16.99 (978-1-4231-9086-8(6)) Disney Pr.
Beck, Barbara. Bill Every Cloud Has a Silver Lining. 2012. 108p. pap. 19.95 (978-1-4626-9718-2(6)) America Star Bks.
Cerone, Diane. Lucy & the Red-Tailed Hawk. Auer, Lois, illus. 2007. 32p. (J). pap. 17.00 (978-0-8059-7565-9(9)) Dorrance Publishing Co., Inc.
Dharma Publishing Staff. The Value of Friends: A Story about Helping Friends in Need. 2nd ed. 2015. (ENG.). 36p. (gr. -1-7). pap. 8.95 (978-0-89800-493-9(4)) Dharma Publishing.
Dickinson, Peter. The Blue Hawk. 2008. 229p. (J). (gr. 5-9). 27.00 (978-0-8446-6478-1(2)) Smith, Peter Pub., Inc.
Gentry, Victory. Grandpa's Fairy Tales: Horatio the Hawk. 2010. pap. 9.95 (978-0-7414-5691-5(5)) Infinity Publishing.
Hamley, Dennis. Hawk's Vision. 2006. 116p. per. (978-1-904529-20-0(8), Back to Front) Solidus.
Johnson, Jaime Gardner. The Ghost of Donley Farm, 1 vol. Klein, Laurie Allen, illus. 2015. (ENG.). 32p. (J). (gr. k-3). 17.95 (978-1-62855-451-9(7)); pap. 9.95 (978-1-62855-459-5(2)) Arbordale Publishing.
Korth, Melanie. The Javelina: Finds Contentment. 2010. 20p. 10.49 (978-1-4520-5485-8(1)) AuthorHouse.
Lee, Prema. Maki's Journey Begins. 2004. (Illus.). (J). per. 11.95 (978-0-9754116-0-5(8)) Magic Wordweaver Pr.
Lispi, Robert. Buddy Hawk: Story of Buddy Hawk. 2005. (J). pap. 8.00 (978-0-8059-6602-2(1)) Dorrance Publishing Co., Inc.
Livingston, Timothy J. & Livingston, Mary A. FireStorm in the Forest: When a Forest Burns. Livingston, Timothy J., illus. 2006. (Illus.). 32p. (J). 19.99 (978-0-9635757-1-5(6)) Red Tail Publishing.
Moses, Albert. The Hawk & the Turtles. Roberts, Pam, illus. 2011. 16p. pap. 24.95 (978-1-4626-4261-8(6)) America Star Bks.
Robertson-Eletto, Joanne. Rocky: The Okeeheelee Bandit. 2013. 48p. pap. 20.99 (978-1-4808-0298-8(0)) Archway Publishing.
Ruiz, John. The Squirrel, the Eagle & the Red Hawk. 2012. 32p. pap. 21.99 (978-1-4691-7970-4(9)) Xlibris Corp.

Vaughn, Richard. Rowena & the Magic Hawk, the First Adventure. 2009. 224p. pap. 14.95 *(978-1-60860-157-8(9),* Eloquent Bks.) Strategic Book Publishing & Rights Agency (SBPRA).

Wainscott, Bud. The Wounded Hawk. 2012. 48p. pap. 11.95 *(978-1-4772-5354-0(8))* AuthorHouse.

HAWTHORNE, NATHANIEL, 1804-1864

Bloom, Harold, ed. Young Goodman Brown. 2005. (Bloom's Modern Critical Interpretations Ser.). (Illus.). 144p. (C). (gr. 9-13). 45.00 *(978-0-7910-8124-2(9),* Chelsea Hse.) Facts On File, Inc.

Diorio, Mary Ann L. A Student's Guide to Nathaniel Hawthorne. 2004. (Understanding Literature Ser.). (Illus.). 160p. (YA). lib. bdg. 29.27 *(978-0-7660-2283-6(8))* Enslow Pubs., Inc.

Johnson, Claudia, ed. Women's Issues in Nathaniel Hawthorne's The Scarlett Letter. 2008. (Social Issues in Literature Ser.). (ENG., Illus.). 224p. (gr. 10-12). 46.40 *(978-0-7377-4262-6(3),* LML02109-243172); pap. 32.00 *(978-0-7377-4263-3(1),* LML02109-243176) Cengage Gale. (Greenhaven Pr., Inc.).

Roberts, Russell. Nathaniel Hawthorne. 2006. (Classic Storytellers Ser.). (Illus.). 48p. (J). (gr. 3-7). lib. bdg. 29.95 *(978-1-58415-454-9(3),* 1259541) Mitchell Lane Pubs., Inc.

Saddleback Educational Publishing Staff, ed. Scarlet Letter. 2011. (Timeless Classics Ser.). (ENG.). 48p. (YA). (gr. 9-12). pupil's gde. ed. 19.95 incl. cd-rom *(978-1-61651-150-0(8))* Saddleback Educational Publishing, Inc.

Sterling, Laurie A. Bloom's How to Write about Nathaniel Hawthorne. 2007. (Bloom's How to Write about Literature Ser.). 344p. (C). (gr. 9-18). 45.00 *(978-0-7910-9481-5(2),* Chelsea Hse.) Facts On File, Inc.

HAYDN, JOSEPH, 1732-1809

Norton, James R. Haydn's World. (Music Throughout History Ser.). 64p. 2009. (gr. 5-6). 58.50 *(978-1-61514-685-7(7),* Rosen Reference) 2007. (Illus.). (J). (gr. 4-7). lib. bdg. 29.25 *(978-1-4042-0727-1(9))* Rosen Publishing Group, Inc., The.

Summerer, Eric Michael. Franz Joseph Haydn. (Primary Source Library of Famous Composers Ser.). 32p. 2009. (gr. 4-4). 42.50 *(978-1-60854-106-5(1))* 2006. (Illus.). (J). (gr. -1-3). lib. bdg. 23.95 *(978-1-4042-2767-5(9))* Rosen Publishing Group, Inc., The. (PowerKids Pr.).

Wheeler, Opal & Deucher, Sybil. Joseph Haydn: the Merry Little Peasant. Greenwalt, Mary, illus. 2005. 118p. per. 13.95 *(978-1-933573-00-7(7))* Zeezok Publishing, LLC.

HAYDN, JOSEPH, 1732-1809—FICTION

Celenza, Anna Harwell. The Farewell Symphony. Kitchel, JoAnn E., illus. 2016. (Once upon a Masterpiece Ser.). (ENG.). 32p. (J). (gr. 1-4). lib. bdg. 16.95 *(978-1-58089-527-9(1))* Charlesbridge Publishing, Inc.

Dunlap, Susanne. The Musician's Daughter. (ENG.). (YA). (gr. 7). 2010. 352p. pap. 8.99 *(978-1-59990-452-8(7),* 9781599904528) 2009. 336p. 16.99 *(978-1-59990-332-3(6),* 9781599903323) Bloomsbury Publishing USA. (Bloomsbury USA Childrens).

HAYES, RUTHERFORD B., 1822-1893

Francis, Sandra. Rutherford B. Hayes. 2008. (Presidents of the U. S. A. Ser.). (ENG., Illus.). 48p. (J). (gr. 3-6). 32.79 *(978-1-60253-048-5(3),* 200687) Child's World, Inc., The.

Levy, Debbie. Rutherford B. Hayes. 2006. (Presidential Leaders Ser.). (Illus.). 112p. (J). (gr. 3-7). lib. bdg. 29.27 *(978-0-8225-1493-0(1),* Lerner Pubns.) Lerner Publishing Group.

Mis, Melody S. How to Draw the Life & Times of Rutherford B. Hayes. 2009. (Kid's Guide to Drawing the Presidents of the United States of America Ser.). 32p. (gr. 4-4). 50.50 *(978-1-61511-159-6(X),* PowerKids Pr.) Rosen Publishing Group, Inc., The.

Otfinoski, Steven & Otfinoski, Steve. Rutherford B. Hayes. 2004. (Encyclopedia of Presidents Ser.). (ENG., Illus.). 110p. (YA). (gr. 5-9). 34.00 *(978-0-516-22866-2(8))* Scholastic Library Publishing.

Rumsch, BreAnn. Rutherford B. Hayes, 1 vol. 2009. (United States Presidents Ser.). (ENG., Illus.). 40p. (YA). (gr. 3-6). 27.07 *(978-1-60453-457-3(5))* ABDO Publishing Co.

Venezia, Mike. Rutherford B. Hayes: Nineteenth President, 1877-1881. Venezia, Mike, illus. 2006. (Getting to Know the U. S. Presidents Ser.). (Illus.). 32p. (J). (gr. 3-7). pap. 7.95 *(978-0-516-25404-3(9))*; (ENG., lib. bdg. 28.00 *(978-0-516-22624-8(X))* Scholastic Library Publishing. (Children's Pr.).

HAZARDOUS WASTES

see also Pollution

Blake, Kevin. Deadly Mine: Libby, Montana. 2017. (Eco-Disasters Ser.). (ENG.). 32p. (J). (gr. 2-7). 19.95 ***(978-1-68402-222-9(3))*** Bearport Publishing Co., Inc.

Facts on File, Inc. Staff, creator. The Hazardous Earth Set, 8-Volumes. 2008. (Hazardous Earth Ser.). (gr. 6-12). 316.00 *(978-0-8160-7828-8(9))* Facts On File, Inc.

Greeley, August. Toxic Waste: Chemical Spills in Our World. (Man-Made Disasters Ser.). 24p. 2009. (gr. 3-3). 42.50 *(978-1-61514-353-5(X))* 2003. (Illus.). (J). lib. bdg. 22.60 *(978-0-8239-6483-3(3))* Rosen Publishing Group, Inc., The. (PowerKids Pr.).

Harmon, Daniel E. Jobs in Environmental Cleanup & Emergency Hazmat Response. 2010. (Green Careers Ser.). 80p. (YA). (gr. 7-12). E-Book 61.20 *(978-1-4488-0132-9(X))* Rosen Publishing Group, Inc., The.

Kallen, Stuart A. Toxic Waste. 2010. (Compact Research Ser.). 96p. (YA). (gr. 7-12). 26.95 *(978-1-60152-124-8(3))* ReferencePoint Pr., Inc.

Kiesbye, Stefan. Nuclear & Toxic Waste. 2010. (At Issue Ser.). (Illus.). 128p. (J). 34.45 *(978-0-7377-4681-5(5))*; pap. 24.45 *(978-0-7377-4682-2(3))* Cengage Gale. (Greenhaven Pr., Inc.).

Parker, Russ. Waste Management Crisis. 2009. (Planet in Crisis Ser.). 32p. (gr. 5-8). (ENG., Illus.). (J). pap. 10.00 *(978-1-4358-0683-2(2))*; (YA). lib. bdg. 25.25 *(978-1-4358-5253-2(2))* Rosen Publishing Group, Inc., The. (Rosen Reference).

Shofner, Melissa Raé. Hazardous Trash. 2017. (Unnatural Disasters Ser.). 32p. (gr. 4-5). pap. 10.50 ***(978-1-5382-0436-8(3))*** Stevens, Gareth Publishing LLLP.

HAZARDOUS WASTES—FICTION

Dunphy, Catherine. Caitlin, 1 vol. 2006. (ENG., Illus.). 184p. (YA). (gr. 5-10). 7.95 *(978-1-55028-923-7(3),* 9781550289237) Lorimer, James & Co., Ltd., Pubs. CAN. Dist: Casemate Pubs. & Bk. Distributors, LLC.

Lasky, Kathryn. Shadows in the Water. 2008. (ENG., Illus.). 224p. (J). (gr. 2-5). pap. 14.95 *(978-0-15-205874-6(5))* Houghton Mifflin Harcourt Publishing Co.

HEALTH

see also Children—Health and Hygiene; Physical Education and Training; Sanitation; Sleep

Aboff, Marcie & Lee, Sally. First Graphics: Myplate & Healthy Eating. Poling, Kyle & Swift, Gary, illus. 2011. (First Graphics: Myplate & Healthy Eating Ser.). (ENG.). 24p. (gr. 1-2). pap. 12.58 *(978-1-4296-7171-2(8))*; lib. bdg. 119.95 *(978-1-4296-6094-5(5))*; pap. 214.20 *(978-1-4296-7172-9(6))* Capstone Press of Coughlan Cos.

Abramovitz, Melissa. 12 Ways to Prevent Disease. 2017. (J). *(978-1-62143-512-9(1))* Pr. Room Editions LLC.

Abramovitz, Melissa & Smibert, Angie. 12 Ways to Prevent Disease. 2016. (Healthy Living Ser.). (ENG., Illus.). 32p. (J). pap. 9.95 *(978-1-63235-388-7(1))* Pr. Room Editions LLC.

Acosta, Jamey & Reid, Stephanie. Health & Safety, 1 vol. 2010. (Early Childhood Themes Ser.). (ENG., Illus.). 16p. (J). (gr. -1-2). pap. 6.99 *(978-1-4333-1808-5(3))*; pap. 19.99 *(978-1-4333-1809-2(1))* Shell Educational Publishing.

Acosta, Jamey & Rice, Dona. Use Your Brain, 1 vol. 2010. (Early Childhood Themes Ser.). (ENG., Illus.). 16p. (J). (gr. -1-2). pap. 6.99 *(978-1-4333-1810-8(5))*; pap. 19.99 *(978-1-4333-1811-5(3))* Shell Educational Publishing.

Adams, Jeanne. Tyler's Safe Day, Everyday Safety for Children. 2009. 24p. pap. 13.50 *(978-1-60860-465-4(9),* Eloquent Bks.) Strategic Book Publishing & Rights Agency (SBPRA).

The Adventures of MolarMan Oral Health Educational Package: MolarMan DVD in English/Spanish/ASL & Bilingual Coloring Workbook in English/Spanish. 2006. (ENG & SPA.). (J). DVD *(978-0-9791794-2-6(4))* Johnson, Gary.

Afrika, Llaila. African Holistic Health. 7th ed. 2004. 584p. pap. 18.95 *(978-1-881316-82-4(3))* A & B Distributors & Pubs. Group.

Allen, Kathy. The Horrible, Miserable Middle Ages: The Disgusting Details about Life During Medieval. 2011. (Disgusting History Ser.). (ENG.). 32p. (gr. 3-4). pap. 47.70 *(978-1-4296-6479-0(7),* Fact Finders) Capstone Press of Coughlan Cos.

—The Horrible, Miserable Middle Ages: The Disgusting Details about Life During Medieval Times. (Disgusting History Ser.). (ENG.). 32p. (gr. 3-4). 2011. pap. 8.10 *(978-1-4296-6350-2(2))* 2010. lib. bdg. 27.32 *(978-1-4296-3958-3(X))* Capstone Press of Coughlan Cos. (Fact Finders).

Allison, Linda, et al. Watch Your Mouth. 2016. (ENG., Illus.). 92p. (J). pap. 9.99 *(978-1-938463-28-0(5))* Bitingduck Pr.

Amos, Janine. Is Helen Pregnant. 2003. (Body Matters Ser.: 1). (ENG., Illus.). 32p. (YA). 19.99 *(978-1-84234-107-0(3))* Evans Brothers, Ltd. GBR. Dist: Independent Pubs. Group.

Anderson, W. M. Talking about Making Good Choices. 2010. (Healthy Living Ser.). (Illus.). 32p. (J). (gr. 3-6). lib. bdg. 26.00 *(978-1-4339-3660-9(7))* Stevens, Gareth Publishing LLLP.

Andrus, Aubre. Bathe, Buff, & Beautify: DIY Crafts & Recipes for Natural Body Care. 2017. (DIY Day Spa Ser.). (ENG.). 48p. (gr. 4-5). lib. bdg. 31.32 *(978-1-5157-3446-8(3))* Capstone Press of Coughlan Cos.

—DIY Day Spa. 2017. (DIY Day Spa Ser.). (ENG.). 48p. (gr. 4-5). 125.28 *(978-1-5157-3452-9(8))* Capstone Press of Coughlan Cos.

Anthony, Mark, et al. Gut Instinct: Diet's Missing Link. 2003. (Illus.). 216p. per. 19.95 *(978-0-9743664-0-1(4))* Leap Forward Pubns.

Antill, Sara. 10 Ways I Can Live A Healthy Life. 2012. (I Can Make a Difference Ser.). (ENG., Illus.). 24p. (J). (gr. 2-5). 22.60 *(978-1-4488-6207-8(8))*; pap. 8.25 *(978-1-4488-6373-0(2))* Rosen Publishing Group, Inc., The. (PowerKids Pr.).

April, Elyse. We Like to Eat Well. Agrell, Lewis, illus. 2010th rev. ed. 2013. (We Like To Ser.). (ENG.). 32p. pap. 9.95 *(978-1-935826-04-0(2))* Kalindi Pr.

—We Like to Eat Well/Nos Gusta Comer Bien. Agrell, Lewis, illus. 2011th alt. ed. 2011. (We Like To Ser.). (ENG.). 32p. pap. 10.95 *(978-1-935826-01-9(8))* Kalindi Pr.

ARISE Foundation & Benson, Susan. Life Skills Curriculum: ARISE Basic Health 101, Book 1. 2011. (Basic Health 101 Ser.). (ENG., Illus.). 88p. (J). (gr. 3-4). pap., wbk. ed. 14.95 *(978-1-58614-031-1(0))* Arise Foundation.

Ashenburg, Katherine. All the Dirt: A History of Getting Clean. Blake, Francis, illus. 2016. (ENG.). 108p. (J). (gr. 3-7). pap. 12.95 *(978-1-55451-789-3(3))* Annick Pr., Ltd. CAN. Dist: Publishers Group West (PGW).

Avian Flu. 2006. (Deadly Diseases & Epidemics Ser.). (Illus.). 88p. (C). (gr. 9-12). lib. bdg. 34.95 *(978-0-7910-8675-9(5),* Chelsea Hse.) Facts On File, Inc.

Ayer, Eleanor H. Everything You Need to Know about Stress. 2009. (Need to Know Library). 64p. (gr. 5-5). 58.50 *(978-1-60854-089-1(8))* Rosen Publishing Group, Inc., The.

Bailey, Megan. Healthy Behaviors. 2013. (Healthy Kids Ser.). (ENG.). 24p. (J). (gr. 1-4). 28.50 *(978-1-62323-536-9(7),* 206269) Child's World, Inc., The.

Baker, Sue. Oh Baby! Stockham, Jess, illus. 2006. (Blanket Babies Ser.). (ENG.). 12p. (J). (gr. -1-k). bds. *(978-1-904550-87-7(8))* Child's Play International Ltd.

Barraclough, Sue. Wash & Clean. 2012. (Healthy Habits Ser.). 24p. (gr. 1-3). lib. bdg. 24.25 *(978-1-59771-310-8(4))* Sea-To-Sea Pubns.

Bartone, John C., Sr. Bioterrorism Potential of Hantaan Virus with Index & Medical Analysis of New Information for Reference & Research: Index & Ana. 2003. 185p. 57.50 *(978-0-7883-3152-7(3),* 0-7883-31523) ABBE Pubs. Assn. of Washington, D.C.

Bellisario, Gina. Take a Bath! My Tips for Keeping Clean. Conger, Holli, illus. 2014. (Cloverleaf Books — My Healthy Habits Ser.). (ENG.). 24p. (gr. k-2). lib. bdg. 23.93 *(978-1-4677-1352-8(X),* Millbrook Pr.) Lerner Publishing Group.

Benchmark Education Company, LLC Staff, compiled by. Good for You! & Personal Health. 2005. spiral bd. 75.00 *(978-1-4108-5808-5(1))* Benchmark Education Co.

—Health & Human Body: Theme Set. 2006. (J). 195.00 *(978-1-4108-7108-4(8))* Benchmark Education Co.

Berger, Melvin & Berger, Gilda. Checkup. 2007. (Illus.). 32p. *(978-0-439-02448-8(X))* Scholastic, Inc.

Berry, Joy. I Love Bathtime. Regan, Dana, illus. 2010. (Teach Me About Ser.). (ENG.). 20p. (J). (gr. k — 1). pap. 5.99 *(978-1-60577-013-0(2))* Berry, Joy Enterprises.

—I Love Being Healthy. Regan, Dana, illus. 2010. (Teach Me About Ser.). (ENG.). 20p. (J). (gr. k — 1). pap. 5.99 *(978-1-60577-005-5(1))* Berry, Joy Enterprises.

—Teach Me about Special Times Nutshell Pack. 2009. (ENG.). 180p. (J). (gr. k — 1). 39.95 *(978-1-60577-035-2(3))* Berry, Joy Enterprises.

Berry, Joy Wilt. A Book about Being Messy. 2005. (Illus.). (J). *(978-0-7172-8577-8(4))* Scholastic, Inc.

Blackburn, Abby. My Little Blue Helmet. 2012. 24p. pap. 14.93 *(978-1-4669-7006-9(5))* Trafford Publishing.

Bodden, Valerie. Dairy. 2015. (J). *(978-1-60818-508-5(7),* Creative Education) Creative Co., The.

—Healthy Plates: Dairy. 2015. (Healthy Plates Ser.). (ENG.). 24p. (J). (gr. 1-3). pap. 9.99 *(978-1-62832-108-1(3),* Creative Paperbacks) Creative Co., The.

Booth. Health Care Science Technology: Career Foundations: Student Motivation. 2004. (gr. 6-12). 208.00 *(978-0-07-829742-7(7))* Glencoe/McGraw-Hill.

Boothroyd, Jennifer. Taste Something New! Giving Different Foods a Try. 2016. (Lightning Bolt Books — Healthy Eating Ser.). (ENG., Illus.). 32p. (J). (gr. 1-3). 26.65 *(978-1-4677-9472-5(4),* Lerner Pubns.) Lerner Publishing Group.

Borgert-Spaniol, Megan. Healthy Eating. 2012. (Eating Right with Myplate Ser.). (ENG., Illus.). 24p. (J). (gr. k-3). lib. bdg. 25.95 *(978-1-60014-757-9(7),* Blastoff! Readers) Bellwether Media.

Boyd, Nicole. Clean & Healthy. 2008. (Real Readers - Upper Emergent Ser.). (ENG., Illus.). 12p. (gr. 1-2). pap. 5.90 *(978-0-8239-8204-2(1))* Rosen Publishing Group, Inc., The.

A Boy's Guide to Growing up - Booklet, 10 per packet. 2005. (Illus.). (J). 63.95 *(978-1-55942-211-6(4))* Witcher Productions.

Bradley, Doug. Needs & Wants. 2012. (InfoMax Readers Ser.). (ENG., Illus.). 16 pp.p. (J). (gr. k-1). pap. 7.00 *(978-1-4488-8947-1(2),* Rosen Classroom) Rosen Publishing Group, Inc., The.

Braun, Eric. Taking Action to Improve People's Health. 2016. (Who's Changing the World? Ser.). (ENG., Illus.). 48p. (J). (gr. 4-6). 33.32 *(978-1-4677-9395-7(7))*; 50.65 *(978-1-4677-9668-2(9),* Lerner Pubns.) Lerner Publishing Group.

Bringsvaerd, Tor Age. When Two Get Up. Soli, Tina, illus. 2009. (When Two Ser.). 36p. (J). (gr. -1-1). 14.95 *(978-0-9815761-4-5(1))* Mackenzie Smiles, LLC.

Bronson, Mary H., et al. Glencoe la Salud. 10th ed. 2004. (Glencoe Health Ser.). (SPA., Illus.). 832p. (gr. 9-12). 114.80 *(978-0-07-862021-8(X),* 007862021X) McGraw-Hill Higher Education.

—Health. 10th ed. 2004. (Glencoe Health Ser.). (ENG., Illus.). 832p. (gr. 9-12). stu. ed. 108.20 *(978-0-07-861211-4(X),* 007861211X) SRA/McGraw-Hill.

—La Salud de los Jóvenes: Curso 2. 3rd ed. 2004. (Teen Health Ser.). (SPA., Illus.). 480p. (gr. 7-8). 89.88 *(978-0-07-861899-4(1),* 0078618991) McGraw-Hill Higher Education.

—Teen Health. 6th ed. 2004. (Teen Health Ser.). (ENG., Illus.). 319p. (gr. 6-8). stu. ed. 85.68 *(978-0-07-861095-0(8),* 0078610958) McGraw-Hill Education.

Brownjohn, Emma. Yes I Can! Be Healthy. Brownjohn, Emma, illus. 2011. (Yes I Can! Ser.). (ENG., Illus.). 18p. (J). (gr. -1-k). 12.99 *(978-1-85707-734-6(2))* Tango Bks. GBR. Dist: Independent Pubs. Group.

Busse, Gregory D. Morphine. Triggle, David J., ed. 2006. (Drugs Ser.). (Illus.). 104p. (C). (gr. 9-12). lib. bdg. 30.00 *(978-0-7910-8551-6(1),* Chelsea Hse.) Facts On File, Inc.

Cain, Marie Mowery. For Your Health. 2013. (Big Books, Blue Ser.). (ENG & SPA., Illus.). 16p. pap. 33.00 *(978-1-59246-003-8(8))* Big Books, by George!

Can Buildings Make You Sick? 2004. (Nova Ser.). (gr. 7-18). 19.95 *(978-1-57807-915-5(2),* WG2217) WGBH Boston Video.

Canino, Kate. Maintaining a Healthy Weight. 2010. (Healthy Habits Ser.). (Illus.). 64p. (YA). (gr. 5-8). pap. 12.95 *(978-1-4488-0609-6(7))*; lib. bdg. 31.95 *(978-1-4358-9439-6(1))* Rosen Publishing Group, Inc., The. (Rosen Reference).

Cardenas, Ernesto A. Healthy Habits. 2009. pap. 4.95 *(978-1-60698-082-8(3))* Milo Educational Bks. & Resources.

—Vegetables for Me! 2009. 19.95 *(978-1-60698-017-0(3))*; pap. 3.95 *(978-1-60698-015-6(7))* Milo Educational Bks. & Resources.

Cassidy, Albert, Jr. & Bennedetti, Eric. The Amazing Adventures of Dr. Snappy & Sam: Dr. Snappy vs. Subluxor. Romanchick, Jennifer, ed. Cassidy, Albert, Jr., illus. 2005. (Illus.). 16p. (J). 9.99 *(978-0-9770527-0-7(2))* All Health Chiropractic Ctrs. Inc.

Cavanagh, Cathy May. Handi-Bear Cares. 2010. 36p. 18.99 *(978-1-4490-9467-6(8))* AuthorHouse.

Cherry Lake Publishing Staff, compiled by. Heathly for Life. 2007. 32p. lib. bdg. 159.60 *(978-1-60279-105-3(8),* 200028) Cherry Lake Publishing.

Christopher, Garrett. Your Amazing Senses: A Content Area Reader-health. 2005. (Emergent (Prek-2) Health Package Ser.). 12p. (gr. k-2). 25.20 *(978-0-8215-7827-8(8))* Sadlier, William H. Inc.

Cicola, Amanda, et al. Health & Safety 1: Gym Class; Shopping for Lunch; Good for You; My Happy Heart; Just Like Me; Staying Safe; Always Brush Your Teeth; A Visit to the Doctor, 8 bks. Simon, Sue A. et al, illus. 2005. (ENG.). 8p. (J). pap. 120.00 *(978-1-893986-26-8(8))* Keep Bks.

Clean & Healthy All Day Long: Limpieza y Salud Todo el Dia Series. 2003. (Limpieza y Salud Todo el Dia Ser.). (Illus.). (J). 96.00 *(978-0-8239-6908-1(8),* Editorial Buenas Letras) Rosen Publishing Group, Inc., The.

Cleland, Jo. Clean Hands, Dirty Hands. 2012. (ENG.). 24p. (gr. k-2). pap. 8.95 *(978-1-61810-213-3(3))* Rourke Educational Media.

Coan, Sharon. Bueno para Mí - Comida Saludable (Good for Me - Healthy Food) 2016. (TIME for KIDS(r) Nonfiction Readers Ser.). (SPA.). 12p. (J). (gr. k-k). 4.99 *(978-1-4938-3032-9(5))* Teacher Created Materials, Inc.

—Good for Me: Healthy Food. 2015. (TIME for KIDS(r) Nonfiction Readers Ser.). (ENG., Illus.). 12p. (gr. k-k). 4.99 *(978-1-4938-2151-8(2))* Teacher Created Materials, Inc.

—Good for Me: Play & Exercise. 2015. (TIME for KIDS(r) Nonfiction Readers Ser.). (ENG., Illus.). 12p. (gr. k-k). 4.99 *(978-1-4938-2152-5(0))* Teacher Created Materials, Inc.

Compton, Leanne, et al. Jump Start 7 & 8: Health & Physical Education. 2007. 336p. pap. 41.00 incl. cd-rom *(978-0-521-70156-3(2))* Cambridge Univ. Pr.

Conklin, Wendy. Safe & Sound: Our Health. 2017. (J). pap. 9.99 ***(978-1-4938-3629-1(3))*** Teacher Created Materials, Inc.

—Safe & Sound: Our Health. 2017. (Time for Kids Nonfiction Readers Ser.). lib. bdg. 20.85 ***(978-0-606-40294-1(2))*** Turtleback Bks.

Connolly, Lorraine. Bad, Bad Germs - Stay Away!!! 2010. 20p. pap. 10.95 *(978-1-4490-4696-5(7))* AuthorHouse.

Conrad, David. Burps, Boogers, & Other Body Functions, 1 vol. 2011. (Health & Your Body Ser.). (ENG.). 24p. (gr. k-1). pap. 7.29 *(978-1-4296-7125-5(4))*; pap. 41.70 *(978-1-4296-7131-6(9))*; lib. bdg. 26.65 *(978-1-4296-6808-8(3))* Capstone Press of Coughlan Cos. (Pebble Plus).

Conrad, Lauren, et al. Beauty. 2012. (ENG., Illus.). 288p. (YA). (gr. 9). 21.99 *(978-0-06-212845-4(0))* HarperCollins Pubs.

Cook, David Fuller, compiled by. A Balanced Approach to Long Life & Vitality, Signature Edition: As Used in Fitness, Wellness, Clinical Weight Loss, & Cardiac Rehabilitation Programs. 2003. (Illus.). 80p. spiral bd. 31.95 *(978-0-9741629-0-4(6))* Cook, David.

Cook, David Fuller, ed. A Balanced Approach to Long Life & Vitality for Christians: As Used in Fitness, Wellness, Clinical Weight Loss, & Cardiac Rehabilitation Programs. 2003. (Illus.). 105p. spiral bd. 33.95 *(978-0-9741629-4-2(9))* Cook, David.

Coping in a Changing World, 6 bks., Set. Incl. Avian Flu. Orr, Tamra B. (Illus.). 2007. lib. bdg. 34.60 *(978-1-4042-0950-3(6))*; Body Piercing & Tattooing: The Hidden Dangers of Body Art. Sawyer, Sarah. 2006. lib. bdg. 34.60 *(978-1-4042-0947-3(6))*; HIV & AIDS. Johanson, Paula. (Illus.). 2007. lib. bdg. 34.60 *(978-1-4042-0948-0(4))*; Obesity. Harmon, Daniel E. 2006. lib. bdg. 34.60 *(978-1-4042-0949-7(2))*; Stress. Bickerstaff, Linda. (Illus.). 2007. lib. bdg. 34.60 *(978-1-4042-0951-0(4))*; Suicide. Giddens, Sandra. 2006. lib. bdg. 34.60 *(978-1-4042-0952-7(2))*; 112p. (YA). (gr. 7-12). 2007. Set lib. bdg. 191.70 *(978-1-4042-1063-9(6))* Rosen Publishing Group, Inc., The.

Cox, Judith. The Wellness Tree. Rogers, Denny, illus. 2003. 32p. (J). (gr. k-4). pap. 2.95 *(978-1-878044-35-8(4))* Mayhaven Publishing, Inc.

Crabtree Publishing, creator. Slim Goodbody's Lighten Up. 2008. (ENG.). 32p. (J). pap. *(978-0-7787-3929-6(5))* Crabtree Publishing Co.

Crewe, Sabrina. In the Home. 2010. (Under the Microscope Ser.). 32p. (gr. 2-4). 30.00 *(978-1-60413-823-8(8),* Chelsea Clubhouse) Facts On File, Inc.

Crockett, Kyle A. Managing Your Weight with Nutrition. Borus, Joshua, ed. 2013. (Understanding Nutrition: a Gateway to Physical & Mental Health Ser.: 11). (Illus.). 48p. (J). (gr. 5-18). 19.95 *(978-1-4222-2881-4(9))* Mason Crest.

—Nutrition & Your Future. Borus, Joshua, ed. 2013. (Understanding Nutrition: a Gateway to Physical & Mental Health Ser.: 11). (Illus.). 48p. (J). (gr. 5-18). 19.95 *(978-1-4222-2885-2(1))* Mason Crest.

—Nutrition for Achievement in Sports & Academics. Borus, Joshua, ed. 2013. (Understanding Nutrition: a Gateway to Physical & Mental Health Ser.). (Illus.). 48p. (J). (gr. 5-18). pap. 9.95 *(978-1-4222-2990-3(4))*; 19.95 *(978-1-4222-2884-5(3))* Mason Crest.

Dahl, Michael. Hello Genius, 4 vols., Set. Vidal, Oriol, illus. Incl. Bunny Eats Lunch. bds. 7.99 *(978-1-4048-5728-5(1))*; Duck Goes Potty. bds. 7.99 *(978-1-4048-5726-1(5))*; Pig Takes a Bath. bds. 7.99 *(978-1-4048-5729-2(X))*; Pony Brushes His Teeth. bds. 7.99 *(978-1-4048-5727-8(3))*; (gr. 1-2). 2010. (Hello Genius Ser.). (ENG., Illus.). 20p. 2009. Set bds. 31.96 *(978-1-4048-6198-5(X))* Picture Window Bks.

Daisy Duck & her Bath. 2004. (Play Pals Ser.). (Illus.). 12p. (J). bds. *(978-1-84229-643-1(4))* Top That! Publishing PLC.

Danielsdottir, Sigrun. Your Body Is Awesome: Body Respect for Children. Bjarkadottir, Björk, illus. 2014. (ENG.). 36p. (J). 17.95 *(978-1-84819-228-7(2),* 2674, Singing Dragon) Kingsley, Jessica Pubs. GBR. Dist: Macmillan Distribution Ltd.

—Your Body Is Brilliant: Body Respect for Children. Bjarkdottir, Bjork, illus. 2014. (ENG.). 36p. (J). 17.95 *(978-1-84819-221-8(5),* 2672, Singing Dragon) Kingsley, Jessica Pubs. GBR. Dist: Macmillan Distribution Ltd.

Degrassi Health: Educational Set. 2004. (Degrassi Junior High Ser.). (gr. 7-18). 99.95 *(978-1-57807-221-7(2),* WG675K) WGBH Boston Video.

Derkazarian, Susan. You Have Head Lice! 2005. (Rookie Read-About Health Ser.). (ENG., Illus.). 32p. (J). (gr. k-2). per. 5.95 *(978-0-516-27920-6(3))*; 20.50 *(978-0-516-25879-9(6))* Scholastic Library Publishing. (Children's Pr.).

Desrocher, Jack, illus. Health Zone, 6 vols., Set. Incl. Eat Right! How You Can Make Good Food Choices. Doeden, Matt. lib. bdg. 30.60 *(978-0-8225-7552-8(3))*; Keep Your Cool! What You Should Know about Stress. Leder, Jane Mersky & Donovan, Sandy. lib. bdg. 30.60 *(978-0-8225-7555-9(8))*; Stay Clear! What You Should Know about Skin Care. Donovan, Sandy. lib. bdg. 30.60 *(978-0-8225-7550-4(7))*; Stay Fit! How You Can Get in Shape. Doeden, Matt. (YA). lib. bdg. 30.60 *(978-0-8225-7553-5(1))*; Stay Safe! How You Can Keep Out of Harm's Way. Nelson, Sara Kirsten. lib. bdg. 30.60 *(978-0-8225-7551-1(5))*; Take a Stand! What You Can Do about Bullying. Golus, Carrie. (YA). lib. bdg. 30.60 *(978-0-8225-7554-2(X))*; (Illus.). 64p. (gr. 4-7). 2008. 2008. Set lib. bdg. 183.60 *(978-0-8225-7549-8(3))* Lerner Publishing Group.

Dickmann, Nancy. Focus on Health. 2016. (Focus on Health Ser.). (ENG.). 32p. (gr. 3-4). 218.56 *(978-1-4914-8256-8(7),* Fact Finders) Capstone Press of Coughlan Cos.

Donohue, Laurie. To the Core: Granola Crumble. 2012. (ENG.). 30p. (J). pap. 14.95 *(978-1-4327-9475-0(2))* Outskirts Pr., Inc.

Donovan, Sandy. Keep Your Cool! What You Should Know about Stress. 2009. pap. 52.95 *(978-0-7613-4685-2(6))* Lerner Publishing Group.

Dorling Kindersley Publishing Staff. Splish! Splash! 2012. (Baby Touch & Feel Ser.). (ENG., Illus.). 14p. (J). (gr. -1 — 1). bds. 5.99 *(978-1-4654-0162-5(8),* DK Children) Dorling Kindersley Publishing, Inc.

Duckworth, Katie. Health. 2004. (Children's Rights Ser.). (J). lib. bdg. 27.10 *(978-1-58340-420-1(1))* Black Rabbit Bks.

Durant, Penny Raife. Sniffles, Sneezes, Hiccups, & Coughs: Level 2. 2005. (DK Readers Ser.). (ENG., Illus.). 32p. (J). (gr. 1-3). pap. 3.99 *(978-0-7566-1106-4(7),* DK Children) Dorling Kindersley Publishing, Inc.

Durrie, Karen. Health. 2011. (J). 27.13 *(978-1-61690-950-5(1))* Weigl Pubs., Inc.

—Health: Arabic-English Bilingual Edition. 2016. (Community Helpers Ser.). (ENG.). (J). (gr. -1-3). 29.99 ***(978-1-61913-903-9(0))*** Weigl Pubs., Inc.

Durrie, Karen. Salud. 2012. (SPA.). (J). *(978-1-61913-210-8(9))* Weigl Pubs., Inc.

Dyer, Janice. Get into Smart Snacks. 2017. (Illus.). 32p. (J). ***(978-0-7787-3642-4(3))*** Crabtree Publishing Co.

E. Z. Writer. I Think I'll Be a Doctor: I Know What to Do. 2012. 24p. pap. 17.99 *(978-1-4685-8016-7(7))* AuthorHouse.

Ebner, Aviva. Health Science Experiments. 2011. (Experiments for Future Scientists Ser.). (Illus.). 160p. (gr. 5-8). 35.00 *(978-1-60413-853-5(X))* Facts On File, Inc.

Edwards, Hazel & Alexander, Goldie. Talking about Illnesses. 2010. (Healthy Living Ser.). (Illus.). 32p. (YA). (gr. 3-6). lib. bdg. 26.00 *(978-1-4339-3657-9(7))* Stevens, Gareth Publishing LLLP.

—Talking about Your Weight. 2010. (Healthy Living Ser.). (Illus.). 32p. (YA). (gr. 3-6). lib. bdg. 26.00 *(978-1-4339-3655-5(0))* Stevens, Gareth Publishing LLLP.

Emerson, Charles P. & Betts, George Herbert. Living at Our Best, Book: Habits of Right Living Series. 2011. 338p. 50.95 *(978-1-258-08164-5(4))* Literary Licensing, LLC.

Emerson, Charles Phillips, et al. Habits for Health, Book: Habits of Right Living Series. 2011. 266p. 47.95 *(978-1-258-07944-4(5))* Literary Licensing, LLC.

Emmer, Rick. Virus Hunter. 2005. (Weird Careers in Science Ser.). (Illus.). 88p. (gr. 5-8). lib. bdg. 25.00 *(978-0-7910-8705-3(0),* Chelsea Hse.) Facts On File, Inc.

Esherick, Joan. Managing Stress. Bridgemohan, Carolyn & Forman, Sara, eds. 2013. (Young Adult's Guide to the Science of Health Ser.: 15). 128p. (J). (gr. 7-18). 24.95 *(978-1-4222-2813-5(4));* (Illus.). pap. 14.95 *(978-1-4222-3002-2(3))* Mason Crest.

Etingoff, Kim. Building a Healthy Diet with the 5 Food Groups. Prock, Lisa Albers, ed. 2014. (On My Plate Ser.: 6). 48p. (J). (gr. 5-18). 20.95 *(978-1-4222-3095-4(3))* Mason Crest.

—Diet Myths: Sorting Through the Hype. Borus, Joshua, ed. 2013. (Understanding Nutrition: a Gateway to Physical & Mental Health Ser.: 11). (Illus.). 48p. (J). (gr. 5-18). 19.95 *(978-1-4222-2876-0(2))* Mason Crest.

—Healthy Alternatives to Sweets & Snacks. Borus, Joshua, ed. 2013. (Understanding Nutrition: a Gateway to Physical & Mental Health Ser.). (Illus.). 48p. (J). (gr. 5-18). pap. 9.95 *(978-1-4222-2992-7(0))* Mason Crest.

—Healthy Fast Foods. Borus, Joshua, ed. 2013. (Understanding Nutrition: a Gateway to Physical & Mental Health Ser.). (Illus.). 48p. (J). (gr. 5-18). pap. 9.95 *(978-1-4222-2988-0(2));* 19.95 *(978-1-4222-2879-1(7))* Mason Crest.

Farnsworth, Vesta J. The House We Live in or the Making of the Body. 2004. reprint ed. pap. 24.95 *(978-1-4179-2036-5(X))* Kessinger Publishing, LLC.

Federer, Jessica Joy. Bobby Bacteria & Friends: Inside UR Body Books Presents. l.t. ed. 2005. (Illus.). 80p. (J). bds. 9.99 *(978-0-9753455-3-5(2))* Amerisearch, Inc.

Ferraro, Bonita. Rules All Around: A Content Area Reader-health. 2005. (Emergent (Prek-2) Health Package Ser.). 12p. (gr. k-2). 25.20 *(978-0-8215-7829-2(4))* Sadlier, William H. Inc.

Fettig, Jamie. The Creator's Manual for Your Body. 2004. per. 14.95 *(978-0-9761555-0-8(8),* 1-773-665-4005) Bazuji Publishing LLC.

Focus on Health. 2015. (Focus on Health Ser.). (ENG.). 32p. (gr. 3-4). 109.28 *(978-1-4914-6801-2(7));* pap. 31.80 *(978-1-4914-7324-5(X))* Capstone Press of Coughlan Cos. (Fact Finders).

Fonda, Jane. Being a Teen: Everything Teen Girls & Boys Should Know about Relationships, Sex, Love, Health, Identity & More. 2014. (ENG., Illus.). 288p. (J). pap. 17.00 *(978-0-8129-7861-2(7),* Random Hse. Trade Paperbacks) Random House Publishing Group.

—Being a Teen: Everything Teen Girls & Boys Should Know about Relationships, Sex, Love, Health, Identity & More. 2014. lib. bdg. 29.40 *(978-0-606-35596-4(0))* Turtleback Bks.

Fox, Nancy. Hide & Seek, No Ticks Please. Seward, Daniel, illus. 2014. (ENG.). 42p. (gr. k-6). pap. 9.95 *(978-1-61448-705-0(7))* Morgan James Publishing.

Foy, Debbie. Bubbles, Tub, Have a Scrub! 2016. (All by Myself Ser.). (ENG., Illus.). 20p. (J). (gr. -1-k). pap. 6.99 *(978-0-7502-9615-1(1),* Wayland) Hachette Children's Group GBR. Dist: Hachette Bk. Group.

Freese, Joan. Tables & Graphs of Healthy Things. 2007. (Math in Our World Ser.). 24p. (gr. 1-2). pap. 8.15 *(978-0-8368-8480-7(9));* (Illus.). lib. bdg. 22.00 *(978-0-8368-8471-5(X))* Stevens, Gareth Publishing LLLP. (Weekly Reader Leveled Readers).

Fromer, Liza & Gerstein, Francine. My Healthy Body. Weissmann, Joe, illus. 2012. (Body Works). (ENG.). 24p. (J). (gr. 1-4). 12.95 *(978-1-77049-312-4(3),* Tundra Bks.) Tundra Bks. CAN. Dist: Penguin Random Hse. LLC.

Furgang, Kathy. Having Healthful Habits & Tener hábitos Sanos: 6 English, 6 Spanish Adaptations. 2011. (ENG & SPA.). (J). 97.00 net. *(978-1-4108-5710-1(7))* Benchmark Education Co.

Gardner, Jane P. Health Science, Vol. 11. Lewin, Russ, ed. 2015. (Science 24/7 Ser.). (Illus.). 48p. (J). (gr. 5). 20.95 *(978-1-4222-3411-2(8))* Mason Crest.

Geis, Patricia. Let's Wash Up! Folch, Sergio, illus. 2009. (Good Habits with Coco & Tula Ser.). 16p. (J). (gr. -1-k). bds. 11.40 *(978-1-60754-410-4(5))* Windmill Bks.

Giddens, Sandra. Making Smart Choices about Food, Nutrition, & Lifestyle. 2009. (Making Smart Choices Ser.). 48p. (gr. 5-5). 53.00 *(978-1-61514-339-9(4),* Rosen Reference) Rosen Publishing Group, Inc., The.

Giddens, Sandra & Giddens, Owen. Making Smart Choices about Food, Nutrition, & Lifestyle. 2008. (Making Smart Choices Ser.). (Illus.). 48p. (YA). (gr. 5-9). lib. bdg. 29.25 *(978-1-4042-1389-0(9))* Rosen Publishing Group, Inc., The.

Gitlin, Marty. The Totally Gross History of Medieval Europe, 01 vols., 1. 2016. (Totally Gross History Ser.). (ENG.). 48p. (J). pap. 11.75 *(978-1-4994-3764-5(1),* Rosen Central) Rosen Publishing Group, Inc., The.

Gleisner, Jenna Lee. My Body Needs Food. 2015. (Healthy Me Ser.). (Illus.). 24p. (J). 27.10 *(978-1-60753-587-4(4))* Amicus Publishing.

—My Body Needs Rest. 2015. (Healthy Me Ser.). (Illus.). 24p. (J). 27.10 *(978-1-60753-588-1(2))* Amicus Publishing.

—My Body Needs to Be Clean. 2015. (Healthy Me Ser.). (Illus.). 24p. (J). 27.10 *(978-1-60753-589-8(0))* Amicus Publishing.

Glencoe McGraw-Hill Staff, et al. Glencoe Health, 3 vols. 9th ed. 2003. (Glencoe Health Ser.). (ENG.). 848p. (gr. 9-12). stu. ed. 111.20 *(978-0-07-826326-2(3),* 0078263263) McGraw-Hill Higher Education.

Glover, David & Glover, Penny. Staying Healthy. 2005. (Humans & Animals Ser.). (Illus.). 30p. (J). (gr. 2-4). lib. bdg. 27.10 *(978-1-58340-693-9(X))* Black Rabbit Bks.

Gogerly, Liz. Keeping Clean. Gordon, Mike, illus. 2008. (Looking after Me Ser.). (ENG.). 32p. (J). (gr. -1-3). pap. *(978-0-7787-4119-0(2));* lib. bdg. *(978-0-7787-4112-1(5))* Crabtree Publishing Co.

Goldsmith, Mike & Chancellor, Deborah. Caring for Our Bodies. 2009. (Now We Know About... Ser.). (ENG., Illus.). 24p. (J). (gr. k-3). pap. *(978-0-7787-4735-2(2));* lib. bdg. *(978-0-7787-4718-5(2))* Crabtree Publishing Co.

Goodacre, Sonia, et al. Cambridge VCE Health & Human Development Units 3 & 4 Bundle. 2nd ed. 2013. (ENG.). pap. *(978-1-107-68809-4(4))* Cambridge Univ. Pr.

Goodbody, Slim. Avoiding Injuries. McGinnis, Ben, illus. Pinchbeck, Chris, photos by. 2007. (Slim Goodbody Good Health Guides). 32p. (J). (gr. 2-6). lib. bdg. 26.00 *(978-0-8368-7739-7(X),* Gareth Stevens Learning Library) Stevens, Gareth Publishing LLLP.

—Keeping Clean. McGinnis, Ben, illus. Pinchbeck, Chris, photos by. 2007. (Slim Goodbody Good Health Guides). 32p. (J). (gr. 2-6). lib. bdg. 26.00 *(978-0-8368-7742-7(X),* Gareth Stevens Learning Library) Stevens, Gareth Publishing LLLP.

Gravelle, Karen & Gravelle, Jennifer. The Period Book: A Girl's Guide to Growing Up. Palen, Debbie, illus. 2017. (ENG.). 144p. (J). pap. 13.99 *(978-1-61963-662-0(X),* 9781619636620, Bloomsbury USA Childrens) Bloomsbury Publishing USA.

Gray, Susan H. Animals Helping to Detect Diseases. 2015. (ENG.). 48p. (J). pap. 6.95 *(978-0-531-21288-2(2),* Orchard Bks.) Scholastic Library Publishing.

Greathouse, Lisa. Eat Healthy, 1 vol. 2011. (Science Readers: a Closer Look Ser.). (ENG., Illus.). 32p. (J). (gr. 3-3). pap. 8.99 *(978-1-4333-3087-2(3))* Teacher Created Materials, Inc.

—Healthy Habits, Healthy You, 1 vol. 2011. (Science Readers: a Closer Look Ser.). (ENG., Illus.). 32p. (J). (gr. 3-3). pap. 8.99 *(978-1-4333-3091-9(1))* Teacher Created Materials, Inc.

—Make It Healthy, 1 vol. 2011. (Science Readers: a Closer Look Ser.). (ENG.). 32p. (J). (gr. 2-2). pap. 8.99 *(978-1-4333-3088-9(1))* Teacher Created Materials, Inc.

Green, Tammy L., et al. Ruby Learns about the World of Wellness. 2005. (ENG., Illus.). 88p. (gr. k-5). pap., stu. ed. 12.00 *(978-0-7360-5756-1(0))* Human Kinetics Pubs.

Green, Tim. Trainer Tim's Camp Fitness. 2012. 40p. pap. 20.99 *(978-1-4772-6052-4(8))* AuthorHouse.

—Trainer Tim's down on the Farm. 2012. 32p. pap. 20.99 *(978-1-4772-9720-9(0))* AuthorHouse.

—Trainer Tim's Gym. 2012. 36p. pap. 20.99 *(978-1-4685-6689-5(X))* AuthorHouse.

—Trainer Tim's Troubled Friend. 2012. 32p. pap. 19.99 *(978-1-4772-0724-6(4))* AuthorHouse.

Greenhaven Press Editors. Mrsa. Williams, Mary E., ed. 2012. (Perspectives on Diseases & Disorders Ser.). (ENG., Illus.). 144p. (gr. 10-12). lib. bdg. 38.95 *(978-0-7377-5779-8(5),* Greenhaven Pr., Inc.) Cengage Gale.

Greenhaven Press Editors & Haugen, David. Health Care Legislation. 2012. (At Issue Ser.). (ENG.). 128p. (gr. 10-12). pap. 27.80 *(978-0-7377-5577-0(6),* Greenhaven Pr., Inc.); lib. bdg. 39.40 *(978-0-7377-5576-3(8))* Cengage Gale.

Greenhaven Press Staff. What Should We Eat? Greenhaven Press, ed. 2016. (At Issue Ser.). (ENG.). 128p. (gr. 10-12). 39.40 *(978-0-7377-7390-3(1),* Greenhaven Pr., Inc.) Cengage Gale.

Griffiths, Andy. What Body Part Is That? A Wacky Guide to the Funniest, Weirdest, & Most Disgustingest Parts of Your Body. Denton, Terry, illus. 2012. (ENG.). 192p. (J). (gr. 3-7). 12.99 *(978-0-312-36790-9(2),* 9780312367909) Feiwel & Friends.

Grow up Healthy. (J). (gr. -1-2). 23.99 *(978-0-8136-4246-8(9))* Modern Curriculum Pr.

Guerber, Hélène Adeline. Yourself & Your House Wonderful. 2012. 330p. pap. 13.50 *(978-1-936639-24-3(6))* St. Augustine Academy Pr.

Guys' Guides. 2005. (Illus.). 48p. (gr. 5-8). lib. bdg. 95.80 *(978-0-8239-4094-3(2))* Rosen Publishing Group, Inc., The.

Guys' Guides, 6 bks. Incl. Real Deal: A Guy's Guide to Being a Guy. Roberts, Jeremy. (YA). lib. bdg. 29.25 *(978-0-8239-3104-0(8),* GUREDE); Stay Cool: A Guy's Guide to Handling Conflict. Hayhurst, Chris. (YA). lib. bdg. 29.25 *(978-0-8239-3159-0(5),* GUSTCO); You Ought to Know: A Guy's Guide to Sex. Kelly, Bill. (J). lib. bdg. 29.25 *(978-0-8239-3084-5(X),* GUYOSH); 48p. (gr. 5-8). 2005. (Illus.). Set lib. bdg. 107.70 o.p. *(978-0-8239-9088-7(5),* GUGUID, Rosen Reference) Rosen Publishing Group, Inc., The.

H Is for Hygiene: H Is for Hope Book Series. 2007. (Illus.). (J). 8.00 *(978-0-9794377-0-0(9))* Turngroup Technologies, LLC.

Hammond, Veronica. Wash Those Hands. 2009. 20p. pap. 9.45 *(978-1-4269-1590-1(X))* Trafford Publishing.

Hand, Carol. 12 Healthy Habits for Life. 2017. (J). *(978-1-62143-506-8(7))* Pr. Room Editions LLC.

Hand, Carol & Mangor, Jodie. 12 Healthy Habits for Life. 2016. (Healthy Living Ser.). (ENG., Illus.). 32p. (J). pap. 9.95 *(978-1-63235-382-5(2))* Pr. Room Editions LLC.

Harcourt School Publishers Staff. Be Active! Program: Health & Fitness. 4th ed. 2004. (Illus.). (gr. k-2). 311.60 *(978-0-15-341407-7(3));* (gr. 3-6). 314.90 *(978-0-15-341408-4(1))* Harcourt Schl. Pubs.

—Health & Fitness: Activity Book. 4th ed. 2003. (gr. -1). pap., act. bk. ed. 4.80 *(978-0-15-341170-0(8))* Harcourt Schl. Pubs.

—Health & Fitness: Resources for Spanish Speakers. 4th ed. 2004. (SPA.). (gr. 1). pap. 20.00 *(978-0-15-341180-9(5));* (gr. 2). pap. 20.00 *(978-0-15-341181-6(3));* (gr. 3). pap. 25.40 *(978-0-15-341182-3(1));* (gr. 4). pap. 25.40 *(978-0-15-341183-0(X));* (gr. 5). pap. 25.40 *(978-0-15-341184-7(8));* (gr. 6). pap. 25.40 *(978-0-15-341185-4(6))* Harcourt Schl. Pubs.

—Health & Fitness 5-Pack: Activity Book. 4th ed. 2003. (gr. -1). act. bk. ed. 23.70 *(978-0-15-341171-7(6))* Harcourt Schl. Pubs.

—Health & Fitness, Grade 3-6. 4th ed. 2003. pap., tchr. ed. 88.20 *(978-0-15-341101-4(5))* Harcourt Schl. Pubs.

—Health & Fitness, Grade K-2. 4th ed. 2003. pap., tchr. ed. 84.80 *(978-0-15-341100-7(7))* Harcourt Schl. Pubs.

Hardyman, Robyn. Healthy Bodies. 2012. (Healthy & Happy Ser.). (Illus.). 32p. (J). (gr. 1-4). lib. bdg. 26.50 *(978-1-4488-5274-1(9))* Rosen Publishing Group, Inc., The.

Harris, Pj. Fat, Fat, What's Wrong with That? The Importance of Diet & Exercise. 2009. 36p. pap. 15.49 *(978-1-4490-2345-4(2))* AuthorHouse.

Hassan, Masood. Madeline & Friends: Fruits & Veggies vs Candy. Lady Josephine, illus. 2010. *(978-0-9812600-6-8(3))* Sapphira Pubns.

Hawkins, Frank C. & Laube, Greta L. B. The Book of Bad Habits for Young (and Not So Young!) Men & Women: How to Chuck the Worst & Turn the Rest to Your Advantage. Hong, Richard, illus. 2010. (ENG.). 148p. (J). (gr. 7). pap. 12.95 *(978-0-9793219-3-1(X))* Big Book Pr., LLC.

Hayes, Marilyn. Jumbo Health Yearbook: Grade 3. (Jumbo Health Ser.). 96p. (J). (gr. 3). 15.95 *(978-0-8209-0063-6(X),* B JHY 3) ESP, Inc.

—Jumbo Health Yearbook: Grade 4. (Jumbo Health Ser.). 96p. (J). (gr. 4). 15.95 *(978-0-8209-0064-3(8),* B JHY 4) ESP, Inc.

Head, Honor. Healthy Eating. 2013. (Let's Read & Talk about Ser.). (Illus.). 32p. (gr. 2-5). 28.50 *(978-1-59771-394-8(5))* Sea-To-Sea Pubns.

—Keeping Clean. 2013. (Let's Read & Talk about Ser.). (Illus.). 32p. (J). (gr. 2-5). 28.50 *(978-1-59771-395-5(3))* Sea-To-Sea Pubns.

Health. 2011. (New Discovering Careers for Your Future Ser.). (Illus.). 128p. (gr. 4-9). 24.95 *(978-0-8160-8051-9(8),* Ferguson Publishing Co.) Facts On File, Inc.

Health Alert, 5 bks., Group 2. Incl. Allergies. Hicks, Terry Allan. (YA). (gr. 4-7). 2005. lib. bdg. 32.79 *(978-0-7614-1918-1(7));* Common Cold. Hicks, Terry Allan. (J). (gr. 3-7). 2006. lib. bdg. 32.79 *(978-0-7614-1913-6(6),* Benchmark Bks.); Eating Disorders. Bjorklund, Ruth. (gr. 4-7). 2005. lib. bdg. 32.79 *(978-0-7614-1914-3(4),* Benchmark Bks.); Food-Borne Illnesses. Bjorklund, Ruth. (YA). (gr. 4-7). 2005. lib. bdg. 32.79 *(978-0-7614-1917-4(9));* Leukemia. Klosterman, Lorrie. (J). (gr. 3-7). 2006. lib. bdg. 32.79 *(978-0-7614-1916-7(0),* Benchmark Bks.); Mononucleosis. Hoffmann, Gretchen. (J). (gr. 3-7). 2006. lib. bdg. 32.79 *(978-0-7614-1915-0(2),* Benchmark Bks.); (Illus.). 64p. 2005. 196.71 *(978-0-7614-1912-9(8),* Benchmark Bks.) Marshall Cavendish Corp.

Health Alert - Group 5, 6 bks., Set. Incl. Chickenpox. Hoffmann, Gretchen. lib. bdg. 32.79 *(978-0-7614-2916-6(6),* Benchmark Bks.); Cystic Fibrosis. Bjorklund, Ruth. lib. bdg. 32.79 *(978-0-7614-2912-8(3),* Benchmark Bks.); Fever. Calamandrei, Camilla. lib. bdg. 32.79 *(978-0-7614-2915-9(8),* Benchmark Bks.); Obesity. Hicks, Terry Allan. lib. bdg. 32.79 *(978-0-7614-2911-1(5),* Benchmark Bks.); Sleep Disorders. Colligan, L. H. (YA). lib. bdg. 32.79 *(978-0-7614-2913-5(1));* Tick-Borne Illnesses. Colligan, L. H. lib. bdg. 32.79 *(978-0-7614-2914-2(X),* Benchmark Bks.); 64p. (gr. 4-18). (Health Alert 5 Ser.). 2008. Set lib. bdg. 196.74 *(978-0-7614-2910-4(7),* Benchmark Bks.) Marshall Cavendish Corp.

Health & the Human Body Classroom Library. (gr. k-2). lib. bdg. 81.95 *(978-0-7368-7134-1(9))* Red Brick Learning.

Health & the Human Body II Classroom Library. (gr. k-2). lib. bdg. 63.95 *(978-0-7368-8825-7(X))* Red Brick Learning.

Health & Your Body. 2010. (Health & Your Body Ser.). (ENG.). 24p. (gr. k-1). lib. bdg. 106.60 *(978-1-4296-5926-0(2),* Pebble Plus) Capstone Press of Coughlan Cos.

Health Matters Field Trip Series, 3 cass.; set. 2004. (NOVA Classroom Field Trips Ser.). (gr. 7-18). tchr. ed. 49.95 *(978-1-57807-639-0(0),* WG1156) WGBH Boston Video.

Health Quest, Set. 2004. (Illus.). 360p. (gr. -1-2). 35.95 *(978-1-58095-929-2(6),* ES9615, Lifepac) Alpha Omega Pubns., Inc.

Health Quest II, 5 vols., Set. 2004. (Illus.). (YA). (gr. 9-12). tchr. ed., stu. ed. 33.95 *(978-0-7403-0182-7(9),* ES9715, Lifepac) Alpha Omega Pubns., Inc.

Healthy Habits, 6 vols., Set. Incl. Blood Pressure Basics. La Bella, Laura. lib. bdg. 31.95 *(978-1-4358-9441-9(3));* Living a Heart-Healthy Life. Wilson, Michael R. lib. bdg. 31.95 *(978-1-4358-9438-9(3));* Maintaining a Healthy Weight. Canino, Kate. lib. bdg. 31.95 *(978-1-4358-9439-6(1));* Understanding Cholesterol. Peterson, Judy Monroe. lib. bdg. 31.95 *(978-1-4358-9440-2(5));* Vitamins & Minerals: Getting the Nutrients Your Body Needs. Watson, Stephanie. lib. bdg. 31.95 *(978-1-4358-9443-3(X));* Your Immune System: Protecting Yourself Against Infection & Illness. Bickerstaff, Linda. lib. bdg. 31.95 *(978-1-4358-9442-6(1));* (YA). (gr. 5-8). (Illus.). 64p. 2010. Set lib. bdg. 175.50 *(978-1-4358-9568-3(1),* Rosen Reference) Rosen Publishing Group, Inc., The.

Heart E Heart & Friends Storybook for Children Ages 3 to 5 Years Old: A Children's Way to a Healthy Lifestyle. 2005. (J). per. 7.95 *(978-0-9762703-3-1(1))* Gilliam, T. & Associates, LLC.

Heart E Heart & Friends Storybook for Children Ages 5 to 8 Years Old: A Children's Way to a Healthy Lifestyle. 2005. (J). per. 6.95 *(978-0-9762703-4-8(X))* Gilliam, T. & Associates, LLC.

Hewitt, Sally. Keeping Healthy. 2015. (ENG.). 24p. (gr. -1-2). 23.99 *(978-1-939581-82-2(6))* QEB Publishing Inc.

Hidalgo-Robert, Alberto. Fat No More: A Teenager's Victory over Obesity. 2012. (J). pap. 16.95 *(978-1-55885-745-2(1),* Piñata Books) Arte Publico Pr.

Holt, Rinehart and Winston Staff. Decisions for Health: Blue Edition. 4th ed. Date not set. (YA). 62.20 *(978-0-03-066817-3(4))* Holt McDougal.

—Decisions for Health Blue. 4th ed. 2005. (Holt Decisions for Health Ser.). (SPA & ENG.). 640p. (gr. 8-8). pap. 85.15 *(978-0-03-068149-3(9))* Houghton Mifflin Harcourt Publishing Co.

—Decisions for Health Blue: Chapter Resource Introduction Booklet. 4th ed. Date not set. pap. 4.20 *(978-0-03-068934-5(1))* Holt McDougal.

—Decisions for Health Blue: Decision-Making. 4th ed. Date not set. pap., wbk. ed. 7.20 *(978-0-03-068356-5(4))* Holt McDougal.

—Decisions for Health Blue, Chptr. 21: Health & Environment. 4th ed. 2004. pap. 11.20 *(978-0-03-068057-1(3))* Holt McDougal.

—Decisions for Health Green. 4th ed. 2004. (SPA.). pap., stu. ed. 11.13 *(978-0-03-068348-0(3))* Holt McDougal.

—Decisions for Health Green. 4th ed. 2005. (Holt Decisions for Health Ser.). (SPA & ENG.). 432p. (gr. 6-6). 85.15 *(978-0-03-068147-9(2))* Houghton Mifflin Harcourt Publishing Co.

—Decisions for Health Green: Chapter Resource Introduction Booklet. 4th ed. Date not set. (YA). pap. 4.20 *(978-0-03-068932-1(5))* Holt McDougal.

—Decisions for Health Green: Decision-Making Workbook. 4th ed. 2004. pap., wbk. ed. 5.60 *(978-0-03-068346-6(7))* Holt McDougal.

—Decisions for Health Red: Chapter Resource Introduction Booklet. 4th ed. Date not set. pap. 4.20 *(978-0-03-068933-8(3))* Holt McDougal.

—Decisions for Health Red: Decision-Making. 4th ed. 2004. pap., wbk. ed. 7.00 *(978-0-03-068351-0(3))* Holt McDougal.

—Decisions for Health Green Chptr. 15: Health & Safety. 4th ed. 2004. pap. 11.20 *(978-0-03-068037-3(9))* Holt McDougal.

—Environmental Science Chptr. 20: Environment & Human Health. 4th ed. Date not set. pap. 11.20 *(978-0-03-068082-3(4))* Holt McDougal.

—Healthcare Blue, Chptr. 20: Consumer Health. 4th ed. 2004. pap. 11.20 *(978-0-03-068056-4(5))* Holt McDougal.

—Holt - Decisions. 4th ed. 2005. (Holt Decisions for Health Ser.). (SPA & ENG.). 480p. (gr. 7-7). 85.15 *(978-0-03-068148-6(0))* Houghton Mifflin Harcourt Publishing Co.

—Holt Science & Technology Chapter 28: Life Science: Staying Healthy. 5th ed. 2004. (Illus.). pap. 12.86 *(978-0-03-030261-9(7))* Holt McDougal.

—A Lifetime of Health: Chapter Resource File Introduction Booklet. 4th ed. Date not set. pap. 4.20 *(978-0-03-068931-4(7))* Holt McDougal.

—A Lifetime of Health: Life Skills. 4th ed. Date not set. pap., wbk. ed. 11.20 *(978-0-03-068117-2(0))* Holt McDougal.

—A Lifetime of Health Chptr. 16: Adolesence & Adulthood. 4th ed. Date not set. pap. 11.20 *(978-0-03-068109-7(X))* Holt McDougal.

—A Lifetime of Health Chptr. 19: Building Relationships. 4th ed. Date not set. pap. 11.20 *(978-0-03-068113-4(8))* Holt McDougal.

—Reading Guide Program Lifehealth Sexual Resource. 4th ed. 2003. cd-rom 59.33 *(978-0-03-066618-6(X))* Holt McDougal.

Honeyman-Lowe, Gina & Lowe, John C. Your Guide to Metabolic Health. 2003. (Illus.). 384p. (YA). per. 24.95 *(978-0-9741238-0-6(3))* McDowell Health-Science Bks., LLC.

Houston, Jack. Jumbo Health Yearbook: Grade 5. (Jumbo Health Ser.). 96p. (J). (gr. 5). 15.95 *(978-0-8209-0065-0(6),* B JHY 5) ESP, Inc.

—Jumbo Health Yearbook: Grade 6. (Jumbo Health Ser.). 96p. (J). (gr. 6). 15.95 *(978-0-8209-0066-7(4),* B JHY 6) ESP, Inc.

—Jumbo Health Yearbook: Grade 7. (Jumbo Health Ser.). 96p. (J). (gr. 7). 15.95 *(978-0-8209-0067-4(2),* B JHY 7) ESP, Inc.

—Jumbo Health Yearbook: Grade 8. (Jumbo Health Ser.). 96p. (YA). (gr. 8). 15.95 *(978-0-8209-0068-1(0),* B JHY 8) ESP, Inc.

Hovius, Christopher. Fitness & Nutrition. McDonnell, Mary Ann & Forman, Sara, eds. 2013. (Young Adult's Guide to the Science of Health Ser.: 15). 128p. (J). (gr. 7-18). 24.95 *(978-1-4222-2809-8(6))* Mason Crest.

Hungry Kids, Healthy Kids. 2005. (Illus.). 32p. per. 3.95 *(978-0-9747133-8-0(4))* Thomas, Frederic Inc.

Hunt, Sara. Stay Fit: Your Guide to Staying Active. 2011. (Healthy Me Ser.). (ENG.). 32p. (gr. 3-4). pap. 47.70 *(978-1-4296-7294-8(3),* Snap Bks.) Capstone Press of Coughlan Cos.

Hunt, Sara, et al. Healthy Me. 2011. (Healthy Me Ser.). (ENG.). 32p. (gr. 3-4). lib. bdg. 111.96 *(978-1-4296-6548-3(3),* Snap Bks.) Capstone Press of Coughlan Cos.

Hunter, Miranda & Hunter, William. Sexually Transmitted Infections. McDonnell, Mary Ann & Forman, Sara, eds. 2013. (Young Adult's Guide to the Science of Health Ser.: 15). 128p. (J). (gr. 7-18). 24.95 *(978-1-4222-2814-2(2))* Mason Crest.

Incredibly Disgusting Food, 4 vols., Set. Incl. Carbonated Beverages: The Incredibly Disgusting Story. Furgang, Adam. (YA). lib. bdg. 29.25 *(978-1-4488-1266-0(6));* Fake Foods: Fried, Fast, & Processed: The Incredibly Disgusting Story. Johanson, Paula. (YA). lib. bdg. 29.25 *(978-1-4488-1269-1(0));* Mystery Meat: Hot Dogs, Sausages, & Lunch Meats. Watson, Stephanie. (J). lib. bdg. 29.25 *(978-1-4488-1268-4(2),* 1323609); Salty & Sugary Snacks: The Incredibly Disgusting Story. Furgang, Adam. (YA). lib. bdg. 29.25 *(978-1-4488-1267-7(4));* (gr. 5-9). 2011. (Incredibly Disgusting Food Ser.). (Illus.). 48p. 2011. Set lib. bdg. 106.00 *(978-1-4488-1390-2(5),* Rosen Reference) Rosen Publishing Group, Inc., The.

Ingredients for a Healthy Life. 2014. (Ingredients for a Healthy Life Ser.). 24p. (J). (gr. 2-5). 135.60 *(978-1-4824-0579-8(2))* Stevens, Gareth Publishing LLLP.

Ivey, Catherine. Totally Amazing Careers in Health Sciences. 2006. (J). 7.80 *(978-0-9753920-9-6(3))* Sally Ride Science.

Jesse, Janeen. The Nail Book: Professional Secrets of Personal Nail Care. l.t. ed. 2004. (Illus.). 120p. (YA). cd-rom

24.95 *(978-0-9748796-1-1(4),* EB030915CD) ProNailTech.com.

Johnson, Gary M., illus. The Adventures of MolarMan: Oral Health Bilingual (English/Spanish) Coloring Workbook. 2006. (ENG & SPA.). (J). *(978-0-9791794-1-9(6))* Johnson, Gary.

Johnson, Kandy & Kids for Health Staff. Health Education Adventure Video Series, Kids for Health: Fifth Grade Facilitator's Manual. 2nd ed. 2006. (Illus.). (J). spiral bd. 175.00 *(978-1-933847-12-2(3))* Kids For Health, Inc.

—Health Education Adventure Video Series, Kids for Health: Fifth Grade Facilitator's Manual/DVD Set. 2nd ed. 2006. (Illus.). spiral bd. 400.00 incl. DVD *(978-1-933847-33-7(6))* Kids For Health, Inc.

—Health Education Adventure Video Series, Kids for Health: First Grade Facilitator's Manual. 2nd ed. 2006. (Illus.). spiral bd. 210.00 *(978-1-933847-08-5(5))* Kids For Health, Inc.

—Health Education Adventure Video Series, Kids for Health: First Grade Facilitator's Manual/DVD Set. 2nd ed. 2006. (Illus.). spiral bd. 475.00 incl. DVD *(978-1-933847-29-0(8))* Kids For Health, Inc.

—Health Education Adventure Video Series, Kids for Health: Fourth Grade Facilitator's Manual. 2nd ed. 2006. (Illus.). spiral bd. 175.00 *(978-1-933847-11-5(5))* Kids For Health, Inc.

—Health Education Adventure Video Series, Kids for Health: Fourth Grade Facilitator's Manual/DVD, DVD. 2nd ed. 2006. (Illus.). spiral bd. 400.00 incl. DVD *(978-1-933847-32-0(8))* Kids For Health, Inc.

—Health Education Adventure Video Series, Kids for Health: Kindergarten Facilitator's Manual. 2nd ed. 2006. (Illus.). spiral bd. 210.00 *(978-1-933847-07-8(7))* Kids For Health, Inc.

—Health Education Adventure Video Series, Kids for Health: Kindergarten Facilitator's Manual/DVD Set. 2nd ed. 2006. (Illus.). spiral bd. 475.00 incl. DVD *(978-1-933847-28-3(X))* Kids For Health, Inc.

—Health Education Adventure Video Series, Kids for Health: Second Grade Facilitator's Manual. 2nd ed. 2006. (Illus.). spiral bd. 210.00 *(978-1-933847-09-2(3))* Kids For Health, Inc.

—Health Education Adventure Video Series, Kids for Health: Second Grade Facilitator's Manual/DVD Set. 2nd ed. 2006. (Illus.). spiral bd. 475.00 incl. DVD *(978-1-933847-30-6(1))* Kids For Health, Inc.

—Health Education Adventure Video Series, Kids for Health: Sixth Grade Facilitator's Manual. 2nd ed. 2006. (Illus.). spiral bd. 175.00 *(978-1-933847-13-9(1))* Kids For Health, Inc.

—Health Education Adventure Video Series, Kids for Health: Sixth Grade Facilitator's Manual/DVD Set. 2nd ed. 2006. (Illus.). spiral bd. 400.00 incl. DVD *(978-1-933847-34-4(4))* Kids For Health, Inc.

—Health Education Adventure Video Series, Kids for Health: Third Grade Facilitator's Manual. 2nd ed. 2006. (Illus.). spiral bd. 210.00 *(978-1-933847-10-8(7))* Kids For Health, Inc.

—Health Education Adventure Video Series, Kids for Health: Third Grade Facilitator's Manual/DVD Set. 2nd ed. 2006. (Illus.). spiral bd. 475.00 incl. DVD *(978-1-933847-31-3(X))* Kids For Health, Inc.

Jones, Tammy. I Am Active. 2009. (Sight Word Readers Set A Ser.). (J). *(978-1-60719-139-1(3))* Newmark Learning LLC.

Joy, Berry. Help Me Learn about Being Messy. 2009. 32p. 7.95 *(978-1-60577-112-0(0))* Berry, Joy Enterprises.

Kalman, Bobbie. I Can Write a Book about How to Be Healthy & Happy. 2012. (ENG.). 32p. (J). *(978-0-7787-7991-9(2))*; pap. *(978-0-7787-8000-7(7))* Crabtree Publishing Co.

—Mi Cuerpo Sano. 2010. (SPA & ENG.). 16p. (J). pap. *(978-0-7787-8563-5(1))*; lib. bdg. *(978-0-7787-8557-6(2))* Crabtree Publishing Co.

Keepin, William, et al. Divine Duality: The Power of Reconciliation Between Women & Men. 2015. (SPA & ENG.). 300p. per. 19.95 *(978-1-890772-74-1(7))* Hohm Pr.

Kelso, Susan. OUCH or AHHH - The Choice IS Easy!, 1 vol. Serpentelli, John, illus. 2009. 47p. pap. 24.95 *(978-1-61546-148-6(5))* America Star Bks.

Kenney, Karen Latchana. What Makes Medical Technology Safer? 2015. (ENG., Illus.). 32p. (J). (gr. 4-6). 26.65 *(978-1-4677-7916-6(4),* Lerner Pubns.) Lerner Publishing Group.

Kessler, David A. Your Food Is Fooling You: How Your Brain Is Hijacked by Sugar, Fat, & Salt. 2012. (ENG., Illus.). 192p. (YA). (gr. 7-12). pap. 10.99 *(978-1-59643-831-6(2),* 9781596438316) Roaring Brook Pr.

Kids for Health Staff & Johnson, Kandy. Health Education Adventure Video Series, Kids for Health: Kindergarten Facilitator's Manual/VHS Set, VHS. 2nd ed. 2006. (Illus.). spiral bd. 475.00 incl. VHS *(978-1-933847-00-9(X))* Kids For Health, Inc.

Kowalski, Kathiann M. National Health Care. 2008. (Open for Debate Ser.). 128p. (gr. 7-18). lib. bdg. 42.79 *(978-0-7614-2943-2(3),* Benchmark Bks.) Marshall Cavendish Corp.

Kray, Peter. The Monster. 2003. 91p. per. 12.95 *(978-0-9715715-1-8(1))* Greenleaf Book Group.

Kreisman, Rachelle. Back off, Sneezy! A Kids' Guide to Staying Well. Haggerty, Tim, illus. 2014. (Start Smart: Health Ser.). 32p. (J). (gr. 1-3). pap. 7.95 *(978-1-937529-68-0(1))* Red Chair Pr.

—What's That Smell? A Kids' Guide to Keeping Clean. Haggerty, Tim, illus. 2014. (Start Smart: Health Ser.). 32p. (J). (gr. 1-3). pap. 7.95 *(978-1-937529-66-6(5))* Red Chair Pr.

Kuskowski, Alex. Cool Body Basics: Healthy & Fun Ways to Care for Your Body, 1 vol. 2012. (Cool Health & Fitness Ser.). (ENG.). 32p. (J). (gr. 3-6). lib. bdg. 27.07 *(978-1-61783-425-7(4),* Checkerboard Library) ABDO Publishing Co.

—Cool Eating: Healthy & Fun Ways to Eat Right, 1 vol. 2012. (Cool Health & Fitness Ser.). (ENG.). 32p. (J). (gr. 3-6). lib. bdg. 27.07 *(978-1-61783-426-4(2),* Checkerboard Library) ABDO Publishing Co.

Landau, Elaine. Head-to-Toe Health, 6 bks., Set. Incl. Asthma. lib. bdg. 28.50 *(978-0-7614-2845-9(3))*; Bites & Stings. lib. bdg. 28.50 *(978-0-7614-2850-3(X))*; Broken Bones. lib. bdg. 28.50 *(978-0-7614-2847-3(X))*; Bumps, Bruises, & Scrapes. lib. bdg. 28.50 *(978-0-7614-2849-7(6))*; Cavities & Toothaches. lib. bdg. 28.50 *(978-0-7614-2848-0(8))*; Common Cold. lib. bdg. 28.50 *(978-0-7614-2844-2(5))*; 32p. (gr. 2-7). (Head-to-Toe Health Ser.). 2008. Set lib. bdg. 171.00 *(978-0-7614-2843-5(7),* Benchmark Bks.) Marshall Cavendish Corp.

Lasslett, Sally, et al. Jump Start 9 & 10: Health & Physical Education. 2007. pap. 32.95 incl. cd-rom *(978-0-521-70167-9(8))* Cambridge Univ. Pr.

Leaf, Munro. How to Be: How to Grow up to Be Healthy, Wealthy, & Wise. 2015. (Rizzoli Classics Ser.). (ENG., Illus.). 104p. (J). (-k). 19.95 *(978-0-7893-3109-0(8))* Universe Publishing.

Leder, Jane Mersky & Donovan, Sandy. Keep Your Cool! What You Should Know about Stress. Desrocher, Jack, illus. 2008. (Health Zone Ser.). (ENG.). 64p. (gr. 4-7). lib. bdg. 30.60 *(978-0-8225-7555-9(8))* Lerner Publishing Group.

Lennon, Liz. I Keep Clean. 2017. (Little Stars,Sea-To-Sea Ser.). (ENG., Illus.). 24p. (J). (gr. -1-k). pap. 6.99 *(978-1-4451-4761-1(0),* Franklin Watts) Hachette Children's Group GBR. Dist: Hachette Bk. Group.

—I Keep Clean. 2013. (Illus.). 25.65 *(978-1-59771-412-9(7))* Sea-To-Sea Pubns.

Lewis, Carole. New First Place Favorites. 2004. 19.99 *(978-0-8307-3231-9(4),* Gospel Light) Gospel Light Pubns.

Libal, Autumn. Fats, Sugars, & Empty Calories: The Fast Food Habit. 2007. (Obesity Ser.). (Illus.). 104p. (YA). (gr. 4-7). lib. bdg. 23.95 *(978-1-59084-943-9(4))* Mason Crest.

Lilly, Melinda. Dirty & Clean. Thompson, Scott M., illus. 2003. 24p. (J). 22.79 *(978-1-58952-636-5(8))* Rourke Educational Media.

Limpieza y Salud Todo el Dia Series, 6 bks., Set. 2003. (SPA., Illus.). (J). lib. bdg. 96.00 *(978-0-8239-6907-4(X),* Editorial Buenas Letras) Rosen Publishing Group, Inc., The.

Llewellyn, Claire. Como Nacen los Bebes? Aprender Sobre Sexualidad. Gordon, Mike, illus. (SPA.). (J). (gr. k-2). pap. *(978-950-24-0944-3(2))* Albatros ARG. Dist: Lectorum Pubns., Inc.

—Me Hace Bien o Mal? Aprender Sobre Medicamentos, Drogas y Salud. Gordon, Mike, illus. (SPA.). (J). (gr. k-2). pap. *(978-950-24-0946-7(9))* Albatros ARG. Dist: Lectorum Pubns., Inc.

—Watch Out! Around Town. Gordon, Mike, illus. 2006. (Watch Out! Bks.). (ENG.). 32p. (J). (gr. -1-2). pap. 7.99 *(978-0-7641-3326-8(8))* Barron's Educational Series, Inc.

—Why Should I Eat Well? Gordon, Mike, illus. 2005. (Why Should I? Bks.). (ENG.). 32p. (J). pap. 7.99 *(978-0-7641-3217-9(2))* Barron's Educational Series, Inc.

—Your Body. 2008. (Look after Yourself Ser.). (Illus.). 30p. (J). (gr. 1-4). lib. bdg. 28.50 *(978-1-59771-096-1(2))* Sea-To-Sea Pubns.

Llewelyn, Claire. Hygiene & Health. 2006. (Qeb Looking after Me Ser.). (Illus.). 24p. (J). (gr. -1-3). lib. bdg. 16.95 *(978-1-59566-194-4(8))* QEB Publishing Inc.

Lluch, Isabel B. & Lluch, Emily. Girls' Guide to Caring for Your Body: Everything You Need to Know - Questions & Answers about Growing Up. 2012. (ENG.). 100p. (J). (gr. 6). pap. 6.95 *(978-1-936061-54-9(6))* WS Publishing.

Macdonald, Margaret. What Keeps Me Healthy? 2014. (Little Books of Answers: Level B Ser.). (Illus.). 16p. (gr. k-2). pap. 7.95 *(978-1-927136-13-3(X))* Three Crows Media NZL. Dist: RiverStream Publishing.

Mackenzie, Catherine. The Deep Black Pond at No 12. 2004. (ENG., Illus.). 160p. (J). mass mkt. 6.99 *(978-1-85792-733-7(8),* 9781857927337) Christian Focus Pubns. GBR. Dist: Bookmasters Distribution.

Manfredini, Becky. Get up & Move! A Content Area Reader-health. 2005. (Emergent (Prek-2) Health Package Ser.). 16p. (gr. k-2). 25.20 *(978-0-8215-7826-1(X))* Sadlier, William H. Inc.

Marshall, Shelley. Super Ben's Dirty Hands: A Book about Healthy Habits. Mahan, Ben, illus. 2010. (Character Education with Super Ben & Molly the Great Ser.). 24p. (J). 22.60 *(978-0-7660-3513-3(1))*; pap. 7.95 *(978-0-7660-3738-0(X),* Enslow Elementary) Enslow Pubs., Inc.

Marsico, Katie. Practice Good Hygiene! 2015. (21st Century Junior Library: Your Healthy Body Ser.). (ENG., Illus.). 24p. (J). (gr. 2-5). 27.07 *(978-1-63188-987-5(7),* 205860) Cherry Lake Publishing.

—Stinky Sanitation Inventions. 2013. (Awesome Inventions You Use Every Day Ser.). (ENG., Illus.). 32p. (gr. 3-6). lib. bdg. 26.60 *(978-1-4677-1090-9(3),* Lerner Pubns.) Lerner Publishing Group.

Mast, Dorcas R. God's Precious Gift. Zimmerman, Suzanne, illus. 2011. 107p. (J). pap. *(978-0-7399-2429-7(X))* Rod & Staff Pubs., Inc.

Mather, Kelly. The Five Keys to Wellness. Schneller, Lisa, illus. 2006. 46p. *(978-0-9787179-8-8(8))* Harmony Healing Hse.

McCaslin, Donna B. My Medical Assistant. 2003. spiral bd. 14.95 *(978-0-9718851-2-7(5))* Leigh, Kimbra.

McConnell, Karen, et al. Health for Life with Web Resources - Cloth. 2014. (ENG., Illus.). 424p. 49.00 *(978-1-4504-3493-5(2))* Human Kinetics Pubs.

McCurry, Chris & Waddington, Emma. Why Do I Have to Eat My Greens? Big Issues for Little People Around Health & Well-Being. Thomas, Louis, illus. 2016. (Life & Soul Library). (ENG.). 32p. (J). (gr. -1-3). 12.99 *(978-1-84780-865-3(4),* Frances Lincoln Children's Bks.) Quarto Publishing Group UK GBR. Dist: Hachette Bk. Group.

McKay, Sindy. We Both Read-Happy & Healthy. 2003. 44p. (J). (gr. 1-2). 7.99 *(978-1-891327-47-6(X))* Treasure Bay, Inc.

Mckenzie, Precious. Buff Ducks. Reasoner, John, illus. 2012. (ENG.). 24p. (gr. k-1). pap. 8.95 *(978-1-61810-304-8(0))* Rourke Educational Media.

McNulty John. I Am Your Health. 2006. (Illus.). 32p. *(978-0-9769580-6-2(6))* I Am Your Playground LLC.

Meiners, Cheri J. & Allen, Elizabeth. Grow Strong! A Book about Healthy Habits. 2016. (Being the Best Me Ser.). (ENG., Illus.). 40p. (J). (gr. -1-2). pap. 9.99 *(978-1-63198-085-5(8))* Free Spirit Publishing, Inc.

Mekonnen, Tsion. I Will Do It! 2011. 28p. pap. 15.99 *(978-1-4628-6580-2(1))* Xlibris Corp.

Merino, Noël. Health Care. Gale Editors, ed. 2010. (Current Controversies Ser.). (ENG.). 224p. (gr. 10-12). 46.40 *(978-0-7377-5099-7(5))*; pap. 32.00 *(978-0-7377-5100-0(2))* Cengage Gale. (Greenhaven Pr., Inc.).

Merki, Mary Bronson & Glencoe McGraw-Hill Staff. Human Sexuality. 9th ed. 2003. (Glencoe Health Ser.). (ENG., Illus.). 139p. (gr. 9-12). stu. ed. 19.72 *(978-0-07-830945-8(X),* 007830945X) McGraw-Hill Higher Education.

Meyer, Susan. Health Issues When You're Transgender. 2016. (Transgender Life Ser.). 00064p. (J). (gr. 6-6). pap. 12.95 *(978-1-4994-6462-7(2))* Rosen Publishing Group, Inc., The.

Miller, Debra A. Medicare. 2012. (Current Controversies Ser.). (ENG.). 224p. (gr. 10-12). pap. 32.00 *(978-0-7377-6240-2(3))*; lib. bdg. 46.40 *(978-0-7377-6239-6(X))* Cengage Gale. (Greenhaven Pr., Inc.).

Miller, Edward. The Monster Health Book: A Guide to Eating Healthy, Being Active & Feeling Great for Monsters & Kids! (ENG., Illus.). 40p. (J). (gr. 2-5). 2008. 7.99 *(978-0-8234-2139-8(2))* 2006. 17.95 *(978-0-8234-1956-2(8))* Holiday Hse., Inc.

Minden, Cecilia. Exercise by the Numbers. 2007. (21st Century Skills Library: Real World Math Ser.). (ENG., Illus.). 32p. (gr. 4-8). lib. bdg. 28.50 *(978-1-60279-010-0(8),* 200063) Cherry Lake Publishing.

—Germ Free. 2010. (21st Century Basic Skills Library: Keep It Clean Ser.). (ENG.). 24p. (gr. k-3). lib. bdg. 22.79 *(978-1-60279-857-1(5),* 200580) Cherry Lake Publishing.

—Keep It Clean: Get Well Soon. 2010. (21st Century Basic Skills Library: Keep It Clean Ser.). (ENG.). 24p. (gr. k-3). lib. bdg. 22.79 *(978-1-60279-858-8(3),* 200582) Cherry Lake Publishing.

—Real World Math: Health & Wellness, 8 vols., Set. Incl. Breakfast by the Numbers. (Illus.). lib. bdg. 28.50 *(978-1-60279-011-7(6),* 200060); Cooking by the Numbers. (Illus.). lib. bdg. 28.50 *(978-1-60279-007-0(8),* 200061); Dinner by the Numbers. (Illus.). lib. bdg. 28.50 *(978-1-60279-013-1(2),* 200062); Exercise by the Numbers. (Illus.). lib. bdg. 28.50 *(978-1-60279-010-0(8),* 200063); Gardening by the Numbers. (Illus.). lib. bdg. 28.50 *(978-1-60279-008-7(6),* 200064); Grocery Shopping by the Numbers. (Illus.). lib. bdg. 28.50 *(978-1-60279-006-3(X),* 200065); Lunch by the Numbers. (Illus.). lib. bdg. 28.50 *(978-1-60279-012-4(4),* 200066); Restaurants by the Numbers. lib. bdg. 28.50 *(978-1-60279-009-4(4),* 200067); (gr. 4-8). 32p. 2007. Set lib. bdg. 159.60 *(978-1-60279-103-9(1),* 200059) Cherry Lake Publishing.

—Time to Wash Up. 2010. (21st Century Basic Skills Library: Keep It Clean Ser.). (ENG.). 24p. (gr. k-3). lib. bdg. 22.79 *(978-1-60279-855-7(9),* 200576) Cherry Lake Publishing.

Mitchell, Melanie. Killing Germs. 2006. (Pull Ahead Books: Health Ser.). (ENG., Illus.). 32p. (gr. k-3). pap. 7.95 *(978-0-8225-2772-5(3))* Lerner Publishing Group.

—Mantenerse Limpio. 2005. (Libros para Avanzar (Pull Ahead Bks.)). (SPA., Illus.). 32p. (J). (gr. 3-7). lib. bdg. 22.60 *(978-0-8225-3168-5(2),* Ediciones Lerner) Lerner Publishing Group.

Murphy, Stuart J. Mighty Maddie. Lum, Bernice, illus. 2004. (MathStart Ser.). 40p. (J). 15.99 *(978-0-06-053159-1(2))*; (ENG.). (gr. -1-3). pap. 5.99 *(978-0-06-053161-4(4))* HarperCollins Pubs.

Murray, Julie. School, 1 vol. 2009. (That's Gross!:A Look at Science Ser.). (ENG., Illus.). 32p. (J). (gr. 2-5). 28.50 *(978-1-60453-557-0(1))* ABDO Publishing Co.

Naden, Corinne J. Health Care: A Right or a Privilege? 2009. (Controversy! Ser.). 112p. (gr. 7-9). lib. bdg. 37.07 *(978-0-7614-4231-8(6))* Marshall Cavendish Corp.

Naik, Anita. My Body, Myself: The Ultimate Health Book for Girls. 2nd rev. ed. 2003. (ENG.). 240p. (J). pap. 8.99 *(978-0-330-34333-6(5),* Macmillan Children's Bks.) Pan Macmillan GBR. Dist: Trafalgar Square Publishing.

Nance, Christopher. Choices. 2003. 80p. (J). pap. 6.00 *(978-0-9648363-4-1(3))* CPI Pubs.

Natterson, Cara. The Care & Keeping of You 2: The Body Book for Older Girls. Masse, Josée, illus. 2013. lib. bdg. 24.50 *(978-0-606-31576-0(4),* Turtleback) Turtleback Bks.

Natural Resources Defense Council Staff, et al. Simple Steps Toward a Healthier Earth. Carpenter, Tad, illus. 2010. (ENG.). 80p. (J). (gr. 3-17). pap., act. bk. ed. 12.99 *(978-0-8118-7141-9(X))* Chronicle Bks. LLC.

Nelson, Robin. Staying Clean. 2006. (Pull Ahead Books: Health Ser.). (ENG., Illus.). 32p. (gr. k-3). pap. 7.95 *(978-0-8225-2773-2(1))* Lerner Publishing Group.

Nuevo Investiguemos 1: Ciencias Naturales y de la Salud. (SPA.). (J). (gr. 1). *(978-958-02-1575-2(8))* Editorial Voluntad S.A. COL. Dist: Distribuidora Norma, Inc.

Nuevo Investiguemos 2: Ciencias Naturales y de la Salud. (SPA.). (J). (gr. 2). *(978-958-02-1576-9(6))* Editorial Voluntad S.A. COL. Dist: Distribuidora Norma, Inc.

Nuevo Investiguemos 3: Ciencias Naturales y de la Salud. (SPA.). (J). (gr. 3). *(978-958-02-1577-6(4))* Editorial Voluntad S.A. COL. Dist: Distribuidora Norma, Inc.

Nuevo Investiguemos 4: Ciencias Naturales y de la Salud. (SPA.). (J). (gr. 4). *(978-958-02-1578-3(2))* Editorial Voluntad S.A. COL. Dist: Distribuidora Norma, Inc.

Nuevo Investiguemos 5: Ciencias Naturales y de la Salud. (SPA.). (J). (gr. 5). *(978-958-02-1579-0(0))* Editorial Voluntad S.A. COL. Dist: Distribuidora Norma, Inc.

Nuevo Investiguemos 6: Ciencias Naturales y de la Salud. (SPA.). *(978-958-02-1534-9(0))* Editorial Voluntad S.A. COL. Dist: Distribuidora Norma, Inc.

Nuevo Investiguemos 7: Ciencias Naturales y de la Salud. (SPA.). (YA). (gr. 7). *(978-958-02-1535-6(9))* Editorial Voluntad S.A. COL. Dist: Distribuidora Norma, Inc.

Nurse Leeda. Healthy Beginnings: Five Ways You Can Stay Healthy! 2012. 28p. pap. 25.00 *(978-1-4772-7451-4(0))* AuthorHouse.

Nygard, Bonnie K., et al. Cody Investigates the World of Wellness. 2005. (ENG., Illus.). 88p. (gr. k-5). pap., stu. ed. 12.00 *(978-0-7360-5578-9(9))* Human Kinetics Pubs.

—Ruby Explores the World of Wellness. 5th rev. ed. 2005. (ENG., Illus.). 88p. (gr. k-5). pap., stu. ed. 12.00 *(978-0-7360-5577-2(0))* Human Kinetics Pubs.

—T. J.'s Adventures in the World of Wellness. 2005. (ENG., Illus.). 88p. (gr. k-5). pap., stu. ed. 12.00 *(978-0-7360-5579-6(7))* Human Kinetics Pubs.

Obesity: Modern-Day Epidemic, 10 vols., Set. Incl. Diet & Your Emotions: The Comfort Food Falsehood. Esherick, Joan. (J). 2004. lib. bdg. 23.95 *(978-1-59084-950-7(7))*; Fats, Sugars, & Empty Calories: The Fast Food Habit. Libal, Autumn. (YA). 2007. lib. bdg. 23.95 *(978-1-59084-943-9(4))*; Medications & Surgeries for Weight Loss: When Dieting Isn't Enough. Hunter, William. (YA). 2007. lib. bdg. 23.95 *(978-1-59084-947-7(7))*; (gr. 4-7). (Illus.). 104p. 2005. Set lib. bdg. 239.50 *(978-1-59084-941-5(8))* Mason Crest.

Oetting, Judy. Germs. Herr, Tad, illus. 2006. (Rookie Reader Skill Set Ser.). (ENG.). 32p. (J). (gr. k-2). pap. 4.95 *(978-0-516-24995-7(9))* Scholastic Library Publishing.

Olson, Gillia M. MyPlate & You, 1 vol. 2011. (Health & Your Body Ser.). (ENG.). 24p. (gr. k-1). pap. 7.29 *(978-1-4296-7129-3(7))*; lib. bdg. 26.65 *(978-1-4296-6809-5(1))*; pap. 41.70 *(978-1-4296-7135-4(1))* Capstone Press of Coughlan Cos. (Pebble Plus).

Olson, Karen. Eat, Run & Live Healthy. Hamelin, Marie-Micheline, illus. 2nd rev. ed. 2009. (Caring for Me Ser.). (ENG.). 20p. (J). pap. 9.95 *(978-1-894778-50-3(2))* Theytus Bks., Ltd. CAN. Dist: Univ. of Toronto Pr.

Olson, Karen W. Healthy Choices, Healthy Lives. Hamelin, Marie-Micheline, illus. (ENG.). 20p. 2005. (J). pap. 10.95 *(978-1-894778-31-2(6))* 2009. pap. 9.95 *(978-1-894778-53-4(7))* Theytus Bks., Ltd. CAN. Dist: Univ. of Toronto Pr.

Oluogbagbemi, Funke. Touch & Count. 2011. 28p. pap. 12.99 *(978-1-4568-2566-9(6))* Xlibris Corp.

Orr, Tamra. Playing Safe, Eating Right: Making Healthy Choices, 1 vol. 2008. (Essential Health: Strong Beautiful Girls Set 1 Ser.). (ENG.). 112p. (J). (gr. 6-12). lib. bdg. 35.64 *(978-1-60453-103-9(7))* ABDO Publishing Co.

Pappas, Diane H. & Covey, Richard D. I'm a Healthy Eater. Estrada, Ric, illus. 2007. (J). *(978-0-545-01424-3(7))* Scholastic, Inc.

—My Healthy Food Pyramid. Estrada, Ric, illus. 2007. (J). pap. *(978-0-545-01429-8(8))* Scholastic, Inc.

Pappas, Diane H., et al. My Trip to the Dentist. Estrada, Ric, illus. 2007. (J). pap. *(978-0-545-01425-0(5))* Scholastic, Inc.

—Why I Need Exercise. Estrada, Ric, illus. 2007. (J). pap. *(978-0-545-01428-1(X))* Scholastic, Inc.

Parker, Vic. Breakfast: Healthy Food Choices, 1 vol. 2014. (Healthy Food Choices Ser.). (ENG.). 32p. (gr. 1-3). lib. bdg. 27.32 *(978-1-4329-9116-6(7),* Heinemann First Library) Heinemann-Raintree.

—Dinner: Healthy Food Choices, 1 vol. 2014. (Healthy Food Choices Ser.). (ENG.). 32p. (gr. 1-3). lib. bdg. 27.32 *(978-1-4329-9118-0(3),* Heinemann First Library) Heinemann-Raintree.

—Healthy Food Choices, 1 vol. 2014. (Healthy Food Choices Ser.). (ENG.). 32p. (gr. 1-3). lib. bdg. 109.28 *(978-1-4329-9120-3(5),* Heinemann First Library) Heinemann-Raintree.

—Lunch: Healthy Food Choices, 1 vol. 2014. (Healthy Food Choices Ser.). (ENG.). 32p. (gr. 1-3). lib. bdg. 27.32 *(978-1-4329-9117-3(5),* Heinemann First Library) Heinemann-Raintree.

—Snacks: Healthy Food Choices, 1 vol. 2014. (Healthy Food Choices Ser.). (ENG.). 32p. (gr. 1-3). lib. bdg. 27.32 *(978-1-4329-9119-7(1),* Heinemann First Library) Heinemann-Raintree.

Peters, Celeste. Health. 2008. (Science Q & A Ser.). (Illus.). 48p. (YA). (gr. 4-8). lib. bdg. 29.05 *(978-1-59036-948-7(3))*; (gr. 5-8). pap. 10.95 *(978-1-59036-949-4(1))* Weigl Pubs., Inc.

Peters, Celeste A. Health. 2016. (J). ***(978-1-5105-2237-4(9))*** SmartBook Media, Inc.

Peters, Celeste A. Health Q & A. 2013. (J). *(978-1-62127-414-8(4))*; pap. *(978-1-62127-420-9(9))* Weigl Pubs., Inc.

Petrie, Kristin. Food & Energy: Striking a Healthy Balance, 1 vol. 2012. (Mission: Nutrition Ser.). (ENG., Illus.). 32p. (YA). (gr. 3-6). 27.07 *(978-1-61783-080-8(1))* ABDO Publishing Co.

—Food as Fuel: Nutrition for Athletes, 1 vol. 2012. (Mission: Nutrition Ser.). (ENG., Illus.). 32p. (YA). (gr. 3-6). 27.07 *(978-1-61783-081-5(X))* ABDO Publishing Co.

Pinnell, Gay Su, et al. Health & Safety 2: Safety First; Don't Be a Couch Potato; Birthday Shots; Just in Case; Time Out; Home Sick; the Eye Doctor; the Big Race, 8 bks., Set. Simon, Sue A. et al, illus. 2005. (ENG.). 8p. (J). pap. 120.00 *(978-1-893986-27-5(6))* Keep Bks.

Platkin, Charles Stuart & Platkin, Charles. Lighten Up: Stay Sane, Eat Great, Lose Weight. 2005. (ENG.). 224p. (YA). (gr. 7-12). 7.99 *(978-1-59514-065-4(4),* Razorbill) Penguin Young Readers Group.

Prevedel, Brenda. Nick Gets Moving. Gulley, Robin R., ed. Gulley Sr, Wayne A., illus. 2013. 32p. pap. 9.99 *(978-0-9886117-1-9(6))* Gulley, Wayne.

Priest, Bonnie. Nancy & the Nutrition Tree. 2008. 28p. pap. 12.95 *(978-1-934925-86-7(1),* Strategic Bk. Publishing) Strategic Book Publishing & Rights Agency (SBPRA).

Purdie, Kate. Personal Hygiene. 2010. (Being Healthy, Feeling Great Ser.). (ENG.). 32p. (J). pap. 10.60 *(978-1-61532-376-0(7),* PowerKids Pr.); (YA). (gr. 3-6). lib. bdg. 26.50 *(978-1-61532-369-2(4))* Rosen Publishing Group, Inc., The.

Raatma, Lucia. Making Smart Choices. 2013. (True Book(tm), a — Guides to Life Ser.). (ENG., Illus.). 48p. (J). lib. bdg. 31.00 *(978-0-531-25524-7(7))*; pap. 6.95 *(978-0-531-23924-7(1))* Scholastic Library Publishing.

Rabe, Tish. Oh, the Things You Can Do That Are Good for You! All about Staying Healthy. Ruiz, Aristides, illus. 2015. (Cat in the Hat's Learning Library). (ENG.). 64p. (J). (gr. k-3). lib. bdg. 13.99 *(978-0-375-91098-2(0),* Random Hse. Bks. for Young Readers) Random Hse. Children's Bks.

Ramos, Pilar. La Invitacion. (SPA.). 32p. (J). 10.00 *(978-84-342-2516-9(6))* Parramon Ediciones S.A. ESP. Dist: Distribuidora Norma, Inc.

Randolph, Joanne. Ambulances/Ambulancias. Alaman, Eduardo, tr. from ENG. 2008. (To the Rescue! / ¡Al Rescate! Ser.). (Illus.). 24p. (J). (gr. 3-7). lib. bdg. 22.60 *(978-1-4042-7670-3(X),* Editorial Buenas Letras) Rosen Publishing Group, Inc., The.

Rau, Dana Meachen. Going Organic: A Healthy Guide to Making the Switch, 1 vol. 2012. (Food Revolution Ser.). (ENG.). 64p. (gr. 6-7). 34.65 *(978-0-7565-4523-9(4))*; pap. 9.10 *(978-0-7565-4528-4(5))* Compass Point Bks. (CPB Grades 4-8).

Raum, Elizabeth. Understanding Health Issues, 15 vols., Set. Incl. I Know Someone with HIV/AIDS. (ENG.). 32p. (gr. 1-3). 2011. pap. 8.29 *(978-1-4329-4570-1(X),* Heinemann First Library); (Understanding Health Issues Ser.). (ENG.). 32p. 2011. Set pap. 24.87 o.p. *(978-1-4329-4584-8(X),* Heinemann First Library) Heinemann-Raintree.

H
I

Ready, Dee. Doctors Help, 1 vol. 2013. (Our Community Helpers Ser.). (ENG.). 24p. (gr. k-1). pap. 6.29 *(978-1-62065-843-7(7))*; pap. 35.70 *(978-1-62065-844-4(5))*; lib. bdg. 21.99 *(978-1-62065-078-3(9))* Capstone Press of Coughlan Cos. (Pebble Bks.).

Reese, Brandon. Draw Me Healthy! Reese, Brandon, illus. 2012. (Illus.). 32p. (J). 7.99 *(978-0-8280-2680-2(7))* Review & Herald Publishing Assn.

Reinke, Beth Bence. Healthy Snacks. 2013. (Healthy Eating with Myplate Ser.). (ENG.). 24p. (J). (gr. 1-4). 28.50 *(978-1-62323-600-7(2)*, 206402) Child's World, Inc., The.

—Sugars & Fats. 2013. (Healthy Eating with Myplate Ser.). (ENG.). 24p. (J). (gr. 1-4). 28.50 *(978-1-62323-601-4(0)*, 206403) Child's World, Inc., The.

Reznick, Jenny. Eating Right: A Content Area Reader. 2005. (Emergent (Prek-2) Health Package Ser.). 20p. (gr. k-2). 25.20 *(978-0-8215-7828-5(6))* Sadlier, William H. Inc.

Rice, Dona Herweck. Comer Bien, 1 vol. 2nd rev. ed. 2012. (Nonfiction Readers Ser.). (SPA.). 20p. (J). (gr. 1-1). pap. 4.99 *(978-1-4333-4430-5(0))* Teacher Created Materials, Inc.

—Delicious & Nutritious, 1 vol. 2011. (Early Childhood Themes Ser.). (ENG.). 16p. (J). (gr. -1-2). pap. 6.99 *(978-1-4333-2369-0(9))*; pap. 19.99 *(978-1-4333-2370-6(2))* Teacher Created Materials, Inc.

—Eating Right, 1 vol. 2nd rev. ed. 2014. (TIME for KIDS(r) Nonfiction Readers Ser.). (ENG., Illus.). 20p. (J). (gr. 1-1). pap. 19.96 *(978-1-4807-1030-6(X))* Shell Educational Publishing.

—Mantenerse Sano, 1 vol. 2nd rev. ed. 2012. (Nonfiction Readers Ser.).Tr. of Staying Healthy. (SPA., Illus.). 20p. (J). (gr. 1-1). pap. 4.99 *(978-1-4333-4428-2(9))* Teacher Created Materials, Inc.

—Staying Healthy, 1 vol. 2nd rev. ed. 2014. (TIME for KIDS(r) Nonfiction Readers Ser.). (ENG., Illus.). 20p. (J). (gr. 1-1). pap. 19.96 *(978-1-4807-1028-3(8))* Shell Educational Publishing.

—Staying Healthy, 1 vol. 2nd rev. ed. 2011. (Nonfiction Readers Ser.). (ENG.). 20p. (J). (gr. 1-1). pap. 4.99 *(978-1-4333-3595-2(6))* Teacher Created Materials, Inc.

Rice, Dona Herwick. Eating Right, 1 vol. 2nd rev. ed. 2011. (Nonfiction Readers Ser.). (ENG.). 20p. (J). (gr. 1-1). pap. 4.99 *(978-1-4333-3597-6(2))* Teacher Created Materials, Inc.

Richard French. Secrets of Health. 2008. 40p. pap. 21.99 *(978-1-4363-1025-3(3))* Xlibris Corp.

Rieger, Linda. A Good Heart. Rieger, Linda, illus. 2007. (Illus.). 20p. (J). *(978-0-9779427-4-9(0))* Pathways into Science.

Riley, Peter. Keeping Healthy. 2016. (Ways into Science Ser.). (ENG., Illus.). 32p. (J). (gr. k-2). pap. 11.99 *(978-1-4451-3484-0(5)*, Franklin Watts) Hachette Children's Group GBR. Dist: Hachette Bk. Group.

Rissman, Rebecca. Going to the Doctor: Comparing Past & Present, 1 vol. 2014. (Comparing Past & Present Ser.). (ENG., Illus.). 24p. (gr. -1-1). lib. bdg. 22.65 *(978-1-4329-8992-7(8)*, Acorn) Heinemann-Raintree.

—Should Bella Go to Bed? Staying Healthy, 1 vol. 2013. (What Would You Do? Ser.). (ENG., Illus.). 24p. (gr. -1-1). pap. 6.29 *(978-1-4329-7256-1(1)*, Acorn) Heinemann-Raintree.

—Should Billy Brush His Teeth? Taking Care of Yourself, 1 vol. 2013. (What Would You Do? Ser.). (ENG., Illus.). 24p. (gr. -1-1). pap. 6.29 *(978-1-4329-7245-5(6))*; lib. bdg. 22.65 *(978-1-4329-7239-4(1))* Heinemann-Raintree. (Acorn).

—Using Myplate. 2012. (Healthy Eating with Myplate Ser.). (ENG.). 24p. (gr. -1-1). pap. 6.29 *(978-1-4329-6985-1(4)*, Acorn) Heinemann-Raintree.

Rissman, Rebecca & Smith, Sian. Keeping Clean, 1 vol. 2012. (Take Care of Yourself! Ser.). (ENG.). 24p. (gr. -1-1). 22.65 *(978-1-4329-6709-3(6))*; pap. 6.29 *(978-1-4329-6716-1(9))* Heinemann-Raintree. (Acorn).

—Staying Safe in the Sun. 2012. (Take Care of Yourself! Ser.). (ENG.). 24p. (gr. -1-1). pap. 35.94 *(978-1-4329-6726-0(6)*, Acorn) Heinemann-Raintree.

Roberts, Jeremy. Drugs & Dieting. 2005. (Drug Abuse Prevention Library). (Illus.). 64p. (YA). (gr. 7-12). lib. bdg. 31.95 *(978-0-8239-3357-0(1))* Rosen Publishing Group, Inc., The.

Roizen, Michael F. & Oz, Mehmet C. Owner's Manual for Teens: A Guide to a Healthy Body & Happy Life. 2011. (ENG.). 464p. pap. 16.99 *(978-0-7432-9258-0(8)*, Free Pr.) Free Pr.

Rooney, Anne. Health & Medicine: The Impact of Science & Technology. 2009. (Pros & Cons Ser.). (ENG.). 64p. (YA). (gr. 5-9). lib. bdg. 35.00 *(978-1-4339-1988-6(5))* Stevens, Gareth Publishing LLLP.

Royston, Angela. Why Do I Wash My Hands? 2012. (My Body Ser.). (ENG., Illus.). 24p. (gr. k-4). pap. 7.95 *(978-1-77092-002-6(1))* Saunders Bk. Co. CAN. Dist: RiverStream Publishing.

Ruff, Kimberly & Sheets, Leslie. Brave Just Like Me. 2011. 32p. 19.95 *(978-1-60888-121-5(0))* Nimble Bks. LLC.

Ruff, Kimberly & Venturi-Pickett, Stacy. Brave Just Like Me. Sheets, Leslie, illus. 2011. 32p. pap. 9.99 *(978-1-60888-106-2(7))* Nimble Bks. LLC.

Rustad, Martha E. H. I Eat Well. 2017. (Healthy Me Ser.). (ENG., Illus.). 24p. (gr. k-1). lib. bdg. 21.99 *(978-1-5157-3983-8(X))* Capstone Press of Coughlan Cos.

Saenger, Stefanie, illus. Grow Healthy Little One. 2007. 24p. (J). pap. 16.95 *(978-0-9796010-0-2(2))* Johnston, Ann.

Salzmann, Mary Elizabeth. Eat Your Vegetables! Healthy Eating Habits, 1 vol. 2014. (Healthy Habits Ser.). (ENG.). 24p. (J). (gr. -1-3). 24.21 *(978-1-62403-529-6(9))* ABDO Publishing Co.

—Healthy Habits, 1 vol. 2014. (Healthy Habits Ser.: 6). (ENG.). 24p. (J). (gr. -1-3). lib. bdg. 145.26 *(978-1-62403-527-2(2)*, SandCastle) ABDO Publishing Co.

—Run! Jump! Play! Healthy Active Habits, 1 vol. 2014. (Healthy Habits Ser.). (ENG.). 24p. (J). (gr. -1-3). 24.21 *(978-1-62403-530-2(2))* ABDO Publishing Co.

—Sleep All Night! Healthy Sleeping Habits, 1 vol. 2014. (Healthy Habits Ser.). (ENG.). 24p. (J). (gr. -1-3). 24.21 *(978-1-62403-531-9(0))* ABDO Publishing Co.

—Take a Bath! Healthy Body Habits, 1 vol. 2014. (Healthy Habits Ser.). (ENG.). 24p. (J). (gr. -1-3). 24.21 *(978-1-62403-532-6(9))* ABDO Publishing Co.

—Wear a Helmet! Healthy Safety Habits, 1 vol. 2014. (Healthy Habits Ser.). (ENG.). 24p. (J). (gr. -1-3). 24.21 *(978-1-62403-533-3(7))* ABDO Publishing Co.

Schaefer, Valorie. The Care & Keeping of You Vol. 1: The Body Book for Younger Girls. 2013. lib. bdg. 24.50 *(978-0-606-31575-3(6)*, Turtleback) Turtleback Bks.

Schrier, Allyson Valentine, et al. Healthy Me. 2011. (Healthy Me Ser.). (ENG.). 32p. (gr. 3-4). pap. 190.80 *(978-1-4296-7300-6(1)*, Snap Bks.) Capstone Press of Coughlan Cos.

Schwartz, Heather E. Stress Less: Your Guide to Managing Stress, 1 vol. 2011. (Healthy Me Ser.). (ENG.). 32p. (gr. 3-4). lib. bdg. 27.99 *(978-1-4296-6547-6(5)*, Snap Bks.) Capstone Press of Coughlan Cos.

Selwyn, Josephine. How Can I Get Fit? 2014. (Little Books of Answers: Level e Ser.). (Illus.). 16p. (gr. k-2). pap. 7.95 *(978-1-927136-43-0(1))* Three Crows Media NZL. Dist: RiverStream Publishing.

Senker, Cath. Exercise & Play. 2008. (Healthy Choices Ser.). (Illus.). 24p. (J). (gr. 3-7). lib. bdg. 22.60 *(978-1-4042-4305-7(4)*, PowerKids Pr.) Rosen Publishing Group, Inc., The.

—Healthy Eating. 2008. (Healthy Choices Ser.). (Illus.). 24p. (J). (gr. 3-7). lib. bdg. 22.60 *(978-1-4042-4303-3(8)*, PowerKids Pr.) Rosen Publishing Group, Inc., The.

—Keeping Clean. 2008. (Healthy Choices Ser.). (Illus.). 24p. (J). (gr. 3-7). lib. bdg. 22.60 *(978-1-4042-4302-6(X)*, PowerKids Pr.) Rosen Publishing Group, Inc., The.

Sesame's: A Giant Coloring Book that teaches Healthy Eating Habits. 2006. (J). 6.99 *(978-1-59949-499-9(X))* Food Marketing Consultants, Inc.

Shajardoust, Masoumeh. Neaty Mitty. 2009. 20p. pap. 10.49 *(978-1-4490-2729-2(6))* AuthorHouse.

Shulman, Stephanie J. The Nose Pickers. 2012. 32p. pap. *(978-0-9841794-1-1(0))* Roxby Media Ltd.

Simons, Rae. At Home in Your Body: Care for the Shape You're In. 2010. (Kids & Obesity Ser.). 48p. (YA). lib. bdg. 19.95 *(978-1-4222-1715-3(9))* Mason Crest.

Slim Goodbody Corp. What's on Myplate? A Guide to Good Nutrition. 2011. (Illus.). 40p. (J). 14.95 *(978-1-887028-63-9(3))* Slim Goodbody Corp.

Slim Goodbody Corp., creator. What's on Myplate? A Guide to Good Nutrition. 2011. (Illus.). 40p. (J). pap. 9.95 *(978-1-887028-62-2(5))* Slim Goodbody Corp.

Sly, Stacey. What Should I Eat? Gentry, Susana, photos by. 2010. (Illus.). 26p. pap. 12.95 *(978-1-60911-432-9(9)*, Eloquent Bks.) Strategic Book Publishing & Rights Agency (SBPRA).

Smart Kids Publishing Staff, creator. Everybody Takes a Bath. 2006. (Rub a Dub Fun in the Tub Ser.). (ENG., Illus.). 10p. (J). (gr. -1). 8.95 *(978-0-8249-6681-2(3)*, Ideal Pubns.) Worthy Publishing.

Smith, Carrie Myers. Fitastic Kids: A Complete Guide to Health & Wellness for Children of All Ages. 2005. 200p. wbk. ed. 18.95 *(978-1-891400-51-3(7))* Sourcebooks, Inc.

Smith, Ian. Going to the Doctor. 2015. (ENG.). 24p. (gr. -1-2). 23.99 *(978-1-939581-81-5(8))* QEB Publishing Inc.

Smith, Liz. A Girl's Guide to Growing up - Booklet, 10 per packet. Perry, Gala, illus. 2005. (J). 63.95 *(978-1-55942-207-9(6))* Witcher Productions.

Sohn, Emily, frwd. Health & Medicine. 2006. (Science News for Kids Ser.). (Illus.). 160p. (gr. 4-6). lib. bdg. 30.00 *(978-0-7910-9122-7(6)*, Chelsea Clubhouse) Facts On File, Inc.

Somervill, Barbara A. Graphing Health & Disease, 1 vol. 2010. (Real World Data Ser.). (ENG., Illus.). 32p. (gr. 3-5). lib. bdg. 29.99 *(978-1-4329-2619-9(5)*, NA-h) Heinemann-Raintree.

Son, John. Relaxation & Yoga. 2016. (True Book(tm), A — Health Ser.). (ENG., Illus.). 48p. (J). lib. bdg. 31.00 *(978-0-531-22847-0(9)*, Children's Pr.) Scholastic Library Publishing.

Spilsbury, Louise. Clean & Healthy. 2012. (Healthy & Happy Ser.). (Illus.). 32p. (J). (gr. 1-4). lib. bdg. 26.50 *(978-1-4488-5277-2(3))* Rosen Publishing Group, Inc., The.

Spilsbury, Richard, et al. Your Body for Life. 2013. (Your Body for Life Ser.). (ENG.). 64p. (gr. 7-8). 215.94 *(978-1-4329-7088-8(7))* Heinemann-Raintree.

Staley, Erin. Improving Community Health & Safety Through Service Learning, 1 vol. 2015. (ENG.). 80p. (YA). 34.60 *(978-1-4777-7955-2(8)*, Rosen Young Adult) Rosen Publishing Group, Inc., The.

Steck-Vaughn Company, creator. Health. 2009. (Fact Matters: Healthy Bodies Ser.). (Illus.). 32p. pap. 8.67 *(978-1-4190-5471-6(6))* Heinemann-Raintree.

Stern, Sam & Stern, Susan. Get Cooking. Campbell, Lorne, photos by. 2009. (ENG., Illus.). 144p. (J). (gr. 5-18). pap. 17.99 *(978-0-7636-3926-6(5))* Candlewick Pr.

Stille, Darlene R. Changing Habits, Living Green. 2011. (Go Green! Ser.). (ENG., Illus.). 32p. (J). (gr. 1-4). lib. bdg. 28.50 *(978-1-60973-169-4(7)*, 201148) Child's World, Inc., The.

Stoyles, Pennie. The A-Z of Health. 2010. (a to Z of Health Ser.). 32p. (gr. 4-7). Vol. 1. lib. bdg. 31.35 *(978-1-59920-541-0(6))* Vol. 2. lib. bdg. 31.35 *(978-1-59920-542-7(4))* Vol. 3. lib. bdg. 31.35 *(978-1-59920-543-4(2))* Vol. 4. lib. bdg. 31.35 *(978-1-59920-544-1(0))* Vol. 6. lib. bdg. 31.35 *(978-1-59920-546-5(7))* Black Rabbit Bks.

Stoyles, Pennie & Pentland, Peter. Medicine & Health. 2011. (Energy in Action Ser.). (Illus.). 32p. (J). (gr. 4). 28.50 *(978-1-60870-568-9(4))* Marshall Cavendish Corp.

Taylor-Butler, Christine. A True Book: Health & the Human Body, 7 vols., Set. Incl. Circulatory System. (Illus.). 31.00 *(978-0-531-16856-1(5))*; Digestive System. (Illus.). 29.00 *(978-0-531-16857-8(3))*; Nervous System. 31.00 *(978-0-531-16861-5(1))*; Respitory System. (Illus.). 31.00 *(978-0-531-16862-2(X))*; 48p. (J). (gr. 3-7). (True Bks.). 2008. Set lib. bdg. 261.00 *(978-0-531-20545-7(2)*, Children's Pr.) Scholastic Library Publishing.

Tecco, Betsy Dru. Food for Fuel: The Connection Between Food & Physical Activity. 2009. (Library of Nutrition Ser.). 48p. (gr. 5-8). 53.00 *(978-1-60853-766-2(8)*, Rosen Reference) Rosen Publishing Group, Inc., The.

Tieck, Sarah. Get Rest, 1 vol. 2012. (ENG.). 32p. 27.07 *(978-1-61783-233-8(2)*, Buddy Bks.) ABDO Publishing Co.

—Keep Clean, 1 vol. 2012. (ENG.). 32p. 27.07 *(978-1-61783-234-5(0)*, Buddy Bks.) ABDO Publishing Co.

Tiller, Jerome. Sammy's Day at the Fair: The Digestive System Featuring Gut Feelings & Reactions. 2004. 48p. (J). lib. bdg. 15.95 *(978-1-59298-046-8(5))* Beaver's Pond Pr., Inc.

Torrisi, Cathy. A Healthy Day. 2011. pap. 39.95 *(978-0-7664-3745-6(0))* Abrams & Co. Pubs., Inc.

Tourville, Amanda Doering. Go Wash Up: Keeping Clean, 1 vol. Rooney, Ronnie, illus. 2008. (How to Be Healthy! Ser.). (ENG.). 24p. (gr. k-2). 26.65 *(978-1-4048-4808-5(8))* Picture Window Bks.

—Lávate. Rooney, Ronnie, illus. 2011. (Cómo Mantenernos Saludables/How to Be Healthy Ser.).Tr. of Go Wash Up. (SPA, MUL & ENG.). 24p. (gr. k-2). 26.65 *(978-1-4048-6892-2(5))* Picture Window Bks.

Troupe, Thomas Kingsley. Kitanai & Filthy Flamingo Wash Up. Christoph, Jamey, illus. 2015. (Kitanai's Healthy Habits Ser.). (ENG.). 24p. (gr. k-2). lib. bdg. 26.65 *(978-1-4795-6081-3(2))* Picture Window Bks.

—Kitanai & Hungry Hare Eat Healthfully. Christoph, Jamey, illus. 2015. (Kitanai's Healthy Habits Ser.). (ENG.). 24p. (gr. k-2). pap. 8.95 *(978-1-4795-6114-8(2))* Picture Window Bks.

—Kitanai's Healthy Habits. Christoph, Jamey, illus. 2015. (Kitanai's Healthy Habits Ser.). (ENG.). 24p. (gr. k-2). lib. bdg. 106.60 *(978-1-4795-6255-8(6))* Picture Window Bks.

A True Book & Trade - Guides to Life. 2013. (True Book™—Guides to Life Ser.). (J). 116.00 *(978-0-531-28843-6(9)*, Children's Pr.) Scholastic Library Publishing.

Turnbull, Stephanie. Why Do We Eat? Haggerty, Tim, illus. 2006. (Beginners Science: Level 2 Ser.). 32p. (J). (gr. 1-3). 4.99 *(978-0-7945-1333-7(6)*, Usborne) EDC Publishing.

Understanding Health Issues, 15 vols., Set. Incl. I Know Someone Who Is Obese. Barraclough, Sue. 27.32 *(978-1-4329-4566-4(1))*; I Know Someone with a Hearing Impairment. Parker, Vic. 27.32 *(978-1-4329-4560-2(2))*; I Know Someone with a Visual Impairment. Parker, Vic. 27.32 *(978-1-4329-4562-6(9))*; I Know Someone with ADHD. Raum, Elizabeth. 27.32 *(978-1-4329-4553-4(X))*; I Know Someone with Allergies. Parker, Vic. 27.32 *(978-1-4329-4555-8(6))*; I Know Someone with Asthma. Parker, Vic. 27.32 *(978-1-4329-4556-5(4))*; I Know Someone with Autism. Barraclough, Sue. 27.32 *(978-1-4329-4563-3(7))*; I Know Someone with Cancer. Barraclough, Sue. 27.32 *(978-1-4329-4564-0(5))*; I Know Someone with Diabetes. Parker, Vic. 27.32 *(978-1-4329-4557-2(2))*; I Know Someone with Eczema. Parker, Vic. 27.32 *(978-1-4329-4559-6(9))*; I Know Someone with Epilepsy. Parker, Vic. 27.32 *(978-1-4329-4561-9(0))*; I Know Someone with HIV/AIDS. Raum, Elizabeth. 27.32 *(978-1-4329-4554-1(8))*; (gr. 1-3). (Understanding Health Issues Ser.). (ENG., Illus.). 32p. 2011. Set lib. bdg. 327.84 *(978-1-4329-4568-8(8)*, Heinemann First Library) Heinemann-Raintree.

Unwin, Mike & Woodward, Kate. What Makes You Ill? Meredith, Susan, ed. Spenceley, Annabel & Chen, Kuo Kang, illus. rev. ed. 2006. (Starting Point Science Ser.). 24p. (J). (gr. -1-3). pap. 4.99 *(978-0-7945-1624-6(6)*, Usborne) EDC Publishing.

Ventura, Marne. 12 Tips for a Healthy Diet. 2017. (J). *(978-1-62143-507-5(5))* Pr. Room Editions LLC.

Ventura, Marne & Ringstad, Arnold. 12 Tips for a Healthy Diet. 2016. (Healthy Living Ser.). (ENG., Illus.). 32p. (J). pap. 9.95 *(978-1-63235-383-2(0))* Pr. Room Editions LLC.

Verdick, Elizabeth. Clean-Up Time/Momento de Arreglar. Heinlen, Marieka, illus. 2017. (Toddler Tools Ser.). (ENG, SPA & MUL.). 24p. (J). bds. 7.95 ***(978-1-63198-154-8(4))*** Free Spirit Publishing, Inc.

Verdick, Elizabeth. Germs Are Not for Sharing. Heinlen, Marieka, illus. 2006. (Best Behavior Ser.).Tr. of Germenes No Son para Compartir. (ENG.). (J). (gr. -1-2). 24p. 7.95 *(978-1-57542-196-4(8))*; 40p. pap. 11.95 *(978-1-57542-197-1(6))* Free Spirit Publishing, Inc.

Verdick, Elizabeth & Heinlen, Marieka. Germs Are Not for Sharing. 2011. (Best Behavior Ser.).Tr. of Germenes No Son para Compartir. (SPA, ENG & MUL.). 24p. (J). (gr. k — 1). 7.95 *(978-1-57542-369-2(3))* Free Spirit Publishing, Inc.

—Germs Are Not for Sharing/Los Gérmenes No Son Para Compartir. 2011. (Best Behavior Ser.). (SPA & ENG.). 40p. (J). (gr. -1-2). pap. 11.95 *(978-1-57542-368-5(5))* Free Spirit Publishing, Inc.

Vogel, Elizabeth. ¡A lavarse las manos! (Washing My Hands) 2009. (Limpieza y salud todo el día (Clean & Healthy All Day Long) Ser.). (SPA.). 24p. (gr. 1-1). 37.50 *(978-1-61514-292-7(4)*, Editorial Buenas Letras) Rosen Publishing Group, Inc., The.

—A Comer Sanamente! 2004. (Limpieza y Salud Todo el Dia Ser.). (SPA & ENG., Illus.). 24p. (J). (gr. -1-2). lib. bdg. 18.75 *(978-0-8239-6612-7(7))* Rosen Publishing Group, Inc., The.

—A Hacer Ejercicio! 2004. (Limpieza y Salud Todo el Dia Ser.). (SPA & ENG., Illus.). 24p. (J). (gr. 1-2). lib. bdg. 18.75 *(978-0-8239-6614-1(3)*, Editorial Buenas Letras) Rosen Publishing Group, Inc., The.

—A Lavarse Las Manos! 2004. (Limpieza y Salud Todo el Dia Ser.). (SPA & ENG., Illus.). 24p. (J). (gr. 1-2). lib. bdg. 18.75 *(978-0-8239-6618-9(6)*, Editorial Buenas Letras) Rosen Publishing Group, Inc., The.

—A Lavarse Los Dientes! 2004. (Limpieza y Salud Todo el Dia Ser.). (SPA & ENG., Illus.). 24p. (J). (gr. 1-2). lib. bdg. 18.75 *(978-0-8239-6620-2(8)*, Editorial Buenas Letras) Rosen Publishing Group, Inc., The.

—Taking Care of My Hair: El Cuidado de Tu Cabello. 2004. (Limpieza y Salud Todo el Dia Ser.). (SPA & ENG., Illus.). 24p. (J). lib. bdg. 18.75 *(978-0-8239-6611-0(9)*, Editorial Buenas Letras) Rosen Publishing Group, Inc., The.

Wainwright, Tabitha. You & an Illness in Your Family. 2005. (Family Matters Ser.). (Illus.). 48p. (YA). (gr. 5-8). lib. bdg. 29.25 *(978-0-8239-3352-5(0))* Rosen Publishing Group, Inc., The.

Wallach, Marlene. The Official Book of Me: Tips for a Lifestyle of Health, Happiness & Wellness. Roe, Monika, illus. 2014. (ENG.). 176p. (J). (gr. 4-8). pap. 9.99 *(978-1-4424-9479-4(4)*, Aladdin) Simon & Schuster Children's Publishing.

Waters, Rosa. Stress & Tension. Croft, Cindy, ed. 2014. (Causes & Effects of Emotions Ser.: 13). 64p. (J). (gr. 7-18). 23.95 *(978-1-4222-3079-4(1))* Mason Crest.

Way, Steve. Fighting Disease. 2011. (Planet SOS Ser.). (Illus.). 48p. (J). (gr. 3-6). pap. 14.05 *(978-1-4339-4971-5(7))*; lib. bdg. 31.95 *(978-1-4339-4970-8(9))* Stevens, Gareth Publishing LLLP. (Gareth Stevens Learning Library).

Webber, Diane. The Skin You're In: Staying Healthy Inside & Out. 2008. (Scholastic Choices Ser.). (ENG.). 112p. (J). (gr. 7-18). pap. 8.95 *(978-0-531-20527-3(4)*, Watts, Franklin); (Illus.). (gr. 3-7). 27.00 *(978-0-531-13869-4(0)*, Children's Pr.) Scholastic Library Publishing.

Weber, Rebecca. Health & Your Body. 2012. (Health & Your Body Ser.). (ENG.). 24p. (gr. k-1). pap. 333.60 *(978-1-4296-8349-4(X))*; pap. 43.74 *(978-1-4296-8348-7(1))*; lib. bdg. 213.20 *(978-1-4296-8140-7(3))*; lib. bdg. 79.95 *(978-1-4296-6838-5(5))* Capstone Press of Coughlan Cos. (Pebble Plus).

—Healthy Habits, 1 vol. 2010. (Health & Your Body Ser.). (ENG.). 24p. (gr. k-1). lib. bdg. 26.65 *(978-1-4296-6611-4(0)*, Pebble Plus) Capstone Press of Coughlan Cos.

—Science & Your Health, 1 vol. (Health & Your Body Ser.). (ENG.). 24p. (gr. k-1). 2011. pap. 7.29 *(978-1-4296-7130-9(0))* 2011. pap. 41.70 *(978-1-4296-7136-1(X))* 2010. lib. bdg. 26.65 *(978-1-4296-6612-1(9))* Capstone Press of Coughlan Cos. (Pebble Plus).

Weber, Rebecca, et al. Health & Your Body. 2011. (Health & Your Body Ser.). (ENG.). 24p. (gr. k-1). pap. 250.20 *(978-1-4296-7138-5(6))*; lib. bdg. 159.90 *(978-1-4296-6839-2(3))*; lib. bdg. 53.30 *(978-1-4296-8568-9(9))*; pap. 41.70 *(978-1-4296-7137-8(8))* Capstone Press of Coughlan Cos. (Pebble Plus).

Weiss, S. I. Coping with the Beauty Myth: A Guide for Real Girls. 2009. (Coping Ser.). 192p. (gr. 7-12). 63.90 *(978-1-61512-014-7(9))* Rosen Publishing Group, Inc., The.

West, Dorothy F. Nutrition, Food, & Fitness. 3rd ed. 2006. (ENG., Illus.). 510p. (gr. 9-12). 62.64 *(978-1-59070-527-8(0))* Goodheart-Willcox Pub.

White, Andrea & Mimi, Vance. Tummies on the Run. Shepperson, Rob, illus. 2012. 32p. pap. 11.95 *(978-1-60898-134-2(7))* namelos llc.

White, Ellen Gould Harmon. The Ministry of Healing. 2005. reprint ed. pap. 42.95 *(978-1-4191-4425-7(1))* Kessinger Publishing, LLC.

White, Nancy. The President's Challenge: A Content Area Reader-health. 2005. (Emergent (Prek-2) Health Package Ser.). 16p. (gr. k-2). 25.20 *(978-0-8215-7830-8(8))* Sadlier, William H. Inc.

Whittaker, Helen. How Toys Roll. 2012. (Toys & Forces Ser.). 32p. (gr. 1-4). lib. bdg. 27.10 *(978-1-59920-468-0(1))* Black Rabbit Bks.

Wilcox, Christine. Teens, Nutrition, & Dieting. 2015. (ENG., Illus.). 80p. (J). lib. bdg. *(978-1-60152-834-6(5))* ReferencePoint Pr., Inc.

William H. Sadlier Staff. From Head to Toes. 2005. (Emergent (Prek-2) Health Package Ser.). 12p. (gr. -1-2). 25.20 *(978-0-8215-7846-9(4))* Sadlier, William H. Inc.

—Play it Safe! 2005. (Emergent (Prek-2) Health Package Ser.). 12p. (gr. -1-1). 25.20 *(978-0-8215-7848-3(0))* Sadlier, William H. Inc.

—Stop Germs. 2005. (Emergent (Prek-2) Health Package Ser.). 12p. (gr. -1-1). 25.20 *(978-0-8215-7850-6(2))* Sadlier, William H. Inc.

Williams, Kara. Frequently Asked Questions about My Pyramid: Eating Right. 2009. (FAQ: Teen Life Ser.). 64p. (gr. 5-6). 58.50 *(978-1-61512-583-8(3))* Rosen Publishing Group, Inc., The.

—Mypyramid: Eating Right. 2007. (FAQ: Teen Life Ser.). (Illus.). 64p. (YA). (gr. 7-12). lib. bdg. 31.95 *(978-1-4042-1974-8(9))* Rosen Publishing Group, Inc., The.

Wilson, Michael R. Living a Heart-Healthy Life. 2010. (Healthy Habits Ser.). 64p. (YA). (ENG.). pap. 12.95 *(978-1-4488-0608-9(9))*; (Illus.). (gr. 5-8). lib. bdg. 31.95 *(978-1-4358-9438-9(3))* Rosen Publishing Group, Inc., The. (Rosen Reference).

Winkler, Peter, et al. Keeping Fit. 2006. (Nonfiction Reading & Writing Workshops Ser.). (ENG., Illus.). 32p. (J). pap. 17.95 *(978-0-7922-8863-3(7))* CENGAGE Learning.

Wood, Ira. Let's Wash Up. 2008. (Rosen Real Readers: Upper Emergent Ser.). (ENG., Illus.). 12p. (gr. 1-2). pap. 5.90 *(978-0-8239-8121-2(5))* Rosen Publishing Group, Inc., The.

Woods, Sadie. I Help at the Store. Aguilera, Aurora, illus. 2017. (Ways I Help Ser.). 24p. (J). (gr. 4-6). pap. 8.25 ***(978-1-5081-5678-9(6)***, PowerKids Pr.) Rosen Publishing Group, Inc., The.

World Health Organization Staff. Quality Assessment Guidebook: A Guide to Assessing Health Services for Adolescent Clients. 2011. (DOCUMENTS for SALE Ser.). (ENG., Illus.). 104p. pap. 24.00 *(978-92-4-159885-9(9))* World Health Organization.

HEALTH—FICTION

Adams, Karen S. Introducing Marlon! Your Cancer-Fighting Friend! A Story to Help a Child Learn How to Use Visual Imagery to Fight Cancer. 2008. 20p. pap. 11.49 *(978-1-4343-7840-8(3))* AuthorHouse.

Allen, Constance. Shake a Leg! Swanson, Maggie, illus. 2010. (Big Bird's Favorites Board Bks.). (ENG.). 24p. (J). (gr. k — 1). bds. 4.99 *(978-0-375-85424-8(X)*, Random Hse. Bks. for Young Readers) Random Hse. Children's Bks.

Almarode, John. Dylan Discovers His Brain ! Norcross, David, illus. 2010. 28p. pap. 12.99 *(978-1-4490-5491-5(9))* AuthorHouse.

Anderson, Peggy Perry. Let's Clean Up! 2012. (Green Light Readers Level 1 Ser.). (ENG., Illus.). 32p. (J). (gr. -1-3). pap. 3.99 *(978-0-547-74562-6(1))* Houghton Mifflin Harcourt Publishing Co.

Andreae, Giles. Morris the Mankiest Monster. McIntyre, Sarah, illus. 2011. (ENG.). 32p. (J). (gr. -1-k). pap. 14.95 *(978-0-552-55935-5(0))* Transworld Publishers Ltd. GBR. Dist: Independent Pubs. Group.

Arnold, Tedd. Dirty Gert. Arnold, Tedd, illus. 2014. (ENG., Illus.). 32p. (J). (gr. 2-5). 6.99 *(978-0-8234-3054-3(5))* Holiday Hse., Inc.

Auerbach, Andrea. Dinnertime. 2012. 28p. pap. 19.99 *(978-1-4772-7169-8(4))* AuthorHouse.

Barchers, Suzanne I. Kip Gets Fit, 1 vol. 2011. (Targeted Phonics Ser.). (ENG.). 16p. (J). (gr. k-2). pap. 5.99 *(978-1-4333-2412-3(1))* Teacher Created Materials, Inc.

—Kip Gets Sick, 1 vol. 2011. (Targeted Phonics Ser.). (ENG., Illus.). 16p. (J). (gr. k-2). pap. 5.99 *(978-1-4333-2422-2(9))* Teacher Created Materials, Inc.

Barron Dc, Philip. Daddy Can't Play Now: A bedtime story of understanding & an introduction to Chiropractic Care. 2009.

(Illus.). 20p. pap. 10.99 (978-1-4490-1818-4(1)) AuthorHouse.

Benenfeld, Rikki. I Go to the Dentist. Rosenfeld, Dina & Leverton, Yossi, eds. Bennenfeld, Rikki, illus. 2011. (Toddler Experience Ser.). (ENG.). 32p. (J). 10.95 (978-1-929628-60-5(9)) Hachai Publishing.

Bernstein, Laurie & Helm, Joanna. Penny the Penguin Has Pku. 2012. 24p. pap. 17.99 (978-1-4772-7226-8(7)) AuthorHouse.

Berry, Ron. My Boo Boo BK. 2009. (ENG., Illus.). 12p. bds. 7.99 (978-0-8249-1403-5(1), Ideal Pubns.) Worthy Publishing.

Birkett, Georgie, illus. Clean It!/¡A Limpiar! 2009. (Helping Hands English/Spanish Edition Ser.). (ENG & SPA.). 24p. (J). (gr. -1-k). pap. (978-1-84643-569-0(2)) Child's Play International Ltd.

Bonilla, Daniel. My Magnificent Horse: An Inspirational. 2005. 76p. pap. 16.95 (978-1-4137-8617-0(0)) PublishAmerica, Inc.

Boutenko, Victoria. Green Smoothie Magic. Korobkina, Katya, illus. 2013. (ENG.). 56p. (J). (gr. -1-3). 12.95 (978-1-58394-601-5(2)) North Atlantic Bks.

Brennan, Sarah. A Dirty Story. Harrison, Harry, illus. 2012. (ENG.). 24p. (J). 21.95 (978-1-937160-26-5(2)) Eliassen Creative.

—An Even Dirtier Story. Harrison, Harry, illus. 2012. (ENG.). 24p. (J). 21.95 (978-1-937160-27-2(0)) Eliassen Creative.

Brenner, Martha F. Montones de Problemas; Stacks of Trouble. 2008. pap. 34.95 (978-1-58013-760-7(1)) Kane Press, Inc.

Brown, Phoenix. I Love to Exercise. Collins, Courtney, illus. 2008. 28p. pap. 24.95 (978-1-60563-727-3(0)) America Star Bks.

Bui, Chris Van. Yummy Yummy for My Tummy, 1 vol. 2009. 14p. pap. 24.95 (978-1-61582-826-5(5)) America Star Bks.

Civardi, Anna. Going to the Doctor Sticker Book. 2009. (First Experiences Sticker Book Ser.). 16p. (J). pap. 6.99 (978-0-7945-2572-9(5), Usborne) EDC Publishing.

Clennell, Bobby. Watch Me Do Yoga. 2010. (ENG., Illus.). 32p. (gr. -1-3). 15.95 (978-1-930485-26-6(3)) Shambhala Pubns., Inc.

Coats, Lucy. Captain Beastlie's Pirate Party. Mould, Chris, illus. 2014. (ENG.). 32p. (J). (gr. -1-2). 15.99 (978-0-7636-7399-4(4), Nosy Crow) Candlewick Pr.

Colbert, Don. The Toxic Detective. 2004. (Illus.). 24p. (J). (gr. k-3). pap. 9.99 (978-1-59185-205-6(6), Charisma Kids) Charisma Media.

Cole, Joanna. My Friend the Doctor. Chambliss, Maxie, illus. 2005. (ENG.). 32p. (J). (gr. -1 — 1). 6.99 (978-0-06-050500-4(1), HarperFestival) HarperCollins Pubs.

Cook, E. Diann. The Andersuns: Jarrell's Sweet Tooth. 2010. 36p. pap. 16.99 (978-1-4490-4997-3(4)) AuthorHouse.

Cousins, Lucy. Maisy Goes to the Hospital. 2009. (Maisy First Experiences Ser.). lib. bdg. 17.20 (978-0-606-06686-0(1), Turtleback) Turtleback Bks.

Cronin, Doreen. Stretch. Menchin, Scott, illus. 2009. (ENG.). 40p. (J). (gr. -1-3). 17.99 (978-1-4169-5341-8(8), Atheneum Bks. for Young Readers) Simon & Schuster Children's Publishing.

Danziger, Paula. Second Grade Rules, Amber Brown. Ross, Tony, illus. 2005. (Amber Brown Ser.). 48p. (gr. k-2). 14.00 (978-0-7569-5521-2(1)) Perfection Learning Corp.

Davidow, Shelley. Spirit of the Mountain, 1 vol. 2003. (ENG.). 144p. (YA). pap. 10.00 (978-0-86315-427-0(1)) Floris Bks. GBR. Dist: SteinerBooks, Inc.

Deem, Saitofi Anne. Myrtle Teachable Moments Series, 16 vols. Incl. Myrtle Learns about Asthma. 8p. (gr. -1-3). pap. 7.95 (978-1-930694-00-2(8)); Myrtle Learns about Dangerous Situations. 8p. (gr. -1-3). pap. 7.95 (978-1-930694-03-3(2)); Myrtle Learns about Diabetes. 12p. (gr. -1-3). pap. 7.95 (978-1-930694-04-0(0)); Myrtle Learns about Hygiene. 8p. (gr. -1-3). pap. 7.95 (978-1-930694-09-5(1)); Myrtle Learns about Lice. 12p. (gr. -1-3). pap. 7.95 (978-1-930694-11-8(3)); Myrtle Learns about Medicine. 8p. (gr. -1-3). pap. 7.95 (978-1-930694-12-5(1)); Myrtle Learns about Safety. 8p. (gr. -1-3). pap. 7.95 (978-1-930694-13-2(X)); Myrtle Learns about Seizures. 8p. (gr. -1-3). pap. 7.95 (978-1-930694-14-9(8)); Myrtle Learns How You Catch an Illness. 8p. (gr. -1-3). pap. 7.95 (978-1-930694-10-1(5)); Myrtle Learns to Eat Well. 12p. (gr. -1-3). pap. 7.95 (978-1-930694-05-7(9)); Myrtle Learns to Get Along. 8p. (gr. -1-3). pap. 7.95 (978-1-930694-08-8(3)); Myrtle Learns to Make Friends. 8p. (gr. -1-3). pap. 7.95 (978-1-930694-07-1(5)); Myrtle Learns to Take Care of Boo Boos. 12p. (gr. -1-3). pap. 7.95 (978-1-930694-01-9(6)); Myrtle Learns Why Exercise Is Important. 8p. pap. 7.95 (978-1-930694-06-4(7)); Myrtle Makes a Choice. 8p. (gr. -1-3). pap. 7.95 (978-1-930694-02-6(4)); Myrtle's Friend Is Very Sick. 8p. (gr. -1-3). pap. 7.95 (978-1-930694-15-6(6)); (J). 1998. (Illus.). Set pap. 114.48 (978-1-930694-16-3(4)) Myrtle Learns.

deRubertis, Barbara. Polly Porcupine's Painting Prize. Alley, R. W., illus. 2011. (Animal Antics A to Z Ser.). 32p. (J). pap. 45.32 (978-0-7613-7662-0(3)) Kane Press, Inc.

Dimari. I See a Healthy Me! 2013. 16p. pap. 7.95 (978-1-4525-8414-0(1), Balboa Pr.) Author Solutions, Inc.

Disney Book Group. Doc McStuffins: Awesome Guy to the Rescue! - Bella's Big Break, 2 bks. in 1. Disney Storybook Art Team, illus. 2015. (ENG.). 48p. (J). (gr. -1-k). pap. 5.99 (978-1-4847-0695-4(1)) Disney Pr.

Disney Book Group Staff. Doc on Call. Disney Storybook Art Team, illus. 2015. (ENG.). 40p. (J). (gr. -1-k). 10.99 (978-1-4847-2187-2(X)) Disney Pr.

Disney Staff. Disney Doc Mcstuffins Happy to Be Healthy! 2014. (Dress-Up Ser.: 4). (ENG.). 24p. (J). (gr. -1-1). 11.99 (978-0-7944-3019-1(8), Reader's Digest Children's Bks.) Studio Fun International.

Dobry, Beth. Why Ronald Fell Apart. 2008. 16p. pap. 8.95 (978-1-59858-687-9(4)) Dog Ear Publishing, LLC.

Downing, Lee. My Organ Buddies. 2010. 32p. (J). pap. 9.95 (978-0-615-32940-6(3)) Orsini Pr.

Dufresne, Didier, et al. Solamente un Poco de Gripe. Vinent, Julia, tr. Modéré, Armelle, illus. 2003. (SPA.). 32p. (J). (gr. k-2). 15.99 (978-84-8470-123-1(9)) Corimbo, Editorial S.L. ESP. Dist: Lectorum Pubns., Inc.

Dusablon, David. Dee Dee's First Shot, 1 vol. Spoerl, Amber, illus. 2009. 17p. pap. 24.95 (978-1-60749-113-2(3)) America Star Bks.

Electra, Agnes. Medical School for Children: Part I. 2011. 46p. pap. 18.00 (978-1-60911-756-6(5), Eloquent Bks.) Strategic Book Publishing & Rights Agency (SBPRA).

Evans, Jan. Repetitive Rhonda. 2007. (Illus.). 29p. (J). 18.95 (978-0-9720176-7-1(4)) Breath & Shadows Productions.

Falk, Kristi & Falk, Daniel. Eartha Gets Well. Peters, Rob, illus. 2012. (ENG.). 30p. (J). 24.95 (978-1-937084-27-1(2), BQB Publishing) Boutique of Quality Books Publishing Co., Inc.

Fapojuwo, Moyo Bukola. Kemi Shows You How to Be A Healthy Kid. 2006. (SPA.). (J). lib. bdg. 5.95 (978-1-59971-225-3(3)) Aardvark Global Publishing.

Fogarty, Laura. I Can Do Anything! 2008. 24p. pap. 24.95 (978-1-60563-501-9(4)) America Star Bks.

Franklin, Shawna. Catching Achoo. 2006. (ENG.). 28p. per. 11.95 (978-1-59800-492-2(1)) Outskirts Pr., Inc.

Galveston, Louise. By the Grace of Todd. 2015. (ENG., Illus.). 272p. (J). (gr. 3-7). pap. 8.99 (978-1-59514-678-6(4), Razorbill) Penguin Young Readers Group.

Gamble, Adam & Jasper, Mark. Good Night Yoga. Chan, Suwin & Blackmore, Katherine, illus. 2016. (Good Night Our World Ser.). (ENG.). 20p. (J). (— 1). bds. 9.95 (978-1-60219-414-4(9)) Good Night Bks.

Gonzalez, Rafael. Cookie Boy! 2011. 20p. pap. 11.99 (978-1-4634-0324-9(0)) AuthorHouse.

Goodman, Larry. Clean up the Glup! 2007. 24p. per. 24.95 (978-1-4241-9141-3(6)) America Star Bks.

Goodrow, Carol. The Treasure of Health & Happiness. Goodrow, Carol, illus. 2006. (ENG., Illus.). 96p. (J). (gr. 4-7). 14.00 (978-1-891369-60-5(1)) Breakaway Bks.

Gosselin, Kim. Smoking Stinks!! Buttner, Thom, illus. 2nd ed. 2009. (Substance Free Kids Ser.). 30p. (J). (gr. -1-3). pap. 16.95 (978-1-891383-20-5(5)) JayJo Bks., LLC.

Greene, Kathi. Betty Gets Ready for the Doctor. 2009. 28p. pap. 15.00 (978-1-4389-4936-9(7)) AuthorHouse.

Grimshaw, Luke. Sniffle, Sneeze, Cough Back Off! Brzozowski, Christina, illus. 2008. 24p. pap. 24.95 (978-1-60703-607-4(X)) America Star Bks.

—Sniffle, Sneeze, Cough... Back Off!, 1 vol. Brzozowski, Christina, illus. 2010. 22p. 24.95 (978-1-4512-1034-7(5)) America Star Bks.

Guest, Elissa Haden. Harriet's Had Enough! Meisel, Paul, illus. 2009. (ENG.). 32p. (J). (gr. -1-2). 15.99 (978-0-7636-3454-4(9)) Candlewick Pr.

Guin, Patricia. Growing Hope. 2017. (ENG.). 40p. 30.00 (978-1-68187-031-1(2)) Bk.Baby Print.

Gutman, Dan. Ms. Leakey Is Freaky! Paillot, Jim, illus. 2011. (My Weird School Daze Ser.: 12). 112p. (J). (gr. 1-5). lib. bdg. 15.89 (978-0-06-170403-1(2)) HarperCollins Pubs.

—Ms. Leakey Is Freaky! No. 12. Paillot, Jim, illus. 2011. (My Weird School Daze Ser.: 12). (ENG.). 112p. (J). (gr. 1-5). pap. 4.99 (978-0-06-170402-4(4)) HarperCollins Pubs.

Hamsa, Bobbie. Dirty Larry. Catanese, Donna, illus. rev. ed. 2003. (Rookie Reader Español Ser.). (ENG.). 24p. (J). (gr. k-2). pap. 4.95 (978-0-516-27493-5(7), Children's Pr.) Scholastic Library Publishing.

Hand, Reuben. The Push Up: Drill Sergeant Bear Volume 2. Fiebiger, John, illus. 2009. 20p. pap. 24.95 (978-1-61546-234-6(1)) America Star Bks.

Harris, Missy. I'm Allergic: Imma Lurgic's Story. 2009. 24p. pap. 12.99 (978-1-4490-1071-3(7)) AuthorHouse.

Heling, Kathryn & Hembrook, Deborah. I Wish I Was Strong Like Manuel. Adamson, Bonnie, illus. 2010. (I Wish Ser.). (ENG.). 32p. (J). (gr. 4-7). pap. 7.95 (978-1-934960-53-0(5), Raven Tree Pr.,Csi) Continental Sales, Inc.

Hewling, Amy Megan. Wishes. 2010. (ENG.). 29p. (978-1-907629-07-5(6)) ShieldCrest.

Hill, Maree. Nurse Nerid. 2011. 28p. pap. 28.03 (978-1-4568-5419-5(4)) Xlibris Corp.

Hill, Terri-Sue. I'm Healthy & Colorful from the Bottom Up. 2013. 40p. pap. 15.95 (978-1-4525-7232-1(1), Balboa Pr.) Author Solutions, Inc.

Hiskey, Iris. Hannah & the Hippo's No Mud Day. 2014. (ENG., Illus.). 32p. (J). (gr. -1-3). 16.99 (978-1-4814-2537-7(4), Simon & Schuster Bks. For Young Readers) Simon & Schuster Bks. For Young Readers.

Hogan, Tamara Anne. Mary Bea Says Why Is for Yog. Tortop, Anil, illus. 2013. 28p. pap. (978-1-922204-06-6(4)) Vivid Publishing.

Holst, Jerome Alphonse. Gretchen & the Gremlins. Krajenbrink Hulin, Yvonne, illus. 2012. 48p. pap. 15.95 (978-0-9794133-5-3(4)) TV Acres Bks.

Huang, Linda & Hoffman, Emily. Why Are You So Strong, Stanley? Stanley Shares with His Friend Walter His Secret to Being Healthy, Happy, & Strong. 2013. (ENG.). 26p. (J). 17.95 (978-1-4787-0359-4(8)) Outskirts Pr., Inc.

Huether, Michael & Huether, Amy. Ju Ju & the Sunblock. 2012. 32p. pap. 10.95 (978-1-60494-729-8(2)) Wheatmark, Inc.

Huisingh, Rosemary. Vocabulary Stories for Toddlers: My Body's Just Right for Me. 2012. (Illus.). 10p. (978-0-7606-1347-4(8)) LinguiSystems, Inc.

Jackson, Armitra L. Eating Safe with Ace & Mace! 2007. 44p. per. 15.95 (978-1-4327-1255-6(1)) Outskirts Pr., Inc.

Jenkins, Henry A. The Adventures of Monkey Squirrel & Frogman: Sand Trap. 2009. 16p. pap. 8.49 (978-1-4343-7827-9(6)) AuthorHouse.

Jones, Christianne C. The Messy One, 1 vol. Martinez-Neal, Juana, illus. 2011. (Little Boost Ser.). (ENG.). 32p. (gr. k-3). lib. bdg. 23.99 (978-1-4048-6651-5(5), Little Boost) Picture Window Bks.

Kay, Sjoukje & Kay, Sjoukje. The Donut Yogi. Vita, Ariela, illus. 2007. (ENG.). 32p. (J). 2.50 (978-0-9789698-1-3(2)) Kay, Sjoukje.

Kelley, Marty. The Messiest Desk. 2009. (J). (978-1-55933-319-1(7)) Zino Pr. Children's Bks.

Klise, Kate. Little Rabbit & the Meanest Mother on Earth. Klise, M. Sarah, illus. 2015. (ENG.). 32p. (J). (gr. -1-3). 6.99 (978-0-544-45611-2(4), HMH Books For Young Readers) Houghton Mifflin Harcourt Publishing Co.

Krumrey, Melanie. Bagels, Buddy, & Me: A Story about Gluten Intolerance & Celiac Disease. 2007. (Illus.). 40p. (J). per. 14.95 (978-0-9797703-0-2(0)) Mustard Seed Pr.

Kubler, Annie. Dinosaur Diner. 2008. (Finger Puppet Bks.). (ENG., Illus.). 24p. (J). (gr. -1-1). (978-1-84643-183-8(2)) Child's Play International Ltd.

Leedy, Loreen. Jack & the Hungry Giant: Eat Right with Myplate. 2013. (ENG., Illus.). 32p. (J). 17.95 (978-0-8234-2602-7(5)) Holiday Hse., Inc.

Leedy, Loreen & Leedy, Loreen. Jack & the Hungry Giant: Eat Right with Myplate. 2015. (ENG.). 32p. (J). (gr. -1-3). 7.99 (978-0-8234-3308-7(0)) Holiday Hse., Inc.

Leigh, Susan K. God I Need to Talt To you About Healthy Eating. 2011. 16p. pap. 1.19 (978-0-7586-2660-8(6)) Concordia Publishing Hse.

Lichtenheld, Tom. What Mess? 2012. (ENG., Illus.). 40p. (J). (gr. -1-3). pap. 7.00 (978-0-316-20123-0(5)) Little, Brown Bks. for Young Readers.

—What Mess? 2012. (J). lib. bdg. 17.20 (978-0-606-26686-4(0), Turtleback) Turtleback Bks.

Lucas, Ian & Medoza, Chris. The Million Year Meal. Cruz, Cheryl, illus. 2012. 32p. (J). 19.95 (978-1-60131-099-6(4)) Big Tent Bks.

Lydon, Jeff. Donald Dent. Behles, Liza, illus. 2003. 34p. (J). per. 10.00 (978-0-9724922-0-1(8)) Authors & Artists Publishers of New York, Inc.

MacDonald, Lisa Lynn. Can't Get Me! 2012. 36p. pap. 20.99 (978-1-4772-7948-9(2)) AuthorHouse.

Macenski, Geraldine. Healthy, Happy Gigi! 2009. 28p. pap. 15.99 (978-1-4415-3644-0(2)) Xlibris Corp.

Mankita, Jay. Elar. 2013. (Illus.). 38p. (J). pap. 9.95 (978-1-935734-49-9(0)) Kitanie Bks.

Marie, Cherry. The President Eats Vegetables & So Do I! 2012. 44p. pap. 12.00 (978-0-9853259-0-9(9)) Professional Publishing Hse. LLC.

Martín Anguita, Carmen & Carmen, Martín Anguita. Cuéntame un Cuento, Que Voy a Comer. Cortazar, Alicia Canas, illus. 2008. (SPA.). 32p. (J). 10.99 (978-84-241-5752-4(4)) Everest Editora ESP. Dist: Lectorum Pubns., Inc.

Massey, David. Torn. 2013. (ENG.). 288p. (J). (gr. 9). 17.99 (978-0-545-49645-2(4)) Scholastic, Inc.

Mattern, Joanne. Batter Up! 2005. (J). pap. (978-1-4108-4193-3(6)) Benchmark Education Co.

Mayer, Mercer & Mayer, Gina. Staying Well. 2013. (Big Little Critter Ser.: 5). (ENG.). 96p. (J). 12.95 (978-1-60746-732-8(1), Premiere) FastPrncil, Inc.

McDaniel, Carren. Fresh Air Friends: The Dangers of Secondhand Smoke. 2012. (ENG.). 33p. (J). pap. 14.95 (978-1-4327-9818-5(9)) Outskirts Pr., Inc.

McDonald, Megan. The Doctor Is In! Reynolds, Peter H., illus. 2010. (Judy Moody Ser.: 5). (ENG.). 176p. (J). (gr. 1-4). 15.99 (978-0-7636-4862-6(0)); pap. 5.99 (978-0-7636-4861-9(2)) Candlewick Pr.

McMullan, Kate. I'm Dirty! McMullan, Jim, illus. 2015. (ENG.). 40p. (J). (gr. -1-3). pap. 6.99 (978-0-06-009295-5(5)) HarperCollins Pubs.

—I'm Dirty! Board Book. McMullan, Jim, illus. 2015. (ENG.). 34p. (J). (gr. -1 — 1). bds. 7.99 (978-0-06-234318-5(1)) HarperCollins Pubs.

McPhate, Paul. The Puggles: The Adventures of Carly & Vinigin. 2006. (ENG.). 48p. per. 16.95 (978-1-4241-4481-5(7)) PublishAmerica, Inc.

Midence, Dominica. Mary's Fairy Learns to Exercise. 2009. 28p. pap. 13.99 (978-1-4389-5003-7(9)) AuthorHouse.

Milway, Katie Smith. Mimi's Village & How Basic Health Care Transformed It. Fernandes, Eugenie, illus. 2012. (CitizenKid Ser.). (ENG.). 32p. (J). (gr. 3-7). 18.95 (978-1-55453-722-8(3)) Kids Can Pr., Ltd. CAN. Dist: Hachette Bk. Group.

Mith with an Itch. 2008. (Illus.). 34p. (J). 10.95 (978-0-9800259-0-3(7)) Dream Weaver Ministries, Inc.

Moncure, Jane Belk. 'Smile,' Says Little Crocodile: A Book about Good Habits. DeSantis, Susan, illus. 2013. (Magic Castle Readers Ser.). (ENG.). 32p. (J). (gr. -1-2). 25.64 (978-1-62323-570-3(7), 206305) Child's World, Inc., The.

Montgomery Gibson, Jane. Oh Forsooth! I've Lost a Tooth! Montgomery Gibson, Jane, illus. 2005. (Illus.). (J). bds. 8.99 (978-1-4183-0021-0(7)) Christ Inspired, Inc.

Morris, Cathy. I'm a Perfectly Normal Kid Who Happens to Have Diabetes! Grunden, Kimberly, illus. 2007. 24p. per. 12.95 (978-1-934246-85-6(9)) Peppertree Pr., The.

Murphy, Stuart J. Happy, Healthy Ajay! 2012. (I See I Learn Ser.). (ENG., Illus.). 32p. (J). (-k). 14.95 (978-1-58089-470-8(4)); pap. 6.95 (978-1-58089-471-5(2)) Charlesbridge Publishing, Inc.

Murray, Diana. Grimelda: the Very Messy Witch. Ross, Heather, illus. 2016. 32p. (J). (gr. -1-3). 16.99 (978-0-06-226448-0(6), Tegen, Katherine Bks) HarperCollins Pubs.

Nancy St. Paul-Martin. Go to the Nurse: Peanut Puffs & Snicker-Doodles. 2009. 28p. pap. 15.49 (978-1-4389-7653-2(4)) AuthorHouse.

Nelson, Jan. Signs of Love. Bohart, Lisa, illus. 2009. 24p. pap. 12.95 (978-1-936051-54-0(0)) Peppertree Pr., The.

NeonSeon. Life of Shouty: Food & Fitness, bk. 2. NeonSeon, illus. 2011. (Life of Shouty Ser.: 2). (ENG., Illus.). 32p. (J). 14.95 (978-0-9842069-1-9(4)) RIXKIN.

North, Laura. Hansel & Gretel & the Green Witch. Jevons, Chris, illus. 2015. (ENG.). 32p. (J). (978-0-7787-1928-1(6)) Crabtree Publishing Co.

North, Merry. Squeaky Clean. 2005. 9p. (978-1-57151-752-4(9)) Playhouse Publishing.

Norton, J. Renae. How Maji Gets Mongo off the Couch! Reed, Cleone, ed. Hayes, Steve & Cole, Amy, illus. 2012. (Maji & Mongo Bks.: 0). (ENG.). 32p. (J). (gr. k-3). 17.95 (978-1-934759-60-8(0)) Reed, Robert D. Pubs.

Oberst M. D., Faap Byron. Brownie Bill & the Health Pirates. 2013. 44p. pap. 20.72 (978-1-4669-9098-2(8)) Trafford Publishing.

Palatini, Margie. Gorgonzola: A Very Stinkysaurus. Bowers, Tim, illus. 2008. (ENG.). 32p. (J). (gr. -1-2). 17.99 (978-0-06-073897-6(9), Tegen, Katherine Bks) HarperCollins Pubs.

Paley, Rebecca, et al. The Body Book for Boys. 2010. (ENG.). 128p. (J). (gr. 5-9). pap. 8.99 (978-0-545-23751-2(3), Scholastic Paperbacks) Scholastic, Inc.

Paoline, Dyann. Cecilia's Fitness Adventure. 2011. 24p. pap. 15.75 (978-1-4634-0797-1(1)) AuthorHouse.

Pappas, Diane H. & Covey, Richard D. It's Good to Be Clean. Estrada, Ric, illus. 2007. (J). pap. (978-0-545-01430-4(1)) Scholastic, Inc.

Parish, Herman. Calling Doctor Amelia Bedelia. Sweat, Lynn, illus. 2004. (Amelia Bedelia Ser.). 64p. (gr. -1-2). 14.00 (978-0-7569-3209-1(2)) Perfection Learning Corp.

Parker, Emma. Blah the Bacteria. 2010. (Illus.). pap. (978-1-877547-46-1(8)) First Edition Ltd.

—Skipping Sally. 2010. (Illus.). pap. (978-1-877561-24-5(X)) First Edition Ltd.

Patrick, Wellman. Mr. Duz Goes to the Doctor. Sam, Kagan, illus. 2007. 24p. (J). 5.95 (978-0-9796226-6-3(2)) MrDuz.com.

Peets, Risa. It's OK to Be Different: An Amazing School Day. 2013. (ENG., Illus.). 76p. (J). pap. 7.99 (978-1-937008-17-8(7)) Heart to Heart Publishing, Inc.

Penner, Lucille Recht. A Limpiar el Campamento; Clean Sweep Campers. 2008. pap. 34.95 (978-1-58013-758-4(X)) Kane Press, Inc.

Racek, Jennifer. Cadberry's Letters. 2008. 33p. 13.90 (978-1-4357-0566-1(1)) Lulu Pr., Inc.

Rainforth, Hannah. Barnaby Bennett, 1 vol. Teo, Ali, illus. 2008. (ENG.). 32p. (J). (gr. -1-3). pap. 5.95 (978-1-59572-156-3(8)) Star Bright Bks., Inc.

Rebecca, Amy. Healthy Habits: The Rainbow Food. 2013. 28p. pap. 24.95 (978-1-63004-021-5(5)) America Star Bks.

Rebein, Alyssa Chase & Chase, Andra. Stanley's "This Is the Life!" Chase, Andra, illus. 2008. (Illus.). (J). (978-1-55942-570-4(9)) Witcher Productions.

Recob, Amy. The BugaBees: Friends with Food Allergies. 2009. (Illus.). 32p. (J). (978-1-59298-279-0(4)) Beaver's Pond Pr., Inc.

Rey, H. A. Race Day. 2010. (Curious George Ser.). (ENG., Illus.). 24p. (J). (gr. -1-3). pap. 3.99 (978-0-547-39361-2(X)) Houghton Mifflin Harcourt Publishing Co.

Ritchey, Melissa. The Kabeezles. 2006. (Illus.). 16p. (J). lib. bdg. 18.95 (978-0-9761128-5-3(X)) KB Bks. & More.

Rodenburg, Michelle. The Good Germ. 2007. (Illus.). 32p. (J). per. 10.95 net. (978-0-9795407-1-4(2)) Grubnedor Pr.

Rosenthal, Amy Krouse. Little Oink. Corace, Jen, illus. aut. ed. 2009. (ENG.). (J). 14.99 (978-0-8118-8331-3(0)) Chronicle Bks. LLC.

Ross, Tony, illus. I Don't Want to Go to Hospital. 2013. (ENG.). 32p. (J). (gr. -1-3). 16.95 (978-1-4677-1155-5(1)) Lerner Publishing Group.

Rossman, Alicia. Miss Lyla's Banana Pancakes to the Rescue! Harkins, Nathan, illus. 2012. 26p. (J). (-18). 19.95 (978-1-61863-342-2(2)) Bookstand Publishing.

Royster, Ka-Sandra. Cough Syrup in Mommy's Hair. 2013. 24p. pap. (978-1-4602-2600-1(3)) FriesenPress.

Rutman, Meredyth & Rutman, Rhett. The Couch Potato Classroom. 2011. 40p. pap. 9.95 (978-1-60047-656-3(2)) Wasteland Pr.

Santillo, LuAnn. Toad. Santillo, LuAnn, ed. 2003. (Half-Pint Kids Readers Ser.). (Illus.). 7p. (gr. -1-1). pap. 1.00 (978-1-59256-107-0(1)) Half-Pint Kids, Inc.

Saunders, Len. Joey the Kangaroo: An Adventure in Exercise. 2010. 32p. pap. 14.95 (978-1-4389-3992-6(2)) AuthorHouse.

—Spunky the Monkey: An Adventure in Exercise. 2010. 32p. pap. 14.95 (978-1-4389-3991-9(4)) AuthorHouse.

Schaefer, Lola M. Loose Tooth. Wickstrom, Sylvie Kantorovitz, illus. 2005. (My First I Can Read Ser.). (ENG.). 32p. (J). (gr. -1-3). pap. 3.99 (978-0-06-052778-5(1)) HarperCollins Pubs.

Schiavi, Sherry. Chelsea's Healthy Secrets. Huffmaster, Elizabeth, illus. 2004. (J). per. 14.95 (978-0-9746378-0-8(7)) Celltrition.

Sherri L. Berner. Healthy Fun with Benjamin & Jasmine: ABCs of the Human Body. Michael A. Cicchetti, illus. 2009. 32p. pap. 12.99 (978-1-4343-8297-9(4)) AuthorHouse.

Sloyer, Elliot. The Safety Pin: Summer Camp Stories. Guiza, Victor, illus. 2014. (ENG.). 32p. (J). 16.95 (978-1-60131-182-5(6), Castlebridge Bks.) Big Tent Bks.

Smart Kids Publishing Staff, creator. Everybody Takes a Bath. 2006. (Rub a Dub Fun in the Tub Ser.). (ENG., Illus.). 10p. (J). (gr. -1). 8.95 (978-0-8249-6681-2(3), Ideal Pubns.) Worthy Publishing.

Spillane, Lisa. Six Healing Sounds with Lisa & Ted: Qigong for Children. Spillane, Lisa, illus. 2011. (ENG., Illus.). 32p. 14.95 (978-1-84819-051-1(4), 4977, Singing Dragon) Kingsley, Jessica Pubs. GBR. Dist: Macmillan Distribution Ltd.

Spinelli, Eileen. Miss Fox's Class Shapes Up. Kennedy, Anne, illus. 2011. (ENG.). 32p. (J). (gr. 1-3). 16.99 (978-0-8075-5171-4(6)) Whitman, Albert & Co.

St. John, Justine. Wilbur the Zucchini-Eating Dragon. 2012. (ENG., Illus.). 24p. (J). pap. 9.99 (978-0-9829256-3-8(8)) SDP Publishing.

Steig, William. Shrek! 2008. (Illus.). (gr. -1-3). 17.00 (978-1-60686-207-0(3)) Perfection Learning Corp.

Stewart, Jennifer J. Close Encounters of a Third-World Kind. 2008. (ENG., Illus.). 181p. (J). (gr. 3-7). 6.95 (978-0-8234-2161-9(9)) Holiday Hse., Inc.

Su'a, Melissa L. What Animals Eat Can Be My Healthy Treat. 2010. 24p. pap. 11.49 (978-1-4389-9078-1(2)) AuthorHouse.

Terry-Todd, Terlene. Sweetie's Healthy Start. 2009. 28p. pap. 12.99 (978-1-60693-829-4(0), Strategic Bk. Publishing) Strategic Book Publishing & Rights Agency (SBPRA).

Thompson, Lauren. Hop, Hop, Jump! Krosoczka, Jarrett J., illus. 2012. (ENG.). 32p. (J). (gr. -1-3). 15.99 (978-1-4169-9745-0(8), McElderry, Margaret K. Bks.) McElderry, Margaret K. Bks.

Thompson, Tamara. Before You Were Born. 2010. 28p. pap. (978-1-84991-205-1(X)) Chipmunkapublishing.

Thomson, Linda. Harry the Hypno-potamus: Metaphorical Tales for the Treatment of Children. 2005. (Illus.). 176p. 44.95 (978-1-904424-57-4(0), 4570) Crown Hse. Publishing.

Toporoff, Debi. Roscoe Goes to the Gym. Butler, Gregory J., illus. 2007.Tr. of Rosco Va Al Gimnasio. (ENG.). 32p. (gr. -1-3). 9.99 (978-1-59979-215-6(X), Creation Hse.) Charisma Media.

Viorst, Judith. Super-Completely & Totally the Messiest! Glasser, Robin Preiss, illus. 2006. (ENG.). 32p. (J). (gr. -1-2). 16.99 (978-1-4169-4200-9(9), Atheneum Bks. for Young Readers) Simon & Schuster Children's Publishing.

Vollmer, Cheryl. A Hungry Lion in My Tummy. Dimitriadis, Nick, illus. 2009. 24p. pap. 9.99 (978-0-9825255-9-3(1), Epigraph Bks.) Monkfish Bk. Publishing Co.

Walker, Nan & Kulling, Monica. The Messiest Room on the Planet. 2009. (Social Studies Connects (r) Ser.). (ENG.). (gr.

k-2). pap. 33.92 *(978-0-7613-4803-0(4))* Lerner Publishing Group.
Walters, Eric. A Reventar: (Stuffed), 1 vol. 2011. (Spanish Soundings Ser.). (SPA.). 144p. (YA). (gr. 8-12). pap. 9.95 *(978-1-55469-861-5(8))* Orca Bk. Pubs. USA.
Whelahan, Marlene. Once upon a Peanut: A true Story... Killian, Sue, illus. 2009. 24p. pap. 12.99 *(978-1-4389-5925-2(7))* AuthorHouse.
Whitford, Rebecca. Sleepy Little Yoga. Selway, Martina, illus. 2007. (ENG.). 28p. (J). (gr. -1 — 1). 13.99 *(978-0-8050-8193-0(3)*, 9780805081930, Holt, Henry & Co. Bks. For Young Readers) Holt, Henry & Co.
Winborne, Mamie Pearl. Sweet Sugar I Got Your Back. 2012. 150p. pap. 13.95 *(978-0-615-58624-3(4))* Professional Publishing Hse. LLC.
Yangas, Angela Marie. The Buggazz: Let There Be Light. 2007. 19.99 *(978-0-9801796-0-6(2))* Binx Bks.
Young, Eugene Randolph, illus. & des. The Food Convention. Young, Eugene Randolph, des. l.t. ed. 2006. 32p. (J). 16.95 *(978-0-9792000-0-7(8))* Les Lum Pubs.
Ziefert, Harriet. Messy Bessie: Where's My Homework? De Muth, Roger, illus. 2007. (J). *(978-1-4287-4707-4(9))* Handprint Bks.

HEALTH, MENTAL

see Mental Health

HEALTH, PUBLIC

see Public Health

HEALTH EDUCATION

Bunting, Lisa, et al. Harcourt Health & Fitness. 2006. (Illus.). 272p. 34.00 *(978-0-15-355122-2(4))*; 328p. 40.95 *(978-0-15-355124-6(0))* Harcourt Schl. Pubs.
E.C Drury Life Skills Class, et al. Viral Avenger: Adventures at Auld College. 2010. 28p. pap. 16.09 *(978-1-4269-2926-7(9))* Trafford Publishing.
Gibbons, Charlie, et al. Graph Links Activity Package for Health. 2003. (Your Health Ser.). (gr. 3-6). 71.90 *(978-0-15-306441-8(2))* Harcourt Schl. Pubs.
—Graph Links Activity Package for Health: Macintosh. 2003. (Your Health Ser.). (gr. 3-6). *(978-0-15-306928-4(7))* Harcourt Schl. Pubs.
—Teacher's Editions. 99th ed. 2003. (Your Health Ser.). (gr. 2-18). tchr. ed. 131.60 *(978-0-15-310146-5(6))*; (gr. 1-18). tchr. ed. 131.60 *(978-0-15-310145-8(8))* Harcourt Schl. Pubs.
Goodrow, Carol. Happy Feet, Healthy Food: Your Child's First Journal of Exercise & Healthy Eating. Goodrow, Carol, illus. 2004. (ENG., Illus.). 112p. (J). 14.00 *(978-1-891369-46-9(6))* Breakaway Bks.
Green, Tammy L., et al. Ruby Explores the World of Wellnss. 2005. (ENG., Illus.). 88p. (gr. k-5). stu. ed. 20.00 *(978-0-7360-6229-9(7))* Human Kinetics Pubs.
—Ruby Learns about the World of Wellness. 2005. (ENG., Illus.). 88p. (gr. k-5). stu. ed. 20.00 *(978-0-7360-6228-2(9))* Human Kinetics Pubs.
—Sydney Travels Through the World of Wellness. 2005. (ENG., Illus.). 88p. (gr. k-5). stu. ed. 20.00 *(978-0-7360-6232-9(7))* Human Kinetics Pubs.
—T. J.'s Adventures in the World of Wellness. 2005. (ENG., Illus.). 88p. (gr. k-5). stu. ed. 20.00 *(978-0-7360-6231-2(9))* Human Kinetics Pubs.
Hand, Carol. 12 Healthy Habits for Life. 2017. (J). *(978-1-62143-506-8(7))* Pr. Room Editions LLC.
Hand, Carol & Mangor, Jodie. 12 Healthy Habits for Life. 2016. (Healthy Living Ser.). (ENG., Illus.). 32p. (J). pap. 9.95 *(978-1-63235-382-5(2))* Pr. Room Editions LLC.
Harcourt School Publishers Staff. Your Health. 3rd ed. 2003. (Your Health Ser.). (Illus.). (gr. 2-18). pupil's gde. ed. 40.60 *(978-0-15-334301-8(X))*; act. bk. ed. 5.70 *(978-0-15-334670-5(1))* Harcourt Schl. Pubs.
Harris, Robie H. It's Perfectly Normal. 2014. lib. bdg. 24.50 *(978-0-606-35863-7(3))* Turtleback Bks.
Helpline: Teen Issues & Answers. 2013. (Helpline: Teen Issues & Answers Ser.). 80p. (YA). (gr. 7-12). 199.50 *(978-1-4488-9459-8(X))* Rosen Publishing Group, Inc., The.
Koniver, Laura. From the Ground Up. Koniver, Laura, illus. 2012. (Illus.). 44p. (J). pap. 16.99 *(978-1-937848-03-3(5))* Do Life Right, Inc.
Marshack, D. L. I'm the Tooth Fairy: Amy's First Visit. 2012. 24p. pap. 17.99 *(978-1-4634-1195-4(2))* AuthorHouse.
Mayo Clinic Health Information, 11 bks., Set. (Illus.). (gr. 8-18). lib. bdg. 329.45 *(978-1-59084-545-5(5))* Mason Crest.
McTavish, Sandra. Life Skills: 225 Ready-to-Use Health Activities for Success & Well-Being (Grades 6-12) 2003. (ENG., Illus.). 284p. pap. 32.95 *(978-0-7879-6959-2(1)*, Jossey-Bass) Wiley, John & Sons, Inc.
Meeks, Linda, et al. Health & Wellness. 2006. (Illus.). 806p. 113.00 *(978-0-07-829857-8(1))* McGraw-Hill Cos., The.
Nygard, Bonnie K., et al. Cody Investigates the World of Wellness. 2005. (ENG., Illus.). 88p. (gr. k-5). stu. ed. 20.00 *(978-0-7360-6230-5(0))* Human Kinetics Pubs.
—WOW! Sydney Travels Through the World of Wellness. 2005. (ENG., Illus.). 88p. (gr. k-5). pap., stu. ed. 12.00 *(978-0-7360-5580-2(0))* Human Kinetics Pubs.
Paonessa, Mary. Growth & Development with Friends, 8 vols. 3rd rev. ed. 2003. (Human Growth & Development Ser.). (Illus.). 41p. (J). (gr. 5-18). pap. 9.00 *(978-0-9711721-0-4(2)*, 388) Paon Pubns.
—Growth & Development with Friends & Family, 8 vols. 3rd rev. ed. 2003. (Human Growth & Development Ser.). (Illus.). 64p. (J). (gr. 6-18). pap. 11.00 *(978-0-9711721-2-8(9)*, 390) Paon Pubns.
—Growth & Development with Friends & School, 8 vols. 3rd ed. 2003. (Human Growth & Development Ser.). (Illus.). (J). (gr. 7-18). 112p. pap., tchr. ed. 15.00 *(978-0-9711721-5-9(3)*, 393); 91p. pap. *(978-0-9711721-4-2(5)*, 392) Paon Pubns.
Rustad, Martha E. H. Healthy Me. 2017. (Healthy Me Ser.). (ENG.). 24p. (gr. k-1). 87.96 *(978-1-5157-4002-5(1)*, Pebble Bks.) Capstone Press of Coughlan Cos.
Santillo, LuAnn. The Doctor. Santillo, LuAnn, ed. 2003. (Half-Pint Kids Readers Ser.). (Illus.). 7p. (J). (gr. -1-1). pap. 1.00 *(978-1-59256-121-6(7))* Half-Pint Kids, Inc.

HEALTH OF CHILDREN

see Children—Health and Hygiene

HEARING

see also Ear

Abbs, Brian, et al. Postcards 1. 2nd ed. 2007. (ENG.). 136p. pap. 27.00 *(978-0-13-179131-2(1))* Pearson ESL.
Aloian, Molly. What Is Hearing? 2013. (ENG., Illus.). 24p. (J). *(978-0-7787-0970-1(1))*; pap. *(978-0-7787-0997-8(3))* Crabtree Publishing Co.
Appleby, Alex. Lo Que Oigo / What I Hear. 2014. (Mis Cinco Sentidos / My Five Senses Ser.). (SPA.). 24p. (J). (gr. k-2). 22.60 *(978-1-4824-0869-0(4))* Stevens, Gareth Publishing LLLP.
—What I Hear. 2014. (My Five Senses Ser.). (Illus.). 24p. (J). (gr. k-2). pap. 8.15 *(978-1-4824-0776-1(0))* Stevens, Gareth Publishing LLLP.
Arif, Amrana. Allah Gave Me Two Ears to Hear. Clarke, Asiya, illus. 2015. (ENG.). 32p. (J). 8.95 *(978-0-86037-353-7(3))* Kube Publishing Ltd. GBR. Dist: Consortium Bk. Sales & Distribution.
Ballard, Carol. How Your Ears Work. 2010. (Your Body at Work Ser.). (ENG.). 32p. (YA). (gr. 2-5). lib. bdg. 26.60 *(978-1-4339-4106-1(6))* Stevens, Gareth Publishing LLLP.
Barnham, Kay. Hearing. 2005. (Our Senses Ser.). (Illus.). 24p. (gr. k-3). lib. bdg. 23.00 *(978-0-8368-4406-1(8)*, Gareth Stevens Learning Library) Stevens, Gareth Publishing LLLP.
Barraclough, Sue. What Can I Hear? 2005. (J). *(978-1-4034-7078-2(2))*; (ENG.). 32p. pap. *(978-1-4034-7084-3(7))* Steck-Vaughn.
Beaumont, S. Baby Senses Hearing. 2005. 12p. bds. *(978-1-905051-46-5(8))* Make Believe Ideas.
Bellamy, Adam. What's That I Hear? 2017. (All about My Senses Ser.). 24p. (J). (gr. k-1). lib. bdg. 22.60 ***(978-0-7660-8603-6(8))*** Enslow Pubs., Inc.
Boothroyd, Jennifer. What Is Hearing? 2009. (Lightning Bolt Books (tm) — Your Amazing Senses Ser.). (ENG.). 32p. (gr. k-2). pap. 7.95 *(978-0-7613-5014-9(4))*; (Illus.). (J). 26.60 *(978-0-7613-4250-2(8)*, Lerner Pubns.) Lerner Publishing Group.
Burstein, John. Have You Heard? Active Listening. 2009. (Slim Goodbody's Life Skills 101 Ser.). (ENG., Illus.). 32p. (J). (gr. 3-6). pap. *(978-0-7787-4806-9(5))*; lib. bdg. *(978-0-7787-4790-1(5))* Crabtree Publishing Co.
Carr, Aaron. El Oido. 2013. (Mis Sentidos Ser.). (SPA., Illus.). 24p. (J). (gr. -1-3). lib. bdg. 27.13 *(978-1-62127-575-6(2)*, AV2 by Weigl) Weigl Pubs., Inc.
Challoner, Jack. Sound: An Investigation. 2008. (Science Investigations Ser.). (Illus.). 32p. (YA). (gr. 4-7). lib. bdg. 26.50 *(978-1-4042-4285-2(6))* Rosen Publishing Group, Inc., The.
Coan, Sharon. Message Received!, 1 vol. (Science Readers: Content & Literacy Ser.). (ENG., Illus.). 24p. (gr. 1-1). 2015. (J). 22.96 *(978-1-4938-1152-6(5))* 2014. pap. 8.99 *(978-1-4807-4565-0(0))* Teacher Created Materials, Inc.
Cobb, Vicki. Perk up Your Ears: Discover Your Sense of Hearing. Lewis, Cynthia, illus. 2003. (Five Senses Ser.). (ENG.). 32p. (gr. 3-5). pap. 7.95 *(978-0-7613-1981-8(6)*, Millbrook Pr.) Lerner Publishing Group.
Dayton, Connor. Hearing. 2014. (Your Five Senses & Your Sixth Sense Ser.). 24p. (J). (gr. k-2). 22.60 *(978-1-4777-3240-3(3)*, PowerKids Pr.) Rosen Publishing Group, Inc., The.
—El Oído / Hearing. De La Vega, Eida, ed. 2014. (Tus Cinco Sentidos y Tu Sexto Sentido / Your Five Senses & Your Sixth Sense Ser.). (SPA & BYN.). 24p. (J). (gr. k-2). 23.60 *(978-1-4777-3268-7(3)*, PowerKids Pr.) Rosen Publishing Group, Inc., The.
Douglas, Lloyd G. My Ears. 2004. (Wel-My Body Ser.). (J). 19.00 *(978-0-516-24062-6(5)*, Children's Pr.) Scholastic Library Publishing.
Dunne, Abbie. Sound. 2016. (Physical Science Ser.). (ENG., Illus.). 24p. (gr. k-1). lib. bdg. 26.65 *(978-1-5157-0940-4(X)*, Pebble Plus) Capstone Press of Coughlan Cos.
Durrie, Karen. Hearing. 2012. (J). *(978-1-61913-309-9(1))*; pap. 12.95 *(978-1-61913-314-3(8))* Weigl Pubs., Inc.
Enslow, Brian. My Ears. 2010. (All about My Body Ser.). (Illus.). 24p. (J). 22.60 *(978-0-7660-3812-7(2))*; pap. 7.95 *(978-1-59845-168-9(5))* Enslow Pubs., Inc. (Enslow Elementary).
Fullick, Ann. Why Do My Ears Pop? Hearing, 1 vol. 2011. (Inside My Body Ser.). (ENG.). 32p. (gr. 3-5). 30.65 *(978-1-4109-4016-2(0)*, NA-r) Heinemann-Raintree.
Furgang, Kathy. My Ears. 2009. (My Body Ser.). 24p. (gr. 3-3). 42.50 *(978-1-61514-687-1(3)*, PowerKids Pr.) Rosen Publishing Group, Inc., The.
Ganeri, Anita. Hearing. 2013. (Senses Ser.). (Illus.). 24p. (gr. k-3). 28.50 *(978-1-59920-851-0(2))* Black Rabbit Bks.
Gray, Susan H. Hearing. 2008. (21st Century Skills Innovation Library: Innovation in Medicine Ser.). (ENG., Illus.). 32p. (gr. 4-8). lib. bdg. 28.50 *(978-1-60279-227-2(5)*, 200158) Cherry Lake Publishing.
Hall, Kirsten. Animal Hearing. 2005. (Animals & Their Senses Ser.). (Illus.). 24p. (gr. k-3). pap. 8.15 *(978-0-8368-4808-3(X))*; lib. bdg. 22.00 *(978-0-8368-4802-1(0))* Stevens, Gareth Publishing LLLP. (Weekly Reader Leveled Readers).
—Animal Hearing/El Oido en los Animales. 2005. (Animals & Their Senses/ Los sentidos de los animales Ser.). (ENG & SPA., Illus.). 24p. (J). (gr. k-3). lib. bdg. 22.00 *(978-0-8368-4814-4(4)*, Weekly Reader Leveled Readers) Stevens, Gareth Publishing LLLP.
Halvorson, Karin. Inside the Ears, 1 vol. 2013. (Super Simple Your Body Ser.). (ENG.). 32p. (J). (gr. k-4). 27.07 *(978-1-61783-610-7(9))* ABDO Publishing Co.
Hewitt, Sally. Hear This! 2008. (Let's Start Science Ser.). (ENG., Illus.). 24p. (J). (gr. 3-7). pap. *(978-0-7787-4058-2(7))* Crabtree Publishing Co.
Hidalgo, Maria. Hearing. 2003. 24p. (J). lib. bdg. 21.35 *(978-1-58340-304-4(3))* Black Rabbit Bks.
Issa, Joanna. What Can I Hear?, 1 vol. 2014. (These Are My Senses Ser.). (ENG., Illus.). 24p. (gr. -1-1). pap. 5.99 *(978-1-4846-0433-5(4)*, Acorn) Heinemann-Raintree.
Jennings, Terry J. Sound. 2009. (J). 28.50 *(978-1-59920-275-4(1))* Black Rabbit Bks.
Kubler, Annie, illus. What Can I Hear? 2011. (Small Senses Ser.). (ENG.). 12p. (J). bds. *(978-1-84643-377-1(0))* Child's Play International Ltd.
Landau, Elaine. The Sense of Hearing. (True Book(tm), a — Health & the Human Body Ser.). (ENG., 48p. (J). 2008. Illus.). (gr. 2-5). 31.00 *(978-0-531-16870-7(0))* 2009. pap. 6.95 *(978-0-531-21832-7(5)*, Children's Pr.) Scholastic Library Publishing.
Lay, Kathryn. Hearing Their Prey: Animals with an Amazing Sense of Hearing, 1 vol. Wald, Christina, illus. 2012. (Sensing Their Prey Ser.). (ENG.). 32p. (J). (gr. -1-4). lib. bdg. 28.50 *(978-1-61641-866-3(4)*, Looking Glass Library) Magic Wagon.
Libra, Anna. Why Does Loud Music Hurt My Ears? An Inside Look at the Ear. 2003. (J). pap. *(978-1-58417-072-3(7))*; lib. bdg. *(978-1-58417-009-9(3))* Lake Street Pubs.
Llewellyn, Claire. Hearing. 2005. (I Know That! Ser.). (Illus.). 24p. (J). (gr. 1-3). lib. bdg. 22.80 *(978-1-932889-47-5(7))* Sea-To-Sea Pubns.
—Sound & Hearing. 2011. (Start-Up Connections Ser.). (ENG., Illus.). 32p. (J). pap. 12.99 *(978-0-237-54364-8(8))* Evans Brothers, Ltd. GBR. Dist: Independent Pubs. Group.
Losacano, Connie. Now I Can Hear! 2009. 16p. pap. 8.49 *(978-1-4490-5270-6(3))* AuthorHouse.
Lowery, Lawrence F. Quiet As a Butterfly. 2017. (I Wonder Why Ser.). (ENG., Illus.). 36p. (J). (gr. k-2). pap. 11.95 *(978-1-68140-354-0(4))* National Science Teachers Assn.
MauleDavid. ARE YOU LISTENING? THE SENSE OF HEARING HIGH BEGINNING BOOK WITH ONLINE ACCESS. 2014. (ENG.). 24p. (J). pap. 9.50 *(978-1-107-63251-6(X))* Cambridge Univ. Pr.
Mayo Clinic Staff, contrib. by. 10 Tips for Better Hearing. 2004. (Compact Guides to Fitness & Health Ser.). (Illus.). 36,52p. (YA). lib. bdg. 15.95 *(978-1-59084-265-2(0))* Mason Crest.
Meachen Rau, Dana. Shhhh... [Scholastic]: A Book about Hearing. Peterson, Rick, illus. 2010. (Amazing Body: the Five Senses Ser.). 24p. pap. 0.56 *(978-1-4048-6541-9(1)*, Nonfiction Picture Bks.) Picture Window Bks.
Milet Publishing Staff. My Bilingual Book-Hearing. 2014. (My Bilingual Book Ser.). (ENG & CHI., Illus.). 28p. (J). (gr. -1-k). 9.95 *(978-1-84059-774-5(7))*; 9.95 *(978-1-84059-785-1(2))*; 9.95 *(978-1-84059-779-0(8))* Milet Publishing.
—My Bilingual Book-Hearing (English-Arabic) 2014. (My Bilingual Book Ser.). (ENG & ARA., Illus.). 28p. (J). (gr. -1-k). 9.95 *(978-1-84059-772-1(0))* Milet Publishing.
—My Bilingual Book-Hearing (English-Bengali) 2014. (My Bilingual Book Ser.). (ENG & BEN., Illus.). 28p. (J). (gr. -1-k). 9.95 *(978-1-84059-773-8(9))* Milet Publishing.
—My Bilingual Book-Hearing (English-Farsi) 2014. (My Bilingual Book Ser.). (ENG & PER., Illus.). 28p. (J). (gr. -1-k). 9.95 *(978-1-84059-775-2(5))* Milet Publishing.
—My Bilingual Book-Hearing (English-French) 2014. (My Bilingual Book Ser.). (ENG & FRE., Illus.). 28p. (J). (gr. -1-k). 9.95 *(978-1-84059-776-9(3))* Milet Publishing.
—My Bilingual Book-Hearing (English-German) 2014. (My Bilingual Book Ser.). (ENG & GER., Illus.). 28p. (J). (gr. -1-k). 9.95 *(978-1-84059-777-6(1))* Milet Publishing.
—My Bilingual Book-Hearing (English-Italian) 2014. (My Bilingual Book Ser.). (ENG & ITA., Illus.). 28p. (J). (gr. -1-k). 9.95 *(978-1-84059-778-3(X))* Milet Publishing.
—My Bilingual Book-Hearing (English-Polish) 2014. (My Bilingual Book Ser.). (ENG, POL & POR., Illus.). 28p. (J). (gr. -1-k). 9.95 *(978-1-84059-780-6(1))* Milet Publishing.
—My Bilingual Book-Hearing (English-Portuguese) 2014. (My Bilingual Book Ser.). (ENG & POR., Illus.). 28p. (J). (gr. -1-k). 9.95 *(978-1-84059-781-3(X))* Milet Publishing.
—My Bilingual Book-Hearing (English-Russian) 2014. (My Bilingual Book Ser.). (ENG & RUS., Illus.). 28p. (J). (gr. -1-k). 9.95 *(978-1-84059-782-0(8))* Milet Publishing.
—My Bilingual Book-Hearing (English-Somali) 2014. (My Bilingual Book Ser.). (ENG & SOM., Illus.). 28p. (J). (gr. -1-k). 9.95 *(978-1-84059-783-7(6))* Milet Publishing.
—My Bilingual Book-Hearing (English-Urdu) 2014. (My Bilingual Book Ser.). (ENG & URD., Illus.). 28p. (J). (gr. -1-k). 9.95 *(978-1-84059-786-8(0))* Milet Publishing.
—My Bilingual Book-Hearing (English-Vietnamese) 2014. (My Bilingual Book Ser.). (ENG & VIE., Illus.). 28p. (J). (gr. -1-k). 9.95 *(978-1-84059-787-5(9))* Milet Publishing.
Mlawer, Teresa, tr. What Do I Hear? / ¿Qué Oigo? Kubler, Annie, illus. 2015. (Small Senses Bilingual Ser.: 5). (ENG & SPA.). 12p. (J). bds. *(978-1-84643-724-3(5))* Child's Play International Ltd.
Mokhemar, Mary Ann. Just for Kids Interactive Auditory Processing Pictures Manual. 2006. (J). 0.00 *(978-0-7606-0665-0(X))* LinguiSystems, Inc.
Morgan, Sally. How Hearing Works. 2010. (Our Senses Ser.). (Illus.). 24p. (J). (gr. -1-2). lib. bdg. 22.60 *(978-1-61532-552-8(2))* Rosen Publishing Group, Inc., The.
—How Hearing Works (Our Senses) 2010. (Our Senses Ser.). 24p. (J). (gr. k-2). pap. 8.25 *(978-1-61532-557-3(3)*, PowerKids Pr.) Rosen Publishing Group, Inc., The.
Murphy, Patricia J. Hearing: Your Ears are the Key to Your Sense of Hearing. 2003. (True Bks.). (ENG.). 48p. (gr. 3-5). pap. 6.95 *(978-0-516-26970-2(4)*, Children's Pr.) Scholastic Library Publishing.
Murray, Julie. I Can Hear, 1 vol. 2016. (ENG., Illus.). 24p. (J). *(978-1-62970-925-3(5)*, 1391205) ABDO Publishing Co.
—Sound & Hearing, 1 vol. 2006. (First Science Ser.). (ENG., Illus.). 24p. (gr. k-4). 25.65 *(978-1-59679-831-1(9)*, Buddy Bks.) ABDO Publishing Co.
Naff, Clayton Farris. Deafness & Hearing Impairment. 2010. (Perspectives on Diseases & Disorders Ser.). (Illus.). 144p. (YA). 38.95 *(978-0-7377-4788-1(9)*, Greenhaven Pr., Inc.) Cengage Gale.
Nelson, Maria. I Can Listen. 2013. 24p. (J). (gr. 1-3). 22.60 *(978-1-4339-9029-8(6))*; pap. 48.90 *(978-1-4339-9031-1(8))*; (ENG., Illus.). pap. 8.15 *(978-1-4339-9030-4(X))* Stevens, Gareth Publishing LLLP.
Nelson, Robin. Hearing. 2005. (First Step Nonfiction Ser.). (Illus.). 24p. (gr. k-2). lib. bdg. 17.27 *(978-0-8225-1264-6(5))* Lerner Publishing Group.
—El Oido. 2006. (Mi Primer Paso al Mundo Real Ser.). (SPA., Illus.). 23p. (J). (gr. 3-7). lib. bdg. 18.60 *(978-0-8225-6221-4(9)*, Ediciones Lerner) Lerner Publishing Group.
—El Oido (Hearing) 2006. (Mi Primer Paso al Mundo Real Ser.). (Illus.). 23p. (J). (gr. -1-3). per. 4.25 *(978-0-8225-6548-2(X)*, Ediciones Lerner) Lerner Publishing Group.
Parker, Steve & Parker, Vic. Having a Hearing Test, 1 vol. 2011. (Growing Up Ser.). (ENG.). 24p. (gr. k-2). 23.32 *(978-1-4329-4799-6(0)*, Heinemann Read & Learn) Heinemann-Raintree.
Phillips, Jillian. The World Around Us! Hearing. 2010. (Dover Coloring Bks.). (ENG., Illus.). 32p. (J). (gr. k-3). pap. 4.99 *(978-0-486-47730-5(4))* Dover Pubns., Inc.
Pryor, Kimberley Jane. Hearing. 2003. (Senses Ser.). (Illus.). 32p. (gr. 2-4). 23.00 *(978-0-7910-7554-8(0)*, Chelsea Hse.) Facts On File, Inc.
Royston, Angela. Sound & Hearing. 2012. (Science Corner Ser.). (Illus.). 24p. (J). (gr. 1-3). lib. bdg. 22.60 *(978-1-4488-5259-8(5))* Rosen Publishing Group, Inc., The.
Roza, Greg. Listen Up: Knowing When & When Not to Speak. 2011. (Communicating with Confidence Ser.). (ENG.). 80p. (YA). (gr. 7-12). pap. 14.15 *(978-1-4488-5516-2(0))*; lib. bdg. 33.25 *(978-1-4488-5515-5(2))* Rosen Publishing Group, Inc., The.
Rustad, Martha E. H. Hearing. 2014. (Illus.). 24p. (J). lib. bdg. 25.65 *(978-1-62031-115-8(1)*, Bullfrog Bks.) Jump! Inc.
Schuh, Mari. The Sense of Hearing. 2007. (Senses Ser.). (ENG., Illus.). 24p. (J). (gr. 2-5). lib. bdg. 25.95 *(978-1-60014-070-9(X))* Bellwether Media.
Sian Revision Vision & Hearing. 2004. (J). *(978-1-59242-079-7(6))* Delta Education, LLC.
Simon, Seymour. Eyes & Ears. 2005. (Illus.). (gr. k-3). 17.00 *(978-0-7569-5398-0(7))* Perfection Learning Corp.
Spilsbury, Louise & Spilsbury, Richard. Shhh! Listen!: Hearing Sounds, 1 vol. HL Studios, H. L., illus. 2014. (Exploring Sound Ser.). (ENG.). 32p. (gr. 2-4). lib. bdg. 30.65 *(978-1-4109-6002-3(1)*, Raintree Perspectives) Heinemann-Raintree.
Stewart, Melissa. Now Hear This! The Secrets of Ears & Hearing. Hamlin, Janet, illus. 2009. (Gross & Goofy Body Ser.). 48p. (gr. 3-4). 29.93 *(978-0-7614-4161-8(1))* Marshall Cavendish Corp.
Tekiela, Stan. Floppers & Loppers, 1 vol. 2013. (Adventure Boardbook Ser.). (ENG.). 22p. (J). (gr. -1-k). bds. 6.95 *(978-1-59193-424-0(9))* Adventure Pubns.
Verdick, Elizabeth & Heinlen, Marieka. Listening Time / Momento para Escuchar. 2016. (Toddler Tools Ser.). (ENG & SPA., Illus.). 24p. (J). bds. 7.95 *(978-1-63198-117-3(X))* Free Spirit Publishing, Inc.
Vogel, Julia. Your Sensational Sense of Hearing. Squier, Robert, illus. 2011. (Sensational Senses Ser.). (ENG.). 32p. (J). (gr. k-3). lib. bdg. 27.07 *(978-1-60954-286-3(X)*, 200815) Child's World, Inc., The.
Wheeler-Toppen, Jodi Lyn. Our Ears Can Hear. 2017. (Our Amazing Senses Ser.). (ENG.). 24p. (gr. k-1). lib. bdg. 21.99 ***(978-1-5157-6713-8(2)***, Pebble Bks.) Capstone Press of Coughlan Cos.
Winnick, Neil. Hearing. 2009. (World of Wonder Ser.). (Illus.). 24p. (J). (gr. 2-4). pap. 8.95 *(978-1-60596-055-5(1))* Weigl Pubs., Inc.
Winnick, Nick. Hearing. 2009. (World of Wonder Ser.). (Illus.). 24p. (J). (gr. 2-4). lib. bdg. 24.45 *(978-1-60596-054-8(3))* Weigl Pubs., Inc.
Woodford, Chris. Experiments with Sound & Hearing. 2010. (Cool Science Ser.). (Illus.). 32p. (J). (gr. 5-6). pap. 10.50 *(978-1-4339-3457-5(4))*; lib. bdg. 28.00 *(978-1-4339-3456-8(6)*, 1309305) Stevens, Gareth Publishing LLLP. (Gareth Stevens Learning Library).
Wouk, Henry. Hearing Disorders. 2010. (Health Alert 7 Ser.). 64p. (YA). (gr. 4-7). 32.79 *(978-0-7614-4817-4(9))* Marshall Cavendish Corp.

HEART

see also Blood—Circulation

Bailey, Jacqui. What Happens When Your Heart Beats? (How Your Body Works). (Illus.). (gr. k-5). 2009. (ENG.). 32p. pap. 10.60 *(978-1-4358-2620-5(5))* 2008. 30p. (J). lib. bdg. 26.50 *(978-1-4042-4430-6(1))* Rosen Publishing Group, Inc., The. (PowerKids Pr.).
Berger, Melvin & Berger, Gilda. Your Heart. 2005. (Illus.). pap. *(978-0-439-77369-0(5))* Scholastic, Inc.
Brett, Flora. Your Circulatory System Works! 2015. (Your Body Systems Ser.). (ENG.). 24p. (gr. 1-2). lib. bdg. 25.32 *(978-1-4914-2063-8(4))* Capstone Press of Coughlan Cos.
Burstein, John. The Amazing Circulatory System: How Does My Heart Work? 2009. (Slim Goodbody's Body Buddies Ser.). (ENG., Illus.). 32p. (J). (gr. 3-5). pap. *(978-0-7787-4431-3(0))* Crabtree Publishing Co.
Caster, Shannon. Heart. 2010. (Body Works Ser.). (Illus.). 24p. (J). pap. 8.25 *(978-1-4358-9828-8(1)*, PowerKids Pr.); (YA). (gr. 2-5). lib. bdg. 22.60 *(978-1-4358-9370-2(0))* Rosen Publishing Group, Inc., The.
Dingles, Molly. Sweet Hearts: Dulce Corazón. Brodie, Neale, illus. 2006. (SPA & ENG.). (J). *(978-1-59646-038-6(5))* Dingles & Co.
Farndon, John. Stickmen's Guide to Your Beating Heart. Dean, Venitia, illus. 2017. (Stickmen's Guides to Your Awesome Body Ser.). (ENG.). 32p. (gr. 3-6). 26.65 ***(978-1-5124-3215-2(6))*** Lerner Publishing Group.
Fitzpatrick, Anne. The Heart. 2003. (Illus.). 24p. (J). lib. bdg. 21.35 *(978-1-58340-308-2(6))* Black Rabbit Bks.
Furgang, Kathy. My Heart. 2009. (My Body Ser.). 24p. (gr. 3-3). 42.50 *(978-1-61514-689-5(X)*, PowerKids Pr.) Rosen Publishing Group, Inc., The.
Guillain, Charlotte. Nuestros Corazones, 1 vol. 2010. (Nuestros Cuerpos Ser.) Tr. of Our Hearts. (SPA.). 24p. (gr. -1-1). 22.65 *(978-1-4329-4295-3(6))*; pap. 6.29 *(978-1-4329-4304-2(9))* Heinemann-Raintree. (Bellota).
—Our Hearts, 1 vol. 2010. (Our Bodies Ser.). (ENG.). 24p. (gr. -1-1). pap. 6.29 *(978-1-4329-3599-3(2)*, Acorn) Heinemann-Raintree.
Halvorson, Karin. Inside the Heart, 1 vol. 2013. (Super Simple Your Body Ser.). (ENG.). 32p. (J). (gr. k-4). lib. bdg. 27.07 *(978-1-61783-612-1(5)*, Super SandCastle) ABDO Publishing Co.
Hewitt, Sally. My Heart & Lungs. 2012. (My Body Ser.). (Illus.). 24p. (gr. k-4). pap. 7.95 *(978-1-926853-98-7(9))* Saunders Bk. Co. CAN. Dist: RiverStream Publishing.
Houghton, Gillian. The Circulatory System. 2007. (How Your Body Works). (ENG., Illus.). 24p. (gr. 3-5). pap. 7.05 *(978-1-4042-2181-9(6)*, PowerKids Pr.) Rosen Publishing Group, Inc., The.
Johnson, Rebecca L. Respiration & Circulation. 2007. (Reading Expeditions Ser.). (ENG., Illus.). 32p. (J). pap. 17.95 *(978-0-7922-4586-5(5))* CENGAGE Learning.
Kingston, Anna & Viegas, Jennifer. The Heart in 3D. 2015. (Human Body In 3D Ser.). (ENG., Illus.). 64p. (J). (gr. 5-6).

32.95 *(978-1-4994-3597-9(5)*, Rosen Central) Rosen Publishing Group, Inc., The.

Libra, Anna. How Do My Cuts Heal? An Inside Look at the Circulatory System. 2003. (J). *(978-1-58417-003-7(4))*; pap. *(978-1-58417-066-2(2))* Lake Street Pubs.

Mason, Paul. Your Hardworking Heart & Spectacular Circulatory System. 2015. (Your Brilliant Body! Ser.). (ENG., Illus.). 32p. (J). (gr. 3-7). lib. bdg. *(978-0-7787-2198-7(1))* Crabtree Publishing Co.

Ollhoff, Jim. The Heart. 2012. (J). *(978-1-61783-255-0(3))* ABDO Publishing Co.

Oxlade, Chris. Why Why Why Does My Heart Begin to Race? 2008. 32p. pap. *(978-1-84810-002-2(7))* Miles Kelly Publishing, Ltd.

—Why Why Why... Does My Heart Begin to Race? 2010. (Why Why Why Ser.). 32p. (J). (gr. 1-6). lib. bdg. 18.95 *(978-1-4222-1587-6(3))* Mason Crest.

Petrie, Kristin. The Circulatory System, 1 vol. 2007. (Human Body Ser.). (ENG., Illus.). 32p. (gr. 4-7). 27.07 *(978-1-59679-709-3(6)*, Checkerboard Library) ABDO Publishing Co.

Randolph, Joanne, ed. Pump It Up: The Heart & Blood. 2017. (Amazing Human Body Ser.). 48p. (J). (gr. 6-6). pap. 11.70 ***(978-0-7660-8985-3(1))*** Enslow Pubs., Inc.

Rieger, Linda. A Good Heart. Rieger, Linda, illus. 2007. (Illus.). 20p. (J). *(978-0-9779427-4-9(0))* Pathways into Science.

Ross, Veronica. Heart. 2004. (Body Ser.). (Illus.). 32p. (J). (gr. -1-3). lib. bdg. 27.10 *(978-1-59389-164-0(4))* Chrysalis Education.

Rustad, Martha E. H. Today Is a Hot Day. 2017. (What Is the Weather Today? Ser.). (ENG., Illus.). 24p. (gr. k-1). lib. bdg. 21.99 *(978-1-5157-4923-3(1)*, Pebble Bks.) Capstone Press of Coughlan Cos.

Schaefer, Lola M. Your Heart. 2011. (Early Connections Ser.). (J). *(978-1-61672-658-4(X))* Benchmark Education Co.

Shaffer, Jody Jensen. My Heart. Alberini, Teresa, illus. 2015. (Inside My Body Ser.). (ENG.). 24p. (J). (gr. 1-3). 19.95 *(978-1-60753-755-7(9))* Amicus Publishing.

Simon, Seymour. The Heart: Our Circulatory System. 2006. (ENG., Illus.). 32p. (J). (gr. k-4). 17.99 *(978-0-06-087720-0(0))*; pap. 6.99 *(978-0-06-087721-7(9)*, Collins) HarperCollins Pubs.

Slike, Janet. Take a Closer Look at Your Heart. 2013. (Take a Closer Look Ser.). (ENG.). 24p. (J). (gr. 2-5). 28.50 *(978-1-62323-547-5(2)*, 206352) Child's World, Inc., The.

Stewart, Melissa. Pump It Up! The Secrets of the Heart & Blood. Hamlin, Janet, illus. 2009. (Gross & Goofy Body Ser.). 48p. (gr. 3-4). 29.93 *(978-0-7614-4164-9(6))* Marshall Cavendish Corp.

Storad, Conrad J. El Aparato Circulatorio. Translations.com Staff, tr. from ENG. 2006. (Libros Sobre el Cuerpo Humano para Madrugadores Ser.). (SPA., Illus.). 48p. (gr. 2-4). lib. bdg. 26.60 *(978-0-8225-6252-8(9))* Lerner Publishing Group.

—El Aparato Circulatorio (the Circulatory System) Translations.com Staff, tr. 2007. (Libros Sobre el Cuerpo Humano para Madrugadores Ser.). (SPA., Illus.). 48p. (gr. 2-4). per. 7.95 *(978-0-8225-6653-3(2))* Lerner Publishing Group.

Taylor-Butler, Christine. The Circulatory System. 2008. (True Book(tm), a — Health & the Human Body Ser.). (ENG., Illus.). 48p. (J). (gr. 3-7). 31.00 *(978-0-531-16856-1(5)*, Children's Pr.) Scholastic Library Publishing.

Williams, Ben. Look Inside: Your Heart & Lungs, 1 vol. 2nd rev. ed. 2011. (Nonfiction Readers Ser.). (ENG.). 28p. (J). (gr. 2-2). pap. 6.99 *(978-1-4333-3636-2(7))* Teacher Created Materials, Inc.

Wilson, Michael R. Living a Heart-Healthy Life. 2010. (Healthy Habits Ser.). 64p. (YA). (ENG.). pap. 12.95 *(978-1-4488-0608-9(9))*; (Illus.). (gr. 5-8). lib. bdg. 31.95 *(978-1-4358-9438-9(3))* Rosen Publishing Group, Inc., The. (Rosen Reference).

World Book, Inc Staff, contrib. by. The Circulatory System. (J). 2013. *(978-0-7166-1842-3(7))* 2006. (Illus.). 48p. *(978-0-7166-4427-9(4))* World Bk., Inc.

Yanez, Alberto. Ekg Rhythms Made Easy. 2011. 92p. pap. 51.99 *(978-1-4568-4355-7(9))* Xlibris Corp.

HEART—DISEASES

Corcoran, Mary K. The Circulatory Story. Czekaj, Jef, illus. 2010. (ENG.). 44p. (J). (gr. 3-7). pap. 7.95 *(978-1-58089-209-4(4))* Charlesbridge Publishing, Inc.

Cut to the Heart. 2004. (NOVA Ser.). (gr. 7-18). 19.95 *(978-1-57807-051-0(1)*, WG2409) WGBH Boston Video.

Dittmer, Lori. Heart Disease. 2011. (Living with Disease Ser.). (Illus.). 48p. (J). (gr. 5-8). lib. bdg. 34.25 *(978-1-60818-075-2(1)*, Creative Education) Creative Co., The.

Gallegos, Rick & Gallegos, Annette. Born with a Broken Heart: Congenital Heart Disease. 2010. 68p. pap. 21.49 *(978-1-4490-3760-4(7))* AuthorHouse.

Markle, Sandra. Faulty Hearts: True Survival Stories. 2010. (Powerful Medicine Ser.). (ENG., Illus.). 48p. (J). (gr. 5-8). lib. bdg. 27.93 *(978-0-8225-8699-9(1))* Lerner Publishing Group.

Murphy, Jim. Breakthrough! How Three People Saved Blue Babies & Changed Medicine Forever. 2015. (ENG., Illus.). 144p. (J). (gr. 5-7). 18.99 *(978-0-547-82183-2(2)*, Clarion Bks.) Houghton Mifflin Harcourt Trade & Reference Pubs.

Peterson, Judy Monroe. Understanding Cholesterol. 2010. (Healthy Habits Ser.). (Illus.). 64p. (YA). (gr. 5-8). pap. 12.95 *(978-1-4488-0610-2(0))*; lib. bdg. 31.95 *(978-1-4358-9440-2(5))* Rosen Publishing Group, Inc., The. (Rosen Reference).

Silverstein, Alvin & Nunn, Laura Silverstein. Heart Disease. 2006. (Twenty-First Century Medical Library). (Illus.). 112p. (YA). (gr. 7-12). lib. bdg. 27.93 *(978-0-7613-3420-0(3))* Lerner Publishing Group.

Spilsbury, Louise & Spilsbury, Richard. The Science of the Heart & Circulatory System. 2017. (Flowchart Smart Ser.). 48p. (gr. 4-5). pap. 84.30 ***(978-1-5382-0683-6(8))*** Stevens, Gareth Publishing LLLP.

Taylor, Robert. Strokes. 2006. (Diseases & Disorders Ser.). (ENG., Illus.). 128p. (gr. 7-12). lib. bdg. 39.90 *(978-1-59018-967-2(1)*, 1256798) Cengage Gale.

HEAT

see also Fire; Temperature; Thermodynamics; Thermometers

Berne, Emma Carlson. Hot! Heat Energy. 2013. (Energy Everywhere Ser.). (ENG., Illus.). 24p. (J). (gr. 3-6). pap. 8.25 *(978-1-4488-9752-0(1))*; lib. bdg. 22.60 *(978-1-4488-9647-9(9))* Rosen Publishing Group, Inc., The. (PowerKids Pr.).

Boothroyd, Jennifer. The Energy That Warms Us: A Look at Heat. 2011. (Lightning Bolt Books Exploring Physical Science Ser.). 32p. pap. 45.32 *(978-0-7613-7647-7(X))*; (ENG.). pap. 7.95 *(978-0-7613-7103-8(6))*; (ENG.). lib. bdg. 26.60 *(978-0-7613-6093-3(X))* Lerner Publishing Group.

Brager, Bruce L. How You Can Use Waste Energy to Heat & Light Your Home. 2009. (Tell Your Parents Ser.). (J). (gr. 4-7). 29.95 *(978-1-58415-765-6(8))* Mitchell Lane Pubs., Inc.

Brent, Lynnette R. I've Discovered Heat! 2008. (Eureka! Ser.). 32p. (gr. 4-18). lib. bdg. 28.50 *(978-0-7614-3196-1(9)*, Benchmark Bks.) Marshall Cavendish Corp.

Challen, Paul C. & Challen, Paul. Drought & Heat Wave Alert! 2004. (Disaster Alert! Ser.). (ENG., Illus.). 32p. (J). pap. *(978-0-7787-1610-5(4))*; lib. bdg. *(978-0-7787-1578-8(7))* Crabtree Publishing Co.

Clark, John O. E. The Basics of Heat. 2014. (Core Concepts Ser.). 96p. (YA). (gr. 7-12). 35.60 *(978-1-4777-7764-0(4))* Rosen Publishing Group, Inc., The.

Coan, Sharon. How Heat Moves, 1 vol. (Science Readers: Content & Literacy Ser.). (ENG., Illus.). 24p. (gr. 1-1). 2015. pap. 22.96 *(978-1-4938-1155-7(X))* 2014. pap. 8.99 *(978-1-4807-4568-1(5))* Teacher Created Materials, Inc.

Corcorane, Ann. Hot & Cold, 1 vol. 2011. (Wonder Readers Emergent Level Ser.). (ENG.). (gr. -1-1). 32p. pap. 5.99 *(978-1-4296-7865-0(8))*; 16p. pap. 35.94 *(978-1-4296-8095-0(4))* Capstone Press of Coughlan Cos. (Wonder Readers).

Dahl, Michael. Hot, Hotter, Hottest: Animals That Adapt to Great Heat. Jensen, Brian, illus. 2005. (Animal Extremes Ser.). (ENG.). 24p. (gr. k-2). lib. bdg. 26.65 *(978-1-4048-1017-4(X))* Picture Window Bks.

Dahl, Michael & Jensen, Brian. Caliente, Más Caliente, Muy Caliente: Animales Que Se Adaptan a Climas Calientes. Translations.com Staff, tr. Dahl, Michael & Jensen, Brian, illus. 2012. (Los Extremos y Los Animales/Animal Extremes Ser.).Tr. of Hot, Hotter, Hottest - Animals That Adapt to Great Heat. (ENG, SPA & MUL., Illus.). 24p. (gr. k-2). lib. bdg. 26.65 *(978-1-4048-7318-6(X))* Picture Window Bks.

Ellse, Mark, et al. Electricity & Thermal Physics. 2nd rev. ed. 2004. (Nelson Advanced Science Ser.). (ENG., Illus.). 152p. (YA). pap. 39.50 *(978-0-7487-7663-4(X))* Nelson Thornes Ltd. GBR. Dist: Trans-Atlantic Pubns., Inc.

Felix, Rebecca. Keeping Cool in Summer. 2014. (21st Century Basic Skills Library: Let's Look at Summer Ser.). (ENG.). 24p. (J). (gr. k-3). 22.79 *(978-1-63137-597-2(0)*, 205171) Cherry Lake Publishing.

Fiedler, Julie. Learning about Heat & Temperature with Graphic Organizers. (Graphic Organizers in Science Ser.). 24p. (gr. 3-4). 2009. 42.50 *(978-1-61513-039-9(X)*, PowerKids Pr.) 2006. (Illus.). (YA). lib. bdg. 22.60 *(978-1-4042-3408-6(X))* Rosen Publishing Group, Inc., The.

Field, Andrea R. Heat. 2012. (Introduction to Physics Ser.). (ENG., Illus.). 80p. (J). (gr. 7-12). lib. bdg. 31.70 *(978-1-61530-838-5(5))* Rosen Publishing Group, Inc., The.

Field, Andrea R., ed. Heat. 2012. (Introduction to Physics Ser.). (ENG., Illus.). 80p. (YA). (gr. 7-12). 63.40 *(978-1-61530-846-0(6))* Rosen Publishing Group, Inc., The.

Gardner, Robert. Sizzling Science Projects with Heat & Energy. LaBaff, Tom, illus. 2006. (Fantastic Physical Science Experiments Ser.). 48p. (J). (gr. 3-4). lib. bdg. 25.27 *(978-0-7660-2586-8(1)*, Enslow Elementary) Enslow Pubs., Inc.

Gish, Melissa. Temperature. 2005. (My First Look at Science Ser.). (Illus.). 24p. (J). (gr. k-3). lib. bdg. 15.95 *(978-1-58341-375-3(8)*, Creative Education) Creative Co., The.

Group/McGraw-Hill, Wright. Heat: Level F, 6 vols. (Take Twostm Ser.). 16p. 29.95 *(978-0-322-08953-2(0))* Wright Group/McGraw-Hill.

Guillain, Charlotte. Caliente o Frío, 1 vol. 2010. (Las Propiedades de Los Materiales Ser.). (SPA.). 24p. (gr. -1-1). 22.65 *(978-1-4329-4239-7(5))*; pap. 6.29 *(978-1-4329-4247-2(6))* Heinemann-Raintree. (Bellota).

HarrisNic. THE SCIENCE OF HEAT LOW INTERMEDIATE BOOK WITH ONLINE ACCESS. 2014. (ENG., Illus.). 24p. (J). pap. 9.50 *(978-1-107-69772-0(7))* Cambridge Univ. Pr.

Hidalgo, Maria. Heat. 2006. (My First Look at Weather Ser.). (Illus.). 24p. (J). (gr. -1-3). lib. bdg. 15.95 *(978-1-58341-449-1(5)*, Creative Education) Creative Co., The.

Holland, Gini. Hot & Cold. 2007. (I Know Opposites Ser.). 16p. (gr. -1-2). pap. 5.30 *(978-0-8368-8299-5(7))*; lib. bdg. 19.00 *(978-0-8368-8294-0(6))* Stevens, Gareth Publishing LLLP. (Weekly Reader Leveled Readers).

—Hot & Cold/Caliente y Frío. 2007. (I Know Opposites/Conceptos Contrarios Ser.). (SPA & ENG.). 16p. (gr. -1-3). lib. bdg. 19.00 *(978-0-8368-8304-6(7)*, Weekly Reader Leveled Readers) Stevens, Gareth Publishing LLLP.

Holt, Rinehart and Winston Staff. Holt Science & Technology Chapter 10: Physical Science: Heat & Heat Technology. 5th ed. 2004. (Illus.). pap. 12.86 *(978-0-03-030401-9(6))* Holt McDougal.

Hughes, Susan. Is It Hot or Cold? 2012. (ENG., Illus.). 24p. (J). *(978-0-7787-2049-2(7))*; pap. *(978-0-7787-2056-0(X))* Crabtree Publishing Co.

Hughes, Tom. Hot & Cold. 2016. (All about Opposites Ser.). (Illus.). 24p. (J). pap. 9.35 *(978-0-7660-8110-9(9))* Enslow Pubs., Inc.

Jeffries, Joyce. Hot & Cold. 2013. (Dinosaur School Ser.). (Illus.). 24p. (gr. -1-1). 22.60 *(978-1-4339-8091-6(6))*; pap. 8.15 *(978-1-4339-8092-3(4))* Stevens, Gareth Publishing LLLP.

Jennings, Terry. Hot & Cold. 2009. (Science Alive Ser.). (Illus.). 32p. (J). (gr. -1-2). pap. *(978-1-897563-55-7(8))* Saunders Bk. Co.

Jennings, Terry J. Hot & Cold. 2009. (J). 28.50 *(978-1-59920-274-7(3))* Black Rabbit Bks.

Kantrowitz, Joseph & Moran, Jeffrey B. Discovering Thermodynamics. 2011. (Scientist's Guide to Physics Ser.). (YA). (gr. 7-12). lib. bdg. 34.60 *(978-1-4488-4701-3(X))* Rosen Publishing Group, Inc., The.

Keiser, Cody. Is It Hot or Is It Cold? Describe & Compare Measurable Attributes. 2013. (InfoMax Math Readers Ser.). (ENG., Illus.). 16p. (J). (gr. k-1). pap. 7.00 *(978-1-4777-2012-7(X)*, Rosen Classroom) Rosen Publishing Group, Inc., The.

Lawrence, Ellen. Heat. 2016. (FUN-Damental Experiments Ser.). (ENG., Illus.). 24p. (J). (gr. -1-3). 17.95 *(978-1-943553-19-8(X))* Bearport Publishing Co., Inc.

Lindeen, Mary. Hot & Cold. 2017. (BeginningtoRead Ser.). (ENG.). 32p. (J). (-2). 22.60 ***(978-1-59953-883-9(0))***; pap. 11.94 ***(978-1-68404-102-2(3))*** Norwood Hse. Pr.

—Sun & Shade. 2017. (BeginningtoRead Ser.). (ENG.). 32p. (J). (-2). 22.60 ***(978-1-59953-872-3(5))***; pap. 11.94 ***(978-1-68404-091-9(4))*** Norwood Hse. Pr.

Lipschultz, Wes. Is It Hot or Cold? Learning to Use a Thermometer. 2009. (Math for the REAL World Ser.). 12p. (gr. 1-2). pap. 5.90 *(978-0-8239-8848-8(1)*, Rosen Classroom) Rosen Publishing Group, Inc., The.

Lockwood, Sophie. Experiment with Heat. 2010. (Explorer Junior Library: Science Explorer Junior Ser.). (ENG.). 32p. (gr. 3-6). lib. bdg. 28.50 *(978-1-60279-843-4(5)*, 200552) Cherry Lake Publishing.

—Super Cool Science Experiments: Heat. 2009. (Explorer Library: Science Explorer Ser.). (ENG., Illus.). 32p. (gr. 4-8). lib. bdg. 28.50 *(978-1-60279-534-1(7)*, 200290) Cherry Lake Publishing.

Mahaney, Ian F. Heat. (Energy in Action Ser.). 24p. 2009. (gr. 3-3). 42.50 *(978-1-61512-258-5(3)*, PowerKids Pr.) 2007. (ENG.). (gr. 3-8). pap. 7.05 *(978-1-4042-2186-4(7)*, PowerKids Pr.) 2007. (Illus.). (YA). (gr. 4-7). lib. bdg. 22.60 *(978-1-4042-3477-2(2))* Rosen Publishing Group, Inc., The.

Marshall Cavendish Benchmark, prod. Hot/Cold. 2nd rev. ed. 2011. (Bookworms 2nd Edition: Opposites Ser.). 16p. (gr. k-1). 21.36 *(978-1-60870-409-5(2))* Marshall Cavendish Corp.

Maurer, Daniel D. Do You Really Want to Burn Your Toast? A Book about Heat. Alberini, Teresa, illus. 2016. (Adventures in Science Ser.). (ENG.). 24p. (J). (gr. k-3). 20.95 *(978-1-60753-961-2(6))* Amicus Publishing.

McPartland, Randall. Understanding the Laws of Thermodynamics. 2015. (J). lib. bdg. *(978-1-62713-429-3(8))* Cavendish Square Publishing.

Murray, Julie. Hot & Cold, 1 vol. 2006. (First Science Ser.). (ENG., Illus.). 24p. (gr. k-4). 25.65 *(978-1-59679-825-0(4)*, Buddy Bks.) ABDO Publishing Co.

Oxlade, Chris. Calentar, 1 vol. 2010. (Materiales Cambiantes Ser.). (SPA.). 32p. (gr. 1-3). 27.32 *(978-1-4329-4429-2(0))*; pap. 8.95 *(978-1-4329-4434-6(7))* Heinemann-Raintree.

—Heating, 1 vol. 2012. (How Does My Home Work? Ser.). (ENG.). 24p. (gr. k-1). lib. bdg. 23.32 *(978-1-4329-6564-8(6)*, Heinemann Read & Learn) Heinemann-Raintree.

Prentice-Hall Staff. Heat Energy. 2nd ed. (Prentice Hall Science Ser.). (J). tchr. ed. 18.97 *(978-0-13-400706-9(9))*; pap., act. bk. ed. *(978-0-13-400722-9(0))* Prentice Hall (Schl. Div.).

Royston, Angela. The Science of Heat. 2016. (Flowchart Smart Ser.). (ENG.). 48p. (J). (gr. 4-5). pap. 14.05 *(978-1-4824-4139-0(X))* Stevens, Gareth Publishing LLLP.

Rustad, Martha E. H. Today Is a Hot Day. 2017. (What Is the Weather Today? Ser.). (ENG., Illus.). 24p. (gr. k-2). pap. 6.29 *(978-1-4966-0946-5(8)*, Pebble Bks.) Capstone Press of Coughlan Cos.

Schmauss, Judy Kentor. Too, Too Hot! Kaminski, Karol, illus. 2006. (Reader's Clubhouse Level 1 Reader Ser.). (ENG.). 24p. (J). (gr. 1-4). pap. 3.99 *(978-0-7641-3285-8(7))* Barron's Educational Series, Inc.

—Too, Too Hot! 2006. (Illus.). 24p. (J). lib. bdg. 11.00 *(978-1-4242-1587-4(0))* Dingles & Co.

Shea, Therese. Heat in Action. 2009. (Real Life Readers Ser.). 12p. (gr. 1-2). pap. 5.90 *(978-1-4042-7899-8(0)*, Rosen Classroom) Rosen Publishing Group, Inc., The.

Sheehan, Thomas F. Para Calentarse, para Refrescarse (Keeping Warm, Keeping Cool) Sarfatti, Esther, tr. 2005. (Ciencia Citadina Ser.). (ENG & SPA., Illus.). 24p. (J). (gr. 3-7). lib. bdg. 21.36 *(978-1-59515-666-2(6))* Rourke Educational Media.

Smith, Sian. Hot & Cold, 1 vol. 2014. (Opposites Ser.). (ENG.). 24p. (gr. -1-1). pap. 5.99 *(978-1-4846-0334-5(6)*, Acorn) Heinemann-Raintree.

Solway, Andrew. Secrets of Heat & Cold. 2010. (Science Secrets Ser.). 32p. (gr. 4). 28.50 *(978-1-60870-138-4(7))* Marshall Cavendish GBR. Dist: Marshall Cavendish Corp.

Steinberg, Lynnae D. What Is Heat Energy? 2017. (Let's Find Out! Forms of Energy Ser.). 32p. (J). (gr. 6-8). pap. 12.90 ***(978-1-68048-701-5(9)***, Britannica Educational Publishing) Rosen Publishing Group, Inc., The.

Stille, Darlene R. Heat, 1 vol. 2012. (Science Behind Ser.). (ENG.). 32p. (gr. 3-3). pap. 8.29 *(978-1-4109-4494-8(8))*; lib. bdg. 30.65 *(978-1-4109-4483-2(2))* Heinemann-Raintree. (Raintree Perspectives).

Stille, Darlene R. & Picture Window Books Staff. La Temperatura: Caliente y Frío. Robledo, Sol, tr. from ENG. Boyd, Sheree, illus. 2007. (Ciencia Asombrosa Ser.). (SPA.). 24p. (gr. k-4). 26.65 *(978-1-4048-3234-3(3))* Picture Window Bks.

Sullivan, Laura L. What Is Heat? 2016. (Unseen Science Ser.). (ENG., Illus.). 32p. (J). (gr. 3-3). pap. 10.58 *(978-1-5026-0910-6(X))* Cavendish Square Publishing.

Sullivan, Navin. Temperature. 2006. (Measure Up! Ser.). (Illus.). 48p. (gr. 4-7). lib. bdg. 31.36 *(978-0-7614-2322-5(2)*, Benchmark Bks.) Marshall Cavendish Corp.

Tanaka, Shelley. The Heat Is On. Beinicke, Steve, illus. (J). pap. 4.99 *(978-1-55054-200-4(1))* Da Capo Pr., Inc.

Taylor, Kim. Heat. (Illus.). 32p. (YA). (gr. 3-18). lib. bdg. 27.10 *(978-1-931983-77-8(1))* Chrysalis Education.

Wadsworth, Pamela. Golwg Gyntaf Ar Egni. 2005. (WEL., Illus.). 24p. pap. *(978-1-85596-257-6(8))* Dref Wen.

Walker, Sally M. El Calor. Translations.com Staff, tr. from ENG. King, Andy, photos by. 2007. (Libros de Energía para madrugadores (Early Bird Energy) Ser.). (SPA., Illus.). 48p. (gr. 2-5). lib. bdg. 26.60 *(978-0-8225-7718-8(6))* Lerner Publishing Group.

—El Calor: Heat. 2008. pap. 52.95 *(978-0-8225-9777-3(2))* Lerner Publishing Group.

—Heat. King, Andy, photos by. 2005. (Early Bird Energy Ser.). (ENG., Illus.). 48p. (gr. 2-5). lib. bdg. 26.60 *(978-0-8225-2459-5(7)*, Lerner Pubns.) Lerner Publishing Group.

—Investigating Heat. 2011. (Searchlight Books How Does Energy Work Ser.). (ENG., Illus.). (gr. 3-5). pap. 51.01 *(978-0-7613-8406-9(5))*; 40p. 27.93 *(978-0-7613-5773-5(4))*; 40p. pap. 8.95 *(978-0-7613-7872-3(3))* Lerner Publishing Group.

World Book, Inc Staff, contrib. by. Heat. 2011. 32p. (J). *(978-0-7166-1425-8(1))* World Bk., Inc.

HEAT—EXPERIMENTS

Canavan, Thomas. Cool Experiments with Heat & Cold. Linley, Adam, illus. 2017. (Mind-Blowing Science Experiments Ser.). 32p. (gr. 4-5). pap. 63.00 ***(978-1-5382-0729-1(X))*** Stevens, Gareth Publishing LLLP.

Cook, Trevor M. Experiments with Heat. 2009. (Science Lab Ser.). (J). (ENG., Illus.). 32p. (gr. 4-6). pap. 10.00 *(978-1-4358-3222-0(1))*; lib. bdg. 26.50 *(978-1-4358-2809-4(7))* Rosen Publishing Group, Inc., The. (PowerKids Pr.).

Gardner, Robert. How Hot Is Hot? Science Projects with Temperature. 2015. (Hot Science Experiments Ser.). 48p. (J). (gr. 3-4). 25.27 *(978-0-7660-6605-2(3))*; pap. 8.95 *(978-0-7660-6606-9(1)*, Enslow Elementary) Enslow Pubs., Inc.

—Really Hot Science Projects with Temperature: How Hot Is It? How Cold Is It? 2003. (Sensational Science Experiments Ser.). (Illus.). 48p. (J). lib. bdg. 25.27 *(978-0-7660-2015-3(0))* Enslow Pubs., Inc.

Gardner, Robert & Kemer, Eric. Easy Genius Science Projects with Temperature & Heat: Great Experiments & Ideas. 2009. (Easy Genius Science Projects Ser.). (Illus.). 128p. (J). (gr. 5-9). lib. bdg. 33.27 *(978-0-7660-2939-2(5))* Enslow Pubs., Inc.

Gardner, Robert & Kemer, Eric. Experiments with Temperature & Heat. 2017. (Science Whiz Experiments Ser.). 128p. (gr. 5-5). lib. bdg. 37.27 ***(978-0-7660-8682-1(8))*** Enslow Pubs., Inc.

Gould, Alan. Convection: A Current Event. Klofkorn, Lisa, illus. Hoyt, Richard, photos by. rev. ed. 2005. (Great Explorations in Math & Science Ser.). 60p. (J). reprint ed. pap. 10.50 *(978-1-931542-05-0(8)*, GEMS) Univ. of California, Berkeley, Lawrence Hall of Science.

Hawkins, Jay. Hot Stuff: The Science of Heat & Cold. 2013. (Big Bang Science Experiments Ser.). (ENG., Illus.). 32p. (gr. 3-6). 26.50 *(978-1-4777-0321-2(7))*; pap. 11.75 *(978-1-4777-0363-2(2))* Windmill Bks.

Magloff, Lisa. Experiments with Heat & Energy. 2010. (Cool Science Ser.). 32p. (J). (gr. 5-6). lib. bdg. 28.00 *(978-1-4339-3450-6(7))*; (Illus.). pap. 10.50 *(978-1-4339-3451-3(5))* Stevens, Gareth Publishing LLLP. (Gareth Stevens Learning Library).

Polinsky, Paige V. Super Simple Experiments with Heat & Cold: Fun & Innovative Science Projects. 2016. (ENG., Illus.). 32p. (J). *(978-1-68078-170-0(7))* ABDO Publishing Co.

Rowe, Brooke. Playing with Solar Heat. Bane, Jeff, illus. 2016. (My Early Library: My Science Fun Ser.). (ENG.). 24p. (J). (gr. k-1). 28.50 *(978-1-63471-031-2(2)*, 208204) Cherry Lake Publishing.

HEAT—FICTION

Albee, Sarah. Fun in the Sun. Williams, Sue, illus. 2006. (Step-By-Step Readers Ser.). (J). pap. *(978-1-59939-058-1(2)*, Reader's Digest Young Families, Inc.) Studio Fun International.

Barclay, Jane. How Hot Was It? Cole, Kathryn, ed. Donato, Janice, illus. (ENG.). 24p. (J). 14.95 *(978-1-894222-70-9(9))* Lobster Pr. CAN. Dist: Univ. of Toronto Pr.

Broach, Elise. Wet Dog! Catrow, David, illus. 2007. (ENG.). 32p. (J). (gr. k-3). pap. 5.99 *(978-0-14-240855-1(7)*, Puffin Books) Penguin Young Readers Group.

Cook, Sherry & Johnson, Terri. Hallie Heat, 26 vols. Kuhn, Jesse, illus. l.t. ed. 2006. (Quirkles — Exploring Phonics through Science Ser.: 8). 32p. (J). 7.99 *(978-1-933815-07-7(8)*, Quirkles, The) Creative 3, LLC.

Frazier, Craig. Stanley Goes for a Drive. 2004. (Stanley Ser.: STAN). (ENG., Illus.). 40p. (J). (gr. -1-7). 15.95 *(978-0-8118-4429-1(3))* Chronicle Bks. LLC.

Layton, Neal. Hot Hot Hot. Layton, Neal, illus. 2004. (ENG., Illus.). 32p. (J). (gr. -1-3). 15.99 *(978-0-7636-2148-3(X))* Candlewick Pr.

Meister, Cari. Buzz Beaker & the Cool Caps, 1 vol. McGuire, Bill, illus. 2011. (Buzz Beaker Bks.). (ENG.). 32p. (gr. 2-3). pap. 6.25 *(978-1-4342-3055-3(4))* Stone Arch Bks.

Van Leeuwen, Jean. Amanda Pig & the Really Hot Day. Schweninger, Ann, illus. 2007. (Oliver & Amanda Ser.). (ENG.). 48p. (J). (gr. 1-3). pap. 3.99 *(978-0-14-240775-2(5)*, Penguin Young Readers) Penguin Young Readers Group.

—Amanda Pig & the Really Hot Day. Schweninger, Ann, illus. 2007. (Oliver & Amanda Ser.). 47p. (J). (gr. -1-3). 11.65 *(978-0-7569-8152-5(2))* Perfection Learning Corp.

HEATHCLIFF (FICTITIOUS CHARACTER)—FICTION

Bingham, J. & Brontë, Emily. Wuthering Heights. 2004. (Paperback Classics Ser.). 144p. (J). pap. 4.95 *(978-0-7945-0573-8(2))* EDC Publishing.

Brontë, Emily. Wuthering Heights. 2004. (Graphic Novels Ser.). (ENG., Illus.). 72p. (J). pap. 7.99 *(978-0-237-52581-1(X))* Evans Brothers, Ltd. GBR. Dist: Independent Pubs. Group.

—Wuthering Heights. Bryant, Clive, ed. Burns, John M., illus. 2011. (ENG.). 160p. lib. bdg. 24.95 *(978-1-907127-80-9(1))* Classical Comics GBR. Dist: Publishers Group West (PGW).

—Wuthering Heights. (Classics Illustrated Ser.). (Illus.). 52p. (YA). pap. 4.95 *(978-1-57209-011-8(1))* Classics International Entertainment, Inc.

—Wuthering Heights. Warner, Darrell, illus. 2004. (Paperback Classics Ser.). 158p. (J). (gr. 5). lib. bdg. 12.95 *(978-1-58086-604-0(2))* EDC Publishing.

HEATING

Plumbing, Heating, Air Conditioning & Refrigeration Student Activity. 2004. (YA). cd-rom *(978-1-57078-954-0(1)*, CEV60033) C E V Multimedia, Ltd.

Thomas, Isabel. Experiments with Heating & Cooling. 2015. (Read & Experiment Ser.). (ENG., Illus.). 32p. (gr. 2-4). 30.65 *(978-1-4109-6839-5(1)*, Raintree Perspectives) Heinemann-Raintree.

HEAVEN

Alcorn, Randy. Tell Me about Heaven. DiCianni, Ron, illus. 2007. 64p. (J). 19.99 *(978-1-58134-853-8(3)*, 1271662) Crossway.

H
I

Alcorn, Randy & Washington, Linda. Heaven for Kids. 2006. (ENG., Illus.). 224p. (J). (gr. 3-7). per. 13.99 *(978-1-4143-1040-4(4)*, Tyndale Kids) Tyndale Hse. Pubs.
Anderson, Carolyn B. Heaven Is a Real Place. 2007. 73p. per. 8.95 *(978-1-59824-512-7(0))* E-BookTime LLC.
Anderson, Debby. Let's Talk about Heaven. 2003. (Illus.). 32p. (J). (gr. -1-2). 12.99 *(978-0-7814-3077-7(1)*, 0781430771) Cook, David C.
Bohlmann, Katharine. Grandpa, Is There a Heaven? Erickson, David, illus. 2008. 32p. pap. 7.49 *(978-0-7586-1478-0(0))* Concordia Publishing Hse.
Bostrom, Kathleen Long. What about Heaven? Kucharik, Elena, illus. 2012. (Little Blessings Ser.). (ENG.). 32p. (J). pap. 3.99 *(978-1-4143-7510-6(7))* Tyndale Hse. Pubs.
Burpo, Todd & Burpo, Sonja. Heaven Is for Real for Kids: A Little Boy's Astounding Story of His Trip to Heaven & Back. 1 vol. 2011. (ENG.). 32p. (J). 14.99 *(978-1-4003-1870-4(X))* Nelson, Thomas Inc.
Burpo, Todd & Vincent, Lynn. Heaven Is for Real for Kids: A Little Boy's Astounding Story of His Trip to Heaven & Back. 2011. (ENG.). 32p. (J). pap. 9.99 *(978-0-7852-3751-8(8))* Nelson, Thomas Inc.
Coulter, Nancy J. When Grandma Went to Heaven. 2009. 36p. pap. 15.49 *(978-1-4389-3424-2(6))* AuthorHouse.
Dent, Jenny. Where Is Heaven? (Spiritual Teachings for Children Ser.). (Illus.). 32p. (J). (gr. k-9). 17.95 *(978-0-85487-052-3(0))* White Eagle Publishing Trust GBR. Dist: DeVorss & Co.
Dlugos, Pamela J. Messages from Heaven: Be a Shining Star. Dlugos, Pamela J., illus. Date not set. (Illus.). 64p. (J). (gr. 4-6). pap. 10.95 *(978-0-9661564-0-9(4))* Rejoyce Pubns.
Dockrey, Donna. Tell Me about A Place Called Heaven. 2010. 32p. pap. 14.50 *(978-0-557-23820-0(X))* Lulu Pr., Inc.
Halteman, Laverne K. Mommy Goes to Heaven. 2003. (Illus.). (J). *(978-0-87813-612-4(6))* Christian Light Pubns., Inc.
Ham, Ken. The Answers Book for Kids, Volume 4: 22 Questions from Kids on Sin, Salvation, & the Christian Life. 2009. (Answers Book for Kids Ser.). (Illus.). 48p. (J). (gr. 3-7). 7.99 *(978-0-89051-528-0(X))* Master Bks.
Lotz, Anne Graham & Graham Lotz, Anne. Heaven God's Promise for Me. 1 vol. Bryant, Laura J., illus. 2011. (ENG.). 40p. (J). 16.99 *(978-0-310-71601-3(2))* Zondervan.
Nystrom, Carolyn. Will I Live Forever? Shilliam, Jo-Anne, illus. 2006. 32p. (J). (gr. -1-3). 11.99 *(978-0-8254-7306-7(3)*, Candle Bks.) Lion Hudson PLC GBR. Dist: Kregel Pubns.
Petkau, Karen S. If Heaven Is So Great, Why Can't I Go Now? 2014. pap. *(978-1-4866-0026-7(3))* Word Alive Pr.
Piper, Don & Murphey, Cecil. 90 Minutes in Heaven: My True Story. 1 vol. 2009. (ENG.). 160p. (J). pap. 9.99 *(978-0-8007-3399-5(1))* Revell.
Rowland, Wilmer. How to Get to Heaven. 2016. (Illus.). (J). *(978-0-7577-5074-8(5))* Word Aflame Pr.
Weldon, Beth. What Does Luke Do in Heaven All Day? 2008. 40p. pap. 17.99 *(978-1-4389-3207-1(3))* AuthorHouse.
Wilkinson, Bruce & Thomas, Mack. A Life God Rewards: Guys Only. ltd. ed. 2006. 96p. bds. 9.99 *(978-1-60142-002-2(1)*, Multnomah) Doubleday Religious Publishing Group, The.

HEAVEN—FICTION

Adornetto, Alexandra. Heaven. 2012. (Halo Trilogy Ser.: 3). (ENG.). 432p. (YA). (gr. 7-12). 17.99 *(978-0-312-65628-7(9))* Feiwel & Friends.
Anderson, Andrea Patrice. Heaven's Diary: Our Gift from God. 2006. 37.00 *(978-0-8059-8845-1(9))* Dorrance Publishing Co., Inc.
Andreae, Giles. Heaven Is Having You. Cabban, Vanessa, illus. 2007. (Padded Board Bks.). 18p. (J). (gr. -1-1). bds. 7.95 *(978-1-58925-820-4(7))* Tiger Tales.
Balestrino, Jerry. Pumpkin the Angel Cat: Pumpkins 1st Mission. 2009. 32p. pap. 13.99 *(978-1-4343-7105-8(0))* AuthorHouse.
Barnes, Kenneth Edward. In Search of A Golden Sparrow. 2011. 124p. (gr. 2-4). 21.23 *(978-1-4634-0878-7(1))*; pap. 12.01 *(978-1-4634-0879-4(X))* AuthorHouse.
Bausley, Alicia. Tucker Goes to Heaven. 2006. 32p. pap. 13.95 *(978-1-59526-457-2(4))* Aeon Publishing Inc.
Bergren, Lisa Tawn. God Gave Us Heaven. 2008. (ENG., Illus.). 40p. (J). (gr. -1-2). 10.99 *(978-1-4000-7446-4(0)*, WaterBrook Pr.) Crown Publishing Group.
Bower, Gary. There's a Party in Heaven! Bower, Jan, illus. 2007. 31p. (J). 11.99 *(978-0-9704621-8-3(2))* Storybook Meadow Publishing.
Cannon, Anita. My Aunt Bonnie: A Child's Story of Love & Loss. 2011. 48p. pap. 20.45 *(978-1-4497-1617-2(2)*, WestBow Pr.) Author Solutions, Inc.
Capehart, Staci. Furry Tails: The Adventures of Mr. Mackie. 2009. 40p. pap. 16.99 *(978-1-4343-6974-1(9))* AuthorHouse.
Capozzola, Christine. Angel from Heaven. Nguyen, Cindy, illus. 2014. (ENG.). 28p. pap. 9.95 *(978-1-63047-189-7(5))* Morgan James Publishing.
Carmona, Bianca L. Gone to Heaven: A children's memior Book. 2011. 20p. pap. 14.95 *(978-1-4634-1517-4(6))* AuthorHouse.
Chen, Wei Dong. Monkey King: The Bane of Heaven. Peng, Chao, illus. 2012. (Monkey King Ser.: 2). (ENG.). 176p. (gr. 5-8). lib. bdg. 29.27 *(978-89-94208-70-1(4))* JR Comics KOR. Dist: Lerner Publishing Group.
Coleman, Pansy J. & Coleman, Jason A. The Wings of an Angel. 2004. 259p. pap. 27.95 *(978-1-4137-2232-1(6))* America Star Bks.
Coppard, A. E. Clorinda Walks in Heaven Stories. 2006. 220p. per. *(978-1-4067-9414-4(7)*, Pomona Pr.) Read Bks.
Crow, Marilee. Does Heaven Get Mail? Snider, K. C., illus. 2008. 24p. pap. 10.95 *(978-1-935137-12-2(3))* Guardian Angel Publishing, Inc.
Curtis, Jessica Lynn. Papa's New Home. Harmon, Steve, illus. 2012. (ENG.). 40p. (J). *(978-0-931674-64-8(6)*, Waldman House Pr.) TRISTAN Publishing, Inc.
Faircloth, M. L. When Will I See Aunt Carole? Ray, Michael, illus. 2012. (J). 26p. 19.95 *(978-1-61863-326-2(0))*; 28p. pap. 9.99 *(978-1-61863-324-8(4))* Bookstand Publishing.
Fleming, Theresa. Going Home with Jesus. 1 vol. Fleming, Yvonne B., illus. 2009. 22p. pap. 24.95 *(978-1-60813-703-9(1))* America Star Bks.
Gooch-Anderson, Stacy. The Legend of the Star. 2009. (Illus.). (J). 15.99 *(978-1-59955-243-9(4))* Cedar Fort, Inc./CFI Distribution.
Harold & I. 2007. (ENG., Illus.). 291p. (J). (gr. 3-8). per. 13.99 *(978-0-7684-2432-4(1))* Send The Light Distribution LLC.
Hippie Bob. God's Cook Book What a Creation! A Hippie Bob Tale. 2009. 24p. pap. 14.99 *(978-1-4389-9834-3(1))* AuthorHouse.
Holbrook, James. Emily I Think I Saw Heaven. Brittingham, Jennifer, illus. 2007. 40p. per. 14.95 *(978-1-934246-56-6(5))* Peppertree Pr., The.
Holyoak, Kathleen & Summers, Sherry. Flowers in Heaven. 2009. 32p. pap. 14.49 *(978-1-4389-4607-8(4))* AuthorHouse.
Huneck, Stephen. Sally Goes to Heaven. 2014. (ENG., Illus.). 48p. (J). (gr. k-2). 18.95 *(978-1-4197-0969-2(0)*, Abrams Bks. for Young Readers) Abrams, Inc.
Joslin, Mary. The Fourth Wise Man. Johnson, Richard, illus. 2007. 28p. (J). (gr. -1-2). 14.99 *(978-0-7814-4545-0(0))* Cook, David C.
Kakkar, Renu. Granny's Return from Heaven as an Incredible Car. 2011. (Illus.). 180p. (gr. 4-6). pap. 14.49 *(978-1-4490-9859-9(2))* AuthorHouse.
Kazmi, Ummul Baneen. Alisha's Heavenly Adventures: It's Magic! 2012. 28p. pap. 19.99 *(978-1-4685-5803-6(X))* AuthorHouse.
Kimmel, Eric A. Even Higher! A Rosh Hashanah Story by I. L. Peretz. Weber, Jill, illus. 2010. (ENG.). 32p. (J). (gr. -1-3). pap. 6.95 *(978-0-8234-2298-2(4))* Holiday Hse., Inc.
Krider, Dave. Do Animals Go to Heaven?. 1 vol. 2009. 49p. pap. 16.95 *(978-1-61546-049-6(7))* America Star Bks.
Lewis, Beverly. What Is Heaven Like? Querin, Pamela, illus. 2006. (ENG.). 32p. (J). (gr. -1-3). 15.99 *(978-0-7642-0184-4(0))* Bethany Hse. Pubs.
Lindsay, Linda. People Heaven. l.t. ed. 2005. (Illus.). (J). 36p. 16.99 *(978-1-59879-020-7(X))*; 26p. per. 11.99 *(978-1-59879-005-4(6))* Lifevest Publishing, Inc.
McLaughlin, Dawn L. Two Tickets to Heaven, Please! 2009. 48p. pap. 16.25 *(978-1-60693-061-8(3)*, Eloquent Bks.) Strategic Book Publishing & Rights Agency (SBPRA).
Mitchell, Lee Ann. Milo the Mighty Protector. 2010. 32p. pap. 12.99 *(978-1-4490-5447-2(1))* AuthorHouse.
MuñOz, Alejandra DáVila. I Want to Paint Heaven. 2011. 28p. pap. 15.00 *(978-1-4567-3685-9(X))* AuthorHouse.
O'Connell, Janet. When They Died, Where Did They Go? 2013. 24p. pap. 12.45 *(978-1-4497-9618-1(4)*, WestBow Pr.) Author Solutions, Inc.
Otenbaker, Audrey Lee. God's Jewel. 2009. 48p. (J). pap. 17.95 *(978-1-4327-3340-7(0))* Outskirts Pr., Inc.
Parrish, Jim. Dog Gone. 2012. 24p. pap. 17.99 *(978-1-4685-6036-7(0))* AuthorHouse.
Pelz, Ramona. My Name Is Mae. Trousdale, Taryn, illus. 2003. (J). per. 9.95 *(978-1-58597-190-9(1))* Leathers Publishing.
Penley, Janet. Boo Boo Kisses from the Littlest Angel. 1 vol. Bartlett, Alyssa Joy, illus. 2010. 34p. 24.95 *(978-1-4489-4539-9(9))* PublishAmerica, Inc.
Phyllis Stella Jadosh. Well Then, You Must Be Lucky. 2011. 24p. pap. 11.95 *(978-1-935268-70-3(8))* Halo Publishing International.
Pinette, Melanie. Looking Up. 2008. 17p. pap. 24.95 *(978-1-60610-905-2(7))* America Star Bks.
Rennich, Lori. When Cooper Got to Heaven. 2011. 28p. pap. 21.99 *(978-1-4568-6199-5(9))* Xlibris Corp.
Robinson, Kim. An Unusual Experience. 2009. 20p. (J). pap. 17.95 *(978-1-4327-3584-5(5))* Outskirts Pr., Inc.
Roesti, Delores. Mareena Maree Mulligan & the Flying Wheelchair: Book 2: The Busybodies. 2008. 102p. pap. 10.95 *(978-0-7414-4477-6(1))* Infinity Publishing.
Rouss, Sylvia. Littlest Tree. Binus, Ari, illus. 2005. 32p. (J). pap. 9.95 *(978-1-932687-26-2(2)*, Devora Publishing) Simcha Media Group.
Shanghai Animation Studio Staff & Tang, Sanmu. Monkey Makes Havoc in Heaven. Xiaozhen, Wu, tr. from CHI. 2010. (Favorite Children's Ser.). (ENG., Illus.). 32p. (J). (gr. -1-3). pap. 5.95 *(978-1-60220-974-9(X))* BetterLink Pr., Inc.
Shaw, Ellie. Together Again. 2012. 24p. pap. 24.95 *(978-1-4626-6427-6(X))* America Star Bks.
Simpson, Clare. My Heaven Book. 2016. (ENG., Illus.). 48p. (J). (gr. -1). 13.99 *(978-1-61261-643-8(7))* Paraclete Pr., Inc.
Smith, Blanche Z. A Gift from God. 2012. 20p. pap. 17.99 *(978-1-4685-8376-2(X))* AuthorHouse.
Turcotte, Michael. Colours Made in Heaven. 1 vol. Turcotte, Derek, illus. 2009. 13p. pap. 24.95 *(978-1-60836-316-2(3))* America Star Bks.
Walker, John Anthony. Frel. 2009. 32p. pap. 12.99 *(978-1-935436-15-7(5))* Rodaian Pr.
Wallace-Lang, Maxine Lois. Sheldon's Adventures in Heaven. Porfirio, Guy, illus. 2003. 48p. (J). 12.99 *(978-0-8280-1508-0(2))* Review & Herald Publishing Assn.
Welsh, Phoebe. Wonder What Do First Day Heaven. 2006. 70p. pap. 16.95 *(978-0-9769618-1-9(4))* Less is More Publishing, LLC.
Wick, Kimberly. Reaching for Heaven. 2009. 36p. pap. 16.99 *(978-1-4389-2268-3(X))* AuthorHouse.
Williams, Amanda Schaefer. Sadie in Heaven. 2012. 28p. pap. 24.95 *(978-1-4626-8802-9(0))* America Star Bks.

HEBREW LANGUAGE

Amery, H. First Thousand Words. rev. ed. 2004. (HEB & ENG.). 64p. (J). 12.99 *(978-0-7945-0029-0(3))* EDC Publishing.
Armeland, Galia. A [Alef] - B [Bet] Yisrael: Aleph Bet Israel. 2009. (HEB & ENG., Illus.). 32p. (J). pap. 10.95 *(978-0-939144-61-7(1))* EKS Publishing Co.
Berlitz Editors. Hebrew Phrase Book. 4th rev. ed. 2003. (Phrase Bks.). (HEB & ENG., Illus.). 224p. 8.95 *(978-2-8315-6927-7(3)*, 569273) Berlitz Publishing.
Blitz, Shmuel. Megilat Ester: The ArtScroll Children's Megillah. Katz, Tova, illus. 2003. (ArtScroll Ser.). (ENG & HEB.). 79p. (J). 16.99 *(978-1-57819-708-8(2)*, MCHH); pap. 10.99 *(978-1-57819-709-5(0)*, MCHP) Mesorah Pubns., Ltd.
Bluedorn, Johannah. Little Bitty Baby Learns Hebrew. Bluedorn, Johannah, illus. 2005. (Illus.). 26p. (J). bds. 12.00 *(978-1-933228-00-6(8))* Trivium Pursuit.
Burke, David. BEAUTY & the BEAST (English to Hebrew - Level 3) Learn HEBREW Through Fairy Tales. 2007. (ENG & HEB.). (J). per. 14.95 incl. audio compact disk *(978-1-891888-94-6(3))* Slangman Publishing.
—Cinderella: Level 1: Learn Hebrew Through Fairy Tales. Obejas, Ofra, tr. Sandoval, Migs, illus. 2006. (Slangman Kids: Level 1 Ser.). (ENG & HEB.). 29p. pap. 14.95 incl. audio compact disk *(978-1-891888-92-2(7))* Slangman Publishing.
—Goldilocks & the 3 Bears: Level 2: Learn Hebrew Through Fairy Tales. Sandoval, Migs, illus. 2006. (Slangman Kids: Level 2 Ser.). (ENG & HEB.). 29p. (J). (gr. -1-3). pap. 14.95 incl. audio compact disk *(978-1-891888-93-9(5))* Slangman Publishing.
Castberg, C. & Adler, Lillian W. The New Reading Hebrew: A Guided Instruction Course. 2004. (Illus.). 126p. (J). 9.98 *(978-0-87441-728-9(7))* Behrman Hse., Inc.
Edwards, Michelle. Alef-Bet. Edwards, Michelle, illus. 2009. (ENG., Illus.). 32p. (J). pap. 10.95 *(978-1-58838-233-7(8)*, NewSouth Bks.) NewSouth, Inc.
Goldeen, Ruth & Goldeen, Bill. Alef-Bet Yoga for Kids. Goldeen, Bill, photos by. 2009. (Israel Ser.). (ENG., Illus.). 32p. (J). (gr. -1-2). 15.95 *(978-0-8225-8756-9(4))*; pap. 7.95 *(978-0-7613-4506-0(X))* Lerner Publishing Group. (Kar-Ben Publishing).
Goldstein, Rose B. Songs to Share. Schloss, E., illus. (ENG & HEB.). 64p. (J). (gr. -1-5). 2.95 *(978-0-8381-0720-1(6)*, 10-720) United Synagogue of America Bk. Service.
Goodman, Marlene. Let's Learn Hebrew Picture Dictionary. 2003. (ENG & HEB., Illus.). 80p. 13.00 *(978-0-07-140825-7(8)*, 0071408258) McGraw-Hill Cos., The.
Groner, Judyth. My First Hebrew Word Book. Marzel, Pépi, illus. 2005. (ENG.). 32p. (J). (gr. -1-2). lib. bdg. 17.95 *(978-1-58013-126-1(3)*, Kar-Ben Publishing) Lerner Publishing Group.
Hazan, Maurice, creator. Hebrew Dialogues Game Level 1. 2005. (HEB.). (J). 126.00 *(978-1-933209-66-1(6))* Symtalk, Inc.
—Hebrew Dialogues Game Level 2. 2005. (HEB.). (J). 126.00 *(978-1-933209-67-8(4))* Symtalk, Inc.
Hewbrew Penmanship. 2006. (C). 10.00 *(978-0-9677313-9-1(9))* Friedman, Yuda.
Hippocrene Books Staff, ed. Hebrew Children's Picture Dictionary: English-Hebrew/Hebrew-English. 2006. (HEB & ENG., Illus.). 114p. pap. 14.95 *(978-0-7818-1163-7(5))* Hippocrene Bks., Inc.
Kaye, Terry, et al. Hebrew Through Prayer, Bk. 1. Siegel, Adam, ed. Ben-Moshe, Jana, illus. 96p. (J). (gr. 4-5). pap. 6.95 *(978-0-87441-563-6(2))* Behrman Hse., Inc.
Let's Learn Aleph-Beis. (Yoni Gold Board Book Ser.). (J). bds. 4.95 *(978-1-58330-149-4(6))* Feldheim Pubs.
Maiben, Dina. Ready, Set... Go Alef Bet! 2012. (Illus.). 96p. (J). *(978-0-87441-860-6(7))* Behrman Hse., Inc.
Michelson, Richard & Gudeon, Karla. The Language of Angels: A Story about the Reinvention of Hebrew. 2017. (ENG., Illus.). 32p. (J). (gr. k-4). lib. bdg. 16.99 *(978-1-58089-636-8(7))* Charlesbridge Publishing, Inc.
Musleah, Rahel & Jarrett, Judy. Apples & Pomegranates: A Family Seder for Rosh Hashanah. 2004. (ENG & HEB., Illus.). 64p. (J). (gr. k-5). pap. 7.95 *(978-1-58013-123-0(9)*, Kar-Ben Publishing) Lerner Publishing Group.
Passport Books Staff, ed. Let's Learn Hebrew. Goodman, Marlene, illus. 2003. (Let's Learn... Picture Dictionary Ser.). (HEB & ENG.). 80p. (J). (gr. 4-7). 11.95 *(978-0-8442-8490-3(4)*, 84904, Passport Bks.) McGraw-Hill Trade.
Rajic, Alex. The Alefbet Illuminated. Rajic, Alex, illus. 2010. (ENG., Illus.). 56p. 0.00 *(978-0-615-38180-0(4))* Cenozoic Pr.
Raz, Rachel. The Colors of Israel. Raz, Rachel, photos by. 2015. (ENG., Illus.). 24p. (J). (gr. -1-2). 7.99 *(978-1-4677-5540-5(0))*; lib. bdg. 17.99 *(978-1-4677-5539-9(7))* Lerner Publishing Group. (Kar-Ben Publishing).
The Rosetta Stone Language Library: Hebrew Level 1. 2005. (J). (gr. 1-18). cd-rom 209.00 *(978-1-883972-76-9(0))* Rosetta Stone Ltd.
Rossel, Seymour. The Storybook Haggadah. 2007. pap. 9.95 *(978-1-932687-59-0(9)*, Pitspopany Pr.) Simcha Media Group.
Sussman, Joni. My First Yiddish Word Book. Marzel, Pepi, illus. 2014. (ENG.). 32p. (J). (gr. -1-2). pap. 12.95 *(978-1-4677-5175-9(8)*, Kar-Ben Publishing) Lerner Publishing Group.
Vocabulary Pt. 2: Sifreinu. Date not set. (Orig.). (J). (gr. 3-18). pap. 1.00 *(978-0-8266-0206-0(1))* Kehot Pubn. Society.
Yacobi, Diana, et al. Sarah, David & YOU Read Hebrew: Book 1. 2005. *(978-0-9761648-1-4(7))* Sarah & David LLC.
Yonay, Shahar & Yonay, Rina. Ha-Mikraah Shel: Osef Kite Keriah Le-Talmidim Ba-Tefutsot: Kolel Targile Lashon U-Fituah Ha-Habah Ve-Havanat Ha-Nikra. 2009. (HEB., Illus.). (J). *(978-0-927580-77-9(2))* Yonay, Shahar.

HEBREWS

see Jews

HEDGEHOGS

Bader, Bonnie. Hedge-Hedgey-Hedgehogs. 2016. (Penguin Young Readers, Level 2 Ser.). (ENG., Illus.). 32p. (J). (gr. 1-2). 3.99 *(978-0-448-48974-2(0)*, Penguin Young Readers) Penguin Young Readers Group.
Borgert-Spaniol, Megan. Baby Hedgehogs. 2015. (Super Cute! Ser.). (ENG., Illus.). 24p. (J). (gr. k-3). lib. bdg. 25.95 *(978-1-62617-217-3(X)*, Blastoff! Readers) Bellwether Media.
Doudna, Kelly. Hilarious Hedgehogs. 1 vol. Nobens, C. A., illus. 2013. (Unusual Pets Ser.). (ENG.). 24p. (J). (gr. -1-3). 24.21 *(978-1-61783-399-1(1))* ABDO Publishing Co.
Dunn, Mary R. Hedgehogs. 1 vol. (Nocturnal Animals Ser.). (ENG., 24p. (gr. k-1). 2011. Illus.). pap. 7.29 *(978-1-4296-6191-7(7))* 2011. pap. 41.70 *(978-1-4296-6360-1(X))* 2010. lib. bdg. 26.65 *(978-1-4296-5284-1(5))* Capstone Press of Coughlan Cos. (Pebble Plus).
Gagne, Tammy. Care for a Pet Hedgehog. 2009. (How to Convince Your Parents You Can ... Ser.). 32p. (J). (gr. 1-4). 25.70 *(978-1-58415-798-4(4))* Mitchell Lane Pubs., Inc.
Goodridge, Teresa. Happy Hedgehogs Stickers. 2015. (Dover Little Activity Books Stickers Ser.). (ENG.). 4p. (J). (gr. k-3). 1.99 *(978-0-486-80319-7(8))* Dover Pubns., Inc.
Gregory, Josh. Hedgehogs. 2015. (ENG., Illus.). 48p. (J). lib. bdg. 29.00 *(978-0-531-21390-2(0)*, Orchard Bks.) Scholastic, Inc.
Harasymiw, Therese. Hedgehogs in the Dark. 2012. (Creatures of the Night Ser.). (Illus.). 24p. (J). (gr. 1-3). pap. 8.15 *(978-1-4339-6374-2(4))* Stevens, Gareth Publishing LLLP.
Hugo, Pierre de, illus. The Hedgehog. 2004. (ENG.). 32p. (J). (gr. k-3). pap. 11.99 *(978-1-85103-354-6(8))* Moonlight Publishing, Ltd. GBR. Dist: Independent Pubs. Group.
James, Lincoln. Hedgehogs Are Not Hogs! 2014. (Confusing Creature Names Ser.). 24p. (J). (gr. 1-3). 22.60 *(978-1-4824-0951-2(8))* Stevens, Gareth Publishing LLLP.
Leach, Michael. Hedgehog. 2009. 32p. (gr. k-5). pap. 10.60 *(978-1-4042-4575-4(8)*, Rosen Classroom); (Illus.). (J). lib. bdg. 25.25 *(978-1-4358-4998-3(1)*, PowerKids Pr.) Rosen Publishing Group, Inc., The.
Markovics, Joyce L. Hedgehog. 2016. (Weird but Cute Ser.). (ENG., Illus.). 24p. (J). (gr. -1-3). lib. bdg. 17.95 *(978-1-62724-846-4(3))* Bearport Publishing Co., Inc.
Matzke, Ann. Hedgehog. 2015. (ENG.). 32p. (gr. 3-6). 32.79 *(978-1-63430-433-7(0))* Rourke Educational Media.
Mulder, Nancy. Caring for Your Hedgehog. 2006. (Caring for Your Pet Ser.). (Illus.). 32p. (J). (gr. 3-7). 9.95 *(978-1-59036-471-0(6))*; lib. bdg. 26.00 *(978-1-59036-470-3(8))* Weigl Pubs., Inc.
Rissman, Rebecca. Hedgehogs: Nocturnal Foragers. 1 vol. 2014. (Night Safari Ser.). (ENG., Illus.). 24p. (gr. k-2). 23.32 *(978-1-4846-0313-0(3)*, Heinemann Read & Learn) Heinemann-Raintree.
Rockwood, Leigh. Tell Me the Difference Between a Porcupine & a Hedgehog. 2013. (How Are They Different? Ser.). (ENG., Illus.). 24p. (J). (gr. k-5). pap. 8.25 *(978-1-4488-9732-2(7))*; lib. bdg. 22.60 *(978-1-4488-9637-0(1))* Rosen Publishing Group, Inc., The. (PowerKids Pr.).
Schuetz, Kari. Hedgehogs. 2013. (Illus.). 24p. (J). *(978-0-531-27650-1(3))*; (ENG.). lib. bdg. 25.95 *(978-1-60014-863-7(8)*, Blastoff! Readers) Bellwether Media.

HEDGEHOGS—FICTION

Alford, Douglas J. & Alford, Pakaket. How Do Hedgehogs Hug? Anderson, Jane A., illus. 2013. 58p. pap. 11.99 *(978-1-62495-071-1(X))* Manufacturing Application Konsulting Engineering (MAKE)in.
Anderson, Lena & Sandin, Joan. Hedgehog, Pig, & the Sweet Little Friend. Sandin, Joan, tr. from SWE. 2007. (Illus.). 32p. (J). (gr. -1-1). 16.00 *(978-91-29-66742-4(9))* R & S Bks. SWE. Dist: Macmillan.
AZ Books. Hedgehog & His Friends. 2013. (Amusing Stories Ser.). (ENG.). 10p. (J). (-k). bds. 7.95 *(978-1-61889-305-5(X))* AZ Bks. LLC.
Bagley, Jessixa. Before I Leave. 2016. (ENG., Illus.). 40p. (J). 17.99 *(978-1-62672-040-4(1)*, 9781626720404) Roaring Brook Pr.
Berg, Brook. What Happened to Marion's Book? Alberg, Nathan, illus. 2003. 48p. (J). (gr. -1-2). per. 16.95 *(978-1-932146-05-9(9)*, Upstart Bks.) Highsmith Inc.
Billows, Denis. Down in Bluebell Wood. 2010. 164p. pap. 11.99 *(978-1-4490-8822-4(8))* AuthorHouse.
Bishop, Poppy. Bear's House of Books. Edgson, Alison, illus. 2017. (ENG.). 32p. (J). (gr. -1-2). 16.99 ***(978-1-68010-038-9(6))*** Tiger Tales.
Brett, Jan. Hedgie Blasts Off! Brett, Jan, illus. 2006. (ENG., Illus.). 32p. (J). (gr. -1-3). 17.99 *(978-0-399-24621-0(5)*, G.P. Putnam's Sons Books for Young Readers) Penguin Young Readers Group.
—El Sombrero. (Buenas Noches Ser.).Tr. of Hat. (SPA.). (J). *(978-958-04-4169-4(3))* Norma S.A.
Butler, M. Christina. One Noisy Night. Macnaughton, Tina, illus. 2016. (ENG.). 32p. (J). (gr. -1-2). 16.99 *(978-1-68010-034-1(3))* Tiger Tales.
—One Snowy Rescue. Macnaughton, Tina, illus. 2015. (ENG.). 32p. (J). (gr. -1-3). 16.99 *(978-1-58925-196-0(2))* Tiger Tales.
—One Special Christmas. Macnaughton, Tina, illus. 2013. (ENG.). 32p. (J). *(978-1-58925-145-8(8))* Tiger Tales.
Calvani, Mayra. Humberto, the Bookworm Hamster. Grady, Kit, illus. 2009. 20p. pap. 10.95 *(978-1-935137-92-4(1))* Guardian Angel Publishing, Inc.
Carr, Elias. Hal y el Nuevo Compañero. Garton, Michael, illus. 2016. (SPA.). (J). ***(978-1-5064-2098-1(2))*** Augsburg Fortress, Pubs.
Chiew, Suzanne. That's What Friends Are For. Pedler, Caroline, illus. 2017. (ENG.). 32p. (J). (gr. -1-2). 16.99 ***(978-1-68010-040-2(8))*** Tiger Tales.
Davies, Caroline & Martin, Sharon. Cotiau Newydd. 2005. (WEL., Illus.). 12p. pap. *(978-1-86101-081-0(8))* Acen Limited.
Dennard, Deborah. Hedgehog Haven: A Story of a British Hedgerow Community. 2005. (Soundprints' Wild Habitats Ser.). (ENG., Illus.). 32p. (J). (gr. 1-4). 8.95 *(978-1-59249-108-7(1)*, SC7020) Soundprints.
—Hedgehog Haven: The Story of an English Hedgerow Community. Hynes, Robert, illus. 2005. (ENG.). (J). (gr. 1-4). 32p. 19.95 *(978-1-56899-989-0(5)*, BC7020); 36p. 15.95 *(978-1-56899-987-6(9)*, B7020); 36p. pap. 6.95 *(978-1-56899-988-3(7)*, S7020) Soundprints.
—Hurry up, Hedgehog! Hynes, Robert, illus. 2003. (Soundprints' Read-and-Discover Ser.). (ENG.). 32p. (gr. -1-1). 12.95 *(978-1-59249-150-6(2)*, PS2012) Soundprints.
—Hurry up, Hedgehog! Hynes, Robert, illus. 2003. (Amazing Animal Adventures Ser.). (ENG.). 32p. (J). (gr. -1-3). per. 3.95 *(978-1-59249-149-0(9)*, S2012) Soundprints.
Dony, John. Henderson the Hedgehog. 2014. (ENG.). 62p. (J). pap. 7.99 *(978-0-9910340-0-0(7))* Dewberry Pr.
Falkenstern, Lisa. A Dragon Moves In. 0 vols. 2011. (ENG.). 32p. (J). (gr. -1-3). 16.99 *(978-0-7614-5947-7(2)*, 9780761459477, Amazon Children's Publishing) Amazon Publishing.
Fergus, Maureen. Buddy & Earl. 1 vol. Sookocheff, Carey, illus. 2015. (Buddy & Earl Ser.: 1). (ENG.). 32p. (J). (gr. -1-2). 16.95 *(978-1-55498-712-2(1))* Groundwood Bks. CAN. Dist: Publishers Group West (PGW).
—Buddy & Earl & the Great Big Baby. 1 vol. Sookocheff, Carey, illus. 2016. (Buddy & Earl Ser.). (ENG.). 32p. (J). (gr. -1-2). 16.95 *(978-1-55498-716-0(4))* Groundwood Bks. CAN. Dist: Publishers Group West (PGW).
—Buddy & Earl Go Exploring. 1 vol. Sookocheff, Carey, illus. 2016. (Buddy & Earl Ser.: 2). (ENG.). 32p. (J). (gr. k-2). 16.95 *(978-1-55498-714-6(8))* Groundwood Bks. CAN. Dist: Publishers Group West (PGW).

Forde, Patricia. Hedgehogs Do Not Like Heights. Dreidemy, Joëlle, illus. 2nd ed. 2016. (Reading Ladder Ser.). (ENG.). 48p. (J). (gr. k-2). 7.99 *(978-1-4052-8211-6(8))* Egmont Bks., Ltd. GBR. Dist: Independent Pubs. Group.

Grout, Claire. Emil & Ordi: Friends for All Time. 2012. 24p. pap. 15.99 *(978-1-4691-6279-9(2))* Xlibris Corp.

Hounslow, Gaynor. Snoop & Sniffly Wiffly - the Tale of Two Hedgehogs: The Children's Book of Wildlife Stories. 2009. (Illus.). 32p. pap. 12.99 *(978-1-4389-6069-2(7))* AuthorHouse.

Isern, Susanna. The Magic Ball of Wool. 2013. (ENG., Illus.). 32p. (J). (gr. -1-k). 16.95 *(978-84-15619-89-5(8))* Eastern National.

Johnson, Amy. Tales of the Forest. 2011. (Illus.). 64p. pap. 13.95 *(978-1-4670-1976-7(3))* AuthorHouse.

Jones, Allan. The Six Crowns: Fair Wind to Widdershins. Chalk, Gary, illus. 2011. (Six Crowns Ser.: 2). 176p. (J). (gr. 2-5). 15.99 *(978-0-06-200626-4(6)*, Greenwillow Bks.) HarperCollins Pubs.

—The Six Crowns: Trundle's Quest. Chalk, Gary, illus. 2011. (Six Crowns Ser.: 1). 176p. (J). (gr. 2-5). pap. 5.99 *(978-0-06-200625-7(8)*, Greenwillow Bks.) HarperCollins Pubs.

Jones, Allan Frewin. Fire over Swallowhaven. Chalk, Gary, illus. 2012. (Six Crowns Ser.: 3). 160p. (J). (gr. 2-5). 15.99 *(978-0-06-200629-5(0)*, Greenwillow Bks.) HarperCollins Pubs.

—Trundle's Quest. Chalk, Gary, illus. 2011. (Six Crowns Ser.: 1). 160p. (J). (gr. 2-5). 15.99 *(978-0-06-200623-3(1)*, Greenwillow Bks.) HarperCollins Pubs.

Lawhead, Stephen R. The Tale of Anabelle Hedgehog. 2003. (Illus.). 112p. pap. 6.99 *(978-0-7459-4677-1(1)*, Lion Books) Lion Hudson PLC GBR. Dist: Trafalgar Square Publishing.

Leigh-Crawford, Lynda. Hovis the Hedgehog: Bonfire Night. 2009. (Illus.). 16p. pap. 9.49 *(978-1-4490-3675-1(9))* AuthorHouse.

Lyons, I. j. April's Pond. 2009. (Illus.). 80p. pap. 11.49 *(978-1-4490-3066-7(1))* AuthorHouse.

Macnaughton, Tina. One Snowy Rescue. 2015. (ENG.). pap. *(978-0-545-92909-7(1))* Scholastic, Inc.

Marie, Lynne. Hedgehog Goes to Kindergarten. Kennedy, Anne, illus. 2011. (J). pap. *(978-0-545-29874-2(1))* Scholastic, Inc.

Martin, Emily. Downpour. Shaughnessy, Mara, illus. 2013. (ENG.). 32p. (J). (gr. -1-k). 14.95 *(978-1-62087-545-2(4)*, 620545, Sky Pony Pr.) Skyhorse Publishing Co., Inc.

Masterson, Hoss. Ball Hog. Alves, Josh, illus. 2017. (Animal All-Stars Ser.). (ENG.). 56p. (gr. 1-3). lib. bdg. 25.32 *(978-1-4965-4308-0(4))* Stone Arch Bks.

McCue, Lisa. HideAway Hedgehog & the Magical Rainbow. 2015. (HideAway Pets Bks.). (ENG., Illus.). 26p. (J). (gr. -1-2). 9.95 *(978-1-4549-1602-4(8))* Sterling Publishing Co., Inc.

McKay, Hilary. Lulu & the Hedgehog in the Rain. Lamont, Priscilla, illus. 2014. (Lulu Ser.: 5). (ENG.). 112p. (J). (gr. 1-5). 13.99 *(978-0-8075-4812-7(X))* Whitman, Albert & Co.

Meadows, Daisy. Emily Prickleback's Clever Idea. 2016. (Magic Animal Friends Ser.: 6). (ENG.). 112p. (J). (gr. 2-5). pap. 4.99 *(978-0-545-90743-9(8)*, Scholastic Paperbacks) Scholastic, Inc.

Muir, Leslie. C. R. Mudgeon. Hector, Julian, illus. 2012. (ENG.). 32p. (J). (gr. -1-3). 15.99 *(978-1-4169-7906-7(9)*, Atheneum Bks. for Young Readers) Simon & Schuster Children's Publishing.

Nosy Crow Staff. Snuggly Puppy Looks for the Perfect Hug: A Tiny Tab Book. Ho, Jannie, illus. 2016. (Tiny Tab Ser.). (ENG.). 8p. (J). (— 1). bds. 7.99 *(978-0-7636-8937-7(8)*, Nosy Crow) Candlewick Pr.

Parker, Amy. How Big Is Love? 2016. (Faith, Hope, Love Ser.). (ENG.). 24p. (J). (gr. -1-k). bds. 9.99 *(978-1-4336-9042-6(X)*, B&H Kids) B&H Publishing Group.

Parker, Emma & Renaud, Marguerite. Hedgehogs. 2010. (Illus.). 16p. pap. *(978-1-877561-80-1(0))* First Edition Ltd.

Paul, Ruth. Hedgehog's Magic Tricks. Paul, Ruth, illus. 2013. (ENG., Illus.). 32p. (J). (gr. -1-2). 12.99 *(978-0-7636-6385-8(9))* Candlewick Pr.

Pfister, Marcus. El Erizo Feliz. Lasconi, Diego, tr. from GER. Pfister, Marcus, illus. 2003.Tr. of Happy Hedgehog. (SPA., Illus.). 32p. (J). (gr. k-3). 15.95 *(978-0-7358-1818-7(5))* North-South Bks., Inc.

Poh, Jennie. Herbie's Big Adventure. Poh, Jennie, illus. 2016. (Fiction Picture Bks.). (ENG., Illus.). 40p. (gr. 1-2). lib. bdg. 23.32 *(978-1-5158-0234-1(5)*, Fiction Picture Bks.) Picture Window Bks.

Puzzuoli, Jon. Wishing to Whistle. 2009. 32p. pap. 17.50 *(978-0-557-10420-8(3))* Lulu Pr., Inc.

Shaskan, Trisha Speed. The Case of the Missing Mola Lisa! Shaskan, Stephen, illus. 2017. (Q & Ray Ser.: 1). (ENG.). 48p. (gr. 2-5). 26.65 *(978-1-5124-1147-8(7)*, Graphic Universe™) Lerner Publishing Group.

Small, Lily. Daisy the Deer. 2017. (Fairy Animals of Misty Wood Ser.). (ENG., Illus.). 144p. (J). pap. 5.99 *(978-1-62779-738-2(6)*, 9781627797382, Holt, Henry & Co. Bks. For Young Readers) Holt, Henry & Co.

—Hailey the Hedgehog. 2016. (Fairy Animals of Misty Wood Ser.). (ENG., Illus.). 144p. (J). pap. 5.99 *(978-1-62779-735-1(1)*, 9781627797351, Holt, Henry & Co. Bks. For Young Readers) Holt, Henry & Co.

—Mia the Mouse, Poppy the Pony, & Hailey the Hedgehog Bindup. Small, Lily, illus. 2016. (Fairy Animals of Misty Wood Ser.). (ENG., Illus.). 416p. (J). pap. 10.99 *(978-1-250-11399-3(7)*, 9781250113993, Holt, Henry & Co. Bks. For Young Readers) Holt, Henry & Co.

Small, Lily. Poppy the Pony & Hailey the Hedgehog Bindup. 2017. (Fairy Animals of Misty Wood Ser.). (ENG., Illus.). 288p. (J). 8.99 ***(978-1-250-13079-2(4)***, 9781250130792, Holt, Henry & Co. Bks. For Young Readers) Holt, Henry & Co.

Stewart, Paul. Un Regalo de Cumpleanos. Riddell, Chris, illus. (SPA.). 30p. (J). (gr. k-2). *(978-84-348-6840-3(7)*, SM30935) SM Ediciones ESP. Dist: Lectorum Pubns., Inc.

Voyer, Dorothy May. Henry Hedgehog's Holiday. 2012. (ENG.). (J). pap. *(978-1-4675-2084-3(5))* Independent Pub.

Weddle, Steve & Weddle, Nikki. Can Hedgehogs Jump? 2011. (Illus.). 28p. pap. 12.52 *(978-1-4520-5751-4(6))* AuthorHouse.

Whitmore, Patrick Charles. Cookie & the Golden Quill. 2012. 202p. pap. *(978-1-78176-738-2(6))* FeedARead.com.

Wilhelm, Hans. Hello, Sun! Wilhelm, Hans, illus. 2005. (Illus.). 32p. (gr. k-2). 15.25 *(978-1-57505-348-6(9))* Lerner Publishing Group.

Williams, Emma Louise. Harry the Hedgehog Loses His Favorite Sock. 2012. 20p. pap. 7.99 *(978-1-939076-00-7(5))* Wiggies, Piggy.

Williams, Jacklyn. Feliz Dia de Gracias, Gus!, 1 vol. Abello, Patricia, tr. from ENG. Cushman, Doug, illus. 2006. (Read-It! Readers en Español: Gus el Erizo Ser.). (SPA.). 32p. (gr. k-3). lib. bdg. 19.99 *(978-1-4048-2690-8(4)*, Easy Readers) Picture Window Bks.

Wilson, Steve. Hedgehugs. Tapper, Lucy, illus. 2015. (Hedgehugs Ser.). (ENG.). 32p. (J). (gr. -1-3). 16.99 *(978-1-62779-404-6(2)*, 9781627794046, Holt, Henry & Co. Bks. For Young Readers) Holt, Henry & Co.

—Hedgehugs & the Hattiepillar. Tapper, Lucy, illus. 2016. (Hedgehugs Ser.). (ENG.). 32p. (J). 16.99 *(978-1-62779-414-5(X)*, 9781627794145, Holt, Henry & Co. Bks. For Young Readers) Holt, Henry & Co.

Wilson, Steve. Hedgehugs: Autumn Hide-And-Squeak. Tapper, Lucy, illus. 2017. (Hedgehugs Ser.). (ENG.). 32p. (J). 16.99 ***(978-1-250-11248-4(6)***, 9781250112484, Holt, Henry & Co. Bks. For Young Readers) Holt, Henry & Co.

Wingate, Frank. Herman the Hedgehog: Bedtime Tales from the Woodland. 2009. (Illus.). 84p. pap. 10.49 *(978-1-4389-9134-4(7))* AuthorHouse.

Yeh, Kat. The Friend Ship. Groenink, Chuck, illus. 2016. (ENG.). 32p. (J). (gr. -1-k). 16.99 *(978-1-4847-0726-5(5))* Disney Pr.

HELICOPTERS

Abramovitz, Melissa. Military Helicopters. 2012. (Military Machines Ser.). (ENG.). 24p. (gr. k-1). pap. 41.70 *(978-1-4296-8314-2(7))*; lib. bdg. 26.65 *(978-1-4296-7574-1(8))* Capstone Press of Coughlan Cos. (Pebble Plus).

Aloian, Molly. Les Hélicoptères. 2010. (FRE.). 32p. (J). pap. *(978-2-89579-523-0(1))* Crabtree Publishing Co.

—Hovering Helicopters. 2010. (Vehicles on the Move Ser.). (ENG.). 32p. (J). (gr. k-3). pap. *(978-0-7787-3062-0(X))*; lib. bdg. *(978-0-7787-3048-4(4))* Crabtree Publishing Co.

Alvarez, Carlos. AH-1W Super Cobras. 2010. (Military Machines Ser.). (ENG., Illus.). 24p. (J). (gr. 3-7). lib. bdg. 25.95 *(978-1-60014-494-3(2)*, Torque Bks.) Bellwether Media.

—AH-6 Little Birds. 2011. (Military Machines Ser.). (ENG., Illus.). 24p. (J). (gr. 3-7). lib. bdg. 25.95 *(978-1-60014-578-0(7)*, Torque Bks.) Bellwether Media.

—CH-46 Sea Knights. 2011. (Military Machines Ser.). (ENG., Illus.). 24p. (J). (gr. 3-7). lib. bdg. 25.95 *(978-1-60014-579-7(5)*, Torque Bks.) Bellwether Media.

—MH-53J Pave Lows. 2009. (Military Machines Ser.). (ENG., Illus.). 24p. (J). (gr. 3-7). lib. bdg. 25.95 *(978-1-60014-281-9(8))* Bellwether Media.

—UH-60 Black Hawks. 2011. (Military Machines Ser.). (ENG., Illus.). 24p. (J). (gr. 3-7). lib. bdg. 25.95 *(978-1-60014-581-0(7)*, Torque Bks.) Bellwether Media.

Apache Helicopter. 2004. (Press-Out & Build Ser.). (Illus.). 24p. (J). per. *(978-1-84229-723-0(6))* Top That! Publishing PLC.

Arnold, Quinn M. Mil Mi-26. 2016. (Illus.). 24p. (J). *(978-1-60818-714-0(4)*, Creative Education) Creative Co., The.

Bender, Lionel. Airplanes & Helicopters. 2006. (J). *(978-1-59389-261-6(6))* Chrysalis Education.

Bledsoe, Karen & Bledsoe, Glen. Helicopters: High-Flying Heroes. 2006. (Mighty Military Machines Ser.). (Illus.). 48p. (J). (gr. 4-10). lib. bdg. 25.27 *(978-0-7660-2663-6(9))* Enslow Pubs., Inc.

Bodden, Valerie. Built for Battle: Helicopters. 2012. (Built for Battle Ser.). (ENG., Illus.). 24p. (J). (gr. 1-3). pap. 7.99 *(978-0-89812-702-7(5)*, Creative Paperbacks) Creative Co., The.

—Helicopters. (J). 2012. (Illus.). 23p. 25.65 *(978-1-60818-127-8(8)*, Creative Education) 2011. (ENG.). 24p. (gr. 1-3). pap. 7.99 *(978-0-89812-576-4(6)*, Creative Paperbacks) 2011. 24p. (gr. k-2). 16.95 *(978-1-60818-005-9(0))* Creative Co., The.

Bone, Emily. Helicopters. 2011. (Discovery Adventures Ser.). 80p. (J). pap. 8.99 *(978-0-7945-2977-2(1)*, Usborne) EDC Publishing.

Boothroyd, Jennifer. How Do Helicopters Work? 2013. (Lightning Bolt Books (tm) — How Flight Works). (ENG., Illus.). 32p. (gr. k-2). pap. 7.95 *(978-1-4677-0784-8(8))*; lib. bdg. 26.60 *(978-0-7613-8966-8(0)*, Lerner Pubns.) Lerner Publishing Group.

Carr, Aaron. Helicopters. 2014. (J). *(978-1-4896-3228-9(X))* Weigl Pubs., Inc.

Colson, Rob Scott. Helicopters. 2013. (Ultimate Machines Ser.). (ENG., Illus.). 24p. (J). (gr. 3-6). pap. 8.25 *(978-1-4777-0115-7(X))*; lib. bdg. 22.60 *(978-1-4777-0065-5(X))* Rosen Publishing Group, Inc., The. (PowerKids Pr.).

Cooke, Tim. Helicopters. 2012. (Ultimate Military Machines Ser.). (Illus.). 32p. (gr. 4-7). lib. bdg. 31.35 *(978-1-59920-821-3(0))* Black Rabbit Bks.

Dartford, Mark. Helicopters. 2003. (Military Hardware in Action Ser.). (ENG., Illus.). 48p. (gr. 5-9). lib. bdg. 25.26 *(978-0-8225-4707-5(4))* Lerner Publishing Group.

David, Jack. Apache Helicopters. 2007. (Military Machines Ser.). (ENG., Illus.). 24p. (J). (gr. 3-7). lib. bdg. 25.95 *(978-1-60014-102-7(1))* Bellwether Media.

—HH-60 Pave Hawk Helicopters. 2008. (Torque Ser.). 24p. (J). (gr. 3-7). 20.00 *(978-0-531-21052-9(9)*, Children's Pr.) Scholastic Library Publishing.

—HH-60 Pavehawk Helicopters. 2008. (Military Machines Ser.). (ENG., Illus.). 24p. (YA). (gr. 3-7). lib. bdg. 25.95 *(978-1-60014-223-9(0))* Bellwether Media.

David West. Helicopter. 2006. (Illus.). 32p. (J). pap. *(978-1-4109-2565-7(X))* Steck-Vaughn.

Eason, Sarah. How Does a Helicopter Work? 2010. (How Does It Work? Ser.). 32p. (J). (gr. 3-6). lib. bdg. 26.00 *(978-1-4339-3465-0(5))*; (Illus.). pap. 10.50 *(978-1-4339-3466-7(3))* Stevens, Gareth Publishing LLLP. (Gareth Stevens Learning Library).

Eden, Paul E. Helicopters. 2006. (Aircraft of the World Ser.). (Illus.). 32p. (gr. 2-6). lib. bdg. 26.00 *(978-0-8368-6904-0(4)*, Gareth Stevens Learning Library) Stevens, Gareth Publishing LLLP.

Ellis, Catherine. Helicopters. (Mega Military Machines Ser.). 24p. 2009. (gr. 1-1). 42.50 *(978-1-61514-635-2(0)*, PowerKids Pr.) 2007. (Illus.). (J). (gr. 3-7). lib. bdg. 22.60 *(978-1-4042-3666-0(X))* Rosen Publishing Group, Inc., The.

—Helicopters/Helicopteros. Brusca, Maria Cristina, tr. 2007. (Mega Military Machines / Megamaquinas Militares Ser.). (ENG & SPA., Illus.). 24p. (J). lib. bdg. 22.60 *(978-1-4042-7621-5(1)*, PowerKids Pr.) Rosen Publishing Group, Inc., The.

—Helicopters/Helicópteros. 2009. (Mega Military Machines/Megamaquinas militares Ser.). (ENG & SPA.). 24p. (gr. 1-1). 42.50 *(978-1-61514-640-6(7)*, Editorial Buenas Letras) Rosen Publishing Group, Inc., The.

Enz, Tammy. Batplanes & Batcopters: The Engineering Behind Batman's Wings, 1 vol. 2014. (Batman Science Ser.). (ENG.). 32p. (gr. 3-4). 27.32 *(978-1-4765-3941-6(3)*, DC Super Heroes) Stone Arch Bks.

Faust, Daniel R. Civilian Drones, 01 vols., 1. 2016. (Drones: Eyes in the Skies Ser.). (ENG., Illus.). 32p. (J). pap. 11.75 *(978-1-5081-4486-1(9)*, PowerKids Pr.) Rosen Publishing Group, Inc., The.

—Entertainment Drones, 01 vols., 1. 2016. (Drones: Eyes in the Skies Ser.). (ENG.). 32p. (J). pap. 11.75 *(978-1-5081-4493-9(1)*, PowerKids Pr.) Rosen Publishing Group, Inc., The.

Finn, Denny Von. AH-1W Super Cobras. 2012. (Military Vehicles Ser.). (ENG., Illus.). 24p. (J). (gr. 3-7). lib. bdg. 25.95 *(978-1-60014-815-6(8)*, Epic Bks.) Bellwether Media.

—Apache Helicopters. 2012. (Military Vehicles Ser.). (ENG., Illus.). 24p. (J). (gr. 3-7). lib. bdg. 25.95 *(978-1-60014-816-3(6)*, Epic Bks.) Bellwether Media.

—MH-53E Sea Dragons. 2014. (Military Vehicles Ser.). (ENG., Illus.). 24p. (J). (gr. 3-7). lib. bdg. 25.95 *(978-1-62617-081-0(9)*, Epic Bks.) Bellwether Media.

—UH-60 Black Hawks. 2013. (Military Vehicles Ser.). (ENG., Illus.). 24p. (J). (gr. 3-7). lib. bdg. 25.95 *(978-1-60014-888-0(3)*, Epic Bks.) Bellwether Media.

Floherty, John Joseph & McGrady, Mike. Whirling Wings: The Story of the Helicopter. 2011. 170p. 41.95 *(978-1-258-05598-1(8))* Literary Licensing, LLC.

Fog City Press Staff, contrib. by. Helicopters. 2009. (Illus.). (J). *(978-1-74089-883-6(4))* Fog City Pr.

Fortuna, Lois. Rescue Helicopters. 2016. (To the Rescue! Ser.). 24p. (J). (gr. k-k). pap. 8.15 *(978-1-4824-4663-0(4))* Stevens, Gareth Publishing LLLP.

Gifford, Clive. Planes & Helicopters. 2012. (ENG.). 24p. (J). *(978-0-7787-7476-1(7))*; (Illus.). pap. *(978-0-7787-7481-5(3))* Crabtree Publishing Co.

Glover, David & Glover, Penny. Planes in Action. 2008. (On the Go Ser.). (Illus.). 24p. (J). (gr. 3-7). lib. bdg. 22.60 *(978-1-4042-4308-8(9)*, PowerKids Pr.) Rosen Publishing Group, Inc., The.

Goldberg, Jan. The C-130 Hercules. 2005. (U. S. Warplanes Ser.). (Illus.). 48p. (YA). (gr. 5-8). lib. bdg. 29.25 *(978-0-8239-3873-5(5))* Rosen Publishing Group, Inc., The.

Goodman, Susan E. Choppers! Doolittle, Michael, photos by. 2004. (Step into Reading Ser.: Vol. 4). (ENG., Illus.). 48p. (J). (gr. 2-4). pap. 3.99 *(978-0-375-82517-0(7)*, Random Hse. Bks. for Young Readers) Random Hse. Children's Bks.

Hamilton, John. AH-64D Apache Longbow. 2012. 32p. 27.07 *(978-1-61783-266-6(9)*, Abdo & Daughters) ABDO Publishing Co.

Hansen, Ole Steen. Helicopters. 2003. (Story of Flight Ser.). (ENG., Illus.). 32p. (J). (gr. 4). pap. *(978-0-7787-1224-4(9))* Crabtree Publishing Co.

Hanson, Anders. Let's Go by Helicopter, 1 vol. 2008. (Let's Go Ser.). (ENG., Illus.). 24p. (J). (gr. k-3). lib. bdg. 24.21 *(978-1-59928-898-7(2)*, SandCastle) ABDO Publishing Co.

Harrison, Paul. Supercopters. 2015. 32p. (gr. 1-5). lib. bdg. 31.35 *(978-1-78404-077-2(0))* Arcturus Publishing GBR. Dist: Black Rabbit Bks.

Helicopters. 2004. (Mega MacHines Ser.). (Illus.). 16p. (J). *(978-2-7643-0201-9(0))* Phidal Publishing, Inc./Editions Phidal, Inc.

Jackson, Kay. Military Helicopters in Action. 2009. (Amazing Military Vehicles Ser.). 24p. (gr. 3-5). (J). pap. 8.25 *(978-1-4358-3158-2(6)*, PowerKids Pr.); (YA). lib. bdg. 22.60 *(978-1-4358-2748-6(1))* Rosen Publishing Group, Inc., The.

Kiland, Taylor Baldwin & Bledsoe, Glen. Military Helicopters: Heroes of the Sky. 2015. (Military Engineering in Action Ser.). (ENG., Illus.). 48p. (J). (gr. 6-6). 27.93 *(978-0-7660-6912-1(5))* Enslow Pubs., Inc.

Kiland, Taylor Baldwin, et al. Military Helicopters: Heroes of the Sky. 2015. (Military Engineering in Action Ser.). (ENG., Illus.). 48p. (J). (gr. 6-6). pap. 11.70 *(978-0-7660-7063-9(8))* Enslow Pubs., Inc.

Langley, Andrew. Helicopters. 2010. (Machines on the Move Ser.). 32p. (J). 28.50 *(978-1-60753-059-6(7))* Amicus Publishing.

—Helicopters. 2012. (Illus.). 32p. (gr. 1-3). pap. 8.95 *(978-1-926722-69-6(8))* Saunders Bk. Co. CAN. Dist: RiverStream Publishing.

Lindeen, Mary. Helicopters. 2007. (Mighty Machines Ser.). (ENG., Illus.). 24p. (J). (gr. k-3). lib. bdg. 25.95 *(978-1-60014-119-5(6))* Bellwether Media.

Loveless, Antony. Apache Helicoper Pilot. 2009. (World's Most Dangerous Jobs Ser.). (ENG., Illus.). 32p. (J). (gr. 3-6). pap. *(978-0-7787-5112-0(0))* Crabtree Publishing Co.

—Apache Helicoper Pilots. 2009. (World's Most Dangerous Jobs Ser.). (ENG., Illus.). 32p. (J). (gr. 3-6). lib. bdg. *(978-0-7787-5098-7(1))* Crabtree Publishing Co.

Loveless, Antony & Oxlade, Chris. Support Helicopter Pilots. 2012. (ENG.). 32p. (J). *(978-0-7787-5102-1(3))*; (The World's Most Dangerous Jobs Ser.: No. 9). pap. *(978-0-7787-5116-8(3))* Crabtree Publishing Co.

Mara, Wil. Helicopter Crew Chief. 2012. (21st Century Skills Library: Cool Military Careers Ser.). (ENG.). 32p. (gr. 4-8). 28.50 *(978-1-61080-449-3(X)*, 202059); pap. 14.21 *(978-1-61080-623-7(9)*, 202233) Cherry Lake Publishing.

Mullins, Matt. How Does It Fly? Helicopter. 2011. (Community Connections: How Does It Fly? Ser.). (ENG.). 24p. (gr. 2-5). lib. bdg. 25.64 *(978-1-61080-065-5(6)*, 201056) Cherry Lake Publishing.

Olien, Rebecca & Olien, Becky. Rescue Helicopters in Action, 1 vol. 2011. (Transportation Zone Ser.). (ENG.). 24p. (gr. 1-2). lib. bdg. 25.32 *(978-1-4296-6850-7(4)*, First Facts) Capstone Press of Coughlan Cos.

Peppas, Lynn. Military Helicopters: Flying into Battle. 2011. (ENG.). 32p. (J). pap. *(978-0-7787-2754-5(8))* Crabtree Publishing Co.

Pettiford, Rebecca. Helicopters. 2017. (Mighty Machines in Action Ser.). (ENG., Illus.). 24p. (J). (gr. k-3). lib. bdg. 25.95 ***(978-1-62617-632-4(9)***, Blastoff! Readers) Bellwether Media.

Randolph, Joanne. Emergency Helicopters. 2008. (To the Rescue! Ser.). (Illus.). 24p. (J). (gr. 3-7). lib. bdg. 22.60 *(978-1-4042-4151-0(5)*, PowerKids Pr.) Rosen Publishing Group, Inc., The.

—Emergency Helicopters/Helicopteros de Emergencia. Alaman, Eduardo, tr. from ENG. 2008. (To the Rescue! / ¡Al Rescate! Ser.). (Illus.). 24p. (J). (gr. -1-3). lib. bdg. 22.60 *(978-1-4042-7672-7(6)*, Editorial Buenas Letras) Rosen Publishing Group, Inc., The.

Riggs, Kate. Helicopters. 2015. (Illus.). 80p. (J). *(978-1-60818-582-5(6)*, Creative Education) Creative Co., The.

—Helicopters: Seedlings. 2016. (Seedlings Ser.). (ENG.). 24p. (J). (gr. k-2). pap. 7.99 *(978-1-62832-187-6(3)*, Creative Paperbacks) Creative Co., The.

Ruck, Colleen. Helicopters. 2011. (My Favorite Machines Ser.). 24p. (gr. 2-5). 28.50 *(978-1-59920-675-2(7))* Black Rabbit Bks.

Schuh, Mari. Helicopters. 2017. (Transportation Ser.). (ENG.). 24p. (gr. k-1). lib. bdg. 21.99 ***(978-1-5157-7304-7(3)***, Pebble Bks.) Capstone Press of Coughlan Cos.

Tieck, Sarah. Helicopters, 1 vol. 2011. (Amazing Vehicles Set 2 Ser.). (ENG., Illus.). 32p. (J). (gr. 2-5). 28.50 *(978-1-61714-697-8(8))* ABDO Publishing Co.

West, David. Helicopters. 2015. (Mechanic Mike's Machines (continuation) Ser.). (Illus.). 24p. (J). (gr. k-3). 27.10 *(978-1-62588-063-5(4))* Black Rabbit Bks.

Wyckoff, Edwin Brit. Helicopter Man: Igor Sikorsky & His Amazing Invention. 2010. (Genius at Work! Great Inventor Biographies Ser.). (Illus.). 32p. (J). 23.94 *(978-0-7660-3445-7(3))* Enslow Pubs., Inc.

Zuehlke, Jeffrey. Helicopters. (Pull Ahead Bks.). (Illus.). 32p. (gr. k-2). 2005. (J). lib. bdg. 22.60 *(978-0-8225-1540-1(7))* 2004. (ENG., pap. 7.95 *(978-0-8225-2382-6(5))* Lerner Publishing Group.

—Helicopters on the Move. 2011. (Lightning Bolt Books Vroom-Vroom Ser.). 32p. pap. 45.32 *(978-0-7613-7618-7(6))*; (ENG.). pap. 7.95 *(978-0-7613-7113-7(3))*; (ENG.). lib. bdg. 26.60 *(978-0-7613-6027-8(1))* Lerner Publishing Group.

HELICOPTERS—FICTION

Coulman, Valerie. When Pigs Fly. l.t. ed. 2012. 63p. (J). pap. *(978-1-4596-3455-8(1))* ReadHowYouWant.com, Ltd.

Faust, Jon. Helicopter Harry & the Copter Kids. 2016. (ENG., Illus.). (J). pap. 9.95 ***(978-0-692-78184-5(6))*** Mother Lode Pr. LLC.

Glass, Andrew. The Wondrous Whirligig: The Wright Brothers¿ First Flying Machine. Glass, Andrew, illus. 2007. (Illus.). 30p. (J). reprint ed. 17.00 *(978-1-4223-6765-0(7))* DIANE Publishing Co.

Hamilton, Kersten & Wells, Rosemary. Yellow Copter. Petrone, Valeria, illus. 2015. (ENG.). 32p. (J). (-k). bds. 16.99 *(978-0-451-46991-5(7)*, Viking Books for Young Readers) Penguin Young Readers Group.

Ketchell, Maureen. The Five & a Half Mystery. 2011. 110p. pap. *(978-1-908105-53-0(4))* Grosvenor Hse. Publishing Ltd.

Kimmel, Elizabeth Cody. My Penguin Osbert in Love. Lewis, H. B., illus. 2010. (ENG.). 48p. (J). (gr. -1-3). 7.99 *(978-0-7636-5001-8(3))* Candlewick Pr.

Kimmel, Elizabeth Cody & Buck, Lewis. My Penguin Osbert in Love, Set. Lewis, H. B., illus. 2008. (ENG.). 48p. (J). (gr. -1-3). 16.99 *(978-0-7636-3032-4(2))* Candlewick Pr.

Mitton, Tony. High-Flying Helicopters. Parker, Ant, illus. 2016. (Amazing Machines Ser.). (ENG.). 24p. 9.99 *(978-0-7534-7290-3(2)*, 9780753472903, Kingfisher) Roaring Brook Pr.

Paul, John. Copters. Young, Bill, illus. 2012. 36p. 24.95 *(978-1-4626-9458-7(6))* America Star Bks.

Rogers, Christopher M., illus. Homer the Helicopter Grand Canyon Adventures. 2007. 72p. (J). 18.95 *(978-0-9786352-3-7(X))* Buscher, Julie W.

Sayres, Brianna Caplan. Where Do Jet Planes Sleep at Night? Slade, Christian, illus. 2017. (ENG.). 32p. (J). (gr. -1-2). 16.99 *(978-0-399-55448-3(3))*; lib. bdg. 19.99 ***(978-0-399-55449-0(1))*** Random Hse. Children's Bks. (Random Hse. Bks. for Young Readers).

Slack, Michael. Elecopter. Slack, Michael, illus. 2013. (ENG., Illus.). 32p. (J). (gr. -1 — 1). 15.99 *(978-0-8050-9304-9(4)*, 9780805093049, Holt, Henry & Co. Bks. For Young Readers) Holt, Henry & Co.

Stiefvater, Maggie. Forever. 2014. (Shiver Ser.: 3). (ENG.). 416p. (J). (gr. 9). pap. 9.99 *(978-0-545-68280-0(0))* Scholastic, Inc.

—Forever. 2014. (Wolves of Mercy Falls Ser.: 3). lib. bdg. 20.85 *(978-0-606-36649-6(0))* Turtleback Bks.

Timothy Nixon. Henry to the Rescue. 2009. (Illus.). 24p. pap. 12.99 *(978-1-4389-4960-4(X))* AuthorHouse.

Top That Publishing Staff, ed. Rescue Helicopter. Dronsfield, Paul, illus. 2007. (Story Book Ser.). (ENG.). 33p. (J). (gr. -1). bds. *(978-1-84666-179-2(X)*, Tide Mill Pr.) Top That! Publishing PLC.

Turner, Jill & Cassettari, Noeline. Happy Helicopters. 2003. (Button Bks.). (Illus.). (J). 12.95 *(978-1-74047-302-6(7))* Book Co. Publishing Pty, Ltd., The AUS. Dist: Penton Overseas, Inc.

Watt, Fiona. Busy Helicopter Book. 2012. (Pull-Back Bks). 10p. (J). ring bd. 24.99 *(978-0-7945-3203-1(9)*, Usborne) EDC Publishing.

HELPFULNESS

Amos, Janine & Spenceley, Annabel. Let's Help Out! 2009. (Best Behavior Ser.). (Illus.). 32p. (J). (gr. -1-2). 22.60 *(978-1-60754-490-6(3))*; pap. 10.55 *(978-1-60754-491-3(1))* Windmill Bks.

Ancona, George. Mis Quehaceres - My Chores. 2005. (Somos Latinos (We Are Latinos) Ser.). (ENG & SPA., Illus.). 32p. (J). (gr. 1-3). lib. bdg. 21.00 *(978-0-516-25291-9(7)*, Children's Pr.) Scholastic Library Publishing.

Appleby, Alex. Dinosaurs Help Out. 2013. (Dinosaur School Ser.). 24p. (J). (gr. k-1). pap. 8.15 *(978-1-4339-9054-0(7))*;

pap. 48.90 (978-1-4339-9055-7(5)); (ENG., Illus.). lib. bdg. 22.60 (978-1-4339-9053-3(9)) Stevens, Gareth Publishing LLLP.

Cavell-Clarke, Steffi. Helping Others. 2017. 24p. (J). (978-0-7787-3703-2(9)) Crabtree Publishing Co.

Clinton, Chelsea. It's Your World: Get Informed, Get Inspired & Get Going! 2015. (ENG., Illus.). 416p. (J). (gr. 5). 18.99 (978-0-399-17612-8(8), Philomel Bks.) Penguin Young Readers Group.

Coan, Sharon. Good for Me: Love. 2015. (TIME for KIDS(r) Nonfiction Readers Ser.). (ENG., Illus.). 12p. (gr. k-k). 4.99 (978-1-4938-2153-2(9)) Teacher Created Materials, Inc.

Dalton, Kippy. Who Can You Help? 2016. (Spring Forward Ser.). (J). (gr. 1). (978-1-4900-3715-8(2)) Benchmark Education Co.

Endres, Hollie J. Helping at School, 6 vols., Set. 2004. (Letter Bks.). (ENG.). 8p. (gr. k-1). pap. 29.70 (978-0-7368-4109-2(1), Letter Bks.) Capstone Press of Coughlan Cos.

—The Letter Mm Set: People Who Help Us, 6 vols. 2004. (Letter Bks.). (ENG.). 8p. (gr. k-1). pap. 29.70 (978-0-7368-4112-2(1), Letter Bks.) Capstone Press of Coughlan Cos.

Fronczak, Blaine. Haley Helps at School. 2013. (Core Math Skills: Numbers & Operations in Base 10 Ser.). 24p. (J). (gr. 1-2). 22.60 (978-1-4777-2225-1(4)); (ENG.). pap. 8.25 (978-1-4777-2097-4(9)) Rosen Publishing Group, Inc., The. (Rosen Classroom).

—Haley Helps at School: Use Place Value & Properties of Operations to Add. 2013. (Rosen Math Readers Ser.). (ENG.). 24p. (J). (gr. 1-2). pap. 49.50 (978-1-4777-2098-1(7), Rosen Classroom) Rosen Publishing Group, Inc., The.

Geis, Patricia. Let's Help! Folch, Sergio, illus. 2009. (Good Habits with Coco & Tula Ser.). 16p. (J). (gr. -1-k). bds. 11.40 (978-1-60754-406-7(7)) Windmill Bks.

Giles, Sophie. The Children's Book of Healthy Habits. Davies, Kate, illus. 2014. (ENG.). 40p. (J). pap. 10.00 (978-1-84135-972-4(6)) Award Pubns. Ltd. GBR. Dist: Parkwest Pubns., Inc.

Glassman, Bruce. Caring. 2009. (Character Counts! Ser.). 48p. (gr. 4-5). 53.00 (978-1-61511-832-8(2)) Rosen Publishing Group, Inc., The.

Goodman, Errol. I Am Helpful. 2011. (Kids of Character Ser.). (Illus.). 24p. (J). (gr. 1-3). pap. 8.15 (978-1-4339-4857-2(5)); lib. bdg. 22.60 (978-1-4339-4856-5(7)) Stevens, Gareth Publishing LLLP.

—I Am Helpful / Soy Acomedida. 2011. (Kids of Character / Chicos con carácter Ser.). (ENG & SPA., Illus.). 24p. (J). (gr. -1-2). 22.60 (978-1-4339-4860-2(5)) Stevens, Gareth Publishing LLLP.

Graham, Cenesha. I Want to Help. 2011. 24p. pap. 14.56 (978-1-4634-1803-8(5)) AuthorHouse.

Gregoire, Maryellen. Help. 2012. (Wonder Readers Emergent Level Ser.). (ENG.). 16p. (gr. -1-1). pap. 35.94 (978-1-4296-9200-7(6), Wonder Readers) Capstone Press of Coughlan Cos.

—Yo Puedo Ayudar (I Can Help) 2012. (Wonder Readers Spanish Emergent Ser.). (SPA.). 16p. (gr. -1-1). pap. 35.94 (978-1-62065-575-7(6)) Capstone Press of Coughlan Cos.

Halloran, Corey. Our Neighborhood Food Drive. 2013. (Core Math Skills: Numbers & Operations in Base 10 Ser.). 24p. (J). (gr. 1-2). 22.60 (978-1-4777-2221-3(1), Rosen Classroom) Rosen Publishing Group, Inc., The.

—Our Neighborhood Food Drive: Extend the Counting Sequence. 2013. (Rosen Math Readers Ser.). (ENG.). 24p. (J). (gr. 1-2). pap. 49.50 (978-1-4777-2068-4(5)); (Illus.). pap. 8.25 (978-1-4777-2067-7(7)) Rosen Publishing Group, Inc., The. (Rosen Classroom).

Harrison, Paul. Let's Work Together. 2011. (Window on the World Ser.). (Illus.). 32p. (978-1-84089-659-6(0)) Zero to Ten, Ltd.

How to Help: A Guide to Giving Back, 8 vols., Set. Incl. Celebrities Giving Back: A Guide to Giving Back. Reusser, Kayleen. lib. bdg. 29.95 (978-1-58415-922-3(7)); Volunteering in School: A Guide to Giving Back. O'Neal, Claire. lib. bdg. 29.95 (978-1-58415-920-9(0)); Ways to Help after a Natural Disaster: A Guide to Giving Back. Saul, Laya. lib. bdg. 29.95 (978-1-58415-917-9(0)); Ways to Help Children with Disabilities: A Guide to Giving Back. Gibson, Karen Bush. lib. bdg. 29.95 (978-1-58415-916-2(2)); Ways to Help Chronically Ill Children: A Guide to Giving Back. Gagne, Tammy. lib. bdg. 29.95 (978-1-58415-919-3(7)); Ways to Help Disadvantaged Youth: A Guide to Giving Back. Saul, Laya. lib. bdg. 29.95 (978-1-58415-918-6(9)); Ways to Help in Your Community: A Guide to Giving Back. O'Neal, Claire. lib. bdg. 29.95 (978-1-58415-921-6(9)); Ways to Help the Elderly: A Guide to Giving Back. Orr, Tamra. lib. bdg. 29.95 (978-1-58415-915-5(4)); (Illus.). 48p. (J). (gr. 4-8). 2010. 2010. Set lib. bdg. 239.60 (978-1-58415-923-0(5)) Mitchell Lane Pubs., Inc.

Jones, Kip. The Power of Bystanders: Willie Bohanon & Friends Learn to Handle Bullying Like a Boss. Isely, Chad, illus. 2015. (ENG.). 32p. (J). pap. 10.95 (978-1-934490-79-2(2)) Boys Town Pr.

Lennon, Liz. I Can Help. 2012. (Little Stars: My Behavior Ser.). (ENG., Illus.). 24p. (J). (gr. -1-3). lib. bdg. 25.65 (978-1-59771-410-5(0)) Sea-To-Sea Pubns.

—My Behaviour - I Can Help. 2017. (Little Stars,Sea-To-Sea Ser.). (ENG., Illus.). 24p. (J). (gr. -1-k). pap. 6.99 (978-1-4451-4764-2(5), Franklin Watts) Hachette Children's Group GBR. Dist: Hachette Bk. Group.

Lindeen, Mary. Helping Others. 2015. (BeginningtoRead Ser.). (ENG., Illus.). 32p. (J). (gr. k-2). pap. 11.94 (978-1-60357-760-1(2)) Norwood Hse. Pr.

—Lend a Hand, 1 vol. 2011. (Wonder Readers Fluent Level Ser.). (ENG.). (gr. -1-2). 32p. pap. 5.99 (978-1-4296-7948-0(4)); 16p. pap. 35.94 (978-1-4296-8119-3(5)) Capstone Press of Coughlan Cos. (Wonder Readers).

Lindeen, Mary & Eunjoo, Jang. Helping Others. 2015. (BeginningtoRead Ser.). (ENG., Illus.). 32p. (J). (gr. k-2). lib. bdg. 22.60 (978-1-59953-700-9(1)) Norwood Hse. Pr.

Mattern, Joanne. Do You Help Others? 2007. (Are You a Good Friend? Ser.). (Illus.). 24p. (gr. k-3). lib. bdg. 22.00 (978-0-8368-8273-5(3), Weekly Reader Leveled Readers) Stevens, Gareth Publishing LLLP.

Mayer, Cassie. Being Helpful, 1 vol. Beech, Mark, illus. 2007. (Citizenship Ser.). (ENG.). 24p. (gr. -1-3). pap. 6.29 (978-1-4034-9493-1(2), Acorn) Heinemann-Raintree.

—Ser Servicial, 1 vol. 2007. (Civismo Ser.). (SPA., Illus.). 24p. (gr. -1-1). pap. 6.29 (978-1-4329-0407-4(8), Bellota) Heinemann-Raintree.

Meiners, Cheri J. Reach Out & Give. Johnson, Meredith, illus. 2006. (Learning to Get Along(r) Ser.). (ENG.). 40p. (J). (gr. 3-7). pap. 10.95 (978-1-57542-204-6(2)) Free Spirit Publishing, Inc.

—Respect & Take Care of Things. Johnson, Meredith, illus. 2004. (Learning to Get Along(r) Ser.). (ENG.). 40p. (J). (gr. -1-3). pap. 10.95 (978-1-57542-160-5(7)) Free Spirit Publishing, Inc.

Michele, Tracey. People Who Help at Car Accidents. 2011. (Learn-Abouts Ser.). (Illus.). 16p. (J). pap. 7.95 (978-1-59920-608-0(0)) Black Rabbit Bks.

—When Can I Help in the Classroom? 2014. (Little Books of Answers: Level C Ser.). (Illus.). 16p. (gr. k-2). pap. 7.95 (978-1-927136-23-2(7)) Three Crows Media NZL. Dist: RiverStream Publishing.

Moerbe, Mary. How Can I Help? God's Calling for Kids - Mini Book. 2014. (ENG., Illus.). (J). pap. 2.49 (978-0-7586-4972-0(X)) Concordia Publishing Hse.

Nelid, Piper. My Family Likes to Help People, 01 vols., 1. 2016. (Rosen REAL Readers: Social Studies Nonfiction / Fiction: Family, Community, & the World Ser.). (ENG.). 8p. (J). pap. 5.46 (978-1-5081-1698-1(9), Rosen Classroom) Rosen Publishing Group, Inc., The.

Nelson, Maria. I Can Volunteer. 2013. (Kids of Character Ser.). 24p. (J). (gr. 1-3). pap. 48.90 (978-1-4339-9039-7(3)); (ENG., Illus.). pap. 8.15 (978-1-4339-9038-0(5)); (ENG., Illus.). lib. bdg. 22.60 (978-1-4339-9037-3(7)) Stevens, Gareth Publishing LLLP.

Nelson, Robin. How Can I Help? A Book about Caring. 2014. (Show Your Character Ser.). (ENG., Illus.). 32p. (gr. 1-3). lib. bdg. 26.60 (978-1-4677-1365-8(1), Lerner Pubns.) Lerner Publishing Group.

Novak, Robby & Montague, Brad. Kid President's Guide to Being Awesome. (J). (gr. 3-7). 2016. 256p. pap. 12.99 (978-0-06-243871-3(9)) 2015. (ENG., Illus.). 240p. 21.99 (978-0-06-235868-4(5)) HarperCollins Pubs.

Oberschneider, Michael. Ollie Outside: Screen-Free Fun. Wolek, Guy, illus. 2016. (ENG.). 32p. (J). (gr. -1-2). pap. 9.99 (978-1-63198-068-8(8)) Free Spirit Publishing, Inc.

Orr, Tamra. Ways to Help the Elderly: A Guide to Giving Back. 2010. (How to Help Ser.). (Illus.). 48p. (J). (gr. 4-8). lib. bdg. 29.95 (978-1-58415-915-5(4)) Mitchell Lane Pubs., Inc.

Paul, Miranda. Whose Hands Are These? A Community Helper Guessing Book. 2016. (ENG., Illus.). 32p. (J). (gr. -1-3). 19.99 (978-1-4677-5214-5(2)); 38.65 (978-1-4677-9726-9(X)) Lerner Publishing Group. (Millbrook Pr.).

—Whose Hands Are These? A Community Helper Guessing Book. Powell, Luciana Navarro, illus. 2016. (Millbrook Picture Bks). (ENG.). 32p. (gr. -1-3). 38.65 (978-1-5124-0738-9(0)) Lerner Publishing Group.

Pryor, Kimberley Jane. Cooperation. 2008. (Values Ser.). 32p. (J). (gr. 1-3). lib. bdg. 18.56 (978-0-7614-3124-4(1)) Marshall Cavendish Corp.

—Helpfulness. 2010. (Values 2 Ser.). 32p. (gr. 1). 18.56 (978-1-60870-144-5(1)) Marshall Cavendish GBR. Dist: Marshall Cavendish Corp.

Rau, Dana Meachen. Kids Top 10 Pet Fish. 2015. (American Humane Association Top 10 Pets for Kids Ser.). 48p. (J). (gr. 3-4). pap. 8.95 (978-0-7660-6641-0(X), Enslow Elementary) Enslow Pubs., Inc.

Schab, Lisa & Gardner, Richard. The Helping, Caring, & Sharing. Schader, Karen, ed. Barr, Steve, illus. 2003. (J). per., wbk. ed. 19.95 (978-1-58815-058-5(5), 67238) Childswork/Childsplay.

Scheunemann, Pam. Cool Jobs for Handy Helpers: Ways to Make Money Doing Home Services, 1 vol. 2011. (Cool Kid Jobs Ser.). (ENG.). 32p. (gr. 3-6). 28.50 (978-1-61613-195-1(0), Checkerboard Library) ABDO Publishing Co.

Shore, Hennie & Gardner, Richard. Helping, Caring, & Sharing Scriptbook. Schader, Karen, ed. 2003. (J). spiral bd. 24.95 (978-1-58815-059-2(3), 67239) Childswork/Childsplay.

Snow, Todd. You Are Helpful. Strong, Melodee, illus. 2008. (You Are Important Ser.). (ENG.). 24p. (J). (gr. -1-3). pap. 8.99 (978-1-934277-23-2(1)) Mam Green Publishing, Inc.

Steinkraus, Kyla. Let's Work Together. 2012. (ENG., Illus.). 24p. (gr. k-2). pap. 8.95 (978-1-61810-268-3(0)) Rourke Educational Media.

World Book, Inc. Staff, contrib. by. Heroes & Helpers: A Supplement to Childcraft: The How & Why Library. 2003. (Illus.). 208p. (J). pap. (978-0-7166-0606-2(2)) World Bk., Inc.

HELPFULNESS—FICTION

Abdo Publishing. Abby & the Book Bunch, 1 vol. 2013. (Abby & the Book Bunch Ser.: 6). (ENG.). 80p. (J). (gr. 2-5). lib. bdg. 162.42 (978-1-61641-911-0(3), Calico Chapter Bks) Magic Wagon.

Adams, Diane. Teacher's Little Helper, 1 vol. Hayashi, Nancy, illus. 2012. (ENG.). 32p. (J). 15.95 (978-1-56145-630-7(6)) Peachtree Pubs.

Adams, Tonya. Sam the Walrus: A Grumpy Day to Play. Johnson, Amber W., illus. 2008. 28p. pap. 24.95 (978-1-60672-861-1(X)) America Star Bks.

Akkari, Hélène. Saving Kanki the Antelope. 2010. 20p. 11.49 (978-1-4520-9156-3(0)) AuthorHouse.

Al-Ghani, K.I. The Red Beast: Controlling Anger in Children with Asperger's Syndrome. Al-Ghani, Haitham, illus. 2008. (K. I. Al-Ghani Children's Colour Story Bks.). (ENG.). 48p. (gr. 3-7). 21.95 (978-1-84310-943-3(3), 1138) Kingsley, Jessica Pubs. GBR. Dist: Macmillan Distribution Ltd.

Alarid, Carilyn & Markel, Marilyn. Hits With His Fist Gives a Helping Hand: Mimbres Children Learn about Caring. 2012. (Illus.). 113p. (J). pap. 16.95 (978-0-86534-508-9(2)) Sunstone Pr.

Albee, Sarah. Max Can Fix That. Schick, Joel, illus. 2006. (Step-By-Step Readers Ser.). (J). pap. (978-1-59939-055-0(8), Reader's Digest Young Families, Inc.) Studio Fun International.

Anderson, Peggy Perry. I Can Help! 2015. (Green Light Readers Level 1 Ser.). (ENG., Illus.). 32p. (J). (gr. 1-4). pap. 3.99 (978-0-544-52801-7(8), HMH Books For Young Readers) Houghton Mifflin Harcourt Publishing Co.

Andrews, Lindsey. I Walk for Water. Bennett, Jerry, illus. 2012. (ENG.). 43p. (J). 16.95 (978-0-615-49668-9(7)) Hilarity Waters Pr.

Anne, Heather. Purple People. 2008. 28p. per. 24.95 (978-1-4241-8458-3(4)) America Star Bks.

Anstee, Ashlyn. No, No, Gnome! Anstee, Ashlyn, illus. 2016. (ENG., Illus.). 40p. (J). (gr. -1-3). 17.99 (978-1-4814-3091-3(2), Simon & Schuster Bks. For Young Readers) Simon & Schuster Bks. For Young Readers.

Applegate, Katherine. Never Glue Your Friends to Chairs. Biggs, Brian, illus. 2008. (Roscoe Riley Rules Ser.: 1). (ENG.). 96p. (J). (gr. 1-5). 15.99 (978-0-06-114882-8(2)); pap. 4.99 (978-0-06-114881-1(4)) HarperCollins Pubs.

Balsley, Tilda & Fischer, Ellen. It's a Mitzvah, Grover! Leigh, Tom, illus. 2013. (ENG.). 24p. (J). (gr. -1-1). 6.95 (978-0-7613-7563-0(5)); lib. bdg. 16.95 (978-0-7613-7562-3(7)) Lerner Publishing Group. (Kar-Ben Publishing).

Bancks, Tristan. Noob, Amateur Dentist. Gorissen, Dean, illus. 2015. (Legends in Their Own Lunchbox Ser.). (ENG.). 56p. (gr. 2-3). pap. 7.99 (978-1-4966-0253-4(6), Legends in Their Own Lunchbox) Capstone Classroom.

Barbari, Nader. Eddy the Elephant. 2010. 32p. pap. 13.99 (978-1-4490-9430-0(9)) AuthorHouse.

Barchers, Suzanne I. What Luck!, 1 vol. 2011. (Targeted Phonics Ser.). (ENG.). 16p. (J). (gr. k-2). pap. 5.99 (978-1-4333-2421-5(0)) Teacher Created Materials, Inc.

Barfield, Asia. My Inspiration. 2009. 14p. 10.70 (978-0-557-05867-9(8)) Lulu Pr., Inc.

Bean, Jonathan. Big Snow. Bean, Jonathan, illus. 2013. (ENG., Illus.). 32p. (J). (gr. -1-1). 16.99 (978-0-374-30696-0(6), 9780374306960, Farrar, Straus & Giroux (BYR)) Farrar, Straus & Giroux.

Beifus, Ruth. Shlavim Classics 2-in-1 Vol. 1: The Best Reward & the Taste of Truth. 2009. 32p. 14.99 (978-1-59826-329-9(3)) Feldheim Pubs.

Bennett, Leonie. Locket Out. Adams, Arlene, illus. 2004. (ENG.). 24p. (J). lib. bdg. 23.65 (978-1-59646-688-3(X)) Dingles & Co.

Berenda, M. J. Helping with Pocket Change. 2011. 24p. pap. 12.95 (978-1-4567-5836-3(5)) AuthorHouse.

Berenstain, Jan & Berenstain, Mike. Mama's Helpers, 1 vol. 2011. (I Can Read! / Berenstain Bears / Good Deed Scouts / Living Lights Ser.). (ENG.). 32p. (J). pap. 3.99 (978-0-310-72099-7(0)) Zonderkidz.

—A Neighbor in Need, 1 vol. 2011. (I Can Read! / Berenstain Bears / Good Deed Scouts / Living Lights Ser.). (ENG.). 32p. (J). (gr. -1-2). pap. 3.99 (978-0-310-72098-0(2)) Zonderkidz.

Berenstain, Jan, et al. The Berenstain Bears Get Involved, 1 vol. 2012. (Berenstain Bears/Living Lights Ser.). (ENG.). 32p. (J). pap. 3.99 (978-0-310-72090-4(7)) Zonderkidz.

Berenstain, Mike. The Berenstain Bears Are SuperBears! Berenstain, Mike, illus. 2015. (I Can Read Level 1 Ser.). (ENG., Illus.). 32p. (J). (gr. -1-3). pap. 3.99 (978-0-06-235008-4(0)) HarperCollins Pubs.

Berglund, Andrea Lloyd. A Good Little Horse: Thunder's Morning Stroll. 2009. 36p. (J). pap. 19.95 (978-1-4327-3822-8(4)) Outskirts Pr., Inc.

Berry, Joy. Being Helpful. 2009. (ENG.). 40p. (J). (gr. -1-k). pap. 7.95 (978-1-60577-218-9(6)) Berry, Joy Enterprises.

Berry, Ron. Let Your Light Shine. 2007. (ENG., Illus.). 16p. (J). (gr. -1-k). bds. 12.99 (978-0-8249-6723-9(2), Ideal Pubns.) Worthy Publishing.

Bettenberg, Barbie. Edgar, the Near-Sighted Eagle. Clement, Marilyn, illus. 2008. 27p. (J). (978-0-9822534-0-3(0)) Cricket XPress of Minnesota.

Beverly-Barrier, Essie. Ouse the Mouse. Allen, Joshua, illus. 2009. 20p. pap. 12.99 (978-1-4389-4518-7(3)) AuthorHouse.

Birkett, Georgie, illus. Clean It!/¡A Limpiar! 2009. (Helping Hands English/Spanish Edition Ser.). (ENG & SPA.). 24p. (J). (gr. -1-k). pap. (978-1-84643-569-0(2)) Child's Play International Ltd.

—Cook It!/¡A Cocinar! 2009. (Helping Hands English/Spanish Edition Ser.). (ENG & SPA.). 24p. (J). (gr. -1-k). pap. (978-1-84643-568-3(4)) Child's Play International Ltd.

—Grow It!/¡A Sembrar! 2009. (Helping Hands English/Spanish Edition Ser.). (ENG & SPA.). 24p. (J). (gr. -1-k). pap. (978-1-84643-570-6(6)) Child's Play International Ltd.

Björkman, Steve. Look Out, Mouse! Björkman, Steve, illus. 2015. (I Like to Read(r) Ser.). (ENG., Illus.). 24p. (J). (gr. -1-3). 6.99 (978-0-8234-3397-1(8)) Holiday Hse., Inc.

Björkman, Steve, illus. Look Out, Mouse! 2015. (I Like to Read(r) Ser.). (ENG.). 24p. (J). (gr. -1-3). 14.95 (978-0-8234-2953-0(9)) Holiday Hse., Inc.

Blackaby, Susan & Haugen, Ryan. Dan Pone la Mesa, 1 vol., Set. Ruíz, Carlos, tr. Haugen, Ryan, illus. 2006. (Read-It! Readers en Español: Story Collection). (ENG & SPA., Illus.). 32p. (gr. -1-3). 21.32 (978-1-4048-1682-4(8), Easy Readers) Picture Window Bks.

Blair, Liza Sparks. Farley Firefly. 2008. 28p. pap. 24.95 (978-1-4241-9598-5(5)) America Star Bks.

Blyton, Enid. Mr Pink-Whistle Interferes. (ENG., Illus.). 112p. (J). pap. 7.99 (978-0-7475-3859-2(X)) Bloomsbury Publishing Plc GBR. Dist: Trafalgar Square Publishing.

Boazu, Elena & Balestrieri, Mauro. Lila's Quest. 2007. 48p. per. 13.95 (978-1-4327-0985-3(2)) Outskirts Pr., Inc.

Borgeson, Grace. Douwlina: A Rhino's Story. 2012. (ENG., Illus.). 32p. 19.95 (978-1-936474-63-9(8), 87298107-73d6-41ce-8918-67bd7c8ae307) Bright Sky Pr.

Bourgeois, Paulette & Clark, Brenda. Franklin Makes a Deal. 2003. (Franklin TV Storybook Ser.). (ENG., Illus.). 32p. (J). (gr. -1-3). 4.95 (978-1-55337-470-1(3)); 10.95 (978-1-55337-469-5(X)) Kids Can Pr., Ltd. CAN. Dist: Hachette Bk. Group.

Bowdish, Lynea. How to Be Nice — & Other Lessons I Didn't Learn. Gray, Leslie, illus. 2006. 47p. (J). pap. (978-1-59336-726-8(0)) Mondo Publishing.

Bowser, Ken. One Wrong Turn. Bowser, Ken, illus. 2016. (Funny Bone Readers: Truck Pals on the Job Ser.). (ENG., Illus.). 24p. (gr. k-2). lib. bdg. 19.99 (978-1-63440-077-0(1), 1401370) Red Chair Pr.

—One Wrong Turn: Helping Those in Need. Bowser, Ken, illus. 2016. (Funny Bone Readers: Truck Pals on the Job Ser.). (ENG., Illus.). 24p. (gr. k-2). 30.65 (978-1-63440-079-4(8)) Red Chair Pr.

Bracken, Beth. Henry Helps Clean His Room, 1 vol. Busby, Ailie, illus. 2012. (Henry Helps Ser.). (ENG.). 24p. (gr. -1 — 1). pap. 5.95 (978-1-4048-7668-2(5)); lib. bdg. 22.65 (978-1-4048-7306-3(6)) Picture Window Bks. (Henry Helps).

—Henry Helps Make Cookies, 1 vol. Busby, Ailie, illus. 2012. (Henry Helps Ser.). (ENG.). 24p. (gr. -1 — 1). pap. 5.95 (978-1-4048-7669-9(3)); lib. bdg. 22.65 (978-1-4048-7303-2(1)) Picture Window Bks. (Henry Helps).

—Henry Helps Plant a Garden, 1 vol. Busby, Ailie, illus. 2012. (Henry Helps Ser.). (ENG.). 24p. (gr. -1 — 1). pap. 5.95 (978-1-4048-7670-5(7)); lib. bdg. 22.65 (978-1-4048-7305-6(8)) Picture Window Bks. (Henry Helps).

—Henry Helps Wash the Car, 1 vol. Busby, Ailie, illus. 2012. (Henry Helps Ser.). (ENG.). 24p. (gr. -1 — 1). pap. 5.95 (978-1-4048-7671-2(5)); lib. bdg. 22.65 (978-1-4048-7304-9(X)) Picture Window Bks. (Henry Helps).

—Henry Helps with Dinner, 1 vol. Busby, Ailie, illus. 2012. (Henry Helps Ser.). (ENG.). 32p. (gr. -1 — 1). pap. 5.95 (978-1-4048-7675-0(8), Henry Helps) Picture Window Bks.

—Henry Helps with Laundry, 1 vol. Busby, Ailie, illus. (Henry Helps Ser.). (ENG.). 24p. (gr. -1 — 1). 2012. pap. 5.95 (978-1-4048-7674-3(X)) 2011. lib. bdg. 22.65 (978-1-4048-6772-7(4)) Picture Window Bks. (Henry Helps).

—Henry Helps with the Baby, 1 vol. Busby, Ailie, illus. (Henry Helps Ser.). (ENG.). 24p. (gr. -1 — 1). 2012. pap. 5.95 (978-1-4048-7672-9(3)) 2011. lib. bdg. 22.65 (978-1-4048-6770-3(8)) Picture Window Bks. (Henry Helps).

—Henry Helps with the Dog, 1 vol. Busby, Ailie, illus. (Henry Helps Ser.). (ENG.). 24p. (gr. -1 — 1). 2012. pap. 5.95 (978-1-4048-7673-6(1)) 2011. lib. bdg. 22.65 (978-1-4048-6771-0(6)) Picture Window Bks. (Henry Helps).

Bradman, Tony. The Wicked Stepmother Helps Out, 1 vol. Warburton, Sarah, illus. 2014. (After Happily Ever After Ser.). (ENG.). 56p. (gr. 2-3). lib. bdg. 25.32 (978-1-4342-7951-4(0), After Happily Ever After) Stone Arch Bks.

Brown, Barbara. The Adventures of Captain Crick, Super Hero. 2011. 28p. pap. 21.99 (978-1-4568-5005-0(9)) Xlibris Corp.

Burns, Joanne. Ollie Oyster's Ouch. 2005. 21p. 8.99 (978-1-4116-5337-5(8)) Lulu Pr., Inc.

Burton, Virginia Lee. Katy & the Big Snow Lap Board Book. 2014. (ENG., Illus.). 38p. (J). (— 1). bds. 11.99 (978-0-544-31717-8(3), HMH Books For Young Readers) Houghton Mifflin Harcourt Publishing Co.

Butler, Jalen. Helping Man: The Beginning. 2012. (ENG.). (J). pap. 12.95 (978-1-4675-2359-2(3)) Independent Pub.

Cabrini, Joe. Chicco's Nicedream Van - Jessica the Superstar. Cabrini, Joe, illus. 2007. (Illus.). 32p. per. (978-0-7552-0301-7(1)) Authors OnLine, Ltd.

Camara-Macauley, Marcella. The Candy Girl. 2008. 32p. pap. 21.99 (978-1-4415-2957-2(8)) Xlibris Corp.

Capucilli, Alyssa Satin. Biscuit Feeds the Pets. Schories, Pat, illus. 2016. (My First I Can Read Ser.). 32p. (J). (gr. -1-3). pap. 3.99 (978-0-06-223696-8(2)) HarperCollins Pubs.

Carmichael, Heather. Ellie Finds a New Home. McFarland, Shea, illus. 2008. (ENG.). 36p. pap. 16.99 (978-1-4389-2976-7(5)) AuthorHouse.

Chapman, Allen. The Radio Boys' First Wireless; or, Winning the Ferberton Prize. 2007. 100p. per. (978-1-4068-4516-7(7)) Echo Library.

Chapmon, Rachelle. Mari. 2009. 148p. pap. 11.99 (978-1-4389-6310-5(6)) AuthorHouse.

Chartier, Doris E. Ben's Desert Journey. 2009. 32p. pap. 14.49 (978-1-4389-7756-0(5)) AuthorHouse.

Child, Lauren. Help! I Really Mean It! 2009. (Charlie & Lola Ser.). (ENG.). 24p. (J). (gr. k-3). mass mkt. 3.99 (978-0-448-45049-0(6), Grosset & Dunlap) Penguin Young Readers Group.

Choyce, Lesley. Sudden Impact. 2006. (Orca Currents Ser.). 104p. (gr. 5-9). 19.95 (978-0-7569-6876-2(3)) Perfection Learning Corp.

Chriss, Granddad. The Adventures of Barazaburg. 2011. 54p. 24.99 (978-1-4568-7988-4(X)); pap. 15.99 (978-1-4568-7987-7(1)) Xlibris Corp.

Clarizio, Laura. If i Had a Magic Carpet. 2005. 48p. pap. 16.95 (978-1-4137-8557-9(3)) America Star Bks.

Cleofas-Moore, Ramona. Tiffany. 2008. 60p. pap. 16.95 (978-1-60474-238-1(0)) America Star Bks.

Clinton, Hillary Rodham. It Takes a Village. Frazee, Marla, illus. 2017. (ENG.). 40p. (J). (gr. -1-3). 19.99 (978-1-4814-3087-6(4), Simon & Schuster/Paula Wiseman Bks.) Simon & Schuster/Paula Wiseman Bks.

Coffelt, Nancy. Aunt Ant Leaves Through the Leaves. Coffelt, Nancy, illus. 2013. (ENG., Illus.). 32p. (J). pap. 7.99 (978-0-8234-2761-1(7)) Holiday Hse., Inc.

—Aunt Ant Leaves Through the Leaves: A Story with Homophones & Homonyms. Coffelt, Nancy, illus. 2012. (ENG., Illus.). 32p. (J). 16.95 (978-0-8234-2353-8(0)) Holiday Hse., Inc.

Coiner, Tea Railene. Hear the Song of the Fairies. 2009. 74p. pap. 19.95 (978-1-61582-833-3(8)) America Star Bks.

Costello, David Hyde. I Can Help. Costello, David Hyde, illus. 2010. (ENG., Illus.). 32p. (J). (gr. -1-1). 15.99 (978-0-374-33526-7(5), 9780374335267, Farrar, Straus & Giroux (BYR)) Farrar, Straus & Giroux.

Crawford, Ruth. Squirrel Boy & Brad: The Storm. 2010. 24p. pap. 12.99 (978-1-4490-1611-1(1)) AuthorHouse.

Crow, Melinda Melton. Rocky & Daisy Wash the Van. Sassin, Eva, illus. 2013. (My Two Dogs Ser.). (ENG.). 32p. (gr. 1-3). pap. 29.70 (978-1-4342-6299-8(5)); (gr. 2-3). pap. 5.95 (978-1-4342-6204-2(9)); (gr. 2-3). lib. bdg. 22.65 (978-1-4342-6010-9(0)) Stone Arch Bks.

Cuff, Ed. D. City of Thieves. 2013. 114p. pap. 7.99 (978-1-61798-076-3(5)) Wild Child Publishing.

Currey, Anna. Truffle Goes to Town. Currey, Anna, illus. 2003. (Illus.). 32p. (YA). (978-1-85602-429-7(6), Pavilion Children's Books) Pavilion Bks.

Cvetkovic, Judith Lynn. Mandy's Lost Adventure. 2008. 48p. per. 24.95 (978-1-4241-9709-5(0)) PublishAmerica, Inc.

Day, Alexandra. Carl & the Kitten. 2011. (My Readers Ser.). (ENG., Illus.). 32p. (J). (gr. -1-1). pap. 4.99 (978-0-312-68197-5(6), 9780312681975) Square Fish.

Denucci, Sharon. Grammie & the Gecko. DeNucci, Corinne, illus. 2008. 40p. pap. 16.99 (978-1-4389-1790-0(2)) AuthorHouse.

Dharma Publishing Staff. Great Gift & the Wish-Fulfilling Gem: A Story about the Wish to Help Others. 2010. (ENG.). 36p. (gr. -1-7). pap. 8.95 *(978-0-89800-600-1(7))* Dharma Publishing.

—Heart of Gold: The Story about the Power of Generosity. 2010. (ENG.). 36p. (gr. -1-7). pap. 8.95 *(978-0-89800-601-8(5))* Dharma Publishing.

Dickson, Louise. The Disappearing Magician. Cupples, Pat, illus. 2007. (Kids Can Read Ser.). (ENG.). 32p. (J). (gr. 1-2). 3.95 *(978-1-55453-034-2(2))* Kids Can Pr., Ltd. CAN. Dist: Hachette Bk. Group.

Dillon, Leo & Dillon, Diane. If Kids Ran the World. Dillon, Leo & Dillon, Diane, illus. 2014. (ENG., Illus.). 32p. (J). 18.99 *(978-0-545-44196-4(X)*, Blue Sky Pr., The) Scholastic, Inc.

Dinardo, Jeff. Mr. Mouse's Motel: Helping Others. Lubach, Peter, illus. 2014. (Funny Bone Readers: Being a Friend Ser.). 24p. (gr. -1-1). pap. 4.99 *(978-1-939656-05-6(2))* Red Chair Pr.

Dixon, Dallas L. Shelby's Collection Day. Williams, Nancy E., ed. Forrest, Grace Metzger, illus. 2013. 24p. (J). pap. 12.98 *(978-1-938526-54-1(6))* Laurus Bks.

Douglas, Kathleen. Johnny, the Unaware Angel. 2007. 108p. per. 19.95 *(978-1-4241-9939-6(5))* PublishAmerica, Inc.

Doyle, Sheldon. Purple Mountain's Majesty. 2008. 224p. pap. 21.95 *(978-1-4357-2017-6(2))* Lulu Pr., Inc.

Dugan, Christine. Muchas Manos Ayudan, 1 vol. rev. ed. 2007. (Building Fluency Through Reader's Theater Ser.). (SPA.). 20p. (J). (gr. 1-2). pap. 6.99 *(978-1-4333-0017-2(6))* Teacher Created Materials, Inc.

Dugin, Andrei. Dragon Feathers. Dugina, Olga, illus. 2010. Orig. Title: Die Drachenfedern. 24p. (J). (gr. k-3). 17.95 *(978-0-86315-774-5(2))* Floris Bks. GBR. Dist: SteinerBooks, Inc.

Durango, Julia. The One-Day House. Diaz, Bianca, illus. 2017. (ENG.). 32p. (J). (gr. -1-2). lib. bdg. 16.99 *(978-1-58089-709-9(6))* Charlesbridge Publishing, Inc.

Dyan, Penelope. Helping Hands. 2011. 34p. pap. 11.95 *(978-1-935630-93-7(8))* Bellissima Publishing, LLC.

—Mikey & Me & the Fly — -the Continuing Story of a Girl & Her Dog. Dyan, Penelope, illus. 2010. (Illus.). 50p. pap. 14.95 *(978-1-935118-94-7(3))* Bellissima Publishing, LLC.

Edwards, Pamela Duncan. The Leprechaun's Gold. Cole, Henry, illus. 2006. (ENG.). 40p. (J). (gr. -1-2). reprint ed. 6.99 *(978-0-06-443878-0(3)*, Tegen, Katherine Bks) HarperCollins Pubs.

Elliott, Linda. When Little Pinkie Gets Her Wings. Switzer, Bobbi, illus. 2007. 28p. per. 11.95 *(978-1-59800-871-5(4))* Outskirts Pr., Inc.

Elliott, Rebecca. Eva's Treetop Festival, Bk. 1. Elliott, Rebecca, illus. 2015. (Owl Diaries: 1). (ENG., Illus.). 80p. (J). (gr. k-2). pap. 4.99 *(978-0-545-68362-3(9))* Scholastic, Inc.

Ellis, Melody A. An Unexpected Hero. 2009. 48p. pap. 16.95 *(978-1-60749-834-6(0))* America Star Bks.

The Elves & the Shoemaker, Level 3. 2016. (Ladybird Readers Ser.). (ENG.). 64p. (J). (gr. 2-4). pap. 9.99 *(978-0-241-25385-4(3))* Penguin Bks., Ltd. GBR. Dist: Independent Pubs. Group.

Evans, Lisa M. Rich Man's Song. Evans, Lisa M., illus. 2017. (Illus.). 36p. (J). 7.99 *(978-0-9745264-2-3(8))* Marquise Publishing.

Falwell, Cathryn. Los Dibujos de David. de La Vega, Eida, tr. from ENG. Falwell, Cathryn, illus. 2005. (SPA., Illus.). 32p. (J). (gr. -1-5). pap. 9.95 *(978-1-58430-258-2(5))* Lee & Low Bks., Inc.

Fields, Terri. One Good Deed. Melmon, Deborah, illus. 2015. (ENG.). 24p. (J). (gr. -1-3). pap. 7.99 *(978-1-4677-3479-0(9)*, Kar-Ben Publishing) Lerner Publishing Group.

—One Good Deed. Melmon, Deborah, illus. 2015. (ENG.). 24p. (J). (gr. -1-3). 17.99 *(978-1-4677-3478-3(0))* Lerner Publishing Group.

Flowers, Luke. Ninja on the Farm (Scholastic Reader, Level 1: Moby Shinobi) 2016. (Scholastic Reader, Level 1 Ser.). (ENG.). 32p. (J). (gr. -1-1). pap. 3.99 *(978-0-545-93537-1(7))* Scholastic, Inc.

Frick, Lisa. "Evie" the Little Jack Russell with Brown Around Her Eyes. 2009. 64p. pap. 31.99 *(978-1-4415-2911-4(X))* Xlibris Corp.

Fruchter, Jason, illus. Friends Help Each Other. 2014. (Daniel Tiger's Neighborhood Ser.). (ENG.). 32p. (J). (gr. -1-k). pap. 3.99 *(978-1-4814-0366-5(4)*, Simon Spotlight) Simon Spotlight.

Gallagher, Diana G. Mice Capades, 1 vol. Juarez, Adriana & Puglisi, Adriana, illus. 2013. (Pet Friends Forever Ser.). (ENG.). 88p. (gr. 1-3). pap. 5.95 *(978-1-4795-1863-0(8))*; lib. bdg. 25.32 *(978-1-4048-7500-5(X))* Picture Window Bks.

Gonick, Larry. Kokopelli & Company in Attack of the Smart Pies. 2005. (ENG., Illus.). 192p. (J). 15.95 *(978-0-8126-2740-4(7))* Cricket Bks.

Grant, Nancy. Maggie & the Backyard Helpers. 2006. (ENG.). 60p. per. 16.95 *(978-1-4241-4373-3(X))* PublishAmerica, Inc.

Griffin, Lydia. BeBa & the Curious Creature Catchers. Lostimolo, Stephanie, illus. l.t. ed. 2006. 32p. (J). 16.95 *(978-0-9770516-0-1(9))* Laffin Minor Pr.

Gruber, Yehudit. The Power of Giving. 2013. 38p. pap. *(978-965-550-204-6(X))* Contento De Semrik.

Gudeon, Adam. Peep & Zeep. 2017. (I Like to Read(r) Ser.). (ENG.). 24p. (J). (gr. -1-3). 14.95 *(978-0-8234-3674-3(8))* Holiday Hse., Inc.

Hall, Bureda Ann Greathouse. Stories of My Little Blue Monkey. 2007. (Illus.). 32p. (J). pap. 15.00 *(978-0-8059-7397-6(4))* Dorrance Publishing Co., Inc.

Hall, Frostie. Dread Champions for the King, Book 2: For the King! 2006. 112p. per. *(978-1-55452-044-2(4))* Essence Publishing.

Hallinan, P. K. Let's Be Helpful. Hallinan, P. K., illus. 2009. (ENG., Illus.). 24p. (J). (gr. -1-2). 8.99 *(978-0-8249-5611-0(7)*, Ideal Pubns.) Worthy Publishing.

—Let's Be Helpful. 2008. (ENG., Illus.). 26p. (J). bds. 7.95 *(978-0-8249-6563-1(9)*, Ideal Pubns.) Worthy Publishing.

Hamilton, Katharine E. Susie at Your Service. 2012. 24p. pap. 17.99 *(978-1-4772-2426-7(2))* AuthorHouse.

Hamilton, Pat. Peaches the Private Eye Poodle: The Missing Muffin Caper. 2008. 32p. pap. 13.50 *(978-1-60693-277-3(2)*, Eloquent Bks.) Strategic Book Publishing & Rights Agency (SBPRA).

Harris, Donna. Ruff Life. 2011. 240p. pap. 17.99 *(978-1-4567-5081-7(X))* AuthorHouse.

Harris, Odis Clinton. Wee Willie & the Lonely Pine. 2008. 23p. pap. 24.95 *(978-1-60563-741-9(6))* America Star Bks.

Harrod-Eagles, Cynthia. Hello Kitty: Garden Party. Hino, Sachiho, illus. 2015. 22p. (J). ***(978-0-545-73447-9(9))*** Scholastic, Inc.

Hayes, Geoffrey. Patrick Eats His Peas & Other Stories. Hayes, Geoffrey, illus. 2013. (ENG., Illus.). 32p. (J). (gr. -1-3). 12.95 *(978-1-935179-34-4(9))* TOON Books / RAW Junior, LLC.

Hayes, Vicki C. Stones, 1 vol. 2016. (Red Rhino Ser.). (ENG.). 68p. (J). (gr. 3-6). pap. 7.95 *(978-1-62250-978-2(1))* Saddleback Educational Publishing, Inc.

HB Staff. Help! Said Jed. 97th ed. 2003. (First-Place Reading Ser.). (gr. 1-18). pap. 16.50 *(978-0-15-308134-7(1))* Harcourt Schl. Pubs.

Heimbuch, Carol Jo. Condor Caper. Martin, Fred, illus. 2008. 128p. pap. 11.50 *(978-1-59330-560-4(5))* Aventine Pr.

Help for Santa. 2006. (Little Elf Set 1 Ser.). (J). 7.33 *(978-1-932570-76-2(4))* Pioneer Valley Bks.

Helvey, Rebecca. Greta's Purpose. Helvey, Rebecca, illus. 2008. (Illus.). 68p. (J). pap. 14.95 *(978-0-9774754-7-6(6))* Spiritbuilding.

Hensley, Sarah M. Helping in My Town. Middleton, Mikell, illus. l.t. ed. 2003. (HRL Big Book Ser.). 8p. (J). (gr. -1-1). pap. 10.95 *(978-1-57332-274-4(1))*; pap. 10.95 *(978-1-57332-275-1(X))* Carson-Dellosa Publishing, LLC. (HighReach Learning, Incorporated).

Herzog, Pearl. The Amazing Fishing Rod. Bodel, Itai, photos by. 2013. (Illus.). 34p. (J). *(978-1-4226-1436-5(0))* Mesorah Pubns., Ltd.

Hickner, Hayden. A Bear & the Bees. 2010. 36p. 15.49 *(978-1-4520-5087-4(2))* AuthorHouse.

Hillert, Margaret. Dear Dragon Helps Out. Schimmell, David, illus. 2012. (BeginningtoRead Ser.). 32p. (J). (-2). lib. bdg. 22.60 *(978-1-59953-505-0(X))* Norwood Hse. Pr.

—Querido Dragón Quiere Ayudar. Fernandez, Queta, tr. from ENG. Schimmell, David, illus. 2014. (BeginningtoRead Ser.).Tr. of Dear Dragon Helps Out. (ENG & SPA.). 32p. (J). (-2). lib. bdg. 22.60 *(978-1-59953-613-2(7))* Norwood Hse. Pr.

Hilliard, Michael. Butter Bee Grows up Too Fast! 2010. 20p. pap. 12.49 *(978-1-4490-7300-8(X))* AuthorHouse.

Hines, Danise. Ziona Learns to Be a Good Samaritan. 2009. 40p. pap. 16.99 *(978-1-4490-1326-4(0))* AuthorHouse.

Hobbs, Leigh. Old Tom, Man of Mystery, 1 vol. Hobbs, Leigh, illus. 2005. (ENG., Illus.). 32p. (J). (gr. -1-3). 16.95 *(978-1-56145-346-7(3))* Peachtree Pubs.

Hockerman, Dennis, illus. The Lion & the Mouse: A Tale about Being Helpful. 2006. (J). 6.99 *(978-1-59939-007-9(8))* Cornerstone Pr.

Holden, Pam. The Gentle Giant, 6 pack. Hatam, Samer, illus. 2009. (Red Rocket Readers Ser.). (ENG.). 16p. (gr. 2-2). pap. *(978-1-877363-81-8(2))* Flying Start Bks.

Horácek, Petr. The Mouse Who Reached the Sky. Horácek, Petr, illus. 2016. (ENG., Illus.). 32p. (J). (-k). 16.99 *(978-0-7636-7916-3(X))* Candlewick Pr.

Houghton, Jill Ziereis. Let's Volunteer. Thompson, Chad, illus. 2013. 28p. pap. 10.95 *(978-1-61244-211-2(0))* Halo Publishing International.

Houghton Mifflin Harcourt Publishing Company Staff. Girl Power 5-Minute Stories. 2015. (5-Minute Stories Ser.). (ENG., Illus.). 224p. (J). (gr. -1-3). 12.99 *(978-0-544-33925-5(8)*, HMH Books For Young Readers) Houghton Mifflin Harcourt Publishing Co.

Howat, Irene, et al. Huw Helpu Pawb. 2005. (Storiau Crefyddol Religious Stories Ser.). (WEL., Illus.). 24p. *(978-1-85994-519-3(8))* Cyhoeddiadau'r Gair.

Hudgins, Larry. My Dog Spike, 1 vol. 2009. 55p. pap. 16.95 *(978-1-60836-421-3(6))* America Star Bks.

Hudson, Phillip. Saying Goodbye, Sam's Love Story. Cook, Jennifer, ed. 2008. (SPA.). 19.95 *(978-0-615-19269-7(6))*; 26p. 19.95 *(978-0-615-19154-6(1))* West Coast Learning Development Center.

Hughan, Judy. The Make Better Story, 1 vol. 2009. 31p. pap. 24.95 *(978-1-60836-754-2(1))* America Star Bks.

Hurwitz, Michele Weber. The Summer I Saved the World ... in 65 Days. 2015. (ENG.). 272p. (J). (gr. 5). pap. 9.99 *(978-0-385-37109-4(8)*, Ember) Random Hse. Children's Bks.

InSeon, Chae. Handy Mr. Hippo. YouDae, Kim, illus. rev. ed. 2014. (MySELF Bookshelf Ser.). (ENG.). 32p. (J). (gr. k-2). pap. 11.94 *(978-1-60357-661-1(4))*; lib. bdg. 25.27 *(978-1-59953-652-1(8))* Norwood Hse. Pr.

Isabella, Jude. The Red Bicycle: The Extraordinary Story of One Ordinary Bicycle. Shin, Simone, illus. 2015. (CitizenKid Ser.). (ENG.). 32p. (J). (gr. 3-7). 18.95 *(978-1-77138-023-2(3))* Kids Can Pr., Ltd. CAN. Dist: Hachette Bk. Group.

Jablonski, Carrie. Spots New Friends. 2012. 20p. pap. 24.95 *(978-1-4626-8398-7(3))* America Star Bks.

Jasnoch, Dorothy. Frankie the Bunny: Helping the Birds. Korzeniowski, Samson O., ed. Jasnoch, Dorothy, illus. 2013. (Illus.). 28p. 17.99 *(978-1-937752-20-0(8))* Owl About Bks. Pub., Inc.

—Frankie the Bunny Helping the Birds. Korzeniowski, Samson, ed. Jasnoch, Dorothy, illus. 2012. (ENG., Illus.). 28p. pap. 12.99 *(978-1-937752-05-7(4))* Owl About Bks. Pub., Inc.

Jenkins, Peter. When Father Christmas Resigned. Jenkins, Sandra, illus. 2012. 36p. pap. *(978-1-908775-94-8(7))* Legend Pr.

Jentsch, R. D. Froggy & Friends Go to the Creek, 1 vol. Jentsch, Joyce Harp, illus. 2009. 41p. pap. 24.95 *(978-1-60836-966-9(8))* America Star Bks.

Jiang, Eva. Eric Loved Fire Trucks. 2013. 28p. pap. 16.09 *(978-1-4669-7117-2(7))* Trafford Publishing.

Joiner, Mica. Petunia Pollie & Her Prolific Purse. 2011. 28p. (gr. -1). pap. 13.59 *(978-1-4567-3400-8(8))* AuthorHouse.

Judge, Chris. The Snow Beast. Judge, Chris, illus. 2015. (ENG., Illus.). 32p. (J). (gr. -1-3). 17.99 *(978-1-4677-9313-1(2))* Andersen Pr. GBR. Dist: Lerner Publishing Group.

Juster, Norton. The Odious Ogre. Feiffer, Jules, illus. 2010. (ENG.). 32p. (J). (gr. -1-2). 17.95 *(978-0-545-16202-9(5)*, Di Capua, Michael) Scholastic, Inc.

Kear, Nicole C. The Fix-It Friends: Have No Fear! Dockray, Tracy, illus. 2017. (Fix-It Friends Ser.). (ENG.). 144p. (J). 16.99 *(978-1-250-11577-5(9)*, 9781250115775) Imprint IND. Dist: Macmillan.

—The Fix-It Friends: Sticks & Stones. Dockray, Tracy, illus. 2017. (Fix-It Friends Ser.: 2). (ENG.). 144p. (J). pap. 5.99 *(978-1-250-08586-3(1)*, 9781250085863) Imprint IND. Dist: Macmillan.

—The Fix-It Friends: the Show Must Go On. Dockray, Tracy, illus. 2017. (Fix-It Friends Ser.: 3). (ENG.). 160p. (J). pap. 5.99 ***(978-1-250-08668-6(X)***, 9781250086686) Imprint IND. Dist: Macmillan.

—The Fix-It Friends: Wish You Were Here. Dockray, Tracy, illus. 2017. (Fix-It Friends Ser.: 4). (ENG.). 160p. (J). pap. 5.99 ***(978-1-250-08670-9(1)***, 9781250086709) Imprint IND. Dist: Macmillan.

Keilbart, L. S. One. Benson, Barbara, illus. 2007. (ENG.). 76p. (J). (gr. k-k). per. *(978-1-85756-610-9(6))* Janus Publishing Co.

Kelley, Khris. Ringo the Helpful Raccoon. Crisenbery, Casey, illus. 2012. 38p. (J). 14.95 *(978-1-937406-70-7(9))* Mascot Bks., Inc.

Kerrin, Jessica Scott. In High Gear! Kelly, Joseph, illus. 2008. (Martin Bridge Ser.). (ENG.). 112p. (J). (gr. 2-5). pap. 6.95 *(978-1-55453-157-8(8))* Kids Can Pr., Ltd. CAN. Dist: Hachette Bk. Group.

Kerwin, Betsy. The Adventures of Floret the Woodland Fairy: The Adventures Begin. 2008. 44p. pap. 18.49 *(978-1-4343-9426-2(3))* AuthorHouse.

Kimmel, Eric A. Even Higher! A Rosh Hashanah Story by I. L. Peretz. Weber, Jill, illus. 2010. (ENG.). 32p. (J). (gr. -1-3). pap. 6.95 *(978-0-8234-2298-2(4))* Holiday Hse., Inc.

King, Frances. The Roundabout Boy. 2012. 28p. pap. 16.50 *(978-1-4772-8059-1(6))* AuthorHouse.

King, Trey. Halloween Rescue! Wang, Sean, illus. 2013. (Lego City Ser.). (ENG.). 24p. (J). (gr. -1-3). 4.99 *(978-0-545-51572-6(6))* Scholastic, Inc.

Kirk, David. Bedtime Story. 2006. (Illus.). 32p. (J). *(978-0-448-44514-4(X))* Penguin Publishing Group.

Klein, Adria F. Hank Hammer, 1 vol. Rowland, Andrew, illus. 2011. (Tool School Ser.). (ENG.). 32p. (gr. 1-2). pap. 6.25 *(978-1-4342-3385-1(5))*; lib. bdg. 22.65 *(978-1-4342-3043-0(0))* Stone Arch Bks.

—Hank Hammer & the Puppy, 1 vol. Rowland, Andrew, illus. 2012. (Tool School Ser.). (ENG.). 32p. (gr. 1-3). pap. 6.25 *(978-1-4342-4233-4(1))*; lib. bdg. 22.65 *(978-1-4342-4020-0(7))* Stone Arch Bks.

—Sammy Saw, 1 vol. Rowland, Andrew, illus. 2011. (Tool School Ser.). (ENG.). 32p. (gr. 1-2). pap. 6.25 *(978-1-4342-3387-5(1))*; lib. bdg. 22.65 *(978-1-4342-3045-4(7))* Stone Arch Bks.

—Sammy Saw & the Campout, 1 vol. Rowland, Andrew, illus. 2012. (Tool School Ser.). (ENG.). 32p. (gr. 1-3). pap. 6.25 *(978-1-4342-4234-1(X))*; lib. bdg. 22.65 *(978-1-4342-4022-4(3))* Stone Arch Bks.

—Sophie Screwdriver, 1 vol. Rowland, Andrew, illus. 2011. (Tool School Ser.). (ENG.). 32p. (gr. 1-2). pap. 6.25 *(978-1-4342-3386-8(3))*; lib. bdg. 22.65 *(978-1-4342-3044-7(9))* Stone Arch Bks.

—Sophie Screwdriver & the Classroom, 1 vol. Rowland, Andrew, illus. 2012. (Tool School Ser.). (ENG.). 32p. (gr. 1-3). pap. 6.25 *(978-1-4342-4235-8(8))*; lib. bdg. 22.65 *(978-1-4342-4021-7(5))* Stone Arch Bks.

—Tia Tape Measure, 1 vol. Rowland, Andrew, illus. 2011. (Tool School Ser.). (ENG.). 32p. (gr. 1-2). pap. 6.25 *(978-1-4342-3388-2(X))*; lib. bdg. 22.65 *(978-1-4342-3046-1(5))* Stone Arch Bks.

—Tia Tape Measure & the Move, 1 vol. Rowland, Andrew, illus. 2012. (Tool School Ser.). (ENG.). 32p. (gr. 1-3). pap. 6.25 *(978-1-4342-4236-5(6))*; lib. bdg. 22.65 *(978-1-4342-4023-1(1))* Stone Arch Bks.

Klett, David E. Rachel & the Wizard of Lake Lure: The Lake Lure Chronicles - Book 2. 2006. (Illus.). (J). lib. bdg. 17.95 *(978-0-9779325-1-1(6))* Five Oaks Pr.

Krakower, Harold. Sugarland: Volume 2 Trouble in Sugarland. 2009. 28p. pap. 12.50 *(978-1-4490-1880-1(7))* AuthorHouse.

Kroll, Steven. The Biggest Christmas Tree Ever. Bassett, Jeni, illus. 2009. (ENG.). 32p. (J). (gr. -1-3). pap. 4.99 *(978-0-545-12119-4(1)*, Cartwheel Bks.) Scholastic, Inc.

Kroll, Virginia. Makayla Cares about Others. Cote, Nancy, illus. 2007. (Way I Act Bks.). (ENG.). 24p. (J). (gr. k-3). lib. bdg. 15.99 *(978-0-8075-4945-2(2))* Whitman, Albert & Co.

LaReau, Kara. The Infamous Ratsos. Myers, Matt, illus. 2017. (Infamous Ratsos Ser.). (ENG.). (J). (gr. k-3). 96p. 14.99 ***(978-0-7636-7637-7(3))***; 64p. pap. 4.99 ***(978-0-7636-9875-1(X))*** Candlewick Pr.

Law, Felicia. Olivia the Orangutan: A Tale of Helpfulness. Spoor, Mike, illus. 2010. (Animal Fair Values Ser.). (ENG.). 32p. (J). (gr. -1-3). pap. 10.55 *(978-1-60754-917-8(4))*; lib. bdg. 22.60 *(978-1-60754-906-2(9))* Windmill Bks.

Lechner, John. Sticky Burr: Adventures in Burrwood Forest. Lechner, John, illus. 2008. (ENG., Illus.). 56p. (J). (gr. 1-4). pap. 7.99 *(978-0-7636-3567-1(7))* Candlewick Pr.

Leffler, Silke & Janisch, Heinz. "I Have a Little Problem" Said the Bear. 2012. (ENG., Illus.). 32p. (J). (gr. -1-3). pap. 8.95 *(978-0-7358-4094-2(6))* North-South Bks., Inc.

Lehman, Barbara. Trainstop. 2008. (ENG., Illus.). 32p. (J). (gr. -1-3). 16.99 *(978-0-618-75640-7(X))* Houghton Mifflin Harcourt Publishing Co.

Lemke, Amy J. & Lemke, Donald B. My Little Bro-Bot, 1 vol. Bradley, Jessica, illus. 2013. (Comics Land Ser.). (ENG.). 32p. (gr. k-2). 7.95 *(978-1-4342-6285-1(5))*; lib. bdg. 25.32 *(978-1-4342-4989-0(1))* Stone Arch Bks.

Levy, Janice. Diva Duck Travels the World, 1 vol. Madden, Colleen M., illus. 2012. (Diva Duck Ser.). (ENG.). 32p. (J). (gr. -1-4). 28.50 *(978-1-61641-888-5(5))* Magic Wagon.

—Flip-Flop & the BFFs, 1 vol. Madden, Colleen M., illus. 2011. (Flip-Flop Adventure Ser.). (ENG.). 32p. (J). (gr. k-3). 28.50 *(978-1-61641-652-2(1))* Magic Wagon.

Lindman. Flicka, Ricka, Dicka & the Strawberries. Lindman, illus. 2013. (Flicka, Ricka, Dicka Ser.). (ENG., Illus.). 32p. (J). (gr. k-3). 9.99 *(978-0-8075-2512-8(X))* Whitman, Albert & Co.

Lindman, Maj. Flicka, Ricka, Dicka & the New Dotted Dresses. 2012. (J). *(978-0-8075-2495-4(6))* Whitman, Albert & Co.

—Flicka, Ricka, Dicka & the New Dotted Dresses. Lindman, Maj, illus. 2012. (Flicka, Ricka, Dicka Ser.). (ENG., Illus.). 32p. (J). (gr. k-3). 9.99 *(978-0-8075-2484-8(0))* Whitman, Albert & Co.

Little, Robert. Fun Day in Mrs. Walker's Class. Galey, Chuck, illus. 2005. 32p. (J). *(978-0-9701863-6-2(3))* Relde Publishing.

Litz, Amanda. Sam & Pam Can & You Can Too! We Can Help Our Mom. Garcia, Cynthia, illus. 2011. 32p. (J). pap. 3.99 *(978-0-9841496-1-2(9))* Traveler's Trunk Publishing LLC.

Loveridge, Pamela. Buzzy Bee. 2012. 24p. pap. 28.03 *(978-1-4797-4802-0(1))* Xlibris Corp.

Lynch, Casey. Mighty Mike Builds a Ball Field, 1 vol. Lynch, Kelly, illus. 2011. (Mighty Mike Ser.). (ENG.). 32p. (gr. -1-2). 28.50 *(978-1-61641-128-2(7)*, Looking Glass Library) ABDO Publishing Co.

—Mighty Mike Builds a Library, 1 vol. Lynch, Kelly, illus. 2011. (Mighty Mike Ser.). (ENG.). 32p. (gr. -1-2). 28.50 *(978-1-61641-129-9(5)*, Looking Glass Library) ABDO Publishing Co.

—Mighty Mike Repairs a Playground, 1 vol. Lynch, Kelly, illus. 2011. (Mighty Mike Ser.). (ENG.). 32p. (gr. -1-2). 28.50 *(978-1-61641-132-9(5)*, Looking Glass Library) ABDO Publishing Co.

—Mighty Mike Saves a School Bus, 1 vol. Lynch, Kelly, illus. 2011. (Mighty Mike Ser.). (ENG.). 32p. (gr. -1-2). 28.50 *(978-1-61641-133-6(3)*, Looking Glass Library) ABDO Publishing Co.

Lynch, Kelly. Mighty Mike Builds a Nature Trail, 1 vol. Lynch, Casey, illus. 2011. (Mighty Mike Ser.). (ENG.). 32p. (gr. -1-2). 28.50 *(978-1-61641-130-5(9)*, Looking Glass Library) ABDO Publishing Co.

Lyon, Nathan W. & Ellis, Kevin L. Sam the Clam. 2010. 28p. pap. 14.95 *(978-1-4520-7784-0(3))* AuthorHouse.

Maclear, Kyo. The Wish Tree. Turnham, Chris, illus. 2016. (ENG.). 40p. (J). (gr. -1 — 1). 16.99 *(978-1-4521-5065-9(6))* Chronicle Bks. LLC.

Maddox, Jake. Dancing Solo, 1 vol. Wood, Katie, illus. 2014. (Jake Maddox Girl Sports Stories Ser.). (ENG.). 72p. (gr. 2-3). 25.32 *(978-1-4342-4142-9(4))* Stone Arch Bks.

Manushkin, Fran. Katie in the Kitchen, 1 vol. Lyon, Tammie, illus. 2010. (Katie Woo Ser.). (ENG.). 32p. (gr. k-2). lib. bdg. 21.32 *(978-1-4048-5724-7(9))* Picture Window Bks.

—Katie Woo & Her Big Ideas, 1 vol. Lyon, Tammie, illus. 2013. (Katie Woo Ser.). (ENG.). 96p. (gr. k-2). pap. 4.95 *(978-1-4795-2026-8(8))* Picture Window Bks.

—Katie Woo Tries Something New. Lyon, Tammie, illus. 2015. (Katie Woo Ser.). (ENG.). 96p. (gr. k-2). pap. 4.95 *(978-1-4795-6182-7(7))* Picture Window Bks.

—Katie's Happy Mother's Day. Lyon, Tammie, illus. 2015. (Katie Woo Ser.). (ENG.). 32p. (gr. k-2). 21.32 *(978-1-4795-6179-7(7))* Picture Window Bks.

Manzano, Sonia. A Box Full of Kittens. Phelan, Matt, illus. 2007. (ENG.). 40p. (J). (gr. -1-3). 17.99 *(978-0-689-83089-1(0)*, Atheneum Bks. for Young Readers) Simon & Schuster Children's Publishing.

Marinaro, Stacy. Carter Finds a Tiger. 2009. 19p. 12.50 *(978-0-578-02365-6(2))* Marinaro, Stacy.

Marvin, Susan. Birthday Dreamz. 2011. 36p. (gr. -1). pap. 15.99 *(978-1-4567-4173-0(X))* AuthorHouse.

Mason, Adrienne. The Drop of Doom. Cupples, Pat, illus. 2007. (Kids Can Read Ser.). (ENG.). 32p. (J). (gr. 1-2). 3.95 *(978-1-55453-036-6(9))*; 14.95 *(978-1-55453-035-9(0))* Kids Can Pr., Ltd. CAN. Dist: Hachette Bk. Group.

Mateboer, Hans. Peter the Cruise Ship - to Alaska. 2007. (Illus.). 32p. (J). 16.95 *(978-0-9759487-2-9(5))* Mateboer, Johannes Aart.

Mathisen, Michael. Abby & the Helping Mommy. Estill, Amy, illus. 2009. 28p. pap. 13.99 *(978-1-4389-5327-4(5))* AuthorHouse.

Mayer, Mercer. Helping Out. 2012. (Big Little Critter Ser.: 2). (ENG., Illus.). 96p. (J). 12.95 *(978-1-60746-071-8(8)*, Premiere) FastPrncil, Inc.

—Just Helping My Dad. Mayer, Mercer, illus. 2011. (My First I Can Read Ser.). (ENG., Illus.). 32p. (J). (gr. -1-3). pap. 3.99 *(978-0-06-083563-7(X))* HarperCollins Pubs.

—Just Helping My Dad. 2011. (Little Critter: I Can Read! Ser.). (J). lib. bdg. 13.55 *(978-0-606-23023-0(8)*, Turtleback) Turtleback Bks.

—Little Critter Fall Storybook Collection. Mayer, Mercer, illus. 2015. (Little Critter Ser.). (ENG., Illus.). 192p. (J). (gr. -1-3). 11.99 *(978-0-06-238032-6(X))* HarperCollins Pubs.

McCabe, Joyce. Flugel Mcdougel, 1 vol. 2010. 20p. 24.95 *(978-1-4512-0779-8(4))* PublishAmerica, Inc.

McGougan, Kathy. Buddy's Christmas Joy. 2011. 20p. pap. 12.95 *(978-1-4634-3763-3(3))* AuthorHouse.

McMahon, Kate. That Touch of Magic. 2009. (ENG.). 112p. (J). pap. 12.95 *(978-1-901737-60-8(8))* Anvil Bks., Ltd. IRL. Dist: Dufour Editions, Inc.

McPhate, Paul J. The Puggle King. 2008. 52p. pap. 16.95 *(978-1-60703-709-5(2))* America Star Bks.

Meister, Cari. Beat Bugs: Penny Lane. 2017. (I Can Read Level 1 Ser.). 32p. (J). (gr. -1-3). pap. 3.99 *(978-0-06-264071-0(2))* HarperCollins Pubs.

M.H.Pruitt. The Adventures of Rexie the Bear. 2009. 16p. pap. 8.99 *(978-1-4490-4211-0(2))* AuthorHouse.

Mighty Mike, 6 vols., Set. Incl. Mighty Mike Builds a Ball Field. Lynch, Casey. Lynch, Kelly, illus. 28.50 *(978-1-61641-128-2(7))*; Mighty Mike Builds a Library. Lynch, Casey. Lynch, Kelly, illus. 28.50 *(978-1-61641-129-9(5))*; Mighty Mike Builds a Nature Trail. Lynch, Kelly. Lynch, Casey, illus. 28.50 *(978-1-61641-130-5(9))*; Mighty Mike Does What's Right! Lynch, Kelly. Lynch, Casey, illus. 28.50 *(978-1-61641-131-2(7))*; Mighty Mike Repairs a Playground. Lynch, Casey. Lynch, Kelly, illus. 28.50 *(978-1-61641-132-9(5))*; Mighty Mike Saves a School Bus. Lynch, Casey. Lynch, Kelly, illus. 28.50 *(978-1-61641-133-6(3))*; (gr. -1-2). (Mighty Mike Ser.). 32p. 2011. 171.00 *(978-1-61641-127-5(9)*, Looking Glass Library) ABDO Publishing Co.

Miller, Pat. Squirrel's New Year's Resolution. Ember, Kathi, illus. 2012. (J). 34.28 *(978-1-61913-135-4(8))* Weigl Pubs., Inc.

—Squirrel's New Year's Resolution. Ember, Kathi, illus. (ENG.). 32p. (J). (gr. k-2). 2017. pap. 7.99 ***(978-0-8075-7592-5(5))*** 2010. 16.99 *(978-0-8075-7591-8(7))* Whitman, Albert & Co.

Misra, Michelle. Secrets & Sapphires. Chaffey, Samantha, illus. 2016. (Angel Wings Ser.: 3). (ENG.). 128p. (J). (gr. 1-4). pap. 5.99 *(978-1-4814-5803-0(5)*, Aladdin) Simon & Schuster Children's Publishing.

Moore, Mel. Mother's Little Helper. 2006. (Illus.). 16p. (J). per. *(978-0-9775919-5-4(6))* Carpe Diem Publishing.

Moser, Lisa. Squirrel's World. Gorbachev, Valeri, illus. 2013. (Candlewick Sparks Ser.). (ENG.). 48p. (J). (gr. k-4). pap. 3.99 *(978-0-7636-6644-6(0))* Candlewick Pr.

Munsch, Robert. Ribbon Rescue. 2007. (J). 12.65 *(978-0-7569-7466-4(6))* Perfection Learning Corp.

Murphy, Stuart J. Percy's Neighborhood. 2013. (I See I Learn Ser.). (ENG.). 32p. (J). (-k). lib. bdg. 14.95 *(978-1-58089-480-7(1))*; (Illus.). pap. 6.95 *(978-1-58089-481-4(X))* Charlesbridge Publishing, Inc.

Murray, Mary, et al. Bob Lends a Helping ... Hand?, 1 vol. 2003. (Big Idea Books / VeggieTales Ser.). (ENG., Illus.). 12p. (J). (gr. -1-1). bds. 4.99 *(978-0-310-70538-3(X))* Zonderkidz.

Muth, Jon J. Zen Ties. Muth, Jon J., illus. 2008. (ENG., Illus.). 40p. (J). (gr. -1-3). 17.99 *(978-0-439-63425-0(3)*, Scholastic Pr.) Scholastic, Inc.

Nanny & I Meet Odie. 2006. (J). lib. bdg. 18.99 *(978-0-9724394-1-1(2))* Sylables.

Neill, Patricia S. Christmas Is a Gift from God. 2008. (Illus.). 24p. (J). 7.00 *(978-0-8059-7845-2(3))* Dorrance Publishing Co., Inc.

Niddrie, June. Fly Ladybird, Fly. 2010. 32p. pap. 16.10 *(978-0-557-31862-9(9))* Lulu Pr., Inc.

O'Donnell, Kerri. Sue Helps Out. 2006. (Neighborhood Readers Ser.). (ENG.). 8p. (gr. -1-3). pap. 5.15 *(978-1-4042-5684-2(9)*, Rosen Classroom) Rosen Publishing Group, Inc., The.

O'Mara, Robert J. Friends Are Special, 1 vol. 2009. 26p. pap. 24.95 *(978-1-60749-087-6(0))* America Star Bks.

O'Neal, Shereka N. Ask for Help! 2012. 28p. pap. 15.99 *(978-1-4691-2758-3(X))* Xlibris Corp.

Osborn, Valerie Huffman. A Week of Bunnies. Osborn, Kimberly, ed. 2007. (ENG., Illus.). 32p. (J). 19.95 *(978-1-932278-25-5(7))* Mayhaven Publishing, Inc.

Parker, Jean Black. Amanda's Helping Hands. 2006. 17.00 *(978-0-8059-9156-7(5))* Dorrance Publishing Co., Inc.

Peine, Jan Muir. Giving Me Away. 2007. (Illus.). 25p. (J). pap. 6.99 *(978-0-9754575-7-3(8))* Ashway Pr.

Pendleton, Claudette M. I'm Mommy's Little Helper. Scott, Christopher L., illus. 2012. 46p. 24.95 *(978-1-4626-9303-0(2))* America Star Bks.

Pilon, Cindy Jett. Joni & the Fallen Star: Helping Children Learn Teamwork. Hazard, John, illus. 2011. (Let's Talk Ser.). (ENG.). 48p. (J). (gr. -1-2). pap. 9.95 *(978-0-88282-353-9(1))* New Horizon Pr. Pubs., Inc.

Piper, Watty. The Little Engine That Could. Hauman, George & Hauman, Doris, illus. deluxe ed. 2009. (Little Engine That Could Ser.). (ENG.). 48p. (J). (gr. -1-2). 17.99 *(978-0-448-45257-9(X)*, Grosset & Dunlap) Penguin Young Readers Group.

Pittar, Gill. Milly, Molly & Sock Heaven. 2004. 28p. *(978-1-86972-015-5(6))* Milly Molly Bks.

—Milly, Molly & Sock Heaven (book W/dolls) 2006. 28p. pap. *(978-1-86972-098-8(9))* Milly Molly Bks.

Porter, Alan J. Cars: The Rookie. Carreres, Albert, illus. 2009. (World of Cars Ser.). (ENG.). 112p. (J). 24.99 *(978-1-60886-522-2(3))* Boom! Studios.

—Cars: the Rookie. Carreres, Albert, illus. 2009. (World of Cars Ser.). (ENG.). 112p. (J). pap. 9.99 *(978-1-934506-84-4(2))* Boom! Studios.

Powell, GinaMarie. Ayiana & the Hurricane Katrina Classmate. Bray, Pamela, illus. 2008. 28p. pap. 24.95 *(978-1-60441-965-8(2))* America Star Bks.

Prentiss, Timothy. A Good Pick. 2006. (Early Explorers Ser.). (J). pap. *(978-1-4108-6111-5(2))* Benchmark Education Co.

Publications International Ltd. Staff, ed. Thomas & Friends: A Busy Day on Sodor. 2009. (Illus.). 18p. (J). bds. 10.98 *(978-1-4127-1735-9(3)*, PIL Kids) Publications International, Ltd.

—Tinkerbell. 2010. 18p. (J). bds. 7.98 *(978-1-60553-697-2(0))* Phoenix International Publications, Inc.

Punnett, Dick. Help Jumbo Escape: A Talk-along Book. Dunnington, Tom, illus. 2nd ed. 2005. (Talk-Along Bks.). 32p. (J). pap. 6.99 *(978-0-9657211-2-7(4))* Tomoka Pr.

Randall, Marilyn. A Hard Nut to Crack. 2009. 36p. pap. 18.95 *(978-0-557-15891-1(5))* Lulu Pr., Inc.

Random House. Santa's Little Helpers (Team Umizoomi) Ostrom, Bob, illus. 2013. (Pictureback(R) Ser.). (ENG.). 16p. (J). (gr. -1-2). 4.99 *(978-0-449-81881-7(0)*, Random Hse. Bks. for Young Readers) Random Hse. Children's Bks.

Reagan, Jean. How to Amaze a Teacher. Wildish, Lee, illus. 2017. (ENG.). 32p. (J). (gr. -1-3). 17.99 *(978-0-553-53825-0(X)*, Knopf Bks. for Young Readers) Random Hse. Children's Bks.

Redbank, Tennant. Lily: Tiana's Helpful Kitten (Disney Princess: Palace Pets) Random House Disney Staff & Matta, Gabriella, illus. 2016. (Stepping Stone Book(TM) Ser.). (ENG.). 64p. (J). (gr. 1-4). 5.99 *(978-0-7364-3393-8(7)*, RH/Disney) Random Hse. Children's Bks.

Reilly, Carmel & Wallace-Mitchell, Jane. Harry Helps Out. 2008. (Rigby Focus Forward: Level E Ser.). (Illus.). 24p. (J). (gr. 4-7). pap. *(978-1-4190-3673-6(4)*, Rigby) Pearson Education Australia.

Ricchiazzi, Lisa Gail. The Adventures of Fella & Dawn: Help One Another. 2012. 20p. pap. 13.77 *(978-1-4669-7170-7(3))* Trafford Publishing.

Rippin, Sally. The Extra-Special Helper. Fukuoka, Aki, illus. 2014. (ENG.). 48p. (J). pap. 4.99 *(978-1-61067-099-9(X))* Kane Miller.

Risco, Elle D. Dora Had a Little Lamb. Savitsky, Steve, illus. 2007. (Dora the Explorer Ser.). (J). (gr. -1-2). 11.65 *(978-0-7569-8294-2(4))* Perfection Learning Corp.

Rodenburg, Michelle. The Good Germ. 2007. (Illus.). 32p. (J). per. 10.95 net. *(978-0-9795407-1-4(2))* Grubnedor Pr.

Ryan, Darlene. Pieces of Me, 1 vol. 2012. (ENG.). 240p. (YA). (gr. 8-12). pap. 12.95 *(978-1-4598-0080-9(X))* Orca Bk. Pubs. USA.

Ryan, Pam Muñoz. Tony Baloney: Buddy Trouble. Fotheringham, Edwin, illus. 2014. (ENG.). 40p. (J). (gr. k-2). 6.99 *(978-0-545-48169-4(4)*, Scholastic Pr.) Scholastic, Inc.

—Tony Baloney: Buddy Trouble. Fotheringham, Ed, illus. 2013. 38p. (J). pap. *(978-0-545-48170-0(8))* Scholastic, Inc.

Rylant, Cynthia. Annie & Snowball & the Prettiest House. Stevenson, Sucie, illus. (Annie & Snowball Ser.: 2). (ENG.). 40p. (J). (gr. k-2). 2008. pap. 3.99 *(978-1-4169-1460-0(9))* 2007. 16.99 *(978-1-4169-0939-2(7))* Simon Spotlight. (Simon Spotlight).

Salmon, Casey. The Adventures of Mabel & Stinky: Mabel, Stinky, & the Terrified Toad. 2009. 44p. pap. 19.99 *(978-1-4389-7454-5(X))* AuthorHouse.

Santillo, LuAnn. Running Fox. Santillo, LuAnn, ed. 2003. (Half-Pint Kids Readers Ser.). (Illus.). 7p. (J). (gr. -1-1). pap. 1.00 *(978-1-59256-079-0(2))* Half-Pint Kids, Inc.

Sateren, Shelley Swanson. Max & Zoe: the Science Fair, 1 vol. Sullivan, Mary, illus. 2013. (Max & Zoe Ser.). (ENG.). 32p. (gr. k-2). pap. 5.19 *(978-1-4795-2330-6(5)*, Max & Zoe) Picture Window Bks.

Saugstad, Edward. Oakee Doakee & the Ego Bomb. 2008. 108p. pap. 19.95 *(978-0-9551503-9-5(6))* Checkpoint Pr. IRL. Dist: Printondemand-worldwide.com.

Scotton, Rob. The Big Helper. 2015. (Splat the Cat 8X8 Ser.). (J). lib. bdg. 13.55 *(978-0-606-36491-1(9))* Turtleback Bks.

Sebring, Janet And Jordan. Every Child Can Be a Hero. 2012. 36p. pap. 21.95 *(978-1-4685-3031-5(3))* AuthorHouse.

Shanghai Animation Studio Staff & Tang, Sanmu. A Deer of Nine Colors. Lee, Yawtsong, tr. from CHI. 2010. (Favorite Children's Ser.). (ENG., Illus.). 32p. (J). (gr. -1-3). pap. 5.95 *(978-1-60220-976-3(6))* BetterLink Pr., Inc.

Shannon, George. Wise Acres. Zemke, Deborah, illus. 2004. (ENG.). 40p. (J). (gr. -1-7). 15.95 *(978-1-59354-041-8(8)*, Handprint Bks.) Chronicle Bks. LLC.

Shannon Simmons. The Community Club: #1 Aubrey & the Fight for LIfe. 2009. 112p. pap. 10.95 *(978-1-4401-7616-6(7))* iUniverse, Inc.

Shea, Bob. Dinosaur vs. Mommy. Shea, Bob, illus. 2015. (Dinosaur vs. Book Ser.). (ENG., Illus.). 40p. (J). (gr. -1-k). 16.99 *(978-1-4231-6086-1(X))* Hyperion Bks. for Children.

Shelton, Dierdre A. Angels Surrounding Me. 2009. 32p. pap. 16.49 *(978-1-4389-4407-4(1))* AuthorHouse.

Singh, Jay. Once upon a Time in a Forest Far Away. 2009. 394p. pap. 33.12 *(978-1-4251-9122-1(3))* Trafford Publishing.

Slegers, Liesbet. Laura Ayuda a Su Mamá/ Laura Helps Her Mom. 2008. 28p. 10.95 *(978-84-263-6492-0(6))* Vives, Luis Editorial (Edelvives) ESP. Dist: Baker & Taylor Bks.

Smith, Diana M. Every Sock Needs a Mate. 2009. 36p. pap. 17.49 *(978-1-4389-2636-0(7))* AuthorHouse.

Smith, Kathy. Helping Hannah. 2010. (Rise & Shine Ser.). (ENG.). 12p. (C). (gr. -1-3). pap. 9.95 *(978-1-4042-6730-5(1))* National Geographic School Publishing, Inc.

Smith, Shirleen L. Not All Heroes Are on TV. 2011. 24p. (gr. -1). pap. 12.45 *(978-1-4497-1721-6(7)*, WestBow Pr.) Author Solutions, Inc.

Snedeker, Erin. The Littlest Elf: Marvin Mcgee & the Candle of Fate. Drotleff, David J., illus. 2010. 44p. pap. 15.50 *(978-1-60911-194-6(X)*, Eloquent Bks.) Strategic Book Publishing & Rights Agency (SBPRA).

Sparks, Favre. Agnes, the Eggless Quail. 2009. 28p. pap. 16.50 *(978-1-60693-491-3(0)*, Strategic Bk. Publishing) Strategic Book Publishing & Rights Agency (SBPRA).

Speak, Steven. Skip & L, Guardian Angel. 2011. 20p. pap. 12.45 *(978-1-4525-3643-9(0))* Get Published.

Steinlage, Ben. Bird Boy. 2011. 290p. pap. 17.95 *(978-1-4327-6667-2(8))* Outskirts Pr., Inc.

Tahir "Z", Zarghuna. The Lazy Froggies. 2012. 28p. (-18). pap. 19.99 *(978-1-4772-8907-5(0))* AuthorHouse.

Talarico Msn, Karen M. My Hands. 2008. 36p. pap. 15.75 *(978-1-4389-3521-8(8))* AuthorHouse.

Telle, Anita. Always Time for Kindness. 2012. (ENG.). (J). pap. *(978-1-4675-2560-2(X))* Independent Pub.

Theobald, Joseph. Marvin Gets Mad! 2013. pap. *(978-0-545-55294-3(X))* Scholastic, Inc.

Thomas Nelson. Playdate Pals Hamster Learns to Help. 2016. (ENG.). 24p. (J). (gr. -1-7). pap. *(978-1-78598-478-5(0))* Make Believe Ideas.

Timbers, James. Salmon & Fuzz in Helping a Friend. 2004. 30p. pap. 24.95 *(978-1-4137-2602-2(X))* PublishAmerica, Inc.

Townsan, Judy. The Wishing Flower, 1 vol. Rosado, Michael, illus. 2009. 13p. pap. 24.95 *(978-1-61546-179-0(5))* America Star Bks.

Trent, Rodney. Sadie Mae's Big Adventure. 2012. 28p. pap. 19.99 *(978-1-4772-6536-9(8))* AuthorHouse.

Urmina, Lisa. Milo & the Green Wagon. 2008. (Illus.). 32p. 15.95 *(978-0-9797429-4-1(3))* Halo Publishing International.

Urbanovic, Jackie. Ducks in a Row. Urbanovic, Jackie & Mathieu, Joe, illus. 2011. (I Can Read Level 1 Ser.). (ENG.). 32p. (J). (gr. k-3). 16.99 *(978-0-06-186438-4(2))*; pap. 3.99 *(978-0-06-186437-7(4))* HarperCollins Pubs.

Uribe, Denise. Queen MacHine. 2012. 24p. pap. 12.56 *(978-1-4669-6083-1(3))* Trafford Publishing.

Verdick, Elizabeth. On-the-Go Time. Heinlen, Marieka, illus. 2011. (Toddler Tools Ser.). (ENG.). 24p. (J). 7.95 *(978-1-57542-379-1(0)*, 1331978) Free Spirit Publishing, Inc.

Voght, Victor A. Fun with Huff & Puff, 1 vol. 2009. 15p. pap. 24.95 *(978-1-60749-853-7(7))* America Star Bks.

Waber, Bernard. Betty's Day Off. Date not set. (J). *(978-0-618-46875-1(7))* Houghton Mifflin Harcourt Publishing Co.

Waddell, Martin. You & Me, Little Bear. 2004. (Illus.). (J). (gr. -1-2). spiral bd. *(978-0-616-01802-6(9))*; spiral bd. *(978-0-616-01803-3(7))* Canadian National Institute for the Blind/Institut National Canadien pour les Aveugles.

Wallace, Carol. Turkeys Together. Rogers, Jaqueline & Rogers, Jacqueline, illus. 2005. (Holiday House Readers: Level 2 Ser.). (ENG.). 40p. (J). (gr. k-3). 15.95 *(978-0-8234-1895-4(2))* Holiday Hse., Inc.

Walshaw, Sam. Lulu Ladybug. 2012. (Illus.). (J). *(978-1-4351-3863-6(5))* Barnes & Noble, Inc.

Watts, Bernadette. The Golden Plate. 2014. (ENG., Illus.). 32p. (J). 17.95 *(978-0-7358-4175-8(6))* North-South Bks., Inc.

The Ways I Help. 2017. (Ways I Help Ser.). 24p. (gr. 4-6). 94.40 *(978-1-5081-5785-4(5))*; pap. 33.00 *(978-1-5081-5797-7(9))* Rosen Publishing Group, Inc., The. (PowerKids Pr.).

Weakley, David. Rowley to the Rescue. 2009. 72p. pap. 24.00 *(978-1-60860-295-7(8)*, Eloquent Bks.) Strategic Book Publishing & Rights Agency (SBPRA).

Wellesley, Rosie. The Very Helpful Hedgehog. Wellesley, Rosie, illus. 2012. (ENG., Illus.). 32p. (J). (gr. -1-k). pap. 11.99 *(978-1-84365-198-7(X)*, Pavilion Children's Books) Pavilion Bks. GBR. Dist: Independent Pubs. Group.

Wenger, Brahm. Dewey's Helping Heart: To Beneift the Larry King Cardiac Foundation. 2009. (ENG.). (J). (gr. -1-2). 18.95 incl. cd-rom *(978-0-9745143-7-6(3))* RandallFraser Publishing.

Wenger, Brahm & Green, Alan. Dewey Doo-It Builds a House: A Children's Story about Habitat for Humanity. 2006. (ENG., Illus.). 32p. (J). (gr. -1-2). 17.95 incl. lp *(978-0-9745143-2-1(2))* RandallFraser Publishing.

—Dewey Doo-It Feeds a Friend. Gillmore, Jean, illus. 2004. (J). *(978-0-9745143-0-7(6))* RandallFraser Publishing.

Weston Woods Staff, creator. A Kiss for Little Bear. 2011. 38.75 *(978-0-439-72739-6(1))*; 18.95 *(978-0-439-72735-8(9))*; 29.95 *(978-0-439-73481-3(9))* Weston Woods Studios, Inc.

Wheatonnovember. The Little Hermit Ant. 2011. 28p. pap. 24.95 *(978-1-4626-3805-5(8))* America Star Bks.

Wheeler, Lisa. Old Cricket. Goembel, Ponder, illus. 2006. 28p. (gr. -1-1). 18.00 *(978-0-7569-6795-6(3))* Perfection Learning Corp.

—Old Cricket. Goembel, Ponder, illus. (ENG.). 32p. (J). (gr. -1-1). 2003. 18.99 *(978-0-689-84510-9(3)*, Atheneum/Richard Jackson Bks.) 2006. reprint ed. 7.99 *(978-1-4169-1855-4(8)*, Atheneum Bks. for Young Readers) Simon & Schuster Children's Publishing.

Williams, C. G., illus. The Incredibly Helpful Helper. 2008. (ENG.). 40p. (J). (gr. -1-k). 14.95 *(978-0-7892-1001-2(0)*, Abbeville Kids) Abbeville Pr., Inc.

Winstead, Rosie. Sprout Helps Out. 2014. (ENG., Illus.). 32p. (J). (gr. -1-k). 16.99 *(978-0-8037-3072-4(1)*, Dial Bks) Penguin Young Readers Group.

Wolf, Linda. Cozy Kitty, 1 vol. 2009. 43p. pap. 24.95 *(978-1-61546-636-8(3))* America Star Bks.

Woods, Candy Godwin. Shimmer Finds Her Gift. 2009. 32p. pap. 13.00 *(978-1-60860-840-9(9)*, Eloquent Bks.) Strategic Book Publishing & Rights Agency (SBPRA).

Woods, Lin. Kenny Can: "Don't Judge Me" 2011. 24p. pap. 15.99 *(978-1-4568-9958-5(9))* Xlibris Corp.

Young, Leslie. Plaid: A Tale of Compassion. 2006. (Illus.). 15p. 9.00 *(978-1-4120-2793-9(4))* Trafford Publishing.

Ziegler, Argentina Palacios, tr. Dora y la Princesa de la Nieve (Dora Saves the Snow Princess) Aikins, Dave, illus. 2008. (Dora la Exploradora Ser.). (SPA.). 24p. (J). (gr. -1-2). pap. 3.99 *(978-1-4169-5870-3(3)*, Libros Para Ninos) Libros Para Ninos.

HELPING BEHAVIOR

see Helpfulness

HEMINGWAY, ERNEST, 1899-1961

Arnold, Quinn M. & Riggs, Kate. Ernest Hemingway. 2017. (Odysseys in Artistry Ser.). (ENG., Illus.). 80p. (J). (gr. 7-11). pap. 14.99 *(978-1-62832-313-9(2)*, Creative Paperbacks) Creative Co., The.

Bloom, Harold. A Farewell to Arms - Ernest Hemingway. 2nd rev. ed. 2009. (Modern Critical Interpretations Ser.). 244p. (C). (gr. 9). 45.00 *(978-0-7910-9624-6(6)*, Chelsea Hse.) Facts On File, Inc.

Bloom, Harold, intro. Nick Adams. 2004. (Bloom's Major Literary Characters Ser.). (Illus.). 177p. (C). (gr. 9-13). 40.00 *(978-0-7910-7885-3(X)*, Chelsea Hse.) Facts On File, Inc.

Boon, Kevin Alexander. Ernest Hemingway: The Sun Also Rises & Other Works. 2007. (Writers & Their Work Ser.). (Illus.). 144p. (gr. 7-18). lib. bdg. 42.79 *(978-0-7614-2590-8(X)*, Benchmark Bks.) Marshall Cavendish Corp.

Bryfonski, Dedria. Male & Female Roles in Ernest Hemingway's: The Sun Also Rises. 2008. (Social Issues in Literature Ser.). (ENG., Illus.). 224p. (gr. 10-12). 46.40 *(978-0-7377-4020-2(5)*, LML02109-239994, Greenhaven Pr., Inc.) Cengage Gale.

Bryfonski, Dedria, ed. Male & Female Roles in Ernest Hemingway's The Sun Also Rises. 2008. (Social Issues in Literature Ser.). (ENG., Illus.). 219p. (YA). (gr. 10-12). 28.45 *(978-0-7377-4021-9(3)*, LML02109-240000, Greenhaven Pr., Inc.) Cengage Gale.

Ernest Hemingway: The Search for Courage. 2014. (ENG.). 236p. (J). (gr. 3-7). pap. 14.95 *(978-1-59077-352-9(7))* Evans, M. & Co., Inc.

Pingelton, Timothy J. Reading & Interpreting the Works of Ernest Hemingway. 2017. (Lit Crit Guides). 160p. (J). (gr. 8-8). lib. bdg. 39.93 ***(978-0-7660-8489-6(2))*** Enslow Pubs., Inc.

Pingelton, Timothy J. A Student's Guide to Ernest Hemingway. 2005. (Understanding Literature Ser.). (Illus.). 160p. (YA). (gr. 7-13). lib. bdg. 29.27 *(978-0-7660-2431-1(8))* Enslow Pubs., Inc.

Reef, Catherine. Ernest Hemingway: A Writer's Life. 2009. (ENG., Illus.). 192p. (J). (gr. 5-7). 20.00 *(978-0-618-98705-4(3))* Houghton Mifflin Harcourt Publishing Co.

Riggs, Kate. Ernest Hemingway. (Illus.). (J). 2016. 80p. *(978-1-60818-717-1(9))* 2008. 48p. 22.95 *(978-1-58341-661-7(7))* Creative Co., The. (Creative Education).

Whiting, Jim. Ernest Hemingway. 2005. (Classic Storytellers Ser.). (Illus.). 48p. (J). (gr. 6-8). lib. bdg. 29.95 *(978-1-58415-376-4(8))* Mitchell Lane Pubs., Inc.

HENRY IV, KING OF FRANCE, 1553-1610

Abbott, J. S. C. History of Henry the Fourth, King of France & Navarre. 335p. reprint ed. 58.00 *(978-0-7950-2170-1(4))* New Library Press LLC.

HENRY VI, KING OF ENGLAND, 1421-1471

Price, Sean Stewart & Price, Sean. Henry VIII: Royal Beheader. 2009. (Wicked History Ser.). (ENG.). 128p. (J). (gr. 6-12). pap. 5.95 *(978-0-531-22173-0(3)*, Children's Pr.) Scholastic Library Publishing.

HENRY VIII, KING OF ENGLAND, 1491-1547

Ashworth, Leon. King Henry VIII. (Illus.). 32p. *(978-0-7451-5289-9(9))*; pap. *(978-0-7540-9012-0(4))* Cherrytree Bks.

Crompton, Samuel Willard. Thomas More: And His Struggles of Conscience. 2005. (Makers of the Middle Ages & Renaissance Ser.). (Illus.). 152p. (J). (gr. 5-8). lib. bdg. 32.95 *(978-0-7910-8636-0(4)*, Chelsea Hse.) Facts On File, Inc.

Graves, Michael A. R. Henry VIII. 2003. (Profiles in Power Ser.). (ENG.). 232p. (C). pap. 27.80 *(978-0-582-38110-0(X))* Longman Publishing.

Guy, John. Henry VIII & His Six Wives. 2004. (Illus.). 32p. (J). (gr. 4-7). pap. 5.95 *(978-1-86007-030-3(2)*, TickTock Books) Octopus Publishing Group GBR. Dist: Independent Pubs. Group.

Prati, Pablo. Enrique VIII. 2004. (Protagonistas Ser.). (SPA.). 96p. (YA). *(978-987-1129-59-1(9))* Grupo Visor E.A.S.A.

Wallace, Susan Helen & Jablonski, Patricia E. Saint Thomas More: Courage, Conscience, & the King. Lachuk, Dani, illus. 2014. (ENG.). 144p. (J). pap. 8.95 *(978-0-8198-9021-4(9))* Pauline Bks. & Media.

HENRY VIII, KING OF ENGLAND, 1491-1547—FICTION

Albritton, Emily. Henry I'm. 2011. 28p. pap. 13.68 *(978-1-4634-4251-4(3))* AuthorHouse.

Castor, H. M. VIII. 2013. (ENG., Illus.). 432p. (YA). (gr. 7). 17.99 *(978-1-4424-7418-5(1)*, Simon & Schuster Bks. For Young Readers) Simon & Schuster Bks. For Young Readers.

Hannah, Martha. The Ghost of Hampton Court. Dowell, Larry, illus. 2006. 32p. (J). 17.95 *(978-0-9779808-0-2(4))* CicadaSun.

Inns, Chris & Woods, Dave. Henry 1/8th. 2014. (ENG., Illus.). 64p. (J). (gr. k-2). pap. 5.99 *(978-1-4083-1361-9(8))* Hodder & Stoughton GBR. Dist: Hachette Bk. Group.

Longshore, Katherine. Gilt. 2013. (ENG.). 432p. (YA). (gr. 7). pap. 9.99 *(978-0-14-242619-7(9)*, Speak) Penguin Young Readers Group.

HENRY THE NAVIGATOR, 1394-1460

Ariganello, Lisa. Henry the Navigator: Prince of Portuguese Exploration. 2006. (In the Footsteps of Explorers Ser.). (ENG., Illus.). 32p. (J). (gr. 4-7). pap. *(978-0-7787-2469-8(7))*; lib. bdg. *(978-0-7787-2433-9(6))* Crabtree Publishing Co.

Gallagher, Aileen. Prince Henry the Navigator: Pioneer of Modern Exploration. rev. ed. (Library of Explorers & Explorationtm Ser.). (Illus.). 112p. (YA). (gr. 5-8). lib. bdg. 31.95 *(978-1-4042-0636-6(1)*, Rosen Reference) Rosen Publishing Group, Inc., The.

Hurwicz, Claude. Henry the Navigator. 2009. (Primary Source Library of Famous Explorers Ser.). 24p. (gr. 4-4). 42.50 *(978-1-60854-124-9(X)*, PowerKids Pr.) Rosen Publishing Group, Inc., The.

HENRY, INFANTE OF PORTUGAL, 1394-1460

see Henry the Navigator, 1394-1460

HENRY, PATRICK, 1736-1799

Adler, David A. A Picture Book of Patrick Henry. Wallner, John et al, illus. 2005. (ENG.). 32p. (J). (gr. k-3). pap. 6.95 *(978-0-8234-1678-3(X))* Holiday Hse., Inc.

Campion, Nardi Reeder. Patrick Henry: Firebrand of the Revolution. Mays, Victor, illus. 2011. 272p. 47.95 *(978-1-258-04065-9(4))* Literary Licensing, LLC.

Espinosa, Rod. Patrick Henry, 1 vol. Espinosa, Rod, illus. 2007. (Bio-Graphics Ser.). (ENG., Illus.). 32p. (gr. 3-6). 28.50 *(978-1-60270-070-3(2)*, Graphic Planet- Nonfiction) ABDO Publishing Co.

Glaser, Jason. Patrick Henry: Liberty or Death. McDonnell, Peter, illus. 2005. (Graphic Biographies Ser.). (ENG.). 32p. (gr. 3-4). 30.65 *(978-0-7368-4970-8(X)*, Graphic Library) Capstone Press of Coughlan Cos.

Harkins, Susan & Harkins, William H. The Life & Times of Patrick Henry. 2006. (Profiles in American History Ser.). (Illus.). 48p. (J). (gr. 4-8). lib. bdg. 29.95 *(978-1-58415-438-9(1))* Mitchell Lane Pubs., Inc.

Heinrichs, Ann. Patrick Henry: Orator & Patriot. 2004. (Our People Ser.). (ENG., Illus.). 32p. (J). (gr. 3-6). 29.93 *(978-1-59296-176-4(2)*, 200648) Child's World, Inc., The.

Jarnow, Jesse. Patrick Henry's Liberty or Death Speech: A Primary Source Investigation. (Great Historic Debates & Speeches Ser.). 64p. 2009. (gr. 5-8). 58.50 *(978-1-61513-120-4(5))* 2004. (Illus.). (J). lib. bdg. 31.95 *(978-1-4042-0152-1(1))* Rosen Publishing Group, Inc., The.

McPherson, Stephanie Sammartino. Liberty or Death: A Story about Patrick Henry. Debon, Nicolas, illus. 2003. (Creative Minds Biographies Ser.). (ENG.). 64p. (gr. 4-8). 22.60 *(978-1-57505-178-9(8))*; pap. 8.95 *(978-0-87614-930-0(1))* Lerner Publishing Group. (Carolrhoda Bks.).

Welch, Catherine A. Patrick Henry. 2006. (History Maker Bios Ser.). (Illus.). 48p. (J). (gr. 3-6). lib. bdg. 26.60 *(978-0-8225-5941-2(2)*, Lerner Pubns.) Lerner Publishing Group.

Weston Woods Staff, creator. Where Was Patrick Henry on the 29th of May? 2011. 38.75 *(978-1-55592-485-0(9))* 2004. 29.95 *(978-1-55592-484-3(0))* 2004. 18.95 *(978-1-55592-483-6(2))* Weston Woods Studios, Inc.

HENRY, PATRICK, 1736-1799—FICTION

Olasky, Susan. Annie Henry: Adventures in the American Revolution. 2005. (Illus.). 528p. (J). pap. 16.99 *(978-1-58134-521-6(6)*, Crossway Bibles) Crossway.

—Annie Henry & the Birth of Liberty. 2011. (J). pap. *(978-1-59638-375-3(5))* P & R Publishing.

—Annie Henry & the Mysterious Stranger. 2003. (Adventures of the American Revolution Ser.: Vol. 3). 144p. (YA). (gr. 3-7). pap. 5.99 *(978-0-89107-907-1(6))* Crossway.

—Annie Henry & the Mysterious Stranger. 2011. (J). pap. *(978-1-59638-376-0(3))* P & R Publishing.

—Annie Henry & the Redcoats. 2011. (J). pap. *(978-1-59638-377-7(1))* P & R Publishing.

—Annie Henry & the Secret Mission. 2011. (J). pap. *(978-1-59638-374-6(7))* P & R Publishing.

Rinaldi, Ann. Or Give Me Death. 2004. (Great Episodes Ser.). 226p. (gr. 5-9). 17.00 *(978-0-7569-3462-0(1))* Perfection Learning Corp.

—Or Give Me Death: A Novel of Patrick Henry's Family. 2004. (Great Episodes Ser.). (ENG.). 240p. (YA). (gr. 7-8). pap. 6.99 *(978-0-15-205076-4(0))* Houghton Mifflin Harcourt Publishing Co.

HENSON, MATTHEW ALEXANDER, 1866-1955

Bedesky, Baron. Peary & Henson: The Race to the North Pole. 2006. (In the Footsteps of Explorers Ser.). (ENG., Illus.). 32p. (J). (gr. 4-7). lib. bdg. *(978-0-7787-2426-1(3))* Crabtree Publishing Co.

Hopkinson, Deborah. Keep On! The Story of Matthew Henson, Co-Discoverer of the North Pole, 1 vol. Alcorn, Stephen, illus. 2009. (ENG.). 36p. (J). (gr. 1-5). 17.95 *(978-1-56145-473-0(7))* Peachtree Pubs.

Johnson, Dolores. Onward: A Photobiography of African-American Polar Explorer Matthew Henson. 2005.

(Photobiographies Ser.). (ENG., Illus.). 64p. (gr. k-3). 27.90 *(978-0-7922-7915-0(8))*; 17.95 *(978-0-7922-7914-3(X))* National Geographic Society. (National Geographic Children's Bks.).

Kramer, Candice. Matthew Henson at the North Pole. 2004. (Reader's Theater Ser.). (J). pap. *(978-1-4108-0798-4(3))* Benchmark Education Co.

Schwartz, Simon. First Man: Reimagining Matthew Henson. Watkinson, Laura, tr. 2015. (ENG., Illus.). 160p. (YA). (gr. 8-12). 31.99 *(978-1-4677-8856-4(2)*, Graphic Universe™) Lerner Publishing Group.

—First Man: The Voyages of Matthew Henson. Watkinson, Laura, tr. from GER. 2015. (ENG., Illus.). 160p. (J). (gr. 8-12). 31.99 *(978-1-4677-5842-0(6)*, Graphic Universe™) Lerner Publishing Group.

Scraper, Katherine. Matthew Henson. 2011. (Early Connections Ser.). (J). *(978-1-61672-563-1(X))* Benchmark Education Co.

Wade, Mary Dodson. Amazing Arctic Explorer Matthew Henson. 2013. (Amazing Americans Ser.). (Illus.). 24p. (J). (gr. k-3). pap. 7.95 *(978-0-7660-5974-0(X)*, Enslow Elementary) Enslow Pubs., Inc.

Weidt, Maryann N. Matthew Henson. 2003. (History Maker Bios Ser.). (Illus.). 48p. (J). (gr. 2-4). 26.60 *(978-0-8225-0397-2(2)*, Lerner Pubns.) Lerner Publishing Group.

HERACLES (GREEK MYTHOLOGY)

see also Hercules (Roman Mythology)

Ehrmann, Johanna. The Labors of Heracles, 1 vol., 1. 2014. (Jr. Graphic Myths: Greek Heroes Ser.). (ENG.). 24p. (J). (gr. 3-6). 26.25 *(978-1-4777-6224-0(8))*; pap. 10.60 *(978-1-4777-6225-7(6))* Rosen Publishing Group, Inc., The. (PowerKids Pr.).

Ford, James Evelyn & Salariya, David. The Twelve Labors of Hercules. Rutherford, Peter, illus. 2013. 32p. (J). *(978-1-4351-5120-8(8))* Barnes & Noble, Inc.

Griffin, Ingrid. The Story of Hercules. 2015. (Stories in the Stars Ser.). (ENG., Illus.). 24p. (J). (gr. 1-2). pap. 8.15 *(978-1-4824-2669-4(2))* Stevens, Gareth Publishing LLLP.

Harris, John. Strong Stuff: Herakles & His Labors. Baseman, Gary, illus. 2005. (ENG.). 32p. (gr. 3-7). 16.95 *(978-0-89236-784-9(9))* Oxford Univ. Pr., Inc.

Hoena, Blake, retold by. The 12 Labors of Hercules: A Graphic Retelling. 2015. (Ancient Myths Ser.). (ENG.). 32p. (gr. 3-4). lib. bdg. 30.65 *(978-1-4914-2071-3(5)*, Graphic Library) Capstone Press of Coughlan Cos.

Jeffrey, Gary. Hercules Fights the Nemean Lion. 2012. (Graphic Mythical Heroes Ser.). (Illus.). 24p. (J). (gr. 3-5). 23.95 *(978-1-4339-7511-0(4))*; pap. 8.15 *(978-1-4339-7512-7(2))* Stevens, Gareth Publishing LLLP. (Gareth Stevens Learning Library).

McCaughrean, Geraldine, retold by. Hercules. 2005. (Heroes Ser.). (ENG.). 152p. (J). (gr. 4-9). 17.95 *(978-0-8126-2737-4(7))* Cricket Bks.

Orr, Tamra. The Monsters of Hercules. 2010. (Monsters in Myth Ser.). (Illus.). 48p. (J). (gr. 4-7). lib. bdg. 29.95 *(978-1-58415-927-8(8))* Mitchell Lane Pubs., Inc.

Storrie, Paul D. Hercules. 2008. pap. 52.95 *(978-0-8225-9454-3(4))* Lerner Publishing Group.

—Hercules. Kurth, Steve, illus. 2007. (Graphic Myths & Legends Ser.). 48p. (J). 26.60 *(978-0-8225-3084-8(8))* Lerner Publishing Group.

—Hercules: Los Doce Trabajos; Hercules: the Twelve Labors. 2008. pap. 52.95 *(978-0-8225-9656-1(3))* Lerner Publishing Group.

—Hercules: Los Doce Trabajos: un Mito Griego. Kurth, Steve & Schulz, Barbara, illus. 2007. (Mitos y leyendas en viñetas (Graphic Myths & Legends) Ser.). (SPA.). 48p. (J). (gr. 4-7). per. 8.95 *(978-0-8225-7967-0(7)*, Ediciones Lerner) Lerner Publishing Group.

—Hercules: The Twelve Labors - A Greek Myth. Kurth, Steve, illus. 2007. (Graphic Myths & Legends Ser.). (ENG.). 48p. (gr. 4-8). per. 8.95 *(978-0-8225-6485-0(8))* Lerner Publishing Group.

—Hercules: The Twelve Labors [a Greek Myth]. Kurth, Steve, illus. 2015. (Graphic Myths & Legends Ser.). (ENG.). 48p. (gr. 4-8). 21.32 *(978-1-4677-5981-6(3)*, Lerner Digital) Lerner Publishing Group.

Van Lente, Fred. Hercules, 1 vol. 2015. (ENG., Illus.). 80p. (J). 35.60 *(978-1-4777-8137-1(4)*, Rosen Young Adult) Rosen Publishing Group, Inc., The.

Whiting, Jim. Hercules. 2007. (Profiles in Greek & Roman Mythology Ser.). (Illus.). 48p. (YA). (gr. 4-7). lib. bdg. 29.95 *(978-1-58415-553-9(1))* Mitchell Lane Pubs., Inc.

HERALDRY

see also Chivalry; Flags; Knights and Knighthood

Avett, Harper. I See the Bald Eagle. 2016. (Symbols of Our Country Ser.). 00024p. (J). (gr. 1-1). 23.60 *(978-1-4994-3051-6(5))*; pap. 8.25 *(978-1-4994-2763-9(8))* Rosen Publishing Group, Inc., The. (PowerKids Pr.).

Crewe, Sabrina. Beavers. 2015. (Canadian Symbols Ser.). (ENG.). 24p. (gr. k-1). 26.65 *(978-1-4914-7091-6(7))* Capstone Press of Coughlan Cos.

Deinard, Jenny. How to Draw Illinois's Sights & Symbols. 2009. (Kid's Guide to Drawing America Ser.). 32p. (gr. k-k). 50.50 *(978-1-61511-060-5(7)*, PowerKids Pr.) Rosen Publishing Group, Inc., The.

—How to Draw Indiana's Sights & Symbols. 2009. (Kid's Guide to Drawing America Ser.). 32p. (gr. k-k). 50.50 *(978-1-61511-063-6(1)*, PowerKids Pr.) Rosen Publishing Group, Inc., The.

—How to Draw Iowa's Sights & Symbols. 2009. (Kid's Guide to Drawing America Ser.). 32p. (gr. k-k). 50.50 *(978-1-61511-064-3(X)*, PowerKids Pr.) Rosen Publishing Group, Inc., The.

—How to Draw Kansas's Sights & Symbols. 2009. (Kid's Guide to Drawing America Ser.). 32p. (gr. k-k). 50.50 *(978-1-61511-065-0(8)*, PowerKids Pr.) Rosen Publishing Group, Inc., The.

—How to Draw Kentucky's Sights & Symbols. 2009. (Kid's Guide to Drawing America Ser.). 32p. (gr. k-k). 50.50 *(978-1-61511-066-7(6)*, PowerKids Pr.) Rosen Publishing Group, Inc., The.

—How to Draw Louisiana's Sights & Symbols. 2009. (Kid's Guide to Drawing America Ser.). 32p. (gr. k-k). 50.50 *(978-1-61511-067-4(4)*, PowerKids Pr.) Rosen Publishing Group, Inc., The.

—How to Draw Maine's Sights & Symbols. 2009. (Kid's Guide to Drawing America Ser.). 32p. (gr. k-k). 50.50 *(978-1-61511-068-1(2)*, PowerKids Pr.) Rosen Publishing Group, Inc., The.

—How to Draw Maryland's Sights & Symbols. 2009. (Kid's Guide to Drawing America Ser.). 32p. (gr. k-k). 50.50 *(978-1-61511-069-8(0)*, PowerKids Pr.) Rosen Publishing Group, Inc., The.

—How to Draw Massachusetts's Sights & Symbols. 2009. (Kid's Guide to Drawing America Ser.). 32p. (gr. k-k). 50.50 *(978-1-61511-070-4(4)*, PowerKids Pr.) Rosen Publishing Group, Inc., The.

—How to Draw Michigan's Sights & Symbols. 2009. (Kid's Guide to Drawing America Ser.). 32p. (gr. k-k). 50.50 *(978-1-61511-071-1(2)*, PowerKids Pr.) Rosen Publishing Group, Inc., The.

DeStefano, Susan. Symbols of America. 2004. (Reading PowerWorks Ser.). (Illus.). 16p. (gr. 1-3). pap. 6.10 *(978-0-7608-9258-9(X))* Sundance/Newbridge Educational Publishing.

Downing, Johnette. Louisiana, the Jewel of the Deep South, 1 vol. Marshall, Julia, illus. 2015. (ENG.). 32p. (J). (gr. k-3). 16.99 *(978-1-4556-2096-8(3))* Pelican Publishing Co., Inc.

Fazzi, Cindy. How to Draw Ireland's Sights & Symbols. 2009. (Kid's Guide to Drawing the Countries of the World Ser.). 48p. (gr. 4-4). 53.00 *(978-1-61511-114-5(X)*, PowerKids Pr.) Rosen Publishing Group, Inc., The.

Fein, E. How to Draw Nevada's Sights & Symbols. 2009. (Kid's Guide to Drawing America Ser.). 32p. (gr. k-k). 50.50 *(978-1-61511-077-3(1)*, PowerKids Pr.) Rosen Publishing Group, Inc., The.

—How to Draw New York's Sights & Symbols. 2009. (Kid's Guide to Drawing America Ser.). 32p. (gr. k-k). 50.50 *(978-1-61511-081-0(X)*, PowerKids Pr.) Rosen Publishing Group, Inc., The.

—How to Draw Oklahoma's Sights & Symbols. 2009. (Kid's Guide to Drawing America Ser.). 32p. (gr. k-k). 50.50 *(978-1-61511-089-6(5)*, PowerKids Pr.) Rosen Publishing Group, Inc., The.

Firestone, Mary, et al. Celebrate America: A Guide to America's Greatest Symbols. Skeens, Matthew, illus. 2010. (American Symbols Ser.). (ENG.). 208p. (gr. 1-2). pap. 15.95 *(978-1-4048-6170-1(X))* Picture Window Bks.

Gaspar, Joe. The Bald Eagle. 2013. (PowerKids Readers: American Symbols Ser.). (Illus.). 24p. (J). (gr. k-2). pap. 8.25 *(978-1-4777-0815-6(4))*; pap. 49.50 *(978-1-4777-0816-3(2))*; lib. bdg. 22.60 *(978-1-4777-0737-1(9))* Rosen Publishing Group, Inc., The. (PowerKids Pr.).

—The Bald Eagle / el Guila Calva. Alamn, Eduardo, ed. 2013. (PowerKids Readers: American Symbols / Smbolos de Amrica Ser.). (ENG & SPA.). 24p. (J). (gr. k-2). 22.60 *(978-1-4777-1205-4(4)*, PowerKids Pr.) Rosen Publishing Group, Inc., The.

Goldsworthy, Kaite. El Aguila de Cabeza Blanca. 2013. (Iconos Americanos Ser.). (SPA., Illus.). 24p. (J). (gr. k-2). lib. bdg. 27.13 *(978-1-62127-617-3(1)*, AV2 by Weigl) Weigl Pubs., Inc.

Gurtler, Janet. Maple Leaf. 2011. 24p. (YA). (gr. 2-4). *(978-1-77071-661-2(0))*; pap. *(978-1-77071-667-4(X))* Weigl Educational Pubs. Ltd.

Herrington, Lisa M. The Bald Eagle. 2014. (Rookie Read-About(r) American Symbols Ser.). (ENG., Illus.). 32p. (J). lib. bdg. *(978-0-531-21564-7(4))* Scholastic Library Publishing.

Kenney, Karen Latchana. The Bald Eagle, 1 vol. Hunt, Judith A., illus. 2011. (Our Nation's Pride Set 2 Ser.). (ENG.). 32p. (J). (gr. 1-4). 28.50 *(978-1-61641-149-7(X))* Magic Wagon.

Keppeler, Jill. Betsy Ross Didn't Create the American Flag: Exposing Myths about US Symbols. 2016. (Exposed! Myths about Early American History Ser.). 00032p. (J). pap. 10.50 *(978-1-4824-5717-9(2))* Stevens, Gareth Publishing LLLP.

Kuedee, Jaycee. How to Draw Minnesota's Sights & Symbols. 2009. (Kid's Guide to Drawing America Ser.). 32p. (gr. k-k). 50.50 *(978-1-61511-072-8(0)*, PowerKids Pr.) Rosen Publishing Group, Inc., The.

—How to Draw Mississippi's Sights & Symbols. 2009. (Kid's Guide to Drawing America Ser.). 32p. (gr. k-k). 50.50 *(978-1-61511-073-5(9)*, PowerKids Pr.) Rosen Publishing Group, Inc., The.

—How to Draw Missouri's Sights & Symbols. 2009. (Kid's Guide to Drawing America Ser.). 32p. (gr. k-k). 50.50 *(978-1-61511-074-2(7)*, PowerKids Pr.) Rosen Publishing Group, Inc., The.

—How to Draw Montana's Sights & Symbols. 2009. (Kid's Guide to Drawing America Ser.). 32p. (gr. k-k). 50.50 *(978-1-61511-075-9(5)*, PowerKids Pr.) Rosen Publishing Group, Inc., The.

Lambert, Nancy. The Star-Spangled Banner. 2016. (Smithsonian Ser.). (ENG., Illus.). 48p. (J). (gr. 3-4). pap. 3.99 *(978-1-101-99607-2(2)*, Penguin Young Readers) Penguin Young Readers Group.

Laplante, Walter. The Presidential Seal. 2015. (Symbols of America Ser.). (ENG.). 24p. (J). (gr. 1-2). pap. 8.15 *(978-1-4824-1886-6(X))* Stevens, Gareth Publishing LLLP.

Masura, Shauna. Digital Badges. 2013. (21st Century Skills Innovation Library: Makers As Innovators Ser.). (ENG.). 32p. (J). (gr. 4-8). 28.50 *(978-1-62431-143-7(1)*, 202892); pap. 14.21 *(978-1-62431-275-5(6)*, 202894) Cherry Lake Publishing.

Mis, M. S. How to Draw New Jersey's Sights & Symbols. 2009. (Kid's Guide to Drawing America Ser.). 32p. (gr. k-k). 50.50 *(978-1-61511-079-7(8)*, PowerKids Pr.) Rosen Publishing Group, Inc., The.

—How to Draw North Dakota's Sights & Symbols. 2009. (Kid's Guide to Drawing America Ser.). 32p. (gr. k-k). 50.50 *(978-1-61511-087-2(9)*, PowerKids Pr.) Rosen Publishing Group, Inc., The.

Mis, Melody S. How to Draw Australia's Sights & Symbols. 2009. (Kid's Guide to Drawing the Countries of the World Ser.). 48p. (gr. 4-4). 53.00 *(978-1-61511-107-7(7)*, PowerKids Pr.) Rosen Publishing Group, Inc., The.

—How to Draw Brazil's Sights & Symbols. 2009. (Kid's Guide to Drawing the Countries of the World Ser.). 48p. (gr. 4-4). 53.00 *(978-1-61511-108-4(5)*, PowerKids Pr.) Rosen Publishing Group, Inc., The.

—How to Draw India's Sights & Symbols. 2009. (Kid's Guide to Drawing the Countries of the World Ser.). 48p. (gr. 4-4). 53.00 *(978-1-61511-113-8(1)*, PowerKids Pr.) Rosen Publishing Group, Inc., The.

—How to Draw Kenya's Sights & Symbols. 2009. (Kid's Guide to Drawing the Countries of the World Ser.). 48p. (gr. 4-4). 53.00 *(978-1-61511-117-6(4)*, PowerKids Pr.) Rosen Publishing Group, Inc., The.

—How to Draw Norway's Sights & Symbols. 2009. (Kid's Guide to Drawing the Countries of the World Ser.). 48p. (gr. 4-4). 53.00 *(978-1-61511-119-0(0)*, PowerKids Pr.) Rosen Publishing Group, Inc., The.

Monroe, Tyler. Bald Eagle. 2013. (U. S. Symbols Ser.). (ENG.). 24p. (gr. k-1). 26.65 *(978-1-4765-3089-5(0))*; pap. 7.95 *(978-1-4765-3538-8(8))* Capstone Press of Coughlan Cos. (Pebble Plus).

—U. S. Symbols. 2013. (U. S. Symbols Ser.). (ENG.). 24p. (gr. k-1). pap. 41.70 *(978-1-4765-3721-4(6))*; lib. bdg. 159.90 *(978-1-4765-3720-7(8))* Capstone Press of Coughlan Cos. (Pebble Plus).

Moore Niver, Heather. Zoom in on the Bald Eagle. 2016. (Zoom in on American Symbols Ser.). 24p. (J). pap. 9.35 *(978-0-7660-8442-1(6))* Enslow Pubs., Inc.

—Zoom in on the Pledge of Allegiance. 2016. (Zoom in on American Symbols Ser.). 24p. (J). pap. 9.35 *(978-0-7660-8438-4(8))* Enslow Pubs., Inc.

Nelson, Maria. The Bald Eagle. 2015. (Symbols of America Ser.). (ENG.). 24p. (J). (gr. 1-2). 22.60 *(978-1-4824-1866-8(5))* Stevens, Gareth Publishing LLLP.

Pearl, Norman. The Pledge of Allegiance, 1 vol. Skeens, Matthew, illus. 2007. (American Symbols Ser.). (ENG.). 24p. (gr. 1-2). 9.95 *(978-1-4048-2647-2(5))* Picture Window Bks.

Peters, S. True. How to Draw New Hampshire's Sights & Symbols. 2009. (Kid's Guide to Drawing America Ser.). 32p. (gr. k-k). 50.50 *(978-1-61511-078-0(X)*, PowerKids Pr.) Rosen Publishing Group, Inc., The.

—How to Draw North Carolina's Sights & Symbols. 2009. (Kid's Guide to Drawing America Ser.). 32p. (gr. k-k). 50.50 *(978-1-61511-084-1(4)*, PowerKids Pr.) Rosen Publishing Group, Inc., The.

—How to Draw Oregon's Sights & Symbols. 2009. (Kid's Guide to Drawing America Ser.). 32p. (gr. k-k). 50.50 *(978-1-61511-090-2(9)*, PowerKids Pr.) Rosen Publishing Group, Inc., The.

Quasha, J. How to Draw Alabama's Sights & Symbols. 2009. (Kid's Guide to Drawing America Ser.). 32p. (gr. k-k). 50.50 *(978-1-61511-043-8(7)*, PowerKids Pr.) Rosen Publishing Group, Inc., The.

—How to Draw Alaska's Sights & Symbols. 2009. (Kid's Guide to Drawing America Ser.). 32p. (gr. k-k). 50.50 *(978-1-61511-044-5(5)*, PowerKids Pr.) Rosen Publishing Group, Inc., The.

Quasha, Jennifer. The Birth & Growth of a Nation: Hands-on Projects about Symbols of American Liberty. 2009. (Great Social Studies Projects Ser.). 24p. (gr. 3-3). 42.50 *(978-1-61513-212-6(0)*, PowerKids Pr.) Rosen Publishing Group, Inc., The.

—How to Draw Arizona's Sights & Symbols. 2009. (Kid's Guide to Drawing America Ser.). 32p. (gr. k-k). 50.50 *(978-1-61511-045-2(3)*, PowerKids Pr.) Rosen Publishing Group, Inc., The.

—How to Draw Arkansas's Sights & Symbols. 2009. (Kid's Guide to Drawing America Ser.). 32p. (gr. k-k). 50.50 *(978-1-61511-046-9(1)*, PowerKids Pr.) Rosen Publishing Group, Inc., The.

—How to Draw California's Sights & Symbols. 2009. (Kid's Guide to Drawing America Ser.). 32p. (gr. k-k). 50.50 *(978-1-61511-047-6(X)*, PowerKids Pr.) Rosen Publishing Group, Inc., The.

—How to Draw Colorado's Sights & Symbols. 2009. (Kid's Guide to Drawing America Ser.). 32p. (gr. k-k). 50.50 *(978-1-61511-050-6(X)*, PowerKids Pr.) Rosen Publishing Group, Inc., The.

—How to Draw Connecticut's Sights & Symbols. 2009. (Kid's Guide to Drawing America Ser.). 32p. (gr. k-k). 50.50 *(978-1-61511-051-3(8)*, PowerKids Pr.) Rosen Publishing Group, Inc., The.

—How to Draw Delaware's Sights & Symbols. 2009. (Kid's Guide to Drawing America Ser.). 32p. (gr. k-k). 50.50 *(978-1-61511-052-0(6)*, PowerKids Pr.) Rosen Publishing Group, Inc., The.

—How to Draw Florida's Sights & Symbols. 2009. (Kid's Guide to Drawing America Ser.). 32p. (gr. k-k). 50.50 *(978-1-61511-054-4(2)*, PowerKids Pr.) Rosen Publishing Group, Inc., The.

—How to Draw Georgia's Sights & Symbols. 2009. (Kid's Guide to Drawing America Ser.). 32p. (gr. k-k). 50.50 *(978-1-61511-057-5(7)*, PowerKids Pr.) Rosen Publishing Group, Inc., The.

—How to Draw Hawaii's Sights & Symbols. 2009. (Kid's Guide to Drawing America Ser.). 32p. (gr. k-k). 50.50 *(978-1-61511-058-2(5)*, PowerKids Pr.) Rosen Publishing Group, Inc., The.

—How to Draw Idaho's Sights & Symbols. 2009. (Kid's Guide to Drawing America Ser.). 32p. (gr. k-k). 50.50 *(978-1-61511-059-9(3)*, PowerKids Pr.) Rosen Publishing Group, Inc., The.

Scholastic, Inc. Staff & Keenan, Sheila. O, Say Can You See? America's Symbols, Landmarks, & Important Words. Boyajian, Ann, illus. 2007. (ENG.). 64p. (J). (gr. -1-3). pap. 6.99 *(978-0-439-59360-1(3)*, Scholastic Nonfiction) Scholastic, Inc.

Silate, Jennifer. The Bald Eagle. 2009. (Primary Sources of American Symbols Ser.). 24p. (gr. 3-3). 42.50 *(978-1-60851-508-0(7)*, PowerKids Pr.) Rosen Publishing Group, Inc., The.

Stanley, Robert E., Sr. Northwest Native Arts: Creative Colors 1, 2 vols. 2003. (Northwest Native Arts Ser.). (Illus.). 32p. (J). (gr. 3-18). pap. 6.95 *(978-0-88839-532-0(9))* Hancock Hse. Pubs.

—Northwest Native Arts: Creative Colors 2, 2 vols., Vol. 3. 2003. (North West Native Arts Ser.). (Illus.). 24p. (J). pap. 5.95 *(978-0-88839-533-7(7))* Hancock Hse. Pubs.

Sundance/Newbridge LLC Staff. Symbols of America. 2004. (Reading PowerWorks Ser.). (gr. 1-3). 37.50 *(978-0-7608-9257-2(1))* Sundance/Newbridge Educational Publishing.

The Symbols of America. 2015. (Symbols of America Ser.). (ENG.). 24p. (J). (gr. 1-2). 135.60 *(978-1-4824-1635-0(2))* Stevens, Gareth Publishing LLLP.

Tecco, Betsy Dru. How to Draw France's Sights & Symbols. 2009. (Kid's Guide to Drawing the Countries of the World Ser.). 48p. (gr. 4-4). 53.00 *(978-1-61511-110-7(7)*, PowerKids Pr.) Rosen Publishing Group, Inc., The.

—How to Draw Germany's Sights & Symbols. 2009. (Kid's Guide to Drawing the Countries of the World Ser.). 48p. (gr. 4-4). 53.00 *(978-1-61511-111-4(5)*, PowerKids Pr.) Rosen Publishing Group, Inc., The.

—How to Draw Italy's Sights & Symbols. 2009. (Kid's Guide to Drawing the Countries of the World Ser.). 48p. (gr. 4-4). 53.00 *(978-1-61511-115-2(8)*, PowerKids Pr.) Rosen Publishing Group, Inc., The.

—How to Draw Japan's Sights & Symbols. 2009. (Kid's Guide to Drawing the Countries of the World Ser.). 48p. (gr. 4-4). 53.00 *(978-1-61511-116-9(6)*, PowerKids Pr.) Rosen Publishing Group, Inc., The.

Tresco, Betsy Dru. How to Draw Hungary's Sights & Symbols. 2009. (Kid's Guide to Drawing the Countries of the World Ser.). 48p. (gr. 4-4). 53.00 *(978-1-61511-112-1(3)*, PowerKids Pr.) Rosen Publishing Group, Inc., The.

Weintraub, A. How to Draw District of Columbia's Sights & Symbols. 2009. (Kid's Guide to Drawing America Ser.). 32p. (gr. k-k). 50.50 *(978-1-61511-053-7(4)*, PowerKids Pr.) Rosen Publishing Group, Inc., The.

—How to Draw Nebraska's Sights & Symbols. 2009. (Kid's Guide to Drawing America Ser.). 32p. (gr. k-k). 50.50 *(978-1-61511-076-6(3)*, PowerKids Pr.) Rosen Publishing Group, Inc., The.

—How to Draw New Mexico's Sights & Symbols. 2009. (Kid's Guide to Drawing America Ser.). 32p. (gr. k-k). 50.50 *(978-1-61511-080-3(1)*, PowerKids Pr.) Rosen Publishing Group, Inc., The.

—How to Draw Ohio's Sights & Symbols. 2009. (Kid's Guide to Drawing America Ser.). 32p. (gr. k-k). 50.50 *(978-1-61511-088-9(7)*, PowerKids Pr.) Rosen Publishing Group, Inc., The.

Yasuda, Anita. The 12 Most Amazing American Monuments & Symbols. 2015. (ENG., Illus.). 32p. (J). pap. 9.95 *(978-1-63235-069-5(6))* RiverStream Publishing.

Zoom in on American Symbols. 2016. (Zoom in on American Symbols Ser.). 24p. (J). lib. bdg. 135.60 *(978-0-7660-8419-3(1))* Enslow Pubs., Inc.

HERBAGE

see Grasses

HERBALS

see Botany; Herbs; Materia Medica

HERBS

Gleason, Carrie. The Biography of Tobacco. 2006. (How Did That Get Here? Ser.). (ENG., Illus.). 32p. (J). (gr. 4-7). lib. bdg. *(978-0-7787-2489-6(1)*, 1259497) Crabtree Publishing Co.

Lundgren, Julie K. Plants As Food, Fuel, & Medicine. 2012. (ENG.). 24p. (gr. 4-5). pap. 8.95 *(978-1-61810-235-5(4))* Rourke Educational Media.

Morgan, Sally. How We Use Plants for Medicine & Health. (How We Use Plants Ser.). (Illus.). 32p. 2009. (ENG.). (gr. 2-5). pap. 10.60 *(978-1-4358-2613-7(2))* 2008. (J). lib. bdg. 26.50 *(978-1-4042-4423-8(9))* Rosen Publishing Group, Inc., The. (PowerKids Pr.).

San Francisco, Carolina Diaz. The Fantastic Herbs. 2013. 26p. pap. 9.95 *(978-1-939289-08-7(4)*, Little Creek Bks.) Jan-Carol Publishing, INC.

HERBS, MEDICAL

see Botany, Medical

HERCULES (ROMAN MYTHOLOGY)

see also Heracles (Greek Mythology)

Griffin, Ingrid. The Story of Hercules. 2015. (Stories in the Stars Ser.). (ENG., Illus.). 24p. (J). (gr. 1-2). pap. 8.15 *(978-1-4824-2669-4(2))* Stevens, Gareth Publishing LLLP.

Hoena, Blake, retold by. The 12 Labors of Hercules: A Graphic Retelling. 2015. (Ancient Myths Ser.). (ENG.). 32p. (gr. 3-4). lib. bdg. 30.65 *(978-1-4914-2071-3(5)*, Graphic Library) Capstone Press of Coughlan Cos.

Orr, Tamra. The Monsters of Hercules. 2010. (Monsters in Myth Ser.). (Illus.). 48p. (J). (gr. 4-7). lib. bdg. 29.95 *(978-1-58415-927-8(8))* Mitchell Lane Pubs., Inc.

Roesser, Blanche. The Story of Leo the Lion. 2015. (Stories in the Stars Ser.). (ENG., Illus.). 24p. (J). (gr. 1-2). pap. 8.15 *(978-1-4824-2673-1(0))* Stevens, Gareth Publishing LLLP.

Rose, Simon. Hercules: The Myth & Science. 2015. (Illus.). 24p. (J). *(978-1-5105-0016-7(2))* SmartBook Media, Inc.

Van Lente, Fred. Hercules, 1 vol. 2015. (ENG., Illus.). 80p. (J). 35.60 *(978-1-4777-8137-1(4)*, Rosen Young Adult) Rosen Publishing Group, Inc., The.

HERCULES (ROMAN MYTHOLOGY)—FICTION

Cartwright, Stephen, illus. Hercules. 2004. (Young Reading Series Two Ser.). 64p. (J). (gr. 2-18). pap. 5.95 *(978-0-7945-0453-3(1)*, Usborne) EDC Publishing.

Collins Morgan, Connie. Hercules on the Bayou, 1 vol. Leonhard, Herb, illus. 2016. (ENG.). 32p. (J). (gr. k-3). 16.99 *(978-1-4556-2185-9(4))* Pelican Publishing Co., Inc.

Evslin, Bernard. Hercules. 2016. (ENG.). 152p. (J). (gr. 3-6). pap. 11.99 *(978-1-5040-3562-0(3))* Open Road Integrated Media, Inc.

Holub, Joan. Play Nice, Hercules! Patricelli, Leslie, illus. 2014. (Mini Myths Ser.). (ENG.). 24p. (J). (gr. -1 — 1). bds. 6.95 *(978-1-4197-0954-8(2)*, Abrams Appleseed) Abrams, Inc.

McMullan, Kate. Get to Work, Hercules!, 1 vol. Zilber, Denis, illus. (Myth-O-Mania Ser.: Bk. 7). (ENG.). 208p. (gr. 4-8). 2011. pap. 5.95 *(978-1-4342-3440-7(1))* 2010. lib. bdg. 25.32 *(978-1-4342-3196-3(8))* Stone Arch Bks. (Myth-O-Mania).

HEREDITY

Anders, Mason. DNA, Genes, & Chromosomes. 2017. (Genetics Ser.). (ENG.). 32p. (gr. 3-4). lib. bdg. 27.32 ***(978-1-5157-7256-9(X))*** Capstone Press of Coughlan Cos.

—Heredity. 2017. (Genetics Ser.). (ENG.). 32p. (gr. 3-4). lib. bdg. 27.32 ***(978-1-5157-7257-6(8))*** Capstone Press of Coughlan Cos.

Benchmark Education Company. Heredity (Teacher Guide) 2005. *(978-1-4108-4650-1(4))* Benchmark Education Co.

H
I

Boothroyd, Jennifer. Eye Color: Brown, Blue, Green, & Other Hues. 2012. (Lightning Bolt Books (tm) — What Traits Are in Your Genes? Ser.). (Illus.). 32p. (gr. k-2). (SPA & ENG.). pap. 7.95 *(978-1-58013-954-0(X))*; (ENG., lib. bdg. 26.60 *(978-0-7613-8938-5(5))* Lerner Publishing Group.

Brannon, Barbara. Discover Heredity. 2005. (J). pap. *(978-1-4108-5136-9(2))* Benchmark Education Co.

Christie, Lee. Basic Heredity: Set Of 6. 2011. (Navigators Ser.). (J). pap. 50.00 net. *(978-1-4108-6238-9(0))* Benchmark Education Co.

—Basic Heredity: Text Pairs. 2008. (Bridges/Navigators Ser.). (J). (gr. 6). 89.00 *(978-1-4108-8431-2(7))* Benchmark Education Co.

Day, Trevor. Genetics: Investigating the Function of Genes & the Science of Heredity. 2012. (Scientific Pathways Ser.). (ENG., Illus.). 48p. (YA). (gr. 5-8). 27.95 *(978-1-4488-7199-5(9)*, Rosen Reference) Rosen Publishing Group, Inc., The.

Genes & Disease Set, 10-Volumes. 2009. (Genes & Disease Ser.). (C). (gr. 9-18). 350.00 *(978-0-7910-9921-6(0)*, Chelsea Hse.) Facts On File, Inc.

Green, Jen. Inheritance of Traits: Why Is My Dog Bigger Than Your Dog?, 1 vol. 2014. (Show Me Science Ser.). (ENG.). 32p. (gr. 3-5). lib. bdg. 30.65 *(978-1-4329-8747-3(X)*, Raintree Perspectives) Heinemann-Raintree.

Hand, Carol. Introduction to Genetics. 2010. (Understanding Genetics Ser.). (ENG.). 80p. (YA). lib. bdg. 33.25 *(978-1-4358-9531-7(2))* Rosen Publishing Group, Inc., The.

Hawley, Ella. Exploring Heredity. 2012. (Let's Explore Life Science Ser.). (ENG., Illus.). 24p. (J). (gr. 3-6). pap. 8.25 *(978-1-4488-6312-9(0))*; lib. bdg. 22.60 *(978-1-4488-6174-3(8))* Rosen Publishing Group, Inc., The. (PowerKids Pr.).

Holt, Rinehart and Winston Staff. Holt Science & Technology Chapter 5: Life Science: Heredity. 5th ed. 2004. (Illus.). pap. 12.86 *(978-0-03-030181-0(5))* Holt McDougal.

Lew, Kristi. Heredity. 2009. (Science Foundations Ser.). (Illus.). 128p. (J). (gr. 7-12). lib. bdg. 35.00 *(978-1-60413-042-3(3))* Facts On File, Inc.

Parsons, Michelle Hyde. Heredity. 2005. (J). pap. *(978-1-4108-4602-0(4))* Benchmark Education Co.

Quinn, Lauren D. Heredity. 2016. (Illus.). 32p. (J). *(978-1-5105-1186-6(5))* SmartBook Media, Inc.

Rice, Dona. All in the Family, 1 vol. rev. ed. 2014. (Science Readers: Content & Literacy Ser.). (ENG., Illus.). 24p. (gr. 1-1). pap. 8.99 *(978-1-4807-4563-6(4))* Teacher Created Materials, Inc.

Silverman, Buffy. Hair Traits: Color, Texture, & More. 2012. (Lightning Bolt Books (tm) — What Traits Are in Your Genes? Ser.). (Illus.). 32p. (gr. k-2). (SPA & ENG.). pap. 7.95 *(978-1-58013-956-4(6))*; (ENG., lib. bdg. 26.60 *(978-0-7613-8941-5(5)*, Lerner Pubns.) Lerner Publishing Group.

Stille, Darlene R. & Ryback, Carol. Heredity. 2007. (Gareth Stevens Vital Science- Life Science Ser.). (Illus.). 48p. (gr. 5-12). lib. bdg. 27.00 *(978-0-8368-8439-5(6)*, Gareth Stevens Secondary Library) Stevens, Gareth Publishing LLLP.

Tweet, Jonathan. Grandmother Fish: A Child's First Book of Evolution. Lewis, Karen, illus. 2016. (ENG.). 40p. (J). 17.99 *(978-1-250-11323-8(7)*, 9781250113238) Feiwel & Friends.

World Book, Inc Staff, contrib. by. Traits & Heredity. 2014. (Illus.). 32p. (J). *(978-0-7166-2827-9(9))* World Bk., Inc.

HERMETISM

see Alchemy; Astrology; Occultism

HERMITS—FICTION

Ballantyne, R. M. Blown to Bits; or, the Lonely Man of Rak. 2006. pap. *(978-1-4065-0515-3(3))* Dodo Pr.

Barry, Jack. The Hermit's Handbook. Leue, Mary, ed. Leue, Mary, illus. Leue, Mary, photos by. 2004. (Philaterra Ser.). 208p. pap. 12.95 *(978-1-878115-14-0(6))* Down-To-Earth-Bks.

Bauer, Joan. Backwater. rev. ed. 2005. (ENG.). 192p. (YA). (gr. 7-12). pap. 7.99 *(978-0-14-240434-8(9)*, Speak) Penguin Young Readers Group.

—Backwater. 2005. 185p. 18.00 *(978-0-7569-5779-7(6))* Perfection Learning Corp.

Clarke, Jane. Sherman Swaps Shells. Parker, Ant, illus. 2003. (Flying Foxes Ser.). (ENG.). 48p. (J). lib. bdg. *(978-0-7787-1485-9(3))* Crabtree Publishing Co.

Gaetz, Dayle Campbell. Crossbow, 1 vol. 2007. (Orca Currents Ser.). (ENG.). 112p. (J). (gr. 5-9). pap. 9.95 *(978-1-55143-841-2(0))*; lib. bdg. 14.95 *(978-1-55143-843-6(7))* Orca Bk. Pubs. USA.

Krejewski, Sandra. The Little Hermit Crab. 2009. 21p. (J). 12.00 *(978-1-60695-004-3(5))* Callanish Pr.

Martin, Lance. The Little Hermit. 2008. 56p. pap. 14.95 *(978-0-9815573-1-1(7))* Highland Pr.

Nervelle, Rosemarie. The Witch of Beaver Creek Mine. 2007. (ENG.). 160p. (J). (gr. 3-7). 14.95 *(978-0-89272-741-4(1))*; 2nd ed. pap. 9.95 *(978-0-89272-763-6(2))* Down East Bks.

Roddy, Lee. The Hermit of Mad River. 2008. (D. J. Dillon Adventure Ser.: No. 9). (J). 8.99 *(978-0-88062-273-8(3))* Mott Media.

Tucker, Valerie Nell. The Hermit's Box. 2009. 36p. pap. 15.49 *(978-1-4490-2285-3(5))* AuthorHouse.

HEROES

see also Courage; Explorers; Mythology; Saints

Allberti, Frances C. Finding Rover. Gremillion, Barry, illus. 2006. (J). per. *(978-0-9785937-1-1(5))* Open Pages Publishing.

American Heroes, Group 2, 6 bks., Set. Incl. Booker T. Washington: Getting into the Schoolhouse. Brimner, Larry Dane. (YA). lib. bdg. 29.93 *(978-0-7614-3063-6(6))*; Chief Crazy Horse: Following a Vision. Brimner, Larry Dane. lib. bdg. 29.93 *(978-0-7614-3061-2(X))*; Eleanor Roosevelt: Making the World a Better Place. Collard, Sneed B., III. lib. bdg. 29.93 *(978-0-7614-3069-8(5))*; John Glenn: Hooked on Flying. Collard, Sneed B., III. (Illus.). (J). lib. bdg. 29.93 *(978-0-7614-3066-7(0))*; Pocahontas: Bridging Two Worlds. Brimner, Larry Dane. lib. bdg. 29.93 *(978-0-7614-3065-0(2))*; Thomas Jefferson: Let Freedom Ring! Collard, Sneed B., III. lib. bdg. 29.93 *(978-0-7614-3067-4(9))*; 48p. (gr. 3-18). 2008. Set lib. bdg. 179.57 *(978-0-7614-3060-5(1)*, Benchmark Bks.) Marshall Cavendish Corp.

Barron, T. A. The Hero's Trail: A Guide for a Heroic Life. 2007. (ENG., Illus.). 192p. (J). (gr. 3-7). 8.99 *(978-0-14-240760-8(7)*, Puffin Books) Penguin Young Readers Group.

Beardsley, Sally. The 10 Bravest Everyday Heroes. 2007. 14.99 *(978-1-55448-488-1(X))* Scholastic Library Publishing.

Beaumont, Steve. How to Draw Warriors. (Drawing Fantasy Art Ser.). 32p. (gr. 4-5). 2009. 50.50 *(978-1-61512-194-6(3)*, PowerKids Pr.) 2007. (Illus.). (J). lib. bdg. 26.50 *(978-1-4042-3858-9(1))* Rosen Publishing Group, Inc., The.

—How to Draw Wizards, Warriors, Orcs & Elves. 2007. (Illus.). 143p. pap. 7.99 *(978-0-7858-2345-2(X)*, Chartwell) Book Sales, Inc.

BeaverSimon. SAVED! HEROES IN EVERYDAY LIFE BEGINNING BOOK WITH ONLINE ACCESS. 2014. (ENG., Illus.). 24p. pap. 7.50 *(978-1-107-64705-3(3))* Cambridge Univ. Pr.

Beck, Glenn. Book of American Heroes. Ajhar, Brian, illus. 2011. (ENG.). 276p. (J). 19.99 *(978-1-4424-2332-9(3)*, Simon & Schuster/Paula Wiseman Bks.) Simon & Schuster/Paula Wiseman Bks.

Berrios, Frank. The Big Book of the DC Super Friends. Golden Books, illus. 2015. (Big Golden Book Ser.). (ENG.). 48p. (J). (gr. k-4). 9.99 *(978-0-553-50773-7(7)*, Golden Bks.) Random Hse. Children's Bks.

Bledsoe, Karen & Bledsoe, Glen. Helicopters: High-Flying Heroes. 2006. (Mighty Military Machines Ser.). (Illus.). 48p. (J). (gr. 4-10). lib. bdg. 25.27 *(978-0-7660-2663-6(9))* Enslow Pubs., Inc.

Bodie, Idella. Heroes & Heroines of the American Revolution. 2004. (Illus.). 48p. (J). pap., instr.'s gde. ed. *(978-0-87844-173-0(5))* Sandlapper Publishing Co., Inc.

—Heroines of the American Revolution. 2003. (Illus.). 99p. (J). pap. 6.95 *(978-0-87844-170-9(0))* Sandlapper Publishing Co., Inc.

Boyer, Crispin. The Book of Heroes: Tales of History's Most Daring Guys. 2016. (ENG., Illus.). 176p. (J). (gr. 3-7). 14.99 *(978-1-4263-2553-3(3)*, National Geographic Children's Bks.) National Geographic Society.

Calcium Staff, contrib. by. The Heroes & Mortals of Greek Mythology, 1 vol. 2011. (Ancient Greek Mythology Ser.). (ENG.). 64p. (gr. 5-7). lib. bdg. 33.99 *(978-0-7565-4480-5(7)*, CPB Grades 4-8) Compass Point Bks.

Callery, Sean. Warriors: The Greatest Fighters in History. 2015. (ENG.). 80p. (J). (gr. 5-9). pap. 10.99 *(978-0-545-85184-8(X))* Scholastic, Inc.

Carroll, Colleen. How Artists See Heroes: Myth, History, War, Everyday. 2003. (How Artists See Ser.). (ENG., Illus.). 48p. (J). (gr. k-7). 12.95 *(978-0-7892-0773-9(7))* Abbeville Pr., Inc.

Ceceri, Kathy. World Myths & Legends: 25 Projects You Can Build Yourself. Braley, Shawn, illus. 2010. (Build It Yourself Ser.). (ENG.). 128p. (J). (gr. 3-7). 21.95 *(978-1-934670-44-6(8))* Octavio Publishing.

Chaline, Eric. Secret Heroes of World War II: Tales of Courage from the Worlds of Espionage & Resistance. 2016. (Illus.). 224p. (YA). **(978-1-4351-6251-8(X))** Metro Bks.

Chilman-Blair, Kim. Superheroes on a Medical Mission, 6 vols., Set 2. Incl. Medikidz Explain ADHD. Taddeo, John. lib. bdg. 29.25 *(978-1-4358-9456-3(1))*; Medikidz Explain Autism. Taddeo, John. lib. bdg. 29.25 *(978-1-4358-9460-0(X))*; Medikidz Explain Depression. Deloache, Shawn. lib. bdg. 29.25 *(978-1-4358-9455-6(3))*; Medikidz Explain HIV. Taddeo, John. lib. bdg. 29.25 *(978-1-4358-9458-7(8))*; Medikidz Explain Sleep Apnea. Deloache, Shawn. lib. bdg. 29.25 *(978-1-4358-9459-4(6))*; Medikidz Explain Swine Flu. lib. bdg. 29.25 *(978-1-4358-9457-0(X))*; (YA). (gr. 5-8). (Illus.). 40p. 2010. Set lib. bdg. 175.50 *(978-1-4358-9570-6(3)*, Rosen Reference) Rosen Publishing Group, Inc., The.

Chin-Lee, Cynthia. Akira to Zoltan: Twenty-Six Men Who Changed the World. Halsey, Megan & Addy, Sean, illus. 2006. (ENG.). 32p. (J). (gr. 3-7). lib. bdg. 15.95 *(978-1-57091-579-6(2))* Charlesbridge Publishing, Inc.

Collard, Sneed B., III. American Heroes, 6 bks., Set. Incl. Abraham Lincoln: A Courageous Leader. 48p. lib. bdg. 29.93 *(978-0-7614-2162-7(9))*; Benjamin Franklin: The Man Who Could Do Just about Anything. 48p. lib. bdg. 29.93 *(978-0-7614-2161-0(0))*; David Crockett: Fearless Frontiersman. 40p. (J). lib. bdg. 28.50 *(978-0-7614-2160-3(2))*; John Adams: Our Second President. 48p. 29.93 *(978-0-7614-2159-7(9))*; Rosa Parks: The Courage to Make a Difference. 48p. lib. bdg. 29.93 *(978-0-7614-2163-4(7))*; Sacagawea: Brave Shoshone Girl. 48p. lib. bdg. 29.93 *(978-0-7614-2166-5(1))*; (Illus.). (gr. 3-7). 2006. 2006. Set lib. bdg. 179.57 *(978-0-7614-2158-0(0)*, Benchmark Bks.) Marshall Cavendish Corp.

Collier, Peter. Choosing Courage: Inspiring Stories of What It Means to Be a Hero. (ENG., Illus.). (J). 2016. 272p. (gr. 4-6). pap. 8.95 *(978-1-57965-705-5(2))* 2015. 240p. 18.95 *(978-1-57965-596-9(3))* Artisan.

Cullis, Megan. Sticker Dressing Heroes. 2012. (Sticker Dressing Ser.). 24p. (J). pap. 8.99 *(978-0-7945-3267-3(5)*, Usborne) EDC Publishing.

Denenberg, Dennis & Roscoe, Lorraine. 50 American Heroes Every Kid Should Meet. rev. ed. 2005. (ENG., Illus.). 128p. (gr. 6-12). pap. 14.95 *(978-0-7613-9548-5(2)*, First Avenue Editions) Lerner Publishing Group.

—50 American Heroes Every Kid Should Meet (2nd Revised Edition) 2016. (ENG., Illus.). 120p. (J). (gr. 6-12). 53.32 *(978-1-5124-1329-8(1)*, Millbrook Pr.) Lerner Publishing Group.

Don, Lari. Girls & Goddesses: Stories of Heroines from Around the World. Greenwood, Francesca, illus. 2016. (World of Stories Ser.). (ENG.). 120p. (J). (gr. 2-6). 26.65 *(978-1-5124-1317-5(8))* Lerner Publishing Group.

Dorling Kindersley Publishing Staff. The Amazing Book of Marvel Spider-Man. 2017. (ENG.). 48p. (J). (gr. k-4). 14.99 ***(978-1-4654-5561-1(2)***, DK Children) Dorling Kindersley Publishing, Inc.

—Marvel the Avengers. 2015. (ENG.). 96p. (J). (gr. 2-5). pap. 12.99 *(978-1-4654-3249-0(3)*, DK Children) Dorling Kindersley Publishing, Inc.

—Ultimate Sticker Collection: DC Comics Wonder Woman. 2017. (Ultimate Sticker Collections). (ENG.). 96p. (J). (gr. 1-4). pap. 12.99 *(978-1-4654-6076-9(4)*, DK Children) Dorling Kindersley Publishing, Inc.

Dorling Kindersley Publishing Staff & Taylor, Victoria. Super-Villains Level 2. 2013. (DK Readers Ser.). (ENG., Illus.). 32p. (J). (gr. 1-3). pap. 3.99 *(978-1-4654-0176-2(8)*, DK Children) Dorling Kindersley Publishing, Inc.

Doyle, Bill H. Behind Enemy Lines. 2009. 135p. (J). pap. *(978-0-545-14705-7(0))* Scholastic, Inc.

Drimmer, Stephanie Warren. The Book of Heroines: Tales of History's Gutsiest Gals. 2016. (ENG., Illus.). 176p. (J). (gr. 3-7). 14.99 *(978-1-4263-2557-1(6)*, National Geographic Children's Bks.) National Geographic Society.

Edgar, Susan E. & Edgar, Kathleen J. 50 American Women of Courage & Vision. 2007. (Illus.). 288p. (J). *(978-1-58865-391-8(9))* Kidsbooks, LLC.

Egan, Tracie. Francisca Alvarez: El ángel de Goliad (Francisca Alvarez: the Angel of Goliad) 2009. (Grandes personajes en la historia de los Estados Unidos (Famous People in American History) Ser.). (SPA.). 32p. (gr. 2-3). 47.90 *(978-1-61512-798-6(4)*, Editorial Buenas Letras) Rosen Publishing Group, Inc., The.

—Francisca Alvarez: The Angel of Goliad. 2009. (Primary Sources of Famous People in American History Ser.). 32p. (gr. 2-3). 47.90 *(978-1-60851-675-9(X))* Rosen Publishing Group, Inc., The.

—Francisca Alvarez: The Angel of Goliad / el ángel de Goliad. 2009. (Famous People in American History/Grandes personajes en la historia de los Estados Unidos Ser.). (ENG & SPA.). 32p. (gr. 2-3). 47.90 *(978-1-61512-544-9(2)*, Editorial Buenas Letras) Rosen Publishing Group, Inc., The.

Fingeroth, David. Age of the Avengers. 2015. (ENG.). 12p. (J). (gr. k-2). 10.99 *(978-0-7944-3270-6(0)*, Reader's Digest Children's Bks.) Studio Fun International.

Fisher-Shumpert, Sharon Y. Sadie's Hero. 2007. 42p. (J). pap. 10.00 *(978-0-9794871-0-1(2))* SYS Publishing.

Fremon, David K. Schindler, Wallenberg, Miep Gies: The Holocaust Heroes. 2014. (Remembering the Holocaust Ser.). 96p. (J). (gr. 6-12). 27.94 *(978-0-7660-6217-7(1))* Enslow Pubs., Inc.

Ganeri, Anita. Heroes of History. Stanton, Joe Todd, illus. 2015. (Heroes of History Ser.). (ENG.). 176p. (J). (gr. 2-4). 11.99 *(978-1-4998-0079-1(7))* Little Bee Books Inc.

Ganeri, Anita & West, David. Heroes of Myths & Legends. 2012. (J). 70.50 *(978-1-4488-5239-0(0))*; pap. 11.75 *(978-1-4488-5238-3(2))*; lib. bdg. 26.50 *(978-1-4488-5200-0(5))* Rosen Publishing Group, Inc., The. (PowerKids Pr.).

Gill, Joel Christian. Strange Fruit Vol. 1: Uncelebrated Narratives from Black History. 2014. (ENG., Illus.). 176p. (YA). (gr. 7). pap. 23.95 *(978-1-938486-29-6(3))* Fulcrum Publishing.

Gray, Peter. Heroes & Villains. 2006. (Drawing Manga Ser.). (Illus.). 32p. (YA). (gr. 3-6). lib. bdg. 26.50 *(978-1-4042-3330-0(X))* Rosen Publishing Group, Inc., The.

—Male Action Figures. 2009. (Drawing Manga Ser.). 32p. (gr. 4-4). 50.50 *(978-1-61512-199-1(4))* Rosen Publishing Group, Inc., The.

Gray, Peter C. Male Action Figures. 2006. (Drawing Manga Ser.). (Illus.). 32p. (YA). (gr. 3-6). lib. bdg. 26.50 *(978-1-4042-3328-7(8))* Rosen Publishing Group, Inc., The.

Guillain, Charlotte. 101 Ways to Be a Great Role Model, 1 vol. 2011. (101 Ser.). (ENG., Illus.). 56p. (gr. 5-9). 34.65 *(978-1-4109-3900-5(6))*; pap. 9.95 *(978-1-4109-4387-3(9))* Heinemann-Raintree. (NA-r).

Halls, Kelly Milner. National Geographic Kids Chapters: Courageous Canine: And More True Stories of Amazing Animal Heroes. 2013. (NGK Chapters Ser.). (ENG., Illus.). 112p. (J). (gr. 2-5). pap. 5.99 *(978-1-4263-1396-7(9)*, National Geographic Children's Bks.) National Geographic Society.

Hamilton, John. Knights & Heroes, 1 vol. 2006. (Fantasy & Folklore Ser.). (ENG., Illus.). 32p. (gr. 5-8). 27.07 *(978-1-59679-336-1(8)*, Abdo & Daughters) ABDO Publishing Co.

—Leaders & Generals of the American Revolution. 2013. (American Revolution Ser.). 32p. (J). (gr. 5-9). lib. bdg. 27.07 *(978-1-61783-681-7(8)*, Abdo & Daughters) ABDO Publishing Co.

Hamilton Wright Mabie. Heroes Every Child Should Know. 2010. (CAM.). 256p. pap. 16.95 *(978-1-4385-3611-8(9)*, Book Jungle) Standard Pubns., Inc.

Hansen, Jim. How to Draw Superheroes. 2009. (Drawing Fantasy Art Ser.). 32p. (gr. 4-5). 50.50 *(978-1-61512-193-9(5)*, PowerKids Pr.) Rosen Publishing Group, Inc., The.

HarperCollins UK Staff. Real Heroes Vol. 2: Courage under Fire. 2011. (ENG., Illus.). 192p. 19.95 *(978-0-00-737903-3(X))* HarperCollins Pubs. Ltd. GBR. Dist: Independent Pubs. Group.

Harris, Laurie Lanzen. Biography for Beginners: Women Who Made a Difference. 2011. (J). lib. bdg. 49.00 *(978-1-931360-43-2(X))* Favorable Impressions.

Hernandez, Daniel. They Call Me a Hero: A Memoir of My Youth. (ENG., Illus.). 240p. (YA). (gr. 7). 2014. pap. 9.99 *(978-1-4424-6235-9(3))* 2013. 17.99 *(978-1-4424-6228-1(0))* Simon & Schuster Bks. For Young Readers. (Simon & Schuster Bks. For Young Readers).

Heroes of Black History. 2015. (Heroes of Black History Ser.). (ENG.). 32p. (J). (gr. 3-4). 159.60 *(978-1-4824-2552-9(1))* Stevens, Gareth Publishing LLLP.

Hoose, Phillip. The Boys Who Challenged Hitler: Knud Pedersen & the Churchill Club. 2015. (ENG., Illus.). 208p. (YA). (gr. 7-12). 19.99 *(978-0-374-30022-7(4)*, 9780374300227, Farrar, Straus & Giroux (BYR)) Farrar, Straus & Giroux.

I'm Going to be the Best Superhero Ever! 2008. (I'm Going to be Storybooks... Ser.). 32p. *(978-1-4075-1585-4(3))* Parragon, Inc.

Johnson, Terri. What Really Happened in Colonial Times: A Collection of Historical Biographies. Dixon, Darla, illus. 2007. (What Really Happened Ser.). 224p. (J). (gr. 4-7). per. 15.95 *(978-1-932786-23-1(6))* Knowledge Quest.

Katz, David Bar. Super Heroes Book of Opposites. 2013. (DC Super Heroes Ser.: 3). (ENG.). 20p. (J). (gr. -1 — 1). bds. 9.99 *(978-1-935703-76-1(5))* Downtown Bookworks.

Kingsley, Charles. Heroes of Greek Mythology. Squire, M H & Mars, E., illus. 2006. (Dover Children's Classics Ser.). (ENG.). 240p. (YA). (gr. 3-12). per. 9.95 *(978-0-486-44854-1(1))* Dover Pubns., Inc.

Kortemeier, Todd. Unsung Heroes of U.S. History. 2017. (Unsung Heroes Ser.). (ENG., Illus.). 32p. (gr. 3-6). 21.95 *(978-1-63235-312-2(1))* Pr. Room Editions LLC.

Landau, Elaine. My Favorite Horses: Spring 2012 New Releases. 2012. (My Favorite Horses Ser.). 24p. (gr. 3-5). lib. bdg. 135.60 *(978-0-7613-4937-2(5)*, Lerner Pubns.) Lerner Publishing Group.

Lang, Leonora Blanche. The Book of Saints & Heroes. Lang, Andrew, ed. Ford, H. J., illus. 2012. 344p. pap. 13.50 *(978-1-936639-18-2(1))* St. Augustine Academy Pr.

Lee, Adrienne. Legendary Warriors. Martin, Cynthia, illus. 2013. (Legendary Warriors Ser.). (ENG.). 32p. (gr. 1-2). 159.90 *(978-1-4765-3628-6(7)*, Blazers) Capstone Press of Coughlan Cos.

LernerClassroom Editors, ed. Teaching Guide for History's Kid Heroes. 2010. pap. 5.95 *(978-0-7613-6695-9(4))* Lerner Publishing Group.

Mabie, H. W., ed. Heroes Every Child Should Know (Yesterday's Classics) 2006. 396p. (J). per. 13.95 *(978-1-59915-097-0(2))* Yesterday's Classics.

Mabie, Hamilton Wright. Heroes Every Child Should Know. 2005. 31.95 *(978-1-4218-0941-0(9))*; 368p. pap. 15.95 *(978-1-59540-641-5(7))* 1st World Publishing, Inc. (1st World Library - Literary Society).

—Heroes Every Child Should Know. 2008. 260p. 25.99 *(978-0-554-31301-6(4))* 2008. 260p. 28.99 *(978-0-554-21998-1(0))* 2006. 268p. pap. 21.99 *(978-1-4264-1392-6(0))* 2006. (ENG.). 258p. pap. 23.99 *(978-1-4264-1445-9(5))* Creative Media Partners, LLC.

—Heroes Every Child Should Know. 2009. 194p. pap. 15.37 *(978-1-4589-5375-9(0))* General Bks. LLC.

—Heroes Every Child Should Know. 2004. reprint ed. pap. 26.95 *(978-1-4191-2360-3(2))*; pap. 1.99 *(978-1-4192-2360-0(7))* Kessinger Publishing, LLC.

—Heroines That Every Child Should Know: T. 2006. (Illus.). pap. 28.95 *(978-1-4286-0305-9(0))* Kessinger Publishing, LLC.

Mabie, Hamilton Wright, ed. Heroes Every Child Should Know. 2007. 260p. per. *(978-1-4065-2954-8(0))* Dodo Pr.

Malala, a Brave Girl from Pakistan/Iqbal, a Brave Boy from Pakistan. 2014. (ENG., Illus.). 40p. (J). (gr. 1-5). 17.99 *(978-1-4814-2294-9(4)*, Beach Lane Bks.) Beach Lane Bks.

March, Julia. Ultimate Sticker Collection: Spider-Man. 2017. (Ultimate Sticker Collections). (ENG.). 96p. (J). (gr. 1-4). pap. 12.99 ***(978-1-4654-6192-6(2)***, DK Children) Dorling Kindersley Publishing, Inc.

Markle, Sandra. Animal Heroes: True Rescue Stories. 2008. (ENG., Illus.). 64p. (gr. 3-8). 29.27 *(978-0-8225-7884-0(0)*, Millbrook Pr.) Lerner Publishing Group.

Markovics, Joyce L. Today's Coast Guard Heroes. 2012. (Acts of Courage: Inside America's Military Ser.). 32p. (J). (gr. 2-7). lib. bdg. 25.27 *(978-1-61772-448-0(3))* Bearport Publishing Co., Inc.

Markovics, Joyce L. & Pushies, Fred J. Today's Army Heroes. 2012. (Acts of Courage: Inside America's Military Ser.). 32p. (J). (gr. 2-7). lib. bdg. 25.27 *(978-1-61772-445-9(9))* Bearport Publishing Co., Inc.

Mattern, Joanne. Super Pets: True Tales of Animal Heroes. 2012. (Illus.). 82p. (J). pap. *(978-0-545-46042-2(5))* Scholastic, Inc.

—True Tales of Courageous Dogs. 2007. 95p. (J). pap. *(978-0-439-02713-7(6))* Scholastic, Inc.

—William Penn. 2010. (Leaders of the Colonial Era Ser.). 112p. (gr. 5-8). 35.00 *(978-1-60413-735-4(5)*, Chelsea Hse.) Facts On File, Inc.

McCann, Michelle Roehm. Boys Who Rocked the World: Heroes from King Tut to Bruce Lee. Hahn, David, illus. 2012. (ENG.). 256p. (J). (gr. 3-7). 18.99 *(978-1-58270-362-6(0))*; pap. 10.99 *(978-1-58270-331-2(0))* Aladdin/Beyond Words.

Mccann, Michelle Roehm. Boys Who Rocked the World: Heroes from King Tut to Shaun White. 2012. lib. bdg. 22.10 *(978-0-606-26897-4(9)*, Turtleback) Turtleback Bks.

McCann, Michelle Roehm & Welden, Amelie. Girls Who Rocked the World: Heroines from Joan of Arc to Mother Teresa. Hahn, Daniel & Hahn, David, illus. 2012. (ENG.). 256p. (J). (gr. 3-7). 19.99 *(978-1-58270-361-9(2))*; pap. 10.99 *(978-1-58270-302-2(7))* Aladdin/Beyond Words.

McGovern, Ann. Native American Heroes: Osceola, Tecumseh & Cochise. 2014. (ENG.). 128p. (J). (gr. 3-7). pap. 4.99 *(978-0-545-46720-9(9)*, Scholastic Nonfiction) Scholastic, Inc.

Meloche, Renee Taft. Heroes for Young Readers Activity Guide Package Books 13-16: Includes: Activity Guide, Audio CD, & Books 13-16. Pollard, Bryan, illus. 2006. (ENG.). 55.94 incl. audio compact disk *(978-1-57658-378-4(3))* YWAM Publishing.

Meltzer, Brad. Heroes for My Daughter. 144p. (J). 2016. (gr. -1-3). 17.99 *(978-0-06-243927-7(8))* 2012. (ENG., Illus.). 19.99 *(978-0-06-190526-1(7))* HarperCollins Pubs.

—Heroes for My Son. 128p. 2016. (J). (gr. -1-3). 17.99 *(978-0-06-243931-4(6))* 2010. (ENG., Illus.). 19.99 *(978-0-06-190528-5(3))* HarperCollins Pubs.

Milner Halls, Kelly. National Geographic Kids Chapters: Courageous Canine: And More True Stories of Amazing Animal Heroes. 2013. (National Geographic Kids Everything Ser.). (ENG., Illus.). 112p. (J). (gr. 2-5). lib. bdg. 14.90 *(978-1-4263-1397-4(7)*, National Geographic Children's Bks.) National Geographic Society.

Native American Heroes. 2015. (Native American Heroes Ser.). (ENG.). 24p. (J). (gr. 1-2). 135.60 *(978-1-4824-2543-7(2))*; pap., pap., pap. 48.90 *(978-1-4824-3486-6(5))* Stevens, Gareth Publishing LLLP.

Obama, Barack. Of Thee I Sing: A Letter to My Daughters. Long, Loren, illus. 2010. (ENG.). 40p. (J). (gr. k-12). 17.99 *(978-0-375-83527-8(X)*, Knopf Bks. for Young Readers) Random Hse. Children's Bks.

O'Malley, Tom. Top Trumps Marvel Heroes. 2008. (Illus.). 192p. pap. *(978-1-84425-477-4(1))* Haynes Manuals, Inc.

Osborne, Mary Pope & Boyce, Natalie Pope. Heroes for All Times. 2014. (Magic Tree House Fact Tracker Ser.: 28). lib. bdg. 16.00 *(978-0-606-35197-3(3))* Turtleback Bks.

—Heroes for All Times: A Nonfiction Companion High Time for Heroes. Murdocca, Sal, illus. 2014. (Magic Tree House - Fact Tracker Ser.: 28). (ENG.). 128p. (J). (gr. 2-5). 6.99 *(978-0-375-87027-9(X)*, Random Hse. Bks. for Young Readers) Random Hse. Children's Bks.

Parham, Jerrill. Boundary Breakers: Remarkable People. 2008. (Illus.). 36p. (J). pap. *(978-0-531-15488-5(2))* Children's Pr., Ltd.

—Boundary Breakers: Remarkable People. 2007. (Shockwave: History & Politics Ser.). (ENG., Illus.). 36p. (J). (gr. 4-8). 25.00 *(978-0-531-17752-5(1),* Children's Pr.) Scholastic Library Publishing.

Petruccio, Steven James. American Heroes Coloring Book. 2013. (ENG.). 48p. (J). (gr. 3-6). pap. 4.99 *(978-0-486-49895-9(6))* Dover Pubns., Inc.

Pochocki, Ethel. Saints & Heroes. Owens, Mary Beth, illus. 2012. 258p. (YA). pap. 15.95 *(978-1-932350-51-7(9))* Bethlehem Bks.

Randolph, Joanne. The Angel of Goliad: Francisca Alvarez & the Texas War for Independence. 2009. (Great Moments in American History Ser.). 32p. (gr. 3-3). 47.90 *(978-1-61513-151-8(5))* Rosen Publishing Group, Inc., The.

Reynolds, Toby & Calver, Paul. Unsung Heroes: Fearless Men & Women Who Changed the World. 2017. (Real Lives Ser.). (ENG., Illus.). 64p. (J). (gr. 4-10). 8.99 *(978-0-7641-6887-1(8))* Barron's Educational Series, Inc.

Rogow, Sally M. Faces of Courage: Young Heroes of World War II. 2008. (ENG., Illus.). 162p. pap. *(978-1-894694-67-4(8))* Granville Island Publishing.

Rosen Publishing Staff. Heroes & Legends, 1 vol. 2015. (Heroes & Legends Ser.). (ENG.). 80p. (YA). 213.60 *(978-1-4777-8171-5(4),* Rosen Young Adult) Rosen Publishing Group, Inc., The.

Rostrom, Laura Lee. My First Book of Mormon Activity Book, Vol. 1. 2011. 64p. pap. 3.99 *(978-1-59955-957-5(9))* Cedar Fort, Inc./CFI Distribution.

Rowe, Brooke. What's Your Superpower? 2016. (Best Quiz Ever Ser.). (ENG., Illus.). 32p. (J). (gr. 4-8). 29.93 *(978-1-63471-108-1(4),* 208543, 45th Parallel Press) Cherry Lake Publishing.

Saunders, Catherine. Are Ewoks Scared of Stormtroopers? 2013. (Star Wars DK Readers Level 1 Ser.). lib. bdg. 13.55 *(978-0-606-35205-5(8))* Turtleback Bks.

Sautter, Aaron. Drawing DC Super Heroes. Doescher, Erik & Levins, Tim, illus. 2015. (Drawing DC Super Heroes Ser.). (ENG.). 32p. (gr. 3-6). lib. bdg. 111.96 *(978-1-4914-2553-4(9),* DC Super Heroes) Stone Arch Bks.

—How to Draw Comic Heroes, 1 vol. Martin, Cynthia, illus. 2007. (Drawing Cool Stuff Ser.). (ENG.). 32p. (gr. 3-4). 27.99 *(978-1-4296-0074-3(8),* Edge Bks.) Capstone Press of Coughlan Cos.

Savery, Annabel. Superheroes. 2012. (It's Amazing Ser.). (Illus.). 32p. (gr. 3-6). lib. bdg. 31.35 *(978-1-59920-692-9(7))* Black Rabbit Bks.

Schiffman, Jessica, illus. Sybil Ludington: Freedom's Brave Rider. 2005. 32p. (J). pap. *(978-0-7367-2931-4(3))* Zaner-Bloser, Inc.

Schuette, Sarah L. A Superhero Cookbook: Simple Recipes for Kids, 1 vol. 2011. (First Cookbooks Ser.). (ENG.). 24p. (gr. 1-2). lib. bdg. 25.32 *(978-1-4296-5998-7(X),* First Facts) Capstone Press of Coughlan Cos.

Schuller, Kathleen. How to Be a Hero - for Boys: Inspiration from Classic Heroes. 2013. 72p. 19.95 *(978-1-4575-1796-9(5));* pap. 9.95 *(978-1-4575-2023-5(0))* Dog Ear Publishing, LLC.

—How to Be a Heroine — -For Girls: Inspiration from Classic Heroines. 2013. 68p. pap. 9.95 *(978-1-4575-1906-2(2))* Dog Ear Publishing, LLC.

—How to Be a Heroine-For Girls: Inspiration from Classic Heroines. Bailey, Melissa, illus. 2013. 68p. 19.95 *(978-1-4575-1649-8(7))* Dog Ear Publishing, LLC.

Sheppard, Si. Heroes & Legends: Set 2. 2015. (Heroes & Legends Ser.). (ENG.). 88p. (YA). (gr. 7-8). 178.00 *(978-1-4994-6193-0(3),* Rosen Young Adult) Rosen Publishing Group, Inc., The.

Smith, Charles R., Jr. 28 Days: Moments in Black History That Changed the World. Evans, Shane W., illus. 2015. (ENG.). 56p. (J). (gr. -1-5). 18.99 *(978-1-59643-820-0(7),* 9781596438200) Roaring Brook Pr.

Sowash, Rick. Heroes of Ohio: 23 True Tales of Courage & Character. 2003. (J). 19.95 *(978-0-9762412-5-6(0));* pap. 11.95 *(978-0-9762412-4-9(2))* Sowash, Rick Publishing Co.

Superheroes of Science. 2015. (Superheroes of Science Ser.). (ENG.). 48p. (J). (gr. 6-6). 191.70 *(978-1-4824-2561-1(0))* Stevens, Gareth Publishing LLLP.

Throp, Claire. Heroes of World War Two. 2015. (Heroes of World War II Ser.). (ENG.). 48p. (gr. 4-6). lib. bdg. 130.60 *(978-1-4109-8049-6(9))* Heinemann-Raintree.

Turner, Tracey. Hard As Nails in Myths & Legends. 2015. (Hard As Nails in History Ser.). (ENG., Illus.). 64p. (J). (gr. 3-7). lib. bdg. *(978-0-7787-1520-7(5))* Crabtree Publishing Co.

Wallace, Archer. Men Who Played the Game. 2003. 127p. 89.00 *(978-0-7950-5139-5(5))* New Library Press LLC.

Wallace, Daniel & Dorling Kindersley Publishing Staff. Superman - The Ultimate Guide to the Man of Steel. 2013. (ENG., Illus.). 200p. (J). (gr. 1-4). 24.99 *(978-1-4654-0875-4(4),* DK Children) Dorling Kindersley Publishing, Inc.

Warriors Around the World. 2016. (Warriors Around the World Ser.). 00048p. (J). (gr. 5-5). 187.95 *(978-1-5081-0291-5(0),* Britannica Educational Publishing) Rosen Publishing Group, Inc., The.

Waters, Fiona. Great Irish Heroes. Marklew, Gilly, illus. 2007. (ENG.). 66p. (J). 23.95 *(978-0-7171-3793-0(7))* M.H. Gill & Co. U. C. IRL. Dist: Dufour Editions, Inc.

Winter, Jonah. Peaceful Heroes. Addy, Sean, illus. 2009. (J). pap. *(978-0-439-62308-7(1),* Levine, Arthur A. Bks.) Scholastic, Inc.

Winter, Jonah & Addy, Sean. Peaceful Heroes. 2009. (ENG., Illus.). 64p. (J). (gr. 4-7). 17.99 *(978-0-439-62307-0(3),* Levine, Arthur A. Bks.) Scholastic, Inc.

World Book, Inc. Staff, contrib. by. Heroes & Helpers: A Supplement to Childcraft: The How & Why Library. 2003. (Illus.). 208p. (J). pap. *(978-0-7166-0606-2(2))* World Bk., Inc.

You Choose: Warriors. 2010. (You Choose: Warriors Ser.). (ENG.). 112p. (gr. 3-4). pap. 83.40 *(978-1-4296-5122-6(9),* You Choose Bks.) Capstone Press of Coughlan Cos.

You Choose: Warriors [Capstone Sole Source]. 2010. (You Choose: Warriors Ser.). 112p. 61.30 *(978-1-4296-5894-2(0),* You Choose Bks.) Capstone Press of Coughlan Cos.

Zalben, Jane Breskin. Paths to Peace: People Who Changed the World. 2006. (ENG., Illus.). 48p. (J). (gr. 3-7). 18.99 *(978-0-525-47734-1(9),* Dutton Books for Young Readers) Penguin Young Readers Group.

Zullo, Allan. Heroes of 9/11. 2011. (Illus.). 181p. (J). pap. *(978-0-545-25506-6(6))* Scholastic, Inc.

—Heroes of Pearl Harbor. 2016. (Ten True Tales Ser.). (ENG., Illus.). 224p. (J). (gr. 3-7). pap. 5.99 *(978-0-545-87276-8(6))* Scholastic, Inc.

—The Rescuers: Kids Who Risked Everything to Save Others. 2006. 135p. pap. *(978-0-439-85483-2(0))* Scholastic, Inc.

—War Heroes: Voices from Iraq. (10 True Tales Ser.). (J). 2014. (ENG.). 160p. (gr. 3-7). pap. 5.99 *(978-0-545-81840-7(0),* Scholastic Nonfiction) 2009. 48p. pap. *(978-0-545-09026-1(1))* Scholastic, Inc.

—World War I Heroes. 2014. 162p. (J). pap. ***(978-0-545-67533-8(2))*** Scholastic, Inc.

Zullo, Allan. 10 True Tales: Heroes Of 9/11. 2015. (Ten True Tales Ser.). (ENG.). 192p. (J). (gr. 3-7). pap. 5.99 *(978-0-545-81813-1(3),* Scholastic Nonfiction) Scholastic, Inc.

HEROES—FICTION

ABDO Publishing Company Staff. Archie Set of 6, 6 vols., Set. 2007. (Archie Ser.). (ENG., Illus.). 80p. 96.84 *(978-1-59961-257-7(7))* Spotlight.

Abnett, Dan & Lanning, Andy. Marvel's Guardians of the Galaxy Prelude. Alves, Wellington et al, illus. 2014. (ENG.). 168p. (J). (gr. 4-17). pap. 14.99 *(978-0-7851-5410-5(8))* Marvel Worldwide, Inc.

Acampora, Michael V. Battle of the Blue Lanterns, 1 vol. Schoening, Dan, illus. 2011. (Green Lantern Ser.). (ENG.). 56p. (gr. 2-3). pap. 4.95 *(978-1-4342-3085-0(6));* lib. bdg. 26.65 *(978-1-4342-2608-2(5))* Stone Arch Bks. (DC Super Heroes).

—Escape from the Orange Lanterns, 1 vol. Schoening, Dan, illus. 2011. (Green Lantern Ser.). (ENG.). 56p. (gr. 2-3). pap. 4.95 *(978-1-4342-3408-7(8),* DC Super Heroes) Stone Arch Bks.

—Red Lanterns' Revenge, 1 vol. Schoening, Dan, illus. 2011. (Green Lantern Ser.). (ENG.). 56p. (gr. 2-3). pap. 4.95 *(978-1-4342-3409-4(6),* DC Super Heroes) Stone Arch Bks.

Acampora, Michael Vincent. Escape from the Orange Lanterns, 1 vol. Schoening, Dan, illus. 2011. (Green Lantern Ser.). (ENG.). 56p. (gr. 2-3). lib. bdg. 26.65 *(978-1-4342-2622-8(0),* DC Super Heroes) Stone Arch Bks.

—Red Lanterns' Revenge, 1 vol. Schoening, Dan, illus. 2011. (Green Lantern Ser.). (ENG.). 56p. (gr. 2-3). lib. bdg. 26.65 *(978-1-4342-2623-5(9),* DC Super Heroes) Stone Arch Bks.

Adpot-a-Hulk. 2003. (J). per. *(978-1-57657-819-3(4))* Paradise Pr., Inc.

Alfaro, Manuel. Super Griego the Great & the Secret Mission to the Moon. Harrington, David, illus. 2009. 40p. pap. 15.95 *(978-1-60844-028-3(1))* Dog Ear Publishing, LLC.

Alger, Horatio. Facing the World. 2006. pap. *(978-1-4065-0704-1(0))* Dodo Pr.

Allen, Gregory G. Chicken Boy: The Amazing Adventures of a Super Hero with Autism. Culver, Dennis, illus. 2012. 32p. pap. 9.99 *(978-0-9853441-0-8(5))* ASD Publishing.

Allvord, Crash & Luiso, Lisa. Heroes of the Diamond. 2011. (J). 14.95 *(978-1-936319-51-0(9))* Mascot Bks., Inc.

Alter, Judy. Sam Houston Is My Hero. 2003. (Chaparral Bks.). (ENG.). 130p. (J). pap. 11.95 *(978-0-87565-277-1(8))* Texas Christian Univ. Pr.

Amara, Phil. The Treehouse Heroes: The Forgotten Beast. Chau, Alina, illus. 2012. (ENG.). 36p. (J). (gr. -1-3). 15.95 *(978-1-59702-034-3(6))* Immedium.

Amma, Jill. The Indaba Tree Odyssey: An African Tale. 2006. 360p. pap. 18.95 *(978-0-7414-3172-1(6))* Infinity Publishing.

Andersen, D. R. The Matter Marvels. 2005. (J). pap. *(978-1-4108-4216-9(9))* Benchmark Education Co.

Anderson, John David. Minion. 2014. (ENG.). 288p. (J). (gr. 3-7). 16.99 *(978-0-06-213311-3(X),* Waldon Pond Pr.) HarperCollins Pubs.

—Sidekicked. (ENG.). (J). (gr. 3-7). 2014. 400p. pap. 6.99 *(978-0-06-213315-1(2))* 2013. 384p. 16.99 *(978-0-06-213314-4(4))* HarperCollins Pubs. (Waldon Pond Pr.).

Anthony, David & Clasman, Charles David. Heroes A2Z #13: (Heroes a to Z): Monkey Monster Truck. Blakeslee, Lys, illus. 2012. 128p. (J). mass mkt. 4.99 *(978-0-9846528-1-5(7))* Sigil Publishing.

Anthony, David & David, Charles. Heroes A2Z #1: (Heroes a to Z): Alien Ice Cream. Blakeslee, Lys, illus. 2007. 128p. (J). pap. 4.99 *(978-0-9728461-8-9(2))* Sigil Publishing.

—Heroes A2Z #2: (Heroes a to Z): Bowling over Halloween: Bowling over Halloween. Blakeslee, Lys, illus. 2007. (Heroes A2Z Ser.). 128p. (J). pap. 4.99 *(978-0-9728461-9-6(0))* Sigil Publishing.

Aptekar, Devan. Darkseid's Revenge. Gordon, Eric A. & Gordon, Steven E., illus. 2012. (ENG.). 24p. (J). (gr. -1-3). pap. 3.99 *(978-0-06-188533-4(9),* HarperFestival) HarperCollins Pubs.

—Darkseid's Revenge. Gordon, Eric A. & Gordon, Steven E., illus. 2012. (Justice League Classic 8X8 Ser.). (J). lib. bdg. 13.55 *(978-0-606-23566-2(3),* Turtleback) Turtleback Bks.

Arnold, Tedd. Buzz Boy & Fly Guy. Arnold, Tedd, illus. 2010. (Fly Guy Ser.: 9). (ENG., Illus.). 32p. (J). (gr. -1-3). 6.99 *(978-0-545-22274-7(5),* Cartwheel Bks.) Scholastic, Inc.

—Buzz Boy & Fly Guy. 2010. (Fly Guy Ser.: 9). lib. bdg. 17.20 *(978-0-606-14841-2(8),* Turtleback) Turtleback Bks.

Aronson, Sarah. Beyond Lucky. 2011. (ENG.). 256p. (J). (gr. 3-7). 16.99 *(978-0-8037-3520-0(0),* Dial Bks) Penguin Young Readers Group.

Attack of the Tagger. unabr. ed. 2006. (Shredderman Ser.: Bk. 2). (Illus.). (J). (gr. 3-6). audio compact disk 28.95 *(978-1-59519-759-7(1))* Live Oak Media.

Avengers Staff, et al. Meet Captain America No. 2. 2011. (Avengers: Earth's Mightiest Heroes! Ser.). (ENG.). 24p. (J). (gr. 1-2). pap. 3.99 *(978-1-4231-4296-6(9))* Marvel Worldwide, Inc.

Bacon, Lee. The Dominion Key. 2014. (Joshua Dread Ser.: 3). (ENG.). 256p. (J). (gr. 4-7). 16.99 *(978-0-385-74382-2(3));* lib. bdg. 19.99 *(978-0-375-99130-1(1))* Random Hse. Children's Bks. (Delacorte Bks. for Young Readers).

—Joshua Dread. 2013. (Joshua Dread Ser.: 1). (ENG.). 272p. (J). (gr. 4-7). 6.99 *(978-0-307-92998-3(1),* Yearling) Random Hse. Children's Bks.

—Joshua Dread: the Dominion Key. 2015. (Joshua Dread Ser.: 3). (ENG.). 256p. (J). (gr. 4-7). 6.99 *(978-0-385-37126-1(8),* Yearling) Random Hse. Children's Bks.

—The Nameless Hero. 2014. (Joshua Dread Ser.: 2). (ENG., Illus.). 304p. (J). (gr. 4-7). 7.99 *(978-0-307-92997-6(3),* Yearling) Random Hse. Children's Bks.

Baltazar, Art. Starro & the Space Dolphins, 1 vol. Baltazar, Art, illus. 2012. (DC Super-Pets Ser.). (ENG., Illus.). 56p. (gr. 2-2). pap. 4.95 *(978-1-4048-7217-2(5),* DC Super-Pets) Picture Window Bks.

Baltazar, Art & Aureliani, Franco. And Now... Braniac!, 1 vol. 2014. (Superman Family Adventures Ser.). (ENG., Illus.). 32p. (gr. 1-2). 22.60 *(978-1-4342-6478-7(5))* Stone Arch Bks.

—And Now... Ma Kent!, 1 vol. 2014. (Superman Family Adventures Ser.). (ENG., Illus.). 32p. (gr. 1-2). 22.60 *(978-1-4342-9006-9(9))* Stone Arch Bks.

—Attack of the Toyman!, 1 vol. 2014. (Superman Family Adventures Ser.). (ENG., Illus.). 32p. (gr. 1-2). 22.60 *(978-1-4342-6476-3(9))* Stone Arch Bks.

—Because You Demanded It... Darkseid!, 1 vol. 2014. (Superman Family Adventures Ser.). (ENG., Illus.). 32p. (gr. 1-2). 22.60 *(978-1-4342-9005-2(0))* Stone Arch Bks.

—Bounty Hunter, 1 vol. Brizuela, Dario, illus. 2012. (Green Lantern: the Animated Ser.). (ENG.). 32p. (gr. 2-3). 22.60 *(978-1-4342-4835-0(6))* Stone Arch Bks.

—By Hook or by Web, 1 vol. Norton, Mike, illus. 2012. (Young Justice Ser.). (ENG.). 32p. (gr. 2-3). 22.60 *(978-1-4342-4556-4(X))* Stone Arch Bks.

—Counterfeits, 1 vol. Brizuela, Dario, illus. 2013. (Green Lantern: the Animated Ser.). (ENG.). 32p. (gr. 2-3). 22.60 *(978-1-4342-5566-2(2))* Stone Arch Bks.

—Enter - Nightwing! Baltazar, Art & Aureliani, Franco, illus. 2012. (Tiny Titans Ser.). (ENG., Illus.). 32p. (gr. 1-2). lib. bdg. 22.60 *(978-1-4342-4540-3(3))* Stone Arch Bks.

—Enter Bizarro!, 1 vol. 2013. (Superman Family Adventures Ser.). (ENG., Illus.). 32p. (gr. 1-2). 22.60 *(978-1-4342-4790-2(2))* Stone Arch Bks.

—General Zod Dogs!, 1 vol. 2014. (Superman Family Adventures Ser.). (ENG., Illus.). 32p. (gr. 1-2). 22.60 *(978-1-4342-6479-4(3))* Stone Arch Bks.

—Goldface Attacks!, 1 vol. Brizuela, Dario, illus. 2014. (Green Lantern: the Animated Ser.). (ENG.). 32p. (gr. 2-3). 22.60 *(978-1-4342-6482-4(3))* Stone Arch Bks.

—Green Lantern: the Animated Series. Brizuela, Dario, illus. 2013. (Green Lantern: the Animated Ser.). (ENG.). 32p. (gr. 2-3). 90.40 *(978-1-4342-8828-8(5))* Stone Arch Bks.

—Hack & You Shall Find, 1 vol. Norton, Mike, illus. 2012. (Young Justice Ser.). (ENG.). 32p. (gr. 2-3). 22.60 *(978-1-4342-4555-7(1))* Stone Arch Bks.

—Haunted, 1 vol. Norton, Mike, illus. 2012. (Young Justice Ser.). (ENG.). 32p. (gr. 2-3). lib. bdg. 22.60 *(978-1-4342-4553-3(5))* Stone Arch Bks.

—Invisible Destroyer. Brizuela, Dario, illus. 2013. (Green Lantern: the Animated Ser.). (ENG.). 32p. (gr. 2-3). 22.60 *(978-1-4342-4796-4(1))* Stone Arch Bks.

—Menace of Metallo! Baltazar, Art, illus. 2013. (Superman Family Adventures Ser.). (ENG., Illus.). 32p. (gr. 1-2). 22.60 *(978-1-4342-4794-0(5))* Stone Arch Bks.

—Monkey Business, 1 vol. Norton, Mike, illus. 2012. (Young Justice Ser.). (ENG.). 32p. (gr. 2-3). 22.60 *(978-1-4342-4554-0(3))* Stone Arch Bks.

—Monkey Metropolis!, 1 vol. Baltazar, Art, illus. 2013. (Superman Family Adventures Ser.). (ENG., Illus.). 32p. (gr. 1-2). 22.60 *(978-1-4342-4791-9(0))* Stone Arch Bks.

—The Mysterious Alien Menace!, 1 vol. 2014. (Superman Family Adventures Ser.). (ENG., Illus.). 32p. (gr. 1-2). 22.60 *(978-1-4342-6477-0(7))* Stone Arch Bks.

—Penguins in the Batcave!, 1 vol. Baltazar, Art & Aureliani, Franco, illus. 2012. (Tiny Titans Ser.). (ENG., Illus.). 32p. (gr. 1-2). 22.60 *(978-1-4342-4539-7(X))* Stone Arch Bks.

—Sidekick City Elementary, 1 vol. Baltazar, Art & Aureliani, Franco, illus. 2012. (Tiny Titans Ser.). (ENG., Illus.). 32p. (gr. 1-2). lib. bdg. 22.60 *(978-1-4342-4528-1(4))* Stone Arch Bks.

—Super-Pets!, 1 vol. Baltazar, Art, illus. 2013. (Superman Family Adventures Ser.). (ENG., Illus.). 32p. (gr. 1-2). 22.60 *(978-1-4342-4792-6(9))* Stone Arch Bks.

—Superman Family Adventures, 1 vol. (Superman Family Adventures Ser.). (ENG.). 32p. (gr. 1-2). 2014. 271.20 *(978-1-4342-8766-3(1))* 2013. 135.60 *(978-1-4342-8829-5(3))* Stone Arch Bks.

—Tiny Titans. Baltazar, Art & Aureliani, Franco, illus. 2013. (Tiny Titans Ser.). (ENG., Illus.). 32p. (gr. 1-2). 113.00 *(978-1-4342-4854-1(2));* 90.40 *(978-1-4342-4853-4(4))* Stone Arch Bks.

—Tiny Titans vs. the Fearsome Five, 1 vol. Baltazar, Art & Aureliani, Franco, illus. 2012. (Tiny Titans Ser.). (ENG., Illus.). 32p. (gr. 1-2). lib. bdg. 22.60 *(978-1-4342-4538-0(1))* Stone Arch Bks.

—Who Is the Purple Superman?, 1 vol. Baltazar, Art, illus. 2013. (Superman Family Adventures Ser.). (ENG., Illus.). 32p. (gr. 1-2). 22.60 *(978-1-4342-4793-3(7))* Stone Arch Bks.

—Young Justice. 2013. (Young Justice Ser.). (ENG.). 32p. (gr. 2-3). 180.80 *(978-1-4342-8835-6(8));* 90.40 *(978-1-4342-8834-9(X))* Stone Arch Bks.

Baltazar, Art & Baltazar, Franco. Aw Yeah Titans! 2013. (Tiny Titans Ser.: 8). lib. bdg. 24.50 *(978-0-606-32095-5(4),* Turtleback) Turtleback Bks.

Baltazar, Art, et al. Campfire Secrets, 1 vol. 2013. (Young Justice Ser.). (ENG.). 32p. (gr. 2-3). 22.60 *(978-1-4342-6037-6(2))* Stone Arch Bks.

—Fears, 1 vol. Jones, Christopher, illus. 2013. (Young Justice Ser.). (ENG.). 32p. (gr. 2-3). 22.60 *(978-1-4342-6038-3(0))* Stone Arch Bks.

—Hal Versus Atrocitus, 1 vol. Brizuela, Dario, illus. 2014. (Green Lantern: the Animated Ser.). (ENG.). 32p. (gr. 2-3). 22.60 *(978-1-4342-6481-7(5))* Stone Arch Bks.

—Trouble in the Arena!, 1 vol. Brizuela, Dario, illus. 2014. (Green Lantern: the Animated Ser.). (ENG.). 32p. (gr. 2-3). 22.60 *(978-1-4342-4787-2(2))* Stone Arch Bks.

—True Colors, 1 vol. Brizuela, Dario, illus. 2013. (Green Lantern: the Animated Ser.). (ENG.). 32p. (gr. 2-3). 22.60 *(978-1-4342-4795-7(3))* Stone Arch Bks.

Baltazar, Arthur & Franco. Aw Yeah Comics! Make Way... for Awesome!, Vol. 3. Baltazar, Arthur et al, illus. 2016. (ENG.). 144p. (J). (gr. 3-7). pap. 12.99 *(978-1-5067-0045-8(4))* Dark Horse Comics.

Bancks, Tristan. Noob & the Librarian Supervillain. Gorissen, Dean, illus. 2015. (Legends in Their Own Lunchbox Ser.). (ENG.). 48p. (gr. 1-2). pap. 7.99 *(978-1-4966-0247-3(1),* Legends in Their Own Lunchbox) Capstone Classroom.

Barichella, Thomas. The Star Snatcher's Planet. 2013. (Little Prince Ser.: 5). (ENG., Illus.). 56p. (J). (gr. 4-8). pap. 7.95 *(978-1-4677-0737-4(6),* Graphic Universe™) Lerner Publishing Group.

Barnhouse, Rebecca. Ring-Giver. 2013. (J). *(978-0-307-98178-3(9))* Random Hse., Inc.

Barton, Chris. Muddymania! Cummings, Troy, illus. 2017. 32p. (J). (gr. -1-3). 17.99 *(978-0-06-234479-3(X))* HarperCollins Pubs.

Beakman, Onk. The Mask of Power: Eruptor Meets the Nightmare King. Geremia, Daniela, illus. 2016. 157p. (J). ***(978-1-5182-2804-9(6),*** Grosset & Dunlap) Penguin Publishing Group.

Beatty, Scott, et al. In the Mouth of the Whale. Vecchio, Luciano, illus. 2015. (Beware the Batman Ser.). (ENG.). 32p. (gr. 2-3). lib. bdg. 22.60 *(978-1-4342-9740-2(3))* Stone Arch Bks.

Becker-Doyle, Eve & Doyle, Evan Brain. Evan Brain's Christmas List & Other Shenanigans: Boy Warrior Fights Evil. Doyle, Evan Brain, illus. 2008. (ENG., Illus.). 64p. pap. 15.95 *(978-0-9794716-3-6(X))* BDA Publishing.

Bee, Stevie J. Cross Your Heart. 2009. 216p. 25.50 *(978-1-60860-133-2(1),* Eloquent Bks.) Strategic Book Publishing & Rights Agency (SBPRA).

Beechen, Adam. Darkseid's Inferno!, 1 vol. Beavers, Ethen, illus. 2013. (Justice League Unlimited Ser.). (ENG.). 32p. (gr. 2-3). 22.60 *(978-1-4342-6043-7(7))* Stone Arch Bks.

—Justice League Unlimited. 2013. (Justice League Unlimited Ser.). (ENG.). 32p. (gr. 2-3). 90.40 *(978-1-4342-8833-2(1));* 180.80 *(978-1-4342-8832-5(3));* 90.40 *(978-1-4342-3936-5(5))* Stone Arch Bks.

Beechen, Adam & Age, Heroic. Mad Mod Is in Vogue!, 1 vol. Vedder, Erik, illus. 2014. (Teen Titans GO! Ser.). (ENG.). 32p. (gr. 2-3). 22.60 *(978-1-4342-9216-2(9))* Stone Arch Bks.

Beechen, Adam & Wong, Walden. In the Dimming Light, 1 vol. Barberi, Carlo, illus. 2013. (Justice League Unlimited Ser.). (ENG.). 32p. (gr. 2-3). 22.60 *(978-1-4342-6042-0(9))* Stone Arch Bks.

—Monitor Duty, 1 vol. Barberi, Carlo, illus. 2013. (Justice League Unlimited Ser.). (ENG.). 32p. (gr. 2-3). 22.60 *(978-1-4342-6041-3(0))* Stone Arch Bks.

—Who Is the Question?, 1 vol. Barberi, Carlo, illus. 2013. (Justice League Unlimited Ser.). (ENG.). 32p. (gr. 2-3). 22.60 *(978-1-4342-6044-4(5))* Stone Arch Bks.

Bell, Sophie. Lilac Attack! 2014. (Ultra Violets Ser.: 3). (ENG., Illus.). 304p. (J). (gr. 3-7). 12.99 *(978-1-59514-648-9(2),* Razorbill) Penguin Young Readers Group.

—Power to the Purple! Battle, Christina, illus. 2013. (Ultra Violets Ser.: 2). (ENG.). 336p. (J). (gr. 3-7). 12.99 *(978-1-59514-647-2(4),* Razorbill) Penguin Young Readers Group.

Belle, Magnolia. Teen Titans Go! - Chillin' Like a Villain. 2015. (ENG., Illus.). 24p. (J). (gr. -1-3). pap. 3.99 *(978-0-316-33329-0(8))* Little, Brown Bks. for Young Readers.

—Teen Titans Go! - Hot Garbage. 2016. (ENG., Illus.). 24p. (J). (gr. -1-3). pap. 3.99 *(978-0-316-26744-1(9))* Little, Brown Bks. for Young Readers.

Bellisario, Gina. Ellie Ultra, 4 vols. Von Innerebner, Jessika, illus. 2016. (Ellie Ultra Ser.). (ENG.). 128p. (gr. 2-3). 103.96 *(978-1-4965-3168-1(X))* Stone Arch Bks.

—An Extra-Ordinary Girl. Von Innerebner, Jessika, illus. 2016. (Ellie Ultra Ser.). (ENG.). 128p. (gr. 2-3). lib. bdg. 25.99 *(978-1-4965-3139-1(6))* Stone Arch Bks.

—Queen of the Spelling Bee. Von Innerebner, Jessika, illus. 2016. (Ellie Ultra Ser.). (ENG.). 128p. (gr. 2-3). lib. bdg. 25.99 *(978-1-4965-3141-4(8))* Stone Arch Bks.

—Super Fluffy to the Rescue. Von Innerebner, Jessika, illus. 2016. (Ellie Ultra Ser.). (ENG.). 128p. (gr. 2-3). lib. bdg. 25.99 *(978-1-4965-3142-1(6))* Stone Arch Bks.

Benedetti, Hervé & Robin, Nicolas. The Planet of the Tortoise Driver. Elyum Studio Staff, illus. 2013. (Little Prince Ser.: 8). (ENG.). 56p. (J). (gr. 4-8). pap. 7.95 *(978-1-4677-0740-4(6),* Graphic Universe™) Lerner Publishing Group.

Benton, Jim. Howard Hubbins Half Hour Hero. 2008. (J). pap. 4.99 *(978-0-06-059774-0(7))* HarperCollins Pubs.

Bergen, Lara. Don't Throw That Away! A Lift-the-Flap Book about Recycling & Reusing. Snyder, Betsy E., illus. 2009. (Little Green Bks.). (ENG.). 14p. (J). (gr. -1-1). bds. 7.99 *(978-1-4169-7517-5(9),* Little Simon) Little Simon.

Bermejo, Lee. The Vigilante Business. 2016. (We Are Robin Ser.: 1). lib. bdg. 26.95 *(978-0-606-38580-0(0))* Turtleback Bks.

Berrios, Frank. Bad Weather! (DC Super Friends) Beavers, Ethen, illus. 2014. (Little Golden Book Ser.). (ENG.). 24p. (J). (-k). 4.99 *(978-0-385-38440-7(8),* Golden Bks.) Random Hse. Children's Bks.

—Batman's Birthday Surprise! (DC Super Friends) Random House & Doescher, Erik, illus. 2016. (Pictureback(R) Ser.). (ENG.). 16p. (J). (gr. -1-2). 4.99 *(978-0-553-53983-7(3),* Random Hse. Bks. for Young Readers) Random Hse. Children's Bks.

Big Guy Books Staff & Duey, Kathleen. Parche, Vol. 3. Gould, Robert, photos by. 2003. (Soldados en el Tiempo: Vol. 3). (SPA & ENG., Illus.). 48p. (J). (gr. k-4). pap. 8.95 *(978-1-929945-37-5(X))* Big Guy Bks., Inc.

Bird, Benjamin. Bubble Trouble! Levins, Tim, illus. 2015. (Amazing Adventures of Superman! Ser.). (ENG.). 32p. (gr. k-2). pap. 3.95 *(978-1-4795-6524-5(5),* DC Super Heroes) Stone Arch Bks.

—Magic Monsters! Levins, Tim, illus. 2015. (Amazing Adventures of Superman! Ser.). (ENG.). 32p. (gr. k-2). pap. 3.95 *(978-1-4795-6525-2(3),* DC Super Heroes) Stone Arch Bks.

—Supergirl's Pet Problem! Levins, Tim, illus. 2015. (Amazing Adventures of Superman! Ser.). (ENG.). 32p. (gr. k-2). pap. 3.95 *(978-1-4795-6523-8(7),* DC Super Heroes) Stone Arch Bks.

—Superman Colors, 1 vol. Beavers, Ethen, illus. 2014. (DC Board Bks.). (ENG.). 20p. (gr. -1 — 1). bds. 5.99 *(978-1-4795-5890-2(7))* Picture Window Bks.

—Wonder Woman ABCs, 1 vol. Beavers, Ethen, illus. 2014. (DC Board Bks.). (ENG.). 20p. (gr. -1 — 1). bds. 5.99 *(978-1-4795-5889-6(3))* Picture Window Bks.

Bird, Benjamin & Siegel, Jerry. Day of the Bizarros! Levins, Tim, illus. 2015. (Amazing Adventures of Superman! Ser.). (ENG.). 32p. (gr. k-2). pap. 3.95 *(978-1-4795-6522-1(9),* DC Super Heroes) Stone Arch Bks.

Blabey, Aaron. The Bad Guys. Blabey, Aaron, illus. 2017. (Bad Guys Ser.: bk.3). (ENG., Illus.). 144p. (J). (gr. 2-5). pap. 5.99 ***(978-1-338-08749-9(5),*** Scholastic Paperbacks) Scholastic, Inc.

—The Bad Guys. (Bad Guys Ser.: 2). (ENG.). 144p. (J). (gr. 2-5). 2017. pap. 5.99 *(978-0-545-91241-9(5))* 2016. pap. 5.99 *(978-0-545-91240-2(7))* Scholastic, Inc. (Scholastic Pr.).

—The Bad Guys. 2016. (Bad Guys Ser.: 1). lib. bdg. 16.00 ***(978-0-606-40039-8(7))*** Turtleback Bks.

Blackman, Malorie. Sinclair, Wonder Bear. Allwright, Deborah, illus. 2005. (Blue Go Bananas Ser.). (ENG.). 48p. (J). (gr. 1-2). lib. bdg. *(978-0-7787-2631-9(2))* Crabtree Publishing Co.

—Sinclair, Wonder Bear. Allwright, Deborah, illus. 2003. (Blue Bananas Ser.). (ENG.). 48p. (J). (gr. k-2). pap. 5.99 *(978-1-4052-0589-4(X))* Egmont Bks., Ltd. GBR. Dist: Independent Pubs. Group.

Blake, Stephanie. Super Bunny. Blake, Stephanie, illus. 2015. (ENG., Illus.). 38p. (J). 15.95 *(978-0-7358-4223-6(X))* North-South Bks., Inc.

Blevins, Wiley. How to Deal with Bullies Superhero-Style: Response to Bullying. Palen, Debbie, illus. 2015. (ENG.). 24p. (gr. k-2). lib. bdg. 19.99 *(978-1-63440-009-1(7))* Red Chair Pr.

Bohls, Steven. Jed & the Junkyard Wars. 2016. (Jed & the Junkyard War Ser.). (ENG.). 304p. (J). (gr. 3-7). 16.99 *(978-1-4847-2923-6(4))* Disney Pr.

Boles, S. Ivan the Invacar Saves the Wobbly Hubcap. Cunningham, Bob, illus. 2014. (J). pap. 7.95 *(978-0-9893267-3-5(X))* People Ink Pr.

Bolton, Chris A. Smash: Trial by Fire. Bolton, Kyle, illus. 2013. (ENG.). 160p. (J). (gr. 4-7). 18.99 *(978-0-7636-5596-9(1))* Candlewick Pr.

Bond, Gwenda. Fallout. 2015. (Lois Lane Ser.). (ENG.). 304p. (gr. 9-12). 16.95 *(978-1-63079-005-9(2))* Switch Pr.

Boniface, William. The Extraordinary Adventures of Ordinary Boy. Gilpin, Stephen, illus. 2008. (Extraordinary Adventures of Ordinary Boy Ser.: 2). (ENG.). 368p. (J). (gr. 3-7). pap. 6.99 *(978-0-06-077469-1(X))* HarperCollins Pubs.

—The Extraordinary Adventures of Ordinary Boy Bk. 3: The Great Powers Outage. Gilpin, Stephen, illus. 2010. (Extraordinary Adventures of Ordinary Boy Ser.: 3). (ENG.). 352p. (J). (gr. 3-7). pap. 7.99 *(978-0-06-077472-1(X))* HarperCollins Pubs.

—The Hero Revealed. Gilpin, Stephen, illus. 2008. (Extraordinary Adventures of Ordinary Boy Ser.: 1). (ENG.). 320p. (J). (gr. 3-7). pap. 6.99 *(978-0-06-077466-0(5))* HarperCollins Pubs.

Boyce, Frank Cottrell. The Astounding Broccoli Boy. 2015. 384p. (J). (gr. 3-7). 16.99 *(978-0-06-240017-8(7),* Walden Pond Pr.) HarperCollins Pubs.

Branch, Ken & Tanguay, Dave. Mr. Who? Mr. Atom! 2015. (Billy Batson & the Magic of Shazam! Ser.). (ENG., Illus.). 32p. (gr. 2-3). lib. bdg. 22.60 *(978-1-4342-9656-6(3))* Stone Arch Bks.

Breen, Steve. Violet the Pilot. 2008. (ENG., Illus.). 32p. (J). (gr. -1-3). 17.99 *(978-0-8037-3125-7(6),* Dial Bks) Penguin Young Readers Group.

Brewis, Alan. Boris Returns A Hero! 2008. 72p. pap. 12.50 *(978-1-4357-4377-9(6))* Lulu Pr., Inc.

Briggs, Andy. Council of Evil. 2009. 1.00 *(978-1-4074-4313-3(5))* Recorded Bks., Inc.

Bright, J. E. Cosmic Clash. Kiernan, Kenny, illus. 2016. (LEGO DC Super Heroes Ser.). (ENG.). 64p. (J). (gr. -1-3). pap. 4.99 *(978-0-545-86801-3(7))* Scholastic, Inc.

—Deepwater Disaster. Schoening, Dan et al, illus. 2011. (DC Super Heroes Ser.). (ENG.). 56p. (gr. 2-3). 26.65 *(978-1-4342-3317-2(0),* DC Super Heroes) Stone Arch Bks.

—The Fastest Pet on Earth, 1 vol. Baltazar, Art, illus. 2011. (DC Super-Pets Ser.). (ENG.). 56p. (gr. 2-2). pap. 4.95 *(978-1-4048-6623-2(X));* lib. bdg. 23.99 *(978-1-4048-6264-7(1))* Picture Window Bks. (DC Super-Pets).

—Heroes of the High Seas, 1 vol. Baltazar, Art, illus. 2011. (DC Super-Pets Ser.). (ENG.). 56p. (gr. 2-2). 23.99 *(978-1-4048-6263-0(3));* pap. 4.95 *(978-1-4048-6621-8(3))* Picture Window Bks. (DC Super-Pets).

—Joker on the High Seas, 1 vol. McManus, Shawn, illus. 2012. (DC Super-Villains Ser.). (ENG.). 56p. (gr. 2-3). pap. 5.95 *(978-1-4342-3895-5(4),* DC Super-villains) Stone Arch Bks.

—The Joker's Magic Mayhem. Vecchio, Luciano, illus. 2016. (Batman & Robin Adventures Ser.). (ENG.). 88p. (gr. 2-3). lib. bdg. 26.65 *(978-1-4965-2538-3(8),* DC Super Heroes) Stone Arch Bks.

—Lex Luthor & the Kryptonite Caverns, 1 vol. Vecchio, Luciano, illus. 2012. (DC Super-Villains Ser.). (ENG.). 56p. (gr. 2-3). pap. 5.95 *(978-1-4342-3896-2(2),* DC Super-villains) Stone Arch Bks.

—Savage Sands, 1 vol. Schoening, Dan, illus. 2011. (Green Lantern Ser.). (ENG.). 56p. (gr. 2-3). pap. 4.95 *(978-1-4342-3405-6(3));* lib. bdg. 26.65 *(978-1-4342-2619-8(0))* Stone Arch Bks. (DC Super Heroes).

—Scarecrow's Nightmare Maze. Vecchio, Luciano, illus. 2016. (Batman & Robin Adventures Ser.). (ENG.). 88p. (gr. 2-3). lib. bdg. 26.65 *(978-1-4965-2537-6(X),* DC Super Heroes) Stone Arch Bks.

—Seed Bank Heist. Beavers, Ethen, illus. 2015. (You Choose Stories: Batman Ser.). (ENG.). 112p. (gr. 2-3). pap. 6.95 *(978-1-4342-9709-9(8))* Stone Arch Bks.

—Teen Titans Go! - Cyborg Circuit Overload. 2015. (ENG., Illus.). 144p. (J). (gr. 1-5). pap. 5.99 *(978-0-316-33336-8(0))* Little, Brown Bks. for Young Readers.

—Teen Titans Go! - Raven Rocks! 2015. (ENG., Illus.). 144p. (J). (gr. 1-5). pap. 5.99 *(978-0-316-37732-4(5))* Little, Brown Bks. for Young Readers.

Bright, J. E. & Loughridge, Lee. The Deadly Dream Machine. Schigiel, Gregg, illus. (Superman Ser.). (ENG.). 56p. (gr. 2-3). 2014. pap. 4.95 *(978-1-4342-2759-1(6))* 2010. lib. bdg. 26.65 *(978-1-4342-1978-7(X))* Stone Arch Bks. (DC Super Heroes).

—Joker on the High Seas, 1 vol. McManus, Shawn, illus. 2012. (DC Super-Villains Ser.). (ENG.). 56p. (gr. 2-3). lib. bdg. 26.65 *(978-1-4342-3794-1(X),* DC Super-villains) Stone Arch Bks.

Bright, J. E., et al. Killer Kaleidoscope, 1 vol. 2011. (Flash Ser.). (ENG., Illus.). 56p. (gr. 2-3). pap. 4.95 *(978-1-4342-3414-8(2));* lib. bdg. 26.65 *(978-1-4342-2628-0(X))* Stone Arch Bks. (DC Super Heroes).

Brighter Child Publishing Staff, creator. Marvel Super Hero Fact Book. 2006. (Marvel Ser.). (Illus.). 12p. (J). bds. 9.95 *(978-1-57791-298-9(5))* Brighter Minds Children's Publishing.

Britten, Adam. Captain Valiant & Me. Hamer, Arthur, illus. 2014. (Captain Valiant Ser.). (ENG.). 160p. (J). (gr. k-3). pap. 9.99 *(978-1-84812-353-3(1))* Bonnier Publishing GBR. Dist: Independent Pubs. Group.

Brouwer, Sigmund. Sewer Rats, 1 vol. 2006. (Orca Currents Ser.). (ENG.). 128p. (J). (gr. 5-9). per. 9.95 *(978-1-55143-488-9(1))* Orca Bk. Pubs. USA.

—Sewer Rats. 2006. (Orca Currents Ser.). 106p. (gr. 4-7). 19.95 *(978-0-7569-6872-4(0))* Perfection Learning Corp.

Brown, Jeff. The U. S. Capital Commotion. Pamintuan, Macky, illus. 2011. (Flat Stanley's Worldwide Adventures Ser.: 9). (ENG.). 112p. (J). (gr. 2-5). pap. 4.99 *(978-0-06-143019-0(6))* HarperCollins Pubs.

—The US Capital Commotion. Pamintuan, Macky, illus. 2011. (Flat Stanley's Worldwide Adventures Ser.: 9). (ENG.). 112p. (J). (gr. 2-5). 15.99 *(978-0-06-157436-8(8))* HarperCollins Pubs.

Buckley, Michael. Attack of the Bullies. (Nerds Ser.). (ENG.). (gr. 3-7). 2013. 336p. (YA). 16.95 *(978-1-4197-0857-2(0))*Bk. 5. 2014. (Illus.). 352p. (J). pap. 7.95 *(978-1-4197-1222-7(5))* Abrams, Inc. (Amulet Bks.).

—The Cheerleaders of Doom, Bk. 3. 2012. (Nerds Ser.). (ENG.). 304p. (YA). (gr. 3-7). pap. 7.95 *(978-1-4197-0414-7(1),* Amulet Bks.) Abrams, Inc.

—NERDS 2: M für Muttersöhnchen. 2011. (SPA.). 260p. (J). (gr. 6-8). pap. 10.99 *(978-987-612-335-8(1))* V&R Editoras.

—Las Porristas del Infierno. 2013. 288p. (J). pap. 11.99 *(978-987-612-627-4(X))* V&R Editoras.

Buehner, Caralyn. Superdog: The Heart of a Hero. Buehner, Mark, illus. 2004. 32p. (J). (gr. -1-3). lib. bdg. 17.89 *(978-0-06-623621-6(5))* HarperCollins Pubs.

Burgess, Starr. Counselor Dynamite: Twas the Day Before Christmas Break. Guiza, Victor, illus. 2012. 28p. (J). 16.95 *(978-1-60131-118-4(4),* Castlebridge Bks.) Big Tent Bks.

—Counselor Dynamite Befuddles the Bullyville Crew. Guiza, Victor, illus. 2013. 52p. (J). 19.95 *(978-1-60131-156-6(7),* Castlebridge Bks.) Big Tent Bks.

Burroughs, Scott, illus. Balloon Blow-Up. 2013. (Hardy Boys: the Secret Files Ser.: 13). (ENG.). 112p. (J). (gr. 1-4). pap. 5.99 *(978-1-4424-5371-5(0),* Aladdin) Simon & Schuster Children's Publishing.

Busiek, Kurt. Marvels: The Platinum Edition Slipcase. 2014. (ENG., Illus.). 512p. (J). (gr. 4-17). 200.00 *(978-0-7851-5471-6(X))* Marvel Worldwide, Inc.

Cabot, Meg. All-American Girl. 2008. (All-American Girl Ser.: 1). (ENG.). 416p. (YA). (gr. 8). pap. 8.99 *(978-0-06-147989-2(6),* HarperTeen) HarperCollins Pubs.

—All-American Girl. 2008. (All-American Girl Ser.: Vol. 1). 398p. (YA). (gr. 7-12). 19.65 *(978-1-4178-2386-4(0),* Turtleback) Turtleback Bks.

—Ready or Not. 2nd ed. 2005. (All-American Girl Ser.: Vol. 2). 256p. (J). (gr. 7-18). lib. bdg. 16.89 *(978-0-06-072451-1(X))* HarperCollins Pubs.

Calle, Juan & Valentino, Serena. Good Dream, Bad Dream: The World's Legendary Heroes Save the Night! 2014. (ENG & SPA., Illus.). 36p. (J). (gr. -1-3). 15.95 *(978-1-59702-103-6(2))* Immedium.

Cannon, Sherrill S. Manner-Man. 2013. 28p. pap. 12.50 *(978-1-62212-478-7(2),* Strategic Bk. Publishing) Strategic Book Publishing & Rights Agency (SBPRA).

Cappoccia, Héloïse. The Planet of the Overhearers. 2013. (Little Prince Ser.: 7). (ENG., Illus.). 56p. (J). (gr. 4-8). pap. 7.95 *(978-1-4677-0739-8(2),* Graphic Universe™) Lerner Publishing Group.

Captain Awesome Gets a Hole-In-One. 2014. (Captain Awesome Ser.: 12). (ENG., Illus.). 128p. (J). (gr. k-4). pap. 5.99 *(978-1-4814-1431-9(3),* Little Simon) Little Simon.

Captain Underpants & the Tyrannical Retaliation of the Turbo Toilet 2000. 2014. (Captain Underpants Ser.: Bk. 11). (ENG., Illus.). 224p. (J). (gr. 2-5). 9.99 *(978-0-545-50490-4(2))* Scholastic, Inc.

Caramagna, Joe. Iron Man & the Armor Wars. 2013. (Iron Man & the Armor Wars Ser.: 4). 24p. (J). (gr. 2-6). lib. bdg. 96.84 *(978-1-61479-163-8(5))* Spotlight.

—Iron Man & the Armor Wars Part 1: Down & Out in Beverly Hills Hosted. 2013. (Iron Man & the Armor Wars Ser.). (Illus.). 24p. (J). (gr. 2-6). lib. bdg. 24.21 *(978-1-61479-164-5(3))* Spotlight.

—Iron Man & the Armor Wars Part 2: The Big Red Machine. 2013. (Iron Man & the Armor Wars Ser.). (Illus.). 24p. (J). (gr. 2-6). lib. bdg. 24.21 *(978-1-61479-165-2(1))* Spotlight.

—Iron Man & the Armor Wars Part 3: How I Learned to Love the Bomb. 2013. (Iron Man & the Armor Wars Ser.). (Illus.). 24p. (J). (gr. 2-6). lib. bdg. 24.21 *(978-1-61479-166-9(X))* Spotlight.

—Iron Man & the Armor Wars Part 4: The Golden Avenger Strikes Back. 2013. (Iron Man & the Armor Wars Ser.). (Illus.). 24p. (J). (gr. 2-6). lib. bdg. 24.21 *(978-1-61479-167-6(8))* Spotlight.

—Marvel Universe Avengers Assemble Volume 2. 2014. (ENG., Illus.). 88p. (J). (gr. -1-17). pap. 9.99 *(978-0-7851-8880-3(0))* Marvel Worldwide, Inc.

—Marvel Universe Guardians of the Galaxy: Cosmic Team-Up. Buscema, Sal, illus. 2014. (ENG.). 96p. (J). (gr. -1-17). pap. 9.99 *(978-0-7851-9031-8(7))* Marvel Worldwide, Inc.

Carbone, Courtney. How to Be a Hero (DC Super Friends) Random House, illus. 2016. (Ultimate Handbook Ser.). (ENG.). 64p. (J). (gr. 1-4). 9.99 *(978-1-101-93958-1(3),* Random Hse. Bks. for Young Readers) Random Hse. Children's Bks.

—Lights Out! (Marvel: Mighty Avengers) Spaziante, Patrick, illus. 2016. (Little Golden Book Ser.). (ENG.). 24p. (J). (-k). 4.99 *(978-0-307-97658-1(0),* Golden Bks.) Random Hse. Children's Bks.

—Supergirl Takes Off! 2016. (Step into Reading Level 2 Ser.). lib. bdg. 14.75 *(978-0-606-38887-0(7))* Turtleback Bks.

—Supergirl Takes off! (DC Super Friends) Random House Editors & Doescher, Erik, illus. 2016. (Step into Reading Ser.). (ENG.). 24p. (J). (gr. -1-1). 4.99 *(978-0-399-55344-8(4),* Random Hse. Bks. for Young Readers) Random Hse. Children's Bks.

—Wonder Woman to the Rescue! 2016. (Step into Reading Level 2 Ser.). lib. bdg. 14.75 *(978-0-606-38476-6(6))* Turtleback Bks.

Cardarelli, Alyn. Captain Virtue & the Champions of Justice. 2012. 38p. pap. 19.99 *(978-1-4685-0955-7(1))* AuthorHouse.

Carroll, Michael. The Ascension, Bk. 2. 2nd ed. 2012. (Super Human Ser.: 2). (ENG.). 400p. (YA). (gr. 7-18). pap. 9.99 *(978-0-14-242109-3(X),* Speak) Penguin Young Readers Group.

—The Awakening, No. 1. 2008. (Quantum Prophecy Ser.: 1). (ENG.). 288p. (J). (gr. 5-6). 8.99 *(978-0-14-241179-7(5),* Puffin Books) Penguin Young Readers Group.

Castro, Nachie. The Man in the Ant Hill, 1 vol. Marvel Illustrators, illus. 2012. (Avengers: Earth's Mightiest Heroes! Ser.). (ENG.). 24p. (J). (gr. -1-4). lib. bdg. 24.21 *(978-1-61479-004-4(3))* Spotlight.

Catanese, P. W. Happenstance Found, No. 1. 2009. (Books of Umber Ser.: 1). (ENG.). 368p. (J). (gr. 3-7). pap. 6.99 *(978-1-4169-5382-1(5),* Aladdin) Simon & Schuster Children's Publishing.

Chabon, Michael. The Astonishing Secret of Awesome Man. Parker, Jake, illus. 2011. (ENG.). 40p. (J). (gr. -1-3). 17.99 *(978-0-06-191462-1(2))* HarperCollins Pubs.

Chanda, J-P. Turtle Rescue! Redondo, Jesus, illus. 2004. (Teenage Mutant Ninja Turtles Ser.). 32p. (J). (gr. 4-7). 11.65 *(978-0-7569-5371-3(5))* Perfection Learning Corp.

Cho, Charles. Age of Ultron: The Reusable Sticker Book. 2015. (ENG., Illus.). 12p. (J). (gr. -1-1). pap. 6.99 *(978-0-316-25642-1(0))* Little, Brown Bks. for Young Readers.

Citra, Becky. Jeremy & the Enchanted Theater. Milne, Jessica, illus. 2004. 64p. (J). lib. bdg. 20.00 *(978-1-4242-1258-3(8))* Fitzgerald Bks.

Clack, Cynthia. Doodles the American Hero. 2007. (ENG., Illus.). 60p. (J). lib. bdg. 20.95 *(978-0-9787533-0-6(5))* Tiger Tale Publishing Co.

CLE, Troy. The Marvelous Effect. 2008. (Marvelous World Ser.: 1). (ENG.). 384p. (J). (gr. 5-9). pap. 8.99 *(978-1-4169-4215-3(7),* Simon & Schuster Bks. For Young Readers) Simon & Schuster Bks. For Young Readers.

Cle, Troy. Olivion's Favorites. 2009. (Marvelous World Ser.: 2). (ENG.). 352p. (J). (gr. 5-9). 14.99 *(978-1-4169-4216-0(5),* Simon & Schuster Bks. For Young Readers) Simon & Schuster Bks. For Young Readers.

Clements, Andrew. About Average. Elliott, Mark, illus. (ENG.). (J). (gr. 3-7). 2014. 144p. pap. 7.99 *(978-1-4169-9725-2(3))* 2012. 128p. 16.99 *(978-1-4169-9724-5(5))* Simon & Schuster Children's Publishing. (Atheneum Bks. for Young Readers).

Clevenger, Lee. IncrediBoy: Be Careful What You Wish. 2004. 267p. (J). pap. 12.95 *(978-0-9764052-0-7(2))* Thomas Max Publishing.

Clocktowerhill Research & Publishing Group. Loyd & Boyd & the Slug Monster of Webster County. 2011. (ENG., Illus.). 104p. (J). 12.99 *(978-0-9832130-0-0(3),* Lucas Violet) Clocktower Hill Research & Publishing Group, LLC.

Coates-Smith, Renee. Bobby's Secret Is Out. 2007. (Illus.). 43p. (J). 12.95 *(978-0-615-14325-5(3))* Imani Productions.

Cobot, Meg. All-American Girl. 2004. 416p. (J). (gr. 7-18). pap. 44.00 incl. audio *(978-0-8072-2281-2(X),* Listening Library) Random Hse. Audio Publishing Group.

Cody, Matthew. Super. (Supers of Noble's Green Ser.). (ENG.). 304p. (J). (gr. 3-7). 2014. 7.99 *(978-0-375-87291-4(4),* Yearling) 2012. 16.99 *(978-0-375-86894-8(1),* Knopf Bks. for Young Readers) Random Hse. Children's Bks.

—Villainous. 2015. (Supers of Noble's Green Ser.). (ENG.). 320p. (J). (gr. 3-7). 6.99 *(978-0-385-75492-7(2),* Yearling) Random Hse. Children's Bks.

Cohen, Alana. Heroes! White, David A., illus. 2011. (Lego City Ser.). (ENG.). 10p. (J). (gr. -1-k). bds. 9.99 *(978-0-545-27439-5(7))* Scholastic, Inc.

Cohen, Ivan & Eltaeb, Gabe. Tattooed Man Trouble!, 1 vol. Vecchio, Luciano, illus. 2014. (Green Lantern: the Animated Ser.). (ENG.). 32p. (gr. 2-3). 22.60 *(978-1-4342-6480-0(7))* Stone Arch Bks.

Cohen, Ivan, et al. Beware the Batman. Vecchio, Luciano & Brizuela, Dario, illus. 2015. (Beware the Batman Ser.). (ENG.). 32p. (gr. 2-3). 90.40 *(978-1-4965-0302-2(3))* Stone Arch Bks.

—Law & Disorder. Vecchio, Luciano, illus. 2015. (Beware the Batman Ser.). (ENG.). 32p. (gr. 2-3). lib. bdg. 22.60 *(978-1-4342-9738-9(1))* Stone Arch Bks.

Colan, Gene & Heck, Don, illus. The Invincible Iron Man. 2014. (ENG.). 264p. (J). (gr. -1-17). pap. 24.99 *(978-0-7851-8843-8(6))* Marvel Worldwide, Inc.

Cole, Bob. Power Reading: Chapter/Sci-Fi/Superhero. Ford, David, illus. 2004. 25p. (J). (gr. 3-4). vinyl bd. 39.95 *(978-1-883186-62-3(5),* PPSFC2) National Reading Styles Institute, Inc.

—Power Reading: Comic Book/Superhero. Ford, David, illus. 2005. 34p. (J). (gr. 2-4). vinyl bd. 29.95 *(978-1-883186-79-1(X),* PPSFC2) National Reading Styles Institute, Inc.

Colfer, Eoin. The Gauntlet. Richardson, Owen & Marvel Press Artist Staff, illus. 2016. (ENG.). 288p. (J). (gr. 3-7). 16.99 *(978-1-4847-4160-3(9),* Marvel Pr.) Disney Publishing Worldwide.

Collins Morgan, Connie. Hercules on the Bayou, 1 vol. Leonhard, Herb, illus. 2016. (ENG.). 32p. (J). (gr. k-3). 16.99 *(978-1-4556-2185-9(4))* Pelican Publishing Co., Inc.

Connolly, MarcyKate. Ravenous. 2016. (Illus.). 416p. (J). (gr. 3-7). 16.99 *(978-0-06-227274-4(8))* HarperCollins Pubs.

Cormier, Robert. Heroes. 2006. (York Notes Ser.). (ENG., Illus.). 112p. pap. *(978-1-4058-3559-6(1))* Pearson Education, Ltd.

Cottringer, Anne. Eliot Jones Midnight Superhero. Smith, Alex T., illus. 2009. 24p. (J). (gr. -1-2). pap. 7.95 *(978-1-58925-416-9(3))* Tiger Tales.

Courage, Nick. The Loudness: A Novel. 2015. (ENG.). 336p. (J). (gr. 3-7). 15.99 *(978-1-63220-414-1(2),* Sky Pony Pr.) Skyhorse Publishing Co., Inc.

Cox, Michael. Johnny Catbiscuit & the Stolen Secrets! Dunn, Gary, illus. 2008. (Johnny Catbiscuit Ser.). (ENG.). 160p. (J). (gr. 2-4). pap. 9.95 *(978-1-4052-3739-0(2))* Egmont Bks., Ltd. GBR. Dist: Independent Pubs. Group.

Crawford, Philip & Crawford, Philip Charles. The Fruit of All Evil. Schoening, Dan, illus. 2014. (Wonder Woman Ser.). (ENG.). 56p. (gr. 2-3). pap. 4.95 *(978-1-4342-2766-9(9),* DC Super Heroes) Stone Arch Bks.

Custard, P. T. Kid Canine - Superhero! Custard, P. T. & Pearson, David, illus. 2008. 32p. (J). 13.95 *(978-0-9785317-1-3(X))* Black Plum Bks.

Dahl, Michael. Bedtime for Batman. Beavers, Ethen, illus. 2016. (DC Super Heroes Ser.). (ENG.). 32p. (gr. -1-2). 15.95 *(978-1-62370-732-3(3));* lib. bdg. 22.65 *(978-1-5158-0652-3(9))* Stone Arch Bks. (DC Super Heroes).

—The Clown Prince of Cards. Vecchio, Luciano, illus. 2016. (Batman Tales of the Batcave Ser.). (ENG.). 40p. (gr. 1-3). lib. bdg. 24.65 *(978-1-4965-4013-3(1),* DC Super Heroes) Stone Arch Bks.

—The Crushing Coin. Vecchio, Luciano, illus. 2016. (Batman Tales of the Batcave Ser.). (ENG.). 40p. (gr. 1-3). lib. bdg. 24.65 *(978-1-4965-4014-0(X),* DC Super Heroes) Stone Arch Bks.

—Dark Tower Rising, 1 vol. Kovar, Ben, illus. 2012. (Troll Hunters Ser.). (ENG.). 112p. (gr. 2-3). lib. bdg. 25.32 *(978-1-4342-3308-0(1),* Troll Hunters) Stone Arch Bks.

—Dino Death-Trap. Vecchio, Luciano, illus. 2016. (Batman Tales of the Batcave Ser.). (ENG.). 40p. (gr. 1-3). lib. bdg. 24.65 *(978-1-4965-4015-7(8),* DC Super Heroes) Stone Arch Bks.

—Fallen Star, 1 vol. Kovar, Ben, illus. 2012. (Troll Hunters Ser.). (ENG.). 112p. (gr. 2-3). lib. bdg. 25.32 *(978-1-4342-3310-3(3),* Troll Hunters) Stone Arch Bks.

—Guardian of Earth, 1 vol. Schoening, Dan, illus. 2011. (Green Lantern Ser.). (ENG.). 56p. (gr. 2-3). pap. 4.95 *(978-1-4342-3081-2(3));* lib. bdg. 26.65 *(978-1-4342-2611-2(5))* Stone Arch Bks. (DC Super Heroes).

—The Last Super Hero, 1 vol. Schoening, Dan, illus. 2011. (Green Lantern Ser.). (ENG.). 56p. (gr. 2-3). pap. 4.95 *(978-1-4342-3082-9(1));* lib. bdg. 26.65 *(978-1-4342-2612-9(3))* Stone Arch Bks. (DC Super Heroes).

—The Lava Crown, 1 vol. Kovar, Ben, illus. 2012. (Troll Hunters Ser.). (ENG.). 112p. (gr. 2-3). lib. bdg. 25.32 *(978-1-4342-3309-7(X),* Troll Hunters) Stone Arch Bks.

—Library of Doom: the Final Chapters. 2015. (Library of Doom: the Final Chapters Ser.). (ENG.). 40p. (gr. 1-3). 95.96 *(978-1-4965-0301-5(5),* Zone Bks.) Stone Arch Bks.

—The Man Behind the Mask, 1 vol. Schoening, Dan, illus. (Batman Ser.). (ENG.). 56p. (gr. 2-3). 2013. pap. 4.95 *(978-1-4342-1730-1(2))* 2009. 26.65 *(978-1-4342-1563-5(6))* Stone Arch Bks. (DC Super Heroes).

—The Marshmallow Mermaid. Crowther, Jeff, illus. 2010. (Graphic Sparks Ser.). (ENG.). 40p. (gr. 1-3). pap. 5.95 *(978-1-4342-2802-4(9),* Graphic Sparks) Stone Arch Bks.

—The Penguin's Power Parasol. Vecchio, Luciano, illus. 2016. (Batman Tales of the Batcave Ser.). (ENG.). 40p. (gr. 1-3). lib. bdg. 24.65 *(978-1-4965-4012-6(3),* DC Super Heroes) Stone Arch Bks.

—Sugar Hero. Crowther, Jeff, illus. (Graphic Sparks Ser.). (ENG.). 40p. (gr. 1-3). 2010. pap. 5.95 *(978-1-4342-2801-7(0))* 2009. lib. bdg. 23.99 *(978-1-4342-1587-1(3))* Stone Arch Bks. (Graphic Sparks).

—Trial of the Amazons, 1 vol. Schoening, Dan, illus. 2010. (Wonder Woman Ser.). (ENG.). 56p. (gr. 2-3). lib. bdg. 26.65 *(978-1-4342-1883-4(X),* DC Super Heroes) Stone Arch Bks.

Dahl, Michael & Loughridge, Lee. The Shrinking City, 1 vol. Schigiel, Gregg, illus. 2009. (Superman Ser.). (ENG.). 56p. (gr. 2-3). 26.65 *(978-1-4342-1569-7(5),* DC Super Heroes) Stone Arch Bks.

—Shrinking City. Schigiel, Gregg, illus. 2013. (Superman Ser.). (ENG.). 56p. (gr. 2-3). pap. 4.95 *(978-1-4342-1735-6(3),* DC Super Heroes) Stone Arch Bks.

Dahl, Michael & Nickel, Scott. The Green Queen of Mean. Crowther, Jeff, illus. 2010. (Graphic Sparks Ser.). (ENG.). 40p. (gr. 1-3). pap. 5.95 *(978-1-4342-2803-1(7),* Graphic Sparks) Stone Arch Bks.

Dahl, Michael, et al. Five Riddles for Robin. Schigiel, Gregg, illus. 2009. (Batman Ser.). (ENG.). 56p. (gr. 2-3). lib. bdg. 26.65 *(978-1-4342-1151-4(7),* DC Super Heroes) Stone Arch Bks.

—Trickster's Bubble Trouble, 1 vol. 2011. (Flash Ser.). (ENG., Illus.). 56p. (gr. 2-3). pap. 4.95 *(978-1-4342-3413-1(4));* lib. bdg. 26.65 *(978-1-4342-2627-3(1))* Stone Arch Bks. (DC Super Heroes).

Dale, Jenny. Husky Hero. Reid, Mick, illus. 2003. 108p. (J). *(978-0-439-54361-3(4))* Scholastic, Inc.

Daley-Prado, M. J. The Super Heroes' in: FIND THAT BUNNY!! 2008. 34p. pap. 17.95 *(978-1-4357-3535-4(8))* Lulu Pr., Inc.

Dambrot, Marc. The Destined: A Hero's Calling. 2008. 116p. pap. 19.95 *(978-1-60474-792-8(7))* America Star Bks.

D'Andrea, Deborah & Borlasca, Hector. Pretend & Play Superhero. 2005. (Illus.). (J). *(978-1-57151-751-7(0))* Playhouse Publishing.

Danko, Dan & Mason, Tom. The Brotherhood of Rotten Babysitters. Gott, Barry, illus. 5th ed. 2005. (ENG.). 144p. (J). (gr. 3-7). pap. 15.99 *(978-0-316-15895-4(X))* Little, Brown Bks. for Young Readers.

David, Lawrence. The Invasion of the Shag Carpet Creature. Gott, Barry, illus. 2004. (Horace Splattly Ser.). 151p. (J). (gr. 4-7). 12.65 *(978-0-7569-2818-6(4))* Perfection Learning Corp.

—The Terror of the Pink Dodo Balloons. Gott, Barry, illus. 2003. (Horace Splattly Ser.). 153p. (J). (gr. 4-7). 12.65 *(978-0-7569-2816-2(8))* Perfection Learning Corp.

David, Peter. Hand in Hand: Part 1. 2013. (Wolverine First Class Set 2 Ser.). (Illus.). 24p. (J). (gr. 2-6). lib. bdg. 24.21 *(978-1-61479-176-8(7))* Spotlight.

—Hand in Hand: Part 2. 2013. (Wolverine First Class Set 2 Ser.). (Illus.). 24p. (J). (gr. 2-6). lib. bdg. 24.21 *(978-1-61479-177-5(5))* Spotlight.

—Rock Gods. 2013. (Wolverine First Class Set 2 Ser.). (Illus.). 24p. (J). (gr. 2-6). lib. bdg. 24.21 *(978-1-61479-180-5(5))* Spotlight.

David, Peter & Van Lente, Fred. Wolverine First Class Set 2. 2013. (Wolverine First Class Set 2 Ser.: 6). 24p. (J). (gr. 2-6). lib. bdg. 145.26 *(978-1-61479-175-1(9))* Spotlight.

Davis, Adam. Avengers: Age of Ultron: Hulk to the Rescue. 2015. (Passport to Reading Level 2 Ser.). (J). lib. bdg. 13.55 *(978-0-606-37215-2(6))* Turtleback Bks.

Davis, Darren. Atlas 123S for Superheroes. 2006. (ENG.). 16p. (J). (gr. -1-12). bds. 5.99 *(978-1-59559-117-3(6))* Left Field,Angel Gate.

—Atlas Gt Planets. 2006. (ENG.). 16p. (J). (gr. -1-12). bds. 5.99 *(978-1-59559-103-6(6))* Left Field,Angel Gate.

Davis, Darren G. & Larner, Bob. Atlas: Greetings from Earth. 2011. (ENG., Illus.). 96p. (J). pap. 7.99 *(978-1-4507-3535-3(5))* Bluewater Productions, Inc.

Davis, Jacky & Soman, David. Ladybug Girl Dresses Up! Soman, David, illus. 2010. (Ladybug Girl Ser.). (ENG., Illus.). 14p. (J). (gr. -1 — 1). bds. 5.99 *(978-0-448-45373-6(8),* Grosset & Dunlap) Penguin Young Readers Group.

DC Comics Staff. DC Super Heroes Storybook Collection. 2012. (ENG., Illus.). 192p. (J). (gr. -1-3). 11.99 *(978-0-06-212398-5(X))* HarperCollins Pubs.

DC Comics Staff & Belle, Magnolia. Teen Titans Go! - The Cruel Giggling Ghoul. 2016. (ENG., Illus.). 24p. (J). (gr. 3-7). pap. 3.99 *(978-0-316-35644-2(1))* Little, Brown Bks. for Young Readers.

DC Super Friends. 2013. (DC Super Friends Ser.). (ENG.). 32p. (gr. 1-2). 180.80 *(978-1-4342-4856-5(9))* Stone Arch Bks.

DC Super Hero Books for Libraries. 2013. (DC Super Heroes Ser.). (ENG.). 3823.26 *(978-1-4342-6566-1(8))* Stone Arch Bks.

DC Super Heroes. 2013. (DC Super Heroes Ser.). (ENG.). 56p. (gr. 2-3). 106.60 *(978-1-4342-6065-9(8))*; 133.25 *(978-1-4342-6064-2(X))* Stone Arch Bks. (DC Super Heroes).

De Bie, Erik Scott. Ghostwalker. 2005. (Fighters Ser.). 318p. *(978-1-4156-3838-5(1))* Wizards of the Coast.

de Campi, Alex. Agent Boo, Vol. 1. 2017. (ENG., Illus.). 96p. pap. 4.99 *(978-1-59816-802-0(9),* 9781598168020) TOKYOPOP, Inc.

DeCarlo, Mike, et al. Captain Boomerang's Comeback!, 1 vol. 2011. (Flash Ser.). (ENG., Illus.). 56p. (gr. 2-3). pap. 4.95 *(978-1-4342-3411-7(8))*; lib. bdg. 26.65 *(978-1-4342-2625-9(5))* Stone Arch Bks. (DC Super Heroes).

—Master of Mirrors!, 1 vol. 2011. (Flash Ser.). (ENG., Illus.). 56p. (gr. 2-3). pap. 4.95 *(978-1-4342-3415-5(0),* DC Super Heroes) Stone Arch Bks.

—Shell Shocker, 1 vol. Doescher, Erik, illus. 2011. (Flash Ser.). (ENG.). 56p. (gr. 2-3). lib. bdg. 26.65 *(978-1-4342-2615-0(8),* DC Super Heroes) Stone Arch Bks.

Defalco, Tom, et al. Thor Epic Collection: War of the Pantheons. Frenz, Ron et al, illus. 2013. (ENG.). 472p. (J). (gr. 4-17). pap. 34.99 *(978-0-7851-8788-2(X))* Marvel Worldwide, Inc.

del Toro, Guillermo & Kraus, Daniel. Trollhunters. Murray, Sean, illus. (Trollhunters Ser.). (ENG.). 320p. (YA). (gr. 7-12). 2016. pap. 9.99 ***(978-1-368-01218-8(3),*** 1380291) 2015. 18.99 *(978-1-4231-2598-3(3),* 1380291) Hyperion Bks. for Children.

DeLand, Maitland. The Great Katie Kate Explains Epilepsy. 2014. (ENG., Illus.). 32p. (J). 14.95 *(978-1-62634-007-7(2),* Greenleaf Book Group Pr.) Greenleaf Book Group.

Dempsey, Kristy. Superhero Instruction Manual. Fearing, Mark, illus. 2016. (ENG.). 40p. (J). (gr. k-3). 16.99 *(978-0-385-75534-4(1),* Knopf Bks. for Young Readers) Random Hse. Children's Bks.

Denton, Terry. The Wooden Cow. Denton, Terry, illus. 2003. (Storymaze Ser.: Vol. 3). (ENG., Illus.). 120p. (J). (gr. 3-6). pap. 11.99 *(978-1-86508-783-2(1))* Allen & Unwin AUS. Dist: Independent Pubs. Group.

Depken, Kristen L. Mighty Troll & Wonder Dragon. Burch, Benjamin, illus. 2016. (Little Golden Book Ser.). (ENG.). 24p. (J). (gr. -1-k). 4.99 *(978-1-101-93149-3(3),* Golden Bks.) Random Hse. Children's Bks.

DeSpain, Pleasant. Tales of Heroes. 2016. (ENG., Illus.). 80p. (J). (gr. 3-4). pap. 9.95 *(978-1-941460-38-2(0))* August Hse. Pubs., Inc.

Dezago, Todd. Casper & the Spectrals TP. 2011. (Illus.). 96p. pap. 7.99 *(978-0-9561259-6-5(4))* Ardden Entertainment GBR. Dist: Diamond Bk. Distributors.

DiCamillo, Kate. Flora & Ulysses: The Illuminated Adventures. Campbell, K. G., illus. (ENG.). (J). (gr. 3-7). 2016. pap. 6.99 *(978-0-7636-8764-9(2))* 2013. 240p. 17.99 *(978-0-7636-6040-6(X))* Candlewick Pr.

—Flora & Ulysses: The Illuminated Adventures. Campbell, K. G., illus. 2016. (ENG.). 256p. (J). (gr. 3-7). 17.20 *(978-0-606-39100-9(2))* Turtleback Bks.

—Flora & Ulysses: The Illuminated Adventures. 2015. lib. bdg. 19.65 *(978-0-606-36861-2(2))* Turtleback Bks.

DiCicco, Sue. Superhero Potty Time. 2011. (ENG., Illus.). 14p. (J). (— 1). bds. 7.99 *(978-0-375-87201-3(9),* Golden Bks.) Random Hse. Children's Bks.

Dillard, Sarah. Extraordinary Warren: A Super Chicken. Dillard, Sarah, illus. 2014. (Pix Ser.). (ENG., Illus.). 64p. (J). (gr. 1-4). 12.99 *(978-1-4424-5340-1(0),* Aladdin) Simon & Schuster Children's Publishing.

Dini, Paul. Men of Steel, 1 vol. Burchett, Rick & Austin, Terry, illus. 2012. (Superman Adventures Ser.). (ENG.). 32p. (gr. 2-3). lib. bdg. 22.60 *(978-1-4342-4549-6(7))* Stone Arch Bks.

DiOrio, Ariel, illus. The Mystery of the Missing Menorahs: A Hanukkah Humdinger! 2007. 52p. (J). pap. 9.95 *(978-0-9659546-4-8(1))* Oak Leaf Systems.

Disney Book Group Staff. Iron Man vs. Titanium Man. Disney Storybook Artists Staff, illus. 2013. (Marvel Super Hero vs. Book Ser.). (ENG.). 24p. (J). (gr. -1-k). pap. 3.99 *(978-1-4231-5469-3(X))* Marvel Worldwide, Inc.

—The Story of Iron Man, Level 2. 2013. (World of Reading Ser.). (ENG., Illus.). 32p. (J). (gr. 1-2). pap. 3.99 *(978-1-4231-5413-6(4))* Marvel Worldwide, Inc.

—These Are the Avengers Level 1 Reader. 2012. (World of Reading Ser.). (ENG.). 32p. (J). (gr. -1-k). pap. 3.99 *(978-1-4231-5398-6(7),* Marvel Pr.) Disney Publishing Worldwide.

—This Is Iron Man. 2012. (World of Reading Ser.). (ENG., Illus.). 32p. (J). (gr. -1-k). pap. 3.99 *(978-1-4231-5412-9(6),* Marvel Pr.) Disney Publishing Worldwide.

—World of Reading This Is Captain America: Level 1. Disney Book Group Staff, illus. 2014. (World of Reading Ser.). (ENG., Illus.). 32p. (J). (gr. -1-k). pap. 3.99 *(978-1-4847-1267-2(6),* Marvel Pr.) Disney Publishing Worldwide.

—5-Minute Marvel Stories. 2012. (5-Minute Stories Ser.). (ENG., Illus.). 192p. (J). (gr. -1 — 1). 12.99 *(978-1-4231-6722-8(8))* Marvel Worldwide, Inc.

Disney Book Group Staff & Macri, Thomas. These Are the X-Men Level 1. Disney Storybook Artists Staff & Bachs, Ramon, illus. 2013. (World of Reading Ser.). (ENG.). 32p. (J). (gr. -1-k). pap. 3.99 *(978-1-4231-7083-9(0))* Marvel Worldwide, Inc.

Disney Book Group Staff & Peterson, Scott. Meet the Marvel Super Heroes: Includes a Poster of Your Favorite Super Heroes! 2013. (ENG., Illus.). 144p. (J). (gr. 1-3). 12.99 *(978-1-4231-6142-4(4))* Marvel Worldwide, Inc.

Disney Book Group Staff & Thomas, Rich. Happy Holidays! From Avengers: Featuring the Voice of Stan Lee. Lim, Ron & Rosenberg, Rachelle, illus. 2014. (ENG.). 48p. (J). (gr. 1-3). 8.99 *(978-1-4847-1227-6(7),* Marvel Pr.) Disney Publishing Worldwide.

Disney Book Group Staff, et al. Shake to Assemble. Disney Book Group Staff et al, illus. 2015. (ENG.). 48p. (J). (gr. -1-k). 12.99 *(978-1-4231-7826-2(2),* Marvel Pr.) Disney Publishing Worldwide.

Disney Editors. Disney Tangled Movie Comic. 2017. (ENG.). 64p. (J). (gr. 4-7). 18.40 *(978-0-606-39085-9(5))* Turtleback Bks.

Disney Press. Avengers: Battle with Ultron. 2015. (Marvel World of Reading Level 2 Ser.). (J). lib. bdg. 13.55 *(978-0-606-36904-6(X))* Turtleback Bks.

Disney Press Editors. Avengers: The New Team. 2015. (Marvel World of Reading Level 1 Ser.). (J). lib. bdg. 13.55 *(978-0-606-36903-9(1))* Turtleback Bks.

DiTocco, Robyn & DiTocco, Tony. The Hero Perseus: A Mad Myth Mystery. 2004. 220p. (gr. 3-12). 19.95 *(978-0-9723429-0-2(7))*; pap. 11.95 *(978-0-9723429-1-9(5))* Brainstorm Pubns., Inc.

Donaldson, Julia. Superworm. Scheffler, Axel, illus. 2014. (ENG.). 32p. (J). (gr. -1-3). 16.99 *(978-0-545-59176-8(7),* Levine, Arthur A. Bks.) Scholastic, Inc.

Doodler, Todd H. Super Fly: The World's Smallest Superhero! 2015. (Super Fly Ser.). (ENG., Illus.). 128p. (J). (gr. k-2). 15.99 *(978-1-61963-379-7(5),* 9781619633797, Bloomsbury USA Childrens) Bloomsbury Publishing USA.

—Super Fly vs. Furious Flea! 2016. (Super Fly Ser.). (ENG., Illus.). 128p. (J). 15.99 *(978-1-61963-385-8(X),* 9781619633858, Bloomsbury USA Childrens) Bloomsbury Publishing USA.

—Super Rawr! Doodler, Todd H., illus. 2016. (ENG., Illus.). 40p. (J). (gr. -1-k). 12.99 *(978-0-545-79969-0(4),* Scholastic Pr.) Scholastic, Inc.

Dorling Kindersley Publishing Staff. Batman's Missions. 2015. (DK Readers Ser.). (ENG.). 64p. (J). (gr. 2-4). pap. 3.99 *(978-1-4654-3014-4(8),* DK Children) Dorling Kindersley Publishing, Inc.

—Super Heroes - Ready for Action! 2013. (LEGO DC Universe DK Readers Ser.). lib. bdg. 13.55 *(978-0-606-31474-9(1),* Turtleback) Turtleback Bks.

—Super-Villains. 2013. (LEGO DC Universe DK Readers Ser.). lib. bdg. 13.55 *(978-0-606-31475-6(X),* Turtleback) Turtleback Bks.

Dorling Kindersley Publishing Staff & Taylor, Victoria. Ready for Action! 2013. (DK Readers Ser.). (ENG., Illus.). 32p. (J). (gr. k-4). pap. 3.99 *(978-1-4654-0174-8(1),* DK Children) Dorling Kindersley Publishing, Inc.

Driscoll, Laura. Real Heroes Don't Wear Capes. 2008. pap. 34.95 *(978-1-58013-764-5(4))* Kane Press, Inc.

—Real Heroes Don't Wear Capes. Wummer, Amy, illus. 2007. (Social Studies Connects). 32p. (J). (gr. -1-3). pap. 5.95 *(978-1-57565-245-0(5))* Kane Press, Inc.

Dyan, Penelope. Mermaids & Wishes for Tails Like Fishes. Dyan, Penelope, illus. 2009. (Illus.). 44p. pap. 11.95 *(978-1-935118-50-3(1))* Bellissima Publishing, LLC.

Dye, Troy & Kelesides, Tom. Goblin Chronicles 01A. 2008. (YA). 3.50 *(978-0-9801314-0-6(5))* Ape Entertainment.

—Goblin Chronicles #1B. 2008. (YA). 3.50 *(978-0-9801314-1-3(3))* Ape Entertainment.

—Goblin Chronicles #2A. 2008. (Illus.). 32p. (J). 3.50 *(978-0-9801314-2-0(1))* Ape Entertainment.

—Goblin Chronicles #2B. 2008. (Illus.). 32p. (J). 3.50 *(978-0-9801314-3-7(X))* Ape Entertainment.

Ebon Research Systems Staff. Dare to Be: Roberto Clemente. l.t. ed. 2003.Tr. of Atrevete a Ser un Heroe. . . Roberto Clemente. (ENG & SPA., Illus.). 22p. 3.99 *(978-0-9648313-5-3(X))* Ebon Research Systems Publishing, LLC.

—Dare to Be Vol. 2: Lessons in the Life of Esperanza. l.t. ed. 2003.Tr. of Atrevete Ser... Un Heroe. (ENG & SPA., Illus.). 16p. (J). 3.99 *(978-0-9648313-4-6(1))* Ebon Research Systems Publishing, LLC.

Eliopoulos, Chris. Mr. Puzzle. Eliopoulos, Chris, illus. 2013. (Mr. Puzzle Ser.). (ENG., Illus.). 40p. (gr. 1-3). 95.96 *(978-1-4342-6347-6(9))* Stone Arch Bks.

—Mr. Puzzle Super Collection!, 1 vol. Eliopoulos, Chris, illus. 2013. (Mr. Puzzle Ser.). (ENG., Illus.). 128p. (gr. 3-6). pap. 7.95 *(978-1-62370-035-5(3))* Capstone Young Readers of Coughlan Cos.

Eliopulos, Nick, et al. Hero Story Collection. 2012. (Step into Reading Level 4 Ser.). lib. bdg. 18.40 *(978-0-606-26791-5(3),* Turtleback) Turtleback Bks.

Eltoukhy, G. N. Fattopia a C: The Tablet Legacy. 2012. 28p. pap. 16.09 *(978-1-4669-3706-2(8))* Trafford Publishing.

Enderle, Dotti. Gingerbread Man Superhero!, 1 vol. Kulka, Joe, illus. 2009. (ENG.). 32p. (J). (gr. k-3). 16.99 *(978-1-58980-521-7(6))* Pelican Publishing Co., Inc.

Escoffier, Michaël. The Day I Lost My Superpowers. Di Giacomo, Kris, illus. 2014. (ENG.). 32p. (J). (gr. -1-3). 16.95 *(978-1-59270-144-5(2))* Enchanted Lion Bks., LLC.

Esquivel, Eric. Carnival Capers! 2016. (LEGO DC Super Heroes Ser.). lib. bdg. 13.55 *(978-0-606-38829-0(X))* Turtleback Bks.

Everheart, Chris, et al. Toys of Terror, 1 vol. 2013. (Superman Ser.). (ENG., Illus.). 56p. (gr. 2-3). pap. 4.95 *(978-1-4342-1374-7(9),* DC Super Heroes) Stone Arch Bks.

Faerber, Jay, et al. Universal Heroes. 2006. (Illus.). 136p. (YA). pap. 13.99 *(978-0-7851-1857-2(8))* Marvel Worldwide, Inc.

Fajardo, Alexis E. Kid Beowulf: The Song of Roland. 2017. lib. bdg. 24.50 ***(978-0-606-40301-6(9))*** Turtleback Bks.

Fan, Nancy Yi. Sword Mountain. 2012. (Swordbird Ser.: 3). (ENG., Illus.). 336p. (J). (gr. 3-7). 16.99 *(978-0-06-165108-3(7))* HarperCollins Pubs.

Farshtey, Greg. The Doom Box. 2012. (LEGO Hero Factory Ser.: 1). lib. bdg. 16.00 *(978-0-606-26768-7(9),* Turtleback) Turtleback Bks.

—Lego DC Super Heroes. 2013. (LEGO DC Super Heroes Ser.). lib. bdg. 19.65 *(978-0-606-32019-1(9),* Turtleback) Turtleback Bks.

—LEGO DC Super Heroes Handbook. 2015. (LEGO DC Super Heroes Ser.). (ENG.). 144p. (J). (gr. -1-3). lib. bdg. 20.85 *(978-0-606-38110-9(4))* Turtleback Bks.

—Mirror World. 2013. (LEGO Hero Factory Ser.: 5). lib. bdg. 16.00 *(978-0-606-32020-7(2),* Turtleback) Turtleback Bks.

Faulkerson, President & CEO Jeffery, Founder. IT's GOOD to BE GOLDEN: Golden Innovations. 2008. 30p. 14.95 *(978-0-615-19351-9(X))* PRACTICAL SOLUTIONS Writing, Editing, Consulting.

—IT's GOOD to BE GOLDEN: the Story of Henry the Heart. 2008. 19p. 14.95 *(978-0-615-19350-2(1))* PRACTICAL SOLUTIONS Writing, Editing, Consulting.

Fein, Eric & Loughridge, Lee. My Frozen Valentine, 1 vol. Schigiel, Gregg, illus. (Batman Ser.). (ENG.). 56p. (gr. 2-3). 2013. pap. 4.95 *(978-1-4342-1731-8(0))* 2009. 26.65 *(978-1-4342-1564-2(4))* Stone Arch Bks. (DC Super Heroes).

Fein, Eric, et al. Catwoman's Halloween Heist, 1 vol. (Batman Ser.). (ENG., Illus.). 56p. (gr. 2-3). 2014. pap. 4.95 *(978-1-4342-2767-6(7))* 2010. lib. bdg. 26.65 *(978-1-4342-2132-2(6))* Stone Arch Bks. (DC Super Heroes).

—The Maker of Monsters, 1 vol. (Batman Ser.). (ENG., Illus.). 56p. (gr. 2-3). 2014. pap. 4.95 *(978-1-4342-2762-1(6))* 2010. lib. bdg. 26.65 *(978-1-4342-1984-8(4))* Stone Arch Bks. (DC Super Heroes).

—Parasite's Power Drain, 1 vol. McManus, Shawn, illus. (Superman Ser.). (ENG.). 56p. (gr. 2-3). 2013. pap. 4.95 *(978-1-4342-2261-9(6))* 2010. lib. bdg. 26.65 *(978-1-4342-1882-7(1))* Stone Arch Bks. (DC Super Heroes).

Ferguson, Adrian. Hamburger Man: Resurrection. 2008. 155p. pap. 17.95 *(978-1-4092-4500-1(4))* Lulu Pr., Inc.

Fialkov, Joshua Hale. X-Men: To Serve & Protect. Coipel, Olivier & Donovan, Deric, illus. 2011. (ENG.). 136p. (J). (gr. 4-17). pap. 14.99 *(978-0-7851-5228-6(8))* Marvel Worldwide, Inc.

Figueroa, Acton. So Not the Drama. 2005. (Illus.). 79p. (J). *(978-1-4156-3929-0(9))* Disney Pr.

Finals Crisis. 2016. (DC Super Hero Girls Ser.: 1). lib. bdg. 20.85 *(978-0-606-38779-8(X))* Turtleback Bks.

Finger, Bill & Cameron, Don. Batman Arkham: Scarecrow. 2016. lib. bdg. 33.05 *(978-0-606-38632-6(7))* Turtleback Bks.

Finnegan, Delphine. Justice League Classic: Mind Games. Roberts, Jeremy et al, illus. 2016. 24p. (J). (gr. -1-3). pap. 3.99 *(978-0-06-236075-5(2),* HarperFestival) HarperCollins Pubs.

Firestone, Carrie. The Unlikelies. 2017. (ENG.). 336p. (YA). (gr. 9-17). 17.99 ***(978-0-316-38286-1(8))*** Little, Brown Bks. for Young Readers.

Fisch, Sholly. April Fools, 1 vol. Brizuela, Dario, illus. 2012. (DC Super Friends Ser.). (ENG.). 32p. (gr. 1-2). lib. bdg. 22.60 *(978-1-4342-4544-1(6))* Stone Arch Bks.

—Challenge of the Super Friends, 1 vol. Brizuela, Dario, illus. 2013. (DC Super Friends Ser.). (ENG.). 32p. (gr. 1-2). lib. bdg. 22.60 *(978-1-4342-4701-8(5))* Stone Arch Bks.

—DC Super Friends. 2013. (DC Super Friends Ser.). (ENG.). 32p. (gr. 1-2). 90.40 *(978-1-4342-4855-8(0))* Stone Arch Bks.

—Hungry for Power, 1 vol. Brizuela, Dario, illus. 2012. (DC Super Friends Ser.). (ENG.). 32p. (gr. 1-2). lib. bdg. 22.60 *(978-1-4342-4541-0(1))* Stone Arch Bks.

—Wanted - The Super Friends. McKenny, Stewart & Moy, Philip, illus. 2012. (DC Super Friends Ser.). (ENG.). 32p. (gr. 1-2). lib. bdg. 22.60 *(978-1-4342-4543-4(8))* Stone Arch Bks.

Fisch, Sholly & Age, Heroic. Happy Birthday, Superman!, 1 vol. Bone, J., illus. 2014. (DC Super Friends Ser.). (ENG.). 32p. (gr. 1-2). 22.60 *(978-1-4342-9222-3(3))* Stone Arch Bks.

—Season of Light, 1 vol. Brizuela, Dario, illus. 2014. (DC Super Friends Ser.). (ENG.). 32p. (gr. 1-2). 22.60 *(978-1-4342-9223-0(1))* Stone Arch Bks.

—Who Is the Mystery Bat-Squad?, 1 vol. Clugston, Chynna, illus. 2014. (DC Super Friends Ser.). (ENG.). 32p. (gr. 1-2). 22.60 *(978-1-4342-9224-7(X))* Stone Arch Bks.

Fisch, Sholly & Ottolini, Horacio. Dinosaur Round-Up, 1 vol. Brizuela, Dario & Staton, Joe, illus. 2012. (DC Super Friends Ser.). (ENG.). 32p. (gr. 1-2). lib. bdg. 22.60 *(978-1-4342-4542-7(X))* Stone Arch Bks.

Fisch, Sholly, et al. The All-New Batman: the Brave & the Bold. 2015. (All-New Batman: the Brave & the Bold Ser.). (ENG., Illus.). 32p. (gr. 2-3). lib. bdg. 90.40 *(978-1-4965-0544-6(1))* Stone Arch Bks.

—Bottle of the Planets. 2015. (All-New Batman: the Brave & the Bold Ser.). (ENG., Illus.). 32p. (gr. 2-3). lib. bdg. 22.60 *(978-1-4342-9658-0(X))* Stone Arch Bks.

—The Bride & the Bold. 2015. (All-New Batman: the Brave & the Bold Ser.). (ENG., Illus.). 32p. (gr. 2-3). lib. bdg. 22.60 *(978-1-4342-9661-0(X))* Stone Arch Bks.

—Clobbered by Clayface! 2015. (All-New Batman: the Brave & the Bold Ser.). (ENG., Illus.). 32p. (gr. 2-3). lib. bdg. 22.60 *(978-1-4342-9663-4(6))* Stone Arch Bks.

—Manhandled by Manhunters! 2015. (All-New Batman: the Brave & the Bold Ser.). (ENG., Illus.). 32p. (gr. 2-3). lib. bdg. 22.60 *(978-1-4342-9662-7(8))* Stone Arch Bks.

—Starro & the Pirates, 1 vol. 2014. (DC Super Friends Ser.). (ENG., Illus.). 32p. (gr. 1-2). 22.60 *(978-1-4342-9225-4(8))* Stone Arch Bks.

—That Holiday Feeling. 2015. (All-New Batman: the Brave & the Bold Ser.). (ENG., Illus.). 32p. (gr. 2-3). lib. bdg. 22.60 *(978-1-4342-9659-7(8))* Stone Arch Bks.

—Through the Looking Glass! 2015. (All-New Batman: the Brave & the Bold Ser.). (ENG., Illus.). 32p. (gr. 2-3). lib. bdg. 22.60 *(978-1-4342-9660-3(1))* Stone Arch Bks.

Flanagan, John. The Battle for Skandia. (Ranger's Apprentice Ser.: 4). (ENG.). (J). (gr. 5-18). 2008. 304p. 18.99 *(978-0-399-24457-5(3),* Philomel Bks.)Bk. 4. 2009. 336p. 8.99 *(978-0-14-241340-1(2),* Puffin Books) Penguin Young Readers Group.

—The Battle for Skandia. 2009. (Ranger's Apprentice Ser.: 4). lib. bdg. 19.65 *(978-0-606-02208-8(2),* Turtleback) Turtleback Bks.

—The Burning Bridge, Bk. 2. 2007. (Ranger's Apprentice Ser.: 2). (ENG.). 304p. (J). (gr. 5-18). 8.99 *(978-0-14-240842-1(5),* Puffin Books) Penguin Young Readers Group.

—The Burning Bridge. 2007. (Ranger's Apprentice Ser.: 2). 262p. lib. bdg. 19.65 *(978-1-4177-9330-3(9),* Turtleback) Turtleback Bks.

—The Icebound Land. 2007. (Ranger's Apprentice Ser.: Bk. 3). 260p. (J). 25.66 *(978-1-4287-4632-9(3),* Follettbound) Follett School Solutions.

—The Icebound Land, Bk. 3. (Ranger's Apprentice Ser.: 3). (ENG.). (J). (gr. 5-18). 2008. 304p. 8.99 *(978-0-14-241075-2(6),* Puffin Books) 2007. 272p. 18.99 *(978-0-399-24456-8(5),* Philomel Bks.) Penguin Young Readers Group.

—The Outcasts. 2011. (Brotherband Chronicles: Bk. 1). (ENG.). (J). (gr. 3-7). 54.99 *(978-1-61657-043-9(1))* Findaway World, LLC.

—The Outcasts. (Brotherband Chronicles Ser.: 1). (ENG.). (J). (gr. 5). 2012. 464p. pap. 8.99 *(978-0-14-242194-9(4),* Puffin Books) 2011. 448p. 18.99 *(978-0-399-25619-6(9),* Philomel Bks.) Penguin Young Readers Group.

—The Outcasts. 2012. (Brotherband Chronicles Ser.: 1). lib. bdg. 19.65 *(978-0-606-26636-9(4),* Turtleback) Turtleback Bks.

—The Royal Ranger. 2014. (Ranger's Apprentice Ser.: 12). (ENG.). 480p. (J). (gr. 5). pap. 8.99 *(978-0-14-242731-6(4),* Puffin Books) Penguin Young Readers Group.

—The Ruins of Gorlan, Bk. 1. 2006. (Ranger's Apprentice Ser.: 1). (ENG.). 288p. (J). (gr. 5-18). 8.99 *(978-0-14-240663-2(5),* Puffin Books) Penguin Young Readers Group.

—The Siege of Macindaw, Bk. 6. (Ranger's Apprentice Ser.: 6). (ENG.). (J). (gr. 5-18). 2010. 336p. 8.99 *(978-0-14-241524-5(3),* Puffin Books) 2009. 304p. 18.99 *(978-0-399-25033-0(6),* Philomel Bks.) Penguin Young Readers Group.

—The Sorcerer of the North, 5 vols., Bk. 5. (Ranger's Apprentice Ser.: 5). (ENG.). (J). (gr. 5-18). 2009. 336p. pap. 8.99 *(978-0-14-241429-3(8),* Puffin Books) 2008. 304p. 18.99 *(978-0-399-25032-3(8),* Philomel Bks.) Penguin Young Readers Group.

—The Sorcerer of the North. 2009. (Ranger's Apprentice Ser.: 5). lib. bdg. 19.65 *(978-0-606-02237-8(6),* Turtleback) Turtleback Bks.

Flanagan, John A. The Tournament at Gorlan. 2016. (Ranger's Apprentice the Early Years Ser.: 1). lib. bdg. 19.65 *(978-0-606-39332-4(3))* Turtleback Bks.

Fleming, Bryn. Cassie & Jasper to the Rescue. 2014. (Range Riders Ser.). (ENG.). 128p. (YA). (gr. 3-7). 23.99 *(978-1-941821-04-6(9),* West Winds Pr.) Graphic Arts Ctr. Publishing Co.

Fliess, Sue. How to Be a Superhero. Dyson, Nikki, illus. 2014. (Little Golden Book Ser.). (ENG.). 24p. (J). (-k). 3.99 *(978-0-385-38737-8(7),* Golden Bks.) Random Hse. Children's Bks.

Flintham, Thomas. Game over, Super Rabbit Boy! a Branches Book (Press Start! #1) 2016. (Press Start! Ser.: 1). (ENG.). 80p. (J). (gr. k-2). pap. 4.99 *(978-1-338-03471-4(5))* Scholastic, Inc.

Fogarty, Paula. Slave of the Lamp. l.t. ed. 2013. 354p. pap. *(978-1-4596-6705-1(0))* ReadHowYouWant.com, Ltd.

Fogg, K. L. Serpent Tide. 2006. 16.95 *(978-1-59156-861-2(7))* Covenant Communications, Inc.

—Widow's Revenge: A Novel. 2007. 355p. (J). *(978-1-59811-319-8(4))* Covenant Communications.

Fontana, Shea. Summer Olympus. 2017. (DC Super Hero Girls Ser.: 3). lib. bdg. 20.85 ***(978-0-606-40123-4(7))*** Turtleback Bks.

Forney, Lane. The Super Power Teens 2: A Blast from the Past. 2010. 137p. pap. 14.99 *(978-0-557-09707-4(X))* Lulu Pr., Inc.

Fox, Gardner. The Atom, Vol. 2. rev. ed. 2003. (ENG., Illus.). 216p. (YA). 49.95 *(978-1-4012-0014-5(1))* DC Comics.

Fox, Jennifer. Team of Heroes. 2014. (Transformers Passport to Reading Ser.). (J). lib. bdg. 13.55 *(978-0-606-35936-8(2))* Turtleback Bks.

—Teen Titans Go! - Brain Food. 2015. (Passport to Reading Level 2 Ser.). (ENG., Illus.). 32p. (J). (gr. -1-3). pap. 3.99 *(978-0-316-33331-3(X))* Little, Brown Bks. for Young Readers.

Foxlee, Karen. Ophelia & the Marvelous Boy. 2014. (ENG.). 240p. (J). (gr. 3-7). 16.99 *(978-0-385-75354-8(3),* Knopf Bks. for Young Readers) Random Hse. Children's Bks.

Frampton, Otis. Red Riding Hood, Superhero. Frampton, Otis, illus. 2015. (Far Out Fairy Tales Ser.). (ENG., Illus.). 40p. (gr. 3-4). lib. bdg. 25.32 *(978-1-4342-9650-4(4))* Stone Arch Bks.

Frenette, Bethany. Burn Bright. 2014. (Dark Star Ser.). (ENG.). 352p. (YA). (gr. 7-12). 17.99 *(978-1-4231-4666-7(2))* Hyperion Bks. for Children.

Fridolfs, Derek. Secret Hero Society- Study Hall of Justice. Nguyen, Dustin, illus. 2016. 176p. (J). pap. ***(978-1-76027-653-9(7))*** Scholastic, Inc.

Friends & Heroes Activity & Coloring Book. 2008. (Friends & Heroes Ser.). (J). pap. *(978-1-4143-2157-8(0),* Tyndale Entertainment) Tyndale Hse. Pubs.

Friesen, Ray. A Cheese Related Mishap & Other Stories. 2005. (Lookit! Ser.). (ENG., Illus.). 100p. per. 8.95 *(978-0-9778177-6-9(X))* Don't Eat Any Bugs Productions.

Frost, Mark. Alliance: The Paladin Prophecy Book 2. 2015. (Paladin Prophecy Ser.: 2). (ENG.). 352p. (YA). (gr. 7). pap. 10.99 *(978-0-375-87108-5(X),* Ember) Random Hse. Children's Bks.

H I

Gaiman, NEil. Odd & the Frost Giants. Riddell, Chris, illus. 2016. 128p. (J). (gr. 3-7). 19.99 (978-0-06-256795-6(0)) HarperCollins Pubs.
—Odd & the Frost Giants. Helquist, Brett, illus. 128p. (J). 2009. (ENG.). (gr. 3-18). 14.99 (978-0-06-167173-9(8)) 2008. lib. bdg. 15.89 (978-0-06-167175-3(4)) HarperCollins Pubs.
Galbraith, Kathryn O. Sparky & Tidbit. Kelley, Gerald, illus. 2015. (Ready-To-Reads Ser.). (ENG.). 40p. (J). (gr. 1-3). pap. 3.99 (978-1-4814-0424-2(5), Simon Spotlight) Simon Spotlight.
Ganz-Schmitt, Sue. Even Superheroes Get Diabetes. Chambers-Goldberg, Micah, illus. 36p. 2011. (gr. -1-3). 22.95 (978-1-59858-303-8(4)) 2007. (J). per. 15.95 (978-1-59858-302-1(6)) Dog Ear Publishing, LLC.
Garza, Xavier. Lucha Libre: The Man in the Silver Mask - A Bilingual Cuento. Garza, Xavier, illus. 2007. (SPA & ENG., Illus.). 40p. (J). (gr. 4-6). pap. 8.95 (978-1-933693-10-1(X)) Cinco Puntos Pr.
—Lucha Libre: The Man in the Silver Mask - A Bilingual Cuento. Crosthwaite, Luis Humberto, tr. Garza, Xavier, illus. 2005. (ENG & SPA., Illus.). 40p. (J). (gr. 4-6). 17.95 (978-0-938317-92-0(X)) Cinco Puntos Pr.
Garza, Xavier, illus. Maximilian & the Mystery of the Guardian Angel. 2011. (Max's Lucha Libre Adventures Ser.). (SPA & ENG.). 160p. (J). (gr. 5-8). pap. 12.95 (978-1-933693-98-9(3)) Cinco Puntos Pr.
Gayton, Sam. Hercufleas. 2016. (ENG.). 272p. (J). (gr. 5-7). 16.99 (978-0-544-63620-0(1)) Houghton Mifflin Harcourt Publishing Co.
Gelin, Antoinette. Captain Underfish: Superhero for the Underworld. 2011. 40p. pap. 25.95 (978-1-4634-2662-0(3)) AuthorHouse.
Gerver, Jane E. The Santa Snatcher. Spaziante, Patrick, illus. 2004. 32p. (J). lib. bdg. 15.00 (978-1-4242-0959-0(5)) Fitzgerald Bks.
Ghiglione, Marco. Ultraheroes Vol. 1: Save the World. Secchi, Riccardo, illus. 2010. (Disney's Hero Squad Ser.). (ENG.). 112p. (J). pap. 9.99 (978-1-60886-543-7(6)) Boom! Studios.
Ghiglione, Marco & Randolph, Grace. Ultraheroes: Save the World. Secchi, Riccardo & Randoplh, Grace, illus. 2010. (Disney's Hero Squad Ser.: 1). (ENG.). 112p. (J). pap. 24.99 (978-1-60886-552-9(5)) Boom! Studios.
Giarrusso, Chris. G-Man Learning to Fly, Vol. 1. 2010. (ENG., Illus.). 96p. (J). pap. 9.99 (978-1-60706-270-7(4), 9781607062707) Image Comics.
—G-Man Volume 2: Cape Crisis: Cape Crisis. 2010. (ENG., Illus.). 128p. (J). pap. 9.99 (978-1-60706-271-4(2), 9781607062714) Image Comics.
Gilroy, Henry. The Clone Wars: Hero of the Confederacy Vol. 1: Breaking Bread with the Enemy!, 1 vol. Koschak, Brian, illus. 2011. (Star Wars: the Clone Wars Ser.: No. 2). (ENG.). 24p. (J). (gr. 7-12). 24.21 (978-1-59961-841-8(9)) Spotlight.
—The Clone Wars: Hero of the Confederacy Vol. 2: A Hero Rises, 1 vol. Koschak, Brian, illus. 2011. (Star Wars: the Clone Wars Ser.: No. 2). (ENG.). 24p. (J). (gr. 7-12). 24.21 (978-1-59961-842-5(7)) Spotlight.
—The Clone Wars: Hero of the Confederacy Vol. 3: the Destiny of Heroes, 1 vol. Koschak, Brian, illus. 2011. (Star Wars: the Clone Wars Ser.: No. 2). (ENG.). 24p. (J). (gr. 7-12). 24.21 (978-1-59961-843-2(5)) Spotlight.
Godwin, Jane. Falling from Grace. 2007. (ENG.). 204p. (J). (gr. 6-12). 16.95 (978-0-8234-2105-3(8)) Holiday Hse., Inc.
Golden Books. The Big Boat Race! (Team Umizoomi) Riley, Kellee, illus. 2012. (Hologramatic Sticker Book Ser.). (ENG.). 48p. (J). (gr. -1-2). pap. 3.99 (978-0-375-86215-1(3), Golden Bks.) Random Hse. Children's Bks.
—Join the Team! (Team Umizoomi) Golden Books, illus. 2012. (Big Coloring Book Ser.). (ENG., Illus.). 48p. (J). (gr. -1-2). pap. 6.99 (978-0-307-93138-2(2), Golden Bks.) Random Hse. Children's Bks.
—Marvel Heroes Little Golden Book Favorites #1 (Marvel) Golden Books, illus. 2016. (Little Golden Book Favorites Ser.). (ENG., Illus.). 80p. (J). (gr. k-k). 7.99 (978-0-307-97653-6(X), Golden Bks.) Random Hse. Children's Bks.
—Really Spaced Out! (Teenage Mutant Ninja Turtles) Golden Books, illus. 2016. (Little Golden Book Ser.). (ENG., Illus.). 24p. (J). (-k). 4.99 (978-1-101-93694-8(0), Golden Bks.) Random Hse. Children's Bks.
Golden Books, illus. DC Super Friends Little Golden Book Favorites (DC Super Friends) 2013. (Little Golden Book Favorites Ser.). (ENG.). 80p. (J). (-k). 6.99 (978-0-449-81621-9(4), Golden Bks.) Random Hse. Children's Bks.
—DC Super Friends Little Golden Book Library (DC Super Friends), 5 vols. 2015. (ENG.). 120p. (J). (-k). 24.95 (978-0-553-50897-0(0), Golden Bks.) Random Hse. Children's Bks.
—Little Golden Book Library, 5 vols. 2016. (ENG.). 24p. (J). (-k). 24.95 (978-0-449-81735-3(0), Golden Bks.) Random Hse. Children's Bks.
—Nine Marvel Super Hero Tales. 2017. (Little Golden Book Treasury Ser.). (ENG.). 224p. (J). (-k). 12.99 (978-1-5247-1783-4(5), Golden Bks.) Random Hse. Children's Bks.
Golden Books Staff. Danger from the Deep. 2009. (Deluxe Coloring Book Ser.). (ENG., Illus.). 96p. (J). (gr. -1-2). pap. 3.99 (978-0-375-85328-9(6), Golden Bks.) Random Hse. Children's Bks.
Golden Books Staff & Random House Staff. Enter the Lair (Teenage Mutant Ninja Turtles) Golden Books Staff & Random House Staff, illus. 2013. (Pictureback(R) Ser.). (ENG., Illus.). 16p. (J). (gr. -1-2). pap. 4.99 (978-0-449-81385-0(1), Random Hse. Bks. for Young Readers) Random Hse. Children's Bks.
Gonnard, Christel. The Planet of the Night Globes. 2013. (Little Prince Ser.: 6). (ENG., Illus.). 56p. (J). (gr. 4-8). pap. 7.95 (978-1-4677-0738-1(4), Graphic Universe™) Lerner Publishing Group.
Gossett, Susan. A True Superhero. 2009. 28p. pap. 16.50 (978-1-4490-3147-3(1)) AuthorHouse.
Gownley, Jim. Amelia vs. the Sneeze Barf: #1, 1 vol. Gownley, Jim, illus. 2011. (Amelia Rules! Ser.). (ENG., Illus.). 36p. 24.21 (978-1-59961-787-9(0)) Spotlight.
Gownley, Jimmy. A Very Ninja Christmas. Gownley, Jimmy, illus. 2009. (Amelia Rules! Ser.). (ENG., Illus.). 80p. (J). (gr. 2-7). pap. 7.99 (978-1-4169-8959-2(5), Atheneum Bks. for Young Readers) Simon & Schuster Children's Publishing.
Grabenstein, Chris. Riley Mack & the Other Known Troublemakers. 2012. (Riley Mack Ser.: 1). (ENG.). 272p. (J). (gr. 3-7). 16.99 (978-0-06-202620-0(8)) HarperCollins Pubs.
—Riley Mack Stirs up More Trouble. 2013. (Riley Mack Ser.: 2). (ENG.). 336p. (J). (gr. 3-7). 16.99 (978-0-06-202622-4(4)) HarperCollins Pubs.
Granson, Steven. Zando. 2009. 124p. pap. 10.95 (978-1-4401-5658-8(1)) iUniverse, Inc.
Green, S. E. Killer Within. 2015. (ENG.). 304p. (YA). (gr. 9). 17.99 (978-1-4814-0288-0(9), Simon Pulse) Simon Pulse.
Greenberger, Robert & Loughridge, Lee. Arctic Attack. Kruse, Jason T., illus. (Batman Ser.). (ENG.). 56p. (gr. 2-3). 2013. pap. 4.95 (978-1-4342-1728-8(0)) 2009. 26.65 (978-1-4342-1561-1(X)) Stone Arch Bks. (DC Super Heroes).
Greenberger, Robert, et al. Robin's First Flight. Schigiel, Gregg, illus. 2013. (Batman Ser.). (ENG.). 56p. (gr. 2-3). pap. 4.95 (978-1-4342-2262-6(4), DC Super Heroes) Stone Arch Bks.
Greene, Daryl C. Benjamin's Dog Joseph: A Three Legged Hero. Akers-Bell, Mary, illus. 2003. 48p. (J). (gr. 2-4). pap. 9.95 (978-0-9700827-4-9(6)); lib. bdg. 17.95 (978-0-9700827-5-6(4)) Densmore-Reid Pubns.
Grey, Mini. Traction Man Is Here! 2012. lib. bdg. 18.40 (978-0-606-26385-6(3), Turtleback) Turtleback Bks.
Gutman, Dan. Funny Boy Meets the Airsick Alien from Andromeda. Dykes, John S., illus. 2012. (Funny Boy Ser.). (ENG.). 136p. (J). (gr. 2-5). pap. 10.99 (978-1-4532-9527-4(5)) Open Road Integrated Media, Inc.
—Funny Boy Versus the Bubble-Brained Barbers from the Big Bang. Dietz, Mike, illus. 2012. (Funny Boy Ser.). (ENG.). 144p. (J). (gr. 2-5). pap. 6.99 (978-1-4532-9532-8(1)) Open Road Integrated Media, Inc.
Guyot, Rebecca. Flyin' Ryan the Rescue Ranger: In: the Puzzleton Storm, 1 vol. 2009. 20p. pap. 24.95 (978-1-60836-856-3(4)) America Star Bks.
Haddix, Margaret Peterson. The Always War. (ENG.). (YA). (gr. 7). 2012. 224p. pap. 8.99 (978-1-4169-9527-2(7)) 2011. 208p. 16.99 (978-1-4169-9526-5(9)) Simon & Schuster Bks. For Young Readers. (Simon & Schuster Bks. For Young Readers).
Haibara, Yak & Haibara, Yak. Sengoku Basara: Samurai Legends Volume 2: Samurai Legends Volume 2, 2 vols. 2013. (ENG., Illus.). 424p. (YA). pap. 19.99 (978-1-926778-59-4(6), 9781926778594) URON Entertainment Corp. CAN. Dist: Diamond Comic Distributors, Inc.
Haines, Lise. Girl in the Arena. 2010. (ENG.). 336p. (YA). (gr. 9-13). pap. 9.99 (978-1-59990-521-1(3), 9781599905211, Bloomsbury USA Childrens) Bloomsbury Publishing USA.
Hale, Bruce. Fat Cat of Underwhere. Hillman, Shane, illus. 2009. (Underwhere Ser.). 176p. (J). pap. 5.99 (978-0-06-085135-4(X)) HarperCollins Pubs.
—Pirates of Underwhere. Hillman, Shane, illus. 2008. (Underwhere Ser.). 164p. (J). (gr. 3-7). lib. bdg. 16.89 (978-0-06-085128-6(7)) HarperCollins Pubs.
—Prince of Underwhere. Hillman, Shane, illus. 2009. (Underwhere Ser.: 1). (ENG.). 176p. (J). (gr. 3-7). pap. 5.99 (978-0-06-085126-2(0)) HarperCollins Pubs.
Hale, Shannon & Hale, Dean. The Princess in Black. Pham, LeUyen, illus. (Princess in Black Ser.). (ENG.). 96p. (J). (gr. k-3). 2015. pap. 6.99 (978-0-7636-7888-3(0)) 2014. 14.99 (978-0-7636-6510-4(X)) Candlewick Pr.
—The Princess in Black. 2015. (Princess in Black Ser.: 1). lib. bdg. 17.20 (978-0-606-36863-6(9)) Turtleback Bks.
—The Princess in Black & the Hungry Bunny Horde. Pham, LeUyen, illus. 2016. (Princess in Black Ser.: 3). (ENG.). (J). (gr. k-3). 96p. pap. 6.99 (978-0-7636-9089-2(9)); 85p. 14.99 (978-0-7636-6513-5(4)) Candlewick Pr.
—The Princess in Black & the Hungry Bunny Horde. Pham, LeUyen, illus. 2016. (Princess in Black Ser.: 3). (ENG.). 85p. (J). (gr. k-3). 17.20 (978-0-606-39109-2(6)) Turtleback Bks.
Hale, Shannon & Hale, Dean. The Princess in Black & the Mysterious Playdate. Pham, LeUyen, illus. 2017. (Princess in Black Ser.: 5). (ENG.). 96p. (J). (gr. k-3). 14.99 **(978-0-7636-8826-4(6))** Candlewick Pr.
Hansen, Justin LaRocca. Brothers Unite. 2016. (Secondhand Heroes Ser.). (ENG., Illus.). 160p. (J). (gr. 3-7). pap. 10.99 (978-0-8037-4094-5(8), Dial Bks) Penguin Young Readers Group.
Hapka, Cathy, pseud, adapted by. Fantastic 4: The Movie Storybook. 2005. (Illus.). 48p. (J). (978-1-4156-0389-5(8)) HarperCollins Pubs.
Hardin, Melinda. Hero Dad, 0 vols. Langdo, Bryan, illus. 2010. (ENG.). 24p. (J). (gr. -1-3). 12.99 (978-0-7614-5713-8(5), 9780761457138, Two Lions) Amazon Publishing.
—Hero Mom. Langdo, Bryan, illus. 2013. 24p. pap. 12.99 (978-1-4778-6645-0(0)) Amazon Publishing.
Harper, Ben. Super Friends: Going Bananas. Random House Staff, illus. 2009. (Step into Reading Ser.). (ENG.). 32p. (J). (gr. -1-1). pap. 3.99 (978-0-375-85613-6(7), Random Hse. Bks. for Young Readers) Random Hse. Children's Bks.
Harper, Charise Mericle. Wedgieman & the Big Bunny Trouble. Shea, Bob, illus. 2014. (Step into Reading Ser.). (ENG.). 48p. (J). (gr. k-3). 3.99 (978-0-307-93073-6(4), Random Hse. Bks. for Young Readers) Random Hse. Children's Bks.
Harris, Todd V. Heroes & Haters. 2008. 75p. pap. 19.95 (978-1-60563-157-8(4)) America Star Bks.
Harvey, Sharon M. One Egg-stra-Ordinary Invention. 2012. (ENG.). 94p. pap. 35.95 (978-1-4327-7210-9(4)) Outskirts Pr., Inc.
Haskell, Rachael. The Biggest Little Hero. 2010. 29p. 15.50 (978-0-615-21356-9(1)) Haskell, Rachael A.
Hatke, Ben. Legends of Zita the Spacegirl. Hatke, Ben, illus. 2012. (Zita the Spacegirl Ser.: 2). (ENG., Illus.). 224p. (J). (gr. 3-7). 19.99 (978-1-59643-806-4(1), 9781596438064); pap. 12.99 (978-1-59643-447-9(3), 9781596434479) Roaring Brook Pr. (First Second Bks.).
—Legends of Zita the Spacegirl. 2012. (Zita the Spacegirl Ser.: 2). (J). lib. bdg. 24.50 (978-0-606-26708-3(5), Turtleback) Turtleback Bks.
Healy, Christopher. The Hero's Guide to Being an Outlaw. Harris, Todd, illus. 2014. (Hero's Guide Ser.: 3). (ENG.). 528p. (J). (gr. 3-7). 16.99 (978-0-06-211848-6(X), Waldon Pond Pr.) HarperCollins Pubs.
—The Hero's Guide to Storming the Castle. Harris, Todd, illus. 2013. (Hero's Guide Ser.: 2). (ENG.). 496p. (J). (gr. 3-7). 16.99 (978-0-06-211845-5(5), Waldon Pond Pr.) HarperCollins Pubs.
Heide, Florence Parry. How to Be a Hero. 2016. (ENG., Illus.). 40p. (J). (gr. k-3). 16.99 (978-1-4521-2710-1(7)) Chronicle Bks. LLC.
Helmer, Marilyn. The Great Garage Sale, 1 vol. Deas, Mike, illus. 2013. (Orca Echoes Ser.). (ENG.). 64p. (J). (gr. 2-3). pap. 6.95 (978-1-4598-0060-1(5)) Orca Bk. Pubs. USA.
Hero in My Eyes. 2006. (J). bds. 21.95 (978-0-9745191-2-8(X)) Lynn Tyner Mitchum & James Rogers.
Heroes in Training. 2003. (J). per. (978-1-57657-823-0(2)) Paradise Pr., Inc.
Herrera, Juan Felipe & Herrera, Juan. La Supermina del Cilantro. Robledo Tapia, Honorio, illus. 2003.Tr. of Super Cilantro Girl. (ENG & SPA.). 32p. (J). 16.95 (978-0-89239-187-5(1)) Lee & Low Bks., Inc.
Higgins, M. G. Fish Boy, 1 vol. 2015. (Red Rhino Ser.). (ENG.). 68p. (J). (gr. 4-6). pap. 7.95 (978-1-62250-953-9(6)) Saddleback Educational Publishing, Inc.
Himekawa, Akira. The Legend of Zelda Box Set, 10 vols. 2011. (ENG., Illus.). 2000p. (J). pap. 79.99 (978-1-4215-4242-3(0)) Viz Media.
—The Legend of Zelda, Vol. 10. Himekawa, Akira, illus. 2010. (ENG., Illus.). 200p. (J). (gr. 2-5). pap. 9.99 (978-1-4215-3724-5(9)) Viz Media.
—The Legend of Zelda, Vol. 5. Himekawa, Akira, illus. 2009. (ENG., Illus.). 200p. (J). pap. 9.99 (978-1-4215-2331-6(0)) Viz Media.
—The Legend of Zelda, Vol. 6. Himekawa, Akira, illus. 2009. (ENG., Illus.). 200p. (J). pap. 9.99 (978-1-4215-2332-3(9)) Viz Media.
—The Legend of Zelda, Vol. 9. Himekawa, Akira, illus. 2010. (ENG., Illus.). 192p. (YA). pap. 9.99 (978-1-4215-2335-4(3)) Viz Media.
Hinds, Gareth. The Odyssey. Hinds, Gareth, illus. 2010. (ENG., Illus.). 256p. (YA). (gr. 7-18). 24.99 (978-0-7636-4266-2(5)); pap. 14.99 (978-0-7636-4268-6(1)) Candlewick Pr.
Hoena, B. A. Livewire! Schoening, Dan, illus. 2010. (J). pap. 34.99 (978-1-4342-1766-0(3)) Stone Arch Bks.
Hoena, Blake. The Riddler's Ransom. Beavers, Ethen, illus. 2015. (You Choose Stories: Batman Ser.). (ENG.). 112p. (gr. 2-3). lib. bdg. 32.65 (978-1-4342-9706-8(3)) Stone Arch Bks.
Hoena, Blake & Hoena, Blake A. Vampires & Veggies. Bardin, Dave, illus. 2016. (Monster Heroes Ser.). (ENG.). 32p. (gr. 1-2). lib. bdg. 21.32 (978-1-4965-3755-3(6)) Stone Arch Bks.
—Zombies & Meatballs. Bardin, Dave, illus. 2016. (Monster Heroes Ser.). (ENG.). 32p. (gr. 1-2). lib. bdg. 21.32 (978-1-4965-3754-6(8)) Stone Arch Bks.
Hoena, Blake A. Livewire!, 1 vol. Schoening, Dan, illus. 2009. (Superman Ser.). (ENG.). 56p. (gr. 2-3). lib. bdg. 26.65 (978-1-4342-1566-6(0), DC Super Heroes) Stone Arch Bks.
Hoena, Blake A. & Hoena, B. A. Livewire!, 1 vol. Schoening, Dan, illus. 2013. (Superman Ser.). (ENG.). 56p. (gr. 2-3). pap. 4.95 (978-1-4342-1733-2(7), DC Super Heroes) Stone Arch Bks.
Hoena, Blake A. & Loughridge, Lee. Cosmic Bounty Hunter, 1 vol. Burchett, Rick, illus. 2010. (Superman Ser.). (ENG.). 56p. (gr. 2-3). lib. bdg. 26.65 (978-1-4342-2133-9(4), DC Super Heroes) Stone Arch Bks.
Holm, Jennifer L. & Holm, Matthew. Captain Disaster. Holm, Jennifer L. & Holm, Matthew, illus. 2012. (Squish Ser.: No. 4). (ENG., Illus.). 96p. (J). (gr. 2-5). pap. 6.99 (978-0-375-84392-1(2)); lib. bdg. 12.99 (978-0-375-93786-6(2)) Random Hse. Children's Bks. (Random Hse. Bks. for Young Readers).
—Captain Disaster. 2012. (Squish Ser.: 4). lib. bdg. 17.20 (978-0-606-26812-7(X), Turtleback) Turtleback Bks.
—Fear the Amoeba. 2014. (Squish Ser.: 6). lib. bdg. 17.20 (978-0-606-36025-8(5)) Turtleback Bks.
—Game On! Holm, Jennifer L. & Holm, Matthew, illus. 2013. (Squish Ser.: No. 5). (ENG., Illus.). 96p. (J). (gr. 2-5). lib. bdg. 12.99 (978-0-307-98300-8(5));No. 5. pap. 6.99 (978-0-307-98299-5(8)) Random Hse. Children's Bks. (Random Hse. Bks. for Young Readers).
—Our Hero. 2005. (Babymouse Ser.: 2). (ENG., Illus.). 96p. (J). (gr. 2-5). pap. 6.99 (978-0-375-83230-7(0)); lib. bdg. 12.99 (978-0-375-93230-4(5)) Random Hse. Children's Bks. (Random Hse. Bks. for Young Readers).
—The Power of the Parasite. Holm, Jennifer L. & Holm, Matthew, illus. 2012. (Squish Ser.: No. 3). (ENG., Illus.). 96p. (J). (gr. 2-5). pap. 6.99 (978-0-375-84391-4(4)); lib. bdg. 12.99 (978-0-375-93785-9(4)) Random Hse. Children's Bks. (Random Hse. Bks. for Young Readers).
—The Power of the Parasite. 2012. (Squish Ser.: 3). lib. bdg. 17.20 (978-0-606-26405-1(1), Turtleback) Turtleback Bks.
—Super Amoeba. Holm, Jennifer L. & Holm, Matthew, illus. 2011. (Squish Ser.: No. 1). (ENG., Illus.). 96p. (J). (gr. 3-7). pap. 6.99 (978-0-375-84389-1(2)); lib. bdg. 12.99 (978-0-375-93783-5(8)) Random Hse. Children's Bks. (Random Hse. Bks. for Young Readers).
Holub, Joan. Play Nice, Hercules! Patricelli, Leslie, illus. 2014. (Mini Myths Ser.). (ENG.). 24p. (J). (gr. -1 — 1). bds. 6.95 (978-1-4197-0954-8(2), Abrams Appleseed) Abrams, Inc.
—Zero the Hero. Lichtenheld, Tom, illus. 2012. (ENG.). 40p. (J). (gr. 1-5). 17.99 (978-0-8050-9384-1(2), 9780805093841, Holt, Henry & Co. Bks. For Young Readers) Holt, Henry & Co.
Holub, Joan & Williams, Suzanne. Hyperion & the Great Balls of Fire. Phillips, Craig, illus. 2013. (Heroes in Training Ser.: 4). (ENG.). 144p. (J). (gr. 1-4). pap. 5.99 (978-1-4424-5269-5(2), Aladdin) Simon & Schuster Children's Publishing.
—Hyperion & the Great Balls of Fire. Phillips, Craig, illus. 2013. (Heroes in Training Ser.: 4). (ENG.). 144p. (J). (gr. 1-4). 16.99 (978-1-4424-5803-1(8), Simon & Schuster/Paula Wiseman Bks.) Simon & Schuster/Paula Wiseman Bks.
—Typhon & the Winds of Destruction. Phillips, Craig, illus. 2013. (Heroes in Training Ser.: 5). (ENG.). 112p. (J). (gr. 1-4). 16.99 (978-1-4424-8844-1(1)); pap. 5.99 (978-1-4424-8842-7(5)) Simon & Schuster Children's Publishing. (Aladdin).
—Typhon & the Winds of Destruction. 2013. (Heroes in Training Ser.: 5). lib. bdg. 16.00 (978-0-606-32330-7(9), Turtleback) Turtleback Bks.
—Uranus & the Bubbles of Trouble. 2015. (Heroes in Training Ser.: 11). lib. bdg. 16.00 (978-0-606-37842-0(1)) Turtleback Bks.
Horning, Mandy Cha'rae. The Defenders: Rise of the Perfected. 2012. 118p. (gr. 10-12). 23.99 (978-1-4772-5327-4(0)); pap. 14.95 (978-1-4772-5328-1(9)) AuthorHouse.
Houser, Jody. Faith. 2016. (Faith Ser.: 1). lib. bdg. 20.85 (978-0-606-38942-6(3)) Turtleback Bks.
Howe, James. The Odorous Adventures of Stinky Dog. Helquist, Brett, illus. 2003. (Tales from the House of Bunnicula Ser.: 6). (ENG.). 112p. (J). (gr. 2-5). 13.99 (978-0-689-85633-4(4), Atheneum Bks. for Young Readers) Simon & Schuster Children's Publishing.
Hubble, Miles & Bryant, Justin. Bob & the Fowl War: Book One in the Poultry Series. 2008. 140p. pap. 11.95 (978-1-4401-0857-0(9)) iUniverse, Inc.
Huber, Randy. Of Heroes & Heroines. 2008. 48p. pap. 16.95 (978-1-4241-5421-0(9)) America Star Bks.
Huelin, Jodi. Batman Versus Bane. Tong, Andie, illus. 2012. (I Can Read Book 2 Ser.). (ENG.). 32p. (J). (gr. -1-3). pap. 3.99 (978-0-06-213224-6(5)) HarperCollins Pubs.
—Tools of the Trade. Gordon, Steven E., illus. 2012. (I Can Read Book 2 Ser.). (ENG.). 32p. (J). (gr. k-3). pap. 3.99 (978-0-06-213223-9(7)) HarperCollins Pubs.
Hueller, Andy. Dizzy Fantastic & Her Flying Bicycle. 2010. (Illus.). 155p. (J). pap. 8.99 (978-1-59955-395-5(3)) Cedar Fort, Inc./CFI Distribution.
Hulk the Hero. 2003. (J). per. (978-1-57657-821-6(6)) Paradise Pr., Inc.
Hulk's Big Mess. 2003. (J). per. (978-1-57657-822-3(4)) Paradise Pr., Inc.
Hulme-Cross, Benjamin. The Egyptian Warrior. 2016. (Warrior Heroes Ser.). (ENG., Illus.). 176p. (J). (gr. 6-9). (978-0-7787-2864-1(1)) Crabtree Publishing Co.
—The Gladiator's Victory. Rinaldi, Angelo, illus. 2015. (ENG.). 160p. (J). (978-0-7787-1764-5(X)) Crabtree Publishing Co.
—The Knight's Enemies. Rinaldi, Angelo, illus. 2015. (ENG.). 160p. (J). (978-0-7787-1765-2(8)) Crabtree Publishing Co.
—The Samurai's Assassin. Rinaldi, Angelo, illus. 2015. (ENG.). 160p. (J). (978-0-7787-1766-9(6)) Crabtree Publishing Co.
—The Viking's Revenge. Rinaldi, Angelo, illus. 2015. (ENG.). 160p. (J). (978-0-7787-1767-6(4)) Crabtree Publishing Co.
Hult, Gene & Bright, J. E. Cat Commander. Vecchio, Luciano, illus. (Dark Knight Ser.). (ENG.). 88p. (gr. 2-3). 2013. pap. 5.95 (978-1-4342-4214-3(5)) 2012. 26.65 (978-1-4342-4088-0(6)) Stone Arch Bks.
Huppert, Beth L. The Tale of the Scarlet Knight. 2013. 24p. pap. 24.95 (978-1-62709-437-5(7)) America Star Bks.
Incomprehensible, Vordak T. & Seegert, Scott. How to Grow up & Rule the World. Martin, John, illus. 2010. (Vordak the Incomprehensible Ser.: No. 1). (ENG.). 208p. (gr. 5-18). 13.99 (978-1-60684-013-9(4), Darby Creek) Lerner Publishing Group.
Irvine, Alex. Phase Two: Marvel's Ant-Man. 2016. (Marvel Cinematic Universe Ser.). (ENG., Illus.). 208p. (J). (gr. 3-7). 10.99 (978-0-316-25638-4(2)) Little, Brown Bks. for Young Readers.
Irvine, Alex & Wyatt, Chris. Phase Two: Marvel's Guardians of the Galaxy. 2015. (Marvel Cinematic Universe Ser.). (ENG.). 192p. (J). (gr. 3-7). 10.99 (978-0-316-25675-9(7)) Little, Brown Bks. for Young Readers.
Jackowski, Rosemarie. Super Duper Diaper-Poopin' Hero. 2011. 24p. pap. 12.99 (978-1-4634-2211-0(3)) AuthorHouse.
Jacobs, Parker, illus. Super Gabba Friends! 2013. (Yo Gabba Gabba! Ser.). (ENG.). 24p. (J). (gr. -1-k). pap. 3.99 (978-1-4424-6184-0(5), Simon Spotlight) Simon Spotlight.
Jacobson, Jennifer Richard. Andy Shane, Hero at Last. Carter, Abby, illus. 2011. (Andy Shane Ser.: 6). (ENG.). 64p. (J). (gr. k-3). pap. 4.99 (978-0-7636-5293-7(8)) Candlewick Pr.
—Hero at Last. Carter, Abby, illus. 2010. (Andy Shane Ser.: 6). (ENG.). 64p. (J). (gr. k-3). 14.99 (978-0-7636-3600-5(2)) Candlewick Pr.
Jacques, Brian. The Angel's Command. 2003. (Castaways of the Flying Dutchman Ser.: No. 2). 1.00 (978-1-4175-5393-8(6)) Recorded Bks., Inc.
Jelenic, Michael. Justice League vs. Bizarro League. 2015. (LEGO DC Super Heroes Chapter Book Ser.). lib. bdg. 14.75 (978-0-606-37794-2(8)) Turtleback Bks.
Jensen, Marion. Almost Super. 2014. (Almost Super Ser.: 1). (ENG.). 256p. (J). (gr. 3-7). 14.99 (978-0-06-220961-0(2)) HarperCollins Pubs.
Jeremiatt, Omani. Paper Boy. Rollins, Bernic, illus. 2003. 40p. (J). (gr. 6-8). pap. 10.00 (978-1-929188-09-3(9)) Morton Bks.
Johnson, Mike. Where No Man Has Gone Before Part 1, 1 vol. 2013. (Star Trek Ser.). (ENG.). 24p. (J). (gr. 6-12). lib. bdg. 24.21 (978-1-61479-161-4(9)) Spotlight.
—Where No Man Has Gone Before Part 2, 1 vol. 2013. (Star Trek Ser.). (ENG.). 24p. (J). (gr. 6-12). lib. bdg. 24.21 (978-1-61479-162-1(7)) Spotlight.
Jones, Brian and Brad. The Righteous Heroes. 2005. 36p. pap. 13.99 (978-1-4116-5423-5(4)) Lulu Pr., Inc.
Jones, Bruce. Captain America Legends: What Price Glory. Rude, Steve, illus. 2003. (Captain America Ser.). 96p. (YA). pap. 9.99 (978-0-7851-1227-3(8)) Marvel Worldwide, Inc.
Jones, Marcia Thornton. Woodford Brave. Whipple, Kevin, illus. 2015. (ENG.). 200p. (J). (gr. 3-7). 16.95 (978-1-62979-305-4(1), Calkins Creek) Boyds Mills Pr.
Joyce, William. E. Aster Bunnymund & the Warrior Eggs at the Earth's Core!, Bk. 2. Joyce, William, illus. 2012. (Guardians Ser.: 2). (ENG., Illus.). 272p. (J). (gr. 2-6). 15.99 (978-1-4424-3050-1(8), Atheneum Bks. for Young Readers) Simon & Schuster Children's Publishing.
Joyce, William & Geringer, Laura. Nicholas St. North & the Battle of the Nightmare King, Bk. 1. Joyce, William, illus. 2011. (Guardians Ser.: 1). (ENG., Illus.). 240p. (J). (gr. 2-6). 15.99 (978-1-4424-3048-8(6), Atheneum Bks. for Young Readers) Simon & Schuster Children's Publishing.
Juaquinito: A Manatee Hero. 2009. (ENG., Illus.). 32p. (J). pap. 7.95 (978-0-9748884-3-9(5)) Little Thoughts For Little Ones Publishing, Inc.
Jules, Jacqueline. Freddie Ramos Makes a Splash. Benitez, Miguel, illus. 2013. (Zapato Power Ser.: Book 4). (ENG.).

96p. (J). (gr. 1-5). pap. 4.99 *(978-0-8075-9486-5(5))* Whitman, Albert & Co.

—Freddie Ramos Makes a Splash Bk. 4. Benítez, Miguel, illus. 2012. (Zapato Power Ser.: Book 4). (ENG.). 96p. (J). (gr. 1-5). 14.99 *(978-0-8075-9485-8(7))* Whitman, Albert & Co.

—Freddie Ramos Zooms to the Rescue. Benitez, Miguel, illus. (Zapato Power Ser.: Book 3). (ENG.). 96p. (J). (gr. 1-5). 2012. pap. 4.99 *(978-0-8075-9484-1(9))*Bk. 3. 2011. 14.99 *(978-0-8075-9482-7(2))* Whitman, Albert & Co.

Jules, Jacqueline & Benítez, Miguel. Freddie Ramos Takes Off. 2010. (Zapato Power Ser.: Book 1). (ENG., Illus.). 88p. (J). (gr. 1-5). 14.99 *(978-0-8075-9480-3(6))* Whitman, Albert & Co.

Jung, Mike. Geeks, Girls, & Secret Identities. Maihack, Mike, illus. 2012. (J). (ENG.). 320p. (gr. 3-7). 16.99 *(978-0-545-33548-5(5))*; pap. *(978-0-545-33549-2(3))* Scholastic, Inc. (Levine, Arthur A. Bks.).

Kahaney, Amelia. The Brokenhearted. 2014. (Brokenhearted Ser.: 1). (ENG.). 368p. (YA). (gr. 8). pap. 9.99 *(978-0-06-223093-5(X)*, HarperTeen) HarperCollins Pubs.

—The Invisible. 2014. (Brokenhearted Ser.: 2). (ENG.). 304p. (YA). (gr. 8). 17.99 *(978-0-06-223192-5(8)*, HarperTeen) HarperCollins Pubs.

Kane, Bob. Comic con & Labor Day. Nguyen, Dustin, illus. 2015. (Batman: Li'l Gotham Ser.). (ENG.). 32p. (gr. 2-3). lib. bdg. 22.60 *(978-1-4342-9736-5(5))* Stone Arch Bks.

—Month of Waters & Independence Day. Nguyen, Dustin, illus. 2015. (Batman: Li'l Gotham Ser.). (ENG.). 32p. (gr. 2-3). lib. bdg. 22.60 *(978-1-4342-9666-5(0))* Stone Arch Bks.

—Sandwich Day & Our Family Album. Nguyen, Dustin, illus. 2015. (Batman: Li'l Gotham Ser.). (ENG.). 32p. (gr. 2-3). lib. bdg. 22.60 *(978-1-4342-9737-2(3))* Stone Arch Bks.

—Tropical Getaway & Bird Watching. Nguyen, Dustin, illus. 2015. (Batman: Li'l Gotham Ser.). (ENG.). 32p. (gr. 2-3). lib. bdg. 22.60 *(978-1-4342-9735-8(7))* Stone Arch Bks.

Kasza, Keiko. Silly Goose's Big Story. Kasza, Keiko, illus. 2012. (ENG., Illus.). 32p. (J). (gr. -1-k). 16.99 *(978-0-399-25542-7(7)*, G.P. Putnam's Sons Books for Young Readers) Penguin Young Readers Group.

Katz, David Bar. My First Wonder Woman Book: Touch & Feel. 2011. (DC Super Heroes Ser.). (ENG.). 12p. (J). (gr. -1). bds. 11.99 *(978-1-935703-13-6(7))* Downtown Bookworks.

Kelley, Gretchen. Superheroes Don't Eat Veggie Burgers. 2016. (ENG.). 272p. (J). 16.99 *(978-1-62779-089-5(6)*, 9781627790895, Holt, Henry & Co. Bks. For Young Readers) Holt, Henry & Co.

Kelly, Joe, et al. Megamind Movie Prequel. 2010. (ENG., Illus.). 52p. (J). pap. 6.95 *(978-1-934944-94-3(7)*, 9781934944943) Ape Entertainment.

Kelly, Neil & Dorling Kindersley Publishing Staff. Glow in the Dark - Marvel Heroes. 2006. (Ultimate Sticker Bks.). (ENG., Illus.). 16p. (J). (gr. k-3). pap. 6.99 *(978-0-7566-2002-8(3)*, DK Children) Dorling Kindersley Publishing, Inc.

—Marvel Heroes. 2006. (Ultimate Sticker Bks.). (ENG., Illus.). 16p. (J). (gr. k-3). pap. 6.99 *(978-0-7566-2000-4(7)*, DK Children) Dorling Kindersley Publishing, Inc.

Kenny, Michael Daedalus. Mr. Strong: Good Thing I Came Along, Vol. 1. Corbera, Gabriel, illus. 2013. (ENG.). 80p. (J). pap. 6.99 *(978-1-4215-4073-3(8))* Viz Media.

kieliszewski, sheila. Superhero. 2009. 24p. 13.70 *(978-0-578-00002-2(4))* Kieliszewski, Shelia.

Kiernan, Kenny, illus. Save the Day! 2013. (J). *(978-1-4844-0146-0(8))* Scholastic, Inc.

King, Trey. Friends & Foes. 2015. (LEGO DC Super Heroes 8X8 Ser.). (Illus.). (J). lib. bdg. 13.55 *(978-0-606-36361-7(0))* Turtleback Bks.

—Friends & Foes! Wang, Sean, illus. 2015. (LEGO DC Super Heroes Ser.: 1). (ENG.). 24p. (J). (gr. -1-3). pap. 3.99 *(978-0-545-78504-4(9))* Scholastic, Inc.

—Race Around the World! Wang, Sean, illus. 2016. (LEGO DC Super Heroes Ser.). (ENG.). 24p. (J). (gr. -1-3). pap. 3.99 *(978-0-545-86797-9(5))* Scholastic, Inc.

King, Wesley. The Incredible Space Raiders from Space! 2015. (ENG., Illus.). 304p. (J). (gr. 3-7). 16.99 *(978-1-4814-2319-9(3)*, Simon & Schuster Bks. For Young Readers) Simon & Schuster Bks. For Young Readers.

Kirby, Stan. Captain Awesome & the Easter Egg Bandit. O'Connor, George, illus. 2015. (Captain Awesome Ser.: 13). (ENG.). 128p. (J). (gr. k-4). pap. 5.99 *(978-1-4814-2558-2(7)*, Little Simon) Little Simon.

—Captain Awesome & the Missing Elephants. O'Connor, George, illus. 2014. (Captain Awesome Ser.: 10). (ENG.). 128p. (J). (gr. k-4). 16.99 *(978-1-4424-8995-0(2))*; pap. 5.99 *(978-1-4424-8994-3(4))* Little Simon. (Little Simon).

—Captain Awesome & the Missing Elephants. 2014. (Captain Awesome Ser.: 10). lib. bdg. 16.00 *(978-0-606-35440-0(9))* Turtleback Bks.

—Captain Awesome & the New Kid. O'Connor, George, illus. 2012. (Captain Awesome Ser.: 3). (ENG.). 128p. (J). (gr. k-4). 16.99 *(978-1-4424-4200-9(X))*; pap. 5.99 *(978-1-4424-4199-6(2))* Little Simon. (Little Simon).

—Captain Awesome & the New Kid. 2012. (Captain Awesome Ser.: 3). lib. bdg. 16.00 *(978-0-606-26324-5(1)*, Turtleback) Turtleback Bks.

—Captain Awesome & the Ultimate Spelling Bee. O'Connor, George, illus. 2013. (Captain Awesome Ser.: 7). (ENG.). 128p. (J). (gr. k-4). 17.99 *(978-1-4424-5156-8(4))*; pap. 5.99 *(978-1-4424-5158-2(0))* Little Simon. (Little Simon).

—Captain Awesome & the Ultimate Spelling Bee. 2013. (Captain Awesome Ser.: 7). lib. bdg. 16.00 *(978-0-606-27035-9(3)*, Turtleback) Turtleback Bks.

—Captain Awesome Gets Crushed. 2013. (Captain Awesome Ser.: 9). lib. bdg. 16.00 *(978-0-606-32331-4(7)*, Turtleback) Turtleback Bks.

—Captain Awesome Goes to Superhero Camp. O'Connor, George, illus. 2015. (Captain Awesome Ser.: 14). (ENG.). 128p. (J). (gr. k-4). pap. 5.99 *(978-1-4814-3153-8(6)*, Little Simon) Little Simon.

—Captain Awesome Meets Super Dude! 2016. (Captain Awesome Ser.: 17). lib. bdg. 16.00 *(978-0-606-38963-1(6))* Turtleback Bks.

—Captain Awesome Meets Super Dude! Super Special. O'Connor, George, illus. 2016. (Captain Awesome Ser.: 17). (ENG.). 160p. (J). (gr. k-4). pap. 5.99 *(978-1-4814-6695-0(X)*, Little Simon) Little Simon.

—Captain Awesome Saves the Winter Wonderland. 2012. (Captain Awesome Ser.: 6). lib. bdg. 16.00 *(978-0-606-26894-3(4)*, Turtleback) Turtleback Bks.

—Captain Awesome, Soccer Star. O'Connor, George, illus. 2012. (Captain Awesome Ser.: 5). (ENG.). 128p. (J). (gr. k-4). 16.99 *(978-1-4424-4332-7(4))*; pap. 5.99 *(978-1-4424-4331-0(6))* Little Simon. (Little Simon).

—Captain Awesome, Soccer Star. 2012. (Captain Awesome Ser.: 5). lib. bdg. 16.00 *(978-0-606-26545-4(7)*, Turtleback) Turtleback Bks.

—Captain Awesome Takes a Dive. O'Connor, George, illus. 2012. (Captain Awesome Ser.: 4). (ENG.). 128p. (J). (gr. k-4). 16.99 *(978-1-4424-4203-0(4))*; pap. 5.99 *(978-1-4424-4202-3(6))* Little Simon. (Little Simon).

—Captain Awesome Takes a Dive. 2012. (Captain Awesome Ser.: 4). lib. bdg. 14.75 *(978-0-606-26325-2(X)*, Turtleback) Turtleback Bks.

—Captain Awesome to the Rescue! 2012. (Captain Awesome Ser.: 1). lib. bdg. 16.00 *(978-0-606-26322-1(5)*, Turtleback) Turtleback Bks.

—Captain Awesome vs. the Evil Babysitter. O'Connor, George, illus. 2014. (Captain Awesome Ser.: 11). (ENG.). 128p. (J). (gr. k-4). pap. 5.99 *(978-1-4814-0446-4(6)*, Little Simon) Little Simon.

—Captain Awesome vs. the Spooky, Scary House. O'Connor, George, illus. 2013. (Captain Awesome Ser.: 8). (ENG.). 128p. (J). (gr. k-2). 16.99 *(978-1-4424-7255-6(3))*; pap. 5.99 *(978-1-4424-7254-9(5))* Little Simon. (Little Simon).

—Captain Awesome vs. the Spooky, Scary House. 2013. (Captain Awesome Ser.: 8). lib. bdg. 16.00 *(978-0-606-32048-1(2)*, Turtleback) Turtleback Bks.

Kirk, David. Captain Sunny Patch. 2006. (Illus.). 32p. (J). *(978-0-448-44515-1(8))* Callaway Editions, Inc.

Klement, Jon. Rush & the Grey Fox: Ready to Rumble. 2007. 96p. per. *(978-1-897217-66-5(8))* Coscom Entertainment.

Knapman, Timothy. Superhero Dad. Berger, Joe, illus. 2016. (ENG.). (J). (gr. -1-2). 15.99 *(978-0-7636-8657-4(3)*, Nosy Crow) Candlewick Pr.

Kochalka, James. The Glorkian Warrior & the Mustache of Destiny. 2016. (Glorkian Warrior Ser.: 3). (ENG., Illus.). 128p. (J). pap. 14.99 *(978-1-62672-022-0(3)*, 9781626720220, First Second Bks.) Roaring Brook Pr.

—The Glorkian Warrior Delivers a Pizza. Kochalka, James, illus. 2014. (Glorkian Warrior Ser.: 1). (ENG., Illus.). 112p. (J). (gr. k-4). pap. 12.99 *(978-1-59643-917-7(3)*, 9781596439177, First Second Bks.) Roaring Brook Pr.

Konigsburg, E. L. The Mysterious Edge of the Heroic World. 2009. (ENG.). 256p. (J). (gr. 5-9). pap. 7.99 *(978-1-4169-5353-1(1)*, Atheneum Bks. for Young Readers) Simon & Schuster Children's Publishing.

Korte, Steve. Beast Boy Bro-Down. 2016. (Teen Titans Go! Chapter Bks.). (J). lib. bdg. 16.00 *(978-0-606-38327-1(1))* Turtleback Bks.

—Mxy's Magical Mayhem. Levins, Tim, illus. 2013. (Man of Steel Ser.). (ENG.). 88p. (gr. 2-3). pap. 5.95 *(978-1-4342-4826-8(7))*; 26.65 *(978-1-4342-4488-8(1))* Stone Arch Bks.

Korté, Steve. Teen Titans Go! - Beast Boy Bro-Down. 2016. (ENG., Illus.). 144p. (J). (gr. 1-5). pap. 5.99 *(978-0-316-26747-2(3))* Little, Brown Bks. for Young Readers.

Korte, Steve. Teen Titans Go! - Starfire Starbomb. 2016. (ENG., Illus.). 144p. (J). (gr. 1-5). pap. 5.99 *(978-0-316-35645-9(X))* Little, Brown Bks. for Young Readers.

Kraatz, Jeramey. The Cloak Society. (Cloak Society Ser.: 1). (ENG.). (J). (gr. 3-7). 2013. 304p. pap. 6.99 *(978-0-06-209548-0(X))* 2012. 288p. 16.99 *(978-0-06-209547-3(1))* HarperCollins Pubs.

—Fall of Heroes. 2014. (Cloak Society Ser.: 3). (ENG.). 320p. (J). (gr. 3-7). 16.99 *(978-0-06-209553-4(6))* HarperCollins Pubs.

—Villains Rising. 2013. (Cloak Society Ser.: 2). (ENG.). 320p. (J). (gr. 3-7). 16.99 *(978-0-06-209550-3(1))* HarperCollins Pubs.

Kroll, Virginia L. Especially Heroes. Ladwig, Tim, illus. 2004. 32p. (J). 16.00 *(978-0-8028-5221-2(1))* Eerdmans, William B. Publishing Co.

Kropp, Paul. One Stormy Night. (Illus.). 88p. *(978-1-897039-10-6(7))* High Interest Publishing (HIP).

Kunkel, Mike. Brother vs. Brother!, 1 vol. Kunkel, Mike, illus. 2014. (Billy Batson & the Magic of Shazam! Ser.). (ENG., Illus.). 32p. (gr. 2-3). 22.60 *(978-1-4342-9228-5(2))* Stone Arch Bks.

—Magic Words!, 1 vol. Kunkel, Mike, illus. 2014. (Billy Batson & the Magic of Shazam! Ser.). (ENG., Illus.). 32p. (gr. 2-3). 22.60 *(978-1-4342-9209-4(6))* Stone Arch Bks.

—Perilous Peril!, 1 vol. Kunkel, Mike, illus. 2014. (Billy Batson & the Magic of Shazam! Ser.). (ENG., Illus.). 32p. (gr. 2-3). 22.60 *(978-1-4342-9227-8(4))* Stone Arch Bks.

—The World's Mightiest Mortal!, 1 vol. Kunkel, Mike, illus. 2014. (Billy Batson & the Magic of Shazam! Ser.). (ENG., Illus.). 32p. (gr. 2-3). 22.60 *(978-1-4342-9226-1(6))* Stone Arch Bks.

Kupperberg, Paul. Dr. Psycho's Circus of Crime, 1 vol. Schoening, Dan, illus. 2014. (Wonder Woman Ser.). (ENG.). 56p. (gr. 2-3). pap. 4.95 *(978-1-4342-2761-4(8)*, DC Super Heroes) Stone Arch Bks.

Kupperberg, Paul & Loughridge, Lee. The Kid Who Saved Superman, 1 vol. Ku, Min Sung, illus. (Superman Ser.). (ENG.). 56p. (gr. 2-3). 2013. pap. 4.95 *(978-1-4342-1937-4(2))* 2009. lib. bdg. 26.65 *(978-1-4342-1936-7(4))* Stone Arch Bks. (DC Super Heroes).

—Meteor of Doom, 1 vol. McManus, Shawn, illus. (Superman Ser.). (ENG.). 56p. (gr. 2-3). 2013. pap. 4.95 *(978-1-4342-1734-9(5))* 2009. lib. bdg. 26.65 *(978-1-4342-1568-0(7))* Stone Arch Bks. (DC Super Heroes).

—The Shadow Masters. Burchett, Rick, illus. (Superman Ser.). (ENG.). 56p. (gr. 2-3). 2014. pap. 4.95 *(978-1-4342-2768-3(5))* 2010. lib. bdg. 26.65 *(978-1-4342-2079-0(6))* Stone Arch Bks. (DC Super Heroes).

Kupperberg, Paul, et al. Bat-Mite's Big Blunder, 1 vol. Schigiel, Gregg, illus. (Batman Ser.). (ENG.). 56p. (gr. 2-3). 2013. pap. 4.95 *(978-1-4342-2255-8(1))* 2010. lib. bdg. 26.65 *(978-1-4342-1877-3(5))* Stone Arch Bks. (DC Super Heroes).

—Super-Villain Showdown, 1 vol. Doescher, Erik, illus. 2013. (Superman Ser.). (ENG.). 56p. (gr. 2-3). pap. 4.95 *(978-1-4342-1736-3(1)*, DC Super Heroes) Stone Arch Bks.

Lagonegro, Melissa. Barbie in Princess Power - Saving the Day! 2015. (Step into Reading Ser.). (ENG., Illus.). 24p. (J). (gr. -1-1). 4.99 *(978-0-553-50890-1(3)*, Random Hse. Bks. for Young Readers) Random Hse. Children's Bks.

Layburn, Joe. Runaways. Williams, John, illus. 2014. (ENG.). 144p. (J). (gr. 4-7). pap. 8.95 *(978-1-84780-080-0(7)*, Frances Lincoln) Quarto Publishing Group UK GBR. Dist: Hachette Bk. Group.

Lean, Sarah. Hero. 2015. (ENG.). 208p. (J). (gr. 3-7). 16.99 *(978-0-06-212238-4(X))* HarperCollins Pubs.

Lederer, Ryan. The Adventures of Captain Candy. 2007. (Illus.). 48p. (J). (gr. 4-7). 15.95 *(978-0-9795852-1-0(X))* Seven Locks Pr.

Lee, Ingrid. The True Story of George. Denis, Stephane, illus. 2004. 62p. (J). lib. bdg. 20.00 *(978-1-4242-1262-0(6))* Fitzgerald Bks.

Lee, Quinlan B. Phonics. 2016. (LEGO DC Super Heroes Ser.). (ENG.). (J). (gr. -1-k). pap. 12.99 *(978-0-545-86802-0(5))* Scholastic, Inc.

Lee, Stan. Balder the Brave. 2013. (Thor: Tales of Asgard Ser.). (Illus.). 24p. (J). (gr. 4-8). lib. bdg. 24.21 *(978-1-61479-169-0(4))* Spotlight.

—Boyhood of Thor! 2013. (Thor: Tales of Asgard Ser.). (Illus.). 24p. (J). (gr. 4-8). lib. bdg. 24.21 *(978-1-61479-170-6(8))* Spotlight.

—Challenge! 2013. (Thor: Tales of Asgard Ser.). (Illus.). 24p. (J). (gr. 4-8). lib. bdg. 24.21 *(978-1-61479-171-3(6))* Spotlight.

—The Fantastic Four. 2013. (ENG., Illus.). 832p. (J). (gr. -1-17). 99.99 *(978-0-7851-8567-3(4))* Marvel Worldwide, Inc.

—The Fantastic Four Omnibus, Vol. 1. 2013. (ENG., Illus.). 848p. (J). (gr. -1-17). 99.99 *(978-0-7851-8566-6(6))* Marvel Worldwide, Inc.

—Quest for the Mystic Mountain! 2013. (Thor: Tales of Asgard Ser.). (Illus.). 24p. (J). (gr. 4-8). lib. bdg. 24.21 *(978-1-61479-172-0(4))* Spotlight.

—Stan Lee's Superhero Christmas. Jessell, Tim, illus. 2nd ed. 2016. (ENG.). (gr. k-2). 27.95 **(978-1-59687-526-5(7)**, ipicturebooks) ibooks, Inc.

—Superhero Christmas. Jessell, Tim, illus. 2004. 32p. (J). (gr. -1-2). 16.89 *(978-0-06-056560-2(8))* HarperCollins Pubs.

—Thor: Tales of Asgard. 2013. (Thor: Tales of Asgard Ser.: 6). 24p. (J). (gr. 4-8). lib. bdg. 145.26 *(978-1-61479-168-3(6))* Spotlight.

—To the Death! 2013. (Thor: Tales of Asgard Ser.). (Illus.). 24p. (J). (gr. 4-8). lib. bdg. 24.21 *(978-1-61479-173-7(2))* Spotlight.

—When Speaks the Dragon! 2013. (Thor: Tales of Asgard Ser.). (Illus.). 24p. (J). (gr. 4-8). lib. bdg. 24.21 *(978-1-61479-174-4(0))* Spotlight.

Lemke, Donald. Batman - Who Is Clayface? Gordon, Steven E. & Gordon, Eric A., illus. 2013. (I Can Read Level 2 Ser.). (ENG.). 32p. (J). (gr. -1-3). pap. 3.99 *(978-0-06-188525-9(8))* HarperCollins Pubs.

—Battle of the Power Ring. 2016. (Justice League Classic: I Can Read! Ser.). (J). lib. bdg. 13.55 *(978-0-606-38159-8(7))* Turtleback Bks.

—Coldfinger: Zinc Alloy. Holgate, Douglas, illus. 2010. (Graphic Sparks Ser.). (ENG.). 40p. (gr. 1-3). pap. 5.95 *(978-1-4342-2314-2(0)*, Graphic Sparks) Stone Arch Bks.

—Justice League Classic: Battle of the Power Ring. Spaziante, Patrick, illus. 2016. (I Can Read Level 2 Ser.). 32p. (J). (gr. -1-3). pap. 3.99 *(978-0-06-234494-6(3))* HarperCollins Pubs.

—Justice League Classic: the Mightiest Magic. Spaziante, Patrick, illus. 2015. (ENG.). 24p. (J). (gr. -1-3). pap. 3.99 *(978-0-06-234490-8(0)*, HarperFestival) HarperCollins Pubs.

—Nightmare in Gotham City. 2015. (Batman 8X8 Storybooks Ser.). (J). lib. bdg. 13.55 *(978-0-606-36952-7(X))* Turtleback Bks.

—Pranking News. 2016. (Justice League Classic: I Can Read! Ser.). (J). lib. bdg. 13.55 *(978-0-606-38772-9(2))* Turtleback Bks.

—Revealed!, 1 vol. Holgate, Douglas, illus. 2008. (Zinc Alloy Ser.). (ENG.). 40p. (gr. 1-3). 23.99 *(978-1-4342-0763-0(3)*, Graphic Sparks) Stone Arch Bks.

—Revealed! Zinc Alloy, 1 vol. Holgate, Douglas, illus. 2008. (Graphic Sparks Ser.). (ENG.). 40p. (gr. 1-3). pap. 5.95 *(978-1-4342-0859-0(1)*, Graphic Sparks) Stone Arch Bks.

—Super Zero, 1 vol. Holgate, Douglas, illus. 2008. (Zinc Alloy Ser.). (ENG.). 40p. (gr. 1-3). 23.99 *(978-1-4342-0762-3(5))*; pap. 5.95 *(978-1-4342-0858-3(3))* Stone Arch Bks. (Graphic Sparks).

—Superman Versus the Silver Banshee. 2013. (Justice League Classic: I Can Read! Ser.). (J). lib. bdg. 13.55 *(978-0-606-27156-1(2)*, Turtleback) Turtleback Bks.

—Superman vs. the Silver Banshee. Smith, Andy, illus. 2013. (I Can Read Level 2 Ser.). (ENG.). 32p. (J). (gr. -1-3). pap. 3.99 *(978-0-06-188524-2(X))* HarperCollins Pubs.

—Who Is Clayface? 2013. (Justice League Classic: I Can Read! Ser.). (J). lib. bdg. 13.55 *(978-0-606-31790-0(2)*, Turtleback) Turtleback Bks.

Lemke, Donald & Loughridge, Lee. Puppet Master's Revenge. Burchett, Rick, illus. 2013. (Batman Ser.). (ENG.). 56p. (gr. 2-3). pap. 4.95 *(978-1-4342-1727-1(2)*, DC Super Heroes) Stone Arch Bks.

Lemke, Donald B. The Amazing Mini-Mutts, 1 vol. Baltazar, Art, illus. 2012. (DC Super-Pets Ser.). (ENG.). 56p. (gr. 2-2). pap. 4.95 *(978-1-4048-7218-9(3))*; lib. bdg. 23.99 *(978-1-4048-6488-7(1))* Picture Window Bks. (DC Super-Pets).

—Coldfinger, 1 vol. Holgate, Douglas, illus. 2009. (Zinc Alloy Ser.). (ENG.). 40p. (gr. 1-3). lib. bdg. 23.99 *(978-1-4342-1586-4(5)*, Graphic Sparks) Stone Arch Bks.

—The Invincible Boy-Bot. 2012. (Zinc Alloy Ser.). (ENG.). 128p. (gr. 1-3). pap. 8.95 *(978-1-4342-4597-7(7))* Stone Arch Bks.

—Spokes on the Water, 1 vol. Holgate, Douglas, illus. 2011. (Bike Rider Ser.). (ENG.). 40p. (gr. 1-3). lib. bdg. 23.99 *(978-1-4342-2537-5(2)*, Graphic Sparks) Stone Arch Bks.

—Superman. Ku, Min Sung, illus. 2014. (DC Super Friends Word Adventures Ser.). (ENG.). 12p. (gr. -1 — 1). bds. 6.99 *(978-1-4795-5243-6(7))* Picture Window Bks.

—Wheelies of Justice, 1 vol. Holgate, Douglas, illus. 2010. (Bike Rider Ser.). (ENG.). 40p. (gr. 1-3). lib. bdg. 23.99 *(978-1-4342-1892-6(9)*, Graphic Sparks) Stone Arch Bks.

—Wonder Woman. Ku, Min Sung, illus. 2014. (DC Super Friends Word Adventures Ser.). (ENG.). 12p. (gr. -1 — 1). bds. 6.99 *(978-1-4795-5244-3(5))* Picture Window Bks.

—Zinc Alloy vs Frankenstein, 1 vol. Holgate, Douglas, illus. (Graphic Sparks Ser.). (ENG.). 40p. (gr. 1-3). 2010. pap. 5.95 *(978-1-4342-1391-4(9))* 2009. lib. bdg. 23.99 *(978-1-4342-1188-0(6))* Stone Arch Bks. (Graphic Sparks).

Lemke, Donald B. & Loughridge, Lee. Mad Hatter's Movie Madness, 1 vol. Schigiel, Gregg, illus. (Batman Ser.). (ENG.). 56p. (gr. 2-3). 2014. pap. 4.95 *(978-1-4342-1675-5(6))* 2010. lib. bdg. 26.65 *(978-1-4342-2131-5(8))* Stone Arch Bks. (DC Super Heroes).

—The Puppet Master's Revenge, 1 vol. Burchett, Rick, illus. 2009. (Batman Ser.). (ENG.). 56p. (gr. 2-3). 26.65 *(978-1-4342-1560-4(1)*, DC Super Heroes) Stone Arch Bks.

Lemke, Donald B., et al. Emperor of the Airwaves, 1 vol. DC Comics Staff, illus. 2013. (Batman Ser.). (ENG.). 56p. (gr. 2-3). pap. 4.95 *(978-1-4342-1364-8(1)*, DC Super Heroes) Stone Arch Bks.

—Emperor of the Airwaves. 2009. (Batman Ser.). (ENG., Illus.). 56p. (gr. 2-3). lib. bdg. 26.65 *(978-1-4342-1153-8(3)*, DC Super Heroes) Stone Arch Bks.

—Fun House of Evil. 2009. (Batman Ser.). (ENG., Illus.). 56p. (gr. 2-3). lib. bdg. 26.65 *(978-1-4342-1145-3(2)*, DC Super Heroes) Stone Arch Bks.

—Wrath of the Weather Wizard, 1 vol. Doescher, Erik, illus. 2011. (Flash Ser.). (ENG.). 56p. (gr. 2-3). pap. 4.95 *(978-1-4342-3090-4(2))*; lib. bdg. 26.65 *(978-1-4342-2613-6(1))* Stone Arch Bks. (DC Super Heroes).

Lethcoe, Jason. The Capture of the Crimson Cape. Lethcoe, Jason, illus. 2006. (Amazing Adventures from Zoom's Academy Ser.). (ENG., Illus.). 144p. (J). (gr. 4-7). pap. 12.95 *(978-0-345-48356-0(1)*, Ballantine Bks.) Random House Publishing Group.

—Zoom's Academy. 2006. (ENG., Illus.). 304p. (J). (gr. 4-7). pap. 14.95 *(978-0-345-49641-6(8)*, Ballantine Bks.) Random House Publishing Group.

Lewis, Gill. Murphy & the Great Surf Rescue. Home, Sarah, illus. 2017. (Puppy Academy Ser.). (ENG.). 128p. (J). 16.99 *(978-1-62779-800-6(5)*, 9781627798006, Holt, Henry & Co. Bks. For Young Readers) Holt, Henry & Co.

Lim, Ronald & Rosenberg, Rachelle, illus. This Is Ant-Man. 2015. 31p. (J). **(978-1-4844-5652-1(1))** Disney Pr.

Linsley, Paul. Blast to the Past! Golden Books, illus. 2015. (Big Golden Book Ser.). (ENG.). 32p. (J). (gr. -1-2). 9.99 *(978-1-101-93464-7(6)*, Golden Bks.) Random Hse. Children's Bks.

Lloyd-Jones, Emily. Deceptive: An Illusive Novel. 2015. (Illusive Ser.: 2). (ENG.). 432p. (YA). (gr. 7-17). 18.00 *(978-0-316-25464-9(9))* Little Brown & Co.

Long, Matty. Super Happy Magic Forest. Long, Matty, illus. 2016. (ENG., Illus.). 32p. (J). (gr. -1-3). 17.99 *(978-0-545-86059-8(8)*, Scholastic Pr.) Scholastic, Inc.

—Super Slug of Doom: A Super Happy Magic Forest Story. Long, Matty, illus. 2017. (ENG., Illus.). 32p. (J). (gr. -1-3). 17.99 *(978-1-338-05435-4(X)*, Scholastic Pr.) Scholastic, Inc.

Loughridge, Lee & Hoena, Blake A. Cosmic Bounty Hunter, 1 vol. Burchett, Rick, illus. 2014. (Superman Ser.). (ENG.). 56p. (gr. 2-3). pap. 4.95 *(978-1-4342-2769-0(3)*, DC Super Heroes) Stone Arch Bks.

Lovhaug, Lewis J. Angel Armor: Just a Boy. 2003. 224p. (YA). pap. 15.95 *(978-0-595-28475-7(2))* iUniverse, Inc.

Lumley, Brian. The Nonesuch & Others. 2009. (Illus.). 122p. (J). (gr. 4-7). 35.00 *(978-1-59606-210-8(X))* Subterranean Pr.

Lupica, Mike. Hero. (ENG.). 304p. (J). (gr. 5-18). 2011. 7.99 *(978-0-14-241960-1(5)*, Puffin Books) 2010. 17.99 *(978-0-399-25283-9(5)*, Philomel Bks.) Penguin Young Readers Group.

—Hero. 2011. lib. bdg. 18.40 *(978-0-606-23142-8(0)*, Turtleback) Turtleback Bks.

Lyga, Barry. Archvillain. 2010. (Archvillain Ser.: 1). (ENG.). 192p. (J). (gr. 3-7). 16.99 *(978-0-545-19649-9(3)*, Scholastic Pr.) Scholastic, Inc.

—Hero Type. 2009. (ENG.). 312p. (YA). (gr. 7). pap. 8.99 *(978-0-547-24877-6(6))* Houghton Mifflin Harcourt Publishing Co.

Lynch, Chris. Hothouse. 2010. (ENG.). 208p. (YA). (gr. 8-18). 16.99 *(978-0-06-167379-5(X)*, HarperTeen) HarperCollins Pubs.

Lynch, Jay. Mo & Jo: Fighting Together Forever. Haspiel, Dean, illus. 2008. (ENG.). 40p. (J). (gr. -1-3). 12.95 *(978-0-9799238-5-2(9))* TOON Books / RAW Junior, LLC.

Lynch, Jay & Haspiel, Dean. Mo & Jo: Fighting Together Forever, 1 vol. 2013. (Toon Bks). (ENG.). 40p. (J). (gr. 2-3). lib. bdg. 27.07 *(978-1-61479-152-2(X))* Spotlight.

Lyons-Reid, Nashika. My Brother the Superhero. 2008. 28p. pap. 15.99 *(978-1-4363-5941-2(4))* Xlibris Corp.

Maberry, Jonathan. The Orphan Army. 2015. (Nightsiders Ser.: 1). (ENG., Illus.). 400p. (J). (gr. 3-7). 16.99 *(978-1-4814-1575-0(1)*, Simon & Schuster Bks. For Young Readers) Simon & Schuster Bks. For Young Readers.

—The Orphan Army. 2016. (Nightsiders Ser.: 1). lib. bdg. 18.40 *(978-0-606-38959-4(8))* Turtleback Bks.

—Vault of Shadows. (Nightsiders Ser.: 2). (ENG.). 464p. (J). (gr. 3-7). 2017. pap. 8.99 *(978-1-4814-1579-8(4))* 2016. (Illus.). 16.99 *(978-1-4814-1578-1(6))* Simon & Schuster Bks. For Young Readers. (Simon & Schuster Bks. For Young Readers).

Macdangereuse, T. T. The Untamed Scoundrel. 2014. (Epic Tales from Adventure Time Ser.). lib. bdg. 17.20 *(978-0-606-35718-0(1))* Turtleback Bks.

Macri, Thomas. The Story of the X-Men Level 2 Reader. Olliffe, Pat, illus. 2013. (World of Reading Ser.). (ENG.). 32p. (J). (gr. 1-3). pap. 3.99 *(978-1-4231-7224-6(8))* Marvel Worldwide, Inc.

—These Are the X-Men. 2013. (Marvel World of Reading Level 1 Ser.). (J). lib. bdg. 13.55 *(978-0-606-32299-7(X)*, Turtleback) Turtleback Bks.

Makura, Sho. Panda Man & the Treasure Hunt. Kato, Haruhi, illus. 2011. (ENG.). 96p. (J). (gr. 1-4). pap. 7.99 *(978-1-4215-3521-0(1))* Viz Media.

—Panda Man vs. Chiwanda. Kato, Haruhi, illus. 2011. (ENG.). 96p. (J). (gr. 1-4). pap. 7.99 *(978-1-4215-3522-7(X))* Viz Media.

Maleev, Alex, et al, illus. The Road to Civil War. 2007. (ENG.). 160p. (YA). (gr. 8-17). pap. 14.99 *(978-0-7851-1974-6(4))* Marvel Worldwide, Inc.

Mangskau, Monica. My Grandpa the Super Hero. 2010. 16p. 9.49 *(978-1-4343-8088-3(2))* AuthorHouse.

Manning, Matthew. Gotham City's Guardian. 2016. (Backstories Ser.). (ENG.). 128p. (J). (gr. 3-7). pap. 5.99 *(978-0-545-86816-7(5))* Scholastic, Inc.

Manning, Matthew K. Catwoman's Nine Lives, 1 vol. Vecchio, Luciano, illus. 2014. (Batman: Comic Chapter Bks.). (ENG.). 88p. (gr. 3-7). 21.32 *(978-1-4342-9132-5(4))* Stone Arch Bks.

—Green Lantern: An Origin Story. Baltazar, Art & Vecchio, Luciano, illus. 2015. (DC Super Heroes Origins Ser.). (ENG.). 48p. (gr. k-2). lib. bdg. 23.99 *(978-1-4342-9730-3(6))* Stone Arch Bks.

—Superman: An Origin Story. Baltazar, Art & Vecchio, Luciano, illus. 2015. (DC Super Heroes Origins Ser.). (ENG.). 48p. (gr. k-2). lib. bdg. 23.99 *(978-1-4342-9728-0(4))* Stone Arch Bks.

Manning, Matthew K. & Sazaklis, John. DC Super Hero Origins. Vecchio, Luciano, illus. 2015. (DC Super Heroes Origins Ser.). (ENG.). 48p. (gr. k-2). lib. bdg. 95.96 *(978-1-4965-0042-7(3),* DC Super Heroes) Stone Arch Bks.

Manning, Matthew K., et al. The Attack of Professor Zoom!, 1 vol. 2011. (Flash Ser.). (ENG., Illus.). 56p. (gr. 2-3). pap. 4.95 *(978-1-4342-3091-1(0));* lib. bdg. 26.65 *(978-1-4342-2614-3(X))* Stone Arch Bks. (DC Super Heroes).

—Little Green Men. (Superman Ser.). (ENG., Illus.). 56p. (gr. 2-3). 2013. pap. 4.95 *(978-1-4342-2259-6(4))* 2010. lib. bdg. 26.65 *(978-1-4342-1881-0(3))* Stone Arch Bks. (DC Super Heroes).

—The Rule of Three. Brizuela, Dario, illus. 2015. (Beware the Batman Ser.). (ENG.). 32p. (gr. 2-3). lib. bdg. 22.60 *(978-1-4342-9739-6(X))* Stone Arch Bks.

—Scarecrow, Doctor of Fear, 1 vol. (Batman Ser.). (ENG., Illus.). 56p. (gr. 2-3). 2014. pap. 4.95 *(978-1-4342-2764-5(2))* 2010. lib. bdg. 26.65 *(978-1-4342-1989-3(5))* Stone Arch Bks. (DC Super Heroes).

—Two-Face's Double Take. McManus, Shawn, illus. (Batman Ser.). (ENG.). 56p. (gr. 2-3). 2013. pap. 4.95 *(978-1-4342-2264-0(0))* 2010. lib. bdg. 26.65 *(978-1-4342-1878-0(3))* Stone Arch Bks. (DC Super Heroes).

Marchese, Stephen, illus. The Flights of Marceau: Week Two. 2007. (ENG.). 60p. (J). 16.95 *(978-0-9797495-1-3(4))* Majestic Eagle Publishing.

Mariconda, Barbara. The Voyage of Lucy P. Simmons. 2012. (Voyage of Lucy P. Simmons Ser.: 1). (ENG.). 256p. (J). (gr. 3-7). 16.99 *(978-0-06-211979-7(6),* Tegen, Katherine Bks) HarperCollins Pubs.

Marko, Cyndi. The Birdy Snatchers. 2014. (Kung Pow Chicken Ser.: 3). (ENG.). 80p. (J). (gr. k-2). 15.99 *(978-0-545-61072-8(9))* Scholastic, Inc.

—The Birdy Snatchers. Marko, Cyndi, illus. 2014. (Kung Pow Chicken Ser.: 3). (ENG., Illus.). 80p. (J). (gr. k-2). pap. 4.99 *(978-0-545-61068-1(0))* Scholastic, Inc.

—The Birdy Snatchers. 2014. (Kung Pow Chicken Ser.: 3). lib. bdg. 14.75 *(978-0-606-35358-8(5))* Turtleback Bks.

—Bok! Bok! Boom! Marko, Cyndi, illus. 2014. (Kung Pow Chicken Ser.: 2). (ENG., Illus.). 80p. (J). (gr. k-2). 15.99 *(978-0-545-61064-3(8));* pap. 4.99 *(978-0-545-61063-6(X))* Scholastic, Inc.

—Bok! Bok! Boom! 2014. (Kung Pow Chicken Ser.: 2). lib. bdg. 14.75 *(978-0-606-35357-1(7))* Turtleback Bks.

—Heroes on the Side. Marko, Cyndi, illus. 2014. (Kung Pow Chicken Ser.: 4). (ENG., Illus.). 80p. (J). (gr. k-2). 15.99 *(978-0-545-61077-3(X));* pap. 4.99 *(978-0-545-61074-2(5))* Scholastic, Inc.

—Heroes on the Side. 2014. (Kung Pow Chicken Ser.: 4). lib. bdg. 14.75 *(978-0-606-36049-4(2))* Turtleback Bks.

—Let's Get Cracking! Marko, Cyndi, illus. 2014. (Kung Pow Chicken Ser.: 1). (ENG., Illus.). 80p. (J). (gr. k-2). 15.99 *(978-0-545-61062-9(1));* pap. 4.99 *(978-0-545-61061-2(3))* Scholastic, Inc.

Marshall, Stacey A. Captain Courage & the Fear-Squishing Shoes. Morse, Michelle, illus. 2012. 16p. pap. 9.95 *(978-1-61633-319-5(7))* Guardian Angel Publishing, Inc.

—Captain Courage & the World's Most Shocking Secret Book 2. Morse, Michelle, illus. 2013. 24p. 19.95 *(978-1-61633-431-4(2))* Guardian Angel Publishing, Inc.

Marvel. Avengers: Age of Ultron: Avengers Save the Day. 2015. (Marvel 8x8s Ser.). (J). lib. bdg. 14.75 *(978-0-606-37214-5(8))* Turtleback Bks.

—Avengers: Age of Ultron: Battle at Avengers Tower. 2015. (Marvel 8x8s Ser.). (J). lib. bdg. 13.55 *(978-0-606-37213-8(X))* Turtleback Bks.

—Captain America - Civil War Reusable Sticker Book. 2016. (ENG., Illus.). 12p. (J). (gr. -1-1). pap. 6.99 *(978-0-316-27145-5(4))* Little, Brown Bks. for Young Readers.

—Captain America: Civil War Junior Novel. 2016. (ENG.). 144p. (J). (gr. 3-7). pap. 6.99 *(978-0-316-27142-4(X))* Little, Brown Bks. for Young Readers.

—Marvel Avengers Assemble: Built for Action. 2015. (ENG.). 24p. (J). (gr. 1-4). pap. 10.99 *(978-0-7944-3392-5(8),* Reader's Digest Children's Bks.) Studio Fun International.

—Marvel Super Heroes Assemble! Tattoos, Fantastic Facts, & Amazing Activites. 2014. (ENG.). 24p. (J). (gr. -1-1). pap. 7.99 *(978-0-7944-3008-5(2),* Reader's Digest Children's Bks.) Studio Fun International.

—Marvel's Avengers 8x8 Bindup. 2016. (ENG.). 192p. (J). (gr. -1-3). 11.99 *(978-0-316-27146-2(2))* Little, Brown Bks. for Young Readers.

—Marvel's Avengers Reader Bindup. 2016. (Passport to Reading Level 2 Ser.). (ENG., Illus.). 192p. (J). (gr. -1-3). pap. 7.99 *(978-0-316-27147-9(0)) Little, Brown Bks. for* Young Readers.

—Marvel's the Avengers Reading Adventures. 2015. (Passport to Reading Level 2 Ser.). (ENG., Illus.). 192p. (J). (gr. -1-3). pap. 7.99 *(978-0-316-25749-7(4))* Little, Brown Bks. for Young Readers.

Marvel & Busse, R. R. I Am Doctor Strange. 2016. (Passport to Reading Level 2 Ser.). (ENG., Illus.). 32p. (J). (gr. -1-3). pap. 3.99 *(978-0-316-27151-6(9))* Little, Brown Bks. for Young Readers.

Marvel & Cho, Charles. The Sorcerer Supreme. 2016. (ENG., Illus.). 24p. (J). (gr. -1-3). pap. 4.99 *(978-0-316-27155-4(1))* Little, Brown Bks. for Young Readers.

Marvel & Davis, Adam. Battle at Avengers Tower. 2015. (ENG., Illus.). 24p. (J). (gr. -1-3). pap. 3.99 *(978-0-316-25643-8(9))* Little, Brown Bks. for Young Readers.

Marvel & Marvel Book Group. This Is the Invincible Iron Man. 2012. (Marvel World of Reading Level 1 Ser.). (J). lib. bdg. 13.55 *(978-0-606-23789-5(5),* Turtleback) Turtleback Bks.

Marvel & Strathearn, Chris. Captain America: Civil War 8x8. 2016. (ENG., Illus.). 24p. (J). (gr. -1-3). pap. 3.99 *(978-0-316-27139-4(X))* Little, Brown Bks. for Young Readers.

Marvel & Wyatt, Chris. Age of Ultron. 2015. (ENG., Illus.). 144p. (J). (gr. 3-7). pap. 6.99 *(978-0-316-25644-5(7))* Little, Brown Bks. for Young Readers.

Marvel, et al. These Are the Avengers. 2012. (Marvel World of Reading Level 1 Ser.). (J). lib. bdg. 13.55 *(978-0-606-23788-8(7),* Turtleback) Turtleback Bks.

Marvel Book Group. Ant-Man: Zombie Repellent: A Mighty Marvel Chapter Book. 2015. (Mighty Marvel Chapter Book Ser.). (ENG.). 128p. (J). (gr. 3-7). pap. 5.99 *(978-1-4847-1449-2(0),* Marvel Pr.) Disney Publishing Worldwide.

—Avengers - Battle with Ultron, Level 2. 2015. (World of Reading Ser.). (ENG.). 32p. (J). (gr. 1-3). pap. 3.99 *(978-1-4847-1448-5(2),* Marvel Pr.) Disney Publishing Worldwide.

—Captain America: An Origin Story. 2014. (Origin Story Ser.). (ENG.). 48p. (J). (gr. 1-3). 8.99 *(978-1-4847-0073-0(2),* Marvel Pr.) Disney Publishing Worldwide.

—Iron-Man 2. 2016. (Read-Along Storybook & CD Ser.). (ENG.). 32p. (J). (gr. -1-k). pap. 6.99 *(978-1-4847-8630-7(0),* Marvel Pr.) Disney Publishing Worldwide.

—Marvel, Level 1: 3 Tales of Action. 2016. (World of Reading Ser.). (ENG.). 96p. (J). (gr. -1-k). pap. 7.99 *(978-1-4847-8747-2(1),* Marvel Pr.) Disney Publishing Worldwide.

—A Mighty Marvel Chapter Book Amazing Adventures! 2016. (Mighty Marvel Chapter Book Ser.: 2). (ENG.). 384p. (J). (gr. 3-7). pap. 11.99 *(978-1-4847-6732-0(2),* Marvel Pr.) Disney Publishing Worldwide.

—Thor Read-Along Storybook & CD. 2016. (Read-Along Storybook & CD Ser.). (ENG.). 32p. (J). (gr. -1-k). pap. 6.99 *(978-1-4847-8173-9(2),* Marvel Pr.) Disney Publishing Worldwide.

—Ultimate Spider-Man - Spider-Man vs Dracula. 2014. (ENG.). 24p. (J). (gr. 3-7). pap. 5.99 *(978-1-4847-1110-1(6),* Marvel Pr.) Disney Publishing Worldwide.

Marvel Book Group Staff & Macri, Thomas. Happy Holidays! from the Avengers. Lim, Ron, illus. 2016. (ENG.). 24p. (J). (gr. 1-3). pap. 5.99 *(978-1-4847-8200-2(3),* Marvel Pr.) Disney Publishing Worldwide.

Marvel Books Group & Macri, Thomas. This Is Wolverine. 2013. (Marvel World of Reading Level 1 Ser.). (J). lib. bdg. 13.55 *(978-0-606-31751-1(1),* Turtleback) Turtleback Bks.

Marvel Comics Staff & Mayer, Kirsten. Age of Ultron: Avengers Save the Day. 2015. (ENG., Illus.). 24p. (J). (gr. -1-3). pap. 4.99 *(978-0-316-25639-1(0))* Little, Brown Bks. for Young Readers.

Marvel Heroes. 2015. *(978-1-4508-9771-6(1),* PIL Kids) Publications International, Ltd.

Marvel Press Group & Disney Book Group Staff. Marvel Super Heroes. Disney Book Group Staff, illus. 2013. (Storybook Collection). (ENG., Illus.). 304p. (J). (gr. -1-k). 15.99 *(978-1-4231-7223-9(X))* Marvel Worldwide, Inc.

Marvel Press Staff & Palacios, Tomas. Suits of Armor. Disney Book Group Staff, illus. 2013. (ENG.). 24p. (J). (gr. -1-k). pap. 3.99 *(978-1-4231-7246-8(9))* Marvel Worldwide, Inc.

Marvel Press Staff, et al. Thor: the Dark World Junior Novel. Disney Book Group Staff, illus. 2013. (ENG.). 128p. (J). (gr. 3-7). pap. 5.99 *(978-1-4231-7245-1(0))* Marvel Worldwide, Inc.

Marvel Staff & Busse, R. R. Captain America: Civil War Reader #2. 2016. (Passport to Reading Level 2 Ser.). (ENG., Illus.). 32p. (J). (gr. -1-3). pap. 3.99 *(978-0-316-27144-8(6))* Little, Brown Bks. for Young Readers.

Marvel Staff & Smith, A. Harrison. Captain America: Civil War Reader #1. 2016. (Passport to Reading Level 1 Ser.). (ENG., Illus.). 32p. (J). (gr. -1-3). pap. 3.99 *(978-0-316-27143-1(8))* Little, Brown Bks. for Young Readers.

Marvel Staff & Wyatt, Chris. Captain America: Civil War Deluxe Junior Novel. 2016. (ENG.). 144p. (J). (gr. 3-7). 9.99 *(978-0-316-27141-7(1))* Little, Brown Bks. for Young Readers.

Marvel Staff, et al. Captain America: Civil War 8x8 W/Add-On. 2016. (ENG.). 24p. (J). (gr. -1-3). pap. 4.99 *(978-0-316-27140-0(3))* Little, Brown Bks. for Young Readers.

Mason, Jane B. Attack of the Cheetah, 1 vol. Schoening, Dan, illus. 2013. (Wonder Woman Ser.). (ENG.). 56p. (gr. 2-3). pap. 4.95 *(978-1-4342-2254-1(3),* DC Super Heroes) Stone Arch Bks.

—Battle Bugs of Outer Space, 1 vol. Baltazar, Art, illus. 2011. (DC Super-Pets Ser.). (ENG.). 56p. (gr. 2-2). pap. 4.95 *(978-1-4048-6848-9(8));* lib. bdg. 23.99 *(978-1-4048-6482-5(2))* Picture Window Bks. (DC Super-Pets).

—Black Manta & the Octopus Army, 1 vol. Vecchio, Luciano, illus. 2012. (DC Super-Villains Ser.). (ENG.). 56p. (gr. 2-3). pap. 5.95 *(978-1-4342-3898-6(9),* DC Super-villains) Stone Arch Bks.

—Super Hero Splash Down, 1 vol. Baltazar, Art, illus. 2011. (DC Super-Pets Ser.). (ENG.). 56p. (gr. 2-2). pap. 4.95 *(978-1-4048-6624-9(8));* lib. bdg. 23.99 *(978-1-4048-6357-6(5))* Picture Window Bks. (DC Super-Pets).

Mason, Jane B., et al. Captain Cold's Arctic Eruption, 1 vol. Doescher, Erik, illus. 2011. (Flash Ser.). (ENG.). 56p. (gr. 2-3). pap. 4.95 *(978-1-4342-3089-8(9));* lib. bdg. 26.65 *(978-1-4342-2617-4(4))* Stone Arch Bks. (DC Super Heroes).

—Ice & Flame, 1 vol. 2011. (Flash Ser.). (ENG., Illus.). 56p. (gr. 2-3). pap. 4.95 *(978-1-4342-3416-2(9));* lib. bdg. 26.65 *(978-1-4342-2630-3(1))* Stone Arch Bks. (DC Super Heroes).

Matheny, Bill, et al. Alfred to the Rescue?! 2015. (Batman Strikes! Ser.). (ENG., Illus.). 32p. (gr. 2-3). lib. bdg. 22.60 *(978-1-4342-9664-1(4))* Stone Arch Bks.

—Bane on the Rampage!, 1 vol. 2014. (Batman Strikes! Ser.). (ENG., Illus.). 32p. (gr. 2-3). 22.60 *(978-1-4342-4788-9(0))* Stone Arch Bks.

—Bane's Breaking In! 2015. (Batman Strikes! Ser.). (ENG., Illus.). 32p. (gr. 2-3). lib. bdg. 22.60 *(978-1-4342-9665-8(2))* Stone Arch Bks.

—The Batman Is on Fire!, 1 vol. 2014. (Batman Strikes! Ser.). (ENG., Illus.). 32p. (gr. 2-3). 22.60 *(978-1-4342-9229-2(0))* Stone Arch Bks.

—Batman Strikes! 2014. (Batman Strikes! Ser.). (ENG., Illus.). 32p. (gr. 2-3). 90.40 *(978-1-4342-8928-5(1))* Stone Arch Bks.

—Catwoman Gets Busted by the Batman, 1 vol. 2014. (Batman Strikes! Ser.). (ENG., Illus.). 32p. (gr. 2-3). 22.60 *(978-1-4342-9211-7(8))* Stone Arch Bks.

—Frozen Solid by Mr. Freeze!, 1 vol. 2014. (Batman Strikes! Ser.). (ENG., Illus.). 32p. (gr. 2-3). 22.60 *(978-1-4342-6472-6(6))* Stone Arch Bks.

—Going... Batty!, 1 vol. 2014. (Batman Strikes! Ser.). (ENG., Illus.). 32p. (gr. 2-3). 22.60 *(978-1-4342-6484-8(X))* Stone Arch Bks.

—In the Clutches of the Penguin!, 1 vol. 2014. (Batman Strikes! Ser.). (ENG., Illus.). 32p. (gr. 2-3). 22.60 *(978-1-4342-6483-1(1))* Stone Arch Bks.

—Joker's Wild!, 1 vol. 2014. (Batman Strikes! Ser.). (ENG., Illus.). 32p. (gr. 2-3). 22.60 *(978-1-4342-6485-5(8))* Stone Arch Bks.

—Man-Bat's Sneak Attack! 2015. (Batman Strikes! Ser.). (ENG., Illus.). 32p. (gr. 2-3). lib. bdg. 22.60 *(978-1-4342-9655-9(5))* Stone Arch Bks.

—Sanity Plea! 2015. (Batman Strikes! Ser.). (ENG., Illus.). 32p. (gr. 2-3). lib. bdg. 22.60 *(978-1-4342-9743-3(8))* Stone Arch Bks.

Mayberry, Michael. Kid Donut: How to Handle Strangers. 2011. 28p. pap. 13.99 *(978-1-4634-3555-4(X))* AuthorHouse.

Mayer, Kirsten. I Am Aquaman. Smith, Andy & Vancata, Brad, illus. 2013. (I Can Read Level 2 Ser.). (ENG.). 32p. (J). (gr. -1-3). pap. 3.99 *(978-0-06-221003-6(3))* HarperCollins Pubs.

—I Am Aquaman. 2013. (Justice League Classic: I Can Read! Ser.). (J). lib. bdg. 13.55 *(978-0-606-31794-8(5),* Turtleback) Turtleback Bks.

Mayer, Mercer. To the Rescue! Mayer, Mercer, illus. 2008. (My First I Can Read Bks.). (ENG., Illus.). 32p. (J). (gr. -1-3). 16.99 *(978-0-06-083548-4(6));* pap. 3.99 *(978-0-06-083547-7(8))* HarperCollins Pubs.

Mazer, Harry. Heroes Don't Run. 2007. (ENG.). 128p. (J). (gr. 3-7). pap. 6.99 *(978-1-4169-3394-6(8),* Simon & Schuster Bks. For Young Readers) Simon & Schuster Bks. For Young Readers.

McCann, Jesse L., et al. Bad Moon Rising, 1 vol. 2014. (Krypto the Superdog Ser.). (ENG., Illus.). 32p. (gr. 1-2). 22.60 *(978-1-4342-6475-6(0))* Stone Arch Bks.

—Crisis of Infinite Kryptos, 1 vol. 2014. (Krypto the Superdog Ser.). (ENG., Illus.). 32p. (gr. 1-2). 22.60 *(978-1-4342-6471-8(8))* Stone Arch Bks.

—Here Comes Krypto, 1 vol. 2014. (Krypto the Superdog Ser.). (ENG., Illus.). 32p. (gr. 1-2). 22.60 *(978-1-4342-4785-8(6))* Stone Arch Bks.

—Houndin' the Mail Carrier!, 1 vol. 2014. (Krypto the Superdog Ser.). (ENG., Illus.). 32p. (gr. 1-2). 22.60 *(978-1-4342-6472-5(6))* Stone Arch Bks.

—The Purr-Fect Crime, 1 vol. 2014. (Krypto the Superdog Ser.). (ENG., Illus.). 32p. (gr. 1-2). 22.60 *(978-1-4342-6474-9(2))* Stone Arch Bks.

—Three Naughty Doggies!, 1 vol. 2014. (Krypto the Superdog Ser.). (ENG., Illus.). 32p. (gr. 1-2). 22.60 *(978-1-4342-6473-2(4))* Stone Arch Bks.

McCaughrean, Geraldine, retold by. Odysseus. 2004. (Heroes Ser.). (ENG., Illus.). 128p. (J). 17.95 *(978-0-8126-2721-3(0))* Cricket Bks.

McCLOUD, Scott. Be Careful What You Wish For... Burchett, Rick & Austin, Terry, illus. 2012. (Superman Adventures Ser.). (ENG.). 32p. (gr. 2-3). lib. bdg. 22.60 *(978-1-4342-4550-2(0))* Stone Arch Bks.

—Distant Thunder, 1 vol. Burchett, Rick & Austin, Terry, illus. 2012. (Superman Adventures Ser.). (ENG.). 32p. (gr. 2-3). 22.60 *(978-1-4342-4551-9(9))* Stone Arch Bks.

—Eye to Eye, 1 vol. Burchett, Rick & Austin, Terry, illus. 2012. (Superman Adventures Ser.). (ENG.). 32p. (gr. 2-3). lib. bdg. 22.60 *(978-1-4342-4552-6(7))* Stone Arch Bks.

McCool, Ben. Souljacker: #2. Rousseau, Craig, illus. 2012. (Captain America: the Korvac Saga Ser.). 24p. (J). (gr. 3-5). lib. bdg. 24.21 *(978-1-61479-020-4(5))* Spotlight.

—The Star Lord: #4. Rousseau, Craig, illus. 2012. (Captain America: the Korvac Saga Ser.). 24p. (J). (gr. 3-5). lib. bdg. 24.21 *(978-1-61479-022-8(1))* Spotlight.

—Strange Days: #1. Rousseau, Craig, illus. 2012. (Captain America: the Korvac Saga Ser.). 24p. (J). (gr. 3-5). lib. bdg. 24.21 *(978-1-61479-019-8(1))* Spotlight.

—The Traveler: #3. Rousseau, Craig, illus. 2012. (Captain America: the Korvac Saga Ser.). 24p. (J). (gr. 3-5). lib. bdg. 24.21 *(978-1-61479-021-1(3))* Spotlight.

McCorkle, Mark & Schooley, Bob. Grudge Match. 2005. (Illus.). 80p. (J). *(978-1-4155-9100-0(8))* Disney Pr.

McCullough, Kelly. School for Sidekicks. 2015. (ENG.). 336p. (J). (gr. 4-9). 16.99 *(978-1-250-03926-2(6),* 9781250039262) Feiwel & Friends.

McGrellis, Barbara. Love Never Fails. 2013. 24p. pap. 10.99 *(978-1-4624-0745-3(5),* Inspiring Voices) Author Solutions, Inc.

McKay, Laurie. Quest Maker. 2016. (Last Dragon Charmer Ser.: 2). (Illus.). 352p. (J). (gr. 3-7). 16.99 *(978-0-06-230846-7(7))* HarperCollins Pubs.

—The Villain Keeper. 2015. (Last Dragon Charmer Ser.: 1). (ENG.). 352p. (J). (gr. 3-7). 16.99 *(978-0-06-230843-6(2))* HarperCollins Pubs.

McKee, David, illus. Elmer & the Birthday Quake. 2013. (ENG.). 32p. (J). (gr. -1-3). 16.95 *(978-1-4677-1117-3(9))* Lerner Publishing Group.

McLeod, Bob. SuperHero ABC. McLeod, Bob, illus. (Illus.). 40p. (J). (gr. -1-3). 2008. (ENG.). pap. 7.99 *(978-0-06-074516-5(9))* 2006. lib. bdg. 18.89 *(978-0-06-074515-8(0))* HarperCollins Pubs.

—Superhero ABC. McLeod, Bob, illus. 2006. (ENG., Illus.). 40p. (J). (gr. -1-3). 17.99 *(978-0-06-074514-1(2))* HarperCollins Pubs.

McMullan, Kate. Get to Work, Hercules!, 1 vol. Zilber, Denis, illus. (Myth-O-Mania Ser.: Bk. 7). (ENG.). 208p. (gr. 4-8). 2011. pap. 5.95 *(978-1-4342-3440-7(1))* 2010. lib. bdg. 25.32 *(978-1-4342-3196-3(8))* Stone Arch Bks. (Myth-O-Mania).

—Myth-O-Mania. 2014. (Myth-O-Mania Ser.). (ENG.). (gr. 4-8). 253.20 *(978-1-4342-9467-8(6),* Myth-O-Mania) Stone Arch Bks.

Meadows, Michelle. Super Bugs. Mayer, Bill, illus. 2016. (ENG.). 40p. (J). (gr. -1-k). 16.99 *(978-0-545-68756-0(X))* Scholastic, Inc.

Meehl, Brian. Suck It Up. 2009. (ENG.). 336p. (YA). (gr. 7). pap. 8.99 *(978-0-440-42091-0(1),* Delacorte Bks. for Young Readers) Random Hse. Children's Bks.

Mercado-López, Larissa. Esteban de Luna, Baby Rescuer / Esteban de Luna, ¡rescatador de Bebés! Pardo DeLange, Alex, illus. 2017. (ENG & SPA.). 32p. (J). (gr. k-3). 17.95 *(978-1-55885-847-3(4),* Piñata Books) Arte Publico Pr.

Meredith, Randy. Marvel Puzzle Peril! 2008. (Marvel Heroes Ser.). (Illus.). 10p. (J). (gr. 1-5). 9.95 *(978-1-57791-377-1(9))* Brighter Minds Children's Publishing.

Miller, William. Joe Louis, My Champion. Pate, Rodney S., illus. 2004. (ENG.). 32p. (J). pap. 10.95 *(978-1-60060-426-3(9))* Lee & Low Bks., Inc.

—Joe Louis, My Champion, 1 vol. Pate, Rodney, tr. Pate, Rodney, illus. 2004. (ENG.). 32p. (J). 16.95 *(978-1-58430-161-5(9))* Lee & Low Bks., Inc.

Moniz, Michael. My Little Superhero. 2013. 42p. 15.95 *(978-1-938083-19-8(9))* Silver Knight Publishing, LLC.

Montijo, Rhode. Chews Your Destiny. Montijo, Rhode, illus. 2017. (Gum Girl Novel Ser.). (ENG., Illus.). 128p. (J). (gr. 1-3). pap. 5.99 *(978-1-4231-5794-6(X))* Hyperion Bks. for Children.

—Chews Your Destiny. 2013. (Gum Girl Novel Ser.). (ENG.). 128p. (J). (gr. -1-3). 14.99 *(978-1-4231-5740-3(0))* Hyperion Pr.

Montoya, Martha, creator. Mi heroe Favorito: Take-Home. 2005. (Los Kitos Ser.). (SPA.). (YA). (gr. 1-3). 15.00 *(978-0-8215-8811-6(7))* Sadlier, William H. Inc.

Moore, Perry. Hero. 2009. (ENG.). 432p. (J). (gr. 5-9). pap. 9.99 *(978-1-4231-0196-3(0))* Hyperion Pr.

Moore, Peter. V Is for Villain. 2014. (ENG.). 336p. (YA). (gr. 7-12). 17.99 *(978-1-4231-5749-6(4))* Hyperion Pr.

Mull, Brandon. Chasing the Prophecy. (Beyonders Ser.: 3). (ENG.). (J). (gr. 3-7). 2014. 528p. pap. 8.99 *(978-1-4169-9797-9(0))* 2013. 512p. 19.99 *(978-1-4169-9796-2(2))* Simon & Schuster Children's Publishing. (Aladdin).

—Seeds of Rebellion. (Beyonders Ser.: 2). (ENG., Illus.). (J). (gr. 3-7). 2013. 528p. pap. 8.99 *(978-1-4169-9795-5(4))* 2012. 512p. 19.99 *(978-1-4169-9794-8(6))* Simon & Schuster Children's Publishing. (Aladdin).

—Seeds of Rebellion. 2012. (Beyonders Ser.: Bk. 2). (ENG., Illus.). 512p. (J). pap. 10.99 *(978-1-4424-4965-7(9),* Simon & Schuster/Paula Wiseman Bks.) Simon & Schuster/Paula Wiseman Bks.

—Seeds of Rebellion. 2013. (Beyonders Ser.: 2). lib. bdg. 19.65 *(978-0-606-27030-4(2),* Turtleback) Turtleback Bks.

—A World Without Heroes. (J). 2011. (Beyonders Ser.: 1). 1.25 *(978-1-4640-0920-4(1))* (Beyonders Ser.: 1). 92.75 *(978-1-4618-0338-6(1))* 2011. (Beyonders Ser.: 1). 124.75 *(978-1-4618-0353-9(5))* 2011. 122.75 *(978-1-4618-0363-8(2))* Recorded Bks., Inc.

—A World Without Heroes. (Beyonders Ser.: 1). (ENG.). (J). (gr. 3-7). 2012. 496p. pap. 8.99 *(978-1-4169-9793-1(8))* 2011. 464p. 19.99 *(978-1-4169-9792-4(X))* Simon & Schuster Children's Publishing. (Aladdin).

—A World Without Heroes. 2011. (Beyonders Ser.: Bk. 1). (ENG.). 464p. (J). pap. 10.99 *(978-1-4424-3530-8(5),* Simon & Schuster/Paula Wiseman Bks.) Simon & Schuster/Paula Wiseman Bks.

—A World Without Heroes. 2012. (Beyonders Ser.: 1). lib. bdg. 19.65 *(978-0-606-23675-1(9),* Turtleback) Turtleback Bks.

—A World Without Heroes; Seeds of Rebellion; Chasing the Prophecy, Set. 2013. (Beyonders Ser.). (ENG., Illus.). 1456p. (J). (gr. 3-7). 59.99 *(978-1-4424-8593-8(0),* Aladdin) Simon & Schuster Children's Publishing.

Murillo, Vinicio. Roderick Roach. 2013. 50p. pap. 10.95 *(978-1-62516-018-8(6),* Strategic Bk. Publishing) Strategic Book Publishing & Rights Agency (SBPRA).

Murphy, Steve & Murphy, Sonia. The Secret. Ostrom, Bob, illus. 2004. (Teenage Mutant Ninja Turtles Ser.). 32p. (J). (gr. k-2). 11.65 *(978-0-7569-5401-7(0))* Perfection Learning Corp.

Muten, Burleigh. Grandfather Mountain: Stories of Gods & Heroes from Many Cultures. Bailey, Sian, illus. 2004. (ENG.). 80p. (J). (gr. 3-6). 19.99 *(978-1-84148-789-2(9))* Barefoot Bks., Inc.

Muth, Jon J. & Buscema, John, illus. Galactus the Devourer. 2014. (ENG.). 184p. (J). (gr. 4-17). pap. 24.99 *(978-0-7851-8562-8(3))* Marvel Worldwide, Inc.

Myers, Bill. My Life as a Supersized Superhero... with Slobber, 1 vol. 2007. (Incredible Worlds of Wally Mcdoogle Ser.: 28). (ENG.). 128p. (gr. 3-7). per. 6.99 *(978-1-4003-0637-4(X))* Nelson, Thomas Inc.

Myklusch, Matt. The End of Infinity. 2013. (Jack Blank Adventure Ser.: 3). (ENG., Illus.). 416p. (J). (gr. 3-7). pap. 8.99 *(978-1-4169-9568-5(4),* Aladdin) Simon & Schuster Children's Publishing.

—Jack Blank & the Imagine Nation. 2010. (Jack Blank Adventure Ser.: Bk. 1). (ENG., Illus.). 480p. (J). (gr. 3-7). 16.99 *(978-1-4169-9561-6(7),* Aladdin) Simon & Schuster Children's Publishing.

—The Secret War. 2012. (Jack Blank Adventure Ser.: 2). (ENG., Illus.). 560p. (J). (gr. 3-7). pap. 7.99 *(978-1-4169-9565-4(X),* Aladdin) Simon & Schuster Children's Publishing.

Nason, Seldon E. The Adventures of Otis & Amigo, Book Two - the President's Request. 2016. (ENG., Illus.). 46p. (J). pap. 11.95 *(978-1-5069-0207-4(3))* First Edition Design eBook Publishing.

Neary, Paul, illus. S. H. I. E. L. D. Nick Fury vs. S. H. I. E. L. D. 2013. (ENG.). 304p. (J). (gr. 4-17). pap. 29.99 *(978-0-7851-8500-0(3))* Marvel Worldwide, Inc.

Nelson, Peter. Herbert's Wormhole: AeroStar & the 3 1/2-Point Plan of Vengeance. Rao, Rohitash, illus. 2013. (Herbert's Wormhole Ser.: 3). (ENG.). 352p. (J). (gr. 3-7). 12.99 *(978-0-06-201220-3(7))* HarperCollins Pubs.

Nickel, Scott. The Incredible Rockhead, 1 vol. Jennings, C. S., illus. 2009. (Incredible Rockhead Ser.). (ENG.). 40p. (gr. 1-3). lib. bdg. 23.99 *(978-1-4342-1591-8(1)*, Graphic Sparks) Stone Arch Bks.

—The Incredible Rockhead vs Papercut!, 1 vol. Jennings, C. S., illus. 2010. (Incredible Rockhead Ser.). (ENG.). 40p. (gr. 1-3). 23.99 *(978-1-4342-1976-3(3)*, Graphic Sparks) Stone Arch Bks.

—Rock, Paper, Scissorlegz. Jennings, C. S., illus. 2012. (Incredible Rockhead Ser.). (ENG.). 128p. (gr. 1-3). pap. 8.95 *(978-1-4342-4596-0(9))* Stone Arch Bks.

Nickel, Scott & Dahl, Michael. The Evil Echo, 1 vol. Crowther, Jeff, illus. 2010. (Princess Candy Ser.). (ENG.). 40p. (gr. 1-3). 23.99 *(978-1-4342-1977-0(1))*; pap. 5.95 *(978-1-4342-2804-8(5))* Stone Arch Bks. (Graphic Sparks).

Nickel, Scott, et al. The Incredible Rockhead & the Spectacular Scissorlegz, 1 vol. Jennings, C. S., illus. 2010. (Incredible Rockhead Ser.). (ENG.). 40p. (gr. 1-3). 23.99 *(978-1-4342-2127-8(X)*, Graphic Sparks) Stone Arch Bks.

Nicklas, James. Study Hall Story. 2008. 146p. pap. 8.84 *(978-1-4357-5691-5(6))* Lulu Pr., Inc.

Nicolle, Malachai. Axe Cop, Vol. 1. 2011. (ENG., Illus.). 144p. (J). (gr. 5-12). pap. 14.99 *(978-1-59582-681-7(5))* Dark Horse Comics.

—Axe Cop, Vol. 3. 2012. (ENG., Illus.). 120p. (J). (gr. 5-12). pap. 14.99 *(978-1-59582-911-5(3))* Dark Horse Comics.

—Bad Guy Earth, Vol. 1. 2011. (ENG., Illus.). 120p. (J). (gr. 5-12). pap. 14.99 *(978-1-59582-825-5(7))* Dark Horse Comics.

Nnabuchi, Afam. Emeka Transforms in the Pit. 2013. 78p. (J). pap. 12.95 *(978-1-4772-9679-0(4))* AuthorHouse.

Novik, Naomi. Will Supervillains Be on the Final? Liberty Vocational. Li, Yishan, illus. 2011. (ENG.). 192p. pap. 10.99 *(978-0-345-51656-5(7)*, Del Rey) Random House Publishing Group.

O'Connor, George. Ker-Splash! O'Connor, George, illus. 2010. (ENG., Illus.). 40p. (J). (gr. -1-3). 19.99 *(978-1-4424-2196-7(7)*, Simon & Schuster Bks. For Young Readers) Simon & Schuster Bks. For Young Readers.

O'Malley, Kevin. Captain Raptor & the Moon Mystery. O'Brien, Patrick, illus. 2005. (Captain Raptor Ser.). (ENG.). 32p. (J). (gr. k-5). 17.99 *(978-0-8027-8935-8(8)*, 9780802789358, Bloomsbury USA Childrens) Bloomsbury Publishing USA.

Orsak, Lane Rockford. Keiko the Fairy, the Kujiki. 2010. 192p. pap. 14.95 *(978-0-557-47206-2(7))* Lulu Pr., Inc.

Otte, John W. Failstate, 1 vol. 2012. (Failstate Ser.: 1). (ENG.). 416p. (YA). pap. 15.99 *(978-1-935929-48-2(8)*, Enclave) Gilead Publishing, LLC.

—Failstate: Legends, 1 vol. 2013. (Failstate Ser.: 2). 464p. (YA). pap. 15.99 *(978-1-935929-94-9(1)*, Enclave) Gilead Publishing, LLC.

Pak, Greg. The Totally Awesome Hulk, Volume 1. 2016. (J). lib. bdg. 30.60 *(978-0-606-38351-6(4))* Turtleback Bks.

Palacios, Tomas. Guardians of the Galaxy: The Story of the Guardians. 2014. (World of Reading Ser.). (ENG.). 32p. (J). (gr. 1-3). pap. 3.99 *(978-1-4847-0065-5(1)*, Marvel Pr.) Disney Publishing Worldwide.

—I Am Ant-Man. 2015. (Illus.). 32p. *(978-0-316-26255-2(2))* Little Brown & Co.

Palacios, Tomas & Hosten, Colin. Guardians of the Galaxy Hallo-Scream Spook-tacular!!! 2016. (ENG.). 24p. (J). (gr. 1-3). pap. 5.99 *(978-1-4847-3214-4(6)*, Marvel Pr.) Disney Publishing Worldwide.

Palacios, Tomas & Marvel Press Book Group. Avengers Top Agents, Most Wanted. 2015. (ENG.). 24p. (J). (gr. 1-3). pap. 4.99 *(978-1-4847-2804-8(1)*, Marvel Pr.) Disney Publishing Worldwide.

Palacios, Tomas & Wong, Clarissa S. Guardians of the Galaxy: These Are the Guardians. 2014. (World of Reading Ser.). (ENG.). 32p. (J). (gr. -1-k). pap. 3.99 *(978-1-4847-0064-8(3)*, Marvel Pr.) Disney Publishing Worldwide.

Parker, Jeff. Ego: The Loving Planet. Santacruz, Juan, illus. 2012. (Avengers Set 3 Ser.). 24p. (J). (gr. 2-6). lib. bdg. 24.21 *(978-1-61479-014-3(0))* Spotlight.

—High Serpent Society. Santacruz, Juan, illus. 2012. (Avengers Set 3 Ser.). 24p. (J). (gr. 2-6). lib. bdg. 24.21 *(978-1-61479-015-0(9))* Spotlight.

—A Not-So-Beautiful Mind. Santacruz, Juan, illus. 2012. (Avengers Set 3 Ser.). 24p. (J). (gr. 2-6). lib. bdg. 24.21 *(978-1-61479-017-4(5))* Spotlight.

Pasko, Martin & Loughridge, Lee. Prankster of Prime Time, 1 vol. Burchett, Rick, illus. (Superman Ser.). (ENG.). 56p. (gr. 2-3). 2014. pap. 4.95 *(978-1-4342-2763-8(4))* 2010. lib. bdg. 26.65 *(978-1-4342-1986-2(0))* Stone Arch Bks. (DC Super Heroes).

Paton, Doug. Terror 911. 90p. pap. *(978-0-9731237-6-0(1))* High Interest Publishing (HIP).

Patterson, James. Public School Superhero. 2015. (ENG., Illus.). 304p. (J). (gr. 3-7). 13.99 *(978-0-316-32214-0(8)*, Jimmy Patterson) Little Brown & Co.

Patterson, James & Tebbetts, Chris. Public School Superhero. Thomas, Cory, illus. 2016. (ENG.). 304p. (J). (gr. 3-7). pap. 7.99 *(978-0-316-26598-0(5)*, Jimmy Patterson) Little Brown & Co.

Patterson, James, et al. Public School Superhero. 2015. *(978-0-316-34231-5(9))* Little, Brown Bks. for Young Readers.

Payne, M. D. Fartsunami. Dockery, Amanda, illus. 2013. (Monster Juice Ser.: 2). (ENG.). 192p. (J). (gr. 3-7). pap. 5.99 *(978-0-448-46227-1(3)*, Grosset & Dunlap) Penguin Young Readers Group.

—Fear the Barfitron. Dockery, Amanda, illus. 2013. (Monster Juice Ser.: 1). (ENG.). 192p. (J). (gr. 3-7). pap. 5.99 *(978-0-448-46226-4(5)*, Grosset & Dunlap) Penguin Young Readers Group.

Peek-a-Boo, Hulk. 2003. (J). per. *(978-1-57657-816-2(X))* Paradise Pr., Inc.

Perritano, John. Battle of the Bots, 1 vol. 2014. (Kid Squad Saves the World Ser.). (ENG.). 112p. (J). (gr. 8-12). lib. bdg. 27.07 *(978-1-62402-037-7(2)*, Calico Chapter Bks.) Magic Wagon.

—The Comet of Doom, 1 vol. Laughead, Mike, illus. 2014. (Kid Squad Saves the World Ser.). (ENG.). 112p. (J). (gr. 8-12). 27.07 *(978-1-62402-038-4(0))* Magic Wagon.

—The Egyptian Prophecy, 1 vol. Laughead, Mike, illus. 2014. (Kid Squad Saves the World Ser.). (ENG.). 112p. (J). (gr. 8-12). 27.07 *(978-1-62402-039-1(9))* Magic Wagon.

—Madness of Captain Cyclops, 1 vol. 2014. (Kid Squad Saves the World Ser.). (ENG.). 112p. (J). (gr. 8-12). lib. bdg. 27.07 *(978-1-62402-040-7(2)*, Calico Chapter Bks) Magic Wagon.

—The Snickerblooms & the Age Bug, 1 vol. Laughead, Mike, illus. 2014. (Kid Squad Saves the World Ser.). (ENG.). 112p. (J). (gr. 8-12). 27.07 *(978-1-62402-041-4(0))* Magic Wagon.

—Warlock Stone, 1 vol. 2014. (Kid Squad Saves the World Ser.). (ENG.). 112p. (J). (gr. 8-12). lib. bdg. 27.07 *(978-1-62402-042-1(9)*, Calico Chapter Bks) Magic Wagon.

Perry Sr., Audie. Heroic Kids of the Inner Dimension, 1 vol. 2010. 73p. pap. 19.95 *(978-1-4489-5037-9(6))* America Star Bks.

Petersen, P. J. Wild River. 2013. (ENG.). 128p. (J). (gr. 4-7). 6.99 *(978-0-375-84624-3(7)*, Yearling) Random Hse. Children's Bks.

Peterson, Doug. LarryBoy Versus the Volcano, 1 vol., No. 9. 2004. (Big Idea Books / LarryBoy Ser.). (ENG., Illus.). 96p. (J). pap. 4.99 *(978-0-310-70728-6(5))* Zonderkidz.

Peterson, Scott. Parasite's Feeding Frenzy, 1 vol. Cavallaro, Mike, illus. 2012. (Man of Steel Ser.). (ENG.). 88p. (gr. 2-3). lib. bdg. 26.65 *(978-1-4342-4099-6(1))*; pap. 5.95 *(978-1-4342-4221-1(8))* Stone Arch Bks.

Petty, J. T. & Pope, Paul. The Fall of the House of West. Rubín, David, illus. 2015. 157p. (J). ***(978-1-5182-0095-3(8)***, First Second Bks.) Roaring Brook Pr.

Pfundstein, Valerie. Veterans: Heroes in Our Neighborhood. Chernesky, Felicia, ed. Anderson, Aaron, illus. 2012. (ENG.). 32p. (J). 18.95 *(978-0-9837186-1-1(X))* Novanglus Publishing, LLC.

Pilkey, Dav. The Adventures of Captain Underpants. Pilkey, Dav, illus. 2013. (Captain Underpants Ser.: 1). (ENG., Illus.). 144p. (J). (gr. 2-5). 9.99 *(978-0-545-49908-8(9))* Scholastic, Inc.

—The Adventures of Captain Underpants. 2004. (Captain Underpants Ser.: No. 1). (J). lib. bdg. 19.95 *(978-0-439-68434-7(X)*, Scholastic, Inc.) Scholastic, Inc.

—The Adventures of Captain Underpants. 2013. (Captain Underpants Color Edition Ser.: 1). lib. bdg. 20.85 *(978-0-606-32441-0(0)*, Turtleback) Turtleback Bks.

—The Adventures of Super Diaper Baby. Pilkey, Dav, illus. 2014. (ENG., Illus.). 144p. (J). (gr. 3-7). 9.99 *(978-0-545-66544-5(2))* Scholastic, Inc.

—The Adventures of Super Diaper Baby. 2004. (J). lib. bdg. 19.95 *(978-0-439-68435-4(8)*, Scholastic, Inc.) Scholastic, Inc.

—The Adventures of Super Diaper Baby. 2014. (Super Diaper Baby Ser.: 1). lib. bdg. 20.85 *(978-0-606-36273-3(8))* Turtleback Bks.

—Big, Bad Battle of the Bionic Booger Boy: The Night of the Nasty Nostril Nuggets. 2003. (Captain Underpants Ser.: 6). (gr. 3-6). lib. bdg. 16.00 *(978-0-613-68836-9(8)*, Turtleback) Turtleback Bks.

—El Capitan Calzoncillos y la Furia de la Supermujer Macroelastica. 2003. (Captain Underpants Ser.: 5). (SPA & ENG., Illus.). 176p. (J). (gr. 2-5). pap. 5.99 *(978-0-439-53820-6(3)*, Scholastic en Espanol) Scholastic, Inc.

—El Capitan Calzoncillos y la Ridicula Historia de los Seres del Inodoro Morado. 2008. (Captain Underpants Ser.). (SPA., Illus.). 176p. (J). (gr. 2-5). pap. 5.99 *(978-0-545-02583-6(4)*, Scholastic en Espanol) Scholastic, Inc.

—Captain Underpants & the Attack of the Talking Toilets. Pilkey, Dav, illus. 2014. (Captain Underpants Ser.: Bk. 2). (ENG., Illus.). 160p. (J). (gr. 2-5). 9.99 *(978-0-545-59932-0(6))* Scholastic, Inc.

—Captain Underpants & the Attack of the Talking Toilets. 2004. (Captain Underpants Ser.: No. 2). (J). lib. bdg. 19.95 *(978-0-439-68436-1(6)*, Scholastic, Inc.) Scholastic, Inc.

—Captain Underpants & the Big, Bad Battle of the Bionic Booger Boy Part 1: The Night of the Nasty Nostril Nuggets. (Captain Underpants Ser.: Bk. 6). (J). 2004. lib. bdg. 19.95 *(978-0-439-68438-5(2)*, Scholastic, Inc.) 2003. (ENG., Illus.). 176p. (gr. 2-5). 18.99 *(978-0-439-37609-9(2))* Scholastic, Inc.

—Captain Underpants & the Big, Bad Battle of the Bionic Booger Boy Part 1: The Night of the Nasty Nostril Nuggets. Pilkey, Dav, illus. 2003. (Captain Underpants Ser.: 6). (ENG., Illus.). 176p. (J). (gr. 2-5). pap. 5.99 *(978-0-439-37610-5(6))* Scholastic, Inc.

—Captain Underpants & the Big, Bad Battle of the Bionic Booger Boy Part 2: The Revenge of the Ridiculous Robo-Boogers. 2004. (Captain Underpants Ser.: Bk. 7). (J). lib. bdg. 19.95 *(978-0-439-68437-8(4)*, Scholastic, Inc.) Scholastic, Inc.

—Captain Underpants & the Big, Bad Battle of the Bionic Booger Boy Part 2: The Revenge of the Ridiculous Robo-Boogers. Pilkey, Dav, illus. 2003. (Captain Underpants Ser.: 7). (ENG., Illus.). 176p. (J). (gr. 2-5). 18.99 *(978-0-439-37611-2(4))*; pap. 5.99 *(978-0-439-37612-9(2))* Scholastic, Inc.

—Captain Underpants & the Big, Bad Battle of the Bionic Booger Boy Part 2: The Revenge of the Ridiculous Robo-Boogers. 2003. (Captain Underpants Ser.: 7). lib. bdg. 16.00 *(978-0-613-68837-6(6)*, Turtleback) Turtleback Bks.

—Captain Underpants & the Invasion of the Incredibly Naughty Cafeteria Ladies from Outer Space: (and the Subsequent Assault of the Equally Evil Lunchroom Zombie Nerds) 2004. (Captain Underpants Ser.: No. 3). (J). lib. bdg. 19.95 *(978-0-439-68439-2(0)*, Scholastic, Inc.) Scholastic, Inc.

—Captain Underpants & the Invasion of the Incredibly Naughty Cafeteria Ladies from Outer Space: Color Edition. 2014. (Captain Underpants Ser.: 3). (ENG., Illus.). 160p. (J). (gr. 2-5). 9.99 *(978-0-545-69470-4(1))* Scholastic, Inc.

—Captain Underpants & the Perilous Plot of Professor Poopypants. (Captain Underpants Ser.: 4). (J). 2015. (ENG.). 160p. (gr. 3). 9.99 *(978-0-545-87187-7(5))* 2004. lib. bdg. 19.95 *(978-0-439-68440-8(4)*, Scholastic, Inc.) Scholastic, Inc.

—Captain Underpants & the Revolting Revenge of the Radioactive Robo-Boxers. Pilkey, Dav, illus. 2013. (Captain Underpants Ser.: 10). (ENG., Illus.). 192p. (J). (gr. 2-5). 9.99 *(978-0-545-17536-4(4))* Scholastic, Inc.

—Captain Underpants & the Revolting Revenge of the Radioactive Robo-Boxers. 2013. (Captain Underpants Ser.: 10). lib. bdg. 20.85 *(978-0-606-31563-0(2)*, Turtleback) Turtleback Bks.

—Captain Underpants & the Sensational Saga of Sir Stinks-a-Lot. Pilkey, Dav, illus. 2015. (Captain Underpants Ser.: 12). (ENG., Illus.). 208p. (J). (gr. 2). 9.99 *(978-0-545-50492-8(9))* Scholastic, Inc.

—Captain Underpants & the Sensational Saga of Sir Stinks-a-Lot. Pilkey, Dav, illus. 2015. (Captain Underpants Ser.: 12). (ENG., Illus.). 208p. (J). (gr. 2). lib. bdg. 20.85 *(978-0-606-37924-3(X))* Turtleback Bks.

—Captain Underpants & the Terrifying Return of Tippy Tinkletrousers. Pilkey, Dav, illus. 2012. (Captain Underpants Ser.: 9). (ENG., Illus.). 304p. (J). (gr. 2-5). 9.99 *(978-0-545-17534-0(8))* Scholastic, Inc.

—Captain Underpants & the Terrifying Return of Tippy Tinkletrousers. 2012. (Captain Underpants Ser.: 9). lib. bdg. 20.85 *(978-0-606-26523-2(6)*, Turtleback) Turtleback Bks.

—Mighty Robot vs. the Mecha-Monkeys from Mars. Santat, Dan, illus. 2014. (Ricky Ricotta Ser.: 4). (ENG.). 144p. (J). (gr. -1-3). pap. 5.99 *(978-0-545-63012-2(6))* Scholastic, Inc.

—Mighty Robot vs. the Mutant Mosquitoes from Mercury. Santat, Dan, illus. 2014. (Ricky Ricotta Ser.: 2). (ENG.). 128p. (J). (gr. -1-3). pap. 5.99 *(978-0-545-63010-8(X))* Scholastic, Inc.

—Mighty Robot vs. the Naughty Nightcrawlers from Neptune. Santat, Dan, illus. 2016. (Ricky Ricotta Ser.: 8). (ENG.). 128p. (J). (gr. -1-3). 15.99 *(978-0-439-37708-9(0))* Scholastic, Inc.

—Ricky Ricotta's Mighty Robot. Santat, Dan, illus. 2014. (Ricky Ricotta Ser.: 1). (ENG.). 112p. (J). (gr. -1-3). pap. 5.99 *(978-0-545-63009-2(6))*; lib. bdg. 15.99 *(978-0-545-63106-8(8))* Scholastic, Inc.

—Ricky Ricotta's Mighty Robot. 2014. (Ricky Ricotta's Mighty Robot Ser.: 1). lib. bdg. 16.00 *(978-0-606-35799-9(8))* Turtleback Bks.

—Ricky Ricotta's Mighty Robot vs. the Jurassic Jackrabbits from Jupiter. Santat, Dan, illus. 2014. (Ricky Ricotta Ser.: 5). (ENG.). 128p. (J). (gr. -1-3). pap. 5.99 *(978-0-545-63013-9(4))* Scholastic, Inc.

—Ricky Ricotta's Mighty Robot vs. the Naughty Nightcrawlers from Neptune. Santat, Dan, illus. 2016. (Ricky Ricotta Ser.: 8). (ENG.). 128p. (J). (gr. -1-3). pap. 5.99 *(978-0-439-37709-6(9))* Scholastic, Inc.

—Ricky Ricotta's Mighty Robot vs. the Unpleasant Penguins from Pluto. Santat, Dan, illus. 2016. (Ricky Ricotta's Mighty Robot Ser.: 9). (ENG.). 128p. (J). (gr. -1-3). 15.99 *(978-0-545-63016-0(9))* Scholastic, Inc.

—Uranium Unicorns from Uranus., Bk. 7. 2015. (Ricky Ricotta Ser.: 7). (ENG., Illus.). 128p. (J). (gr. -1-3). pap. 5.99 *(978-0-545-63015-3(0))* Scholastic, Inc.

—The Voodoo Vultures from Venus. Santat, Dan, illus. 2014. (Ricky Ricotta Ser.: 3). (ENG.). 128p. (J). (gr. -1-3). pap. 5.99 *(978-0-545-63011-5(8))* Scholastic, Inc.

Pilutti, Deb. Ten Rules of Being a Superhero. Pilutti, Deb, illus. 2014. (ENG., Illus.). 32p. (J). (gr. -1-2). 17.99 *(978-0-8050-9759-7(7)*, 9780805097597, Holt, Henry & Co. Bks. For Young Readers) Holt, Henry & Co.

Pinto, Ferando. Little Heroes. 2012. (ENG.). (J). pap. 14.99 *(978-1-4507-8573-0(5))* Independent Pub.

Pitchford, Dean. Captain Nobody. 2010. (ENG.). 208p. (J). (gr. 3-7). 6.99 *(978-0-14-241667-9(3)*, Puffin Books) Penguin Young Readers Group.

Pope, Paul & Petty, J. T. The Rise of Aurora West. Rubín, David, illus. 2014. (Battling Boy Ser.). (ENG.). 160p. (J). (gr. 5-12). pap. 9.99 *(978-1-62672-009-1(6)*, 9781626720091, First Second Bks.) Roaring Brook Pr.

Pope, Paul, et al. The Fall of the House of West. 2015. (J). lib. bdg. 20.85 *(978-0-606-37806-2(5))* Turtleback Bks.

Powell, Martin A., et al. The Fog of Fear. 2009. (Batman Ser.). (ENG., Illus.). 56p. (gr. 2-3). lib. bdg. 26.65 *(978-1-4342-1154-5(1)*, DC Super Heroes) Stone Arch Bks.

—The Stolen Superpowers, 1 vol. Burchett, Rick, illus. 2013. (Superman Ser.). (ENG.). 56p. (gr. 2-3). pap. 4.95 *(978-1-4342-1373-0(0)*, DC Super Heroes) Stone Arch Bks.

—The Stolen Superpowers. 2009. (Superman Ser.). (ENG., Illus.). 56p. (gr. 2-3). lib. bdg. 26.65 *(978-1-4342-1160-6(6)*, DC Super Heroes) Stone Arch Bks.

Publications International Ltd. Staff, ed. Captain America Large Play a Sound. 2011. 24p. (J). 14.98 *(978-1-4508-1608-3(8))* Publications International, Ltd.

—Green Lantern Large Play a Sound. 2011. 24p. (J). 12.98 *(978-1-4508-1606-9(1))* Publications International, Ltd.

—Look & Find: Myths & Heroes. 2011. 24p. (J). 7.98 *(978-1-4508-0665-7(1))* Publications International, Ltd.

—Look & Find - Captain America: The First Avenger. 2011. 24p. (J). 3.75 net. *(978-1-4508-1877-3(3))* Phoenix International Publications, Inc.

—Look & Find Green Lantern. 2011. 24p. (J). 7.98 *(978-1-4508-1179-8(5))* Publications International, Ltd.

—Marvel Heroes. 2007. (J). 9.98 *(978-1-4127-8449-8(2))* Phoenix International Publications, Inc.

—Marvel Heroes. 2007. (J). 7.10 *(978-1-4127-6665-4(6))* Publications International, Ltd.

Puckett, Kelley. Batman's Dark Secret. Muth, Jon J., illus. 2015. (ENG.). 32p. (J). (gr. k-2). 17.99 *(978-0-545-86755-9(X)*, Scholastic Pr.) Scholastic, Inc.

Pukac, Michael & Stephen, Marchesi, illus. The Flights of Marceau: Week Three. 2008. (ENG.). 64p. (J). 16.95 *(978-0-9797495-2-0(2))* Majestic Eagle Publishing.

Pushker, Gloria Teles & Tarman, Mel. Toby Belfer Learns about Heroes & Martyrs, 1 vol. Henriquez, Emile, illus. 2009. (Toby Belfer Ser.). (ENG.). 128p. (J). (gr. 3-7). 14.95 *(978-1-58980-647-4(6))* Pelican Publishing Co., Inc.

Random House. DC Super Friends 5-Minute Story Collection (DC Super Friends) Random House, illus. 2016. (ENG., Illus.). 160p. (J). (-k). 12.99 *(978-0-399-55219-9(7)*, Random Hse. Bks. for Young Readers) Random Hse. Children's Bks.

—DC Super Hero Girls Activity Journal (DC Super Hero Girls) Random House, illus. 2017. (Official Guide Ser.). (ENG., Illus.). 160p. (J). (gr. 2-4). 13.99 *(978-1-5247-1845-9(9)*, Random Hse. Bks. for Young Readers) Random Hse. Children's Bks.

Random House Disney Staff. Big Hero 6. Random House Disney Staff, illus. 2014. (Little Golden Book Ser.). (ENG., Illus.). 24p. (J). (-k). 4.99 *(978-0-7364-3168-2(3)*, Golden Bks.) Random Hse. Children's Bks.

—Planes: Fire & Rescue (Disney Planes: Fire & Rescue) Random House Disney Staff, illus. 2014. (Little Golden Book Ser.). (ENG., Illus.). 24p. (J). (-k). 4.99 *(978-0-7364-3166-8(7)*, Golden/Disney) Random Hse. Children's Bks.

Random House Disney Staff & Fontana, Shea. Super Hero High Yearbook! (DC Super Hero Girls) Random House Disney Staff, illus. 2016. (ENG., Illus.). 96p. (J). (gr. 3-7). pap. 9.99 *(978-1-5247-0106-2(8)*, Random Hse. Bks. for Young Readers) Random Hse. Children's Bks.

Random House Editors. Too Much Ooze! (Teenage Mutant Ninja Turtles) Random House Editors & Spaziante, Patrick, illus. 2015. (Step into Reading Ser.). (ENG.). 24p. (J). (gr. -1-1). 4.99 *(978-0-553-50866-6(0)*, Random Hse. Bks. for Young Readers) Random Hse. Children's Bks.

Random House Staff. Riddle Me This! Random House Staff, illus. 2010. (Pictureback(R) Ser.). (ENG., Illus.). 24p. (J). (gr. -1-2). pap. 3.99 *(978-0-375-84747-9(2)*, Random Hse. Bks. for Young Readers) Random Hse. Children's Bks.

—Saved by the Shell! 2012. lib. bdg. 13.55 *(978-0-606-26800-4(6)*, Turtleback) Turtleback Bks.

Random House Staff, illus. Hero Story Collection (DC Super Friends) 2012. (Step into Reading Ser.). (ENG.). 160p. (J). (gr. -1-1). pap. 7.99 *(978-0-375-87298-3(1)*, Random Hse. Bks. for Young Readers) Random Hse. Children's Bks.

Raney, Tom, et al, illus. The Infinity War. 2006. (ENG.). 400p. (J). (gr. 4-17). pap. 29.99 *(978-0-7851-2105-3(6))* Marvel Worldwide, Inc.

Ransom, Candice. The Rescue Adventure of Stenny Green, Hindenburg Crash Eyewitness. Hammond, Ted & Carbajal, Richard, illus. 2011. (History's Kid Heroes Ser.). 32p. pap. 51.02 *(978-0-7613-7638-5(0)*, Graphic Universe™); (ENG.). (gr. 3-5). 26.60 *(978-0-7613-6178-7(2))*; (ENG.). (gr. 3-5). pap. 8.95 *(978-0-7613-7070-3(6)*, Graphic Universe™) Lerner Publishing Group.

—The Underground Adventure of Arly Dunbar, Cave Explorer. Hammond, Ted & Carbajal, Richard Pimentel, illus. 2011. (History's Kid Heroes Set III Ser.). pap. 51.02 *(978-0-7613-7640-8(2)*, Graphic Universe™) Lerner Publishing Group.

—The Underground Adventure of Arly Dunbar, Cave Explorer. Hammond, Ted & Carbajal, Richard, illus. 2011. (History's Kid Heroes Ser.). (ENG.). 32p. (J). (gr. 3-5). (J). 26.60 *(978-0-7613-6182-4(0))*; pap. 8.95 *(978-0-7613-7074-1(9)*, Graphic Universe™) Lerner Publishing Group.

Reader's Digest Staff. Rise of the Guardians: Worlds of Wonder. Primeau, Chuck, illus. deluxe ed. 2012. (ENG.). 24p. (J). (gr. k-2). 19.99 *(978-0-7944-2803-7(7))* Reader's Digest Assn., Inc., The.

Reid, James. Your Guide to Superheroes, 1 vol. 2013. (Fiction Readers Ser.). (ENG., Illus.). 28p. (J). (gr. 2-2). pap. 6.99 *(978-1-4333-5566-0(3))* Shell Educational Publishing.

Remender, Rick. Uncanny Avengers - Avenge the Earth, Vol. 4. 2014. (ENG., Illus.). 136p. (J). (gr. 4-17). 24.99 *(978-0-7851-5423-5(X))* Marvel Worldwide, Inc.

Revenge of the Bully. 2014. (How to Beat the Bully Ser.). (ENG., Illus.). 288p. (J). (gr. 3-7). 17.99 *(978-1-4424-5677-8(9)*, Simon & Schuster/Paula Wiseman Bks.) Simon & Schuster/Paula Wiseman Bks.

Reynolds, Aaron & Rash, Andy. Superhero School. Rash, Andy, illus. 2009. (ENG., Illus.). 32p. (J). (gr. k-2). 17.99 *(978-1-59990-166-4(8)*, 9781599901664, Bloomsbury USA Childrens) Bloomsbury Publishing USA.

RH Disney Staff & Scollon, Bill. Fight to the Finish! RH Disney Staff & Disney Storybook Art Team, illus. 2014. (Step into Reading Ser.). (ENG.). 48p. (J). (gr. k-3). 3.99 *(978-0-7364-3189-7(6)*, RH/Disney) Random Hse. Children's Bks.

Richards, George. The Great Australian Super-Hero: Now You See Him, Now You Don't. 2012. 152p. pap. 12.95 *(978-1-4759-4245-3(1))* iUniverse, Inc.

Richardson, Mike. Dark Horse Heroes, Vol. 1. Dark Horse Comics Staff & Warner, Christopher S., eds. Hughes, Adam, illus. 2008. (ENG.). 488p. pap. 24.95 *(978-1-59307-734-1(3))* Dark Horse Comics.

Riordan, Rick. The House of Hades. 2013. (Heroes of Olympus Ser.). (ENG.). 608p. (J). (gr. 5-17). 19.99 *(978-1-4231-4672-8(7))* Hyperion Pr.

Riordan, Rick & Venditti, Robert. Heroes of Olympus, Book One the Lost Hero: the Graphic Novel. Powell, Nathan, illus. 2014. (Heroes of Olympus Ser.). (ENG.). 192p. (J). (gr. 5-9). pap. 12.99 *(978-1-4231-6325-1(7))* Hyperion Bks. for Children.

Rjk. Little Hero's Frown. Stubbing, Lori, illus. 2012. 36p. pap. 24.95 *(978-1-4626-7786-3(X))* America Star Bks.

Roberts, Daniel. The Super Hero Club. 2008. 36p. pap. 16.99 *(978-1-4389-0454-2(1))* AuthorHouse.

Robinson, T. J. The Academy Defenders. 2nd ed. 2012. 326p. pap. 14.99 *(978-1-936850-76-1(1))* Rhemalda Publishing.

Rocco, John. Blizzard. Rocco, John, illus. 2014. (ENG., Illus.). 40p. (J). (gr. -1-k). 17.99 *(978-1-4231-7865-1(3))* Disney Pr.

—Super Hair-O & the Barber of Doom. Rocco, John, illus. 2013. (ENG., Illus.). 32p. (J). (gr. -1-4). 16.99 *(978-1-4231-2189-3(9))* Disney Pr.

Rodda, Emily. Deltora Quest #7: the Valley of the Lost. 2012. (Deltora Quest Ser.). (ENG.). 160p. (J). (gr. 3-7). pap. 5.99 *(978-0-545-46027-9(1))* Scholastic, Inc.

—Return to Del. 2012. (Deltora Quest Ser.). (ENG.). 160p. (J). (gr. 3-7). pap. 5.99 *(978-0-545-46028-6(X))* Scholastic, Inc.

—Rowan & the Ice Creepers. 2003. (Rowan of Rin Ser.). 272p. (J). (gr. 3-18). 15.99 *(978-0-06-029780-0(8))* HarperCollins Pubs.

—Rowan & the Travelers. 2004. (Rowan of Rin Ser.). (ENG.). 192p. (J). (gr. 3-18). pap. 6.99 *(978-0-06-056072-0(X)*, Greenwillow Bks.) HarperCollins Pubs.

—Rowan & the Zebak. 2003. (Rowan of Rin Ser.). (ENG., Illus.). 208p. (J). (gr. 2-18). pap. 5.99 *(978-0-06-441024-3(2)*, Harper Trophy) HarperCollins Pubs.

—Rowan of Rin. 2004. (Rowan of Rin Ser.). (ENG., Illus.). 176p. (J). (gr. 3-18). pap. 6.99 *(978-0-06-056071-3(1)*, Greenwillow Bks.) HarperCollins Pubs.

H
I

Rodriguez, Alfredo. Redfoot. O'Reilly, Sean Patrick, ed. 2011. (Illus.). 43p. pap. 8.95 *(978-1-926914-59-6(7))* Arcana Studio, Inc.

Rodriguez, Cindy L. Heroes Were Made On 9/11, 1 vol. Elliott, Joyce L., illus. 2010. 26p. 24.95 *(978-1-4489-6070-5(3))* PublishAmerica, Inc.

Roman, Dave. Zero Gravity. Roman, Dave, illus. 2011. (Astronaut Academy Ser.: 1). (ENG., Illus.). 192p. (J). (gr. 5-9). pap. 9.99 *(978-1-59643-620-6(4),* 9781596436206, First Second Bks.) Roaring Brook Pr.

Rosen, Lucy. I Am Bane. Cohn, Scott, illus. 2012. (Dark Knight Rises Ser.). (ENG.). 24p. (J). (gr. -1-2). pap. 3.99 *(978-0-06-213222-2(9),* HarperFestival) HarperCollins Pubs.

—Justice League: Meet the Justice League. Gordon, Eric A. & Gordon, Steven E., illus. 2013. (I Can Read Level 2 Ser.). (ENG.). 32p. (J). (gr. -1-3). pap. 3.99 *(978-0-06-221002-9(5))* HarperCollins Pubs.

—Meet the Teen Titans. 2014. (Passport to Reading Level 2 Ser.). (J). lib. bdg. 13.55 *(978-0-606-35934-4(6))* Turtleback Bks.

—Superman's Superpowers. Tong, Andie, illus. 2013. (I Can Read Level 2 Ser.). (ENG.). 32p. (J). (gr. -1-3). pap. 3.99 *(978-0-06-223597-8(4))* HarperCollins Pubs.

Rouse, Lidany, compiled by. The Children's Letters to Their Hero. 2012. 58p. pap. 16.99 *(978-1-58275-319-5(9))* Aaron Bk. Publishing.

Rudnick, Elizabeth. Hulk Versus the World, 1 vol. Marvel Illustrators, illus. 2012. (Avengers: Earth's Mightiest Heroes! Ser.). (ENG.). 24p. (J). (gr. -1-4). lib. bdg. 24.21 *(978-1-61479-002-0(7))* Spotlight.

—Iron Man Is Born, 1 vol. Marvel Illustrators, illus. 2012. (Avengers: Earth's Mightiest Heroes! Ser.). (ENG.). 24p. (J). (gr. -1-4). lib. bdg. 24.21 *(978-1-61479-003-7(5))* Spotlight.

—Thor the Mighty, 1 vol. Marvel Illustrators, illus. 2012. (Avengers: Earth's Mightiest Heroes! Ser.). (ENG.). 24p. (J). (gr. -1-4). lib. bdg. 24.21 *(978-1-61479-005-1(1))* Spotlight.

Rust, Ned. Patrick Griffin's First Birthday on Ith. 2017. (Patrick Griffin & the Three Worlds Ser.: 2). (ENG.). 304p. (J). 16.99 *(978-1-62672-344-3(3),* 9781626723443) Roaring Brook Pr.

—Patrick Griffin's Last Breakfast on Earth. 2016. (Patrick Griffin & the Three Worlds Ser.: 1). (ENG.). 416p. (J). 16.99 *(978-1-62672-342-9(7),* 9781626723429) Roaring Brook Pr.

Salisbury, Graham. Hero of Hawaii. Rogers, Jacqueline, illus. 2012. (Calvin Coconut Ser.). (ENG.). 160p. (J). (gr. 2-5). pap. 6.99 *(978-0-375-86505-3(5),* Yearling) Random Hse. Children's Bks.

Sanders, Stephanie S. Villain School: Hero in Disguise. 2012. (ENG.). 240p. (YA). (gr. 5-8). 15.99 *(978-1-59990-907-3(3),* 9781599909073, Bloomsbury USA Childrens) Bloomsbury Publishing USA.

Sanderson, Brandon. Alcatraz Versus the Shattered Lens. 2016. (Alcatraz Versus the Evil Librarians Ser.: 4). (ENG.). 336p. (J). 16.99 *(978-0-7653-7900-9(7),* 9780765379009, Starscape) Doherty, Tom Assocs., LLC.

Santat, Dan, illus. Mighty Robot vs. the Stupid Stinkbugs from Saturn. 2015. (Ricky Ricotta Ser.: 6). (ENG.). 128p. (J). (gr. -1-3). 15.99 *(978-0-545-63121-1(1))* Scholastic, Inc.

—Stupid Stinkbugs from Saturn. 2015. (Ricky Ricotta Ser.: 6). (ENG.). 128p. (J). (gr. -1-3). pap. 5.99 *(978-0-545-63014-6(2))* Scholastic, Inc.

Santos, Ray. Justice League Classic: I Am Green Lantern. Gordon, Steven E. & Gordon, Eric A., illus. 2013. (I Can Read Level 2 Ser.). (ENG.). 32p. (J). (gr. -1-3). pap. 3.99 *(978-0-06-221006-7(8))* HarperCollins Pubs.

Satterwhite, William. Stealth, Vol. 1. 2005. 44p. (YA). pap. 5.75 *(978-1-4116-2395-8(9))* Lulu Pr., Inc.

Savage, Stephen. Supertruck. Savage, Stephen, illus. 2015. (ENG., Illus.). 32p. (J). (gr. -1-1). 12.99 *(978-1-59643-821-7(5),* 9781596438217) Roaring Brook Pr.

Sazaklis, John. Barnyard Brainwash, 1 vol. Baltazar, Art, illus. 2012. (DC Super-Pets Ser.). (ENG.). 56p. (gr. 2-2). pap. 4.95 *(978-1-4048-7213-4(2));* lib. bdg. 23.99 *(978-1-4048-6483-2(0))* Picture Window Bks. (DC Super-Pets).

—Batman: An Origin Story. Baltazar, Art & Vecchio, Luciano, illus. 2015. (DC Super Heroes Origins Ser.). (ENG.). 48p. (gr. k-2). lib. bdg. 23.99 *(978-1-4342-9727-3(6))* Stone Arch Bks.

—Battle - Battle in Metropolis. Smith, Andy & Vancata, Brad, illus. 2013. (ENG.). 24p. (J). (gr. -1-3). pap. 3.99 *(978-0-06-188537-2(1),* HarperFestival) HarperCollins Pubs.

—Battle in Metropolis. 2013. (Justice League Classic 8X8 Ser.). lib. bdg. 13.55 *(978-0-606-31827-3(5),* Turtleback) Turtleback Bks.

—Day of Doom. 2013. (Justice League Classic: I Can Read! Ser.). (J). lib. bdg. 13.55 *(978-0-606-32162-4(4),* Turtleback) Turtleback Bks.

—Guardians of the Galaxy (Marvel: Guardians of the Galaxy) Borkowski, Michael & Atiyeh, Michael, illus. 2016. (Little Golden Book Ser.). (ENG.). 24p. (J). (-k). 4.99 *(978-0-399-55096-6(8),* Golden Bks.) Random Hse. Children's Bks.

—The Hopping Hero, 1 vol. Baltazar, Art, illus. 2011. (DC Super-Pets Ser.). (ENG.). 56p. (gr. 2-2). pap. 4.95 *(978-1-4048-6843-4(7));* lib. bdg. 23.99 *(978-1-4048-6477-1(6))* Picture Window Bks. (DC Super-Pets).

—I Am the Flash. 2014. (Justice League Classic: I Can Read! Ser.). (J). lib. bdg. 13.55 *(978-0-606-35073-0(X),* Turtleback) Turtleback Bks.

—Justice League Classic - I Am the Flash. Gordon, Steven E. & Gordon, Eric A., illus. 2014. (I Can Read Level 2 Ser.). (ENG.). 32p. (J). (gr. -1-3). pap. 3.99 *(978-0-06-221005-0(X))* HarperCollins Pubs.

—Royal Rodent Rescue, 1 vol. Baltazar, Art, illus. 2011. (DC Super-Pets Ser.). (ENG.). 56p. (gr. 2-2). pap. 4.95 *(978-1-4048-6622-5(1));* lib. bdg. 23.99 *(978-1-4048-6307-1(9))* Picture Window Bks. (DC Super-Pets).

—Salamander Smackdown. Baltazar, Art, illus. 2011. (DC Super-Pets Ser.). (ENG.). 56p. (gr. 2-2). pap. 4.95 *(978-1-4048-6844-1(5),* DC Super-Pets) Picture Window Bks.

—Salamander Smackdown!, 1 vol. Baltazar, Art, illus. 2011. (DC Super-Pets Ser.). (ENG.). 56p. (gr. 2-2). lib. bdg. 23.99 *(978-1-4048-6478-8(4),* DC Super-Pets) Picture Window Bks.

—Wonder Woman: An Origin Story. Baltazar, Art & Vecchio, Luciano, illus. 2015. (DC Super Heroes Origins Ser.). (ENG.). 48p. (gr. k-2). lib. bdg. 23.99 *(978-1-4342-9729-7(2))* Stone Arch Bks.

Sazaklis, John & Merkel, Joe F. Day of the Undead. Tong, Andie, illus. 2013. (ENG.). 24p. (J). (gr. -1-3). pap. 3.99 *(978-0-06-220999-3(X),* HarperFestival) HarperCollins Pubs.

Sazaklis, John & Vancata, Brad. Superman: Day of Doom. Smith, Andy, illus. 2013. 29p. (YA). *(978-1-4844-0620-5(6))* Harper & Row Ltd.

Scholastic & Rusu, Meredith. The Secret Shopkin. 2016. (Shopkins Ser.: 3). (ENG.). 24p. (J). (gr. -1-3). pap. 4.99 *(978-1-338-03297-0(6))* Scholastic, Inc.

Scholastic Editors. Space Justice! 2015. (LEGO DC Super Heroes Ser.). lib. bdg. 13.55 *(978-0-606-37077-6(3))* Turtleback Bks.

Scholastic Editors, ed. Last Laugh! 2013. (LEGO DC Super Heroes Ser.). lib. bdg. 13.55 *(978-0-606-32018-4(0),* Turtleback) Turtleback Bks.

Scholastic, Inc. Staff. Space Justice! 2015. (LEGO DC Super Heroes Ser.). (ENG., Illus.). 32p. (J). (gr. -1-3). pap. 3.99 *(978-0-545-82556-6(3))* Scholastic, Inc.

Scholastic, Inc. Staff, contrib. by. Collector's Sticker Book. 2011. (Lego Ninjago Ser.). (ENG.). 16p. (J). (gr. 2-5). pap. 6.99 *(978-0-545-35630-5(X))* Scholastic, Inc.

Scholastic, Inc. Staff, ed. Save the Day. 2013. (LEGO DC Super Heroes Ser.). lib. bdg. 13.55 *(978-0-606-32017-7(2),* Turtleback) Turtleback Bks.

Scholastic, Inc. Staff & Kogge, Michael. Cross Fire. 2016. (Batman vs. Superman: Dawn of Justice Ser.). (ENG.). 144p. (J). (gr. 2-5). pap. 5.99 *(978-0-545-91630-1(5))* Scholastic, Inc.

Scholastic, Inc. Staff & Marsham, Liz. Movie Flip Book. 2016. (Batman vs. Superman: Dawn of Justice Ser.). (ENG.). 112p. (J). (gr. 3-7). pap. 9.99 *(978-0-545-91627-1(5))* Scholastic, Inc.

Scholastic, Inc. Staff & Wheeler, Alex. Hostage. 2009. (Star Wars: Rebel Force Ser.: 2). (ENG.). 176p. (J). (gr. 3-7). 6.99 *(978-0-545-11218-5(4))* Scholastic, Inc.

Scholastic, Inc. Staff, et al. Attack of the Legion of Doom! 2016. (LEGO DC Super Heroes Ser.). (ENG.). 64p. (J). (gr. 2-5). pap. 4.99 *(978-0-545-86799-3(1))* Scholastic, Inc.

Seabrook, Heather. Lego Chima - Heroes' Quest. 2014. (DK Reader Level 2 Ser.). lib. bdg. 13.55 *(978-0-606-35732-6(7))* Turtleback Bks.

Sebring, Janet And Jordan. Every Child Can Be a Hero. 2012. 36p. pap. 21.95 *(978-1-4685-3031-5(3))* AuthorHouse.

Secchi, Richard & Salati, Giorgio. Race for the Ultrapods, Vol. 2. Turconi, Stefano et al, illus. 2010. (Disney's Hero Squad Ser.). (ENG.). 128p. (J). (gr. 4-7). pap. 9.99 *(978-1-60886-560-4(6))* Boom! Studios.

Seidman, David, et al. Deadly Double. 2013. (Superman Ser.). (ENG., Illus.). 56p. (gr. 2-3). pap. 4.95 *(978-1-4342-1726-4(4),* DC Super Heroes) Stone Arch Bks.

Seydou, Garba B. The One Man Army. 2012. 58p. pap. 16.95 *(978-1-4626-8958-3(2))* America Star Bks.

Shanower, Eric. Oz: Road to Oz. 2013. (ENG., Illus.). 136p. (J). (gr. -1-17). pap. 16.99 *(978-0-7851-6405-0(7))* Marvel Worldwide, Inc.

Shea, Lisa. Meet Chase the Police-Bot. 2013. (Transformers Passport to Reading Ser.). (J). lib. bdg. 13.55 *(978-0-606-31736-8(8),* Turtleback) Turtleback Bks.

Shealy, Dennis & Random House Staff. Heroes United! - Attack of the Robot! Doescher, Erik et al, illus. 2008. (Pictureback(R) Ser.). (ENG.). 32p. (J). (gr. -1-2). pap. 4.99 *(978-0-375-84409-6(0),* Random Hse. Bks. for Young Readers) Random Hse. Children's Bks.

Siegel, Jerry, et al. Adventures of Superman. Gordon, Steven E. et al, illus. 2013. 125p. (J). *(978-1-4351-5063-8(5))* Barnes & Noble, Inc.

Siegel, Mark & Siegel, Alexis. The Sand Warrior. Bouma, Xanthe et al, illus. 2017. (5 Worlds Ser.: 1). (ENG.). 256p. (J). (gr. 3-7). 18.99 ***(978-1-101-93586-6(3))***; pap. 12.99 ***(978-1-101-93588-0(X))***; lib. bdg. 21.99 ***(978-1-101-93587-3(1))*** Random Hse. Children's Bks. (Random Hse. Bks. for Young Readers).

—The Sand Warrior. Bouma, Xanthe et al, illus. 2017. (5 Worlds Ser.: 1). lib. bdg. 24.50 ***(978-0-606-40243-9(8))*** Turtleback Bks.

Siglain, Michael. Captain America - The Winter Soldier: Rescue at Sea. 2014. (ENG.). 24p. (J). (gr. 3-7). pap. 4.99 *(978-1-4847-0537-7(8),* Marvel Pr.) Disney Publishing Worldwide.

Simonson, Louise. Monster Magic, 1 vol. Schoening, Dan, illus. (Wonder Woman Ser.). (ENG.). 56p. (gr. 2-3). 2013. pap. 4.95 *(978-1-4342-2260-2(8))* 2010. lib. bdg. 26.65 *(978-1-4342-1884-1(8))* Stone Arch Bks. (DC Super Heroes).

Simonson, Louise, et al. Bizarro Is Born!, 1 vol. Doescher, Erik, illus. (Superman Ser.). (ENG.). 56p. (gr. 2-3). 2013. pap. 4.95 *(978-1-4342-1725-7(6))* 2009. 26.65 *(978-1-4342-1567-3(9))* Stone Arch Bks. (DC Super Heroes).

Simonson, Walter. Thor by Walter Simonson Volume 3. 2013. (ENG., Illus.). 264p. (J). (gr. 4-17). pap. 29.99 *(978-0-7851-8462-1(7))* Marvel Worldwide, Inc.

Sipe, Kelly. What It Takes to Be a Hero. 2012. 24p. pap. 12.45 *(978-1-4624-0326-4(3),* Inspiring Voices) Author Solutions, Inc.

Slack, Michael. Elecopter. Slack, Michael, illus. 2013. (ENG., Illus.). 32p. (J). (gr. -1 — 1). 15.99 *(978-0-8050-9304-9(4),* 9780805093049, Holt, Henry & Co. Bks. For Young Readers) Holt, Henry & Co.

Slott, Dan & Templeton, Ty. Batman Adventures. Templeton, Ty, illus. 2013. (Batman Adventures Ser.). (ENG., Illus.). 32p. (gr. 2-3). 158.20 *(978-1-4342-8837-0(4))* Stone Arch Bks.

Slott, Dan, et al. Masquerade in Red!, 1 vol. 2013. (Batman Adventures Ser.). (ENG.). 32p. (gr. 2-3). 22.60 *(978-1-4342-6036-9(4))* Stone Arch Bks.

—Phantasm Strikes!, 1 vol. Burchett, Rick, illus. 2013. (Batman Adventures Ser.). (ENG.). 32p. (gr. 2-3). 22.60 *(978-1-4342-6035-2(6))* Stone Arch Bks.

—Playing with Matches, 1 vol. Burchett, Rick, illus. 2013. (Batman Adventures Ser.). (ENG.). 32p. (gr. 2-3). 22.60 *(978-1-4342-6034-5(8))* Stone Arch Bks.

—Target: Deadshot!, 1 vol. Templeton, Ty, illus. 2013. (Batman Adventures Ser.). (ENG.). 32p. (gr. 2-3). 22.60 *(978-1-4342-6033-8(X))* Stone Arch Bks.

Smith, Alex T. Claude in the City, 1 vol. Smith, Alex T., illus. (Claude Ser.). (ENG., Illus.). 96p. (J). (gr. 2-4). 2015. pap. 7.95 *(978-1-56145-843-1(0))* 2013. 12.95 *(978-1-56145-697-0(7))* Peachtree Pubs.

Smith, Nerissia. Prince de'Mario's Adventure, 1 vol. Dartes, Staci, illus. 2009. 29p. pap. 24.95 *(978-1-61582-972-9(5))* America Star Bks.

Smith, Shirleen L. Not All Heroes Are on TV. 2011. 24p. (gr. -1). pap. 12.45 *(978-1-4497-1721-6(7),* WestBow Pr.) Author Solutions, Inc.

Smith, William D. Becoming a Superhero: Adventures of an American Superhero. 2008. 128p. per. 13.95 *(978-1-4327-2071-1(6))* Outskirts Pr., Inc.

Snider, Brandon T. Teen Titans Go! 2016. (ENG., Illus.). 24p. (J). (gr. 3-7). pap. 5.99 *(978-0-316-37726-3(0))* Little, Brown Bks. for Young Readers.

Sniegoski, Tom. Quest for the Spark. Smith, Jeff, illus. (Bone Ser.). (ENG.). (J). (gr. 3-7). 2012. 240p. pap. 10.99 *(978-0-545-14104-8(4))*Bk. 2. 2012. 240p. 26.99 *(978-0-545-14103-1(6))*Bk. 3. 2013. 288p. pap. 10.99 *(978-0-545-14106-2(0))*No. 3. 2013. 288p. 22.99 *(978-0-545-14105-5(2))* Scholastic, Inc. (Graphix).

—Quest for the Spark. (Bone: Quest for the Spark Ser.: 3). 2013. lib. bdg. 22.10 *(978-0-606-31497-8(0))* 2012. lib. bdg. 22.10 *(978-0-606-23947-9(2))* Turtleback Bks. (Turtleback).

Sniegoski, Tom & Smith, Jeff. Quest for the Spark, Bk. 1. Smith, Jeff, illus. 2011. (BONE: Quest for the Spark Ser.: 1). (ENG., Illus.). 224p. (J). (gr. 3-7). 26.99 *(978-0-545-14101-7(X),* Graphix) Scholastic, Inc.

Sohmer, Ryan. Least I Could Do Beginnings Volume 1: Look at Me: Look at Me. 2010. 32p. 19.95 *(978-0-9812163-3-1(1))* Blind Ferret Entertainment CAN. Dist: Diamond Bk. Distributors.

Solomons, David. My Gym Teacher Is an Alien Overlord. Ferguson, Laura Ellen, illus. 2016. (ENG.). 288p. (J). (gr. 3-7). 16.99 *(978-0-451-47494-0(5),* Viking Books for Young Readers) Penguin Young Readers Group.

Sonishi, Kenji. Leave It to PET!, Vol. 2. Sonishi, Kenji, illus. 2009. (ENG., Illus.). 196p. (J). pap. 7.99 *(978-1-4215-2650-8(6))* Viz Media.

—Leave It to PET!, Vol. 4. Sonishi, Kenji, illus. 2010. (ENG., Illus.). 192p. (J). pap. 7.99 *(978-1-4215-2652-2(2))* Viz Media.

Sonneborn, Scott. Attack of the Invisible Cats, 1 vol. Baltazar, Art, illus. 2011. (DC Super-Pets Ser.). (ENG.). 56p. (gr. 2-2). pap. 4.95 *(978-1-4048-6847-2(X));* lib. bdg. 23.99 *(978-1-4048-6481-8(4))* Picture Window Bks. (DC Super-Pets).

—Beware Our Power! Schoening, Dan, illus. 2011. (J). lib. bdg. (ENG.). 56p. (gr. 2-3). pap. 4.95 *(978-1-4342-3086-7(4),* DC Super Heroes) Stone Arch Bks.

—Captain Cold & the Blizzard Battle, 1 vol. McManus, Shawn, illus. 2012. (DC Super-Villains Ser.). (ENG.). 56p. (gr. 2-3). pap. 5.95 *(978-1-4342-3897-9(0),* DC Super-villains) Stone Arch Bks.

—Catwoman's Classroom of Claws. Schoening, Dan, illus. (Batman Ser.). (ENG.). 56p. (gr. 2-3). 2013. pap. 4.95 *(978-1-4342-1732-5(9))* 2009. lib. bdg. 26.65 *(978-1-4342-1565-9(2))* Stone Arch Bks. (DC Super Heroes).

—Deep Space Hijack. Schoening, Dan, illus. (Superman Ser.). (ENG.). 56p. (gr. 2-3). 2013. pap. 4.95 *(978-1-4342-2257-2(8))* 2010. lib. bdg. 26.65 *(978-1-4342-1880-3(5))* Stone Arch Bks. (DC Super Heroes).

—Moon Bandits. Cavallaro, Mike & DC Comics Staff, illus. 2013. (Man of Steel Ser.). (ENG.). 88p. (gr. 2-3). 26.65 *(978-1-4342-4093-4(2))* Stone Arch Bks.

—The Moon Bandits. Cavallaro, Mike, illus. 2013. (Man of Steel Ser.). (ENG.). 88p. (gr. 2-3). pap. 5.95 *(978-1-4342-4223-5(4))* Stone Arch Bks.

—Partners in Peril. Smith, Andy & Vancata, Brad, illus. 2013. (ENG.). 24p. (J). (gr. -1-3). pap. 3.99 *(978-0-06-221007-4(6),* HarperFestival) HarperCollins Pubs.

—Prisoner of the Penguin!, 1 vol. Vecchio, Luciano, illus. 2014. (Batman: Comic Chapter Bks.). (ENG.). 88p. (gr. 3-7). 21.32 *(978-1-4342-9131-8(6))* Stone Arch Bks.

—Prisoner of the Ring, 1 vol. Schoening, Dan, illus. 2011. (Green Lantern Ser.). (ENG.). 56p. (gr. 2-3). pap. 4.95 *(978-1-4342-3410-0(X));* lib. bdg. 26.65 *(978-1-4342-2624-2(7))* Stone Arch Bks. (DC Super Heroes).

Sonneborn, Scott & Loughridge, Lee. Captain Cold & the Blizzard Battle, 1 vol. McManus, Shawn, illus. 2012. (DC Super-Villains Ser.). (ENG.). 56p. (gr. 2-3). lib. bdg. 26.65 *(978-1-4342-3796-5(6),* DC Super-villains) Stone Arch Bks.

Sonneborn, Scott, et al. Killer Croc Hunter, 1 vol. (Batman Ser.). (ENG., Illus.). 56p. (gr. 2-3). 2013. pap. 4.95 *(978-1-4342-2258-9(6))* 2010. lib. bdg. 26.65 *(978-1-4342-1876-6(7))* Stone Arch Bks. (DC Super Heroes).

—Shell Shocker, 1 vol. Doescher, Erik, illus. 2011. (Flash Ser.). (ENG.). 56p. (gr. 2-3). pap. 4.95 *(978-1-4342-3092-8(9),* DC Super Heroes) Stone Arch Bks.

Sonneveld, Stephen. The Prince of Destiny. 2007. 56p. pap. 30.50 *(978-0-615-16784-8(5))* Splendid Torch.

Spaziante, Patrick. Too Much Ooze! 2015. (Step into Reading Level 2 Ser.). lib. bdg. 14.75 *(978-0-606-36399-0(8))* Turtleback Bks.

Stanek, Robert, pseud. The Art of Ruin Mist: Heroes & Villains. 2007. (ENG.). 60p. (YA). per. 16.00 *(978-1-57545-163-3(8))* RP Media.

Stauffacher, Sue & Love, Comfort. Wireman. 2007. (Illus.). 159p. (J). pap. *(978-0-9709811-4-1(7))* Grand Valley State Univ.

Steele, Michael A. High-Tech Terror, 1 vol. Schoening, Dan, illus. 2011. (Green Lantern Ser.). (ENG.). 56p. (gr. 2-3). pap. 4.95 *(978-1-4342-3084-3(8));* lib. bdg. 26.65 *(978-1-4342-2609-9(3))* Stone Arch Bks. (DC Super Heroes).

—Web of Doom, 1 vol. Schoening, Dan, illus. 2011. (Green Lantern Ser.). (ENG.). 56p. (gr. 2-3). lib. bdg. 26.65 *(978-1-4342-2621-1(2),* DC Super Heroes) Stone Arch Bks.

Steele, Michael Anthony. Web of Doom, 1 vol. Schoening, Dan, illus. 2011. (Green Lantern Ser.). (ENG.). 56p. (gr. 2-3). pap. 4.95 *(978-1-4342-3407-0(X),* DC Super Heroes) Stone Arch Bks.

Stein, Erin K. I Am Wonder Woman. Farley, Rick, illus. 2010. (I Can Read Level 2 Ser.). (ENG.). 32p. (J). (gr. -1-3). pap. 3.99 *(978-0-06-188517-4(7))* HarperCollins Pubs.

Stein, Tammar. The Six-Day Hero. 2017. (ENG.). 256p. (gr. 4-7). 16.99 ***(978-1-5124-5871-8(6))***; (J). *(978-1-5124-2855-1(8))* Lerner Publishing Group. (Kar-Ben Publishing).

Stephens, Sarah. Midway Monkey Madness, 1 vol. Baltazar, Art, illus. 2011. (DC Super-Pets Ser.). (ENG.). 56p. (gr. 2-2). pap. 4.95 *(978-1-4048-6619-5(1));* lib. bdg. 23.99 *(978-1-4048-6305-7(2))* Picture Window Bks. (DC Super-Pets).

—Pooches of Power!, 1 vol. Baltazar, Art, illus. 2011. (DC Super-Pets Ser.). (ENG.). 56p. (gr. 2-2). pap. 4.95 *(978-1-4048-6620-1(5));* lib. bdg. 23.99 *(978-1-4048-6306-4(0))* Picture Window Bks. (DC Super-Pets).

Stephens, Sarah Hines. Backward Bowwow, 1 vol. Baltazar, Art, illus. 2011. (DC Super-Pets Ser.). (ENG.). 56p. (gr. 2-2). pap. 4.95 *(978-1-4048-6845-8(3));* lib. bdg. 23.99 *(978-1-4048-6480-1(6))* Picture Window Bks. (DC Super-Pets).

—Creature of Chaos. Schoening, Dan, illus. (Wonder Woman Ser.). (ENG.). 56p. (gr. 2-3). 2013. pap. 4.95 *(978-1-4342-2256-5(X))* 2010. lib. bdg. 26.65 *(978-1-4342-1885-8(6))* Stone Arch Bks. (DC Super Heroes).

—Night of the Scaredy Crows, 1 vol. Baltazar, Art, illus. 2012. (DC Super-Pets Ser.). (ENG.). 56p. (gr. 2-2). pap. 4.95 *(978-1-4048-7663-7(4));* lib. bdg. 23.99 *(978-1-4048-6492-4(X))* Picture Window Bks. (DC Super-Pets).

—Super-Pets Showdown, 1 vol. Baltazar, Art, illus. 2012. (DC Super-Pets Ser.). (ENG.). 56p. (gr. 2-2). pap. 4.95 *(978-1-4048-7216-5(7));* lib. bdg. 23.99 *(978-1-4048-6486-3(5))* Picture Window Bks. (DC Super-Pets).

—Superpowered Pony, 1 vol. Baltazar, Art, illus. 2011. (DC Super-Pets Ser.). (ENG.). 56p. (gr. 2-2). pap. 4.95 *(978-1-4048-6846-5(1));* lib. bdg. 23.99 *(978-1-4048-6479-5(2))* Picture Window Bks. (DC Super-Pets).

Stephens, Sarah Hines & Hines-Stephens, Sarah. Rumble in the Rainforest, 1 vol. Schoening, Dan, illus. (Wonder Woman Ser.). (ENG.). 56p. (gr. 2-3). 2014. pap. 4.95 *(978-1-4342-2765-2(0))* 2010. 26.65 *(978-1-4342-1992-3(5))* Stone Arch Bks. (DC Super Heroes).

Stephenson, Norman E. God's Blood: The Fate of the Lost Templar Treasure. 2007. 176p. per. 13.95 *(978-0-595-47539-1(6))* iUniverse, Inc.

Sternin, Joshua & Ventimilia, Jeffrey. Teenage Mutant Ninja Turtles: Pizza Party! 2014. (Step into Reading Level 2 Ser.). lib. bdg. 13.55 *(978-0-606-36282-5(7))* Turtleback Bks.

Stewart, Yale. Alien Superman!, 1 vol. Stewart, Yale, illus. 2014. (Amazing Adventures of Superman! Ser.). (ENG., Illus.). 32p. (gr. k-2). lib. bdg. 25.32 *(978-1-4795-5733-2(1),* DC Super Heroes) Stone Arch Bks.

—Battle of the Super Heroes!, 1 vol. Stewart, Yale, illus. 2014. (Amazing Adventures of Superman! Ser.). (ENG., Illus.). 32p. (gr. k-2). 25.32 *(978-1-4795-5731-8(5),* DC Super Heroes) Stone Arch Bks.

—Creatures from Planet X!, 1 vol. Stewart, Yale, illus. 2014. (Amazing Adventures of Superman! Ser.). (ENG., Illus.). 32p. (gr. k-2). lib. bdg. 25.32 *(978-1-4795-5734-9(X),* DC Super Heroes) Stone Arch Bks.

—Escape from Future World!, 1 vol. Stewart, Yale, illus. 2014. (Amazing Adventures of Superman! Ser.). (ENG., Illus.). 32p. (gr. k-2). lib. bdg. 25.32 *(978-1-4795-5732-5(3),* DC Super Heroes) Stone Arch Bks.

Stiefvater, Maggie. Forever. 2014. (Shiver Ser.: 3). (ENG.). 416p. (J). (gr. 9). pap. 9.99 *(978-0-545-68280-0(0))* Scholastic, Inc.

Stilton, Geronimo. Flood Mission. 2015. (Illus.). 117p. (J). *(978-0-545-92010-0(8))* Scholastic, Inc.

—Geronimo Stilton Heromice Bk. 3: Flood Mission. 2015. (Illus.). 128p. (J). pap. *(978-0-545-66814-9(X))* Scholastic, Inc.

Stilton, Geronimo, et al. Robot Attack. Usai, Luca & Verzini, Daniele, illus. 2015. 117p. (J). *(978-0-545-86796-2(7))* Scholastic, Inc.

Stock, Lisa. DK Readers L2: Star Wars: Rey to the Rescue! 2017. (Star Wars DK Readers Level 2 Ser.). lib. bdg. 13.55 ***(978-0-606-39899-2(6))*** Turtleback Bks.

Stone Arch Books. April Showers & Cinco de Mayo, 1 vol. Nguyen, Dustin, illus. 2014. (Batman: Li'l Gotham Ser.). (ENG.). 32p. (gr. 2-3). 22.60 *(978-1-4342-9220-9(7))* Stone Arch Bks.

—Christmas & New Year's Eve, 1 vol. Nguyen, Dustin, illus. 2014. (Batman: Li'l Gotham Ser.). (ENG.). 32p. (gr. 2-3). 22.60 *(978-1-4342-9217-9(7))* Stone Arch Bks.

—Halloween & Thanksgiving, 1 vol. Nguyen, Dustin, illus. 2014. (Batman: Li'l Gotham Ser.). (ENG.). 32p. (gr. 2-3). 22.60 *(978-1-4342-9208-7(8))* Stone Arch Bks.

—Mother's Day & Father's Day, 1 vol. Nguyen, Dustin, illus. 2014. (Batman: Li'l Gotham Ser.). (ENG.). 32p. (gr. 2-3). 22.60 *(978-1-4342-9221-6(5))* Stone Arch Bks.

—St. Patrick's Day & Easter, 1 vol. Nguyen, Dustin, illus. 2014. (Batman: Li'l Gotham Ser.). (ENG.). 32p. (gr. 2-3). 22.60 *(978-1-4342-9219-3(3))* Stone Arch Bks.

—Valentine's Day & the Lunar New Year, 1 vol. Nguyen, Dustin, illus. 2014. (Batman: Li'l Gotham Ser.). (ENG.). 32p. (gr. 2-3). 22.60 *(978-1-4342-9218-6(5))* Stone Arch Bks.

Strohm, Keith Francis. Bladesinger. 2006. (Fighters Ser.). (Illus.). 312p. *(978-1-4156-6627-2(X))* Wizards of the Coast.

Strong, Jeremy. Bungleman. Mosedale, Julian, illus. 2007. (Collins Big Cat Ser.). (ENG.). 96p. (J). (gr. 2-3). pap. 8.99 *(978-0-00-723063-9(4))* HarperCollins Pubs. Ltd. GBR. Dist: Independent Pubs. Group.

Sturm, James, et al. Characters in Action! Sturm, James, illus. 2013. (Adventures in Cartooning Ser.). (ENG., Illus.). 64p. (J). (gr. 1-5). pap. 10.99 *(978-1-59643-732-6(4),* 9781596437326, First Second Bks.) Roaring Brook Pr.

Sumerak, Marc. Ororo: Before the Storm. Barberi, Carlo, illus. 2012. (Ororo: Before the Storm Ser.). 24p. (J). (gr. 2-6). lib. bdg. 24.21 *(978-1-61479-026-6(4));* lib. bdg. 24.21 *(978-1-61479-024-2(8));* lib. bdg. 24.21

(978-1-61479-027-3(2)); lib. bdg. 24.21 (978-1-61479-025-9(6)) Spotlight.

Sutton, Laurie S. Batman vs. the Penguin. Vecchio, Luciano, illus. 2013. (Dark Knight Ser.). (ENG.). 88p. (gr. 2-3). pap. 5.95 (978-1-4342-4825-1(9)) Stone Arch Bks.

—Cheetah & the Purrfect Crime, 1 vol. Vecchio, Luciano, illus. 2012. (DC Super-Villains Ser.). (ENG.). 56p. (gr. 2-3). pap. 5.95 (978-1-4342-3900-6(4)); lib. bdg. 26.65 (978-1-4342-3799-6(0)) Stone Arch Bks. (DC Super-villains).

—Clayface's Slime Spree. Vecchio, Luciano, illus. 2016. (Batman & Robin Adventures Ser.). (ENG.). 88p. (gr. 2-3). lib. bdg. 26.65 (978-1-4965-2536-9(1), DC Super Heroes) Stone Arch Bks.

—The Dark Knight: the Penguin's Crime Wave. Vecchio, Luciano, illus. 2013. (ENG.). (J). (gr. 4-7). pap. 35.70 (978-1-4342-4872-5(0)) Stone Arch Bks.

—Demons of Deep Space. Vecchio, Luciano, illus. 2012. (Man of Steel Ser.). (ENG.). 88p. (gr. 2-3). lib. bdg. 26.65 (978-1-4342-4098-9(3)); pap. 5.95 (978-1-4342-4220-4(X)) Stone Arch Bks.

—Fear the Shark, 1 vol. Schoening, Dan, illus. 2011. (Green Lantern Ser.). (ENG.). 56p. (gr. 2-3). pap. 4.95 (978-1-4342-3406-3(1)); lib. bdg. 26.65 (978-1-4342-2620-4(4)) Stone Arch Bks. (DC Super Heroes).

—The Joker's Dozen. Beavers, Ethen, illus. 2015. (You Choose Stories: Batman Ser.). (ENG.). 112p. (gr. 2-3). lib. bdg. 32.65 (978-1-4342-9707-5(1)) Stone Arch Bks.

—Killer Croc of Doom! Vecchio, Luciano, illus. (Dark Knight Ser.). (ENG.). 88p. (gr. 2-3). 2013. pap. 5.95 (978-1-4342-4215-0(3)) 2012. 26.65 (978-1-4342-4097-2(5)) Stone Arch Bks.

—The Light King Strikes!, 1 vol. Schoening, Dan, illus. 2011. (Green Lantern Ser.). (ENG.). 56p. (gr. 2-3). pap. 4.95 (978-1-4342-3083-6(X)); lib. bdg. 26.65 (978-1-4342-2610-5(7)) Stone Arch Bks. (DC Super Heroes).

—Night of a Thousand Doomsdays, 1 vol. Vecchio, Luciano, illus. 2013. (Man of Steel Ser.). (ENG.). 88p. (gr. 2-3). 26.65 (978-1-4342-4487-1(3)) Stone Arch Bks.

—Night of a Thousand Doomsdays. Vecchio, Luciano, illus. 2013. (Man of Steel Ser.). (ENG.). 88p. (gr. 2-3). pap. 5.95 (978-1-4342-4827-5(5)) Stone Arch Bks.

—The Penguin's Crime Wave, 1 vol. Vecchio, Luciano, illus. 2013. (Dark Knight Ser.). (ENG.). 88p. (gr. 2-3). lib. bdg. 26.65 (978-1-4342-4485-7(7)) Stone Arch Bks.

—The Planet Collector, 1 vol. Vecchio, Luciano, illus. 2014. (Superman: Comic Chapter Bks.). (ENG.). 88p. (gr. 3-7). 21.32 (978-1-4342-9133-2(2)) Stone Arch Bks.

—The Real Man of Steel, 1 vol. Vecchio, Luciano, illus. 2014. (Superman: Comic Chapter Bks.). (ENG.). 88p. (gr. 3-7). 21.32 (978-1-4342-9134-9(0)) Stone Arch Bks.

—Sinestro & the Ring of Fear, 1 vol. McManus, Shawn, illus. 2012. (DC Super-Villains Ser.). (ENG.). 56p. (gr. 2-3). pap. 5.95 (978-1-4342-3899-3(7), DC Super-villains) Stone Arch Bks.

—Sword of the Dragon, 1 vol. Schoening, Dan, illus. (Wonder Woman Ser.). (ENG.). 56p. (gr. 2-3). 2014. pap. 4.95 (978-1-4342-2760-7(X)) 2010. 26.65 (978-1-4342-1979-4(8)) Stone Arch Bks. (DC Super Heroes).

Sutton, Laurie S. & Bright, J. E. Batman & Robin Adventures. Vecchio, Luciano, illus. 2016. (Batman & Robin Adventures Ser.). (ENG.). 88p. (gr. 2-3). 106.60 (978-1-4965-2551-2(5), DC Super Heroes) Stone Arch Bks.

Sutton, Laurie S. & Loughridge, Lee. Sinestro & the Ring of Fear, 1 vol. McManus, Shawn, illus. 2012. (DC Super-Villains Ser.). (ENG.). 56p. (gr. 2-3). lib. bdg. 26.65 (978-1-4342-3798-9(2), DC Super-villains) Stone Arch Bks.

Sutton, Laurie S., et al. The Dark Knight. 2013. (Dark Knight Ser.). (ENG.). 88p. (gr. 2-3). 106.60 (978-1-4342-4810-7(0)); 213.20 (978-1-4342-4809-1(7)); pap. 47.60 (978-1-4342-4862-6(3)); pap. 23.80 (978-1-4342-4861-9(5)) Stone Arch Bks. (DC Super Heroes).

—Gorilla Warfare, 1 vol. Doescher, Erik, illus. 2011. (Flash Ser.). (ENG.). 56p. (gr. 2-3). pap. 4.95 (978-1-4342-3087-4(2), DC Super Heroes) Stone Arch Bks.

—Master of Mirrors!, 1 vol. 2011. (Flash Ser.). (ENG., Illus.). 56p. (gr. 2-3). lib. bdg. 26.65 (978-1-4342-2629-7(8), DC Super Heroes) Stone Arch Bks.

Tanguay, Dave. Come Together! Vaughns, Byron, illus. 2015. (Billy Batson & the Magic of Shazam! Ser.). (ENG.). 32p. (gr. 2-3). lib. bdg. 22.60 (978-1-4342-9744-0(6)) Stone Arch Bks.

—Deception Reception! Vaughns, Byron, illus. 2015. (Billy Batson & the Magic of Shazam! Ser.). (ENG.). 32p. (gr. 2-3). lib. bdg. 22.60 (978-1-4342-9742-6(X)) Stone Arch Bks.

—Fire Fire Everywhere! Vaughns, Byron, illus. 2015. (Billy Batson & the Magic of Shazam! Ser.). (ENG.). 32p. (gr. 2-3). lib. bdg. 22.60 (978-1-4342-9745-7(4)) Stone Arch Bks.

—The Legacy of Mr. Banjo! Vaughns, Byron, illus. 2015. (Billy Batson & the Magic of Shazam! Ser.). (ENG.). 32p. (gr. 2-3). lib. bdg. 22.60 (978-1-4342-9746-4(2)) Stone Arch Bks.

Tardif, Elizabeth. A Bunny Named Apple. Buehrle, Jacquelyn, illus. 2011. 28p. pap. 24.95 (978-1-4560-0946-5(X)) America Star Bks.

Teitelbaum, Michael. Cine en casa: Heroes de Cine: Movie Theater: Marvel Heroes. 2007. (Cine en casa Disney Ser.). (Illus.). 46p. (J). (978-970-718-535-7(X), Silver Dolphin en Español) Advanced Marketing, S. de R. L. de C. V.

—Meet the Super Heroes. 2009. (Justice League Classic: I Can Read! Ser.). (J). lib. bdg. 13.55 (978-0-606-06941-0(0), Turtleback) Turtleback Bks.

—Tale of Zuko. Spaziante, Patrick, illus. 2008. (Avatar Ser.). (ENG.). 96p. (J). (gr. 2-6). pap. 5.99 (978-1-4169-4984-8(4), Simon Spotlight/Nickelodeon) Simon Spotlight/Nickelodeon.

Templeton, Ty & Slott, Dan. Free Man, 1 vol. Templeton, Ty, illus. 2012. (Batman Adventures Ser.). (ENG., Illus.). 32p. (gr. 2-3). lib. bdg. 22.60 (978-1-4342-4558-8(6)) Stone Arch Bks.

—My Boyfriend's Back, 1 vol. Templeton, Ty, illus. 2012. (Batman Adventures Ser.). (ENG., Illus.). 32p. (gr. 2-3). lib. bdg. 22.60 (978-1-4342-4559-5(4)) Stone Arch Bks.

—Need to Know, 1 vol. Templeton, Ty, illus. 2012. (Batman Adventures Ser.). (ENG., Illus.). 32p. (gr. 2-3). lib. bdg. 22.60 (978-1-4342-4560-1(8)) Stone Arch Bks.

—No Asylum, 1 vol. Templeton, Ty, illus. 2012. (Batman Adventures Ser.). (ENG., Illus.). 32p. (gr. 2-3). lib. bdg. 22.60 (978-1-4342-4557-1(8)) Stone Arch Bks.

Tennapel, Doug. Cardboard. 2012. lib. bdg. 24.50 (978-0-606-26212-5(1), Turtleback) Turtleback Bks.

Terrell, Brandon. Summer Freeze! Beavers, Ethen, illus. 2015. (You Choose Stories: Batman Ser.). (ENG.). 112p. (gr. 2-3). lib. bdg. 32.65 (978-1-4342-9708-2(X)) Stone Arch Bks.

Thomas, Jim. Super Slam Turtles! Spaziante, Patrick, illus. 2005. 22p. (J). lib. bdg. 15.00 (978-1-4242-0971-2(4)) Fitzgerald Bks.

Thomas, Rich. The Amazing Spider-Man: An Origin Story, 1 vol. Clark, Jeff, illus. 2012. (Marvel Origins Ser.). (ENG.). 48p. (J). (gr. -1-4). lib. bdg. 24.21 (978-1-61479-007-5(8)) Spotlight.

Thomas, Rich, Jr. The Avengers: An Origin Story. Olliffe, Pat, illus. 2nd ed. 2013. (Origin Story Ser.). (ENG.). 48p. (J). (gr. 1-3). 8.99 (978-1-4231-8308-2(8)) Marvel Worldwide, Inc.

Thomas, Rich. The Courageous Captain America: An Origin Story, 1 vol. Semeiks, Val, illus. 2012. (Marvel Origins Ser.). (ENG.). 48p. (J). (gr. -1-4). lib. bdg. 24.21 (978-1-61479-008-2(6)) Spotlight.

—The Invincible Iron Man: An Origin Story, 1 vol. Rousseau, Craig, illus. 2012. (Marvel Origins Ser.). (ENG.). 48p. (J). (gr. -1-4). lib. bdg. 24.21 (978-1-61479-010-5(8)) Spotlight.

—The Mighty Avengers: An Origin Story. Olliffe, Pat, illus. 2012. (Origin Story Ser.). (ENG.). 48p. (J). (gr. 1-3). 8.99 (978-1-4231-4841-8(X), Marvel Pr.) Disney Publishing Worldwide.

—The Mighty Thor: An Origin Story, 1 vol. Clark, Jeff, illus. 2012. (Marvel Origins Ser.). (ENG.). 48p. (J). (gr. -1-4). lib. bdg. 24.21 (978-1-61479-011-2(6)) Spotlight.

—Spider-Man: Attack of the Heroes. 2014. (Mighty Marvel Chapter Bks.). (J). lib. bdg. 16.00 (978-0-606-35271-0(6)) Turtleback Bks.

—Spider-Man: Attack of the Heroes: A Marvel Chapter Book. Disney Book Group, illus. 2014. (Mighty Marvel Chapter Book Ser.: 1). (ENG.). 128p. (J). (gr. 1-3). pap. 5.99 (978-1-4231-4301-7(9), Marvel Pr.) Disney Publishing Worldwide.

—Thor: An Origin Story. Olliffe, Pat, illus. 2013. (Origin Story Ser.). (ENG.). 48p. (J). (gr. 1-3). 8.99 (978-1-4231-7215-4(9)) Marvel Worldwide, Inc.

—The Uncanny X-Men: An Origin Story, 1 vol. The Storybook Art Group, illus. 2012. (Marvel Origins Ser.). (ENG.). 48p. (J). (gr. -1-4). lib. bdg. 24.21 (978-1-61479-012-9(4)) Spotlight.

Thomas, Rich, Jr. & Siglain, Michael. Captain America: The Tomorrow Army. Disney Book Group Staff et al, illus. 2014. (Mighty Marvel Chapter Book Ser.: 2). (ENG.). 144p. (J). (gr. 1-3). pap. 5.99 (978-1-4231-4303-1(5), Marvel Pr.) Disney Publishing Worldwide.

Thompson, Mike. Chicken Boy & the Wrath of Dr. Dimwad. Thompson, Mike, illus. 2008. (Illus.). 102p. (J). per. 9.95 (978-0-9799216-0-5(0)) Thompson Original Productions LLC.

Thornburg, Michael. The Monster Kids' Adventures: The Retur. 2005. pap. 19.95 (978-1-4137-8556-2(5)) PublishAmerica, Inc.

Tillworth, Mary. Barbie in Princess Power. 2015. (Little Golden Book Ser.). (ENG., Illus.). 24p. (J). (-k). 4.99 (978-0-553-50741-6(9), Golden Bks.) Random Hse. Children's Bks.

Titan Books Staff, et al. Monsters vs. Aliens: the M Files. Dalton, Alex & Laguna, Fabio, illus. 2009. (ENG.). 48p. pap. 4.95 (978-1-84856-281-3(0), Titan Bks.) Titan Bks. Ltd. GBR. Dist: Penguin Random Hse. LLC.

Tobin, Richard K. Skating on Thick Ice. LeBlanc, Rebecca, ed. Chapman, Jesse, illus. 2013. 122p. (J). pap. 12.00 (978-1-929882-96-0(3)) Biographical Publishing Co.

Tong, Andie, illus. Justice League Reading Collection. 2017. (I Can Read Level 2 Ser.). (ENG.). 160p. (J). (gr. -1-3). pap. 16.99 (978-0-06-229187-5(4)) HarperCollins Pubs.

Top That Publishing Staff, ed. Halfpipe Heroes. 2004. (Wicked Tattoos Ser.). (Illus.). 16p. (J). pap. (978-1-84510-111-4(1)) Top That! Publishing PLC.

Toriyama, Akira & Jones, Gerard. Dragon Ball, Vol. 4. 2009. (Dragon Ball Ser.: 4). (ENG.). 80p. (Orig.). (J). pap. 4.99 (978-1-4215-2948-6(3)) Viz Media.

—Dragon Ball in Danger! 2009. (Dragon Ball Ser.: 2). (ENG.). 80p. (J). pap. 4.99 (978-1-4215-2946-2(7)) Viz Media.

Torres, J. Power Lunch Book 1: First Course: First Course. 2011. (ENG., Illus.). 40p. (J). 12.99 (978-1-934964-70-5(0), 9781934964705) Oni Pr., Inc.

—The Secret of the Doomsday Design!, 1 vol. Bone, J., illus. 2013. (Batman: the Brave & the Bold Ser.). (ENG.). 32p. (gr. 2-3). 22.60 (978-1-4342-4707-0(4)) Stone Arch Bks.

Torres, J., et al. The Beast Boy Who Cried Wolf, 1 vol. 2014. (Teen Titans GO! Ser.). (ENG., Illus.). 32p. (gr. 2-3). 22.60 (978-1-4342-6433-6(5)) Stone Arch Bks.

—Blackfire's Back!, 1 vol. 2014. (Teen Titans GO! Ser.). (ENG., Illus.). 32p. (gr. 2-3). 22.60 (978-1-4342-9215-5(0)) Stone Arch Bks.

—Demo, 1 vol. 2014. (Teen Titans GO! Ser.). (ENG., Illus.). 32p. (gr. 2-3). 22.60 (978-1-4342-4789-6(9)) Stone Arch Bks.

—Lame, 1 vol. 2014. (Teen Titans GO! Ser.). (ENG., Illus.). 32p. (gr. 2-3). 22.60 (978-1-4342-6467-1(X)) Stone Arch Bks.

—Monster Zit!, 1 vol. 2014. (Teen Titans GO! Ser.). (ENG., Illus.). 32p. (gr. 2-3). 22.60 (978-1-4342-9213-1(4)) Stone Arch Bks.

—My Crummy Valentine, 1 vol. 2014. (Teen Titans GO! Ser.). (ENG., Illus.). 32p. (gr. 2-3). 22.60 (978-1-4342-6468-8(8)) Stone Arch Bks.

—Thunder & Lightning Strike!, 1 vol. 2014. (Teen Titans GO! Ser.). (ENG., Illus.). 32p. (gr. 2-3). 22.60 (978-1-4342-9214-8(2)) Stone Arch Bks.

Travis, Lucille. The Far Journey. 2009. 160p. (J). (gr. 4-7). 8.99 (978-1-60682-023-0(0)) BJU Pr.

Trine, Greg. Attack of the Valley Girls. Montijo, Rhode, illus. 6th ed. 2008. (Melvin Beederman, Superhero Ser.: 6). (ENG.). 144p. (J). (gr. 2-5). pap. 8.99 (978-0-8050-8161-9(5), 9780805081619) Square Fish.

—The Brotherhood of the Traveling Underpants. Montijo, Rhode, illus. 7th ed. 2009. (Melvin Beederman, Superhero Ser.: 7). (ENG.). 144p. (J). (gr. 2-5). pap. 8.99 (978-0-8050-8163-3(1), 9780805081633) Square Fish.

—The Brotherhood of the Traveling Underpants. 2009. (Melvin Beederman Superhero Ser.: 7). (J). lib. bdg. 19.65 (978-0-606-01751-0(8), Turtleback) Turtleback Bks.

—The Curse of the Bologna Sandwich. Montijo, Rhode, illus. 2006. (Melvin Beederman, Superhero Ser.: 1). (ENG.). 144p. (J). (gr. 2-5). pap. 8.99 (978-0-8050-7836-7(3), 9780805078367) Square Fish.

—Dinos Are Forever. Dormer, Frank W., illus. 2014. (Adventures of Jo Schmo Ser.: 1). (ENG.). 112p. (J). (gr. 1-4). pap. 5.99 (978-0-544-00325-5(X), HMH Books For Young Readers) Houghton Mifflin Harcourt Publishing Co.

—The Fake Cape Caper. Montijo, Rhode, illus. 5th rev. ed. 2007. (Melvin Beederman, Superhero Ser.: 5). (ENG.). 144p. (J). (gr. 2-5). pap. 8.99 (978-0-8050-8159-6(3), 9780805081596) Square Fish.

—The Grateful Fred. Montijo, Rhode, illus. 3rd rev. ed. 2006. (Melvin Beederman, Superhero Ser.: 3). (ENG.). 144p. (J). (gr. 2-5). pap. 8.99 (978-0-8050-7922-7(X), 9780805079227) Square Fish.

—Invasion from Planet Dork. Montijo, Rhode, illus. 2010. (Melvin Beederman, Superhero Ser.: 8). (ENG.). 144p. (J). (gr. 2-7). pap. 8.99 (978-0-8050-8167-1(4), 9780805081671) Square Fish.

—Pinkbeard's Revenge. Dormer, Frank W., illus. (Adventures of Jo Schmo Ser.: 4). (ENG.). 128p. (J). (gr. 1-4). 2015. pap. 5.99 (978-0-544-45601-3(7), HMH Books For Young Readers) 2013. 12.99 (978-0-547-80797-3(X)) Houghton Mifflin Harcourt Publishing Co.

—The Revenge of the McNasty Brothers. Montijo, Rhode, illus. 2nd rev. ed. 2006. (Melvin Beederman, Superhero Ser.: 2). (ENG.). 144p. (J). (gr. 2-5). pap. 8.99 (978-0-8050-7837-4(1), 9780805078374) Square Fish.

—Shifty Business. Dormer, Frank W., illus. (Adventures of Jo Schmo Ser.: 3). (ENG.). 112p. (J). (gr. 1-4). 2014. pap. 5.99 (978-0-544-33911-8(8), HMH Books For Young Readers) 2013. 12.99 (978-0-547-80796-6(1)) Houghton Mifflin Harcourt Publishing Co.

—Terror in Tights. Montijo, Rhode, illus. 4th rev. ed. 2007. (Melvin Beederman, Superhero Ser.: 4). (ENG.). 144p. (J). (gr. 2-5). pap. 8.99 (978-0-8050-7924-1(6), 9780805079241) Square Fish.

—Wyatt Burp Rides Again. Dormer, Frank W., illus. 2014. (Adventures of Jo Schmo Ser.: 2). (ENG.). 112p. (J). (gr. 1-4). pap. 5.99 (978-0-544-01899-0(0), HMH Books For Young Readers) Houghton Mifflin Harcourt Publishing Co.

Trumbauer, Lisa. Standoff: Remembering the Alamo, 1 vol. Schoonover, Brent, illus. 2008. (Historical Fiction Ser.). (ENG.). 56p. (gr. 2-3). pap. 6.25 (978-1-4342-0849-1(4), Graphic Flash) Stone Arch Bks.

Tsang, Evonne & Jimenez, Adan. Hero City. BarÓN, Lara & Torres, German, illus. 2012. (Twisted Journeys (r) Ser.: 22). (ENG.). 112p. (J). (gr. 4-7). pap. 7.95 (978-1-57505-945-7(2), Graphic Universe™) Lerner Publishing Group.

—Hero City. Barón, Lara & Torres, German, illus. 2012. (Twisted Journeys (r) Ser.: 22). (ENG.). 112p. (J). (gr. 4-7). lib. bdg. 27.93 (978-0-7613-4595-4(7), Graphic Universe™) Lerner Publishing Group.

Tulien, Sean. The Black Masquerade. Vecchio, Luciano, illus. 2013. (Dark Knight Ser.). (ENG.). 88p. (gr. 2-3). pap. 5.95 (978-1-4342-4824-4(0)); lib. bdg. 26.65 (978-1-4342-4486-4(5)) Stone Arch Bks.

Tulien, Sean, et al. Clock King's Time Bomb, 1 vol. Schoening, Dan, illus. 2011. (Flash Ser.). (ENG.). 56p. (gr. 2-3). pap. 4.95 (978-1-4342-3412-4(6)); lib. bdg. 26.65 (978-1-4342-2626-6(3)) Stone Arch Bks. (DC Super Heroes).

—Shadow of the Sun, 1 vol. 2011. (Flash Ser.). (ENG., Illus.). 56p. (gr. 2-3). pap. 4.95 (978-1-4342-3088-1(0), DC Super Heroes) Stone Arch Bks.

Turner, Henry. Ask the Dark. (ENG.). 256p. (YA). (gr. 9). 2016. pap. 9.99 (978-0-544-81353-3(7), HMH Books For Young Readers) 2015. 17.99 (978-0-544-30827-5(1), Clarion Bks.) Houghton Mifflin Harcourt Publishing Co.

Turner, Katharine. Reptile Rampage. Gordon, Eric A. & Gordon, Steven E., illus. 2012. (I Can Read Level 2 Ser.). (ENG.). 32p. (J). (gr. -1-3). pap. 3.99 (978-0-06-188521-1(5)) HarperCollins Pubs.

—Reptile Rampage. 2012. (Justice League Classic: I Can Read! Ser.). (J). lib. bdg. 13.55 (978-0-606-23593-8(0), Turtleback) Turtleback Bks.

Twinkle Books. Terrible Tommy. 2006. (J). 14.98 (978-0-9792992-6-1(8)) Twinkle Bks.

Tzvieli, Neta. The Private Eyes & the Mysterious Submarine. 2009. 149p. 17.99 (978-1-59826-286-5(6)) Feldheim Pubs.

Urey, Gary. Super Schnoz & the Gates of Smell. Long, Ethan, illus. (Super Schnoz Ser.: 1). (ENG.). 160p. (J). (gr. 3-7). 2015. pap. 6.99 (978-0-8075-7560-4(7)) 2013. 14.99 (978-0-8075-7555-0(0)) Whitman, Albert & Co.

—Super Schnoz & the Invasion of the Snore Snatchers. Frawley, Keith, illus. 2014. (Super Schnoz Ser.: 2). (ENG.). 160p. (J). (gr. 3-7). 14.99 (978-0-8075-7557-4(7)) Whitman, Albert & Co.

Van Der Heide, Iris. A Strange Day. ten Cate, Marijke, illus. 2007. (ENG.). 24p. (J). (gr. -1-3). 16.95 (978-1-932425-94-9(2), Lemniscaat) Boyds Mills Pr.

Van Draanen, Wendelin. Attack of the Tagger. Biggs, Brian, illus. unabr. ed. 2006. (Shredderman Ser.: Bk. 2). (J). (gr. 3-6). audio 24.95 (978-1-59519-758-0(3)) Live Oak Media.

—Attack of the Tagger. Biggs, Brian, illus. 2006. (Shredderman Ser.: Bk. 2). (ENG.). 176p. (J). (gr. 1-4). 6.99 (978-0-440-41913-6(1), Yearling) Random Hse. Children's Bks.

—Enemy Spy. Biggs, Brian, illus. 2006. (Shredderman Ser.: Bk. 4). (ENG.). 192p. (J). (gr. 1-4). 6.99 (978-0-440-41915-0(8), Yearling) Random Hse. Children's Bks.

—Meet the Gecko. Biggs, Brian, illus. 2006. (Shredderman Ser.: Bk. 3). (ENG.). 176p. (J). (gr. 1-4). 5.99 (978-0-440-41914-3(X), Yearling) Random Hse. Children's Bks.

—Secret Identity. Biggs, Brian, illus. 2006. (Shredderman Ser.: Bk. 1).Tr. of Al Haqiqa Wara ¿Al Fatak¿. (ENG.). 144p. (J). (gr. 1-4). reprint ed. 6.99 (978-0-440-41912-9(3), Yearling) Random Hse. Children's Bks.

—Shredderman: Secret Identity. Biggs, Brian, illus. unabr. ed. 2006. (Shredderman Ser.: Bk. 1).Tr. of Shredderman - Al Haqiqa Wara ¿Al Fatak¿. (J). (gr. 2-4). audio 24.95 (978-1-59519-762-7(1)) Live Oak Media.

—Shredderman: Secret Identity. unabr. ed. 2006. (Shredderman Ser.: Bk. 1).Tr. of Shredderman - Al Haqiqa Wara ¿Al Fatak¿. (Illus.). (J). (gr. 2-4). pap. 28.95 incl. audio compact disk (978-1-59519-763-4(X)) Live Oak Media.

Van Lente, Fred. The Pack: Part 1. 2013. (Wolverine First Class Set 2 Ser.). (Illus.). 24p. (J). (gr. 2-6). lib. bdg. 24.21 (978-1-61479-178-2(3)) Spotlight.

—The Pack: Part 2. 2013. (Wolverine First Class Set 2 Ser.). (Illus.). 24p. (J). (gr. 2-6). lib. bdg. 24.21 (978-1-61479-179-9(1)) Spotlight.

—Substitute. 2013. (Wolverine First Class Set 2 Ser.). (Illus.). 24p. (J). (gr. 2-6). lib. bdg. 24.21 (978-1-61479-181-2(3)) Spotlight.

Vega, Diego. The Iron Brand. 2007. (Young Zorro Ser.). 240p. (YA). (gr. 3-7). pap. 6.99 (978-0-06-083947-5(3), Rayo) HarperCollins Pubs.

Venditti, Robert. Attack of the Alien Horde. Higgins, Dusty, illus. 2015. (Miles Taylor & the Golden Cape Ser.: 1). (ENG.). 304p. (J). (gr. 4-7). 16.99 (978-1-4814-0542-3(X)) Simon & Schuster, Inc.

Vergo, Franny. Jonathan Ray & His Superhero Pack: Be Bully-Free. 2012. 44p. pap. 18.50 (978-1-4772-4558-3(8)) AuthorHouse.

Verne, Jules. Michael Strogoff. 2006. 408p. pap. 26.45 (978-1-59462-432-2(1), Book Jungle) Standard Pubns., Inc.

Vicary, Tim. Grace Darling. Oxford University Press Staff & Bassett, Jennifer, eds. 3rd ed. 2008. (ENG., Illus.). 64p. 10.00 (978-0-19-479061-1(4)) Oxford Univ. Pr., Inc.

Vidal, Séverine. Mega Bunny. Barroux, Stephane, illus. 2015. (Mega Hero Bks.). (ENG.). 28p. (J). (gr. k-2). 12.95 (978-1-77085-638-7(2), 9781770856387) Firefly Bks., Ltd.

—Mega Mouse. Barroux, Stephane, illus. 2015. (Mega Hero Bks.). (ENG.). 28p. (J). (gr. k-2). 12.95 (978-1-77085-639-4(0), 9781770856394) Firefly Bks., Ltd.

—Mega Pig. Barroux, Stephane, illus. 2015. (Mega Hero Bks.). (ENG.). 28p. (J). (gr. k-2). 12.95 (978-1-77085-636-3(6), 9781770856363) Firefly Bks., Ltd.

—Mega Wolf. Barroux, Stephane, illus. 2015. (Mega Hero Bks.). (ENG.). 28p. (J). (gr. k-2). 12.95 (978-1-77085-637-0(4), 9781770856370) Firefly Bks., Ltd.

Vincent, Patti. The Village Heroes Meet the Dragon. 2008. 44p. pap. 19.95 (978-1-4389-1764-1(3)) AuthorHouse.

Voigt, Cynthia. The Tale of Oriel. 2015. (Tales of the Kingdom Ser.: 3). (ENG., Illus.). 544p. (YA). (gr. 7). 19.99 (978-1-4814-0323-8(0), Atheneum Bks. for Young Readers) Simon & Schuster Children's Publishing.

Waid, Mark. City of Incredibles, Vol. 2. Takara, Marcio, illus. 2010. (Incredibles Ser.). (ENG.). 112p. (J). 24.99 (978-1-60886-529-1(0)) Boom! Studios.

—Incorruptible. Takara, Marcio, illus. 2012. (ENG.). 128p. Vol. 6. (Incorruptible Ser.: 6). (gr. 10). pap. 16.99 (978-1-60886-084-5(1)) Vol. 7. (gr. 9). pap. 16.99 (978-1-60886-085-2(X)) Boom! Studios.

—The Incredibles: City of Incredibles, Vol. 2. Takara, Marcio, illus. 2010. (Incredibles Ser.). (ENG.). 112p. (J). pap. 9.99 (978-1-60886-503-1(7)) Boom! Studios.

Waid, Mark & Walker, Landry. Revenge from Below. Takara, Marcio, illus. 2010. (Incredibles Ser.). (ENG.). 112p. (J). (gr. 3-6). pap. 9.99 (978-1-60886-518-5(5)) Boom! Studios.

Walker, Landry. Secrets & Lies. Takara, Marcio, illus. 2010. (Incredibles Ser.). 112p. (J). (gr. 3-8). pap. 9.99 (978-1-60886-583-3(5)) Boom! Studios.

—Supergirl: Cosmic Adventures of the 8th Grade. 2016. lib. bdg. 24.50 (978-0-606-38776-7(5)) Turtleback Bks.

Walker, Landry Q. Supergirl: Cosmic Adventures in the 8th Grade. Jones, Eric, illus. 2013. (Supergirl: Cosmic Adventures in the 8th Grade Ser.). (ENG.). 32p. (gr. 2-3). lib. bdg. 135.60 (978-1-4342-8830-1(7)); lib. bdg. 45.20 (978-1-4342-8831-8(5)); lib. bdg. 45.20 (978-1-4342-4367-6(2)) Stone Arch Bks.

Walker, Landry Q. & Mason, Joey. Evil in a Skirt! #5, 1 vol. Jones, Eric, illus. 2013. (Supergirl: Cosmic Adventures in the 8th Grade Ser.). (ENG.). 32p. (gr. 2-3). 22.60 (978-1-4342-6045-1(3)) Stone Arch Bks.

—Off to Save the Day..., No. 6. Jones, Eric, illus. 2013. (Supergirl: Cosmic Adventures in the 8th Grade Ser.). (ENG.). 32p. (gr. 2-3). 22.60 (978-1-4342-6046-8(1)) Stone Arch Bks.

Walsh, Melanie. Isaac & His Amazing Asperger Superpowers! Walsh, Melanie, illus. 2016. (ENG., Illus.). 32p. (J). (gr. -1-2). 16.99 (978-0-7636-8121-0(0)) Candlewick Pr.

Walsh, Sheila. Will, God's Mighty Warrior, 1 vol. Johnson, Meredith, illus. 2006. (Will, God's Mighty Warrior Ser.: 1). (ENG.). 32p. (gr. -1-3). 14.99 (978-1-4003-0805-7(4)) Nelson, Thomas Inc.

Walt, G. L. Heroes All Around. 2011. 28p. pap. 15.99 (978-1-4568-8825-1(0)) Xlibris Corp.

Waters, Zack C. Blood Moon Rider. 2006. (Florida Historical Fiction for Youth Ser.). (ENG.). 126p. (J). (gr. 4-9). 13.95 (978-1-56164-350-9(5)) Pineapple Pr., Inc.

Watson, Andi. Quest. Yuji, Iwahara, illus. 2004. (Marvel Heroes Ser.). 120p. (YA). pap. 13.99 (978-0-7851-1298-3(7)) Marvel Worldwide, Inc.

Watts, Fraces. The Middle Sheep. Watson, Judy, illus. 2010. (ENG.). 80p. (J). (gr. 2-5). pap. 6.00 (978-0-8028-5368-4(4)) Eerdmans, William B. Publishing Co.

Watts, Frances. Extraordinary Ernie & Marvelous Maud. Watson, Judy, illus. 2010. (ENG.). 80p. (J). (gr. 2-5). pap. 6.00 (978-0-8028-5363-9(3), Eerdmans Bks For Young Readers) Eerdmans, William B. Publishing Co.

Wax, Wendy. Meet Leatherhead. Spaziante, Patrick, illus. 2005. 22p. (J). lib. bdg. 15.00 (978-1-4242-0972-9(2)) Fitzgerald Bks.

Wayne, Matt. Attack of the Virtual Villains. Moy, Philip, illus. 2012. (Batman: the Brave & the Bold Ser.). (ENG.). 32p. (gr. 2-3). lib. bdg. 22.60 (978-1-4342-4546-5(2)) Stone Arch Bks.

—Menace of the Time Thief, 1 vol. Suriano, Andy & Davis, Dan W., illus. 2012. (Batman: the Brave & the Bold Ser.). (ENG.). 32p. (gr. 2-3). lib. bdg. 22.60 (978-1-4342-4548-9(9)) Stone Arch Bks.

—Panic of the Composite Creatures. Suriano, Andy & Davis, Dan W., illus. 2012. (Batman: the Brave & the Bold Ser.). (ENG.). 32p. (gr. 2-3). lib. bdg. 22.60 (978-1-4342-4545-8(4)) Stone Arch Bks.

—President Batman, 1 vol. Suriano, Andy & Davis, Dan W., illus. 2012. (Batman: the Brave & the Bold Ser.). (ENG.). 32p. (gr. 2-3). lib. bdg. 22.60 (978-1-4342-4547-2(0)) Stone Arch Bks.

Weigel, Jeff. Atomic Ace & the Robot Rampage. Weigel, Jeff, illus. 2006. (ENG., Illus.). 32p. (J). (gr. 1-5). 6.95 (978-0-8075-0485-7(8)); 15.95 (978-0-8075-0484-0(X)) Whitman, Albert & Co.

Weisman, Greg, et al. Rabbit Holes, 1 vol. Davis, Dan, illus. 2013. (Young Justice Ser.). (ENG.). 32p. (gr. 2-3). 22.60 (978-1-4342-6039-0(9)) Stone Arch Bks.

—Wonderland, 1 vol. Jones, Christopher, illus. 2013. (Young Justice Ser.). (ENG.). 32p. (gr. 2-3). 22.60 (978-1-4342-6040-6(2)) Stone Arch Bks.

Weitzman, Jacqueline Preiss. Superhero Joe. Barrett, Ron, illus. 2011. (ENG.). 32p. (J). (gr. -1-3). 16.99 (978-1-4169-9157-1(3), Simon & Schuster/Paula Wiseman Bks.) Simon & Schuster/Paula Wiseman Bks.

—Superhero Joe & the Creature Next Door. Barrett, Ron, illus. 2013. (ENG.). 32p. (J). (gr. -1-3). 16.99 (978-1-4424-1268-2(2), Simon & Schuster Bks. For Young Readers) Simon & Schuster Bks. For Young Readers.

West, Tracey, adapted by. Jack in! MegaMan! 2006. 59p. (J). (978-0-439-76837-5(3)) Scholastic, Inc.

Westlake, Donald E. The Risk Profession. 2009. 60p. pap. 7.95 (978-1-60664-380-8(0)) Rodgers, Alan Bks.

Wetterer, Margaret K. The Midnight Adventure of Kate Shelley, Train Rescuer. 2010. pap. 51.02 (978-0-7613-6919-6(8)) Lerner Publishing Group.

—The Midnight Adventure of Kate Shelley, Train Rescuer. Trover, Zachary, illus. 2010. (History's Kid Heroes Ser.). (ENG.). 32p. (gr. 3-5). 26.60 (978-0-7613-6173-2(1)); pap. 8.95 (978-0-7613-6192-3(8), Graphic Universe™) Lerner Publishing Group.

Wetterer, Margaret K. & Wetterer, Charles M. The Snowshoeing Adventure of Milton Daub, Blizzard Trekker. 2010. pap. 51.02 (978-0-7613-6921-9(X)) Lerner Publishing Group.

—The Snowshoeing Adventure of Milton Daub, Blizzard Trekker. Trover, Zachary, illus. 2010. (History's Kid Heroes Ser.). (ENG.). 32p. (gr. 3-5). pap. 8.95 (978-0-7613-6194-7(4), Graphic Universe™); lib. bdg. 26.60 (978-0-7613-6175-6(8)) Lerner Publishing Group.

Wheeler, Lisa. When Pigs Fly. Ansley, Frank, illus. 2005. (Fitch & Chip Ser.). 48p. (gr. 1-3). 14.00 (978-0-7569-5472-7(X)) Perfection Learning Corp.

—When Pigs Fly. Ansley, Frank, illus. 2003. (Fitch & Chip Ser.: 2). (ENG.). 48p. (J). (gr. 1-3). 16.99 (978-0-689-84951-0(6), Atheneum/Richard Jackson Bks.) Simon & Schuster Children's Publishing.

Wildsmith, Brian. The Little Wood Duck, 1 vol. 2007. (ENG., Illus.). 32p. (J). (gr. -1-3). 16.95 (978-1-59572-042-9(1)) Star Bright Bks., Inc.

—The Little Wood Duck, 1 vol. Wildsmith, Brian, illus. 2006. (ENG., Illus.). 32p. (J). pap. 6.95 (978-1-59572-049-8(9)) Star Bright Bks., Inc.

Willis, Jeanne. Supercat vs the Party Pooper (Supercat, Book 2) 2015. (Supercat Ser.: 2). (ENG.). 208p. (J). 5.99 (978-0-00-811040-6(9), HarperCollins Children's Bks.) HarperCollins Pubs. Ltd. GBR. Dist: HarperCollins Pubs.

Wilson, A. c. & Wilson, A. C. Ambersil - the Legacy of Mr Harrison. 2011. 496p. pap. (978-1-908105-45-5(3)) Grosvenor Hse. Publishing Ltd.

Windham, Ryder. Island of Lost Masks. 2015. lib. bdg. 16.00 (978-0-606-37793-5(X)) Turtleback Bks.

Wolfman, Marv. Nova Classic Volume 3. Buscema, John et al, illus. 2014. (ENG.). 304p. (J). (gr. 4-17). pap. 34.99 (978-0-7851-8552-9(6)) Marvel Worldwide, Inc.

Wong, Clarissa S. The Story of the Guardians of the Galaxy. 2014. (Marvel World of Reading Level 2 Ser.). (J). lib. bdg. 13.55 (978-0-606-35279-6(1)) Turtleback Bks.

Wrecks, Billy. Ant-Man. Spaziante, Patrick, illus. 2016. (Little Golden Book Ser.). (ENG.). 24p. (J). (-k). 4.99 (978-0-399-55097-3(6), Golden Bks.) Random Hse. Children's Bks.

—Batman's Hero Files (DC Super Friends) Random House Editors et al, illus. 2015. (Step into Reading Ser.). (ENG.). 24p. (J). (gr. -1-1). 4.99 (978-0-553-50808-6(3), Random Hse. Bks. for Young Readers) Random Hse. Children's Bks.

—The Big Freeze (Marvel) Borkowski, Michael & Atiyen, Michael, illus. 2016. (Little Golden Book Ser.). (ENG.). 24p. (J). (-k). 4.99 (978-0-307-97656-7(4), Golden Bks.) Random Hse. Children's Bks.

—Big Heroes! (DC Super Friends) Golden Books Staff, illus. 2011. (Little Golden Book Ser.). (ENG.). 24p. (J). (gr. -1-2). 4.99 (978-0-375-87237-2(X), Golden Bks.) Random Hse. Children's Bks.

—Bizarro Day! 2013. (Step into Reading Level 2 Ser.). lib. bdg. 13.55 (978-0-606-26971-1(1), Turtleback) Turtleback Bks.

—Bizarro Day! (DC Super Friends) Legramandi, Francesco, illus. 2013. (Step into Reading Ser.). (ENG.). 32p. (J). (gr. k-3). pap. 3.99 (978-0-307-98119-6(3), Random Hse. Bks. for Young Readers) Random Hse. Children's Bks.

—Catch Catwoman! 2013. (Step into Reading Level 2 Ser.). lib. bdg. 13.55 (978-0-606-32196-9(9), Turtleback) Turtleback Bks.

—Crime Wave! 2012. (Step into Reading Level 2 Ser.). lib. bdg. 13.55 (978-0-606-23739-0(9), Turtleback) Turtleback Bks.

—Crime Wave! (DC Super Friends) Schoening, Dan, illus. 2012. (Step into Reading Ser.). (ENG.). 32p. (J). (gr. -1-1). pap. 3.99 (978-0-375-86898-6(4), Random Hse. Bks. for Young Readers) Random Hse. Children's Bks.

—Eye of the Dragon (Marvel: Iron Man) Spaziante, Patrick, illus. 2016. (Little Golden Book Ser.). (ENG.). 24p. (J). (-k). 4.99 (978-0-307-97654-3(8), Golden Bks.) Random Hse. Children's Bks.

—Heroes vs. Villains/Space Chase! (DC Super Friends) Doescher, Erik et al, illus. 2013. (Pictureback(R) Ser.). (ENG.). 32p. (J). (gr. -1-2). pap. 4.99 (978-0-307-97616-1(5), Random Hse. Bks. for Young Readers) Random Hse. Children's Bks.

—The Invincible Iron Man. Golden Books Staff & Spaziante, Patrick, illus. 2016. (Little Golden Book Ser.). (ENG.). 24p. (J). (gr. k-k). 4.99 (978-0-307-93064-4(5), Golden Bks.) Random Hse. Children's Bks.

—The Mighty Avengers (Marvel: the Avengers) Spaziante, Patrick, illus. 2016. (Little Golden Book Ser.). (ENG.). 24p. (J). (gr. k-k). 4.99 (978-0-307-93109-2(9), Golden Bks.) Random Hse. Children's Bks.

—Reptile Rumble! 2014. (Step into Reading Level 2 Ser.). lib. bdg. 13.55 (978-0-606-35541-4(3)) Turtleback Bks.

—The Super Friends Save Christmas/Race to the North Pole! Random House Staff, illus. 2012. (Pictureback(R) Ser.). (ENG.). 32p. (J). (gr. -1-2). pap. 4.99 (978-0-307-97946-9(6), Random Hse. Bks. for Young Readers) Random Hse. Children's Bks.

—Super-Pets! Golden Books Staff & Beavers, Ethen, illus. 2016. (Little Golden Book Ser.). (ENG.). 24p. (J). (gr. -1-k). 4.99 (978-0-553-53923-3(X), Golden Bks.) Random Hse. Children's Bks.

—Superman! (DC Super Friends) Beavers, Ethen, illus. 2013. (Little Golden Book Ser.). (ENG.). 24p. (J). (-k). 4.99 (978-0-307-93195-5(1), Golden Bks.) Random Hse. Children's Bks.

Wrecks, Billy & Kaplan, Arie. Doctor Strange Little Golden Book (Marvel: Doctor Strange) Golden Books et al, illus. 2017. (Little Golden Book Ser.). (ENG.). 24p. (J). (-k). 4.99 (978-1-101-93865-2(X), Golden Bks.) Random Hse. Children's Bks.

Wyatt, Chris. Falcon: Fight or Flight: A Mighty Marvel Chapter Book. Grummett, Tom, illus. 2015. (Mighty Marvel Chapter Book Ser.). (ENG.). 128p. (J). (gr. 3-7). pap. 5.99 (978-1-4847-1529-1(2), Marvel Pr.) Disney Publishing Worldwide.

—Meet the Marvel Super Heroes. Lim, Ron, illus. 2nd ed. 2015. (ENG.). 160p. (J). (gr. 1-3). 12.99 (978-1-4847-0670-1(6), Marvel Pr.) Disney Publishing Worldwide.

Wyatt, Chris 'Doc'. Bravest Warriors: The Great Core Caper, Vol.1. Howell, Corin, illus. 2014. (ENG.). 112p. (J). pap. 7.99 (978-1-4215-7539-1(6)) Viz Media.

X-Men. 2003. (J). (978-1-57657-859-9(3)) Paradise Pr., Inc.

Yamagata, Ishio. Rokka: Braves of the Six Flowers, Vol. 1 (light Novel) 2017. (Rokka: Braves of the Six Flowers (Light Novel) Ser.: 1). (ENG., Illus.). 224p. (gr. 8-17). pap. 14.00 (978-0-316-50141-5(7), Yen Pr.) Orbit.

Yang, Gene Luen. The Shadow Hero. Liew, Sonny, illus. 2014. (ENG.). 176p. (YA). (gr. 7-12). pap. 17.99 (978-1-59643-697-8(2), 9781596436978, First Second Bks.) Roaring Brook Pr.

—The Shadow Hero. Liew, Sonny, illus. 2014. (YA). lib. bdg. 30.60 (978-0-606-35521-6(9)) Turtleback Bks.

Yee, Lisa. Batgirl at Super Hero High. Random House, illus. 2017. (ENG.). 240p. (J). (gr. 3-7). 13.99 (978-1-101-94065-5(4), Random Hse. Bks. for Young Readers) Random Hse. Children's Bks.

—Supergirl at Super Hero High. Random House Staff, illus. 2016. (ENG.). 240p. (J). (gr. 3-7). 13.99 (978-1-101-94062-4(X), Random Hse. Bks. for Young Readers) Random Hse. Children's Bks.

Yolen, Jane. A Plague of Unicorns, 1 vol. 2016. (ENG.). 192p. (J). pap. 7.99 (978-0-310-74611-9(6)) Zonderkidz.

—A Plague of Unicorns. 2015. (J). pap. (978-0-310-74610-2(8)) Zondervan.

Yolen, Jane & Harris, Robert J. Atalanta & the Arcadian Beast. 2003. (Young Heroes Ser.: Bk. 3). 256p. (J). 15.99 (978-0-06-029454-0(X)) HarperCollins Pubs.

York, M. J. The Constellation Hercules: The Story of the Hero. Morrow, J. T., illus. 2013. (Constellations Ser.). (ENG.). 32p. (J). (gr. 2-5). 29.93 (978-1-62323-486-7(7), 206254) Child's World, Inc., The.

Yourgrau, Barry. Another Nastybook: The Curse of the Tweeties. DeJesus, Robert, illus. 2006. 171p. (J). (gr. 5-9). lib. bdg. 13.89 (978-0-06-057982-1(X), Cotler, Joanna Books) HarperCollins Pubs.

—Nasty Book. 2005. (ENG.). 192p. (J). (gr. 5-9). 11.99 (978-0-06-057978-4(1)) HarperCollins Pubs.

—Nastybook. 2007. (ENG.). 192p. (J). (gr. 5-9). pap. 5.99 (978-0-06-057980-7(3), Harper Trophy) HarperCollins Pubs.

Zahler, Diane. A True Princess. (ENG.). (J). (gr. 3-7). 2012. 208p. pap. 6.99 (978-0-06-182503-3(4)) 2011. 192p. 15.99 (978-0-06-182501-9(8)) HarperCollins Pubs.

Zinn, Bridget. Poison. 2014. (ENG.). 288p. (YA). (gr. 7-12). pap. 9.99 (978-1-4231-5330-6(8)) Hyperion Bks. for Children.

Zusak, Markus. Cartas Cruzadas. 2012. (Vintage Espanol Ser.). (SPA.). 384p. (YA). (gr. 7). pap. 14.95 (978-0-307-95145-8(6), Vintage Espanol) Knopf Doubleday Publishing Group.

—I Am the Messenger. 2009. 10.52 (978-0-7848-2491-7(6), Everbind) Marco Bk. Co.

—I Am the Messenger. 2006. 21.00 (978-0-7569-7034-5(2)) Perfection Learning Corp.

—I Am the Messenger. (ENG.). 368p. (YA). (gr. 7). 2005. 16.95 (978-0-375-83099-0(5)) 2006. (Illus.). reprint ed. pap. 10.99 (978-0-375-83667-1(5)) Random Hse. Children's Bks. (Knopf Bks. for Young Readers).

—I Am the Messenger. (J). 2007. 1.25 (978-1-4281-2308-3(3)) 2007. 77.75 (978-1-4281-2309-0(1)) 2006. 74.75 (978-1-4281-2311-3(3)) Recorded Bks., Inc.

HEROINES

see Heroes; Women in the Bible

HEROISM

see Courage; Heroes

HERONS

Stoughton, K. Come along on a Tour: With Angel & Henry. 2007. (Illus.). 16p. (J). 11.95 (978-0-9768442-8-0(1)) GWF Publishing & Henry's Helpers.

HERONS—FICTION

Buchwald, Emilie. Floramel & Esteban. Robinson, Charles, illus. 2009. (ENG.). 80p. (J). (gr. 1-6). 16.95 (978-1-57131-688-2(4)) Milkweed Editions.

Claremont, Chris. X-Men Forever. 2011. (ENG., Illus.). 120p. (J). (gr. 4-17). pap. 16.99 (978-0-7851-4665-0(2)) Marvel Worldwide, Inc.

Hadithi, Mwenye & Kennaway, Adrienne. Laughing Giraffe. 2009. (ENG., Illus.). 32p. (J). (gr. k-2). 8.99 (978-0-340-94520-9(6)) Hodder & Stoughton GBR. Dist: Hachette Bk. Group.

Jewett, Sarah Orne. A White Heron. Alvord, Douglas, illus. 2005. (ENG.). 32p. (J). pap. 10.95 (978-1-56792-287-5(2)) Godine, David R. Pub.

McGaw, Wayne T. T-Boy of the Bayou. Crespo, George, illus. 2003. 32p. (J). (gr. -1-3). 15.95 (978-0-87614-648-4(5), Carolrhoda Bks.) Lerner Publishing Group.

Percy, Graham. The Heron & the Fish. Percy, Graham, illus. 2009. (Aesop's Fables Ser.). (ENG., Illus.). 32p. (J). (gr. k-3). 28.50 (978-1-60253-202-1(8), 200037) Child's World, Inc., The.

Ramírez, Antonio. Napí, 1 vol. Domi, illus. 2004. (SPA.). 40p. (J). 15.95 (978-0-88899-611-4(X)) Groundwood Bks. CAN. Dist: Publishers Group West (PGW).

Schmidt-Kyanka, Anita. Sapsucker Blues: The Story of an Endearing Family of Great Blue Herons. 2013. 48p. pap. 20.99 (978-1-4808-0250-6(6)) Archway Publishing.

Watts, Kevin Bradley. Ben & the Mysterious Sound: Series: the Adventures of Tug Boat Ben. 2007. (Illus.). 32p. (J). (978-0-9782625-2-5(2)); pap. (978-0-9782625-1-8(4)) Alderney Publishing, Inc.

Yeoman, John. The Heron & the Crane. Blake, Quentin, illus. 2011. (ENG.). 32p. (J). (gr. -1-k). pap. 13.99 (978-1-84939-200-6(5)) Andersen Pr. GBR. Dist: Independent Pubs. Group.

HERSCHEL, CAROLINE LUCRETIA, 1750-1848

Robinson, Ella May. Stars in Her Heart. 2005. 127p. per. 10.95 (978-1-57258-318-4(5)) TEACH Services, Inc.

HERSCHEL, WILLIAM, SIR, 1738-1822

Robinson, Ella May. Stars in Her Heart. 2005. 127p. per. 10.95 (978-1-57258-318-4(5)) TEACH Services, Inc.

Sherman, Josepha. Uranus. 2009. (Space!). 64p. (gr. 5-18). lib. bdg. 32.79 (978-0-7614-4248-6(0)) Marshall Cavendish Corp.

HERSHEY, MILTON SNAVELY, 1857-1945

Benge, Janet & Benge, Geoff. Milton Hershey: More Than Chocolate. 2012. (ENG.). (YA). pap. 9.99 (978-1-932096-82-8(5)) Emerald Bks.

Buckley, James, Jr. Who Was Milton Hershey? Hammond, Ted, illus. 2013. (Who Was? Ser.). (ENG.). 112p. (J). (gr. 3-7). 5.99 (978-0-448-47936-1(2), Grosset & Dunlap) Penguin Young Readers Group.

Buckley, James. Who Was Milton Hershey? 2013. (Who Was... ? Ser.). lib. bdg. 16.00 (978-0-606-34163-9(3), Turtleback) Turtleback Bks.

Eboch, M. M. Milton Hershey: Young Chocolatier. Henderson, Meryl, illus. 2008. (Childhood of Famous Americans Ser.). (ENG.). 224p. (J). (gr. 3-7). pap. 6.99 (978-1-4169-5569-6(0), Simon & Schuster/Paula Wiseman Bks.) Simon & Schuster/Paula Wiseman Bks.

Green, Sara. Hershey's. (Hershey's Ser.). 24p. (J). (gr. 3-8). 2017. pap. 7.99 **(978-1-61891-248-0(8))** 2015. (ENG., Illus.). lib. bdg. 25.95 (978-1-62617-206-7(4)) Bellwether Media. (Pilot Bks.).

Mattern, Joanne. Milton Hershey: Hershey's Chocolate Creator, 1 vol. (Food Dudes Set 1 Ser.). (ENG.). 32p. (gr. 3-6). 2014. lib. bdg. 27.07 (978-1-62403-494-7(2), Checkerboard Library) 2011. (Illus.). (J). 27.07 (978-1-61613-557-7(3)) ABDO Publishing Co.

Schuette, Sarah L. Milton Hershey, 1 vol. 2014. (Business Leaders Ser.). (ENG.). 24p. (gr. k-1). lib. bdg. 21.99 (978-1-4765-9640-2(9), Pebble Bks.) Capstone Press of Coughlan Cos.

Sutcliffe, Jane. Milton Hershey. Parlin, Tim, illus. 2003. (History Maker Biographies Ser.). (ENG.). 48p. (gr. 3-6). 27.93 (978-0-8225-0247-0(X), Lerner Pubns.) Lerner Publishing Group.

HESSE, HERMANN, 1877-1962

Hesse, Hermann. Bajo la Rueda. 2003.Tr. of Unterm Rad. (SPA.). bds. 6.98 (978-968-6769-57-9(9)) Epoca, Editorial, S.A. de C.V. MEX. Dist: Giron Bks.

HIAWATHA, ACTIVE 15TH CENTURY

Schomp, Virginia. Hiawatha & the Great Peace. 2013. 32p. (J). (gr. 6-9). 28.50 (978-1-60870-440-8(8)); pap. 10.58 (978-1-62712-015-9(7)) Cavendish Square Publishing.

Taylor, C. J. Peace Walker: The Legend of Hiawatha & Tekanawita. 2004. (ENG., Illus.). 48p. (J). (gr. 2-4). 15.95 (978-0-88776-547-6(5), Tundra Bks.) Tundra Bks. CAN. Dist: Penguin Random Hse. LLC.

HIBERNATION

see Animals—Hibernation

HICCUPS—FICTION

Albee, Sarah. Hic! Brannon, Tom, illus. 2006. (Step-By-Step Readers Ser.). (J). pap. (978-1-59939-061-1(2), Reader's Digest Young Families, Inc.) Studio Fun International.

Bentley, Tadgh. Little Penguin Gets the Hiccups. Bentley, Tadgh, illus. 2015. (ENG., Illus.). 40p. (J). (gr. -1-3). 17.99 (978-0-06-233536-4(7)) HarperCollins Pubs.

Child, Lauren. I Can't Stop Hiccuping! 2010. (Charlie & Lola Ser.). lib. bdg. 13.55 (978-0-606-10629-0(4), Turtleback) Turtleback Bks.

Cuyler, Margery. Skeleton for Dinner. Terry, Will, illus. 2013. (ENG.). 32p. (J). (gr. -1-3). 16.99 (978-0-8075-7398-3(1)) Whitman, Albert & Co.

Dearing, Ruth. Tommy & the Hiccups. 2013. 44p. pap. 10.00 (978-0-9843487-9-4(4)) Painting the Pages Publishing.

Delgato, Carolyn A. Jiggy & his Hiccups, 1 vol. 2010. 30p. 24.95 (978-1-4512-0927-3(4)) PublishAmerica, Inc.

Depken, Kristen L. Dragon Hiccups. Burch, Benjamin, illus. 2015. (Little Golden Book Ser.). (ENG.). 24p. (J). (-k). 4.99 (978-0-553-52310-2(4), Golden Bks.) Random Hse. Children's Bks.

Derubertis, Barbara. Hanna Hippo's Horrible Hiccups. 2010. pap. 45.32 (978-0-7613-6510-5(9)) Kane Press, Inc.

deRubertis, Barbara. Hanna Hippo's Horrible Hiccups. Alley, R. W., illus. 2010. (Animal Antics A to Z Ser.). 32p. (J). (gr. -1-3). pap. 7.95 (978-1-57565-312-9(5)); lib. bdg. 22.60 (978-1-57565-319-8(2)) Kane Press, Inc.

deRubertis, Barbara & DeRubertis, Barbara. Hanna Hippo's Horrible Hiccups. Alley, R. W., illus. 2012. (Animal Antics A to Z Ser.). 32p. (J). (gr. 2 — 1). cd-rom 7.95 (978-1-57565-401-0(6)) Kane Press, Inc.

Disney Book Group. Doc Mcstuffins a Good Case of the Hiccups: Book with DVD. Disney Storybook Art Team, illus. 2015. (ENG.). 32p. (J). (gr. -1-k). 9.99 (978-1-4847-0687-9(0)) Disney Pr.

Hannah's Hiccups: Individual Title Six-Packs. (gr. k-1). 23.00 (978-0-7635-8831-1(8)) Rigby Education.

Hepfler, Caroline Ann. Huckleberrys Hiccups. 2009. 20p. pap. 11.25 (978-1-60693-917-8(3), Strategic Bk. Publishing) Strategic Book Publishing & Rights Agency (SBPRA).

Higgins, Kitty. Wild Bill Hiccups. 2005. (J). pap. (978-1-4108-4213-8(4)) Benchmark Education Co.

Larson, Angela. Harry Hiccers: Friends of A Feether. 2012. pap. (978-1-4507-7996-8(4)) Independent Pub.

Little, Penny. Baby Bear's Birthday Hiccups! Jones, Lara, illus. 2008. (ENG.). 32p. (J). (gr. 2-4). 24.50 (978-0-230-53029-4(X), Macmillan) Pan Macmillan GBR. Dist: Trans-Atlantic Pubns., Inc.

Magee, Helen. A Ghost Called Clarence. l.t. ed. 2007. pap. (978-1-905665-66-2(0)) Pollinger In Print.

Martin, Janelle. Lexis, the Hiccupping Lion. 2013. 12p. pap. 7.95 (978-1-4908-0545-0(1), WestBow Pr.) Author Solutions, Inc.

McKee, David. Zebra's Hiccups. McKee, David, illus. 2009. (ENG., Illus.). 32p. (J). (gr. k-k). pap. 10.99 (978-1-84270-923-8(2)) Andersen Pr. GBR. Dist: Independent Pubs. Group.

Mills, David. Mei Ling's Hiccups. Brazell, Derek, illus. 2004. (CHI & ENG.). 32p. (J). pap. (978-1-85269-703-7(2)) Mantra Lingua.

—Mei Ling's Hiccups: Higgadii Mii Linig. Brazell, Derek, illus. 2004. (ENG & SOM.). 32p. (J). pap. (978-1-85269-564-4(1)) Mantra Lingua.

Newman, Tracy. Shabbat Hiccups. Exelby, Ilana, illus. 2016. (ENG.). 32p. (J). (gr. -1-3). 16.99 (978-0-8075-7312-9(4)) Whitman, Albert & Co.

Powell, Jillian. Hiccups!, 1 vol. Chambers, Mark A., illus. 2013. (Start Reading Ser.). (ENG.). 24p. (gr. k-1). pap. 7.95 (978-1-4765-4103-7(5)) Capstone Press of Coughlan Cos.

Sterling, Holly. Hiccups! 2016. (ENG., Illus.). 32p. (J). 17.99 (978-1-84780-674-1(0), Frances Lincoln Children's Bks.) Quarto Publishing Group UK GBR. Dist: Littlehampton Bk Services, Ltd.

Watson-Dubisch, Carolyn. Bug-a-boo, 1. l.t. ed. 2006. (Illus.). 32p. (J). per. 9.95 (978-0-9779295-1-1(5)) Medusa Road Pr.

Zenz, Aaron. The Hiccupotamus, 0 vols. 2009. (ENG.). 32p. (J). (gr. -1-2). 12.99 (978-0-7614-5622-3(8), 9780761456223, Amazon Children's Publishing) Amazon Publishing.

HICKOK, WILD BILL, 1837-1876

Fein, Eric. High Noon: Wild Bill Hickok & the Code of the Old West. 2009. (Great Moments in American History Ser.). 32p. (gr. 3-3). 47.90 (978-1-61513-145-7(0)) Rosen Publishing Group, Inc., The.

Green, Carl R. & Sanford, William R. Wild Bill Hickok. rev. ed. 2008. (Outlaws & Lawmen of the Wild West, Revised Edition Ser.). (Illus.). 48p. (J). (gr. 5-18). lib. bdg. 25.27 (978-0-7660-3177-7(2)) Enslow Pubs., Inc.

Phillips, Larissa. Wild Bill Hickok: Legend of the American Wild West. 2004. (Primary Sources of Famous People in American History Ser.). (ENG., Illus.). 32p. (gr. 4-8). pap. 10.00 (978-0-8239-4194-0(9)) Rosen Publishing Group, Inc., The.

—Wild Bill Hickok: Legend of the American Wild West / Leyenda del oeste Americano. 2009. (Famous People in American History/Grandes personajes en la historia de los Estados Unidos Ser.). (ENG & SPA.). 32p. (gr. 2-3). 47.90 (978-1-61512-557-9(4), Editorial Buenas Letras) Rosen Publishing Group, Inc., The.

—Wild Bill Hickok: Legend of the Wild West. 2009. (Primary Sources of Famous People in American History Ser.). 32p. (gr. 2-3). 47.90 (978-1-60851-740-4(3)) Rosen Publishing Group, Inc., The.

—Wild Bill Hickok: Leyenda del oeste Americano. 2004. (Grandes personajes en la historia de los Estados Unidos Ser.). (SPA.). 32p. (gr. 3-6). pap. 10.00 (978-0-8239-4240-4(6), Rosen Classroom) Rosen Publishing Group, Inc., The.

—Wild Bill Hickok: Leyenda del oeste americano (Wild Bill Hickok: Legend of the American Wild West) 2009. (Grandes personajes en la historia de los Estados Unidos (Famous People in American History) Ser.). (SPA.). 32p. (gr. 2-3). 47.90 (978-1-61512-810-5(7), Editorial Buenas Letras) Rosen Publishing Group, Inc., The.

Wild Bill Hickok. 2010. (Legends of the Wild West Ser.). (Illus.). 112p. (gr. 6-12). 35.00 (978-1-60413-593-0(X), Chelsea Hse.) Facts On File, Inc.

HIDES AND SKINS

Boothroyd, Jennifer. Fur. 2011. (First Step Nonfiction / Body Coverings Ser.). pap. 33.92 (978-0-7613-8608-7(4)); (ENG.). 24p. pap. 6.95 (978-0-7613-7828-0(6)); (ENG., Illus.). 24p. lib. bdg. 23.93 (978-0-7613-5786-5(6)) Lerner Publishing Group.

HIEROGLYPHICS

see also Picture-Writing

Coulter, Lavrie. Secrets in Stone: All about Maya Hieroglyphs. English, Sarah Jane, illus. 2003. 48p. (gr. 4-8). 18.00 (978-0-7567-9000-4(X)) DIANE Publishing Co.

Fine, Jil. Mayan Writing in Mesoamerica. 2003. (Writing in the Ancient World Ser.). (Illus.). 24p. (J). lib. bdg. 22.60 (978-0-8239-6511-3(2), PowerKids Pr.) Rosen Publishing Group, Inc., The.

Greeley, August. Mayan Writing in Mesoamerica. 2009. (Writing in the Ancient World Ser.). 24p. (gr. 3-3). 42.50 (978-1-60854-903-0(8), PowerKids Pr.) Rosen Publishing Group, Inc., The.

Harper, Ellen. Fun with Egyptian Symbols Stencils. 2003. (Dover Stencils Ser.). (ENG., Illus.). 6p. (J). (gr. 1-4). pap. 1.99 (978-0-486-43109-3(6)) Dover Pubns., Inc.

Rumford, James. Seeker of Knowledge: The Man Who Deciphered Egyptian Hieroglyphs. 2003. (Rise & Shine Ser.). (ENG., Illus.). 32p. (C). (gr. -1-3). pap. 11.95 (978-0-618-33345-5(2)) National Geographic School Publishing, Inc.

HI-FI SYSTEMS

see High-Fidelity Sound Systems

HIGH-FIDELITY SOUND SYSTEMS

Matthews, John. DVDs. 2008. (21st Century Skills Library: Global Products Ser.). (ENG., Illus.). 32p. (gr. 4-8). lib. bdg. 28.50 (978-1-60279-253-1(4), 200120) Cherry Lake Publishing.

HIGH SCHOOL EDUCATION

see Education, Secondary

HIGH SCHOOLS

Bluestein, Jane & Katz, Eric. High School's Not Forever. 2005. (ENG., Illus.). 250p. (gr. 8-12). pap. 12.95 *(978-0-7573-0256-5(4))* Health Communications, Inc.

Creating Your High School Portfolio: An Interactive Guide for Documenting & Planning Your Education, Career, & Life. 2003. 160p. 10.95 *(978-1-56370-906-7(6),* J9066, JIST Works) JIST Publishing.

Friedman, Hannah. Everything Sucks: Losing My Mind & Finding Myself in a High School Quest for Cool. 2009. (ENG.). 264p. (YA). (gr. 8-12). pap. 12.95 *(978-0-7573-0775-1(2),* HCI Teens) Health Communications, Inc.

Greenhaven Press Editors. The Columbine School Shootings. 2012. (Perspectives on Modern World History Ser.). (ENG., Illus.). 224p. (J). (gr. 10-12). lib. bdg. 42.45 *(978-0-7377-5788-0(4),* Greenhaven Pr., Inc.) Cengage Gale.

Long, Trish. If You Can Survive High School, You Can Survive Anything! 2010. 116p. pap. 12.00 *(978-1-4520-6334-8(6))* AuthorHouse.

MacKay, Jennifer. The Columbine School Shootings. 2010. (Crime Scene Investigations Ser.). (Illus.). 128p. (YA). (gr. 7-12). 35.45 *(978-1-4205-0138-4(0))* Cengage Gale.

Messina, Noreen E. Teenwork: Four Teens Tell All: A Guide for Finding Jobs. 2005. (Illus.). 126p. (gr. 6-12). per. 12.75 *(978-1-59070-598-8(X))* Goodheart-Willcox Pub.

Miller, Mara. School Desegregation & the Story of the Little Rock Nine. 2008. (From Many Cultures, One History Ser.). (Illus.). 128p. (J). (gr. 3-7). lib. bdg. 33.27 *(978-0-7660-2835-7(6))* Enslow Pubs., Inc.

Roselius, J. Chris. Surviving School: Managing School & Career Paths, 1 vol. 2010. (Essential Health: a Guy's Guide Ser.). (ENG.). 112p. (J). (gr. 6-12). lib. bdg. 35.64 *(978-1-61613-544-7(1))* ABDO Publishing Co.

HIGH SPEED AERODYNAMICS

see Aerodynamics, Supersonic

HIGH-SPEED AERONAUTICS

see also Aerodynamics, Supersonic; Rockets (Aeronautics)

Farndon, John. Megafast Planes. Edwards, Mat & Pyke, Jeremy, illus. 2016. (Megafast Ser.). (ENG.). 32p. (J). (gr. 3-6). lib. bdg. 26.65 *(978-1-4677-9365-0(5))* Lerner Publishing Group.

Harkins, Susan Sales. Breaking the Sound Barrier: The Story of Chuck Yeager. 2005. (Monumental Milestones Ser.). (Illus.). 48p. (YA). (gr. 4-7). lib. bdg. 29.95 *(978-1-58415-398-6(9),* 1244924) Mitchell Lane Pubs., Inc.

HIGHER EDUCATION

see Education, Higher

HIGHWAY ACCIDENTS

see Traffic Accidents

HIGHWAY CONSTRUCTION

see Roads

HIGHWAY TRANSPORTATION

see Transportation, Automotive

HIGHWAYMEN

see Robbers and Outlaws

HIGHWAYS

see Roads; Streets

HIJACKING OF AIRCRAFT

Buell, Tonya. The Crash of United Flight 93 on September 11, 2001. 2005. (Terrorist Attacks Ser.). (Illus.). 64p. (YA). (gr. 7-12). lib. bdg. 31.95 *(978-0-8239-3857-5(3))* Rosen Publishing Group, Inc., The.

—The Crash of United Flight 93 on September 11 2001. 2009. (Terrorist Attacks Ser.). 64p. (gr. 5-5). 58.50 *(978-1-60853-316-9(6))* Rosen Publishing Group, Inc., The.

Dunstan, Simon. Entebbe: The Most Daring Raid of Israel's Special Forces. 2011. (Most Daring Raids in History Ser.). (Illus.). 64p. (YA). (gr. 7-12). 31.95 *(978-1-4488-1868-6(0))* Rosen Publishing Group, Inc., The.

Lusted, Marcia Amidon. The D. B. Cooper Hijacking, 1 vol. 2012. (Unsolved Mysteries (el) Ser.). (ENG.). 112p. (J). (gr. 6-12). lib. bdg. 35.64 *(978-1-61783-301-4(0),* Essential Library) ABDO Publishing Co.

Streissguth, Tom. The D. B. Cooper Hijacking. 2015. (Unsolved Mysteries Ser.). (ENG.). 24p. (J). (gr. 1-4). 28.50 *(978-1-63407-072-0(0),* 208909) Child's World, Inc., The.

Wright, John. The U. S. Transportation Security Administration. 2004. (Rescue & Prevention Ser.). (Illus.). 96p. (YA). (gr. 7-18). lib. bdg. 22.95 *(978-1-59084-412-0(2))* Mason Crest.

HIJACKING OF AIRCRAFT—FICTION

Moss, Miriam. Girl on a Plane. 2017. (ENG.). 288p. (YA). (gr. 7). pap. 9.99 ***(978-1-328-74207-0(5),*** HMH Books For Young Readers) Houghton Mifflin Harcourt Publishing Co.

Peretti, Frank E. Trapped at the Bottom of the Sea. 2004. (Cooper Kids Adventure Ser.: No. 4). 144p. (gr. 4-7). 5.99 *(978-0-89107-594-3(1));* Vol. 4. (J). (gr. 3-6). pap. 6.99 *(978-1-58134-621-3(2))* Crossway.

HIKING

see also Backpacking; Walking

Beattie, Amy & Coppin, Sara. Hiking, 01 vols., 1. 2016. (Outdoor Life Ser.). (ENG., Illus.). 64p. (J). 32.95 *(978-1-4994-6231-9(X),* Rosen Young Adult) Rosen Publishing Group, Inc., The.

Bodden, Valerie. Hiking. 2009. (Active Sports Ser.). 24p. (J). (gr. 1-5). lib. bdg. 24.25 *(978-1-58341-698-3(6),* Creative Education) Creative Co., The.

Cefrey, Holly. Let's Take a Hike! Converting Fractions to Decimals. 2009. (PowerMath Ser.). (ENG., Illus.). 24p. (J). (gr. 3-4). pap. 8.25 *(978-0-8239-8928-7(3),* PowerKids Pr.) Rosen Publishing Group, Inc., The.

Champion, Neil. Camping & Hiking. 2011. (Get Outdoors Ser.). (Illus.). 32p. (J). (gr. 4-6). lib. bdg. 25.25 *(978-1-4488-3295-8(0),* PowerKids Pr.) Rosen Publishing Group, Inc., The.

—Wild Trail: Hiking & Camping. 2013. (Illus.). 32p. (J). lib. bdg. 28.50 *(978-1-59920-809-1(1))* Black Rabbit Bks.

Eckart, Edana. I Can Go Hiking. 2003. (Wel-Sports Ser.). (ENG., Illus.). 24p. (J). 19.00 *(978-0-516-24276-7(8));* (gr. -1-2). pap. 4.95 *(978-0-516-24368-9(3))* Scholastic Library Publishing. (Children's Pr.).

Famous American Trails. (Illus.). (J). (gr. 3-6). 103.50 *(978-0-8239-7289-0(5),* Reading Power) Rosen Publishing Group, Inc., The.

Fitzsimmons, Kakie. Anna Goes Hiking: Discover Hiking & Explore Nature. l.t. ed. 2007. (Bur Bur & Friends Ser.). (Illus.). 40p. (J). (gr. 3-7). lib. bdg. 14.95 *(978-0-9777121-7-5(6))* IGI Pr.

Flowers, Pam & Farnsworth, Bill. Ellie's Long Walk: The True Story of Two Friends on the Appalachian Trail. 2012. (ENG., Illus.). 32p. (J). (gr. -1-3). pap. 11.99 *(978-0-88240-885-9(2),* West Winds Pr.) Graphic Arts Ctr. Publishing Co.

Frisch, Nate. Hiking. 2017. (J). *(978-1-60818-688-4(1),* Creative Education) Creative Co., The.

Green, Sara. Hiking. 2012. (Outdoor Adventures Ser.). (ENG., Illus.). 24p. (J). (gr. 3-8). lib. bdg. 25.95 *(978-1-60014-800-2(X),* Pilot Bks.) Bellwether Media.

Hanna, Dawn. Best Hikes & Walks of Southwestern British Columbia, 1 vol., Vol. 1. 2nd rev. ed. 2006. (ENG., Illus.). 360p. (gr. 4). per. 21.95 *(978-1-55105-455-1(8),* 1551054558) Lone Pine Publishing USA.

The Hiking & Camping Coloring Book. 2004. (J). mass mkt. *(978-0-9745863-8-0(2))* Cypress Knees Publishing.

Hiking Together: Fourth Grade Guided Comprehension Level K. (On Our Way to English Ser.). (gr. 4-18). 34.50 *(978-0-7578-7145-0(3))* Rigby Education.

Kids Can Press Staff. This Is Daniel Cook on a Hike. Li, Karen, ed. 2006. (This Is Daniel Cook Ser.). (ENG., Illus.). 24p. (J). (gr. -1-1). 4.95 *(978-1-55453-080-9(6))* Kids Can Pr., Ltd. CAN. Dist: Hachette Bk. Group.

Klein, Adam G. Hiking, 1 vol. 2008. (Outdoor Adventure! Ser.). (ENG.). 32p. (gr. k-6). 27.07 *(978-1-59928-959-5(8),* Checkerboard Library) ABDO Publishing Co.

Laplante, Walter. The Appalachian Trail. 2016. (Road Trip Ser.). (Illus.). 24p. (J). (gr. 3-2). pap. 8.15 *(978-1-4824-4673-9(1))* Stevens, Gareth Publishing LLLP.

Lundgren, Julie K. Hiking. 2009. (Illus.). 24p. (J). (gr. 4-8). lib. bdg. 27.07 *(978-1-60694-366-3(9))* Rourke Educational Media.

Martins, Isabel Minhós & Mad. What's That Noise? 2016. (ENG., Illus.). 40p. (J). (gr. -1-2). 19.95 *(978-1-84976-429-2(8))* Tate Publishing, Ltd. GBR. Dist: Abrams, Inc.

Mason, Paul. Hiking & Camping: The World's Top Hikes & Camping Spots, 1 vol. 2011. (Passport to World Sports Ser.). (ENG.). 32p. (gr. 3-4). lib. bdg. 27.99 *(978-1-4296-6863-7(6),* Edge Bks.) Capstone Press of Coughlan Cos.

McKinney, John. Hiking & Backpacking, Vol. 10. 2016. (Great Outdoors! Ser.). (Illus.). 48p. (J). (gr. 5). 20.95 *(978-1-4222-3569-0(6))* Mason Crest.

Morey, Allan. Hiking. 2017. (Great Outdoors Ser.). (ENG.). 32p. (J). (gr. 1-3). pap. 9.99 *(978-1-68152-079-7(6))* Amicus.

—Hiking. 2016. (Great Outdoors Ser.). (ENG.). 32p. (J). (gr. 1-4). 20.95 *(978-1-60753-800-4(8))* Amicus Publishing.

Norris, Ashley P. Watson. How to Hike Like a Pro. 2014. (Outdoor Sports Skills Ser.). (Illus.). 48p. (J). (gr. 4-10). 14.95 *(978-1-62285-138-6(2))* Enslow Pubs., Inc.

Rae, Cheri & McKinney, John. Hiking. 2007. (21st Century Skills Library: Healthy for Life Ser.). (ENG.). 32p. (gr. 4-8). pap. 14.21 *(978-1-60279-086-5(8),* 200647) Cherry Lake Publishing.

Richardson, Gillian. Hiking. (J). 2013. *(978-1-62127-355-4(5))* 2013. pap. *(978-1-62127-361-5(X))* 2007. (Illus.). 24p. (gr. 4-7). lib. bdg. 24.45 *(978-1-59036-659-2(X))* 2007. (Illus.). 24p. (gr. 4-7). per. 8.95 *(978-1-59036-660-8(3))* Weigl Pubs., Inc.

Shea, Therese. The Bigfoot Trail. 2014. (Scariest Places on Earth Ser.). 24p. (J). (gr. 2-5). pap. 8.15 *(978-1-4824-0928-4(3))* Stevens, Gareth Publishing LLLP.

Slade, Suzanne. Let's Go Hiking. (Adventures Outdoors Ser.). 32p. 2009. (gr. 4-5). 47.90 *(978-1-61511-270-8(7))* 2007. (Illus.). (J). (gr. 3-7). lib. bdg. 25.25 *(978-1-4042-3651-6(1))* Rosen Publishing Group, Inc., The. (PowerKids Pr.).

Tieck, Sarah. Hiking, 1 vol. 2013. (Move Your Body Ser.). (ENG.). 32p. (J). (gr. 2-5). 27.07 *(978-1-61783-562-9(5))* ABDO Publishing Co.

Turnbull, Stephanie. Hiking. 2016. (Adventure Sports Ser.). 24p. (gr. 2-6). 28.50 *(978-1-62588-384-1(6),* Smart Apple Media) Black Rabbit Bks.

York, M. J. Hiking. 2014. (Great Outdoors Ser.). (ENG.). 24p. (J). (gr. 2-5). 28.50 *(978-1-62687-330-8(5),* 207170) Child's World, Inc., The.

HILL, BARNEY

Cheatham, Mark. Aliens! 2012. (Jr. Graphic Monster Stories Ser.). (ENG.). 24p. (J). (gr. 3-6). pap. 10.60 *(978-1-4488-6403-4(8));* lib. bdg. 25.25 *(978-1-4488-6222-1(1))* Rosen Publishing Group, Inc., The. (PowerKids Pr.).

HILLARY, EDMUND, SIR, 1919-2008

Bodden, Valerie. To the Top of Mount Everest. (Great Expeditions Ser.). (Illus.). 48p. (J). 2012. (ENG.). (gr. 4-7). pap. 12.00 *(978-0-89812-668-6(1))* 2011. (gr. 5-8). lib. bdg. 34.25 *(978-1-60818-070-7(0))* Creative Co., The. (Creative Education).

Coburn, Broughton. Triumph on Everest: A Photobiography of Sir Edmund Hillary. 2003. (Photobiographies Ser.). (ENG., Illus.). 64p. (J). (gr. 5). pap. 7.95 *(978-0-7922-7932-7(8),* National Geographic Children's Bks.) National Geographic Society.

Crompton, Samuel Willard. Sir Edmund Hillary. 2009. (Great Explorers Ser.). (Illus.). 112p. (J). (gr. 6-12). 30.00 *(978-1-60413-420-9(8),* Chelsea Hse.) Facts On File, Inc.

Elish, Dan. Edmund Hillary: First to the Top. 2006. (Great Explorations Ser.). (Illus.). 80p. (J). (gr. 3-7). lib. bdg. 32.79 *(978-0-7614-2224-2(2),* Benchmark Bks.) Marshall Cavendish Corp.

Helfand, Lewis. Conquering Everest: The Lives of Edmund Hillary & Tenzing Norgay. Tayal, Amit, illus. 2011. (Campfire Graphic Novels Ser.). (ENG.). 96p. (YA). (gr. 5-12). pap. 12.99 *(978-93-80741-24-6(3),* Campfire) Steerforth Pr.

Herman, Gail & Amatrula, Michele. Climbing Everest (Totally True Adventures) 2015. (Totally True Adventures Ser.). (ENG., Illus.). 112p. (J). (gr. 2-5). 4.99 *(978-0-553-50986-1(1),* Random Hse. Bks. for Young Readers) Random Hse. Children's Bks.

Hyde, Natalie. Conquering Everest. 2013. (ENG., Illus.). 48p. (J). pap. *(978-0-7787-1175-9(7))* Crabtree Publishing Co.

Johnson, Robin. Conquering Everest. 2013. (ENG., Illus.). 48p. (J). *(978-0-7787-1167-4(6))* Crabtree Publishing Co.

Jones, Brenn. Learning about Teamwork from the Lives of Sir Edmund Hillary & Tenzing Norgay. 2009. (Character Building Book Ser.). (gr. 2-3). 42.50 *(978-1-60854-968-9(2),* PowerKids Pr.) Rosen Publishing Group, Inc., The.

Trussell-Cullen, Alan. Edmund Hillary. 2009. pap. 13.25 *(978-1-60559-058-5(4))* Hameray Publishing Group, Inc.

Whipple, Heather. Hillary & Norgay: To the Top of Mount Everest. 2007. (In the Footsteps of Explorers Ser.). (ENG., Illus.). 32p. (J). (gr. 3-7). lib. bdg. *(978-0-7787-2418-6(2));* pap. *(978-0-7787-2454-4(9))* Crabtree Publishing Co.

Yomtov, Nel. Amelia Earhart Flies Across the Atlantic. 2015. (Extraordinary Explorers Ser.). (ENG., Illus.). 24p. (J). (gr. 3-7). lib. bdg. 29.95 *(978-1-62617-290-6(0),* Black Sheep) Bellwether Media.

—Edmund Hillary Reaches the Top of Everest. 2015. (Extraordinary Explorers Ser.). (ENG., Illus.). 24p. (J). (gr. 3-7). lib. bdg. 29.95 *(978-1-62617-291-3(9),* Black Sheep) Bellwether Media.

HIMALAYA MOUNTAINS

Aloian, Molly. The Himalayas. 2011. (ENG., Illus.). 48p. (J). pap. *(978-0-7787-7569-0(0));* (gr. 4-7). lib. bdg. *(978-0-7787-7562-1(3))* Crabtree Publishing Co.

Chapman, Simon. Himalayas - Bottom to Top. 2017. (ENG., Illus.). 80p. (J). pap. 9.99 ***(978-0-00-820900-1(6))*** HarperCollins Pubs. Ltd. GBR. Dist: Independent Pubs. Group.

Chapman, Simon. In the Himalayas. Chapman, Simon, illus. 2005. (Illus.). 103p. (J). lib. bdg. 20.00 *(978-1-4242-0626-1(X))* Fitzgerald Bks.

Currie, Stephen. The Himalayas. 2004. (Exploration & Discovery Ser.). (ENG., Illus.). 112p. (J). (gr. 7-10). 30.85 *(978-1-59018-497-4(1),* Lucent Bks.) Cengage Gale.

Maynard, Charles W. The Himalayas. (Great Mountain Ranges of the World Ser.). 24p. 2009. (gr. 3-3). 42.50 *(978-1-61513-170-9(1))* 2004. (Illus.). (J). lib. bdg. 22.60 *(978-0-8239-6694-3(1))* Rosen Publishing Group, Inc., The. (PowerKids Pr.).

Nagda, Ann Whitehead. World above the Clouds: A Story of a Himalayan Ecosystem. Kratter, Paul, illus. 2005. (Wild Habitats Ser.: Vol. 18). (ENG.). 36p. (J). (gr. 1-4). 19.95 *(978-1-56899-880-0(5),* BC7017); 15.95 *(978-1-56899-878-7(3),* B7017); pap. 6.95 *(978-1-56899-879-4(1),* S7017) Soundprints.

Publishers, Wayland & Newland, Sonya. Climbing the Himalayan Mountains. 2016. (Travelling Wild Ser.). (ENG., Illus.). 32p. (J). (gr. 4-6). 17.99 *(978-0-7502-9864-3(2),* Wayland) Hachette Children's Group GBR. Dist: Hachette Bk. Group.

Reeve, Penny. Himalayan Adventures. 2005. (Adventure Ser.). (ENG., Illus.). 96p. (J). (gr. 3-7). per. 8.99 *(978-1-84550-080-1(6),* 9781845500801, CF4Kids) Christian Focus Pubns. GBR. Dist: Bookmasters Distribution.

Reynolds, Jan. Himalaya, 1 vol. 2007. (Vanishing Cultures Ser.). (ENG., Illus.). 32p. (J). (gr. 4-7). 16.95 *(978-1-60060-144-6(8));* 9.95 *(978-1-60060-129-3(4))* Lee & Low Bks., Inc.

Somervill, Barbara A. The Magnificent Himalayas. 2004. (Geography of the World Ser.). (ENG., Illus.). 32p. (J). (gr. 3-6). 28.50 *(978-1-59296-332-4(3),* 200265) Child's World, Inc., The.

Tarbox, A. D. A Mountain Food Chain: Nature's Bounty. 2nd ed. 2015. (Illus.). 80p. (J). *(978-1-60818-540-5(0),* Creative Education) Creative Co., The.

HIMALAYA MOUNTAINS—FICTION

Allende, Isabel. Kingdom of the Golden Dragon. 2009. (City of the Beasts Ser.: Bk. 2).Tr. of Reino del Dragón de Oro. (ENG.). 480p. pap. 14.99 *(978-0-06-182512-5(3),* Harper Perennial) HarperCollins Pubs.

—Kingdom of the Golden Dragon. Peden, Margaret Sayers, tr. from SPA. 2005. (City of the Beasts Ser.: Bk. 2).Tr. of Reino del Dragón de Oro. (ENG.). 464p. (J). (gr. 5-12). pap. 10.99 *(978-0-06-058944-8(2),* Rayo) HarperCollins Pubs.

Burchett, Jan & Vogler, Sara. Avalanche Alert, 1 vol. Le Feyer, Diane, illus. (Wild Rescue Ser.). (ENG.). 152p. (gr. 3-6). 2013. 9.95 *(978-1-4342-4893-0(3))* 2012. 25.32 *(978-1-4342-3772-9(9))* Stone Arch Bks.

De Munnik, Hema. Bhole: Adventures of a Young Yogi. 2006. (ENG., Illus.). 352p. (J). (gr. 3-7). per. 18.95 *(978-81-88157-37-2(6))* Lotus Pr.

Delgado, Josep Francesc. Nima, El Sherpa. 2003. (SPA.). 168p. *(978-84-8453-060-2(4),* PT31196) Ediciones del Bronce ESP. Dist: Lectorum Pubns., Inc.

Earhart, Kristin. Mountain Mission (Race the Wild #6) 2016. (Race the Wild Ser.: 6). (ENG.). 144p. (J). (gr. 2-5). pap. 4.99 *(978-0-545-94065-8(6),* Scholastic Paperbacks) Scholastic, Inc.

Fujita, Rima. Save the Himalayas. 2011. (ENG, JPN & TIB., Illus.). 44p. 19.95 *(978-1-935548-09-6(3))* One Peace Bks., Inc.

Gunter, Miles & Shannon, Kelsey. Yeti vs. Vampire. 2012. (Illus.). 96p. (YA). pap. 12.95 *(978-0-9822253-5-6(0))* Antarctic Pr., Inc.

Ibbotson, Eva. The Abominables. Robinson, Fiona, illus. 2013. (ENG.). 272p. (J). (gr. 3-7). 16.95 *(978-1-4197-0789-6(2),* Amulet Bks.) Abrams, Inc.

—The Abominables. Robinson, Fiona, illus. 2014. (ENG.). 288p. (J). (gr. 3-7). pap. 8.95 *(978-1-4197-1215-9(2),* Amulet Bks.) Abrams, Inc.

Kerr, P. B., pseud. The Five Fakirs of Faizabad. 2011. (Children of the Lamp Ser.: Vol. 6). (ENG.). 448p. (J). (gr. 3-7). pap. 8.99 *(978-0-545-12659-5(2),* Scholastic Paperbacks) Scholastic, Inc.

Mills, Judith Christine. Carew. rev. ed. 2007. (ENG., Illus.). 248p. (J). (gr. 6). per. 7.95 *(978-1-55263-788-3(3))* Leaf Storm Pr.

Naga, Ann Whitehead. World above the Clouds: A Story of a Himalayan Ecosystem. 2005. (Soundprints' Wild Habitats Ser.). (ENG., Illus.). 36p. (J). (gr. 1-4). 8.95 *(978-1-59249-105-6(7),* SC7017) Soundprints.

Nelson, Peter. Creature Keepers & the Burgled Blizzard-Bristles. Rao, Rohitash, illus. 2016. (Creature Keepers Ser.: 3). 336p. (J). (gr. 3-7). 12.99 *(978-0-06-223647-0(4))* HarperCollins Pubs.

Spudich, Giulietta. The Amber Giant. 2017. 142p. (J). pap. 7.99 ***(978-1-941429-49-5(1))*** Handersen Publishing.

Sundance/Newbridge LLC Staff. The Abominable Snowman. 2005. (Choose Your Own Adventure Ser.). (gr. 4-8). pap. 5.50 *(978-0-7608-9693-8(3))* Sundance/Newbridge Educational Publishing.

HINDUISM

see also Yoga

Blake, Philip. We Are Hindus. 2016. (ENG., Illus.). 32p. (J). (gr. 4-6). pap. 11.99 *(978-1-4451-3889-3(1),* Franklin Watts) Hachette Children's Group GBR. Dist: Hachette Bk. Group.

Chopra, Deepak. Fire in the Heart: A Spiritual Guide for Teens. 2006. (ENG., Illus.). 208p. (YA). (gr. 7-12). pap. 14.99 *(978-0-689-86217-5(2),* Simon & Schuster Bks. For Young Readers) Simon & Schuster Bks. For Young Readers.

Cooper, Alison. Facts about Hinduism. 2010. (World Religions Ser.). (ENG.). 48p. (YA). lib. bdg. 29.25 *(978-1-61532-321-0(X),* Rosen Reference) Rosen Publishing Group, Inc., The.

Das, Rasamandala. Hinduism. 2007. (Atlas of World Faiths/Arcturus Ser.). (Illus.). 48p. (YA). (gr. 7-12). lib. bdg. 32.80 *(978-1-59920-057-6(0))* Black Rabbit Bks.

—Hinduism. 2005. (Religions of the World Ser.). (Illus.). 48p. (gr. 5-12). pap. 14.05 *(978-0-8368-5873-0(5));* lib. bdg. 31.00 *(978-0-8368-5867-9(0))* Stevens, Gareth Publishing LLLP. (Gareth Stevens Secondary Library).

Demi. The Fantastic Adventures of Krishna. Demi, illus. 2013. (ENG., Illus.). 44p. (J). (gr. -1-3). 19.95 *(978-1-937786-05-2(6),* Wisdom Tales) World Wisdom, Inc.

Dicker, Katie & Vekaria, Alka. I Belong to the Hindu Faith. 2009. (I Belong Ser.). (Illus.). 24p. (J). (ENG.). pap. 8.25 *(978-1-4358-8620-9(8),* PowerKids Pr.); (gr. 1-4). lib. bdg. 22.60 *(978-1-4358-3033-2(4))* Rosen Publishing Group, Inc., The.

Doherty, Vrinda & Valmiki. Prince Rama of the Solar Dynasty Pt. 1: Prince in Exile, the Journey Begins. Doherty, Ann, illus. 2011. (ENG.). 212p. 29.95 *(978-0-9817273-1-8(X))* Torchlight Publishing.

Elby, Tristan. Hinduism. 2017. (ENG.). 40p. (J). (gr. 6-9). pap. 11.99 ***(978-0-00-822775-3(6))*** HarperCollins Pubs. Ltd. GBR. Dist: Independent Pubs. Group.

Elby, Tristan & McKain, Neil. World Religions: Hinduism, Buddhism & Sikhism. 2017. (ENG.). 120p. (J). (gr. 6-9). pap. 29.99 ***(978-0-00-822769-2(1))*** HarperCollins Pubs. Ltd. GBR. Dist: Independent Pubs. Group.

Ganeri, Anita. Hindu Festivals Through the Year. 2003. (Year of Festivals Ser.). 30p. (J). lib. bdg. 24.25 *(978-1-58340-372-3(8))* Black Rabbit Bks.

—Hindu Stories. Phillips, Rachael, illus. 2014. (Storyteller Ser.). (ENG.). 32p. (J). (gr. 2-4). pap. 10.99 *(978-1-78388-008-9(2))* Tulip Books GBR. Dist: Independent Pubs. Group.

—The Ramayana & Other Hindu Texts. 2003. 30p. (J). lib. bdg. 24.25 *(978-1-58340-242-9(X))* Black Rabbit Bks.

Gerner, Katy. Hinduism. 2008. (Religions Around the World Ser.). 32p. (gr. 3-18). lib. bdg. 18.56 *(978-0-7614-3166-4(7),* Benchmark Bks.) Marshall Cavendish Corp.

Hawker, Frances & Resi, Putu. Hinduism in Bali. Campbell, Bruce, photos by. 2009. (ENG., Illus.). 32p. (J). (gr. 3-6). *(978-0-7787-5008-6(6));* pap. *(978-0-7787-5025-3(6))* Crabtree Publishing Co.

Jani, Mahendra & Jani, Vandana. What You Will See Inside a Hindu Temple. Bhargava, Neirah & Dave, Vijay, photos by. 2005. (What You Will See Inside ... Ser.). (ENG., Illus.). 32p. (J). (gr. 3-7). 17.99 *(978-1-59473-116-7(0),* 9781594731167, Skylight Paths Publishing) LongHill Partners, Inc.

Johari, Harish & Sperling, Vatsala. How Parvati Won the Heart of Shiva. Weltevrede, Pieter, illus. 2004. (Classic Indian Stories for Children Ser.). (ENG.). 32p. (J). (gr. -1-6). 15.95 *(978-1-59143-042-1(9),* Bear Cub Bks.) Bear & Co.

Jones, Constance A. & Ryan, James D. Encyclopedia of Hinduism. 2007. (Encyclopedia of World Religions Ser.). (Illus.). 592p. (C). (gr. 9). per. 21.95 *(978-0-8160-7336-8(8),* Checkmark Bks.) Facts On File, Inc.

Kelkar, Gauri. Little Monk's Durga. 2011. (ENG., Illus.). 60p. 14.95 *(978-81-8328-190-4(7))* Wisdom Tree IND. Dist: SCB Distributors.

—Little Monk's Lakshmi. 2011. (ENG., Illus.). 60p. 14.95 *(978-81-8328-191-1(5))* Wisdom Tree IND. Dist: SCB Distributors.

—Little Monk's Parvati. 2011. (ENG.). 60p. 14.95 *(978-81-8328-192-8(3))* Wisdom Tree IND. Dist: SCB Distributors.

—Little Monk's Saraswati. 2011. (ENG.). 60p. 14.95 *(978-81-8328-189-8(3))* Wisdom Tree IND. Dist: SCB Distributors.

Kerner, Stuart, et al. Hinduism. 2012. (Illus.). 72p. (gr. 7-9). pap. 29.50 *(978-1-4441-2222-0(3))* Hodder Education Group GBR. Dist: Trans-Atlantic Pubns., Inc.

Krishnaswami, Uma. The Broken Tusk: Stories of the Hindu God Ganesha. 2006. (ENG., Illus.). 128p. (J). (gr. 3-7). per. 16.95 *(978-0-87483-806-0(1))* August Hse. Pubs., Inc.

Marsico, Katie. Hinduism. 2017. (21st Century Skills Library: Global Citizens: World Religions Ser.). (ENG., Illus.). 32p. (J). (gr. 4-7). lib. bdg. 29.93 *(978-1-63472-157-8(8),* 209200) Cherry Lake Publishing.

Parker-Rock, Michelle. Diwali: The Hindu Festival of Lights, Feasts, & Family. 2004. (Finding Out about Holidays Ser.). (Illus.). 48p. (J). lib. bdg. 25.27 *(978-0-7660-2235-5(8))* Enslow Pubs., Inc.

Patel, Sanjay J. & Haynes, Emily. Ganesha's Sweet Tooth. 2012. (ENG., Illus.). 40p. (J). (gr. -1-3). 16.99 *(978-1-4521-0362-4(3))* Chronicle Bks. LLC.

Peppas, Lynn. Holi. 2009. (Celebrations in My World Ser.). (ENG., Illus.). 32p. (J). (gr. k-2). pap. *(978-0-7787-4771-0(9));* (gr. 1-3). *(978-0-7787-4753-6(0))* Crabtree Publishing Co.

Pomaska, Anna. My First Mandalas Coloring Book. 2008. (Dover Coloring Bks.). (ENG., Illus.). 32p. (J). (gr. -1-2). 3.99 *(978-0-486-46556-2(X))* Dover Pubns., Inc.

Prime, Ranchor. Hinduism. (Illus.). 64p. (YA). (gr. 4-18). lib. bdg. 29.95 *(978-1-59389-129-9(6))* Chrysalis Education.

Rajan, Gayatri. The Story of Santoshi Devi. (Illus.). 40p. (Orig.). (J). (gr. k-6). pap. *(978-0-9644226-0-5(3))* Buddhi Pubns.

Rangan, Nalini. Hinduism. 2017. (J). ***(978-1-4222-3818-9(0))*** Mason Crest.

H
I

Rossi, Ann. India. 2007. (Reading Expeditions Ser.). (ENG., Illus.). 24p. (J). pap. 14.95 *(978-0-7922-4537-7(7))* CENGAGE Learning.

See & Paint: Gods & Goddesses. 18p. (J). (gr. -1-5). 2.95 *(978-81-7120-245-4(4))* Sri Ramakrishna Math IND. Dist: Vedanta Pr.

Senker, Cath. Hinduism: Signs, Symbols, Stories. 2009. (Religious Signs, Symbols, & Stories Ser.). (Illus.). 32p. (J). (ENG.). pap. 10.00 *(978-1-4358-3046-2(6))*; lib. bdg. 25.25 *(978-1-4358-3038-7(5))* Rosen Publishing Group, Inc., The. (PowerKids Pr.).

—My Hindu Year. 2007. (Year of Religious Festivals Ser.). (Illus.). 32p. (J). (gr. 1-4). lib. bdg. 25.25 *(978-1-4042-3731-5(3))* Rosen Publishing Group, Inc., The.

Sperling, Vatsala. The Magical Adventures of Krishna: How a Mischief Maker Saved the World. Weltevrede, Pieter, illus. 2nd ed. 2009. (ENG.). 32p. (J). (gr. -1-6). 15.95 *(978-1-59143-110-7(7))*, Bear Cub Bks.) Bear & Co.

Stegenga, Wil. Sacred Yantra Coloring Book. 2009. (Dover Design Coloring Bks.). (ENG., Illus.). 32p. (gr. 3-5). pap. 3.99 *(978-0-486-47081-8(4))* Dover Pubns., Inc.

Wallace, Holly. Hinduism: Babu's Story. 2013. (Our World of Faith Ser.). (Illus.). 32p. (J). (gr. 3-6). *(978-1-84898-616-9(5)*, TickTock Books) Octopus Publishing Group.

White, Bender Richardson. Hinduism. 4th rev. ed. 2009. (World Religions Ser.). (Illus.). 144p. (J). (gr. 6-12). 40.00 *(978-1-60413-108-6(X)*, Chelsea Hse.) Facts On File, Inc.

Woods, Christopher & McClintic, Ben, illus. Where's Hanuman? 2009. (ENG.). 32p. (gr. 3-18). 9.95 *(978-0-9779785-8-8(3))* Torchlight Publishing.

Young, Serinity. Hinduism. 2006. (World Religions Ser.). (Illus.). 144p. (gr. 7-7). lib. bdg. 42.79 *(978-0-7614-2116-0(5)*, Benchmark Bks.) Marshall Cavendish Corp.

HIP-HOP MUSIC

see Rap (Music)

HIPPIES—FICTION

Gutman, Dan. Mr. Louie Is Screwy! Paillot, Jim, illus. 2007. (My Weird School Ser.: 20). (ENG.). 112p. (J). (gr. 1-5). pap. 4.99 *(978-0-06-123479-8(6))* HarperCollins Pubs.

Horvath, Polly. Mr. & Mrs. Bunny: Detectives Extraordinaire! Blackall, Sophie, illus. 2012. (ENG.). 256p. (J). (gr. 3-7). 16.99 *(978-0-375-86755-2(4)*, Schwartz & Wade Bks.) Random Hse. Children's Bks.

Johnson, J. J. This Girl Is Different. 1 vol. 2011. (ENG.). 288p. (YA). (gr. 7-11). 16.95 *(978-1-56145-578-2(4))* Peachtree Pubs.

Ostow, Micol. Family. (ENG.). 384p. (J). (gr. 9). 2013. pap. 9.99 *(978-1-60684-393-2(1))* 2011. 17.99 *(978-1-60684-155-6(6))* Lerner Publishing Group. (Carolrhoda Lab™).

Partridge, Elizabeth. Dogtag Summer. (ENG.). 240p. (YA). (gr. 3-12). 2012. pap. 7.99 *(978-1-59990-829-8(8)*, 9781599908298) 2011. 16.99 *(978-1-59990-183-1(8)*, 9781599901831) Bloomsbury Publishing USA. (Bloomsbury USA Childrens).

Pikey, Mikey. The Diamond Tree. 2007. 378p. pap. 31.95 *(978-1-84728-234-7(2))* Lulu Pr., Inc.

Ziegler, Jennifer. How Not to Be Popular. 2010. (ENG.). 348p. (YA). (gr. 7). mass mkt. 8.99 *(978-0-440-24024-2(7)*, Delacorte Bks. for Young Readers) Random Hse. Children's Bks.

HIPPOCRATES

Gow, Mary. The Greatest Doctor of Ancient Times: Hippocrates & His Oath. 2009. (Great Minds of Ancient Science & Math Ser.). (Illus.). 128p. (J). (gr. 4-7). lib. bdg. 33.27 *(978-0-7660-3118-0(7))* Enslow Pubs., Inc.

Jankowski, Connie. Hippocrates: Making the Way for Medicine. 1 vol. 2007. (Science Readers Ser.). (ENG.). 32p. (J). (gr. 3-3). pap. 8.99 *(978-0-7439-0596-1(2))* Shell Educational Publishing.

Lusted, Marcia. Hippocrates. 2017. (Junior Biography From Ancient Civilization Ser.). (gr. 4-6). 29.95 *(978-1-68020-030-0(5))* Mitchell Lane Pubs., Inc.

Whiting, Jim. The Life & Times of Hippocrates. 2006. (Biography from Ancient Civilizations Ser.). (Illus.). 48p. (J). (gr. 3-7). lib. bdg. 29.95 *(978-1-58415-512-6(4)*, 1259600) Mitchell Lane Pubs., Inc.

HIPPOPOTAMUS

AZ Books, creator. Hello, I'm Hippo! 2012. (Who Lives in the Book? Ser.). (ENG., Illus.). 10p. (J). (gr. -1-k). bds. 11.95 *(978-1-61889-212-6(6))* AZ Bks. LLC.

Barbe-Julien, Colette. Little Hippopotamuses. 2005. (Born to Be Wild Ser.). (Illus.). 24p. (gr. k-3). lib. bdg. 23.00 *(978-0-8368-4736-9(9)*, Gareth Stevens Learning Library) Stevens, Gareth Publishing LLLP.

Borgert-Spaniol, Megan. Baby Hippos. 2015. (Super Cute! Ser.). (ENG., Illus.). 24p. (J). (gr. k-3). lib. bdg. 25.95 *(978-1-62617-218-0(8)*, Blastoff! Readers) Bellwether Media.

Brannon, Cecelia H. Baby Hippos at the Zoo. 2016. (All about Baby Zoo Animals Ser.). (ENG.). 24p. (J). (gr. k-1). pap. 9.35 *(978-0-7660-7145-2(6))*; (Illus.). lib. bdg. 22.60 *(978-0-7660-7148-3(0))* Enslow Pubs., Inc.

Carr, Aaron. Hippo. 2014. (Illus.). 24p. (J). *(978-1-62127-283-0(4))* Weigl Pubs., Inc.

Clarke, Penny. Hippos. 2009. (Scary Creatures Ser.). (ENG., Illus.). 32p. (J). (gr. 3-5). 27.00 *(978-0-531-21671-2(3)*, Children's Pr.); pap. 8.95 *(978-0-531-21042-0(1)*, Watts, Franklin) Scholastic Library Publishing.

Claybourne, Anna. Hippo. 2012. (Animals on the Edge Ser.). (ENG., Illus.). 48p. (gr. 3-8). pap. 12.00 *(978-1-4081-4961-4(3)*, 9781408149614, Bloomsbury USA Childrens) Bloomsbury Publishing USA.

Cunningham, Kevin. Egrets & Hippos. 2016. (21st Century Junior Library: Better Together Ser.). (ENG., Illus.). 24p. (J). (gr. 2-5). 27.07 *(978-1-63471-081-7(9)*, 208403) Cherry Lake Publishing.

DiSiena, Laura Lyn & Eliot, Hannah. Hippos Can't Swim: And Other Fun Facts. Oswald, Pete, illus. 2014. (Did You Know? Ser.). (ENG.). 32p. (J). (gr. -1-3). 17.99 *(978-1-4424-9352-0(6))*; pap. 5.99 *(978-1-4424-9324-7(0))* Little Simon. (Little Simon).

Doudna, Kelly. It's a Baby Hippopotamus!, 1 vol. 2009. (Baby African Animals Ser.). (ENG., Illus.). 24p. (J). (gr. k-3). lib. bdg. 24.21 *(978-1-60453-155-8(X)*, SandCastle) ABDO Publishing Co.

Edwards, Roberta. Best Friends: The True Story of Owen & Mzee. Schwartz, Carol, illus. 2007. (Penguin Young Readers, Level 2 Ser.). (ENG.). 32p. (J). (gr. 1-2). mass mkt. 3.99 *(978-0-448-44567-0(0)*, Penguin Young Readers) Penguin Young Readers Group.

—Best Friends: The True Story of Owen & Mzee. Schwartz, Carol, illus. 2007. (All Aboard Science Reader Ser.). 32p. (gr. -1-3). 14.00 *(978-0-7569-8167-9(0))* Perfection Learning Corp.

Evento, Susan. The Mighty Hippopotamus. 2003. (Illus.). 32p. (J). pap. 6.00 *(978-1-59034-493-4(6))* Mondo Publishing.

Gannij, Joan. Hidden Hippo. Beaton, Clare, illus. 2011. (ENG.). 32p. (J). (gr. -1-2). pap. 6.99 *(978-1-84686-533-6(6))* Barefoot Bks., Inc.

Gareth Stevens Editorial Staff. Hippos. 2004. (All about Wild Animals Ser.). (Illus.). 32p. (gr. k-4). lib. bdg. 26.00 *(978-0-8368-4118-3(2)*, Gareth Stevens Learning Library) Stevens, Gareth Publishing LLLP.

Gish, Melissa. Hippopotamuses. 2013. (Illus.). 48p. (J). 35.65 *(978-1-60818-288-6(6)*, Creative Education) Creative Co., The.

—Living Wild: Hippos. 2014. (Living Wild Ser.). (ENG., Illus.). 48p. (J). (gr. 4-7). pap. 12.00 *(978-0-89812-841-3(2)*, Creative Paperbacks) Creative Co., The.

Green, Jen. Hippopotamus. 2009. (Illus.). 52p. (J). *(978-0-7172-6297-7(9))* Grolier, Ltd.

Gregory, Josh. Hippopotamuses. 2016. (Nature's Children Ser.). (ENG., Illus.). 48p. (J). pap. 6.95 *(978-0-531-21933-1(X)*, Children's Pr.) Scholastic Library Publishing.

Hatkoff, Craig, et al. Owen & Mzee: The Language of Friendship. Greste, Peter, photos by. 2007. (Owen & Mzee Ser.). (ENG., Illus.). 40p. (J). (gr. -1-3). 18.99 *(978-0-439-89959-8(1)*, Scholastic Pr.) Scholastic, Inc.

—Owen & Mzee: The True Story of a Remarkable Friendship. Greste, Peter, illus. 2006. (Owen & Mzee Ser.). (ENG.). 40p. (J). (gr. -1-3). 17.99 *(978-0-439-82973-1(9)*, Scholastic Pr.) Scholastic, Inc.

Heos, Bridget. Do You Really Want to Meet a Hippopotamus? Fabbri, Daniele, illus. 2017. (Do You Really Want to Meet... Wild Animals? Ser.). (ENG.). 24p. (J). (gr. 1-3). pap. 8.99 *(978-1-68152-117-6(2))* Amicus.

—Do You Really Want to Meet a Hippopotamus? Fabbri, Daniele, illus. 2016. (Do You Really Want to Meet... Wild Animals? Ser.). (ENG.). 24p. (J). (gr. k-3). 20.95 *(978-1-60753-946-9(2))* Amicus Publishing.

Hippos. 2003. (J). per. *(978-1-57657-944-2(1))* Paradise Pr., Inc.

Hippos: Individual Title Six-Packs. (Story Steps Ser.). (gr. k-2). 32.00 *(978-0-7635-9618-7(3))* Rigby Education.

Huge Hippos. 2013. (Great Big Animals Ser.). 24p. (J). (gr. k-2). pap. 48.90 *(978-1-4339-9438-8(0))* Stevens, Gareth Publishing LLLP.

Jango-Cohen, Judith. Hippopotamuses. 2006. (Animals Animals Ser.). (Illus.). 48p. (gr. 3-7). lib. bdg. 29.93 *(978-0-7614-2238-9(2)*, Benchmark Bks.) Marshall Cavendish Corp.

London, Jonathan. Hippos Are Huge! Trueman, Matthew, illus. (Read & Wonder Ser.). (ENG.). 32p. (J). (gr. k-3). 2017. 6.99 *(978-0-7636-7952-1(6))* 2015. 16.99 *(978-0-7636-6592-0(4))* Candlewick Pr.

Lunis, Natalie. Hippo: River Horse. 2016. (Animal Loudmouths Ser.). (ENG.). 24p. (J). (gr. k-3). pap. 7.95 ***(978-1-944998-45-5(4))*** Bearport Publishing Co., Inc.

—Hippo — River Horse. 2011. (Animal Loudmouths: Noisy Animals Ser.). 24p. (J). (gr. k-3). lib. bdg. 22.61 *(978-1-61772-275-2(8))* Bearport Publishing Co., Inc.

—Hippopotamus. 2016. (J). lib. bdg. *(978-1-62724-820-4(X))* Bearport Publishing Co., Inc.

Marsico, Katie. Hippopotamuses. 2012. (21st Century Basic Skills Library: Baby Zoo Animals Ser.). (ENG.). 24p. (gr. k-3). 22.79 *(978-1-61080-458-5(9)*, 202068); pap. 12.79 *(978-1-61080-632-9(8)*, 202242) Cherry Lake Publishing.

Masterson, Josephine. A Hippo's Home. 2015. (Rosen REAL Readers: STEM & STEAM Collection). (ENG.). 8p. pap. 5.46 *(978-1-4994-9635-2(4)*, Rosen Classroom) Rosen Publishing Group, Inc., The.

Murray, Julie. Hippopotamuses. 1 vol. 2012. (ENG.). 32p. 28.50 *(978-1-61783-220-8(0)*, Big Buddy Bks.) ABDO Publishing Co.

Nagelhout, Ryan. Huge Hippos. 2013. (Great Big Animals Ser.). 24p. (J). (gr. k-2). pap. 8.15 *(978-1-4339-9437-1(2))*; (ENG., Illus.). lib. bdg. 22.60 *(978-1-4339-9436-4(4))* Stevens, Gareth Publishing LLLP.

—Huge Hippos / Grandes Hipopótamos. 2013. (Great Big Animals / Superanimales Ser.). (SPA.). 24p. (J). (gr. k-2). 22.60 *(978-1-4339-9440-1(2))* Stevens, Gareth Publishing LLLP.

Owens, Henry. How to Track a Hippo. 1. 2014. (Scatalog: a Kid's Field Guide to Animal Poop Ser.). (ENG.). 24p. (J). (gr. k-5). 23.60 *(978-1-61533-888-7(8)*, Windmill Bks.) Rosen Publishing Group, Inc., The.

Owings, Lisa. The Hippopotamus. 2011. (Nature's Deadliest Ser.). (ENG., Illus.). 24p. (YA). (gr. 3-8). lib. bdg. 25.95 *(978-1-60014-666-4(X)*, Pilot Bks.) Bellwether Media.

—Meet a Baby Hippo. 2015. (ENG., Illus.). 32p. (J). (gr. k-2). 26.65 *(978-1-4677-8115-2(0)*, Lerner Pubns.) Lerner Publishing Group.

Page, Robin & Jenkins, Steve. How to Clean a Hippopotamus: A Look at Unusual Animal Partnerships. Jenkins, Steve, illus. 2010. (ENG., Illus.). 32p. (J). (gr. 1-4). 17.99 *(978-0-547-24515-7(7))* Houghton Mifflin Harcourt Publishing Co.

Pelusey, Michael & Pelusey, Jane. Rhinoceroses & Hippopotamuses. 2008. (Zoo Animals Ser.). 32p. (gr. 2-3). lib. bdg. 18.56 *(978-0-7614-3150-3(0)*, Benchmark Bks.) Marshall Cavendish Corp.

Pingry, Patricia A. Baby Hippopotamus. Sharp, Chris, illus. 2004. 26p. (J). bds. 6.95 *(978-0-8249-6554-9(X)*, Ideal Pubns.) Worthy Publishing.

Rake, Jody Sullivan. Hippos: In the Wild. 2010. (Killer Animals Ser.). (ENG.). 32p. (gr. 1-2). lib. bdg. 26.65 *(978-1-4296-4010-7(3)*, Blazers) Capstone Press of Coughlan Cos.

Reade, Clara. Hippos. 2012. (PowerKids Readers: Safari Animals Ser.). (ENG., Illus.). 24p. (J). (gr. k-2). pap. 8.25 *(978-1-4488-7472-9(6))*; lib. bdg. 22.60 *(978-1-4488-7392-0(4))* Rosen Publishing Group, Inc., The. (PowerKids Pr.).

Reher, Matt. Hippos Eat. 2015. (1G Science Ser.). (ENG., Illus.). 28p. (J). pap. 5.99 *(978-1-63437-156-8(9))* American Reading Co.

Riggs, Kate. Hippopotamuses. 2016. (Amazing Animals Ser.). (Illus.). 24p. (J). (ENG.). (gr. 1-3). pap. 8.99 *(978-1-62832-218-7(7)*, Creative Paperbacks); 28.95 *(978-1-60818-612-9(1)*, Creative Education) Creative Co., The.

Ring, Susan. Herbie. 2009. (J). *(978-1-60596-662-5(2))*; *(978-1-60596-661-8(4))* Weigl Pubs., Inc.

—Project Hippopotamus. Kissock, Heather & Marshall, Diana, eds. 2003. (Zoo Life Ser.). (Illus.). 24p. (J). pap. 8.95 *(978-1-59036-057-6(5))* Weigl Pubs., Inc.

—Project Hippopotamus. 2003. (Zoo Babies Ser.). (Illus.). 24p. (J). (gr. 2-4). lib. bdg. 24.45 *(978-1-59036-013-2(3))* Weigl Pubs., Inc.

Schuetz, Kari. Hippopotamuses. 2011. (Animal Safari Ser.). (ENG., Illus.). 24p. (J). (gr. k-3). lib. bdg. 25.95 *(978-1-60014-606-0(6)*, Blastoff! Readers) Bellwether Media.

Scott, Jonathan & Scott, Angela. Africa's Big Three. Scott, Jonathan & Scott, Angela, illus. 2006. (Collins Big Cat Ser.). (ENG., Illus.). 56p. (J). (gr. 2-2). pap. 6.99 *(978-0-00-718693-8(2))* HarperCollins Pubs. Ltd. GBR. Dist: Independent Pubs. Group.

Shea, Therese. 20 Fun Facts about Hippos. 2012. (Fun Fact File: Animals! Ser.). (ENG.). 32p. (J). (gr. 2-5). pap. 10.50 *(978-1-4339-6519-7(4))*; lib. bdg. 25.25 *(978-1-4339-6517-3(8))* Stevens, Gareth Publishing LLLP. (Gareth Stevens Learning Library).

Smith, Lucy. Hippos: Huge & Hungry. 2009. 24p. (YA). pap. 8.25 *(978-1-4358-3280-0(9))* Rosen Publishing Group, Inc., The.

Stone, Tanya Lee. Hippos. 2003. (Wild Wild World Ser.). 24p. (YA). 24.94 *(978-1-56711-815-5(1)*, Blackbirch Pr., Inc.) Cengage Gale.

Storad, Conrad J. Hippos. 2005. (Early Bird Nature Bks.). (ENG., Illus.). 48p. (gr. 2-5). lib. bdg. 26.60 *(978-0-8225-2869-2(X)*, Lerner Pubns.) Lerner Publishing Group.

Taylor, Trace. You Think You Know Hippos. Taylor, Trace, illus. 2008. (1-3Y Wild Animals Ser.). (ENG., Illus.). 24p. (J). (gr. k-2). pap. 5.99 *(978-1-59301-267-0(5))* American Reading Co.

Ticktock Media, Ltd. Staff. What Do Hippos Do? 2008. (What Do Animals Do? Ser.). (ENG.). 10p. (J). (gr. k — 1). bds. 4.95 *(978-1-84696-791-7(0)*, TickTock Books) Octopus Publishing Group GBR. Dist: Independent Pubs. Group.

Turnbull, Stephanie. Hippo. 2015. (Big Beasts Ser.). (Illus.). 24p. (gr. k-3). 28.50 *(978-1-62588-165-6(7))* Black Rabbit Bks.

—Hippo. 2015. (ENG., Illus.). 24p. (J). pap. 8.95 *(978-1-77092-213-6(X))* RiverStream Publishing.

Von Zumbusch, Amelie. Hippos. 2007. (Safari Animals Ser.). (Illus.). 24p. (J). (gr. 3-7). lib. bdg. 22.60 *(978-1-4042-3617-2(1)*, PowerKids Pr.) Rosen Publishing Group, Inc., The.

von Zumbusch, Amelie. Hippos. 2009. (Safari Animals Ser.). 24p. (gr. 1-1). 42.50 *(978-1-60852-952-0(5)*, PowerKids Pr.) Rosen Publishing Group, Inc., The.

Von Zumbusch, Amelie. Hippos/Hipopótamos. 2007. (Safari Animals / Animales de Safari Ser.). (SPA & ENG., Illus.). 24p. (J). (gr. k-3). lib. bdg. 22.60 *(978-1-4042-7607-9(6)*, PowerKids Pr.) Rosen Publishing Group, Inc., The.

von Zumbusch, Amelie. Hippos/Hipopótamos. 2009. (Safari Animals/Animales de safari Ser.). 24p. (gr. 1-1). 42.50 *(978-1-60852-977-3(0)*, Editorial Buenas Letras) Rosen Publishing Group, Inc., The.

Walker, Sally M. Hippos. rev. ed. 2008. (Nature Watch Ser.). (ENG.). 48p. (gr. 4-8). 27.93 *(978-0-8225-7512-2(4)*, Lerner Pubns.) Lerner Publishing Group.

Wilsdon, Christina. Hippopotamus. 2006. (Illus.). 45p. (J). *(978-1-59939-077-2(9)*, Reader's Digest Young Families, Inc.) Studio Fun International.

—Hippopotamuses. 2009. (Amazing Animals Ser.). 48p. (J). (gr. 2-6). pap. 10.50 *(978-1-4339-2123-0(5)*, Gareth Stevens Learning Library); (YA). (gr. 3-6). lib. bdg. 28.00 *(978-0-8368-9119-5(8))* Stevens, Gareth Publishing LLLP.

HIPPOPOTAMUS—FICTION

Andrade, Maria J. Why Dear Mrs Sullivan Is Distressed! 2012. 30p. 19.95 *(978-0-9706347-8-8(1))* Clara Publishing.

Bauer, Marion Dane. A Mama for Owen. Butler, John, illus. 2007. (ENG.). 32p. (J). (gr. -1-3). 17.99 *(978-0-689-85787-4(X)*, Simon & Schuster Bks. For Young Readers) Simon & Schuster Bks. For Young Readers.

Baugh, Ayana Sala. Loopiehotamus, the Chihuahua Who Thinks He Is a Hippopotamus: A Loopiehotamus Christmas. 2012. 32p. pap. 19.99 *(978-1-4685-8111-9(2))* AuthorHouse.

—Loopiehotamus, the Chihuahua Who Thinks He Is a Hippopotamus: His Life. 2011. 24p. pap. 16.99 *(978-1-4567-4002-3(4))* AuthorHouse.

—Loopiehotamus, the Chihuahua Who Thinks He Is a Hippopotamus Book: His Journey. 2011. 20p. pap. 14.99 *(978-1-4634-3437-3(5))* AuthorHouse.

Bedford, David & Worthington, Leonie. Who's Laughing? 2007. (Illus.). 16p. pap. *(978-1-921272-11-0(2))* Little Hare Bks. AUS. Dist: HarperCollins Pubs. Australia.

Benchmark Education Co., LLC. Happy Hippo Holiday Big Book. 2014. (Shared Reading Foundations Ser.). (J). (gr. -1). *(978-1-4509-9425-5(3))* Benchmark Education Co.

Bloom, Becky. Leo & Lester. Biet, Pascal, illus. 2003. (J). 32p. 15.95 *(978-1-59034-582-5(7))*; 33p. pap. *(978-1-59034-583-2(5))* Mondo Publishing.

Boniface, William. Lights Out, Night's Out. Kirkova, Milena, illus. 2011. (ENG.). 24p. (J). pap. 6.99 *(978-1-4494-0236-5(4))* Andrews McMeel Publishing.

Bonwill, Ann. I Am Not a Copycat! Rickerty, Simon, illus. 2013. (ENG.). 32p. (J). (gr. -1-1). 15.99 *(978-1-4424-8053-7(X))* Simon & Schuster Children's Publishing.

Boynton, Sandra. Belly Button Book! (Lap Edition) 2011. (ENG., Illus.). 24p. (J). (gr. k — 1). bds. 11.95 *(978-0-7611-6618-4(1)*, 16618) Workman Publishing Co., Inc.

—Hippos Go Berserk! Boynton, Sandra, illus. 2009. (ENG., Illus.). 32p. (J). 9.99 *(978-1-4169-9619-4(2)*, Little Simon) Little Simon.

—Your Personal Penguin. 2006. (ENG., Illus.). 24p. (J). (gr. k — 1). bds. 6.95 *(978-0-7611-4372-7(6)*, 14372) Workman Publishing Co., Inc.

Brez, Lisa. Hickerdoodle Meets a Chigger. l.t. ed. 2004. (Illus.). 40p. (J). per. 6.99 *(978-0-9743758-5-4(3))* Red Engine Pr.

Brown, Jami L. Poot: The Pink Boy. 2011. 24p. pap. 16.99 *(978-1-4634-2283-7(0))* AuthorHouse.

Burningham, John. Tug-of-War. Burningham, John, illus. 2013. (ENG., Illus.). 32p. (J). (gr. k-3). 16.99 *(978-0-7636-6575-3(4))* Candlewick Pr.

Charlesworth, Liza & Scholastic, Inc. Staff. The Happy Hippos. Mahoney, Daniel J., illus. 2005. (Number Tales Ser.). (ENG.). 16p. (J). (gr. -1-1). pap. 2.99 *(978-0-439-69023-2(4))* Scholastic, Inc.

Chiarini, Chynna. Hippy Potto's Travel Adventure. 2010. 48p. pap. 11.99 *(978-1-4520-3447-8(8))* AuthorHouse.

Crow, Kristyn. Hello, Hippo! Goodbye, Bird! Bernatene, Poly, illus. 2016. (ENG.). 32p. (J). (gr. -1-2). 15.99 *(978-0-553-50990-8(X)*, Knopf Bks. for Young Readers) Random Hse. Children's Bks.

Dahl, Michael. Hippo Says "Excuse Me" Vidal, Oriol, illus. 2011. (Hello Genius Ser.). (ENG.). 20p. (gr. 1-2). bds. 7.99 *(978-1-4048-6787-1(2))* Picture Window Bks.

Davis, Martine. There's a Red Hippo at My Door. 2012. 24p. pap. 13.99 *(978-1-4772-8070-6(7))* AuthorHouse.

Delval, Marie-Hélène. Hippopo va se Baigner. 12.95 *(978-2-227-75604-5(7))* Bayard Editions FRA. Dist: Distribooks, Inc.

Denis, Kasey. Henry the Hippo. 2012. 24p. pap. 17.99 *(978-1-4772-6558-1(9))* AuthorHouse.

Derubertis, Barbara. Hanna Hippo's Horrible Hiccups. 2010. pap. 45.32 *(978-0-7613-6510-5(9))* Kane Press, Inc.

deRubertis, Barbara. Hanna Hippo's Horrible Hiccups. Alley, R. W., illus. 2010. (Animal Antics A to Z Ser.). 32p. (J). (gr. -1-3). pap. 7.95 *(978-1-57565-312-9(5))*; lib. bdg. 22.60 *(978-1-57565-319-8(2))* Kane Press, Inc.

deRubertis, Barbara & DeRubertis, Barbara. Hanna Hippo's Horrible Hiccups. Alley, R. W., illus. 2012. (Animal Antics A to Z Ser.). 32p. (J). (gr. 2 — 1). cd-rom 7.95 *(978-1-57565-401-0(6))* Kane Press, Inc.

Durber, Matt & Brooks, Felicity. Muddy Hippo. Wells, Rachel, illus. 2007. (Play Bks). 10p. (J). (gr. -1-k). bds. 10.99 *(978-0-7945-1688-8(2)*, Usborne) EDC Publishing.

Elschner, Géraldine. The Little Hippo: A Children's Book Inspired by Egyptian Art. Klauss, Anja, illus. 2014. (ENG.). 32p. (J). (gr. -1-3). 14.95 *(978-3-7913-7167-2(3))* Prestel Verlag GmbH & Co KG. DEU. Dist: Penguin Random Hse. LLC.

Finke, Margot. Ruthie & the Hippo's Fat Behind. Snider, K. C., illus. 2010. 16p. pap. 10.95 *(978-1-61633-059-0(7))* Guardian Angel Publishing, Inc.

Fliess, Sue. A Dress for Me!, 0 vols. Laughead, Mike, illus. 2012. (ENG.). 24p. (J). (gr. k-3). 12.99 *(978-0-7614-6148-7(5)*, 9780761461487, Amazon Children's Publishing) Amazon Publishing.

—Shoes for Me!, 0 vols. Laughead, Mike, illus. 2011. (ENG.). 24p. (J). (gr. -1-3). 12.99 *(978-0-7614-5825-8(5)*, 9780761458258, Amazon Children's Publishing) Amazon Publishing.

Foust, Cindy. Harry, harry Hippo. 2006. (J). 12.94 *(978-0-9749220-8-9(0))* Alpha-kidZ.

Friden, Chris. Bathtime with Bubbles. Zapater Oliva, Carlos & Depew, Robert, illus. 2008. (J). *(978-0-9801849-2-1(4))* Haydenburri Lane.

Gannij, Joan. Hidden Hippo. Beaton, Clare, illus. 2009. (ENG.). 24p. (J). (gr. -1-k). 7.99 *(978-1-84686-329-5(5))* Barefoot Bks., Inc.

Gazarik, Rebecca Renee. The Caribbean Caribou's Ancient Discovery. Patterson, Aaron James, ed. Gazarik, Rebecca Renee, illus. 2012. (Illus.). 36p. (J). *(978-0-9802258-2-2(5))* Gazarik, Rebecca.

Green, John Patrick. Hippopotamister. 2016. (ENG., Illus.). 96p. (J). 17.99 *(978-1-62672-200-2(5)*, 9781626722002, First Second Bks.) Roaring Brook Pr.

Harper, Jamie. Miss Mingo & the First Day of School. Harper, Jamie, illus. 2009. (ENG., Illus.). 32p. (J). (gr. -1-3). pap. 6.99 *(978-0-7636-4134-4(0))* Candlewick Pr.

Harris, Dee. I Am Not a Hippopotamus, I Am a Little Girl. Book. Bohart, Lisa, illus. 2011. 24p. pap. 12.95 *(978-1-61493-005-1(8))* Peppertree Pr., The.

Harrison, Kenny. Hide & Seek Harry at the Playground. Harrison, Kenny, illus. 2015. (ENG., Illus.). 20p. (J). (-k). bds. 6.99 *(978-0-7636-7347-5(1))* Candlewick Pr.

—Hide & Seek Harry on the Farm. Harrison, Kenny, illus. 2015. (ENG., Illus.). 20p. (J). (-k). bds. 6.99 *(978-0-7636-7370-3(6))* Candlewick Pr.

Hippo Pot & Hippo Tot, Set. A,6 Packs. (Supersonic Phonics Ser.). (gr. k-3). 29.00 *(978-0-7635-0532-5(3))* Rigby Education.

Hiskey, Iris. Hannah & the Hippo's No Mud Day. 2014. (ENG., Illus.). 32p. (J). (gr. -1-3). 16.99 *(978-1-4814-2537-7(4)*, Simon & Schuster Bks. For Young Readers) Simon & Schuster Bks. For Young Readers.

Horowitz, Dave. A Monkey among Us. Horowitz, Dave, illus. 2004. (Illus.). 40p. (J). (gr. -1-1). 14.99 *(978-0-06-054335-8(3)*, HarperFestival) HarperCollins Pubs.

Hoyes, Amy & Reimann, A. J. Happy the Hippo: Eats Healthy Food. Stewart, K. L., illus. 2013. 24p. pap. 9.99 *(978-1-938743-08-5(3))* Reimann Bks.

InSeon, Chae. Handy Mr. Hippo. YouDae, Kim, illus. rev. ed. 2014. (MySELF Bookshelf Ser.). (ENG.). 32p. (J). (gr. k-2). pap. 11.94 *(978-1-60357-661-1(4))*; lib. bdg. 25.27 *(978-1-59953-652-1(8))* Norwood Hse. Pr.

Jones, Shelley V. & Sprick, Marilyn. Turtle in the Tuba: Read Well Level K Unit 8 Storybook. McDonnell, Kevin, illus. 2004. (Read Well Level K Ser.). 20p. *(978-1-57035-672-8(6))* Cambium Education, Inc.

Landstrom, Lena. A Hippo's Tale. Sandin, Joan, tr. from SWE. 2007. (Illus.). 32p. (J). (gr. -1-1). 15.00 *(978-91-29-66603-8(1))* R & S Bks. SWE. Dist: Macmillan.

—The New Hippos. Sandin, Joan, tr. from SWE. 2003. (Illus.). 32p. (J). 15.00 *(978-91-29-65823-1(3))* R & S Bks. SWE. Dist: Macmillan.

Law, Felicia. Hudson the Hippo: A Tale of Self-Control. Danson, Lesley, illus. 2010. (Animal Fair Values Ser.). (ENG.). 32p. (J). (gr. -1-3). pap. 10.55

(978-1-60754-913-0(1)); lib. bdg. 22.60 (978-1-60754-904-8(2)) Windmill Bks.

Lester, Helen. Hurty Feelings. Munsinger, Lynn, illus. 2007. (ENG.). 32p. (J). (gr. -1-3). 7.99 (978-0-618-84062-5(1)) Houghton Mifflin Harcourt Publishing Co.

—Hurty Feelings. Munsinger, Lynn, illus. 2014. (Laugh-Along Lessons Ser.). (ENG.). 32p. (J). (gr. -1-3). 8.99 (978-0-544-10622-2(9)) Houghton Mifflin Harcourt Publishing Co.

London, Jonathan. Here Comes Doctor Hippo: A Little Hippo Story. Eduar, Gilles, illus. (Little Hippo Ser.). (ENG.). 32p. (J). (gr. -1-k). 2013. pap. 6.95 (978-1-62091-595-0(2)) 2012. 15.95 (978-1-59078-851-6(6)) Boyds Mills Pr.

—Here Comes Firefighter Hippo. Eduar, Gilles, illus. 2013. (Little Hippo Ser.). (ENG.). 32p. (J). (gr. -1-1). 15.95 (978-1-59078-968-1(7)) Boyds Mills Pr.

Long, Olivia. Hortense, the Happy Hippo. Long, Olivia, illus. Date not set. (Kaleidoscope Ser.). (Illus.). 32p. (J). (gr. -1-4). (978-1-880042-03-8(7)) Shelf-Life Bks.

Mack, Jeff. Hippo & Rabbit. Mack, Jeff, illus. 2011. (Scholastic Reader Level 1 Ser.). (ENG., Illus.). 32p. (J). (gr. -1-2). pap. 3.99 (978-0-545-27445-6(1), Cartwheel Bks.) Scholastic, Inc.

—Hippo & Rabbit in Brave Like Me. Mack, Jeff, illus. 2011. (Scholastic Reader Level 1 Ser.). (ENG., Illus.). 32p. (J). (gr. -1-2). pap. 3.99 (978-0-545-28360-1(4), Cartwheel Bks.) Scholastic, Inc.

Marshall, James. George & Martha No. 4: The Best of Friends Early Reader. 2011. (Green Light Readers Level 2 Ser.). (ENG., Illus.). 32p. (J). (gr. -1-3). pap. 4.99 (978-0-547-51988-3(5)) Houghton Mifflin Harcourt Publishing Co.

—George & Martha Early Reader. 2010. (Green Light Readers Level 2 Ser.). (ENG., Illus.). 24p. (J). (gr. -1-3). pap. 4.99 (978-0-547-40624-4(X)) Houghton Mifflin Harcourt Publishing Co.

—George & Martha Two Great Friends Early Reader. 2010. (Green Light Readers Level 2 Ser.). (ENG., Illus.). 32p. (J). (gr. -1-3). pap. 4.99 (978-0-547-40625-1(8)) Houghton Mifflin Harcourt Publishing Co.

—Rise & Shine No. 5. 2011. (George & Martha Ser.). (ENG., Illus.). 40p. (J). (gr. -1-3). pap. 4.99 (978-0-547-57687-9(0)) Houghton Mifflin Harcourt Publishing Co.

—Round & Round, No. 3. 2011. (Green Light Readers Level 2 Ser.). (ENG., Illus.). 32p. (J). (gr. -1-3). pap. 3.99 (978-0-547-51982-1(6)) Houghton Mifflin Harcourt Publishing Co.

May, Stephan. Leo the Entrepreneurial Hippo. 2008. (Illus.). 56p. pap. 10.95 (978-1-4401-0480-0(8)) iUniverse, Inc.

May, Tessa. Bella Wishes. Rodriguez, Dave, illus. 2004. 35p. pap. 13.95 incl. audio compact disk (978-0-9759325-0-6(0)) CarLou Interactive Media & Publishing.

McKee, David. Elmer & the Hippos. McKee, David, illus. 2010. (Andersen Press Picture Bks). (ENG., Illus.). 32p. (J). (gr. -1-3). 16.95 (978-0-7613-6442-9(0)) Lerner Publishing Group.

MCP Staff. Where Can a Hippo Hide?, Level 4, Bk. 36. (J). (gr. -1-3). 24.50 (978-0-8136-1966-8(1)) Modern Curriculum Pr.

Merchant, Brenda C. Huga Huga Hippo. l.t. ed. 2010. (Illus.). 49p. (J). 26.00 (978-0-9845023-0-1(0)) A-Gator Publishing.

Metzger, Steve & Antonini, Gabriele, illus. Huggapotamus. 2011. (J). (978-0-545-34352-7(6)) Scholastic, Inc.

Moncure, Jane Belk. Yes, No, Little Hippo: A Book about Safety. DeSantis, Susan, illus. 2013. (Magic Castle Readers Ser.). (ENG.). 32p. (J). (gr. -1-2). 25.64 (978-1-62323-571-0(5), 206306) Child's World, Inc., The.

Nœ–ez, Marisa. CHOCOLATE. 2007. (ENG., Illus.). 36p. (J). 17.95 (978-84-96788-83-1(0)) OQO, Editora ESP. Dist: Baker & Taylor Bks.

Nesquens, Daniel & Schimel, Lawrence. Mister H. Lozano, Luciano, illus. 2015. (ENG.). 61p. (J). 14.00 (978-0-8028-5440-7(0), Eerdmans Bks For Young Readers) Eerdmans, William B. Publishing Co.

Nussbaum, Ben. Toko the Hippo. Wenzel, Gregory, illus. 2006. (ENG.). 36p. (J). 14.99 (978-1-59249-577-1(X)); 8.95 (978-1-59249-580-1(X)); pap. 2.95 (978-1-59249-579-5(6)); pap. 6.95 (978-1-59249-578-8(8)) Soundprints.

Oguneye, Kunle. Sikulu & Harambe by the Zambezi River: An African Vversion of the Good Samaritan Story. McCorkindale, Bruce & Youtsey, Scott, illus. 2008. 32p. (J). (gr. -1-5). 14.99 (978-0-9777382-4-3(8)) Blue Brush Media.

Olson, Denise. Geoff the Green Hippo: A Children's Book about Adoption. 2011. 16p. (gr. -1). pap. 14.99 (978-1-4567-6951-2(0)) AuthorHouse.

Parker, Emma. Missy Hip Hoppo. 2010. (Illus.). 16p. pap. (978-1-877561-56-6(8)) First Edition Ltd.

Plourde, Lynn. You're Doing That in the Talent Show?! Cornelison, Sue, illus. 2016. (ENG.). 32p. (J). (gr. -1-k). 16.99 (978-1-4847-1491-1(1)) Disney Pr.

—You're Wearing That to School?! Cornelison, Sue, illus. 2013. (ENG.). 32p. (J). (gr. -1-3). 16.99 (978-1-4231-5510-2(6)) Disney Pr.

Ralls, Ken. Henrietta Hippo Learns to Dance. McQuitty, LaVonia Corbin, illus. 2nd ed. 2013. 24p. (J). 15.00 (978-0-9884125-3-8(5)) Scribe's Closet Pubns., The.

Reece, William James. The Great Hippo Migration. 2007. 92p. per. 19.95 (978-1-4241-9770-5(8)) America Star Bks.

Reitze, Glenn Logan. Ernie the Easter Hippopotamus: A Comic Adventure for Anytime. Reitze, Glenn Logan, illus. 2007. (ENG., Illus.). 48p. (J). lib. bdg. 19.95 (978-0-88265-040-1(8), Fine Art Editions) North American International.

Reitze, Glenn Logan, illus. & text. Ernie the Easter Hippotamus: A Comic Adventure for Anytime. Reitze, Glenn Logan, text. 2007. (J). pap. (978-0-88265-041-8(6)) North American International.

Renert, Gerry. Nathan Saves Summer. Bradshaw, Carrie Anne, illus. 2010. (ENG.). 32p. (J). (gr. -1-3). 16.95 (978-1-934960-76-9(4), Raven Tree Pr.,Csi) Continental Sales, Inc.

—Nathan Saves Summer/Nathan Rescata el Verano. Bradshaw, Carrie Anne, illus. 2010. (ENG & SPA.). 32p. (J). (gr. -1-3). 16.95 (978-1-934960-74-5(8), Raven Tree Pr.,Csi) Continental Sales, Inc.

Rimes, Rebecca. Hippie Hippopotamus. 2011. 24p. (gr. 10-12). pap. 12.74 (978-1-4634-0855-8(2)) AuthorHouse.

Rogers, Alan. Higher & Higher. 2004. (Little Giants Ser.). (Illus.). 16p. (J). (gr. -1-k). 5.95 (978-1-58728-153-2(8), Two-Can Publishing) T&N Children's Publishing.

Rossacci, Jacob. Harold the Hippo Learns to Sing. 2003. (J). 8.95 (978-1-932205-74-9(8)) Word Association Pubs.

Rox, John. I Want a Hippopotamus for Christmas. Whatley, Bruce, illus. 2005. 32p. (J). (gr. -1-3). 17.99 (978-0-06-052942-0(3)) HarperCollins Pubs.

Safari Press Staff, ed. Book Buddy - Hippo with Story Book. (Illus.). 10p. (J). (gr. -1-3). pap. (978-1-881469-86-5(7)) Safari, Ltd.

Samoun, Abigail. How Hippo Says Hello! Watts, Sarah, illus. 2014. (Little Traveler Ser.). (ENG.). 22p. (J). (gr. -1-k). bds. 6.95 (978-1-4549-0820-3(3)) Sterling Publishing Co., Inc.

Scott, Chay L. Henry the Hippo. 2012. 32p. pap. 32.70 (978-1-4797-1168-0(3)) Xlibris Corp.

Shea, Bob. Oh, Daddy! Shea, Bob, illus. 2010. (ENG., Illus.). 40p. (J). (gr. -1-1). 16.99 (978-0-06-173080-1(7)) HarperCollins Pubs.

Shepherd, Donna J. Dotty's Topsy Tale. Collier, Kevin Scott, illus. 2009. 16p. pap. 9.95 (978-1-935137-55-9(7)) Guardian Angel Publishing, Inc.

Shimberg, Elaine Fantle. Helga, the Hippopotamouse. Walling, Sandy Seeley, illus. 2008. (ENG.). 36p. (J). 7.95 (978-0-9741940-4-2(2)) Abernathy Hse. Publishing.

Shum, Benson. Holly's Day at the Pool: A Walt Disney Animation Studios Artist Showcase. Shum, Benson, illus. 2017. (Walt Disney Animation Studios Artist Showcase Ser.). (ENG., Illus.). 40p. (J). (gr. -1-k). 16.99 (978-1-4847-0938-2(1)) Disney Pr.

Stockland, Patricia M. Tiger Toothache, 1 vol. Haugen, Ryan, illus. 2008. (Safari Friends Ser.). (ENG.). 32p. (gr. -1-3). 28.50 (978-1-60270-087-1(7), Looking Glass Library) ABDO Publishing Co.

Sundberg, Angela M., et al. The Pottamus Family & the Unhappy Pottamus. Sundberg, Angela M. et al, illus. 2007. (J). pap. 16.00 (978-0-8059-7478-2(4)) Dorrance Publishing Co., Inc.

Tidd, Louise Vitellaro. Can a Hippo Hop? Brown, Kevin, illus. 2006. (ENG.). 24p. (gr. k-2). pap. 8.95 (978-1-57874-043-7(6), Kaeden Bks.) Kaeden Corp.

Tilby, Ginny. You Should, You Should. 2013. (ENG.). 32p. (J). (gr. k-3). 16.95 (978-1-938301-70-4(6)) Familius LLC.

Towle, Barbara E. How Timbo & Trevor Got Together. Spellman, Susan, illus. 2007. (ENG.). 38p. (J). (gr. -1-3). 19.95 (978-1-933002-21-7(2)) PublishingWorks.

Trodd, Mark. Hippo in the Stable. 2012. 36p. pap. 32.70 (978-1-4797-1561-9(1)) Xlibris Corp.

Trotter, Bob. Up the Wooden Hill: Bedtime Stories for Little Ones. Edgar, Barrie, illus. 2011. 98p. pap. 17.99 (978-1-60976-139-4(1), Eloquent Bks.) Strategic Book Publishing & Rights Agency (SBPRA).

Twohy, Mike. Mouse & Hippo. Twohy, Mike, illus. 2017. (ENG., Illus.). 32p. (J). (gr. -1-3). 17.99 (978-1-4814-5124-6(3), Simon & Schuster/Paula Wiseman Bks.) Simon & Schuster/Paula Wiseman Bks.

Whittington, Joseph. The Hippopotamus Who Didn't Like Himself. 2011. 32p. (gr. -1). pap. 12.99 (978-1-4389-7882-6(0)) AuthorHouse.

Wild, Margaret. Kiss Kiss! Strevens-Marzo, Bridget, illus. 2004. 26p. pap. (978-1-877003-51-6(4)) Little Hare Bks. AUS. Dist: HarperCollins Pubs. Australia.

—Kiss Kiss! Strevens-Marzo, Bridget, illus. 2004. (ENG.). 24p. (J). (gr. -1-1). 14.99 (978-0-689-86279-3(2), Simon & Schuster Bks. For Young Readers) Simon & Schuster Bks. For Young Readers.

Wild, Margaret & Strevens-Marzo, Bridget. Kiss, Kiss Box Set. 2006. (Illus.). 24p. (J). (978-1-921049-25-5(1)) Little Hare Bks. AUS. Dist: HarperCollins Pubs. Australia.

William H. Sadlier Staff. A Hippo in June's Tub, Vol. 2. 2005. (Early Library). (gr. k-2). 24.00 net. (978-0-8215-8958-8(X)) Sadlier, William H. Inc.

Willis, Jeanne. Hippospotamus. Ross, Tony, illus. 2012. (Andersen Press Picture Bks). (ENG.). 32p. (J). (gr. -1-3). 16.95 (978-1-4677-0316-1(8)) Lerner Publishing Group.

Wilson, Karma. Hilda Must Be Dancing. Watts, Suzanne, illus. (ENG.). 32p. (J). (gr. -1-3). 2008. 7.99 (978-1-4169-5083-7(4)) 2004. 17.99 (978-0-689-84788-2(2)) McElderry, Margaret K. Bks. (McElderry, Margaret K. Bks.).

Yolen, Jane. Hip Hippos. van Kampen, Vlasta, illus. 2008. (ENG.). 18p. (J). bds. (978-1-55470-009-7(4)) Me to We.

—One Hippo Hops. van Kampen, Vlasta, illus. 2008. (ENG.). 18p. (J). (gr. -1-k). bds. (978-1-55470-007-3(8)) Me to We.

—Sad, Mad, Glad Hippos. van Kampen, Vlasta, illus. 2008. (ENG.). 18p. (J). (gr. -1-k). bds. (978-1-55470-008-0(6)) Me to We.

Yunger, Joshua. Hippo & Monkey. 2012. (Adventures of Hippo & Monkey Ser.: 1). (ENG., Illus.). 48p. (J). (gr. 1-3). 19.95 (978-1-59373-107-6(8)) Bunker Hill Publishing, Inc.

Zenz, Aaron. The Hiccupotamus, 0 vols. 2009. (ENG.). 32p. (J). (gr. -1-2). 12.99 (978-0-7614-5622-3(8), 9780761456223, Amazon Children's Publishing) Amazon Publishing.

HIROSHIMA-SHI (JAPAN)

Bodden, Valerie. The Bombing of Hiroshima & Nagasaki. 2007. (Days of Change Ser.). (Illus.). 48p. (J). (gr. 4-7). lib. bdg. 31.35 (978-1-58341-545-0(9), Creative Education) Creative Co., The.

—The Bombing of Hiroshima & Nagasaki: Days of Change. 2015. (Illus.). 80p. (J). (978-1-60818-525-2(7), Creative Education) Creative Co., The.

—The Bombing of Hiroshima & Nagasaki: Odysseys in History. 2016. (Odysseys in History Ser.). (ENG., Illus.). 80p. (J). (gr. 7-10). pap. 14.99 (978-1-62832-126-5(1), Creative Paperbacks) Creative Co., The.

Coerr, Eleanor. Sadako & the Thousand Paper Cranes. Himler, Ronald, illus. 2004. (Puffin Modern Classics Ser.). (ENG.). 80p. (J). (gr. 3-7). pap. 6.99 (978-0-14-240113-2(7), Puffin Books) Penguin Young Readers Group.

Eleanor, Coerr. Sadako & the Thousand Paper Cranes. 2014. (Puffin Modern Classics Ser.). (ENG.). 80p. (J). (gr. 3-7). 10.24 (978-1-63245-199-6(9)) Lectorum Pubns., Inc.

Kaelberer, Angie Peterson & Langley, Andrew. Hiroshima & Nagasaki. 2017. (Eyewitness to World War II Ser.). (ENG.). 112p. (gr. 5-7). lib. bdg. 35.99 **(978-0-7565-5584-9(1)**, CPB Grades 4-8) Compass Point Bks.

Lawton, Clive A. Hiroshima: The Story of the First Atom Bomb. 60th anniv. ed. 2004. (Watts Nonfiction Ser.). (ENG., Illus.). 48p. (J). (gr. 5-18). 18.99 (978-0-7636-2271-8(0)) Candlewick Pr.

Orr, Tamra. The Atom Bomb: Creating & Exploding the First Nuclear Weapon. (Library of Weapons of Mass Destruction Ser.). 64p. 2009. (gr. 5-5). 58.50 (978-1-60853-955-0(5)) 2004. (Illus.). (J). lib. bdg. 31.95 (978-1-4042-0292-4(7)) Rosen Publishing Group, Inc., The.

Peppas, Lynn. Hiroshima & Nagasaki. 2013. (ENG., Illus.). 48p. (J). (978-0-7787-1171-1(4)); pap. (978-0-7787-1179-7(X)) Crabtree Publishing Co.

Poolos, J. The Atomic Bombings of Hiroshima & Nagasaki. 2008. (Great Historic Disasters Ser.). (Illus.). 128p. (gr. 5-8). 35.00 (978-0-7910-9738-0(2), Chelsea Hse.) Facts On File, Inc.

Redmond, Shirley Raye. Hiroshima. 2009. (J). (978-1-58415-784-7(4)) Mitchell Lane Pubs., Inc.

Ross, Stewart. Hiroshima. 2011. (Place in History Ser.). 48p. (YA). (gr. 5-9). lib. bdg. 34.25 (978-1-84837-674-8(X)) Arcturus Publishing GBR. Dist: Black Rabbit Bks.

Smibert, Angie. 12 Incredible Facts about the Dropping of the Atomic Bombs. 2015. (Turning Points in US History Ser.). (ENG., Illus.). 32p. (J). (gr. 3-5). 19.95 (978-1-63235-129-6(3), 12-Story Library) Pr. Room Editions LLC.

HIROSHIMA-SHI (JAPAN)—FICTION

Burkinshaw, Kathleen. The Last Cherry Blossom. 2016. (J). **(978-1-63450-618-2(9))** Skyhorse Publishing Co., Inc.

Duras, Marguerite. Hiroshima Mon Amour, Level B.Tr. of Hiroshima My Love. (FRE.). (YA). (gr. 7-12). 9.95 (978-0-88436-998-1(6), 40308) EMC/Paradigm Publishing.

Jafa, Manorama. Sadako of Hiroshima (English) 2013. (ENG.). 16p. pap. 4.95 (978-93-5036-084-2(5)) Ratna, Sagar Pvt. Ltd. IND. Dist: Midpoint Trade Bks., Inc.

Manale, Shizumi Shigeto & Marshall, Richard. Running with Cosmos Flowers: The Children of Hiroshima, 1 vol. 2014. (ENG., Illus.). 152p. (YA). (gr. 8-8). 16.99 (978-1-4556-1966-5(3)) Pelican Publishing Co., Inc.

Nilsson, Troy, 2nd. Hiroshima Stones: The Shadow Stones of Hiroshima - a Story of Love & War. Nilsson, Troy, 2nd, illus. collector's aut. ed. 2003. Orig. Title: Hiroshima Stones. (Illus.). 248p. (YA). 24.95 (978-0-9724771-1-6(X), Nilsson, Troy) Nilsson Media.

HISPANIC AMERICANS

Here are entered works on United States citizens of Latin American descent. Works on citizens of Latin American countries are entered under Latin Americans. Works on citizens of Latin American countries in the United States are entered under Latin Americans—United States.

ABDO Publishing Company Staff. Hispanic American History, 1 vol. 2011. (Hispanic American History Ser.). (ENG., Illus.). 32p. 162.42 (978-1-61783-051-8(8), Abdo & Daughters) ABDO Publishing Co.

Abrams, Dennis. America Ferrera. 2010. (Great Hispanic Heritage Ser.). (Illus.). 112p. (gr. 6-12). 35.00 (978-1-60413-967-9(6), Chelsea Hse.) Facts On File, Inc.

Ancona, George. Mi Escuela: My School. 2004. (Somos Latino (We Are Latinos) Ser.). 21.00 (978-0-516-23686-5(5), Watts, Franklin) Scholastic Library Publishing.

—Mis Quehaceres - My Chores. 2005. (Somos Latinos (We Are Latinos) Ser.). (ENG & SPA., Illus.). 32p. (J). (gr. 1-3). lib. bdg. 21.00 (978-0-516-25291-9(7), Children's Pr.) Scholastic Library Publishing.

Arkham, Thomas. Latino American Civil Rights. 2012. (J). pap. (978-1-4222-2336-9(1)) Mason Crest.

—Latino American Civil Rights. Limón, José E., ed. 2012. (Hispanic Americans: Major Minority Ser.). 64p. (J). (gr. 4). 22.95 (978-1-4222-2319-2(1)) Mason Crest.

—Latino Americans & Their Jobs. 2013. (Illus.). 64p. (J). pap. (978-1-4222-2340-6(X)) Mason Crest.

—Latino Americans & Their Jobs. Limón, José E., ed. 2012. (Hispanic Americans: Major Minority Ser.). (Illus.). 64p. (J). (gr. 4). 22.95 (978-1-4222-2323-9(X)) Mason Crest.

—Latinos Today. 2013. (Illus.). 64p. (J). pap. (978-1-4222-2344-4(2)) Mason Crest.

—Latinos Today. Limón, José E., ed. 2012. (Hispanic Americans: Major Minority Ser.). (Illus.). 64p. (J). (gr. 4). 22.95 (978-1-4222-2327-7(2)) Mason Crest.

Brown, Monica. My Name Is Celia: The Life of Celia Cruz. López, Rafael, illus. 2004.Tr. of Me Llamo Celia - La Vida de Celia Cruz. (ENG, SPA & MUL.). 32p. (J). (gr. k-3). 15.95 (978-0-87358-872-0(X)) Cooper Square Publishing Llc.

Buckley, Annie. Ellen Ochoa. 2007. (21st Century Skills Library: Life Skills Biographies Ser.). (ENG., Illus.). 48p. (gr. 4-8). lib. bdg. 31.36 (978-1-60279-075-9(2), 200041) Cherry Lake Publishing.

Clapper, Kathryn N. Irma Rangel, 1 vol. 2014. (Great Women in History Ser.). (ENG., Illus.). 24p. (gr. k-1). lib. bdg. 21.99 (978-1-4914-0538-3(4), Pebble Bks.) Capstone Press of Coughlan Cos.

Cockcroft, James D. Latinos in Beisbol. 2004. (Illus.). 207p. (J). (gr. 4-9). reprint ed. pap. 10.00 (978-0-7567-7347-2(4)) DIANE Publishing Co.

Cofer, Judith Ortiz, ed. Riding Low on the Streets of Gold: Latino Literature for Young Adults. 2003. (Illus.). 192p. (J). pap. 14.95 (978-1-55885-380-5(4), Piñata Books) Arte Publico Pr.

Cornell, Kari. Mars Science Lab Engineer Diana Trujillo. 2016. (STEM Trailblazer Bios Ser.). (ENG., Illus.). 32p. (J). (gr. 2-5). pap. 8.99 (978-1-4677-9721-4(9), Lerner Pubns.) Lerner Publishing Group.

Cruz, Barbara C. The Fight for Latino Civil Rights. 2015. (Our Shared History Ser.). (ENG., Illus.). 128p. (J). (gr. 7-7). lib. bdg. 37.27 (978-0-7660-7006-6(9)) Enslow Pubs., Inc.

Cruz, Bàrbara C. Triumphs & Struggles for Latino Civil Rights. 2008. (From Many Cultures, One History Ser.). (Illus.). 128p. (J). (gr. 5-18). lib. bdg. 33.27 (978-0-7660-2804-3(6)) Enslow Pubs., Inc.

Davies, Gill. Hispanic America 1490s - the Present. Aronson, Marc, ed. 2005. (National Geographic Timelines Ser.). (Illus.). 64p. (J). 27.90 (978-0-7922-7077-5(0)) CENGAGE Learning.

—Hispanic America 1490s- the Present. Aronson, Marc, ed. 2005. (National Geographic Timelines Ser.). (Illus.). 64p. (J). 17.95 (978-0-7922-6455-2(X)) CENGAGE Learning.

DePietro, Frank. Latino Americans & Immigration Laws. 2013. (Illus.). 64p. pap. (978-1-4222-2338-3(8)) Mason Crest.

—Latino Americans & Immigration Laws. Limón, José E., ed. 2012. (Hispanic Americans: Major Minority Ser.). (Illus.). 64p. (J). (gr. 4). 22.95 (978-1-4222-2321-5(3)) Mason Crest.

—Latino Americans & Religion. 2013. (Illus.). 64p. (J). pap. (978-1-4222-2339-0(6)) Mason Crest.

—Latino Americans & Religion. Limón, José E., ed. 2012. (Hispanic Americans: Major Minority Ser.). (Illus.). 64p. (J). (gr. 4). 22.95 (978-1-4222-2322-2(1)) Mason Crest.

—Latino Arts in the United States. Limón, José E., ed. 2012. (Hispanic Americans: Major Minority Ser.). (Illus.). 64p. (J). (gr. 4). 22.95 (978-1-4222-2324-6(8)) Mason Crest.

—Latino Migrant Workers. 2013. (Illus.). 64p. (J). pap. (978-1-4222-2343-7(4)) Mason Crest.

—Latino Migrant Workers. Limón, José E., ed. 2012. (Hispanic Americans: Major Minority Ser.). (Illus.). 64p. (J). (gr. 4). 22.95 (978-1-4222-2326-0(4)) Mason Crest.

—Spain Arrives in the Americas. 2012. (Illus.). 64p. (J). pap. (978-1-4222-2341-3(8)) Mason Crest.

Doak, Robin Santos. Fighting for American Values: 1941-1985. Overmyer-Velazquez, Mark, ed. 2007. (Latino-American History Ser.). (Illus.). 106p. (YA). (gr. 5-9). lib. bdg. 35.00 (978-0-8160-6444-1(X)) Facts On File, Inc.

—Struggling to Become American: 1899-1940. Overmyer-Velazquez, Mark, ed. 2006. (Latino-American History Ser.). (Illus.). 106p. (YA). (gr. 5-9). lib. bdg. 35.00 (978-0-8160-6443-4(1)) Facts On File, Inc.

Engle, Margarita. Bravo! Poems About Amazing Hispanics. López, Rafael, illus. 2017. (ENG.). 48p. (J). 18.99 (978-0-8050-9876-1(3), 9780805098761, Holt, Henry & Co. Bks. For Young Readers) Holt, Henry & Co.

Exceptional Latinos. 2015. (Exceptional Latinos Ser.). (ENG.). 24p. (J). (gr. 3-4). 135.60 (978-0-7660-6672-4(X)); pap., pap., pap. 336.60 (978-0-7660-6673-1(8)); pap., pap., pap. 56.10 (978-0-7660-7051-6(4)) Enslow Pubs., Inc.

Facts on File, Inc. Staff, creator. A to Z of Latino Americans Set, 4 vols. 2007. (A to Z of Latino Americans Ser.). (Illus.). 304p. (C). (gr. 9). 180.00 (978-0-8160-7431-0(3)) Facts On File, Inc.

Family Stories: Ten Stories. 2005. (SPA & ENG., Illus.). 27p. (J). pap. (978-0-9716580-8-0(0)) Lectura Bks.

Gagne, Tammy. What Its Like to Be Sonia Sotomayor. de la Vega, Eida, tr. from SPA. 2010. (What It's Like to Be/Que se Siente al Ser Ser.). (ENG & SPA., Illus.). 32p. (J). (gr. -1-2). lib. bdg. 25.70 (978-1-58415-853-0(0)) Mitchell Lane Pubs., Inc.

Gallagher, Brigid. Sonia Sotomayor, 1 vol. 2014. (Extraordinary Women Ser.). (ENG., Illus.). 48p. (gr. 6-6). pap. 9.95 (978-1-4109-5954-6(6)); lib. bdg. 32.65 (978-1-4109-5946-1(5)) Heinemann-Raintree.

García, Luis. Johan Santana. 2012. (Superstars of Baseball ENGLISH Ser.). 32p. (J). (gr. 4). 19.95 (978-1-4222-2695-7(6)); (SPA., Illus.). 19.95 (978-1-4222-2642-1(5)) Mason Crest.

Garza, Carmen Lomas, illus. In My Family. 2011.Tr. of En Mi Familia. (ENG & SPA.). 32p. (C). (gr. 1-4). pap. 24.95 (978-0-89239-163-9(4)) National Geographic School Publishing, Inc.

Gibson, Karen. What It's Like to Be George Lopez. de la Vega, Eida, tr. from ENG. 2011. (What It's Like to Be... = Que Se Sienta Al Ser... Ser.). (SPA., Illus.). 32p. (J). (gr. -1-2). lib. bdg. 25.70 (978-1-58415-991-9(X)) Mitchell Lane Pubs., Inc.

—What It's Like to Be Jennifer Lopez. de la Vega, Eida, tr. from ENG. 2011. (What It's Like to Be... = Que Se Sienta Al Ser... Ser.). (SPA., Illus.). 32p. (J). (gr. -1-2). lib. bdg. 25.70 (978-1-58415-990-2(1)) Mitchell Lane Pubs., Inc.

Gitlin, Martin. Sonia Sotomayor: Supreme Court Justice, 1 vol. 2010. (Essential Lives Set 5 Ser.). (ENG.). 112p. (J). (gr. 6-12). lib. bdg. 35.64 (978-1-61613-518-8(2)) ABDO Publishing Co.

Gravenhorst, Edna Campos. Ay, Mijo! Why Do You Want to Be an Engineer? 2007. 155p. (978-0-9745346-3-3(3)) Big River Distribution.

The Great Hispanic Heritage. (Illus.). (gr. 6-12). lib. bdg. (978-0-7910-8049-8(8), Chelsea Hse.) Facts On File, Inc.

Grolier Publishing Company Staff, contrib. by. Hispanic American Biographies, 8 vols. 2006. (Illus.). (J). (978-0-7172-6128-4(X)); (978-0-7172-6129-1(8)); (978-0-7172-6130-7(1)); (978-0-7172-6131-4(X)); (978-0-7172-6132-1(8)); (978-0-7172-6126-0(3)); (978-0-7172-6127-7(1)); (978-0-7172-6125-3(5)) Grolier, Ltd.

—Hispanic American Biographies, 8 vols., Set. 2006. (Illus.). (J). (gr. 6-18). 499.00 (978-0-7172-6124-6(7)) Scholastic Library Publishing.

Guzmán, Lila & Guzmán, Rick. Ellen Ochoa: La Primera Astronauta Latina. 2014. (Latinos Famosos Ser.). 32p. (gr. 2). pap. 7.95 (978-0-7660-6086-9(1)) Enslow Pubs., Inc.

—George Lopez: Comedian & TV Star. 2006. (Famous Latinos Ser.). (Illus.). 32p. (J). (gr. 3-4). lib. bdg. 23.94 (978-0-7660-2644-5(2), Enslow Elementary) Enslow Pubs., Inc.

—George Lopez: Comediante y Estrella de TV. 2007. (Latinos Famosos Ser.). (Illus.). 32p. (J). (gr. 4-7). lib. bdg. 23.94 (978-0-7660-2680-3(9), Enslow Elementary) Enslow Pubs., Inc.

—George Lopez: Latino King of Comedy. 2008. (Latino Biography Library). (Illus.). 128p. (J). (gr. k-6). lib. bdg. 33.27 (978-0-7660-2968-2(9)) Enslow Pubs., Inc.

Hansen-Krening, Nancy, et al, eds. Kaleidoscope: A Multicultural Booklist for Grades K-8. 4th ed. 2003. (NCTE Bibliography Ser.). (Illus.). 118p. (J). pap. 30.95 (978-0-8141-2539-7(5), 25395) National Council of Teachers of English.

Hernández, Roger E. The Civil War, 1840s-1890s. 2008. (Hispanic America Ser.). 80p. (gr. 5-18). lib. bdg. 34.21 (978-0-7614-2939-5(5), Benchmark Bks.) Marshall Cavendish Corp.

—1898 to World War II. 2009. (Hispanic America 2 Ser.). 80p. (gr. 5). 34.21 (978-0-7614-4176-2(X)) Marshall Cavendish Corp.

Herrera, Juan Felipe. Portraits of Hispanic American Heroes. Colón, Raúl, illus. 2014. (ENG.). 96p. (J). (gr. 3-7). 19.99 (978-0-8037-3809-6(9), Dial Bks) Penguin Young Readers Group.

Hile, Kevin. Cesar Chavez. 2008. (Twentieth Century's Most Influential Hispanics Ser.). (ENG., Illus.). 96-128p. (gr. 7-10). 34.80 *(978-1-4205-0094-3(5)*, Lucent Bks.) Cengage Gale.

Hollihan, Kerrie Logan. Hispanic Heritage Month: Mes de la Herencia Hispana. Sanz, Ma Pilar, tr. 2010. (Latin American Celebrations & Festivals / Celebraciones y Festivales en Latinoamérica Ser.). (ENG & SPA., Illus.). 24p. (YA). (gr. 2-5). lib. bdg. 22.60 *(978-1-4358-9364-1(6))* Rosen Publishing Group, Inc., The.

Hunter, Miranda. Latino Americans & Immigration Laws: Crossing the Border. 2007. (Hispanic Heritage Ser.). (Illus.). 112p. (YA). (gr. 4-7). lib. bdg. 22.95 *(978-1-59084-939-2(6))* Mason Crest.

—Story of Latino Civil Rights: Fighting for Justice. 2007. (Hispanic Heritage Ser.). (Illus.). 112p. (YA). lib. bdg. 22.95 *(978-1-59084-934-7(5))* Mason Crest.

Hurst, Heidi. Jennifer Lopez. 2003. (People in the News Ser.). (Illus.). 112p. (J). 32.45 *(978-1-59018-325-0(8)*, Lucent Bks.) Cengage Gale.

Influential Latinos. 2015. (Influential Latinos Ser.). (ENG.). 128p. (J). (gr. 7-7). 223.62 *(978-0-7660-6698-4(3))* Enslow Pubs., Inc.

Jaffe, Elizabeth Dana. Ellen Ochoa. 2004. (Rookie Biography Ser.). (Illus.). 31p. 20.50 *(978-0-516-21721-5(6)*, Children's Pr.) Scholastic Library Publishing.

Jones, Jen. A Reader's Guide to Gary Soto's Taking Sides. 2010. (Multicultural Literature Ser.). (Illus.). 128p. (YA). (gr. 8-18). 33.27 *(978-0-7660-3168-5(3))* Enslow Pubs., Inc.

Juarez, Christine. Ellen Ochoa. 2016. (Great Hispanic & Latino Americans Ser.). (ENG.). 24p. (gr. k-1). lib. bdg. 21.99 *(978-1-5157-1888-8(3)*, Pebble Bks.) Capstone Press of Coughlan Cos.

—Great Hispanic & Latino Americans. 2016. (Great Hispanic & Latino Americans Ser.). (ENG.). 24p. (gr. k-1). 131.94 *(978-1-5157-1931-1(6)*, Pebble Bks.) Capstone Press of Coughlan Cos.

—John Danny Olivas. 2016. (Great Hispanic & Latino Americans Ser.). (ENG.). 24p. (gr. k-1). lib. bdg. 21.99 *(978-1-5157-1890-1(5)*, Pebble Bks.) Capstone Press of Coughlan Cos.

Keedle, Jayne. Ellen Ochoa. 2009. (People We Should Know Ser.). 32p. (gr. 3-5). (J). lib. bdg. 31.00 *(978-1-4339-0019-8(X))*; pap. 10.50 *(978-1-4339-0159-1(5))* Stevens, Gareth Publishing LLLP. (Gareth Stevens Learning Library).

Kingston, Anna. Respecting the Contributions of Latino Americans. 2012. (Stop Bullying Now! Ser.). (ENG., Illus.). 24p. (J). (gr. 3-6). 22.60 *(978-1-4488-7449-1(1))*; pap. 8.25 *(978-1-4488-7522-1(6))* Rosen Publishing Group, Inc., The. (PowerKids Pr.).

Krull, Kathleen. Sonia Sotomayor: I'll Be the Judge of That! Dominguez, Angela N., illus. 2015. (Women Who Broke the Rules Ser.). (ENG.). 48p. (J). (gr. 1-4). 16.99 *(978-0-8027-3797-7(8)*, 9780802737977, Bloomsbury USA Childrens) Bloomsbury Publishing USA.

Latino American Biographies. (YA). (gr. 6-12). pap. 14.50 *(978-0-8359-0849-8(6))* Globe Fearon Educational Publishing.

Lee, Sally. Freddie Prinze, Jr: From Shy Guy to Movie Star. 2008. (Latino Biography Library). (Illus.). 128p. (J). (gr. k-6). lib. bdg. 33.27 *(978-0-7660-2965-1(4))* Enslow Pubs., Inc.

Libal, Autumn. Women in the Hispanic World. 2006. (Women's Issues, Global Trends Ser.). (Illus.). 112p. (YA). lib. bdg. 22.95 *(978-1-59084-858-6(6))* Mason Crest.

Marquez, Heron. Latin Sensations. (Biography Ser.). (Illus.). 112p. (gr. 6-12). 2005. lib. bdg. 27.93 *(978-0-8225-4993-2(X))* 2003. (YA). pap. 7.95 *(978-0-8225-9695-0(4)*, Lerner Pubns.) Lerner Publishing Group.

Marsh, Carole. The Best Book of Hispanic Biographies. 2003. (Fiesta! Siesta! And All the Rest-a! Ser.). 32p. (J). (gr. 3-8). pap. 7.95 *(978-0-635-02116-8(1))* Gallopade International.

—The BIG Book of Hispanic Activities. 2003. (Fiesta! Siesta! And All the Rest-a! Ser.). 48p. (J). (gr. 2-6). pap. 9.95 *(978-0-635-02115-1(3))* Gallopade International.

—Celebrating Hispanic Heritage: 20 Days of Activities, Reading, Recipes, Parties, Plays & More. 2003. (Fiesta! Siesta! And All the Rest-a! Ser.). 24p. (J). (gr. 1-8). pap. 5.95 *(978-0-635-02119-9(6))* Gallopade International.

—Ellen Ochoa: First Hispanic American Woman in Space: First Hispanic American Woman in Space. 2003. 12p. (gr. k-4). 2.95 *(978-0-635-02138-0(2))* Gallopade International.

—Hispanic Heritage Coloring Book. 2003. 24p. (gr. k-2). pap. 3.95 *(978-0-635-02117-5(X))* Gallopade International.

—Hispanic Trivia: The Hispanic Experience A to Z! 2003. (Fiesta! Siesta! And All the Rest-a! Ser.). 32p. (J). (gr. 3-8). pap. 7.95 *(978-0-635-02118-2(8))* Gallopade International.

McElroy, Lisa Tucker. Alberto Gonzales: Attorney General. 2006. (Gateway Biographies Ser.). (Illus.). 48p. (J). (gr. 4-8). lib. bdg. 23.93 *(978-0-8225-3418-1(5))* Lerner Publishing Group.

McIntosh, Kenneth. The Latino Religious Experience: People of Faith & Vision. 2007. (Hispanic Heritage Ser.). (Illus.). 112p. (YA). (gr. 4-7). lib. bdg. 22.95 *(978-1-59084-933-0(7))* Mason Crest.

—Latinos Today: Facts & Figures. 2007. (Hispanic Heritage Ser.). (Illus.). 112p. (YA). (gr. 4-7). lib. bdg. 22.95 *(978-1-59084-940-8(X))* Mason Crest.

McPherson, Stephanie Sammartino. Sonia Sotomayor: Supreme Court Justice. 2015. (Exceptional Latinos Ser.). (ENG., Illus.). 24p. (J). (gr. 3-4). pap. 9.35 *(978-0-7660-6722-6(X))* Enslow Pubs., Inc.

Media Projects, Inc., Staff. Student Almanac of Hispanic American History, 2 vols., Vol. 1. 2003. (Illus.). 144p. (C). (gr. 6-8). stu. ed. 101.00 *(978-0-313-32605-9(3)*, MS2605, Greenwood) ABC-CLIO, LLC.

Mintzer, Richard. Latino Americans in Sports, Film, Music & Government: Trailblazers. 2007. (Hispanic Heritage Ser.). (Illus.). 112p. (YA). (gr. 4-7). lib. bdg. 22.95 *(978-1-59084-936-1(1))* Mason Crest.

Miriam Colon, Actriz y Fundadora de Teatro. 2003. 94.95 *(978-0-8136-9219-7(9))*; pap. 48.95 *(978-0-8136-9207-4(5))* Modern Curriculum Pr.

Monnig, Alex. Albert Pujols: Groundbreaking Slugger, 1 vol. 2012. (Playmakers Ser.). (ENG.). 32p. (J). (gr. 3-6). 27.07 *(978-1-61783-294-9(4))* ABDO Publishing Co.

Nickle's, Greg. The Hispanics: We Came to North America. 2006. (Illus.). 32p. (J). (gr. 4-8). reprint ed. 19.00 *(978-0-7567-9903-8(1))* DIANE Publishing Co.

Ochoa, George & Smith, Carter. Atlas of Hispanic-American History. 2nd rev. ed. 2008. (Multicultural Atlas Ser.). (Illus.). 250p. (C). (gr. 9-18). 95.00 *(978-0-8160-7092-3(X))* Facts On File, Inc.

Ollhoff, Jim. Conflicts & Independence, 1 vol. 2011. (Hispanic American History Ser.). (ENG., Illus.). 32p. (YA). (gr. 5-9). 27.07 *(978-1-61783-054-9(2))* ABDO Publishing Co.

—Freedom & the Future, 1 vol. 2011. (Hispanic American History Ser.). (ENG., Illus.). 32p. (YA). (gr. 5-9). 27.07 *(978-1-61783-056-3(9))* ABDO Publishing Co.

—Identity & Civil Rights, 1 vol. 2011. (Hispanic American History Ser.). (ENG., Illus.). 32p. (YA). (gr. 5-9). 27.07 *(978-1-61783-057-0(7))* ABDO Publishing Co.

Olmstead. Hispanic-American Biographies Series, 5 vols., Set 1. 2004. (Illus.). 125.43 *(978-1-4109-0715-8(5))* Harcourt Schl. Pubs.

Otfinoski, Steven. The New Republic. 2008. (Hispanic America Ser.). 80p. (gr. 5-18). lib. bdg. 34.21 *(978-0-7614-2938-8(7)*, Benchmark Bks.) Marshall Cavendish Corp.

—1990-2010. 2009. (Hispanic America 2 Ser.). 80p. (gr. 5). 34.21 *(978-0-7614-4180-9(8))* Marshall Cavendish Corp.

Paige, Joy. Ellen Ochoa: The First Hispanic Woman in Space. (Library of Astronaut Biographies Ser.). 112p. (gr. 5-8). 2009. 63.90 *(978-1-60853-520-0(7))* 2004. (Illus.). lib. bdg. 34.60 *(978-0-8239-4457-6(3))* Rosen Publishing Group, Inc., The. (Rosen Reference).

Palmer, Bill. Trailblazing Latino Americans. 2012. (J). pap. *(978-1-4222-2348-2(5))* Mason Crest.

—Trailblazing Latino Americans. Limón, José E., ed. 2012. (Hispanic Americans: Major Minority Ser.). 64p. (J). (gr. 4). 22.95 *(978-1-4222-2331-4(0))* Mason Crest.

Petrillo, Valerie. A Kid's Guide to Latino History: More Than 50 Activities. 2009. (Kid's Guide Ser.). (ENG.). 224p. (J). (gr. 2-4). pap. 16.95 *(978-1-55652-771-5(3))* Chicago Review Pr., Inc.

PRESS, Celebration. Ellen Ochoa: Reaching for the Stars. 2003. (ENG.). (J). (gr. 2-5). pap., stu. ed. 34.95 *(978-0-673-62081-1(6)*, Celebration Pr.) Pearson Schl.

Rodríguez Gonzalez, Tania. Adrián Beltré. 2012. (Superstars of Baseball ENGLISH Ser.). 32p. (J). (gr. 4). 19.95 *(978-1-4222-2682-7(4))*; (SPA.). 19.95 *(978-1-4222-2629-2(8))* Mason Crest.

—Alex Rodriguez. 2012. (Superstars of Baseball ENGLISH Ser.). 32p. (J). (gr. 4). 19.95 *(978-1-4222-2674-2(3))*; (SPA., Illus.). 19.95 *(978-1-4222-2621-6(2))* Mason Crest.

—Bartolo Colón. 2012. (Superstars of Baseball ENGLISH Ser.). 32p. (J). (gr. 4). 19.95 *(978-1-4222-2687-2(5))*; (SPA., Illus.). 19.95 *(978-1-4222-2634-6(4))* Mason Crest.

—Carlos Beltrán. 2012. (Superstars of Baseball ENGLISH Ser.). 32p. (J). (gr. 4). 19.95 *(978-1-4222-2699-5(9))*; (SPA., Illus.). 19.95 *(978-1-4222-2646-9(8))* Mason Crest.

—Carlos Peña. 2012. (Superstars of Baseball SPANISH Ser.). (SPA.). 32p. (J). (gr. 4). 19.95 *(978-1-4222-2625-4(5))* Mason Crest.

—Francisco Cordero. 2012. (Superstars of Baseball SPANISH Ser.). 32p. (J). (gr. 4). (SPA.). 19.95 *(978-1-4222-2637-7(9))*; 19.95 *(978-1-4222-2690-2(5))* Mason Crest.

—Francisco Liriano. 2012. (Superstars of Baseball ENGLISH Ser.). 32p. (J). (gr. 4). 19.95 *(978-1-4222-2692-6(1))*; (SPA., Illus.). 19.95 *(978-1-4222-2639-1(5))* Mason Crest.

—Hanley Ramirez. 2012. (Superstars of Baseball ENGLISH Ser.). 32p. (J). (gr. 4). 19.95 *(978-1-4222-2675-9(1))*; (SPA., Illus.). 19.95 *(978-1-4222-2622-3(0))* Mason Crest.

—Jhonny Peralta. 2012. (Superstars of Baseball ENGLISH Ser.). 32p. (J). (gr. 4). 19.95 *(978-1-4222-2686-5(7))*; (SPA., Illus.). 19.95 *(978-1-4222-2633-9(6))* Mason Crest.

—José Bautista. 2012. (Superstars of Baseball ENGLISH Ser.). 32p. (J). (gr. 4). 19.95 *(978-1-4222-2685-8(9))*; (SPA., Illus.). 19.95 *(978-1-4222-2632-2(8))* Mason Crest.

—José Valverde. 2012. (Superstars of Baseball SPANISH Ser.). (SPA., Illus.). 32p. (J). (gr. 4). 19.95 *(978-1-4222-2641-4(7))* Mason Crest.

—Juan Uribe. 2012. (Superstars of Baseball ENGLISH Ser.). 32p. (J). (gr. 4). 19.95 *(978-1-4222-2671-1(9))*; (SPA., Illus.). 19.95 *(978-1-4222-2618-6(2))* Mason Crest.

—Miguel Batista. 2012. (Superstars of Baseball ENGLISH Ser.). 32p. (J). (gr. 4). 19.95 *(978-1-4222-2689-6(1))*; (SPA., Illus.). 19.95 *(978-1-4222-2636-0(0))* Mason Crest.

—Miguel Tejada. 2012. (Superstars of Baseball ENGLISH Ser.). 32p. (J). (gr. 4). 19.95 *(978-1-4222-2672-8(7))*; (SPA., Illus.). 19.95 *(978-1-4222-2619-3(0))* Mason Crest.

—Nelson Cruz. 2012. (Superstars of Baseball ENGLISH Ser.). 32p. (J). (gr. 4). 19.95 *(978-1-4222-2691-9(3))*; (SPA., Illus.). 19.95 *(978-1-4222-2638-4(7))* Mason Crest.

—Placido Polanco. 2012. (Superstars of Baseball SPANISH Ser.). (SPA.). 32p. (J). (gr. 4). 19.95 *(978-1-4222-2624-7(7))* Mason Crest.

—Rafael Furcal. 2012. (Superstars of Baseball ENGLISH Ser.). 32p. (J). (gr. 4). 19.95 *(978-1-4222-2688-9(3))*; (SPA., Illus.). 19.95 *(978-1-4222-2635-3(2))* Mason Crest.

—Robinson Canó. 2012. (Superstars of Baseball ENGLISH Ser.). 32p. (J). (gr. 4). 19.95 *(978-1-4222-2683-4(2))* Mason Crest.

—Ubaldo Jiménez. 2012. (Superstars of Baseball ENGLISH Ser.). 32p. (J). (gr. 4). 19.95 *(978-1-4222-2680-3(8))*; (SPA & ENG., Illus.). 19.95 *(978-1-4222-2627-8(1))* Mason Crest.

—Vladimir Guerrero. 2012. (Superstars of Baseball ENGLISH Ser.). (Illus.). 32p. (J). (gr. 4). 19.95 *(978-1-4222-2681-0(6))*; (SPA & ENG., 19.95 *(978-1-4222-2628-5(X))* Mason Crest.

—Yadier Molina. 2012. (Superstars of Baseball ENGLISH Ser.). 32p. (J). (gr. 4). 19.95 *(978-1-4222-2698-8(0))*; (SPA., Illus.). 19.95 *(978-1-4222-2645-2(X))* Mason Crest.

Rodríguez Gonzalez, Tania & Rodriguez, Tania. Placido Polanco. 2012. (Superstars of Baseball ENGLISH Ser.). 32p. (J). (gr. 4). 19.95 *(978-1-4222-2677-3(8))* Mason Crest.

Rodríguez Salazar, Tania. Aramis Ramirez. 2012. 32p. (J). (Illus.). *(978-1-4222-2670-4(0))*; (gr. 4). 19.95 *(978-1-4222-2693-3(X))* Mason Crest.

—Carlos Peña. 2012. (Superstars of Baseball ENGLISH Ser.). 32p. (J). (gr. 4). 19.95 *(978-1-4222-2678-0(6))* Mason Crest.

Salqueiro, Adolfo. Carlos Gonzalez. 2012. (Superstars of Baseball ENGLISH Ser.). 32p. (J). (gr. 4). 19.95 *(978-1-4222-2696-4(4))*; (SPA.). 19.95 *(978-1-4222-2643-8(3))* Mason Crest.

Savage, Jeff. Mark Sanchez. 2011. (Amazing Athletes Ser.). (ENG., Illus.). 32p. (gr. 2-5). lib. bdg. 25.26 *(978-0-7613-7673-6(9))* Lerner Publishing Group.

Schraff, Anne E. Ellen Ochoa: Astronaut & Inventor. 2009. (Latino Biography Library). (Illus.). 128p. (J). (gr. 6-18). lib. bdg. 33.27 *(978-0-7660-3163-0(2))* Enslow Pubs., Inc.

—Jaime Escalante: Inspirational Math Teacher. 2008. (Latino Biography Library). (Illus.). 128p. (J). (gr. k-6). lib. bdg. 33.27 *(978-0-7660-2967-5(0))* Enslow Pubs., Inc.

Schwartz, Heather E. Astronaut Ellen Ochoa. 2017. (STEM Trailblazer Bios Ser.). (ENG.). 32p. (J). (gr. 2-5). pap. 8.99 ***(978-1-5124-5627-1(6))***; (Illus.). 26.65 ***(978-1-5124-3449-1(3)***, Lerner Pubns.) Lerner Publishing Group.

Schweitzer, Karen. Americans of South American Heritage. (Successful Americans Ser.). 64p. (YA). 2009. (gr. 9-12). 22.95 *(978-1-4222-0526-6(6))* 2007. (gr. 7-18). pap. 9.95 *(978-1-4222-0861-8(3))* Mason Crest.

Seidman, David. Creating a New Future: 1986 to Present. Overmyer-Velazquez, Mark, ed. 2007. (Latino-American History Ser.). (Illus.). 106p. (YA). (gr. 5-9). lib. bdg. 35.00 *(978-0-8160-6445-8(8))* Facts On File, Inc.

Sharp, Anne Wallace. Nancy Lopez. 2008. (Twentieth Century's Most Influencial Hispanics Ser.). (ENG., Illus.). 96-128p. (gr. 7-10). 34.80 *(978-1-4205-0060-8(0)*, Lucent Bks.) Cengage Gale.

Shea, John. Outsiders. 2011. (J). *(978-0-531-22556-1(9))* Scholastic, Inc.

Shichtman, Sandra H. Sonia Sotomayor. 2011. (Supreme Court Justices Ser.). (Illus.). 111p. 28.95 *(978-1-59935-156-8(0))* Reynolds, Morgan Inc.

Silverstone, Michael. Latino Legends: Hispanics in Major League Baseball. 2003. (High Five Reading - Green Ser.). (ENG., Illus.). 48p. (gr. 3-4). per. 9.00 *(978-0-7368-2832-1(X)*, High Five Reading (RBL)) Capstone Press of Coughlan Cos.

Sosa, Carlos. Celebrations. 2007. (Familia Banderas Ser.). (Illus.). 48p. (J). (gr. 3-7). per. 9.95 *(978-1-933669-11-3(X))* Literary Architects, LLC.

—Cultures. 2007. (Familia Banderas Ser.). (Illus.). 48p. (J). (gr. 3-7). per. 9.95 *(978-1-933669-12-0(8))* Literary Architects, LLC.

Sosa, Carlos & Castaneda, Patricia. Celebrations: La Familia Banderas. 2006. (Illus.). 48p. (J). pap. 9.95 *(978-1-933669-03-8(9))* Literary Architects, LLC.

—Cultures: La Familia Banderas. 2006. (Illus.). 48p. (J). pap. 9.95 *(978-1-933669-04-5(7))* Literary Architects, LLC.

Stewart, Mark & Kennedy, Mike. Latino Baseball's Finest Fielders/Las Mas Destacados Guantes del Beisbol Latino. Kalmanovitz, Manuel, tr. from ENG. 2003. (En Fuego Ser.). (ENG & SPA., Illus.). 48p. (J). (gr. 5-18). pap. 9.95 *(978-0-7613-1749-4(X))* Lerner Publishing Group.

—Latino Baseball's Hottest Hitters. Kalmanovitz, Manuel, tr. 2003. (En Fuego Ser.). (SPA & ENG., Illus.). 48p. (J). (gr. 5-18). pap. 9.95 *(978-0-7613-1775-3(9))* Lerner Publishing Group.

Tieck, Sarah. Jennifer Lopez: Famous Entertainer, 1 vol. 2012. (Big Buddy Biographies Ser.). (ENG.). 32p. (J). (gr. 2-5). 28.50 *(978-1-61783-225-3(1))* ABDO Publishing Co.

Tol, Alex Van. Sonia Sotomayor: U.S. Supreme Court Justice. 2010. (Crabtree Groundbreaker Biographies Ser.). (ENG., Illus.). 112p. (J). pap. *(978-0-7787-2546-6(4))* Crabtree Publishing Co.

Tonatiuh, Duncan. Separate Is Never Equal: Sylvia Mendez & Her Family's Fight for Desegregation. 2014. (ENG., Illus.). 40p. (J). (gr. 1-4). 18.95 *(978-1-4197-1054-4(0)*, Abrams Bks. for Young Readers) Abrams, Inc.

Torres, John. Sonia Sotomayor: First Latina Supreme Court Justice. 2015. (Influential Latinos Ser.). (ENG., Illus.). 128p. (J). (gr. 7-7). 37.27 *(978-0-7660-7001-1(8))* Enslow Pubs., Inc.

Van Tol, Alex. Sonia Sotomayor: U. S. Supreme Court Justice. 2010. (Crabtree Groundbreaker Biographies Ser.). (ENG., Illus.). 112p. (J). (gr. 5-8). lib. bdg. *(978-0-7787-2537-4(5))* Crabtree Publishing Co.

Watson, Marilyn Myrick. Raul Castro: Arizona's First Hispanic Governor. 2007. (J). *(978-0-9790826-5-8(X))*; *(978-0-9790826-6-5(8))* Acacia Publishing, Inc.

Weber, Rebecca. Ellen Ochoa. 2011. (Early Connections Ser.). (J). *(978-1-61672-550-1(8))* Benchmark Education Co.

Wheeler, Jill C. Jennifer Lopez. 2003. (Star Tracks Ser.). (Illus.). 64p. (J). (gr. 3-8). lib. bdg. 27.07 *(978-1-57765-770-5(5))* ABDO Publishing Co.

—Julia Alvarez, 1 vol. 2012. (Children's Authors Set 6 Ser.). (ENG., Illus.). 24p. (YA). (gr. 2-5). 25.65 *(978-1-61783-045-7(3))* ABDO Publishing Co.

Williams, Zella. America Ferrera: Award-Winning Actress. 2010. (Hispanic Headliners Ser.). (ENG.). 24p. (J). pap. 8.25 *(978-1-4488-1478-7(2))*; lib. bdg. 22.60 *(978-1-4488-1473-2(1))* Rosen Publishing Group, Inc., The. (PowerKids Pr.).

—America Ferrera: Award-Winning Actress = Estrella de la Pantalla. 2010. (Hispanic Headliners / Hispanos en Las Noticias Ser.). (ENG & SPA.). 24p. (J). (gr. 2-5). lib. bdg. 22.60 *(978-1-4488-0713-0(1))* Rosen Publishing Group, Inc., The.

—Mark Sanchez: Quarterback on the Rise - Mariscal de Campo en Ascenso. 2010. (Hispanic Headliners / Hispanos en Las Noticias Ser.). (ENG & SPA.). 24p. (J). (gr. 2-5). 22.60 *(978-1-4488-1171-7(6))* Rosen Publishing Group, Inc., The.

—Sonia Sotomayor: Supreme Court Justice. 2010. (Hispanic Headliners Ser.). (ENG.). 24p. (J). pap. 8.25 *(978-1-4488-1474-9(X))*; lib. bdg. 22.60 *(978-1-4488-1455-8(3))* Rosen Publishing Group, Inc., The. (PowerKids Pr.).

Woog, Adam. Jennifer Lopez. 2008. (Great Hispanic Heritage Ser.). (Illus.). 117p. (gr. 6-12). lib. bdg. 35.00 *(978-0-7910-9724-3(2)*, Chelsea Hse.) Facts On File, Inc.

Worth, Richard. 1950s to 1960s. 2009. (Hispanic America 2 Ser.). 80p. (gr. 5). 34.21 *(978-0-7614-4177-9(8))* Marshall Cavendish GBR. Dist: Marshall Cavendish Corp.

—The 1970s to the 1980s. 2009. (Hispanic America 2 Ser.). 80p. (gr. 5). 34.21 *(978-0-7614-4178-6(6))* Marshall Cavendish Corp.

Zermeno C., Francisco. Caft Chronicles. 2007. 96p. per. 17.95 *(978-0-915745-98-2(4))* Floricanto Pr.

HISPANIC AMERICANS—FICTION

Altman, Linda Jacobs. El Camino de Amelia. 2004. (SPA., Illus.). (J). (gr. k-3). spiral bd. *(978-0-616-14603-3(5))* Canadian National Institute for the Blind/Institut National Canadien pour les Aveugles.

Anaya, Rudolfo. ChupaCabra & the Roswell UFO. 2008. (ENG.). 144p. (YA). (gr. 9-18). 9.95 *(978-0-8263-4469-4(0))* Univ. of New Mexico Pr.

—Curse of the ChupaCabra. 2013. (ENG.). 176p. (YA). pap. 19.95 *(978-0-8263-4115-0(2))* Univ. of New Mexico Pr.

Arena, Jen. Marta! Big & Small. Dominguez, Angela, illus. 2016. (ENG & SPA.). 32p. (J). 16.99 *(978-1-62672-243-9(9)*, 9781626722439) Roaring Brook Pr.

Argueta, Jorge. Moony Luna. Gómez, Elizabeth, illus. 2013.Tr. of Luna, Lunita Lunera. (ENG & SPA.). 32p. (J). pap. 9.95 *(978-0-89239-306-0(8)*, Children's Book Press) Lee & Low Bks., Inc.

Arntson, Steven. The Wrap-Up List. 2014. (ENG.). 240p. (YA). (gr. 7). pap. 8.99 *(978-0-544-23264-8(X)*, HMH Books For Young Readers) Houghton Mifflin Harcourt Publishing Co.

Bacigalupi, Paolo. Zombie Baseball Beatdown. (ENG.). (J). (gr. 3-7). 2014. 320p. pap. 7.99 *(978-0-316-22079-8(5))* 2013. 304p. 17.00 *(978-0-316-22078-1(7))* Little, Brown Bks. for Young Readers.

Benavidez, Max. Historia de Carlito/ Carlito's Story. 2008. 121p. pap. 8.95 *(978-1-60448-004-7(1))* Lectura Bks.

Bencastro, Mario. A Promise to Keep. Giersbach-Rascon, Susan, tr. from SPA. 2005. 134p. (J). (gr. 3-7). pap. 9.95 *(978-1-55885-457-4(6)*, Piñata Books) Arte Publico Pr.

Bertrand, Diane Gonzales. The F Factor. 2010. 256p. (YA). (gr. 6-18). pap. 12.95 *(978-1-55885-598-4(X)*, Piñata Books) Arte Publico Pr.

Bertrand, Diane Gonzales & Ventura, Gabriela Baeza. A Bean & Cheese Taco Birthday / un Cumpleaños con Tacos de Frijoles con Queso. Trujillo, Robert, illus. 2015. (SPA & ENG.). 32p. (J). (gr. k-3). 17.95 *(978-1-55885-812-1(1))* Arte Publico Pr.

Bowe, Julie. Birthday Glamour! 2015. (Victoria Torres, Unfortunately Average Ser.). (ENG.). 160p. (gr. 4-4). lib. bdg. 26.65 *(978-1-4965-0533-0(6))* Stone Arch Bks.

—Curve Ball. 2017. (Victoria Torres, Unfortunately Average Ser.). (ENG.). 160p. (gr. 4-4). pap. 5.95 *(978-1-4965-3820-8(X))*; lib. bdg. 26.65 *(978-1-4965-3818-5(8))* Stone Arch Bks.

—Dance Fever. 2017. (Victoria Torres, Unfortunately Average Ser.). (ENG.). 160p. (gr. 4-4). lib. bdg. 26.65 *(978-1-4965-3819-2(6))* Stone Arch Bks.

—Face the Music. 2015. (Victoria Torres, Unfortunately Average Ser.). (ENG.). 160p. (gr. 4-4). pap. 5.95 *(978-1-4965-0538-5(7))* Stone Arch Bks.

—Formula for Friends. 2015. (Victoria Torres, Unfortunately Average Ser.). (ENG.). 160p. (gr. 4-4). pap. 5.95 *(978-1-4965-0539-2(5))* Stone Arch Bks.

—So Much Drama. 2016. (Victoria Torres, Unfortunately Average Ser.). (ENG., Illus.). 160p. (gr. 4-4). pap. 5.95 *(978-1-4965-3807-9(2))*; lib. bdg. 26.65 *(978-1-4965-3799-7(8))* Stone Arch Bks.

—Vicka for President! 2016. (Victoria Torres, Unfortunately Average Ser.). (ENG., Illus.). 160p. (gr. 4-4). lib. bdg. 26.65 *(978-1-4965-3800-0(5))* Stone Arch Bks.

Bozarth, Jan. Zally's Book. Burden, Andrea, illus. 2010. (Fairy Godmother Academy Ser.: No. 3). (ENG.). 208p. (J). (gr. 3-7). pap. 6.99 *(978-0-375-85185-8(2)*, Yearling) Random Hse. Children's Bks.

Brown, Monica. Lola Levine & the Ballet Scheme. 2016. (Lola Levine Ser.: 3). (ENG., Illus.). 112p. (J). (gr. 1-5). 14.99 *(978-0-316-25844-9(X))* Little, Brown Bks. for Young Readers.

—Marisol McDonald & the Clash Bash/Marisol Mddonald y la Fiesta Sin Igual. Palacios, Sara, illus. 2013. (Marisol Mcdonald Ser.). (ENG & SPA.). 40p. (J). 18.95 *(978-0-89239-273-5(8))* Lee & Low Bks., Inc.

—Marisol Mcdonald & the Monster: Marisol Mcdonald y el Monstruo. Palacios, Sara, illus. 2016. (Marisol Mcdonald Ser.). (ENG & SPA.). 32p. (J). (gr. k-3). 18.95 *(978-0-89239-326-8(2))* Lee & Low Bks., Inc.

—Marisol Mcdonald Doesn't Match / Marisol Mcdonald no Combina. Palacios, Sara, illus. 2013. (Marisol Mcdonald Ser.). (SPA & ENG.). 32p. (J). (gr. -1-3). 17.95 *(978-0-89239-235-3(5))* Lee & Low Bks., Inc.

Broyles, Anne. Arturo & the Navidad Birds, 1 vol. Lewis, K. E., illus. 2013. (ENG & SPA.). 32p. (J). (gr. k-3). 16.99 *(978-1-4556-1801-9(2))* Pelican Publishing Co., Inc.

Calle, Juan & Valentino, Serena. Good Dream, Bad Dream: The World's Legendary Heroes Save the Night! 2014. (ENG & SPA., Illus.). 36p. (J). (gr. -1-3). 15.95 *(978-1-59702-103-6(2))* Immedium.

Caraballo, Samuel. Estas Manos: Manitas de Mi Familia. Costello, Shawn, illus. 2014.Tr. of These Hands: My Family's Hands. (ENG & SPA.). (J). 17.95 *(978-1-55885-795-7(8)*, Piñata Books) Arte Publico Pr.

—My Big Sister / Mi Hermana Mayor. Muraida, Thelma, illus. 2012. (ENG & SPA.). (J). (gr. 3-8). 16.95 *(978-1-55885-750-6(8)*, Piñata Books) Arte Publico Pr.

Carlson, Lori M., ed. Voices in First Person: Reflections on Latino Identity. Morais, Flavio, illus. Rivera-Ortiz, Manuel, photos by. 2008. (ENG.). 96p. (YA). (gr. 7-18). 17.99 *(978-1-4169-0635-3(5)*, Atheneum Bks. for Young Readers) Simon & Schuster Children's Publishing.

Carson, Diana Pastora. All the Muchos in the World: A Special Story about Love. Pruitt, Ginny, illus. 2006. 32p. (J). pap. 8.95 *(978-0-8198-0779-3(6))* Pauline Bks. & Media.

Cervantes, Angela. Allie, First at Last. 2016. (ENG.). 208p. (J). (gr. 3-7). 16.99 *(978-0-545-81223-8(2)*, Scholastic Pr.) Scholastic, Inc.

Chambers, Veronica & Clampet, Jason. Papi's Bodega. Miyares, Daniel, illus. 2013. (J). *(978-1-4231-0125-3(1))* Disney Pr.

Christopher, Matt. Centerfield Ballhawk. Beier, Ellen, illus. 2009. (New Peach Street Mudders Sports Library). 64p. (J). (gr. 2-4). lib. bdg. 23.93 *(978-1-59953-317-9(0))* Norwood Hse. Pr.

Cofer, Judith Ortiz. ¡A Bailar! / Let's Dance! Rodriguez, Christina Ann, illus. 2011. (ENG & SPA.). (J). 16.95 *(978-1-55885-698-1(6)*, Piñata Books) Arte Publico Pr.

Córdova, Zoraida. Labyrinth Lost. (Brooklyn Brujas Ser.: 1). (ENG.). (YA). (gr. 8-12). 2017. 352p. pap. 10.99

(978-1-4926-2316-8(4)) 2016. 336p. 17.99 *(978-1-4926-2094-5(7)*, 9781492620945) Sourcebooks, Inc.

Corpi, Lucha & Fields, Lisa. The Triple Banana Split Boy/El Nino Goloso. Corpi, Lucha & Fields, Lisa, illus. 2009. (SPA & ENG., Illus.). 32p. (J). (gr. -1-4). 16.95 *(978-1-55885-504-5(1))* Arte Publico Pr.

Cortez, Sarah, ed. You Don't Have a Clue: Latino Mystery Stories for Teens. 2011. 320p. (YA). (gr. 6-18). pap. *(978-1-55885-692-9(7))* Arte Publico Pr.

Cumpiano, Ina & Ramirez, Jose. Quinito, Day & Night. 2008.Tr. of Quinito, Dia y Noche. (SPA & ENG., Illus.). 24p. (J). (gr. -1-3). 16.95 *(978-0-89239-226-1(6))* Lee & Low Bks., Inc.

De Anda, Diane. A Day without Sugar / un día sin Azúcar. Baeza Ventura, Gabriela, tr. Montecalvo, Janet, illus. 2012. (SPA & ENG.). (J). 17.95 *(978-1-55885-702-5(8)*, Piñata Books) Arte Publico Pr.

DeAnda, Diane. The Monster in the Mattress & Other Stories: El Monstruo en el Colchón y Otros Cuentos. 2011. (SPA & ENG., Illus.). 90p. (J). (gr. 3-7). pap. 9.95 *(978-1-55885-693-6(5)*, Piñata Books) Arte Publico Pr.

dePaola, Tomie. Adelita: A Mexican Cinderella Story. dePaola, Tomie, illus. 2004. (SPA & ENG., Illus.). 40p. (J). (gr. -1-3). pap. 6.99 *(978-0-14-240187-3(0)*, Puffin Books) Penguin Young Readers Group.

Doerrfeld, Cori. A Perfect View. Doerrfeld, Cori & Page, Tyler, illus. 2017. (Cici: a Fairy's Tale Ser.: 3). (ENG.). 48p. (J). (gr. 2-5). 26.65 *(978-1-4677-6154-3(0))*; pap. 7.99 *(978-1-5124-3068-4(4))*; E-Book 19.99 ***(978-1-5124-2700-4(4)***, 9781512427004) Lerner Publishing Group. (Graphic Universe™).

—Truth in Sight. Doerrfeld, Cori & Page, Tyler, illus. 2016. (Cici: a Fairy's Tale Ser.: 2). (ENG.). 48p. (J). (gr. 2-5). lib. bdg. 26.65 *(978-1-4677-6153-6(2)*, Graphic Universe™) Lerner Publishing Group.

Dorros, Arthur. Papá & Me. Gutierrez, Rudy, illus. 2008. (ENG.). 32p. (J). (gr. -1-3). 16.99 *(978-0-06-058156-5(5)*, Rayo) HarperCollins Pubs.

Dower, Laura. Gabi & the Great Big Bakeover. Lazuli, Lilly, illus. 160p. 2017. (J). *(978-1-4747-2213-1(X))* 2016. (ENG.). (gr. 4-5). lib. bdg. 26.65 *(978-1-4965-3119-3(1))* Stone Arch Bks.

Duncan, Alexandra. Blight. 2017. 400p. (YA). (gr. 8). 17.99 *(978-0-06-239699-0(4)*, Greenwillow Bks.) HarperCollins Pubs.

Engle, Margarita. Mountain Dog. Ivanov, Aleksey & Ivanov, Olga, illus. 2013. (ENG.). 224p. (J). (gr. 3-7). 17.99 *(978-0-8050-9516-6(0)*, 9780805095166, Holt, Henry & Co. Bks. For Young Readers) Holt, Henry & Co.

—Mountain Dog. Ivanov, Aleksey & Ivanov, Olga, illus. 2014. (ENG.). 240p. (J). (gr. 3-7). pap. 7.99 *(978-1-250-04424-2(3)*, 9781250044242) Square Fish.

English, Karen. Don't Feed the Geckos! The Carver Chronicles, Book Three. Freeman, Laura, illus. 2016. (Carver Chronicles Ser.). (ENG.). 144p. (J). (gr. 1-4). pap. 5.99 *(978-0-544-81083-9(X)*, HMH Books For Young Readers) Houghton Mifflin Harcourt Publishing Co.

Eschberger, Beverly. The Elephants in the Land of Enchantment: An Elephant Family Adventure. Gower, Jim, illus. 2009. 96p. (J). pap. 3.99 *(978-1-932926-02-6(X)*, Kinkajou Pr.) Artemesia Publishing, LLC.

Fernandez, Giselle. Gigi & the Birthday Ring. Petersen, Sheli, illus. 2005. (J). *(978-1-56492-358-5(4))* Laredo Publishing Co., Inc.

Ficklin, Jonene H. The Garden Gate. 2005. (YA). 14.95 *(978-0-9761188-2-4(3))* Victor's Crown Publishing.

Flor Ada, Alma. Celebra el Ano Nuevo Chino con la Familia Fong. 2006. (Cuentos para Celebrar / Stories to Celebrate Ser.). (Illus.). 30p. (gr. k-6). per. 11.95 *(978-1-59820-114-7(X)*, Alfaguara) Santillana USA Publishing Co., Inc.

—Celebrate Chinese New Year with the Fong Family. Castro, Mima, illus. 2006. (Cuentos para Celebrar / Stories to Celebrate Ser.). 30p. (gr. k-6). per. 11.95 *(978-1-59820-126-0(3))* Santillana USA Publishing Co., Inc.

—Celebrate Christmas & Three Kings Day with Pablo & Carlitos. Torres, Walter, illus. 2006. (Cuentos para Celebrar / Stories to Celebrate Ser.). 30p. (gr. k-6). per. 11.95 *(978-1-59820-136-9(0))* Santillana USA Publishing Co., Inc.

—Quiero Ayudar! Dominguez, Angela, illus. 2010.Tr. of Let Me Help! (ENG & SPA.). 32p. (J). (gr. -1-3). 16.95 *(978-0-89239-232-2(0))* Lee & Low Bks., Inc.

Fontes, Justine. Benito Runs. (Surviving Southside Ser.). (ENG.). 104p. (YA). (gr. 6-12). 2015. 34.65 *(978-1-4677-6008-9(0)*, Lerner Digital) 2011. pap. 7.95 *(978-0-7613-6165-7(0))* 2011. lib. bdg. 27.93 *(978-0-7613-6151-0(0))* Lerner Publishing Group.

Frances, Barbara. Lottie's Adventure: A Kidnapping Unraveled. 2007. 180p. pap. 12.95 *(978-0-615-16787-9(X))* Positive Imaging, LLC.

Galindo, Claudia & Pluecker, John. Do You Know the Cucuy? Conoces Al Cucuy? Coombs, Jonathan, illus. 2008. (SPA & ENG.). 32p. (J). (gr. -1-2). 16.95 *(978-1-55885-492-5(4)*, Piñata Books) Arte Publico Pr.

Gallagher, Diana G. Advice about Family: Claudia Cristina Cortez Uncomplicates Your Life. Garvey, Brann, illus. 2010. (Claudia Cristina Cortez Ser.). (ENG.). 80p. (gr. 2-3). pap. 6.10 *(978-1-4342-2250-3(0)*, Claudia Cristina Cortez) Stone Arch Bks.

—Advice about Friends: Claudia Cristina Cortez Uncomplicates Your Life. Garvey, Brann, illus. 2010. (Claudia Cristina Cortez Ser.). (ENG.). 80p. (gr. 2-3). pap. 6.10 *(978-1-4342-2251-0(9)*, Claudia Cristina Cortez) Stone Arch Bks.

—Advice about School: Claudia Cristina Cortez Uncomplicates Your Life. Garvey, Brann, illus. 2010. (Claudia Cristina Cortez Ser.). (ENG.). 80p. (gr. 2-3). pap. 6.10 *(978-1-4342-2252-7(7))*; 26.65 *(978-1-4342-1905-3(4))* Stone Arch Bks. (Claudia Cristina Cortez).

—Advice about Work & Play: Claudia Cristina Cortez Uncomplicates Your Life. Garvey, Brann, illus. 2010. (Claudia Cristina Cortez Ser.). (ENG.). 80p. (gr. 2-3). pap. 6.10 *(978-1-4342-2253-4(5))*; 26.65 *(978-1-4342-1908-4(9))* Stone Arch Bks. (Claudia Cristina Cortez).

—Bad Luck Bridesmaid: The Complicated Life of Claudia Cristina Cortez, 1 vol. Garvey, Brann, illus. 2009. (Claudia Cristina Cortez Ser.). (ENG.). 88p. (gr. 2-3). 26.65 *(978-1-4342-1573-4(3)*, Claudia Cristina Cortez) Stone Arch Bks.

—Beach Blues: The Complicated Life of Claudia Cristina Cortez, 1 vol. Garvey, Brann, illus. 2008. (Claudia Cristina Cortez Ser.). (ENG.). 88p. (gr. 2-3). pap. 6.10 *(978-1-4342-0869-9(9)*, Claudia Cristina Cortez) Stone Arch Bks.

—Beware! The Complicated Life of Claudia Cristina Cortez, 1 vol. Garvey, Brann, illus. 2009. (Claudia Cristina Cortez Ser.). (ENG.). 88p. (gr. 2-3). 26.65 *(978-1-4342-1575-8(X)*, Claudia Cristina Cortez) Stone Arch Bks.

—Friends Forever? The Complicated Life of Claudia Cristina Cortez, 1 vol. Garvey, Brann, illus. 2008. (Claudia Cristina Cortez Ser.). (ENG.). 88p. (gr. 2-3). pap. 6.10 *(978-1-4342-0868-2(0))*; lib. bdg. 26.65 *(978-1-4342-0772-2(2))* Stone Arch Bks. (Claudia Cristina Cortez).

—Party! The Complicated Life of Claudia Cristina Cortez, 1 vol. Garvey, Brann, illus. 2008. (Claudia Cristina Cortez Ser.). (ENG.). 88p. (gr. 2-3). pap. 6.10 *(978-1-4342-0867-5(2))*; lib. bdg. 26.65 *(978-1-4342-0771-5(4))* Stone Arch Bks. (Claudia Cristina Cortez).

—Pool Problem: The Complicated Life of Claudia Cristina Cortez, 1 vol. Garvey, Brann, illus. 2009. (Claudia Cristina Cortez Ser.). (ENG.). 88p. (gr. 2-3). 26.65 *(978-1-4342-1577-2(6)*, Claudia Cristina Cortez) Stone Arch Bks.

—Vote! The Complicated Life of Claudia Cristina Cortez, 1 vol. Garvey, Brann, illus. 2008. (Claudia Cristina Cortez Ser.). (ENG.). 88p. (gr. 2-3). pap. 6.10 *(978-1-4342-0866-8(4))*; lib. bdg. 26.65 *(978-1-4342-0770-8(6))* Stone Arch Bks. (Claudia Cristina Cortez).

Garza, Xavier. The Donkey Lady Fights la Llorona & Other Stories / la Señora Asno Se Enfrenta a la Llorona y Otros Cuentos. Álvarez, Mayra E., tr. 2015. (ENG & SPA., Ilus.). 144p. (J). (gr. 3-6). pap. 9.95 *(978-1-55885-816-9(4)*, Piñata Books) Arte Publico Pr.

—Rooster Joe & the Bully / el Gallo Joe y el Abusón. 2016. (ENG & SPA.). 128p. (J). (gr. 5-8). pap. 9.95 *(978-1-55885-835-0(0)*, Piñata Books) Arte Publico Pr.

Garza, Xavier, illus. The Great & Mighty Nikko. 2015. (ENG.). 32p. (J). pap. 7.95 *(978-1-935955-83-2(7))*; (gr. -1-4). 16.95 *(978-1-935955-82-5(9))* Cinco Puntos Pr.

Gershator, David & Gershator, Phillis. Bread Is for Eating. Shaw-Smith, Emma, illus. 2003. (ENG & SPA.). 25p. (J). (gr. k-4). reprint ed. 16.00 *(978-0-7567-9033-2(6))* DIANE Publishing Co.

Gonzales Bertrand, Diane. There's a Name for This Feeling / Hay un Nombre para lo Que Siento. Baeza Ventura, Gabriela, tr. 2014. (ENG & SPA.). 72p. (J). pap. 10.95 *(978-1-55885-784-1(2)*, Piñata Books) Arte Publico Pr.

Gonzales, Felipe C. Little Folk Stories & Tales by Don Pablo: Bilingual Stories in Spanish & English = Chistes y Cuentos de Don Pablo: Cuentos Bilingües en Español e Inglés. 2010. (SPA & ENG.). (J). pap. 24.95 *(978-0-86534-772-4(7))* Sunstone Pr.

Gonzalez, Maya Christina. My Colors, My World. Gonzalez, Maya Christina, illus. 2013.Tr. of Mis Colores, Mi Mundo. (ENG & SPA., Illus.). 32p. (J). pap. 9.95 *(978-0-89239-278-0(9)*, Children's Book Press) Lee & Low Bks., Inc.

Gonzalez, Rigoberto & González, Rigoberto. Soledad Sigh-Sighs. Ibarra, Rosa, illus. 2014.Tr. of Soledad Suspiros. (ENG & SPA.). 32p. (J). pap. 8.95 *(978-0-89239-309-1(2)*, Children's Book Press) Lee & Low Bks., Inc.

Green, D. L. Kaitlyn & the Competition. 2016. (Babysitter Chronicles Ser.). (ENG.). 160p. (gr. 4-7). pap. 6.95 *(978-1-4914-8861-4(1))* Stone Arch Bks.

Haugaard, Kay. No Place. 2nd ed. 2007. (ENG., Illus.). 140p. (J). (gr. 2-8). per. 6.95 *(978-1-57131-675-2(2))* Milkweed Editions.

Hernandez, David. Suckerpunch. 2007. (ENG.). 224p. (YA). (gr. 9-18). 17.99 *(978-0-06-117330-1(4)*, HarperTeen) HarperCollins Pubs.

Ibarra, Maria Teresa Ornelas. Penny & Me. 2006. (J). 4.95 *(978-0-9774306-6-6(9))* Acacia Publishing, Inc.

Jones, Jen. Lissa & the Fund-Raising Funk, No. 3. 2011. (Team Cheer Ser.). (ENG.). 112p. (gr. 4-4). lib. bdg. 25.32 *(978-1-4342-2996-0(3)*, Team Cheer) Stone Arch Bks.

—Lissa & the Fund-Raising Funk: # 3, 1 vol. 2012. (Team Cheer Ser.). (ENG.). 112p. (gr. 4-4). pap. 7.19 *(978-1-4342-4251-8(X)*, Team Cheer) Stone Arch Bks.

Jones, Patrick. Bridge. 2014. (Alternative Ser.). (ENG.). 96p. (YA). (gr. 6-12). lib. bdg. 27.93 *(978-1-4677-3903-0(0))* Lerner Publishing Group.

—Guarding Secrets. 2015. (J). 9.99 *(978-1-4677-7694-3(7))*; (ENG.). 96p. (gr. 6-12). lib. bdg. 27.99 *(978-1-4677-5801-7(9))* Lerner Publishing Group.

—Triangle Choke. 2013. (Dojo Ser.). (ENG.). 136p. (YA). (gr. 6-12). pap. 7.95 *(978-1-4677-1487-7(9))*; lib. bdg. 27.93 *(978-1-4677-0630-8(2))* Lerner Publishing Group. (Darby Creek).

Jones, Patrick & Clark, Marshunna. Duty or Desire. 2016. (Unbarred Ser.). (ENG.). 112p. (YA). (gr. 6-12). lib. bdg. 27.99 *(978-1-5124-0002-1(5)*, Darby Creek) Lerner Publishing Group.

—Duty or Desire. 2016. (Unbarred Ser.). (ENG.). 112p. (YA). (gr. 6-12). pap. 7.99 *(978-1-5124-0089-2(0)*, Darby Creek) Lerner Publishing Group.

—Duty or Desire. 2016. (Unbarred Ser.). (ENG.). 112p. (YA). (gr. 6-12). 42.65 *(978-1-5124-0090-8(4)*, Darby Creek) Lerner Publishing Group.

Jules, Jacqueline. Abuela's Birthday. Smith, Kim, illus. 2015. (Sofia Martinez Ser.). (ENG.). 32p. (gr. k-2). lib. bdg. 21.32 *(978-1-4795-5775-2(7)*, Sofia Martinez) Picture Window Bks.

—Abuela's Special Letters. Smith, Kim, illus. 2017. (Sofia Martinez Ser.). (ENG.). 32p. (gr. k-2). lib. bdg. 21.32 *(978-1-5158-0728-5(2)*, Sofia Martinez) Picture Window Bks.

—The Beach Trip. Smith, Kim, illus. 2016. (Sofia Martinez Ser.). (ENG.). 32p. (gr. k-2). lib. bdg. 21.32 *(978-1-4795-8719-3(2)*, Sofia Martinez) Picture Window Bks.

—Freddie Ramos Makes a Splash. Benitez, Miguel, illus. 2013. (Zapato Power Ser.: Book 4). (ENG.). 96p. (J). (gr. 1-5). pap. 4.99 *(978-0-8075-9486-5(5))* Whitman, Albert & Co.

—Freddie Ramos Makes a Splash Bk. 4. Benítez, Miguel, illus. 2012. (Zapato Power Ser.: Book 4). (ENG.). 96p. (J). (gr. 1-5). 14.99 *(978-0-8075-9485-8(7))* Whitman, Albert & Co.

—Freddie Ramos Springs into Action. Benitez, Miguel, illus. 2011. (Zapato Power Ser.: Book 2). (ENG.). 96p. (J). (gr. 1-5). pap. 4.99 *(978-0-8075-9483-4(0))* Whitman, Albert & Co.

—Freddie Ramos Stomps the Snow. Benitez, Miguel, illus. 2014. (Zapato Power Ser.: Book 5). (ENG.). 96p. (J). (gr. 1-5). 14.99 *(978-0-8075-9487-2(3))* Whitman, Albert & Co.

—Freddie Ramos Takes Off, Bk. 1. Benitez, Miguel, illus. 2011. (Zapato Power Ser.: Book 1). (ENG.). 88p. (J). (gr. 1-5). pap. 4.99 *(978-0-8075-9479-7(2))* Whitman, Albert & Co.

—Freddie Ramos Zooms to the Rescue. Benitez, Miguel, illus. (Zapato Power Ser.: Book 3). (ENG.). 96p. (J). (gr. 1-5). 2012. pap. 4.99 *(978-0-8075-9484-1(9))*Bk. 3. 2011. 14.99 *(978-0-8075-9482-7(2))* Whitman, Albert & Co.

—Lights Out. Smith, Kim, illus. 2016. (Sofia Martinez Ser.). (ENG.). 32p. (gr. k-2). lib. bdg. 21.32 *(978-1-4795-8718-6(4))* Picture Window Bks.

—The Marigold Mess. Smith, Kim, illus. 2015. (Sofia Martinez Ser.). (ENG.). 32p. (gr. k-2). lib. bdg. 21.32 *(978-1-4795-5776-9(5)*, Sofia Martinez) Picture Window Bks.

—The Missing Mouse. Smith, Kim, illus. 2015. (Sofia Martinez Ser.). (ENG.). 32p. (gr. k-2). lib. bdg. 21.32 *(978-1-4795-5774-5(9)*, Sofia Martinez) Picture Window Bks.

—My Family Adventure. Smith, Kim, illus. 2015. (Sofia Martinez Ser.). (ENG.). 96p. (gr. k-2). pap. 4.95 *(978-1-4795-5790-5(0)*, Sofia Martinez) Picture Window Bks.

—My Vida Loca. Smith, Kim, illus. 2016. (Sofia Martinez Ser.). (ENG.). 96p. (gr. k-2). pap. 4.95 *(978-1-4795-8720-9(6)*, Sofia Martinez) Picture Window Bks.

—Picture Perfect. Smith, Kim, illus. 2015. (Sofia Martinez Ser.). (ENG.). 32p. (gr. k-2). lib. bdg. 21.32 *(978-1-4795-5773-8(0)*, Sofia Martinez) Picture Window Bks.

—The Secret Recipe. Smith, Kim, illus. 2016. (Sofia Martinez Ser.). (ENG.). 32p. (gr. k-2). lib. bdg. 21.32 *(978-1-4795-8717-9(6)*, Sofia Martinez) Picture Window Bks.

—Shopping Trip Trouble Smith, Kim, illus. 2017. (Sofia Martinez Ser.). (ENG.). 32p. (gr. k-2). lib. bdg. 21.32 *(978-1-5158-0729-2(0)*, Sofia Martinez) Picture Window Bks.

—Singing Superstar. Smith, Kim, illus. 2016. (Sofia Martinez Ser.). (ENG.). 32p. (gr. k-2). lib. bdg. 21.32 *(978-1-4795-8716-2(8)*, Sofia Martinez) Picture Window Bks.

Karre, Elizabeth. The Fight. 2013. (Surviving Southside Ser.). (ENG.). 128p. (YA). (gr. 6-12). pap. 7.95 *(978-1-4677-0709-1(0))*; lib. bdg. 27.93 *(978-1-4677-0596-7(9))* Lerner Publishing Group.

Klein, Adria F. Max Celebra el Ano Nuevo Chino, 1 vol. Robledo, Sol, tr. from ENG. Gallagher-Cole, Mernie, illus. 2007. (Read-It! Readers en Español: la Vida de Max Ser.). (SPA.). 24p. (gr. -1-3). lib. bdg. 21.32 *(978-1-4048-3794-2(9)*, Easy Readers) Picture Window Bks.

—Max Come Al Aire Libre, 1 vol. Robledo, Sol, tr. from ENG. Gallagher-Cole, Mernie, illus. 2007. (Read-It! Readers en Español: la Vida de Max Ser.). (SPA.). 24p. (gr. -1-3). lib. bdg. 21.32 *(978-1-4048-3795-9(7)*, Easy Readers) Picture Window Bks.

—Max Goes to School. Gallagher-Cole, Mernie, illus. 2007. (Read-It! Readers: the Life of Max Ser.). (ENG.). 24p. (gr. -1-2). per. 3.95 *(978-1-4048-3059-2(6)*, Easy Readers) Picture Window Bks.

—Max Goes to the Barber. Gallagher-Cole, Mernie, illus. 2007. (Read-It! Readers: the Life of Max Ser.). (ENG.). 24p. (gr. -1-2). per. 3.95 *(978-1-4048-3060-8(X)*, Easy Readers) Picture Window Bks.

—Max Goes to the Dentist. Gallagher-Cole, Mernie, illus. 2007. (Read-It! Readers: the Life of Max Ser.). (ENG.). 24p. (gr. -1-2). per. 3.95 *(978-1-4048-3061-5(8)*, Easy Readers) Picture Window Bks.

—Max Goes to the Doctor, 1 vol. Gallagher-Cole, Mernie, illus. 2007. (Read-It! Readers: the Life of Max Ser.). (ENG.). 24p. (gr. -1-2). lib. bdg. 21.32 *(978-1-4048-3680-8(2))*; per. 3.95 *(978-1-4048-3686-0(1)*, 1274408) Picture Window Bks. (Easy Readers).

—Max Goes to the Farm, 1 vol. Gallagher-Cole, Mernie, illus. 2007. (Read-It! Readers: the Life of Max Ser.). (ENG.). 24p. (gr. -1-2). lib. bdg. 21.32 *(978-1-4048-3678-5(0)*, Easy Readers) Picture Window Bks.

—Max Goes to the Farmers' Market, 1 vol. Gallagher-Cole, Mernie, illus. 2009. (Read-It! Readers: the Life of Max Ser.). (ENG.). 24p. (gr. -1-2). 21.32 *(978-1-4048-5263-1(8)*, Easy Readers) Picture Window Bks.

—Max Goes to the Fire Station, 1 vol. Gallagher-Cole, Mernie, illus. 2009. (Read-It! Readers: the Life of Max Ser.). (ENG.). 24p. (gr. -1-2). 21.32 *(978-1-4048-5266-2(2)*, Easy Readers) Picture Window Bks.

—Max Goes to the Library. Gallagher-Cole, Mernie, illus. (Read-It! Readers: the Life of Max Ser.). (ENG.). 24p. (gr. -1-2). 2007. per. 3.95 *(978-1-4048-3062-2(6))* 2005. lib. bdg. 21.32 *(978-1-4048-1182-9(6))* Picture Window Bks. (Easy Readers).

—Max Goes to the Nature Center, 1 vol. Gallagher-Cole, Mernie, illus. 2009. (Read-It! Readers: the Life of Max Ser.). (ENG.). 24p. (gr. -1-2). 21.32 *(978-1-4048-5269-3(7)*, Easy Readers) Picture Window Bks.

—Max Goes to the Playground, 1 vol. Gallagher-Cole, Mernie, illus. 2007. (Read-It! Readers: the Life of Max Ser.). (ENG.). 24p. (gr. -1-2). lib. bdg. 21.32 *(978-1-4048-3681-5(0)*, Easy Readers) Picture Window Bks.

—Max Goes to the Recycling Center, 1 vol. Gallagher-Cole, Mernie, illus. 2009. (Read-It! Readers: the Life of Max Ser.). (ENG.). 24p. (gr. -1-2). 21.32 *(978-1-4048-5272-3(7)*, Easy Readers) Picture Window Bks.

—Max Goes to the Zoo, 1 vol. Gallagher-Cole, Mernie, illus. 2007. (Read-It! Readers: the Life of Max Ser.). (ENG.). 24p. (gr. -1-2). lib. bdg. 21.32 *(978-1-4048-3677-8(2))*; per. 3.95 *(978-1-4048-3683-9(7))* Picture Window Bks. (Easy Readers).

—Max Se Queda a Dormir, 1 vol. Robledo, Sol, tr. from ENG. Gallagher-Cole, Mernie, illus. 2007. (Read-It! Readers en Español: la Vida de Max Ser.). (SPA.). 24p. (gr. -1-3). lib. bdg. 21.32 *(978-1-4048-3797-3(3)*, Easy Readers) Picture Window Bks.

—Max Va a la Biblioteca, 1 vol. Lozano, Clara, tr. Gallagher-Cole, Mernie, illus. 2007. (Read-It! Readers en Español: la Vida de Max Ser.). (SPA.). 24p. (gr. -1-3). per. 3.95 *(978-1-4048-3036-3(7)*, Easy Readers) Picture Window Bks.

—Max Va a la Escuela, 1 vol. Lozano, Clara, tr. Gallagher-Cole, Mernie, illus. 2007. (Read-It! Readers en Español: la Vida de Max Ser.). (SPA.). 24p. (gr. -1-3). per. 3.95 *(978-1-4048-3037-0(5)*, Easy Readers) Picture Window Bks.

—Max Va a la Peluqueria, 1 vol. Lozano, Clara, tr. Gallagher-Cole, Mernie, illus. 2007. (Read-It! Readers en Español: la Vida de Max Ser.). (SPA.). 24p. (gr. -1-3). per. 3.95 *(978-1-4048-3038-7(3)*, Easy Readers) Picture Window Bks.

—Max Va Al Dentista, 1 vol. Lozano, Clara, tr. Gallagher-Cole, Mernie, illus. 2007. (Read-It! Readers en Español: la Vida de Max Ser.). (SPA.). 24p. (gr. -1-3). per. 3.95 *(978-1-4048-3039-4(1)*, Easy Readers) Picture Window Bks.

—Max Va Al Doctor. Lozano, Clara, tr. from ENG. Gallagher-Cole, Mernie, illus. 2008. (Read-It! Readers en Español: la Vida de Max Ser.). (SPA.). 24p. (gr. -1-3). per. 3.95 *(978-1-4048-4584-8(4)*, Easy Readers) Picture Window Bks.

—Max y la Fiesta de Adopcion, 1 vol. Robledo, Sol, tr. from ENG. Gallagher-Cole, Mernie, illus. 2007. (Read-It! Readers en Español: la Vida de Max Ser.). (SPA.). 24p. (gr. -1-3). lib. bdg. 21.32 *(978-1-4048-3793-5(0)*, Easy Readers) Picture Window Bks.

—Max's Fun Day, 1 vol. Gallagher-Cole, Mernie, illus. 2007. (Read-It! Readers: the Life of Max Ser.). (ENG.). 24p. (gr. -1-2). lib. bdg. 21.32 *(978-1-4048-3150-6(9)*, 1265797, Easy Readers) Picture Window Bks.

Kraus, Joanna H. A Night of Tamales & Roses. Caravela, Elena, illus. 2007. (ENG.). 32p. (J). (gr. -1-3). 15.95 *(978-0-9726614-4-7(1))* Shenanigan Bks.

Lachtman, Ofelia Dumas. Pepita & the Bully: Pepita y la Peleonera. Baeza Ventura, Gabriela, tr. Pardo DeLange, Alex, illus. 2011. (SPA & ENG.). 32p. (J). (gr. -1-3). 16.95 *(978-1-55885-689-9(7)*, Piñata Books) Arte Publico Pr.

—Pepita on Pepper Street/Pepita en la Calle Pepper. Monsivais, Maria Estela, tr. from ENG. Delange, Alex Pardo, illus. 2008. (SPA & ENG.). 32p. (J). (gr. -1-3). 16.95 *(978-1-55885-443-7(6)*, Piñata Books) Arte Publico Pr.

—Pepita Packs Up: Pepita Empaca. Ventura, Gabriela Baeza, tr. from ENG. Delange, Alex Pardo, illus. 2005. 48p. (J). (gr. -1-k). lib. bdg. 16.95 *(978-1-55885-431-4(2)*, Piñata Books) Arte Publico Pr.

—The Trouble with Tessa. 2005. 122p. (J). (gr. 3-7). per. 9.95 *(978-1-55885-448-2(7)*, Piñata Books) Arte Publico Pr.

Laínez, René Colato. Mamá the Alien: Mamá la Extraterrestre. Lacámara, Laura, illus. 2016. (ENG & SPA.). 32p. (J). (gr. 1-4). 17.95 *(978-0-89239-298-8(3))* Lee & Low Bks., Inc.

—The Tooth Fairy Meets el Ratón Pérez. Lintern, Tom, illus. 2010. (ENG.). 32p. (J). (gr. -1-2). 15.99 *(978-1-58246-296-7(8)*, Tricycle Pr.) Random Hse. Children's Bks.

—Waiting for Papá/Esperando a Papá. Accardo, Anthony, illus.Tr. of Esperando a Papa. (ENG & SPA.). 32p. (gr. 1-3). 16.95 *(978-1-55885-403-1(7)*, Piñata Books) Arte Publico Pr.

Langan, Paul. The Fallen. 2006. (Bluford Ser.: No. 11). 144p. (YA). (gr. 7-18). pap. 4.95 *(978-1-59194-066-1(4))* Townsend Pr.

Liberts, Jennifer. Go, Go, Trucks! Yamada, Mike, illus. 2017. (Step into Reading Ser.). (ENG.). 32p. (J). (gr. -1-1). 3.99 ***(978-0-399-54951-9(X))***; lib. bdg. 12.99 ***(978-0-399-54952-6(8))*** Random Hse. Children's Bks. (Random Hse. Bks. for Young Readers).

Littman, Sarah Darer. Life, After. 2010. (ENG.). 288p. (J). (gr. 7-18). 17.99 *(978-0-545-15144-3(9)*, Scholastic Pr.) Scholastic, Inc.

López, Diana. Ask My Mood Ring How I Feel. 2013. (ENG.). 336p. (J). (gr. 3-7). 17.00 *(978-0-316-20996-0(1))* Little Brown & Co.

—Ask My Mood Ring How I Feel. 2014. (ENG.). 352p. (J). (gr. 3-7). pap. 7.99 *(978-0-316-20994-6(5))* Little, Brown Bks. for Young Readers.

Lord, Cynthia. A Handful of Stars. (ENG.). 192p. (J). (gr. 3-7). 2017. pap. 6.99 ***(978-0-545-70028-3(0))*** 2015. 16.99 *(978-0-545-70027-6(2))* Scholastic, Inc. (Scholastic Pr.).

Lozano, José. Little Chanclas. 2015. (ENG & SPA., Illus.). 32p. (J). (gr. k-3). 16.95 *(978-1-935955-85-6(3))* Cinco Puntos Pr.

Lynch, Janet Nichols. Messed Up. 2009. (ENG.). 320p. (YA). (gr. 7-18). 17.95 *(978-0-8234-2185-5(6))* Holiday Hse., Inc.

Manning, Maurie J. Kitchen Dance. Manning, Maurie J., illus. 2008. (ENG., Illus.). 32p. (J). (gr. -1-3). 17.99 *(978-0-618-99110-5(7))* Houghton Mifflin Harcourt Publishing Co.

Manushkin, Fran. Pedro & the Shark. Lyon, Tammie, illus. 2017. (Pedro Ser.). (ENG.). 32p. (gr. k-2). lib. bdg. 21.32 *(978-1-5158-0873-2(4))* Pedro Pubns. GBR. Dist: Capstone Pub.

—Pedro, First-Grade Hero. Lyon, Tammie, illus. 2016. (Pedro Ser.). (ENG.). 96p. (gr. k-2). pap. 4.95 *(978-1-5158-0112-2(8))* Pedro Pubns. GBR. Dist: Capstone Pub.

—Pedro for President. Lyon, Tammie, illus. 2016. (Pedro Ser.). (ENG.). 32p. (gr. k-2). lib. bdg. 21.32 *(978-1-5158-0087-3(3))* Pedro Pubns. GBR. Dist: Capstone Pub.

—Pedro Goes Buggy. Lyon, Tammie, illus. 2016. (Pedro Ser.). (ENG.). 32p. (gr. k-2). lib. bdg. 21.32 *(978-1-5158-0085-9(7))* Pedro Pubns. GBR. Dist: Capstone Pub.

—Pedro's Big Goal. Lyon, Tammie, illus. 2016. (Pedro Ser.). (ENG.). 32p. (gr. k-2). lib. bdg. 21.32 *(978-1-5158-0086-6(5))* Pedro Pubns. GBR. Dist: Capstone Pub.

—Pedro's Mystery Club. Lyon, Tammie, illus. 2016. (Pedro Ser.). (ENG.). 32p. (gr. k-2). lib. bdg. 21.32 *(978-1-5158-0084-2(9))* Pedro Pubns. GBR. Dist: Capstone Pub.

Manzano, Sonia. A Box Full of Kittens. Phelan, Matt, illus. 2007. (ENG.). 40p. (J). (gr. -1-3). 17.99 *(978-0-689-83089-1(0)*, Atheneum Bks. for Young Readers) Simon & Schuster Children's Publishing.

Marcantonio, Patricia Santos, et al. Red Ridin' in the Hood: And Other Cuentos. Alarcão, Renato, illus. 2005. (ENG.). 192p. (J). (gr. 2-5). 17.99 *(978-0-374-36241-6(6)*, 9780374362416, Farrar, Straus & Giroux (BYR)) Farrar, Straus & Giroux.

Martelli, Dawn. Like Me. Wharton, Jennifer Heyd, illus. 2004. (J). *(978-1-893516-01-4(6))* Our Child Pr.

Martinez, Claudia Guadalupe. Pig Park. 2014. (ENG.). 248p. (J). 15.95 *(978-1-935955-76-4(4))* Cinco Puntos Pr.
—The Smell of Old Lady Perfume. 2008. (ENG., Illus.). 248p. (J). (gr. 4-9). 15.95 *(978-1-933693-18-7(5))* Cinco Puntos Pr.
Martínez, Claudia Guadalupe. Smell of Old Lady Perfume. 2011. (ENG., Illus.). 256p. (J). (gr. 4-10). pap. 7.95 *(978-1-933693-88-0(6))* Cinco Puntos Pr.
Mateo, José Manuel. Migrant. Pedro, Javier Martínez, illus. 2014. (ENG & SPA.). 22p. (J). (gr. 3-7). 19.95 *(978-1-4197-0957-9(7),* Abrams Bks. for Young Readers) Abrams, Inc.
McConnie Zapater, Beatriz. Fiesta. Ortega, Jose, illus. 2005. (Multicultural Celebrations Ser.). 32p. (J). 4.95 *(978-1-59373-009-3(8))* Bunker Hill Publishing, Inc.
McCormack, Caren McNelly. The Fiesta Dress: A Quinceanera Tale. 0 vols. Aviles, Martha, illus. 2012. (ENG.). 42p. (J). (gr. k-4). pap. 7.99 *(978-0-7614-6236-1(8),* 9780761462361, Amazon Children's Publishing) Amazon Publishing.
McDonald, Kirsten. The Big Rain, 1 vol. Meza, Erika, illus. 2016. (Carlos & Carmen Ser.). (ENG.). 32p. (J). (gr. k-3). 27.07 *(978-1-62402-137-4(9))* Magic Wagon.
—The Green Surprise, 1 vol. Meza, Erika, illus. 2016. (Carlos & Carmen Ser.). (ENG.). 32p. (J). (gr. k-3). 27.07 *(978-1-62402-138-1(7))* Magic Wagon.
—The Nighttime Noise, 1 vol. Meza, Erika, illus. 2016. (Carlos & Carmen Ser.). (ENG.). 32p. (J). (gr. k-3). 27.07 *(978-1-62402-139-8(5))* Magic Wagon.
—The One-Tire House, 1 vol. Meza, Erika, illus. 2016. (Carlos & Carmen Ser.). (ENG.). 32p. (J). (gr. k-3). 27.07 *(978-1-62402-140-4(9))* Magic Wagon.
—The Perfect Piñatas. 2016. (Carlos & Carmen Set 3 Ser.). (ENG.). (gr. -1-3). lib. bdg. 27.07 ***(978-1-62402-183-1(2))*** ABDO Publishing Co.
—The Pet Show Problem. 2016. (Carlos & Carmen Set 3 Ser.). (ENG., Illus.). (J). (gr. -1-3). lib. bdg. 27.07 ***(978-1-62402-184-8(0))*** ABDO Publishing Co.
—The Sandy Weekend, 1 vol. Meza, Erika, illus. 2016. (ENG.). 32p. (J). 27.07 *(978-1-62402-142-8(5))* Magic Wagon.
—The Sparkly Night. 2016. (Carlos & Carmen Set 3 Ser.). (ENG., Illus.). (J). (gr. -1-3). lib. bdg. 27.07 ***(978-1-62402-185-5(9))*** ABDO Publishing Co.
—Tio Time, 1 vol. Meza, Erika, illus. 2016. (ENG.). 32p. (J). *(978-1-62402-143-5(3))* Magic Wagon.
—The Wobbly Wheels, 1 vol. Meza, Erika, illus. 2016. (ENG.). 32p. (J). *(978-1-62402-144-2(1))* Magic Wagon.
—The Yummy Mistake. Meza, Erika, illus. 2016. (ENG.). 32p. (J). *(978-1-62402-145-9(X))* Magic Wagon.
McManis, Margaret. Olé! Cinco de Mayo!, 1 vol. Harrington, David, illus. 2013. (ENG.). 32p. (J). (gr. k-3). 16.99 *(978-1-4556-1754-8(7))* Pelican Publishing Co., Inc.
Medina, Meg. Tia Isa Quiere un Carro. Munoz, Claudio, illus. 2012.Tr. of Tia Isa Wants a Car. (SPA.). 32p. (J). (gr. -1-2). pap. 6.99 *(978-0-7636-5751-2(4))* Candlewick Pr.
—Tía Isa Quiere un Carro. 2012.Tr. of Tia Isa Wants a Car. (SPA.). lib. bdg. 17.20 *(978-0-606-23801-4(8),* Turtleback) Turtleback Bks.
—Tia Isa Wants a Car. Munoz, Claudio, illus. 2016. (ENG.). 32p. (J). (gr. -1-2). 6.99 *(978-0-7636-5752-9(2))* Candlewick Pr.
—Tia Isa Wants a Car. Muñoz, Claudio, illus. 2011. (ENG.). 32p. (J). (gr. -1-2). 15.99 *(978-0-7636-4156-6(1))* Candlewick Pr.
Miller-Lachmann, Lyn. Once upon a Cuento. 2003. (ENG.). 256p. pap. 18.95 *(978-1-880684-99-3(3))* Curbstone Pr.
Montes, Marisa. A Crazy Mixed-Up Spanglish Day. Cepeda, Joe, illus. 2004. (Get Ready for Gabi Ser.). 120p. (gr. 2-5). 14.00 *(978-0-7569-3403-3(6))* Perfection Learning Corp.
—A Crazy Mixed-Up Spanglish Day. Cepeda, Joe, illus. 2003. (Get Ready for Gabi Ser.). 128p. (J). 12.95 *(978-0-439-51710-2(9),* Scholastic Paperbacks) Scholastic, Inc.
Montijo, Rhode. Chews Your Destiny. Montijo, Rhode, illus. 2017. (Gum Girl Novel Ser.). (ENG., Illus.). 128p. (J). (gr. 1-3). pap. 5.99 *(978-1-4231-5794-6(X))* Hyperion Bks. for Children.
—Chews Your Destiny. 2013. (Gum Girl Novel Ser.). (ENG.). 128p. (J). (gr. -1-3). 14.99 *(978-1-4231-5740-3(0))* Hyperion Pr.
Mora, Pat. Let's Eat! - ¡A Comer! Suarez, Maribel, illus. 2008. (My Family: Mi Familia Ser.). (SPA & ENG.). 24p. (J). (gr. -1-3). 12.99 *(978-0-06-085038-8(8),* Rayo) HarperCollins Pubs.
Mora, Pat & Parra, John. Gracias/Thanks. 2005. (ENG & SPA., Illus.). 32p. (J). (gr. k-5). 17.95 *(978-1-60060-258-0(4))* Lee & Low Bks., Inc.
Namm, Diane. Pick a Pet. Suarez, Maribel, tr. Suarez, Maribel, illus. 2004. (My First Reader Ser.). (ENG.). 31p. (J). 18.50 *(978-0-516-24417-4(5),* Children's Pr.) Scholastic Library Publishing.
Nikola-Lisa, W. My Teacher Can Teach... Anyone! Galindo, Felipe, illus. 2004. (ENG.). 32p. (J). (gr. -1-2). 16.95 *(978-1-58430-163-9(5));* pap. 9.95 *(978-1-60060-276-4(2))* Lee & Low Bks., Inc.
Older, Daniel José. Shadowshaper. (ENG.). (J). 2016. 320p. (gr. 7). pap. 9.99 *(978-1-338-03247-5(X))* 2015. 304p. (gr. 9). 17.99 *(978-0-545-59161-4(9))* Scholastic, Inc.
Quintero, Sofia. Efrain's Secret. 2011. (ENG.). 276p. (YA). (gr. 9). pap. 8.99 *(978-0-440-24062-4(X),* Ember) Random Hse. Children's Bks.
—Show & Prove. 2015. (ENG.). 352p. (YA). (gr. 7). 17.99 *(978-0-375-84707-3(3),* Knopf Bks. for Young Readers) Random Hse. Children's Bks.
Ramos, Dania. Who's Ju? 2015. (ENG.). 174p. (J). pap. 9.95 *(978-1-937997-61-8(8))* Northampton Hse.
Ricci, Christine. Say Cheese! Savitsky, Steven, illus. 2004. (Dora the Explorer Ser.). (ENG.). 24p. (J). pap. 3.99 *(978-0-689-86496-4(5),* Simon Spotlight/Nickelodeon) Simon Spotlight/Nickelodeon.
Rice, David & Rice, David Talbot. Crazy Loco. Clayton, Christian, illus. 2003. (ENG.). 144p. (YA). (gr. 7-11). 6.99 *(978-0-14-250056-9(9),* Speak) Penguin Young Readers Group.
Rivera-Ashford, Roni Capin. My Tata's Remedies - Los Remedios de Mi Tata. Castro L., Antonio, illus. 2015. (ENG & SPA.). 40p. (J). (gr. 1-6). pap. 8.95 *(978-1-935955-89-4(6))* Cinco Puntos Pr.
Rivera, Lilliam. The Education of Margot Sanchez. 2017. (ENG., Illus.). 304p. (YA). (gr. 9). 17.99 *(978-1-4814-7211-1(9),* Simon & Schuster Bks. For Young Readers) Simon & Schuster Bks. For Young Readers.
Robleda, Margarita. Paco: A Latino Boy in the U.S. 2004. (Paco & María Ser.). (SPA.). 36p. (gr. 3-5). pap. 13.95 *(978-1-59437-560-6(7),* Alfaguara) Santillana USA Publishing Co., Inc.
Rodriguez, Cindy L. When Reason Breaks. 2015. (ENG.). 304p. (YA). (gr. 7-12). 17.99 *(978-1-61963-412-1(0),* 9781619634121, Bloomsbury USA Childrens) Bloomsbury Publishing USA.
Rodriguez, Luis J. It Doesn't Have to Be This Way. Galvez, Daniel, illus. 2013. (ENG & SPA.). 32p. (J). pap. 9.95 *(978-0-89239-203-2(7))* Lee & Low Bks., Inc.
Roper, Robert, illus. Dora Goes to School. 2004. (Dora the Explorer Ser.: Vol. 8). (ENG.). 24p. (J). pap. 3.99 *(978-0-689-86494-0(9),* Simon Spotlight/Nickelodeon) Simon Spotlight/Nickelodeon.
Rosas, Marcelino. Afuera: A Young Latino's Journey. 2013. 226p. (YA). pap. 12.99 *(978-0-9859437-0-7(X))* Proud Peacock Publishing.
Rose, Judith Robbins. Look Both Ways in the Barrio Blanco. 2015. (ENG.). 352p. (J). (gr. 5). 16.99 *(978-0-7636-7235-5(1))* Candlewick Pr.
Ruiz-Flores, Lupe. The Battle of the Snow Cones/La Guerra de las Raspas. 2010. (SPA.). 32p. (J). (gr. -1-3). 16.95 *(978-1-55885-575-5(0),* Piñata Books) Arte Publico Pr.
Saldana, Theresa. The Almost Murder & Other Stories. 2008. (ENG.). 144p. (YA). (gr. 6-18). pap. 10.95 *(978-1-55885-507-6(6),* Piñata Books) Arte Publico Pr.
Sánchez-Korrol, Virginia. A Surprise for Teresita / una Sorpresa para Teresita. Flores, Carolyn Dee, illus. 2016. (ENG & SPA.). 32p. (J). (gr. k-3). 17.95 *(978-1-55885-831-2(8),* Piñata Books) Arte Publico Pr.
Sanders, Jeane F. Ramón. 2008. 100p. pap. 19.95 *(978-1-60610-768-3(2))* America Star Bks.
Schraff, Anne. Dark Secrets, 1 vol. unabr. ed. 2011. (Urban Underground Ser.). (ENG.). 201p. (YA). (gr. 9-12). pap. 9.95 *(978-1-61651-267-5(9))* Saddleback Educational Publishing, Inc.
—Leap of Faith, 1 vol. unabr. ed. 2011. (Urban Underground Ser.). (ENG.). 201p. (YA). (gr. 9-12). pap. 9.95 *(978-1-61651-588-1(0))* Saddleback Educational Publishing, Inc.
—The Petition. 2008. (Passages Ser.). 103p. (J). (gr. 4-6). lib. bdg. 13.95 *(978-0-7569-8391-8(6))* Perfection Learning Corp.
—The Stranger, 1 vol. unabr. ed. 2011. (Urban Underground Ser.). (ENG.). 200p. (YA). (gr. 9-12). pap. 9.95 *(978-1-61651-266-8(0))* Saddleback Educational Publishing, Inc.
—Time of Courage, 1 vol. unabr. ed. 2011. (Urban Underground Ser.). (ENG.). 197p. (YA). (gr. 9-12). pap. 9.95 *(978-1-61651-270-5(9))* Saddleback Educational Publishing, Inc.
—To Catch a Dream, 1 vol. unabr. ed. 2011. (Urban Underground Ser.). (ENG.). 198p. (YA). (gr. 9-12). pap. 9.95 *(978-1-61651-269-9(5))* Saddleback Educational Publishing, Inc.
—The Unforgiven, 1 vol. unabr. ed. 2011. (Urban Underground Ser.). (ENG.). 198p. (YA). (gr. 9-12). pap. 9.95 *(978-1-61651-586-7(4))* Saddleback Educational Publishing, Inc.
—Waters Edge, 1 vol. unabr. ed. 2011. (Urban Underground Ser.). (ENG.). 197p. (YA). (gr. 9-12). pap. 9.95 *(978-1-61651-589-8(9))* Saddleback Educational Publishing, Inc.
Schraff, Anne E. Deliverance, 1 vol. unabr. ed. 2011. (Urban Underground Ser.). (ENG.). 198p. (YA). (gr. 9-12). pap. 9.95 *(978-1-61651-587-4(2))* Saddleback Educational Publishing, Inc.
Siegal, Ida. Undercover! (Emma Is on the Air #4) 2016. (Emma Is on the Air Ser.: 4). (ENG.). 128p. (J). (gr. 2-5). pap. 4.99 *(978-0-545-68710-2(1),* Scholastic Paperbacks) Scholastic, Inc.
Silvera, Adam. They Both Die at the End. 2017. 384p. (YA). (gr. 9). 17.99 ***(978-0-06-245779-0(9))*** HarperCollins Pubs.
Simon, Charnan. Shattered Star. 2015. (Surviving Southside Ser.). (ENG.). 104p. (YA). (gr. 6-12). 34.65 *(978-1-4677-6011-9(0),* Lerner Digital) Lerner Publishing Group.
Soto, Gary. Accidental Love. 2008. (ENG., Illus.). 192p. (YA). (gr. 7). pap. 9.99 *(978-0-15-206113-5(4))* Houghton Mifflin Harcourt Publishing Co.
Stamper, Judith Bauer. The Quinceañera. Varma, Ishan, illus. 2010. (J). *(978-1-60617-121-9(6))* Teaching Strategies, LLC.
Starr, Meg. Alicia's Happy Day, 1 vol. Van Wright, Cornelius & Hu, Ying-Hwa, illus. 2003. (ENG.). 32p. (J). pap. 5.95 *(978-1-932065-06-0(7))* Star Bright Bks., Inc.
—Alicia's Happy Day, 1 vol. Hu, Ying-Hwa & Van Wright, Cornelius, illus. 2003. (ENG.). 32p. (J). (gr. -1-3). 15.95 *(978-1-887734-85-1(6))* Star Bright Bks., Inc.
—Alicia's Happy Day (Spanish/English), 1 vol. Fiol, Maria, tr. from ENG. Van Wright, Cornelius & Hu, Ying-Hwa, illus. 2007. (SPA & ENG.). 32p. (J). (gr. k-3). pap. 6.95 *(978-1-59572-116-7(9))* Star Bright Bks., Inc.
—Alicia's Happy Day (Spanish/English), 1 vol. Fiol, Maria, tr. Van Wright, Cornelius & Hu, Ying-Hwa, illus. 2007. (ENG.). 32p. (J). (gr. -1-3). 15.95 *(978-1-59572-115-0(0))* Star Bright Bks., Inc.
Stewart, Jennifer J. The Twelve Days of Christmas in Arizona. Avril, Lynne, illus. 2010. (Twelve Days of Christmas in America Ser.). (ENG.). 40p. (J). (gr. k). 12.95 *(978-1-4027-7036-4(7))* Sterling Publishing Co., Inc.
Terrell, Brandon. The Cursed Stage. Epelbaum, Mariano, illus. 2017. (Snoops, Inc Ser.). (ENG.). 112p. (gr. 4-6). lib. bdg. 26.65 *(978-1-4965-4346-2(7))* Stone Arch Bks.
—Tracking Champ. Epelbaum, Mariano, illus. 2017. (Snoops, Inc Ser.). (ENG.). 112p. (gr. 4-6). lib. bdg. 26.65 *(978-1-4965-4348-6(3))* Stone Arch Bks.
—The Vanishing Treasure. Epelbaum, Mariano, illus. 2017. (Snoops, Inc Ser.). (ENG.). 112p. (gr. 4-6). lib. bdg. 26.65 *(978-1-4965-4345-5(9))* Stone Arch Bks.
Thong, Roseanne Greenfield. Green Is a Chile Pepper. 2016. (J). lib. bdg. 18.40 *(978-0-606-39431-4(1))* Turtleback Bks.
—Green Is a Chile Pepper: A Book of Colors. 2014. (Multicultural Shapes & Colors Ser.). (Illus.). 40p. (J). lib. bdg. 28.50 *(978-1-60753-707-6(9))* Amicus Publishing.
—Green Is a Chile Pepper: A Book of Colors. Parra, John, illus. 2014. (ENG & SPA.). 40p. (J). (gr. -1-k). 16.99 *(978-1-4521-0203-0(1))* Chronicle Bks. LLC.
—Round Is a Tortilla. Parra, John, illus. 2015. (ENG.). 40p. (J). (gr. -1-k). 7.99 *(978-1-4521-4568-6(7))* Chronicle Bks. LLC.
—Round Is a Tortilla: A Book of Shapes. 2014. (Multicultural Shapes & Colors Ser.). (Illus.). 40p. (J). lib. bdg. 28.50 *(978-1-60753-566-9(1))* Amicus Publishing.
—Round Is a Tortilla: A Book of Shapes. Parra, John, illus. 2013. (ENG.). 40p. (J). (gr. -1-k). 16.99 *(978-1-4521-0616-8(9))* Chronicle Bks. LLC.
Torres, Jennifer. Finding the Music, 1 vol. Alarcão, Renato, illus. 2015.Tr. of En Pos de la Música. (ENG & SPA.). 40p. (J). 18.95 *(978-0-89239-291-9(6))* Lee & Low Bks., Inc.
Van Draanen, Wendelin. The Gecko & Sticky: the Power Potion. Gilpin, Stephen, illus. 2011. (Gecko & Sticky Ser.). (ENG.). 240p. (J). (gr. 3-7). 6.99 *(978-0-440-42245-7(0),* Yearling) Random Hse. Children's Bks.
—The Greatest Power. Gilpin, Stephen, illus. 2011. (Gecko & Sticky Ser.: Bk. 1). (ENG.). 208p. (J). (gr. 3-7). 7.99 *(978-0-440-42243-3(4),* Yearling) Random Hse. Children's Bks.
—Sinister Substitute. Gilpin, Stephen, illus. (Gecko & Sticky Ser.: Bk. 3). (ENG.). 224p. (J). (gr. 3-7). 2011. 7.99 *(978-0-440-42244-0(2),* Yearling) 2010. 12.99 *(978-0-375-84378-5(7),* Knopf Bks. for Young Readers) Random Hse. Children's Bks.
Velasquez, Eric. Looking for Bongo. 2017. (ENG.). 32p. (J). (gr. -1-1). 6.99 *(978-0-8234-3767-2(1))* Holiday Hse., Inc.
—Looking for Bongo. Velasquez, Eric, illus. 2016. (ENG., Illus.). 32p. (J). (gr. -1-1). 16.95 *(978-0-8234-3565-4(2))* Holiday Hse., Inc.
Velásquez, Gloria. Rudy's Memory Walk. 2009. (Roosevelt High School Ser.). 140p. (YA). (gr. 6-18). pap. 9.95 *(978-1-55885-593-9(9))* Arte Publico Pr.
Ventura, Marne. Edgy Estella Aces the Sleepover Party. Trinidad, Leo, illus. 2016. (Worry Warriors Ser.). (ENG.). 96p. (gr. 2-4). lib. bdg. 25.99 *(978-1-4965-3610-5(X))* Stone Arch Bks.
Vicente, Alidis. The Case of the Three Kings / el Caso de Los Reyes Magos: The Flaca Files / Los Expedientes de Flaca. 2016. (Flaca Files / Los Expedientes de Flaca Ser.). (MUL, ENG & SPA., Illus.). 96p. (J). (gr. 3-6). pap. 9.95 *(978-1-55885-822-0(9),* Piñata Books) Arte Publico Pr.
Villareal, Ray. On the Other Side of the Bridge. 2014. (ENG.). 227p. (J). pap. 11.95 *(978-1-55885-802-2(4),* Piñata Books) Arte Publico Pr.
Voorhees, Coert. On the Free. 2017. (ENG.). 280p. (YA). (gr. 9-12). 17.99 ***(978-1-5124-2913-8(9))*** Lerner Publishing Group.
Weller, Frances Ward. The Day the Animals Came: A Story of Saint Francis Day. Long, Loren, illus. 2006. 35p. (J). (gr. k-4). reprint ed. 17.00 *(978-1-4223-5396-7(6))* DIANE Publishing Co.
Willson, Sarah. Dora's Halloween Adventure. Savitsky, Steven, illus. 2003. (Dora the Explorer Ser.). (ENG.). 14p. (J). bds. 5.99 *(978-0-689-85844-4(2),* Simon Spotlight/Nickelodeon) Simon Spotlight/Nickelodeon.
Witte, Anna. El Fandango de Lola. Archer, Micha, illus. 2011. (SPA.). 32p. (J). (gr. k-5). 9.99 *(978-1-84686-359-2(7))* Barefoot Bks., Inc.
—Lola's Fandango. Masse, Josée & Archer, Micha, illus. 2011. (ENG.). 48p. (J). 16.99 *(978-1-84686-174-1(8))* Barefoot Bks., Inc.
Wright, Bil. Putting Makeup on the Fat Boy. (ENG., 240p. (YA). (gr. 7). 2012. Illus.). pap. 9.99 *(978-1-4169-4004-3(9))* 2011. 16.99 *(978-1-4169-3996-2(2))* Simon & Schuster Bks. For Young Readers. (Simon & Schuster Bks. For Young Readers).
Yoo, Paula. Want to Play? Ng-Benitez, Shirley, illus. 2016. (Confetti Kids Ser.). (ENG.). 32p. (J). (gr. k-2). 14.95 *(978-1-62014-250-9(3))* Lee & Low Bks., Inc.
Zemke, Deborah. The Curse of Einstein's Pencil. 2017. (Bea Garcia Ser.: 2). (ENG., Illus.). 144p. (J). (gr. 1-4). 15.99 *(978-0-8037-4155-3(3),* Dial Bks) Penguin Young Readers Group.
—My Life in Pictures. 2016. (Bea Garcia Ser.). (ENG., Illus.). 144p. (J). (gr. 1-3). 14.99 *(978-0-8037-4154-6(5),* Dial Bks) Penguin Young Readers Group.
—My Life in Pictures. 2017. (Bea Garcia Ser.: 1). lib. bdg. 18.40 ***(978-0-606-40083-1(4))*** Turtleback Bks.
Zepeda, Gwendolyn & Ventura, Gabriela Baeza. Growing up with Tamales: Los Tamales de Ana. Ward, April, illus. 2008. (SPA & ENG.). 32p. (J). (gr. -1-2). 16.95 *(978-1-55885-493-2(2),* Piñata Books) Arte Publico Pr.
—Sunflowers/Girasoles. Gambino, Alisha Ann Guadalupe, illus. 2009. (SPA & ENG.). 32p. (J). (gr. -1-2). 16.95 *(978-1-55885-267-9(0),* Piñata Books) Arte Publico Pr.

HISPANO-AMERICAN WAR, 1898

see Spanish-American War, 1898

HISTOCHEMISTRY

see Biochemistry

HISTOLOGY

see Anatomy; Anatomy, Comparative; Cells

HISTORIANS

see also Archaeologists

Bendick, Jeanne. Herodotus & the Road to History. Bendick, Jeanne, illus. 2009. (Illus.). (J). pap. 13.95 *(978-1-932350-20-3(9))* Bethlehem Bks.
Bertrand, Diane Gonzales. Ricardo's Race/la Carrera de Ricardo. Viegas-Barros, Rocio, tr. from ENG. Accardo, Anthony, illus. 2007. (SPA.). 32p. (J). (gr. -1-2). 16.95 *(978-1-55885-481-9(9))* Arte Publico Pr.
Durden, Robert F. The Life of Carter G. Woodson: Father of African-American History. 2014. (Legendary African Americans Ser.). (Illus.). 96p. (J). (gr. 6-12). pap. 10.95 *(978-0-7660-6123-1(X))* Enslow Pubs., Inc.
Durden, Robert Franklin. The Life of Carter G.Woodson: Father of African-American History. 2014. (Legendary African Americans Ser.). 96p. (J). (gr. 6-12). 27.94 *(978-0-7660-6122-4(1))* Enslow Pubs., Inc.
Levene, Rebecca. Captain Cook. Cuzik, David, illus. 2005. (Usborne Famous Lives Gift Bks.). 61p. (J). (gr. -1-3). 8.95 *(978-0-7945-1051-0(5),* Usborne) EDC Publishing.
McKissack, Patricia C. & McKissack, Fredrick L. Carter G. Woodson: Black History Pioneer. 2013. (Famous African Americans Ser.). 24p. (J). (gr. k-3). pap. 7.95 *(978-1-4644-0195-4(0),* Enslow Elementary) Enslow Pubs., Inc.
Shirley, David. Alex Haley: Author. 2005. (Black Americans of Achievement Ser.). (Illus.). 112p. (gr. 6-12). 35.00 *(978-0-7910-8249-2(0),* Chelsea Hse.) Facts On File, Inc.
Whiting, Jim. The Life & Times of Thucydides. 2008. (Biography from Ancient Civilizations Ser.). (Illus.). 48p. (J). (gr. 4-8). lib. bdg. 29.95 *(978-1-58415-698-7(8))* Mitchell Lane Pubs., Inc.
Woelfle, Gretchen. Write on, Mercy! The Secret Life of Mercy Otis Warren. Wallner, Alexandra, illus. 2012. (ENG.). 40p. (J). (gr. 3). 16.95 *(978-1-59078-822-6(2),* Calkins Creek) Boyds Mills Pr.

HISTORIC BUILDINGS

Chapman, Tony. Buildings, Bridges, & Landmarks: a Complete History. 2016. (ENG., Illus.). 118p. pap. 19.99 *(978-1-62686-556-3(6),* Thunder Bay Pr.) Readerlink Distribution Services, LLC.
Collins. Collins Fascinating Facts - Amazing Places. rev. ed. 2016. (Collins Fascinating Facts Ser.). (ENG.). 72p. (J). (gr. 1-3). pap. 10.99 *(978-0-00-816919-0(5))* HarperCollins Pubs. Ltd. GBR. Dist: Independent Pubs. Group.
Drez, Jennifer & Bumstead, Robin. Goodnight Cowtown. Voight, Lisa, illus. 2012. 40p. (J). 17.95 *(978-0-615-54492-2(4))* Petit Chou Chou, LLC.
Hamilton, Robert. Encyclopedia of Amazing Places: Discover Famous Wonders of the World. 2012. (Illus.). 224p. (J). *(978-1-4351-4347-0(7))* Barnes & Noble, Inc.
Hibbert, Adam. World Wonders. 2010. (Unpredictable Nature Ser.). 48p. (J). (gr. 3-18). lib. bdg. 19.95 *(978-1-4222-2008-5(7))* Mason Crest.
Jaskol, Julie & Lewis, Brian. City of Angels: In & Around Los Angeles. Kleven, Elisa, illus. 2008. (J). *(978-1-883318-85-7(8))* Angel City Pr.
Kawa, Katie. America's Oddest Buildings. 2016. (Weird America Ser.). 00032p. (J). pap. 10.50 ***(978-1-4824-5739-1(3))*** Stevens, Gareth Publishing LLLP.
Kumar, Monica. Jay & Juhi: Taj Mahal Kee Saahsik Khoj. Aggarwal, Madhu, tr. Sona & Jacob, illus. 2008.Tr. of Jay & Juhi: the Taj Mahal Adventure. (HIN & ENG.). 32p. (J). pap. 14.99 *(978-0-9797191-4-1(3))* MeeraMasi, Inc.
Look Inside [Capstone Sole Source]. 2010. (Look Inside Ser.). 24p. lib. bdg. 143.94 *(978-1-4296-5869-0(X),* Pebble Plus) Capstone Press of Coughlan Cos.
Maynard, Charles W. Castillo de San Marcos. 2009. (Famous Forts Throughout American History Ser.). 24p. (gr. 3-4). 42.50 *(978-1-61512-514-2(0),* PowerKids Pr.) Rosen Publishing Group, Inc., The.
—Fort McHenry. 2009. (Famous Forts Throughout American History Ser.). 24p. (gr. 3-4). 42.50 *(978-1-61512-519-7(1),* PowerKids Pr.) Rosen Publishing Group, Inc., The.
—Fort Sumter. 2009. (Famous Forts Throughout American History Ser.). 24p. (gr. 3-4). 42.50 *(978-1-61512-520-3(5),* PowerKids Pr.) Rosen Publishing Group, Inc., The.
National Geographic Learning Staff. Famous Landmarks, Level 3. 2011. (World Windows Ser.). (ENG.). 16p. stu. ed. 9.95 *(978-1-133-56616-8(2))* Cengage Heinle.
Prior, Jennifer. America's Man-Made Landmarks. rev. ed. 2014. (Primary Source Readers Content & Literacy Ser.). (ENG., Illus.). 32p. (gr. 3-3). pap. 8.99 *(978-1-4333-7370-1(X))* Teacher Created Materials, Inc.
Rubbino, Salvatore. A Walk in New York. Rubbino, Salvatore, illus. (ENG., Illus.). 40p. (J). (gr. -1-3). 2017. 8.99 ***(978-0-7636-9510-1(6))*** 2009. 16.99 *(978-0-7636-3855-9(2))* Candlewick Pr.
Rubin, Donna. Log Cabin Kitty. Halbower, Susan J., illus. 2012. 56p. pap. 20.00 *(978-0-87565-503-1(3))* Texas Christian Univ. Pr.
Seeley, M. H. America's Oddest Historical Moments. 2016. (Weird America Ser.). 00032p. (J). pap. 10.50 ***(978-1-4824-5751-3(2))*** Stevens, Gareth Publishing LLLP.
Simonds, Lucy. Wonders of the World. 2007. (Trackers-Math Ser.). (gr. 2-5). pap. 5.00 *(978-1-59055-925-3(8))* Pacific Learning, Inc.
Skewes, John. San Francisco ABC. 2016. (Larry Gets Lost Ser.). (ENG., Illus.). 32p. (J). (-k). 14.99 *(978-1-57061-994-6(8),* Little Bigfoot) Sasquatch Bks.
Skewes, John & Mullin, Michael. Larry Gets Lost in Los Angeles. Skewes, John, illus. 2009. (Larry Gets Lost Ser.). (ENG., Illus.). 32p. (J). (gr. -1-2). 17.99 *(978-1-57061-568-9(3),* Little Bigfoot) Sasquatch Bks.
—Larry Gets Lost in New York City. Skewes, John, illus. 2010. (Larry Gets Lost Ser.). (ENG., Illus.). 32p. (J). (gr. -1-2). 17.99 *(978-1-57061-620-4(5),* Little Bigfoot) Sasquatch Bks.
—Larry Gets Lost in San Francisco. Skewes, John, illus. 2009. (Larry Gets Lost Ser.). (ENG., Illus.). 32p. (J). (gr. -1-2). 17.99 *(978-1-57061-567-2(5),* Little Bigfoot) Sasquatch Bks.
Sterling Children's, Sterling & Schader Lee, Susan. Secrets of Our Nation's Capital: Weird & Wonderful Facts about Washington, DC. 2016. (ENG., Illus.). 160p. (J). (gr. 1-3). 8.95 *(978-1-4549-2003-8(3))* Sterling Publishing Co., Inc.
Van Vleet, Carmella. Seven Wonders of the World: Discover Amazing Monuments to Civilization with 20 Projects. Rizvi, Farah, illus. 2011. (Build It Yourself Ser.). (ENG.). 128p. (J). (gr. 3-7). 21.95 *(978-1-934670-82-8(0));* pap. 15.95 *(978-1-936313-73-0(1))* Open City Bks.
Wood, Ira. Fort Sumter: Where the Civil War Began. 2009. (Reading Room Collection 1 Ser.). 16p. (gr. 2-3). 37.50 *(978-1-60851-944-6(9),* PowerKids Pr.) Rosen Publishing Group, Inc., The.

HISTORIC BUILDINGS—FICTION

Cann, Kate. Consumed. (ENG.). 336p. (J). (gr. 9). 2012. pap. 9.99 *(978-0-545-26387-0(5))* 2011. 16.99 *(978-0-545-26388-7(3))* Scholastic, Inc.
—Possessed. (ENG.). 336p. (J). (gr. 9-9). 2011. pap. 9.99 *(978-0-545-12813-1(7))* 2010. 16.99 *(978-0-545-12812-4(9))* Scholastic, Inc.
Clark, Mary Higgins. The Magical Christmas Horse. Minor, Wendell, illus. 2011. (ENG.). 40p. (J). (gr. -1-3). 17.99 *(978-1-4169-9478-7(5),* Simon & Schuster/Paula Wiseman Bks.) Simon & Schuster/Paula Wiseman Bks.

Fairlie, Emily. The Magician's Bird. Caparo, Antonio Javier, illus. 2014. (Tuckernuck Mysteries Ser.: 2). (ENG.). 288p. (J). (gr. 3-7). pap. 6.99 (978-0-06-211894-3(3), Tegen, Katherine Bks) HarperCollins Pubs.
—The Magician's Bird. 2013. (Tuckernuck Mysteries Ser.: 2). (ENG.). 288p. (J). (gr. 3-7). 16.99 (978-0-06-211893-6(5), Tegen, Katherine Bks) HarperCollins Pubs.
Gordon, Amy. Twenty Gold Falcons. (ENG.). 240p. (J). (gr. 3-7). 2012. pap. 8.99 (978-0-8234-2656-0(4)) 2010. 16.95 (978-0-8234-2252-4(6)) Holiday Hse., Inc.
Marsh, Carole. The Mystery in New York City. 2009. (Real Kids, Real Places Ser.). (Illus.). 146p. (J). lib. bdg. 18.99 (978-0-635-06998-6(9), Marsh, Carole Mysteries) Gallopade International.
—The Mystery of the Biltmore House. 25th ed. 2009. (Real Kids, Real Places Ser.). 148p. (J). 18.99 (978-0-635-06989-4(X), Marsh, Carole Mysteries) Gallopade International.
—The White House Christmas Mystery. 2009. (Real Kids, Real Places Ser.). 146p. (J). 18.99 (978-0-635-06996-2(2), Marsh, Carole Mysteries) Gallopade International.
Mullin, Michael & Skewes, John. Larry Gets Lost in the Twin Cities. Skewes, John, illus. 2012. (Larry Gets Lost Ser.). (ENG., Illus.). 32p. (J). (gr. -1-2). 17.99 (978-1-57061-754-6(6), Little Bigfoot) Sasquatch Bks.
Skewes, John & Mullin, Michael. Larry Gets Lost in Boston. Skewes, John, illus. 2013. (Larry Gets Lost Ser.). (ENG., Illus.). 32p. (J). (gr. -1-2). 17.99 (978-1-57061-793-5(7), Little Bigfoot) Sasquatch Bks.
—Larry Gets Lost in Chicago. Skewes, John, illus. 2010. (Larry Gets Lost Ser.). (ENG., Illus.). 32p. (J). (gr. -1-2). 16.99 (978-1-57061-619-8(1), Little Bigfoot) Sasquatch Bks.
Tyre, Lisa Lewis & Airgood, Ellen. Last in a Long Line of Rebels. 2015. (ENG.). 288p. (J). (gr. 5). 16.99 (978-0-399-16838-3(9), Nancy Paulsen Books) Penguin Young Readers Group.

HISTORIC SITES

see also Historic Buildings; Monuments

Bauman, Amy & Durman, Laura. Personalities & Places. 2010. (CC: Native North Americans Ser.). 112p. (gr. 6-12). 42.80 (978-1-933834-81-8(1)) Brown Bear Bks.
Bryant, Tamera. This Land Is Your Land. 2004. (ZB Reads Trio Books). (Illus.). v, 57p. (gr. 3-5). pap. 4.50 (978-0-7367-1784-7(6)) Zaner-Bloser, Inc.
—We Remember: State Monuments & Historic Sites. 2004. (ZB Reads Trio Books). (Illus.). iii, 43p. (gr. 3-5). pap., tchr. ed. 4.50 (978-0-7367-1783-0(8)) Zaner-Bloser, Inc.
Burnham, Brad. Qumran Caves: Hiding Place for the Dead Sea Scrolls. 2009. (Famous Caves of the World Ser.). 24p. (gr. 3-4). 42.50 (978-1-61512-499-2(3), PowerKids Pr.) Rosen Publishing Group, Inc., The.
Burns Knight, Margy. Talking Walls: Discover Your World, 1 vol. Sibley O'Brien, Anne, illus. 2017. (ENG.). 64p. (gr. 2-7). pap. 9.95 (978-0-88448-576-6(5), 884576) Tilbury Hse. Pubs.
Collins. Collins Fascinating Facts - Amazing Places. rev. ed. 2016. (Collins Fascinating Facts Ser.). (ENG.). 72p. (J). (gr. 1-3). pap. 10.99 (978-0-00-816919-0(5)) HarperCollins Pubs. Ltd. GBR. Dist: Independent Pubs. Group.
Crispiels, Giada, illus. Wildlife of New York Coloring Book: A Five-Borough Coloring Book. 2016. (ENG.). 60p. 14.95 (978-0-7892-1255-9(2)) Abbeville Pr., Inc.
Crypts, Tombs, & Secret Rooms. 2017. (Crypts, Tombs, & Secret Rooms Ser.). 48p. (gr. 4-5). pap. 84.30 **(978-1-5382-0606-5(4))**; lib. bdg. 191.70 **(978-1-5382-0605-8(6))** Stevens, Gareth Publishing LLLP.
Dickerson, Joy E. Pack & Go. 2004. (ZB Reads Trio Books). (Illus.). iii, 75p. (gr. 3-5). pap. 5.00 (978-0-7367-1785-4(4)) Zaner-Bloser, Inc.
Eggers, Dave. Her Right Foot. Ojala, Eiko & Harris, Shawn, illus. 2017. (ENG.). 104p. (J). (gr. k-3). 19.99 **(978-1-4521-6281-2(6))** Chronicle Bks. LLC.
Firestone, Mary, et al. Celebrate America: A Guide to America's Greatest Symbols. Skeens, Matthew, illus. 2010. (American Symbols Ser.). (ENG.). 208p. (gr. 1-2). pap. 15.95 (978-1-4048-6170-1(X)) Picture Window Bks.
Freedman, Jeri. Historical Villages, 01 vols., 1. 2016. (Role-Playing for Fun & Profit Ser.). (ENG.). 48p. (J). pap. 11.75 (978-1-4994-3724-9(2), Rosen Central) Rosen Publishing Group, Inc., The.
George, Enzo. Newgrange Burial Chamber. 2017. (Crypts, Tombs, & Secret Rooms Ser.). 48p. (gr. 4-5). pap. 84.30 **(978-1-5382-0641-6(2))** Stevens, Gareth Publishing LLLP.
Gillis, Jennifer Blizin. Restored Villages. 2007. (Field Trips Ser.). (Illus.). 24p. (J). (gr. 2-5). lib. bdg. 27.07 (978-1-60044-563-7(2)) Rourke Educational Media.
Goldish, Meish. Colonial Williamsburg. 2016. (American Places: from Vision to Reality Ser.). (ENG.). 32p. (J). (gr. 2-7). 19.95 (978-1-944102-46-3(9)) Bearport Publishing Co., Inc.
Graphic Expeditions. 2010. (Graphic Expeditions Ser.). 32p. lib. bdg. 293.20 (978-1-4296-5860-7(6), Graphic Library) Capstone Press of Coughlan Cos.
Greathouse, Lisa E. & Kuligowski, Stephanie. ¡Sin Resolver! Lugares Misteriosos. 2017. (TIME for Kids en Español - Level 4 Ser.). (SPA.). 48p. (gr. 4-4). lib. bdg. 31.99 (978-1-5157-5133-5(3)) Time for Kids Inc AUS. Dist: Capstone Pub.
Hamilton, Robert. Encyclopedia of Amazing Places: Discover Famous Wonders of the World. 2012. (Illus.). 224p. (J). (978-1-4351-4347-0(7)) Barnes & Noble, Inc.
Henzel, Cynthia Kennedy. Taj Mahal, 1 vol. 2011. (Troubled Treasures: World Heritage Sites Ser.). (ENG., Illus.). 32p. (J). (gr. 3-6). 27.07 (978-1-61613-568-3(9)) ABDO Publishing Co.
Hibbert, Adam. World Wonders. 2010. (Unpredictable Nature Ser.). 48p. (J). (gr. 3-18). lib. bdg. 19.95 (978-1-4222-2008-5(7)) Mason Crest.
Hurd, Owen. Chicago History for Kids: Triumphs & Tragedies of the Windy City Includes 21 Activities. 2007. (For Kids Ser.). (ENG., Illus.). 192p. (J). (gr. 4-7). pap. 16.95 (978-1-55652-654-1(7)) Chicago Review Pr., Inc.
Jaskol, Julie & Lewis, Brian. City of Angels: In & Around Los Angeles. Kleven, Elisa, illus. 2008. (J). (978-1-883318-85-7(8)) Angel City Pr.
Joseph, Frank. Archaeological Discoveries of Ancient America, 1 vol., 1. 2014. (Discovering Ancient America Ser.). (ENG.). 296p. (YA). (gr. 7-12). 38.25 (978-1-4777-2809-3(0)) Rosen Publishing Group, Inc., The.
Lindeen, Mary. History Rocks!, 1 vol. (Wonder Readers: Social Studies). (ENG.). (gr. -1-2). 2012. 20p. lib. bdg. 22.65 (978-1-4296-9614-2(1)) 2011. 16p. pap. 35.94 (978-1-4296-8262-6(0)) 2011. 32p. pap. 5.99 (978-1-4296-7927-5(1)) Capstone Press of Coughlan Cos. (Wonder Readers).
National Geographic Learning Staff. Famous Landmarks, Level 3. 2011. (World Windows Ser.). (ENG.). 16p. stu. ed. 9.95 (978-1-133-56616-8(2)) Cengage Heinle.
Niver, Heather Moore. 20 Fun Facts about US Monuments. 2013. (Fun Fact File: US History! Ser.). 32p. (J). (gr. 3-6). pap. 10.50 (978-1-4339-9209-4(4)); pap. 63.00 (978-1-4339-9210-0(8)) Stevens, Gareth Publishing LLLP.
Niver, Heather Moore & Moore Niver, Heather. 20 Fun Facts about US Monuments. 2013. 32p. (J). (gr. 3-6). 25.25 (978-1-4339-9208-7(6)) Stevens, Gareth Publishing LLLP.
Price, Denise D. Freedom Trail Pop up Book of Boston. 2015. (ENG., Illus.). 17p. (J). 29.99 (978-0-9907781-0-3(X)) White Dharma Ltd.
Prior, Jennifer. America's Man-Made Landmarks. rev. ed. 2014. (Primary Source Readers Content & Literacy Ser.). (ENG., Illus.). 32p. (gr. 3-3). pap. 8.99 (978-1-4333-7370-1(X)) Teacher Created Materials, Inc.
Putnam, Jeff. National Monuments: Events & Times. 2004. (ZB Reads Trio Books). (Illus.). iii, 75p. (gr. 4-6). pap. 5.00 (978-0-7367-1787-8(0)) Zaner-Bloser, Inc.
Rudolph, Ellen K. Willi Gets a History Lesson: In Virginia's Historic Triangle. Rudolph, Ellen K., photos by. 2007. (ENG., Illus.). 80p. pap. 24.00 (978-0-9791348-0-7(3)) EKR Pubns.
Scholastic, Inc. Staff & Keenan, Sheila. O, Say Can You See? America's Symbols, Landmarks, & Important Words. Boyajian, Ann, illus. 2007. (ENG.). 64p. (J). (gr. -1-3). pap. 6.99 (978-0-439-59360-1(3), Scholastic Nonfiction) Scholastic, Inc.
Schwartz, Heather E. & Salzano, Tammi. Around the World: An Amazing World. 2009. (Illus.). 48p. (J). pap. (978-0-545-17229-5(2)) Scholastic, Inc.
Skewes, John & Mullin, Michael. Larry Gets Lost in Los Angeles. Skewes, John, illus. 2009. (Larry Gets Lost Ser.). (ENG., Illus.). 32p. (J). (gr. -1-2). 17.99 (978-1-57061-568-9(3), Little Bigfoot) Sasquatch Bks.
—Larry Gets Lost in New York City. Skewes, John, illus. 2010. (Larry Gets Lost Ser.). (ENG., Illus.). 32p. (J). (gr. -1-2). 17.99 (978-1-57061-620-4(5), Little Bigfoot) Sasquatch Bks.
—Larry Gets Lost in San Francisco. Skewes, John, illus. 2009. (Larry Gets Lost Ser.). (ENG., Illus.). 32p. (J). (gr. -1-2). 17.99 (978-1-57061-567-2(5), Little Bigfoot) Sasquatch Bks.
Smith, Tod G., contrib. by. Graphic Expeditions, 10 vols., Set. Incl. Getting to the Bottom of Global Warming: An Isabel Soto Investigation. Collins, Terry. Schulz, Barbara, illus. lib. bdg. 30.65 (978-1-4296-3972-9(5)); Mesa Verde Cliff Dwellers: An Isabel Soto Archaeology Adventure. Collins, Terry. Anderson, Bill, illus. lib. bdg. 30.65 (978-1-4296-3971-2(7)); Searching for UFOs: An Isabel Soto Investigation. Sautter, Aaron. lib. bdg. 30.65 (978-1-4296-3974-3(1)); Secrets of Martial Arts: An Isabel Soto History Adventure. Harbo, Christopher L. lib. bdg. 30.65 (978-1-4296-3973-6(3)); (gr. 3-4). (Graphic Expeditions Ser.). (ENG.). 32p. 2010. Set lib. bdg. 306.50 o.p. (978-1-4296-4449-5(4), Graphic Library) Capstone Press of Coughlan Cos.
Stern, Steven L. Wretched Ruins. 2010. (Scary Places Ser.). (Illus.). 32p. (YA). (gr. 4-7). lib. bdg. 25.27 (978-1-936087-55-6(3)) Bearport Publishing Co., Inc.
Tectum, compiled by. Our Amazing World: Discover cultural sites 1, from the Unesco World Heritage, 1 vol. 2011. (ENG.). 32p. 14.95 (978-90-79761-06-7(0)) Tectum B.V.B.A. BEL. Dist: Innovative Logistics.
Tectum Publishers Staff, compiled by. Our Amazing World: Discover cultural sites 2, from the Unesco World Heritage, 1 vol. 2011. (ENG.). 32p. 14.95 (978-90-79761-07-4(9)) Tectum B.V.B.A. BEL. Dist: Innovative Logistics.
Van Vleet, Carmella. Seven Wonders of the World: Discover Amazing Monuments to Civilization with 20 Projects. Rizvi, Farah, illus. 2011. (Build It Yourself Ser.). (ENG.). 128p. (J). (gr. 3-7). 21.95 (978-1-934670-82-8(0)); pap. 15.95 (978-1-936313-73-0(1)) Open City Bks.
Williams, Brian. World Wonders. 2010. (What About... Ser.). (Illus.). 40p. (J). (gr. 6-8). lib. bdg. 19.95 (978-1-4222-1567-8(9)) Mason Crest.
Woods, Michael & Woods, Mary B. Seven Wonders of Ancient Asia. 2008. (Seven Wonders Ser.). (ENG., Illus.). 80p. (gr. 5-8). lib. bdg. 33.26 (978-0-8225-7569-6(8)) Lerner Publishing Group.
Yasuda, Anita. The 12 Most Amazing American Monuments & Symbols. 2015. (ENG., Illus.). 32p. (J). pap. 9.95 (978-1-63235-069-5(6)) RiverStream Publishing.
—The 12 Most Amazing American Monuments & Symbols. 2014. (ENG., Illus.). 32p. (J). (978-1-63235-009-1(2)) Pr. Room Editions LLC.

HISTORIC SITES—FICTION

Andrews, Jane. Ten Boys Who Lived on the Road from Long Ago to Now (Yesterday's Classics) 2006. (J). 9.95 (978-1-59915-064-2(6)) Yesterday's Classics.
Farber, E. S. Fish Finelli (Book 1) Seagulls Don't Eat Pickles. Beene, Jason, illus. 2014. (Fish Finelli Ser.). (ENG.). 168p. (J). (gr. 3-7). pap. 6.99 (978-1-4521-2853-5(7)) Chronicle Bks. LLC.
Farber, Erica. Fish Finelli: Seagulls Don't Eat Pickles. Beene, Jason, illus. 2013. (Fish Finelli Ser.). (ENG.). 155p. (J). (gr. 2-5). 15.99 (978-1-4521-0820-9(X)) Chronicle Bks. LLC.
Franks, Melissa. Warped! An Adventure Through Time Bk. 1: A What-a-saur? 2008. 96p. pap. 19.95 (978-1-60703-636-4(3)) America Star Bks.
Marsh, Carole. The Mystery on the Great Wall of China: Beijing, China. 2009. (Around the World in 80 Mysteries Ser.). (Illus.). 132p. (J). lib. bdg. 18.99 (978-0-635-07014-2(6), Marsh, Carole Mysteries) Gallopade International.
Skewes, John & Mullin, Michael. Larry Gets Lost in Chicago. Skewes, John, illus. 2010. (Larry Gets Lost Ser.). (ENG., Illus.). 32p. (J). (gr. -1-2). 16.99 (978-1-57061-619-8(1), Little Bigfoot) Sasquatch Bks.
Wagner, Lloyd S. Ghosts at Gettysburg: An Oliver Family Adventure. 2007. 144p. per. 11.95 (978-0-595-46877-5(2)) iUniverse, Inc.

HISTORICAL ATLASES

see Historical Geography—Maps

HISTORICAL CHRONOLOGY

see Chronology, Historical

HISTORICAL DICTIONARIES

see History—Dictionaries

HISTORICAL GEOGRAPHY

Huey, Lois Miner. American Archaeology Uncovers the Westward Movement. 2009. (American Archaeology Ser.). (Illus.). 64p. (J). (gr. 5-6). 31.36 (978-0-7614-4265-3(0)) Marshall Cavendish Corp.
Samuels, Charlie. Mapping the Physical World. 2017. (Mapping in the Modern World Ser.). (ENG.). 32p. (J). **(978-0-7787-3236-5(3))**; pap. **(978-0-7787-3242-6(8))** Crabtree Publishing Co.
Spickert, Diane Nelson. Earthsteps: A Rock's Journey Through Time. Wallace, Marianne D., illus. 2010. (ENG.). 32p. (J). (gr. -1-3). pap. 9.95 (978-1-55591-730-2(5)) Fulcrum Publishing.

HISTORICAL GEOGRAPHY—MAPS

Adams, Simon. The Kingfisher Atlas of World History: A Pictoral Guide to the World's People & Events, 10000BCE-Present. 2016. (ENG.). 192p. (J). 24.99 (978-0-7534-7294-1(5), 9780753472941, Kingfisher) Roaring Brook Pr.
Axelrod-Contrada, Joan. A Historical Atlas of Colonial America. 2009. (United States: Historical Atlases of the Growth of a New Nation Ser.). 64p. (gr. 5-5). 61.20 (978-1-60854-251-2(3)) Rosen Publishing Group, Inc., The.
Hammon, Inc. Staff, ed. Historical Atlas of the World. 5th rev. ed. 2007. (Atlas Ser.). (Illus.). 72p. (gr. 9-12). pap. 11.95 (978-0-8437-1391-6(7), 713917) Hammond World Atlas Corp.
Romano, Amy. A Historical Atlas of Jordan. 2009. (Historical Atlases of South Asia, Central Asia, & the Middle East Ser.). 64p. (gr. 6-6). 61.20 (978-1-61513-322-2(4)) Rosen Publishing Group, Inc., The.

HISTORICAL POETRY

Alexander, Elizabeth. Praise Song for the Day. Diaz, David, illus. 2012. (ENG.). 32p. (J). (gr. 1-5). 16.99 (978-0-06-192663-1(9), Tegen, Katherine Bks) HarperCollins Pubs.
Sheppard, Keith. Welcome to the Crazyverse: A Collection of Comic Poems about Famous People in History. 2012. (Illus.). 108p. pap. (978-1-904808-85-5(9)) Evertype.

HISTORIOGRAPHY

see also Historians

Collins UK & Collins KS3 Staff. KS3 History. 2014. (ENG.). 216p. (YA). (gr. 6-9). pap. 16.95 (978-0-00-756289-3(6)) HarperCollins Pubs. Ltd. GBR. Dist: Independent Pubs. Group.
Freeburg, Jessica. Tangled History. 2016. (Tangled History Ser.). (ENG.). 112p. (gr. 3-4). 255.92 (978-1-5157-3353-9(X)) Capstone Press of Coughlan Cos.
Graphic History. 2016. (Graphic History Ser.). (ENG.). 32p. (gr. 3-4). lib. bdg. 582.35 (978-1-5157-4019-3(6), Graphic Library) Capstone Press of Coughlan Cos.
Hunter, Nick. History Around You, 1 vol. 2014. (History at Home Ser.). (ENG., Illus.). 32p. (gr. 1-3). 27.32 (978-1-4846-0230-0(7), Heinemann First Library) Heinemann-Raintree.
—History at Home, 1 vol. 2014. (History at Home Ser.). (ENG.). 32p. (gr. 1-3). 81.96 (978-1-4846-0233-1(1), Heinemann First Library) Heinemann-Raintree.
—Talking about the Past, 1 vol. 2014. (History at Home Ser.). (ENG., Illus.). 32p. (gr. 1-3). 27.32 (978-1-4846-0232-4(3)); pap. 7.99 (978-1-4846-0236-2(6)) Heinemann-Raintree. (Heinemann First Library).
Kalman, Bobbie. I Can Write a Book about History. 2012. (ENG.). 32p. (J). (978-0-7787-7990-2(4)); pap. (978-0-7787-7999-5(8)) Crabtree Publishing Co.
Kimmel, Allison Crotzer, et al. Primary Source History. 2016. (Primary Source History Ser.). (ENG.). 32p. (gr. 3-4). 218.56 (978-1-4914-8502-6(7), Fact Finders) Capstone Press of Coughlan Cos.
Langley, Andrew, et al. Days of Decision. 2013. (Days of Decision Ser.). (ENG.). 64p. (gr. 7-8). pap. 59.94 (978-1-4329-7646-0(X)); lib. bdg. 179.95 (978-1-4329-7639-2(7)) Heinemann-Raintree.
Let's Find Out! Primary Sources. 2016. (Let's Find Out! Primary Sources Ser.). 00032p. (J). (gr. 2-3). 195.60 (978-1-5081-0281-6(3), Britannica Educational Publishing) Rosen Publishing Group, Inc., The.
Micklos, John, Jr. & Webb, Sarah Powers. Primary Source History. 2016. (Primary Source History Ser.). (ENG.). 32p. (gr. 3-4). pap. 31.80 (978-1-4914-8503-3(5), Fact Finders) Capstone Press of Coughlan Cos.
Wills, Adele. Texts Through History. 2004. (Routledge a Level English Guides). (ENG., Illus.). (C). 96p. 95.00 (978-0-415-31909-6(9)); 94p. per. 25.95 (978-0-415-31910-2(2), RU26770) Routledge.

HISTORY, ANCIENT

see also Archaeology; Bible; Civilization

Ancient World History: Patterns of Interaction. 2005. (gr. 6-12). tchr. ed. (978-0-618-37681-0(X), 2-00462) Holt McDougal.
Ancient World History: Patterns of Interaction: EEdition Plus Online. (gr. 6-12). 2005. (978-0-618-42268-5(4), 2-00681) 2003. (978-0-618-19413-1(4), 2-70055) Holt McDougal.
Ancient World History: Patterns of Interaction: EEdition Plus Online with purchase of print Pupil's Edition-1 Year. 2005. (gr. 6-12). (978-0-618-42278-4(1), 2-00683) Holt McDougal.
Awfully Ancient. 2015. (Awfully Ancient Ser.). (ENG.). 32p. (J). (gr. 5-5). 159.60 (978-1-4824-2560-4(2)); pap., pap., pap. 63.00 (978-1-4824-3439-2(3)) Stevens, Gareth Publishing LLLP.
Back in Time. 2017. (Back in Time Ser.). 48p. (gr. 5-6). pap. 70.20 **(978-0-7660-9030-9(2))**; lib. bdg. 167.58 **(978-0-7660-9029-3(9))** Enslow Pubs., Inc.
Bauer, Susan Wise. Ancient Times Vol. 1: From the Earliest Nomads to the Last Roman Emperor. West, Jeff, illus. 2nd rev. ed. 2006. (ENG.). 338p. 24.95 (978-1-933339-01-6(2), 333901) Well-Trained Mind Pr.
Beck, Roger B., et al. Ancient World History: Patterns of Interaction. l.t. ed. 2006. (Illus.). 840p. (gr. 9-12). 83.76 (978-0-618-37679-7(8), 2-00460) Holt McDougal.
Benchmark Education Company, LLC Staff, compiled by. Early River Civilizations. 2006. spiral bd. 330.00 (978-1-4108-7011-7(1)) 2005. (J). spiral bd. 265.00 (978-1-4108-5773-6(5)) Benchmark Education Co.
—Early River Civilizations: Theme Set. 2006. (J). 183.00 (978-1-4108-7139-8(8)) Benchmark Education Co.
—Social Studies Theme: Early River Civilizations. 2005. spiral bd. 115.00 (978-1-4108-5325-7(X)) Benchmark Education Co.
Bensinger, Henry. The Ancient Greek Economy. 2013. (Spotlight on Ancient Civilizations: Greece Ser.). (ENG.). 24p. (J). (gr. 3-4). 23.60 (978-1-4777-0771-5(9)); (Illus.). pap. 10.00 (978-1-4777-0875-0(8)) Rosen Publishing Group, Inc., The. (PowerKids Pr.).
Berry, Bob, illus. Ancient Times: Step-by-Step Instructions for 18 Ancient Characters & Civilzations. 2013. (Learn to Draw Ser.). (ENG.). 40p. (J). (gr. 1-3). pap. 4.95 (978-1-60058-310-0(5), 1600583105) Quarto Publishing Group USA.
Bingham, Jane. Encyclopedia of Ancient World. 2004. (History Encyclopedias Ser.). (Illus.). 400p. (J). 39.95 (978-0-7945-0364-2(0), Usborne) EDC Publishing.
Bingham, Jane, et al. Encyclopedia of the Ancient World. 2007. (Usborne Internet-Linked Encyclopedia Ser.). (Illus.). 400p. (J). pap. 19.99 (978-0-7945-1141-8(4), Usborne) EDC Publishing.
Bluedorn, Harvey & Bluedorn, Laurie. Ancient History from Primary Sources: A Literary Timeline. 2003. (Illus.). 223p. per. 59.00 (978-0-9743616-4-2(X)) Trivium Pursuit.
Bradley, Pamela. The Ancient World Transformed: Societies, Personalities & Historical Periods from Egypt, Greece & Rome. 2014. (ENG.). pap. 49.50 (978-1-107-67443-1(3)) Cambridge Univ. Pr.
Burgan, Michael. You Choose: History. 2013. (You Choose: History Ser.). (ENG.). 112p. (gr. 3-4). pap. 27.80 (978-1-4765-3761-0(5), You Choose Bks.) Capstone Press of Coughlan Cos.
Burgan, Michael, et al. You Choose: History. 2013. (You Choose: History Ser.). (ENG.). 112p. (gr. 3-4). 127.96 (978-1-4765-0470-4(9), You Choose Bks.) Capstone Press of Coughlan Cos.
Chandler, Fiona & McCaffrey, Susie. The Usborne Internet-Linked Ancient World. 2005. (Illus.). 96p. (978-0-439-78503-7(0)) Scholastic, Inc.
Church, Alfred J. Stories of the East from Herodotus. 2009. (Illus.). 230p. pap. 10.95 (978-1-59915-386-5(6)) Yesterday's Classics.
Collins UK Publishing Staff & Collins KS3 Staff. KS3 History. 2014. (ENG.). 144p. (YA). (gr. 6-9). pap. 12.95 (978-0-00-756288-6(8)) HarperCollins Pubs. Ltd. GBR. Dist: Independent Pubs. Group.
Corr, Kendra & Coletti, Sharon. The Ancient Greeks: I Think: It's Elementary! 2013. pap. 29.95 (978-1-938275-05-0(5)) InspirEd Educators.
Cottrell, George. Ancient Greece. 2017. (Unlocking Ancient Civilizations Ser.). (J). (gr. 4-5). pap. 63.00 **(978-1-5345-2030-1(9))**; 32p. pap. 10.50 **(978-1-5345-2029-5(5))**; 32p. lib. bdg. 27.25 **(978-1-5345-2031-8(7))** Greenhaven Publishing LLC. (KidHaven Publishing).
Cox, Phil Roxbee & Reid, Struan. Who Were the First People? 2004. (Starting Point History Ser.). (Illus.). 32p. (J). pap. 4.95 (978-0-7945-0339-0(X), Usborne) EDC Publishing.
—Who Were the First People? Wood, Gerald, illus. rev. ed. 2006. (Starting Point History Ser.). 32p. (J). (gr. 1). lib. bdg. 12.95 (978-1-58086-499-2(6)) EDC Publishing.
Crandell, Joyce & Bauer, Susan Wise. Ancient Times: From the Earliest Nomads to the Last Roman Emperor. West, Jeff, illus. 3rd ed. 2006. (ENG.). 322p. pap., act. bk. ed. 36.95 (978-1-933339-05-4(5), 333905) Well-Trained Mind Pr.
Crypts, Tombs, & Secret Rooms. 2017. (Crypts, Tombs, & Secret Rooms Ser.). 48p. (gr. 4-5). lib. bdg. 191.70 **(978-1-5382-0605-8(6))** Stevens, Gareth Publishing LLLP.
Dixon, Darla, illus. What Really Happened in Ancient Times: A Collection of Historical Biographies, 4. 2007. (What Really Happened Ser.). 240p. per. 15.95 (978-1-932786-21-7(X)) Knowledge Quest.
Education.com. History & Me: A Workbook of Historic Figures & Family Research. 2015. (ENG.). 96p. (J). (gr. 2-2). pap. 7.99 (978-0-486-80263-3(9)) Dover Pubns., Inc.
Exploring the Ancient & Medieval Worlds. 2015. (Exploring the Ancient & Medieval Worlds Ser.). (ENG.). 160p. (YA). (gr. 8-8). 456.40 (978-1-5026-0374-6(8)) Cavendish Square Publishing.
Garbe, Suzanne, et al. Dangerous History. 2013. (Dangerous History Ser.). (ENG.). 32p. (gr. 3-4). lib. bdg. 111.96 (978-1-62065-969-4(7), Edge Bks.) Capstone Press of Coughlan Cos.
Great Empires. 2015. (Great Empires Ser.). (ENG.). 48p. (J). (gr. 7-7). 188.16 (978-1-5026-0382-1(9)) Cavendish Square Publishing.
Harvey, Gill & Reid, Struan. Encyclopedia of Ancient Egypt. 2004. (History Encyclopedias Ser.). (Illus.). 144p. (J). (gr. 4-18). lib. bdg. 27.95 (978-1-58086-387-2(6)) EDC Publishing.
Haywood, John, ed. The Illustrated History Encyclopedia Everyday Life in the Ancient World: How People Lived & Worked Through the Ages. 2015. (ENG., Illus.). 256p. pap. 13.99 (978-1-86147-457-5(1), Armadillo) Anness Publishing GBR. Dist: National Bk. Network.
Haywood, John, et al, eds. Children's Encyclopedia of the Ancient World. 2013. (ENG., Illus.). 512p. (J). (gr. 3-7). pap. 17.99 (978-1-84322-995-7(1), Armadillo) Anness Publishing GBR. Dist: National Bk. Network.
Hindley, Judy, et al. Time Traveler: Visit Medieval Times, the Viking Age, the Roman World & Ancient Egypt. rev. ed. 2004. (Time Travelers Bks.). (Illus.). 130p. (J). (gr. 3-6). 22.95 (978-0-7460-3365-4(6)) EDC Publishing.
Holmes & Thom. The First Vertebrates. 2008. (Prehistoric Earth Ser.). (Illus.). 188p. (YA). (gr. 9-12). 35.00 (978-0-8160-5958-4(6)) Facts On File, Inc.
Holt, Rinehart and Winston Staff. The Human Journey: The Ancient World: Online Edition. 3rd ed. 2003. 75.93 (978-0-03-072543-2(7)) Holt McDougal.

Howitt, Carolyn. The British Museum Quiz Book. 2004. (Illus.). 80p. (J). pap. *(978-0-7141-3035-4(4))* British Museum Pr.

Hunt, Norman Bancroft. Living in the Ancient World. 2008. (Living in the Ancient World Ser.). 576p. (gr. 6-12). 175.00 *(978-0-8160-6336-9(2))* Facts On File, Inc.

Hurdman, Charlotte, et al. Living History: What Life Was Like in Ancient Times. 2011. (ENG., Illus.). 512p. (J). (gr. -1-12). 17.99 *(978-1-84322-937-7(4))* Anness Publishing GBR. Dist: National Bk. Network.

Johnson, Terri. What Really Happened in Colonial Times: A Collection of Historical Biographies. Dixon, Darla, illus. 2007. (What Really Happened Ser.). 224p. (J). (gr. 4-7). per. 15.95 *(978-1-932786-23-1(6))* Knowledge Quest.

Kemp, Ellwood W. Streams of History. 2008. 100p. pap. 7.95 *(978-1-59915-259-2(2))*; 72p. pap. 7.95 *(978-1-59915-258-5(4))*; 88p. pap. 7.95 *(978-1-59915-257-8(6))* Yesterday's Classics.

—Streams of History: Early Civilizations (Yesterday's Classics) 2008. 84p. per. 7.95 *(978-1-59915-254-7(1))* Yesterday's Classics.

Little, Frances Delanoy. Ancient Stories from the Dardanelles 1924. 2004. reprint ed. pap. 30.95 *(978-1-4179-7641-6(1))* Kessinger Publishing, LLC.

Macdonald, Fiona, et al. The Incredible Ancient History Book Box: Includes Fascinating Facts, 120 Step-by-Step Projects & over 3000 Amazing Pictures, 8 vols. 2012. (ENG., Illus.). 64p. (J). (gr. 3-7). pap. 20.00 *(978-1-84322-800-4(9))* Anness Publishing GBR. Dist: National Bk. Network.

Maier, Kimberly. History Odyssey, Ancients - Level Three. 2006. (YA). ring bd. 38.00 *(978-0-9766057-6-8(7))* Pandia Pr.

Malam, John. Dig It: History from Objects, 4 vols., Set. Incl. Egyptians. lib. bdg. 26.50 *(978-1-4488-3283-5(7))*; Greeks. lib. bdg. 26.50 *(978-1-4488-3284-2(5))*; Romans. lib. bdg. 26.50 *(978-1-4488-3285-9(3))*; Vikings. lib. bdg. 26.50 *(978-1-4488-3286-6(1))*; (YA). (gr. 2-5). (Dig It: History from Objects Ser.). (Illus.). 32p. 2011. Set lib. bdg. 101.00 *(978-1-4488-3306-1(X)*, PowerKids Pr.) Rosen Publishing Group, Inc., The.

Meister, Cari. Totally Wacky Facts about Ancient History. 2016. (Mind Benders Ser.). (ENG., Illus.). 112p. (gr. 1-3). lib. bdg. 23.32 *(978-1-4914-8385-5(7))* Capstone Press of Coughlan Cos.

Merrill, Yvonne Y. Ancient People Vol. 2: Art Activities about Minoans, Mycenaeans, Trojans, Ancient Greeks, Etruscans, & Romans. Simpson, Mary, illus. 2nd ed. 2004. (Hands-on Ser.). (ENG.). 88p. (J). (gr. 3-7). pap. 20.00 *(978-0-9643177-9-6(6))* KK.

Millard, A. & Sims, L. A Visitor's Guide to the Ancient World. 2004. (Time Tours Ser.). (Illus.). 192p. (J). pap. 17.95 *(978-0-7945-0461-8(2))* EDC Publishing.

Miller, Reagan & Richardson, Hazel. Arts & Culture in the Ancient World. 2011. (ENG., Illus.). 32p. (J). *(978-0-7787-1732-4(1))* Crabtree Publishing Co.

—Arts & Culture in the Ancient World. Crabtree Publishing Co. Staff, ed. 2011. (Life in the Ancient World Ser.: No. 1). (ENG., Illus.). 32p. (J). (gr. 5-8). pap. *(978-0-7787-1739-3(9))* Crabtree Publishing Co.

Morris, Neil. Ancient World. 2003. (Knowledge Masters Ser.). (Illus.). 32p. (YA). pap. incl. cd-rom *(978-1-903954-49-2(5)*, Pavilion Children's Books) Pavilion Bks.

National Geographic Learning Staff. In Times Long Ago. 2012. Vol. 3928. (ENG., Illus.). 16p. (C). (gr. -1-2). pap. 5.95 *(978-1-57471-133-2(4)*, 3928) National Geographic School Publishing, Inc.

Page, Jason. Castles & Dungeons. 2008. (Factastic Journey Ser.). (Illus.). 32p. (J). (gr. k-7). pap. 8.95 *(978-1-59905-239-7(3))* Saddleback Educational Publishing, Inc.

Race for History. (Race for History Ser.). (ENG.). 32p. (gr. 3-4). 2011. pap. 190.80 *(978-1-4296-6417-2(7))* 2010. pap. 24.30 *(978-1-4296-6249-9(2))* Capstone Press of Coughlan Cos. (Fact Finders).

Race for History, 4 vols., Set. Incl. Who Reached the South Pole First? Llanas, Sheila Griffin. lib. bdg. 27.32 *(978-1-4296-3344-4(1))*; Who Really Created Democracy? Leavitt, Amie Jane. lib. bdg. 27.32 *(978-1-4296-3343-7(3))*; Who Really Discovered America? Asselin, Kristine Carlson. lib. bdg. 27.32 *(978-1-4296-3342-0(5))*; Who Really Discovered Electricity? Leavitt, Amie Jane. lib. bdg. 27.32 *(978-1-4296-3345-1(X))*; (gr. 3-4). (Race for History Ser.). (ENG.). 32p. 2010. Set lib. bdg. 109.28 *(978-1-4296-5400-5(7)*, Fact Finders) Capstone Press of Coughlan Cos.

Raum, Elizabeth. The Aztec Empire: An Interactive History Adventure. 2012. (You Choose: Historical Eras Ser.). (ENG.). 112p. (gr. 3-4). pap. 41.70 *(978-1-4296-9475-9(0)*, You Choose Bks.) Capstone Press of Coughlan Cos.

Rector, Rebecca Kraft. The Early River Valley Civilizations. 2016. (First Humans & Early Civilizations Ser.). 64p. (J). (gr. 6-6). pap. 12.95 *(978-1-4994-6326-2(X))* Rosen Publishing Group, Inc., The.

Reid, S. & Chisholm, J. Who Built the Pyramids? rev. ed. 2004. (Starting Point History Ser.). (Illus.). 32p. (J). pap. 4.95 *(978-0-7945-0343-7(8)*, Usborne) EDC Publishing.

Rice, Dona. Chicas y Chicos Malos Del Mundo Antiguo. 2016. (TIME for Kids en Español - Level 5 Ser.). (SPA.). 64p. (gr. 5-5). lib. bdg. 31.99 *(978-1-5157-2953-2(2))* Time for Kids Inc AUS. Dist: Capstone Pub.

Rice, Dona Herweck. Bad Guys & Gals of the Ancient World, 1 vol. 2nd rev. ed. 2013. (Nonfiction Readers Ser.). (ENG.). 64p. (J). (gr. 5-5). pap. 10.99 *(978-1-4333-4904-1(3))*; (Illus.). pap. 31.96 *(978-1-4333-7427-2(7))* Teacher Created Materials, Inc.

Rojas, Emilio. La Simple Historia de un Cualquiera: No Siempre Es Cualquier Historia. 2003. (SPA.). 205p. (YA). 15.95 *(978-968-6966-02-2(1))* EDITER'S Publishing Hse. MEX. Dist: EDITER'S Publishing Hse.

Scholastic, Inc. Staff, contrib. by. Short Plays for Building Fluency: Famous Americans - 22 Reproducible Plays That Build Fluency, Vocabulary, & Comprehension. 2008. (Short Plays for Building Fluency Ser.). (ENG.). 200p. pap. 19.99 *(978-0-545-07216-8(6)*, Teaching Resources) Scholastic, Inc.

Scholastic Library Publishing. The Ancient World. 2012. (J). 306.00 *(978-0-531-24524-8(1)*, Children's Pr.) Scholastic Library Publishing.

Spielvogel, Jackson J., et al. World History Journey Across Time: The Early Ages, Course 1. 2004. (MS Wh Jat Early Age V-1 (ga) Ser.). (ENG., Illus.). 568p. (gr. 6-9). stu. ed. 87.56 *(978-0-07-860309-9(9)*, 0078603099) McGraw-Hill Higher Education.

Stefoff, Rebecca. The Ancient Mediterranean World. 2004. (World Historical Atlases Ser.). (Illus.). 48p. (gr. 5). 26.95 *(978-0-7614-1641-8(2)*, Benchmark Bks.) Marshall Cavendish Corp.

Synge, M. B. On the Shores of the Great Sea, Book I of the Story of the World. 2007. 212p. 21.99 *(978-1-60206-619-9(1))*; per. 14.99 *(978-1-60206-618-2(3))* Cosimo, Inc.

—On the Shores of the Great Sea (Yesterday's Classics) Synge, E. M., illus. l.t. ed. 2006. 240p. (J). per. 11.95 *(978-1-59915-013-0(1))* Yesterday's Classics.

Unearthing Ancient Worlds, 8 vols., Set. Incl. Angkor Wat. Behnke, Alison. lib. bdg. 30.60 *(978-0-8225-7585-6(X))*; Easter Island. Capek, Michael. (YA). lib. bdg. 30.60 *(978-0-8225-7583-2(3))*; Emperor Qin's Terra Cotta Army. Capek, Michael. (Illus.). lib. bdg. 30.60 *(978-0-8225-7507-8(8))*; Machu Picchu. Kops, Deborah. lib. bdg. 30.60 *(978-0-8225-7584-9(1))*; Palenque. Kops, Deborah. (Illus.). (J). lib. bdg. 30.60 *(978-0-8225-7504-7(3))*; Pompeii. Sonneborn, Liz. (Illus.). lib. bdg. 30.60 *(978-0-8225-7505-4(1))*; Tomb of King Tutankhamen. Woods, Michael & Woods, Mary B. (Illus.). lib. bdg. 30.60 *(978-0-8225-7506-1(X))*; Troy. Kerns, Ann. lib. bdg. 30.60 *(978-0-8225-7582-5(5))*; 80p. (gr. 5-8). 2008. (Unearthing Ancient Worlds Ser.). (ENG.). 2008. Set lib. bdg. 214.20 *(978-0-8225-7503-0(5)*, Twenty-First Century Bks.) Lerner Publishing Group.

Van Loon, Hendrik Willem. Ancient Man. 2008. (Illus.). 128p. pap. 6.99 *(978-1-59605-800-2(5)*, Cosimo Classics) Cosimo, Inc.

—Ancient Man. 2004. reprint ed. pap. 1.99 *(978-1-4192-0682-5(6))*; pap. 15.95 *(978-1-4191-0682-8(1))* Kessinger Publishing, LLC.

—Ancient Man: The Beginning of Civilizations. 2007. (Illus.). 128p. per. *(978-1-4065-4732-0(8))* Dodo Pr.

—Ancient Man: The Beginning of Civilizations. 2007. 88p. per. *(978-1-4068-3815-2(2))* Echo Library.

What You Didn't Know about History: Set 3. 2015. (What You Didn't Know about History Ser.). (ENG.). 24p. (J). (gr. 2-3). 135.60 *(978-1-4824-1641-1(7))* Stevens, Gareth Publishing LLLP.

Whitfield, Cathy. History Odyssey, Ancients (level One) 2007. ring bd. 31.00 *(978-0-9766057-8-2(3))* Pandia Pr.

Woolf, Alex. Encounters with the Past. 2014. (Encounters with the Past Ser.). 32p. (J). (gr. 3-6). 159.60 *(978-1-4824-0906-2(2))* Stevens, Gareth Publishing LLLP.

You Choose: Historical Eras Spring 2011. 2010. (You Choose: Historical Eras Ser.). (ENG.). 112p. (gr. 3-4). 63.98 *(978-1-4296-5982-6(3)*, You Choose Bks.) Capstone Press of Coughlan Cos.

You Choose: History. 2011. (You Choose: History Ser.). (ENG.). 112p. (gr. 3-4). pap. 1000.80 *(978-1-4296-6442-4(8)*, You Choose Bks.) Capstone Press of Coughlan Cos.

You Choose: Historical Eras. 2010. (You Choose: Historical Eras Ser.). (ENG.). 112p. (gr. 3-4). pap. 13.90 *(978-1-4296-6278-9(6)*, You Choose Bks.) Capstone Press of Coughlan Cos.

You Choose: Historical Eras Classroom Collection. 2011. (You Choose: Historical Eras Ser.). (ENG.). 112p. (gr. 3-4). pap. 250.20 *(978-1-4296-6443-1(6)*, You Choose Bks.) Capstone Press of Coughlan Cos.

You Choose: History. 2010. (You Choose: History Ser.). (ENG.). 112p. (gr. 3-4). 63.98 *(978-1-4296-5482-1(1)*, You Choose Bks.) Capstone Press of Coughlan Cos.

HISTORY, ANCIENT—FICTION

Capstone Press. Truth & Rumors Fall 2010, 1 vol. 2010. (Truth & Rumors Ser.). (ENG.). 32p. lib. bdg. 159.90 *(978-1-4296-5907-9(6)*, Edge Bks.) Capstone Press of Coughlan Cos.

Corr, Janice. The Aussie Time Travellers & the Cave of the Opal Eyed Snake. 2005. (Illus.). 112p. pap. 13.50 *(978-1-4120-4621-3(1))* Trafford Publishing.

De Pauw, Linda Grant. In Search of Molly Pitcher. 2007. 164p. 30.00 *(978-1-4303-1345-8(5))* Lulu Pr., Inc.

Grey, Christopher Peter & Grey, Christopher. Leonardo's Shadow: Or, My Astonishing Life As Leonardo Da Vinci's Servant. 2008. (ENG.). 400p. (YA). (gr. 7). pap. 12.99 *(978-1-4169-0544-8(8)*, Atheneum Bks. for Young Readers) Simon & Schuster Children's Publishing.

Helfand, Lewis. 400 BC: The Story of the Ten Thousand. Singh, Lalit Kumar, illus. 2011. (Campfire Graphic Novels Ser.). (ENG.). 72p. (YA). (gr. 5-12). pap. 9.99 *(978-93-80028-61-3(X)*, Campfire) Steerforth Pr.

Hillyer, V. M. A Child's History of the World. 2012. 460p. 29.99 *(978-1-60796-533-6(X))* Meirovich, Igal.

Keun, Irmgard. Child of All Nations. Hofmann, Michael, tr. from GER. 2008. (ENG.). 208p. (gr. 4-13). 23.95 *(978-1-59020-099-5(3)*, 902099) Overlook Pr., The.

Morris, Charles. Historic Tales the Romance of Reality Spanish America. 2017. (ENG., Illus.). act. bk. ed. incl. cd-rom *(978-1-892824-26-4(4))* AFCHRON.

Mracek, Ann. Friendship Flies the Sun: The Ancient Egyptian Legend of Scarab Beetle. l.t. ed. 2005. (DAN., Illus.). 32p. (J). per. 15.99 *(978-0-9766488-0-2(6))* Mracek, Ann.

Nelson, Marilyn. Pemba's Song. 2008. (ENG.). 112p. (J). (gr. 7-18). 16.99 *(978-0-545-02076-3(X)*, Scholastic Pr.) Scholastic, Inc.

Reformation & Enlightenment. 2004. (Stories in History Ser.). (gr. 6-12). *(978-0-618-14223-1(1)*, 2-00243) Holt McDougal.

Truth & Rumors, 1 vol. 2010. (Truth & Rumors Ser.). (ENG.). 32p. (gr. 3-4). lib. bdg. 139.95 *(978-1-4296-4749-6(3)*, Edge Bks.) Capstone Press of Coughlan Cos.

HISTORY—ATLASES

see Historical Geography—Maps

HISTORY, BIBLICAL

see Bible—History of Biblical Events

HISTORY—CHRONOLOGY

see Chronology, Historical

HISTORY, CHURCH

see Church History

HISTORY—CRITICISM

see Historiography

HISTORY—DICTIONARIES

Chandler, Fiona. The Usborne Internet-Linked First Encyclopedia of History. 2004. (First Encyclopedias Ser.). (Illus.). 64p. (J). pap. 9.99 *(978-0-7945-0386-4(1)*, Usborne) EDC Publishing.

Chandler, Fiona, et al. The Usborne First Encyclopedia of History. Hancock, David, illus. 2005. 64p. (J). *(978-0-439-78717-8(3))* Scholastic, Inc.

Farndon, John, et al. The History Encyclopedia: Follow the Development of Human Civilization Around the World. 2016. (ENG., Illus.). 512p. (J). (gr. -1-12). pap. 14.99 *(978-1-86147-708-8(2)*, Armadillo) Anness Publishing GBR. Dist: National Bk. Network.

Lemberg, David S. & Canby, Courtlandt. Encyclopedia of Historic Places, 3 vols. 2nd rev. ed. 2007. (Facts on File Library of World History). (Illus.). 1644p. (C). (gr. 9-12). 300.00 *(978-0-8160-5344-5(8))* Facts On File, Inc.

HISTORY—HISTORIOGRAPHY

see Historiography

HISTORY, MILITARY

see Military History

HISTORY—MISCELLANEA

ABDO Publishing. Mysteries of History. 2016. (Mysteries of History Ser.: 6). (ENG.). 48p. (J). (gr. 3-6). lib. bdg. 196.74 *(978-1-68078-021-5(2))* ABDO Publishing Co.

BBC. A History of Humankind. 2016. (ENG., Illus.). 176p. (YA). 16.99 *(978-1-4059-2653-9(8)*, 9781405926539) Penguin Bks., Ltd. GBR. Dist: Diamond Comic Distributors, Inc.

Blackwood, Gary L. Enigmatic Events. 2005. (Unsolved History Ser.). (Illus.). 80p. (gr. 6-7). lib. bdg. 23.95 *(978-0-7614-1889-4(X)*, Benchmark Bks.) Marshall Cavendish Corp.

Blackwood, Gary L. & Follett, Katherine. Enigmatic Events. 2009. (Benchmark Rockets: History's Mysteries Ser.). 32p. (gr. 3). 28.50 *(978-0-7614-4358-2(4))* Marshall Cavendish GBR. Dist: Marshall Cavendish Corp.

Bragg, Georgia. How They Choked: Failures, Flops, & Flaws of the Awfully Famous. O'Malley, Kevin, illus. 2016. (ENG.). 208p. (J). pap. 9.99 *(978-1-68119-216-1(0)*, 9781681192161, Bloomsbury USA Childrens) Bloomsbury Publishing USA.

Chandler, Matt. Dangerous Times: History's Most Troubled Eras. 2013. (Dangerous History Ser.). (ENG.). 32p. (gr. 3-4). 27.99 *(978-1-4765-0126-0(2)*, Edge Bks.) Capstone Press of Coughlan Cos.

Coster, Patience. Really Horrible History Jokes, 1. 2014. (Really Horrible Jokes Ser.). (ENG.). 32p. (J). (gr. k-3). pap. 10.00 *(978-1-4777-9083-0(7)*, Windmill Bks.) Rosen Publishing Group, Inc., The.

Coster, Patience & King, Karen. Really Horrible History Jokes, 1. 2014. (Really Horrible Jokes Ser.). (ENG.). 32p. (J). (gr. k-3). 26.25 *(978-1-4777-9082-3(9)*, Windmill Bks.) Rosen Publishing Group, Inc., The.

Doomed! 2015. (Doomed! Ser.). (ENG.). 32p. (J). (gr. 4-5). pap., pap., pap. 63.00 *(978-1-4824-3457-6(1))* Stevens, Gareth Publishing LLLP.

Eaton, Gale. A History of Ambition in 50 Hoaxes, 1 vol. 2016. (History In 50 Ser.: 0). (ENG., Illus.). 272p. (gr. 6-12). 24.95 *(978-0-88448-465-3(3)*, 884465) Tilbury Hse. Pubs.

Forest, Christopher. The World's Wackiest History. 2015. (Library of Weird Ser.). (ENG., Illus.). 32p. (gr. 3-4). lib. bdg. 27.99 *(978-1-4914-2018-8(9))* Capstone Press of Coughlan Cos.

Gay, Kathlyn & Blundell, Nigel. The World's Worst Mistakes. 2016. (Making Headlines Ser.). 160p. (J). lib. bdg. 39.93 *(978-0-7660-8367-7(5))* Enslow Pubs., Inc.

Gifford, Clive. Killer History: A Gruesome & Grisly Trip Through the Past. 2013. (ENG.). 144p. (YA). (gr. 4-6). 9.99 *(978-1-62145-029-0(5))* Reader's Digest Assn., Inc., The.

Greathouse, Lisa & Kuligowski, Stephanie. Unsolved! Mysterious Events, 1 vol. 2nd rev. ed. 2012. (Nonfiction Readers Ser.). (ENG., Illus.). 48p. (J). (gr. 4-4). pap. 9.99 *(978-1-4333-4827-3(6))* Teacher Created Materials, Inc.

Gunderson, Jessica, et al. Tangled History. 2015. (Tangled History Ser.). (ENG.). 112p. (gr. 3-4). 127.96 *(978-1-4914-7418-1(1))* Capstone Press of Coughlan Cos.

Hawkins, Jay. Really Horrible History Facts. 2013. (Really Horrible Facts Ser.). 32p. (J). (gr. k-3). pap. 60.00 *(978-1-61533-810-8(1))*; pap. 10.00 *(978-1-61533-809-2(8))* Windmill Bks.

Hibbert, Clare. A Brief Illustrated History of Exploration. 2017. (Brief Illustrated History Ser.). (ENG.). 32p. (gr. 3-5). lib. bdg. 27.32 *(978-1-5157-2522-0(7)*, Fact Finders) Capstone Press of Coughlan Cos.

Hinman, Bonnie. Fascinating History. 2018. (ENG.). 32p. (gr. 3-6). 31.35 ***(978-1-63235-420-4(9)***, 12-Story Library) Pr. Room Editions LLC.

History Exposed. 2016. (History Exposed Ser.). 224p. (gr. 9-9). lib. bdg. 330.00 *(978-1-5026-1993-8(8))* Cavendish Square Publishing.

Hughes, Susan & Wandelmaier, Michael. Case Closed? Nine Mysteries Unlocked by Modern Science. Wandelmaier, Michael, illus. 2013. (ENG., Illus.). 88p. (J). (gr. 3-7). pap. 12.95 *(978-1-55453-363-3(5))* Kids Can Pr., Ltd. CAN. Dist: Hachette Bk. Group.

Lassieur, Allison. Unsolved Historical Mysteries. 2015. (Unsolved Mystery Files Ser.). (ENG., Illus.). 32p. (gr. 3-4). pap. 7.95 *(978-1-4914-4340-8(5))* Capstone Press of Coughlan Cos.

LernerClassroom Editors, ed. Teaching Guide for History Speaks. 2010. pap. 5.95 *(978-0-7613-6689-8(X))* Lerner Publishing Group.

Loewen, Nancy & Skelley, Paula. Go Go Global. 2015. (Go Go Global Ser.). (ENG.). 32p. (gr. 1-2). 109.28 *(978-1-4914-6655-1(3)*, Aplus Bks.) Capstone Press of Coughlan Cos.

Mason, Paul. Did the Romans Eat Chips? And Other Questions about History, 1 vol. 2013. (Questions You Never Thought You'd Ask Ser.). (ENG., Illus.). 32p. (gr. 1-3). 29.99 *(978-1-4109-5198-4(7))*; pap. 8.95 *(978-1-4109-5204-2(5))* Heinemann-Raintree. (Read Me!).

Meister, Cari. Wacky Facts about History. 2016. (Mind Benders Ser.). (ENG., Illus.). 240p. (gr. 1-3). pap. 7.95 *(978-1-4914-8391-6(1))* Capstone Press of Coughlan Cos.

Merrell, Patrick. Uncle John's iFlush - Hurtling Thru History Bathroom Reader for Kids Only! 2013. (ENG., Illus.). 96p. (J). (gr. 1-6). 12.95 *(978-1-60710-904-4(2)*, Portable Pr.) Readerlink Distribution Services, LLC.

O'Hearn, Michael. History Debate: A Rip-Roaring Game of Either-Or Questions. 2012. (This or That? Ser.). (ENG., Illus.). 32p. (gr. 3-4). 27.99 *(978-1-4296-8414-9(3))* Capstone Press of Coughlan Cos.

—History Debate: A Rip-Roaring Game of Either/Or Questions. 2012. (This or That? Ser.). (ENG., Illus.). 32p. (gr. 3-4). pap. 8.29 *(978-1-4296-9274-8(X))* Capstone Press of Coughlan Cos.

Our Shared History. 2015. (Our Shared History Ser.). (ENG.). 128p. (J). (gr. 7-7). 223.62 *(978-0-7660-6699-1(1))* Enslow Pubs., Inc.

Payne, Jan, et al. Attila the Hun Was Killed by a Nosebleed: And Other Facts about History. 2016. (True or False? Ser.). (Illus.). 48p. (J). (gr. 3-3). pap. 11.70 *(978-0-7660-7724-9(1))* Enslow Pubs., Inc.

Powell, Marie. Unsolved! 2015. (ENG., Illus.). 32p. (J). *(978-0-7787-8073-1(2))* Crabtree Publishing Co.

Rice, Dona Herweck. Unsolved! History's Mysteries, 1 vol. 2nd rev. ed. 2012. (TIME for KIDS(r) Nonfiction Readers Ser.). (ENG.). 48p. (J). (gr. 4-4). pap. 9.99 *(978-1-4333-4829-7(2))* Teacher Created Materials, Inc.

The Rise & Fall of Empires. 2016. (Rise & Fall of Empires Ser.). 64p. (gr. 6-6). 172.25 *(978-1-4777-8553-9(1))*; pap. 64.75 *(978-1-4994-6427-6(4))* Rosen Publishing Group, Inc., The. (Rosen Young Adult).

Rowe, Brooke. What Decade Do You Belong In? 2016. (Illus.). 32p. (J). *(978-1-63470-508-0(4))* Cherry Lake Publishing.

Samuels, Charlie. Conspiracy! 2013. (ENG.). 32p. (J). *(978-0-7787-1126-1(9))*; pap. *(978-0-7787-1130-8(7))* Crabtree Publishing Co.

Schwartz, Heather E. & Salzano, Tammi. Around the World: An Amazing World. 2009. (Illus.). 48p. (J). pap. *(978-0-545-17229-5(2))* Scholastic, Inc.

Sherman, Patrice. The Case of the Train Without Wheels & Other True History Mysteries for You to Solve, 1 vol. 2012. (Seriously True Mysteries Ser.). (ENG.). 32p. (gr. 3-4). lib. bdg. 27.32 *(978-1-4296-7626-7(4)*, Fact Finders) Capstone Press of Coughlan Cos.

Simmons, Alex. Mysteries of the Past: A Chapter Book. 2005. (True Tales Ser.). (ENG., Illus.). 48p. (J). (gr. 2-4). lib. bdg. 22.50 *(978-0-516-25184-4(8)*, Children's Pr.) Scholastic Library Publishing.

Snedding, Robert, et al. A Brief Illustrated History. 2017. (Brief Illustrated History Ser.). (ENG.). 32p. (gr. 3-5). 163.92 *(978-1-5157-2524-4(3)*, Fact Finders) Capstone Press of Coughlan Cos.

Swain, Gwenyth & Gitlin, Martin. You Choose: History. 2012. (You Choose: History Ser.). (ENG.). 112p. (gr. 3-4). 63.98 *(978-1-4296-6591-9(2))*; pap. 1084.20 *(978-1-4296-8486-6(0))*; pap. 13.90 *(978-1-4296-9513-8(7))* Capstone Press of Coughlan Cos. (You Choose Bks.).

Tangled History, 6 vols. 2016. (Tangled History Ser.). (ENG.). 112p. (gr. 3-4). 191.94 *(978-1-4914-8467-8(5))* Capstone Press of Coughlan Cos.

Terrell, Brandon. 12 Unsolved Mysteries. 2017. (Scary & Spooky Ser.). (ENG.). 32p. (J). (gr. 3-6). 21.95 *(978-1-63235-298-9(2))* Pr. Room Editions LLC.

Vickers, Rebecca. Every Possession Has a History, 1 vol. 2014. (Everything Has a History Ser.). (ENG., Illus.). 64p. (gr. 7-8). pap. 10.95 *(978-1-4329-9591-1(X))*; lib. bdg. 35.99 *(978-1-4329-9586-7(3))* Heinemann-Raintree.

Vonne, Mira. Gross History. 2017. (Gross History Ser.). (ENG.). 32p. (gr. 1-2). 159.90 *(978-1-5157-4200-5(8)*, Blazers) Capstone Press of Coughlan Cos.

Webb, Sarah Powers. Perspectives on History. 2015. (Perspectives on History Ser.). (ENG.). 32p. (gr. 3-4). lib. bdg. 54.64 *(978-1-4914-2456-8(7)*, Fact Finders) Capstone Press of Coughlan Cos.

Woolf, Alex. The Impact of Technology in History & Archaeology. 2015. (Impact of Technology Ser.). (ENG., Illus.). 56p. (gr. 6-9). pap. 9.49 *(978-1-4846-2642-9(7))* Heinemann-Raintree.

Yenne, Bill. 100 Men Who Shaped World History. 2015. (ENG., Illus.). 100p. pap. 7.95 *(978-0-912517-05-6(0))* Bluewood Bks.

Yomtov, Nel, et al. Perspectives on History. 2015. (Perspectives on History Ser.). (ENG.). 32p. (gr. 3-4). lib. bdg. 163.92 *(978-1-4914-2457-5(5)*, Fact Finders) Capstone Press of Coughlan Cos.

HISTORY, MODERN

Here are entered works covering the period after 1453.

see also Civilization, Modern; Reformation; Renaissance

ABDO Publishing Company Staff. Essential Events Set 7. 2011. (Essential Events Set 7 Ser.: 8). (ENG., Illus.). 112p. (J). (gr. 6-12). lib. bdg. 285.12 *(978-1-61783-095-2(X)*, Essential Library) ABDO Publishing Co.

Bailey, Viola & Wise, Ella. Victorian Times. Date not set. (Focus on History Ser.). (Illus.). 64p. (J). pap. 129.15 *(978-0-582-18240-0(9))* Addison-Wesley Longman, Ltd. GBR. Dist: Trans-Atlantic Pubns., Inc.

Bauer, Susan Wise & Johnson, Barbara Allen. The Story of the World: History for the Classical Child. unabr. ed. 2005. (ENG.). 1p. 55.95 *(978-0-9742391-2-5(7))* Open Texture.

Beller, Susan Provost. The History Puzzle: How We Know What We Know about the Past. 2006. (ENG., Illus.). 128p. (gr. 7-12). lib. bdg. 26.60 *(978-0-7613-2877-3(7))* Lerner Publishing Group.

Berndl, Klaus & Hattstein, Markus. The Contemporary World: From 1945 to the 21st Century. 2012. (Witness to History: A Visual Chronicle of the World Ser.). (ENG., Illus.). 200p. (J). (gr. 7-12). 46.50 *(978-1-4488-7225-1(1))* Rosen Publishing Group, Inc., The.

Bingham, Marjorie. An Age of Empires, 1200-1750. 2006. 32.95 *(978-0-19-522268-5(7))* Oxford Univ. Pr., Inc.

Bingham, Marjorie Wall. An Age of Empires, 1200-1750. 2005. (Medieval & Early Modern World Ser.: 4). (ENG., Illus.). 160p. (YA). 32.95 *(978-0-19-517839-5(4))* Oxford Univ. Pr., Inc.

Burgan, Michael & Doeden, Matt. You Choose: Modern History, 1 vol. 2014. (You Choose: Modern History Ser.). (ENG.). 112p. (gr. 3-4). 63.98 *(978-1-4914-0362-4(4)*, You Choose Bks.) Capstone Press of Coughlan Cos.

Clare, John D. Cold War & After. 2nd rev. ed. 2005. (Illus.). 64p. pap. 26.50 *(978-0-340-81480-2(2)*, Hodder Education) Hodder Education Group GBR. Dist: Trans-Atlantic Pubns., Inc.

—A World Study after 1900. 2003. (Illus.). 96p. pap. 29.50 *(978-0-340-86912-3(7)*, Hodder Education) Hodder Education Group GBR. Dist: Trans-Atlantic Pubns., Inc.

Corrigan, Jim. The 1900s Decade in Photos: A Decade of Discovery. 2010. (Amazing Decades in Photos Ser.). (Illus.). 64p. (J). (gr. 5-9). lib. bdg. 29.27 *(978-0-7660-3129-6(2))* Enslow Pubs., Inc.

—The 1910s Decade in Photos: A Decade That Shook the World. 2010. (Amazing Decades in Photos Ser.). (Illus.). 64p. (J). (gr. 5-9). lib. bdg. 29.27 *(978-0-7660-3130-2(6))* Enslow Pubs., Inc.

—The 1920s Decade in Photos: The Roaring Twenties. 2010. (Amazing Decades in Photos Ser.). (Illus.). 64p. (J). (gr. 5-9). lib. bdg. 29.27 *(978-0-7660-3131-9(4))* Enslow Pubs., Inc.

—The 1930s Decade in Photos: Depression & Hope. 2010. (Amazing Decades in Photos Ser.). (Illus.). 64p. (J). (gr. 5-9). lib. bdg. 29.27 *(978-0-7660-3132-6(2))* Enslow Pubs., Inc.

—The 1940s Decade in Photos: A World at War. 2010. (Amazing Decades in Photos Ser.). (Illus.). 64p. (J). (gr. 5-9). lib. bdg. 29.27 *(978-0-7660-3133-3(0))* Enslow Pubs., Inc.

—The 1950s Decade in Photos: The American Decade. 2010. (Amazing Decades in Photos Ser.). (Illus.). 64p. (J). (gr. 5-9). lib. bdg. 29.27 *(978-0-7660-3134-0(9))* Enslow Pubs., Inc.

—The 1960s Decade in Photos: Love, Freedom, & Flower Power. 2010. (Amazing Decades in Photos Ser.). (Illus.). 64p. (J). (gr. 5-9). lib. bdg. 29.27 *(978-0-7660-3135-7(7))* Enslow Pubs., Inc.

—The 1970s Decade in Photos: Protest & Change. 2010. (Amazing Decades in Photos Ser.). (Illus.). 64p. (J). (gr. 5-9). lib. bdg. 29.27 *(978-0-7660-3136-4(5))* Enslow Pubs., Inc.

—The 1980s Decade in Photos: The Triumph of Democracy. 2010. (Amazing Decades in Photos Ser.). (Illus.). 64p. (J). (gr. 5-9). lib. bdg. 29.27 *(978-0-7660-3137-1(3))* Enslow Pubs., Inc.

—The 1990s Decade in Photos: The Rise of Technology. 2010. (Amazing Decades in Photos Ser.). (Illus.). 64p. (J). (gr. 5-9). lib. bdg. 29.27 *(978-0-7660-3138-8(1))* Enslow Pubs., Inc.

—The 2000s Decade in Photos: A New Millennium. 2010. (Amazing Decades in Photos Ser.). (Illus.). 64p. (J). (gr. 5-9). lib. bdg. 29.27 *(978-0-7660-3139-5(X))* Enslow Pubs., Inc.

DeMarco, Neil. A World Study after 1900. 2003. (Illus.). 96p. pap. 29.50 *(978-0-340-86913-0(5)*, Hodder Education) Hodder Education Group GBR. Dist: Trans-Atlantic Pubns., Inc.

DeMarco, Neil & Aylett, J. F. Cold War & After. 2nd rev. ed. 2005. (Illus.). 64p. pap. 32.50 *(978-0-340-81479-6(9))* Hodder Education Group GBR. Dist: Trans-Atlantic Pubns., Inc.

Desmarais, Kathleen. History Odyssey, Early Modern (level Two) 2007. ring bd. 38.00 *(978-0-9766057-9-7(1))* Pandia Pr.

Dwyer, Helen. The Early Modern World, 1492 to 1783. 2010. (CC: Atlas of World History Ser.). 112p. (gr. 6-12). 42.80 *(978-1-933834-68-9(4))* Brown Bear Bks.

Essential Facts. 2004. (I-Quest Ser.). (J). *(978-1-84229-753-7(8))* Top That! Publishing PLC.

Fardon, John. 1000 Things You Should Know about Modern History. 2004. (1000 Things You Should Know about Ser.). (Illus.). 64p. (YA). (gr. 5-18). lib. bdg. 19.95 *(978-1-59084-468-7(8))* Mason Crest.

Finger, Brad. 13 Photos Children Should Know. 2011. (ENG., Illus.). 48p. (J). (gr. 3-7). 14.95 *(978-3-7913-7047-7(2))* Prestel Verlag GmbH & Co KG. DEU. Dist: Penguin Random Hse. LLC.

Foster, Genevieve. The World of William Penn. 2008. (Illus.). 192p. (J). pap. *(978-1-893103-30-6(7))* Beautiful Feet Bks.

—The Year of the Horseless Carriage, 1801. 2008. (Illus.). 95p. *(978-1-893103-31-3(5))* Beautiful Feet Bks.

Group/McGraw-Hill, Wright. Castle Life in the Middle Ages, 6 vols. (Book2WebTM Ser.). (gr. 4-8). 36.50 *(978-0-322-04449-4(9))* Wright Group/McGraw-Hill.

Hanes, Sharon M., et al. Cold War: Biographies, 2.0. 2003. (Cold War Reference Library). (Illus.). (J). (ENG.). 474p. 191.00 *(978-0-7876-7663-6(2))*; xxxv, 473p. *(978-0-7876-7665-0(9))*; xxxv, 473p. *(978-0-7876-7664-3(0))* Cengage Gale. (UXL).

History: Student Testing Kit. 2004. (Illus.). (J). (gr. 1-8). stu. ed. 5.00 *(978-0-7403-0043-1(1)*, HD001); (YA). (gr. 7-12). stu. ed. 5.00 *(978-0-7403-0044-8(X)*, HD002) Alpha Omega Pubns., Inc.

Hollingsworth, Tamara. Unforgettable News Reports, 1 vol. 2nd rev. ed. 2013. (TIME for KIDS(r) Nonfiction Readers Ser.). (ENG., Illus.). 64p. (J). (gr. 5-5). pap. 10.99 *(978-1-4333-4945-4(0))* Teacher Created Materials, Inc.

Huff, Toby E. An Age of Science & Revolutions, 1600-1800. (Illus.). 2006. 173p. (J). 32.95 *(978-0-19-522269-2(5))* 2005. (ENG., 176p. (YA). (gr. 7-18). lib. bdg. 32.95 *(978-0-19-517724-4(X))* Oxford Univ. Pr., Inc.

Hughes, Shirley. A Brush with the Past, 1900-1950: The Years That Changed Our Lives. 2005. (ENG., Illus.). 112p. (gr. 5-18). 45.00 *(978-0-370-32839-3(6))* Random Hse. GBR. Dist: Independent Pubs. Group.

Knebel, Arthur & Udelhoven, Hermann-Josef. The Modern Era through World War II: From the 18th Century To 1945. 2012. (Witness to History: A Visual Chronicle of the World Ser.). (ENG., Illus.). 200p. (J). (gr. 7-12). 46.50 *(978-1-4488-7224-4(3))* Rosen Publishing Group, Inc., The.

Kovacs, Charles. The Age of Revolution, 1 vol. 2003. (ENG.). 240p. (YA). pap. 19.95 *(978-0-86315-395-2(X))* Floris Bks. GBR. Dist: SteinerBooks, Inc.

Levy, Patricia. From Punk Rock to Perestroika: The Mid 1970s to the Mid 1980s. 2005. (Modern Eras Uncovered Ser.). (Illus.). 56p. (J). pap. *(978-1-4109-1798-0(3))* Steck-Vaughn.

—From Speakeasies to Stalinism: The 1920s to the Mid-1930s. 2005. (Modern Eras Uncovered Ser.). (Illus.). 56p. (J). pap. *(978-1-4109-1794-2(0))* Steck-Vaughn.

—Modern Eras Uncovered: From Beatlemania to Watergate. 2005. (Modern Eras Uncovered Ser.). (Illus.). 56p. (J). *(978-1-84443-965-2(8))*; *(978-1-84443-955-3(0))* Steck-Vaughn.

—Modern Eras Uncovered: From Compact Discs to the Gulf War. 2005. (Modern Eras Uncovered Ser.). (Illus.). 56p. (J). *(978-1-84443-967-6(4))*; *(978-1-84443-957-7(7))* Steck-Vaughn.

—Modern Eras Uncovered: From Punk Rock to Perestroika. 2005. (Modern Eras Uncovered Ser.). (Illus.). 56p. (J). *(978-1-84443-966-9(6))*; *(978-1-84443-956-0(9))* Steck-Vaughn.

—Modern Eras Uncovered: From the World Wide Web to September 11. 2005. (Modern Eras Uncovered Ser.). (Illus.). 56p. (J). *(978-1-84443-968-3(2))* Steck-Vaughn.

Levy, Patricia & Sheehan, Sean. From Compact Discs to the Gulf War: The Mid 1980s to the Early 1990s. 2005. (Modern Eras Uncovered Ser.). (Illus.). 56p. (J). pap. *(978-1-4109-1799-7(1))* Steck-Vaughn.

—From the World Wide Web to September 11: The Early 1990s to 2001. 2005. (Modern Eras Uncovered Ser.). (Illus.). 56p. (J). pap. *(978-1-4109-1800-0(9))* Steck-Vaughn.

—Modern Eras Uncovered: From the World Wide Web to September 11. 2005. (Modern Eras Uncovered Ser.). (Illus.). 56p. (J). *(978-1-84443-958-4(5))* Steck-Vaughn.

Mann, Charles. 1493 for Young People: From Columbus's Voyage to Globalization. 2016. (For Young People Ser.). (ENG., Illus.). 416p. (J). (gr. 7). pap. 18.95 *(978-1-60980-663-7(6)*, Triangle Square) Seven Stories Pr.

Meister, Cari. Totally Wacky Facts about Modern History. 2016. (Mind Benders Ser.). (ENG., Illus.). 112p. (gr. 1-3). lib. bdg. 23.32 *(978-1-4914-8386-2(5))* Capstone Press of Coughlan Cos.

Monumental Milestones: Great Events of Modern Times, 22 vols., Set. Incl. Assassination of John F. Kennedy 1963. Harkins, Susan Sales & Harkins, William H. (YA). (gr. 4-7). 2007. lib. bdg. 29.95 *(978-1-58415-540-9(X))*; Blitzrieg! Hitler's Lightning War. Rice, Earle, Jr. (YA). (gr. 4-7). 2007. lib. bdg. 29.95 *(978-1-58415-542-3(6))*; Breaking the Sound Barrier: The Story of Chuck Yeager. Harkins, Susan Sales. (YA). (gr. 4-7). 2005. lib. bdg. 29.95 *(978-1-58415-398-6(9)*, 1244924); Civil Rights Movement. Murcia, Rebecca Thatcher. (YA). (gr. 4-7). 2005. lib. bdg. 29.95 *(978-1-58415-401-3(2))*; Creation of Isreal. Whiting, Jim. (YA). (gr. 4-7). 2007. lib. bdg. 29.95 *(978-1-58415-538-6(8))*; Cuban Missile Crisis: The Cold War Goes Hot. Whiting, Jim. (YA). (gr. 4-7). 2005. lib. bdg. 29.95 *(978-1-58415-404-4(7))*; Dawn of Aviation: The Story of the Wright Brothers. Orr, Tamra B. (YA). (gr. 4-7). 2005. lib. bdg. 29.95 *(978-1-58415-396-2(2)*, 1244922); Disaster in the Indian Ocean, Tsunami 2004. Torres, John Albert. (YA). (gr. 4-7). 2005. lib. bdg. 29.95 *(978-1-58415-344-3(X))*; Exploring the North Pole: The Story Robert Edwin Peary & Matthew Henson. Sherman, Josepha. (J). (gr. 4-7). 2005. lib. bdg. 29.95 *(978-1-58415-402-0(0))*; Fall of the Berlin Wall. Tracy, Kathleen. (YA). (gr. 4-7). 2005. lib. bdg. 29.95 *(978-1-58415-405-1(5))*; Fall of the Soviet Union 1991. Harkins, Susan Sales & Harkins, William H. (YA). (gr. 4-7). 2007. lib. bdg. 29.95 *(978-1-58415-539-3(6))*; Hurricane Katrina & the Devastation of New Orleans 2005. Torres, John Albert. (YA). (gr. 4-7). 2006. lib. bdg. 29.95 *(978-1-58415-473-0(X))*; Overview of World War I. Whiting, Jim. (YA). (gr. 4-7). 2006. lib. bdg. 29.95 *(978-1-58415-471-6(3))*; Russian Revolution 1917. Whiting, Jim. (YA). (gr. 4-7). 2007. lib. bdg. 29.95 *(978-1-58415-537-9(X))*; Scopes Monkey Trial. Whiting, Jim. (YA). (gr. 4-7). 2006. lib. bdg. 29.95 *(978-1-58415-468-6(3))*; Sinking of the Titanic. Whiting, Jim. (J). (gr. 3-7). 2006. lib. bdg. 29.95 *(978-1-58415-472-3(1))*; Story of the Attack on Pearl Harbor. Whiting, Jim. (YA). (gr. 4-7). 2005. lib. bdg. 29.95 *(978-1-58415-397-9(0))*; Story of the Great Depression. Gedney, Mona K. (YA). (gr. 4-7). 2005. lib. bdg. 29.95 *(978-1-58415-403-7(9))*; Story of the Holocaust. Whiting, Jim. (YA). (gr. 4-7). 2005. lib. bdg. 29.95 *(978-1-58415-400-6(4))*; Top Secret: The Story of the Manhattan Project. Tracy, Kathleen. (YA). (gr. 4-7). 2005. lib. bdg. 29.95 *(978-1-58415-399-3(7))*; Vietnam War. Gibson, Karen Bush. (J). (gr. 4-8). 2007. lib. bdg. 29.95 *(978-1-58415-541-6(8))*; Watergate Scandal. Tracy, Kathleen. (YA). (gr. 4-7). 2006. lib. bdg. 29.95 *(978-1-58415-470-9(5))*; (Illus.). 48p. (Monumental Milestones Ser.). 2007. Set lib. bdg. 658.90 *(978-1-58415-543-0(4))* Mitchell Lane Pubs., Inc.

Morris, Neil. Modern World Leaders. 2003. (History Makers (Chrysalis) Ser.). (Illus.). 48p. (J). (gr. 5-18). lib. bdg. 29.95 *(978-1-932333-79-4(7))* Chrysalis Education.

Nardo, Don, et al. Whoops! a History of Bad Days. 2017. (Whoops! a History of Bad Days Ser.). (ENG.). 48p. (gr. 5-8). 133.28 *(978-1-4109-8577-4(6))* Heinemann-Raintree.

Perritano, John. Education, Poverty, & Inequality. 2017. (Illus.). 64p. (J). *(978-1-4222-3634-5(X))* Mason Crest.

—The Making of the Modern World: 1945 to the Present: Culture & Customs in a Connected World, Vol. 9. 2016. (Making of the Modern World: 1945 to the Present Ser.: Vol. 9). (ENG., Illus.). 64p. (J). (gr. 7-12). 23.95 *(978-1-4222-3635-2(8))* Mason Crest.

Robson, David. The Decade of The 2000s. 2011. (Understanding World History Ser.). (ENG., Illus.). 96p. (YA). (gr. 7-12). lib. bdg. 27.95 *(978-1-60152-187-3(1))* ReferencePoint Pr., Inc.

Ryan, James G. & Schlup, Leonard, eds. Historical Dictionary of The 1940s. 2006. (ENG., Illus.). 648p. (C). 158.00 *(978-0-7656-0440-8(X)*, Y182788) Routledge.

Scott, Janine. The Two Great Wars. 2007. (Shockwave: History & Politics Ser.). (ENG., Illus.). 36p. (J). (gr. 4-6). lib. bdg. 25.00 *(978-0-531-17756-3(4)*, Children's Pr.) Scholastic Library Publishing.

Sheehan, Sean. From Beatlemania to Watergate: The Early 1960s to the Mid 1970s. 2005. (Modern Eras Uncovered Ser.). (Illus.). 56p. (J). pap. *(978-1-4109-1797-3(5))* Steck-Vaughn.

—From Jessie Owens to Hiroshima: The Mid 1930s to 1945. 2005. (Modern Eras Uncovered Ser.). (Illus.). 56p. (J). pap. *(978-1-4109-1795-9(9))* Steck-Vaughn.

—From Television to the Berlin Wall: The Mid-1940s to the Early 1960s. 2005. (Modern Eras Uncovered Ser.). (Illus.). 56p. (J). pap. *(978-1-4109-1796-6(7))* Steck-Vaughn.

—From the Wright Brothers to the Treaty of Versailles: The 1900s to 1918. 2005. (Modern Eras Uncovered Ser.). (Illus.). 56p. (J). pap. *(978-1-4109-1793-5(2))* Steck-Vaughn.

—Modern Eras Uncovered: From Jesse Owens to Hiroshima. 2005. (Modern Eras Uncovered Ser.). (Illus.). 56p. (J). *(978-1-84443-962-1(3))*; *(978-1-84443-952-2(6))* Steck-Vaughn.

—Modern Eras Uncovered: From Speakeasies to Stalinism. 2005. (Modern Eras Uncovered Ser.). (Illus.). 56p. (J). *(978-1-84443-961-4(5))* Steck-Vaughn.

—Modern Eras Uncovered: From Television to the Berlin Wall. 2005. (Modern Eras Uncovered Ser.). (Illus.). 56p. (J). *(978-1-84443-963-8(1))* Steck-Vaughn.

—Modern Eras Uncovered: From the Wright Brothers to the Treaty of Versailles. 2005. (Modern Eras Uncovered Ser.). (Illus.). 56p. (J). *(978-1-84443-960-7(7))*; *(978-1-84443-950-8(X))* Steck-Vaughn.

Sheehan, Sean & Levy, Pat. Modern Eras Uncovered: From Speakeasies to Stalinism. 2005. (Modern Eras Uncovered Ser.). (Illus.). 56p. (J). *(978-1-84443-951-5(8))* Steck-Vaughn.

—Modern Eras Uncovered: From Television to the Berlin Wall. 2005. (Modern Eras Uncovered Ser.). (Illus.). 56p. (J). pap. *(978-1-84443-953-9(4))* Steck-Vaughn.

Smith, Bonnie G. & Kelley, Donald R. The Medieval & Early Modern World: Primary Sources & Reference Volume. 2006. 32.95 *(978-0-19-522300-2(4))* Oxford Univ. Pr., Inc.

—The Medieval & Early Modern World: Primary Sources & Reference Volume. 2005. (Medieval & Early Modern World Ser.). (ENG., Illus.). 176p. (YA). 32.95 *(978-0-19-517848-7(3))* Oxford Univ. Pr., Inc.

Spilsbury, Louise. Industrialization & Empire, 1783 to 1914. 2010. (CC: Atlas of World History Ser.). 112p. (gr. 6-12). 42.80 *(978-1-933834-69-6(2))* Brown Bear Bks.

—World Wars & Globalization, 1914 to 2010. 2010. (Curriculum Connections: Atlas of World History Ser.). 39.95 *(978-1-933834-70-2(6))* Brown Bear Bks.

Tames, Richard. The 1920s. 2005. (Picture History of the 20th Century (Sea to Sea) Ser.). (Illus.). 48p. (YA). (gr. 7-12). lib. bdg. 29.95 *(978-1-932889-70-3(1))* Sea-To-Sea Pubns.

Tougas, Shelley, et al. Captured History. 2013. (Captured History Ser.). (ENG.). 64p. (gr. 5-7). 69.30 *(978-0-7565-4721-9(0))*; 207.90 *(978-0-7565-4722-6(9))*; pap. 18.20 *(978-0-7565-4718-9(0))* Compass Point Bks. (CPB Grades 4-8).

Whitfield, Cathy. History Odyssey, Early Modern - Level One. 2006. (J). ring bd. 31.00 *(978-0-9766057-5-1(9))* Pandia Pr.

Wiesner-Hanks, Merry E. An Age of Voyages, 1350-1600. 2005. (Medieval & Early Modern World Ser.: 5). (ENG., Illus.). 192p. (YA). (gr. 7-18). lib. bdg. 32.95 *(978-0-19-517672-8(3))* Oxford Univ. Pr., Inc.

Wiesner, Merry E. An Age of Voyages, 1450-1600. 2006. (Illus.). 189p. 32.95 *(978-0-19-522264-7(4))* Oxford Univ. Pr., Inc.

Wilson, John. Failed Hope: The Story of the Lost Peace. 2012. (Stories of Canada Ser.: 14). (ENG., Illus.). 120p. (J). pap. 18.99 *(978-1-4597-0345-2(6))* Dundurn CAN. Dist: Ingram Publisher Services.

—Failed Hope: The Story of the Lost Peace (Large Print 16pt) 2013. 180p. pap. *(978-1-4596-6314-5(4))* ReadHowYouWant.com, Ltd.

HISTORY, NATURAL

see Natural History

HISTORY, NAVAL

see Naval History

see names of countries with the subdivision History, Naval e. g. United States—History, Naval

HISTORY—POETRY

see Historical Poetry

HISTORY—SOURCES

Clapper, Nikki Bruno. Learning about Primary Sources. 2015. (Media Literacy for Kids Ser.). (ENG., Illus.). 24p. (gr. k-1). lib. bdg. 26.65 *(978-1-4914-6050-4(4))* Capstone Press of Coughlan Cos.

Downey, Glen R. The 10 Most Significant Documents in History. 2008. 14.99 *(978-1-55448-547-5(9))* Scholastic Library Publishing.

Fontichiaro, Kristin. Find Out Firsthand: Using Primary Sources. 2012. (Explorer Junior Library: Information Explorer Junior Ser.). (ENG.). 24p. (gr. 1-4). 28.50 *(978-1-61080-487-5(2)*, 202097) Cherry Lake Publishing.

—Super Smart Information Strategies: Go Straight to the Source. 2010. (Explorer Library: Information Explorer Ser.). (ENG.). 32p. (gr. 4-8). pap. 14.21 *(978-1-61080-257-4(8)*, 200905); lib. bdg. 28.50 *(978-1-60279-640-9(8)*, 200343) Cherry Lake Publishing.

Langston-George, Rebecca, et al. Primary Source History. 2015. (Primary Source History Ser.). (ENG.). 32p. (gr. 3-4). lib. bdg. 109.28 *(978-1-4914-1855-0(9)*, Fact Finders) Capstone Press of Coughlan Cos.

Loh-Hagan, Virginia. Time Capsule. 2017. (D. I. Y. Make It Happen Ser.). (ENG., Illus.). 32p. (J). (gr. 4-8). lib. bdg. 29.93 *(978-1-63472-146-2(2)*, 209156, 45th Parallel Press) Cherry Lake Publishing.

Spence, Kelly & Barghoorn, Linda. Be a Photograph Detective. 2017. (Be a Document Detective Ser.). (ENG., Illus.). 24p. (J). ***(978-0-7787-3066-8(2))*** Crabtree Publishing Co.

—Be a Speech Detective. 2017. (Be a Document Detective Ser.). (ENG., Illus.). 24p. (J). ***(978-0-7787-3079-8(4))*** Crabtree Publishing Co.

Spence, Kelly & Burns, Kylie. Be a Diary Detective. 2017. (Be a Document Detective Ser.). (ENG., Illus.). 24p. (J). ***(978-0-7787-3053-8(0))*** Crabtree Publishing Co.

—Be an Artifact Detective. 2017. (Be a Document Detective Ser.). (ENG., Illus.). 24p. (J). ***(978-0-7787-3039-2(5))*** Crabtree Publishing Co.

Tait, Leia. Primary Sources. 2007. (Social Studies Essential Skills Ser.). (Illus.). 24p. (J). lib. bdg. 24.45 *(978-1-59036-763-6(4))*; (gr. 4-7). per. 8.95 *(978-1-59036-764-3(2))* Weigl Pubs., Inc.

HISTORY, UNIVERSAL

see World History

HISTORY—YEARBOOKS

Dorling Kindersley Publishing Staff. History Year by Year. 2013. (ENG.). 320p. (J). (gr. 4-7). 24.99 *(978-1-4654-1418-2(5)*, DK Children) Dorling Kindersley Publishing, Inc.

HISTORY IN ART

Harris, Nathaniel. Stories Behind the Art: Wall Paintings. 2016. (Stories in Art Ser.). (ENG., Illus.). 32p. (J). (gr. 2-4). pap. 11.99 *(978-0-7502-9446-1(9)*, Wayland) Hachette Children's Group GBR. Dist: Hachette Bk. Group.

Spilsbury, Richard. Stained Glass Windows. 2016. (ENG., Illus.). 32p. (J). (gr. 4-6). pap. 11.99 *(978-0-7502-9450-8(7)*, Wayland) Hachette Children's Group GBR. Dist: Hachette Bk. Group.

—Stories Behind the Art - Sculpture. 2017. (Stories in Art Ser.). (ENG., Illus.). 32p. (J). (gr. 4-6). pap. 11.99 *(978-0-7502-9486-7(8)*, Wayland) Hachette Children's Group GBR. Dist: Hachette Bk. Group.

HISTRIONICS

see Acting; Theater

HITCHHIKING

see Walking

HITLER, ADOLF, 1889-1945

Adolf Hitler & Nazi Germany. 2006. (World Leaders Ser.). (Illus.). 176p. (gr. 3-7). lib. bdg. 28.95 *(978-1-931798-78-5(8))* Reynolds, Morgan Inc.

Altman, Linda Jacobs. Adolf Hitler: Evil Mastermind of the Holocaust. 2005. (Holocaust Heroes & Nazi Criminals Ser.). (Illus.). 160p. (YA). (gr. 7-13). lib. bdg. 29.27 *(978-0-7660-2533-2(0))* Enslow Pubs., Inc.

—Adolf Hitler & the Rise of the Third Reich. 2016. (People & Events That Changed the World Ser.). (ENG., Illus.). 112p. (J). (gr. 7-8). 37.27 *(978-0-7660-7175-9(8))* Enslow Pubs., Inc.

—Hitler, Goebbels, Himmler: The Nazi Holocaust Masterminds. 2014. (Remembering the Holocaust Ser.). 96p. (J). (gr. 6-12). pap. 10.95 *(978-0-7660-6198-9(1))* Enslow Pubs., Inc.

—Hitler, Goebbles, Himmler: The Nazi Holocaust Masterminds. 2014. (Remembering the Holocaust Ser.). (Illus.). 96p. (J). (gr. 6-12). 27.94 *(978-0-7660-6197-2(3))* Enslow Pubs., Inc.

—Hitler's Rise to Power & the Holocaust. 2003. (Holocaust in History Ser.). (Illus.). 128p. (J). (gr. 5-12). lib. bdg. 26.60 *(978-0-7660-1991-1(8))* Enslow Pubs., Inc.

Bartoletti, Susan Campbell. Hitler Youth: Growing up in Hitler's Shadow. 2005. (ENG., Illus.). 176p. (J). (gr. 7). 21.99 *(978-0-439-35379-3(3))* Scholastic, Inc.

Benchmark Education Company. Three Twentieth Century Dictators (Teacher Guide) 2004. *(978-1-4108-2593-3(0))* Benchmark Education Co.

Beyer, Mark. Heinrich Muller: Gestapo Chief. 2005. (Holocaust Biographies Ser.). (Illus.). 112p. (YA). (gr. 7-12). lib. bdg. 34.60 *(978-0-8239-3376-1(8))* Rosen Publishing Group, Inc., The.

—Heinrich Müller: Gestapo Chief. 2009. (Holocaust Biographies Ser.). 112p. (gr. 7-12). 63.90 *(978-1-61513-386-4(0))* Rosen Publishing Group, Inc., The.

Buckley, James, Jr. Adolf Hitler. 2017. (History's Worst Ser.). (ENG., Illus.). 208p. (J). (gr. 3-7). pap. 7.99 ***(978-1-4814-7942-4(3)***, Aladdin) Simon & Schuster Children's Publishing.

Darman, Peter, ed. World War II Begins. 2012. (World War II Ser.). (ENG., Illus.). 64p. (J). (gr. 7-12). lib. bdg. 31.95 *(978-1-4488-9232-7(5))* Rosen Publishing Group, Inc., The.

Daynes, Katie. Adolf Hitler. 2006. (Usborne Famous Lives Gift Bks.). (Illus.). 64p. (J). (gr. 2-5). 8.99 *(978-0-7945-1261-3(5)*, Usborne) EDC Publishing.

Dufner, Annette. The Rise of Adolf Hitler. 2003. (At Issue in History Ser.). (ENG., Illus.). 144p. (YA). 26.70 *(978-0-7377-1519-4(7))*; pap. 35.75 *(978-0-7377-1518-7(9))* Cengage Gale. (Greenhaven Pr., Inc.).

Ellis, Catherine & Roberts, Jeremy. Adolf Hitler, 01 vols., 1. 2016. (Holocaust Ser.). (ENG., Illus.). 112p. (J). 35.60 *(978-1-4994-6248-7(4)*, Rosen Young Adult) Rosen Publishing Group, Inc., The.

Freeman, Charles. The Rise of the Nazis. 2005. (How Did It Happen? Ser.). (ENG., Illus.). 48p. (gr. 7-10). lib. bdg. 36.70 *(978-1-59018-608-4(7)*, Lucent Bks.) Cengage Gale.

—Why Did the Rise of the Nazis Happen? 2010. (Moments in History Ser.). (Illus.). 48p. (YA). (gr. 5-9). lib. bdg. 31.95 *(978-1-4339-4175-7(9))*; (ENG., (J). (gr. 6-8). pap. 14.05 *(978-1-4339-4176-4(7)*, Gareth Stevens Secondary Library) Stevens, Gareth Publishing LLLP.

Giblin, James Cross. The Life & Death of Adolf Hitler. 2015. (ENG., Illus.). 256p. (J). (gr. 5-7). pap. 9.99 *(978-0-544-45591-7(6)*, HMH Books For Young Readers) Houghton Mifflin Harcourt Publishing Co.

—The Life & Death of Adolf Hitler. 2015. lib. bdg. 20.85 *(978-0-606-36830-8(2))* Turtleback Bks.

Gottfried, Ted. Children of the Slaughter: Young People of the Holocaust. Alcorn, Stephen, illus. (Holocaust History Ser.). 112p. (YA). (gr. 7-12). 22.95 *(978-1-58013-202-2(2)*, Kar-Ben Publishing) Lerner Publishing Group.

—Nazi Germany: The Face of Tyranny. Alcorn, Stephen, illus. (Holocaust History Ser.). 112p. (YA). (gr. 7-12). 22.95 *(978-1-58013-203-9(0)*, Kar-Ben Publishing) Lerner Publishing Group.

Gutsche, Henry. Hitler's Willing Warrior. 190p. (YA). (gr. 7-18). 9.99 *(978-0-88092-520-4(5))* Royal Fireworks Publishing Co.

Jukes, Geoffrey & O'Neill, Robert John. World War II: The Eastern Front 1941-1945. 2010. (World War II: Essential Histories Ser.). (Illus.). 96p. (YA). (gr. 9-12). lib. bdg. 33.25 *(978-1-4358-9134-0(1))* Rosen Publishing Group, Inc., The.

Krammer, Arnold. Hitler in Paris: How a Photograph Shocked a World at War, 1 vol. 2014. (Captured World History Ser.). (ENG.). 64p. (gr. 5-7). lib. bdg. 34.65 *(978-0-7565-4733-2(4)*, CPB Grades 4-8) Compass Point Bks.

Malam, John. Hitler Invades Poland. 2007. (Dates with History Ser.). (ENG., Illus.). 48p. (J). pap. 9.99 *(978-1-84234-535-1(4))* Evans Brothers, Ltd. GBR. Dist: Independent Pubs. Group.

Marcovitz, Hal. The Rise of the Nazis. 2014. (Understanding World History Ser.). (ENG., Illus.). 96p. (J). lib. bdg. *(978-1-60152-654-0(7))* ReferencePoint Pr., Inc.

McCormick, Patricia. The Plot to Kill Hitler: Dietrich Bonhoeffer: Pastor, Spy, Unlikely Hero. 2016. (Illus.). 192p. (J). (gr. 3). 18.99 *(978-0-06-241108-2(X))* HarperCollins Pubs.

O'Reilly, Bill. Hitler's Last Days: The Death of the Nazi Regime & the World's Most Notorious Dictator. 2015. (Illus.). 320p. (J). pap. *(978-1-62779-455-8(7))*; (ENG., (gr. 5-9). 19.99 *(978-1-62779-396-4(6)*, 9781627793964, Holt, Henry & Co. Bks. For Young Readers) Holt, Henry & Co.

H I

—Hitler's Last Days: The Death of the Nazi Regime & the World's Most Notorious Dictator. Barcellona, Christine, ed. 2017. (ENG.). 336p. (J). pap. 12.99 *(978-1-250-08859-8(3)*, 9781250088598) Square Fish.

Price, Sean Stewart. Adolf Hitler. 2010. (Wicked History Ser.). (ENG.). 128p. (J). (gr. 6-12). pap. 5.95 *(978-0-531-22357-4(4))*; (Illus.). 31.00 *(978-0-531-20757-4(9))* Scholastic Library Publishing. (Watts, Franklin).

Rice, Earle, Jr. Blitzrieg! Hitler's Lightning War. 2007. (Monumental Milestones Ser.). (Illus.). 48p. (YA). (gr. 4-7). lib. bdg. 29.95 *(978-1-58415-542-3(6))* Mitchell Lane Pubs., Inc.

Roxburgh, Ellis. Adolf Hitler vs. Winston Churchill: Foes of World War II. 2015. (History's Greatest Rivals Ser.). (ENG.). 48p. (J). (gr. 6-8). lib. bdg. 31.95 *(978-1-4824-2205-4(0))* Stevens, Gareth Publishing LLLP.

Ruby, India. Three Twentieth Century Dictators: Set Of 6. 2011. (Navigators Ser.). (J). pap. 50.00 net. *(978-1-4108-2578-0(7))* Benchmark Education Co.

Vander Hook, Sue. Adolf Hitler: German Dictator, 1 vol. 2011. (Essential Lives Set 6 Ser.). (ENG., Illus.). 112p. (J). (gr. 6-12). lib. bdg. 35.64 *(978-1-61714-781-4(8)*, Essential Library) ABDO Publishing Co.

Woolf, Alex. The Rise of Nazi Germany. 2004. (Questioning History Ser.). (J). lib. bdg. 28.50 *(978-1-58340-442-3(2))* Black Rabbit Bks.

Wukovits, John F. World War II in Europe. 2004. (World History Ser.). (ENG., Illus.). 112p. (gr. 7-10). 34.95 *(978-1-59018-185-0(9)*, Lucent Bks.) Cengage Gale.

Zdrok, Jodie L. 1880-1900 (Events That Changed the World) 2004. (gr. 10-12). 22.45 *(978-0-7377-2038-9(7)*, Greenhaven Pr., Inc.) Cengage Gale.

HOAXES

see Impostors and Imposture

HOBBIES

see also Collectors and Collecting; Handicraft

Arnosky, Jim. Beachcombing: Exploring the Seashore. 2014. (ENG.). 32p. (J). (gr. 2-5). 8.99 *(978-0-14-751163-8(1)*, Puffin Books) Penguin Young Readers Group.

Bozzo, Linda & Library. At Play in the Past, Present, & Future. 2010. (Imagining the Future Ser.). (Illus.). 24p. (J). lib. bdg. 22.60 *(978-0-7660-3436-5(4)*, Enslow Elementary) Enslow Pubs., Inc.

Bullivant, Cecil. Every Boys Book of Hobbies. 2006. 544p. per. *(978-1-4067-9704-6(9)*, Hesperides Pr.) Read Bks.

Forest, Christopher. The Kids' Guide to Collecting Stuff, 1 vol. 2010. (Kids' Guides). (ENG.). 32p. (gr. 3-4). lib. bdg. 27.99 *(978-1-4296-5442-5(2)*, Edge Bks.) Capstone Press of Coughlan Cos.

French, Cathy. You Can Make a Memory Scrapbook. 2011. (Early Connections Ser.). (J). *(978-1-61672-565-5(6))* Benchmark Education Co.

Gilpin, Rebecca. Fairy Things to Make & Do Kid Kit. McCafferty, Jan, illus. 2004. (Kid Kits Ser.). 32p. (J). 15.99 *(978-1-58086-731-3(6))*; 15.99 *(978-1-58086-727-6(8))* EDC Publishing. (Usborne).

Harbo, Christopher. Easy Origami Scrapbooking: An Augmented Reality Crafting Experience. 2017. (Origami Crafting 4D Ser.). (ENG., Illus.). 24p. (gr. 1-2). lib. bdg. 26.65 *(978-1-5157-3584-7(2)*, First Facts) Capstone Press of Coughlan Cos.

Hobby Time! 2017. (Hobby Time! Ser.). 32p. (gr. 9-9). 165.00 ***(978-1-4994-3400-2(6))***; pap. 70.50 ***(978-1-5081-5366-5(3))*** Rosen Publishing Group, Inc., The. (PowerKids Pr.).

Holden, Pam. Things to Do. 2015. (ENG., Illus.). 16p. (-1). pap. *(978-1-77654-119-5(7)*, Red Rocket Readers) Flying Start Bks.

Hyde, Margaret O. & Keene, Frances W. Hobby Fun Book: For Grade School Boys & Girls. 2010. (Dover Children's Activity Bks.). (ENG.). 128p. (J). (gr. 2-5). pap. 8.99 *(978-0-486-47839-5(4))* Dover Pubns., Inc.

Ikids Staff. Made with Love for Mom. Kalis, Jennifer, illus. 2008. (ENG.). 24p. (J). (gr. 1-17). 7.99 *(978-1-58476-660-5(3)*, IKIDS) Innovative Kids.

My Cool Hobbies. (Girls' World Ser.). 16p. (J). *(978-2-7643-0144-9(8))* Phidal Publishing, Inc./Editions Phidal, Inc.

Ripley Entertainment Staff, contrib. by. Fun & Games. 2010. (Ripley's Believe It or Not Ser.). 36p. (YA). (gr. 3-18). lib. bdg. 19.95 *(978-1-4222-1534-0(2))* Mason Crest.

Ripley's Believe It or Not, 16 vols., Set. Incl. All Consuming. Ripley Entertainment. (YA). (gr. 3-18). lib. bdg. 19.95 *(978-1-4222-1536-4(9))*; Amazing Earth. Ripley Entertainment. (YA). (gr. 3-18). lib. bdg. 19.95 *(978-1-4222-1539-5(3))*; Animal Antics. Ripley Entertainment Staff, contrib. by. (YA). (gr. 3-18). lib. bdg. 19.95 *(978-1-4222-1535-7(0))*; Arts & Entertainment. Ripley's Entertainment Inc Staff, contrib. by. (J). (gr. 5-18). lib. bdg. 19.95 *(978-1-4222-1530-2(X))*; Beyond Belief. Ripley Entertainment. (YA). (gr. 3-18). lib. bdg. 19.95 *(978-1-4222-1537-1(7))*; Beyond Understanding. Ripley Entertainment. (YA). (gr. 3-18). lib. bdg. 19.95 *(978-1-4222-1531-9(8))*; Body & Mind. Ripley Entertainment Staff, contrib. by. (YA). (gr. 3-18). lib. bdg. 19.95 *(978-1-4222-1532-6(6))*; Extraordinary Animals. Ripley Entertainment Staff, contrib. by. (YA). (gr. 3-18). lib. bdg. 19.95 *(978-1-4222-1533-3(4))*; Fun & Games. Ripley Entertainment Staff, contrib. by. (YA). (gr. 3-18). lib. bdg. 19.95 *(978-1-4222-1534-0(2))*; Life in the Fast Lane. Ripley Entertainment. (YA). (gr. 3-18). lib. bdg. 19.95 *(978-1-4222-1538-8(5))*; Off the Wall. Ripley Entertainment. (YA). (gr. 3-18). lib. bdg. 19.95 *(978-1-4222-1542-5(3))*; Taking Life to Extremes. Ripley Entertainment. (YA). (gr. 3-18). lib. bdg. 19.95 *(978-1-4222-1540-1(7))*; Totally Obsessed. Ripley Entertainment. (YA). (gr. 3-18). lib. bdg. 19.95 *(978-1-4222-1541-8(5))*; Was That a Good Idea? Ripley Entertainment. (YA). (gr. 3-18). lib. bdg. 19.95 *(978-1-4222-1543-2(1))*; What Are You Like? Ripley Entertainment. (YA). (gr. 3-18). lib. bdg. 19.95 *(978-1-4222-1544-9(X))*; Wonders of Science. Ripley Entertainment. (YA). (gr. 3-18). lib. bdg. 19.95 *(978-1-4222-1545-6(8))*; 36p. 2010. 2010. 319.20 *(978-1-4222-1529-6(6))* Mason Crest.

Rowe, Brooke. What Club Should You Try? 2015. (Illus.). 32p. (J). *(978-1-63470-033-7(3))* Cherry Lake Publishing.

Rue, Nancy N. The Fun-Finder Book: It's a God Thing!, 1 vol. 2003. (Lily Ser.). (ENG.). 112p. (J). pap. 7.99 *(978-0-310-70258-0(5))* Zondervan.

Salzmann, Mary Elizabeth. Money for Hobbies, 1 vol. 2010. (Your Piggy Bank: A Guide to Spending & Saving for Kids! Ser.). (ENG.). 24p. (J). (gr. k-3). 27.07 *(978-1-61641-030-8(2))* Magic Wagon.

Spilsbury, Louise. Coastal Treasure Hunter. 2010. (ENG.). 32p. (J). pap. *(978-0-7787-9928-3(X))* Crabtree Publishing Co.

Stern, Sam & Stern, Susan. Get Cooking. Campbell, Lorne, photos by. 2009. (ENG., Illus.). 144p. (J). (gr. 5-18). pap. 17.99 *(978-0-7636-3926-6(5))* Candlewick Pr.

Ventura, Marne & Laughlin, Kara L. 10 Things to Do, 1 vol. 2014. (10 Things to Do Ser.). (ENG.). 32p. (gr. 1-2). 109.28 *(978-1-4765-9902-1(5)*, Aplus Bks.) Capstone Press of Coughlan Cos.

Wilkes, Angela. Activities for All Year Round. 2004. (Activities for All Year Round Ser.). (ENG.). 96p. (J). 7.95 *(978-0-7945-0770-1(0)*, Usborne) EDC Publishing.

World Book, Inc Staff, contrib. by. Things I Like. 2010. (J). *(978-0-7166-7743-7(1))* World Bk., Inc.

HOBBIES—FICTION

Bourgeois, Paulette & Clark, Brenda. Franklin's Trading Cards. 2003. (Kids Can Read Ser.). (ENG., Illus.). 32p. (J). (gr. 1-2). 3.95 *(978-1-55337-464-0(9))*; 14.95 *(978-1-55337-463-3(0))* Kids Can Pr., Ltd. CAN. Dist: Hachette Bk. Group.

Enderle, Dotti. Beyond the Grave: An Up2U Mystery Adventure, 1 vol. Uhles, Mary, illus. 2013. (Up2U Adventures Ser.). (ENG.). 80p. (J). (gr. 2-5). 27.07 *(978-1-61641-964-6(4)*, Calico Chapter Bks) Magic Wagon.

Jennings, Sharon. Franklin's Trading Cards. Jeffrey, Sean et al, illus. 2003. 32p. (J). *(978-0-439-41816-4(X))* Scholastic, Inc.

Lockley, Belinda. Sometimes I Think of the Fish in the Sea. 2008. 16p. pap. 24.95 *(978-1-60474-844-4(3))* America Star Bks.

Polacco, Patricia. Rotten Richie & the Ultimate Dare. Polacco, Patricia, illus. 2006. (ENG., Illus.). 48p. (J). (gr. k-3). 17.99 *(978-0-399-24531-2(6)*, Philomel Bks.) Penguin Young Readers Group.

Watterson, William. Die Welt der Wunder. Bartoszko, Alexandra, tr. from ENG. (Calvin & Hobbes Ser.: Vol. 16). (GER., Illus.). 64p. (J). pap. *(978-3-8105-0365-7(7))* Kruger, Wolfgang Verlag, GmbH DEU. Dist: International Bk. Import Service, Inc.

HOCKEY

Adams, Carly. Queens of the Ice: They Were Fast, They Were Fierce, They Were Teenage Girls, 1 vol. 2011. (Lorimer Recordbooks Ser.). (ENG., Illus.). 136p. (YA). (gr. 7-12). 9.95 *(978-1-55277-720-6(0)*, 9781552777206) Lorimer, James & Co., Ltd., Pubs. CAN. Dist: Casemate Pubs. & Bk. Distributors, LLC.

Anthony, David. Girls Play Field Hockey. 2016. (Girls Join the Team Ser.). 24p. (J). (gr. 3-3). 23.60 *(978-1-4994-2099-9(4))*; pap. 8.25 *(978-1-4994-2097-5(8))* Rosen Publishing Group, Inc., The. (PowerKids Pr.).

Barber, Jim. Toronto Maple Leafs: Stories of Canada's Legendary Team. 2006. (Junior Amazing Stories Ser.). (ENG., Illus.). 96p. pap. *(978-1-55439-714-3(6))* Altitude Publishing Canada Ltd.

Barth, Katrin & Nordmann, Lutz. Learning Field Hockey. 2007. (Illus.). 152p. (J). (gr. 4-7). pap. 14.95 *(978-1-84126-210-9(2))* Meyer & Meyer Sport, Ltd. GBR. Dist: Cardinal Pubs. Group.

Bird, Nicky & Duncan, Peter. Hockey Alphabet Book, 1 vol. 2016. (IThink Ser.: 3). (ENG., Illus.). 64p. (J). pap. 6.99 ***(978-1-897206-06-5(2)***, 9781897206065) Folklore Publishing CAN. Dist: Lone Pine Publishing USA.

Biskup, Agnieszka. Hockey: How It Works. 2010. (Science of Sports (Sports Illustrated for Kids) Ser.). (ENG.). 48p. (gr. 3-4). pap. 59.70 *(978-1-4296-5109-7(1))* Capstone Press of Coughlan Cos.

Borth, Teddy. Hockey: Great Moments, Records, & Facts, 1 vol. 2014. (Great Sports Ser.). (ENG., Illus.). 24p. (J). (gr. 2-4). lib. bdg. 28.50 *(978-1-62970-691-7(4))* ABDO Publishing Co.

Brignall, Richard. Summit Series '72: Eight Games That Put Canada on Top of World Hockey, 1 vol. 2011. (Lorimer Recordbooks Ser.). (ENG., Illus.). 152p. (J). (gr. 7-12). 16.95 *(978-1-55277-884-5(3)*, 9781552778845) Lorimer, James & Co., Ltd., Pubs. CAN. Dist: Casemate Pubs. & Bk. Distributors, LLC.

Brown, Jonatha A. Hockey. 2004. (My Favorite Sport Ser.). (Illus.). 24p. (gr. 1-4). pap. 8.15 *(978-0-8368-4347-7(9))*; lib. bdg. 22.00 *(978-0-8368-4340-8(1))* Stevens, Gareth Publishing LLLP. (Weekly Reader Leveled Readers).

Burgan, Michael. Miracle on Ice: How a Stunning Upset United a Country. 2016. (Captured History Sports Ser.). (ENG.). 64p. (gr. 5-7). pap. 8.95 *(978-0-7565-5294-7(X))*; lib. bdg. 34.65 *(978-0-7565-5290-9(7))* Compass Point Bks. (CPB Grades 4-8).

Burgan, Michael, et al. Hockey Superstars, 4 vols. 2015. (Hockey Superstars Ser.). (ENG.). 32p. (gr. 3-9). 139.95 *(978-1-4914-6963-7(3))* Capstone Press of Coughlan Cos.

Capstone Press. Cool Sports Facts. 2010. (Cool Sports Facts Ser.). (ENG.). 32p. lib. bdg. 119.95 *(978-1-4296-5945-1(9)*, Pebble Plus) Capstone Press of Coughlan Cos.

Caughill, Jeff. The Good Old Hockey Game. 2012. 28p. pap. *(978-1-105-58056-7(3))* Lulu.com.

Chandler, Matt. The Science of Hockey: The Top Ten Ways Science Affects the Game. 2016. (Top 10 Science Ser.). (ENG., Illus.). 32p. (gr. 3-4). lib. bdg. 27.99 *(978-1-4914-8221-6(4))* Capstone Press of Coughlan Cos.

Clay, Kathryn. Cool Hockey Facts. 2011. (Cool Sports Facts Ser.). (ENG.). 24p. (gr. k-1). pap. 41.70 *(978-1-4296-7392-1(3)*, Pebble Plus) Capstone Press of Coughlan Cos.

Cole, Stephen. Xtreme Hockey. 2008. (ENG.). 32p. (J). (gr. 1-7). 21.50 *(978-1-4169-7467-3(9)*, Atheneum Bks. for Young Readers) Simon & Schuster Children's Publishing.

Connolly, Helen. Field Hockey: Rules, Tips, Strategy, & Safety. 2009. (Sports from Coast to Coast Ser.). 48p. (gr. 6-6). 53.00 *(978-1-60853-123-3(6)*, Rosen Reference) Rosen Publishing Group, Inc., The.

Crosby, Sidney, et al. Sidney Crosby. 2015. (Quotes from the Greatest Athletes Ser.). (ENG., Illus.). 24p. (J). lib. bdg. 12.95 *(978-1-4896-3377-4(4)*, AV2 by Weigl) Weigl Pubs., Inc.

Crossingham, John & Kalman, Bobbie. Slap Shot Hockey. 2008. (Sports Starters Ser.). (ENG., Illus.). 32p. (J). (gr. 3-7). pap. *(978-0-7787-3174-0(X))*; lib. bdg. *(978-0-7787-3142-9(1))* Crabtree Publishing Co.

Cruickshank, Don. Calgary Flames. 2011. (Illus.). 24p. (gr. k-2). *(978-1-77071-640-7(8))*; pap. *(978-1-77071-654-4(8))* Weigl Educational Pubs. Ltd.

—Les Canadiens de Montréal: Les Equipes de Hockey du Canada. Karvonen, Tanjah, tr. from ENG. 2011. (FRE., Illus.). 24p. (gr. k-2). *(978-1-77071-424-3(3))* Weigl Educational Pubs. Ltd.

—Les Canucks de Vancouver: Les Equipes de Hockey du Canada. Karvonen, Tanjah, tr. from ENG. 2011. (FRE., Illus.). 24p. (gr. k-2). *(978-1-77071-427-4(8))* Weigl Educational Pubs. Ltd.

—Edmonton Oilers. 2011. (Illus.). 24p. (gr. k-2). *(978-1-77071-641-4(6))*; pap. *(978-1-77071-655-1(6))* Weigl Educational Pubs. Ltd.

—Les Flames de Calgary: Les Equipes de Hockey du Canada. Karvonen, Tanjah, tr. from ENG. 2011. (FRE., Illus.). 24p. (gr. k-2). *(978-1-77071-422-9(7))* Weigl Educational Pubs. Ltd.

—Les Maple Leafs de Toronto: Les Equipes de Hockey du Canada. Karvonen, Tanjah, tr. from ENG. 2011. (FRE., Illus.). 24p. (gr. k-2). *(978-1-77071-426-7(X))* Weigl Educational Pubs. Ltd.

—Montreal Canadiens. 2011. (Illus.). 24p. (gr. k-2). *(978-1-77071-642-1(4))*; pap. *(978-1-77071-656-8(4))* Weigl Educational Pubs. Ltd.

—Les Oilers D'Edmonton: Les Equipes de Hockey du Canada. Karvonen, Tanjah, tr. from ENG. 2011. (FRE., Illus.). 24p. (gr. k-2). *(978-1-77071-423-6(5))* Weigl Educational Pubs. Ltd.

—Ottawa Senators. 2011. (Illus.). 24p. (gr. k-2). *(978-1-77071-643-8(2))* Weigl Educational Pubs. Ltd.

—Les Sénateurs D'Ottawa: Les Equipes de Hockey du Canada. Karvonen, Tanjah, tr. from ENG. 2011. (FRE., Illus.). 24p. (gr. k-2). *(978-1-77071-425-0(1))* Weigl Educational Pubs. Ltd.

—Toronto Maple Leafs. 2011. (Illus.). 24p. (gr. k-2). *(978-1-77071-644-5(0))*; pap. *(978-1-77071-658-2(0))* Weigl Educational Pubs. Ltd.

—Vancouver Canucks. 2011. (Illus.). 24p. (gr. k-2). *(978-1-77071-645-2(9))*; pap. *(978-1-77071-659-9(9))* Weigl Educational Pubs. Ltd.

Danakas, John & Brignall, Richard. Small Town Glory. 2006. (Recordbooks Ser.). (ENG., Illus.). 120p. (J). (gr. 4-6). *(978-1-55028-961-9(6))* Lorimer, James & Co., Ltd., Pubs. CAN. Dist: Casemate Pubs. & Bk. Distributors, LLC.

—Small Town Glory: The Story of the Kenora Thistles' Remarkable Quest for the Stanley Cup, 1 vol. 2006. (Lorimer Recordbooks Ser.). (ENG., Illus.). 120p. (J). (gr. 4-6). 9.95 *(978-1-55028-943-5(8)*, 9781550289435) Lorimer, James & Co., Ltd., Pubs. CAN. Dist: Casemate Pubs. & Bk. Distributors, LLC.

Derr, Aaron. Hockey: An Introduction to Being a Good Sport. Kelly, Jim, illus. 2017. (Start Smart (tm) — Sports Ser.). (ENG.). 32p. (J). (gr. k-3). lib. bdg. 26.65 *(978-1-63440-131-9(X))*; 39.99 ***(978-1-63440-143-2(3))*** Red Chair Pr.

Doeden, Matt. All about Hockey. 2015. (All about Sports Ser.). (ENG., Illus.). 32p. (gr. 1-2). 27.32 *(978-1-4914-1996-0(2))* Capstone Press of Coughlan Cos.

Doeden, Matt, et al. Hockey Superstars. 2015. (Hockey Superstars Ser.). (ENG.). 32p. (gr. 3-4). lib. bdg. 111.96 *(978-1-4914-2561-9(X))* Capstone Press of Coughlan Cos.

Dolphin, Colleen. Ice Hockey by the Numbers, 1 vol. 2010. (Team Sports by the Numbers Ser.). (ENG.). 24p. (J). (gr. k-3). lib. bdg. 24.21 *(978-1-60453-770-3(1)*, SandCastle) ABDO Publishing Co.

Donaldson, Chelsea. Hayley Wickenheiser, 1 vol. 2014. (Canadian Biographies Ser.). (ENG.). 24p. (gr. k-1). 26.65 *(978-1-4914-1958-8(X)*, Pebble Plus) Capstone Press of Coughlan Cos.

Dunn, Joe. Miracle on Ice, 1 vol. Dunn, Ben, illus. 2007. (Graphic History Ser.). (ENG.). 32p. (gr. 3-6). 28.50 *(978-1-60270-077-2(X)*, Graphic Planet- Nonfiction) ABDO Publishing Co.

Durrie, Karen. Al Hockey. 2012. (J). *(978-1-61913-201-6(X))* Weigl Pubs., Inc.

—Hockey. 2011. (J). 27.13 *(978-1-61690-940-6(4))*; *(978-1-61690-586-6(7))* Weigl Pubs., Inc.

Egan, Tracie. Field Hockey. 2005. (Sports from Coast to Coast Ser.). (Illus.). 48p. (J). (gr. 5-8). lib. bdg. 26.50 *(978-1-4042-0182-8(3))* Rosen Publishing Group, Inc., The.

Ervin, Phil. 12 Reasons to Love Hockey. 2018. (ENG.). 32p. (gr. 3-6). 31.35 ***(978-1-63235-428-0(4)***, 12-Story Library) Pr. Room Editions LLC.

Foley, Mike. Hockey. King, Andy, photos by. 2005. (Play-by-Play Ser.). (Illus.). 80p. (J). (gr. 4-8). pap. 7.95 *(978-0-8225-9878-7(7))* Lerner Publishing Group.

Frederick, Shane. The Best of Everything Hockey Book, 1 vol. (All-Time Best of Sports Ser.). (ENG.). 64p. (gr. 3-4). 2011. pap. 8.95 *(978-1-4296-6328-1(6))* 2011. pap. 53.70 *(978-1-4296-6455-4(X))* 2010. lib. bdg. 34.65 *(978-1-4296-5469-2(4))* Capstone Press of Coughlan Cos.

—Fantasy Hockey Math: Using Stats to Score Big in Your League. 2016. (Fantasy Sports Math Ser.). (ENG., Illus.). 32p. (gr. 3-4). lib. bdg. 27.99 *(978-1-5157-2159-8(0))* Capstone Press of Coughlan Cos.

—Hockey: The Math of the Game. 2011. (Sports Math Ser.). (ENG.). 48p. (gr. 5-6). pap. 47.70 *(978-1-4296-7322-8(2))* Capstone Press of Coughlan Cos.

—Hockey Stats & the Stories Behind Them: What Every Fan Needs to Know. 2016. (Sports Stats & Stories Ser.). (ENG., Illus.). 48p. (gr. 4-6). lib. bdg. 31.99 *(978-1-4914-8217-9(6))* Capstone Press of Coughlan Cos.

—Hockey's Record Breakers. 2017. (Record Breakers Ser.). (ENG., Illus.). 32p. (gr. 3-4). lib. bdg. 27.32 *(978-1-5157-3758-2(6))* Capstone Press of Coughlan Cos.

—The Technology of Hockey, 1 vol. 2013. (High-Tech Sports Ser.). (ENG.). 48p. (gr. 3-9). pap. 8.95 *(978-1-62065-912-0(3))*; pap. 53.70 *(978-1-62065-913-7(1))*; lib. bdg. 31.99 *(978-1-4296-9954-9(X))* Capstone Press of Coughlan Cos.

—The Ultimate Collection of Pro Hockey Records, 1 vol. 2012. (For the Record Ser.). (ENG., 64p. (gr. 4-6). Illus.). pap. 8.95 *(978-1-4296-9434-6(3))*; pap. 53.70 *(978-1-4296-9435-3(1))*; (Illus.). lib. bdg. 34.65 *(978-1-4296-8579-5(4))* Capstone Press of Coughlan Cos.

—Ultimate Collection of Pro Hockey Records 2015, 1 vol. 2014. (ENG.). 128p. (gr. 4-6). 14.95 *(978-1-4914-1962-5(8))* Capstone Press of Coughlan Cos.

—The Ultimate Guide to Pro Hockey Teams. 2010. (Ultimate Pro Team Guides (Sports Illustrated for Kids) Ser.). (ENG.). 72p. (gr. 3-4). pap. 53.70 *(978-1-4296-5736-5(7))* Capstone Press of Coughlan Cos.

—Wacky Hockey Trivia: Fun Facts for Every Fan. 2016. (Wacky Sports Trivia Ser.). (ENG., Illus.). 32p. (gr. 3-4). lib. bdg. 27.99 *(978-1-5157-1991-5(X))* Capstone Press of Coughlan Cos.

Frederick, Shane & Wacholtz, Anthony. Hockey: The Math of the Game, 1 vol. 2011. (Sports Math Ser.). (ENG.). 48p. (gr. 5-6). pap. 8.19 *(978-1-4296-7321-1(4))*; lib. bdg. 31.99 *(978-1-4296-6570-4(X))* Capstone Press of Coughlan Cos.

Frisch, Aaron. New York Islanders. 2004. (Stanley Cup Champions Ser.). (Illus.). 32p. (J). lib. bdg. *(978-1-58341-276-3(X)*, Creative Education) Creative Co., The.

Gitlin, Martin. Hockey, 1 vol. 2012. (ENG.). 64p. 32.79 *(978-1-61783-144-7(1)*, SportsZone) ABDO Publishing Co.

—The Stanley Cup: All about Pro Hockey's Biggest Event, 1 vol. 2012. (Winner Takes All Ser.). (ENG., 32p. (gr. 3-4). Illus.). pap. 7.19 *(978-1-4296-9440-7(8))*; pap. 41.70 *(978-1-4296-9441-4(6))* Capstone Press of Coughlan Cos.

—The Stanley Cup: All about Pro Hockey's Biggest Event, 1 vol. 2012. (Winner Takes All Ser.). (ENG., Illus.). 32p. (gr. 3-4). lib. bdg. 27.99 *(978-1-4296-6575-9(0))* Capstone Press of Coughlan Cos.

Glave, Tom. Incredible Hockey Records. 2016. (Incredible Sports Records Ser.). (ENG.). 24p. (J). (gr. 2-5). 28.50 *(978-1-5038-0889-8(0)*, 210678) Child's World, Inc., The.

Goodman, Michael E. Detroit - Red Wings. 2011. (NHL: History & Heroes Ser.). (ENG., Illus.). 48p. (J). (gr. 5-17). pap. 9.99 *(978-1-897563-17-5(5)*, Creative Paperbacks) Creative Co., The.

—Philadelphia - Flyers. 2011. (NHL: History & Heroes Ser.). (ENG., Illus.). 48p. (J). (gr. 5-17). pap. 9.99 *(978-1-897563-20-5(5)*, Creative Paperbacks) Creative Co., The.

—The Story of the Montreal Canadiens. (NHL: History & Heroes Ser.). (gr. 5-17). 2011. (ENG., Illus.). 48p. (J). pap. 9.99 *(978-1-897563-18-2(3)*, Creative Paperbacks) 2008. (YA). 22.95 *(978-1-58341-618-1(8))* Creative Co., The.

—The Story of the New York Rangers. 2011. (NHL: History & Heroes Ser.). (ENG., Illus.). 48p. (J). (gr. 5-17). pap. 9.99 *(978-1-897563-19-9(1)*, Creative Paperbacks) Creative Co., The.

Graves, Will. Martin Brodeur. 2016. (Illus.). 32p. *(978-1-62143-283-8(1))* Pr. Room Editions LLC.

—Sidney Crosby. 2016. (Illus.). 32p. (J). *(978-1-62143-284-5(X))* Pr. Room Editions LLC.

Groenendyk, Doretta. Hockey Morning Noon & Night, 1 vol. 2015. (ENG., Illus.). 32p. (J). (gr. k-2). pap. 12.95 *(978-1-927502-30-3(6))* Acorn Pr., The CAN. Dist: Orca Bk. Pubs. USA.

Gürth, Per-Henrik. First Hockey Words. Gürth, Per-Henrik, illus. 2014. (ENG., Illus.). 32p. (J). (gr. -1-k). 15.95 *(978-1-77138-114-7(0))* Kids Can Pr., Ltd. CAN. Dist: Hachette Bk. Group.

Hawkins, Jeff. Playing Pro Hockey. 2014. (Playing Pro Sports Ser.). (ENG., Illus.). 64p. (gr. 4-8). lib. bdg. 26.60 *(978-1-4677-3847-7(6)*, Lerner Pubns.) Lerner Publishing Group.

Hetrick, Hans. Outrageous Hockey Rivalries. 2015. (Sports Rivalries Ser.). (ENG., Illus.). 32p. (gr. 3-4). lib. bdg. 27.99 *(978-1-4914-2027-0(8))* Capstone Press of Coughlan Cos.

Hoena, B. A. The Science of Hockey with Max Axiom, Super Scientist. 2015. (Science of Sports with Max Axiom Ser.). (ENG., Illus.). 32p. (gr. 3-4). lib. bdg. 30.65 *(978-1-4914-6086-3(5))* Capstone Press of Coughlan Cos.

Hoena, Blake. Hockey. 2015. (J). lib. bdg. 25.65 *(978-1-62031-180-6(1)*, Bullfrog Bks.) Jump! Inc.

—The Science of Hockey with Max Axiom, Super Scientist. Cacau, Caio, illus. 2015. (Science of Sports with Max Axiom Ser.). (ENG.). 32p. (gr. 3-4). pap. 7.95 *(978-1-4914-6090-0(3)*, Graphic Library) Capstone Press of Coughlan Cos.

Huberts, Al. Hockey Canada's Learn All about Hockey: Color & Activity. Bailey, Frank, illus. 2012. (Rule 1, Sports Color & Activity Bks.). (ENG.). 176p. (J). (gr. -1-3). pap. 9.99 *(978-1-77049-436-7(7)*, Fenn-Tundra) Tundra Bks. CAN. Dist: Penguin Random Hse. LLC.

Hurley, Michael. Ice Hockey, 1 vol. 2013. (Fantastic Sports Facts Ser.). (ENG., Illus.). 32p. (gr. 1-3). pap. 8.29 *(978-1-4109-5113-7(8))*; lib. bdg. 29.99 *(978-1-4109-5106-9(5))* Heinemann-Raintree. (Read Me!).

Hurtig, Jennifer. Field Hockey. 2013. (J). *(978-1-62127-317-2(2))*; pap. *(978-1-62127-322-6(9))* Weigl Pubs., Inc.

—For the Love of Field Hockey. 2006. (For the Love of Sports Ser.). (Illus.). 24p. (J). (gr. 3-7). lib. bdg. 24.45 *(978-1-59036-400-0(7))*; per. 8.95 *(978-1-59036-401-7(5))* Weigl Pubs., Inc.

Irwin, Sue. Safety Stars: Players Who Fought to Make the Hard-Hitting Game of Professional Hockey Safer, 1 vol. 2015. (Lorimer Recordbooks Ser.). (ENG., Illus.). 136p. (YA). (gr. 7-12). pap. 9.95 *(978-1-4594-0846-3(2)*, 9781459408463) Lorimer, James & Co., Ltd., Pubs. CAN. Dist: Casemate Pubs. & Bk. Distributors, LLC.

Johnson, Robin. Ice Hockey & Curling. 2009. (Winter Olympic Sports Ser.). (ENG., Illus.). 32p. (J). (gr. 3-6). lib. bdg. *(978-0-7787-4023-0(4))* Crabtree Publishing Co.

Johnstone, Robb. Hockey. 2009. (In the Zone Ser.). 24p. (J). (gr. 3-5). pap. 8.95 *(978-1-60596-131-6(0))*; (Illus.). lib. bdg. 24.45 (978-1-60596-130-9(2)) Weigl Pubs., Inc.

Jordan, Christopher. Hockey 123. 2011. (My First NHL Book Ser.). (ENG.). 30p. (J). (gr. k-k). bds. 6.95 *(978-1-77049-347-6(6)*, Fenn-Tundra) Tundra Bks. CAN. Dist: Penguin Random Hse. LLC.

—Hockey 123: My First NHL Book. 2010. (My First NHL Bks.). (ENG., Illus.). 30p. (J). (gr. -1). bds. *(978-1-55168-367-6(9))* Me to We.

—Hockey ABC. 2010. (My First NHL Bks.). (ENG., Illus.). 30p. (J). (gr. -1). bds. *(978-1-55168-365-2(2))* Me to We.
—Hockey ABC. 2011. (My First NHL Book Ser.). (ENG.). 30p. (J). (gr. k-k). bds. 6.95 *(978-1-77049-346-9(8),* Fenn-Tundra) Tundra Bks. CAN. Dist: Penguin Random Hse. LLC.
—Hockey Animals. 2011. (My First NHL Book Ser.). (ENG., Illus.). 24p. (J). (-k). bds. 8.99 *(978-1-77049-317-9(4));* bds. 6.95 *(978-1-77049-344-5(1),* Fenn-Tundra) Tundra Bks. CAN. Dist: Random Hse., Inc., Penguin Random Hse. LLC.
—Hockey Colors. 2011. (My First NHL Book Ser.). (ENG.). 30p. (J). (gr. k-k). bds. 6.95 *(978-1-77049-349-0(2),* Fenn-Tundra) Tundra Bks. CAN. Dist: Penguin Random Hse. LLC.
—Hockey Colours. 2010. (My First NHL Bks.). (ENG., Illus.). 30p. (J). (gr. -1). bds. *(978-1-55168-368-3(7))* Me to We.
—Hockey Colours. 2011. (ENG., Illus.). 30p. (J). (-k). bds. 8.99 *(978-1-77049-322-3(0))* Tundra Bks. CAN. Dist: Random Hse., Inc.
—Hockey Opposites. 2011. (My First NHL Book Ser.). (ENG., Illus.). 30p. (J). (-k). bds. 8.99 *(978-1-77049-318-6(2));* bds. 6.95 *(978-1-77049-345-2(X),* Fenn-Tundra) Tundra Bks. CAN. Dist: Random Hse., Inc., Penguin Random Hse. LLC.
—Hockey Shapes. 2010. (My First NHL Bks.). (ENG., Illus.). 30p. (J). (gr. -1). bds. *(978-1-55168-370-6(9))* Me to We.
—Hockey Shapes. 2011. (My First NHL Book Ser.). (ENG., Illus.). 30p. (J). (-k). bds. 8.99 *(978-1-77049-321-6(2));* bds. 6.95 *(978-1-77049-348-3(4),* Fenn-Tundra) Tundra Bks. CAN. Dist: Random Hse., Inc., Penguin Random Hse. LLC.
Kawa, Katie. Hockey's Greatest Records, 1 vol. 2015. (ENG., Illus.). 32p. (J). lib. bdg. 26.25 *(978-1-4994-0228-5(7),* PowerKids Pr.) Rosen Publishing Group, Inc., The.
Kennedy, Mike. Ice Hockey. 2003. (Watts Library). (Illus.). 64p. (J). 25.50 *(978-0-531-12273-0(5),* Watts, Franklin) Scholastic Library Publishing.
Killcoyne, Hope Lourie. Hockey & Its Greatest Players, 1 vol. 2015. (ENG.). 80p. (YA). 31.70 *(978-1-62275-586-8(3),* Britannica Educational Publishing) Rosen Publishing Group, Inc., The.
Kopp, Megan. Hockey. 2011. (J). (gr. 4-6). pap. 13.95 *(978-1-61690-706-8(1),* AV2 by Weigl); (Illus.). 32p. (YA). (gr. 2-5). 28.55 *(978-1-61690-701-3(0))* Weigl Pubs., Inc.
Kortemeier, Todd. Pro Hockey by the Numbers. 2016. (Illus.). 32p. (J). pap. *(978-1-4914-9069-3(1))* Capstone Press of Coughlan Cos.
Kortemeier, Tom. Pro Hockey by the Numbers. 2016. (Pro Sports by the Numbers Ser.). (ENG., Illus.). 32p. (gr. 3-4). lib. bdg. 27.99 *(978-1-4914-9057-0(8),* Edge Bks.) Capstone Press of Coughlan Cos.
Labrecque, Ellen. The Science of a Slap Shot. 2015. (21st Century Skills Library: Full-Speed Sports Ser.). (ENG., Illus.). 32p. (J). (gr. 4-7). 29.93 *(978-1-63362-584-6(2),* 206520) Cherry Lake Publishing.
Latimer, Clay. VIP Pass to a Pro Hockey Game Day: From the Locker Room to the Press Box (and Everything in Between), 1 vol. (Game Day (Sports Illustrated for Kids) Ser.). (ENG.). 32p. (gr. 3-4). 2011. pap. 8.19 *(978-1-4296-6286-4(7))* 2011. pap. 47.70 *(978-1-4296-6450-9(9))* 2010. lib. bdg. 27.99 *(978-1-4296-5464-7(3))* Capstone Press of Coughlan Cos.
Laughlin, Kara L. Hockey. 2016. (Beginning Sports Ser.). (ENG.). 24p. (J). (gr. k-3). 27.07 *(978-1-5038-0777-8(0),* 210605) Child's World, Inc., The.
LeClair, Danielle. Sidney Crosby: Ma Vie. Karvonen, Tanjah, tr. from ENG. 2011. (FRE., Illus.). 24p. (YA). (gr. 2-4). *(978-1-77071-430-4(8))* Weigl Educational Pubs. Ltd.
Leclaire, Danielle. Sidney Crosby. 2010. (Illus.). 24p. *(978-1-77071-596-7(7));* pap. *(978-1-77071-602-5(5))* Weigl Educational Pubs. Ltd.
Lindeen, Mary. Let's Play Hockey! 2015. (BeginningtoRead Ser.). (ENG., Illus.). 32p. (J). (gr. k-2). lib. bdg. 22.60 *(978-1-59953-686-6(2))* Norwood Hse. Pr.
—Let's Play Hockey. 2015. (BeginningtoRead Ser.). (ENG.). 32p. (J). (gr. k-2). pap. 11.94 *(978-1-60357-746-5(7))* Norwood Hse. Pr.
MacDonald, James. Hockey Skills: How to Play Like a Pro. 2008. (How to Play Like a Pro Ser.). (Illus.). 48p. (J). (gr. 3-6). lib. bdg. 25.27 *(978-0-7660-3207-1(8))* Enslow Pubs., Inc.
Mahaney, Ian F. The Math of Hockey. 2011. (J). 49.50 *(978-1-4488-2699-5(3),* PowerKids Pr.); pap. 8.25 *(978-1-4488-2698-8(5),* PowerKids Pr.); (gr. 2-5). lib. bdg. 22.60 *(978-1-4488-2556-1(3))* Rosen Publishing Group, Inc., The.
Mattern, Joanne. I Know Hockey. 2013. (21st Century Basic Skills Library: I Know Sports Ser.). (ENG., Illus.). 24p. (J). (gr. k-3). 22.79 *(978-1-62431-401-8(5),* 202724); pap. 12.79 *(978-1-62431-477-3(5),* 202726) Cherry Lake Publishing.
McAuliffe, Bill. Colorado - Avalanche. 2011. (NHL: History & Heroes Ser.). (ENG., Illus.). 48p. (J). (gr. 5-17). pap. 9.99 *(978-1-897563-16-8(7),* Creative Paperbacks) Creative Co., The.
—The NHL - History & Heroes: The\Story of the Toronto Maple Leafs. 2008. (NHL: History & Heroes Ser.). (Illus.). 42p. (YA). (gr. 5-9). 22.95 *(978-1-58341-621-1(8))* Creative Co., The.
—The Story of the Colorado Avalanche. 2008. (NHL: History & Heroes Ser.). (Illus.). 42p. (YA). (gr. 5-9). 22.95 *(978-1-58341-616-7(1))* Creative Co., The.
—Toronto - Maple Leafs. 2011. (NHL: History & Heroes Ser.). (ENG., Illus.). 48p. (J). (gr. 5-17). pap. 9.99 *(978-1-897563-21-2(3),* Creative Paperbacks) Creative Co., The.
McClellan, Ray. Hockey. 2009. (My First Sports Ser.). (ENG., Illus.). 24p. (J). (gr. 2-5). lib. bdg. 25.95 *(978-1-60014-330-4(X),* Blastoff! Readers) Bellwether Media.
McFarlane, Brian. Peter Puck's Big Book of Hockey: Fascinating Facts about the World's Fastest Team Sport. 2011. (ENG., Illus.). 208p. pap. *(978-1-55168-351-5(2))* Me to We.
McFee, Shane. Let's Play Ice Hockey. (Let's Get Active Ser.). 24p. 2009. (gr. 2-3). 42.50 *(978-1-61514-254-5(1))* 2008. (Illus.). (J). (gr. 3-7). lib. bdg. 22.60 *(978-1-4042-4195-4(7))* Rosen Publishing Group, Inc., The. (PowerKids Pr.).
McIntyre, Abigael. An Insider's Guide to Field Hockey, 1 vol. 2015. (ENG.). 48p. (YA). 30.25 *(978-1-4777-8073-2(4),* Rosen Reference) Rosen Publishing Group, Inc., The.
McKinley, Michael. Ice Time: The Story of Hockey. 2006. (ENG., Illus.). 80p. (J). (gr. k-12). 18.95 *(978-0-88776-762-3(1),* Tundra Bks.) Tundra Bks. CAN. Dist: Penguin Random Hse. LLC.
McMahon, Dave. Girls Play to Win Hockey. 2010. (Girls Play to Win Ser.). 64p. (J). (gr. 3-6). lib. bdg. 27.93 *(978-1-59953-390-2(1))* Norwood Hse. Pr.
Miller, Raymond H. Jaromir Jagr. 2003. (Stars of Sports Ser.). (ENG., Illus.). 48p. (J). 27.50 *(978-0-7377-1539-2(1),* Greenhaven Pr., Inc.) Cengage Gale.
Nagelhout, Ryan. Becoming a Pro Hockey Player. 2015. (Going Pro Ser.). (ENG.). 32p. (J). (gr. 3-4). pap. 10.50 *(978-1-4824-2066-1(X));* (Illus.). lib. bdg. 26.60 *(978-1-4824-2067-8(8))* Stevens, Gareth Publishing LLLP.
—Hockey: Who Does What? 2017. (Sports: What's Your Position? Ser.). 32p. (J). (gr. 3-4). pap. 10.50 ***(978-1-5382-0429-0(0))*** Stevens, Gareth Publishing LLLP.
—I Love Hockey. 2014. (My Favorite Sports Ser.). (Illus.). 24p. (J). (gr. k-2). 22.60 *(978-1-4824-0731-0(0))* Stevens, Gareth Publishing LLLP.
—Me Encanta el Hockey / I Love Hockey. 2014. (My Favorite Sports Ser.). (SPA & ENG., Illus.). 24p. (J). (gr. k-2). 22.60 *(978-1-4824-0853-9(8))* Stevens, Gareth Publishing LLLP.
—The Science of Hockey. 2015. (Sports Science Ser.). (ENG., Illus.). 32p. (J). (gr. 4-5). pap. 10.00 *(978-1-4994-1070-9(0),* PowerKids Pr.) Rosen Publishing Group, Inc., The.
—Talk Like a Hockey Player. 2016. (Let's Talk Sports! Ser.). 00032p. (J). pap. 10.50 ***(978-1-4824-5704-9(0))*** Stevens, Gareth Publishing LLLP.
Nagelhout, Ryan. 20 Fun Facts about Hockey. 2016. (Fun Fact File: Sports! Ser.). (ENG.). 32p. (J). (gr. 2-3). lib. bdg. 25.25 *(978-1-4824-3980-9(8));* (Illus.). pap. 10.50 *(978-1-4824-3978-6(6))* Stevens, Gareth Publishing LLLP.
Napier, Matt. Hat Tricks Count: A Hockey Number Book. Rose, Melanie, illus. rev. ed. 2005. (Sports Ser.). (ENG.). 40p. (J). (gr. k-5). 16.95 *(978-1-58536-163-2(1))* Sleeping Bear Pr.
—Hockey Numbers. Rose, Melanie, illus. (Numbers & Counting Ser.). (ENG.). 2009. 14p. 11.75 *(978-1-58536-495-4(9))* 2007. 22p. (J). (gr. -1-1). 7.99 *(978-1-58536-346-9(4))* Sleeping Bear Pr.
—Little Hockey. 2012. (Little Sports Ser.). (ENG., Illus.). 22p. (J). 7.95 *(978-1-58536-712-2(5))* Sleeping Bear Pr.
—Z Is for Zamboni: A Hockey Alphabet. Rose, Melanie, illus. 2015. (Av2 Fiction Readalong 2016 Ser.). (ENG.). (J). (gr. -1-1). lib. bdg. 34.28 *(978-1-4896-3771-0(0),* AV2 by Weigl) Weigl Pubs., Inc.
—1, 2, 3 Cheers for the Toronto Maple Leafs! An Official Toronto Maple Leafs Counting Book. Rose, Melanie, illus. 2016. (ENG.). 32p. (J). (gr. -1-2). 19.99 *(978-1-77049-801-3(X),* Fenn-Tundra) Tundra Bks. CAN. Dist: Penguin Random Hse. LLC.
Nichols, John. The NHL - History & Heroes: The Story of the Boston Bruins. 2011. (NHL: History & Heroes Ser.). (ENG., Illus.). 48p. (J). (gr. 5-17). pap. 9.99 *(978-1-897563-14-4(0),* Creative Paperbacks) Creative Co., The.
—Philadelphia Flyers. 2004. (Stanley Cup Champions Ser.). (Illus.). 32p. (J). lib. bdg. *(978-1-58341-279-4(4),* Creative Education) Creative Co., The.
Nicholson, Lorna Schultz. Pink Power: The First Women's Hockey World Champions. 2007. (Recordbooks Ser.). (ENG., Illus.). 128p. (YA). (gr. 3-8). *(978-1-55028-989-3(6))* Lorimer, James & Co., Ltd., Pubs. CAN. Dist: Casemate Pubs. & Bk. Distributors, LLC.
—Winning Gold: Canada's Incredible 2002 Olympic Victory in Women's Hockey, 1 vol. 2010. (Lorimer Recordbooks Ser.). (ENG., Illus.). 112p. (J). (gr. 8-12). 16.95 *(978-1-55277-473-1(2),* 9781552774731) Lorimer, James & Co., Ltd., Pubs. CAN. Dist: Casemate Pubs. & Bk. Distributors, LLC.
Omoth, Tyler. First Source to Hockey: Rules, Equipment, & Key Playing Tips. 2016. (First Sports Source Ser.). (ENG., Illus.). 24p. (gr. 1-2). lib. bdg. 25.32 *(978-1-4914-8423-4(3),* First Facts) Capstone Press of Coughlan Cos.
Otten, Jack. Hockey Sobre Hielo. 2004. (Entrenamiento Deportivo (Sports Training) Ser.). (SPA & ENG., Illus.). 24p. (J). lib. bdg. 22.60 *(978-0-8239-6847-3(2),* Editorial Buenas Letras) Rosen Publishing Group, Inc., The.
—Hockey sobre hielo (Ice Hockey) 2009. (Entrenamiento deportivo (Sports Training) Ser.). 24p. (gr. 1-2). 42.50 *(978-1-61512-270-7(2),* Editorial Buenas Letras) Rosen Publishing Group, Inc., The.
—Ice Hockey. 2009. (Sports Training Ser.). 24p. (gr. 1-2). 42.50 *(978-1-60853-187-5(2),* PowerKids Pr.) Rosen Publishing Group, Inc., The.
Peters, Chris. Girls' Hockey, 1 vol. 2013. (Girls' SportsZone Ser.). (ENG., Illus.). 48p. (J). (gr. 3-6). lib. bdg. 32.79 *(978-1-61783-987-0(6),* SportsZone) ABDO Publishing Co.
—Great Moments in Olympic Ice Hockey, 1 vol. 2014. (Great Moments in Olympic Sports Ser.). (ENG.). 64p. (gr. 10-14). lib. bdg. 32.79 *(978-1-62403-395-7(4),* SportsZone) ABDO Publishing Co.
—Stanley Cup Finals, 1 vol. 2013. (Sports' Great Championships Ser.). (ENG.). 64p. (J). (gr. 4-6). lib. bdg. 32.79 *(978-1-61783-672-5(9),* SportsZone) ABDO Publishing Co.
Pritchard, Phil. Travels with Stanley. 2007. (ENG., Illus.). 144p. (J). *(978-1-55168-297-6(4))* Fenn, H. B. & Co., Ltd.
Rausch, David. National Hockey League. 2014. (Major League Sports Ser.). (ENG.). 24p. (J). (gr. 3-7). 25.95 *(978-1-62617-137-4(8),* Epic Bks.) Bellwether Media.
Ross, Dalton. The Top Teams Ever: Football, Baseball, Basketball & Hockey Winners. 2005. (Sports Illustrated for Kids Books Ser.). (Illus.). 176p. (YA). (gr. 7-12). lib. bdg. 33.25 *(978-0-8239-3693-9(7))* Rosen Publishing Group, Inc., The.
—The Top Teams Ever: Football, Baseball, Basketball, & Hockey Winners. 2009. (Sports Illustrated for Kids Bks). 176p. (gr. 7-12). 63.90 *(978-1-60853-156-1(2))* Rosen Publishing Group, Inc., The.
Ross, Jesse Paul & Puzzling Sports Institute Staff. Slapshot Hockey Quizbook: 50 Fun Games Brought to You by the Puzzling Sports Institute. unabr. ed. 2009. (ENG.). 80p. pap. 8.95 *(978-0-88971-234-8(4))* Nightwood Editions CAN. Dist: Midpoint Trade Bks., Inc.
Roytman, Arkady. GOAL! the Hockey Coloring Book. 2013. (Dover Coloring Bks.). (ENG.). 32p. (J). (gr. 2-5). pap. 3.99 *(978-0-486-49889-8(1))* Dover Pubns., Inc.
Roza, Greg. Hockey. 2012. (On the Team Ser.). (ENG.). 24p. (J). (gr. 2-5). pap. 8.15 *(978-1-4339-6450-3(3));* lib. bdg. 22.60 *(978-1-4339-6448-0(1))* Stevens, Gareth Publishing LLLP. (Gareth Stevens Learning Library).
—Sidney Crosby. 2011. (Today's Sports Greats Ser.). (Illus.). 32p. (gr. 4-6). (J). pap. 10.50 *(978-1-4339-5876-2(7),* Gareth Stevens Learning Library); (YA). lib. bdg. 26.60 *(978-1-4339-5874-8(0))* Stevens, Gareth Publishing LLLP.
Sandler, Michael. Hockey: Miracle on Ice. 2006. (Upsets & Comebacks Ser.). (Illus.). 32p. (YA). (gr. 3-6). lib. bdg. 25.27 *(978-1-59716-168-8(3))* Bearport Publishing Co., Inc.
Savage, Jeff. Hockey Super Stats. 2017. (Pro Sports Stats Ser.). (ENG.). 32p. (J). (gr. 3-6). 27.99 ***(978-1-5124-3411-8(6))*** Lerner Publishing Group.
—Super Hockey Infographics. 2015. (Super Sports Infographics Ser.). (ENG., Illus.). 32p. (J). (gr. 3-5). lib. bdg. 26.65 *(978-1-4677-5234-3(7),* Lerner Pubns.) Lerner Publishing Group.
—Super Hockey Infographics. Kulihin, Vic, illus. 2015. (Super Sports Infographics Ser.). (ENG.). 32p. (J). (gr. 3-5). pap. 8.99 *(978-1-4677-7577-9(0),* Lerner Pubns.) Lerner Publishing Group.
—Top 25 Hockey Skills, Tips, & Tricks. 2011. (Top 25 Sports Skills, Tips, & Tricks Ser.). (Illus.). 48p. (J). (gr. 2-5). lib. bdg. 25.27 *(978-0-7660-3869-1(6));* (gr. 4-18). pap. 8.95 *(978-1-59845-357-7(2))* Enslow Pubs., Inc.
Schuette, Sarah L. Hockey Scramble: A Spot-It Challenge, 1 vol. 2013. (Spot It Ser.). (ENG.). 32p. (gr. 1-2). lib. bdg. 27.32 *(978-1-62065-063-9(0),* Aplus Bks.) Capstone Press of Coughlan Cos.
Schuh, Mari C. Hockey. 2017. (Spot Sports Ser.). (ENG.). 16p. (gr. k-3). 17.95 ***(978-1-68151-088-0(X))*** Amicus Publishing.
Schultz Nicholson, Lorna. Fighting for Gold: The Story of Canada's Sledge Hockey Paralympic Gold, 1 vol. 2009. (Lorimer Recordbooks Ser.). (ENG., Illus.). 128p. (gr. 8-12). 9.95 *(978-1-55277-030-6(3),* 9781552770306); (YA). 16.95 *(978-1-55277-031-3(1))* Lorimer, James & Co., Ltd., Pubs. CAN. Dist: Casemate Pubs. & Bk. Distributors, LLC.
—Pink Power: The First Women's Hockey World Champions, 1 vol. 2007. (Lorimer Recordbooks Ser.). (ENG., Illus.). 128p. (J). (gr. 3-8). 9.95 *(978-1-55028-987-9(X),* 9781550289879) Lorimer, James & Co., Ltd., Pubs. CAN. Dist: Casemate Pubs. & Bk. Distributors, LLC.
Schwartz, Heather E. Top Ice Hockey Tips. 2017. (Top Sports Tips Ser.). (ENG., Illus.). 32p. (gr. 3-4). lib. bdg. 27.99 *(978-1-5157-4723-9(9),* Snap Bks.) Capstone Press of Coughlan Cos.
Sharp, Anne Wallace. Ice Hockey. 2010. (Science Behind Sports Ser.). 112p. (YA). (gr. 7-12). 34.45 *(978-1-4205-0281-7(6))* Cengage Gale.
Shea, Kevin. H Is for Hockey. 2013. (ENG.). (J). pap. *(978-1-58536-891-4(1))* Sleeping Bear Pr.
—H Is for Hockey: An NHL Alumni Alphabet. Dewar, Ken, illus. 2012. (ENG.). 32p. (J). (gr. 1-5). 16.95 *(978-1-58536-794-8(X)); (978-1-58536-814-3(8))* Sleeping Bear Pr.
Siemasz, Greg. Hockey, 1 vol. 2013. (Winter Sports Ser.). (ENG., Illus.). 48p. (gr. 3-6). pap. 6.95 *(978-1-4109-5457-2(9));* 32.65 *(978-1-4109-5451-0(X))* Heinemann-Raintree.
Skog, Jason. Chicago - Blackhawks. 2011. (NHL: History & Heroes Ser.). (ENG., Illus.). 48p. (J). (gr. 5-17). pap. 9.99 *(978-1-897563-15-1(9),* Creative Paperbacks) Creative Co., The.
—The NHL: The\Story of the Chicago Blackhawks. 2008. (NHL: History & Heroes Ser.). (Illus.). 42p. (YA). (gr. 5-9). 22.95 *(978-1-58341-615-0(3))* Creative Co., The.
Sterling Publishing Co., Inc. My First Hockey Book. 2016. (First Sports Ser.). (ENG., Illus.). 22p. (J). (— 1). bds. 6.95 *(978-1-4549-1974-2(4))* Sterling Publishing Co., Inc.
Stewart, Mark. The Boston Bruins. Gibbons, Denis, ed. 2014. (Team Spirit Ser.). (ENG.). 48p. (J). (gr. 3-6). lib. bdg. 29.27 *(978-1-59953-616-3(1))* Norwood Hse. Pr.
—The Chicago Blackhawks. Gibbons, Denis, ed. 2014. (Team Spirit Ser.). (ENG.). 48p. (J). (gr. 3-6). lib. bdg. 29.27 *(978-1-59953-617-0(X))* Norwood Hse. Pr.
—The Colorado Avalanche. Gibbons, Denis, ed. 2014. (Team Spirit Ser.). (ENG.). 48p. (J). (gr. 3-6). lib. bdg. 29.27 *(978-1-59953-618-7(8))* Norwood Hse. Pr.
—The Detroit Red Wings. Gibbons, Denis, ed. 2014. (Team Spirit Ser.). (ENG.). 48p. (J). (gr. 3-6). lib. bdg. 29.27 *(978-1-59953-619-4(6))* Norwood Hse. Pr.
—The Edmonton Oilers. Gibbons, Denis, ed. 2014. (Team Spirit Ser.). (ENG.). 48p. (J). (gr. 3-6). lib. bdg. 29.27 *(978-1-59953-620-0(X))* Norwood Hse. Pr.
—The Los Angeles Kings. Gibbons, Denis, ed. 2014. (Team Spirit Ser.). (ENG.). 48p. (J). (gr. 3-6). lib. bdg. 29.27 *(978-1-59953-621-7(8))* Norwood Hse. Pr.
—The Montreal Canadiens. Gibbons, Denis, ed. 2014. (Team Spirit Ser.). (ENG.). 48p. (J). (gr. 3-6). lib. bdg. 29.27 *(978-1-59953-622-4(6))* Norwood Hse. Pr.
—The New Jersey Devils. Gibbons, Denis, ed. 2014. (Team Spirit Ser.). (ENG.). 48p. (J). (gr. 3-6). lib. bdg. 29.27 *(978-1-59953-623-1(4))* Norwood Hse. Pr.
—The New York Rangers. Gibbons, Denis, ed. 2014. (Team Spirit Ser.). (ENG.). 48p. (J). (gr. 3-6). lib. bdg. 29.27 *(978-1-59953-624-8(2))* Norwood Hse. Pr.
—The Philadelphia Flyers. Gibbons, Denis, ed. 2014. (Team Spirit Ser.). (ENG.). 48p. (J). (gr. 3-6). lib. bdg. 29.27 *(978-1-59953-625-5(0))* Norwood Hse. Pr.
—The Pittsburgh Penguins. Gibbons, Denis, ed. 2014. (Team Spirit Ser.). (ENG.). 48p. (J). (gr. 3-6). lib. bdg. 29.27 *(978-1-59953-626-2(9))* Norwood Hse. Pr.
—The Toronto Maple Leafs. Gibbons, Denis, ed. 2014. (Team Spirit Ser.). (ENG.). 48p. (J). (gr. 3-6). lib. bdg. 29.27 *(978-1-59953-627-9(7))* Norwood Hse. Pr.
—The Vancouver Canucks. Gibbons, Denis, ed. 2014. (Team Spirit Ser.). (ENG.). 48p. (J). (gr. 3-6). lib. bdg. 29.27 *(978-1-59953-628-6(5))* Norwood Hse. Pr.
Stewart, Mark & Kennedy, Mike. Score! The Action & Artistry of Hockey's Magnificent Moment. 2010. (Spectacular Sports Ser.). (ENG., Illus.). 64p. (gr. 5-12). lib. bdg. 33.27 *(978-0-8225-8753-8(X))* Lerner Publishing Group.
Storden, Thom. Amazing Hockey Records, 1 vol. 2014. (Epic Sports Records Ser.). (ENG.). 32p. (gr. 1-2). lib. bdg. 26.65 *(978-1-4914-0742-4(5))* Capstone Press of Coughlan Cos.
Stubbs, Dave. Our Game: The History of Hockey in Canada. 2008. 56p. (J). (gr. 3-5). 14.95 *(978-1-897073-89-6(5))* Lobster Pr. CAN. Dist: Orca Bk. Pubs. USA.
Stuckey, Rachel. Up Your Game on & off the Ice. 2014. (ENG., Illus.). 32p. (J). pap. *(978-0-7787-0723-3(7))* Crabtree Publishing Co.
Suen, Anastasia. La historia del hockey (the Story of Hockey) 2009. (Historia de los deportes (Sports History) Ser.). (SPA.). 24p. (gr. 2-2). 42.50 *(978-1-61513-313-0(5),* Editorial Buenas Letras) Rosen Publishing Group, Inc., The.
Swope, Bob. Teach'n Beginning Offensive Ice Hockey Drills, Plays, & Games Free Flow Handbook. 2013. 90p. pap. 19.95 *(978-0-9911151-1-2(2))* Jacobob Pr., LLC.
Teach'n Beginning Defensive Ice Hockey Drills, Plays, & Games Free Flow Handbook. 2013. 132p. pap. 16.95 *(978-0-9911151-9-8(8))* Jacobob Pr., LLC.
Thomas, Keltie. How Hockey Works. Hall, Greg & Owlkids Books Inc. Staff, illus. 2nd ed. 2006. (How Sports Work Ser.). (ENG.). 64p. (J). (gr. 4-7). pap. 10.95 *(978-1-897066-65-2(1),* Maple Tree Pr.) Owlkids Bks. Inc. CAN. Dist: Publishers Group West (PGW).
Tiffany, Sean, illus. Hockey. 2008. (Sticker Stories Ser.). (ENG.). 16p. (J). (gr. -1-2). 5.99 *(978-0-448-44902-9(1),* Grosset & Dunlap) Penguin Young Readers Group.
Trusdell, Brian. Miracle on Ice, 1 vol. 2014. (Greatest Events in Sports History Ser.). (ENG., Illus.). 48p. (J). (gr. 3-6). lib. bdg. 32.79 *(978-1-62403-597-5(3),* SportsZone) ABDO Publishing Co.
Ulmer, Michael. M Is for Maple Leafs. Rose, Melanie, illus. 2014. (ENG.). 32p. (J). 19.95 *(978-1-77049-798-6(6),* Tundra Bks.) Tundra Bks. CAN. Dist: Penguin Random Hse. LLC.
—S Is for the Stanley Cup: A Hockey Championship Alphabet. Benoit, Renné & Lyons, Chris, illus. 2017. (ENG.). 32p. (J). (gr. 1-4). 16.99 *(978-1-58536-972-0(1),* 204226) Sleeping Bear Pr.
Vanderhoof, Gabrielle. Hockey. 2010. (Getting the Edge Ser.). 96p. (YA). lib. bdg. 24.95 *(978-1-4222-1735-1(3))* Mason Crest.
VandeVoorde, Jay. Muskegon Lumberjacks-the Life of a Hockey Puck! 2011. 56p. (gr. 2-4). pap. 11.99 *(978-1-4634-1736-9(5))* AuthorHouse.
Wacholtz, Anthony. Picture a Slap Shot: A Hockey Drawing Book, 1 vol. Ray, Mike, illus. 2013. (Drawing with Sports Illustrated Kids Ser.). (ENG.). 64p. (gr. 5-7). 33.99 *(978-1-4765-3105-2(6))* Capstone Press of Coughlan Cos.
Waxman, Laura Hamilton. Ice Hockey & Curling. 2017. (Winter Olympic Sports Ser.). (ENG.). 32p. (J). (gr. 2-5). pap. 9.99 *(978-1-68152-180-0(6))* Amicus.
—Ice Hockey & Curling. 2017. (Winter Olympic Sports Ser.). (ENG.). 32p. (gr. 1-4). 20.95 *(978-1-68151-149-8(5))* Amicus Publishing.
Weakland, Mark. Hockey Counting, 1 vol. 2013. (SI Kids Rookie Bks.). (ENG.). 32p. (gr. 1-2). 27.32 *(978-1-4765-0226-7(9))* Capstone Press of Coughlan Cos.
—Hockey Patterns, 1 vol. (SI Kids Rookie Bks.). (ENG.). (gr. 1-2). 2014. 20p. bds. 7.95 *(978-1-4765-3580-7(9))* 2013. 32p. 27.32 *(978-1-4765-0227-4(7))* Capstone Press of Coughlan Cos.
—Hockey Shapes, 1 vol. (SI Kids Rookie Bks.). (ENG., (gr. 1-2). 2014. Illus.). 20p. bds. 7.95 *(978-1-4765-3578-4(7))* 2013. 32p. 27.32 *(978-1-4765-0225-0(0))* Capstone Press of Coughlan Cos.
—SI Kids Rookie Books: Football & Hockey. 2013. (SI Kids Rookie Bks.). (ENG.). (gr. 1-2). 32p. lib. bdg. 163.92 *(978-1-4765-3744-3(5));* 20p. bds. 39.75 *(978-1-4765-3743-6(7))* Capstone Press of Coughlan Cos.
—SI Kids Rookie Books: Hockey. 2013. (SI Kids Rookie Bks.). (ENG.). (gr. 1-2). 32p. lib. bdg. 81.96 *(978-1-4765-0469-8(5));* 20p. bds. 15.90 *(978-1-4765-3742-9(9))* Capstone Press of Coughlan Cos.
Winters, Jaime. Breakaway! The History of Hockey. 2014. (ENG., Illus.). 32p. (J). *(978-0-7787-0752-3(0))* Crabtree Publishing Co.
—Center Ice: The Stanley Cup. 2014. (ENG., Illus.). 32p. (J). pap. *(978-0-7787-0707-3(5))* Crabtree Publishing Co.
Wiseman, Blaine. Stanley Cup. 2011. 24p. (YA). (gr. 2-4). *(978-1-77071-665-0(3));* pap. *(978-1-77071-671-1(8))* Weigl Educational Pubs. Ltd.
—Stanley Cup. 2013. (J). *(978-1-62127-368-4(7));* pap. *(978-1-62127-373-8(3))* Weigl Pubs., Inc.
Wiseman, Blaine & Tait, Leia. Hockey Records. 2010. (Record Breakers Ser.). (Illus.). 24p. (YA). (gr. 3-6). lib. bdg. 27.13 *(978-1-61690-112-7(8));* (J). (gr. 4-6). pap. 12.95 *(978-1-61690-113-4(6))* Weigl Pubs., Inc.
Wood, Alix. You Can Be an Ice-Skater, Vol. 1. 2014. (Let's Get Moving! Ser.). (ENG.). 32p. (J). (gr. 3-4). 26.60 *(978-1-4824-0283-4(1))* Stevens, Gareth Publishing LLLP.
Wright, John. Hockey. 2005. (Sports Injuries Ser.). (Illus.). 64p. (YA). lib. bdg. 19.95 *(978-1-59084-634-6(6))* Mason Crest.
Zweig, Eric. Boston Bruins. 2017. (Illus.). 32p. (J). ***(978-0-7787-3426-0(9))*** Crabtree Publishing Co.
—Chicago Blackhawks. 2017. (Illus.). 32p. (J). ***(978-0-7787-3427-7(7))*** Crabtree Publishing Co.
—Detroit Red Wings. 2017. (Illus.). 32p. (J). ***(978-0-7787-3438-3(2))*** Crabtree Publishing Co.
—Long Shot: How the Winnipeg Falcons Won the First Olympic Hockey Gold, 1 vol. 2007. (Lorimer Recordbooks Ser.). (ENG., Illus.). 112p. (gr. 4-6). (J). 9.95 *(978-1-55028-974-9(8),* 9781550289749); *(978-1-55028-975-6(6))* Lorimer, James & Co., Ltd., Pubs. CAN. Dist: Casemate Pubs. & Bk. Distributors, LLC.
—Montreal Canadiens. 2017. (Illus.). 32p. (J). ***(978-0-7787-3439-0(0))*** Crabtree Publishing Co.
—New York Rangers. 2017. (Illus.). 32p. (J). ***(978-0-7787-3440-6(4))*** Crabtree Publishing Co.
—Toronto Maple Leafs. 2017. (Illus.). 32p. (J). ***(978-0-7787-3441-3(2))*** Crabtree Publishing Co.
Zweig, Eric. Tough Guys: Hockey Rivals in Times of War & Disaster, 1 vol. 2009. (Lorimer Recordbooks Ser.). (ENG., Illus.). 144p. (YA). (gr. 8-12). 16.95 *(978-1-55277-428-1(7),* 9781552774281); 9.95 *(978-1-55277-423-6(6),* 9781552774236) Lorimer, James & Co., Ltd., Pubs. CAN. Dist: Casemate Pubs. & Bk. Distributors, LLC.

HOCKEY—BIOGRAPHY

Bradley, Michael. Pro Hockey's Underdogs: Players & Teams Who Shocked the Hockey World. 2017. (Sports Shockers! Ser.). (ENG.). 32p. (gr. 3-4). lib. bdg. 27.99 ***(978-1-5157-8045-8(7))*** Capstone Press of Coughlan Cos.

H
I

Brehm, Mike. Rising Stars: The 10 Best Young Players in the NHL. 2009. (Sports Illustrated for Kids Bks). 176p. (gr. 7-12). 63.90 *(978-1-60853-151-6(1))* Rosen Publishing Group, Inc., The.

Brehm, Mike & Russo, Michael. Rising Stars: The 10 Best Young Players in the NHL. 2005. (Sports Illustrated for Kids Books Ser.). (Illus.). 176p. (YA). (gr. 7-12). lib. bdg. 33.25 *(978-0-8239-3575-8(2))* Rosen Publishing Group, Inc., The.

Burgan, Michael. Sidney Crosby. 2015. (Hockey Superstars Ser.). (ENG.). 32p. (gr. 3-4). lib. bdg. 27.99 *(978-1-4914-2138-3(X))* Capstone Press of Coughlan Cos.

Burns, Kylie. Sidney Crosby. 2013. (ENG., Illus.). 32p. (J). *(978-0-7787-0038-8(0))*; pap. *(978-0-7787-0068-5(2))* Crabtree Publishing Co.

Campbell, Cassie. H. E. A. R. T. 2007. (ENG., Illus.). 108p. (J). (gr. 2-9). pap. *(978-1-55168-315-7(6))* Me to We.

Crosby, Sidney, et al. Sidney Crosby. 2015. (Quotes from the Greatest Athletes Ser.). (ENG., Illus.). 24p. (J). lib. bdg. 28.55 *(978-1-4896-3376-7(6)*, AV2 by Weigl) Weigl Pubs., Inc.

Doeden, Matt. Carey Price. 2015. (Hockey Superstars Ser.). (ENG.). 32p. (gr. 3-4). lib. bdg. 27.99 *(978-1-4914-2140-6(1))* Capstone Press of Coughlan Cos.

—Phil Kessel. 2015. (Hockey Superstars Ser.). (ENG., Illus.). 32p. (gr. 3-9). pap. 7.95 *(978-1-4914-9022-8(5))*; lib. bdg. 27.99 *(978-1-4296-8278-7(7))* Capstone Press of Coughlan Cos.

—Sidney Crosby: Hockey Superstar. 2012. (Superstar Athletes Ser.). (ENG.). 24p. (gr. 1-2). pap. 7.29 *(978-1-4296-8005-9(9))*; pap. 41.70 *(978-1-4296-8495-8(X))*; lib. bdg. 25.32 *(978-1-4296-7684-7(1))* Capstone Press of Coughlan Cos.

—Stars of Hockey, 1 vol. 2014. (Sports Stars Ser.). (ENG.). 24p. (gr. k-1). lib. bdg. 26.65 *(978-1-4765-3960-7(X)*, Pebble Plus) Capstone Press of Coughlan Cos.

—Steven Stamkos. 2015. (Hockey Superstars Ser.). (ENG.). 32p. (gr. 3-4). lib. bdg. 27.99 *(978-1-4914-2139-0(8))* Capstone Press of Coughlan Cos.

—Wayne Gretzky. (Sports Heroes & Legends Ser.). (ENG.). (gr. 5-12). 2008. pap. 56.72 *(978-0-8225-9401-7(3))* 2007. (Illus.). 120p. lib. bdg. 30.60 *(978-0-8225-7165-0(X))* Lerner Publishing Group.

Feldman, Heather. Wayne Gretzky: Hockey Star. 2009. (Sports Superstars Ser.). 24p. (gr. 1-1). 42.50 *(978-1-60853-184-4(8)*, PowerKids Pr.) Rosen Publishing Group, Inc., The.

Florence, Melanie. Jordin Tootoo: The Highs & Lows in the Journey of the First Inuit to Play in the NHL, 1 vol. 2010. (Lorimer Recordbooks Ser.). (ENG., Illus.). 104p. (YA). (gr. 7-12). lib. bdg. 16.95 *(978-1-55277-531-8(3)*, 9781552775318); mass mkt. 9.95 *(978-1-55277-529-5(1)*, 9781552775295) Lorimer, James & Co., Ltd., Pubs. CAN. Dist: Casemate Pubs. & Bk. Distributors, LLC.

Frederick, Shane. Alexander Ovechkin. 2015. (Hockey Superstars Ser.). (ENG.). 32p. (gr. 3-4). lib. bdg. 27.99 *(978-1-4914-2141-3(X))* Capstone Press of Coughlan Cos.

—Hockey Legends in the Making, 1 vol. 2014. (Legends in the Making Ser.). (ENG.). 32p. (gr. 3-4). lib. bdg. 27.99 *(978-1-4765-4065-8(9))* Capstone Press of Coughlan Cos.

—John Tavares. 2015. (Hockey Superstars Ser.). (ENG., Illus.). 32p. (gr. 3-9). pap. 7.95 *(978-1-4914-9025-9(X))*; lib. bdg. 27.99 *(978-1-62065-158-2(0))* Capstone Press of Coughlan Cos.

—Jonathan Toews: Hockey Superstar, 1 vol. 2014. (Superstar Athletes Ser.). (ENG.). 24p. (gr. 1-2). pap. 7.29 *(978-1-4765-9432-3(5))*; lib. bdg. 25.32 *(978-1-4765-9427-9(9))* Capstone Press of Coughlan Cos.

—Side-By-Side Hockey Stars: Comparing Pro Hockey's Greatest Players, 1 vol. 2014. (Side-By-Side Sports Ser.). (ENG.). 48p. (gr. 4-6). lib. bdg. 27.99 *(978-1-4765-6166-0(4))* Capstone Press of Coughlan Cos.

—Six Degrees of Sidney Crosby: Connecting Hockey Stars. 2015. (Six Degrees of Sports Ser.). (ENG.). 48p. (gr. 3-4). lib. bdg. 31.99 *(978-1-4914-2143-7(6))* Capstone Press of Coughlan Cos.

—Who's Who of Pro Hockey: A Guide to the Game's Greatest Players. 2015. (Who's Who of Pro Sports Ser.). (ENG., Illus.). 32p. (gr. 3-4). lib. bdg. 27.99 *(978-1-4765-5797-7(7))* Capstone Press of Coughlan Cos.

Gitlin, Marty. Patrick Kane: Hockey Star. 2017. (Biggest Names in Sports (hardcover) Ser.). (ENG., Illus.). 32p. (J). (gr. 4-7). lib. bdg. 28.50 ***(978-1-63517-042-9(7)***, Focus Readers) North Star Editions.

Grabowski, John F. Detroit Redwings. 2003. (Great Sports Teams Ser.). (ENG., Illus.). 112p. (J). 30.85 *(978-1-59018-269-7(3)*, Lucent Bks.) Cengage Gale.

Graves, Will. Best Hockey Players of All Time, 1 vol. 2014. (Sports' Best Ever Ser.). (ENG.). 64p. (gr. 3-6). lib. bdg. 32.79 *(978-1-62403-620-0(1)*, SportsZone) ABDO Publishing Co.

Greve, Tom. Hockey Goalies. 2009. (Playmakers Ser.). (Illus.). 24p. (YA). (gr. 3-6). lib. bdg. 27.07 *(978-1-60694-331-1(6))* Rourke Educational Media.

Hammer, Maxwell. Sidney Crosby: NHL MVP & Champion. 2015. (Today's MVPs & Champions Ser.). (ENG.). 24p. (J). (gr. 2-5). 27.07 *(978-1-63143-740-3(2)*, 208575) Child's World, Inc., The.

Haugen, Brenda. Johnathan Toews. 2015. (Hockey Superstars Ser.). (ENG., Illus.). 32p. (gr. 3-9). lib. bdg. 27.99 *(978-1-62065-157-5(2))* Capstone Press of Coughlan Cos.

—Jonathan Toews. 2015. (Hockey Superstars Ser.). (ENG.). 32p. (gr. 3-9). pap. 7.95 *(978-1-4914-9024-2(1))* Capstone Press of Coughlan Cos.

Herman, Gail & dePaola, Tomie. Who Is Wayne Gretzky? Hammond, Ted & Harrison, Nancy, illus. 2015. (Who Was? Ser.). (ENG.). 112p. (J). (gr. 3-7). 5.99 *(978-0-448-48321-4(1)*, Grosset & Dunlap) Penguin Young Readers Group.

Herman, Gail & Harrison, Nancy. Who Is Wayne Gretzky? 2015. (Who Is...? Ser.). lib. bdg. 16.00 *(978-0-606-36595-6(8))* Turtleback Bks.

Kirkpatrick, Rob. Wayne Gretzky: Hockey All-Star. 2009. (Great Record Breakers in Sports Ser.). 24p. (gr. 3-3). 42.50 *(978-1-61513-192-1(2)*, PowerKids Pr.) Rosen Publishing Group, Inc., The.

Kortemeier, Todd. Jonathan Toews. 2016. (Illus.). 32p. (J). *(978-1-62143-289-0(0))* Pr. Room Editions LLC.

—Superstars of the NHL. 2016. (Pro Sports Superstars Ser.). (ENG., Illus.). 24p. (J). (gr. 1-4). 20.95 *(978-1-60753-938-4(1))* Amicus Publishing.

Maurer, Tracy Nelson. Jonathan Toews. 2015. (Famous Athletes Ser.). (ENG., Illus.). 24p. (gr. k-1). lib. bdg. 26.65 *(978-1-4914-6235-5(3))* Capstone Press of Coughlan Cos.

McMahon, Dave. Alex Ovechkin: NHL Superstar, 1 vol. 2011. (Playmakers Ser.). (ENG., Illus.). 32p. (YA). (gr. 3-6). 27.07 *(978-1-61714-750-0(8))* ABDO Publishing Co.

—Sidney Crosby: Hockey's Golden Boy, 1 vol. 2011. (Playmakers Ser.). (ENG., Illus.). 32p. (J). (gr. 3-6). 27.07 *(978-1-61714-745-6(1))* ABDO Publishing Co.

Morrison, Jessica. Wayne Gretzky: Greatness on Ice. 2010. (Crabtree Groundbreaker Biographies Ser.). (ENG., Illus.). 112p. (J). pap. *(978-0-7787-2548-0(0))*; (gr. 5-8). lib. bdg. *(978-0-7787-2539-8(1))* Crabtree Publishing Co.

Mortillaro, Nicole. Connor Mcdavid. 2015. (Hockey Superstars Ser.). (ENG., Illus.). 32p. (gr. 3-9). lib. bdg. 27.99 *(978-1-4914-9021-1(7))* Capstone Press of Coughlan Cos.

—Jarome Iginla: How the NHL's First Black Captain Gives Back, 1 vol. 2010. (Lorimer Recordbooks Ser.). (ENG., Illus.). 112p. (gr. 7-12). (YA). lib. bdg. 16.95 *(978-1-55277-542-4(9)*, 9781552775424); (J). mass mkt. 9.95 *(978-1-55277-541-7(0)*, 9781552775417) Lorimer, James & Co., Ltd., Pubs. CAN. Dist: Casemate Pubs. & Bk. Distributors, LLC.

—Something to Prove: The Story of Hockey Tough Guy Bobby Clarke, 1 vol. 2010. (Lorimer Recordbooks Ser.). (ENG., Illus.). 96p. (gr. 8-12). 16.95 *(978-1-55277-481-6(3)*, 9781552774816); pap. 9.95 *(978-1-55277-480-9(5)*, 9781552774809) Lorimer, James & Co., Ltd., Pubs. CAN. Dist: Casemate Pubs. & Bk. Distributors, LLC.

—Willie O'Ree: The Story of the First Black Player in the NHL, 1 vol. 2012. (Lorimer Recordbooks Ser.). (ENG., Illus.). (YA). (gr. 7-12). 118p. 16.95 *(978-1-4594-0196-9(4)*, 9781459401969); 120p. pap. 9.95 *(978-1-4594-0195-2(6)*, 9781459401952) Lorimer, James & Co., Ltd., Pubs. CAN. Dist: Casemate Pubs. & Bk. Distributors, LLC.

Myers, Jess. Hockey Record Breakers, 1 vol. 2016. (ENG., Illus.). 48p. (J). ***(978-1-62403-848-8(4)***, SportsZone) ABDO Publishing Co.

Nagelhout, Ryan. Sidney Crosby. 2016. (Sports MVPs Ser.). 24p. (J). (gr. 2-1). 22.60 *(978-1-4824-4643-2(X))* Stevens, Gareth Publishing LLLP.

Nagle, Jeanne. Sidney Crosby: One of the NHL's Top Scorers. 2015. (Living Legends of Sports Ser.). (ENG.). 48p. (J). (gr. 5-6). pap. 14.05 *(978-1-68048-125-9(8)*, Britannica Educational Publishing) Rosen Publishing Group, Inc., The.

—Sidney Crosby: The NHL's Top Scorer. 2015. (Living Legends of Sports Ser.). (ENG., Illus.). 48p. (J). (gr. 5-6). 25.85 *(978-1-68048-124-2(X)*, Britannica Educational Publishing) Rosen Publishing Group, Inc., The.

NHLPA. We Are the Goal Scorers: The Top Point Leaders of the NHL. 2013. (NHLPA/NHL We Are the Players Ser.). (ENG.). 72p. (J). (gr. 2-5). 12.99 *(978-1-77049-461-9(8)*, Fenn-Tundra) Tundra Bks. CAN. Dist: Penguin Random Hse. LLC.

—We Are the Goalies: The Top Netminders of the NHL. 2013. (NHLPA/NHL We Are the Players Ser.). (ENG.). 72p. (J). (gr. 2-5). 12.99 *(978-1-77049-459-6(6)*, Fenn-Tundra) Tundra Bks. CAN. Dist: Penguin Random Hse. LLC.

Nicholson, Lorna Schultz. Winning Gold: Canada's Incredible 2002 Olympic Victory in Women's Hockey, 1 vol. 2009. (Lorimer Recordbooks Ser.). (ENG., Illus.). 112p. (J). (gr. 8-12). pap. 9.95 *(978-1-55277-472-4(4)*, 9781552774724) Lorimer, James & Co., Ltd., Pubs. CAN. Dist: Casemate Pubs. & Bk. Distributors, LLC.

Rivkin, Jennifer. Hockey Superstars: Past, Present, & Future. 2014. (ENG., Illus.). 32p. (J). pap. *(978-0-7787-0715-8(6))* Crabtree Publishing Co.

Romanuk, Paul. Le Hockey Ses Supervedettes 2004-2005. annuals 2004. (FRE., Illus.). (J). pap. *(978-0-439-96134-9(3))* Scholastic Canada, Ltd.

—Hockey Superstars 2004-2005. annuals 2004. (ENG., Illus.). 48p. (J). pap. *(978-0-439-96133-2(5))* Scholastic Canada, Ltd.

Rossiter, Sean. Dominik Hasek. 2003. (Hockey Heroes Ser.). (Illus.). 44p. (gr. 5-9). 6.95 *(978-1-55054-679-8(1))* Da Capo Pr., Inc.

—Mario Lemieux. 2003. (Hockey Heroes Ser.). (Illus.). 64p. pap. 12.95 *(978-1-55054-870-9(0))* Da Capo Pr., Inc.

Savage, Jeff. Alex Ovechkin. 2011. (Amazing Athletes Set VIII Ser.). pap. 45.32 *(978-0-7613-8601-8(7))*; (ENG.). 32p. (gr. 2-5). pap. 7.95 *(978-0-7613-7818-1(9))*; (ENG.). 32p. (gr. 2-5). lib. bdg. 25.26 *(978-0-7613-7672-9(0))* Lerner Publishing Group.

—Sidney Crosby. 2009. (Amazing Athletes Ser.). (J). (gr. 2-5). 23.93 *(978-0-7613-4054-6(8))*; pap. 40.95 *(978-0-7613-4780-4(1))* Lerner Publishing Group.

Schwartzenberger, Tina. Don Cherry. 2010. (Illus.). 24p. *(978-1-77071-625-4(4))*; pap. *(978-1-77071-626-1(2))* Weigl Educational Pubs. Ltd.

Shapiro, Howard. Hockey Player for Life. 2008. (Forever Friends Ser.). (ENG.). 128p. (gr. 3-9). pap. 12.95 *(978-0-595-51785-5(4))* Animal Media Group LLC.

Sutoski, Jennifer. Carey Price. 2015. (Canadian Biographies Ser.). (ENG., Illus.). 24p. (gr. k-1). lib. bdg. 26.65 *(978-1-4914-7835-6(7)*, Pebble Plus) Capstone Press of Coughlan Cos.

Tieck, Sarah. Sidney Crosby: Hockey Champion, 1 vol. 2011. (Big Buddy Biographies Set 6 Ser.). (ENG., Illus.). 32p. (J). (gr. 2-5). 28.50 *(978-1-61714-702-9(8))* ABDO Publishing Co.

Zweig, Eric. Dominant Defensemen. 2014. (Hockey Hall of Fame Kids Ser.). (ENG., Illus.). 48p. (J). (gr. 4-7). pap. 6.99 *(978-1-77085-430-7(4)*, 9781770854307) Firefly Bks., Ltd.

—Great Goalies. 2014. (Hockey Hall of Fame Kids Ser.). (ENG., Illus.). 48p. (J). (gr. 4-7). pap. 7.99 *(978-1-77085-431-4(2)*, 9781770854314) Firefly Bks., Ltd.

—Star Power: The Legend & Lore of Cyclone Taylor, 1 vol. 2007. (Lorimer Recordbooks Ser.). (ENG., Illus.). 104p. (YA). (gr. 4-8). 8.95 *(978-1-55028-995-4(0)*, 9781550289954); *(978-1-55028-997-8(7))* Lorimer, James & Co., Ltd., Pubs. CAN. Dist: Casemate Pubs. & Bk. Distributors, LLC.

—Super Scorers. 2014. (Hockey Hall of Fame Kids Ser.). (ENG., Illus.). 48p. (J). (gr. 4-7). pap. 7.99 *(978-1-77085-429-1(0)*, 9781770854291) Firefly Bks., Ltd.

HOCKEY—FICTION

Aryal, Aimee. Let's Go, Broncos! 2008. (YA). 14.95 *(978-1-932888-75-1(6))* Mascot Bks., Inc.

Atkins, Ben. The Breakaway Kid. Woods, Vanessa, illus. 2nd rev. ed. 2005. (ENG.). 32p. (J). per. 8.00 *(978-0-9768653-0-8(0))* Summer Day Publishing, LLC.

Bailey, Linda. The Farm Team. Slavin, Bill, illus. 2008. (ENG.). 32p. (J). (gr. -1-2). pap. 7.95 *(978-1-55453-317-6(1))* Kids Can Pr., Ltd. CAN. Dist: Hachette Bk. Group.

Beveridge, Cathy. Offside. 2006. (ENG.). 336p. mass mkt. 9.95 *(978-1-894345-25-5(8))* Thistledown Pr., Ltd. CAN. Dist: Univ. of Toronto Pr.

Bogart, Mike. Ice Warriors, 1 vol. 2010. 72p. pap. 19.95 *(978-1-4489-3885-8(6))* America Star Bks.

Borer, Christopher. Patrick & Hatrick, 1 vol. McDonald, Patrick, illus. 2010. 44p. pap. 24.95 *(978-1-4489-7978-3(1))* PublishAmerica, Inc.

Bossley, Michele Martin. Goon Squad, 1 vol. 2003. (Lorimer Sports Stories Ser.). (ENG.). 104p. (J). (gr. 4-8). 8.95 *(978-1-55028-808-7(3)*, 9781550288087); 16.95 *(978-1-55028-809-4(1)*, 9781550288094) Lorimer, James & Co., Ltd., Pubs. CAN. Dist: Casemate Pubs. & Bk. Distributors, LLC.

Bradley, Sandra. Henry Holton Takes the Ice. Palacios, Sara, illus. 2015. (ENG.). 40p. (J). (gr. k-3). 16.99 *(978-0-8037-3856-0(0)*, Dial Bks) Penguin Young Readers Group.

Brennan, Ashley Logan. Hockey! Hockey! 2012. 24p. pap. 17.99 *(978-1-4772-7146-9(5))* AuthorHouse.

Brouwer, Sigmund. Blazer Drive, 1 vol. 2007. (Orca Sports Ser.). (ENG.). 176p. (YA). (gr. 6-10). per. 9.95 *(978-1-55143-717-0(1))* Orca Bk. Pubs. USA.

—Chief Honor, 1 vol. 2008. (Orca Sports Ser.). (ENG.). 176p. (YA). (gr. 6-10). pap. 9.95 *(978-1-55143-915-0(8))* Orca Bk. Pubs. USA.

—Hitmen Triumph, 1 vol. 2007. (Orca Sports Ser.). (ENG.). 168p. (YA). (gr. 6-10). per. 9.95 *(978-1-55143-873-3(9))* Orca Bk. Pubs. USA.

—Rebel Glory, 1 vol. 2006. (Orca Sports Ser.). (ENG., Illus.). 176p. (YA). (gr. 6-10). per. 9.95 *(978-1-55143-631-9(0))* Orca Bk. Pubs. USA.

—Thunderbird Spirit, 1 vol. 2008. (Orca Sports Ser.). (ENG.). 192p. (YA). (gr. 6-10). pap. 9.95 *(978-1-55469-045-9(5))* Orca Bk. Pubs. USA.

—Tiger Threat, 1 vol. 2006. (Orca Sports Ser.). (ENG.). 176p. (YA). (gr. 6-10). per. 9.95 *(978-1-55143-639-5(6))* Orca Bk. Pubs. USA.

—Timberwolf Challenge, 1 vol. Griffiths, Dean, illus. 2008. (Orca Echoes Ser.). (ENG.). 64p. (J). (gr. 2-3). pap. 6.95 *(978-1-55143-730-9(9))* Orca Bk. Pubs. USA.

—Timberwolf Chase, 1 vol. Griffiths, Dean, illus. 2006. (Orca Echoes Ser.). (ENG.). 64p. (J). (gr. 2-3). per. 6.95 *(978-1-55143-548-0(9))* Orca Bk. Pubs. USA.

—Timberwolf Hunt, 1 vol. Griffiths, Dean, illus. 2007. (Orca Echoes Ser.). (ENG.). 64p. (J). (gr. 2-3). per. 6.95 *(978-1-55143-726-2(0))* Orca Bk. Pubs. USA.

—Timberwolf Prey, 1 vol. Ross, Graham, illus. 2010. (Orca Echoes Ser.). (ENG.). 64p. (J). (gr. 2-3). pap. 6.95 *(978-1-55469-109-8(5))* Orca Bk. Pubs. USA.

—Timberwolf Revenge, 1 vol. Griffiths, Dean, illus. 2006. (Orca Echoes Ser.). (ENG.). 64p. (J). (gr. 2-3). per. 6.95 *(978-1-55143-544-2(6))* Orca Bk. Pubs. USA.

—Timberwolf Tracks, 1 vol. Ross, Graham, illus. 2009. (Orca Echoes Ser.). (ENG.). 64p. (J). (gr. 2-3). pap. 6.95 *(978-1-55143-734-7(1))* Orca Bk. Pubs. USA.

—Timberwolf Trap, 1 vol. Griffiths, Dean, illus. 2007. (Orca Echoes Ser.). (ENG.). 64p. (J). (gr. 2-3). per. 6.95 *(978-1-55143-722-4(8))* Orca Bk. Pubs. USA.

—Winter Hawk Star, 1 vol. 2007. (Orca Sports Ser.). (ENG.). 160p. (YA). (gr. 6-10). per. 9.95 *(978-1-55143-869-6(0))* Orca Bk. Pubs. USA.

Brouwer, Sigmund & Gingras, Gaston. La Revanche des Loups Gris, 1 vol. Griffiths, Dean, illus. 2011. (Loups Gris Ser.). (FRE.). 72p. (J). (gr. 2-3). pap. 6.95 *(978-1-4598-0011-3(7))* Orca Bk. Pubs. USA.

Browne, Susan Chalker. Freddy's Hockey Hero, 1 vol. Rose, Hilda, illus. 2010. (ENG.). 32p. (J). (gr. k-3). 10.95 *(978-1-897174-62-3(4)*, Tuckamore Bks.) Creative Bk. Publishing CAN. Dist: Orca Bk. Pubs. USA.

Burke, Christina. Melvin et le Grand Match de Hockey. Minguet, Anne, tr. Franfou, illus. 2013. 52p. *(978-0-9918561-3-8(9))*; pap. *(978-0-9918561-2-1(0))* Stars Aligned Publishing.

Casciano, Christie & Moziak, Rose Mary Casciano, illus. Haunted Hockey in Lake Placid. 2012. 72p. (J). pap. *(978-1-59531-040-8(1))* North Country Bks., Inc.

—The Puck Hog. 2011. 44p. (J). pap. 9.95 *(978-1-59531-037-8(1))* North Country Bks., Inc.

Charles, Norma. Chasing a Star. 2009. (ENG., Illus.). 182p. (YA). (gr. 5-8). pap. *(978-1-55380-077-4(X))* Ronsdale Pr.

Christopher, Matt. Body Check. 2003. (ENG.). 144p. (J). (gr. 3-7). pap. 5.99 *(978-0-316-13405-7(8))* Little, Brown Bks. for Young Readers.

—Body Check. 2004. (Matt Christopher Sports Ser.). 138p. (gr. 3-7). 15.00 *(978-0-7569-2984-8(9))* Perfection Learning Corp.

—Face-Off. 2005. (Sports Classics III Ser.). 119p. (J). lib. bdg. 15.00 *(978-1-59054-755-7(1))* Fitzgerald Bks.

—The Hockey Machine. 2008. (New Matt Christopher Sports Library). 128p. (J). (gr. 4-6). lib. bdg. 26.60 *(978-1-59953-214-1(X))* Norwood Hse. Pr.

—Ice Magic. 2007. (New Matt Christopher Sports Library). 128p. (J). (gr. 4-6). lib. bdg. 26.60 *(978-1-59953-112-0(7))* Norwood Hse. Pr.

—Inline Skater. 2005. (Sports Classics IV Ser.). 153p. (J). lib. bdg. 15.00 *(978-1-59054-759-5(4))* Fitzgerald Bks.

—Roller Hockey Radicals. 2005. (Sports Classics III Ser.). 157p. (J). lib. bdg. 15.00 *(978-1-59054-767-0(5))* Fitzgerald Bks.

—Roller Hockey Rumble. Koelsch, Michael, tr. Koelsch, Michael, illus. 3rd ed. 2004. (ENG.). 64p. (J). (gr. 1-4). pap. 13.99 *(978-0-316-73755-5(0))* Little, Brown Bks. for Young Readers.

Crawley, Oksanna. So, You Be Keon & I'll Be Mahovlich. 2009. 28p. pap. 13.99 *(978-1-4490-0243-5(9))* AuthorHouse.

Dahl, Michael. Goodnight Hockey. Forshay, Christina, illus. 2015. (Sports Illustrated Kids Bedtime Bks.). (ENG.). 32p. (gr. -1-2). lib. bdg. 22.60 *(978-1-4795-6526-9(1))* Capstone Press of Coughlan Cos.

Diersch, Sandra. No Contact, 1 vol. 2008. (Lorimer Sports Stories Ser.). (ENG.). 136p. (J). (gr. 4-8). 16.95 *(978-1-55277-025-2(7)*, 9781552770252); 8.95 *(978-1-55277-024-5(9)*, 9781552770245) Lorimer, James & Co., Ltd., Pubs. CAN. Dist: Casemate Pubs. & Bk. Distributors, LLC.

Dunbar, Helene. These Gentle Wounds. 2014. (ENG.). 312p. (YA). pap. 11.99 *(978-0-7387-4027-0(6)*, Flux) North Star Editions.

Durkin, Shawn & Doherty, Catherine. Shola's Game: A Novel. (Illus.). 93p. *(978-1-897039-17-5(4))* High Interest Publishing (HIP).

Einstein, James Allan. Hockey Jokes for Kids, 1 vol. 2014. (ENG.). 120p. (J). pap. 9.95 *(978-1-926700-47-2(3)*, 9781926700472) Blue Bike Bks. CAN. Dist: Lone Pine Publishing USA.

Eyre, Lindsay. The Mean Girl Meltdown. 2015. (Sylvie Scruggs Ser.: 2). (ENG., Illus.). 160p. (J). (gr. 2-5). pap. 5.99 *(978-0-545-62030-7(9)*, Levine, Arthur A. Bks.) Scholastic, Inc.

Ferguson, Donald. Chums of Scranton High at Ice Hockey. 2006. 25.95 *(978-1-4218-2936-4(3))*; pap. 10.95 *(978-1-4218-3036-0(1))* 1st World Publishing, Inc.

Fidler, Mark. Pond Puckster. 2nd ed. 2003. 148p. (J). (gr. 4-8). reprint ed. pap. 11.95 *(978-0-9721839-0-1(6))* BLR Bks.

—Two Faced Forward. 2005. 145p. (J). (gr. 4-8). pap. 11.95 *(978-0-9721839-3-2(0))* BLR Bks.

FitzGerald, Dawn. Getting in the Game. 2007. (ENG.). 144p. (J). (gr. 4-8). pap. 16.99 *(978-0-312-37753-3(3)*, 9780312377533) Square Fish.

Fletcher, Erin. All Laced Up. 2016. (ENG., Illus.). (YA). (gr. 7). pap. 15.99 ***(978-1-68281-316-4(9))*** Entangled Publishing, LLC.

The Flying Hockey Stick. 2007. (Illus.). 64p. (J). (gr. -1-3). 18.95 *(978-1-930900-31-8(7))* Purple Hse. Pr.

Forsyth, C. A. & Forsyth, Christine. Two on One, 1 vol. 2005. (Lorimer Sports Stories Ser.: 83). (ENG.). 112p. (J). (gr. 4-8). 8.95 *(978-1-55028-900-8(4)*, 9781550289008) Lorimer, James & Co., Ltd., Pubs. CAN. Dist: Casemate Pubs. & Bk. Distributors, LLC.

Forsyth, Christine. Two on One, 1 vol. 2005. (Lorimer Sports Stories Ser.: 83). (ENG.). 112p. (J). (gr. 4-8). 16.95 *(978-1-55028-901-5(2)*, 9781550289015) Lorimer, James & Co., Ltd., Pubs. CAN. Dist: Casemate Pubs. & Bk. Distributors, LLC.

Geddes, Diana E. Hockey Practice. Palmer, Kate S., illus. 2005. (ENG.). 12p. (gr. k-2). pap. 7.95 *(978-1-57874-001-7(0)*, Kaeden Bks.) Kaeden Corp.

Grocki, Jennifer. From A to Zamboni, the Alphabet Hockey Style! Flyers Edition. Lendway, Andy, illus. 2007. 32p. (J). 16.95 *(978-0-9793833-0-4(7))* Team Kidz, Inc.

Hellman, Charles S. The Hockey Bully. Tiritilli, Robert A., illus. 2013. 34p. pap. 9.25 *(978-0-935938-23-4(0))* LuckySports.

Hendrickson, David H. Cracking the Ice. 2011. (YA). 365p. (gr. 9-18). 16.95 *(978-1-934813-55-3(9))*; 366p. *(978-1-934813-56-0(7))* Westside Bks.

Hillert, Margaret. I Did It, Dear Dragon. Schimmell, David, illus. 2009. (BeginningtoRead Ser.). 32p. (J). (gr. k-2). lib. bdg. 22.60 *(978-1-59953-295-0(6))* Norwood Hse. Pr.

Hotte, Sylvain. Power Forward. Roberts, Casey, tr. 2012. (Break Away Ser.). (ENG., Illus.). 180p. (YA). (gr. 8). pap. 16.95 *(978-1-926824-42-0(3))* Baraka Bks. CAN. Dist: Independent Pubs. Group.

Hurcomb, Fran. Going Places, 1 vol. 2008. (Orca Young Readers Ser.). (ENG.). 128p. (J). (gr. 3-6). pap. 7.95 *(978-1-55469-019-0(6))* Orca Bk. Pubs. USA.

Hyman, Zachary. Hockey Hero. Pullen, Zachary, illus. 2015. (ENG.). 40p. (J). (gr. 1-4). 17.99 *(978-1-77049-630-9(0)*, Tundra Bks.) Tundra Bks. CAN. Dist: Penguin Random Hse. LLC.

Johnson, Jeremy. Rallo's Goal. 2016. (What's Your Dream? Ser.). (ENG.). 96p. (gr. 3-4). lib. bdg. 25.32 *(978-1-4965-3444-6(1))* Capstone Press of Coughlan Cos.

Klein, Abby. Don't Sit on My Lunch! Mckinley, John & McKinley, John, illus. 2005. (Ready, Freddy! Ser.: 4). (ENG.). 96p. (J). (gr. -1-3). 5.99 *(978-0-439-55602-6(3)*, Blue Sky Pr., The) Scholastic, Inc.

Kreie, Chris. There Are No Figure Eights in Hockey. Santillan, Jorge H., illus. 2010. (Sports Illustrated Kids Victory School Superstars Ser.). (ENG.). 56p. (gr. 1-3). pap. 5.95 *(978-1-4342-2808-6(8))* Stone Arch Bks.

Leonetti, Mike. My Leafs Sweater. 2004. (Illus.). (J). (gr. k-5). spiral bd. *(978-0-616-01700-5(6))* Canadian National Institute for the Blind/Institut National Canadien pour les Aveugles.

—Wendel & the Great One. Banning, Greg, illus. 2008. 383p. *(978-1-55192-812-8(4))* Raincoast Bk. Distribution.

Lewman, David. SpongeBob's Slap Shot. Moore, Harry, illus. 2008. (SpongeBob SquarePants Ser.). (ENG.). 24p. (J). (gr. -1-3). pap. 3.99 *(978-1-4169-6153-6(4)*, Simon Spotlight/Nickelodeon) Simon Spotlight/Nickelodeon.

—Spongebob's Slap Shot. 2014. (Spongebob Squarepants 8X8 Ser.). lib. bdg. 13.55 *(978-0-606-36280-1(0))* Turtleback Bks.

Lueders, Tamara Devitre. Hoagie, the Hockey Turtle. 2005. (ENG., Illus.). 33p. (J). per. 15.99 *(978-1-4257-0169-7(8))* Xlibris Corp.

Lynch, Chris. Iceman. 2013. (ENG.). (YA). (gr. 7). 160p. 16.99 *(978-1-4424-6002-7(4))*; 176p. pap. 9.99 *(978-1-4424-6001-0(6))* Simon & Schuster Bks. For Young Readers. (Simon & Schuster Bks. For Young Readers).

MacGregor, Roy. The Complete Screech Owls, Vol. 1. 2005. (ENG.). 488p. (J). (gr. 3-7). pap. 15.95 *(978-0-7710-5484-6(X)*, Screech Owls) McClelland & Stewart CAN. Dist: Penguin Random Hse. LLC.

—Face-Off at the Alamo. 2013. (Screech Owls Ser.). (ENG.). 176p. (J). (gr. 4-7). pap. 8.95 *(978-1-77049-418-3(9)*, Tundra Bks.) Tundra Bks. CAN. Dist: Penguin Random Hse. LLC.

—The Ghost of the Stanley Cup. 2013. (Screech Owls Ser.). (ENG.). 176p. (J). (gr. 4-7). pap. 8.99 *(978-1-77049-416-9(2)*, Tundra Bks.) Tundra Bks. CAN. Dist: Penguin Random Hse. LLC.

—The Highest Number in the World. Despres, Genevieve, illus. 2014. (ENG.). 32p. (J). (gr. 1-4). 17.99

(978-1-77049-575-3(4), Tundra Bks.) Tundra Bks. CAN. Dist: Penguin Random Hse. LLC.

—Mystery at Lake Placid. 2013. (Screech Owls Ser.). (ENG.). 272p. (J). (gr. 4-7). pap. 8.95 *(978-1-77049-413-8(8)*, Tundra Bks.) Tundra Bks. CAN. Dist: Penguin Random Hse. LLC.

—The Night They Stole the Stanley Cup. 2013. (Screech Owls Ser.). (ENG.). 176p. (J). (gr. 4-7). pap. 8.99 *(978-1-77049-414-5(6)*, Tundra Bks.) Tundra Bks. CAN. Dist: Penguin Random Hse. LLC.

—Panic in Pittsburgh. 2013. (Screech Owls Ser.). (ENG.). 176p. (J). (gr. 4-7). pap. 8.95 *(978-1-77049-419-0(7)*, Tundra Bks.) Tundra Bks. CAN. Dist: Penguin Random Hse. LLC.

—Peril at the World's Biggest Hockey Tournament. 2008. (ENG.). 160p. (YA). (gr. 3-7). mass mkt. 6.99 *(978-0-7710-5607-9(9)*, Screech Owls) McClelland & Stewart CAN. Dist: Penguin Random Hse. LLC.

—Peril at the World's Biggest Hockey Tournament. 2013. (Screech Owls Ser.). (ENG.). 208p. (J). (gr. 4-7). pap. 8.99 *(978-1-77049-417-6(0)*, Tundra Bks.) Tundra Bks. CAN. Dist: Penguin Random Hse. LLC.

—The Secret of the Deep Woods, No. 17. 2003. (ENG.). 128p. (J). (gr. 4-18). mass mkt. 4.95 *(978-0-7710-5646-8(X)*, Screech Owls) McClelland & Stewart CAN. Dist: Penguin Random Hse. LLC.

—Sudden Death in New York City. 2013. (Screech Owls Ser.). (ENG.). 176p. (J). (gr. 4-7). pap. 8.95 *(978-1-77049-415-2(4)*, Tundra Bks.) Tundra Bks. CAN. Dist: Penguin Random Hse. LLC.

MacLeod, J.E.. Waiting to Score. 2011. 8.42 *(978-1-934813-17-1(6))* Westside Bks.

Maddox, Jake. Backup Goalie, 1 vol. Tiffany, Sean, illus. 2008. (Jake Maddox Sports Stories Ser.). (ENG.). 72p. (gr. 2-3). pap. 5.95 *(978-1-4342-0517-9(7))*; lib. bdg. 25.32 *(978-1-4342-0467-7(7))* Stone Arch Bks.

—Face-Off, 1 vol. Tiffany, Sean, illus. 2006. (Jake Maddox Sports Stories Ser.). (ENG.). 72p. (gr. 2-3). lib. bdg. 25.32 *(978-1-59889-063-1(8))* Stone Arch Bks.

—Face-Off, 1 vol. Tiffany, Sean, illus. 2006. (Jake Maddox Sports Stories Ser.). (ENG.). 72p. (gr. 2-3). pap. 5.95 *(978-1-59889-237-6(1))* Stone Arch Bks.

—Field Hockey Firsts, 1 vol. Mourning, Tuesday, illus. 2009. (Jake Maddox Girl Sports Stories Ser.). (ENG.). 72p. (gr. 2-3). 25.32 *(978-1-4342-1606-9(3))* Stone Arch Bks.

—Hockey Meltdown, 1 vol. Tiffany, Sean, illus. 2011. (Jake Maddox Sports Stories Ser.). (ENG.). 72p. (gr. 2-3). pap. 5.95 *(978-1-4342-3426-1(6))*; lib. bdg. 25.32 *(978-1-4342-2990-8(4))* Stone Arch Bks.

—Power Play. 2016. (Jake Maddox JV Girls Ser.). (ENG.). 96p. (gr. 3-4). lib. bdg. 25.99 *(978-1-4965-3673-0(8))* Stone Arch Bks.

—Slap-Shot Slump. 2015. (Jake Maddox JV Ser.). (ENG.). 96p. (gr. 3-4). lib. bdg. 25.99 *(978-1-4342-9635-1(0))* Stone Arch Bks.

Mantell, Paul, text. Cool As Ice: Cool As Ice: the #1 Sports Series for Kids. 2005. (Sports Classics III Ser.). 148p. (J). lib. bdg. 15.00 *(978-1-59054-751-9(9))* Fitzgerald Bks.

McDine, Donna M. Hockey Agony. Hammond, Julie, illus. 2013. 20p. pap. 9.95 *(978-1-61633-360-7(X))* Guardian Angel Publishing, Inc.

McFarlane, Brian. The Hockey Book. 11th ed. 2008. (Mitchell Brothers Ser.). (ENG.). 200p. (J). (gr. 3-7). per. *(978-1-55168-312-6(1))* Magma.

—The Kapuskasing Kids. 12th ed. 2008. (Mitchell Brothers Ser.). (ENG.). 200p. (J). (gr. 3-7). pap. *(978-1-55168-285-3(0))* Magma.

—On the Hockey Highway, Vol. 2. 2nd ed. 2007. (Mitchell Brothers Ser.). (ENG.). 220p. (J). (gr. 2-7). pap. *(978-1-55168-245-7(1))* Magma.

—Peter Puck & the Stolen Stanley Cup. Storey, Geri, illus. 2015. (Adv. Hockey's Greatest Mascot Ser.). (ENG.). 64p. (J). (gr. 1-4). 10.99 *(978-1-77049-581-4(9)*, Fenn-Tundra) Tundra Bks. CAN. Dist: Penguin Random Hse. LLC.

—Season of Surprises. 9th ed. 2008. (Mitchell Brothers Ser.). (ENG.). 184p. (J). (gr. 3-7). pap. *(978-1-55168-300-3(8))* Me to We.

—Stanley Cup Dream. 6th ed. 2007. (Mitchell Brothers Ser.). (ENG.). 200p. (J). (gr. 3-7). pap. *(978-1-55168-259-4(1))* Magma.

McFarlane, Leslie. Leslie Mcfarlane's Hockey Stories, 2 vols. 2006. (ENG., Illus.). 176p. (J). 13.95 *(978-1-55263-848-4(0))* Leaf Storm Pr.

—McGonigle Scores! 2006. (ENG.). 256p. (J). pap. 9.95 *(978-1-55263-834-7(0))* Leaf Storm Pr.

McGugan, Jim. Bridge 6. 2004. (Illus.). (J). (gr. k-3). spiral bd. *(978-0-616-01721-0(9))* Canadian National Institute for the Blind/Institut National Canadien pour les Aveugles.

McKnight, Marty. Jim Nasium. 2015. (Jim Nasium Ser.). (ENG.). 88p. (gr. 2-3). 101.28 *(978-1-4965-2010-4(6))* Stone Arch Bks.

—Jim Nasium Is a Hockey Hazard. Jones, Chris B., illus. 2015. (Jim Nasium Ser.). (ENG.). 88p. (gr. 2-3). pap. 5.95 *(978-1-4965-0524-8(7))* Stone Arch Bks.

McMahon, Patricia. The Mystery of the Morphing Hockey Stick. Manders, John, illus. 2004. 138p. (J). lib. bdg. 15.38 *(978-1-4242-0403-8(8))* Fitzgerald Bks.

Mizzoni, Chris. The Sterling Seven, Hockey's First Team Ever. 2009. 24p. pap. 11.99 *(978-1-4490-2739-1(3))* AuthorHouse.

Nicholson, Lorna Schultz. Delaying the Game, 1 vol. 2005. (Lorimer Sports Stories Ser.). (ENG.). 112p. (J). (gr. 4-8). 16.95 *(978-1-55028-895-7(4)*, 9781550288957) Lorimer, James & Co., Ltd., Pubs. CAN. Dist: Casemate Pubs. & Bk. Distributors, LLC.

—Puckster Goes to the Olympics. Findley, Kelly, illus. 2013. (ENG.). 24p. (J). (gr. -1-3). pap. 6.99 *(978-1-77049-594-4(0)*, Fenn-Tundra) Tundra Bks. CAN. Dist: Penguin Random Hse. LLC.

—Puckster's First Hockey Tournament. Findley, Kelly, illus. 2012. (ENG.). 24p. (J). (gr. -1-3). pap. 6.99 *(978-1-77049-457-2(X)*, Fenn-Tundra) Tundra Bks. CAN. Dist: Penguin Random Hse. LLC.

—Puckster's First Hockey Tryout. Findley, Kelly, illus. 2013. (ENG.). 24p. (J). (gr. -1-3). pap. 6.99 *(978-1-77049-596-8(7)*, Fenn-Tundra) Tundra Bks. CAN. Dist: Penguin Random Hse. LLC.

—Too Many Men, 1 vol. 2006. (Lorimer Sports Stories Ser.). (ENG.). 128p. (J). (gr. 4-8). 16.95 *(978-1-55028-949-7(7)*, 9781550289497) Lorimer, James & Co., Ltd., Pubs. CAN. Dist: Casemate Pubs. & Bk. Distributors, LLC.

Nicholson, Lorna Schultz & Schultz Nicholson, Lorna. Against the Boards, 1 vol. 2005. (Lorimer Sports Stories Ser.). (ENG.). 112p. (J). (gr. 4-8). 9.95 *(978-1-55028-864-3(4)*, 9781550288643) Lorimer, James & Co., Ltd., Pubs. CAN. Dist: Casemate Pubs. & Bk. Distributors, LLC.

Nilsson, Bo Sigvard. Come on, Brian! A Young Boy's Struggle to Play in an All-Star Hockey Tournament. 2012. 56p. (gr. 4-6). pap. 8.95 *(978-1-4502-9301-3(8))* iUniverse, Inc.

Parkhurst, Johanna. Thanks a Lot, John Leclair. 2016. (Here's to You, Zeb Pike Ser.). (ENG., Illus.). (YA). pap. 14.99 ***(978-1-63477-428-4(0)***, Harmony Ink Pr.) Dreamspinner Pr.

Paulsen, Gary & Paulsen, Jim. Field Trip. 2015. (ENG.). 128p. (J). (gr. 5). 12.99 *(978-0-553-49674-1(3)*, Lamb, Wendy Bks.) Random Hse. Children's Bks.

Poulsen, David A. Blind Date. 2nd rev. ed. 2008. (Lawrence High Yearbook Ser.). (ENG.). 96p. (J). (gr. 2-7). pap. *(978-1-55263-933-7(9))* Me to We.

Publications International Ltd. Staff. For the Love of Hockey BK Brick. 2008. 320p. 12.98 *(978-1-4127-1535-5(0)*, PIL Kids) Publications International, Ltd.

Random House. SpongeBob's Slap Shot (SpongeBob SquarePants) Random House, illus. 2014. (Pictureback(R) Ser.). (ENG., Illus.). 24p. (J). (gr. -1-2). 3.99 *(978-0-385-37852-9(1)*, Random Hse. Bks. for Young Readers) Random Hse. Children's Bks.

Russell, Nancy. Rink of Dreams. rev. ed. 2008. (ENG.). 252p. (J). pap. *(978-1-55263-935-1(5))* Magma.

Schultz Nicholson, Lorna. Northern Star, 1 vol. 2006. (Lorimer Sports Stories Ser.). (ENG.). 112p. (J). (gr. 4-8). 16.95 *(978-1-55028-911-4(X)*, 9781550289114); 9.95 *(978-1-55028-910-7(1)*, 9781550289107) Lorimer, James & Co., Ltd., Pubs. CAN. Dist: Casemate Pubs. & Bk. Distributors, LLC.

—Roughing, 1 vol. 2004. (Lorimer Sports Stories Ser.). (ENG.). 112p. (J). (gr. 4-8). 16.95 *(978-1-55028-859-9(8)*, 9781550288599) Lorimer, James & Co., Ltd., Pubs. CAN. Dist: Casemate Pubs. & Bk. Distributors, LLC.

—Too Many Men, 1 vol. 2006. (Lorimer Sports Stories Ser.). (ENG.). 128p. (J). (gr. 4-8). 8.95 *(978-1-55028-948-0(9)*, 9781550289480) Lorimer, James & Co., Ltd., Pubs. CAN. Dist: Casemate Pubs. & Bk. Distributors, LLC.

Schwartz, Ellen. Yossi's Goal, 1 vol. 2006. (Orca Young Readers Ser.). (ENG., Illus.). 144p. (J). (gr. 3-6). per. 6.95 *(978-1-55143-492-6(X))* Orca Bk. Pubs. USA.

Scudamore, Beverly. Misconduct, 1 vol. 2004. (Lorimer Sports Stories Ser.: 72). (ENG.). 112p. (J). (gr. 4-8). 16.95 *(978-1-55028-855-1(5)*, 9781550288551); 8.95 *(978-1-55028-854-4(7)*, 9781550288544) Lorimer, James & Co., Ltd., Pubs. CAN. Dist: Casemate Pubs. & Bk. Distributors, LLC.

Shaw, Mary. Brady Brady & the B Team, 12 vols. Temple, Chuck, illus. l.t. ed. 2006. 32p. (J). per. *(978-1-897169-09-4(4))* Brady Brady, Inc.

—Brady Brady & the Big Mistake, 11vols. Temple, Chuck, illus. l.t. ed. 2004. 32p. (J). per. *(978-0-9735557-4-5(2))* Brady Brady, Inc.

—Brady Brady & the Great Exchange, 11 vols. Temple, Chuck, illus. l.t. ed. 2003. 32p. (J). per. *(978-0-9735557-5-2(0))* Brady Brady, Inc.

—Brady Brady & the Great Rink, 11 vols. Temple, Chuck, illus. l.t. ed. 2004. 32p. (J). per. *(978-0-9735557-0-7(X))* Brady Brady, Inc.

—Brady Brady & the MVP, 11 vols. Temple, Chuck, illus. l.t. ed. 2004. 32p. (J). per. *(978-0-9735557-7-6(7))* Brady Brady, Inc.

—Brady Brady & the Puck on the Pond, 11 vols. Temple, Chuck, illus. l.t. ed. 2005. 32p. (J). per. *(978-1-897169-07-0(8))* Brady Brady, Inc.

—Brady Brady & the Runaway Goalie, 11 vols. Temple, Chuck, illus. l.t. ed. 2004. 32p. (J). per. *(978-0-9735557-1-4(8))* Brady Brady, Inc.

—Brady Brady & the Singing Tree, 11 vols. Temple, Chuck, illus. l.t. ed. 2004. 32p. (J). per. *(978-0-9735557-3-8(4))* Brady Brady, Inc.

—Brady Brady & the Twirlin' Torpedo, 11 vols. Temple, Chuck, illus. l.t. ed. 2004. 32p. (J). per. *(978-0-9735557-2-1(6))* Brady Brady, Inc.

Sherman, Harold Morrow. Flying Heels & Other Hockey Stories. 2011. 264p. 47.95 *(978-1-258-08063-1(X))* Literary Licensing, LLC.

Skuy, David. Off the Crossbar. 2005. (Illus.). 182p. (J). (gr. 4-7). per. 14.95 *(978-1-59411-105-1(7))* Writers' Collective, The.

Sollinger, Emily. Bob the Builder. 2016. (Passport to Reading Level 1 Ser.). (ENG.). 32p. (J). (gr. -1-3). pap. 3.99 *(978-0-316-27296-4(5))* Little, Brown Bks. for Young Readers.

Stelmach, Orest. The Boy Who Stole from the Dead, 0 vols. 2014. (Nadia Tesla Ser.: 2). (ENG.). 366p. pap. 14.95 *(978-1-4778-0948-8(1)*, 9781477809488, Thomas & Mercer) Amazon Publishing.

Stewart, Kenneth. The Drop of the Puck. 2012. 24p. pap. 24.95 *(978-1-4626-7682-8(0))* America Star Bks.

Swan, Bill. Deflection!, 1 vol. 2004. (Lorimer Sports Stories Ser.: 71). (ENG.). 112p. (J). (gr. 4-8). 16.95 *(978-1-55028-853-7(9)*, 9781550288537) Lorimer, James & Co., Ltd., Pubs. CAN. Dist: Casemate Pubs. & Bk. Distributors, LLC.

Tobin, Richard K. Skating on Thick Ice. LeBlanc, Rebecca, ed. Chapman, Jesse, illus. 2013. 122p. (J). pap. 12.00 *(978-1-929882-96-0(3))* Biographical Publishing Co.

Trifunov, David. Ice Time, 1 vol. 2015. (Lorimer Sports Stories Ser.). (ENG.). 120p. (J). (gr. 4-8). pap. 9.95 *(978-1-4594-0854-8(3)*, 9781459408548) Lorimer, James & Co., Ltd., Pubs. CAN. Dist: Casemate Pubs. & Bk. Distributors, LLC.

Troupe, Thomas Kingsley. Ghostly Goalie. Faber, Rudy, illus. 2016. (Hauntiques Ser.). (ENG.). 128p. (gr. 4-6). lib. bdg. 25.32 *(978-1-4965-3544-3(8))* Stone Arch Bks.

Truckey, Don. The Adventures of Caraway Kim... Right Wing. 2008. (ENG.). 256p. (J). pap. 10.95 *(978-1-897235-43-0(7))* Thistledown Pr., Ltd. CAN. Dist: Univ. of Toronto Pr.

Ulrich, Maureen. Power Plays, 1 vol. 2007. (ENG.). 304p. (YA). (gr. 8-12). 10.95 *(978-1-55050-379-1(0))* Coteau Bks. CAN. Dist: Orca Bk. Pubs. USA.

Vandervelde, Beatrice. Home Ice, 1 vol. 2004. (Lorimer Sports Stories Ser.: 76). (ENG.). 104p. (J). (gr. 4-8). 16.95 *(978-1-55028-863-6(6)*, 9781550288636) Lorimer, James & Co., Ltd., Pubs. CAN. Dist: Casemate Pubs. & Bk. Distributors, LLC.

VanRiper, Justin & VanRiper, Gary. The Pond Hockey Challenge. 2012. (Adirondack Kids Ser.: Vol. 12). (Illus.). 96p. (J). pap. 9.95 *(978-0-9826250-2-6(2))* Adirondack Kids Pr.

Walsh, Ann. Shabash! 2nd ed. 2008. (ENG.). 112p. (J). (gr. 4-8). pap. 11.99 *(978-1-55002-829-4(4)*, Sandcastle Bks.) Dundurn CAN. Dist: Ingram Publisher Services.

Weber, Lori. My Granny Loves Hockey. Liska, Eliska, illus. 2014. (ENG.). 32p. (J). (gr. -1-3). 16.95 *(978-1-927018-43-9(9))* Simply Read Bks. CAN. Dist: Ingram Publisher Services.

Weston Woods Staff, creator. Ready, Freddy! #4: Don't Sit on My Lunch! 2011. 20.95 *(978-0-545-05006-7(5))* Weston Woods Studios, Inc.

Wheeler, Lisa. Dino-Hockey. Gott, Barry, illus. 2007. (Carolrhoda Picture Bks.). (ENG.). 32p. (J). (gr. k-3). 16.95 *(978-0-8225-6191-0(3)*, Carolrhoda Bks.) Lerner Publishing Group.

Yomtov, Nel & Fuentes, Benny. Reality Check, 1 vol. Sandoval, Gerardo, illus. 2010. (Sports Illustrated Kids Graphic Novels Ser.). (ENG.). 56p. (gr. 2-3). pap. 7.19 *(978-1-4342-2294-7(2))*; 26.65 *(978-1-4342-1912-1(7))* Stone Arch Bks.

Zamboni Brez. 2003. 183p. (J). (gr. 4-8). pap. 11.95 *(978-0-9721839-1-8(4))* BLR Bks.

Zweig, Eric. Fever Season. 2009. (ENG.). 256p. (YA). (gr. 4-18). pap. 10.99 *(978-1-55488-432-2(2)*, Dundurn Pr.) Dundurn CAN. Dist: Ingram Publisher Services.

HOGS

see Pigs

HOGWARTS SCHOOL OF WITCHCRAFT AND WIZARDRY (IMAGINARY ORGANIZATION)—FICTION

Rowling, J. K. Harrius Potter et Philosophi Lapis. Needham, Peter, tr. from ENG. 2003. (Harry Potter Ser.).Tr. of Harry Potter & the Philosopher's Stone. (LAT & ENG., Illus.). 256p. (YA). (gr. 7). 29.99 *(978-1-58234-825-4(1)*, 9781582348254, Bloomsbury USA Childrens) Bloomsbury Publishing USA.

—Harry Potter à l'École des Sorciers. Menard, Jean-François, tr. from ENG. 2007. (Harry Potter Ser.: Year 1).Tr. of Harry Potter & the Sorcerer's Stone. 311p. (J). per. 14.95 *(978-2-07-061236-9(8))* Gallimard, Editions FRA. Dist: Distribooks, Inc.

—Harry Potter & the Chamber of Secrets. 2009. 9.64 *(978-0-7848-1444-4(9)*, Everbind) Marco Bk. Co.

—Harry Potter & the Chamber of Secrets. unabr. ed. 2004. (Harry Potter Ser.: Year 2). 352p. (J). (gr. 3-18). pap. 46.00 incl. audio *(978-0-8072-8207-6(3)*, S YA 137 SP, Listening Library) Random Hse. Audio Publishing Group.

—Harry Potter & the Chamber of Secrets. (Harry Potter Ser.: 2). (J). 2006. 1.25 *(978-1-4193-8079-2(6))* 2003. 78.75 *(978-1-4025-6698-1(0))* Recorded Bks., Inc.

—Harry Potter & the Chamber of Secrets. (Harry Potter Ser.: Year 2). (RUS., Illus.). 28.95 *(978-5-8451-0947-7(7))* Rosmen-Izdat RUS. Dist: Distribooks, Inc.

—Harry Potter & the Chamber of Secrets. Kay, Jim, illus. 2016. (Harry Potter Ser.: 2). (ENG.). 272p. (J). (gr. 3). 39.99 *(978-0-545-79132-8(4))*; 275.00 *(978-1-338-11986-2(9))* Scholastic, Inc. (Levine, Arthur A. Bks.).

—Harry Potter & the Chamber of Secrets. l.t. ed. 2003. (Harry Potter Ser.: Year 2). (ENG.). 466p. pap. 13.95 *(978-1-59413-001-4(9))* Thorndike Pr.

—Harry Potter & the Chamber of Secrets. 2013. (Harry Potter (Kazu Kibuishi Illustrations) Ser.: 2). lib. bdg. 24.50 *(978-0-606-32346-8(5)*, Turtleback) Turtleback Bks.

—Harry Potter & the Deathly Hallows. (Illus.). 2008. 832p. pap. *(978-0-7475-9586-1(0))* 2007. (ENG., 608p. *(978-0-7475-9106-1(7))* Bloomsbury Publishing Plc.

—Harry Potter & the Deathly Hallows. braille ed. 2007. (Harry Potter Ser.: Year 7). (J). (gr. 4-7). 34.99 *(978-0-939173-57-0(3))* National Braille Pr.

—Harry Potter & the Deathly Hallows. 2010. 25.00 *(978-1-60686-882-9(9))* Perfection Learning Corp.

—Harry Potter & the Deathly Hallows, 17 vols. 2007. (Harry Potter Ser.: 7). (YA). 129.79 *(978-1-4281-6654-7(8))*; 131.75 *(978-1-4281-6652-3(1))* Recorded Bks., Inc.

—Harry Potter & the Deathly Hallows. GrandPré, Mary, illus. (Harry Potter Ser.: 7). (ENG.). (J). 2009. 784p. (gr. 4-7). pap. 14.99 *(978-0-545-13970-0(8)*, Levine, Arthur A. Bks.) 2007. 784p. (gr. 5-9). 34.99 *(978-0-545-01022-1(5))* 2007. 816p. (gr. 4-7). 65.00 *(978-0-545-02937-7(6)*, Levine, Arthur A. Bks.) Scholastic, Inc.

—Harry Potter & the Deathly Hallows. l.t. ed. 2009. (ENG.). 970p. pap. 14.95 *(978-1-59413-355-8(7)*, Large Print Pr.) 2007. (Harry Potter Ser.: Year 7). (Illus.). 969p. (J). (gr. 4-7). 34.95 *(978-0-7862-9665-1(8))* Thorndike Pr.

—Harry Potter & the Deathly Hallows. (Harry Potter (Kazu Kibuishi Illustrations) Ser.: 7). 2013. lib. bdg. 29.40 *(978-0-606-32351-2(1))* 2009. lib. bdg. 26.95 *(978-0-606-00420-6(3))* Turtleback Bks. (Turtleback).

—Harry Potter & the Deathly Hallows. Bar-hillel, Gili, tr. from ENG. 2007. (Harry Potter Ser.: Year 7). (HEB., Illus.). 568p. (J). (gr. 4-7). pap. *(978-965-482-635-8(6))* Yediot Aharonot Bks., Miscal.

—Harry Potter & the Goblet of Fire. 2009. 10.24 *(978-0-7848-1587-8(9)*, Everbind) Marco Bk. Co.

—Harry Potter & the Goblet of Fire. (Harry Potter Ser.: 4). (J). 2006. 1.25 *(978-1-4193-8531-5(3))* 2003. 101.75 *(978-1-4025-6702-5(2))* Recorded Bks., Inc.

—Harry Potter & the Goblet of Fire. GrandPré, Mary, illus. l.t. ed. 2003. (Harry Potter Ser.: Vol. 4). (ENG.). 936p. pap. 11.66 *(978-1-59413-003-8(5))* Thorndike Pr.

—Harry Potter & the Goblet of Fire. 2013. (Harry Potter (Kazu Kibuishi Illustrations) Ser.: 4). lib. bdg. 26.95 *(978-0-606-32348-2(1)*, Turtleback) Turtleback Bks.

—Harry Potter & the Half-Blood Prince. 2005. (ENG.). cd-rom *(978-0-7475-8258-8(0))* Bloomsbury Publishing Plc.

—Harry Potter & the Half-Blood Prince, 9 vols. braille ed. 2005. (Harry Potter Ser.: Year 6). (J). (gr. 4-8). 29.99 *(978-0-939173-39-6(5)*, HALF) National Braille Pr.

—Harry Potter & the Half-Blood Prince. GrandPré, Mary, illus. 2006. (Harry Potter Ser.: Year 6). 652p. (gr. 4-8). 23.00 *(978-0-7569-6765-9(1))* Perfection Learning Corp.

—Harry Potter & the Half-Blood Prince. (Harry Potter Ser.: 6). (J). 2007. 1.25 *(978-1-4193-5430-4(2))* 2006. 110.75 *(978-1-4193-5436-6(1))* 2006. 193.75 *(978-1-4193-5432-8(9))* 2005. 113.75 *(978-1-4193-5434-2(5))* Recorded Bks., Inc.

—Harry Potter & the Half-Blood Prince. GrandPré, Mary, illus. (Harry Potter Ser.: 6). (ENG.). 672p. (J). (gr. 4-8). 2005. 29.99 *(978-0-439-78454-2(9))* 2006. reprint ed. per. 12.99 *(978-0-439-78596-9(0))* Scholastic, Inc. (Levine, Arthur A. Bks.).

—Harry Potter & the Half-Blood Prince. (Illus.). (J). (gr. 4-7). 2007. (ENG.). 832p. per. 14.95 *(978-1-59413-221-6(6))* 2005. (Harry Potter Ser.: Year 6). 831p. 29.95 *(978-0-7862-7745-2(9))* Thorndike Pr. (Large Print Pr.).

—Harry Potter & the Half-Blood Prince. 2013. (Harry Potter (Kazu Kibuishi Illustrations) Ser.: 6). lib. bdg. 26.95 *(978-0-606-32350-5(3)*, Turtleback) Turtleback Bks.

—Harry Potter & the Half Blood Prince - Chinese Language. 2005. (Harry Potter Ser.: Year 6). (CHI.). 496p. (YA). (gr. 4-8). pap. 28.95 *(978-7-02-005323-0(8)*, HAP06) People's Literature Publishing Hse. CHN. Dist: Chinasprout, Inc.

—Harry Potter & the Order of the Phoenix. (ENG.). 768p. (J). (gr. 6-10). pap. *(978-0-7475-6107-1(9))* Bloomsbury Publishing Plc.

—Harry Potter & the Order of the Phoenix. 2008. *(978-977-14-2697-4(4))* Nahdat Misr Bkshop for Printing and Pubs.

—Harry Potter & the Order of the Phoenix, 13 vols. braille ed. 2003. (Harry Potter Ser.: Year 5). (YA). 29.99 *(978-0-939173-38-9(7))* National Braille Pr.

—Harry Potter & the Order of the Phoenix. 2003. (Harry Potter Ser.: Year 5). (CHI.). 575p. (YA). pap. 26.95 *(978-7-02-004327-9(5)*, HAP05) People's Literature Publishing Hse. CHN. Dist: Chinasprout, Inc.

—Harry Potter & the Order of the Phoenix. 2004. (Harry Potter Ser.). 870p. (gr. 4-6). 16.49 *(978-0-7569-4163-5(6))* Perfection Learning Corp.

—Harry Potter & the Order of the Phoenix. 2003. (ENG.). 768p. *(978-1-55192-570-7(2))* Raincoast Bk. Distribution.

—Harry Potter & the Order of the Phoenix. GrandPré, Mary, illus. (Harry Potter Ser.: 5). (ENG.). (J). (gr. 3-7). 2004. 896p. mass mkt. 12.99 *(978-0-439-35807-1(8)*, Scholastic Paperbacks) 2003. 870p. 29.99 *(978-0-439-35806-4(X))* Scholastic, Inc.

—Harry Potter & the Order of the Phoenix. l.t. ed. 2003. (Harry Potter Ser.: Year 5). 1093p. 29.95 *(978-0-7862-5778-2(4)*, Large Print Pr.) Thorndike Pr.

—Harry Potter & the Order of the Phoenix. GrandPré, Mary, illus. l.t. ed. 2003. (Thorndike Young Adult Ser.). (ENG.). 1232p. (J). (gr. 4-7). per. 14.95 *(978-1-59413-112-7(0)*, Large Print Pr.) Thorndike Pr.

—Harry Potter & the Order of the Phoenix. (Harry Potter (Kazu Kibuishi Illustrations) Ser.: 5). 2013. lib. bdg. 26.95 *(978-0-606-32349-9(X))* 2004. lib. bdg. 24.50 *(978-0-613-99916-8(9))* Turtleback Bks. (Turtleback).

—Harry Potter & the Philosopher's Stone. 2014. (ENG., Illus.). 352p. *(978-1-4088-5589-8(5))* Bloomsbury Publishing Plc.

—Harry Potter & the Prisoner of Azkaban. 2009. 9.64 *(978-0-7848-1542-7(9)*, Everbind) Marco Bk. Co.

—Harry Potter & the Prisoner of Azkaban. 2005. (Harry Potter Ser.: Year 3). (CHI.). 260p. (YA). pap. 16.95 *(978-7-02-003345-4(8)*, HAP03) People's Literature Publishing Hse. CHN. Dist: Chinasprout, Inc.

—Harry Potter & the Prisoner of Azkaban, 10 vols. 2003. (Harry Potter Ser.: 3). (J). 84.75 *(978-1-4025-6700-1(6))* Recorded Bks., Inc.

—Harry Potter & the Prisoner of Azkaban. l.t. ed. 2003. (Harry Potter Ser.: Year 3). (ENG.). 592p. pap. 13.95 *(978-1-59413-002-1(7)*, Large Print Pr.) Thorndike Pr.

—Harry Potter & the Prisoner of Azkaban. 2013. (Harry Potter (Kazu Kibuishi Illustrations) Ser.: 3). lib. bdg. 24.50 *(978-0-606-32347-5(3)*, Turtleback) Turtleback Bks.

—Harry Potter & the Sorcerer's Stone. 2014. (ENG.). lthr. 79.00 *(978-1-62715-772-8(7))* Leatherbound Bestsellers.

—Harry Potter & the Sorcerer's Stone. 2009. 8.44 *(978-0-7848-2438-2(X))*; 10.84 *(978-0-7848-1357-7(4))* Marco Bk. Co. (Everbind).

—Harry Potter & the Sorcerer's Stone. 2003. (Harry Potter Ser.: Year 1). (CHI.). 191p. (YA). pap. 14.95 *(978-7-02-003343-0(1)*, HAP01) People's Literature Publishing Hse. CHN. Dist: Chinasprout, Inc.

—Harry Potter & the Sorcerer's Stone. (Harry Potter Ser.: 1). (J). 2004. 1.25 *(978-1-4025-6757-5(X))* 2003. 80.75 *(978-1-4025-6696-7(4))* Recorded Bks., Inc.

—Harry Potter & the Sorcerer's Stone. Kay, Jim, illus. 2015. (Harry Potter Ser.: 1). (ENG.). 256p. (J). (gr. 3). 39.99 *(978-0-545-79035-2(2)*, Levine, Arthur A. Bks.) Scholastic, Inc.

—Harry Potter & the Sorcerer's Stone, Bk. 1. 2013. (Harry Potter Ser.: 1). (ENG., Illus.). 336p. (J). (gr. 4). pap. 12.99 *(978-0-545-58288-9(1))* Scholastic, Inc.

—Harry Potter & the Sorcerer's Stone. 2013. (Harry Potter (Kazu Kibuishi Illustrations) Ser.: 1). lib. bdg. 24.50 *(978-0-606-32345-1(7)*, Turtleback) Turtleback Bks.

—Harry Potter e a Camara Secreta. (Harry Potter Ser.: Year 2).Tr. of Harry Potter & the Chamber of Secrets. (POR.). pap. 28.95 *(978-85-325-1166-9(X))* Rocco, Editora, Ltda BRA. Dist: Distribooks, Inc.

—Harry Potter e a Pedra Filosofal. (Harry Potter Ser.: Year 1).Tr. of Harry Potter & the Philospher's Stone. (POR.). pap. 28.95 *(978-85-325-1101-0(5))* Rocco, Editora, Ltda BRA. Dist: Distribooks, Inc.

—Harry Potter e a Prisioneiro de Azkaban. (Harry Potter Ser.: Year 3).Tr. of Harry Potter & the Prisioner of Azkaban. (POR.). pap. 29.95 *(978-85-325-1206-2(2))* Rocco, Editora, Ltda BRA. Dist: Distribooks, Inc.

—Harry Potter e il Prigioniero di Azkaban. (Harry Potter Ser.: Year 3).Tr. of Harry Potter & the Prisioner of Azkaban. (ITA.). pap. 32.95 *(978-88-7782-852-1(8))* Salani ITA. Dist: Distribooks, Inc.

—Harry Potter e o Cálice de Fogo. (Harry Potter Ser.: Year 4).Tr. of Harry Potter & the Goblet of Fire. (POR.). pap. 38.95 *(978-85-325-1252-9(6))* Rocco, Editora, Ltda BRA. Dist: Distribooks, Inc.

—Harry Potter et la Coupe de Feu. (Harry Potter Ser.: Year 4).Tr. of Harry Potter & the Goblet of Fire. (FRE., Illus.). 766p. pap. 19.95 *(978-2-07-054351-9(X))* Gallimard, Editions FRA. Dist: Distribooks, Inc.

—Harry Potter y el Prisionero de Azkaban. 2004. (Harry Potter Ser.: Year 3).Tr. of Harry Potter & the Prisioner of Azkaban. (SPA., Illus.). 360p. (gr. 3-18). 17.95 (978-84-7888-519-0(6), SAL1889) Emece Editores ESP. Dist: Lectorum Pubns., Inc.

—Harry Potter y la Camara Secreta. 2004. (Harry Potter Ser.: Year 2).Tr. of Harry Potter & the Chamber of Secrets. (SPA., Illus.). 288p. (YA). (gr. 3-18). 15.95 (978-84-7888-495-7(5), SAL4595) Emece Editores ESP. Dist: Lectorum Pubns., Inc.

—Harry Potter y la Piedra Filosofal. 2004. (Harry Potter Ser.: Year 1).Tr. of Harry Potter & the Sorcerer's Stone. (SPA., Illus.). 256p. (YA). (gr. 7-18). 15.95 (978-84-7888-445-2(9), SAL2819) Emece Editores ESP. Dist: Lectorum Pubns., Inc.

Rowling, J. K. & Scholastic, Inc. Staff. Harry Potter. 2007. (Harry Potter Ser.: Years 1-7). (ENG.). (J). (gr. 3-7). 205.93 (978-0-545-04425-7(1), Levine, Arthur A. Bks.) Scholastic, Inc.

HOISTING MACHINERY

see also Cranes, Derricks, etc.; Elevators

Reinke, Beth. Cranes Lift! 2017. (Bumba Books (tm) — Construction Zone Ser.). (ENG.). (J). (gr. -1-1). pap. 6.99 **(978-1-5124-5542-7(3))**; (Illus.). lib. bdg. 25.32 **(978-1-5124-3356-2(X))** Lerner Publishing Group.

HOLIDAY COOKING

see also Christmas Cooking

Cornell, Kari A., ed. Holiday Cooking Around the World. Wolfe, Robert L. & Wolfe, Diane, illus. Wolfe, Robert L. & Wolfe, Diane, photos by. 2nd rev. exp. ed. 2003. (Easy Menu Ethnic Cookbooks). 72p. (J). (gr. 5-12). pap. 7.95 (978-0-8225-4159-2(9)) Lerner Publishing Group.

Kuskowski, Alex. Super Simple Holiday Cookies: Easy Cookie Recipes for Kids!, 1 vol. 2016. (Super Simple Cookies Ser.). (ENG., Illus.). 32p. (J). (gr. k-4). 27.07 (978-1-62403-949-2(9)) ABDO Publishing Co.

Labat, Yancey C., illus. Fun Foods for Holidays! 2007. 56p. (J). (978-0-439-83229-8(2)) Scholastic, Inc.

Price, Pamela S. Cool Holiday Treats: Easy Recipes for Kids to Bake, 1 vol. 2010. (Cool Baking Ser.). (ENG.). 32p. (gr. 3-6). 28.50 (978-1-60453-776-5(0), Checkerboard Library) ABDO Publishing Co.

Publications International Ltd. Staff, ed. Jello Simply Stunning Holiday Desserts. 2008. spiral bd. 3.98 (978-1-4127-2866-9(5)) Publications International, Ltd.

Raabe, Emily. A Hanukkah Holiday Cookbook. 2009. (Festive Foods for the Holidays Ser.). 24p. (gr. 3-3). 42.50 (978-1-61512-595-1(7), PowerKids Pr.) Rosen Publishing Group, Inc., The.

—A Kwanzaa Holiday Cookbook. 2009. (Festive Foods for the Holidays Ser.). 24p. (gr. 3-3). 42.50 (978-1-61512-596-8(5), PowerKids Pr.) Rosen Publishing Group, Inc., The.

Rauchwerger, Lisa. Chocolate Chip Challah: And Other Twists on the Jewish Holiday Table. Rauchwerger, Lisa, illus. 2004. (Illus.). 127p. (J). (gr. k-3). pap. 17.95 (978-0-8074-0700-4(3), 510606) URJ Pr.

Rigg, Annie & Woram, Catherine. Fun Christmas Crafts to Make & Bake: Over 60 Festive Projects to Make with Your Kids. 2012. (ENG., Illus.). 160p. (978-1-84975-273-2(7)) Ryland Peters & Small.

Strand, Jessica & Massman-Johnson, Tammy. Kids in the Holiday Kitchen. 2008. (J). (978-0-8118-6135-9(X)) Chronicle Bks. LLC.

Strand, Jessica, et al. Kids in the Holiday Kitchen. 2008. (ENG., Illus.). 96p. (gr. 8-17). pap. 16.95 (978-0-8118-6139-7(2)) Chronicle Bks. LLC.

Tabs, Judy & Steinberg, Barbara. Matzah Meals: A Passover Cookbook for Kids. Hauser, Bill, illus. 2004. (Passover Ser.). (ENG.). 64p. (J). (gr. 3-5). pap. 7.95 (978-1-58013-086-8(0), Kar-Ben Publishing) Lerner Publishing Group.

Tuminelly, Nancy. Cool Holiday Food Art: Easy Recipes That Make Food Fun to Eat!, 1 vol. 2011. (Cool Food Art Ser.). (ENG., Illus.). 32p. (J). (gr. 3-6). 28.50 (978-1-61613-365-8(1), Checkerboard Library) ABDO Publishing Co.

—Super Simple Holiday Treats: Easy No-Bake Recipes for Kids, 1 vol. 2010. (Super Simple Cooking Ser.). (ENG.). 32p. (gr. 3-6). 27.07 (978-1-61613-386-3(4), Super SandCastle) ABDO Publishing Co.

Vega, Ali. Witches' Brew & Other Horrifying Party Foods. 2017. (Little Kitchen of Horrors Ser.). (ENG.). 32p. (J). (gr. 2-5). 12.99 **(978-1-5124-3777-5(8)**, Lerner Pubns.); 39.99 **(978-1-5124-3776-8(X)**, Lerner Pubns.); 39.99 **(978-1-5124-2808-7(6)**, Lerner Pubns.); (Illus.). 26.65 (978-1-5124-2576-5(1)) Lerner Publishing Group.

Webb, Lois Sinaiko & Roten, Lindsay Grace. Holidays of the World Cookbook for Students, 1 vol. 2nd rev. ed. 2011. (C). 496p. pap. 36.00 (978-0-313-39790-5(2), A2878P); (Illus.). 442p. 105.00 (978-0-313-38393-9(6), A2878C) ABC-CLIO, LLC.

Zakon, Miriam. Kids' Kosher Cookbook. 2005. (Illus.). 111p. (J). 16.99 (978-1-56871-376-2(2)) Targum Pr., Inc.

HOLIDAY DECORATIONS

Barchers, Suzanne. The Big Book of Holidays & Cultural Celebrations. rev. ed. 2013. (Classroom Resources Ser.). (ENG., Illus.). 296p. (gr. k-2). pap. 19.99 (978-1-4258-1046-7(2)) Shell Educational Publishing.

Bledsoe, Karen E. Chinese New Year Crafts. 2005. (Fun Holiday Crafts Kids Can Do! Ser.). (Illus.). 32p. (J). lib. bdg. 23.94 (978-0-7660-2347-5(8), Enslow Elementary) Enslow Pubs., Inc.

—Fun Chinese New Year Crafts. 2015. (Kid Fun Holiday Crafts! Ser.). 32p. (J). (gr. 3-4). 23.94 (978-0-7660-6240-5(6)) Enslow Pubs., Inc.

Corwin, Judith Hoffman. Kwanzaa Crafts: A Holiday Craft Book. 2004. (Illus.). 48p. (J). (gr. k-4). reprint ed. pap. 6.00 (978-0-7567-7711-1(9)) DIANE Publishing Co.

Daning, Tom. Fun-To-Make Crafts for Halloween. 2005. (Illus.). 63p. (J). (978-0-329-43124-2(2)) Boyds Mills Pr.

Dickinson, Gill. Creative Crafts for Kids. 2013. (ENG.). 256p. pap. 14.99 (978-0-600-62710-4(1), Hamlyn) Octopus Publishing Group GBR. Dist: Hachette Bk. Group.

Erlbach, Arlene & Erlbach, Herb. Fun Mother's Day Crafts. 2015. (Kid Fun Holiday Crafts! Ser.). 32p. (J). (gr. 3-4). 23.94 (978-0-7660-6245-0(7)) Enslow Pubs., Inc.

—Fun Thanksgiving Day Crafts. 2015. (Kid Fun Holiday Crafts! Ser.). 32p. (J). (gr. 3-4). 23.94 (978-0-7660-6250-4(3)) Enslow Pubs., Inc.

—Fun Valentine's Day Crafts. 2015. (Kid Fun Holiday Crafts! Ser.). 32p. (J). (gr. 3-4). 23.94 (978-0-7660-6255-9(4)) Enslow Pubs., Inc.

Erlbach, Arlene & Erlbach, Herbert. Mother's Day Crafts. 2005. (Fun Holiday Crafts Kids Can Do! Ser.). (Illus.). 32p. (J). lib. bdg. 23.94 (978-0-7660-2348-2(6), Enslow Elementary) Enslow Pubs., Inc.

Felix, Rebecca. Mini Holiday Crafts. 2017. (Mini Makers Ser.). (ENG.). 32p. (J). (gr. 2-5). 12.99 **(978-1-5124-3837-6(5)**, Lerner Pubns.); 39.99 **(978-1-5124-3836-9(7)**, Lerner Pubns.); 39.99 **(978-1-5124-2811-7(6)**, Lerner Pubns.); (Illus.). 26.65 (978-1-5124-2633-5(4)) Lerner Publishing Group.

Fun for Little Hands Series, 7 bks., Set. 2003. (Illus.). (J). 21.33 (978-0-929371-92-4(5), Kar-Ben Publishing) Lerner Publishing Group.

Gnojewski, Carol. Cinco de Mayo Crafts. 2005. (Fun Holiday Crafts Kids Can Do! Ser.). (Illus.). 32p. (J). lib. bdg. 23.94 (978-0-7660-2344-4(3), Enslow Elementary) Enslow Pubs., Inc.

—Earth Day Crafts. 2005. (Fun Holiday Crafts Kids Can Do! Ser.). (Illus.). 32p. (J). lib. bdg. 23.94 (978-0-7660-2346-8(X), Enslow Elementary) Enslow Pubs., Inc.

Harbo, Christopher L. Easy Holiday Origami, 1 vol. 2010. (Easy Origami Ser.). (ENG.). 24p. (gr. 1-2). lib. bdg. 25.32 (978-1-4296-5387-9(6), First Facts) Capstone Press of Coughlan Cos.

Hardyman, Robyn. Origami Fun: Holidays. 2017. (Origami Fun Ser.). (ENG., Illus.). 24p. (YA). (gr. 3-7). lib. bdg. 25.95 **(978-1-62617-711-6(2))** Bellwether Media.

Holland, Gini. Holiday Crafts. 2013. (From Trash to Treasure Ser.). 32p. (J). (gr. 3-6). 26.50 (978-1-4777-1286-3(0)); pap. 11.75 (978-1-4777-1366-2(2)) Rosen Publishing Group, Inc., The. (PowerKids Pr.).

McGee, Randel. Celebrate Chinese New Year with Paper Crafts. 2015. (Celebrate Holidays with Paper Crafts Ser.). 48p. (J). (gr. 3-4). 25.27 (978-0-7660-6350-1(X)) Enslow Pubs., Inc.

—Celebrate Day of the Dead with Paper Crafts. 2015. (Celebrate Holidays with Paper Crafts Ser.). 48p. (J). (gr. 3-4). 25.27 (978-0-7660-6360-0(7)) Enslow Pubs., Inc.

—Celebrate Halloween with Paper Crafts. 2015. (Celebrate Holidays with Paper Crafts Ser.). 48p. (J). (gr. 3-4). 25.27 (978-0-7660-6365-5(8)) Enslow Pubs., Inc.

—Celebrate Kwanzaa with Paper Crafts. 2015. (Celebrate Holidays with Paper Crafts Ser.). 48p. (J). (gr. 3-4). 25.27 (978-0-7660-6370-9(4)) Enslow Pubs., Inc.

—Celebrate Valentine's Day with Paper Crafts. 2015. (Celebrate Holidays with Paper Crafts Ser.). 48p. (J). (gr. 3-4). 25.27 (978-0-7660-6375-4(5)) Enslow Pubs., Inc.

—Paper Crafts for Chinese New Year. (Paper Craft Fun for Holidays Ser.). (Illus.). 48p. (J). (gr. 3-4). 2012. pap. 8.95 (978-1-4644-0319-4(8)) 2008. lib. bdg. 25.27 (978-0-7660-2950-7(6)) Enslow Pubs., Inc. (Enslow Elementary).

—Paper Crafts for Day of the Dead. (Paper Craft Fun for Holidays Ser.). (Illus.). 48p. (J). (gr. 3-4). 2012. pap. 8.95 (978-1-4644-0323-1(6)) 2008. lib. bdg. 25.27 (978-0-7660-2951-4(4)) Enslow Pubs., Inc. (Enslow Elementary).

—Paper Crafts for Halloween. 2012. (Paper Craft Fun for Holidays Ser.). (Illus.). 48p. (J). (gr. 3-4). pap. 8.95 (978-1-4644-0325-5(2), Enslow Elementary) Enslow Pubs., Inc.

—Paper Crafts for Kwanzaa. 2012. (Paper Craft Fun for Holidays Ser.). (Illus.). 48p. (J). (gr. 3-4). pap. 8.95 (978-1-4644-0327-9(9), Enslow Elementary) Enslow Pubs., Inc.

—Paper Crafts for Valentine's Day. 2012. (Paper Craft Fun for Holidays Ser.). (Illus.). 48p. (J). (gr. 3-4). pap. 8.95 (978-1-4644-0329-3(5), Enslow Elementary) Enslow Pubs., Inc.

Mercer, Abbie. Happy New Year. (Holiday Fun Ser.). 24p. 2009. (gr. 2-3). 42.50 (978-1-61513-376-5(3), PowerKids Pr.) 2007. (Illus.). (J). (gr. 3-7). lib. bdg. 22.60 (978-1-4042-3808-4(5)) Rosen Publishing Group, Inc., The.

—Happy Valentine's Day. 2007. (Holiday Fun Ser.: Vol. 4). (Illus.). 24p. (J). (gr. 3-7). lib. bdg. 22.60 (978-1-4042-3809-1(3)) Rosen Publishing Group, Inc., The.

Muehlenhardt, Amy Bailey. Thanksgiving Crafts, 1 vol. Takvorian, Nadine, illus. 2010. (Thanksgiving Ser.). (ENG.). 24p. (gr. 1-2). lib. bdg. 27.32 (978-1-4048-6282-1(X)) Picture Window Bks.

Numeroff, Laura Joffe. Easter Egg Designs. Date not set. (J). 7.99 (978-0-694-01419-4(2)) HarperCollins Pubs.

Owen, Ruth. Holiday Crafts. 2013. (From Trash to Treasure Ser.). 32p. (J). (gr. 3-6). pap. 70.50 (978-1-4777-1367-9(0), PowerKids Pr.) Rosen Publishing Group, Inc., The.

Rau, Dana Meachen. Creating Thanksgiving Crafts. Petelinsek, Kathleen, illus. 2013. (How-To Library). (ENG.). 32p. (J). (gr. 3-6). 28.50 (978-1-62431-148-2(2), 202912); pap. 14.21 (978-1-62431-280-9(2), 202914) Cherry Lake Publishing.

—Creating Winter Crafts. Petelinsek, Kathleen, illus. 2013. (How-To Library). (ENG.). 32p. (J). (gr. 3-6). 28.50 (978-1-62431-150-5(4), 202920); pap. 14.21 (978-1-62431-282-3(9), 202922) Cherry Lake Publishing.

Robinson, Fay. Father's Day Crafts. 2005. (Fun Holiday Crafts Kids Can Do! Ser.). (Illus.). 32p. (J). lib. bdg. 23.94 (978-0-7660-2343-7(5), Enslow Elementary) Enslow Pubs., Inc.

—Halloween Crafts. 2004. (Fun Holiday Crafts Kids Can Do! Ser.). (Illus.). 32p. (J). lib. bdg. 23.94 (978-0-7660-2236-2(6)) Enslow Pubs., Inc.

Ross, Kathy. All New Crafts for Halloween. Leonard, Barbara, illus. 2003. (All New Holiday Crafts for Kids Ser.). 48p. lib. bdg. 23.90 (978-0-7613-2554-3(9), Millbrook Pr.) Lerner Publishing Group.

—All New Crafts for Halloween. Leonard, Barbara & Holm, Sharon, illus. 2003. (All New Holiday Crafts for Kids Ser.). (ENG.). 48p. (gr. k-3). pap. 7.95 (978-0-7613-1577-3(2), Millbrook Pr.) Lerner Publishing Group.

—All New Crafts for Mother's Day & Father's Day. Holm, Sharon Lane, illus. 2007. (All New Holiday Crafts for Kids Ser.). (ENG.). 48p. (gr. k-3). per. 7.95 (978-0-8225-6368-6(1), First Avenue Editions) Lerner Publishing Group.

—All New Crafts for Thanksgiving. Holm, Sharon Lane, illus. 2005. 48p. (gr. k-2). (J). per. 7.95 (978-0-7613-2394-5(5), First Avenue Editions); (ENG.). lib. bdg. 25.26 (978-0-7613-2922-0(6), Millbrook Pr.) Lerner Publishing Group.

—More of the Best Holiday Crafts Ever! Holm, Sharon Lane, illus. 2005. 160p. (J). (gr. k-4). bds. 19.95 (978-0-7613-2345-7(7)) Lerner Publishing Group.

Skillicorn, Helen. Spooky Crafts. 2010. (Creative Crafts for Kids Ser.). 32p. (J). (gr. 2-5). lib. bdg. 28.00 (978-1-4339-3564-0(3)); (Illus.). pap. 10.50 (978-1-4339-3565-7(1)) Stevens, Gareth Publishing LLLP. (Gareth Stevens Learning Library).

Speechley, Greta. Valentine Crafts. 2010. (Creative Crafts for Kids Ser.). 32p. (J). (gr. 2-5). lib. bdg. 28.00 (978-1-4339-3600-5(3)); (Illus.). pap. 10.50 (978-1-4339-3598-5(8)) Stevens, Gareth Publishing LLLP. (Gareth Stevens Learning Library).

Strand, Jessica. Holiday Crafting & Baking with Kids: Gifts, Sweets, & Treats for the Whole Family! Herring, Aimée, photos by. 2011. (ENG., Illus.). 128p. (gr. 13-17). pap. 19.95 (978-1-4521-0109-5(4)) Chronicle Bks. LLC.

Strand, Jessica & Massman-Johnson, Tammy. Kids in the Holiday Kitchen. 2008. (J). (978-0-8118-6135-9(X)) Chronicle Bks. LLC.

Strand, Jessica, et al. Kids in the Holiday Kitchen. 2008. (ENG., Illus.). 96p. (gr. 8-17). pap. 16.95 (978-0-8118-6139-7(2)) Chronicle Bks. LLC.

Visca, Curt & Visca, Kelley. How to Draw Cartoon Holiday Symbols. 2004. (Kid's Guide to Drawing Ser.). (Illus.). 24p. (YA). (gr. 2-5). lib. bdg. 25.25 (978-0-8239-6726-1(3)) Rosen Publishing Group, Inc., The.

HOLIDAYS

see also Fasts and Feasts

also names of holidays, e.g. Fourth of July

ABDO Publishing Company. Holidays Set 1. 2003. (Holidays Set 1 Ser.). (gr. k-4). 153.90 (978-1-57765-950-1(3), Buddy Bks.) ABDO Publishing Co.

ABDO Publishing Company Staff. Holidays II. 2005. (Holidays Set 2 Ser.). (gr. k-4). 162.42 (978-1-59197-584-7(0), Buddy Bks.) ABDO Publishing Co.

—Holidays Set 3. 2011. (Holidays Set 3 Ser.). (Illus.). 24p. 153.90 (978-1-61783-037-2(2), Buddy Bks.) ABDO Publishing Co.

ABDO Publishing Company Staff & Dash, Meredith. National Holidays. 2014. (National Holidays Ser.: 6). (ENG.). 24p. (J). (gr. 4-8). lib. bdg. 171.00 (978-1-62970-042-7(8)) ABDO Publishing Co.

Abramovitz, Melissa & Cella, Clara. Let's Celebrate. 2012. (Let's Celebrate Ser.). (ENG.). 24p. (gr. k-1). pap. 250.20 (978-1-4296-9395-0(9)); lib. bdg. 159.90 (978-1-4296-9169-7(7)) Capstone Press of Coughlan Cos. (Pebble Plus).

Adler, David A. The Story of Hanukkah. Weber, Jill, illus. 2012. (ENG.). 32p. (J). (gr. -1-2). pap. 6.99 (978-0-8234-2547-1(9)) Holiday Hse., Inc.

Allen, Heather. BOOST Earth Day Is Every Day! Activity Book. 2013. (BOOST Educational Ser.). (ENG.). 48p. (J). (gr. 3-5). pap. 5.99 (978-0-486-49433-3(0)) Dover Pubns., Inc.

Aloian, Molly. Canada Day. 2009. (Celebrations in My World Ser.). (ENG., Illus.). 32p. (J). (gr. k-2). pap. (978-0-7787-4770-3(0)); (gr. 1-3). (978-0-7787-4752-9(2)) Crabtree Publishing Co.

—Cultural Traditions in Australia. 2012. (ENG.). 32p. (J). (978-0-7787-7516-4(X)); (Illus.). pap. (978-0-7787-7521-8(6)) Crabtree Publishing Co.

—Cultural Traditions in Brazil. 2012. (ENG.). 32p. (J). lib. bdg. (978-0-7787-7583-6(6)); (Illus.). pap. (978-0-7787-7590-4(9)) Crabtree Publishing Co.

—Cultural Traditions in Canada. 2014. (ENG., Illus.). 32p. (J). (978-0-7787-0297-9(9)) Crabtree Publishing Co.

—Cultural Traditions in Israel. 2014. (ENG., Illus.). 32p. (J). (978-0-7787-0303-7(7)) Crabtree Publishing Co.

—Cultural Traditions in Russia. 2012. (ENG.). 32p. (J). pap. (978-0-7787-7595-9(X)); lib. bdg. (978-0-7787-7588-1(7)) Crabtree Publishing Co.

—Cultural Traditions in South Africa. 2014. (ENG., Illus.). 32p. (J). (978-0-7787-0304-4(5)) Crabtree Publishing Co.

—Cultural Traditions in Thailand. 2012. (ENG.). 32p. (J). (978-0-7787-7519-5(4)); (Illus.). pap. (978-0-7787-7524-9(0)) Crabtree Publishing Co.

—Cultural Traditions in the United States. 2014. (ENG., Illus.). 32p. (J). (978-0-7787-0305-1(3)) Crabtree Publishing Co.

—Remembrance Day. 2010. (ENG., Illus.). 32p. (J). (978-0-7787-4765-9(4)); pap. (978-0-7787-4783-3(2)) Crabtree Publishing Co.

Aloian, Molly & Peppas, Lynn. Cultural Traditions in Mexico. 2012. (ENG.). 32p. (J). lib. bdg. (978-0-7787-7587-4(9)) Crabtree Publishing Co.

Aloian, Molly & Peppas, Lynne. Cultural Traditions in Mexico. 2012. (ENG.). 32p. (J). pap. (978-0-7787-7594-2(1)) Crabtree Publishing Co.

American Holidays. 2004. (Illus.). lib. bdg. 7.95 (978-0-8225-4780-8(5)) Lerner Publishing Group.

Amstutz, Lisa J. Diwali. 2017. (Holidays Around the World Ser.). (ENG.). 24p. (gr. k-1). lib. bdg. 21.99 (978-1-5157-4853-3(7), Pebble Bks.) Capstone Press of Coughlan Cos.

—Holidays Around the World. 2017. (Holidays Around the World Ser.). (ENG.). 24p. (gr. k-1). 131.94 (978-1-5157-4881-6(2), Pebble Bks.) Capstone Press of Coughlan Cos.

Ancona, George. Mis Fiestas: My Celebrations. 2005. (Somos Latinos (We Are Latinos) Ser.).Tr. of My Celebrations. (ENG & SPA., Illus.). 32p. (J). (gr. 1-3). lib. bdg. 21.00 (978-0-516-25290-2(9)) Scholastic Library Publishing.

Appleby, Alex. Feliz Da de la Tierra! / Happy Earth Day!, Vol. 1. 2014. (¡Felices Fiestas! / Happy Holidays! Ser.). (SPA & BYN.). 24p. (J). (gr. k-k). 22.60 (978-1-4339-9956-7(0)) Stevens, Gareth Publishing LLLP.

—Happy Earth Day!, Vol. 1. 2014. (Happy Holidays! Ser.). 24p. (J). (gr. k-k). (ENG.). 22.60 (978-1-4339-9935-2(8)); pap. 8.15 (978-1-4339-9937-6(4)) Stevens, Gareth Publishing LLLP.

—Happy Valentine's Day!, Vol. 1. 2014. (Happy Holidays! Ser.). (Illus.). 24p. (J). (gr. k-k). (ENG.). 22.60 (978-1-4339-9951-2(X)); pap. 8.15 (978-1-4339-9953-6(6)) Stevens, Gareth Publishing LLLP.

Ard, Catherine. Origami Holidays. 2015. (Amazing Origami Ser.). (ENG.). 32p. (J). (gr. 2-3). 26.60 (978-1-4824-2200-9(X)) Stevens, Gareth Publishing LLLP.

Berendes, Mary. Holidays & Celebrations (Los Días de Fiestas y Las Celebraciones) Petelinsek, Kathleen, illus. 2008. (WordBooks/Libros de Palabras Ser.). (SPA & ENG.). 24p. (J). (gr. k-3). 25.64 (978-1-59296-991-3(7), 201093) Child's World, Inc., The.

Besel, Jennifer M. Holiday Sketchbook. Makuc, Lucy, illus. 2013. (Holiday Sketchbook Ser.). (ENG.). (gr. 1-2). 40p. pap. 19.80 (978-1-4765-3653-8(8)); 24p. lib. bdg. 101.28 (978-1-4765-3652-1(X)) Capstone Press of Coughlan Cos. (First Facts).

Best Holiday Books, 17 bks., Set. (Illus.). (J). (gr. 1-4). lib. bdg. 322.15 (978-0-89490-337-3(3)) Enslow Pubs., Inc.

Betances, Abigail. American Holidays. 2009. (Real Life Readers Ser.). 12p. (gr. 1-2). pap. 5.90 (978-1-4042-7911-7(3), Rosen Classroom) Rosen Publishing Group, Inc., The.

Birenbaum, Barbara. Groundhog Willie's Shadow. 2006. (Story Within a Story Ser.). (ENG., Illus.). 32p. (J). (gr. 3-5). (978-0-935343-74-8(1)) Peartree (r).

—Groundhogs Across America: Story Within a Story(c). 2016. (ENG., Illus.). 44p. (J). (gr. 2-5). 21.00 (978-0-935343-44-1(X)) Peartree (r).

Bix, Jasper. Winter Holidays. 2016. (Winter Fun Ser.). (ENG., Illus.). 24p. (J). (gr. k-k). pap. 8.15 (978-1-4824-3763-8(5)) Stevens, Gareth Publishing LLLP.

Blitz, Shmuel & Katz, Tova. Artscroll Children's Machzor: [ha-Mahazor Ha-Rishon: Rosh Ha-Shanah Ve-Yom Kipur]. 2009. (HEB., Illus.). 96p. (978-1-4226-0910-1(3)) Mesorah Pubns., Ltd.

Bodden, Valerie. Thanksgiving. 2005. (My First Look at Holidays Ser.). (Illus.). 24p. (J). (gr. k-3). lib. bdg. 15.95 (978-1-58341-370-8(7), Creative Education) Creative Co., The.

Boothroyd, Jennifer. Holidays. 2006. (First Step Nonfiction - We Are Alike & Different Ser.). (ENG., Illus.). 8p. (gr. -1-1). pap. 4.95 (978-0-8225-5728-9(2), Lerner Pubns.) Lerner Publishing Group.

Braun, Eric. Plan a Holiday Party. 2014. (Party Time! Ser.). (ENG., Illus.). 32p. (gr. 4-8). lib. bdg. 26.60 (978-1-4677-3834-7(4), Lerner Pubns.) Lerner Publishing Group.

Bredeson, Carmen. St. Patrick's Day. 2003. (Rookie Read-About Holidays Ser.). (Illus.). 32p. (J). 20.50 (978-0-516-25857-7(5), Children's Pr.) Scholastic Library Publishing.

Brill, Marlene Targ. El Día de los Veteranos. Fitzpatrick, Julia, tr. from ENG. Wang, Qi Z., Illus. 2005. (Yo Solo - Festividades (on My Own - Holidays) Ser.). (SPA.). 48p. (gr. 2-4). lib. bdg. 25.26 (978-0-8225-3120-3(8)) Lerner Publishing Group.

—Veterans Day. Wang, Qi Z., illus. 2005. (On My Own Holidays Ser.). (ENG.). 48p. (gr. 2-4). pap. 6.95 (978-1-57505-766-8(2)) Lerner Publishing Group.

Brode, Robyn. April;abril. 2009. (Months of the Year/Meses del año Ser.). (ENG & SPA.). 24p. (J). (gr. -1-3). pap. 8.15 (978-1-4339-2109-4(X), Weekly Reader Leveled Readers) Stevens, Gareth Publishing LLLP.

—April/Abril. 2009. (Months of the Year/Meses del año Ser.). (ENG & SPA.). 24p. (J). (gr. -1-3). lib. bdg. 22.00 (978-1-4339-1932-9(X), Weekly Reader Leveled Readers) Stevens, Gareth Publishing LLLP.

—December. 2nd rev. ed. 2009. (Months of the Year Ser.). 24p. (J). (gr. -1-3). pap. 8.15 (978-1-4339-2105-6(7)); lib. bdg. 22.00 (978-1-4339-1928-2(1)) Stevens, Gareth Publishing LLLP. (Weekly Reader Leveled Readers).

—December;diciembre. 2009. (Months of the Year/Meses del año Ser.). (ENG & SPA.). 24p. (J). (gr. -1-3). pap. 8.15 (978-1-4339-2117-9(0), Weekly Reader Leveled Readers) Stevens, Gareth Publishing LLLP.

—December/Diciembre. 2009. (Months of the Year/Meses del año Ser.). (ENG & SPA.). 24p. (J). (gr. -1-3). lib. bdg. 22.00 (978-1-4339-1940-4(0), Weekly Reader Leveled Readers) Stevens, Gareth Publishing LLLP.

—February;febrero. 2009. (Months of the Year/Meses del año Ser.). (ENG & SPA.). 24p. (J). (gr. -1-3). pap. 8.15 (978-1-4339-2107-0(3), Weekly Reader Leveled Readers) Stevens, Gareth Publishing LLLP.

—February/Febrero. 2009. (Months of the Year/Meses del año Ser.). (ENG & SPA.). 24p. (J). (gr. -1-3). lib. bdg. 22.00 (978-1-4339-1930-5(3), Weekly Reader Leveled Readers) Stevens, Gareth Publishing LLLP.

—January;enero. 2009. (Months of the Year/Meses del año Ser.). (ENG & SPA.). 24p. (J). (gr. -1-3). pap. 8.15 (978-1-4339-2106-3(5), Weekly Reader Leveled Readers) Stevens, Gareth Publishing LLLP.

—January/Enero. 2009. (Months of the Year/Meses del año Ser.). (ENG & SPA.). 24p. (J). (gr. -1-3). lib. bdg. 22.00 (978-1-4339-1929-9(X), Weekly Reader Leveled Readers) Stevens, Gareth Publishing LLLP.

—July;julio. 2009. (Months of the Year/Meses del año Ser.). (ENG & SPA.). 24p. (J). (gr. -1-3). pap. 8.15 (978-1-4339-2112-4(X), Weekly Reader Leveled Readers) Stevens, Gareth Publishing LLLP.

—July/Julio. 2009. (Months of the Year/Meses del año Ser.). (ENG & SPA.). 24p. (J). (gr. -1-3). lib. bdg. 22.00 (978-1-4339-1935-0(4), Weekly Reader Leveled Readers) Stevens, Gareth Publishing LLLP.

—June;junio. 2009. (Months of the Year/Meses del año Ser.). (ENG & SPA.). 24p. (J). (gr. -1-3). pap. 8.15 (978-1-4339-2111-7(1), Weekly Reader Leveled Readers) Stevens, Gareth Publishing LLLP.

—June/Junio. 2009. (Months of the Year/Meses del año Ser.). (ENG & SPA.). 24p. (J). (gr. -1-3). lib. bdg. 22.00 (978-1-4339-1934-3(6), Weekly Reader Leveled Readers) Stevens, Gareth Publishing LLLP.

—March;marzo. 2009. (Months of the Year/Meses del año Ser.). (ENG & SPA.). 24p. (J). (gr. -1-3). pap. 8.15 (978-1-4339-2108-7(1), Weekly Reader Leveled Readers) Stevens, Gareth Publishing LLLP.

—March/Marzo. 2009. (Months of the Year/Meses del año Ser.). (ENG & SPA.). 24p. (J). (gr. -1-3). lib. bdg. 22.00 (978-1-4339-1931-2(1), Weekly Reader Leveled Readers) Stevens, Gareth Publishing LLLP.

—May;mayo. 2009. (Months of the Year/Meses del año Ser.). (ENG & SPA.). 24p. (J). (gr. -1-3). pap. 8.15 *(978-1-4339-2110-0(3),* Weekly Reader Leveled Readers) Stevens, Gareth Publishing LLLP.
—May/Mayo. 2009. (Months of the Year/Meses del año Ser.). (ENG & SPA.). 24p. (J). (gr. -1-3). lib. bdg. 22.00 *(978-1-4339-1933-6(8),* Weekly Reader Leveled Readers) Stevens, Gareth Publishing LLLP.
—November;noviembre. 2009. (Months of the Year/Meses del año Ser.). (ENG & SPA.). 24p. (J). (gr. -1-3). pap. 8.15 *(978-1-4339-2116-2(2),* Weekly Reader Leveled Readers) Stevens, Gareth Publishing LLLP.
—November/Noviembre. 2009. (Months of the Year/Meses del año Ser.). (ENG & SPA.). 24p. (J). (gr. -1-3). lib. bdg. 22.00 *(978-1-4339-1939-8(7),* Weekly Reader Leveled Readers) Stevens, Gareth Publishing LLLP.
—October. 2nd rev. ed. 2009. (Months of the Year Ser.). 24p. (J). (gr. -1-3). pap. 8.15 *(978-1-4339-2103-2(0));* lib. bdg. 22.00 *(978-1-4339-1926-8(5))* Stevens, Gareth Publishing LLLP. (Weekly Reader Leveled Readers).
—October;octubre. 2009. (Months of the Year/Meses del año Ser.). (ENG & SPA.). 24p. (J). (gr. -1-3). pap. 8.15 *(978-1-4339-2115-5(4),* Weekly Reader Leveled Readers) Stevens, Gareth Publishing LLLP.
—October/Octubre. 2009. (Months of the Year/Meses del año Ser.). (ENG & SPA.). 24p. (J). (gr. -1-3). lib. bdg. 22.00 *(978-1-4339-1938-1(9),* Weekly Reader Leveled Readers) Stevens, Gareth Publishing LLLP.
—September;septiembre. 2009. (Months of the Year/Meses del año Ser.). (ENG & SPA.). 24p. (J). (gr. -1-3). pap. 8.15 *(978-1-4339-2114-8(6),* Weekly Reader Leveled Readers) Stevens, Gareth Publishing LLLP.
—September/Septiembre. 2009. (Months of the Year/Meses del año Ser.). (ENG & SPA.). 24p. (J). (gr. -1-3). lib. bdg. 22.00 *(978-1-4339-1937-4(0),* Weekly Reader Leveled Readers) Stevens, Gareth Publishing LLLP.
Brode, Robyn & Nations, Susan. April. 2nd rev. ed. 2009. (Months of the Year Ser.). (ENG.). 24p. (J). (gr. -1-3). pap. 8.15 *(978-1-4339-2097-4(2));* lib. bdg. 22.00 *(978-1-4339-1920-6(6))* Stevens, Gareth Publishing LLLP. (Weekly Reader Leveled Readers).
—February. 2nd rev. ed. 2009. (Months of the Year Ser.). (ENG.). 24p. (J). (gr. -1-3). pap. 8.15 *(978-1-4339-2095-0(6));* lib. bdg. 22.00 *(978-1-4339-1918-3(4))* Stevens, Gareth Publishing LLLP. (Weekly Reader Leveled Readers).
—January. 2nd rev. ed. 2009. (Months of the Year Ser.). (ENG.). 24p. (J). (gr. -1-3). pap. 8.15 *(978-1-4339-2094-3(8));* lib. bdg. 22.00 *(978-1-4339-1917-6(6))* Stevens, Gareth Publishing LLLP. (Weekly Reader Leveled Readers).
—July. 2nd rev. ed. 2009. (Months of the Year Ser.). (ENG.). 24p. (J). (gr. -1-3). pap. 8.15 *(978-1-4339-2100-1(6));* lib. bdg. 22.00 *(978-1-4339-1923-7(0))* Stevens, Gareth Publishing LLLP. (Weekly Reader Leveled Readers).
—June. 2nd rev. ed. 2009. (Months of the Year Ser.). (ENG.). 24p. (J). (gr. -1-3). pap. 8.15 *(978-1-4339-2099-8(9));* lib. bdg. 22.00 *(978-1-4339-1922-0(2))* Stevens, Gareth Publishing LLLP. (Weekly Reader Leveled Readers).
—March. 2nd rev. ed. 2009. (Months of the Year Ser.). (ENG.). 24p. (J). (gr. -1-3). pap. 8.15 *(978-1-4339-2096-7(4));* lib. bdg. 22.00 *(978-1-4339-1919-0(2))* Stevens, Gareth Publishing LLLP. (Weekly Reader Leveled Readers).
—May. 2nd rev. ed. 2009. (Months of the Year Ser.). (ENG.). 24p. (J). (gr. -1-3). pap. 8.15 *(978-1-4339-2098-1(0));* lib. bdg. 22.00 *(978-1-4339-1921-3(4))* Stevens, Gareth Publishing LLLP. (Weekly Reader Leveled Readers).
—November. 2nd rev. ed. 2009. (Months of the Year Ser.). (ENG.). 24p. (J). (gr. -1-3). pap. 8.15 *(978-1-4339-2104-9(9));* lib. bdg. 22.00 *(978-1-4339-1927-5(3))* Stevens, Gareth Publishing LLLP. (Weekly Reader Leveled Readers).
—September. 2nd rev. ed. 2009. (Months of the Year Ser.). (ENG.). 24p. (J). (gr. -1-3). pap. 8.15 *(978-1-4339-2102-5(2));* lib. bdg. 22.00 *(978-1-4339-1925-1(7))* Stevens, Gareth Publishing LLLP. (Weekly Reader Leveled Readers).
Broslavick, Chris & Pichler, Tony. Totally Lent! A Teen's Journey to Easter 2007. 2006. (Illus.). 64p. pap. 5.95 *(978-1-933178-44-8(2))* Pflaum Publishing Group.
—Totally Lent! A Teen's Journey to Easter 2008. 2007. (Illus.). 64p. (YA). (gr. 8-12). pap. 5.95 *(978-1-933178-72-1(8))* Pflaum Publishing Group.
Brown, Jo Ann. Fat Tuesday. 2012. (Illus.). 34p. pap. 19.99 *(978-1-62230-353-3(9))* Salem Author Services.
Bullard, Lisa. Cloverleaf Books#8482; - Holidays & Special Day. 2012. (Holidays & Special Day Ser.). (Illus.). 24p. (J). (gr. k-2). lib. bdg. 107.69 *(978-0-7613-5061-3(6),* Millbrook Pr.) Lerner Publishing Group.
—Cloverleaf Books#8482; - Holidays & Special Days: 6Pack Set. Saunders, Katie, illus. 2012. (Holidays & Special Days Ser.). 24p. (J). (gr. k-2). pap. 237.69 *(978-0-7613-9252-1(1),* Millbrook Pr.) Lerner Publishing Group.
—Cloverleaf Books#8482; - Holidays & Special Days: Single Copy Set. Saunders, Katie, illus. 2012. (Holidays & Special Days Ser.). 24p. (J). (gr. k-2). pap. 39.62 *(978-0-7613-9251-4(3),* Millbrook Pr.) Lerner Publishing Group.
Burns, Kylie. Cultural Traditions in Kenya. 2015. (ENG., Illus.). 32p. (J). *(978-0-7787-8063-2(5))* Crabtree Publishing Co.
Burton, Margie, et al. Celebrations Around the World. 2011. (Early Connections Ser.). (J). *(978-1-61672-516-7(8))* Benchmark Education Co.
Cabello-Argandona, Roberto. Cinco de Mayo: An Illustrated History. 2008. (Nuestra Historia Ser.). 208p. pap. 24.95 *(978-1-888205-05-3(9))* Floricanto Pr.
Catalani, Dorothy Kon & Catalani, Jim. Wethechildren, Future Leaders - Patriotic 123. Stephens, Joan Wilson, illus. 2010. 16p. pap. 10.95 *(978-1-936343-19-5(3))* Peppertree Pr., The.
Celebrations. 2016. (Celebrations Ser.). 00024p. (J). (gr. 1-1). 94.40 *(978-1-4994-2627-4(5),* PowerKids Pr.) Rosen Publishing Group, Inc., The.
Celebrations & Rituals Around the World Set, 5 vol. set. 2003. (gr. 4-8). 154.00 *(978-0-7166-5020-1(7))* World Bk., Inc.
Cella, Clara. Groundhog Day, 1 vol. 2012. (Let's Celebrate Ser.). (ENG., Illus.). 24p. (gr. k-1). lib. bdg. 26.65 *(978-1-4296-8731-7(2),* Pebble Plus) Capstone Press of Coughlan Cos.
—Memorial Day. 2012. (Let's Celebrate Ser.). (ENG.). 24p. (gr. k-1). pap. 41.70 *(978-1-4296-9391-2(6));* (Illus.). 26.65 *(978-1-4296-8732-4(0));* (Illus.). pap. 7.29 *(978-1-4296-9390-5(8))* Capstone Press of Coughlan Cos. (Pebble Plus).
Cella, Clara & Abramovitz, Melissa. Let's Celebrate. 2012. (Let's Celebrate Ser.). (ENG.). 24p. (gr. k-1). pap. 14.58 *(978-1-4296-9394-3(0),* Pebble Plus) Capstone Press of Coughlan Cos.
Chan, Hingman. Celebrating Chinese New Year: An Activity Book, Second Edition. Yoon, Selina & Chen, Michael Yoon, eds. 2009. (Illus.). 32p. (J). (gr. k-5). pap., act. bk. ed. 8.95 *(978-1-932457-04-9(6),* Asia for Kids) Infini Pr., LLC.
Charleston, Janice. Our Country's Holidays. 2012. (I'm an American Citizen Ser.). (ENG., Illus.). 24p. (J). (gr. 1-3). 22.60 *(978-1-4488-8587-9(6),* PowerKids Pr.) Rosen Publishing Group, Inc., The.
Clark Sawyer, J. Holiday Colors: Our Favorite Days. 2015. (Illus.). 24p. (J). lib. bdg. *(978-1-62724-325-4(9))* Bearport Publishing Co., Inc.
—Los Colores de Las Celebraciones: Nuestros Días Favoritos. 2014. (Los Colores Cuentan una Historia Ser.). (SPA.). 24p. (J). (gr. -1-3). lib. bdg. 23.93 *(978-1-62724-467-1(0))* Bearport Publishing Co., Inc.
Cohn, Scotti. Big Cat, Little Kitty, 1 vol. Detwiler, Susan, illus. 2011. (ENG.). 32p. (J). (gr. -1-3). 16.95 *(978-1-60718-124-8(X));* pap. 8.95 *(978-1-60718-134-7(7))* Arbordale Publishing.
Conger, Holli, illus. Cultural Holidays, 6 vols., Set. Incl. Chinese New Year. Marsico, Katie. 28.50 *(978-1-60270-600-2(X));* Christmas. Owens, L. L. 28.50 *(978-1-60270-601-9(8));* Cinco de Mayo. Owens, L. L. 28.50 *(978-1-60270-602-6(6));* Hanukkah. Owens, L. L. 28.50 *(978-1-60270-603-3(4));* Ramadan. Anderson, Sheila. 28.50 *(978-1-60270-605-7(0));* (gr. -1-4). (Cultural Holidays Ser.). (Illus.). 32p. 2009. 171.00 *(978-1-60270-599-9(2),* Looking Glass Library- Nonfiction) Magic Wagon.
Coppendale, Jean. Special Holidays. 2006. (Illus.). 32p. (YA). (gr. 1-18). lib. bdg. 27.10 *(978-1-931983-98-3(4))* Chrysalis Education.
Cox, Tracey M. Shaping up the Year. Bell, Samantha, illus. 2009. 24p. pap. 10.95 *(978-1-935137-73-3(5))* Guardian Angel Publishing, Inc.
Dalrymple, Lisa. Cultural Traditions in South Korea. 2016. (ENG., Illus.). 32p. (J). lib. bdg. *(978-0-7787-8088-5(0))* Crabtree Publishing Co.
Dash, Meredith. Día de Los Veteranos de Guerra. 2015. (Días Festivos Ser.). (SPA., Illus.). 24p. (gr. k-1). pap. 7.95 *(978-1-4966-0421-7(0))* Capstone Classroom.
—Veterans Day, 1 vol. 2014. (National Holidays Ser.). (ENG., Illus.). 24p. (J). (gr. 4-8). lib. bdg. 28.50 *(978-1-62970-048-9(7))* ABDO Publishing Co.
Dawson, Emily C. Holidays & Celebrations. 2010. (Special Days Ser.). 24p. 25.65 *(978-1-60753-030-5(9))* Amicus Publishing.
Dayton, Connor. Memorial Day. 2012. (American Holidays Ser.). (ENG., Illus.). 24p. (J). (gr. k-3). pap. 8.25 *(978-1-4488-6244-3(2));* lib. bdg. 22.60 *(978-1-4488-6143-9(8))* Rosen Publishing Group, Inc., The. (PowerKids Pr.).
—Memorial Day: Día de Los Caídos. Alamán, Eduardo, tr. from ENG. 2012. (American Holidays / Celebraciones en los Estados Unidos Ser.). (SPA & ENG., Illus.). 24p. (J). (gr. k-3). lib. bdg. 22.60 *(978-1-4488-6709-7(6),* PowerKids Pr.) Rosen Publishing Group, Inc., The.
—Veterans Day. 2012. (American Holidays Ser.). (ENG., Illus.). 24p. (J). (gr. k-3). pap. 8.25 *(978-1-4488-6250-4(7));* lib. bdg. 22.60 *(978-1-4488-6146-0(2))* Rosen Publishing Group, Inc., The. (PowerKids Pr.).
—Veterans Day: Día de Los Veteranos. Alamán, Eduardo, tr. from ENG. 2012. (American Holidays / Celebraciones en los Estados Unidos Ser.). (SPA & ENG.). 24p. (gr. k-3). lib. bdg. 22.60 *(978-1-4488-6712-7(6),* PowerKids Pr.) Rosen Publishing Group, Inc., The.
de la Vega, Eida, tr. Celebrath with Me/Celebra Conmigo, 4 vols., Set. Incl. Christmas/Navidad. Hinman, Christmas. lib. bdg. 25.70 *(978-1-58415-864-6(6));* Independence Day/Día de la Independencia. Scholl, Elizabeth. lib. bdg. 25.70 *(978-1-58415-862-2(X));* Memorial Day/Día de los Caídos. Orr, Tamra. lib. bdg. 25.70 *(978-1-58415-863-9(8));* Thanksgiving/Accion de Gracias. Hinman, Bonnie. lib. bdg. 25.70 *(978-1-58415-861-5(1));* (Illus.). 32p. (J). (gr. -1-2). 2010. (SPA.). 2010. Set lib. bdg. 102.00 *(978-1-58415-865-3(4))* Mitchell Lane Pubs., Inc.
Dia De los Veteranos, 18 vols., Set. Incl. Año Nuevo Chino. Dickmann, Nancy. (Illus.). pap. 6.29 *(978-1-4329-5399-7(0));* Día de las Elecciones. Rissman, Rebecca. (Illus.). pap. 6.29 *(978-1-4329-5412-3(1));* Diwali. Dickmann, Nancy. pap. 6.29 *(978-1-4329-5400-0(8));* Janucá. Dickmann, Nancy. pap. 6.29 *(978-1-4329-5401-7(6));* Navidad. Dickmann, Nancy. pap. 6.29 *(978-1-4329-5396-6(6));* Pascua. Dickmann, Nancy. (Illus.). pap. 6.29 *(978-1-4329-5397-3(4));* Ramadán y el Eid Al-Fitr. Dickmann, Nancy. (Illus.). pap. 6.29 *(978-1-4329-5398-0(2));* (gr. -1-1). (Fiestas Ser.). (SPA.). 24p. 2011. Set pap. 44.03 *(978-1-4329-5414-7(8),* Bellota) Heinemann-Raintree.
Dean, Sheri. Martin Luther King, Jr. Day. 2010. (Our Country's Holidays Ser.). (ENG.). 24p. (J). (gr. k-3). pap. 8.15 *(978-1-4339-3918-1(5));* lib. bdg. 22.60 *(978-1-4339-3917-4(7))* Stevens, Gareth Publishing LLLP.
—Memorial Day. 2010. (Our Country's Holidays Ser.). (ENG.). 24p. (J). (gr. k-3). pap. 8.15 *(978-1-4339-3921-1(5));* lib. bdg. 22.60 *(978-1-4339-3920-4(7))* Stevens, Gareth Publishing LLLP.
—Memorial Day (Día de Los Caídos) 2006. (Our Country's Holidays/ Las fiestas de nuestra nacion Ser.). (SPA., Illus.). 24p. (gr. k-3). pap. 8.15 *(978-0-8368-6528-8(6),* Weekly Reader Leveled Readers) Stevens, Gareth Publishing LLLP.
—Presidents' Day. 2010. (Our Country's Holidays Ser.). (ENG.). 24p. (J). (gr. k-3). pap. 8.15 *(978-1-4339-3924-2(X));* lib. bdg. 22.60 *(978-1-4339-3923-5(1))* Stevens, Gareth Publishing LLLP.
Demi Staff. Happy, Happy Chinese New Year! 2003. (ENG., Illus.). 24p. (J). (gr. -1-2). 8.99 *(978-0-375-82642-9(4),* Knopf Bks. for Young Readers) Random Hse. Children's Bks.
DeRubertis, Barbara. Let's Celebrate Earth Day. 2015. (Holidays & Heroes Ser.). (ENG., Illus.). 32p. (J). (gr. 1-4). pap. 7.95 *(978-1-57565-651-9(5))* Kane Press, Inc.
—Let's Celebrate Memorial Day. 2016. (Holidays & Heroes Ser.). (ENG., Illus.). 32p. (J). (gr. 1-4). pap. 7.95 *(978-1-57565-831-5(3))* Kane Press, Inc.
—Let's Celebrate Veterans Day. 2014. (Holidays & Heroes Ser.). (Illus.). 32p. (J). (gr. 1-3). pap. 7.95 *(978-1-57565-653-3(1))* Kane Press, Inc.
DeSpain, Pleasant. Tales of Holidays, Vol. 5. Bell, Don, illus. 2005. (Books of Nine Lives: Vol. 5). (ENG.). 80p. (J). (gr. 3-6). 14.95 *(978-0-87483-667-7(0))* August Hse. Pubs., Inc.
Día del Árbol, 18 vols., Set. Incl. Día de las Elecciones. Rissman, Rebecca. (Illus.). 22.65 *(978-1-4329-5393-5(1));* Diwali. Dickmann, Nancy. 22.65 *(978-1-4329-5381-2(8));* Janucá. Dickmann, Nancy. 22.65 *(978-1-4329-5382-9(6));* Ramadán y el Eid Al-Fitr. Dickmann, Nancy. (Illus.). 22.65 *(978-1-4329-5379-9(6));* (gr. -1-1). (Fiestas Ser.). (SPA.). Illus.). 24p. 2011. Set lib. bdg. 113.25 *(978-1-4329-5395-9(8),* Bellota) Heinemann-Raintree.
Dickmann, Nancy. Año Nuevo Chino, 1 vol. 2011. (Fiestas Ser.). (SPA & ENG., Illus.). 24p. (gr. -1-1). pap. 6.29 *(978-1-4329-5399-7(0),* Bellota) Heinemann-Raintree.
—Diwali, 1 vol. 2011. (Fiestas Ser.). (SPA & ENG.). 24p. (gr. -1-1). 22.65 *(978-1-4329-5381-2(8));* pap. 6.29 *(978-1-4329-5400-0(8))* Heinemann-Raintree. (Bellota).
Ditchfield, Christin. Memorial Day. 2003. (True Bks.). (ENG., Illus.). 48p. (J). 25.00 *(978-0-516-22783-2(1),* Children's Pr.) Scholastic Library Publishing.
Dolphin, Colleen. April Fools' Day to Z Day: Holidays from A to Z, 1 vol. 2009. (Let's Learn A to Z Ser.). (ENG., Illus.). 32p. (J). (gr. -1-2). 27.07 *(978-1-60453-495-5(8))* ABDO Publishing Co.
Dorling Kindersley Publishing Staff. Baby's First Thanksgiving. 2017. (ENG.). 14p. (J). (— 1). bds. 5.99 ***(978-1-4654-6349-4(6),*** DK Children) Dorling Kindersley Publishing, Inc.
—Celebrations Around the World. 2008. 16p. (J). (gr. k-5). 2.49 *(978-0-7566-3316-5(8))* Dorling Kindersley Publishing, Inc.
—Pop-Up Peekaboo Pumpkin. 2017. (ENG.). 12p. (J). (— 1). bds. 9.99 *(978-1-4654-5276-4(1),* DK Children) Dorling Kindersley Publishing, Inc.
Douglass, Susan L. Ramadan. Reeves, Jeni, illus. (On My Own Holidays Ser.). 48p. (gr. 2-4). 2004. (J). lib. bdg. 25.26 *(978-0-87614-932-4(8))* 2003. (ENG.). pap. 6.95 *(978-1-57505-584-8(8))* Lerner Publishing Group.
Dworkin, Motoko. A Year in Japan: Folktales, Songs & Art for the Classroom. 2nd ed. 2012. (Illus.). 151p. pap. 26.95 *(978-0-9836716-1-9(3))* Paradise Copies, Inc.
Evans, Lucas. A Year of Happy Holidays. 2012. 36p. pap. 24.99 *(978-1-300-19923-6(7))* Lulu Pr., Inc.
Feldman, Jean R. & Karapetkova, Holly. Earth Day (Tune, Clap Your Hands Together) Lap Book. 2010. (ENG., Illus.). 12p. (gr. -1-k). 9.95 *(978-1-61590-218-7(X))* Rourke Educational Media.
Ferreira, Bailey & Ferreira, Ann Devine. Bailey Enjoys His First Holiday Season. 2011. 32p. 17.50 *(978-1-4269-5814-4(5))* Trafford Publishing.
Ferry, Sharon. Granddad Bud: A Veterans Day Story. 2010. 36p. 12.99 *(978-1-4520-5029-4(5))* AuthorHouse.
Festive Foods for the Holidays. (Illus.). (J). (gr. k-5). 119.70 *(978-0-8239-7182-4(1))* Rosen Publishing Group, Inc., The.
Fishman, Cathy Goldberg. Hanukkah. Young, Mary O'Keefe, illus. 2004. (On My Own Holidays Ser.). 48p. (J). (gr. 2-4). lib. bdg. 25.26 *(978-1-57505-195-6(8))* Lerner Publishing Group.
—On Sukkot & Simchat Torah. Hall, Melanie, illus. 2006. (ENG.). 32p. (J). (gr. -1-4). lib. bdg. 17.95 *(978-1-58013-165-0(4),* Kar-Ben Publishing) Lerner Publishing Group.
—Passover. Marshall, Ann & Reeves, Jeni, illus. 2006. (On My Own Holidays Ser.). (ENG.). 48p. (gr. 2-4). 25.26 *(978-1-57505-656-2(9))* Lerner Publishing Group.
—Passover. Reeves, Jeni, illus. 2006. (On My Own Holidays Ser.). (ENG.). 48p. (gr. 2-4). per. 6.95 *(978-1-57505-695-1(X),* First Avenue Editions) Lerner Publishing Group.
Foran, Jill. Christmas. 2003. (Celebrating Cultures Ser.). (Illus.). 24p. (J). lib. bdg. 24.45 *(978-1-59036-091-0(5))* Weigl Pubs., Inc.
—Hanukkah. 2003. (Celebrating Cultures Ser.). (Illus.). 24p. (J). lib. bdg. 24.45 *(978-1-59036-092-7(3))* Weigl Pubs., Inc.
—Martin Luther King Jr. Day. 2004. (American Holidays Ser.). (Illus.). 24p. (J). lib. bdg. 24.45 *(978-1-59036-107-8(5));* (gr. 1-3). per. 8.95 *(978-1-59036-167-2(9))* Weigl Pubs., Inc.
Gallagher, Debbie. Family Celebrations. 2008. (Families Ser.). 32p. (gr. 1-2). lib. bdg. 18.56 *(978-0-7614-3133-6(0),* Benchmark Bks.) Marshall Cavendish Corp.
Garcia, James. Cinco de Mayo: A Mexican Holiday about Unity & Pride. 2003. (Proud Heritage: the Hispanic Library). (ENG., Illus.). 40p. (J). (gr. 3-6). 29.93 *(978-1-56766-174-3(2),* 200003) Child's World, Inc., The.
Gerace, Frank E. & Leslie, Clare Walker. The Ancient Celtic Festivals: And How We Celebrate Them Today. 2nd ed. 2008. (ENG., Illus.). 64p. (J). (gr. 4-7). pap. 12.95 *(978-1-59477-256-6(8))* Inner Traditions International, Ltd.
Gibbons, Gail. Groundhog Day! Gibbons, Gail, illus. 2007. (ENG., Illus.). 32p. (J). (gr. -1-3). pap. 7.99 *(978-0-8234-2116-9(3))* Holiday Hse., Inc.
—Thanksgiving Is... 2004. (ENG., Illus.). 32p. (J). tchr. ed. 17.95 *(978-0-8234-1849-7(9))* Holiday Hse., Inc.
Gilchrist, Cherry. A Calendar of Festivals. Cann, Helen, illus. 2006. 79p. (J). (gr. 4-8). reprint ed. pap. 10.00 *(978-1-4223-5551-0(9))* DIANE Publishing Co.
Gillespie, Katie. Halloween. 2015. (Let's Celebrate American Holidays Ser.). (ENG.). (J). lib. bdg. 27.13 *(978-1-4896-3621-8(8),* AV2 by Weigl) Weigl Pubs., Inc.
—Ramadan. 2015. (Let's Celebrate American Holidays Ser.). (ENG.). (J). lib. bdg. 27.13 *(978-1-4896-3633-1(1),* AV2 by Weigl) Weigl Pubs., Inc.
—Veterans' Day. 2015. (Let's Celebrate American Holidays Ser.). (ENG.). (J). lib. bdg. 27.13 *(978-1-4896-3637-9(4),* AV2 by Weigl) Weigl Pubs., Inc.
Glazer, Devorah. A Touch of the High Holidays: A Touch & Feel Book. Seva, illus. 2006. 16p. (J). bds. 7.95 *(978-0-8266-0020-2(4))* Merkos L'Inyonei Chinuch.
Gleason, Carrie. Day of the Dead. 2008. (Celebrations in My World Ser.). (ENG., Illus.). 32p. (J). (gr. k-3). pap. *(978-0-7787-4297-5(0));* lib. bdg. *(978-0-7787-4279-1(2))* Crabtree Publishing Co.
Gleisner, Jenna Lee. We Celebrate Cinco de Mayo in Spring. 2014. (21st Century Basic Skills Library: Let's Look at Spring Ser.). (ENG., Illus.). 24p. (J). (gr. k-3). pap. 12.79 *(978-1-62431-684-5(0),* 203141) Cherry Lake Publishing.
—We Celebrate Earth Day in Spring. 2014. (21st Century Basic Skills Library: Let's Look at Spring Ser.). (ENG., Illus.). 24p. (J). (gr. k-3). 22.79 *(978-1-62431-658-6(1),* 203144) Cherry Lake Publishing.
Gnojewski, Carol. Celebrating Cinco de Mayo. 2012. (Celebrating Holidays Ser.). 48p. (J). (gr. 3-18). 25.27 *(978-0-7660-4032-8(1),* Enslow Elementary) Enslow Pubs., Inc.
—Day of the Dead: A Latino Celebration of Family & Life. 2005. (Finding Out about Holidays Ser.). (Illus.). 48p. (J). lib. bdg. 23.93 *(978-0-7660-1780-1(X),* Enslow Elementary) Enslow Pubs., Inc.
—Kwanzaa: Seven Days of African-American Pride. 2004. (Finding Out about Holidays Ser.). (Illus.). 48p. (J). lib. bdg. 25.27 *(978-0-7660-2209-6(9))* Enslow Pubs., Inc.
—Ramadan: A Muslim Time of Fasting, Prayer, & Celebration. 2004. (Finding Out about Holidays Ser.). (Illus.). 48p. (J). (gr. 2-5). lib. bdg. 25.27 *(978-0-7660-2275-1(7))* Enslow Pubs., Inc.
Gosman, Gillian. Simple Machines & Holidays. 2014. (Simple Machines Everywhere Ser.). 24p. (J). (gr. k-3). pap. 49.50 *(978-1-4777-6643-9(X),* PowerKids Pr.) Rosen Publishing Group, Inc., The.
Grack, Rachel. Cinco de Mayo. 2017. (Celebrating Holidays! Ser.). (ENG.). 24p. (J). (gr. k-3). lib. bdg. 25.95 ***(978-1-62617-617-1(5),*** Blastoff! Readers) Bellwether Media.
—Groundhog Day. 2017. (Celebrating Holidays! Ser.). (ENG.). 24p. (J). (gr. k-3). lib. bdg. 25.95 ***(978-1-62617-620-1(5),*** Blastoff! Readers) Bellwether Media.
—Veterans Day. 2017. (Celebrating Holidays! Ser.). (ENG., Illus.). 24p. (J). (gr. k-3). lib. bdg. 25.95 ***(978-1-62617-624-9(8),*** Blastoff! Readers) Bellwether Media.
Gregoire, Maryellen. Fun Days! 2011. (Wonder Readers Emergent Level Ser.). (ENG.). 32p. (gr. -1-1). pap. 5.99 *(978-1-4296-7836-0(4),* Wonder Readers) Capstone Press of Coughlan Cos.
Gregory, Helen. Celebrations Around the World, 1 vol. (Wonder Readers Next Steps: Social Studies). (ENG.). (gr. -1-1). 2013. 20p. lib. bdg. 22.65 *(978-1-4765-0040-9(1))* 2011. 32p. pap. 5.99 *(978-1-4296-7799-8(6))* 2011. 16p. pap. 35.94 *(978-1-4296-8075-2(X))* Capstone Press of Coughlan Cos. (Wonder Readers).
Grolier Educational Staff, contrib. by. Argentina. 2003. (Illus.). 32p. (J). 309.00 *(978-0-7172-5788-1(6),* Grolier) Scholastic Library Publishing.
Grosshauser, Peter, illus. My Week. 2010. (My World Ser.). (ENG.). 24p. (J). (gr. -1-1). lib. bdg. 22.60 *(978-1-60754-951-2(4))* Windmill Bks.
Hall, Dorothy & Daniel, Marie. Guess the Covered Word for Seasons & Holidays. 2003. (Four Blocks Ser.). 48p. pap. 25.99 *(978-0-88724-125-3(5))* Four Blocks.
Hallinan, P. K. Holidays & Special Feelings, 8 bks. (Illus.). (J). lib. bdg. 108.60 *(978-1-56674-909-1(3))* Forest Hse. Publishing Co., Inc.
Halpern, Chaiky, illus. The Hamentash That Ran Away. (J). (gr. -1-4). 2.95 *(978-0-87306-250-3(7))* Feldheim Pubs.
Hamilton, Lynn. Memorial Day. 2015. (Illus.). 24p. (J). *(978-1-5105-0114-0(2))* SmartBook Media, Inc.
—Memorial Day. (American Celebrations Ser.). (Illus.). 24p. (J). 2010. (gr. 3-5). pap. 11.95 *(978-1-60596-778-3(5))* 2010. (gr. 3-5). lib. bdg. 25.70 *(978-1-60596-771-4(8))* 2004. lib. bdg. 24.45 *(978-1-59036-105-4(9))* 2004. (gr. 1-3). per. 8.95 *(978-1-59036-168-9(7))* Weigl Pubs., Inc.
—Presidents' Day. 2004. (American Holidays Ser.). (Illus.). 24p. (J). (gr. 1-3). lib. bdg. 24.45 *(978-1-59036-108-5(3));* per. 8.95 *(978-1-59036-169-6(5))* Weigl Pubs., Inc.
Harasymiw, Therese. World Holidays. 2009. (Real Life Readers Ser.). 24p. (gr. 3-4). pap. 8.25 *(978-1-4358-0129-5(6),* Rosen Classroom) Rosen Publishing Group, Inc., The.
Harrison, Lorraine. My Fourth of July. 2012. (InfoMax Readers Ser.). (ENG., Illus.). 24p. (J). (gr. 1-2). pap. 8.25 *(978-1-4488-9046-0(2),* Rosen Classroom) Rosen Publishing Group, Inc., The.
Harte, May. Halloween. 2009. (My Library of Holidays Ser.). 24p. (gr. 1-1). 37.50 *(978-1-61514-694-9(6),* PowerKids Pr.) Rosen Publishing Group, Inc., The.
—Halloween. Gonzalez, Tomas, tr. from ENG. 2004. (My Library of Holidays). (SPA & ENG., Illus.). 24p. (J). (gr. 1-2). lib. bdg. 16.00 *(978-1-4042-7529-4(0),* 1219514, PowerKids Pr.) Rosen Publishing Group, Inc., The.
—Thanksgiving. 2009. (My Library of Holidays Ser.). 24p. (gr. 1-1). 37.50 *(978-1-61514-697-0(0),* PowerKids Pr.) Rosen Publishing Group, Inc., The.
Haugen, Brenda. Holidays & Celebrations, 8 vols. Ouren, Todd, illus. Incl. Thanksgiving. (ENG., Illus.). 24p. (gr. k-3). 2003. 26.65 *(978-1-4048-0191-2(X));* (Holidays & Celebrations Ser.). (ENG.). Illus.). 24p. 2003. 26.65 o.p. *(978-1-4048-0190-5(1))* Picture Window Bks.
—Thanksgiving. Ouren, Todd, illus. 2003. (Holidays & Celebrations Ser.). (ENG.). 24p. (gr. k-3). 26.65 *(978-1-4048-0191-2(X))* Picture Window Bks.
Hayashi, Leslie Ann. Celebrating Holidays in Hawaii. Bishop, Kathleen Wong, illus. 2010. (ENG.). 36p. (J). 14.95 *(978-1-56647-914-1(2))* Mutual Publishing LLC.
Hayes, Amy. Celebrate Earth Day. 2015. (J). pap. *(978-1-62713-483-5(2))* Cavendish Square Publishing.
—Celebrate Memorial Day. 2015. (J). pap. *(978-1-62713-474-3(3))* Cavendish Square Publishing.
Heiligman, Deborah. Celebrate Diwali: With Sweets, Lights, & Fireworks. 2008. (Holidays Around the World Ser.). (ENG., Illus.). 32p. (J). (gr. 1-4). 6.95 *(978-1-4263-0291-6(6),* National Geographic Children's Bks.) National Geographic Society.
—Celebrate Independence Day: With Parades, Picnics, & Fireworks. 2007. (Holidays Around the World Ser.). (ENG., Illus.). 32p. (J). (gr. 2-5). lib. bdg. 23.90 *(978-1-4263-0075-2(1),* National Geographic Children's Bks.) National Geographic Society.
—Celebrate Rosh Hashanah & Yom Kippur: With Honey, Prayers, & the Shofar. 2007. (Holidays Around the World

H
I

Ser.). (ENG., Illus.). 32p. (J). (gr. 2-5). 15.95 (978-1-4263-0076-9(X)); lib. bdg. 23.90 (978-1-4263-0077-6(8)) National Geographic Society. (National Geographic Children's Bks.).

Heiligman, Deborah & Dennis, Matthew. Celebrate Independence Day: With Parades, Picnics, & Fireworks. 2007. (Holidays Around the World Ser.). (ENG., Illus.). 32p. (J). (gr. 2-5). 15.95 (978-1-4263-0074-5(3), National Geographic Children's Bks.) National Geographic Society.

Heiligman, Deborah & Yavari, Neguin. Celebrate Ramadan & Eid Al-Fitr: With Praying, Fasting, & Charity. 2009. (Holidays Around the World Ser.). (ENG., Illus.). 32p. (J). (gr. 1-4). 6.95 (978-1-4263-0476-7(5), National Geographic Children's Bks.) National Geographic Society.

Heinrichs, Ann. Cinco de Mayo. Petelinsek, Kathleen, illus. 2013. (Holidays & Celebrations Ser.). (ENG.). 32p. (J). (gr. k-3). 27.07 (978-1-62323-505-5(7), 206277) Child's World, Inc., The.

—Father's Day. Alley, R. W., illus. 2013. (Holidays & Celebrations Ser.). (ENG.). 32p. (J). (gr. k-3). 27.07 (978-1-62323-506-2(5), 206279) Child's World, Inc., The.

Heller, Daryl. Hanukkah / Jánuca. 2009. (My Library of Holidays / Mi biblioteca de celebraciones Ser.). (ENG & SPA.). 24p. (gr. 1-1). 37.50 (978-1-61514-701-4(2), Editorial Buenas Letras) Rosen Publishing Group, Inc., The.

—Hanukkah/Januca. 2004. (My Library of Holidays). (SPA & ENG., Illus.). 24p. (J). (gr. k-1). lib. bdg. 16.00 (978-1-4042-7525-6(8), PowerKids Pr.) Rosen Publishing Group, Inc., The.

—Kwanzaa. 2009. (My Library of Holidays Ser.). 24p. (gr. 1-1). 37.50 (978-1-61514-696-3(2), PowerKids Pr.) Rosen Publishing Group, Inc., The.

—Kwanzaa / Kwanzaa. 2009. (My Library of Holidays / Mi biblioteca de celebraciones Ser.). (ENG & SPA.). 24p. (gr. 1-1). 37.50 (978-1-61514-702-1(0), Editorial Buenas Letras) Rosen Publishing Group, Inc., The.

Herrington, Lisa M. Groundhog Day. 2013. (ENG.). 32p. (J). 23.00 (978-0-531-27203-9(6)); pap. 5.95 (978-0-531-27353-1(9)) Scholastic Library Publishing.

—Martin Luther King Jr. Day. 2013. (Rookie Read-About(tm) Holidays Ser.). (ENG.). 32p. (J). 25.00 (978-0-531-27205-3(2)); pap. 5.95 (978-0-531-27355-5(5)) Scholastic Library Publishing.

Hibbert, Clare. My Busy Day. Raga, Sylvia, illus. 2011. (Busy Times Ser.). (ENG.). 24p. (J). 19.99 (978-0-237-54263-4(3)) Evans Brothers, Ltd. GBR. Dist: Independent Pubs. Group.

Holidays & Celebrations Set, 10-Volumes. 2009. (Holidays & Celebrations Ser.). (gr. 5-8). 400.00 (978-1-60413-645-6(6), Chelsea Hse.) Facts On File, Inc.

Holidays & Culture [Really Good Stuff]. 2011. (Holidays & Culture Ser.). 24p. pap. 41.70 (978-1-4296-6087-7(2), First Facts) Capstone Press of Coughlan Cos.

Holidays & Festivals, 1 vol., Set. Incl. Chinese New Year. Dickmann, Nancy. (Illus.). pap. 6.29 (978-1-4329-4069-0(4)); Christmas. Dickmann, Nancy. pap. 6.29 (978-1-4329-4066-9(X)); Diwali. Dickmann, Nancy. (Illus.). pap. 6.29 (978-1-4329-4070-6(8)); Easter. Dickmann, Nancy. (Illus.). pap. 6.29 (978-1-4329-4067-6(8)); Election Day. Rissman, Rebecca. pap. 6.29 (978-1-4329-4082-9(1)); Hanukkah. Dickmann, Nancy. (Illus.). pap. 6.29 (978-1-4329-4071-3(6)); Ramadan & Id-Ul-Fitr. Dickmann, Nancy. pap. 6.29 (978-1-4329-4068-3(6)); (gr. -1-1). (Holidays & Festivals Ser.). (ENG.). 24p. 2010. Set pap. 107.10 o.p. (978-1-4329-4084-3(8), Acorn) Heinemann-Raintree.

Holidays Classroom Library. (gr. k-2). lib. bdg. 54.95 (978-0-7368-7143-3(8)) Red Brick Learning.

Holidays Complete Program. (gr. k-2). 311.95 (978-0-7368-7153-2(5)) Red Brick Learning.

Holidays of the Church Year. (Imagine That! Activity Bks.). (Illus.). 48p. (J). pap. 5.95 (978-0-87162-836-7(8), E2302) Warner Pr., Inc.

Houghton, Gillian. Christmas. 2009. (My Library of Holidays Ser.). 24p. (gr. 1-1). 37.50 (978-1-61514-692-5(X), PowerKids Pr.) Rosen Publishing Group, Inc., The.

—Easter. 2009. (My Library of Holidays Ser.). 24p. (gr. 1-1). 37.50 (978-1-61514-693-2(8), PowerKids Pr.) Rosen Publishing Group, Inc., The.

Howse, Jennifer. Boxing Day: Canadian Celebrations. 2010. (Illus.). 24p. (978-1-77071-637-7(8)) Weigl Educational Pubs. Ltd.

Hoyt-Goldsmith, Diane. Celebrating Chinese New Year. Migdale, Lawrence, photos by. (ENG., Illus.). 32p. (J). (gr. 4-6). pap. 6.95 (978-0-8234-1520-5(1)) Holiday Hse., Inc.

—Cinco de Mayo: Celebrating the Traditions of Mexico. Migdale, Lawrence, illus. 2008. (ENG.). 32p. (J). (gr. 3-7). 16.95 (978-0-8234-2107-7(4)) Holiday Hse., Inc.

Hudak, Heather C. Election Day with Code. 2012. (American Celebrations Ser.). (ENG., Illus.). 24p. (J). (gr. 3-5). pap. 12.95 (978-1-61913-866-7(2), AV2 by Weigl) Weigl Pubs., Inc.

Hutto, Rebekah McLeod. The Day When God Made the Church. 2016. (ENG., Illus.). 48p. (J). (gr. -1-8). pap. 15.99 (978-1-61261-564-6(3)) Paraclete Pr., Inc.

Hyde, Natalie. Cultural Traditions in Sweden. 2015. (ENG., Illus.). 32p. (J). (978-0-7787-8064-9(3)) Crabtree Publishing Co.

Ingalls, Ann. Christmas Traditions Around the World. Chavarri, Elisa, illus. 2013. (World Traditions Ser.). (ENG.). 32p. (J). (gr. k-3). 28.50 (978-1-61473-425-3(9), 205130) Child's World, Inc., The.

Isbell, Hannah. Groundhog Day. 2016. (Story of Our Holidays Ser.). (Illus.). 32p. (J). pap. 10.52 (978-0-7660-8332-5(2)) Enslow Pubs., Inc.

Ishii, Minako. Girls' Day/Boys' Day. Ishii, Minako, photos by. 2007. (Illus.). 64p. (J). (gr. 4-7). 16.95 (978-1-57306-274-9(X)) Bess Pr., Inc.

Jackson, Ellen B. The Summer Solstice. 2003. (Illus.). 32p. (J). (gr. 3-6). pap. 7.95 (978-0-7613-1985-6(9), Millbrook Pr.) Lerner Publishing Group.

Jango-Cohen, Judith. Chinese New Year. Chin, Jason, illus. 2010. (ENG.). 48p. (C). (gr. 2-4). pap. 11.95 (978-1-57505-763-7(8)) National Geographic School Publishing, Inc.

Jeffries, Joyce. Dinosaur Holidays. 2014. (Dinosaur School Ser.). 24p. (J). (gr. -1-1). pap. 8.15 (978-1-4824-0737-2(X)) Stevens, Gareth Publishing LLLP.

Kain, Kathleen. All about Holidays. Mahan, Ben, illus. 2004. (Treasure Tree Ser.). 32p. (J). (978-0-7166-1644-3(0)) World Bk., Inc.

—All about Holidays: With Inspector McQ. Mahan, Ben, illus. 2004. (Early Literacy Library). 32p. (J). (gr. 2-5). 219.00 (978-0-7166-1647-4(5)) World Bk., Inc.

Kaplan, Leslie C. Chinese New Year. (Library of Holidays Ser.). 24p. 2009. (gr. 2-3). 42.50 (978-1-60853-707-5(2)) 2004. (Illus.). (J). lib. bdg. 22.60 (978-0-8239-6658-5(5)) Rosen Publishing Group, Inc., The. (PowerKids Pr.).

—Flag Day. 2004. (Library of Holidays Ser.). (Illus.). 24p. (J). lib. bdg. 22.60 (978-0-8239-6659-2(3), PowerKids Pr.) Rosen Publishing Group, Inc., The.

—Independence Day. 2009. (Library of Holidays Ser.). 24p. (gr. 2-3). 42.50 (978-1-60853-713-6(7), PowerKids Pr.) Rosen Publishing Group, Inc., The.

—Martin Luther King Jr. Day. (Library of Holidays Ser.). 24p. 2009. (gr. 2-3). 42.50 (978-1-60853-714-3(5)) 2004. (Illus.). (J). lib. bdg. 22.60 (978-0-8239-6661-5(5)) Rosen Publishing Group, Inc., The. (PowerKids Pr.).

—Veterans Day. 2009. (Library of Holidays Ser.). 24p. (gr. 2-3). 42.50 (978-1-60853-718-1(8), PowerKids Pr.) Rosen Publishing Group, Inc., The.

Kenney, Karen Latchana. Memorial Day, 1 vol. Hunt, Judith A., illus. 2011. (Our Nation's Pride Set 2 Ser.). (ENG.). 32p. (J). (gr. 1-4). 28.50 (978-1-61641-152-7(X)) Magic Wagon.

Kessel, Joyce K. Halloween. Carlson, Nancy, illus. 2007. (Yo Solo - Festividades (on My Own - Holidays) Ser.). (SPA.). (gr. 2-4). pap. 39.62 (978-0-8225-9676-9(8)) Lerner Publishing Group.

Kimmel, Eric A. Wonders & Miracles: A Passover Companion. Kimmel, Eric A., illus. 2004. (Wonders & Miracles Ser.). (ENG., Illus.). 144p. (J). 21.99 (978-0-439-07175-8(5)) Scholastic, Inc.

Kindersley, Barnabas & Kindersley, Anabel, photos by. Celebraciones. 2005.Tr. of Celebrations. (SPA., Illus.). (J). (gr. 1-4). 18.95 (978-0-9628720-5-1(9)) Iaconi, Mariuccia Bk. Imports.

Kinney, Ada. Happy Father's Day! 2016. (Celebrations Ser.). 00024p. (J). (gr. 1-1). pap. 8.25 (978-1-4994-2668-7(2), PowerKids Pr.) Rosen Publishing Group, Inc., The.

Klebanow, Barbara & Fischer, Sara. American Holidays: Exploring Traditions, Customs, & Backgrounds. 2nd ed. 2005. (gr. 4-12). pap., stu. ed. 16.50 (978-0-86647-196-1(0)) Pro Lingua Assocs., Inc.

Knudsen, Shannon. Easter Around the World. Erickson, David, illus. 2005. (On My Own Holidays Ser.). (ENG.). 48p. (gr. 2-4). 25.26 (978-1-57505-655-5(0)) Lerner Publishing Group.

—La Pascua en Todo el Mundo. Erickson, David L., illus. 2007. (Yo Solo - Festividades (on My Own - Holidays) Ser.). 48p. (J). (gr. k-5). (SPA.). lib. bdg. 25.26 (978-0-8225-7791-1(7)); per. 6.95 (978-0-8225-7794-2(1)) Lerner Publishing Group.

—La Pascua en Todo el Mundo; Easter Around the World. 2008. pap. 40.95 (978-0-8225-9677-6(6)) Lerner Publishing Group.

Kropf, Latifa Berry. It's Hanukkah Time! Cohen, Tod, photos by. 2011. (Hanukkah Ser.). (ENG., Illus.). 24p. (J). (gr. -1-1). pap. 8.95 (978-0-7613-8306-2(9), Kar-Ben Publishing) Lerner Publishing Group.

—It's Sukkah Time. Cohen, Tod, illus. Cohen, Tod, photos by. 2003. (Sukkot & Simchat Torah Ser.). 24p. (J). (gr. -1-1). 12.95 (978-1-58013-084-4(4), Kar-Ben Publishing) Lerner Publishing Group.

—It's Sukkah Time! Cohen, Tod, photos by. 2012. (Sukkot & Simchat Torah Ser.). (ENG., Illus.). 24p. (J). (gr. -1-1). 9.95 (978-1-4677-0741-1(4), Kar-Ben Publishing) Lerner Publishing Group.

Landau, Elaine. Celebrating Earth Day. 2012. (Celebrating Holidays Ser.). (Illus.). 48p. (J). (gr. 3-4). pap. 8.95 (978-1-59845-401-7(3), Enslow Elementary) Enslow Pubs., Inc.

—Celebrating St. Patrick's Day. 2012. (Celebrating Holidays Ser.). (Illus.). 48p. (J). (gr. 3-4). pap. 8.95 (978-1-59845-402-4(1), Enslow Elementary) Enslow Pubs., Inc.

—Celebrating Veterans Day. 2012. (Celebrating Holidays Ser.). 48p. (J). (gr. 3-4). (Illus.). pap. 8.95 (978-1-59845-403-1(X)); 25.27 (978-0-7660-4036-6(4)) Enslow Pubs., Inc. (Enslow Elementary).

—Easter: Parades, Chocolates, & Celebration. 2004. (Finding Out about Holidays Ser.). (Illus.). 48p. (J). lib. bdg. 25.27 (978-0-7660-2172-3(6)) Enslow Pubs., Inc.

—What Is St. Patrick's Day? 2011. (I Like Holidays! Ser.). (Illus.). 24p. (J). (gr. k-18). pap. 7.95 (978-1-59845-291-4(6), Enslow Elementary) Enslow Pubs., Inc.

—What Is Veterans Day? 2011. (I Like Holidays! Ser.). (Illus.). 24p. (J). (gr. k-18). pap. 7.95 (978-1-59845-290-7(8), Enslow Elementary); (gr. 1-4). lib. bdg. 22.60 (978-0-7660-3705-2(3)) Enslow Pubs., Inc.

Larkin, Jean. Totally Lent! A Child's Journey to Easter 2007. 2006. (Illus.). 64p. pap. 5.95 (978-1-933178-46-2(9)) Pflaum Publishing Group.

—Totally Lent! A Child's Journey to Easter 2008. 2007. (Illus.). 64p. (J). (gr. 4-7). pap. 5.95 (978-1-933178-70-7(1)) Pflaum Publishing Group.

—Totally Lent! A Kid's Journey to Easter 2007. 2006. (Illus.). 64p. pap. 5.95 (978-1-933178-45-5(0)) Pflaum Publishing Group.

Lawrence, Ellen. Celebrations & Special Days. 2015. (My World Your World Ser.). (ENG.). 24p. (J). (gr. -1-3). lib. bdg. 23.93 (978-1-910549-00-1(2)) Bearport Publishing Co., Inc.

Lee, Michelle. Holi. 2016. (World's Greatest Celebrations Ser.). (ENG., Illus.). 32p. (gr. 3-8). 27.99 (978-1-62920-572-4(9)) Scobre Pr. Corp.

Lee, Sally. Holiday Histories. 2015. (Holiday Histories Ser.). (ENG.). 24p. (gr. k-1). 106.60 (978-1-4914-6922-4(6), Pebble Plus) Capstone Press of Coughlan Cos.

Lehman, LaLonnie. The Boar's Head Festival: A Christmas Celebration. Halbower, Susan J., illus. 2015. (ENG.). 32p. 22.95 (978-0-87565-626-7(9)) Texas Christian Univ. Pr.

Lerner Publishing Group Staff. On My Own Holidays: Classroom Set. 2005. (Illus.). (J). (gr. 2-4). 70.95 (978-0-8225-2768-8(5)) Lerner Publishing Group.

Levy, Janey. Juneteenth: Celebrating the End of Slavery. 2009. (Reading Room Collection 2 Ser.). 24p. (gr. 3-4). 42.50 (978-1-60851-976-7(7), PowerKids Pr.) Rosen Publishing Group, Inc., The.

Lindeen, Mary. Happy Groundhog Day! 2015. (BeginningtoRead Ser.). (ENG., Illus.). 32p. (J). (gr. k-2). lib. bdg. 22.60 (978-1-59953-688-0(9)) Norwood Hse. Pr.

—St. Patrick's Day. 2015. (BeginningtoRead Ser.). (ENG.). 32p. (J). (gr. k-2). pap. 11.94 (978-1-60357-747-2(5)) Norwood Hse. Pr.

Lowery, Linda. Cinco de Mayo. Knutson, Barbara, illus. 2005. (On My Own Holidays Ser.). 48p. (J). (gr. k-3). per. 6.95 (978-1-57505-764-4(6)); (gr. 2-4). 25.26 (978-1-57505-654-8(2)) Lerner Publishing Group.

—El Cinco de Mayo. Knutson, Barbara, illus. 2005. (Yo Solo - Festividades (on My Own - Holidays) Ser.). (SPA.). 48p. (J). (gr. 2-4). per. 6.95 (978-0-8225-3119-7(4)); (gr. 3-7). lib. bdg. 25.26 (978-0-8225-3118-0(6)) Lerner Publishing Group.

—Day of the Dead. Knutson, Barbara, illus. 2003. (On My Own Holidays Ser.). (ENG.). 48p. (gr. 2-4). pap. 6.95 (978-1-57505-581-7(3)); lib. bdg. 25.26 (978-0-87614-914-0(X)) Lerner Publishing Group.

—El Dia de los Muertos. Knutson, Barbara, illus. 2005. (Yo Solo Festividades Ser.).Tr. of Day of the Dead. (SPA.). 48p. (J). (gr. 2-4). per. 5.95 (978-0-8225-3123-4(2)) Lerner Publishing Group.

—El Dia de los Muertos. Translations.com Staff, tr. Knutson, Barbara, illus. 2005. (Yo Solo - Festividades (on My Own - Holidays) Ser.).Tr. of Day of the Dead. (SPA & ENG.). 48p. (gr. 2-4). lib. bdg. 25.26 (978-0-8225-3122-7(4)) Lerner Publishing Group.

—Earth Day. Bergherr, Mary, illus. rev. ed. 2003. (On My Own Holidays Ser.). (ENG.). 48p. (gr. 2-4). (J). lib. bdg. 25.26 (978-1-57505-700-2(X)); pap. 6.95 (978-1-57505-620-3(8)) Lerner Publishing Group.

Maile, Ruby. Why Are You Having A Party? 2014. (Little Books of Answers: Level B Ser.). (Illus.). 16p. (gr. k-2). pap. 7.95 (978-1-927136-10-2(5)) Three Crows Media NZL. Dist: RiverStream Publishing.

Margaret, Amy. Halloween. 2009. (Library of Holidays Ser.). 24p. (gr. 2-3). 42.50 (978-1-60853-712-9(9), PowerKids Pr.) Rosen Publishing Group, Inc., The.

—Presidents' Day. 2009. (Library of Holidays Ser.). 24p. (gr. 2-3). 42.50 (978-1-60853-716-7(1), PowerKids Pr.) Rosen Publishing Group, Inc., The.

Marsico, Katie. Chinese New Year, 1 vol. Conger, Holli, illus. 2009. (Cultural Holidays Ser.). (ENG.). 32p. (gr. -1-4). 28.50 (978-1-60270-600-2(X), Looking Glass Library- Nonfiction) Magic Wagon.

Mattern, Joanne. Celebrate Cinco de Mayo. 2006. (Celebrate Holidays Ser.). (Illus.). 104p. (J). (gr. 5-6). lib. bdg. 33.27 (978-0-7660-2579-0(9)) Enslow Pubs., Inc.

Matters, Print & Blackwell, Amy Hackney. Independence Days. 2009. (Holidays & Celebration Ser.). (Illus.). 112p. (gr. 5-8). 40.00 (978-1-60413-101-7(2), Chelsea Hse.) Facts On File, Inc.

—Lent, Yom Kippur, & Other Atonement Days. 2009. (Holidays & Celebration Ser.). (Illus.). 112p. (gr. 5-8). 40.00 (978-1-60413-100-0(4), Chelsea Hse.) Facts On File, Inc.

McCune, Susan. Memorial Day, 01 vols., 1. 2016. (Rosen REAL Readers: Social Studies Nonfiction / Fiction: Family, Community, & the World Ser.). (ENG.). 12p. (J). pap. 6.33 (978-1-5081-1773-5(X), Rosen Classroom) Rosen Publishing Group, Inc., The.

McGovern, Ann. Why it's a Holiday. 2011. 68p. pap. 10.95 (978-1-4502-4530-2(7)) iUniverse, Inc.

McKissack, Fredrick L. & McKissack, Lisa Beringer. Cinco de Mayo-Count & Celebrate! 2009. (Holidays—Count & Celebrate! Ser.). (Illus.). 32p. (J). (gr. k-3). lib. bdg. 23.94 (978-0-7660-3104-3(7)) Enslow Pubs., Inc.

Medina, Conni. Make a Chinese New Year Dragon, 1 vol. 2nd rev. ed. 2014. (TIME for KIDS(r) Nonfiction Readers Ser.). (ENG., Illus.). 20p. (J). (gr. 1-1). pap. 19.96 (978-1-4807-1026-9(1)) Shell Educational Publishing.

Mills, Nathan & Charleston, Janice. Our Country's Holidays. 2012. (Rosen Readers Ser.). (ENG., Illus.). 24p. (J). (gr. 1-2). pap. 49.50 (978-1-4488-8834-4(4)); pap. 8.25 (978-1-4488-8833-7(6)) Rosen Publishing Group, Inc., The. (Rosen Classroom).

Mills, Nathan & Englund, Frederick. Celebrating Our Holidays. 2012. (Rosen Readers Ser.). (ENG., Illus.). 16p. (J). (gr. k-1). pap. 7.00 (978-1-4488-8743-9(7), Rosen Classroom) Rosen Publishing Group, Inc., The.

MoonRattles. Heritage Holiday Activity Guide: Seventh Lunar Month. 2007. (Illus.). 52p. (J). spiral bd. (978-0-9790920-5-3(1)) MoonRattles.

Morey, Allan. Veterans Day. Bernstein, Galia, illus. 2017. (Holidays in Rhythm & Rhyme Ser.). (ENG.). 24p. (gr. 1-3). 33.99 **(978-1-68410-059-0(3))** Cantata Learning.

Morganelli, Adrianna. Cultural Traditions in Argentina. 2016. (ENG., Illus.). 32p. (J). lib. bdg. (978-0-7787-8086-1(4)) Crabtree Publishing Co.

Morrison, Jessica. Saint-Jean-Baptiste Day. 2010. (Illus.). 24p. (978-1-55388-616-7(X)); pap. (978-1-55388-617-4(8)) Weigl Educational Pubs. Ltd.

Mortensen, Lori. Veterans Day. 2016. (Spring Forward Ser.). (J). (gr. 1). (978-1-4900-9391-8(5)) Benchmark Education Co.

Murphy, Charles. Celebrations Around the World. 2016. (Adventures in Culture Ser.). 00024p. (J). pap. 8.15 **(978-1-4824-5575-5(7))** Stevens, Gareth Publishing LLLP.

Murray, Julie. Chinese New Year, 1 vol. 2005. (Buddy Book Ser.). (ENG., Illus.). 24p. (gr. k-4). 25.65 (978-1-59197-585-4(9), Buddy Bks.) ABDO Publishing Co.

—Cinco de Mayo, 1 vol. 2005. (Buddy Book Ser.). (ENG., Illus.). 24p. (gr. k-4). 25.65 (978-1-59197-586-1(7), Buddy Bks.) ABDO Publishing Co.

—Independence Day, 1 vol. 2005. (Buddy Book Ser.). (ENG., Illus.). 24p. (gr. k-4). 25.65 (978-1-59197-588-5(3), Buddy Bks.) ABDO Publishing Co.

—Martin Luther King, Jr. Day, 1 vol. 2005. (Buddy Book Ser.). (ENG., Illus.). 24p. (gr. k-4). 25.65 (978-1-59197-589-2(1), Buddy Bks.) ABDO Publishing Co.

—President's Day, 1 vol. 2005. (Buddy Book Ser.). (ENG., Illus.). 24p. (gr. k-4). 25.65 (978-1-59197-590-8(5), Buddy Bks.) ABDO Publishing Co.

—Veterans Day, 1 vol. 2011. (Holidays Set 3 Ser.). (ENG., Illus.). 24p. (J). (gr. 1-4). 25.65 (978-1-61783-043-3(7)) ABDO Publishing Co.

Musleah, Rahel & Jarrett, Judy. Apples & Pomegranates: A Family Seder for Rosh Hashanah. 2004. (ENG & HEB., Illus.). 64p. (J). (gr. k-5). pap. 7.95 (978-1-58013-123-0(9), Kar-Ben Publishing) Lerner Publishing Group.

Nelson, Robin. Earth Day. 2003. (First Step Nonfiction Ser.). (Illus.). 24p. (J). (gr. -1-3). pap. 5.95 (978-0-8225-1320-9(X)); (gr. k-2). lib. bdg. 18.60 (978-0-8225-1283-7(1)) Lerner Publishing Group.

—Martin Luther King, Jr. Day. 2003. (First Step Nonfiction Ser.). (Illus.). 24p. (J). (gr. k-2). lib. bdg. 18.60 (978-0-8225-1282-0(3)) Lerner Publishing Group.

—Veterans Day. 2005. (First Step Nonfiction Ser.). (Illus.). (J). (gr. k-2). 23p. lib. bdg. 18.60 (978-0-8225-2617-9(4)); (ENG., 24p. pap. 6.95 (978-0-8225-5379-3(1)) Lerner Publishing Group. (Lerner Pubns.).

O'Brien, Joan. Holidays Around the World. 2006. (Dover Holiday Coloring Book Ser.). (ENG., Illus.). 32p. (J). (gr. 3-8). 3.95 (978-0-486-45161-9(5)) Dover Pubns., Inc.

O'Connor, Rachel. Halloween / Halloween. 2009. (My Library of Holidays / Mi biblioteca de celebraciones Ser.). (ENG & SPA.). 24p. (gr. 1-1). 37.50 (978-1-61514-700-7(4), Editorial Buenas Letras) Rosen Publishing Group, Inc., The.

Orr, Tamra. Memorial Day/Dia de los Caidos. de la Vega, Eida, tr. from ENG. 2010. (Celebrate with Me/Celebra Conmigo Ser.). (ENG & SPA., Illus.). 32p. (J). (gr. -1-2). lib. bdg. 25.70 (978-1-58415-863-9(8)) Mitchell Lane Pubs., Inc.

Otto, Carolyn. Celebrate Cinco de Mayo: With Fiestas, Music, & Dance. 2008. (Holidays Around the World Ser.). (ENG., Illus.). 32p. (J). (gr. 1-4). 23.90 (978-1-4263-0216-9(9)); 15.95 (978-1-4263-0215-2(0)) National Geographic Society. (National Geographic Children's Bks.).

—Celebremos el Cinco de Mayo: Con Fiestas, Musica y Baile. 2008. (Holidays Around the World Ser.). (SPA., Illus.). 32p. (J). (gr. 1-4). 15.95 (978-1-4263-0363-0(7), National Geographic Children's Bks.) National Geographic Society.

Otto, Carolyn B. Celebrate Kwanzaa: With Cadels, a Comminity & the Fruits of the Harvest. 2017. (Holidays Around the World Ser.). (ENG., Illus.). 32p. (J). (gr. 1-4). pap. 7.99 **(978-1-4263-2849-7(4)**, National Geographic Children's Bks.) National Geographic Society.

—Holidays Around the World: Celebrate Kwanzaa. 2017. (Holidays Around the World Ser.). (ENG.). 32p. (J). (gr. 1-4). lib. bdg. 17.90 **(978-1-4263-2850-3(8)**, National Geographic Children's Bks.) National Geographic Society.

Our Holidays. 2015. (Our Holidays Ser.). (ENG.). 24p. (J). (gr. 1-1). 145.26 (978-1-5026-0310-4(1)); 49.32 (978-1-5026-0330-2(6)) Cavendish Square Publishing.

Owens, L. L. Cinco de Mayo, 1 vol. Conger, Holli, illus. 2009. (Cultural Holidays Ser.). (ENG.). 32p. (gr. -1-4). 28.50 (978-1-60270-602-6(6), Looking Glass Library- Nonfiction) Magic Wagon.

Parker-Rock, Michelle. Diwali: The Hindu Festival of Lights, Feasts, & Family. 2004. (Finding Out about Holidays Ser.). (Illus.). 48p. (J). lib. bdg. 25.27 (978-0-7660-2235-5(8)) Enslow Pubs., Inc.

Parnell, Declan. All about Birthdays, 01 vols., 1. 2016. (Rosen REAL Readers: Social Studies Nonfiction / Fiction: Family, Community, & the World Ser.). (ENG.). 8p. (J). pap. 5.46 (978-1-5081-1686-8(5), Rosen Classroom) Rosen Publishing Group, Inc., The.

Peppas, Lynn. Cultural Traditions in China. 2012. (ENG.). 32p. (J). pap. (978-0-7787-7591-1(7)); lib. bdg. (978-0-7787-7584-3(4)) Crabtree Publishing Co.

—Cultural Traditions in Egypt. 2012. (ENG., Illus.). 32p. (J). pap. (978-0-7787-7522-5(4)) Crabtree Publishing Co.

—Cultural Traditions in France. 2014. (ENG., Illus.). 32p. (J). (978-0-7787-0302-0(9)) Crabtree Publishing Co.

—Cultural Traditions in Germany. 2015. (ENG., Illus.). 32p. (J). (978-0-7787-8060-1(0)) Crabtree Publishing Co.

—Cultural Traditions in Greece. 2012. (ENG.). 32p. (J). (978-0-7787-7518-8(6)); (Illus.). pap. (978-0-7787-7523-2(2)) Crabtree Publishing Co.

—Cultural Traditions in Iran. 2015. (ENG., Illus.). 32p. (J). (978-0-7787-8061-8(9)) Crabtree Publishing Co.

—Cultural Traditions in Jamaica. 2015. (ENG., Illus.). 32p. (J). (978-0-7787-8062-5(7)) Crabtree Publishing Co.

—Cultural Traditions in Japan. 2012. (ENG.). 32p. (J). pap. (978-0-7787-7593-5(3)); lib. bdg. (978-0-7787-7586-7(0)) Crabtree Publishing Co.

—Cultural Traditions in the United Kingdom. 2014. (ENG., Illus.). 32p. (J). (978-0-7787-0301-3(0)) Crabtree Publishing Co.

—Election Day. 2010. (Celebrations in My World Ser.). (ENG.). 32p. (J). (gr. k-3). pap. (978-0-7787-4932-5(0)) Crabtree Publishing Co.

—Groundhog Day. 2010. (Celebrations in My World Ser.). (ENG.). 32p. (J). (gr. k-3). (978-0-7787-4926-4(6)); pap. (978-0-7787-4933-2(9)) Crabtree Publishing Co.

—Juneteenth. 2010. (Celebrations in My World Ser.). (ENG.). 32p. (J). (gr. k-3). pap. (978-0-7787-4935-6(5)) Crabtree Publishing Co.

—Presidents' Day. 2009. (Celebrations in My World Ser.). (ENG., Illus.). 32p. (J). (gr. k-2). pap. (978-0-7787-4774-1(3)); (gr. 1-3). (978-0-7787-4756-7(5)) Crabtree Publishing Co.

—Victoria Day. 2012. (ENG.). 32p. (J). (978-0-7787-4088-9(9)); pap. (978-0-7787-4093-3(5)) Crabtree Publishing Co.

Peppas, Lynn & Aloian, Molly. Cultural Traditions in India. 2012. (ENG.). 32p. (J). pap. (978-0-7787-7592-8(5)); lib. bdg. (978-0-7787-7585-0(2)) Crabtree Publishing Co.

Pettiford, Rebecca. El Año Nuevo Chino. 2015.Tr. of Chinese New Year. (SPA., Illus.). 24p. (J). lib. bdg. (978-1-62031-239-1(5), Bullfrog Bks.) Jump! Inc.

—Chinese New Year. 2015. (Illus.). 24p. (J). (gr. k-3). lib. bdg. (978-1-62031-184-4(4), Bullfrog Bks.) Jump! Inc.

—Día de Los Veteranos. 2015.Tr. of Veterans Day. (SPA & ENG., Illus.). 24p. (J). lib. bdg. (978-1-62031-245-2(X), Bullfrog Bks.) Jump! Inc.

—Diwali. 2014. (Illus.). 24p. (J). lib. bdg. 25.65 (978-1-62031-132-5(1), Bullfrog Bks.) Jump! Inc.

—Veterans Day. 2015. xvi, 287p. (J). lib. bdg. (978-1-62031-188-2(7), Bullfrog Bks.) Jump! Inc.

Pfeifer, Alice Ann. Totally Lent! A Kid's Journey to Easter 2008. 2007. (Illus.). 64p. pap. 5.95 (978-1-933178-71-4(X)) Pflaum Publishing Group.

Pingry, Patricia A. The Easter Story. Utt, Mary Ann, illus. (ENG.). (J). 2006. 32p. (gr. -1-3). per. 3.95

(978-0-8249-5531-1(5)) 2003. 26p. bds. 6.95 *(978-0-8249-4231-1(0))* Worthy Publishing. (Ideal Pubns.).

—The Story of Easter. Wells, Lorraine, illus. 2006. (ENG.). 26p. (gr. -1-k). 12.95 *(978-0-8249-6649-2(X)*, Ideal Pubns.) Worthy Publishing.

Ponto, Joanna. Veterans Day. 2016. (Story of Our Holidays Ser.). (Illus.). 32p. (J). (gr. 3-3). pap. 10.52 *(978-0-7660-7638-9(5))* Enslow Pubs., Inc.

Pratt, Laura. Mother's Day: Canadian Celebrations. 2010. (Illus.). 24p. *(978-1-77071-631-5(9))*; pap. *(978-1-77071-632-2(7))* Weigl Educational Pubs. Ltd.

Rabe, Tish. A Very Crabby Christmas. Aikins, Dave, illus. 2012. (Little Golden Book Ser.). (ENG.). 24p. (J). (gr. k-k). 4.99 *(978-0-307-97623-9(8)*, Golden Bks.) Random Hse. Children's Bks.

Reynolds, Jan. Celebrate! Connections among Cultures, 1 vol. Reynolds, Jan, photos by. 2006. (ENG., Illus.). 32p. (J). pap. 9.95 *(978-1-60060-452-2(8))* Lee & Low Bks., Inc.

—Connections among Cultures. 2006. (ENG., Illus.). 32p. (J). (gr. k-4). 16.95 *(978-1-58430-253-7(4))* Lee & Low Bks., Inc.

Richards, Jon. Vacations & Holidays. 2005. (How Things Have Changed Ser.). (Illus.). 32p. (J). (gr. 3-7). lib. bdg. 27.10 *(978-1-59389-197-8(0))* Chrysalis Education.

Rissman, Rebecca. Election Day, 1 vol. 2010. (Holidays & Festivals Ser.). (ENG.). 24p. (gr. -1-1). 22.65 *(978-1-4329-4063-8(5))*; pap. 6.29 *(978-1-4329-4082-9(1))* Heinemann-Raintree. (Acorn).

Rivera Lassén, Carmen & Maldonado, Victor. Los tres reyes a Caballo. Alvarez, Mrinali, illus. 2005. (SPA.). 28p. (J). 8.95 *(978-0-8477-1552-7(3))* Univ. of Puerto Rico Pr.

Roberts, Russell. Holidays & Celebrations in Colonial America. 2006. (Building America Ser.). (Illus.). 48p. (J). (gr. 3-7). lib. bdg. 29.95 *(978-1-58415-467-9(5))* Mitchell Lane Pubs., Inc.

Robinson, Fay. Celebrating Chinese New Year. 2012. (Celebrating Holidays Ser.). (Illus.). 48p. (J). (gr. 3-4). pap. 8.95 *(978-1-59845-398-0(X))*; lib. bdg. 25.27 *(978-0-7660-4031-1(3))* Enslow Pubs., Inc. (Enslow Elementary).

Rodgers, Kelly. Remembering Our Heroes: Veterans Day, 1 vol. rev. ed. 2014. (Primary Source Readers Content & Literacy Ser.). (ENG., Illus.). 32p. (gr. 3-3). pap. 8.99 *(978-1-4333-7363-3(7))* Teacher Created Materials, Inc.

Romulo, Liana. Filipino Celebrations: A Treasury of Feasts & Festivals. Dandan-Albano, Corazon, illus. 2012. (ENG.). 48p. (J). (gr. k-4). 16.95 *(978-0-8048-3821-4(6))* Tuttle Publishing.

Roop, Peter & Roop, Connie. Let's Celebrate St. Patrick's Day. Connelly, Gwen, illus. 2003. 32p. (J). (gr. 3-6). pap. 6.95 *(978-0-7613-1782-1(1))*; lib. bdg. 22.90 *(978-0-7613-2505-5(0))* Lerner Publishing Group. (Millbrook Pr.).

Rydaker, Ewa. Lucia Morning in Sweden. Lewis, Anne Gillespie, ed. Stahlberg, Carina, illus. 2014. (ENG.). 35p. (J). (gr. -1-3). pap. 8.99 *(978-1-935666-65-3(7))* Nodin Pr.

San Vicente, Luis, illus. The Festival of Bones / el Festival de Las Calaveras. 2014. (ENG.). 32p. (J). 7.95 *(978-1-941026-03-8(6))* Cinco Puntos Pr.

Sanna, Ellyn. Folk Festivals. 2004. (North American Folklore Ser.). (Illus.). 112p. (J). (gr. 7-18). lib. bdg. 22.95 *(978-1-59084-340-6(1))* Mason Crest.

Santella, Andrew. The First Thanksgiving. 2003. (Cornerstones of Freedom Ser.). (ENG., Illus.). 48p. (YA). (gr. 4-7). 26.00 *(978-0-516-24204-0(0))* Scholastic Library Publishing.

Scholastic, Inc. Staff. Seasons & Holidays: 40 Instant & Adorable Patterns for Bulletin Boards, Class Books, Newsletters, Stationery, & More. 2004. (Biggie Patterns Ser.). (ENG.). 48p. (gr. -1-3). pap. 10.99 *(978-0-439-46840-4(X))* Scholastic, Inc.

Scholl, Elizabeth. Independence Day/Dia de la Independencia. de la Vega, Eida, tr. from ENG. 2010. (Celebrate with Me/Celebra Conmigo Ser.). (ENG & SPA., Illus.). 32p. (J). (gr. -1-2). lib. bdg. 25.70 *(978-1-58415-862-2(X))* Mitchell Lane Pubs., Inc.

Sebra, Richard. It's Cinco de Mayo! 2017. (Bumba Books (tm) — It's a Holiday! Ser.). (ENG.). 24p. (J). (gr. -1-1). 12.99 ***(978-1-5124-3693-8(3)**, Lerner Pubns.)*; 38.65 ***(978-1-5124-2745-5(4)**, Lerner Pubns.)*; 38.65 ***(978-1-5124-3692-1(5)**, Lerner Pubns.)*; (Illus.). 25.32 *(978-1-5124-2566-6(4))* Lerner Publishing Group.

A Second Birthday: 6 Small Books. (Greetings Ser.: Vol. 2). 24p. (gr. 2-3). 31.00 *(978-0-7635-9414-5(8))* Rigby Education.

A Second Birthday: Big Book. (Greetings Ser.: Vol. 2). 24p. (gr. 2-3). 31.00 *(978-0-7635-5698-3(X))* Rigby Education.

Selwyn, Josephine. What Holidays Do You Have? 2014. (Little Books of Answers: Level d Ser.). (Illus.). 16p. (gr. k-2). pap. 7.95 *(978-1-927136-30-0(X))* Three Crows Media NZL. Dist: RiverStream Publishing.

Simonds, Lucy. Celebrations. 2007. (Trackers-Math Ser.). (gr. 2-5). pap. 5.00 *(978-1-59055-919-2(3))* Pacific Learning, Inc.

Smith, Maximilian. The Story of Cinco de Mayo. 2016. (History of Our Holidays Ser.). (ENG.). 24p. (J). (gr. 1-2). pap. 8.15 *(978-1-4824-3898-7(4))* Stevens, Gareth Publishing LLLP.

—What Is Groundhog Day? 2016. (History of Our Holidays Ser.). (ENG., Illus.). 24p. (J). (gr. 1-2). pap. 8.15 *(978-1-4824-3832-1(1))* Stevens, Gareth Publishing LLLP.

Snedeker, Gus. Celebrations Throughout the Year: Holiday Folklore. 2013. 48p. (J). pap. *(978-1-4222-2506-6(2))* Mason Crest.

—Celebrations Throughout the Year: Holiday Folklore. Jabbour, Alan, ed. 2012. (North American Folklore for Youth Ser.). 48p. (J). (gr. 4). 19.95 *(978-1-4222-2495-3(3))* Mason Crest.

Sosa, Carlos. Celebrations. 2007. (Familia Banderas Ser.). (Illus.). 48p. (J). (gr. 3-7). per. 9.95 *(978-1-933669-11-3(X))* Literary Architects, LLC.

Sosa, Carlos & Castaneda, Patricia. Celebrations: La Familia Banderas. 2006. (Illus.). 48p. (J). pap. 9.95 *(978-1-933669-03-8(9))* Literary Architects, LLC.

Spence, Kelly. Cultural Traditions in the Netherlands. 2016. (ENG., Illus.). 32p. (J). *(978-0-7787-8089-2(9))* Crabtree Publishing Co.

The Story of Our Holidays: Set 2. 2016. (Story of Our Holidays Ser.). 32p. (gr. 3-3). pap. 94.68 *(978-0-7660-7992-2(9))*; lib. bdg. 227.43 *(978-0-7660-7496-5(X))* Enslow Pubs., Inc.

The Story of Our Holidays: Set 3. 2016. (Story of Our Holidays Ser.). 32p. (J). lib. bdg. 176.89 *(978-0-7660-8410-0(8))* Enslow Pubs., Inc.

Sullivan, Erin Ash. Holidays Around the World: Set Of 6. 2010. (Navigators Ser.). (J). pap. 44.00 net. *(978-1-4108-6244-0(5))* Benchmark Education Co.

—Holidays Around the World: Text Pairs. 2008. (Bridges/Navigators Ser.). (J). (gr. 3). 94.00 *(978-1-4108-8362-9(0))* Benchmark Education Co.

Swain, Gwenyth. Celebrating. 2011. (Small World Ser.). (Illus.). 24p. bds. *(978-1-84089-674-9(4))* Zero to Ten, Ltd.

Tait, Leia. Cinco de Mayo. 2015. (Illus.). 24p. (J). *(978-1-5105-0108-9(8))* SmartBook Media, Inc.

—Cinco de Mayo. 2006. (American Holidays Ser.). (Illus.). 24p. (J). (gr. 3-7). lib. bdg. 24.45 *(978-1-59036-460-4(0))*; per. 8.95 *(978-1-59036-463-5(5))* Weigl Pubs., Inc.

Tang, Sanmu. Celebrating the Chinese New Year. Ying, Wu, tr. from CHI. 2010. (Chinese Festivals Ser.). (ENG., Illus.). 32p. (J). (gr. -1-3). pap. 4.95 *(978-1-60220-958-9(8))* BetterLink Pr., Inc.

Thong, Roseanne Greenfield. Dia de los Muertos. Ballesteros, Carles, illus. 2015. (ENG & SPA.). 32p. (J). (gr. -1-3). 16.99 *(978-0-8075-1566-2(3))* Whitman, Albert & Co.

Tomljanovic, Tatiana. Ramadan. 2012. (American Celebrations (Weigl) Ser.). (ENG., Illus.). 24p. (J). (gr. 3-5). lib. bdg. 27.13 *(978-1-61913-865-0(4)*, AV2 by Weigl) Weigl Pubs., Inc.

—Ramadan with Code. 2012. (American Celebrations Ser.). (ENG., Illus.). 24p. (J). (gr. 3-5). pap. 12.95 *(978-1-61913-868-1(9)*, AV2 by Weigl) Weigl Pubs., Inc.

Tourville, Amanda Doering. Veteran's Day, 1 vol. Ouren, Todd, illus. 2008. (Our Nation's Pride Ser.). (ENG.). 32p. (gr. -1-3). 28.50 *(978-1-60270-117-5(2)*, Looking Glass Library-Nonfiction) Magic Wagon.

Tran, Kim-Lan & Millar, Louise. Tet: The New Year. Vo-Dinh, Mai, illus. 2005. (Multicultural Celebrations Ser.). 32p. (J). 4.95 *(978-1-59373-012-3(8))* Bunker Hill Publishing, Inc.

Troum, Carole. The Sharing Chair: Tell about your holiday In... 2009. 60p. pap. 21.99 *(978-1-4389-5239-0(2))* AuthorHouse.

Trueit, Trudi Strain. Martin Luther King, Jr. Day. Snyder, Joel, illus. 2013. (Holidays & Celebrations Ser.). (ENG.). 32p. (J). (gr. k-3). 27.07 *(978-1-62323-509-3(X)*, 206283) Child's World, Inc., The.

Trueit, Trudi Strain & Strain-Trueit, Trudi. Diwali. rev. ed. 2006. (Rookie Read-About Holidays Ser.). (ENG., Illus.). 32p. (J). (gr. 1-2). pap. 5.95 *(978-0-531-11835-1(5)*, Children's Pr.) Scholastic Library Publishing.

—Earth Day. rev. ed. 2006. (Rookie Read-About Holidays Ser.). (ENG., Illus.). 32p. (J). (gr. 1-2). pap. 5.95 *(978-0-531-11836-8(3)*, Children's Pr.) Scholastic Library Publishing.

Urrutia, Maria Cristina & Orozco, Rebeca. Cinco de Mayo: Yesterday & Today. 2006. (SPA., Illus.). 29p. (J). (gr. 4-8). reprint ed. 16.00 *(978-1-4223-5464-3(4))* DIANE Publishing Co.

Venter, Sahm. Freedom Day: 27 April. 2008. (Exploring Our National Days Ser.). (ENG.). 70p. 20.95 *(978-1-77009-349-2(4))* Jacana Media ZAF. Dist: Independent Pubs. Group.

—Youth Day June 16. 2007. (Exploring Our National Days Ser.). (ENG., Illus.). 72p. (gr. 4-7). 20.95 *(978-1-77009-235-8(8))* Jacana Media ZAF. Dist: Independent Pubs. Group.

Wade, Mary Dodson. Cinco de Mayo. 2003. (Rookie Read-About Holidays Ser.). (ENG., Illus.). 32p. (J). (gr. 1-2). pap. 5.95 *(978-0-516-27489-8(9)*, Children's Pr.) Scholastic Library Publishing.

—Presidents' Day: Honoring the Birthdays of Washington & Lincoln. 2004. (Finding Out about Holidays Ser.). (Illus.). 48p. (J). lib. bdg. 25.27 *(978-0-7660-2234-8(X))* Enslow Pubs., Inc.

Walker, Robert. Veterans Day. 2010. (ENG., Illus.). 32p. (J). *(978-0-7787-4767-3(0))*; pap. *(978-0-7787-4785-7(9))* Crabtree Publishing Co.

Washington, De'borah L. Fairytale Holiday 1 And. 2011. 24p. pap. 13.95 *(978-1-4567-6408-1(X))* AuthorHouse.

Watson, Yolanda. Which Holiday Is It?, 6 vols., Set. 2003. (Phonics Readers 1-36 Ser.). (ENG.). 8p. (gr. k-1). pap. 29.70 *(978-0-7368-3210-6(6)*, Phonics Readers) Capstone Press of Coughlan Cos.

Webb, Lois Sinaiko & Roten, Lindsay Grace. Holidays of the World Cookbook for Students, 1 vol. 2nd rev. ed. 2011. (Illus.). 442p. (C). 105.00 *(978-0-313-38393-9(6)*, A2878C) ABC-CLIO, LLC.

Weston Woods Staff, creator. The Day of the Dead / el Día de Los Muertos. 2011. (ENG & SPA.). 38.75 *(978-0-545-42607-7(3))*; 29.95 *(978-0-545-37417-0(0))*; 18.95 *(978-0-545-42606-0(5))* Weston Woods Studios, Inc.

Williams, Colleen Madonna Flood. My Adventure on Father's Day. 2007. 44p. (J). 8.99 *(978-1-59092-547-8(5))* Blue Forge Pr.

—My Adventure on Groundhog Day. 2009. (ENG.). 44p. (J). 8.99 *(978-1-59092-548-5(3))* Blue Forge Pr.

—My Adventure on Martin Luther King Jr. Day. 2009. (ENG.). 44p. (J). 8.99 *(978-1-59092-551-5(3))* Blue Forge Pr.

—My Adventure on President's Day. 2007. 44p. (J). 8.99 *(978-1-59092-555-3(6))* Blue Forge Pr.

—My Adventure on St. Patrick's Day. 2007. 44p. (J). 8.99 *(978-1-59092-556-0(4))* Blue Forge Pr.

—My Adventure on Veteran's Day. 2006. 44p. (J). 8.99 *(978-1-59092-559-1(9))* Blue Forge Pr.

Wiseman, Blaine. Father's Day: Canadian Celebrations. 2010. (Illus.). 24p. *(978-1-77071-634-6(3))*; pap. *(978-1-77071-635-3(1))* Weigl Educational Pubs. Ltd.

World Book, Inc Staff, contrib. by. National Celebrations. 2009. (Illus.). 46p. (J). *(978-0-7166-5043-0(6))* World Bk., Inc.

World Book, Inc. Staff, contrib. by. Winter Celebrations. 2003. (World Book's Celebrations & Rituals Around the World Ser.). (Illus.). 46p. (J). *(978-0-7166-5013-3(4))* World Bk., Inc.

Worsley, Arlene. Veterans Day. 2015. (Illus.). 24p. (J). *(978-1-5105-0118-8(5))* SmartBook Media, Inc.

—Veterans Day. 2010. (American Celebrations Ser.). (Illus.). 24p. (J). (gr. 3-5). pap. 11.95 *(978-1-60596-932-9(X))* Weigl Pubs., Inc.

York, M. J. Celebrating Earth Day. 2017. (Welcome, Spring! Ser.). (ENG.). 24p. (J). (gr. -1-2). lib. bdg. 27.07 *(978-1-5038-1652-7(4)*, 211504) Child's World, Inc., The.

Yu, Ling. Cooking the Chinese Way. 2nd rev. exp. ed. 2003. (Easy Menu Ethnic Cookbooks). (Illus.). 72p. (J). (gr. 5-12). pap. 7.95 *(978-0-8225-4160-8(2))* Lerner Publishing Group.

Zemlicka, Shannon. Easter Around the World. Erickson, David, illus. 2005. (On My Own Holidays Ser.). 48p. (J). (gr. k-3). pap. 6.95 *(978-1-57505-765-1(4))* Lerner Publishing Group.

Zocchi, Judy. On Chinese New Year. Wallis, Rebecca, illus. 2005. (Holiday Happenings Ser.). 32p. (J). pap. 10.95 *(978-1-59646-188-8(8))*; lib. bdg. 21.65 *(978-1-891997-55-6(6))* Dingles & Co.

—On Chinese New Year/el Año Nuevo Chino. Wallis, Rebecca, illus. 2005. (Holiday Happenings Ser.).Tr. of Año Nuevo Chino. (ENG & SPA.). 32p. (J). pap. 10.95 *(978-1-59646-190-1(X))*; lib. bdg. 21.65 *(978-1-891997-56-3(4))* Dingles & Co.

—On Christmas Eve. Wallis, Rebecca, illus. 2005. (Holiday Happenings Ser.). 32p. (J). lib. bdg. 21.65 *(978-1-891997-47-1(5))* Dingles & Co.

—On Easter Morning. Wallis, Rebecca, illus. 2005. (Holiday Happenings Ser.). (ENM.). 32p. (J). lib. bdg. 21.65 *(978-1-891997-41-9(6))* Dingles & Co.

—On Halloween Night. Wallis, Rebecca, illus. 2005. (Holiday Happenings Ser.). (ENG.). 32p. (J). lib. bdg. 21.65 *(978-1-891997-77-8(7))* Dingles & Co.

—On Independence Day. Wallis, Rebecca, illus. 2005. (Holiday Happenings Ser.). 32p. (J). per. 10.95 *(978-1-59646-209-0(4))* Dingles & Co.

—On Independence Day/el día de la Independencia. Wallis, Rebecca, illus. 2005. (Holiday Happenings Ser.).Tr. of día de la Independencia. (ENG & SPA.). 32p. (J). per. 10.95 *(978-1-59646-211-3(6))* Dingles & Co.

—On Saint Patrick's Day. Wallis, Rebecca, illus. 2005. (Holiday Happenings Ser.). (ENG.). 32p. (J). lib. bdg. 21.65 *(978-1-891997-39-6(4))* Dingles & Co.

—On Thanksgiving Day. Wallis, Rebecca, illus. 2004. (Holiday Happenings Ser.). (ENM.). 32p. (J). lib. bdg. 21.65 *(978-1-891997-74-7(2))* Dingles & Co.

—On Three Kings Day. Wallis, Rebecca, illus. 2005. (Holiday Happenings Ser.). 32p. (J). pap. 10.95 *(978-1-59646-204-5(3))*; lib. bdg. 21.65 *(978-1-891997-53-2(X))*; per. 10.95 *(978-1-59646-205-2(1))* Dingles & Co.

—On Three Kings Day/el día de los tres Reyes Magos. Wallis, Rebecca, illus. 2005. (Holiday Happenings Ser.).Tr. of día de los tres Reyes Magos. (ENG & SPA.). 32p. (J). pap. 10.95 *(978-1-59646-206-9(X))*; lib. bdg. 21.65 *(978-1-891997-54-9(8))*; per. 10.95 *(978-1-59646-207-6(8))* Dingles & Co.

—On Valentine's Day. Wallis, Rebecca, illus. 2005. (Holiday Happenings Ser.). 32p. (J). lib. bdg. 21.65 *(978-1-891997-79-2(3))* Dingles & Co.

HOLIDAYS—DRAMA

Halligan, Terry. Funny Skits & Sketches. Behr, Joyce, illus. unabr. ed. 2003. 128p. (YA). (gr. 4-12). pap. 15.00 *(978-0-88734-688-0(X))* Players Pr., Inc.

HOLIDAYS—FICTION

Abdelsalam, Lisa. A Song for Me: A Muslim Holiday Story. Nielsen, Janet Marie, illus. 2006. 34p. (J). *(978-0-9755975-1-4(5))* Abdelsalam Corp.

Abramson, Jill & O'Connor, Jane. Holiday Helper. Melmon, Deborah, illus. 2014. (Penguin Young Readers, Level 2 Ser.). (ENG.). 32p. (J). (gr. 1-3). pap. 3.99 *(978-0-448-45677-5(X)*, Penguin Young Readers) Penguin Young Readers Group.

Accord Publishing Staff. Santa's Workshop: A Mini Animotion Book. Idle, Molly, illus. 2011. (ENG.). 12p. (J). 9.99 *(978-1-4494-0834-3(6))* Andrews McMeel Publishing.

Ahlstrom, Leonard. Christmas Shoes for Children. 2004. pap. 7.99 *(978-0-9714147-1-6(8))* Point To Point Publishing.

Albrecht, Sally K., et al. Snow Way Out! A Vacation in Winter's Wonderland: A Mini-Musical for Unison & 2-Part Voices. 2009. (ENG.). 68p. pap. 34.99 *(978-0-7390-5835-0(5))* Alfred Publishing Co., Inc.

Alemagna, Beatrice, creator. The Wonderful Fluffy Little Squishy. 2015. (ENG., Illus.). 48p. (J). (gr. -1-3). 18.95 *(978-1-59270-180-3(9))* Enchanted Lion Bks., LLC.

Alexander, Louise. My Little Pony: Happy Haunting. 2016. (ENG.). 24p. (J). (gr. -1-3). 8.99 *(978-0-316-36150-7(X))* Little, Brown Bks. for Young Readers.

Allan, Patsy. Tessa the Runaway Teapot. 2012. 36p. pap. 32.70 *(978-1-4797-2706-3(7))* Xlibris Corp.

Anne-Marie-Mugwe. Cobjay's Summer Holiday & How to Catch a Squirrel. 2013. (Illus.). 36p. pap. 22.88 *(978-1-4817-8223-4(1))* AuthorHouse.

Ashford, Jeron. Winter Candle. Schuett, Stacey, illus. 2014. (ENG.). 28p. (J). (gr. -1-6). 16.95 *(978-1-939547-10-1(5))* Creston Bks.

Ashman, Linda. Over the River & Through the Wood: A Holiday Adventure. Smith, Kim, illus. 2015. (ENG.). 32p. (J). (gr. -1). 14.95 *(978-1-4549-1024-4(0))* Sterling Publishing Co., Inc.

Awdry, W. Thomas's Christmas Delivery. Stubbs, Tommy, illus. 2004. (Sparkle Storybook Ser.). (ENG.). 32p. (J). (gr. -1-2). 8.99 *(978-0-375-82877-5(X)*, Random Hse. Bks. for Young Readers) Random Hse. Children's Bks.

Baier, Hiltrud. Greta in Schweden. 2009. 114p. pap. *(978-3-8391-2523-6(5))* Books on Demand GmbH.

Baker, Keith. Hap-Pea All Year! Baker, Keith, illus. 2016. (Peas Ser.). (ENG., Illus.). 40p. (J). (gr. -1-3). 17.99 *(978-1-4814-5854-2(X)*, Beach Lane Bks.) Beach Lane Bks.

Barbo, Maria S. The Velveteen Rabbit Christmas. Hague, Michael, illus. 2013. (My Readers Ser.). (ENG.). 32p. (J). (gr. -1-1). 15.99 *(978-1-250-01768-0(8)*, 9781250017680) Square Fish.

Beauvais, Clémentine. The Very Royal Holiday. Moor, Becka, illus. 2017. (ENG.). 224p. (J). pap. 10.99 *(978-1-4088-6394-7(4)*, 9781408863947, Bloomsbury USA Childrens) Bloomsbury Publishing USA.

Bell, Frank & Bowler, Colin. Panda Patrol Go on Holiday. Seaman, Paul, illus. 2004. 24p. pap. 7.00 *(978-1-84161-083-2(6))* Ravette Publishing, Ltd. GBR. Dist: Parkwest Pubns., Inc.

Bentley, Dawn. Gingerbread Man. 2005. (Holiday Sparklers Book Ser.). (ENG., Illus.). 10p. (J). 4.95 *(978-1-58117-163-1(3)*, Intervisual/Piggy Toes) Bendon, Inc.

Berenstain, Mike, illus. The Berenstain Bears' Holiday Cookbook: Cub-Friendly Cooking with an Adult, 1 vol. 2016. (Berenstain Bears/Living Lights Ser.). (ENG.). 96p. (J). 12.99 *(978-0-310-75399-5(6))* Zonderkidz.

Berenstain, Stan & Berenstain, Jan. The Berenstain Bears & the Mama's Day Surprise. 2004. (First Time Books Ser.). (ENG., Illus.). 32p. (J). (gr. -1-2). pap. 4.99 *(978-0-375-81132-6(X)*, Random Hse. Bks. for Young Readers) Random Hse. Children's Bks.

Berrow, G. M. My Little Pony: Princess Cadance & the Spring Hearts Garden. 2016. (Princess Collection). (ENG., Illus.). 160p. (J). (gr. 3-7). 9.99 *(978-0-316-38930-3(7))* Little, Brown Bks. for Young Readers.

Bickel, Karla. Easter Lights. Bickel, Karla, illus. l.t. ed. 2004. (Illus.). 16p. (J). (gr. -1-6). pap. 5.00 *(978-1-891452-14-7(2)*, 7) Heart Arbor Bks.

Birney, Betty G. Winter According to Humphrey. 2013. (Humphrey Ser.: 9). (ENG.). 176p. (J). (gr. 3-7). pap. 5.99 *(978-0-14-242759-0(4)*, Puffin Books) Penguin Young Readers Group.

—Winter According to Humphrey. 2013. (According to Humphrey Ser.: 9). lib. bdg. 16.00 *(978-0-606-32138-9(1)*, Turtleback) Turtleback Bks.

Bischoff, Marlene A. Charming Chirp. 2013. 26p. pap. 13.95 *(978-1-4796-0132-5(2))* TEACH Services, Inc.

Blake, Jon. Holiday Mania at the House of Fun. Roberts, David, illus. 2007. (ENG.). 128p. (J). (gr. k-2). pap. 6.95 *(978-0-340-93129-5(9))* Hachette Children's Group GBR. Dist: Hachette Bk. Group.

Blumberg, Margie. Avram's Gift. McGaw, Laurie, illus. (ENG.). 48p. 2005. (YA). pap. 11.95 *(978-0-9624166-3-7(0))* 2003. (J). (gr. 3-18). 15.95 *(978-0-9624166-2-0(2))* MB Publishing, LLC.

Boudreaux, Amanda. A Birthday Breakfast. 2012. 24p. pap. 17.99 *(978-1-62230-383-0(0))* Salem Author Services.

Bridwell, Norman. Clifford's Happy Easter. 2011. (Clifford's Big Ideas Ser.). (Illus.). (gr. -1). 14.00 *(978-1-60686-966-6(3))* Perfection Learning Corp.

Brown, Kathryn. Freddy the Brave. 2010. 43p. pap. 12.50 *(978-1-4461-2959-3(4))* Lulu Pr., Inc.

Brown, Margaret Wise. A Pussycat's Christmas. Mortimer, Anne, illus. 2009. (ENG.). 32p. (J). (gr. k-4). 9.99 *(978-0-06-186978-5(3)*, Tegen, Katherine Bks) HarperCollins Pubs.

Brown-Wood, Janay & Burris, Priscilla. Grandma's Tiny House. 2017. (ENG., Illus.). 32p. (J). (-k). lib. bdg. 16.99 *(978-1-58089-712-9(6))* Charlesbridge Publishing, Inc.

Browne, Susan Chalker. Hey Freddy, It's Canada's Birthday!, 1 vol. Rose, Hilda, illus. 2009. (ENG.). 32p. (J). (gr. k-5). 10.95 *(978-1-897174-39-5(X)*, Tuckamore Bks) Creative Bk. Publishing CAN. Dist: Orca Bk. Pubs. USA.

Browning, Tom & Moore, Clement C. The Night Before Christmas. 2009. (ENG., Illus.). 48p. (J). (gr. k). 14.95 *(978-1-4027-5484-5(1)*, Sterling Innovation) Sterling Publishing Co., Inc.

Brownlow, Brooke. The Magic of Old Oak Hill. 2005. 48p. pap. 16.95 *(978-1-4241-0223-5(5))* PublishAmerica, Inc.

Bunting, Eve. A Perfect Father's Day. Meddaugh, Susan, illus. 2016. (ENG.). 40p. (J). (gr. -1-3). 8.99 *(978-0-544-70900-3(4)*, HMH Books For Young Readers) Houghton Mifflin Harcourt Publishing Co.

Burkhart, Jessica. Masquerade. 2012. (Canterwood Crest Ser.: 16). (ENG.). 256p. (J). (gr. 4-7). pap. 7.99 *(978-1-4424-3655-8(7)*, Aladdin) Simon & Schuster Children's Publishing.

Caine, Paul. Jake's Journey. 2010. 68p. pap. 10.49 *(978-1-4520-0508-9(7))* AuthorHouse.

Cann, Kate. Mediterranean Holiday: Or, How I Moved to a Tiny Island & Found the Love of My Life. 2007. (ENG.). 416p. (YA). (gr. 9-12). pap. 5.99 *(978-0-06-115216-0(1)*, HarperTeen) HarperCollins Pubs.

Capucilli, Alyssa Satin. Biscuit Loves Father's Day. Schories, Pat & Young, Mary O'Keefe, illus. 2004. (ENG.). 20p. (J). (gr. -1-1). pap. 6.99 *(978-0-06-009463-8(X)*, HarperFestival) HarperCollins Pubs.

—Biscuit Loves Mother's Day. Schories, Pat & Young, Mary O'Keefe, illus. 2004. (ENG.). 20p. (J). (gr. -1-1). pap. 6.99 *(978-0-06-009462-1(1)*, HarperFestival) HarperCollins Pubs.

Carr, Annie Roe. Nan Sherwood's Winter Holidays. 2007. 124p. per. *(978-1-4068-4397-2(0))* Echo Library.

Chapman, Brenda. Hiding in Hawk's Creek. 2006. (Jennifer Bannon Mystery Ser.: 2). (ENG.). 144p. (YA). per. 9.95 *(978-1-894917-24-7(3)*, Napoleon & Co.) Dundurn CAN. Dist: Ingram Publisher Services.

Chelkowski, Lisa. The Sisters' Christmas Tale. 2009. 44p. pap. 21.99 *(978-1-4415-3577-1(2))* Xlibris Corp.

Chiarello, Robin Taylor. The Blue Lobster's Holiday! Bohart, Lisa, illus. 2012. 40p. pap. 16.95 *(978-1-61493-053-2(8))* Peppertree Pr., The.

Ching, Tokie. Boy's Day in Hawaii. Arai, Setsuo, illus. 2008. 32p. (J). 12.95 *(978-1-56647-852-6(9))* Mutual Publishing LLC.

—Girl's Day in Hawaii with Yuki Chan. 2006. 40p. (J). 14.95 *(978-1-56647-820-5(0))* Mutual Publishing LLC.

A Christmas Tradition. 2007. 69p. pap. 16.26 *(978-1-4303-1458-5(3))* Lulu Pr., Inc.

Clarizio, Laura. If I Had a Magic Carpet III: Haunted Holidays. 2008. 73p. pap. 19.95 *(978-1-60563-240-7(6))* America Star Bks.

Cohn, Rachel & Levithan, David. The Twelve Days of Dash & Lily. 2016. (ENG.). 224p. (YA). (gr. 7). 17.99 *(978-0-399-55380-6(0)*, Knopf Bks. for Young Readers) Random Hse. Children's Bks.

Cookie Jar Entertainment Inc Staff. It's a Happy Holiday! 2007. 32p. (J). mass mkt. 4.99 *(978-1-60095-271-5(2)*, Doodlebops) Cookie Jar.

Cooper, Alexandra. Spin the Dreidel! Gévry, Claudine, illus. 2004. (ENG.). 14p. (J). (gr. -1-2). bds. 7.99 *(978-0-689-86430-8(2)*, Little Simon) Little Simon.

Cornell-Castle, Violet R. Santa's Elves. 2008. 32p. pap. 18.65 *(978-1-4363-5899-6(X))* Xlibris Corp.

Cox, Judy. Cinco de Mouse-O! Ebbeler, Jeffrey, illus. 2010. (SPA & ENG.). 32p. (J). (gr. -1-3). 16.95 *(978-0-8234-2194-7(5))* Holiday Hse., Inc.

—Go to Sleep, Groundhog. Meisel, Paul, illus. 2003. (ENG.). 32p. (gr. k-3). tchr. ed. 17.95 *(978-0-8234-1645-5(3))* Holiday Hse., Inc.

H I

Crispian. Mystery on the Tambo River. 2011. 120p. (gr. 4-6). 20.95 *(978-1-4502-6506-5(5))*; pap. 10.95 *(978-1-4502-6504-1(9))* iUniverse, Inc.

Crowley-Ranelli, D. Holiday Island: Santa in a Bathing Suit? 2009. 56p. pap. 9.95 *(978-1-60860-268-1(0)*, Eloquent Bks.) Strategic Book Publishing & Rights Agency (SBPRA).

DaColl, Ivar. El Dia de Muertos. 2004.Tr. of Day of the Dead. (SPA., Illus.). (J). 14.95 *(978-1-930332-44-7(0))* Lectorum Pubns., Inc.

Dauth, Freya. Zoe & the Albatross. 2012. 140p. pap. 11.99 *(978-1-4525-0304-2(4))* Balboa Pr.

Davenport, Kathy. Holly's Chocolate Heart. 2011. 40p. 17.49 *(978-1-4567-1520-5(8))* AuthorHouse.

David, Erica. Christmas with Krabby Klaws. Martinez, Heather, illus. 2010. (SpongeBob SquarePants Ser.). (ENG.). 16p. (J). pap. 5.99 *(978-1-4424-0805-0(7)*, Simon Spotlight/Nickelodeon) Simon Spotlight/Nickelodeon.

Dearle, Anne Crofton. Ginger Cat. 2011. (Illus.). 92p. pap. 12.10 *(978-1-4567-7484-4(0))* AuthorHouse.

DeJong, Meindert. Una Gata Casi Blanca. (SPA.). (YA). (gr. 5-8). pap. *(978-84-279-3385-9(1)*, NG3487) Noguer y Caralt Editores, S. A. ESP. Dist: Lectorum Pubns., Inc.

dePaola, Tomie. Strega Nona's Gift. dePaola, Tomie, illus. 2011. (ENG., Illus.). 32p. (J). (gr. -1-3). 17.99 *(978-0-399-25649-3(0)*, Nancy Paulsen Books) Penguin Young Readers Group.

Depken, Kristen & Depken, Kristen L. One, Two... Boo! Gévry, Claudine, illus. 2009. (ENG.). 12p. (J). (gr. -1 — 1). bds. 3.99 *(978-0-375-84418-8(X)*, Golden Bks.) Random Hse. Children's Bks.

Depken, Kristen L. Merry Christmas, Pocoyo (Pocoyo) Random House, illus. 2013. (Glitter Board Book Ser.). (ENG.). 12p. (J). (— 1). bds. 6.99 *(978-0-449-81903-6(5)*, Random Hse. Bks. for Young Readers) Random Hse. Children's Bks.

Deshpande, Shashi. 3 Novels. 2006. 379p. *(978-0-14-333511-5(1)*, Puffin) Penguin Publishing Group.

DeSpain, Pleasant. Tales of Holidays. 2016. (ENG., Illus.). 80p. (J). (gr. 3-4). pap. 9.95 *(978-1-941460-39-9(9))* August Hse. Pubs., Inc.

Dickens, Charles. A Christmas Carol. 2004. (Aladdin Classics Ser.). (ENG.). 128p. (Orig.). (J). pap. 5.99 *(978-0-689-87180-1(5)*, Simon & Schuster/Paula Wiseman Bks.) Simon & Schuster/Paula Wiseman Bks.

Disney Book Group Staff & Higginson, Sheila Sweeny. My Huggy Valentine. Disney Storybook Art Team, illus. 2013. (ENG.). 24p. (J). (gr. -1-k). pap. 5.99 *(978-1-4847-0425-7(8))* Disney Pr.

Disney Book Group Staff & LaRose, Melinda. Jake & the Never Land Pirates - Winter Never Land. Disney Storybook Art Team, illus. 2014. (ENG.). 12p. (J). (gr. -1-k). bds. 7.99 *(978-1-4231-9424-8(1))* Disney Pr.

Dorling Kindersley Publishing Staff & Saunders, Catherine. Summer Adventures, Level 3. 2013. (DK Readers Ser.). (ENG.). 48p. (J). (gr. 2-4). pap. 3.99 *(978-1-4654-0259-2(4)*, DK Children) Dorling Kindersley Publishing, Inc.

Dove, Karen. A Gift for Santa. 2012. 50p. 23.99 *(978-1-61996-793-9(6))*; pap. 12.99 *(978-1-61996-792-2(8))* Salem Author Services.

Dower, Laura. For Emme, Baked with Love. Lazuli, Lilly, illus. 2016. (Dessert Diaries). (ENG.). 160p. (gr. 4-5). pap. 5.95 *(978-1-4965-4142-0(1))* Stone Arch Bks.

Dragovich, Joe. The Empty Hook. 2013. (ENG.). 36p. pap. 13.95 *(978-1-4497-7819-4(4)*, WestBow Pr.) Author Solutions, Inc.

Duncan, Billy. A Haunting Good Time, 1 vol. 2009. 48p. pap. 16.95 *(978-1-60836-120-5(9))* America Star Bks.

Ediger, Max. Caleb & Shalev. 2010. 36p. pap. 13.95 *(978-1-60860-808-9(5)*, Eloquent Bks.) Strategic Book Publishing & Rights Agency (SBPRA).

Elliott, Rebecca. Warm Hearts Day: A Branches Book. Elliott, Rebecca, illus. 2016. (Owl Diaries: 5). (ENG., Illus.). 80p. (J). (gr. k-2). pap. 4.99 *(978-1-338-04280-1(7))* Scholastic, Inc.

Ellis, Rolant. Cyfres Cled: Castell Marwolaeth Boenus AC Erchyll. 2005. (WEL., Illus.). 75p. pap. *(978-0-86243-377-2(0))* Y Lolfa.

Evans, Zoe. Holiday Spirit. Barrager, Brigette, illus. 2011. (Cheer! Ser.: 3). (ENG.). 224p. (J). (gr. 3-7). pap. 6.99 *(978-1-4424-3362-5(0)*, Simon Spotlight) Simon Spotlight.

Facey, Paulet. Annie & the Washpan of Ripe Bananas. 2012. 24p. pap. 15.99 *(978-1-4797-2659-2(1))* Xlibris Corp.

Falki, Pamela Marie. The Perfect Christmas Tree: Petrie & Toby's Holiday Adventure. 2009. 24p. pap. 11.49 *(978-1-4343-9983-0(4))* AuthorHouse.

Falla, Lynne. World of the Weeples: Sophie & the Weeples. 2012. 24p. pap. 15.99 *(978-1-4771-2078-1(5))* Xlibris Corp.

Fedatova, Marina, illus. The 12 Elves: A New Christmas Tradition. 2010. (ENG.). 18p. (J). (gr. -1-k). bds. 12.99 *(978-1-4424-1684-0(X)*, Little Simon) Little Simon.

Feldman, Thea & Auerbach, Annie. The Snow Family: A Winter's Tale. Alderson, Lisa, illus. 2005. 12p. (J). 13.00 *(978-0-7567-9460-6(9))* DIANE Publishing Co.

Fisch, Sholly & Age, Heroic. Season of Light, 1 vol. Brizuela, Dario, illus. 2014. (DC Super Friends Ser.). (ENG.). 32p. (gr. 1-2). 22.60 *(978-1-4342-9223-0(1))* Stone Arch Bks.

Fliess, Sue. How to Trap a Leprechaun. Randall, Emma, illus. 2017. (ENG.). 32p. (J). (gr. -1-k). 16.99 *(978-1-5107-0670-5(4)*, Sky Pony Pr.) Skyhorse Publishing Co., Inc.

Flor Ada, Alma. Celebrate Martin Luther King, Jr. Day with Mrs. Park's Class. Weiss, Monica, illus. 2006. (Stories to Celebrate Ser.). 30p. (gr. k-6). per. 11.95 *(978-1-59820-125-3(5)*, Alfaguara) Santillana USA Publishing Co., Inc.

Florence, Debbi Michiko. Jasmine Toguchi, Super Sleuth. Vukovic, Elizabet, illus. 2017. (J). pap. ***(978-0-374-30414-0(9))*** Farrar, Straus & Giroux.

Frederick, Heather Vogel. Home for the Holidays. (Mother-Daughter Book Club Ser.). (ENG.). (J). (gr. 4-9). 2012. 384p. pap. 8.99 *(978-1-4424-0686-5(0))* 2011. 352p. 18.99 *(978-1-4424-0685-8(2))* Simon & Schuster Bks. For Young Readers. (Simon & Schuster Bks. For Young Readers).

Freeman, Don. Spring Is Here, Corduroy! McCue, Lisa, illus. 2007. (Corduroy Ser.). (ENG.). 16p. (J). (gr. -1-k). 6.99 *(978-0-448-44461-1(5)*, Grosset & Dunlap) Penguin Young Readers Group.

Gaetz, Dayle Campbell. Spoiled Rotten, 1 vol. 2005. (Orca Currents Ser.). (ENG.). 128p. (J). (gr. 5-9). per. 9.95 *(978-1-55143-474-2(1))* Orca Bk. Pubs. USA.

Garland, Michael. King Puck. Garland, Michael, illus. 2007. (Illus.). 32p. (J). (gr. -1-3). (ENG.). 16.99 *(978-0-06-084809-5(X))*; lib. bdg. 18.99 *(978-0-06-084810-1(3))* HarperCollins Pubs.

Garofoli, Viviana, illus. Halloween Hugs: A HUGS Book. 2014. (Hugs Book Ser.: 6). (ENG.). 10p. (J). (gr. -1-k). bds. 9.99 *(978-0-7944-3240-9(9))* Reader's Digest Assn., Inc., The.

Garratt, Irene Joyce. Andrew's Activities: Two in One Stories. 2009. (Illus.). 20p. pap. 10.49 *(978-1-4389-4235-3(4))* AuthorHouse.

Gemmell, N. J. Coco Banjo & the Super Wow Surprise. 2017. (Coco Banjo Ser.: 3). (ENG.). 192p. (J). (gr. 1-3). 9.99 ***(978-0-85798-737-2(2))*** Random Hse. Australia AUS. Dist: Independent Pubs. Group.

Glickman, Susan. Bernadette in the Doghouse, 1 vol. 2011. (Lunch Bunch Ser.). (ENG., Illus.). 122p. (J). (gr. 2-4). pap. 8.95 *(978-1-897187-92-0(0))* Second Story Pr. CAN. Dist: Orca Bk. Pubs. USA.

Golden Books. Barbie Fall 2016 Holiday Movie Hologramatic Sticker Book (Barbie) 2016. (Hologramatic Sticker Book Ser.). (ENG.). 64p. (J). (gr. -1-2). pap. 4.99 *(978-0-399-54957-1(9)*, Golden Bks.) Random Hse. Children's Bks.

—It's Time for Christmas! (Bubble Guppies) Golden Books, illus. 2014. (Big Coloring Book Ser.). (ENG., Illus.). 48p. (J). (gr. -1-2). pap. 6.99 *(978-0-385-38409-4(2)*, Golden Bks.) Random Hse. Children's Bks.

Golden Books Staff, et al. Christmas Favorites. Catusanu, Mircea & Wilkin, Eloise, illus. 2009. (Little Golden Book Favorites Ser.). (ENG.). 80p. (J). (gr. -1-2). 6.99 *(978-0-375-85778-2(8)*, Golden Bks.) Random Hse. Children's Bks.

Gordon, Ellen. A Verseful of Jewish Holidays. Katz, Avi, illus. 2008. 24p. pap. 9.95 *(978-965-7344-47-7(6))* Mazo Pubs.

Gordon, Sylvia. Further Adventures of the Potty Wizard & His Cat, Muddles. 2009. (Illus.). 60p. pap. 10.49 *(978-1-4389-6819-3(1))* AuthorHouse.

Griffin, Adele & Sheinmel, Courtney. Agnes & Clarabelle Celebrate! Palacios, Sara, illus. 2017. (Agnes & Clarabelle Ser.). (ENG.). 80p. (J). 9.99 *(978-1-61963-217-2(9)*, 9781619632172, Bloomsbury USA Childrens) Bloomsbury Publishing USA.

Gruber, Daveda. More Tales of a Tiny Dog. 2009. 71p. pap. 32.50 *(978-1-4092-6657-0(5))* Lulu Pr., Inc.

Gutman, Dan. Bunny Double, We're in Trouble! 2014. (My Weird School Ser.). (J). lib. bdg. 16.00 *(978-0-606-35055-6(1)*, Turtleback) Turtleback Bks.

Hamlyn, Jean. Clumsy Daisy Goes on Holiday: Book 3. 2010. (Illus.). 40p. pap. 18.49 *(978-1-4520-1025-0(0))* AuthorHouse.

Hannigan, Kate. Cupcake Cousins, Book 3 Winter Wonders. Hughes, Brooke Boynton, illus. 2017. (Cupcake Cousins Ser.). (ENG.). 240p. (J). (gr. 3-7). pap. 6.99 ***(978-1-4847-2363-0(5))*** Hyperion Bks. for Children.

Hapka, Catherine, pseud. Holiday in Enchancia. 2013. (Sofia the First Ser.). (J). lib. bdg. 24.50 *(978-0-606-32289-8(2)*, Turtleback) Turtleback Bks.

Hapka, Catherine, pseud & Disney Book Group Staff. Holiday in Enchancia. Disney Storybook Art Team, illus. 2013. (ENG.). 40p. (J). (gr. -1-k). 12.99 *(978-1-4231-8396-9(7))* Disney Pr.

Hapka, Cathy, pseud. Picture Me Christmas Princess. Hill, Heather C. & Roush, April, illus. 2003. (Picture Me Holiday Ser.). 10p. (J). (gr. -1-18). bds. 6.99 *(978-1-57151-571-1(2))* Playhouse Publishing.

Harris, John. Jingle Bells: How the Holiday Classic Came to Be, 1 vol. Gustavson, Adam, illus. 2011. (ENG.). 32p. (J). 16.95 *(978-1-56145-590-4(3))* Peachtree Pubs.

Harrod-Eagles, Cynthia. The Changeling. 2010. 195p. pap. 18.50 *(978-1-4452-5850-8(1))* Lulu Pr., Inc.

Harvey, Jacqueline. Alice-Miranda Holds the Key. Yinfoo, Anne, illus. 2017. (Alice-Miranda Ser.: 15). (ENG.). 384p. (J). (gr. 3-7). 9.99 ***(978-0-14-378070-0(0))*** Random Hse. Australia AUS. Dist: Independent Pubs. Group.

Harvey, Pam & Panckridge, Michael. Ghost of a Chance. 2007. 208p. *(978-0-207-20063-2(7))* HarperCollins Pubs. Australia.

Hayes, Karel. The Christmas Visitors. 2013. (ENG., Illus.). 32p. (J). (gr. -1-3). 16.95 *(978-1-60893-248-1(6))* Down East Bks.

Henry, Henther French. Life, Liberty & the Pursuit of Jellybeans: A Fourth of July Story. Henry, Henther French, illus. 2004. (Claire's Holiday Adventures Ser.). (ENG., Illus.). 32p. (J). (gr. k-4). 15.95 *(978-0-9706341-6-0(1))* Cubbie Blue Publishing.

—Life, Liberty & the Pursuit of Jellybeans: An Independence Day Story. Henry, Henther French, illus. 2004. (Claire's Holiday Adventures Ser.). (ENG., Illus.). 32p. (J). (gr. k-4). 16.95 *(978-0-9706341-5-3(3))* Cubbie Blue Publishing.

Hillert, Margaret. Fun Days. (J). 4.95 *(978-0-87895-678-4(6))* Modern Curriculum Pr.

—Fun Days. Roraback, Robin, illus. 2016. (BeginningtoRead Ser.). (ENG.). 32p. (J). (gr. -1-2). 22.60 *(978-1-59953-815-0(6))*; pap. 11.94 *(978-1-60357-977-3(X))* Norwood Hse. Pr.

Hohn, Nadia L. & Luxbacher, Irene. Malaika's Costume, 1 vol. 2016. (ENG., Illus.). 32p. (J). (gr. -1-2). 18.95 *(978-1-55498-754-2(7))* Groundwood Bks. CAN. Dist: Publishers Group West (PGW).

Holub, Joan. Dragon Dance: A Chinese New Year. Huang, Benrei, illus. 2003. (Lift-The-Flap, Puffin Ser.). (ENG.). 16p. (J). (gr. -1-k). pap. 6.99 *(978-0-14-240000-5(9)*, Puffin Books) Penguin Young Readers Group.

Hotchkiss, Gerry. Emily & the Lost City of Urgup: An Adventure in Arabia. 2012. 112p. 20.95 *(978-1-4759-3764-0(4))*; pap. 10.95 *(978-1-4759-3762-6(8))* iUniverse, Inc.

Howse, Jennifer. Le Lendemain de Noël: Les Célébrations Canadiennes. Karvonen, Tanjah, tr. from ENG. 2011. (FRE.). 24p. (gr. k-3). *(978-1-77071-395-6(6))* Weigl Educational Pubs. Ltd.

Hull, Norman. Joyce's Holiday in France. 2011. 96p. (gr. -1). pap. 9.99 *(978-1-4634-3694-0(7))* AuthorHouse.

Hyde, Margaret. Mo Smells the Holidays: A Scentsational Journey. Giacomini, Amanda, illus. 2009. (Mo's Nose Ser.). (ENG.). 24p. (J). (gr. k-k). 17.95 *(978-0-9816255-3-9(3))* Mo's Nose, LLC.

Jalali, Reza. Moon Watchers: Shirin's Ramadan Miraacle. 2017. lib. bdg. 19.60 ***(978-0-606-40159-3(8))*** Turtleback Bks.

Jalali, Reza. Moon Watchers: Shirin's Ramadan Miracle, 1 vol. Sibley O'Brien, Anne, illus. 2017. (ENG.). 32p. (gr. 1-7). pap. 8.95 *(978-0-88448-587-2(0)*, 884587) Tilbury Hse. Pubs.

Jansen, Karen. Mardi Gras in New Orleans: An Alphabet Book. 2008. 32p. pap. 13.99 *(978-1-4389-1543-2(8))* AuthorHouse.

Jitchotvisut, Donna M. Mittens for Christmas. 2009. 376p. 31.95 *(978-1-4401-0372-8(0))*; pap. 21.95 *(978-1-4401-0370-4(4))* iUniverse, Inc.

Julie, Aunt. Paddleduck! Julie, A Little Girl from Texas. 2011. 56p. (gr. 2-4). pap. 8.95 *(978-1-4269-2584-9(0))* Trafford Publishing.

Kane, Bob. Comic con & Labor Day. Nguyen, Dustin, illus. 2015. (Batman: Li'l Gotham Ser.). (ENG.). 32p. (gr. 2-3). lib. bdg. 22.60 *(978-1-4342-9736-5(5))* Stone Arch Bks.

Karpinski, David. Sarah's Christmas Presence. 2006. 58p. pap. 8.95 *(978-0-7414-3411-1(3))* Infinity Publishing.

Katz, Karen. Counting Christmas. Katz, Karen, illus. 2007. (Classic Board Bks.). (ENG., Illus.). 32p. (J). (gr. -1-1). bds. 7.99 *(978-1-4169-3624-4(6)*, Little Simon) Little Simon.

—Grandpa & Me. Katz, Karen, illus. 2004. (ENG., Illus.). 14p. (J). (gr. -1-k). bds. 6.99 *(978-0-689-86644-9(5)*, Little Simon) Little Simon.

Keep, Richard. Clatter Bash! A Day of the Dead Celebration, 1 vol. Keep, Richard, illus. (ENG., Illus.). 32p. (J). (gr. k-3). 2008. pap. 7.95 *(978-1-56145-461-7(3))* 2004. 15.95 *(978-1-56145-322-1(6))* Peachtree Pubs.

Kennedy, Bryan. Charlie's Favorite Christmas. 2012. 26p. pap. 5.95 *(978-0-9885358-0-0(7))* Bryan-Kennedy Entertainment, LLC.

Kimmelman, Leslie. The Very Crowded Sukkah, 0 vols. 2013. (ENG.). 32p. (J). (gr. -1-k). 17.99 *(978-1-4778-1716-2(6)*, 9781477817162, Amazon Children's Publishing) Amazon Publishing.

Kimpton, Diana. Princess Ellie's Royal Jamboree No. 11. Finlay, Lizzie, illus. 11th ed. 2008. (ENG.). 96p. (gr. 1-4). pap. 3.99 *(978-1-4231-1531-1(7))* Hyperion Pr.

—Princess Ellie's Snowy Ride. Finlay, Lizzie, illus. 2007. (Pony-Crazed Princess Ser.). 90p. (J). 11.65 *(978-0-7569-8352-9(5))* Perfection Learning Corp.

Kinton, P. D. Wishing for Wizards & Chips for Te. 2010. 28p. pap. *(978-1-907211-26-3(8))* Grosvenor Hse. Publishing Ltd.

Kirk, David. Happy Heartwood Day. 2005. (Illus.). (J). *(978-1-4156-3888-0(8)*, Grosset & Dunlap) Penguin Publishing Group.

Kleinberg, Naomi. Have Yourself a Furry Little Christmas. Womble, Louis, illus. 2007. (ENG.). 12p. (J). (gr. k — 1). bds. 4.99 *(978-0-375-84133-0(4)*, Random Hse. Bks. for Young Readers) Random Hse. Children's Bks.

Kline, Suzy. Horrible Harry & the Holidaze. Remkiewicz, Frank, illus. 2004. (Horrible Harry Ser.). (ENG.). 80p. (J). (gr. 2-4). 4.99 *(978-0-14-240205-4(2)*, Puffin Books) Penguin Young Readers Group.

Kraft, Erik P. Lenny & Mel. Kraft, Erik P., illus. 2012. (Ready-for-Chapters Ser.). (ENG., Illus.). 64p. (J). (gr. 2-5). pap. 6.99 *(978-0-689-85891-8(4)*, Aladdin) Simon & Schuster Children's Publishing.

Krulik, Nancy. Love Stinks! John and Wendy Staff, illus. 2004. (Katie Kazoo, Switcheroo Ser.: 15). (ENG.). 80p. (J). (gr. 2-4). pap. 4.99 *(978-0-448-43640-1(X)*, Grosset & Dunlap) Penguin Young Readers Group.

Kubler, Annie. Wheels on the Bus, 15 vols. Kubler, Annie, illus. 2005. (ENG, TUR & MUL., Illus.). 14p. (J). bds. *(978-1-84444-980-4(7))* Mantra Lingua.

—Wheels on the Bus, 15 vols. 2005. (ENG, SPA & MUL., Illus.). 14p. (J). bds. *(978-1-84444-979-8(3))* Mantra Lingua.

—Wheels on the Bus, 15 vols. Kubler, Annie, illus. 2005. (ENG, SOM & MUL., Illus.). 14p. (J). bds. *(978-1-84444-978-1(5))* Mantra Lingua.

—Wheels on the Bus, 15 vols. 2005. (Illus.). 14p. (J). (POR, ENG & MUL.). bds. *(978-1-84444-977-4(7))*; (PAN, ENG & MUL., bds. *(978-1-84444-976-7(9))* Mantra Lingua.

—Wheels on the Bus, 15 vols. Kubler, Annie, illus. 2005. (Illus.). 14p. (J). (ENG, FRE & MUL.). bds. *(978-1-84444-974-3(2))*; (CHI, ENG & MUL., bds. *(978-1-84444-973-6(4))*; (ENG, CHI & MUL., bds. *(978-1-84444-972-9(6))*; (ENG, HIN & MUL., bds. *(978-1-84444-975-0(0))*; (BEN, ENG & MUL., bds. *(978-1-84444-971-2(8))*; (ARA, ENG & MUL., bds. *(978-1-84444-970-5(X))*; (URD, ENG & MUL., bds. *(978-1-84444-981-1(5))* Mantra Lingua.

Kurtz, John. Claus Kids Stickers. 2011. (Dover Little Activity Books Stickers Ser.). (ENG.). 4p. (J). (gr. k-3). pap. 1.50 *(978-0-486-48294-1(4))* Dover Pubns., Inc.

—Claus Kids Super Sticker Book: A Year-Round Christmas Celebration. 2011. (Dover Sticker Bks.). (ENG., Illus.). 6p. (J). (gr. k-5). 7.99 *(978-0-486-48295-8(2))* Dover Pubns., Inc.

Kyrja, et al. Rupert's Tales: The Wheel of the Year Beltane, Litha, Lammas, & Mabon, 1 vol. 2011. (ENG., Illus.). 64p. (J). 19.99 *(978-0-7643-3689-8(4)*, 9780764336898, Schiffer Publishing Ltd) Schiffer Publishing, Ltd.

Lanton, Sandy. Lots of Latkes: A Hanukkah Story. Redenbaugh, Vicki Jo, illus. 2003. (ENG.). 32p. (J). (gr. -1-3). 14.95 *(978-1-58013-091-2(7)*, Kar-Ben Publishing) Lerner Publishing Group.

Laterra, Joann. Halloween Crossing. 2004. 127p. (YA). pap. 14.95 *(978-0-7414-2101-2(1))* Infinity Publishing.

Lau, Barbara & Nesbitt, Kris. Sokita Celebrates the New Year: A Cambodian American Holiday. Chatterley, Cedric N., photos by. 2004. (Illus.). 32p. (J). per. 9.95 *(978-0-9747456-0-2(X))* Greensboro Historical Museum, Inc.

Lee, Zaina. Sun Takes a Holiday. 2009. 28p. pap. 13.99 *(978-1-4389-9992-0(5))* AuthorHouse.

Lionheart, Amelia. The Dolphin Heptad. 2009. 200p. (gr. 4-6). pap. 14.95 *(978-1-4401-8028-6(8))* iUniverse, Inc.

Llewellyn, Claire. Splash!, 1 vol. Beard, Lauren, illus. 2013. (Start Reading Ser.). (ENG.). 24p. (gr. k-1). pap. 7.95 *(978-1-4765-3186-1(2))*; pap. 41.94 *(978-1-4765-3232-5(X))* Capstone Press of Coughlan Cos.

Lowes, Tom, illus. Casey's Four Holiday Celebrations. l.t. ed. 2003. 38p. (J). 16.95 *(978-0-9722099-9-1(9)*, C4HC) Caseys World Bks.

Luenn, Nancy. A Gift for Abuelita/Un Regalo para Abuelita: Celebrating the Day of the Dead/En Celebration del Dia de los Muertos. Chapman, Robert, illus. 2004.Tr. of Un Regalo para Abuelita: En Celebration del Dia de los Muertos. (ENG, SPA & MUL.). 32p. (J). (gr. k-3). 15.95 *(978-0-87358-688-7(3))* Cooper Square Publishing Llc.

Maccarone, Grace. Turkey Day. Manders, John, illus. 2010. (Scholastic Reader Level 1 Ser.). (ENG.). 32p. (J). (gr. -1-3). pap. 3.99 *(978-0-545-12001-2(2)*, Cartwheel Bks.) Scholastic, Inc.

Macri, Thomas. Avengers: Happy Holidays! 2016. (Marvel 8x8s Ser.). (J). lib. bdg. 16.00 ***(978-0-606-39176-4(2))*** Turtleback Bks.

Mae, Darcie. Sammy & Robert Go Home for the Holidays. 2011. 44p. pap. 24.95 *(978-1-4560-5702-2(2))* America Star Bks.

Man-Kong, Mary. Holiday Style (Barbie) 2014. (Big Coloring Book Ser.). (ENG.). 48p. (J). (gr. -1-2). pap. 6.99 *(978-0-385-38339-4(8)*, Golden Bks.) Random Hse. Children's Bks.

Mara, Cate. The Great Kieranski & the Bardbuy. 2012. 114p. pap. *(978-0-9873204-2-1(4))* Breedles Publishing.

Margaret Penrose. Dorothy Dale's Queer Holidays. l.t. ed. 2007. (ENG.). 174p. pap. 21.99 *(978-1-4264-8931-0(5))* Creative Media Partners, LLC.

Marion, L. K. Summer Holiday with Funny Bunny. 2012. 32p. pap. 17.25 *(978-1-4669-6475-4(8))* Trafford Publishing.

May, Eleanor. The Best Mother's Day Ever. Pilz, M. H., illus. 2010. (Social Studies Connects Ser.). 32p. (J). (gr. 1-3). pap. 5.95 *(978-1-57565-299-3(4))* Kane Press, Inc.

Mayer, Mercer. It's Earth Day!, No. 5. Mayer, Mercer, illus. 2008. (Little Critter Ser.: No. 5). (ENG., Illus.). 24p. (J). (gr. -1-2). pap. 3.99 *(978-0-06-053959-7(3)*, HarperFestival) HarperCollins Pubs.

McDaniel, Lurlene. Starry, Starry Night: Three Holiday Stories. 2011. (ENG.). 272p. (YA). (gr. 7). pap. 8.99 *(978-0-385-74045-6(X)*, Ember) Random Hse. Children's Bks.

McGinty, Alice B. Rabbi Benjamin's Buttons. Reinhardt, Jennifer Black, illus. (ENG.). 32p. (J). (gr. -1-3). 2017. pap. 7.99 *(978-1-58089-433-3(X))* 2014. lib. bdg. 17.95 *(978-1-58089-432-6(1))* Charlesbridge Publishing, Inc.

McManis, Margaret. Olé! Cinco de Mayo!, 1 vol. Harrington, David, illus. 2013. (ENG.). 32p. (J). (gr. k-3). 16.99 *(978-1-4556-1754-8(7))* Pelican Publishing Co., Inc.

McNamara, Margaret. Martin Luther King Jr. Day. Gordon, Mike, illus. 2007. (Robin Hill School Ser.). (ENG.). 32p. (J). (gr. -1-1). pap. 3.99 *(978-1-4169-3494-3(4)*, Simon Spotlight) Simon Spotlight.

McOmber, Rachel B., ed. Bags... Bags (Holidays) rev. ed. (Illus.). (J). *(978-0-944991-98-5(X))* Swift Learning Resources.

—McOmber Phonics Storybooks: Boyer's Toy Store. rev. ed. (Illus.). (J). *(978-0-944991-69-5(6))* Swift Learning Resources.

Meachen Rau, Dana. Holiday Time. 2004. (Compass Point Early Reader Ser.). (J). 18.60 *(978-0-7565-0571-4(2))* Compass Point Bks.

Meadows, Daisy. Destiny the Rock Star Fairy. 2011. (Rainbow Magic Ser.). (ENG., Illus.). 176p. (J). (gr. 2-5). pap. 6.99 *(978-0-545-27056-4(1)*, Scholastic Paperbacks) Scholastic, Inc.

—Stella the Star Fairy. Ripper, Georgie, illus. 2008. (Rainbow Magic Ser.). (ENG.). 192p. (J). (gr. -1-3). pap. 6.99 *(978-0-545-06776-8(6)*, Scholastic Paperbacks) Scholastic, Inc.

Menge, Dawn. Queen Vernita Visits the Blue Ice Mountains. 2009. 32p. (J). pap. 19.95 *(978-1-4327-1169-6(5))* Outskirts Pr., Inc.

Miller-Stehr, Felicia. Are You Chanukah or Christmas? 2008. 32p. pap. 17.99 *(978-1-4343-9517-7(0))* AuthorHouse.

Minaki, Christina. Zoe's Extraordinary Holiday Adventures, 1 vol. 2007. (ENG.). 116p. (J). (gr. 2-5). pap. 8.95 *(978-1-897187-26-5(2))* Second Story Pr. CAN. Dist: Orca Bk. Pubs. USA.

Mitchell, Carolann. The Song of the Snow. 2011. 68p. (gr. 4-6). pap. 8.95 *(978-0-595-46609-2(5))* iUniverse, Inc.

Moncure, Jane Belk. Mousekin's Special Day: A Book about Special Days. Gallagher-Cole, Mernie, illus. 2013. (Magic Castle Readers Ser.). (ENG.). 32p. (J). (gr. -1-2). 25.64 *(978-1-62323-586-4(3)*, 206321) Child's World, Inc., The.

Moore, Clement C. C'Etait la Veille de Noel. Santore, Charles, illus. 2012. (FRE.). 48p. (J). 18.95 *(978-1-60433-300-8(6)*, Applesauce Pr.) Cider Mill Pr. Bk. Pubs., LLC.

Mora, Pat. Book Fiesta! Celebrate Children's Day. López, Rafael, illus. 2009.Tr. of Celebremos el Día de los Niños, el Día de los Libros. (SPA & ENG.). 40p. (J). (gr. -1-1). 17.99 *(978-0-06-128877-7(2)*, Rayo) HarperCollins Pubs.

—Book Fiesta! Celebrate Children's Day/Book Day; Celebremos el Dia de Los Ninos/el Dia de Los Libros. López, Rafael, illus. 2016. 40p. (J). (gr. -1-1). pap. 6.99 *(978-0-06-128878-4(0))* HarperCollins Pubs.

Mora, Pat & Ventura, Gabriela Baeza. The Remembering Day / el Día de Los Muertos. Casilla, Robert, illus. 2015. (SPA & ENG.). 32p. (J). (gr. k-3). 17.95 *(978-1-55885-805-3(9)*, Piñata Books) Arte Publico Pr.

Morley, Elizabeth. Let Sleeping Hedgehogs Spy. 2013. (Illus.). 154p. pap. *(978-1-78299-107-6(7))* FeedARead.com.

Morrison, Jessica. La Fête du Travail: Les Célébrations Canadiennes. Karvonen, Tanjah, tr. from ENG. 2011. (FRE.). 24p. (gr. k-3). *(978-1-77071-397-0(2))* Weigl Educational Pubs. Ltd.

—Le Jour de la SaintJeanBaptiste: Les Célébrations Canadiennes. Karvonen, Tanjah, tr. from ENG. 2011. (FRE.). 24p. (gr. k-3). *(978-1-77071-399-4(9))* Weigl Educational Pubs. Ltd.

Moss, Miriam. Matty Takes Off! Simmons, Jane, illus. 2008. (Matty & Milly Ser.). (ENG.). 32p. (J). (gr. -1-k). 19.95 *(978-1-84270-701-2(9))* Andersen Pr. GBR. Dist: Independent Pubs. Group.

Multicultural Staff. Ravi's Diwali Surprise Story P. (J). 48.95 *(978-0-8136-2338-2(3))* Modern Curriculum Pr.

Murrell, Belinda. Lulu Bell's: Fantastic Holiday Fun. 2016. (Lulu Bell Ser.). (ENG., Illus.). 384p. (J). (gr. 1-3). pap. 9.99 *(978-1-925324-37-2(0))* Random Hse. Australia AUS. Dist: Independent Pubs. Group.

—Lulu Bell's Amazing Animal Adventures. 2016. (Lulu Bell Ser.). (ENG., Illus.). 384p. (J). (gr. 1-3). pap. 9.99 *(978-1-925324-35-8(4))* Random Hse. Australia AUS. Dist: Independent Pubs. Group.

My Holiday Dress. 2003. (J). per. *(978-1-57657-929-9(8))* Paradise Pr., Inc.

Naifeh, Ted. Courtney Crumrin Volume 4: Monstrous Holiday Special Edition: Monstrous Holiday Special Edition. 2013. (ENG., Illus.). 128p. (YA). 24.99 *(978-1-934964-92-7(1)*, 9781934964927) Oni Pr., Inc.

Neale, J. B. In the Shadow of the Guillotine. 2008. 180p. pap. 13.95 *(978-1-4092-0391-9(3))* Lulu Pr., Inc.

Nicholls, Claire. In it to win It. 2011. 160p. (gr. 4-6). pap. 14.09 *(978-1-4567-7994-8(X))* AuthorHouse.

Novesky, Amy. Mister & Lady Day: Billie Holiday & the Dog Who Loved Her. Newton, Vanessa Brantley, illus. 2013. (ENG.). 32p. (J). (gr. -1-3). 16.99 *(978-0-15-205806-7(0))* Houghton Mifflin Harcourt Publishing Co.

Olcott, Frances Jenkins. Good Stories for Great Holidays. Lt. ed. 2006. (ENG.). 324p. pap. 24.99 *(978-1-4264-1125-0(1))* Creative Media Partners, LLC.

—Good Stories for Holidays. 2004. reprint ed. pap. 1.99 *(978-1-4192-2211-5(2))*; pap. 27.95 *(978-1-4191-2211-8(8))* Kessinger Publishing, LLC.

Owens, Donna. NIBBLES:VOLUME 3, Nibbles enjoys the Holidays. 2008. 38p. pap. 14.95 *(978-1-4357-4715-9(1))* Lulu Pr., Inc.

Parragon Staff. Celebrate the Year with Winnie the Pooh. 2010. (Disney Diecut Classics). 72p. (J). (gr. -1-1). *(978-1-4075-8902-2(4))* Parragon, Inc.

Pascual, Emilio. Dias de Reyes Magos. Serrano, Javier U., illus. 4th ed. 2003. (SPA.). 158p. *(978-84-207-9079-4(6)*, GS4140) Grupo Anaya, S.A. ESP. Dist: Lectorum Pubns., Inc.

Peanuts Picture Books. 2013. (Peanuts Picture Bks.: 5). (ENG.). 24-48p. (J). (gr. -1-4). lib. bdg. 121.05 *(978-1-61479-028-0(0))* ABDO Publishing Co.

Pearce, Margaret. A Belinda Robinson Novel Book 2: Belinda & the Holidays It Rained. 2013. 78p. pap. *(978-1-922233-22-6(6))* Writers Exchange E-Publishing.

Perkins, Stephanie. My True Love Gave to Me: Twelve Holiday Stories. (ENG., Illus.). 336p. (YA). 2016. pap. 10.99 *(978-1-250-05931-4(3)*, 9781250059314) 2014. (gr. 8-12). 18.99 *(978-1-250-05930-7(5)*, 9781250059307) St. Martin's Pr. (St. Martin's Griffin).

Peyo. Smurfs Mini Library: Rise & Shine; Happy Smurfdays; Fun & Games; Making Music; Whatever the Weather. Peyo, illus. 2014. (Smurfs Classic Ser.). (ENG., Illus.). 70p. (J). (gr. -1-2). bds. 6.99 *(978-1-4424-9543-2(X)*, Simon Spotlight) Simon Spotlight.

Pfeffer, Z. My Yom Tov Album. 2004. (Illus.). 105p. (J). 16.95 *(978-1-931681-58-2(9))* Israel Bookshop Pubns.

Pilkey, Dav. The Dumb Bunnies' Easter. 2008. (Dumb Bunnies Ser.). (ENG., Illus.). 32p. (J). (gr. -1-3). pap. 6.99 *(978-0-545-00880-8(8)*, Scholastic Paperbacks) Scholastic, Inc.

—Dumb Bunnies' Easter. Pilkey, Dav, illus. 2009. (Dumb Bunnies Ser.). (ENG., Illus.). 32p. (J). (gr. -1-3). 16.99 *(978-0-545-03946-8(0))* Scholastic, Inc.

Prime, Derek. Sarah & Paul Go on Holiday Again: Discover about Being a Christian. 2006. (Sarah & Paul Ser.). (ENG., Illus.). 128p. (J). per. 6.99 *(978-1-84550-162-4(4)*, 94175d0d-6922-46f5-bc95-9e8edf2f526c) Christian Focus Pubns. GBR. Dist: Bookmasters Distribution.

Reader's Digest Staff & Gold, Gina. Bunny Hugs. 2013. (Hugs Book Ser.). (ENG.). 10p. (J). (gr. -1-k). bds. 4.99 *(978-0-7944-2784-9(7))* Studio Fun International.

Rey, H. A. Hooray for Halloween, Curious George. 2016. (Curious George Ser.). (ENG., Illus.). 24p. (J). (gr. -1-3). 9.99 *(978-0-544-69956-4(4)*, HMH Books For Young Readers) Houghton Mifflin Harcourt Publishing Co.

Richardson, Bernard. Freddy Weller's Holiday. 2011. 50p. 24.99 *(978-1-4628-9548-9(4))*; pap. 15.99 *(978-1-4628-9547-2(6))* Xlibris Corp.

Rigby Education Staff. Dad's Pasta. (Sails Literacy Ser.). (Illus.). 16p. (gr. 2-3). 27.00 *(978-0-7635-9951-5(4)*, 699514C99) Rigby Education.

Rinaldi, Ann. Come Juneteenth. 2009. (ENG., Illus.). 256p. (YA). (gr. 7). pap. 7.99 *(978-0-15-206392-4(7))* Houghton Mifflin Harcourt Publishing Co.

Roberts, Bethany. Fourth of July Mice ! 2004. (ENG., Illus.). 32p. (J). (gr. -1-1). tchr. ed. 13.00 *(978-0-618-31367-9(2)*, Clarion Bks.) Houghton Mifflin Harcourt Trade & Reference Pubs.

Ruiz-Flores, Lupe. Lupita's First Dance / el Primer Baile de Lupita. Baeza Ventura, Gabriela, tr. Utomo, Gabhor, illus. 2013. (SPA.). 32p. (J). 17.95 *(978-1-55885-772-8(9)*, Piñata Books) Arte Publico Pr.

Ryles, Donald. The Magic Holiday Forest. 2008. 40p. pap. 8.95 *(978-1-4357-4772-2(0))* Lulu Pr., Inc.

Sanders, Jeane F. Ramón. 2008. 100p. pap. 19.95 *(978-1-60610-768-3(2))* America Star Bks.

Sansone, V. K. WANTED: Children for Toys. 2009. 32p. pap. 14.98 *(978-0-557-16717-3(5))* Lulu Pr., Inc.

Santomero, Angela C. Happy Halloween, Daniel Tiger! Style Guide Staff & Fruchter, Jason, illus. 2014. (Daniel Tiger's Neighborhood Ser.). (ENG.). 14p. (J). (gr. -1-2). bds. 6.99 *(978-1-4814-0429-7(6)*, Simon Spotlight) Simon Spotlight.

Sam, Amélie & Trouillot, Virgile. Happy Holidays. 2009. (Groove High Ser.). (Illus.). 112p. (YA). (gr. 5-8). 31.95 *(978-1-60754-526-2(8))*; pap. 15.25 *(978-1-60754-527-9(6))* Windmill Bks.

Schulman, Janet. 10 Trim-the-Tree'ers. Davick, Linda, illus. 2011. (ENG.). 32p. (J). (gr. -1 — 1). bds. 6.99 *(978-0-375-87302-7(3)*, Knopf Bks. for Young Readers) Random Hse. Children's Bks.

Schulz, Charles M. Peanuts Holiday Box Set. 2010. (Miniature Editions Ser.). (ENG.). 128p. 9.95 *(978-0-7624-3958-4(0))* Running Pr. Bk. Pubs.

Scott, Shirley A. The Adventures of Jack & Dobbie: Doggie Holidays. 2011. 40p. pap. 17.95 *(978-1-4567-3426-8(1))* AuthorHouse.

Sedgwick, Patricia Louise. Santa's Key. deluxe ed. 2004. (Illus.). 12.95 incl. audio compact disk *(978-0-9688190-1-2(X))* F. D. & D. Corp. CAN. Dist: Hushion Hse. Publishing, Ltd.

Sewer, Anecia. Why Transfer Day, Anyway? Samuel, Karen, illus. 2007. 16p. (J). 15.99 *(978-0-9752986-0-2(7))* Research Institute Pr., The.

Shannon, Terry Miller. Reindeer Holiday. 2016. (Spring Forward Ser.). (J). (gr. 1). *(978-1-4900-9390-1(7))* Benchmark Education Co.

Shea, Therese. Flag Day. 2006. (Neighborhood Readers Ser.). (ENG.). 16p. (gr. 1-3). pap. 6.50 *(978-1-4042-7144-9(9)*, Rosen Classroom) Rosen Publishing Group, Inc., The.

Sherman, Marcia A. The Splendid, Blended Family. 2007. 24p. 13.95 *(978-0-615-17159-3(1))* Pumpkin Seeds Pr.

Shore, Diane Z. This Is the Feast. Lloyd, Megan, illus. 2011. (ENG.). 32p. (J). (gr. -1-3). pap. 6.99 *(978-0-06-443850-6(3))* HarperCollins Pubs.

Sicks, Linda. Nick's Holiday Celebration. Messing, Dave, illus. 2010. (Importance of Family Ser.). 40p. (J). 18.95 *(978-1-936193-05-9(1))* Nick The Cat, LLC.

Silverhardt, Lauryn. SpongeBob SpookyPants. Style Guide Staff, illus. 2004. (SpongeBob SquarePants Ser.). (ENG.). 16p. (J). bds. 5.99 *(978-0-689-87320-1(4)*, Simon Spotlight/Nickelodeon) Simon Spotlight/Nickelodeon.

Skinner, Daphne. Palapalooza. Smath, Jerry, illus. 2006. (Social Studies Connects). 32p. (J). (gr. -1-3). pap. 5.95 *(978-1-57565-163-7(7))* Kane Press, Inc.

Slegers, Liesbet. Happy Easter! Slegers, Liesbet, illus. 2012. (ENG., Illus.). 30p. (J). (gr. k — 1). 15.95 *(978-1-60537-114-6(9))* Cobblestone Publishing Co.

Smith, Cliff. New Magical Holiday Stories. 2005. pap. 31.99 *(978-1-4134-7971-3(5))* Xlibris Corp.

Smith, S. C. Mabell. Ethel Morton's Holidays. 2007. 112p. 94.99 *(978-1-4280-7692-1(1))*; per. 88.99 *(978-1-4280-7699-0(9))* IndyPublish.com.

Snowflake Day! 2014. (Daniel Tiger's Neighborhood Ser.). (ENG., Illus.). 14p. (J). (gr. -1-k). bds. 5.99 *(978-1-4814-1771-6(1)*, Simon Spotlight) Simon Spotlight.

Sparks, Favre. The Ugly Brown Cup. 2013. 12p. pap. 9.00 *(978-1-62516-468-1(8)*, Strategic Bk. Publishing) Strategic Book Publishing & Rights Agency (SBPRA).

Spelvin, Justin. Blue's Big Parade! Chernichaw, Ian, illus. 2005. (Blue's Clues Ser.). (ENG.). 24p. (J). pap. 3.99 *(978-0-689-87673-8(4)*, Simon Spotlight/Nickelodeon) Simon Spotlight/Nickelodeon.

Spinner, Stephanie. The Nutcracker. Malone, Peter, illus. 2015. (ENG.). 40p. (J). (gr. -1-2). lib. bdg. 20.99 *(978-0-553-52465-9(8)*, Knopf Bks. for Young Readers) Random Hse. Children's Bks.

Stanley, Diane. Thanksgiving on Plymouth Plantation. Berry, Holly, illus. 2004. (Time-Traveling Twins Ser.). (ENG.). 48p. (J). (gr. k-5). 16.99 *(978-0-06-027069-8(1))* HarperCollins Pubs.

Stern, Ricki. Mission Impossible. Date not set. (Beryl E. Bean Ser.: Vol. 3). (Illus.). (J). lib. bdg. 15.89 *(978-0-06-028773-3(X)*, Harper Trophy) HarperCollins Pubs.

Stevens, Michael J. Silver Spitfire. 2010. 164p. pap. *(978-1-907652-13-4(2))* Grosvenor Hse. Publishing Ltd.

Stilton, Geronimo. Save the White Whale! 2011. (ENG.). 128p. (J). (gr. 2-5). pap. 7.99 *(978-0-545-10377-0(0)*, Scholastic Paperbacks) Scholastic, Inc.

—A Very Merry Christmas. 2008. (Geronimo Stilton Ser.: 35). (ENG.). 128p. (J). (gr. 2-5). pap. 7.99 *(978-0-545-02135-7(9)*, Scholastic Paperbacks) Scholastic, Inc.

Stone Arch Books. April Showers & Cinco de Mayo, 1 vol. Nguyen, Dustin, illus. 2014. (Batman: Li'l Gotham Ser.). (ENG.). 32p. (gr. 2-3). 22.60 *(978-1-4342-9220-9(7))* Stone Arch Bks.

—Christmas & New Year's Eve, 1 vol. Nguyen, Dustin, illus. 2014. (Batman: Li'l Gotham Ser.). (ENG.). 32p. (gr. 2-3). 22.60 *(978-1-4342-9217-9(7))* Stone Arch Bks.

—Halloween & Thanksgiving, 1 vol. Nguyen, Dustin, illus. 2014. (Batman: Li'l Gotham Ser.). (ENG.). 32p. (gr. 2-3). 22.60 *(978-1-4342-9208-7(8))* Stone Arch Bks.

—Mother's Day & Father's Day, 1 vol. Nguyen, Dustin, illus. 2014. (Batman: Li'l Gotham Ser.). (ENG.). 32p. (gr. 2-3). 22.60 *(978-1-4342-9221-6(5))* Stone Arch Bks.

—St. Patrick's Day & Easter, 1 vol. Nguyen, Dustin, illus. 2014. (Batman: Li'l Gotham Ser.). (ENG.). 32p. (gr. 2-3). 22.60 *(978-1-4342-9219-3(3))* Stone Arch Bks.

—Valentine's Day & the Lunar New Year, 1 vol. Nguyen, Dustin, illus. 2014. (Batman: Li'l Gotham Ser.). (ENG.). 32p. (gr. 2-3). 22.60 *(978-1-4342-9218-6(5))* Stone Arch Bks.

Stuart, Carrie. Chinese New Year. 2006. (Neighborhood Readers Ser.). (ENG.). 12p. (gr. -1-3). pap. 5.90 *(978-1-4042-6461-8(2)*, Rosen Classroom) Rosen Publishing Group, Inc., The.

Swallow, Pamela Curtis & Swallow, Pamela C. Groundhog Gets a Say. Bunkus, Denise, illus. 2007. (ENG.). 40p. (J). (gr. k-3). pap. 6.99 *(978-0-14-240896-4(4)*, Puffin Books) Penguin Young Readers Group.

Thaler, Mike. St. Patrick's Day from the Black Lagoon. Lee, Jared, illus. 2011. 61p. (J). *(978-0-545-27328-2(5))* Scholastic, Inc.

Tooth, Lucy. Star the Tooth Fairy Takes A Holiday to Visit Santa at the North Pole! 2010. 40p. 17.95 *(978-0-557-41623-3(X))* Lulu Pr., Inc.

Tuxford, Jenny & Brazier, Jenny. Fredd Boggitt & the Loch Ness Monster. 2009. 152p. pap. 11.99 *(978-1-4389-9593-9(8))* AuthorHouse.

Tyre, Greg R. Fun with Sockie. 2009. 28p. pap. 14.99 *(978-1-4490-0105-6(X))* AuthorHouse.

Ulker, Munise. Little Batul's Eid Celebration: The Most Pleasant Festival of Sacrifice. 2013. (ENG., Illus.). 32p. (J). (gr. -1-3). pap. 6.95 *(978-1-59784-294-5(X))* Tughra Bks.

Universal & King, Trey. Phil Saves the Holidays! 2016. (ENG., Illus.). 24p. (J). (gr. -1-3). 8.99 *(978-0-316-36149-1(6))* Little, Brown Bks. for Young Readers.

Van Syckle, A. & Schwartz, Josh. The OC: 'twas the Night Before Chrismukkah. 2005. 206p. (YA). *(978-1-4156-3915-3(9))* Scholastic, Inc.

Varacchi, Barbara. Desiree & Daisy Mae & All That Love. 2012. 24p. pap. 17.99 *(978-1-4685-6146-3(4))* AuthorHouse.

Verma, Jatinder. The Story of Divaali. Mistry, Nilesh, illus. 2007. (ENG.). 40p. (J). (gr. -1-3). pap. 7.99 *(978-1-84686-131-4(4))* Barefoot Bks., Inc.

Vojta, Pat Stemper. Mr. Groundhog Wants the Day Off/El Senor Marmota Quiere el Dia Libre. Leviskiy, Olga, illus. 2010. (ENG & SPA.). 32p. (J). (gr. 4-7). 16.95 *(978-1-934960-77-6(2)*, Raven Tree Pr.,Csi) Continental Sales, Inc.

Wade, Mary Dodson & National Geographic Learning Staff. El Dia de los Muertos. 2010. (Rise & Shine Ser.).Tr. of Day of the Dead. (ENG., Illus.). 32p. (C). (gr. 1-2). pap. 9.95 *(978-0-516-27354-9(X))* National Geographic School Publishing, Inc.

Warren, G. A. Starr Light & the Christmas Story. Ciesinska, Izabela, illus. 2009. 32p. (J). 14.95 *(978-1-935268-09-3(0))* Halo Publishing International.

Waters, George T. The Perfect Little Pumpkin. Duquet, Guy J., illus. Lt. ed. 2006. 30p. (J). per. 14.95 *(978-1-59879-286-7(5))* Lifevest Publishing, Inc.

Waters, Kate. Lion Dancer: Ernie Wan's Chinese New Year. Cooper, Martha & Slovenz-Low, Madeline, illus. 2010. (Rise & Shine Ser.). (ENG.). 40p. (C). (gr. -1-3). pap. 9.95 *(978-0-590-43047-0(5))* National Geographic School Publishing, Inc.

Waters, Tony. Cinnamon's Busy Year. Waters, Tony, illus. 2003. (Illus.). 32p. (J). (gr. -1-3). pap. 5.95 *(978-0-9710278-2-4(X))* All About Kids Publishing.

Weatherford, Carole Boston. Celebremos Juneteenth! de La Vega, Eida, tr. from ENG. Buchanan, Yvonne, illus. 2007. (SPA.). 32p. (J). (gr. -1-3). pap. 7.95 *(978-1-60060-247-4(9))* Lee & Low Bks., Inc.

Wells, Carolyn. Two Little Women on a Holiday. 2004. reprint ed. pap. 22.95 *(978-1-4191-9150-3(0))* Kessinger Publishing, LLC.

—Two Little Women on A Holiday. 2004. reprint ed. pap. 1.99 *(978-1-4192-9150-0(5))* Kessinger Publishing, LLC.

Wesley, Valerie Wilson. Willimena Rules: 9 Steps to the Best, Worst, Greatest Hiliday Ever! 2015. (ENG.). (J). (gr. 2-5). pap. 6.00 *(978-1-933491-17-2(5))* Just Us Bks., Inc.

Whitman Guszcza, Helen Suzanne. Little Lilli & Willy Live Here. 2012. (Illus.). 80p. pap. 19.95 *(978-1-4575-1026-7(X))* Dog Ear Publishing, LLC.

Whittingham, Stephen. The Best Summer Holiday. 2012. 100p. pap. 8.99 *(978-1-4525-0425-4(3))* Balboa Pr.

Wilkins, Phil Cole. Dragog & the Seven Weeks of Summer. 2012. 164p. (gr. -1). pap. 15.60 *(978-1-4567-8998-5(8))* AuthorHouse.

Wilkinson, Richard. Wilkinson Tales: A Collection of Holiday Short Stories for Young People. 2009. 80p. pap. 26.49 *(978-1-4490-0902-1(6))* AuthorHouse.

Wilson, A. c. & Wilson, A. C. Ambersil - the Legacy of Mr Harrison. 2011. 496p. pap. *(978-1-908105-45-5(3))* Grosvenor Hse. Publishing Ltd.

Wilson, Pamela J. Tales from Tubblewood Too. 2009. (Illus.). 164p. 23.50 *(978-1-4389-4064-9(5))* AuthorHouse.

—Tales from Tubblewood Too: Miss Duck to the Rescue. 2009. (Illus.). 164p. pap. 13.50 *(978-1-4389-4063-2(7))* AuthorHouse.

Woods, Cindy Smith. The Happy, Happy Christmas Book. 2011. 58p. pap. 16.95 *(978-1-4626-4064-5(8))* America Star Bks.

Worsham, Adria F. Max Celebrates Cinco de Mayo, 1 vol. Gallagher-Cole, Mernie, illus. 2008. (Read-It! Readers: the Life of Max Ser.). (ENG.). 24p. (gr. -1-2). lib. bdg. 21.32 *(978-1-4048-4759-0(6)*, Easy Readers) Picture Window Bks.

Wright, Amber. Celebrate! Your Inner Star. 2011. 94p. pap. 19.95 *(978-1-4560-5171-6(7))* America Star Bks.

Yim, Natasha. Goldy Luck & the Three Pandas. Zong, Grace, illus. (ENG.). 32p. (J). (gr. -1-3). 2015. pap. 7.95 *(978-1-58089-653-5(7))* 2014. lib. bdg. 16.95 *(978-1-58089-652-8(9))* Charlesbridge Publishing, Inc.

Zucker, Jonny. Lighting a Lamp: A Diwali Story. Cohen, Jan Barger, illus. 2004. (Festival Time Ser.). (ENG.). 24p. (J). pap. 8.99 *(978-0-7641-2670-3(9))* Barron's Educational Series, Inc.

HOLIDAYS—POETRY

Brooks, Marie, et al. Pet Poems & Special Days Poems. 2008. (Illus.). 32p. (J). lib. bdg. 23.65 *(978-1-59646-598-5(0))* Dingles & Co.

Duggan, Paul. Deux Squelettes au Téléphone. Sylvestre, Daniel, illus. 2004. (Picture Bks.). (FRE.). 32p. (J). (gr. 4). *(978-2-89021-677-8(2))* Diffusion du livre Mirabel (DLM).

Koontz, Dean. Every Day's a Holiday: Amusing Rhymes for Happy Times. Parks, Phil, illus. 2003. 144p. (J). 18.89 *(978-0-06-008585-8(1))* HarperCollins Pubs.

Lewis, J. Patrick. Kooky Crumbs: Poems in Praise of Dizzy Days. Uhles, Mary, illus. 2016. (ENG.). 32p. (J). 12.99 *(978-1-61067-371-6(9))* Kane Miller.

Low, Elizabeth Cothen. Big Book of Seasons, Holidays, & Weather: Rhymes, Fingerplays, & Songs for Children. 2011. (ENG., Illus.). 156p. E-Book *(978-1-59884-624-9(8)*, Libraries Unlimited) ABC-CLIO, LLC.

Pilkey, Dav. 'Twas the Night Before Thanksgiving. 2004. (Bookshelf Ser.). (ENG.). 32p. (J). (gr. -1-k). pap. 6.99 *(978-0-439-66937-5(5)*, Scholastic Paperbacks) Scholastic, Inc.

Public Domain Staff. Five Little Pumpkins. Yaccarino, Dan, illus. 2003. (ENG.). 16p. (J). (gr. -1-k). pap. 6.99 *(978-0-694-01177-3(0)*, HarperFestival) HarperCollins Pubs.

HOLLYWOOD (LOS ANGELES, CALIF.)—FICTION

Alender, Katie. Famous Last Words. 2014. (ENG.). 320p. (J). (gr. 7). 18.99 *(978-0-545-63997-2(2))* Scholastic, Inc.

Baker, Ken. Finding Forever. 2015. (ENG.). 256p. (YA). (gr. 2-17). pap. 9.95 *(978-0-7624-5594-2(2)*, Running Pr. Kids) Running Pr. Bk. Pubs.

Belshe, Judy. The Fry Family Goes to Hollywood. 2007. (Illus.). 50p. (J). spiral bd. 10.00 *(978-0-9655530-4-9(3))* Snuggle Up Bks.

Blumenthal, Deborah. Charlie Hits It Big. Brunkus, Denise, illus. 2008. 32p. (J). (gr. -1). lib. bdg. 17.89 *(978-0-06-056354-7(0))* HarperCollins Pubs.

Bonin, Liane. Pretty on the Outside: Fame Unlimited. 2007. 288p. (YA). pap. 9.99 *(978-0-451-22122-3(2)*, N A L Trade) Penguin Publishing Group.

Bradley, F. T. The Alias Men. 2015. (Double Vision Ser.: 3). (ENG.). 256p. (J). (gr. 3-7). pap. 6.99 *(978-0-06-210444-1(6))* HarperCollins Pubs.

—Double Vision: The Alias Men. 2014. (Double Vision Ser.: 3). (ENG.). 256p. (J). (gr. 3-7). 16.99 *(978-0-06-210443-4(8))* HarperCollins Pubs.

Callaghan, Cindy. Lost in Hollywood. 2016. (Mix Ser.). (ENG., Illus.). 240p. (J). (gr. 4-8). pap. 7.99 *(978-1-4814-6571-7(6)*, Aladdin) Simon & Schuster Children's Publishing.

Calonita, Jen. Family Affairs. 2009. (Secrets of My Hollywood Life Ser.: 3). (ENG.). 352p. (YA). (gr. 7-17). pap. 7.99 *(978-0-316-11800-2(1)*, Poppy) Little, Brown Bks. for Young Readers.

—On Location. 2008. (Secrets of My Hollywood Life Ser.: 2). (ENG.). 256p. (YA). (gr. 7-17). per. 7.99 *(978-0-316-15440-6(7)*, Poppy) Little, Brown Bks. for Young Readers.

—Secrets of My Hollywood Life. 2007. (Secrets of My Hollywood Life Ser.: 1). (ENG.). 256p. (J). (gr. 7-17). per. 19.99 *(978-0-316-15443-7(1)*, Poppy) Little, Brown Bks. for Young Readers.

Cheaney, J. B. I Don't Know How the Story Ends. 2015. (ENG.). 288p. (J). (gr. 4-7). 16.99 *(978-1-4926-0944-5(7)*, 9781492609445, Sourcebooks Jabberwocky) Sourcebooks, Inc.

Coleman, Rowan. Hollywood Star. 2011. (ENG.). 320p. (J). (gr. 6-9). pap. 11.99 *(978-0-00-724433-1(9))* HarperCollins Pubs. Ltd. GBR. Dist: HarperCollins Pubs.

Conrad, Lauren. Starstruck. (YA). 2013. (Fame Game Ser.: 2). (ENG.). 320p. (gr. 9). pap. 10.99 *(978-0-06-207982-4(4))* 2012. (Fame Game Ser.: 2). (ENG.). 304p. (gr. 9). 18.99 *(978-0-06-207980-0(8))* 2012. 352p. pap. *(978-0-06-220964-1(7))* HarperCollins Pubs.

Crane, Caprice. Confessions of a Hater. 2014. (ENG.). 384p. (YA). (gr. 8). pap. 9.99 *(978-1-250-04433-4(2)*, 9781250044334) Square Fish.

Decter, Ed & Burns, Laura J. Hot Mess. 2010. (Chloe Gamble Ser.). (ENG.). 368p. (YA). (gr. 9-18). pap. 16.99 *(978-1-4169-5437-8(6)*, Simon Pulse) Simon Pulse.

DeVillers, Julia & Roy, Jennifer. Double Feature. 2012. (Mix Ser.). (ENG.). 288p. (J). (gr. 4-8). pap. 7.99 *(978-1-4424-3403-5(1)*, Aladdin) Simon & Schuster Children's Publishing.

Doctorow, Cory. Pirate Cinema. 2012. (ENG.). 384p. (YA). (gr. 8-13). 19.99 *(978-0-7653-2908-0(5)*, 9780765329080, Tor Teen) Doherty, Tom Assocs., LLC.

Frees, Jessie Lynch. Jackie Winquackey & Her 43 Cats Go to Hollywood. Gebr, Jaroslav, illus. 2005. 32p. (J). 14.99 *(978-0-9760553-0-3(9))* Tizbit Books, LLC.

Gentry, Brad. The Hollywood Princess. 2009. 40p. pap. 20.99 *(978-1-4490-3545-7(0))* AuthorHouse.

Handford, Martin. Where's Waldo? in Hollywood. Handford, Martin, illus. 2007. (Where's Waldo? Ser.). (ENG., Illus.). 32p. (J). (gr. k-4). pap. 7.99 *(978-0-7636-3501-5(4))* Candlewick Pr.

Hare, Mimi & Naylor, Clare. The First Assistant: A Continuing Tale from Behind the Hollywood Curtain. 2007. (ENG.). 288p. (gr. 12-18). 14.00 *(978-0-452-28836-2(3)*, Plume) Penguin Publishing Group.

Harrison, Lisi. Dial L for Loser. 2008. (Clique Novels Ser.). 268p. 20.00 *(978-1-60686-291-9(X))* Perfection Learning Corp.

John, Antony. Imposter. 2015. (ENG.). 320p. (YA). (gr. 7). 17.99 *(978-0-8037-4124-9(3)*, Dial Bks) Penguin Young Readers Group.

Kerston, Caroline. Hollywood Harry. 2005. 28.00 *(978-0-8059-9458-2(0))* Dorrance Publishing Co., Inc.

Klise, Kate. Hollywood, Dead Ahead. Klise, M. Sarah, illus. (43 Old Cemetery Road Ser.: 5). (ENG.). 144p. (J). (gr. 2-5). 2014. pap. 6.99 *(978-0-544-33661-2(5)*, HMH Books For Young Readers) 2013. 15.99 *(978-0-547-85283-6(5))* Houghton Mifflin Harcourt Publishing Co.

Lane, Dakota. Gothic Lolita: A Mystical Thriller. Lane, Dakota, illus. 2008. (ENG., Illus.). 208p. (YA). (gr. 7-18). 17.99 *(978-1-4169-1396-2(3)*, Atheneum Bks. for Young Readers) Simon & Schuster Children's Publishing.

Langston, Laura. Hot New Thing, 1 vol. 2014. (Orca Limelights Ser.). (ENG.). 136p. (J). (gr. 6-9). pap. 9.95 *(978-1-4598-0431-9(7))* Orca Bk. Pubs. USA.

Locklear, Morgan & Locklear, Jennifer. Exposure. 2014. (ENG.). 271p. pap. 19.99 *(978-1-62342-121-2(7))* Omnific Publishing.

Marsh, Carole. The Mystery at Hollywood. 2011. (Carole Marsh Mysteries Ser.). (J). pap. 7.99 *(978-0-635-07959-6(3)*, Marsh, Carole Mysteries) Gallopade International.

McCoy, Mary. Dead to Me. 2015. (ENG.). 304p. (YA). (gr. 7-12). 17.99 *(978-1-4231-8712-7(1))* Hyperion Bks. for Children.

McDonald, Abby. Jane Austen Goes to Hollywood. (ENG.). 336p. (YA). (gr. 9). 2015. pap. 8.99 *(978-0-7636-7669-8(1))* 2013. 17.99 *(978-0-7636-5508-2(2))* Candlewick Pr.

McDonald, Megan. Judy Moody Goes to Hollywood: Behind the Scenes with Judy Moody & Friends. Reynolds, Peter H. & Candlewick Press Staff, illus. 2011. (Judy Moody Ser.). (ENG.). 160p. (J). (gr. 1-4). 14.99 *(978-0-7636-5551-8(1))* Candlewick Pr.

Muszynski, Julie. Henley in Hollywood. 2015. (ENG., Illus.). 56p. 20.00 *(978-0-9905320-0-2(3))* Glitterati, Inc.

Patterson, James & Grabenstein, Chris. I Totally Funniest: A Middle School Story. Park, Laura, illus. 2015. (J). 320p. *(978-0-316-26161-6(0))*; (ENG.). 336p. (gr. 3-7). 13.99 *(978-0-316-40593-5(0)*, Jimmy Patterson) Little Brown & Co.

Pfeffer, Susan Beth. Revenge of the Aztecs. 2004. 118p. (J). lib. bdg. 16.92 *(978-1-4242-0763-3(0))* Fitzgerald Bks.

Pinkwater, Daniel M. The Yggyssey: How Iggy Wondered What Happened to All the Ghosts, Found Out Where They Went, & Went There. 2010. (ENG., Illus.). 256p. (J). (gr. 5-7). pap. 6.99 *(978-0-547-32865-2(6))* Houghton Mifflin Harcourt Publishing Co.

Reisfeld, Randi. No Strings Attached: CC (Cape Cod); Partiers Preferred. 2013. (ENG., Illus.). 624p. (YA). (gr. 9). pap. 9.99 *(978-1-4424-5978-6(6)*, Simon Pulse) Simon Pulse.

Rottenberg, David Ira & Rottenberg, David Ira. Gwendolyn Goes Hollywood. Anderson, Lesley, illus. 2011. 40p. (J). 16.99 *(978-0-910291-11-8(X))* Cedar Crest Bks.

Ruditis, P. J. Love, Hollywood Style. 2013. (Romantic Comedies Ser.). (ENG., Illus.). 272p. (YA). (gr. 7). pap. 13.99 *(978-1-4814-1539-2(5)*, Simon Pulse) Simon Pulse.

Savage, Derek. Cool Cat Loves Going Green. 2010. (Cool Cat Ser.: Vol. 2).Tr. of Cool Cat le gusta Cuidar el Medio Ambiente. (ENG & SPA., Illus.). 32p. (J). 7.95 *(978-0-9673000-4-7(5))* Blue Thunder Bks.

H

I

Serle, Rebecca. Famous in Love. 2014. (ENG.). 336p. (YA). (gr. 7-17). 18.00 *(978-0-316-36632-8(3),* Poppy) Little, Brown Bks. for Young Readers.
—Truly Madly Famously. 2015. (Famous in Love Ser.: 2). (ENG.). 320p. (YA). (gr. 7-17). 18.00 *(978-0-316-36640-3(4),* Poppy) Little, Brown Bks. for Young Readers.
Shankman, Adam & Sullivan, Laura L. Girl about Town. 2016. (ENG., Illus.). 336p. (YA). (gr. 9). 17.99 *(978-1-4814-4787-4(4),* Atheneum Bks. for Young Readers) Simon & Schuster Children's Publishing.
Shankman, Adam & Sullivan, Laura L. Murder among the Stars. 2017. (YA). pap. ***(978-1-4814-4791-1(2))***; (ENG., Illus.). 320p. (gr. 9). 17.99 ***(978-1-4814-4790-4(4))*** Simon & Schuster Children's Publishing. (Atheneum Bks. for Young Readers).
Shukert, Rachel. Starstruck. 2013. (ENG.). 352p. (YA). (gr. 7). 17.99 *(978-0-385-74108-8(1),* Delacorte Pr.) Random Hse. Children's Bks.
Simone, Ni-Ni & Abrams, Amir. Get Ready for War. 2013. (Hollywood High Ser.: 2). (ENG., Illus.). 288p. (YA). (gr. 9). pap. 9.95 *(978-0-7582-7355-0(X),* K-Teen/Dafina) Kensington Publishing Corp.
—Get Ready for War. 2013. (Hollywood High Ser.: 2). 423p. (YA). lib. bdg. 20.80 *(978-0-606-27305-3(0),* Turtleback) Turtleback Bks.
—Lights, Love, & Lip Gloss. 2014. (Hollywood High Ser.: 4). (ENG., Illus.). 240p. (YA). (gr. 13). pap. 9.95 *(978-0-7582-8854-7(9),* K-Teen) Kensington Publishing Corp.
—Put Your Diamonds Up. 2014. (Hollywood High Ser.: 3). (ENG., Illus.). 256p. (YA). (gr. 13). pap. 16.00 *(978-0-7582-8852-3(2),* K-Teen) Kensington Publishing Corp.
Smallman, Steve. Santa Is Coming to Hollywood. Dunn, Robert, illus. 2015. (ENG.). 32p. (J). (-3). 9.99 *(978-1-4926-2664-0(3),* Sourcebooks Jabberwocky) Sourcebooks, Inc.
Steel, Danielle. Pretty Minnie in Hollywood. Valiant, Kristi, illus. 2016. (ENG.). 32p. (J). (gr. -1-2). 17.99 *(978-0-553-53755-0(5),* Doubleday Bks. for Young Readers) Random Hse. Children's Bks.
Stevenson, Steve. The Hollywood Intrigue. 2015. (Agatha Girl of Mystery Ser.: 9). lib. bdg. 16.00 *(978-0-606-37544-3(9))* Turtleback Bks.
—The Hollywood Intrigue #9. Turconi, Stefano, illus. 2015. (Agatha: Girl of Mystery Ser.: 9). (ENG.). 144p. (J). (gr. 3-7). 5.99 *(978-0-448-48680-2(6),* Grosset & Dunlap) Penguin Young Readers Group.
Stilton, Thea. Thea Stilton & the Hollywood Hoax. 2016. (Thea Stilton Ser.: 23). lib. bdg. 18.40 *(978-0-606-38799-6(4))* Turtleback Bks.
Stokes, K. Lynn. Clouded Visions. 2008. 208p. 24.95 *(978-0-595-51980-4(6))*; pap. 14.95 *(978-0-595-53217-9(9))* iUniverse, Inc.
Strasser, Todd. Famous. (ENG.). 272p. (YA). (gr. 7). 2013. pap. 9.99 *(978-1-4424-5418-7(0))* 2011. 15.99 *(978-1-4169-7511-3(X))* Simon & Schuster Bks. For Young Readers. (Simon & Schuster Bks. For Young Readers).
Summy, Barrie. I So Don't Do Famous. 2012. (ENG.). 304p. (J). (gr. 5). 7.99 *(978-0-385-73791-3(2),* Yearling) Random Hse. Children's Bks.
Van Draanen, Wendelin. Sammy Keyes & the Hollywood Mummy. 2008. (Sammy Keyes Ser.: Bk. 6). (J). 64.99 *(978-1-60640-641-0(8))* Findaway World, LLC.
Vaughan, Christina. Artie Goes to Hollywood. 2007. 32p. (J). cd-rom *(978-0-9798242-0-3(6))* Castlebrook Pubns.
Wolf, Elisabeth. Lulu in la la Land. 2013. (Lulu in la la Land Ser.: 1). (ENG.). 272p. (J). (gr. 3-6). pap. 6.99 *(978-1-4022-8504-2(3),* 9781402285042, Sourcebooks Jabberwocky) Sourcebooks, Inc.
Zettel, Sarah. Golden Girl. 2013. (American Fairy Trilogy Ser.: Bk. 2). (ENG.). 320p. (YA). (gr. 7). 17.99 *(978-0-375-86939-6(5),* Random Hse. Bks. for Young Readers) Random Hse. Children's Bks.

HOLMES, OLIVER WENDELL, 1841-1935

Littlefield, Sophie W. & Wiecek, William. Oliver Wendell Holmes Jr: The Supreme Court & American Legal Thought. 2005. (Library of American Lives & Times). (Illus.). 112p. (J). (gr. -1-3). lib. bdg. 34.60 *(978-1-4042-2652-4(4),* PowerKids Pr.) Rosen Publishing Group, Inc., The.

HOLMES, SHERLOCK (FICTITIOUS CHARACTER)—FICTION

Adler, Irene. The Dark Lady, 1 vol. Bruno, Iacopo, illus. 2014. (Sherlock, Lupin, & Me Ser.). (ENG.). 240p. (gr. 4-8). 12.95 *(978-1-62370-040-9(X))* Capstone Young Readers of Coughlan Cos.
—The Mystery of the Scarlet Rose. McGuinness, Nanette, tr. from ITA. Bruno, Iacopo, illus. 2015. (Sherlock, Lupin, & Me Ser.). (ENG.). 256p. (gr. 4-8). lib. bdg. 26.65 *(978-1-4342-6524-1(2))* Stone Arch Bks.
—Sherlock, Lupin, & Me, 1 vol. Bruno, Iacopo, illus. 2014. (Sherlock, Lupin, & Me Ser.). (ENG.). 240p. (gr. 4-8). 53.30 *(978-1-4342-9602-3(4))* Stone Arch Bks.
—The Soprano's Last Song, 1 vol. Iacopo, Bruno & Bruno, Iacopo, illus. 2014. (Sherlock, Lupin, & Me Ser.). (ENG.). 240p. (gr. 4-8). lib. bdg. 26.65 *(978-1-4342-6522-7(6))* Stone Arch Bks.
Bevins, Pegi & Doyle, Arthur Conan. Sherlock Holmes. 2003. (Retold Classics Anthologies Ser.). (Illus.). 282p. (J). pap. 9.99 *(978-0-7891-5931-1(7))* Perfection Learning Corp.
Cosson, M. J. Sherlock Holmes & A Scandal in Bohemia. rev. ed. 2010. pap. 39.62 *(978-0-7613-6954-7(6))* Lerner Publishing Group.
—Sherlock Holmes & the Adventure at the Abbey Grange. 2nd rev. ed. 2010. pap. 39.62 *(978-0-7613-6957-8(0))* Lerner Publishing Group.
—Sherlock Holmes & the Adventure of the Blue Gem. 3rd rev. ed. 2010. pap. 39.62 *(978-0-7613-6959-2(7))* Lerner Publishing Group.
—Sherlock Holmes & the Adventure of the Speckled Band. 5th rev. ed. 2010. pap. 39.62 *(978-0-7613-6962-2(7))* Lerner Publishing Group.
—Sherlock Holmes & the Adventure of the Sussex Vampire. 6th rev. ed. 2010. pap. 39.62 *(978-0-7613-6963-9(5))* Lerner Publishing Group.
Doyle, Arthur Conan. Adv of the Devils Foot. 2010. (Illus.). 254p. (J). pap. *(978-4-591-11698-2(0))* Fukuinkan Shoten.
—The Adventures & the Memoirs of Sherlock Holmes. McKowen, Scott, illus. 2004. (Sterling Unabridged Classics Ser.). (ENG.). 576p. (J). (gr. 5). 14.95 *(978-1-4027-1453-5(X))* Sterling Publishing Co., Inc.
—Adventures of Sherlock Holmes. 2008. (Bring the Classics to Life Ser.). (ENG., Illus.). 72p. (gr. 5-12). pap., act. bk. ed. 10.95 *(978-1-55576-064-9(3),* EDCTR-504B) EDCON Publishing Group.
—The Boys' Sherlock Holmes. Haycraft, Howard, ed. 2011. 366p. 51.95 *(978-1-258-00844-4(0))* Literary Licensing, LLC.
—The Extraordinary Cases of Sherlock Holmes. 2010. (Puffin Classics Ser.). (ENG.). 304p. (J). (gr. 5-7). pap. 5.99 *(978-0-14-133004-4(X),* Puffin Books) Penguin Young Readers Group.
—The Hound of the Baskervilles. 2004. (Fast Track Classics Ser.). (Illus.). 48p. (J). pap. *(978-0-237-52402-9(3))* Evans Brothers, Ltd.
—The Hound of the Baskervilles. Harvey, Bob, illus. 2004. (Paperback Classics Ser.). 158p. (J). (gr. 5). lib. bdg. 12.95 *(978-1-58086-605-7(0))* EDC Publishing.
—The Hound of the Baskervilles. 2008. (Bring the Classics to Life Ser.). (Illus.). 72p. (gr. 5-12). pap., act. bk. ed. 10.95 *(978-0-931334-67-2(5),* EDCTR-502B) EDCON Publishing Group.
—The Hound of the Baskervilles. 2012. (Puffin Classics Ser.). (ENG.). 256p. (J). (gr. 5). pap. 5.99 *(978-0-14-132939-0(4),* Puffin Books) Penguin Young Readers Group.
—The Man with the Twisted Lip - Lego - the Adventures of Sherlock Holmes. Macaluso, James, illus. 2014. (ENG.). pap. *(978-1-78092-698-8(7))* MX Publishing, Ltd.
—El Sabueso de Los Baskerville, 1 vol. Ferran, Adriana & Ferran, Daniel, illus. 2010. (Classic Fiction Ser.). (SPA.). 72p. (gr. 2-3). 27.99 *(978-1-4342-2325-8(6),* Graphic Revolve en Español) Stone Arch Bks.
—Sherlock Holmes. 2003. (Retold Ser.). (Illus.). 282p. (J). (gr. 7-18). 15.99 *(978-0-7569-1196-6(6))* Perfection Learning Corp.
—Sherlock Holmes & the Adventure of Black Peter. Rohrbach, Sophie & Morrow, J. T., illus. 2012. (On the Case with Holmes & Watson Ser.). 48p. (J). (gr. 4-6). pap. 39.62 *(978-0-7613-9274-3(2))*; (ENG.). pap. 6.95 *(978-0-7613-7100-7(1))* Lerner Publishing Group. (Graphic Universe™).
—Sherlock Holmes & the Adventure of the Cardboard Box. Rohrbach, Sophie & Morrow, J. T., illus. 2012. (On the Case with Holmes & Watson Ser.). 48p. (J). (gr. 4-6). pap. 39.62 *(978-0-7613-9275-0(0))*; (ENG.). pap. 6.95 *(978-0-7613-7098-7(6))* Lerner Publishing Group. (Graphic Universe™).
—Sherlock Holmes & the Adventure of the Three Garridebs. Rohrbach, Sophie & Morrow, J. T., illus. 2012. (On the Case with Holmes & Watson Ser.). 48p. (J). (gr. 4-6). pap. 39.62 *(978-0-7613-9276-7(9))*; (ENG.). pap. 6.95 *(978-0-7613-7099-4(4))* Lerner Publishing Group. (Graphic Universe™).
—Sherlock Holmes & the Boscombe Valley Mystery. Rohrbach, Sophie & Morrow, J. T., illus. 2011. (On the Case with Holmes & Watson Ser.: 10). (ENG.). 48p. (J). (gr. 4-6). 27.93 *(978-0-7613-7089-5(7))*; pap. 6.95 *(978-0-7613-7097-0(8))* Lerner Publishing Group. (Graphic Universe™).
—Sherlock Holmes & the Case of the Hound of the Baskervilles. Vogel, Malvina G., ed. Marcos, Pablo, illus. 2006. 237p. (YA). (gr. 4-8). 10.00 *(978-0-7567-9834-5(5))* DIANE Publishing Co.
—Sherlock Holmes & the Gloria Scott. Rohrbach, Sophie & Morrow, J. T., illus. 2012. (On the Case with Holmes & Watson Ser.: 14). (ENG.). 48p. (J). (gr. 4-6). lib. bdg. 27.93 *(978-0-7613-7093-2(5))* Lerner Publishing Group.
—Sherlock Holmes & the Gloria Scott. Rohrbach, Sophie & Morrow, J. T., illus. 2012. (On the Case with Holmes & Watson Ser.). 48p. (J). (gr. 4-6). pap. 39.62 *(978-0-7613-9277-4(7))*; (ENG.). pap. 6.95 *(978-0-7613-7101-4(X))* Lerner Publishing Group. (Graphic Universe™).
—A Study in Scarlet & Other Sherlock Holmes Adventures. 2011. (Oxford Children's Classics Ser.). (ENG.). 320p. (YA). 9.95 *(978-0-19-273283-5(8))* Oxford Univ. Pr., Inc.
Goodwin, Vincent. The Adventure of the Blue Carbuncle, 1 vol. Dunn, Ben, illus. 2012. (Graphic Novel Adventures of Sherlock Holmes Set 2 Ser.). (ENG.). 48p. (J). (gr. 3-8). lib. bdg. 29.93 *(978-1-61641-891-5(5),* Graphic Planet) Magic Wagon.
—The Adventure of the Cardboard Box, 1 vol. Dunn, Ben, illus. 2013. (Graphic Novel Adventures of Sherlock Holmes Set 3 Ser.). (ENG.). 48p. (J). (gr. 3-8). lib. bdg. 29.93 *(978-1-61641-971-4(7),* Graphic Planet) Magic Wagon.
—The Adventure of the Copper Beeches, 1 vol. Dunn, Ben, illus. 2012. (Graphic Novel Adventures of Sherlock Holmes Set 2 Ser.). (ENG.). 48p. (J). (gr. 3-8). lib. bdg. 29.93 *(978-1-61641-892-2(3),* Graphic Planet) Magic Wagon.
—The Adventure of the Dying Detective, 1 vol. Dunn, Ben, illus. 2013. (Graphic Novel Adventures of Sherlock Holmes Set 3 Ser.). (ENG.). 48p. (J). (gr. 3-8). lib. bdg. 29.93 *(978-1-61641-972-1(5),* Graphic Planet) Magic Wagon.
—The Adventure of the Engineer's Thumb, 1 vol. Dunn, Ben, illus. 2012. (Graphic Novel Adventures of Sherlock Holmes Set 2 Ser.). (ENG.). 48p. (J). (gr. 3-8). lib. bdg. 29.93 *(978-1-61641-893-9(1),* Graphic Planet) Magic Wagon.
—The Adventure of the Priory School, 1 vol. Dunn, Ben, illus. 2013. (Graphic Novel Adventures of Sherlock Holmes Set 3 Ser.). (ENG.). 48p. (J). (gr. 3-8). lib. bdg. 29.93 *(978-1-61641-973-8(3),* Graphic Planet) Magic Wagon.
—The Adventure of the Red Circle, 1 vol. Dunn, Ben, illus. 2013. (Graphic Novel Adventures of Sherlock Holmes Set 3 Ser.). (ENG.). 48p. (J). (gr. 3-8). lib. bdg. 29.93 *(978-1-61641-974-5(1),* Graphic Planet) Magic Wagon.
—The Adventure of the Second Stain, 1 vol. Dunn, Ben, illus. 2013. (Graphic Novel Adventures of Sherlock Holmes Set 3 Ser.). (ENG.). 48p. (J). (gr. 3-8). lib. bdg. 29.93 *(978-1-61641-975-2(X),* Graphic Planet) Magic Wagon.
—The Adventure of the Six Napoleons, 1 vol. Dunn, Ben, illus. 2013. (Graphic Novel Adventures of Sherlock Holmes Set 3 Ser.). (ENG.). 48p. (J). (gr. 3-8). lib. bdg. 29.93 *(978-1-61641-976-9(8),* Graphic Planet) Magic Wagon.
—The Adventure of the Solitary Cyclist, 1 vol. Dunn, Ben, illus. 2012. (Graphic Novel Adventures of Sherlock Holmes Set 2 Ser.). (ENG.). 48p. (J). (gr. 3-8). lib. bdg. 29.93 *(978-1-61641-894-6(X),* Graphic Planet) Magic Wagon.
—The Adventure of the Three Students, 1 vol. Dunn, Ben, illus. 2012. (Graphic Novel Adventures of Sherlock Holmes Set 2 Ser.). (ENG.). 48p. (J). (gr. 3-8). lib. bdg. 29.93 *(978-1-61641-895-3(8),* Graphic Planet) Magic Wagon.
—The Adventure of Wisteria Lodge, 1 vol. Dunn, Ben, illus. 2012. (Graphic Novel Adventures of Sherlock Holmes Set 2 Ser.). (ENG.). 48p. (J). (gr. 3-8). lib. bdg. 29.93 *(978-1-61641-896-0(6),* Graphic Planet) Magic Wagon.
Lane, Andrew. Death Cloud. 2012. (ENG.). (YA). (gr. 7-12). 64.99 *(978-1-4272-2800-0(0))* Findaway World, LLC.
—Death Cloud. 2011. (Sherlock Holmes: the Legend Begins Ser.: 1). (ENG.). 336p. (YA). (gr. 7-12). pap. 10.99 *(978-0-312-56371-4(X),* 9780312563714) Square Fish.
—Death Cloud. l.t. ed. 2011. (Young Sherlock Holmes Ser.). 367p. 23.99 *(978-1-4104-3971-0(2))* Thorndike Pr.
—Death Cloud. 2011. (Sherlock Holmes: the Legend Begins Ser.: 1). (YA). lib. bdg. 22.10 *(978-0-606-23781-9(X),* Turtleback) Turtleback Bks.
—Fire Storm. 2013. (Sherlock Holmes: the Legend Begins Ser.: 4). (ENG.). 352p. (YA). (gr. 7-12). 17.99 *(978-0-374-32311-0(9),* 9780374323110, Farrar, Straus & Giroux (BYR)) Farrar, Straus & Giroux.
—Knife Edge. 2015. (Sherlock Holmes: the Legend Begins Ser.: 6). (ENG.). 320p. (YA). (gr. 7). 18.99 *(978-0-374-38011-3(2),* 9780374380113, Farrar, Straus & Giroux (BYR)) Farrar, Straus & Giroux.
Mack, Tracy & Citrin, Michael. The Fall of the Amazing Zalindas. 2006. (Illus.). 259p. (J). *(978-1-4287-0951-5(7),* Orchard Bks.) Scholastic, Inc.
—Fall of the Amazing Zalindas. 2009. (Sherlock Holmes & the Baker St. Irregulars Ser.: 1). (ENG.). 272p. (J). (gr. 3-7). 6.99 *(978-0-545-06939-7(4),* Scholastic Paperbacks) Scholastic, Inc.
Peacock, Shane. Becoming Holmes: The Boy Sherlock Holmes, His Final Case. (Boy Sherlock Holmes Ser.). (ENG., Illus.). 252p. (YA). (gr. 5). 2014. pap. 9.99 *(978-1-77049-768-9(4))* 2012. 19.95 *(978-1-77049-232-5(1))* Tundra Bks. CAN. (Tundra Bks.). Dist: Penguin Random Hse. LLC.
—Death in the Air. (Boy Sherlock Holmes Ser.). (ENG., Illus.). (YA). (gr. 5-9). 2009. 254p. pap. 9.95 *(978-0-88776-928-3(4))* 2008. 264p. 19.95 *(978-0-88776-851-4(2))* Tundra Bks. CAN. (Tundra Bks.). Dist: Penguin Random Hse. LLC.
—The Dragon Turn. 2013. (Boy Sherlock Holmes Ser.). (ENG., Illus.). 242p. (J). (gr. 5-9). pap. 9.95 *(978-1-77049-411-4(1),* Tundra Bks.) Tundra Bks. CAN. Dist: Penguin Random Hse. LLC.
—The Dragon Turn: The Boy Sherlock Holmes, His Fifth Case. 2011. (Boy Sherlock Holmes Ser.). (ENG., Illus.). 228p. (J). (gr. 5-9). pap. 19.95 *(978-1-77049-231-8(3),* Tundra Bks.) Tundra Bks. CAN. Dist: Penguin Random Hse. LLC.
—Eye of the Crow. 2009. (Boy Sherlock Holmes Ser.). (ENG., Illus.). 272p. (YA). (gr. 5-9). pap. 10.99 *(978-0-88776-919-1(5),* Tundra Bks.) Tundra Bks. CAN. Dist: Penguin Random Hse. LLC.
—Eye of the Crow: The Boy Sherlock Holmes, His 1st Case. 2007. (Boy Sherlock Holmes Ser.). (ENG.). 264p. (YA). (gr. 5-9). 19.95 *(978-0-88776-850-7(4),* Tundra Bks.) Tundra Bks. CAN. Dist: Penguin Random Hse. LLC.
—The Secret Fiend. 2010. (Boy Sherlock Holmes Ser.). (ENG.). 256p. (YA). (gr. 5-9). 19.95 *(978-0-88776-853-8(9),* Tundra Bks.) Tundra Bks. CAN. Dist: Penguin Random Hse. LLC.
—The Secret Fiend: The Boy Sherlock Holmes, His Fourth Case. 2012. (Boy Sherlock Holmes Ser.). (ENG., Illus.). 262p. (YA). (gr. 5-9). pap. 9.95 *(978-1-77049-385-8(9),* Tundra Bks.) Tundra Bks. CAN. Dist: Penguin Random Hse. LLC.
—Vanishing Girl: The Boy Sherlock Holmes, His 3rd Case. 2010. (Boy Sherlock Holmes Ser.). (ENG., Illus.). 326p. (YA). (gr. 5-9). pap. 11.99 *(978-1-77049-234-9(8),* Tundra Bks.) Tundra Bks. CAN. Dist: Penguin Random Hse. LLC.
—Vanishing Girl: The Boy Sherlock Holmes, His Third Case. 2009. (Boy Sherlock Holmes Ser.). (ENG., Illus.). 320p. (YA). (gr. 5-9). 19.95 *(978-0-88776-852-1(0),* Tundra Bks.) Tundra Bks. CAN. Dist: Penguin Random Hse. LLC.
Shaw, Murray & Cosson, M. J. Sherlock Holmes & a Scandal in Bohemia. Rohrbach, Sophie, illus. 2010. (On the Case with Holmes & Watson Ser.: 1). (ENG.). 48p. (J). (gr. 4-6). pap. 6.95 *(978-0-7613-6197-8(9),* Graphic Universe™) Lerner Publishing Group.
—Sherlock Holmes & the Adventure at the Abbey Grange. Rohrbach, Sophie, illus. 2010. (On the Case with Holmes & Watson Ser.: 2). (ENG.). 48p. (J). (gr. 4-6). pap. 6.95 *(978-0-7613-6200-5(2),* Graphic Universe™) Lerner Publishing Group.
—Sherlock Holmes & the Adventure of the Blue Gem. Rohrbach, Sophie, illus. 2010. (On the Case with Holmes & Watson Ser.: 3). (ENG.). 48p. (J). (gr. 4-6). pap. 6.95 *(978-0-7613-6202-9(9),* Graphic Universe™) Lerner Publishing Group.
—Sherlock Holmes & the Adventure of the Dancing Men. Rohrbach, Sophie, illus. 2010. (On the Case with Holmes & Watson Ser.: 4). (ENG.). 48p. (J). (gr. 4-6). pap. 6.95 *(978-0-7613-6199-2(5),* Graphic Universe™) Lerner Publishing Group.
—Sherlock Holmes & the Adventure of the Speckled Band. Rohrbach, Sophie, illus. 2010. (On the Case with Holmes & Watson Ser.: 5). (ENG.). 48p. (J). (gr. 4-6). pap. 6.95 *(978-0-7613-6198-5(7),* Graphic Universe™) Lerner Publishing Group.
—Sherlock Holmes & the Adventure of the Sussex Vampire. Rohrbach, Sophie, illus. 2010. (On the Case with Holmes & Watson Ser.: 6). (ENG.). 48p. (J). (gr. 4-6). pap. 6.95 *(978-0-7613-6201-2(0),* Graphic Universe™) Lerner Publishing Group.
Storck, Patrick. Muppet Sherlock Holmes. Mebberson, Amy, illus. 2011. (Muppet Show Ser.). 128p. pap. 9.99 *(978-1-60886-613-7(0))* Boom! Studios.
Unglick, Richard. Sherlock Holmes: the Hound of the Baskervilles. 2016. (Playmobil Ser.). (ENG.). 96p. (J). (gr. 1-7). 19.95 *(978-1-63322-078-2(8),* Walter Foster Jr) Quarto Publishing Group USA.
Vanneman, Alan. Sherlock Holmes & the Giant Rat of Sumatra. 2003. (Otto Penzler Bks.). (ENG.). 304p. pap. 15.00 *(978-0-7867-1125-3(6))* Westview Pr.
Viney, Peter. The Case of the Dead Batsman, 7. 2013. (Garnet Oracle Readers Ser.). (Illus.). 40p. pap., stu. ed. 4.50 *(978-1-907575-21-1(9))* Garnet Education GBR. Dist: Garnet Publishing, Ltd.
Whitehouse, Howard. The Faceless Fiend: Being the Tale of a Criminal Mastermind, His Masked Minions & a Princess with a Butter Knife, Involving Explosives & a Certain Amount of Pushing & Shoving. Slavin, Bill, illus. 2007. (Mad Misadventures of Emmaline & Rubberbones Ser.). (ENG.). 272p. (J). (gr. 4-7). 7.95 *(978-1-55453-180-6(2))* Kids Can Pr., Ltd. CAN. Dist: Hachette Bk. Group.
Williams, Anthony, illus. The Hound of the Baskervilles. 2014. (ENG.). 32p. pap. 8.95 *(978-1-78404-357-5(5))* Arcturus Publishing GBR. Dist: Bookmasters Distribution.

HOLOCAUST, JEWISH (1939-1945)

Abramson, Ann. Who Was Anne Frank? Harrison, Nancy, illus. 2007. (Who Was? Ser.). (ENG.). 112p. (J). (gr. 3-7). pap. 5.99 *(978-0-448-44482-6(8),* Grosset & Dunlap) Penguin Young Readers Group.
—Who Was Anne Frank? Harrison, Nancy, illus. 2007. (Who Was... ? Ser.). 103p. (gr. 2-6). 15.00 *(978-0-7569-8166-2(2))* Perfection Learning Corp.
—Who Was Anne Frank? Harrison, Nancy, illus. 2007. (Who Was... ? Ser.). 103p. (J). (gr. 4-7). 16.00 *(978-1-4177-6854-7(1),* Turtleback) Turtleback Bks.
Allen, John. Holocaust Survivors. 2015. (ENG., Illus.). 80p. (J). lib. bdg. 28.95 *(978-1-60152-848-3(5))* ReferencePoint Pr., Inc.
Altman, Linda Jacobs. Adolf Hitler: Evil Mastermind of the Holocaust. 2005. (Holocaust Heroes & Nazi Criminals Ser.). (Illus.). 160p. (YA). (gr. 7-13). lib. bdg. 29.27 *(978-0-7660-2533-2(0))* Enslow Pubs., Inc.
—Adolf Hitler & the Rise of the Third Reich. 2016. (People & Events That Changed the World Ser.). (ENG., Illus.). 112p. (J). (gr. 7-8). 37.27 *(978-0-7660-7175-9(8))* Enslow Pubs., Inc.
—Crimes & Criminals of the Holocaust. 2004. (Holocaust in History Ser.). (Illus.). 104p. (J). lib. bdg. 26.60 *(978-0-7660-1995-9(0))* Enslow Pubs., Inc.
—Escape-Teens on the Run: Primary Sources from the Holocaust. 2010. (True Stories of Teens in the Holocaust Ser.). (Illus.). 128p. (YA). (gr. 9-12). 33.27 *(978-0-7660-3270-5(1))* Enslow Pubs., Inc.
—The Forgotten Victims of the Holocaust. 2003. (Holocaust in History Ser.). (Illus.). 104p. (J). (gr. 5-12). lib. bdg. 27.94 *(978-0-7660-1993-5(4))* Enslow Pubs., Inc.
—Hidden Teens, Hidden Lives: Primary Sources from the Holocaust. 2010. (True Stories of Teens in the Holocaust Ser.). (Illus.). 128p. (YA). (gr. 9-12). 33.27 *(978-0-7660-3271-2(X))* Enslow Pubs., Inc.
—Hitler, Goebbels, Himmler: The Nazi Holocaust Masterminds. 2014. (Remembering the Holocaust Ser.). 96p. (J). (gr. 6-12). pap. 10.95 *(978-0-7660-6198-9(1))* Enslow Pubs., Inc.
—Hitler, Goebbles, Himmler: The Nazi Holocaust Masterminds. 2014. (Remembering the Holocaust Ser.). (Illus.). 96p. (J). (gr. 6-12). 27.94 *(978-0-7660-6197-2(3))* Enslow Pubs., Inc.
—Hitler's Rise to Power & the Holocaust. 2003. (Holocaust in History Ser.). (Illus.). 128p. (J). (gr. 5-12). lib. bdg. 26.60 *(978-0-7660-1991-1(8))* Enslow Pubs., Inc.
—Impact of the Holocaust. 2004. (Holocaust in History Ser.). (Illus.). 104p. (J). lib. bdg. 26.60 *(978-0-7660-1996-6(9))* Enslow Pubs., Inc.
—The Jewish Victims of the Holocaust. 2003. (Holocaust in History Ser.). (Illus.). 104p. (J). (gr. 5-12). lib. bdg. 27.94 *(978-0-7660-1992-8(6))* Enslow Pubs., Inc.
—Resisters & Rescuers: Standing up Against the Holocaust. 2003. (Holocaust in History Ser.). (Illus.). 104p. (J). (gr. 5-12). lib. bdg. 27.94 *(978-0-7660-1994-2(2))* Enslow Pubs., Inc.
—The Warsaw Ghetto Uprising: Striking a Blow Against the Nazis. 2011. (Holocaust Through Primary Sources Ser.). (Illus.). 128p. (J). (gr. 6-18). pap. 10.95 *(978-1-59845-347-8(5))*; (gr. 9-12). lib. bdg. 33.27 *(978-0-7660-3320-7(1))* Enslow Pubs., Inc.
—Warsaw, Lodz, Vilna: The Holocaust Ghettos. 2014. (Remembering the Holocaust Ser.). 96p. (J). (gr. 6-12). pap. 10.95 *(978-0-7660-6208-5(2))*; (Illus.). 27.94 *(978-0-7660-6207-8(4))* Enslow Pubs., Inc.
Ashby, Ruth. Anne Frank: Young Diarist. 2005. 186p. (J). lib. bdg. 18.46 *(978-1-4242-2208-7(7))* Fitzgerald Bks.
Axelrod, Toby. Hans & Sophie Scholl: German Resisters of the White Rose. 2005. (Holocaust Biographies Ser.). (Illus.). 112p. (YA). (gr. 7-12). lib. bdg. 34.60 *(978-0-8239-3316-7(4),* HBHOBI) Rosen Publishing Group, Inc., The.
Bartoletti, Susan Campbell. Hitler Youth: Growing up in Hitler's Shadow. 2005. (ENG., Illus.). 176p. (J). (gr. 7). 21.99 *(978-0-439-35379-3(3))* Scholastic, Inc.
Bascomb, Neal. The Nazi Hunters: How a Team of Spies & Survivors Captured the World's Most Notorious Nazi. 2013. (ENG., Illus.). 256p. (J). (gr. 7). 17.99 *(978-0-545-43099-9(2),* Levine, Arthur A. Bks.) Scholastic, Inc.
Bayer, Linda N. Elie Wiesel: Spokesman for Remembrance. 2005. (Holocaust Biographies Ser.). (Illus.). 112p. (J). (gr. 7-12). lib. bdg. 34.60 *(978-0-8239-3306-8(7),* HBWIES) Rosen Publishing Group, Inc., The.
Beyer, Mark. Emmanuel Ringelblum: Historian of the Warsaw Ghetto. (Holocaust Biographies Ser.). 112p. (gr. 7-12). 2009. 63.90 *(978-1-61513-384-0(4))* 2005. (Illus.). (YA). lib. bdg. 34.60 *(978-0-8239-3375-4(X))* Rosen Publishing Group, Inc., The.
—Heinrich Muller: Gestapo Chief. 2005. (Holocaust Biographies Ser.). (Illus.). 112p. (YA). (gr. 7-12). lib. bdg. 34.60 *(978-0-8239-3376-1(8))* Rosen Publishing Group, Inc., The.
—Heinrich Müller: Gestapo Chief. 2009. (Holocaust Biographies Ser.). 112p. (gr. 7-12). 63.90 *(978-1-61513-386-4(0))* Rosen Publishing Group, Inc., The.
Bisson, Michelle. Hedy's Journey The True Story of a Hungarian Girl Fleeing the Holocaust. Ramon, El Primo, illus. 2017. (Encounter: Narrative Nonfiction Picture Bks.). (ENG.). 40p. (gr. 5-6). 15.95 ***(978-1-5157-8222-3(0))*** Encounter Bks.

Blohm, Craig E. Holocaust Camps & Killing Centers. 2015. (ENG., Illus.). 80p. (J). lib. bdg. *(978-1-60152-842-1(6))* ReferencePoint Pr., Inc.

—Holocaust Rescue & Liberation. 2015. (ENG., Illus.). 80p. (J). lib. bdg. *(978-1-60152-844-5(2))* ReferencePoint Pr., Inc.

—Holocaust Resistance. 2015. (ENG., Illus.). 80p. (J). lib. bdg. *(978-1-60152-846-9(9))* ReferencePoint Pr., Inc.

Bloom, Harold, ed. & tr. Literature of the Holocaust. Bloom, Harold, tr. 2003. (Bloom's Period Studies). (Illus.). 350p. (C). (gr. 9-13). 45.00 *(978-0-7910-7677-4(6),* Chelsea Hse.) Facts On File, Inc.

Boas, Jacob. We Are Witnesses: Five Diaries of Teenagers Who Died in the Holocaust. 2009. (ENG.). 208p. (YA). (gr. 6-10). pap. 9.99 *(978-0-312-53567-4(8),* 9780312535674) Square Fish.

Bodden, Valerie. The Holocaust. 2007. (Days of Change Ser.). (Illus.). 48p. (J). (gr. 4-7). lib. bdg. 31.35 *(978-1-58341-547-4(5),* Creative Education) Creative Co., The.

Bornstein, Michael & Holinstat, Debbie Bornstein. Survivors Club: The True Story of a Very Young Prisoner of Auschwitz. 2017. (Illus.). (J). (ENG.). 352p. 16.99 *(978-0-374-30571-0(4),* 9780374305710, Farrar, Straus & Giroux (BYR)); xviii, 348p. pap. *(978-1-250-11875-2(1))* Farrar, Straus & Giroux.

Brandman, Bronia & Bierman, Carol. The Girl Who Survived: A True Story of the Holocaust. 2010. 91p. (J). pap. *(978-0-545-17574-6(7))* Scholastic, Inc.

Brezina, Corona. Nazi Architects of the Holocaust. 2014. (Documentary History of the Holocaust Ser.). 80p. (YA). (gr. 7-12). 34.25 *(978-1-4777-7597-4(8))* Rosen Publishing Group, Inc., The.

Brophy Down, Susan. Irena Sendler: Bringing Life to Children of the Holocaust. 2012. (ENG.). 112p. (J). pap. *(978-0-7787-2556-5(1));* (Illus.). *(978-0-7787-2553-4(7))* Crabtree Publishing Co.

Brown, Jonatha A. Anne Frank. 2004. (People to Know Ser.). (Illus.). 24p. (gr. 1-4). lib. bdg. 22.00 *(978-0-8368-4309-5(6),* Weekly Reader Leveled Readers) Stevens, Gareth Publishing LLLP.

—Anne Frank. Acosta, Tatiana & Gutierrez, Guillermo, trs. 2004. (Gente Que Hay Que Conocer Ser.). (SPA., Illus.). 24p. (gr. 1-4). lib. bdg. 22.00 *(978-0-8368-4351-4(7),* Weekly Reader Leveled Readers) Stevens, Gareth Publishing LLLP.

Brown, Jonatha A. & Goff, Elizabeth Hudson. Anne Frank. Floor, Guus & Timmons, Jonathan, illus. 2006. (Graphic Biographies (World Almanac Library (Firm))). 32p. (gr. 5-8). lib. bdg. 27.00 *(978-0-8368-6196-9(5))* Stevens, Gareth Publishing LLLP.

Buchignani, Walter. Tell No One Who You Are: The Hidden Childhood of Régine Miller. 2008. (ENG., Illus.). 192p. (J). (gr. 4-7). pap. 12.95 *(978-0-88776-817-0(2),* Tundra Bks.) Tundra Bks. CAN. Dist: Penguin Random Hse. LLC.

Byers, Ann. Anti-Semitism & the Final Solution: The Holocaust Overview. 2014. (Remembering the Holocaust Ser.). 96p. (J). (gr. 6-12). pap. 10.95 *(978-0-7660-6193-4(0))* Enslow Pubs., Inc.

—Auschwitz, Bergen-Belsen, Treblinka: The Holocaust Camps. 2014. (Remembering the Holocaust Ser.). 96p. (J). (gr. 6-12). 27.94 *(978-0-7660-6212-2(0));* pap. 10.95 *(978-0-7660-6213-9(9))* Enslow Pubs., Inc.

—Courageous Teen Resisters: Primary Sources from the Holocaust. 2010. (True Stories of Teens in the Holocaust Ser.). (Illus.). 128p. (YA). (gr. 9-12). 33.27 *(978-0-7660-3269-9(8))* Enslow Pubs., Inc.

—Kristallnacht & Living in Nazi Germany. 2014. (Documentary History of the Holocaust Ser.). 80p. (YA). (gr. 7-12). 34.25 *(978-1-4777-7595-0(1))* Rosen Publishing Group, Inc., The.

—Oskar Schindler: Saving Jews from the Holocaust. 2005. (Holocaust Heroes & Nazi Criminals Ser.). (Illus.). 160p. (J). (gr. 6-12). lib. bdg. 27.93 *(978-0-7660-2534-9(9))* Enslow Pubs., Inc.

—Remembering the Holocaust: Anti-Semitism & the "Final Solution": The Holocaust Overview. 2014. (Remembering the Holocaust Ser.). (Illus.). 96p. (J). (gr. 6-12). 27.94 *(978-0-7660-6192-7(2))* Enslow Pubs., Inc.

—Rescuing the Danish Jews: A Heroic Story from the Holocaust. 2011. (Holocaust Through Primary Sources Ser.). (Illus.). 128p. (J). (gr. 6-18). pap. 10.95 *(978-1-59845-343-0(2));* (gr. 9-12). lib. bdg. 33.27 *(978-0-7660-3321-4(X))* Enslow Pubs., Inc.

—Saving Children from the Holocaust: The Kindertransport. 2011. (Holocaust Through Primary Sources Ser.). (Illus.). 128p. (J). (gr. 6-18). pap. 10.95 *(978-1-59845-344-7(0));* (gr. 9-12). lib. bdg. 33.27 *(978-0-7660-3323-8(6))* Enslow Pubs., Inc.

—Trapped-Youth in the Nazi Ghettos: Primary Sources from the Holocaust. 2010. (True Stories of Teens in the Holocaust Ser.). (Illus.). 128p. (YA). (gr. 9-12). 33.27 *(978-0-7660-3272-9(8))* Enslow Pubs., Inc.

—Youth Destroyed-The Nazi Camps: Primary Sources from the Holocaust. 2010. (True Stories of Teens in the Holocaust Ser.). (Illus.). 128p. (YA). (gr. 9-12). 33.27 *(978-0-7660-3273-6(6))* Enslow Pubs., Inc.

Callahan, Kerry P. Mordechai Anielewicz: Hero of the Warsaw Ghetto Uprising. (Holocaust Biographies Ser.). 112p. (gr. 7-12). 2009. 63.90 *(978-1-61513-389-5(5))* 2005. (Illus.). (YA). lib. bdg. 34.60 *(978-0-8239-3377-8(6))* Rosen Publishing Group, Inc., The.

Cohen-Janca, Irène. Mister Doctor: Janusz Korczak & the Orphans of the Warsaw Ghetto. Quarello, Maurizio A. C., illus. 2016. (ENG.). 68p. (J). 12.95 *(978-1-55451-861-6(X))* Annick Pr., Ltd. CAN. Dist: Publishers Group West (PGW).

Cohen, Robert Z. Jewish Resistance Against the Holocaust. 2014. (Documentary History of the Holocaust Ser.). (Illus.). 80p. (YA). (gr. 7-12). 34.25 *(978-1-4777-7601-8(X))* Rosen Publishing Group, Inc., The.

Crispin, M. Guyle. Holocaust: A Q&A Guide to Help Young Adults Really Understand the Holocaust. 2006. (ENG., Illus.). 230p. per. 46.99 *(978-0-7618-3542-4(3))* Univ. Pr. of America, Inc.

Darman, Peter, ed. The Holocaust & Life under Nazi Occupation. 2012. (World War II Ser.). (ENG., Illus.). 64p. (YA). (gr. 7-12). lib. bdg. 31.95 *(978-1-4488-9235-8(X))* Rosen Publishing Group, Inc., The.

Deem, James M. Auschwitz: Voices from the Death Camp. 2011. (Holocaust Through Primary Sources Ser.). (Illus.). 128p. (J). (gr. 6-18). pap. 10.95 *(978-1-59845-346-1(7));* (gr. 9-12). lib. bdg. 33.27 *(978-0-7660-3322-1(8))* Enslow Pubs., Inc.

DeSaix, Deborah Durland & Ruelle, Karen Gray. Peter's War. DeSaix, Deborah Durland, illus. Date not set. (Illus.). (J). *(978-0-8234-2416-0(2))* Holiday Hse., Inc.

A Documentary History of the Holocaust. 2014. (Documentary History of the Holocaust Ser.). 80p. (YA). (gr. 7-12). 274.00 *(978-1-4777-7613-1(3))* Rosen Publishing Group, Inc., The.

Dolan, Sean. Adolf Eichmann: Engineer of Death. 2005. (Holocaust Biographies Ser.). (Illus.). 112p. (YA). (gr. 7-12). lib. bdg. 34.60 *(978-0-8239-3308-2(3),* HBEICH) Rosen Publishing Group, Inc., The.

Downing, David. Aftermath & Remembrance. 2005. (World Almanac Library of the Holocaust). (Illus.). 48p. (gr. 5-12). lib. bdg. 31.00 *(978-0-8368-5948-5(0),* Gareth Stevens Secondary Library) Stevens, Gareth Publishing LLLP.

—Nazi Death Camps. 2005. (World Almanac Library of the Holocaust). (Illus.). 48p. (gr. 5-12). lib. bdg. 31.00 *(978-0-8368-5947-8(2),* Gareth Stevens Secondary Library) Stevens, Gareth Publishing LLLP.

—Origins of the Holocaust. 2005. (World Almanac Library of the Holocaust). (Illus.). 48p. (gr. 5-12). lib. bdg. 31.00 *(978-0-8368-5943-0(X),* Gareth Stevens Secondary Library) Stevens, Gareth Publishing LLLP.

Draper, Allison Stark. Pastor Andre Trocme: Spiritual Leader of the French Village, Le Chambon. 2005. (Holocaust Biographies Ser.). (Illus.). 112p. (YA). (gr. 7-12). lib. bdg. 34.60 *(978-0-8239-3378-5(4))* Rosen Publishing Group, Inc., The.

—Pastor André Trocmé: Spiritual Leader of the French Village le Chambon. 2009. (Holocaust Biographies Ser.). 112p. (gr. 7-12). 63.90 *(978-1-61513-390-1(9))* Rosen Publishing Group, Inc., The.

Elie Wiesel's Night. 2009. (Bloom's Guides). 136p. (C). (gr. 9-18). 30.00 *(978-1-60413-198-7(5),* Chelsea Hse.) Facts On File, Inc.

Ellis, Catherine & Roberts, Jeremy. Adolf Hitler, 01 vols., 1. 2016. (Holocaust Ser.). (ENG., Illus.). 112p. (J). 35.60 *(978-1-4994-6248-7(4),* Rosen Young Adult) Rosen Publishing Group, Inc., The.

Experiencing Eras & Events: Experiencing the Holocaust, 2 vols. 2003. (ENG., Illus.). 466p. (J). lib. bdg. 191.00 *(978-0-7876-5414-6(0),* GML00502-173636, UXL) Cengage Gale.

Finkelstein, Norman H. Remember Not to Forget: A Memory of the Holocaust. Hokanson, Lois & Hokanson, Lars, illus. 2004. (ENG.). 32p. pap. 12.95 *(978-0-8276-0770-5(9))* Jewish Pubn. Society.

Fishkin, Rebecca Love. Heroes of the Holocaust, 1 vol. 2011. (Holocaust Ser.). (ENG.). 64p. (gr. 6-7). pap. 9.10 *(978-0-7565-4443-0(2));* lib. bdg. 33.99 *(978-0-7565-4391-4(6))* Compass Point Bks. (CPB Grades 4-8).

Fitzgerald, Stephanie. Children of the Holocaust, 1 vol. 2011. (Holocaust Ser.). (ENG.). 64p. (gr. 6-7). lib. bdg. 33.99 *(978-0-7565-4390-7(8),* CPB Grades 4-8) Compass Point Bks.

Forest, Jim. Silent As a Stone: Mother Maria of Paris & the Trash Can Rescue. Pancheshnaya, Dasha, illus. 2007. (ENG.). 32p. (J). 18.00 *(978-0-88141-314-4(3))* St. Vladimir's Seminary Pr.

Frank, Ana. The Diary of a Anne Frank. adapted ed. pap., tchr. ed. 4.95 *(978-0-8359-0138-3(6))* Globe Fearon Educational Publishing.

—The Diary of a Anne Frank. 241p. (J). (gr. 4-6). pap. 4.99 *(978-0-8072-1363-6(2),* Listening Library) Random Hse. Audio Publishing Group.

Freeburg, Jessica. Fight for Survival: The Story of the Holocaust. 2016. (Tangled History Ser.). (ENG., Illus.). 112p. (gr. 3-4). lib. bdg. 31.99 *(978-1-4914-8454-8(3))* Capstone Press of Coughlan Cos.

Freedman, Jeri. The Warsaw Ghetto & Uprising. 2014. (Documentary History of the Holocaust Ser.). 80p. (YA). (gr. 7-12). 34.25 *(978-1-4777-7605-6(2))* Rosen Publishing Group, Inc., The.

Fremon, David K. Schindler, Wallenberg, Miep Gies: The Holocaust Heroes. 2014. (Remembering the Holocaust Ser.). 96p. (J). (gr. 6-12). 27.94 *(978-0-7660-6217-7(1))* Enslow Pubs., Inc.

Friedman, Laurie. Angel Girl. Amit, Ofra, illus. 2008. 32p. (J). (gr. 3-7). 16.95 *(978-0-8225-8739-2(4),* Carolrhoda Bks.) Lerner Publishing Group.

Gitlin, Martin. The Holocaust, 1 vol. 2010. (Essential Events Set 5 Ser.). (ENG.). 112p. (J). (gr. 6-12). lib. bdg. 35.64 *(978-1-61613-683-3(9))* ABDO Publishing Co.

Goff, Elizabeth Hudson & Brown, Jonatha A. Anne Frank. 2006. (Graphic Biographies (World Almanac Library (Firm))). (Illus.). 32p. (gr. 5-8). pap. 10.50 *(978-0-8368-6248-5(1))* Stevens, Gareth Publishing LLLP.

Gottfried, Ted. Children of the Slaughter: Young People of the Holocaust. Alcorn, Stephen, illus. (Holocaust History Ser.). 112p. (YA). (gr. 7-12). 22.95 *(978-1-58013-202-2(2),* Kar-Ben Publishing) Lerner Publishing Group.

—Deniers of the Holocaust: Who They Are, What They Do, Why They Do It. Alcorn, Stephen, illus. (Holocaust History Ser.). 112p. (YA). (gr. 7-12). 22.95 *(978-1-58013-200-8(6),* Kar-Ben Publishing) Lerner Publishing Group.

—Heroes of the Holocaust. Alcorn, Stephen, illus. (Holocaust History Ser.). 112p. (YA). (gr. 7-12). 22.95 *(978-1-58013-222-0(7),* Kar-Ben Publishing) Lerner Publishing Group.

—Nazi Germany: The Face of Tyranny. Alcorn, Stephen, illus. (Holocaust History Ser.). 112p. (YA). (gr. 7-12). 22.95 *(978-1-58013-203-9(0),* Kar-Ben Publishing) Lerner Publishing Group.

Greek, Joe. Righteous Gentiles: Non-Jews Who Fought Against Genocide. 2014. (Documentary History of the Holocaust Ser.). 80p. (YA). (gr. 7-12). 34.25 *(978-1-4777-7611-7(7))* Rosen Publishing Group, Inc., The.

Greenfeld, Howard. A Promise Fulfilled: Theodor Herzl, Chaim Weizmann, David Ben-Gurion, & the Creation of the State of Israel. 2005. (Illus.). 144p. (J). (gr. 7-18). 19.89 *(978-0-06-051505-8(8))* HarperCollins Pubs.

Griscom, Laura, illus. The Boy Named 27091: A Teenager's Struggle for Survival during the Holocaust. 2007. (J). lib. bdg. 6.95 *(978-0-9633705-4-9(5))* Share Publishing.

Gruenbaum, Michael. Somewhere There Is Still a Sun: A Memoir of the Holocaust. 2015. (ENG., Illus.). 384p. (J). (gr. 5-9). 17.99 *(978-1-4424-8486-3(1),* Aladdin) Simon & Schuster Children's Publishing.

Gruenbaum, Michael & Hasak-Lowy, Todd. Somewhere There Is Still a Sun: A Memoir of the Holocaust. 2017. (ENG., Illus.). 384p. (J). (gr. 5-9). pap. 8.99 *(978-1-4424-8487-0(X),* Simon & Schuster/Paula Wiseman Bks.) Simon & Schuster/Paula Wiseman Bks.

Haugen, David M. & Musser, Susan. The Holocaust. 2011. (Perspectives on Modern World History Ser.). (Illus.). 224p. (J). (gr. 10-18). lib. bdg. 42.45 *(978-0-7377-5258-8(0),* Greenhaven Pr., Inc.) Cengage Gale.

Heims, Neil. Reading the Diary of Anne Frank. 2005. (Engaged Reader Ser.). (Illus.). 104p. (gr. 5-8). lib. bdg. 25.00 *(978-0-7910-8829-6(4),* Chelsea Hse.) Facts On File, Inc.

Herman, Gail. What Was the Holocaust? 2018. (What Was... ? Ser.). lib. bdg. 16.00 ***(978-0-606-40113-5(X))*** Turtleback Bks.

Hermann, Spring. Anne Frank: Hope in the Shadows of the Holocaust. 2005. (Holocaust Heroes & Nazi Criminals Ser.). (Illus.). 160p. (YA). (gr. 6-12). lib. bdg. 29.27 *(978-0-7660-2531-8(4))* Enslow Pubs., Inc.

Hillman, Laura. I Will Plant You a Lilac Tree: A Memoir of a Schindler's List Survivor. 2005. (ENG., Illus.). 256p. (YA). (gr. 7). 16.95 *(978-0-689-86980-8(0),* Atheneum Bks. for Young Readers) Simon & Schuster Children's Publishing.

—I Will Plant You a Lilac Tree: A Memoir of a Schindler's List Survivor. 2008. (ENG., Illus.). 288p. (YA). (gr. 9-12). mass mkt. 7.99 *(978-1-4169-5366-1(3),* Simon Pulse) Simon Pulse.

Hodgson, Julie. Polly Mae. 2006. 115p. 20.00 *(978-1-4116-6340-4(3))* Lulu Pr., Inc.

Hoffman, Betty N. Liberation: Stories of Survival from the Holocaust. 2011. (Holocaust Through Primary Sources Ser.). (Illus.). 128p. (J). (gr. 6-18). pap. 10.95 *(978-1-59845-348-5(3));* (gr. 9-12). lib. bdg. 33.27 *(978-0-7660-3319-1(8))* Enslow Pubs., Inc.

Hollingsworth, Tamara. Anne Frank: A Light in the Dark, 1 vol. 2nd rev. ed. 2012. (TIME for KIDS(r) Nonfiction Readers Ser.). (ENG.). 48p. (J). (gr. 4-4). pap. 9.99 *(978-1-4333-4865-5(9))* Teacher Created Materials, Inc.

The Holocaust, 4 vols., Set. Incl. Children of the Holocaust. Fitzgerald, Stephanie. lib. bdg. 33.99 *(978-0-7565-4390-7(8));* Heroes of the Holocaust. Fishkin, Rebecca Love. lib. bdg. 33.99 *(978-0-7565-4391-4(6));* Legacy of the Holocaust. Skog, Jason. lib. bdg. 33.99 *(978-0-7565-4393-8(2));* (gr. 6-7)., CPB Grades 4-8 (Holocaust Ser.). (ENG.). 64p. 2011. Set lib. bdg. 101.97 *(978-0-7565-4394-5(0))* Compass Point Bks.

Holocaust Biographies. 2005. (Illus.). 112p. (gr. 7-12). lib. bdg. 319.20 *(978-0-8239-3912-1(X))* Rosen Publishing Group, Inc., The.

Holocaust Biographies, 8 bks., Set 1. Incl. Adolf Eichmann: Engineer of Death. Dolan, Sean. (YA). lib. bdg. 34.60 *(978-0-8239-3308-2(3),* HBEICH); Elie Wiesel: Spokesman for Remembrance. Bayer, Linda N. (J). lib. bdg. 34.60 *(978-0-8239-3306-8(7),* HBWIES); Hans & Sophie Scholl: German Resisters of the White Rose. Axelrod, Toby. (YA). lib. bdg. 34.60 *(978-0-8239-3316-7(4),* HBHOBI); Hermann Goering: Hitler's Second in Command. Ramen, Fred. (YA). lib. bdg. 34.60 *(978-0-8239-3307-5(5),* HBGORI); 112p. (gr. 7-12). (Illus.). 2005. Set lib. bdg. 212.00 *(978-0-8239-9121-1(0),* HBHOBI); Set lib. bdg. 212.00 *(978-0-8239-9424-3(4))* Rosen Publishing Group, Inc., The.

Houghton, Sarah. Elie Wiesel: A Holocaust Survivor Cries Out for Peace. 2003. (High Five Reading - Green Ser.). (ENG., Illus.). 48p. (J). (gr. 3-4). per. 9.00 *(978-0-7368-2833-8(8),* High Five Reading (RBL)) Capstone Press of Coughlan Cos.

—Elie Wiesel Set: A Holocaust Survivor Cries Out for Peace, 6. 2003. (High Five Reading - Green Ser.). (ENG.). 48p. (gr. 3-4). pap. 54.00 *(978-0-7368-2843-7(5),* High Five Reading (RBL)) Capstone Press of Coughlan Cos.

Idzikowski, Lisa. Raoul Wallenberg: Rescuer of Hungarian Jews During the Holocaust. 2017. (J). ***(978-1-5383-8118-2(4));*** pap. ***(978-1-5383-8117-5(6))*** Rosen Publishing Group, Inc., The.

Jaegermann, Judith. My Childhood in the Holocaust. 2004. (Illus.). 59p. (YA). per. 9.95 *(978-965-90462-2-5(7))* Mazo Pubs.

Johnson, Stephen, ed. From the Holocaust to Healing the World. 2003. per. 7.95 *(978-0-9659781-1-8(7))* Holocaust Museum Houston.

Kacer, Kathy. The Magician of Auschwitz, 1 vol. Newland, Gillian, illus. 2014. (ENG.). 32p. (J). (gr. 3-5). 18.95 *(978-1-927583-46-3(2))* Second Story Pr. CAN. Dist: Orca Bk. Pubs. USA.

Kacer, Kathy, ed. We Are Their Voice: Young People Respond to the Holocaust, 1 vol. 2012. (Holocaust Remembrance Ser.). (ENG.). 160p. (J). (gr. 6-8). pap. 16.95 *(978-1-926920-77-1(5))* Second Story Pr. CAN. Dist: Orca Bk. Pubs. USA.

Kaelberer, Angie Peterson & Fitzgerald, Stephanie. Kristallnacht. 2017. (Eyewitness to World War II Ser.). (ENG.). 112p. (gr. 5-7). lib. bdg. 35.99 ***(978-0-7565-5583-2(3),*** CPB Grades 4-8) Compass Point Bks.

Koestler-Grack, Rachel. Elie Wiesel: Witness for Humanity. 2009. (Life Portraits Ser.). (Illus.). 112p. (J). (gr. 7-12). lib. bdg. 36.00 *(978-1-4339-0054-9(8),* 1293616) Stevens, Gareth Publishing LLLP.

Kor, Eva Mozes & Buccieri, Lisa Rojany. Surviving the Angel of Death: The True Story of a Mengele Twin in Auschwitz. 2012. (ENG.). 175p. (J). (gr. 6). pap. 8.95 *(978-1-933718-57-6(9))* Tanglewood Pr.

—Surviving the Angel of Death: The True Story of a Mengele Twin in Auschwitz. 2012. lib. bdg. 19.60 *(978-0-606-23838-0(7),* Turtleback) Turtleback Bks.

Kor, Eva Mozes, et al. Surviving the Angel of Death: The Story of a Mengele Twin in Auschwitz. 2009. (ENG., Illus.). 141p. (J). (gr. 6-18). 14.95 *(978-1-933718-28-6(5))* Tanglewood Pr.

Kramer, Ann. Anne Frank: The Young Writer Who Told the World Her Story. 2009. (National Geographic World History Biographies Ser.). (ENG., Illus.). 64p. (J). (gr. 3-7). 7.99 *(978-1-4263-0414-9(5),* National Geographic Children's Bks.) National Geographic Society.

Landau, Abraham, et al. Branded on My Arm & in My Soul: A Holocaust Memoir. 2011. (Illus.). 144p. 50.00 *(978-0-932027-20-7(2))* Spinner Pubns., Inc.

—Branded on My Arm & in My Soul: The Holocaust Memoir of Abraham Landau. 2011. (Illus.). 144p. pap. 25.00 *(978-0-932027-19-1(9))* Spinner Pubns., Inc.

Laub, Frima. Between the Shadows. Laub, Frima & Uhlig, Elizabeth, illus. 2009. 81p. (J). pap. 12.95 *(978-0-9815345-2-7(X))* Marble Hse. Editions.

—Between the Shadows. Uhlig, Elizabeth, illus. 2007. (J). pap. 12.95 *(978-0-9786745-2-6(9))* Marble Hse. Editions.

Lee, Carol Ann. Anne Frank & the Children of the Holocaust. 2008. (ENG., Illus.). 256p. (J). (gr. 5-18). 7.99 *(978-0-14-241069-1(1),* Puffin Books) Penguin Young Readers Group.

Lensky, Mordechai. A Physician Inside the Warswa Ghetto. 2009. 257p. (YA). pap. 27.50 *(978-0-9814686-3-1(2))* Yad Vashem Pubns. ISR. Dist: Coronet Bks.

Levine, Ellen. Darkness over Denmark: The Danish Resistance & the Rescue of the Jews. 2005. (ENG., Illus.). 178p. (YA). (gr. 7-18). pap. 14.95 *(978-0-8234-1755-1(7))* Holiday Hse., Inc.

Levine, Karen. Hana's Suitcase: A True Story, 1 vol. (Holocaust Remembrance Ser.: Vol. 3). (ENG., Illus.). 2013. 120p. (J). (gr. 6-8). pap. 16.95 *(978-1-896764-55-9(X))* 2005. 124p. (gr. 4-18). pap. 19.95 incl. audio compact disk *(978-1-896764-61-0(4))* Second Story Pr. CAN. Dist: Orca Bk. Pubs. USA.

—Hana's Suitcase Anniversary Album, 1 vol. 2013. (Holocaust Remembrance Ser.). (ENG., Illus.). 176p. (J). (gr. 6-8). 24.95 *(978-1-926920-36-8(8))* Second Story Pr. CAN. Dist: Orca Bk. Pubs. USA.

—La Maleta de Hana: Un Relato Verídico. Kosmal, Mariana, tr. from ENG. 2006. (SPA., Illus.). 113p. (YA). (gr. 8-12). per. 10.40 *(978-1-933032-01-6(4),* LC33993) Lectorum Pubns., Inc.

Levy, Patricia. The Holocaust. 2003. (Questioning History Ser.). (J). lib. bdg. 28.50 *(978-1-58340-267-2(5))* Black Rabbit Bks.

Leyson, Leon. The Boy on the Wooden Box: How the Impossible Became Possible ... on Schindler's List. (ENG., Illus.). (J). (gr. 4-9). 2015. 256p. pap. 9.99 *(978-1-4424-9782-5(3))* 2013. 240p. 17.99 *(978-1-4424-9781-8(5))* Simon & Schuster Children's Publishing. (Atheneum Bks. for Young Readers).

—The Boy on the Wooden Box: How the Impossible Became Possible ... on Schindler's List. 2015. lib. bdg. 19.65 *(978-0-606-36097-5(2))* Turtleback Bks.

Lobel, Anita. No Pretty Pictures: A Child of War. 2008. (ENG.). 288p. (J). (gr. 5). pap. 7.99 *(978-0-06-156589-2(X),* Greenwillow Bks.) HarperCollins Pubs.

—No Pretty Pictures: A Child of War. 2008. (J). (gr. 5-8). lib. bdg. 18.40 *(978-0-613-28590-2(5),* Turtleback) Turtleback Bks.

Lombardo, Jennifer & Robson, David. The Horrors of Auschwitz. 2017. (World History Ser.). 104p. (YA). (gr. 7-7). 39.90 ***(978-1-5345-6054-3(8),*** Lucent Pr.) Greenhaven Publishing LLC.

Lowery, Zoe & Norton, James R. The Nazi Regime & the Holocaust. 2016. (Bearing Witness: Genocide & Ethnic Cleansing in the Modern World Ser.). 64p. (J). (gr. 6-6). 34.45 *(978-1-5081-7163-8(7))* Rosen Publishing Group, Inc., The.

Lowery, Zoe & Roberts, Jeremy. Oscar Schindler, 01 vols., 1. 2016. (Holocaust Ser.). (ENG., Illus.). 112p. (J). 35.60 *(978-1-4994-6252-4(2),* Rosen Young Adult) Rosen Publishing Group, Inc., The.

Ludwig, Trudy. Gifts from the Enemy. Orback, Craig, illus. 2014. (HumanKIND Project Ser.). (ENG.). 32p. (gr. 2-7). 16.95 *(978-1-935952-97-8(8))* White Cloud Pr.

Mara, Wil. Kristallnacht: Nazi Persecution of the Jews in Europe. 2009. (Perspectives on Ser.). 112p. (gr. 7). 39.93 *(978-0-7614-4026-0(7))* Marshall Cavendish Corp.

Marcovitz, Hal. The Rise of the Nazis. 2014. (Understanding World History Ser.). (ENG., Illus.). 96p. (J). lib. bdg. *(978-1-60152-654-0(7))* ReferencePoint Pr., Inc.

Mazzeo, Tilar J. Irena's Children. 2016. (ENG., Illus.). 272p. (J). (gr. 5-7). 17.99 *(978-1-4814-4991-5(5),* McElderry, Margaret K. Bks.) McElderry, Margaret K. Bks.

McArthur, Debra. Raoul Wallenberg: Rescuing Thousands from the Nazis' Grasp. 2005. (Holocaust Heroes & Nazi Criminals Ser.). (Illus.). 160p. (J). (gr. 6-12). lib. bdg. 27.93 *(978-0-7660-2530-1(6))* Enslow Pubs., Inc.

McDowell, Pamela. Anne Frank. 2014. (J). *(978-1-4896-2456-7(2))* Weigl Pubs., Inc.

Meyer, Susan. Nazi Concentration Camps: A Policy of Genocide. 2014. (Documentary History of the Holocaust Ser.). (Illus.). 80p. (J). (gr. 7-12). 34.25 *(978-1-4777-7603-2(6))* Rosen Publishing Group, Inc., The.

Miklowitz, Gloria. Anne Frank. 2009. pap. 13.25 *(978-1-60559-053-0(3))* Hameray Publishing Group, Inc.

Mochizuki, Ken. Pasajea la Libertad. 2004. (SPA., Illus.). (J). (gr. k-4). spiral bd. *(978-0-616-03091-2(6))* Canadian National Institute for the Blind/Institut National Canadien pour les Aveugles.

—Passage to Freedom: The Sugihara Story. 2005. 19.45 *(978-0-7569-4773-6(1))* Perfection Learning Corp.

Mochizuki, Ken & Lee, Dom. Passage to Freedom: The Sugihara Story. 2010. (Rise & Shine Ser.). (ENG., Illus.). 32p. (C). pap. 14.95 *(978-1-58430-157-8(0))* National Geographic School Publishing, Inc.

Moore, Ann & Culpin, Christopher. The Holocaust. 2003. (Illus.). 64p. pap. 26.00 *(978-0-7195-7709-3(8));* pap., tchr. ed. 62.50 *(978-0-7195-7710-9(1))* Hodder Education Group GBR. (Hodder Education). Dist: Trans-Atlantic Pubns., Inc.

Moore, Lisa. Elie Wiesel: Surviving the Holocaust, Speaking Out Against Genocide. 2005. (Holocaust Heroes & Nazi Criminals Ser.). (Illus.). 160p. (J). (gr. 7-12). lib. bdg. 27.93 *(978-0-7660-2576-9(4))* Enslow Pubs., Inc.

Nelson, Sheila. Never Again: Survivors of the Holocaust. (Survivors Ser.). (J). 2010. 128p. (gr. 7-12). 24.95 *(978-1-4222-0459-7(6))* 2009. 129p. pap. 24.95 *(978-1-4222-1472-5(9))* Mason Crest.

Norton, James. The Holocaust: Jews, Germany, & the National Socialists. 2009. (Genocide in Modern Times Ser.). 64p. (gr. 6-6). 58.50 *(978-1-61512-677-4(5))* Rosen Publishing Group, Inc., The.

H
I

Norton, James R. The Holocaust: Jews, Germany, & the National Socialists. 2008. (Genocide in Modern Times Ser.). (Illus.). 64p. (YA). (gr. 9-12). lib. bdg. 31.95 *(978-1-4042-1821-5(1))* Rosen Publishing Group, Inc., The.

Opdyke, Irene Gut. In My Hands: Memories of a Holocaust Rescuer. 2004. (ENG., Illus.). 304p. (YA). (gr. 9). mass mkt. 7.99 *(978-0-553-49411-2(2)*, Laurel Leaf) Random Hse. Children's Bks.

—In My Hands: Memories of a Holocaust Rescuer. 2016. (ENG., Illus.). 288p. (YA). (gr. 9). pap. 10.99 *(978-0-553-53884-7(5)*, Ember) Random Hse. Children's Bks.

Opdyke, Irene Gut & Armstrong, Jennifer. In My Hands: Memories of a Holocaust Rescuer. pap. *(978-0-385-72870-6(0))* Knopf Doubleday Publishing Group.

—In My Hands: Memories of a Holocaust Rescuer. 2009. 9.14 *(978-0-7848-2512-9(2))*; 14.72 *(978-0-7848-2511-2(4))* Marco Bk. Co. (Everbind).

Oshiro, Beverly & Sachs, Ruth. Adolf Eichmann, 01 vols., 1. 2016. (Holocaust Ser.). (ENG., Illus.). 112p. (J). 35.60 *(978-1-4994-6246-3(8)*, Rosen Young Adult) Rosen Publishing Group, Inc., The.

Owlkids Books Inc. Staff & Arato, Rona. The Last Train: A Holocaust Story. 2013. (ENG., Illus.). 144p. (J). (gr. 6). 16.95 *(978-1-926973-62-3(3))* Owlkids Bks. Inc. CAN. Dist: Publishers Group West (PGW).

Parks, Peggy J. Anne Frank. 2016. (ENG.). 80p. (J). (gr. 5-12). 38.60 *(978-1-60152-946-6(5))* ReferencePoint Pr., Inc.

Peppas, Lynn. The Holocaust. 2015. (ENG.). 48p. (J). *(978-0-7787-1548-1(5))* Crabtree Publishing Co.

Perl, Lila & Lazan, Marion Blumenthal. Four Perfect Pebbles: A True Story of the Holocaust. 2016. 160p. (J). (gr. 7-7). pap. 6.99 *(978-0-06-248996-8(8)*, Greenwillow Bks.) HarperCollins Pubs.

Phillips, Dee. Holocaust. 2014. (Yesterday's Voices Ser.). (YA). lib. bdg. 19.60 *(978-0-606-35581-0(2))* Turtleback Bks.

Poole, Josephine. Ana Frank. Barrett, Angela, illus. 2005. (SPA.). 32p. (J). (gr. 3-4). 17.99 *(978-1-930332-87-4(4))* Lectorum Pubns., Inc.

Ramen, Fred. Hermann Goering: Hitler's Second in Command. 2005. (Holocaust Biographies Ser.). (Illus.). 112p. (YA). (gr. 7-12). lib. bdg. 34.60 *(978-0-8239-3307-5(5)*, HBGORI) Rosen Publishing Group, Inc., The.

—Hermann Goring: Hitler's Second-in-Command. 2009. (Holocaust Biographies Ser.). 112p. (gr. 7-12). 63.90 *(978-1-61513-387-1(9))* Rosen Publishing Group, Inc., The.

Rappaport, Doreen. Beyond Courage: The Untold Story of Jewish Resistance During the Holocaust. 2012. (ENG., Illus.). 240p. (J). (gr. 5). 22.99 *(978-0-7636-2976-2(6))* Candlewick Pr.

Robbins, Trina. Lily Renée, Escape Artist: From Holocaust Survivor to Comic Book Pioneer. Timmons, Anne & Oh, Mo, illus. 2011. (Single Titles Ser.). (ENG.). 96p. (J). (gr. 5-8). pap. 7.95 *(978-0-7613-8114-3(7))*; lib. bdg. 29.27 *(978-0-7613-6010-0(7))* Lerner Publishing Group. (Graphic Universe™).

Robson, David. Auschwitz. 2009. (World History Ser.). (ENG., Illus.). 128p. (J). (gr. 7-10). 34.95 *(978-1-4205-0131-5(3)*, Lucent Bks.) Cengage Gale.

Rogow, Sally M. Faces of Courage: Young Heroes of World War II. 2008. (ENG., Illus.). 162p. pap. *(978-1-894694-67-4(8))* Granville Island Publishing.

Rossel, Seymour. The Holocaust: An End to Innocence. 2012. (J). *(978-1-60280-203-2(3))* Ktav Publishing Hse., Inc.

Roy, Jennifer. Jars of Hope: How One Woman Helped Save 2,500 Children During the Holocaust. Owenson, Meg, illus. 2015. (Encounter: Narrative Nonfiction Picture Bks.). (ENG.). 32p. (gr. 3-5). lib. bdg. 27.32 *(978-1-4914-6072-6(5))* Encounter Bks.

Rubin, Susan Goldman. The Anne Frank Case: Simon Wiesenthal's Search for the Truth. Farnsworth, Bill, illus. 2009. (ENG.). 40p. (J). (gr. 5-18). 18.95 *(978-0-8234-2109-1(0))* Holiday Hse., Inc.

—Irena Sendler & the Children of the Warsaw Ghetto. Farnsworth, Bill, illus. 2011. (ENG.). 40p. (J). (gr. 1-5). 18.95 *(978-0-8234-2251-7(8))* Holiday Hse., Inc.

Rubin, Susan Goldman & Weissberger, Ela. The Cat with the Yellow Star: Coming of Age in Terezin. (ENG., Illus.). 40p. 2008. (J). (gr. 3-9). pap. 8.99 *(978-0-8234-2154-1(6))* 2006. (YA). (gr. 8-12). 16.95 *(978-0-8234-1831-2(6))* Holiday Hse., Inc.

Ruelle, Karen Gray. The Grand Mosque of Paris: A Story of How Muslims Rescued Jews During the Holocaust. DeSaix, Deborah Durland, illus. 2010. (ENG.). 40p. (J). (gr. 3-18). pap. 8.95 *(978-0-8234-2304-0(2))* Holiday Hse., Inc.

—Hidden on the Mountain: Stories of Children Sheltered from the Nazis in le Chambon. DeSaix, Deborah Durland, illus. 2007. (ENG.). 272p. (J). (gr. 5-18). 24.95 *(978-0-8234-1928-9(2))* Holiday Hse., Inc.

Russo, Marisabina. Always Remember Me: How One Family Survived World War II. Russo, Marisabina, illus. 2005. (ENG., Illus.). 48p. (J). (gr. 1-5). 19.99 *(978-0-689-86920-4(7)*, Atheneum Bks. for Young Readers) Simon & Schuster Children's Publishing.

Sachs, Ruth. Adolf Eichmann: Engineer of Death. 2009. (Holocaust Biographies Ser.). 112p. (gr. 7-12). 63.90 *(978-1-61513-380-2(1))* Rosen Publishing Group, Inc., The.

Schloss, Eva & Powers, Barbara. The Promise: The Moving Story of a Family in the Holocaust. Yaron, Sophie, illus. 2006. (ENG.). 160p. (J). (gr. 13-18). 10.99 *(978-0-14-132081-6(8))* Penguin Bks., Ltd. GBR. Dist: Independent Pubs. Group.

Schroeder, Peter W. & Schroeder-Hildebrand, Dagmar. Six Million Paper Clips: The Making of a Children's Holocaust Memorial. 2005. (Illus.). (J). (gr. 3-7). 48p. 17.95 *(978-1-58013-169-8(7))*; (ENG., 64p. pap. 8.95 *(978-1-58013-176-6(X))* Lerner Publishing Group. (Kar-Ben Publishing).

Senker, Cath. Fs: On the Frontline Surviving the Holocaust. 2005. (Illus.). 48p. (J). *(978-1-84443-694-1(2))*; pap. *(978-1-84443-701-6(9))* Steck-Vaughn.

Sheehan, Sean. Auschwitz. 2011. (Place in History Ser.). 48p. (YA). (gr. 5-9). lib. bdg. 34.25 *(978-1-84837-672-4(3))* Arcturus Publishing GBR. Dist: Black Rabbit Bks.

—The Holocaust. 2005. (How Did It Happen? Ser.). (ENG., Illus.). 48p. (YA). (gr. 7-10). lib. bdg. 32.10 *(978-1-59018-607-7(9)*, Lucent Bks.) Cengage Gale.

—Why Did the Holocaust Happen? 2010. (Moments in History Ser.). (Illus.). 48p. (YA). (gr. 5-9). lib. bdg. 31.95 *(978-1-4339-4172-6(4))*; (gr. 6-8). pap. 14.05 *(978-1-4339-4173-3(2)*, Gareth Stevens Secondary Library) Stevens, Gareth Publishing LLLP.

Singer, Flora M. Flora - I Was but A Child. 2007. 180p. (J). pap. 26.50 *(978-0-9760739-8-7(6))* Yad Vashem Pubns. ISR. Dist: Coronet Bks.

Skog, Jason. The Legacy of the Holocaust, 1 vol. 2011. (Holocaust Ser.). (ENG.). 64p. (gr. 6-7). pap. 9.10 *(978-0-7565-4444-7(0))*; lib. bdg. 33.99 *(978-0-7565-4393-8(2))* Compass Point Bks. (CPB Grades 4-8).

Soumerai, Eve Nussbaum & Schulz, Carol D. A Voice from the Holocaust, 1 vol. 2003. (Voices of Twentieth-Century Conflict Ser.). (Illus.). 144p. (C). 46.00 *(978-0-313-32358-4(5)*, GR2358, Greenwood) ABC-CLIO, LLC.

Spielman, Gloria. Janusz Korczak's Children. Archambault, Matthew, illus. 2007. (Kar-Ben for Older Readers Ser.). 40p. (J). (gr. 3-7). lib. bdg. 17.95 *(978-1-58013-255-8(3))*; (ENG.). pap. 7.95 *(978-0-8225-7050-9(5))* Lerner Publishing Group. (Kar-Ben Publishing).

Steele, D. Kelley. Would You Salute? One Child's Story of the Holocaust. Rickenbaker, Becky Hyatt, illus. 2006. 48p. (J). (gr. 4-6). 22.95 *(978-0-9711534-2-4(6))* Hidden Path Pubn., Inc.

Stillman, Lorry & Holocaust Human Rights Center of Maine. The Spirit That Moves Us: Using Literature, Art, & Music to Teach about the Holocaust at the Secondary & College Level, 1 vol., Vol. 3. 3rd ed. 2003. (Spirit That Moves Us Ser.). (ENG., Illus.). 220p. pap. 19.95 *(978-0-88448-230-7(8))* Tilbury Hse. Pubs.

Streissguth, Tom. Adolf Eichmann: Executing the Final Solution. 2005. (Holocaust Heroes & Nazi Criminals Ser.). (Illus.). 160p. (YA). (gr. 7-13). lib. bdg. 29.27 *(978-0-7660-2575-2(6))* Enslow Pubs., Inc.

Taylor, Peter Lane. The Secret of Priest's Grotto: A Holocaust Survival Story. 2007. (Holocaust Ser.). (Illus.). 64p. (J). (gr. 3-7). lib. bdg. 18.95 *(978-1-58013-260-2(X)*, Kar-Ben Publishing) Lerner Publishing Group.

Taylor, Peter Lane & Nicola, Christos. The Secret of Priest's Grotto: A Holocaust Survival Story. 2007. (Holocaust Ser.). (ENG., Illus.). 64p. (YA). (gr. 5-12). per. 8.95 *(978-1-58013-261-9(8)*, Kar-Ben Publishing) Lerner Publishing Group.

Throp, Claire. The Horrors of the Holocaust. 2017. (Deadly History Ser.). (ENG.). 48p. (gr. 3-4). lib. bdg. 33.32 ***(978-1-4846-4166-8(3)**, Heinemann InfoSearch)* Heinemann-Raintree.

Throp, Claire. Resisting the Nazis. 2015. (Heroes of World War II Ser.). (ENG., Illus.). 48p. (gr. 4-6). 32.65 *(978-1-4109-8045-8(6))* Heinemann-Raintree.

Toll, Nelly S. Behind the Secret Window: A Memoir of a Hidden Childhood During World War II. 2003. (ENG.). 176p. (J). (gr. 3-7). 5.99 *(978-0-14-230241-5(4)*, Puffin Books) Penguin Young Readers Group.

Topek, Susan R. Ten Good Rules. Schanzer, Rosalyn, illus. 2004. (General Jewish Interest Ser.). 24p. (J). (gr. -1-1). pap. 6.95 *(978-0-929371-30-6(5)*, Kar-Ben Publishing) Lerner Publishing Group.

Uschan, Michael V. The Holocaust. 2005. (World History Ser.). (ENG., Illus.). 112p. (YA). (gr. 7-10). lib. bdg. 33.45 *(978-1-59018-252-9(9)*, Lucent Bks.) Cengage Gale.

Van Maarsen, Jacqueline. A Friend Called Anne: One Girl's Story of War, Peace, & a Unique Friendship with Anne Frank. 2007. (Illus.). 163p. (J). (gr. 5-9). 14.65 *(978-0-7569-8146-4(8))* Perfection Learning Corp.

Van Maarsen, Jacqueline & Lee, Carol Ann. A Friend Called Anne. 2007. (ENG., Illus.). 176p. (J). (gr. 3-7). 6.99 *(978-0-14-240719-6(4)*, Puffin Books) Penguin Young Readers Group.

Vander Zee, Ruth. Erika's Story. Innocenti, Roberto, illus. 2003. (ENG.). 24p. (J). (gr. 1-3). 19.99 *(978-1-56846-176-2(3))* Creative Co., The.

Vaughan, Marcia. Irena's Jars of Secrets, 1 vol. Mazellan, Ron, illus. 2011. (ENG.). 40p. (J). 18.95 *(978-1-60060-439-3(0))* Lee & Low Bks., Inc.

Vaughan, Marcia & Mazellan, Ron. Irena's Jars of Secrets. 2015. (ENG.). (J). pap. 10.95 *(978-1-62014-252-3(X))* Lee & Low Bks., Inc.

Wagner, Heather Lehr. Elie Wiesel: Messenger of Peace. 2007. (Modern Peacemakers Ser.). (Illus.). 112p. (YA). (gr. 9-12). lib. bdg. 30.00 *(978-0-7910-9220-0(8))* Facts On File, Inc.

Watts, Irene N. & Boraks-Nemetz, Lillian, compiled by. Tapestry of Hope: Holocaust Writing for Young People. 2003. (ENG., Illus.). 256p. (J). (gr. 5-18). 18.95 *(978-0-88776-638-1(2)*, Tundra Bks.) Tundra Bks. CAN. Dist: Penguin Random Hse. LLC.

Waxman, Laura Hamilton. Anne Frank. 2009. (History Maker Biographies Ser.). (ENG.). 48p. (gr. 3-6). 27.93 *(978-0-7613-4221-2(4)*, Lerner Pubns.) Lerner Publishing Group.

Whiting, Jim. Anne Frank. 2007. (What's So Great About... ? Ser.). (Illus.). 32p. (YA). (gr. 2-4). lib. bdg. 25.70 *(978-1-58415-581-2(7))* Mitchell Lane Pubs., Inc.

—The Story of the Holocaust. 2005. (Monumental Milestones Ser.). (Illus.). 48p. (YA). (gr. 4-7). lib. bdg. 29.95 *(978-1-58415-400-6(4))* Mitchell Lane Pubs., Inc.

Williams, Brenda & Williams, Brian. Saving the Persecuted. 2015. (Heroes of World War II Ser.). (ENG., Illus.). 48p. (gr. 4-6). 32.65 *(978-1-4109-8046-5(4))* Heinemann-Raintree.

Willis, Laurie. The Holocaust. 2009. (Social Issues Firsthand Ser.). (ENG., Illus.). 192p. (YA). (gr. 10-12). lib. bdg. 33.75 *(978-0-7377-4255-8(0)*, LML02109-243168, Greenhaven Pr., Inc.) Cengage Gale.

Winkelstein, Steven Paul. Brisko: A True Tale of Holocaust Survival. Juliano, Dana, illus. 2014. 104p. (J). *(978-0-9824498-6-8(0))* Mystic Waters Publishing.

Words for All Time: Students Letters to Holocaust Survivors. 2008. (YA). mass mkt. 19.95 *(978-0-9793771-6-7(1))* ComteQ Publishing.

Worth, Richard. Heinrich Himmler: Murderous Architect of the Holocaust. 2005. (Holocaust Heroes & Nazi Criminals Ser.). (Illus.). 160p. (YA). (gr. 7-13). lib. bdg. 27.93 *(978-0-7660-2532-5(2))* Enslow Pubs., Inc.

Ziemian, Joseph. The Cigarette Sellers of Three Crosses Square. 2005. (Library of Holocaust Testimonies Ser.). (Illus.). 168p. pap. 24.95 *(978-0-85303-686-9(1))* Vallentine Mitchell Pubs. GBR. Dist: ISBS Publisher Services.

Zullo, Allan & Bovsun, Mara. Heroes of the Holocaust: True Stories of Rescues by Teens. 2005. (Illus.). 183p. (J). *(978-0-439-67608-3(8))* Scholastic, Inc.

HOLOCAUST, JEWISH (1939-1945)—FICTION

Aaron, Chester. Gideon. 2009. (ENG., Illus.). 190p. (YA). pap. 12.99 *(978-1-934841-62-4(5)*, Zumaya Thresholds) Zumaya Pubns. LLC.

Appelfeld, Aharon. Adam & Thomas. Green, Jeffrey M., tr. from HEB. Dumas, Philippe, illus. 2017. (ENG.). 160p. (J). (gr. 3-7). pap. 14.95 *(978-1-60980-744-3(8)*, Triangle Square) Seven Stories Pr.

Arato, Rona. The Ship to Nowhere, 1 vol. 2016. (Holocaust Remembrance Ser.). (ENG.). 144p. (J). (gr. 6-8). pap. 14.95 *(978-1-77260-018-6(0))* Second Story Pr. CAN. Dist: Orca Bk. Pubs. USA.

Boyne, John. The Boy in the Striped Pajamas. (ENG.). (YA). (gr. 7). 2006. 224p. 17.99 *(978-0-385-75106-3(0))* 2008. 240p. pap. 9.99 *(978-0-385-75189-6(3))* Fickling, David Bks. GBR. Dist: Penguin Random Hse. LLC.

—The Boy in the Striped Pajamas. 2011. 10.54 *(978-0-7848-3514-2(4)*, Everbind) Marco Bk. Co.

—The Boy in the Striped Pajamas. 2008. 215p. (gr. 7-12). 20.00 *(978-0-7569-8943-9(4))* Perfection Learning Corp.

—The Boy in the Striped Pajamas. 2007. (ENG.). 224p. (YA). (gr. 7-18). pap. 9.99 *(978-0-385-75153-7(2)*, Ember) Random Hse. Children's Bks.

—The Boy in the Striped Pajamas. rev. l.t. ed. 2007. (Thorndike Literacy Bridge Ser.). 247p. (YA). (gr. 7-12). 23.95 *(978-0-7862-9425-1(6))* Thorndike Pr.

—The Boy in the Striped Pajamas. 2007. 215p. (YA). (gr. 7-12). 20.85 *(978-1-4178-1823-5(9)*, Turtleback) Turtleback Bks.

—The Boy in the Striped Pajamas (Deluxe Illustrated Edition) Jeffers, Oliver, illus. 2016. (ENG.). 352p. (YA). (gr. 7). 18.99 *(978-0-399-55931-0(0)*, Knopf Bks. for Young Readers) Random Hse. Children's Bks.

Cerrito, Angela. The Safest Lie. 2015. (ENG.). 192p. (J). (gr. 3-7). 16.95 *(978-0-8234-3310-0(2))* Holiday Hse., Inc.

Chapman, Fern Schumer. Is It Night or Day? 2010. (ENG.). 224p. (J). (gr. 5-9). 17.99 *(978-0-374-17744-7(9)*, 9780374177447, Farrar, Straus & Giroux (BYR)) Farrar, Straus & Giroux.

Clark, Kathy. The Choice, 1 vol. 2015. (Holocaust Remembrance Ser.). (ENG., Illus.). 200p. (J). (gr. 6-8). pap. 14.95 *(978-1-927583-65-4(9))* Second Story Pr. CAN. Dist: Orca Bk. Pubs. USA.

—Guardian Angel House, 1 vol. 2009. (Holocaust Remembrance Ser.). (ENG., Illus.). 180p. (J). (gr. 4-8). pap. 14.95 *(978-1-897187-58-6(0))* Second Story Pr. CAN. Dist: Orca Bk. Pubs. USA.

Codell, Esmé Raji. Vive la Paris. 2006. (ENG.). 224p. (gr. 4-7). 15.99 *(978-0-7868-5124-9(4))* Hyperion Pr.

Cohen-Janca, Irène. Mister Doctor: Janusz Korczak & the Orphans of the Warsaw Ghetto. Quarello, Maurizio A. C., illus. 2015. (ENG.). 68p. (J). (gr. 4-7). 24.95 *(978-1-55451-715-2(X)*, 9781554517152) Annick Pr., Ltd. CAN. Dist: Publishers Group West (PGW).

Dauvillier, Loïc & Salsedo, Greg. Hidden. Lizano, Marc, illus. 2014. (ENG.). 80p. (J). (gr. 1-5). 16.99 *(978-1-59643-873-6(8)*, 9781596438736, First Second Bks.) Roaring Brook Pr.

Dostis, Isaac & Haddad Ikonomopoulos, Marcia. Ten Gold Medals: Glory or Freedom. 2005. (Illus.). ii, 72p. (J). *(978-0-8197-0770-3(8))* Bloch Publishing Co.

Dunlop, Ed. Escape to Liechtenstein. 2003. (Young Refugees Ser.). 152p. (J). (gr. 3-7). per. 7.49 *(978-1-59166-013-2(0))* BJU Pr.

—The Incredible Rescues. Halverson, Tom, illus. 2003. 166p. (J). (gr. 4-7). 7.49 *(978-1-59166-012-5(2))* BJU Pr.

Engle, Margarita. Tropical Secrets: Holocaust Refugees in Cuba. 2009. (ENG.). 208p. (YA). (gr. 7-12). 23.99 *(978-0-8050-8936-3(5)*, 9780805089363, Holt, Henry & Co. Bks. For Young Readers) Holt, Henry & Co.

Fitzgerald, Laura Marx. Under the Egg. (ENG.). 256p. (J). (gr. 3-7). 2015. 7.99 *(978-0-14-242765-1(9)*, Puffin Books) 2014. 16.99 *(978-0-8037-4001-3(8)*, Dial Bks) Penguin Young Readers Group.

Flegg, Aubrey. In the Claws of the Eagle Vol. 3. 2006. (Louise Trilogy Ser.: 03). (ENG.). 288p. (J). pap. 12.95 *(978-0-86278-827-8(7))* O'Brien Pr., Ltd., The IRL. Dist: Dufour Editions, Inc.

Fleischman, Sid. The Entertainer & the Dybbuk. 2009. (ENG.). 192p. (J). (gr. 4-9). pap. 6.99 *(978-0-06-177140-8(6)*, Greenwillow Bks.) HarperCollins Pubs.

Florida-James, Mark. Berlin Wolf. 2013. (ENG.). 336p. pap. *(978-1-78306-005-4(0))* Troubador Publishing Ltd.

Friedman, D. Dina. Escaping into the Night. 2009. (ENG.). 208p. (J). (gr. 5-9). pap. 9.99 *(978-1-4169-8648-5(0)*, Simon & Schuster Bks. For Young Readers) Simon & Schuster Bks. For Young Readers.

Gleitzman, Morris. Then. 2013. (Once Ser.: 2). (ENG.). 224p. (YA). (gr. 7). pap. 9.99 *(978-1-250-00341-6(5)*, 9781250003416) Square Fish.

Gottesfeld, Jeff. The Tree in the Courtyard: Looking Through Anne Frank's Window. McCarty, Peter, illus. 2016. (ENG.). 40p. (J). (gr. k-3). 17.99 *(978-0-385-75397-5(7))*; lib. bdg. 20.99 *(978-0-385-75398-2(5))* Random Hse. Children's Bks. (Knopf Bks. for Young Readers).

Gratz, Alan, et al. Prisoner B-3087. 2013. (ENG.). 272p. (J). (gr. 4-7). 16.99 *(978-0-545-45901-3(X)*, Scholastic Pr.) Scholastic, Inc.

Hausfater, Rachel. The Little Boy Star: An Allegory of the Holocaust. Zimmerman, Joelle, tr. from FRE. Latyk, Olivier, illus. 2006. (ENG.). 32p. (J). (gr. 4-7). 16.95 *(978-1-59687-172-4(5))* IBks., Inc.

—The Little Boy Star: An Allegory of the Holocaust. Latyk, Olivier, illus. 2nd ed. 2017. (ENG.). (J). (gr. k-3). 19.95 ***(978-1-59687-542-5(9)**, ipicturebooks)* ibooks, Inc.

Hesse, Monica. Girl in the Blue Coat. (ENG.). 320p. (gr. 7-17). 2017. (YA). pap. 9.99 *(978-0-316-26063-3(0))* 2016. 17.99 *(978-0-316-26060-2(6))* 2016. (YA). E-Book *(978-0-316-26064-0(9))* Little, Brown Bks. for Young Readers.

—Girl in the Blue Coat. 2017. (YA). lib. bdg. 20.85 ***(978-0-606-39918-0(6))*** Turtleback Bks.

Heuvel, Eric & Miller, Lorraine T. A Family Secret. Miller, Lorraine T., tr. from DUT. Heuvel, Eric, illus. 2009. (ENG., Illus.). 64p. (J). (gr. 5-9). pap. 11.99 *(978-0-374-42265-3(6)*, 9780374422653) Square Fish.

Joffo, Joseph. A Bag of Marbles: The Graphic Novel. 2013. 128p. pap. 29.27 *(978-1-4677-1651-2(0))* Lerner Publishing Group.

—A Bag of Marbles: The Graphic Novel. Gauvin, Edward, tr. Bailly, Vincent, illus. 2013. (ENG.). 128p. (gr. 7-12). pap. 9.95 *(978-1-4677-1516-4(6))*; lib. bdg. 29.27 *(978-1-4677-0700-8(7))* Lerner Publishing Group. (Graphic Universe™).

Kacer, Kathy. The Diary of Laura's Twin, 1 vol. 2008. (Holocaust Remembrance Ser.). (ENG., Illus.). 208p. (J). (gr. 4-8). pap. 14.95 *(978-1-897187-39-5(4))* Second Story Pr. CAN. Dist: Orca Bk. Pubs. USA.

—Shanghai Escape, 1 vol. 2013. (Holocaust Remembrance Ser.). (ENG.). 204p. (J). (gr. 6-8). pap. 14.95 *(978-1-927583-10-4(1))* Second Story Pr. CAN. Dist: Orca Bk. Pubs. USA.

Karlin, Ann. Another Time - Another Place. Mazo, Chaim, ed. 2010. 96p. pap. 12.95 *(978-965-7344-68-2(9))* Mazo Pubs.

Katies Choice. 2005. (YA). per. *(978-1-59872-217-8(4))* Instant Pub.

Kaurin, Marianne. Almost Autumn. Hedger, Rosie, tr. from NOR. 2017. (ENG.). 288p. (J). (gr. 7). 17.99 *(978-0-545-88965-0(0)*, Levine, Arthur A. Bks.) Scholastic, Inc.

Kerr, Judith. When Hitler Stole Pink Rabbit. (SPA.). 172p. (J). 11.95 *(978-84-204-3201-4(6))* Santillana USA Publishing Co., Inc.

—When Hitler Stole Pink Rabbit. 2009. (gr. 3-6). lib. bdg. 17.20 *(978-0-8085-9123-8(1)*, Turtleback) Turtleback Bks.

Kositsky, Lynne. The Thought of High Windows. 2004. (ENG.). 176p. (J). (gr. 7-9). 6.95 *(978-1-55337-622-4(6))* Kids Can Pr., Ltd. CAN. Dist: Hachette Bk. Group.

Lawton, Wendy. A La Sombra de Su Mano, 1 vol. 2009. Orig. Title: Shadow of His Hand. (SPA.). 160p. pap. 4.99 *(978-0-8254-1379-7(6)*, Editorial Portavoz) Kregel Pubns.

Lawton, Wendy G. Shadow of His Hand: A Story Based on the Life of Holocaust Survivor Anita Dittman. 2004. (Daughters of the Faith Ser.). (ENG.). 160p. (J). (gr. 3). pap. 7.99 *(978-0-8024-4074-7(6))* Moody Pubs.

Lehman, Theodore H. Defying Odds. 2014. (YA). pap. *(978-1-935604-63-1(5))* Gaon Bks.

Lewis, J. Patrick. The Wren & the Sparrow. Nayberg, Yevgenia, illus. 2014. (J). 6.99 *(978-1-4677-6210-6(5)*, Kar-Ben Publishing) Lerner Publishing Group.

Lowenstein, Sallie Claire. Waiting for Eugene. 2006. (Illus.). 201p. (J). *(978-1-4156-6166-6(9))* Book Wholesalers, Inc.

MacDonald, Maryann. Odette's Secrets. 2013. (ENG., Illus.). 240p. (YA). (gr. 5-8). 16.99 *(978-1-59990-750-5(X)*, 9781599907505, Bloomsbury USA Childrens) Bloomsbury Publishing USA.

Mazer, Norma Fox. Good Night, Maman. 2006. 185p. (J). (gr. k-4). reprint ed. 16.00 *(978-1-4223-5862-7(3))* DIANE Publishing Co.

—Good Night, Maman. 2010. (ENG., Illus.). 192p. (J). (gr. 5-7). pap. 12.95 *(978-0-15-206173-9(8))* Houghton Mifflin Harcourt Publishing Co.

McKay, Sharon E. End of the Line. 2014. (ENG., Illus.). 128p. (J). (gr. 4-6). pap. 12.95 *(978-1-55451-658-2(7)*, 9781554516582) Annick Pr., Ltd. CAN. Dist: Publishers Group West (PGW).

Orlev, Uri. Run, Boy, Run. Halkin, Hillel, tr. 10th ed. 2007. (ENG.). 192p. (YA). (gr. 5-18). 7.99 *(978-0-618-95706-4(5))* Houghton Mifflin Harcourt Publishing Co.

Perl, Lila. Isabel's War. 2014. (ENG.). 224p. (J). (gr. 2-7). pap. 12.95 *(978-1-939601-27-8(4))* Ig Publishing, Inc.

—Lilli's Quest. 2015. (ENG.). 224p. (J). (-9). pap. 12.95 *(978-1-939601-53-7(3))* Ig Publishing, Inc.

Pressler, Mirjam. Malka. Murdoch, Brian, tr. 2005. 280p. (YA). (gr. 7-12). 13.65 *(978-0-7569-5217-4(4))* Perfection Learning Corp.

Pryor, Bonnie. Simon's Escape: A Story of the Holocaust. 2010. (Historical Fiction Adventures (HFA) Ser.). (Illus.). 160p. (J). pap. 10.95 *(978-1-59845-216-7(9))*; (gr. 3-6). 29.27 *(978-0-7660-3388-7(0))* Enslow Pubs., Inc.

Pushker, Gloria Teles & Tarman, Mel. Toby Belfer Learns about Heroes & Martyrs, 1 vol. Henriquez, Emile, illus. 2009. (Toby Belfer Ser.). (ENG.). 128p. (J). (gr. 3-7). 14.95 *(978-1-58980-647-4(6))* Pelican Publishing Co., Inc.

Roy, Jennifer. Yellow Star, 0 vols. 2014. (ENG.). 256p. (gr. 5-7). pap. 9.99 *(978-0-7614-6310-8(0)*, 9780761463108, Amazon Children's Publishing) Amazon Publishing.

Sax, Aline. The War Within These Walls. 2013. (ENG., Illus.). 176p. (YA). 17.00 *(978-0-8028-5428-5(1)*, Eerdmans Bks For Young Readers) Eerdmans, William B. Publishing Co.

Schmidt, Gary D. Mara's Stories: Glimmers in the Darkness. 2008. (ENG.). 160p. (YA). (gr. 5-9). per. 14.99 *(978-0-312-37388-7(0)*, 9780312373887) Square Fish.

Sharenow, Robert. The Berlin Boxing Club. 2012. (ENG.). 432p. (YA). (gr. 8). pap. 9.99 *(978-0-06-157970-7(X)*, HarperTeen) HarperCollins Pubs.

—The Berlin Boxing Club. 2012. (YA). lib. bdg. 20.85 *(978-0-606-26871-4(5)*, Turtleback) Turtleback Bks.

Simon, Tanya & Simon, Richard. Oskar & the Eight Blessings. Siegel, Mark, illus. 2015. (ENG.). 40p. (J). (gr. -1-3). 17.99 *(978-1-59643-949-8(1)*, 9781596439498) Roaring Brook Pr.

Spinelli, Jerry. Milkweed. 2010. (ENG.). 240p. (YA). (gr. 7). pap. 9.99 *(978-0-375-86147-5(5)*, Ember) Random Hse. Children's Bks.

Spradlin, Michael P. The Enemy Above. 2016. (ENG.). 240p. (J). (gr. 3-7). 16.99 *(978-0-545-85782-6(1)*, Scholastic Pr.) Scholastic, Inc.

Surber, Mary Brigid. The Last Stork Summer. 2015. (ENG.). 128p. pap. 13.95 *(978-1-78279-934-6(2)*, Top Hat Bks.) Hunt, John Publishing Ltd. GBR. Dist: National Bk. Network.

Tarshis, Lauren. I Survived the Nazi Invasion 1944. 2014. (I Survived Ser.: 9). (ENG.). 112p. (J). (gr. 2-5). pap. 4.99 *(978-0-545-45938-9(9))* Scholastic, Inc.

—I Survived the Nazi Invasion 1944. 2014. (I Survived . Ser.: No. 9). lib. bdg. 14.75 *(978-0-606-35397-7(6))* Turtleback Bks.

Vander Zee, Ruth. Erika's Story. Innocenti, Roberto, illus. 2013. (ENG.). 24p. (J). (gr. 1-3). pap. 10.99 *(978-0-89812-891-8(9),* Creative Paperbacks) Creative Co., The.

Vander Zee, Ruth & Sneider, Marian. Eli Remembers. Farnsworth, Bill, illus. 2007. (ENG.). 32p. (J). (gr. -1-3). 18.00 *(978-0-8028-5309-7(9),* Eerdmans Bks For Young Readers) Eerdmans, William B. Publishing Co.

Watts, Irene N. Good-Bye Marianne: A Story of Growing up in Nazi Germany. Shoemaker, Kathryn E., illus. 2008. (ENG.). 128p. (J). (gr. 4-7). pap. 12.95 *(978-0-88776-830-9(X),* Tundra Bks.) Tundra Bks. CAN. Dist: Penguin Random Hse. LLC.

—Touched by Fire. 2013. (ENG., Illus.). 202p. (YA). (gr. 5-9). 17.95 *(978-1-77049-524-1(X),* Tundra Bks.) Tundra Bks. CAN. Dist: Penguin Random Hse. LLC.

Whitney, Kim Ablon. The Other Half of Life. 2010. (ENG.). 256p. (YA). (gr. 7). mass mkt. 7.99 *(978-0-375-84422-5(8),* Laurel Leaf) Random Hse. Children's Bks.

Williams, Laura E. Behind the Bedroom Wall. Goldstein, A. Nancy, illus. 2005. (Historical Fiction for Young Readers Ser.). (ENG.). 184p. (J). (gr. 3-7). per. 8.00 *(978-1-57131-658-5(2))* Milkweed Editions.

—Behind the Bedroom Wall. Goldstein, A. Nancy, illus. 2006. 169p. (gr. -1-7). 17.45 *(978-0-7569-6389-7(3))* Perfection Learning Corp.

The Winter Horses. 2014. (ENG., Illus.). 288p. (YA). (gr. 7). 16.99 *(978-0-385-75543-6(0),* Knopf Bks. for Young Readers) Random Hse. Children's Bks.

Wiseman, Eva. Kanada. 2006. (ENG., Illus.). 264p. (YA). (gr. 5). pap. 9.95 *(978-0-88776-729-6(X),* Tundra Bks.) Tundra Bks. CAN. Dist: Penguin Random Hse. LLC.

Wiviott, Meg. Benno & the Night of Broken Glass. Bisaillon, Josée, illus. 2010. (ENG.). 32p. (J). (gr. 2-5). pap. 7.95 *(978-0-8225-9975-3(9));* lib. bdg. 17.95 *(978-0-8225-9929-6(5))* Lerner Publishing Group. (Kar-Ben Publishing).

Yolen, Jane. The Devil's Arithmetic. 2004. (Puffin Modern Classics Ser.). (ENG.). 176p. (J). (gr. 5-3). pap. 7.99 *(978-0-14-240109-5(9),* Puffin Books) Penguin Young Readers Group.

—Stone Angel. Green, Katie May, illus. 2015. (ENG.). 40p. (J). (gr. k-3). 16.99 *(978-0-399-16741-6(2),* Philomel Bks.) Penguin Young Readers Group.

HOLOCAUST SURVIVORS

Here are entered works on persons who survived the Jewish Holocaust of 1939-1945, with emphasis on their lives since 1945.

Allen, John. Holocaust Survivors. 2015. (ENG., Illus.). 80p. (J). lib. bdg. 28.95 *(978-1-60152-848-3(5))* ReferencePoint Pr., Inc.

Altman, Linda Jacobs. Hidden Teens, Hidden Lives: Primary Sources from the Holocaust. 2010. (True Stories of Teens in the Holocaust Ser.). (Illus.). 128p. (YA). (gr. 9-12). 33.27 *(978-0-7660-3271-2(X))* Enslow Pubs., Inc.

Bayer, Linda N. Elie Wiesel: Spokesman for Remembrance. 2005. (Holocaust Biographies Ser.). (Illus.). 112p. (J). (gr. 7-12). lib. bdg. 34.60 *(978-0-8239-3306-8(7),* HBWIES) Rosen Publishing Group, Inc., The.

Berne, Emma Carlson. Escaping the Nazis on the Kindertransport. 2017. (Encounter: Narrative Nonfiction Stories Ser.). (ENG., Illus.). 112p. (gr. 3-4). lib. bdg. 29.99 *(978-1-5157-4545-7(7))* Capstone Press of Coughlan Cos.

Bisson, Michelle. Hedy's Journey The True Story of a Hungarian Girl Fleeing the Holocaust. Ramon, El Primo, illus. 2017. (Encounter: Narrative Nonfiction Picture Bks.). (ENG.). 40p. (gr. 5-6). 15.95 ***(978-1-5157-8222-3(0))*** Encounter Bks.

Brandman, Bronia & Bierman, Carol. The Girl Who Survived: A True Story of the Holocaust. 2010. 91p. (J). pap. *(978-0-545-17574-6(7))* Scholastic, Inc.

Colbert, David. Anne Frank. 2008. (10 Days Ser.). (ENG., Illus.). 160p. (J). (gr. 3-8). pap. 7.99 *(978-1-4169-6445-2(2),* Aladdin) Simon & Schuster Children's Publishing.

Currie, Stephen. Escapes from Nazi Persecution. 2003. (Great Escapes Ser.). (ENG., Illus.). 112p. (J). 30.85 *(978-1-59018-279-6(0),* Lucent Bks.) Cengage Gale.

Downing, David. Aftermath & Remembrance. 2005. (World Almanac Library of the Holocaust). (Illus.). 48p. (gr. 5-12). lib. bdg. 31.00 *(978-0-8368-5948-5(0),* Gareth Stevens Secondary Library) Stevens, Gareth Publishing LLLP.

Gertner, Sheina Sachar. The Tree Stood Still. 2006. 96p. per. 9.95 *(978-1-58939-886-3(6))* Virtualbookworm.com Publishing, Inc.

Gottfried, Ted. Children of the Slaughter: Young People of the Holocaust. Alcorn, Stephen, illus. (Holocaust History Ser.). 112p. (YA). (gr. 7-12). 22.95 *(978-1-58013-202-2(2),* Kar-Ben Publishing) Lerner Publishing Group.

Harris, Samuel R. Sammy Child Survivor of the Holocaust. 2005. (Illus.). 128p. pap. 14.95 *(978-0-9759253-0-0(X))* Harris, Samuel.

Hay, Jeff. The Holocaust. Greenhaven Press Editors, ed. 2014. (Genocide & Persecution Ser.). (ENG., Illus.). 240p. (gr. 10-12). lib. bdg. 42.00 *(978-0-7377-6897-8(5),* Greenhaven Pr., Inc.) Cengage Gale.

Hoffman, Betty N. Liberation: Stories of Survival from the Holocaust. 2011. (Holocaust Through Primary Sources Ser.). (Illus.). 128p. (J). (gr. 6-18). pap. 10.95 *(978-1-59845-348-5(3));* (gr. 9-12). lib. bdg. 33.27 *(978-0-7660-3319-1(8))* Enslow Pubs., Inc.

Houghton, Sarah. Elie Wiesel: A Holocaust Survivor Cries Out for Peace. 2003. (High Five Reading - Green Ser.). (ENG., Illus.). 48p. (J). (gr. 3-4). per. 9.00 *(978-0-7368-2833-8(8),* High Five Reading (RBL)) Capstone Press of Coughlan Cos.

—Elie Wiesel Set: A Holocaust Survivor Cries Out for Peace, 6. 2003. (High Five Reading - Green Ser.). (ENG.). 48p. (gr. 3-4). pap. 54.00 *(978-0-7368-2843-7(5),* High Five Reading (RBL)) Capstone Press of Coughlan Cos.

Johnson, Stephen, ed. From the Holocaust to Healing the World. 2003. per. 7.95 *(978-0-9659781-1-8(7))* Holocaust Museum Houston.

Kemeny, Esther. On the Shores of Darkness: The Memoir of Esther Kemeny Haller, Heather, ed. 2003. (Illus.). 144p. per. *(978-0-9743961-7-0(6))* Haller Company, The.

Lobel, Anita. No Pretty Pictures: A Child of War. 2008. (ENG.). 288p. (J). (gr. 5). pap. 7.99 *(978-0-06-156589-2(X),* Greenwillow Bks.) HarperCollins Pubs.

Ludwig, Trudy. Gifts from the Enemy. Orback, Craig, illus. 2014. (HumanKIND Project Ser.). (ENG.). 32p. (gr. 2-7). 16.95 *(978-1-935952-97-8(8))* White Cloud Pr.

MacKenzie, Catherine. Corrie Ten Boo - Are All of the Watches Safe? Ammassari, Rita, illus. 2011. (Little Lights Ser.). (ENG.). 24p. (J). (gr. -1-2). 7.99 *(978-1-84550-109-9(8),* 8f71ca06-a3ed-4fbd-93f4-7acda1909291) Christian Focus Pubns. GBR. Dist: Bookmasters Distribution.

Moore, Lisa. Elie Wiesel: Surviving the Holocaust, Speaking Out Against Genocide. 2005. (Holocaust Heroes & Nazi Criminals Ser.). (Illus.). 160p. (J). (gr. 7-12). lib. bdg. 27.93 *(978-0-7660-2576-9(4))* Enslow Pubs., Inc.

Nelson, Sheila. Never Again: Survivors of the Holocaust. (Survivors Ser.). (J). 2010. 128p. (gr. 7-12). 24.95 *(978-1-4222-0459-7(6))* 2009. 129p. pap. 24.95 *(978-1-4222-1472-5(9))* Mason Crest.

Rubin, Susan Goldman. The Anne Frank Case: Simon Wiesenthal's Search for the Truth. Farnsworth, Bill, illus. 2009. (ENG.). 40p. (J). (gr. 5-18). 18.95 *(978-0-8234-2109-1(0))* Holiday Hse., Inc.

Schloss, Eva & Powers, Barbara. The Promise: The Moving Story of a Family in the Holocaust. Yaron, Sophie, illus. 2006. (ENG.). 160p. (J). (gr. 13-18). 10.99 *(978-0-14-132081-6(8))* Penguin Bks., Ltd. GBR. Dist: Independent Pubs. Group.

Singer, Flora M. Flora - I Was but A Child. 2007. 180p. (J). pap. 26.50 *(978-0-9760739-8-7(6))* Yad Vashem Pubns. ISR. Dist: Coronet Bks.

Strauss, Gwen. The Hiding Game, 1 vol. Leonhard, Herb, illus. 2017. 40p. (J). (gr. 2-5). 17.99 *(978-1-4556-2265-8(6))* Pelican Publishing Co., Inc.

Thomson, Ruth. Terezin: Voices from the Holocaust. 2013. (ENG., Illus.). 64p. (YA). (gr. 5-9). pap. 9.99 *(978-0-7636-6466-4(9))* Candlewick Pr.

Vander Zee, Ruth. Erika's Story. Innocenti, Roberto, illus. 2003. (ENG.). 24p. (J). (gr. 1-3). 19.99 *(978-1-56846-176-2(3))* Creative Co., The.

Wagner, Heather Lehr. Elie Wiesel: Messenger of Peace. 2007. (Modern Peacemakers Ser.). (Illus.). 112p. (YA). (gr. 9-12). lib. bdg. 30.00 *(978-0-7910-9220-0(8))* Facts On File, Inc.

Words for All Time: Students Letters to Holocaust Survivors. 2008. (YA). mass mkt. 19.95 *(978-0-9793771-6-7(1))* ComteQ Publishing.

Yeatts, Tabatha. Weisel, Wiesenthal, Klarsfeld: The Holocaust Survivors. 2014. (Remembering the Holocaust Ser.). 96p. (J). (gr. 6-12). 27.94 *(978-0-7660-6202-3(3))* Enslow Pubs., Inc.

—Wiesel, Wiesenthal, Klarsfeld: The Holocaust Survivors. 2014. (Remembering the Holocaust Ser.). 96p. (J). (gr. 6-12). pap. 10.95 *(978-0-7660-6203-0(1))* Enslow Pubs., Inc.

Zullo, Allan. Survivors: True Stories of Children in the Holocaust. 2005. (Survivors Ser.). (ENG., Illus.). 208p. (J). (gr. 3-7). 6.99 *(978-0-439-66996-2(0),* Scholastic Paperbacks) Scholastic, Inc.

HOLOCAUST SURVIVORS—FICTION

Bowen, Joshua. A Boy Called Jesse. 2008. (Illus.). 20p. (J). lib. bdg. 9.95 *(978-0-9778290-7-1(3))* Midwest Wrtng.

Bowen, Michael Dale. Edwarda Opatowska Saved My Life! 2008. (Illus.). 16p. (J). lib. bdg. 9.95 *(978-0-9778290-6-4(5))* Midwest Wrtng.

Dalager, Stig. David's Story. 2010. (ENG., Illus.). 280p. (J). pap. 18.95 *(978-1-906582-04-3(1))* Aurora Metro Pubns. Ltd. GBR. Dist: Consortium Bk. Sales & Distribution.

Fried, Leah. Where Is Shimmele? Ruppaport, Aviva, tr. from HEB. 2003. (Illus.). 318p. (YA). (gr. 6-8). 20.00 *(978-1-885220-31-8(6))* Moznaim Publishing Corp.

Gleitzman, Morris. Now. 2012. (Once Ser.: 3). (ENG.). 192p. (YA). (gr. 7). 16.99 *(978-0-8050-9378-0(8),* 9780805093780, Holt, Henry & Co. Bks. For Young Readers) Holt, Henry & Co.

—Now. 2013. (Once Ser.: 3). (ENG.). 192p. (YA). (gr. 7). pap. 9.99 *(978-1-250-03417-5(5),* 9781250034175) Square Fish.

Headley, Julia. Yanina Ballerina. 2008. (Illus.). 17p. (J). lib. bdg. 9.95 *(978-0-9778290-8-8(1))* Midwest Wrtng.

Lewis, J. Patrick. The Wren & the Sparrow. Nayberg, Yevgenia, illus. 2014. (J). 6.99 *(978-1-4677-6210-6(5),* Kar-Ben Publishing) Lerner Publishing Group.

Mazer, Norma Fox. Good Night, Maman. 2006. 185p. (J). (gr. k-4). reprint ed. 16.00 *(978-1-4223-5862-7(3))* DIANE Publishing Co.

—Good Night, Maman. 2010. (ENG., Illus.). 192p. (J). (gr. 5-7). pap. 12.95 *(978-0-15-206173-9(8))* Houghton Mifflin Harcourt Publishing Co.

McMillan, Frank. Cezanne Is Missing. 2006. (ENG.). 323p. (YA). (gr. 7). per. 14.95 *(978-0-9711359-4-9(0))* Cambridge Hse. Publishing Co., LLC.

Meyer, Molly. Never Alone a Girl of Hope. 2008. (Illus.). 24p. (J). lib. bdg. 9.95 *(978-0-9778290-4-0(9))* Midwest Wrtng.

Papemy, Myra. The Greenies. 2007. (ENG.). 304p. (J). mass mkt. 6.99 *(978-0-00-639356-6(X),* Harper Trophy) HarperCollins Pubs.

Scholzen, Barbara. Jolanta & Her 2,500 Kids12. 2008. (Illus.). 12p. (J). lib. bdg. 9.95 *(978-0-9778290-9-5(X))* Midwest Wrtng.

Svoboda, Megan. Esther Katz a Girl of Hope. 2008. (Illus.). 20p. (J). lib. bdg. 9.95 *(978-0-9778290-5-7(7))* Midwest Wrtng.

Wild, Margaret. Let the Celebrations Begin. Vivas, Julie, illus. 2014. (ENG.). 40p. (J). (gr. 2-5). 16.99 *(978-0-7636-7013-9(8))* Candlewick Pr.

Wiviott, Meg. Paper Hearts. 2015. (ENG., Illus.). 352p. (YA). (gr. 7). 17.99 *(978-1-4814-3983-1(9),* McElderry, Margaret K. Bks.) McElderry, Margaret K. Bks.

Zail, Suzy. Playing for the Commandant. 2014. (ENG.). 256p. (YA). (gr. 7). 16.99 *(978-0-7636-6403-9(0))* Candlewick Pr.

HOLY GRAIL

see Grail

HOLY ROMAN EMPIRE

Bhote, Themina. Charlemagne: Life & Times of an Early Medieval Emperor. 2004. (Leaders of the Middle Ages Ser.). (Illus.). 112p. (YA). (gr. 5-9). lib. bdg. 34.60 *(978-1-4042-0161-3(0))* Rosen Publishing Group, Inc., The.

—Charlemagne: The Life & Times of an Early Medieval Emperor. 2009. (Leaders of the Middle Ages Ser.). 112p. (gr. 5-8). 66.50 *(978-1-61513-896-8(X),* Rosen Reference) Rosen Publishing Group, Inc., The.

Gagne, Tammy. Charlemagne. 2017. (Junior Biography From Ancient Civilization Ser.). (gr. 4-6). 29.95 *(978-1-68020-020-1(8))* Mitchell Lane Pubs., Inc.

Gelfand, Dale Evva. Charlemagne. 2003. (Ancient World Leaders Ser.). (Illus.). 112p. (gr. 6-12). 30.00 *(978-0-7910-7224-0(X),* Chelsea Hse.) Facts On File, Inc.

McKinley, Herald. Persia, the Rise of Islam, & the Holy Roman Empire. 2015. (Exploring the Ancient & Medieval Worlds Ser.). (ENG., Illus.). 160p. (J). (gr. 8-8). 45.64 *(978-1-5026-0677-8(1))* Cavendish Square Publishing.

Schlesinger, Arthur M., Jr., intro. Ancient World Leaders. (Illus.). (gr. 6-12). lib. bdg. *(978-0-7910-8056-6(0),* Chelsea Hse.) Facts On File, Inc.

Whiting, Jim. The Life & Times of Charlemagne. 2005. (Biography from Ancient Civilizations Ser.). (Illus.). 48p. (J). (gr. 4-8). lib. bdg. 29.95 *(978-1-58415-346-7(6))* Mitchell Lane Pubs., Inc.

HOLY SCRIPTURES

see Bible

HOLY SEE

see Catholic Church; Popes

HOME

see also Home Economics; Marriage

The Big Picture: Homes. 2011. (Big Picture: Homes Ser.). (ENG.). 24p. (gr. 1-2). pap. 166.80 *(978-1-4296-6734-0(6),* First Facts) Capstone Press of Coughlan Cos.

Endres, Hollie J. The Letter Hh Set: Homes, 6 vols. 2004. (Letter Bks.). (ENG.). 8p. (gr. k-1). pap. 29.70 *(978-0-7368-4107-8(5),* Letter Bks.) Capstone Press of Coughlan Cos.

Hinkler Books, creator. 101 First Words: At Home. 2011. (101 First Words Ser.). (Illus.). 16p. (J). (gr. -1). bds. 7.99 *(978-1-74184-819-9(9))* Hinkler Bks. Pty, Ltd. AUS. Dist: Ideals Pubns.

Jones, Tammy. My Home. 2009. (Sight Word Readers Set A Ser.). (J). 3.49 net. *(978-1-60719-144-5(X))* Newmark Learning LLC.

Lawrence, Ellen. A Place to Call Home. 2015. (My World Your World Ser.). (ENG.). 24p. (J). (gr. -1-3). lib. bdg. 23.93 *(978-1-910549-02-5(9))* Bearport Publishing Co., Inc.

Levete, Sarah. Taking Action Against Family Breakups. 2010. (Taking Action Ser.). (ENG.). 48p. (YA). pap. 11.75 *(978-1-61532-311-1(2),* Rosen Reference); (gr. 5-9). lib. bdg. 29.25 *(978-1-61532-310-4(4))* Rosen Publishing Group, Inc., The.

Litchfield, Jo. At Home. rev. ed. 2013. (First Words Board Bks). 12p. (J). ring bd. 6.99 *(978-0-7945-2617-7(9),* Usborne) EDC Publishing.

Marsico, Katie. Good Manners at Home, 1 vol. Haslam, John, illus. 2009. (Good Manners Matter! Ser.). (ENG.). 32p. (J). (gr. -1-2). 28.50 *(978-1-60270-607-1(7))* Magic Wagon.

Milet Publishing Staff. Home. 2011. (My First Bilingual Book Ser.). (ENG., Illus.). 24p. (J). (gr. k — 1). bds. 7.99 *(978-1-84059-642-7(2));* bds. 7.99 *(978-1-84059-646-5(5))* Milet Publishing.

—Home - My First Bilingual Book. 2011. (My First Bilingual Book Ser.). (Illus.). 24p. (J). (gr. k — 1). (ENG.). bds. 7.99 *(978-1-84059-653-3(8));* (ENG., bds. 7.99 *(978-1-84059-654-0(6));* (SPA & ENG., bds. 8.99 *(978-1-84059-652-6(X));* (ENG., bds. 8.99 *(978-1-84059-645-8(7));* (ENG., bds. 7.99 *(978-1-84059-641-0(4))* Milet Publishing.

—Home (English-Arabic) 2011. (My First Bilingual Book Ser.). (ENG., Illus.). 24p. (J). (gr. k — 1). bds. 7.99 *(978-1-84059-640-3(6))* Milet Publishing.

—Home (English-French) 2011. (My First Bilingual Book Ser.). (FRE & ENG., Illus.). 24p. (J). (gr. k — 1). bds. 8.99 *(978-1-84059-644-1(9))* Milet Publishing.

—Home (English-Polish) 2011. (My First Bilingual Book Ser.). (ENG & POR., Illus.). 24p. (J). (gr. k — 1). bds. 7.99 *(978-1-84059-648-9(1))* Milet Publishing.

—Home (English-Portuguese) 2011. (My First Bilingual Book Ser.). (ENG., Illus.). 24p. (J). (gr. k — 1). bds. 7.99 *(978-1-84059-649-6(X))* Milet Publishing.

—My First Bilingual Book - Home. 2011. (My First Bilingual Book Ser.). (ENG., Illus.). 24p. (J). (gr. k — 1). bds. 7.99 *(978-1-84059-643-4(0));* bds. 7.99 *(978-1-84059-647-2(3))* Milet Publishing.

—My First Bilingual Book-Home (English-Russian) 2011. (My First Bilingual Book Ser.). (ENG., Illus.). 24p. (J). (gr. k — 1). bds. 7.99 *(978-1-84059-650-2(3))* Milet Publishing.

—My First Bilingual Book-Home (English-Somali) 2011. (My First Bilingual Book Ser.). (ENG., Illus.). 24p. (J). (gr. k — 1). bds. 7.99 *(978-1-84059-651-9(1))* Milet Publishing.

—My First Bilingual Book-Home (English-Vietnamese) 2011. (My First Bilingual Book Ser.). (ENG., Illus.). 24p. (J). (gr. k — 1). bds. 8.99 *(978-1-84059-655-7(4))* Milet Publishing.

Miller, Amanda. This Is the Way We Help at Home. 2009. (Scholastic News Nonfiction Readers Ser.). (ENG.). 24p. (J). (gr. 1-2). pap. 6.95 *(978-0-531-21441-1(9),* Children's Pr.); lib. bdg. 22.00 *(978-0-531-21340-7(4))* Scholastic Library Publishing.

Nunn, Daniel. ABCs at Home, 1 vol. 2012. (Everyday Alphabet Ser.). (ENG.). 32p. (gr. -1-k). pap. 9.95 *(978-1-4109-4736-9(X));* lib. bdg. 25.32 *(978-1-4109-4731-4(9))* Heinemann-Raintree.

Nunn, Daniel & Smith, Sian. Manners at Home, 1 vol. 2012. (Oh, Behave! Ser.). (ENG.). 24p. (gr. -1-1). lib. bdg. 22.65 *(978-1-4329-6636-2(7),* Acorn) Heinemann-Raintree.

Oaks, Kristen M. My Home Can Be a Holy Place. Burr, Dan, illus. 2015. (J). 18.99 *(978-1-62972-099-9(2))* Deseret Bk. Co.

Parramón, José María. Mi Calle. Borday, Irene, illus. (Coleccion Estoy En...).Tr. of My Street. (SPA.). 32p. (J). (gr. k-3). 6.36 *(978-84-342-1003-5(7))* Parramon Ediciones S.A. ESP. Dist: Lectorum Pubns., Inc.

—Mi Casa. Borday, Irene, illus. (Coleccion Estoy En...).Tr. of My House. (SPA.). 32p. (J). (gr. k-3). 6.36 *(978-84-342-1002-8(9))* Parramon Ediciones S.A. ESP. Dist: Lectorum Pubns., Inc.

—Mi Jardin. Borday, Irene, illus. (Coleccion Estoy En...).Tr. of My Garden. (SPA.). 32p. (J). (gr. k-3). 6.36 *(978-84-342-1005-9(3))* Parramon Ediciones S.A. ESP. Dist: Lectorum Pubns., Inc.

Parramón, José María & Bordoy, Irene. Mi Calle.Tr. of My Street. (SPA., Illus.). (J). (gr. -1-1). 6.95 *(978-958-04-1277-9(4))* Norma S.A. COL. Dist: Distribuidora Norma, Inc.

Rotner, Shelley & Goldblas, Amy. Home. Rotner, Shelley, photos by. 2010. (Shelley Rotner's Early Childhood Library Ser.). (ENG., Illus.). 32p. (gr. -1-2). lib. bdg. 25.26 *(978-0-7613-4605-0(8))* Lerner Publishing Group.

Star Bright Books. My First Words at Home, 1 vol. 2011. (ENG.). 20p. (J). (gr. -1). bds. 6.95 *(978-1-59572-281-2(5))* Star Bright Bks., Inc.

—My First Words at Home (Burmese Karen/English), 1 vol. 2012. (KAR & ENG., Illus.). 20p. (J). 6.95 *(978-1-59572-373-4(0))* Star Bright Bks., Inc.

—My First Words at Home (Burmese/English), 1 vol. 2012. (BUR & ENG., Illus.). 20p. (J). 6.95 *(978-1-59572-372-7(2))* Star Bright Bks., Inc.

—My First Words at HOME (Spanish/English), 1 vol. 2011. (ENG.). 32p. (J). bds. 6.95 *(978-1-59572-282-9(3))* Star Bright Bks., Inc.

Stella, Gaia. Welcome to My House: A Collection of First Words. 2017. (ENG., Illus.). 48p. (J). (gr. -1-k). 17.99 ***(978-1-4521-5792-4(8))*** Chronicle Bks. LLC.

Weitzman, Elizabeth. Let's Talk about Staying in a Shelter. 2004. (Let's Talk Library). (Illus.). 24p. (J). lib. bdg. 22.60 *(978-0-8239-6812-1(X),* PowerKids Pr.) Rosen Publishing Group, Inc., The.

Yates, Vicki. Life at Home. 2016. (Then & Now Ser.). (ENG.). 24p. pap. 6.29 *(978-1-4846-3778-4(X),* Acorn) Heinemann-Raintree.

HOME—FICTION

Allen, Nancy. Everyone Has a Home. 2015. (ENG.). 24p. (gr. k-3). 28.50 *(978-1-63430-365-1(2))* Rourke Educational Media.

Anderson, Renae. Upon the Heads of the Children. 2009. 236p. 25.75 *(978-1-60860-483-8(7),* Strategic Bk. Publishing) Strategic Book Publishing & Rights Agency (SBPRA).

Auch, M. J. Wing Nut. 2008. (ENG.). 256p. (J). (gr. 5-9). pap. 14.99 *(978-0-312-38420-3(3),* 9780312384203) Square Fish.

Baker, Jeannie. Home. Baker, Jeannie, illus. 2004. (ENG., Illus.). 32p. (J). (gr. k-5). 16.99 *(978-0-06-623935-4(4),* Greenwillow Bks.) HarperCollins Pubs.

Banks, Kate. The Cat Who Walked Across France. Hallensleben, Georg, illus. 2004. (ENG.). 40p. (J). (gr. -1-2). 18.99 *(978-0-374-39968-9(9),* 9780374399689, Farrar, Straus & Giroux (BYR)) Farrar, Straus & Giroux.

Beranek, Malinda. Rocky, the Country Squirrel. 2008. 12p. pap. 24.95 *(978-1-60563-018-2(7))* America Star Bks.

Berenstain, Jan & Berenstain, Mike. God Bless Our Home, 1 vol. 2012. (Berenstain Bears/Living Lights Ser.). (ENG., Illus.). 32p. (J). pap. 3.99 *(978-0-310-72089-8(3))* Zonderkidz.

Berenstain, Stan & Berenstain, Jan. Berenstain Bears' Home Sweet Tree. 2013. (ENG.). 32p. (J). (-3). 9.99 *(978-1-4022-9085-5(3),* Sourcebooks Jabberwocky) Sourcebooks, Inc.

Berkes, Marianne. Anybody Home?, 1 vol. Dickinson, Rebecca, illus. 2013. (ENG.). 32p. (J). (gr. -1-3). 17.95 *(978-1-60718-618-2(7),* 9781607186182); pap. 9.95 *(978-1-60718-630-4(6))* Arbordale Publishing.

Biddulph, Rob. Blown Away. Biddulph, Rob, illus. 2015. (ENG., Illus.). 40p. (J). (gr. -1-3). 17.99 *(978-0-06-236724-2(2))* HarperCollins Pubs.

Blackstone, Stella. Cleo on the Move. Mockford, Caroline, illus. 2013. (ENG.). 24p. (J). (gr. -1-k). pap. 6.99 *(978-1-78285-057-1(0))* Barefoot Bks., Inc.

Bode, N. E. The Anybodies. Ferguson, Peter, illus. 2005. (ENG.). 288p. (J). (gr. 5-8). reprint ed. pap. 6.99 *(978-0-06-055737-9(0))* HarperCollins Pubs.

Bonniol, Magali. El Ogro De Mariuchi. 2003. (SPA.). 40p. *(978-84-8470-112-5(3))* Corimbo, Editorial S.L.

Bradford, Wade. Why Do I Have to Make My Bed? van der Sterre, Johnanna, illus. 2011. (ENG.). 32p. (J). (gr. -1-2). 16.99 *(978-1-58246-327-8(1),* Tricycle Pr.) Random Hse. Children's Bks.

Brown, Margaret Wise. Home for a Bunny. Williams, Garth, illus. 2003. (Big Little Golden Book Ser.). (ENG.). 32p. (J). (gr. -1-k). reprint ed. 9.99 *(978-0-307-10546-2(6),* Golden Bks.) Random Hse. Children's Bks.

Brown, Petra. When the Wind Blew. Brown, Petra, illus. 2017. (ENG., Illus.). 32p. (J). (gr. k-3). 16.99 *(978-1-58536-969-0(1),* 204234) Sleeping Bear Pr.

Cantu, Sarah. The Dogs that Follow their Detective Dreams. Adventure No. 1: Find a New Home. 2008. 48p. pap. 20.95 *(978-0-615-18600-9(9))* Cantu, Ricardo.

Carpenter, Joyce M. An Unexpected Friend. 2010. 24p. 11.49 *(978-1-4520-0758-8(6))* AuthorHouse.

Cassidy, Anne. Innocent. 2014. (ENG.). 192p. (YA). (gr. 7). pap. 8.99 *(978-0-340-88200-9(X))* Hodder & Stoughton GBR. Dist: Hachette Bk. Group.

Centineo Durrett, Marjorie. Stick People Stories. 2009. 20p. pap. 10.49 *(978-1-4490-2856-5(X))* AuthorHouse.

Cheeseboro, Tyrese. Why Did Ronald Break the Rules? Rules at Home & Rules at School! 2010. 28p. 12.49 *(978-1-4490-8871-2(6))* AuthorHouse.

Cogan, Karen. Pancho Finds A Home. Davidson, Blanche, illus. 2007. 32p. (J). 19.95 *(978-1-929115-16-7(4))* Azro Pr., Inc.

Colbert, Catherine McNulty. Downsize Your Parents! Tips for Moving from a 2400 Sq Ft Home into an 800 Sq Ft Home. 2009. 34p. pap. 9.00 *(978-1-935125-48-8(6))* Robertson Publishing.

Cole, Henry. A Nest for Celeste: A Story about Art, Inspiration, & the Meaning of Home. Cole, Henry, illus. (Nest for Celeste Ser.: 1). (ENG., Illus.). 352p. (J). (gr. 3-7). 2012. pap. 6.99 *(978-0-06-170412-3(1))* 2010. 16.99 *(978-0-06-170410-9(5))* HarperCollins Pubs. (Tegen, Katherine Bks).

Cole, Joanna & Van Horn, William. Ca C'est Chez Moi.Tr. of This is the Place for Me. (FRE.). (J). 6.99 *(978-0-590-71919-3(X))* Scholastic, Inc.

CourseCrafters Staff, des. Interactive Storybooks - This Is My House. 2003. (J). spiral bd. 14.95 *(978-1-58605-964-4(5))* LeapFrog Enterprises, Inc.

H
I

Deacon, Alexis. A Place to Call Home. Schwarz, Viviane, illus. 2011. (ENG.). 40p. (J). (gr. -1-2). 16.99 *(978-0-7636-5360-6(8))* Candlewick Pr.
Derksen, Barbara Ann. Scruffles Finds a Home. 2007. *(978-1-59872-935-1(7))* Instant Pub.
Dowell, Frances O'Roark. Where I'd Like to Be. 2004. (Aladdin Fiction Ser.). 232p. (gr. 5-9). 17.00 *(978-0-7569-4357-8(4))* Perfection Learning Corp.
—Where I'd Like to Be. (ENG.). (J). (gr. 5-9). 2003. Illus.). 240p. 17.99 *(978-0-689-84420-1(4))* 2004. 256p. reprint ed. pap. 7.99 *(978-0-689-87067-5(1))* Simon & Schuster Children's Publishing. (Atheneum Bks. for Young Readers).
—Where I'd Like to Be. l.t. ed. 2003. 162p. (J). 22.95 *(978-0-7862-5741-6(5))* Thorndike Pr.
Duey, Kathleen. The Journey Home. Rayyan, Omar, illus. 2003. (Unicorn's Secret Ser.: 8). (ENG.). 80p. (J). (gr. 2-5). pap. 5.99 *(978-0-689-85374-6(2),* Aladdin) Simon & Schuster Children's Publishing.
Eastman, P. D. El Mejor Nido. Mlawer, Teresa, tr. from ENG. 2005.Tr. of Best Nest. (SPA., Illus.). 64p. (J). (gr. k-2). 9.99 *(978-1-930332-84-3(X),* LC33270) Lectorum Pubns., Inc.
Edwards, Julie Andrews. Mandy. Westerman, Johanna, illus. 2nd ed. 2006. (Julie Andrews Collection). (ENG.). 320p. (J). (gr. 3-7). 17.99 *(978-0-06-113162-2(8));* pap. 6.99 *(978-0-06-120707-5(1))* HarperCollins Pubs.
Ellis, Carson. Home. 2015. (ENG., Illus.). 40p. (J). (gr. -1-3). 16.99 *(978-0-7636-6529-6(0))* Candlewick Pr.
Faulkner, Keith. Who's Home? McEwan, Joseph, illus. 12p. (J). (gr. -1). pap. 4.99 *(978-1-881445-33-3(X))* Sandvik Publishing.
Florence, Leigh Anne. The Adoption. Asher, James, illus. 2003. (Woody: the Kentucky Wiener Ser.). 32p. (J). (gr. -1-3). per. 12.95 *(978-0-9741417-0-1(4))* HotDiggetyDog Pr.
Foster, Thelma Louise Elisher. A Brand New House. 2011. 24p. pap. 15.99 *(978-1-4568-4803-3(8))* Xlibris Corp.
Fraser, Lynne. Henry's New Home. Fraser, Jess, illus. 2007. (J). cd-rom 9.99 *(978-0-9795190-9-3(8))* Color & Learn.
Frost, Helen. Keesha's House. 2011. 9.46 *(978-0-7848-3534-0(9),* Everbind) Marco Bk. Co.
—Keesha's House. 2013. (ENG.). 144p. (YA). (gr. 7-12). pap. 9.99 *(978-0-312-64127-6(3),* 9780312641276) Square Fish.
Giles, S. A. A Home for All: How a Little Puppy Finds a Home. 2006. 20.00 *(978-0-8059-9076-8(3))* Dorrance Publishing Co., Inc.
Gownley, Jimmy. Amelia in Joy & Wonder, 1 vol. 2013. (Amelia Rules! Set 2 Ser.). (ENG.). 36p. (J). (gr. 3-6). 24.21 *(978-1-61479-072-3(8))* Spotlight.
Green, Margaret. Ty Finds a New Home. 2017. (Dinotrux 8X8 Ser.). (J). lib. bdg. 14.75 *(978-0-606-39190-0(8))* Turtleback Bks.
Grubman, Bonnie. Oy Vey! Life in a Shoe. Mottram, Dave, illus. 2016. (J). *(978-1-68115-515-9(X))* Behrman Hse., Inc.
Halfmann, Janet. Hermit Crab's Home: Safe in a Shell. Dacey, Bob, illus. 2007. (ENG.). 32p. (J). pap. 6.95 *(978-1-59249-733-1(0))* Soundprints.
—Hermit Crab's Home: Safe in a Shell. Dacey, Bob & Bandelin, Debra, illus. 2007. (Smithsonian Oceanic Collection). (ENG.). 32p. (J). (gr. -1-3). 16.95 *(978-1-59249-732-4(2))* Soundprints.
Harris, Teresa E. The Perfect Place. 2014. (ENG.). 272p. (J). (gr. 5-7). 17.99 *(978-0-547-25519-4(5))* Houghton Mifflin Harcourt Publishing Co.
Hensley, Terri Anne. Henry's new Home. 2007. (J). per. 6.95 *(978-0-9789057-1-2(7))* Huntington Ludlow Media Group.
Holczer, Tracy. The Secret Hum of a Daisy. 2014. (ENG.). 320p. (J). (gr. 5). 16.99 *(978-0-399-16393-7(X),* G.P. Putnam's Sons Books for Young Readers) Penguin Young Readers Group.
Howard, Jennifer. Lucy & the Land of Lost Socks. 2009. 56p. pap. 10.49 *(978-1-4389-5362-5(3))* AuthorHouse.
I Am A Dog. 2008. (Illus.). 26p. 24.95 *(978-0-9801054-0-7(4))* Teahouse of Danger.
Jackson, Tyrone. Save Our Home. 2006. (ENG.). 88p. per. 16.95 *(978-1-4241-0875-6(6))* PublishAmerica, Inc.
Jewl, Terry. The Pixies in Home Sweet Home. 2012. 24p. pap. 24.95 *(978-1-4626-5585-4(8))* America Star Bks.
Jokisch, Kimberly. I Have Two Homes. 2009. 24p. pap. 11.99 *(978-1-4389-2823-4(8))* AuthorHouse.
Kittinger, Jo S. The House on Dirty-Third Street, 1 vol. González, Thomas, illus. 2012. (ENG.). 32p. (J). 16.95 *(978-1-56145-619-2(5))* Peachtree Pubs.
Kline, Trish & Donev, Mary. Coming Home: KA Reader 8. 2007. (Illus.). 32p. (J). per. 20.00 *(978-1-934307-01-4(7))* Ghost Hunter Productions.
Lasky, Kathryn. Felix Takes the Stage. Gilpin, Stephen, illus. (Deadlies Ser.). (ENG.). 144p. (J). (gr. 2-5). 2011. pap. 5.99 *(978-0-545-11730-2(5),* Scholastic Paperbacks) 2010. 15.99 *(978-0-545-11681-7(3),* Scholastic Pr.) Scholastic, Inc.
Lewis, J. Patrick & Zappitello, Beth. First Dog. Bowers, Tim, illus. 2009. (ENG.). 32p. (J). (gr. k-6). 15.95 *(978-1-58536-467-1(3))* Sleeping Bear Pr.
Lindquist, Jennie D. Little Silver House. Williams, Garth, illus. 2008. (J). (gr. 2-6). 21.00 *(978-0-8446-6190-2(2))* Smith, Peter Pub., Inc.
Lloyd-Jones, Sally & Dyer, Jane. The House That's Your Home. 2015. (ENG., Illus.). 40p. (J). (gr. -1-2). 17.99 *(978-0-375-85884-0(9),* Schwartz & Wade Bks.) Random Hse. Children's Bks.
Long, Julie Anne. A Notorious Countess Confesses: Pennyroyal Green Series. 2012. (Pennyroyal Green Ser.: 7). (ENG.). 384p. mass mkt. 5.99 *(978-0-06-211802-8(1),* Avon Bks.) HarperCollins Pubs.
Lorimer, Janet. No Place Like Home, 1 vol. unabr. ed. 2010. (Q Reads Ser.). (ENG.). 32p. (YA). (gr. 9-12). pap. 6.95 *(978-1-61651-203-3(2))* Saddleback Educational Publishing, Inc.
Love, Mary. Mama's House. 2005. 44p. per. 23.99 *(978-1-4257-0254-0(6))* Xlibris Corp.
Luna, James, et al. The Place Where You Live / el Lugar Donde Vives. Muraida, Thelma, illus. 2015. (SPA & ENG.). 32p. (J). (gr. k-3). 17.95 *(978-1-55885-813-8(X))* Arte Publico Pr.
MacKay, Lisa. Nick Finds a Home. 2009. 32p. pap. 12.99 *(978-1-4490-3245-6(1))* AuthorHouse.
MacKinnon, Art. Chloe's Great Blue Adventure. 2011. 36p. pap. 16.86 *(978-1-4634-1704-8(7))* AuthorHouse.
Maris, Ron. Pwy Sy 'na? 2005. (WEL., Illus.). 17p. *(978-0-900439-79-7(3))* Gwasg Carreg Gwalch.
Martin, Ann M. Needle & Thread. Andreasen, Dan, illus. 2007. 205p. (J). pap. *(978-0-545-03660-3(7))* Scholastic, Inc.
Mazur, Cathy. Stanley Seagull. Gedrich, Colleen, illus. 2011. 32p. (J). 16.95 *(978-0-9837418-1-7(6));* pap. 7.95 *(978-0-9837418-0-0(8))* Tribute Bks.
McHugh, Rosetta. Poodiky Oglethorpe. 2009. 20p. pap. 24.95 *(978-1-60749-086-9(2))* America Star Bks.
McInnes, Nicole. Brianna on the Brink. 2013. (ENG.). 176p. (YA). (gr. 10). 16.95 *(978-0-8234-2741-3(2))* Holiday Hse., Inc.
McPhail, David. The Searcher & Old Tree. McPhail, David, illus. 2011. (ENG., Illus.). 32p. (J). (gr. -1-2). pap. 7.95 *(978-1-58089-224-7(8))* Charlesbridge Publishing, Inc.
Michalak, Jamie. The Coziest Place. Davis, Jon, illus. 2013. (ENG.). 32p. (J). (gr. -1-k). 14.99 *(978-1-58925-121-2(0))* Tiger Tales.
Michels, Dia L. Look What I See! Where Can I Be? At Home. Bowles, Michael J. N., photos by. 2005. (ENG., Illus.). 32p. (J). (gr. -1-12). 9.95 *(978-1-930775-06-0(7))* Platypus Media, L.L.C.
Navarro, Cece P. My Cherry Tree House. 2008. 16p. pap. 24.95 *(978-1-60474-415-6(4))* America Star Bks.
Neilson, Ginger. Gunter the Underwater Elephant. Neilson, Ginger, illus. 2011. (Illus.). 32p. pap. 15.99 *(978-0-9832740-2-5(9))* 4RV Publishing, LLC.
Novak, Ali. My Life with the Walter Boys. 2014. (ENG.). 368p. (YA). (gr. 7-12). pap. 10.99 *(978-1-4022-9786-1(6),* 9781402297861) Sourcebooks, Inc.
O'Reilly, Jane. The Notations of Cooper Cameron. 2017. (ENG.). 320p. (J). (gr. 3-5). 17.99 ***(978-1-5124-0415-9(2),*** Carolrhoda Bks.) Lerner Publishing Group.
O'Ryan, Ray. Return to Earth! Kraft, Jason, illus. 2015. (Galaxy Zack Ser.: 10). (ENG.). 128p. (J). (gr. k-4). pap. 5.99 *(978-1-4814-2181-2(6),* Little Simon) Little Simon.
Pierre, Eileen. It's Not Easy Being Mean. 2010. 56p. pap. 10.00 *(978-1-60860-929-1(4),* Eloquent Bks.) Strategic Book Publishing & Rights Agency (SBPRA).
Pinkwater, Daniel M. Beautiful Yetta: The Yiddish Chicken. Pinkwater, Jill, illus. 2010. (ENG.). 32p. (J). (gr. -1-2). 17.99 *(978-0-312-55824-6(4),* 9780312558246) Feiwel & Friends.
Pollak, Dale. Velocity: From the Front Line to the Bottom Line. 2010. (ENG.). 144p. 29.95 *(978-0-9760095-7-3(9))* New Year Publishing.
Prater, Cindy. Kelsie's Potty Adventure. Williams, Denny, illus. 2006. 40p. per. 19.95 *(978-1-59858-271-0(2))* Dog Ear Publishing, LLC.
Reasoner, Charles. The 3 Blind Mice Inside the Spooky Scary & Creepy Haunted House. Reasoner, Charles, illus. 2007. (Story Book Ser.). (Illus.). 10p. (J). (gr. -1-3). bds. *(978-1-84666-381-9(4),* Tide Mill Pr.) Top That! Publishing PLC.
Reilly, Carmel & Stewart, Christen. More Like Home. 2008. (Rigby Focus Forward: Level P Ser.). (Illus.). 24p. (J). (gr. 4-7). pap. *(978-1-4190-3854-9(0),* Rigby) Pearson Education Australia.
Rey, H. A. Builds a Home. 2011. (Curious George Ser.). (ENG., Illus.). 24p. (J). (gr. -1-3). 6.99 *(978-0-547-59410-1(0))* Houghton Mifflin Harcourt Publishing Co.
Riad, Hala. Twinkie Has a New Home. 2011. 24p. pap. 14.93 *(978-1-4269-7120-4(6))* Trafford Publishing.
Riphagen, Loes, illus. Animals Home Alone. 2011. (ENG.). 32p. (J). (gr. -1-3). 15.95 *(978-1-934734-55-1(1))* Seven Footer Pr.
Ross, Tony. I Want to Go Home! Ross, Tony, illus. 2014. (Illus.). 32p. (J). (gr. -1-3). 16.95 *(978-1-4677-5095-0(6))* Lerner Publishing Group.
Rouncville, Bibi. Sea Bugs & Moose Eggs. 2009. 52p. pap. 9.50 *(978-1-4357-4004-4(1))* Lulu Pr., Inc.
Rowen, Amy & Rowen, Tyla Marie. Waggin' Tales. 2003. 182p. (YA). 23.95 *(978-0-595-66087-2(8));* pap. 13.95 *(978-0-595-29955-3(5))* iUniverse, Inc.
Sally, Zak. Sammy the Mouse #2 (Ignatz) 2008. (ENG.). 32p. pap. 7.95 *(978-1-56097-999-9(2))* Fantagraphics Bks.
Sanchez, Juanita L. Pancho the Green Parrot Lays an Egg, 1 vol. Ramirez, Samuel, illus. 2009. 24p. pap. 24.95 *(978-1-61546-150-9(7))* America Star Bks.
Sand-Eveland, Cyndi. A Tinfoil Sky. 2012. (ENG., Illus.). 218p. (YA). (gr. 5-9). 17.95 *(978-1-77049-277-6(1),* Tundra Bks.) Tundra Bks. CAN. Dist: Penguin Random Hse. LLC.
Shreeve, Elizabeth. Hector Springs Loose. Levy, Pamela R., illus. 2004. (Ready-For-Chapters Ser.). (ENG.). 80p. (J). (gr. 1-4). pap. 3.99 *(978-0-689-86414-8(0),* Simon & Schuster/Paula Wiseman Bks.) Simon & Schuster/Paula Wiseman Bks.
Sisco, K. B. Jackpot's Tail. 2008. (ENG.). 32p. pap. 15.99 *(978-1-4196-4475-7(0))* CreateSpace Independent Publishing Platform.
Skinner, Tina. Christopher Wren Avian Architect, 1 vol. LouLou, illus. 2008. (ENG.). 32p. (J). 15.99 *(978-0-7643-3169-5(8),* 9780764331695) Schiffer Publishing, Ltd.
Smith, Linda. The Inside Tree. Brown, Kathryn, illus. Date not set. 32p. (J). (gr. -1-3). 5.99 *(978-0-06-443542-0(3))* HarperCollins Pubs.
Snyder, Lavinia Branca. Going Home: The Little Stories of Manoosh & Baloosh. 2003. (Illus.). 24p. (J). mass mkt. *(978-1-932233-01-8(6))* Aurora Libris Corp.
Squires, R. L. Peaches & Cream, 1 vol. Collier, Kevin Scott, illus. 2009. 31p. pap. 24.95 *(978-1-60749-164-4(8))* America Star Bks.
Stamm, Peter & Bauer, Jutta. When We Lived in Uncle's Hat. Schumman, Nani & Connolly, Kate, trs. from GER. 2006. (ENG., Illus.). 39p. (J). (gr. k-2). pap. 16.95 *(978-1-905341-04-7(0))* WingedChariot Pr. GBR. Dist: Independent Pubs. Group.
Stead, Philip C. A Home for Bird. Stead, Philip C., illus. 2012. (ENG., Illus.). 32p. (J). (gr. -1-3). 17.99 *(978-1-59643-711-1(1),* 9781596437111) Roaring Brook Pr.
Sullivan, Kevin & Morgan, Elizabeth. Anne's New Home. 2010. (Anne of Green Gables Picture Bks.). (ENG.). 32p. (J). (gr. k-2). pap. 4.95 *(978-0-9736803-7-9(7))* Davenport Pr. CAN. Dist: Independent Pubs. Group.
Swarbrick, David E. Peggy's Play House. 2011. 24p. pap. 24.95 *(978-1-4626-1989-4(4))* America Star Bks.
Thomas, Linda. The Cats of Dogwood Lane: Daisy Finds a Home. 2009. 28p. pap. 15.00 *(978-1-4389-3831-8(4))* AuthorHouse.
Thomas, Lori. The Daisy Family. 2008. 16p. pap. 24.95 *(978-1-60610-274-9(5))* America Star Bks.
Townsend, Peter. Shelly & Muffin's Big Lesson Learned. 2008. 11p. pap. 24.95 *(978-1-60672-379-1(0))* America Star Bks.
Tubb, Kristin O'Donnell. Selling Hope. 2010. (ENG.). 224p. (YA). (gr. 5-9). 29.99 *(978-0-312-61122-4(6),* 9780312611224) Feiwel & Friends.
U. S. National Geographic Society Staff. Anybody Home? 2008. (Mama Mirabelle Ser.). (ENG., Illus.). 24p. (J). (gr. -1-2). pap. 3.99 *(978-1-4263-0303-6(3));* lib. bdg. 11.90 *(978-1-4263-0304-3(1))* National Geographic Society. (National Geographic Children's Bks.).
Vezeau, Sheila. Sky, the Blue Bunny. Ostrowski, Justin, illus. 2012. 16p. pap. 24.95 *(978-1-4626-7533-3(6))* America Star Bks.
Villines, Carol. Clean Your Room. Villines, Leo, illus. 2008. 20p. pap. 24.95 *(978-1-60441-166-9(X))* America Star Bks.
Walker, Mary. The Flower Tree. 2010. (Illus.). 50p. pap. 12.95 *(978-1-4327-3588-3(8))* Outskirts Pr., Inc.
Williams, Vera B. Home at Last. Raschka, Chris, illus. 2016. 40p. (J). (gr. -1-3). 17.99 *(978-0-06-134973-7(9),* Greenwillow Bks.) HarperCollins Pubs.
Willis-Gould, Glennis. Dad's New Shed. 2013. 44p. pap. 20.45 *(978-1-4525-1027-9(X),* Balboa Pr.) Author Solutions, Inc.
Wolbrueck, Cherri. Amy Finds a Home. 2008. 36p. pap. 21.99 *(978-1-4363-7237-4(2))* Xlibris Corp.
Wong, Janet S. Homegrown House. Lewis, E. B., illus. 2009. (ENG.). 40p. (J). (gr. -1-3). 16.99 *(978-0-689-84718-9(1),* McElderry, Margaret K. Bks.) McElderry, Margaret K. Bks.
Younger, Mary. You're Not A Ladybird You've Got No Spots. 2011. (Illus.). 24p. 14.09 *(978-1-4567-7082-2(9))* AuthorHouse.
Yum, Hyewon. This Is Our House. Yum, Hyewon, illus. 2013. (ENG., Illus.). 36p. (J). (gr. -1-2). 16.99 *(978-0-374-37487-7(2),* 9780374374877, Farrar, Straus & Giroux (BYR)) Farrar, Straus & Giroux.

HOME AND SCHOOL

How to Convince Your Parents You Can..., 20 vols., Set. Incl. Care for a Kitten. Bearce, Stephanie. (J). 2009. 25.70 *(978-1-58415-803-5(4));* Care for a Pet Bunny. Harkins, Susan Sales & Harkins, William H. (Illus.). (J). 2008. lib. bdg. 25.70 *(978-1-58415-659-8(7));* Care for a Pet Chameleon. Whiting, Jim. (Illus.). (YA). 2007. lib. bdg. 25.70 *(978-1-58415-605-5(8));* Care for a Pet Chimpanzee. Leavitt, Amie Jane. (Illus.). (J). 2007. lib. bdg. 25.70 *(978-1-58415-607-9(4));* Care for a Pet Chinchilla. Leavitt, Amie Jane. (Illus.). (J). 2009. lib. bdg. 25.70 *(978-1-58415-799-1(2));* Care for a Pet Ferret. Orr, Tamra. (Illus.). (YA). 2008. lib. bdg. 25.70 *(978-1-58415-660-4(0));* Care for a Pet Guinea Pig. Bearce, Stephanie. (J). 2009. 25.70 *(978-1-58415-797-7(6));* Care for a Pet Hamster. Smalley, Carol Parenzan. (J). 2009. 25.70 *(978-1-58415-804-2(2));* Care for a Pet Hedgehog. Gagne, Tammy. (J). 2009. 25.70 *(978-1-58415-798-4(4));* Care for a Pet Horse. O'Neal, Claire. (Illus.). (YA). 2008. lib. bdg. 25.70 *(978-1-58415-662-8(7));* Care for a Pet Mouse. Leavitt, Amie Jane. (Illus.). (J). 2007. lib. bdg. 25.70 *(978-1-58415-606-2(6));* Care for a Pet Parrot. LaRoche, Amelia. (Illus.). (J). 2009. lib. bdg. 25.70 *(978-1-58415-795-3(X));* Care for a Pet Snake. Whiting, Jim. (Illus.). (YA). 2007. lib. bdg. 25.70 *(978-1-58415-604-8(X));* Care for a Pet Sugar Glider. Leavitt, Amie Jane. (Illus.). (J). 2009. lib. bdg. 25.70 *(978-1-58415-800-4(X));* Care for a Pet Tarantula. Leavitt, Amie Jane. (Illus.). (J). 2007. lib. bdg. 25.70 *(978-1-58415-603-1(1));* Care for a Potbellied Pig. Orr, Tamra. (Illus.). (YA). 2008. lib. bdg. 25.70 *(978-1-58415-661-1(9));* Care for a Puppy. Adams, Michelle Medlock. (J). 2009. 25.70 *(978-1-58415-802-8(6));* Care for a Racing Pigeon. Gagne, Tammy. (J). 2009. 25.70 *(978-1-58415-801-1(8));* Care for a Wild Chincoteague Pony. Boone, Mary. (Illus.). (YA). 2008. lib. bdg. 25.70 *(978-1-58415-663-5(5));* Care for a Wolfdog. Gagne, Tammy. (J). 2009. 25.70 *(978-1-58415-796-0(8));* 32p. (gr. 1-4). 2010. Set lib. bdg. 514.00 *(978-1-58415-805-9(0))* Mitchell Lane Pubs., Inc.
Marsh, Carole. Heroes & Helpers Resource Book for Teachers & Parents. 2004. 48p. (gr. 2-8). pap. 12.95 *(978-0-635-01101-5(8))* Gallopade International.

HOME DECORATION

see Interior Decoration

HOME ECONOMICS

see also Consumer Education; Cooking; Dairying; Entertaining; Food; Fuel; Furniture; Heating; House Cleaning; Interior Decoration; Sewing; Shopping

Antill, Sara. 10 Ways I Can Help My Family. 2012. (I Can Make a Difference Ser.). (ENG.). 24p. (J). (gr. 2-5). pap. 8.25 *(978-1-4488-6367-9(8));* lib. bdg. 22.60 *(978-1-4488-6204-7(3))* Rosen Publishing Group, Inc., The. (PowerKids Pr.).
Beco, Alice. Cool Careers Without College for People Who Love Houses. 2006. (Cool Careers Without College Ser.). (Illus.). 144p. (YA). (gr. 7-12). lib. bdg. 35.95 *(978-1-4042-0753-0(8))* Rosen Publishing Group, Inc., The.
—Cool Careers Without College for People who Love Houses. 2009. (Cool Careers Without College Ser.). 144p. (gr. 6-6). 66.50 *(978-1-61511-967-7(1))* Rosen Publishing Group, Inc., The.
Behnke, Alison. Can Rats Swim from Sewers into Toilets? And Other Questions about Your Home. 2010. (Is That a Fact? Ser.). (ENG.). 40p. (gr. 4-6). lib. bdg. 26.60 *(978-0-7613-4914-3(6))* Lerner Publishing Group.
Boothroyd, Jennifer. From Washboards to Washing Machines: How Homes Have Changed. 2011. (Comparing Past & Present Ser.). pap. 7.95 *(978-0-7613-7839-6(1));* pap. 45.32 *(978-0-7613-8394-9(8));* (ENG., Illus.). 32p. lib. bdg. 26.60 *(978-0-7613-6747-5(0))* Lerner Publishing Group.
Bozzo, Linda & Library. Houses of the Past, Present, & Future. 2010. (Imagining the Future Ser.). (Illus.). 24p. (J). lib. bdg. 22.60 *(978-0-7660-3433-4(X),* Enslow Elementary) Enslow Pubs., Inc.
Chastain, Zachary. Home Sweet Home: Around the House in the 1800s. 2009. (Daily Life in America in the 1800s Ser.). 64p. (YA). (gr. 7-18). pap. 9.95 *(978-1-4222-1854-9(6));* lib. bdg. 22.95 *(978-1-4222-1781-8(7))* Mason Crest.
Fortuna, Lois. Let's Clean Up! 2016. (We Can Do It! Ser.). (ENG.). 24p. (J). (gr. k-k). pap. 8.15 *(978-1-4824-3813-0(5))* Stevens, Gareth Publishing LLLP.
Foundations for Living, Set. 2004. 47.95 *(978-0-7403-0371-5(6),* Lifepac) Alpha Omega Pubns., Inc.
Gaarder-Juntti, Oona. Shapes at Home, 1 vol. 2013. (Shapes Everywhere Ser.). (ENG.). 24p. (gr. k-4). lib. bdg. 25.65 *(978-1-61783-411-0(4),* Super SandCastle) ABDO Publishing Co.
Home Economics, 11 vols., Set. 2004. (Illus.). (YA). (gr. 9-12). tchr. ed., stu. ed. 51.95 *(978-0-7403-0162-9(4),* ES9815, Lifepac) Alpha Omega Pubns., Inc.
Kalman, Bobbie. What Are My Jobs? 2010. (My World Ser.). (ENG., Illus.). 16p. (J). (gr. k-2). *(978-0-7787-9434-9(2));* pap. *(978-0-7787-9478-3(4))* Crabtree Publishing Co.
Kowalski, Kathiann M. Be Smart about Shopping: The Critical Consumer & Civic Financial Responsibility. 2014. (Be Smart about Money & Financial Literacy Ser.). 48p. (J). lib. bdg. 22.60 *(978-0-7660-4283-4(9))* Enslow Pubs., Inc.
Mills, Nathan & Ridolfi, Isabella. Sue Goes to the Store. 2012. (Rosen Readers Ser.). (ENG., Illus.). 16p. (J). (gr. k-1). pap. 7.00 *(978-1-4488-8737-8(2),* Rosen Classroom) Rosen Publishing Group, Inc., The.
Our Homes. 2007. (J). *(978-1-933834-15-3(3))* Brown Bear Books.
Richards, Jon. In the Home. 2005. (How Things Have Changed Ser.). (Illus.). 32p. (J). (gr. 3-7). lib. bdg. 27.10 *(978-1-59389-198-5(9))* Chrysalis Education.
Rissman, Rebecca. Counting at Home, 1 vol. 2012. (I Can Count! Ser.). (ENG.). 24p. (gr. -1-k). pap. 9.95 *(978-1-4329-6699-7(5));* lib. bdg. 25.32 *(978-1-4329-6694-2(4))* Heinemann-Raintree.
Robinson, Sharon, et al. Home Economics. 2007. (Illus.). 96p. pap. 29.50 *(978-0-340-92711-3(9),* Hodder Education) Hodder Education Group GBR. Dist: Trans-Atlantic Pubns., Inc.
Scholastic Choices, 4 vols., Set. Incl. I Did It Without Thinking: True Stories about Impulsive Decisions That Changed Lives. Hugel, Bob. (gr. 3-7). 27.00 *(978-0-531-13868-7(2));* Sisters & Brothers: The Ultimate Guide to Understanding Your Siblings & Yourself. Winchester, Elizabeth Siris & Siris-Winchester, Elizabeth. (gr. 7-12). 27.00 *(978-0-531-13870-0(4));* Skin You're In: Staying Healthy Inside & Out. Webber, Diane. (gr. 3-7). 27.00 *(978-0-531-13869-4(0));* Totally Tolerant: Spotting & Stopping Prejudice. Webber, Diane & Mandel, Laurie. (gr. 7-12). 27.00 *(978-0-531-13867-0(4));* (Illus.). 112p. (J)., Children's Pr. 2008. Set lib. bdg. 108.00 o.p. *(978-0-531-20440-5(5),* Watts, Franklin) Scholastic Library Publishing.
Solis, Lisa V. Classroom Cupboard: Lessons, Activities & Culinary Concoctions for Kids, 1 vol. 2003. (Illus.). 160p. (C). pap. 28.00 *(978-1-56308-957-2(2),* LU9572, Libraries Unlimited) ABC-CLIO, LLC.
The Book Company, ed. Home. (Sparkle Bks.). (ENG.). 10p. (J). bds. 4.99 *(978-1-74047-330-9(2))* Book Co. Publishing Pty, Ltd., The AUS. Dist: Penton Overseas, Inc.
Ticktock Media, Ltd. Staff. Little Helper. 2009. (Busy Tots Ser.). (ENG.). 10p. (J). (gr. -1-k). bds. 6.95 *(978-1-84696-798-6(8),* TickTock Books) Octopus Publishing Group GBR. Dist: Independent Pubs. Group.

HOME ECONOMICS—ACCOUNTING

see also Finance, Personal

McCune, Susan. Our Family Budget, 01 vols., 1. 2016. (Rosen REAL Readers: Social Studies Nonfiction / Fiction: Family, Community, & the World Ser.). (ENG.). 12p. (J). pap. 6.33 *(978-1-5081-1737-7(3),* Rosen Classroom) Rosen Publishing Group, Inc., The.
Orman, Suze. The Adventures of Billy & Penny. Travis, Kathy, illus. 2017. (ENG.). 40p. 14.99 *(978-1-4019-5304-1(2))* Hay Hse., Inc.

HOME ECONOMICS—VOCATIONAL GUIDANCE

Beco, Alice. Cool Careers Without College for People Who Love Houses & Apartments. 2017. (Cool Careers Without College Ser.). 112p. (gr. 12-12). 38.45 ***(978-1-5081-7538-4(1),*** Rosen Young Adult) Rosen Publishing Group, Inc., The.
Greenberger, Robert. Cool Careers Without College for People Who Love to Organize, Manage, & Plan. (Cool Careers Without College Ser.). 144p. 2009. (gr. 6-6). 66.50 *(978-1-61511-978-3(7))* 2006. (Illus.). (YA). (gr. 7-12). lib. bdg. 35.95 *(978-1-4042-0752-3(X))* Rosen Publishing Group, Inc., The.

HOME EDUCATION

see Self-Culture

HOME MISSIONS

see Missions

HOME REPAIRING

see Houses—Repairing

HOME STUDY COURSES

see Self-Culture

HOMELESS PERSONS

see also Homelessness

Bringle, Jennifer. Homelessness in America Today. 2010. (In the News Ser.). (ENG.). 64p. (YA). pap. 12.95 *(978-1-4488-1683-5(1));* (gr. 7-12). lib. bdg. 31.95 *(978-1-4358-9451-8(0))* Rosen Publishing Group, Inc., The.
Fields, Julianna. Kids Growing up Without a Home. 2010. (Changing Face of Modern Families Ser.). (Illus.). 64p. (YA). (gr. 5-18). lib. bdg. 22.95 *(978-1-4222-1498-5(2))* Mason Crest.
Huff, Tim, illus. The Cardboard Shack Beneath the Bridge. 2007. 31p. *(978-1-897186-09-1(6))* Castle Quay Bks. Canada.
Latchana Kenney, Karen. The Hidden Story of Homelessness, 1 vol., 1. 2014. (Undercover Story Ser.). (ENG.). 48p. (J). (gr. 5-8). 30.25 *(978-1-4777-2797-3(3),* Rosen Reference) Rosen Publishing Group, Inc., The.
Lüsted, Marcia Amidon. Coping with Homelessness. 2017. (J). ***(978-1-5081-7691-6(4))*** Rosen Publishing Group, Inc., The.
Lynette, Rachel. What to Do When Your Family Loses Its Home. 2010. (Let's Work It Out Ser.). 24p. (J). (ENG.). pap. 8.25 *(978-1-4358-9766-3(8),* PowerKids Pr.); (Illus.). (gr. 2-5).

lib. bdg. 22.60 *(978-1-4358-9339-9(5))* Rosen Publishing Group, Inc., The.
Weitzman, Elizabeth. Let's Talk about Staying in a Shelter. 2009. (Let's Talk Library). 24p. (gr. 2-3). 42.50 *(978-1-60853-452-4(9),* PowerKids Pr.) Rosen Publishing Group, Inc., The.

HOMELESS PERSONS—FICTION

Acioli, Socorro. The Head of the Saint. Hahn, Daniel, tr. from POR. Snell, Alexis, illus. 2016. (ENG.). 192p. (YA). (gr. 7). 16.99 *(978-0-553-53792-5(X),* Delacorte Pr.) Random Hse. Children's Bks.
Alger, Horatio. The Young Outlaw: Or, Adrift in the Streets. 2004. (Illus.). 15.90 *(978-1-4145-0294-6(X))* Pavilion Pr., Inc.
Anderson, Natalie C. City of Saints & Thieves. 2017. (ENG.). 432p. (YA). (gr. 7). 18.99 *(978-0-399-54758-4(4),* G.P. Putnam's Sons Books for Young Readers) Penguin Young Readers Group.
Applegate, Katherine. Crenshaw. 2015. (ENG.). 256p. (J). (gr. 5-9). 16.99 *(978-1-250-04323-8(9),* 9781250043238) Feiwel & Friends.
—Crenshaw. 2017. (ENG.). 272p. (J). pap. 7.99 ***(978-1-250-09166-6(7),*** 9781250091666) Square Fish.
—Crenshaw. 2017. (J). lib. bdg. 18.40 ***(978-0-606-40539-3(9))*** Turtleback Bks.
—Crenshaw. 2016. (SPA.). 192p. (J). (gr. 5-8). pap. 13.99 *(978-987-747-067-3(5))* V&R Editoras.
Avi. City of Orphans. Ruth, Greg, illus. (ENG.). 368p. (J). (gr. 5-9). 2012. pap. 8.99 *(978-1-4169-7108-5(4),* Atheneum Bks. for Young Readers) 2011. 17.99 *(978-1-4169-7102-3(5),* Atheneum/Richard Jackson Bks.) Simon & Schuster Children's Publishing.
Balliett, Blue. Hold Fast. 2015. (ENG.). 288p. (J). (gr. 3-7). pap. 6.99 *(978-0-545-29989-3(6),* Scholastic Paperbacks) Scholastic, Inc.
Barclift, Betty. Gypsy Summer: A Novel. 2003. 160p. (J). pap. 7.99 *(978-0-8254-2038-2(5))* Kregel Pubns.
Barrett, Mary Brigid. Shoebox Sam, 1 vol. Morrison, Frank, illus. 2011. (ENG.). 32p. (J). 15.99 *(978-0-310-71549-8(0))* Zonderkidz.
Bauer, Joan. Almost Home. (ENG.). (J). (gr. 5). 2013. 288p. pap. 7.99 *(978-0-14-242748-4(9),* Puffin Books) 2012. 272p. 16.99 *(978-0-670-01289-3(0),* Viking Books for Young Readers) Penguin Young Readers Group.
Berenstain, Jan & Berenstain, Mike. Help the Homeless, 1 vol. 2012. (I Can Read! / Berenstain Bears / Good Deed Scouts / Living Lights Ser.). (ENG., Illus.). 32p. (J). pap. 3.99 *(978-0-310-72102-4(4))* Zonderkidz.
Bliss, Bryan. No Parking at the End Times. 2015. (ENG.). 272p. (YA). (gr. 9). 17.99 *(978-0-06-227541-7(0),* Greenwillow Bks.) HarperCollins Pubs.
Booth, Coe. Tyrell. 2011. 9.04 *(978-0-7848-3385-8(0),* Everbind) Marco Bk. Co.
Bowler, Tim. Playing Dead. 2010. (Blade Ser.: 1). (ENG.). 256p. (YA). (gr. 9-18). 7.99 *(978-0-14-241600-6(2),* Speak) Penguin Young Readers Group.
Bowsher, Melodie. My Lost & Found Life. 2006. (ENG.). 320p. (YA). (gr. 9-13). 16.95 *(978-1-58234-736-3(0),* 9781582347363, Bloomsbury USA Childrens) Bloomsbury Publishing USA.
Brenner, Summer. Ivy, Homeless in San Francisco. Bowes, Brian, illus. 2nd ed. 2011. (ENG.). 176p. (J). (gr. 4-7). pap. 15.00 *(978-1-60486-317-8(X))* PM Pr.
Bukiet, Melvin Jules. Undertown. 2013. (ENG.). 304p. (J). (gr. 3-7). 17.95 *(978-1-4197-0589-2(X),* Amulet Bks.) Abrams, Inc.
Carey, Janet Lee. The Double Life of Zoe Flynn. 2007. (ENG.). 240p. (J). (gr. 3-7). pap. 12.95 *(978-1-4169-6754-5(0),* Simon & Schuster/Paula Wiseman Bks.) Simon & Schuster/Paula Wiseman Bks.
Cassidy, Sara. Skylark, 1 vol. 2014. (Orca Soundings Ser.). (ENG.). 136p. (YA). (gr. 8-12). pap. 9.95 *(978-1-4598-0590-3(9))* Orca Bk. Pubs. USA.
Chitty, Joan E. Charlie Macaffee: Search for the Genie's Body. 2005. 267p. pap. 27.95 *(978-1-4241-0007-1(0))* PublishAmerica, Inc.
Choyce, Lesley. Crash, 1 vol. 2013. (Orca Soundings Ser.). (ENG.). 136p. (YA). (gr. 8-12). pap. 9.95 *(978-1-4598-0522-4(4));* lib. bdg. 16.95 *(978-1-4598-0525-5(9))* Orca Bk. Pubs. USA.
Clements, Andrew. Room One: A Mystery or Two. Elliott, Mark, illus. 2008. (ENG.). 192p. (J). (gr. 3-7). pap. 7.99 *(978-0-689-86687-6(9),* Atheneum Bks. for Young Readers) Simon & Schuster Children's Publishing.
—Room One: A Mystery or Two. Blair, Chris & Elliott, Mark, illus. 2006. (ENG.). 176p. (J). (gr. 3-7). 17.99 *(978-0-689-86686-9(0),* Atheneum Bks. for Young Readers) Simon & Schuster Children's Publishing.
Cuff, Ed. D. City of Thieves. 2013. 114p. pap. 7.99 *(978-1-61798-076-3(5))* Wild Child Publishing.
Cupala, Holly. Don't Breathe a Word. 2012. (ENG.). 320p. (YA). (gr. 9). pap. 8.99 *(978-0-06-176669-5(0),* HarperTeen) HarperCollins Pubs.
De Palma, Toni. Under the Banyan Tree. 2007. (ENG.). 192p. (YA). (gr. 7-18). 16.95 *(978-0-8234-1965-4(7))* Holiday Hse., Inc.
de Vigan, Delphine. No & Me. Miller, George, tr. from FRE. 2010. (ENG.). 256p. (YA). (gr. 7-12). 16.99 *(978-1-59990-479-5(9),* 9781599904795, Bloomsbury USA Childrens) Bloomsbury Publishing USA.
DiCamillo, Kate. Great Joy. Ibatoulline, Bagram, illus. 2010. (ENG.). 32p. (J). (gr. -1-3). 8.99 *(978-0-7636-4996-8(1))* Candlewick Pr.
Duey, Kathleen. Castle Avamir. Rayyan, Omar, illus. 2004. (Unicorn's Secret Ser.). 73p. (gr. 2-5). 15.00 *(978-0-7569-3357-9(9))* Perfection Learning Corp.
Ellis, Deborah. No Ordinary Day, 1 vol. (ENG.). (J). (gr. 3-7). 2014. 160p. pap. 9.95 *(978-1-55498-108-3(5))* 2011. 144p. 16.95 *(978-1-55498-134-2(4))* Groundwood Bks. CAN. Dist: Publishers Group West (PGW).
—No Ordinary Day. 2013. 164p. pap. *(978-1-4596-6451-7(5))* ReadHowYouWant.com, Ltd.
Fitzpatrick, Deb. At My Door. 2016. (ENG.). 128p. (J). (gr. 2-4). 9.95 *(978-1-925162-70-7(2))* Fremantle Pr. AUS. Dist: Independent Pubs. Group.
Fogelin, Adrian. Anna Casey's Place in the World. 2003. (ENG.). 224p. (J). (gr. 3-7). pap. 7.95 *(978-1-56145-295-8(5),* Q32694) Peachtree Pubs.
Freeman, Ruth. One Good Thing about America. Honesta, Kathrin, illus. 2017. (ENG.). 160p. (J). (gr. 3-6). 16.95 *(978-0-8234-3695-8(0))* Holiday Hse., Inc.
Frost, C. Amethyst. Mourning under the Bridge. 2012. 280p. pap. 9.99 *(978-0-9847236-2-1(5))* Frost, C. A.
Genhart, Michael. I See You. Lew-Vriethoff, Joanne, illus. 2017. 40p. (J). 15.95 ***(978-1-4338-2758-7(1),*** Magination Pr.) American Psychological Assn.
Glasgow, Kathleen. Girl in Pieces. 2016. (ENG.). 416p. (YA). (gr. 9). lib. bdg. 21.99 *(978-1-101-93473-9(5),* Delacorte Pr.) Random House Publishing Group.
—Girl in Pieces. 2016. (ENG.). 416p. (YA). (gr. 9). 18.99 *(978-1-101-93471-5(9),* Delacorte Pr.) Random Hse. Children's Bks.
Grace, Kathleen. The Perfect Pug. 2011. 24p. pap. 24.95 *(978-1-4512-7557-5(9))* America Star Bks.
Grantner, Anne M. & Haggart, Gary. Without a Home. Hannon, Kenneth, photos by. 2003. (Illus.). 35p. (YA). (gr. 5-18). pap. 12.95 *(978-0-9740929-0-4(8))* Shelter of Flint, Inc.
Gray, P. J. Trippin' 2015. (Trippin' Ser.: 1). (YA). lib. bdg. 19.60 *(978-0-606-36833-9(7))* Turtleback Bks.
—Trippin' Book 1, 1 vol. 2015. (Trippin' Ser.). (ENG.). 64p. (YA). (gr. 9-12). 8.95 *(978-1-62250-931-7(5))* Saddleback Educational Publishing, Inc.
Griffin, Paul. Ten Mile River. 2011. (ENG.). 208p. (YA). (gr. 7-18). 7.99 *(978-0-14-241983-0(4),* Speak) Penguin Young Readers Group.
Grimes, Nikki. Rich. Christie, R. Gregory, illus. 2009. (Dyamonde Daniel Book Ser.: 2). (ENG.). 112p. (J). (gr. 2-4). 12.99 *(978-0-399-25176-4(6),* G.P. Putnam's Sons Books for Young Readers) Penguin Young Readers Group.
Gunning, Monica. A Shelter in Our Car. Pedlar, Elaine, illus. 2013. (ENG.). 32p. (J). pap. 9.95 *(978-0-89239-308-4(4),* Children's Book Press) Lee & Low Bks., Inc.
Halahmy, Miriam. Behind Closed Doors. 2017. (ENG.). 208p. (J). (gr. 9). 16.95 *(978-0-8234-3641-5(1));* ***(978-0-8234-3792-4(2))*** Holiday Hse., Inc.
Hesse, Karen. Brooklyn Bridge. Sheban, Chris, illus. 2011. (ENG.). 256p. (J). (gr. 5-9). pap. 9.99 *(978-0-312-67428-1(7),* 9780312674281) Square Fish.
Hobbs, Valerie. Maggie & Oliver or a Bone of One's Own. Thermes, Jennifer, illus. 2013. (ENG.). 208p. (J). (gr. 3-7). pap. 6.99 *(978-1-250-01672-0(X),* 9781250016720) Square Fish.
Holm, M. S. The Arborist. Sayles, Susana, illus. 2007. (ENG.). 104p. (J). 16.95 *(978-0-9796199-1-5(2));* pap. 11.95 *(978-0-9796199-3-9(9))* Great West Publishing. (Sentry Bks.).
Hubbard, Jim. Lives Turned Upside Down: Homeless Children in Their Own Words & Photographs. 2007. (ENG.). 40p. (J). (gr. 4-6). pap. 12.99 *(978-1-4169-6838-2(5),* Simon & Schuster/Paula Wiseman Bks.) Simon & Schuster/Paula Wiseman Bks.
Hyde, Catherine Ryan. Becoming Chloe. 2008. (ENG.). 224p. (YA). (gr. 9). pap. 8.99 *(978-0-375-83260-4(2),* Knopf Bks. for Young Readers) Random Hse. Children's Bks.
Kaufman, Sashi. The Other Way Around. 288p. (YA). (gr. 8-12). 2017. (ENG.). pap. 9.99 ***(978-1-5124-8177-8(7),*** Carolrhoda Bks.) 2014. 17.95 *(978-1-4677-0262-1(5))* Lerner Publishing Group.
Kirby, Susan E. A No-Fuss Christmas. 2010. (J). *(978-1-60682-059-9(1))* BJU Pr.
Kowalski, William. Just Gone, 1 vol. 2013. (Rapid Reads Ser.). (ENG.). 128p. pap. 9.95 *(978-1-4598-0327-5(2),* Raven Bks.) Literations.
—The Way It Works, 1 vol. 2010. (Rapid Reads Ser.). (ENG.). 128p. pap. 9.95 *(978-1-55469-367-2(5),* Raven Bks.) Literations.
Krulik, Nancy E. Revenge of the Killer Worms. 2015. (George Brown, Class Clown Ser.: 16). lib. bdg. 14.75 *(978-0-606-37545-0(7))* Turtleback Bks.
Landowne, Youme. Selavi, That Is Life: A Haitian Story of Hope. Landowne, Youme, illus. 2004. (ENG., Illus.). 40p. (J). (gr. k-2). 17.95 *(978-0-938317-84-5(9))* Cinco Puntos Pr.
Lupica, Mike. Fast Break. 2015. (ENG.). 272p. (J). (gr. 5-8). 17.99 *(978-0-399-25606-6(7),* Philomel Bks.) Penguin Publishing Group.
—Fast Break. 2016. (ENG.). 288p. (J). (gr. 5). pap. 8.99 *(978-1-101-99783-3(4),* Puffin Books) Penguin Young Readers Group.
—Fast Break. 2016. (ENG.). 288p. (J). (gr. 5). 19.65 *(978-0-606-39313-3(7))* Turtleback Bks.
Lynch, Chris. Killing Time in Crystal City. 2015. (ENG., Illus.). 240p. (YA). (gr. 7). 17.99 *(978-1-4424-4011-1(2),* Simon & Schuster Bks. For Young Readers) Simon & Schuster Bks. For Young Readers.
Mathews, Leslie. I Am a Bear. Dumont, Jean-françois, illus. 2015. (ENG.). 34p. (J). 16.00 *(978-0-8028-5447-6(8),* Eerdmans Bks For Young Readers) Eerdmans, William B. Publishing Co.
Matthews, L. S. Lexi. 2008. 200p. (J). pap. *(978-0-385-73575-9(8),* Delacorte Pr) Random House Publishing Group.
McClintock, Norah. Out of the Cold. 2012. (Robyn Hunter Mysteries Ser.: 4). (ENG.). 232p. (YA). (gr. 6-12). pap. 8.95 *(978-0-7613-9396-2(X),* Darby Creek); lib. bdg. 27.93 *(978-0-7613-8314-7(X))* Lerner Publishing Group.
McClure, Wendy. Wanderville. 2014. (Wanderville Ser.: 1). (ENG.). (J). (gr. 3-7). 240p. pap. 7.99 *(978-1-59514-701-1(2));* 224p. 16.99 *(978-1-59514-700-4(4))* Penguin Young Readers Group. (Razorbill).
McNeal, Laura. Dark Water. 2011. (ENG.). 324p. (YA). (gr. 7). pap. 9.99 *(978-0-375-84330-3(2),* Ember) Random Hse. Children's Bks.
Mikkelsen, Jon. Race for Home. Lueth, Nathan, illus. 2008. (We Are Heroes Ser.). (ENG.). 40p. (gr. 2-3). lib. bdg. 23.99 *(978-1-4342-0786-9(2),* Keystone Bks.) Stone Arch Bks.
Millard, Glenda. A Small Free Kiss in the Dark. 2010. (ENG.). 192p. (YA). (gr. 7-18). pap. 16.95 *(978-0-8234-2264-7(X))* Holiday Hse., Inc.
Mills, Charles. The Great Sleepy-Time Stew Rescue. 2004. (Honors Club Story Ser.: Vol. 4). (Illus.). 127p. (J). 7.99 *(978-0-8163-2009-7(8))* Pacific Pr. Publishing Assn.
Moore, Stephanie. Better Than Picture Perfect. 2014. (Sharp Sisters Ser.: 2). (ENG.). 160p. (YA). (gr. 6-12). pap. 7.95 *(978-1-4677-4486-7(7),* Darby Creek) Lerner Publishing Group.
Moses, Shelia P. Joseph. (ENG.). (YA). (gr. 7). 2010. 208p. pap. 8.99 *(978-1-4169-9442-8(4))* 2008. (Illus.). 176p. 16.99 *(978-1-4169-1752-6(7))* McElderry, Margaret K. Bks. (McElderry, Margaret K. Bks.).
O'Connor, Barbara. How to Steal a Dog. 2009. (ENG.). 192p. (J). (gr. 3-7). pap. 6.99 *(978-0-312-56112-3(1),* 9780312561123) Square Fish.
Paulsen, Gary. Paintings from the Cave: Three Novellas. (ENG.). (YA). (gr. 7-7). 2012. 174p. pap. 8.99 *(978-0-553-49466-2(X),* Ember) 2011. 176p. 15.99 *(978-0-385-74684-7(9),* Lamb, Wendy Bks.) Random Hse. Children's Bks.
Phillips, Gin. The Hidden Summer. 2014. (ENG.). 208p. (J). (gr. 5). pap. 7.99 *(978-0-14-242568-8(0),* Puffin Books) Penguin Young Readers Group.
Pyron, Bobbie. The Dogs of Winter. 2014. (ENG.). 320p. (J). (gr. 5-9). pap. 7.99 *(978-0-545-39931-9(9),* Levine, Arthur A. Bks.) Scholastic, Inc.
Quick, Matthew. Sorta Like a Rock Star. 2011. (ENG.). 384p. (YA). (gr. 7-17). pap., pap. 10.99 *(978-0-316-04353-3(2))* Little, Brown Bks. for Young Readers.
Quintanilla, Billie. Never Again a Homeless Christmas! 2012. 28p. 24.95 *(978-1-62709-069-8(X))* America Star Bks.
Rapp, Adam. 33 Snowfish. Ering, Timothy Basil, illus. 2006. (ENG.). 192p. (YA). (gr. 9-12). per. 7.99 *(978-0-7636-2917-5(0))* Candlewick Pr.
Rhodes, Jewell Parker. Towers Falling. 2016. (ENG., Illus.). 240p. (J). (gr. 3-7). 16.99 *(978-0-316-26222-4(6))* Little, Brown Bks. for Young Readers.
Rhuday-Perkovich, Olugbemisola. 8th Grade Super Zero. 2011. (ENG.). 336p. (J). (gr. 4-7). pap. 7.99 *(978-0-545-09725-3(8),* Levine, Arthur A. Bks.) Scholastic, Inc.
Riordan, Rick. The Sword of Summer. l.t. ed. 2015. (Magnus Chase & the Gods of Asgard Ser.: Bk. 1). (ENG.). 698p. 24.99 *(978-1-4104-8316-4(9))* Cengage Gale.
—The Sword of Summer. (Magnus Chase & the Gods of Asgard Ser.: Bk. 1). (ENG.). (J). 2017. 544p. (gr. 3-7). pap. 9.99 *(978-1-4231-6337-4(0))* 2015. 512p. (gr. 5-9). 19.99 *(978-1-4231-6091-5(6))* Hyperion Bks. for Children.
—The Sword of Summer. Rocco, John, illus. ltd. ed. 2015. (Magnus Chase & the Gods of Asgard Ser.: Bk. 1). (ENG.). 512p. (J). (gr. 5-9). 100.00 *(978-1-4847-1871-1(2))* Hyperion Bks. for Children.
—The Sword of Summer. 2017. (Magnus Chase & the Gods of Asgard Ser.: 1). (J). lib. bdg. 20.85 ***(978-0-606-39972-2(0))*** Turtleback Bks.
Rooftoppers. 2014. (ENG., Illus.). 304p. (J). (gr. 3-7). pap. 7.99 *(978-1-4424-9059-8(4),* Simon & Schuster Bks. For Young Readers) Simon & Schuster Bks. For Young Readers.
Rundell, Katherine. Rooftoppers. Fan, Terry, illus. 2013. (ENG.). 288p. (J). (gr. 3-7). 16.99 *(978-1-4424-9058-1(6),* Simon & Schuster Bks. For Young Readers) Simon & Schuster Bks. For Young Readers.
Sachar, Louis. Buracos. pap. 29.95 *(978-85-336-1280-8(X))* Livraria Martins Editora BRA. Dist: Distribooks, Inc.
—Holes. 2008. (KOR., Illus.). 334p. (J). pap. *(978-89-364-5602-3(4))* Chang-jag and Bipyeong Co.
—Holes. 10th ed. 2008. (ENG., Illus.). 272p. (J). (gr. 4-8). 18.99 *(978-0-374-33266-2(5),* 9780374332662, Farrar, Straus & Giroux (BYR)) Farrar, Straus & Giroux.
—Holes. 2008. (ENG.). (J). 39.99 *(978-0-7393-7103-9(7))* Findaway World, LLC.
—Holes. 2014. (CHI & ENG.). 246p. (J). (gr. 4-8). pap. *(978-7-5442-7158-5(7))* Fukuinkan Shoten.
—Holes. 2009. 9.14 *(978-0-7848-1394-2(9),* Everbind) Marco Bk. Co.
—Holes. 240p. (J). (gr. 4-6). pap. 5.99 *(978-0-8072-8073-7(9),* Listening Library) Random Hse. Audio Publishing Group.
—Holes, 4 vols. (J). 2006. 46.75 *(978-1-4193-6136-4(8))* 2004. 1.25 *(978-1-4025-6758-2(8))* Recorded Bks., Inc.
—Holes. l.t. ed. 2003. 288p. pap. 10.95 *(978-0-7862-6190-1(0))* Thorndike Pr.
Scott, Earnestine E. Little Mike's Family: A Novel for Second & Third Graders. 2012. 30p. 24.95 *(978-1-4626-6018-6(5))* America Star Bks.
Seskin, Steve & Shamblin, Allen. A Chance to Shine. Christie, R. & Christie, Gregory, illus. 2006. (ENG.). 30p. (J). (gr. -1-2). 16.99 *(978-1-58246-167-0(8),* Tricycle Pr.) Random Hse. Children's Bks.
Shamblin, Seskin & National Geographic Learning Staff. A Chance to Shine. Christie, R. Gregory, illus. 2008. (ENG.). 32p. (C). (gr. -1-2). pap. 12.95 *(978-1-58246-304-9(2))* National Geographic School Publishing, Inc.
Sher, Emil. Young Man with Camera. Wyman, David, photos by. 2015. (ENG., Illus.). 240p. (J). (gr. 7). 17.99 *(978-0-545-54131-2(X),* Levine, Arthur A. Bks.) Scholastic, Inc.
Smith, Julie. Hearts for the Homeless. 2012. 28p. pap. 19.99 *(978-1-4685-5602-5(9))* AuthorHouse.
Spalding, Esta. Knock about with the Fitzgerald-Trouts. Smith, Sydney, illus. 2017. (ENG.). 320p. (J). (gr. 3-7). 16.99 *(978-0-316-29860-5(3))* Little, Brown Bks. for Young Readers.
—Look Out for the Fitzgerald-Trouts. Smith, Sydney, illus. 2016. (ENG.). 256p. (J). (gr. 3-7). 16.99 *(978-0-316-29858-2(1))* Little, Brown Bks. for Young Readers.
Strasser, Todd. No Place. 2014. (ENG., Illus.). 272p. (YA). (gr. 7). 17.99 *(978-1-4424-5721-8(X),* Simon & Schuster Bks. For Young Readers) Simon & Schuster Bks. For Young Readers.
Stryker, Robin. Goldie, the Homeless Calico Cat. Rubino, Alisa A., illus. 2005. (J). pap. *(978-0-932991-35-5(1))* Place In The Woods, The.
Taylor, Shirley A. The Stable Boy. Hall, Wendell E., illus. 2012. (ENG.). 40p. (J). (gr. 2-17). 17.95 *(978-1-935166-79-5(4))* Parkhurst Brothers, Inc., Pubs.
Thomas, Jacquelin. Split Ends. 2010. (ENG.). 272p. pap. 17.99 *(978-1-4165-9879-4(0))* Pocket Books.
Upjohn, Rebecca. Lily & the Paper Man, 1 vol. Benoit, Renne & Second Story Press Staff, illus. 2007. (ENG.). 24p. (J). (gr. k-3). 15.95 *(978-1-897187-19-7(X))* Second Story Pr. CAN. Dist: Orca Bk. Pubs. USA.
Van Draanen, Wendelin. Runaway. 2012. (ENG.). 272p. (YA). (gr. 5). pap. 9.99 *(978-0-307-97597-3(5),* Ember) Random Hse. Children's Bks.
—Sammy Keyes & the Sisters of Mercy. 2008. (Sammy Keyes Ser.: Bk. 3). (J). 59.99 *(978-1-60640-646-5(9))* Findaway World, LLC.
Villareal, Ray. On the Other Side of the Bridge. 2014. (ENG.). 227p. (J). pap. 11.95 *(978-1-55885-802-2(4),* Piñata Books) Arte Publico Pr.
Wallace, Barbara Brooks. Secret in St. Something. 2003. (ENG., Illus.). 160p. (J). (gr. 3-7). pap. 9.95 *(978-0-689-85601-3(6),* Aladdin) Simon & Schuster Children's Publishing.
Williams, Michael. Now Is the Time for Running. 2013. (ENG.). 240p. (YA). (gr. 7-17). pap. 10.99 *(978-0-316-07788-0(7))* Little, Brown Bks. for Young Readers.
Wolk, Lauren. Wolf Hollow. 2016. (ENG.). 304p. (J). (gr. 5-7). 16.99 *(978-1-101-99482-5(7),* Dutton Books for Young Readers) Penguin Young Readers Group.
Yee, Paul. Money Boy. 2013. 192p. pap. *(978-1-4596-6450-0(7))* ReadHowYouWant.com, Ltd.

HOMELESSNESS

see also Homeless Persons

Bringle, Jennifer. Homelessness in America Today. 2010. (In the News Ser.). (ENG.). 64p. (YA). pap. 12.95 *(978-1-4488-1683-5(1));* (gr. 7-12). lib. bdg. 31.95 *(978-1-4358-9451-8(0))* Rosen Publishing Group, Inc., The.
Cartlidge, Cherese. Homeless Youth. 2016. (ENG., Illus.). 80p. (J). (gr. 5-12). *(978-1-60152-978-7(3))* ReferencePoint Pr., Inc.
Conrad, Colleen Mullen. Reggie's Place: The Story of How One Boy's Life Made A Difference for Homeless Youth. 2011. (ENG.). 36p. (J). pap. 19.95 *(978-1-4327-7803-3(X));* pap. 24.95 *(978-1-4327-7839-2(0))* Outskirts Pr., Inc.
Furgang, Kathy. Ending Hunger & Homelessness Through Service Learning, 1 vol. 2015. (ENG.). 80p. (YA). 34.60 *(978-1-4777-7959-0(0),* Rosen Young Adult) Rosen Publishing Group, Inc., The.
Gerdes, Louise. The Homless. 2007. (Opposing Viewpoints Ser.). (ENG., Illus.). 240p. (YA). (gr. 10-12). 29.45 *(978-0-7377-3655-7(0),* LML02109-234136, Greenhaven Pr., Inc.) Cengage Gale.
Harrison, Jean. Home. 2004. (Children's Rights Ser.). (J). lib. bdg. 27.10 *(978-1-58340-418-8(X))* Black Rabbit Bks.
Huff, Tim, illus. The Cardboard Shack Beneath the Bridge. 2007. 31p. *(978-1-897186-09-1(6))* Castle Quay Bks. Canada.
Latchana Kenney, Karen. The Hidden Story of Homelessness, 1 vol., 1. 2014. (Undercover Story Ser.). (ENG.). 48p. (J). (gr. 5-8). 30.25 *(978-1-4777-2797-3(3),* Rosen Reference) Rosen Publishing Group, Inc., The.
Lüsted, Marcia Amidon. Coping with Homelessness. 2017. (J). ***(978-1-5081-7691-6(4))*** Rosen Publishing Group, Inc., The.
Lüsted, Marcia Amidon. I Am Homeless, Now What? 2016. (Teen Life 411 Ser.). 00112p. (J). (gr. 7-7). 37.10 *(978-1-5081-7187-4(4))* Rosen Publishing Group, Inc., The.
Merino, Noël. Poverty & Homelessness. Greenhaven Press Editors, ed. 2014. (Current Controversies Ser.). (ENG., Illus.). 224p. (gr. 10-12). lib. bdg. 46.40 *(978-0-7377-6886-2(X),* Greenhaven Pr., Inc.) Cengage Gale.
—Poverty & Homelessness. Greenhaven Press Editors & Gale Editors, eds. 2014. (Current Controversies Ser.). (ENG., Illus.). 224p. (gr. 7-12). pap. 32.00 *(978-0-7377-6887-9(8),* Greenhaven Pr., Inc.) Cengage Gale.
Poole, H. W. Homelessness & Families, Vol. 12. 2016. (Families Today Ser.). (Illus.). 48p. (J). (gr. 5). 20.95 *(978-1-4222-3616-1(1))* Mason Crest.
Rotner, Shelley & Goldblas, Amy. Home. Rotner, Shelley, photos by. 2010. (Shelley Rotner's Early Childhood Library Ser.). (ENG., Illus.). 32p. (gr. -1-2). lib. bdg. 25.26 *(978-0-7613-4605-0(8))* Lerner Publishing Group.
Schauer, Pete, ed. Homelessness & Street Crime. 2017. (Current Controversies Ser.). (ENG.). (YA). (gr. 10-12). pap. 32.00 ***(978-1-5345-0093-8(6))*** Greenhaven Publishing LLC.
Schauer, Peter J. Homelessness & Street Crime. 2017. (J). ***(978-1-5345-0095-2(2))*** Greenhaven Publishing LLC.
Thompson, Tamara. Homelessness. Greenhaven Press Editors, ed. 2012. (Opposing Viewpoints Ser.). (ENG., Illus.). 224p. (gr. 10-12). 48.80 *(978-0-7377-5939-6(9));* pap. 33.80 *(978-0-7377-5940-2(2),* Greenhaven Pr., Inc.) Cengage Gale.
Walker, Ida. Homelessness. 2013. (Introducing Issues with Opposing Viewpoints Ser.). (ENG., Illus.). 144p. (gr. 10-12). 42.00 *(978-0-7377-3851-3(0),* Greenhaven Pr., Inc.) Cengage Gale.
Yasuda, Anita. Hannah Taylor. 2011. 24p. (YA). (gr. 2-4). *(978-1-77071-646-9(7));* pap. *(978-1-77071-650-6(5))* Weigl Educational Pubs. Ltd.
—Hannah Taylor: Ma Vie. Karvonen, Tanjah, tr. from ENG. 2011. (FRE., Illus.). 24p. (YA). (gr. 2-4). *(978-1-77071-434-2(0))* Weigl Educational Pubs. Ltd.

HOMELESSNESS—FICTION

Auch, Mary Jane. A Dog on His Own. 2009. (ENG., Illus.). 160p. (J). (gr. 3-7). pap. 7.95 *(978-0-8234-2243-2(7))* Holiday Hse., Inc.
Bromley, Anne C. & Casilla, Robert. The Lunch Thief, 1 vol. 2010. (ENG., Illus.). 32p. (gr. 3-7). 16.95 *(978-0-88448-311-3(8),* 884311) Tilbury Hse. Pubs.
Byrne, Michael. Lottery Boy. 2016. (ENG.). 304p. (YA). (gr. 7). 16.99 *(978-0-7636-7996-5(8))* Candlewick Pr.
Easton, Kelly. Walking on Air. 2010. (ENG.). 240p. (YA). (gr. 7). pap. 11.99 *(978-1-4424-1437-2(5),* McElderry, Margaret K. Bks.) McElderry, Margaret K. Bks.
Falk, Karen. Tacianna & the Endless Ball of String. 2006. 83p. pap. 19.95 *(978-1-4241-3287-4(8))* PublishAmerica, Inc.
Flake, Sharon G. Begging for Change. rev. ed. 2007. (ENG.). 256p. (J). (gr. 7-12). pap. 7.99 *(978-1-4231-0384-4(X),* Jump at the Sun) Hyperion Bks. for Children.
—Money Hungry. Disney Press Staff, illus. rev. ed. 2007. (ENG.). 192p. (J). (gr. 5-9). pap. 8.99 *(978-1-4231-0386-8(6),* Jump at the Sun) Hyperion Bks. for Children.
Goodwin, Catherine. Seeking Shelter. 2006. (ENG., Illus.). 156p. (J). per. *(978-1-55380-033-0(8))* Ronsdale Pr.

H
I

Greene, Janice. No Exit, 1 vol. unabr. ed. 2010. (Q Reads Ser.). (ENG.). 32p. (YA). (gr. 9-12). pap. 6.95 *(978-1-61651-202-6(4))* Saddleback Educational Publishing, Inc.

Hill, Kirkpatrick. Do Not Pass Go. 2007. (ENG.). 240p. (J). (gr. 4-9). 16.99 *(978-1-4169-1400-6(5))*, McElderry, Margaret K. Bks.) McElderry, Margaret K. Bks.

Holmes, S. D. The Adventures of Mister. 2009. 56p. pap. 23.99 *(978-1-4389-3786-1(5))* AuthorHouse.

King, Stephen Michael. Mutt Dog! King, Stephen Michael, illus. 2005. (Illus.). 32p. (J). *(978-1-86504-636-5(1))*; pap. *(978-1-86504-637-2(X))* Scholastic, Inc. (Scholastic Pr.).

Kowalski, William. Just Gone, 1 vol. 2013. (Rapid Reads Ser.). (ENG.). 128p. pap. 9.95 *(978-1-4598-0327-5(2))*, Raven Bks.) Literations.

Lachenmeyer, Nathaniel. Broken Beaks. Ingpen, Robert R., illus. 2005. 32p. (J). 15.95 *(978-0-85572-335-4(1))* Warwick Publishing CAN. Dist: Two Rivers Distribution.

Mango's Quest: The story of a home lost & Found. 2008. 4.95 *(978-0-9724425-8-9(8))*, White Tiger Pr.) Homes for the Homeless Institute, Inc.

McCalla Njee, Lena. Ivan Gets a Dream House. 2012. 46p. pap. 13.99 *(978-0-9829630-4-3(1))* Minna Pr.

Miller, Janet. Little House on the Highway - a Story of a Homeless Family & School Bullying. 2011. 200p. pap. 19.95 *(978-1-257-83540-9(8))* Lulu Pr., Inc.

Moore, Stephanie Perry. Better Than Picture Perfect. 2014. (Sharp Sisters Ser.: 2). (ENG.). 160p. (YA). (gr. 6-12). lib. bdg. 27.93 *(978-1-4677-3725-8(9))* Lerner Publishing Group.

Nunez, Ralph da Costa & Ellison, Jesse Andrews. Voyage to Shelter Cove. Simon, Madeline Gerstein, illus. 2005. (J). pap. 5.00 *(978-0-9724425-3-4(7))* Homes for the Homeless Institute, Inc.

Ottenbreit, Sharon. Only One Toy Allowed. 2010. 32p. pap. 15.99 *(978-0-557-36426-8(4))* Lulu Pr., Inc.

Qualls, Millie Marie. Miss Cooney & Her New Home. 2012. 24p. 24.95 *(978-1-4626-7426-8(7))* America Star Bks.

Reece, Julie. Crux. 2012. (ENG.). 298p. (YA). pap. 14.99 *(978-1-937744-06-9(X))* J. Taylor Publishing.

Richter, Jutta. Beyond the Station Lies the Sea. Brailovsky, Anna, tr. from GER. 2009. (ENG.). 96p. (J). (gr. 2-7). 14.00 *(978-1-57131-690-5(6))* Milkweed Editions.

Ruffo, J.I. HOMELESS: LEYENDAS DE LA INJUSTICIA SOCIAL. 2015. (SPA., Illus.). 280p. pap. *(978-84-16359-31-8(8))* Punto Rojo Libros, S.L.

Snyder, Sandy. There's Only One I in Charlie. Ferrenburg, Susie, illus. 2011. 48p. pap. 24.95 *(978-1-4626-4086-7(9))* America Star Bks.

Taylor, Pat Eytcheson. Scamper Tangles with Christmas. 2012. 56p. pap. 15.00 *(978-0-9845630-4-3(0))* Catch-A-Winner Publishing.

Voyage to Shelter Cove. 2006. (Illus.). (J). pap., act. bk. ed. 2.00 *(978-0-9724425-5-8(3))*, White Tiger Pr.) Homes for the Homeless Institute, Inc.

Wessel-Estes, Pam. A Quilt & a Home. 2012. 36p. pap. 14.95 *(978-1-4575-1489-0(3))*; 24.95 *(978-1-4575-1490-6(7))* Dog Ear Publishing, LLC.

HOMER—ADAPTATIONS

Colum, Padraic. The Children's Homer: The Adventures of Odysseus & the Tale of Troy. 2011. 144p. pap. 7.95 *(978-1-61382-004-9(6))* Simon & Brown.

Redmond, Diane. The Odyssey, Vol. 4. Smith, Barry, illus. unabr. ed. 2003. (Curtain Up Ser.: Vol. 4). (ENG.). 48p. (J). (gr. 1-4). pap. 15.00 *(978-0-7136-4628-3(4))*, A&C Black) Bloomsbury Publishing Plc GBR. Dist: Players Pr., Inc.

HOMER, WINSLOW, 1836-1910

Venezia, Mike. Winslow Homer. Venezia, Mike, illus. 2004. (Getting. . Know Artists Ser.). (ENG., Illus.). 32p. (J). (gr. 3-4). pap. 6.95 *(978-0-516-26979-5(8))*, Children's Pr.) Scholastic Library Publishing.

HOMES

see Houses

HOMESTEAD LAW

Porterfield, Jason. The Homestead Act of 1862. 2005. (Primary Sources in American History Ser.). (Illus.). 64p. (J). (gr. 5-8). lib. bdg. 31.95 *(978-1-4042-0178-1(5))* Rosen Publishing Group, Inc., The.

—The Homestead Act Of 1862: A Primary Source History of the Settlement of the American Heartland in the Late 19th Century. 2009. (Primary Sources in American History Ser.). 64p. (gr. 5-8). 58.50 *(978-1-60851-496-0(X))* Rosen Publishing Group, Inc., The.

HOMOSEXUALITY

Apelqvist, Eva. LGBTQ Families: The Ultimate Teen Guide. 2013. (It Happened to Me Ser.: 37). (ENG., Illus.). 208p. 55.00 *(978-0-8108-8536-3(0))* Scarecrow Pr., Inc.

Barrett, John E. Some Assembly Required: The Not-So-Secret Life of a Transgender Teen. 2014. (ENG., Illus.). 256p. (YA). (gr. 8). 17.99 *(978-1-4814-1675-7(8))*, Simon & Schuster Bks. For Young Readers) Simon & Schuster Bks. For Young Readers.

Bausum, Ann. Stonewall: Breaking Out in the Fight for Gay Rights. 2015. (ENG., Illus.). 128p. (YA). (gr. 7). 16.99 *(978-0-670-01679-2(9))*, Viking Books for Young Readers) Penguin Young Readers Group.

Berlatsky, Noah. Homosexuality. 2011. (Global Viewpoints Ser.). 224p. (J). lib. bdg. 40.45 *(978-0-7377-5191-8(6))*; (ENG.). (gr. 12-12). pap. 31.70 *(978-0-7377-5192-5(4))* Cengage Gale. (Greenhaven Pr., Inc.).

Bernay, Emma, ed. Homosexuality. 2007. (Introducing Issues with Opposing Viewpoints Ser.). (ENG., Illus.). 151p. (YA). (gr. 7-12). lib. bdg. 36.95 *(978-0-7377-3852-0(9))* Cengage Gale.

Bily, Cynthia A. Gay Marriage. Gale, ed. 2014. (Introducing Issues with Opposing Viewpoints Ser.). (ENG., Illus.). 144p. (J). (gr. 10-12). lib. bdg. 42.00 *(978-0-7377-6923-4(8))*, Greenhaven Pr., Inc.) Cengage Gale.

Brezina, Corona. Coming Out As Transgender. 2016. (Transgender Life Ser.). 00064p. (J). (gr. 6-6). pap. 12.95 *(978-1-5081-7179-9(3))* Rosen Publishing Group, Inc., The.

Butt, Sheila K. Does God Love Michael's Two Daddies. Perkins, Ken, illus. 2007. (ENG.). 16p. (J). pap. 7.95 *(978-0-932859-94-5(1))* Apologetics Pr., Inc.

Connors, Paul. Homosexuality. 2007. (Current Controversies Ser.). (ENG., Illus.). 224p. (gr. 10-12). 46.40 *(978-0-7377-3721-9(2))* Cengage Gale.

Connors, Paul G. Homosexuality. 2007. (Current Controversies Ser.). (ENG., Illus.). 224p. (gr. 10-12). pap. 32.00 *(978-0-7377-3722-6(0))*, Greenhaven Pr., Inc.) Cengage Gale.

Cronn-Mills, Kirstin & Nelson, Alex Jackson. LGBTQ+ Athletes Claim the Field: Striving for Equality. 2016. (ENG., Illus.). 104p. (YA). (gr. 7-12). 51.99 *(978-1-5124-1139-3(6))*, Twenty-First Century Bks.) Lerner Publishing Group.

Dawson, James. This Book Is Gay. 2015. (ENG., Illus.). 272p. (YA). (gr. 8-12). 16.99 *(978-1-4926-1782-2(2))* Sourcebooks, Inc.

Dawson, James & Dawson, Juno. This Book Is Gay. 2015. (ENG., Illus.). 272p. (YA). (gr. 8-12). pap. 10.99 *(978-1-4926-1783-9(0))*, 9781492617839) Sourcebooks, Inc.

Friedman, Lauri S., ed. Gays in the Military. 2011. (Writing the Critical Essay: an Opposing Viewpoints Guide Ser.). (Illus.). 128p. (J). (gr. 9-12). 33.75 *(978-0-7377-5912-9(7))* Cengage Gale.

—Sexual Orientation. 2012. (Introducing Issues with Opposing Viewpoints Ser.). (ENG., Illus.). 144p. (J). (gr. 7-10). lib. bdg. 36.95 *(978-0-7377-6281-5(0))*, Greenhaven Pr., Inc.) Cengage Gale.

The Gallup's Guide to Modern Gay, Lesbian, & Transgender Lifestyle, 15 vols., Set. Incl. Being Gay, Staying Healthy. Seba, Jaime. 64p. pap. 9.95 *(978-1-4222-1864-8(3))*; Gay & Lesbian Role Models. Seba, Jaime A. 64p. pap. 9.95 *(978-1-4222-1867-9(8))*; Gay Believers: Homosexuality & Religion. Sanna, Emily. 64p. pap. 9.95 *(978-1-4222-1868-6(6))*; Gay Characters in Theatre, Movies, & Television: New Roles, New Attitudes. Seba, Jaime. 64p. pap. 9.95 *(978-1-4222-2013-9(3))*; Gay Issues & Politics: Marriage, the Military, & Work Place Discrimination. Seba, Jaime A. 64p. pap. 9.95 *(978-1-4222-1869-3(4))*; Gay People of Color: Facing Prejudices, Forging Identities. Seba, Jaime. 64p. pap. 9.95 *(978-1-4222-1877-8(5))*; Gays & Mental Health: Fighting Depression, Saying No to Suicide. Seba, Jaime. 64p. pap. 9.95 *(978-1-4222-1870-9(8))*; Homophobia: From Social Stigma to Hate Crimes. Hunt, Jamie. 64p. pap. 9.95 *(978-1-4222-1871-6(6))*; Homosexuality Around the World: Safe Havens, Cultural Challenges. Seba, Jaime. 64p. pap. 9.95 *(978-1-4222-1872-3(4))*; New Generation of Homosexuality: Modern Trends in Gay & Lesbian Communities. Palmer, Bill. 64p. pap. 9.95 *(978-1-4222-1873-0(2))*; Smashing the Stereotypes: What Does It Mean to Be Gay, Lesbian, Bisexual, or Transgender? Seba, Jaime A. 64p. pap. 9.95 *(978-1-4222-1874-7(0))*; Statistical Timeline & Overview of Gay Life. Chastain, Zachary. 96p. pap. 9.95 *(978-1-4222-1875-4(9))*; What Causes Sexual Orientation? Genetics, Biology, Psychology. Palmer, Bill. 64p. pap. 9.95 *(978-1-4222-1876-1(7))*; (YA). (gr. 7-18). 2009. (Illus.). 64p. 2011. Set pap. 149.25 *(978-1-4222-1863-1(5))*, 1317845); Set lib. bdg. 344.25 *(978-1-4222-1758-0(2))*, 1317845) Mason Crest.

Heitkamp, Kristina Lyn. Gay-Straight Alliances: Networking with Other Teens & Allies. 2017. (LGBTQ+ Guide to Beating Bullying Ser.). 64p. (J). (gr. 12-11). 34.45 ***(978-1-5081-7427-1(X))***; pap. 12.95 ***(978-1-5081-7426-4(1))*** Rosen Publishing Group, Inc., The. (Rosen Young Adult).

Henneberg, Susan, ed. LGBT Rights. 2017. (Current Controversies Ser.). 224p. (YA). (gr. 10-12). pap. 32.00 ***(978-1-5345-0035-8(9))***; lib. bdg. 46.40 ***(978-1-5345-0019-8(7))*** Greenhaven Publishing LLC. (Greenhaven Publishing).

Hill, Katie Rain. Rethinking Normal: A Memoir in Transition. 2014. (ENG., Illus.). 272p. (YA). (gr. 8). 17.99 *(978-1-4814-1823-2(8))*, Simon & Schuster Bks. For Young Readers) Simon & Schuster Bks. For Young Readers.

Hillstrom, Kevin. Gay Marriage. Greenhaven Press Editors, ed. 2014. (Hot Topics Ser.). (ENG., Illus.). 128p. (gr. 7-10). lib. bdg. 39.40 *(978-1-4205-0870-3(9))*, Lucent Bks.) Cengage Gale.

Hillstrom, Laurie Collier. The Stonewall Riots. 2016. (Defining Moments Ser.). (Illus.). 240p. (J). 60.00 *(978-0-7808-1442-4(8))* Omnigraphics, Inc.

Hollander, Barbara Gottfried. Harvey Milk: The First Openly Gay Elected Official in the United States. 2017. (J). ***(978-1-5383-8093-2(5))***, Rosen Young Adult) Rosen Publishing Group, Inc., The.

Hudson, David L. Gay Rights. 2004. (Point/Counterpoint Ser.). (Illus.). 112p. (C). (gr. 9-13). 35.00 *(978-0-7910-8094-8(3))*, Chelsea Hse.) Facts On File, Inc.

Huegel, Kelly. GLBTQ: The Survival Guide for Gay, Lesbian, Bisexual, Transgender, & Questioning Teens. 2nd rev. ed. 2011. (ENG.). 240p. (YA). (gr. 7-18). pap. 15.99 *(978-1-57542-363-0(4))* Free Spirit Publishing, Inc.

Hunt, Jamie. Homophobia: From Social Stigma to Hate Crimes. 2009. (Gallup's Guide to Modern Gay, Lesbian, & Transgender Lifestyle Ser.). 64p. (YA). (gr. 7-18). pap. 9.95 *(978-1-4222-1871-6(6))*; lib. bdg. 22.95 *(978-1-4222-1752-8(3))* Mason Crest.

Hurt, Avery Elizabeth. Working with Your School to Create a Safe Environment. 2017. (LGBTQ+ Guide to Beating Bullying Ser.). 64p. (J). (gr. 12-11). pap. 12.95 ***(978-1-5081-7433-2(4))***, Rosen Young Adult) Rosen Publishing Group, Inc., The.

Kafka, Tina. Gay Rights. 2006. (Hot Topics Ser.). (ENG., Illus.). 128p. (gr. 7-12). lib. bdg. 39.40 *(978-1-59018-637-4(0))* Cengage Gale.

Kaster, Jeffrey. What Catholic Teens Should Know about Homosexuality. Larking, Jean K., ed. 2004. (What Catholic Teens Should Know Ser.). (Illus.). 8p. (YA). 7.95 *(978-0-89837-236-6(4))*, 441010) Pflaum Publishing Group.

Kingston, Anna. Respecting the Contributions of LGBT Americans. 2012. (Stop Bullying Now! Ser.). (ENG., Illus.). 24p. (J). (gr. 3-6). pap. 8.25 *(978-1-4488-7519-1(6))*; lib. bdg. 22.60 *(978-1-4488-7446-0(7))* Rosen Publishing Group, Inc., The. (PowerKids Pr.).

Klein, Rebecca T. Transgender Rights & Protections. 2016. (Transgender Life Ser.). 00064p. (J). (gr. 6-6). pap. 12.95 *(978-1-4994-6458-0(4))* Rosen Publishing Group, Inc., The.

Levithan, David & Merrell, Billy. The Full Spectrum: A New Generation of Writing about Gay, Lesbian, Bisexual, Transgender, Questioning, & Other Identities. 2006. (ENG., Illus.). 336p. (YA). (gr. 7-12). per. 9.99 *(978-0-375-83290-1(4))*, Ember) Random Hse. Children's Bks.

The LGBTQ+ Guide to Beating Bullying. 2017. (LGBTQ+ Guide to Beating Bullying Ser.). 64p. (gr. 12-11). 172.25 ***(978-1-4994-6643-0(9))***; pap. 64.75 ***(978-1-4994-6645-4(5))*** Rosen Publishing Group, Inc., The. (Rosen Young Adult).

Mapua, Jeff. Lana Wachowski. 2016. (Transgender Pioneers Ser.). 112p. (J). (gr. 6-6). 37.10 *(978-1-5081-7160-7(2))* Rosen Publishing Group, Inc., The.

Marcovitz, Hal. Teens & Gay Issues. 2008. (Gallup Youth Survey, Major Issues & Trends Ser.). (Illus.). 112,128p. (YA). (gr. 7-9). lib. bdg. 22.95 *(978-1-59084-873-9(X))* Mason Crest.

—Teens & LGBT Issues. Developed in Association with the Gallup Organization Staff, ed. 2013. (Gallup Youth Survey: Major Issues & Trends Ser.: 14). 112p. (J). (gr. 7-18). 24.95 *(978-1-4222-2953-8(X))* Mason Crest.

Mayo, Jeanne. Uncensored: Dating, Friendship, & Sex. 2007. (Illus.). 237p. (YA). (gr. 7-12). per. 14.99 *(978-1-57794-821-6(1))* Harrison House Pubs.

Orr, Tamra. Home & Family Relationships. 2010. (Teens: Being Gay, Lesbian, Bisexual, or Transgender Ser.). (Illus.). 80p. (YA). (gr. 7-12). lib. bdg. 33.25 *(978-1-4358-3579-5(4))* Rosen Publishing Group, Inc., The.

Palmer, Bill. A New Generation of Homosexuality: Modern Trends in Gay & Lesbian Communities. 2009. (Gallup's Guide to Modern Gay, Lesbian, & Transgender Lifestyle Ser.). 64p. (YA). (gr. 7-18). pap. 9.95 *(978-1-4222-1873-0(2))*; lib. bdg. 22.95 *(978-1-4222-1754-2(X))* Mason Crest.

—What Causes Sexual Orientation? Genetics, Biology, Psychology. 2009. (Gallup's Guide to Modern Gay, Lesbian, & Transgender Lifestyle Ser.). 64p. (YA). (gr. 7-18). pap. 9.95 *(978-1-4222-1876-1(7))*; lib. bdg. 22.95 *(978-1-4222-1757-3(4))* Mason Crest.

Payment, Simone. Friendship, Dating, & Relationships. 2010. (Teens: Being Gay, Lesbian, Bisexual, or Transgender Ser.). (Illus.). 80p. (YA). (gr. 7-12). lib. bdg. 33.25 *(978-1-4358-3578-8(6))* Rosen Publishing Group, Inc., The.

Penne, Barbra. Transgender Role Models & Pioneers. 2016. (Transgender Life Ser.). 00064p. (J). (gr. 6-6). pap. 12.95 *(978-1-5081-7183-6(1))* Rosen Publishing Group, Inc., The.

Penne, Barbra & Renehan, Patrick. Your Rights As an LGBTQ+ Teen. 2017. (LGBTQ+ Guide to Beating Bullying Ser.). 64p. (J). (gr. 12-11). pap. 12.95 ***(978-1-5081-7437-0(7))***, Rosen Young Adult) Rosen Publishing Group, Inc., The.

Petrikowski, Nicki Peter. Critical Perspectives on Gender Identity. 2016. (Analyzing the Issues Ser.). 208p. (J). (gr. 8-8). 47.93 *(978-0-7660-7672-3(5))* Enslow Pubs., Inc.

Pitman, Gayle E. When You Look Out the Window: How Phyllis Lyon & Del Martin Built a Community. Lyles, Christopher, illus. 2017. (J). ***(978-1-4338-2736-5(0))***, Magination Pr.) American Psychological Assn.

Pohlen, Jerome. Gay & Lesbian History for Kids: The Century-Long Struggle for LGBT Rights, with 21 Activities. 2015. (For Kids Ser.). (ENG., Illus.). 192p. (J). (gr. 4). pap. 17.95 *(978-1-61373-082-9(9))* Chicago Review Pr., Inc.

Poole, H. W. LGBT Families, Vol. 12. 2016. (Families Today Ser.). (Illus.). 48p. (J). (gr. 5). 20.95 *(978-1-4222-3619-2(6))* Mason Crest.

Prager, Sarah. Queer, There, & Everywhere: 23 People Who Changed the World. O'Ferrall, Zoë More, illus. 2017. 272p. (YA). (gr. 8). 17.99 *(978-0-06-247431-5(6))* HarperCollins Pubs.

Rodger, Ellen. Jazz Jennings: Voice for LGBTQ Youth. 2017. (Illus.). 32p. (J). ***(978-0-7787-3419-2(6))*** Crabtree Publishing Co.

Rodi, Robert & Ross, Laura. Coming Out & Seeking Support, Vol. 10. Jennings, Kevin, ed. 2016. (Living Proud! Growing up LGBTQ Ser.). (Illus.). 64p. (J). (gr. 7). 23.95 *(978-1-4222-3503-4(3))* Mason Crest.

—Confronting Stereotypes, Vol. 10. Jennings, Kevin, ed. 2016. (Living Proud! Growing up LGBTQ Ser.). 64p. (J). (gr. 7). 23.95 *(978-1-4222-3509-6(2))* Mason Crest.

—Engaging with Politics, Vol. 10. Jennings, Kevin, ed. 2016. (Living Proud! Growing up LGBTQ Ser.). 64p. (J). (gr. 7). 23.95 *(978-1-4222-3504-1(1))* Mason Crest.

—Facing Homophobia, Vol. 10. Jennings, Kevin, ed. 2016. (Living Proud! Growing up LGBTQ Ser.). 64p. (J). (gr. 7). 23.95 *(978-1-4222-3508-9(4))* Mason Crest.

—Finding Community, Vol. 10. Jennings, Kevin, ed. 2016. (Living Proud! Growing up LGBTQ Ser.). 64p. (J). (gr. 7). 23.95 *(978-1-4222-3505-8(X))* Mason Crest.

—Keeping Physically Healthy, Vol. 10. Jennings, Kevin, ed. 2016. (Living Proud! Growing up LGBTQ Ser.). 64p. (J). (gr. 7). 23.95 *(978-1-4222-3506-5(8))* Mason Crest.

—Keeping Physically Healthy: Growing up LGBTQ. 2017. (Illus.). 63p. (J). *(978-1-4222-3501-0(7))* Mason Crest.

—Living with Religion & Faith, Vol. 10. Jennings, Kevin, ed. 2016. (Living Proud! Growing up LGBTQ Ser.). (Illus.). 64p. (J). (gr. 7). 23.95 *(978-1-4222-3507-2(6))* Mason Crest.

—Staying Mentally Healthy, Vol. 10. Jennings, Kevin, ed. 2016. (Living Proud! Growing up LGBTQ Ser.). (Illus.). 64p. (J). (gr. 7). 23.95 *(978-1-4222-3510-2(6))* Mason Crest.

—Understanding Sexual Orientation & Gender Identity, Vol. 10. Jennings, Kevin, ed. 2016. (Living Proud! Growing up LGBTQ Ser.). (Illus.). 64p. (J). (gr. 7). 23.95 *(978-1-4222-3511-9(4))* Mason Crest.

Roleff, Tamara, ed. Homosexuality. 2011. (Issues That Concern You Ser.). (Illus.). 144p. (YA). (gr. 9-12). 36.95 *(978-0-7377-5904-4(6))* Cengage Gale.

Rosenthal, Beth. Gay Parenting. 2012. (Opposing Viewpoints Ser.). (ENG., Illus.). 224p. (gr. 10-12). lib. bdg. 48.80 *(978-0-7377-6422-2(8))*, Greenhaven Pr., Inc.) Cengage Gale.

Rosenthal, Beth, ed. Gay Parenting. 2012. (Opposing Viewpoints Ser.). (ENG., Illus.). 240p. (gr. 10-12). pap. 29.45 *(978-0-7377-6423-9(6))*, Greenhaven Pr., Inc.) Cengage Gale.

Sanna, Emily. Gay Believers: Homosexuality & Religion. 2009. (Gallup's Guide to Modern Gay, Lesbian, & Transgender Lifestyle Ser.). 64p. (YA). (gr. 7-18). pap. 9.95 *(978-1-4222-1868-6(6))* Mason Crest.

Seba, Jaime. Being Gay, Staying Healthy. 2009. (Gallup's Guide to Modern Gay, Lesbian, & Transgender Lifestyle Ser.). 64p. (YA). (gr. 7-18). pap. 9.95 *(978-1-4222-1864-8(3))*; (Illus.). lib. bdg. 22.95 *(978-1-4222-1744-3(2))* Mason Crest.

—Coming Out: Telling Family & Friends. 2009. (Gallup's Guide to Modern Gay, Lesbian, & Transgender Lifestyle Ser.). (Illus.). 64p. (YA). (gr. 7-18). lib. bdg. 22.95 *(978-1-4222-1745-0(0))* Mason Crest.

—Homosexuality Around the World: Safe Havens, Cultural Challenges. 2009. (Gallup's Guide to Modern Gay, Lesbian, & Transgender Lifestyle Ser.). 64p. (YA). (gr. 7-18). pap. 9.95 *(978-1-4222-1872-3(4))*; (Illus.). lib. bdg. 22.95 *(978-1-4222-1753-5(1))* Mason Crest.

Seba, Jaime A. Gay & Lesbian Role Models. 2009. (Gallup's Guide to Modern Gay, Lesbian, & Transgender Lifestyle Ser.). 64p. (YA). (gr. 7-18). pap. 9.95 *(978-1-4222-1867-9(8))* Mason Crest.

—Smashing the Stereotypes: What Does It Mean to Be Gay, Lesbian, Bisexual, or Transgender? 2009. (Gallup's Guide to Modern Gay, Lesbian, & Transgender Lifestyle Ser.). (Illus.). 64p. (YA). (gr. 7-18). lib. bdg. 22.95 *(978-1-4222-1755-9(8))* Mason Crest.

Snow, Judith E. How It Feels to Have a Gay or Lesbian Parent: A Book by Kids for Kids of All Ages. 2004. (ENG., Illus.). (C). 136p. 140.00 *(978-1-56023-419-7(9))*, HW14434); 130p. pap. 35.95 *(978-1-56023-420-3(2))*, HW14375) Routledge.

Staley, Erin. Laverne Cox. 2016. (Transgender Pioneers Ser.). 112p. (J). (gr. 6-6). 37.10 *(978-1-5081-7159-1(9))* Rosen Publishing Group, Inc., The.

Teens: Being Gay, Lesbian, Bisexual, or Transgender, 4 vols., Set. Incl. Friendship, Dating, & Relationships. Payment, Simone. lib. bdg. 33.25 *(978-1-4358-3578-8(6))*; GLBT Teens & Society. Nagle, Jeanne. lib. bdg. 33.25 *(978-1-4358-3581-8(6))*; Home & Family Relationships. Orr, Tamra. lib. bdg. 33.25 *(978-1-4358-3579-5(4))*; Life at School & in the Community. Worth, Richard. lib. bdg. 33.25 *(978-1-4358-3580-1(8))*; (YA). (gr. 7-12). 2010. (Illus.). 80p. 2010. Set lib. bdg. 122.40 *(978-1-4358-3611-2(1))* Rosen Publishing Group, Inc., The.

Thompson, Tamara. Transgender People. 2015. (At Issue Ser.). (ENG.). 128p. (gr. 10-12). pap. 27.80 *(978-0-7377-7192-3(5))*, Greenhaven Pr., Inc.) Cengage Gale.

Thrash, Maggie. Honor Girl: A Graphic Memoir. Thrash, Maggie, illus. 2015. (ENG., Illus.). 272p. (YA). (gr. 9). 19.99 *(978-0-7636-7382-6(X))* Candlewick Pr.

—Honor Girl: A Graphic Memoir. 2017. lib. bdg. 26.95 ***(978-0-606-39843-5(0))*** Turtleback Bks.

Watson, Stephanie. Gay Rights Movement, 1 vol. 2013. (Essential Library of Social Change Ser.). (ENG.). 112p. (J). (gr. 6-12). lib. bdg. 35.64 *(978-1-61783-887-3(X))*, Essential Library) ABDO Publishing Co.

Woods, Sara. Identifying As Transgender. 2016. (Transgender Life Ser.). 00064p. (J). (gr. 6-6). pap. 12.95 *(978-1-4994-6456-6(8))* Rosen Publishing Group, Inc., The.

Worth, Richard. Life at School & in the Community. 2010. (Teens: Being Gay, Lesbian, Bisexual, or Transgender Ser.). (Illus.). 80p. (YA). (gr. 7-12). lib. bdg. 33.25 *(978-1-4358-3580-1(8))* Rosen Publishing Group, Inc., The.

HOMOSEXUALITY—FICTION

Albertalli, Becky. Simon vs. the Homo Sapiens Agenda. (YA). (gr. 9). 2016. 336p. pap. 10.99 *(978-0-06-234868-5(X))*; 2015. (ENG.). 320p. 17.99 *(978-0-06-234867-8(1))* HarperCollins Pubs.

—The Upside of Unrequited. 2017. 352p. (YA). (gr. 9). 17.99 *(978-0-06-234870-8(1))* HarperCollins Pubs.

Allen, Skye. Pretty Peg. 2016. (ENG., Illus.). (J). 27.99 ***(978-1-63533-064-9(5))***, Harmony Ink Pr.) Dreamspinner Pr.

Atwood, D. E. If We Shadows. 2016. (ENG., Illus.). (J). 24.99 ***(978-1-63533-033-5(5))*** 2014. 240p. pap. 14.99 *(978-1-62798-820-9(3))* Dreamspinner Pr. (Harmony Ink Pr.).

Bach, Ari. Gudsriki. 2016. (ENG., Illus.). (YA). 32.99 ***(978-1-63533-022-9(X))***, Harmony Ink Pr.) Dreamspinner Pr.

Bach, Tamara. Girl from Mars. Tanaka, Shelley, tr. from GER. 2008. (ENG.). 160p. (J). (gr. 8). 16.95 *(978-0-88899-724-1(8))* Groundwood Bks. CAN. Dist: Publishers Group West (PGW).

Balkovec, Lisa. Setting It Straight. 2006. (YA). per. 13.95 *(978-1-932172-24-9(6))* McKenna Publishing Group.

Barakiva, Michael. One Man Guy. 2014. (ENG.). 272p. (YA). (gr. 7). 17.99 *(978-0-374-35645-3(9))*, Farrar, Straus & Giroux (BYR)) Farrar, Straus & Giroux.

Barnes, David-Matthew. Fifty Yards & Holding. 2015. (ENG.). 264p. (gr. 7). pap. 11.95 *(978-1-62639-081-2(9))*, 1384972) Bold Strokes Bks.

Beam, Cris. I Am J. 2012. (ENG.). 352p. (YA). (gr. 10-17). pap. 10.99 *(978-0-316-05360-0(0))* Little, Brown Bks. for Young Readers.

Beauty of the Broken. 2014. (ENG., Illus.). 368p. (YA). (gr. 9). 17.99 *(978-1-4814-0709-0(0))*, Simon Pulse) Simon Pulse.

Benincasa, Sara. Great. 2014. (ENG.). 272p. (YA). (gr. 9). 17.99 *(978-0-06-222269-5(4))*, HarperTeen) HarperCollins Pubs.

Bick, Ilsa J. The Sin-Eater's Confession. Elyum Studio, illus. 2014. (ENG.). 296p. (YA). (gr. 9-12). pap. 9.95 *(978-1-4677-3705-0(4))*, Carolrhoda Lab™) Lerner Publishing Group.

—The Sin-Eater's Confession. 2013. (ENG.). 296p. (YA). (gr. 9-12). 17.95 *(978-0-7613-5687-5(8))* Lerner Publishing Group.

Birdsall, Bridget. Double Exposure. alt. ed. 2016. (ENG.). 284p. (J). (gr. 6). pap. 9.99 *(978-1-5107-1158-7(9))*, Sky Pony Pr.) Skyhorse Publishing Co., Inc.

Bonaste, Sophie. The Sacrifices We Make. 2016. (ENG., Illus.). (J). 24.99 ***(978-1-63477-975-3(4))***, Harmony Ink Pr.) Dreamspinner Pr.

Brown, Jaye Robin. Georgia Peaches & Other Forbidden Fruit. 2016. 432p. (YA). (gr. 9). 17.99 *(978-0-06-227098-6(2))*, HarperTeen) HarperCollins Pubs.

Burch, Christian. Hit the Road, Manny: A Manny Files Novel. 2008. (ENG.). 240p. (J). (gr. 3-7). 16.99 *(978-1-4169-2812-6(X))*, Atheneum Bks. for Young Readers) Simon & Schuster Children's Publishing.

Burd, Nick. The Vast Fields of Ordinary. 2009. (ENG.). 320p. (YA). (gr. 9-18). 16.99 *(978-0-8037-3340-4(2))*, Dial Bks) Penguin Young Readers Group.

Burns, A. M. Guardians. 2016. (ENG., Illus.). (J). 24.99 ***(978-1-63533-021-2(1))***, Harmony Ink Pr.) Dreamspinner Pr.

Burns, A. M. & Ricci, Caitlin. Running with the Pack. 2016. (ENG., Illus.). (YA). pap. 14.99 ***(978-1-63477-063-7(3))***, Harmony Ink Pr.) Dreamspinner Pr.

Burton, Hallie. For a Price. 2016. (ENG., Illus.). (J). 24.99 ***(978-1-63533-017-5(3)**, Harmony Ink Pr.) Dreamspinner Pr.

—Tapestry. 2016. (ENG., Illus.). (J). 27.99 ***(978-1-63533-078-6(5))*** 2013. 276p. pap. 16.99 *(978-1-62380-355-1(1))* Dreamspinner Pr. (Harmony Ink Pr.).

Burton, Hallie. Tapestry [Library Edition]. 2013. 276p. pap. 16.99 *(978-1-62380-926-3(6)*, Harmony Ink Pr.) Dreamspinner Pr.

Carlson, Melody. Bright Purple: Color Me Confused. 2006. (Truecolors Ser.: 10). (ENG.). 224p. (YA). (gr. 4-7). per. 14.99 *(978-1-57683-950-8(8)*, Th1nk Bks.) NavPress Publishing Group.

Cart, Michael, et al. How Beautiful the Ordinary. 2009. (ENG.). 368p. (YA). (gr. 9-18). 17.99 *(978-0-06-115498-0(9)*, HarperTeen) HarperCollins Pubs.

Carter, Caela. My Best Friend, Maybe. 2014. (ENG.). 352p. (YA). (gr. 9). 17.99 *(978-1-59990-970-7(7)*, 9781599909707, Bloomsbury USA Childrens) Bloomsbury Publishing USA.

Chambers, Aidan. Postcards from No Man's Land. 2004. (ENG.). 320p. (YA). (gr. 9-18). reprint ed. 8.99 *(978-0-14-240145-3(5)*, Speak) Penguin Young Readers Group.

Cohn, Rachel & Levithan, David. Naomi & Ely's No Kiss List. 2008. (ENG.). 256p. (YA). (gr. 9). pap. 9.99 *(978-0-375-84441-6(4)*, Ember) Random Hse. Children's Bks.

Dawn, Nyrae. The History of Us. (ENG., Illus.). 2016. (YA). (gr. 9-12). 24.99 ***(978-1-63477-968-5(1))*** 2015. 184p. (J). pap. 14.99 *(978-1-63476-179-6(0))* Dreamspinner Pr. (Harmony Ink Pr.).

—Turn the World Upside Down. 2016. (ENG., Illus.). (YA). pap. 14.99 ***(978-1-63477-418-5(3)**, Harmony Ink Pr.) Dreamspinner Pr.

DEKELB-RITTENHOUSE, Diane. Immortal Longings. 2012. (ENG.). 340p. (J). (gr. 7). pap. 14.95 *(978-0-9845318-4-4(X))* Tiny Stachel Pr.

Demcak, Andrew. Ghost Songs. 2016. (ENG., Illus.). (J). 24.99 ***(978-1-63533-019-9(X))*** 2014. 210p. pap. 14.99 *(978-1-62798-795-0(9))* Dreamspinner Pr. (Harmony Ink Pr.).

—A Little Bit Langston. 2016. (ENG., Illus.). (YA). (gr. 9-12). 24.99 ***(978-1-63477-928-9(2)**, Harmony Ink Pr.) Dreamspinner Pr.

Dinnison, Kris. You & Me & Him. (ENG.). 288p. (YA). (gr. 9). 2016. pap. 8.99 *(978-0-544-67175-1(9))* 2015. 17.99 *(978-0-544-30112-2(9))* Houghton Mifflin Harcourt Publishing Co. (HMH Books For Young Readers).

Donovan, Stacey. Who I Am Keeps Happening. 2004. (YA). *(978-0-7636-1988-6(4))* Candlewick Pr.

dos Santos, Steven. The Culling. 2013. (Torch Keeper Ser.: 1). (ENG.). 432p. (YA). pap. 9.99 *(978-0-7387-3537-5(X)*, Flux) North Star Editions.

Elmendorf, Dana. South of Sunshine. 2016. (ENG.). 256p. (YA). (gr. 8-12). 16.99 *(978-0-8075-7568-0(2))* Whitman, Albert & Co.

Erich, James. Seidman [Library Edition]. 2012. 210p. pap. 14.99 *(978-1-62380-904-1(5)*, Harmony Ink Pr.) Dreamspinner Pr.

Erno, Jeff. You Belong with Me. 2016. (ENG., Illus.). (J). 24.99 ***(978-1-63477-998-2(3))*** 2013. 164p. pap. 14.99 *(978-1-62380-533-3(3))* Dreamspinner Pr. (Harmony Ink Pr.).

Erno, Jeff. You Belong with Me [Library Edition]. 2013. 164p. pap. 14.99 *(978-1-62380-922-5(3)*, Harmony Ink Pr.) Dreamspinner Pr.

Evangelista, Kate. No Holding Back. 2016. (Dodge Cove Trilogy Ser.). (ENG.). 256p. (YA). pap. 9.99 *(978-1-250-10062-7(3)*, 9781250100627) Feiwel & Friends.

Farizan, Sara. Tell Me Again How a Crush Should Feel. 2014. (ENG.). 304p. (YA). (gr. 9-12). 16.95 *(978-1-61620-284-2(X)*, 73284) Algonquin Bks. of Chapel Hill.

Farrey, Brian. With or Without You. 2011. (ENG., Illus.). 368p. (YA). (gr. 11-18). pap. 8.99 *(978-1-4424-0699-5(2)*, Simon Pulse) Simon Pulse.

Federle, Tim. The Great American Whatever. (ENG.). (YA). (gr. 9). 2017. 304p. pap. 10.99 *(978-1-4814-0410-5(5))* 2016. (Illus.). 288p. E-Book *(978-1-4814-0411-2(3))* 2016. (Illus.). 288p. 17.99 *(978-1-4814-0409-9(1))* Simon & Schuster Bks. For Young Readers. (Simon & Schuster Bks. For Young Readers).

Finneyfrock, Karen. The Sweet Revenge of Celia Door. 2014. (ENG.). 288p. (YA). (gr. 7). pap. 9.99 *(978-0-14-750995-6(5)*, Speak) Penguin Young Readers Group.

Fleet, Suki. The Glass House. 2016. (ENG., Illus.). (J). 24.99 ***(978-1-63477-966-1(5)**, Harmony Ink Pr.) Dreamspinner Pr.

Floreen, Tim. Tattoo Atlas. 2016. (ENG., Illus.). 384p. (YA). (gr. 9). 17.99 *(978-1-4814-3280-1(X)*, Simon Pulse) Simon Pulse.

Ford, Michael Thomas. Suicide Notes. 2010. (ENG.). 304p. (YA). (gr. 9). pap. 9.99 *(978-0-06-073757-3(3)*, HarperTeen) HarperCollins Pubs.

Freely, Jessica. All the Colors of Love. 2016. (ENG., Illus.). (YA). (gr. 9-12). 24.99 ***(978-1-63477-932-6(0)**, Harmony Ink Pr.) Dreamspinner Pr.

Gaines, Sara. Noble Falling. 2016. (ENG., Illus.). (J). 24.99 ***(978-1-63533-052-6(1)**, Harmony Ink Pr.) Dreamspinner Pr.

Gant, Gene. The Battle for Jericho [Library Edition]. 2013. 240p. pap. 14.99 *(978-1-62380-917-1(7)*, Harmony Ink Pr.) Dreamspinner Pr.

—The Thunder in His Head. 2016. (ENG., Illus.). (YA). (gr. 8-12). 24.99 ***(978-1-63477-978-4(9)**, Harmony Ink Pr.) Dreamspinner Pr.

Gant, Gene. The Thunder in His Head [Library Edition]. 2012. 200p. (-18). pap. 14.99 *(978-1-62380-903-4(7)*, Harmony Ink Pr.) Dreamspinner Pr.

Gant, Gene & Erno, Jeff. The Battle for Jericho. 2016. (ENG., Illus.). (J). 24.99 ***(978-1-63477-961-6(4)**, Harmony Ink Pr.) Dreamspinner Pr.

Garden, Nancy. Annie on My Mind. 2007. (ENG., Illus.). 272p. (YA). (gr. 7-12). pap. 9.99 *(978-0-374-40011-8(3)*, 9780374400118) Square Fish.

Gideon, Francis. The Santa Hoax. 2016. (ENG., Illus.). (YA). pap. 16.99 ***(978-1-63477-426-0(4)**, Harmony Ink Pr.) Dreamspinner Pr.

Girard, M-E. Girl Mans Up. 2016. 384p. (YA). (gr. 9). 17.99 *(978-0-06-240417-6(2)*, HarperTeen) HarperCollins Pubs.

González, Rigoberto. Antonio's Card: La Tarjeta de Antonio. Álvarez, Cecilia, illus. 2016. (ENG & SPA.). (J). pap. 9.95 *(978-0-89239-387-9(4)*, Children's Book Press) Lee & Low Bks., Inc.

González, Rigoberto & Alvarez, Cecilia Concepcion. Antonio's Card/la Tarjeta de Antonio. 2013. (ENG & SPA., Illus.). 32p. (J). 17.95 *(978-0-89239-204-9(5))* Lee & Low Bks., Inc.

Goode, John. End of the Innocence. 2016. (ENG., Illus.). (J). 29.99 ***(978-1-63533-008-3(4)**, Harmony Ink Pr.) Dreamspinner Pr.

—Tales from Foster High. 2016. (ENG., Illus.). (YA). 24.99 ***(978-1-63533-077-9(7)**, Harmony Ink Pr.) Dreamspinner Pr.

Goode, John & Morgan, J.G. The Unseen Tempest. (ENG., Illus.). (YA). 2016. (Lords of Arcadia Ser.: Vol. 3). (gr. 8-12). 24.99 ***(978-1-63477-980-7(0))*** 2014. 248p. pap. 14.99 *(978-1-63216-189-5(3))* Dreamspinner Pr. (Harmony Ink Pr.).

Graham, H. Rachelle. Cursed. 2012. (ENG.). 264p. (gr. 7). pap. 13.95 *(978-1-59493-296-0(4))* Bella Bks., Inc.

Green, John. Will Grayson, Will Grayson. 2011. lib. bdg. 22.10 *(978-0-606-15358-4(6)*, Turtleback) Turtleback Bks.

Green, John & Levithan, David. Will Grayson, Will Grayson. 2015. (SPA.). 336p. (YA). (gr. 7). pap. 12.95 *(978-1-101-91070-2(4)*, Vintage Espanol) Knopf Doubleday Publishing Group.

—Will Grayson, Will Grayson. (ENG., (YA). (gr. 9-18). 2011. Illus.). 352p. 10.99 *(978-0-14-241847-5(1)*, Speak) 2010. 320p. 17.99 *(978-0-525-42158-0(0)*, Dutton Books for Young Readers) Penguin Young Readers Group.

Greene, Bette. The Drowning of Stephan Jones. 2012. 220p. pap. 9.99 *(978-0-9834681-3-4(3))* Greene & Sandell.

Haan, Linda de & Nijland, Stern. King & King. Haan, Linda de & Nijland, Stern, illus. 2003. (ENG., Illus.). 32p. (J). (gr. k-3). 15.99 *(978-1-58246-061-1(2)*, Tricycle Pr.) Random Hse. Children's Bks.

Hale, Samantha. Everything Changes. 2014. (ENG.). 264p. (J). (gr. 7). pap. 11.95 *(978-1-62639-303-5(6))* Bold Strokes Bks.

Hall, John. Is He or Isn't He? 2006. (ENG.). 304p. (YA). (gr. 9). pap. 8.99 *(978-0-06-078747-9(3)*, HarperTeen) HarperCollins Pubs.

Hartinger, Brent. Geography Club. (ENG.). 240p. 2003. (J). 17.99 *(978-0-06-001221-2(8))* 2004. (YA). (gr. 9). reprint ed. pap. 9.99 *(978-0-06-001223-6(4)*, HarperTeen) HarperCollins Pubs.

—Split Screen: Attack of the Soul-Sucking Brain Zombies; Bride of the Soul-Sucking Brain Zombies. 2007. 304p. (YA). (gr. 9-12). lib. bdg. 17.89 *(978-0-06-082409-9(3)*, HarperTeen) HarperCollins Pubs.

Hawke, Jay Jordan. Onwaachige the Dreamer. 2016. (ENG., Illus.). (YA). 24.99 ***(978-1-63533-058-8(0)**, Harmony Ink Pr.) Dreamspinner Pr.

—Pukawiss the Outcast. 2016. (ENG., Illus.). (J). 24.99 ***(978-1-63533-066-3(1))*** 2014. 204p. pap. 14.99 *(978-1-62798-646-5(4))* Dreamspinner Pr. (Harmony Ink Pr.).

—A Scout Is Brave. 2nd ed. 2016. (ENG., Illus.). (J). 24.99 ***(978-1-63477-929-6(0)**, Harmony Ink Pr.) Dreamspinner Pr.

Helms, Rhonda. Promposal. 2015. (ENG., Illus.). 224p. (YA). (gr. 7). pap. 9.99 *(978-1-4814-2231-4(6)*, Simon Pulse) Simon Pulse.

Hoblin, Paul & Hueller, Patrick. Archenemy. 2013. (Counterattack Ser.). (ENG.). 112p. (YA). (gr. 6-12). pap. 7.95 *(978-1-4677-0721-3(X))* Lerner Publishing Group.

Hoffmann, Lou. Key of Behliseth. 2nd ed. 2016. (ENG., Illus.). (J). 27.99 ***(978-1-63533-037-3(8)**, Harmony Ink Pr.) Dreamspinner Pr.

Hopkins, Ellen. The You I've Never Known. 2017. (ENG., Illus.). 608p. (YA). (gr. 9). 18.99 *(978-1-4814-4290-9(2)*, McElderry, Margaret K. Bks.) McElderry, Margaret K. Bks.

Howe, James. Totally Joe. 2007. (Misfits Ser.). (ENG.). 224p. (J). (gr. 4-8). pap. 7.99 *(978-0-689-83958-0(8)*, Atheneum Bks. for Young Readers) Simon & Schuster Children's Publishing.

Hubert. Adrian & the Tree of Secrets. 2014. (ENG., Illus.). 128p. (gr. 6). pap. 18.95 *(978-1-55152-556-3(9))* Arsenal Pulp Pr. CAN. Dist: Consortium Bk. Sales & Distribution.

Hutchinson, Shaun David. The Five Stages of Andrew Brawley. Larsen, Christine, illus. 2015. (ENG.). 304p. (YA). (gr. 7). 17.99 *(978-1-4814-0310-8(9)*, Simon Pulse) Simon Pulse.

—Fml. 2013. (ENG.). 304p. (YA). (gr. 9). pap. 9.99 *(978-1-4424-3287-1(X)*, Simon Pulse) Simon Pulse.

—We Are the Ants. 2016. (ENG., Illus.). 464p. (YA). (gr. 9). 17.99 *(978-1-4814-4963-2(X)*, Simon Pulse) Simon Pulse.

Irwin, Judy. What's It to You? 2013. 106p. pap. *(978-0-9877088-7-8(2))* Irwin, Judy.

Isensee, Rik. We're Not Alone. 2016. (ENG.). 164p. (gr. 6-12). pap. 10.99 *(978-1-5040-2702-1(7))* Open Road Integrated Media, Inc.

Jacobson, Jennifer Richard. Stained. 2005. (ENG., Illus.). 208p. (YA). (gr. 8-18). 16.95 *(978-0-689-86745-3(X)*, Atheneum/Richard Jackson Bks.) Simon & Schuster Children's Publishing.

Jay, Annabelle. Starsong. 2017. (Sun Dragon Ser.: Vol. 3). (ENG., Illus.). (YA). pap. 14.99 ***(978-1-63533-246-9(X)**, Harmony Ink Pr.) Dreamspinner Pr.

Jones, Patrick. Combat Zone. 2015. (ENG.). 96p. (YA). (gr. 6-12). pap. 7.99 *(978-1-4677-8094-0(4))* Lerner Publishing Group.

Juby, Susan. Another Kind of Cowboy. 2007. 344p. (YA). lib. bdg. 6.99 *(978-0-06-076521-7(6)*, HarperTeen) HarperCollins Pubs.

Kadence, Sam. Evolution. 2013. 230p. pap. 14.99 *(978-1-62380-410-7(8)*, Harmony Ink Pr.) Dreamspinner Pr.

—On the Right Track. 2016. (ENG., Illus.). (YA). (gr. 9-12). 24.99 ***(978-1-63533-057-1(2))*** 2013. 184p. pap. 14.99 *(978-1-62798-069-2(5))* Dreamspinner Pr. (Harmony Ink Pr.).

Keane, Danni. No Big Deal. (ENG., Illus.). (J). 2016. 24.99 ***(978-1-63533-051-9(3))*** 2015. 186p. pap. 14.99 *(978-1-63216-723-1(9))* Dreamspinner Pr. (Harmony Ink Pr.).

Kennedy, C. Omorphi. Girault, Bénédicte, tr. 2016. (ENG., Illus.). (J). 34.99 ***(978-1-63533-055-7(6)**, Harmony Ink Pr.) Dreamspinner Pr.

—Slaying Isidore's Dragons. (ENG., Illus.). (J). 2016. 32.99 ***(978-1-63533-073-1(4))*** 2015. 350p. pap. 17.99 *(978-1-63476-001-0(8))* Dreamspinner Pr. (Harmony Ink Pr.).

—Tharros. 2016. (ENG., Illus.). (YA). 32.99 ***(978-1-63477-958-6(4)**, Harmony Ink Pr.) Dreamspinner Pr.

Kennedy, Sean. The Ongoing Reformation of Micah Johnson. 2016. (ENG., Illus.). (YA). 24.99 ***(978-1-63477-972-2(X)**, Harmony Ink Pr.) Dreamspinner Pr.

Kerick, Mia. Intervention. 2016. (ENG., Illus.). (J). 24.99 ***(978-1-63533-036-6(X)**, Harmony Ink Pr.) Dreamspinner Pr.

—Intervention [Library Edition]. 2014. 230p. pap. 14.99 *(978-1-62798-336-5(8)*, Harmony Ink Pr.) Dreamspinner Pr.

—Not Broken, Just Bent. 2016. (ENG., Illus.). (J). 24.99 ***(978-1-63533-054-0(8)**, Harmony Ink Pr.) Dreamspinner Pr.

—Not Broken, Just Bent [Library Edition]. 2014. 180p. pap. 14.99 *(978-1-62798-529-1(8)*, Harmony Ink Pr.) Dreamspinner Pr.

—The Red Sheet. 2016. (ENG., Illus.). (J). 24.99 ***(978-1-63477-974-6(6))*** 2014. 190p. pap. 14.99 *(978-1-62798-715-8(0))* Dreamspinner Pr. (Harmony Ink Pr.).

—Us Three. 2016. (ENG., Illus.). (J). 24.99 ***(978-1-63477-989-0(4))*** 2014. 180p. pap. 14.99 *(978-1-62798-908-4(0))* Dreamspinner Pr. (Harmony Ink Pr.).

King, Jeremy Jordan. In Stone: A Grotesque Faerie Tale. 2012. (ENG.). 264p. (gr. 7). pap. 11.95 *(978-1-60282-761-5(3))* Bold Strokes Bks.

Klise, James. Love Drugged. 2010. (ENG.). 312p. (YA). (gr. 7-18). pap. 9.95 *(978-0-7387-2175-0(1)*, Flux) North Star Editions.

Kluger, Steve. My Most Excellent Year: A Novel of Love, Mary Poppins, & Fenway Park. 2009. (ENG.). 416p. (YA). (gr. 7-18). 9.99 *(978-0-14-241343-2(7)*, Speak) Penguin Young Readers Group.

Knowles, Jo. See You at Harry's. 2012. (ENG., Illus.). 310p. (J). (gr. 5). 16.99 *(978-0-7636-5407-8(8))* Candlewick Pr.

Kocek, Sara. Promise Me Something. 2015. (ENG.). 320p. (YA). (gr. 8-12). pap. 9.99 *(978-0-8075-6643-5(8))* Whitman, Albert & Co.

Koehler, Christopher. Poz. (ENG., Illus.). (J). 2016. 24.99 ***(978-1-63533-063-2(7))*** 2015. 200p. pap. 14.99 *(978-1-63216-368-4(3))* Dreamspinner Pr. (Harmony Ink Pr.).

Koertge, Ronald. Boy Girl Boy. 2007. (ENG., Illus.). 180p. (YA). (gr. 9-18). pap. 12.95 *(978-0-15-205865-4(6))* Houghton Mifflin Harcourt Publishing Co.

Koja, Kathe. Talk. 2008. (ENG.). 144p. (YA). (gr. 7-12). per. 16.99 *(978-0-312-37605-5(7)*, 9780312376055) Square Fish.

Konigsberg, Bill. Honestly Ben. 2017. (ENG.). 336p. (J). (gr. 9). 17.99 *(978-0-545-85826-7(7))* Scholastic, Inc.

—Openly Straight. (ENG.). 336p. (J). (gr. 9). 2015. pap. 9.99 *(978-0-545-79865-5(5))* 2013. 17.99 *(978-0-545-50989-3(0))* Scholastic, Inc. (Levine, Arthur A. Bks.).

Laughton, Geoff. By the Creek. 2016. (ENG., Illus.). (J). 24.99 ***(978-1-63477-945-6(2)**, Harmony Ink Pr.) Dreamspinner Pr.

Lavoie, Jennifer. Andy Squared. 2012. (ENG.). 264p. (J). (gr. 7). pap. 11.95 *(978-1-60282-743-1(5))* Bold Strokes Bks.

—The First Twenty. 2015. (ENG.). 264p. (J). (gr. 7). pap. 11.95 *(978-1-62639-414-8(8))* Bold Strokes Bks.

Lee, M. C. The Shadow Operation. 2016. (Center Ser.). (ENG., Illus.). (YA). pap. 16.99 ***(978-1-63477-430-7(2)**, Harmony Ink Pr.) Dreamspinner Pr.

—You Don't Know Jack. 2016. (ENG., Illus.). (J). 24.99 ***(978-1-63477-999-9(1)**, Harmony Ink Pr.) Dreamspinner Pr.

Levithan, David. Hold Me Closer: The Tiny Cooper Story. 2015. (ENG.). 208p. (YA). (gr. 9). 17.99 *(978-0-525-42884-8(4)*, Dutton Books for Young Readers) Penguin Young Readers Group.

—Love Is the Higher Law. 2010. (ENG.). 176p. (YA). (gr. 7). pap. 9.99 *(978-0-375-83469-1(9)*, Knopf Bks. for Young Readers) Random Hse. Children's Bks.

—Two Boys Kissing. (ENG.). (YA). (gr. 9). 2015. 224p. pap. 9.99 *(978-0-307-93191-7(9)*, Ember) 2013. 208p. 16.99 *(978-0-307-93190-0(0)*, Knopf Bks. for Young Readers) Random Hse. Children's Bks.

—Two Boys Kissing. 2015. lib. bdg. 20.85 *(978-0-606-37273-2(3))* Turtleback Bks.

—Wide Awake. 2008. (ENG.). 240p. (YA). (gr. 9). pap. 8.99 *(978-0-375-83467-7(2)*, Knopf Bks. for Young Readers) Random Hse. Children's Bks.

Levithan, David & LaCour, Nina. You Know Me Well. 2016. (ENG.). 256p. (YA). 18.99 *(978-1-250-09864-1(5)*, 9781250098641, St. Martin's Griffin) St. Martin's Pr.

Levy, Dana Alison. The Family Fletcher Takes Rock Island. (ENG.). 272p. (J). (gr. 4-7). 2017. 6.99 ***(978-0-553-52133-7(0)**, Yearling) 2016. 16.99 *(978-0-553-52130-6(6)*, Delacorte Bks. for Young Readers) Random Hse. Children's Bks.

Lieberman, Leanne. Gravity. 1 vol. 2008. (ENG.). 280p. (YA). (gr. 7-12). pap. 12.95 *(978-1-55469-049-7(8))* Orca Bk. Pubs. USA.

Linn, Laurent. Draw the Line. Linn, Laurent, illus. 2016. (ENG., Illus.). 528p. (YA). (gr. 7). 17.99 *(978-1-4814-5280-9(0)*, McElderry, Margaret K. Bks.) McElderry, Margaret K. Bks.

Lippincott, Robin & Watts, Julia. Rufus + Syd. 2016. (ENG., Illus.). (YA). 24.99 ***(978-1-63533-069-4(6)**, Harmony Ink Pr.) Dreamspinner Pr.

Lo, Malinda. Huntress. 2012. (ENG.). 416p. (YA). (gr. 10-17). pap. 11.99 *(978-0-316-03999-4(3))* Little, Brown Bks. for Young Readers.

Lou, Rachel. The Bridge. 2016. (ENG., Illus.). (YA). (gr. 8-12). 24.99 ***(978-1-63477-964-7(9)**, Harmony Ink Pr.) Dreamspinner Pr.

Lynch, Katherine E. & Radclyffe, eds. OMGQueer. 2012. (ENG.). 264p. (J). (gr. 7). pap. 9.95 *(978-1-60282-682-3(X))* Bold Strokes Bks.

Lynne, Zoe. Carnival - Chattanooga. 2016. (ENG., Illus.). (J). 24.99 ***(978-1-63477-947-0(9)**, Harmony Ink Pr.) Dreamspinner Pr.

—That Witch! 2016. (ENG., Illus.). (J). 24.99 ***(978-1-63477-959-3(2))*** 2013. 204p. pap. 14.99 *(978-1-62380-692-7(5))* Dreamspinner Pr. (Harmony Ink Pr.).

Lynne, Zoe. That Witch! [Library Edition]. 2013. 204p. pap. 14.99 *(978-1-62380-927-0(4)*, Harmony Ink Pr.) Dreamspinner Pr.

Lyon, George Ella. Sonny's House of Spies. 2007. (ENG.). 304p. (J). (gr. 6-9). pap. 14.95 *(978-1-4169-6815-3(6)*, Simon & Schuster/Paula Wiseman Bks.) Simon & Schuster/Paula Wiseman Bks.

Lyons, Ella. Marian. 2016. (ENG., Illus.). (YA). pap. 14.99 ***(978-1-63477-420-8(5)**, Harmony Ink Pr.) Dreamspinner Pr.

Malloy, Brian. Twelve Long Months. 2010. (ENG.). 320p. (J). (gr. 7). 9.99 *(978-0-439-87763-3(6)*, Scholastic Paperbacks) Scholastic, Inc.

Marino, Peter. Magic & Misery. 2009. (ENG.). 272p. (YA). (gr. 9-18). 17.95 *(978-0-8234-2133-6(3))* Holiday Hse., Inc.

Marshak, Flo. Grandma Punch Is: A Woman, a Mother, a Grandma, a Professional & a Lesbian. 2012. 32p. pap. 24.95 *(978-1-4626-8176-1(X))* PublishAmerica, Inc.

Martin, Rj. The Body. 2016. (ENG., Illus.). (YA). 27.99 ***(978-1-63477-962-3(2)**, Harmony Ink Pr.) Dreamspinner Pr.

McCormack, Devon. When Ryan Came Back. 2016. (ENG., Illus.). (J). 24.99 ***(978-1-63477-994-4(0)**, Harmony Ink Pr.) Dreamspinner Pr.

McNamara, Brian. Bottled up Secret. 2014. (ENG.). 264p. (J). (gr. 7). pap. 11.95 *(978-1-62639-209-0(9))* Bold Strokes Bks.

—Breaking up Point. 2015. (ENG.). 36p. (YA). (gr. 9). pap. 11.95 *(978-1-62639-430-8(X))* Bold Strokes Bks.

Medina, Nico. Fat Hoochie Prom Queen. 2008. (ENG.). 320p. (YA). (gr. 9-18). pap. 8.99 *(978-1-4169-3603-9(3)*, Simon Pulse) Simon Pulse.

Michaels, Robbie. Caught in the Middle. 2016. (Caught in the ACT Ser.: Vol. 2). (ENG., Illus.). (YA). 24.99 ***(978-1-63477-951-7(7)**, Harmony Ink Pr.) Dreamspinner Pr.

Miller, Sam J. The Art of Starving. 2017. 384p. (YA). (gr. 8). 17.99 ***(978-0-06-245671-7(7)**, HarperTeen) HarperCollins Pubs.

Moskowitz, Hannah. Gone, Gone, Gone. 2012. (ENG., Illus.). 288p. (YA). (gr. 9). 16.99 *(978-1-4424-5312-8(5))*; pap. 9.99 *(978-1-4424-0753-4(0))* Simon Pulse. (Simon Pulse).

Mulhall, MB. Heavyweight. 2016. (ENG., Illus.). (J). 24.99 ***(978-1-63533-026-7(2))*** 2014. 230p. pap. 14.99 *(978-1-62798-712-7(6))* Dreamspinner Pr. (Harmony Ink Pr.).

Murphy, Julie. Ramona Blue. (YA). (gr. 8). 2018. (ENG.). 448p. pap. 9.99 ***(978-0-06-241836-4(X))*** 2017. 432p. 17.99 *(978-0-06-241835-7(1))* HarperCollins Pubs.

Myracle, Lauren. Kissing Kate. 2007. (ENG.). 208p. (YA). (gr. 7-18). 7.99 *(978-0-14-240869-8(7)*, Speak) Penguin Young Readers Group.

Nelson, Jandy. I'll Give You the Sun. 2015. (CHI.). 384p. (YA). (gr. 9). pap. *(978-986-359-180-1(7))* Ecus Publishing Hse.

—I'll Give You the Sun. 2014. (ENG.). 384p. (YA). (gr. 9). 17.99 *(978-0-8037-3496-8(4)*, Dial Bks) Penguin Publishing Group.

—I'll Give You the Sun. 2015. (ENG.). 400p. (YA). (gr. 9-12). pap. 10.99 *(978-0-14-242576-3(1)*, Speak) Penguin Young Readers Group.

—I'll Give You the Sun. 2015. (ENG.). 400p. (YA). (gr. 9). 21.30 *(978-1-68065-512-4(4))* Perfection Learning Corp.

—I'll Give You the Sun. 2015. lib. bdg. 22.10 *(978-0-606-37572-6(4))* Turtleback Bks.

Ness, Patrick. Release. 2017. 288p. (YA). (gr. 9). 17.99 ***(978-0-06-240319-3(2)**, HarperTeen) HarperCollins Pubs.

Newman, Lesléa. Heather Has Two Mommies. Cornell, Laura, illus. 2015. (ENG.). 32p. (J). (gr. -1-2). 16.99 *(978-0-7636-6631-6(9))* Candlewick Pr.

Oelschlager, Vanita. A Tale of Two Daddies. Blackwood, Kristin, illus. 2010. (ENG.). 42p. (J). (gr. -1-3). 15.95 *(978-0-9819714-5-2(8))*; pap. 8.95 *(978-0-9819714-6-9(6))* VanitaBooks.

O'Shea, M.J. Loveblood. 2016. (ENG., Illus.). (J). 27.99 ***(978-1-63533-044-1(0)**, Harmony Ink Pr.) Dreamspinner Pr.

Ostrovski, Emil. Away We Go. 2016. 272p. (YA). (gr. 9). 17.99 *(978-0-06-223855-9(8)*, Greenwillow Bks.) HarperCollins Pubs.

Page, Winter. Breaking Free. 2016. (ENG., Illus.). (J). 24.99 ***(978-1-63477-943-2(6))*** 2014. 180p. pap. 14.99 *(978-1-62798-914-5(5))* Dreamspinner Pr. (Harmony Ink Pr.).

Parker, Madison. Play Me, I'm Yours. 2016. (ENG., Illus.). (J). 24.99 ***(978-1-63533-062-5(9))*** 2013. 244p. pap. 14.99 *(978-1-62380-449-7(3))* Dreamspinner Pr. (Harmony Ink Pr.).

Parker, Madison. Play Me, I'm Yours [Library Edition]. 2013. 244p. pap. 14.99 *(978-1-62380-919-5(3)*, Harmony Ink Pr.) Dreamspinner Pr.

Parkhurst, Johanna. Here's to You, Zeb Pike [Library Edition]. 2014. 180p. pap. 14.99 *(978-1-62798-526-0(3)*, Harmony Ink Pr.) Dreamspinner Pr.

Parkhurst, Johanna. Thanks a Lot, John Leclair. 2016. (Here's to You, Zeb Pike Ser.). (ENG., Illus.). (YA). pap. 14.99 ***(978-1-63477-428-4(0)**, Harmony Ink Pr.) Dreamspinner Pr.

Parkinson, Will. Pitch. 2016. (ENG., Illus.). (J). 24.99 ***(978-1-63533-061-8(0))*** 2013. 190p. pap. 14.99 *(978-1-62798-034-0(2))* Dreamspinner Pr. (Harmony Ink Pr.).

—Wet Paint. 2016. (ENG., Illus.). (J). 24.99 ***(978-1-63477-993-7(2)**, Harmony Ink Pr.) Dreamspinner Pr.

Payne, K. E. Because of Her. 2014. (ENG.). 264p. (J). (gr. 7). pap. 11.95 *(978-1-62639-049-2(5))* Bold Strokes Bks.

—Me@You.com. 2012. (ENG.). 288p. (J). (gr. 7). pap. 13.95 *(978-1-60282-592-5(0))* Bold Strokes Bks.

Pearce, Jackson. As You Wish. (ENG.). 304p. (YA). (gr. 8). 2010. pap. 8.99 *(978-0-06-166154-9(6))* 2009. 16.99 *(978-0-06-166152-5(X))* HarperCollins Pubs. (HarperTeen).

Peck, Dale. Sprout. 2009. (ENG.). 288p. (YA). (gr. 9-12). 16.99 *(978-1-59990-160-2(9)*, 9781599901602, Bloomsbury USA Childrens) Bloomsbury Publishing USA.

Peck, Richard. The Best Man, 5 vols. (ENG.). (J). 2017. 44.95 ***(978-0-525-48687-9(9)**, Puffin Books) 2017. 256p. (gr. 4-7). 8.99 ***(978-0-14-751579-7(3)**, Puffin Books) 2016. 240p. (gr. 4-7). 16.99 *(978-0-8037-3839-3(0)*, Dial Bks) Penguin Young Readers Group.

Penn, Astor. All the Devils Here. 2016. (ENG., Illus.). (YA). (gr. 8-12). 24.99 ***(978-1-63477-933-3(9)**, Harmony Ink Pr.) Dreamspinner Pr.

Peters, Julie Anne. Rage: A Love Story. 2010. (ENG.). 306p. (YA). (gr. 9). pap. 9.99 *(978-0-375-84411-9(2)*, Knopf Bks. for Young Readers) Random Hse. Children's Bks.

Philips, L. Perfect Ten. 2017. (ENG.). 352p. (YA). (gr. 9). 17.99 *(978-0-425-28811-5(0)*, Viking Books for Young Readers) Penguin Young Readers Group.

Pitman, Gayle E. This Day in June. Litten, Kristyna, illus. 2013. (J). *(978-1-4338-1658-1(X))*; pap. *(978-1-4338-1659-8(8))* American Psychological Assn. (Magination Pr.).

Plum-Ucci, Carol. What Happened to Lani Garver. 2004. (ENG.). 336p. (YA). (gr. 9). reprint ed. pap. 9.99 *(978-0-15-205088-7(4))* Houghton Mifflin Harcourt Publishing Co.

Polacco, Patricia. In Our Mothers' House. Polacco, Patricia, illus. 2009. (ENG., Illus.). 48p. (J). (gr. 1-3). 17.99

H I

(978-0-399-25076-7(X), Philomel Bks.) Penguin Young Readers Group.

Quintero, Isabel. Gabi, a Girl in Pieces. 2014. (ENG.). 208p. (J). pap. 11.95 (978-1-935955-95-5(0)); (YA). 17.95 (978-1-935955-94-8(2)) Cinco Puntos Pr.

Ramsey, Jo. Ball Caps & Khakis. 2016. (ENG., Illus.). (YA). 24.99 **(978-1-63477-938-8(X))**; 180p. (J). pap. 14.99 (978-1-63477-034-7(X)) Dreamspinner Pr. (Harmony Ink Pr.).

—Blue Jeans & Sweatshirts. 2016. (ENG., Illus.). (J). 24.99 **(978-1-63477-942-5(8)**, Harmony Ink Pr.) Dreamspinner Pr.

—Shoulder Pads & Flannel. 2016. (ENG., Illus.). (J). 24.99 **(978-1-63533-072-4(6)**, Harmony Ink Pr.) Dreamspinner Pr.

Reed, Emily. Fairy Tales for Modern Queers. (ENG., Illus.). (J). 2016. 24.99 **(978-1-63533-012-0(2))** 2015. 180p. pap. 14.99 (978-1-63216-720-0(4)) Dreamspinner Pr. (Harmony Ink Pr.).

Reed, Emily. Fairy Tales for Modern Queers [Library Edition]. 2015. (ENG., Illus.). 180p. (J). pap. 14.99 (978-1-63216-721-7(2), Harmony Ink Pr.) Dreamspinner Pr.

Regan, Anne, ed. Harmonious Hearts 2016: Stories from the Young Author Challenge. 2016. (Harmonious Hearts Ser.). (ENG., Illus.). (YA). pap. 17.99 **(978-1-63477-834-3(0)**, Harmony Ink Pr.) Dreamspinner Pr.

Reid, Raziel. When Everything Feels Like the Movies. 2015. (ENG., Illus.). 176p. (J). (gr. 6). pap. 15.95 (978-1-55152-574-7(7)) Arsenal Pulp Pr. CAN. Dist: Consortium Bk. Sales & Distribution.

Ricci, Caitlin. Head above Water. 2016. (Robbie & Sam Ser.: Vol. 2). (ENG., Illus.). (YA). pap. 14.99 **(978-1-63477-424-6(8)**, Harmony Ink Pr.) Dreamspinner Pr.

—Weathering the Storm. 2016. (ENG., Illus.). (J). 24.99 **(978-1-63477-992-0(4))** Dreamspinner Pr.

Richardson, Justin & Parnell, Peter. And Tango Makes Three. Cole, Henry, illus. 2005. (ENG.). 32p. (J). (gr. -1-3). 17.99 (978-0-689-87845-9(1), Simon & Schuster Bks. For Young Readers) Simon & Schuster Bks. For Young Readers.

—And Tango Makes Three: 10th Anniversary Edition. Cole, Henry, illus. 10th ed. 2015. (ENG.). 40p. (J). (gr. -1-3). 17.99 (978-1-4814-4884-0(6), Simon & Schuster Bks. For Young Readers) Simon & Schuster Bks. For Young Readers.

Rosas, Marcelino. Afuera: A Young Latino's Journey. 2013. 226p. (YA). pap. 12.99 (978-0-9859437-0-7(X)) Proud Peacock Publishing.

Rudetsky, Seth. The Rise & Fall of a Theater Geek. 2015. (ENG.). 288p. (YA). (gr. 7). pap. 9.99 (978-0-449-81672-1(9), Random Hse. Bks. for Young Readers) Random Hse. Children's Bks.

Rumble. 2014. (ENG., Illus.). 560p. (YA). (gr. 9). 19.99 (978-1-4424-8284-5(2), McElderry, Margaret K. Bks.) McElderry, Margaret K. Bks.

Ryan, Hope. The Geek & His Artist. 2016. (ENG., Illus.). (J). 29.99 **(978-1-63477-965-4(7)**, Harmony Ink Pr.) Dreamspinner Pr.

Ryan, P E. Saints of Augustine. 2007. 308p. (YA). (gr. 7-18). 16.99 (978-0-06-085810-0(9)); lib. bdg. 17.89 (978-0-06-085811-7(7)) HarperCollins Pubs. (HarperTeen).

Ryan, Patrick. Gemini Bites. 2011. (ENG.). 240p. (J). (gr. 7-8). 17.99 (978-0-545-22128-3(5), Scholastic Pr.) Scholastic, Inc.

—In Mike We Trust. 2009. 321p. (J). lib. bdg. 17.89 (978-0-06-085814-8(1), HarperTeen) HarperCollins Pubs.

Ryan, Sara. Empress of the World. 2003. (ENG.). 304p. (YA). (gr. 9-18). 8.99 (978-0-14-250059-0(3), Speak) Penguin Young Readers Group.

Sáenz, Benjamin Alire. Aristotle & Dante Discover the Secrets of the Universe. (ENG., Illus.). 368p. (YA). (gr. 7). 2014. pap. 12.99 (978-1-4424-0893-7(6)) 2012. 21.99 (978-1-4424-0892-0(8)) Simon & Schuster Bks. For Young Readers. (Simon & Schuster Bks. For Young Readers).

Sanchez, Alex. Boyfriends with Girlfriends. (ENG.). 224p. (YA). (gr. 7). 2012. pap. 10.99 (978-1-4169-3775-3(7)) 2011. 16.99 (978-1-4169-3773-9(0)) Simon & Schuster Bks. For Young Readers. (Simon & Schuster Bks. For Young Readers).

—Getting It. Mehta, Sangeeta, ed. 2007. (ENG., Illus.). 240p. (YA). (gr. 7-12). pap. 8.99 (978-1-4169-0898-2(6), Simon & Schuster Bks. For Young Readers) Simon & Schuster Bks. For Young Readers.

—The God Box. Del Rosario, Michael, ed. 2009. (ENG., Illus.). 272p. (YA). (gr. 7). pap. 10.99 (978-1-4169-0900-2(1), Simon & Schuster Bks. For Young Readers) Simon & Schuster Bks. For Young Readers.

—Rainbow Boys. 2003. (ENG., Illus.). 262p. (YA). (gr. 7). pap. 9.99 (978-0-689-85770-6(5), Simon & Schuster Bks. For Young Readers) Simon & Schuster Bks. For Young Readers.

—Rainbow High. 2005. (ENG., Illus.). 266p. (YA). (gr. 7). reprint ed. pap. 11.99 (978-0-689-85478-1(1), Simon & Schuster Bks. For Young Readers) Simon & Schuster Bks. For Young Readers.

—Rainbow Road. 2007. (ENG., Illus.). 266p. (YA). (gr. 7-12). pap. 11.99 (978-1-4169-1191-3(X), Simon & Schuster Bks. For Young Readers) Simon & Schuster Bks. For Young Readers.

—So Hard to Say. Weiss, Jennifer, ed. 2006. (ENG., Illus.). 232p. (YA). (gr. 7-12). reprint ed. pap. 11.99 (978-1-4169-1189-0(8), Simon & Schuster Bks. For Young Readers) Simon & Schuster Bks. For Young Readers.

Sanchez, Alex & Louth, Jack. Rainbow Road. 2005. (ENG., Illus.). 256p. (J). (gr. 7). 16.95 (978-0-689-86565-7(1), Simon & Schuster Bks. For Young Readers) Simon & Schuster Bks. For Young Readers.

Sandberg, Winter. Private Display of Affection [Library Edition]. 2014. 210p. pap. 14.99 (978-1-62798-537-6(9), Harmony Ink Pr.) Dreamspinner Pr.

Sanders, Russell. All You Need Is Love. 2017. 220p. pap. 14.99 **(978-1-63533-321-3(0)**, Harmony Ink Pr.) Dreamspinner Pr.

Schemery, Beau. The Last Blade. 2016. (ENG., Illus.). (J). 32.99 **(978-1-63477-969-2(X))** 2013. 350p. pap. 17.99 (978-1-62380-453-4(1)) Dreamspinner Pr. (Harmony Ink Pr.).

—The 7th of London. 2016. (ENG., Illus.). (J). 32.99 **(978-1-63477-960-9(6)**, Harmony Ink Pr.) Dreamspinner Pr.

Schiffer, Miriam B. Stella Brings the Family. Clifton-Brown, Holly, illus. 2015. (ENG.). 36p. (J). (gr. k-3). 16.99 (978-1-4521-1190-2(1)) Chronicle Bks. LLC.

Schmatz, Pat. Mousetraps. Hauser, Bill, illus. 2008. (ENG.). 192p. (YA). (gr. 7-12). 17.95 (978-0-8225-8657-9(6), Carolrhoda Bks.) Lerner Publishing Group.

Self, Jeffery. Drag Teen. 2016. (ENG.). 272p. (YA). (gr. 9). 17.99 (978-0-545-82993-9(3), PUSH) Scholastic, Inc.

Setterington, Ken. Mom & Mum Are Getting Married!, 1 vol. Priestley, Alice, illus. 2004. (ENG.). 24p. (J). (gr. -1-3). 15.95 (978-1-896764-84-9(3)) Second Story Pr. CAN. Dist: Orca Bk. Pubs. USA.

Sharpe, Tess. Far from You. 2014. (ENG.). 352p. (YA). (gr. 9-17). 17.99 (978-1-4231-8462-1(9)) Hyperion Bks. for Children.

Shraya, Vivek. God Loves Hair. Neufeld, Juliana, illus. 2014. (ENG.). 112p. (gr. 6). pap. 18.95 (978-1-55152-543-3(7), 399) Arsenal Pulp Pr. CAN. Dist: Consortium Bk. Sales & Distribution.

Siegert, Mia. Jerkbait. 2016. (ENG.). 350p. (YA). (gr. 8). pap. 14.99 (978-1-63163-066-8(0), Jolly Fish Pr.) North Star Editions.

Silvera, Adam. More Happy Than Not. (ENG.). (YA). (gr. 9). 2016. 336p. pap. 10.99 (978-1-61695-677-6(1)) 2015. 304p. 18.99 (978-1-61695-560-1(0)) Soho Pr., Inc. (Soho Teen).

Silvera, Adam. They Both Die at the End. 2017. 384p. (YA). (gr. 9). 17.99 **(978-0-06-245779-0(9))** HarperCollins Pubs.

Sloan, Brian. A Really Nice Prom Mess. 2008. (ENG., Illus.). 320p. (YA). (gr. 9-12). pap. 8.99 (978-1-4169-5389-0(2), Simon & Schuster Bks. For Young Readers) Simon & Schuster Bks. For Young Readers.

—Tale of Two Summers. 2014. (ENG., Illus.). 256p. (YA). (gr. 7). pap. 12.99 (978-1-4169-5794-2(4), Simon & Schuster Bks. For Young Readers) Simon & Schuster Bks. For Young Readers.

Sobat, Gail Sidonie. Chance to Dance for You. 2011. (ENG.). 176p. pap. 14.95 (978-1-926531-11-3(6), Great Plains Teen Fiction) Great Plains Pubns. CAN. Dist: Publishers Group Canada.

Sones, Sonya. One of Those Hideous Books Where the Mother Dies. (ENG., (YA). (gr. 7). 2013. Illus.). 288p. pap. 9.99 (978-1-4424-9383-4(6)) 2005. 272p. reprint ed. pap. 7.99 (978-1-4169-0788-6(2)) Simon & Schuster Bks. For Young Readers. (Simon & Schuster Bks. For Young Readers).

St. James, James. Freak Show. 2008. (ENG.). 304p. (YA). (gr. 9-18). 8.99 (978-0-14-241231-2(7), Puffin Bks) Penguin Young Readers Group.

Stein, Brynn. Ray of Sunlight. 2016. (ENG., Illus.). (J). (gr. 7). 24.99 **(978-1-63533-068-7(8)**, Harmony Ink Pr.) Dreamspinner Pr.

Stevens, Tracey. Chalice of the Goddess. Snowden, Susan, ed. Stevens, Tracey, illus. 2004. (Illus.). 313p. (YA). per. 17.95 (978-0-9719628-4-2(7)) Amazing Dreams Publishing.

Stevenson, Robin. Big Guy, 1 vol. 2008. (Orca Soundings Ser.). (ENG.). (YA). (gr. 8-12). 112p. 16.95 (978-1-55143-912-9(3)); 128p. pap. 9.95 (978-1-55143-910-5(7)) Orca Bk. Pubs. USA.

—Inferno, 1 vol. 2009. (ENG.). 240p. (YA). (gr. 7-12). pap. 12.95 (978-1-55469-077-0(3)) Orca Bk. Pubs. USA.

—Under Threat. 2016. (Orca Soundings Ser.). lib. bdg. 20.80 (978-0-606-38702-6(1)) Turtleback Bks.

Stoddard, T. R. Don't Ask, Don't Tell. 2012. 184p. (-18). pap. (978-1-909402-09-6(5)) Vamptasy Publishing.

Sugiura, Misa. It's Not Like It's a Secret. 2017. 400p. (YA). (gr. 8). 17.99 (978-0-06-247341-7(7), HarperTeen) HarperCollins Pubs.

Tamaki, Mariko. Saving Montgomery Sole. 2016. (ENG.). 240p. (YA). 17.99 (978-1-62672-271-2(4), 9781626722712) Roaring Brook Pr.

—Saving Montgomery Sole. 2017. (ENG.). 240p. (YA). pap. 9.99 (978-1-250-10440-3(8), 9781250104403) Square Fish.

Thorne, Jenn Marie. The Inside of Out. 2016. (ENG.). 400p. (YA). (gr. 7). 17.99 (978-0-8037-4058-7(1), Dial Bks) Penguin Young Readers Group.

Thrash, Maggie. Honor Girl. Thrash, Maggie, illus. 2017. (ENG., Illus.). 272p. (YA). (gr. 9). pap. 14.99 (978-0-7636-8755-7(3)) Candlewick Pr.

Topol, Carolyn LeVine. Run for It All. 2016. (ENG., Illus.). (YA). pap. 14.99 **(978-1-63477-065-1(X)**, Harmony Ink Pr.) Dreamspinner Pr.

Tregay, Sarah. Fan Art. DeJesus, Melissa, illus. 2014. (ENG.). 368p. (YA). (gr. 8). 17.99 (978-0-06-224315-7(2), Tegen, Katherine Bks) HarperCollins Pubs.

U'Nique, Mystique Ann. Reg, Dave & Zach. 2013. 24p. pap. 24.95 (978-1-62709-972-1(7)) PublishAmerica, Inc.

Van Rooyen, Suzanne. Obscura Burning. 2nd ed. 2016. (ENG., Illus.). (YA). pap. 14.99 **(978-1-63477-422-2(1)**, Harmony Ink Pr.) Dreamspinner Pr.

Wallace, Kim. Erik & Isabelle Junior Year at Foresthill High. 2006. (Foresthill High Ser.). 227p. (YA). (gr. 9). per. 12.00 (978-0-9755848-2-8(0)) Foglight Pr.

Ward, Kaitlin. Bleeding Earth. 2016. (ENG.). 256p. (YA). 17.99 (978-0-9864484-8-5(6)) Adaptive Studios.

Westerfeld, Scott. Afterworlds. 2014. (ENG., Illus.). 608p. (YA). (gr. 9). 19.99 (978-1-4814-2234-5(0), Simon Pulse) Simon Pulse.

Whaley, John Corey. Highly Illogical Behavior. 2016. (ENG.). 256p. (YA). (gr. 9). 17.99 (978-0-525-42818-3(6), Dial Bks) Penguin Young Readers Group.

—Highly Illogical Behavior. 2017. lib. bdg. 22.10 **(978-0-606-40099-2(0))** Turtleback Bks.

Wheeler, Elizabeth. Asher's Out. 2015. (ENG.). 264p. (J). (gr. 7). pap. 11.95 (978-1-62639-411-7(3)) Bold Strokes Bks.

Wilke, Daria & Schwartz, Marian. Playing a Part. 2015. (ENG.). 176p. (J). (gr. 7). 18.99 (978-0-545-72607-8(7)) Scholastic, Inc.

Williams, Julie. Drama Queens in the House. 2014. (ENG.). 432p. (YA). (gr. 7). 17.99 (978-1-59643-735-7(9), 9781596437357) Roaring Brook Pr.

Wilson, Martin. We Now Return to Regular Life. 2017. (ENG.). 384p. (YA). (gr. 9). 17.99 **(978-0-7352-2782-8(9)**, Dial Bks) Penguin Young Readers Group.

Wilson, Martin. What They Always Tell Us. 2010. (ENG.). 304p. (YA). (gr. 9). pap. 8.99 (978-0-385-73508-7(1), Delacorte Bks. for Young Readers) Random Hse. Children's Bks.

Wittlinger, Ellen. Love & Lies: Marisol's Story. (ENG.). (YA). 2009. 272p. (gr. 7). pap. 8.99 (978-1-4169-7914-2(X)) 2008. 256p. (gr. 9-18). 16.99 (978-1-4169-1623-9(7)) Simon & Schuster Bks. For Young Readers. (Simon & Schuster Bks. For Young Readers).

Woodson, Jacqueline. From the Notebooks of Melanin Sun. 2011. 9.68 (978-0-7848-3512-8(8)) 2009. 7.84 (978-0-7848-2356-9(1)) Marco Bk. Co. (Everbind).

—From the Notebooks of Melanin Sun. 2010. (ENG.). 176p. (J). (gr. 5-18). 7.99 (978-0-14-241641-9(X), Puffin Books) Penguin Young Readers Group.

—From the Notebooks of Melanin Sun. 2003. (Point Ser.). (ENG.). 141p. (YA). (gr. 7). 13.65 (978-0-7807-7292-2(X)) Perfection Learning Corp.

—The House You Pass on the Way. 2010. (ENG.). 160p. (YA). (gr. 7-18). 8.99 (978-0-14-241706-5(8), Puffin Books) Penguin Young Readers Group.

Wright, Bil. Putting Makeup on the Fat Boy. (ENG., 240p. (YA). (gr. 7). 2012. Illus.). pap. 9.99 (978-1-4169-4004-3(9)) 2011. 16.99 (978-1-4169-3996-2(2)) Simon & Schuster Bks. For Young Readers. (Simon & Schuster Bks. For Young Readers).

X, Sulayman & Sulayman, X. Tears of a Dragon. 2nd ed. 2016. (ENG., Illus.). (J). 29.99 **(978-1-63533-079-3(3)**, Harmony Ink Pr.) Dreamspinner Pr.

Zubro, Mark. Gentle. 2016. (ENG., Illus.). (YA). pap. 14.99 **(978-1-944770-29-7(1))** MLR Pr., LLC.

HONDURAS

Dendinger, Roger E. & Gritzner, Charles F. Honduras. 2nd rev. ed. 2011. (Modern World Nations Ser.). 112p. (gr. 6-12). 35.00 (978-1-61753-046-3(8), Chelsea Hse.) Facts On File, Inc.

Nazario, Sonia. La Travesía de Enrique. 2015. (ENG & SPA.). 304p. (YA). (gr. 7). pap. 9.99 (978-0-553-53554-9(4), Ember) Random Hse. Children's Bks.

Shields, Charles J. Honduras. 2010. (Central America Today Ser.). 63p. (YA). (gr. 7-18). pap. 9.95 (978-1-4222-0716-1(1)); (Illus.). (gr. 9-12). 21.95 (978-1-4222-0649-2(1)) Mason Crest.

—Honduras, Vol. 8. Henderson, James D., ed. 2015. (Discovering Central America: History, Politics, & Culture Ser.). (Illus.). 64p. (J). (gr. 7). lib. bdg. 22.95 (978-1-4222-3290-3(5)) Mason Crest.

Sjonger, Rebecca. Cultural Traditions in Honduras. 2017. 32p. (J). **(978-0-7787-8096-0(1))** Crabtree Publishing Co.

Zuchora-Walske, Christine. Honduras in Pictures. 2009. (Visual Geography Series, Second Ser.). (ENG.). 80p. (gr. 5-12). 31.93 (978-1-57505-960-0(6)) Lerner Publishing Group.

Zwiren, Shira. Honduras. 2016. (Countries We Come From Ser.). (ENG.). 32p. (J). (gr. -1-3). lib. bdg. 19.95 (978-1-944102-70-8(1)) Bearport Publishing Co., Inc.

HONESTY

see also Truthfulness and Falsehood

Aloian, Molly. Live It: Honesty. 2009. (Crabtree Character Sketches Ser.). (ENG., Illus.). 32p. (J). (gr. 3-6). pap. (978-0-7787-4914-1(2)); lib. bdg. (978-0-7787-4881-6(2)) Crabtree Publishing Co.

Amoroso, Cynthia. Honesty. 2013. (Values to Live By Ser.). (ENG.). 24p. (J). (gr. -1-2). 25.64 (978-1-62323-520-8(0), 206291) Child's World, Inc., The.

Amos, Janine & Spenceley, Annabel. Let's Own Up. 2009. (Best Behavior Ser.). (Illus.). 32p. (J). (gr. -1-2). 22.60 (978-1-60754-503-3(9)); pap. 10.55 (978-1-60754-505-7(5)) Windmill Bks.

Andersen, Jill. Honesty Is an Important Value in Our Family. 2016. (Rosen REAL Readers: Social Studies Nonfiction / Fiction: Family, Community, & the World Ser.). 12p. (gr. 1-k). pap. 6.33 (978-1-5081-2326-2(8), Rosen Classroom) Rosen Publishing Group, Inc., The.

Barraclough, Sue. Honestidad, 1 vol. 2010. (Explorar el Civismo Ser.). (SPA.). 32p. (gr. 1-3). 27.32 (978-1-4329-4458-2(4)); pap. 8.29 (978-1-4329-4466-7(5)) Heinemann-Raintree.

—Honesty. 2016. (Exploring Citizenship Ser.). (ENG.). 32p. pap. 8.29 (978-1-4846-3994-8(4), Heinemann First Library) Heinemann-Raintree.

Berry, Joy. Help Me Be Good about Cheating. 2009. (Help Me Be Good Ser.). 32p. pap. 7.95 (978-1-60577-123-6(6)) Berry, Joy Enterprises.

Berry, Joy Wilt. A Book about Cheating. 2005. (Illus.). (J). (978-0-7172-8583-9(9)) Scholastic, Inc.

—A Book about Lying. 2005. (Illus.). (J). (978-0-7172-8576-1(6)) Scholastic, Inc.

Braun, Eric. Fatal Faults: The Story of the Challenger Explosion. 2015. (Tangled History Ser.). (ENG., Illus.). 112p. (gr. 3-4). lib. bdg. 31.99 (978-1-4914-7077-0(1)) Capstone Press of Coughlan Cos.

Burch, Regina G. & Donovan Guntly, Jenette. I Can Tell the Truth. Motoyama, Keiko, illus. 2004. (Doing the Right Thing Ser.). 16p. (J). (gr. -1-2). lib. bdg. 20.00 (978-0-8368-4249-4(9), Gareth Stevens Learning Library) Stevens, Gareth Publishing LLLP.

Character Ed Says Honesty Counts. 2006. (J). 4.95 (978-1-55548-057-8(8), 678) Human Relations Media.

Currie, Stephen. Cheating. 2007. (Ripped from the Headlines Ser.). (YA). (gr. 7-12). 23.95 (978-1-60217-011-7(8)) Erickson Pr.

Donaghey, Reese. Telling the Truth. 2015. (Illus.). 23p. (J). lib. bdg. (978-1-4824-1730-2(8)) Stevens, Gareth Publishing LLLP.

Donahue, Jill Lynn. Ser Honesto. Previn, Stacey, illus. 2011. (¡Así Debemos Ser!/Way to Be! Ser.).Tr. of Being Honest. (ENG, SPA & MUL.). 24p. (gr. -1-2). lib. bdg. 26.65 (978-1-4048-6689-8(2)) Picture Window Bks.

Doudna, Kelly. Honestly!, 1 vol. Craig, Diane, ed. 2007. (Character Concepts Ser.). (ENG., Illus.). 24p. (J). (gr. k-3). lib. bdg. 24.21 (978-1-59928-735-5(8), SandCastle) ABDO Publishing Co.

Eason, Sarah. Come Clean, Carlos: Tell the Truth. 2013. (You Choose Ser.). (Illus.). 32p. (J). lib. bdg. 23.94 (978-0-7660-4306-0(1), Enslow Elementary) Enslow Pubs., Inc.

—Hand It over, Harry: Don't Steal. 2013. (You Choose Ser.). (Illus.). 32p. (J). 23.94 (978-0-7660-4308-4(8), Enslow Elementary) Enslow Pubs., Inc.

Erroll, Mark. I Am Honest. 2011. (Kids of Character Ser.). (Illus.). 24p. (J). (gr. 1-3). pap. 8.15 (978-1-4339-4863-3(X)); lib. bdg. 22.60 (978-1-4339-4862-6(1)) Stevens, Gareth Publishing LLLP.

—I Am Honest / Soy Honesto. 2011. (Kids of Character / Chicos con carácter Ser.). (ENG & SPA., Illus.). 24p. (J). (gr. -1-2). 22.60 (978-1-4339-4866-4(4)) Stevens, Gareth Publishing LLLP.

Gordon, Sharon. Decimos la Verdad. 2006. (Bookworms Ser.). (SPA & ENG., Illus.). 24p. (gr. k-1). lib. bdg. 15.95 (978-0-7614-2362-1(1), Benchmark Bks.) Marshall Cavendish Corp.

—We Tell the Truth. (J). 2007. pap. 6.99 (978-0-7614-3277-7(9)) 2005. (ENG & SPA., Illus.). 24p. (gr. 3-7). lib. bdg. 22.79 (978-0-7614-1996-9(9), Benchmark Bks.) Marshall Cavendish Corp.

—We Tell the Truth/Decimos la Verdad. 2006. (Bookworms Ser.). (ENG & SPA., Illus.). 24p. (gr. k-1). lib. bdg. 15.95 (978-0-7614-2442-0(3)) Marshall Cavendish Corp.

Greve, Meg. Integrity. 2012. (ENG.). 24p. (gr. k-2). pap. 8.95 (978-1-61810-270-6(2)) Rourke Educational Media.

Hicks, Kelli L. Honesty. 2012. (ENG., Illus.). 24p. (gr. k-2). pap. 8.95 (978-1-61810-265-2(6)) Rourke Educational Media.

Kiesbye, Stefan. Cheating. 2010. (Social Issues Firsthand Ser.). (ENG.). 192p. (gr. 10-12). 38.30 (978-0-7377-5009-6(X), Greenhaven Pr., Inc.) Cengage Gale.

[Kurtz] Character Education Set 2. 2010. (Character Education Ser.). pap. 41.70 (978-1-4296-5040-3(0), Bridgestone Bks.) Capstone Press of Coughlan Cos.

Larsen, Carolyn. Playing Fair: A Book about Cheating. O'Connor, Tim, illus. 2016. (Growing God's Kids Ser.). (ENG.). 32p. (J). pap. 4.99 (978-0-8010-0943-3(X)) Baker Bks.

Manolis, Kay & Leslie, Tonya. Abraham Lincoln: A Life of Honesty. 2007. (People of Character Ser.). (ENG., Illus.). 24p. (J). (gr. 2-5). lib. bdg. 25.95 (978-1-60014-091-4(2)) Bellwether Media.

Marshall, Shelley. Molly the Great Tells the Truth: A Book about Honesty. Mahan, Ben, illus. 2010. (Character Education with Super Ben & Molly the Great Ser.). 24p. (J). 22.60 (978-0-7660-3520-1(4)); pap. 7.95 (978-0-7660-3745-8(2), Enslow Elementary) Enslow Pubs., Inc.

Martineau, Susan & Jinny, Johnson. What's It Like to Be... Grasshopper? Sanzi, Desiderio, illus. 2011. (What's It Like to Be... ? Ser.). 24p. (J). (gr. -1-k). 25.65 (978-1-60753-193-7(3)) Amicus Publishing.

Mayer, Cassie. Being Honest, 1 vol. Beech, Mark, illus. 2007. (Citizenship Ser.). (ENG.). 24p. (gr. -1-3). pap. 6.29 (978-1-4034-9492-4(4), Acorn) Heinemann-Raintree.

—Ser Honesto, 1 vol. 2007. (Civismo Ser.). (SPA., Illus.). 24p. (gr. -1-1). pap. 6.29 (978-1-4329-0406-7(X), Bellota) Heinemann-Raintree.

Mead, David. Little Abe Lincoln Learns a Lesson in Honesty: Honesty. Sharp, Chris, illus. 2003. (American Virtues for Kids Ser.). (J). bds. 6.95 (978-0-9746440-0-4(5), Ideal Pubns.) Worthy Publishing.

Meiners, Cheri J. Be Honest & Tell the Truth. Johnson, Meredith, illus. 2007. (Learning to Get Along(r) Ser.). (ENG.). 40p. (gr. -1-3). pap. 10.95 (978-1-57542-258-9(1)) Free Spirit Publishing, Inc.

Parks, Peggy J. Teens & Cheating. 2015. (ENG., Illus.). 96p. (J). lib. bdg. (978-1-60152-766-0(7)) ReferencePoint Pr., Inc.

Ponto, Joanna. Being Honest. 2015. (J). (978-0-7660-6633-5(9)) Enslow Pubs., Inc.

Pryor, Kimberley Jane. Honesty. 2008. (Values Ser.). 32p. (gr. 1-2). lib. bdg. 18.56 (978-0-7614-3125-1(X), Benchmark Bks.) Marshall Cavendish Corp.

—Integrity. 2010. (Values 2 Ser.). 32p. (gr. 1). 18.56 (978-1-60870-145-2(X)) Marshall Cavendish GBR. Dist: Marshall Cavendish Corp.

Rissman, Rebecca. Excuses, Excuses!, 1 vol. Plage, Stella, illus. 2013. (Excuses, Excuses! Ser.). (ENG.). 24p. (gr. -1-k). pap. 9.95 (978-1-4329-7669-9(9), NA-h) Heinemann-Raintree.

Rondina, Catherine. Lying: Deal with It Straight Up, 1 vol. Workman, Dan, illus. 2006. (Lorimer Deal with It Ser.). (ENG.). 32p. (J). (gr. 4-6). pap. 12.95 (978-1-55028-906-0(3), 9781550289060) Lorimer, James & Co., Ltd., Pubs. CAN. Dist: Casemate Pubs. & Bk. Distributors, LLC.

Rosenthal, Beth. Cheating. 2007. (Introducing Issues with Opposing Viewpoints Ser.). (Illus.). 141p. (YA). (gr. 7-12). lib. bdg. 36.95 (978-0-7377-3802-5(2)) Cengage Gale.

Salzmann, Mary Elizabeth. I Am Honest. 2003. (Building Character Ser.). (ENG., Illus.). 24p. (J). (gr. k-3). lib. bdg. 24.21 (978-1-57765-828-3(0), SandCastle) ABDO Publishing Co.

Szumski, Bonnie. Cheating. rev. ed. 2014. (Matters of Opinion Ser.). (ENG.). 64p. (J). (gr. 4-6). pap. 14.60 (978-1-60357-585-0(5)); lib. bdg. 27.93 (978-1-59953-605-7(6)) Norwood Hse. Pr.

Walker, Robert. Live It: Integrity. 2009. (ENG., Illus.). 32p. (J). (gr. 3-6). lib. bdg. (978-0-7787-4886-1(3)) Crabtree Publishing Co.

Welbourn, Shannon. Step Forward with Integrity. 2016. (Step Forward! Ser.). (ENG., Illus.). 24p. (J). (gr. 2-5). (978-0-7787-2788-0(2)) Crabtree Publishing Co.

Wilmore, Kathy. Muhammad Ali: With a Discussion of Honesty. 2003. (Values in Action Ser.). (J). (978-1-59203-065-1(3)) Learning Challenge, Inc.

Wittrock, Jeni. How Honest Are You?, 1 vol. 2011. (Friendship Quizzes Ser.). (ENG.). 32p. (gr. 3-4). lib. bdg. 27.99 (978-1-4296-6542-1(4), Snap Bks.) Capstone Press of Coughlan Cos.

HONESTY—FICTION

Abdulaya, Lina. Once upon a Time in Oromiy: Sheekko Sheekoo. 2011. 52p. pap. 22.28 (978-1-4567-6540-8(X)) AuthorHouse.

Abercrombie, Barbara. The Show-and-Tell Lion. Cravath, Lynne Avril & Avril, Lynne, illus. 2006. (ENG.). 32p. (J). (gr. -1-2). 17.99 (978-0-689-86408-7(6), McElderry, Margaret K. Bks.) McElderry, Margaret K. Bks.

Alger, Horatio. Five Hundred Dollars: Or: Jacob Marlowe's Secret. 2007. (ENG.). 192p. per. 19.99 (978-1-4346-5063-4(4)); 206p. per. 22.99 (978-1-4346-5064-1(2)) Creative Media Partners, LLC.

Amato, Mary. The Naked Mole-Rat Letters. (ENG., Illus.). 208p. (J). 2007. (gr. 4-7). pap. 7.99 (978-0-8234-2098-8(1)) 2005. 16.95 (978-0-8234-1927-2(4)) Holiday Hse., Inc.

Anne, Heather. Purple People. 2008. 28p. per. 24.95 (978-1-4241-8458-3(4)) America Star Bks.

Atchison, David C. The Adventures of Black Bart: Dry Bones. 2008. 84p. pap. 7.94 *(978-0-615-20238-9(1))* Black Bart Bks.

Barnholdt, Lauren. Aces Up. 2010. (ENG.). 288p. (YA). (gr. 7). pap. 9.99 *(978-0-385-73874-3(9)*, Ember) Random Hse. Children's Bks.

—Devon Delaney Should Totally Know Better. 2009. (Mix Ser.). (ENG.). 288p. (J). (gr. 4-8). pap. 6.99 *(978-1-4169-8019-3(9)*, Aladdin) Simon & Schuster Children's Publishing.

Basye, Dale E. Fibble. Dob, Bob, illus. 2012. (Heck Ser.). (ENG.). 384p. (J). (gr. 4-7). pap. 6.99 *(978-0-375-85679-2(X)*, Yearling) Random Hse. Children's Bks.

Berger, Joe. The Pudding Problem. Berger, Joe, illus. 2017. (Lyttle Lies Ser.: 1). (ENG., Illus.). 240p. (J). (gr. 3-7). 13.99 ***(978-1-4814-7083-4(3)***, McElderry, Margaret K. Bks.) McElderry, Margaret K. Bks.

Bowen, Fred. Touchdown Trouble, 1 vol. 2009. (Fred Bowen Sports Story Ser.). (ENG.). 128p. (J). (gr. 2-7). pap. 5.95 *(978-1-56145-497-6(4))* Peachtree Pubs.

—Winners Take All, 1 vol. 2009. (All-Star Sports Story Ser.). (ENG., Illus.). 112p. (J). pap. 5.95 *(978-1-56145-512-6(1))* Peachtree Pubs.

Breathed, Berkeley. Edwurd Fudwupper Fibbed Big. Breathed, Berkeley, illus. 2003. (ENG., Illus.). 40p. (J). (gr. 1-4). pap. 8.00 *(978-0-316-14425-4(8))* Little, Brown Bks. for Young Readers.

Brightwood, Laura, illus. The Woodsman & His Ax. Brightwood, Laura, . 2007. (J). DVD *(978-1-934409-07-7(3))* 3-C Institute for Social Development.

Brisson, Pat. The Summer My Father Was Ten. Shine, Andrea, illus. 2014. 32p. pap. 8.00 *(978-1-61003-366-4(3))* Center for the Collaborative Classroom.

Brown, Marc. Arthur's Classroom Fib. 2007. (Arthur Step into Reading Ser.). lib. bdg. 13.55 *(978-1-4177-7281-0(6)*, Turtleback) Turtleback Bks.

Bulion, Leslie. Uncharted Waters, 1 vol. (ENG.). 192p. (J). (gr. 3-7). 2009. pap. 7.95 *(978-1-56145-485-3(0))* 2006. 14.95 *(978-1-56145-365-8(X))* Peachtree Pubs.

Cabot, Meg. Pants on Fire. (YA). 2008. (ENG.). 288p. (gr. 8). pap. 9.99 *(978-0-06-088017-0(1))* 2007. (ENG.). 272p. (gr. 7-10). 16.99 *(978-0-06-088015-6(5))* 2007. 260p. (gr. 7-10). lib. bdg. 17.89 *(978-0-06-088016-3(3))* HarperCollins Pubs. (HarperTeen).

Caplan, Frank A. The Donkey Who Lost His Tail. 2010. (Illus.). 20p. 12.49 *(978-1-4520-2778-4(1))* AuthorHouse.

Carlson, Nancy. Harriet & the Garden. 2nd rev. ed. 2004. (ENG., Illus.). 32p. (J). (gr. k-2). pap. 6.95 *(978-1-57505-612-8(7))* Lerner Publishing Group.

Carlson, Nancy, tr. & illus. Harriet & the Garden. Carlson, Nancy, illus. 2nd rev. ed. 2005. (Nancy Carlson's Neighborhood Ser.). 32p. (gr. k-2). 15.95 *(978-1-57505-710-1(7))* Lerner Publishing Group.

Carty, Amy. The Little Girl Who Lied: The Importance of Honesty. Williams, Nancy E., ed. Gau Family Studio, illus. 2013. 40p. (J). pap. 16.98 *(978-1-938526-69-5(4))* Laurus Bks.

Choldenko, Gennifer. Notes from a Liar & Her Dog. 2003. (ENG.). 240p. (J). (gr. 3-7). pap. 7.99 *(978-0-14-250068-2(2)*, Puffin Books) Penguin Young Readers Group.

—Notes from a Liar & Her Dog. 2004. 224p. (J). (gr. 4-7). pap. 38.00 incl. audio *(978-0-8072-2097-9(3)*, Listening Library) Random Hse. Audio Publishing Group.

Clark, Kent & Snider, Brandon T. Peter Powers & the League of Lying Lizards! Bardin, Dave, illus. 2017. (Peter Powers Ser.: 4). (ENG.). 128p. (J). (gr. 1-5). 15.99 ***(978-0-316-54640-9(2))*** Little, Brown Bks. for Young Readers.

Cocca-Leffler, Maryann. Princess Kim & Too Much Truth. 2012. (J). 34.28 *(978-1-61913-121-7(8))* Weigl Pubs., Inc.

—Princess Kim & Too Much Truth. Cocca-Leffler, Maryann, illus. 2011. (ENG., Illus.). 32p. (J). (gr. 1-3). 16.99 *(978-0-8075-6618-3(7))* Whitman, Albert & Co.

Cole, Kathryn. Fifteen Dollars & Thirty-Five Cents: A Story about Choices, 1 vol. Leng, Qin, illus. 2015. (I'm a Great Little Kid Ser.). (ENG.). 24p. (J). (gr. 1-3). 15.95 *(978-1-927583-82-1(9))* Second Story Pr. CAN. Dist: Orca Bk. Pubs. USA.

Cook, Julia. Well, I Can Top That! Dufalla, Anita, illus. 2014. (ENG.). 32p. (J). pap. 10.95 *(978-1-934490-57-0(1))* Boys Town Pr.

Cosgrove, Stephen. Flynn "Flea" Flicker: Sticking to the Truth. Arroyo, Fian, illus. 2004. (J). *(978-1-58804-353-5(3))* P C I Education.

Costello, Judi. Gertrude & the Creature. Bouthyette, Valerie, illus. 2008. 28p. pap. 24.95 *(978-1-60672-737-9(0))* America Star Bks.

Coville, Bruce. The Skull of Truth: A Magic Shop Book. Lippincott, Gary A., illus. 2007. (Magic Shop Book Ser.: 4). (ENG.). 208p. (J). (gr. 5-7). pap. 7.99 *(978-0-15-206084-8(7))* Houghton Mifflin Harcourt Publishing Co.

Dee, Barbara. Truth or Dare. (ENG.). (J). (gr. 4-8). 2017. 272p. pap. 7.99 ***(978-1-4814-5969-3(4))*** 2016. (Illus.). 256p. 16.99 *(978-1-4814-5968-6(6))* Simon & Schuster Children's Publishing. (Aladdin).

Defosse, Rosana Curiel. Santiago & the Fox of Hatsune. Barradas, Leticia, illus. (SPA.). 32p. (J). (gr. 3-5). pap. 7.95 *(978-970-29-0134-1(0))* Santillana USA Publishing Co., Inc.

Demi. The Empty Pot. Demi, illus. 2007. (ENG., Illus.). 32p. (J). (gr. -1-3). pap. 25.99 *(978-0-8050-8227-2(1)*, 9780805082272, Holt, Henry & Co. Bks. For Young Readers) Holt, Henry & Co.

Denman, K. L. Agent Angus, 1 vol. 2012. (Orca Currents Ser.). (ENG.). 128p. (J). (gr. 5-9). 16.95 *(978-1-4598-0104-2(0))*; pap. 9.95 *(978-1-4598-0103-5(2))* Orca Bk. Pubs. USA.

Dickens, Charles. Oliver Twist: With a Discussion of Honesty. 2003. (Values in Action Illustrated Classics Ser.). (J). *(978-1-59203-051-4(3))* Learning Challenge, Inc.

Diggle, David Mark. Melanie: Honestly Finds Herself Out of Her Depth. Diggle, Daniel James, illus. 2011. 24p. (J). pap. *(978-0-9871657-1-8(2))* Diggle de Doo Productions Pty, Ltd.

Dubose, Sarah. Uncharted Waters. 2013. 440p. pap. *(978-1-4596-6282-7(2))* ReadHowYouWant.com, Ltd.

Dungy, Tony & Dungy, Lauren. Here Comes the Parade! Newton, Vanessa Brantley, illus. 2014. (Tony & Lauren Dungy Ready-To-Reads Ser.). (ENG.). 32p. (J). (gr. k-2). pap. 3.99 *(978-1-4424-5469-9(5)*, Simon Spotlight) Simon Spotlight.

—The Missing Cupcake Mystery. Newton, Vanessa Brantley, illus. 2013. (Tony & Lauren Dungy Ready-To-Reads Ser.). (ENG.). 32p. (J). (gr. k-2). 16.99 *(978-1-4424-5464-4(4))*; pap. 3.99 *(978-1-4424-5463-7(6))* Simon Spotlight. (Simon Spotlight).

—The Missing Cupcake Mystery. 2013. (Simon & Schuster Ready-To-Read Level 2 Ser.). lib. bdg. 13.55 *(978-0-606-27055-7(8)*, Turtleback) Turtleback Bks.

Earnhardt, Donna W. & Castellani, Andrea. Being Frank. 2012. (ENG., Illus.). 32p. (J). (gr. k-2). 16.95 *(978-1-936261-19-2(7))* Flashlight Pr.

Easton, Tom. Pirates Can Be Honest, 01 vols., 1. 2016. (Pirate Pals Ser.). (ENG.). 32p. (J). pap. 10.00 *(978-1-5081-9141-4(7)*, Windmill Bks.) Rosen Publishing Group, Inc., The.

Elias, Megan J. Stir It Up: Home Economics in American Culture. 2010. (ENG., Illus.). 240p. (C). pap. 22.50 *(978-0-8122-2121-3(4))* Univ. of Pennsylvania Pr.

Farrell, Darren. Doug-Dennis & the Flyaway Fib. 2010. (ENG.). 40p. (J). (gr. k-3). 16.99 *(978-0-8037-3437-1(9)*, Dial Bks) Penguin Young Readers Group.

Feldkamp, Jim And Cate. The Adventures of Tommy & Clara on Mount Catherine. 2008. 32p. pap. 14.49 *(978-1-4389-1366-7(4))* AuthorHouse.

Fields, Jan. Meri Mercer Doesn't Lie, Mostly, 1 vol. 2014. (Meri's Mirror Ser.). (ENG., Illus.). 80p. (J). (gr. 2-5). lib. bdg. 27.07 *(978-1-62402-009-4(7)*, Calico Chapter Bks) Magic Wagon.

Fletcher, Ralph. Spider Boy. 2009. (ENG.). 192p. (J). (gr. 5-7). pap. 6.99 *(978-0-547-24820-2(2))* Houghton Mifflin Harcourt Publishing Co.

Foreman, Michael. Norman's Ark. Foreman, Michael, illus. 2006. (Tiger Tales Ser.). (Illus.). 24p. (J). (gr. -1-3). pap. 6.95 *(978-1-58925-401-5(5))* Tiger Tales.

Franklin, Jo. I'm an Alien & I Want to Go Home. Kelley, Marty, illus. 2015. (ENG.). 192p. (J). (gr. 5-7). 16.99 *(978-0-544-44295-5(4))* Houghton Mifflin Harcourt Publishing Co.

—I'M an Alien & I Want to Go Home! Kelley, Marty, illus. 2017. (ENG.). 192p. (J). (gr. 5-7). pap. 6.99 *(978-0-544-93824-3(0)*, HMH Books For Young Readers) Houghton Mifflin Harcourt Publishing Co.

Friedman, Laurie. Honestly, Mallory! 2009. pap. 34.95 *(978-0-7613-4788-0(7))* Lerner Publishing Group.

—Honestly, Mallory! Pollak, Barbara, illus. (Mallory Ser.: 8). (ENG.). 160p. (J). (gr. 2-5). 2008. pap. 5.95 *(978-1-58013-840-6(3)*, First Avenue Editions) 2007. 15.95 *(978-0-8225-6193-4(X)*, Carolrhoda Bks.) Lerner Publishing Group.

Gantos, Jack. Practice Makes Perfect for Rotten Ralph. Rubel, Nicole, illus. 2009. (Rotten Ralph Rotten Readers Ser.: 2). (ENG.). 48p. (J). (gr. 1-3). pap. 8.99 *(978-0-374-40002-6(4)*, 9780374400026) Square Fish.

Gemmen, Heather. But It's True. Lagares, Luciano, illus. 2004. (Tough Stuff for Kids Ser.). 36p. (J). (gr. 4-7). pap., pap. 5.99 *(978-0-7814-4033-2(5)*, 0781440335) Cook, David C.

Gewirtz, Adina Rishe. Zebra Forest. (ENG., 208p. (J). (gr. 4-7). 2014. Illus.). pap. 7.99 *(978-0-7636-7166-2(5))* 2013. 15.99 *(978-0-7636-6041-3(8))* Candlewick Pr.

Giff, Patricia Reilly. The Big Whopper. Bright, Alasdair, illus. 2010. (Zigzag Kids Ser.). (ENG.). 80p. (J). (gr. 1-4). pap. 4.99 *(978-0-553-49469-3(4)*, Yearling) Random Hse. Children's Bks.

Greene, Stephanie. Owen Foote, Super Spy. Weston, Martha, illus. 2005. (ENG.). 96p. (J). (gr. 1-4). pap. 8.95 *(978-0-618-55159-0(X))* Houghton Mifflin Harcourt Publishing Co.

Gunderson, Jessica. I Broke into Gymnastics Camp, 1 vol. Santillan, Jorge H., illus. 2012. (Sports Illustrated Kids Victory School Superstars Ser.). (ENG.). 56p. (gr. 1-3). pap. 5.95 *(978-1-4342-3869-6(5))*; lib. bdg. 26.65 *(978-1-4342-2245-9(4))* Stone Arch Bks.

Hale, Bruce. Trouble Is My Beeswax. 2004. (Chet Gecko Mystery Ser.). (Illus.). 111p. (gr. 3-7). 16.00 *(978-0-7569-3488-0(5))* Perfection Learning Corp.

Hall, Kirsten. Little Lies: All about Math. Luedecke, Bev, illus. 2003. (Beastieville Ser.). 32p. (J). 19.50 *(978-0-516-22896-9(X)*, Children's Pr.) Scholastic Library Publishing.

Hall, Martha Gamble. A Note from Sant. 2008. 16p. pap. 10.99 *(978-1-4389-2308-6(2))* AuthorHouse.

Hallinan, P. K. Let's Be Honest. (ENG., Illus.). 24p. (J). 2008. (gr. -1-3). lib. bdg. 8.99 *(978-0-8249-5580-9(3))* 2003. bds. 8.75 *(978-0-8249-5478-9(5))* Worthy Publishing. (Ideal Pubns.).

Hamilton, Elizabeth L. Jeremy Rabbit's Honesty Pie. 2003. (Character Critters Ser.: No. 2). (Illus.). 32p. (J). (gr. -1-3). per. 5.95 *(978-0-9713749-5-9(3)*, Character-in-Action) Quiet Impact, Inc.

Hamilton, Tim. The Big Fib. Hamilton, Tim, illus. (I Like to Read(r) Ser.). (ENG., Illus.). 24p. (J). (gr. -1-3). 2015. 6.99 *(978-0-8234-3312-4(9))* 2014. 14.95 *(978-0-8234-2939-4(3))* Holiday Hse., Inc.

Hardie, Jill. The Sparkle Egg. Kornacki, Christine, illus. 2014. 32p. (J). 16.99 *(978-0-8249-5664-6(8)*, Ideal Pubns.) Worthy Publishing.

Harper, Charise Mericle. Just Grace & the Super Sleepover. 2014. (Just Grace Ser.: 11). (ENG., Illus.). 208p. (J). (gr. 1-4). 15.99 *(978-0-544-04584-2(X))* Houghton Mifflin Harcourt Publishing Co.

Harris, Amber. Wisteria Jane. Hoyt, Ard, illus. 2015. (Wisteria Jane Book Ser.). (ENG.). 32p. (J). (gr. -1-3). 16.95 *(978-1-60554-411-3(6))* Redleaf Pr.

Hayes, Joe. Juan Verdades - El Hombre Que No Sabía Mentir. Fiedler, Joseph Daniel, illus. 2011.Tr. of Juan Verdades/The Man Who Couldn't Tell a Lie. (SPA & ENG.). 32p. (J). (gr. 3-6). pap. 8.95 *(978-1-933693-70-5(3))* Cinco Puntos Pr.

Hershey, Mary. My Big Sister Is So Bossy She Says You Can't Read This Book. 2006. (ENG., Illus.). 176p. (J). (gr. 3-7). per. 6.99 *(978-0-553-48797-8(3)*, Yearling) Random Hse. Children's Bks.

Holmes, Andy. Tipper Tells a Lie, 1 vol. de Giorgi, Sergio, illus. 2014. (ENG.). 22p. (J). bds. 9.99 *(978-0-529-11213-2(2))* Nelson, Thomas Inc.

Holub, Joan. Don't Get Lost, Odysseus! Patricelli, Leslie, illus. 2016. (Mini Myths Ser.). (ENG.). 24p. (J). (gr. -1 — 1). bds. 6.95 *(978-1-4197-1897-7(5)*, Abrams Appleseed) Abrams, Inc.

—Good Job, Athena! Patricelli, Leslie, illus. 2016. (Mini Myths Ser.). (ENG.). 24p. (J). (gr. -1 — 1). bds. 6.95 *(978-1-4197-1898-4(3)*, Abrams Appleseed) Abrams, Inc.

Houran, Lori Haskins. Greetings, Sharkling! Warrick, Jessica, illus. 2016. (How to Be an Earthling (r) Ser.: 2). (ENG.). 64p. (gr. 1-3). 22.65 *(978-1-57565-821-6(6))* Kane Press, Inc.

—Greetings, Sharkling! Honesty. Warrick, Jessica, illus. 2016. (How to Be an Earthling (r) Ser.: 2). (ENG.). 64p. (gr. 1-3). 34.65 *(978-1-57565-823-0(2))* Kane Press, Inc.

Howell, Trisha Adelena. The Adventures of Melon & Turnip. Lopez, Paul, illus. 2004. 32p. 15.95 *(978-1-931210-04-1(7))* Howell Canyon Pr.

Jeffrey, Sarah. Me & My Invisible Guy, 0 vols. 2013. (ENG.). 256p. (YA). (gr. 7-11). 15.99 *(978-1-4778-1636-3(4)*, 9781477816363, Amazon Children's Publishing) Amazon Publishing.

Jenkins, Jerry B. & Fabry, Chris. Stolen Secrets. 2005. (Red Rock Mysteries Ser.: 2). (ENG., Illus.). 224p. (YA). (gr. -1-7). pap. 6.99 *(978-1-4143-0141-9(3)*, Tyndale Kids) Tyndale Hse. Pubs.

Johnson, Darlington. Layla the Ladybug - "Honesty" 2011. 24p. pap. 15.99 *(978-1-4568-5214-6(0))* Xlibris Corp.

Jones, Christianne C. Hello, Goodbye, & a Very Little Lie, 1 vol. Battuz, Christine, illus. (Little Boost Ser.). (ENG.). 32p. (gr. k-3). 2012. 7.95 *(978-1-4048-7498-5(4))* 2010. lib. bdg. 23.99 *(978-1-4048-6167-1(X))* Picture Window Bks. (Little Boost).

Kaplan, Michael B. Betty Bunny Didn't Do It. Jorisch, Stéphane, illus. 2013. (Betty Bunny Ser.). (ENG.). 32p. (J). (gr. -1-k). 16.99 *(978-0-8037-3858-4(7)*, Dial Bks) Penguin Young Readers Group.

Karras, Kim. Accidentally Me. 2016. (ENG.). (YA). pap. 15.99 *(978-1-4621-1867-0(4)*, Sweetwater Bks.) Cedar Fort, Inc./CFI Distribution.

Kats, Jewel. Miss Popular Steals the Show: Girls in Wheelchairs Rule! Stenton, Murray, illus. 2014. 37p. (J). pap. 14.95 *(978-1-61599-236-2(7))* Loving Healing Pr., Inc.

Kelsey, Annie. Pippa Morgan's Diary. Larsen, Kate, illus. 2015. (Pippa Morgan's Diary Ser.: 1). (ENG.). 160p. (J). (gr. 3-7). 12.99 *(978-1-4926-2328-1(8)*, 9781492623281, Sourcebooks Jabberwocky) Sourcebooks, Inc.

Kent, Renee Holmes. Tell the Truth, Cassie, Vol. 6. 2004. (Adventures in Misty Falls Ser.: Vol. 6). (Illus.). 100p. (J). (gr. 4-7). pap. 4.99 *(978-1-56309-452-1(5)*, N007110) New Hope Pubs.

Keplinger, Kody. Lying Out Loud: a Companion to the DUFF. 2016. (ENG.). 304p. (J). (gr. 9). pap. 9.99 *(978-0-545-83110-9(5)*, Scholastic Paperbacks) Scholastic, Inc.

Kim, YeShil. Tortoise & Hare. Kheiriyeh, Rashin, illus. 2014. (MySELF Bookshelf Ser.). (ENG.). 32p. (J). (gr. k-2). pap. 11.94 *(978-1-60357-700-7(9))*; lib. bdg. 25.27 *(978-1-59953-665-1(X))* Norwood Hse. Pr.

Kline, Suzy. Horrible Harry & the Mud Gremlins. Remkiewicz, Frank, illus. 2004. (Horrible Harry Ser.). 50p. (gr. 2). 14.00 *(978-0-7569-2815-5(X))* Perfection Learning Corp.

Laboy, Gloria J. Sally Learns Honesty. 2008. 20p. pap. 13.95 *(978-1-4327-2553-2(X))* Outskirts Pr., Inc.

Larbalestier, Justine. Liar. 2010. (ENG.). 384p. (YA). (gr. 9-13). pap. 10.99 *(978-1-59990-519-8(1)*, 9781599905198, Bloomsbury USA Childrens) Bloomsbury Publishing USA.

Latimer, Àlex. The Boy Who Cried Ninja, 1 vol. Latimer, Àlex, illus. 2011. (ENG., Illus.). 32p. (J). (gr. -1-3). 15.95 *(978-1-56145-579-9(2))* Peachtree Pubs.

—The Boy Who Cried Ninja. 2014. lib. bdg. 18.40 *(978-0-606-35511-7(1))* Turtleback Bks.

Leibenkop, T. The Sovereign of the Northern Winds. 2009. 30p. pap. 13.50 *(978-1-60693-847-8(9)*, Eloquent Bks.) Strategic Book Publishing & Rights Agency (SBPRA).

Leigh-Anna Tehan. Beyond All Imagination: The First Souvenir. Paul Reising, illus. 2009. 44p. pap. 18.49 *(978-1-4389-6452-2(8))* AuthorHouse.

Leigh, Tom, illus. Pinocchio: A Tale of Honesty. 2006. (J). 6.99 *(978-1-59939-005-5(1))* Cornerstone Pr.

Levins, Sandra. Eli's Lie-O-Meter: A Story about Telling the Truth. Ebbeler, Jeffrey, illus. 2010. 32p. (J). (gr. -1-3). 14.95 *(978-1-4338-0735-0(1))*; pap. 9.95 *(978-1-4338-0736-7(X))* American Psychological Assn. (Magination Pr.).

Lichtman, Wendy. Secrets, Lies, & Algebra. 2008. (Do the Math Ser.: 1). (ENG., Illus.). 208p. (YA). (gr. 8-8). pap. 6.99 *(978-0-06-122957-2(1)*, Greenwillow Bks.) HarperCollins Pubs.

Lynch, Chris. Little Blue Lies. 2014. (ENG.). 224p. (YA). (gr. 7). 17.99 *(978-1-4424-4008-1(2)*, Simon & Schuster Bks. For Young Readers) Simon & Schuster Bks. For Young Readers.

Mackall, Dandi Daley. Double Trouble, 1 vol. Wolf, Claudia, illus. 2011. (I Can Read! / a Horse Named Bob Ser.). (ENG.). 32p. (J). pap. 3.99 *(978-0-310-71785-0(X))* Zonderkidz.

Maddox, Jake. Victory Vault, 1 vol. Pulsar Studios Staff, illus. 2011. (Jake Maddox Girl Sports Stories Ser.). (ENG.). 72p. (gr. 2-3). 25.32 *(978-1-4342-2498-9(8))* Stone Arch Bks.

Magoon, Scott. The Boy Who Cried Bigfoot! Magoon, Scott, illus. 2013. (ENG., Illus.). 48p. (J). (gr. -1-3). 17.99 *(978-1-4424-1257-6(7)*, Simon & Schuster Bks. For Young Readers) Simon & Schuster/Paula Wiseman Bks.

Mallon, Lynn & Marshall, Jennifer. It Pays to Be Honest. 2010. 28p. pap. 11.95 *(978-1-60594-440-1(8)*, Llumina Pr.) Aeon Publishing Inc.

Manushkin, Fran. The Big Lie, 1 vol. Lyon, Tammie, illus. 2009. (Katie Woo Ser.). (ENG.). 32p. (gr. k-2). 21.32 *(978-1-4048-5497-0(5))* Picture Window Bks.

Manushkin, Fran & Lyon, Tammie. La Gran Mentira, 1 vol. Lyon, Tammie, illus. 2012. (Katie Woo en Español Ser.). (SPA., Illus.). 32p. (gr. k-2). pap. 6.95 *(978-1-4048-7678-1(2))*; lib. bdg. 21.32 *(978-1-4048-7522-7(0))* Picture Window Bks.

Marino, Nan. Neil Armstrong Is My Uncle & Other Lies Muscle Man McGinty Told Me. 2012. (ENG.). 176p. (J). (gr. 3-7). pap. 6.99 *(978-0-312-66548-7(2)*, 9780312665487) Square Fish.

Mayer, Mercer. It's True, 1 vol. 2013. (ENG.). 24p. (J). pap. 3.99 *(978-1-4003-2247-3(2))* Nelson, Thomas Inc.

—It's True!, 1 vol. 2013. (ENG., Illus.). 24p. (J). bds. 9.99 *(978-1-4003-2246-6(4))* Nelson, Thomas Inc.

McCafferty, Megan. Thumped. 2013. (Bumped Ser.: 2). (ENG.). 304p. (YA). (gr. 8). pap. 8.99 *(978-0-06-196277-6(5))* HarperCollins Pubs.

McClintock, Norah. Snitch, 1 vol. 2005. (Orca Soundings Ser.). (ENG.). 128p. (YA). (gr. 8-12). per. 9.95 *(978-1-55143-484-1(9))* Orca Bk. Pubs. USA.

McConnaughhay, JoDee H. Tell the Truth, Tyler. Urbanovic, Jackie, illus. 2014. (Happy Day Ser.). (ENG.). 16p. (J). pap. 2.49 *(978-1-4143-9468-8(3))* Tyndale Hse. Pubs.

McDonald, Joyce. Shades of Simon Gray. 2003. (Readers Circle Ser.). 245p. (YA). 14.15 *(978-0-7569-1880-4(4))* Perfection Learning Corp.

McFadden, Jennifer. Rusty My Playful Cat. 2010. 24p. pap. 11.49 *(978-1-4490-5101-3(4))* AuthorHouse.

McKissack, Patricia C., et al. The Honest-to-Goodness Truth. Potter, Giselle, illus. 2003. (ENG.). 40p. (J). (gr. -1-3). 7.99 *(978-0-689-85395-1(5)*, Aladdin) Simon & Schuster Children's Publishing.

McLaurin, Corey F. Larry, Lisa & the Missing Kite, 1 vol. Dixon, Corey, illus. 2009. 20p. pap. 24.95 *(978-1-61546-590-3(1))* America Star Bks.

Messer, Celeste M. The Boy Who Cried Wolf. Hoeffner, Deb, illus. 2004. 82-92p. 4.95 *(978-0-9702171-9-6(6))* AshleyAlan Enterprises.

Mitchell, Todd. The Secret to Lying. (ENG., Illus.). 336p. (YA). (gr. 9). 2011. pap. 7.99 *(978-0-7636-5620-1(8))* 2010. 17.99 *(978-0-7636-4084-2(0))* Candlewick Pr.

Morgan, Melissa J. Reality Bites, 15 vols. 2007. (Camp Confidential Ser.: 15). (ENG.). 160p. (J). (gr. 3-7). pap. 4.99 *(978-0-448-44539-7(5)*, Grosset & Dunlap) Penguin Young Readers Group.

Myers, Bill. My Life As a Prickly Porcupine from the Planet Pluto, 1 vol. 2004. (Incredible Worlds of Wally Mcdoogle Ser.: 23). (ENG.). 128p. pap. 6.99 *(978-0-8499-5994-3(2))* Nelson, Thomas Inc.

Norman, Donna Marie. Just a Swim? Widowati, Marini, illus. 2008. 29p. pap. 24.95 *(978-1-60672-182-7(8))* America Star Bks.

O'Connor, Jane. Fancy Nancy: My Family History. Glasser, Robin Preiss et al, illus. 2010. (I Can Read Level 1 Ser.). (ENG.). 32p. (J). (gr. -1-3). 16.99 *(978-0-06-188270-8(4))* HarperCollins Pubs.

—My Family History. Glasser, Robin Preiss et al, illus. 2010. (I Can Read Level 1 Ser.). (ENG.). 32p. (J). (gr. -1-3). pap. 3.99 *(978-0-06-188271-5(2))* HarperCollins Pubs.

—My Family History. 2010. (Fancy Nancy - I Can Read! Ser.). (J). lib. bdg. 13.55 *(978-0-606-14988-4(0)*, Turtleback) Turtleback Bks.

Palatini, Margie. Isabella for Real. Pham, LeUyen, illus. 2016. (ENG.). 208p. (J). (gr. 5-7). 16.99 *(978-0-544-14846-8(0)*, HMH Books For Young Readers) Houghton Mifflin Harcourt Publishing Co.

Parker, David. I Tell the Truth! Goodnow, Patti, illus. 2004. (J). pap. *(978-0-439-62808-2(3))* Scholastic, Inc.

Paulsen, Gary. Liar, Liar. 2012. (ENG.). 128p. (J). (gr. 3-7). 6.99 *(978-0-375-86611-1(6)*, Yearling) Random Hse. Children's Bks.

Penn, Tony. The Misadventures of Michael Mcmichaels: The Angry Alligator, Vol. 1. Martin, Brian, illus. 2016. (ENG.). 96p. (J). pap. 7.95 *(978-1-934490-94-5(6))* Boys Town Pr.

Penn, Tony. The Misadventures of Michael Mcmichaels: The Creepy Campers, vol. 3. Martin, Brian, illus. 2017. (Michael Mcmichaels Ser.: 3). (ENG.). 84p. (J). pap. 7.95 ***(978-1-944882-10-5(3))*** Boys Town Pr.

Pinocchio: A Classic Story about Honesty. 2003. (Illus.). 32p. per. 3.95 *(978-0-9747133-2-8(5)*, Values to Live By Classic Stories) Thomas, Frederic Inc.

Pitcock, Tiffany. Just Friends. 2017. (ENG.). 320p. (YA). pap. 10.99 *(978-1-250-08405-7(9)*, 9781250084057) Feiwel & Friends.

Plato's Journey: Evaluation Guide. 2006. (J). *(978-1-55942-421-9(4))* Witcher Productions.

Poydar, Nancy. Zip, Zip... Homework. Poydar, Nancy, illus. 2008. (ENG., Illus.). 32p. (J). (gr. -1-3). 16.95 *(978-0-8234-2090-2(6))* Holiday Hse., Inc.

Rahaman, Vashanti. Divali Rose. Akib, Jamel, illus. 2008. (ENG.). 32p. (J). (gr. 2-4). 16.95 *(978-1-59078-524-9(X))* Boyds Mills Pr.

Rankin, Laura. Ruthie & the (Not So) Teeny Tiny Lie. Rankin, Laura, illus. 2007. (ENG., Illus.). 32p. (J). (gr. -1-3). 17.99 *(978-1-59990-010-0(6)*, 9781599900100, Bloomsbury USA Childrens) Bloomsbury Publishing USA.

Reinhardt, Dana. Harmless. 2008. (ENG.). 240p. (YA). (gr. 9). pap. 8.99 *(978-0-553-49497-6(X)*, Ember) Random Hse. Children's Bks.

—Tell Us Something True. 2016. (ENG.). 208p. (YA). (gr. 9). lib. bdg. 20.99 *(978-0-375-99066-3(6)*, Lamb, Wendy Bks.) Random Hse. Children's Bks.

Reiss, Kathryn. The Tangled Web: A Julie Mystery. Tibbles, Jean-Paul, illus. 2009. (ENG.). 168p. (J). (gr. 4-18). 10.95 *(978-1-59369-475-3(X))*; pap. 6.95 *(978-1-59369-476-0(8))* American Girl Publishing, Inc.

Robins, Eleanor. Don't Get Caught, 1 vol. unabr. ed. 2011. (Choices Ser.). (ENG.). 52p. (YA). (gr. 9-12). 7.95 *(978-1-61651-592-8(9))* Saddleback Educational Publishing, Inc.

—Easy Pass, 1 vol. unabr. ed. 2011. (Choices Ser.). (ENG.). 51p. (YA). (gr. 9-12). 7.95 *(978-1-61651-596-6(1))* Saddleback Educational Publishing, Inc.

—No Limits, 1 vol. unabr. ed. 2011. (Choices Ser.). (ENG.). 52p. (YA). (gr. 9-12). 7.95 *(978-1-61651-598-0(8))* Saddleback Educational Publishing, Inc.

Roderick, Judith A. Charlie the Cat: Charlie Teaches Others a Lesson about Honesty. 2011. 24p. pap. 11.60 *(978-1-4634-1920-2(1))* AuthorHouse.

Rodríguez, Orlando A. Valores Morales y Buenos Hábitos — Rangel, Mario Hugo, illus. 2003. (SPA.). 32p. (J). *(978-0-311-38595-9(8))* Baptist Spanish Publishing Hse./Casa Bavtista de Publicaciones: Mundo Hispano.

Ross, Jill. What's the Matter, Mr. Ticklebritches? Pruitt, Gwendolyn, illus. 2010. (ENG.). 70p. (J). (gr. 3-7). pap. 9.95 *(978-1-59825-948-3(2))* Shenanigans Series.

Rowley, M'lin. The Silver Coat. 2009. (Knights of Right Ser.: Bk. 2). 71p. (J). (gr. 1-5). pap. 6.99 *(978-1-60641-104-9(7),* Shadow Mountain) Shadow Mountain Publishing.

Ryan, Patrick. In Mike We Trust. 2009. 321p. (J). lib. bdg. 17.89 *(978-0-06-085814-8(1),* HarperTeen) HarperCollins Pubs.

Scheel, Morgan Lee. The Fabulous Glitter Girl. Sbandelli, Angela, illus. 2017. (ENG.). 54p. (J). pap. 9.95 *(978-1-63047-998-5(5))* Morgan James Publishing.

Schooley, Bob & McCorkle, Mark. Liar of Kudzu. 2008. (ENG.). 192p. (J). (gr. 5-9). pap. 9.99 *(978-1-4169-1489-1(7),* Simon & Schuster Bks. For Young Readers) Simon & Schuster Bks. For Young Readers.

Schumacher, Julie. The Book of One Hundred Truths. 2008. (Yearling Bks.). (ENG.). 192p. (J). (gr. 3-7). 6.99 *(978-0-440-42085-9(7),* Yearling) Random Hse. Children's Bks.

Seal, Vickie Di-Ann. Edgar Tells the Truth. 2012. 26p. 24.95 *(978-1-4626-0976-5(7))* America Star Bks.

Shepard, Sara. Ali's Pretty Little Lies. 2013. (Pretty Little Liars Companion Novel Ser.). (ENG.). 320p. (YA). (gr. 9). pap. 9.99 *(978-0-06-223337-0(8),* HarperTeen) HarperCollins Pubs.

—Ali's Pretty Little Lies. 2013. (Pretty Little Liars Ser.). (YA). lib. bdg. 20.85 *(978-0-606-35048-8(9),* Turtleback) Turtleback Bks.

Sierra, Judy. Tell the Truth, B. B. Wolf. Seibold, J. Otto, illus. 2010. (ENG.). 40p. (J). (gr. -1-2). 16.99 *(978-0-375-85620-4(X),* Knopf Bks. for Young Readers) Random Hse. Children's Bks.

Sommer, Carl. The Great Deception. Noé, illus. 2009. (Quest for Success Ser.). (ENG.). 40p. (YA). pap. 4.95 *(978-1-57537-279-2(7));* lib. bdg. 12.95 *(978-1-57537-254-9(1))* Advance Publishing, Inc.

—The Great Deception(El Gran Engaño) Noé, illus. 2009. (Quest for Success Bilingual Ser.). (ENG & SPA.). 72p. (YA). lib. bdg. 14.95 *(978-1-57537-228-0(2))* Advance Publishing, Inc.

Springer, Kristina. My Fake Boyfriend Is Better Than Yours. 2013. (ENG.). 208p. (YA). (gr. 6-9). pap. 6.99 *(978-0-312-64159-7(1),* 9780312641597) Square Fish.

Steinkraus, Kyla. Nobody's Watching. Dufalla, Anita, illus. 2012. (ENG.). 24p. (gr. 2-3). pap. 8.95 *(978-1-61810-328-4(8))* Rourke Educational Media.

Stevens, Janet & Crummel, Susan Stevens. Jackalope. 2003. (ENG., Illus.). 56p. (J). (gr. -1-3). 17.00 *(978-0-15-216736-3(6))* Houghton Mifflin Harcourt Publishing Co.

Stevenson, Robin. Big Guy, 1 vol. 2008. (Orca Soundings Ser.). (ENG.). (YA). (gr. 8-12). 112p. 16.95 *(978-1-55143-912-9(3));* 128p. pap. 9.95 *(978-1-55143-910-5(7))* Orca Bk. Pubs. USA.

Tayleur, Karen. Liar! The True Story of David Mortimore Baxter. Garvey, Brann, illus. 2007. (David Mortimore Baxter Ser.). (ENG.). 80p. (gr. 2-3). per. 6.05 *(978-1-59889-206-2(1),* David Mortimore Baxter) Stone Arch Bks.

—The Truth! David Mortimore Baxter Comes Clean, 1 vol. Garvey, Brann, illus. 2006. (David Mortimore Baxter Ser.). (ENG.). 96p. (gr. 2-3). lib. bdg. 26.65 *(978-1-59889-078-5(6),* David Mortimore Baxter) Stone Arch Bks.

Terry, Anne. Honest Bob, the Dog, Has a Tea Party. 2013. 30p. pap. 9.83 *(978-1-62884-761-1(1))* Speedy Publishing LLC.

Terry Anne. Honest Bob, the Dog, Tells the Truth. 2013. 26p. pap. 9.66 *(978-1-63022-211-6(9))* Speedy Publishing LLC.

To Be Perfectly Honest: A Novel Based on an Untrue Story. 2014. (ENG., Illus.). 496p. (YA). (gr. 7). pap. 11.99 *(978-0-689-87605-9(X),* Simon & Schuster Bks. For Young Readers) Simon & Schuster Bks. For Young Readers.

Tym, Kate. Tell the Truth. 2008. (Manners Ser.). (Illus.). 24p. (J). (gr. -1-1). lib. bdg. 16.95 *(978-1-59566-588-1(9))* QEB Publishing Inc.

Updale, Eleanor. Johnny Swanson. 2012. (ENG.). 384p. (J). (gr. 3-7). 8.99 *(978-0-385-75228-2(8),* Yearling) Random Hse. Children's Bks.

Van Gorder, Vivian Ezeife. Master Kofi & Friskey the Dog. 2012. 20p. pap. 17.99 *(978-1-4772-6817-9(0))* AuthorHouse.

Villareal, Ray. Who's Buried in the Garden? 2009. 160p. (YA). (gr. 6-18). pap. 10.95 *(978-1-55885-546-5(7),* Piñata Books) Arte Publico Pr.

Wallace, Patrick. Jared: Boy from the Bottom. Boller, David, illus. 2003. 153p. (J). per. *(978-0-9740753-0-3(2))* Heritage Youth, Inc.

Westling, Vicki Diane. Finders Keepers: Sam & Friends. 2010. 40p. pap. 16.99 *(978-1-4520-2215-4(1))* AuthorHouse.

Weston, Carol. Ava XOX. 2016. (Ava & Pip Ser.: 3). (ENG.). 208p. (J). (gr. 5-8). 15.99 *(978-1-4926-2077-8(7),* 9781492620778, Sourcebooks Jabberwocky) Sourcebooks, Inc.

Wiggins, Thalia. Greg & the Cheat Sheets, 1 vol. Tate, Don, illus. 2012. (Making Choices: the Mcnair Cousins Ser.). (ENG.). 64p. 27.07 *(978-1-61641-630-0(0),* Calico Chapter Bks) Magic Wagon.

Wilhelm, Hans. Tyrone the Double Dirty Rotten Cheater. (FRE.). (J). pap. 6.99 *(978-0-590-74141-5(1))* Scholastic, Inc.

Wilson, Rosalee. Elijah the Penguin. 2007. 60p. pap. 16.95 *(978-0-9798154-8-5(7))* Living Waters Publishing Co.

Wittlinger, Ellen. Love & Lies: Marisol's Story. (ENG.). (YA). 2009. 272p. (gr. 7). pap. 8.99 *(978-1-4169-7914-2(X))* 2008. 256p. (gr. 9-18). 16.99 *(978-1-4169-1623-9(7))* Simon & Schuster Bks. For Young Readers. (Simon & Schuster Bks. For Young Readers).

HONEY

see also Bees

Cunningham, Kevin. Honeyguide Birds & Ratels. 2016. (21st Century Junior Library: Better Together Ser.). (ENG., Illus.). 24p. (J). (gr. 2-5). 27.07 *(978-1-63471-086-2(X),* 208423) Cherry Lake Publishing.

Dawson, Emily C. How Bees Make Honey. 2010. (Our Animal World Ser.). 24p. (J). 25.65 *(978-1-60753-012-1(0))* Amicus Publishing.

Ellison, Virginia H. The Winnie-the-Pooh Cookbook. Shepard, Ernest H., illus. 2010. (Winnie-The-Pooh Ser.). (ENG.). 112p. (J). (gr. 3-7). 19.99 *(978-0-525-42359-1(1),* Dutton Books for Young Readers) Penguin Young Readers Group.

Felix, Rebecca. What Do Bees Do in Summer? 2014. (21st Century Basic Skills Library: Let's Look at Summer Ser.). (ENG., Illus.). 24p. (J). (gr. k-3). pap. 12.79 *(978-1-63137-646-7(2),* 205188) Cherry Lake Publishing.

Ghione, Yvette & Gagnon, Celeste, creators. This Is Daniel Cook Making Honey. 2007. (This Is Daniel Cook Ser.). (ENG., Illus.). 24p. (J). (gr. -1-1). 4.95 *(978-1-55453-086-1(5))* Kids Can Pr., Ltd. CAN. Dist: Hachette Bk. Group.

Gibbons, Gail. Honey Makers. 2014. 17.00 *(978-1-63419-706-9(2))* Perfection Learning Corp.

Milton, Joyce. Honeybees. Mueller, Peter R. & Mueller, Pete, illus. 2003. (Penguin Young Readers, Level 3 Ser.). (ENG.). 48p. (J). (gr. 1-3). pap. 3.99 *(978-0-448-42846-8(6),* Penguin Young Readers) Penguin Young Readers Group.

Murray, Julie. Flower to Honey, 1 vol. 2006. (Beginning to End Ser.). (ENG., Illus.). 24p. (gr. k-4). 25.65 *(978-1-59679-836-6(X),* Buddy Bks.) ABDO Publishing Co.

Nelson, Robin. From Flower to Honey. (Start to Finish, Second Series: Nature's Cycles Ser.). 24p. (gr. k-3). 2012. (ENG.). pap. 39.62 *(978-0-7613-9292-7(0))* 2012. (ENG.). pap. 6.95 *(978-0-7613-8574-5(6))* 2012. (ENG.). lib. bdg. 23.93 *(978-0-7613-6563-1(X))* 2003. (Illus.). (J). lib. bdg. 18.60 *(978-0-8225-0717-8(X))* Lerner Publishing Group.

Pattrick, Steve. Bees & Honey: KinderFacts Individual Title Six-Packs. (Kinderstarters Ser.). 8p. (gr. -1-1). 21.00 *(978-0-7635-8740-6(0))* Rigby Education.

Rockwell, Anne F. & Rockwell. Honey in a Hive. Schindler, S. D., illus. 2005. (Let's-Read-And-Find-Out Science 2 Ser.). (ENG.). 40p. (J). (gr. k-4). pap. 5.99 *(978-0-06-445204-5(2))* HarperCollins Pubs.

Schuh, Mari. Honeybees. 2013. (ENG., Illus.). 24p. (J). lib. bdg. 25.65 *(978-1-62031-051-9(1))* Jump! Inc.

Spilsbury, Louise. How Bees Make Honey. 2011. (Big Picture: Food Ser.). (ENG.). 24p. (J). (gr. 1-2). pap. 41.70 *(978-1-4296-6728-9(1),* First Facts) Capstone Press of Coughlan Cos.

Stewart, Melissa. How Do Bees Make Honey? 2008. (Tell Me Why, Tell Me How Ser.). (Illus.). 32p. (gr. 3-18). lib. bdg. 29.93 *(978-0-7614-2923-4(9),* Benchmark Bks.) Marshall Cavendish Corp.

Sullivan, Martha. If You Love Honey. Morrison, Cathy, illus. 2015. (ENG.). 32p. (J). (gr. k-4). 16.95 *(978-1-58469-533-2(1))* Dawn Pubns.

HONG KONG (CHINA)

Kagda, Falaq & Koh, Magdalene. Hong Kong. 2nd rev. ed. 2008. (Cultures of the World Ser.). 144p. (gr. 6-18). lib. bdg. 42.79 *(978-0-7614-3034-6(2),* Benchmark Bks.) Marshall Cavendish Corp.

Morrissey, Tricia. H Is for Hong Kong: A Primer in Pictures. Briel, Elizabeth, illus. 2009. (Alphabetical World Ser.). (CHI & ENG.). 36p. (J). (gr. k-4). 12.95 *(978-1-934159-13-2(1))* ThingsAsian Pr.

Sasek, Miroslav. This Is Hong Kong. 2007. (This Is ... Ser.). (ENG., Illus.). 64p. (J). (gr. 2-12). 17.95 *(978-0-7893-1560-1(2))* Universe Publishing.

Scott, Janine. Living in Hong Kong: Set Of 6. 2010. (Early Connections Ser.). (J). pap. 37.00 net. *(978-1-4108-1075-5(5))* Benchmark Education Co.

Somervill, Barbara A. Hong Kong. 2015. (ENG., Illus.). 144p. (J). lib. bdg. *(978-0-531-21698-9(5),* Orchard Bks.) Scholastic, Inc.

Torres, John Albert. Hong Kong. 2009. (J). *(978-1-58415-792-2(5))* Mitchell Lane Pubs., Inc.

HONG KONG (CHINA)—FICTION

Alexander, Lyndi. Windmills. 2013. 248p. (J). pap. 14.99 *(978-1-61271-226-0(6))* Zumaya Pubns. LLC.

Bollback, Anthony G. Capture of the Twin Dragon. 2012. 152p. pap. 8.99 *(978-0-9849359-1-8(6))* Finding the Cause, LLC.

—Hijacked. 2012. 176p. pap. 8.99 *(978-0-9849359-5-6(9))* Finding the Cause, LLC.

—Smugglers in Hong Kong. 2012. 156p. pap. 8.99 *(978-0-9849359-0-1(8))* Finding the Cause, LLC.

—The Tiger Shark Strikes Again. 2012. 172p. pap. 8.99 *(978-0-9849359-4-9(0))* Finding the Cause, LLC.

Carson, John & Carson, Marlene. Ramblin' Rose: The Chinese Fortune Cookie. 2008. 291p. pap. 8.99 *(978-0-9800034-1-3(5))* BBM Bks.

Crotty, Martha. Hong Kong Kitty. Thurn, Gwen & Thurn, David Ryan, illus. 2005. (J). per. 14.00 *(978-0-9766017-0-8(2))* Ironcreek Pr.

De Laurentiis, Giada. Hong Kong! #3. Gambatesa, Francesca, illus. 2014. (Recipe for Adventure Ser.: 3). (ENG.). 144p. (J). (gr. 2-5). 6.99 *(978-0-448-46258-5(3));* 16.99 *(978-0-448-48040-4(9))* Penguin Young Readers Group. (Grosset & Dunlap).

Gurden, Gloria. Wersel Goes to Hong Kong. 2012. 84p. (gr. 2-4). pap. 11.11 *(978-1-4669-4083-3(2))* Trafford Publishing.

Horowitz, Anthony. Necropolis, 9 vols. 2009. (Gatekeepers Ser.: 4). (J). 92.75 *(978-1-4407-0430-7(9));* 122.75 *(978-1-4407-0434-5(1));* 120.75 *(978-1-4407-0436-9(8));* 90.75 *(978-1-4407-0432-1(5));* 1.25 *(978-1-4407-0439-0(2));* 254.75 *(978-1-4407-0431-4(7))* Recorded Bks., Inc.

—Necropolis. (Gatekeepers Ser.: 4). (ENG.). 400p. (J). (gr. 3-7). 2011. pap. 8.99 *(978-0-439-68006-6(9),* Scholastic Paperbacks) 2009. 17.99 *(978-0-439-68003-5(4),* Scholastic Pr.) Scholastic, Inc.

—Necropolis. 2009. 400p. pap. *(978-1-4063-2108-1(7))* Walker Bks., Ltd.

Jones, Gareth P. The Clan of the Scorpion. Finlayson, Luke, illus. 2013. (Ninja Meerkats Ser.: 1). (ENG.). 128p. (J). (gr. 2-4). pap. 5.99 *(978-1-250-01664-5(9),* 9781250016645) Square Fish.

Leloup, Roger. The Dragon of Hong Kong - Yoko Tsuno, Vol. 5. 2010. (Yoko Tsuno Ser.: 5). (ENG., Illus.). 46p. (J). (gr. 3-17). pap. 11.95 *(978-1-84918-041-2(5))* CineBook GBR. Dist: National Bk. Network.

McOmber, Rachel B., ed. McOmber Phonics Storybooks: A Package from Hong Kong. rev. ed. (Illus.). (J). *(978-0-944991-61-9(0))* Swift Learning Resources.

Paul, Naomi. Code Name Komiko. 2014. (Illus.). 288p. (YA). (gr. 6-12). pap. 10.95 *(978-1-62324-024-0(7));* 285p. 19.95 *(978-1-62324-023-3(9))* Enslow Pubs., Inc.

Roberge, Tracy. Jacob & Alec Move to Hong Kong. 2011. 32p. pap. 17.99 *(978-1-257-01739-3(X))* Lulu Pr., Inc.

Rosenberg, Michael. Chilly Goes to Hong Kong & China: Another Chilly the Toy Polar Bear Adventure. 2013. 36p. pap. 13.95 *(978-1-62212-841-9(9),* Strategic Bk. Publishing) Strategic Book Publishing & Rights Agency (SBPRA).

Russell, Ching Yeung. Tofu Quilt. (ENG.). 136p. (J). 2016. (gr. 4-7). pap. 10.95 ***(978-1-62014-354-4(2))*** 2009. (gr. 3-8). 16.95 *(978-1-60060-423-2(4))* Lee & Low Bks., Inc.

Sedgwick, Julian. The Black Dragon. Moffett, Patricia, illus. 2016. (Mysterium Ser.: 1). (ENG.). 352p. (gr. 4-8). 18.99 *(978-1-4677-7567-0(3));* 38.65 *(978-1-4677-9555-5(0))* Lerner Publishing Group. (Carolrhoda Bks.).

Smith, Icy. Three Years & Eight Months. Kindert, Jennifer C., illus. 2013. (J). *(978-0-9856237-8-4(0))* East West Discovery Pr.

Tilley. Damaged. 2011. (ENG.). 260p. (gr. 9-13). pap. 11.95 *(978-988-18967-0-4(3))* Haven Bks.

Tilley, Adrian. The Spider's Web. 2010. (ENG.). 232p. (YA). (gr. 4-7). pap. 11.95 *(978-988-18094-5-2(2))* Haven Bks.

Uncle Markie. Piglette & Bobo in the New Territories. 2003. (YA). ring bd. 9.95 *(978-1-933129-06-8(9))* Studio 403.

Vittachi, Nury & Ros, Laura, contrib. by. Thomas Beckham Wang & Other Stories. 2006. 112p. per. *(978-988-99021-0-0(9))* Chameleon Pr.

HOOVER, HERBERT, 1874-1964

King, David C. Herbert Hoover. 2009. (Presidents & Their Times 3 Ser.). 96p. (gr. 6). 34.21 *(978-0-7614-3626-3(X))* Marshall Cavendish Corp.

Rumsch, BreAnn. Herbert Hoover, 1 vol. 2009. (United States Presidents Ser.). (ENG., Illus.). 40p. (YA). (gr. 3-6). 27.07 *(978-1-60453-458-0(3))* ABDO Publishing Co.

Ruth, Amy. Herbert Hoover. 2004. (Presidential Leaders Ser.). (Illus.). 112p. (J). (gr. 6-12). lib. bdg. 29.27 *(978-0-8225-0821-2(4))* Lerner Publishing Group.

Souter, Gerry & Souter, Janet. Herbert Hoover. 2008. (Presidents of the U. S. A. Ser.). (ENG., Illus.). 48p. (J). (gr. 3-6). 32.79 *(978-1-60253-059-1(9),* 200698) Child's World, Inc., The.

Wilson, Natashya. How to Draw the Life & Times of Herbert Hoover. (Kid's Guide to Drawing the Presidents of the United States of America Ser.). 32p. 2009. (gr. 4-4). 50.50 *(978-1-61511-144-2(1),* PowerKids Pr.) 2007. (Illus.). (YA). (gr. 2-5). 26.50 *(978-1-4042-3007-1(6))* Rosen Publishing Group, Inc., The.

HOOVER, J. EDGAR (JOHN EDGAR), 1895-1972

Aronson, Marc. Master of Deceit: J. Edgar Hoover & America in the Age of Lies. 2012. (ENG., Illus.). 230p. (J). (gr. 9). 25.99 *(978-0-7636-5025-4(0))* Candlewick Pr.

HOOVER DAM (ARIZ. AND NEV.)

DuTemple, Lesley A. The Hoover Dam. 2003. (Great Building Feats Ser.). (ENG., Illus.). 96p. (gr. 5-9). 27.93 *(978-0-8225-4691-7(4))* Lerner Publishing Group.

Gabriel, Luke. The Hoover Dam. 2014. (United States Landmarks Ser.). (ENG.). 24p. (J). (gr. 1-4). 27.07 *(978-1-62323-956-5(7),* 206731) Child's World, Inc., The.

Graham, Ian. You Wouldn't Want to Work on the Hoover Dam! An Explosive Job You'd Rather Not Do. Antram, David, illus. 2012. (You Wouldn't Want to... Ser.). (ENG.). 32p. (J). pap. 9.95 *(978-0-531-20946-2(6),* Watts, Franklin); lib. bdg. 29.00 *(978-0-531-20871-7(0))* Scholastic Library Publishing.

Halls, Kelly Milner. The Story of the Hoover Dam: A History Perspectives Book. 2014. (Perspectives Library). (ENG., Illus.). 32p. (J). (gr. 4-8). 28.50 *(978-1-62431-668-5(9),* 203236) Cherry Lake Publishing.

Mann, Elizabeth. The Hoover Dam: The Story of Hard Times, Tough People & the Taming of a Wild River. Witschonke, Alan, illus. 2006. (Wonders of the World Book Ser.). (ENG.). 48p. (J). (gr. 4-8). pap. 9.95 *(978-1-931414-13-5(0),* 9781931414135) Mikaya Pr.

Masterson, Josephine. At the Hoover Dam. 2015. (Rosen REAL Readers: STEM & STEAM Collection). (ENG.). 12p. (gr. 1-2). pap. 6.33 *(978-1-4994-9884-4(5),* Rosen Classroom) Rosen Publishing Group, Inc., The.

Miller, Heather. The Hoover Dam. 2014. (Great Idea Ser.). (ENG., Illus.). 48p. (J). (gr. 4-6). lib. bdg. 26.60 *(978-1-59953-595-1(5))* Norwood Hse. Pr.

Murray, Julie. Hoover Dam, 1 vol. 2005. (All Aboard America Ser.). (ENG., Illus.). 24p. (gr. k-4). 25.65 *(978-1-59197-506-9(9),* Buddy Bks.) ABDO Publishing Co.

Ringstad, Arnold. The Building of the Hoover Dam. 2017. (Engineering That Made America Ser.). (ENG.). 32p. (J). (gr. 3-6). lib. bdg. 28.50 *(978-1-5038-1637-4(0,* 211153) Child's World, Inc., The.

Roza, Greg. The Hoover Dam: Applying Problem-Solving Strategies. (Math for the Real World Ser.). 32p. 2009. (ENG., Illus.). (gr. 6-7). pap. 10.00 *(978-1-4042-6065-8(X))* 2009. (gr. 5-5). 47.90 *(978-1-60851-369-7(6),* PowerKids Pr.) 2006. (Illus.). (YA). (gr. 5-9). lib. bdg. 25.25 *(978-1-4042-3356-0(3))* Rosen Publishing Group, Inc., The.

Zuehlke, Jeffrey. The Hoover Dam. 2009. (Lightning Bolt Books (tm) — Famous Places Ser.). (ENG.). 32p. (gr. k-2). 26.60 *(978-0-8225-9408-6(0),* Lerner Pubns.) Lerner Publishing Group.

HORMONES

Canavan, Thomas. Fit & Healthy: Heart, Lungs, & Hormones. 2015. (How Your Body Works). (ENG.). 32p. (J). (gr. 4-4). pap. 10.00 *(978-1-4994-1224-6(X),* PowerKids Pr.) Rosen Publishing Group, Inc., The.

Kim, Melissa L. The Endocrine & Reproductive Systems. 2003. (Human Body Library). (Illus.). 48p. (J). (gr. 4-10). lib. bdg. 25.27 *(978-0-7660-2020-7(7))* Enslow Pubs., Inc.

McLaughlin, Marc, et al. How Cells Send, Receive, & Process Information, 1 vol. 2015. (ENG.). 64p. (YA). 31.70 *(978-1-62275-800-5(5),* Britannica Educational Publishing) Rosen Publishing Group, Inc., The.

Perritano, John. Performance-Enhancing Drugs: Steroids, Hormones, & Supplements, Vol. 13. Becker, Sara, ed. 2016. (Drug Addiction & Recovery Ser.). (Illus.). 64p. (J). (gr. 7). 23.95 *(978-1-4222-3609-3(9))* Mason Crest.

HORN (MUSICAL INSTRUMENT)

Feldstein, Sandy & Clark, Larry. Barbara Allen - Horn in F Solo with Piano Acc. W/CD. 2005. (YA). pap. 9.95 *(978-1-932895-62-9(0))* PlayinTime Productions, Inc.

Froseth, James O. Horn in F Home Helper First Lessons at School & at Home. 2005. 20p. 7.95 *(978-1-57999-502-7(0),* M577) G I A Pubns., Inc.

HORNADAY, WILLIAM TEMPLE, 1854-1937

Caper, William. American Bison: A Scary Prediction. 2007. (America's Animal Comebacks Ser.). (Illus.). 32p. (YA). (gr. 2-5). lib. bdg. 25.27 *(978-1-59716-504-4(2))* Bearport Publishing Co., Inc.

HORNETS

Hayes, Amy. Hornets. 2015. (Things That Sting Ser.). (ENG., Illus.). 24p. (J). (gr. 2-3). lib. bdg. 22.60 *(978-1-4824-1698-5(0))* Stevens, Gareth Publishing LLLP.

Markle, Sandra. Hornets. 2008. pap. 52.95 *(978-1-58013-281-7(2))* Lerner Publishing Group.

—Hornets: Incredible Insect Architects. 2008. (Insect World Ser.). (ENG., Illus.). 48p. (J). (gr. 4-8). lib. bdg. 27.93 *(978-0-8225-7297-8(4),* Lerner Pubns.) Lerner Publishing Group.

Pallotta, Jerry. Hornet vs. Wasp. Bolster, Rob, illus. 2013. 32p. (J). pap. *(978-0-545-45190-1(6))* Scholastic, Inc.

HOROLOGY

see Clocks and Watches; Sundials

HOROSCOPES

see Astrology

HORROR STORIES

Aber, Linda. The Chiller Thrillers: Attack of the Leaping Lizards. Roe, David, illus. 2012. (Chiller Thrillers Ser.). (ENG.). 96p. (J). (gr. 4-6). pap. 7.99 *(978-0-7944-2566-1(6))* Reader's Digest Assn., Inc., The.

Adaptor. Graphic Horror Set 3. 2014. (Graphic Horror Set 3 Ser.: 6). 32p. (J). (gr. 5-8). lib. bdg. 171.00 *(978-1-62402-012-4(7),* Graphic Planet) Magic Wagon.

Ahlberg, Allan & Ahlberg, Janet. It Was a Dark & Stormy Night. (ENG., Illus.). 80p. (J). pap. 8.95 *(978-0-14-130027-6(2))* Penguin Bks., Ltd. GBR. Dist: Trafalgar Square Publishing.

Aikawa, Yu. Dark Edge, Vol. 6. Aikawa, Yu, illus. 2006. (Dark Edge Ser.). (ENG., Illus.). 200p. (YA). pap. 9.95 *(978-1-59796-026-7(6))* DrMaster Pubns. Inc.

Alender, Katie. As Dead as It Gets. 2013. (Bad Girls Don't Die Ser.). (ENG.). 448p. (J). (gr. 7-17). pap. 9.99 *(978-1-4231-3778-8(7))* Hyperion Pr.

—Bad Girls Don't Die. 2010. (ENG.). 352p. (J). (gr. 7-17). pap. 8.99 *(978-1-4231-0877-1(9))* Hyperion Pr.

—The Dead Girls of Hysteria Hall. (ENG.). 336p. (J). (gr. 7). 2016. pap. 9.99 *(978-1-338-03239-0(9))* 2015. 18.99 *(978-0-545-63999-6(9))* Scholastic, Inc.

—From Bad to Cursed. 2012. (ENG.). 448p. (YA). (gr. 7-17). pap. 9.99 *(978-1-4231-3777-1(9))* Hyperion Pr.

Allan, Tony. True Ghost Stories. rev. ed. 2004. (True Adventure Stories Ser.). 144p. (J). pap. 4.99 *(978-0-7945-0274-4(1),* Usborne) EDC Publishing.

Allan, Tony & Dowswell, Paul. True Ghost Stories. 2004. (True Adventure Stories Ser.). (Illus.). 122p. (J). (gr. 5). lib. bdg. 12.95 *(978-1-58086-601-9(8))* EDC Publishing.

Almond, David. Clay. 2008. (ENG.). 272p. (YA). (gr. 7-12). pap. 8.99 *(978-0-440-42013-2(X),* Delacorte Bks. for Young Readers) Random Hse. Children's Bks.

Anderson, Jodi Lynn. The Vanishing Season. 2014. (ENG.). 272p. (YA). (gr. 9). 17.99 *(978-0-06-200327-0(5),* HarperTeen) HarperCollins Pubs.

Anderson, M. T. Thirsty. 2008. (ENG., Illus.). 256p. (YA). (gr. 7). pap. 8.99 *(978-0-7636-3895-5(1))* Candlewick Pr.

—Zombie Mommy. Cyrus, Kurt, illus. 2012. (Pals in Peril Tale Ser.). (ENG.). 224p. (J). (gr. 5-9). pap. 6.99 *(978-1-4424-5440-8(7),* Beach Lane Bks.) Beach Lane Bks.

Anderson, Michael. Woolly Bargains: A Scary Story for Young People. 2013. (ENG.). 27p. (J). pap. 22.95 *(978-1-4787-0654-0(6))* Outskirts Pr., Inc.

Andrews, V. C. Garden of Shadows. 2010. (ENG.). 368p. (YA). (gr. 9). pap. 9.99 *(978-1-4424-0643-8(7),* Simon Pulse) Simon Pulse.

—If There Be Thorns/Seeds of Yesterday. 2010. (ENG.). 816p. (YA). (gr. 9). pap. 14.99 *(978-1-4424-0656-8(9),* Simon Pulse) Simon Pulse.

Arevamirp, Esile & Primavera, Elise. Fred & Anthony Meet the Demented Super-Degerm-O Zombie. Primavera, Elise, illus. 2007. (ENG., Illus.). 128p. (J). (gr. 2-6). pap. 4.99 *(978-0-7868-3680-2(6))* Hyperion Pr.

Atwater-Rhodes, Amelia. The Den of Shadows Quartet. 2009. (ENG.). 608p. (YA). (gr. 7). pap. 11.99 *(978-0-385-73894-1(3),* Ember) Random Hse. Children's Bks.

Atwood, Megan. Last Desserts. 2011. (Night Fall Ser.). (ENG.). 120p. (YA). (gr. 6-12). pap. 7.95 *(978-0-7613-7811-2(1));* lib. bdg. 27.93 *(978-0-7613-7744-3(1))* Lerner Publishing Group.

Auxier, Jonathan. The Night Gardener. (ENG.). (YA). (gr. 3-7). 2015. 384p. pap. 8.95 *(978-1-4197-1531-0(3))* 2014. 368p. 16.95 *(978-1-4197-1144-2(X))* Abrams, Inc. (Amulet Bks.).

—The Night Gardener. 2015. (J). lib. bdg. 19.60 *(978-0-606-36891-9(4))* Turtleback Bks.

Avi. School of the Dead. 288p. (J). (gr. 3-7). 2017. pap. 6.99 ***(978-0-06-174086-2(1))*** 2016. 16.99 *(978-0-06-174085-5(3))* HarperCollins Pubs.

—School of the Dead. 2017. (ENG.). (J). (gr. 3-7). lib. bdg. 17.20 ***(978-0-606-40053-4(2))*** Turtleback Bks.

Avi. The Seer of Shadows. 2009. (ENG.). 224p. (J). (gr. 4-7). pap. 6.99 *(978-0-06-000017-2(1))* HarperCollins Pubs.

AZ Books Staff & Evans, Olivia. Haunted Castle. Shumovich, Nadezhda, ed. 2012. (Terribly Funny Monsters Ser.). (ENG., Illus.). 10p. (J). bds. 15.95 *(978-1-61889-134-1(0))* AZ Bks. LLC.

Bachmann, Stefan, et al. The Cabinet of Curiosities: 36 Tales Brief & Sinister. Jansson, Alexander, illus. 2014. (ENG.). 496p. (J). (gr. 3-7). 16.99 *(978-0-06-233105-2(1));* pap. 6.99 *(978-0-06-231314-0(2))* HarperCollins Pubs. (Greenwillow Bks.).

Bacigalupi, Paolo. Zombie Baseball Beatdown. 2014. (ENG.). 320p. (J). (gr. 3-7). pap. 7.99 *(978-0-316-22079-8(5))* Little, Brown Bks. for Young Readers.

Baker, Chandler. Teen Frankenstein. 2016. (High School Horror Ser.: 1). (ENG.). 368p. (YA). 17.99 *(978-1-250-05874-4(0),* 9781250058744) Feiwel & Friends.

—Teen Frankenstein. 2017. (High School Horror Ser.: 1). (ENG.). 336p. (YA). pap. 9.99 *(978-1-250-06887-3(8),* 9781250068873) Square Fish.

—Teen Hyde: High School Horror. 2017. (High School Horror Ser.: 2). (ENG.). 272p. (YA). 17.99 *(978-1-250-05875-1(9),* 9781250058751) Feiwel & Friends.

Baker, Monica S. Freestyle, 1 vol. 2010. (ENG., Illus.). 160p. (J). 14.99 *(978-0-7643-3538-9(3)*, 9780764335389) Schiffer Publishing, Ltd.

Balawajder, Thomas, et al. The Ultimate Homework Survival Guide: A Reality Horror Production. Wise, Noreen, ed. 2nd ed. 2003. (Illus.). 64p. (J). per. 6.95 *(978-1-58584-559-0(0))* Huckleberry Pr.

Ballarini, Joe. A Babysitter's Guide to Monster Hunting #1. To, Vivienne, illus. 2017. (Babysitter's Guide to Monsters Ser.: 1). 352p. (J). (gr. 3-7). 13.99 *(978-0-06-243783-9(6)*, Tegen, Katherine Bks) HarperCollins Pubs.

Bannister, illus. The Calling. 2010. (Elsewhere Chronicles Ser.: Bk. 4). 48p. (J). (gr. 2-5). lib. bdg. 27.93 *(978-0-7613-6068-1(9)*, Graphic Universe™) Lerner Publishing Group.

Baptiste, Tracey. The Jumbies. 2015. (ENG.). 240p. (J). (gr. 3-7). 15.95 *(978-1-61620-414-3(1))* Algonquin Bks. of Chapel Hill.

Baptiste, Tracey. The Rise of the Jumbies. 2017. (Jumbies Ser.). (ENG.). 256p. (J). (gr. 3-7). 16.95 ***(978-1-61620-665-9(9))*** Algonquin Bks. of Chapel Hill.

Barker, Clive. The Thief of Always. 2008. (ENG.). 288p. pap. 15.99 *(978-0-06-168426-5(0)*, Harper Perennial) HarperCollins Pubs.

Baron, Ruth. Defriended. 2013. 248p. (J). pap. *(978-0-545-56761-9(0))* Scholastic, Inc.

Barraclough, Lindsey. Long Lankin. (ENG.). 464p. (YA). (gr. 7). 2014. pap. 9.99 *(978-0-7636-6937-9(7))* 2012. (Illus.). 16.99 *(978-0-7636-5808-3(1))* Candlewick Pr.

—The Mark of Cain. 2016. (ENG.). 496p. (YA). (gr. 9). 17.99 *(978-0-7636-7864-7(3))* Candlewick Pr.

Bass, Guy. Stitch Head. Williamson, Pete, illus. 2013. (Stitch Head Ser.). (ENG.). 192p. (gr. 3-4). pap. 262.80 *(978-1-62370-161-1(9))* Capstone Young Readers of Coughlan Cos.

Bass, Patrik Henry. The Zero Degree Zombie Zone. Craft, Jerry, illus. 2014. (ENG.). 144p. (J). (gr. 3-7). 16.99 *(978-0-545-13210-7(X)*, Scholastic Pr.) Scholastic, Inc.

Bates, Penny. A Murder of Crows. 2004. (Shades Ser.). 60p. (J). pap. *(978-0-237-52648-1(4))* Evans Brothers, Ltd.

Baudet, Stephanie. New Library of Horror: Dracula. 128p. (J). pap. 7.95 *(978-0-233-99578-6(1))* Andre Deutsch GBR. Dist: Trans-Atlantic Pubns., Inc.

Baughan, Michael Gray. Stephen King. 2009. (Who Wrote That? Ser.). (Illus.). 112p. (gr. 6-12). 35.00 *(978-0-7910-9852-3(4)*, Chelsea Hse.) Facts On File, Inc.

Baxter, Nicola, retold by. Terrifying Tales: Nine Stories of Spine-Tingling Suspense. 2013. (ENG., Illus.). 80p. (J). (gr. 3-7). pap. 9.99 *(978-1-84322-927-8(7))* Anness Publishing GBR. Dist: National Bk. Network.

Beatty, Robert. Serafina & the Black Cloak. (Serafina Ser.). (ENG.). (J). (gr. 3-7). 2016. 320p. pap. 7.99 *(978-1-4847-1187-3(4))* 2015. 304p. 16.99 *(978-1-4847-0901-6(2))* Hyperion Bks. for Children.

—Serafina & the Black Cloak. 2016. (J). lib. bdg. 18.40 *(978-0-606-38336-3(0))* Turtleback Bks.

—Serafina & the Splintered Heart. 2017. (Serafina Ser.: bk.3). (ENG.). 368p. (J). (gr. 3-7). 16.99 ***(978-1-4847-7504-2(X))*** Hyperion Bks. for Children.

—Serafina & the Twisted Staff. (Serafina Ser.). (ENG.). (J). (gr. 3-7). 2017. 400p. pap. 7.99 ***(978-1-4847-7806-7(5))*** 2016. 384p. 16.99 *(978-1-4847-7503-5(1))* Hyperion Bks. for Children.

—Serafina & the Twisted Staff. 2017. (J). lib. bdg. 18.40 ***(978-0-606-39977-7(1))*** Turtleback Bks.

Beaudoin, Sean. The Infects. (ENG.). 384p. (YA). (gr. 9). 2014. pap. 8.99 *(978-0-7636-7160-0(6))* 2012. (Illus.). 16.99 *(978-0-7636-5947-9(9))* Candlewick Pr.

Becker, Tom. Lifeblood. 2010. (Darkside Ser.: 2). (ENG.). 288p. (J). (gr. 7). 7.99 *(978-0-545-03746-4(8)*, Orchard Bks.) Scholastic, Inc.

Bedard, Tony. Route 666 Traveler: Highway of Horror. Moline, Karl et al, illus. 2004. (Route 666 Traveler Ser.). 160p. (YA). pap. 9.95 *(978-1-59314-041-0(X))* CrossGeneration Comics, Inc.

Bell, Alex. Frozen Charlotte. 2016. (ENG.). 304p. (J). (gr. 7). 18.99 *(978-0-545-94108-2(3)*, Scholastic Pr.) Scholastic, Inc.

Bellairs, John. The Curse of the Blue Figurine (A Johnny Dixon Mystery: Book One) 2011. 150p. pap. 15.95 *(978-1-61756-324-9(2))* Open Road Integrated Media, Inc.

—The Mummy, the Will, & the Crypt (A Johnny Dixon Mystery: Book Two) 2011. 126p. pap. 14.95 *(978-1-61756-328-7(5))* Open Road Integrated Media, Inc.

Benson, E. F. The Confession of Charles Linkworth. 2004. reprint ed. pap. 1.99 *(978-1-4192-5738-4(2))* Kessinger Publishing, LLC.

Beraducci, Deborah. Tyler's Halloween Horror, 1 vol. Eyre, Jane, illus. 2009. 22p. pap. 24.95 *(978-1-4489-2133-1(3))* America Star Bks.

Berenstain, Stan & Berenstain, Jan. The Berenstain Bears Go on a Ghost Walk. Berenstain, Jan, illus. 2005. (Berenstain Bears Ser.). (ENG., Illus.). 32p. (J). (gr. -1-2). 10.99 *(978-0-06-057399-7(6))*; pap. 3.99 *(978-0-06-057383-6(X))* HarperCollins Pubs. (HarperFestival).

Berkshire, Mary Ann. The Black Glove Rises. 2012. 44p. 19.95 *(978-1-4626-7242-4(6))* America Star Bks.

—Midnight Scream: The Black Glove Book 3. 2013. 66p. pap. 17.95 *(978-1-4560-2505-2(8))* America Star Bks.

Berry, Ron. Beware the Haunted House. Sharp, Chris, illus. 2008. (ENG.). 12p. (J). (gr. -1-k). bds. 12.99 *(978-0-8249-1815-6(0)*, Ideal Pubns.) Worthy Publishing.

Best, Rosie. Skulk. 2013. (ENG.). 400p. (J). pap. 9.99 *(978-1-908844-70-5(1)*, Strange Chemistry) Watkins Media Limited GBR. Dist: Penguin Random Hse. LLC.

Bible, Jake. ScareScapes Book Two: Systems Failure! 2016. (ScareScapes Ser.: 2). (ENG.). 144p. (J). pap. 6.99 *(978-1-68261-162-3(0))* Simon & Schuster.

Bichoman Vuelve de la Tumba. (Fantasmas de Fear Street Coleccion). (SPA.). (YA). (gr. 5-8). pap. 7.95 *(978-950-04-1718-1(9)*, EM9292) Emecé Editores S.A. ARG. Dist: Planeta Publishing Corp., Lectorum Pubns., Inc.

Bick, Ilsa J. The Dickens Mirror. 2015. (Dark Passages Ser.: 2). (ENG.). 576p. (YA). (gr. 9-12). 18.99 *(978-1-5124-0177-6(3)*, Carolrhoda Lab™) Lerner Publishing Group.

—Monsters. 2014. (ENG.). 688p. (J). (gr. 9). pap. 9.99 *(978-1-60684-544-8(6)*, Carolrhoda Lab™) Lerner Publishing Group.

—White Space, Bk. 1. 2014. (Dark Passages Ser.: Bk. 1). (ENG.). 560p. (J). (gr. 9). 18.99 *(978-1-60684-419-9(9))* Lerner Publishing Group.

Bick, Ilsa J. & Ilsa, Bick. The Dickens Mirror. 2017. (Dark Passages Ser.: 2). (ENG.). 576p. (YA). (gr. 9-12). 9.99 *(978-1-5124-4144-4(9)*, Carolrhoda Bks.) Lerner Publishing Group.

Bickle, Laura. The Outside. (ENG.). 320p. (YA). (gr. 7). 2014. pap. 8.99 *(978-0-544-33635-3(6)*, HMH Books For Young Readers) 2013. 16.99 *(978-0-544-00013-1(7))* Houghton Mifflin Harcourt Publishing Co.

Billings, Tirrea. The Monster in the Basement. 2010. 12p. pap. 10.99 *(978-1-4490-2817-6(9))* AuthorHouse.

Black, Jenna. Night Magic. 2017. (Nightstruck Ser.). (ENG.). 288p. (YA). 17.99 *(978-0-7653-8006-7(4)*, 9780765380067, Tor Teen) Doherty, Tom Assocs., LLC.

Blake, Kendare. Anna Dressed in Blood. 2012. (Anna Dressed in Blood Ser.: 1). (YA). lib. bdg. 22.10 *(978-0-606-26252-1(0)*, Turtleback) Turtleback Bks.

—Girl of Nightmares. (Anna Dressed in Blood Ser.: 2). (ENG.). 336p. (YA). (gr. 8). 2014. pap. 9.99 *(978-0-7653-2868-7(2)*, 9780765328687) 2012. 17.99 *(978-0-7653-2866-3(6)*, 9780765328663) Doherty, Tom Assocs., LLC. (Tor Teen).

—Girl of Nightmares. l.t. ed. 2012. (ENG.). 412p. 23.99 *(978-1-4104-5206-1(9))* Thorndike Pr.

Blakley-Cartwright, Sarah & Johnson, David Leslie. Red Riding Hood. 2011. (ENG.). 352p. (YA). (gr. 10-17). pap. 9.99 *(978-0-316-17604-0(4)*, Poppy) Little, Brown Bks. for Young Readers.

Blevins, Wiley. Cinderella & the Vampire Prince. Cox, Steve, illus. 2016. (Scary Tales Retold Ser.). (ENG.). 24p. (gr. k-3). lib. bdg. 23.99 *(978-1-63440-090-9(9))* Red Chair Pr.

—Hansel & Gretel & the Haunted Hut. Cox, Steve, illus. 2016. (Scary Tales Retold Ser.). (ENG.). 24p. (gr. k-3). pap. 6.99 *(978-1-63440-097-8(6))* Red Chair Pr.

—Hansel & Gretel & the Haunted Hut. Cox, Steve, illus. 2016. (Scary Tales Retold Ser.). (ENG.). 24p. (gr. k-3). lib. bdg. 23.99 *(978-1-63440-096-1(8))* Red Chair Pr.

—Little Dead Riding Hood. Cox, Steve, illus. 2016. (Scary Tales Retold Ser.). (ENG.). 24p. (gr. k-3). lib. bdg. 23.99 *(978-1-63440-102-9(6))* Red Chair Pr.

Bloomfield, Charlotte. Corridor of Doors. 2013. 130p. pap. *(978-1-909411-28-9(0))* Mauve Square Publishing.

Blue, Elly. Pedal Zombies. 2015. (Bikes in Space Ser.: 3). (ENG., Illus.). 160p. pap. 9.95 *(978-1-62106-562-3(6)*, Elly Blue Publishing) Microcosm Publishing.

Blue Moon. 2014. (Dead City Ser.: 2). (ENG., Illus.). 336p. (J). (gr. 4-8). pap. 7.99 *(978-1-4424-4132-3(1)*, Aladdin) Simon & Schuster Children's Publishing.

Boggs, Danielle. The Snow Globe. 2008. 55p. pap. 16.95 *(978-1-60703-588-6(X))* America Star Bks.

BookSource Staff, compiled by. Lights, Camera... Zombies! 2013. (Hardy Boys: Secret Files Ser.: 12). lib. bdg. 14.75 *(978-0-606-32033-7(4)*, Turtleback) Turtleback Bks.

Boos, Ben. Fantasy: An Artist's Realm. Boos, Ben, illus. 2010. (ENG., Illus.). 96p. (J). (gr. 5-9). 19.99 *(978-0-7636-4056-9(5))* Candlewick Pr.

Bosworth, Jennifer. The Killing Jar. 2016. (ENG.). 352p. (YA). 17.99 *(978-0-374-34137-4(0)*, 9780374341374, Farrar, Straus & Giroux (BYR)) Farrar, Straus & Giroux.

Bourgeois, Paulette & Clark, Brenda. Franklin's Library Book. 2005. (Kids Can Read Ser.). (ENG., Illus.). 32p. (J). (gr. 1-2). 3.95 *(978-1-55337-713-9(3))*; 14.95 *(978-1-55337-712-2(5))* Kids Can Pr., Ltd. CAN. Dist: Hachette Bk. Group.

Bovi, J. K. Wicked Haints: A Savannah Ghost Story, 1 vol. 2013. (ENG., Illus.). 128p. (J). pap. 16.99 *(978-0-7643-4383-4(1)*, 9780764343834) Schiffer Publishing, Ltd.

Bowen, Carl & Poe, Edgar Allen. The Murders in the Rue Morgue, 1 vol. Dimaya, Emerson & Calero, Dennis, illus. 2013. (Edgar Allan Poe Graphic Novels Ser.). (ENG.). 72p. (gr. 2-3). 27.99 *(978-1-4342-3033-1(3))*; pap. 6.10 *(978-1-4342-4259-4(5))* Stone Arch Bks.

Bracegirdle, P. J. Sinister Scenes. (Joy of Spooking Ser.). (ENG.). 320p. (J). (gr. 3-7). 2012. pap. 6.99 *(978-1-4169-3421-9(9))* 2011. 15.99 *(978-1-4169-3420-2(0))* McElderry, Margaret K. Bks. (McElderry, Margaret K. Bks.).

—Unearthly Asylum. (Joy of Spooking Ser.). (ENG.). (J). (gr. 3-7). 2011. 320p. pap. 5.99 *(978-1-4169-3419-6(7))* 2010. 304p. 15.99 *(978-1-4169-3418-9(9))* McElderry, Margaret K. Bks. (McElderry, Margaret K. Bks.).

Bradman, Tony. Final Cut. 2004. (Illus.). 87p. *(978-0-439-79597-5(4))* Scholastic, Inc.

Brancatelli, Joe, et al. Creepy Archives Volume 18. Simon, Philip, ed. 2014. (ENG., Illus.). 288p. 49.99 *(978-1-61655-269-5(7))* Dark Horse Comics.

Brege, K. B. Abominable Snowman A Frozen Nightmare! 2009. (Mick Morris Myth Solver Ser.: No. 5). (Illus.). 156p. (J). pap. 6.99 *(978-0-9774119-4-8(X))* Team B Creative LLC.

—Ghost Board Posse London Screaming! 2008. (Ghost Board Posse Ser.: No. 1). (Illus.). 207p. (YA). pap. 6.99 *(978-0-9774119-6-2(6))* Team B Creative LLC.

Brennan, Sarah Rees. Unmade. 2014. (Lynburn Legacy Ser.: Bk. 3). (ENG., Illus.). 384p. (YA). (gr. 7). 17.99 *(978-0-375-87043-9(1)*, Random Hse. Bks. for Young Readers) Random Hse. Children's Bks.

—Unspoken. (Lynburn Legacy Ser.: Bk. 1). (ENG.). (YA). (gr. 7). 2012. 384p. 18.99 *(978-0-375-87041-5(5)*, Random Hse. Bks. for Young Readers)Bk. 1. 2013. 400p. pap. 8.99 *(978-0-375-87103-0(9)*, Ember) Random Hse. Children's Bks.

—Untold. Fochesato, Giorgio, illus. 2013. (Lynburn Legacy Ser.: Bk. 2). (ENG.). 384p. (YA). (gr. 7). 18.99 *(978-0-375-87042-2(3)*, Random Hse. Bks. for Young Readers) Random Hse. Children's Bks.

Brereton, Dan, et al. Buffy the Vampire Slayer Omnibus, 7 vols., Vol. 1. Golden, Christopher, illus. 2007. (Buffy the Vampire Slayer Ser.). (ENG.). 408p. pap. 24.99 *(978-1-59307-784-6(X))* Dark Horse Comics.

Brewer, Heather. The Cemetery Boys. 2015. (ENG.). 288p. (YA). (gr. 8). 17.99 *(978-0-06-230788-0(6)*, HarperTeen) HarperCollins Pubs.

—The Cemetery Boys. 2016. (YA). lib. bdg. 20.85 *(978-0-606-38741-5(2))* Turtleback Bks.

—Chronicles of Vladimir Tod, 2 vols. 2009. (Chronicles of Vladimir Tod Ser.: 2). (ENG.). 288p. (YA). (gr. 7-18). 8.99 *(978-0-14-241342-5(9)*, Speak) Penguin Young Readers Group.

—Eighth Grade Bites. Laud, Julia, illus. 2013. (Chronicles of Vladimir Tod Ser.: 1). (ENG.). 144p. (YA). (gr. 7). pap. 12.99 *(978-0-8037-3811-9(0)*, Dial Bks) Penguin Young Readers Group.

—Eighth Grade Bites. 2008. (Chronicles of Vladimir Tod Ser.: 1). (ENG.). 192p. (YA). (gr. 7). 8.99 *(978-0-14-241187-2(6)*, Speak) Penguin Young Readers Group.

—Eleventh Grade Burns, 4 vols. 2010. (Chronicles of Vladimir Tod Ser.: 4). (ENG.). 320p. (YA). (gr. 7-18). 8.99 *(978-0-14-241647-1(9)*, Speak); 4th ed. 16.99 *(978-0-525-42243-3(9)*, Dutton Books for Young Readers) Penguin Young Readers Group.

—First Kill. 2012. (Slayer Chronicles Ser.: 1). (ENG.). 336p. (YA). (gr. 7). pap. 8.99 *(978-0-14-242196-3(0)*, Speak) Penguin Young Readers Group.

—First Kill. 2012. (Slayer Chronicles Ser.: 1). lib. bdg. 19.65 *(978-0-606-26670-3(4)*, Turtleback) Turtleback Bks.

—Tenth Grade Bleeds. Preseault, N., ed. 2010. (Chronicles of Vladimir Tod Ser.: 3). (ENG.). 304p. (YA). (gr. 7-18). pap. 8.99 *(978-0-14-241560-3(X)*, Speak) Penguin Young Readers Group.

—Tenth Grade Bleeds. 2009. (Chronicles of Vladimir Tod Ser.: 3). (ENG., Illus.). 304p. (YA). (gr. 7-18). 16.99 *(978-0-525-42135-1(1)*, Dutton Books for Young Readers) Penguin Young Readers Group.

—Tenth Grade Bleeds. 2010. (Chronicles of Vladimir Tod Ser.: 03). lib. bdg. 19.65 *(978-0-606-10594-1(8)*, Turtleback) Turtleback Bks.

—The Chronicles of Vladimir Tod. 2011. (Chronicles of Vladimir Tod Ser.: 5). (ENG.). 336p. (YA). (gr. 7-18). 8.99 *(978-0-14-241752-2(1)*, Speak) Penguin Young Readers Group.

—Twelfth Grade Kills. 5th ed. 2010. (Chronicles of Vladimir Tod Ser.: 5). (ENG.). 340p. (YA). (gr. 7-18). 16.99 *(978-0-525-42224-2(2)*, Dutton Books for Young Readers) Penguin Young Readers Group.

Brezenoff, Steve. Bites, 1 vol. Pinelli, Amerigo, illus. 2013. (Ravens Pass Ser.). (ENG.). 96p. (gr. 2-3). pap. 6.15 *(978-1-4342-6217-2(0))* Stone Arch Bks.

—Bites. 2013. (Ravens Pass Ser.). (ENG.). 96p. (gr. 2-3). pap. 35.70 *(978-1-4342-6289-9(8))* Stone Arch Bks.

—Bites, 1 vol. Pinelli, Amerigo, illus. 2013. (Ravens Pass Ser.). (ENG.). 96p. (gr. 2-3). lib. bdg. 25.32 *(978-1-4342-4617-2(5))* Stone Arch Bks.

—Cheaters. 2013. (Ravens Pass Ser.). (ENG.). 96p. (gr. 2-3). pap. 35.70 *(978-1-4342-6291-2(X))* Stone Arch Bks.

—Cheaters, 1 vol. Pinelli, Amerigo, illus. 2013. (Ravens Pass Ser.). (ENG.). 96p. (gr. 2-3). lib. bdg. 25.32 *(978-1-4342-4616-5(7))* Stone Arch Bks.

—Curses for Sale, 1 vol. Percival, Tom, illus. 2012. (Ravens Pass Ser.). (ENG.). 96p. (gr. 2-3). pap. 6.15 *(978-1-4342-4209-9(9))*; lib. bdg. 25.32 *(978-1-4342-3763-7(X))* Stone Arch Bks.

—Lost Island, 1 vol. Pinelli, Amerigo, illus. 2013. (Ravens Pass Ser.). (ENG.). 96p. (gr. 2-3). pap. 6.15 *(978-1-4342-6214-1(6))* Stone Arch Bks.

—Lost Island. 2013. (Ravens Pass Ser.). (ENG.). 96p. (gr. 2-3). pap. 35.70 *(978-1-4342-6290-5(1))* Stone Arch Bks.

—Lost Island, 1 vol. Pinelli, Amerigo, illus. 2013. (Ravens Pass Ser.). (ENG.). 96p. (gr. 2-3). lib. bdg. 25.32 *(978-1-4342-4614-1(0))* Stone Arch Bks.

—The Mummy at Midnight. Prothero, Tiffany, illus. 2008. (Shade Bks.). (ENG.). 80p. (gr. 2-3). 25.32 *(978-1-4342-0797-5(8)*, Shade Bks.) Stone Arch Bks.

—New in Town, 1 vol. Percival, Tom, illus. 2012. (Ravens Pass Ser.). (ENG.). 96p. (gr. 2-3). pap. 6.15 *(978-1-4342-4210-5(2))*; lib. bdg. 25.32 *(978-1-4342-3793-4(1))* Stone Arch Bks.

—No Place Like Home, 1 vol. Pinelli, Amerigo, illus. 2013. (Ravens Pass Ser.). (ENG.). 96p. (gr. 2-3). pap. 6.15 *(978-1-4342-6215-8(4))* Stone Arch Bks.

—No Place Like Home. 2013. (Ravens Pass Ser.). (ENG.). 96p. (gr. 2-3). pap. 35.70 *(978-1-4342-6292-9(8))* Stone Arch Bks.

—No Place Like Home, 1 vol. Pinelli, Amerigo, illus. 2013. (Ravens Pass Ser.). (ENG.). 96p. (gr. 2-3). lib. bdg. 25.32 *(978-1-4342-4615-8(9))* Stone Arch Bks.

—Ravens Pass. 2013. (Ravens Pass Ser.). (ENG.). 96p. (gr. 2-3). 202.56 *(978-1-4342-6053-6(4))*; 101.28 *(978-1-4342-6054-3(2))*; pap. 47.60 *(978-1-4342-6294-3(4))*; pap. 285.60 *(978-1-4342-6293-6(6))*; pap. 23.80 *(978-1-4342-6295-0(2))* Stone Arch Bks.

—The Sleeper, 1 vol. Percival, Tom, illus. 2012. (Ravens Pass Ser.). (ENG.). 96p. (gr. 2-3). pap. 6.15 *(978-1-4342-4211-2(0))*; lib. bdg. 25.32 *(978-1-4342-3792-7(3))* Stone Arch Bks.

—Witch Mayor, 1 vol. Percival, Tom, illus. 2012. (Ravens Pass Ser.). (ENG.). 96p. (gr. 2-3). pap. 6.15 *(978-1-4342-4212-9(9))*; lib. bdg. 25.32 *(978-1-4342-3791-0(5))* Stone Arch Bks.

Brian, Kate. Endless (a Shadowlands Novel) 2014. (Shadowlands Ser.). (ENG.). 336p. (YA). (gr. 7-12). 17.99 *(978-1-4231-6485-2(7))* Hyperion Bks. for Children.

—Hereafter (a Shadowlands Novel) 2014. (Shadowlands Ser.). (ENG.). 336p. (YA). (gr. 9-17). pap. 9.99 *(978-1-4231-6526-2(8))* Hyperion Bks. for Children.

—Shadowlands. 2013. (Shadowlands Ser.). (ENG.). 352p. (YA). (gr. 9-17). pap. 9.99 *(978-1-4231-6525-5(X))* Hyperion Pr.

Bright, Rachel. Love Monster & the Scary Something. 2016. (ENG., Illus.). 32p. (J). 17.99 *(978-0-374-34691-1(7)*, 9780374346911, Farrar, Straus & Giroux (BYR)) Farrar, Straus & Giroux.

Brothers Washburn Staff, contrib. by. Mojave Green: Dimensions in Death. 2014. (Dimensions in Death Ser.: 2). (ENG.). 328p. (YA). (gr. 7). pap. 14.99 *(978-1-939967-85-5(6)*, Jolly Fish Pr.) North Star Editions.

Brown, Roberta Simpson. Scared in School. 2005. (ENG.). 141p. (J). (gr. 6-9). pap. 8.95 *(978-0-87483-496-3(1))* August Hse. Pubs., Inc.

—Scariest Stories Ever Told. 2016. (ENG.). 260p. (J). (gr. 4-6). pap. 9.95 *(978-1-939160-99-7(5))* August Hse. Pubs., Inc.

Bruchac, Joseph. Bearwalker. Comport, Sally Wern, illus. 2010. (ENG.). 240p. (J). (gr. 5). pap. 6.99 *(978-0-06-112315-3(3))* HarperCollins Pubs.

—Skeleton Man. Comport, Sally Wern, illus. 2003. (Skeleton Man Ser.: 1). (ENG.). 128p. (J). (gr. 5-18). pap. 5.99 *(978-0-06-440888-2(4))* HarperCollins Pubs.

—Skeleton Man. Comport, Sally Wern, illus. 2003. 114p. (J). (gr. 5). 12.65 *(978-0-7569-3399-9(4))* Perfection Learning Corp.

—Whisper in the Dark. Comport, Sally Wern, illus. 2009. (ENG.). 192p. (J). (gr. 5). pap. 6.99 *(978-0-06-058089-6(5))* HarperCollins Pubs.

Brush Creations & Holmes, A. M. X. Robbie Virtual vs. Vlad the Vampire: Book 1. 2007. 56p. pap. 9.95 *(978-0-7414-3621-4(3))* Infinity Publishing.

Bryant, Clive, ed. Sweeney Todd: The Demon Barber of Fleet Street. Shalvey, Declan et al, illus. 2012. (ENG.). 176p. pap. 16.95 *(978-1-907127-09-0(7)*, Classical Comics, Ltd.); pap. 16.95 *(978-1-907127-10-6(0)*, Classical Comics, Ltd.); (gr. 9). lib. bdg. 24.95 *(978-1-907127-82-3(8))* Classical Comics GBR. Dist: Publishers Group West (PGW).

Buchanan, Andrea J. Gift. 2012. (ENG.). 326p. (YA). (gr. 7-12). pap. 9.99 *(978-1-4532-2023-8(2)*, Open Road Media E-riginal) Open Road Integrated Media, Inc.

Buckingham, Royce. The Dead Boys. 2010. (ENG.). 208p. (J). (gr. 5-18). 16.99 *(978-0-399-25222-8(3)*, G.P. Putnam's Sons Books for Young Readers) Penguin Young Readers Group.

Bunting, Eve. The Lambkins. Keegan, Jonathan, illus. 2005. 192p. (J). (gr. 5-18). (ENG.). 15.99 *(978-0-06-059906-5(5))*; lib. bdg. 16.89 *(978-0-06-059907-2(3))* HarperCollins Pubs. (Cotler, Joanna Books).

—Night of the Gargoyles. Wiesner, David, illus. 2014. 32p. pap. 8.00 *(978-1-61003-176-9(8))* Center for the Collaborative Classroom.

Burke, Anjalena. Siren: Book 3 of the Dead End Series, 1 vol. 2010. 66p. pap. 19.95 *(978-1-4489-5795-8(8))* America Star Bks.

Burke, Anjalena Anita. Ghost: The Dead End Series Book 1, 1 vol. 2009. 73p. pap. 16.95 *(978-1-61582-686-5(6))* PublishAmerica, Inc.

Burt, Steve. Even Odder: More Stories to Chill the Heart. Hagerman, Jessica, illus. 2003. 144p. pap. 14.95 *(978-0-9741407-0-4(8))* Burt, Steven E.

—Oddest Yet: Even More Stories to Chill the Heart. Hagerman, Jessica, illus. 2004. 144p. (gr. 5-18). pap. 14.95 *(978-0-9741407-1-1(6))* Burt, Steven E.

Butler, Dori Hillestad. The Secret Room. 2015. (Haunted Library: 5). (Illus.). 128p. (J). lib. bdg. 16.00 *(978-0-606-36768-4(3))* Turtleback Bks.

Cabot, Meg. Haunted. 2004. (Mediator Ser.: No. 5). (ENG.). 288p. (J). (gr. 7-18). pap. 6.99 *(978-0-06-447278-4(7)*, Harper Trophy) HarperCollins Pubs.

Cabot, Meg, et al. Prom Nights from Hell. 2010. (ENG.). 336p. (YA). (gr. 9). pap. 9.99 *(978-0-06-197600-1(8)*, HarperTeen) HarperCollins Pubs.

Caine, Rachel, pseud. Carpe Corpus. 2009. (Morganville Vampires Ser.: 6). (ENG.). 256p. (YA). (gr. 9-18). mass mkt. 7.99 *(978-0-451-22719-5(0)*, Berkley) Penguin Publishing Group.

—Fade Out. 2009. (Morganville Vampires Ser.: Bk. 7). 256p. (YA). lib. bdg. 20.00 *(978-1-4242-4701-1(2))* Fitzgerald Bks.

—Fade Out. 2009. (Morganville Vampires Ser.: 7). (ENG.). 256p. (YA). (gr. 9-18). mass mkt. 7.99 *(978-0-451-22866-6(9)*, Berkley) Penguin Publishing Group.

—Feast of Fools. 2008. (Morganville Vampires Ser.: Bk. 4). 256p. (YA). lib. bdg. 20.00 *(978-1-4242-4702-8(0))* Fitzgerald Bks.

—Feast of Fools. 2008. (Morganville Vampires Ser.: 4). (ENG.). 256p. (YA). (gr. 9-18). mass mkt. 7.99 *(978-0-451-22463-7(9)*, Berkley) Penguin Publishing Group.

Campbell, Suzy. The Hidden Graveyard. 2011. 62p. pap. 19.95 *(978-1-4560-4265-3(3))* America Star Bks.

Capstone Press. Scary Stories, 1 vol. 2010. (Scary Stories Ser.). (ENG.). 32p. lib. bdg. 106.60 *(978-1-4296-5914-7(9)*, Edge Bks.) Capstone Press of Coughlan Cos.

Carman, Patrick. Thirteen Days to Midnight. 2011. (ENG.). 304p. (J). (gr. 7-17). pap. 10.99 *(978-0-316-00404-6(9))* Little, Brown Bks. for Young Readers.

—3:15 Season One Things That Go Bump in the Night. 2011. (3:15 Ser.: 1). (ENG.). 176p. (J). (gr. 5-9). 12.99 *(978-0-545-38475-9(3))* Scholastic, Inc.

Carman, Patrick & Studios, P. c. The Crossbones. 2010. (Skeleton Creek Ser.: 3). (ENG.). 224p. (J). (gr. 3-7). 14.99 *(978-0-545-24994-2(5))* Scholastic, Inc.

Carmitchel, Andrew. A Wizard on Oak Street. 2007. 68p. per. 8.95 *(978-0-595-47849-1(2))* iUniverse, Inc.

Carnevale, Michael. The Hotel Coolidge. 2007. 91p. pap. 10.95 *(978-0-7414-3752-5(X))* Infinity Publishing.

Carpenter, Michelle D. More No Fear here Six Scary Stories to Thrill You & the Kids + Extras. 2004. 61p. per. 9.99 *(978-1-4116-1706-3(1))* Lulu Pr., Inc.

—No Fear Here Five Scary Stories to Thrill You & the Kids. 2004. 85p. per. 6.54 *(978-1-4116-1579-3(4))* Lulu Pr., Inc.

Carr, Elias & Karre, Andrew. The Combination. 2011. (Night Fall Ser.). (ENG.). 120p. (YA). (gr. 6-12). pap. 7.95 *(978-0-7613-7810-5(3))* Lerner Publishing Group.

Carretero, Mónica. HAUNTED HOUSES HANDBOOK. 2013. (Handbooks Ser.). (ENG., Illus.). 32p. (J). (gr. k-2). *(978-84-15241-05-8(4))* D P & G Military Pubs.

Carter, Rebecca. Moonlit Daydreams. 2010. 71p. pap. 11.99 *(978-0-557-35588-4(5))* Lulu Pr., Inc.

Cary, Kate. Bloodline. 2006. (ENG.). 352p. (YA). (gr. 7-12). 9.99 *(978-1-59514-078-4(6)*, Razorbill) Penguin Young Readers Group.

—Reckoning. 2008. (ENG.). 320p. (YA). (gr. 7-18). pap. 9.99 *(978-1-59514-179-8(0)*, Razorbill) Penguin Young Readers Group.

La Casa de los Alaridos. (Fantasmas de Fear Street Coleccion). (SPA.). (YA). (gr. 5-8). pap. 7.95 *(978-950-04-1870-6(3)*, EM10013) Emecé Editores S.A. ARG. Dist: Planeta Publishing Corp., Lectorum Pubns., Inc.

Cascone, Annette & Cascone, Gina. Grave Secrets. 2014. (Deadtime Stories Ser.). (ENG.). 192p. (J). (gr. 3-7). pap. 6.99 *(978-0-7653-3071-0(7)*, 9780765330710, Starscape) Doherty, Tom Assocs., LLC.

—Little Magic Shop of Horrors. 2013. (Deadtime Stories Ser.: 5). (ENG.). 192p. (J). (gr. 3-7). pap. 6.99 *(978-0-7653-3069-7(5)*, 9780765330697, Starscape) Doherty, Tom Assocs., LLC.

H I

—The Witching Game. (Deadtime Stories Ser.). (ENG.). 192p. (J). (gr. 3-7). 2014. pap. 6.99 (978-0-7653-3072-7(5), 9780765330727) 2012. mass mkt. 5.99 (978-0-7653-6972-7(9), 9780765369727) Doherty, Tom Assocs., LLC. (Starscape).

Cascone, Gina & Cascone, Annette. Little Magic Shop of Horrors. 2012. (Deadtime Stories Ser.: 5). (ENG.). 192p. (J). (gr. 3-7). 14.99 (978-0-7653-3075-8(X), 9780765330758, Starscape) Doherty, Tom Assocs., LLC.

Casey, Joe. Haunt, Vol. 4. 2012. (ENG., Illus.). 140p. (YA). pap. 14.99 (978-1-60706-588-3(6), 9781607065883) Image Comics.

Castro, Adam-Troy. Gustav Gloom & the Four Terrors. Margiotta, Kristen, illus. 2013. (Gustav Gloom Ser.: 3). (ENG.). 248p. (J). (gr. 3-7). 12.99 (978-0-448-45835-9(7), Grosset & Dunlap) Penguin Young Readers Group.

—Gustav Gloom & the Nightmare Vault, No. 2. Margiotta, Kristen, illus. 2013. (Gustav Gloom Ser.: 2). (ENG.). 248p. (J). (gr. 3-7). 12.99 (978-0-448-45834-2(9), Grosset & Dunlap) Penguin Young Readers Group.

—Gustav Gloom & the Nightmare Vault #2. Margiotta, Kristen, illus. 2014. (Gustav Gloom Ser.: 2). (ENG.). 248p. (J). (gr. 3-7). 7.99 (978-0-448-48329-0(7), Grosset & Dunlap) Penguin Young Readers Group.

—Gustav Gloom & the People Taker. Margiotta, Kristen, illus. 2012. (Gustav Gloom Ser.: 1). (ENG.). 232p. (J). (gr. 3-7). 12.99 (978-0-448-45833-5(0), Grosset & Dunlap) Penguin Young Readers Group.

Castro, Adam-Troy & dePaola, Tomie. Gustav Gloom & the Cryptic Carousel #4. Margiotta, Kristen, illus. 2015. (Gustav Gloom Ser.: 4). (ENG.). 248p. (J). (gr. 3-7). 7.99 (978-0-448-48719-9(5), Grosset & Dunlap) Penguin Young Readers Group.

—Gustav Gloom & the Inn of Shadows #5. Margiotta, Kristen, illus. 2015. (Gustav Gloom Ser.: 5). (ENG.). 248p. (J). (gr. 3-7). bds. 12.99 (978-0-448-46458-9(6), Grosset & Dunlap) Penguin Young Readers Group.

Caswell, Brian. Double Exposure. 2005. 240p. (YA). pap. (978-0-7022-3533-7(4)) Univ. of Queensland Pr.

Cawthon, Scott & Breed-Wrisley, Kira. The Silver Eyes. 2016. (Five Nights at Freddy's Ser.: 1). (ENG.). 400p. (J). (gr. 7-7). pap. 9.99 (978-1-338-13437-7(X)) Scholastic, Inc.

—The Silver Eyes. 2016. (Five Nights at Freddy's Ser.: bk.1). (YA). lib. bdg. 20.85 **(978-0-606-39982-1(8))** Turtleback Bks.

—The Twisted Ones. 2017. (Five Nights at Freddy's Ser.: bk.2). (ENG.). 304p. (YA). (gr. 7-7). pap. 9.99 **(978-1-338-13930-3(4))** Scholastic, Inc.

Chabert, Jack. The Locker Ate Lucy! Ricks, Sam, illus. 2014. (Eerie Elementary — Branches Ser.: bk.2). (ENG.). 96p. (J). (gr. 1-3). 15.99 (978-0-545-62396-4(0)); pap. 4.99 (978-0-545-62395-7(2)) Scholastic, Inc.

—The Locker Ate Lucy! 2014. (Eerie Elementary — Branches Ser.: bk.2). (ENG.). (J). lib. bdg. 14.75 (978-0-606-36052-4(2)) Turtleback Bks.

—Recess Is a Jungle! Ricks, Sam, illus. 2016. (Eerie Elementary — Branches Ser.: bk.3). (ENG.). 96p. (J). (gr. 1-3). 15.99 (978-0-545-87353-6(3)) Scholastic, Inc.

—School Freezes Over! Ricks, Sam, illus. 2016. (Eerie Elementary — Branches Ser.: bk.5). (ENG.). 96p. (J). (gr. 1-3). pap. 4.99 (978-0-545-87373-4(8)) Scholastic, Inc.

—The School Is Alive! Ricks, Sam, illus. 2014. (Eerie Elementary — Branches Ser.: bk.1). (ENG.). 96p. (J). (gr. 1-3). 15.99 (978-0-545-62393-3(6)); pap. 4.99 (978-0-545-62392-6(8)) Scholastic, Inc.

—The School Is Alive! 2014. (Eerie Elementary — Branches Ser.: bk.1). (ENG.). (J). lib. bdg. 14.75 (978-0-606-35822-4(6)) Turtleback Bks.

—The Science Fair Is Freaky! Ricks, Sam, illus. 2016. (Eerie Elementary — Branches Ser.: bk.4). (ENG.). 96p. (J). (gr. 1-3). pap. 4.99 (978-0-545-87368-0(1)) Scholastic, Inc.

—The Science Fair Is Freaky! 2016. (Eerie Elementary — Branches Ser.: bk.4). (ENG.). (J). lib. bdg. 14.75 (978-0-606-38806-1(0)) Turtleback Bks.

Chalifoux, Lisa M. Bravery Is like Love. Perras, Marielle, illus. 2009. 24p. pap. 10.99 (978-1-4269-0942-9(X)) Trafford Publishing.

Chalmers, Jason. Camp Sacrowee. 2011. 84p. pap. 19.95 (978-1-4241-7494-2(5)) America Star Bks.

Chan, Marty. Barnabas Bigfoot: Bone Eater. 2013. (ENG.). 112p. (gr. 8-11). pap. 10.95 (978-1-927068-43-4(6)) Thistledown Pr., Ltd. CAN. Dist: Univ. of Toronto Pr.

Chandler, Elizabeth. The Deep End of Fear. 2008. (Dark Secrets Ser.: 4). (ENG.). 320p. (J). (gr. 7). pap. 13.99 (978-1-4169-7142-9(4), Simon Pulse) Simon Pulse.

—Legacy of Lies - Don't Tell. 2009. (Dark Secrets Ser.: 1). (ENG., Illus.). 496p. (YA). (gr. 7-18). pap. 9.99 (978-1-4169-9461-9(0), Simon Pulse) Simon Pulse.

—No Time to Die - The Deep End of Fear No. 2. 2010. (Dark Secrets Ser.: 2). (ENG.). 624p. (YA). (gr. 7). pap. 9.99 (978-1-4169-9462-6(9), Simon Pulse) Simon Pulse.

Charles, Veronika Martenova. Don't Eat That! Parkins, David, illus. 2008. (Easy-To-Read Spooky Tales Ser.). (ENG.). 56p. (J). (gr. k-3). pap. 5.95 (978-0-88776-857-6(1), Tundra Bks.) Tundra Bks. CAN. Dist: Penguin Random Hse. LLC.

—Don't Enter the House! Parkins, David, illus. 2008. (Easy-To-Read Spooky Tales Ser.). (ENG.). 56p. (J). (gr. k-3). pap. 5.95 (978-0-88776-856-9(3), Tundra Bks.) Tundra Bks. CAN. Dist: Penguin Random Hse. LLC.

—Don't Forget! Parkins, David, illus. 2008. (Easy-To-Read Spooky Tales Ser.). (ENG.). 56p. (J). (gr. k-3). pap. 5.95 (978-0-88776-859-0(8), Tundra Bks.) Tundra Bks. CAN. Dist: Penguin Random Hse. LLC.

—Don't Go in There! Parkins, David, illus. 2007. (Easy-To-Read Spooky Tales Ser.). (ENG.). 56p. (J). (gr. k-3). pap. 5.95 (978-0-88776-781-4(8), Tundra Bks.) Tundra Bks. CAN. Dist: Penguin Random Hse. LLC.

—Don't Go into the Forest! Parkins, David, illus. 2007. (Easy-To-Read Spooky Tales Ser.). (ENG.). 56p. (J). (gr. k-3). pap. 5.95 (978-0-88776-778-4(8), Tundra Bks.) Tundra Bks. CAN. Dist: Penguin Random Hse. LLC.

—Don't Go near the Water! Parkins, David, illus. 2007. (Easy-To-Read Spooky Tales Ser.). (ENG.). 56p. (J). (gr. k-3). pap. 5.95 (978-0-88776-780-7(X), Tundra Bks.) Tundra Bks. CAN. Dist: Penguin Random Hse. LLC.

—Don't Open the Door! Parkins, David, illus. 2007. (Easy-To-Read Spooky Tales Ser.). (ENG.). 56p. (J). (gr. k-3). pap. 5.95 (978-0-88776-779-1(6), Tundra Bks.) Tundra Bks. CAN. Dist: Penguin Random Hse. LLC.

—Don't Talk to Strangers! Parkins, David, illus. 2008. (Easy-To-Read Spooky Tales Ser.). (ENG.). 56p. (J). (gr. k-3). pap. 5.95 (978-0-88776-847-7(4), Tundra Bks.) Tundra Bks. CAN. Dist: Penguin Random Hse. LLC.

—Don't Touch That! Parkins, David, illus. 2008. (Easy-To-Read Spooky Tales Ser.). (ENG.). 56p. (J). (gr. k-3). pap. 5.95 (978-0-88776-858-3(X), Tundra Bks.) Tundra Bks. CAN. Dist: Penguin Random Hse. LLC.

—Don't Walk Alone at Night! Parkins, David, illus. 2007. (Easy-To-Read Spooky Tales Ser.). (ENG.). 56p. (J). (gr. k-3). pap. 5.95 (978-0-88776-782-1(6), Tundra Bks.) Tundra Bks. CAN. Dist: Penguin Random Hse. LLC.

Chowdary, Daddala Vineesha. The Locket of Moonstone. 2013. 120p. (gr. 10-12). 30.95 (978-1-4828-1234-3(7)); pap. 11.95 (978-1-4828-1235-0(5)) Author Solutions, Inc. (PartridgeIndia).

Chupeco, Rin. The Girl from the Well. 2014. (ENG.). 272p. (YA). (gr. 9-12). 16.99 (978-1-4022-9218-7(X), 9781402292187) Sourcebooks, Inc.

—The Suffering. 2015. (ENG.). 320p. (YA). (gr. 8-12). 16.99 (978-1-4926-2983-2(9), 9781492629832) Sourcebooks, Inc.

Clare, Cassandra. City of Bones. (Mortal Instruments Ser.: Bk. 1). (ENG., Illus.). (YA). (gr. 9). 2015. 544p. pap. 13.99 (978-1-4814-5592-3(3)) 2007. 496p. 21.99 (978-1-4169-1428-0(5)) 2015. 544p. pap. 13.99 (978-1-4814-7030-8(2)) McElderry, Margaret K. Bks. (McElderry, Margaret K. Bks.).

—City of Bones. 2008. (Mortal Instruments Ser.: Bk. 1). 485p. (gr. 9-12). 23.00 (978-1-60686-361-9(4)) Perfection Learning Corp.

—City of Bones, 12 vols. 2007. (Mortal Instruments Ser.: 1). (YA). 131.75 (978-1-4281-5454-4(X)); 120.75 (978-1-4281-5450-6(7)); 1.25 (978-1-4281-5445-2(0)); 286.75 (978-1-4281-5449-0(3)); 122.75 (978-1-4281-5448-3(5)); 133.75 (978-1-4281-5452-0(3)) Recorded Bks., Inc.

—City of Bones. 2013. (The Mortal Instruments Ser.: Bk. 1). pap. (978-1-4424-9306-3(2)) Simon & Schuster, Inc.

—City of Bones. l.t. ed. 2008. (Mortal Instruments Ser.: 1). 629p. (YA). 31.95 (978-1-4104-0958-4(9)) Thorndike Pr.

—City of Bones. 2015. (Mortal Instruments Ser.: Bk. 1). 544p. (YA). lib. bdg. 25.75 (978-0-606-37731-7(X)) Turtleback Bks.

—City of Heavenly Fire. 2014. (Mortal Instruments Ser.: No. 6). (ENG., Illus.). 752p. (YA). (gr. 9). 24.99 (978-1-4424-1689-5(0), McElderry, Margaret K. Bks.) McElderry, Margaret K. Bks.

—City of Lost Souls. (Mortal Instruments Ser.: Bk. 5). (ENG., (YA). (gr. 9). 2015. Illus.). 592p. pap. 13.99 (978-1-4814-5600-5(8)) 2012. 544p. 21.99 (978-1-4424-1686-4(6)) McElderry, Margaret K. Bks. (McElderry, Margaret K. Bks.).

—City of Lost Souls, 16 vols. 2012. (Mortal Instruments Ser.: Bk. 5). (YA). 135.75 (978-1-4640-3948-5(8)); 133.75 (978-1-4640-3952-2(6)); 133.75 (978-1-4640-3951-5(8)); 317.75 (978-1-4640-3949-2(6)) Recorded Bks., Inc.

—City of Lost Souls. 2015. (Mortal Instruments Ser.: Bk. 5). 592p. (YA). lib. bdg. 25.75 (978-0-606-37736-2(0)) Turtleback Bks.

—City of Lost Souls. 2012. 512p. pap. (978-1-4063-3760-0(9)) Walker Bks., Ltd.

Clare, Cassandra, et al. The Bane Chronicles. Clare, Cassandra, ed. 2014. (Bane Chronicles Ser.). (ENG., Illus.). 528p. (YA). (gr. 9). 22.99 (978-1-4424-9599-9(5), McElderry, Margaret K. Bks.) McElderry, Margaret K. Bks.

—Tales from the Shadowhunter Academy. (Tales from the Shadowhunter Academy Ser.). (ENG.). (YA). (gr. 9). 2017. 704p. pap. 14.99 **(978-1-4814-4326-5(7))** 2016. (Illus.). 672p. 23.99 (978-1-4814-4325-8(9)) McElderry, Margaret K. Bks. (McElderry, Margaret K. Bks.).

Clark, Mary Higgins. Ghost Ship. Minor, Wendell, illus. 2007. (ENG.). 40p. (J). (gr. 1-5). 17.99 (978-1-4169-3514-8(2), Simon & Schuster/Paula Wiseman Bks.) Simon & Schuster/Paula Wiseman Bks.

Clasicos de Terror, Vol. I. (Clasicos Juveniles Coleccion). (SPA.). (YA). (gr. 5-8). pap. (978-950-11-1282-5(9), SG4721) Sigmar ARG. Dist: Lectorum Pubns., Inc.

Clasicos de Terror III. (Coleccion Clasicos Juveniles). (SPA.). (YA). (gr. 5-8). (978-950-11-1617-5(4)) Sigmar ARG. Dist: Lectorum Pubns., Inc.

Classic Goosebumps & Stine, R. L. Be Careful What You Wish For. 2009. (Classic Goosebumps Ser.: 7). (ENG.). 160p. (J). (gr. 3-7). 6.99 (978-0-545-03524-8(4), Scholastic Paperbacks) Scholastic, Inc.

—The Curse of the Mummy's Tomb. 2009. (Classic Goosebumps Ser.: 6). (ENG.). 160p. (J). (gr. 3-7). 6.99 (978-0-545-03523-1(6), Scholastic Paperbacks) Scholastic, Inc.

—Say Cheese & Die! 2009. (Classic Goosebumps Ser.: 8). (ENG.). 160p. (J). (gr. 3-7). 6.99 (978-0-545-03525-5(2), Scholastic Paperbacks) Scholastic, Inc.

Clement-Moore, Rosemary. Hell Week. 2009. (Maggie Quinn: Girl vs Evil Ser.). (ENG.). 336p. (YA). (gr. 9). pap. 9.99 (978-0-385-73415-8(8), Delacorte Bks. for Young Readers) Random Hse. Children's Bks.

—Prom Dates from Hell. 2008. (Maggie Quinn: Girl vs Evil Ser.). (ENG.). 320p. (YA). (gr. 9). pap. 8.99 (978-0-385-73413-4(1), Delacorte Bks. for Young Readers) Random Hse. Children's Bks.

Climer, Steven Lee. Young of Heart. 2006. (YA). pap. (978-0-9790649-5-1(3)) Mardi Gras Publishing, LLC.

Cohen, Marina. The Doll's Eye. 2017. (ENG.). 208p. (J). 16.99 (978-1-62672-204-0(8), 9781626722040) Roaring Brook Pr.

—The Inn Between. Watts, Sarah, illus. 2016. (ENG.). 208p. (J). 16.99 (978-1-62672-202-6(1), 9781626722026) Roaring Brook Pr.

Colandro, Lucille. There Was an Old Lady Who Swallowed a Bat! Lee, Jared, illus. 2005. (ENG.). 32p. (J). (gr. -1-3). pap. 6.99 (978-0-439-73766-1(4), Cartwheel Bks.) Scholastic, Inc.

Common, Gabriel. The Demon of Basile High: The Return of Cassius. 2007. 132p. per. 11.95 (978-1-4327-0664-7(0)) Outskirts Pr., Inc.

Cooney, Caroline B. Freeze Tag. 2016. (ENG.). 160p. (J). (gr. 7-12). pap. 11.99 (978-1-5040-3555-2(0)) Open Road Integrated Media, Inc.

—The Stranger. 2016. (ENG.). 164p. (J). (gr. 7-12). pap. 11.99 (978-1-5040-3557-6(7)) Open Road Integrated Media, Inc.

—Twins. 2016. (ENG.). 150p. (J). (gr. 7-12). pap. 11.99 (978-1-5040-3559-0(3)) Open Road Integrated Media, Inc.

Cooper, Louise. Short & Scary! 2014. (ENG., Illus.). 96p. (J). 10.95 (978-0-19-278190-1(1)) Oxford Univ. Pr., Inc.

Cormier, Robert. El Sindrome de la Ternura. Palmer, Magdalena, tr. 2005. (Escritura desatada Ser.).Tr. of Tenderness. (SPA.). 208p. (YA). pap. 11.95 (978-84-666-0160-3(0)) Ediciones B ESP. Dist: Independent Pubs. Group.

Cormier, Shawn P. NiDemon. 2005. (YA). per. 12.95 (978-0-9740151-1-8(3)) Pine View Pr.

Coville, Bruce. Odds Are Good: An Oddly Enough & Odder Than Ever Omnibus. 2006. (ENG., Illus.). 352p. (YA). (gr. 7-12). pap. 16.95 (978-0-15-205716-9(1)) Houghton Mifflin Harcourt Publishing Co.

Creagh, Kelly. Enshadowed. 2012. (ENG., Illus.). 448p. (YA). (gr. 7). 17.99 (978-1-4424-0204-1(0), Atheneum Bks. for Young Readers) Simon & Schuster Children's Publishing.

—Enshadowed: A Nevermore Book. 2013. (ENG., Illus.). 464p. (YA). (gr. 7). pap. 9.99 (978-1-4424-0206-5(7)) Simon & Schuster Children's Publishing.

—Nevermore. (ENG., Illus.). (YA). (gr. 9). 2011. 576p. pap. 9.99 (978-1-4424-0201-0(6)) 2010. 560p. 17.99 (978-1-4424-0200-3(8)) Simon & Schuster Children's Publishing. (Atheneum Bks. for Young Readers).

—Oblivion. 2015. (ENG.). 448p. (YA). (gr. 7). 18.99 (978-1-4424-3627-5(1)) Simon & Schuster Children's Publishing.

Cresse, Peter. The Bloody Hand. 2009. (Illus.). 40p. pap. 18.95 (978-1-4389-2161-7(6)) AuthorHouse.

Croall, Marie P. School of Evil. Carruthers, Sandy, illus. 2010. (Twisted Journeys (r) Ser.: 13). (ENG.). 112p. (J). (gr. 4-7). pap. 7.95 (978-0-8225-9271-6(1), Graphic Universe™); lib. bdg. 27.93 (978-0-8225-9263-1(0)) Lerner Publishing Group.

Crossley-Holland, Kevin. Enchantment: Fairy Tales, Ghost Stories & Tales of Wonder. Chichester Clark, Emma, illus. 2003. 128p. (YA). reprint ed. 22.00 (978-0-7567-6961-1(2)) DIANE Publishing Co.

Crowell, Peter Thomas. Haunted Mountain: The Tales of True Adventure, Book Two. 2006. (J). 19.95 (978-0-9740290-8-5(4)) Crowell, Peter T. Pubns.

Cummings, Troy. Attack of the Shadow Smashers. 2013. (Notebook of Doom Ser.: 3). (ENG.). 96p. (J). (gr. 1-3). pap. 4.99 (978-0-545-55297-4(4)) Scholastic, Inc.

—Attack of the Shadow Smashers. 2013. (Notebook of Doom Ser.: 3). lib. bdg. 14.75 (978-0-606-32369-7(4), Turtleback) Turtleback Bks.

—Charge of the Lightning Bugs. Cummings, Troy, illus. 2015. (Notebook of Doom Ser.: 8). (ENG., Illus.). 96p. (J). (gr. 1-3). 15.99 (978-0-545-79554-8(0)); pap. 4.99 (978-0-545-79555-5(9)) Scholastic, Inc.

—Chomp of the Meat-Eating Vegetables. 2014. (Notebook of Doom Ser.: 4). (ENG.). 96p. (J). (gr. 1-3). 15.99 (978-0-545-55300-1(8)); (Illus.). pap. 4.99 (978-0-545-55299-8(0)) Scholastic, Inc.

—Chomp of the Meat-Eating Vegetables. 2014. (Notebook of Doom Ser.: 4). lib. bdg. 14.75 (978-0-606-35362-5(3)) Turtleback Bks.

—Day of the Night Crawlers. 2013. (Notebook of Doom Ser.: 2). (ENG.). 96p. (J). (gr. 1-3). 15.99 (978-0-545-49324-6(2)); pap. 4.99 (978-0-545-49325-3(0)); E-Book (978-0-545-49327-7(7)) Scholastic, Inc.

—Day of the Night Crawlers. 2013. (Notebook of Doom Ser.: 2). lib. bdg. 14.75 (978-0-606-32368-0(6), Turtleback) Turtleback Bks.

—Flurry of the Snombies. 2015. (Notebook of Doom Ser.: 7). (ENG., Illus.). 96p. (J). (gr. 1-3). 15.99 (978-0-545-79551-7(6)); pap. 4.99 (978-0-545-79550-0(8)) Scholastic, Inc.

—March of the Vanderpants. 2017. (Notebook of Doom — Branches Ser.: 12). lib. bdg. 14.75 **(978-0-606-40192-0(X))** Turtleback Bks.

—The Notebook of Doom #6: Pop of the Bumpy Mummy (a Branches Book) - Library Edition. 2014. (Notebook of Doom Ser.: 6). (ENG.). 96p. (J). (gr. 1-3). 15.99 (978-0-545-69899-3(5)) Scholastic, Inc.

—The Notebook of Doom Collection, Bks. 1-3. Cummings, Troy, illus. 2016. (Notebook of Doom Ser.). (ENG., Illus.). 288p. (J). (gr. 1-3). pap. 9.99 (978-1-338-10199-7(4)) Scholastic, Inc.

—Pop of the Bumpy Mummy. Cummings, Troy, illus. 2014. (Notebook of Doom Ser.: 6). (ENG., Illus.). 96p. (J). (gr. 1-3). pap. 4.99 (978-0-545-69898-6(7)) Scholastic, Inc.

—Rise of the Balloon Goons. 2013. (Notebook of Doom Ser.: 1). (ENG., Illus.). 96p. (J). (gr. 1-3). 15.99 (978-0-545-49322-2(6)); pap. 4.99 (978-0-545-49323-9(4)) Scholastic, Inc.

—Snap of the Super-Goop. 2016. (Notebook of Doom Ser.: 10). lib. bdg. 14.75 (978-0-606-38805-4(2)) Turtleback Bks.

—Snap of the Super-Goop: A Branches Book. Cummings, Troy, illus. 2016. (Notebook of Doom Ser.: 1). (ENG., Illus.). 96p. (J). (gr. 1-3). 15.99 (978-0-545-86500-5(X)) Scholastic, Inc.

—Snap of the Super-Goop - A Branches Book. Cummings, Troy, illus. 2016. (Notebook of Doom Ser.: 1). (ENG., Illus.). 96p. (J). (gr. 1-3). pap. 4.99 (978-0-545-86499-2(2)) Scholastic, Inc.

—Sneeze of the Octo-Schnozz: a Branches Book (the Notebook of Doom #11) 2016. (Notebook of Doom Ser.: 11). (ENG.). 96p. (J). (gr. 1-3). pap. 4.99 (978-1-338-03448-6(0)) Scholastic, Inc.

—Whack of the P-Rex. 2014. (Notebook of Doom Ser.: 5). (ENG.). 96p. (J). (gr. 1-3). pap. 4.99 (978-0-545-69895-5(2)) Scholastic, Inc.

Cunningham, Mary. Curse of the Bayou. 2007. (Cynthia's Attic Ser.). 157p. (J). per. 9.99 (978-1-59080-575-6(5)) Echelon Press Publishing.

Cushman, Doug. Dirk Bones & the Mystery of the Haunted House. Cushman, Doug, illus. 2009. (I Can Read Level 1 Ser.). (ENG., Illus.). 32p. (J). (gr. k-3). pap. 3.99 (978-0-06-073767-2(0)) HarperCollins Pubs.

Cusick, Richie Tankersley. It Begins - Rest in Peace, Vol. 1. 2012. (Unseen Ser.: 1). (ENG.). 576p. (YA). (gr. 7). pap. 7.99 (978-0-14-242336-3(X), Speak) Penguin Young Readers Group.

—Someone at the Door. 2013. (ENG., Illus.). 256p. (Orig.). (YA). (gr. 7). pap. 16.99 (978-1-4814-0163-0(7), Simon Pulse) Simon Pulse.

—The Unseen 2 Rest in Peace. 2005. (Unseen Ser.: 2). (ENG.). 304p. (YA). (gr. 7-7). 8.99 (978-0-14-240464-5(0), Speak) Penguin Young Readers Group.

—The Unseen IV. 2005. (Point Horror Ser.). 400p. pap. (978-0-439-96345-9(1)) Scholastic, Inc.

—The Unseen Volume 2: Blood Brothers/Sin & Salvation. 2012. (Unseen Ser.: 2). (ENG.). 640p. (YA). (gr. 7). pap. 7.99 (978-0-14-242337-0(8), Speak) Penguin Young Readers Group.

Dahl, Michael. Blood in the Library, 1 vol. Kendall, Bradford, illus. 2011. (Return to the Library of Doom Ser.). (ENG.). 72p. (gr. 1-3). lib. bdg. 23.99 (978-1-4342-3228-1(X), Zone Bks.) Stone Arch Bks.

—Blood Shark! Sinkovec, Igor, illus. 2015. (Igor's Lab of Fear Ser.). (ENG.). 40p. (gr. 1-3). lib. bdg. 23.99 (978-1-4965-0456-2(9)) Stone Arch Bks.

—The Book That Ate My Brother, 1 vol. Kendall, Bradford, illus. 2010. (Return to the Library of Doom Ser.). (ENG.). 72p. (gr. 1-3). lib. bdg. 23.99 (978-1-4342-2144-5(X), Zone Bks.) Stone Arch Bks.

—The Boy Who Was It: And Other Scary Tales. Bonet, Xavier, illus. 2016. (Michael Dahl's Really Scary Stories Ser.). (ENG.). 72p. (gr. 2-3). lib. bdg. 25.32 (978-1-4965-3772-0(6)) Stone Arch Bks.

—Brain Invaders. Catling, Andy, illus. 2016. (Igor's Lab of Fear Ser.). (ENG.). 40p. (gr. 1-3). lib. bdg. 23.99 (978-1-4965-3526-9(X)) Stone Arch Bks.

—Dark Tower Rising, 1 vol. Kovar, Ben, illus. 2012. (Troll Hunters Ser.). (ENG.). 112p. (gr. 2-3). lib. bdg. 25.32 (978-1-4342-3308-0(1), Troll Hunters) Stone Arch Bks.

—Death Sentence. Evergreen, Nelson, illus. 2015. (Library of Doom: the Final Chapters Ser.). (ENG.). 40p. (gr. 1-3). 23.99 (978-1-4342-9678-8(4)) Stone Arch Bks.

—Dictionary of 1,000 Rooms, 1 vol. Kendall, Bradford, illus. 2011. (Return to the Library of Doom Ser.). (ENG.). 72p. (gr. 1-3). lib. bdg. 23.99 (978-1-4342-3229-8(8), Zone Bks.) Stone Arch Bks.

—The Doll That Waved Goodbye: And Other Scary Tales. Bonet, Xavier, illus. 2015. (Michael Dahl's Really Scary Stories Ser.). (ENG.). 72p. (gr. 2-3). lib. bdg. 25.32 (978-1-4965-0595-8(6)) Stone Arch Bks.

—Don't Open It! Kendall, Bradford, illus. 2016. 40p. (J). (978-1-4747-1054-1(9)) Stone Arch Bks.

—Electric Claw. Catling, Andy, illus. 2016. (Igor's Lab of Fear Ser.). (ENG.). 40p. (gr. 1-3). lib. bdg. 23.99 (978-1-4965-3527-6(8)) Stone Arch Bks.

—Fallen Star, 1 vol. Kovar, Ben, illus. 2012. (Troll Hunters Ser.). (ENG.). 112p. (gr. 2-3). lib. bdg. 25.32 (978-1-4342-3310-3(3), Troll Hunters) Stone Arch Bks.

—Frightmares: A Creepy Collection of Scary Stories. Bonet, Xavier, illus. 2015. (Michael Dahl's Really Scary Stories Ser.). (ENG.). 224p. (gr. 2-3). pap. 8.95 (978-1-4965-0598-9(0)) Stone Arch Bks.

—Frightmares 2: More Scary Stories for the Fearless Reader. Bonet, Xavier, illus. 2016. (Michael Dahl's Really Scary Stories Ser.). (ENG.). 224p. (gr. 2-3). pap. 8.95 (978-1-4965-4136-9(7)) Stone Arch Bks.

—Frightmares 3: Even More Scary Stories to Read If You Dare. Bonet, Xavier, illus. 2017. (Michael Dahl's Really Scary Stories Ser.). (ENG.). 224p. (gr. 2-3). pap. 8.95 **(978-1-4965-4915-0(5))** Stone Arch Bks.

—Ghost Writer, 1 vol. Kendall, Bradford, illus. 2011. (Return to the Library of Doom Ser.). (ENG.). 72p. (gr. 1-3). lib. bdg. 23.99 (978-1-4342-3230-4(1), Zone Bks.) Stone Arch Bks.

—The Girl in the Graveyard: And Other Scary Tales. Bonet, Xavier, illus. 2017. (Michael Dahl's Really Scary Stories Ser.). (ENG.). 72p. (gr. 2-3). lib. bdg. 25.32 **(978-1-4965-4901-3(5))** Stone Arch Bks.

—The Goblin in the Grass: And Other Scary Tales. Bonet, Xavier, illus. 2016. (Michael Dahl's Really Scary Stories Ser.). (ENG.). 72p. (gr. 2-3). lib. bdg. 25.32 (978-1-4965-3773-7(4)) Stone Arch Bks.

—Igor's Lab of Fear, 4 vols. 2015. (Igor's Lab of Fear Ser.). (ENG.). 40p. (gr. 1-3). lib. bdg. 95.96 (978-1-4965-2031-9(9)) Stone Arch Bks.

—A Jar of Eyeballs. Sinkovec, Igor, illus. 2015. (Igor's Lab of Fear Ser.). (ENG.). 40p. (gr. 1-3). lib. bdg. 23.99 (978-1-4965-0455-5(0)) Stone Arch Bks.

—Killer App, 1 vol. Kendall, Bradford, illus. 2011. (Return to the Library of Doom Ser.). (ENG.). 72p. (gr. 1-3). lib. bdg. 23.99 (978-1-4342-3231-1(X), Zone Bks.) Stone Arch Bks.

—The Last Word. Kendall, Bradford, illus. 2016. 40p. (J). (978-1-4747-1055-8(7)) Stone Arch Bks.

—The Lava Crown, 1 vol. Kovar, Ben, illus. 2012. (Troll Hunters Ser.). (ENG.). 112p. (gr. 2-3). lib. bdg. 25.32 (978-1-4342-3309-7(X), Troll Hunters) Stone Arch Bks.

—The Library Claw: And Other Scary Tales. Bonet, Xavier, illus. 2017. (Michael Dahl's Really Scary Stories Ser.). (ENG.). 72p. (gr. 2-3). lib. bdg. 25.32 **(978-1-4965-4902-0(3))** Stone Arch Bks.

—Library of Doom: the Final Chapters. Kendall, Bradford, illus. 2016. (Library of Doom: the Final Chapters Ser.). (ENG.). 40p. (gr. 1-3). 191.92 (978-1-4965-2574-1(4), Zone Bks.) Stone Arch Bks.

—The Lost Page. Evergreen, Nelson, illus. 2015. (Library of Doom: the Final Chapters Ser.). (ENG.). 40p. (gr. 1-3). 23.99 (978-1-4342-9679-5(2)) Stone Arch Bks.

—Lost Skeleton. Catling, Andy, illus. 2016. (Igor's Lab of Fear Ser.). (ENG.). 40p. (gr. 1-3). lib. bdg. 23.99 (978-1-4965-3529-0(4)) Stone Arch Bks.

—Maze Monster. Catling, Andy, illus. 2016. (Igor's Lab of Fear Ser.). (ENG.). 40p. (gr. 1-3). lib. bdg. 23.99 (978-1-4965-3528-3(6)) Stone Arch Bks.

—Michael Dahl's Really Scary Stories. Bonet, Xavier, illus. 2016. (Michael Dahl's Really Scary Stories Ser.). (ENG.). 72p. (gr. 2-3). 202.56 (978-1-4965-3805-5(6)) Stone Arch Bks.

—Michael Dahl's Really Scary Stories, 4 vols. 2015. (Michael Dahl's Really Scary Stories Ser.). (ENG.). 72p. (gr. 2-3). 101.28 (978-1-4965-2016-6(5)) Stone Arch Bks.

—The Monster in the Mailbox: And Other Scary Tales. Bonet, Xavier, illus. 2016. (Michael Dahl's Really Scary Stories Ser.).

(ENG.). 72p. (gr. 2-3). lib. bdg. 25.32 *(978-1-4965-3771-3(8))* Stone Arch Bks.

—The Night Octopus: And Other Scary Tales. Bonet, Xavier, illus. 2017. (Michael Dahl's Really Scary Stories Ser.). (ENG.). 72p. (gr. 2-3). lib. bdg. 25.32 ***(978-1-4965-4899-3(X))*** Stone Arch Bks.

—Night of the Scrawler. Kendall, Bradford, illus. 2016. 40p. (J). *(978-1-4747-1056-5(5))* Stone Arch Bks.

—Ooze Is It? Sinkovec, Igor, illus. 2015. (Igor's Lab of Fear Ser.). (ENG.). 40p. (gr. 1-3). lib. bdg. 23.99 *(978-1-4965-0457-9(7))* Stone Arch Bks.

—The Phantom on the Phone & Other Scary Tales. Bonet, Xavier, illus. 2015. (Michael Dahl's Really Scary Stories Ser.). (ENG.). 72p. (gr. 2-3). lib. bdg. 25.32 *(978-1-4965-0597-2(2))* Stone Arch Bks.

—Rats on the Page, 1 vol. Kendall, Bradford, illus. 2010. (Return to the Library of Doom Ser.). (ENG.). 72p. (gr. 1-3). lib. bdg. 23.99 *(978-1-4342-2147-6(4),* Zone Bks.) Stone Arch Bks.

—The Sea of Lost Books, 1 vol. Kendall, Bradford, illus. 2010. (Return to the Library of Doom Ser.). (ENG.). 72p. (gr. 1-3). lib. bdg. 23.99 *(978-1-4342-2142-1(3),* Zone Bks.) Stone Arch Bks.

—Shadow Shoes: And Other Scary Tales. Bonet, Xavier, illus. 2017. (Michael Dahl's Really Scary Stories Ser.). (ENG.). 72p. (gr. 2-3). lib. bdg. 25.32 ***(978-1-4965-4900-6(7))*** Stone Arch Bks.

—The Spine Tingler. Evergreen, Nelson, illus. 2015. (Library of Doom: the Final Chapters Ser.). (ENG.). 40p. (gr. 1-3). 23.99 *(978-1-4342-9680-1(6))* Stone Arch Bks.

—The Stranger on the Stairs: And Other Scary Tales. Bonet, Xavier, illus. 2015. (Michael Dahl's Really Scary Stories Ser.). (ENG.). 72p. (gr. 2-3). lib. bdg. 25.32 *(978-1-4965-0594-1(8))* Stone Arch Bks.

—Thesaurus Rex. Kendall, Bradford, illus. 2016. 40p. (J). *(978-1-4747-1057-2(3))* Stone Arch Bks.

—Tome Raider. Evergreen, Nelson, illus. 2015. (Library of Doom: the Final Chapters Ser.). (ENG.). 40p. (gr. 1-3). 23.99 *(978-1-4342-9677-1(6))* Stone Arch Bks.

—The Vampire Chapter, 1 vol. Kendall, Bradford, illus. 2010. (Return to the Library of Doom Ser.). (ENG.). 72p. (gr. 1-3). 23.99 *(978-1-4342-2143-8(1),* Zone Bks.) Stone Arch Bks.

—The Voice in the Boys' Room & Other Scary Tales. Bonet, Xavier, illus. 2015. (Michael Dahl's Really Scary Stories Ser.). (ENG.). 72p. (gr. 2-3). lib. bdg. 25.32 *(978-1-4965-0596-5(4))* Stone Arch Bks.

—Werewolf Skin. Sinkovec, Igor, illus. 2015. (Igor's Lab of Fear Ser.). (ENG.). 40p. (gr. 1-3). lib. bdg. 23.99 *(978-1-4965-0458-6(5))* Stone Arch Bks.

—Zombie Cupcakes: And Other Scary Tales. Bonet, Xavier, illus. 2016. (Michael Dahl's Really Scary Stories Ser.). (ENG.). 72p. (gr. 2-3). lib. bdg. 25.32 *(978-1-4965-3774-4(2))* Stone Arch Bks.

—Zombie in the Library, 1 vol. Kendall, Bradford, illus. 2010. (Return to the Library of Doom Ser.). (ENG.). 72p. (gr. 1-3). lib. bdg. 23.99 *(978-1-4342-2145-2(8),* Zone Bks.) Stone Arch Bks.

Darke, J. A. Attack of the Mud Creatures. Evergreen, Nelson, illus. 2015. (Spine Shivers Ser.). (ENG.). 128p. (gr. 3-4). lib. bdg. 26.65 *(978-1-4965-0220-9(5))* Stone Arch Bks.

—Do Not Watch. Evans, Neil, illus. 2016. (Spine Shivers Ser.). (ENG.). 128p. (gr. 3-4). lib. bdg. 26.65 *(978-1-4965-3071-4(3))* Stone Arch Bks.

—Fade to Black. Evans, Neil, illus. 2016. (Spine Shivers Ser.). (ENG.). 128p. (gr. 3-4). lib. bdg. 26.65 *(978-1-4965-3070-7(5))* Stone Arch Bks.

—The Grin in the Dark. Evergreen, Nelson, illus. 2015. (Spine Shivers Ser.). (ENG.). 128p. (gr. 3-4). lib. bdg. 26.65 *(978-1-4965-0217-9(5))* Stone Arch Bks.

—The Screaming Bridge. Evergreen, Nelson, illus. 2015. (Spine Shivers Ser.). (ENG.). 128p. (gr. 3-4). lib. bdg. 26.65 *(978-1-4965-0219-3(1))* Stone Arch Bks.

—Tech Fury. Evergreen, Nelson, illus. 2015. (Spine Shivers Ser.). (ENG.). 128p. (gr. 3-4). lib. bdg. 26.65 *(978-1-4965-0218-6(3))* Stone Arch Bks.

Datlow, Ellen & Windling, Terri. Teeth: Vampire Tales. 2011. (ENG.). 480p. (YA). (gr. 8-18). 17.99 *(978-0-06-193515-2(8));* pap. 9.99 *(978-0-06-193514-5(X))* HarperCollins Pubs.

Dave, Matt. Supercool Snotman, No. 8. Baines, Nigel, illus. (ENG.). 112p. pap. *(978-1-84738-288-7(6))* Simon & Schuster, Ltd.

Davidson, Danica. The Armies of Herobrine: An Unofficial Overworld Adventure, Book Five. 2016. (Unofficial Overworld Adventure Ser.). (ENG.). 112p. (J). (gr. 1-7). pap. 7.99 *(978-1-5107-1620-9(3),* Sky Pony Pr.) Skyhorse Publishing Co., Inc.

Davie, Jan. Stairway to the Stars. 2005. 76p. pap. *(978-1-84401-569-6(6))* Athena Pr.

Davies, Anna. Followers. 2014. (ENG.). 224p. (J). (gr. 9). pap. 9.99 *(978-0-545-51196-4(8))* Scholastic, Inc.

Dawson, James. Hollow Pike. 2012. (ENG.). 320p. (YA). (gr. 7-17). 8.99 *(978-1-78062-128-9(0),* Orion Children's Bks.) Hachette Children's Group GBR. Dist: Hachette Bk. Group.

del Toro, Guillermo & Kraus, Daniel. Trollhunters. Murray, Sean, illus. (Trollhunters Ser.). (ENG.). 320p. (YA). (gr. 7-12). 2016. pap. 9.99 ***(978-1-368-01218-8(3),*** 1380291) 2015. 18.99 *(978-1-4231-2598-3(3),* 1380291) Hyperion Bks. for Children.

Delaney, Joseph. The Dark Army. 2017. 416p. (YA). (gr. 8). pap. 9.99 ***(978-0-06-233457-2(3),*** Greenwillow Bks.) HarperCollins Pubs.

—Fury of the Seventh Son, Bk. 13. Arrasmith, Patrick, illus. (Last Apprentice Ser.: 13). (ENG.). 480p. (YA). (gr. 8). 2015. pap. 9.99 *(978-0-06-219232-5(9))* 2014. 17.99 *(978-0-06-219231-8(0))* HarperCollins Pubs. (Greenwillow Bks.).

—Ghost Prison. (ENG.). 112p. (YA). (gr. 6-12). 2014. pap. 5.99 *(978-1-4926-0174-6(8))* 2013. 12.99 *(978-1-4022-9318-4(6),* 9781402293184) Sourcebooks, Inc.

—Grimalkin the Witch Assassin Bk. 9, Bk. 9. Arrasmith, Patrick, illus. 2012. (Last Apprentice Ser.: 9). (ENG.). 400p. (YA). (gr. 8). 17.99 *(978-0-06-208207-7(8),* Greenwillow Bks.) HarperCollins Pubs.

—The Last Apprentice Bk. 8: Rage of the Fallen. Arrasmith, Patrick, illus. 2012. (Last Apprentice Ser.: 8). (ENG.). 416p. (YA). (gr. 8). pap. 9.99 *(978-0-06-202758-0(1),* Greenwillow Bks.) HarperCollins Pubs.

—The Last Apprentice - I Am Alice, Bk. 12. Arrasmith, Patrick, illus. 2013. (Last Apprentice Ser.: 12). (ENG.). 448p. (YA). (gr. 8). 17.99 *(978-0-06-171513-6(1),* Greenwillow Bks.) HarperCollins Pubs.

—The Last Apprentice: the Spook's Bestiary: The Guide to Creatures of the Dark. Heller, Julek, illus. 2014. (Last Apprentice Short Fiction Ser.: 3). (ENG.). 240p. (YA). (gr. 8). pap. 8.99 *(978-0-06-208115-5(2),* Greenwillow Bks.) HarperCollins Pubs.

—Lure of the Dead. Arrasmith, Patrick, illus. 2013. (Last Apprentice Ser.: 10). (ENG.). 448p. (YA). (gr. 8). pap. 9.99 *(978-0-06-202762-7(X),* Greenwillow Bks.) HarperCollins Pubs.

—A New Darkness. 2014. (ENG.). 352p. (YA). (gr. 8). 17.99 *(978-0-06-233453-4(0),* Greenwillow Bks.) HarperCollins Pubs.

—Rise of the Huntress Bk. 7, Bk. 7. Arrasmith, Patrick, illus. 2011. (Last Apprentice Ser.: 7). (ENG.). 464p. (YA). (gr. 8). pap. 9.99 *(978-0-06-171512-9(3),* Greenwillow Bks.) HarperCollins Pubs.

—The Seventh Son, Bks. 1 & 2. 2014. (Last Apprentice Ser.). (ENG.). 704p. (J). (gr. 8). pap. 10.99 *(978-0-06-220970-2(1),* Greenwillow Bks.) HarperCollins Pubs.

—Slither, Bk. 11. 2013. (Last Apprentice Ser.: 11). (ENG.). 416p. (YA). (gr. 8). 17.99 *(978-0-06-219234-9(5),* Greenwillow Bks.) HarperCollins Pubs.

—The Spook's Bestiary: The Guide to Creatures of the Dark. Heller, Julek, illus. 2011. (Last Apprentice Short Fiction Ser.: 3). (ENG.). 240p. (YA). (gr. 8). 16.99 *(978-0-06-208114-8(4),* Greenwillow Bks.) HarperCollins Pubs.

Dennard, Susan. A Darkness Strange & Lovely. (Something Strange & Deadly Trilogy Ser.: 2). (ENG.). (YA). (gr. 9). 2014. 432p. pap. 9.99 *(978-0-06-208330-2(9))* 2013. 416p. 17.99 *(978-0-06-208329-6(5))* HarperCollins Pubs. (HarperTeen).

—Something Strange & Deadly. (Something Strange & Deadly Trilogy Ser.: 1). (ENG.). (YA). (gr. 9). 2013. 416p. pap. 9.99 *(978-0-06-208327-2(9))* 2012. 400p. 17.99 *(978-0-06-208326-5(0))* HarperCollins Pubs. (HarperTeen).

Derek the Ghost Staff. Monsters on the March. Fischer, Scott M., illus. 2012. (Scary School Ser.: 2). (ENG.). 256p. (J). (gr. 3-7). 15.99 *(978-0-06-196095-6(0))* HarperCollins Pubs.

Despain, Bree. The Dark Divine. 2009. (ENG.). 384p. (J). (gr. 7-18). 17.99 *(978-1-60684-057-3(6),* Carolrhoda Lab™) Lerner Publishing Group.

Despeyroux, Denise & Poe, Edgar Allen. Dark Graphic Tales by Edgar Allan Poe. Serratosa, Miquel, illus. 2012. (Dark Graphic Novels Ser.). 96p. (J). (gr. 5-9). 31.94 *(978-0-7660-4086-1(0))* Enslow Pubs., Inc.

Diggins, Matthew. Andrew & the Secret Gallery. Diggins, Matthew, illus. 2007. (Illus.). 30p. (J). (gr. 1-5). 15.95 *(978-1-60108-016-5(6))* Red Cygnet Pr.

Disney Book Group. Tales from the Haunted Mansion: Volume II: Midnight at Madame Leota's. 2017. (Tales from the Haunted Mansion Ser.: 2). (ENG.). 208p. (J). (gr. 3-7). 14.99 ***(978-1-4847-1471-3(7))*** Disney Pr.

Disney Book Group Staff & Brooke, Samantha. Gravity Falls Happy Summerween! / the Convenience Store... of Horrors! 2014. (ENG.). 48p. (J). (gr. 1-3). pap. 5.99 *(978-1-4847-1078-4(9))* Disney Pr.

Dolan, Elys. The Mystery of the Haunted Farm. Dolan, Elys, illus. 2016. (ENG., Illus.). (J). (gr. -1-3). 17.99 *(978-0-7636-8658-1(1),* Nosy Crow) Candlewick Pr.

Dolan, Penny. Two Ghost Stories. Tambellini, Stefano, illus. 2015. (Collins Big Cat Ser.). (ENG.). 48p. (J). (gr. 3-4). pap. 9.95 *(978-0-00-812780-0(8))* HarperCollins Pubs. Ltd. GBR. Dist: Independent Pubs. Group.

Dompieri, Patricia Lynn. Lemon Bee & Other Peculiar Tales. 2013. 136p. pap. 11.95 *(978-1-4787-2240-3(1))* Outskirts Pr., Inc.

Donbavand, Tommy. Attack of the Trolls. 2012. (Scream Street Ser.: 8). (ENG., Illus.). 128p. (J). (gr. 3-7). pap. 5.99 *(978-0-7636-5760-4(3))* Candlewick Pr.

—Blood of the Witch. 2009. (Scream Street Ser.: 2). (ENG., Illus.). 128p. (J). (gr. 3-7). pap. 5.99 *(978-0-7636-4607-3(5))* Candlewick Pr.

—Blood of the Witch: Book 2, 1 vol. Cartoon Saloon, illus. 2012. (ENG.). 120p. (J). 24.21 *(978-1-59961-993-4(8),* Chapter Bks.) Spotlight.

—Claw of the Werewolf, Bk. 6. Cartoon Saloon Staff, illus. 2010. (Scream Street Ser.: 6). (ENG.). 128p. (J). (gr. 3-7). pap. 5.99 *(978-0-7636-4638-7(5))* Candlewick Pr.

—Claw of the Werewolf: Book 6, 1 vol. Cartoon Saloon, illus. 2012. (ENG.). 120p. (J). 24.21 *(978-1-59961-997-2(0),* Chapter Bks.) Spotlight.

—Fang of the Vampire: Book 1, 1 vol. Cartoon Saloon, illus. 2012. (ENG.). 129p. (J). 24.21 *(978-1-59961-992-7(X),* Chapter Bks.) Spotlight.

—Flame of the Dragon. Donbavand, Tommy, illus. 2015. (Scream Street Ser.: 13). (ENG., Illus.). 192p. (J). (gr. 3-7). pap. 5.99 *(978-0-7636-5765-9(4))* Candlewick Pr.

—Flesh of the Zombie, Bk. 4. Cartoon Saloon Staff, illus. 2010. (Scream Street Ser.: 4). (ENG.). 128p. (J). (gr. 3-7). pap. 5.99 *(978-0-7636-4637-0(7))* Candlewick Pr.

—Flesh of the Zombie: Book 4, 1 vol. Cartoon Saloon, illus. 2012. (ENG.). 120p. (J). 24.21 *(978-1-59961-995-8(4),* Chapter Bks.) Spotlight.

—Heart of the Mummy, Bk. 3. Cartoon Saloon Staff, illus. 2010. (Scream Street Ser.: 3). (ENG.). 128p. (J). (gr. 3-7). pap. 5.99 *(978-0-7636-4636-3(9))* Candlewick Pr.

—Heart of the Mummy: Book 3, 1 vol. Cartoon Saloon, illus. 2012. (ENG.). 120p. (J). 24.21 *(978-1-59961-994-1(6),* Chapter Bks.) Spotlight.

—Invasion of the Normals. 2012. (Scream Street Ser.: 7). (ENG., Illus.). 128p. (J). (gr. 3-7). pap. 5.99 *(978-0-7636-5759-8(X))* Candlewick Pr.

—Skull of the Skeleton, Bk. 5. Cartoon Saloon Staff, illus. 2010. (Scream Street Ser.: 5). (ENG.). 128p. (J). (gr. 3-7). pap. 5.99 *(978-0-7636-4635-6(0))* Candlewick Pr.

—Skull of the Skeleton: Book 5, 1 vol. Cartoon Saloon, illus. 2012. (ENG.). 120p. (J). 24.21 *(978-1-59961-996-5(2),* Chapter Bks.) Spotlight.

—Terror of the Nightwatchman. 2014. (Scream Street Ser.: 9). (ENG.). 128p. (J). (gr. 3-7). pap. 5.99 *(978-0-7636-5761-1(1))* Candlewick Pr.

Dorsey, Angela. The Time Thief. 2011. (ENG.). 144p. (YA). (gr. 6). pap. 9.99 *(978-1-926607-27-6(9),* Napoleon & Co.) Dundum CAN. Dist: Ingram Publisher Services.

Dower, Laura. They Came from Planet Q. Schlafman, Dave, illus. 2010. (Monster Squad Ser.: 4). (ENG.). 144p. (J). (gr. 2-4). pap. 5.99 *(978-0-448-44915-9(3),* Grosset & Dunlap) Penguin Young Readers Group.

Downie, David. Horrible Stories My Dad Told Me. Nanevich, Julia, tr. Seroya, Tea, illus. 2012. 44p. pap. *(978-1-922159-90-8(5))* Blue Peg Publishing.

—Horrible Stories My Dad Told Me. Ivanova, Kalina, tr. Seroya, Tea, illus. 2012. 42p. pap. *(978-1-922159-96-0(4))* Blue Peg Publishing.

—Horrible Stories My Dad Told Me. M, Akiko, tr. Seroya, Tea, illus. 2012. 44p. pap. *(978-1-922159-94-6(8))* Blue Peg Publishing.

—Horrible Stories My Dad Told Me. Tatsi, Andreanna, tr. Seroya, Tea, illus. 2012. 44p. pap. *(978-1-922159-95-3(6))* Blue Peg Publishing.

—Horrible Stories My Dad Told Me. Seroya, Tea, illus. 2012. 42p. pap. *(978-0-9873501-0-7(2))* Blue Peg Publishing.

Dracula. (J). 9.95 *(978-1-56156-373-9(0))* Kidsbooks, LLC.

Drago, Ty. The Undertakers: The Rise of the Corpses. 2011. (ENG.). 480p. (J). (gr. 5-8). 13.99 *(978-1-4022-4785-9(0),* 9781402247859, Sourcebooks Jabberwocky) Sourcebooks, Inc.

Dragon, Laura Roach, ed. Bayou Bogeyman: Presents Hoodoo & Voodoo, 1 vol. 2016. (ENG.). 200p. (J). (gr. 3-7). pap. 9.95 *(978-1-4556-2173-6(0))* Pelican Publishing Co., Inc.

Duke, Shirley. Unthinkable. 2010. (Night Fall Ser.). (ENG.). 112p. (YA). (gr. 6-12). 27.93 *(978-0-7613-6142-8(1));* pap. 7.95 *(978-0-7613-6157-2(X))* Lerner Publishing Group.

Dunn, Joeming. Cask of Amontillado, 1 vol. 2014. (Graphic Horror Set 3 Ser.). (ENG.). 32p. (J). (gr. 5-8). lib. bdg. 28.50 *(978-1-62402-015-5(1),* Graphic Planet) Magic Wagon.

—Raven, 1 vol. 2014. (Graphic Horror Set 3 Ser.). (ENG.). 32p. (J). (gr. 5-8). lib. bdg. 28.50 *(978-1-62402-017-9(8),* Graphic Planet) Magic Wagon.

Dunne, Colin. Werewolf. 128p. (J). pap. 7.95 *(978-0-233-99580-9(3))* Andre Deutsch GBR. Dist: Trans-Atlantic Pubns., Inc.

Duval, Alex. Ritual. 2007. (Vampire Beach Ser.). (ENG.). 208p. (YA). (gr. 9-12). mass mkt. 5.99 *(978-1-4169-1168-5(5),* Simon Pulse) Simon Pulse.

Eboch, Chris. The Ghost on the Stairs. 2009. (Haunted Ser.). (ENG.). 176p. (J). (gr. 3-7). pap. 5.99 *(978-1-4169-7548-9(9),* Aladdin) Simon & Schuster Children's Publishing.

—The Riverboat Phantom. 2009. (Haunted Ser.). (ENG.). 192p. (J). (gr. 3-7). pap. 5.99 *(978-1-4169-7549-6(7),* Aladdin) Simon & Schuster Children's Publishing.

Ecton, Emily. Boots & Pieces. 2008. (ENG.). 240p. (J). (gr. 3-7). pap. 11.99 *(978-1-4169-6167-3(4),* Aladdin) Simon & Schuster Children's Publishing.

Edquist, Patrick. Zombie Penguins of the Antarctic. 2011. 40p. pap. 16.99 *(978-1-4567-6291-9(5))* AuthorHouse.

Eggleton, Hazel. Ghost of Widdecot Manor. 2013. 184p. pap. *(978-1-909734-07-4(1))* ThornBerry Publishing UK.

Elfakir, Mahamad Ali. Blueberry Bubble Gum. 2013. 44p. 16.95 *(978-0-578-10978-7(6))* Elfa Bks.

Enderle, Dotti. Beyond the Grave: An Up2U Mystery Adventure, 1 vol. Uhles, Mary, illus. 2013. (Up2U Adventures Ser.). (ENG.). 80p. (J). (gr. 2-5). 27.07 *(978-1-61641-964-6(4),* Calico Chapter Bks) Magic Wagon.

—Clawed! An Up2U Horror Adventure, 1 vol. To, Vivienne, illus. 2013. (Up2U Adventures Ser.). (ENG.). 80p. (J). (gr. 2-5). lib. bdg. 27.07 *(978-1-61641-965-3(2),* Calico Chapter Bks) Magic Wagon.

Escott, John & Pearson Education Staff. Ghost of Genny Castle. 2nd ed. 2008. (ENG., Illus.). 48p. pap. 11.99 *(978-1-4058-6953-9(4))* Pearson Education.

Fahy, Thomas. Sleepless. 2010. (ENG.). 224p. (YA). (gr. 7). pap. 8.99 *(978-1-4169-5902-1(5),* Simon & Schuster Bks. For Young Readers) Simon & Schuster Bks. For Young Readers.

—The Unspoken. 2008. (ENG.). 176p. (YA). (gr. 7-18). 15.99 *(978-1-4169-4007-4(3),* Simon & Schuster Bks. For Young Readers) Simon & Schuster Bks. For Young Readers.

Fahy, Thomas Richard & Fahy, Thomas. Sleepless. 2009. (ENG.). 224p. (YA). (gr. 7-18). 15.99 *(978-1-4169-5901-4(7),* Simon & Schuster Bks. For Young Readers) Simon & Schuster Bks. For Young Readers.

Fallenstein, J. Graffiti. 2017. (Midnight Ser.). (ENG.). 88p. (YA). (gr. 6-12). 26.65 *(978-1-5124-2767-7(5));* 12.99 ***(978-1-5124-3489-7(2),*** Darby Creek); 39.99 ***(978-1-5124-3488-0(4),*** Darby Creek); 39.99 ***(978-1-5124-2787-5(X),*** Darby Creek) Lerner Publishing Group.

—S. O. S. 2017. (Midnight Ser.). (ENG.). 104p. (YA). (gr. 6-12). lib. bdg. 26.65 *(978-1-5124-2770-7(5),* Darby Creek) Lerner Publishing Group.

—S. O. S. 2017. (Midnight Ser.). (ENG.). 104p. (YA). (gr. 6-12). 12.99 ***(978-1-5124-3492-7(2));*** 39.99 ***(978-1-5124-2790-5(X));*** 39.99 ***(978-1-5124-3491-0(4))*** Lerner Publishing Group. (Darby Creek).

—The Witching Hour. 2017. (Midnight Ser.). (ENG.). 96p. (YA). (gr. 6-12). 26.65 *(978-1-5124-2771-4(3));* 12.99 ***(978-1-5124-3498-9(1),*** Darby Creek); 39.99 ***(978-1-5124-3497-2(3),*** Darby Creek); 39.99 ***(978-1-5124-2791-2(8),*** Darby Creek) Lerner Publishing Group.

Fangorn. Little Horrors. 2004. (Illus.). 32p. (J). (gr. -1-3). pap. 9.99 *(978-1-86007-130-0(9),* TickTock Books) Octopus Publishing Group GBR. Dist: Independent Pubs. Group.

Fantich, Susanna. A Cat's Tale. 2012. 210p. 33.99 *(978-1-4582-0527-8(4));* pap. 15.99 *(978-1-4582-0525-4(8))* Author Solutions, Inc. (Abbott Pr.).

Feasey, Steve. Blood Wolf: Wereling Book #3. 2011. (Wereling Ser.: 3). (ENG.). 304p. (YA). (gr. 7). pap. 12.99 *(978-0-312-65352-1(2),* 9780312653521) Feiwel & Friends.

—Dark Moon. 2011. (Wereling Ser.: 2). (ENG.). 336p. (YA). (gr. 7-18). pap. 18.99 *(978-0-312-64643-1(7),* 9780312646431) Feiwel & Friends.

Ferguson, Dwayne. Ghost Ranch: The Legend of Mad Jake, 2004. (Kid Caramel: Bk. 4). (J). pap. 4.50 *(978-0-940975-17-0(3),* Sankofa Bks.) Just Us Bks., Inc.

Fienberg, Anna & Fienberg, Barbara. Tashi & the Haunted House. Gamble, Kim, illus. 9th ed. 2007. (Tashi Ser.). (ENG.). 64p. (Orig.). (J). (gr. k-2). pap. 8.99 *(978-1-74114-953-1(3))* Allen & Unwin AUS. Dist: Independent Pubs. Group.

Fischer, Rusty. Zombies Don't Cry. 2011. (Living Dead Love Story Ser.: 1). (ENG.). 371p. (YA). (gr. 6-18). pap. 9.95 *(978-1-60542-382-1(3),* Gold Medallion) Medallion Pr., Inc.

Fischman, Sheila, tr. from FRE. The Flying Canoe. Oberman, Sheldon & Cohen, Sheldon, illus. 2004. (ENG.). 24p. (J). (gr. 3-7). 15.95 *(978-0-88776-636-7(6),* Tundra Bks.) Tundra Bks. CAN. Dist: Penguin Random Hse. LLC.

Fisher, Sam. Scare Scape. 2015. (ENG.). 352p. (J). (gr. 3-7). 12.99 *(978-0-545-74497-3(0),* Scholastic Pr.) Scholastic, Inc.

Fleischman, Sid. The Entertainer & the Dybbuk. 2009. (ENG.). 192p. (J). (gr. 4-9). pap. 6.99 *(978-0-06-177140-8(6),* Greenwillow Bks.) HarperCollins Pubs.

Flitcroft, Jean. The Chupacabra. 2014. (Cryptid Files Ser.: No. 2). 232p. (gr. 4-8). (J). lib. bdg. 27.93 *(978-1-4677-3265-9(6));* (ENG.). (YA). pap. 7.95 *(978-1-4677-3483-7(7))* Lerner Publishing Group. (Darby Creek).

—The Loch Ness Monster. 2014. (Cryptid Files Ser.: No. 1). 192p. (gr. 4-8). (J). lib. bdg. 27.93 *(978-1-4677-2602-3(8));* (ENG.). (YA). pap. 7.95 *(978-1-4677-3481-3(0))* Lerner Publishing Group. (Darby Creek).

—The Pacific Giants. 2014. (Cryptid Files Ser.: No. 3). 240p. (gr. 4-8). (J). lib. bdg. 27.93 *(978-1-4677-3266-6(4));* (ENG.). (YA). pap. 7.95 *(978-1-4677-3485-1(3))* Lerner Publishing Group. (Darby Creek).

Frade, B. A. Clone Camp! 2017. (Tales from the Scaremaster Ser.: 3). (ENG.). 176p. (J). (gr. 3-7). pap. 5.99 *(978-0-316-31727-6(6))* Little, Brown Bks. for Young Readers.

Francis, Azra Daniel. Grampa's Stories. 2013. 232p. *(978-1-4602-2688-9(7))* FriesenPress.

—Grandpa's Stories. 2013. 232p. pap. *(978-1-4602-2689-6(5))* FriesenPress.

Freeman, J. Miller. Creak in the Night - Mystery of the Crypts. Lavender, Todd, illus. 2012. 74p. pap. 9.99 *(978-0-9850410-1-4(3))* Akmaeon Publishing, LLC.

Frost, Heather. Guardians. 2013. (Seers - Trilogy Ser.: Vol. 3). (ENG.). 424p. (J). (gr. 8-12). pap. 17.99 *(978-1-4621-1035-3(5),* Sweetwater Bks.) Cedar Fort, Inc./CFI Distribution.

Fukuda, Andrew. The Hunt. 2012. (Hunt Trilogy Ser.: 1). (ENG.). 304p. (YA). (gr. 7). pap. 11.99 *(978-1-250-00529-8(9),* 9781250005298); 17.99 *(978-1-250-00514-4(0),* 9781250005144) St. Martin's Pr. (St. Martin's Griffin).

Furie, Peter. Numchucks' Curse. 2005. (Cyber Screams Ser.). 189p. (YA). (gr. 8-12). per. 12.95 *(978-0-9772927-0-7(3))* Bangzoom Pubs.

Gaiman, NEil. Coraline. 2003. (FRE.). (J). (gr. 5-8). pap. ***(978-2-226-14019-7(0))*** Albin-Michel, Editions.

—Coraline. McKean, Dave, illus. (P. S. Ser.). (ENG.). 2006. 192p. (gr. 6-8). pap. 12.99 *(978-0-06-113937-6(8),* William Morrow Paperbacks) 2004. 224p. (J). (gr. 3-7). pap. 8.99 *(978-0-06-057591-5(3))* HarperCollins Pubs.

—Coraline, 12 Copies. 2003. (J). pap. 71.88 *(978-0-06-056895-5(X));* pap. 71.88 *(978-0-06-057152-8(7))* HarperCollins Pubs.

—Coraline. 2003. 162p. (gr. 7-9). 17.00 *(978-0-7569-1568-1(6))* Perfection Learning Corp.

—Coraline. McKean, Dave, illus. 2007. 151p. (J). (gr. 6-8). 60.00 *(978-1-59606-147-7(2))* Subterranean Pr.

—CORALINE. 2009. (SPA.). 160p. (YA). pap. 12.95 *(978-84-9838-237-2(8))* Publicaciones y Ediciones Salamandra, S.A. ESP. Dist: Spanish Pubs., LLC.

—CORALINE. 2009. (SPA.). 188p. (YA). 20.95 *(978-84-92429-74-5(7))* Roca Editorial ESP. Dist: Spanish Pubs., LLC.

—Coraline. 3rd ed. 2003. (SPA., Illus.). 160p. *(978-84-7888-579-4(X),* 1952) Emece Editores.

—Coraline. McKean, Dave, illus. movie tie-in ed. 2008. (ENG.). 176p. (J). (gr. 3). pap. 6.99 *(978-0-06-164969-1(4),* HarperFestival) HarperCollins Pubs.

—Coraline. 2012. (J). (gr. 5-8). lib. bdg. 18.40 *(978-0-613-67322-8(0),* Turtleback) Turtleback Bks.

—Coraline. McKean, Dave, illus. 10th anniv. ed. 2012. (HarperClassics Ser.). (ENG.). 208p. (J). (gr. 3-7). pap. 7.99 *(978-0-380-80734-5(3))* HarperCollins Pubs.

—Coraline: Reading Group Guide. McKean, Dave, illus. *(978-0-06-056878-8(X))* HarperCollins Pubs.

—The Graveyard Book Graphic Novel. 2015. (J). Vol. 1. lib. bdg. 20.85 *(978-0-606-37613-6(5))* Vol. 2. lib. bdg. 20.85 *(978-0-606-37614-3(3))* Turtleback Bks.

Gaines, Bill, et al. The Vault of Horror, Vol. 3. Chabon, Daniel, ed. Craig, Johnny, illus. 2014. (ENG.). 200p. 49.99 *(978-1-61655-292-3(1))* Dark Horse Comics.

Gallardo, Adam J. Zombified. 2015. (Zombie Apocalypse Ser.). (ENG.). 352p. (YA). (gr. 13). pap. 9.95 *(978-1-61773-100-6(5),* K-Teen) Kensington Publishing Corp.

Gammell, Stephen, illus. More Scary Stories to Tell in the Dark. 80p. (J). (gr. 4-6). pap. 4.95 *(978-0-8072-1424-4(8),* Listening Library) Random Hse. Audio Publishing Group.

Gantos, Jack. The Love Curse of the Rumbaughs. 2008. (ENG.). 192p. (YA). (gr. 9-12). pap. 14.99 *(978-0-312-38052-6(6),* 9780312380526) Square Fish.

Gareth Stevens Publishing, creator. Cursed Creatures. 2006. (Ghost Stories Ser.). (Illus.). 128p. (gr. 3-7). lib. bdg. 31.00 *(978-0-8368-6821-0(8),* Gareth Stevens Learning Library) Stevens, Gareth Publishing LLLP.

—The Doomed & the Dead. 2006. (Ghost Stories Ser.). (Illus.). 128p. (gr. 3-7). lib. bdg. 31.00 *(978-0-8368-6822-7(6),* Gareth Stevens Learning Library) Stevens, Gareth Publishing LLLP.

—From the Grave. 2006. (Ghost Stories Ser.). (Illus.). 128p. (gr. 3-7). lib. bdg. 31.00 *(978-0-8368-6823-4(4),* Gareth Stevens Learning Library) Stevens, Gareth Publishing LLLP.

Garner, Em. Contaminated. (ENG.). 336p. (J). (gr. 7). 2014. pap. 9.99 *(978-1-60684-542-4(X))* 2013. 17.99 *(978-1-60684-354-3(0))* Lerner Publishing Group. (Carolrhoda Lab™).

H I

—Contaminated 2 - Mercy Mode. 2014. (ENG.). 341p. (J). (gr. 7). 17.99 (978-1-60684-356-7(7), Carolrhoda Lab™) Lerner Publishing Group.
—Mercy Mode. 2017. (Contaminated Ser.: 2). (ENG.). 341p. (J). (gr. 7-12). 9.99 (978-1-5124-4143-7(0), Carolrhoda Bks.) Lerner Publishing Group.
Garvey, Amy. Glass Heart. 2012. (Cold Kiss Ser.: 2). (ENG.). 320p. (YA). (gr. 8). 17.99 (978-0-06-199624-5(6), HarperTeen) HarperCollins Pubs.
Garza, Xavier. The Donkey Lady Fights la Llorona & Other Stories / la Señora Asno Se Enfrenta a la Llorona y Otros Cuentos. Álvarez, Mayra E., tr. 2015. (ENG & SPA., Illus.). 144p. (J). (gr. 3-6). pap. 9.95 (978-1-55885-816-9(4), Piñata Books) Arte Publico Pr.
Gauthier, Bertrand. Les Tenebres Piegees, Vol. RJ 65. Jorisch, Stéphane, illus. 2003. (Roman Jeunesse Ser.). (FRE.). 96p. (YA). (gr. 4-7). pap. (978-2-89021-292-3(0)) Diffusion du livre Mirabel (DLM).
Geist, Ken. We're Going on a Spooky Ghost Hunt. Francis, Guy, illus. 2017. (StoryPlay Ser.). (ENG.). 32p. (J). (gr. -1 — 1). 5.99 (978-1-338-14189-4(9), Cartwheel Bks.) Scholastic, Inc.
Gerani, Gary. Dinosaurs Attack. Trimpe, Herb et al, illus. 2014. (ENG.). 136p. pap. 19.99 (978-1-61377-862-3(7), 9781613778623) Idea & Design Works, LLC.
Gerrold, David, et al. Diary of a Stinky Dead Kid, No. 8. Hack, Robert et al, illus. 2009. (Tales from the Crypt Graphic Novels Ser.). (ENG.). 96p. (J). (gr. 5-12). pap. 7.95 (978-1-59707-163-5(3), 9781597071635); 12.95 (978-1-59707-164-2(1), 9781597071642) Papercutz.
—Wickeder. Parker, Rick et al, illus. 2010. (Tales from the Crypt Graphic Novels Ser.). (ENG.). 64p. (J). (gr. 5-12). pap. 6.99 (978-1-59707-215-1(X), 9781597072151); 10.99 (978-1-59707-216-8(8), 9781597072168) Papercutz.
Giangregorio, Anthony. Only the Young Survive: An Apocalyptic Tale. 2011. 110p. pap. 6.99 (978-1-935458-89-0(2)) Living Dead Pr.
—Zombies Are Cool. Collins, Andrew Dawe, illus. 2013. 38p. pap. 9.99 (978-1-61199-073-7(4)) Living Dead Pr.
—Zombies Are People Too! 2013. 42p. pap. 7.99 (978-1-61199-072-0(6)) Living Dead Pr.
Gibbons, Alan. Renegade. 2010. (ENG., Illus.). 336p. (YA). (gr. 7-17). 8.99 (978-1-4440-0079-5(9), Orion Children's Bks.) Hachette Children's Group GBR. Dist: Hachette Bk. Group.
Gibson, Jo. Obsessed. 2014. (ENG.). 384p. (YA). (gr. 13). pap. 9.95 (978-1-61773-238-6(9), K-Teen) Kensington Publishing Corp.
Gier, Kerstin. Dream a Little Dream. Bell, Anthea, tr. from GER. 2015. (Silver Trilogy Ser.: 1). (ENG.). 336p. (YA). (gr. 7). 17.99 (978-1-62779-027-7(6), 9781627790277, Holt, Henry & Co. Bks. For Young Readers) Holt, Henry & Co.
—Dream On. Bell, Anthea, tr. from GER. 2016. (Silver Trilogy Ser.: 2). (ENG.). 336p. (YA). 17.99 (978-1-62779-079-6(9), 9781627790796, Holt, Henry & Co. Bks. For Young Readers) Holt, Henry & Co.
—Just Dreaming. Bell, Anthea, tr. from GER. 2017. (Silver Trilogy Ser.). (ENG.). 368p. (YA). 18.99 (978-1-62779-080-2(2), 9781627790802, Holt, Henry & Co. Bks. For Young Readers) Holt, Henry & Co.
Gifford, P. S. Dr. Offig's Lessons from the Dark Side, Volume 1. 2008. (ENG.). 176p. (YA). pap. 10.95 (978-0-9801506-2-9(0)) BRP Publishing Group.
Gilbert, Jeff. Trick or Shriek. 2006. 72p. pap. 5.97 (978-0-9646781-1-8(X)) Hairball Pr.
Goddard, Drew, et al. No Future for You, 8 vols., Vol. 2. Jeanty, Georges et al, illus. 2008. (Buffy the Vampire Slayer Ser.). (ENG.). 320p. pap. 15.99 (978-1-59307-963-5(X)) Dark Horse Comics.
Goebel, Jenny. Grave Images. 2013. (ENG.). 208p. (J). (gr. 3-7). 16.99 (978-0-545-51930-4(6), Scholastic Pr.) Scholastic, Inc.
Goodwin, Vincent. Body-Snatcher, 1 vol. 2014. (Graphic Horror Set 3 Ser.). (ENG.). 32p. (J). (gr. 5-8). lib. bdg. 28.50 (978-1-62402-013-1(5), Graphic Planet) Magic Wagon.
—Call of Cthulhu, 1 vol. 2014. (Graphic Horror Set 3 Ser.). (ENG., Illus.). 32p. (J). (gr. 5-8). lib. bdg. 28.50 (978-1-62402-014-8(3), Graphic Planet) Magic Wagon.
—Moonlit Road, 1 vol. 2014. (Graphic Horror Set 3 Ser.). (ENG.). 32p. (J). (gr. 5-8). lib. bdg. 28.50 (978-1-62402-016-2(X), Graphic Planet) Magic Wagon.
—Wendigo, 1 vol. 2014. (Graphic Horror Set 3 Ser.). (ENG.). 32p. (J). (gr. 5-8). lib. bdg. 28.50 (978-1-62402-018-6(6), Graphic Planet) Magic Wagon.
Graham, Oakley. Monster Mayhem. Wilson, Jessica, illus. 2016. (Doodle Wars Ser.). (ENG.). 100p. (J). (gr. k-3). pap. 12.99 (978-1-84956-731-2(X)) Top That! Publishing PLC GBR. Dist: Independent Pubs. Group.
Grant, Donna. Hungrige Begierde. 2014.Tr. of The Hunger. (GER.). pap. 5.99 (978-1-942017-15-8(4)) DL Grant, LLC.
Grant, John & Stocks, Mike. Classic Horror. 2004. 432p. (J). 12.95 (978-0-7945-0616-2(X), Usborne) EDC Publishing.
Grant, Michael. Hunger. (Gone Ser.: 2). (ENG.). 608p. (YA). (gr. 8-18). 2014. pap. 9.99 (978-0-06-144908-6(3)) 2009. (Illus.). 17.99 (978-0-06-144906-2(7)) HarperCollins Pubs. (Tegen, Katherine Bks).
Grant, Tess. Flying in the Dark. 2013. 186p. pap. 10.99 (978-1-62237-167-9(4)) Turquoise Morning Pr.
Graves, Annie. The Demon Babysitter. McElhinney, Glenn, illus. 2015. (Nightmare Club Ser.: 7). (ENG.). 64p. (J). (gr. 2-5). pap. 6.99 (978-1-4677-6041-6(2), Darby Creek); lib. bdg. 25.32 (978-1-4677-4355-6(0)) Lerner Publishing Group.
—A Dog's Breakfast. McElhinney, Glenn, illus. 2015. (Nightmare Club Ser.: 1). (ENG.). 64p. (J). (gr. 2-5). pap. 6.99 (978-1-4677-6042-3(0)); lib. bdg. 25.32 (978-1-4677-4350-1(X)) Lerner Publishing Group.
—Frankenkids. 2015. (Nightmare Club Ser.: 5). (ENG., Illus.). 64p. (J). (gr. 2-5). pap. 6.99 (978-1-4677-6043-0(9)) Lerner Publishing Group.
—Frankenkids. McElhinney, Glenn, illus. 2015. (Nightmare Club Ser.: 5). (ENG.). 64p. (J). (gr. 2-5). lib. bdg. 25.32 (978-1-4677-4352-5(6)) Lerner Publishing Group.
—Guinea Pig Killer. McElhinney, Glenn, illus. 2015. (Nightmare Club Ser.: 4). (ENG.). 64p. (J). (gr. 2-5). pap. 6.99 (978-1-4677-6044-7(7)); lib. bdg. 25.32 (978-1-4677-4351-8(8)) Lerner Publishing Group.
—The Hatching. McElhinney, Glenn, illus. 2015. (Nightmare Club Ser.: 8). (ENG.). 64p. (J). (gr. 2-5). pap. 6.99 (978-1-4677-6045-4(5), Darby Creek); lib. bdg. 25.32 (978-1-4677-4354-9(2)) Lerner Publishing Group.
—Help! My Brother's a Zombie. McElhinney, Glenn, illus. 2015. (J). (Nightmare Club Ser.: 2). (ENG.). 64p. (gr. 2-5). lib. bdg. 25.32 (978-1-4677-4348-8(8)); 6.99 (978-1-4677-7871-8(0)) Lerner Publishing Group.
—Mirrored. 2015. (Nightmare Club Ser.: 3). (ENG., Illus.). 64p. (J). (gr. 2-5). pap. 6.99 (978-1-4677-6047-8(1)) Lerner Publishing Group.
—Mirrored. McElhinney, Glenn, illus. 2015. (Nightmare Club Ser.: 3). (ENG.). 64p. (J). (gr. 2-5). lib. bdg. 25.32 (978-1-4677-4349-5(6)) Lerner Publishing Group.
—The Wolfling's Bite. McElhinney, Glenn, illus. 2015. (Nightmare Club Ser.: 6). (ENG.). 64p. (J). (gr. 2-5). pap. 6.99 (978-1-4677-6048-5(X), Darby Creek); lib. bdg. 25.32 (978-1-4677-4353-2(4)) Lerner Publishing Group.
Graves, Damien. The Cat Lady. 2007. (Midnight Library). (Illus.). 168p. (J). (gr. 4-7). 13.65 (978-0-7569-8324-6(X)) Perfection Learning Corp.
—The Deadly Catch. 2008. (Midnight Library). (Illus.). 170p. (J). (gr. 4-7). 13.65 (978-0-7569-8824-1(1)) Perfection Learning Corp.
—I Can See You. 2010. (Midnight Library Ser.). 160p. (J). 15.10 (978-1-60686-248-3(0)) Perfection Learning Corp.
Graves, Judith. Second Skin. 2011. 280p. (J). pap. 16.99 (978-1-61603-006-3(2)) Leap Bks.
—Under My Skin. Cox, Val, illus. 2010. 328p. (YA). (gr. 8-18). pap. 16.99 (978-1-61603-000-1(3)) Leap Bks.
Gray, C. M. Infected. 2nd ed. 2016. (Zombiefied Ser.: 02). 192p. pap. 5.99 (978-0-7333-3422-1(9)) ABC Bks. AUS. Dist: HarperCollins Pubs.
Gray, Claudia. Afterlife. 2012. (Evernight Ser.: 4). (ENG.). 384p. (YA). (gr. 8). pap. 9.99 (978-0-06-128451-9(3), HarperTeen) HarperCollins Pubs.
—Balthazar. (Evernight Ser.: 5). (ENG.). (YA). (gr. 8). 2013. 400p. pap. 9.99 (978-0-06-196119-9(1)) 2012. 384p. 17.99 (978-0-06-196118-2(3)) HarperCollins Pubs. (HarperTeen).
—Evernight. 2009. (Evernight Ser.: 1). (ENG.). 352p. (YA). (gr. 8). pap. 8.99 (978-0-06-128444-1(0), HarperTeen) HarperCollins Pubs.
—Hourglass. 2011. (Evernight Ser.: 3). (ENG.). 368p. (YA). (gr. 8). pap. 8.99 (978-0-06-128448-9(3), HarperTeen) HarperCollins Pubs.
—Sorceress. 2015. (Spellcaster Ser.: 3). (ENG.). 352p. (YA). (gr. 8). 17.99 (978-0-06-196124-3(8), HarperTeen) HarperCollins Pubs.
—Spellcaster. 2013. (Spellcaster Ser.: 1). (ENG.). 400p. (YA). (gr. 8). 17.99 (978-0-06-196120-5(5), HarperTeen) HarperCollins Pubs.
—Stargazer. (Evernight Ser.: 2). (ENG.). (YA). (gr. 8). 2010. 352p. pap. 8.99 (978-0-06-128446-5(7)) 2009. 336p. 17.99 (978-0-06-128440-3(8)) HarperCollins Pubs. (HarperTeen).
—Steadfast. (Spellcaster Ser.: 2). (ENG.). (YA). (gr. 8). 2015. 368p. pap. 9.99 (978-0-06-196123-6(X)) 2014. 352p. 17.99 (978-0-06-196122-9(1)) HarperCollins Pubs. (HarperTeen).
Gray, Keith. Creepers. 2004. (ENG.). 192p. (YA). (gr. 7-9). per. 14.99 (978-0-09-947564-4(2)) Transworld Publishers Ltd. GBR. Dist: Independent Pubs. Group.
Greenburg, Dan. Don't Count on Dracula. Davis, Jack E., illus. 2004. (Zack Files Ser.). 58p. lib. bdg. 15.00 (978-0-7569-2236-8(4)) Perfection Learning Corp.
Grey, Jacob. Ferals. 2015. (Ferals Ser.: 1). (ENG.). 288p. (J). (gr. 3-7). 16.99 (978-0-06-232103-9(X)) HarperCollins Pubs.
Griffin, Bethany. The Fall. 2014. (ENG.). 432p. (YA). (gr. 9). 17.99 (978-0-06-210785-5(2), Greenwillow Bks.) HarperCollins Pubs.
Guardino, Dawn M. Nightmare Echoes: Short Scary Stories for Young Teens. 2003. 108p. 22.95 (978-1-4107-8325-7(1)); pap. 11.45 (978-1-4107-8324-0(3)) AuthorHouse.
Gunhus, Jeff. Jack Templar Monster Hunter. 2012. 196p. pap. 10.95 (978-0-9884259-0-3(4)) Seven Guns Pr.
Gutman, Dan. The Million Dollar Strike. 2004. 176p. (J). lib. bdg. 18.46 (978-1-4242-2107-3(2)) Fitzgerald Bks.
—The Million Dollar Strike. 2006. 176p. (J). (gr. 3-7). 13.65 (978-0-7569-7023-9(7)) Perfection Learning Corp.
Hahn, Mary Downing. Deep & Dark & Dangerous. 2008. (ENG.). 192p. (J). (gr. 5-7). pap. 7.99 (978-0-547-07645-4(2)) Houghton Mifflin Harcourt Publishing Co.
—Look for Me by Moonlight. 2008. (ENG.). 208p. (YA). (gr. 7). pap. 7.99 (978-0-547-07616-4(9)) Houghton Mifflin Harcourt Publishing Co.
—One for Sorrow: A Ghost Story. 2017. (ENG.). 304p. (J). (gr. 5-7). 16.99 (978-0-544-81809-5(1)) Houghton Mifflin Harcourt Publishing Co.
—Took: A Ghost Story. 2016. (ENG.). 272p. (J). (gr. 5-7). pap. 7.99 (978-0-544-81310-6(3), HMH Books For Young Readers) Houghton Mifflin Harcourt Publishing Co.
Hallinan, P. K. Today Is Halloween! Hallinan, P. K., illus. 2008. (ENG., Illus.). 26p. (J). (gr. -1-k). bds. 6.99 (978-0-8249-1805-7(3), Ideal Pubns.) Worthy Publishing.
Hamilton, Martha & Weise, Mutch. Scared Witless: Thirteen Eerie Tales to Tell. Pope, Kevin, illus. 2015. (ENG.). 64p. (J). (gr. 3-6). pap. 8.95 (978-1-939160-95-9(2)) August Hse. Pubs., Inc.
Hankins, Jim. Teddy Scares Volume 3. 2008. (Illus.). 52p. (YA). pap. 6.95 (978-0-9791050-2-9(1)) Ape Entertainment.
Hansen, Lynne. The Change: Heritage of Horror Series. 2004. (Heritage of Horror Ser.: 2). 108p. (YA). pap. 9.00 (978-0-7599-4491-6(1)) Hard Shell Word Factory.
Hapka, Catherine, pseud. Plants vs. Zombies: Save Your Brains! 2014. (I Can Read Level 2 Ser.). (ENG.). 32p. (J). (gr. -1-3). pap. 3.99 (978-0-06-229496-8(2)) HarperCollins Pubs.
Hapka, Cathy, pseud. Dawn of the Dead. 2014. 181p. (J). pap. (978-0-545-58840-9(5)) Scholastic, Inc.
Harper, Benjamin & Poe, Edgar Allen. The Tell-Tale Heart, 1 vol. Calero, Dennis, illus. 2013. (Edgar Allan Poe Graphic Novels Ser.). (ENG.). 72p. (gr. 2-3). lib. bdg. 27.99 (978-1-4342-3023-2(6)) Stone Arch Bks.
HarperCollins Publishers Ltd. Staff, et al. Origins No. 5. 2010. (Vampire Diaries: Stefan's Diaries: 1). (ENG.). 256p. (YA). (gr. 9-18). pap. 9.99 (978-0-06-200393-5(3), HarperTeen) HarperCollins Pubs.
Harris, Ashley Rae. The Prank. 2011. (Night Fall Ser.). (ENG.). 120p. (YA). (gr. 6-12). pap. 7.95 (978-0-7613-7814-3(6)); lib. bdg. 27.93 (978-0-7613-7747-4(6)) Lerner Publishing Group.
Hart, Jeff. Eat, Brains, Love. 2013. (Eat, Brains, Love Ser.: 1). (ENG.). 352p. (YA). (gr. 8). pap. 9.99 (978-0-06-220034-1(8), HarperTeen) HarperCollins Pubs.
—Undead with Benefits. 2014. (Eat, Brains, Love Ser.: 2). (ENG.). 416p. (YA). (gr. 8). pap. 9.99 (978-0-06-220036-5(4), HarperTeen) HarperCollins Pubs.
Hartzell, Andy. Fox Bunny Funny. 2007. (ENG., Illus.). 104p. pap. 10.00 (978-1-891830-97-6(X), 9781891830976) Top Shelf Productions.
Harwood, Kelsey. Still Alive. 2012. 144p. pap. 9.99 (978-1-60820-746-6(3)) MLR Pr., LLC.
Hawthorne, Nathaniel. The House of the Seven Gables, 1 vol. Fisher, Scott, illus. 2011. (Calico Illustrated Classics Ser.). (ENG.). 112p. (J). (gr. 3-6). 27.07 (978-1-60270-746-7(4)) Magic Wagon.
Hayes, Christine. The Mothman's Curse. Hindle, James K., illus. 2015. (ENG.). 320p. (J). (gr. 3-7). 15.99 (978-1-62672-027-5(4), 9781626720275) Roaring Brook Pr.
—Mothman's Curse. 2016. (J). lib. bdg. 18.40 (978-0-606-39560-1(1)) Turtleback Bks.
Heller, Jason & Stine, R. L. Slappy's Revenge: Twisted Tricks from the World's Smartest Dummy. 2015. (ENG., Illus.). 96p. (J). (gr. 2-7). pap. 8.99 (978-0-545-82125-4(8)) Scholastic, Inc.
Helquist, Brett, illus. Scary Stories 3: More Tales to Chill Your Bones. 2011. 109p. (J). pap. (978-0-545-38507-7(5)) Scholastic, Inc.
Henderson, Jason. The Triumph of Death. 2012. (Alex Van Helsing Ser.: 3). (ENG.). 320p. (YA). (gr. 8). 17.99 (978-0-06-195103-9(X), HarperTeen) HarperCollins Pubs.
—Vampire Rising. 2010. (Alex Van Helsing Ser.: 1). (ENG.). 256p. (YA). (gr. 8-18). 16.99 (978-0-06-195099-5(8), HarperTeen) HarperCollins Pubs.
—Voice of the Undead. 2011. (Alex Van Helsing Ser.: 2). (ENG.). 304p. (YA). (gr. 8). 16.99 (978-0-06-195101-5(3), HarperTeen) HarperCollins Pubs.
Herbert, James. The Rats. 2003. (Rats Ser.: Bk. 1). (ENG.). 208p. (J). 32.50 (978-0-333-76118-2(9)) Macmillan Pubs., Ltd. GBR. Dist: Trafalgar Square Publishing.
Herren, Greg. Dark Tide. 2014. (ENG.). 264p. (J). (gr. 7). pap. 11.95 (978-1-62639-197-0(1)) Bold Strokes Bks.
Hicks, Faith Erin & Druckmann, Neil. The Last of Us: American Dreams. Wright, Brendan, ed. 2013. (ENG., Illus.). 96p. pap. 16.99 (978-1-61655-212-1(3)) Dark Horse Comics.
Higgins, F. E. The Lunatic's Curse. 2011. (ENG.). 352p. (J). (gr. 5-9). 29.99 (978-0-312-56682-1(4), 9780312566821) Feiwel & Friends.
Higgins, M. G. The Lost House. 2014. (Red Rhino Ser.). (J). lib. bdg. 18.40 (978-0-606-36202-3(9)) Turtleback Bks.
Higgins, Nadia. Down, Zombie, Down! Zombie Zappers Book 4. 2014. (Zombie Zappers Ser.). 64p. (J). (gr. 5-9). pap. 9.95 (978-1-62285-016-7(5)) Enslow Pubs., Inc.
—Zombie Camp: Zombie Zappers Book 1. 2014. (Zombie Zappers Ser.). 64p. (J). (gr. 5-9). pap. 9.95 (978-1-62285-000-6(9)) Enslow Pubs., Inc.
—Zombie Field Day: Zombie Zappers Book 2. 2014. (Zombie Zappers Ser.). 64p. (J). (gr. 5-9). pap. 9.95 (978-1-62285-006-8(8)) Enslow Pubs., Inc.
—The Zombie Next Door: Zombie Zappers Book 3. 2014. (Zombie Zappers Ser.). 64p. (J). (gr. 5-9). pap. 9.95 (978-1-62285-011-2(4)) Enslow Pubs., Inc.
Higson, Charlie. The Dead (new Cover) (an Enemy Novel) 2014. (Enemy Novel Ser.). (ENG.). 512p. (YA). (gr. 9-17). pap. 9.99 (978-1-4847-2145-2(4)) Hyperion Bks. for Children.
—The End (an Enemy Novel) (Enemy Novel Ser.). (ENG.). 512p. (YA). (gr. 9-17). 2017. pap. 9.99 (978-1-4847-3291-5(X)) 2016. 17.99 (978-1-4847-1695-3(7)) Hyperion Bks. for Children.
—The Enemy (new Cover) (an Enemy Novel) 2014. (Enemy Novel Ser.). (ENG.). 448p. (YA). (gr. 9-17). pap. 9.99 (978-1-4847-2146-9(2)) Hyperion Bks. for Children.
—The Fallen (an Enemy Novel) 2014. (Enemy Novel Ser.). (ENG.). 544p. (YA). (gr. 9-17). 17.99 (978-1-4231-6566-8(7)) Disney Pr.
—The Fallen (an Enemy Novel) 2015. (Enemy Novel Ser.). (ENG.). 560p. (YA). (gr. 9-17). pap. 9.99 (978-1-4231-6636-8(1)) Hyperion Bks. for Children.
—The Fear (new Cover) (an Enemy Novel) 2014. (Enemy Novel Ser.). (ENG.). 496p. (YA). (gr. 9-17). pap. 9.99 (978-1-4847-2144-5(6)) Hyperion Bks. for Children.
—The Hunted (an Enemy Novel) 2015. (Enemy Novel Ser.: 6). (ENG.). 464p. (YA). (gr. 9-17). 17.99 (978-1-4231-6567-5(5)) Hyperion Bks. for Children.
—The Sacrifice. 2013. (Enemy Novel Ser.). (ENG.). 496p. (YA). (gr. 9-17). 17.99 (978-1-4231-6565-1(9)) Hyperion Pr.
—The Sacrifice (an Enemy Novel) 2014. (Enemy Novel Ser.). (ENG.). 512p. (YA). (gr. 9-17). pap. 9.99 (978-1-4231-6635-1(3)) Hyperion Bks. for Children.
Hill, Will. The Rising: A Department 19 Novel. 2013. (Department Nineteen Ser.: 2). (ENG.). 592p. (YA). (gr. 9). pap. 9.99 (978-1-59514-629-8(6), Razorbill) Penguin Young Readers Group.
—Zero Hour. 2015. (Department 19 Ser.: 4). (ENG.). 704p. (J). pap. 9.99 (978-0-00-750584-5(1), HarperCollins Children's Bks.) HarperCollins Pubs. Ltd. GBR. Dist: HarperCollins Pubs.
Hoblin, Paul & Hueller, Patrick. Foul. 2011. (Night Fall Ser.). (ENG.). 120p. (YA). (gr. 6-12). pap. 7.95 (978-0-7613-7813-6(8)); lib. bdg. 27.93 (978-0-7613-7746-7(8)) Lerner Publishing Group.
Hodgson, William Hope. The Sea Horses. 2004. reprint ed. pap. 1.99 (978-1-4192-8166-2(6)) Kessinger Publishing, LLC.
Holder, Nancy & Viguié, Debbie. Crusade. (Crusade Ser.). (ENG.). (YA). (gr. 9). 2011. 496p. pap. 9.99 (978-1-4169-9803-7(9)) 2010. 480p. 16.99 (978-1-4169-9802-0(0)) Simon Pulse. (Simon Pulse).
—Damned. 2011. (Crusade Ser.). (ENG.). 544p. (YA). (gr. 9). pap. 9.99 (978-1-4169-9805-1(5), Simon Pulse) Simon Pulse.
—Vanquished. 2012. (Crusade Ser.). (ENG.). 496p. (YA). (gr. 9). 16.99 (978-1-4169-9806-8(3)); pap. 9.99 (978-1-4169-9807-5(1)) Simon Pulse. (Simon Pulse).
Holt, Simon. The Devouring #2: Soulstice. 2010. (Devouring: Book 2 Ser.). (ENG.). 288p. (YA). (gr. 7-17). pap. 19.99 (978-0-316-03574-3(2)) Little, Brown Bks. for Young Readers.
Hopkins, Howard. The Nightmare Club #3: the Willow Witch. 2009. 104p. pap. 9.98 (978-0-578-00361-0(9)) Golden Perils Pr.
Horowitz, Anthony. Bloody Horowitz. 2011. (ENG.). 336p. (J). (gr. 5-18). 6.99 (978-0-14-241874-1(9), Puffin Books) Penguin Young Readers Group.
—The Complete Horowitz Horror. 2008. (ENG.). 448p. (J). (gr. 3-7). 7.99 (978-0-14-241162-9(0), Puffin Books) Penguin Young Readers Group.
Horror, 10 vols. 2005. (Double Fastback Ser.). (J). (gr. 6-12). 64p. pap. 54.95 (978-0-13-024469-7(4)); 32p. pap. 54.95 (978-0-13-024451-2(1)) Globe Fearon Educational Publishing.
Hotel Horror. (Fantasmas de Fear Street Coleccion). (SPA.). (YA). (gr. 5-8). Vol. 1. pap. 7.95 (978-950-04-2091-4(0), EM11732) Vol. 2. pap. 7.95 (978-950-04-2092-1(9), EM11736) Emecé Editores S.A. ARG. Dist: Planeta Publishing Corp., Lectorum Pubns., Inc.
House, August. The August House Book of Scary Stories: Spooky Tales for Telling Out Loud. 2016. (ENG., Illus.). 144p. (J). (gr. 5-9). pap. 9.95 (978-1-941460-41-2(0)) August Hse. Pubs., Inc.
Howard, Kate. Goosebumps Movie: Night of the Living Monsters. 2015. (Goosebumps Ser.). lib. bdg. 14.75 (978-0-606-37764-5(6)) Turtleback Bks.
—Goosebumps the Movie: Night of the Living Monsters. 2015. (ENG.). 48p. (J). (gr. 2-5). pap. 4.99 (978-0-545-82254-1(8)) Scholastic, Inc.
Howard, Lee. Scooby-Doo & the High Tech House of the Future, 1 vol. 2016. (Scooby-Doo Comic Readers Ser.). (ENG.). 32p. (J). (gr. k-3). lib. bdg. 24.21 (978-1-61479-452-3(9), Graphic Planet) Magic Wagon.
—Scooby-Doo & the Unnatural, 1 vol. 2016. (Scooby-Doo Comic Readers Ser.). (ENG.). 32p. (J). (gr. k-3). lib. bdg. 24.21 (978-1-61479-453-0(7), Graphic Planet) Magic Wagon.
—Scooby-Doo in Mummy Scares Best, 1 vol. 2016. (Scooby-Doo Comic Readers Ser.). (ENG.). 32p. (J). (gr. k-3). lib. bdg. 24.21 (978-1-61479-455-4(3), Graphic Planet) Magic Wagon.
Hughes, Dawn Marie. Deadwood: Haunted Stories. 2006. 94p. pap. 16.95 (978-1-4241-2600-2(2)) PublishAmerica, Inc.
Hulme-Cross, Benjamin. The House of Memories. Evergreen, Nelson, illus. 2015. (Dark Hunter Ser.). (ENG.). 64p. (J). (gr. 4-8). pap. 4.99 (978-1-4677-8085-8(5)) Lerner Publishing Group.
—The Marsh Demon. Evergreen, Nelson, illus. 2015. (Dark Hunter Ser.). (ENG.). 64p. (J). (gr. 4-8). 17.32 (978-1-4677-8658-4(6)) Lerner Publishing Group.
—The Red Thirst. Evergreen, Nelson, illus. 2015. (Dark Hunter Ser.). (ENG.). 64p. (J). (gr. 4-8). pap. 4.99 (978-1-4677-8088-9(X)) Lerner Publishing Group.
—Ship of Death. Evergreen, Nelson, illus. 2015. (Dark Hunter Ser.). (ENG.). 64p. (J). (gr. 4-8). pap. 4.99 (978-1-4677-8090-2(1)) Lerner Publishing Group.
—The Stone Witch. Evergreen, Nelson, illus. 2015. (Dark Hunter Ser.). (ENG.). 64p. (J). (gr. 4-8). pap. 4.99 (978-1-4677-8089-6(8)) Lerner Publishing Group.
—Wolf Trap. Evergreen, Nelson, illus. 2015. (Dark Hunter Ser.). (ENG.). 64p. (J). (gr. 4-8). pap. 4.99 (978-1-4677-8086-5(3)) Lerner Publishing Group.
Hunter, Erin. Midnight. Richardson, Owen & Stevenson, Dave, illus. 2015. (Warriors: the New Prophecy Ser.: 1). (ENG.). 352p. (J). (gr. 3-7). pap. 7.99 (978-0-06-236702-0(1)) HarperCollins Pubs.
Huntington, Geoffrey. Blood Moon. 2013. (Ravenscliff Ser.: 3). (ENG.). 260p. pap. 17.99 (978-1-62681-169-0(5)) Diversion Publishing Corp.
Hutchison, Barry. Mr Mumbles, 1. 2010. (Invisible Fiends Ser.: 1). (ENG.). 288p. (J). 8.99 (978-0-00-731515-4(5), HarperCollins Children's Bks.) HarperCollins Pubs. Ltd. GBR. Dist: HarperCollins Pubs.
Imaginism Studios Inc. Staff & Disney Storybook Art Team, illus. Vampirina Going Batty. 2017. (ENG.). 24p. (J). (gr. -1-k). pap. 5.99 (978-1-368-00619-4(1)) Disney Pr.
International Thriller Writers Association Staff. Fear: 13 Stories of Suspense & Horror. Stine, R. L., ed. 2010. (ENG.). 320p. (YA). (gr. 7-18). 16.99 (978-0-525-42168-9(8), Dutton Books for Young Readers) Penguin Young Readers Group.
Invisible Man. (ARA., Illus.). 100p. (YA). pap. 5.95 (978-0-86685-741-3(9), LDL934) Librairie du Liban Pubns. FRA. Dist: International Bk. Ctr., Inc.
Ireland, Kenneth. The Ghost Train. 2004. 126p. (J). 5.00 (978-1-84161-032-0(1)) Ravette Publishing, Ltd. GBR. Dist: Parkwest Pubns., Inc.
—Sleep Well. 2004. 126p. (J). 5.00 (978-1-84161-030-6(5)) Ravette Publishing, Ltd. GBR. Dist: Parkwest Pubns., Inc.
—The Werewolf Mask. 2004. 126p. (J). 5.00 (978-1-84161-033-7(X)) Ravette Publishing, Ltd. GBR. Dist: Parkwest Pubns., Inc.
Irving, Washington, et al. Halloween Classics, Vol. 23. Pomplun, Tom, ed. 2012. (ENG., Illus.). 144p. (YA). pap. 17.95 (978-0-9825630-5-2(1), 9780982563052) Eureka Productions.
Jablonski, Carla. Shadow of the Sphinx. 2007. (Charmed Ser.). (ENG.). 192p. (YA). pap. 14.95 (978-1-4169-6756-9(7), Gallery Bks.) Gallery Bks.
Jackson, Steve. House of Hell. 2006. (Fighting Fantasy Gamebooks Ser.). 320p. mass mkt. 6.99 (978-0-7434-9297-3(8)) Simon & Schuster, Inc.
Jacob, C. W. The Tipperary Bird. 2009. (Illus.). 40p. pap. 18.99 (978-1-4389-5212-3(0)) AuthorHouse.
Jacobs, W. W. The Monkey's Paw. 2010. (Creative Short Stories Ser.). (Illus.). 32p. (J). (gr. 5-18). 19.95 (978-1-58341-919-9(5), Creative Education) Creative Co., The.
James, M. R. OXFORD BOOKWORMS. STAGE 4: THE UNIQUE GRAVE SHORT STORIES EDITION 08. 3rd ed. 2008. (ENG., Illus.). 96p. 9.38 (978-0-19-479191-5(2)) Oxford Univ. Pr., Inc.
Jarvis, Robin. Dancing Jax. 2012. (ENG., Illus.). 576p. (YA). 8.99 (978-0-00-745341-2(8), HarperCollins Children's Bks.) HarperCollins Pubs. Ltd. GBR. Dist: HarperCollins Pubs.
Jasper, Rick & Reece, Richard. The Late Bus. 2011. (Night Fall Ser.). (ENG.). 112p. (YA). (gr. 6-12). pap. 7.95

(978-0-7613-7812-9(X)); lib. bdg. 27.93 *(978-0-7613-7745-0(X))* Lerner Publishing Group.

—Skin. 2010. (Night Fall Ser.). (ENG.). 112p. (YA). (gr. 6-12). 27.93 *(978-0-7613-6143-5(X))*; pap. 7.95 *(978-0-7613-6158-9(8))* Lerner Publishing Group.

—Thaw. 2010. (Night Fall Ser.). (ENG.). 112p. (YA). (gr. 6-12). 27.93 *(978-0-7613-6145-9(6))*; pap. 7.95 *(978-0-7613-6161-9(8))* Lerner Publishing Group.

Jeanty, Georges, et al. The Core, Vol. 5. Allie, Scott & Hahn, Sierra, eds. 2014. (ENG., Illus.). 168p. pap. 17.99 *(978-1-61655-254-1(9))* Dark Horse Comics.

Jefford, Nikki. Aurora Sky: Vampire Hunter, Vol. 1. 2013. 260p. pap. 10.99 *(978-1-939997-48-7(8))* Boyce, S. M.

Jepson, Gill. Out of Time 2: Raven's Hoard. 2012. (ENG., Illus.). 168p. pap. *(978-1-78088-322-9(6))* Troubador Publishing Ltd.

Jessup, VonDa. Wanda the Witch at the Happy Haunted House. 2008. (Illus.). 44p. pap. 18.50 *(978-1-60693-149-3(0)*, Eloquent Bks.) Strategic Book Publishing & Rights Agency (SBPRA).

Jinks, Catherine. Eloise. 2007. (Allie's Ghost Hunters Ser.: Bk. 3). (ENG.). 180p. (Orig.). (J). (gr. 4-7). pap. 11.99 *(978-1-74114-659-2(3))* Allen & Unwin AUS. Dist: Independent Pubs. Group.

—Eustace. 2007. (Allie's Ghost Hunters Ser.: Bk. 2). (ENG.). 168p. (J). (gr. 4-7). pap. 11.99 *(978-1-74114-660-8(7))* Allen & Unwin AUS. Dist: Independent Pubs. Group.

Johnson, Alaya Dawn. Detective Frankenstein. Ota, Yuko, illus. 2011. (Twisted Journeys (r) Ser.: 17). (ENG.). 112p. (J). (gr. 4-7). pap. 7.95 *(978-0-8225-8943-3(5))*; pap. 45.32 *(978-0-7613-7613-2(5))*; lib. bdg. 27.93 *(978-0-8225-8942-6(7))* Lerner Publishing Group. (Graphic Universe™).

Johnson, Hal. Fearsome Creatures of the Lumberwoods: 20 Chilling Tales from the Wilderness. Mead, Tom, illus. 2015. (ENG.). 176p. (J). (gr. 3-8). 14.95 *(978-0-7611-8461-4(9))* Workman Publishing Co., Inc.

Johnson, Liliane & Dufton, Jo S. Children's Chillers & Thrillers. Bruhn, Joan Z., illus. 136p. (Orig.). (J). pap. 10.00 *(978-0-930069-04-9(8))* Jasmine Pr.

Jolley, Dan. My Boyfriend Bites, 3 vols., No. 3. Martinez, Alitha E., illus. 2011. (My Boyfriend Is a Monster Ser.: 3). (ENG.). 128p. (YA). (gr. 7-12). 29.27 *(978-0-7613-5599-1(5))* Lerner Publishing Group.

—My Boyfriend Is a Monster - My Boyfriend Bites. Martinez, Alitha E., illus. 2011. (My Boyfriend Is a Monster Ser.: 3). (ENG.). 128p. (YA). (gr. 7-12). pap. 9.95 *(978-0-7613-7078-9(1)*, Graphic Universe™) Lerner Publishing Group.

—Wrapped up in You. Nourigat, Natalie, illus. 2012. (My Boyfriend Is a Monster Ser.: 6). (ENG.). 128p. (YA). (gr. 7-12). pap. 9.95 *(978-0-8225-9425-3(0)*, Graphic Universe™) Lerner Publishing Group.

Jones, Allan Frewin. The Wreckers. 2003. (ENG.). 163p. (J). mass mkt. *(978-0-330-36810-0(9)*, Pan) Pan Macmillan.

Jones, Darynda. Death & the Girl He Loves. 2013. (Darklight Ser.: 3). (ENG.). 272p. (YA). (gr. 8-12). pap. 9.99 *(978-0-312-62522-1(7)*, 9780312625221, St. Martin's Griffin) St. Martin's Pr.

Jude, Sarah. The May Queen Murders. 2017. (ENG.). 304p. (YA). (gr. 9). pap. 9.99 *(978-0-544-93725-3(2)*, HMH Books For Young Readers) Houghton Mifflin Harcourt Publishing Co.

Kagawa, Julie. The Immortal Rules. 2013. (Blood of Eden Ser.: 1). lib. bdg. 20.85 *(978-0-606-26947-6(9)*, Turtleback) Turtleback Bks.

Kane, Christy. Tales of the Sisters Kane. 2006. (Illus.). 96p. (J). (gr. 4-7). 20.00 *(978-0-9778949-4-9(0))* Baby Tattoo Bks.

Kaplan, Bruce Eric. Monsters Eat Whiny Children. Kaplan, Bruce Eric, illus. 2010. (ENG., Illus.). 40p. (J). (gr. -1-3). 17.99 *(978-1-4169-8689-8(8)*, Simon & Schuster Bks. For Young Readers) Simon & Schuster Bks. For Young Readers.

Karlsson, Val. The Protectors. 2010. (Night Fall Ser.). (ENG.). 112p. (YA). (gr. 6-12). 27.93 *(978-0-7613-6144-2(8))*; pap. 7.95 *(978-0-7613-6159-6(6))* Lerner Publishing Group.

Kayla Taylor. Fatal Elements: Book 1. 2009. 368p. pap. 20.95 *(978-1-4401-8495-6(X))* iUniverse, Inc.

Keating, T. P. Bleeding Hearts: the Diary of a Country Vampire. 2005. 272p. (YA). pap. 12.48 *(978-1-4116-4815-9(3))* Lulu Pr., Inc.

Keswick, Kitty. Freaksville. Cox, Val, illus. 2010. 328p. (YA). (gr. 8-12). pap. 16.99 *(978-1-61603-001-8(1))* Leap Bks.

Kiarie, Vivian W. The Waltz, the Weasel & the Lair. 2008. 50p. pap. 16.95 *(978-1-60474-265-7(8))* America Star Bks.

Kidwell, Justina. The Haunted Tree House, the Ghost Town, & the Dark Reaper: The Kent Boys' Adventures, 1 vol. 2009. 48p. pap. 16.95 *(978-1-60813-234-8(X))* America Star Bks.

Kiernan, Celine. Into the Grey. 2014. (ENG.). 304p. (YA). (gr. 7). 16.99 *(978-0-7636-7061-0(8))* Candlewick Pr.

King, Kirsty. My New Friends. 2005. 52p. pap. *(978-1-84401-576-4(9))* Athena Pr.

Kingsley, Ron D. Stories from the Life of Ronnie Kaye: Monsters. 2013. (ENG.). 125p. (YA). pap. 8.95 *(978-1-4787-1121-6(3))* Outskirts Pr., Inc.

Kirkman, Robert. Call to Arms. 2016. (Walking Dead Ser.: 26). lib. bdg. 26.95 *(978-0-606-39079-8(0))* Turtleback Bks.

—No Turning Back, Vol. 25. 2016. (Walking Dead Ser.: 25). lib. bdg. 26.95 *(978-0-606-38027-0(2))* Turtleback Bks.

Kitchel, Samantha. The Beauty in the Beasts. 2013. 186p. pap. 12.99 *(978-1-300-48245-1(1))* Lulu Pr., Inc.

Klause, Annette Curtis. Blood & Chocolate. 2007. (ENG.). 288p. (YA). (gr. 7). pap. 9.99 *(978-0-385-73421-9(2)*, Ember) Random Hse. Children's Bks.

Kloepfer, John. Empire State of Slime. DeGrand, Ned & DeGrand, David, illus. 2013. (Zombie Chasers Ser.: 4). (ENG.). 208p. (J). (gr. 3-7). 16.99 *(978-0-06-223095-9(6))* HarperCollins Pubs.

—Nothing Left to Ooze. DeGrand, David, illus. 2014. (Zombie Chasers Ser.: 5). (ENG.). (J). (gr. 3-7). 240p. pap. 6.99 *(978-0-06-223099-7(9))*; 224p. 16.99 *(978-0-06-223098-0(0))* HarperCollins Pubs.

—The Zombie Chasers - Zombies of the Caribbean. DeGrand, David, illus. 2014. (Zombie Chasers Ser.: 6). (ENG.). 224p. (J). (gr. 3-7). 16.99 *(978-0-06-229024-3(X))* HarperCollins Pubs.

Knudsen, Michelle. Evil Librarian. 2014. (ENG.). 352p. (YA). (gr. 9). 16.99 *(978-0-7636-6038-3(8))* Candlewick Pr.

Kopp, Megan. Scary Folktales, 1 vol. 2010. (Scary Stories Ser.). (ENG.). 32p. (gr. 3-4). lib. bdg. 27.99 *(978-1-4296-4571-3(7)*, Edge Bks.) Capstone Press of Coughlan Cos.

Kraus, Daniel. Scowler. 2014. (ENG.). 304p. (YA). (gr. 9). pap. 9.99 *(978-0-385-74310-5(6)*, Ember) Random Hse. Children's Bks.

Krovatin, Christopher. Entombed. 2014. (Gravediggers Ser.: 3). (ENG.). 320p. (J). (gr. 3-7). 16.99 *(978-0-06-207746-2(5)*, Tegen, Katherine Bks) HarperCollins Pubs.

—Terror Cove. 2013. (Gravediggers Ser.: 2). (ENG.). 368p. (J). (gr. 3-7). 16.99 *(978-0-06-207743-1(0)*, Tegen, Katherine Bks) HarperCollins Pubs.

—Venomous. Yates, Kelly, illus. 2008. (ENG.). 336p. (YA). (gr. 8-18). 16.99 *(978-1-4169-2487-6(6)*, Atheneum Bks. for Young Readers) Simon & Schuster Children's Publishing.

Kurtagich, Dawn. And the Trees Crept In. 2016. (ENG.). 352p. (YA). (gr. 10-17). 17.99 *(978-0-316-29870-4(0))* Little, Brown Bks. for Young Readers.

L'Allier, Peter Wesley Thomas. Rotten Robbie & the Legend of Wanabinoo. 2006. (Illus.). 215p. 18.95 *(978-0-9724022-8-6(4))* TangleTown Media Inc.

Lancaster, Susan. The Caves & the Skull. 2004. 160p. pap. *(978-0-9730350-1-8(3))* Snosrap Publishing.

Lancett, Peter. The Bridge of Dark Tears. 2008. (Dark Man Ser.). (ENG., Illus.). 48p. pap. *(978-1-84167-746-0(9))* Ransom Publishing Ltd.

—The Bridge of Dark Tears, 1 vol. unabr. ed. 2011. (Dark Man Ser.). (ENG.). 47p. (YA). (gr. 9-12). 7.95 *(978-1-61651-294-1(6))* Saddleback Educational Publishing, Inc.

—The Dark Dreams, 1 vol. unabr. ed. 2010. (Dark Man Ser.). (ENG.). 34p. (YA). (gr. 9-12). pap. 7.95 *(978-1-61651-017-6(X))* Saddleback Educational Publishing, Inc.

—The Dark Garden. 2008. (Dark Man Ser.). (ENG., Illus.). 48p. pap. *(978-1-84167-750-7(7))* Ransom Publishing Ltd.

—The Dark Garden, 1 vol. unabr. ed. 2011. (Dark Man Ser.). (ENG.). 47p. (YA). (gr. 9-12). 7.95 *(978-1-61651-298-9(9))* Saddleback Educational Publishing, Inc.

—The Dark Glass, 1 vol. unabr. ed. 2010. (Dark Man Ser.). (ENG.). 34p. (YA). (gr. 9-12). pap. 7.95 *(978-1-61651-018-3(8))* Saddleback Educational Publishing, Inc.

—The Dark Music. 2008. (Dark Man Ser.). (ENG., Illus.). 48p. pap. *(978-1-84167-749-1(3))* Ransom Publishing Ltd.

—The Dark Music, 1 vol. unabr. ed. 2011. (Dark Man Ser.). (ENG.). 47p. (YA). (gr. 9-12). 7.95 *(978-1-61651-297-2(0))* Saddleback Educational Publishing, Inc.

—The Dark River. 2008. (Dark Man Ser.). (ENG., Illus.). 48p. pap. *(978-1-84167-745-3(0))* Ransom Publishing Ltd.

—The Dark River, 1 vol. unabr. ed. 2011. (Dark Man Ser.). (ENG.). 47p. (YA). (gr. 9-12). 7.95 *(978-1-61651-293-4(8))* Saddleback Educational Publishing, Inc.

—The Dark Side of Magic, 1 vol. unabr. ed. 2010. (Dark Man Ser.). (ENG.). 34p. (YA). (gr. 9-12). pap. 7.95 *(978-1-61651-019-0(6))* Saddleback Educational Publishing, Inc.

—The Dark Waters of Time, 1 vol. unabr. ed. 2010. (Dark Man Ser.). (ENG.). 34p. (YA). (gr. 9-12). pap. 7.95 *(978-1-61651-020-6(X))* Saddleback Educational Publishing, Inc.

—The Past Is Dark. 2008. (Dark Man Ser.). (ENG., Illus.). 48p. pap. *(978-1-84167-747-7(7))* Ransom Publishing Ltd.

—The Past Is Dark, 1 vol. unabr. ed. 2011. (Dark Man Ser.). (ENG.). 47p. (YA). (gr. 9-12). 7.95 *(978-1-61651-295-8(4))* Saddleback Educational Publishing, Inc.

—Playing the Dark Game. 2008. (Dark Man Ser.). (ENG., Illus.). 48p. pap. *(978-1-84167-748-4(5))* Ransom Publishing Ltd.

Langley, Jan. The Captain & Harry: A Trembling Tail of Thieves. Robinson, Susan, illus. 2006. 30p. (J). (gr. 4-7). pap. 10.95 *(978-1-892384-23-2(X))* Avery Color Studios, Inc.

Lansdale, John L., et al. Something Wicca This Way Comes, No. 7. Romberger, James et al, illus. 7th ed. 2009. (Tales from the Crypt Graphic Novels Ser.: 7). (ENG.). 96p. (J). (gr. 5-12). 12.95 *(978-1-59707-151-2(X)*, 9781597071512) Papercutz.

Latham, William. Scary Stories of Stamford. 2009. 51p. pap. 9.99 *(978-1-4357-6032-5(8))* Lulu Pr., Inc.

Lauren, Christina. The House. 2015. (ENG., Illus.). 384p. (YA). (gr. 9). 18.99 *(978-1-4814-1371-8(6))* Simon & Schuster Children's Publishing.

Lawrence, P. Anthony. Jessie & Fumbling Giant. 2013. 28p. pap. 24.95 *(978-1-63000-899-4(0))* America Star Bks.

Le Fanu, J. Sheridan. Madam Crowl's Ghost & the Dead Sexton. 2004. reprint ed. pap. 1.99 *(978-1-4192-3188-9(X))*; pap. 15.95 *(978-1-4191-3188-2(5))* Kessinger Publishing, LLC.

Le Guin, Ursula K. Catwings. Schindler, S. D., illus. 2003. (Catwings Ser.: No. 1). (ENG.). 48p. (J). (gr. -1-3). 5.99 *(978-0-439-55189-2(7))* Scholastic, Inc.

Leach, Maria. The Thing at the Foot of the Bed & Other Scary Tales. Werth, Kurt, illus. 2016. (ENG.). 128p. (J). (gr. 2-5). pap. 7.99 *(978-0-486-80786-7(X))* Dover Pubns., Inc.

Leiber, Fritz. Gonna Roll the Bones. Wiesner, David, illus. 2004. 32p. (J). *(978-0-689-03637-8(X))*; 16.95 *(978-0-689-03591-3(8))* ibooks, Inc. (Milk & Cookies).

Leigh, Suzie. The Glitter Man. 2010. 164p. 22.95 *(978-1-4520-1266-7(0))*; pap. 12.95 *(978-1-4520-1267-4(9))* AuthorHouse.

Lenhard, Elizabeth. Drop-Dead Gorgeous. 2014. 186p. (J). pap. *(978-0-545-58951-2(7))* Scholastic, Inc.

Leoni, Gail. Shudders! Horrible Things Kids Love to Be Afraid Of. 2011. 44p. pap. 24.95 *(978-1-4626-5323-2(5))* America Star Bks.

Leroux, Gaston. Graphic Horror, 6 vols., Set 2. Espinosa, Rod, illus. Incl. Phantom of the Opera. (Illus.). 32p. (gr. 5-8). 2009. 28.50 *(978-1-60270-679-8(4)*, Graphic Planet- Fiction); (Graphic Horror Set 2 Ser.). (Illus.). 32p. 2009. 171.00 *(978-1-60270-675-0(1)*, Graphic Planet- Fiction) ABDO Publishing Co.

—The Phantom of the Opera, 1 vol. Fisher, Scott, illus. 2011. (Calico Illustrated Classics Ser.). (ENG.). 112p. (J). (gr. 3-6). 27.07 *(978-1-60270-749-8(9))* Magic Wagon.

—The Phantom of the Opera. Howell, Troy, illus. 2008. (Classic Starts(tm) Ser.). (ENG.). 160p. (J). (gr. 2-4). 6.95 *(978-1-4027-4580-5(X))* Sterling Publishing Co., Inc.

Lettrick, Robert. The Murk. Disney Storybook Art Team, illus. 2015. (ENG.). 320p. (J). (gr. 5-9). 16.99 *(978-1-4231-8695-3(8))* Hyperion Bks. for Children.

Leveen, Tom. Sick. 2013. (ENG.). 288p. (YA). (gr. 9-17). 18.95 *(978-1-4197-0805-3(8)*, Amulet Bks.) Abrams, Inc.

Lewis, Richard. The Demon Queen. 2012. (ENG.). 240p. (YA). (gr. 7). pap. 11.99 *(978-1-4169-3590-2(8)*, Simon & Schuster Bks. For Young Readers) Simon & Schuster Bks. For Young Readers.

Lewman, David. Proud to Be a Ghostbuster. 2016. (Simon & Schuster Ready-To-Read Level 3 Ser.). lib. bdg. 13.55 *(978-0-606-38994-5(6))* Turtleback Bks.

Liggett, Kim. The Last Harvest. 2017. (ENG.). 352p. (YA). 17.99 *(978-0-7653-8098-2(6)*, 9780765380982, Tor Teen) Doherty, Tom Assocs., LLC.

Lim, Andrew. Tales from the Kopitiam. (Paranormal Singapore Ser.: Vol. 4). (ENG.). 2009. 1p. pap. 9.95 *(978-981-08-1081-8(4))* Vol. 3. 3rd ed. 2008. 160p. pap. 9.95 *(978-981-08-1080-1(6))* Monsoon Bks. Pte. Ltd. SGP. Dist: Tuttle Publishing, National Bk. Network.

Link, Kelly. Pretty Monsters. 2010. (ENG., Illus.). 416p. (YA). (gr. 7-18). 9.99 *(978-0-14-241672-3(X)*, Speak) Penguin Young Readers Group.

Liparulo, Robert. House of Dark Shadows, 1 vol. 2009. (Dreamhouse Kings Ser.: 1). (ENG.). 304p. pap. 9.99 *(978-1-59554-727-9(4))* Nelson, Thomas Inc.

—Watcher in the Woods, 1 vol. 2009. (Dreamhouse Kings Ser.: 2). (ENG.). 304p. pap. 9.99 *(978-1-59554-728-6(2))* Nelson, Thomas Inc.

Litwin, Laura Baskes. Write Horror Fiction in 5 Simple Steps. 2012. (Creative Writing in 5 Simple Steps Ser.). (Illus.). 48p. (J). (gr. 5-9). 25.27 *(978-0-7660-3836-3(X))* Enslow Pubs., Inc.

Loeb, Jeph. The Witching Hour. rev. ed. 2009. (ENG., Illus.). 160p. (YA). pap. 19.99 *(978-1-56389-945-4(0))* DC Comics.

Loewen, Nancy. Share a Scare: Writing Your Own Scary Story, 1 vol. Lyles, Christopher, illus. 2009. (Writer's Toolbox Ser.). (ENG.). 32p. (gr. 2-4). pap. 8.95 *(978-1-4048-5700-1(1))* Picture Window Bks.

Loiske, Jennifer. Black Diamond. 2013. 246p. (J). pap. 13.61 *(978-1-291-30145-8(3))* Lulu Pr., Inc.

Lovecraft, H. P. At the Mountains of Madness. 2014. (Fantastic Fiction Ser.). (ENG., Illus.). 192p. pap. 9.99 *(978-0-85775-693-0(1)*, d0401421-7cac-407d-94f3-6481a680334f) Flame Tree Publishing GBR. Dist: Bookmasters Distribution.

Lubar, David. Attack of the Vampire Weenies: And Other Warped & Creepy Tales. 2011. (Weenies Stories Ser.). (ENG.). 224p. (J). (gr. 4-7). 15.99 *(978-0-7653-2345-3(1)*, 9780765323453, Starscape) Doherty, Tom Assocs., LLC.

—The Battle of the Red Hot Pepper Weenies: And Other Warped & Creepy Tales. 2010. (Weenies Stories Ser.). (ENG.). 192p. (J). (gr. 4-7). mass mkt. 5.99 *(978-0-7653-6075-5(6)*, 9780765360755; Starscape) Doherty, Tom Assocs., LLC.

—Beware the Ninja Weenies: And Other Warped & Creepy Tales. (Weenies Stories Ser.). (ENG.). 192p. (J). (gr. 4-7). 2013. mass mkt. 5.99 *(978-0-7653-6879-9(X)*, 9780765368799) 2012. 15.99 *(978-0-7653-3213-4(2)*, 9780765332134) Doherty, Tom Assocs., LLC. (Starscape).

—The Bully Bug: A Monsterrific Tale. 2014. (Monsterrific Tales Ser.). (ENG., Illus.). 144p. (J). (gr. 3-7). 24.99 *(978-0-7653-3082-6(2)*, 9780765330826, Starscape) Doherty, Tom Assocs., LLC.

—Curse of the Campfire Weenies: And Other Warped & Creepy Tales. 2008. (Weenies Stories Ser.). (ENG.). 208p. (J). (gr. 4-9). mass mkt. 5.99 *(978-0-7653-5771-7(2)*, 9780765357717, Starscape) Doherty, Tom Assocs., LLC.

—Extremities: Stories of Death, Murder, & Revenge. 2014. (ENG.). 208p. (YA). (gr. 8-12). pap. 9.99 *(978-0-7653-3461-9(5)*, 9780765334619, Tor Teen) Doherty, Tom Assocs., LLC.

—The Gloomy Ghost. 2014. (Monsterrific Tales Ser.). (ENG., Illus.). 144p. (J). (gr. 3-7). 15.99 *(978-0-7653-3080-2(6)*, 9780765330802, Starscape) Doherty, Tom Assocs., LLC.

—Invasion of the Road Weenies. 2006. (Weenies Stories Ser.). (ENG.). 192p. (J). (gr. 4-7). mass mkt. 5.99 *(978-0-7653-5325-2(3)*, 9780765353252, Starscape) Doherty, Tom Assocs., LLC.

—Wipeout of the Wireless Weenies. 2015. (Weenies Stories Ser.). (ENG.). 176p. (J). (gr. 3-7). pap. 8.99 *(978-0-7653-8058-6(7)*, 9780765380586, Starscape) Doherty, Tom Assocs., LLC.

—Wipeout of the Wireless Weenies: And Other Warped & Creepy Tales. 2014. (Weenies Stories Ser.). (ENG., Illus.). 176p. (J). (gr. 4-7). 15.99 *(978-0-7653-3214-1(0)*, 9780765332141, Starscape) Doherty, Tom Assocs., LLC.

Lumley, Brian. The Nonesuch & Others. 2009. (Illus.). 122p. (J). (gr. 4-7). 35.00 *(978-1-59606-210-8(X))* Subterranean Pr.

Lurie, Susan & Stine, R. L. Monster Survival Guide. 2015. (ENG., Illus.). 96p. (J). (gr. 3-8). pap. 7.99 *(978-0-545-82126-1(6))* Scholastic, Inc.

Lusted, Marcia Amidon. How to Analyze the Works of Stephen King, 1 vol. 2010. (Essential Critiques Set 1 Ser.). (ENG.). 112p. (J). (gr. 6-12). lib. bdg. 35.64 *(978-1-61613-536-2(0)*, Essential Library) ABDO Publishing Co.

Maberry, Jonathan. Bits & Pieces. 2015. (Rot & Ruin Ser.: 5). (ENG., Illus.). 592p. (YA). (gr. 7). 19.99 *(978-1-4814-4418-7(2))* Simon & Schuster Children's Publishing.

—Fire & Ash. 2013. (Rot & Ruin Ser.: 4). (ENG., Illus.). 544p. (YA). (gr. 7). 18.99 *(978-1-4424-3992-4(0)*, Simon & Schuster Bks. For Young Readers) Simon & Schuster Bks. For Young Readers.

—Rot & Ruin, 11 vols. 2010. (Rot & Ruin Ser.: 1). (J). 122.75 *(978-1-4498-3356-5(X))*; 90.75 *(978-1-4498-3354-1(3))*; 1.25 *(978-1-4498-3360-2(8))*; 120.75 *(978-1-4498-3358-9(6))*; 256.75 *(978-1-4498-3353-4(5))* Recorded Bks., Inc.

—Rot & Ruin. (Rot & Ruin Ser.: 1). (ENG.). (YA). (gr. 7). 2011. 480p. pap. 11.99 *(978-1-4424-0233-1(4))* 2010. 464p. 17.99 *(978-1-4424-0232-4(6))* Simon & Schuster Bks. For Young Readers. (Simon & Schuster Bks. For Young Readers).

—Rot & Ruin. 2011. (Rot & Ruin Ser.: 1). lib. bdg. 23.30 *(978-0-606-23292-0(3)*, Turtleback) Turtleback Bks.

—The Rot & Ruin Collection: Rot & Ruin; Dust & Decay; Flesh & Bone, Fire & Ash. 2013. (Rot & Ruin Ser.). (ENG., Illus.). 2016p. (YA). (gr. 7). 72.99 *(978-1-4424-9770-2(X)*, Simon & Schuster Bks. For Young Readers) Simon & Schuster Bks. For Young Readers.

MacHale, D. J. The Black. (Morpheus Road Ser.: 2). (ENG.). (J). (gr. 5-9). 2012. 432p. pap. 9.99 *(978-1-4169-6520-6(3))* 2011. 416p. 18.99 *(978-1-4169-6517-6(3))* Simon & Schuster Children's Publishing. (Aladdin).

—The Blood. (Morpheus Road Ser.: 3). (ENG.). 384p. (J). (gr. 5-9). 2013. pap. 8.99 *(978-1-4169-6521-3(1))* 2012. 17.99 *(978-1-4169-6518-3(1))* Simon & Schuster Children's Publishing. (Aladdin).

—The Light. 2010. (Morpheus Road Ser.: 1). (ENG.). 352p. (J). (gr. 5-9). pap. 9.99 *(978-1-4169-6519-0(X)*, Aladdin) Simon & Schuster Children's Publishing.

—The Light. 2010. (Morpheus Road Ser.: 1). (ENG.). 352p. (J). (gr. 5-18). 17.99 *(978-1-4169-6516-9(5)*, Simon & Schuster/Paula Wiseman Bks.) Simon & Schuster/Paula Wiseman Bks.

MacLennan, Cathy. Spooky Spooky Spooky! 2009. (ENG., Illus.). 32p. (J). (gr. -1-1). 16.95 *(978-1-906250-67-6(7))* Boxer Bks., Ltd. GBR. Dist: Sterling Publishing Co., Inc.

Magic Wagon Staff. Ghost Detectors Set 2, 1 vol. 2012. (Ghost Detectors Ser.: 6). (ENG., Illus.). 80p. 162.42 *(978-1-61641-622-5(X)*, Calico Chapter Bks) Magic Wagon.

Mahy, Margaret. Don't Read This! And Other Tales of the Unnatural. 2004. (ENG., Illus.). 208p. (J). reprint ed. pap. 7.95 *(978-1-932425-25-3(X)*, Lemniscaat) Boyds Mills Pr.

Maneru, Maria, et al. Mis Primeros Relatos de Miedo. Jos, Luis Telleria, illus. 2004. 312p. (J). *(978-968-13-3782-7(4))* Editorial Diana, S.A. MEX. Dist: Lectorum Pubns., Inc.

Manning, Matthew K. & Poe, Edgar Allen. The Fall of the House of Usher, 1 vol. Jimenz, Jim & Calero, Dennis, illus. 2013. (Edgar Allan Poe Graphic Novels Ser.). (ENG.). 72p. (gr. 2-3). 27.99 *(978-1-4342-3024-9(4))*; pap. 6.10 *(978-1-4342-4258-7(7))* Stone Arch Bks.

Mariotte, Jeff. Fall. 2004. (Witch Season Ser.). (ENG.). 320p. (YA). (gr. 9). mass mkt. 5.99 *(978-0-689-86724-8(7)*, Simon Pulse) Simon Pulse.

Marquitz, Tim. Skulls. Milner, Isaac, ed. Lucero, Jessica, illus. 2011. pap. 13.25 *(978-1-61572-354-6(4))* Damnation Bks.

Marrone, Amanda. Devoured. 2009. (ENG.). 304p. (YA). (gr. 9-18). pap. 9.99 *(978-1-4169-7890-9(9)*, Simon Pulse) Simon Pulse.

Martin, T. Michael. The End Games. 2014. (ENG.). 400p. (YA). (gr. 9). pap. 9.99 *(978-0-06-220181-2(6))* HarperCollins Pubs.

Marvel Book Group. Ant-Man: Zombie Repellent: A Mighty Marvel Chapter Book. 2015. (Mighty Marvel Chapter Book Ser.). (ENG.). 128p. (J). (gr. 3-7). pap. 5.99 *(978-1-4847-1449-2(0)*, Marvel Pr.) Disney Publishing Worldwide.

Marvel Book Group & Behling, Steve. Marvel Monsters Unleashed: the Gruesome Gorgilla! Marvel Press Artist, (IL, illus. 2017. (Marvel Monsters Unleashed! Ser.). (ENG.). 176p. (J). (gr. 3-7). pap. 6.99 ***(978-1-368-00248-6(X)***, Marvel Pr.) Disney Publishing Worldwide.

Mary-Todd, Jonathan. Lock-In. 2011. (Night Fall Ser.). (ENG.). 112p. (YA). (gr. 6-12). pap. 7.95 *(978-0-7613-7815-0(4))*; lib. bdg. 27.93 *(978-0-7613-7743-6(3))* Lerner Publishing Group.

Massie, Elizabeth. Ameri-Scares: New York. 2013. 148p. pap. 12.99 *(978-1-937530-55-6(8))* Crossroad Pr.

Masters, Anthony. Scary Tales to Tell in the Dark. 2012. (ENG.). 136p. pap. 13.99 *(978-1-4482-0502-8(6)*, 9781448205028, Bloomsbury Reader) Bloomsbury Publishing Plc GBR. Dist: Macmillan.

May, Elizabeth. The Fallen Kingdom: Book Three of the Falconer Trilogy. 2017. (Falconer Ser.: 3). (ENG.). 400p. (YA). 18.99 ***(978-1-4521-2883-2(9))*** Chronicle Bks. LLC.

May, Elizabeth. The Vanishing Throne. 2016. (Falconer Ser.: 2). (ENG., Illus.). 458p. (YA). (gr. 7-12). 17.99 *(978-1-4521-2882-5(0))* Chronicle Bks. LLC.

Mayhall, Robin. He Loves Me, He Loves Me Not. Cella, Kristen & Tiede, Dirk, illus. 2013. (My Boyfriend Is a Monster Ser.: 7). (ENG.). 128p. (YA). (gr. 7-12). lib. bdg. 29.27 *(978-0-7613-6005-6(0)*, Graphic Universe™) Lerner Publishing Group.

—He Loves Me, He Loves Me Not. Cella, Kristen et al, illus. 2013. (My Boyfriend Is a Monster Ser.: 7). (ENG.). 128p. (YA). (gr. 7-12). pap. 9.95 *(978-0-7613-8548-6(7)*, Graphic Universe™) Lerner Publishing Group.

McBride, Lish. Firebug. 2014. (ENG.). 336p. (YA). (gr. 9-12). 17.99 *(978-0-8050-9862-4(3)*, 9780805098624, Holt, Henry & Co. Bks. For Young Readers) Holt, Henry & Co.

McCarthy, Kai. Unpredictable Prophecies. 2012. 324p. 29.95 *(978-1-4626-7644-6(8))* America Star Bks.

McChiller, BBH. Monster Moon: Curse of Zala Manor. 2009. 192p. (J). (gr. 3-6). 15.95 *(978-1-933277-10-3(6))* Stargazer Publishing Co.

McCune, D. J. Death & Co. 2013. (Death & Co Ser.: 1). (ENG.). 288p. (YA). (gr. 8). pap. 11.99 *(978-1-4714-0092-6(1))* Bonnier Publishing GBR. Dist: Independent Pubs. Group.

McGann, Oisín. The Evil Hairdo. 2006. (Forbidden Files Ser.). (ENG., Illus.). 80p. (J). pap. 10.95 *(978-0-86278-940-4(0))* O'Brien Pr., Ltd., The IRL. Dist: Dufour Editions, Inc.

—The Poison Factory. 2006. (Forbidden Files Ser.). (ENG., Illus.). 96p. (J). pap. 10.95 *(978-0-86278-941-1(9))* O'Brien Pr., Ltd., The IRL. Dist: Dufour Editions, Inc.

McGeddon, R. Zombies! McGeddon, R. & Littler, Jamie, illus. 2016. (Disaster Diaries: 2). (ENG.). 192p. (J). 9.99 *(978-1-250-09084-3(9)*, 9781250090843) Imprint IND. Dist: Macmillan.

McGee, Joe. Peanut Butter & Brains. Santoso, Charles, illus. 2015. (ENG.). 32p. (J). (gr. -1-3). 16.95 *(978-1-4197-1247-0(0)*, Abrams Bks. for Young Readers) Abrams, Inc.

McKay, Kirsty. Undead. (ENG.). (J). 2013. 288p. (gr. 7). pap. 9.99 *(978-0-545-38189-5(4))* 2012. 272p. (gr. 9). 17.99 *(978-0-545-38188-8(6))* Scholastic, Inc. (Chicken Hse., The).

—Unfed. 2015. (Undead Ser.: 2). (YA). 1.25 *(978-1-4906-3511-8(4))* Recorded Bks., Inc.

McKissack, Patricia C. The Dark-Thirty: Southern Tales of the Supernatural. Pinkney, Brian, illus. 2004. 122p. (J). (gr. 5-8). reprint ed. pap. 17.00 *(978-0-7567-7601-5(5))* DIANE Publishing Co.

—The Dark-Thirty: Southern Tales of the Supernatural. Pinkney, Brian, illus. 2006. (ENG.). 128p. (J). (gr. 3-7). 18.95 *(978-0-679-81863-2(4)*, Knopf Bks. for Young Readers) Random Hse. Children's Bks.

McMurtry, Ken. Zombie Penpal. 2010. (Illus.). 144p. (J). pap. 6.99 *(978-1-933390-34-5(4))* Chooseco LLC.

McNeil, Gretchen. Possess. (ENG.). (YA). (gr. 8). 2012. 400p. pap. 9.99 *(978-0-06-206072-3(4))* 2011. 384p. 17.99 *(978-0-06-206071-6(6))* HarperCollins Pubs.

—Ten. (ENG.). (YA). (gr. 8). 2013. 320p. pap. 9.99 *(978-0-06-211879-0(X))* 2012. 304p. 17.99 *(978-0-06-211878-3(1))* HarperCollins Pubs.

Mead, Richelle. Shadow Kiss. 2008. (Vampire Academy Ser.: 3). (ENG.). 448p. (YA). (gr. 7-18). pap. 10.99 *(978-1-59514-197-2(9)*, Razorbill) Penguin Publishing Group.

Miller, Whitney A. The Crimson Gate. 2015. (ENG.). 312p. (YA). pap. 9.99 *(978-0-7387-4204-5(X)*, Flux) North Star Editions.

—The Violet Hour. 2014. (ENG.). 312p. (YA). pap. 9.99 *(978-0-7387-3721-8(6)*, Flux) North Star Editions.

Mind Grabber. 64p. (YA). (gr. 6-12). pap. *(978-0-8224-2335-5(9))* Globe Fearon Educational Publishing.

Monahan, Hillary. Bloody Mary, Book 2 Mary: Unleashed. (Bloody Mary Ser.). (ENG.). 256p. (YA). (gr. 7-12). 2016. pap. 9.99 *(978-1-4231-8694-6(X))* 2015. 17.99 *(978-1-4231-8539-0(0))* Hyperion Bks. for Children.

—Mary: The Summoning. 2014. (Bloody Mary Ser.). (ENG.). 256p. (YA). (gr. 7-12). 16.99 *(978-1-4231-8519-2(6))* Hyperion Bks. for Children.

—Summoning. 2015. (Bloody Mary Ser.). (ENG.). 272p. (YA). (gr. 7-12). pap. 9.99 *(978-1-4231-8693-9(1))* Hyperion Bks. for Children.

Moro, Robin, et al, illus. Read Aloud Spooky Stories. 2006. 320p. (J). (gr. 4-7). 15.98 *(978-0-7853-6338-5(6)*, 7159100) Publications International, Ltd.

Moulton, Courtney Allison. Angelfire. 2011. (Angelfire Ser.: 1). (ENG.). 464p. (YA). (gr. 8-18). 17.99 *(978-0-06-200232-7(5)*, Tegen, Katherine Bks) HarperCollins Pubs.

—My Soul to Reap. 2011. (YA). lib. bdg. 17.89 *(978-0-06-200234-1(1))* HarperCollins Pubs.

—Wings of the Wicked. 2012. (Angelfire Ser.: 2). (ENG.). 528p. (YA). (gr. 9). 17.99 *(978-0-06-200236-5(8)*, Tegen, Katherine Bks) HarperCollins Pubs.

Munday, Evan. Dial M for Moma. 2013. (Dead Kid Detective Agency Ser.). (ENG., Illus.). 320p. (J). (gr. 3-8). pap. 11.95 *(978-1-77041-073-2(2))* Purple Bear Bks., Inc.

Murphy, Lisa. Little Vampire. 2009. 262p. pap. 16.95 *(978-1-4092-9494-8(3))* Lulu Pr., Inc.

Mutis, Álvaro. La Mansión de Araucaíma: Diario de Lecumberri. (SPA.). (J). 8.00 *(978-958-04-6975-9(X))* Norma S.A. COL. Dist: Distribuidora Norma, Inc.

My Teacher Is an Alien Collection. 2014. (My Teacher Bks.). (ENG., Illus.). 736p. (J). (gr. 3-7). pap. 27.99 *(978-1-4814-1594-1(8)*, Aladdin) Simon & Schuster Children's Publishing.

Nance, Andrew. Return to Daemon Hall: Evil Roots. Polhemus, Coleman, illus. 2011. (ENG.). 256p. (YA). (gr. 7-12). 18.99 *(978-0-8050-8748-2(6)*, Holt, Henry & Co. Bks. For Young Readers) Holt, Henry & Co.

Nardone, Frank. Something's Brewing in Salem. 2013. 164p. pap. 9.99 *(978-0-9884024-1-6(6))* Dragon Tree Bks.

Nass, Marcia & Campisi, Stephanie. Mini Mysteries & Kooky Spookies. Innes, Calvin, illus. 2007. 176p. per. 6.99 *(978-0-9795364-2-7(1))* Chowder Bay Bks.

Newbound, Andrew. Ghoul Strike! 2010. (ENG.). 320p. (J). (gr. 3-7). 16.99 *(978-0-545-22938-8(3)*, Chicken Hse., The) Scholastic, Inc.

Newton-Perry, Linda. Eye of the Beast. 2009. 62p. pap. 7.98 *(978-0-557-06333-8(7))* Lulu Pr., Inc.

Night, P. J. Best Friends Forever. 2012. (You're Invited to a Creepover Ser.: 6). (ENG.). 160p. (J). (gr. 3-7). pap. 6.99 *(978-1-4424-4150-7(X)*, Simon Spotlight) Simon Spotlight.

—Best Friends Forever. 2012. (Creepover Ser.: 6). lib. bdg. 17.20 *(978-0-606-26336-8(5)*, Turtleback) Turtleback Bks.

—Don't Move a Muscle! 2016. (You're Invited to a Creepover Ser.: 21). (ENG., Illus.). 160p. (J). (gr. 3-7). pap. 6.99 *(978-1-4814-2922-1(1)*, Simon Spotlight) Simon Spotlight.

—Don't Move a Muscle! 2016. (Creepover Ser.: 21). lib. bdg. 17.20 *(978-0-606-38974-7(1))* Turtleback Bks.

—Home, Sweet Haunt. 2013. (You're Invited to a Creepover Ser.: 15). (ENG., Illus.). 160p. (J). (gr. 3-7). pap. 6.99 *(978-1-4424-7240-2(5)*, Simon Spotlight) Simon Spotlight.

—Is She for Real? 2012. (Creepover Ser.: 7). lib. bdg. 17.20 *(978-0-606-26340-5(3)*, Turtleback) Turtleback Bks.

—It's All Downhill from Here. 2012. (You're Invited to a Creepover Ser.: 10). (ENG.). 160p. (J). (gr. 3-7). pap. 5.99 *(978-1-4424-5285-5(4)*, Simon Spotlight) Simon Spotlight.

—It's All Downhill from Here. 2012. (Creepover Ser.: 10). lib. bdg. 16.00 *(978-0-606-26896-7(0)*, Turtleback) Turtleback Bks.

—No Trick-Or-Treating!, 1 vol. 2013. (You're Invited to a Creepover Ser.). (ENG.). 192p. (J). (gr. 3-6). lib. bdg. 24.21 *(978-1-61479-061-7(2)*, Essential Library) ABDO Publishing Co.

—No Trick-Or-Treating! 2012. (Creepover Ser.: 9). lib. bdg. 17.20 *(978-0-606-26337-5(3)*, Turtleback) Turtleback Bks.

—No Trick-or-Treating! Superscary Superspecial. 2012. (You're Invited to a Creepover Ser.: 9). (ENG.). 208p. (J). (gr. 3-7). pap. 6.99 *(978-1-4424-5053-0(3)*, Simon Spotlight) Simon Spotlight.

—Off the Wall. 2013. (You're Invited to a Creepover Ser.: 14). (ENG., Illus.). 160p. (J). (gr. 3-7). pap. 5.99 *(978-1-4424-7238-9(3)*, Simon Spotlight) Simon Spotlight.

—Read It & Weep! 2013. (You're Invited to a Creepover Ser.: 13). (ENG., Illus.). 160p. (J). (gr. 3-7). pap. 5.99 *(978-1-4424-5987-8(5)*, Simon Spotlight) Simon Spotlight.

—Ready for a Scare?, 1 vol. 2013. (You're Invited to a Creepover Ser.). (ENG.). 160p. (J). (gr. 3-6). lib. bdg. 24.21 *(978-1-61479-062-4(0)*, Essential Library) ABDO Publishing Co.

—Ready for a Scare? 2011. (You're Invited to a Creepover Ser.: 3). (ENG.). 160p. (J). (gr. 3-7). pap. 6.99 *(978-1-4424-2903-1(8)*, Simon Spotlight) Simon Spotlight.

—Ready for a Scare? 2011. (Creepover Ser.: 3). lib. bdg. 17.20 *(978-0-606-23747-5(X)*, Turtleback) Turtleback Bks.

—The Show Must Go On! 2011. (You're Invited to a Creepover Ser.: 4). (ENG.). 160p. (J). (gr. 3-7). pap. 6.99 *(978-1-4424-2905-5(4)*, Simon Spotlight) Simon Spotlight.

—Show Must Go On!, 1 vol. 2013. (You're Invited to a Creepover Ser.). (ENG.). 160p. (J). (gr. 3-6). lib. bdg. 24.21 *(978-1-61479-063-1(9)*, Essential Library) ABDO Publishing Co.

—The Show Must Go On! 2011. (Creepover Ser.: 4). lib. bdg. 16.00 *(978-0-606-23748-2(8)*, Turtleback) Turtleback Bks.

—The Terror Behind the Mask. 2014. (You're Invited to a Creepover Ser.: 19). (ENG., Illus.). 160p. (J). (gr. 3-7). pap. 6.99 *(978-1-4814-0460-0(1)*, Simon Spotlight) Simon Spotlight.

—There's Something Out There, 1 vol. 2013. (You're Invited to a Creepover Ser.). (ENG.). 160p. (J). (gr. 3-6). lib. bdg. 24.21 *(978-1-61479-064-8(7)*, Essential Library) ABDO Publishing Co.

—There's Something Out There. 2011. (You're Invited to a Creepover Ser.: 5). (ENG.). 160p. (J). (gr. 3-7). pap. 6.99 *(978-1-4424-4148-4(8)*, Simon Spotlight) Simon Spotlight.

—Together Forever. 2012. (You're Invited to a Creepover Ser.: 8). (ENG.). 160p. (J). (gr. 3-7). pap. 5.99 *(978-1-4424-5159-9(9)*, Simon Spotlight) Simon Spotlight.

—Together Forever. 2012. (Creepover Ser.: 8). lib. bdg. 16.00 *(978-0-606-26339-9(X)*, Turtleback) Turtleback Bks.

—Truth or Dare ..., 1 vol. 2013. (You're Invited to a Creepover Ser.). (ENG.). 160p. (J). (gr. 3-6). lib. bdg. 24.21 *(978-1-61479-065-5(5)*, Essential Library) ABDO Publishing Co.

—What a Doll! 2013. (You're Invited to a Creepover Ser.: 12). (ENG.). 160p. (J). (gr. 3-7). pap. 6.99 *(978-1-4424-5985-4(9)*, Simon Spotlight) Simon Spotlight.

—Will You Be My Friend? 2015. (Creepover Ser.: 20). lib. bdg. 17.20 *(978-0-606-37136-0(2))* Turtleback Bks.

—Your Worst Nightmare. 2013. (You're Invited to a Creepover Ser.: 17). (ENG., Illus.). 160p. (J). (gr. 3-7). pap. 6.99 *(978-1-4424-8235-7(4)*, Simon Spotlight) Simon Spotlight.

—Your Worst Nightmare. 2013. (Creepover Ser.: 17). lib. bdg. 17.20 *(978-0-606-32324-6(4)*, Turtleback) Turtleback Bks.

Noyes, Deborah, ed. Gothic! 2006. (ENG.). 256p. (YA). (gr. 9-12). per. 8.99 *(978-0-7636-2737-9(2))* Candlewick Pr.

—The Restless Dead: Ten Original Stories of the Supernatural. 2007. (ENG., Illus.). 272p. (YA). (gr. 7-12). 16.99 *(978-0-7636-2906-9(5))* Candlewick Pr.

Nye, Alex. Chill, 1 vol. 2006. (ENG., Illus.). 176p. (J). 11.95 *(978-0-86315-546-8(4))* Floris Bks. GBR. Dist: SteinerBooks, Inc.

Nykko. Book Six: The Tower of Shadows. Bannister, illus. 2013. (Elsewhere Chronicles Ser.: 6). (ENG.). 48p. (J). (gr. 4-8). pap. 6.95 *(978-1-4677-1517-1(4))*; lib. bdg. 27.93 *(978-1-4677-1233-0(7))* Lerner Publishing Group.

—The Elsewhere Chronicles. 2009. (Elsewhere Chronicles Ser.). (ENG.). (J). (gr. 4-8). pap. 39.62 *(978-0-7613-5088-0(8))*;Pack, Set. pap. 237.69 *(978-0-7613-5090-3(X))* Lerner Publishing Group.

—The Parting. Bannister, illus. 2011. (Elsewhere Chronicles Ser.: 5). (ENG.). 48p. (J). (gr. 4-8). pap. 6.95 *(978-0-7613-7524-1(4))* Lerner Publishing Group.

—The Parting, Bk. 5. Bannister, illus. 2011. (Elsewhere Chronicles Ser.: 5). (ENG.). 48p. (J). (gr. 4-8). lib. bdg. 27.93 *(978-0-7613-6632-4(6))* Lerner Publishing Group.

Odentz, Howard. Dead. 2013. 272p. pap. 14.95 *(978-1-61194-299-6(3)*, Bell Bridge Bks.) BelleBks., Inc.

Odentz, Howard. Wicked Dead. 2016. (ENG., Illus.). (YA). pap. 15.95 ***(978-1-61194-712-0(X))*** BelleBks., Inc.

Oh, Ellen. Spirit Hunters. 2017. (Spirit Hunters Ser.: 1). 288p. (J). (gr. 3-7). 16.99 ***(978-0-06-243008-3(4))*** HarperCollins Pubs.

O'Hara, Mo. The Fin-Tastic Fish-Sitter. Jagucki, Marek, illus. 2016. (My Big Fat Zombie Goldfish Ser.). (ENG.). 40p. (J). (gr. -1-2). 16.99 *(978-1-250-06523-0(2)*, 9781250065230) Feiwel & Friends.

—Fins of Fury. Jagucki, Marek, illus. 2015. (My Big Fat Zombie Goldfish Ser.: Bk. 3). (ENG.). 224p. (J). (gr. 2-5). 12.99 *(978-1-250-02921-8(X)*, 9781250029218) Feiwel & Friends.

—My Big Fat Zombie Goldfish. Jagucki, Marek, illus. 2014. (My Big Fat Zombie Goldfish Ser.: 1). (ENG.). 208p. (J). (gr. 2-5). pap. 6.99 *(978-1-250-05215-5(7)*, 9781250052155) Square Fish.

Olin, Sean. Killing Britney. 2005. (ENG.). 240p. (YA). (gr. 9-12). pap. 9.99 *(978-0-689-87778-0(1)*, Simon Pulse) Simon Pulse.

Oliver, Lin & Winkler, Henry. There's a Zombie in My Bathtub. 2015. (Here's Hank Ser.: 5). lib. bdg. 16.00 *(978-0-606-36767-7(5))* Turtleback Bks.

Oppel, Kenneth. The Nest. Klassen, Jon, illus. (ENG.). (J). (gr. 5). 2016. 272p. pap. 7.99 *(978-1-4814-3233-7(8))* 2015. 256p. 16.99 *(978-1-4814-3232-0(X))* Simon & Schuster Bks. For Young Readers. (Simon & Schuster Bks. For Young Readers).

—Such Wicked Intent. (ENG., 320p. (YA). (gr. 7). 2012. Illus.). 16.99 *(978-1-4424-0318-5(7))*Bk. 2. 2013. pap. 9.99 *(978-1-4424-0319-2(5))* Simon & Schuster Bks. For Young Readers. (Simon & Schuster Bks. For Young Readers).

Orme, David & Orme, David. Vampires. 2008. (ENG., Illus.). 36p. pap. *(978-1-84167-692-0(6))* Ransom Publishing Ltd.

O'Shei, Tim. Creepy Urban Legends, 1 vol. 2010. (Scary Stories Ser.). (ENG.). 32p. (gr. 3-4). lib. bdg. 27.99 *(978-1-4296-4572-0(5)*, Edge Bks.) Capstone Press of Coughlan Cos.

Ostow, Micol. Amity. 2014. (ENG.). 362p. (J). (gr. 9). 18.99 *(978-1-60684-156-3(4)*, Carolrhoda Lab™) Lerner Publishing Group.

Paiba, Helen. Scary Stories for 7 Year Olds. 2017. (ENG., Illus.). 256p. (J). (gr. 2-4). pap. 8.99 *(978-1-5098-1832-7(4))* Pan Macmillan GBR. Dist: Independent Pubs. Group.

Paiba, Helen, compiled by. Scary Stories for Nine Year Olds. (ENG., Illus.). 256p. (J). (gr. 4). pap. 8.99 *(978-0-330-37492-7(3)*, Pan) Pan Macmillan GBR. Dist: Trafalgar Square Publishing.

Palmer, Michele. Ghosts & Golems: Haunting Tales of the Supernatural. Black, Theodor, illus. 2003. (ENG.). 128p. pap. 9.95 *(978-0-8276-0763-7(6))* Jewish Pubn. Society.

Paradine, Mike. King of Toys. 2006. 83p. pap. 19.95 *(978-1-4241-2694-1(0))* America Star Bks.

Parker, Jeff, et al. Wonderland, Vol. 1. Allie, Scott & Hahn, Sierra, eds. 2013. (ENG., Illus.). 144p. pap. 17.99 *(978-1-61655-145-2(3))* Dark Horse Comics.

Parker, Steve. Skeleton. Dorling Kindersley Publishing Staff, ed. 2004. (DK Eyewitness Bks.). (ENG., Illus.). 72p. (J). (gr. 3-7). 16.99 *(978-0-7566-0727-2(2)*, DK Children) Dorling Kindersley Publishing, Inc.

Parrish, Anya. Damage. 2011. (ENG.). 288p. (YA). pap. 9.95 *(978-0-7387-2700-4(8)*, Flux) North Star Editions.

Pasqualini, Rosie. Nantarctica: Twilight-Water. 2008. 62p. pap. 6.98 *(978-0-557-00921-3(9))* Lulu Pr., Inc.

Patrick, David. Nero Demare & the Legend of the Vampires. 2007. 284p. (YA). per. 17.95 *(978-0-595-42014-8(1))* iUniverse, Inc.

Pearce, Bryony. The Weight of Souls. 2013. (ENG.). 288p. (YA). 17.99 *(978-1-908844-64-4(7)*, Strange Chemistry) Watkins Media Limited GBR. Dist: Penguin Random Hse. LLC.

Pearson Education Staff. Room in the Tower & Other Stories. 2nd ed. 2008. (ENG., Illus.). 48p. pap. 11.99 *(978-1-4058-6962-1(3))* Pearson Education.

Peck, Richard. Three Quarters Dead. 2011. (ENG.). 224p. (YA). (gr. 7-18). 7.99 *(978-0-14-241942-7(7)*, Speak) Penguin Young Readers Group.

Penn-Coughin, O. They're Coming for You: Scary Stories that Scream to be Read. 2009. (J). per. *(978-0-9816836-0-7(6))* You Come Too Publishing.

Perkins, T. J. On Forbidden Ground: Sequel to Mystery of the Attic. 2006. (Illus.). 112p. (YA). 10.99 *(978-0-9777538-7-1(5))* GumShoe Press.

Perritano, John. Warlock Stone, 1 vol. 2014. (Kid Squad Saves the World Ser.). (ENG.). 112p. (J). (gr. 8-12). lib. bdg. 27.07 *(978-1-62402-042-1(9)*, Calico Chapter Bks) Magic Wagon.

Perro Monstruoso. (Fantasmas de Fear Street Coleccion). (SPA.). (YA). (gr. 5-8). pap. 7.95 *(978-950-04-1930-7(0)*, EM0316) Emecé Editores S.A. ARG. Dist: Planeta Publishing Corp., Lectorum Pubns., Inc.

Perry, Glyn & Parry, Glyn. Invisible Girl. 2003. 160p. (YA). pap. 15.25 *(978-1-920731-48-9(2))* Fremantle Pr. AUS. Dist: Independent Pubs. Group.

Peterson, Brandon & Brereton, Dan. Giant Killer. 2006. (ENG., Illus.). 128p. (YA). pap. 14.99 *(978-1-58240-539-1(5)*, 9781582405391) Image Comics.

Peterson, Megan Cooley. Super Scary Stuff. 2016. (Super Scary Stuff Ser.). (ENG.). 24p. (gr. 1-2). 101.28 *(978-1-5157-0293-1(6)*, First Facts) Capstone Press of Coughlan Cos.

Petrucha, Stefan. Devil in the Details. 2003. (ENG., Illus.). 48p. (gr. 11-18). pap. 6.95 *(978-0-9726443-7-2(7)*, 9780972644372) Moonstone.

Petrucha, Stefan & Pendleton, Thomas. Prey. 2008. (Wicked Dead Ser.). (ENG.). 208p. (J). (gr. 7-18). pap. 9.99 *(978-0-06-113853-9(3)*, HarperTeen) HarperCollins Pubs.

Philbrick, Rodman & Hamett, Lynn. Le Demier Cauchemar Bk. 3: The Final Nightmare.Tr. of Maison de la Rue du Cerisier: Le Demier Cauchemar. (FRE.). (YA). pap. 5.99 *(978-0-590-24676-7(3))* Scholastic, Inc.

—L' Ensorcellement Bk. 1: The Haunting.Tr. of Maison de la Rue du Cerisier: L'Ensorcellement. (FRE.). (YA). pap. 5.99 *(978-0-590-24674-3(7))* Scholastic, Inc.

—La Terreur Bk. 2: The Horror.Tr. of Maison de la Rue du Cerisier: La Terreur. (FRE.). (YA). pap. 5.99 *(978-0-590-24675-0(5))* Scholastic, Inc.

Phillips, Dee. The Deadly Secret of Room 113. 2016. (Cold Whispers II Ser.). (ENG.). 32p. (J). (gr. 2-6). 19.95 *(978-1-944102-32-6(9))* Bearport Publishing Co., Inc.

—Doomed on Death Row. 2016. (Cold Whispers II Ser.). (ENG.). 32p. (J). (gr. 2-6). 19.95 *(978-1-944102-35-7(3))* Bearport Publishing Co., Inc.

—Fright at the Freemont Library. 2016. (Cold Whispers II Ser.). (ENG.). 32p. (J). (gr. 2-6). 19.95 *(978-1-944102-36-4(1))* Bearport Publishing Co., Inc.

—The Ghostly Secret of Lakeside School. 2016. (Cold Whispers II Ser.). (ENG.). 32p. (J). (gr. 2-6). 19.95 *(978-1-944102-33-3(7))* Bearport Publishing Co., Inc.

—Nightmare in the Hidden Morgue. 2016. (Cold Whispers II Ser.). (ENG.). 32p. (J). (gr. 2-6). 19.95 *(978-1-944102-34-0(5))* Bearport Publishing Co., Inc.

—Terror in the Underground Tunnel. 2016. (Cold Whispers II Ser.). (ENG.). 32p. (J). (gr. 2-6). 19.95 *(978-1-944102-37-1(X))* Bearport Publishing Co., Inc.

—Trapped in the Abandoned Hospital. 2016. (Cold Whispers II Ser.). (ENG.). 32p. (J). (gr. 2-6). 19.95 *(978-1-944102-31-9(0))* Bearport Publishing Co., Inc.

—The Vampire's Lair. 2016. (Cold Whispers II Ser.). (ENG.). 32p. (J). (gr. 2-6). 19.95 *(978-1-944102-30-2(2))* Bearport Publishing Co., Inc.

Pike, Christopher, pseud. Chain Letter: Chain Letter; the Ancient Evil. 2013. (ENG., Illus.). 496p. (J). (gr. 9). pap. 12.99 *(978-1-4424-7215-0(4)*, Simon Pulse) Simon Pulse.

—The Cold People. 2015. (Spooksville Ser.: 5). (ENG., Illus.). 128p. (J). (gr. 3-7). pap. 6.99 *(978-1-4814-1061-8(X)*, Aladdin) Simon & Schuster Children's Publishing.

—The Dark Corner. 2015. (Spooksville Ser.: 7). (ENG., Illus.). 128p. (J). (gr. 3-7). pap. 5.99 *(978-1-4814-1074-8(1)*, Aladdin) Simon & Schuster Children's Publishing.

—Deepest Desires, Instant Remorse No. 2, Bk. 2. 2010. (Thirst Ser.: 2). (ENG.). 608p. (YA). (gr. 9). pap. 11.99 *(978-1-4169-8309-5(0)*, Simon Pulse) Simon Pulse.

—The Hidden Beast. 2016. (Spooksville Ser.: 12). (ENG., Illus.). 112p. (J). (gr. 3-7). 16.99 *(978-1-4814-1095-3(4))*; pap. 7.99 *(978-1-4814-1093-9(8))* Simon & Schuster Children's Publishing. (Aladdin).

—The Hollow Skull. (Illus.). (J). 14.00 *(978-0-671-55060-8(8)*, Simon & Schuster Bks. For Young Readers) Simon & Schuster Bks. For Young Readers.

—Remember Me: Her Death Will Not Go Unpunished... 2010. (Remember Me Ser.: Vols. 1-3). (ENG., Illus.). 848p. (YA). (gr. 9). pap. 9.99 *(978-1-4424-0596-7(1)*, Simon Pulse) Simon Pulse.

—Road to Nowhere. 2011. (ENG.). 256p. (YA). (gr. 8). pap. 10.99 *(978-1-4424-3106-5(7)*, Simon Pulse) Simon Pulse.

—The Secret Path. 2014. (Spooksville Ser.: 1). (ENG., Illus.). 128p. (J). (gr. 3-7). pap. 6.99 *(978-1-4814-1049-6(0)*, Aladdin) Simon & Schuster Children's Publishing.

—The Shadow of Death. 2011. (Thirst Ser.: 4). (ENG., Illus.). 528p. (YA). (gr. 9). pap. 10.99 *(978-1-4424-1319-1(0)*, Simon Pulse) Simon Pulse.

—Thirst, 3 vols. 2013. (Thirst Ser.). (ENG.). 1744p. (YA). (gr. 9). pap. 30.99 *(978-1-4424-8375-0(X)*, Simon Pulse) Simon Pulse.

—To Die For. 2010. (ENG.). 416p. (J). (gr. 9-9). pap. 9.99 *(978-0-545-26434-1(0))* Scholastic, Inc.

—The Wicked Cat. 2015. (Spooksville Ser.: 10). (ENG., Illus.). 128p. (J). (gr. 3-7). pap. 6.99 *(978-1-4814-1086-1(5)*, Aladdin) Simon & Schuster Children's Publishing.

—The Wicked Cat. 2015. (Spooksville Ser.: 10). lib. bdg. 17.20 *(978-0-606-37851-2(0))* Turtleback Bks.

—The Wishing Stone. 2015. (Spooksville Ser.: 9). (ENG., Illus.). 128p. (J). (gr. 3-7). pap. 6.99 *(978-1-4814-1083-0(0)*, Aladdin) Simon & Schuster Children's Publishing.

—The Wishing Stone. 2015. (Spooksville Ser.: 9). lib. bdg. 17.20 *(978-0-606-37852-9(9))* Turtleback Bks.

—The Witch's Revenge. 2015. (Spooksville Ser.: 6). (ENG., Illus.). 128p. (J). (gr. 3-7). pap. 6.99 *(978-1-4814-1069-4(5)*, Aladdin) Simon & Schuster Children's Publishing.

Pirotta, Saviour. The Ghosts Who Danced: And Other Spooky Stories from Around the World. Hess, Paul, illus. 2015. (ENG.). 64p. (J). (gr. 1-5). 22.99 *(978-1-84780-435-8(7)*, Frances Lincoln) Quarto Publishing Group UK GBR. Dist: Hachette Bk. Group.

Plum-Ucci, Carol. The She. 2005. (ENG., Illus.). 372p. (YA). (gr. 9-12). reprint ed. pap. 19.99 *(978-0-15-205453-3(7))* Houghton Mifflin Harcourt Publishing Co.

Pluth, Lisa Anderson. A Haunting in Little River. 2011. 94p. pap. 19.95 *(978-1-4560-9700-4(8))* America Star Bks.

Poblocki, Dan. The Book of Bad Things. 2014. (ENG.). 256p. (J). (gr. 5-9). 16.99 *(978-0-545-64553-9(0)*, Scholastic Pr.) Scholastic, Inc.

—The Gathering. 2016. (Shadow House Ser.: 1). (ENG., Illus.). 224p. (J). (gr. 3-7). 12.99 *(978-0-545-92550-1(9)*, Scholastic Pr.) Scholastic, Inc.

—The Haunting of Gabriel Ashe. (ENG.). 288p. (J). (gr. 5-9). 2015. pap. 7.99 *(978-0-545-40271-2(9))* 2013. 16.99 *(978-0-545-40270-5(0))* Scholastic, Inc. (Scholastic Pr.).

—The House on Stone's Throw Island. 2015. (ENG.). 272p. (J). (gr. 5-9). 16.99 *(978-0-545-64556-0(5)*, Scholastic Pr.) Scholastic, Inc.

—The Nightmarys. 2011. (ENG.). 336p. (J). (gr. 3-7). pap. 7.99 *(978-0-375-84257-3(8)*, Yearling) Random Hse. Children's Bks.

Poblocki, Dan. No Way Out. 2017. (Shadow House Ser.: 3). (ENG.). 224p. (J). (gr. 3-7). lib. bdg. 16.99 ***(978-1-338-14859-6(1))***; (Illus.). 12.99 ***(978-0-545-92552-5(5))*** Scholastic, Inc.

Poe, Edgar Allen. Edgar Allan Poe. McConnell, James, illus. 2004. (Great American Short Stories Ser.). 80p. (gr. 4-7). lib. bdg. 24.00 *(978-0-8368-4254-8(5)*, Gareth Stevens Learning Library) Stevens, Gareth Publishing LLLP.

—Edgar Allan Poe's Tales of Mystery & Madness. Grimly, Gris, illus. 2004. (ENG.). 144p. (J). (gr. 5-9). 19.99 *(978-0-689-84837-7(4)*, Atheneum Bks. for Young Readers) Simon & Schuster Children's Publishing.

—The Raven & Other Writings. 2003. (Aladdin Classics Ser.). (ENG.). 448p. (J). (gr. 4-7). pap. 7.99 *(978-0-689-86352-3(7)*, Aladdin) Simon & Schuster Children's Publishing.

—The Stories of Edgar Allan Poe. McKowen, Scott, illus. 2010. (Sterling Unabridged Classics Ser.). (ENG.). 344p. (J). (gr. 5-18). 14.95 *(978-1-4027-7325-9(0))* Sterling Publishing Co., Inc.

—Tales of Mystery & Imagination. Jones, Barry, illus. 2004. (Paperback Classics Ser.). 144p. (J). pap. 4.95 *(978-0-7945-0186-0(9)*, Usborne) EDC Publishing.

—TALES OF TERROR LEVEL 3 LOWER-INTERMEDIATE. 2009. (ENG., Illus.). 80p. pap. 12.75 *(978-84-8323-532-4(3))* Cambridge Univ. Pr.

—The Tell-Tale Heart & Other Stories. Grimly, Gris, illus. 2011. (ENG.). 144p. (J). (gr. 6-9). pap. 12.99 *(978-1-4169-5026-4(5)*, Atheneum Bks. for Young Readers) Simon & Schuster Children's Publishing.

Poe, Edgar Allen & Harper, Benjamin. The Tell-Tale Heart, 1 vol. Calero, Dennis, illus. 2013. (Edgar Allan Poe Graphic Novels Ser.). (ENG.). 72p. (gr. 2-3). pap. 6.10 *(978-1-4342-4261-7(7))* Stone Arch Bks.

Poe, Edgar Allen, et al. The Fall of the House of Usher & Other Writings: Poems, Tales, Essays, & Reviews. (Classics Illustrated Ser.). (Illus.). 52p. (YA). pap. 4.95 *(978-1-57209-014-9(6))* Classics International Entertainment, Inc.

Ponti, James. Blue Moon. 2013. (Dead City Ser.: 2). (ENG., Illus.). 336p. (J). (gr. 4-8). 17.99 *(978-1-4424-4131-6(3)*, Aladdin) Simon & Schuster Children's Publishing.

—Dark Days. 2015. (Dead City Ser.: 3). (ENG., Illus.). 304p. (J). (gr. 3-7). 17.99 *(978-1-4814-3636-6(8)*, Aladdin) Simon & Schuster Children's Publishing.

Poole, Diamond Catherine Cheyenne. Leslie the Old Hag Who Collected Souls. 2012. 32p. pap. 24.95 *(978-1-4626-6196-1(3))* America Star Bks.

Preller, James. Good Night, Zombie. Bruno, Iacopo, illus. 2013. (Scary Tales Ser.: 3). (ENG.). 112p. (J). (gr. 2-5). pap. 5.99 *(978-1-250-01891-5(9)*, 9781250018915) Feiwel & Friends.

—Home Sweet Horror. Bruno, Iacopo, illus. 2013. (Scary Tales Ser.: 1). (ENG.). 112p. (J). (gr. 2-5). pap. 5.99 *(978-1-250-01887-8(0)*, 9781250018878) Feiwel & Friends.

—Home Sweet Horror. 2013. (Scary Tales Ser.: 1). (J). lib. bdg. 16.00 *(978-0-606-31893-8(3)*, Turtleback) Turtleback Bks.

—I Scream, You Scream! Bruno, Iacopo, illus. 2013. (Scary Tales Ser.: 2). (ENG.). 112p. (J). (gr. 2-5). 14.99 *(978-1-250-01888-5(9)*, 9781250018885); pap. 5.99 *(978-1-250-01889-2(7)*, 9781250018892) Feiwel & Friends.

—Nightmareland. Bruno, Iacopo, illus. 2014. (Scary Tales Ser.: 4). (ENG.). 112p. (J). (gr. 2-5). 15.99 *(978-1-250-01892-2(7)*, 9781250018922) Feiwel & Friends.

—Swamp Monster. Bruno, Iacopo, illus. 2015. (Scary Tales Ser.: 6). (ENG.). 96p. (J). (gr. 2-5). 15.99 *(978-1-250-04097-8(3)*, 9781250040978) Feiwel & Friends.

Prentice, Justin & Prentice, Jeff. It Can Be Scary When You Move. 2012. 28p. pap. 24.95 *(978-1-4626-9753-3(4))* America Star Bks.

Priestley, Chris. The Dead Men Stood Together. 2015. (ENG., Illus.). 272p. (YA). (gr. 3-6). pap. 12.99 *(978-1-4088-4302-4(1),* 9781408843024, Bloomsbury USA Childrens) Bloomsbury Publishing USA.

—The Dead of Winter. 2012. (ENG., Illus.). 224p. (YA). (gr. 7-12). 16.99 *(978-1-59990-745-1(3),* 9781599907451, Bloomsbury USA Childrens) Bloomsbury Publishing USA.

—Tales of Terror from the Black Ship. Roberts, David, illus. 2008. (Tales of Terror Ser.: 1). (ENG.). 256p. (YA). (gr. 3-6). 12.99 *(978-1-59990-290-6(7),* 9781599902906, Bloomsbury USA Childrens) Bloomsbury Publishing USA.

Primavera, Elise & Arevamirp, Esile. Fred & Anthony Escape from the Netherworld. Primavera, Elise, illus. 2007. (ENG., Illus.). 128p. (J). (gr. 2-6). pap. 4.99 *(978-0-7868-3678-9(4))* Hyperion Pr.

Prose, Francine. The Turning. 2012. (ENG.). 256p. (YA). (gr. 8). 17.99 *(978-0-06-199966-6(0),* HarperTeen) HarperCollins Pubs.

Punter, Russell. Monsters, Stories Of. 2004. (Young Reading Series One Ser.). 48p. (J). (gr. 2-18). pap. 5.95 *(978-0-7945-0757-2(3),* Usborne) EDC Publishing.

Rand, Johnathan. Amer Ch Double Thrillers. 2010. 256p. pap. 6.99 *(978-1-893699-26-7(9))* AudioCraft Publishing, Inc.

—American Chillers #1 Michigan Mega-Monsters. 2003. (American Chillers Ser.). (YA). pap. 5.99 *(978-1-893699-19-9(6))* AudioCraft Publishing, Inc.

—American Chillers #23 Wicked Velociraptors of West Virginia. 2008. 208p. (J). pap. 5.99 *(978-1-893699-94-6(3))* AudioCraft Publishing, Inc.

—American Chillers #24 Haunting in New Hampshire. 2008. 208p. (J). pap. 5.99 *(978-1-893699-96-0(X))* AudioCraft Publishing, Inc.

Randall, Thomas. The Waking: Dreams of the Dead. 2nd ed. 2010. (ENG., Illus.). 304p. (YA). (gr. 7-18). pap. 8.99 *(978-1-59990-585-3(X),* 9781599905853, Bloomsbury USA Childrens) Bloomsbury Publishing USA.

Randall, Thomas & Golden, Christopher. Spirits of the Noh. 2011. (ENG.). 272p. (YA). (gr. 7-18). pap. 9.99 *(978-1-59990-251-7(6),* 9781599902517, Bloomsbury USA Childrens) Bloomsbury Publishing USA.

Really Scary Stuff [Capstone Sole Source]. 2010. (Really Scary Stuff Ser.). 24p. lib. bdg. 95.96 *(978-1-4296-5877-5(0),* First Facts) Capstone Press of Coughlan Cos.

Reilly, Hope. The Ghost Horse at Cove House: A Book about the Strength of Friendship. 2013. 32p. pap. 13.00 *(978-1-61204-666-2(5),* Strategic Bk. Publishing) Strategic Book Publishing & Rights Agency (SBPRA).

Reiner, Carl. Tell Me Another Scary Story... but Not Too Scary! Bennett, James & Bennett, Carl A., illus. 2009. (ENG.). 32p. (J). (gr. 4-7). 16.95 *(978-1-59777-630-1(0))* Phoenix Bks., Inc.

Reiss, Kathryn. Pale Phoenix. 2003. (ENG., Illus.). 336p. (J). (gr. 5-7). pap. 15.95 *(978-0-15-204927-0(4))* Houghton Mifflin Harcourt Publishing Co.

Riad, Hala. Haunted Backyard. 2012. 24p. 24.95 *(978-1-4626-2530-7(4))* America Star Bks.

Rich, Susan. Half-Minute Horrors. (ENG.). 160p. (J). (gr. 5). 2011. pap. 5.99 *(978-0-06-183381-6(9))* 2009. (Illus.). 14.99 *(978-0-06-183379-3(7))* HarperCollins Pubs.

Richards, Natalie D. One Was Lost. (ENG., (YA). (gr. 7-12). 2017. Illus.). 23.99 ***(978-1-4926-6232-7(1))*** 2016. 320p. pap. 10.99 *(978-1-4926-1574-3(9),* 9781492615743) Sourcebooks, Inc.

Riddle, Waide. The Chocolate Man: A Children's Horror Tale. 2003. 24p. (J). 9.95 *(978-0-9724619-1-7(4))* Passage Publishing.

Ridley, R. W. Banshee Worm King. 2012. 242p. pap. 9.99 *(978-0-9792067-5-7(8))* Middleburry Hse. Publishing.

—Dēlon City: Book Two of the Oz Chronicles. 2006. (YA). per. 9.99 *(978-0-9792067-0-2(7))* Middleburry Hse. Publishing.

Roach. Monstrous Stories #1: Night of the Zombie Goldfish. 2013. (Monstrous Stories Ser.). (ENG.). 64p. (J). (gr. 2-5). pap. 4.99 *(978-0-545-42554-4(9),* Scholastic Paperbacks) Scholastic, Inc.

Roberts, Jeyn. When They Fade. 2016. (ENG.). 352p. (YA). (gr. 9). 17.99 *(978-0-385-75413-2(2),* Knopf Bks. for Young Readers) Random Hse. Children's Bks.

Robinson, Aquila. Septic Zombie - a Short Story. 2012. 28p. pap. 4.99 *(978-0-9840423-6-4(9))* Breakneck Media.

Rocklin, Joanne. This Book Is Haunted. Adinolfi, JoAnn, illus. 2003. (I Can Read Level 1 Ser.). (ENG.). 48p. (J). (gr. k-3). pap. 3.99 *(978-0-06-444261-9(6))* HarperCollins Pubs.

Rodriguez, David. Shadowgirls - Season One. Nelson, Angela, ed. 2013. (ENG., Illus.). 240p. (YA). 29.95 *(978-0-9832161-1-7(8),* 9780983216117) Th3rd World Studios.

Rodríguez, Pedro. Chilling Tales of Horror: Dark Graphic Short Stories. 2012. (Dark Graphic Novels Ser.). (Illus.). 96p. (J). (gr. 5-9). 31.94 *(978-0-7660-4085-4(2))* Enslow Pubs., Inc.

Rogers, Kelly. Buyer Beware, 1 vol. Peterschmidt, Betsy, illus. 2016. (ENG.). 48p. (J). lib. bdg. 28.50 *(978-1-62402-167-1(0))* Magic Wagon.

—The House Sitters, 1 vol. Peterschmidt, Betsy, illus. 2016. (ENG.). 48p. (J). lib. bdg. *(978-1-62402-168-8(9))* Magic Wagon.

—The Key, 1 vol. Peterschmidt, Betsy, illus. 2016. (ENG.). 48p. (J). lib. bdg. *(978-1-62402-169-5(7))* Magic Wagon.

—Study Group. Peterschmidt, Betsy, illus. 2016. (ENG.). 48p. (J). lib. bdg. *(978-1-62402-170-1(0))* Magic Wagon.

Rollins, Danielle. Burning. 2016. (ENG.). 352p. (YA). 17.99 *(978-1-61963-738-2(3),* 9781619637382, Bloomsbury USA Childrens) Bloomsbury Publishing USA.

Rosas, Beverly. The Hand That Scared Jenny. Davis, Jeff, illus. 2008. 47p. pap. 24.95 *(978-1-4241-9138-3(6))* PublishAmerica, Inc.

Roux, Madeleine. Catacomb. (Asylum Ser.: 3). (YA). (gr. 9). 2016. 352p. pap. 9.99 *(978-0-06-236406-7(5))* 2015. (ENG.). 336p. 17.99 *(978-0-06-236405-0(7))* HarperCollins Pubs.

—Sanctum. 2014. (Illus.). 343p. (YA). *(978-0-06-235182-1(6))* Harper & Row Ltd.

—Sanctum. 2014. (Asylum Ser.: 2). (ENG., Illus.). 352p. (YA). (gr. 9). 17.99 *(978-0-06-222099-8(3))* HarperCollins Pubs.

Rowe, W. W. & Filius, Charles A. Things Alive! & Other Freaky Secrets. 2012. 140p. pap. 12.95 *(978-0-615-66672-3(8))* Charwood Pubns.

Ruby, Lois. The Doll Graveyard. 2014. (Hauntings Ser.). lib. bdg. 17.20 *(978-0-606-35810-1(2))* Turtleback Bks.

Ruby, Lois. The Secret Grave: a Hauntings Novel. 2017. (ENG.). 256p. (J). (gr. 3-7). pap. 6.99 ***(978-0-545-93250-9(5),*** Scholastic Paperbacks) Scholastic, Inc.

Ruiz Zafón, Carlos. Marina. 2009. (Best Seller (Edebe) Ser.). (SPA.). 286p. pap. *(978-84-236-8726-8(0))* Edebé.

Ryan, Carrie. The Dark & Hollow Places. (Forest of Hands & Teeth Ser.: Bk. 3). (ENG.). 384p. (YA). (gr. 9). 2012. pap. 8.99 *(978-0-385-73860-6(9),* Ember) 2011. 17.99 *(978-0-385-73859-0(5),* Delacorte Bks. for Young Readers) Random Hse. Children's Bks.

—The Dead-Tossed Waves. 2011. (Forest of Hands & Teeth Ser.: Bk. 2). (J). 59.99 *(978-1-61707-144-7(7))* Findaway World, LLC.

—The Dead-Tossed Waves. (Forest of Hands & Teeth Ser.: Bk. 2). (ENG.). (YA). (gr. 9). 2011. 432p. pap. 9.99 *(978-0-385-73685-5(1))* 2010. 416p. 17.99 *(978-0-385-73684-8(3))* Random Hse. Children's Bks. (Delacorte Bks. for Young Readers).

—The Forest of Hands & Teeth. 2011. (Forest of Hands & Teeth Ser.: Bk. 1). (YA). 59.99 *(978-1-61707-145-4(5))* Findaway World, LLC.

—The Forest of Hands & Teeth. 2010. (Forest of Hands & Teeth Ser.: Bk. 1). (ENG.). 310p. (gr. 9-12). 20.00 *(978-1-60686-909-3(4))* Perfection Learning Corp.

—The Forest of Hands & Teeth. 2010. (Forest of Hands & Teeth Ser.: Bk. 1). (ENG.). 336p. (YA). (gr. 9-18). pap. 9.99 *(978-0-385-73682-4(7),* Ember) Random Hse. Children's Bks.

—The Forest of Hands & Teeth. 2010. (Forest of Hands & Teeth Ser.: Bk. 1). lib. bdg. 20.85 *(978-0-606-23881-6(6),* Turtleback) Turtleback Bks.

Saddlewick, A. B. Horror Holiday. Horne, Sarah, illus. 2013. (Monstrous Maud Ser.: 5). (ENG.). 128p. (J). (gr. k-2). pap. 6.99 *(978-1-78055-172-2(X))* O'Mara, Michael Bks., Ltd. GBR. Dist: Independent Pubs. Group.

Sage, Angie. Frognapped. Pickering, Jimmy, illus. 2008. (Araminta Spookie Ser.: 3). (ENG.). 224p. (J). (gr. 2-5). pap. 6.99 *(978-0-06-077489-9(4),* Tegen, Katherine Bks) HarperCollins Pubs.

Sala, Richard. Cat Burglar Black. Sala, Richard, illus. 2009. (ENG., Illus.). 128p. (J). (gr. 6-9). pap. 17.99 *(978-1-59643-144-7(X),* 9781596431447, First Second Bks.) Roaring Brook Pr.

San Souci, Robert D. Dare to Be Scared: Thirteen Stories to Chill & Thrill. Ouimet, David, illus. 2003. (Dare to Be Scared Ser.). (ENG.). 144p. (J). (gr. 3-7). 17.95 *(978-0-8126-2688-9(5))* Cricket Bks.

—Dare to Be Scared 4: Thirteen More Tales of Terror. Ouimet, David, illus. 2009. (Dare to Be Scared Ser.: 4). (ENG.). 229p. (J). (gr. 2-9). 17.95 *(978-0-8126-2754-1(7))* Cricket Bks.

—Haunted Houses. Murphy, Kelly & Revoy, Antoine, illus. 2012. (Are You Scared Yet? Ser.). (ENG.). 304p. (J). (gr. 4-7). pap. 10.99 *(978-0-312-55136-0(3),* 9780312551360) Square Fish.

—More Short & Shivery: Thirty Terrifying Tales. Coville, Katherine, illus. 2015. (ENG.). 224p. (J). (gr. 3-7). 6.99 *(978-0-440-41857-3(7),* Yearling) Random Hse. Children's Bks.

—Triple-Dare to Be Scared: Thirteen Further Freaky Tales. Ouimet, David, illus. 2007. (Dare to Be Scared Ser.). (ENG.). 240p. (J). (gr. 2-9). 16.95 *(978-0-8126-2749-7(0))* Cricket Bks.

Sander, Sonia. Scooby-Doo & the International Express. 2009. (Illus.). 32p. (J). pap. *(978-0-545-16283-8(1))* Scholastic, Inc.

—Scooby-Doo in Food Fight!, 1 vol. 2016. (Scooby-Doo Comic Readers Ser.). (ENG.). 32p. (J). (gr. k-3). lib. bdg. 24.21 *(978-1-61479-454-7(5),* Graphic Planet) Magic Wagon.

Sane, Justin. Heart of a Corpse; an Undead Engagement Part One. Sane, Justin, illus. 2012. (Illus.). 34p. pap. 5.95 *(978-1-59362-243-5(0),* Slave Labor Graphics) Slave Labor Bks.

Sauer, Tammi. Mostly Monsterly. Magoon, Scott, illus. 2010. (ENG.). 40p. (J). (gr. -1-3). 17.99 *(978-1-4169-6110-9(0),* Simon & Schuster/Paula Wiseman Bks.) Simon & Schuster/Paula Wiseman Bks.

Savage, J. Scott. Making the Team. Holgate, Doug, illus. 2015. (Case File 13 Ser.: 2). (ENG.). 288p. (J). (gr. 3-7). pap. 6.99 *(978-0-06-213335-9(7))* HarperCollins Pubs.

Scaletta, Kurtis. The Tanglewood Terror. (ENG.). 272p. (J). 2012. (gr. 4-7). 7.99 *(978-0-375-86542-8(X),* Yearling) 2011. (gr. 3-7). 16.99 *(978-0-375-86758-3(9),* Knopf Bks. for Young Readers) Random Hse. Children's Bks.

Scary Stories, 1 vol. 2010. (Scary Stories Ser.). (ENG.). 32p. (gr. 3-4). lib. bdg. 111.96 *(978-1-4296-4575-1(X),* Edge Bks.) Capstone Press of Coughlan Cos.

Scary Stories Treasury Lenticular Cover. 2007. 80p. *(978-1-4054-9871-5(4))* Parragon, Inc.

Schemery, Beau. The Last Blade. 2016. (ENG., Illus.). (J). 32.99 ***(978-1-63477-969-2(X))*** 2013. 350p. pap. 17.99 *(978-1-62380-453-4(1))* Dreamspinner Pr. (Harmony Ink Pr.).

Schkolnik, Saul. Cuentos de Terror, de Magia y de Otras Cosas Extranas. (SPA.). (YA). (gr. 5-8). pap. *(978-956-13-1319-4(7),* AB0160) Bello, Andres CHL. Dist: Lectorum Pubns., Inc.

Scholastic, Inc. Staff & Stine, R. L. Write Your Fright. 2011. (Goosebumps Horrorland Ser.). (ENG.). 64p. 12.99 *(978-0-545-33295-8(8),* Scholastic Paperbacks) Scholastic, Inc.

Schroeder, Lisa. I Heart You, You Haunt Me. 2008. (ENG.). 240p. (YA). (gr. 9). pap. 10.99 *(978-1-4169-5520-7(8),* Simon Pulse) Simon Pulse.

Schwartz, Alvin. More Scary Stories to Tell in the Dark. 2010. (Scary Stories Ser.: 2). (J). lib. bdg. 16.00 *(978-0-606-14981-5(3),* Turtleback) Turtleback Bks.

—Scary Stories 3: More Tales to Chill Your Bones. Helquist, Brett, illus. 2011. (Scary Stories Ser.). (ENG.). 128p. (J). (gr. 4-18). 16.99 *(978-0-06-083523-1(0));* pap. 5.99 *(978-0-06-083524-8(9))* HarperCollins Pubs.

—Scary Stories Box Set, 3 vols. Helquist, Brett, illus. 2011. (Scary Stories Ser.). (ENG.). 128p. (J). (gr. 4). pap. 14.99 *(978-0-06-198093-0(5))* HarperCollins Pubs.

Schwartz, Alvin & Alvin, Schwartz. Historias de Miedo. Irving, George S., illus. 2003. (Historias de Miedo Scary Stories to Tell in the Dark Ser.). (SPA.). 120p. (YA). (gr. 5-8). pap. 11.99 *(978-84-241-8662-3(1))* Everest Editora ESP. Dist: Lectorum Pubns., Inc.

—Historias de Miedo 2: Relatos Espeluznantes para No Dejarte Dormir. Irving, George S., illus. 2003. (Historias de Miedo Scary Stories to Tell in the Dark Ser.).Tr. of More Scary Stories to Tell in the Dark. (SPA.). 112p. (YA). (gr. 5-8). pap. 11.99 *(978-84-241-8663-0(X))* Everest Editora ESP. Dist: Lectorum Pubns., Inc.

—Historias de Miedo 3: Relatos Aterradores para Helarte la Sangre. Irving, George S., illus. 2003. (Historias de Miedo Scary Stories to Tell in the Dark Ser.).Tr. of Scary Stories 3: More Tales to Chill Your Bones. (SPA.). 128p. (YA). (gr. 5-8). pap. 11.99 *(978-84-241-8664-7(8))* Everest Editora ESP. Dist: Lectorum Pubns., Inc.

Schwartz, Alvin. In a Dark, Dark Room & Other Scary Stories (reillustrated) Rivas, Victor, illus. 2017. (I Can Read Level 2 Ser.). 64p. (J). (gr. -1-3). 16.99 ***(978-0-06-264338-4(X));*** pap. 3.99 ***(978-0-06-264337-7(1))*** HarperCollins Pubs.

—More Scary Stories to Tell in the Dark. Gammell, Stephen, illus. 2017. (Scary Stories Ser.: 2). 112p. (J). (gr. 3-7). pap. 6.99 ***(978-0-06-268285-7(7))*** HarperCollins Pubs.

—Scary Stories 3. Gammell, Stephen, illus. 2017. (Scary Stories Ser.: 3). 128p. (J). (gr. 3-7). pap. 6.99 ***(978-0-06-268287-1(3))*** HarperCollins Pubs.

—Scary Stories Paperback Box Set: Scary Stories to Tell in the Dark, More Scary Stories, Scray Stories 3. Gammell, Stephen, illus. 2017. (Scary Stories Ser.). 368p. (J). (gr. 3-7). pap. 20.97 ***(978-0-06-268289-5(X))*** HarperCollins Pubs.

Scieszka, Jon & Gidwitz, Adam. Terrifying Tales. 2015. (Guys Read Ser.). (J). lib. bdg. 17.20 *(978-0-606-37615-0(1))* Turtleback Bks.

Scieszka, Jon, et al. Guys Read: Terrifying Tales. 2015. (Guys Read Ser.: 6). (ENG., Illus.). 288p. (J). (gr. 3-7). 16.99 *(978-0-06-238558-1(5),* Walden Pond Pr.) HarperCollins Pubs.

Scott, Chris. Unseen. 2012. 86p. pap. 19.95 *(978-1-4626-8786-2(5))* America Star Bks.

Sedgwick, Marcus. The Book of Dead Days. 2006. (ENG.). 288p. (YA). (gr. 5-12). reprint ed. per. 7.99 *(978-0-385-74704-2(7),* Lamb, Wendy Bks.) Random Hse. Children's Bks.

Seeley, Tim. Bloodstrike Vol. 1: Reborn under a Bad Sign. 2012. (ENG., Illus.). 160p. (YA). pap. 14.99 *(978-1-60706-625-5(4),* 9781607066255) Image Comics.

Seifert, Brandon. Witch Doctor Volume 2: Mal Practice TP: Mal Practice TP. 2013. (ENG., Illus.). 176p. (YA). pap. 14.99 *(978-1-60706-693-4(9),* 9781607066934) Image Comics.

Shan, Darren, pseud. Allies of the Night. 2005. (Cirque du Freak Ser.: 8). (ENG., Illus.). 256p. (J). (gr. 7-17). pap. 10.99 *(978-0-316-11437-0(5))* Little, Brown Bks. for Young Readers.

—Angels. 2013. (Zom-B Ser.: 4). (ENG.). 192p. (gr. 7-17). 15.00 *(978-0-316-21414-8(0))* Little, Brown Bks. for Young Readers.

—Bec. 2008. (ENG.). 256p. (YA). (gr. 10-17). pap. 10.00 *(978-0-316-01390-1(0))* Little, Brown Bks. for Young Readers.

—Birth of a Killer. 2011. (Saga of Larten Crepsley Ser.: 1). (ENG.). 288p. (YA). (gr. 10-17). pap. 10.99 *(978-0-316-07862-7(X))* Little, Brown Bks. for Young Readers.

—Brothers to the Death. 2013. (Saga of Larten Crepsley Ser.: 4). (ENG.). 272p. (YA). (gr. 10-17). pap. 10.00 *(978-0-316-07871-9(9))* Little, Brown Bks. for Young Readers.

—Dark Calling. 2010. (ENG.). 224p. (YA). (gr. 10-17). pap. 10.00 *(978-0-316-04872-9(0))* Little, Brown Bks. for Young Readers.

—Death's Shadow. 2009. (ENG.). 240p. (YA). (gr. 10-17). pap. 10.00 *(978-0-316-00382-7(4))* Little Brown & Co.

—Demon Apocalypse. 2009. (ENG.). 208p. (YA). (gr. 10-17). pap. 9.99 *(978-0-316-00380-3(8))* Little, Brown Bks. for Young Readers.

—Demon Thief. 2007. (ENG.). 256p. (YA). (gr. 10-17). per. 10.00 *(978-0-316-01238-6(6))* Little, Brown Bks. for Young Readers.

—Gladiator. 2014. (Zom-B Ser.: 6). (ENG., Illus.). 176p. (YA). (gr. 7-17). 15.00 *(978-0-316-21407-0(8))* Little Brown & Co.

—Hunters of the Dusk. 2005. (Cirque du Freak Ser.: 7). (ENG., Illus.). 224p. (J). (gr. 7-17). pap. 10.99 *(978-0-316-60211-2(6))* Little, Brown Bks. for Young Readers.

—Hunters of the Dusk. 2005. (Cirque du Freak Ser.: 7). (J). lib. bdg. 22.10 *(978-1-4177-3731-4(X),* Turtleback) Turtleback Bks.

—Killers of the Dawn, 9. 2004. (ENG.). 192p. *(978-0-00-713781-7(8))* HarperCollins Pubs. Australia.

—Killers of the Dawn. 2006. (Cirque du Freak Ser.: 9). (ENG., Illus.). 224p. (J). (gr. 7-17). per. 10.99 *(978-0-316-10654-2(2))* Little, Brown Bks. for Young Readers.

—The Lake of Souls, 10. 2004. (Darren Shan Saga: Bk. 10). (ENG.). 224p. *(978-0-00-715919-2(6))* HarperCollins Pubs. Australia.

—The Lake of Souls. 2006. (Cirque du Freak Ser.: 10). (ENG., Illus.). 272p. (J). (gr. 7-17). per. 10.99 *(978-0-316-01665-0(9))* Little, Brown Bks. for Young Readers.

—Lord Loss. 2005. (Demonata Ser.: Bk. 1). (Illus.). 272p. *(978-0-00-719321-9(1))* HarperCollins Pubs. Australia.

—Lord Loss. 2006. (ENG.). 240p. (J). (gr. 10-17). per. 10.99 *(978-0-316-01233-1(5))* Little, Brown Bks. for Young Readers.

—Lord Loss. 2006. (Demonata Ser.: 1). (J). 22.10 *(978-1-4177-8308-3(7),* Turtleback) Turtleback Bks.

—Lord of the Shadows, 11. 2005. (Darren Shan Saga: Bk. 11). (ENG.). 192p. *(978-0-00-715920-8(X))* HarperCollins Pubs. Australia.

—Lord of the Shadows. 2007. (Cirque du Freak Ser.: 11). (ENG., Illus.). 256p. (J). (gr. 7-17). per. 10.99 *(978-0-316-01661-2(6))* Little, Brown Bks. for Young Readers.

—Lord of the Shadows. 2007. (Cirque du Freak Ser.: 11). (J). lib. bdg. 22.10 *(978-1-4177-7441-8(X),* Turtleback) Turtleback Bks.

—Ocean of Blood. 2012. (Saga of Larten Crepsley Ser.: 2). (ENG.). 272p. (YA). (gr. 10-17). pap. 10.99 *(978-0-316-07867-2(0))* Little, Brown Bks. for Young Readers.

—Palace of the Damned. (Saga of Larten Crepsley Ser.: 3). (ENG.). (YA). (gr. 10-17). 2012. 272p. pap. 10.00 *(978-0-316-07869-6(7))* 2011. 256p. 17.99 *(978-0-316-07870-2(0))* Little, Brown Bks. for Young Readers.

—Slawter. 2007. (ENG.). 240p. (J). (gr. 10-17). pap. 10.99 *(978-0-316-01388-8(9))* Little, Brown Bks. for Young Readers.

—Sons of Destiny, 12. 2005. (Darren Shan Saga: Bk. 12). (ENG.). 208p. *(978-0-00-715921-5(8))* HarperCollins Pubs. Australia.

—Sons of Destiny. 2007. (Cirque du Freak Ser.: 12). (ENG., Illus.). 272p. (J). (gr. 7-17). per. 9.99 *(978-0-316-01663-6(2))* Little, Brown Bks. for Young Readers.

—Sons of Destiny. 2012. (Cirque du Freak, the Manga Ser.: 12). lib. bdg. 24.55 *(978-0-606-26471-6(X),* Turtleback) Turtleback Bks.

—Trials of Death. 2004. (Cirque du Freak Ser.: 5). (ENG., Illus.). 224p. (J). (gr. 7-17). pap. 10.99 *(978-0-316-60395-9(3))* Little, Brown Bks. for Young Readers.

—Tunnels of Blood. 2003. (Cirque du Freak Ser.: 3). (ENG., Illus.). 240p. (J). (gr. 7-17). pap. 10.99 *(978-0-316-60608-0(1))* Little, Brown Bks. for Young Readers.

—Tunnels of Blood. 2003. (Cirque du Freak Ser.: 3). (J). (gr. 3-6). lib. bdg. 20.85 *(978-0-613-71782-3(1),* Turtleback) Turtleback Bks.

—Vampire Mountain. 2003. (Cirque du Freak Ser.: 4). (ENG., Illus.). 208p. (J). (gr. 7-17). pap. 10.99 *(978-0-316-60542-7(5))* Little, Brown Bks. for Young Readers.

—Vampire Mountain. 2003. (Cirque du Freak Ser.: 4). (J). (gr. 5-8). lib. bdg. 22.10 *(978-0-613-71781-6(3),* Turtleback) Turtleback Bks.

—The Vampire Prince. 2004. (Cirque du Freak Ser.: 6). (ENG., Illus.). 208p. (J). (gr. 7-17). pap. 10.99 *(978-0-316-60274-7(4))* Little, Brown Bks. for Young Readers.

—The Vampire Prince. 2004. (Cirque du Freak Ser.: 6). (J). lib. bdg. 19.65 *(978-1-4177-3732-1(8),* Turtleback) Turtleback Bks.

—Wolf Island. 2010. (ENG.). 216p. (YA). (gr. 10-17). pap. 10.00 *(978-0-316-04881-1(X))* Little, Brown Bks. for Young Readers.

—Zom-B. Pleece, Warren, illus. 2016. (ENG.). 208p. (YA). (gr. 7-17). 15.00 *(978-0-316-33845-5(1))* Little Brown & Co.

—Zom-B. 2015. (Zom-B Ser.: 11). (ENG., Illus.). 192p. (gr. 7-17). 15.99 *(978-0-316-21409-4(4))* Little Brown & Co.

—Zom-B. (Zom-B Ser.: 1). (ENG.). (YA). (gr. 7-17). 2012. 192p. 15.99 *(978-0-316-21440-7(X))*Bk. 10. 2015. (Illus.). 208p. 15.99 *(978-0-316-21422-3(1))* Vol. 8. 2014. (Illus.). 192p. 15.99 *(978-0-316-21429-2(9))* Little, Brown Bks. for Young Readers.

—Zom-B Baby. 2013. (Zom-B Ser.: 5). (ENG.). 176p. (YA). (gr. 7-17). 15.00 *(978-0-316-21420-9(5))* Little, Brown Bks. for Young Readers.

—Zom-B Chronicles. 2014. (Zom-B Ser.). (ENG.). 560p. (YA). (gr. 7-17). pap. 13.00 *(978-0-316-28489-9(0))* Little, Brown Bks. for Young Readers.

—The Zom-B Chronicles #2. 2015. (Zom-B Ser.). (ENG., Illus.). 544p. (J). (gr. 7-17). pap. 13.00 *(978-0-316-30073-5(X))* Little, Brown Bks. for Young Readers.

—Zom-B City. 2013. (Zom-B Ser.: 3). (ENG.). 176p. (YA). (gr. 7-17). 15.00 *(978-0-316-21436-0(1))* Little, Brown Bks. for Young Readers.

—Zom-B Family. 2014. (Zom-B Ser.: 9). (ENG.). 208p. (YA). (gr. 7-17). 15.00 *(978-0-316-21434-6(5))* Little Brown & Co.

—Zom-B Underground. 2013. (Zom-B Ser.: 2). (ENG., Illus.). 192p. (YA). (gr. 7-17). 14.99 *(978-0-316-21412-4(4))* Little, Brown Bks. for Young Readers.

Sheff, Nic. Harmony House. 2016. 304p. (J). (gr. 9). 17.99 *(978-0-06-233709-2(2),* HarperTeen) HarperCollins Pubs.

Shelley, Mary. Frankenstein. Akib, Jamel, illus. 2006. (Classic Starts(tm) Ser.). (ENG.). 160p. (J). (gr. 2-4). 6.95 *(978-1-4027-2666-8(X))* Sterling Publishing Co., Inc.

—Frankenstein. 2009. (Foundation Classics Ser.). (Illus.). 56p. (J). (gr. 5-9). lib. bdg. 27.95 *(978-1-60754-848-5(8))* Windmill Bks.

—Frankenstein, 1 vol. Ho, Jason, illus. 2007. (Graphic Horror Ser.). (ENG.). 32p. (gr. 4-7). 28.50 *(978-1-60270-059-8(1),* Graphic Planet- Fiction) ABDO Publishing Co.

—Frankenstein. Irving, Frazer, illus. 2005. 176p. (gr. 3-7). 21.00 *(978-0-7569-5809-1(1))* Perfection Learning Corp.

—Frankenstein. 2010. (ENG., Illus.). 28p. 29.95 *(978-0-7893-2085-8(1))* Universe Publishing.

—Frankenstein. Williams, Anthony, illus. 2014. (ENG.). 32p. pap. 8.95 *(978-1-78404-356-8(7))* Arcturus Publishing GBR. Dist: Bookmasters Distribution.

—Frankenstein. abr. ed. 2010. (Dover Classic Stories Coloring Book Ser.). (ENG.). 48p. (J). (gr. 3-8). pap. 4.99 *(978-0-486-47415-1(1))* Dover Pubns., Inc.

—Frankenstein: The Graphic Novel. 2010. (Classic Graphic Novel Collection). (ENG., Illus.). 144p. (YA). (gr. 7-12). 34.80 *(978-1-4205-0374-6(X))* Cengage Gale.

—Frankenstein: With a Discussion of Tolerance. Clift, Eva, tr. Clift, Eva, illus. 2003. (Values in Action Illustrated Classics Ser.). (J). *(978-1-59203-048-4(3))* Learning Challenge, Inc.

—Gris Grimly's Frankenstein. Grimly, Gris, illus. 2013. (ENG.). 208p. (YA). (gr. 8). 24.99 *(978-0-06-186297-7(5))* HarperCollins Pubs.

—Gris Grimly's Frankenstein. Grimly, Gris, illus. 2015. (ENG.). 208p. (YA). (gr. 8). pap. 16.99 *(978-0-06-186298-4(3))* HarperCollins Pubs.

—Ladybird Classics - Frankenstein. 2016. (Ladybird Classics Ser.). (ENG., Illus.). 72p. (J). (gr. k-3). 11.99 *(978-0-7232-9706-2(1))* Penguin Bks., Ltd. GBR. Dist: Independent Pubs. Group.

Shelley, Mary & Shelley, Mary. Frankenstein. (J). 9.95 *(978-1-56156-309-8(9))* Kidsbooks, LLC.

Shelley, Mary, et al. Frankenstein. 2004. (ENG.). 112p. pap. 20.00 (978-0-582-82301-3(3)) Pearson Education, Ltd. GBR. Dist: Trans-Atlantic Pubns., Inc.

Shusterman, Neal. Darkness Creeping: Twenty Twisted Tales. 2007. (ENG.). 304p. (J). (gr. 3-7). 7.99 (978-0-14-240721-9(6), Puffin Books) Penguin Young Readers Group.

—Full Tilt. 2004. (ENG.). 208p. (YA). (gr. 7). mass mkt. 8.99 (978-0-689-87325-6(5), Simon Pulse) Simon Pulse.

—Scorpion Shards. 2013. (Star Shards Chronicles Ser.: 1). (ENG., Illus.). (YA). (gr. 7). 240p. 17.99 (978-1-4424-5836-9(4)); 256p. pap. 9.99 (978-1-4424-5114-8(9)) Simon & Schuster Bks. For Young Readers. (Simon & Schuster Bks. For Young Readers).

—Shattered Sky. 2013. (Star Shards Chronicles Ser.: 3). (ENG., Illus.). 544p. (YA). (gr. 7). 17.99 (978-1-4424-5835-2(6)); pap. 9.99 (978-1-4424-5117-9(3)) Simon & Schuster Bks. For Young Readers. (Simon & Schuster Bks. For Young Readers).

—Thief of Souls. 2013. (Star Shards Chronicles Ser.: 2). (ENG., Illus.). (YA). (gr. 7). 304p. 17.99 (978-1-4424-5837-6(2)); 320p. pap. 9.99 (978-1-4424-5112-4(2)) Simon & Schuster Bks. For Young Readers. (Simon & Schuster Bks. For Young Readers).

Shutter. 2015. (ENG.). 384p. (YA). (gr. 8-12). 17.99 (978-1-250-04467-9(7)) Feiwel & Friends.

Sierra, Sergio A. & Shelley, Mary. Frankenstein by Mary Shelley. Ribas, Meritxell, illus. 2012. (Dark Graphic Novels Ser.). 96p. (J). (gr. 5-9). 31.94 (978-0-7660-4084-7(4)) Enslow Pubs., Inc.

Silberstein, James. The Night Crystal Mcgoober Had Seven Heads. 2004. 132p. 21.95 (978-0-595-66716-1(3)) iUniverse, Inc.

Skillchecks for Horror. 2005. (Double Fastback Ser.). (J). (gr. 6-12). 64p. pap. 5.95 (978-0-13-024476-5(7)); 32p. pap. 5.95 (978-0-13-024459-8(7)) Globe Fearon Educational Publishing.

Skogen, Jennifer. Burning #1. 1 vol. 2015. (Haunting of Grey Hills Ser.). (ENG.). 216p. (YA). (gr. 9-12). lib. bdg. 27.13 (978-1-68076-029-3(7), Epic Pr.) ABDO Publishing Co.

—Distant Deep #5. 2015. (Haunting of Grey Hills Ser.). (ENG.). 200-216p. (YA). (gr. 9-12). lib. bdg. 27.13 (978-1-68076-033-0(5), Epic Pr.) ABDO Publishing Co.

Slade, Arthur. Northern Frights Trilogy. 2014. 352p. (YA). (gr. 8). pap. 8.99 (978-0-06-233289-9(9)) HarperCollins Pubs.

Sleator, William. The Boy Who Couldn't Die. 2005. (ENG.). 184p. (J). (gr. 7-17). pap. 8.95 (978-0-8109-8790-6(2)) Abrams, Inc.

Smith, Alexander Gordon. Death Sentence. 2011. (Escape from Furnace Ser.: 3). (ENG.). 272p. (YA). (gr. 7-11). 17.99 (978-0-374-32494-0(8), 9780374324940, Farrar, Straus & Giroux (BYR)) Farrar, Straus & Giroux.

—Death Sentence. 2012. (Escape from Furnace Ser.: 3). (ENG.). 288p. (YA). (gr. 7-11). pap. 10.99 (978-0-312-67441-0(4), 9780312674410) Square Fish.

—Execution. 2012. (Escape from Furnace Ser.: 5). (ENG.). 320p. (YA). (gr. 7-11). 16.99 (978-0-374-36224-9(6), 9780374362249, Farrar, Straus & Giroux (BYR)) Farrar, Straus & Giroux.

—Execution. 2013. (Escape from Furnace Ser.: 5). (ENG.). 336p. (YA). (gr. 7-11). pap. 10.99 (978-1-250-02942-3(2), 9781250029423) Square Fish.

—Fugitives. 2012. (Escape from Furnace Ser.: 4). (ENG.). 288p. (YA). (gr. 7-11). 17.99 (978-0-374-32484-1(0), 9780374324841, Farrar, Straus & Giroux (BYR)) Farrar, Straus & Giroux.

—Fugitives. 2012. (Escape from Furnace Ser.: 4). (ENG.). 304p. (YA). (gr. 7-11). pap. 10.99 (978-1-250-00339-3(3), 9781250003393) Square Fish.

—The Fury. 2013. (ENG.). 688p. (YA). (gr. 7). 19.99 (978-0-374-32495-7(6), 9780374324957, Farrar, Straus & Giroux (BYR)) Farrar, Straus & Giroux.

—Hellfighters. 2016. (Devil's Engine Ser.: 2). (ENG.). 320p. (YA). 18.99 (978-0-374-30172-9(7), 9780374301729, Farrar, Straus & Giroux (BYR)) Farrar, Straus & Giroux.

—Solitary. 2010. (Escape from Furnace Ser.: 2). (ENG.). 240p. (YA). (gr. 7-11). 17.99 (978-0-374-32492-6(1), 9780374324926, Farrar, Straus & Giroux (BYR)) Farrar, Straus & Giroux.

—Solitary. 2011. (Escape from Furnace Ser.: 2). (ENG.). 256p. (YA). (gr. 7-11). pap. 10.99 (978-0-312-67476-2(7), 9780312674762) Square Fish.

Smith, Caighlan. Children of Icarus. 2016. (ENG.). 312p. (gr. 9-10). 16.95 (978-1-63079-057-8(5)) Switch Pr.

Smith, L. J. Destiny Rising. 2013. (Vampire Diaries: the Hunters Ser.: 3). (ENG.). 416p. (YA). (gr. 9). pap. 9.99 (978-0-06-201774-1(8), HarperTeen) HarperCollins Pubs.

—The Forbidden Game: The Hunter - The Chase - The Kill. 2010. (Forbidden Game Ser.: Bks. 1-3). (ENG.). 768p. (YA). (gr. 7). pap. 10.99 (978-1-4169-8940-0(4), Simon Pulse) Simon Pulse.

—The Hunt. 2013. (Secret Circle Ser.: 5). (ENG.). 288p. (YA). (gr. 8). pap. 9.99 (978-0-06-213043-3(9), HarperTeen) HarperCollins Pubs.

—Moonsong. 2012. (Vampire Diaries: the Hunters Ser.: 2). (ENG.). 400p. (YA). (gr. 9). 17.99 (978-0-06-201770-3(5), HarperTeen) HarperCollins Pubs.

Smith, L. J. & Clark, Aubrey. Unseen. 0 vols. 2013. (Vampire Diaries: the Salvation Ser.: 1). (ENG.). 306p. (YA). (gr. 7-9). pap. 9.99 (978-1-4778-0967-9(8), 9781477809679, 47North) Amazon Publishing.

Smith, L. J. & Williamson, Kevin. The Compelled. 2012. (Vampire Diaries: Stefan's Diaries: 6). (ENG.). 256p. (YA). (gr. 9). pap. 10.99 (978-0-06-211398-6(4), HarperTeen) HarperCollins Pubs.

Smith, L. J., et al. Bloodlust. 2011. (Vampire Diaries: Stefan's Diaries: 2). (ENG.). 256p. (YA). (gr. 9-18). pap. 9.99 (978-0-06-200394-2(1), HarperTeen) HarperCollins Pubs.

Smolanoff, Michael. The Scary Kids Club. 2010. 172p. 29.99 (978-1-4535-4146-3(2)); pap. 19.99 (978-1-4535-4145-6(4)) Xlibris Corp.

Smythe, R. R. Into the Woods. 2007. 122p. (YA). per. 7.49 net. (978-0-9787139-4-2(X), Pandora) Highland Pr. Publishing.

Sniegoski, Thomas E. Monstrous. 2017. (Savage Ser.). (ENG., Illus.). 448p. (YA). (gr. 9). 18.99 (**978-1-4814-7718-5(8)**, Simon Pulse) Simon Pulse.

Sniegoski, Tom. Monstrous. 2017. (YA). pap. (**978-1-4814-7719-2(6)**, Simon Pulse) Simon Pulse.

Spine Shivers. 2015. (Spine Shivers Ser.). (ENG.). 128p. (gr. 3-4). pap. 27.80 (978-1-4965-2209-2(5)) Stone Arch Bks.

The Spirits Within: A Millersburg Novel. 2006. (YA). per. 7.99 (978-0-9765478-2-2(1)) Stone Acres Publishing Co.

Steele, S. The Tell Me a Story Book. 2007. 116p. per. 13.99 (978-1-4259-7993-5(9)) AuthorHouse.

Steensland, Mark. Behind the Bookcase. Murphy, Kelly, illus. 2013. (ENG.). 288p. (J). (gr. 3-7). 6.99 (978-0-385-74072-2(7), Yearling) Random Hse. Children's Bks.

Stefoff, Rebecca. Stephen King. 2010. (Today's Writers & Their Works). 128p. (gr. 7-18). 42.79 (978-0-7614-4122-9(0)) Marshall Cavendish Corp.

Steve, Behling. Marvel Monsters Unleashed: Beware the Glop! Marvel Press Artist Staff, illus. 2017. (Marvel Monsters Unleashed! Ser.). (ENG.). 176p. (J). (gr. 3-7). pap. 6.99 (**978-1-368-00247-9(1)**, Marvel Pr.) Disney Publishing Worldwide.

Stevenson, Robert Louis. Classics Illustrated #7: Dr. Jekyll & Mr. Hyde. 2009. (Classics Illustrated Graphic Novels Ser.). (ENG., Illus.). 56p. (J). (gr. 3-9). 9.95 (978-1-59707-171-0(4), 9781597071710) Papercutz.

—Dr. Jekyll & Mr. Hyde. 2008. (Bring the Classics to Life Ser.). (ENG., Illus.). 72p. (gr. 4-12). pap., act. bk. ed. 10.95 (978-0-931334-50-4(0), EDCTR-402B) EDCON Publishing Group.

—Dr Jekyll & Mr Hyde. Lubach, Vanessa, illus. 2014. (Classics of Science Fiction Ser.). (ENG.). 64p. pap. 6.95 (978-1-906230-15-9(3)) Real Reads Ltd. GBR. Dist: Casemate Pubs. & Bk. Distributors, LLC.

—Dr. Jekyll & Mr. Hyde. 2009. (Foundation Classics Ser.). (Illus.). 56p. (J). (gr. 5-9). lib. bdg. 27.95 (978-1-60754-849-2(6)) Windmill Bks.

—Dr. Jekyll & Mr. Hyde. 2006. (Reader's Workshop Ser.). (ENG.). 64p. (C). pap. 17.95 (978-0-7362-3140-4(4)) CENGAGE Learning.

—Dr. Jekyll & Mr. Hyde. 1 vol. 2010. (Illustrated Classics Ser.). (ENG., Illus.). 64p. (YA). (gr. 9-12). per. 9.95 (978-1-56254-894-0(8)) Saddleback Educational Publishing, Inc.

—The Strange Case of Dr. Jekyll & Mr. Hyde. (Classics Illustrated Ser.). (Illus.). 52p. (YA). pap. 4.95 (978-1-57209-008-8(1)) Classics International Entertainment, Inc.

—The Strange Case of Dr. Jekyll & Mr. Hyde. Andrews, Gary, illus. 2008. (Fast Track Classics Ser.). (ENG.). 48p. pap. 10.00 (978-1-4190-5082-4(6)) Steck-Vaughn.

—The Strange Case of Dr. Jekyll & Mr. Hyde. McKowen, Scott, illus. 2011. (Sterling Unabridged Classics Ser.). (ENG.). 96p. (J). 9.95 (978-1-4027-8402-6(3)) Sterling Publishing Co., Inc.

—The Strange Case of Dr. Jekyll & Mr. Hyde. Akib, Jamel, illus. 2006. (Classic Starts(tm) Ser.). (ENG.). 160p. (J). (gr. 2-4). 6.95 (978-1-4027-2667-5(8), 1252057) Sterling Publishing Co., Inc.

—Strange Case of Dr. Jekyll & Mr. Hyde. Kennedy, Cam, illus. 2008. (ENG.). 48p. (YA). (gr. 5). pap. 11.95 (978-0-88776-882-8(2), Tundra Bks.) Tundra Bks. CAN. Dist: Penguin Random Hse. LLC.

—The Strange Case of Dr. Jekyll & Mr. Hyde: With a Discussion of Moderation. Clift, Eva, tr. Clift, Eva, illus. 2003. (Values in Action Illustrated Classics Ser.). (J). (978-1-59203-053-8(X)) Learning Challenge, Inc.

—The Strange Case of Dr. Jekyll & Mr. Hyde (Quality Library Classics) 2008. (YA). pap. 14.95 (978-1-57545-703-1(2)) RP Media.

Stevenson, Robert Louis & Venable, Alan. The Strange Case of Dr. Jekyll & Mr. Hyde. 2005. (Classic Literature Ser.). 108p. pap. 9.95 (978-1-4105-0119-6(1)); pap., E-Book 69.00 incl. audio compact disk (978-1-4105-0117-2(5)) Johnston, Don Inc.

Stewart, Paul & Riddell, Chris. Barnaby Grimes: Legion of the Dead. 2012. (Barnaby Grimes Ser.). (ENG.). 240p. (J). (gr. 4-7). 6.99 (978-0-385-73699-2(1), Yearling) Random Hse. Children's Bks.

Stilton, Geronimo. Fright Night. 2013. (Creepella Von Cacklefur Ser.: 5). (ENG.). 128p. (J). (gr. 2-5). pap. 7.99 (978-0-545-39349-2(3), Scholastic Paperbacks) Scholastic, Inc.

—Meet Me in Horrorwood. 2011. (Geronimo Stilton — Creepella Von Cacklefur Ser.: 2). (Illus.). 112p. (J). lib. bdg. 18.40 (978-0-606-22947-0(7), Turtleback) Turtleback Bks.

Stine, R. L. The Adventures of Shrinkman. 0 vols. unabr. ed. 2012. (ENG.). 140p. (J). (gr. 3-7). pap. 4.99 (978-1-61218-328-2(X), 9781612183282, Amazon Children's Publishing) Amazon Publishing.

—Attack of the Graveyard Ghouls. 2015. (Goosebumps Ser.: 31). lib. bdg. 17.20 (978-0-606-37069-1(2)) Turtleback Bks.

—Be Careful What You Wish For. 2009. (Goosebumps Ser.: 7). lib. bdg. 17.20 (978-0-606-00242-4(1), Turtleback) Turtleback Bks.

—Beware! R. L. Stine Picks His Favorite Scary Stories. 2004. (ENG., Illus.). 224p. (J). (gr. 3-18). pap. 6.99 (978-0-06-055547-4(5)) HarperCollins Pubs.

—The Birthday Party of No Return! 2012. (Goosebumps Hall of Horrors Ser.: 6). (ENG.). 160p. (J). (gr. 3-7). pap. 6.99 (978-0-545-28938-2(6), Scholastic Paperbacks) Scholastic, Inc.

—The Birthday Party of No Return. 2012. (Goosebumps HorrorLand: Hall of Horrors Ser.: 6). lib. bdg. 17.20 (978-0-606-23932-5(4), Turtleback) Turtleback Bks.

—The Blob That Ate Everyone. 2015. (Goosebumps Ser.: 28). lib. bdg. 17.20 (978-0-606-37071-4(4)) Turtleback Bks.

—Bound Galley - Haunted Mask Lives! Date not set. (J). pap. (978-0-06-449214-0(1), Harper Trophy) HarperCollins Pubs.

—Broken Hearts. 2011. (Fear Street Superchillers Ser.: Bk. 3). (ENG.). 224p. (YA). (gr. 7). pap. 10.99 (978-1-4424-4273-3(5), Simon Pulse) Simon Pulse.

—Claws! 2011. (Goosebumps Hall of Horrors Ser.: 1). (ENG.). 160p. (J). (gr. 3-7). pap. 6.99 (978-0-545-28933-7(5), Scholastic Paperbacks) Scholastic, Inc.

—The Confession. 2005. (Fear Street Ser.: Bk. 39). (ENG.). 160p. (YA). (gr. 7). pap. 7.99 (978-1-4169-0322-2(4), Simon Pulse) Simon Pulse.

—The Creatures from Beyond Beyond. 0 vols. unabr. ed. 2012. (ENG.). 144p. (J). (gr. 2-4). pap. 4.99 (978-1-61218-327-5(1), 9781612183275, Amazon Children's Publishing) Amazon Publishing.

—Creep from the Deep. 2008. (Goosebumps HorrorLand Ser.: No. 2). 137p. (gr. 4-7). 17.00 (978-0-7569-8815-9(2)) Perfection Learning Corp.

—Creep from the Deep. 2008. (Goosebumps Horrorland Ser.: 2). (ENG.). 160p. (J). (gr. 3-7). 6.99 (978-0-439-91870-1(7), Scholastic Paperbacks) Scholastic, Inc.

—The Curse of the Mummy's Tomb. 2009. (Goosebumps Ser.: 6). lib. bdg. 17.20 (978-0-606-00243-1(X), Turtleback) Turtleback Bks.

—Darkest Dawn. 2005. (Fear Street Nights Ser.: No. 3). 182p. (YA). lib. bdg. 20.00 (978-1-4242-0994-1(3)) Fitzgerald Bks.

—Darkest Dawn. 2012. (Fear Street Nights Ser.: 3). (ENG.). 192p. (YA). (gr. 7). pap. 9.99 (978-1-4424-6058-4(X), Simon Pulse) Simon Pulse.

—The Dead Boyfriend. 2016. 288p. (YA). pap. (**978-1-250-11199-9(4)**, Dunne, Thomas Bks.) St. Martin's Pr.

—The Dead Boyfriend: A Fear Street Novel. 2016. (Fear Street Ser.). (ENG.). 288p. (YA). 18.99 (978-1-250-05895-9(3), 9781250058959) St. Martin's Pr.

—Deep Trouble. 2008. (Classic Goosebumps Ser.: 2). (ENG.). 144p. (J). (gr. 3-7). 6.99 (978-0-545-03519-4(8), Scholastic Paperbacks) Scholastic, Inc.

—Don't Scream! 2012. (J). 137p. (978-0-545-48408-4(1)); (Goosebumps Hall of Horrors Ser.: 5). (ENG.). 160p. (gr. 3-7). pap. 6.99 (978-0-545-28937-5(8), Scholastic Paperbacks) Scholastic, Inc.

—Don't Stay up Late: A Fear Street Novel. 2015. (Fear Street Ser.). (ENG.). 304p. (YA). (gr. 7-12). 17.99 (978-1-250-05162-2(2), 9781250051622, St. Martin's Griffin) St. Martin's Pr.

—Dr. Maniac vs. Robby Schwartz. 2008. (Goosebumps Horrorland Ser.: 5). (ENG.). 160p. (J). (gr. 3-7). pap. 6.99 (978-0-439-91873-2(1), Scholastic Paperbacks) Scholastic, Inc.

—Dr. Maniac Will See You Now. 2013. (Goosebumps Most Wanted Ser.: 5). (ENG.). 160p. (J). (gr. 3-7). pap. 6.99 (978-0-545-41802-7(X), Scholastic Paperbacks) Scholastic, Inc.

—Dr. Maniac Will See You Now. 2013. (Goosebumps Most Wanted Ser.: 5). lib. bdg. 17.20 (978-0-606-32376-5(7), Turtleback) Turtleback Bks.

—Escape from HorrorLand. 2009. (Goosebumps Horrorland Ser.: 11). (ENG.). 160p. (J). (gr. 3-7). 6.99 (978-0-439-91879-4(0), Scholastic Paperbacks) Scholastic, Inc.

—Escape from Horrorland. 2009. (Goosebumps HorrorLand Ser.: 11). lib. bdg. 17.20 (978-0-606-05355-6(7), Turtleback) Turtleback Bks.

—Fear Street Super Thriller: Party Games & Don't Stay up Late. 2015. (Fear Street Ser.). (ENG.). 592p. (YA). (gr. 7-12). pap. 11.99 (978-1-250-07693-9(5), 9781250076939, St. Martin's Griffin) St. Martin's Pr.

—Fear Street Super Thriller - Secrets: The Lost Girl & Can You Keep a Secret. 2 bks. in 1. 2016. (Fear Street Ser.). (ENG.). 544p. (YA). pap. 11.99 (978-1-250-09648-7(0), 9781250096487) St. Martin's Pr.

—Al Final de la Noche. Alonso, Victoria, tr. 2005. (Escritura desatada Ser.). (SPA & ENG.). 216p. (YA). (gr. 7). 17.95 (978-84-666-0772-8(2)) Ediciones B ESP. Dist: Independent Pubs. Group.

—First Evil. 2011. (Fear Street Cheerleaders Ser.: 1). (ENG.). 176p. (YA). (gr. 9). pap. 9.99 (978-1-4424-3086-0(9), Simon Pulse) Simon Pulse.

—The Five Masks of Dr. Scream. 2011. (Goosebumps Hall of Horrors Ser.: 3). (ENG.). 192p. (J). (gr. 3-7). pap. 7.99 (978-0-545-28936-8(X), Scholastic Paperbacks) Scholastic, Inc.

—Frankenstein's Dog. 2013. (Goosebumps Most Wanted Ser.: 4). 136p. (J). lib. bdg. 17.20 (978-0-606-32006-1(7), Turtleback) Turtleback Bks.

—Ghost Beach. 2010. (Classic Goosebumps Ser.: 15). (ENG.). 160p. (J). (gr. 3-7). 6.99 (978-0-545-17803-7(7), Scholastic Paperbacks) Scholastic, Inc.

—Ghost Beach. 2003. (Goosebumps Ser.: No. 22). (gr. 5-8). 14.75 (978-0-613-70848-7(2), Turtleback) Turtleback Bks.

—Goosebumps. 2015. (Goosebumps Ser.). (ENG.). 736p. (J). (gr. 3-7). pap. 29.99 (978-0-545-84730-8(3)) Scholastic, Inc.

—Goosebumps Wanted: the Haunted Mask. 2013. (Goosebumps: Wanted Ser.). (ENG.). 240p. (J). (gr. 3-7). pap. 6.99 (978-0-545-41797-6(X), Scholastic Paperbacks) Scholastic, Inc.

—The Haunted Car. 2015. (Goosebumps Ser.: 30). lib. bdg. 17.20 (978-0-606-37073-8(0)) Turtleback Bks.

—The Haunted Mask. 2013. lib. bdg. 17.20 (978-0-606-32005-4(9), Turtleback) Turtleback Bks.

—The Haunter. 2016. (Goosebumps Most Wanted Special Edition Ser.: 4). (ENG.). 192p. (J). (gr. 3-7). pap. 7.99 (978-0-545-82545-0(8), Scholastic Paperbacks) Scholastic, Inc.

—The Haunter. 2016. (Goosebumps Most Wanted Ser.). lib. bdg. 18.40 (978-0-606-38784-2(6)) Turtleback Bks.

—The Haunting Hour. movie tie-in ed. 2011. (ENG.). 160p. (J). (gr. 3). pap. 5.99 (978-0-06-210691-9(0)) HarperCollins Pubs.

—Heads, You Lose. 2010. (Goosebumps HorrorLand Ser.: No. 15). 160p. (J). pap. (978-1-4071-1636-5(3)) Scholastic, Inc.

—Help! We Have Strange Powers! 2009. (Goosebumps Horrorland Ser.: 10). (ENG.). 160p. (J). (gr. 3-7). 6.99 (978-0-439-91878-7(2), Scholastic Paperbacks) Scholastic, Inc.

—Help! We Have Strange Powers! 2009. (Goosebumps HorrorLand Ser.: 10). lib. bdg. 17.20 (978-0-606-05347-1(6), Turtleback) Turtleback Bks.

—Here Comes the Shaggedy. 2016. (Goosebumps: Most Wanted Ser.: 9). (ENG., Illus.). 160p. (J). (gr. 3-7). pap. 6.99 (978-0-545-82547-4(4), Scholastic Paperbacks) Scholastic, Inc.

—Here Comes the Shaggedy. 2016. (Goosebumps Most Wanted Ser.: 9). (Illus.). 140p. (J). lib. bdg. 17.20 (978-0-606-38587-9(8)) Turtleback Bks.

—How I Got My Shrunken Head. 2009. (Classic Goosebumps Ser.: 10). (ENG.). 144p. (J). (gr. 3-7). 6.99 (978-0-545-03518-7(X), Scholastic Paperbacks) Scholastic, Inc.

—How I Got My Shrunken Head. 2009. (Goosebumps Ser.: 10). lib. bdg. 17.20 (978-0-606-00245-5(6), Turtleback) Turtleback Bks.

—How I Met My Monster. 2013. (Goosebumps: Most Wanted Ser.: 3). (ENG.). 160p. (J). (gr. 3-7). pap. 6.99 (978-0-545-41800-3(3), Scholastic Paperbacks) Scholastic, Inc.

—Killer's Kiss. 2005. (Fear Street Ser.: Bk. 42). (ENG.). 160p. (YA). (gr. 7). pap. 7.99 (978-1-4169-0320-8(8), Simon Pulse) Simon Pulse.

—Little Shop of Hamsters. 2010. (Goosebumps Horrorland Ser.: 14). (ENG.). 160p. (J). (gr. 3-7). 6.99 (978-0-545-16195-4(9), Scholastic Paperbacks) Scholastic, Inc.

—Midnight Games. 2005. (Fear Street Nights Ser.: No. 2). 183p. (YA). lib. bdg. 20.00 (978-1-4242-1119-7(0)) Fitzgerald Bks.

—Midnight Games. 2005. (Fear Street Nights Ser.: 2). (ENG.). 160p. (YA). (gr. 7). pap. 6.99 (978-0-689-87865-7(6), Simon Pulse) Simon Pulse.

—A Midsummer Night's Scream. 2013. (ENG.). 256p. (YA). (gr. 7). 17.99 (978-1-250-02434-3(X), 9781250024343) Feiwel & Friends.

—A Midsummer Night's Scream. 2014. (ENG.). 256p. (YA). (gr. 7-12). pap. 10.99 (978-1-250-04434-1(0), 9781250044341) Square Fish.

—Monster Blood. 2008. (Classic Goosebumps Ser.: 3). (ENG.). 144p. (J). (gr. 3-7). 6.99 (978-0-545-03520-0(1), Scholastic Paperbacks) Scholastic, Inc.

—Monster Blood for Breakfast! 2008. (Goosebumps Horrorland Ser.: 3). (ENG.). 144p. (J). (gr. 3-7). pap. 6.99 (978-0-439-91871-8(5), Scholastic Paperbacks) Scholastic, Inc.

—Movie Novel. Scholastic, Inc. Staff, illus. 2015. (ENG.). 144p. (J). (gr. 3-8). pap. 5.99 (978-0-545-82124-7(X)) Scholastic, Inc.

—Mutacion Fatal. 2003. (SPA.). pap. (978-0-590-01798-5(5)) Scholastic GBR. Dist: Lectorum Pubns., Inc.

—My Alien Parents. 0 vols. unabr. ed. 2012. (ENG.). 60p. (J). (gr. 3-7). pap. 4.99 (978-1-61218-325-1(5), 9781612183251, Amazon Children's Publishing) Amazon Publishing.

—The New Girl. 2006. (Fear Street Ser.: Bk. 1). (ENG., Illus.). 176p. (YA). (gr. 7-12). mass mkt. 7.99 (978-1-4169-1810-3(8), Simon Pulse) Simon Pulse.

—A Night in Terror Tower. 2009. (Classic Goosebumps Ser.: 12). (ENG.). 160p. (J). (gr. 3-7). 6.99 (978-0-545-15887-9(7), Scholastic Paperbacks) Scholastic, Inc.

—Night of the Giant Everything. 2011. (Goosebumps Hall of Horrors Ser.: 2). (ENG.). 160p. (J). (gr. 3-7). pap. 6.99 (978-0-545-28935-1(1), Scholastic Paperbacks) Scholastic, Inc.

—Night of the Living Dummy. 2008. (Classic Goosebumps Ser.: 1). (ENG.). 160p. (J). (gr. 3-7). 6.99 (978-0-545-03517-0(1), Scholastic Paperbacks) Scholastic, Inc.

—Night of the Puppet People. 2015. 136p. (J). (**978-1-4806-9296-1(4)**) Scholastic, Inc.

—Night of the Puppet People. 2015. (Goosebumps Most Wanted Ser.: 8). lib. bdg. 17.20 (978-0-606-37792-8(1)) Turtleback Bks.

—Night of the Puppet People (Goosebumps Most Wanted #8) 2015. (Goosebumps: Most Wanted Ser.: 8). (ENG.). 160p. (J). (gr. 3-7). pap. 6.99 (978-0-545-62775-7(3), Scholastic Paperbacks) Scholastic, Inc.

—Night of the Werecat. 2011. (R. L. Stine's Ghosts of Fear Street Ser.). (ENG.). 128p. (J). (gr. 3-7). pap. 4.99 (978-1-4424-2698-6(5), Aladdin) Simon & Schuster Children's Publishing.

—Nightmare Hour. movie tie-in ed. 2011. (ENG.). 160p. (J). (gr. 3). pap. 5.99 (978-0-06-210692-6(9)) HarperCollins Pubs.

—One Day at Horrorland. 2008. (Classic Goosebumps Ser.: 5). (ENG.). 144p. (J). (gr. 3-7). 6.99 (978-0-545-03522-4(8), Scholastic Paperbacks) Scholastic, Inc.

—Padres de Otra Dimension. (Fantasmas de Fear Street Coleccion). (SPA.). (YA). (gr. 5-8). pap. 7.95 (978-950-04-1963-5(7), EM10792) Emecé Editores S.A. ARG. Dist: Planeta Publishing Corp., Lectorum Pubns., Inc.

—Party Games: A Fear Street Novel. 2014. (Fear Street Ser.). (ENG.). 288p. (YA). (gr. 7-12). 17.99 (978-1-250-05161-5(4), 9781250051615, St. Martin's Griffin) St. Martin's Pr.

—The Perfect Date. 2005. (Fear Street Ser.). (ENG.). 160p. (YA). (gr. 7). pap. 7.99 (978-1-4169-0323-9(2), Simon Pulse) Simon Pulse.

—Phantom of the Auditorium. 2011. (Classic Goosebumps Ser.: 20). (ENG.). 160p. (J). (gr. 3-7). pap. 6.99 (978-0-545-29836-0(9), Scholastic Paperbacks) Scholastic, Inc.

—Please Don't Feed the Vampire! A Give Yourself Goosebumps Book. 2015. (Classic Goosebumps Ser.: 32). (ENG.). 144p. (J). (gr. 3-7). pap. 6.99 (978-0-545-82887-1(2), Scholastic Paperbacks) Scholastic, Inc.

—Return of the Mummy. 2010. (Classic Goosebumps Ser.: 18). (ENG.). 160p. (J). (gr. 3-7). pap. 6.99 (978-0-545-17794-8(4), Scholastic Paperbacks) Scholastic, Inc.

—Revenge of the Living Dummy. 2008. (Goosebumps Horrorland Ser.: 1). (ENG.). 144p. (J). (gr. 3-7). 6.99 (978-0-439-91869-5(3), Scholastic Paperbacks) Scholastic, Inc.

—Revenge of the Living Dummy. 2008. (Goosebumps HorrorLand Ser.: 1). 128p. (gr. 4-7). lib. bdg. 17.20 (978-1-4178-1891-4(3), Turtleback) Turtleback Bks.

—Revenge of the Shadow People & the Bugman Lives! Twice Terrifying Tales. 2010. (R. L. Stine's Ghosts of Fear Street Ser.). (ENG.). 240p. (J). (gr. 3-7). pap. 6.99 (978-1-4424-0802-9(2), Aladdin) Simon & Schuster Children's Publishing.

—The Rich Girl. 2005. (Fear Street Ser.: Bk. 45). (ENG.). 144p. (YA). (gr. 7). pap. 6.99 (978-1-4169-0324-6(0), Simon Pulse) Simon Pulse.

—Rotten School - Dudes, the School Is Haunted! Park, Trip, illus. 2009. (Rotten School Ser.: No. 7). 128p. (J). pap. 4.99 *(978-0-06-078820-9(8),* Harper Trophy) HarperCollins Pubs.
—Say Cheese - And Die Screaming! 2008. (Goosebumps HorrorLand Ser.: No. 8). (Illus.). 125p. lib. bdg. 17.00 *(978-1-60686-344-2(4))* Perfection Learning Corp.
—Say Cheese - And Die Screaming! 2009. (Goosebumps Horrorland Ser.: 8). (ENG.). 160p. (J). (gr. 3-7). 6.99 *(978-0-439-91876-3(6),* Scholastic Paperbacks) Scholastic, Inc.
—Say Cheese & Die. 2009. (Goosebumps Ser.: 8). lib. bdg. 17.20 *(978-0-606-00247-9(2),* Turtleback) Turtleback Bks.
—Say Cheese & Die Screaming! 2009. (Goosebumps HorrorLand Ser.: 8). lib. bdg. 17.20 *(978-0-606-06886-4(4),* Turtleback) Turtleback Bks.
—Scarecrow Walks at Midnight. 2010. (Classic Goosebumps Ser.: 16). (ENG.). 160p. (J). (gr. 3-7). 6.99 *(978-0-545-17801-3(0),* Scholastic Paperbacks) Scholastic, Inc.
—The Scream of the Haunted Mask. 2008. (Goosebumps Horrorland Ser.: 4). (ENG.). 160p. (J). (gr. 3-7). pap. 6.99 *(978-0-439-91872-5(3),* Scholastic Paperbacks) Scholastic, Inc.
—Secret Admirer. 2006. (Fear Street Ser.: Bk. 37). (ENG.). 160p. (YA). (gr. 7). mass mkt. 7.99 *(978-1-4169-0820-3(X),* Simon Pulse) Simon Pulse.
—A Shocker on Shock Street. 2015. (Goosebumps Ser.: 23). lib. bdg. 17.20 *(978-0-606-37064-6(1))* Turtleback Bks.
—Slappy New Year! 2010. (Goosebumps Horrorland Ser.: 18). (ENG.). 160p. (J). (gr. 3-7). pap. 6.99 *(978-0-545-16199-2(1),* Scholastic Paperbacks) Scholastic, Inc.
—Slappy's Tales of Horror. 2015. (Goosebumps Graphix Ser.). lib. bdg. 24.50 *(978-0-606-37761-4(1))* Turtleback Bks.
—Slappy's Tales of Horror (Goosebumps Graphix) Roman, Dave et al, illus. 2015. (Goosebumps Graphix Ser.). (ENG.). 176p. (J). (gr. 3-7). pap. 12.99 *(978-0-545-83595-4(X),* Graphix) Scholastic, Inc.
—Son of Slappy. 2013. (Goosebumps Most Wanted Ser.: 2). (ENG.). 160p. (J). (gr. 3-7). pap. 6.99 *(978-0-545-41799-0(6),* Scholastic Paperbacks) Scholastic, Inc.
—Son of Slappy. 2013. (Goosebumps Most Wanted Ser.: 2). lib. bdg. 17.20 *(978-0-606-31533-3(0),* Turtleback) Turtleback Bks.
—Stay Away from the Tree House & Eye of the Fortuneteller: Twice Terrifying Tales. 2009. (R. L. Stine's Ghosts of Fear Street Ser.). (ENG., Illus.). 224p. (J). (gr. 3-7). pap. 7.99 *(978-1-4169-9137-3(9),* Aladdin) Simon & Schuster Children's Publishing.
—Stay Out of the Basement. 2011. (Classic Goosebumps Ser.: 22). (ENG.). 160p. (J). (gr. 3-7). pap. 6.99 *(978-0-545-29838-4(5),* Scholastic Paperbacks) Scholastic, Inc.
—The Streets of Panic Park. 2009. (Goosebumps Horrorland Ser.: 12). (ENG.). 160p. (J). (gr. 3-7). 6.99 *(978-0-439-91880-0(4),* Scholastic Paperbacks) Scholastic, Inc.
—The Streets of Panic Park. 2009. (Goosebumps HorrorLand Ser.: 12). lib. bdg. 17.20 *(978-0-606-05366-2(2),* Turtleback) Turtleback Bks.
—Switched. 2006. (Fear Street Ser.: Bk. 32). (ENG.). 160p. (YA). (gr. 7). mass mkt. 7.99 *(978-1-4169-1375-7(0),* Simon Pulse) Simon Pulse.
—Three Faces of Me, 0 vols. unabr. ed. 2012. (ENG.). 86p. (J). (gr. 3-7). pap. 4.99 *(978-1-61218-326-8(3),* 9781612183268, Amazon Children's Publishing) Amazon Publishing.
—Vampire Breath. 2011. (Classic Goosebumps Ser.: 21). (ENG.). 160p. (J). (gr. 3-7). pap. 6.99 *(978-0-545-29837-7(7),* Scholastic Paperbacks) Scholastic, Inc.
—Wanted: The Haunted Mask. 2012. (Goosebumps Ser.). (ENG.). 240p. (J). (gr. 3-7). 15.99 *(978-0-545-41793-8(7),* Scholastic Paperbacks) Scholastic, Inc.
—Weirdo Halloween. 2010. (Goosebumps HorrorLand Ser.: No. 16). 240p. (J). pap. *(978-1-4071-1637-2(1))* Scholastic, Inc.
—Welcome to Camp Nightmare. 2010. (Classic Goosebumps Ser.: 14). (ENG.). 160p. (J). (gr. 3-7). 6.99 *(978-0-545-15889-3(3),* Scholastic Paperbacks) Scholastic, Inc.
—Welcome to Camp Slither. 2009. (Goosebumps Horrorland Ser.: 9). (ENG.). 160p. (J). (gr. 3-7). 6.99 *(978-0-439-91877-0(4),* Scholastic Paperbacks) Scholastic, Inc.
—Welcome to Camp Slither. 2009. (Goosebumps HorrorLand Ser.: 9). lib. bdg. 17.20 *(978-0-606-05345-7(X),* Turtleback) Turtleback Bks.
—Welcome to Dead House. 2010. (Classic Goosebumps Ser.: 13). (ENG.). 160p. (J). (gr. 3-7). 6.99 *(978-0-545-15888-6(5),* Scholastic Paperbacks) Scholastic, Inc.
—Welcome to Dead House. 2010. (Goosebumps Ser.: 13). lib. bdg. 17.20 *(978-0-606-14077-5(8),* Turtleback) Turtleback Bks.
—Werewolf of Fever Swamp. 2009. (Classic Goosebumps Ser.: 11). (ENG.). 160p. (J). (gr. 3-7). 6.99 *(978-0-545-15886-2(9),* Scholastic Paperbacks) Scholastic, Inc.
—The Werewolf of Fever Swamp. (Goosebumps Ser.: 11). 2009. lib. bdg. 17.20 *(978-0-606-00241-7(3))* 2003. (gr. 5-8). 14.75 *(978-0-613-68300-5(5))* Turtleback Bks. (Turtleback).
—When the Ghost Dog Howls. 2010. (Goosebumps Horrorland Ser.: 13). (ENG.). 160p. (J). (gr. 3-7). 6.99 *(978-0-545-16194-7(0),* Scholastic Paperbacks) Scholastic, Inc.
—When the Ghost Dog Howls. 2010. (Goosebumps HorrorLand Ser.: 13). lib. bdg. 17.20 *(978-0-606-07124-6(5),* Turtleback) Turtleback Bks.
—Why I Quit Zombie School. 2011. (Goosebumps Hall of Horrors Ser.: 4). (ENG.). 160p. (J). (gr. 3-7). pap. 6.99 *(978-0-545-28932-0(7),* Scholastic Paperbacks) Scholastic, Inc.
—Wizard of Ooze. 2010. (Goosebumps Horrorland Ser.: 17). (ENG.). 160p. (J). (gr. 3-7). pap. 6.99 *(978-0-545-16198-5(3),* Scholastic Paperbacks) Scholastic, Inc.
—Yo Fui un Zombi. (Fear Street Ser.). (SPA.). (YA). (gr. 7-18). pap. 7.95 *(978-950-04-2027-3(9),* EM10970) Emecé Editores S.A. ARG. Dist: Planeta Publishing Corp., Lectorum Pubns., Inc.
—You Can't Scare Me! 2010. (Classic Goosebumps Ser.: 17). (ENG.). 160p. (J). (gr. 3-7). pap. 6.99 *(978-0-545-17796-2(0),* Scholastic Paperbacks) Scholastic, Inc.
—Zombie Halloween. 2014. (Goosebumps Most Wanted Special Edition Ser.: 1). (ENG.). 192p. (J). (gr. 3-7). pap. 7.99 *(978-0-545-62776-4(1),* Scholastic Paperbacks) Scholastic, Inc.
—Zombie Town, 0 vols. unabr. ed. 2012. (ENG.). 74p. (J). (gr. 3-7). pap. 4.99 *(978-1-61218-329-9(8),* 9781612183299, Amazon Children's Publishing) Amazon Publishing.
—The 12 Screams of Christmas. 2014. (Goosebumps Most Wanted Special Edition Ser.: 2). (ENG.). 192p. (J). (gr. 3-7). pap. 7.99 *(978-0-545-62777-1(X),* Scholastic Paperbacks) Scholastic, Inc.
—The 12 Screams of Christmas. 2014. (Goosebumps Most Wanted Ser.). lib. bdg. 18.40 *(978-0-606-36066-1(2))* Turtleback Bks.
—The 13th Warning, 0 vols. unabr. ed. 2012. (ENG.). 76p. (J). (gr. 3-7). pap. 4.99 *(978-1-61218-330-5(1),* 9781612183305, Amazon Children's Publishing) Amazon Publishing.
—30 Tales to Give You Goosebumps. 2004. 391p. (J). *(978-0-7607-5680-5(5))* Scholastic, Inc.
Stoker, Bram. Dracula. 2009. (Foundation Classics Ser.). (Illus.). 56p. (J). (gr. 5-9). lib. bdg. 27.95 *(978-1-60754-847-8(X))* Windmill Bks.
—Dracula. Gilbert, Anne Yvonne, illus. 2010. (ENG.). 96p. (J). (gr. 7-18). 19.99 *(978-0-7636-4793-3(4),* Templar) Candlewick Pr.
—Dracula, 1 vol. Simon, Ute, illus. 2011. (Calico Illustrated Classics Ser.: No. 3). (ENG.). 112p. (J). (gr. 3-6). 27.07 *(978-1-61641-101-5(5))* Magic Wagon.
—Dracula. Bryant, Clive, ed. Johnson, Staz et al, illus. 2012. (ENG.). 144p. (gr. 6). pap. 16.95 *(978-1-906332-67-9(3),* Classical Comics, Ltd.); pap. 16.95 *(978-1-906332-68-6(1))* Classical Comics GBR. Dist: Publishers Group West (PGW).
—Dracula. Williams, Anthony, illus. 2014. (ENG.). 32p. 8.95 *(978-1-78404-355-1(9))* Arcturus Publishing GBR. Dist: Bookmasters Distribution.
—Dracula. Kliros, Thea, illus. abr. ed. 2011. (Dover Children's Thrift Classics Ser.). (ENG.). 96p. (J). (gr. 3-8). reprint ed. pap. 4.00 *(978-0-486-29567-1(2))* Dover Pubns., Inc.
—Dracula. McKowen, Scott, illus. 2010. (Sterling Unabridged Classics Ser.). (ENG.). 416p. (J). (gr. 5-18). 14.95 *(978-1-4027-7324-2(2))* Sterling Publishing Co., Inc.
—Dracula: Retold from the Bram Stoker Original. Akib, Jamel, illus. 2007. (Classic Starts(tm) Ser.). (ENG.). 160p. (J). (gr. 2-4). 6.95 *(978-1-4027-3690-2(8))* Sterling Publishing Co., Inc.
—Mummy, 1 vol. Miroglio, Brian, illus. 2007. (Graphic Horror Ser.). (ENG.). 32p. (gr. 3-7). 28.50 *(978-1-60270-061-1(3),* Graphic Planet- Fiction) ABDO Publishing Co.
Stolarz, Laurie. Return to the Dark House. 2016. (Dark House Ser.). (ENG., Illus.). 320p. (YA). (gr. 7-12). pap. 9.99 *(978-1-4231-9473-6(X))* Hyperion Bks. for Children.
Stolarz, Laurie Faria. Return to the Dark House. 2015. (Dark House Ser.). (ENG., Illus.). 364p. (YA). (gr. 7-12). 17.99 *(978-1-4231-8173-6(5))* Hyperion Bks. for Children.
—Welcome to the Dark House. 2014. (Dark House Ser.). (ENG., Illus.). 368p. (YA). (gr. 7-12). 16.99 *(978-1-4231-8172-9(7))* Hyperion Bks. for Children.
Storm, Falcon. Natalie the Not-So-Nasty: Tales from upon A. Time Series. 2013. (ENG.). 82p. pap. 9.95 *(978-1-62253-072-4(1))* Evolved Publishing.
Storrie, Paul D. Made for Each Other, 2 vols. Cowgur, Eldon, illus. 2011. (My Boyfriend Is a Monster Ser.: 2). (ENG.). 128p. (YA). (gr. 7-12). 29.27 *(978-0-7613-5601-1(0))* Lerner Publishing Group.
—#02 Made for Each Other. Cowgur, Eldon, illus. 2011. (My Boyfriend Is a Monster Ser.). 128p. (YA). pap. 56.72 *(978-0-7613-7604-0(6),* Graphic Universe™) Lerner Publishing Group.
Strand, Jeff. A Bad Day for Voodoo. 2012. (ENG.). 272p. (YA). (gr. 7-12). pap. 11.99 *(978-1-4022-6680-5(4),* 9781402266805) Sourcebooks, Inc.
Strange, Jason. Basement of the Undead, 1 vol. Parks, Phil, illus. 2011. (Jason Strange Ser.). (ENG.). 72p. (gr. 2-3). pap. 6.25 *(978-1-4342-3433-9(9));* lib. bdg. 25.32 *(978-1-4342-3234-2(4))* Stone Arch Bks.
—The Demon Card, 1 vol. Evergreen, Nelson & Kendall, Bradford, illus. 2012. (Jason Strange Ser.). (ENG.). 72p. (gr. 2-3). pap. 6.25 *(978-1-4342-3884-9(9));* lib. bdg. 25.32 *(978-1-4342-3296-0(4))* Stone Arch Bks.
—Faceless Friend, 1 vol. Parks, Phil, illus. 2011. (Jason Strange Ser.). (ENG.). 72p. (gr. 2-3). pap. 6.25 *(978-1-4342-3431-5(2));* lib. bdg. 25.32 *(978-1-4342-3232-8(8))* Stone Arch Bks.
—Full Moon Horror, 1 vol. Parks, Phil & Dal Lago, Alberto, illus. 2011. (Jason Strange Ser.). (ENG.). 72p. (gr. 2-3). pap. 6.25 *(978-1-4342-3434-6(7));* lib. bdg. 25.32 *(978-1-4342-3235-9(2))* Stone Arch Bks.
—The Graveyard Plot, 1 vol. Evergreen, Nelson & Kendall, Bradford, illus. 2012. (Jason Strange Ser.). (ENG.). 72p. (gr. 2-3). pap. 6.25 *(978-1-4342-3886-3(5))* Stone Arch Bks.
—The Mothman's Shadow, 1 vol. Parks, Phil, illus. 2011. (Jason Strange Ser.). (ENG.). 72p. (gr. 2-3). pap. 6.25 *(978-1-4342-3093-5(7))* Stone Arch Bks.
—The Mothman's Shadow, 1 vol. Soleiman, Serg & Parks, Phil, illus. 2011. (Jason Strange Ser.). (ENG.). 72p. (gr. 2-3). lib. bdg. 25.32 *(978-1-4342-2965-6(3))* Stone Arch Bks.
—Strays, 1 vol. Evergreen, Nelson & Kendall, Bradford, illus. 2012. (Jason Strange Ser.). (ENG.). 72p. (gr. 2-3). pap. 6.25 *(978-1-4342-3883-2(0));* lib. bdg. 25.32 *(978-1-4342-3295-3(6))* Stone Arch Bks.
—Text 4 Revenge, 1 vol. Parks, Phil & Dal Lago, Alberto, illus. 2011. (Jason Strange Ser.). (ENG.). 72p. (gr. 2-3). pap. 6.25 *(978-1-4342-3432-2(0));* lib. bdg. 25.32 *(978-1-4342-3233-5(6))* Stone Arch Bks.
—Zombie Winter, 1 vol. Parks, Phil, illus. 2011. (Jason Strange Ser.). (ENG.). 72p. (gr. 2-3). pap. 6.25 *(978-1-4342-3095-9(3))* Stone Arch Bks.
—Zombie Winter, 1 vol. Soleiman, Serg & Parks, Phil, illus. 2011. (Jason Strange Ser.). (ENG.). 72p. (gr. 2-3). lib. bdg. 25.32 *(978-1-4342-2964-9(5))* Stone Arch Bks.
—23 Crow's Perch, 1 vol. Evergreen, Nelson & Kendall, Bradford, illus. 2012. (Jason Strange Ser.). (ENG.). 72p. (gr. 2-3). pap. 6.25 *(978-1-4342-3885-6(7));* lib. bdg. 25.32 *(978-1-4342-3297-7(2))* Stone Arch Bks.
Strasser, Todd. Nighttime: Too Dark to See. Cushman, Doug, illus. 2008. 79p. (J). *(978-0-439-80068-6(4))* Scholastic, Inc.
—Too Dark to See. Cushman, Doug, illus. 2009. (Nighttime Ser.). (ENG.). 80p. (J). (gr. 2-5). 4.99 *(978-0-545-12476-8(X),* Scholastic Paperbacks) Scholastic, Inc.
Stratton, Steve. Plainridge. 2013. 182p. (J). pap. 12.95 *(978-1-61314-170-0(X),* Innovo Pr.) Innovo Publishing, LLC.
Stroud, Jonathan. Buried Fire. 2004. 332p. (J). pap. *(978-0-7818-5794-9(5))* Hippocrene Bks., Inc.
Stroud, Jonathan. Lockwood & Co. 2017. (Lockwood & Co Ser.). (ENG.). 480p. (J). (gr. 3-7). pap. 7.99 ***(978-1-4847-1190-3(4))*** Hyperion Bks. for Children.
Suen, Anastasia. The Scary Night: A Robot & Rico Story, 1 vol. Laughead, Mike, illus. 2009. (Robot & Rico Ser.). (ENG.). 32p. (gr. 1-2). pap. 6.25 *(978-1-4342-1752-3(3))* Stone Arch Bks.
Summers, Courtney. This Is Not a Test. 2012. (ENG.). 336p. (YA). (gr. 8). pap. 10.99 *(978-0-312-65674-4(2),* 9780312656744, St. Martin's Griffin) St. Martin's Pr.
Szpirglas, Jeff. Evil Eye. 2013. 192p. pap. *(978-0-9867914-7-5(4))* Star Crossed Pr.
Tagg, Christine. Who Will You Meet on Scary Street? Nine Pop-up Nightmares! Fuge, Charles, illus. 2004. 20p. (J). reprint ed. 15.00 *(978-0-7567-8003-6(9))* DIANE Publishing Co.
Tamura, Yumi. Book of Justice. Tamura, Yumi, illus. 2003. (Chicago Ser.: Vol. 2). (ENG., Illus.). 200p. pap. 15.95 *(978-1-56931-829-4(8))* Viz Media.
Taylor, Corey. House of Gold & Bones. Hahn, Sierra, ed. 2013. (ENG., Illus.). 104p. pap. 14.99 *(978-1-61655-287-9(5))* Dark Horse Comics.
Taylor, Drew Hayden. The Night Wanderer: A Native Gothic Novel. Wyatt, Michael, illus. 2007. (ENG.). 228p. (YA). (gr. 7-12). 21.95 *(978-1-55451-100-6(3),* 9781554511006); 5th ed. pap. 12.95 *(978-1-55451-099-3(6),* 9781554510993) Annick Pr., Ltd. CAN. Dist: Publishers Group West (PGW).
Taylor, Greg. Killer Pizza. 2011. (ENG.). 368p. (YA). (gr. 5-9). pap. 10.99 *(978-0-312-67485-4(6),* 9780312674854) Square Fish.
—Killer Pizza: the Slice. 2012. (ENG.). 368p. (YA). (gr. 5-9). pap. 10.99 *(978-1-250-00478-9(0),* 9781250004789) Square Fish.
Taylor, Sean. I Want to Be in a Scary Story. Jullien, Jean, illus. 2017. (ENG.). 32p. (J). (-k). 15.99 ***(978-0-7636-8953-7(X))*** Candlewick Pr.
Teitelbaum, Michael. The Curse of the Haunted House. 2015. (Cold Whispers Ser.). (ENG., Illus.). 32p. (J). (gr. 2-6). lib. bdg. 26.60 *(978-1-62724-806-8(4))* Bearport Publishing Co., Inc.
—The Ghastly Ghost Town. 2015. (Cold Whispers Ser.). (ENG., Illus.). 32p. (J). (gr. 2-6). lib. bdg. 26.60 *(978-1-62724-811-2(0))* Bearport Publishing Co., Inc.
—The Ghost at the Grand Inn. 2015. (Cold Whispers Ser.). (ENG., Illus.). 32p. (J). (gr. 2-6). lib. bdg. 26.60 *(978-1-62724-808-2(0))* Bearport Publishing Co., Inc.
—Night of the Gravedigger. 2015. (Cold Whispers Ser.). (ENG., Illus.). 32p. (J). (gr. 2-6). lib. bdg. 26.60 *(978-1-62724-805-1(6))* Bearport Publishing Co., Inc.
—The Phantom Pharaoh. 2015. (Cold Whispers Ser.). (ENG., Illus.). 32p. (J). (gr. 2-6). lib. bdg. 26.60 *(978-1-62724-810-5(2))* Bearport Publishing Co., Inc.
The Born Storytellers. Eye of the Tiger: A Born Storyteller Collection of Fantasy & Horror Stories. Price, Kevin, ed. 2013. (Illus.). 232p. (J). pap. *(978-0-9872559-7-6(5))* Logorythm.
Thomas, Jesse Lee. The Ghost House. Daily, Rick, illus. 2011. 30p. pap. 16.00 *(978-1-4349-8472-2(9),* RoseDog Bks.) Dorrance Publishing Co., Inc.
Thomas, Roy, text. Dracula. 2010. (ENG., Illus.). 208p. (gr. 10-17). 19.99 *(978-0-7851-4905-7(8))* Marvel Worldwide, Inc.
Thompson, Jill. Scary Godmother Comic Book Stories. 2011. (ENG., Illus.). 312p. (J). (gr. 5). pap. 24.99 *(978-1-59582-723-4(4))* Dark Horse Comics.
Thornhill, Gail. The Secret Life of Truly Jones. 2003. 196p. (J). pap. 12.99 *(978-1-58832-081-0(2))* Unlimited Publishing LLC.
Tingle, Tim & Moore, Doc. More Spooky Texas Tales. Benas, Jeanne A., illus. 2010. (ENG.). 104p. (J). (gr. 4-7). lib. bdg. 18.95 *(978-0-89672-700-7(9))* Texas Tech Univ. Pr.
Townsend, John. Hunter's Moon. 2004. (Shades Ser.). 64p. (J). pap. *(978-0-237-52647-4(6))* Evans Brothers, Ltd.
Tres Deseos Malignos. (Fear Street Ser.). (SPA.). (YA). (gr. 7-18). pap. 7.95 *(978-950-04-1891-1(6))* Emecé Editores S.A. ARG. Dist: Planeta Publishing Corp., Lectorum Pubns., Inc.
Triple-Decker, 3 vols., Set. pap. 20.00 *(978-0-9657367-4-9(1))* Less Pr.
Tsang, Evonne. I Love Him to Pieces. Görrissen, Janina, illus. 2011. (My Boyfriend Is a Monster Ser.: 1). (ENG.). 128p. (YA). (gr. 7-12). 29.27 *(978-0-7613-6004-9(2))* Lerner Publishing Group.
—#01 I Love Him to Pieces. Görrissen, Janina, illus. 2011. (My Boyfriend Is a Monster Ser.). 128p. (YA). pap. 56.72 *(978-0-7613-7602-6(X),* Graphic Universe™) Lerner Publishing Group.
Tucholke, April Genevieve. Between the Devil & the Deep Blue Sea. 2014. (ENG.). 384p. (YA). (gr. 9). pap. 9.99 *(978-0-14-242321-9(1),* Speak) Penguin Young Readers Group.
—Between the Spark & the Burn. (ENG.). (YA). (gr. 7). 2015. 352p. pap. 9.99 *(978-0-14-750939-0(4),* Speak) 2014. 336p. 17.99 *(978-0-8037-4047-1(6),* Dial Bks) Penguin Young Readers Group.
—Slasher Girls & Monster Boys. 2015. (ENG.). 400p. (YA). (gr. 7-12). 17.99 *(978-0-8037-4173-7(1),* Dial Bks) Penguin Publishing Group.
—Slasher Girls & Monster Boys. 2016. (ENG.). 400p. (YA). (gr. 7). pap. 10.99 *(978-0-14-751408-0(8),* Speak) Penguin Young Readers Group.
Tulien, Sean & Poe, Edgar Allen. The Pit & the Pendulum, 1 vol. Fabul, J. C. & Calero, Dennis, illus. 2013. (Edgar Allan Poe Graphic Novels Ser.). (ENG.). 72p. (gr. 2-3). pap. 6.10 *(978-1-4342-4260-0(9));* lib. bdg. 27.99 *(978-1-4342-4024-8(X))* Stone Arch Bks.
Turner, J. R. School's Out 4-Ever. 2009. (Extreme Hauntings Ser.). 278p. (YA). pap. 13.99 *(978-1-59080-680-7(8),* Quake) Echelon Press Publishing.
Urrea, Lourdes. Athon Labar. rev. ed. 2006. (Ediciones Castillo Castillo Del Terror Ser.). (SPA & ENG.). 136p. (J). (gr. 6-9). pap. 6.95 *(978-970-20-0309-0(1))* Castillo, Ediciones, S. A. de C. V. MEX. Dist: Macmillan.
Urrea, Lourdes, et al. En Busca de Dracu. 2005. (Ediciones Castillo Castillo Del Terror Ser.).Tr. of Looking for Dracu. (SPA.). (J). (gr. 2-6). pap. 7.95 *(978-970-20-0339-7(3))* Castillo, Ediciones, S. A. de C. V. MEX. Dist: Iaconi, Mariuccia Bk. Imports.
—Piel de Gallina. 2005. (Ediciones Castillo Castillo Del Terror Ser.).Tr. of Chicken Bumps. (SPA.). (J). (gr. 2-6). pap. 7.95 *(978-970-20-0292-5(3))* Castillo, Ediciones, S. A. de C. V. MEX. Dist: Iaconi, Mariuccia Bk. Imports.
—El Secreto Gitano. 2005. (Ediciones Castillo Castillo Del Terror Ser.).Tr. of Gypsy Secret. (SPA.). (J). (gr. 2-6). pap. 7.95 *(978-970-20-0310-6(5))* Castillo, Ediciones, S. A. de C. V. MEX. Dist: Iaconi, Mariuccia Bk. Imports.
Van Etten, Chris. Wickedpedia. 2014. (ENG.). 224p. (J). (gr. 9). pap. 9.99 *(978-0-545-41587-3(X))* Scholastic, Inc.
Van Lente, Fred, et al. Tales from the Crypt. Todd, Mort et al, illus. 2009. (Tales from the Crypt Graphic Novels Ser.: 6). (ENG.). 96p. (J). (gr. 5-12). 12.95 *(978-1-59707-137-6(4),* 9781597071376) Papercutz.
Vande Velde, Vivian. All Hallows' Eve: 13 Stories. 2010. (ENG., Illus.). 240p. (YA). (gr. 7). pap. 8.99 *(978-0-15-206473-0(7))* Houghton Mifflin Harcourt Publishing Co.
—Being Dead. 2003. (ENG.). 224p. (YA). (gr. 7-12). pap. 8.99 *(978-0-15-204912-6(6))* Houghton Mifflin Harcourt Publishing Co.
Vanhee, Jason. Engines of the Broken World. 2013. (ENG.). 272p. (YA). (gr. 7). 16.99 *(978-0-8050-9629-3(9),* 9780805096293, Holt, Henry & Co. Bks. For Young Readers) Holt, Henry & Co.
—Engines of the Broken World. 2014. (ENG.). 288p. (YA). (gr. 7). pap. 9.99 *(978-1-250-05082-3(0),* 9781250050823) Square Fish.
Vanholme, Virginie. Malevolence & Mandrake. 2nd ed. 2009. (Scared to Death Ser.: 2). (ENG., Illus.). 48p. (gr. 3-17). pap. 11.95 *(978-1-905460-77-9(5))* CineBook GBR. Dist: National Bk. Network.
Vargo, Tim. Unbound: A Tale of Temptation & Terror. 2003. 242p. pap. 12.95 *(978-1-930008-04-5(X))* Willowgate Pr.
Varley, Dax. The Crow. Proctor, Jon, illus. 2016. (ENG.). 48p. (J). lib. bdg. *(978-1-62402-160-2(3))* Magic Wagon.
—Graveyard Dirt. Proctor, Jon, illus. 2016. (ENG.). 48p. (J). lib. bdg. *(978-1-62402-158-9(1))* Magic Wagon.
—Hideout. Proctor, Jon, illus. 2016. (ENG.). 48p. (J). lib. bdg. 28.50 *(978-1-62402-157-2(3))* Magic Wagon.
—The Locket. Proctor, Jon, illus. 2016. (ENG.). 48p. (J). lib. bdg. *(978-1-62402-159-6(X))* Magic Wagon.
Vaughn, Carrie. Swords V Cthulhu. Bullington, Jesse & Tanzer, Molly, eds. 2016. (ENG., Illus.). 368p. pap. 13.99 *(978-1-908983-09-1(4))* Stone Skin Pr. GBR. Dist: Independent Pubs. Group.
Vaught, Susan. Insanity. 2014. (ENG.). 384p. (YA). (gr. 9). 17.99 *(978-1-59990-784-0(4),* 9781599907840, Bloomsbury USA Childrens) Bloomsbury Publishing USA.
Vega, Danielle. The Merciless. 2014. (Merciless Ser.: 1). (ENG.). 288p. (YA). (gr. 9). 17.99 *(978-1-59514-722-6(5),* Razorbill) Penguin Young Readers Group.
—The Merciless II: The Exorcism of Sofia Flores. 2016. (Merciless Ser.: 2). (ENG.). 320p. (YA). (gr. 9). 17.99 *(978-1-59514-726-4(8),* Razorbill) Penguin Young Readers Group.
Vega, Danielle & Loftin, Nikki. The Merciless. 2015. (Merciless Ser.: 1). (ENG.). 304p. (YA). (gr. 9). pap. 10.99 *(978-1-59514-723-3(3),* Razorbill) Penguin Young Readers Group.
—Survive the Night. 2015. (DUT & ENG.). 272p. (YA). (gr. 9). 17.99 *(978-1-59514-724-0(1),* Razorbill) Penguin Young Readers Group.
Verano, M. Diary of a Haunting. (Diary of a Haunting Ser.). (ENG., Illus.). (YA). (gr. 9). 2016. 336p. pap. 10.99 *(978-1-4814-3068-5(8))* 2015. 320p. 17.99 *(978-1-4814-3069-2(6))* Simon Pulse. (Simon Pulse).
Verstraete, Majanka. Fright Train: Weirdville. l.t. ed. 2013. 3. (ENG.). 88p. (gr. 2-6). pap. 9.95 *(978-1-62253-069-4(1))* Evolved Publishing.
—House of Horrors: Weirdville. l.t. ed. 2013. 2. (ENG.). 90p. (gr. 2-6). pap. 9.95 *(978-1-62253-067-0(5))* Evolved Publishing.
Vincent, Bruno. School for Villains, 1. 2013. (Tumblewater Ser.). (ENG., Illus.). 314p. (J). (gr. 4-7). pap. 8.99 *(978-0-330-47953-0(9))* Pan Macmillan GBR. Dist: Independent Pubs. Group.
Vita. Head in the Clouds. 2004. (Illus.). 108p. pap. 44.50 *(978-0-9760062-0-6(0))* Magic Woman Pubns.
Walker, Chris, creator. Collision Course Goad by Zombienose. 2005. (Illus.). 60p. (YA). 13.95 *(978-0-9768670-0-5(1))* Icecat Bks.
Walker, Landry. Little Gloomy Super Scary Monster Show Volume 1. 2008. (ENG., Illus.). 104p. pap. 9.95 *(978-1-59362-103-2(5),* 9781593621032) Slave Labor Bks.
Wallace, Barbara Brooks. Peppermints in the Parlor. unabr. ed. 2004. (Illus.). 208p. (J). (gr. 3-7). pap. 36.00 incl. audio *(978-0-8072-8785-9(7),* YA267SP, Listening Library) Random Hse. Audio Publishing Group.
—Peppermints in the Parlor. 2005. (ENG.). 208p. (J). (gr. 3-7). pap. 7.99 *(978-0-689-87417-8(0),* Aladdin) Simon & Schuster Children's Publishing.
Wallace, Kali. Shallow Graves. (YA). (gr. 9). 2017. 384p. pap. 9.99 ***(978-0-06-236621-4(1))*** 2016. 368p. 17.99 *(978-0-06-236620-7(3))* HarperCollins Pubs. (Tegen, Katherine Bks).
Wallace, Rich. A Deadly Fall. Volpari, Daniela, illus. 2016. 48p. (J). *(978-1-62402-147-3(6))* Magic Wagon.
—The Room of Woe: An Up2U Horror Adventure, 1 vol. Emroca Flores, Jose, illus. 2015. (ENG.). 80p. (J). *(978-1-62402-094-0(1))* Magic Wagon.

Walters, Eric. Visions. 2011. (ENG.). 208p. (J). pap. (978-1-55455-122-4(6)) Fitzhenry & Whiteside, Ltd.

Warnasuriya, Chandrani. Spooky Tales from the Orient: Tales of Ogres, Demons, Ghosts, Spells, Charms & the Enchanted, 1 vol. 2009. 167p. pap. 24.95 (978-1-61546-978-9(8)) America Star Bks.

Washburn, Berk, et al. Fatal Green. 2016. (Dimensions in Death Ser.: 3). (ENG.). 292p. (YA). (gr. 7). pap. 17.99 (978-1-63163-034-7(2), Jolly Fish Pr.) North Star Editions.

Watson, Stephanie. The Club. 2010. (Night Fall Ser.). (ENG.). 112p. (YA). (gr. 6-12). 27.93 (978-0-7613-6147-3(2)); pap. 7.95 (978-0-7613-6162-6(6)) Lerner Publishing Group.

—Messages from Beyond. 2010. (Night Fall Ser.). (ENG.). 112p. (YA). (gr. 6-12). 27.93 (978-0-7613-6146-6(4)); pap. 7.95 (978-0-7613-6160-2(X)) Lerner Publishing Group.

Watts, Julia. Kindred Spirits. 2008. (ENG.). 147p. (gr. 3-18). pap. 8.95 (978-0-9667359-9-4(4)) Harren Communications, LLC.

Webb, Margot & Chorpash, Marci. My Grandmommy Is Shrinking. 2003. 60p. pap. 8.95 (978-0-595-29143-4(0)) iUniverse, Inc.

Weird & Spooky Tales. Date not set. (Illus.). 192p. (J). (gr. 3-8). pap. 13.95 (978-0-87460-391-0(9)) Lion Bks.

Wendling, Peter. The Magic of the Dark Ravine. Durie, Sally, illus. 2011. 36p. pap. 13.95 (978-1-60976-933-8(3), Eloquent Bks.) Strategic Book Publishing & Rights Agency (SBPRA).

West, Carly Anne. The Bargaining. 2015. (ENG., Illus.). 416p. (YA). (gr. 9). 17.99 (978-1-4424-4182-8(8), Simon Pulse) Simon Pulse.

West, Tracey. Plant Your Path. 2013. (Plants vs. Zombies Ser.). (ENG.). 144p. (J). (gr. 1-5). pap. 5.99 (978-0-06-229494-4(6), HarperFestival) HarperCollins Pubs.

Weyn, Suzanne. The Cursed Scarab. 2015. (Hauntings: the Haunted Museum Ser.: 4). lib. bdg. 17.20 (978-0-606-37076-9(5)) Turtleback Bks.

—Dr. Frankenstein's Daughters. 2013. (ENG.). 256p. (J). (gr. 7). 17.99 (978-0-545-42533-9(6), Scholastic Pr.) Scholastic, Inc.

—The Pearl Earring. 2014. (Hauntings: the Haunted Museum Ser.: 3). lib. bdg. 17.20 (978-0-606-36326-6(2)) Turtleback Bks.

White, Aaron D. Creek Babies. 2013. 44p. pap. 16.95 (978-1-63000-671-6(8)) America Star Bks.

Whitehouse, Howard. Zombie Elementary: The Real Story. 2017. (ENG.). 256p. (J). (gr. 4-7). pap. 7.99 (978-1-77049-609-5(2), Tundra Bks.) Tundra Bks. CAN. Dist: Penguin Random Hse. LLC.

Whiting, Jim. Really Scary Stuff, 4 vols., Set. Incl. Scary Ghosts. lib. bdg. 25.32 (978-1-4296-3967-5(9)); Scary Monsters. lib. bdg. 25.32 (978-1-4296-3968-2(7)); Scary Places. lib. bdg. 25.32 (978-1-4296-3970-5(9)); (gr. 1-2). (Really Scary Stuff Ser.). (ENG.). 24p. 2010. Set lib. bdg. 75.96 (978-1-4296-4417-4(6), First Facts) Capstone Press of Coughlan Cos.

Wignall, K. J. Alchemy. Book Two of the Mercian Trilogy: Alchemy. 2012. (ENG.). 336p. (J). (gr. 7). 17.99 (978-1-60684-265-2(X), Carolrhoda Lab™) Lerner Publishing Group.

—Blood: Book One of the Mercian Trilogy. 2012. (ENG.). 272p. (J). (gr. 7). pap. 9.99 (978-1-60684-387-1(7), Carolrhoda Lab™) Lerner Publishing Group.

Will You Be My Friend? 2015. (You're Invited to a Creepover Ser.: 20). (ENG., Illus.). 160p. (J). (gr. 3-7). pap. 6.99 (978-1-4424-9731-3(9), Simon Spotlight) Simon Spotlight.

Winters, Cat. In the Shadow of Blackbirds. 2014. (ENG., Illus.). 416p. (YA). (gr. 7-17). pap. 8.95 (978-1-4197-1023-0(0), Amulet Bks.) Abrams, Inc.

Wood, Dick. Boris Karloff Tales of Mystery Archives Volume 5. 2011. (ENG., Illus.). 232p. 49.99 (978-1-59582-615-2(7)) Dark Horse Comics.

Wright, Terry. The One-Eyed Monster. 2006. 48p. pap. 16.95 (978-1-4241-3696-4(2)) PublishAmerica, Inc.

Xu, Lei. Cavern of the Blood Zombies. Mok, Kathy, tr. 2011. (Graver Robbers' Chronicles Ser.). (ENG.). 240p. pap. 9.95 (978-1-934159-31-6(X)) ThingsAsian Pr.

Yambar, Chris, ed. Edison's Frankenstein 1910. Bihun, Robb, illus. 2003. (YA). mass mkt. 7.95 (978-1-929515-27-1(8)) Comic Library International.

Yancey, Rick. The Curse of the Wendigo. 2011. (Monstrumologist Ser.: 2). (ENG.). 464p. (YA). (gr. 9). pap. 12.99 (978-1-4169-8451-1(8), Simon & Schuster Bks. For Young Readers) Simon & Schuster Bks. For Young Readers.

—The Final Descent. 2013. (Monstrumologist Ser.: 4). (ENG., Illus.). 320p. (YA). (gr. 9). 18.99 (978-1-4424-5153-7(X), Simon & Schuster Bks. For Young Readers) Simon & Schuster Bks. For Young Readers.

—The Isle of Blood. (Monstrumologist Ser.: 3). (ENG.). 560p. (YA). (gr. 9). 2012. pap. 12.99 (978-1-4169-8453-5(4)) 2011. (Illus.). 18.99 (978-1-4169-8452-8(6)) Simon & Schuster Bks. For Young Readers. (Simon & Schuster Bks. For Young Readers).

—The Monstrumologist Collection: Monstrumologist; Curse of the Wendigo; Isle of Blood; Final Descent. 2014. (Monstrumologist Ser.). (ENG., Illus.). 1808p. (YA). (gr. 9). pap. 46.99 (978-1-4814-3012-8(2), Simon & Schuster Bks. For Young Readers) Simon & Schuster Bks. For Young Readers.

Yeager, Graham. Diablo: The Third Millersburg Novel. 2006. 145p. (YA). per. 7.99 (978-0-9765478-4-6(8)) Stone Acres Publishing Co.

—Stone Hedge: The Fourth Millersburg Novel. 2006. 142p. (YA). per. 7.99 (978-0-9765478-6-0(4)) Stone Acres Publishing Co.

Young, J. E. Horror in Space. Huddleston, Courtney, illus. 2011. (Twisted Journeys (r) Ser.: 18). (ENG.). 112p. (J). (gr. 4-7). pap. 7.95 (978-0-8225-9273-0(8), Graphic Universe™) Lerner Publishing Group.

Young, Timothy. They're Coming!, 1 vol. 2012. (ENG., Illus.). 32p. (J). 16.99 (978-0-7643-4225-7(8), 9780764342257) Schiffer Publishing, Ltd.

You're Invited to a Creepover. 2013. (You're Invited to a Creepover Ser.: 6). (J). (gr. 3-6). lib. bdg. 145.26 (978-1-61479-060-0(4)) ABDO Publishing Co.

Zafón, Carlos Ruiz. The Watcher in the Shadows. (ENG.). (YA). (gr. 7-17). 2014. 288p. pap. 10.99 (978-0-316-04475-2(X)) 2013. 272p. 18.00 (978-0-316-04476-9(8)) Little, Brown Bks. for Young Readers.

Zander, R. W. When the Zombies Come Marchin' Home. 2003. 158p. (J). (978-0-439-39868-8(1)) Scholastic, Inc.

Zornow, Jeff. Werewolf, 1 vol. Zornow, Jeff, illus. 2007. (Graphic Horror Ser.). (ENG., Illus.). 32p. (gr. 3-7). 28.50 (978-1-60270-062-8(1), Graphic Planet- Fiction) ABDO Publishing Co.

HORSE

see Horses

HORSE RACING

Broyles, Janell. Barrel Racing. (World of Rodeo Ser.). 48p. 2009. (gr. 6-6). 53.00 (978-1-60854-300-7(5), Rosen Reference) 2006. (Illus.). (YA). (gr. 4-7). lib. bdg. 29.25 (978-1-4042-0543-7(8)) Rosen Publishing Group, Inc., The.

Buckley, James. Who Was Seabiscuit? Copeland, Gregory, illus. 2015. 105p. (J). (978-1-4844-6962-0(3), Grosset & Dunlap) Penguin Publishing Group.

—Who Was Seabiscuit? 2015. (Who Was... ? Ser.). lib. bdg. 16.00 (978-0-606-37557-3(0)) Turtleback Bks.

Buckley, James, et al. Who Was Seabiscuit? Copeland, Gregory, illus. 2015. (Who Was? Ser.). (ENG.). 112p. (J). (gr. 3-7). 5.99 (978-0-448-48309-2(2), Grosset & Dunlap) Penguin Young Readers Group.

Curry, Marion. Horse & Pony Competitions. 2006. (Horses & Ponies Ser.). (Illus.). 32p. (gr. 2-6). lib. bdg. 23.00 (978-0-8368-6834-0(X), Gareth Stevens Learning Library) Stevens, Gareth Publishing LLLP.

Fishman, Jon M. American Pharoah. 2016. (Amazing Athletes Ser.). (ENG., Illus.). 32p. (J). (gr. 2-5). 7.99 (978-1-5124-0877-5(8)); 26.65 (978-1-5124-0829-4(8)); 39.99 (978-1-5124-0831-7(X)); 39.99 (978-1-5124-0876-8(X)) Lerner Publishing Group. (Lerner Pubns.).

Green, John. Great Racehorses. 2006. (Dover Nature Coloring Book Ser.). (ENG., Illus.). 32p. (J). (gr. 3-5). pap. 3.99 (978-0-486-45162-6(3)) Dover Pubns., Inc.

Hamilton, S. L. Kentucky Derby. 2013. (Xtreme Races Ser.). 32p. (J). (gr. 3-9). lib. bdg. 27.07 (978-1-61783-695-4(8), Abdo & Daughters) ABDO Publishing Co.

Hubbard, Crystal. The Last Black King of the Kentucky Derby: The Story of Jimmy Winkfield. McGuire, Robert, illus. 2008. (ENG.). 40p. (J). (gr. 1-6). 17.95 (978-1-58430-274-2(7)) Lee & Low Bks., Inc.

Hubbard, Crystal & McGuire, Robert. The Last Black King of the Kentucky Derby. 2005. (ENG., Illus.). 40p. (J). pap. 11.95 (978-1-60060-891-9(4)) Lee & Low Bks., Inc.

Martin, Martha. Steeplechase. 2009. (ENG., Illus.). 32p. (J). (gr. 3-6). lib. bdg. (978-0-7787-4981-3(9)); (gr. 4-5). pap. (978-0-7787-4997-4(5)) Crabtree Publishing Co.

McCarthy, Meghan. Seabiscuit: The Wonder Horse. McCarthy, Meghan, illus. 2008. (ENG., Illus.). 40p. (J). (gr. -1-3). 16.99 (978-1-4169-3360-1(3), Simon & Schuster/Paula Wiseman Bks.) Simon & Schuster/Paula Wiseman Bks.

Scanlan, Lawrence. The Big Red Horse: The Story of Secretariat & the Loyal Groom Who Loved Him. 2010. 176p. (J). (gr. 4-7). pap. 7.99 (978-0-06-202669-9(0)); (ENG., Illus.). pap. 9.99 (978-0-00-639352-8(7)) HarperCollins Pubs.

Shea, Therese. Racing Horses. 2011. (Horsing Around Ser.). (Illus.). 24p. (J). (gr. 2-5). pap. 8.15 (978-1-4339-4636-3(X), Gareth Stevens Learning Library); lib. bdg. 22.60 (978-1-4339-4635-6(1)) Stevens, Gareth Publishing LLLP.

Spoilyourhorse Com Staff. SpoilYourHorse. com Horse Bits: A Study Guide for Beginning Rider & Instructor. 2003. 142p. (YA). pap. 14.95 (978-0-595-27996-8(1)) iUniverse, Inc.

Turnbull, Stephanie. Racehorses. 2015. (My Favorite Horses Ser.). 24p. (gr. 2-5). 28.50 (978-1-62588-182-3(7)) Black Rabbit Bks.

—Racehorses. 2015. (ENG., Illus.). 24p. (J). pap. 8.95 (978-1-77092-228-0(8)) RiverStream Publishing.

Valentine, Billy, compiled by & comment. Dear Smarty: A Collection of Letters Written to Smarty Jones by Children, Families & Other Animals from Across America. Valentine, Billy, comment. 2nd ed. 2005. 152p. (YA). pap. 19.95 (978-0-9763935-0-4(6), 1214) Braveheart Pr., LLC.

Young, Rae. Drawing Barrel Racers & Other Speedy Horses, 1 vol. Q2AMedia Services Private Ltd, Q2AMedia Services, illus. 2014. (Drawing Horses Ser.). (ENG.). 32p. (gr. 3-4). lib. bdg. 27.99 (978-1-4765-3994-2(4), Snap Bks.) Capstone Press of Coughlan Cos.

HORSE RACING—FICTION

Alltheway bay. 2004. (YA). per. 7.95 (978-0-9749320-0-2(0)) Bay Horse Creations LLC.

Archer, Colleen Rutherford. Galloping Goldrush: The Journey Begins. Stafford, Susan, ed. 2005. (J). per. 11.95 (978-0-9740841-5-2(8)) K&B Products.

Bagnold, Enid. National Velvet. 2013. (ENG.). 320p. (J). (gr. 3-12). pap. 7.99 (978-0-486-49297-1(4)) Dover Pubns., Inc.

Bates, Michelle. Racing Vacation. 2017. (Sandy Lane Stables Ser.). (ENG.). 128p. (YA). pap. 5.99 **(978-0-7945-3914-6(9)**, Usborne) EDC Publishing.

Bradley, Lisa. Abby Wize: Awa. 2010. 304p. 29.99 (978-1-4520-2491-2(X)); pap. 19.99 (978-1-4520-2490-5(1)) AuthorHouse.

Brown, Jeff. The Midnight Ride of Flat Revere. Pamintuan, Macky, illus. 2016. (Flat Stanley's Worldwide Adventures Ser.: 13). (ENG.). 112p. (J). (gr. 1-5). 14.75 (978-0-606-39266-2(1)) Turtleback Bks.

Chandler, Ann. Siena Summer, 1 vol. 2009. (ENG., Illus.). 142p. (YA). (gr. 6-9). pap. 12.95 (978-1-896580-17-3(3)) Tradewind Bks. CAN. Dist: Orca Bk. Pubs. USA.

Chellis, Marie. The Hayburner, 1 vol. 2010. 60p. pap. 19.95 (978-1-4512-9053-0(5)) America Star Bks.

Clarke, Nancy & Muire, Penny. Stormy Hill's Challenge. 2013. 248p. 26.00 (978-1-62212-803-7(6), Strategic Bk. Publishing) Strategic Book Publishing & Rights Agency (SBPRA).

Dawson, JoAnn. Willie to the Rescue. 2006. 264p. 15.95 (978-0-9746561-0-6(0)); pap. 8.95 (978-0-9746561-2-0(7)) FT Richards Publishing.

Dorling Kindersley Publishing Staff. Let's Go Riding! 2013. (DK Reader Level 2 Ser.). lib. bdg. 13.55 (978-0-606-31477-0(6), Turtleback) Turtleback Bks.

Dorsey, Angela. Summer of Desperate Races. 2013. 126p. pap. (978-1-927100-28-8(3)) Enchanted Pony Bks.

Gregg, Stacy. The Girl Who Rode the Wind. 2016. (ENG.). 336p. (J). (gr. 4). 6.99 (978-0-00-818923-5(4), HarperCollins Children's Bks.) HarperCollins Pubs. Ltd. GBR. Dist: HarperCollins Pubs.

Hambleton, Anne. Raja: Story of a Racehorse. Peggykauffman.com Staff & Kauffman, Margaret, illus. 2011. (ENG.). 272p. (J). (gr. 4-7). pap. 12.95 (978-0-615-54029-0(5)) Old Bow Publishing.

Hart, Alison. Gabriel's Horses, 1 vol. 2007. (Racing to Freedom Trilogy). (ENG.). 160p. (J). (gr. 3-7). 14.95 (978-1-56145-398-6(6)) Peachtree Pubs.

—Gabriel's Triumph, 1 vol. 2007. (Racing to Freedom Trilogy). (ENG.). 160p. (J). (gr. 3-7). 14.95 (978-1-56145-410-5(9)) Peachtree Pubs.

Hector, Rachel. Re-Ride. 2003. 149p. (YA). pap. 11.95 (978-0-595-26707-1(6), Writers Club Pr.) iUniverse, Inc.

Helidoniotis, Kathy. Horse Mad Heroes. 2007. 272p. (J). (978-0-7322-8423-7(6)) HarperCollins Pubs. Australia.

Henry, Marguerite. Gaudenzia, Pride of the Palio. Ward, Lynd, illus. 2014. (ENG.). 304p. (J). (gr. 3-7). pap. 5.99 (978-1-4814-0397-9(4), Aladdin) Simon & Schuster Children's Publishing.

Huttoe, Norma. Rusty - the Kissing Horse. 2008. 28p. pap. 12.49 (978-1-4389-0227-2(1)) AuthorHouse.

James, Will. The Dark Horse. 2003. (Illus.). 288p. 35.00 (978-0-87842-484-9(9), 818) Mountain Pr. Publishing Co., Inc.

—The Dark Horse, Vol. 1. James, Will, illus. rev. ed. (Illus.). 288p. (J). (gr. 4). pap. (978-0-87842-486-3(5), 817) Mountain Pr. Publishing Co., Inc.

Jarmes, Jon Jeffery. Jason Post: Magic at the Downs. 2006. (YA). 19.95 (978-0-9770483-0-4(6)) Speech Publishing Hse.

Kelly, Lynda. The Most Horrible Pony! 2013. 202p. pap. (978-1-903053-36-2(6)) Kelly Pubns.

Kelso, Mary Jean. Cowboy James. Snider, K. C., illus. 2011. 24p. pap. 10.95 (978-1-61633-174-0(7)); 19.95 (978-1-61633-178-8(X)) Guardian Angel Publishing, Inc.

Lambert, Joyce. Slick 'n Slide. Metzger, Jan, illus. 2008. 36p. 9.95 (978-0-9801146-0-7(8)) Lamweg Publishing.

Lawrence, D. H. The Rocking-Horse Winner. 2010. (Illus.). 40p. (J). 19.95 (978-1-58341-924-3(1), Creative Education) Creative Co., The.

Long, Loren & Bildner, Phil. Horsin' Around. Long, Loren, illus. 2009. (Sluggers Ser.: 2). (ENG., Illus.). 224p. (J). (gr. 3-7). pap. 8.99 (978-1-4169-1888-2(4), Simon & Schuster Bks. For Young Readers) Simon & Schuster Bks. For Young Readers.

Lyon, Jane & Bailey, Karen. Primerica: A Home for the Brave. 2011. (ENG., Illus.). 40p. (J). (gr. k-5). 16.95 (978-1-58150-341-8(5), Eclipse Pr.) Blood-Horse, Inc., The.

Marsh, Carole. The Mystery at the Kentucky Derby. 2009. (Real Kids, Real Places Ser.). (Illus.). 146p. (J). lib. bdg. 18.99 (978-0-635-07002-9(2), Marsh, Carole Mysteries) Gallopade International.

McCall Smith, Alexander. Harriet Bean & the League of Cheats. 2006. (Harriet Bean Ser.: 2). (J). 106.75 (978-1-4281-0376-4(7)) Recorded Bks., Inc.

Meadows, Daisy. Helena the Horse-Riding Fairy. 2010. (Sports Fairies Ser.: 1). (ENG.). 80p. (J). (gr. 2-5). 4.99 (978-0-545-20252-7(3), Scholastic Paperbacks) Scholastic, Inc.

Neri, Greg. Grand Theft Horse: A Graphic Novel. Wilkin, Corban, illus. 2016. (YA). (978-1-4677-9463-3(5), Graphic Universe™) Lerner Publishing Group.

Platt, Chris. Willow King, 1 vol. 2010. (ENG.). 192p. (J). (gr. 3-7). pap. 6.95 (978-1-56145-549-2(0)) Peachtree Pubs.

Sargent, Dave & Sargent, Pat. Brandy: (Blue Roan) Beauty Is Inside, 30 vols., Vol. 5. Lenoir, Jane, illus. 2003. (Saddle up Ser.: Vol. 5). 42p. (J). lib. bdg. 23.60 (978-1-56763-799-1(X)); mass mkt. 10.95 (978-1-56763-800-4(7)) Ozark Publishing.

Sewell, Anna. Black Beauty. l.t. ed. 2010. (ENG.). 260p. pap. 22.95 (978-1-4104-2390-0(5), Kennebec Large Print) Cengage Gale.

Shaw, J. M. Molly's Stallion. 2010. (J). pap. (978-0-88092-769-7(0)) Royal Fireworks Publishing Co.

Snelling, Lauraine. Golden Filly, No. 1. 2009. (ENG.). 624p. (J). pap. 16.00 (978-0-7642-0737-2(7)) Bethany Hse. Pubs.

—Golden Filly Collection 2. 2009. (ENG.). 624p. (J). pap. 16.00 (978-0-7642-0738-9(5)) Bethany Hse. Pubs.

Song, Amira. Horse Lovers Forever. 2012. 64p. pap. (978-1-4602-0144-2(2)) FriesenPress.

St. John, Lauren. Kentucky Thriller. Dean, David, illus. 2014. (Jóvenes Lectores. Los Misterios de Laura Ser.). (SPA.). 248p. (J). (gr. 4-7). pap. 8.95 (978-84-8343-271-6(4), Bambu, Editorial) Combel Editorial, S.A. ESP. Dist: Independent Pubs. Group.

Stevenson, James. Runaway Horse! Date not set. (J). 15.99 (978-0-06-051978-0(9)); 16.89 (978-0-06-051979-7(7)) HarperCollins Pubs.

Stiefvater, Maggie. The Scorpio Races. 2013. lib. bdg. 22.10 (978-0-606-31501-2(2), Turtleback) Turtleback Bks.

Timmons, Robbie. Twoey & the Goat. 2008. (ENG., Illus.). 192p. (J). (gr. 1-7). 15.95 (978-1-58726-517-4(6), Mitten Pr.) Ann Arbor Editions LLC.

Volponi, Paul. Homestretch. 2009. (ENG.). 160p. (YA). (gr. 7-18). 16.99 (978-1-4169-3987-0(3), Atheneum Bks. for Young Readers) Simon & Schuster Children's Publishing.

HORSEBREAKING

see Horses—Training

HORSEMANSHIP

see also Rodeos

Akyroyd, Clarissa. Native American Horsemanship. Johnson, Troy, ed. 2013. (Native American Life Ser.: 15). 64p. (J). (gr. 5-18). 19.95 (978-1-4222-2971-2(8)) Mason Crest.

Bailey, Diane. Horseback Riding, Vol. 10. 2016. (Great Outdoors! Ser.: Vol. 10). (ENG., Illus.). 48p. (J). (gr. 5-8). 20.95 (978-1-4222-3570-6(X)) Mason Crest.

Barth, Katrin & Sieber, Antonia. Learning Horseback Riding. 2005. (Learning ... Training ... Ser.). (Illus.). 136p. pap. 14.95 (978-1-84126-153-9(X)) Meyer & Meyer Sport, Ltd. GBR. Dist: Cardinal Pubs. Group.

—Training Horseback Riding. 2005. (Learning ... Training ... Ser.). (Illus.). 152p. pap. 14.95 (978-1-84126-156-0(4)) Meyer & Meyer Sport, Ltd. GBR. Dist: Cardinal Pubs. Group.

Behrens, Janice. Let's Talk Swimming. 2008. (Scholastic News Nonfiction Readers Ser.). (ENG.). 24p. (J). pap. 6.95 (978-0-531-20425-2(1)) Scholastic Library Publishing.

Blackledge, Annabel. Let's Go Riding, Level 2. 2005. (DK Readers Ser.). (ENG., Illus.). 32p. (J). (gr. 1-3). pap. 3.99 (978-0-7566-1694-6(8), DK Children) Dorling Kindersley Publishing, Inc.

Bodden, Valerie. Horsing Around: Riding Horses. 2014. (Horsing Around Ser.). (ENG.). 24p. (J). (gr. 1-3). pap. 7.99 (978-0-89812-834-5(X), Creative Paperbacks) Creative Co., The.

—Horsing Around: Showing Horses. 2014. (Horsing Around Ser.). (ENG.). 24p. (J). (gr. 1-3). pap. 7.99 (978-0-89812-835-2(8), Creative Paperbacks) Creative Co., The.

—Horsing Around: Training Horses. 2014. (Horsing Around Ser.). (ENG.). 24p. (J). (gr. 1-3). pap. 7.99 (978-0-89812-836-9(6), Creative Paperbacks) Creative Co., The.

—Showing Horses. 2013. (Illus.). 24p. (J). 25.65 (978-1-60818-472-9(2), Creative Education) Creative Co., The.

Bratton, Donna Bowman. Saddle Up! Riding & Competitions for Horse Lovers, 1 vol. 2014. (Crazy about Horses Ser.). (ENG., Illus.). 32p. (gr. 3-4). 27.99 (978-1-4914-0711-0(5), Snap Bks.) Capstone Press of Coughlan Cos.

Calder, Kate. L'Équitation. 2009. (Sans Limites Ser.). (FRE., Illus.). 32p. (J). pap. 9.95 (978-2-89579-232-1(1)) Bayard Canada Livres CAN. Dist: Crabtree Publishing Co.

Dancer, Audrey & Behrens, Janice. Let's Talk Riding. 2008. (ENG., Illus.). 24p. (J). 22.00 (978-0-531-13826-7(7), Children's Pr.) Scholastic Library Publishing.

Dickins, Rosie & Pratt, Leonie. Horse & Pony Treasury. Sims, Lesley, ed. Young, Norman & Ablett, Barry, illus. 2006. (Horse & Pony Treasury Ser.). 93p. (J). 19.99 (978-0-7945-1431-0(6), Usborne) EDC Publishing.

Doucet, Alexandra. Going to a Horse Show: Equestrian Showing. 2009. 28p. pap. 14.68 (978-1-4490-4870-9(6)) AuthorHouse.

Dowdy, Penny. Cross Country & Endurance. 2009. (Horsing Around Ser.). (ENG.). 32p. (J). (gr. 4-5). pap. (978-0-7787-4996-7(7)); (Illus.). (gr. 3-6). lib. bdg. (978-0-7787-4980-6(0)) Crabtree Publishing Co.

—Dressage. 2009. (ENG., Illus.). 32p. (J). (gr. 3-6). lib. bdg. (978-0-7787-4978-3(9)); (gr. 4-5). pap. (978-0-7787-4994-3(0)) Crabtree Publishing Co.

Draper, Allison Stark. Trail Riding: Have Fun, Be Smart. 2005. (Explore the Outdoors Ser.). (Illus.). 64p. (YA). (gr. 7-12). lib. bdg. 31.95 (978-0-8239-3170-5(6), EOTRRI) Rosen Publishing Group, Inc., The.

Draper, Judith. My First Horse & Pony Show & Games. 2007. (J). (978-0-7534-6038-2(6), Kingfisher) Roaring Brook Pr.

Draper, Judith & Roberts, Matthew. My First Horse & Pony Book: From Breeds & Bridles to Jophpurs & Jumping. 2005. (My First Horse & Pony Ser.). (ENG., Illus.). 48p. (J). (gr. k-3). 11.99 (978-0-7534-5878-5(0), 9780753458785, Kingfisher) Roaring Brook Pr.

Edom, H. & Sims, L. Starting Riding. rev. ed. 2004. (First Skills Ser.). (Illus.). 32p. (J). (ENG.). pap. 4.99 (978-0-7945-0441-0(8)); lthr. 12.99 (978-1-58086-544-9(5)) EDC Publishing.

Gaydon, S. Activators Riding. (Illus.). 128p. pap. 8.99 (978-0-340-71517-8(0)) Hodder & Stoughton GBR. Dist: Trafalgar Square Publishing.

Gray, Susan H. Horse Shows. 2013. 48p. (J). (gr. 4-8). 29.93 (978-1-60870-838-3(1)); pap. 12.93 (978-1-62712-088-3(2)) Cavendish Square Publishing.

Harvey, G. & Dickens, R. Little Book of Riding & Pony Care. rev. ed. 2004. (Complete Book of Riding & Pony Care Ser.). (ENG., Illus.). 144p. (J). 7.95 (978-0-7945-0611-7(9)) EDC Publishing.

—Riding & Pony Care. 2004. (Complete Book of Riding & Pony Care Ser.). (Illus.). (J). (gr. 3-18). (ENG.). 1p. pap. 15.95 (978-0-7945-0181-5(8), Usborne); 144p. lib. bdg. 23.95 (978-1-58086-422-0(8)) EDC Publishing.

Humphrys-Dunne, Deanie. Tails of Sweetbrier. Humphrys-Bajaj, Holly, illus. 2013. 82p. pap. 9.95 (978-1-61286-182-1(2)) Avid Readers Publishing Group.

Jeffrey, Laura S. Choosing a Horse: How to Choose & Care for a Horse. 2013. (American Humane Association Pet Care Ser.). 48p. (J). (gr. 3-18). lib. bdg. 25.27 (978-0-7660-4083-0(6)); pap. 8.95 (978-1-4644-0218-0(3), Enslow Elementary) Enslow Pubs., Inc.

—Horses: How to Choose & Care for a Horse. 2004. (American Humane Pet Care Library). (Illus.). 48p. (J). lib. bdg. 25.27 (978-0-7660-2519-6(5)) Enslow Pubs., Inc.

Johnson, Robin. Show Jumping. 2009. (ENG., Illus.). 32p. (J). (gr. 3-6). lib. bdg. (978-0-7787-4979-0(7)); (gr. 4-5). pap. (978-0-7787-4995-0(9)) Crabtree Publishing Co.

Jones, Viola & Draper, Allison Stark. Trail Riding, 01 vols., 1. 2016. (Outdoor Life Ser.). (ENG., Illus.). 64p. (J). 32.95 (978-1-4994-6239-5(5), Rosen Young Adult) Rosen Publishing Group, Inc., The.

Kids Riding with Confidence: Fun Lessons to Keep Young Riders Safe, Calm & Around Horses. 2014. (ENG., Illus.). 32p. (J). (gr. k-5). (978-1-57076-706-7(8)) Verlhac Editions.

Kimball, Cheryl. Horse Showing for Kids: Training, Grooming, Trailering, Apparel, Tack, Competing, Sportsmanship. 2004. (ENG., Illus.). 160p. (J). (gr. 4-10). pap. 16.95 (978-1-58017-501-2(5), 67501) Storey Publishing, LLC.

Kissock, Heather. Horseback Riding. (J). 2013. (978-1-62127-356-1(3)) 2013. pap. (978-1-62127-362-2(8)) 2007. (Illus.). 24p. (gr. 4-7). lib. bdg. 24.45 (978-1-59036-661-5(1)) 2007. (Illus.). 24p. (gr. 4-7). per. 8.95 (978-1-59036-662-2(X)) Weigl Pubs., Inc.

Kolpin, Molly & Bratton, Donna Bowman. Crazy about Horses: Everything Horse Lovers Needs to Know, 1 vol. 2014. (Crazy about Horses Ser.). (ENG., Illus.). 112p. (gr. 3-4). pap. 12.95 (978-1-4914-0713-4(1), Snap Bks.) Capstone Press of Coughlan Cos.

Kras, Sara Louise. Horse Riding. 2013. 48p. (J). (gr. 4-8). 29.93 (978-1-60870-837-6(3)) Cavendish Square Publishing.

Kras, Sarah Louise. Horse Riding. 2013. (Horses Ser.). 48p. (J). (gr. 4-8). pap. 12.93 (978-1-62712-087-6(4)) Cavendish Square Publishing.

Krementz, Jill. A Very Young Rider. Krementz, Jill, photos by. 2006. (Illus.). 124p. (gr. 4-7). 24.95 (978-0-9755516-2-2(0)) DreamHse. Publishing Inc.

Marsico, Katie. Therapy Horses. 2013. 48p. (J). (gr. 4-8). 29.93 *(978-1-60870-839-0(X))* Cavendish Square Publishing.
Martin, Martha. Steeplechase. 2009. (ENG., Illus.). 32p. (J). (gr. 3-6). lib. bdg. *(978-0-7787-4981-3(9))*; (gr. 4-5). pap. *(978-0-7787-4997-4(5))* Crabtree Publishing Co.
—Trail Riding. 2009. (ENG., Illus.). 32p. (J). (gr. 3-6). lib. bdg. *(978-0-7787-4982-0(7))*; (gr. 4-5). pap. *(978-0-7787-4998-1(3))* Crabtree Publishing Co.
Needham, Kate. Pony Guide. 2006. (Illus.). 31p. (J). *(978-0-439-78703-1(3))* Scholastic, Inc.
Newhouse, Maxwell. The RCMP Musical Ride. 2004. (ENG., Illus.). 24p. (J). (gr. k-12). 15.95 *(978-0-88776-683-1(8),* Tundra Bks.) Tundra Bks. CAN. Dist: Penguin Random Hse. LLC.
Pakizer, Debi & Sears, Mary A. Vaulting: The Art of Gymnastics on Horseback. Anderson, Julia & Barnette, Jackie, eds. Sears, Mary A., illus. (Illus.). 24p. (Orig.). (J). (gr. k-6). pap. 5.00 *(978-0-9639785-6-1(X))* Sears, M.A.
PONY, compiled by. The Little Horse Book. 2007. (YA). pap. *(978-1-933343-58-7(3))* Stabenfeldt Inc.
Pony Club. 2012. (Illus.). 120p. (J). ***(978-1-4351-4412-5(0))*** Barnes & Noble, Inc.
Ransford, Sandy. The Kingfisher Illustrated Horse & Pony Encyclopedia. rev. ed. 2010. (ENG., Illus.). 224p. (J). (gr. 5-9). 24.99 *(978-0-7534-6485-4(3),* 9780753464854, Kingfisher) Roaring Brook Pr.
Richter, Judy. Riding for Kids: Stable Care, Equipment, Tack, Clothing, Longeing, Lessons, Jumping, Showing. 2003. (ENG., Illus.). 144p. (J). (gr. 4-8). pap. 16.95 *(978-1-58017-510-4(4),* 67510) Storey Publishing, LLC.
Riding: Level I, 6 vols. (Wonder Worldtm Ser.). 16p. 29.95 *(978-0-7802-2024-9(2))* Wright Group/McGraw-Hill.
Sarkisian, K. I Have a Horse: Learning the H Sound. 2009. (PowerPhonics Ser.). 24p. (gr. 1-1). 39.90 *(978-1-60851-449-6(8),* PowerKids Pr.) Rosen Publishing Group, Inc., The.
Smith, Lucy. The Usborne Book of Horses & Ponies. Gray, Miranda & Trotter, Stuart, illus. 2006. 32p. (J). pap. *(978-0-439-88983-4(9))* Scholastic, Inc.
Spiotta-DiMare, Loren. Therapy Horses: Horses That Heal. 2014. (Horses That Help with the American Humane Association Ser.). 48p. (J). lib. bdg. 25.27 *(978-0-7660-4217-9(0),* Enslow Elementary) Enslow Pubs., Inc.
Talbert, Marc. Ahold of the Reins. Date not set. 124p. (J). (gr. 3-7). pap. 6.99 *(978-0-06-440950-6(3))* HarperCollins Pubs.
—Holding the Reins: A Ride Through Cowgirl Life. Van Cleve, Barbara, photos by. 2003. (Illus.). 112p. (J). (gr. 3-7). 16.99 *(978-0-06-029255-3(5))* HarperCollins Pubs.
Turnbull, Stephanie. Show Horses. 2015. (ENG., Illus.). 24p. (J). pap. 8.95 *(978-1-77092-229-7(6))* RiverStream Publishing.
Ward, Lesley. Jumping for Kids. 2007. (ENG., Illus.). 144p. (J). (gr. 4-10). pap. 16.95 *(978-1-58017-672-9(0),* 67672) Storey Publishing, LLC.
Wright, John. Equestrian Sport. 2005. (Sports Injuries Ser.). (Illus.). 64p. (YA). lib. bdg. 19.95 *(978-1-59084-629-2(X))* Mason Crest.

HORSEMANSHIP—FICTION

Aunt Connye. The Riding Game. 2008. 24p. pap. 11.99 *(978-1-4343-7742-5(3))* AuthorHouse.
Bates, Michelle. Horse for the Summer. 2010. (Sandy Lane Stables Ser.). 128p. (J). pap. 4.99 *(978-0-7945-2539-2(3),* Usborne) EDC Publishing.
—Horse in Danger. (Sandy Lane Stables Ser.). 2017. (ENG.). 128p. (YA). pap. 5.99 ***(978-0-7945-3915-3(7))*** 2009. (Illus.). 114p. (J). (gr. 5). pap. 4.99 *(978-0-7945-2530-9(X))* EDC Publishing. (Usborne).
Bates, Michelle. Midnight Horse. rev. ed. 2011. (Sandy Lane Stables Ser.). 128p. (J). pap. 4.99 *(978-0-7945-2529-3(6),* Usborne) EDC Publishing.
Bentley, Sue. Riding Rescue. 2013. (Magic Ponies Ser.: 6). lib. bdg. 14.75 *(978-0-606-32119-8(5),* Turtleback) Turtleback Bks.
Bloomberg, Georgina & Hapka, Catherine. Rein It In. 2013. (a Circuit Ser.). (ENG.). 240p. (YA). (gr. 7). pap. 9.99 *(978-1-61963-102-1(4),* 9781619631021, Bloomsbury USA Childrens) Bloomsbury Publishing USA.
Brooke, Lauren. All or Nothing. 2007. (Chestnut Hill Ser.: No. 6). 184p. (J). lib. bdg. 15.38 *(978-1-4242-1719-9(9))* Fitzgerald Bks.
—The New Class. 2005. (Chestnut Hill Ser.: No. 1). 212p. (J). (gr. 4-7). lib. bdg. 12.65 *(978-0-7569-6479-5(2))* Perfection Learning Corp.
Bryant, Bonnie. Horse Play. 2007. (Saddle Club(R) Ser.: No. 7). (ENG.). 144p. (J). (gr. 3-7). 5.99 *(978-0-553-15754-3(X),* Yearling) Random Hse. Children's Bks.
Burkhart, Jessica. Comeback. 2012. (Canterwood Crest Ser.: 15). lib. bdg. 18.40 *(978-0-606-26312-2(8),* Turtleback) Turtleback Bks.
—Elite Ambition. 2010. (Canterwood Crest Ser.: 10). (ENG.). 224p. (J). (gr. 4-8). pap. 7.99 *(978-1-4424-0382-6(9),* Aladdin) Simon & Schuster Children's Publishing.
—Home for Christmas. 2013. (Canterwood Crest Ser.). lib. bdg. 18.40 *(978-0-606-32322-2(8),* Turtleback) Turtleback Bks.
—Masquerade. 2012. (Canterwood Crest Ser.: 16). lib. bdg. 18.40 *(978-0-606-26887-5(1),* Turtleback) Turtleback Bks.
—Unfriendly Competition. 2011. (Canterwood Crest Ser.: 12). (ENG.). 192p. (J). (gr. 4-8). pap. 7.99 *(978-1-4424-0386-4(1),* Aladdin) Simon & Schuster Children's Publishing.
Burkhart, Jessica & Haley, Patricia. Chosen: Super Special. 2011. (Canterwood Crest Ser.). (ENG.). 304p. (J). (gr. 5-8). pap. 7.99 *(978-1-4424-1946-9(6),* Aladdin) Simon & Schuster Children's Publishing.
Circle of Blue. 2006. (J). *(978-1-933343-37-2(0),* PONY) Stabenfeldt Inc.
Citra, Becky. Sam's Ride, 1 vol. Meissner, Amy, illus. 2009. (Orca Echoes Ser.). (ENG.). 64p. (J). (gr. 2-3). pap. 6.95 *(978-1-55469-160-9(5))* Orca Bk. Pubs. USA.
Cole, Cathleen. Four Seasons Stables: A Saddle Seat Rid. 2006. 53p. pap. 16.95 *(978-1-4241-3430-4(7))* PublishAmerica, Inc.
Dale, Jay. Daisy Wants to Go Riding, 1 vol. Draycott, Michelle, illus. 2012. (Wonder Words Ser.). (ENG.). 32p. (gr. k-2). pap. 5.99 *(978-1-4296-8920-5(X),* Engage Literacy) Capstone Press of Coughlan Cos.
Dorsey, Angela. Spring of the Poacher's Moon. 2012. 124p. pap. *(978-1-927100-16-5(X))* Enchanted Pony Bks.
—Summer of Wild Hearts. 2012. 128p. pap. *(978-1-927100-18-9(6))* Enchanted Pony Bks.
Edge, Laura Bufano. Wild West Dreams. 2006. (J). pap. *(978-0-88092-623-2(6))*; lib. bdg. *(978-0-88092-622-5(8))* Royal Fireworks Publishing Co.
Feld, Ellen F. Rimfire: The Barrel Racing Morgan Horse. Mellin, Jeanne, illus. 2009. (ENG.). 206p. (J). pap. 9.95 *(978-0-9709002-1-0(X))* Willow Bend Publishing.
Gaard, Betty. Jericho Ride. 2003. (Illus.). 165p. (J). pap. 8.99 *(978-1-57924-968-7(X))* BJU Pr.
Galbraith, Julie. Stable Ground: The Riding Series #1. 2013. 136p. pap. *(978-1-927794-05-0(6))* Lechner Syndications.
Gerlach, Elizabeth K. Apples for Cheyenne: A Story about Autism, Horses & Friendship. 2010. (ENG., Illus.). 44p. (J). (gr. k-4). pap. 11.95 *(978-1-935274-22-3(8))* Future Horizons, Inc.
Goril, Cindy. Lacey's Legacy: Stretch's Story. Jamison, Sharon, illus. 2013. 28p. (J). pap. 12.95 *(978-1-935188-56-8(9))* Star Publish LLC.
Green, D. L. Sparkling Jewel. Wallis, Emily, illus. 2015. (Silver Pony Ranch Ser.: 1). (ENG.). 96p. (J). (gr. 1-3). pap. 4.99 *(978-0-545-79765-8(9))* Scholastic, Inc.
—Sweet Buttercup. Wallis, Emily, illus. 2016. (Silver Pony Ranch Ser.: 2). (ENG.). 96p. (J). (gr. 1-3). 15.99 *(978-0-545-79770-2(5))* Scholastic, Inc.
Greene, Kimberly. My Life on TV. 2011. (My Sister's a Pop Star Ser.). 320p. (J). pap. 5.99 *(978-0-7945-2901-7(1),* Usborne) EDC Publishing.
Gregg, Stacy. Flame & the Rebel Riders, 9. 2015. (Pony Club Secrets Ser.: 9). (ENG., Illus.). 240p. (J). (gr. 4-7). 8.99 *(978-0-00-729929-4(X),* HarperCollins Children's Bks.) HarperCollins Pubs. Ltd. GBR. Dist: HarperCollins Pubs.
—Nightstorm & the Grand Slam, 12. 2016. (Pony Club Secrets Ser.: 12). (ENG., Illus.). 272p. (J). (gr. 4-7). 7.99 *(978-0-00-729932-4(X),* HarperCollins Children's Bks.) HarperCollins Pubs. Ltd. GBR. Dist: HarperCollins Pubs.
—Showjumpers, 2. 2010. (Pony Club Rivals Ser.: 2). (ENG.). 272p. (J). (gr. 4-7). pap. 7.99 *(978-0-00-733344-8(7),* HarperCollins Children's Bks.) HarperCollins Pubs. Ltd. GBR. Dist: HarperCollins Pubs.
—Stardust & the Daredevil Ponies, 4. 2015. (Pony Club Secrets Ser.: 4). (ENG., Illus.). 240p. (J). pap. 6.99 *(978-0-00-724516-1(5),* HarperCollins Children's Bks.) HarperCollins Pubs. Ltd. GBR. Dist: HarperCollins Pubs.
—Victory & the All-Stars Academy. 2015. (Pony Club Secrets Ser.: 8). (ENG., Illus.). 288p. (J). (gr. 4-7). 6.99 *(978-0-00-727033-0(X),* HarperCollins Children's Bks.) HarperCollins Pubs. Ltd. GBR. Dist: HarperCollins Pubs.
Griffin, Kitty. The Ride: The Legend of Betsy Dowdy. Priceman, Marjorie, illus. 2010. (ENG.). 40p. (J). (gr. -1-3). 16.99 *(978-1-4169-2816-4(2),* Atheneum Bks. for Young Readers) Simon & Schuster Children's Publishing.
Haas, Jessie. Birthday Pony. Apple, Margot, illus. 2004. 80p. (J). (gr. 2-18). 15.99 *(978-0-06-057359-1(7))* HarperCollins Pubs.
Hamilton, Sable. Free Spirit. 2015. (Stardust Stables Ser.). (ENG.). 160p. (gr. 3-6). lib. bdg. 22.65 *(978-1-4342-9792-1(6))* Stone Arch Bks.
—A Star Is Born. 2015. (Stardust Stables Ser.). (ENG.). 160p. (gr. 3-6). lib. bdg. 22.65 *(978-1-4342-9790-7(X))* Stone Arch Bks.
—Stardust Stables. 2015. (Stardust Stables Ser.). (ENG.). 160p. (gr. 3-6). lib. bdg. 67.95 *(978-1-4965-0112-7(8),* Stardust Stables) Stone Arch Bks.
—Wildfire. 2015. (Stardust Stables Ser.). (ENG.). 160p. (gr. 3-6). lib. bdg. 22.65 *(978-1-4342-9791-4(8))* Stone Arch Bks.
Hapka, Catherine, pseud. Back in the Saddle. 2016. (Marguerite Henry's Ponies of Chincoteague Ser.: 7). (ENG., Illus.). 192p. (J). (gr. 3-7). pap. 6.99 *(978-1-4814-5993-8(7),* Aladdin) Simon & Schuster Children's Publishing.
—Blue Ribbon Summer. 2014. (Marguerite Henry's Ponies of Chincoteague Ser.: 2). (ENG., Illus.). 208p. (J). (gr. 3-7). pap. 6.99 *(978-1-4814-0339-9(7),* Aladdin) Simon & Schuster Children's Publishing.
—Moonlight Mile. 2015. (Marguerite Henry's Ponies of Chincoteague Ser.: 4). (ENG., Illus.). 192p. (J). (gr. 3-7). pap. 6.99 *(978-1-4814-0345-0(1),* Aladdin) Simon & Schuster Children's Publishing.
—The New Pony. Kennedy, Anne, illus. 2013. (I Can Read Level 2 Ser.). (ENG.). 32p. (J). (gr. -1-3). 16.99 *(978-0-06-208674-7(X))* HarperCollins Pubs.
—True Riders. 2015. (Marguerite Henry's Ponies of Chincoteague Ser.: 6). (ENG., Illus.). 192p. (J). (gr. 3-7). 17.99 *(978-1-4814-3972-5(3),* Aladdin) Simon & Schuster Children's Publishing.
—A Winning Gift. 2015. (Marguerite Henry's Ponies of Chincoteague Ser.: 5). (ENG., Illus.). 192p. (J). (gr. 3-7). pap. 6.99 *(978-1-4814-3968-8(5),* Aladdin) Simon & Schuster Children's Publishing.
Hapka, Catherine, pseud & Bloomberg, Georgina. The A Circuit. 2011. (a Circuit Ser.). (ENG.). 288p. (YA). (gr. 7-12). 16.99 *(978-1-59990-641-6(4),* 9781599906416); pap. 9.99 *(978-1-59990-634-8(1),* 9781599906348) Bloomsbury Publishing USA. (Bloomsbury USA Childrens).
—My Favorite Mistake: An a Circuit Novel. 2012. (a Circuit Ser.). (ENG.). 256p. (YA). pap. 9.99 *(978-1-59990-642-3(2),* 9781599906423, Bloomsbury USA Childrens) Bloomsbury Publishing USA.
—Off Course. 2012. (a Circuit Ser.). (ENG.). 256p. (YA). (gr. 7-12). pap. 9.99 *(978-1-59990-909-7(X),* 9781599909097, Bloomsbury USA Childrens) Bloomsbury Publishing USA.
Helidoniotis, Kathy. Horse Mad Western. 2008. 272p. *(978-0-7322-8424-4(4))* HarperCollins Pubs. Australia.
Henry, Marguerite. White Stallion of Lipizza. 2015. (ENG., Illus.). 208p. (J). (gr. 3-7). 19.99 *(978-1-4814-0392-4(3),* Aladdin) Simon & Schuster Children's Publishing.
—White Stallion of Lipizza. Dennis, Wesley, illus. 2014. (ENG.). 192p. (J). (gr. 3-7). pap. 7.99 *(978-1-4814-0391-7(5),* Aladdin) Simon & Schuster Children's Publishing.
Holub, Joan & Williams, Suzanne. Poseidon & the Sea of Fury. Phillips, Craig, illus. 2012. (Heroes in Training Ser.: 2). (ENG.). 128p. (J). (gr. 1-4). 16.99 *(978-1-4424-5798-0(8))*; pap. 5.99 *(978-1-4424-5265-7(X))* Simon & Schuster Children's Publishing. (Aladdin).
Howard, Cheryl Lynne. Captured by Love: A Wild Horse Story Based on Psalm 139. 2011. 48p. pap. 11.00 *(978-1-4567-1822-0(3))* AuthorHouse.
Huws, Emily. Nid Fy Mai I. Lawrie, Robin, illus. 2005. (WEL.). 64p. pap. *(978-1-84512-025-2(6))* Cymdeithas Lyfrau Ceredigion.
Irving, Washington. The Legend of Sleepy Hollow. 2012. (ENG., Illus.). 32p. pap. 9.95 *(978-0-7624-4619-3(6),* Running Pr. Minature Editions) Running Pr. Bk. Pubs.
Jakobs, D. Holly, Jolly Harmony. 2013. (Passport to Reading Level 2 Ser.). (J). lib. bdg. 14.75 *(978-0-606-32276-8(0),* Turtleback) Turtleback Bks.
Juby, Susan. Another Kind of Cowboy. 2007. 344p. (YA). lib. bdg. 6.99 *(978-0-06-076521-7(6),* HarperTeen) HarperCollins Pubs.
Keene, Carolyn. Mystery of the Midnight Rider. 2013. (Nancy Drew Diaries: 3). (ENG.). 208p. (J). (gr. 1-7). pap. 6.99 *(978-1-4424-7860-2(8),* Aladdin) Simon & Schuster Children's Publishing.
—Nancy Drew Diaries 3-Books-In-1! Curse of the Arctic Star; Strangers on a Train; Mystery of the Midnight Rider. 2016. (Nancy Drew Diaries). (ENG., Illus.). 592p. (J). (gr. 3-7). pap. 8.99 *(978-1-4814-8554-8(7),* Aladdin) Simon & Schuster Children's Publishing.
Kelly, Bernadette. Courage to Ride, 1 vol. 2010. (Ridgeview Riding Club Ser.). (ENG.). 144p. (gr. 4-5). 25.32 *(978-1-4342-1931-2(3))* Stone Arch Bks.
—If Wishes Were Horses, 1 vol. 2010. (Ridgeview Riding Club Ser.). (ENG.). 144p. (Orig.). (gr. 4-5). 25.32 *(978-1-4342-1929-9(1))* Stone Arch Bks.
—Leap of Faith, 1 vol. 2010. (Ridgeview Riding Club Ser.). (ENG.). 144p. (gr. 4-5). 25.32 *(978-1-4342-1932-9(1))* Stone Arch Bks.
—Team Challenge, 1 vol. 2010. (Ridgeview Riding Club Ser.). (ENG.). 144p. (Orig.). (gr. 4-5). 25.32 *(978-1-4342-1930-5(5))* Stone Arch Bks.
Kendall, Jane F. Maestoso Petra. Sanderson, Ruth, illus. 2010. (Horse Diaries: No. 4). (ENG.). 160p. (J). (gr. 3-7). pap. 7.99 *(978-0-375-85842-0(3),* Random Hse. Bks. for Young Readers) Random Hse. Children's Bks.
Kenneally, Miranda. Racing Savannah, 1 vol. unabr. ed. 2015. (Hundred Oaks Ser.: Bk. 4). (ENG.). (YA). (gr. 7-9). 14.99 *(978-1-5012-1560-5(4),* 9781501215605, Audible Studios on Brilliance Audio) Brilliance Publishing, Inc.
—Racing Savannah. 2013. (Hundred Oaks Ser.: Bk. 4). (ENG.). 304p. (YA). (gr. 7-12). pap. 9.99 *(978-1-4022-8476-2(4),* 9781402284762) Sourcebooks, Inc.
Krulik, Nancy. Horsing Around. John and Wendy Staff, illus. 2009. (Katie Kazoo, Switcheroo Ser.: 30). (ENG.). 80p. (J). (gr. 2-4). pap. 3.99 *(978-0-448-44677-6(4),* Grosset & Dunlap) Penguin Young Readers Group.
Lyne, Jennifer H. Catch Rider. (ENG.). 288p. (YA). (gr. 7). 2014. pap. 8.99 *(978-0-544-30182-5(X),* HMH Books For Young Readers) 2013. (Illus.). 16.99 *(978-0-547-86871-4(5))* Houghton Mifflin Harcourt Publishing Co.
Mackall, Dandi Daley. You & Your Horse: How to Whisper Your Way into Your Horse's Life. O'Connor, Jeff, illus. 2009. (ENG.). 160p. (J). (gr. 4-8). pap. 5.99 *(978-1-4169-6449-0(5),* Aladdin) Simon & Schuster Children's Publishing.
Maddox, Jake. Horseback Hopes, 1 vol. Mourning, Tuesday, illus. 2009. (Jake Maddox Girl Sports Stories Ser.). (ENG.). 72p. (gr. 2-3). 25.32 *(978-1-4342-1214-6(9))* Stone Arch Bks.
Man-Kong, Mary. I Can Be a Horse Rider. 2012. (Barbie Step into Reading Level 1 Ser.). lib. bdg. 13.55 *(978-0-606-23721-5(6),* Turtleback) Turtleback Bks.
—I Can Be a Horse Rider (Barbie) RH Disney Staff & An, Jiyoung, illus. 2012. (Step into Reading Ser.). (ENG.). 32p. (J). (gr. -1-1). pap. 3.99 *(978-0-375-97030-6(4),* Random Hse. Bks. for Young Readers) Random Hse. Children's Bks.
Mayfield, Holly. Melvin: A True Story with a Happy Ending. Gilman, Sara, illus. 2013. 38p. pap. 9.99 *(978-0-9892711-9-6(6))* Mindstir Media.
McCarthy, Peggy & Rivers, Julia. Tough Break: The Barn Girls. 2012. (ENG.). 132p. pap. 10.95 *(978-1-4327-9122-3(2))* Outskirts Pr., Inc.
McKain, Kelly. Megan & Mischief. 2008. (Pony Camp Diaries: Vol. 1). 96p. (J). (gr. 3-5). 3.99 *(978-1-56148-646-5(9),* Good Bks.) Skyhorse Publishing Co., Inc.
—Poppy & Prince. 2008. (Pony Camp Diaries: Vol. 2). 96p. (J). (gr. 3-5). 3.99 *(978-1-56148-647-2(7),* Good Bks.) Skyhorse Publishing Co., Inc.
McLoon, Linda Snow. Crown Prince. 2013. (ENG.). 272p. (gr. 6-9). pap. *(978-1-57076-546-9(4))* Verlhac Editions.
—Crown Prince Challenged. 2012. (Brookmeade Young Riders Ser.: 2). (ENG.). 384p. (YA). (gr. 6-9). pap. *(978-1-57076-545-2(6))* Verlhac Editions.
Mullarkey, Lisa. The Campfire Capers, 1 vol. 2014. (Storm Cliff Stables Ser.). (ENG., Illus.). 112p. (J). (gr. 7-11). 27.07 *(978-1-62402-049-0(6))* Magic Wagon.
—Gold Medal Glitch, 1 vol. 2014. (Storm Cliff Stables Ser.). (ENG., Illus.). 112p. (J). (gr. 7-11). 27.07 *(978-1-62402-050-6(X))* Magic Wagon.
—Horsenapped!, 1 vol. 2014. (Storm Cliff Stables Ser.). (ENG., Illus.). 112p. (J). (gr. 7-11). 27.07 *(978-1-62402-051-3(8))* Magic Wagon.
Murphy, Patricia J. Horse Club. 2013. (DK Adventures Ser.). (ENG.). 128p. (J). (gr. 3-7). 16.99 *(978-1-4654-1811-1(3))*; pap. 5.99 *(978-1-4654-1723-7(0))* Dorling Kindersley Publishing, Inc. (DK Children).
Platt, Chris. Astra, 1 vol. 2010. (ENG.). 176p. (J). (gr. 3-7). 15.95 *(978-1-56145-541-6(5))* Peachtree Pubs.
Primavera, Elise. Libby of High Hopes. Primavera, Elise, illus. 2012. (Libby of High Hopes Ser.). (ENG., Illus.). 192p. (J). (gr. 2-5). 14.99 *(978-1-4169-5542-9(9),* Simon & Schuster/Paula Wiseman Bks.) Simon & Schuster/Paula Wiseman Bks.
—Project Blue Ribbon. Primavera, Elise, illus. 2015. (Libby of High Hopes Ser.). (ENG., Illus.). 288p. (J). (gr. 2-5). 16.99 *(978-1-4169-5543-6(7),* Simon & Schuster Bks. For Young Readers) Simon & Schuster Bks. For Young Readers.
Redmond, Diane. The Most Beautiful Horse in the World. 2007. (YA). *(978-1-933343-60-0(5))* Stabenfeldt Inc.
Rippin, Sally. The Bumpy Ride: Hey Jack! Spartels, Stephanie, illus. 2014. (ENG.). 48p. (J). pap. 4.99 *(978-1-61067-187-3(2))* Kane Miller.
Romansky, Sally Rosenberg. Invincible. Ott, Margot Janet, illus. 2006. (J). pap. 8.95 *(978-0-9723729-4-7(6))* Imagination Stage, Inc.
Simon, Jenne. LEGO Friends: Andrea's New Horse. Ku, Min Sung, illus. 2014. (LEGO Friends Ser.). (ENG.). 24p. (J). (gr. -1-3). pap. 3.99 *(978-0-545-78391-0(7))* Scholastic, Inc.
Smedley, Frank E. Frank Fairlegh: Scenes from the Life of a Private Pupil. 2007. (ENG.). 570p. per. 30.99 *(978-1-4346-4557-9(6))*; 640p. per. 45.75 *(978-1-4346-4558-6(4))* Creative Media Partners, LLC.
St. John, Lauren. The One Dollar Horse. 2013. (ENG.). 240p. (J). (gr. 4-7). pap. ***(978-1-4440-0636-0(3),*** Orion Children's Bks.) Hachette Children's Group GBR. Dist: Hachette Bk. Group.
Stamm, Linda J. Lilly & Zander: A Children's Story about Equine-Assisted Activities. Whitaker, Suzanne, illus. 2014. (J). pap. *(978-1-938313-03-5(8))* Graphite Pr.
Taylor, Lori. What to Do When Your Hoof Turns Blue!!! Taylor, Lori, illus. I.t. ed. 2006. (Illus.). 28p. (J). pap. 20.99 *(978-1-59879-220-1(2))* Lifevest Publishing, Inc.
Wedekind, Annie. A Horse of Her Own. 2009. (ENG.). 288p. (YA). (gr. 5-9). pap. 8.99 *(978-0-312-58146-6(7),* 9780312581466) Square Fish.
Weyn, Suzanne. Learning to Fly. 2010. 176p. (J). pap. *(978-1-4071-1742-3(4))* Scholastic, Inc.
Ziegesar, Cecily von. Dark Horses. 2016. (ENG.). 336p. (YA). (gr. 9). 18.99 *(978-1-61695-517-5(1),* Soho Teen) Soho Pr., Inc.
Zöller, Elisabeth & Kolloch, Brigitte. Antonia, the Horse Whisperer: The Rosenburg Riding Stables, Volume 1. Gotzen-Beek, Betina, illus. 2014. (ENG.). 96p. (J). (gr. 2-7). 9.95 *(978-1-62636-383-0(8),* Sky Pony Pr.) Skyhorse Publishing Co., Inc.

HORSES

see also Ponies

All about Horses: Everything a Horse-Crazy Girl Needs to Know, 1 vol. 2014. (Crazy about Horses Ser.). (ENG., Illus.). 32p. (gr. 3-4). lib. bdg. 27.99 *(978-1-4914-0710-3(7),* Snap Bks.) Capstone Press of Coughlan Cos.
Amoroso, Cynthia & Noyed, Bob. Horses. 2016. (In the Barnyard Ser.). (ENG.). 24p. (J). (gr. k-3). 27.07 *(978-1-5038-0828-7(9),* 210672) Child's World, Inc., The.
Andrekson, Judy. Brigadier: Gentle Hero. Parkins, David, illus. 2009. (True Horse Stories Ser.). (ENG.). 96p. (J). (gr. 4-7). pap. 7.95 *(978-0-88776-904-7(7),* Tundra Bks.) Tundra Bks. CAN. Dist: Penguin Random Hse. LLC.
—Fosta: Marathon Master. Parkins, David, illus. 2008. (True Horse Stories Ser.). (ENG.). 104p. (J). (gr. 4-7). pap. 7.95 *(978-0-88776-838-5(5),* Tundra Bks.) Tundra Bks. CAN. Dist: Penguin Random Hse. LLC.
—JB Andrew: Mustang Magic. Parkins, David, illus. 2008. (True Horse Stories Ser.). (ENG.). 88p. (J). (gr. 4-7). pap. 7.95 *(978-0-88776-837-8(7),* Tundra Bks.) Tundra Bks. CAN. Dist: Penguin Random Hse. LLC.
—Little Squire: The Jumping Pony. Parkins, David, illus. 2007. (True Horse Stories Ser.). (ENG.). 80p. (J). (gr. 4-7). pap. 7.99 *(978-0-88776-770-8(2),* Tundra Bks.) Tundra Bks. CAN. Dist: Penguin Random Hse. LLC.
—Miskeen: The Dancing Horse. Parkins, David, illus. 2007. (True Horse Stories Ser.). (ENG.). 96p. (J). (gr. 4-7). pap. 7.95 *(978-0-88776-771-5(0),* Tundra Bks.) Tundra Bks. CAN. Dist: Penguin Random Hse. LLC.
Antill, Sara. A Horse's Life. 2012. (Illus.). 24p. (J). 49.50 *(978-1-4488-5109-6(2),* 1329322, PowerKids Pr.); pap. 8.25 *(978-1-4488-5108-9(4),* 1329322, PowerKids Pr.); lib. bdg. 22.60 *(978-1-4488-4980-2(2),* 1329322) Rosen Publishing Group, Inc., The.
Apte, Sunita. Police Horses. 2007. (Horse Power Ser.). (Illus.). 32p. (YA). (gr. 2-5). lib. bdg. 25.27 *(978-1-59716-401-6(1))* Bearport Publishing Co., Inc.
Arnold, Jude. The Lipizzan Reunion: A True Story. 2009. 48p. pap. 19.49 *(978-1-4389-7060-8(9))* AuthorHouse.
Ashe, E. Happy Horse: A Children's Book of Horses. Ashe, E., illus. 2003. (Illus.). 18p. (J). bds. 12.95 *(978-0-9727849-0-0(X),* 0-9727849-0-X) Happy Horse Publishing, Ltd.
Baker, Brynn. Military Heroes. 2015. (Military Heroes Ser.). (ENG.). 32p. (gr. 3-4). 109.28 *(978-1-4914-6806-7(8),* Fact Finders) Capstone Press of Coughlan Cos.
Baldwin, Elizabeth. Horses. 2009. (Crabtree Contact Ser.). (ENG., Illus.). 32p. (J). (gr. 4-7). pap. *(978-0-7787-3797-1(7))*; lib. bdg. *(978-0-7787-3775-9(6))* Crabtree Publishing Co.
Ball, Ashley. My Horse Samson. 2011. (J). *(978-0-938467-10-6(7))* Headline Bks., Inc.
Barbe-Julien, Colette. Little Horses. 2006. (Born to Be Wild Ser.). (Illus.). 24p. (J). (gr. k-3). lib. bdg. 23.00 *(978-0-8368-6167-9(1),* Gareth Stevens Learning Library) Stevens, Gareth Publishing LLLP.
Bardenhagen-Ludlow, Deborah. A Visit to the Neighbors: Mommy, Do You Think Horses Can Talk to Each Other? 2012. 24p. pap. 17.99 *(978-1-4772-8310-3(2))* AuthorHouse.
Barnes, Julia. Horses at Work. 2006. (Animals at Work Ser.). (Illus.). 32p. (J). (gr. 3-6). lib. bdg. 26.00 *(978-0-8368-6225-6(2),* Gareth Stevens Learning Library) Stevens, Gareth Publishing LLLP.
Behling, Silke. Get to Know Horse Breeds: The 100 Best-Known Breeds. 2014. (Get to Know Cat, Dog, & Horse Breeds Ser.). 144p. (J). 33.27 *(978-0-7660-4259-9(6))*; pap. 10.95 *(978-1-4644-0461-0(5))* Enslow Pubs., Inc.
Bell, N. W. The Great American Horse Book: A Childrens Guide to Horse's. I.t. ed. 2003.Tr. of Gran Libro Del Calballo Americano. (SPA., Illus.). 32p. (J). 10.99 *(978-0-9729753-0-8(6))* Really Big Coloring Bks., Inc.
Bennett, Kathy. Pony Pointers: How to Safely Care for Your Horse or Pony. Peterson, Carol A., illus. 2004. 48p. (J). per. 7.99 *(978-0-9763209-0-6(8))* Trail Trotters Bk. Ranch.
Beylon, Cathy. Let's Color Together — Horses & Ponies. 2014. (ENG., Illus.). 64p. (J). (gr. -1-3). pap. 3.99 *(978-0-486-77974-4(2))* Dover Pubns., Inc.
Biniok, Janice. Your First Horse. 2012. (J). *(978-1-61900-003-2(2))*; pap. *(978-1-61900-004-9(0))* Eldorado Ink.

H
I

Blazeman, Christopher. Horses up Close, 1 vol. 2nd rev. ed. 2014. (TIME for KIDS(r) Nonfiction Readers Ser.). (ENG., Illus.). 28p. (J). (gr. 2-2). pap. 23.96 (978-1-4807-1044-3(X)) Shell Educational Publishing.

—Horses up Close, 1 vol. 2nd rev. ed. 2011. (Nonfiction Readers Ser.). (ENG.). 28p. (J). (gr. 2-2). pap. 6.99 (978-1-4333-3617-1(0)) Teacher Created Materials, Inc.

Bodden, Valerie. Caring for Horses. 2013. (Horsing Around (Creative Education) Ser.). (ENG., Illus.). 24p. (J). (gr. -1-3). 25.65 (978-1-60818-470-5(6), Creative Education) Creative Co., The.

—Horsing Around: Caring for Horses. 2014. (Horsing Around Ser.). (ENG.). 24p. (J). (gr. 1-3). pap. 7.99 (978-0-89812-833-8(1), Creative Paperbacks) Creative Co., The.

—Horsing Around: Riding Horses. 2014. (Horsing Around Ser.). (ENG.). 24p. (J). (gr. 1-3). pap. 7.99 (978-0-89812-834-5(X), Creative Paperbacks) Creative Co., The.

—Horsing Around: Showing Horses. 2014. (Horsing Around Ser.). (ENG.). 24p. (J). (gr. 1-3). pap. 7.99 (978-0-89812-835-2(8), Creative Paperbacks) Creative Co., The.

—Riding Horses. 2013. (Horsing Around (Creative Education) Ser.). (ENG., Illus.). 24p. (J). (gr. -1-3). 25.65 (978-1-60818-471-2(4), Creative Education) Creative Co., The.

—Showing Horses. 2013. (Illus.). 24p. (J). 25.65 (978-1-60818-472-9(2), Creative Education) Creative Co., The.

Bozzo, Linda. Mi Primer Caballo. 2008. (My First Pet Bilingual Library from the American Humane Association Ser.).Tr. of My First Horse. (ENG & SPA., Illus.). 32p. (J). (gr. 1-3). lib. bdg. 23.94 (978-0-7660-3035-0(0)) Enslow Pubs., Inc.

—My First Horse. 2007. (My First Pet Library from the American Humane Association Ser.). (Illus.). 32p. (J). (gr. 1-2). lib. bdg. 23.94 (978-0-7660-2753-4(8), Enslow Elementary) Enslow Pubs., Inc.

Brack, Susan. Horsing Around! Stickers. 2011. (Dover Little Activity Books Stickers Ser.). (ENG.). 8p. (J). (gr. k-3). pap. 1.50 (978-0-486-48186-9(7)) Dover Pubns., Inc.

Bratton, Donna Bowman. From Head to Tail: All about Horse Care, 1 vol. 2014. (Crazy about Horses Ser.). (ENG., Illus.). 32p. (gr. 3-4). 27.99 (978-1-4914-0709-7(3), Snap Bks.) Capstone Press of Coughlan Cos.

Brazen Horse. 2006. (J). (978-1-933343-30-3(3), PONY) Stabenfeldt Inc.

Brecke, Nicole & Stockland, Patricia M. Horses You Can Draw. Brecke, Nicole, illus. 2009. (Ready, Set, Draw! Ser.). (ENG., Illus.). 32p. (gr. 2-4). lib. bdg. 25.26 (978-0-7613-4160-4(9), Millbrook Pr.) Lerner Publishing Group.

Brenan-Leitner, Rita. The Legend of Cricket. the Horse by the Side of the Road. 2013. 34p. pap. 12.95 (978-1-61170-153-1(8)) Robertson Publishing.

Brett, Flora. A Horse's View of the World. 2015. (Pet Perspectives Ser.). (ENG., Illus.). 24p. (gr. 1-2). lib. bdg. 25.32 (978-1-4914-5044-4(4)) Capstone Press of Coughlan Cos.

Bright, Michael. Wild Horses. 2015. (ENG., Illus.). 64p. 12.99 (978-1-86147-464-3(4), Armadillo) Anness Publishing GBR. Dist: National Bk. Network.

Buckley, James. Who Was Seabiscuit? Copeland, Gregory, illus. 2015. 105p. (J). (978-1-4844-6962-0(3), Grosset & Dunlap) Penguin Publishing Group.

—Who Was Seabiscuit? 2015. (Who Was... ? Ser.). lib. bdg. 16.00 (978-0-606-37557-3(0)) Turtleback Bks.

Buckley, James, et al. Who Was Seabiscuit? Copeland, Gregory, illus. 2015. (Who Was? Ser.). (ENG.). 112p. (J). (gr. 3-7). 5.99 (978-0-448-48309-2(2), Grosset & Dunlap) Penguin Young Readers Group.

Bull, Peter, illus. Horses. Date not set. (Old MacDonald Stickers Ser.). 16p. (J). 2.98 (978-0-7525-7060-0(9)) Parragon, Inc.

Busy Kids Horses & Ponies Sticker Activity Book. 2008. (Busy Kids Ser.). (Illus.). 12p. (J). (gr. -1-3). pap. (978-1-84610-722-1(9)) Make Believe Ideas.

Calhoun, Kelly. Crines Majestuosas (Majestic Manes) Caballo (Horse) 2016. (Adivina (Guess What) Ser.). (SPA., Illus.). 24p. (J). (gr. k-2). 28.50 (978-1-63471-450-1(4), 208863) Cherry Lake Publishing.

—Majestic Manes: Horse. 2015. (Guess What Ser.). (ENG., Illus.). 24p. (J). (gr. k-2). pap. 12.79 (978-1-63362-711-6(X), 206685) Cherry Lake Publishing.

Carr, Aaron. Horses. 2014. (Illus.). 24p. (J). (978-1-62127-232-8(X)) Weigl Pubs., Inc.

Carraway, Rose. Horses on the Farm. 2012. (Farm Animals Ser.). (Illus.). 24p. (gr. k-2). 69.20 (978-1-4339-8055-8(X)); (J). 22.60 (978-1-4339-7356-7(1)); (J). pap. 8.15 (978-1-4339-7357-4(X)) Stevens, Gareth Publishing LLLP.

—Horses on the Farm / Caballos de Granja. 2012. (Farm Animals / Animales de granja Ser.). (SPA & ENG., Illus.). 24p. (J). (gr. k-2). 22.60 (978-1-4339-7400-7(2)) Stevens, Gareth Publishing LLLP.

Clark, Katie. Police Horses. 2013. (We Work! Animals with Jobs Ser.). (Illus.). 24p. (J). (gr. -1-3). lib. bdg. 21.32 (978-1-61772-896-9(9)) Bearport Publishing Co., Inc.

Clough, Paige. Nosey Rosey. 2016. (ENG.). 32p. (J). 16.95 (978-1-942945-35-2(3), 9781942945352) Bright Sky Pr.

Clutton-Brock, Juliet. DK Eyewitness Books: Horse. 2016. (DK Eyewitness Bks.). (ENG., Illus.). 72p. (J). (gr. 3-7). pap. 9.99 (978-1-4654-5174-3(9), 1405883, DK Children) Dorling Kindersley Publishing, Inc.

—Horse. 2016. (DK Eyewitness Bks.). (ENG., Illus.). 72p. (J). (gr. 3-7). lib. bdg. 19.99 (978-1-4654-5175-0(7), 1405883, DK Children) Dorling Kindersley Publishing, Inc.

Collard, Sneed B., III. The World Famous Miles City Bucking Horse Sale. 2010. 64p. 18.00 (978-0-9844460-0-1(1)) Bucking Horse Bks.

Criscione, Rachel Damon. The Appaloosa. (Library of Horses Ser.). 24p. (gr. 3-3). 2009. 42.50 (978-1-60853-719-8(6)) 2006. (Illus.). (J). lib. bdg. 22.60 (978-1-4042-3450-5(0)) Rosen Publishing Group, Inc., The. (PowerKids Pr.).

—The Miniature Horse. 2009. (Library of Horses Ser.). 24p. (gr. 3-3). 42.50 (978-1-60853-720-4(X), PowerKids Pr.) Rosen Publishing Group, Inc., The.

—The Morgan. (Library of Horses Ser.). 24p. (gr. 3-3). 2009. 42.50 (978-1-60853-721-1(8)) 2006. (Illus.). (J). lib. bdg. 22.60 (978-1-4042-3451-2(9)) Rosen Publishing Group, Inc., The. (PowerKids Pr.).

—The Mustang. (Library of Horses Ser.). 24p. (gr. 3-3). 2009. 42.50 (978-1-60853-722-8(6)) 2006. (Illus.). (J). lib. bdg. 22.60 (978-1-4042-3452-9(7)) Rosen Publishing Group, Inc., The. (PowerKids Pr.).

—The Palomino. (Library of Horses Ser.). 24p. (gr. 3-3). 2009. 42.50 (978-1-60853-723-5(4)) 2006. (Illus.). (J). lib. bdg. 22.60 (978-1-4042-3449-9(7)) Rosen Publishing Group, Inc., The. (PowerKids Pr.).

—The Quarter Horse. 2006. (Library of Horses Ser.). (Illus.). 24p. (J). (gr. 3-7). lib. bdg. 22.60 (978-1-4042-3448-2(9), PowerKids Pr.) Rosen Publishing Group, Inc., The.

Crisp, Marty. Everything Horse. 2005. (Kids Faqs Ser.). (ENG., Illus.). 64p. (J). (gr. 3-6). pap. 7.95 (978-1-55971-921-6(4)) Cooper Square Publishing Llc.

Curry, Marion. Horse & Pony Basics. 2006. (Horses & Ponies Ser.). (Illus.). 32p. (gr. 2-6). lib. bdg. 23.00 (978-0-8368-6831-9(5), Gareth Stevens Learning Library) Stevens, Gareth Publishing LLLP.

—Horse & Pony Breeds. 2006. (Horses & Ponies Ser.). (Illus.). 32p. (gr. 2-6). lib. bdg. 23.00 (978-0-8368-6832-6(3), Gareth Stevens Learning Library) Stevens, Gareth Publishing LLLP.

—Horse & Pony Care. 2006. (Horses & Ponies Ser.). (Illus.). 32p. (gr. 2-6). lib. bdg. 23.00 (978-0-8368-6833-3(1), Gareth Stevens Learning Library) Stevens, Gareth Publishing LLLP.

—1000 Facts on Horses. 2004. (Illus.). 224p. (J). (978-0-7607-6084-0(5)) Barnes & Noble, Inc.

de la Bédoyere, Camilla. Horses & Ponies. 2015. (100 Facts You Should Know Ser.). (ENG., Illus.). 48p. (J). (gr. 4-5). pap. 14.05 (978-1-4824-3199-5(8)) Stevens, Gareth Publishing LLLP.

Dearborn-Watts/Dearborn, Ana/Dorothy. La Pouliche Princesse Louise. 2008. (FRE.). 32p. pap. 7.00 (978-1-896543-38-3(3)) DreamCatcher Publishing CAN. Dist: Univ. of Toronto Pr.

Decaire, Carmale, ed. Girls & Their Horses. Clar, David, illus. 2006. (ENG.). 64p. (J). (gr. 4-7). pap. 8.95 (978-1-59369-209-4(9)) American Girl Publishing, Inc.

Dell, Pamela. Appaloosas. 2014. (Majestic Horses Ser.). (ENG.). 24p. (J). (gr. 2-5). 28.50 (978-1-62687-002-4(0), 206791) Child's World, Inc., The.

—Arabians. 2014. (Majestic Horses Ser.). (ENG.). 24p. (J). (gr. 2-5). 28.50 (978-1-62687-003-1(9), 206792) Child's World, Inc., The.

—Clydesdales. 2014. (Majestic Horses Ser.). (ENG.). 24p. (J). (gr. 2-5). 28.50 (978-1-62687-004-8(7), 206793) Child's World, Inc., The.

—Mustangs. 2014. (Majestic Horses Ser.). (ENG.). 24p. (J). (gr. 2-5). 28.50 (978-1-62687-005-5(5), 206794) Child's World, Inc., The.

—Przewalski's Horses. 2014. (Majestic Horses Ser.). (ENG.). 24p. (J). (gr. 2-5). 28.50 (978-1-62687-006-2(3), 206795) Child's World, Inc., The.

—Thoroughbreds. 2014. (Majestic Horses Ser.). (ENG.). 24p. (J). (gr. 2-5). 28.50 (978-1-62687-008-6(X), 206797) Child's World, Inc., The.

Dicker, Katie. Horses. 2014. (Farm Animals Ser.). (Illus.). 24p. (gr. 2-5). 28.50 (978-1-62588-022-2(7)) Black Rabbit Bks.

Dickins, Rosie & Pratt, Leonie. Horse & Pony Treasury. Sims, Lesley, ed. Young, Norman & Ablett, Barry, illus. 2006. (Horse & Pony Treasury Ser.). 93p. (J). 19.99 (978-0-7945-1431-0(6), Usborne) EDC Publishing.

Dolphin, Colleen. Happy Horses, 1 vol. 2011. (Farm Pets Ser.). (ENG., Illus.). 24p. (J). (gr. k-3). lib. bdg. 24.21 (978-1-61613-372-6(4)) ABDO Publishing Co.

Dorling Kindersley Publishing Staff. Horses. 2013. (Pocket Genius Ser.). (ENG.). 160p. (J). (gr. 3-7). 7.99 (978-1-4654-0881-5(9), DK Children) Dorling Kindersley Publishing, Inc.

—Horses & Ponies. 2014. (Eye Wonder Ser.). (ENG.). 56p. (J). (gr. k-4). 10.99 (978-1-4654-1564-6(5), DK Children) Dorling Kindersley Publishing, Inc.

—Pocket Genius: Horses. 2016. (Pocket Genius Ser.). (ENG., Illus.). 160p. (J). (gr. 3-7). pap. 4.99 (978-1-4654-4587-2(0), DK Children) Dorling Kindersley Publishing, Inc.

—Ponies & Horses. 2009. (DK Readers Ser.). (ENG.). 32p. (J). (gr. -1-1). 3.99 (978-0-7566-4295-2(7), DK Children) Dorling Kindersley Publishing, Inc.

—Ultimate Sticker Book: Horses & Ponies. 2017. (Ultimate Sticker Bks.). (ENG.). 32p. (J). (gr. k-2). pap. 6.99 (978-1-4654-5692-2(9), DK Children) Dorling Kindersley Publishing, Inc.

Dorling Kindersley Publishing Staff & Woodward, John. Horses: The Ultimate Treasury. 2012. (ENG.). 160p. (J). (gr. 3-7). 19.99 (978-0-7566-9801-0(4), DK Children) Dorling Kindersley Publishing, Inc.

Downey, Fairfax. Famous Horses of the Civil War. Chapman, Frederick T., illus. 2011. 128p. 40.95 (978-1-258-00351-7(1)) Literary Licensing, LLC.

Doyle, Sheri. Horses, 1 vol. 2012. (Farm Animals Ser.). (ENG., Illus.). 24p. (gr. k-1). lib. bdg. 26.65 (978-1-4296-8648-8(0), Pebble Plus) Capstone Press of Coughlan Cos.

Dyan, Penelope. The Comeback Kids — Book 11 — The Wild Mustangs. Weigand, John D., photos by. 2013. (Illus.). 34p. pap. 14.95 (978-1-61477-078-7(6)) Bellissima Publishing, LLC.

Esseltine, Bruce. At the Horse Farm. 2016. (Fun on the Farm Ser.). 00024p. (J). pap. 8.15 (978-1-4824-5524-3(2)) Stevens, Gareth Publishing LLLP.

Farley, Terri. Wild at Heart: Mustangs & the Young People Fighting to Save Them. Farlow, Melissa, photos by. 2015. (ENG., Illus.). 208p. (J). (gr. 5-7). 19.99 (978-0-544-39294-6(9), HMH Books For Young Readers) Houghton Mifflin Harcourt Publishing Co.

Farrell, Russell & Mueller, Peter. All about Horses & Pets. 2010. (All about Drawing Ser.). 80p. (J). 34.25 (978-1-936309-06-1(8)) Quarto Publishing Group USA.

Felber, Bill. The Horse in War. 2005. (Horse Library). (Illus.). 64p. (gr. 5-8). 125.00 (978-0-7910-6650-8(9), Chelsea Hse.) Facts On File, Inc.

Felton, Harold W. A Horse Named Justin Morgan. Fisher, Leonard Everett, illus. 2011. 162p. 41.95 (978-1-258-07855-3(4)) Literary Licensing, LLC.

Fetty, Margaret. Fire Horses. 2008. (Horse Power Ser.). (Illus.). 32p. (J). (gr. 2-5). lib. bdg. 25.27 (978-1-59716-626-3(X), 1277577) Bearport Publishing Co., Inc.

—Show Horses. 2007. (Horse Power Ser.). (Illus.). 32p. (YA). (gr. 2-5). lib. bdg. 25.27 (978-1-59716-399-6(6)) Bearport Publishing Co., Inc.

Fishman, Jon M. American Pharoah. 2016. (Amazing Athletes Ser.). (ENG., Illus.). 32p. (J). (gr. 2-5). 7.99 (978-1-5124-0877-5(8)); 26.65 (978-1-5124-0829-4(8)); 39.99 (978-1-5124-0831-7(X)); 39.99 (978-1-5124-0876-8(X)) Lerner Publishing Group. (Lerner Pubns.).

Frazel, Ellen. The Appaloosa Horse. 2011. (Horse Breed Roundup Ser.). (ENG., Illus.). 24p. (YA). (gr. 3-8). lib. bdg. 25.95 (978-1-60014-655-8(4), Pilot Bks.) Bellwether Media.

—The Clydesdale Horse. 2011. (Horse Breed Roundup Ser.). (ENG., Illus.). 24p. (YA). (gr. 3-8). lib. bdg. 25.95 (978-1-60014-657-2(0), Pilot Bks.) Bellwether Media.

—The Spanish Mustang. 2011. (Horse Breed Roundup Ser.). (ENG., Illus.). 24p. (YA). (gr. 3-8). lib. bdg. 25.95 (978-1-60014-659-6(7), Pilot Bks.) Bellwether Media.

Frydenborg, Kay. Wild Horse Scientists. (Scientists in the Field Ser.). (ENG., Illus.). 80p. (J). (gr. 5-7). 2014. pap. 9.99 (978-0-544-25746-7(4), HMH Books For Young Readers) 2012. 18.99 (978-0-547-51831-2(5)) Houghton Mifflin Harcourt Publishing Co.

Funston, Sylvia. The Kids' Horse Book. 2005. (ENG., Illus.). 72p. (J). (gr. 3-6). pap. 7.95 (978-1-897066-37-9(6), Maple Tree Pr.) Owlkids Bks. Inc. CAN. Dist: Publishers Group West (PGW).

Gaff, Jackie. I Wonder Why Horses Wear Shoes. 2011. (I Wonder Why Ser.). (ENG., Illus.). 32p. (J). (gr. k-3). pap. 6.99 (978-0-7534-6526-4(4), 9780753465264, Kingfisher) Roaring Brook Pr.

Ganeri, Anita. Winnie's Guide to Caring for Your Horse or Pony, 1 vol. Peterson, Rick, illus. 2013. (Pets' Guides). (ENG.). 32p. (gr. 1-3). pap. 8.29 (978-1-4329-7141-0(7)); lib. bdg. 27.32 (978-1-4329-7134-2(4)) Heinemann-Raintree. (Heinemann First Library).

Gibbons, Gail. Horses! Gibbons, Gail, illus. 2005. (ENG., Illus.). 32p. (gr. k-3). tchr. ed. 17.95 (978-0-8234-1703-2(4)) Holiday Hse., Inc.

—Horses! 2004. (ENG., Illus.). 32p. (J). (gr. -1-3). 7.99 (978-0-8234-1875-6(8)) Holiday Hse., Inc.

Gibbs, Maddie. Horses, 1 vol. 2015. (ENG., Illus.). 24p. (J). lib. bdg. 23.60 (978-1-4994-0143-1(4), PowerKids Pr.) Rosen Publishing Group, Inc., The.

—Los Caballos / Horses, 1 vol. 2015. (Amigos de la Granja / Farmyard Friends Ser.). (ENG & SPA.). 24p. (J). 23.60 (978-1-4994-0267-4(8), PowerKids Pr.) Rosen Publishing Group, Inc., The.

Gilkerson, Patricia. My Adventure with Wild Horses. 2006. 44p. (J). 8.99 (978-1-59092-312-2(X)) Blue Forge Pr.

Gish, Melissa. Living Wild: Wild Horses. 2015. (Living Wild Ser.). (ENG.). 48p. (J). (gr. 5-8). pap. 12.00 (978-1-62832-006-0(0), Creative Paperbacks) Creative Co., The.

—Wild Horses. 2014. 46p. (978-1-60818-420-0(X), Creative Education) Creative Co., The.

Glaser, Rebecca Stromstad. Horses Neigh. 2016. (ENG., Illus.). 14p. (J). (gr. -1 — 1). bds. 7.99 (978-1-68152-126-8(1)) Amicus.

Gordon, Sharon. Guess Who Runs. 2004. (Bookworms: Guess Who Ser.). (SPA & ENG., Illus.). 31p. (J). (gr. 3-7). lib. bdg. 21.36 (978-0-7614-1763-7(X), Benchmark Bks.) Marshall Cavendish Corp.

—Guess Who Runs: Adivina Quién Corre. 2007. (Bookworms — Bilingual Editions: Guess Who/Adivina Quien 2 Ser.). (SPA & ENG.). 32p. (gr. k-2). 15.95 (978-0-7614-2885-5(2)); 15.95 (978-0-7614-2868-8(2)) Marshall Cavendish Corp.

Grack, Rachel. The American Paint Horse. 2011. (Horse Breed Roundup Ser.). (ENG., Illus.). 24p. (YA). (gr. 3-8). lib. bdg. 25.95 (978-1-60014-652-7(X), Pilot Bks.) Bellwether Media.

—The American Saddlebred Horse. 2011. (Horse Breed Roundup Ser.). (ENG., Illus.). 24p. (YA). (gr. 3-8). lib. bdg. 25.95 (978-1-60014-654-1(6), Pilot Bks.) Bellwether Media.

Graubart, Norman D. Horses in American History. 2014. (How Animals Shaped History Ser.). (Illus.). 24p. (J). (gr. k-5). 23.60 (978-1-4777-6761-0(4)); pap. 49.50 (978-1-4777-6627-9(8)); pap. 8.25 (978-1-4777-6762-7(2)) Rosen Publishing Group, Inc., The. (PowerKids Pr.).

Green, Emily K. Horses. 2007. (Farm Animals Ser.). (ENG., Illus.). 24p. (J). (gr. k-3). lib. bdg. 25.95 (978-1-60014-067-9(X)) Bellwether Media.

Green, John. Big Book of Horses to Color. 2006. (Dover Nature Coloring Book Ser.). (ENG., Illus.). 160p. (gr. 3-8). 7.95 (978-0-486-45178-7(X)) Dover Pubns., Inc.

—Favorite Horses. 2005. (Dover Nature Coloring Book Ser.). (ENG., Illus.). 32p. (J). (gr. 3-8). 3.99 (978-0-486-44010-1(9)) Dover Pubns., Inc.

—Horse Anatomy. 2006. (Dover Nature Coloring Book Ser.). (ENG., Illus.). 32p. (gr. 6-8). 3.99 (978-0-486-44813-8(4)) Dover Pubns., Inc.

—Horses of the Old West. 2007. (Dover Nature Coloring Book Ser.). (ENG., Illus.). 32p. (gr. 3-8). 3.99 (978-0-486-45675-1(7)) Dover Pubns., Inc.

—Horses Tattoos. 2003. (Dover Tattoos Ser.). (ENG., Illus.). 2p. (J). (gr. 1-4). pap. 1.99 (978-0-486-43029-4(4)) Dover Pubns., Inc.

—Wonderful World of Horses Coloring Book. 2005. (Dover Nature Coloring Book Ser.). (ENG., Illus.). 32p. (J). (gr. 3-5). 3.99 (978-0-486-44465-9(1)) Dover Pubns., Inc.

Green, Sara. The Arabian Horse. 2011. (Horse Breed Roundup Ser.). (ENG., Illus.). 24p. (YA). (gr. 3-8). lib. bdg. 25.95 (978-1-60014-656-5(2), Pilot Bks.) Bellwether Media.

—The Belgian Horse. 2012. (Horse Breed Roundup Ser.). (ENG., Illus.). 24p. (J). (gr. 3-8). lib. bdg. 25.95 (978-1-60014-736-4(4), Pilot Bks.) Bellwether Media.

—The Friesian Horse. 2012. (Horse Breed Roundup Ser.). (ENG., Illus.). 24p. (J). (gr. 3-8). lib. bdg. 25.95 (978-1-60014-737-1(2), Pilot Bks.) Bellwether Media.

—The Lipizzan Horse. 2012. (Horse Breed Roundup Ser.). (ENG., Illus.). 24p. (J). (gr. 3-8). lib. bdg. 25.95 (978-1-60014-738-8(0), Pilot Bks.) Bellwether Media.

—The Lipizzan Horse. 2012. (ENG., Illus.). 24p. 23.00 (978-0-531-20877-9(X), Children's Pr.) Scholastic Library Publishing.

—The Morgan Horse. 2012. (Horse Breed Roundup Ser.). (ENG., Illus.). 24p. (J). (gr. 3-8). lib. bdg. 25.95 (978-1-60014-739-5(9), Pilot Bks.) Bellwether Media.

—The Relgian Horse. 2012. (ENG., Illus.). 24p. 23.00 (978-0-531-20875-5(3), Children's Pr.) Scholastic Library Publishing.

—The Tennessee Walking Horse. 2011. (Horse Breed Roundup Ser.). (ENG., Illus.). 24p. (YA). (gr. 3-8). lib. bdg. 25.95 (978-1-60014-660-2(0), Pilot Bks.) Bellwether Media.

—The Thoroughbred Horse. 2011. (Horse Breed Roundup Ser.). (ENG., Illus.). 24p. (YA). (gr. 3-8). lib. bdg. 25.95 (978-1-60014-661-9(9), Pilot Bks.) Bellwether Media.

Greenwood, Mark. Midnight. Lessac, Frané, illus. 2015. (ENG.). 32p. (J). (gr. k-4). 16.99 (978-0-7636-7466-3(4)) Candlewick Pr.

Haas, Jessie. Horse Crazy! 1,001 Fun Facts, Craft Projects, Games, Activities, & Know-How for Horse-Loving Kids. 2009. (ENG., Illus.). 376p. (J). (gr. 3-8). pap. 16.95 (978-1-60342-154-6(8), 62154) Storey Publishing, LLC.

Hanley, Shirley. Horse Memories of Luck Ahead. 2010. 24p. pap. 15.99 (978-1-4500-5429-4(3)) Xlibris Corp.

Hansard, Peter. A Field Full of Horses. Lilly, Kenneth, illus. 2008. (Read, Listen, & Wonder Ser.). (ENG.). 32p. (J). (gr. -1-3). pap. 8.99 (978-0-7636-3828-3(5)) Candlewick Pr.

Hanson, Anders. Handsome Horses, 1 vol. 2007. (Perfect Pets Ser.). (ENG., Illus.). 24p. (J). (gr. k-3). lib. bdg. 24.21 (978-1-59928-750-8(1), SandCastle) ABDO Publishing Co.

Hapka, Catherine, pseud. Snowman: The True Story of a Champion. 2016. (ENG., Illus.). 160p. (J). (gr. 3-7). 17.99 (978-1-4814-7812-0(5), Aladdin) Simon & Schuster Children's Publishing.

Head, Honor. Horses & Ponies. 2007. (QEB Know Your Pet Ser.). (Illus.). 32p. (J). lib. bdg. 19.95 (978-1-59566-219-4(7)) QEB Publishing Inc.

Hendrix, Emilia. Horses & Foals. 2016. (Animal Family Ser.). (ENG., Illus.). 24p. (J). (gr. k-k). pap. 8.15 (978-1-4824-3775-1(9)) Stevens, Gareth Publishing LLLP.

Henry, Marguerite. Album of Horses. Dennis, Wesley, illus. 2015. (ENG.). 208p. (J). (gr. 3-7). 19.99 (978-1-4814-4258-9(9), Aladdin) Simon & Schuster Children's Publishing.

Heos, Bridget. Do You Really Want a Horse? Longhi, Katya, illus. 2013. (Do You Really Want a Pet? Ser.). (ENG.). 24p. (gr. 1-4). 27.10 (978-1-60753-207-1(7)) Amicus Publishing.

Hibbert, Clare. If You Were a Horse. 2013. (If You Were A... Ser.). 32p. (gr. 2-5). 31.35 (978-1-59920-964-7(0)) Black Rabbit Bks.

Higgins, Melissa. Sgt. Reckless - The War Horse: Korean War Hero. Iglesias, Álvaro, illus. 2014. (Animal Heroes Ser.). (ENG.). 32p. (gr. k-2). 28.65 (978-1-4795-5462-1(6)) Picture Window Bks.

Hiley, Lisa & Langrish, Bob. The Horse Breeds Poster Book. 2003. (ENG., Illus.). 64p. (J). (gr. 2-8). pap. 10.95 (978-1-58017-507-4(4), 67507) Storey Publishing, LLC.

Hinds, Kathryn. Scythians & Sarmatians. 2009. (Barbarians! Ser.). 80p. (gr. 6). 35.64 (978-0-7614-4072-7(0)) Marshall Cavendish GBR. Dist: Marshall Cavendish Corp.

Hodgkins, Fran. Horses. 2009. (FACT ATLAS Ser.). 72p. (J). pap. 13.99 (978-0-8416-1094-1(0)) Hammond World Atlas Corp.

Holub, Joan. Why Do Horses Neigh? DiVito, Anna, illus. 2003. (Penguin Young Readers, Level 3 Ser.). (ENG.). 48p. (J). (gr. 1-3). pap. 3.99 (978-0-14-230119-7(1), Penguin Young Readers) Penguin Young Readers Group.

Hong, Chen Jiang. The Magic Horse of Han Gan. Bedrick, Claudia Z., tr. from FRE. 2006. (ENG., Illus.). 38p. (J). (gr. -1-3). 16.95 (978-1-59270-063-9(2)) Enchanted Lion Bks., LLC.

Hood, Karen Jean Matsko. Gaited Horse Activity & Coloring Book. Whispering Pine Press International, ed. Artistic Design Service Staff, illus. 2014. (Hood Activity & Coloring Book Ser.). 160p. (J). bk. 4. spiral bd. 21.95 (978-1-59649-628-6(2)) Vol. 4. (ENG.). per. 19.95 (978-1-59210-591-5(2)) Whispering Pine Pr. International, Inc.

—Gaited Horse Activity & Coloring Book-English/German/Spanish Edition. Whispering Pine Press International, Inc. Staff, ed. Artistic Book and Web Design, illus. 2010. (ENG, GER & SPA.). 160p. (J). per. 19.95 (978-1-59649-522-7(7)) Whispering Pine Pr. International, Inc.

—Gaited Horse Journal: A Daily Journal, Bk.4. Whispering Pine Press International, Inc. Staff, ed. Artistic Design Services Staff, illus. 2014. (Children's Journal Series). 160p. (J). 19.95 (978-1-59434-790-0(5)); per. 13.95 (978-1-59434-791-7(3)); spiral bd. 15.95 (978-1-59434-795-5(6)) Whispering Pine Pr. International, Inc.

—Icelandic Horse Activity & Coloring Book, Vol. 6. Whispering Pine Press International, ed. Artistic Design Service Staff, illus. 2nd ed. 2014. (Educational Activity & Coloring Book Ser.). (ENG, ICE & GER.). 160p. (J). spiral bd. 21.95 (978-1-59649-364-3(X)) Whispering Pine Pr. International, Inc.

—Icelandic Horse Activity & Coloring Book: Activity & Coloring Book, Vol. 6. Whispering Pine Press International, ed. Artistic Design Service Staff, illus. 2014. (Hood Activity & Coloring Book Ser.). (ENG, GER & ICE.). 160p. (J). per. 19.95 (978-1-59210-595-3(5)) Whispering Pine Pr. International, Inc.

Horses & Ponies. 2009. (Reference Readers Ser.). 32p. (978-1-4075-1835-0(6)) Parragon, Inc.

Hucks, Doris. I Am a Shining Star. 2011. 36p. pap. 18.00 (978-1-4634-1916-5(3)) AuthorHouse.

Hudak, Heather C. Thumbelina. 2008. (Inspiring Animals Ser.). (Illus.). 24p. (J). (gr. 2-4). pap. 8.95 (978-1-59036-855-8(X)); lib. bdg. 24.45 (978-1-59036-854-1(1)) Weigl Pubs., Inc.

Hutchings, Amy. What Happens at a Horse Farm? ¿Qué Pasa en una Granja de Caballos? 2008. (Where People Work Ser.). 24p. (gr. -1-3). pap. 8.15 (978-0-8368-9373-1(5), Weekly Reader Leveled Readers) Stevens, Gareth Publishing LLLP.

—What Happens at a Horse Farm? (¿Qué Pasa en una Granja de Caballos?) 2008. (Where People Work Ser.). (SPA & ENG.). 24p. (gr. -1-3). pap. 8.15 (978-0-8368-9379-3(4), Weekly Reader Leveled Readers) Stevens, Gareth Publishing LLLP.

Ipcar, Dahlov. Horses of Long Ago. 2014. (ENG., Illus.). 64p. (J). (gr. -1-5). 19.95 (978-1-60893-323-5(7)) Down East Bks.

—World Full of Horses. 2014. (ENG., Illus.). 36p. (J). (gr. -1-3). 17.95 *(978-1-60893-314-3(8))* Down East Bks.

Jackson, Shelley Ann & Crosby, Jeff. Harness Horses, Bucking Broncos & Pit Ponies: A History of Horse Breeds. Jackson, Shelley Ann & Crosby, Jeff, illus. 2011. (ENG., Illus.). 74p. (J). (gr. k-12). 19.95 *(978-0-88776-986-3(1)*, Tundra Bks.) Tundra Bks. CAN. Dist: Penguin Random Hse. LLC.

Jackson, Tom. Wild Horses. 2008. (Nature's Children Ser.). (Illus.). 52p. (J). *(978-0-7172-6265-6(0))* Grolier, Ltd.

Jeffrey, Laura S. Choosing a Horse: How to Choose & Care for a Horse. 2013. (American Humane Association Pet Care Ser.). 48p. (J). (gr. 3-18). lib. bdg. 25.27 *(978-0-7660-4083-0(6))*; pap. 8.95 *(978-1-4644-0218-0(3)*, Enslow Elementary) Enslow Pubs., Inc.

—Horses: How to Choose & Care for a Horse. 2004. (American Humane Pet Care Library). (Illus.). 48p. (J). lib. bdg. 25.27 *(978-0-7660-2519-6(5))* Enslow Pubs., Inc.

Jepperson, Richard. Two Fires in the Night: The Third Part of the Crazy Horse Chronicles. Mundie, Ken, illus. 2003. viii, 56p. (YA). (gr. 7-12). 16.95 *(978-0-9672012-2-1(5))* String of Beads Pubns.

Johnson, Robin. Show Jumping. 2009. (ENG., Illus.). 32p. (J). (gr. 3-6). lib. bdg. *(978-0-7787-4979-0(7))* Crabtree Publishing Co.

Kahn, Sarah, ed. 50 Horses & Ponies to Spot. Jackson, Ian, illus. 2009. (Spotter's Cards Ser.). 52p. (J). 9.99 *(978-0-7945-2171-4(1)*, Usborne) EDC Publishing.

Kalman, Bobbie. Baby Horses. 2008. (It's Fun to Learn about Baby Animals Ser.). (ENG., Illus.). 24p. (J). (gr. 3-7). pap. *(978-0-7787-3972-2(4))* Crabtree Publishing Co.

Kalman, Bobbie & Levigne, Heather. Que es un Caballo? 2006. (Ciencia de los Seres Vivos Ser.). (ENG & SPA.). 32p. (J). (gr. 2-3). pap. *(978-0-7787-8812-6(1))* Crabtree Publishing Co.

—¿Qué Es un Caballo? 2006. (Ciencia de los Seres Vivos Ser.). (ENG & SPA., Illus.). 32p. (J). lib. bdg. *(978-0-7787-8766-2(4))* Crabtree Publishing Co.

Kavanaugh, Missy & Gurman, Sarah, texts. Horses. 2009. (Illus.). (J). *(978-1-4351-1781-5(6))* Barnes & Noble, Inc.

Keaster, Diane W. Chickadee - the Traveler, 11 vols. Page, Debbie, illus. l.t. ed. 2004. (ZC Horses: Vol. 8). (ENG.). 80p. (J). per. 7.95 *(978-0-9721496-7-9(8))* ZC Horses Series of Children's Bks.

—Darby - the Cow Dog, 9 vols. Page, Debbie et al, illus. l.t. ed. 2005. (ZC Horses: 9). (ENG.). 68p. (J). per. 7.95 *(978-0-9721496-8-6(6))* ZC Horses Series of Children's Bks.

—Leroy - the Stallion, 25 vols. Page, Debbie, illus. l.t. ed. 2003. (ZC Horses: 6). (ENG.). 79p. (J). per. 7.95 *(978-0-9721496-5-5(1))* ZC Horses Series of Children's Bks.

—Sonny - the Spectacular. Becker, Toni, illus. l.t. ed. 2006. (ZC Horses: Vol. 9). (ENG.). 80p. (J). per. 7.95 *(978-0-9721496-9-3(4))* ZC Horses Series of Children's Bks.

Kelly, Miles. 100 Facts Horses & Ponies. 2017. (ENG.). pap. ***(978-1-78617-013-2(2))*** Miles Kelly Publishing, Ltd.

Khan, Sarah. Little Book of Horses & Ponies. Lambert, Stephen, illus. 2010. (Miniature Editions Ser.). 64p. (YA). (gr. 3-18). 6.99 *(978-0-7945-2791-4(4)*, Usborne) EDC Publishing.

Kimball, Cheryl. Horse Showing for Kids: Training, Grooming, Trailering, Apparel, Tack, Competing, Sportsmanship. 2004. (ENG., Illus.). 160p. (J). (gr. 4-10). pap. 16.95 *(978-1-58017-501-2(5)*, 67501) Storey Publishing, LLC.

Kitts, Wendy. Sable Island: The Wandering Sandbar, 1 vol. 2012. (ENG., Illus.). 96p. (J). (gr. 2-4). pap. 15.95 *(978-1-55109-865-4(2))* Nimbus Publishing, Ltd. CAN. Dist: Orca Bk. Pubs. USA.

Kolpin, Molly. Favorite Horses: Breeds Girls Love, 1 vol. 2014. (Crazy about Horses Ser.). (ENG., Illus.). 32p. (gr. 3-4). lib. bdg. 27.99 *(978-1-4914-0708-0(5)*, Snap Bks.) Capstone Press of Coughlan Cos.

Kolpin, Molly & Bratton, Donna Bowman. Crazy about Horses, 1 vol. 2014. (Crazy about Horses Ser.). (ENG.). 32p. (gr. 3-4). 111.96 *(978-1-4914-0712-7(3)*, Snap Bks.) Capstone Press of Coughlan Cos.

—Crazy about Horses: Everything Horse Lovers Needs to Know, 1 vol. 2014. (Crazy about Horses Ser.). (ENG., Illus.). 112p. (gr. 3-4). pap. 12.95 *(978-1-4914-0713-4(1)*, Snap Bks.) Capstone Press of Coughlan Cos.

Krisher, Trudy. An Affectionate Farewell: the Story of Old Abe & Old Bob. Dodson, Bert, illus. 2015. (ENG.). 32p. (J). (gr. 1-2). 17.95 *(978-1-59373-155-7(8))* Bunker Hill Publishing, Inc.

Kummer, Patricia K. Working Horses. 2013. 48p. (J). (gr. 4-8). 29.93 *(978-1-60870-840-6(3))* Cavendish Square Publishing.

Landau, Elaine. Appaloosas Are My Favorite! 2012. (My Favorite Horses Ser.). (ENG.). 24p. (gr. 3-5). lib. bdg. 22.60 *(978-0-7613-6535-8(4)*, Lerner Pubns.) Lerner Publishing Group.

—Arabians Are My Favorite! 2012. (My Favorite Horses Ser.). (ENG.). 24p. (gr. 3-5). lib. bdg. 22.60 *(978-0-7613-4938-9(3)*, Lerner Pubns.) Lerner Publishing Group.

—Lipizzans Are My Favorite! 2012. (My Favorite Horses Ser.). (ENG.). 24p. (gr. 3-5). lib. bdg. 22.60 *(978-0-7613-6533-4(8)*, Lerner Pubns.) Lerner Publishing Group.

—Morgan Horses Are My Favorite! 2012. (My Favorite Horses Ser.). (ENG.). 24p. (gr. 3-5). lib. bdg. 22.60 *(978-0-7613-6536-5(2)*, Lerner Pubns.) Lerner Publishing Group.

Langrish, Bob. Horses & Friends Poster Book. 2004. (ENG., Illus.). 64p. (J). (gr. 3-8). pap. 10.95 *(978-1-58017-580-7(5)*, 67580) Storey Publishing, LLC.

Langrish, Bob, et al, photos by. Dream Horses. 2004. (ENG., Illus.). 64p. (J). (gr. 2-8). pap. 10.95 *(978-1-58017-574-6(0)*, 67574) Storey Publishing, LLC.

Ledu, Stephanie. We Both Read-the Horse Lover's Book. Hudrisier, Cecile, illus. 2009. 44p. (J). 9.95 *(978-1-60115-019-6(9))* Treasure Bay, Inc.

Ledu, Stéphanie. We Both Read-The Horse Lover's Book. Hudrisier, Cecile, illus. 2009. 44p. (J). pap. 4.99 *(978-1-60115-020-2(2))* Treasure Bay, Inc.

Linde, Barbara M. Appaloosas. 2012. (Horsing Around Ser.). (ENG.). 24p. (J). (gr. 2-5). pap. 8.15 *(978-1-4339-6458-9(9))*; lib. bdg. 22.60 *(978-1-4339-6456-5(2))* Stevens, Gareth Publishing LLLP. (Gareth Stevens Learning Library).

—Arabian Horses. 2012. (Horsing Around Ser.). (ENG.). 24p. (J). (gr. 2-5). pap. 8.15 *(978-1-4339-6462-6(7))*; lib. bdg. 22.60 *(978-1-4339-6460-2(0))* Stevens, Gareth Publishing LLLP. (Gareth Stevens Learning Library).

—Clydesdales. 2012. (Horsing Around Ser.). (ENG.). 24p. (J). (gr. 2-5). pap. 8.15 *(978-1-4339-6466-4(X))*; lib. bdg. 22.60 *(978-1-4339-6464-0(3))* Stevens, Gareth Publishing LLLP. (Gareth Stevens Learning Library).

—Famous Horses. 2011. (Horsing Around Ser.). (Illus.). 24p. (J). (gr. 2-5). pap. 8.15 *(978-1-4339-4624-0(6)*, Gareth Stevens Learning Library); lib. bdg. 22.60 *(978-1-4339-4623-3(8))* Stevens, Gareth Publishing LLLP.

—Miniature Horses. 2011. (Horsing Around Ser.). (Illus.). 24p. (J). (gr. 2-5). lib. bdg. 22.60 *(978-1-4339-4631-8(9))* Stevens, Gareth Publishing LLLP.

Littlefield, Cindy A. & Littlefield. Horse Games & Puzzles for Kids: 102 Brainteasers, Word Games, Jokes & Riddles, Picture Puzzlers, Matches & Logic Tests for Horse-Loving Kids. 2004. (Storey's Games & Puzzles Ser.). (ENG., Illus.). 144p. (J). (gr. 3-8). pap. 9.95 *(978-1-58017-538-8(4)*, 67538) Storey Publishing, LLC.

Lomberg, Michelle. Caring for Your Horse. 2004. (Caring for Your Pet Ser.). (Illus.). 32p. (J). (gr. 4-7). per. 9.95 *(978-1-59036-152-8(0))*; lib. bdg. 26.00 *(978-1-59036-117-7(2))* Weigl Pubs., Inc.

—Horse. 2009. (My Pet Ser.). (Illus.). 32p. (J). (gr. 3-5). pap. 9.95 *(978-1-60596-093-7(4))*; lib. bdg. 26.00 *(978-1-60596-092-0(6))* Weigl Pubs., Inc.

Lomberg, Michelle & Gillespie, Katie. Horse. 2015. (J). *(978-1-4896-2966-1(1))* Weigl Pubs., Inc.

Lunis, Natalie. Miniature Horses. 2009. (Peculiar Pets Ser.). (Illus.). 24p. (YA). (gr. 2-5). lib. bdg. 22.61 *(978-1-59716-861-8(0))* Bearport Publishing Co., Inc.

Lynch, Annabelle. Horses & Foals. 2017. (Animals & Their Babies Ser.). (Illus.). 24p. (gr. k-3). 28.50 ***(978-1-62588-417-6(6)***, Smart Apple Media) Black Rabbit Bks.

Lyons, Jane & Bailey, Karen. Skipingo Home: A Thoroughbred's Second Chance. Gordon, Susie, illus. 2009. (ENG.). 40p. (J). (gr. -1-3). 16.95 *(978-1-58150-205-3(2)*, Eclipse Pr.) Blood-Horse, Inc., The.

Mack, Gail. Horses. 2009. (Great Pets 3 Ser.). 48p. (gr. 3). 29.93 *(978-0-7614-4147-2(6))* Marshall Cavendish GBR. Dist: Marshall Cavendish Corp.

Macken, JoAnn Early. Horses. 2nd rev. ed. 2009. (Animals That Live on the Farm Ser.). (ENG.). 24p. (J). (gr. -1-3). pap. 8.15 *(978-1-4339-2467-5(6))*; lib. bdg. 22.60 *(978-1-4339-2398-2(X))* Stevens, Gareth Publishing LLLP. (Weekly Reader Leveled Readers).

—Horses;Los Caballos. 2nd rev. ed. 2009. (Animals That Live on the Farm/Animales que viven en la granja Ser.). (ENG & SPA.). 24p. (J). (gr. -1-3). pap. 8.15 *(978-1-4339-2474-3(9))*; lib. bdg. 22.60 *(978-1-4339-2430-9(7))* Stevens, Gareth Publishing LLLP. (Weekly Reader Leveled Readers).

MacLeod, Elizabeth. Galloping Through History: Incredible True Horse Stories. 2015. (ENG., Illus.). 88p. (J). (gr. 4-7). pap. 14.95 *(978-1-55451-699-5(4)*, 9781554516995) Annick Pr., Ltd. CAN. Dist: Publishers Group West (PGW).

Magby, Meryl. Mustangs. 2012. (American Animals Ser.). (ENG., Illus.). 24p. (J). (gr. k-3). lib. bdg. 22.60 *(978-1-4488-6178-1(0))*; pap. 8.25 *(978-1-4488-6315-0(5)*, PowerKids Pr.) Rosen Publishing Group, Inc., The.

Make Believe Ideas, creator. Lift Stick & Learn Horse & Pony. 2006. (Lift Stick & Learn Ser.). (Illus.). 12p. (J). (gr. -1-k). pap. *(978-1-84610-283-7(9))* Make Believe Ideas.

Marsico, Katie. Horse Rescue. 2013. 48p. (J). (gr. 4-8). 29.93 *(978-1-60870-836-9(5))*; pap. 12.93 *(978-1-62712-086-9(6))* Cavendish Square Publishing.

—Wild Horses. 2013. (Nature's Children Ser.). (ENG.). 48p. (J). 28.00 *(978-0-531-20983-7(0))*; pap. 6.95 *(978-0-531-24309-1(5))* Scholastic Library Publishing. (Children's Pr.).

Mason, Paul. Horses & Ponies. Elsom, Clare, illus. 2013. (Animal Family Albums Ser.). (ENG.). 32p. (gr. 2-4). pap. 8.29 *(978-1-4109-4942-4(7))*; 30.65 *(978-1-4109-4937-0(0))* Heinemann-Raintree. (Raintree Perspectives).

Mattern, Joanne. Mounted Police. 2009. (Working Together Ser.). 24p. (gr. 1-2). 42.50 *(978-1-60854-831-6(7)*, PowerKids Pr.) Rosen Publishing Group, Inc., The.

—Policía montada (Mounted Police) 2009. (Trabajo en grupo (Working Together) Ser.). (SPA.). 24p. (gr. 1-2). 42.50 *(978-1-60854-578-0(4)*, Editorial Buenas Letras) Rosen Publishing Group, Inc., The.

Matzke, Ann. Mini Horse. 2015. (ENG.). 32p. (gr. 3-6). 32.79 *(978-1-63430-434-4(9))* Rourke Educational Media.

McCarthy, Meghan. Seabiscuit: The Wonder Horse. McCarthy, Meghan, illus. 2008. (ENG., Illus.). 40p. (J). (gr. -1-3). 16.99 *(978-1-4169-3360-1(3)*, Simon & Schuster/Paula Wiseman Bks.) Simon & Schuster/Paula Wiseman Bks.

McClendon, Kimberli A. Have You Heard? Jesus Walks on Water. 2012. 30p. pap. 13.99 *(978-1-4497-4179-2(7)*, WestBow Pr.) Author Solutions, Inc.

McNeil, Niki, et al. HOCPP1036 Horses. 2005. spiral bd. 19.50 *(978-1-60308-036-1(8))* In the Hands of a Child.

Meister, Cari. Horses. 2012. (Illus.). 24p. (J). lib. bdg. 25.65 *(978-1-62031-004-5(X))* Jump! Inc.

Mercer, Abbie. Horses on a Farm. 2009. (Barnyard Animals Ser.). 24p. (J). (ENG.). pap. 8.25 *(978-1-4042-8065-6(0))*; (Illus.). lib. bdg. 22.60 *(978-1-4042-8052-6(9))* Rosen Publishing Group, Inc., The. (PowerKids Pr.).

Metz, Lorijo. Arabian Horses. 2012. (World of Horses Ser.). (ENG., Illus.). 24p. (J). (gr. k-5). pap. 8.25 *(978-1-4488-7499-6(8))*; lib. bdg. 22.60 *(978-1-4488-7426-2(2))* Rosen Publishing Group, Inc., The. (PowerKids Pr.).

—Clydesdales. 2012. (World of Horses Ser.). (ENG., Illus.). 24p. (J). (gr. k-5). pap. 8.25 *(978-1-4488-7500-9(5))*; lib. bdg. 22.60 *(978-1-4488-7427-9(0))* Rosen Publishing Group, Inc., The. (PowerKids Pr.).

—Friesians. 2012. (World of Horses Ser.). (ENG., Illus.). 24p. (J). (gr. k-5). 22.60 *(978-1-4488-7431-6(9))*; pap. 8.25 *(978-1-4488-7504-7(8))* Rosen Publishing Group, Inc., The. (PowerKids Pr.).

—Lipizzans. 2012. (World of Horses Ser.). (ENG., Illus.). 24p. (J). (gr. k-5). 22.60 *(978-1-4488-7428-6(9))*; pap. 8.25 *(978-1-4488-7501-6(3))* Rosen Publishing Group, Inc., The. (PowerKids Pr.).

—Lusitanos. 2012. (World of Horses Ser.). (ENG., Illus.). 24p. (J). (gr. k-5). 22.60 *(978-1-4488-7430-9(0))*; pap. 8.25 *(978-1-4488-7503-0(X))* Rosen Publishing Group, Inc., The. (PowerKids Pr.).

—Thoroughbreds. 2012. (World of Horses Ser.). (ENG., Illus.). 24p. (J). (gr. k-5). 22.60 *(978-1-4488-7429-3(7))*; pap. 8.25 *(978-1-4488-7502-3(1))* Rosen Publishing Group, Inc., The. (PowerKids Pr.).

Mezzanotte, Jim. Police. 2010. (Working Animals Ser.). 64p. (gr. 5-18). 28.50 *(978-1-60870-166-7(2))* Marshall Cavendish Corp.

Mickle, Shelley Fraser. Barbaro: America's Horse. 2007. (ENG., Illus.). 160p. (J). (gr. 3-7). pap. 9.99 *(978-1-4169-4865-0(1)*, Simon & Schuster/Paula Wiseman Bks.) Simon & Schuster/Paula Wiseman Bks.

Milbourne, Anna. Horses & Ponies. Gaudenzi, Giacinto & Haggerty, Tim, illus. 2006. (Beginners Nature: Level 1 Ser.). 32p. (J). (gr. k-2). 4.99 *(978-0-7945-1397-9(2)*, Usborne) EDC Publishing.

Minden, Cecilia. Farm Animals: Horses. 2009. (21st Century Junior Library: Farm Animals Ser.). (ENG., Illus.). 24p. (gr. 2-4). lib. bdg. 25.64 *(978-1-60279-541-9(X)*, 200274) Cherry Lake Publishing.

—Foals Grow up to Be Horses. 2010. (21st Century Basic Skills Library: Animals Grow Up Ser.). (ENG.). 24p. (gr. k-3). lib. bdg. 22.79 *(978-1-60279-853-3(2)*, 200572) Cherry Lake Publishing.

Mobley, W. Lenore. Enjoy the Journey: Of Women & Their Horses along the Snake River Plain. 2011. 220p. (gr. -1 — 1). pap. 17.50 *(978-1-4567-6954-3(5))* AuthorHouse.

Monahan, Erin. Arabian Horses (Caballos Árabes) Strictly Spanish Translation Services Staff, tr. from ENG. 2012. (Cabollos/Horses Ser.). (ENG & MUL.). 24p. (gr. k-1). lib. bdg. 21.99 *(978-1-4296-9226-7(X))* Capstone Press of Coughlan Cos.

Monahan, Erin & O'Brien, Kim. Caballos/Horses. Strictly Spanish, LLC., tr. 2012. (Cabollos/Horses Ser.). (MUL.). 24p. (gr. k-1). lib. bdg. 109.95 *(978-1-4296-9229-8(4))* Capstone Press of Coughlan Cos.

Moody, Ralph. American Horses. O'Keeffe, Neil, illus. 2004. (ENG.). 185p. pap. 14.95 *(978-0-8032-8301-5(6)*, MOOAMX, Bison Bks.) Univ. of Nebraska Pr.

Morgan, Sally. Horses. 2012. (Pets Plus Ser.). (Illus.). 32p. (gr. 3-6). lib. bdg. 31.35 *(978-1-59920-702-5(8))* Black Rabbit Bks.

—Wild Horses: Animal Lives Series. 2008. (J). lib. bdg. 18.95 *(978-1-59566-539-3(0))* QEB Publishing Inc.

Mudpuppy Press Staff. Magic Horses 100-piece Puzzle. 2005. (J). 12.99 *(978-0-7353-0512-0(9))* Galison.

Murray, Julie. Arabian Horses, 1 vol. 2003. (Buddy Book Ser.). (ENG.). 24p. (J). (gr. 1-4). 25.65 *(978-1-57765-701-9(2))* ABDO Publishing Co.

—Clydesdale Horses, 1 vol. 2005. (Animal Kingdom Set Ii Ser.). (ENG., Illus.). 24p. (gr. k-4). 25.65 *(978-1-59197-306-5(6)*, Buddy Bks.) ABDO Publishing Co.

—Crime-Fighting Animals, 1 vol. 2009. (Going to Work:Animal Edition Ser.). (ENG., Illus.). 32p. (J). (gr. 2-5). 27.07 *(978-1-60453-561-7(X))* ABDO Publishing Co.

—Horses, 1 vol. 2015. (ENG., Illus.). 24p. (J). 27.07 *(978-1-62970-941-3(7))* ABDO Publishing Co.

—Pinto Horses, 1 vol. 2005. (Animal Kingdom Set Ii Ser.). (ENG., Illus.). 24p. (gr. k-4). 25.65 *(978-1-59197-331-7(7)*, Buddy Bks.) ABDO Publishing Co.

My Little Pony Staff. I Love to Draw! Design & Draw Your Favorite Ponies with Stickers, Stencils, & More! 2013. (Learn Drawing Ser.: 1). (ENG.). 48p. (J). (gr. 1-4). pap. 8.99 *(978-0-7944-2852-5(5))* Reader's Digest Assn., Inc., The.

Nagle, Jeanne. Working Horses. 2011. (Horsing Around Ser.). (Illus.). 24p. (J). (gr. 2-5). pap. 8.15 *(978-1-4339-4644-8(0)*, Gareth Stevens Learning Library); lib. bdg. 22.60 *(978-1-4339-4643-1(2))* Stevens, Gareth Publishing LLLP.

Nathan, Sandy. Tecolote: The Little Horse That Could. 2011. (Illus.). 44p. (J). pap. 14.95 *(978-0-9762809-9-6(X))* Vilasa Pr.

National Geographic Kids Staff. Ponies & Horses. 2015. (NG Sticker Activity Bks.). (ENG.). 56p. (J). (gr. -1-3). pap., act. bk. ed. 6.99 *(978-1-4263-1902-0(9)*, National Geographic Children's Bks.) National Geographic Society.

Nelson, Robin. From Foal to Horse. (Start to Finish, Second Series: Nature's Cycles Ser.). (ENG.). 24p. (gr. k-3). 2012. pap. 6.95 *(978-0-7613-8675-9(0))* 2012. lib. bdg. 23.93 *(978-0-7613-8672-8(6))* 2003. (Illus.). lib. bdg. 19.93 *(978-0-8225-0941-7(5))* Lerner Publishing Group.

—Horses. 2009. pap. 34.95 *(978-0-7613-4093-5(9))*; (ENG.). 24p. 23.93 *(978-0-7613-4058-4(0)*, Lerner Pubns.) Lerner Publishing Group.

Nelson, Su. I'm No Dummy! 2011. 44p. pap. 18.50 *(978-1-4634-3500-4(2))* AuthorHouse.

Niven, Felicia Lowenstein & Library Association Staff. Learning to Care for a Horse. 2010. (Beginning Pet Care with American Humane Ser.). (Illus.). 48p. (J). 25.27 *(978-0-7660-3196-8(9)*, Enslow Elementary) Enslow Pubs., Inc.

Noble, Marty. 3-D Coloring Book — Horses. 2014. (Dover 3-D Coloring Book Ser.). (ENG., Illus.). 32p. (J). (gr. 2). pap. 5.99 *(978-0-486-49474-6(8))* Dover Pubns., Inc.

O'Brien, Kim. Caballos Paint. Strictly Spanish Translation Services Staff, tr. from ENG. 2012. (Cabollos/Horses Ser.).Tr. of American Paint Horses. (SPA, ENG & MUL.). 24p. (gr. k-1). lib. bdg. 21.99 *(978-1-4296-9225-0(1))* Capstone Press of Coughlan Cos.

—Caballos Pura Sangre. Strictly Spanish Translation Services Staff, tr. from ENG. 2012. (Cabollos/Horses Ser.).Tr. of Thoroughbred Horses. (SPA & MUL.). 24p. (gr. k-1). lib. bdg. 21.99 *(978-1-4296-9227-4(8))* Capstone Press of Coughlan Cos.

Olson, Bethany. Baby Horses. 2013. (Super Cute! Ser.). (ENG., Illus.). 24p. (J). (gr. k-3). lib. bdg. 25.95 *(978-1-60014-928-3(6)*, Blastoff! Readers) Bellwether Media.

Ondov, Rebecca E. My Horse Diary for Girls: What I Love about Horses. 2016. (ENG.). 160p. (J). 9.99 *(978-0-7369-6615-3(3))* Harvest Hse. Pubs.

O'Neal, Claire. Care for a Pet Horse. 2008. (How to Convince Your Parents You Can ... Ser.). (Illus.). 32p. (YA). (gr. 1-4). lib. bdg. 25.70 *(978-1-58415-662-8(7))* Mitchell Lane Pubs., Inc.

Osborne, Mary Pope & Boyce, Natalie Pope. Horse Heroes: Stallion by Starlight. Murdocca, Sal, illus. 2013. (Magic Tree House - Fact Tracker Ser.: 27). (ENG.). 128p. (J). (gr. 2-5). 6.99 *(978-0-375-87026-2(1)*, Random Hse. Bks. for Young Readers) Random Hse. Children's Bks.

Osborne, Mary Pope, et al. Horse Heroes. 2013. (Magic Tree House Fact Tracker Ser.: 27). lib. bdg. 16.00 *(978-0-606-26995-7(9)*, Turtleback) Turtleback Bks.

Otfinoski, Steven. Horses. 2009. (Animals Animals 10 Ser.). 48p. (gr. 3). 29.93 *(978-0-7614-3974-5(9))* Marshall Cavendish Corp.

Owen, Ruth. Horses. 2011. (World's Smartest Animals Ser.). (ENG., Illus.). 32p. (J). (gr. k-5). 26.50 *(978-1-61533-378-3(9))*; pap. 11.75 *(978-1-61533-418-6(1))* Windmill Bks.

Packard, Mary. Working Horses. 2007. (Horse Power Ser.). (Illus.). 32p. (J). (gr. 2-5). lib. bdg. 25.27 *(978-1-59716-403-0(8))* Bearport Publishing Co., Inc.

Parker, Steve & Kelly, Miles. 100 Facts on Horses & Ponies. 2010. (Illus.). 48p. pap. *(978-1-84236-985-2(7))* Miles Kelly Publishing, Ltd.

Perkins, Sheila. Horses & Ponies. 2015. (Scholastic Reader, Level 3 Ser.). (ENG.). 32p. (J). (gr. 1-3). pap. 3.99 *(978-0-545-88959-9(6)*, Scholastic Paperbacks) Scholastic, Inc.

Peterson, Cris. Wild Horses: Black Hills Sanctuary. Upitis, Alvis, photos by. 2009. (ENG., Illus.). 32p. (J). (gr. 4-6). pap. 11.95 *(978-1-59078-799-1(4))* Boyds Mills Pr.

Peyton, K. M. Horses. 2009. (Wild Reads Ser.). (ENG., Illus.). 32p. (YA). (gr. k). pap. 4.95 *(978-0-19-911972-1(4))* Oxford Univ. Pr., Inc.

Pickeral, Tamsin. The Encyclopedia of Horses & Ponies. 2003. 384p. (YA). pap. 19.95 *(978-0-7525-8277-1(1))* Parragon, Inc.

Pinnington, Andrea. The Horse & Pony Creativity Book. 2013. (Creativity Bks.). (ENG., Illus.). 80p. (J). (gr. 1-6). pap. 12.99 *(978-1-4380-0127-2(4))* Barron's Educational Series, Inc.

PONY, compiled by. The Little Horse Book. 2007. (YA). pap. *(978-1-933343-58-7(3))* Stabenfeldt Inc.

Rajczak, Kristen. Thoroughbreds. 2012. (Horsing Around Ser.). (ENG., Illus.). 24p. (J). (gr. 2-5). pap. 8.15 *(978-1-4339-6478-7(3))*; lib. bdg. 22.60 *(978-1-4339-6476-3(7))* Stevens, Gareth Publishing LLLP. (Gareth Stevens Learning Library).

Randolph, Joanne. My Friend the Miniature Horse. 2010. (Curious Pet Pals Ser.). (ENG., Illus.). 24p. (J). (gr. k-3). pap. 8.15 *(978-1-60754-984-0(0))*; lib. bdg. 22.60 *(978-1-60754-976-5(X))* Windmill Bks.

Ransford, Sandy. The Kingfisher Illustrated Horse & Pony Encyclopedia. rev. ed. 2010. (ENG., Illus.). 224p. (J). (gr. 5-9). 24.99 *(978-0-7534-6485-4(3)*, 9780753464854, Kingfisher) Roaring Brook Pr.

Redmond, Shirley Raye. Blind Tom: The Horse Who Helped Build the Great Railroad. Bradley, Lois, illus. 2009. (J). pap. 10.00 *(978-0-87842-558-7(6))* Mountain Pr. Publishing Co., Inc.

Regan, Lisa. Horses. Jackson, Ian, illus. 2010. (I Love Animals Ser.). (ENG.). 24p. (J). (gr. 1-5). pap. 8.15 *(978-1-61533-234-2(0))*; lib. bdg. 22.60 *(978-1-61533-228-1(6))* Windmill Bks.

Reid, Struan. Dictionary of horses & ponies - internet Linked. Khan, Aziz, illus. rev. ed. 2004. 128p. (J). pap. 14.95 *(978-0-7945-0843-2(X)*, Usborne) EDC Publishing.

Riggs, Kate. Amazing Animals: Wild Horses. 2015. (Amazing Animals Ser.). (ENG.). 24p. (J). (gr. 1-3). pap. 8.99 *(978-1-62832-093-0(1)*, Creative Paperbacks) Creative Co., The.

—Seedlings: Wild Horses. 2017. (Seedlings Ser.). (ENG.). 24p. (J). (gr. -1-1). pap. 7.99 ***(978-1-62832-485-3(6)***, Creative Paperbacks) Creative Co., The.

—Wild Horses. (J). 2017. ***(978-1-60818-870-3(1))*** 2015. *(978-1-60818-493-4(5))* Creative Co., The. (Creative Education).

Rockwood, Leigh. Horses Are Smart! 2010. (Super Smart Animals Ser.). (Illus.). 24p. (J). pap. 8.25 *(978-1-4358-9838-7(9)*, PowerKids Pr.); (gr. 2-5). lib. bdg. 22.60 *(978-1-4358-9399-3(9))* Rosen Publishing Group, Inc., The.

Rumsch, BreAnn. Arabian Horses, 1 vol. 2011. (Horses Set 1 *2011 Ser.). (ENG.). 24p. (J). (gr. 2-5). 25.65 *(978-1-61613-418-1(6))* ABDO Publishing Co.

—Clydesdale Horses, 1 vol. 2011. (Horses Set 1 *2011 Ser.). (ENG.). 24p. 25.65 *(978-1-61613-419-8(4)*, Checkerboard Library) ABDO Publishing Co.

—Palomino Horses, 1 vol. 2011. (Horses Set 1 *2011 Ser.). (ENG.). 24p. 25.65 *(978-1-61613-420-4(8)*, Checkerboard Library) ABDO Publishing Co.

—Pinto Horses, 1 vol. 2011. (Horses Set 1 *2011 Ser.). (ENG.). 24p. 25.65 *(978-1-61613-421-1(6)*, Checkerboard Library) ABDO Publishing Co.

—Shetland Ponies, 1 vol. 2011. (Horses Set 1 *2011 Ser.). (ENG.). 24p. 25.65 *(978-1-61613-422-8(4)*, Checkerboard Library) ABDO Publishing Co.

—Thoroughbred Horses, 1 vol. 2011. (Horses Set 1 *2011 Ser.). (ENG.). 24p. 25.65 *(978-1-61613-423-5(2)*, Checkerboard Library) ABDO Publishing Co.

Sandler, Michael. Military Horses. 2007. (Horse Power Ser.). (Illus.). 32p. (YA). (gr. 2-5). lib. bdg. 25.27 *(978-1-59716-402-3(X))* Bearport Publishing Co., Inc.

—Race Horses. 2007. (Horse Power Ser.). (Illus.). 32p. (J). (gr. 2-5). lib. bdg. 25.27 *(978-1-59716-398-9(8))* Bearport Publishing Co., Inc.

Sarkisian, K. I Have a Horse: Learning the H Sound. 2009. (PowerPhonics Ser.). 24p. (gr. 1-1). 39.90 *(978-1-60851-449-6(8)*, PowerKids Pr.) Rosen Publishing Group, Inc., The.

Scanlan, Lawrence. The Big Red Horse: The Story of Secretariat & the Loyal Groom Who Loved Him. 2010. 176p. (J). (gr. 4-7). pap. 7.99 *(978-0-06-202669-9(0))*; (ENG., Illus.). pap. 9.99 *(978-0-00-639352-8(7))* HarperCollins Pubs.

Sexton, Colleen. Caring for Your Horse. 2010. (Pet Care Library). (ENG., Illus.). 24p. (J). (gr. 2-5). lib. bdg. 25.95 *(978-1-60014-469-1(1)*, Blastoff! Readers) Bellwether Media.

Shea, Therese. Racing Horses. 2011. (Horsing Around Ser.). (Illus.). 24p. (J). (gr. 2-5). pap. 8.15 *(978-1-4339-4636-3(X)*, Gareth Stevens Learning Library); lib. bdg. 22.60 *(978-1-4339-4635-6(1))* Stevens, Gareth Publishing LLLP.

Shew, David & Orttenburger, Rhonda Shew. Midway Dreams. 2014. (ENG.). 36p. pap. 15.95 *(978-1-4908-0295-4(9)*, WestBow Pr.) Author Solutions, Inc.

Shulman, Mark. Horsing Around. Nethery, Susan, illus. 2005. (Storytime Stickers Ser.). (ENG.). 16p. (J). (gr. k-2). pap. 5.95 *(978-1-4027-1808-3(X))* Sterling Publishing Co., Inc.
Silverman, Buffy. Can You Tell a Horse from a Pony? 2012. (Animal Look-Alikes Ser.). 32p. (gr. k-2). pap. 45.32 *(978-0-7613-9256-9(4))*; (ENG.). pap. 7.95 *(978-0-7613-8554-7(1))*; (ENG.). lib. bdg. 26.60 *(978-0-7613-6740-6(3)*, Lerner Pubns.) Lerner Publishing Group.
—Meet a Baby Horse. 2016. (Lightning Bolt Books (tm) — Baby Farm Animals Ser.). (ENG., Illus.). 32p. (J). (gr. 1-3). 26.65 *(978-1-5124-0801-0(8))* Lerner Publishing Group.
Silverman, Buffy. Mini Horses. 2017. (J). ***(978-1-5124-8304-8(4))*** Lerner Publishing Group.
Silverstein, Alvin, et al. Miniature Horses: Cool Pets! Kelley, Gerald, illus. 2012. (Far-Out & Unusual Pets Ser.). 48p. (J). (gr. 3-4). pap. 8.95 *(978-1-4644-0125-1(X))*; 25.27 *(978-0-7660-3880-6(7))* Enslow Pubs., Inc. (Enslow Elementary).
Simon, Seymour. Horses. Simon, Seymour, illus. 2017. (ENG., Illus.). 32p. (J). (gr. 1-5). pap. 6.99 *(978-0-06-446256-3(0))* HarperCollins Pubs.
—Horses. 2006. (ENG., Illus.). 40p. (J). (gr. 1-5). 17.99 *(978-0-06-028944-7(9))* HarperCollins Pubs.
Sly, Debby. Fun with Ponies & Horses: Training, Riding, Grooming, Games. 2003. (Illus.). 128p. (J). pap. *(978-1-59258-018-7(1))* Hylas Publishing.
Smith, L. The Usborne Book of Horses & Ponies. rev. ed. 2004. (Young Nature Ser.). (Illus.). 32p. (Orig.). (J). pap. 6.95 *(978-0-7945-0850-0(2)*, Usborne) EDC Publishing.
Smith, Lucy. The Usborne Book of Horses & Ponies. Gray, Miranda & Trotter, Stuart, illus. 2006. 32p. (J). pap. *(978-0-439-88983-4(9))* Scholastic, Inc.
Spiotta-DiMare, Loren. Draft Horses: Horses That Work. 2014. (Horses That Help with the American Humane Association Ser.). 48p. (J). lib. bdg. 25.27 *(978-0-7660-4220-9(0)*, Enslow Elementary) Enslow Pubs., Inc.
—Therapy Horses: Horses That Heal. 2014. (Horses That Help with the American Humane Association Ser.). 48p. (J). lib. bdg. 25.27 *(978-0-7660-4217-9(0)*, Enslow Elementary) Enslow Pubs., Inc.
Stafford, Susan, ed. Horse Tales for the Soul, Vol. 5. 2004. (Horse Tales for the Soul Ser.: 5). 160p. per. 19.95 *(978-0-9740841-1-4(5))* K&B Products.
Staub, Frank J. Running Free: America's Wild Horses. Staub, Frank J., photos by. 2006. (Prime (Elementary) Ser.). (Illus.). 48p. (J). (gr. 3-4). lib. bdg. 25.27 *(978-0-7660-2670-4(1))* Enslow Pubs., Inc.
Steele-Staccio, Eva & Klutz Editors. The Marvelous Book of Magical Horses: Dress up Paper Horses & Their Fairy Friends. 2011. (ENG.). 56p. (J). (gr. 1-1). spiral bd. 19.99 *(978-1-59174-926-4(3))* Klutz.
Stockland, Patricia M. In the Horse Stall, 1 vol. Ouren, Todd, illus. 2007. (Barnyard Buddies Ser.). (ENG.). 24p. (gr. -1-2). 27.07 *(978-1-60270-024-6(9)*, Looking Glass Library-Nonfiction) Magic Wagon.
Stoddard, Rosie & Marshall, Phillip. Horse: The Essential Guide for Young Equestrians. Hamilton, Libby, ed. Allsopp, Sophie et al, illus. 2008. (Genuine & Moste Authentic Guide Ser.: 4). (ENG.). 32p. (J). (gr. 1-4). 16.99 *(978-0-7636-3547-3(2))* Candlewick Pr.
Stone, Lynn M. Arabian Horses. 2007. (Eye to Eye with Horses (High Interest) Ser.). (Illus.). 24p. (J). (gr. 3-6). lib. bdg. 27.07 *(978-1-60044-581-1(0))* Rourke Educational Media.
—Paint Horses. 2007. (Eye to Eye with Horses (High Interest) Ser.). (Illus.). 24p. (J). (gr. 3-6). lib. bdg. 27.07 *(978-1-60044-582-8(9))* Rourke Educational Media.
Stubblefield, Karen. Anna & Chen. 2003. 37p. pap. 24.95 *(978-1-4137-0350-4(X))* PublishAmerica, Inc.
The Sunday Horse: Individual Title Six-Packs. (Action Packs Ser.). 120p. (gr. 3-5). 44.00 *(978-0-7635-8435-1(5))* Rigby Education.
Swanson, Diane. Wild Horses. 2004. (Welcome to the World of Animals Ser.). (Illus.). 32p. (gr. 1-4). lib. bdg. 24.00 *(978-0-8368-4026-1(7)*, Gareth Stevens Learning Library) Stevens, Gareth Publishing LLLP.
Swinney, Nicola Jane. I Love Horses & Ponies. 2014. (Illus.). 120p. (J). pap. *(978-1-4351-5535-0(1))* Barnes & Noble, Inc.
Swinney, Nicola Jane. My Little Book of Horses & Ponies. Langrish, Bob, illus. 2016. 64p. (J). ***(978-1-4351-6349-2(4))*** Barnes & Noble, Inc.
Szymanski, Lois. The True Story of Miracle Man, 1 vol. 2013. (ENG., Illus.). 48p. (J). pap. 14.99 *(978-0-7643-4420-6(X)*, 9780764344206) Schiffer Publishing, Ltd.
Thatcher, Henry. Clydesdales & Miniature Horses, 1 vol., 1. 2014. (Big Animals, Small Animals Ser.). (ENG.). 32p. (J). (gr. k-5). 26.25 *(978-1-4777-6102-1(0)*, PowerKids Pr.) Rosen Publishing Group, Inc., The.
Thomas, Isabel. Handy Horse Projects. 2015. (Pet Projects Ser.). (ENG., Illus.). 32p. (gr. 3-5). 27.99 *(978-1-4109-8065-6(0)*, Snap Bks.) Capstone Press of Coughlan Cos.
Thronson, Lloyd. White Rockets with Four Hooves. 2011. 38p. pap. 16.95 *(978-1-4560-6910-0(1))* America Star Bks.
Top That Publishing Staff, ed. Wacky Pony. 2004. (Wacky Animals Ser.). (Illus.). 10p. (J). pap. *(978-1-84510-092-6(1))* Top That! Publishing PLC.
Toufexis, George. Ultimate Horse-Athon Facts & Activity Book. 2013. (ENG.). 48p. (J). (gr. 3-8). pap. 4.99 *(978-0-486-49184-4(6))* Dover Pubns., Inc.
Tracqui, Valérie. Face-to-Face with the Horse: Faster Than the Wind. Delaborde, Gilles, photos by. 2004. (Face to Face Ser.). (Illus.). 28p. (J). (gr. -1-2). 9.95 *(978-1-57091-450-8(8))* Charlesbridge Publishing, Inc.
Trueit, Trudi Strain. Horse Care. 2013. 48p. (J). (gr. 4-8). 29.93 *(978-1-60870-835-2(7))*; pap. 12.93 *(978-1-62712-085-2(8))* Cavendish Square Publishing.
Turnbull, Stephanie. Show Horses. 2015. (My Favorite Horses Ser.). (Illus.). 24p. (gr. 2-5). 28.50 *(978-1-62588-183-0(5)*, 1381111) Black Rabbit Bks.
—Sports Horses. 2015. (My Favorite Horses Ser.). (Illus.). 24p. (gr. 2-5). 28.50 *(978-1-62588-184-7(3))* Black Rabbit Bks.
—Sports Horses. 2015. (ENG., Illus.). 24p. (J). pap. 8.95 *(978-1-77092-230-3(X))* RiverStream Publishing.
—Wild Horses. 2015. (My Favorite Horses Ser.). 24p. (gr. 2-5). 28.50 *(978-1-62588-185-4(1))* Black Rabbit Bks.
—Wild Horses. 2015. (ENG., Illus.). 24p. (J). pap. 8.95 *(978-1-77092-231-0(8))* RiverStream Publishing.
—Working Horses. 2015. (My Favorite Horses Ser.). 24p. (gr. 2-5). 28.50 *(978-1-62588-180-9(0))* Black Rabbit Bks.
—Working Horses. 2015. (ENG., Illus.). 24p. (J). pap. 8.95 *(978-1-77092-226-6(1))* RiverStream Publishing.
Twine, Alice. Horses. (Baby Animals Ser.). 24p. 2009. (gr. 1-1). 42.50 *(978-1-61511-490-0(4)*, PowerKids Pr.) 2007. (Illus.). (J). (gr. -1-3). lib. bdg. 22.60 *(978-1-4042-3774-2(7))* Rosen Publishing Group, Inc., The.
—Horses/Caballos. 2009. (Baby Animals/Animales bebé Ser.). (SPA.). 24p. (gr. 1-1). 42.50 *(978-1-61511-502-0(1)*, Editorial Buenas Letras) Rosen Publishing Group, Inc., The.
—Horses/Caballos. Obregon, Jose Maria, tr. 2007. (Baby Animals / Animales Bebé Ser.). (ENG & SPA., Illus.). 24p. (J). (gr. -1-3). lib. bdg. 22.60 *(978-1-4042-7630-7(0)*, Editorial Buenas Letras) Rosen Publishing Group, Inc., The.
Ulmer, Michael. H Is for Horse: An Equestrian Alphabet. vanFrankenhuyze, Gijsbert, illus. rev. ed. 2004. (Sports Ser.). (ENG.). 40p. (J). (gr. -1-5). 17.95 *(978-1-58536-213-4(1))* Sleeping Bear Pr.
—H Is for Horse: An Equestrian Alphabet. Frankenhuyzen, Gijsbert van, illus. 2015. (Av2 Fiction Readalong 2016 Ser.). (ENG.). (J). (gr. 1-4). lib. bdg. 34.28 *(978-1-4896-3750-5(8)*, AV2 by Weigl) Weigl Pubs., Inc.
Uttridge, Sarah. Horses Around the World. 2014. (Animals Around the World Ser.). (Illus.). 32p. (gr. 2-5). 31.35 *(978-1-62588-193-9(2))* Black Rabbit Bks.
Van Cleaf, Kristin. American Paint Horses, 1 vol. 2006. (Horses Set 2 Ser.). (ENG., Illus.). 24p. (gr. k-6). 25.65 *(978-1-59679-313-2(9)*, Checkerboard Library) ABDO Publishing Co.
—Miniature Horses, 1 vol. 2006. (Horses Set 2 Ser.). (ENG., Illus.). 24p. (gr. k-6). 25.65 *(978-1-59679-315-6(5)*, Checkerboard Library) ABDO Publishing Co.
—Mustang Horses, 1 vol. 2006. (Horses Set 2 Ser.). (ENG., Illus.). 24p. (gr. k-6). 25.65 *(978-1-59679-316-3(3)*, Checkerboard Library) ABDO Publishing Co.
—Przewalski's Horses, 1 vol. 2006. (Horses Set 2 Ser.). (ENG., Illus.). 24p. (gr. k-6). 25.65 *(978-1-59679-317-0(1)*, Checkerboard Library) ABDO Publishing Co.
—Quarter Horses, 1 vol. 2006. (Horses Set 2 Ser.). (ENG., Illus.). 24p. (gr. k-6). 25.65 *(978-1-59679-318-7(X)*, Checkerboard Library) ABDO Publishing Co.
Vogel, Julia. Wild Horses. 2004. (Our Wild World Ser.). (ENG., Illus.). 48p. (J). (gr. 2-5). pap. 7.95 *(978-1-55971-882-0(X))* Cooper Square Publishing Llc.
Von Kessel, Carola. Understanding Horses with Caddie. Guhe, Irmtraud, illus. 2004. (ENG.). 32p. (J). (gr. 4). 13.95 *(978-3-86127-948-8(7))* Cadmos Verlag GmbH DEU. Dist: Independent Pubs. Group.
Walker, Kathryn. See How Horses & Ponies Grow. 2009. (See How They Grow Ser.). (J). (gr. k-3). (ENG., Illus.). 24p. pap. 8.25 *(978-1-4358-2881-0(X))*; lib. bdg. 22.60 *(978-1-4358-2832-2(1))* Rosen Publishing Group, Inc., The. (PowerKids Pr.).
Walter Foster Creative Team, ed. All about Drawing Horses & Pets. 2008. (All about Drawing Ser.). (ENG., Illus.). 80p. (J). (gr. 1-3). pap. 9.95 *(978-1-60058-580-7(9)*, 1600585809) Quarto Publishing Group USA.
Watson, Mary Gordon. Beds & Bedding. Vincer, Carole, illus. 2nd ed. 2006. (Threshold Picture Guides: 9). (ENG.). 24p. (Orig.). (gr. 3-18). pap. *(978-1-872082-69-1(6)*, Allen, J. A. & Company, Limited) Hale, Robert Ltd.
Wendorf, Sarah. A Is for Appaloosa! 2005. 24p. (J). 8.13 *(978-1-4116-3235-6(4))* Lulu Pr., Inc.
West, David. Dawn Horse. Poluzzi, Alessandro, illus. 2017. (Graphic Prehistoric Animals Ser.). 32p. (gr. 3-7). lib. bdg. 31.35 *(978-1-62588-407-7(9))* Black Rabbit Bks.
Wild Horses: Individual Title Six-Packs. (Action Packs Ser.). 120p. (gr. 3-5). 44.00 *(978-0-7635-8434-4(7))* Rigby Education.
Wilsdon, Christina. For Horse-Crazy Girls Only: Everything You Want to Know about Horses. Underhill, Alecia, illus. 2010. (ENG.). 160p. (J). (gr. 3-6). 16.99 *(978-0-312-60323-6(1)*, 9780312603236) Feiwel & Friends.
—Horses. 2007. (J). *(978-1-59939-075-8(2)*, Reader's Digest Young Families, Inc.) Studio Fun International.
Wolf, Linda Little. The Great Spirit Horse, 1 vol. 2nd ed. 2003. (ENG., Illus.). 152p. (J). (gr. 3-6). pap. 10.95 *(978-1-58980-123-3(7))* Pelican Publishing Co., Inc.
The Wonder of Horses. 2013. (Illus.). 47p. (J). *(978-1-61628-788-7(8))* Fog City Pr.
Wood, Alix. Miniature Horses. 2016. (Mini Animals Ser.). 00032p. (J). (gr. 2-3). pap. 10.00 *(978-1-4994-8161-7(6)*, Windmill Bks.) Rosen Publishing Group, Inc., The.
Woodward, John & Dorling Kindersley Publishing Staff. Horses: The Ultimate Treasury. 2014. (ENG.). 160p. (J). (gr. 3-7). pap. 14.99 *(978-1-4654-1850-0(4)*, DK Children) Dorling Kindersley Publishing, Inc.
Workman Publishing Company Staff. The Horse Farm. Graham, Lindsay, illus. 2004. (ENG.). 18p. (J). (gr. -1). pap., tchr. ed. 7.95 *(978-1-58017-583-8(X)*, 67583) Storey Publishing, LLC.
Workman Publishing, Workman. Eyelike Stickers: Horses. 2016. (Eyelike Stickers Ser.). (ENG., Illus.). 12p. (J). (gr. -1-12). 6.95 *(978-0-7611-8724-0(3))* Workman Publishing Co., Inc.
World Book, Inc Staff, contrib. by. Arabians & Other Horses. 2007. (World Book's Animals of the World Ser.). (Illus.). 64p. (J). *(978-0-7166-1331-2(X))* World Bk., Inc.
Worth, Bonnie. If I Ran the Horse Show: All about Horses. Ruiz, Aristides & Mathieu, Joe, illus. 2012. (Cat in the Hat's Learning Library). (ENG.). 48p. (J). (gr. k-3). 9.99 *(978-0-375-86683-8(3)*, Random Hse. Bks. for Young Readers) Random Hse. Children's Bks.
Wynne, Patricia J. The Evolution of the Horse. 2008. (Dover Nature Coloring Book Ser.). (ENG., Illus.). 32p. (J). (gr. 3-5). pap. 3.99 *(978-0-486-46795-5(3))* Dover Pubns., Inc.
Yerxa, Leo. Ancient Thunder. 1 vol. 2012. (ENG., Illus.). 40p. (J). (gr. -1-3). 9.95 *(978-1-55498-127-4(1))* Groundwood Bks. CAN. Dist: Publishers Group West (PGW).
Yorks, Sharon Lene. Finals Bound. 2003. (Cloverleaf Ser.: Bk. 2). (Illus.). 240p. (J). (gr. 6-18). pap. 5.99 *(978-0-9720132-2-2(9))* Tumbleweed Publishing.
Young, Rae. Drawing Friesians & Other Beautiful Horses, 1 vol. Q2AMedia Services Private Ltd, Q2AMedia Services, illus. 2014. (Drawing Horses Ser.). (ENG.). 32p. (gr. 3-4). lib. bdg. 27.99 *(978-1-4765-3996-6(0)*, Snap Bks.) Capstone Press of Coughlan Cos.
—Drawing Horses, 1 vol. Q2AMedia Services Private Ltd, Q2AMedia Services, illus. 2014. (Drawing Horses Ser.). (ENG.). 32p. (gr. 3-4). lib. bdg. 167.94 *(978-1-4765-4667-4(3)*, Snap Bks.) Capstone Press of Coughlan Cos.
—Drawing Mustangs & Other Wild Horses, 1 vol. Q2AMedia Services Private Ltd, Q2AMedia Services, illus. 2014. (Drawing Horses Ser.). (ENG.). 32p. (gr. 3-4). lib. bdg. 27.99 *(978-1-4765-4002-3(0)*, Snap Bks.) Capstone Press of Coughlan Cos.
—Drawing Thoroughbreds & Other Elegant Horses, 1 vol. Q2AMedia Services Private Ltd, Q2AMedia Services, illus. 2014. (Drawing Horses Ser.). (ENG.). 32p. (gr. 3-4). lib. bdg. 27.99 *(978-1-4765-3993-5(6)*, Snap Bks.) Capstone Press of Coughlan Cos.

HORSES—FICTION

Abercrombie, Josephine. Charlie the Horse. Vincent, Benjamin, illus. 2004. (J). 15.99 *(978-0-9769648-0-3(5))* J A Interests, Inc.
Abrahamson, Bobbie. Sunflower: A Pony's Story. 2012. 36p. pap. *(978-1-105-60309-9(1))* Lulu.com.
Adams, Jean Ekman. Clarence & the Purple Horse Bounce into Town. Adams, Jean Ekman, illus. 2003. (Illus.). 32p. (J). (gr. -1-3). 15.95 *(978-0-87358-826-3(6)*, Rising Moon Bks. for Young Readers) Northland Publishing.
—A Cowgirl & her Horse. 2011. (Illus.). 32p. (J). 15.95 *(978-1-933855-71-4(1))* Rio Nuevo Pubs.
Adams, Katharine. Blackthorn. 2011. 222p. 44.95 *(978-1-258-06889-9(3))* Literary Licensing, LLC.
Aiken, Joan. Snow Horse & Other Stories. 2004. *(978-0-7136-7654-9(X)*, A&C Black) Bloomsbury Publishing Plc.
Alberto, Daisy. A Horse & a Hero. Random House Disney Staff, illus. 2011. (Step into Reading Ser.). (ENG.). 32p. (J). (gr. k-3). pap. 3.99 *(978-0-7364-2746-3(5)*, RH/Disney) Random Hse. Children's Bks.
Alexander, Samantha. Jodie. (ENG., Illus.). 128p. mass mkt. 6.99 *(978-0-330-36836-0(2)*, Pan) Pan Macmillan GBR. Dist: Trafalgar Square Publishing.
Allen, Jean. Esmerelda Finds a Friend. 2012. 24p. 24.95 *(978-1-4626-5127-6(5))* America Star Bks.
Allthewaybay. 2004. (YA). per. 7.95 *(978-0-9749320-0-2(0))* Bay Horse Creations LLC.
Altieri, Marion. Claude, the Clumsy Clydesdale. Romero, Gina, illus. 2011. (Alpha Mare Ser.: Vol. 1). 42p. (J). 16.47 *(978-0-9840418-0-0(X))*; pap. 14.47 *(978-0-9840418-1-7(8))* Caballo Pr. of Ann Arbor. (Caballito Children's Bks.).
Alvarez, Jennifer Lynn. The Guardian Herd: Windborn. McClellan, David, illus. 2017. (Guardian Herd Ser.: 4). 432p. (J). (gr. 3-7). pap. 6.99 ***(978-0-06-228616-1(1))*** HarperCollins Pubs.
Amateau, Gigi. Chancey of the Maury River. 2010. (ENG., Illus.). 256p. (J). (gr. 4-7). pap. 6.99 *(978-0-7636-4523-6(0))* Candlewick Pr.
—Dante: Horses of the Maury River Stables. 2016. (Horses of the Maury River Ser.). (ENG.). 320p. (J). (gr. 3-7). pap. 6.99 *(978-0-7636-8754-0(5))* Candlewick Pr.
—Dante of the Maury River. 2015. (Horses of the Maury River Ser.). (ENG.). 320p. (J). (gr. 3-7). 15.99 *(978-0-7636-7004-7(9))* Candlewick Pr.
—Macadoo of the Maury River. (Horses of the Maury River Ser.). (ENG.). (J). (gr. 4-7). 2015. 208p. pap. 6.99 *(978-0-7636-7670-4(5))* 2013. 192p. 15.99 *(978-0-7636-3766-8(1))* Candlewick Pr.
Amery, Heather. New Pony. Cartwright, Stephen, illus. rev. ed. 2004. (Farmyard Tales Readers Ser.). 16p. (J). pap. 5.95 *(978-0-7945-0787-9(5)*, Usborne) EDC Publishing.
Anderson, C. W. Blaze & Thunderbolt. (J). (gr. 1-4). 22.75 *(978-0-8446-7167-3(3))* Smith, Peter Pub., Inc.
Anderson, Laurie Halse. Trickster. 2008. (Vet Volunteers Ser.: 3). (ENG.). 144p. (J). (gr. 3-7). 6.99 *(978-0-14-241083-7(7)*, Puffin Books) Penguin Young Readers Group.
Anderson, Michael, Jr. Blaze & the Lost Quarry. (J). (gr. 1-4). 22.75 *(978-0-8446-7001-0(4))* Smith, Peter Pub., Inc.
Animal I Can Hear s/s - Horse. 2005. (J). bds. *(978-1-4194-0059-9(2))* Paradise Pr., Inc.
Anton, Jackie. Backyard Horse Tales Sox: 2nd Edition. 2012. 124p. pap. 11.99 *(978-1-4575-0949-0(0))* Dog Ear Publishing, LLC.
Arena, Jacqueline. Horsing Around. Maddock, Monika, illus. 2005. (Girlz Rock! Ser.). (J). pap. *(978-1-59336-703-9(1))* Mondo Publishing.
Armstrong, Jennifer. Magnus at the Fire. Smith, Owen, illus. 2005. (ENG.). 32p. (J). (gr. k-3). 18.99 *(978-0-689-83922-1(7)*, Simon & Schuster Bks. For Young Readers) Simon & Schuster Bks. For Young Readers.
Atwater, Jillene. Small & Sassy. DeBroeck, Sarah, illus. 2011. 36p. pap. 24.95 *(978-1-4489-8374-2(6))* America Star Bks.
AZ Books Staff. Hello, I'm Horse! Gorbachenok, Ekaterina, ed. 2012. (Who Lives in the Book? Ser.). (ENG.). 10p. (J). (-k). bds. 11.95 *(978-1-61889-069-6(7))* AZ Bks. LLC.
—Horse's Farm. Potapenko, Olga, ed. 2012. (Talking Plush Animals Ser.). (ENG.). 10p. (J). (gr. -1-k). bds. 10.95 *(978-1-61889-112-9(X))* AZ Bks. LLC.
Babbitt, Ellen C. Jataka Tales I & II. 2008. 80p. pap. 9.95 *(978-1-60459-517-8(5))* Wilder Pubns., Corp.
Baglio, Ben M. Colt on Christmas Eve. Baum, Ann & Lasher, Mary Ann, illus. 2005. 142p. (J). pap. *(978-0-439-77522-9(1))* Scholastic, Inc.
—Lost in the Snow. Ettlinger, Doris, illus. 2007. 153p. (J). *(978-0-439-87144-0(1))* Scholastic, Inc.
Bagnold, Enid. National Velvet. 2013. (ENG.). 320p. (J). (gr. 3-12). pap. 7.99 *(978-0-486-49297-1(4))* Dover Pubns., Inc.
Ballard, George Anne. White Fire, the Indian Boy. James, Melody, illus. 2012. 24p. pap. 12.00 *(978-0-9855312-3-2(1))* Bolton Publishing LLC.
Ballard MacKenzie, Laurie. Margarit: One Fair Lady. 2012. 26p. 21.95 *(978-1-4575-1459-3(1))* Dog Ear Publishing, LLC.
Banks, Radine. Nochi Come Back. 2006. 112p. per. 12.20 *(978-1-4120-8803-9(8))* Trafford Publishing.
Barchers, Suzanne I. Luce & Duke, 1 vol. 2011. (Targeted Phonics Ser.). (ENG., Illus.). 16p. (J). (gr. k-2). pap. 5.99 *(978-1-4333-2919-7(0))* Teacher Created Materials, Inc.
Barnes, Laura T. Ernest's Special Christmas. Camburn, Carol A., illus. 2003. (Ernest Ser.). 36p. (J). (gr. k-3). 17.95 *(978-0-9674681-3-6(2))* Barnesyard Bks.
Barr, Gordon. The Beginning. 2005. 67p. (J). (gr. 3-8). pap. *(978-0-9730093-2-3(2))* Barr, Gordon Ltd.
Bates, M. Horse in Danger. 2004. (Sandy Lane Stables Ser.). (ENG.). 118p. (J). pap. 4.99 *(978-0-7945-0502-8(3))* EDC Publishing.
—Strangers at the Stables. 2004. (Sandy Lane Stables Ser.). (J). (ENG.). 118p. pap. 4.99 *(978-0-7945-0503-5(1))*; 100p. lib. bdg. 12.99 *(978-1-58086-580-7(1))* EDC Publishing.
Bates, Michelle. Dream Pony. 2010. (Sandy Lane Stables Ser.). 100p. (J). pap. 4.99 *(978-0-7945-2537-8(7)*, Usborne) EDC Publishing.
—A Horse for the Summer. 2006. (Sandy Lane Stables Ser.). (J). (gr. 5). 108p. lib. bdg. 12.95 *(978-1-58086-557-9(7))*; (ENG., Illus.). 110p. per. 4.95 *(978-0-7945-0501-1(5)*, Usborne) EDC Publishing.
—Horse in Danger. (Sandy Lane Stables Ser.). 2017. (ENG.). 128p. (YA). pap. 5.99 ***(978-0-7945-3915-3(7))*** 2009. (Illus.). 114p. (J). (gr. 5). pap. 4.99 *(978-0-7945-2530-9(X))* EDC Publishing. (Usborne).
—Midnight Horse. (J). 2003. (ENG.). 118p. pap. 4.99 *(978-0-7945-0506-6(6))* 2011. 128p. pap. 4.99 *(978-0-7945-2529-3(6))* EDC Publishing. (Usborne).
—The Perfect Pony. 2004. (Sandy Lane Stables Ser.). 112p. (J). (gr. 5). lib. bdg. 12.95 *(978-1-58086-574-6(7))* EDC Publishing.
—The Perfect Pony. 2004. (Illus.). 112p. (J). *(978-0-439-63994-1(8))* Scholastic, Inc.
Bates, Michelle. Strangers at the Stables. 2017. (Sandy Lane Stables Ser.). (ENG.). 128p. (YA). pap. 5.99 ***(978-0-7945-3916-0(5)***, Usborne) EDC Publishing.
Battlecry Forever! 2007. (J). *(978-1-933343-45-7(1)*, PONY) Stabenfeldt Inc.
Beatty, Hetty Burlingame. Blitz. Tolford, Joshua, illus. 2012. 124p. 40.95 *(978-1-258-25354-7(2))*; pap. 25.95 *(978-1-258-25430-8(1))* Literary Licensing, LLC.
Beekman, Kelley Lee. Sir Eli & the Halloween Dragon: The Legend of the Toasted Marshmallow. 2006. 55p. pap. 16.95 *(978-1-4241-4047-3(1))* PublishAmerica, Inc.
Belgue, Nancy. Casey Little, Yo-Yo Queen, 1 vol. 2005. (Orca Young Readers Ser.). (ENG., Illus.). 128p. (J). (gr. 3-6). per. 5.95 *(978-1-55143-357-8(5))* Orca Bk. Pubs. USA.
Bentley, Sue. A Twinkle of Hooves. 2013. (Magic Ponies Ser.: 3). lib. bdg. 14.75 *(978-0-606-31678-1(7)*, Turtleback) Turtleback Bks.
Beobi & the Magic Coloring Book at the Horse Stables. 2006. (J). 3.99 *(978-0-9743847-5-7(5))* Cohn, Tricia.
Berglund, Andrea Lloyd. A Good Little Horse: Thunder's Morning Stroll. 2009. 36p. (J). pap. 19.95 *(978-1-4327-3822-8(4))* Outskirts Pr., Inc.
Bethell, Zillah. A Whisper of Horses. 2017. (ENG.). 352p. (J). 16.99 *(978-1-250-09394-3(5)*, 9781250093943) Feiwel & Friends.
Bettino, Teresa Adele. The Adventures of Sugarbabe & Thunder. 2013. 34p. pap. 12.00 *(978-0-9742842-0-0(3))* Bettino, Teresa Adele.
Bevis, Brittany. Two Foals, a Dash of Sprinkles & a Cherry on Top! Talley, Pam, illus. 2011. 32p. (J). 18.47 *(978-0-9824766-7-3(1))*; pap. 18.47 *(978-0-9824766-8-0(X))* Caballo Pr. of Ann Arbor. (Caballito Children's Bks.).
Billups, Ruth A. No Place for a Horse. 2008. 48p. pap. 16.95 *(978-1-60703-118-5(3))* America Star Bks.
Bischoff, Marlene A. Charming Chirp. 2013. 26p. pap. 13.95 *(978-1-4796-0132-5(2))* TEACH Services, Inc.
Björkman, Steve, illus. Look Out, Mouse! 2015. (I Like to Read(r) Ser.). (ENG.). 24p. (J). (gr. -1-3). 14.95 *(978-0-8234-2953-0(9))* Holiday Hse., Inc.
Black, Pam, illus. Candee Bar. 42p. (J). 2007. spiral bd. *(978-0-9800791-2-8(8))* 2nd rev. ed. 2008. spiral bd. 18.95 *(978-0-9800791-3-5(6))* Moores Publishing.
Blake, Edna L. & Boatwright, Edith. Grandma & her Amazing Colt, Dripper! Allen, Kathy, illus. 2005. 50p. (J). 12.00 *(978-0-9668906-3-1(9))* Blake, Edna.
Blanck, Cathy. A Party for Arty. 2004. (Illus.). 32p. (J). pap. *(978-0-9753059-0-4(5))* Red Barn Reading Inc.
Boer, Paula. Brumbies. Evans, Rowena, illus. 2011. (ENG.). 148p. pap. 14.99 *(978-0-615-56093-9(8))* IFWG Publishing Inc.
Bolognese, Don. The Warhorse. Bolognese, Don, illus. 2010. (ENG., Illus.). 176p. (J). (gr. 5-9). pap. 9.99 *(978-1-4424-2942-0(9)*, Simon & Schuster Bks. For Young Readers) Simon & Schuster Bks. For Young Readers.
Bonnell, Kris. Mmm, Apples. 2006. (J). pap. 3.95 *(978-1-933727-22-6(5))* Reading Reading Bks., LLC.
Book Buddy: Horse with Story Book. Orig. Title: Child's Play. (Illus.). 10p. (J). (gr. -1-3). reprint ed. *(978-1-881469-75-9(1))* Safari, Ltd.
Bossley, Michele Martin. Jumper, 1 vol. 2006. (Orca Sports Ser.). (ENG.). 160p. (YA). (gr. 6-10). per. 9.95 *(978-1-55143-620-3(5))* Orca Bk. Pubs. USA.
Botelho, R. J. Elizabeth & Equines: G. A. R. T. H. V (Genetically Altered Radically Transformed Human), 1 vol. 2009. 105p. pap. 19.95 *(978-1-61582-952-1(0))* America Star Bks.
Boudin, Jonathan. The Little Red Riding Book. Adrian, Marti, illus. 2012. (ENG.). 94p. (J). (gr. 2-4). pap. 8.95 *(978-0-9736330-3-0(4))* JB Max Publishing CAN. Dist: Independent Pubs. Group.
Bover, Annie. Mooncorn. 2013. (Illus.). 20p. pap. *(978-1-909465-18-3(6))* Cloister Hse. Pr., The.
Bradley, Lisa. Abby Wize: Awa. 2010. 304p. 29.99 *(978-1-4520-2491-2(X))*; pap. 19.99 *(978-1-4520-2490-5(1))* AuthorHouse.
Branson, Terri & Wilks, Jackie. Mirror of the Carousel. lt. ed. 2006. (Illus.). 24p. (J). per. 14.99 *(978-0-9765786-8-0(9))* Dragonfly Publishing, Inc.
Breen, Krista Michelle. Hardware - the Trouble with Phillip. 2013. 160p. pap. *(978-0-9735241-1-6(1))* Groundskeeper's Cottage.
—Quicksand: The Mysterious Disappearance of Dakotaroo. 2012. pap. *(978-0-9735241-0-9(3))* Groundskeeper's Cottage.
Brennan, Sarah. The Tale of a Dark Horse. 2013. (ENG., Illus.). 32p. (J). 24.95 *(978-1-937160-57-9(2))* Eliassen Creative.

Brent, Isabelle. The Christmas Horse & the Three Wise Men. 2016. (ENG., Illus.). 28p. (J). (gr. k-3). 17.95 *(978-1-937786-61-8(7),* Wisdom Tales) World Wisdom, Inc.
Brinegar, R. L. Ron. Pokey: The Fastest Horse on the Ranch. 2007. 33p. pap. 8.95 *(978-0-7414-4078-5(4))* Infinity Publishing.
Brocker, Susan. Restless Spirit. 2007. 176p. *(978-1-86950-623-0(5))* HarperCollins Pubs. Australia.
Brooke, Lauren. All or Nothing. 2007. (Chestnut Hill Ser.: No. 6). 184p. (J). lib. bdg. 15.38 *(978-1-4242-1719-9(9))* Fitzgerald Bks.
Brooks, Heather. Bonnies: Healing Hearts. 2009. 240p. pap. 4.99 *(978-0-06-169915-3(2))* HarperCollins Pubs.
—Hercules: A Matter of Trust. 2009. (Running Horse Ridge Ser.: 2). (ENG.). 224p. (J). (gr. 5-18). pap. 6.99 *(978-0-06-142981-1(3))* HarperCollins Pubs.
—Sapphire - New Horizons. 2009. (Running Horse Ridge Ser.: 1). (ENG.). 208p. (J). (gr. 5-18). pap. 4.99 *(978-0-06-142980-4(5))* HarperCollins Pubs.
Brown, Corinne. Wishful Watoosi: The Horse That Wished He Wasn't. 2012. (ENG., Illus.). 32p. (J). 16.95 *(978-0-9721057-2-9(7),* 3000) Cowgirl Peg Enterprises.
Brown, Liz. Dark Ryder. Mclanson, Matt, illus. 2004. (New Series Canada). 91p. (J). pap. *(978-1-897039-02-1(6))* High Interest Publishing (HIP).
Brown, Ruth & Sewell, Anna. Black Beauty. Brown, Ruth, illus. 2016. (ENG., Illus.). 32p. (J). (gr. -1-3). 17.99 *(978-1-5124-1619-0(3))* Andersen Pr. GBR. Dist: Lerner Publishing Group.
Bruckner, Tai. Lemon Path Encounter, 1 vol. Bruckner, Wes, illus. 2009. 15p. pap. 24.95 *(978-1-60836-407-7(0))* America Star Bks.
Bryant, Bonnie. Horse Play. 2007. (Saddle Club(R) Ser.: No. 7). (ENG.). 144p. (J). (gr. 3-7). 5.99 *(978-0-553-15754-3(X),* Yearling) Random Hse. Children's Bks.
Burkhart, Jessica. Behind the Bit. 2009. (Canterwood Crest Ser.: 3). (ENG.). 272p. (J). (gr. 4-8). pap. 7.99 *(978-1-4169-5842-0(8),* Aladdin) Simon & Schuster Children's Publishing.
—Best Enemies. 2009. (Canterwood Crest Ser.: 5). (ENG.). 272p. (J). (gr. 4-8). pap. 7.99 *(978-1-4169-9037-6(2),* Aladdin) Simon & Schuster Children's Publishing.
—Canterwood Crest Stable of Stories: Take the Reins; Chasing Blue; Behind the Bit; Triple Fault. 2014. (Canterwood Crest Ser.). (ENG., Illus.). 1088p. (J). (gr. 4-8). pap. 31.99 *(978-1-4814-1474-6(7),* Aladdin) Simon & Schuster Children's Publishing.
—Chasing Blue. 2009. (Canterwood Crest Ser.: 2). (ENG.). 272p. (J). (gr. 4-8). pap. 7.99 *(978-1-4169-5841-3(X),* Aladdin) Simon & Schuster Children's Publishing.
—Comeback. 2012. (Canterwood Crest Ser.: 15). (ENG.). 208p. (J). (gr. 5-8). pap. 7.99 *(978-1-4424-1952-0(0),* Aladdin) Simon & Schuster Children's Publishing.
—Comeback. 2012. (Canterwood Crest Ser.: 15). lib. bdg. 18.40 *(978-0-606-26312-2(8),* Turtleback) Turtleback Bks.
—Famous. 2013. (Canterwood Crest Ser.: 18). (ENG.). 240p. (J). (gr. 4-7). pap. 7.99 *(978-1-4424-3659-6(X),* Aladdin) Simon & Schuster Children's Publishing.
—Home for Christmas. 2013. (Canterwood Crest Ser.). lib. bdg. 18.40 *(978-0-606-32322-2(8),* Turtleback) Turtleback Bks.
—Home for Christmas: Super Special. 2013. (Canterwood Crest Ser.). (ENG., Illus.). 240p. (J). (gr. 4-8). pap. 7.99 *(978-1-4424-3661-9(1),* Aladdin) Simon & Schuster Children's Publishing.
—Home Sweet Drama. 2010. (Canterwood Crest Ser.: 8). (ENG.). 240p. (J). (gr. 4-8). pap. 7.99 *(978-1-4169-9040-6(2),* Aladdin) Simon & Schuster Children's Publishing.
—Jealousy. 2013. (Canterwood Crest Ser.: 17). (ENG.). 208p. (J). (gr. 4-7). pap. 7.99 *(978-1-4424-3657-2(3),* Aladdin) Simon & Schuster Children's Publishing.
—Jealousy. 2013. (Canterwood Crest Ser.: 17). lib. bdg. 17.20 *(978-0-606-27032-8(9),* Turtleback) Turtleback Bks.
—Little White Lies. 2009. (Canterwood Crest Ser.: 6). (ENG.). 240p. (J). (gr. 4-8). pap. 7.99 *(978-1-4169-9038-3(0),* Aladdin) Simon & Schuster Children's Publishing.
—Masquerade. 2012. (Canterwood Crest Ser.: 16). lib. bdg. 18.40 *(978-0-606-26887-5(1),* Turtleback) Turtleback Bks.
—Popular. 2012. (Canterwood Crest Ser.: 14). (ENG.). 272p. (J). (gr. 4-8). pap. 7.99 *(978-1-4424-1950-6(4),* Aladdin) Simon & Schuster Children's Publishing.
—Popular. 2012. (Canterwood Crest Ser.: 14). lib. bdg. 18.40 *(978-0-606-26311-5(X),* Turtleback) Turtleback Bks.
—Rival Revenge. 2010. (Canterwood Crest Ser.: 7). (ENG.). 240p. (J). (gr. 4-8). pap. 7.99 *(978-1-4169-9039-0(9),* Aladdin) Simon & Schuster Children's Publishing.
—Scandals, Rumors, Lies. 2010. (Canterwood Crest Ser.: 11). (ENG.). 192p. (J). (gr. 4-8). pap. 7.99 *(978-1-4424-0384-0(5),* Aladdin) Simon & Schuster Children's Publishing.
—Scandals, Rumors, Lies. 2010. (Canterwood Crest Ser.: 11). lib. bdg. 18.40 *(978-0-606-15241-9(5),* Turtleback) Turtleback Bks.
—Triple Fault. 2009. (Canterwood Crest Ser.: 4). (ENG.). 288p. (J). (gr. 4-8). pap. 7.99 *(978-1-4169-5843-7(6),* Aladdin) Simon & Schuster Children's Publishing.
—Unfriendly Competition. 2011. (Canterwood Crest Ser.: 12). (ENG.). 192p. (J). (gr. 4-8). pap. 7.99 *(978-1-4424-0386-4(1),* Aladdin) Simon & Schuster Children's Publishing.
—Wild Hearts. 2015. (If Only... Ser.). (ENG.). 368p. (YA). (gr. 7). 17.99 *(978-1-61963-258-5(6),* 9781619632585, Bloomsbury USA Childrens) Bloomsbury Publishing USA.
Burkhart, Jessica & Haley, Patricia. Chosen: Super Special. 2011. (Canterwood Crest Ser.). (ENG.). 304p. (J). (gr. 5-8). pap. 7.99 *(978-1-4424-1946-9(6),* Aladdin) Simon & Schuster Children's Publishing.
Burkhart, Kiersi & Keyser, Amber J. One Brave Summer. 2017. (Quartz Creek Ranch Ser.). (ENG.). 224p. (J). (gr. 4-8). 27.99 *(978-1-4677-9254-7(3))* Lerner Publishing Group.
—Shy Girl & Shy Guy. 2017. (Quartz Creek Ranch Ser.). (ENG.). 240p. (gr. 4-8). 27.99 *(978-1-4677-9253-0(5),* Carolrhoda Bks.) Lerner Publishing Group.
Burks, Brian. Corre con Caballos. Vinos, Maria, tr. Pelaez, Ricardo, illus. 2003. (la Orilla Del Viento Ser.). (SPA.). 96p. (J). per. 7.50 *(978-968-16-7057-3(4),* 168) Fondo de Cultura Economica USA.
Burton, Chanel & Burton, Chanel. Wildancer Takes First: Wildancer Wins First Place. 2012. 44p. pap. 15.00 *(978-1-60976-164-6(2),* Strategic Bk. Publishing) Strategic Book Publishing & Rights Agency (SBPRA).
Burton, Virginia Lee. Calico the Wonder Horse. gif. ed. 2016. (ENG., Illus.). 64p. (J). (gr. -1-3). 14.99 *(978-0-547-57572-8(6),* HMH Books For Young Readers) Houghton Mifflin Harcourt Publishing Co.
Calvert, J. Oliver. Honey Childrens Series Honey Meets the Prince Book One. 2006. (J). 15.77 *(978-0-9771318-1-5(5))* Hope Harvest Publishing.
Campbell-Fells. Blue Ribbon Girls. 2005. 145p. pap. 13.95 *(978-0-7414-2593-5(9))* Infinity Publishing.
Campbell, Joanna, pseud. Star of Shadowbrook Farm. 2008. (YA). *(978-1-933343-77-8(X))* Stabenfeldt Inc.
Carpenter Czerw, Nancy. Friends on the Farm. Berlin, Rose Mary & Bauer, Dana, illus. 2006. (Itty & Bitty Ser.). (ENG.). 32p. (J). (gr. -1-3). 15.95 *(978-0-9755618-3-6(9))* McWitty Pr., Inc.
—Two Miniature Horses. Bauer, Dana, illus. 2006. (Itty & Bitty Ser.). (ENG.). 32p. (J). (gr. -1-3). 15.95 *(978-0-9755618-2-9(0))* McWitty Pr., Inc.
Carr, Debra. The Curry Comb Caper. Carr, Stephen, illus. 2006. 48p. per. 8.95 *(978-1-933912-59-2(6))* Westview Publishing Co., Inc.
Carter, Anne Laurel. Out of the Deeps, 1 vol. Debon, Nicolas, illus. 2008. (ENG.). 32p. (J). (gr. -1-3). 19.95 *(978-1-55143-559-6(4))* Orca Bk. Pubs. USA.
Cartwright, Stephen. Little Book of Train Stories. rev. ed. 2011. (Farmyard Tales Readers Ser.). 64p. (J). ring bd. 8.99 *(978-0-7945-3070-9(2),* Usborne) EDC Publishing.
Casaluci, Stacy Manning. Miracles Love a Believer. 2011. 32p. pap. 13.00 *(978-1-61204-094-3(2),* Eloquent Bks.) Strategic Book Publishing & Rights Agency (SBPRA).
Casanova, Mary. Stealing Thunder. 2014. (Fesler-Lampert Minnesota Heritage Ser.). (ENG.). 144p. pap. 9.95 *(978-0-8166-9210-1(6))* Univ. of Minnesota Pr.
Castlemon, Harry. Sportsmans Club in the Saddle. 2006. pap. 30.95 *(978-1-4286-5231-6(0))* Kessinger Publishing, LLC.
Caudle, P. L. The Tale of Strawberry Snow, 1 vol. Simmonds, Frank H., illus. 2012. (ENG.). 48p. (J). 16.99 *(978-0-7643-4076-5(X),* 9780764340765) Schiffer Publishing, Ltd.
Chaconas, Dori. Pennies in a Jar, 1 vol. Lewin, Ted, illus. 2007. (ENG.). 32p. (J). (gr. 1-5). 16.95 *(978-1-56145-422-8(2))* Peachtree Pubs.
Chandler, Andrew Robert. Horatio the Half-Hooved Horse. 2003. (J). per. *(978-1-59196-438-4(5))* Instant Pub.
Chandler, Ann. Siena Summer, 1 vol. 2009. (ENG., Illus.). 142p. (YA). (gr. 6-9). pap. 12.95 *(978-1-896580-17-3(3))* Tradewind Bks. CAN. Dist: Orca Bk. Pubs. USA.
Charles, Valerie. The Dancing Light. 2013. 118p. pap. *(978-1-84944-167-4(7))* UKUnpublished.
Chasing Gold. 2014. (Marguerite Henry's Ponies of Chincoteague Ser.: 3). (ENG., Illus.). 192p. (J). (gr. 3-7). pap. 6.99 *(978-1-4814-0342-9(7),* Aladdin) Simon & Schuster Children's Publishing.
Chatel, Kim. Clip-Clop, Tippity-Tap French Vocabulary on the Farm. Bullock, Kathleen, illus. 2011. 24p. pap. 10.95 *(978-1-61633-136-8(4))* Guardian Angel Publishing, Inc.
—Horse Camp. 2011. 28p. 19.95 *(978-1-61633-145-0(3));* pap. 11.95 *(978-1-61633-146-7(1))* Guardian Angel Publishing, Inc.
Chellis, Marie. The Hayburner, 1 vol. 2010. 60p. pap. 19.95 *(978-1-4512-9053-0(5))* America Star Bks.
Chester, Laura. Hiding Glory. Lippincott, Gary A., illus. 2007. (ENG.). 160p. (J). (gr. 3-7). 18.95 *(978-1-59543-616-0(2))* Willow Creek Pr., Inc.
Childs, Barbara. Sammy & the Cow Bird. 2009. 48p. pap. 21.99 *(978-1-4389-8025-6(6))* AuthorHouse.
Chin, Oliver. The Year of the Horse: Tales from the Chinese Zodiac. Wood, Jennifer, illus. 2013. (Tales from the Chinese Zodiac Ser.: 8). (ENG.). 36p. (J). (gr. -1-3). 15.95 *(978-1-59702-080-0(X))* Immedium.
Christie, Caroline. Silver Heels: A Story of Blackfeet Indians at Glacier National Park. Wilde, George, illus. 2011. 162p. 41.95 *(978-1-258-00441-5(0))* Literary Licensing, LLC.
Christmas Colt. 2006. (J). *(978-1-933343-36-5(2),* PONY) Stabenfeldt Inc.
Circle of Blue. 2006. (J). *(978-1-933343-37-2(0),* PONY) Stabenfeldt Inc.
Citra, Becky. Missing, 1 vol. 2011. (ENG.). 184p. (J). (gr. 4-7). pap. 9.95 *(978-1-55469-345-0(4))* Orca Bk. Pubs. USA.
Clancy, Kaycee. Sky Painters. 2007. 41p. per. 11.95 *(978-0-9776777-8-8(8))* Legacy Publishing Services, Inc.
Clarke, Nancy & Muire, Penny. Stormy Hill's Challenge. 2013. 248p. 26.00 *(978-1-62212-803-7(6),* Strategic Bk. Publishing) Strategic Book Publishing & Rights Agency (SBPRA).
Clear the Hurdles, Sara! 2005. (J). *(978-1-933343-01-3(X),* PONY) Stabenfeldt Inc.
Clough, Paige. The Jumping Orie Story. Yates, Bridget & Ward, Karen, illus. 2015. (J). *(978-1-942945-24-6(8))* Bright Sky Pr.
—The Jumping Orie Story. Yates, Bridget & Ward, Karen, illus. 2015. (J). ***(978-0-9915511-2-5(5))*** Rule 2 Bks.
Cole, Cathleen. Four Seasons Stables: A Saddle Seat Rid. 2006. 53p. pap. 16.95 *(978-1-4241-3430-4(7))* PublishAmerica, Inc.
—The Night Mare of Four Seasons Stables. 2008. 76p. pap. 19.95 *(978-1-60703-860-3(9))* America Star Bks.
Coleman, Claudia. Yo Yo & the Great Flood. 2008. 100p. pap. 22.95 *(978-1-60145-606-9(9))* Booklocker.com, Inc.
Coles, Chantel. Valentina: Lisa's Dream Come True. 2005. 50p. pap. 16.95 *(978-1-4137-9771-8(7))* PublishAmerica, Inc.
Compton, Dawn. Leave 'Em Standing. 2005. (Illus.). pap. 12.95 *(978-1-932196-73-3(0))* WordWright.biz, Inc.
Coné, Robert. The Candy Bandit Strikes Again! Baker, David, illus. 2011. 28p. pap. 24.95 *(978-1-4560-8019-8(9))* America Star Bks.
Conroe, Lindy. Rockafella Jones & the Hidden Treasure. Riette, Susanne, illus. 2011. 108p. (J). pap. 10.95 *(978-1-935199-00-7(5))* Blue Mustang Pr.
Cook, Sherry & Johnson, Terri. Hallie Heat, 26 vols. Kuhn, Jesse, illus. l.t. ed. 2006. (Quirkles — Exploring Phonics through Science Ser.: 8). 32p. (J). 7.99 *(978-1-933815-07-7(8),* Quirkles, The) Creative 3, LLC.
Coons, Anita. What about Me? 2003. (Illus.). 96p. (J). (gr. k-8). per. 10.95 *(978-1-930648-56-2(1))* Goose River Pr.
Cooper, Margaret. The Christmas Horse. Bohart, Lisa, illus. 2008. 32p. pap. 12.95 *(978-0-9821654-9-2(8))* Peppertree Pr., The.
Cooper, Nelle. Princess Lil. 2013. 82p. (J). pap. 9.00 *(978-1-936442-16-4(7))* Fresh Ink Group.
Cooper, Page. Amigo, Circus Horse. Pitz, Henry, illus. 2011. 240p. 46.95 *(978-1-258-06394-8(8))* Literary Licensing, LLC.
Corgliano, K. L. Millie & Me, 1 vol. 2009. 29p. pap. 24.95 *(978-1-60813-935-4(2))* America Star Bks.
—Millie & Me Fourth Grade Field Day. 2012. 44p. pap. 13.99 *(978-0-615-56735-8(5))* K.L.Corgliano.
Cosgrove, Stephen. Jalopy. James, Robin, illus. 2016. (Serendipity Ser.: 21). (ENG.). 32p. (Orig.). (J). (gr. k-4). pap. 7.95 *(978-1-941437-32-2(X))* Heritage Builders, LLC.
—Nitter Pitter. James, Robin, illus. 2015. (Serendipity Ser.: 20). (ENG.). 32p. (J). (gr. k-4). pap. 7.95 *(978-1-941437-38-4(9))* Heritage Builders, LLC.
—Sooty-Foot. James, Robin, illus. 2015. (Serendipity Ser.: 21). (ENG.). 32p. (J). (gr. k-4). pap. 7.95 *(978-1-941437-30-8(3))* Heritage Builders, LLC.
Costain, Meredith. Stella, Circus Star. McGowan, Shane, illus. 2015. (Legends in Their Own Lunchbox Ser.). (ENG.). 56p. (gr. 2-3). pap. 7.99 *(978-1-4966-0255-8(2),* Legends in Their Own Lunchbox) Capstone Classroom.
Cowley, Joy. Miss Doll & Friends: Rocking Race. Bordicchia, Gaia, illus. 2014. (ENG.). 8p. pap. *(978-0-927244-64-0(0),* Joy Cowley Club) Flying Start Bks.
Craig, Jenny. I Believe in Genevieve. Edelson, Wendy, illus. 2013. (ENG.). 40p. (J). (gr. -1-3). 16.95 *(978-1-62157-085-1(1),* Regnery Kids) Regnery Publishing, Inc., An Eagle Publishing Co.
Crane, Crankey. Horse Book. 2006. 23p. (J). 12.99 *(978-1-4116-7116-4(3))* Lulu Pr., Inc.
Crazy Dream Horse. 2005. 19.95 net. *(978-0-9749501-0-5(6))* Inheritance Pr., Inc.
Culverwell, C. Ellen. The Horse Lady. 2009. (J). pap. *(978-0-88092-723-9(2));* lib. bdg. *(978-0-88092-722-2(4))* Royal Fireworks Publishing Co.
Curry, Kenneth. Star & Peanut. 2007. (Illus.). 22p. (J). 10.95 *(978-0-9798364-9-7(2))* Curry Brothers Publishing Group.
Cyr, Joe. Two Happy Stories. Owen, Ramon, illus. 2007. 36p. per. 12.95 *(978-1-934246-73-5(5))* Peppertree Pr., The.
Czerw, Nancy Carpenter. Itty & Bitty - On the Road. Berlin, Rose Mary, illus. 2008. (Itty & Bitty Ser.: 3). (ENG.). 32p. (J). (gr. -1-3). 16.95 *(978-0-9755618-4-3(7))* McWitty Pr., Inc.
Dahlstrom, S. J. Green Colt, No. 4. 2016. (Adventures of Wilder Good Ser.). (ENG.). 162p. (J). (gr. 3). pap. 8.95 *(978-1-58988-114-3(1))* Dry, Paul Bks., Inc.
Dailey, Reid. Ross the Reader & the Adventure of the Pirate's Treasure. Edgerley, Ross, illus. 2009. 44p. pap. 16.95 *(978-1-59858-900-9(8))* Dog Ear Publishing, LLC.
Dale, Jay. Daisy Wants to Go Riding, 1 vol. Draycott, Michelle, illus. 2012. (Wonder Words Ser.). (ENG.). 32p. (gr. k-2). pap. 5.99 *(978-1-4296-8920-5(X),* Engage Literacy) Capstone Press of Coughlan Cos.
—Pippa & the Flowers, 1 vol. Draycott, Michelle, illus. 2012. (Wonder Words Ser.). (ENG.). 32p. (gr. k-2). pap. 5.99 *(978-1-4296-8908-3(0),* Engage Literacy) Capstone Press of Coughlan Cos.
Daley, James. Great Horse Stories. 2010. (Dover Children's Classics Ser.). (ENG.). 240p. (J). (gr. 3-5). pap. 7.99 *(978-0-486-47669-8(3))* Dover Pubns., Inc.
Dalmatian Press Staff, adapted by. Black Beauty. 2003. (ENG.). 128p. (C). pap. 16.95 *(978-0-7593-9884-9(4),* Cengage Learning) CENGAGE Learning.
Dalton, Linda J. The Mystery of the Broomstick Horse. 2012. 116p. 29.99 *(978-1-4797-4781-8(5));* pap. 19.99 *(978-1-4797-4780-1(7))* Xlibris Corp.
Dammier, Patti. Got Carrots? Rescued Horse: The Winter Vacation. 2012. 142p. 21.95 *(978-1-4759-2842-6(4));* pap. 11.95 *(978-1-4759-2840-2(8))* iUniverse, Inc.
Dana, Barbara. Spencer & His Friends. 2014. (ENG., Illus.). 128p. (J). (gr. 3-7). pap. 13.99 *(978-1-4814-3754-7(2),* Atheneum Bks. for Young Readers) Simon & Schuster Children's Publishing.
Dance, Jennifer. Paint. 2015. (ENG.). 248p. (J). pap. 12.99 *(978-1-4597-2868-4(8))* Dundurn CAN. Dist: Ingram Publisher Services.
Dangerous Summer 3. 2007. (J). *(978-1-933343-50-1(8),* PONY) Stabenfeldt Inc.
Darling, Fiona. The Horse's Curse. 2003. 144p. (J). pap. 7.95 *(978-0-86327-904-1(X))* Wolfhound Pr. IRL. Dist: Interlink Publishing Group, Inc.
Darragh, Jill. Milly Feather. Gamble, Gael, illus. 2013. 64p. pap. *(978-0-473-26560-1(5))* Rangitawa Publishing.
Davis, Joyce E. Fancy the Prancing Horse. 2003. (Illus.). 24p. 10.95 *(978-1-58597-180-0(4))* Leathers Publishing.
Davis, Susan Page. Sarah's Long Ride. 2007. (Piper Ranch Ser.). 173p. (J). (gr. 3-7). per. 8.99 *(978-1-59166-737-7(2))* BJU Pr.
Decola, Diane. Butterfly. 2008. 180p. pap. 15.99 *(978-1-4389-0715-4(X))* AuthorHouse.
DeGrasse, Samantha. Taber Is Beautiful. McPherson, Melinda, illus. 2011. 28p. pap. 12.56 *(978-1-4269-5825-0(0))* Trafford Publishing.
DeJong, Meindert. La Colina Que Canta. (SPA., Illus.). 120p. (YA). (gr. 5-8). *(978-84-279-3434-4(3),* NG3494) Noguer y Caralt Editores, S. A. ESP. Dist: Lectorum Pubns., Inc.
DeLaCroix, Alice. The Best Horse Ever. Himler, Ronald, illus. 2010. (ENG.). 80p. (J). (gr. 1-5). 15.95 *(978-0-8234-2254-8(2))* Holiday Hse., Inc.
Delafontaine, Ariane. Prince des Montagnes. 2012. 190p. pap. 38.59 *(978-1-291-11264-1(2))* Lulu Pr., Inc.
Dembo, Jaiden. Finding Strider. 2010. 52p. pap. 15.54 *(978-0-557-39981-9(5))* Lulu Pr., Inc.
Demeritt, Mary Anne. The Twilight Ride of the Pink Fairy. Daniel, Ellen, illus. 2006. 36p. (J). pap. 17.95 *(978-1-58597-410-8(2))* Leathers Publishing.
Dempsey, Tami. We Are a Champion! 2010. 36p. pap. 15.49 *(978-1-4490-8102-7(9))* AuthorHouse.
Dengler-McKerchar, Rosemarie. Australia's History in Rhyme - Part 19: Gold Fever. 2005. (J). *(978-1-933343-00-6(1),* PONY) Stabenfeldt Inc.
Denman, K. L. Spiral, 1 vol. 2008. (Orca Soundings Ser.). (ENG.). (YA). (gr. 8-12). 112p. 16.95 *(978-1-55143-932-7(8));* 128p. pap. 9.95 *(978-1-55143-930-3(1))* Orca Bk. Pubs. USA.
Denton, P. J. Pony Party! Denos, Julia, illus. 5th ed. 2008. (Sleepover Squad Ser.: 5). (ENG.). 96p. (J). (gr. 1-4). pap. 4.99 *(978-1-4169-5931-1(9),* Aladdin) Simon & Schuster Children's Publishing.
Depken, Kristen L. Island of the Lost Horses (Dora & Friends) Aikins, David, illus. 2015. (Step into Reading Ser.). (ENG.). 24p. (J). (gr. -1-1). 4.99 *(978-0-553-52093-4(8),* Random Hse. Bks. for Young Readers) Random Hse. Children's Bks.
Di Fabbio, Nancy. Midnight Magic: Be Careful What You Wish For! 2011. 240p. (gr. 4-6). 25.95 *(978-1-4502-9147-7(3));* pap. 15.95 *(978-1-4502-9145-3(7))* iUniverse, Inc.
Diablo - A Day Like Any Other. 2007. (J). *(978-1-933343-43-3(5),* PONY) Stabenfeldt Inc.
Diablo - Race Against Time. 2006. (J). *(978-1-933343-29-7(X),* PONY) Stabenfeldt Inc.
Diablo's Double. 2005. (J). *(978-1-933343-02-0(8),* PONY) Stabenfeldt Inc.
Diaz, Katacha. Wild Horse Country. Casale, Paul, illus. (Wild Reading Adventures! Ser.). (ENG.). (J). 2005. 32p. (gr. -1-2). 8.95 *(978-1-59249-220-6(7),* SC7105) 2005. 36p. (gr. -1-2). 15.95 *(978-1-59249-137-7(5),* B7105) 2005. 36p. (gr. -1-2). pap. 6.95 *(978-1-59249-138-4(3),* S7105) 2005. 32p. (gr. -1-3). 19.95 *(978-1-59249-219-0(3),* BC7105) 2003. 36p. (gr. 2-2). pap. 2.95 *(978-1-59249-139-1(1),* S7155) Soundprints.
Diaz, Katacha & Bosson, Jo-Ellen. Wild Horse Country. Casale, Paul, illus. 2005. (Wild Reading Adventures! Ser.). (ENG.). 36p. (J). (gr. -1-2). 9.95 *(978-1-59249-140-7(5),* PS7155) Soundprints.
DiCamillo, Kate. Leroy Ninker Saddles Up. Van Dusen, Chris, illus. (Tales from Deckawoo Drive Ser.: Vol. 1). (ENG.). 96p. (J). (gr. 1-4). 2015. pap. 5.99 *(978-0-7636-8012-1(5))* 2014. 12.99 *(978-0-7636-6339-1(5))* Candlewick Pr.
—Leroy Ninker Saddles Up. 2015. (Tales from Deckawoo Drive Ser.: 1). lib. bdg. 16.00 *(978-0-606-36868-1(X))* Turtleback Bks.
Dickerson, Karle. The Forgotten Filly. 2008. (YA). *(978-1-933343-79-2(6))* Stabenfeldt Inc.
Dillon, Eilis. The Island of Horses. 2004. (New York Review Children's Collection). (ENG.). 224p. (J). (gr. 4-7). 17.95 *(978-1-59017-102-8(0),* NYR Children's Collection) New York Review of Bks., Inc., The.
Distler, Christine A. Pegasus: The Introduction. 2005. 84p. pap. 11.95 *(978-1-59113-763-4(2))* Booklocker.com, Inc.
Dodgson, Y. K. The Day the Horse Was Free. T. W. Zimmerman, illus. 2004. 16p. (J). 11.95 *(978-0-9748091-0-6(1))* Alaska Avenue Pr.
—The Day the Horse Was Free. Zimmerman, T. W., illus. rev. ed. 2005. 24p. (J). 11.95 *(978-0-9748091-1-3(X))* Alaska Avenue Pr.
Dorling Kindersley Publishing Staff & Saunders, Catherine. Let's Go Riding!, Level 2. 2013. (DK Readers Ser.). (ENG.). 32p. (J). (gr. 1-3). pap. 3.99 *(978-1-4654-0261-5(6),* DK Children) Dorling Kindersley Publishing, Inc.
Dorsey, Angela. Abandoned. 2012. 142p. pap. *(978-1-927100-12-7(7))* Enchanted Pony Bks.
—Autumn in Snake Canyon. 2012. 122p. pap. *(978-1-927100-23-3(2))* Enchanted Pony Bks.
—Autumn of Angels. 2013. 128p. pap. *(978-1-927100-30-1(5))* Enchanted Pony Bks.
—Fighting Chance. 2008. (J). *(978-1-933343-78-5(8))* Stabenfeldt Inc.
—Horse Angel Comic: Rough Diamond. 2007. (YA). pap. *(978-1-933343-66-2(4))* Stabenfeldt Inc.
—Horse Angel Comic - the Desert King. 2008. (J). pap. *(978-1-933343-82-2(6))* Stabenfeldt Inc.
—Silver Dream. 2007. (YA). *(978-1-933343-64-8(8))* Stabenfeldt Inc.
—Spring of Secrets. 2012. 122p. pap. *(978-1-927100-26-4(7))* Enchanted Pony Bks.
—Spring of the Poacher's Moon. 2012. 124p. pap. *(978-1-927100-16-5(X))* Enchanted Pony Bks.
—Summer of Wild Hearts. 2012. 128p. pap. *(978-1-927100-18-9(6))* Enchanted Pony Bks.
—Winter of Sinking Waters. 2012. 130p. pap. *(978-1-927100-25-7(9))* Enchanted Pony Bks.
—Winter of the Crystal Dances. 2012. 138p. pap. *(978-1-927100-14-1(3))* Enchanted Pony Bks.
—Winter of the Whinnies Brigade. 2013. 120p. pap. *(978-1-927100-32-5(1))* Enchanted Pony Bks.
Dorsey, Angela & Miller, Marina. Sun Catcher. 2012. 108p. pap. *(978-1-927100-10-3(0))* Enchanted Pony Bks.
Doty, Jean Slaughter. If Wishes Were Horses. 2012. (ENG.). 132p. (YA). (gr. 7). pap. 7.99 *(978-1-4424-8606-5(6),* Simon & Schuster Bks. For Young Readers) Simon & Schuster Bks. For Young Readers.
Douthwaite, Wendy. The Orange Pony. 2003. (ENG., Illus.). 96p. (J). (gr. 2-7). mass mkt. 6.99 *(978-0-330-33631-4(2),* Pan) Pan Macmillan GBR. Dist: Trafalgar Square Publishing.
Dowley-Wise, Justine. A Pig Called Harriet. 2008. (ENG.). 112p. pap. 31.99 *(978-1-4389-3388-7(6))* AuthorHouse.
Doyle, Malachy. Horse. Rinaldi, Angelo, illus. 2008. (ENG.). 32p. (J). (gr. k-4). 17.99 *(978-1-4169-2467-8(1),* McElderry, Margaret K. Bks.) McElderry, Margaret K. Bks.
Dudney, Emma Mae. The Runaway. 2008. 144p. pap. 9.95 *(978-0-9800854-0-2(3))* Authors' Discovery Cooperation, Inc.
Duey, Kathleen. Castle Avamir. Rayyan, Omar, illus. 2003. (Unicorn's Secret Ser.: 7). (ENG.). 80p. (J). (gr. 2-5). pap. 5.99 *(978-0-689-85372-2(6),* Simon & Schuster/Paula Wiseman Bks.) Simon & Schuster/Paula Wiseman Bks.
—Lara & the Moon-Colored Filly, Bk. 2. 2nd ed. 2005. (Hoofbeats Ser.: 6). (ENG.). 136p. (J). (gr. 3-7). pap. 4.99 *(978-0-14-240231-3(1),* Puffin Books) Penguin Young Readers Group.
—True Heart. Rayyan, Omar, illus. 2005. 76p. (J). lib. bdg. 15.00 *(978-1-59054-920-9(1))* Fitzgerald Bks.
—True Heart. Rayyan, Omar, illus. 2003. (Unicorn's Secret Ser.: 6). (ENG.). 80p. (J). (gr. 2-5). pap. 6.99 *(978-0-689-85370-8(X),* Aladdin) Simon & Schuster Children's Publishing.

H

Duey, Kathleen & Grosset and Dunlap Staff. Katie & the Mustang, Bk. 1. 2004. (Hoofbeats Ser.: 1). (ENG.). 144p. (J). (gr. 3-7). pap. 5.99 *(978-0-14-240090-6(4),* Puffin Books) Penguin Young Readers Group.

Duffy, Martin. Peg Leg Gus. 2007. (J). pap. *(978-0-9785853-3-4(X))* Ogma Pr.

Duncan, James Carl. Lucy — the Colt That Went to the Belmont Stakes. 2012. 40p. pap. 20.99 *(978-1-4772-5489-9(7))* AuthorHouse.

Dutton, Stella. Pinto the Chisholm Pony: 150th Chisholm Trail Edition. anniv. collector's ed. 2017. (ENG., Illus.). 62p. (J). (gr. -1-6). 39.99 *(978-0-9790832-9-7(X))* 405 Pubns.

Dyan, Penelope. The Last Mustang. 2013. 94p. pap. 8.95 *(978-1-61477-077-0(8))* Bellissima Publishing, LLC.

Earhart, Kristin. Buttercup Mystery. Geddes, Serena, illus. 2015. (Marguerite Henry's Misty Inn Ser.: 2). (ENG.). 128p. (J). (gr. 2-5). pap. 5.99 *(978-1-4814-1416-6(X),* Aladdin) Simon & Schuster Children's Publishing.

—Roscoe & the Pony Parade. Gurney, John Steven, illus. 2008. (Little Apple Ser.). 88p. (J). *(978-0-545-08094-1(0))* Scholastic, Inc.

—Runaway Pony. Geddess, Serena, illus. 2015. (Marguerite Henry's Misty Inn Ser.: 3). (ENG.). 128p. (J). (gr. 2-5). pap. 5.99 *(978-1-4814-1419-7(4),* Aladdin) Simon & Schuster Children's Publishing.

—Runaway Pony. 2015. (Marguerite Henry's Misty Inn Ser.: 3). lib. bdg. 16.00 *(978-0-606-37835-2(9))* Turtleback Bks.

—Welcome Home! Geddes, Serena, illus. 2015. (Marguerite Henry's Misty Inn Ser.: 1). (ENG.). 128p. (J). (gr. 2-5). 16.99 *(978-1-4814-1414-2(3),* Aladdin) Simon & Schuster Children's Publishing.

—Welcome Home! 2015. (Marguerite Henry's Misty Inn Ser.: 1). lib. bdg. 16.00 *(978-0-606-37126-1(5))* Turtleback Bks.

Earhart, Kristin & Geddes, Serena. Welcome Home!; Buttercup Mystery; Runaway Pony; Finding Luck. 2016. (Marguerite Henry's Misty Inn Ser.). (ENG., Illus.). 512p. (J). (gr. 2-5). pap. 23.99 *(978-1-4814-7012-4(4),* Aladdin) Simon & Schuster Children's Publishing.

Earl, Cheri Pray & Williams, Carol Lynch. The Rescue Begins in Delaware. Oliphant, Manelle, illus. 2013. (Just in Time Ser.: 1). (ENG.). 144p. (J). (gr. 3-7). pap. 9.95 *(978-1-938301-74-2(9))* Familius LLC.

East, Cathy. Anna Sewell's Black Beauty. Wald, Christina, illus. 2009. (Penguin Young Readers, Level 4 Ser.: No. 3). (ENG.). 48p. (J). (gr. 3-4). pap. 3.99 *(978-0-448-45190-9(5),* Penguin Young Readers) Penguin Young Readers Group.

Ebers, Georg. The Greylock. 2004. reprint ed. pap. 1.99 *(978-1-4192-6506-8(7));* pap. 15.95 *(978-1-4191-6506-1(2))* Kessinger Publishing, LLC.

Echo of Hooves. 2005. (J). *(978-1-933343-10-5(9),* PONY) Stabenfeldt Inc.

Edge, Laura Bufano. Wild West Dreams. 2006. (J). pap. *(978-0-88092-623-2(6));* lib. bdg. *(978-0-88092-622-5(8))* Royal Fireworks Publishing Co.

Edmonds, Lin. Patric the Pony & the Race for Freedom. 2011. 32p. pap. 15.50 *(978-1-4670-3662-7(5))* AuthorHouse.

—Patric the Pony & the Shining Star. 2010. 36p. pap. 17.49 *(978-1-4520-7389-7(9))* AuthorHouse.

—Patric the Pony Finds a Friend. Connors, Mary, illus. 2009. 32p. pap. 12.99 *(978-1-4389-5167-6(1))* AuthorHouse.

Eleanor, Coalson. Simon Says Run. 2006. (Illus.). (J). 8.95 *(978-1-56167-944-7(5))* American Literary Pr.

Erin, K. c. Blueberry Pie: The Adventures of Blueberry Bear & Her Friends. Sloane, Roxy, illus. 2009. 40p. pap. 16.99 *(978-1-4389-7592-4(9))* AuthorHouse.

Esparza-Vela, Mary. The Smiling Burro. Motz, Mike, illus. 2012. 16p. pap. 9.95 *(978-1-61633-323-2(5))* Guardian Angel Publishing, Inc.

Evans, Margaret. The Tale of Rainbow's End. 2007. pap. 11.00 *(978-0-8059-8716-4(9))* Dorrance Publishing Co., Inc.

Eveleigh, Victoria. Katy's Pony Challenge. 2016. (Katy's Exmoor Ponies Ser.). (ENG., Illus.). 144p. (J). (gr. 2-4). 7.99 *(978-1-4440-1451-8(X),* Orion Children's Bks.) Hachette Children's Group GBR. Dist: Hachette Bk. Group.

Fabian, Ingrid. The Black Arabian Foal. 2011. (Illus.). 53p. pap. 15.95 *(978-1-84624-530-5(3))* Book Guild, Ltd. GBR. Dist: Trans-Atlantic Pubns., Inc.

Fals, Mary. The Chosen Colt. 2009. 40p. pap. 18.49 *(978-1-4389-9417-8(6))* AuthorHouse.

Farley, Steve. The Black Stallion & the Lost City. 2012. (Black Stallion Ser.). (ENG.). 256p. (J). (gr. 4-7). 6.99 *(978-0-375-87208-2(6),* Yearling) Random Hse. Children's Bks.

Farley, Steven. The Black Stallion & the Shape-Shifter. 2010. (Black Stallion Ser.). (ENG.). 272p. (J). (gr. 3-7). 8.99 *(978-0-375-84532-1(1),* Yearling) Random Hse. Children's Bks.

Farley, Terri. Desert Dancer. 2003. (Phantom Stallion Ser.: 7). (ENG., Illus.). 240p. (J). (gr. 5-18). pap. 5.99 *(978-0-06-053725-8(6))* HarperCollins Pubs.

—Desert Dancer. 2003. (Phantom Stallion Ser.). (Illus.). 234p. (J). (gr. 5-9). 12.65 *(978-0-7569-3561-0(X))* Perfection Learning Corp.

—Free Again. 2003. (Phantom Stallion Ser.). (Illus.). 218p. (J). 12.65 *(978-0-7569-3560-3(1))* Perfection Learning Corp.

—Heartbreak Bronco. 2004. 227p. (J). lib. bdg. 16.92 *(978-1-4242-0830-2(0))* Fitzgerald Bks.

—Phantom Stallion - Wild Horse Island Bk. 2: The Shining Stallion. 2007. (Phantom Stallion: Wild Horse Island Ser.: 2). (ENG., Illus.). 224p. (J). (gr. 5-9). pap. 4.99 *(978-0-06-081543-1(4))* HarperCollins Pubs.

—Phantom Stallion Box Set: The Wild One; Mustang Moon; Dark Sunshine. Call, Greg, illus. 2004. (Phantom Stallion Ser.). 704p. (J). (gr. 5-18). pap. 14.99 *(978-0-06-059504-3(3),* HarperCollins) HarperCollins Pubs.

—Rain Forest Rose Bk. 3. 2007. (Phantom Stallion: Wild Horse Island Ser.: 3). (ENG.). 224p. (J). (gr. 5-18). pap. 4.99 *(978-0-06-088616-5(1))* HarperCollins Pubs.

—Wild Honey No. 22. 2006. (Phantom Stallion Ser.: 22). (ENG., Illus.). 320p. (J). (gr. 5). pap. 4.99 *(978-0-06-081539-4(6))* HarperCollins Pubs.

—The Wild One. 2007. (Phantom Stallion Ser.). (ENG.). 224p. (J). (gr. 5-9). pap. 1.99 *(978-0-06-133928-8(8))* HarperCollins Pubs.

Farley, Walter. The Black Stallion. Ward, Keith, illus. 2008. (Black Stallion Ser.). (ENG.). 288p. (J). (gr. 3-7). 15.99 *(978-0-375-85582-5(3),* Random Hse. Bks. for Young Readers) Random Hse. Children's Bks.

Faust, Lauren. The Magic Begins, Vol. 1. 2013. (My Little Pony Ser.). (ENG., Illus.). 112p. (J). (gr. 2-5). pap. 7.99 *(978-1-61377-754-1(X),* 9781613777541) Idea & Design Works, LLC.

Feld, Ellen F. Annie: The Mysterious Morgan Horse. Mellin, Jeanne, illus. 2007. 206p. (J). per. 9.95 *(978-0-9709002-9-6(5))* Willow Bend Publishing.

—Blackjack: Dreaming of a Morgan Horse, 4 vols. Mellin, Jeanne, illus. 3rd rev. ed. 2007. 235p. (J). (gr. 4-6). per. 9.95 *(978-0-9709002-8-9(7))* Willow Bend Publishing.

—Rimfire: The Barrel Racing Morgan Horse. Mellin, Jeanne, illus. 2009. (ENG.). 206p. (J). pap. 9.95 *(978-0-9709002-1-0(X))* Willow Bend Publishing.

—Robin: The Lovable Morgan Horse, 4 vols. Mellin, Jeanne, illus. 2005. (ENG.). 204p. (J). (gr. 4-6). per. 9.95 *(978-0-9709002-5-8(2))* Willow Bend Publishing.

Feldman, Lowell S. Little Falabella the Magical Horse. 2006. 92p. (gr. 1-1). pap. 31.99 *(978-1-4257-1869-5(8))* Xlibris Corp.

Fenwick, Carol. Jennell & the Horse in the Enchanted Valley. 2011. 32p. pap. 12.95 *(978-1-4634-4445-7(1))* AuthorHouse.

Ferrell, Miralee. A Horse for Kate. 2015. (Horses & Friends Ser.: 1). (ENG.). 208p. (J). pap. 7.99 *(978-0-7814-1114-1(9))* Cook, David C.

—Silver Spurs. 2015. (Horses & Friends Ser.: 2). (ENG.). 240p. (J). pap. 7.99 *(978-0-7814-1113-4(0))* Cook, David C.

Ferrone, John M. Margo & the Trail Ride. Ferrone, John M., photos by. Date not set. (Illus.). 36p. (J). (gr. -1-5). pap. 16.95 *(978-1-928811-05-3(1))* Story Stuff, Inc.

Finch, Kate. On with the Show! 2014. (Pet Hotel Ser.: 4). lib. bdg. 14.75 *(978-0-606-35201-7(5))* Turtleback Bks.

—Pet Hotel #4: on with the Show! Gurney, John Steven & Jessell, Tim, illus. 2014. (Pet Hotel Ser.: 4). (ENG.). 96p. (J). (gr. 2-5). pap. 4.99 *(978-0-545-50184-2(9),* Scholastic Paperbacks) Scholastic, Inc.

Finn, Mary. Belladonna. 2011. (ENG., Illus.). 384p. (YA). (gr. 7-18). 16.99 *(978-0-7636-5106-0(0))* Candlewick Pr.

Flannigan, Liz. Starlight Grey. Docampo, Valeria, illus. 2013. (Magic Stories Ser.). (ENG.). 48p. (J). (gr. 1-4). pap. 8.99 *(978-1-84686-778-1(9))* Barefoot Bks., Inc.

Fleischman, Sid. The Midnight Horse. Sís, Peter, illus. 2004. (ENG.). 96p. (J). (gr. 3-7). pap. 5.99 *(978-0-06-072216-6(9),* Greenwillow Bks.) HarperCollins Pubs.

Fleming, Bryn. Cassie & Jasper to the Rescue. 2014. (Range Riders Ser.). (ENG.). 128p. (YA). (gr. 3-7). pap. 9.99 *(978-0-88240-992-4(1),* West Winds Pr.) Graphic Arts Ctr. Publishing Co.

Flood, Nancy Bo. Soldier Sister, Fly Home. Begay, Shonto, illus. 2016. (ENG.). 176p. (YA). (gr. 5). lib. bdg. 16.95 *(978-1-58089-702-0(9))* Charlesbridge Publishing, Inc.

A Foal Is Born. 2007. (J). *(978-1-933343-46-4(X),* PONY) Stabenfeldt Inc.

Francois, Betsy. The Horse Who Thinks She's a Cat. 2011. 24p. pap. 15.99 *(978-1-4653-4322-2(9))* Xlibris Corp.

Frantic Flight. 2005. (J). *(978-1-933343-07-5(9),* PONY) Stabenfeldt Inc.

Freedom's Whisper. 2007. (J). *(978-1-933343-52-5(4),* PONY) Stabenfeldt Inc.

Freisinger, Vickie. Reno Does Chores, 1 vol. 2009. 36p. pap. 24.95 *(978-1-60813-027-6(4))* America Star Bks.

The Frog Who Thought He Was a Horse: Individual Title Six-Packs. (Literatura 2000 Ser.). (gr. 2-3). 33.00 *(978-0-7635-0225-6(1))* Rigby Education.

Fuerst, Jeffrey B. The Old Gray Mare. Currant, Gary, illus. 2010. (Rising Readers Ser.). (J). 3.49 *(978-1-60719-692-1(1))* Newmark Learning LLC.

Funnell, Pippa. Solo the Super Star. 2010. (ENG., Illus.). 96p. 9.99 *(978-1-84255-714-3(9))* Orion Publishing Group, Ltd. GBR. Dist: Hachette Bk. Group.

—Team Magic. 2016. (Tilly's Horse, Magic Ser.). (ENG.). 128p. (J). (gr. 4-6). 6.99 *(978-1-4440-1204-0(5),* Orion Children's Bks.) Hachette Children's Group GBR. Dist: Hachette Bk. Group.

Furman, A. L., ed. Horse Stories: Young Readers. Geer, Charles, illus. 2011. 192p. 42.95 *(978-1-258-09836-0(9))* Literary Licensing, LLC.

Gaither, Doug. The Lonely Mare, 1 vol. 2010. 22p. pap. 24.95 *(978-1-4489-5871-9(7))* PublishAmerica, Inc.

Galing, Ed. Tony. Stead, Erin E., illus. 2017. (ENG.). 32p. (J). 16.99 *(978-1-62672-308-5(7),* 9781626723085) Roaring Brook Pr.

Gallagher, Diana G. Monica & the Worst Horse Ever, 1 vol. 2010. (Monica Ser.). (ENG.). 88p. (gr. 2-3). 26.65 *(978-1-4342-1981-7(X))* Stone Arch Bks.

Gallegos, Michael. Three Royal Horses. 2012. 24p. pap. 24.95 *(978-1-62709-266-1(8))* America Star Bks.

Garcia, Marina, et al. Mateo de Paseo por el Museo. 2003. (SPA., Illus.). 36p. (J). 17.95 *(978-84-8488-068-4(0))* Serres, Ediciones, S. L. ESP. Dist: Lectorum Pubns., Inc.

Garcia, Nasario. Grandpa Lolo's Navajo Saddle Blanket: La Tilma de Abuelito Lolo. Moeller, Richard, illus. Moeller, Richard, photos by. 2012. (J). *(978-0-8263-5078-7(X));* 61p. pap. *(978-0-8263-5080-0(1));* (SPA.). 72p. pap. *(978-0-8263-5079-4(8))* Univ. of New Mexico Pr.

Garland, Sherry. Best Horse on the Force, 1 vol. 2006. (ENG.). 112p. (J). (gr. 3-7). per. 7.95 *(978-1-58980-437-1(6))* Pelican Publishing Co., Inc.

Garlick, Nicholas. Storm Horse. 2017. (J). pap. ***(978-0-545-90415-5(3))*** Scholastic, Inc.

Gemeinhart, Dan. Some Kind of Courage. 2016. (ENG.). 240p. (J). (gr. 3-7). 16.99 *(978-0-545-66577-3(9),* Scholastic Pr.) Scholastic, Inc.

George, Joshua. Horses & Unicorns. Green, Barry, illus. 2017. (Scratch & Draw Ser.). (ENG.). 56p. (J). (gr. k-2). 12.99 ***(978-1-78700-073-5(7))*** Top That! Publishing PLC GBR. Dist: Independent Pubs. Group.

The Ghost Horse of Meadow Green. 2005. (J). *(978-1-933343-03-7(6),* PONY) Stabenfeldt Inc.

Gibson, Sylvia Scott & Gibson, James E. Latawnya the Naughty Horse Two, 1 vol. Gibson, Gregory V., illus. 2010. 22p. 24.95 *(978-1-4489-7859-5(9))* PublishAmerica, Inc.

Giff, Patricia Reilly. Wild Girl. 2011. (ENG.). 160p. (J). (gr. 3-7). pap. 6.99 *(978-0-440-42177-1(2),* Yearling) Random Hse. Children's Bks.

Glaeser, Patricia Heinz. A New Day for Foal. 2007. 40p. per. 24.95 *(978-1-4241-8342-5(1))* America Star Bks.

Goble, Paul. The Girl Who Loved Wild Horses. 2015. 32p. pap. 8.00 *(978-1-61003-619-1(0))* Center for the Collaborative Classroom.

Goodman, Eli. The White Horse. Fisher, Brenda Beck, illus. 2016. (ENG.). 68p. (J). pap. 12.95 *(978-1-63047-932-9(2))* Morgan James Publishing.

Goodspeed, Judy. Saddle Up. 2007. (Illus.). 24p. (J). (ENG.). 14.99 *(978-0-9794660-7-6(5));* 24.99 *(978-0-9794660-0-7(8));* per. 12.99 *(978-0-9794660-1-4(6))* Dragonfly Publishing, Inc.

Goril, Cindy. Lacey's Legacy: Stretch's Story. Jamison, Sharon, illus. 2013. 28p. (J). pap. 12.95 *(978-1-935188-56-8(9))* Star Publish LLC.

Gragg, Karla. Memphis Learns the Hard Way. Unger, Erin, illus. 2013. 28p. pap. 6.95 *(978-0-9818396-7-7(3))* True Horizon Publishing.

Grandma, Sue. Rocky the Rocking Horse. 2010. 24p. 12.99 *(978-1-4520-7333-0(3))* AuthorHouse.

Grant, K. M. Blood Red Horse. 2006. (DeGranville Trilogy Ser.). (ENG.). 320p. (YA). (gr. 5-9). per. 10.99 *(978-0-8027-7734-8(1),* 9780802777348, Bloomsbury USA Childrens) Bloomsbury Publishing USA.

Green, Ann L. Sgt. Dusty's New Home. 2006. (J). 15.95 *(978-0-9795397-0-1(6))* Liferays Publishing.

The Green Horse Summer. 2006. (J). *(978-1-933343-28-0(1),* PONY) Stabenfeldt Inc.

Gregg, Stacy. The Auditions, 1. 2010. (Pony Club Rivals Ser.: 1). (ENG.). 288p. (J). (gr. 4-7). 7.99 *(978-0-00-733343-1(9),* HarperCollins Children's Bks.) HarperCollins Pubs. Ltd. GBR. Dist: HarperCollins Pubs.

—The Blaze & the Dark Rider. 2014. (Pony Club Secrets Ser.: 2). (ENG., Illus.). 256p. (J). pap. 6.99 *(978-0-00-724517-8(3),* HarperCollins Children's Bks.) HarperCollins Pubs. Ltd. GBR. Dist: HarperCollins Pubs.

—Destiny & the Wild Horses, 3. 2015. (Pony Club Secrets Ser.: 3). (ENG., Illus.). 256p. (J). pap. 6.99 *(978-0-00-724518-5(1),* HarperCollins Children's Bks.) HarperCollins Pubs. Ltd. GBR. Dist: HarperCollins Pubs.

—Flame & the Rebel Riders, 9. 2015. (Pony Club Secrets Ser.: 9). (ENG., Illus.). 240p. (J). (gr. 4-7). 8.99 *(978-0-00-729929-4(X),* HarperCollins Children's Bks.) HarperCollins Pubs. Ltd. GBR. Dist: HarperCollins Pubs.

—Fortune & the Golden Trophy. 2015. (Pony Club Secrets Ser.: 7). (ENG., Illus.). 240p. (J). (gr. 4-7). pap. 8.99 *(978-0-00-727032-3(1),* HarperCollins Children's Bks.) HarperCollins Pubs. Ltd. GBR. Dist: HarperCollins Pubs.

—The Island of Lost Horses. 2015. (ENG.). 320p. (J). pap. 6.99 *(978-0-00-758027-9(4),* HarperCollins Children's Bks.) HarperCollins Pubs. Ltd. GBR. Dist: HarperCollins Pubs.

—Mystic & the Midnight Ride, 1. 2014. (Pony Club Secrets Ser.: 1). (ENG., Illus.). 208p. (J). pap. 6.99 *(978-0-00-724519-2(X),* HarperCollins Children's Bks.) HarperCollins Pubs. Ltd. GBR. Dist: HarperCollins Pubs.

—Nightstorm & the Grand Slam, 12. 2016. (Pony Club Secrets Ser.: 12). (ENG., Illus.). 272p. (J). (gr. 4-7). 7.99 *(978-0-00-729932-4(X),* HarperCollins Children's Bks.) HarperCollins Pubs. Ltd. GBR. Dist: HarperCollins Pubs.

—Riding Star, 3. 2011. (Pony Club Rivals Ser.: 3). (ENG.). 304p. (J). (gr. 4-7). pap. 7.99 *(978-0-00-733345-5(5),* HarperCollins Children's Bks.) HarperCollins Pubs. Ltd. GBR. Dist: HarperCollins Pubs.

—Showjumpers, 2. 2010. (Pony Club Rivals Ser.: 2). (ENG.). 272p. (J). (gr. 4-7). pap. 7.99 *(978-0-00-733344-8(7),* HarperCollins Children's Bks.) HarperCollins Pubs. Ltd. GBR. Dist: HarperCollins Pubs.

—Storm & the Silver Bridle. 2015. (Pony Club Secrets Ser.: 6). (ENG., Illus.). 240p. (J). pap. 6.99 *(978-0-00-727031-6(3),* HarperCollins Children's Bks.) HarperCollins Pubs. Ltd. GBR. Dist: HarperCollins Pubs.

—Victory & the All-Stars Academy. 2015. (Pony Club Secrets Ser.: 8). (ENG., Illus.). 288p. (J). (gr. 4-7). 6.99 *(978-0-00-727033-0(X),* HarperCollins Children's Bks.) HarperCollins Pubs. Ltd. GBR. Dist: HarperCollins Pubs.

Grooms, Molly. We Are Puppies. 2005. 40p. bds. *(978-90-5843-815-7(5))* YoYo Bks.

Grosgebauer, Clare Ham. Snickerdoodle & the Roller-Skating Horse! Rissing, Karen, illus. 3rd ed. 2005. 36p. (J). (gr. -1-3). 12.99 *(978-0-9741888-4-3(0))* Small Wonders Enterprises.

Grovet, Heather. Beanie, the Horse That Wasn't a Horse. 2004. 95p. (J). 6.99 *(978-0-8163-2053-0(5))* Pacific Pr. Publishing Assn.

Guest, Elissa Haden. Iris & Walter. Davenier, Christine, illus. 2006. (Iris & Walter Ser.). 43p. (gr. 1-4). 15.95 *(978-0-7569-7008-6(3))* Perfection Learning Corp.

—Iris & Walter & the Birthday Party. Davenier, Christine, illus. 2013. (Green Light Readers Level 3 Ser.). (ENG.). 44p. (J). (gr. 1-4). pap. 3.99 *(978-0-544-10498-3(6))* Houghton Mifflin Harcourt Publishing Co.

Guibert, Emmanuel. The Thunder Horse. 2013. (Ariol Ser.: 2). (J). lib. bdg. 24.50 *(978-0-606-31910-2(7),* Turtleback) Turtleback Bks.

Gundel, Jean. The Mystery Key at Camp Green Meadow. Robertson, R. H., illus. 2011. (J). pap. 14.95 *(978-1-59571-730-6(7))* Word Association Pubs.

Gunderson, Jessica. The Horse on the Hill: A Story of Ancient India, 1 vol. Hu, Caroline, illus. 2009. (Read-It! Chapter Books: Historical Tales Ser.). (ENG.). 64p. (gr. 2-4). 22.65 *(978-1-4048-5222-8(0),* Chapter Readers) Picture Window Bks.

Gunter, Frances. Golden Horseshoe, Vol. 1. 2003. (YA). per. 9.95 *(978-0-9710389-1-2(0))* Elk River Pr.

—Golden Horseshoe 2, Vol. 2. 2003. (Illus.). 95p. (J). per. 9.95 *(978-0-9710389-2-9(9))* Elk River Pr.

Haas, Jessie. Bramble & Maggie: Give & Take. Friend, Alison, illus. 2013. (ENG.). 56p. (J). (gr. k-3). 14.99 *(978-0-7636-5021-6(8))* Candlewick Pr.

—Bramble & Maggie: Horse Meets Girl. Friend, Alison, illus. 2013. (Candlewick Sparks Ser.). (ENG.). 56p. (J). (gr. k-3). pap. 3.99 *(978-0-7636-6251-6(8))* Candlewick Pr.

—Bramble & Maggie Give & Take. Friend, Alison, illus. 2015. (Candlewick Sparks Ser.). (ENG.). 56p. (J). (gr. k-4). pap. 3.99 *(978-0-7636-7787-9(6))* Candlewick Pr.

—Bramble & Maggie: Snow Day. Friend, Alison, illus. 2016. (ENG.). 56p. (J). (gr. k-3). 14.99 *(978-0-7636-7364-2(1))* Candlewick Pr.

—Bramble & Maggie Spooky Season. Friend, Alison, illus. 2016. (Candlewick Sparks Ser.). (ENG.). 56p. (J). (gr. k-3). pap. 3.99 *(978-0-7636-8743-4(X))* Candlewick Pr.

—Horse Meets Girl. Friend, Alison, illus. 2012. (ENG.). 56p. (J). (gr. k-3). 14.99 *(978-0-7636-4955-5(4))* Candlewick Pr.

—Saige. Davis, Sarah, illus. 2012. (American Girl Today Ser.: Bk. 1). lib. bdg. 17.15 *(978-0-606-31568-5(3),* Turtleback) Turtleback Bks.

—Saige Paints the Sky. Davis, Sarah, illus. 2012. (American Girl Today Ser.: Bk. 2). lib. bdg. 17.15 *(978-0-606-31569-2(1),* Turtleback) Turtleback Bks.

Haas, Jessie & Wedekind, Annie. Mercury's Flight: The Story of a Lipizzaner Stallion. 2011. (Breyer Horse Collection: 4). (ENG.). 128p. (J). (gr. 4-7). pap. 9.99 *(978-0-312-64451-2(5),* 9780312644512) Feiwel & Friends.

Haffner, Kirstin. Born to Be Free. 2006. 133p. pap. 11.95 *(978-1-4116-8471-3(0))* Lulu Pr., Inc.

Hahn, Cathe. Step Up!, 1 vol. Artley, Bob, illus. 2005. (ENG.). 32p. (J). (gr. k-3). 16.99 *(978-1-58980-214-8(4))* Pelican Publishing Co., Inc.

Half Moon Ranch: Rodeo Rocky. 2006. (J). *(978-1-933343-40-2(0),* PONY) Stabenfeldt Inc.

Half Moon Ranch: Wild Horses. 2006. (J). *(978-1-933343-33-4(8),* PONY) Stabenfeldt Inc.

Halls, Kelly Milner. Blazing Courage. Parks, Phil, illus. 2015. (ENG.). 96p. (J). (gr. 4-8). lib. bdg. 25.32 *(978-1-4677-7219-8(4));* (Animal Rescues Ser.: 1). 6.99 *(978-1-4677-8990-5(9))* Lerner Publishing Group. (Darby Creek).

Halvorson, Marilyn. Blue Moon. 2004. (Orca Soundings Ser.). 109p. (gr. 4-7). 19.95 *(978-0-7569-4285-4(3))* Perfection Learning Corp.

Hambleton, Anne. Raja: Story of a Racehorse. Peggykauffman.com Staff & Kauffman, Margaret, illus. 2011. (ENG.). 272p. (J). (gr. 4-7). pap. 12.95 *(978-0-615-54029-0(5))* Old Bow Publishing.

Hamilton, Sable. Free Spirit. 2015. (Stardust Stables Ser.). (ENG.). 160p. (gr. 3-6). lib. bdg. 22.65 *(978-1-4342-9792-1(6))* Stone Arch Bks.

—A Star Is Born. 2015. (Stardust Stables Ser.). (ENG.). 160p. (gr. 3-6). lib. bdg. 22.65 *(978-1-4342-9790-7(X))* Stone Arch Bks.

—Stardust Stables. 2015. (Stardust Stables Ser.). (ENG.). 160p. (gr. 3-6). lib. bdg. 67.95 *(978-1-4965-0112-7(8),* Stardust Stables) Stone Arch Bks.

—Wildfire. 2015. (Stardust Stables Ser.). (ENG.). 160p. (gr. 3-6). lib. bdg. 22.65 *(978-1-4342-9791-4(8))* Stone Arch Bks.

Han, Jia. My Name Is Zedonk. 2017. (ENG.). 40p. (J). (gr. -1-2). 16.95 *(978-1-941529-53-9(4),* Plum Blossom Bks.) Parallax Pr.

Hapka, Catherine, pseud. Blue Ribbon Day. Kennedy, Anne, illus. 2013. (I Can Read Level 2 Ser.). (ENG.). 32p. (J). (gr. -1-3). 16.99 *(978-0-06-208677-8(4));* pap. 3.99 *(978-0-06-208676-1(6))* HarperCollins Pubs.

—The Camping Trip. 2014. (Pony Scouts: I Can Read! Ser.). (J). lib. bdg. 13.55 *(978-0-606-35069-3(1),* Turtleback) Turtleback Bks.

—Chasing Gold. 2014. (Ponies of Chincoteague Ser.: 3). lib. bdg. 17.20 *(978-0-606-36099-9(9))* Turtleback Bks.

—Horse Diaries #12: Luna. Sanderson, Ruth, illus. 2015. (Horse Diaries). (ENG.). 160p. (J). (gr. 3-7). lib. bdg. 12.99 *(978-0-553-53371-2(1),* Random Hse. Bks. for Young Readers) Random Hse. Children's Bks.

—Jingle Bells. Sanderson, Ruth, illus. 2014. (Horse Diaries). (ENG.). 208p. (J). (gr. 3-7). pap. 7.99 *(978-0-385-38484-1(X),* Random Hse. Bks. for Young Readers) Random Hse. Children's Bks.

—Jingle Bells. 2014. (Horse Diaries: 11). lib. bdg. 18.40 *(978-0-606-36024-1(7))* Turtleback Bks.

—Moonlight Mile. 2015. (Marguerite Henry's Ponies of Chincoteague Ser.: 4). (ENG., Illus.). 192p. (J). (gr. 3-7). pap. 6.99 *(978-1-4814-0345-0(1),* Aladdin) Simon & Schuster Children's Publishing.

—Moonlight Mile. 2015. (Ponies of Chincoteague Ser.: 4). lib. bdg. 17.20 *(978-0-606-36307-5(6))* Turtleback Bks.

—Pony Crazy. Kennedy, Anne, illus. 2010. (I Can Read Level 2 Ser.). (ENG.). 32p. (J). (gr. -1-3). pap. 3.99 *(978-0-06-125535-9(1))* HarperCollins Pubs.

—Really Riding! Kennedy, Anne, illus. 2010. (I Can Read Level 2 Ser.). (ENG.). 32p. (J). (gr. -1-3). pap. 3.99 *(978-0-06-125538-0(6))* HarperCollins Pubs.

—Yatimah. Sanderson, Ruth, illus. 2011. (Horse Diaries). (ENG.). 176p. (J). (gr. 3-7). pap. 7.99 *(978-0-375-86719-4(8),* Random Hse. Bks. for Young Readers) Random Hse. Children's Bks.

Hapka, Catherine, pseud & Hapka, Cathy. Elska. Griffin-Scott, Janet & Sanderson, Ruth, illus. 2009. (Horse Diaries: No. 1). (ENG.). 144p. (J). (gr. 3-7). pap. 7.99 *(978-0-375-84732-5(4),* Random Hse. Bks. for Young Readers) Random Hse. Children's Bks.

Harlow, Joan Hiatt. Midnight Rider. 2006. (ENG.). 384p. (J). (gr. 4-9). pap. 8.99 *(978-0-689-87010-1(8),* McElderry, Margaret K. Bks.) McElderry, Margaret K. Bks.

Harrison, Paula. The Magic Rings. 2013. (Rescue Princesses Ser.: 6). lib. bdg. 14.75 *(978-0-606-32373-4(2),* Turtleback) Turtleback Bks.

Hart, Alison. Bell's Star. Sanderson, Ruth, illus. 2009. (Horse Diaries: No. 2). (ENG.). 144p. (J). (gr. 3-7). pap. 7.99 *(978-0-375-85204-6(2),* Random Hse. Bks. for Young Readers) Random Hse. Children's Bks.

—Gabriel's Horses, 1 vol. 2007. (Racing to Freedom Trilogy). (ENG.). 160p. (J). (gr. 3-7). 14.95 *(978-1-56145-398-6(6))* Peachtree Pubs.

—Gabriel's Journey, 1 vol. (Racing to Freedom Ser.). (ENG.). 160p. (J). 2011. pap. 4.99 *(978-1-56145-530-0(X))* 2008. (Illus.). (gr. 3-7). 14.95 *(978-1-56145-442-6(7))* Peachtree Pubs.

—Risky Chance. Sanderson, Ruth, illus. 2011. (Horse Diaries). (ENG.). 176p. (J). (gr. 3-7). pap. 7.99 *(978-0-375-86833-7(X),* Random Hse. Bks. for Young Readers) Random Hse. Children's Bks.

—Whirlwind. 2010. (ENG.). 272p. (YA). (gr. 7-8). pap. 8.99 *(978-0-375-86005-8(3),* Laurel Leaf) Random Hse. Children's Bks.

Hart, Julie Anne. Miss Molly Mare. 2011. 16p. 8.50 *(978-1-4520-5172-7(0))* AuthorHouse.

Harvey, Pam & Panckridge, Michael. Into the Fire. 2008. 192p. (J). *(978-0-207-20061-8(0))* HarperCollins Pubs. Australia.

Havice, L. K. Peanut the Tiny Horse. Bessey, Brandan, illus. 2012. 50p. *(978-1-4602-0956-1(7))*; pap. *(978-1-4602-0954-7(0))* FriesenPress.

Havill, Juanita. Call the Horse Lucky. Lane, Nancy, illus. 2010. (ENG.). 24p. (J). (gr. k-3). 16.95 *(978-0-940719-10-1(X))* Gryphon Pr., The.

Hawkins, Al. April Is Born: Adventures of a New Quarter Horse Filly. Erickson, Terri, illus. l.t. ed. 2004. 24p. (J). pap. 9.50 *(978-0-9640056-5-5(4))* Arrowhead Publishing.

Haynali, Carolyn A. (Nesto). Goldie: The little horse that didn't Listen. 2011. 20p. pap. 12.90 *(978-1-4634-4765-6(5))* AuthorHouse.

Heaton, Layce D. The Many Tracks of Lap'n Tap, 1. Heaton, Layce D., illus. 2006. (Illus.). 32p. (J). lib. bdg. 18.95 *(978-0-9761128-3-9(3))* KB Bks. & More.

Heimbuch, Carol. Shadow Stallion. 2011. 170p. pap. 11.50 *(978-1-59330-693-9(8))* Aventine Pr.

Heimbuch, Carol Jo. Condor Caper. Martin, Fred, illus. 2008. 128p. pap. 11.50 *(978-1-59330-560-4(5))* Aventine Pr.

Heinz, Brian J. Cheyenne Medicine Hat. Manchess, Gregory, illus. 2004. (ENG.). 32p. (J). (gr. 1-3). 19.95 *(978-1-56846-181-6(X))* Creative Co., The.

Helidoniotis, Kathy. Horse Mad Academy. 2006. 176p. *(978-0-7322-8422-0(8))* HarperCollins Pubs. Australia.

—Horse Mad Heroes. 2007. 272p. (J). *(978-0-7322-8423-7(6))* HarperCollins Pubs. Australia.

—Horse Mad Summer. 2006. 224p. *(978-0-7322-8421-3(X))* HarperCollins Pubs. Australia.

—Horse Mad Western. 2008. 272p. *(978-0-7322-8424-4(4))* HarperCollins Pubs. Australia.

—Totally Horse Mad. 2006. 240p. *(978-0-7322-8420-6(1))* HarperCollins Pubs. Australia.

Helsel, Sandra. Pokey & the Rooster. Snyder, Joe, illus. 2009. 28p. pap. 9.95 *(978-0-9818488-1-5(8))* Ajoyin Publishing, Inc.

Hendershot, Eric. A Horse for Christmas. 2012. pap. 8.99 *(978-1-4621-1078-0(9))* Cedar Fort, Inc./CFI Distribution.

Hendry, Frances. Quest for a Kelpie. l.t. ed. 2007. 248p. per. *(978-1-905665-17-4(2))* Pollinger In Print.

Henrietta: Not Everybody Wears Horseshoes. 2004. (Illus.). 32p. (J). 6.99 *(978-0-9744520-1-2(7))* Glitter Creek, Inc.

Henry, Marguerite. Black Gold. Dennis, Wesley, illus. 2016. (ENG.). 208p. (J). (gr. 3-7). 19.99 *(978-1-4814-6212-9(1)*, Aladdin) Simon & Schuster Children's Publishing.

—Justin Morgan Had a Horse. 2011. 8.32 *(978-0-7848-3468-8(7)*, Everbind) Marco Bk. Co.

—Justin Morgan Had a Horse. Dennis, Wesley, illus. (ENG.). 176p. (J). (gr. 3-7). 2015. 19.99 *(978-1-4814-2562-9(5))* 2006. pap. 7.99 *(978-1-4169-2785-3(9))* Simon & Schuster Children's Publishing. (Aladdin).

—Justin Morgan Had a Horse. 2003. (J). (gr. 3-8). 20.25 *(978-0-8446-7245-8(9))* Smith, Peter Pub., Inc.

—King of the Wind: The Story of the Godolphin Arabian. unabr. ed. 2004. 173p. (J). (gr. 4-7). pap. 38.00 incl. audio *(978-0-8072-8697-5(4)*, YA239SP, Listening Library) Random Hse. Audio Publishing Group.

—King of the Wind: The Story of the Godolphin Arabian. 2015. (ENG., Illus.). 192p. (J). (gr. 3-7). 19.99 *(978-1-4814-2133-1(6)*, Aladdin) Simon & Schuster Children's Publishing.

—King of the Wind: The Story of the Godolphin Arabian. Dennis, Wesley, illus. 2006. (ENG.). 176p. (J). (gr. 3-7). pap. 7.99 *(978-1-4169-2786-0(7)*, Aladdin) Simon & Schuster Children's Publishing.

—Marguerite Henry Treasury of Horses Set: Misty of Chincoteague; Justin Morgan Had a Horse; King of the Wind. Dennis, Wesley, illus. 2007. (ENG.). 528p. (J). (gr. 3-7). pap. 21.99 *(978-1-4169-3954-2(7)*, Aladdin) Simon & Schuster Children's Publishing.

—Misty's Twilight. Haus Grandpre, Karen, illus. 2016. (ENG.). 144p. (J). (gr. 3-7). 19.99 *(978-1-4814-5221-2(5)*, Aladdin) Simon & Schuster Children's Publishing.

—Misty's Twilight. Grandpré, Karen Haus, illus. 2007. (ENG.). 144p. (J). (gr. 3-7). pap. 6.99 *(978-1-4169-2787-7(5)*, Aladdin) Simon & Schuster Children's Publishing.

—San Domingo. Lougheed, Robert, illus. 2016. (ENG.). 288p. (J). (gr. 3-7). 19.99 *(978-1-4814-6211-2(3)*, Aladdin) Simon & Schuster Children's Publishing.

—Stormy, Misty's Foal. Dennis, Wesley, illus. (ENG.). (J). (gr. 3-7). 2015. 256p. 19.99 *(978-1-4814-2561-2(7))* 2007. 224p. pap. 6.99 *(978-1-4169-2788-4(3))* Simon & Schuster Children's Publishing. (Aladdin).

—White Stallion of Lipizza. 2015. (ENG., Illus.). 208p. (J). (gr. 3-7). 19.99 *(978-1-4814-0392-4(3)*, Aladdin) Simon & Schuster Children's Publishing.

—White Stallion of Lipizza. Dennis, Wesley, illus. 2014. (ENG.). 192p. (J). (gr. 3-7). pap. 7.99 *(978-1-4814-0391-7(5)*, Aladdin) Simon & Schuster Children's Publishing.

Hensler, K. Why Worry? The Adventures of Bay/Bob/A/Loo/Bop Everything in Moderation. 2008. 48p. pap. 24.95 *(978-1-60610-813-0(1))* America Star Bks.

Henson, Heather. Dream of Night. 2010. (ENG.). 224p. (J). (gr. 3-7). 15.99 *(978-1-4169-4899-5(6)*, Atheneum Bks. for Young Readers) Simon & Schuster Children's Publishing.

Henson, Heather. The Whole Sky. 2017. (ENG., Illus.). 256p. (J). (gr. 5-7). 16.99 ***(978-1-4424-1405-1(7)***, Atheneum/Caitlyn Dlouhy Books) Simon & Schuster Children's Publishing.

Hermes, Patricia. Black Cloud, No. 8. Sheckels, Astrid, illus. 2012. (Horse Diaries). (ENG.). 176p. (J). (gr. 3-7). pap. 7.99 *(978-0-375-86881-8(X)*, Random Hse. Bks. for Young Readers) Random Hse. Children's Bks.

—Black Cloud. 2012. (Horse Diaries: 8). lib. bdg. 18.40 *(978-0-606-26553-9(8)*, Turtleback) Turtleback Bks.

—Emma Dilemma, the Nanny, & the Best Horse Ever, 0 vols. Carter, Abby, illus. 2013. (Emma Dilemma Ser.: 6). (ENG.). 144p. (J). (gr. 3-6). pap. 9.99 *(978-1-4778-1633-2(X)*, 9781477816332, Amazon Children's Publishing) Amazon Publishing.

—Koda. Sanderson, Ruth, illus. 2009. (Horse Diaries: No. 3). (ENG.). 160p. (J). (gr. 3-7). pap. 7.99 *(978-0-375-85199-5(2)*, Random Hse. Bks. for Young Readers) Random Hse. Children's Bks.

Heti, Sheila. We Need a Horse. Rojas, Clare, illus. 2011. (ENG.). 32p. (J). (gr. k-6). 16.95 *(978-1-936365-40-1(5))* McSweeney's Publishing.

Hickman, Rachel. One Silver Summer. 2016. (ENG.). 272p. (J). (gr. 9). 17.99 *(978-0-545-80892-7(8)*, Scholastic Pr.) Scholastic, Inc.

Hickox, Rebecca. Per & the Dala Horse. Gilbert, Yvonne, illus. 2003. 32p. (J). pap. 8.95 *(978-1-57534-034-0(8))* Skandisk, Inc.

Hicks, Angie, illus. The Fairy Horse. 2012. (ENG.). 24p. (J). 9.95 *(978-1-84135-834-5(7))* Award Pubns. Ltd. GBR. Dist: Parkwest Pubns., Inc.

Higginson, Hadley. Keeker & the Pony Camp Catastrophe, Bk. 5. Perrett, Lisa, illus. 2007. (Keeker & the Sneaky Pony Ser.: KEEK). (ENG.). 56p. (J). (gr. k-3). per. 4.99 *(978-0-8118-5597-6(X))* Chronicle Bks. LLC.

Hill, Janet Muirhead. The Horse & the Crow: A Miranda & Starlight Story. 2015. (ENG.). 268p. (J). pap. 13.00 *(978-1-937849-27-6(9))* Raven Publishing Inc. of Montana.

—Horses for Sale: A Miranda & Starlight Story. 2016. (ENG., Illus.). 192p. (YA). pap. 12.00 *(978-1-937849-32-0(5))* Raven Publishing Inc. of Montana.

—Miranda & Starlght. 2013. (J). cd-rom 19.00 *(978-1-937849-08-5(2))* Raven Publishing Inc. of Montana.

—Miranda & Starlight: (the Starlight Books, 1) Revised Edition, 6 vols. Lehmkuhl, Pat, illus. 2nd rev. ed. 2003. (Starlight Bks.: 1). 168p. (J). (gr. 3-7). per. 9.00 *(978-0-9714161-4-7(1))* Raven Publishing Inc. of Montana.

Hill, Susan & Sewell, Anna. Black Beauty & the Thunderstorm. Farnsworth, Bill, illus. 2011. (My Readers Ser.). (ENG.). 48p. (J). (gr. 1-3). pap. 3.99 *(978-0-312-64721-6(2)*, 9780312647216) Square Fish.

Hinton, S. E. Taming the Star Runner. 2013. (ENG.). 192p. (YA). (gr. 7). pap. 7.99 *(978-0-385-37666-2(9)*, Delacorte Pr.) Random Hse. Children's Bks.

Hoban, Russell. Rosie's Magic Horse. Blake, Quentin, illus. 2013. (ENG.). 40p. (J). (gr. -1-3). 15.99 *(978-0-7636-6400-8(6))* Candlewick Pr.

Hobbs, Will. The Big Wander. 2004. (Illus.). 181p. (J). (gr. 5-9). 13.65 *(978-0-7569-4970-9(X))* Perfection Learning Corp.

Hodgson, Julie. Juno & the Windwalker. 2010. 40p. pap. 18.95 *(978-1-4461-4244-8(2))* Lulu Pr., Inc.

—Miniature Horse Tales. 2005. 37p. (J). 15.00 *(978-1-4116-4144-0(2))* Lulu Pr., Inc.

Hogan Ii, Haywood. The Horse, the Dog, & the Bird. 2012. 24p. pap. 16.95 *(978-1-4685-7633-7(X))* AuthorHouse.

Holmes, Victoria. The Horse from the Sea. 2005. (ENG.). 320p. (J). (gr. 5-18). 15.99 *(978-0-06-052028-1(0))* HarperCollins Pubs.

—The Horse from the Sea: An Epic Horse Story. 2005. 320p. (J). (gr. k-9). lib. bdg. 16.89 *(978-0-06-052029-8(9))* HarperCollins Pubs.

—Rider in the Dark: An Epic Horse Story. 2004. (Illus.). 320p. (J). (gr. 5-18). (ENG.). 15.99 *(978-0-06-052025-0(6))*; lib. bdg. 16.89 *(978-0-06-052026-7(4))* HarperCollins Pubs.

Holt, Stephen. The Whistling Stallion. Crowell, Pers, illus. 2011. 224p. 44.95 *(978-1-258-10199-2(8))* Literary Licensing, LLC.

Holub, Joan & Williams, Suzanne. Poseidon & the Sea of Fury. Phillips, Craig, illus. 2012. (Heroes in Training Ser.: 2). (ENG.). 128p. (J). (gr. 1-4). 16.99 *(978-1-4424-5798-0(8))*; pap. 5.99 *(978-1-4424-5265-7(X))* Simon & Schuster Children's Publishing. (Aladdin).

Honderich, Lou. Ricki. 2013. 170p. pap. 10.99 *(978-0-9856906-6-3(6))* Mockingbird Lane Pr.

Horowitz, Dave. Little Big Horse. 2014. (Scholastic Reader Level 1 Ser.). lib. bdg. 13.55 *(978-0-606-35375-5(5))* Turtleback Bks.

Horse Angel - Chica's Story. 2007. (J). *(978-1-933343-48-8(6)*, PONY) Stabenfeldt Inc.

Horse Angel - Ride into Fear. 2005. (J). *(978-1-933343-11-2(7)*, PONY) Stabenfeldt Inc.

Horse Angel - Run Wild. 2006. (J). *(978-1-933343-26-6(5)*, PONY) Stabenfeldt Inc.

A Horse Called Trouble. 2006. (J). *(978-1-933343-34-1(6)*, PONY) Stabenfeldt Inc.

Horse Sense. 2005. 44p. (J). 3.99 *(978-0-9763213-2-3(7))* OHC Group LLC.

Hourlier, Sylvaine. Blacky & the Enchanted Mountain, 1 vol. 2010. 48p. pap. 16.95 *(978-1-4512-1140-5(6))* America Star Bks.

Howard, Cheryl Lynne. Captured by Love: A Wild Horse Story Based on Psalm 139. 2011. 48p. pap. 11.00 *(978-1-4567-1822-0(3))* AuthorHouse.

Howard, Victoria. The Adventures of Max & Molly: A Love Story about a Dog & a Horse. 2012. 52p. pap. 24.99 *(978-1-4772-4866-9(8))* AuthorHouse.

Hubler, Marsha. Blue Ribbon Champ, 1 vol. rev. ed. 2010. (Keystone Stables Ser.). (ENG.). 112p. (J). pap. 7.99 *(978-0-310-71797-3(3))* Zonderkidz.

—A Horse to Love, 1 vol. ed. 2009. (Keystone Stables Ser.). (ENG.). 144p. (J). pap. 4.99 *(978-0-310-71792-8(2))* Zonderkidz.

—Leading the Way, 1 vol. 2010. (Keystone Stables Ser.). (ENG.). 128p. (J). pap. 7.99 *(978-0-310-71796-6(5))* Zonderkidz.

—The Long Ride Home, 1 vol. 2010. (Keystone Stables Ser.). (ENG.). 144p. (J). pap. 7.99 *(978-0-310-71692-1(6))* Zonderkidz.

—On the Victory Trail, 1 vol. rev. ed. 2009. (Keystone Stables Ser.). (ENG.). 144p. (J). pap. 7.99 *(978-0-310-71793-5(0))* Zonderkidz.

—Southern Belle's Special Gift, 1 vol. 2009. (Keystone Stables Ser.). (ENG.). 128p. (J). pap. 7.99 *(978-0-310-71794-2(9))* Zonderkidz.

—Summer Camp Adventure, 1 vol. 2009. (Keystone Stables Ser.). (ENG.). 128p. (J). pap. 7.99 *(978-0-310-71795-9(7))* Zonderkidz.

—Whispering Hope, 1 vol., Bk. 7. 2010. (Keystone Stables Ser.). (ENG.). 144p. (J). pap. 7.99 *(978-0-310-71691-4(8))* Zonderkidz.

Hucklesby, Jill. Samphire Song. 2013. (ENG.). 296p. (J). (gr. 3-7). 16.99 *(978-0-8075-7224-5(1))* Whitman, Albert & Co.

Hughes, Holly. Hoofbeats of Danger. 2009. (Mysteries Through Time Ser.). 144p. (YA). (gr. 4-8). 31.95 *(978-1-60754-176-9(9))*; pap. 15.25 *(978-1-60754-177-6(7))* Windmill Bks.

Hughes, Jenny. Dark Horse. 2014. (ENG.). 224p. (J). (gr. 3-7). pap. 9.95 *(978-1-62124-010-5(X))* Breakaway Bks.

—Fantasy Horse. 2013. (ENG.). 192p. (J). (gr. 3-7). pap. 9.95 *(978-1-62124-004-4(5))* Breakaway Bks.

—A Horse by Any Other Name. 2014. (ENG.). 224p. (J). (gr. 3-7). pap. 9.95 *(978-1-62124-009-9(6))* Breakaway Bks.

—Horse in the Diary. 2014. (ENG.). 128p. (J). (gr. 3-7). pap. 9.95 *(978-1-62124-014-3(2))* Breakaway Bks.

—Horse in the Mirror. 2014. (ENG.). 128p. (J). (gr. 3-7). pap. 9.95 *(978-1-62124-012-9(6))* Breakaway Bks.

—The Horse in the Portrait. 2008. (YA). *(978-1-933343-72-3(9))* Stabenfeldt Inc.

—Horse in the Portrait. 2014. (ENG.). 128p. (J). (gr. 3-7). pap. 9.95 *(978-1-62124-013-6(4))* Breakaway Bks.

—Legend of the Island Horse. 2013. (ENG.). 224p. (J). (gr. 3-7). pap. 9.95 *(978-1-62124-007-5(X))* Breakaway Bks.

—Model Horse. 2013. (ENG.). 192p. (gr. 3-7). pap. 9.95 *(978-1-62124-002-0(9))* Breakaway Bks.

—Mystery at Black Horse Farm. 2013. (ENG.). 144p. (J). (gr. 3-7). pap. 9.95 *(978-1-62124-003-7(7))* Breakaway Bks.

—Sea Horses. 2013. (ENG., Illus.). 224p. (J). (gr. 3-7). pap. 9.95 *(978-1-62124-006-8(1))* Breakaway Bks.

Hungry Horse: Individual Title Six-Packs. (Literatura 2000 Ser.). (gr. 1-2). 28.00 *(978-0-7635-0057-3(7))* Rigby Education.

Hyde, Heidi Smith. Feivel's Flying Horses. van der Sterre, Johanna, illus. 2010. (ENG.). 32p. (J). (gr. k-4). lib. bdg. 17.95 *(978-0-7613-3957-1(4)*, Kar-Ben Publishing) Lerner Publishing Group.

If Wishes Were Horses. 2007. (J). *(978-1-933343-53-2(2)*, PONY) Stabenfeldt Inc.

ImageBooks Staff. Little Horse: Finger Puppet Book. Put, Klaartje van der, illus. 2013. (Little Finger Puppet Board Bks.). (ENG.). 12p. (J). (gr. -1 — 1). bds. 6.99 *(978-1-4521-1249-7(5))* Chronicle Bks. LLC.

Inny. Epiphany Rose-the Message. 2006. pap. 8.99 *(978-1-60034-097-0(0))* Salem Author Services.

Ipcar, Dahlov. One Horse Farm, 1 vol. Ipcar, Dahlov, illus. 2011. (ENG., Illus.). 36p. (J). 17.95 *(978-1-934031-39-1(9)*, 9c1cb594-de8e-4edf-b155-de5e1e50fbce) Islandport Pr., Inc.

Jackson, Gabrielle E. Peggy Stewart. 2007. 176p. per. *(978-1-4065-1803-0(4))* Dodo Pr.

James, Andrea. Adventures at Ja-Mar Farms: Pup-Pup, Padluck & PIG Take a Walk in the Wet Woods, 1 vol. 2010. 48p. 24.95 *(978-1-4512-1005-7(1))* PublishAmerica, Inc.

James M.A., Deborah. Tangerine, Spark, & Rainbow's Story. 2012. 44p. pap. 21.99 *(978-1-4685-4956-0(1))* AuthorHouse.

James, Will. The Dark Horse. 2003. (Illus.). 288p. 35.00 *(978-0-87842-484-9(9)*, 818) Mountain Pr. Publishing Co., Inc.

—The Dark Horse, Vol. 1. James, Will, illus. rev. ed. (Illus.). 288p. (J). (gr. 4). pap. *(978-0-87842-486-3(5)*, 817) Mountain Pr. Publishing Co., Inc.

—My First Horse, Vol. 1. rev. ed. (Illus.). 48p. (J). (gr. 4). 16.00 *(978-0-87842-488-7(1)*, 819) Mountain Pr. Publishing Co., Inc.

—Smokey Vol. 1: The Cowhorse. rev. ed. (Tumbleweed Ser.). (Illus.). 260p. (J). (gr. 4-7). 36.00 *(978-0-87842-414-6(8)*, 805) Mountain Pr. Publishing Co., Inc.

—Smoky Cowhorse, the Cowhorse. 2011. 9.00 *(978-0-7848-3460-2(1)*, Everbind) Marco Bk. Co.

—Smoky, the Cow Horse. 2003. (J). (gr. 3-8). 20.50 *(978-0-8446-7247-2(5))* Smith, Peter Pub., Inc.

—Smoky the Cowhorse. 2008. (ENG., Illus.). 336p. (J). (gr. 3-7). pap. 8.99 *(978-1-4169-4941-1(0)*, Aladdin) Simon & Schuster Children's Publishing.

—Young Cowboy. rev. ed. 2004. (Illus.). 88p. (J). (gr. 4-7). 15.00 *(978-0-87842-419-1(9)*, 806) Mountain Pr. Publishing Co., Inc.

Jan, Young. Starting the Colt. 2014. (ENG.). 174p. (J). pap. 12.00 *(978-1-937849-10-8(4))* Raven Publishing Inc. of Montana.

Jazynka, Kitson. Boys Camp: Nate's Story. Orback, Craig, illus. 2015. (ENG.). 144p. (J). (gr. 1-5). pap. 9.95 *(978-1-62914-806-9(7)*, Sky Pony Pr.) Skyhorse Publishing Co., Inc.

—Nate's Story, Bk. 2. Orback, Craig, illus. 2013. (ENG.). 144p. (J). (gr. 2-5). 14.95 *(978-1-62087-981-8(6)*, 620981, Sky Pony Pr.) Skyhorse Publishing Co., Inc.

Jeffers, Karen. Tosh. 2013. 26p. pap. 13.95 *(978-1-4787-0255-9(9))* Outskirts Pr., Inc.

Jennings, Terri & Gold, Paul Daniel. Cadbury's Big Move. 2007. 52p. per. 19.95 *(978-1-4327-0705-7(1))* Outskirts Pr., Inc.

Jensen, Barb E. A Horse Named Summertime. 2007. 224p. per. 13.95 *(978-1-60264-113-6(7))* Virtualbookworm.com Publishing, Inc.

Johnson, Christopher L. I Don't Have Crooked Legs. 2013. 130p. 28.99 *(978-1-4497-8355-6(4))*; pap. 11.99 *(978-1-4497-8356-3(2))* Author Solutions, Inc. (WestBow Pr.).

Johnson, Joanne Gail. Donkey & the Racehorse. Ferris, Carole Anne, illus. 2011. (ENG.). 48p. pap. 12.00 *(978-0-230-02552-3(8)*, Macmillan) Pan Macmillan GBR. Dist: Macmillan.

Johnson, Mar. Jack the Mighty Steed. 2011. 88p. pap. 19.95 *(978-1-4560-4916-4(X))* America Star Bks.

Johnston, Annie Fellows. The Little Colonel's House Party. Meynell, Louis, illus. 2007. 176p. per. *(978-1-4065-3514-3(1))* Dodo Pr.

Jones, Wendy Lou. Quest for Golden Downs. 2013. 246p. pap. 10.95 *(978-0-9777110-2-4(1))* Royal Knight Inc.

Juby, Susan. Another Kind of Cowboy. 2007. 344p. (YA). lib. bdg. 6.99 *(978-0-06-076521-7(6)*, HarperTeen) HarperCollins Pubs.

Judybee. Queen Amina of Zari: Queens of Africa Book 1. LittlePinkPebble, illus. 2011. 28p. pap. *(978-1-908218-43-8(6))* MX Publishing, Ltd.

Jupin, David Perez, illus. Love. 2013. 20p. pap. 11.95 *(978-1-937504-67-0(0))* Worthy Shorts.

K, U. The Palomino. 2008. (J). pap. *(978-1-933343-89-1(3))* Stabenfeldt Inc.

Kahler, Janet C. 1918 Covered Wagon Adventure. 2006. (Illus.). 94p. per. 10.95 *(978-1-57258-444-0(0)*, 945-6305) TEACH Services, Inc.

Kane, Doug. Ariel's Journey. 2008. 256p. pap. 8.95 *(978-0-9817234-0-2(3))* Blue Ink Pr.

Kasten, Victoria. Mighty Stallion. 2005. (Illus.). 70p. (J). per. 8.95 *(978-0-9788850-0-7(7))* Kasten, Victoria.

—Mighty Stallion 2 Fury's Journey. 2006. (Illus.). 72p. (J). per. 8.95 *(978-0-9788850-1-4(5))* Kasten, Victoria.

—Mighty Stallion 3 Glory's Legend. 2006. (ENG., Illus.). (J). per. 8.95 *(978-0-9788850-2-1(3))* Kasten, Victoria.

—Mighty Stallion 4 Dancer's Dream. 2007. (Illus.). (J). per. 8.95 *(978-0-9788850-3-8(1))* Kasten, Victoria.

—Mighty Stallion 5 A Stallion's Heart. Briggs, Scott, photos by. 2007. (Illus.). (J). per. 8.95 *(978-0-9788850-5-2(8))* Kasten, Victoria.

Kaya Does It Her Way. 2007. (J). *(978-1-933343-47-1(8)*, PONY) Stabenfeldt Inc.

Keaster, Diane. Tawny-The Beauty. Page, Debbie, illus. 2013. 70p. pap. 7.95 *(978-0-9791719-2-5(X))* ZC Horses Series of Children's Bks.

Keene, Carolyn. Nancy Drew Diaries 3-Books-In-1! Curse of the Arctic Star; Strangers on a Train; Mystery of the Midnight Rider. 2016. (Nancy Drew Diaries). (ENG., Illus.). 592p. (J). (gr. 3-7). pap. 8.99 *(978-1-4814-8554-8(7)*, Aladdin) Simon & Schuster Children's Publishing.

—Unicorn Uproar. Pamintuan, Macky, illus. 2009. (Nancy Drew & the Clue Crew Ser.: 22). (ENG.). 96p. (J). (gr. 1-4). pap. 4.99 *(978-1-4169-7810-7(0)*, Aladdin) Simon & Schuster Children's Publishing.

Kelly, Bernadette. Courage to Ride, 1 vol. 2010. (Ridgeview Riding Club Ser.). (ENG.). 144p. (gr. 4-5). 25.32 *(978-1-4342-1931-2(3))* Stone Arch Bks.

—If Wishes Were Horses, 1 vol. 2010. (Ridgeview Riding Club Ser.). (ENG.). 144p. (Orig.). (gr. 4-5). 25.32 *(978-1-4342-1929-9(1))* Stone Arch Bks.

—Leap of Faith, 1 vol. 2010. (Ridgeview Riding Club Ser.). (ENG.). 144p. (gr. 4-5). 25.32 *(978-1-4342-1932-9(1))* Stone Arch Bks.

—Team Challenge, 1 vol. 2010. (Ridgeview Riding Club Ser.). (ENG.). 144p. (Orig.). (gr. 4-5). 25.32 *(978-1-4342-1930-5(5))* Stone Arch Bks.

Kelly, Bernadette & Ward, Krista. Norton's First Show, 1 vol. Alger, Liz, illus. 2013. (Pony Tales Ser.). (ENG.). 56p. (gr. 2-2). pap. 5.05 *(978-1-4795-2068-8(3)*, Chapter Readers) Picture Window Bks.

—Who Stole Norton?, 1 vol. Alger, Liz, illus. 2009. (Pony Tales Ser.). (ENG.). 56p. (gr. 2-2). lib. bdg. 21.32 *(978-1-4048-5503-8(3)*, Chapter Readers) Picture Window Bks.

Kelly, Lynda. Arab Dream Horse, Not. 2013. 188p. pap. *(978-1-903053-38-6(2))* Kelly Pubns.

Kelso, Mary Jean. The Adventures of Andy & Spirit: Book 1. Snider, K. C., illus. 2010. 64p. pap. 9.95 *(978-1-61633-069-9(4))* Guardian Angel Publishing, Inc.

—Andy & Spirit Go to the Fair. Snider, K. C., illus. 2008. 24p. pap. 10.95 *(978-1-935137-03-0(4))* Guardian Angel Publishing, Inc.

Kemp, Mary Kay. The Adventures of Jimmy Joe & Tippy Toe: Show & Tell. 2011. 20p. (gr. 1-2). pap. 14.00 *(978-1-4567-6170-7(6))* AuthorHouse.

Kendall, Christine. Riding Chance. 2016. (ENG.). 224p. (J). (gr. 5-9). 16.99 *(978-0-545-92404-7(9)*, Scholastic Pr.) Scholastic, Inc.

Kendall, Jane. Tennessee Rose. 2012. (Horse Diaries: 9). lib. bdg. 18.40 *(978-0-606-26554-6(6)*, Turtleback) Turtleback Bks.

Kendall, Jane F. Maestoso Petra. Sanderson, Ruth, illus. 2010. (Horse Diaries: No. 4). (ENG.). 160p. (J). (gr. 3-7). pap. 7.99 *(978-0-375-85842-0(3)*, Random Hse. Bks. for Young Readers) Random Hse. Children's Bks.

—Tennessee Rose. Sheckels, Astrid, illus. 2012. (Horse Diaries). (ENG.). 160p. (J). (gr. 3-7). pap. 7.99 *(978-0-375-87006-4(7)*, Random Hse. Bks. for Young Readers) Random Hse. Children's Bks.

Kenneally, Miranda. Racing Savannah, 1 vol. unabr. ed. 2015. (Hundred Oaks Ser.: Bk. 4). (ENG.). (YA). (gr. 7-9). 14.99 *(978-1-5012-1560-5(4)*, 9781501215605, Audible Studios on Brilliance Audio) Brilliance Publishing, Inc.

—Racing Savannah. 2013. (Hundred Oaks Ser.: Bk. 4). (ENG.). 304p. (YA). (gr. 7-12). pap. 9.99 *(978-1-4022-8476-2(4)*, 9781402284762) Sourcebooks, Inc.

Kenworthy, Mary. Tid Bit. 2004. 59p. pap. 16.95 *(978-1-4137-5231-1(4))* America Star Bks.

Kessler, Jackie Morse. Breath. 2013. (Riders of the Apocalypse Ser.: 4). (ENG.). 336p. (YA). (gr. 7). pap. 8.99 *(978-0-547-97043-1(9))* Houghton Mifflin Harcourt Publishing Co.

—Hunger. 2010. (Riders of the Apocalypse Ser.: 1). (ENG.). 192p. (YA). (gr. 7-18). pap. 9.99 *(978-0-547-34124-8(5))* Houghton Mifflin Harcourt Publishing Co.

Ketchen, Susan. Born That Way. 2009. (ENG.). 176p. (YA). (gr. 7-10). pap. 12.95 *(978-0-88982-254-2(9))* Oolichan Bks. CAN. Dist: Univ. of Toronto Pr.

Keyser, Amber J. & Burkhart, Kiersi. One Brave Summer. 2017. (Quartz Creek Ranch Ser.). (ENG.). 224p. (gr. 4-8). 35.99 ***(978-1-5124-0892-8(1)***, Darby Creek) Lerner Publishing Group.

—Shy Girl & Shy Guy. 2017. (Quartz Creek Ranch Ser.). (ENG.). 240p. (gr. 4-8). 35.99 ***(978-1-4677-9569-2(0)***, Darby Creek) Lerner Publishing Group.

Kilgras, Heidi & Parker, Jessie. Barbie - Horse Show Champ. Wolcott, Karen, illus. 2009. (Step into Reading Ser.). (ENG.). 32p. (J). (gr. -1-1). pap. 3.99 *(978-0-375-84701-1(4)*, Random Hse. Bks. for Young Readers) Random Hse. Children's Bks.

Kimpton, Diana. Pony-Crazed Princess: Princess Ellie's Mystery. Finlay, Lizzie, illus. 3rd rev. ed. 2006. (ENG.). 96p. (gr. 1-4). pap. 3.99 *(978-0-7868-4872-0(3))* Hyperion Pr.

Kirk, Ruth Lynn. Charlie Ate My Hat! 2004. 32p. pap. 7.99 *(978-0-9675410-2-0(6))* Shamrock Pr.

Klimo, Kate. Cinders. Sanderson, Ruth, illus. 2016. (Horse Diaries). (ENG.). 176p. (J). (gr. 3-7). pap. 7.99 *(978-1-101-93690-0(8)*, Random Hse. Bks. for Young Readers) Random Hse. Children's Bks.

Knapp, Jodi. The Adventures of Kelly & Lucky: The Beginning. 2010. 76p. pap. 20.99 *(978-1-60976-090-8(5)*, Eloquent Bks.) Strategic Book Publishing & Rights Agency (SBPRA).

Koops, Sheena. Voice of the Valley, 1 vol. 2006. (ENG.). 224p. (YA). (gr. 8-12). per. 8.95 (978-1-55143-514-5(4)) Orca Bk. Pubs. USA.

Kravetz, Nathan. A Horse of Another Color. 2011. 68p. (gr. 4-6). pap. 10.95 (978-1-4620-0591-8(8)) iUniverse, Inc.

Kressley, Carson. You're Different & That's Super. Lee, Jared, illus. 2005. (ENG.). 64p. (J). (gr. -1-3). 14.99 (978-1-4169-0070-2(5), Simon & Schuster Bks. For Young Readers) Simon & Schuster Bks. For Young Readers.

Kristina Simmons. Winter Beauty. 2010. 192p. pap. 13.95 (978-1-4401-4449-3(4)) iUniverse, Inc.

Kumin, Maxine. Oh, Harry! Moser, Barry, illus. 2011. (ENG.). 32p. (J). (gr. -1-3). 16.99 (978-1-59643-439-4(2), 9781596434394) Roaring Brook Pr.

Lagonegro, Melissa & RH Disney Staff. A Horse to Love: An Enchanted Stables Story. Disney Storybook Artists Staff, illus. 2007. (Pictureback(R) Ser.). (ENG.). 16p. (J). (gr. -1-2). pap. 3.99 (978-0-7364-2504-9(7), RH/Disney) Random Hse. Children's Bks.

Lambert, Joyce. Slick 'n Slide. Metzger, Jan, illus. 2008. 36p. 9.95 (978-0-9801146-0-7(8)) Lamweg Publishing.

Lanisek, Bill. Tony the Pony. 2011. 24p. pap. 15.99 (978-1-4568-3368-8(5)) Xlibris Corp.

Lao, Samantha. The Scared Panda. 2009. 20p. pap. 10.49 (978-1-4389-9226-6(2)) AuthorHouse.

Lara, Mike. A Boy & a Horse. 2011. 40p. pap. 21.99 (978-1-4628-8024-9(X)) Xlibris Corp.

Lardone, Lilia. Caballero Negro. (Torre de Papel Ser.). (SPA.). (J). (gr. 4-18). 7.95 (978-958-04-5052-8(8)) Norma S.A. COL. Dist: Distribuidora Norma, Inc.

Larson, Susan. Sam (a Pastoral) 2012. (ENG.). 220p. (YA). pap. 12.95 (978-0-9826069-9-5(0)) Savvy Pr.

Lasky, Kathryn. Escape. 2014. (Horses of the Dawn Ser.: 1). (ENG.). 240p. (J). (gr. 3-7). 16.99 (978-0-545-39716-2(2), Scholastic Pr.) Scholastic, Inc.

—The Escape. 2014. (Horses of the Dawn Trilogy Ser.: 1). lib. bdg. 17.20 (978-0-606-36034-0(4)) Turtleback Bks.

—Horses of the Dawn #1: the Escape. 2014. (Horses of the Dawn Ser.: 1). (ENG.). 240p. (J). (gr. 3-7). pap. 6.99 (978-0-545-39730-8(8), Scholastic Pr.) Scholastic, Inc.

—Star Rise. 2014. (Horses of the Dawn Ser.: 2). (ENG., Illus.). 208p. (J). (gr. 3-7). 16.99 (978-0-545-39717-9(0), Scholastic Pr.) Scholastic, Inc.

—Star Rise. 2015. (Horses of the Dawn Trilogy Ser.: 2). lib. bdg. 17.20 (978-0-606-37785-0(9)) Turtleback Bks.

—Wild Blood. 2016. (Horses of the Dawn Ser.: 3). (ENG., Illus.). 208p. (J). (gr. 3-7). 16.99 (978-0-545-68300-5(9), Scholastic Pr.) Scholastic, Inc.

—Wild Blood. 2016. (Horses of the Dawn Trilogy Ser.: 3). (ENG.). 195p. (J). (gr. 3-7). 17.20 (978-0-606-39120-7(7)) Turtleback Bks.

Lauer, Lucy S. A Horse Named Kat. 2006. 272p. (YA). per. 7.95 (978-0-9713497-3-5(8)) Cave Hollow Pr.

Lawrence, D. H. The Rocking-Horse Winner. 2010. (Illus.). 40p. (J). 19.95 (978-1-58341-924-3(1), Creative Education) Creative Co., The.

Lawson, Robert. Mr. Revere & I. 2003. (J). (gr. 4-8). 22.75 (978-0-8446-7258-8(0)) Smith, Peter Pub., Inc.

Layos, Alexandra. An Almost True Horse Tale. Bauer, Dana, illus. I.t. ed. 2003. 20p. (J). (gr. 1-5). pap. 8.95 (978-0-9655501-3-0(3)) Saddle & Bridle, Inc.

—Timeless: Blue Ribbon Days #2, 2, 2. 2005. (Illus.). 128p. (YA). pap. 10.95 (978-0-9655501-4-7(1)) Saddle & Bridle, Inc.

Lean, Sarah. A Hundred Horses. (ENG.). (J). (gr. 3-7). 2015. 240p. pap. 6.99 (978-0-06-212230-8(4)) 2014. 224p. 16.99 (978-0-06-212229-2(0)) HarperCollins Pubs. (Tegen, Katherine Bks).

Lee, Betsy B. The Buggy That Boogied Away. Lee, Sarah Ann, illus. 2006. 24p. (J). pap. 6.95 (978-0-9720267-7-2(0)) Learning Abilities Bks.

—Whoa, Wiggle-Worm: A Little Lemon Book about an Overly Active Child, 1 bk. Varnedoe, Catharine E., illus. I.t. ed. 2003. 24p. (J). pap. 7.95 (978-0-9720267-3-4(8)) Learning Abilities Bks.

Lee, Dakota. Flash of Freedom. 2009. 128p. pap. 11.95 (978-0-595-52557-7(1)) iUniverse, Inc.

Lee, Josie D. & Myers, Glenice. Reno & the Rodeo. 2010. 108p. 21.49 (978-1-4490-7315-2(8)); pap. 10.99 (978-1-4490-7316-9(6)) AuthorHouse.

Lee, Mary Ellen. Danny & Life on Bluff Point: Blizzard of '95 revised Edition. 2009. 160p. (gr. 4-7). pap. 12.95 (978-0-595-53308-4(6)) iUniverse, Inc.

Lee, Patty. Three Dogs & a Horse Named Blue. Lee, Jack, illus. 2009. 80p. pap. 10.49 (978-1-4389-9685-1(3)) AuthorHouse.

Legend of the Island Horse. 2006. (J). (978-1-933343-22-8(2)) Stabenfeldt Inc.

Lehmkuhl, Pat, illus. Starlight, Star Bright: (the Starlight Books, 3), 6 vols. 2003. (Starlight Bks.: Bk. 3). 192p. (J). (gr. 3-7). per. 12.00 (978-0-9714161-2-3(5)) Raven Publishing Inc. of Montana.

Leigh, S. Dream Pony. 2004. (Sandy Lane Stables Ser.). (J). (ENG.). 118p. pap. 4.95 (978-0-7945-0500-4(7)); 100p. lib. bdg. 12.95 (978-1-58086-556-2(9)) EDC Publishing.

Leland, Toni M. Christa Joins a Horse Club: Second in Christa Duncan Series. Leland, Toni M., illus. 2004. Orig. Title: Christa Joins 4-H. (Illus.). (J). pap. 6.95 (978-1-887932-49-3(6), SmallHorse Pr.) Equine Graphics Publishing Group.

Lester, Alison. The Circus Horse. Harvey, Roland, illus. 2009. (ENG.). 64p. (J). (gr. k-3). pap. 4.99 (978-0-8118-6656-9(4)) Chronicle Bks. LLC.

—Running with the Horses. 2011. (ENG., Illus.). 32p. (J). (gr. k-3). 16.95 (978-0-7358-4002-7(4)) North-South Bks., Inc.

—The Snow Pony. 2006. (ENG.). 208p. (J). (gr. 5-7). pap. 12.95 (978-0-618-77125-7(5)) Houghton Mifflin Harcourt Publishing Co.

Lester, Alison & Harvey, Roland. The Silver Horse Switch. 2009. (ENG., Illus.). 64p. (J). (gr. k-3). pap. 4.99 (978-0-8118-6554-8(1)) Chronicle Bks. LLC.

Lewin, Betsy. Good Night, Knight. Lewin, Betsy, illus. 2015. (I Like to Read(r) Ser.). (ENG., Illus.). 24p. (J). (gr. -1-3). 14.95 (978-0-8234-3206-6(8)); 6.99 (978-0-8234-3315-5(3)) Holiday Hse., Inc.

Lewis, Steve, Sr. The Course of a Horse. 2006. (J). 65.00 (978-1-59971-897-2(9)) Aardvark Global Publishing.

Light, Carol, illus. Oops, a Curious Horse Story Telling Board. 2003. (J). (978-0-9745803-4-0(1)) Little Big Tomes.

Liguori, Anthony J. Vienna & Venture: Tales from the Equine Side. 2011. 72p. pap. 10.70 (978-1-4269-5036-0(5)) Trafford Publishing.

Limbaugh, Rush H., III & Limbaugh, Kathryn Adams. Rush Revere & the American Revolution. 2014. (ENG.). 256p. 19.99 (978-1-4767-8987-3(8), Threshold Editions) Threshold Editions.

—Rush Revere & the American Revolution. Hiers, Christopher, illus. 2014. 244p. (J). pap. (978-1-4767-8989-7(4), Threshold Editions) Threshold Editions.

Lindgren, Astrid. Do You Know Pippi Longstocking? Dyssegaard, Elisabeth Kallick, tr. Nyman, Ingrid, illus. 2005. 32p. (J). pap. 4.95 (978-91-29-66203-0(6)) R & S Bks. SWE. Dist: Macmillan.

Little Pony's Secret. (Glitter Books... Ser.). 24p. (978-1-4054-9471-7(9)) Parragon, Inc.

Lodge, Jo. Cosy Cuddlers: Horse, 4. 2006. (ENG., Illus.). 8p. (J). (gr. -1-k). 7.99 (978-0-333-98753-7(5)) Macmillan Pubs., Ltd. GBR. Dist: Trafalgar Square Publishing.

Long, Loren. An Otis Christmas. Long, Loren, illus. 2013. (Otis Ser.: Bk. 4). (ENG., Illus.). 40p. (J). (gr. -1-2). 17.99 (978-0-399-16395-1(6), Philomel Bks.) Penguin Publishing Group.

—An Otis Christmas. Long, Loren, illus. 2016. (Otis Ser.). (ENG., Illus.). 38p. (J). (gr. -1-2). bds. 8.99 (978-0-399-54811-6(4), Philomel Bks.) Penguin Young Readers Group.

Long, Olivia. A Horse of a Different Color. Long, Olivia, illus. Date not set. (Kaleidoscope Ser.). (Illus.). 32p. (J). (gr. -1-4). 9.95 (978-1-880042-01-4(0), SL12451) Shelf-Life Bks.

Lorenzo, Lucia Ann. Lucky, My Best Friend. 2012. 24p. pap. 17.99 (978-1-4772-8087-4(1)) AuthorHouse.

Lost in the Wilderness. 2006. (J). (978-1-933343-39-6(7), PONY) Stabenfeldt Inc.

Lottridge, Celia. Ticket to Curlew, 1 vol. 2nd ed. 2007. (ENG.). 144p. (J). (gr. 2-7). pap. 8.95 (978-0-88899-843-9(0)) Groundwood Bks. CAN. Dist: Publishers Group West (PGW).

Lubner, Susan. A Horse's Tale: A Colonial Williamsburg Adventure. Moore, Margie, illus. 2008. (ENG.). 32p. (J). (gr. -1-1). 17.95 (978-0-8109-9490-4(9), Abrams Bks. for Young Readers) Abrams, Inc.

Luce, Catherine. The Milk Horse. Snider, K. C., illus. 2011. 20p. pap. 10.95 (978-1-61633-168-9(2)) Guardian Angel Publishing, Inc.

Lyle-Soffe, Shari. A Horse of Course. Ruble, Eugene, illus. 2009. 20p. pap. 10.95 (978-1-935137-82-5(4)) Guardian Angel Publishing, Inc.

Lyon, Jane & Bailey, Karen. Primerica: A Home for the Brave. 2011. (ENG., Illus.). 40p. (J). (gr. k-5). 16.95 (978-1-58150-341-8(5), Eclipse Pr.) Blood-Horse, Inc., The.

MacDonald, Anne Louise. The Ghost Horse of Meadow Green. 2005. (ENG., Illus.). 208p. (J). (gr. 5-9). 6.95 (978-1-55337-637-8(4)) Kids Can Pr., Ltd. CAN. Dist: Hachette Bk. Group.

MacGregor, Helen. Gnasher, Delta & the Biscuits. 2009. 48p. pap. 10.49 (978-1-4389-1367-4(2)) AuthorHouse.

MacHado, Ana Maria. Mi Reino Por un Caballo. (SPA.). pap. 11.95 (978-950-07-2222-3(4)) Editorial Sudamericana S.A. ARG. Dist: Distribooks, Inc.

Mackall, Dandi Daley. Bob's Great Escape, 1 vol. Wolf, Claudia, illus. 2011. (I Can Read! / a Horse Named Bob Ser.). (ENG.). 32p. (J). pap. 3.99 (978-0-310-71784-3(1)) Zonderkidz.

—Buckskin Bandit. 2004. (Winnie the Horse Gentler Ser.: 8). (ENG., Illus.). 224p. (J). mass mkt. 5.99 (978-0-8423-8724-8(2), Tyndale Kids) Tyndale Hse. Pubs.

—Dark Horse. 2009. (Starlight Animal Rescue Ser.: 4). (ENG.). 224p. (J). (gr. 3-7). mass mkt. 5.99 (978-1-4143-1271-2(7), Tyndale Kids) Tyndale Hse. Pubs.

—Double Trouble, 1 vol. Wolf, Claudia, illus. 2011. (I Can Read! / a Horse Named Bob Ser.). (ENG.). 32p. (J). pap. 3.99 (978-0-310-71785-0(X)) Zonderkidz.

—Friendly Foal. 2004. (Winnie the Horse Gentler Ser.: 7). (ENG.). 224p. (J). mass mkt. 5.99 (978-0-8423-8723-1(4), Tyndale Kids) Tyndale Hse. Pubs.

—A Horse Named Bob, 1 vol. Wolf, Claudia, illus. 2011. (I Can Read! / a Horse Named Bob Ser.). (ENG.). 32p. (J). pap. 3.99 (978-0-310-71782-9(5)) Zonderkidz.

—A Perfect Pony, 1 vol. Wolf, Claudia, illus. 2011. (I Can Read! / a Horse Named Bob Ser.). (ENG.). 32p. (J). pap. 3.99 (978-0-310-71783-6(3)) Zonderkidz.

—That's My Colt: An Easter Tale. Ellison, Chris, illus. 2008. 24p. (J). (gr. -1). 13.49 (978-0-7586-1423-0(3)) Concordia Publishing Hse.

—You & Your Horse: How to Whisper Your Way into Your Horse's Life. O'Connor, Jeff, illus. 2009. (ENG.). 160p. (J). (gr. 4-8). pap. 5.99 (978-1-4169-6449-0(5), Aladdin) Simon & Schuster Children's Publishing.

MacKay, Lisa. Nick Finds a Home. 2009. 32p. pap. 12.99 (978-1-4490-3245-6(1)) AuthorHouse.

MacLean, Heather. The Moonicorn Fairies. 2011. 40p. pap. (978-1-77067-687-9(2)) FriesenPress.

MacLeod, Elizabeth. Bunny the Brave War Horse: Based on a True Story. Lafrance, Marie, illus. 2014. (ENG.). 32p. (J). (gr. 1-3). 16.95 (978-1-77138-024-9(1)) Kids Can Pr., Ltd. CAN. Dist: Hachette Bk. Group.

Maddox, Jake & Berne, Emma Carlson. Horseback Hurdles, 1 vol. Wood, Katie, illus. 2012. (Jake Maddox Girl Sports Stories Ser.). (ENG.). 72p. (gr. 2-3). pap. 5.95 (978-1-4342-3905-1(5)); lib. bdg. 25.32 (978-1-4342-3294-6(8)) Stone Arch Bks.

The Magical Horses Vol. 2000: A Fairy Tale for the Young & the Young at Heart. I.t. ed. 2005. (Illus.). 127p. (J). per. (978-0-9738625-0-8(5)) Blue Cat Publishing.

Magness, Lee. Silver Dasher. 2003. 164p. pap. 12.95 (978-0-595-29043-7(4)) iUniverse, Inc.

Magpie, Lance White, reader. The Girl Who Loved Wild Horses. 2003. (Richard Jackson Books (Atheneum Hardcover) Ser.). (Illus.). (J). (gr. -1-2). 28.95 incl. audio compact disk (978-1-59112-752-9(1)) Live Oak Media.

Man-Kong, Mary. Barbie Loves Horses (Barbie) Duarte, Pamela, illus. 2013. (Color Plus Stencil Ser.). (ENG.). 64p. (J). (gr. -1-2). pap. 5.99 (978-0-449-81612-7(5), Golden Bks.) Random Hse. Children's Bks.

Manushkin, Fran. Cowgirl Katie, 1 vol. Lyon, Tammie, illus. 2014. (Katie Woo Ser.). (ENG.). 32p. (gr. k-2). lib. bdg. 21.32 (978-1-4795-2174-6(4)) Picture Window Bks.

The Many Tracks of Lap'n Tap. 2007. (J). per. 10.95 (978-0-9761128-4-6(1)) KB Bks. & More.

Marchese, Stephen, illus. The Flights of Marceau: Week Two. 2007. (ENG.). 60p. (J). 16.95 (978-0-9797495-1-3(4)) Majestic Eagle Publishing.

Marlow, Herb. Sundancer. Newberry, Loretta, illus. 2004. 56p. (J). lib. bdg. 21.95 (978-1-893595-39-2(0)); per. 14.95 (978-1-893595-41-5(2)) Four Seasons Bks., Inc.

Marlow, Susan K. Andi Saddles Up, 1 vol. 2017. (Circle C Stepping Stones Ser.: 1). 112p. (J). pap. 7.99 **(978-0-8254-4430-2(6))** Kregel Pubns.

—Andrea Carter & the Dangerous Decision, 1 vol. 2007. (Circle C Adventures Ser.). 144p. (J). pap. 7.99 (978-0-8254-3357-3(6)) Kregel Pubns.

—Andrea Carter & the Family Secret, 1 vol. 2008. (Circle C Adventures Ser.). 144p. (J). pap. 7.99 (978-0-8254-3365-8(7)) Kregel Pubns.

—Andrea Carter's Tales from the Circle C Ranch, 1 vol. 2015. (Illus.). 160p. (J). pap. 7.99 (978-0-8254-4379-4(2)) Kregel Pubns.

—The Last Ride: An Andrea Carter Book, 1 vol. 2016. (Circle C Milestones Ser.: 3). 176p. (YA). pap. 9.99 (978-0-8254-4369-5(5)) Kregel Pubns.

—Thick As Thieves: An Andrea Carter Book, 1 vol. 2015. (Circle C Milestones Ser.: 1). 176p. (YA). pap. 9.99 (978-0-8254-4367-1(9)) Kregel Pubns.

Marrs, Christie, creator. The Perfect Gift: I B Hoofinit's Horse Tales. I.t. ed. 2004. (Illus.). 57p. (J). mass mkt. 5.99 (978-1-928890-19-5(9)) I. B. Hoofinit Co.

Marsh, Carole. The Mystery at the Kentucky Derby. 2009. (Real Kids, Real Places Ser.). (Illus.). 146p. (J). lib. bdg. 18.99 (978-0-635-07002-9(2), Marsh, Carole Mysteries) Gallopade International.

Martelly, Ameline. Flor. 2011. 92p. pap. 31.99 (978-1-4653-4715-2(1)) Xlibris Corp.

Martin, Jacqueline Briggs. The Finest Horse in Town. Gaber, Susan, illus. 2003. 32p. (J). 17.95 (978-1-930900-27-1(9)) Purple Hse. Pr.

Martinello, Marian L. Ready's Gifts. 2003. (Illus.). 158p. (YA). (gr. 8-18). per. 12.95 (978-0-9724113-0-1(5)) MindCatcher Pr.

Martone, Ginny. The White Stallion. 2006. (ENG.). 60p. per. 16.95 (978-1-4241-4332-0(2)) PublishAmerica, Inc.

Mary E. Gale. Mountain Boy in the City. 2009. 136p. 21.95 (978-1-4401-6771-3(0)); pap. 11.95 (978-1-4401-6773-7(7)) iUniverse, Inc.

Mastro, M. L. Return to Baladah. 2011. 88p. (gr. 10-12). pap. 9.99 (978-1-4520-7377-4(5)) AuthorHouse.

Matty & the Moonlight Horse. 2005. (J). (978-1-933343-06-8(0), PONY) Stabenfeldt Inc.

Mayfield, Holly. Melvin: A True Story with a Happy Ending. Gilman, Sara, illus. 2013. 38p. pap. 9.99 (978-0-9892711-9-6(6)) Mindstir Media.

McCaughrean, Geraldine. El Caballo de Madera. Barroso, Paz, tr. Ross, Tony, illus. 2005. (Mythology Series Collection Mitos Ser.).Tr. of Wooden Horse (Pandora's Box). (SPA.). 50p. (J). (gr. 2-3). 9.95 (978-84-348-6432-0(0)) SM Ediciones ESP. Dist: Iaconi, Mariuccia Bk. Imports.

McClean, Will. Go, Bluey Go! Tummyre, Dustin, illus. 2003. 32p. (J). 14.95 (978-1-57072-252-3(8)) Overmountain Pr.

McConchie, Lyn. Autumn of the Wild Poney. 2012. (ENG.). 126p. (YA). pap. 12.00 (978-1-936021-40-6(4), Banana Oil Bks.) Cyberwizard Productions.

McCormic, Maxine Griffith. Casey's Hoof Prints. Christensen, D. J., illus. 2006. (ENG.). 72p. (J). pap. 14.95 (978-1-59299-217-1(X)) Inkwater Pr.

McCully, Emily Arnold. Wonder Horse: The True Story of the World's Smartest Horse. McCully, Emily Arnold, illus. 2010. (ENG., Illus.). 32p. (J). (gr. -1-3). 17.99 (978-0-8050-8793-2(1), 9780805087932, Holt, Henry & Co. Bks. For Young Readers) Holt, Henry & Co.

McDaniel, Lurlene. A Horse for Mandy. 2004. 80p. (J). (gr. 3-5). pap. 4.99 (978-1-58196-011-2(5), Darby Creek) Lerner Publishing Group.

McDonald, Ann-Eve. I Can't Go to School Today, My Horses Might Escape. 2004. (J). (978-0-9770158-0-1(7)) BeachWalk Bks. Inc.

McGarvey, A. J. Loyalty Unbroken: A Mustang's Tale. 2011. (Illus.). 84p. pap. 12.52 (978-1-4520-5162-8(3)) AuthorHouse.

McGeorge, Constance W. Chestnut, 1 vol. Whyte, Mary, illus. 2004. (ENG.). 32p. (J). 16.95 (978-1-56145-321-4(8)) Peachtree Pubs.

McGovern, Suzanne. Gator & Pete - More Alike Than It Seems. Bizjak, Donna, illus. 2007. (J). 13.99 (978-0-9792558-0-9(5)) Hatch Ideas, Inc.

McKissack, Patricia C. Away West. James, Gordon C. & James, Gordon, illus. 2006. (Scraps of Time Ser.). (ENG.). 144p. (J). (gr. 3-7). 5.99 (978-0-14-240688-5(0), Puffin Books) Penguin Young Readers Group.

McLoon, Linda Snow. Crown Prince. 2013. (ENG.). 272p. (gr. 6-9). pap. (978-1-57076-546-9(4)) Verlhac Editions.

—Crown Prince Challenged. 2012. (Brookmeade Young Riders Ser.: 2). (ENG.). 384p. (YA). (gr. 6-9). pap. (978-1-57076-545-2(6)) Verlhac Editions.

McMahon, V. Karen. I Saw a White Horse Today. Bailey, Loretta Dovell, illus. Black, Janet, photos by. 2011. 28p. pap. 24.95 (978-1-4626-0282-7(7)) America Star Bks.

McMullin, Neridah & McLean, Andrew. Fabish: The Horse That Braved a Bushfire. 2016. (ENG.). 32p. (J). (gr. 1-4). 18.99 (978-1-925266-86-3(9)) Allen & Unwin AUS. Dist: Independent Pubs. Group.

Meek, S. P. Pagan: A Border Patrol Horse. 2011. 254p. 46.95 (978-1-258-08439-4(2)) Literary Licensing, LLC.

Meigs, Elizabeth Bleecker. The White Winter: A Story of Scarlet Hill. Chapman, Frederick T., illus. 2011. 208p. 44.95 (978-1-258-08230-7(6)) Literary Licensing, LLC.

Melton, Cheri. Baby Wild Horses of the Comstock. 2010. 20p. 13.77 (978-1-4269-1916-9(6)) Trafford Publishing.

Memories of Grace. 2009. (ENG.). 95p. pap. 15.95 (978-0-9814648-6-2(6)) Inkwell Books LLC.

Merry, Margaret. The Adventures of Princess the Pony. 2009. 64p. pap. 19.50 (978-1-60860-936-9(7), Eloquent Bks.) Strategic Book Publishing & Rights Agency (SBPRA).

Miller, Albert G. Fury & the White Mare. 2011. 186p. 42.95 (978-1-258-07408-1(7)) Literary Licensing, LLC.

Miller, Holly & Schwartzkopf, Jere. A Horse Named Princess: Hola Princess Adios Thistle. 2009. 48p. pap. 17.49 (978-1-4343-6976-5(5)) AuthorHouse.

Miller, J. Cris. Stories to Read to Children: The Pony & the Unicorn & 3 other Stories, 8 vols., Vol. 1. 2007. (Illus.). 80p. (J). 19.95 (978-0-9725308-2-8(7)) Miller, J. Cris & Assocs.

Miller, Sibley. Heads Up, Horses! 2009. (Wind Dancers Ser.: 5). (ENG., Illus.). 80p. (J). (gr. 1-4). pap. 16.99 (978-0-312-56220-5(9), 9780312562205) Feiwel & Friends.

—Horse Magic - Or Not? Chang, Tara Larsen & Gershman, Jo, illus. 2011. (Wind Dancers Ser.: 12). (ENG.). 80p. (J). (gr. 1-4). pap. 16.99 (978-0-312-60545-2(5), 9780312605452) Feiwel & Friends.

—A Horse, of Course! Chang, Tara Larsen & Gershman, Jo, illus. 2009. (Wind Dancers Ser.: 7). (ENG.). 80p. (J). (gr. 1-4). pap. 16.99 (978-0-312-56402-5(3), 9780312564025) Feiwel & Friends.

—A Horse's Best Friend. Chang, Tara Larsen & Gershman, Jo, illus. 2011. (Wind Dancers Ser.: 9). (ENG.). 80p. (J). (gr. 1-4). pap. 6.99 (978-0-312-60542-1(0), 9780312605421) Feiwel & Friends.

—Horses Her Way. Chang, Tara Larsen & Gershman, Jo, illus. 2009. (Wind Dancers Ser.: 6). (ENG.). 80p. (J). (gr. 1-4). pap. 16.99 (978-0-312-56279-3(9), 9780312562793) Feiwel & Friends.

—Horsey Trails. Chang, Tara Larsen & Gershman, Jo, illus. 2011. (Wind Dancers Ser.: 11). (ENG.). 80p. (J). (gr. 1-4). pap. 16.99 (978-0-312-60544-5(7), 9780312605445) Feiwel & Friends.

—Hungry as a Horse. 2009. (Wind Dancers Ser.: 8). (ENG., Illus.). 80p. (J). (gr. 1-4). pap. 6.99 (978-0-312-56403-2(1), 9780312564032) Feiwel & Friends.

—Merry-Go-Horses. Chang, Tara Larsen & Gershman, Jo, illus. 2011. (Wind Dancers Ser.: 10). (ENG.). 80p. (J). (gr. 1-4). pap. 6.99 (978-0-312-60543-8(9), 9780312605438) Feiwel & Friends.

Miller, Sibley & Lenhard, Elizabeth. The Horse Must Go On. Chang, Tara Larsen & Gershman, Jo, illus. 2008. (Wind Dancers Ser.: 3). (ENG.). 80p. (J). (gr. 1-4). pap. 11.99 (978-0-312-38282-7(0), 9780312382827) Feiwel & Friends.

—Horses' Night Out. Chang, Tara Larsen & Gershman, Jo, illus. 2008. (Wind Dancers Ser.: 4). (ENG.). 80p. (J). (gr. 1-4). pap. 16.99 (978-0-312-38283-4(9), 9780312382834) Feiwel & Friends.

—If Wishes Were Horses. Chang, Tara Larsen & Gershman, Jo, illus. 2008. (Wind Dancers Ser.: 1). (ENG.). 80p. (J). (gr. 1-4). pap. 7.99 (978-0-312-38280-3(4), 9780312382803) Feiwel & Friends.

Mini Cuentos: Relampago, Caballo Salvaje, Pelirrojo y Tania.Tr. of Mini Faiy Tales: Lightning the Wild Horse. (SPA.). (J). (gr. k-4). 4.98 (978-970-607-620-5(4)) Larousse, Ediciones, S. A. de C. V. MEX. Dist: Continental Bk. Co., Inc.

Moeri, Louise. The Devil in Ol' Rosie. 2009. (ENG.). 208p. (J). (gr. 3-6). pap. 10.99 (978-1-4424-0202-7(4), Atheneum Bks. for Young Readers) Simon & Schuster Children's Publishing.

Monninger, Joseph. Finding Somewhere. 2012. (ENG.). 240p. (YA). (gr. 7). pap. 8.99 (978-0-375-89755-9(0), Ember) Random Hse. Children's Bks.

Monroe Donovan, Jane. Winter's Gift. Monroe Donovan, Jane, illus. 2004. (Holiday Ser.). (ENG., Illus.). 32p. (J). 16.95 (978-1-58536-231-8(X)) Sleeping Bear Pr.

Monson, Lois. God Is for Every Day(r) - Horse Dreams: Teach-A-Child Companion Book with VCD, 2 vols., Vol. 2. JoySoul Corporation, illus. Monson, Lois, photos by. 2006. 24p. (J). spiral bd. 14.95 (978-0-9727786-9-5(1)) JoySoul Corp.

—God Is for Every Day(r) - Horse Dreams: Teach-a-Child Companion Book/DVD Set. Monson, Lois, photos by. 2008. (Illus.). 28p. (J). ring bd. 14.95 (978-0-9727786-8-8(3)) JoySoul Corp.

Montgomery, Rutherford G. The Capture of the Golden Stallion. (J). 22.95 (978-0-8488-0132-8(6)) Amereon Ltd.

—The Golden Stallion's Victory. (J). 20.95 (978-0-8488-0133-5(4)) Amereon Ltd.

Moore, Judith. Jessica the Furry Baroo. Brown, Karen, illus. 2007. 44p. per. 14.95 (978-1-59858-364-9(6)) Dog Ear Publishing, LLC.

Morck, Irene. Tough Trails, 1 vol. 2003. (Orca Soundings Ser.). (ENG.). 128p. (YA). (gr. 8-12). pap. 9.95 (978-1-55143-271-7(4)) Orca Bk. Pubs. USA.

Morey, Walt. Year of the Black Pony. 2006. (Living History Library). 171p. (J). (gr. 4-7). pap. 11.95 (978-1-932350-08-1(X)) Bethlehem Bks.

Morneau, Ronald E. Moondancer's Adventures. Rodstrom, Terri, illus. 2011. 28p. pap. 24.95 (978-1-4626-2590-1(8)) America Star Bks.

Morpurgo, Michael. Farm Boy. Foreman, Michael, illus. 2007. (ENG.). 76p. (J). (gr. 4-7). pap. 15.99 (978-1-84365-090-4(8)) Pavilion Bks. GBR. Dist: Independent Pubs. Group.

—War Horse. 2nd ed. 2013. (ENG., Illus.). 72p. pap. 9.38 (978-0-19-424982-9(4)) Oxford Univ. Pr., Inc.

—War Horse. 2010. (ENG.). 176p. (J). (gr. 3-7). pap. 7.99 (978-0-439-79664-4(4), Scholastic Pr.) Scholastic, Inc.

—The White Horse of Zennor & other Stories. 2nd ed. 2012. (ENG.). 160p. (J). (gr. 4-7). pap. 7.99 (978-1-4052-5675-9(3)) Egmont Bks., Ltd. GBR. Dist: Independent Pubs. Group.

Mudpuppy Press Staff. Magic Horses Seal & Send Stationery. 2005. (Illus.). (J). 7.99 (978-0-7353-0098-9(4)) Galison.

Mullarkey, Lisa. Battle of the Bunks, 1 vol. Franco, Paula, illus. 2016. (ENG.). 112p. (J). lib. bdg. (978-1-62402-162-6(X)) Magic Wagon.

—Carly, 1 vol. Franco, Paula, illus. 2016. (Pony Girls Ser.). (ENG.). 112p. (J). (gr. 1-4). 27.07 (978-1-62402-127-5(1)) Magic Wagon.

—Daniela, 1 vol. Franco, Paula, illus. 2016. (Pony Girls Ser.). (ENG.). 112p. (J). (gr. 1-4). 27.07 (978-1-62402-128-2(X)) Magic Wagon.

—A Feast of Fun, 1 vol. Franco, Paula, illus. 2016. (ENG.). 112p. (J). lib. bdg. (978-1-62402-163-3(8)) Magic Wagon.

—A Filming Fiasco, 1 vol. Franco, Paula, illus. 2016. (ENG.). 112p. (J). lib. bdg. (978-1-62402-164-0(6)) Magic Wagon.

—Gabriela, 1 vol. Franco, Paula, illus. 2016. (Pony Girls Ser.). (ENG.). 112p. (J). (gr. 1-4). 27.07 (978-1-62402-129-9(8)) Magic Wagon.

—Gold Medal Glitch, 1 vol. 2014. (Storm Cliff Stables Ser.). (ENG., Illus.). 112p. (J). (gr. 7-11). 27.07 (978-1-62402-050-6(X)) Magic Wagon.

—Hopes in Hiding, 1 vol. Franco, Paula, illus. 2016. (ENG.). 112p. (J). lib. bdg. (978-1-62402-165-7(4)) Magic Wagon.

—Kianna, 1 vol. Franco, Paula, illus. 2016. (Pony Girls Ser.). (ENG.). 112p. (J). (gr. 1-4). 27.07 (978-1-62402-130-5(1)) Magic Wagon.

—Trail Ride Troubles, 1 vol. 2014. (Storm Cliff Stables Ser.). (ENG.). 112p. (J). (gr. 7-11). lib. bdg. 27.07 (978-1-62402-052-0(6), Calico Chapter Bks) Magic Wagon.

Murphy, Bud. Wild Stallion. Moyers, William, illus. 2011. 176p. 42.95 (978-1-258-05633-9(X)) Literary Licensing, LLC.

Murray, Jean. Madhead the Crazy Horse. 2015. (ENG., Illus.). 43p. (J). (gr. 4-6). mass mkt. 13.95 (978-1-78554-955-7(3), 526cdd1d-e583-45ea-8f1f-012dfba496b4) Austin, Stan AUS. Dist: Bookmasters Distribution.

My Pony. (Early Intervention Levels Ser.). 23.10 (978-0-7362-0018-9(5)) CENGAGE Learning.

Mystic Tide. 2007. (J). (978-1-933343-44-0(3), PONY) Stabenfeldt Inc.

Nation, Kay. Jamie Learns to Love. 2006. pap. 10.00 (978-1-4257-0534-3(0)) Xlibris Corp.

Nelson, Birgitta. The Sacking of Visby. 2011. 150p. 30.00 (978-1-257-05686-6(7)); pap. 14.99 (978-1-257-05680-4(8)) Lulu Pr., Inc.

Nelson, Karen, creator. Crystal Brave: Literature Theme Unit. 2012. (Illus.). 48p. spiral bd. 19.99 (978-1-930584-02-0(4)) Progreso Publishing Group , LLC.

Nelson, S. D. Gift Horse: A Lakota Story. 2016. (ENG., Illus.). 40p. (gr. -1-3). pap. 9.95 (978-1-4197-2064-2(3), Abrams Bks. for Young Readers) Abrams, Inc.

Nelson, Suzanne. The Horseshoe. Nowak, Cheri, illus. 2012. (J). 14.95 (978-1-937406-49-3(0)) Mascot Bks., Inc.

Neri, Greg. Grand Theft Horse: A Graphic Novel. Wilkin, Corban, illus. 2016. (YA). (978-1-4677-9463-3(5), Graphic Universe™) Lerner Publishing Group.

Nesbit, Troy. Sand Dune Pony, Vol. 2013. (Wilderness Mystery Ser.). (ENG., Illus.). 248p. (J). (gr. 3-7). pap. 12.95 (978-1-58979-811-3(2)) Taylor Trade Publishing.

Newhall, Mary & Campbell, Joanna. Bridal Dreams. 2005. (Thoroughbred Ser.). (Illus.). 163p. (gr. 3-7). 15.00 (978-0-7569-5359-1(6)) Perfection Learning Corp.

—Samantha's Irish Luck. 2005. (Thoroughbred Ser.). (Illus.). 156p. (gr. 3-7). 15.00 (978-0-7569-5350-8(2)) Perfection Learning Corp.

Nguyen-Tuong, Karine. Arnold the Smiling Horse. 2004. (ENG., Illus.). 44p. (J). pap. (978-0-9713890-7-6(1)) Outer Banks Pr.

Nicoll, David. Bean on the Farm. 2012. 24p. pap. 15.99 (978-1-4691-7837-0(0)) Xlibris Corp.

Nolan, Tina. The Homeless Foal. Chernyshova, Anna, illus. 2017. (Animal Rescue Center Ser.). (ENG.). 112p. (J). (gr. 1-3). pap. 4.99 **(978-1-58925-498-5(8))** Tiger Tales.

O'Brien, Anne. Patches in Her Dreams: An Alaskan Children's Story. 2012. (Illus.). 14p. (J). 8.50 (978-0-9830764-5-2(6)) Northbooks.

Odgers, Darrel & Odgers, Sally. The Mare's Tale. Dawson, Janine, illus. 2009. (Pet Vet Ser.: 2). 96p. (J). (gr. 2-6). pap. 4.99 (978-1-935279-02-0(5)) Kane Miller.

O'Grady, Standish Hayes. The Pursuit of the Gilla Decair & His Horse. 2004. reprint ed. pap. 1.99 (978-1-4192-7950-8(5)) Kessinger Publishing, LLC.

O'Hara, Mary. My Friend Flicka Book. 2005. (Charming Classics). (ENG.). 352p. pap. 6.99 (978-0-06-084595-7(3)) HarperCollins Pubs.

Ohi, Ruth. Chicken, Pig, Cow Horse Around. Ohi, Ruth, illus. 2010. (Chicken, Pig, Cow Ser.). (ENG., Illus.). 32p. (J). (gr. -1-k). 19.95 (978-1-55451-245-4(X), 9781554512454) Annick Pr., Ltd. CAN. Dist: Publishers Group West (PGW).

Ohi, Ruth, illus. Chicken, Pig, Cow Horse Around. 3rd ed. 2010. (Chicken, Pig, Cow Ser.). (ENG.). 32p. (J). (gr. -1-k). pap. 6.95 (978-1-55451-244-7(1), 9781554512447) Annick Pr., Ltd. CAN. Dist: Publishers Group West (PGW).

Oja, L. G. Little Miss Izzy's Adventures - Miss Izzy & the Monsters. 2013. 24p. pap. (978-1-4602-1421-3(8)) FriesenPress.

Oldfield, Jenny. Crazy Horse. 2009. (Horses of Half Moon Ranch Ser.: 3). (ENG.). 160p. (J). (gr. 4-7). pap. 9.99 (978-1-4022-1702-9(1), Sourcebooks Jabberwocky) Sourcebooks, Inc.

—Half Moon Ranch: Johnny Mohawk. 2008. (YA). (978-1-933343-74-7(5)) Stabenfeldt Inc.

—Midnight Lady. 2009. (Horses of Half Moon Ranch Ser.: 5). (ENG.). 176p. (J). (gr. 4-7). pap. 5.99 (978-1-4022-1704-3(8), Sourcebooks Jabberwocky) Sourcebooks, Inc.

—Wild Horses. 2008. (Horses of Half Moon Ranch Ser.: 1). (ENG.). 160p. (J). (gr. 4-7). pap. 7.99 (978-1-4022-1327-4(1), Sourcebooks Jabberwocky) Sourcebooks, Inc.

Oracle of the Horses. 2005. (YA). per. (978-0-615-12836-8(X)) Miller, Don G.

O'Reilly, Basha. Count Pompeii - Stallion of the Steppes. 2005. (Illus.). pap. 9.99 (978-1-59048-007-6(4)) Long Riders' Guild Pr., The.

Orman, Roscoe. Ricky & Mobo. 2013. 34p. pap. 9.95 (978-1-62901-048-9(0)) Inkwater Pr.

Orme, Helen. Horsing Around. 2008. (Siti's Sisters Ser.). (ENG., Illus.). 36p. pap. (978-1-84167-685-2(3)) Ransom Publishing Ltd.

Orr, Wendy. Stolen! - A Pony Called Pebbles. Castelao, Patricia, illus. 2012. (Rainbow Street Shelter Ser.: 5). (ENG.). 128p. (J). (gr. 2-5). pap. 5.99 (978-0-8050-9504-3(7), 9780805095043, Holt, Henry & Co. Bks. For Young Readers) Holt, Henry & Co.

—Stolen! - A Pony Called Pebbles. 2012. (Rainbow Street Shelter Ser.: 5). (J). lib. bdg. 16.00 (978-0-606-26719-9(0), Turtleback) Turtleback Bks.

Osborne, Mary Pope. Stallion by Starlight. Murdocca, Sal, illus. (Magic Tree House Merlin Mission Ser.: No. 21). (ENG.). (J). (gr. 2-5). 2014. 144p. pap. 5.99 (978-0-307-98044-1(8)) 2013. 128p. lib. bdg. 15.99 (978-0-307-98042-7(1)) Random Hse. Children's Bks. (Random Hse. Bks. for Young Readers).

Osborne, Mary Pope & McPhail, David. Moonhorse. Saelig, S. M., illus. 2016. (ENG.). 40p. (J). (gr. -1-2). 16.99 (978-0-394-88960-3(6), Knopf Bks. for Young Readers) Random Hse. Children's Bks.

Osorio, Marta. El Caballito Que Queria Volar. (SPA.). 48p. (J). (gr. 3-5). 9.45 (978-84-305-6075-2(0)) Susaeta Ediciones, S.A. ESP. Dist: Lectorum Pubns., Inc.

Osorio, Marta & Marta, Osorio. El Caballito Que Queria Volar. (SPA., Illus.). 110p. (J). (978-84-392-8111-5(0)) Gaviota Ediciones ESP. Dist: Lectorum Pubns., Inc.

Palma, B. El Dorado: A Palo Alto Adventure. 2012. 136p. (gr. -1). 23.99 (978-1-4634-3110-5(4)); pap. 13.99 (978-1-4634-3111-2(2)) AuthorHouse.

Palmer, Connie. I Will Run Free No More, 1 vol. 2009. 49p. pap. 16.95 (978-1-4489-7122-0(5)) America Star Bks.

Papp, Robert, illus. A Horse Named Dragon. 2008. (Boxcar Children Mysteries Ser.: 114). (ENG.). 128p. (J). (gr. 1-5). lib. bdg. 14.99 (978-0-8075-5571-2(1)); per. 5.99 (978-0-8075-5572-9(X)) Whitman, Albert & Co.

Parsons, Pateh. Lickitysplit, the Handicapped Horse. 2008. 36p. pap. 24.95 (978-1-60563-933-8(8)) America Star Bks.

Patterson, Sadie. Old Pete & Dan. 2010. 16p. 8.49 (978-1-4490-1489-6(5)) AuthorHouse.

Pauly, Heather E. Kon: The Bay Painted Stallion. 2010. 60p. pap. 12.99 (978-1-4490-4895-2(1)) AuthorHouse.

Pearce, Margaret. Jumping into Trouble Book 3: Missing! a Horse. 2013. 66p. pap. (978-1-922066-61-9(3)) Writers Exchange E-Publishing.

—Jumping into Trouble Series Book 1: Wanted! a Horse. 2013. 108p. pap. (978-1-922066-59-6(1)) Writers Exchange E-Publishing.

Pearl, Alexa. The #1: Big Secret. Sordo, Paco, illus. 2017. (Tales of Sasha Ser.: 1). (ENG.). 112p. (J). (gr. 1-3). pap. 5.99 (978-1-4998-0389-1(3)) Little Bee Books Inc.

—#2: Journey Beyond the Trees. Sordo, Paco, illus. 2017. (Tales of Sasha Ser.: 2). (ENG.). 112p. (J). (gr. 1-3). pap. 5.99 (978-1-4998-0391-4(5)) Little Bee Books Inc.

Pearson, Carol Lynn. Summer of Truth. 2007. 104p. per. 9.99 (978-1-59955-046-6(6)) Cedar Fort, Inc./CFI Distribution.

Peck, Robert Newton. Horse Thief. 2003. 277p. (YA). (gr. 7). 13.65 (978-0-7569-1461-5(2)) Perfection Learning Corp.

Perez, Marlene. A Rainbow Year. 2004. (Shared Connections Ser.). (J). instr.'s gde. ed. 27.00 (978-1-4108-1603-0(6)) Benchmark Education Co.

Perry, Charles. The Legend of Scarface. Perry, Charles, photos by. 2005. (ENG., Illus.). 12p. (J). 5.75 (978-1-57274-752-4(8), 2764, Bks. for Young Learners) Owen, Richard C. Pubs., Inc.

Pescatore, Faith. A Bell for Justin. 2009. 56p. pap. 10.99 (978-1-4389-6821-6(3)) AuthorHouse.

Peters, Karen Lynn. If I Only Had a Horse. 2013. 36p. 16.99 (978-0-9894748-4-9(4)) Mindstir Media.

Peterson, Shelley. Sundancer. Drake, Marybeth, illus. rev. ed. 2007. (ENG.). 264p. (YA). (gr. 7-12). pap. 7.95 (978-1-55263-842-2(1)) Leaf Storm Pr.

Peterson, Shelley. Sundancer: The Saddle Creek Series. 2017. (Saddle Creek Ser.: 2). (ENG.). 408p. (YA). pap. 12.99 **(978-1-4597-3948-2(5))** Dundurn CAN. Dist: Ingram Publisher Services.

Petit, Karen. The Mystery of the Stolen Stallion. 2007. (Illus.). 246p. (J). per. 14.95 (978-0-9794420-4-9(4)) Red Letter Pr.

Peyton, K. M. No Turning Back IR. 2013. pap. 5.99 (978-0-7945-3148-5(2), Usborne) EDC Publishing.

—Stealaway. Wyatt, David, illus. 2004. (ENG.). 96p. (J). 12.95 (978-0-8126-2722-0(9)) Cricket Bks.

Phillips, Beth Ann. Crystal Kingdom, 1 vol. 2009. 63p. pap. 19.95 (978-1-60813-003-0(7)) America Star Bks.

Phillips, Valerie A. A Wish upon a Star. 2010. 28p. pap. 14.99 (978-1-4520-7712-3(6)) AuthorHouse.

Pierro, Rita. A Horse in the House, 1 vol. French, David, illus. 2009. 29p. pap. 24.95 (978-1-60836-410-7(0)) America Star Bks.

Pierson, Jan. The Haunted Horse of Gold Hill. 2005. (Ghostowners Ser.: Vol. 4). (Illus.). 109p. (J). per. 9.95 (978-0-9721800-3-0(6)) WildWest Publishing.

Pinnington, Andrea. Horse & Pony Pocket Activity Fun & Games: Games & Puzzles, Fold-Out Scenes, Patterned Paper, Stickers! 2014. (Pocket Activity Fun & Games Ser.). (ENG.). 96p. (J). (gr. 1-5). pap. 7.99 (978-1-4380-0446-4(X)) Barron's Educational Series, Inc.

Pinter, Sarah. Electra. 2003. 134p. 21.95 (978-0-595-65843-5(1)); pap. 11.95 (978-0-595-28742-0(5)) iUniverse, Inc.

Pistole, Katy. Flying High. 2003. (Illus.). 126p. (J). 7.99 (978-0-8163-1942-8(1)) Pacific Pr. Pubns.

Platt, Chris. Astra, 1 vol. 2010. (ENG.). 176p. (J). (gr. 3-7). 15.95 (978-1-56145-541-6(5)) Peachtree Pubs.

—Moon Shadow. 2006. (ENG.). 176p. (J). (gr. 3-7). 14.95 (978-1-56145-382-5(X)) Peachtree Pubs.

—Star Gazer, 1 vol. 2011. (ENG.). 144p. (J). (gr. 3-7). 14.95 (978-1-56145-596-6(2), Peachtree Junior) Peachtree Pubs.

—Storm Chaser, 1 vol. 2009. (ENG.). 160p. (J). (gr. 3-7). 15.95 (978-1-56145-496-9(6)) Peachtree Pubs.

—Willow King, 1 vol. 2010. (ENG.). 192p. (J). (gr. 3-7). pap. 6.95 (978-1-56145-549-2(0)) Peachtree Pubs.

—Wind Dancer, 1 vol. 2014. (ENG.). 176p. (J). (gr. 3-6). 15.95 (978-1-56145-736-6(1)) Peachtree Pubs.

Plez, Josey. My Adventures with Granny Roo - Riding Jessy. 2011. 24p. pap. 19.95 (978-1-4626-3139-1(8)) America Star Bks.

Polglase, Pamela. Handy & Dandy. 2008. 182p. pap. 15.96 (978-0-557-02578-7(8)); 27.76 (978-1-4357-4588-9(4)) Lulu Pr., Inc.

Pony Farm Mystery. 2006. (J). (978-1-933343-25-9(7), PONY) Stabenfeldt Inc.

The Pony Trek. 2005. (J). (978-1-933343-08-2(7), PONY) Stabenfeldt Inc.

The Pony Winter. 2007. (J). (978-1-933343-42-6(7), PONY) Stabenfeldt Inc.

Popsicle, Patty. Crack-a-Doodle Horse Tales: A Tale about Biting. 2011. 24p. (gr. -1). pap. 12.99 (978-1-4343-5157-9(2)) AuthorHouse.

—Crack-a-doodle Horse Tales: A Tale about Pinching. 2011. 24p. (gr. -1). pap. 12.99 (978-1-4389-4289-6(3)) AuthorHouse.

—Crack-a-doodle Horse Tales: A Tale about Pulling Hair. 2011. 24p. (gr. -1). pap. 12.99 (978-1-4520-6096-5(7)) AuthorHouse.

Porta, Bill K. Rusty the Rescue Horse. 2011. 24p. pap. 11.32 (978-1-4520-4452-1(X)) AuthorHouse.

Porte, Barbara Ann. Harry's Pony. Abolafia, Yossi, illus. 2003. (I Can Read Bks.). 64p. (J). 16.89 (978-0-06-050658-2(X)) HarperCollins Pubs.

Porter, Amber Leann. To Be a Champion. 2008. 31p. pap. 24.95 (978-1-60610-222-0(2)) PublishAmerica, Inc.

Porter, Pamela. Sky, 1 vol. Gerber, Mary Jane, illus. 2005. (ENG.). 88p. (J). (gr. 3-5). pap. 9.95 (978-0-88899-607-7(1), Libros Tigrillo) Groundwood Bks. CAN. Dist: Publishers Group West (PGW).

Potter, Ellen. Piper Green & the Fairy Tree: the Sea Pony. Leng, Qin, illus. 2016. (Piper Green & the Fairy Tree Ser.). (ENG.). 128p. (J). (gr. 2-4). 14.99 (978-0-553-49931-5(9), Knopf Bks. for Young Readers) Random Hse. Children's Bks.

Potter, Tina M. The Horse Story. 2005. 36p. (J). pap. 9.65 (978-1-4116-5761-8(6)) Lulu Pr., Inc.

Price, Margaret. Chillipop. 2009. 196p. pap. 18.95 (978-1-4490-0958-8(1)) AuthorHouse.

Primavera, Elise. Libby of High Hopes. Primavera, Elise, illus. 2012. (Libby of High Hopes Ser.). (ENG., Illus.). 192p. (J). (gr. 2-5). 14.99 (978-1-4169-5542-9(9), Simon & Schuster/Paula Wiseman Bks.) Simon & Schuster/Paula Wiseman Bks.

—Libby of High Hopes. 2015. lib. bdg. 17.20 (978-0-606-37846-8(4)) Turtleback Bks.

—Project Blue Ribbon. Primavera, Elise, illus. 2015. (Libby of High Hopes Ser.). (ENG., Illus.). 288p. (J). (gr. 2-5). 16.99 (978-1-4169-5543-6(7), Simon & Schuster Bks. For Young Readers) Simon & Schuster Bks. For Young Readers.

Pukac, Michael & Stephen, Marchesi, illus. The Flights of Marceau: Week Three. 2008. (ENG.). 64p. (J). 16.95 (978-0-9797495-2-0(2)) Majestic Eagle Publishing.

Pullein-Thompson, Christine. Phantom Horse. 2012. (ENG., Illus.). 176p. (J). pap. 9.95 (978-1-84135-820-8(7)) Award Pubns. Ltd. GBR. Dist: Parkwest Pubns., Inc.

—Phantom Horse Comes Home. 2012. (ENG., Illus.). 176p. (J). pap. 9.95 (978-1-84135-822-2(3)) Award Pubns. Ltd. GBR. Dist: Parkwest Pubns., Inc.

—Phantom Horse Disappears. 2012. (ENG., Illus.). 176p. (J). pap. 9.95 (978-1-84135-821-5(5)) Award Pubns. Ltd. GBR. Dist: Parkwest Pubns., Inc.

—Phantom Horse in Danger. 2012. (ENG., Illus.). 176p. (J). pap. 9.95 (978-1-84135-824-6(X)) Award Pubns. Ltd. GBR. Dist: Parkwest Pubns., Inc.

—Phantom Horse Island Mystery. 2012. (ENG., Illus.). 176p. (J). pap. 9.95 (978-1-84135-825-3(8)) Award Pubns. Ltd. GBR. Dist: Parkwest Pubns., Inc.

—Wait for Me. 2012. (ENG., Illus.). 176p. (J). pap. 9.95 (978-1-84135-823-9(1)) Award Pubns. Ltd. GBR. Dist: Parkwest Pubns., Inc.

Rae, Navah. A Job for Comet. 2011. 28p. pap. 24.95 (978-1-4626-0913-0(9)) America Star Bks.

Raine, Amelie. Mallomar Goes to the Moon. 2010. 32p. pap. 12.99 (978-1-4490-1392-9(9)) AuthorHouse.

—The Misadventures of Mallomar the Horse. 2009. 32p. pap. 12.99 (978-1-4389-8371-4(9)) AuthorHouse.

Raine, Bonnie. Islands. MacMenamin, John, illus. 2003. 48p. (J). per. (978-1-931456-74-6(7)) Athena Pr.

Ramsey, Calvin Alexander & Stroud, Bettye. Belle, the Last Mule at Gee's Bend: A Civil Right's Story. 2016. lib. bdg. 18.40 (978-0-606-37938-0(X)) Turtleback Bks.

Randerath, Jeanette & Winterhager, Randerath -. ¡vuela, Yoa, Vuela! 2012. (SPA.). 32p. (J). (gr. 2-3). pap. 19.99 (978-84-261-3918-4(3)) Juventud, Editorial ESP. Dist: Lectorum Pubns., Inc.

Ransom, Candice. The Life-Saving Adventure of Sam Deal, Shipwreck Rescuer. Trover, Zachary, illus. 2010. (History's Kid Heroes Ser.). (ENG.). 32p. (gr. 3-5). pap. 8.95 (978-0-7613-6196-1(0), Graphic Universe™); lib. bdg. 26.60 (978-0-7613-6177-0(4)) Lerner Publishing Group.

Rattlesnake Rock. 2006. (J). (978-1-933343-16-7(8)) Stabenfeldt Inc.

Redmond, Diane. The Most Beautiful Horse in the World. 2007. (YA). (978-1-933343-60-0(5)) Stabenfeldt Inc.

Reed, Sharon. Tara: Prairie Horse Series. 2006. pap. 14.00 (978-0-8059-7091-3(6)) Dorrance Publishing Co., Inc.

Reekie, Jocelyn. The Week of the Horse. 2004. 4p. pap., tchr. ed. (978-1-55192-707-7(1)) Raincoast Bk. Distribution CAN. Dist: Publishers Group West (PGW).

Reid, Mayne. WarTrail or the Hunt of the Wild Horse A. 2006. (Illus.). pap. 40.95 (978-1-4286-5282-8(5)) Kessinger Publishing, LLC.

Reilly, Hope. The Ghost Horse at Cove House: A Book about the Strength of Friendship. 2013. 32p. pap. 13.00 (978-1-61204-666-2(5), Strategic Bk. Publishing) Strategic Book Publishing & Rights Agency (SBPRA).

Renfrew, Regan. Orphans of the Heart: A Young Girl & a Paint Filly Heal Each Other's Broken Hearts. 2013. (ENG.). 163p. (YA). pap. 12.95 (978-1-4787-1686-0(X)) Outskirts Pr., Inc.

Revere, John J. The Little Brown Horse. Harvancik, Monica, illus. 2011. 34p. 17.95 (978-1-4327-8146-0(4)) Outskirts Pr., Inc.

Reznik, Anastassia, ed. The Little Horse Gornok: Russian Fairy Tale. 2009. 40p. pap. 18.95 (978-1-4343-9830-7(7)) AuthorHouse.

Rhema, Dan. Bluegrass Breeze. Leonard, Michael, illus. 2004. (J). per. 19.95 (978-0-9729835-1-8(1)) Mesquite Tress Pr., LLC.

Richards, Laura E. The Wooing of Calvin Parks. 2004. reprint ed. pap. 28.95 (978-1-4179-2877-4(8)) Kessinger Publishing, LLC.

Richter, Abigail. I See a Horse! 2006. (Neighborhood Readers Ser.). (ENG.). 16p. (gr. 1-3). pap. 6.50 (978-1-4042-7248-4(8), Rosen Classroom) Rosen Publishing Group, Inc., The.

Riddle, A. E. All about Blade, 1 vol. 2009. 48p. pap. 16.95 (978-1-60836-984-3(6)) PublishAmerica, Inc.

Riordan, Betty J. The Imaginary Journeys of Bj & Dobbin. 2008. 108p. pap. 11.99 (978-1-60647-432-7(4)) Salem Author Services.

Rising, Janet. Stables S. O. S. The Pony Whisperer. 2012. (ENG.). 192p. (J). (gr. 5-7). pap. 6.99 (978-1-4022-3957-1(2), Sourcebooks Jabberwocky) Sourcebooks, Inc.

Robertson, Keith. Ticktock & Jim: Famous Horse Stories. Dennis, Wesley, illus. 2011. 250p. 46.95 (978-1-258-10102-2(5)) Literary Licensing, LLC.

Robinson, Whitney A. Horse Diaries #14: Calvino. Sanderson, Ruth, illus. 2017. (Horse Diaries: 12). (ENG.). 160p. (J). (gr. 3-7). pap. 7.99 (978-1-101-93779-2(3), Random Hse. Bks. for Young Readers) Random Hse. Children's Bks.

Rocking Horse. 2004. (J). per. (978-1-57657-382-2(6)) Paradise Pr., Inc.

Rogers, Anne. PRINCE & the APPLE TREE. 2008. 32p. pap. 23.50 (978-1-4092-1035-1(9)) Lulu Pr., Inc.

Romig, Hilary. Meet Ruby & Louise. 2009. 16p. pap. 8.49 (978-1-4389-4609-2(0)) AuthorHouse.

Rose, Eilidh. I'm Just a Little Horse. Orkrania, Alexia, illus. 2014. (ENG.). 12p. (gr. -1). (978-1-78244-589-0(7)) Top That! Publishing PLC.

Ross, Tony & Willis, Jeanne. Dozy Mare. 2005. (ENG., Illus.). 32p. (J). (gr. k-2). 17.95 (978-1-84270-386-1(2)) Andersen Pr. GBR. Dist: Independent Pubs. Group.

Rottman, S. L. Hero, 1 vol. 2007. (ENG.). 144p. (YA). (gr. 7-18). (978-1-56145-427-3(3)) Peachtree Pubs.

Rueda, Claudia. La Suerte de Ozu. 2003. (Los Primerisimos Ser.). (SPA.). 32p. (J). pap. 7.50 (978-968-16-7051-1(5)) Fondo de Cultura Economica USA.

Russel, Mary. Flickertail & Paint, Barnyard Sleuths, 1 vol. 2010. 96p. pap. 19.95 (978-1-4489-7248-7(5)) America Star Bks.

Ryan, Pam Muñoz & McInerney, Kathleen. Paint the Wind. 2009. (ENG.). 352p. (J). (gr. 3-7). pap. 7.99 (978-0-545-10176-9(X), Scholastic Paperbacks) Scholastic, Inc.

Salter, Kay. Fifteenth Summer: The Sarah Bowers Series. 2011. 188p. (gr. -1). 24.99 (978-1-4567-6380-0(6)); pap. 15.99 (978-1-4567-6381-7(4)) AuthorHouse.

Sanderson, Nancy. Summer of the Dancing Horse. 2010. 200p. pap. 14.49 (978-1-4520-6891-6(7)) AuthorHouse.

—Summer of the Painted Horse. 2009. 188p. pap. 14.49 (978-1-4490-2312-6(6)) AuthorHouse.

Sanderson, Whitney. Golden Sun. Sanderson, Ruth, illus. 2010. (Horse Diaries). (ENG.). 160p. (J). (gr. 3-7). pap. 7.99 (978-0-375-86194-9(7), Random Hse. Bks. for Young Readers) Random Hse. Children's Bks.

Santillo, LuAnn. Trot, Trot. Santillo, LuAnn, ed. 2003. (Half-Pint Kids Readers Ser.). (Illus.). 7p. (J). (gr. -1-1). pap. 1.00 (978-1-59256-067-7(9)) Half-Pint Kids, Inc.

Sargent, Dave & Denton, Ivan. Misty's Miracle No. 4: Overcome Fear, 6 vols. Denton, Ivan, illus. 2004. (Illus.). 36p. (J). pap. 10.95 (978-1-59381-005-4(9)) Ozark Publishing.

Sargent, Dave & Sargent, Pat. Bashful: (Dusty Dun) Be Brave. Lenoir, Jane, illus. 2003. (Saddle up Ser.: Vol. 1). 42p. (J). pap. 10.95 (978-1-56763-684-0(5)); lib. bdg. 23.60 (978-1-56763-683-3(7)) Ozark Publishing.

—Bo: (Linebacked Orange Dun) Be Happy, 30 vols., Vol. 4. Lenoir, Jane, illus. 2003. (Saddle up Ser.: Vol. 4). 42p. (J). lib. bdg. 23.60 (978-1-56763-685-7(3)); mass mkt. 10.95 (978-1-56763-686-4(1)) Ozark Publishing.

—Brandy: (Blue Roan) Beauty Is Inside, 30 vols., Vol. 5. Lenoir, Jane, illus. 2003. (Saddle up Ser.: Vol. 5). 42p. (J). lib. bdg. 23.60 (978-1-56763-799-1(X)); mass mkt. 10.95 (978-1-56763-800-4(7)) Ozark Publishing.

—Buttons: (Muddy Dun) Have Courage, Vol. 9. Lenoir, Jane, illus. 2003. (Saddle up Ser.: Vol. 9). 42p. (J). pap. 10.95 (978-1-56763-688-8(8)); lib. bdg. 23.60 (978-1-56763-687-1(X)) Ozark Publishing.

—Chick: (Chocolate Chestnut) Be Loyal, 30 vols., Vol. 16. Lenoir, Jane, illus. 2003. (Saddle up Ser.: Vol. 16). 42p. (J). pap. 10.95 (978-1-56763-678-9(0)); lib. bdg. 23.60 (978-1-56763-677-2(2)) Ozark Publishing.

—Cricket: (Seal Brown) Do Your Best, 30. Lenoir, Jane, illus. 2003. (Saddle up Ser.: Vol. 20). 42p. (J). 20. lib. bdg. 22.60 (978-1-56763-649-9(7)) Vol. 20. pap. 10.95 (978-1-56763-650-5(0)) Ozark Publishing.

—Duke: (Dappled Palomino) Good Behavior, 30 vols., Vol. 23. Lenoir, Jane, illus. 2003. (Saddle up Ser.: Vol. 23). 42p. (J). pap. 10.95 (978-1-56763-682-6(9)); lib. bdg. 23.60 (978-1-56763-681-9(0)) Ozark Publishing.

—Dusty: (Grey Sabino) Be Helpful, 30 vols., Vol. 24. Lenoir, Jane, illus. 2003. (Saddle up Ser.: Vol. 24). 42p. (J). pap. 10.95 (978-1-56763-808-0(2)); lib. bdg. 23.60 (978-1-56763-807-3(4)) Ozark Publishing.

—Freckles: (Flea-bitten Grey) Be Proud of Old Glory, 30 vols., Vol. 26. Lenoir, Jane, illus. 2003. (Saddle up Ser.: Vol. 26). 42p. (J). pap. 10.95 (978-1-56763-810-3(4)); lib. bdg. 23.60 (978-1-56763-809-7(0)) Ozark Publishing.

—Ginger: (Lilac Roan) Be Likeable, 30 vols., Vol. 27. Lenoir, Jane, illus. 2003. (Saddle up Ser.: Vol. 27). 42p. (J). pap. 10.95 (978-1-56763-812-7(0)); lib. bdg. 23.60 (978-1-56763-811-0(2)) Ozark Publishing.

—Goober: (Silver Dapple) Appreciate Others, 30 vols., Vol. 29. Lenoir, Jane, illus. 2003. (Saddle up Ser.: Vol. 29). 42p. (J). lib. bdg. 23.60 (978-1-56763-689-5(6)) Ozark Publishing.

—Goober: (Sliver Dapple) Appreciate Others, 30 vols., Vol. 29. Lenoir, Jane, illus. 2004. (Saddle up Ser.: Vol. 29). 42p. (J). pap. 10.95 (978-1-56763-690-1(X)) Ozark Publishing.

—Grady: (Dappled Grey) Proud to Be an American, 30 vols., Vol. 30. Lenoir, Jane, illus. 2003. (Saddle up Ser.: Vol. 30). 42p. (J). lib. bdg. 23.60 (978-1-56763-813-4(9)) Ozark Publishing.

—Grady: Proud to Be an American, 30 vols. Lenoir, Jane, illus. 2003. (Saddle up Ser.: Vol. 30). 42p. (J). pap. 10.95 (978-1-56763-814-1(7)) Ozark Publishing.

—Gus: (Slate Grullo) Be Thankful, 30 vols., Vol. 32. Lenoir, Jane, illus. 2003. (Saddle up Ser.: Vol. 32). 42p. (J). lib. bdg. 23.60 (978-1-56763-693-2(4)); pap. 10.95 (978-1-56763-694-9(2)) Ozark Publishing.

—Hondo: (Silver Dun) Look for Good in Others, 30 vols., Vol. 34. Lenoir, Jane, illus. 2003. (Saddle up Ser.: Vol. 34). 42p. (J). pap. 10.95 (978-1-56763-802-8(3)); lib. bdg. 23.60 (978-1-56763-801-1(5)) Ozark Publishing.

—Hoot: (Grullo) Be Creative, 30. Lenoir, Jane, illus. 2003. (Saddle up Ser.: Vol. 35). 42p. (J). 35. pap. 6.95 (978-1-56763-696-3(9)) Vol. 35. lib. bdg. 23.60 (978-1-56763-695-6(0)) Ozark Publishing.

—Lily: (Lilac Dun) A Second Chance, 30 vols., Vol. 38. Lenoir, Jane, illus. 2003. (Saddle up Ser.: Vol. 38). 42p. (J). pap.

H
I

10.95 *(978-1-56763-698-7(5))*; lib. bdg. 23.60 *(978-1-56763-697-0(7))* Ozark Publishing.

—Mack: (Medicine Hat Paint) Be a Leader, 30 vols., Vol. 39. Lenoir, Jane, illus. 2003. (Saddle up Ser.: Vol. 39). 42p. (J). pap. 10.95 *(978-1-56763-700-7(0))* Ozark Publishing.

—Nick: (Linebacked Claybank Dun) Crime Does Not Pay, 30 vols., Vol. 42. Lenoir, Jane, illus. 2003. (Saddle up Ser.: Vol. 42). 42p. (J). pap. 10.95 *(978-1-56763-702-1(7))*; lib. bdg. 23.60 *(978-1-56763-701-4(9))* Ozark Publishing.

—Nubbin: (Linebacked Apricot Dun) Freedom, 30 vols., Vol. 43. Lenoir, Jane, illus. 2003. (Saddle up Ser.: Vol. 43). 42p. (J). pap. 10.95 *(978-1-56763-704-5(3))*; lib. bdg. 23.60 *(978-1-56763-703-8(5))* Ozark Publishing.

—Pete: (Pink-skinned Palomino) Be a Hero, 30 vols., Vol. 46. Lenoir, Jane, illus. 2003. (Saddle up Ser.: Vol. 46). 42p. (J). lib. bdg. 23.60 *(978-1-56763-707-6(8))* Ozark Publishing.

—Pete: Pink-skinned Palomino) Be a Hero, 30 vols., Vol. 46. Lenoir, Jane, illus. 2003. (Saddle up Ser.: Vol. 46). 42p. (J). pap. 10.95 *(978-1-56763-708-3(6))* Ozark Publishing.

—Ranger: (Olive Grullo) Be Honest, 30 vols., Vol. 48. Lenoir, Jane, illus. 2003. (Saddle up Ser.: Vol. 48). 42p. (J). pap. 10.95 *(978-1-56763-710-6(8))*; lib. bdg. 23.60 *(978-1-56763-709-0(4))* Ozark Publishing.

—Rascal: (Red Dun) Responsible Leadership, 30 vols., Vol. 49. Lenoir, Jane, illus. 2003. (Saddle up Ser.: Vol. 49). 42p. (J). pap. 10.95 *(978-1-56763-712-0(4))* Ozark Publishing.

—Rocky: (Blue-eyed Palomino) Be Free, 30 vols., Vol. 51. Lenoir, Jane, illus. 2003. (Saddle up Ser.: Vol. 51). 42p. (J). lib. bdg. 23.60 *(978-1-56763-713-7(2))* Ozark Publishing.

—Rusty: (Red Roan) Be Strong & Brave, 30 vols., Vol. 52. Lenoir, Jane, illus. 2003. (Saddle up Ser.: Vol. 52). 42p. (J). pap. 10.95 *(978-1-56763-804-2(X))*; lib. bdg. 23.60 *(978-1-56763-803-5(1))* Ozark Publishing.

—Sonny: (Linebacked Yellow Dun) Have Orderly Manners, 30 vols., Vol. 54. Lenoir, Jane, illus. 2003. (Saddle up Ser.: Vol. 54). 42p. (J). lib. bdg. 23.60 *(978-1-56763-715-1(9))* Ozark Publishing.

—Sonny: (Linebacked Yllow Dun) Have Orderly Manners, 30 vols., Vol. 54. Lenoir, Jane, illus. 2003. (Saddle up Ser.: Vol. 54). 42p. (J). pap. 10.95 *(978-1-56763-716-8(7))* Ozark Publishing.

—Whiskers: (Roan) Pride & Peace, 30 vols., Vol. 59. Lenoir, Jane, illus. 2003. (Saddle up Ser.: Vol. 59). 42p. (J). pap. 10.95 *(978-1-56763-806-6(6))* Ozark Publishing.

—White Thunder: I'm a Leader, 56 vols., Vol. 6. Huff, Jeane, illus. 2nd rev. ed. 2003. (Animal Pride Ser.: 6). 42p. (J). lib. bdg. 20.95 *(978-1-56763-769-4(8))* Ozark Publishing.

—Zeb: (Zebra Dun) Be Prepared, 30 vols., Vol. 60. Lenoir, Jane, illus. 2003. (Saddle up Ser.: Vol. 60). 42p. (J). pap. 10.95 *(978-1-56763-718-2(3))*; lib. bdg. 23.60 *(978-1-56763-717-5(5))* Ozark Publishing.

Savage, Bridgette Z. Fly Like the Wind. Savage, Charles J., ed. Savage, Bridgette Z., illus. Savage, Charles J., photos by. 2005. (ENG., Illus.). 112p. (YA). (gr. 5). per. 16.99 *(978-0-9771494-0-7(4))* Buckbeech Studios.

Scaletta, Jane. Kimbo's First Horse Show, 1 vol. 2008. (ENG., Illus.). 52p. pap. 24.95 *(978-1-60474-480-4(4))* America Star Bks.

Scardamaglia, Christine. Paso Joe. 2012. 28p. pap. 19.99 *(978-1-4772-6166-8(4))* AuthorHouse.

Schindel, John. Busy Horsies. Lark, Casi, photos by. 2007. (Busy Book Ser.). (ENG., Illus.). 20p. (J). (gr. k — 1). bds. 6.99 *(978-1-58246-223-3(2))*, Tricycle Pr.) Random Hse. Children's Bks.

Schnetzler, Pattie L. Widdermaker. Sealock, Rick, illus. 2005. 32p. (gr. k-2). 15.95 *(978-0-87614-647-7(7))* Lerner Publishing Group.

Schorr, Titus. May's Horse, 01 vols., 1. 2016. (Rosen REAL Readers: STEM & STEAM Collection). (ENG.). 8p. (J). pap. 5.46 *(978-1-5081-1449-9(8))*, Rosen Classroom) Rosen Publishing Group, Inc., The.

Schultz, Jan Neubert. Horse Sense: The Story of Will Sasse, His Horse Star & the Outlaw Jesse James. 2005. (Adventures in Time Ser.). (Illus.). 180p. (J). (gr. 4-8). 15.95 *(978-1-57505-998-3(3))* Lerner Publishing Group.

Scorned. 2005. (J). *(978-1-933343-09-9(5))*, PONY) Stabenfeldt Inc.

Scott, Elizabeth M. It's Rodeo Time! With Mamma Scottie & the Kids. 2009. 52p. pap. 24.99 *(978-1-4490-1750-7(9))* AuthorHouse.

Scott, Michele. Dark Harmony: A Vivienne Taylor Horse Lover's Mystery, 0 vols. 2014. (Fairmont Riding Academy Ser.: 2). (ENG.). 384p. (YA). (gr. 7-12). pap. 9.99 *(978-1-4778-4726-8(X))*, 9781477847268, Amazon Children's Publishing) Amazon Publishing.

—Perfect Harmony: A Vivienne Taylor Horse Lover's Mystery, 0 vols. 2014. (Fairmont Riding Academy Ser.). (ENG.). 274p. (YA). (gr. 7-9). pap. 9.99 *(978-1-4778-4779-4(0))*, 9781477847794, Skyscape) Amazon Publishing.

—Silent Harmony, 0 vols. unabr. ed. 2013. (Fairmont Riding Academy Ser.: 1). (ENG.). 256p. (YA). (gr. 7-12). pap. 9.99 *(978-1-4778-1713-1(1))*, 9781477817131, Amazon Children's Publishing) Amazon Publishing.

Scott, Victoria. Titans. 2017. (ENG.). 320p. (J). (gr. 7). pap. 9.99 *(978-1-338-09555-5(2))*, Scholastic Pr.) Scholastic, Inc.

Seabag-Montefiore, Mary. Black Beauty (Picture Book) Marks, Alan, illus. 2008. (Picture Book Classics Ser.). 24p. (J). 9.99 *(978-0-7945-2250-6(5))*, Usborne) EDC Publishing.

Seabag-Montefiore, Mary, retold by. Black Beauty with CD. 2008. (Young Reading Gift Books with CD Ser.). 64p. (J). 9.99 *(978-0-7945-2170-7(3))*, Usborne) EDC Publishing.

Secret in the Stable. 2008. (Illus.). 32p. *(978-0-545-02924-7(4))* Scholastic, Inc.

Seeley, Bonnie L. Sun & Ponies, Wind & Sky. Seeley, Douglas A., illus. Lidard, Kelly, photos by. 2004. 32p. (J). lib. bdg. 11.95 *(978-0-9728380-1-6(5))* Seecraft Publishing.

Seredy, Kate. The Chestry Oak. 2015. (Illus.). 253p. (J). pap. 12.95 *(978-1-930900-81-3(3))* Purple Hse. Pr.

Sewell, Anna. Black Beauty. 2005. 27.95 *(978-1-4218-0905-2(2))*, 1st World Library - Literary Society) 1st World Publishing, Inc.

—Black Beauty. (J). 21.95 *(978-0-88411-065-1(6))* Amereon Ltd.

—Black Beauty. 2016. (ENG., Illus.). (J). (gr. 4-7). 26.95 ***(978-1-354-25151-5(2))***; 25.95 ***(978-1-354-25150-8(4))*** Creative Media Partners, LLC.

—Black Beauty. 2005. 92p. per. 4.95 *(978-1-4209-2539-5(3))* Digireads.com Publishing.

—Black Beauty. Marks, Alan, illus. 2006. (Usborne Young Reading Ser.). 64p. (J). (gr. 2-5). 8.99 *(978-0-7945-1193-7(7))*, Usborne) EDC Publishing.

—Black Beauty. 2008. (Bring the Classics to Life Ser.). (Illus.). 72p. (gr. 2-12). pap., act. bk. ed. 10.95 *(978-0-931334-51-1(9))*, EDCTR201B) EDCON Publishing Group.

—Black Beauty. 2010. (Folio Junior Ser.: Vol. 63188). (FRE.). (J). (gr. 3-6). pap. ***(978-2-07-063188-9(5))*** Gallimard, Editions.

—Black Beauty. 2006. (My First Classics Ser.). 112p. (J). (gr. k-3). pap. 4.99 *(978-0-06-079148-3(9))*, HarperFestival) HarperCollins Pubs.

—Black Beauty. (Illus.). 192p. (J). 9.95 *(978-1-56156-310-4(2))* Kidsbooks, LLC.

—Black Beauty. 2012. (ENG., Illus.). (J). (gr. 4-7). 34.99 ***(978-1-365-03063-5(6))***; pap. 11.99 ***(978-1-365-03068-0(7))*** Lulu Pr., Inc.

—Black Beauty. (Charm Book Classics Ser.). 32p. *(978-1-4054-9108-2(6))* Parragon, Inc.

—Black Beauty. Aldous, Kate, illus. 2003. 288p. (J). 9.98 *(978-1-4054-1675-7(0))* Parragon, Inc.

—Black Beauty. Hough, Charlotte, illus. 2008. (Puffin Classics Ser.). (ENG.). 288p. (J). (gr. 3-7). 5.99 *(978-0-14-132103-5(2))*, Puffin Books) Penguin Young Readers Group.

—Black Beauty. 2005. (Illus.). 176p. (gr. 3-7). 21.00 *(978-0-7569-5808-4(3))* Perfection Learning Corp.

—Black Beauty. (J). 8.97 *(978-0-13-052329-7(1))* Prentice Hall PTR.

—Black Beauty. 2013. (ENG.). 320p. (J). (gr. 4-7). pap. 10.99 *(978-0-09-957293-0(1))* Random Hse. GBR. Dist: Independent Pubs. Group.

—Black Beauty. 2011. (ENG., Illus.). (J). 14.99 ***(978-1-61382-629-4(X))*** Simon & Brown.

—Black Beauty. McKowen, Scott, illus. 2004. (Sterling Unabridged Classics Ser.). (ENG.). 208p. (J). (gr. 5). 9.95 *(978-1-4027-1452-8(1))* Sterling Publishing Co., Inc.

—Black Beauty. Corvino, Lucy, illus. 2005. (Classic Starts(tm) Ser.). (ENG.). 160p. (J). (gr. 2-4). 6.95 *(978-1-4027-1144-2(1))* Sterling Publishing Co., Inc.

—Black Beauty. 2007. (Illus.). 96p. (J). *(978-0-545-03332-9(2))* Scholastic, Inc.

—Black Beauty. Lt. ed. 2010. (ENG.). 260p. pap. 22.95 *(978-1-4104-2390-0(5))*, Kennebec Large Print) Cengage Gale.

—Black Beauty. (J). reprint ed. lib. bdg. 48.00 *(978-0-7426-1042-2(X))* Classic Bks.

—Black Beauty. deluxe ed. 2005. (Charming Classics). 288p. (J). pap. 9.99 *(978-0-06-075770-0(1))*, HarperFestival) HarperCollins Pubs.

—Black Beauty. 2004. reprint ed. pap. 1.99 *(978-1-4192-1018-1(1))*; pap. 15.95 *(978-1-4191-1018-4(7))* Kessinger Publishing, LLC.

—Black Beauty, 2 vols., Set. Lt. ed. (YA). (gr. 8-18). reprint ed. 10.00 *(978-0-89064-017-3(3))* National Assn. for Visually Handicapped.

—Black Beauty. Lt. ed. 2004. (Large Print Ser.). 268p. 25.00 *(978-1-58287-619-1(3))* North Bks.

—Black Beauty. unabr. ed. 2004. (Chrysalis Childrens Classics Ser.). (Illus.). 190p. (YA). pap. *(978-1-84365-062-1(2))*, Pavilion Children's Books) Pavilion Bks.

—Black Beauty: And a Discussion of Kindness. Martin, Richard, illus. 2003. (Values in Action Illustrated Classics Ser.). 191p. (J). *(978-1-59203-028-6(9))* Learning Challenge, Inc.

—Black Beauty: The Autobiography of a Horse. 2016. 193p. (J). pap. *(978-1-5124-0214-8(1))*, First Avenue Editions) Lerner Publishing Group.

—Black Beauty, Young Folks' Edition - Abridged with Original Illustrations. 2011. 112p. *(978-1-84902-394-8(8))* Benediction Classics.

—Black Beauty's Early Days in the Meadow. Donovan, Jane Monroe, illus. rev. ed. 2006. (ENG.). 32p. (J). (gr. k-6). 15.95 *(978-1-58536-296-7(4))* Sleeping Bear Pr.

Sewell, Anna & Ladybird Books Staff. Black Beauty. Matyjaszek, Kasia, illus. 2015. (Ladybird Classics Ser.). (ENG.). 72p. (J). (gr. k-3). 8.99 *(978-1-4093-1124-9(4))* Penguin Bks., Ltd. GBR. Dist: Independent Pubs. Group.

Sewell, Anna & Toaspern, H. Black Beauty. 2016. (ENG., Illus.). (J). (gr. 4-7). 24.95 ***(978-1-354-43640-0(7))*** Creative Media Partners, LLC.

Shakespeare, Strawberry. Hope's Horse: The Mystery of Shadow Ridge. 2013. 94p. pap. 11.97 *(978-0-9774335-6-8(0))* Diamond Star Pr.

Sharkey-Wilmot. The Mysterious Golden Horse. 2007. 168p. 22.95 *(978-0-595-69325-2(3))*; per. 12.95 *(978-0-595-45162-3(4))* iUniverse, Inc.

Sharon, Janusz. When Horses Could Fly: And Other Fantastic Tales. Kathy, Newell-Worby, illus. 2007. 80p. (J). pap. 19.95 *(978-0-9658533-6-1(5))* Amigo Pubns., Inc.

Shaw, Esther. The Winter Mare. 2005. (ENG., Illus.). 198p. pap. *(978-1-84401-447-7(9))* Athena Pr.

Shaw, J. M. Molly's Stallion. 2010. (J). pap. *(978-0-88092-769-7(0))* Royal Fireworks Publishing Co.

Shefelman, Janice J. & Shefelman, Tom, illus. Son of Spirit Horse. 2004. 74p. (J). *(978-1-57168-833-0(1))*, Eakin Pr.) Eakin Pr.

Shepherd, JaiLeen. Anan: Lea's Special Friend — Part II of the Lea Trilogy. 2006. (J). per. 15.95 *(978-1-889743-55-4(0))* Robbie Dean Pr.

—Lea's Song: The Life of a Special Little Horse. 2006. (J). per. 13.95 *(978-1-889743-54-7(2))* Robbie Dean Pr.

Shepherd, Megan. The Secret Horses of Briar Hill. 2016. (ENG., Illus.). 240p. (J). (gr. 5). 16.99 *(978-1-101-93975-8(3))*, Delacorte Bks. for Young Readers) Random Hse. Children's Bks.

Sherman, Josepha. Magic Hoofbeats: Horse Tales from Many Lands. Wingerter, Linda, illus. 2004. (ENG.). 80p. (J). 19.99 *(978-1-84148-091-6(6))* Barefoot Bks., Inc.

Shorrock, Anne. The Secret Adventures of Amelia & Rainbow. 2008. 36p. pap. 15.95 *(978-1-60693-011-3(7))*, Eloquent Bks.) Strategic Book Publishing & Rights Agency (SBPRA).

Siamon, Sharon. Secrets in the Sand. 2007. (J). *(978-1-933343-27-3(3))*, PONY) Stabenfeldt Inc.

Sieweke, Susan. The Spirit of Hope. 2008. 36p. pap. 16.00 *(978-1-4389-0514-3(9))* AuthorHouse.

Silverman, Erica. Cowgirl Kate & Cocoa. Lewin, Betsy, illus. (Cowgirl Kate & Cocoa Ser.). (ENG.). 44p. (J). (gr. 1-4). 2006. pap. 5.95 *(978-0-15-205660-5(2))* 2005. 15.00 *(978-0-15-202124-5(8))* Houghton Mifflin Harcourt Publishing Co.

—Cowgirl Kate & Cocoa. Lewin, Betsy, illus. 2007. (Cowgirl Kate & Cocoa Ser.). (gr. 1-4). 15.95 *(978-0-7569-8043-6(7))* Perfection Learning Corp.

—Cowgirl Kate & Cocoa: Horse in the House. Lewin, Betsy, illus. 2010. (Cowgirl Kate & Cocoa Ser.). (ENG.). 44p. (J). (gr. 1-4). pap. 5.99 *(978-0-547-31672-7(0))* Houghton Mifflin Harcourt Publishing Co.

—Cowgirl Kate & Cocoa: Partners. Lewin, Betsy, illus. 2007. (Cowgirl Kate & Cocoa Ser.). (ENG.). 44p. (J). (gr. 1-4). pap. 5.95 *(978-0-15-206010-7(3))* Houghton Mifflin Harcourt Publishing Co.

—Cowgirl Kate & Cocoa: Rain or Shine. Lewin, Betsy, illus. 2009. (Cowgirl Kate & Cocoa Ser.). (ENG.). 44p. (J). (gr. 1-4). pap. 5.99 *(978-0-15-206602-4(0))* Houghton Mifflin Harcourt Publishing Co.

—Cowgirl Kate & Cocoa: Spring Babies. Lewin, Betsy, illus. 2011. (Cowgirl Kate & Cocoa Ser.: 6). (ENG.). 40p. (J). (gr. 1-4). pap. 5.99 *(978-0-547-56685-6(9))* Houghton Mifflin Harcourt Publishing Co.

—Favorite Stories from Cowgirl Kate & Cocoa: Partners. Lewin, Betsy, illus. 2013. (Cowgirl Kate & Cocoa — Green Light Readers Ser.). (ENG.). 22p. (J). (gr. -1-3). lib. bdg. 13.55 *(978-0-606-33983-4(3))*, Turtleback) Turtleback Bks.

—Favorite Stories from Cowgirl Kate & Cocoa: Rain or Shine. Lewin, Betsy, illus. 2013. (Green Light Readers Level 2 Ser.). (ENG.). 24p. (J). (gr. 1-4). pap. 3.99 *(978-0-544-10502-7(8))* Houghton Mifflin Harcourt Publishing Co.

—Favorite Stories from Cowgirl Kate & Cocoa: School Days. Lewin, Betsy, illus. 2014. (Green Light Readers Level 2 Ser.). (ENG.). 32p. (J). (gr. 1-4). 12.99 *(978-0-544-23017-0(5))*, HMH Books For Young Readers) Houghton Mifflin Harcourt Publishing Co.

—Favorite Stories from Cowgirl Kate & Cocoa: Spring Babies. Lewin, Betsy, illus. 2016. (Green Light Readers Level 2 Ser.). (ENG.). 32p. (J). (gr. 1-4). 3.99 *(978-0-544-66844-7(8))*, HMH Books For Young Readers) Houghton Mifflin Harcourt Publishing Co.

—Horse in the House. Lewin, Betsy, illus. 2009. (Cowgirl Kate & Cocoa Ser.). (ENG.). 44p. (J). (gr. 1-4). 15.00 *(978-0-15-205390-1(5))* Houghton Mifflin Harcourt Publishing Co.

—Partners. Lewin, Betsy, illus. 2007. (Cowgirl Kate & Cocoa Ser.). pap. 7.93 *(978-1-4189-5237-2(0))* Houghton Mifflin Harcourt Trade & Reference Pubs.

—Partners. Lewin, Betsy, illus. 2007. (Cowgirl Kate & Cocoa Ser.). (gr. 1-4). 15.95 *(978-0-7569-8042-9(9))* Perfection Learning Corp.

—School Days. Lewin, Betsy, illus. 2008. (Cowgirl Kate & Cocoa Ser.). (ENG.). 48p. (J). (gr. 1-4). pap. 5.95 *(978-0-15-206130-2(4))* Houghton Mifflin Harcourt Publishing Co.

Silverman, Erica & Lewin, Betsy. Favorite Stories from Cowgirl Kate & Cocoa. 2013. (Green Light Readers Level 2 Ser.). (ENG., Illus.). 32p. (J). (gr. 1-4). pap. 3.99 *(978-0-544-02267-6(X))* Houghton Mifflin Harcourt Publishing Co.

—Favorite Stories from Cowgirl Kate & Cocoa Partners. 2013. (Green Light Readers Level 2 Ser.). (ENG., Illus.). 24p. (J). (gr. 1-4). pap. 3.99 *(978-0-544-02265-2(3))* Houghton Mifflin Harcourt Publishing Co.

Simon, Jenne. Andrea's New Horse. 2014. lib. bdg. 13.55 *(978-0-606-36362-4(9))* Turtleback Bks.

Sireau, Christine. Theo: The Blue Rider Pigeon. Tannenbaum, Rose, illus. 2005. 20p. (J). (gr. -1-3). pap. 15.00 *(978-0-88010-561-3(5))* SteinerBooks, Inc.

Sisco, Joann Ellen. Bonnie from Blue Mountain: 1. 2012. 88p. pap. 13.95 *(978-1-4772-7070-7(1))* AuthorHouse.

Smee, Nicola. Jingle-Jingle. 2008. (ENG., Illus.). 32p. (J). (gr. -1-1). 14.95 *(978-1-906250-08-9(1))* Boxer Bks., Ltd. GBR. Dist: Sterling Publishing Co., Inc.

Smiley, Jane. Gee Whiz. Clayton, Elaine, illus. 2013. (Horses of Oak Valley Ranch Ser.: Bk. 5). (ENG.). 272p. (J). (gr. 5). 16.99 *(978-0-375-86969-3(7))*, Knopf Bks. for Young Readers) Random Hse. Children's Bks.

—Gee Whiz, Bk. 5. 2014. (Horses of Oak Valley Ranch Ser.: Bk. 5). (ENG.). 272p. (J). (gr. 5). 7.99 *(978-0-375-87132-0(2))*, Yearling) Random Hse. Children's Bks.

—The Georges & the Jewels. 2010. (Horses of Oak Valley Ranch Ser.: Bk. 1). (ENG.). 240p. (J). (gr. 5). 6.99 *(978-0-375-86228-1(5))*, Yearling) Random Hse. Children's Bks.

—A Good Horse. 2011. (Horses of Oak Valley Ranch Ser.: Bk. 2). (ENG.). 256p. (J). (gr. 5). 6.99 *(978-0-375-86230-4(7))*, Yearling) Random Hse. Children's Bks.

—Pie in the Sky. 2013. (Horses of Oak Valley Ranch Ser.). (ENG.). 272p. (J). (gr. 5). 6.99 *(978-0-375-87131-3(4))*, Yearling) Random Hse. Children's Bks.

—True Blue. 2012. (Horses of Oak Valley Ranch Ser.: Bk. 3). (ENG.). 304p. (J). (gr. 5). 6.99 *(978-0-375-86232-8(3))*, Yearling) Random Hse. Children's Bks.

Smith, Emilie & Tejada, Marguerita. Viva Zapata!, 1 vol. Czernecki, Stefan, illus. 2009. (ENG.). 32p. (J). (gr. -1-3). 14.95 *(978-1-896580-55-5(6))* Tradewind Bks. CAN. Dist: Orca Bk. Pubs. USA.

Smith, Kathy. New Shoes for Chili Bean: Adventures of a Little Red Mule. 2011. 28p. (J). pap. 30.95 *(978-1-4327-6965-9(0))*; pap. 19.95 *(978-1-4327-6524-8(8))* Outskirts Pr., Inc.

Smith, Molly K. Cassie's Guardian Angel. 2009. 24p. pap. 17.50 *(978-1-4490-4065-9(9))* AuthorHouse.

Smith, Valerie H. The Spirit Stories: A Series of Short Stories for Children. 2007. 64p. per. 8.95 *(978-1-59824-450-2(7))* E-BookTime LLC.

Snelling, Lauraine. What about Cimmaron? 2008. (J). 8.99 *(978-1-59166-872-5(7))* BJU Pr.

Sneve, Virginia Driving Hawk. High Elk's Treasure. 2003. (EMC Masterpiece Series Access Editions). (Illus.). xxv, 110p. (J). 10.99 *(978-0-8219-2414-3(1))*, 35370) EMC/Paradigm Publishing.

Spanabel, H. A. Skyler & the Skunks. 2009. 48p. pap. *(978-1-84923-954-7(1))* YouWriteOn.

Springer, Nancy. The Boy on a Black Horse. 2010. (ENG.). 176p. (YA). (gr. 7). pap. 9.99 *(978-1-4424-1353-5(0))*, Atheneum Bks. for Young Readers) Simon & Schuster Children's Publishing.

Squiers, Connie. The Copper Colt. 2013. 94p. pap. 7.95 *(978-1-937829-78-0(2))*, Total Publishing & Media) Yorkshire Publishing Group.

St. John, Lauren. Kentucky Thriller. Dean, David, illus. 2014. (Jóvenes Lectores. Los Misterios de Laura Ser.). (SPA.). 248p. (J). (gr. 4-7). pap. 8.95 *(978-84-8343-271-6(4))*, Bambu, Editorial) Combel Editorial, S.A. ESP. Dist: Independent Pubs. Group.

St. John, Lauren. The One Dollar Horse. 2013. (ENG.). 240p. (J). (gr. 4-7). pap. ***(978-1-4440-0636-0(3))***, Orion Children's Bks.) Hachette Children's Group GBR. Dist: Hachette Bk. Group.

Stabenfeldt. Secrets in the Sand. 2007. (J). *(978-1-933343-51-8(6))*, PONY) Stabenfeldt Inc.

Stabenfeldt, prod. Starshine Legacy 2: Comic Book. 2007. (YA). *(978-1-933343-56-3(7))* Stabenfeldt Inc.

Stafford, Susan. Pocket Pegasus. 2012. (ENG.). 120p. pap. *(978-1-894377-32-4(X))* Breakwater Bks., Ltd.

Standish, Burt L. Frank Merriwell's Horse. Rudman, Jack, ed. 2003. (Frank Merriwell Ser.). pap. 9.95 *(978-0-8373-9146-5(6))* Merriwell, Frank Inc.

Stanley, Dean. The Horsosaurus. France, Mark, illus. 2008. 32p. pap. 14.62 *(978-1-4251-8158-1(9))* Trafford Publishing.

Starfall Education. My Horse Glory. Starfall Education, ed. 2004. (ENG., Illus.). 8p. (J). pap. *(978-1-59577-013-4(5))* Starfall Education.

Starshine Legacy 1. 2006. (J). *(978-1-933343-38-9(9))*, PONY) Stabenfeldt Inc.

Steers, Billy. Tractor Mac Arrives at the Farm. (Tractor Mac Ser.). (ENG., Illus.). (J). 2016. 24p. pap. 4.99 *(978-0-374-30536-9(6))*, 9780374305369) 2015. 32p. (gr. -1-k). 8.99 *(978-0-374-30102-6(6))*, 9780374301026) Farrar, Straus & Giroux. (Farrar, Straus & Giroux (BYR)).

Stein, David Ezra. Cowboy Ned & Andy. Stein, David Ezra, illus. (ENG., Illus.). 32p. (J). (gr. -1-1). 2011. 6.99 *(978-1-4424-3619-0(0))* 2006. 16.99 *(978-1-4169-0041-2(1))* Simon & Schuster/Paula Wiseman Bks. (Simon & Schuster/Paula Wiseman Bks.).

Stephens, Sarah Hines. Superpowered Pony, 1 vol. Baltazar, Art, illus. 2011. (DC Super-Pets Ser.). (ENG.). 56p. (gr. 2-2). pap. 4.95 *(978-1-4048-6846-5(1))*; lib. bdg. 23.99 *(978-1-4048-6479-5(2))* Picture Window Bks. (DC Super-Pets).

Stevenson, James. Runaway Horse! Date not set. (J). 15.99 *(978-0-06-051978-0(9))*; 16.89 *(978-0-06-051979-7(7))* HarperCollins Pubs.

Stiefvater, Maggie. The Scorpio Races. (ENG.). (J). (gr. 9). 2013. 448p. pap. 10.99 *(978-0-545-22491-8(8))*, Scholastic Paperbacks) 2011. 416p. 17.99 *(978-0-545-22490-1(X))*, Scholastic Pr.) Scholastic, Inc.

Strong, Frances Dinkins. Beth's Fella. Payne, Kay, illus. 2006. 112p. (J). pap. 9.95 *(978-0-9720267-6-5(2))* Learning Abilities Bks.

Stuckenschneider, Chris. Twist of Fate: The Miracle Colt & His Friends. 2009. (Illus.). 32p. (J). 16.95 *(978-1-933370-73-6(4))* Reedy Pr.

Sulkowski, Jennifer Suzanne. A Pony Named Napoleon. 2013. 74p. 30.95 *(978-1-59299-979-8(4))*; pap. 22.95 *(978-1-59299-978-1(6))* Inkwater Pr.

Summers, Mark. The Riddle Horse. Summers, Mark, illus. 2016. (ENG., Illus.). 32p. (J). (gr. 1-3). 18.99 *(978-1-56846-291-2(3))*, Creative Editions) Creative Co., The.

Sundberg, Peggy. Isabelle Lives a Dream. Wiles, Pat, illus. Lt. ed. 2003. (ENG.). 32p. (J). 11.95 *(978-0-9721057-1-2(9))* Cowgirl Peg Enterprises.

—Okey-Dokey Oakie. Wiles, Pat, illus. 2008. (ENG.). 32p. (J). pap. 11.95 *(978-0-9721057-7-4(8))*, Cowgirl Peg Bks.) Cowgirl Peg Enterprises.

—Shortstuff Bucks!, 3 vols. 2005. (ENG., Illus.). 32p. (J). 17.95 *(978-0-9721057-4-3(3))*, 3000) Cowgirl Peg Enterprises.

Swick, Carmen D. Patch Land Adventures Book 2 Camping at Mimi's Ranch. Lambert, Page, ed. Manfre, Joey, illus. 2012. 40p. pap. 12.99 *(978-0-9831380-1-3(X))* Presbeau Publishing, Inc.

Szymanski, Lois. Wild Colt, 1 vol. Kantjas, Linda, illus. 2012. (ENG.). 40p. (J). 16.99 *(978-0-7643-3975-2(3))*, 9780764339752) Schiffer Publishing, Ltd.

Szymanski, Lois K. A Pony to the Rescue. 2007. (Charming Ponies Ser.). 96p. (J). (gr. 2-5). pap. 4.99 *(978-0-06-128869-2(1))*, HarperFestival) HarperCollins Pubs.

—The True Story of Sea Feather, 1 vol. 2010. (ENG., Illus.). 48p. (J). pap. 14.99 *(978-0-7643-3609-6(6))*, 9780764336096) Schiffer Publishing, Ltd.

Taeryn, M. S. Chosen Four: The Faelan Prophecies, Book One. 2010. 444p. (gr. 10-12). pap. 23.95 *(978-1-4502-4797-9(0))*; (J). 33.95 *(978-1-4502-5634-6(1))* iUniverse, Inc.

Tapler, Judy. Santa Horse. Kohler, Michelle, illus. 2008. 36p. pap. 16.99 *(978-1-4389-2290-4(6))* AuthorHouse.

Taschek, Karen. Horse of Seven Moons. 2005. (ENG., Illus.). 192p. (YA). pap. 14.95 *(978-0-8263-3215-8(3))* Univ. of New Mexico Pr.

—The Risen Horse. 2010. (ENG.). 248p. (YA). (gr. 7-18). pap. 15.95 *(978-0-8263-4837-1(8))* Univ. of New Mexico Pr.

Tate, Nikki. Razor's Edge, 1 vol. 2009. (Orca Sports Ser.). (ENG.). 168p. (YA). (gr. 6-10). pap. 9.95 *(978-1-55469-167-8(2))* Orca Bk. Pubs. USA.

—Venom, 1 vol. 2009. (Orca Sports Ser.). (ENG.). 176p. (YA). (gr. 6-10). pap. 9.95 *(978-1-55469-071-8(4))* Orca Bk. Pubs. USA.

Tayler, Sandra. Hold on to Your Horses. Call, Angela, illus. 2008. 32p. (J). per. 15.00 *(978-0-9779074-8-9(1))* Tayler Corp., The.

Taylor, Lori. What to Do When Your Hoof Turns Blue!!! Taylor, Lori, illus. Lt. ed. 2006. (Illus.). 28p. (J). pap. 20.99 *(978-1-59879-220-1(2))* Lifevest Publishing, Inc.

Teitelbaum, Michael. Tale of Zuko. Spaziante, Patrick, illus. 2008. (Avatar Ser.). (ENG.). 96p. (J). (gr. 2-6). pap. 5.99 *(978-1-4169-4984-8(4))*, Simon Spotlight/Nickelodeon) Simon Spotlight/Nickelodeon.

Tetlow, Karin. Harry the Carousel Horse. Guze, Tessa, illus. 2012. 32p. pap. 15.96 *(978-0-615-55671-0(X))* Juping Horse Pr.
Thomas, David, ed. Teenage Horse Stories. Osborne, Richard, illus. 2011. 252p. 46.95 *(978-1-258-09866-7(0))* Literary Licensing, LLC.
Thompson, Kate. Highway Robbery. Dress, Robert & Duddle, Johnny, illus. 2009. (ENG.). 128p. (J). (gr. 5-18). 15.99 *(978-0-06-173034-4(3),* Greenwillow Bks.) HarperCollins Pubs.
—I'm Just a Little Horse. Green, Barry, illus. 2017. (Googley-Eye Bks.). (ENG.). 12p. (J). (gr. -1-k). bds. 7.99 *(978-1-78445-868-3(6))* Top That! Publishing PLC GBR. Dist: Independent Pubs. Group.
—Most Wanted. 2010. (ENG.). 144p. (J). (gr. 3-18). 15.99 *(978-0-06-173037-5(8),* Greenwillow Bks.) HarperCollins Pubs.
Thompson, Marilyn. Adopting Liberty the Mustang. 2008. 17p. pap. 24.95 *(978-1-4241-9639-5(6))* America Star Bks.
Thorpe, Kiki. From the Mist. Christy, Jana, illus. 2013. (Stepping Stone Book Series: No. 4). (ENG.). 128p. (J). (gr. 1-4). 5.99 *(978-0-7364-2797-5(X),* RH/Disney) Random Hse. Children's Bks.
Tiddle, Deanna Hessedal. Apartment Horse & Friends. 2003. 62p. (J). pap. 9.95 *(978-0-7414-1724-4(3))* Infinity Publishing.
Timmons, Robbie. Twoey & the Goat. 2008. (ENG., Illus.). 192p. (J). (gr. 1-7). 15.95 *(978-1-58726-517-4(6),* Mitten Pr.) Ann Arbor Editions LLC.
Tomlinson, Theresa. Voyage of the Snake Lady. 2007. 385p. (YA). (gr. 7-12). lib. bdg. 18.89 *(978-0-06-084740-1(9),* Eos) HarperCollins Pubs.
Toresen, Eli B. Summer with Prince. 2007. (YA). *(978-1-933343-68-6(0),* PONY) Stabenfeldt Inc.
—Yearbook Trouble at the Riding Camp. 2007. (YA). *(978-1-933343-67-9(2))* Stabenfeldt Inc.
Torrel, Wendy. GUARDIAN of DREAMS (1st Edition) Klingbeil, Kendall, illus. l.t. ed. 2004. 32p. (J). 14.95 *(978-0-9746890-0-5(9));* pap. 10.95 *(978-0-9746890-1-2(7))* White Tulip Publishing.
Tribolet, Leslie L. Danny's Tale: Adventures of an Arabian Horse in his Own Words. 2010. (Illus.). 112p. 24.95 *(978-1-4490-6065-7(X));* pap. 14.95 *(978-1-4490-6064-0(1))* AuthorHouse.
Turninelly, Nancy. Horse Shoes, 1 vol. Nobens, Cheryl A., illus. 2006. (Animal Tales Ser.). (ENG.). 24p. (J). (gr. k-3). lib. bdg. 24.21 *(978-1-59679-943-1(9),* SandCastle) ABDO Publishing Co.
—Horse Shoes. Nobens, C. A., illus. 2006. (Fact & Fiction Ser.). 24p. (J). pap. 48.42 *(978-1-59679-944-8(7))* ABDO Publishing Co.
—Los Zapatos de la Potranca, 1 vol. Nobens, C. A., illus. 2007. (Cuentos de Animales Ser.). (SPA & ENG.). 24p. (J). (gr. k-3). lib. bdg. 24.21 *(978-1-59928-677-8(7),* SandCastle) ABDO Publishing Co.
Turnbull, Ann. El Caballo de Arena. Foreman, Michael, illus. (Barril Sin Fondo Ser.).Tr. of Sand Horse. (SPA.). (J). (gr. 3-5). pap. *(978-968-6465-00-6(6))* Casa de Estudios de Literatura y Talleres Artisticos Amaquemecan A.C. MEX. Dist: Lectorum Pubns., Inc.
Tyler, Sandy. Herkimer's Big Day: Herkimer the Police Horse Meets a Young Girl Named Sammy. Williams, Brian, illus. 2012. (ENG.). 22p. (J). pap. 20.95 *(978-1-4327-9005-9(6))* Outskirts Pr., Inc.
Tyrrell, Helen. Nora & the Dancing Horse. 2003. 231p. (J). pap. 14.95 *(978-0-7414-1349-9(3))* Infinity Publishing.
Ulrich, Ann Carol. The Mystery at Hickory Hill: Annette Vetter Adventure #1. 2006. (Illus.). 196p. (YA). per. 9.95 *(978-0-944851-25-8(8))* Earth Star Pubns.
Valeska, Jon & Fripp, Jean. Thunder & the Pirates. Fripp, Jean, ed. Laroche, Bridget, illus. 2004. 32p. (J). (gr. k-4). 5.99 *(978-0-9701008-9-4(2))* Bicast, Inc.
Van Camp, Richard. What's the Most Beautiful Thing You Know about Horses? Littlechild, George, illus. 2013. (ENG.). 32p. (J). pap. 9.95 *(978-0-89239-185-1(5))* Lee & Low Bks., Inc.
Vinsh, Aara J. Ben, the Miracle Horse, 1 vol. 2010. 193p. pap. 24.95 *(978-1-4489-7591-4(3))* America Star Bks.
Virant, Janice. T-Bone the Flying Horse. 2013. (ENG.). 26p. (J). pap. 10.95 *(978-1-4327-5951-3(5))* Outskirts Pr., Inc.
Volponi, Paul. Homestretch. 2009. (ENG.). 160p. (YA). (gr. 7-18). 16.99 *(978-1-4169-3987-0(3),* Atheneum Bks. for Young Readers) Simon & Schuster Children's Publishing.
von Rosenberg, Byron. Dale the Uniclyde: An adventure in Friendship. Parrott, Heather, illus. 2007. 22p. (J). 11.95 *(978-0-9759858-6-1(8))* Red Mountain Creations.
Wade, Judith. Faelen, the Horse from the Sea. 2007. 107p. (J). mass mkt. 5.99 *(978-0-9728958-5-9(X))* Riley Pr.
Wagner, Elaine. Racin' Jason. Kaszonyi, Janet, illus. 2009. (Racin' Jason Ser.). (ENG.). 52p. (gr. 2-3). pap. 10.95 *(978-1-894778-73-2(1))* Theytus Bks., Ltd. CAN. Dist: Univ. of Toronto Pr.
Wallace, Bill. Beauty. 2007. (ENG.). 192p. (J). (gr. 3-7). pap. 6.99 *(978-1-4169-4942-8(9),* Simon & Schuster/Paula Wiseman Bks.) Simon & Schuster/Paula Wiseman Bks.
Wallace, Sharolyn. The Adventures of Bruce, Ben & Gerry: Bruce's Dream. 2012. 28p. pap. 17.99 *(978-1-4772-0249-4(8))* AuthorHouse.
—The Adventures of Bruce, Ben & Gerry: Training Day. 2012. 24p. pap. 17.99 *(978-1-4772-5397-7(1))* AuthorHouse.
Wallen, Virginia. Sonny & Sammy. 2006. 17.00 *(978-0-8059-9809-2(8))* Dorrance Publishing Co., Inc.
Walsh, Ann. Horse Power, 1 vol. 2007. (Orca Currents Ser.). (ENG.). (J). (gr. 5-9). 128p. pap. 9.95 *(978-1-55143-881-8(X));* 112p. lib. bdg. 14.95 *(978-1-55143-883-2(6))* Orca Bk. Pubs. USA.
Warner, Penny. The Mystery of the Missing Mustangs. 2012. 107p. (J). *(978-0-88166-411-9(1))* Meadowbrook Pr.
Warren, Tania Catherine. All about Charlie Horse: Charlie Horse & His Adventures. Warren, Steven Mathew, illus. 2012. 26p. 24.95 *(978-1-4626-5442-0(8))* America Star Bks.
Watch Out, Sara! 2006. (J). *(978-1-933343-35-8(4),* PONY) Stabenfeldt Inc.
Watters, Sandy. Love, Hope & Faith Play Seek & Find! A Positive Word, Horse in the House Series Book. 2013. 40p. pap. 16.95 *(978-1-4497-8183-5(7),* WestBow Pr.) Author Solutions, Inc.
Weale, David. Everything That Shines. McNevin, Dale, illus. (ENG.). 24p. pap. 6.95 *(978-0-9698606-8-6(4))* Acorn Pr., The CAN. Dist: Goose Lane Editions.
Webster, Amye. Shell's Journey. 2013. 162p. pap. 9.99 *(978-0-9891510-2-3(6))* Zebra Ginkgo.
Wedding, Linda. The Blue-Eyed, Tri-Colored American Paint: A Lesson in Trust for Baby. 2008. 44p. pap. 24.95 *(978-1-4241-9925-9(5))* America Star Bks.
Wedekind, Annie. A Horse of Her Own. 2009. (ENG.). 288p. (YA). (gr. 5-9). pap. 8.99 *(978-0-312-58146-6(7),* 9780312581466) Square Fish.
—Samirah's Ride: The Story of an Arabian Filly. 2010. (Breyer Horse Collection: 3). (ENG.). 128p. (J). (gr. 4-7). pap. 14.99 *(978-0-312-62268-8(6),* 9780312622688) Feiwel & Friends.
Wedekind, Annie & Haas, Jessie. Wild Blue: The Story of a Mustang Appaloosa. Wedekind, Annie, illus. 2009. (Breyer Horse Collection: 1). (ENG., Illus.). 128p. (J). (gr. 4-7). pap. 5.99 *(978-0-312-59917-1(X),* 9780312599171) Feiwel & Friends.
Weed, Thurlow R. Camel Fables from the Sailors of the Sudan. 2004. 84p. pap. 15.95 *(978-0-7414-2229-3(8))* Infinity Publishing.
Wehrmeijer, Annelien. Sophie & Daisy. van de Liejgraaf, Deborah, illus. 2014. (My Best Friend & Me Ser.). (ENG.). 10p. (J). (gr. -1 — 1). bds. 7.99 *(978-0-7641-6664-8(6))* Barron's Educational Series, Inc.
Wells, Misty. Hank the Horse. 2012. 20p. pap. 15.99 *(978-1-4685-7968-0(1))* AuthorHouse.
Wells, Rosemary. Ivy Takes Care. LaMarche, Jim, illus. (ENG.). 208p. (J). (gr. 3-7). 2015. pap. 6.99 *(978-0-7636-7660-5(8))* 2013. 15.99 *(978-0-7636-5352-1(7))* Candlewick Pr.
West, Tracey. Hermes & the Horse with Wings. 2017. (Heroes in Training Ser.: 13). lib. bdg. 16.00 ***(978-0-606-39738-4(8))*** Turtleback Bks.
Weyn, Suzanne. Daring to Dream. 2010. 163p. (J). *(978-0-545-23330-9(5))* Scholastic, Inc.
—Learning to Fly. 2010. 176p. (J). pap. *(978-1-4071-1742-3(4))* Scholastic, Inc.
Whint, Ana Lee. Espalemit. 2003. (ENG.). 112p. pap. 9.95 *(978-0-595-26259-5(7),* Writers Club Pr.) iUniverse, Inc.
Whipp, Jo. Otis & Baby Jean. Whipp, Katie, illus. 2012. 26p. 24.95 *(978-1-4626-5049-1(X))* America Star Bks.
White, Julie. High Fences, 1 vol. 2008. (ENG.). 192p. (J). (gr. 4-7). per. 9.95 *(978-1-55039-163-3(1))* Sono Nis Pr. CAN. Dist: Orca Bk. Pubs. USA.
Whyte, Janet M. Rescue Rider, 1 vol. 2011. (Lorimer Sports Stories Ser.). (ENG.). 136p. (J). (gr. 4-8). pap. 9.95 *(978-1-55277-868-5(1),* 9781552778685) Lorimer, James & Co., Ltd., Pubs. CAN. Dist: Casemate Pubs. & Bk. Distributors, LLC.
Wickham, Kimberly, illus. Angels & Horses. 2007. 128p. per. 12.85 *(978-1-4251-0215-9(8))* Trafford Publishing.
—Summer of Magic Horses. 2007. 134p. 12.85 *(978-1-4251-3012-1(7))* Trafford Publishing.
Wilbur, Helen L. Finnegan & Fox: The Ten-Foot Cop. Manders, John, illus. 2013. (ENG.). 32p. (J). (gr. 1-4). 16.95 *(978-1-58536-784-9(2),* 202354) Sleeping Bear Pr.
Wiley, Elizabeth. Carousel Horse: Keiry. 2012. 124p. pap. 35.98 *(978-1-4669-3796-3(3))* Trafford Publishing.
Williams, Kelly Ann. Pye. 2010. 36p. pap. 11.50 *(978-1-4452-8438-5(3))* Lulu Pr., Inc.
Williams, Susan. Wind Rider. 2006. 309p. (J). (gr. 5-9). 16.99 *(978-0-06-087236-6(5))* HarperCollins Pubs.
Williams, Ursula Moray. Adventures of the Little Wooden Horse. Brisley, Joyce Lankester, illus. 2013. (ENG.). 256p. (J). (gr. -1-2). 15.99 *(978-0-230-75495-9(3))* Pan Macmillan GBR. Dist: Independent Pubs. Group.
Williams, Valerie. The Funny Dreams of Dennis the Dartmoor Pony. 2010. (Illus.). 24p. 12.99 *(978-1-4520-0504-1(4))* AuthorHouse.
Wilson, Diane Lee. Firehorse. (ENG.). 336p. (YA). (gr. 7). 2010. pap. 8.99 *(978-1-4424-0331-4(4))* 2006. (Illus.). 17.99 *(978-1-4169-1551-5(6))* McElderry, Margaret K. Bks. (McElderry, Margaret K. Bks.).
—I Rode a Horse of Milk White Jade. 2010. (ENG.). 272p. (J). (gr. 4-10). pap. 9.99 *(978-1-4022-4027-0(9),* Sourcebooks Jabberwocky) Sourcebooks, Inc.
—Raven Speak. (ENG.). 256p. (YA). (gr. 7). 2011. pap. 8.99 *(978-1-4169-8654-6(5))* 2010. 16.99 *(978-1-4169-8653-9(7))* McElderry, Margaret K. Bks. (McElderry, Margaret K. Bks.).
—To Ride the Gods' Own Stallion. 2010. (ENG.). 256p. (J). (gr. 4-10). pap. 11.99 *(978-1-4022-4028-7(7),* Sourcebooks Jabberwocky) Sourcebooks, Inc.
Wilson, Essdale. Horses, Tigers & Neighbors. 2007. 160p. per. 24.95 *(978-1-4241-5811-9(7))* America Star Bks.
Wilson, Karma. Horseplay! McMullan, Jim, illus. 2012. (ENG.). 40p. (gr. -1-3). 16.99 *(978-0-316-93842-6(4))* Little Brown & Co.
Wing, Carol. Lio the Carousel Horse. Moen, Ruth, illus. 2010. (ENG.). 32p. (J). (gr. -1-2). 14.95 *(978-1-933067-37-7(3))* Beachhouse Publishing, LLC.
Wink, Edward. A Horse's Tale. 2013. 32p. pap. 24.95 *(978-1-63000-147-6(3))* America Star Bks.
The Winter Horses. 2014. (ENG., Illus.). 288p. (YA). (gr. 7). 16.99 *(978-0-385-75543-6(0),* Knopf Bks. for Young Readers) Random Hse. Children's Bks.
Winters, John. Gramps' Children's Stories. 2007. 60p. pap. 6.96 *(978-1-4357-0038-3(4))* Lulu Pr., Inc.
Wojciechowska, Maia. A Kingdom in a Horse. 143p. (YA). (gr. 5-18). pap. 4.50 *(978-0-8072-1391-9(8),* Listening Library) Random Hse. Audio Publishing Group.
Wojciechowska, Maia & Manna, Sal. A Kingdom in a Horse. 2012. (ENG.). 160p. (J). (gr. 2-7). pap. 9.95 *(978-1-61608-481-3(2),* 608481, Sky Pony Pr.) Skyhorse Publishing Co., Inc.
Wolf, Carla. Moving Towards a Dream. 2006. 91p. pap. 19.95 *(978-1-4241-5444-9(8))* America Star Bks.
Wolfe, Jane. Hungry Horse. Benham, Tors, illus. 2016. (ENG.). 8p. bds. 6.99 *(978-1-84322-721-2(5),* Armadillo) Anness Publishing GBR. Dist: National Bk. Network.
Wonderley, Stanley. A Boy & His Horse. 2012. 19.95 *(978-0-7414-7806-1(4));* pap. 11.95 *(978-0-7414-7805-4(6))* Infinity Publishing.
Woodard, Amy. The Day the Teacher Rode a Horse to School. 2008. 24p. pap. 24.95 *(978-1-60441-736-4(6))* America Star Bks.
Woodford, Pamela. Lilly & Harry. 2013. (Brighter Little Minds Ser.). (ENG., Illus.). 24p. (J). pap. 10.95 *(978-1-871305-79-1(9))* Orpen Pr. IRL. Dist: Dufour Editions, Inc.
Wooster, Devin Ann. Barbie Fall 2016 Holiday Movie Deluxe Step into Reading (Barbie) 2016. (Step into Reading Ser.). (ENG., Illus.). 24p. (J). (gr. -1-1). pap. 4.99 *(978-1-101-93995-6(8),* Random Hse. Bks. for Young Readers) Random Hse. Children's Bks.
—Horses to the Rescue. 2016. (Barbie Step into Reading Level 2 Ser.). (ENG., Illus.). 24p. (J). (gr. -1-1). 14.75 *(978-0-606-39352-2(8))* Turtleback Bks.
Worm, Piet. Three Little Horses. 2007. (Illus.). 61p. (J). (gr. -1-3). 18.95 *(978-1-930900-36-3(8))* Purple Hse. Pr.
Wyont, Wanda. Sunbeam. Huskins, Suzanne Hallier, illus. 2006. 32p. (J). 12.50 *(978-1-933251-07-3(7))* Parkway Pubs., Inc.
Xiong, Kim, illus. Paper Horse. 2008. (ENG & CHI.). 37p. (J). 18.95 *(978-1-60603-003-5(5))* Better Chinese LLC.
Yeoman, John. The Young Performing Horse. Blake, Quentin, illus. 2016. (ENG.). 32p. (J). (-k). pap. 9.99 *(978-1-78344-375-8(8))* Andersen Pr. GBR. Dist: Independent Pubs. Group.
Yolen, Jane. Centaur Rising. 2014. (ENG.). 272p. (J). (gr. 3-7). 16.99 *(978-0-8050-9664-4(7),* 9780805096644, Holt, Henry & Co. Bks. For Young Readers) Holt, Henry & Co.
Young, Andrea. Finny & the Boy from Horse Mountain. 2013. (ENG.). 320p. (J). (gr. 6-8). 16.95 *(978-1-62087-682-4(5),* 620682, Sky Pony Pr.) Skyhorse Publishing Co., Inc.
Young, Ed & Adams, Tracey. The Lost Horse: A Chinese Folktale. 2004. (ENG., Illus.). 32p. (J). (gr. -1-3). pap. 7.00 *(978-0-15-205023-8(X))* Houghton Mifflin Harcourt Publishing Co.
Young, Heather. Norman. 2012. 36p. pap. 21.99 *(978-1-4797-1356-1(2))* Xlibris Corp.
Young, Jan. Starting the Colt. 2014. 173p. (J). *(978-1-937849-11-5(2))* Raven Publishing Inc. of Montana.
Young, Kimberly Rich. A Horse Is a Horse. 2008. 40p. pap. 24.95 *(978-1-4241-9755-2(4))* America Star Bks.
Zahler, Thomas F., et al. Pony Tales, Vol. 1. Curnow, Bobby, illus. 2013. (My Little Pony Ser.). (ENG.). 152p. pap. 19.99 *(978-1-61377-740-4(X),* 9781613777404) Idea & Design Works, LLC.
Zoller, Elisabeth & Kolloch, Brigitte. Antonia & the Big Competition: The Rosenburg Riding Stables, Volume 2. Gotzen-Beek, Betina, illus. 2014. (ENG.). 92p. (J). (gr. 2-7). 9.95 *(978-1-62873-597-0(X),* Sky Pony Pr.) Skyhorse Publishing Co., Inc.
Zöller, Elisabeth & Kolloch, Brigitte. Antonia, the Horse Whisperer: The Rosenburg Riding Stables, Volume 1. Gotzen-Beek, Betina, illus. 2014. (ENG.). 96p. (J). (gr. 2-7). 9.95 *(978-1-62636-383-0(8),* Sky Pony Pr.) Skyhorse Publishing Co., Inc.

HORSES—HISTORY

Friddell, Claudia. Goliath: Hero of the Great Baltimore Fire. Howell, Troy, illus. 2010. (True Stories Ser.). (ENG.). 32p. (J). (gr. 1-4). 17.95 *(978-1-58536-455-8(X),* 202179) Sleeping Bear Pr.
Henry, Marguerite. King of the Wind: The Story of the Godolphin Arabian. 2011. 8.32 *(978-0-7848-3456-5(3),* Everbind) Marco Bk. Co.
Hogner, Dorothy Childs. Our American Horse. Hogner, Nils, illus. 2015. (ENG.). 128p. (J). (gr. 3-12). pap. 5.99 *(978-0-486-78441-0(X))* Dover Pubns., Inc.
The Horse, of Course: Individual Title Six-Packs. (Action Packs Ser.). 128p. (gr. 3-5). 44.00 *(978-0-7635-3308-3(4))* Rigby Education.
Linde, Barbara M. Horses in History. 2011. (Horsing Around Ser.). (Illus.). 24p. (J). (gr. 2-5). pap. 8.15 *(978-1-4339-4628-8(9),* Gareth Stevens Learning Library); lib. bdg. 22.60 *(978-1-4339-4627-1(0))* Stevens, Gareth Publishing LLLP.
McCormick, Patricia. Sergeant Reckless: The True Story of the Little Horse Who Became a Hero. Bruno, Iacopo, illus. 2017. 40p. (J). (gr. 1-5). 17.99 ***(978-0-06-229259-9(5))*** HarperCollins Pubs.
Patent, Dorothy Hinshaw. Decorated Horses. Brett, Jeannie, illus. 2015. (ENG.). 48p. (J). (gr. 3-7). 17.95 *(978-1-58089-362-6(7))* Charlesbridge Publishing, Inc.
—The Horse & the Plains Indians: A Powerful Partnership. Munoz, William, photos by. 2012. (ENG., Illus.). 112p. (J). (gr. 5-7). 17.99 *(978-0-547-12551-0(8))* Houghton Mifflin Harcourt Publishing Co.

HORSES—PICTORIAL WORKS

Carroll, Colleen. Horses. 2008. (How Artists See Jr.: Ser.). (ENG., Illus.). 18p. (J). (gr. -1-k). bds. 7.95 *(978-0-7892-0975-7(6),* Abbeville Kids) Abbeville Pr., Inc.
Chester, Laura & DeMari, Donna. Heartbeat for Horses. 2007. (ENG., Illus.). 192p. 29.95 *(978-1-59543-443-2(7))* Willow Creek Pr., Inc.
Langrish, Bob, et al, photos by. Dream Horses. 2004. (ENG., Illus.). 64p. (J). (gr. 2-8). pap. 10.95 *(978-1-58017-574-6(0),* 67574) Storey Publishing, LLC.
Momatiuk, Yva. Face to Face with Wild Horses. Eastcott, John, photos by. 2009. (Face to Face with Animals Ser.). (ENG., Illus.). 32p. (J). (gr. 2-5). 16.95 *(978-1-4263-0466-8(8));* lib. bdg. 25.90 *(978-1-4263-0467-5(6))* National Geographic Society. (National Geographic Children's Bks.).
Peter Pauper Press, Inc., creator. Scratch & Sketch Horses (Trace-Along) An Art Activity Book for Artistic Horse Lovers of All Ages. 2016. (ENG.). (J). 14.99 ***(978-1-4413-2251-7(5))*** Peter Pauper Pr. Inc.

HORSES—POETRY

Chester, Laura & DeMari, Donna. Heartbeat for Horses. 2007. (ENG., Illus.). 192p. 29.95 *(978-1-59543-443-2(7))* Willow Creek Pr., Inc.
Frost, Robert. The Runaway. Lang, Glenna, illus. Date not set. (ENG.). 32p. pap. 9.95 *(978-1-56792-243-1(0))* Godine, David R. Pub.

HORSES—TRAINING

Bodden, Valerie. Horsing Around: Training Horses. 2014. (Horsing Around Ser.). (ENG.). 24p. (J). (gr. 1-3). pap. 7.99 *(978-0-89812-836-9(6),* Creative Paperbacks) Creative Co., The.
—Training Horses. 2013. (Horsing Around (Creative Education) Ser.). (ENG., Illus.). 24p. (J). (gr. -1-3). 25.65 *(978-1-60818-473-6(0),* Creative Education) Creative Co., The.
Bowman, Donna Janell. Step Right Up: How Doc & Jim Key Taught the World about Kindness, 1 vol. Minter, Daniel, illus. 2016. (ENG.). 48p. (J). (gr. 2-8). 19.95 *(978-1-62014-148-9(5))* Lee & Low Bks., Inc.
Bratton, Donna Bowman. Saddle Up! Riding & Competitions for Horse Lovers, 1 vol. 2014. (Crazy about Horses Ser.). (ENG., Illus.). 32p. (gr. 3-4). 27.99 *(978-1-4914-0711-0(5),* Snap Bks.) Capstone Press of Coughlan Cos.
Degn, Bibi. My Horse, My Friend: Hands-On Ttouch Training for Kids. Joseph, Lilliana, tr. 2011. (ENG.). 32p. (J). (gr. 2-4). 14.95 *(978-1-57076-481-3(6))* Trafalgar Square Bks.
Eschbach, Andrea & Eschbach, Markus. How to Speak Horse: A Horse-Crazy Kid's Guide to Reading Body Language, Understanding Behavior, & Talking Back with Simple Groundwork Lessons. 2012. (ENG.). 32p. (J). (gr. 2-4). *(978-1-57076-532-2(4))* Verlhac Editions.
Spiotta-DiMare, Loren. Performing Horses: Horses That Entertain. 2014. (Horses That Help with the American Humane Association Ser.). 48p. (J). lib. bdg. 25.27 *(978-0-7660-4219-3(7),* Enslow Elementary) Enslow Pubs., Inc.
—Police Horses: Horses That Protect. 2014. (Horses That Help with the American Humane Association Ser.). 48p. (J). lib. bdg. 25.27 *(978-0-7660-4218-6(9),* Enslow Elementary) Enslow Pubs., Inc.
Weatherwax, Barbara. Gaited Games: Activities for the Young Gaited Horse Fancier. Weatherwax, Barbara, illus. 2004. (Illus.). 50p. (J). (gr. 1-8). 10.00 *(978-0-9740793-2-5(4))* Markwin Pr.

HORSES IN MOTION PICTURES

Goldish, Meish. Hollywood Horses. 2008. (Horse Power Ser.). (Illus.). 32p. (J). (gr. 2-5). lib. bdg. 25.27 *(978-1-59716-627-0(8))* Bearport Publishing Co., Inc.

HORSESHOE CRABS

Crenson, Victoria. Horseshoe Crabs & Shorebirds: The Story of a Food Web, 1 vol. Cannon, Annie, illus. 2003. (ENG.). 32p. (J). (gr. 3-5). 16.95 *(978-0-7614-5115-0(3))* Marshall Cavendish Corp.
High Tide for Horseshoe Crabs. 2015. (ENG., Illus.). 40p. (J). (gr. -1-2). lib. bdg. 16.95 *(978-1-58089-604-7(9))* Charlesbridge Publishing, Inc.

HORTICULTURE

see Gardening

HOSPITAL ADMINISTRATION

see Hospitals—Administration

HOSPITALITY

see Entertaining

HOSPITALS

see also Medical Centers

Amos, Janine. Going to the Hospital. 2009. (Changes Ser.). (Illus.). 32p. (J). (gr. k-2). 22.60 *(978-1-60754-484-5(9));* (gr. 2-5). pap. 10.55 *(978-1-60754-486-9(5))* Windmill Bks.
Anderson, Nancy. The Hospital in My City. 2016. (Rosen REAL Readers: Social Studies Nonfiction / Fiction: Family, Community, & the World Ser.). 8p. (gr. 1-k). pap. 5.46 *(978-1-5081-2263-0(6),* Rosen Classroom) Rosen Publishing Group, Inc., The.
Carr, Aaron. The Hospital. 2014. (Illus.). 24p. (J). *(978-1-62127-345-5(8))* Weigl Pubs., Inc.
Clendening, John. Veterinary Hospitals. 2014. (Animal Rescue Ser.). 32p. (J). (gr. 3-6). lib. bdg. 26.25 *(978-1-4777-7023-8(2),* PowerKids Pr.) Rosen Publishing Group, Inc., The.
Doeden, Matt. The Haunted Sanatorium: A Chilling Interactive Adventure. 2017. (You Choose: Haunted Places Ser.). (ENG., Illus.). 112p. (gr. 3-4). lib. bdg. 31.99 *(978-1-5157-3651-6(2),* You Choose Bks.) Capstone Press of Coughlan Cos.
Dyan, Penelope. The Little Hospital Book. Quinn, Courtney, illus. 2008. 108p. 19.95 *(978-1-935118-09-1(9));* pap. 8.95 *(978-1-935118-08-4(0))* Bellissima Publishing, LLC.
Enz, Tammy. Hidden Worlds, 4 vols., Set. Incl. Behind the Racks: Exploring the Secrets of a Shopping Mall. lib. bdg. 26.65 *(978-1-4296-3386-4(7));* Beyond the Bars: Exploring the Secrets of a Police Station. lib. bdg. 26.65 *(978-1-4296-3377-2(8));* Under the Lights: Exploring the Secrets of a Sports Stadium. lib. bdg. 26.65 *(978-1-4296-3376-5(X));* (gr. 1-2). (Hidden Worlds Ser.). (ENG.). 32p. 2010. Set lib. bdg. 79.95 *(978-1-4296-3777-0(3),* Blazers) Capstone Press of Coughlan Cos.
Gordon, Sharon. Que Hay Dentro de un Hospital? 2006. (Bookworms Ser.). (SPA & ENG., Illus.). 32p. (gr. 1-2). lib. bdg. 15.95 *(978-0-7614-2394-2(X))* Marshall Cavendish Corp.
—What's Inside a Hospital? 2007. (J). pap. 37.75 *(978-0-7614-3347-7(3))* Marshall Cavendish Corp.
—What's Inside a Hospital?/Que Hay Dentro de un Hospital? 2006. (Bookworms Ser.). (ENG & SPA., Illus.). 32p. (gr. 1-2). lib. bdg. 15.95 *(978-0-7614-2474-1(1))* Marshall Cavendish Corp.
Hidden Worlds [Capstone Sole Source]. 2010. (Hidden Worlds Ser.). 32p. lib. bdg. 101.28 *(978-1-4296-5865-2(7),* Blazers) Capstone Press of Coughlan Cos.
Hospital. 2007. (Busy Books Large Ser.). 5p. *(978-1-4054-9501-1(4)); (978-1-4054-9497-7(2))* Parragon, Inc.
Kalman, Bobbie. Hospital Workers in the Emergency Room. 2004. (My Community & Its Helpers Ser.). (ENG., Illus.). 32p. (J). pap. *(978-0-7787-2123-9(X))* Crabtree Publishing Co.
Keogh, Josie. A Trip to the Hospital. 2012. (PowerKids Readers: My Community Ser.). (ENG., Illus.). 24p. (J). (gr. k-2). pap. 8.25 *(978-1-4488-7486-6(6));* lib. bdg. 22.60 *(978-1-4488-7407-1(6))* Rosen Publishing Group, Inc., The. (PowerKids Pr.).
—A Trip to the Hospital / de visita en el Hospital. Alamán, Eduardo, tr. from ENG. 2012. (PowerKids Readers: My Community / Mi comunidad Ser.). (ENG & SPA., Illus.). 24p. (J). (gr. k-2). 22.60 *(978-1-4488-7831-4(4),* Editorial Buenas Letras) Rosen Publishing Group, Inc., The.
Koll, Hilary, et al. Using Math in the ER. 2006. (Mathworks!). (Illus.). 32p. (gr. 2-6). pap. 10.50 *(978-0-8368-6769-5(6));* lib. bdg. 26.00 *(978-0-8368-6762-6(9))* Stevens, Gareth Publishing LLLP. (Gareth Stevens Learning Library).

H
I

Kreisman, Rachelle. Places We Go: A Kids' Guide to Community Sites. Haggerty, Tim, illus. 2015. (Start Smart: Community Ser.). (ENG.). 32p. (gr. 1-3). 26.65 *(978-1-937529-36-9(3))* Red Chair Pr.

Lucas, Derek. Why We Need Hospitals. 2012. (InfoMax Readers Ser.). (ENG., Illus.). 24p. (J). (gr. 1-2). pap. 8.25 *(978-1-4488-9010-1(1)*, Rosen Classroom) Rosen Publishing Group, Inc., The.

Manolis, Kay. Ambulances. 2008. (Mighty Machines Ser.). (ENG., Illus.). 24p. (J). (gr. k-3). lib. bdg. 25.95 *(978-1-60014-176-8(5))* Bellwether Media.

Murphy, Patricia. Everything You Need to Know about Staying in the Hospital. (Need to Know Library). 64p. 2009. (gr. 5-5). 58.50 *(978-1-60854-088-4(X))* 2005. (Illus.). (YA). (gr. 7-12). 31.95 *(978-0-8239-3325-9(3))* Rosen Publishing Group, Inc., The.

Murray, Julie. Hospital, 1 vol. 2009. (That's Gross!:A Look at Science Ser.). (ENG., Illus.). 32p. (J). (gr. 2-5). 28.50 *(978-1-60453-556-3(3))* ABDO Publishing Co.

Parker, Steve & Parker, Vic. Going to the Hospital, 1 vol. 2011. (Growing Up Ser.). (ENG.). 24p. (gr. k-2). 23.32 *(978-1-4329-4797-2(4)*, Heinemann Read & Learn) Heinemann-Raintree.

Rhatigan, Joe. Get a Job at the Hospital. 2016. (Bright Futures Press: Get a Job Ser.). (ENG., Illus.). 32p. (J). (gr. 4-6). 29.93 *(978-1-63471-907-0(7)*, 208949) Cherry Lake Publishing.

Rose, Deborah Lee. Jimmy the Joey: The True Story of an Amazing Koala Rescue. Rose, Deborah Lee, photos by. 2013. (ENG., Illus.). 32p. (J). (gr. -1-3). lib. bdg. 25.90 *(978-1-4263-1372-1(1)*, National Geographic Children's Bks.) National Geographic Society.

Rose, Deborah Lee & Kelly, Susan. Jimmy the Joey: The True Story of an Amazing Koala Rescue. Kelly, Susan, photos by. 2013. (ENG., Illus.). 32p. (J). (gr. -1-3). 16.95 *(978-1-4263-1371-4(3)*, National Geographic Children's Bks.) National Geographic Society.

Rosenberg, Pam. Ugh! Icky, Sticky, Gross Stuff in the Hospital. Ramos, Beatriz Helena, illus. 2007. (Icky, Sticky, Gross-Out Bks.). (ENG.). 24p. (J). (gr. 3-6). 27.07 *(978-1-59296-897-8(X)*, 200356) Child's World, Inc., The.

—Working at a Hospital. 2008. (21st Century Junior Library: Careers Ser.). (ENG., Illus.). 24p. (gr. 2-5). lib. bdg. 27.07 *(978-1-60279-264-7(X)*, 200169) Cherry Lake Publishing.

Rosinsky, Natalie M. A Hospital. 2003. 24p. (J). lib. bdg. 21.35 *(978-1-58340-327-3(2))* Black Rabbit Bks.

Schuh, Mari. Community Helpers at the Hospital. 2016. (Community Helpers on the Scene Ser.). (ENG., Illus.). 24p. (gr. k-1). lib. bdg. 21.99 *(978-1-5157-2397-4(6)*, Pebble Bks.) Capstone Press of Coughlan Cos.

Steffora, Tracey. Math at the Hospital, 1 vol. 2013. (Math on the Job Ser.). (ENG., Illus.). 24p. (gr. k-2). pap. 6.29 *(978-1-4329-7159-5(X))*; lib. bdg. 22.65 *(978-1-4329-7152-6(2))* Heinemann-Raintree. (Acorn).

Williams, Dinah. Abandoned Insane Asylums. 2008. (Scary Places Ser.). (Illus.). 32p. (YA). (gr. 4-7). lib. bdg. 25.27 *(978-1-59716-575-4(1))* Bearport Publishing Co., Inc.

—Shuttered Horror Hospitals. (Scary Places Ser.). 32p. (gr. 4-8). 2017. (ENG.). (J). 8.95 ***(978-1-68402-608-1(3))*** 2011. (YA). lib. bdg. 25.27 *(978-1-61772-148-9(4))* Bearport Publishing Co., Inc.

Wood, Alix. Abandoned Hospitals. 2016. (World's Scariest Places Ser.). 00032p. (J). pap. 10.50 ***(978-1-4824-5897-8(7))*** Stevens, Gareth Publishing LLLP.

Woolf, Alex. A Photographic View of Hospitals. 2016. (Past in Pictures Ser.). (ENG., Illus.). 32p. (J). (gr. 4-6). pap. 11.99 *(978-0-7502-8354-0(8)*, Wayland) Hachette Children's Group GBR. Dist: Hachette Bk. Group.

HOSPITALS—ADMINISTRATION

Cortino, Becky. From the Heart: Injecting Healing Humor in the Healthcare Setting. 2009. 58p. (YA). mass mkt. 15.00 *(978-0-9799093-2-0(5))* Heart 4 Clowning Pr., A.

Hanson, Anne E. Ambulances in Action, 1 vol. 2011. (Transportation Zone Ser.). (ENG.). 24p. (gr. 1-2). lib. bdg. 25.32 *(978-1-4296-6827-9(X)*, First Facts) Capstone Press of Coughlan Cos.

HOSPITALS—EMPLOYEES

Colby, Jennifer. Hospital. 2016. (21st Century Junior Library: Explore a Workplace Ser.). (ENG.). 24p. (J). (gr. 2-5). 27.07 *(978-1-63471-074-9(6)*, 208375) Cherry Lake Publishing.

Jaynie R. Wood, M. s. & Jo Berkus. Going to the Hospital What Will I See? And Who are Those People Wearing Funny Clothes? 2009. (Illus.). 44p. pap. 18.49 *(978-1-4389-3862-2(4))* AuthorHouse.

Kalman, Bobbie. Hospital Workers in the Emergency Room. 2004. (My Community & Its Helpers Ser.). (ENG., Illus.). 32p. (J). pap. *(978-0-7787-2123-9(X))* Crabtree Publishing Co.

Mills, Nathan & Stevens, Alex. Who Works at the Hospital? 2012. (Rosen Readers Ser.). (ENG., Illus.). 24p. (J). (gr. 1-2). pap. 8.25 *(978-1-4488-8791-0(7)*, Rosen Classroom) Rosen Publishing Group, Inc., The.

HOSPITALS—FICTION

Accardo, Reba, told to. Surgery for Me? 2005. (J). pap. 8.00 *(978-0-8059-6697-8(8))* Dorrance Publishing Co., Inc.

Adler, David A. The Valentine Baby Mystery. Natti, Susanna, illus. 25th ed. 2006. (Cam Jansen Ser.: 25). (ENG.). 80p. (J). (gr. 2-5). 4.99 *(978-0-14-240694-6(5)*, Puffin Books) Penguin Young Readers Group.

Aker, Don. The First Stone. 2014. 304p. (YA). (gr. 8). pap. 7.99 *(978-0-06-231349-2(5))* HarperCollins Pubs.

Alender, Katie. The Dead Girls of Hysteria Hall. 2015. (ENG.). 336p. (J). (gr. 7). 18.99 *(978-0-545-63999-6(9))* Scholastic, Inc.

Baglio, Ben M. Colt on Christmas Eve. Baum, Ann & Lasher, Mary Ann, illus. 2005. 142p. (J). pap. *(978-0-439-77522-9(1))* Scholastic, Inc.

—Corgi in the Cupcakes. Baum, Ann, illus. 2008. 142p. (J). pap. *(978-0-439-02533-1(8))* Scholastic, Inc.

Ballard, Alexandra. What I Lost. 2017. (ENG., Illus.). 400p. (YA). 17.99 *(978-0-374-30463-8(7)*, 9780374304638, Farrar, Straus & Giroux (BYR)) Farrar, Straus & Giroux.

Benedis-Grab, Daphne. Clementine for Christmas. 2015. (ENG.). 256p. (J). (gr. 3-7). 16.99 *(978-0-545-83951-8(3)*, Scholastic Pr.) Scholastic, Inc.

Berenstain, Mike. Hospital Friends. 2015. (Berenstain Bears Ser.). (J). lib. bdg. 13.55 *(978-0-606-36932-9(5))* Turtleback Bks.

Blance, Ellen & Cook, Tony. Monster Goes to the Hospital. Date not set. (Illus.). 40p. pap. 129.15 *(978-0-582-19305-5(2))* Addison-Wesley Longman, Ltd. GBR. Dist: Trans-Atlantic Pubns., Inc.

Bourgeois, Paulette. Franklin Goes to the Hospital. 2004. (Illus.). (J). (gr. -1-2). spiral bd. *(978-0-616-03024-0(X))*; spiral bd. *(978-0-616-04547-3(6))* Canadian National Institute for the Blind/Institut National Canadien pour les Aveugles.

Bryce, Celia. Anthem for Jackson Dawes. 2013. (ENG.). 240p. (YA). (gr. 7-12). 16.99 *(978-1-59990-975-2(8)*, 9781599909752, Bloomsbury USA Childrens) Bloomsbury Publishing USA.

Bucki, Jo Dee & O'Malley, John. Maya Visits a Hospital: Love Is the Best Medicine, 110 vols. Hicks, Mindy, ed. Matthews, Ashley, illus. l.t. ed. 2007. 32p. (J). per. 4.95 *(978-0-9769069-0-2(2))* TAOH Inspired Education, LLC.

Busby, Cylin. Blink Once. 2012. (ENG.). 304p. (YA). (gr. 7-12). 17.99 *(978-1-59990-818-2(2)*, 9781599908182, Bloomsbury USA Childrens) Bloomsbury Publishing USA.

Campbell-Fells. Blue Ribbon Girls. 2005. 145p. pap. 13.95 *(978-0-7414-2593-5(9))* Infinity Publishing.

Carey, Becky. Wilma Goes to the Hospital. 2007. (Illus.). (J). 9.95 *(978-0-9791331-0-7(6))* Carey, Rebecca.

Chand, Vimi. The World of Peanut Butter Jelly Boy: Peanut Butter Jelly Boy's Stay in the Hospital, 1 vol. 2010. 44p. 24.95 *(978-1-4489-5610-4(2))* PublishAmerica, Inc.

Choyce, Lesley. Sudden Impact, 1 vol. 2005. (Orca Currents Ser.). (ENG.). 128p. (J). (gr. 5-9). per. 9.95 *(978-1-55143-476-6(8))* Orca Bk. Pubs. USA.

—Sudden Impact. 2006. (Orca Currents Ser.). 104p. (gr. 5-9). 19.95 *(978-0-7569-6876-2(3))* Perfection Learning Corp.

Civardi, Anne. Going to the Hospital. 2009. (First Experiences Sticker Bks). 18p. (J). pap. 6.99 *(978-0-7945-2431-9(1)*, Usborne) EDC Publishing.

—Going to the Hospital. Bates, Michelle, ed. Cartwright, Stephen, illus. rev. ed. 2005. (Usborne First Experiences Ser.). 16p. (J). (gr. -1-3). per. 4.99 *(978-0-7945-1006-0(X)*, Usborne) EDC Publishing.

Couloumbis, Audrey. Jake. 2011. (ENG.). 176p. (J). (gr. 3-7). pap. 6.99 *(978-0-375-85631-0(5)*, Yearling) Random Hse. Children's Bks.

Cousins, Lucy. Maisy Goes to the Hospital. Cousins, Lucy, illus. 2009. (Maisy Ser.). (ENG., Illus.). 32p. (J). (gr. k-k). pap. 6.99 *(978-0-7636-4372-0(6))* Candlewick Pr.

—Maisy Goes to the Hospital. 2009. (Maisy First Experiences Ser.). lib. bdg. 17.20 *(978-0-606-06686-0(1)*, Turtleback) Turtleback Bks.

Davis, David. Nurse's Night Before Christmas, 1 vol. Rice, James, illus. 2003. (Night Before Christmas Ser.). (ENG.). 32p. (J). (gr. k-3). 16.99 *(978-1-58980-152-3(0))* Pelican Publishing Co., Inc.

Disney Book Group. Doc Mcstuffins Welcome to Mcstuffinsville. Disney Storybook Art Team, illus. 2016. (ENG.). 24p. (J). (gr. -1-k). bds. 8.99 *(978-1-4847-4677-6(5))* Disney Pr.

Ditmars, Maribeth R. The Bald-Headed Princess: Cancer, Chemo, & Courage. 2010. 80p. (J). (gr. 3-8). 14.95 *(978-1-4338-0737-4(8))*; pap. 9.95 *(978-1-4338-0738-1(6))* American Psychological Assn. (Magination Pr.).

Dyer, K. C. Ms. Zephyr's Notebook. 2007. (ENG., Illus.). 206p. (YA). (gr. 7). pap. 12.99 *(978-1-55002-691-7(7)*, Boardwalk Bks.) Dundurn CAN. Dist: Ingram Publisher Services.

Edge, Christopher. Twelve Minutes to Midnight. 2014. (Penelope Tredwell Mysteries Ser.: Book 1). (ENG.). 256p. (J). (gr. 3-7). 16.99 *(978-0-8075-8133-9(X))* Whitman, Albert & Co.

Fisher, Terri. The Adventures of Grandma Terri: Grandma Terri's Hospital Visit. 2012. 24p. pap. 13.95 *(978-1-4685-4647-7(3))* AuthorHouse.

Ford, Michael Thomas. Suicide Notes. 2010. (ENG.). 304p. (YA). (gr. 9). pap. 9.99 *(978-0-06-073757-3(3)*, HarperTeen) HarperCollins Pubs.

Golden Books. The Doctor Is In! Unten, Eren, illus. 2012. (Little Golden Book Ser.). (ENG.). 24p. (J). (gr. k-k). 4.99 *(978-0-307-97588-1(6)*, Golden Bks.) Random Hse. Children's Bks.

Greenwood, Anna. The Children at St Bartholomew's Hospital. 2008. 172p. pap. 13.95 *(978-1-4401-0558-6(8))* iUniverse, Inc.

Grovet, Heather. What's Wrong with Rusty. 2004. (Review Kids Ser.). 144p. (J). pap. 7.99 *(978-0-8280-1756-5(5))* Review & Herald Publishing Assn.

Halpern, Julie. Get Well Soon. 2009. (ENG.). 224p. (YA). (gr. 7-12). pap. 9.99 *(978-0-312-58148-0(3)*, 9780312581480) Square Fish.

Hayatian, MaryAnn. The Flower Child. 2009. 32p. 20.00 *(978-0-557-06445-8(7))* Lulu Pr., Inc.

Hayles, Marsha. Breathing Room. 2013. (ENG., Illus.). 272p. (J). (gr. 5-9). pap. 9.99 *(978-1-250-03411-3(6)*, 9781250034113) Square Fish.

Hillert, Margaret. Dear Dragon Goes to the Hospital. Schimmell, David, illus. rev. ed. 2014. (BeginningtoRead Ser.). (ENG.). 32p. (J). (gr. k-2). pap. 11.94 *(978-1-60357-422-8(0))*; lib. bdg. 22.60 *(978-1-59953-581-4(5))* Norwood Hse. Pr.

Hoban, Russell. Jim's Lion. Deacon, Alexis, illus. 2014. (ENG.). 64p. (J). (gr. 1-4). 15.99 *(978-0-7636-6517-3(7))* Candlewick Pr.

Hodkin, Michelle. The Retribution of Mara Dyer. 2014. (Mara Dyer Trilogy: Vol. 3). (ENG., Illus.). 480p. (YA). (gr. 9). 18.99 *(978-1-4424-8423-8(3)*, Simon & Schuster Bks. For Young Readers) Simon & Schuster Bks. For Young Readers.

Holliday, Susan. Riding the Storm. l.t. ed. 2007. 164p. per. *(978-1-905665-22-8(9))* Pollinger In Print.

Hopkins, Ellen. Impulse. (ENG.). (YA). (gr. 9-12). 2008. 688p. pap. 12.99 *(978-1-4169-0357-4(7))* 2007. 672p. 22.99 *(978-1-4169-0356-7(9))* McElderry, Margaret K. Bks. (McElderry, Margaret K. Bks.).

Hutchinson, Shaun David. The Five Stages of Andrew Brawley. Larsen, Christine, illus. 2015. (ENG.). 304p. (YA). (gr. 7). 17.99 *(978-1-4814-0310-8(9)*, Simon Pulse) Simon Pulse.

Jean, Emiko. We'll Never Be Apart. 2015. (ENG.). 288p. (YA). (gr. 9). 17.99 *(978-0-544-48200-5(X)*, HMH Books For Young Readers) Houghton Mifflin Harcourt Publishing Co.

Johnson, Lindsay Lee. Worlds Apart. 2005. (ENG.). 168p. (J). (gr. 6-9). 16.95 *(978-1-932425-28-4(4)*, Lemniscaat) Boyds Mills Pr.

Johnson, Mo. Noah's Garden: When Someone You Love Is in the Hospital. Josse, Annabelle, illus. 2010. (ENG.). 32p. (J). (gr. -1-2). 15.99 *(978-0-7636-4782-7(9))* Candlewick Pr.

Kent, Renee Holmes. Robyn to the Rescue, Vol. 5. 2004. (Adventures in Misty Falls Ser.: Vol. 5). (Illus.). 100p. (J). (gr. 4-7). pap. 4.99 *(978-1-56309-451-4(7)*, N007109) New Hope Pubs.

Kerr, Judith. MOG & the V. E. T. Kerr, Judith, illus. 2005. (ENG., Illus.). 32p. (J). (gr. k-2). pap. 9.99 *(978-0-00-717128-6(5)*, HarperCollins Children's Bks.) HarperCollins Pubs. Ltd. GBR. Dist: HarperCollins Pubs.

Ladd, Debbie. Nurse Robin's Hats. Nakasone, Shaun, illus. 2006. 52p. (J). 16.95 *(978-0-9727615-3-6(5))* Deb on Air Bks.

Mayer, Mercer. My Trip to the Hospital, No. 5. Mayer, Mercer, illus. 2005. (Little Critter Ser.). (ENG., Illus.). 24p. (J). (gr. -1-2). pap. 3.99 *(978-0-06-053949-8(6)*, HarperFestival) HarperCollins Pubs.

McCarthy, Cori. You Were Here. 2016. (ENG., Illus.). 400p. (YA). (gr. 8-12). 17.99 *(978-1-4926-1704-4(0)*, 9781492617044) Sourcebooks, Inc.

McCormick, Patricia. Cut. 2011. (ENG.). 176p. (J). (gr. 7-7). pap. 8.99 *(978-0-545-29079-1(1)*, PUSH) Scholastic, Inc.

—Purple Heart. (ENG.). (YA). (gr. 8). 2011. 224p. pap. 9.99 *(978-0-06-173092-4(0))* 2009. 208p. 16.99 *(978-0-06-173090-0(4))* HarperCollins Pubs.

McMurchy-Barber, Gina & Zweig, Eric. Free as a Bird. 2010. (ENG., Illus.). 176p. (YA). (gr. 6-8). pap. 10.99 *(978-1-55488-447-6(0)*, Dundurn Pr.) Dundurn CAN. Dist: Ingram Publisher Services.

Meister, Cari. Moopy the Underground Monster, 1 vol. Messner, Dennis, illus. 2009. (Monster Friends Ser.). (ENG.). 32p. (gr. 2-3). 22.65 *(978-1-4342-1630-4(6))* Stone Arch Bks.

Morgan, Allen. Matthew & the Midnight Hospital. 2004. (Illus.). (J). (gr. k-3). spiral bd. *(978-0-616-01529-2(1))* Canadian National Institute for the Blind/Institut National Canadien pour les Aveugles.

Nickel, Laura. Alexander's Hospital Stay. 2004. 45p. pap. 24.95 *(978-1-4137-3060-9(4))* PublishAmerica, Inc.

Olson, Cynthia J. Kiera's Cry, 1 vol. 2009. 151p. pap. 24.95 *(978-1-60749-280-1(6))* America Star Bks.

Parr, Susan Sherwood. Christopher's Adventures: Chris Visits the Hospital, Vol. 2. Paraschiv, Doina, illus. 2nd alt. ed. 2013. (ENG.). 24p. (J). pap. 8.95 *(978-0-9827998-8-8(8)*, KID-E Bks.) Word Prodns.

Poblocki, Dan. The Ghost of Graylock. (ENG.). 272p. (J). (gr. 5-9). 2014. pap. 7.99 *(978-0-545-40269-9(7)*, Scholastic Paperbacks) 2012. 16.99 *(978-0-545-40268-2(9)*, Scholastic Pr.) Scholastic, Inc.

Post, Cynthia W. Carrie Flower: Goes to the Hospital. 2011. pap. 12.95 *(978-0-7414-6461-3(6))* Infinity Publishing.

Rey, H. A. & Rey, Margret. Curious George Goes to the Hospital (Special Edition) 2017. (Curious George Ser.). (ENG., Illus.). 56p. (J). (gr. -1-3). 17.99 *(978-0-544-76408-8(0)*, HMH Books For Young Readers) Houghton Mifflin Harcourt Publishing Co.

Rey, H. A., et al. Merry Christmas, Curious George. Young, Mary O'Keefe, illus. 2012. (Curious George Ser.). (ENG.). 32p. (J). (gr. -1-3). 9.99 *(978-0-547-76054-4(X))* Houghton Mifflin Harcourt Publishing Co.

Rey, Margret & Rey, H. A. Curious George Goes to the Hospital, 1 vol. 2008. (Curious George Ser.). (ENG., Illus.). 48p. (J). (gr. -1-3). audio compact disk 10.95 *(978-0-618-80063-6(8))* Houghton Mifflin Harcourt Publishing Co.

Ross, Tony. No Quiero Ir al Hospital. 2004.Tr. of I Don't Want to Go to Hospital. (SPA., Illus.). (J). 6.50 *(978-84-348-7752-8(X))* SM Ediciones ESP. Dist: Lectorum Pubns., Inc.

Ross, Tony, illus. I Don't Want to Go to Hospital. 2013. (ENG.). 32p. (J). (gr. -1-3). 16.95 *(978-1-4677-1155-5(1))* Lerner Publishing Group.

Sawyer, Ruth. The Primrose Ring. l.t. ed. 2007. 116p. pap. 19.99 *(978-1-4346-4248-6(8))* Creative Media Partners, LLC.

—The Primrose Ring. 2007. 104p. per. *(978-1-4065-3881-6(7))* Dodo Pr.

Schossow, Peter. Where Is Grandma? Schossow, Peter, illus. 2017. (ENG., Illus.). 64p. (J). (gr. k-5). 17.99 ***(978-1-77657-154-3(1))*** Gecko Pr. NZL. Dist: Lerner Publishing Group.

Seamon, Hollis. Somebody up There Hates You: A Novel. 2013. (ENG.). 256p. (YA). (gr. 8-12). 16.95 *(978-1-61620-260-6(2)*, 73260) Algonquin Bks. of Chapel Hill.

Shahan, Sherry. Skin & Bones. 2014. (ENG.). 272p. (YA). (gr. 8-12). 16.99 *(978-0-8075-7397-6(3))* Whitman, Albert & Co.

Shepherd, Megan. The Secret Horses of Briar Hill. 2016. (ENG., Illus.). 240p. (J). (gr. 5). 16.99 *(978-1-101-93975-8(3)*, Delacorte Bks. for Young Readers) Random Hse. Children's Bks.

Slanina, Anne M. Baby Brother Goes to the Hospital. Agnew, Alicia, illus. 2007. (Adventures of Annie Mouse Ser.: Bk. 2). 28p. (J). 18.99 *(978-0-9793379-1-8(7))*; per. 9.99 *(978-0-9793379-0-1(9))* Annie Mouse Bks.

Smith, Alex T. Claude in the City, 1 vol. Smith, Alex T., illus. (Claude Ser.). (ENG., Illus.). 96p. (J). (gr. 2-4). 2015. pap. 7.95 *(978-1-56145-843-1(0))* 2013. 12.95 *(978-1-56145-697-0(7))* Peachtree Pubs.

Snow, C. P. Last Things. 2008. (Strangers & Brothers Ser.: 11). (ENG.). 394p. pap. 19.95 *(978-1-84232-432-5(2))* House of Stratus, Inc. GBR. Dist: Gardners Bks. Ltd.

Sobat, Gail Sidonie. Gravity Journal. 2008. (ENG.). 162p. (YA). (gr. 15-18). pap. 14.95 *(978-1-894283-78-6(3))* Great Plains Pubns. CAN. Dist: Publishers Group Canada.

Spurling, Wesley. Gerry the Giraffe. 2009. 36p. pap. 16.99 *(978-1-4389-4223-0(0))* AuthorHouse.

Stanek, Robert, pseud. The Bugville Critters Rush to the Hospital. 2008. (ENG., Illus.). (J). 32p. per. 9.95 *(978-1-57545-150-3(6))*; 52p. per. 19.95 *(978-1-57545-126-8(3))* RP Media.

—The Bugville Critters Vacation Surprise: Buster Bee's School Days #3. 2008. (ENG., Illus.). 68p. (J). per. 18.95 *(978-1-57545-172-5(7))* RP Media.

—Rush to the Hospital. 2008. (ENG., Illus.). 32p. (J). pap. 5.59 *(978-1-57545-192-3(1))* RP Media.

Steers, Billy. Tractor Mac Tune-Up. 2015. (Tractor Mac Ser.). (ENG., Illus.). 32p. (J). (gr. -1-2). 8.99 *(978-0-374-30108-8(5)*, 9780374301088, Farrar, Straus & Giroux (BYR)) Farrar, Straus & Giroux.

Stewart, H. E. The Patched Heart: A Gift of Friendship & Caring, 1 vol. 2010. (ENG., Illus.). 32p. (J). (gr. -1-3). 19.95 *(978-0-9693852-5-7(0))* Tudor Hse. GBR. Dist: Orca Bk. Pubs. USA.

Stilton, Geronimo. Merry Christmas, Geronimo! Wolf, Matt, illus. 2004. (Geronimo Stilton Ser.: No. 12). 113p. (J). lib. bdg. 10.00 *(978-1-4242-0281-2(7))* Fitzgerald Bks.

Stockham, Jessica, illus. Visiting the Hospital. 2011. (First Time Ser.). (ENG.). 24p. (J). (gr. 2-2). pap. *(978-1-84643-336-8(3))* Child's Play International Ltd.

Thiel, Annie. Dakota's Mom Goes to the Hospital. Edwards, William M. & Marjoribanks, Karen, illus. 2006. (Playdate Kids Ser.). 32p. (J). (gr. -1-3). 14.95 *(978-1-933721-03-3(0))* Playdate Kids Publishing.

Thiel Annie. The Playdate Kids Dakota's Mom Goes to the Hospital 2ED 2007. 2007. 32p. 12.95 *(978-1-933721-30-9(8))*; pap. 6.95 *(978-1-933721-26-2(X))* Playdate Kids Publishing.

Turner, Kathy. Bobby Magilacahde's Trip to the Hospital. 2010. 16p. 8.49 *(978-1-4520-5874-0(1))* AuthorHouse.

Vizzini, Ned. It's Kind of a Funny Story. 2007. (ENG.). 464p. (YA). (gr. 7-12). per. 9.99 *(978-0-7868-5197-3(X))* Disney Publishing Worldwide.

—It's Kind of a Funny Story. 2007. (YA). lib. bdg. 20.85 *(978-1-4178-1818-1(2)*, Turtleback) Turtleback Bks.

Wakem, Samantha. Milly's Magic Play House: The Hospital, 1 vol. Herridge, Debbie, illus. 2010. 20p. 24.95 *(978-1-4489-5114-7(3))* PublishAmerica, Inc.

Walden, Pamela Charlene. Puff Bear Goes to the Hospital. 2013. 44p. pap. 9.99 *(978-1-62839-470-2(6))* Salem Author Services.

Watt, Fiona. Complete Book of First Experiences. rev. ed. 2011. (First Experiences Ser.). 144p. (J). ring bd. 19.99 *(978-0-7945-2948-2(8)*, Usborne) EDC Publishing.

Wells, Helen. Cherry Ames, Army Nurse. 2005. (Cherry Ames Nurse Stories Ser.: Bk. 3). 224p. (J). (gr. 4-7). 14.95 *(978-0-9771597-2-7(8))* Springer Publishing Co., Inc.

—Cherry Ames, Chief Nurse. 2005. (Cherry Ames Nurse Stories Ser.: Bk. 4). 224p. (YA). (gr. 8-12). 14.95 *(978-0-9771597-3-4(6))* Springer Publishing Co., Inc.

—Cherry Ames, Senior Nurse. 2005. (Cherry Ames Nurse Stories Ser.: Bk. 2). 224p. (J). (gr. 4-7). 14.95 *(978-0-9771597-1-0(X))* Springer Publishing Co., Inc.

—Cherry Ames, Student Nurse. 2005. (Cherry Ames Nurse Stories Ser.: Bk. 1). 224p. (J). (gr. 4-7). 14.95 *(978-0-9771597-0-3(1))* Springer Publishing Co., Inc.

—Cherry Ames Veteran's Nurse. 2006. (Cherry Ames Nurse Stories Ser.). 224p. (J). (gr. 3-7). 14.95 *(978-0-8261-0400-7(2))* Springer Publishing Co., Inc.

West, Carly Anne. The Murmurings. 2013. (ENG.). 384p. (YA). (gr. 9). 16.99 *(978-1-4424-4179-8(8)*, Simon Pulse) Simon Pulse.

Westling, Vicki Diane. Hannibal Goes to the Hospital: A Sam & Friends Book. 2011. 32p. pap. 15.99 *(978-1-4634-0997-5(4))* AuthorHouse.

White, Paul. Jungle Doctor's Crooked Dealings. 2011. (Flamingo Fiction 9-13s Ser.). (ENG., Illus.). 144p. (J). (gr. 5-7). pap. 8.99 *(978-1-84550-299-7(X)*, 9b21af6e-da89-4bc5-b0d9-5ce6419b0795) Christian Focus Pubns. GBR. Dist: Bookmasters Distribution.

—Jungle Doctor's Enemies. 2011. (Flamingo Fiction 9-13s Ser.). (ENG., Illus.). 160p. (J). (gr. 5-7). pap. 8.99 *(978-1-84550-300-0(7)*, c2552503-49be-450c-84cc-9ec522751da8) Christian Focus Pubns. GBR. Dist: Bookmasters Distribution.

Williams, Carol Lynch. The Haven: A Novel. 2014. (ENG.). 224p. (YA). (gr. 7). 18.99 *(978-0-312-69871-3(2)*, 9780312698713, St. Martin's Griffin) St. Martin's Pr.

HOSTESSES, AIRLINE

see Flight Attendants

HOT RODS

see Automobile Racing; Automobiles

HOTELS, MOTELS, ETC.

Finn, Denny Von. Stanley Hotel. 2013. (Scariest Places on Earth Ser.). (ENG., Illus.). 24p. (J). (gr. 3-7). lib. bdg. 25.95 *(978-1-60014-950-4(2)*, Torque Bks.) Bellwether Media.

Lassieur, Allison. Stanley Hotel: A Chilling Interactive Adventure. 2017. (You Choose: Haunted Places Ser.). (ENG., Illus.). 112p. (gr. 3-4). lib. bdg. 31.99 *(978-1-5157-3650-9(4)*, You Choose Bks.) Capstone Press of Coughlan Cos.

Lunis, Natalie. Eerie Inns. 2014. (Scary Places Ser.). 32p. (J). (gr. 4-8). lib. bdg. 25.27 *(978-1-62724-090-1(X))* Bearport Publishing Co., Inc.

Mara, Wil. The Innkeeper. 2010. (Colonial People Ser.). 48p. (gr. 3-18). 29.93 *(978-0-7614-4796-2(2))* Marshall Cavendish Corp.

Parvis, Sarah. Haunted Hotels. (Scary Places Ser.). 32p. (gr. 4-8). 2017. (ENG.). (J). 8.95 ***(978-1-68402-602-9(4))*** 2008. (Illus.). (YA). lib. bdg. 25.27 *(978-1-59716-574-7(3))* Bearport Publishing Co., Inc.

Wood, Alix. Spooky Hotels. 2016. (World's Scariest Places Ser.). 00032p. (J). pap. 10.50 ***(978-1-4824-5916-6(7))*** Stevens, Gareth Publishing LLLP.

HOTELS, MOTELS, ETC.—FICTION

Adler, David A. Cam Jansen & the Catnapping Mystery. Natti, Susanna, illus. 2005. (Cam Jansen Ser.). 58p. (gr. 2-5). 14.00 *(978-0-7569-5045-3(7))* Perfection Learning Corp.

Alger, Horatio. Joe the Hotel Boy. 2006. pap. *(978-1-4065-0712-6(1))* Dodo Pr.

—Joe the Hotel Boy: Or, Winning Out by Pluck. 2007. 164p. pap. 19.99 *(978-1-4346-5069-6(3))*; 172p. pap. 21.99 *(978-1-4346-5070-2(7))* Creative Media Partners, LLC.

Anderson, M. T. The Clue of the Linoleum Lederhosen. Cyrus, Kurt, illus. 2010. (Pals in Peril Tale Ser.). (ENG.). (J). (gr. 5-9). 256p. 17.99 *(978-1-4424-0697-1(6))*; 272p. pap. 6.99 *(978-1-4424-0702-2(6))* Beach Lane Bks. (Beach Lane Bks.).

At Your Service. 2014. (Mix Ser.). (ENG., Illus.). 272p. (J). (gr. 4-8). pap. 7.99 *(978-1-4814-0283-5(8)*, Aladdin) Simon & Schuster Children's Publishing.

Averill, Esther. The Hotel Cat. Averill, Esther, illus. 2005. (New York Review Children's Collection Ser.). (ENG., Illus.). 180p. (J). (gr. k-4). 17.95 *(978-1-59017-159-2(4)*, NYR Children's Collection) New York Review of Bks., Inc., The.

Avi. City of Orphans. Ruth, Greg, illus. 2011. (ENG.). 368p. (J). (gr. 5-9). 17.99 *(978-1-4169-7102-3(5)*, Atheneum/Richard Jackson Bks.) Simon & Schuster Children's Publishing.

Baker, Kage. The Hotel under the Sand. Law, Stephanie Pui-Mun, illus. 2009. (ENG.). 179p. (J). (gr. 2-7). pap. *(978-1-892391-89-6(9))* Tenmen, Edition, Horst Tenmen.

Beck, Andrea. Pierre in the Air!, 1 vol. Beck, Andrea, illus. 2011. (Pierre le Poof Ser.: 3). (ENG., Illus.). 32p. (J). (gr. -1-3). 19.95 *(978-1-55469-032-9(3))* Orca Bk. Pubs. USA.

Bemelmans, Ludwig. The Golden Basket. 2016. (ENG., Illus.). 96p. (J). (gr. 1-5). pap. 9.99 *(978-0-486-80717-1(7))* Dover Pubns., Inc.

Beverly, Cleary. The Mouse & the Motorcycle. 2014. (Mouse & the Motorcycle Ser.). (ENG.). 208p. (J). (gr. 2-5). 11.24 *(978-1-63245-245-0(6))* Lectorum Pubns., Inc.

Bond, Gwenda & Rowe, Chistopher. The Lost Legacy. Thomas, Glenn, illus. 2017. (Supernormal Sleuthing Service Ser.: 1). 416p. (J). (gr. 3-7). 16.99 *(978-0-06-245994-7(5)*, Greenwillow Bks.) HarperCollins Pubs.

Carman, Patrick. Floors, Bk. 1. 2013. (Floors Ser.: 1). (ENG.). 272p. (J). (gr. 3-7). pap. 6.99 *(978-0-545-46092-7(1)*, Scholastic Paperbacks) Scholastic, Inc.

—Floors #3: the Field of Wacky Inventions. 2015. (Floors Ser.: 3). (ENG.). 224p. (J). (gr. 3-7). pap. 6.99 *(978-0-545-79859-4(0)*, Scholastic Paperbacks) Scholastic, Inc.

Carnevale, Michael. The Hotel Coolidge. 2007. 91p. pap. 10.95 *(978-0-7414-3752-5(X))* Infinity Publishing.

Cartwright, Nancy & Jones, Joanna. Henry's Adventure at the Franklin Hotel. Feterl, Bill, illus. 2011. (YA). lib. bdg. *(978-0-913062-44-9(8))* Fenwyn Pr.

Cohen, Marina. The Inn Between. Watts, Sarah, illus. 2016. (ENG.). 208p. (J). 16.99 *(978-1-62672-202-6(1)*, 9781626722026) Roaring Brook Pr.

Dahl, Michael. The Assistant Vanishes!, 1 vol. Weber, Lisa K., illus. 2013. (Hocus Pocus Hotel Ser.). (ENG.). 112p. (gr. 2-3). lib. bdg. 25.32 *(978-1-4342-4101-6(7))* Stone Arch Bks.

—Hocus Pocus Hotel, 1 vol. Weber, Lisa K., illus. 2014. (Hocus Pocus Hotel Ser.). (ENG.). 128p. (gr. 2-3). 50.64 *(978-1-4342-8937-7(0))* Stone Arch Bks.

—Hocus Pocus Hotel. 2013. (Hocus Pocus Hotel Ser.). (ENG.). 112p. (gr. 2-3). 101.28 *(978-1-4342-4821-3(6))*; 50.64 *(978-1-4342-4820-6(8))* Stone Arch Bks.

—Hocus Pocus Hotel, 1 vol. Weber, Lisa K., illus. 2012. (Hocus Pocus Hotel Ser.). (ENG.). 216p. (gr. 2-3). 10.95 *(978-1-4342-4253-2(6))* Stone Arch Bks.

—Out the Rear Window, 1 vol. Weber, Lisa K., illus. 2012. (Hocus Pocus Hotel Ser.). (ENG.). 112p. (gr. 2-3). lib. bdg. 25.32 *(978-1-4342-4038-5(X))* Stone Arch Bks.

—The Prisoners of the Thirteenth Floor, 1 vol. Weber, Lisa K., illus. 2014. (Hocus Pocus Hotel Ser.). (ENG.). 128p. (gr. 2-3). 25.32 *(978-1-4342-6508-1(0))* Stone Arch Bks.

—The Return of Abracadabra, 1 vol. Weber, Lisa K., illus. 2013. (Hocus Pocus Hotel Ser.). (ENG.). 208p. (gr. 2-3). 10.95 *(978-1-4342-4721-6(X))* Stone Arch Bks.

—The Thirteenth Mystery, 1 vol. Weber, Lisa K., illus. 2014. (Hocus Pocus Hotel Ser.). (ENG.). 224p. (gr. 2-3). 10.95 *(978-1-4342-6509-8(9))* Stone Arch Bks.

—To Catch a Ghost, 1 vol. Weber, Lisa K., illus. 2012. (Hocus Pocus Hotel Ser.). (ENG.). 112p. (gr. 2-3). lib. bdg. 25.32 *(978-1-4342-4100-9(9))* Stone Arch Bks.

—The Trouble with Abracadabra, 1 vol. Weber, Lisa K., illus. 2013. (Hocus Pocus Hotel Ser.). (ENG.). 112p. (gr. 2-3). lib. bdg. 25.32 *(978-1-4342-4102-3(5))* Stone Arch Bks.

—The Wizard & the Wormhole, 1 vol. Weber, Lisa K., illus. 2014. (Hocus Pocus Hotel Ser.). (ENG.). 128p. (gr. 2-3). 25.32 *(978-1-4342-6507-4(2))* Stone Arch Bks.

del Rio, Tania. Warren the 13th & the All-Seeing Eye. Staehle, Will, illus. 2015. (Warren The 13th Ser.: 1). (ENG.). 224p. (J). (gr. 5). 16.95 *(978-1-59474-803-5(9))* Quirk Bks.

Demetrios, Heather. I'll Meet You There. 2015. (ENG.). 400p. (YA). (gr. 9). 17.99 *(978-0-8050-9795-5(3)*, 9780805097955, Holt, Henry & Co. Bks. For Young Readers) Holt, Henry & Co.

Deutsch, Stacia, adapted by. Hotel Transylvania 2: Movie Novelization. 2015. (Illus.). 141p. (J). *(978-1-4806-9404-0(5)*, Simon Spotlight) Simon Spotlight.

Dinardo, Jeff. Mr. Mouse's Motel: Helping Others. Lubach, Peter, illus. 2014. (Funny Bone Readers: Being a Friend Ser.). 24p. (gr. -1-1). pap. 4.99 *(978-1-939656-05-6(2))* Red Chair Pr.

d'Lacey, Chris. Icefire. d'Lacey, Chris, illus. 2007. (Last Dragon Chronicles Ser.: 2). (Illus.). lib. bdg. 19.65 *(978-1-4177-9138-5(1)*, Turtleback) Turtleback Bks.

Evatt, Harriet. The Secret of the Old Coach Inn. Stone, David, illus. 2011. 190p. 42.95 *(978-1-258-08239-0(X))* Literary Licensing, LLC.

Evelyn. Lucy the Elephant & Sami the Mouse: A Bedtime Story. Conforti, John W., tr. Conforti, John W., illus. 2003. (J). *(978-0-9740115-0-9(9))* WeBeANS Corp.

—Lucy the Elephant & Sami the Mouse: The Birthday Party. Conforti, John W., illus. 2004. (J). *(978-0-9740115-1-6(7))* WeBeANS Corp.

Ferrier, Florian, et al. The Ghosts in the Clouds. Ferrier, Katherine, illus. 2017. (Hotel Strange Ser.: 4). (ENG.). 40p. (gr. 2-5). 26.65 *(978-1-4677-8587-7(3)*, Graphic Universe™) Lerner Publishing Group.

Ferrier, Katherine & Ferrier, Florian. His Royal Majesty of the Mushrooms. Ferrier, Katherine, illus. 2016. (Hotel Strange Ser.: 3). (ENG., Illus.). 40p. (J). (gr. 2-5). lib. bdg. 26.65 *(978-1-4677-8586-0(5)*, Graphic Universe™) Lerner Publishing Group.

Finch, Kate. On with the Show! Gurney, John Steven, illus. 2014. 76p. (J). *(978-1-4242-5954-0(1))* Scholastic, Inc.

—On with the Show! 2014. (Pet Hotel Ser.: 4). lib. bdg. 14.75 *(978-0-606-35201-7(5))* Turtleback Bks.

—Pet Hotel #4: on with the Show! Gurney, John Steven & Jessell, Tim, illus. 2014. (Pet Hotel Ser.: 4). (ENG.). 96p. (J). (gr. 2-5). pap. 4.99 *(978-0-545-50184-2(9)*, Scholastic Paperbacks) Scholastic, Inc.

Frazier, Angie. The Midnight Tunnel: A Suzanna Snow Mystery. 2011. (ENG.). 288p. (J). (gr. 3-7). 17.99 *(978-0-545-20862-8(9)*, Scholastic Pr.) Scholastic, Inc.

George, Kallie. Fall. Graegin, Stephanie, illus. 2017. (Heartwood Hotel Ser.). (ENG.). 176p. (J). (gr. 2-5). 14.99 ***(978-1-4847-3161-1(1))*** Disney Pr.

—The Greatest Gift. 2017. (Heartwood Hotel Ser.: 2). (J). lib. bdg. 16.00 ***(978-0-606-39967-8(4))*** Turtleback Bks.

—Heartwood Hotel, Book 1 a True Home. Graegin, Stephanie, illus. 2017. (Heartwood Hotel Ser.). (ENG.). 176p. (J). (gr. 2-5). pap. 5.99 ***(978-1-4847-4638-7(4))*** Hyperion Bks. for Children.

Grabenstein, Chris. Beach Party Surf Monkey. Allen, Brooke A., illus. 2017. (Welcome to Wonderland Ser.: 2). (ENG.). 320p. (J). (gr. 3-7). 13.99 *(978-0-553-53610-2(9)*, Random Hse. Bks. for Young Readers) Random Hse. Children's Bks.

—Home Sweet Motel. Allen, Brooke, illus. 2016. (Welcome to Wonderland Ser.: 1). (ENG.). 304p. (J). (gr. 3-7). 13.99 *(978-0-553-53602-7(8)*, Random Hse. Bks. for Young Readers) Random Hse. Children's Bks.

Graham, Alastair. Full Moon Soup. 2007. (Illus.). 32p. (J). (gr. k-3). 12.95 *(978-1-905417-54-4(3))* Boxer Bks., Ltd. GBR. Dist: Sterling Publishing Co., Inc.

Graham, Alistair. Full Moon Soup. Graham, Alistair, illus. 2003. (Full Moon Soup & Full Moon Afloat Ser.). (Illus.). 32p. (YA). pap. *(978-1-85602-071-8(1)*, Pavilion Children's Books) Pavilion Bks.

Graham, Denise R. Curse of the Lost Grove. 2005. (Knights of the Silver Dragon Ser.: Bk. 10). (Illus.). 177p. (J). *(978-1-4156-3841-5(1)*, Mirrorstone) Wizards of the Coast.

Grossinger, Tania. Jackie & Me: A Very Special Friendship. Esperanza, Charles George, illus. 2013. (ENG.). 32p. (J). (gr. -1-3). 16.95 *(978-1-62087-683-1(3)*, 620683, Sky Pony Pr.) Skyhorse Publishing Co., Inc.

Hahn, Mary Downing. All the Lovely Bad Ones. 2009. (ENG.). 192p. (J). (gr. 2-5). pap. 7.99 *(978-0-547-24878-3(4))* Houghton Mifflin Harcourt Publishing Co.

—Look for Me by Moonlight. 2008. (ENG.). 208p. (YA). (gr. 7). pap. 7.99 *(978-0-547-07616-4(9))* Houghton Mifflin Harcourt Publishing Co.

Higgins, Ryan T. Hotel Bruce. Higgins, Ryan T., illus. 2016. (Mother Bruce Ser.). (ENG., Illus.). 48p. (J). (gr. -1-k). 17.99 *(978-1-4847-4362-1(8))* Hyperion Bks. for Children.

Higginson, Sheila Sweeny & Deutsch, Stacia, adapted by. Hotel Transylvania 2 Movie Novelization. 2015. (Hotel Transylvania 2 Ser.). (ENG., Illus.). 144p. (J). (gr. 3-7). pap. 6.99 *(978-1-4814-4819-2(6)*, Simon Spotlight) Simon Spotlight.

Hobbs, Leigh. The Big Book of Mr Badger. 2016. (Mr Badger Ser.). (ENG., Illus.). 324p. (J). (gr. 2-4). pap. 12.99 *(978-1-76011-243-1(7))* Allen & Unwin AUS. Dist: Independent Pubs. Group.

Holt, Kimberly Willis. Blooming at the Texas Sunrise Motel. Rosenberry, Vera, illus. 2017. (ENG.). 336p. (J). 16.99 *(978-1-62779-324-7(0)*, 9781627793247, Holt, Henry & Co. Bks. For Young Readers) Holt, Henry & Co.

Hotel Horror. (Fantasmas de Fear Street Coleccion). (SPA.). (YA). (gr. 5-8). Vol. 1. pap. 7.95 *(978-950-04-2091-4(0)*, EM11732) Vol. 2. pap. 7.95 *(978-950-04-2092-1(9)*, EM11736) Emecé Editores S.A. ARG. Dist: Planeta Publishing Corp., Lectorum Pubns., Inc.

John Philip Duck. 2004. (J). 29.95 incl. audio compact disk *(978-0-8045-4127-5(2))*; 27.95 incl. audio *(978-0-8045-6932-3(0))* Spoken Arts, Inc.

Johnson, Maureen. Scarlett Fever. (ENG.). 352p. (J). (gr. 7-7). 2011. pap. 9.99 *(978-0-545-09633-1(2))* 2010. 16.99 *(978-0-439-89928-4(1))* Scholastic, Inc.

—Suite Scarlett. 2009. (ENG.). 368p. (J). (gr. 3-7). 8.99 *(978-0-545-09632-4(4))* Scholastic, Inc.

Kasdan, Mallory. Ella. Chin, Marcos, illus. 2015. (ENG.). 56p. (J). (gr. k-3). bds. 17.99 *(978-0-670-01675-4(6)*, Viking Books for Young Readers) Penguin Young Readers Group.

Kopetz, Mark. Red Herrings at Rock Island: A Door County Mystery. 2005. 15.00 *(978-0-940473-42-3(9))* Caxton, Wm Ltd.

Kovacs, Deborah. Catie Copley. Williams, Jared T., illus. 2007. (ENG.). 32p. (J). (gr. -1-3). 17.95 *(978-1-56792-332-2(1))* Godine, David R. Pub.

—Catie Copley's Great Escape. Williams, Jared T., illus. 2009. (J). 17.95 *(978-1-56792-382-7(8))*; (ENG.). 32p. (gr. -1-3). 17.95 *(978-1-56792-379-7(8))* Godine, David R. Pub.

Liebig, Nelda Johnson. Carrie & the Boarding House. 2005. 127p. (J). (gr. 3-7). 10.95 *(978-1-883953-35-5(9))* Great Lakes Literary, LLC.

Maher, Liam & May, Gin. Ghost Story. 2013. 20p. pap. 9.95 *(978-1-61633-428-4(2))* Guardian Angel Publishing, Inc.

McClatchy, Lisa. Eloise & the Snowman, 1 vol. Lyon, Tammie, illus. 2016. (ENG.). 32p. (J). ***(978-1-61479-402-8(2))*** Spotlight.

McClatchy, Lisa & Thompson, Kay. Eloise's New Bonnet. Lyon, Tammie Speer & Lyon, Tammie, illus. 2007. (Eloise Ser.). (ENG.). 32p. (J). (gr. -1-1). pap. 3.99 *(978-0-689-87452-9(9)*, Simon Spotlight) Simon Spotlight.

Medina, Andre, illus. Meet the Monsters. 2015. (Hotel Transylvania 2 Ser.). (ENG.). 16p. (J). (gr. -1-3). pap. 5.99 *(978-1-4814-4802-4(1)*, Simon Spotlight) Simon Spotlight.

Melton, Marcia. The Boarding House. Doran, Fran, illus. 2012. 153p. (J). pap. 12.00 *(978-1-937849-03-0(1))* Raven Publishing Inc. of Montana.

Milford, Kate. Ghosts of Greenglass House. 2017. (ENG., Illus.). 464p. (J). (gr. 5-7). 17.99 ***(978-0-544-99146-0(X)***, Clarion Bks.) Houghton Mifflin Harcourt Trade & Reference Pubs.

Milford, Kate. Greenglass House. 2015. (CHI.). 352p. (J). (gr. 5-7). pap. *(978-986-320-886-0(8))* Commonwealth Publishing Co., Ltd.

—Greenglass House. Zollars, Jaime, illus. (ENG.). (J). (gr. 5-7). 2016. 400p. pap. 7.99 *(978-0-544-54028-6(X)*, HMH Books For Young Readers) 2014. 384p. 17.99 *(978-0-544-05270-3(6))* Houghton Mifflin Harcourt Publishing Co.

—Greenglass House. 2016. lib. bdg. 18.40 *(978-0-606-38908-2(3))* Turtleback Bks.

Naylor, Phyllis Reynolds. Bernie Magruder & the Bats in the Belfry. 2004. (ENG., Illus.). 144p. (J). (gr. 3-7). pap. 7.99 *(978-0-689-85067-7(0)*, Atheneum Bks. for Young Readers) Simon & Schuster Children's Publishing.

Nixon & Brush. Champagne with a Corpse. (Thumbprint Mysteries Ser.). 32.86 *(978-0-8092-0420-5(7))* McGraw-Hill/Contemporary.

O'Connor, Barbara. Greetings from Nowhere. 2008. (ENG.). 208p. (J). (gr. 5-8). 17.99 *(978-0-374-39937-5(9)*, 9780374399375, Farrar, Straus & Giroux (BYR)) Farrar, Straus & Giroux.

Odanaka, Barbara. A Crazy Day at the Critter Café. White, Lee, illus. 2009. (ENG.). 32p. (J). (gr. -1-3). 17.99 *(978-1-4169-3914-6(8)*, McElderry, Margaret K. Bks.) McElderry, Margaret K. Bks.

Paratore, Coleen Murtagh. The Cupid Chronicles. 2008. (Wedding Planner's Daughter Ser.). (ENG.). 224p. (J). (gr. 4-8). pap. 6.99 *(978-1-4169-5484-2(8)*, Aladdin) Simon & Schuster Children's Publishing.

—Willa by Heart. 2008. (Wedding Planner's Daughter Ser.). (ENG.). 240p. (J). (gr. 3-7). 15.99 *(978-1-4169-4076-0(6)*, Simon & Schuster Bks. For Young Readers) Simon & Schuster Bks. For Young Readers.

—Willa by Heart. 2009. (Wedding Planner's Daughter Ser.). (ENG.). 240p. (J). (gr. 4-8). pap. 6.99 *(978-1-4169-7470-3(9)*, Aladdin) Simon & Schuster Children's Publishing.

—Wish I Might: From the Life of Willa Havisham. 2010. (ENG.). 176p. (J). (gr. 5-9). 16.99 *(978-0-545-09406-1(2)*, Scholastic Pr.) Scholastic, Inc.

Pearson, Mary E. A Room on Lorelei Street. 2008. (ENG.). 288p. (YA). (gr. 9-13). pap. 19.99 *(978-0-312-38019-9(4)*, 9780312380199) Square Fish.

Pinkwater, Daniel M. The Yggyssey: How Iggy Wondered What Happened to All the Ghosts, Found Out Where They Went, & Went There. 2010. (ENG., Illus.). 256p. (J). (gr. 5-7). pap. 6.99 *(978-0-547-32865-2(6))* Houghton Mifflin Harcourt Publishing Co.

Polacco, Patricia. John Philip Duck. Polacco, Patricia, illus. 2004. (ENG., Illus.). 48p. (J). (gr. k-4). 17.99 *(978-0-399-24262-5(7)*, Philomel Bks.) Penguin Young Readers Group.

Ripley's Believe It or Not Editors. Haunted Hotel. 2011. (Ripley RBI Ser.). 128p. (J). pap. 4.99 *(978-1-893951-65-5(0))* Ripley Entertainment, Inc.

Roberts, Willo Davis. Rebel. 2005. 153p. (J). (gr. 3-7). 13.65 *(978-0-7569-5076-7(7))* Perfection Learning Corp.

Rossell, Judith. Withering-By-Sea. Rossell, Judith, illus. 2017. (ENG., Illus.). 288p. (J). (gr. 3-7). pap. 7.99 *(978-1-4814-4368-5(2))* Simon & Schuster Children's Publishing.

Ruby, Lois. Rebel Spirits. 2013. (ENG.). 304p. (J). (gr. 7). 17.99 *(978-0-545-42623-7(5))*; 292p. (YA). *(978-0-545-55282-0(6))* Scholastic, Inc.

Rylant, Cynthia. Old Town in the Green Groves. 2007. (Little House Ser.). (ENG.). 192p. (J). (gr. 3-7). pap. 6.99 *(978-0-06-088546-5(7))* HarperCollins Pubs.

Scattergood, Augusta. The Way to Stay in Destiny. 2015. (ENG.). 192p. (J). (gr. 3-7). 16.99 *(978-0-545-53824-4(6)*, Scholastic Pr.) Scholastic, Inc.

Stern, A. J. Funny Business, 4 vols. Marts, Doreen Mulryan, illus. 2011. (Frankly, Frannie Ser.: 4). (ENG.). 128p. (J). (gr. 1-3). pap. 5.99 *(978-0-448-45540-2(4)*, Grosset & Dunlap) Penguin Young Readers Group.

Stilton, Geronimo. Surf's up Geronimo. 2005. (Geronimo Stilton Ser.: No. 20). (ENG., Illus.). 128p. (J). (gr. 2-5). 7.99 *(978-0-439-69143-7(5)*, Scholastic Paperbacks) Scholastic, Inc.

—This Hotel Is Haunted! 2012. (Geronimo Stilton Ser.: Bk. 50). (ENG., Illus.). 128p. (J). (gr. 2-5). pap. 7.99 *(978-0-545-34102-8(7)*, Scholastic Paperbacks) Scholastic, Inc.

Swanson Sateren, Shelley. Adventures at Hound Hotel. Melmon, Deborah, illus. 2016. (Adventures at Hound Hotel Ser.). (ENG.). 72p. (gr. 2-3). 202.56 *(978-1-5158-0078-1(4)*, Adventures at Hound Hotel) Picture Window Bks.

Teitelbaum, Michael. The Ghost at the Grand Inn. 2015. (Cold Whispers Ser.). (ENG., Illus.). 32p. (J). (gr. 2-6). lib. bdg. 26.60 *(978-1-62724-808-2(0))* Bearport Publishing Co., Inc.

Thompson, Kay. Eloise at the Wedding. Lyon, Tammie Speer, illus. 2006. (Eloise Ser.). (ENG.). 32p. (J). (gr. -1-1). pap. 3.99 *(978-0-689-87449-9(9)*, Simon Spotlight) Simon Spotlight.

Thompson, Kay & Brenner, Marie. Kay Thompson's Eloise: The Absolutely Essential 50th Anniversary Edition: A Book for Precocious Grown-Ups. Knight, Hilary, illus. 2007. 84p. (J). reprint ed. 20.00 *(978-1-4223-6789-6(4))* DIANE Publishing Co.

Trumbauer, Lisa. Mountain Manor Mystery. Hawkes, Kevin, illus. 2006. 96p. (J). pap. *(978-1-59034-810-9(9))* Mondo Publishing.

Turnage, Sheila. The Ghosts of Tupelo Landing. 2014. (Mo & Dale Mysteries Ser.). (ENG.). 368p. (J). (gr. 5). 16.99 *(978-0-8037-3671-9(1)*, Kathy Dawson Books) Penguin Young Readers Group.

—The Ghosts of Tupelo Landing. 2015. lib. bdg. 18.40 *(978-0-606-36773-8(X))* Turtleback Bks.

Vail, Emily Blake. The Grey Ghost of the Pharaoh. Barbra K. Mudd, illus. 2004. 176p. (YA). per. 8.99 *(978-0-935087-27-7(3))* Wright Publishing, Inc.

Vernick, Shirley Reva. The Black Butterfly. 2014. (ENG.). 226p. (J). 19.95 *(978-1-935955-79-5(9))* Cinco Puntos Pr.

Webb, Holly. The Case of the Feathered Mask: The Mysteries of Maisie Hitchins, Book 4. Lindsay, Marion, illus. 2017. (Mysteries of Maisie Hitchins Ser.: 4). (ENG.). 176p. (J). (gr. 2-5). pap. 5.99 *(978-0-544-94884-6(X)*, HMH Books For Young Readers) Houghton Mifflin Harcourt Publishing Co.

—The Case of the Secret Tunnel. Lindsay, Marion, illus. 2016. (Mysteries of Maisie Hitchins Ser.: 5). (ENG.). 176p. (J). (gr. 2-5). 15.99 *(978-0-544-81554-4(8)*, HMH Books For Young Readers) Houghton Mifflin Harcourt Publishing Co.

Webb, Holly & Lindsay, Marion. The Case of the Stolen Sixpence. Lindsay, Marion, illus. 2014. (Mysteries of Maisie Hitchins Ser.: 1). (ENG., Illus.). 176p. (J). (gr. 2-5). 14.99 *(978-0-544-33928-6(2)*, HMH Books For Young Readers) Houghton Mifflin Harcourt Publishing Co.

Webster, Jean. Jerry. 2008. 108p. 22.95 *(978-1-60664-939-8(6))*; pap. 9.95 *(978-1-60664-060-9(7))* Aegypan.

Weiss, Ellen. Eloise & the Very Secret Room. Lyon, Tammie Speer & Lyon, Tammie, illus. 2006. (Eloise Ser.). (ENG.). 32p. (J). (gr. -1-1). pap. 3.99 *(978-0-689-87450-5(2)*, Simon Spotlight) Simon Spotlight.

—Eloise & the Very Secret Room, 1 vol. Lyon, Tammie, illus. 2016. (ENG.). 32p. (J). ***(978-1-61479-403-5(0))*** Spotlight.

White, Ruth. The Treasure of Way down Deep. 2013. (ENG.). 176p. (J). (gr. 5-9). 16.99 *(978-0-374-38067-0(8)*, 9780374380670, Farrar, Straus & Giroux (BYR)) Farrar, Straus & Giroux.

Whitney, A. D. T. Sights & Insights: Patience Strong's Story of over the Way. Vol. 1. 2006. 356p. per. 26.99 *(978-1-4255-3625-1(5))* Michigan Publishing.

—Sights & Insights: Patience Strong's Story of over the Way. Vol. 2. 2006. 344p. per. 23.99 *(978-1-4255-3480-6(5))* Michigan Publishing.

Young, Suzanne. Hotel for the Lost. 2016. (ENG., Illus.). 304p. (YA). (gr. 9). pap. 10.99 *(978-1-4814-2301-4(0)*, Simon Pulse) Simon Pulse.

—Hotel Ruby. 2015. (ENG., Illus.). 288p. (YA). (gr. 9). 17.99 *(978-1-4814-2300-7(2)*, Simon Pulse) Simon Pulse.

HOUDINI, HARRY, 1874-1926

Adler, David A. & Adler, Michael S. A Picture Book of Harry Houdini. Matt, Collins, illus. 2010. (ENG.). 32p. (J). (gr. -1-3). pap. 7.99 *(978-0-8234-2302-6(6))* Holiday Hse., Inc.

—A Picture Book of Harry Houdini. Collins, Matt, illus. 2009. (ENG.). 32p. (J). (gr. -1-3). 17.95 *(978-0-8234-2059-9(0))* Holiday Hse., Inc.

Biskup, Agnieszka. Houdini: The Life of the Great Escape Artist, 1 vol. Kinsella, Pat, illus. 2011. (American Graphic Ser.). (ENG.). 32p. (gr. 3-4). pap. 8.10 *(978-1-4296-6268-0(9))*; pap. 47.70 *(978-1-4296-6435-6(5))* Capstone Press of Coughlan Cos. (Graphic Library).

Carlson, Laurie M. Harry Houdini for Kids: His Life & Adventures with 21 Magic Tricks & Illusions. 2009. (For Kids Ser.). (ENG., Illus.). 144p. (J). (gr. 4-7). pap. 18.95 *(978-1-55652-782-1(9))* Chicago Review Pr., Inc.

Cobb, Vicki & Dorling Kindersley Publishing Staff. Harry Houdini: A Photographic Story of a Life. 2005. (DK Biography Ser.). (ENG., Illus.). 128p. (J). (gr. 5-12). pap. 6.99 *(978-0-7566-1245-0(4)*, DK Children) Dorling Kindersley Publishing, Inc.

Fleischman, Sid. Escape! The Story of the Great Houdini. (Illus.). (J). 2008. (ENG.). 240p. (gr. 3-7). pap. 8.99 *(978-0-06-085096-8(5)*, Greenwillow Bks.) 2006. (ENG., 224p. (gr. 3-7). 19.99 *(978-0-06-085094-4(9)*, Greenwillow Bks.) 2006. 210p. (gr. 4-8). lib. bdg. 19.89 *(978-0-06-085095-1(7))* HarperCollins Pubs.

Kimmel, Eric A. A Spotlight for Harry. Madsen, Jim, illus. 2010. (Stepping Stone Book Ser.). (ENG.). 112p. (J). (gr. 2-5). pap. 4.99 *(978-0-375-85696-9(X)*, Random Hse. Bks. for Young Readers) Random Hse. Children's Bks.

Kraske, Robert. Harry Houdini. 2015. 72p. pap. 7.00 *(978-1-61003-493-7(7))* Center for the Collaborative Classroom.

MacLeod, Elizabeth. Harry Houdini. Mantha, John, illus. 2009. (Kids Can Read Ser.). (ENG.). 32p. (J). (gr. 1-3). 3.95 *(978-1-55453-299-5(X))*; 14.95 *(978-1-55453-298-8(1))* Kids Can Pr., Ltd. CAN. Dist: Hachette Bk. Group.

—Harry Houdini: A Magical Life. 2005. (Snapshots: Images of People & Places in History Ser.). (ENG., Illus.). 32p. (J). (gr. 3-7). 6.95 *(978-1-55337-770-2(2))* Kids Can Pr., Ltd. CAN. Dist: Hachette Bk. Group.

Piehl, Janet. Harry Houdini. 2009. (History Maker Biographies Ser.). (gr. 3-6). 26.60 *(978-1-58013-705-8(9)*, Lerner Pubns.) Lerner Publishing Group.

Saddleback Educational Publishing Staff, ed. Houdini, 1 vol. unabr. ed. 2008. (Graphic Biographies Ser.). (ENG., Illus.). 25p. (YA). (gr. 9-12). pap. 7.95 *(978-1-59905-224-3(5))* Saddleback Educational Publishing, Inc.

Weaver, Janice. Harry Houdini: The Legend of the World's Greatest Escape Artist. Lane, Chris, illus. 2011. (ENG.). 48p. (J). (gr. 3-7). 18.95 *(978-1-4197-0014-9(6)*, Abrams Bks. for Young Readers) Abrams, Inc.

HOUSE-BOATS

see Houseboats

HOUSE CLEANING

Bensinger, Lou. Tiny Invaders in Your Home. 2010. (Tiny Invaders Ser.). (Illus.). 24p. (J). pap. 8.25 *(978-1-4358-9846-2(X)*, PowerKids Pr.) Rosen Publishing Group, Inc., The.

Berry, Joy. Clean Your Room. 2009. (Fun & Easy Way Ser.). (ENG.). 52p. (J). (gr. 1-5). pap. 7.95 *(978-1-60577-312-4(3))* Berry, Joy Enterprises.

Burton, Margie, et al. Cleaning My Room. 2011. (Early Connections Ser.). (J). *(978-1-61672-483-2(8))* Benchmark Education Co.

Nelson, Robin. How I Clean My Room. 2014. (First Step Nonfiction - Responsibility in Action Ser.). (ENG., Illus.). 24p. (gr. k-2). lib. bdg. 23.93 *(978-1-4677-3634-3(1)*, Lerner Pubns.) Lerner Publishing Group.

Swain, Gwenyth. Tidy Up! 2011. (Small World Ser.). (Illus.). 24p. bds. *(978-1-84089-676-3(0))* Zero to Ten, Ltd.

Uboh, Victoria. Let's Clean My Room !! 2005. 28p. per. 19.99 *(978-1-4208-8585-9(5))* AuthorHouse.

HOUSE DECORATION

see Interior Decoration

HOUSE FLIES

see Flies

HOUSE FURNISHINGS

see Interior Decoration

HOUSE PAINTING

La Bella, Laura. Careers in Painting & Wall Covering, 01 vols., 1. 2016. (Essential Careers Ser.). (ENG.). 80p. (J). 34.25 *(978-1-4994-6219-7(0)*, Rosen Young Adult) Rosen Publishing Group, Inc., The.

HOUSE REPAIRING

see Houses—Repairing

HOUSEBOATS

Smith, Sian. Homes That Move, 1 vol. 2013. (Where We Live Ser.). (ENG.). 24p. (gr. -1-1). pap. 6.95 *(978-1-4329-8072-6(6)*, Acorn) Heinemann-Raintree.

HOUSEBOATS—FICTION

Dunn, Joeming & Dunn, Ben, illus. Houseboat Mystery. 2011. (Boxcar Children Graphic Novels Ser.: 16). (ENG.). 32p. (J). (gr. 1-5). pap. 6.99 *(978-0-8075-3395-6(5))* Whitman, Albert & Co.

Harper, Suzanne. A Mischief of Mermaids. 2013. (Unseen World of Poppy Malone Ser.: 3). (ENG.). 288p. (J). (gr. 3-7). 16.99 *(978-0-06-199613-9(0)*, Greenwillow Bks.) HarperCollins Pubs.

Kessler, Liz. The Tail of Emily Windsnap. Gibb, Sarah, illus. 2012. (Emily Windsnap Ser.: 1). (ENG.). 224p. (J). (gr. 3-7). pap. 5.99 *(978-0-7636-6020-8(5))* Candlewick Pr.

—The Tail of Emily Windsnap. 2012. (Emily Windsnap Ser.: 1). lib. bdg. 16.00 *(978-0-606-25544-8(3)*, Turtleback) Turtleback Bks.

Rathborne, St. George. The House Boat Boys; or, Drifting down to the Sunny South. 2007. 108p. per. *(978-1-4068-3747-6(4))* Echo Library.

Walden, Walter. Boy Scouts Afloat. 2005. (Illus.). pap. 27.95 *(978-1-885529-48-0(1))* Stevens Publishing.

Winfield, Arthur M. The Rover Boys on the River. 2007. 248p. 26.95 *(978-1-4218-4139-7(8))*; per. 11.95 *(978-1-4218-4237-0(8))* 1st World Publishing, Inc. (1st World Library - Literary Society).

—The Rover Boys on the River or the Search for the Missing. 2006. (ENG.). 272p. per. 27.95 *(978-1-4286-4115-0(7))* Kessinger Publishing, LLC.

HOUSEHOLD APPLIANCES

see Household Equipment and Supplies

HOUSEHOLD APPLIANCES, ELECTRIC

How things Work: Level Q, 6 vols., Vol. 3. (Explorers Ser.). 32p. (gr. 3-6). 44.95 *(978-0-7699-0620-1(6))* Shortland Pubns. (U. S. A.) Inc.

Jan's New Fan: KinderReaders Individual Title, 6 Packs. (Kinderstarters Ser.). 8p. (gr. -1-1). 21.00 *(978-0-7635-8666-9(8))* Rigby Education.

Kachur, Matthew. Our Current World & Nuestro mundo Eléctrico: 6 English, 6 Spanish Adaptations. 2011. (ENG & SPA.). (J). 89.00 net. *(978-1-4108-5680-7(1))* Benchmark Education Co.

McGough, Roger. Until I Met Dudley: How Everyday Things Really Work. Riddell, Chris, illus. 2012. (ENG.). 32p. (J). (gr. -1-2). pap. 8.99 *(978-1-84780-350-4(4)*, Frances Lincoln) Quarto Publishing Group UK GBR. Dist: Hachette Bk. Group.

Rigby Education Staff. Fans. (Illus.). 8p. (J). bds. 3.95 *(978-0-7635-6492-6(3)*, 764923C99) Rigby Education.

HOUSEHOLD BUDGET

see Home Economics—Accounting

HOUSEHOLD EMPLOYEES—FICTION

Angleberger, Tom. Horton Halfpott: Or, the Fiendish Mystery of Smugwick Manor - Or, the Loosening of M'Lady Luggertuck's Corset. (ENG., Illus.). (J). (gr. 3-7). 2012. 240p. pap. 7.99 *(978-1-4197-0169-6(X))* 2011. 224p. 16.95 *(978-0-8109-9715-8(0))* Abrams, Inc. (Amulet Bks.).

Auxier, Jonathan. The Night Gardener. (ENG.). (YA). (gr. 3-7). 2015. 384p. pap. 8.95 *(978-1-4197-1531-0(3))* 2014. 368p. 16.95 *(978-1-4197-1144-2(X))* Abrams, Inc. (Amulet Bks.).

—The Night Gardener. 2015. (J). lib. bdg. 19.60 *(978-0-606-36891-9(4))* Turtleback Bks.

Barbieri, Gladys. A Charmed Life / una Vida con Suerte. Field, Lisa, illus. 2016. (MUL, ENG & SPA.). 32p. (J). (gr. k-3). 17.95 *(978-1-55885-827-5(X)*, Piñata Books) Arte Publico Pr.

Bradbury, Jennifer. A Moment Comes. 2013. (ENG., Illus.). 288p. (YA). (gr. 7). 17.99 *(978-1-4169-7876-3(3))* Simon & Schuster Children's Publishing.

Buckey, Sarah Masters. Clue in the Castle Tower: A Samantha Mystery. Ross, Peg, ed. Giovine, Sergio, illus. 2011. (ENG.). 184p. (YA). (gr. 4-18). pap. 6.95 *(978-1-59369-752-5(X))* American Girl Publishing, Inc.

Budhos, Marina. Tell Us We're Home. 2011. (ENG.). 320p. (YA). (gr. 7). pap. 9.99 *(978-1-4424-2128-8(2)*, Atheneum Bks. for Young Readers) Simon & Schuster Children's Publishing.

Cann, Kate. Consumed. (ENG.). 336p. (J). (gr. 9). 2012. pap. 9.99 *(978-0-545-26387-0(5))* 2011. 16.99 *(978-0-545-26388-7(3))* Scholastic, Inc.

—Possessed. (ENG.). 336p. (J). (gr. 9-9). 2011. pap. 9.99 *(978-0-545-12813-1(7))* 2010. 16.99 *(978-0-545-12812-4(9))* Scholastic, Inc.

Coats, J. Anderson. The Wicked & the Just. 2013. (ENG.). 352p. (YA). (gr. 7). pap. 9.99 *(978-0-544-02221-8(1))* Houghton Mifflin Harcourt Publishing Co.

Dunkle, Clare B. The House of Dead Maids. Arrasmith, Patrick, illus. 2011. (ENG.). 176p. (YA). (gr. 7-12). pap. 16.99 *(978-0-312-55155-1(X)*, 9780312551551) Square Fish.

Enderle, Dotti. Grow a Ghost!, 1 vol. McWilliam, Howard, illus. 2016. (ENG.). 80p. (J). *(978-1-62402-100-8(X))* Magic Wagon.

Fitzgerald, Laura Marx. The Gallery. 2016. (ENG.). 336p. (J). (gr. 5-7). 16.99 *(978-0-525-42865-7(8)*, Dial Bks) Penguin Young Readers Group.

Glines, Abbi. Breathe. 2013. (Sea Breeze Ser.). (ENG., Illus.). 352p. (YA). (gr. 11). 17.99 *(978-1-4424-8870-0(0))*; pap. 9.99 *(978-1-4424-8869-4(7))* Simon Pulse. (Simon Pulse).

—Breathe. 2011. 166p. (gr. 8-12). pap. 9.99 *(978-1-61798-004-6(8))* Wild Child Publishing.

Hale, Marian. The Goodbye Season. 2009. (ENG.). 288p. (YA). (gr. 7-12). 16.99 *(978-0-8050-8855-7(5)*, 9780805088557, Holt, Henry & Co. Bks. For Young Readers) Holt, Henry & Co.

Harlow, Joan Hiatt. Midnight Rider. 2006. (ENG.). 384p. (J). (gr. 4-9). pap. 8.99 *(978-0-689-87010-1(8)*, McElderry, Margaret K. Bks.) McElderry, Margaret K. Bks.

Hooper, Mary. Newes from the Dead. 2010. (ENG., Illus.). 272p. (YA). (gr. 9-13). pap. 16.99 *(978-0-312-60864-4(0)*, 9780312608644) Square Fish.

Hughes, Shirley. Daisy Saves the Day. Hughes, Shirley, illus. 2015. (ENG., Illus.). 32p. (J). (gr. k-4). 16.99 *(978-0-7636-7323-9(4))* Candlewick Pr.

Kimmel, Eric A. The Golem's Latkes, 0 vols. Jasinski, Aaron, illus. 2011. (ENG.). 40p. (J). (gr. k-3). 17.99 *(978-0-7614-5904-0(9)*, 9780761459040, Amazon Children's Publishing) Amazon Publishing.

Kraegel, Kenneth. The Song of Delphine. Kraegel, Kenneth, illus. 2015. (ENG., Illus.). 40p. (J). (gr. k-3). 15.99 *(978-0-7636-7001-6(4))* Candlewick Pr.

Lasky, Kathryn. Hannah. 2011. (Daughters of the Sea Ser.: 1). (ENG.). 320p. (J). (gr. 7-7). pap. 9.99 *(978-0-545-23803-8(X))* Scholastic, Inc.

Lee, Y. S. Rivals in the City. 2015. (Agency Ser.). (ENG.). 304p. (YA). (gr. 7). 16.99 *(978-0-7636-5914-1(2))* Candlewick Pr.

—The Traitor in the Tunnel. 2012. (Agency Ser.: 3). (ENG., Illus.). 384p. (YA). (gr. 7). 16.99 *(978-0-7636-5316-3(0))* Candlewick Pr.

Levine, Phyllis. Matilda. 2007. (ENG.). 108p. per. 12.95 *(978-1-60047-079-0(3))* Wasteland Pr.

Lewis, Ali. Timber Creek Station. 2016. (ENG.). 240p. (YA). (gr. 6-12). 18.99 *(978-1-4677-8117-6(7))*; 35.99 *(978-1-4677-8816-8(3)*, Carolrhoda Lab™) Lerner Publishing Group.

Lois, Lowry. Anastasia Asusordenes. 2003. (Anastasia Krupnik Ser.).Tr. of Anastasia at Your Order. (SPA.). 120p. (J). 9.95 *(978-84-239-7073-5(6))* Espasa Calpe, S.A. ESP. Dist: Planeta Publishing Corp.

—Anastasia at Your Service. (Anastasia Krupnik Ser.). 149p. (J). (gr. 4-6). pap. 3.99 *(978-0-8072-1409-1(4)*, Listening Library) Random Hse. Audio Publishing Group.

MacColl, Michaela & Chronicle Books Staff. A Novel of Intrigue & Romance. 2010. (ENG., Illus.). 368p. (YA). (gr. 7-17). 16.99 *(978-0-8118-7300-0(5))* Chronicle Bks. LLC.

Mariconda, Barbara. Lucy at Sea. 2013. (Voyage of Lucy P. Simmons Ser.: 2). (ENG.). 320p. (J). (gr. 3-7). 16.99 *(978-0-06-211993-3(1)*, Tegen, Katherine Bks) HarperCollins Pubs.

—The Voyage of Lucy P. Simmons. 2074. (ENG.). 256p. (J). (gr. 3-7). 6.99 *(978-0-06-211980-3(X)*, Tegen, Katherine Bks) HarperCollins Pubs.

Milord, Susan. The Ghost on the Hearth. Dabcovich, Lydia, illus. 2003. (Vermont Folklife Center Children's Book Ser.). (ENG.). 32p. (J). (gr. -1-3). 15.95 *(978-0-916718-18-3(2))* Vermont Folklife Ctr.

Murdock, Catherine Gilbert. Wisdom's Kiss. 2013. (ENG.). 320p. (YA). (gr. 7). pap. 8.99 *(978-0-547-85540-0(0))* Houghton Mifflin Harcourt Publishing Co.

—Wisdom's Kiss: A Thrilling & Romantic Adventure, Incorporating Magic, Villany, & a Cat. 2011. (ENG.). 304p. (YA). (gr. 7). 16.99 *(978-0-547-56687-0(5))* Houghton Mifflin Harcourt Publishing Co.

Parish, Herman. Amelia Bedelia Chapter Book #10: Amelia Bedelia Ties the Knot. Avril, Lynne, illus. 2016. (Amelia Bedelia Ser.). 160p. (J). (gr. 1-5). pap. 4.99 *(978-0-06-233416-9(6)*, Greenwillow Bks.) HarperCollins Pubs.

—Amelia Bedelia, Cub Reporter. Sweat, Lynn, illus. 2012. (I Can Read Level 2 Ser.). (ENG.). 64p. (J). (gr. -1-3). 16.99 *(978-0-06-209510-7(2))*; pap. 3.99 *(978-0-06-209509-1(9))* HarperCollins Pubs. (Greenwillow Bks.).

—Amelia Bedelia Talks Turkey. Sweat, Lynn, illus. 2008. (Amelia Bedelia Ser.). (ENG.). 64p. (J). (gr. k-4). 16.99 *(978-0-06-084352-6(7)*, Greenwillow Bks.) HarperCollins Pubs.

—Amelia Bedelia Talks Turkey. Parish, Herman & Sweat, Lynn, illus. 2008. (Amelia Bedelia Ser.). 64p. (J). (gr. k-4). lib. bdg. 17.89 *(978-0-06-084353-3(5)*, Greenwillow Bks.) HarperCollins Pubs.

—Calling Doctor Amelia Bedelia. Sweat, Lynn, illus. 2004. (I Can Read Level 2 Ser.). (ENG.). 64p. (J). (gr. k-3). pap. 3.99 *(978-0-06-008780-7(3)*, Greenwillow Bks.) HarperCollins Pubs.

—Calling Doctor Amelia Bedelia. Sweat, Lynn, illus. 2004. (Amelia Bedelia Ser.). 64p. (gr. -1-2). 14.00 *(978-0-7569-3209-1(2))* Perfection Learning Corp.

Parish, Peggy. Amelia Bedelia. Siebel, Fritz, illus. 50th ed. 2012. (I Can Read Level 2 Ser.). (ENG.). 64p. (J). (gr. k-3). pap. 3.99 *(978-0-06-444155-1(5)*, Greenwillow Bks.) HarperCollins Pubs.

—Amelia Bedelia. Siebel, Fritz, illus. 2012. (Amelia Bedelia: I Can Read! Ser.: 1). (J). (gr. 1-3). lib. bdg. 13.55 *(978-0-88103-916-0(0)*, Turtleback) Turtleback Bks.

—Amelia Bedelia & the Baby. Sweat, Lynn, illus. 2004. (I Can Read Level 2 Ser.). (ENG.). 64p. (J). (gr. k-3). pap. 3.99 *(978-0-06-051105-0(2)*, Greenwillow Bks.) HarperCollins Pubs.

—Amelia Bedelia Goes Camping. Sweat, Lynn, illus. 2003. (I Can Read Level 2 Ser.). (ENG.). 64p. (J). (gr. k-3). pap. 3.99 *(978-0-06-051106-7(0)*, Greenwillow Bks.) HarperCollins Pubs.

—Amelia Bedelia Goes Camping. 2003. (Amelia Bedelia: I Can Read! Ser.: 10). (J). (gr. k-3). lib. bdg. 13.55 *(978-0-613-62664-4(8)*, Turtleback) Turtleback Bks.

—Amelia Bedelia's Family Album. Sweat, Lynn, illus. 2003. (I Can Read Level 2 Ser.). (ENG.). 48p. (J). (gr. k-3). pap. 3.99 *(978-0-06-051116-6(8)*, Greenwillow Bks.) HarperCollins Pubs.

—Amelia Bedelia's Family Album. 2003. (Amelia Bedelia: I Can Read! Ser.: 12). (J). (gr. k-3). lib. bdg. 13.55 *(978-0-613-62129-8(8)*, Turtleback) Turtleback Bks.

—Good Work, Amelia Bedelia. Sweat, Lynn, illus. 2003. (I Can Read Level 2 Ser.). (ENG.). 64p. (J). (gr. k-3). pap. 3.99 *(978-0-06-051115-9(X)*, Greenwillow Bks.) HarperCollins Pubs.

—Good Work, Amelia Bedelia. 2003. (Amelia Bedelia: I Can Read! Ser.: 6). (J). (gr. k-3). lib. bdg. 13.55 *(978-0-613-68343-2(9)*, Turtleback) Turtleback Bks.

Qamar, Amjed. Beneath My Mother's Feet. (ENG.). 208p. (YA). (gr. 7). 2011. pap. 10.99 *(978-1-4424-1451-8(0))* 2008. 16.99 *(978-1-4169-4728-8(0))* Simon & Schuster Children's Publishing. (Atheneum Bks. for Young Readers).

Rasheed, Leila. Diamonds & Deceit. 2014. (At Somerton Ser.). (ENG.). 432p. (YA). (gr. 7-12). 17.99 *(978-1-4231-7118-8(7))* Hyperion Bks. for Children.

Rothenberger, Suzanne. Mattie: Life at Paddock Mansion. 2013. 136p. pap. 9.95 *(978-0-9890509-4-4(7))* Garland City Bks. of Watertown.

Sharafeddine, Fatima. The Servant, 1 vol. 2017. (ENG.). 160p. (J). (gr. 6). pap. 9.95 *(978-1-55498-308-7(8))* Groundwood Bks. CAN. Dist: Publishers Group West (PGW).

Skye, obert. Pillage. (YA). 2010. (Pillage Ser.: 1). (ENG.). 320p. (gr. 7). mass mkt. 7.99 *(978-1-60641-680-8(4))* 2008. (Illus.). 352p. 17.95 *(978-1-59038-922-5(0))* Shadow Mountain Publishing. (Shadow Mountain).

Stevermer, Caroline. Magic below Stairs. 2011. (ENG.). 208p. (J). (gr. 3-7). 6.99 *(978-0-14-241871-0(4)*, Puffin Books) Penguin Young Readers Group.

Stuber, Barbara. Crossing the Tracks. (ENG.). 272p. (YA). (gr. 7). 2011. pap. 8.99 *(978-1-4169-9704-7(0))* 2010. 16.99 *(978-1-4169-9703-0(2))* McElderry, Margaret K. Bks. (McElderry, Margaret K. Bks.).

Sullivan, Laura L. Love by the Morning Star. 2014. (ENG.). 320p. (YA). (gr. 7-12). 17.99 *(978-0-547-68951-7(9)*, HMH Books For Young Readers) Houghton Mifflin Harcourt Publishing Co.

Umansky, Kaye. Clover Twig & the Perilous Path. Wright, Johanna, illus. 2013. (ENG.). 272p. (J). (gr. 3-7). pap. 7.99 *(978-1-250-02727-6(6)*, 9781250027276) Square Fish.

Warburton, Carol. Edge of Night: A Novel. 2004. (Illus.). 278p. pap. 14.95 *(978-1-59156-013-5(6))* Covenant Communications, Inc.

Webb, Holly. Rose. 2013. (Rose Ser.: 1). (ENG.). 240p. (J). (gr. 3-6). pap. 6.99 *(978-1-4022-8581-3(7)*, 9781402285813, Sourcebooks Jabberwocky) Sourcebooks, Inc.

Whitby, Adele. Camille's Story 1910. 2015. (Secrets of the Manor Ser.: 7). (ENG., Illus.). 160p. (J). (gr. 3-7). pap. 6.99 *(978-1-4814-3988-6(X)*, Simon Spotlight) Simon Spotlight.

Zahler, Diane. The Thirteenth Princess. 2011. (ENG.). 272p. (J). (gr. 3-7). pap. 6.99 *(978-0-06-182500-2(X))* HarperCollins Pubs.

HOUSEHOLD EQUIPMENT AND SUPPLIES

see also Household Appliances, Electric

Bidder, Jane. Inventions We Use at Home. 2006. (Everyday Inventions Ser.). (Illus.). 32p. (gr. 1-4). lib. bdg. 26.00 *(978-0-8368-6898-2(6)*, Gareth Stevens Learning Library) Stevens, Gareth Publishing LLLP.

Blaxland, Wendy. Knives & Forks. 2008. (How Are They Made? Ser.). 32p. (gr. 4-18). lib. bdg. 18.56 *(978-0-7614-3805-2(X)*, Benchmark Bks.) Marshall Cavendish Corp.

—Mugs & Plates. 2008. (How Are They Made? Ser.). 32p. (gr. 4-18). lib. bdg. 18.56 *(978-0-7614-3809-0(2)*, Benchmark Bks.) Marshall Cavendish Corp.

Boothroyd, Jennifer. From Washboards to Washing Machines: How Homes Have Changed. 2011. (Comparing Past & Present Ser.). pap. 45.32 *(978-0-7613-8394-9(8))*; pap. 7.95 *(978-0-7613-7839-6(1))*; (ENG., Illus.). 32p. lib. bdg. 26.60 *(978-0-7613-6747-5(0))* Lerner Publishing Group.

Eck, Kristin. Opuestas en mi Casa. 2009. (Board Books en Espanol Ser.). (SPA.). 16p. (gr. k-k). 23.90 *(978-1-61511-640-9(0)*, Editorial Buenas Letras) Rosen Publishing Group, Inc., The.

Humberstone, Eliot. Everyday Things. rev. ed. 2007. (Explainers Ser.). (Illus.). 95p. (J). (gr. 4-7). 14.99 *(978-0-7945-1808-0(7)*, Usborne) EDC Publishing.

Litchfield, Jo. Home. Litchfield, Jo & Allen, Francesca, illus. 2006. (Usborne Look & Say Ser.). 12p. (J). (gr. -1-k). bds. 7.99 *(978-0-7945-1425-9(1)*, Usborne) EDC Publishing.

Lunis, Natalie. Household Inventions: From Toilets to Toasters. 2006. (Which Came First? Ser.). (Illus.). 32p. (YA). (gr. 3-6). lib. bdg. 25.27 *(978-1-59716-131-2(4))* Bearport Publishing Co., Inc.

MacDonald, Margaret. Kitchen Machines. 2011. (Learn-Abouts: Level 10 Ser.). (Illus.). 16p. (J). pap. 7.95 *(978-1-59920-602-8(1))* Black Rabbit Bks.

Meachen Rau, Dana. Chefs. 2007. (Tools We Use Ser.). (Illus.). 32p. (gr. k-2). lib. bdg. 15.95 *(978-0-7614-2657-8(4)*, Benchmark Bks.) Marshall Cavendish Corp.

—Chefs/Los Chefs. 2007. (Tools We Use/Instrumentos de Trabajo Ser.). (SPA & ENG., Illus.). 32p. (gr. k-2). lib. bdg. 15.95 *(978-0-7614-2822-0(4)*, Benchmark Bks.) Marshall Cavendish Corp.

—Los Chefs. 2007. (Instrumentos de Trabajo Ser.). (SPA & ENG., Illus.). 32p. (gr. k-2). lib. bdg. 15.95 *(978-0-7614-2798-8(8)*, Benchmark Bks.) Marshall Cavendish Corp.

Our Homes. 2007. (J). *(978-1-933834-15-3(3))* Brown Bear Books.

Oxlade, Chris. Gadgets & Games, 1 vol. 2013. (Design & Engineering for STEM Ser.). (ENG., Illus.). 56p. (gr. 6-8). pap. 9.99 *(978-1-4329-7036-9(4)*, NA-h); lib. bdg. 34.65 *(978-1-4329-7031-4(3))* Heinemann-Raintree.

—Screws. 2009. (Simple Machines (Smart Apple Media Paperback) Ser.). (Illus.). 32p. (J). (gr. k-2). pap. 7.95 *(978-1-59920-202-0(6))* Black Rabbit Bks.

Rau, Dana Meachen. Chefs. 2007. (J). pap. 6.99 *(978-0-7614-3290-6(6))* Marshall Cavendish Corp.

Richards, Jon. In the Home. 2005. (How Things Have Changed Ser.). (Illus.). 32p. (J). (gr. 3-7). lib. bdg. 27.10 *(978-1-59389-198-5(9))* Chrysalis Education.

Ridley, Sarah. A Metal Can. 2006. (How It's Made Ser.). (Illus.). 32p. (gr. 1-4). lib. bdg. 26.00 *(978-0-8368-6702-2(5)*, Gareth Stevens Learning Library) Stevens, Gareth Publishing LLLP.

Thomas, Danita & Thomas, John E. The Ultimate Book of Holiday Kid Concoctions: More Than 50 Wacky, Wild, & Crazy Concoctions for All Occasions. 2006. (Ultimate Book of Kid Concoctions Ser.). (Illus.). 80p. (J). (gr. 4-7). per. 14.99 *(978-0-8054-4445-2(9))* B&H Publishing Group.

—The Ultimate Book of Kid Concoctions. 2006. (Illus.). 80p. (J). (gr. 4-7). per. 14.99 *(978-0-8054-4443-8(2))* B&H Publishing Group.

World Book, Inc Staff, contrib. by. Durable Goods. 2008. 64p. (J). *(978-0-7166-1408-1(1))* World Bk., Inc.

HOUSEHOLD EXPENSES

see Home Economics—Accounting

HOUSEHOLD MANAGEMENT

see Home Economics

HOUSEHOLD MOVING

see Moving, Household

HOUSEKEEPING

see Home Economics

HOUSES

Here are entered general works on houses.

see also Apartment Houses; Building; Building—Repair and Reconstruction

Anderson, Judith. Looking at Settlements. 2007. (Geography Skills/Watts Ser.). (Illus.). 46p. (J). (gr. 4-7). lib. bdg. 32.80 *(978-1-59920-052-1(X))* Black Rabbit Bks.

Awa, Solomon. Igluvigaliurniq Qamusiurnirlu: How to Build an Iglu & a Qamutiik, 1 vol. Breithaupt, Andrew, illus. 2013. (ENG.). 32p. (J). (gr. 3-6). 9.95 *(978-1-927095-31-7(X))* Inhabit Media Inc. CAN. Dist: Independent Pubs. Group.

Barber, Nicola. Homes Around the World. 2007. (ENG., Illus.). 32p. (J). *(978-0-7787-3541-0(9))* Crabtree Publishing Co.

—Homes on the Move. 2007. (Homes Around the World Ser.). (ENG., Illus.). 32p. (J). (gr. 4-7). pap. *(978-0-7787-3556-4(7))* Crabtree Publishing Co.

—Homes on the Water. 2007. (Homes Around the World Ser.). (ENG., Illus.). 32p. (J). (gr. 3-7). pap. *(978-0-7787-3559-5(1))* Crabtree Publishing Co.

—Island Homes. 2007. (Homes Around the World Ser.). (ENG., Illus.). 32p. (J). (gr. 4-7). pap. *(978-0-7787-3555-7(9))*; lib. bdg. *(978-0-7787-3543-4(5))* Crabtree Publishing Co.

—Mountain Homes. 2007. (Homes Around the World Ser.). (ENG., Illus.). 32p. (J). (gr. 3-7). pap. *(978-0-7787-3557-1(5))*; lib. bdg. *(978-0-7787-3545-8(1))* Crabtree Publishing Co.

—Village Homes. 2007. (Homes Around the World Ser.). (ENG., Illus.). 32p. (J). (gr. 3-7). pap. *(978-0-7787-3558-8(3))*; lib. bdg. *(978-0-7787-3546-5(X))* Crabtree Publishing Co.

Bass, Hester Thompson. So Many Houses. Arzoumanian, Alik, illus. 2007. (Rookie Reader Repetitive Text Ser.). 32p. (gr. k-2). 14.95 *(978-0-7569-8049-8(6))* Perfection Learning Corp.

Berendes, Mary. House/la Casa. Petelinsek, Kathleen, illus. 2008. (WordBooks/Libros de Palabras Ser.). (SPA & ENG.). 24p. (J). (gr. k-3). 25.64 *(978-1-59296-992-0(5)*, 201094) Child's World, Inc., The.

Bloomsbury USA. Baby's First Words: Home. 2016. (ENG., Illus.). 10p. (J). (— 1). bds. 5.99 *(978-1-61963-824-2(X)*, 9781619638242, Bloomsbury Activity Bks.) Bloomsbury Publishing USA.

Bowers, Jenny. Sticker Style: House. Bowers, Jenny, illus. 2015. (ENG., Illus.). 12p. (J). (gr. k-3). pap. 12.99 *(978-0-7636-7983-5(6)*, Big Picture Press) Candlewick Pr.

Bozzo, Linda & Library. Houses of the Past, Present, & Future. 2010. (Imagining the Future Ser.). (Illus.). 24p. (J). lib. bdg. 22.60 *(978-0-7660-3433-4(X)*, Enslow Elementary) Enslow Pubs., Inc.

Brooks, F. & Litchfield, J. En Casa. 2004.Tr. of At Home. (SPA., Illus.). 10p. (J). 4.95 *(978-0-7460-4825-2(4))* EDC Publishing.

Bullard, Lisa. My Home, Your Home. Becker, Paula, illus. 2015. (Cloverleaf Books (tm) — Alike & Different Ser.). (ENG.). 24p. (gr. k-2). pap. 6.99 *(978-1-4677-6032-4(3)*, Millbrook Pr.) Lerner Publishing Group.

Burton, Margie, et al. Homes Around the World. 2011. (Early Connections Ser.). (J). *(978-1-61672-293-7(2))* Benchmark Education Co.

Butterfield, Moira. Homes Around the World. 2016. (Children Like Us Ser.). (ENG.). 32p. (J). (gr. 3-3). pap. 10.58 *(978-1-5026-0842-0(1))* Cavendish Square Publishing.

Cane, Ella. Homes in My World, 1 vol. 2013. (My World Ser.). (ENG.). 24p. (gr. k-1). 21.99 *(978-1-4765-3118-2(8))*; pap. 6.95 *(978-1-4765-3460-2(8))* Capstone Press of Coughlan Cos. (Pebble Bks.).

Carle, Eric. My Very First Book of Animal Homes. Carle, Eric, illus. 2007. (ENG., Illus.). 20p. (J). (gr. -1 — 1). bds. 5.99 *(978-0-399-24647-0(9)*, Philomel Bks.) Penguin Young Readers Group.

Chastain, Zachary. Home Sweet Home: Around the House in the 1800s. 2009. (Daily Life in America in the 1800s Ser.). 64p. (YA). (gr. 7-18). pap. 9.95 *(978-1-4222-1854-9(6))*; lib. bdg. 22.95 *(978-1-4222-1781-8(7))* Mason Crest.

Crabtree, Marc. Meet My Neighbor, the Builder. 2009. (Meet my Neighbor Ser.). (ENG., Illus.). 24p. (J). (gr. k-2). lib. bdg. *(978-0-7787-4570-9(8))* Crabtree Publishing Co.

Diemer, Lauren. Igloos. 2010. (Illus.). 24p. *(978-1-77071-578-3(9))*; pap. *(978-1-77071-585-1(1))* Weigl Educational Pubs. Ltd.

Emberley, Rebecca. My Room/Mi Cuarto. 2005. (SPA & ENG., Illus.). 10p. (J). (gr. -1 — 1). bds. 6.99 *(978-0-316-00052-9(3))* Little, Brown Bks. for Young Readers.

Gaarder-Juntti, Oona. What in the World Is a Green Home?, 1 vol. 2010. (Super SandCastle Ser.). (ENG., Illus.). 24p. 25.65 *(978-1-61613-189-0(6)*, 1315120, Super SandCastle) ABDO Publishing Co.

Gallagher, Debbie. Family Homes. 2008. (Families Ser.). 32p. (gr. 1-2). lib. bdg. 18.56 *(978-0-7614-3136-7(5)*, Benchmark Bks.) Marshall Cavendish Corp.

Gillis, Jennifer Blizin. Hogares para Todos/Homes for Everyone. Alemián, Manuel, tr. 2006. (My Neighborhood Discovery Library). (SPA & ENG., Illus.). 24p. (J). (gr. 3-7). lib. bdg. 22.79 *(978-1-60044-290-2(0))* Rourke Educational Media.

Giulieri, Anne. The Secret Tree House, 1 vol. Boyer, Susy, illus. 2012. (Engage Literacy Green Ser.). (ENG.). 32p. (gr. k-2). pap. 5.99 *(978-1-4296-8999-1(4)*, Engage Literacy) Capstone Press of Coughlan Cos.

Gordon, Sharon. At Home (Mi Casa), 6 bks., Set. Incl. At Home by the Ocean/Mi Casa Junto Al Mar. lib. bdg. 15.95 *(978-0-7614-2456-7(3))*; At Home in the City/Mi Casa en la Ciudad. lib. bdg. 15.95 *(978-0-7614-2452-9(0))*; At Home in the Desert/Mi Casa en el Desierto. lib. bdg. 15.95 *(978-0-7614-2453-6(9))*; At Home on the Farm/Mi Casa en la Granja. lib. bdg. 15.95 *(978-0-7614-2454-3(7))*; At Home on the Mountain/Mi Casa en la Montana. lib. bdg. 15.95 *(978-0-7614-2455-0(5))*; At Home on the Ranch/Mi Casa en el Rancho. lib. bdg. 15.95 *(978-0-7614-2458-1(X))*; (Illus.). 32p. (gr. k-2). (Bookworms — Bilingual Editions: at Home/Mi Casa Ser.). (ENG & SPA.). 2006. Set lib. bdg. 95.70 *(978-0-7614-2451-2(2))* Marshall Cavendish Corp.

Gosman, Gillian. Simple Machines in Your Home. 2014. (Simple Machines Everywhere Ser.). 24p. (J). (gr. k-3). pap. 49.50 *(978-1-4777-6644-6(8)*, PowerKids Pr.) Rosen Publishing Group, Inc., The.

Grant, Donald, et al. La Casa. (SPA., Illus.). 40p. (J). *(978-84-348-3728-7(5)*, CA9913) SM Ediciones.

Gregory, Cam. Who Lives Here? 2014. (Little Books of Answers: Level a Ser.). (Illus.). 16p. (gr. k-2). pap. 7.95 *(978-1-927136-01-0(6))* Three Crows Media NZL. Dist: RiverStream Publishing.

Gregory, Helen. All about Homes. 2011. (Wonder Readers Early Level Ser.). (ENG.). 16p. (gr. -1-1). pap. 35.94 *(978-1-4296-8066-0(0)*, Wonder Readers) Capstone Press of Coughlan Cos.

Guin, Valerie. Where We Live. 2005. (One World (Smart Apple Media) Ser.). (Illus.). 30p. (J). (gr. 3-6). lib. bdg. 27.10 *(978-1-58340-698-4(0))* Black Rabbit Bks.

Gustafson, Angela. Imagine a House: A Journey to Fascinating Houses Around the World. 2003. (What a World We Live in Ser.). (Illus.). 32p. (J). (gr. k-6). lib. bdg. 16.95 *(978-0-9726849-0-3(5))* Out of the Box.

Hardyman, Robyn. How a Solar-Powered Home Works. 2013. (EcoWorks Ser.). 32p. (J). (gr. 3-5). pap. 10.50 *(978-1-4339-9549-1(2),* Gareth Stevens Learning Library); pap. 63.00 *(978-1-4339-9550-7(6));* (ENG., Illus.). lib. bdg. 26.60 *(978-1-4339-9548-4(4))* Stevens, Gareth Publishing LLLP.

Hemmel, David. Living in the Key West Style Anywhere: A Complete Guide to Planning a Home in the Charming Key West Style. 2004. (Illus.). 144p. per. 24.95 *(978-0-9745637-0-1(6))* Duval Publishing.

Herrington, Lisa M. Totally Strange Buildings. 2017. (Rookie Amazing America(tm) Ser.). (ENG., Illus.). 32p. (J). pap. 5.95 *(978-0-531-22591-2(7),* Children's Pr.) Scholastic Library Publishing.

Hewitt, Sally. Homes. 2010. (Starting Geography Ser.). 32p. (J). (gr. 2-5). 28.50 *(978-1-60753-125-8(9))* Amicus Publishing.

Hicks, Kelli. What Happens When You Flush? 2014. (ENG.). 24p. (gr. k-3). 28.50 *(978-1-62717-648-4(9))* Rourke Educational Media.

Home: A Memoir of My Early Years. (Butterfly Bks.). (ARA., Illus.). 15p. (J). 11.95 *(978-0-86685-615-7(3),* LDL6153) International Bk. Ctr., Inc.

Houses: Individual Title Six-Packs. (gr. 1-2). 22.00 *(978-0-7635-9161-8(0))* Rigby Education.

Houses: KinderFacts Individual Title Six-Packs. (Kinderstarters Ser.). 8p. (gr. -1-1). 21.00 *(978-0-7635-8745-1(1))* Rigby Education.

James, Lincoln. Native American Homes. 2009. (Real Life Readers Ser.). 24p. (gr. 3-4). pap. 8.25 *(978-1-4358-0127-1(X),* Rosen Classroom) Rosen Publishing Group, Inc., The.

Jensen, Patricia. My House. Becker, Wayne, illus. 2003. (My First Reader Ser.). (ENG.). 32p. (J). 18.50 *(978-0-516-22934-8(6),* Children's Pr.) Scholastic Library Publishing.

Jones, Rob Lloyd. See Inside Houses Long Ago. 2010. (See Inside Board Bks.). 16p. (J). (gr. 2). bds. 12.99 *(978-0-7945-2815-7(5),* Usborne) EDC Publishing.

Kalman, Bobbie. Esta Es Mi Casa. 2010. (SPA & ENG.). 16p. (J). pap. *(978-0-7787-8586-6(6));* lib. bdg. *(978-0-7787-8560-6(2))* Crabtree Publishing Co.

Kane, Barry & Kane, Tracy. Fairy Houses ... Everywhere! 2006. (Fairy Houses Ser.). (ENG., Illus.). 56p. (J). (gr. -1-k). 14.95 *(978-0-9708104-4-1(X))* Light-Beams Publishing.

Kreger, Claire. Homes: From Start to Finish. Carney, Patrick, illus. Carney, Patrick, photos by. 2003. 32p. (J). 24.95 *(978-1-4103-0169-7(9),* Blackbirch Pr., Inc.) Cengage Gale.

Lacey, Saskia. How to Build a House: A Colossal Adventure of Construction, Teamwork, & Friendship. Sodomka, Martin, illus. 2016. (Technical Tales Ser.). (ENG.). 64p. (J). (gr. 1-3). 14.95 *(978-1-63322-141-3(5),* Walter Foster Jr) Quarto Publishing Group USA.

Laroche, Giles. If You Lived Here: Houses of the World. 2011. (ENG., Illus.). 32p. (J). (gr. 1-4). 17.99 *(978-0-547-23892-0(4))* Houghton Mifflin Harcourt Publishing Co.

Laval, Thierry. Look & Find at Home. 2017. (Mini Look & Find Ser.). (ENG.). 14p. (J). 9.95 ***(978-0-531-23082-4(1),*** Children's Pr.) Scholastic Library Publishing.

Lawrence, Ellen. Building with Poop. 2017. (Scoop on Poop Ser.). (ENG.). (J). (gr. -1-3). lib. bdg. 17.95 ***(978-1-68402-247-2(9))*** Bearport Publishing Co., Inc.

Lennon, Liz. What I Like - Where I Live. 2017. (Little Stars Ser.). (ENG., Illus.). 24p. (J). (gr. -1-k). pap. 6.99 *(978-1-4451-4769-7(6),* Franklin Watts) Hachette Children's Group GBR. Dist: Hachette Bk. Group.

Lindeen, Mary. Where People Live, 1 vol. 2011. (Wonder Readers Fluent Level Ser.). (ENG.). 32p. (gr. -1-2). pap. 5.99 *(978-1-4296-7975-6(1),* Wonder Readers) Capstone Press of Coughlan Cos.

Loewen, Nancy & Skelley, Paula. Homes of the World. 2015. (Go Go Global Ser.). (ENG., Illus.). 32p. (gr. 1-2). lib. bdg. 27.32 *(978-1-4914-3919-7(X))* Capstone Press of Coughlan Cos.

MacDonald, Margaret. Homes of the Past. 2011. (Learn-Abouts Ser.). (Illus.). 16p. (J). pap. 7.95 *(978-1-59920-645-5(5))* Black Rabbit Bks.

—What Are Houses Made Of? 2011. (Learn-Abouts Ser.). (Illus.). 16p. (J). pap. 7.95 *(978-1-59920-620-2(X))* Black Rabbit Bks.

Manning, Jack. American Indian Homes, 1 vol. 2014. (American Indian Homes Ser.). (ENG.). 24p. (gr. 1-2). 101.28 *(978-1-4914-0326-6(8),* First Facts) Capstone Press of Coughlan Cos.

—Igloos, 1 vol. 2014. (American Indian Homes Ser.). (ENG.). 24p. (gr. 1-2). lib. bdg. 25.32 *(978-1-4914-0314-3(4))* Capstone Press of Coughlan Cos.

McCormick, Rosie. Homes. 2003. (Starters Ser.). 24p. (J). lib. bdg. 21.35 *(978-1-58340-261-0(6))* Black Rabbit Bks.

Michele, Tracey. From Plan to House. 2011. (Illus.). 16p. (J). pap. 7.95 *(978-1-59920-623-3(4))* Black Rabbit Bks.

Morgan, Sally. How We Use Plants for Shelter. 2009. (How We Use Plants Ser.). 32p. (gr. 2-5). pap. 10.60 *(978-1-4358-2612-0(4),* Rosen Classroom) Rosen Publishing Group, Inc., The.

Musselwhite, Helen. Little Houses: A Counting Book. 2015. (ENG., Illus.). 32p. (J). (gr. -1-k). 15.95 *(978-1-78067-613-5(1))* King, Laurence Publishing GBR. Dist: Hachette Bk. Group.

My House. 2003. (J). per. *(978-1-57657-175-0(0))* Paradise Pr., Inc.

Nelson, Maria. Gross Things in Your House. 2012. (That's Gross! Ser.). (Illus.). 24p. (J). (gr. 2-5). 22.60 *(978-1-4339-7123-5(2));* pap. 8.15 *(978-1-4339-7124-2(0))* Stevens, Gareth Publishing LLLP. (Gareth Stevens Learning Library).

Nelson, Robin. Where Is My Home? 2005. (First Step Nonfiction Ser.). (Illus.). 24p. (gr. k-2). lib. bdg. 17.27 *(978-0-8225-0189-3(9))* Lerner Publishing Group.

Nelson, Robin & National Geographic Learning Staff. Where Is My Home? 2012. (ENG.). 24p. (C). (gr. k-2). pap. 10.95 *(978-0-8225-1978-2(X))* National Geographic School Publishing, Inc.

Newhouse, Maxwell. The House That Max Built. 2008. (ENG., Illus.). 24p. (J). (gr. -1-1). 18.95 *(978-0-88776-774-6(5),* Tundra Bks.) Tundra Bks. CAN. Dist: Penguin Random Hse. LLC.

O'Connell, Eleanor. Homes Around the World. 2016. (Adventures in Culture Ser.). 00024p. (J). pap. 8.15 ***(978-1-4824-5586-1(2))*** Stevens, Gareth Publishing LLLP.

Petty, Kate. Homes. 2006. (World Show-And-Tell Ser.). (ENG., Illus.). 32p. (J). (gr. -1-1). 14.95 *(978-1-58728-547-9(9));* pap. 8.95 *(978-1-58728-548-6(7))* Cooper Square Publishing Llc.

Raum, Elizabeth. Homes: From Caves to Eco-Pods. 2010. (Timeline History Ser.). (ENG., Illus.). 32p. (gr. 3-5). 29.99 *(978-1-4329-3802-4(9),* NA-h) Heinemann-Raintree.

—The Scoop on Clothes, Homes, & Daily Life in Colonial America, 1 vol. 2011. (Life in the American Colonies Ser.). (ENG.). 32p. (gr. 3-4). 27.32 *(978-1-4296-6138-6(0),* Fact Finders) Capstone Press of Coughlan Cos.

Rice, Dona Herweck. Homes Around the World, 1 vol. 2nd rev. ed. 2014. (TIME for KIDS(r) Nonfiction Readers Ser.). (ENG., Illus.). 20p. (J). (gr. 1-1). pap. 19.96 *(978-1-4807-1031-3(8))* Shell Educational Publishing.

Rickards, Lynne. Houses & Homes Red Band. 2016. (Cambridge Reading Adventures Ser.). (ENG.). 16p. pap. 6.56 *(978-1-107-54949-4(3))* Cambridge Univ. Pr.

Rigby Education Staff. Let's Sleep. (Sails Literacy Ser.). (Illus.). 16p. (gr. 1-2). 27.00 *(978-0-7635-9887-7(9),* 698879C99) Rigby Education.

Rosa-Mendoza, Gladys. My House/Mi Casa. Borlasca, Hector, illus. 2007. (English Spanish Foundations Ser.). (gr. -1-1). per. 19.95 *(978-1-931398-84-8(4))* Me+Mi Publishing.

Rosenberg, Pam. Yecch! Icky, Sticky, Gross Stuff in Your House. Ramos, Beatriz Helena, illus. 2007. (Icky, Sticky, Gross-Out Bks.). (ENG.). 24p. (J). (gr. 3-6). 27.07 *(978-1-59296-898-5(8),* 200357) Child's World, Inc., The.

Rotner, Shelley & Goldblas, Amy. Home. Rotner, Shelley, photos by. 2010. (Shelley Rotner's Early Childhood Library Ser.). (ENG., Illus.). 32p. (gr. -1-2). lib. bdg. 25.26 *(978-0-7613-4605-0(8))* Lerner Publishing Group.

Schaefer, Adam R. Homes Around the World. Freeman, Marcia S., ed. 2006. (Living in My World Ser.). (Illus.). 8p. (J). (gr. 3-7). pap. 5.95 *(978-1-59515-967-0(3))* Rourke Educational Media.

Skinner, Tina. Log & Timber Frame Homes, 1 vol. 2003. (ENG., Illus.). 224p. (gr. 10-13). 44.95 *(978-0-7643-1754-5(7),* 9780764317545) Schiffer Publishing, Ltd.

Smith, Alastair, ed. Homes & Houses Then & Now. 2004. (Then & Now Flip Flaps Ser.). (SPA & ENG., Illus.). 1p. (J). (gr. 2-18). pap. 7.95 *(978-0-7460-3100-1(9))* EDC Publishing.

Smith, Paula. Homes in Different Places. 2015. (Learning about Our Global Community Ser.). (ENG.). 24p. (J). *(978-0-7787-2012-6(8))* Crabtree Publishing Co.

Smith, Sian. City Homes, 1 vol. 2013. (Where We Live Ser.). (ENG.). 24p. (gr. -1-1). 22.65 *(978-1-4329-8065-8(3));* pap. 6.95 *(978-1-4329-8070-2(X))* Heinemann-Raintree. (Acorn).

—Where We Live. 2013. (Where We Live Ser.). (ENG.). 24p. (gr. -1-1). pap. 23.96 *(978-1-4329-8074-0(2));* lib. bdg. 67.95 *(978-1-4329-8069-6(6))* Heinemann-Raintree. (Acorn).

Spilsbury, Louise & Spilsbury, Richard. Houses & Homes. 2013. (Start-Up Connections Ser.). (ENG., Illus.). 32p. (J). pap. 12.99 *(978-0-237-54372-3(9))* Evans Brothers, Ltd. GBR. Dist: Independent Pubs. Group.

Stamper, Judith Bauer. House, Sweet House. 2010. (J). *(978-1-60617-137-0(2))* Teaching Strategies, LLC.

Stiles, David. Forts for Kids. 2011. (ENG., Illus.). 96p. pap. 16.95 *(978-0-7627-6453-2(8),* Lyons Pr.) Globe Pequot Pr., The.

Taylor, Saranne. Ancient Homes. Chiacchiera, Moreno & Todd, Michelle, illus. 2014. (ENG.). 32p. (J). *(978-0-7787-1437-8(3))* Crabtree Publishing Co.

—Futuristic Homes. Chiacchiera, Moreno & Todd, Michelle, illus. 2014. (ENG.). 32p. (J). *(978-0-7787-1439-2(X))* Crabtree Publishing Co.

—Green Homes. Chiacchiera, Moreno & Todd, Michelle, illus. 2014. (ENG.). 32p. (J). *(978-0-7787-1452-1(7))* Crabtree Publishing Co.

VanTassell - Luto, Ceneca. The Other White House. 2011. 28p. (gr. -1). pap. 14.95 *(978-1-4567-4052-8(0))* AuthorHouse.

Walker, Sally. Ghost Walls: The Story of a 17th-Century Colonial Homestead. 2014. (Illus.). 136p. (J). (gr. 6-12). lib. bdg. 20.95 *(978-0-7613-5408-6(5),* Carolrhoda Bks.) Lerner Publishing Group.

Watson, Donna. Houses: Past & Present. 2005. (ENG., Illus.). 24p. (J). (gr. 3-3). pap. 5.97 net. *(978-0-328-13351-2(5),* Scott Foresman) Pearson Schl.

Wright, Craig, ed. Where People Live. 2010. (ENG., Illus.). 16p. act. bk. ed. 4.06 *(978-0-19-440172-2(3))* Oxford Univ. Pr., Inc.

HOUSES—FICTION

Ables, Troy. Around This Old House. 2004. 20p. pap. 24.95 *(978-1-4137-3169-9(4))* PublishAmerica, Inc.

Alex, Smith. Home. Alex, Smith, illus. 2010. (ENG., Illus.). 32p. (J). (gr. -1-2). 15.95 *(978-1-58925-088-5(5))* Tiger Tales.

Amato, Anne McCoy. Moving Shelly: A Novel. 2010. 148p. (gr. 4-6). pap. 12.95 *(978-1-4502-2584-7(5))* iUniverse, Inc.

Auxier, Jonathan. The Night Gardener. (ENG.). (YA). (gr. 3-7). 2015. 384p. pap. 8.95 *(978-1-4197-1531-0(3))* 2014. 368p. 16.95 *(978-1-4197-1144-2(X))* Abrams, Inc. (Amulet Bks.).

—The Night Gardener. 2015. (J). lib. bdg. 19.60 *(978-0-606-36891-9(4))* Turtleback Bks.

Avila, Juan Casas. DOS Casos de Casas y Algunas Otras Cosas. Jimenez, Leticia Serrano, illus. rev. ed. 2006. (Castillo de la Lectura Verde Ser.). (SPA & ENG.). 72p. (J). (gr. 2-4). pap. 7.95 *(978-970-20-0175-1(7))* Castillo, Ediciones, S. A. de C. V. MEX. Dist: Macmillan.

Bagley, Jessixa. Laundry Day. 2017. (ENG., Illus.). 32p. (J). 17.99 *(978-1-62672-317-7(6),* 9781626723177) Roaring Brook Pr.

The Barnabys' New House, 6 Packs. (Literatura 2000 Ser.). (gr. 1-2). 28.00 *(978-0-7635-0458-8(0))* Rigby Education.

Bartolome, Teresita Africano. We Lost Our House, 1 vol. 2010. 24p. 24.95 *(978-1-4489-7338-5(4))* PublishAmerica, Inc.

Bigham, Madge A. Little Folks' Land. Ripperton, Lisa M., ed. 2009. 452p. pap. 15.95 *(978-1-59915-375-9(0))* Yesterday's Classics.

Blair, Candice. Rosie's Pink House, 1 vol. Cato, Andrea, illus. 2010. 18p. 24.95 *(978-1-4489-4619-8(0))* America Star Bks.

Blakemore, Megan Frazer. The Water Castle. 2014. (ENG.). 368p. (YA). (gr. 3-8). pap. 7.99 *(978-0-8027-3593-5(2),* 9780802735935, Bloomsbury USA Childrens) Bloomsbury Publishing USA.

Blance, Ellen & Cook, Tony. Monster Cleans His House. Date not set. (Illus.). 16p. pap. 129.15 *(978-0-582-18590-6(4))* Addison-Wesley Longman, Ltd. GBR. Dist: Trans-Atlantic Pubns., Inc.

—Monster Looks for a House. Date not set. (Illus.). 16p. pap. 129.15 *(978-0-582-18589-0(0))* Addison-Wesley Longman, Ltd. GBR. Dist: Trans-Atlantic Pubns., Inc.

Blazin' Hot: Coloring/Activity Book (English) 2005. (Illus.). (J). 2.99 *(978-0-9770455-0-1(1))* Mighty Kids Media.

Blazin' Hot: Picture Book (English) 8x8. 2006. (J). 5.99 *(978-1-933934-29-7(8))* Mighty Kids Media.

Blazin' Hot Picture Book (English) 2005. (Illus.). (J). 5.99 *(978-0-9765953-9-7(7))* Mighty Kids Media.

Bomgaars, Sharon. The Best Clubhouse Ever. 2009. 232p. 24.99 *(978-1-4259-9307-8(9))* AuthorHouse.

Bone, Jody. The Little House That Grew. 2012. 36p. pap. 15.49 *(978-1-4669-5857-9(X))* Trafford Publishing.

Bonner, P. A. I Can Make a Difference: All Around My House. 2009. (ENG.). 14p. 8.95 *(978-1-58117-919-4(7),* Intervisual/Piggy Toes) Bendon, Inc.

Bratun, Katy. Gingerbread Mouse. Bratun, Katy, illus. 2007. (ENG., Illus.). 32p. (J). (gr. -1-3). per. 6.99 *(978-0-06-009082-1(0))* HarperCollins Pubs.

Brezenoff, Steve. Burning Secrets, 1 vol. Vue, Tou, illus. (Vortex Bks.). (ENG.). 112p. (gr. 2-3). 2008. pap. 7.19 *(978-1-59889-920-7(1))* 2007. 26.65 *(978-1-59889-854-5(X))* Stone Arch Bks. (Vortex Bks.).

—The Ride That Was Really Haunted, 1 vol. Calo, Marcos, illus. 2011. (Field Trip Mysteries Ser.). (ENG.). 88p. (gr. 2-3). pap. 6.10 *(978-1-4342-3427-8(4));* lib. bdg. 25.32 *(978-1-4342-3224-3(7))* Stone Arch Bks.

Brian, Kate, pseud. The Book of Spells. 2010. (Private Ser.: Bk. 13). (ENG.). 336p. (YA). (gr. 9-18). 17.99 *(978-1-4424-1236-1(4),* Simon & Schuster Bks. For Young Readers) Simon & Schuster Bks. For Young Readers.

Brightwood, Laura, illus. The House That Talked to Itself. 2006. (J). *(978-0-9779290-3-0(5))* 3-C Institute for Social Development.

Brignaud, Pierre, illus. Caillou - My First Dictionary. rev. ed. 2007. (My First Dictionary Ser.). (ENG.). 16p. (J). (gr. -1-k). bds. 12.95 *(978-2-89450-627-1(9))* Caillouet, Gerry.

Britan, Denise G. Harry Meets Sam. 2011. 24p. pap. 12.99 *(978-1-4628-6756-1(1))* Xlibris Corp.

Burton, Virginia Lee. The Little House. Burton, Virginia Lee, illus. 2009. (ENG., Illus.). 42p. (J). (gr. -1 — 1). bds. 7.99 *(978-0-547-13104-7(6))* Houghton Mifflin Harcourt Publishing Co.

—The Little House, 1 vol. (Read along Book & CD Ser.). (ENG., Illus.). 44p. (J). (gr. -1-3). 2007. audio compact disk 10.99 *(978-0-618-91651-1(2))* 70th anniv. ed. 2012. lib. bdg. 17.99 *(978-0-547-79044-2(9))* Houghton Mifflin Harcourt Publishing Co.

Carberry, Marie. This Is My House!, 1 vol. 2010. 20p. pap. 24.95 *(978-1-61546-991-8(5))* America Star Bks.

Carey, Edward. Lungdon: Book Three. 2016. (Iremonger Trilogy Ser.: 0). (ENG.). 512p. (YA). (gr. 5-12). pap. 11.99 *(978-1-4683-1306-2(1),* 461306) Overlook Pr., The.

Carle, Eric. A House for Hermit Crab. Carle, Eric, illus. 2014. (World of Eric Carle Ser.). (ENG., Illus.). 32p. (J). (gr. k-2). pap. 3.99 *(978-1-4814-0915-5(8),* Simon Spotlight) Simon Spotlight.

Charbonnel-Bojman, Severine. What's in My House? 2012. (ENG., Illus.). 256p. (J). (gr. -1-k). 9.95 *(978-1-77085-113-9(5),* 9781770851139) Firefly Bks., Ltd.

Chausse, Sylvie. Los Gatos de Maria Tatin. Crozat, Francois, illus. 2003. (SPA.). 32p. (J). (gr. k-2). *(978-84-8418-067-8(0),* ZZ30446) Zendrera Zariquiey, Editorial ESP. Dist: Lectorum Pubns., Inc.

Cleaning House. 2003. (J). per. *(978-1-57657-964-0(6))* Paradise Pr., Inc.

Columbus, Chris & Vizzini, Ned. Battle of the Beasts. 2014. (House of Secrets Ser.: 2). (ENG.). 480p. (J). (gr. 3-7). 17.99 *(978-0-06-219249-3(3))* HarperCollins Pubs.

—House of Secrets. 2015. (House of Secrets Ser.: Vol. 1). (KOR.). 580p. (J). *(978-89-491-7127-2(9))* Biryongso Publishing Co.

—House of Secrets. Call, Greg, illus. (House of Secrets Ser.: 1). (J). 2014. (ENG.). 512p. (gr. 3-7). pap. 7.99 *(978-0-06-219247-9(7))* 2013. (ENG.). 496p. (gr. 3-7). 17.99 *(978-0-06-219246-2(9))* 2013. 490p. *(978-0-06-225964-6(4))* HarperCollins Pubs.

—House of Secrets. 2014. (House of Secrets Ser.: 1). (J). lib. bdg. 18.40 *(978-0-606-35070-9(5),* Turtleback) Turtleback Bks.

Corlyn, Ron. The House That Grew. 2013. 24p. pap. 24.95 *(978-1-63000-118-6(X))* America Star Bks.

Cowley, Joy. Meanies in the House. 2009. pap. 8.25 *(978-1-60559-227-5(7))* Hameray Publishing Group, Inc.

Crisanaz, Catherine M. The Best House for Molly. 2008. 36p. per. 24.95 *(978-1-4241-9093-5(2))* America Star Bks.

Cuqui. The Little House Without Windows: A Casinha sem Janelas. 2008. 124p. pap. 11.00 *(978-1-4343-7876-7(4))* AuthorHouse.

Curry, Jane Louise. The Egyptian Box. 2008. (ENG.). 196p. (J). (gr. 4-6). pap. 10.95 *(978-1-4169-7140-5(8),* Simon & Schuster/Paula Wiseman Bks.) Simon & Schuster/Paula Wiseman Bks.

Daniel, Susan Spence. The House That Wanted a Family. 2012. 32p. pap. 13.99 *(978-1-4624-0081-2(7),* Inspiring Voices) Author Solutions, Inc.

Del Moral, Susana. La Casa de Violet. Zaidi, Nadeem, illus. 2005. (Baby Einstein: Libros de Carton Ser.). (SPA.). 10p. (J). (gr. -1). bds. *(978-970-718-305-6(5),* Silver Dolphin en Español) Advanced Marketing, S. de R. L. de C. V.

Dietrich, Sean, illus. Hansel & Gretel: The Graphic Novel, 1 vol. 2008. (Graphic Spin Ser.). (ENG.). 40p. (gr. 1-3). 25.32 *(978-1-4342-0767-8(6),* Graphic Revolve) Stone Arch Bks.

Donaldson, Julia. A Squash & a Squeeze. Scheffler, Axel, illus. 2016. (ENG.). 32p. (J). (gr. -1-k). 16.99 *(978-1-338-05220-6(9))* Scholastic, Inc.

Dooling, Sandra. Haunted Houses!, 1 vol., 1. 2014. (Jr. Graphic Monster Stories Ser.). (ENG.). 24p. (J). (gr. 3-6). 26.25 *(978-1-4777-6199-1(3),* PowerKids Pr.) Rosen Publishing Group, Inc., The.

Dunning, John Harris & Singh, Nikhil. Salem Brownstone: All along the Watchtowers. Singh, Nikhil, illus. 2010. (ENG., Illus.). 96p. (YA). (gr. 7-18). 18.99 *(978-0-7636-4735-3(7))* Candlewick Pr.

Durand, Delphine. My House. Adams, Sarah, tr. from FRE. 2007. (ENG., Illus.). 44p. (J). (gr. k-2). 12.95 *(978-1-905341-09-2(1))* WingedChariot Pr. GBR. Dist: Independent Pubs. Group.

Ellis, Carson. Home. 2015. (ENG., Illus.). 40p. (J). (gr. -1-3). 16.99 *(978-0-7636-6529-6(0))* Candlewick Pr.

Fitch, Sheree. There's a Mouse in My House! braille ed. 2004. (Illus.). (J). (gr. k-3). spiral bd. *(978-0-616-07235-6(X));* spiral bd. *(978-0-616-07234-9(1))* Canadian National Institute for the Blind/Institut National Canadien pour les Aveugles.

Fleming, Candace. Tippy-Tippy-Tippy, Hide! Karas, G. Brian, illus. 2007. (ENG.). 40p. (J). (gr. -1-3). 17.99 *(978-0-689-87479-6(0),* Atheneum Bks. for Young Readers) Simon & Schuster Children's Publishing.

Fox, Alex. Windsock Wesley & His Wild & Wonderful Weather MacHine, Living in Cloud. Bazzoni, Lainie M. A., illus. 2010. 48p. pap. 16.50 *(978-1-60911-873-0(1),* Eloquent Bks.) Strategic Book Publishing & Rights Agency (SBPRA).

Freedman, Deborah. This House, Once. Freedman, Deborah, illus. 2017. (ENG., Illus.). 40p. (J). (gr. -1-3). 17.99 *(978-1-4814-4284-8(8))* Simon & Schuster Children's Publishing.

Fultion, T. C. Jan the Cleaning Lady. 2009. 20p. pap. 10.95 *(978-1-60860-447-0(0),* Strategic Bk. Publishing) Strategic Book Publishing & Rights Agency (SBPRA).

Funaro, Gregory. Alistair Grim's Odditorium. 2015. (Alistair Grim Ser.). (ENG.). (J). (gr. 3-7). 448p. pap. 7.99 *(978-1-4847-0899-6(7));* (Illus.). 432p. 16.99 *(978-1-4847-0006-8(6))* Hyperion Bks. for Children.

—Alistair Grim's Odditorium. 2015. (J). lib. bdg. 18.40 *(978-0-606-37399-9(3))* Turtleback Bks.

Gaiman, NEil. Los Lobos de la Pared. McKean, Dave, illus. 2006.Tr. of Wolves in the Wall. (SPA.). 64p. 22.95 *(978-1-59497-222-5(2))* Public Square Bks.

Gaston, Sharon D. Clean Your Own House & Misery Loves Company. 2009. 40p. pap. 18.50 *(978-1-4389-7831-4(6))* AuthorHouse.

Giacomucci, Carol. A New Home. 2006. 23p. pap. 10.95 *(978-0-7414-3498-2(9))* Infinity Publishing.

Golden Books Staff. The House That Jack Built. Miller, J. P., illus. 2008. (Little Golden Book Ser.). (ENG.). 24p. (J). (gr. -1-2). 4.99 *(978-0-375-83530-8(X),* Golden Bks.) Random Hse. Children's Bks.

Goodhart, Pippa. House that Jack Built. Parker, Andy, illus. 2004. (ENG.). 24p. (J). lib. bdg. 23.65 *(978-1-59646-700-2(2))* Dingles & Co.

Grabo, Carl. The Cat in Grandfather's House. 2008. 120p. 23.95 *(978-1-60664-842-1(X));* pap. 10.95 *(978-1-60664-087-6(9))* Aegypan.

Greene, Janice. The Eye of the Hurricane, 1 vol. unabr. ed. 2010. (Q Reads Ser.). (ENG.). 32p. (YA). (gr. 9-12). pap. 6.95 *(978-1-61651-191-3(5))* Saddleback Educational Publishing, Inc.

—The House on the Hill, 1 vol. unabr. ed. 2010. (Q Reads Ser.). (ENG.). 32p. (YA). (gr. 9-12). pap. 6.95 *(978-1-61651-192-0(3))* Saddleback Educational Publishing, Inc.

Group/McGraw-Hill, Wright. The New House: Level H, 6 vols. (Take Twostm Ser.). 16p. 29.95 *(978-0-322-09000-2(8))* Wright Group/McGraw-Hill.

Gwent (Wales), Staff Development Unit Staff & Acen Staff, contrib. by. Croeso I Gartref Llew. 2005. (WEL., Illus.). 8p. pap. *(978-1-874049-34-0(3))* Acen Limited.

Halam, Ann. The Shadow on the Stairs. 2012. (Stoke Books Titles Ser.). 64p. (J). (gr. 5-8). pap. 7.95 *(978-1-78112-016-3(1));* lib. bdg. 22.60 *(978-1-78112-015-6(3))* Stoke Bks.

Hawthorne, Nathaniel. The House of the Seven Gables, 1 vol. Fisher, Scott, illus. 2011. (Calico Illustrated Classics Ser.). (ENG.). 112p. (J). (gr. 3-6). 27.07 *(978-1-60270-746-7(4))* Magic Wagon.

Hayes, Malcolm. The Dreamcatchers. 2006. 282p. pap. 20.14 *(978-1-4120-8320-1(6))* Trafford Publishing.

Heather Heath Pruett. The Happy House. 2012. 24p. 24.95 *(978-1-4626-6081-0(9))* America Star Bks.

Hébert, Marie-Francine. Une Maison dans la Baleine. Germain, Philippe, illus. 2003. (Premier Roman Ser.). (FRE.). 64p. (J). (gr. 2-5). pap. *(978-2-89021-240-4(8))* Diffusion du livre Mirabel (DLM).

Higgins, M. G. The Lost House. 2014. (Red Rhino Ser.). (J). lib. bdg. 18.40 *(978-0-606-36202-3(9))* Turtleback Bks.

Hilburn, Dora. Between. 2015. 247p. (YA). pap. *(978-1-56825-175-2(0))* Rainbow Bks., Inc.

Hill, Eric. Spot Ayuda en la Casa. (SPA.). pap. 4.95 *(978-950-07-1968-1(1))* Editorial Sudamericana S.A. ARG. Dist: Distribooks, Inc.

—Spot en Casa. (SPA.). pap. 4.95 *(978-950-07-1962-9(2))* Editorial Sudamericana S.A. ARG. Dist: Distribooks, Inc.

Hoberman, Mary Ann. A House Is a House for Me. Fraser, Betty, illus. 2007. (ENG.). 48p. (J). (gr. -1-1). pap. 7.99 *(978-0-14-240773-8(9),* Puffin Books) Penguin Young Readers Group.

Hooser, Betty. A Flying House for Entertainment. 2012. 28p. pap. 24.95 *(978-1-4626-7582-1(4))* America Star Bks.

Hopkins, William J. The Sandman: His House Stories (Yesterday's Classics) 2009. 136p. pap. 8.95 *(978-1-59915-304-9(1))* Yesterday's Classics.

I Can Say- Around the House. 2005. (J). bds. *(978-1-4194-0036-0(3))* Paradise Pr., Inc.

Irwin, Inez Haynes. Maida's Little House. 2004. reprint ed. pap. 27.95 *(978-1-4179-4236-7(3))* Kessinger Publishing, LLC.

H
I

Jackson, Mike. The Best Dog House Ever! 2013. (Step into Reading Level 1 Ser.). lib. bdg. 13.55 (978-0-606-26981-0(9), Turtleback) Turtleback Bks.
James, Catherine. The Sad Little House. Collier, Kevin Scott, illus. 2008. 24p. pap. 10.95 (978-1-935137-06-1(9)) 2006. 28p. (J). E-Book 9.95 incl. cd-rom (978-1-933090-18-4(9)) Guardian Angel Publishing, Inc.
Jensen, Patricia. My House. 2004. (My First Reader Ser.). (ENG.). 32p. (J). (gr. k-1). pap. 3.95 (978-0-516-24636-9(4), Children's Pr.) Scholastic Library Publishing.
Johnson, Fran. Mystery House. 2008. 152p. 22.60 (978-1-4389-3152-4(2)); pap. 12.30 (978-1-4389-3153-1(0)) AuthorHouse.
Kelaita, Lynda. Some Houses Are White. 2009. 32p. pap. 10.95 (978-1-935125-44-0(3)) Robertson Publishing.
Keller, Holly. What I See. 2003. (Green Light Readers Level 1 Ser.). (ENG., Illus.). 24p. (J). (gr. -1-3). pap. 3.95 (978-0-15-204854-9(5)) Houghton Mifflin Harcourt Publishing Co.
Kent, Lorna, illus. In My House. 2004. 8p. (J). bds. 3.99 (978-1-85854-086-3(0)) Brimax Books Ltd. GBR. Dist: Byeway Bks.
Kimmelman, Leslie. The Very Crowded Sukkah, 0 vols. 2013. (ENG.). 32p. (J). (gr. -1-k). 17.99 (978-1-4778-1716-2(6), 9781477817162, Amazon Children's Publishing) Amazon Publishing.
King, Kirsty. My New Friends. 2005. 52p. pap. (978-1-84401-576-4(9)) Athena Pr.
Kirk, Bill. My Grandma's Kitchen Rules. Movshina, Marina, illus. 2009. 24p. pap. 10.95 (978-1-935137-88-7(3)) Guardian Angel Publishing, Inc.
Kirk, Daniel. Library Mouse: Home Sweet Home. 2013. (ENG., Illus.). 40p. (J). (gr. 1-4). 17.95 (978-1-4197-0544-1(X), Abrams Bks. for Young Readers) Abrams, Inc.
Klise, Kate. Greetings from the Graveyard. Klise, M. Sarah, illus. (43 Old Cemetery Road Ser.). (ENG.). 160p. (J). (gr. 2-5). 2015. pap. 6.99 (978-0-544-54010-1(7)) 2014. 15.99 (978-0-544-10567-6(2)) Houghton Mifflin Harcourt Publishing Co. (HMH Books For Young Readers).
—Over My Dead Body. Klise, M. Sarah, illus. 2011. (43 Old Cemetery Road Ser.: Bk. 2). (ENG.). 128p. (J). (gr. 2-5). pap. 6.99 (978-0-547-57713-5(3)) Houghton Mifflin Harcourt Publishing Co.
Kohara, Kazuno. Ghosts in the House! Kohara, Kazuno, illus. 2010. (ENG., Illus.). 32p. (J). (gr. -1-1). pap. 7.99 (978-0-312-60886-6(1), 9780312608866) Square Fish.
Kooser, Ted. House Held up by Trees. Klassen, Jon, illus. 2012. (ENG.). 32p. (J). (gr. -1-3). 16.99 (978-0-7636-5107-7(9)) Candlewick Pr.
Lael, Anita. The Little Brick House. Gresham, Delia, illus. 2012. 32p. pap. 24.95 (978-1-4626-9374-0(1)); 30p. 24.95 (978-1-4626-5972-2(1)) America Star Bks.
Laing, Marilyn. Why the Turtle & the Snail Carried their Houses on Their Back. 2011. 24p. pap. 13.50 (978-1-4567-3154-0(8)) AuthorHouse.
Landa, Norbert. The Secret House of Papa Mouse. Turk, Hanne, illus. 2004. (Picture Books/Quality Time Ser.). 32p. (gr. k-3). lib. bdg. 26.00 (978-0-8368-4106-0(9), Gareth Stevens Learning Library) Stevens, Gareth Publishing LLLP.
Laura Grey Wahl. The Magic Town of Stuart Easterly. 2009. 16p. pap. 15.00 (978-1-4389-4703-7(8)) AuthorHouse.
Lavigne, Guy & Godbout, Real. La Maison du Pendu. 2003. (Roman Jeunesse Ser.). (Illus.). 96p. (YA). (gr. 4-7). pap. (978-2-89021-328-9(5)) Diffusion du livre Mirabel (DLM).
Lee, Tammie. House. 2009. 36p. pap. 24.95 (978-1-61546-045-8(4)) America Star Bks.
Léger, Diane Carmel. Emily Carr's Attic, 1 vol. Léger, Michael, illus. 2008. (ENG.). 32p. (J). (gr. -1-3). pap. 9.95 (978-1-55143-958-7(1)) Orca Bk. Pubs. USA.
Leija-Sysak, Viviana. My House Is Full of Light. 2008. 20p. 11.50 (978-1-4357-1606-3(X)) Lulu Pr., Inc.
Leray, Merrill. The House of Lady Chase. 2009. 70p. pap. 15.99 (978-1-4415-4381-3(3)) Xlibris Corp.
Lewis, Clarajane. The House on the Hill. 2012. (Illus.). 26p. pap. 12.00 (978-1-78035-399-9(5), Fastprint Publishing) Upfront Publishing Ltd. GBR. Dist: Printondemand-worldwide.com.
Liparulo, Robert. Gatekeepers, 1 vol. 2009. (Dreamhouse Kings Ser.: 3). (ENG.). 320p. pap. 9.99 (978-1-59554-729-3(0)) Nelson, Thomas Inc.
—House of Dark Shadows, 1 vol. 2009. (Dreamhouse Kings Ser.: 1). (ENG.). 304p. pap. 9.99 (978-1-59554-727-9(4)) Nelson, Thomas Inc.
Lodico, Cheryl. The Wacky World of Winnie & Willie. 2007. 14.00 (978-0-8059-8362-3(7)) Dorrance Publishing Co., Inc.
Lorimer, Janet. Look to the Light, 1 vol. unabr. ed. 2010. (Q Reads Ser.). (ENG.). 32p. (YA). (gr. 9-12). pap. 6.95 (978-1-61651-193-7(1)) Saddleback Educational Publishing, Inc.
Low, Alice. Blueberry Mouse. Friend, David Michael, tr. Friend, David Michael, illus. 2004. (J). 15.95 (978-1-59336-111-2(4)); pap. (978-1-59336-112-9(2)) Mondo Publishing.
MacDonald, Betty Bard. The Squeaky Door. Date not set. 32p. (J). (gr. -1-1). pap. 4.99 (978-0-06-443566-6(0)) HarperCollins Pubs.
MacDonald, Margaret Read. The Squeaky Door. DePalma, Mary Newell, illus. 2006. (ENG.). 40p. (J). (gr. -1-1). 16.99 (978-0-06-028373-5(4)) HarperCollins Pubs.
MacLachlan, Patricia. Kindred Souls. 2013. (ENG.). 144p. (J). (gr. 1-5). pap. 5.99 (978-0-06-052299-5(2), Tegen, Katherine Bks) HarperCollins Pubs.
Mahy, Margaret. The Magician of Hoad. 2010. (ENG.). 432p. (YA). (gr. 9). pap. 9.99 (978-1-4169-7808-4(9), McElderry, Margaret K. Bks.) McElderry, Margaret K. Bks.
Marie, Christina. Where Would I Live?, 1 vol. 2010. 18p. 24.95 (978-1-4489-7584-6(0)) PublishAmerica, Inc.
Marino, Gianna. Too Tall Houses. 2012. (ENG.). 40p. (J). (gr. -1-k). 16.99 (978-0-670-01314-2(5), Viking Books for Young Readers) Penguin Young Readers Group.
Martin, Ann M. Ten Rules for Living with My Sister. 2012. (ENG.). 256p. (J). (gr. 4-7). pap. 7.99 (978-1-250-01021-6(7), 9781250010216) Square Fish.
McGuirk, Leslie. The Moogees Move House. McGuirk, Leslie, illus. 2012. (ENG., Illus.). 32p. (J). (gr. -1-2). 14.99 (978-0-7636-5558-7(9)) Candlewick Pr.
Meachen Rau, Dana. My Special Space. Kim, Julie J., illus. 2003. (Rookie Readers Ser.). 32p. (J). 19.50 (978-0-516-22881-5(1), Children's Pr.) Scholastic Library Publishing.
Miller, Sibley & Lenhard, Elizabeth. Horse Happy. Chang, Tara Larsen & Gershman, Jo, illus. 2008. (Wind Dancers Ser.: 2). (ENG.). 80p. (J). (gr. 1-4). pap. 7.99 (978-0-312-38281-0(2), 9780312382810) Feiwel & Friends.
Mitch, Karlie. The Green Stone House, 1 vol. 2010. 94p. pap. 16.95 (978-1-61546-305-3(4)) PublishAmerica, Inc.
Mongredien, Sue. Oliver Moon's Fangtastic Sleepover. 2011. (Oliver Moon Ser.). 92p. (J). pap. 4.99 (978-0-7945-3094-5(X), Usborne) EDC Publishing.
Montgomery, L. M. Ana y la Casa de Sus Suenos. (Coleccion "Ana, la de Tejas Verdes").Tr. of Anne's House of Dreams. (SPA.). 256p. (YA). (gr. 5-8). (978-84-7888-637-1(0), SAL8825) Emece Editores ESP. Dist: Lectorum Pubns., Inc.
Montgomery, Lewis B. The Case of the Haunted Haunted House, Vol. 3. Wummer, Amy, illus. 2009. (Milo & Jazz Mysteries Ser.). 96p. (J). (gr. k-3). 22.60 (978-1-57565-297-9(8)); (ENG.). (gr. 3-7). pap. 6.95 (978-1-57565-295-5(1)) Kane Press, Inc.
Moore, Kelly, et al. Neverwas. 2014. (Amber House Ser.: 2). (ENG.). 320p. (J). (gr. 9). 17.99 (978-0-545-43418-8(1), Levine, Arthur A. Bks.) Scholastic, Inc.
Mould, Chris. The Icy Hand. Mould, Chris, illus. 2008. (Something Wickedly Weird Ser.: 2). (ENG., Illus.). 176p. (J). (gr. 5-9). 9.95 (978-1-59643-385-4(X), 9781596433854) Roaring Brook Pr.
Munro, Rosemary. The House That Flew to the Seaside. 2016. (ENG., Illus.). 32p. (J). pap. (978-1-78222-442-6(4)) Paragon Publishing, Rothersthorpe.
Murray, Marjorie Dennis. Halloween Night. Dorman, Brandon, illus. 2013. (ENG.). 40p. (J). (gr. k-4). pap. 6.99 (978-0-06-185773-7(4), Greenwillow Bks.) HarperCollins Pubs.
My Home: Individual Title Six-Packs. (Chiquilibros Ser.). (gr. k-1). 23.00 (978-0-7635-0447-2(5)) Rigby Education.
My House: Individual Title Six-Packs. (Literatura 2000 Ser.). (gr. 1-2). 28.00 (978-0-7635-0142-6(5)) Rigby Education.
The New House, 6, Pack. (Sails Literacy Ser.). 16p. (gr. k-18). 27.00 (978-0-7635-4447-8(7)) Rigby Education.
Night, P. J. Home, Sweet Haunt. 2013. (Creepover Ser.: 15). lib. bdg. 16.00 (978-0-606-32047-4(4), Turtleback) Turtleback Bks.
Olson, Norah. What the Dead Want. 2016. (Illus.). 304p. (YA). (gr. 8). 17.99 (978-0-06-241011-5(3), Tegen, Katherine Bks) HarperCollins Pubs.
Parker, Emma. Chuck the Chilli. 2010. (Illus.). pap. (978-1-877547-92-8(1)) First Edition Ltd.
Perez, Monica, et al. Curious George Builds a Home. 2006. (Curious George Ser.). (ENG., Illus.). 24p. (J). (gr. -1-3). 4.99 (978-0-618-72395-9(1)) Houghton Mifflin Harcourt Publishing Co.
Peterson, Sheryl. The Best Part of a Sauna, 1 vol. Dupre, Kelly, illus. 2013. (ENG.). 32p. (J). (gr. 1-2). pap. 9.95 (978-0-9883508-1-6(5)) Raven Productions, Inc.
Phillips, Dee. Dare, 1 vol. unabr. ed. 2011. (Right Now! Ser.). (ENG.). 45p. (YA). (gr. 9-12). pap. 8.95 (978-1-61651-246-0(6)) Saddleback Educational Publishing, Inc.
Pitman, Colin. The House That Talked. 2012. (Illus.). 78p. pap. 13.66 (978-1-4772-2639-1(7)) AuthorHouse.
Priestley, Chris. The Dead of Winter. 2012. (ENG., Illus.). 224p. (YA). (gr. 7-12). 16.99 (978-1-59990-745-1(3), 9781599907451, Bloomsbury USA Childrens) Bloomsbury Publishing USA.
Puppy's House. Date not set. (Illus.). (J). bds. 4.98 (978-1-4054-0787-8(5)) Parragon, Inc.
Pybus, Judith. The Ladder. 2009. 136p. pap. 10.99 (978-1-4490-0298-5(6)) AuthorHouse.
Raquel, Israel & Sissom, Carol. Help Mommy Clean-Up! 2006. (Help Mommy Clen-Up! Ser.: Vol. 1). (Illus.). 16p. (J). mass mkt. 7.99 (978-1-4243-2034-9(8)) Independent Publisher Services.
Reid, James. Dinosaur House, 1 vol. rev. ed. 2013. (Fiction Readers Ser.). (ENG., Illus.). 12p. (J). (gr. 1-1). pap. 4.99 (978-1-4333-5459-5(4)); pap. 12.96 (978-1-4807-1138-9(1)) Shell Educational Publishing.
Repta, Jennifer. The Three Little Houses. 2013. 16p. pap. 12.68 (978-1-4669-7898-0(8)) Trafford Publishing.
Rey, H. A. Builds a Home. 2011. (Curious George Ser.). (ENG., Illus.). 24p. (J). (gr. -1-3). 6.99 (978-0-547-59410-1(0)) Houghton Mifflin Harcourt Publishing Co.
Robeson, K. S. Chloe & Bia Bk. 2: Tales from Wind Creek. 2003. 96p. per. 8.95 (978-0-9723530-1-4(1)) Falcor Bks.
Rockwell, Anne. Let's Go to the Hardware Store. Iwai, Melissa, illus. 2016. (ENG.). 32p. (J). 16.99 (978-0-8050-8738-3(9), 9780805087383, Holt, Henry & Co. Bks. For Young Readers) Holt, Henry & Co.
Romig, Hilary. Mrs Crumbs' Trunk. 2009. 24p. pap. 12.99 (978-1-4490-0466-8(0)) AuthorHouse.
Root, Phyllis. The House That Jill Built: A Pop-up Book. Durand, Delphine, illus. 2007. 18p. (J). reprint ed. 16.00 (978-1-4223-6756-8(8)) DIANE Publishing Co.
Rosen, Michael. This Is Our House. Graham, Bob, illus. 2005. (ENG.). 32p. (J). (gr. -1-2). 7.99 (978-0-7636-2816-1(6)) Candlewick Pr.
Rudy, Maggie & Abrams, Pam. The House That Mouse Built. Wolf, Bruce, photos by. 2011. (ENG., Illus.). 32p. (J). (gr. -1). 14.99 (978-1-935703-25-9(0)) Downtown Bookworks.
Rylant, Cynthia. Let's Go Home: The Wonderful Things about a House. Halperin, Wendy Anderson, illus. 2005. (ENG.). 32p. (J). (gr. -1-3). 7.99 (978-1-4169-0839-5(0), Simon & Schuster Bks. For Young Readers) Simon & Schuster Bks. For Young Readers.
Scarry, Richard. Mi Casa.Tr. of My Home. (SPA., Illus.). (J). 6.95 (978-950-04-0715-1(9)) Emecé Editores S.A. ARG. Dist: Planeta Publishing Corp.
—Mi Casa. Scarry, Richard, illus. 2003. (Richard Scarry Ser.).Tr. of My Home. (SPA., Illus.). (J). (gr. -1-3). pap. (978-970-690-845-2(5)) Planeta Mexicana Editorial S. A. de C. V.
Schieldt, Corine. Somebody's Gotta Get Rid of That Vacuum. Schieldt, Jodi, illus. 2008. 24p. per. 24.95 (978-1-4241-9121-5(1)) America Star Bks.
Scott, Jeanette B. Three Story House. 2005. 48p. pap. 10.00 (978-1-4134-6430-6(0)) Xlibris Corp.
Seuss, Dr., tr. & illus. Come Over to My House. Seuss, Dr., illus. Date not set. (J). lib. bdg. 11.99 (978-0-679-98255-5(8)); (gr. -1-3). 7.99 (978-0-679-88255-8(3)) Random Hse. Children's Bks. (Random Hse. Bks. for Young Readers).
Shea, Therese. A House for Mouse. 2006. (Neighborhood Readers Ser.). (ENG.). 8p. (gr. -1-3). pap. 5.15 (978-1-4042-5672-9(5), Rosen Classroom) Rosen Publishing Group, Inc., The.
Shreeve, Elizabeth. Hector Afloat. Levy, Pamela R., illus. 2004. 71p. (J). lib. bdg. 15.00 (978-1-4242-0902-6(1)) Fitzgerald Bks.
Silverman, Erica. Horse in the House. Lewin, Betsy, illus. 2009. (Cowgirl Kate & Cocoa Ser.). (ENG.). 44p. (J). (gr. 1-4). 15.00 (978-0-15-205390-1(5)) Houghton Mifflin Harcourt Publishing Co.
Smith, Adelene Keeler. Sophie Gets Curtains! 2010. 28p. (J). pap. 12.99 (978-1-4520-8943-0(4)) AuthorHouse.
Snyder, Zilpha Keatley. The Treasures of Weatherby. 2008. (ENG.). 240p. (J). (gr. 3-7). pap. 7.99 (978-1-4169-1399-3(8), Atheneum Bks. for Young Readers) Simon & Schuster Children's Publishing.
Staehli, Melissa. Charlie's Gingerbread House. Rottinger, Amy, illus. 2012. 24p. pap. 11.95 (978-1-61244-063-7(0)) Halo Publishing International.
Stanley the Builder, 1 vol. 2014. (Stanley Ser.). (ENG., Illus.). 32p. (J). (gr. -1-2). 14.95 (978-1-56145-801-1(5)) Peachtree Pubs.
Steinhöfel, Andreas & Wright, Chantal. The Spaghetti Detectives. 2011. (ENG.). 176p. (J). (gr. 3-7). 16.99 (978-0-545-28975-7(0), Chicken Hse., The) Scholastic, Inc.
Stelten, Gene. A House for Wally & Me. Johnson, Chelsea, illus. 2009. 32p. (J). 13.95 (978-1-935130-13-0(7)) Grateful Steps.
Stewart, Mark R. Malcolm's Cubby House. Swope, Brenda, illus. 2011. 28p. pap. 24.95 (978-1-4560-0958-8(3)) America Star Bks.
Stine, R. L. First Evil. 2011. (Fear Street Cheerleaders Ser.: 1). (ENG.). 176p. (YA). (gr. 9). pap. 9.99 (978-1-4424-3086-0(9), Simon Pulse) Simon Pulse.
—Welcome to Dead House. 2010. (Goosebumps Ser.: 13). lib. bdg. 17.20 (978-0-606-14077-5(8), Turtleback) Turtleback Bks.
Stoddart, Heidi Jardine. East to the Sea, 1 vol. 2007. (ENG., Illus.). 32p. (J). (gr. -1-2). pap. 10.95 (978-1-55109-577-6(7)) Nimbus Publishing, Ltd. CAN. Dist: Orca Bk. Pubs. USA.
Stone Arch Books (Firm: Afton, Minn.) Staff. Hansel & Gretel: The Graphic Novel, 1 vol. Dietrich, Sean, illus. 2008. (Graphic Spin Ser.). (ENG.). 40p. (gr. 1-3). pap. 5.95 (978-1-4342-0863-7(X), Graphic Revolve) Stone Arch Bks.
Sutton, Margaret. The Unfinished House, No. 11. Doane, Pelagie, illus. 2008. (Judy Bolton Mysteries Ser.). (ENG.). 264p. (gr. 4-7). pap. 14.95 (978-1-4290-9031-5(6)) Applewood Bks.
Swanson, Susan Marie. The House in the Night. Krommes, Beth, illus. (ENG.). (J). 2011. 36p. (gr. k — 1). bds. 7.99 (978-0-547-57769-2(9)) 2008. 40p. (gr. -1-3). 17.99 (978-0-618-86244-3(7)) Houghton Mifflin Harcourt Publishing Co.
Swegles, Maryanne. Digging for Bottles. 2005. (Illus.). 28p. (J). 15.00 (978-0-9768418-0-7(0)) Hydrangea Pr.
Taylor, Di. Moving House. 2010. (ENG., Illus.). 20p. 4.81 (978-0-19-440082-4(4)) Oxford Univ. Pr., Inc.
Taylor, Dorothy L. Abigail's New Home. Schimmel, Beth, illus. (Valley View Farm Tales Ser.). 20p. (J). (gr. k-3). 7.50 (978-0-9610640-0-6(5)) Taylor, Dorothy Loring.
Teddy Bear-House. 2003. (J). per. (978-1-57657-162-0(9)) Paradise Pr., Inc.
Themerson, Stefan & Wright, Barbara. Mr Rouse Builds His House. 2014. (ENG., Illus.). 148p. (J). (gr. -1-3). 12.95 (978-1-84976-154-3(X)) Tate Publishing, Ltd. GBR. Dist: Abrams, Inc.
Thomas, Mikey. The Mouse & the House. 2012. 24p. pap. 24.95 (978-1-4626-7854-9(8)) America Star Bks.
Troulis, Jennifer. Penelope & Priscilla: And the Enchanted House of Whispers. 2nd ed. 2004. (Illus.). 229p. per. 13.95 (978-0-9768602-0-4(1)) Twin Monkeys Pr.
Tullgren, Tom. Journey to Imagiland. 2012. 320p. pap. 17.95 (978-1-62141-272-4(5)) Booklocker.com, Inc.
Ugon, Gabriela Armand. El Secreto de la Casa Gris. (SPA.). (J). 8.95 (978-958-04-7349-7(8)) Norma S.A. COL. Dist: Distribuidora Norma, Inc.
Unsworth, Tania. Brightwood. 2016. (ENG.). 272p. (J). (gr. 4-7). 16.95 (978-1-61620-330-6(7)) Algonquin Bks. of Chapel Hill.
Van Dusen, Chris. If I Built a House. 2012. (ENG.). 32p. (J). (-k). 17.99 (978-0-8037-3751-8(3), Dial Bks) Penguin Young Readers Group.
Van Patter, Bruce. Farley Found It! 2006. (ENG., Illus.). 32p. (J). (gr. -1-1). 17.95 (978-1-59078-351-1(4)) Boyds Mills Pr.
Vincolisi, Marnie. The House Who Found Its Home. Clarke, Benjamin S., illus. 2013. 32p. pap. 10.95 (978-0-9823732-3-1(6)) Light Internal Publishing.
Volkmer, Todd. Stacey Mcduver's House. 2005. 19p. (J). 12.38 (978-1-4116-6425-8(6)) Lulu Pr., Inc.
Walker-Renner, Christa. Santa's Magic. 2009. 20p. pap. 11.00 (978-1-4389-8206-9(2)) AuthorHouse.
Watson-Dubisch, Carolyn. Night of the Armadillos, 1. Watson-Dubisch, Carolyn, illus. I.t. ed. 2006. (Illus.). 32p. (J). per. 9.95 (978-0-9779295-2-8(3)) Medusa Road Pr.
West, Carly Anne. The Bargaining. 2015. (ENG., Illus.). 416p. (YA). (gr. 9). 17.99 (978-1-4424-4182-8(8), Simon Pulse) Simon Pulse.
West, Jacqueline. The Second Spy. 2013. (Books of Elsewhere Ser.: 3). lib. bdg. 18.40 (978-0-606-31698-9(1), Turtleback) Turtleback Bks.
—The Second Spy, Vol. 3. Bernatene, Poly, illus. 2012. (Books of Elsewhere Ser.: 3). (ENG.). 304p. (J). (gr. 5-18). 16.99 (978-0-8037-3689-4(4), Dial Bks) Penguin Young Readers Group.
—The Shadows. 2011. (Books of Elsewhere Ser.: 1). (ENG.). 272p. (J). (gr. 5-7). 7.99 (978-0-14-241872-7(2), Puffin Books) Penguin Young Readers Group.
—The Shadows. Bernatene, Poly, illus. 2010. (Books of Elsewhere Ser.: 1). (ENG.). 256p. (J). (gr. 5-18). 16.99 (978-0-8037-3440-1(9), Dial Bks) Penguin Young Readers Group.
—The Shadows. I.t. ed. 2010. (Books of Elsewhere Ser.: Vol. 1). (ENG.). 268p. 23.99 (978-1-4104-3139-4(8)) Thorndike Pr.
—The Shadows. 2011. (Books of Elsewhere Ser.: 1). lib. bdg. 17.20 (978-0-606-23070-4(X), Turtleback) Turtleback Bks.
—The Strangers. Bernatene, Poly, illus. 2014. (Books of Elsewhere Ser.: 4). (ENG.). 336p. (J). (gr. 5). pap. 7.99 (978-0-14-242575-6(3), Puffin Books) Penguin Young Readers Group.
Weston Woods Staff, creator. The Little House. 2011. 18.95 (978-0-439-72746-4(4)); 38.75 (978-0-439-72748-8(0)) Weston Woods Studios, Inc.
—This Is the House That Jack Built. 2011. 38.75 (978-0-439-78426-9(3)); 18.95 (978-0-439-78424-5(7)) Weston Woods Studios, Inc.
Williams, Raymond. The House of Useful Things. 2012. (Illus.). 44p. pap. 13.50 (978-1-78035-396-8(0), Fastprint Publishing) Upfront Publishing Ltd. GBR. Dist: Printondemand-worldwide.com.
Wilson, Mark A. The Old Man's Secret Friend, 1 vol. 2009. 19p. pap. 19.95 (978-1-61582-315-4(8)) PublishAmerica, Inc.
Wingart, Ramona A. Where Is Brother Beaver?, 1 vol. 2010. 30p. 24.95 (978-1-4489-4773-7(1)) PublishAmerica, Inc.
The Worst House, 6 Packs. (Bookweb Ser.). 32p. (gr. 3-18). 34.00 (978-0-7635-3930-6(9)) Rigby Education.
Wright, Betty Ren. Princess for a Week. Rogers, Jacqueline, illus. 2007. (ENG.). 160p. (J). (gr. 4-7). pap. 6.95 (978-0-8234-2111-4(2)) Holiday Hse., Inc.
Wright, Susan. Grandma's Haunted House. 2007. 64p. per. 16.95 (978-1-4241-0466-6(1)) PublishAmerica, Inc.
Yeager, Graham. Stone Hedge: The Fourth Millersburg Novel. 2006. 142p. (YA). per. 7.99 (978-0-9765478-6-0(4)) Stone Acres Publishing Co.
Yum, Hyewon. This Is Our House. Yum, Hyewon, illus. 2013. (ENG., Illus.). 36p. (J). (gr. -1-2). 16.99 (978-0-374-37487-7(2), 9780374374877, Farrar, Straus & Giroux (BYR)) Farrar, Straus & Giroux.
Ziefert, Harriet. Messy Bessie: Where's My Homework? De Muth, Roger, illus. 2007. (J). (978-1-4287-4707-4(9)) Handprint Bks.

HOUSES—REPAIRING

Beco, Alice. Cool Careers Without College for People who Love Houses. 2009. (Cool Careers Without College Ser.). 144p. (gr. 6-6). 66.50 (978-1-61511-967-7(1)) Rosen Publishing Group, Inc., The.

HOUSES OF ANIMALS

see Animals—Habitations

HOUSING

see also Apartment Houses; City Planning; Homelessness

Boudreau, Hélène, et al. Life in a Residential City. 2010. (Learn about Urban Life Ser.). (ENG., Illus.). 32p. (J). (gr. 3-6). pap. (978-0-7787-7403-7(1)); lib. bdg. (978-0-7787-7393-1(0)) Crabtree Publishing Co.
Crewe, Sabrina. In the Home. 2010. (Under the Microscope Ser.). 32p. (gr. 2-4). 30.00 (978-1-60413-823-8(8), Chelsea Clubhouse) Facts On File, Inc.
Guillain, Charlotte. Coping with Moving Away, 1 vol. 2011. (Real Life Issues Ser.). (ENG.). 48p. (gr. 6-8). 32.65 (978-1-4329-4764-4(8)) Heinemann-Raintree.
Hopkinson, Deborah. Shutting Out the Sky: Life in the Tenements of New York, 1880-1924. 2003. (ENG., Illus.). 144p. (J). (gr. 3-7). 19.99 (978-0-439-37590-0(8), Orchard Bks.) Scholastic, Inc.
Kennedy, Robert. Spanish Words in the House, Vol. 1. 2014. (Learn My Language! Spanish Ser.). 24p. (J). (gr. 1-2). (ENG.). 22.60 (978-1-4824-0360-2(9)); pap. 8.15 (978-1-4824-0363-3(3)) Stevens, Gareth Publishing LLLP.
Landau, Jennifer. Smart Strategies for Sharing, Subletting, & Renting an Apartment. 2014. (Financial Security & Life Success for Teens Ser.). (Illus.). 80p. (J). (gr. 7-12). pap. 14.15 (978-1-4777-7632-2(X)) Rosen Publishing Group, Inc., The.
McDowell, Tina. At Home Around the World. 2003. (Rosen Real Readers: Upper Emergent Ser.). (ENG., Illus.). 12p. (gr. 1-2). pap. 5.90 (978-0-8239-6363-8(2)) Rosen Publishing Group, Inc., The.
Miller, Jake. Who's Who in a Public Housing Community. (Communities at Work Ser.). 24p. (gr. 2-2). 2009. 42.50 (978-1-61511-898-4(5)) 2005. (Illus.). (J). lib. bdg. 22.60 (978-1-4042-2786-6(5)) 2005. (ENG., Illus.). pap. 8.25 (978-1-4042-5026-0(3)) Rosen Publishing Group, Inc., The. (PowerKids Pr.).
Nunn, Daniel. Homes, 1 vol. 2012. (Why Living Things Need Ser.). (ENG., Illus.). 24p. (gr. -1-1). pap. 6.29 (978-1-4329-5921-0(2), Acorn) Heinemann-Raintree.
Oxlade, Chris. Homes, 1 vol. 2012. (Science Behind Ser.). (ENG.). 32p. (gr. 3-3). pap. 8.29 (978-1-4109-4499-3(9)); lib. bdg. 30.65 (978-1-4109-4488-7(3)) Heinemann-Raintree. (Raintree Perspectives).
Parker, Steve & Parker, Vic. Moving, 1 vol. 2011. (Growing Up Ser.). (ENG.). 24p. (gr. k-2). 23.32 (978-1-4329-4800-9(8), Heinemann Read & Learn) Heinemann-Raintree.
Rice, Dona Herweck. Homes Around the World, 1 vol. 2nd rev. ed. 2014. (TIME for KIDS(r) Nonfiction Readers Ser.). (ENG., Illus.). 20p. (J). (gr. 1-1). pap. 19.96 (978-1-4807-1031-3(8)) Shell Educational Publishing.
Rubel, David. If I Had a Hammer: Building Homes & Hope with Habitat for Humanity. 2009. (ENG., Illus.). 160p. (J). (gr. 5-8). 19.99 (978-0-7636-4701-8(2)) Candlewick Pr.
Smith, Sian. Rural Homes, 1 vol. 2013. (Where We Live Ser.). (ENG.). 24p. (gr. -1-1). 22.65 (978-1-4329-8066-5(1)); pap. 6.95 (978-1-4329-8071-9(8)) Heinemann-Raintree. (Acorn).
Suen, Anastasia. Habitat for Humanity. 2009. (Helping Organizations Ser.). 24p. (gr. 2-2). 42.50 (978-1-61513-259-1(7), PowerKids Pr.) Rosen Publishing Group, Inc., The.
—Habitat Para la Humanidad. 2004. (Organizaciones de Ayuda (Helping Organizations) Ser.). (SPA & ENG., Illus.). 24p. (J). (gr. 3-6). lib. bdg. 22.60 (978-0-8239-6857-2(X), Editorial Buenas Letras) Rosen Publishing Group, Inc., The.
—Hábitat para la Humanidad (Habitat for Humanity) 2009. (Organizaciones de ayuda (Helping Organizations) Ser.). (SPA.). 24p. (gr. 2-2). 42.50 (978-1-60851-145-7(6), Editorial Buenas Letras) Rosen Publishing Group, Inc., The.

HOUSING—FICTION

Charles, Norma. Boxcar Kid. 2008. (ENG.). 120p. (YA). (gr. 6-7). pap. 11.99 (978-1-55002-755-6(7)) Dundum CAN. Dist: Ingram Publisher Services.

Geronimo Stilton Staff. Mouse House Hunter. 2015. (Geronimo Stilton Ser.: 61). (ENG.). 128p. (J). (gr. 2-5). pap. 7.99 (978-0-545-83554-1(2), Scholastic Paperbacks) Scholastic, Inc.

Liparulo, Robert. Watcher in the Woods, 1 vol. 2009. (Dreamhouse Kings Ser.: 2). (ENG.). 304p. pap. 9.99 (978-1-59554-728-6(2)) Nelson, Thomas Inc.

Mikkelsen, Jon. The Empty Room. Lueth, Nathan, illus. 2008. (We Are Heroes Ser.). (ENG.). 40p. (gr. 2-3). lib. bdg. 23.99 (978-1-4342-0791-3(9), Keystone Bks.) Stone Arch Bks.

Stilton, Geronimo. Mouse House Hunter. 2015. (Geronimo Stilton Ser.: 61). lib. bdg. 18.40 (978-0-606-37780-5(8)) Turtleback Bks.

West, Jacqueline. The Strangers. Bernatene, Poly, illus. 2013. (Books of Elsewhere Ser.: 4). (ENG.). 320p. (J). (gr. 5). 16.99 (978-0-8037-3690-0(8), Dial Bks) Penguin Young Readers Group.

HOUSTON, SAM, 1793-1863

Bodden, Valerie. Samuel Houston: Army Leader & Historic Politician, 1 vol. 2010. (Military Heroes Ser.). (ENG.). 112p. (J). (gr. 6-12). lib. bdg. 35.64 (978-1-60453-962-2(3)) ABDO Publishing Co.

Caravantes, Peggy. American in Texas: The Story of Sam Houston. 2004. (Notable Americans Ser.). (Illus.). 144p. (YA). (gr. 6-12). 23.95 (978-1-931798-19-8(2)) Reynolds, Morgan Inc.

Harkins, Susan Sales & Harkins, William H. Sam Houston. 2006. (What's So Great About... ? Ser.). (Illus.). 32p. (J). (gr. 2-4). lib. bdg. 25.70 (978-1-58415-482-2(9)) Mitchell Lane Pubs., Inc.

Mattern, Joanne. Sam Houston: A Fearless Statesman, 1 vol. 2012. (Primary Source Readers Ser.). (ENG.). 32p. (J). (gr. 3-3). pap. 8.99 (978-1-4333-5049-8(1)) Teacher Created Materials, Inc.

Miller, Barbara Kiely. Sam Houston. 2007. (Grandes Personajes (Great Americans) Ser.). 24p. (gr. 1-4). (SPA.). pap. 8.15 (978-0-8368-8336-7(5)); pap. 8.15 (978-0-8368-8323-7(3)); lib. bdg. 22.00 (978-0-8368-8316-9(0)); (SPA., Illus.). lib. bdg. 22.00 (978-0-8368-8329-9(2)) Stevens, Gareth Publishing LLLP. (Weekly Reader Leveled Readers).

Sanford, William R. & Green, Carl R. Sam Houston: Courageous Texas Hero. 2012. (Courageous Heroes of the American West Ser.). (Illus.). 48p. (J). pap. 8.95 (978-1-4644-0092-6(X)); (gr. 5-18). lib. bdg. 22.60 (978-0-7660-4009-0(7)) Enslow Pubs., Inc.

Turner, Carolyn. Sam Houston. 2010. pap. 9.95 (978-1-61690-066-3(0)); 24p. (J). (gr. 2-4). lib. bdg. 25.70 (978-1-61690-065-6(2)) Weigl Pubs., Inc.

Wade, Mary Dodson. Sam Houston: Standing Firm. Fisher Hein, Joy, illus. 2009. (ENG.). 24p. (J). (gr. k-2). 16.95 (978-1-933979-13-7(5), b21386f0-913f-4469-aac4-6dc1e0ccf68c) Bright Sky Pr.

Wade, Mary Dodson & Finney, Pat. Sam Houston: I Am Houston. Finney, Pat, illus. 2009. (ENG., Illus.). 64p. (J). (gr. 4-7). 16.95 (978-1-933979-37-3(2), 69142d3c-afed-48b8-9ae8-3c9533f77117) Bright Sky Pr.

Woodward, Mac. Sam Houston: For Texas & the Union. 2009. (Library of American Lives & Times Ser.). 112p. (gr. 5-5). 69.20 (978-1-60853-504-0(5)) Rosen Publishing Group, Inc., The.

Woodward, Walter M. Sam Houston: For Texas & the Union. 2005. (Library of American Lives & Times). (Illus.). 112p. (YA). (gr. 4-8). lib. bdg. 34.60 (978-0-8239-5739-2(X)) Rosen Publishing Group, Inc., The.

HOUSTON, SAM, 1793-1863—FICTION

Kelly, David A. The Astro Outlaw. Meyers, Mark, illus. 2012. (Ballpark Mysteries Ser.: Bk. 4). (ENG.). 112p. (J). (gr. 1-4). pap. 4.99 (978-0-375-86883-2(6), Random Hse. Bks. for Young Readers) Random Hse. Children's Bks.

Sargent, Dave & Sargent, Pat. Grady: (Dappled Grey) Proud to Be an American, 30 vols., Vol. 30. Lenoir, Jane, illus. 2003. (Saddle up Ser.: Vol. 30). 42p. (J). lib. bdg. 23.60 (978-1-56763-813-4(9)) Ozark Publishing.

—Grady: Proud to Be an American, 30 vols. Lenoir, Jane, illus. 2003. (Saddle up Ser.: Vol. 30). 42p. (J). pap. 10.95 (978-1-56763-814-1(7)) Ozark Publishing.

HOUSTON ASTROS (BASEBALL TEAM)

Gilbert, Sara. The Story of the Houston Astros. 2011. (J). 35.65 (978-1-60818-042-4(5), Creative Education) Creative Co., The.

Kennedy, Mike & Stewart, Mark. Meet the Astros. 2010. (Smart about Sports Ser.). 24p. (J). (gr. k-3). lib. bdg. 22.60 (978-1-59953-370-4(7)) Norwood Hse. Pr.

Roselius, J. Chris. Houston Astros, 1 vol. (Inside MLB Ser.). (ENG., 48p. (gr. 3-6). 2011. Illus.). (YA). lib. bdg. 32.79 (978-1-61714-045-7(7)) 2014. lib. bdg. 32.79 (978-1-62403-471-8(3), SportsZone) ABDO Publishing Co.

Stewart, Mark. The Houston Astros. 2012. (Team Spirit Ser.). 48p. (J). (gr. 3-6). lib. bdg. 29.27 (978-1-59953-483-1(5)) Norwood Hse. Pr.

HOUSTON OILERS (FOOTBALL TEAM)

Frisch, Aaron. The History of the Tennessee Titans. 2004. (NFL Today Ser.). (Illus.). 32p. (YA). (gr. 5-9). 18.95 (978-1-58341-316-6(2)) Creative Co., The.

HOVERCRAFT

see Ground-Effect Machines

HOWL, THE MAGICIAN (FICTITIOUS CHARACTER)—FICTION

Jones, Diana Wynne. Howl's Moving Castle. 2008. (World of Howl Ser.: 1). (ENG.). 448p. (J). (gr. 3-7). pap. 7.99 (978-0-06-147878-9(4), Greenwillow Bks.) HarperCollins Pubs.

—Howl's Moving Castle. 2009. 9.00 (978-0-7848-2484-9(3), Everbind) Marco Bk. Co.

—Howl's Moving Castle, 8 vols. 2008. (YA). 101.75 (978-1-4361-5953-1(9)); 179.75 (978-1-4361-5948-7(2)); 104.75 (978-1-4361-5951-7(2)); 1.25 (978-1-4361-5944-9(X)); 78.75 (978-1-4361-5947-0(4)); 75.75 (978-1-4361-5949-4(0)) Recorded Bks., Inc.

HUDSON, HENRY, -1611

Cooke, Tim. Explore with Henry Hudson. 2014. (ENG., Illus.). 32p. (J). (978-0-7787-1246-6(X)); pap. (978-0-7787-1258-9(3)) Crabtree Publishing Co.

Donohue, Moira Rose. Henry Hudson. 2014. (Illus.). 24p. (J). (978-1-938813-16-0(2)) State Standards Publishing, LLC.

Gleason, Carrie. Henry Hudson: Seeking the Northwest Passage. 2005. (In the Footsteps of Explorers Ser.). (ENG., Illus.). 32p. (J). (gr. -1-9). pap. (978-0-7787-2444-5(1)) Crabtree Publishing Co.

Gould, Jane H. Henry Hudson. 2013. (Jr. Graphic Famous Explorers Ser.). (ENG., Illus.). 24p. (J). (gr. 3-6). pap. 10.60 (978-1-4777-0127-0(3)); lib. bdg. 25.25 (978-1-4777-0071-6(4)) Rosen Publishing Group, Inc., The. (PowerKids Pr.).

Hazelton, Amie. Henry Hudson: An Explorer of the Northwest Passage. 2017. (World Explorers Ser.). (ENG., Illus.). 32p. (gr. 3-4). lib. bdg. 27.32 (978-1-5157-4205-0(9)) Capstone Press of Coughlan Cos.

Marsh, Carole. Henry Hudson. 2004. 12p. (gr. k-4). 2.95 (978-0-635-02379-7(2)) Gallopade International.

Molzahn, Arlene Bourgeois. Henry Hudson: Explorer of the Hudson River. 2003. (Explorers! Ser.). (Illus.). 48p. (J). lib. bdg. 25.27 (978-0-7660-2070-2(3)) Enslow Pubs., Inc.

Otfinoski, Steven. Henry Hudson: In Search of the Northwest Passage. 2006. (Great Explorations Ser.). (Illus.). 80p. (J). (gr. 3-7). lib. bdg. 32.79 (978-0-7614-2225-9(0), Benchmark Bks.) Marshall Cavendish Corp.

Petrie, Kristin. Henry Hudson, 1 vol. 2007. (Explorers Set 2 Ser.). (ENG., Illus.). 32p. (gr. 4-7). 27.07 (978-1-59679-741-3(X), Checkerboard Library) ABDO Publishing Co.

Sherman, Josepha. Henry Hudson: English Explorer of the Northwest Passage. (Library of Explorers & Exploration Ser.). 112p. (gr. 5-8). 2009. 66.50 (978-1-60853-605-4(X)) 2003. (Illus.). (J). lib. bdg. 34.60 (978-0-8239-3620-5(1)) Rosen Publishing Group, Inc., The. (Rosen Reference).

—Henry Hudson: Exploring the Northwest Passage. 2015. (Incredible Explorers Ser.). (ENG., Illus.). 64p. (J). (gr. 7-7). 34.21 (978-1-5026-0127-8(3)) Cavendish Square Publishing.

Smalley, Carol Parenzan. Henry Hudson. 2006. (What's So Great About... ? Ser.). (Illus.). 32p. (J). (gr. 2-4). lib. bdg. 25.70 (978-1-58415-479-2(9)) Mitchell Lane Pubs., Inc.

Toth, Henrietta. Henry Hudson. 2016. (Spotlight on Explorers & Colonization Ser.). 00048p. (J). (gr. 6-6). pap. 11.75 (978-1-5081-7222-2(6)) Rosen Publishing Group, Inc., The.

Waxman, Laura Hamilton. A Journey with Henry Hudson. 2017. (Primary Source Explorers Ser.). (ENG.). 40p. (J). (gr. 3-5). 30.65 (978-1-5124-0774-7(7)) Lerner Publishing Group.

Weaver, Janice. Hudson. Craig, David, illus. 2010. (ENG.). 48p. (J). (gr. 3-7). 22.95 (978-0-88776-814-9(8), Tundra Bks.) Tundra Bks. CAN. Dist: Penguin Random Hse. LLC.

Young, Jeff C. Henry Hudson: Discoverer of the Hudson River. 2009. (Great Explorers of the World Ser.). (Illus.). 112p. (J). (gr. 7-12). lib. bdg. 33.27 (978-1-59845-123-8(5)) Enslow Pubs., Inc.

HUDSON RIVER AND VALLEY

Baron, Robert C. & Locker, Thomas. Hudson: The Story of a River. Locker, Thomas, illus. 2004. (ENG., Illus.). 32p. (J). (gr. 3). 17.95 (978-1-55591-512-4(4)) Fulcrum Publishing.

Childress, Diana. Along the Hudson. 2003. (Rivers of North America Ser.). (J). lib. bdg. 34.93 (978-0-8225-4697-9(3), Lerner Pubns.) Lerner Publishing Group.

Harmon, Daniel E. Hudson River. 2004. (Rivers in American Life & Times Ser.). (Illus.). 120p. (C). (gr. 9-13). 32.50 (978-0-7910-7727-6(6), Chelsea Hse.) Facts On File, Inc.

Hazelton, Amie. Henry Hudson: An Explorer of the Northwest Passage. 2017. (World Explorers Ser.). (ENG., Illus.). 32p. (gr. 3-4). lib. bdg. 27.32 (978-1-5157-4205-0(9)) Capstone Press of Coughlan Cos.

Talbott, Hudson. River of Dreams: The Story of the Hudson River. Talbott, Hudson, illus. 2009. (ENG., Illus.). 40p. (J). (gr. 1-3). 17.99 (978-0-399-24521-3(9), G.P. Putnam's Sons Books for Young Readers) Penguin Young Readers Group.

Wood, Ian. The Hudson River. 2003. (Rivers of North America Ser.). (Illus.). 32p. (gr. 2-6). lib. bdg. 26.00 (978-0-8368-3755-1(X), Gareth Stevens Learning Library) Stevens, Gareth Publishing LLLP.

HUDSON'S BAY COMPANY

Andra-Warner, Elle. Hudson's Bay Company Adventures: Tales of Canada's Early Fur Traders. 2006. (Amazing Stories Ser.). (ENG.). 96p. (J). pap. 9.95 (978-1-55439-700-6(6), 9781554397006) Lorimer, James & Co., Ltd., Pubs. CAN. Dist: Casemate Pubs. & Bk. Distributors, LLC.

Bailey, Katharine. Radisson & des Groseilliers: Fur Traders of the North. 2006. (In the Footsteps of Explorers Ser.). (ENG., Illus.). 32p. (J). (gr. 3-7). lib. bdg. (978-0-7787-2422-3(0), 1253444); (gr. 4-7). pap. (978-0-7787-2458-2(1), 1253444) Crabtree Publishing Co.

HUGGINS, HENRY (FICTITIOUS CHARACTER)—FICTION

Cleary, Beverly. Henry & Beezus. Darling, Louis et al, illus. 2014. (Henry Huggins Ser.: 2). (ENG.). 224p. (J). (gr. 3-7). 16.99 (978-0-688-21383-1(9)); 50th anniv. ed. pap. 6.99 (978-0-380-70914-4(7)) HarperCollins Pubs.

—Henry & Beezus. (Henry Huggins Ser.). 192p. (J). (gr. 1-4). pap. 4.99 (978-0-8072-1484-8(1), Listening Library) Random Hse. Audio Publishing Group.

—Henry & Ribsy. Darling, Louis et al, illus. 2014. (Henry Huggins Ser.: 3). (ENG.). (J). (gr. 3-7). 192p. 16.99 (978-0-688-21382-4(0)); 50th anniv. ed. 208p. pap. 6.99 (978-0-380-70917-5(1)) HarperCollins Pubs.

—The Henry & Ribsy Box Set: Henry Huggins, Henry & Ribsy, Ribsy. 2015. (Henry Huggins Ser.). (ENG.). 624p. (J). (gr. 3-7). pap. 18.99 (978-0-06-236063-2(9)) HarperCollins Pubs.

—Henry & the Clubhouse. Darling, Louis et al, illus. 2014. (Henry Huggins Ser.: 5). (ENG.). 224p. (J). (gr. 3-7). 16.99 (978-0-688-21381-7(2)); pap. 7.99 (978-0-380-70915-1(5)) HarperCollins Pubs.

—Henry & the Paper Route. Darling, Louis et al, illus. 2014. (Henry Huggins Ser.: 4). (ENG.). 224p. (J). (gr. 3-7). 16.99 (978-0-688-21380-0(4)); reprint ed. pap. 7.99 (978-0-380-70921-2(X)) HarperCollins Pubs.

—Henry Huggins. Darling, Louis et al, illus. 2014. (Henry Huggins Ser.: 1). (ENG.). 208p. (J). (gr. 3-7). 16.99 (978-0-688-21385-5(5)) HarperCollins Pubs.

—Henry Huggins, 1 vol. Darling, Louis, illus. 2004. (Henry Huggins Ser.: 1). (SPA.). 160p. (J). (gr. 3-7). pap. 7.99 (978-0-06-073600-2(3)) HarperCollins Pubs.

—Henry Huggins. Darling, Louis et al, illus. 50th anniv. ed. 2016. (Henry Huggins Ser.: 1). (ENG.). 208p. (J). (gr. 3-7). pap. 6.99 (978-0-380-70912-0(0)) HarperCollins Pubs.

—Ribsy. Darling, Louis et al, illus. 2014. (Henry Huggins Ser.: 6). (ENG.). 240p. (J). (gr. 3-7). 16.99 (978-0-688-21662-7(5)); pap. 7.99 (978-0-380-70955-7(4)) HarperCollins Pubs.

HUGHES, LANGSTON, 1902-1967

Anderson, Jennifer Joline. Langston Hughes, 1 vol. 2013. (Great American Authors Ser.). (ENG.). 48p. (J). (gr. 3-6). lib. bdg. 32.79 (978-1-61783-718-0(0)) ABDO Publishing Co.

Anthony, David H. Langston Hughes: Harlem Renaissance Writer, 1 vol. 2011. (Primary Source Readers Ser.). (ENG., Illus.). 32p. (J). (gr. 4-4). pap. 8.99 (978-1-4333-1520-6(3)) Teacher Created Materials, Inc.

Berry, S. L. Langston Hughes. 2014. lib. bdg. 35.65 (978-1-60818-327-2(0)) Creative Co., The.

—Voices in Poetry: Langston Hughes. 2015. (Voices in Poetry Ser.). (ENG.). 48p. (J). (gr. 5-8). pap. 12.00 (978-1-62832-055-8(9), Creative Paperbacks) Creative Co., The.

Gallagher, Brigid. Langston Hughes, 1 vol. 2012. (American Biographies Ser.). (ENG.). 48p. (gr. 4-6). pap. 9.95 (978-1-4329-6466-5(6), NA-h) Heinemann-Raintree.

Gibson, Karen Bush. Langston Hughes. 2007. (Poets & Playwrights Ser.). (Illus.). 112p. (J). (gr. 3-7). lib. bdg. 37.10 (978-1-58415-431-0(4)) Mitchell Lane Pubs., Inc.

Hudson, Katura J. & Hudson, Cheryl Willis. Langston's Legacy: 101 Ways to Celebrate the Life & Work of Langston Hughes. Hudson, Stephan, photos by. 2004. (Illus.). 48p. (J). (gr. 4-18). pap. 7.95 (978-0-940975-99-6(8), Sankofa Bks.) Just Us Bks., Inc.

Rhynes, Martha E. I, Too, Sing America: The Story of Langston Hughes. 2004. (World Writers Ser.). (Illus.). 144p. (YA). (gr. 6-12). 23.95 (978-1-883846-89-3(7), First Biographies) Reynolds, Morgan Inc.

Roby, Cynthia A. & Rohan, Rebecca. Langston Hughes. 2016. (Artists of the Harlem Renaissance Ser.). (ENG.). 128p. (J). (gr. 9-9). lib. bdg. 45.64 (978-1-5026-1064-5(7)) Cavendish Square Publishing.

Shull, Jodie A. Langston Hughes: Life Makes Poems. 2006. (African-American Biography Library). (Illus.). 128p. (J). (gr. 6-12). lib. bdg. 33.27 (978-0-7660-2468-7(7)) Enslow Pubs., Inc.

Wallace, Maurice O. Langston Hughes: The Harlem Renaissance. 2007. (Writers & Their Work Ser.). (Illus.). 144p. (J). (gr. 4-7). lib. bdg. 39.93 (978-0-7614-2591-5(8), Benchmark Bks.) Marshall Cavendish Corp.

HULL HOUSE (CHICAGO, ILL.)

Owens, Tom. Immigrants & Neighbors. 2003. (Illus.). 40p. pap. 8.00 (978-0-7891-5850-5(7)) Perfection Learning Corp.

HUMAN-ANIMAL RELATIONSHIPS

see also Animals And Civilization

Albee, Sarah. Bugged: How Insects Changed History. Leighton, Robert, illus. 2014. (ENG.). 176p. (J). (gr. 3-6). pap. 17.99 (978-0-8027-3422-8(7), 9780802734228, Bloomsbury USA Childrens) Bloomsbury Publishing USA.

Baker, Joan. A Tale of Two Beagles. 2013. 16p. pap. 7.95 (978-1-4908-1539-8(2), WestBow Pr.) Author Solutions, Inc.

Boothroyd, Jennifer. People & the Environment. 2008. (First Step Nonfiction - Ecology Ser.). (Illus.). 23p. (J). (gr. -1-3). lib. bdg. 18.60 (978-0-8225-8601-2(0), Lerner Pubns.); pap. 34.95 (978-0-8225-9357-7(2)) Lerner Publishing Group.

Bowman, Donna Janell. Step Right Up: How Doc & Jim Key Taught the World about Kindness, 1 vol. Minter, Daniel, illus. 2016. (ENG.). 48p. (J). (gr. 2-8). 19.95 (978-1-62014-148-9(5)) Lee & Low Bks., Inc.

Bozzo, Linda. When Parrots Speak. 2017. (Animal Emotions Ser.). 32p. (J). (gr. 3-3). pap. 10.52 **(978-0-7660-8864-1(2))**; lib. bdg. 25.27 **(978-0-7660-8621-0(6))** Enslow Pubs., Inc.

Brouwer, Sigmund. Innocent Heroes. 2017. (ENG., Illus.). 208p. (J). (gr. 4-7). 16.99 (978-1-101-91846-3(2), Tundra Bks.) Tundra Bks. CAN. Dist: Penguin Random Hse. LLC.

Brunke, Dawn Baumann. Animal Voices, Animal Guides: Discover Your Deeper Self Through Communication with Animals. 2nd ed. 2009. (ENG.). 256p. pap. 16.00 (978-1-59143-098-8(4)) Bear & Co.

—Awakening to Animal Voices: A Teen Guide to Telepathic Communication with All Life. 2004. (ENG., Illus.). 272p. (YA). (gr. 7-12). pap. 14.95 (978-0-89281-136-6(6), Healing Arts Pr.) Inner Traditions International, Ltd.

Cass, Liz. Ouisa & the Big People. 2012. (ENG., Illus.). 77p. (978-1-907629-35-8(1)) ShieldCrest.

Cohn, Jessica. Una Mano a la Pata: Protegiendo Los Animales. 2017. (TIME for Kids en Español - Level 4 Ser.). (SPA., Illus.). 48p. (gr. 4-4). lib. bdg. 31.99 (978-1-5157-5148-9(1)) Time for Kids Inc AUS. Dist: Capstone Pub.

Collins, Ellen. A Biography: My Life As a Basset Hound (2005. 51p. pap. 16.95 (978-1-4137-8776-4(2)) America Star Bks.

Cowcher, Helen. Desert Elephants, 1 vol. Cowcher, Helen, illus. 2011. (ENG., Illus.). 40p. (J). (gr. k-3). 16.99 (978-0-374-31774-4(7), 9780374317744, Farrar, Straus & Giroux (BYR)) Farrar, Straus & Giroux.

Cox, Lynne. Elizabeth, Queen of the Seas. Floca, Brian, illus. 2014. (ENG.). 48p. (J). (gr. -1-3). 20.99 (978-0-375-95888-5(6)); 17.99 (978-0-375-85888-8(1)) Random Hse. Children's Bks. (Schwartz & Wade Bks.).

Dee, Joan. Bertie. 2012. (Illus.). 48p. pap. 9.60 (978-1-909300-01-9(2)) Action Publishing Technology Ltd GBR. Dist: Printondemand-worldwide.com.

Downer, Ann. Wild Animal Neighbors: Sharing Our Urban World. 2013. 64p. pap. 24.95 (978-1-4677-1663-5(4)); (ENG., Illus.). (gr. 5-12). 33.27 (978-0-7613-9021-3(9), Twenty-First Century Bks.) Lerner Publishing Group.

Earley, Chris. Falcons in the City: The Story of a Peregine Family. Massey, Luke, photos by. 2016. (ENG., Illus.). 48p. (J). (gr. 4-8). pap. 9.95 (978-1-77085-803-9(2), 9781770858039) Firefly Bks., Ltd.

Ekberg, Jodi & Lisman, Jaclyn. The Adventures of Cain & Frankie: The Husky Brothers - the Beginning. 2013. 24p. pap. 13.97 (978-1-62212-529-6(0), Strategic Bk. Publishing) Strategic Book Publishing & Rights Agency (SBPRA).

Fleury, Rick & Staehr, Linda. Rainbows for Buckerou. 2013. 24p. pap. 10.95 (978-1-4497-8775-2(4), WestBow Pr.) Author Solutions, Inc.

Ford, Gabrielle & Thomson, Sarah. Gabe & Izzy: Standing up for America's Bullied. 2014. (ENG., Illus.). 192p. (J). (gr. 5). pap. 8.99 (978-0-14-750994-9(7), Puffin Books) Penguin Young Readers Group.

Fornaro, Claire. The Puppy Factory Guide to Dog Care: The Absolute to the Zany of Dog Care. 2009. 28p. pap. 13.50 (978-1-4251-6597-0(4)) Trafford Publishing.

Gallina, Danielle. Dear God, Are There Any Flies in Heaven? Foy, Denis, illus. 2013. (ENG.). (J). 15.98 (978-1-62086-380-0(4)) Mascot Bks., Inc.

Gill, Shelley. Gabe. Scheff, Marc, illus. 2016. (ENG.). 64p. (J). (gr. 3-7). lib. bdg. 12.95 (978-1-57091-354-9(4)) Charlesbridge Publishing, Inc.

Green, Joanne. The Story of Thumper the Cleft-Affected Bunny. 2008. 56p. pap. (978-1-897512-14-2(7)) Saga Bks.

Green, Sara. Military Dogs. 2013. (Dogs to the Rescue! Ser.). (ENG., Illus.). 24p. (J). (gr. 3-8). lib. bdg. 25.95 (978-1-60014-956-6(1), Pilot Bks.) Bellwether Media.

Hammond, Charmaine. Toby, the Pet Therapy Dog, & His Hospital Friends. Prevac, Rose Anne, illus. 2011. (ENG.). 36p. (J). pap. 12.99 (978-0-9836045-0-1(9), Kendahl Hse. Pr.) Youngs, Bettie Bks.

—Toby, the Pet Therapy Dog, Says Be a Buddy, Not a Bully. 2013. (ENG., Illus.). 34p. (J). pap. 12.99 (978-0-9836045-4-9(1)) Youngs, Bettie Bks.

—Toby, the Pet Therapy Dog, Says Be a Buddy Not a Bully. Prevec, Rose Anne, illus. 2013. (ENG.). (J). pap. 12.95 (978-0-9836045-5-6(X), Kendahl Hse. Pr.) Youngs, Bettie Bks.

Hansen, Keli. Nala's Story. 2009. 130p. pap. 19.95 (978-1-60749-816-2(2)) America Star Bks.

Hargreaves, Susan. Animal Hero Kids: Voices for the Voiceless. 2014. (Illus.). 284p. (J). pap. 27.95 (978-0-615-99522-9(5)) Animal Hero Kids.

Hart, Anne. Dogs with Careers: Ten Happy-Ending Stories of Purpose & Passion. 2007. 348p. per. 19.95 (978-0-595-47474-5(8), ASJA Pr.) iUniverse, Inc.

Herglotz, Pam Herglotz. Ichabod & the Chipmunks. 2010. 40p. pap. 17.91 (978-0-557-19218-2(8)) Lulu Pr., Inc.

Hodge, Susie. Artists & Their Pets: True Stories of Famous Artists & Their Animal Friends. Lemay, Violet, illus. 2017. (ENG.). 192p. (J). (gr. 2-5). 14.95 **(978-1-946064-01-1(7))** Duo Pr. LLC.

Holt, Carmen & Jim. Betun: The Story of a Rascalero As Told by His Companeros. 2012. 28p. pap. 19.99 (978-1-4772-6665-6(8)) AuthorHouse.

Howard, Denise. Jameela's Big Adventure. 2009. 84p. pap. 10.49 (978-1-4490-5355-0(6)) AuthorHouse.

Hussl Krassnig, Gloria. What a Family. 2006. (Illus.). 114p. 23.95 (978-0-9791468-0-0(1)) Hussl, Gloria.

Jenkins, Steve. Never Smile at a Monkey: And 17 Other Important Things to Remember. Jenkins, Steve, illus. 2009. (ENG., Illus.). 32p. (J). (gr. -1-3). 17.99 (978-0-618-96620-2(X)) Houghton Mifflin Harcourt Publishing Co.

Johnson, Nancy Carole. Pierre, the Turtle Who Went to College. 2008. 24p. pap. 10.95 (978-1-4327-2614-0(5)) Outskirts Pr., Inc.

Kalman, Bobbie. My Dog Likes Me. 2010. (My World Ser.). (ENG.). 16p. (J). (gr. k-3). (978-0-7787-9499-8(7)); pap. (978-0-7787-9524-7(1)) Crabtree Publishing Co.

Katz, Jon. Meet the Dogs of Bedlam Farm. Katz, Jon, photos by. 2011. (ENG., Illus.). 32p. (J). (gr. -1-3). 17.99 (978-0-8050-9219-6(6), 9780805092196, Holt, Henry & Co. Bks. For Young Readers) Holt, Henry & Co.

Kimmelman, Leslie. A Dog Named Honey. 2005. (IOpeners Ser.). (Illus.). 8p. (J). pap. 7.56 (978-0-7652-5144-2(2)) Celebration Pr.

King, Vickie. Search Dogs & You, a Wilderness Safety Guide from American Search Dogs. 2009. 32p. pap. 13.00 (978-1-60860-105-9(6), Strategic Bk. Publishing) Strategic Book Publishing & Rights Agency (SBPRA).

Krisher, Trudy. An Affectionate Farewell: the Story of Old Abe & Old Bob. Dodson, Bert, illus. 2015. (ENG.). 32p. (J). (gr. 1-2). 17.95 (978-1-59373-155-7(8)) Bunker Hill Publishing, Inc.

Lawrence-Loughlin, Amy. For the Love of Gus: A True Rescue to Riches Tale. 2012. 36p. pap. 15.49 (978-1-4669-5371-0(3)) Trafford Publishing.

Leonard, Dion. Finding Gobi: The True Story of One Little Dog's Big Journey. 2017. (ENG.). 208p. (J). pap. 14.99 **(978-0-7180-7531-6(5))** Nelson, Thomas Inc.

Levy, Debbie & Panza, Rosana. Dozer's Run: A True Story of a Dog & His Race. Opie, David, illus. 2014. (ENG.). 32p. (J). (gr. 1-4). 16.99 (978-1-58536-896-9(2), 203665) Sleeping Bear Pr.

Love, Ann & Drake, Jane. Talking Tails: The Incredible Connection Between People & Their Pets. Slavin, Bill, illus. (ENG.). 80p. (J). (gr. 4-7). 2012. pap. 9.95 (978-1-77049-359-9(X)) 2010. 22.95 (978-0-88776-884-2(9)) Tundra Bks. CAN. (Tundra Bks.). Dist: Penguin Random Hse. LLC.

Lucky (The Cat). My 9 8 7 6 5 4 3 2 1 Lives: A Cat's Tail of Her near Death & Life Experiences. 2009. 52p. pap. 22.49 (978-1-4490-0076-9(2)) AuthorHouse.

Lunis, Natalie. Comfort Dogs. 2014. (Dog Heroes Ser.). (ENG., Illus.). 32p. (J). (gr. 2-7). lib. bdg. 25.27 (978-1-62724-287-5(2)) Bearport Publishing Co., Inc.

Mansfield, Monica. When You Have to Say Goodbye: Loving & Letting Go of Your Pet. Peterson, Lennie, illus. 2011. (ENG.). 32p. (J). (gr. k). 8.95 (978-0-9831032-1-9(6), BeanPole Bks.) Harren Communications, LLC.

Marrin, Albert. Oh Rats! Mordan, C. B., illus. 2014. (ENG.). 112p. (J). (gr. 5). pap. 8.99 (978-0-14-751281-9(6), Puffin Books) Penguin Young Readers Group.

—Oh, Rats! The Story of Rats & People. 2006. (ENG., Illus.). 48p. (J). (gr. 5-18). 16.99 (978-0-525-47762-4(4), Dutton Books for Young Readers) Penguin Young Readers Group.

Marsico, Katie. How Do We Live Together? Coyotes. 2010. (Community Connections: How Do We Live Together? Ser.).

(ENG.). 24p. (gr. 2-5). lib. bdg. 25.64 (978-1-60279-621-8(1), 200325) Cherry Lake Publishing.

—How Do We Live Together? Hawks. 2010. (Community Connections: How Do We Live Together? Ser.). (ENG.). 24p. (gr. 2-5). lib. bdg. 25.64 (978-1-60279-624-9(6), 200327) Cherry Lake Publishing.

—How Do We Live Together? Rabbits. 2010. (Community Connections: How Do We Live Together? Ser.). (ENG.). 24p. (gr. 2-5). lib. bdg. 25.64 (978-1-60279-622-5(X), 200329) Cherry Lake Publishing.

—How Do We Live Together? Turtles. 2010. (Community Connections: How Do We Live Together? Ser.). (ENG.). 24p. (gr. 2-5). lib. bdg. 25.64 (978-1-60279-623-2(8), 200332) Cherry Lake Publishing.

—Therapy Horses. 2013. 48p. (J). (gr. 4-8). 29.93 (978-1-60870-839-0(X)) Cavendish Square Publishing.

Milanowski, Lorraine. Holly the Lucky Little Kitten. 2009. 20p. pap. 10.49 (978-1-4490-0380-7(X)) AuthorHouse.

Moberg, Julia. Animal Heroes: The Wolves, Camels, Elephants, Dogs, Cats, Horses, Penguins, Dolphins, & Other Remarkable Animals That Proved They Are Man's Best Friend. Albrecht Studios, Jeff, illus. 2017. (ENG.). 96p. (J). (gr. 2-7). 14.95 (978-1-63322-159-8(8), Moondance) Quarto Publishing Group USA.

Mobley, W. Lenore. Enjoy the Journey: Of Women & Their Horses along the Snake River Plain. 2011. 220p. (gr. -1 — 1). pap. 17.50 (978-1-4567-6954-3(5)) AuthorHouse.

Morgan, Lynne. Crackers. 2007. (Illus.). 60p. per. 9.99 (978-0-9795935-0-5(6), Eloquent Bks.) Strategic Book Publishing & Rights Agency (SBPRA).

Murphy, Frank. George Washington & the General's Dog. Walz, Richard, illus. 2015. 48p. pap. 5.00 (978-1-61003-605-4(0)) Center for the Collaborative Classroom.

—George Washington & the General's Dog. 2003. (J). 1.25 (978-1-4025-4103-2(1)) Recorded Bks., Inc.

National Geographic Kids Staff. Animal Friendship! Collection: Amazing Stories of Animal Friends & the Humans That Love Them. 2015. (NGK Chapters Ser.). (ENG.). 336p. (J). (gr. 2-5). pap. 14.99 (978-1-4263-2022-4(1), National Geographic Children's Bks.) National Geographic Society.

—Funny Animals! Collection: Amazing Stories of Hilarious Animals & Surprising Talents. 2015. (NGK Chapters Ser.). (ENG., Illus.). 336p. (J). (gr. 2-5). pap. 14.99 (978-1-4263-2024-8(8), National Geographic Children's Bks.) National Geographic Society.

—To the Rescue! Collection: Amazing Stories of Courageous Animals & Animal Rescues. 2015. (NGK Chapters Ser.). (ENG.). 336p. (J). (gr. 2-5). pap. 14.99 (978-1-4263-2023-1(X), National Geographic Children's Bks.) National Geographic Society.

National Geographic Kids Staff & Donohue, Moira Rose. Kangaroo to the Rescue! And More True Stories of Amazing Animal Heroes. 2015. (NGK Chapters Ser.). (ENG.). 112p. (J). (gr. 2-5). pap. 5.99 (978-1-4263-1913-6(4)); lib. bdg. 14.90 (978-1-4263-1915-0(0)) National Geographic Society. (National Geographic Children's Bks.).

Newman, Aline Alexander. Cat Tales: True Stories of Kindness & Companionship with Kitties. 2017. (ENG., Illus.). 160p. (J). (gr. k-12). 12.99 (978-1-4263-2734-6(X), National Geographic Children's Bks.) National Geographic Society.

—Lucky Leopards! 2014. (NGK Chapters Ser.). (ENG., Illus.). 112p. (J). (gr. 2-5). lib. bdg. 14.90 (978-1-4263-1458-2(2), National Geographic Children's Bks.) National Geographic Society.

—Lucky Leopards! And More True Stories of Amazing Animal Rescues! 2014. (NGK Chapters Ser.). (ENG., Illus.). 112p. (J). (gr. 2-5). pap. 5.99 (978-1-4263-1457-5(4), National Geographic Children's Bks.) National Geographic Society.

Newman, Aline Alexander & Weitzman, Gary. How to Speak Cat: A Guide to Decoding Cat Language. 2015. (ENG., Illus.). 176p. (J). (gr. 3-7). pap. 12.99 (978-1-4263-1863-4(4), National Geographic Children's Bks.) National Geographic Society.

Norris, A. Smokey the Kitten - A True Story. 2007. 264p. pap. 4.95 (978-1-4184-7028-9(7)) AuthorHouse.

O'Connell, Caitlin. Bridge to the Wild: Behind the Scenes at the Zoo. Rodwell, Timothy, photos by. 2016. (ENG., Illus.). 208p. (J). (gr. 5-7). 18.99 (978-0-544-27739-7(2), HMH Books For Young Readers) Houghton Mifflin Harcourt Publishing Co.

Olsson, Elizabeth. The Tiny Pink House. 2010. 24p. 19.95 (978-1-4520-1203-2(2)) AuthorHouse.

Orcutt, Cherie. A Beautiful Husky Needs a Home. Frongia, Daniela, illus. 2012. 32p. pap. 21.00 (978-1-4685-7156-1(7)) AuthorHouse.

Paderewski, Elliot. Plants, Animals, & People Live Together. 2016. (Rosen REAL Readers: STEM & STEAM Collection). 8p. (gr. 1-k). pap. 5.46 (978-1-5081-2398-9(5), Rosen Classroom) Rosen Publishing Group, Inc., The.

Patent, Dorothy Hinshaw. The Horse & the Plains Indians: A Powerful Partnership. Munoz, William, photos by. 2012. (ENG., Illus.). 112p. (J). (gr. 5-7). 17.99 (978-0-547-12551-0(8)) Houghton Mifflin Harcourt Publishing Co.

Paulsen, Gary. This Side of Wild. Jessell, Tim, illus. 2015. (ENG.). 144p. (J). (gr. 5). 16.99 (978-1-4814-5150-5(2), Simon & Schuster Bks. For Young Readers) Simon & Schuster Bks. For Young Readers.

—This Side of Wild: Mutts, Mares, & Laughing Dinosaurs. Jessell, Tim, illus. 2016. (ENG.). 160p. (J). (gr. 5). pap. 7.99 (978-1-4814-5151-2(0), Simon & Schuster Bks. For Young Readers) Simon & Schuster Bks. For Young Readers.

Peters, Gregory N. Real Animal Heroes, 1 vol. 2014. (Real World Adventures Ser.). (ENG.). 48p. (gr. 4-12). 31.99 (978-1-4765-8532-1(6)) Capstone Press of Coughlan Cos.

Quigley, Karen. Everyone Loves Elwood. 2007. (Illus.). 42p. (YA). 15.00 (978-0-9800449-1-1(X)) Quigley, Karen.

Raatma, Lucia. How Do We Live Together? Deer. 2010. (Community Connections: How Do We Live Together? Ser.). (ENG.). 24p. (gr. 2-5). lib. bdg. 25.64 (978-1-60279-618-8(1), 200326) Cherry Lake Publishing.

—How Do We Live Together? Mountain Lions. 2010. (Community Connections: How Do We Live Together? Ser.). (ENG.). 24p. (gr. 2-5). lib. bdg. 25.64 (978-1-60279-625-6(4), 200328) Cherry Lake Publishing.

—How Do We Live Together? Raccoons. 2010. (Community Connections: How Do We Live Together? Ser.). (ENG.). 24p. (gr. 2-5). lib. bdg. 25.64 (978-1-60279-619-5(X), 200330) Cherry Lake Publishing.

—How Do We Live Together? Snakes. 2010. (Community Connections: How Do We Live Together? Ser.). (ENG.). 24p. (gr. 2-5). lib. bdg. 25.64 (978-1-60279-620-1(3), 200331) Cherry Lake Publishing.

Rankin, Renee. Miss Lantz & Sadey: First in the Series of Little Sunshines Life Journey. 2013. 44p. pap. 16.95 (978-1-63000-412-5(X)) America Star Bks.

Rau, Harry the Cat. 2009. 28p. pap. 15.99 (978-1-4389-3876-9(4)) AuthorHouse.

Rayburn, Scooter. Animal Friends for You! Let's Be Friends! 2011. 16p. pap. (978-1-4269-8944-5(X)) Trafford Publishing (UK) Ltd.

Rayyan, Omar, illus. My Kitten's First Year. 2008. (ENG.). 24p. (J). (gr. -1-3). 12.99 (978-0-8249-5572-4(2), Ideal Pubns.) Worthy Publishing.

Reilly, Cherie Brooks. Feathered & Furry Friends at the Farm. 2012. 108p. (gr. -1). pap. 11.92 (978-1-4669-4095-6(6)) Trafford Publishing.

Rice, Dona. Please Don't Feed the Animals. 2015. (Building Fluency Through Reader's Theater Ser.). (ENG., Illus.). 32p. (gr. 3-3). pap. 7.99 (978-1-4938-1288-2(2)) Teacher Created Materials, Inc.

Richmond, Marianne R. Goodbye, Faithful Friend: Remembering Your Dog with Love. 2005. (ENG., Illus.). 40p. (YA). 7.95 (978-0-9770000-1-2(X), Marianne Richmond Studios, Inc.) Sourcebooks, Inc.

Richter, Ian. Chloe the Cat. 2013. 24p. pap. 12.45 (978-1-4525-8111-8(8), Balboa Pr.) Author Solutions, Inc.

Ritthaler, Lynn. Pepper. 2012. 142p. (gr. -1). 23.99 (978-1-4772-8009-6(X)); pap. 14.95 (978-1-4772-8010-2(3)) AuthorHouse.

Ross, Samuel B., Jr. The Extraordinary Spirit of Green Chimneys: Connecting Children & Animals to Create Hope. 2011. (ENG., Illus.). 268p. 24.95 (978-1-55753-580-1(9), f4620000-a1e9-429e-8b9a-e198a58f775f) Purdue Univ. Pr.

Schaefer, Peggy. More Stories of Dogs. 2005. (Illus.). 205p. 12.95 (978-0-8249-4639-5(1), Ideal Pubns.) Worthy Publishing.

Seaver Keith, Emily. A Home for Webby. Seaver Keith, Emily, illus. 2008. (Illus.). 23p. (J). (gr. -1-3). 16.95 (978-0-9728646-1-9(X)) Bangzoom Pubs.

Shields, Amy. Best Friends Forever! And More True Stories of Animal Friendships. 2013. (NGK Chapters Ser.). (ENG., Illus.). 112p. (J). (gr. 2-5). pap. 5.99 (978-1-4263-0935-9(X)); lib. bdg. 14.90 (978-1-4263-0954-0(6)) National Geographic Society. (National Geographic Children's Bks.).

Simms, Rk. Me & My Dog, Petey. 2008. 32p. pap. 19.99 (978-1-4363-2842-5(X)) Xlibris Corp.

Simonds, Lucy. People & Pets. 2007. (Trackers-Math Ser.). (gr. 2-5). pap. 5.00 (978-1-59055-920-8(7)) Pacific Learning, Inc.

Stanley, Sheryl. Hank Becomes a Hero. 2009. 40p. pap. 18.49 (978-1-4389-6081-4(6)) AuthorHouse.

Steward, Martha. Darby's Story: The Life of an Adopted Dog. 2009. 36p. pap. 15.95 (978-1-4490-2775-9(X)) AuthorHouse.

Stockburger, Susan. Adventures of Sugar Pie! 2011. 20p. (gr. -1). pap. 11.00 (978-1-4567-5356-6(8)) AuthorHouse.

Stone, Kelly P. What Do Pets Do When They Go up to Heaven?, 1 vol. Stone, Kelly P. & Stone, Joyce M., illus. 2009. 13p. pap. 24.95 (978-1-61546-212-4(0)) America Star Bks.

Tait, Leia. Pecorino. 2008. (Inspiring Animals Ser.). (Illus.). 24p. (J). (gr. 2-4). pap. 8.95 (978-1-59036-859-6(2)); lib. bdg. 24.45 (978-1-59036-858-9(4)) Weigl Pubs., Inc.

Unruh, Cindy. Sierra, the Black Lab Who Loved to Eat: (a True Story) Krehbiel, Angie, illus. 2012. 32p. pap. 24.95 (978-1-4626-5537-3(8)) America Star Bks.

Weintraub, Robert. No Better Friend: A Man, a Dog, & Their Incredible True Story of Friendship & Survival in World War II. 2016. (ENG., Illus.). 304p. (J). (gr. 5-17). 16.99 (978-0-316-34467-8(2)) Little, Brown Bks. for Young Readers.

Wells, Melisa. Remembering Ruby: For Families Living Beyond the Loss of a Pet. 2007. 60p. per. 9.95 (978-1-4327-0351-6(X)) Outskirts Pr., Inc.

White-Adams, Beverly & Adams, Rusty. The Adventures of Rusty: Rusty Goes to Virginia Vol. 1. 2011. 32p. pap. (978-1-4269-8935-3(0)) Trafford Publishing (UK) Ltd.

HUMAN-ANIMAL RELATIONSHIPS—FICTION

Aaron, Chester. An American Ghost. 2011. (YA). pap. (978-1-936144-28-0(X)) Zumaya Pubns. LLC.

Abramson, Jill & O'Connor, Jane. Holiday Helper. Melmon, Deborah, illus. 2014. (Penguin Young Readers, Level 2 Ser.). (ENG.). 32p. (J). (gr. 1-3). pap. 3.99 (978-0-448-45677-5(X), Penguin Young Readers) Penguin Young Readers Group.

Adams, Jean Ekman. A Cowgirl & her Horse. 2011. (Illus.). 32p. (J). 15.95 (978-1-933855-71-4(1)) Rio Nuevo Pubs.

Allen, Page. Madison's Descent: A Child's Journey. (Illus.). (J). 2006. pap. 25.00 (978-0-9752516-2-1(7)) 2004. lib. bdg. 60.00 (978-0-9752516-1-4(9)) Otis & Randolph Pr.

Amundson, Susan D. Three Little Lambs — Somewhere. Geiken, Brenda Joy, illus. 2006. 40p. (J). (978-1-59984-002-4(2)) Bluedoor, llc.

Angus, Sam. Soldier Dog. 2014. (ENG.). 272p. (J). (gr. 4-7). pap. 7.99 (978-1-250-04417-4(0), 9781250044174) Square Fish.

Anyanwu, Francis Eze. The Awesome Dog: How the Dog Became Man's Best Friend. 2011. 73p. pap. 14.95 (978-1-4327-5666-6(4)) Outskirts Pr., Inc.

Armstrong, Kelley. The Gathering. (Darkness Rising Ser.: 1). (YA). (gr. 8). 2012. 384p. pap. 9.99 (978-0-06-179703-3(0)) 2011. 368p. 17.99 (978-0-06-179702-6(2)) HarperCollins Pubs.

—The Gathering. (Darkness Rising Ser.: Bk. 1). (YA). 1.25 (978-1-4498-6189-5(X)); 100.75 (978-1-4498-6186-5(5)); 2013. 102.75 (978-1-4498-6184-1(9)) Recorded Bks., Inc.

Aubry, Cécile. Belle & Sebastien: The Child of the Montains. Norminton, Gregory, tr. from FRE. Stephens, Helen, illus. 2016. (ENG.). 200p. (J). 10.99 (978-1-84749-591-4(5), 9781847495914, Alma Classics) Bloomsbury Publishing USA.

Baker, E. D. Dragon Kiss. 2nd ed. 2009. (Tales of the Frog Princess Ser.). (ENG.). 288p. (YA). (gr. 5-8). 16.99 (978-1-59990-348-4(2), 9781599903484, Bloomsbury USA Childrens) Bloomsbury Publishing USA.

Baldwin, Christopher. Little Dee & the Penguin. 2016. (ENG., Illus.). 128p. (J). (gr. 3-7). pap. 10.99 (978-0-8037-4108-9(1), Dial Bks) Penguin Young Readers Group.

Ballantyne, Robert Michael. Jarwin & Cuffy. l.t. ed. 2007. (ENG.). 102p. pap. 19.99 (978-1-4346-3724-6(7)) Creative Media Partners, LLC.

Banks, Anna. Of Poseidon. 2013. (Syrena Legacy Ser.: 1). (ENG.). 384p. (YA). (gr. 8-12). pap. 10.99 (978-1-250-02736-8(5), 9781250027368) Square Fish.

Baraba, Joseph Frank. Dusty. 2006. 59p. pap. 16.95 (978-1-4241-2018-5(7)) PublishAmerica, Inc.

Barbre, Mark. A Cat Named Friend. Smith, Brody, illus. 2008. 18p. (J). pap. 9.95 (978-0-615-20414-7(7)) Edgar Road Publishing.

Barger, Caroline. The Roundup. 2008. 12p. per. 24.95 (978-1-4241-8845-1(8)) America Star Bks.

Barnett, Mac. The Skunk. McDonnell, Patrick, illus. 2015. (ENG.). 40p. (J). (gr. -1-3). 17.99 (978-1-59643-966-5(1), 9781596439665) Roaring Brook Pr.

Barreto, Sonia. Onyx. Switzer, Bobbi, illus. 2008. 36p. pap. 13.95 (978-1-4327-1787-2(1)) Outskirts Pr., Inc.

Barrows, Annie. Bound to Be Bad. 2009. (Ivy & Bean Ser.: 5). (J). lib. bdg. 16.00 (978-0-606-14473-5(0), Turtleback) Turtleback Bks.

—Ivy + Bean Bound to Be Bad. Blackall, Sophie, illus. (Ivy & Bean Ser.: IVYB). (ENG.). (J). (gr. 1-5). 2009. 128p. pap. 5.99 (978-0-8118-6857-0(5)) 2008. 124p. 14.99 (978-0-8118-6265-3(8)) Chronicle Bks. LLC.

Barrows, Annie & Blackall, Sophie. Ivy + Bean Bound to Be Bad, 1 vol. 2011. (Ivy & Bean Ser.). (ENG., Illus.). 128p. (J). (gr. 1-4). 24.21 (978-1-59961-932-3(6)) Spotlight.

Barrows, Marjorie. Little Duck. Myers, Marie Honre, illus. 2011. 50p. 35.95 (978-1-258-08897-2(5)) Literary Licensing, LLC.

Barton, Brittney B. Piper & Pickle: Smile. Young, Susan, illus. 2013. 68p. 18.99 (978-0-9856336-0-8(3)) P2 Publishing.

Beil, Michael D. Lantern Sam & the Blue Streak Bandits. 2015. (ENG., Illus.). 288p. (J). (gr. 3-7). pap. 7.99 (978-0-385-75320-3(9), Yearling) Random Hse. Children's Bks.

Bentley, Sue. The Perfect Secret. 2014. (Magic Puppy Ser.: 14). lib. bdg. 14.75 (978-0-606-35686-2(X)) Turtleback Bks.

—The Perfect Secret #14. Swan, Angela & Farley, Andrew, illus. 2014. (Magic Puppy Ser.: 14). (ENG.). 128p. (J). (gr. 1-3). 5.99 (978-0-448-46799-3(2), Grosset & Dunlap) Penguin Young Readers Group.

Birney, Betty G. Secrets According to Humphrey. 2015. (Humphrey Ser.: 10). (ENG.). 160p. (J). (gr. 3-7). 5.99 (978-0-14-751431-8(2), Puffin Books) Penguin Young Readers Group.

Blade, Adam. Chasing Evil. (Chronicles of Avantia Ser.). (ENG.). 176p. (J). (gr. 3-7). 2013. pap. 5.99 (978-0-545-36157-6(5), Scholastic Paperbacks) 2012. 15.99 (978-0-545-36158-3(3), Scholastic Pr.) Scholastic, Inc.

—First Hero. 2012. (Chronicles of Avantia Ser.). (ENG.). 176p. (J). (gr. 3-7). 15.99 (978-0-545-36160-6(5), Scholastic Pr.) Scholastic, Inc.

Blanks, Morgan Georgia. The Desert Island. 2008. 52p. pap. 20.49 (978-1-4343-9006-6(3)) AuthorHouse.

Blaylock, Janet. Crissy LeeAnn's Life. 2008. 33p. pap. 13.50 (978-1-4357-5437-9(9)) Lulu Pr., Inc.

Bolton, Nicola Joanne. Jasper. 2009. 58p. pap. 10.50 (978-1-4092-4609-1(4)) Lulu Pr., Inc.

Borgo, Lacy Finn. Big Mama's Baby. Cote, Nancy, illus. 2007. (ENG.). 32p. (J). (gr. k-2). 15.95 (978-1-59078-187-6(2)) Boyds Mills Pr.

Botelho, R. J. Elizabeth & Equines: G. A. R. T. H. V (Genetically Altered Radically Transformed Human), 1 vol. 2009. 105p. pap. 19.95 (978-1-61582-952-1(0)) America Star Bks.

Bow, Erin. Plain Kate. (ENG.). 320p. (J). (gr. 7-7). 2012. pap. 9.99 (978-0-545-16665-2(9)) 2010. 17.99 (978-0-545-16664-5(0)) Scholastic, Inc. (Levine, Arthur A. Bks.).

Bowen, Anne. Scooter in the Outside. Carter, Abby, illus. 2012. (ENG.). 32p. (J). 16.95 (978-0-8234-2326-2(3)) Holiday Hse., Inc.

Briley, Jennifer Lenore. Justin's Journey. 2008. 48p. pap. 16.95 (978-1-60672-150-6(X)) America Star Bks.

Broach, Elise. James to the Rescue. Murphy, Kelly, illus. 2015. (Masterpiece Adventures Ser.: 2). (ENG.). 112p. (J). (gr. 1-4). 15.99 (978-1-62779-316-2(X), 9781627793162, Holt, Henry & Co. Bks. For Young Readers) Holt, Henry & Co.

—Masterpiece. 2010. 18.00 (978-1-60686-888-1(8)) Perfection Learning Corp.

—Masterpiece. Murphy, Kelly, illus. 2010. (ENG.). 320p. (J). (gr. 4-7). pap. 7.99 (978-0-312-60870-5(5), 9780312608705) Square Fish.

—Masterpiece. 2010. (J). lib. bdg. 18.40 (978-0-606-14604-3(0), Turtleback) Turtleback Bks.

—The Miniature World of Marvin & James. Murphy, Kelly, illus. 2014. (Masterpiece Adventures Ser.: 1). (ENG.). 112p. (J). (gr. 1-4). 15.99 (978-0-8050-9190-8(4), 9780805091908, Holt, Henry & Co. Bks. For Young Readers) Holt, Henry & Co.

—Trouble at School for Marvin & James. Murphy, Kelly, illus. 2017. (Masterpiece Adventures Ser.: 3). (ENG.). 112p. (J). 15.99 (978-1-62779-318-6(6), 9781627793186, Holt, Henry & Co. Bks. For Young Readers) Holt, Henry & Co.

Brodien-Jones, Christine. The Owl Keeper. Kneen, Maggie, illus. 2011. (ENG.). 320p. (J). (gr. 3-7). 8.99 (978-0-385-73815-6(3), Yearling) Random Hse. Children's Bks.

Brodsky, Kathy. Just Sniffing Around. Bennett, Cameron, illus. 2009. (ENG.). 40p. 19.99 (978-0-578-03620-5(7)) Helpingwords.

Brown, Adam. The Adventures of Wormie Wormington Book Three: Wormie & the Snowball. Smart, Andy, illus. 2013. 48p. pap. (978-0-9919196-3-5(7)) Beckon Creative.

—The Adventures of Wormie Wormington Book Two: Wormie & the Kite. Smart, Andy, illus. 2013. 48p. pap. (978-0-9919196-2-8(9)) Beckon Creative.

Brown, Adam & Smart, Andy. The Adventures of Wormie Wormington Book One: Wormie & the Fish. Smart, Andy, illus. 2013. (Illus.). 50p. pap. (978-0-9919196-0-4(2)) Beckon Creative.

Brown, Tricia. Bobbie the Wonder Dog: A True Story. Porter, Cary, illus. 2016. (ENG.). 32p. (J). 16.99 (978-1-943328-36-9(6), West Winds Pr.) Graphic Arts Ctr. Publishing Co.

Browne, Anthony. Little Beauty. Browne, Anthony, illus. 2010. (ENG., Illus.). 32p. (J). (gr. -1-2). pap. 6.99 (978-0-7636-4967-8(8)) Candlewick Pr.

—Little Beauty. 2010. lib. bdg. 17.20 (978-0-606-14714-9(4), Turtleback) Turtleback Bks.

Bryan, Suzanne. Bonkers Finds His Way Home. 2008. 45p. pap. 7.54 (978-1-4357-4461-5(6)) Lulu Pr., Inc.

Buchwald, Claire. Max Talks to Me. Ritz, Karen, illus. 2007. (Sit! Stay! Read! Ser.). (ENG.). 24p. (J). (gr. k-2). 16.95 (978-0-940719-03-3(7)) Gryphon Pr., The.

Buffalo, Tom And Tracey. Loganæs Big Night Out. 2008. 24p. pap. 11.99 (978-1-4389-1893-8(3)) AuthorHouse.

Burgess, Thornton W. Adventures of Bob White. Cady, Harrison, illus. 2011. (Dover Children's Thrift Classics Ser.). (ENG.). 96p. (J). (gr. k-3). pap. 3.00 (978-0-486-48109-8(3)) Dover Pubns., Inc.

Burkhart, Jessica. Triple Fault. 2009. (Canterwood Crest Ser.: 4). (ENG.). 288p. (J). (gr. 4-8). pap. 7.99 (978-1-4169-5843-7(6), Aladdin) Simon & Schuster Children's Publishing.

Burkhart, Kiersi & Keyser, Amber J. Shy Girl & Shy Guy. 2017. (Quartz Creek Ranch Ser.). (ENG.). 240p. (gr. 4-8). 27.99 (978-1-4677-9253-0(5), Carolrhoda Bks.) Lerner Publishing Group.

Burlingham, Abi. Best Friends. Everitt-Stewart, Andy, illus. 2009. (Stories to Grow with Ser.). 24p. (J). (gr. -1-2). 22.60 (978-1-60754-475-3(X)); pap. 8.15 (978-1-60754-476-0(8)) Windmill Bks.

Bushell, Abby. Pc Rob Has a Very Important Job: Talking about Strangers. 2010. (Illus.). 20p. pap. 10.49 (978-1-4490-6628-4(3)) AuthorHouse.

Butler, Debra Rae. BenjiB. 2008. 24p. pap. 24.95 (978-1-60441-484-4(7)) America Star Bks.

Byrne, John Patrick. Donald & Benoit. Byrne, John Patrick, illus. 2011. (ENG., Illus.). 64p. (J). (gr. 2-5). 17.95 (978-0-7893-2084-1(3)) Universe Publishing.

Cameron, W. Bruce. Ellie's Story: A Dog's Purpose Novel. 2015. (Dog's Purpose Ser.). (ENG., Illus.). 208p. (J). (gr. 3-7). 16.99 (978-0-7653-7469-1(2), 9780765374691, Starscape) Doherty, Tom Assocs., LLC.

Campbell, Howard. A Dog Named Pavlov: Un Perro Llamado Pavlov. McCloskey, Kevin, illus. 2010. 44p. (J). pap. (978-0-9790350-4-3(X)) Star Fire.

Carbone, Courtney. Palace Pets: Snuggle Buddies. 2014. (Step into Reading Level 2 Ser.). lib. bdg. 13.55 (978-0-606-35193-5(0)) Turtleback Bks.

—Snuggle Buddies. Random House Disney Staff, illus. 2014. (Step into Reading Ser.). (ENG.). 32p. (J). (gr. -1-1). 3.99 (978-0-7364-3155-2(1)); lib. bdg. 12.99 (978-0-7364-8158-8(3)) Random Hse. Children's Bks. (RH/Disney).

Carmichael, Clay. Wild Things. (ENG.). (J). 2012. 184p. (gr. 5-8). pap. 9.95 (978-1-59078-914-8(8)) 2009. 248p. (gr. 4-6). 18.95 (978-1-59078-627-7(0), Front Street) Boyds Mills Pr.

—Wild Things, 6 vols. 2010. (J). 77.75 (978-1-4498-0632-3(5)) Recorded Bks., Inc.

Carmody, Isobelle. The Farseekers. 2003. (Obernewtyn Chronicles: Bk. 2). (Illus.). 316p. (J). 13.65 (978-0-7569-4608-1(5)) Perfection Learning Corp.

Carter, Aimée. Simon Thorn & the Viper's Pit. 2017. (Simon Thorn Ser.). (ENG.). 304p. (J). 16.99 (978-1-61963-715-3(4), 9781619637153, Bloomsbury USA Childrens) Bloomsbury Publishing USA.

—Simon Thorn & the Wolf's Den. 2017. (Simon Thorn Ser.). (ENG.). 336p. (J). pap. 7.99 (978-1-61963-706-1(5), 9781619637061, Bloomsbury USA Childrens) Bloomsbury Publishing USA.

Cast, P. C. Moon Chosen. 2016. (Tales of a New World Ser.: 1). (ENG., Illus.). 608p. (YA). (gr. 7-12). 18.99 (978-1-250-10072-6(0), 9781250100726, St. Martin's Griffin) St. Martin's Pr.

Cervantes, Angela. Gaby, Lost & Found. 2015. (Wish Ser.). (ENG.). 224p. (J). (gr. 3-7). pap. 6.99 (978-0-545-79863-1(9), Scholastic Paperbacks) Scholastic, Inc.

Chapman, Linda. Twilight Magic. Kronheimer, Ann, illus. 2008. 149p. (J). pap. (978-0-545-03160-8(5)) Scholastic, Inc.

Chaud, Benjamin. Farewell Floppy. 2015. (ENG., Illus.). 40p. (J). (gr. -1-k). 17.99 (978-1-4521-3734-6(X)) Chronicle Bks. LLC.

Chew, Ruth. No Such Thing as a Witch. 2013. (Matter-Of-Fact Magic Book Ser.). (ENG., Illus.). 128p. (J). (gr. 2-5). 5.99 (978-0-449-81562-5(5)); 15.99 (978-0-449-81559-5(5)) Random Hse. Children's Bks. (Random Hse. Bks. for Young Readers).

Chicatelli, Joy. Bailey's Heartstrings. Rottinger, Amy, illus. 2011. 28p. pap. 12.95 (978-1-935268-96-3(1)) Halo Publishing International.

Chick, Bryan. Riddles & Danger. 2011. (Secret Zoo Ser.: 3). (ENG.). 288p. (J). (gr. 3-7). 16.99 (978-0-06-198927-8(4), Greenwillow Bks.) HarperCollins Pubs.

—The Secret Zoo: Raids & Rescues. (Secret Zoo Ser.: 5). (ENG.). 272p. (J). (gr. 3-7). 2014. pap. 6.99 (978-0-06-219229-5(9)) 2013. 16.99 (978-0-06-219228-8(0)) HarperCollins Pubs. (Greenwillow Bks.).

—Traps & Specters. 2013. (Secret Zoo Ser.: 4). (ENG.). 320p. (J). (gr. 3-7). pap. 6.99 (978-0-06-219223-3(X), Greenwillow Bks.) HarperCollins Pubs.

Christelow, Eileen. Letters from a Desperate Dog. 2006. (ENG., Illus.). 32p. (J). (gr. 1-4). 16.99 (978-0-618-51003-0(6)) Houghton Mifflin Harcourt Publishing Co.

Clark, Ruth E. Airport Mouse. Jones, Phil, illus. 2008. (ENG.). 32p. (J). (gr. -1-3). 15.95 (978-0-9792963-2-1(3)) Hibiscus Publishing.

Clarke, Nancy & Muire, Penny. Stormy Hill's Challenge. 2013. 248p. 26.00 (978-1-62212-803-7(6), Strategic Bk. Publishing) Strategic Book Publishing & Rights Agency (SBPRA).

Coe, Victoria J. Fenway & Hattie & the Evil Bunny Gang. 2017. (Fenway & Hattie Ser.). (ENG.). 192p. (J). (gr. 3-7). 16.99 (978-1-101-99633-1(1), G.P. Putnam's Sons Books for Young Readers) Penguin Young Readers Group.

Coffman, Jan. A Common Bond. 2008. 73p. pap. 19.95 *(978-1-60672-302-9(2))* America Star Bks.
Cole, Henry. A Nest for Celeste: A Story about Art, Inspiration, & the Meaning of Home. Cole, Henry, illus. (Nest for Celeste Ser.: 1). (ENG., Illus.). 352p. (J). (gr. 3-7). 2012. pap. 6.99 *(978-0-06-170412-3(1))* 2010. 16.99 *(978-0-06-170410-9(5))* HarperCollins Pubs. (Tegen, Katherine Bks).
Conroy, Kathy. Life Through a Dog's Eyes: The Adventures of Ralph. 2008. (ENG.). 44p. pap. 19.69 *(978-1-4343-8465-2(9))* AuthorHouse.
Cooper, Elisha. Homer. Cooper, Elisha, illus. 2012. (ENG., Illus.). 32p. (J). (gr. -1-3). 16.99 *(978-0-06-201248-7(7),* Greenwillow Bks.) HarperCollins Pubs.
Coover, Colleen & Tobin, Paul. Adventure Time: The Flip Side. 2014. lib. bdg. 33.05 *(978-0-606-36120-0(0))* Turtleback Bks.
Corder, Zizou. Lionboy. 2004. (ENG., Illus.). 304p. (J). (gr. 3-7). reprint ed. pap. 8.99 *(978-0-14-240226-9(5),* Puffin Books) Penguin Young Readers Group.
—Lionboy: The Truth. 2006. (ENG., Illus.). 240p. (J). (gr. 3-7). 7.99 *(978-0-14-240705-9(4),* Puffin Books) Penguin Young Readers Group.
Corgliano, K. L. Millie & Me, 1 vol. 2009. 29p. pap. 24.95 *(978-1-60813-935-4(2))* America Star Bks.
Corlett, William. The Door in the Tree. 2010. (Magician's House Quartet Ser.: 2). (ENG.). 304p. (YA). (gr. 5-8). pap. 13.99 *(978-1-4424-1414-3(6),* Simon Pulse) Simon Pulse.
—The Steps up the Chimney. 2011. (Magician's House Quartet Ser.: 1). (ENG.). 288p. (YA). (gr. 7). pap. 13.99 *(978-1-4424-2935-2(6),* Simon Pulse) Simon Pulse.
Coville, Katherine. Ivy. 2017. (ENG.). 144p. (J). (gr. 2-5). lib. bdg. 19.99 *(978-0-553-53976-9(0),* Knopf Bks. for Young Readers) Random Hse. Children's Bks.
Cox, Denise L. Ginger Is Adopted, 1 vol. 2010. 26p. pap. 24.95 *(978-1-61582-892-0(3))* PublishAmerica, Inc.
Creech, Sharon. Moo. 288p. (J). (gr. 3-7). 2017. pap. 6.99 ***(978-0-06-241526-4(3))*** 2016. 16.99 *(978-0-06-241524-0(7))* 2016. lib. bdg. 17.89 *(978-0-06-241525-7(5))* HarperCollins Pubs.
—Moo. 2017. lib. bdg. 17.20 ***(978-0-606-40402-0(3))*** Turtleback Bks.
Cressey, Roger. The Talking Giraffe. Cressey, Roger, illus. 2013. (Illus.). 118p. pap. *(978-1-78222-143-2(3))* Paragon Publishing, Rothersthorpe.
Cunningham, S. C. Ginormous Joe's Broken Bark. 2009. 48p. pap. 21.90 *(978-1-4490-3116-9(1))* AuthorHouse.
Dadey, Debbie. Great Green Gator Graduation. Lucas, Margeaux, illus. 2006. (Swamp Monster in Third Grade Ser.). 58p. (J). pap. *(978-0-439-79401-5(3))* Scholastic, Inc.
Damitz, Charlie. Diving for el Corazon. Diefendorf, Cathy, illus. 2007. (ENG.). 101p. (J). pap. 7.95 *(978-0-9744446-3-5(4))* All About Kids Publishing.
Davis, Bertha. Jay's Friend Kitty Brew Jumbo Coloring & Activity Book. Bowman, Todd A., illus. 2013. 26p. pap. 9.99 *(978-0-9899472-1-3(1))* Kids At Heart Publishing, LLC.
Davis, Beth. Sago, A Very Special Service Dog: N/a. Schilling, Deborah, illus. 2011.Tr. of N/a. 28p. (J). 15.00 *(978-0-9822974-9-0(1));* lib. bdg. 24.00 *(978-0-9822974-8-3(3))* Rolemommy.
Davis, Christine. The Shelter Dog. Davis, Christine, illus. 2008. (Illus.). 32p. (J). (gr. -1-3). 11.95 *(978-0-9659225-4-8(5))* Lighthearted Pr., Inc.
Davis, Jim, et al. A Game of Cat & Mouse. Dargaud Media Staff & Ellipsanime Staff, illus. 2012. (Garfield Graphic Novels Ser.). (ENG.). 32p. (J). (gr. 1-6). 7.99 *(978-1-59707-300-4(8),* 9781597073004) Papercutz.
Dawley, Linda. Wee Mac. 2014. (ENG.). 146p. (J). pap. *(978-0-9941011-8-1(X),* The Little Red Hen Community Pr.) CCB Publishing.
Dawson, Joy. Maggie, the Color-Blind Cow: A loving heart — -that didn't see Color. 2006. (ENG., Illus.). 36p. (J). per. 12.95 *(978-1-59800-892-0(7))* Outskirts Pr., Inc.
Day, Alexandra. Carl's Snowy Afternoon. Day, Alexandra, illus. 2009. (Carl Ser.). (ENG., Illus.). 32p. (J). (gr. -1-1). 13.99 *(978-0-374-31086-8(6),* 9780374310868, Farrar, Straus & Giroux (BYR)) Farrar, Straus & Giroux.
Day, Kathleen. The Sweet Song of Rainbow Bird. 2012. 32p. pap. 14.75 *(978-1-4669-3555-6(3))* Trafford Publishing.
Dean, Sara. The Puppy Who Found a Boy, 1 vol. Hacker, Randy, illus. 2009. 13p. pap. 24.95 *(978-1-61546-278-0(3))* America Star Bks.
DeGreeff, Davy. Tommy Bomani: Land of Legend, 1 vol. Brookins, Sam, illus. 2010. (Tommy Bomani: Teen Warrior Ser.: Bk. 2). (ENG.). 112p. (gr. 3-8). 27.07 *(978-1-60270-698-9(0),* Calico Chapter Bks) Magic Wagon.
—Tommy Bomani: Shape-Shifter, 1 vol. Brookins, Sam, illus. 2010. (Tommy Bomani: Teen Warrior Ser.: Bk. 1). (ENG.). 112p. (gr. 3-8). 27.07 *(978-1-60270-697-2(2),* Calico Chapter Bks) Magic Wagon.
Demarest, Jeannie. My Best Friend Troubles. 2009. 28p. pap. 21.99 *(978-1-4415-3236-7(6))* Xlibris Corp.
Dérib & Jeffrey, Erica. Yakari & Great Eagle. 2007. (Yakari Ser.: 1). (ENG., Illus.). 48p. (J). (gr. 4-7). per. 11.95 *(978-1-905460-04-5(X))* CineBook GBR. Dist: National Bk. Network.
Deutsch, Stacia & Cohon, Rhody. Lucky Phoo. 2013. 182p. pap. *(978-1-927792-28-5(2))* Imajin Bks.
DiCamillo, Kate. Gracias a Winn-Dixie. 2010.Tr. of Because of Winn-Dixie. (SPA.). 152p. (gr. 4-6). pap. 12.99 *(978-84-279-3265-4(0))* Noguer y Caralt Editores, S. A. ESP. Dist: Lectorum Pubns., Inc.
Disney Book Group Staff & Marsoli, Lisa Ann. World of Reading: Sofia the First the Missing Necklace: Level Pre-1. Disney Storybook Art Team, illus. 2014. (World of Reading Ser.). (ENG.). 32p. (J). (gr. -1-k). pap. 3.99 *(978-1-4231-7164-5(0))* Disney Pr.
Dolheguy, Heather. Meg & Mr Biggs - the Magic Cat. 2008. 64p. 32.78 *(978-1-4092-2382-5(5))* Lulu Pr., Inc.
Donaldson, Julia. The Quick Brown Fox Cub. 2006. (Red Bananas Ser.). (ENG., Illus.). 48p. (J). (gr. -1-3). lib. bdg. *(978-0-7787-1080-6(7))* Crabtree Publishing Co.
Donofrio, Beverly. Where's Mommy? McClintock, Barbara, illus. 2014. (Mary & the Mouse Ser.). (ENG.). 32p. (J). (gr. -1-2). 17.99 *(978-0-375-84423-2(6),* Schwartz & Wade Bks.) Random Hse. Children's Bks.
Douglass, E. The Squirrel Friends Adventures: The Monster & the Great Storm. 2013. 100p. 19.95 *(978-1-4759-6640-4(7));* pap. 9.95 *(978-1-4759-6638-1(5))* iUniverse, Inc.
Dowell, Frances O'Roark. The Second Life of Abigail Walker. (ENG., Illus.). (J). (gr. 3-7). 2013. 272p. pap. 5.99 *(978-1-4424-0594-3(5))* 2012. 240p. 16.99 *(978-1-4424-0593-6(7))* Simon & Schuster Children's Publishing. (Atheneum Bks. for Young Readers).
Dugan, Karen. Always Blue for Chicu. Dugan, Karen, illus. 2010. (ENG., Illus.). 32p. (J). (gr. k-2). 16.95 *(978-0-940719-09-5(6))* Gryphon Pr., The.
Dunbar, Polly. Penguin. Dunbar, Polly, illus. 2010. (ENG., Illus.). 40p. (J). (gr. -1-3). pap. 6.99 *(978-0-7636-4972-2(4))* Candlewick Pr.
Duncan, Daniel. South. 2017. (ENG., Illus.). 40p. (J). (gr. k-2). 17.95 *(978-1-4197-2299-8(9),* Abrams Bks. for Young Readers) Abrams, Inc.
Duncan-Pauley, Chadney. A Bull's Paradise. 2009. 32p. pap. 15.60 *(978-0-557-17660-1(3))* Lulu Pr., Inc.
Dyan, Penelope. Vita Mccafee Mckay, Cat Rescuer. Dyan, Penelope, illus. 2009. (Illus.). 44p. pap. 11.95 *(978-1-935118-53-4(6))* Bellissima Publishing, LLC.
Easton, Kelly. The Outlandish Adventures of Liberty Aimes. Swearingen, Greg, illus. 2011. (ENG.). 224p. (J). (gr. 3-7). pap. 6.99 *(978-0-375-83772-2(8),* Yearling) Random Hse. Children's Bks.
Edwards, Lori. Fire Fawn. 2013. 58p. pap. 8.99 *(978-1-4525-7703-6(X),* Balboa Pr.) Author Solutions, Inc.
Edwards, Nicholas & White, Ellen Emerson. The Rescue. 2009. (Dog Whisperer Ser.: 1). (ENG.). 224p. (J). (gr. 3-7). pap. 9.99 *(978-0-312-36768-8(6),* 9780312367688) Square Fish.
Eichler, Darlene. Where's the Kitty. Wyles, Betty, illus. 2013. 52p. pap. 18.95 *(978-0-9893063-1-7(3))* ProsePress.
Eichler, Ken. Swift Eagle's Vision Quest, 1 vol. 2009. 95p. pap. 19.95 *(978-1-60703-649-4(5))* America Star Bks.
Engle, Margarita. Mountain Dog. Ivanov, Aleksey & Ivanov, Olga, illus. 2013. (ENG.). 224p. (J). (gr. 3-7). 17.99 *(978-0-8050-9516-6(0),* 9780805095166, Holt, Henry & Co. Bks. For Young Readers) Holt, Henry & Co.
—Mountain Dog. Ivanov, Aleksey & Ivanov, Olga, illus. 2014. (ENG.). 240p. (J). (gr. 3-7). pap. 7.99 *(978-1-250-04424-2(3),* 9781250044242) Square Fish.
Estep, Lorena. Puddles on the Floor. Thayne, Tamira Ci, illus. 2008. 24p. 15.95 *(978-0-615-21952-3(7))* Who Chains You.
Etcheberry-Morton, Mary Jean. Oui Oui Oui of the Pyrenees. 2012. (Illus.). 125p. (J). pap. 10.95 *(978-1-935709-26-8(7))* Ctr. for Basque Studies.
Fabrizio, Anthony. The Last Forest, 1 vol. 2009. 64p. pap. 19.95 *(978-1-61546-861-4(7))* America Star Bks.
Fauske, Tore. Sid. 2009. (Illus.). 104p. pap. 10.99 *(978-1-4389-6533-8(8))* AuthorHouse.
Faust, Laurie, illus. A New Home for Honey. 2006. (Adventures of Honey Ser.). (J). pap. 9.95 *(978-0-9789227-0-2(0))* Weeping Willow Publishing.
Feagins, Sistah L. E. T. M. E. TELL'YA Bernadine. Hakim & Terrance Shadow Mystery ! 2009. 68p. pap. 15.72 *(978-0-557-09041-9(5))* Lulu Pr., Inc.
Felix, Erica. Jay-Bee & Me. 2013. 20p. pap. 24.95 *(978-1-62709-205-0(6))* America Star Bks.
Ferguson, J. M. Bubbles the Little Pig, 1 vol. 2008. (ENG.). 44p. 24.95 *(978-1-60474-229-9(1))* America Star Bks.
Fidler, Kathleen. Flash the Sheepdog. 3rd rev. ed. (ENG., Illus.). 176p. 12.00 *(978-0-86315-581-9(2))* Floris Bks. GBR. Dist: SteinerBooks, Inc.
Filipina, Monika. All about Cats. Filipina, Monika, illus. 2017. (Child's Play Library). (ENG., Illus.). 32p. (J). pap. *(978-1-84643-933-9(7))* Child's Play International Ltd.
Filippello, Michael. In a Place Called Barrontippeny. 2008. 24p. pap. 24.95 *(978-1-60813-295-9(1))* America Star Bks.
Fleck, Denise. Don't Judge a Book by Its Cover. Chin, Lili, illus. 2013. 24p. pap. 14.99 *(978-1-4575-1758-7(2))* Dog Ear Publishing, LLC.
Fletcher, Susan. Dadblamed Union Army Cow. Root, Kimberly Bulcken, illus. 2016. (ENG.). 32p. (J). (gr. k-3). 7.99 *(978-0-7636-8770-0(7))* Candlewick Pr.
The Flower Pot Bunnies Return. 2006. (J). *(978-0-9755390-2-6(7))* Fifth Ave Pr.
Formento, Alison. These Bees Count! Snow, Sarah, illus. 2012. (These Things Count! Ser.). (ENG.). 32p. (J). (gr. -1-3). 16.99 *(978-0-8075-7868-1(1))* Whitman, Albert & Co.
Francis, Anwen. Siani Shetland. 2008. (ENG.). 84p. (J). pap. 9.95 *(978-1-905762-62-0(3))* Parthian Bks. GBR. Dist: Independent Pubs. Group.
Frederick, Heather Vogel. The Black Paw. 2013. (Spy Mice Ser.: 1). (ENG., Illus.). 224p. (J). (gr. 3-6). pap. 7.99 *(978-1-4424-6701-9(0),* Simon & Schuster Bks. For Young Readers) Simon & Schuster Bks. For Young Readers.
Freeman, Martha. The Orphan & the Mouse. McPhail, David, illus. 2014. (ENG.). 176p. (J). (gr. 3-7). 16.95 *(978-0-8234-3167-0(3))* Holiday Hse., Inc.
Frith, Nicholas John. Hello, Mr. Dodo! 2017. (ENG.). 32p. (J). (gr. -1-3). 17.99 *(978-1-338-08939-4(0))* Scholastic, Inc.
Fuentes, Peggy Jo. Boogoos, the Calico Kitty. 2009. 16p. pap. 24.95 *(978-1-60836-914-0(5))* America Star Bks.
Funnell, Pippa. Solo the Super Star. 2010. (ENG., Illus.). 96p. 9.99 *(978-1-84255-714-3(9))* Orion Publishing Group, Ltd. GBR. Dist: Hachette Bk. Group.
—Team Magic. 2016. (Tilly's Horse, Magic Ser.). (ENG.). 128p. (J). (gr. 4-6). 6.99 *(978-1-4440-1204-0(5),* Orion Children's Bks.) Hachette Children's Group GBR. Dist: Hachette Bk. Group.
Fussell, Sandy. Sad, the Dog. Suwannakit, Tull, illus. 2015. (ENG.). 32p. (J). (gr. -1-2). 15.99 *(978-0-7636-7826-5(0))* Candlewick Pr.
Gale, Eric Kahn. The Zoo at the Edge of the World. Nielson, Sam, illus. 2015. (ENG.). 240p. (J). (gr. 3-7). pap. 6.99 *(978-0-06-212517-0(6))* HarperCollins Pubs.
Gallico, Paul. The Abandoned. 2013. (ENG.). 320p. (J). (gr. 4-7). 15.95 *(978-1-59017-626-9(X),* NYR Children's Collection) New York Review of Bks., Inc., The.
Gardner, Sara. Emma & the Dinosaur. 2013. 26p. pap. 16.99 *(978-1-4525-8441-6(9),* Balboa Pr.) Author Solutions, Inc.
Gemeinhart, Dan. The Honest Truth. 2015. (ENG.). 240p. (J). (gr. 3-7). pap. 6.99 *(978-0-545-66574-2(4));* 16.99 *(978-0-545-66573-5(6))* Scholastic, Inc. (Scholastic Pr.).
George, Jean Craighead. Ice Whale. Hendrix, John, illus. 2015. (ENG.). 224p. (J). (gr. 4-7). 7.99 *(978-0-14-242741-5(1),* Puffin Books) Penguin Young Readers Group.
Gipson, Fred. Old Yeller. Date not set. 192p. (J). 20.95 *(978-0-8488-2273-6(0))* Amereon Ltd.
—Old Yeller. 2003. (Trophy Bk.). (ENG.). 192p. (J). (gr. 5-18). pap. 6.99 *(978-0-06-440382-5(3))* HarperCollins Pubs.
—Old Yeller. 2009. (Perennial Classics Ser.). 132p. (gr. 4-7). 20.85 *(978-0-613-85744-4(5),* Turtleback) Turtleback Bks.
Gipson, Fred & Polson, Steven. Old Yeller. 2009. (Perennial Classics Ser.). (ENG., Illus.). 144p. (gr. 4-7). pap. 12.99 *(978-0-06-093547-4(2),* Harper Perennial) HarperCollins Pubs.
Glazer, Maryann. The Adventures of Teddy Bark-Lee: Teddy Goes to the Doctor. 2009. 28p. pap. 13.99 *(978-1-4490-2836-7(5))* AuthorHouse.
Goetze, Jutta. Howl. 2007. 96p. (YA). pap. *(978-1-4207-0740-3(X))* Sundance/Newbridge Educational Publishing.
Golding, Julia. The Chimera's Curse, 0 vols. 2010. (Companions Quartet Ser.: 4). (ENG.). 320p. (J). (gr. 4-7). pap. 9.99 *(978-0-7614-5726-8(7),* 9780761457268, Amazon Children's Publishing) Amazon Publishing.
—The Gorgon's Gaze, 0 vols., Bk. 2. 2010. (Companions Quartet Ser.: 2). (ENG.). 320p. (J). (gr. 4-7). pap. 9.99 *(978-0-7614-5653-7(8),* 9780761456537, Amazon Children's Publishing) Amazon Publishing.
—Mines of the Minotaur, 0 vols., Bk. 3. unabr. ed. 2010. (Companions Quartet Ser.: 3). (ENG.). 288p. (J). (gr. 5-9). pap. 9.99 *(978-0-7614-5796-1(8),* 9780761457961, Amazon Children's Publishing) Amazon Publishing.
—Secret of the Sirens, 0 vols. 2009. (Companions Quartet Ser.: 1). (ENG.). 368p. (J). (gr. 4-7). pap. 9.99 *(978-0-7614-5617-9(1),* 9780761456179, Amazon Children's Publishing) Amazon Publishing.
Goniwicha, William. Spike a Relli: The Mini Doberman. 2009. 28p. pap. 13.99 *(978-1-4389-5678-7(9))* AuthorHouse.
Good Dog... Not So Good Dog. 2007. (J). *(978-0-9793568-1-0(4))* Merlin, Debbi.
Gordon, Janice Knuth. The Eager Bunny. 2009. 60p. (J). pap. 27.95 *(978-1-4327-3673-6(6))* Outskirts Pr., Inc.
Gotsch, Connie. Belle's Trial. Cogan, John, illus. 2010. (ENG & ABK.). 150p. (J). pap. 8.99 *(978-1-932926-12-5(7),* Kinkajou Pr.) Artemesia Publishing, LLC.
Gottesfeld, Jeff. The Cat Whisperer, 1 vol. 2015. (Red Rhino Ser.). (ENG.). 72p. (J). (gr. 3-6). mass mkt. 7.95 *(978-1-62250-955-3(2))* Saddleback Educational Publishing, Inc.
Greene, Jacqueline Dembar. Speak up, Tommy! Melmon, Deborah, illus. 2012. (Kar-Ben Favorites Ser.). (ENG.). 32p. (J). (gr. -1-3). lib. bdg. 17.95 *(978-0-7613-7497-8(3),* Kar-Ben Publishing) Lerner Publishing Group.
Gregg, Stacy. The Girl Who Rode the Wind. 2016. (ENG.). 336p. (J). (gr. 4). 6.99 *(978-0-00-818923-5(4),* HarperCollins Children's Bks.) HarperCollins Pubs. Ltd. GBR. Dist: HarperCollins Pubs.
Grey, C. R. Animas, Book One Legacy of the Claw. Madsen, Jim, illus. 2015. (Animas Ser.). (ENG.). 320p. (J). (gr. 3-7). pap. 7.99 *(978-1-4231-8466-9(1))* Hyperion Bks. for Children.
—Animas, Book Two Flight of the King. 2015. (Animas Ser.). (ENG., Illus.). 304p. (J). (gr. 3-7). 16.99 *(978-1-4231-8343-3(6))* Hyperion Bks. for Children.
—Legacy of the Claw. Madsen, Jim, illus. 2014. (Animas Ser.). (ENG.). 304p. (J). (gr. 3-7). 16.99 *(978-1-4231-8038-8(0))* Disney Pr.
Grinnell, Suzanne. Where Is Beau? Peter, Joshua, illus. 2008. 24p. pap. 12.99 *(978-1-59858-612-1(2))* Dog Ear Publishing, LLC.
Grover, Jan Zita. A Home for Dakota. 2008. (Sit! Stay! Read! Ser.). (ENG., Illus.). 24p. (J). (gr. k-2). 16.95 *(978-0-940719-05-7(3))* Gryphon Pr., The.
Guzman, Lila. Kichi in Jungle Jeopardy. Johnson, Regan, illus. (J). 2007. (ENG.). 135p. (gr. 2-7). pap. 8.95 *(978-0-9769417-2-9(4))* 2006. 144p. 13.95 *(978-0-9769417-1-2(6))* Blooming Tree Pr.
Haas, Jessie. Bramble & Maggie: Give & Take. Friend, Alison, illus. 2013. (ENG.). 56p. (J). (gr. k-3). 14.99 *(978-0-7636-5021-6(8))* Candlewick Pr.
—Bramble & Maggie Give & Take. Friend, Alison, illus. 2015. (Candlewick Sparks Ser.). (ENG.). 56p. (J). (gr. k-4). pap. 3.99 *(978-0-7636-7787-9(6))* Candlewick Pr.
Hale, Rachael. Baby's Best Friend. 2011. (ENG.). 20p. (J). (gr. -1 — 1). bds. 6.99 *(978-0-316-12962-6(3))* Little, Brown Bks. for Young Readers.
Hamilton, John. Dog Friday. 2010. (Illus.). 60p. pap. 21.99 *(978-1-4490-9468-3(6))* AuthorHouse.
Hansell, Robin. Mason & Monkey's Big Adventure. 2013. 52p. pap. 23.99 *(978-1-4808-0254-4(9))* Archway Publishing.
Happel, Roberta L. Lynd. 2009. 16p. pap. 8.99 *(978-1-4389-4088-5(2))* AuthorHouse.
Harlan. My Best Friend. 2011. 28p. pap. 9.95 *(978-1-4327-7164-5(7))* Outskirts Pr., Inc.
Harper, Jessica. A Place Called Kindergarten. Karas, G. Brian, illus. 2008. (ENG.). 32p. (J). (gr. -1-k). pap. 6.99 *(978-0-14-241174-2(4),* Puffin Books) Penguin Young Readers Group.
Harrinsson, Nelson. Mario, Donkey Cuco & the Mango Tree. 2011. 48p. pap. 24.95 *(978-1-4560-4911-9(9))* America Star Bks.
Harrison, Megan Bernadette. The Adventures of Kitty Tom & Blossom: Book One. 2009. 36p. pap. 24.95 *(978-1-60749-257-3(1))* America Star Bks.
Harrison, Mette Ivie. The Princess & the Bear. 2010. (ENG.). 352p. (YA). (gr. 8). pap. 8.99 *(978-0-06-155316-5(6),* HarperTeen) HarperCollins Pubs.
—The Princess & the Hound. 2008. (ENG.). 432p. (YA). (gr. 8). pap. 8.99 *(978-0-06-113189-9(X),* HarperTeen) HarperCollins Pubs.
Haworth, Katie. Petunia Paris's Parrot. Williamson, Jo, illus. 2017. (ENG.). 40p. (J). (gr. -1-3). 17.99 *(978-1-4998-0437-9(7))* Little Bee Books Inc.
Hayes, Joe. My Pet Rattlesnake. 2014. (ENG., Illus.). 32p. (J). 16.95 *(978-1-935955-61-0(6));* pap. 7.95 *(978-1-935955-62-7(4))* Cinco Puntos Pr.
Hearne, Betsy. The Canine Connection: Stories about Dogs & People. 2007. (ENG.). 128p. (YA). (gr. 7). pap. 8.95 *(978-1-4169-6817-7(2),* Simon Pulse) Simon Pulse.
Heible, Bev. A Collection of Short Tails. 2012. 60p. 17.95 *(978-1-62709-686-7(8));* pap. 17.95 *(978-1-62709-343-9(5))* America Star Bks.
Henson, Heather. The Whole Sky. 2017. (ENG., Illus.). 256p. (J). (gr. 5-7). 16.99 ***(978-1-4424-1405-1(7),*** Atheneum/Caitlyn Dlouhy Books) Simon & Schuster Children's Publishing.
Hermes, Patricia. Black Cloud, No. 8. Sheckels, Astrid, illus. 2012. (Horse Diaries). (ENG.). 176p. (J). (gr. 3-7). pap. 7.99 *(978-0-375-86881-8(X),* Random Hse. Bks. for Young Readers) Random Hse. Children's Bks.
—Black Cloud. 2012. (Horse Diaries: 8). lib. bdg. 18.40 *(978-0-606-26553-9(8),* Turtleback) Turtleback Bks.
Herzog, Mary Ann. The Buddy Tails. 2008. 49p. pap. 16.95 *(978-1-60441-760-9(9))* America Star Bks.
High, Linda Oatman. One Amazing Elephant. 2017. 272p. (J). (gr. 3-7). 16.99 *(978-0-06-245583-3(4))* HarperCollins Pubs.
Hill, Amye Rose. The Amazing Mr. Buddy. 10th ed. 2005. (Illus.). (J). 6.99 *(978-0-9769234-0-4(8))* Zany Angel Projects LLC.
Hill, Janet Muirhead. Miranda & Starlight: (the Starlight Books, 1) Revised Edition, 6 vols. Lehmkuhl, Pat, illus. 2nd rev. ed. 2003. (Starlight Bks.: 1). 168p. (J). (gr. 3-7). per. 9.00 *(978-0-9714161-4-7(1))* Raven Publishing Inc. of Montana.
Hill, Meggan. Nico & Lola: Kindness Shared Between a Boy & a Dog. Graunke, Susan M., illus. 2010. (ENG.). 40p. (J). (gr. -1-3). 16.99 *(978-0-06-199043-4(4))* HarperCollins Pubs.
Hipp, Helen C. A Different Kind of Safari. Diaco, Paula Tedford, ed. Glass, Hilary Ann Love, illus. 2013. 32p. 17.95 *(978-0-9890134-0-6(5))* A Different Kind of Safari LLC.
Hodges, Meredith. Jasper: The Story of a Mule. Shields, Bonnie, illus. 2003. 245p. (J). (gr. k-7). 39.95 *(978-0-9702309-8-0(2))* Lucky 3 Ranch, Inc.
Holliday, Andrea. Squissy, the Little Grey Squirrel That Got a Second Chance. 2013. 28p. pap. 24.95 *(978-1-4626-9788-5(7))* America Star Bks.
Holmes, S. D. The Adventures of Mister. 2009. 56p. pap. 23.99 *(978-1-4389-3786-1(5))* AuthorHouse.
Hooker, Adele. Sailor the Cat. Gwinner, Patricia, illus. 2011. 24p. pap. 24.95 *(978-1-4560-8026-6(1))* America Star Bks.
Howe, Peter. Waggit's Tale. Rayyan, Omar, illus. 2009. (Waggit Ser.: 1). (ENG.). 304p. (J). (gr. 5). pap. 6.99 *(978-0-06-124263-2(2))* HarperCollins Pubs.
Hughes, Susan. Bailey. 2016. (Puppy Pals Ser.: 1). (ENG.). 112p. (J). (gr. 2-5). pap. 5.99 *(978-1-4926-3394-5(1),* 9781492633945, Sourcebooks Jabberwocky) Sourcebooks, Inc.
Ibbotson, Eva. One Dog & His Boy. 2012. (ENG.). 288p. (J). (gr. 3-7). 16.99 *(978-0-545-35196-6(0),* Scholastic Pr.) Scholastic, Inc.
Idle, Molly. Flora & the Chicks. 2017. (ENG., Illus.). 20p. (J). bds. 9.99 *(978-1-4521-4657-7(8))* Chronicle Bks. LLC.
—Flora & the Peacocks. 2016. (ENG., Illus.). 40p. (J). (gr. -1-k). 17.99 *(978-1-4521-3816-9(8))* Chronicle Bks. LLC.
—Flora & the Penguin. 2014. (ENG., Illus.). 40p. (J). (gr. -1-k). 16.99 *(978-1-4521-2891-7(X))* Chronicle Bks. LLC.
Idle, Molly, illus. Flora & the Flamingo. 2013. (ENG.). 44p. (J). (gr. -1-1). 17.99 *(978-1-4521-1006-6(9))* Chronicle Bks. LLC.
Ingle, Annie & Klimo, Kate. Dog Diaries #2: Buddy. Jessell, Tim, illus. 2013. (Dog Diaries). (ENG.). 160p. (J). (gr. 2-5). pap. 7.99 *(978-0-307-97904-9(0),* Random Hse. Bks. for Young Readers) Random Hse. Children's Bks.
Inkpen, Mick. I Will Love You Anyway. Inkpen, Chloe, illus. 2016. (ENG.). 32p. (J). (gr. -1-1). 17.99 *(978-1-4814-7099-5(X),* Aladdin) Simon & Schuster Children's Publishing.
Iserles, Inbali. The Taken. 2015. (Foxcraft Ser.). (ENG., Illus.). 272p. (J). (gr. 3-7). 16.99 *(978-0-545-69081-2(1),* Scholastic Pr.) Scholastic, Inc.
Iserles, Inbali, illus. The Taken. 2015. 252p. (J). pap. ***(978-0-545-91869-5(3),*** Scholastic Pr.) Scholastic, Inc.
Jackson, Ellen. Abe Lincoln Loved Animals. Ettlinger, Doris, illus. 2013. (AV2 Fiction Readalong Ser.: Vol. 56). (ENG.). 32p. (J). 34.28 *(978-1-62127-864-1(6),* AV2 by Weigl) Weigl Pubs., Inc.
Jacques, Brian. Voyage of Slaves: A Tale from the Castaways of the Flying Dutchman. 2007. (ENG.). 320p. (gr. 12-18). 7.99 *(978-0-441-01528-3(X),* Ace Bks.) Penguin Publishing Group.
Jeffrey, Leonard J. Journeys of the Mind-Book. 2011. 116p. (J). pap. *(978-1-4269-9333-6(1))* Trafford Publishing (UK) Ltd.
Jennings, Patrick. We Can't All Be Rattlesnakes. 2011. (ENG.). 144p. (J). (gr. 3-7). pap. 5.99 *(978-0-06-082117-3(5))* HarperCollins Pubs.
Jensen, Barb E. A Horse Named Summertime. 2007. 224p. per. 13.95 *(978-1-60264-113-6(7))* Virtualbookworm.com Publishing, Inc.
(Jerry) Deal, Gerald R. Famous Dog Chowski. 2013. 44p. pap. 20.72 *(978-1-4669-9707-3(9))* Trafford Publishing.
Job. The River of Forgetfulness. Dérib, illus. 2013. (Yakari Ser.: 10). (ENG.). 48p. pap. 11.95 *(978-1-84918-140-2(3))* CineBook GBR. Dist: National Bk. Network.
—Yakari & Nanabozo. Derib, illus. 2014. (Yakari Ser.: 11). (ENG.). 48p. pap. 11.95 *(978-1-84918-177-8(2))* CineBook GBR. Dist: National Bk. Network.
—Yakari & the Coyote. Dérib, illus. 2012. (Yakari Ser.: 9). (ENG.). 48p. (J). (gr. 1-6). pap. 11.95 *(978-1-84918-101-3(2))* CineBook GBR. Dist: National Bk. Network.
Johnson, Gwen & Johnson, Carl. The Treasure of Diamond's Shoal. Lt. ed. 2007. (ENG., Illus.). 24p. (J). 8.95 *(978-0-9795860-0-2(3))* Fish Tales Publishing.
Johnson, Varian. The Return. 2016. (Spirit Animals: Fall of the Beasts Ser.: 3). (ENG.). 192p. (J). (gr. 3-7). 12.99 *(978-0-545-84207-5(7))* Scholastic, Inc.
Johnston, Tony. A Small Thing ... but Big. Hooper, Hadley, illus. 2016. (ENG.). 40p. (J). 17.99 *(978-1-62672-256-9(0),* 9781626722569) Roaring Brook Pr.
K. Elizabeth, Sterling. Austin's First Puppy. 2007. 48p. (J). pap. 10.95 *(978-0-7414-3263-6(3))* Infinity Publishing.
Kadohata, Cynthia. Cracker! The Best Dog in Vietnam. (ENG.). 320p. (J). (gr. 5-9). 2008. pap. 8.99 *(978-1-4169-0638-4(X))* 2007. (Illus.). 18.99 *(978-1-4169-0637-7(1))* Simon & Schuster Children's Publishing. (Atheneum Bks. for Young Readers).
Kanata, Konami. Chi's Sweet Home, Volume 12. 2015. (Chi's Sweet Home Ser.). (ENG., Illus.). 176p. (J). (gr. 2-5). pap.

H
I

13.95 *(978-1-941220-25-2(8),* Vertical) Kodansha America, Inc.

Katis, Michael. Cheech the Pup: With Illustrations by Sharyn Crownover. 2008. pap. 17.00 *(978-0-8059-7915-2(8))* Dorrance Publishing Co., Inc.

Kats, Jewel. Jenny & Her Dog Both Fight Cancer: A Tale of Chemotherapy & Caring. 2015. (J). pap. *(978-1-61599-279-9(0))* Loving Healing Pr., Inc.

Kehret, Peg & the Cat, Pete. Trapped! 2008. (Pete the Cat Ser.). (ENG.). 192p. (J). (gr. 3-7). 5.99 *(978-0-14-241189-6(2),* Puffin Books) Penguin Young Readers Group.

Kelly, Bernadette & Ward, Krista. Naughty Norton, 1 vol. Alger, Liz, illus. 2013. (Pony Tales Ser.). (ENG.). 56p. (gr. 2-2). pap. 5.05 *(978-1-4795-2067-1(5),* Chapter Readers) Picture Window Bks.

—Norton's First Show, 1 vol. Alger, Liz, illus. 2013. (Pony Tales Ser.). (ENG.). 56p. (gr. 2-2). pap. 5.05 *(978-1-4795-2068-8(3),* Chapter Readers) Picture Window Bks.

Kelly, Lynda. Arab Dream Horse, Not. 2013. 188p. pap. *(978-1-903053-38-6(2))* Kelly Pubns.

Kelso, Mary Jean. The Adventures of Andy & Spirit: Book 1. Snider, K. C., illus. 2010. 64p. pap. 9.95 *(978-1-61633-069-9(4))* Guardian Angel Publishing, Inc.

—Andy & Spirit Go to the Fair. Snider, K. C., illus. 2008. 24p. pap. 10.95 *(978-1-935137-03-0(4))* Guardian Angel Publishing, Inc.

Kendall, Christine. Riding Chance. 2016. (ENG.). 224p. (J). (gr. 5-9). 16.99 *(978-0-545-92404-7(9),* Scholastic Pr.) Scholastic, Inc.

Kendall, Stan P. Samson Gets a Family. 2005. 22p. (J). 13.50 *(978-1-4116-5756-4(X))* Lulu Pr., Inc.

Kerr, M. E., pseud. Snakes Don't Miss Their Mothers. 2003. (ENG.). 208p. (J). 15.99 *(978-0-06-052624-5(6))* HarperCollins Pubs.

Kerr, Mike. Mike & a Lynx Named Kitty. Vitt, Karren, illus. 2nd rev. ed. 2006. 112p. per. 13.50 *(978-1-931195-36-2(6))* KiwE Publishing, Ltd.

Keyser, Amber J. & Burkhart, Kiersi. Shy Girl & Shy Guy. 2017. (Quartz Creek Ranch Ser.). (ENG.). 240p. (gr. 4-8). 35.99 ***(978-1-4677-9569-2(0),*** Darby Creek) Lerner Publishing Group.

Kieslich, Anita Hilliker. Friends Forever: Adventures of Henderson. 2010. 32p. pap. 14.49 *(978-1-4490-7997-0(0))* AuthorHouse.

Kim, Aram. Cat on the Bus. Kim, Aram, illus. 2016. (ENG., Illus.). 32p. (J). (gr. -1-1). 16.95 *(978-0-8234-3647-7(0))* Holiday Hse., Inc.

King, Terrie. The Six-Toed Dog & the Big-Headed Puppy. 2008. 104p. pap. 19.95 *(978-1-60672-765-2(6))* America Star Bks.

Kipling, Rudyard. The White Seal. Jones, Chuck, illus. 2006. (ENG.). 32p. (J). (gr. -1-3). 8.95 *(978-0-8249-6598-3(1),* Ideal Pubns.) Worthy Publishing.

Kirsch, Amanda. Honor Bound. 2013. pap. 11.95 *(978-1-59433-375-0(0))* Publication Consultants.

Klimo, Kate. Buddy. 2013. (Dog Diaries: 2). lib. bdg. 18.40 *(978-0-606-27000-7(0),* Turtleback) Turtleback Bks.

Klimo, Kate. Tiny Tim. Jessell, Tim, illus. 2017. (Dog Diaries: 11). (ENG.). 176p. (J). (gr. 2-5). pap. 7.99 ***(978-0-399-55131-4(X))***; lib. bdg. 12.99 ***(978-0-399-55132-1(8))*** Random Hse. Children's Bks. (Random Hse. Bks. for Young Readers).

Klise, Kate. Stay: A Girl, a Dog, a Bucket List. Klise, M. Sarah, illus. 2017. (ENG.). 32p. (J). 17.99 *(978-1-250-10714-5(8),* 9781250107145) Feiwel & Friends.

Kneen, Maggie, illus. Some Pig! A Charlotte's Web Picture Book. 2006. (Charlotte's Web Ser.). 32p. (J). (gr. k-2). 17.89 *(978-0-06-078162-0(9))* HarperCollins Pubs.

Knight-Mudie, Karen. Yarns from Yandilla. 2013. 344p. pap. *(978-0-9875697-0-7(8))* Davey, Mary Stella.

Knk Adventures. Ruth & Her Shepherd. 2012. 40p. pap. *(978-1-4602-0309-5(7))* FriesenPress.

Koch, Janet Marie. Hallie's Best Birthday. 2008. 48p. pap. 24.95 *(978-1-60610-812-3(3))* America Star Bks.

Koertge, Ronald. Strays. 2010. (ENG., Illus.). 176p. (YA). (gr. 9). pap. 7.99 *(978-0-7636-4377-5(7))* Candlewick Pr.

Koja, Kathe. Straydog. 2004. (ENG.). 128p. (YA). (gr. 7-18). reprint ed. 7.99 *(978-0-14-240071-5(8),* Speak) Penguin Young Readers Group.

Kornechak, Marilyn Gilbert. Paisano Pete: Snake-Killer Bird. Eckhardt, Jason C., illus. 2003. 100p. (J). (gr. 3-7). per. 11.95 *(978-1-57168-770-8(X),* Eakin Pr.) Eakin Pr.

Korte, Steve. Curse of the Stage Fright. Neely, Scott, illus. 2016. (Scooby-Doo Comic Chapter Bks.). (ENG.). 88p. (gr. 3-7). pap. 5.95 *(978-1-4965-3587-0(1))* Capstone Press of Coughlan Cos.

Krone, Thelma Smith. Sadie. Snader, Gregory, illus. 2008. 6p. (J). pap. 7.95 *(978-1-934696-02-6(1),* Shooting Star Edition) American Literary Pr.

Krulik, Nancy & dePaola, Tomie. Pup Art #9. Braun, Sebastien, illus. 2015. (Magic Bone Ser.: 9). (ENG.). 128p. (J). (gr. 1-3). bds. 4.99 *(978-0-448-48749-6(7),* Grosset & Dunlap) Penguin Young Readers Group.

Kuhlman, Evan. Hank's Big Day: The Story of a Bug. Groenink, Chuck, illus. 2016. (ENG.). 40p. (J). (gr. -1-2). 16.99 *(978-0-553-51150-5(5),* Schwartz & Wade Bks.) Random Hse. Children's Bks.

Kumar, Navina Magesh. Haley's Wish. 2011. 28p. pap. 12.99 *(978-1-4567-6318-3(0))* AuthorHouse.

Kurtz, Carmen. Brun. (SPA.). 128p. (YA). (gr. 5-8). *(978-84-279-3367-5(3))* Noguer y Caralt Editores, S. A. ESP. Dist: Lectorum Pubns., Inc.

Labatt, Mary. Lake Monster Mix-Up. Rioux, Jo-Anne, illus. 2009. (Sam & Friends Mystery Ser.). (ENG.). 96p. (J). (gr. 2-5). 7.95 *(978-1-55337-302-5(2))*; 16.95 *(978-1-55337-822-8(9))* Kids Can Pr., Ltd. CAN. Dist: Hachette Bk. Group.

LaBree Stute, Lela. Summer Pugs. 2010. 44p. pap. 19.99 *(978-0-557-41763-6(5))* Lulu Pr., Inc.

Laird, Lisa J. I'm the Only One Who Loves Cliff the Goat. 2009. 48p. pap. 19.49 *(978-1-4389-5660-2(6))* AuthorHouse.

Lalla, C. R. Wiggles & Wags Tale: Coming Home. 2009. (Illus.). 24p. pap. 15.99 *(978-1-59858-789-0(7))* Dog Ear Publishing, LLC.

Lamb, Braden. Adventure Time. Paroline, Shelli, illus. 2014. (Adventure Time Ser.: 3). (ENG.). 128p. (J). (gr. 4). 34.99 *(978-1-60886-347-1(6))* Boom! Studios.

Landau, Jeff. Saying Goodbye to Sophie. 2006. (Illus.). 48p. (J). per. 9.95 *(978-0-9728389-2-4(9))* InnerRESOURCES Pubns.

Larson, Kirby. Duke. 2013. (Dogs of World War II Ser.). (ENG.). 240p. (J). (gr. 3-7). 16.99 *(978-0-545-41637-5(X),* Scholastic Pr.) Scholastic, Inc.

Lasky, Kathryn. Hawksmaid: The Untold Story of Robin Hood & Maid Marian. 2011. (ENG.). 320p. (J). (gr. 5). pap. 6.99 *(978-0-06-000072-1(4))* HarperCollins Pubs.

—Star Rise. 2014. (Horses of the Dawn Ser.: 2). (ENG., Illus.). 208p. (J). (gr. 3-7). 16.99 *(978-0-545-39717-9(0),* Scholastic Pr.) Scholastic, Inc.

Lawrence, Duane. Sammy Squirrel & Rodney Raccoon. Clover, Gordon, illus. 2007. (ENG.). 106p. pap. *(978-1-894694-54-4(6))* Granville Island Publishing.

Lawson, Rob, illus. Duke Finds a Home. 2006. (Duke's Tails Ser.). 32p. (J). *(978-0-9779308-0-7(7))* Bush Brothers & Co.

Le Bec, Yann & Le Bec, Gwendal. Raymond. 2017. (ENG.). 32p. (J). (gr. -1-2). 16.99 *(978-0-7636-8950-6(5))* Candlewick Pr.

Lee, Jenny. Elvis & the Underdogs: Secrets, Secret Service, & Room Service. Light, Kelly, illus. 2015. (Elvis & the Underdogs Ser.: 2). (ENG.). 352p. (J). (gr. 3-7). pap. 6.99 *(978-0-06-223557-2(5))* HarperCollins Pubs.

Leth, Kate. Adventure Time Vol. 4. 2014. lib. bdg. 24.50 *(978-0-606-36119-4(7))* Turtleback Bks.

Lettich, Sheldon, et al. Max: Best Friend, Hero, Marine. 2015. (ENG.). 256p. (J). (gr. 3-7). pap. 6.99 *(978-0-06-242039-8(9))* HarperCollins Pubs.

Levin, Jack E. & Levin, Norma R. My Dog Spot. Levin, Jack E. & Levin, Norma R., illus. 2016. (ENG., Illus.). 40p. (J). (gr. -1-3). 17.99 *(978-1-4814-6907-4(X),* Aladdin) Simon & Schuster Children's Publishing.

Lewis, Gill. Pip & the Paw of Friendship. Home, Sarah, illus. 2017. (Puppy Academy Ser.). (ENG.). 128p. (J). pap. 5.99 *(978-1-250-09285-4(X),* 9781250092854, Holt, Henry & Co. Bks. For Young Readers) Holt, Henry & Co.

Lewis, J. M. The Adventures of Gabby & Coyote Girl. 2007. 64p. per. 7.95 *(978-1-4327-1511-3(9))* Outskirts Pr., Inc.

Lewman, David. Secret Life of Pets. Random House, illus. 2016. (Deluxe Junior Novel Ser.). (ENG.). 144p. (J). (gr. 2-5). 9.99 *(978-0-399-55490-2(4),* Random Hse. Bks. for Young Readers) Random Hse. Children's Bks.

Liepelt, Juanita. Blue: The Luckiest Dog in the World. Kasy, Frank, illus. 2008. 48p. 19.95 *(978-0-9791317-0-7(7),* Realitlys Bks.) RealitylsBooks.com, Inc.

Litwin, Mike. The Big Cowhuna. Litwin, Mike, illus. 2015. (Welcome to Bermooda! Ser.: 3). (ENG., Illus.). 160p. (J). (gr. 1-5). 14.99 *(978-0-8075-8720-1(6))* Whitman, Albert & Co.

—Crown of the Cowibbean. Litwin, Mike, illus. 2014. (Welcome to Bermooda! Ser.: 2). (ENG., Illus.). 144p. (J). (gr. 1-5). 14.99 *(978-0-8075-8719-5(2))* Whitman, Albert & Co.

Lloyd, Stacy K. A Girl & Her Dog. 2005. 32p. pap. 12.00 *(978-1-4116-1359-1(7))* Lulu Pr., Inc.

London, C. Alexander. Blood in the Water. 2014. (Tides of War Ser.: 1). (ENG.). 224p. (J). (gr. 5-9). pap. 5.99 *(978-0-545-66298-7(2),* Scholastic Paperbacks) Scholastic, Inc.

—Honor Bound. 2014. (Tides of War Ser.: 2). (ENG.). 224p. (J). (gr. 5-9). pap. 5.99 *(978-0-545-66301-4(6),* Scholastic Paperbacks) Scholastic, Inc.

London, Jack. Colmillo Blanco. 2003. (Advanced Reading Ser.: Vol. 56).Tr. of White Fang. (SPA., Illus.). 268p. (J). (gr. 4-7). 11.95 *(978-84-239-9030-6(3))* Espasa Calpe, S.A. ESP. Dist: Planeta Publishing Corp.

—Colmillo Blanco.Tr. of White Fang. (SPA.). (J). 8.00 *(978-958-04-7143-1(6))* Norma S.A. COL. Dist: Distribuidora Norma, Inc.

—Colmillo Blanco. 2006. (Clasicos Juveniles Ser.).Tr. of White Fang. (SPA., Illus.). 279p. pap. 13.95 *(978-84-263-5246-0(4))* Vives, Luis Editorial (Edelvives) ESP. Dist: Lectorum Pubns., Inc.

—White Fang, 1 vol. VanArsdale, Anthony, illus. 2011. (Calico Illustrated Classics Ser.: No. 3). (ENG.). 112p. (J). (gr. 3-6). 27.07 *(978-1-61641-112-1(0))* Magic Wagon.

Lukkarinen, Ritva. Amy. Vainio, Pirkko, illus. 2009. (ENG.). 30p. (J). (gr. -1-k). 16.95 *(978-1-60537-058-3(4))* Cobblestone Publishing Co.

Lutz II, William. A Frog from Anoratum. 2008. 124p. pap. 11.00 *(978-0-615-18287-2(9))* Lutz, William G.

Lynch, Chris. Cyberia. 2008. (Cyberia Ser.: 1). (ENG.). 160p. (J). (gr. 3-7). 16.99 *(978-0-545-02793-9(4),* Scholastic Pr.) Scholastic, Inc.

—Monkey See, Monkey Don't. 2009. (Cyberia Ser.: 2). (ENG.). 144p. (J). (gr. 3-7). 16.99 *(978-0-545-02794-6(2),* Scholastic Pr.) Scholastic, Inc.

MacDonald, Anne Louise. Seeing Red. 2009. (ENG.). 224p. (J). (gr. 5-9). 17.95 *(978-1-55453-291-9(4))* Kids Can Pr., Ltd. CAN. Dist: Hachette Bk. Group.

MacDonald, Anne Louise & Wahl, Charis. Seeing Red. 2009. (ENG.). 224p. (J). (gr. 5-9). 8.95 *(978-1-55453-292-6(2))* Kids Can Pr., Ltd. CAN. Dist: Hachette Bk. Group.

MacDonald, James. Levi, Adventures of a Police Dog. 2005. (Illus.). 96p. (J). 16.95 *(978-0-9716923-1-2(9))* Regency Hse., Ltd.

MacLachlan, Patricia. Waiting for the Magic. Bates, Amy June, illus. 2012. (ENG.). 176p. (J). (gr. 3-7). pap. 6.99 *(978-1-4169-2746-4(8),* Atheneum Bks. for Young Readers) Simon & Schuster Children's Publishing.

—White Fur Flying. (ENG., Illus.). (J). (gr. 2-6). 2014. 144p. pap. 7.99 *(978-1-4424-2172-1(X))* 2013. 128p. 15.99 *(978-1-4424-2171-4(1))* McElderry, Margaret K. Bks. (McElderry, Margaret K. Bks.).

Maddox, Jake & Berne, Emma Carlson. Horseback Hurdles, 1 vol. Wood, Katie, illus. 2012. (Jake Maddox Girl Sports Stories Ser.). (ENG.). 72p. (gr. 2-3). pap. 5.95 *(978-1-4342-3905-1(5))*; lib. bdg. 25.32 *(978-1-4342-3294-6(8))* Stone Arch Bks.

Madison's Descent: A Child's Journey. collector's ed. 2004. (J). 75.00 *(978-0-9752516-0-7(0))* Otis & Randolph Pr.

Mafera, Sandra. Cloud of Dauphin Island. 2009. 28p. pap. 12.49 *(978-1-4389-5159-1(0))* AuthorHouse.

Malone, Cheryl Lawton. Dario & the Whale. Masseva, Bistra, illus. 2016. (ENG.). 32p. (J). (gr. -1-3). 16.99 *(978-0-8075-1463-4(2))* Whitman, Albert & Co.

Manzel, Michael, illus. Moby's Tale. 2004. 248p. (YA). pap. 19.95 *(978-0-9746345-0-0(6))* River of Life Publishing.

Marchese, Allison Marie. Patty's Best Friend. 2008. (Illus.). 16p. (J). 7.00 *(978-0-8059-7533-8(0))* Dorrance Publishing Co., Inc.

Marsoli, Lisa Ann. The Missing Necklace. 2014. (Sofia the First World of Reading Ser.). (J). lib. bdg. 13.55 *(978-0-606-35912-2(5))* Turtleback Bks.

Martinello, Marian L. Ready's Gifts. 2003. (Illus.). 158p. (YA). (gr. 8-18). per. 12.95 *(978-0-9724113-0-1(5))* MindCatcher Pr.

Mary, Agnes. The Story of Sammie. 2011. 28p. pap. 15.99 *(978-1-4568-7771-2(2))* Xlibris Corp.

Mary Barr. The Ditch Dog the Hedge Cat. 2009. 108p. pap. 10.95 *(978-1-4401-5558-1(5))* iUniverse, Inc.

Mason, Alexis. Just an Ordinary Little Dog: Barnaby's Story. Bunch, Paul, illus. 2010. (J). *(978-0-9755280-4-4(1))* Insight Technical Education.

Masson, J. Moussaieff. The Cat Who Came in from the Cold: A Fable. 2004. 107p. *(978-0-345-47867-2(3),* Ballantine Bks.) Random House Publishing Group.

McBride, Anthony & McBride, Autumn. The Lost Cat. 2007. (Illus.). pap. 11.00 *(978-1-56411-540-9(2),* CB Publishing & Design) UBUS Communications Systems.

McCoy, Tanya. If My Best Friend was an Elephant, 1 vol. 2010. 20p. 24.95 *(978-1-4512-1063-7(9))* PublishAmerica, Inc.

McCully, Emily Arnold. Clara: The (Mostly) True Story of the Rhinoceros Who Dazzled Kings, Inspired Artists, & Won the Hearts of Everyone . . . While She Ate Her Way up & down a Continent! McCully, Emily Arnold, illus. 2016. (ENG., Illus.). 48p. (J). (gr. -1-3). 17.99 *(978-0-553-52246-4(9),* Schwartz & Wade Bks.) Random Hse. Children's Bks.

McCurry, Meryl. Monto. 2009. 28p. pap. 13.99 *(978-1-4490-1403-2(8))* AuthorHouse.

Mcghee, Alison. Pablo & Birdy. Juan, Ana, illus. 2017. (ENG.). 304p. (J). (gr. 3-7). 17.99 ***(978-1-4814-7026-1(4),*** Atheneum/Caitlyn Dlouhy Books) Simon & Schuster Children's Publishing.

McGovern, Cammie. Chester & Gus. 2017. 272p. (J). (gr. 3-7). 16.99 *(978-0-06-233068-0(3))* HarperCollins Pubs.

McGreal, Sue. Jimmy Fox's Great Pet Adventure. 2013. 68p. pap. *(978-1-78299-607-1(9))* FeedARead.com.

McKinley, Robin. Pegasus. 2010. (ENG.). 416p. (YA). (gr. 7-18). 18.99 *(978-0-399-24677-7(0),* G.P. Putnam's Sons Books for Young Readers) Penguin Young Readers Group.

McKoin, Cathy Taylor. Little Pup Finds a Home! 2009. 28p. pap. 15.99 *(978-1-4415-3407-1(5))* Xlibris Corp.

McMillin, Jack D. The Water Dog. Nevarez, Lisa D., illus. 2011. 24p. pap. 24.95 *(978-1-4626-0544-6(3))* America Star Bks.

Meadows, Daisy. Amelia Sparklepaw's Party Problem. 2016. (Magic Animal Friends Special Edition Ser.). (ENG.). 176p. (J). (gr. 2-5). pap. 6.99 *(978-0-545-94080-1(X),* Scholastic Pr.) Scholastic, Inc.

—Chloe Slipperslide's Secret. 2016. (Magic Animal Friends Ser.: 11). lib. bdg. 14.75 *(978-0-606-38801-6(X))* Turtleback Bks.

—Grace Woollyhop's Musical Mystery. 2016. (Magic Animal Friends Ser.: 12). lib. bdg. 14.75 *(978-0-606-38802-3(8))* Turtleback Bks.

—Rosie Gigglepip's Lucky Escape. 2016. (Magic Animal Friends Ser.: 8). (ENG., Illus.). 112p. (J). (gr. 2-5). pap. 4.99 *(978-0-545-90747-7(0),* Scholastic Paperbacks) Scholastic, Inc.

—Sophie Flufftail's Brave Plan. 2016. (Magic Animal Friends Ser.: 5). (ENG., Illus.). 112p. (J). (gr. 2-5). pap. 4.99 *(978-0-545-90741-5(1),* Scholastic Paperbacks) Scholastic, Inc.

Meadows, Daisy & Scott, Lisa Ann. Amelia Sparklepaw's Party Problem. 2016. (Magic Animal Friends Ser.). (ENG.). 176p. (J). (gr. 2-5). 17.20 *(978-0-606-39140-5(1))* Turtleback Bks.

Mean Margaret. 2014. (ENG., Illus.). 176p. (J). (gr. 2-7). 16.99 *(978-1-4814-1014-4(8),* Atheneum Bks. for Young Readers) Simon & Schuster Children's Publishing.

Metz, Melinda. Raven's Point. 2005. pap. *(978-0-06-052373-2(5))* HarperCollins Canada, Ltd.

Miles, Ellen. Champ. 2016. (Puppy Place Ser.: 43). (ENG.). 96p. (J). (gr. 2-5). pap. 4.99 *(978-0-545-85727-7(9),* Scholastic Paperbacks) Scholastic, Inc.

—Champ. 2016. (Puppy Place Ser.: 43). (ENG.). 96p. (J). (gr. 2-5). 14.75 *(978-0-606-39138-2(X))* Turtleback Bks.

—Cooper. 2014. (Puppy Place Ser.: 35). lib. bdg. 14.75 *(978-0-606-36060-9(3))* Turtleback Bks.

—Lola. 2017. (Puppy Place Ser.: 45). lib. bdg. 14.75 ***(978-0-606-40168-5(7))*** Turtleback Bks.

—Nala. 2016. 89p. (J). ***(978-1-4844-8019-9(8))*** Scholastic, Inc.

—Nala (the Puppy Place #41) 2016. (Puppy Place Ser.: 41). (ENG.). 96p. (J). (gr. 2-5). pap. 4.99 *(978-0-545-85723-9(6),* Scholastic Paperbacks) Scholastic, Inc.

—The Puppy Place #35: Cooper. 2014. (Puppy Place Ser.: 35). (ENG.). 96p. (J). (gr. 2-5). pap. 4.99 *(978-0-545-60382-9(X),* Scholastic Paperbacks) Scholastic, Inc.

Miranda, Edward. A Ribbon for Diego. Bohart, Lisa, illus. 2008. 28p. pap. 12.95 *(978-0-9821654-5-4(5))* Peppertree Pr., The.

Miyazaki, Hayao. Ponyo Picture Book, Vol. 1. Miyazaki, Hayao, illus. 2009. (ENG., Illus.). 152p. (J). (gr. 2-7). 19.99 *(978-1-4215-3065-9(1))* Viz Media.

Molloy, Sheila. Jack - King of the Dogs. Steed, Tobias, ed. Molloy, Michael, illus. 2004. (Jack Ser.: 1). (ENG.). 100p. (J). (gr. 4-7). pap. 9.99 *(978-1-904872-30-6(1),* Can of Worms Kids Pr.) Can of Worms Pr. GBR. Dist: Independent Pubs. Group.

Morpurgo, Michael. Little Foxes. 2nd ed. 2009. (ENG., Illus.). 208p. (J). (gr. 2-4). pap. 11.99 *(978-1-4052-3339-2(7))* Egmont Bks., Ltd. GBR. Dist: Independent Pubs. Group.

—Shadow. 2012. (ENG.). 192p. (J). (gr. 5-9). 16.99 *(978-0-312-60659-6(1),* 9780312606596) Feiwel & Friends.

Morris, Kyle. Watching the Puppy Grow. 2017. (Text Connections Guided Close Reading Ser.). (J). (gr. 1). *(978-1-4900-1805-8(0))* Benchmark Education Co.

Muir-Chase, Marlene. Miranda the Mallard from Moose Jaw, 1 vol. 2009. 31p. pap. 24.95 *(978-1-60749-255-9(5))* America Star Bks.

Mull, Brandon, et al. Tales of the Fallen Beasts. 2016. (Spirit Animals Ser.). (ENG.). 192p. (J). (gr. 3-7). 12.99 *(978-0-545-90129-1(4))* Scholastic, Inc.

Muller, Seth. Keepers of the WindClaw Chronicles: The Day of Storms, 3 vols., Vol. 2. Dubay, Tayloe, ed. Whitethorne, Bahe, Jr., illus. 2nd ed. 2010. 224p. (J). pap. 12.95 *(978-1-893354-10-4(5))* Salina Bookshelf Inc.

—Keepers of the WindClaw Chronicles: The Mockingbird's Manual. Tayloe, McConnell Dubay, ed. Whitethorne, Bahe, Jr., illus. 2009. (ENG.). 128p. (J). (gr. 4-7). pap. 12.95 *(978-1-893354-04-3(0))* Salina Bookshelf Inc.

Nastari, Nadine, illus. Mr. TLC (Three-Legged Cat) 2007. 36p. (J). spiral bd. 14.95 *(978-0-9798387-5-0(4))* Nastari, Nadine.

Naylor, Phyllis Reynolds. The Shiloh Collection: Shiloh; Saving Shiloh; Shiloh Season; Shiloh Christmas. 2016. (Shiloh Quartet Ser.: 6). (ENG., Illus.). 688p. (J). (gr. 3-7). pap. 31.99 *(978-1-4814-8677-4(2),* Atheneum/Caitlyn Dlouhy Books) Simon & Schuster Children's Publishing.

Neal, Michael. Bonnie's Rescue: A Courageous Critters« Series Book. 2009. 56p. pap. 8.95 *(978-1-4401-1237-9(1))* iUniverse, Inc.

Neffen, Marjorie E. Bashful the Brown-Eyed Dog Gets a Home. 2013. 36p. pap. 24.95 *(978-1-4626-9881-3(6))* America Star Bks.

Nesquens, Daniel & Schimel, Lawrence. Mister H. Lozano, Luciano, illus. 2015. (ENG.). 61p. (J). 14.00 *(978-0-8028-5440-7(0),* Eerdmans Bks For Young Readers) Eerdmans, William B. Publishing Co.

Newhall, Mary & Campbell, Joanna. Samantha's Irish Luck. 2005. (Thoroughbred Ser.). (Illus.). 156p. (gr. 3-7). 15.00 *(978-0-7569-5350-8(2))* Perfection Learning Corp.

Newman, Lesléa. Ketzel, the Cat Who Composed. Bates, Amy June, illus. 2015. (ENG.). 40p. (J). (gr. k-3). 16.99 *(978-0-7636-6555-5(X))* Candlewick Pr.

Nilsen, Morten. Snyder: The Pig's Tale. Osenchakov, Yuri, illus. 2007. 116p. 24.95 *(978-0-9774906-0-8(2))* Counterbalance Bks.

Norrie, Louise Rosalyn. The Adventures of Flat Cat. 2011. 144p. 29.99 *(978-1-4628-9397-3(X))* Xlibris Corp.

North, Poppy. The Ruby Stone. 2013. 52p. pap. 15.99 *(978-1-4797-6920-9(7))* Xlibris Corp.

North, Ryan. Adventure Time, Vol. 2. Paroline, Shelli & Lamb, Braden, illus. 2013. (Adventure Time Ser.: 1). (ENG.). 128p. (J). (gr. 4). 34.99 *(978-1-60886-321-1(2))* Boom! Studios.

—Adventure Time Vol. 2. Paroline, Shelli & Lamb, Braden, illus. 2013. (Adventure Time Ser.). (ENG.). 112p. (J). (gr. 4). pap. 14.99 *(978-1-60886-323-5(9))* Boom! Studios.

—Adventure Time Vol. 3. Paroline, Shelli & Lamb, Braden, illus. 2013. (Adventure Time Ser.). (ENG.). 112p. (J). (gr. 4). pap. 14.99 *(978-1-60886-317-4(4))* Boom! Studios.

North, Ryan & Lamb, Branden. Adventure Time, Vol. 1. Paroline, Shelli, illus. 2012. (Adventure Time Ser.). (ENG.). 128p. (J). (gr. 4). pap. 14.99 *(978-1-60886-280-1(1))* Boom! Studios.

Nowra, Louis. Into That Forest. 2013. 162p. 16.99 *(978-1-4778-6725-9(2))* Amazon Publishing.

Noyes, William H., Jr. Mittens. 2008. 36p. pap. 24.95 *(978-1-4241-9440-7(7))* America Star Bks.

Nussbaum, Ben. Toko the Hippo. Wenzel, Gregory, illus. 2006. (ENG.). 36p. (J). 8.95 *(978-1-59249-580-1(X))*; 14.99 *(978-1-59249-577-1(X))*; pap. 2.95 *(978-1-59249-579-5(6))*; pap. 6.95 *(978-1-59249-578-8(8))* Soundprints.

O'Connor, Barbara. Wish. 2016. (ENG.). 240p. (J). 16.99 *(978-0-374-30273-3(1),* 9780374302733, Farrar, Straus & Giroux (BYR)) Farrar, Straus & Giroux.

Oldham, Lacy. A Dog Named Timmy, 1 vol. 2009. 52p. pap. 16.95 *(978-1-4489-1707-5(7))* PublishAmerica, Inc.

O'Neill, Rachael. Do You Want a Hug, Honey Bunny? O'Neill, Rachael, illus. 2008. (Tiger Tales Ser.). (Illus.). 12p. (J). (gr. -1-k). 8.95 *(978-1-58925-829-7(0))* Tiger Tales.

Orenstein, Denise Gosliner. Dirt. 2017. (J). pap. ***(978-0-545-92586-0(X),*** Scholastic Pr.) Scholastic, Inc.

Osborne, Joey N. Boxes, Boxes, Everywhere Boxes, 1 vol. 2009. 32p. pap. 24.95 *(978-1-60749-732-5(8))* America Star Bks.

Osborne, Mary Pope, et al. Buenos Días, Gorilas. Murdocca, Sal, illus. 2014. 26. (SPA.). 88p. (J). (gr. 2-4). pap. 5.99 *(978-1-933032-93-1(6))* Lectorum Pubns., Inc.

Oulton, Harry. A Pig Called Heather. 2015. (ENG.). 192p. (J). (gr. 3-7). 16.95 *(978-0-8234-3290-5(4))* Holiday Hse., Inc.

Oulton, Harry. The Return of a Pig Called Heather. 2017. (Pig Called Heather Ser.: 2). (ENG., Illus.). 192p. (J). (gr. 4-7). pap. 8.99 ***(978-1-84812-473-8(2))*** Bonnier Publishing GBR. Dist: Independent Pubs. Group.

Page, Louise. Furballs' Fables. 2008. 100p. pap. 17.50 *(978-1-4092-1068-9(5))* Lulu Pr., Inc.

Patchett, Mary Elwyn. Ajax: Golden Dog of the Australian Bush. Tansley, Eric, illus. 2011. 172p. 42.95 *(978-1-258-01103-1(4))* Literary Licensing, LLC.

Patenaude, Jeremy, et al. Playful Puppy. 2014. (DK Readers Ser.). (ENG.). 32p. (J). (gr. k-4). pap. 3.99 *(978-1-4654-1999-6(3),* DK Children) Dorling Kindersley Publishing, Inc.

Patrick, Ella. Rapunzel Finds a Friend (Disney Princess) Thomas, Jeffrey, illus. 2016. (ENG.). 32p. (J). (gr. -1-2). 7.99 *(978-0-7364-3388-4(0),* RH/Disney) Random Hse. Children's Bks.

Patterson, Sadie. Old Pete & Dan. 2010. 16p. 8.49 *(978-1-4490-1489-6(5))* AuthorHouse.

Pauly, Heather E. Kon: The Bay Painted Stallion. 2010. 60p. pap. 12.99 *(978-1-4490-4895-2(1))* AuthorHouse.

Paver, Michelle. Ghost Hunter. Taylor, Geoff, illus. 2011. (Chronicles of Ancient Darkness Ser.: 6). 304p. (J). (gr. 5). pap. 7.99 *(978-0-06-072842-7(6),* Tegen, Katherine Bks) HarperCollins Pubs.

—Gods & Warriors. 2013. (Gods & Warriors Ser.: 1). (ENG.). 336p. (J). (gr. 5). pap. 8.99 *(978-0-14-242284-7(3),* Puffin Books) Penguin Young Readers Group.

PC Treasures Staff, prod. Little Red Riding Hood. 2007. (J). *(978-1-60072-031-4(5))* PC Treasures, Inc.

Pearson, Betty Jean. Learn with Ladee: A Service Dog. 2008. 30p. pap. 24.95 *(978-1-4241-9507-7(1))* America Star Bks.

Peck, Richard. Secrets at Sea. 2012. (ENG.). 272p. (J). (gr. 3-7). pap. 7.99 *(978-0-14-242183-3(9),* Puffin Books) Penguin Young Readers Group.

—Secrets at Sea. Murphy, Kelly, illus. 2011. (ENG.). 256p. (J). (gr. 3-7). 16.99 *(978-0-8037-3455-5(7)*, Dial Bks) Penguin Young Readers Group.

Pelley, Kathleen T. Raj the Bookstore Tiger. Keiser, Paige, illus. 2011. (ENG.). 32p. (J). (gr. -1-3). 15.95 *(978-1-58089-230-8(2))* Charlesbridge Publishing, Inc.

Pennypacker, Sara. Pax. Klassen, Jon, illus. 2016. (ENG.). (J). (gr. 3-3). 16.99 ***(978-0-06-245703-5(9))*** Blackstone Audio, Inc.

—Pax. Klassen, Jon, illus. 2016. 288p. (J). (gr. 3-7). 16.99 *(978-0-06-237701-2(9))* HarperCollins Pubs.

—Pax. 2017. (SPA.). lib. bdg. 29.35 ***(978-0-606-40010-7(9))*** Turtleback Bks.

—PAX: UNA HISTORIA DE PAZ Y AMISTAD. 2017. (SPA.). 304p. (gr. -1-2). pap. 16.95 ***(978-84-15594-95-6(X)***, Nube De Tinta) Penguin Random House Grupo Editorial ESP. Dist: Two Rivers Distribution.

Perry, Rex. Coco's Girls. Perry, Rex, illus. 2008. (ENG., Illus.). 36p. (YA). per. 12.95 *(978-0-9740212-1-8(0))* Cedar Grove Bks.

Peruski, Steven. My Friend & Teacher Sammie. 2006. (ENG., Illus.). (YA). 21.99 *(978-0-615-13428-4(9))* Compassion Pets Publishing.

Phillips, Azelin. Quicksilver. 2010. 32p. pap. 14.49 *(978-1-4490-4522-7(7))* AuthorHouse.

Phillips, Kelly. Macs the Wonder Dog. 2008. 21p. pap. 24.95 *(978-1-4241-8937-3(3))* America Star Bks.

Phillips, Ruby Ann. Pet Psychic. Isik, Semur, illus. 2015. (Krystal Ball Ser.). (ENG.). 112p. (gr. 2-3). lib. bdg. 25.32 *(978-1-4795-5875-9(3))* Picture Window Bks.

Pierce, Tamora. Emperor Mage. 2015. (Immortals Ser.: 3). (ENG., Illus.). 368p. (YA). (gr. 7). pap. 10.99 *(978-1-4814-4026-4(8))* Simon & Schuster Children's Publishing.

—Emperor Mage. 2005. (Immortals Ser.: 3). (ENG.). 384p. (YA). (gr. 7). pap. 7.99 *(978-1-4169-0337-6(2)*, Simon Pulse) Simon Pulse.

—The Realms of the Gods. 2005. (Immortals Ser.: No. 4). 347p. (gr. 7-12). 18.00 *(978-0-7569-5775-9(3))* Perfection Learning Corp.

—Wild Magic. 2005. (Immortals Ser.: No. 1). (Illus.). 362p. (gr. 7-12). 18.00 *(978-0-7569-5508-3(4))* Perfection Learning Corp.

—Wolf-Speaker. 2005. (Immortals Ser.: No. 2). 344p. (gr. 7-12). 18.00 *(978-0-7569-5509-0(2))* Perfection Learning Corp.

—Wolf-Speaker. 2015. (Immortals Ser.: 2). (ENG., Illus.). 352p. (YA). (gr. 7). pap. 10.99 *(978-1-4814-4024-0(1))* Simon & Schuster Children's Publishing.

Polacco, Patricia. Ginger & Petunia. Polacco, Patricia, illus. 2007. (ENG., Illus.). 40p. (J). (gr. -1-3). 17.99 *(978-0-399-24539-8(1)*, Philomel Bks.) Penguin Young Readers Group.

Polglase, Pamela. Handy & Dandy. 2008. 182p. 27.76 *(978-1-4357-4588-9(4))* Lulu Pr., Inc.

Pollard, Tara. Season's Christmas Quest: The Dog's Story. 2012. 138p. (gr. 1-1). 21.95 *(978-1-4759-4008-4(4))*; pap. 11.95 *(978-1-4759-4009-1(2))* iUniverse, Inc.

Posner-Sanchez, Andrea. Cuddly Princess Pals. Random House Disney Staff, illus. 2014. (Pictureback(R) Ser.). (ENG.). 24p. (J). (gr. -1-2). 3.99 *(978-0-7364-3135-4(7)*, RH/Disney) Random Hse. Children's Bks.

Powell, Gail. The Adventures of Harold J. Kat. 2008. 40p. pap. 16.99 *(978-1-4259-6334-7(X))* AuthorHouse.

Powell, Glenda. Cassie & Mr. Ant. Mitchell, Hazel, illus. 2008. 30p. (J). (gr. -1-3). per. 7.95 *(978-0-9779445-6-9(5))* Zoe Life Publishing.

Powell, Jillian. Hurry up, Pony!, 1 vol. Colnaghi, Stefania, illus. 2013. (Start Reading Ser.). (ENG.). 24p. (gr. k-1). pap. 7.95 *(978-1-4765-4105-1(1))* Capstone Press of Coughlan Cos.

Pratchett, Terry. The Amazing Maurice & His Educated Rodents. 2008. (Discworld Novels Ser.). 368p. (YA). (gr. 8-18). pap. 8.99 *(978-0-06-001235-9(8))* HarperCollins Pubs.

—The Amazing Maurice & His Educated Rodents. 2003. (ENG.). 340p. (gr. 7). 19.00 *(978-0-7569-1458-5(2))* Perfection Learning Corp.

—The Amazing Maurice & His Educated Rodents. 2008. (Discworld Ser.: 33). (YA). (gr. 5-8). 19.65 *(978-0-613-65757-0(8)*, Turtleback) Turtleback Bks.

Price, Justine. The Dreams of a Puppy. 2013. 28p. pap. 24.95 *(978-1-63000-049-3(3))* America Star Bks.

Price, Reynolds. A Perfect Friend. 2013. (ENG.). (J). pap. 4.99 *(978-0-689-83148-5(X)*, Simon & Schuster/Paula Wiseman Bks.) Simon & Schuster/Paula Wiseman Bks.

Prineas, Sarah. Heart of the Land. 2017. (Spirit Animals: Fall of the Beasts Ser.: 5). (ENG.). 192p. (J). (gr. 3-7). 12.99 ***(978-1-338-11665-6(7))*** Scholastic, Inc.

—Heart of the Land (Spirit Animals: Fall of the Beasts, Book 5) 2017. (Spirit Animals: Fall of the Beasts Ser.: 5). (ENG.). 192p. (J). (gr. 3-7). 16.99 ***(978-1-338-18981-0(6))*** Scholastic, Inc.

Publications International Ltd. Staff, ed. Up & down! Play-a-Sound Book & Huggable Kai-lan. 2010. (J). 14.98 *(978-1-4127-5591-7(3))* Publications International, Ltd.

Pullein-Thompson, Christine. Phantom Horse. 2012. (ENG., Illus.). 176p. (J). pap. 9.95 *(978-1-84135-820-8(7))* Award Pubns. Ltd. GBR. Dist: Parkwest Pubns., Inc.

—Phantom Horse Comes Home. 2012. (ENG., Illus.). 176p. (J). pap. 9.95 *(978-1-84135-822-2(3))* Award Pubns. Ltd. GBR. Dist: Parkwest Pubns., Inc.

—Phantom Horse Disappears. 2012. (ENG., Illus.). 176p. (J). pap. 9.95 *(978-1-84135-821-5(5))* Award Pubns. Ltd. GBR. Dist: Parkwest Pubns., Inc.

—Phantom Horse Island Mystery. 2012. (ENG., Illus.). 176p. (J). pap. 9.95 *(978-1-84135-825-3(8))* Award Pubns. Ltd. GBR. Dist: Parkwest Pubns., Inc.

—Wait for Me. 2012. (ENG., Illus.). 176p. (J). pap. 9.95 *(978-1-84135-823-9(1))* Award Pubns. Ltd. GBR. Dist: Parkwest Pubns., Inc.

Pyatt, K. C. Rebekah As Her Journey Begins. 2008. 60p. pap. 9.95 *(978-1-933912-00-4(6))* Westview Publishing Co., Inc.

Pyron, Bobbie. The Dogs of Winter. 2014. (ENG.). 320p. (J). (gr. 5-9). pap. 7.99 *(978-0-545-39931-9(9)*, Levine, Arthur A. Bks.) Scholastic, Inc.

—A Dog's Way Home. 2012. (ENG.). 336p. (J). (gr. 3-7). pap. 6.99 *(978-0-06-198672-7(0)*, Tegen, Katherine Bks) HarperCollins Pubs.

—A Dog's Way Home. Jessell, Tim, illus. 2011. (ENG.). 336p. (J). (gr. 3-7). 16.99 *(978-0-06-198674-1(7)*, Tegen, Katherine Bks) HarperCollins Pubs.

Rakusin, Sudie. Dear Calla Roo... Love, Savannah Blue No. 2: A Letter about Getting Sick & Feeling Better. Rakusin, Sudie, illus. 2003. (Illus.). 32p. (J). (gr. -1-4). 16.95 *(978-0-9664805-3-5(8))* Winged Willow Pr.

Rankine-Van Wassenhoven, Jacqueline. A Frog Named Waldor. Zhang, Annie, illus. 2008. 20p. per. 24.95 *(978-1-4241-9926-6(3))* America Star Bks.

Rao, Sirish. The Old Animals' Forest Band. Bai, Durga, illus. 2008. 40p. (J). (gr. -1-3). *(978-81-86211-41-0(1))* Tara Publishing.

Redbank, Tennant. Beauty: Aurora's Sleepy Kitten. Random House Disney Staff, illus. 2014. (Stepping Stone Book Ser.). (ENG.). 64p. (J). (gr. 2-5). 5.99 *(978-0-7364-3266-5(3)*, RH/Disney) Random Hse. Children's Bks.

—Beauty the Sleepiest Kitty. Random House Disney Staff, illus. 2014. (Stepping Stone Book(TM) Ser.). (ENG.). 64p. (J). (gr. 1-4). lib. bdg. 12.99 *(978-0-7364-8163-2(X)*, RH/Disney) Random Hse. Children's Bks.

Redd, Faye V. Mia & Her Kitten Sophie. 2008. 24p. pap. 11.49 *(978-1-4343-9835-2(8))* AuthorHouse.

Reisfeld, Randi & Gilmour, H. B. What the Dog Said. 2012. (ENG.). 256p. (YA). (gr. 4-14). 16.99 *(978-1-59990-702-4(X)*, 9781599907024, Bloomsbury USA Childrens) Bloomsbury Publishing USA.

Reynolds, Alison. A Year with Marmalade. McKenzie, Heath, illus. 2013. (ENG.). 40p. (J). (gr. -1-1). 15.99 *(978-1-4424-8105-3(6)*, Little Simon) Little Simon.

Richardson, Michelle Y. Kaito: Shedding Tears. 2010. 104p. (J). pap. 9.95 *(978-1-4502-5267-6(2))* iUniverse, Inc.

Richter, Jutta. The Cat: Or, How I Lost Eternity. Brailovsky, Anna, tr. from GER. Berner, Rotraut Susanne, illus. 2007. (ENG.). 80p. (J). (gr. 1-6). 14.00 *(978-1-57131-676-9(0))* Milkweed Editions.

Rising, Janet. Pony Whisperer. 2010. (ENG.). 208p. (J). (gr. 4-7). pap. 6.99 *(978-1-4022-3952-6(1)*, Sourcebooks Jabberwocky) Sourcebooks, Inc.

Ritz, C. Tiger's World: Growing Up. 2013. 72p. pap. *(978-1-77097-596-5(9))* FriesenPress.

Roba, Jean. Bored Silly with Billy. 2010. (Billy & Buddy Ser.: 2). (ENG., Illus.). 48p. (J). (gr. 3-17). pap. 11.95 *(978-1-84918-049-8(0))* CineBook GBR. Dist: National Bk. Network.

Roberts, Shelly. Sissy & the Old Crow. 2006. (Illus.). 36p. (J). per. 18.00 *(978-0-9789798-2-9(6)*, 978-9789798-2-9) Blackbird's World Publishing Co.

—Sissy & the Old Crow (Coloring Book) 2006. (Illus.). 36p. (J). per. 6.50 *(978-0-9789798-3-6(4)*, 978-0-9789798-3-6) Blackbird's World Publishing Co.

Robinson, Fiona. The Useful Moose: A Truthful, Moose-Full Tale. 2004. (ENG., Illus.). 32p. (J). (gr. -1-3). 15.95 *(978-0-8109-4925-6(3))* Abrams, Inc.

Roche, Louise. The Amazing Adventures of Libby Lightfoot: Book 1: Book 1. 2011. 40p. 17.50 *(978-1-4567-3443-5(1))* AuthorHouse.

Root, Laura L. Quail in My Garden: Book One of Adventures in My Garden. 2012. 64p. pap. 26.99 *(978-1-4490-6963-6(0))* AuthorHouse.

Rose, D. M. A Tail of Friendship: The Psychiatrist Is In. 2012. 34p. 24.95 *(978-1-4626-5240-2(9))* America Star Bks.

Rosen, Michael J. The Tale of Rescue. Fellows, Stan, illus. 2015. (ENG.). 112p. (J). (gr. 5). 14.99 *(978-0-7636-7167-9(3))* Candlewick Pr.

Rostoker-Gruber, Karen & Isaacs, Ronald H. Farmer Kobi's Hanukkah Match. Decker, C. B., illus. 2015. (J). *(978-1-68115-501-2(X))*; pap. *(978-0-87441-924-5(7))* Behrman Hse., Inc.

Rovan, Joan. Patches the Cow-Cat. 2008. 32p. pap. 16.50 *(978-1-4357-3480-7(7))* Lulu Pr., Inc.

Rozanski, Bonnie. Borderline. 2007. (ENG.). 208p. (YA). (gr. 10). pap. 22.95 *(978-0-88984-293-9(0))* Porcupine's Quill, Inc. CAN. Dist: Univ. of Toronto Pr.

Rubin, Adam. Those Darn Squirrels! Salmieri, Daniel, illus. 2008. (ENG.). 32p. (J). (gr. -1-3). 17.99 *(978-0-547-00703-8(5))* Houghton Mifflin Harcourt Publishing Co.

—Those Darn Squirrels Fly South. Salmieri, Daniel, illus. 2012. (ENG.). 32p. (J). (gr. -1-3). 17.99 *(978-0-547-67823-8(1))* Houghton Mifflin Harcourt Publishing Co.

Russell, Christopher. Dogboy. 2006. 272p. (J). (gr. 5). 15.99 *(978-0-06-084116-4(8)*, Greenwillow Bks.) HarperCollins Pubs.

—Hunted. 2007. (J). (gr. 5-9). 254p. 15.99 *(978-0-06-084119-5(2))*; 272p. lib. bdg. 16.89 *(978-0-06-084120-1(6)*, Greenwillow Bks.) HarperCollins Pubs.

Salamon, Julie. Cat in the City. Weber, Jill, illus. 2014. (ENG.). 208p. (J). (gr. 3-7). 16.99 *(978-0-8037-4056-3(5)*, Dial Bks) Penguin Young Readers Group.

—Mutt's Promise. Weber, Jill, illus. 2016. (ENG.). 256p. (J). (gr. 3-7). 16.99 *(978-0-525-42778-0(3)*, Dial Bks) Penguin Young Readers Group.

Salisbury, Graham. Calvin Coconut: Man Trip. Rogers, Jacqueline, illus. 2013. (Calvin Coconut Ser.). (ENG.). 144p. (J). (gr. 2-5). pap. 6.99 *(978-0-375-86507-7(1)*, Yearling) Random Hse. Children's Bks.

Sandusky, Thomas & Hill, Kathy. Spidy the Spider Monkey. Johnson, Gretchen, illus. 2009. 32p. pap. 12.95 *(978-0-9823002-5-1(5))* Peppertree Pr., The.

Sargent, Dave, et al. A Puppy for Bobby, 10 vols. 2004. (Learn to Read Ser.: 10). (Illus.). 18p. (J). pap. 10.95 *(978-1-56763-818-9(X))* Ozark Publishing.

Scardamaglia, Christine. Paso Joe. 2012. 28p. pap. 19.99 *(978-1-4772-6166-8(4))* AuthorHouse.

Senior, Patricia. Pip & the Magic Flute. 2008. (Illus.). 40p. pap. 18.49 *(978-1-4389-0023-0(6))* AuthorHouse.

Sensel, Joni. Bears Barge In. Bivins, Christopher, illus. 2003. 32p. (J). (gr. -1-18). 14.95 *(978-0-9701195-0-6(X))* Dream Factory Bks.

Shamaley, Rochelle. Buddy Finds a Home. 2013. 28p. pap. 19.99 *(978-1-4817-0315-4(3))* AuthorHouse.

Sheckels, Astrid, illus. Nic & Nellie, 1 vol. 2013. (ENG.). 32p. (J). (gr. 1-4). 17.95 *(978-1-934031-52-0(6)*, 9781934031520) Islandport Pr., Inc.

Shivkumar, Suganthi Mahadevan. Every Dog Has His Day! 2016. (ENG.). 46p. (J). (gr. 4-6). 10.95 *(978-1-78554-946-5(4)*, 5d07ae3b-b677-4afc-a359-000168d67c3a) Austin, Stan AUS. Dist: Bookmasters Distribution.

Shotz, Jennifer Li. Hero - Rescue Mission. 2017. (Hero Ser.: 3). 192p. (J). (gr. 3-7). pap. 7.99 ***(978-0-06-256045-2(X))*** HarperCollins Pubs.

Shyba, Jessica. Bathtime with Theo & Beau. 2016. (ENG., Illus.). 40p. (J). 16.99 *(978-1-250-05907-9(0)*, 9781250059079) Feiwel & Friends.

Siegel, Randy. My Snake Blake. Bloch, Serge, illus. 2012. (ENG.). 32p. (J). (gr. -1-1). 16.99 *(978-1-59643-584-1(4)*, 9781596435841) Roaring Brook Pr.

Sievert, Jean & Cloninger, Shirley. Gabriel the Gordian Angel. 2009. 60p. pap. 21.99 *(978-1-4490-1254-0(X))* AuthorHouse.

Sieweke, Susan. The Spirit of Hope. 2008. 36p. pap. 16.00 *(978-1-4389-0514-3(9))* AuthorHouse.

Simmons Bell, Linda. Kylie & Mr Whiskers. 2009. 20p. pap. 13.00 *(978-1-4389-3555-3(2))* AuthorHouse.

Sleigh, Barbara. Carbonel & Calidor: Being the Further Adventures of a Royal Cat. Front, Charles, illus. 2009. (ENG.). 224p. (J). (gr. 4-7). 17.95 *(978-1-59017-333-6(3)*, NYR Children's Collection) New York Review of Bks., Inc., The.

Smiley, Jeremy. Chester: Little Turtle, Big Adventure, 1 vol. 2009. 36p. pap. 24.95 *(978-1-60703-489-6(1))* America Star Bks.

Smith, Claude Clayton. The Gull That Lost the Sea. Cathcart, Sharyn, illus. 2008. (ENG.). 34p. pap. 5.95 *(978-0-9667359-7-0(8)*, BeanPole Bks.) Harren Communications, LLC.

Smith, Jodene Lynn & Thompson, Chad. Beh, Beh, Borreguito Negro, 1 vol. rev. ed. 2010. (Early Childhood Themes Ser.). (SPA., Illus.). 16p. (J). (gr. -1-2). pap. 6.99 *(978-1-4333-2094-1(0))*; pap. 19.99 *(978-1-4333-2095-8(9))* Shell Educational Publishing.

Smith, Louise C. Mr. Stubbs: Autobiography of a Clever Cat. 2008. pap. 9.00 *(978-0-8059-8691-4(X))* Dorrance Publishing Co., Inc.

Smith-Mansell, Dana. The Smith Family's New Puppy: Helping Children Cope with a New Family Member. Voerg, Kathy, illus. 2008. (Let's Talk Ser.). (ENG.). 48p. (J). (gr. -1-4). pap. 8.95 *(978-0-88282-327-0(2))* New Horizon Pr. Pubs., Inc.

Smith, Molly K. Cassie's Guardian Angel. 2009. 24p. pap. 17.50 *(978-1-4490-4065-9(9))* AuthorHouse.

Smith, Sherry. The Wolf & the Shield: An Adventure with Saint Patrick. McNally, Nicholas, illus. 2016. 118p. (J). pap. *(978-0-8198-8356-8(5))* Pauline Bks. & Media.

Smith, William. Frankie & Earnie Meet, 1 vol. 2009. pap. 24.95 *(978-1-60749-333-4(0))* America Star Bks.

Snyder, Sandy. There's Only One I in Charlie. Ferrenburg, Susie, illus. 2011. 48p. pap. 24.95 *(978-1-4626-4086-7(9))* America Star Bks.

Sommer, A. M. Tucker's Birthday. 2007. 56p. (gr. 2-2). per. 15.99 *(978-1-4257-8987-9(0))* Xlibris Corp.

Soros, Barbara. Tenzin's Deer. Mayer, Danuta, illus. 2007. (ENG.). 32p. (J). (gr. 2-4). pap. 7.99 *(978-1-84686-130-7(6))* Barefoot Bks., Inc.

Spencer, Frances Mcneil. Dee & the Dog: Home at Last. 2012. 90p. (gr. 4-6). pap. 13.95 *(978-1-4772-6709-7(3))* AuthorHouse.

St. John, Lauren. Dolphin Song. 2009. (ENG.). 272p. (J). (gr. 3-7). 7.99 *(978-0-14-241375-3(5)*, Puffin Books) Penguin Young Readers Group.

—The Elephant's Tale. 2011. (ENG.). 240p. (J). (gr. 3-7). 6.99 *(978-0-14-241879-6(X)*, Puffin Books) Penguin Young Readers Group.

Standifer, Charlcy. Butch the One-Of-a-Kind Dog. 2013. 32p. 25.99 *(978-1-4582-1118-7(5)*, Abbott Pr.) Author Solutions, Inc.

Stangl, Katrin, illus. Strong As a Bear. 2016. (ENG.). 40p. (J). (gr. -1-3). 16.95 *(978-1-59270-198-8(1))* Enchanted Lion Bks., LLC.

Starling, Landa. If You Sleep with a Cat on Your Head. Formelio, Lorri, illus. 2008. 27p. pap. 24.95 *(978-1-60703-318-9(6))* America Star Bks.

Stein, David Ezra. I'm My Own Dog. Stein, David Ezra, illus. 2014. (ENG., Illus.). 32p. (J). (gr. -1-3). 15.99 *(978-0-7636-6139-7(2))* Candlewick Pr.

—I'm My Own Dog. 2014. 38.75 *(978-1-4906-4052-5(5))*; 36.75 *(978-1-4906-4378-6(8))* Recorded Bks., Inc.

Stein, Garth. Enzo - Races in the Rain! Alley, R. W., illus. 2014. (ENG.). 40p. (J). (gr. -1-3). 17.99 *(978-0-06-229533-0(0))* HarperCollins Pubs.

—Enzo & the Fourth of July Races. Alley, R. W., illus. 2017. 40p. (J). (gr. -1-3). 17.99 *(978-0-06-238059-3(1))* HarperCollins Pubs.

—Racing in the Rain: My Life as a Dog. 2011. (ENG., Illus.). 304p. (J). (gr. 3-7). 16.99 *(978-0-06-201574-7(5))*; pap. 6.99 *(978-0-06-201576-1(1))* HarperCollins Pubs.

Stephens, R. David. My Animal Friends, 1 vol. Shoemaker, Kathryn, illus. 2003. (ENG.). 32p. (J). (gr. k-3). pap. 6.95 *(978-1-896580-74-6(2))* Tradewind Bks. CAN. Dist: Orca Bk. Pubs. USA.

Stiefvater, Maggie. Forever. (Shiver Ser.: 3). (ENG.). (J). (gr. 9). 2014. 416p. pap. 9.99 *(978-0-545-68280-0(0))* 2011. 400p. 17.99 *(978-0-545-25908-8(8)*, Scholastic Pr.) Scholastic, Inc.

—Forever. l.t. ed. 2011. (Shiver Trilogy: Bk. 3). (ENG.). 598p. 23.99 *(978-1-4104-3606-1(3))* Thorndike Pr.

—Forever. 2014. (Wolves of Mercy Falls Ser.: 3). lib. bdg. 20.85 *(978-0-606-36649-6(0))* Turtleback Bks.

—Hunted, Bk. 2. 2014. (Spirit Animals Ser.: 2). (ENG., Illus.). 192p. (J). (gr. 3-7). 12.99 *(978-0-545-52244-1(7))* Scholastic, Inc.

—Linger. 2014. (Shiver Ser.). (ENG.). (YA). (gr. 9). lib. bdg. 20.60 ***(978-1-68065-091-4(2))*** Perfection Learning Corp.

—Linger. (Shiver Ser.: 2). (ENG.). (J). (gr. 9). 2014. 384p. pap. 9.99 *(978-0-545-68279-4(7))* 2010. 368p. 17.99 *(978-0-545-12328-0(3)*, Scholastic Pr.) Scholastic, Inc.

—Linger. l.t. ed. 2011. (Shiver Trilogy: Bk. 2). (ENG.). 488p. 23.99 *(978-1-4104-3447-0(8))* Thorndike Pr.

—Shiver. 2011. (Shiver Trilogy: Bk. 1). 9.64 *(978-0-7848-3572-2(1)*, Everbind) Marco Bk. Co.

—Shiver. (ENG.). (gr. 9). 2014. (Shiver Ser.). (YA). lib. bdg. 20.60 ***(978-1-68065-090-7(4))*** 2010. (Shiver Trilogy: Bk. 1). 392p. 20.00 *(978-1-60686-750-1(4))* Perfection Learning Corp.

—Shiver. (Shiver Ser.: 1). (ENG.). (J). 2014. 416p. (gr. 9). pap. 9.99 *(978-0-545-68278-7(9))* 2009. 400p. (gr. 7-18). 17.99 *(978-0-545-12326-6(7)*, Scholastic Pr.) Scholastic, Inc.

—Shiver. l.t. ed. 2010. (Shiver Trilogy: Bk. 1). (ENG.). 506p. 23.95 *(978-1-4104-2667-3(X))* Thorndike Pr.

—Shiver. 2014. (Wolves of Mercy Falls Ser.: 1). lib. bdg. 20.85 *(978-0-606-36647-2(4))* Turtleback Bks.

—Sinner. 2015. (Shiver Ser.). (ENG.). 368p. (J). (gr. 9). pap. 10.99 *(978-0-545-65459-3(9))* Scholastic, Inc.

Stiefvater, Maggie & Scholastic, Inc. Staff. Shiver; Linger; Forever. 2011. (Shiver Ser.). (ENG.). (J). (gr. 9-9). 52.97 *(978-0-545-32686-5(9)*, Scholastic Pr.) Scholastic, Inc.

Stone, Jeff. Monkey. 2006. (Five Ancestors Ser.: Bk. 2). (ENG.). 208p. (J). (gr. 3-7). per. 6.99 *(978-0-375-83074-7(X)*, Yearling) Random Hse. Children's Bks.

—Tiger. 2006. (Five Ancestors Ser.: Bk. 1). (ENG., Illus.). 208p. (J). (gr. 3-7). reprint ed. 6.99 *(978-0-375-83072-3(3)*, Yearling) Random Hse. Children's Bks.

Strelkoff, Tatiana. Jeremy & the Crow Nation. Martin, Bobi, ed. 2003. (Changer Ser.: Vol. 2). (Illus.). 128p. (Orig.). (J). (gr. 7-12). pap. 6.95 *(978-0-945522-04-1(5)*, 2204-5) Rebecca Hse.

Strouse, Benjamin. Hey, Boy. Phelan, Jennifer, illus. 2014. (ENG.). 40p. (J). pap. 7.95 *(978-1-4575-3341-9(3))* Dog Ear Publishing, LLC.

—Hey, Boy. Phelan, Jennifer, illus. 2017. (ENG.). 48p. (J). (gr. -1-3). 15.99 ***(978-1-4814-7101-5(5)***, McElderry, Margaret K. Bks.) McElderry, Margaret K. Bks.

Strow, Lorie. The Shimmers. 2011. 32p. pap. 21.99 *(978-1-4568-8133-7(7))* Xlibris Corp.

Sundberg, Peggy. Jazmine's Incredible Story. Wiles, Pat, illus. 2006. 32p. (J). 16.95 *(978-0-9721057-5-0(1)*, Cowgirl Peg Bks.) Cowgirl Peg Enterprises.

Swiney, Wendy D. Harvey's Very Favorite Place. 2009. 20p. pap. 12.99 *(978-1-4389-6547-5(8))* AuthorHouse.

Talbott, Hudson. From Wolf to Woof. Talbott, Hudson, illus. 2016. (ENG., Illus.). 40p. (J). (gr. k-3). 16.99 *(978-0-399-25404-8(8)*, Nancy Paulsen Books) Penguin Young Readers Group.

Tate Kuelling, Judy. The Hitchhiker. 2009. 20p. pap. 10.49 *(978-1-4389-5144-7(2))* AuthorHouse.

Tennapel, Doug. Tommysaurus Rex. 2013. (ENG., Illus.). 144p. (J). (gr. 4-7). pap. 10.99 *(978-0-545-48383-4(2)*, Graphix) Scholastic, Inc.

TenNapel, Doug. Tommysaurus Rex. 2013. (ENG., Illus.). 144p. (J). (gr. 3-7). 19.99 *(978-0-545-48382-7(4)*, Graphix) Scholastic, Inc.

Terri, Branson. Brother Dragon. l.t. ed. 2007. (ENG., Illus.). 24p. (J). 14.99 *(978-0-9787421-9-5(2))* Dragonfly Publishing, Inc.

Thames, Fiona. A Dog's Mad Dash for Home. 2008. 32p. pap. 24.95 *(978-1-4241-8672-3(2))* America Star Bks.

Thebo, Mimi. Dreaming the Bear. 2017. (YA). pap. *(978-0-399-55753-8(9))* Earthscan Canada.

Tirgari, Simin. Color of the Heart. 2011. 84p. pap. 8.95 *(978-1-4620-4966-0(4))* iUniverse, Inc.

Tofield, Simon, creator. Simon's Cat off to the Vet ... & Other Adventures. 2015. (ENG., Illus.). 240p. 27.95 *(978-1-61775-402-9(1))* Akashic Bks.

Trumbo, Stephen. Friends of the Forest. 2008. 39p. pap. 24.95 *(978-1-60563-781-5(5))* America Star Bks.

Ts'o, Pauline. Whispers of the Wolf. 2015. (ENG., Illus.). 40p. (J). (gr. k-3). 16.95 *(978-1-937786-45-8(5)*, Wisdom Tales) World Wisdom, Inc.

Tubb, Kristin O'Donnell. A Dog Like Daisy. 2017. 192p. (J). (gr. 3-7). 16.99 *(978-0-06-246324-1(1)*, Tegen, Katherine Bks) HarperCollins Pubs.

Vail, Rochelle Kelly. Critters: A Dog's Tale. 2007. 140p. per. 11.95 *(978-1-4327-0826-9(0))* Outskirts Pr., Inc.

Van Dusen, Chris. The Circus Ship. Van Dusen, Chris, illus. 2015. (ENG., Illus.). 40p. (J). (gr. -1-3). 6.99 *(978-0-7636-5592-1(9))* Candlewick Pr.

—The Circus Ship Big Book. 2011. (ENG., Illus.). 40p. (J). (gr. -1-3). pap. 24.99 *(978-0-7636-5593-8(7))* Candlewick Pr.

Van Gorder, Vivian Ezeife. Master Kofi & Friskey the Dog. 2012. 20p. pap. 17.99 *(978-1-4772-6817-9(0))* AuthorHouse.

Vande Velde, Vivian. Smart Dog. 2007. (ENG., Illus.). 160p. (J). (gr. 5-7). pap. 7.99 *(978-0-15-206172-2(X))* Houghton Mifflin Harcourt Publishing Co.

Velle, Tori. Jake the Snake. 2009. 40p. pap. 16.99 *(978-1-4490-4431-2(X))* AuthorHouse.

Velmans, Hester. Isabel of the Whales. 2006. (ENG.). 192p. (J). (gr. 3-7). per. 6.99 *(978-0-440-42025-5(3)*, Yearling) Random Hse. Children's Bks.

Verrett, Michael. It Followed Me Home Can I Keep It? 2010. 35p. pap. 10.00 *(978-0-557-28827-4(4))* Lulu Pr., Inc.

—It Followed Me Home Can I Keep It? (full Color) 2010. 35p. pap. 19.00 *(978-0-557-29796-2(6))* Lulu Pr., Inc.

Villasenor, Victor. Little Crow to the Rescue/el Cuervito al Rescate. Munoz, Elizabeth Cummins, tr. Alcantara, Felipe Ugalde, illus. 2005. (SPA & ENG.). 32p. (J). (gr. -1-3). pap. 16.95 *(978-1-55885-430-7(4)*, Piñata Books) Arte Publico Pr.

Voake, Steve. Daisy Dawson & the Secret Pond. Meserve, Jessica, illus. 2010. (Daisy Dawson Ser.: 2). (ENG.). 96p. (J). (gr. 1-4). pap. 5.99 *(978-0-7636-4730-8(6))* Candlewick Pr.

—Daisy Dawson Is on Her Way! Meserve, Jessica, illus. 2009. (Daisy Dawson Ser.: 1). (ENG.). 112p. (J). (gr. 1-4). pap. 5.99 *(978-0-7636-4294-5(0))* Candlewick Pr.

—Daisy Dawson on the Farm. Meserve, Jessica, illus. 2013. (Daisy Dawson Ser.). (ENG.). 96p. (J). (gr. 1-4). pap. 5.99 *(978-0-7636-6340-7(9))* Candlewick Pr.

Vujadinovic, Nenad. Ronny. Fur, Emil, illus. 2007. (POL & ENG.). 32p. (J). pap. 12.95 *(978-1-60195-105-2(1))* International Step by Step Assn.

Waines, Frances Drummond. Humpi, the Orphan Camel, 1 vol. 2010. 104p. pap. 19.95 *(978-1-4489-3963-3(1))* America Star Bks.

Wainwright, Debra. That Kind of Dog. 2009. (ENG., Illus.). 32p. (J). (gr. k-2). 16.95 *(978-0-9792035-4-1(6))* Pleasant St. Pr.

Wales, Dirk. Jack London's Dog. Moser, Barry, illus. 2008. 64p. (YA). (gr. 5-9). 17.95 *(978-0-9632459-3-9(7))* Great Plains Pr.
Wall, Billy James. The Mystery of Marcy & the Stony Squirrel. 2009. 40.00 *(978-1-61584-580-4(1))* Independent Pub.
Wall, Laura. Goose on the Farm. Wall, Laura, illus. 2016. (Illus.). 48p. (J). (gr. -1-3). 12.99 *(978-0-06-232439-9(X))* HarperCollins Pubs.
Walsh, Barbara. Sammy in the Sky. Wyeth, Jamie, illus. 2011. (ENG.). 32p. (J). (gr. -1-3). 16.99 *(978-0-7636-4927-2(9))* Candlewick Pr.
Wang, Gabrielle. The Wishbird. 2013. (ENG.). 200p. (YA). (gr. 7). 12.99 *(978-0-14-330752-5(5))* Penguin Books Australia AUS. Dist: Independent Pubs. Group.
Ward, Lindsay. Rosco vs. the Baby. Ward, Lindsay, illus. 2016. (ENG., Illus.). 32p. (J). (gr. -1-3). 17.99 *(978-1-4814-3657-1(0),* Simon & Schuster Bks. For Young Readers) Simon & Schuster Bks. For Young Readers.
Warner, Jodi. Shia's Tail 2. 2012. 24p. pap. 10.95 *(978-1-4624-0369-1(7),* Inspiring Voices) Author Solutions, Inc.
Watson, K. R. Little Gabby Meets Her New Family. 2008. 44p. pap. 17.99 *(978-1-4389-1767-2(8))* AuthorHouse.
Weathers, Marlon. Henry Baldpate & His Treetop Friends. 2008. 24p. pap. 24.95 *(978-1-60672-923-6(3))* America Star Bks.
Webb, Holly. Harry the Homeless Puppy. Williams, Sophy, illus. 2015. (Pet Rescue Adventures Ser.). (ENG.). 128p. (J). (gr. 2-6). pap. 4.99 *(978-1-58925-474-9(0))* Tiger Tales.
—Jessie the Lonely Puppy. Williams, Sophy, illus. 2015. (Pet Rescue Adventures Ser.). (ENG.). 128p. (J). (gr. 2-6). pap. 4.99 *(978-1-58925-473-2(2))* Tiger Tales.
—Kitten Nobody Wanted. Williams, Sophy, illus. 2015. (Pet Rescue Adventures Ser.). (ENG.). 128p. (J). (gr. 2-6). lib. bdg. 19.99 *(978-1-58925-182-3(2))* Tiger Tales.
—Lost in the Snow. Williams, Sophy, illus. 2015. (Pet Rescue Adventures Ser.). (ENG.). 128p. (J). (gr. 2-6). pap. 4.99 *(978-1-58925-472-5(4));* lib. bdg. 19.99 *(978-1-68010-004-4(1))* Tiger Tales.
—The Lost Puppy. Williams, Sophy, illus. 2016. (Pet Rescue Adventures Ser.). (ENG.). 128p. (J). (gr. 2-6). pap. 4.99 *(978-1-58925-491-6(0))* Tiger Tales.
—The Missing Kitten. Williams, Sophy, illus. 2016. (Pet Rescue Adventures Ser.). (ENG.). 128p. (J). (gr. 2-6). pap. 4.99 *(978-1-58925-488-6(0))* Tiger Tales.
—The Scruffy Puppy. Williams, Sophy, illus. 2016. (Pet Rescue Adventures Ser.). (ENG.). 128p. (J). (gr. 2-6). pap. 4.99 *(978-1-58925-490-9(2))* Tiger Tales.
Webb, James, Jr. They Call Me Giz. 2012. 72p. pap. 28.99 *(978-1-4772-3761-8(5))* AuthorHouse.
Wedekind, Annie. Samirah's Ride: The Story of an Arabian Filly. 2010. (Breyer Horse Collection: 3). (ENG.). 128p. (J). (gr. 4-7). pap. 14.99 *(978-0-312-62268-8(6),* 9780312622688) Feiwel & Friends.
Wegelius, Jakob. The Murderer's Ape. 2017. (ENG.). 624p. (YA). (gr. 7). 17.99 *(978-1-101-93175-2(2),* Delacorte Pr.) Random Hse. Children's Bks.
Wegelius, Jakob & Graves, Peter. The Murderer's Ape. 2017. (YA). lib. bdg. *(978-1-101-93176-9(0),* Delacorte Pr) Random House Publishing Group.
Wendling, Peter. Matthew Leads the Animal Parade, 1 vol. 2010. 30p. 24.95 *(978-1-4512-1836-7(2))* PublishAmerica, Inc.
West, Denis. Sam of the Forest Railway. 2012. 66p. pap. 13.50 *(978-1-78035-361-6(8),* Fastprint Publishing) Upfront Publishing Ltd. GBR. Dist: Printondemand-worldwide.com.
Whispers from the Bay. 2008. 224p. (YA). 22.95 *(978-0-9794454-0-8(X))* Tkac, John Enterprises LLC.
Wickham, Kimberly, illus. Summer of Magic Horses. 2007. 134p. 12.85 *(978-1-4251-3012-1(7))* Trafford Publishing.
Widmayer, Paul. Jake & the Cowboy Hat. 2013. 24p. pap. 12.45 *(978-1-4908-1233-5(4),* WestBow Pr.) Author Solutions, Inc.
Wilkerson, Dawn. Katie & Katoa Travel down the River. 2009. 48p. pap. 16.95 *(978-1-61582-862-3(1))* America Star Bks.
Willems, Mo. The Pigeon Wants a Puppy! Willems, Mo, illus. 2008. (Pigeon Ser.). (ENG., Illus.). 40p. (J). (gr. -1-k). 16.99 *(978-1-4231-0960-0(0))* Hyperion Pr.
Williams, Susan. Wind Rider. 2006. 309p. (J). (gr. 5-9). 16.99 *(978-0-06-087236-6(5))* HarperCollins Pubs.
Wilson, Annemarie. What Could Have Happened to Max? 2008. 56p. pap. 14.95 *(978-1-59858-683-1(1))* Dog Ear Publishing, LLC.
Wilson, Elizabeth & de los Heros, Luis. Chifa Chi's Little Adventure in Cuzco & MacHu Picchu. 2012. 42p. pap. 21.99 *(978-1-105-20126-4(0))* Lulu Pr., Inc.
Wolfe, Linda, illus. Across the Road. 2008. 32p. (J). 10.00 *(978-0-937179-16-1(7))* Blue Scarab Pr.
Yamanushi, Toshiko. The Deer King. Tani, Toshihiko, illus. 2014. (J). 8.95 *(978-1-935523-70-3(8))* World Tribune Pr.
Zelaya, Carol. Emily Waits for Her Family. Metcalf, Kristin, illus. 2007. (Emily the Chickadee Ser.). 32p. (J). (gr. 2-3). 14.95 *(978-0-9796265-0-0(1))* Richlee Publishing.
Zera, Beata. Little Puppy Swifty & Elle. 2008. 64p. pap. 21.99 *(978-1-4257-6703-7(6))* Xlibris Corp.

HUMAN BEINGS

Brooks, Susie. People: Discover Great Art & Create Your Own! 2013. (Get into Art Ser.). (ENG., Illus.). 32p. (J). (gr. 2-9). 14.99 *(978-0-7534-7059-6(4),* 9780753470596, Kingfisher) Roaring Brook Pr.
Catalano, Angela. Community Space: How Land & Weather Shape Communities. 2005. (Communities at Work Ser.). (ENG., Illus.). 24p. (gr. 2-3). pap. 8.25 *(978-1-4042-5022-2(0),* PowerKids Pr.) Rosen Publishing Group, Inc., The.
Challen, Paul C. Migration in the 21st Century: How Will Globalization & Climate Change Affect Migration & Settlement? 2010. (Investigating Human Migration & Settlement Ser.). (ENG., Illus.). 48p. (J). (gr. 5-8). *(978-0-7787-5181-6(3));* pap. *(978-0-7787-5196-0(1))* Crabtree Publishing Co.
Dodge Cummings, Judy. Human Migration: Investigate the Global Journey of Humankind. Casteel, Tom, illus. 2016. (Inquire & Investigate Ser.). (ENG.). 128p. (gr. 6-10). 22.95 *(978-1-61930-371-3(X))* Open City Bks.
Endres, Hollie J. The Letter Mm Set: People Who Help Us, 6 vols. 2004. (Letter Bks.). (ENG.). 8p. (gr. k-1). pap. 29.70 *(978-0-7368-4112-2(1),* Letter Bks.) Capstone Press of Coughlan Cos.
Gagne, Tammy & Willis, John. Migration & Settlement. 2017. (J). ***(978-1-5105-2179-7(8),*** Berkley) Penguin Publishing Group.
Hirsch, Rebecca E. Climate Migrants: On the Move in a Warming World. 2016. (ENG., Illus.). 88p. (YA). (gr. 7-12). 35.99 *(978-1-4677-9341-4(8));* 53.32 *(978-1-5124-1145-4(0))* Lerner Publishing Group. (Twenty-First Century Bks.).
LaBaff, Stephanie. Draw Cartoon People in 4 Easy Steps: Then Write a Story. LaBaff, Tom, illus. 2012. (Drawing in 4 Easy Steps Ser.). 48p. (J). (gr. 3-18). 25.27 *(978-0-7660-3843-1(2))* Enslow Pubs., Inc.
Labaff, Stephanie. Draw Cartoon People in 4 Easy Steps: Then Write a Story. LaBaff, Tom, illus. 2012. (Drawing in 4 Easy Steps Ser.). 48p. (J). (gr. 3-18). pap. 8.95 *(978-1-4644-0016-2(4),* Enslow Elementary) Enslow Pubs., Inc.
Nishida, Masaki. Drawing Manga Martial Arts Figures. 2009. (How to Draw Manga Ser.). 24p. (gr. 3-3). 47.90 *(978-1-61513-440-3(9),* PowerKids Pr.) Rosen Publishing Group, Inc., The.
People Are Living Things: Individual Title Six-Packs. (gr. k-1). 23.00 *(978-0-7635-9038-3(X))* Rigby Education.
Rand, Casey. DNA & Heredity, 1 vol. 2010. (Investigating Cells Ser.). (ENG., Illus.). 48p. (J). (gr. 3-6). 33.32 *(978-1-4329-3880-2(0),* Heinemann InfoSearch) Heinemann-Raintree.
Richards, Jon. The Human World. Simkins, Ed, illus. 2013. (World in Infographics Ser.). (ENG.). 32p. (J). (gr. 3-7). 15.95 *(978-1-926973-94-4(1))* Owlkids Bks. Inc. CAN. Dist: Publishers Group West (PGW).
Rigby Education Staff. Spikes, Scales & Armor. (Sails Literacy Ser.). (Illus.). 16p. (gr. 1-2). 27.00 *(978-0-7635-9919-5(0),* 699190C99) Rigby Education.
Romero, Libby. Characteristics of People. 2006. (J). pap. *(978-1-4108-6482-6(0))* Benchmark Education Co.
Rushworth, Gary. What Makes a Human a Human? Set Of 6. 2011. (Navigators Ser.). (J). pap. 48.00 net. *(978-1-4108-6231-0(3))* Benchmark Education Co.
Stille, Darlene R. Protecting Animals. 2011. (Go Green! Ser.). (ENG.). 32p. (J). (gr. 1-4). lib. bdg. 28.50 *(978-1-60973-174-8(3),* 201153) Child's World, Inc., The.
Sundance/Newbridge LLC Staff. Being Human. 2007. (Early Science Ser.). (gr. k-3). 18.95 *(978-1-4007-6513-3(7));* pap. 6.10 *(978-1-4007-6509-6(9))* Sundance/Newbridge Educational Publishing.
Tanaka, Shelley. A Great Round Wonder: My Book of the World. Perna, Debi, illus. (J). 4.99 *(978-1-55054-213-4(3))* Da Capo Pr., Inc.
Walker, Robert. Pushes & Pulls: Why Do People Migrate? 2010. (Investigating Human Migration & Settlement Ser.). (ENG., Illus.). 48p. (J). (gr. 5-8). *(978-0-7787-5183-0(X));* pap. *(978-0-7787-5198-4(8))* Crabtree Publishing Co.
World Book, Inc Staff, contrib. by. Encyclopedia of Human Beings, 2 vols. 2014. (Illus.). (J). *(978-0-7166-7520-4(X))* World Bk., Inc.

HUMAN BEINGS—EFFECT OF ENVIRONMENT ON

see also Human Skin Color

Aitken, Stephen. People. 2013. (Climate Crisis Ser.). 64p. (J). (gr. 5-8). pap. 15.28 *(978-1-62712-041-8(6));* (Illus.). 31.36 *(978-1-60870-461-3(0))* Cavendish Square Publishing.
Catalano, Angela. Community Space: How Land & Weather Shape Communities. (Communities at Work Ser.). 24p. 2009. (gr. 2-2). 42.50 *(978-1-61511-893-9(4),* PowerKids Pr.) 2005. (Illus.). (YA). (gr. 1-4). lib. bdg. 22.60 *(978-1-4042-2783-5(0))* Rosen Publishing Group, Inc., The.
Creative Media Applications Staff, contrib. by. The Human Body & the Environment: How Our Surroundings Affect Our Health, 4 vols. 2003. (Middle School Reference Ser.). (Illus.). 576p. (C). (gr. 6-8). 195.00 *(978-0-313-32558-8(6),* MS2558, Greenwood) ABC-CLIO, LLC.
Daly, James & Zuckerman, Amy. 2030: A Day in the Life of Tomorrow's Kids. Manders, John, illus. 2009. (ENG.). 32p. (J). (gr. 1-3). 16.99 *(978-0-525-47860-7(4),* Dutton Books for Young Readers) Penguin Young Readers Group.
Desonie, Dana. Humans & the Natural Environment. 2008. (Our Fragile Planet Ser.). (Illus.). 210p. (YA). (gr. 7-12). 35.00 *(978-0-8160-6220-1(X))* Facts On File, Inc.
Greene, Carol. I Love Our People. 2012. (I Love Our Earth Ser.). (Illus.). 24p. (J). pap. 7.95 *(978-1-4644-0136-7(5));* (gr. 3-4). 22.60 *(978-0-7660-4041-0(0))* Enslow Pubs., Inc. (Enslow Elementary).
Levin, Judy. Life at a High Altitude. 2009. (Life in Extreme Environments Ser.). 64p. (gr. 5-8). 53.00 *(978-1-61514-268-2(1),* Rosen Reference) Rosen Publishing Group, Inc., The.
Morgan, Anne. The Smallest Carbon Footprint in the Land & Other Eco-Tales. McKinnon, Gay, illus. 2012. 80p. pap. *(978-1-922120-23-6(5),* IP Kidz) Interactive Pubns. Pty, Ltd.
Paraire, Philippe & Collin, Marie-Marthe. El Medio Ambiente Explicado a los Ninos. (SPA., Illus.). 62p. (J). (gr. 3-5). *(978-84-406-5512-7(6),* EB1713) Ediciones B ESP. Dist: Lectorum Pubns., Inc.
Rustad, Martha E. H. People in Spring, 1 vol. 2012. (All about Spring Ser.). (ENG.). 24p. (gr. k-1). pap. 7.29 *(978-1-4296-9361-5(4));* pap. 41.70 *(978-1-4296-9359-2(2));* (Illus.). lib. bdg. 26.65 *(978-1-4296-8657-0(X))* Capstone Press of Coughlan Cos. (Pebble Plus).
Vermond, Kira. Why We Live Where We Live. McLaughlin, Julie, illus. 2014. (ENG.). 48p. (J). (gr. 4-6). 17.95 *(978-1-77147-011-7(9),* Owlkids) Owlkids Bks. Inc. CAN. Dist: Publishers Group West (PGW).

HUMAN BEINGS—INFLUENCE ON NATURE

see Nature—Effect of Human Beings on

HUMAN BEINGS—ORIGIN

see also Anatomy, Comparative; Evolution; Prehistoric Peoples

Anderson, Dale. How Do We Know the Nature of Human Origins. 2009. (Great Scientific Questions & the Scientists Who Answered Them Ser.). 112p. (gr. 7-12). 63.90 *(978-1-61513-202-7(3))* Rosen Publishing Group, Inc., The.
—How Do We Know the Nature of Humankind. 2005. (Great Scientific Questions & the Scientists Who Answered Them Ser.). (Illus.). 112p. (J). (gr. 7-12). lib. bdg. 34.60 *(978-1-4042-0077-7(0))* Rosen Publishing Group, Inc., The.
Harris, Nicholas. The First Humans. Dennis, Peter, illus. 2006. 31p. (J). *(978-0-7607-7528-8(1))* backpackbook.
Heitkamp, Kristina Lyn. The Rift Valley & the Archaeological Evidence of the First Humans. 2016. (First Humans & Early Civilizations Ser.). 64p. (J). (gr. 6-6). pap. 12.95 *(978-1-4994-6318-7(9))* Rosen Publishing Group, Inc., The.
Kortemeier, Todd. Discovering the Origin of Human Life. 2017. (Science Frontiers Ser.). (ENG., Illus.). 32p. (J). (gr. 3-6). 21.95 *(978-1-63235-376-4(8))* Pr. Room Editions LLC.
Rignstad, Arnold. Discovering the Origin of Human Life. 2016. (Science Frontiers Ser.). (ENG., Illus.). 32p. (J). pap. 9.95 *(978-1-63235-393-1(8),* 12-Story Library) Pr. Room Editions LLC.
Stefoff, Rebecca. Humans: An Evolutionary History, 4 vols., Set. Incl. First Humans. (YA). (gr. 8-18). lib. bdg. 37.07 *(978-0-7614-4184-7(0));* Ice Age Neanderthals. (gr. 7-18). 37.07 *(978-0-7614-4186-1(7));* Modern Humans. (gr. 7-18). lib. bdg. 37.07 *(978-0-7614-4187-8(5));* Origins. (gr. 7-18). lib. bdg. 37.07 *(978-0-7614-4183-0(2));* 112p. 2009. 2010. Set lib. bdg. 148.29 o.p. *(978-0-7614-4181-6(6))* Marshall Cavendish Corp.
Yasuda, Anita. N Gua Mends the Sky: A Chinese Flood Myth. 2014. (Short Tales Chinese Myths Ser.). 32p. (J). (gr. 3-6). lib. bdg. 24.21 *(978-1-62402-033-9(X),* Short Tales) Magic Wagon.

HUMAN BODY

see also Anatomy; Physiology

Alexander, Heather. Human Body. Lozano, Andres, illus. 2017. (Life on Earth Ser.). (ENG.). 16p. (J). (gr. -1-1). bds. 12.99 *(978-1-84780-906-3(5),* Wide Eyed Editions) Quarto Publishing Group UK GBR. Dist: Hachette Bk. Group.
All about Me. 2008. (Sliding Word Books... Ser.). 7p. *(978-1-4075-1590-8(X))* Parragon, Inc.
The Amazing Body - The Five Senses, 5 vols. 2005. (Amazing Body: the Five Senses Ser.). (ENG., Illus.). 24p. (gr. k-3). 53.30 *(978-1-4048-1000-6(5))* Picture Window Bks.
The Amazing Human Body. 2017. (Amazing Human Body Ser.). 48p. (gr. 6-6). pap. 70.20 ***(978-0-7660-9033-0(7));*** lib. bdg. 167.58 ***(978-0-7660-9032-3(9))*** Enslow Pubs., Inc.
The Amazing Human Body, 6 bks., Set. Incl. Circulatory System. Bjorklund, Ruth. lib. bdg. 34.21 *(978-0-7614-3053-7(9));* Digestive System. Hoffmann, Gretchen. lib. bdg. 34.21 *(978-0-7614-3058-2(X));* Endocrine System. Klosterman, Lorrie. lib. bdg. 34.21 *(978-0-7614-3055-1(5));* Immune System. Klosterman, Lorrie. lib. bdg. 34.21 *(978-0-7614-3054-4(7));* Skeletal System. Haywood, Karen. lib. bdg. 34.21 *(978-0-7614-3056-8(3));* Skin. Klosterman, Lorrie. lib. bdg. 34.21 *(978-0-7614-3057-5(1));* 80p. (gr. 5-18). (Amazing Human Body Ser.). 2008. Set lib. bdg. 205.26 *(978-0-7614-3052-0(0),* Benchmark Bks.) Marshall Cavendish Corp.
Andrews, Barbara. The Circulatory System. 2006. (J). pap. *(978-1-4108-6510-6(X))* Benchmark Education Co.
—Discover the Circulatory System. 2006. (J). pap. *(978-1-4108-6513-7(4))* Benchmark Education Co.
Arnold, Nick. Huesos, Sangre y Otros Pedazos del Cuerpo. De Saulles, Tony, illus. 2003. (Coleccion Esa Horrible Cienca). (SPA.). 156p. (YA). (gr. 5-8). *(978-84-272-2051-5(0),* ML8311) Molino, Editorial ESP. Dist: Lectorum Pubns., Inc.
Ascension Press, creator. Theology of the Body for Teens Student Workbook: Discovering God's Plan for Love & Life. 2006. (Illus.). 210p. per. 14.95 *(978-1-932927-86-3(7))* Ascension Pr.
Ashour, Monica. Every Body Is a Gift: God Made Us to Love. Kaminski, Karol, illus. 2015. (J). 12.95 *(978-0-8198-2376-2(7))* Pauline Bks. & Media.
—Every Body Is Smart: God Helps Me Listen & Choose. Kaminski, Karol, illus. 2015. (J). 12.95 *(978-0-8198-2372-4(4))* Pauline Bks. & Media.
—Everybody Has a Body: God Made Boys & Girls. Kaminski, Karol, illus. 2015. (J). 12.95 *(978-0-8198-2368-7(6))* Pauline Bks. & Media.
Atlas de Anatomia. (Conoce y Cuida Tu Cuerpo Ser.). (SPA., Illus.). 32p. (YA). 32.00 *(978-84-342-1963-2(8))* Parramon Ediciones S.A. ESP. Dist: Distribuidora Norma, Inc.
Avison, Brigid. I Wonder Why I Sleep: And Other Questions about My Body. 2011. (I Wonder Why Ser.). (ENG., Illus.). 32p. (J). (gr. k-3). pap. 6.99 *(978-0-7534-6525-7(6),* 9780753465257, Kingfisher) Roaring Brook Pr.
AZ Books Staff. About the Human Body. Petrovskaya, Olga, ed. 2012. (Million Whys Ser.). (ENG.). 12p. (J). (gr. -1-4). bds. 18.95 *(978-1-61889-058-0(1))* AZ Bks. LLC.
Bailey, Gerry & Way, Steve. Body & Health. 2009. (Simply Science Ser.). (Illus.). 32p. (YA). (gr. 3-6). lib. bdg. 26.00 *(978-1-4339-0030-3(0))* Stevens, Gareth Publishing LLLP.
Bailey, Jacqui. What Happens When You Move? 2008. (How Your Body Works Ser.). (Illus.). 30p. (J). lib. bdg. 26.50 *(978-1-4042-4426-9(3),* PowerKids Pr.) Rosen Publishing Group, Inc., The.
Balcerzak, Kara Garbe. Bizarre Things We've Done to Our Bodies. 2015. (History of the Bizarre Ser.). (ENG., Illus.). 32p. (gr. 3-4). lib. bdg. 27.99 *(978-1-4914-4268-5(9),* Edge Bks.) Capstone Press of Coughlan Cos.
Barnes, Kate & Weston, Steve. The Human Body. 2012. (ENG., Illus.). 48p. (J). 15.00 *(978-1-899762-85-9(X))* Award Pubns. Ltd. GBR. Dist: Parkwest Pubns., Inc.
Barraclough, Sue. My Body. 2009. (Me & My World Ser.). (Illus.). 24p. (J). (gr. -1-2). pap. 8.15 *(978-1-60754-062-5(2));* lib. bdg. 22.60 *(978-1-60754-057-1(6))* Windmill Bks.
Basher, Simon & Green, Dan. Human Body: A Book with Guts! Basher, Simon, illus. 2011. (Basher Science Ser.). (ENG., Illus.). 128p. (J). (gr. 5-10). pap. 8.99 *(978-0-7534-6501-1(9),* 9780753465011, Kingfisher) Roaring Brook Pr.
Bayden, Maya & Toriello, James. The Stomach in 3D. 2015. (Human Body In 3D Ser.). (ENG., Illus.). 64p. (J). (gr. 5-6). 32.95 *(978-1-4994-3613-6(0),* Rosen Central) Rosen Publishing Group, Inc., The.
Beck, Paul. El Cuerpo Humano. Fairman, Jennifer, illus. 2007. (SPA.). 48p. (J). (gr. k-5). *(978-970-718-436-7(1),* Silver Dolphin en Español) Advanced Marketing, S. de R. L. de C. V.
Becker, Jack & Sherman, Josepha. The Upper Limbs in 3D. 2015. (Human Body In 3D Ser.). (ENG., Illus.). 64p. (J). (gr. 5-6). 32.95 *(978-1-4994-3617-4(3),* Rosen Central) Rosen Publishing Group, Inc., The.
Beevor, Lucy. Brains, Body, Bones! 2017. (Brains, Body, Bones! Ser.). (ENG.). 32p. (gr. 3-5). 122.60 *(978-1-4109-8598-9(9),* Raintree Perspectives) Heinemann-Raintree.
Benchmark Education Company, LLC Staff, compiled by. Health & Human Body: Theme Set. 2006. (J). 195.00 *(978-1-4108-7108-4(8))* Benchmark Education Co.
—Human Body. 2006. spiral bd. 640.00 *(978-1-4108-6789-6(7))* Benchmark Education Co.
—The Human Body. 2006. spiral bd. 330.00 *(978-1-4108-7020-9(0))* 2005. (J). spiral bd. 265.00 *(978-1-4108-5763-7(8))* Benchmark Education Co.
—Human Body: Theme Set. 2006. (J). 147.00 *(978-1-4108-7079-7(0))* Benchmark Education Co.
—The Human Body: Theme Set. 2006. (J). 215.00 *(978-1-4108-7133-6(9))* Benchmark Education Co.
Berger, Melvin & Berger, Gilda. Your Body. 2005. (Illus.). pap. *(978-0-439-77363-8(6))* Scholastic, Inc.
Bjorklund, Ruth. Cystic Fibrosis. 2008. (Health Alert Ser.). 64p. (gr. 4-18). lib. bdg. 32.79 *(978-0-7614-2912-8(3),* Benchmark Bks.) Marshall Cavendish Corp.
Black, Lisa M. My Amazing Hands. 2011. 28p. pap. 24.95 *(978-1-4560-6480-8(0))* America Star Bks.
Body Bugs. 2013. (Earth's Grossest Animals Ser.). 32p. (J). (gr. k-5). pap. 60.00 *(978-1-61533-782-8(2),* PowerKids Pr.) Rosen Publishing Group, Inc., The.
Boothroyd, Jennifer. Facial Features: Freckles, Earlobes, Noses, & More. 2012. (Lightning Bolt Books (tm) — What Traits Are in Your Genes? Ser.). (SPA & ENG., Illus.). 32p. (gr. k-2). pap. 7.95 *(978-1-58013-955-7(8))* Lerner Publishing Group.
Bradley, Timothy. Increíble pero Real - Anatomías Asquerosas. 2017. (TIME for Kids en Español - Level 4 Ser.). (SPA.). 48p. (gr. 4-4). lib. bdg. 31.99 *(978-1-5157-5141-0(4))* Time for Kids Inc AUS. Dist: Capstone Pub.
Bradley, Timothy J. Strange but True: Gross Anatomy, 1 vol. 2nd rev. ed. 2012. (Nonfiction Readers Ser.). (ENG.). 48p. (J). (gr. 4-4). pap. 9.99 *(978-1-4333-4860-0(8))* Teacher Created Materials, Inc.
Bredeson, Carmen. Weird but True Human Body Facts. 2011. (Weird but True Science Ser.). (Illus.). 24p. (J). (gr. k-18). pap. 7.95 *(978-1-59845-369-0(6),* Enslow Elementary); (gr. 5-9). lib. bdg. 22.60 *(978-0-7660-3865-3(3))* Enslow Pubs., Inc.
Brown, Carron. Shine-A-light: The Human Body. Saunders, Rachel, illus. 2016. (ENG.). 36p. (J). 12.99 *(978-1-61067-465-2(0))* Kane Miller.
Brown, Jonatha A. Animal Heads & Necks. 2006. (Why Animals Look Different Ser.). (Illus.). 24p. (gr. 1-4). pap. 8.15 *(978-0-8368-6866-1(8));* lib. bdg. 22.00 *(978-0-8368-6861-6(7))* Stevens, Gareth Publishing LLLP. (Weekly Reader Leveled Readers).
Bruhn, Aron. The Human Body. Ito, Joel & Kemly, Kathleen, illus. 2010. (Inside Ser.). (ENG.). 48p. (gr. 4-6). pap. 9.95 *(978-1-4027-7779-0(5))* Sterling Publishing Co., Inc.
—Inside Human Body. Ito, Joel & Kemly, Kathleen Hadam, illus. 2010. (Inside Ser.). (ENG.). 48p. (gr. 4-6). 16.95 *(978-1-4027-7091-3(X))* Sterling Publishing Co., Inc.
Bryan, Jenny. El Milagro del Nacimiento: Una Ventana Transparente. (Colección Ventana Transparente). (SPA., Illus.). 18p. (J). (gr. 3-5). 29.95 *(978-950-11-1027-2(3),* SGM273) Sigmar ARG. Dist: AIMS International Bks., Inc., Lectorum Pubns., Inc.
Building Blocks of Science: Human Bodyworks Teacher's Guide (Firsthand Learning) 2007. ring bd. *(978-0-89278-337-3(0))* Carolina Biological Supply Co.
Building Blocks of Science: Human Bodyworks Unit Kit (Firsthand Learning) 2007. ring bd. *(978-0-89278-332-8(X))* Carolina Biological Supply Co.
Bullion, Leslie. Random Body Parts, 1 vol. Lowery, Mike, illus. 2015. (ENG.). 48p. (J). (gr. 3-6). 14.95 *(978-1-56145-737-3(X))* Peachtree Pubs.
Bulletpoints Human Body. 2005. (Illus.). (J). per. 4.99 *(978-1-933581-03-3(4))* Byeway Bks.
Burstein, John. Dynamic Digestive System: How Does My Stomach Work? 2009. (Slim Goodbody's Body Buddies Ser.). (ENG., Illus.). 32p. (J). (gr. 3-5). pap. *(978-0-7787-4429-0(9))* Crabtree Publishing Co.
—The Dynamic Digestive System: How Does My Stomach Work? 2009. (Slim Goodbody's Body Buddies Ser.). (ENG., Illus.). 32p. (J). (gr. 3-5). lib. bdg. *(978-0-7787-4415-3(9))* Crabtree Publishing Co.
—The Remarkable Respiratory System: How Do My Lungs Work? 2009. (Slim Goodbody's Body Buddies Ser.). (ENG., Illus.). 32p. (J). (gr. 3-5). lib. bdg. *(978-0-7787-4416-0(7))* Crabtree Publishing Co.
Burton, Margie, et al. Your Body & Tu Cuerpo: 6 English, 6 Spanish Adaptations. 2011. (J). spiral bd. 75.00 net. *(978-1-4108-5634-0(8))* Benchmark Education Co.
Butler, Chris, illus. My Body. 2010. (My World Ser.).Tr. of Mi Cuerpo. (ENG.). 24p. (J). (gr. -1-1). pap. 8.15 *(978-1-61533-027-0(5));* lib. bdg. 22.60 *(978-1-60754-947-5(6))* Windmill Bks.
Butterfield, Moira & Jacobs, Pat. The Human Body. 2016. (Know It All Ser.). (ENG., Illus.). 32p. (J). (gr. 5-5). pap. 10.58 *(978-1-5026-0898-7(7),* 1398903) Cavendish Square Publishing.
Caballero, D., tr. Esa Eres Tu y Este Soy Yo. Rubel, Doris, illus. 2006. (Junior (Silver Dolphin) Ser.). (SPA.). 16p. (J). (gr. -1). 9.95 *(978-970-718-346-9(2))* Readerlink Distribution Services, LLC.
Cagliano, Stefano. El Cuerpo Humano. (Coleccion Hiperlibros de la Ciencia). (SPA.). 196p. (YA). (gr. 5-8). *(978-84-7131-938-8(1),* EDI30282) Editex, Editorial S.A. ESP. Dist: Lectorum Pubns., Inc.
Calabresi, Linda. Human Body. 2008. (Insiders Ser.). (ENG., Illus.). 64p. (J). (gr. 3-7). 17.99 *(978-1-4169-3861-3(3),* Simon & Schuster Bks. For Young Readers) Simon & Schuster Bks. For Young Readers.
Canavan, Thomas. How Your Body Works: The Ultimate Illustrated Guide. 2015. (ENG.). 128p. (J). (gr. 2). pap. 9.99 *(978-0-486-79744-1(9))* Dover Pubns., Inc.
—Ready for Action: Bones & Muscles. 2015. (How Your Body Works). (ENG.). 32p. (J). (gr. 4-4). pap. 10.00

(978-1-4994-1230-7(4), PowerKids Pr.) Rosen Publishing Group, Inc., The.

—What Makes Your Heart Beat Faster? Questions about Internal Organs. 2016. (Human Body FAQ Ser.). 00032p. (J). (gr. 3-3). pap. 10.00 (978-1-4994-3170-4(8), PowerKids Pr.) Rosen Publishing Group, Inc., The.

Capicola, Anthony. Sweat! 2017. (Your Body at Its Grossest Ser.). 24p. (gr. 1-2). pap. 8.15 **(978-1-4824-6476-4(4))** Stevens, Gareth Publishing LLLP.

Cardenas, Ernesto A. Two by Two. 2009. 19.95 (978-1-60698-014-9(9)); pap. 3.95 (978-1-60698-012-5(2)) Milo Educational Bks. & Resources.

Carolan. This Is My Piko. Carolan, Joanna, illus. 2009. 58p. 17.95 incl. audio compact disk (978-0-9715333-0-1(X)) Banana Patch Pr.

Carothers, Sue & Henke, Elizabeth. Human Body: Fun Activities, Experiments, Investigations, & Observations! 2003. (Skills for Success Ser.). (ENG.). 128p. (gr. 2-3). pap. 16.99 (978-0-88724-953-2(1), CD-4328) Carson-Dellosa Publishing, LLC.

—Human Body, Grades 4 - 6: Fun Activities, Experiments, Investigations, & Observations! Hall, Milton, illus. 2003. (Skills for Success Ser.). (ENG.). 128p. (gr. 4-6). pap. 16.99 (978-0-88724-954-9(X), CD-4329) Carson-Dellosa Publishing, LLC.

Cassan, Adolfo. Inside the Human Body. 2005. (Inside the Human Body Ser.). (Illus.). 32p. (gr. 4-6). 112.00 (978-0-7910-9086-2(8), Chelsea Clubhouse) Facts On File, Inc.

Caviezel, Giovanni. My Own Human Body. Mesturini, Cristina, illus. 2012. (Little People Shape Bks.). (ENG.). 10p. (J). (gr. k-2). bds. 8.99 (978-0-7641-6570-2(4)) Barron's Educational Series, Inc.

Chambers, Catherine. See for Yourself: Body Science. 2010. (Crabtree Connections Ser.). (ENG.). 24p. (J). (gr. 3-6). (978-0-7787-9950-4(6)); pap. (978-0-7787-9972-6(7)) Crabtree Publishing Co.

Chandler, Fiona. First Encyclopedia of the Human Body: Internet-Linked. Hancock, David & Woodcock, John, illus. 2004. (Usborne First Encyclopedia Library). 64p. (J). (gr. 3-18). lib. bdg. 17.95 (978-1-58086-653-8(0), Usborne) EDC Publishing.

—First Encyclopedia of the Human Body - Internet Linked. Hancock, David, illus. 2004. (First Encyclopedias Ser.). (ENG.). 64p. (J). (gr. 3-18). pap. 9.99 (978-0-7945-0695-7(X), Usborne) EDC Publishing.

—First Encyclopedia of the Human Body II. rev. ed. 2011. (First Encyclopedias Ser.). 64p. (J). pap. 9.99 (978-0-7945-3060-0(5), Usborne) EDC Publishing.

—The Usborne Little Encyclopedia of the Human Body: Internet-Linked. Hancock, David & Woodcock, John, illus. 2006. 64p. (J). (gr. 4-7). 6.99 (978-0-7945-1094-7(9), Usborne) EDC Publishing.

Chang, Heidi. The Skin on Your Body, 1 vol. 2015. (ENG.). 32p. (J). 23.45 (978-1-62275-644-5(4), Britannica Educational Publishing) Rosen Publishing Group, Inc., The.

Charlesworth, Liza. Human Body Set: Exciting Nonfiction Books That Build Kids' Vocabularies. 2009. (Science Vocabulary Readers Set Ser.). (ENG.). (gr. 1-2). 69.99 (978-0-545-14918-1(5), Teaching Resources) Scholastic, Inc.

Claybourne, A. Complete Book of the Human Body. 2004. (J). 96p. lib. bdg. 22.95 (978-1-58086-617-0(4), Usborne); (ENG., Illus.). 112p. pap. 14.95 (978-0-7945-0628-5(3)) EDC Publishing.

Claybourne, Anna. Compl Bk of the Human Body - Internet Linked. rev. ed. 2006. 112p. (J). pap. 14.99 (978-0-7945-1557-7(6), Usborne) EDC Publishing.

—Human Body. 2016. (Mind Webs Ser.). (ENG., Illus.). 32p. (J). (gr. 4-6). pap. 11.99 (978-0-7502-8972-6(4), Wayland) Hachette Children's Group GBR. Dist: Hachette Bk. Group.

—Smelly Farts & Other Body Horrors. 2014. (ENG.). 32p. (J). (978-0-7787-1404-0(7)) Crabtree Publishing Co.

Close, Edward. Body Basics, 1 vol., 1. 2014. (Discovery Education: How It Works). (ENG.). 32p. (gr. 3-6). 26.25 (978-1-4777-6309-4(0), PowerKids Pr.) Rosen Publishing Group, Inc., The.

Cobb, Vicki. Your Body Battles A Stomachache. 2009. pap. 40.95 (978-0-7613-4621-0(X)) Lerner Publishing Group.

Cohen, Robert Z. The Stomach & Intestines in Your Body, 1 vol. 2015. (ENG.). 32p. (J). 23.45 (978-1-62275-632-2(0), Britannica Educational Publishing) Rosen Publishing Group, Inc., The.

Cole, Joanna. Inside the Human Body. Degen, Bruce, illus. 2011. (Magic School Bus Ser.). (ENG.). (J). (gr. 2-5). 9.99 (978-0-545-24083-3(2)); pap. 18.99 incl. audio compact disk (978-0-545-24086-4(7)) Scholastic, Inc.

Collins. Collins Fascinating Facts - Human Body. rev. ed. 2016. (Collins Fascinating Facts Ser.). (ENG., Illus.). 72p. (J). (gr. 1-3). pap. 10.99 (978-0-00-816925-1(X)) HarperCollins Pubs. Ltd. GBR. Dist: Independent Pubs. Group.

Columbo, Luann. Explore the Human Body. Zukerman, Craig & Fairman, Jennifer, illus. 2016. (Explore Ser.). (ENG.). 16p. (J). (gr. 2). 21.95 (978-1-62686-396-5(2), Silver Dolphin Bks.) Readerlink Distribution Services, LLC.

Conrad, David. Burps, Boogers, & Other Body Functions, 1 vol. 2011. (Health & Your Body Ser.). (ENG.). 24p. (gr. k-1). pap. 7.29 (978-1-4296-7125-5(4)); lib. bdg. 26.65 (978-1-4296-6808-8(3)) Capstone Press of Coughlan Cos. (Pebble Plus).

Coss, Lauren. Weird-But-True Facts about the Human Body. Gallagher-Cole, Mernie, illus. 2013. (Weird-But-True Facts Ser.). (ENG.). 32p. (J). (gr. 2-5). 28.50 (978-1-61473-419-2(4), 205123) Child's World, Inc., The.

Crawford, Sheryl Ann & Harris, Lauren. Human Body: 20 Short, Reproducible Plays That Teach Key Concepts, Expand Vocabulary, & Build Fluency. 2009. (ENG.). 64p. (gr. 1-2). pap. 11.99 (978-0-545-15430-7(8), Teaching Resources) Scholastic, Inc.

Crewe, Sabrina. In Your Body. 2010. (Under the Microscope Ser.). 32p. (gr. 2-4). 30.00 (978-1-60413-825-2(4), Chelsea Clubhouse) Facts On File, Inc.

Crispin, Sam. Pee & Poop! 2017. (Your Body at Its Grossest Ser.). 24p. (gr. 1-2). pap. 8.15 **(978-1-4824-6465-8(9))** Stevens, Gareth Publishing LLLP.

Croker, Mark. Atlas del Cuerpo Humano. (SPA., Illus.). 64p. (YA). 19.95 (978-950-11-0888-0(0), SGM8880) Sigmar ARG. Dist: Continental Bk. Co., Inc.

El Cuerpo. 2003. (Megabites Ser.). (SPA., Illus.). (J). pap. 8.95 (978-0-9715256-7-2(6)) Planeta Publishing Corp.

El Cuerpo Humano: Una Ventana Transparente. (Colección Ventana Transparente). (SPA., Illus.). 17p. (J). (gr. 3-5). 27.95 (978-950-11-0926-9(7), SGM9267) Sigmar ARG. Dist: Continental Bk. Co., Inc., Lectorum Pubns., Inc.

Cuida Tu Cuerpo. (Conoce y Cuida Tu Cuerpo Ser.). (SPA.). 32p. (YA). 32.00 (978-84-342-1880-2(1)) Parramon Ediciones S.A. ESP. Dist: Distribuidora Norma, Inc.

Curry, Don L. How Do Your Lungs Work? 2004. (Rookie Read-About Health Ser.). (ENG.). 32p. (J). (gr. k-2). pap. 5.95 (978-0-516-27856-8(8), Children's Pr.) Scholastic Library Publishing.

Da Silva, Rosa. The 10 Most Uncontrollable Functions of the Body. 2008. (J). 14.99 (978-1-55448-531-4(2)) Scholastic Library Publishing.

Daniels, Patricia, et al. Ultimate Body-Pedia: An Amazing Inside-Out Tour of the Human Body. 2014. (ENG., Illus.). 272p. (J). (gr. 2-5). 24.99 (978-1-4263-1721-7(2), National Geographic Children's Bks.) National Geographic Society.

—Ultimate Bodypedia: An Amazing Inside-Out Tour of the Human Body. 2014. (ENG.). 272p. (J). (gr. 2-5). lib. bdg. 33.90 (978-1-4263-1722-4(0), National Geographic Children's Bks.) National Geographic Society.

Danielsdottir, Sigrun. Your Body Is Awesome: Body Respect for Children. Bjarkadottir, Björk, illus. 2014. (ENG.). 36p. (J). 17.95 (978-1-84819-228-7(2), 2674, Singing Dragon) Kingsley, Jessica Pubs. GBR. Dist: Macmillan Distribution Ltd.

—Your Body Is Brilliant: Body Respect for Children. Bjarkadottir, Bjork, illus. 2014. (ENG.). 36p. (J). 17.95 (978-1-84819-221-8(5), 2672, Singing Dragon) Kingsley, Jessica Pubs. GBR. Dist: Macmillan Distribution Ltd.

Daynes, Katie. See Inside Your Body. King, Colin, illus. 2006. 15p. (J). (gr. -1-3). bds. 12.99 (978-0-7945-1233-0(X), Usborne) EDC Publishing.

De la Bédoyère, Camilla. Human Body. (Ripley Twists Ser.). 48p. (J). (gr. 3-18). 2010. lib. bdg. 19.95 (978-1-4222-1830-3(9)) 2009. (Illus.). pap. 8.95 (978-1-4222-2068-9(0)) Mason Crest.

de la Bedoyere, Camilla. The Ultimate Interactive Guide to the Human Body. 2016. (ENG., Illus.). 48p. (J). (gr. 1). spiral bd. 19.95 (978-1-62686-569-3(8), Silver Dolphin Bks.) Readerlink Distribution Services, LLC.

de la Bédoyere, Camilla. 3-D Explorer: Human Body. 2015. (3D Explorers Ser.). (ENG., Illus.). 32p. (J). (gr. 1). 19.95 (978-1-62686-433-7(0), Silver Dolphin Bks.) Readerlink Distribution Services, LLC.

Del Moral, Susana. Baby Da Vinci, Mi Cuerpo. Zaidi, Nadeem, illus. 2006. (Baby Einstein Ser.). (SPA.). 6p. (J). (gr. -1-k). bds. (978-970-718-455-8(8), Silver Dolphin en Español) Advanced Marketing, S. de R. L. de C. V.

del Moral Zavariz, Susana & Zaidi, Nadeem. El Concurso: Un Libro con Espejos. 2006. (SPA., Illus.). 5p. (J). (gr. -1-k). bds. (978-970-718-458-9(2), Silver Dolphin en Español) Advanced Marketing, S. de R. L. de C. V.

DePalma, Vanessa. This Is My Body: A Safety for Little Girls. Depalma, Victoria, illus. 2003. 15p. (J). (gr. -1-4). (978-0-9728135-0-1(0)) DePalma, Vanessa.

Dods, Emma. Wow! Surprising Facts about the Human Body. Aspinall, Marc, illus. 2014. (Wow! Ser.). (ENG.). 32p. (J). (gr. k-3). 8.99 (978-0-7534-7185-2(X), 9780753471852, Kingfisher) Roaring Brook Pr.

Dolphin, Colleen. Armpits to Zits: The Body from A to Z, 1 vol. Craig, Diane, ed. 2007. (Let's See A to Z Ser.). (ENG., Illus.). 32p. (gr. -1-3). 27.07 (978-1-59928-884-0(2), Super SandCastle) ABDO Publishing Co.

Dompierre, Judith. Body & Body Functions. 2011. 32p. pap. 24.95 (978-1-4560-6442-6(8)) America Star Bks.

Donovan, Sandy. Rumble & Spew: Gross Stuff in Your Stomach & Intestines. Slack, Michael H., illus. 2009. (Gross Body Science Ser.). (ENG.). 48p. (gr. 3-5). lib. bdg. 29.27 (978-0-8225-8899-3(4)) Lerner Publishing Group.

Dorling Kindersley Publishing Staff. Amazing Pop-Up Human Body. 2016. (ENG., Illus.). 32p. (J). (gr. k-4). 21.99 (978-1-4654-5306-8(7), DK Children) Dorling Kindersley Publishing, Inc.

—Baby Faces. 2016. (ENG., Illus.). 14p. (J). (— 1). bds. 5.99 (978-1-4654-4466-0(1), DK Children) Dorling Kindersley Publishing, Inc.

—DK Adventures: a Trip Through the Body: A Trip Through the Body. 2015. (DK Adventures Ser.). (ENG.). 128p. (J). (gr. 3-7). 16.99 (978-1-4654-2932-2(8), DK Children) Dorling Kindersley Publishing, Inc.

—DK Findout! Human Body. 2017. (DK Find Out! Ser.). (ENG.). 64p. (J). (gr. 1-4). pap. 10.99 **(978-1-4654-6308-1(9)**, DK Children) Dorling Kindersley Publishing, Inc.

—Eyes, Nose, Toes Peekaboo! 2008. (ENG.). 12p. (J). (gr. -1-k). bds. 6.99 (978-0-7566-3759-0(7), DK Children) Dorling Kindersley Publishing, Inc.

—First Human Body Encyclopedia. 2005. (ENG., Illus.). 128p. (J). (gr. 3-7). 16.99 (978-0-7566-0997-9(6), DK Children) Dorling Kindersley Publishing, Inc.

—Human Body. (Eye Wonder Ser.). (ENG.). (J). 2013. 56p. (gr. k-4). 10.99 (978-1-4654-0906-5(8)) 2013. (Illus.). 160p. (gr. 3-7). 7.99 (978-1-4654-0882-2(7)) 2012. (Illus.). 256p. (gr. 2-5). 24.99 (978-0-7566-9307-7(1)) Dorling Kindersley Publishing, Inc. (DK Children).

—Human Body! 2017. (ENG.). 208p. (J). (gr. 4-7). 24.99 **(978-1-4654-6239-8(2)**, DK Children) Dorling Kindersley Publishing, Inc.

—My First Body. 2016. (ENG., Illus.). 36p. (J). (— 1). bds. 5.99 (978-1-4654-4492-9(0), DK Children) Dorling Kindersley Publishing, Inc.

—Super Human Encyclopedia. 2014. (ENG., Illus.). 208p. (J). (gr. 3-7). 24.99 (978-1-4654-2445-7(8), DK Children) Dorling Kindersley Publishing, Inc.

—A Trip Through the Body. 2015. (DK Adventures Ser.). (ENG.). 128p. (J). (gr. 3-7). pap. 5.99 (978-1-4654-2933-9(6), DK Children) Dorling Kindersley Publishing, Inc.

—Ultimate Factivity Collection: Human Body. 2016. (ENG.). 96p. (J). (gr. 1-4). pap. 12.99 (978-1-4654-4506-3(4), DK Children) Dorling Kindersley Publishing, Inc.

Dorling Kindersley Publishing Staff & Winston, Robert. Utterly Amazing Human Body. 2015. (ENG., Illus.). 32p. (J). (gr. 3-7). 19.99 (978-1-4654-2920-9(4), DK Children) Dorling Kindersley Publishing, Inc.

Doudna, Kelly. Stand Up!, 1 vol. 2007. (Character Concepts Ser.). (ENG., Illus.). 24p. (J). (gr. k-3). lib. bdg. 24.21 (978-1-59928-742-3(0), SandCastle) ABDO Publishing Co.

Douglas, Lloyd G. My Mouth. 2004. (Welcome Bks.). (ENG.). 24p. (J). (gr. -1-2). pap. 4.95 (978-0-516-22131-1(0), Children's Pr.) Scholastic Library Publishing.

Dowdy, Penny. Body Math. 2008. (Math Alive! Ser.). 32p. (gr. 4-18). lib. bdg. 28.50 (978-0-7614-3215-9(9), Benchmark Bks.) Marshall Cavendish Corp.

Dunn, Joeming. Graphic Adventures: The Human Body, 6 vols., Set. Espinosa, Rod, illus. Incl. Brain: A Graphic Novel Tour. Espinosa, Rod. 28.50 (978-1-60270-683-5(2)); Eyes: A Graphic Novel Tour. 28.50 (978-1-60270-684-2(0)); Heart: A Graphic Novel Tour. Espinosa, Rod. 28.50 (978-1-60270-685-9(9)); Kidneys: A Graphic Novel Tour. 28.50 (978-1-60270-686-6(7)); Liver: A Graphic Novel Tour. 28.50 (978-1-60270-687-3(5)); Lungs: A Graphic Novel Tour. 28.50 (978-1-60270-688-0(3)); (J). (gr. 3-6). (Graphic Body Ser.). (Illus.). 32p. 2009. 171.00 (978-1-60270-682-8(4), Graphic Planet- Nonfiction) ABDO Publishing Co.

Editors of Kingfisher. Incredible Human Body. 2016. (Fast Facts Ser.). (ENG., Illus.). 32p. (J). pap. 6.99 (978-0-7534-7301-6(1), 9780753473016, Kingfisher) Roaring Brook Pr.

Editors of Time Magazine. TIME Your Body. 2013. (ENG., Illus.). 112p. (gr. 11-17). 29.95 (978-1-61893-083-5(4), Time Bks.) Time Inc. Bks.

Edmunds, Kate, illus. Dry Bones. 2009. (Classic Books with Holes Big Book Ser.). (ENG.). 16p. (J). (gr. -1-1). (978-1-84643-210-1(3)) Child's Play International Ltd.

—Dry Bones W/ 2009. (Classic Books with Holes US Soft Cover with CD Ser.). (ENG.). 16p. (J). pap. incl. audio compact disk (978-1-84643-259-0(6)) Child's Play International Ltd.

Encyclopaedia Britannica, Inc. Staff, compiled by. Britannica Illustrated Science Library: Human Body, 16 vols. 2008. (Illus.). (J). 29.95 (978-1-59339-390-8(3)); 29.95 (978-1-59339-391-5(1)) Encyclopaedia Britannica, Inc.

—Learning about Our Bodies. 2008. 49.95 (978-1-59339-660-2(0)) Encyclopaedia Britannica, Inc.

—The Respiratory System. 2008. 49.95 (978-1-59339-558-2(2)) Encyclopaedia Britannica, Inc.

Ending & Extending Life. 2010. (Contemporary Issues in Science Ser.). (Illus.). 240p. (YA). (gr. 7-12). 35.00 (978-0-8160-6205-8(6)) Facts On File, Inc.

Enslow, Brian. My Body. 2010. (All about My Body Ser.). (Illus.). 24p. (J). 22.60 (978-0-7660-3811-0(4)); pap. 7.95 (978-1-59845-172-6(3)) Enslow Pubs., Inc. (Enslow Elementary).

—My Mouth. 2010. (All about My Body Ser.). (Illus.). 24p. (J). 22.60 (978-0-7660-3815-8(7)); pap. 7.95 (978-1-59845-171-9(5)) Enslow Pubs., Inc. (Enslow Elementary).

—My Nose. 2010. (All about My Body Ser.). (Illus.). 24p. (J). pap. 7.95 (978-1-59845-170-2(7), Enslow Elementary) Enslow Pubs., Inc.

Esherick, Joan. Looking & Feeling Good in Your Body. Garcia, Victor, ed. 2014. (Understanding Obesity Ser.: 10). (Illus.). 104p. (J). (gr. 7-18). lib. bdg. 24.95 (978-1-4222-3063-3(5)) Mason Crest.

Extraordinary Bodies. 2014. (Ripleys Believe It or Not! Download the Weird Ser.: 8). 36p. (J). (gr. 4-18). lib. bdg. 20.95 (978-1-4222-3150-0(X)) Mason Crest.

Fact Atlas: Human Body. 2009. (FACT ATLAS Ser.). 72p. (J). 14.95 (978-0-8437-1980-2(X)) Hammond World Atlas Corp.

Farndon, John. Stuff You Need to Know about the Human Body. Hutchinson, Tim, illus. 2017. (ENG.). 80p. (J). (gr. 4-12). pap. 14.95 **(978-1-77085-981-4(0)**, 9781770859814) Firefly Bks., Ltd.

Federer, Jessica Joy. Bobby Bacteria & Friends: Inside UR Body Books Presents. l.t. ed. 2005. (Illus.). 80p. (J). bds. 9.99 (978-0-9753455-3-5(2)) Amerisearch, Inc.

Fernandez, A. & Fernandez, Q. Hooray for My Nose. (Hooray for My Senses Ser.). (Illus.). (J). 19.27 (978-1-58952-375-3(X)) Rourke Educational Media.

Fletcher, Patricia. Why Do People Have Chins? And Other Curious Human Adaptations. 2017. (Odd Adaptations Ser.). 32p. (J). (gr. 3-4). pap. 10.50 **(978-1-5382-0397-2(9))** Stevens, Gareth Publishing LLLP.

Flowchart Smart: Set 2. 2017. (Flowchart Smart Ser.). 48p. (gr. 4-5). pap. 84.30 **(978-1-5382-0778-9(8))**; lib. bdg. 191.70 **(978-1-5382-0612-6(9))** Stevens, Gareth Publishing LLLP.

Fornari, Giuliano, illus. Panoramas Human Body. 2006. (J). (978-0-7607-8155-5(9)) backpackbook.

Freed, Kira. Artificial Limbs. 2016. (Miracles of Medicine Ser.). 00048p. (J). pap. 14.05 **(978-1-4824-6096-4(3))** Stevens, Gareth Publishing LLLP.

French, Cathy. Cells & Las Células: 6 English, 6 Spanish Adaptations. 2011. (ENG & SPA.). (J). 101.00 net. (978-1-4108-5726-2(3)) Benchmark Education Co.

Friedman, Lauri S., ed. Body Image. 2012. (Introducing Issues with Opposing Viewpoints Ser.). (ENG., Illus.). 144p. (gr. 7-10). lib. bdg. 36.95 (978-0-7377-6273-0(X), Greenhaven Pr., Inc.) Cengage Gale.

Fromer, Liza & Gerstein, Francine. My Achy Body. Weissmann, Joe, illus. 2011. (Body Works). (ENG.). 24p. (J). (gr. 1-4). 12.95 (978-1-77049-204-2(6), Tundra Bks.) Tundra Bks. CAN. Dist: Penguin Random Hse. LLC.

—My Healthy Body. Weissmann, Joe, illus. 2012. (Body Works). (ENG.). 24p. (J). (gr. 1-4). 12.95 (978-1-77049-312-4(3), Tundra Bks.) Tundra Bks. CAN. Dist: Penguin Random Hse. LLC.

—My Itchy Body. Weissmann, Joe, illus. 2012. (Body Works). (ENG.). 24p. (J). (gr. 1-4). 12.95 (978-1-77049-311-7(5), Tundra Bks.) Tundra Bks. CAN. Dist: Penguin Random Hse. LLC.

—My Messy Body. Weissmann, Joe, illus. 2011. (Body Works). (ENG.). 24p. (J). (gr. 1-4). 12.95 (978-1-77049-202-8(X), Tundra Bks.) Tundra Bks. CAN. Dist: Penguin Random Hse. LLC.

—My Noisy Body. Weissmann, Joe, illus. 2011. (Body Works). (ENG.). 24p. (J). (gr. 1-4). 12.95 (978-1-77049-201-1(1), Tundra Bks.) Tundra Bks. CAN. Dist: Penguin Random Hse. LLC.

—My Stretchy Body. Weissmann, Joe, illus. 2011. (Body Works). (ENG.). 24p. (J). (gr. 1-4). 12.95 (978-1-77049-203-5(8), Tundra Bks.) Tundra Bks. CAN. Dist: Penguin Random Hse. LLC.

Furgang, Kathy. My Nose. 2009. (My Body Ser.). 24p. (gr. 3-3). 42.50 (978-1-61514-691-8(1), PowerKids Pr.) Rosen Publishing Group, Inc., The.

Gallavotti, Barbara. El Cuerpo Humano en Acción. (Coleccion Bravo). (SPA., Illus.). 76p. (978-84-7131-904-3(7), EDI30261) Editex, Editorial S.A. ESP. Dist: Lectorum Pubns., Inc.

—The Human Body in Action. Shapiro, Brett, tr. from ITA. Inklink, Studio, illus. 2004. 123p. (J). (gr. 4-8). reprint ed. pap. 9.00 (978-0-7567-8334-1(8)) DIANE Publishing Co.

Galvin, Laura Gates. Human Body A to Z. MacDonald, Judy, illus. 2012. (ENG.). 40p. 9.95 (978-1-60727-296-0(2)) Soundprints.

Ganeri, Anita. Human Body. 2013. (Kingfisher Readers Ser.). (ENG., Illus.). 32p. (J). (gr. k-3). 12.99 (978-0-7534-6962-0(6), 9780753469620, Kingfisher) Roaring Brook Pr.

—Make & Move: Human Body. 2016. (Make & Move Ser.). (ENG., Illus.). 28p. (J). (gr. k). 19.95 (978-1-62686-489-4(6), Silver Dolphin Bks.) Readerlink Distribution Services, LLC.

Gardner, Robert. Easy Genius Science Projects with the Human Body: Great Experiments & Ideas. 2008. (Easy Genius Science Projects Ser.). (Illus.). 112p. (J). (gr. 5-9). lib. bdg. 33.27 (978-0-7660-2927-9(1)) Enslow Pubs., Inc.

—Experiments with the Human Body. 2017. (Science Whiz Experiments Ser.). 128p. (J). (gr. 5-5). lib. bdg. 37.27 **(978-0-7660-8684-5(4))** Enslow Pubs., Inc.

Gardner, Robert. Human Body Experiments Using Fingerprints, Hair, Muscles, & More: One Hour or Less Science Experiments. 2012. (Last-Minute Science Projects Ser.). (Illus.). 48p. (J). (gr. 5-18). 25.27 (978-0-7660-3958-2(7)) Enslow Pubs., Inc.

Gestalten. My Body: The Human Body in Illustrations. Section Graphics Golden Staff, illus. 2016. (ENG.). 48p. (J). (gr. 3-7). 24.95 (978-3-89955-712-1(3)) Die Gestalten Verlag DEU. Dist: Penguin Random Hse. LLC.

Glencoe McGraw-Hill Staff. Human Body Systems. 2nd ed. 2004. (Glen Sci: Human Body Systems Ser.). (ENG., Illus.). 280p. (gr. 6-8). lib. bdg., stu. ed. 32.40 (978-0-07-861743-0(X), 007861743X) McGraw-Hill Higher Education.

Goddard, Jolyon. Inside the Human Body. 2010. (Invisible Worlds Ser.). 48p. (gr. 4). 28.50 (978-0-7614-4190-8(5)) Marshall Cavendish Corp.

Gordon, Sharon. My Stomach. 2004. (Bookworms Ser.). (ENG & SPA., Illus.). 31p. (J). 21.36 (978-0-7614-1782-8(6)) Marshall Cavendish Corp.

—What's Inside? (¿Qué Hay Dentro?), 6 bks., Set. Incl. Que Hay Dentro de una Estacion de Policia? / What's Inside a Police Station? lib. bdg. 15.95 (978-0-7614-2476-5(8)); Whats Inside a Fire Truck? (¿Qué Hay Dentro de un Camión de Bomberos?) lib. bdg. 15.95 (978-0-7614-2472-7(5)); What's Inside a Firehouse/Que Hay Dentro de un Cuartel de Bomberos? lib. bdg. 15.95 (978-0-7614-2473-4(3)); What's Inside a Hospital?/Que Hay Dentro de un Hospital? lib. bdg. 15.95 (978-0-7614-2474-1(1)); What's Inside a Police Car/Que Hay Dentro de un Carro de Policia? lib. bdg. 15.95 (978-0-7614-2475-8(X)); What's Inside an Ambulance?/Que Hay Dentro de una Ambulancia? lib. bdg. 15.95 (978-0-7614-2471-0(7)); (Illus.). 32p. (gr. 1-2). (Bookworms — Bilingual Editions: What's Inside?/¿Que Hay Dentro? Ser.). (ENG & SPA.). 2006. Set lib. bdg. 95.70 (978-0-7614-2469-7(5)) Marshall Cavendish Corp.

Gottlieb. The Human Body. 2004. (Wonders of Science Ser.). (ENG.). (gr. 7-12). 176p. pap., tchr. ed. 27.70 (978-0-7398-9182-7(0)); (Illus.). 144p. pap. 24.55 (978-0-7398-9176-6(6)) Houghton Mifflin Harcourt Publishing Co.

Grace, Catherine O'Neill. How & Why: A Kids' Book about the Body. Barr, Loel, illus. 2011. (J). (978-0-89043-231-0(7)) Consumers Union of U. S., Inc.

Grade 1 Know Your Body Student Workbook. 3rd rev. ed. 2006. 70p. 5.99 (978-0-7575-2852-1(X)) Kendall Hunt Publishing Co.

Grade 2 Know Your Body Student Workbook. 3rd rev. ed. 2006. 76p. 8.95 (978-0-7575-2871-2(6)) Kendall Hunt Publishing Co.

Grade 3 Know Your Body Student Workbook. 3rd rev. ed. 2006. 76p. 8.95 (978-0-7575-2877-4(5)) Kendall Hunt Publishing Co.

Grade 5 Know Your Body Student Textbook. 3rd rev. ed. 2007. 294p. pap. 19.95 (978-0-7575-2951-1(8)) Kendall Hunt Publishing Co.

Grade 6 Know Your Body Student Textbook. 3rd rev. ed. 2007. 314p. pap. 19.95 (978-0-7575-2950-4(X)) Kendall Hunt Publishing Co.

Gray, Susan H. The Muscular System. 2014. (Human Body Ser.). (ENG.). 24p. (J). (gr. 2-5). 28.50 (978-1-62687-336-0(4), 207176) Child's World, Inc., The.

—The Respiratory System. 2014. (Human Body Ser.). (ENG.). 24p. (J). (gr. 2-5). 28.50 (978-1-62687-338-4(0), 207178) Child's World, Inc., The.

—The Skeletal System. 2014. (Human Body Ser.). (ENG.). 24p. (J). (gr. 2-5). 28.50 (978-1-62687-339-1(9), 207179) Child's World, Inc., The.

Green, Emily & Manolis, Kay. The Circulatory System. 2009. (Body Systems Ser.). (ENG., Illus.). 24p. (J). (gr. 2-5). lib. bdg. 25.95 (978-1-60014-242-0(7)) Bellwether Media.

Green, Meghan & Lankford, Ronald D., Jr. Body Image & Body Shaming. 2017. (Hot Topics Ser.). 112p. (J). (gr. 7-7). lib. bdg. 39.40 **(978-1-5345-6016-1(5)**, Lucent Pr.) Greenhaven Publishing LLC.

Green-Warren, Loretta M. Counting, Rhyming & Body Parts. 2010. 24p. 12.99 (978-1-4490-8408-0(7)) AuthorHouse.

Griffiths, Andy. What Body Part Is That? A Wacky Guide to the Funniest, Weirdest, & Most Disgustingest Parts of Your Body. Denton, Terry, illus. 2012. (ENG.). 192p. (J). (gr. 3-7).

H
I

12.99 (978-0-312-36790-9(2), 9780312367909) Feiwel & Friends.

Guillain, Charlotte. Our Bodies, 5 vols., Set. Incl. Our Blood. pap. 6.29 (978-1-4329-3604-4(2)); Our Bones. pap. 6.29 (978-1-4329-3605-1(0)); Our Brains. pap. 6.29 (978-1-4329-3601-3(8)); Our Hearts. pap. 6.29 (978-1-4329-3599-3(2)); Our Lungs. pap. 6.29 (978-1-4329-3603-7(4)); Our Muscles. (Illus.). pap. 6.29 (978-1-4329-3602-0(6)); Our Skin. pap. 6.29 (978-1-4329-3606-8(9)); Our Stomachs. pap. 6.29 (978-1-4329-3600-6(X)); (gr. -1-1). (Our Bodies Ser.). (ENG.). 24p. 2010. Set pap. 50.32 (978-1-4329-3607-5(7)); Set lib. bdg. 135.90 (978-1-4329-3598-6(4)) Heinemann-Raintree. (Acorn).

Gul, Hasibe, et al. My Wonderful Body. 2011. (ENG.). 16p. (J). (gr. -1 — 1). pap. 3.95 (978-1-59784-241-9(9)) Tughra Bks.

Gunzi, Christiane. My Body. Murrell, Deborah, ed. 2015. (ENG., Illus.). 34p. (J). 7.99 (978-1-906572-22-8(4)) Award Pubns. Ltd. GBR. Dist: Parkwest Pubns., Inc.

Hale, Ohara. Who Did It? Who Farted? Who Burped? Who Pooped? Who Peed? Who Sneezed?, 5 vols. 2014. (ENG., Illus.). 50p. (J). (-k). 14.95 (978-1-57687-681-7(0), powerHouse Bks.) powerHouse Cultural Entertainment, Inc.

Harcourt School Publishers, creator. Human Body. 2006. (Illus.). 24p. (J). pap. 6.00 (978-0-15-364950-9(X)) Harcourt Schl. Pubs.

Harper, P. Thandi Hicks. Hip-Hop Development. 2005. (978-1-887191-02-9(X)) Youth Popular Culture Institute, Inc.

Harris, Ashley Rae. Girl in the Mirror: Understanding Physical Changes, 1 vol. 2008. (Essential Health: Strong Beautiful Girls Set 1 Ser.). (ENG.). 112p. (J). (gr. 6-12). lib. bdg. 35.64 (978-1-60453-100-8(2)) ABDO Publishing Co.

Harris, Robie H. Sexo... Que Es? 2003. (SPA., Illus.). (YA). (gr. 7-8). pap. (978-84-95040-35-0(2), RR7144) Serres, Ediciones, S. L. ESP. Dist: Lectorum Pubns., Inc.

—Who Has What? All about Girls' Bodies & Boys' Bodies. Westcott, Nadine Bernard, illus. 2011. (Let's Talk about You & Me Ser.). (ENG.). 32p. (J). (gr. -1-2). 15.99 (978-0-7636-2931-1(6)) Candlewick Pr.

Hawkins, Jay. Really Horrible Body Facts. 2013. (Really Horrible Facts Ser.). 32p. (J). (gr. k-3). 25.25 (978-1-61533-743-9(1)); pap. 10.00 (978-1-61533-803-0(9)); pap. 60.00 (978-1-61533-804-7(7)) Windmill Bks.

Health & the Human Body Classroom Library. (gr. k-2). lib. bdg. 81.95 (978-0-7368-7134-1(9)) Red Brick Learning.

Health & the Human Body II Classroom Library. (gr. k-2). lib. bdg. 63.95 (978-0-7368-8825-7(X)) Red Brick Learning.

Healthy Head, Hands & Hearts. 2008. (Illus.). 36p. (J). pap. 6.00 (978-0-9815308-1-9(8)) Amazement Square.

Heath, Beverly C. My Parts Equal Me! Floyd, John, Jr., illus. 2005. 15p. (J). (gr. -1). bds. 5.95 (978-0-9752860-2-9(1)) OurRainbow Pr., LLC.

Heos, Bridget. The Brain in Your Body, 1 vol. 2015. (ENG., Illus.). 32p. (J). 23.45 (978-1-62275-636-0(3), Britannica Educational Publishing) Rosen Publishing Group, Inc., The.

Hewitt, Sally. My Digestive System. 2012. (My Body Ser.). (ENG., Illus.). 24p. (gr. k-4). pap. 7.95 (978-1-926853-97-0(0)) Saunders Bk. Co. CAN. Dist: RiverStream Publishing.

Higgins, Melissa. We All Look Different. 2012. (Celebrating Differences Ser.). (ENG.). 24p. (gr. k-1). pap. 41.70 (978-1-4296-8323-4(6), Pebble Plus) Capstone Press of Coughlan Cos.

Hightower, Melvin. Earwax & Boogers! 2017. (Your Body at Its Grossest Ser.). 24p. (gr. 1-2). pap. 8.15 **(978-1-4824-6461-0(6))** Stevens, Gareth Publishing LLLP.

—Pus & Scabs! 2017. (Your Body at Its Grossest Ser.). 24p. (gr. 1-2). pap. 8.15 **(978-1-4824-6469-6(1))** Stevens, Gareth Publishing LLLP.

Hindley, Judy. Eyes, Nose, Fingers, & Toes: A First Book All about You. Granström, Brita, illus. 2004. (ENG.). 24p. (J). (gr. k-k). bds. 6.99 (978-0-7636-2383-8(0)) Candlewick Pr.

Hirsch, Rebecca E. The Human Microbiome: The Germs That Keep You Healthy. 2016. (ENG., Illus.). 112p. (gr. 7-12). (J). 34.65 (978-1-4677-8568-6(7)); (YA). 51.99 (978-1-5124-1140-9(X), Twenty-First Century Bks.) Lerner Publishing Group.

Holland, Simon. Human Body. Cosgrove, Lee, illus. 2015. (Lie Detector Ser.). (ENG.). 32p. (gr. k-3). pap. 5.95 (978-1-4795-8515-1(7)) Picture Window Bks.

Holt, Rinehart and Winston Staff. Decisions for Health Red Chptr. 16: Your Changing Body. 4th ed. 2004. pap. 11.20 (978-0-03-068043-4(3)) Holt McDougal.

—Holt Science & Technology Chapter 22: Life Science: Body Organization. 5th ed. 2004. (Illus.). pap. 12.86 (978-0-03-030238-1(2)) Holt McDougal.

—Holt Science & Technology Chapter 24: Life Science: Digestive & Urinary Systems. 5th ed. 2004. (Illus.). pap. 12.86 (978-0-03-030241-1(2)) Holt McDougal.

Hook, Sue & Jackson, Carolyn, eds. All about People: How We Grow, How Our Bodies Work, & How We Feel. 2005. (Illus.). 93p. (J). (gr. k-4). reprint ed. 20.00 (978-0-7567-8683-0(5)) DIANE Publishing Co.

Houghton, Gillian. Bones: The Skeletal System. 2006. (Body Works Ser.). (Illus.). 24p. (YA). (gr. 2-5). lib. bdg. 22.60 (978-1-4042-3473-4(X)) Rosen Publishing Group, Inc., The.

—The Skeletal System. 2007. (How Your Body Works). (ENG., Illus.). 24p. (gr. 3-5). pap. 7.05 (978-1-4042-2182-6(4), PowerKids Pr.) Rosen Publishing Group, Inc., The.

How the Body Works, 10 bks., Big Bk. Set. (J). 230.00 (978-0-8136-2946-9(2)) Modern Curriculum Pr.

How Your Body Works. 2015. (How Your Body Works). (ENG.). 32p. (J). (gr. 4-4). pap., pap., pap. 360.00 (978-1-4994-1600-8(8), PowerKids Pr.) Rosen Publishing Group, Inc., The.

Human Body. 2014. (DK Eyewitness Bks.). (ENG.). 72p. (J). (gr. 3-7). lib. bdg. 19.99 (978-1-4654-2620-8(5), DK Children) Dorling Kindersley Publishing, Inc.

The Human Body: How It Works Set, 11-Volumes. 2009. (Human Body: How It Works Ser.). (C). (gr. 9-18). 385.00 (978-0-7910-9915-5(6), Chelsea Hse.) Facts On File, Inc.

The Human Body: Level O, 6 vols. (Explorers Ser.). 32p. (gr. 3-6). 44.95 (978-0-7699-0599-0(4)) Shortland Pubns. (U. S. A.) Inc.

Human Body Encyclopedia. (Children's Reference Ser.). 224p. 15.99 (978-1-4075-0562-6(9)) Parragon, Inc.

Human Body FAQ. 2016. (Human Body FAQ Ser.). 00032p. (J). (gr. 3-3). 157.50 (978-1-5081-5342-9(6), PowerKids Pr.) Rosen Publishing Group, Inc., The.

The Human Body In 3D. 2015. (Human Body In 3D Ser.). (ENG.). 64p. (J). (gr. 5-6). pap., pap., pap. 777.00 (978-1-4777-8629-1(5), Rosen Central) Rosen Publishing Group, Inc., The.

Human Body Systems Lesson Plans & Blackline Masters (National Version) 2009. (Journeys Ser.). 20.00 (978-1-4042-9530-8(5), Rosen Classroom) Rosen Publishing Group, Inc., The.

Inside My Body, 10 vols., Set. Incl. How Do My Muscles Get Strong? Muscles & Exercise. Parker, Steve. pap. 7.99 (978-1-4109-4028-5(4)); What Happens to Broken Bones? Bones. Ballard, Carol. pap. 8.95 (978-1-4109-4022-3(5)); Why Do I Have Periods? Menstruation & Puberty. Thomas, Isabel. pap. 7.99 (978-1-4109-4026-1(8)); (gr. 3-5). (Inside My Body Ser.). (ENG.). 32p. 2011. Set pap. 24.93 (978-1-4109-4031-5(4)); Set lib. bdg. 306.50 (978-1-4109-4020-9(9)) Heinemann-Raintree. (NA-r).

Inside the Human Body, 6 vols. (Book2WebTM Ser.). (gr. 4-8). 36.50 (978-0-322-02979-8(1)) Wright Group/McGraw-Hill.

Irvine, Ron S. ABC's of Your Body, 1 vol. 2010. 30p. pap. 24.95 (978-1-4489-7747-5(9)) PublishAmerica, Inc.

It's Amazing: It's Amazing Package. 2003. 125.95 (978-0-673-61613-5(4)) Celebration Pr.

Jango-Cohen, Judith. El Aparato Respiratorio (the Respiratory System) Translations.com Staff, tr. 2007. (Libros Sobre el Cuerpo Humano para Madrugadores Ser.). (SPA., Illus.). 48p. (gr. 2-4). per. 7.95 (978-0-8225-6652-6(4)) Lerner Publishing Group.

Jenkins, Pete. Nose. Quintanilla, Hazel, illus. 2017. (I See, I Saw Ser.). (ENG.). (J). (gr. k-1). 28.51 **(978-1-68342-153-5(1))** Rourke Educational Media.

—Toes. Quintanilla, Hazel, illus. 2017. (I See, I Saw Ser.). (ENG.). (J). (gr. k-1). 28.51 **(978-1-68342-151-1(5))** Rourke Educational Media.

Jenkins, Steve. Actual Size. 2011. (ENG., Illus.). 28p. (J). (gr. 1-4). pap. 7.99 (978-0-547-51291-4(0)) Houghton Mifflin Harcourt Publishing Co.

Jerome, Kate Boehm. More Science of You. 2007. (Reading Expeditions Ser.). (ENG., Illus.). 24p. (J). pap. 14.95 (978-0-7922-4566-7(0)) CENGAGE Learning.

Jeunesse, Gallimard & Peyrols, Sylvaine. The Human Body. Peyrols, Sylvaine, illus. 2007. (First Discovery Book Ser.). (ENG., Illus.). 24p. (J). (gr. -1-k). pap. 5.99 (978-0-439-91088-0(9)) Scholastic, Inc.

Johnson, Rebecca L. El Aparato Digestivo. Translations.com Staff, tr. 2006. (Libros Sobre el Cuerpo Humano para Madrugadores Ser.). (ENG & SPA., Illus.). 48p. (gr. 2-4). lib. bdg. 26.60 (978-0-8225-6253-5(7)) Lerner Publishing Group.

—El Aparato Digestivo (the Digestive System) Translations.com Staff, tr. 2007. (Libros Sobre el Cuerpo Humano para Madrugadores Ser.). (SPA., Illus.). 48p. (gr. 2-4). per. 7.95 (978-0-8225-6649-6(4)) Lerner Publishing Group.

—The Digestive System. 2005. (Early Bird Body Systems Ser.). (Illus.). 48p. (J). (gr. 2-4). lib. bdg. 25.26 (978-0-8225-1247-9(5)) Lerner Publishing Group.

—Your Muscular System. 2012. (Searchlight Books — How Does Your Body Work? Ser.). (ENG., Illus.). 40p. (gr. 3-5). pap. 8.95 (978-1-58013-961-8(2)) Lerner Publishing Group.

Jones, Ayesha. Allah Gave Me a Tongue to Taste. Stratford, Stevan, illus. 2016. (ENG.). 32p. (J). 8.95 (978-0-86037-338-4(X)) Kube Publishing Ltd. GBR. Dist: Consortium Bk. Sales & Distribution.

Jones, Peter. Complete Guides Human Body. 2012. (ENG.). 144p. (J). (978-1-4351-4407-1(4)) Barnes & Noble, Inc.

K/H (Kyb). Grade K Know Your Body Student Workbook. 3rd rev. ed. 2006. 66p. 8.95 (978-0-7575-2760-9(4)) Kendall Hunt Publishing Co.

Katz, Karen & Bauer, Marion Dane. Baby's Box of Fun! A Karen Katz Lift-the-Flap Gift Set - Where Is Baby's Bellybutton? - Where Is Baby's Mommy? - Toes, Ears, & Nose! Katz, Karen, illus. gif. ed. 2004. (ENG., Illus.). 44p. (J). (gr. -1 — 1). bds. 17.99 (978-0-689-03862-4(3), Little Simon) Little Simon.

Kenney, Karen Latchana. Peeking under Your Skin. Wood, Steven, illus. 2016. (What's Beneath Ser.). (ENG.). 32p. (gr. -1-3). lib. bdg. 27.32 (978-1-4795-8668-4(4)) Picture Window Bks.

Kerrod, Robin & Parker, Steve. Find Out about the Body. 2013. (ENG., Illus.). 64p. (J). (gr. 2-7). 9.99 (978-1-84322-870-7(X)) Anness Publishing GBR. Dist: National Bk. Network.

Kingfisher Editors & Dods, Emma. Surprising Facts about the Human Body. Aspinall, Marc, illus. 2014. (Wow! Ser.). (ENG.). 32p. (J). (gr. k-3). 15.99 (978-0-7534-7118-0(3), 9780753471180, Kingfisher) Roaring Brook Pr.

Kirk, Bill. Muscles Make Us Move. Ruble, Eugene, illus. 2011. 32p. pap. 10.95 (978-1-61633-134-4(8)) Guardian Angel Publishing, Inc.

—Tissue Tantra: The Sum of Our Parts Series Book 9. Ruble, Eugene, illus. 2013. 28p. pap. 10.95 (978-1-61633-448-2(7)) Guardian Angel Publishing, Inc.

Klosterman, Lorrie. The Excretory System. 2009. (Amazing Human Body 2 Ser.). 80p. (gr. 5). 34.21 (978-0-7614-4037-6(2)) Marshall Cavendish GBR. Dist: Marshall Cavendish Corp.

Know Your Body Grade K Kit. 3rd rev. ed. 2006. pap. 249.95 (978-0-7575-2566-7(0)) Kendall Hunt Publishing Co.

Koerper und Ihre Berechnung I. (Duden-Schuelerhilfen Ser.). (GER.). 96p. (YA). (gr. 5-8). (978-3-411-04291-3(5)) Bibliographisches Institut & F. A. Brockhaus AG DEU. Dist: International Bk. Import Service, Inc.

Koerper und Ihre Berechnung II. (Duden-Schuelerhilfen Ser.). (GER.). 96p. (YA). (gr. 9-10). (978-3-411-05161-8(2)) Bibliographisches Institut & F. A. Brockhaus AG DEU. Dist: International Bk. Import Service, Inc.

Kolpin, Molly. My Silly Body. 2015. (My Silly Body Ser.). (ENG.). 24p. (gr. k-1). lib. bdg. 106.60 (978-1-4914-2563-3(6), Pebble Plus) Capstone Press of Coughlan Cos.

Kolpin, Molly, et al. First Graphics: Body Systems. Jones, Chris B., illus. 2012. (First Graphics: Body Systems Ser.). (ENG.). 24p. (gr. 1-2). pap. 25.16 (978-1-4296-9332-5(0)); lib. bdg. 71.97 (978-1-4296-9158-1(1)) Capstone Press of Coughlan Cos.

Korb, Rena B. & Weinhaus, Anthony J. My Mouth, 1 vol. Simard, Remy, illus. 2010. (My Body Ser.). (ENG.). 32p. (J). (gr. k-3). 28.50 (978-1-60270-806-8(1)) Magic Wagon.

—My Stomach, 1 vol. Simard, Remy, illus. 2010. (My Body Ser.). (ENG.). 32p. (J). (gr. k-3). 28.50 (978-1-60270-810-5(X)) Magic Wagon.

Kranking, Kathy. Mini & Mighty: Teeny Tiny Animals. 2007. (Illus.). 32p. (J). (978-0-439-02574-4(5)) Scholastic, Inc.

Krohmer, Randolph W. The Reproductive System. 2009. (Human Body: How It Works Ser.). (Illus.). 160p. (C). (gr. 9-18). 35.00 (978-1-60413-373-8(2), Chelsea Hse.) Facts On File, Inc.

Kudlinski, Kathleen V. Boy, Were We Wrong about the Human Body! Tilley, Debbie, illus. 2015. (ENG.). 32p. (J). (gr. -1-3). 16.99 (978-0-8037-3792-1(0), Dial Bks) Penguin Young Readers Group.

Ladybird. The Human Body, Level 4. 2016. (Read It Yourself with Ladybird Ser.). (ENG., Illus.). 48p. (J). pap. 9.99 (978-0-241-23767-0(X)) Penguin Bks., Ltd. GBR. Dist: Independent Pubs. Group.

—The Human Body-Read It Yourself with Ladybird, Level 4. 2016. (Read It Yourself with Ladybird Ser.). (ENG., Illus.). 48p. (J). 5.99 (978-0-241-23768-7(8)) Penguin Bks., Ltd. GBR. Dist: Independent Pubs. Group.

Landau, Elaine. Nosebleeds. 2009. (Head-to Toe Health 2 Ser.). 32p. (gr. 2). 28.50 (978-0-7614-3503-7(4)) Marshall Cavendish GBR. Dist: Marshall Cavendish Corp.

Larimore, Walt, et al. Lintball Leo's Not-So-Stupid Questions about Your Body, 1 vol. Phillips, Mike, illus. 2003. (ENG.). 128p. (J). pap. 7.99 (978-0-310-70545-1(2)) Zonderkidz.

Lataif, Nicole. Siempre Tú: Un Libro Sobre Tu Cuerpo y Tu Alma. Pérez, Karen H., tr. from ENG. Rojas, Mary, illus. 2014.Tr. of Forever You: a Book about Your Body & Soul. (SPA.). (J). pap. 9.95 (978-0-8198-9009-2(X)) Pauline Bks. & Media.

Lazoo Publishing Staff. All about Faces. Miyakoshi, Junko, tr. from JPN. 2009. (ENG., Illus.). 28p. (gr. -1). 14.95 (978-1-934734-06-3(3)) Seven Footer Pr.

Lerner Publishing Group Staff. Body Systems: Classroom Set. 2005. (Illus.). (J). (gr. 2-4). 46.95 (978-0-8225-2347-5(7)) Lerner Publishing Group.

LernerClassroom Editors. Early Bird Body Systems Teaching Guide. 2009. pap. 7.95 (978-0-8225-2324-6(8)) Lerner Publishing Group.

Lew, Kristi. Farts, Vomit, & Other Functions That Help Your Body, 1 vol. 2010. (Nasty (but Useful!) Science Ser.). (ENG.). 32p. (gr. 3-4). lib. bdg. 27.32 (978-1-4296-4539-3(3), Fact Finders) Capstone Press of Coughlan Cos.

Li, Maggie. The Amazing Human Body Detectives: Facts, Myths & Quirks of the Body. 2016. (ENG., Illus.). 32p. (J). (gr. k-3). 15.99 (978-1-84365-297-7(8), Pavilion) Pavilion Bks. GBR. Dist: Independent Pubs. Group.

Llewellyn, Claire. Your Body. 2008. (Look after Yourself Ser.). (Illus.). 30p. (J). (gr. 1-4). lib. bdg. 28.50 (978-1-59771-096-1(2)) Sea-To-Sea Pubns.

Lodge, Jo. Baby's Very First Book: Faces: A Rag/cloth Book about Faces with Mirror, Crinkly Pages & High-Contrast Images. 2016. (ENG., Illus.). 8p. (J). 10.99 **(978-1-5098-0705-5(5))** Pan Macmillan GBR. Dist: Independent Pubs. Group.

Macaulay, David. The Way We Work: Getting to Know the Amazing Human Body. 2008. (ENG., Illus.). 336p. (J). (gr. 5-7). 35.00 (978-0-618-23378-6(4)) Houghton Mifflin Harcourt Publishing Co.

Macdonald, Fiona. You Wouldn't Want to Live Without Pain! Antram, David, illus. 2016. (You Wouldn't Want to Live Without... Ser.). (ENG.). 32p. (J). lib. bdg. 29.00 (978-0-531-21491-6(5), Watts, Franklin) Scholastic Library Publishing.

Macnair, Patricia. Everything You Need to Know about the Human Body. (Everything You Need to Know Ser.). (ENG., Illus.). 160p. (J). (gr. k-4). 2014. pap. 10.99 (978-0-7534-7168-5(X), 9780753471685) 2011. 12.99 (978-0-7534-6686-5(4), 9780753466865) Roaring Brook Pr. (Kingfisher).

Maldonado, Premier. Cuerpo. 2006. (SPA., Illus.). 14.99 (978-0-9727886-4-9(6)) Osmosis, LLC.

Manolis, Kay. Blastoff! Readers - Body Systems, 6 vols., Set. Incl. Circulatory System. 20.00 (978-0-531-21701-6(9)); Digestive System. 20.00 (978-0-531-21702-3(7)); Muscular System. 20.00 (978-0-531-21703-0(5)); Nervous System. 20.00 (978-0-531-21704-7(3)); Respiratory System. 20.00 (978-0-531-21705-4(1)); Skeletal System. 20.00 (978-0-531-21706-1(X)); (Illus.). 24p. (J). (gr. k-3). 2009. 2009. Set lib. bdg. 120.00 (978-0-531-27900-7(6), Children's Pr.) Scholastic Library Publishing.

Margulies, Sheldon. The Fascinating Body: How It Works. 2004. (ENG., Illus.). 424p. (J). pap. 43.95 (978-1-57886-076-0(8)) Scarecrow Pr., Inc.

Martin, Michael. Bodyworx Vacation Bible School. 2003. cd-rom (978-0-9709763-5-2(6)) Return To The Word.

Martin, Ruth. Little Explorers: My Amazing Body. Sanders, Allan, illus. 2015. (Little Explorers Ser.). (ENG.). 18p. (J). (gr. -1-3). 9.99 (978-1-4998-0040-1(1)) Little Bee Books Inc.

Mason, Paul. Can You Lick Your Own Elbow? And Other Questions about the Human Body, 1 vol. 2013. (Questions You Never Thought You'd Ask Ser.). (ENG.). 32p. (gr. 1-3). 29.99 (978-1-4109-5201-1(0)); pap. 8.95 (978-1-4109-5207-3(X)) Heinemann-Raintree. (Read Me!).

—The Fact or Fiction Behind Human Bodies. 2016. (Fact or Phony? Ser.). (ENG.). 96p. (J). (gr. 5-6). lib. bdg. 33.25 (978-1-4824-4264-9(7)) Stevens, Gareth Publishing LLLP.

Maynard, Christopher, et al. How Your Body Works. 2004. (Knowledge Masters Plus Ser.). (Illus.). 32p. (YA). pap. incl. cd-rom (978-1-903954-44-7(4), Pavilion Children's Books) Pavilion Bks.

McNeil, Niki, et al. HOCPP 1066 Human Body. 2006. spiral bd. 22.00 (978-1-60308-066-8(X)) In the Hands of a Child.

—HOCPP 1122 Healthy Bodies. 2006. spiral bd. 12.50 (978-1-60308-122-1(4)) In the Hands of a Child.

Meachen Rau, Dana. El Corazon y la Sangre. 2006. (Bookworms Ser.). (SPA & ENG., Illus.). 32p. (gr. 1-2). lib. bdg. 15.95 (978-0-7614-2404-8(0)) Marshall Cavendish Corp.

—My Heart & Blood/el Corazon y la Sangre. 2006. (Bookworms Ser.). (ENG & SPA., Illus.). 32p. (gr. 1-2). lib. bdg. 15.95 (978-0-7614-2482-6(2)) Marshall Cavendish Corp.

—My Lungs/Los Pulmones. 2006. (Bookworms Ser.). (ENG & SPA., Illus.). 32p. (gr. 1-2). lib. bdg. 15.95 (978-0-7614-2483-3(0)) Marshall Cavendish Corp.

—Los Pulmones. 2006. (Bookworms Ser.). (SPA & ENG., Illus.). 31p. (J). (gr. 3-7). lib. bdg. 22.79 (978-0-7614-2405-5(9)) Marshall Cavendish Corp.

—What's Inside Me? (¿Qué Hay Dentro de Mí?), 6 bks., Set. Incl. My Bones & Muscles/Huesos y Musculos. lib. bdg. 15.95 (978-0-7614-2479-6(2)); My Brain/el Cerebro. lib. bdg. 15.95 (978-0-7614-2480-2(6)); My Heart & Blood/el Corazon y la Sangre. lib. bdg. 15.95 (978-0-7614-2482-6(2)); My Lungs/Los Pulmones. lib. bdg. 15.95 (978-0-7614-2483-3(0)); My Skin/la Piel. lib. bdg. 15.95 (978-0-7614-2484-0(9)); My Stomach/el Estomago. lib. bdg. 15.95 (978-0-7614-2485-7(7)); (Illus.). 32p. (gr. 1-2). (Bookworms — Bilingual Editions: What's Inside Me?/¿Que Hay Dentro de Mi? Ser.). (ENG & SPA.). 2006. Set lib. bdg. 95.70 (978-0-7614-2477-2(6)) Marshall Cavendish Corp.

Media, Cont. The Human Body. 2008. (ENG., Illus.). 96p. (YA). 17.99 (978-1-931703-02-4(7)) Creative Publishing Consultants.

—Our Body. 2008. (ENG., Illus.). 48p. (YA). 12.99 (978-1-931703-12-3(4)) Creative Publishing Consultants.

Meredith, Susan. What's Inside You? rev. ed. 2007. 24p. (J). pap. 4.99 (978-0-7945-1625-3(4), Usborne) EDC Publishing.

Miller, Margaret. Baby Faces. Miller, Margaret, photos by. 2009. (Look Baby! Bks.). (ENG., Illus.). 14p. (J). (gr. -1 — 1). bds. 4.99 (978-1-4169-7887-9(9), Little Simon) Little Simon.

Miller, Sara Swan. All Kinds of Noses. 2007. (All Kinds Of Ser.). (Illus.). 48p. (gr. 3-3). lib. bdg. 29.93 (978-0-7614-2522-9(5)) Marshall Cavendish Corp.

Modern Publishing Staff. Look at Me! 2007. (Illus.). (J). (gr. -1-3). bds. 4.99 (978-0-7666-2607-2(5)) Modern Publishing.

Molino & AWAN, SHEILA. Mi Primer Libro Del Cuerpo Humano. (SPA., Illus.). pap. 12.95 (978-84-272-1734-8(X)) Molino, Editorial ESP. Dist: Distribooks, Inc.

Montgomery, Heather L. Why Do My Teeth Fall Out? And Other Questions Kids Have about the Human Body, 1 vol. Davis, Jon, illus. 2011. (Kids' Questions Ser.). (ENG.). 24p. (gr. 1-2). pap. 7.49 (978-1-4048-6534-1(9)) Picture Window Bks.

Morgan, Philip. Moving Your Body. 2010. (How Your Body Works). 32p. (YA). (gr. 4-7). 28.50 (978-1-60753-054-1(6)) Amicus Publishing.

—Moving Your Body. 2012. (Illus.). 32p. (gr. 4-7). pap. 8.95 (978-1-926722-64-1(7)) Saunders Bk. Co. CAN. Dist: RiverStream Publishing.

Morgan, Sally. How Smell Works. 2010. (Our Senses Ser.). 24p. (J). (gr. k-2). pap. 8.25 (978-1-61532-561-0(1), PowerKids Pr.); (Illus.). (gr. -1-2). lib. bdg. 22.60 (978-1-61532-554-2(9)) Rosen Publishing Group, Inc., The.

—Inside Your Mouth & Other Body Parts. 2006. (Hidden Habitats Ser.). (J). (978-1-59389-282-1(9)) Chrysalis Education.

Morrison, Ben. The Digestive System. 2009. (Insider's Guide to the Body Ser.). 48p. (gr. 5-8). 53.00 (978-1-61513-582-0(0), Rosen Reference) Rosen Publishing Group, Inc., The.

A Mosaic of Magical Information, 10 vols., Set. Incl. Birds. Johnson, Jinny. (Illus.). 2004. lib. bdg. 19.95 (978-1-59084-447-2(5)); Cats & Kittens. Parker, Steve. (Illus.). 2010. 19.95 (978-1-4222-1987-4(9)); Dogs & Puppies. De la Bédoyère, Camilla. 2010. 19.95 (978-1-4222-1988-1(7)); Human Body. Parker, Steve. 2010. 19.95 (978-1-4222-1989-8(5)); Inventions. Brewer, Duncan. (Illus.). 2010. 19.95 (978-1-4222-1990-4(9)); T-Rex. Parker, Steve. (Illus.). 2010. 19.95 (978-1-4222-1991-1(7)); 100 Things You Should Know about the Wild West. Langley, Andrew. (Illus.). 2004. lib. bdg. 19.95 (978-1-59084-458-8(0)); 48p. (YA). (gr. 3-18). 2011. Set lib. bdg. 199.50 (978-1-4222-1992-8(5)) Mason Crest.

Mullins, Patty Rutland. All about You with Inspector McQ. Holub, Joan, illus. 2004. (Treasure Tree Ser.). 32p. (J). (978-0-7166-1646-7(7)) World Bk., Inc.

Murray, Julie. The Body, 1 vol. 2009. (That's Gross! A Look at Science Ser.). (ENG., Illus.). 32p. (J). (gr. 2-5). 28.50 (978-1-60453-554-9(7)) ABDO Publishing Co.

—Your Body. 2016. (Your Body Ser.: 6). (ENG.). 24p. (J). (gr. k-2). lib. bdg. 162.42 (978-1-68080-155-2(4)) ABDO Publishing Co.

Murrell, Deborah & Brooks, Susie. Human Body Lift-The-Flap. Lewis, Anthony, illus. 2014. (Lift-The-Flap Tab Bks.). (ENG.). 16p. (J). (gr. k-1). bds. 9.99 (978-0-7534-7060-2(8), 9780753470602, Kingfisher) Roaring Brook Pr.

My Body: Individual Title Six-Packs. (Discovery World Ser.). 12p. (gr. k-1). 28.00 (978-0-7635-8450-4(9)) Rigby Education.

My Body Does Strange Stuff! 2013. (My Body Does Strange Stuff! Ser.). 24p. (J). (gr. 1-3). 135.60 (978-1-4339-9673-3(1)); pap. 293.40 (978-1-4339-9764-8(9)); pap. 48.90 (978-1-4339-9763-1(0)) Stevens, Gareth Publishing LLLP.

Nagelhout, Ryan. The Heart & Blood in Your Body, 1 vol. 2015. (ENG.). 32p. (J). 23.45 (978-1-62275-640-7(1), Britannica Educational Publishing) Rosen Publishing Group, Inc., The.

National Geographic Kids Staff. All about Me. 2014. (Look & Learn Ser.). (ENG.). 24p. (J). (-k). bds. 6.99 (978-1-4263-1483-4(3), National Geographic Children's Bks.) National Geographic Society.

—Weird but True! Human Body: 300 Outrageous Facts about Your Awesome Anatomy. 2017. (ENG., Illus.). 208p. (J). (gr. 3-7). pap. 7.99 (978-1-4263-2726-1(9), National Geographic Children's Bks.) National Geographic Society.

Nervensystem und Sinnesorgane: Fachliche Inhalte und Uebungsaufgaben. 2nd ed. (Duden Abiturhilfen Ser.). (GER.). 112p. (YA). (gr. 12-13). (978-3-411-04152-7(8)) Bibliographisches Institut & F. A. Brockhaus AG DEU. Dist: International Bk. Import Service, Inc.

Nettleton, Pamela Hill. Gurgles & Growls: Learning about Your Stomach. Shipe, Becky, illus. 2004. (Amazing Body Ser.). (ENG.). 24p. (gr. k-3). per. 8.95 (978-1-4048-0504-0(4)) Picture Window Bks.

Northrup, Christiane. Beautiful Girl: Celebrating the Wonders of Your Body. 2013. (ENG., Illus.). 28p. 14.95 (978-1-4019-3403-3(X)) Hay Hse., Inc.

Nuestro Cuerpo Habla, 6 vols., Vol. 3. (Explorers. Exploradores Nonfiction Sets Ser.). (SPA.). (gr. 3-6). *(978-0-7699-0657-7(5))* Shortland Pubns. (U. S. A.) Inc.

Okido. Head to Toe: My Body & How It Works. 2012. (ENG., Illus.). 64p. (J). (gr. -1-3). 19.95 *(978-0-500-65005-9(5), 565005)* Thames & Hudson.

Omoto, Garrett, illus. Ke Kino - The Body. 2006. Orig. Title: Ke Kino. (HAW.). 16p. (J). 8.95 *(978-1-933835-02-0(8))* Partners in Development Foundation.

Osburn, Mary Rose. I Know Body Parts. 2016. (What I Know Ser.). 00024p. (J). pap. 8.15 *(978-1-4824-5453-6(X))* Stevens, Gareth Publishing LLLP.

O'Sullivan, Robyn. Your 206 Bones, 32 Teeth, & Other Body Math. 2006. (Science Chapters Ser.). (ENG., Illus.). 48p. (J). (gr. 1-4). lib. bdg. 17.90 *(978-0-7922-5955-8(6),* National Geographic Children's Bks.) National Geographic Society.

Our Busy Bodies, 6, Pack. (gr. k-1). 23.00 *(978-0-7635-9049-9(5))* Rigby Education.

Owen, Ruth. What Happens When I Eat? 2013. (My Body: Inside & Out! Ser.). 24p. (J). (gr. -1-3). lib. bdg. 23.93 *(978-1-909673-26-7(9))* Ruby Tuesday Books Limited GBR. Dist: Bearport Publishing Co., Inc.

—What Happens When I Grow? 2013. (My Body: Inside & Out! Ser.). 24p. (J). (gr. -1-3). lib. bdg. 23.93 *(978-1-909673-32-8(3))* Ruby Tuesday Books Limited GBR. Dist: Bearport Publishing Co., Inc.

—What Happens When I Move? 2013. (My Body: Inside & Out! Ser.). 24p. (J). (gr. -1-3). lib. bdg. 23.93 *(978-1-909673-28-1(5))* Ruby Tuesday Books Limited GBR. Dist: Bearport Publishing Co., Inc.

—What Happens When I Sleep? 2013. (My Body: Inside & Out! Ser.). 24p. (J). (gr. -1-3). lib. bdg. 23.93 *(978-1-909673-30-4(7))* Ruby Tuesday Books Limited GBR. Dist: Bearport Publishing Co., Inc.

Oxlade, Chris. Why Why Why Does My Heart Begin to Race? 2008. 32p. pap. *(978-1-84810-002-2(7))* Miles Kelly Publishing, Ltd.

—Why Why Why... Does My Heart Begin to Race? 2010. (Why Why Why Ser.). 32p. (J). (gr. 1-6). lib. bdg. 18.95 *(978-1-4222-1587-6(3))* Mason Crest.

Parker, Steve. The Human Body. 2010. (Mosaic of Magical Information Ser.). 48p. (YA). (gr. 3-18). 19.95 *(978-1-4222-1989-8(5))* Mason Crest.

—Human Body. 2013. (Illus.). 48p. (J). *(978-1-4351-5091-1(0))* Barnes & Noble, Inc.

—The Human Body Book. 2nd ed. 2013. (ENG., Illus.). 288p. 40.00 *(978-1-4654-0213-4(6),* DK) Dorling Kindersley Publishing, Inc.

—What about the Human Body. 2008. 40p. pap. *(978-1-84810-070-1(1))* Miles Kelly Publishing, Ltd.

Pérols, Sylvaine & Perols, Sylvaine. El Cuerpo. (Coleccion Mundo Maravilloso). (SPA., Illus.). 24p. (J). (gr. 2-4). *(978-84-348-6321-7(9),* SM30013) SM Ediciones ESP. Dist: Lectorum Pubns., Inc.

Petreycik, Rick. Headaches. 2006. (Health Alert Ser.). (Illus.). 64p. (J). (gr. 3-7). lib. bdg. 31.36 *(978-0-7614-2210-5(2),* Benchmark Bks.) Marshall Cavendish Corp.

Peyrols, Sylvaine. The Body. Peyrols, Sylvaine, illus. 2012. (ENG., Illus.). 36p. (J). (gr. -1-k). spiral bd. 12.99 *(978-1-85103-396-6(3))* Moonlight Publishing, Ltd. GBR. Dist: Independent Pubs. Group.

Pinnington, Andrea. Mi Cuerpo. 2012. (Scholastic Explora Tu Mundo Ser.). (SPA.). 32p. (J). (gr. -1-3). 7.99 *(978-0-545-45885-6(4),* Scholastic en Espanol) Scholastic, Inc.

—My Body. 2012. (Scholastic Discover More Ser.). (ENG., Illus.). 32p. (J). (gr. -1-3). 7.99 *(978-0-545-34514-9(6),* Scholastic Reference) Scholastic, Inc.

Pinnington, Andrea & Lamprell, Penny. My Body. 2012. (J). lib. bdg. *(978-0-531-22952-1(1))* Scholastic, Inc.

Podesto, Martine. The Body. 2008. (My Science Notebook Ser.). (Illus.). 104p. (YA). (gr. 5-9). lib. bdg. 31.00 *(978-0-8368-9212-3(7))* Stevens, Gareth Publishing LLLP.

Powell, Jillian. Sore Throat. 2008. (Feeling Sick? Ser.). (Illus.). 23p. (J). (gr. 1-4). lib. bdg. 27.10 *(978-1-84234-473-6(0))* Cherrytree Pubns., Inc.

Publications International Ltd. Staff, ed. Electronic Time for Learning: The Human Body. 2010. 120p. 18.98 *(978-1-4127-9854-9(X),* PIL Kids) Publications International, Ltd.

Qamaruddin, Rizwana. Allah Gave Me a Nose to Smell. Stratford, Stevan, illus. 2015. (ENG.). 32p. (J). 8.95 *(978-0-86037-333-9(9))* Kube Publishing Ltd. GBR. Dist: Consortium Bk. Sales & Distribution.

¿Que Hay Dentro de Mi? (Coleccion Primeros Pasos en la Ciencia). (SPA.). (J). (gr. 1-3). pap. *(978-950-724-156-7(6),* LMA8219) Lumen ARG. Dist: Lectorum Pubns., Inc.

¿Que Te Hace Enferma? (Coleccion Primeros Pasos en la Ciencia). (SPA., Illus.). (J). (gr. 1-3). *(978-950-724-495-7(6),* LMA8227) Lumen ARG. Dist: Lectorum Pubns., Inc.

Rabe, Tish. Inside Your Outside! All about the Human Body. Ruiz, Aristides, illus. 2003. (Cat in the Hat's Learning Library). (ENG.). 48p. (J). (gr. -1-3). 9.99 *(978-0-375-81100-5(1),* Random Hse. Bks. for Young Readers) Random Hse. Children's Bks.

Rajczak, Kristen. Freaky Stories about Our Bodies. 2015. (Freaky True Science Ser.). (ENG.). 32p. (J). (gr. 4-5). 26.60 *(978-1-4824-2962-6(4))* Stevens, Gareth Publishing LLLP.

Rake, Jody Sullivan. Why Feet Smell & Other Gross Facts about Your Body, 1 vol. 2012. (Gross Me Out Ser.). (ENG.). 24p. (gr. 1-2). pap. 7.29 *(978-1-4296-7955-8(7));* pap. 41.70 *(978-1-4296-8377-7(5));* lib. bdg. 25.32 *(978-1-4296-7610-6(8))* Capstone Press of Coughlan Cos. (First Facts).

Randolph, Joanne. Whose Nose Is This? 2009. (Animal Clues Ser.). (Illus.). 24p. (J). lib. bdg. 22.60 *(978-1-4042-4451-1(4),* PowerKids Pr.) Rosen Publishing Group, Inc., The.

—Whose Nose Is This? De Quién Es Esta Nariz? 2009. (Animal Clues / ¿Adivina de Quién Es? Ser.). (SPA & ENG., Illus.). 24p. (J). lib. bdg. 22.60 *(978-1-4358-2528-4(4),* PowerKids Pr.) Rosen Publishing Group, Inc., The.

Randolph, Joanne, ed. Microbes: The Good, the Bad, & the Ugly. 2017. (Amazing Human Body Ser.). 48p. (J). (gr. 6-6). pap. 11.70 ***(978-0-7660-8997-6(5))*** Enslow Pubs., Inc.

Reader's Digest Editors. God Made You. 2004. (Small Miracles Ser.: No. 1). 12p. (J). 5.99 *(978-1-4003-0314-4(1))* Nelson, Thomas Inc.

Reher, Matt & Taylor Fonzone. Top 10 Most Disgusting Facts about the Human Body. 2016. (2R Science Ser.). (ENG.). 32p. (J). pap. 5.99 ***(978-1-63437-603-7(X))*** American Reading Co.

—Top 10 Most Disgusting Facts about the Human Body (FSTK ONLY) 2016. (2r Fstk Ser.). (ENG.). 32p. (J). pap. 5.99 ***(978-1-63437-664-8(1))*** American Reading Co.

Reid, Stephanie. My Body, 1 vol. 2011. (Early Childhood Themes Ser.). (ENG.). 16p. (J). (gr. -1-2). pap. 6.99 *(978-1-4333-2367-6(2));* pap. 19.99 *(978-1-4333-2368-3(0))* Teacher Created Materials, Inc.

Reilly, Kathleen M. The Human Body: 25 Fantastic Projects Illuminate How the Body Works. Braley, Shawn, illus. 2008. (Build It Yourself Ser.). (ENG.). 128p. (J). (gr. 3-7). pap. 15.95 *(978-1-934670-24-8(3))* Octavio Publishing.

Rhatigan, Joe. Ouch! The Weird & Wild Ways Your Body Deals with Agonizing Aches, Ferocious Fevers, Lousy Lumps, Crummy Colds, Bothersome Bites, Breaks, Bruises & Burns & Makes Them Feel Better! Owsley, Anthony, illus. 2015. (ENG.). 80p. (J). (gr. 4-7). pap. 9.95 *(978-1-62354-053-1(4))* Charlesbridge Publishing, Inc.

Rice, Dona. Marvelous Me: My Face. 2015. (TIME for KIDS(r) Nonfiction Readers Ser.). (ENG., Illus.). 12p. (gr. k-k). 4.99 *(978-1-4938-2150-1(4))* Teacher Created Materials, Inc.

—Marvelous Me: My Feet. 2015. (TIME for KIDS(r) Nonfiction Readers Ser.). (ENG., Illus.). 12p. (gr. k-k). 4.99 *(978-1-4938-2149-5(0))* Teacher Created Materials, Inc.

—Marvelous Me: My Hands. 2015. (TIME for KIDS(r) Nonfiction Readers Ser.). (ENG., Illus.). 12p. (gr. k-k). 4.99 *(978-1-4938-2148-8(2))* Teacher Created Materials, Inc.

—Soy Maravilloso. 2016. (Nonfiction Readers Ser.). (SPA.). 12p. (J). (gr. k-k). pap. 4.99 *(978-1-4938-3029-9(5));* (Illus.). pap. 4.99 *(978-1-4938-3030-5(9))* Teacher Created Materials, Inc.

Richards, Jon. The Human Body. Simkins, Ed, illus. 2013. (World in Infographics Ser.). (ENG.). 32p. (J). (gr. 3-7). 15.95 *(978-1-926973-93-7(3))* Owlkids Bks. Inc. CAN. Dist: Publishers Group West (PGW).

RIGBY. Inside Our Bodies: Fourth Grade Class Collection Books. 2003. (Rigby on Our Way to English Ser.). (ENG.). 32p. (gr. 4-4). pap. 48.75 *(978-0-7578-4344-0(1))* Rigby Education.

Rigby Education Staff. Discovery World: My Body. (Discovery World Ser.). (Illus.). 12p. (gr. k-1). 23.00 *(978-0-7635-2697-9(5))* Rigby Education.

—Head, Shoulders, Knees & Toes. (Illus.). (J). suppl. ed. 20.00 *(978-0-7635-6429-2(X),* 764299C99) Rigby Education.

Ring, Susan. Body: An Interactive & 3-D Exploration. Graham, Michele, illus. 2008. (ENG.). 20p. (J). (gr. 2). 19.95 *(978-1-58117-801-2(8),* Intervisual/Piggy Toes) Bendon, Inc.

Ripley Entertainment Staff, contrib. by. Body & Mind. 2010. (Ripley's Believe It or Not Ser.). 36p. (YA). (gr. 3-18). lib. bdg. 19.95 *(978-1-4222-1532-6(6))* Mason Crest.

Ripley Publishing Staff & Ripley Entertainment, Inc Staff, contrib. by. Body Tales. 2013. (Illus.). 36p. (J). pap. *(978-1-4222-2792-3(8))* Mason Crest.

Ripley's Believe It or Not Editors & Ripley's Believe It Or Not! Staff. Ripley Twists: Human Body PORTRAIT EDN. 2014. (Twist Ser.). (ENG.). 48p. (J). 12.95 *(978-1-893951-84-6(7))* Ripley Entertainment, Inc.

Ripley's Believe It Or Not! Staff. Body Bizarre. 2012. (Ripley's Disbelief & Shock Ser.). 36p. (J). (gr. 3-4). 19.95 *(978-1-4222-2563-9(1))* Mason Crest.

—Body Tales. 2013. (Ripley's Believe It or Not! Strikingly True Ser.: 8). 36p. (J). (gr. 4-18). 19.95 *(978-1-4222-2775-6(8))* Mason Crest.

—Seeing Is Believing. 2012. (Ripley's Disbelief & Shock Ser.). 36p. (J). (gr. 3-4). 19.95 *(978-1-4222-2564-6(X))* Mason Crest.

Roberts, Christa. Guinness World Records: Amazing Body Records! 100 Mind-Blowing Body Records from Around the World! 2016. (J). lib. bdg. 16.00 *(978-0-606-38192-5(9))* Turtleback Bks.

Rockett, Paul. 100 Trillion Good Bacteria Living in the Human Body. Ruffle, Mark, illus. 2015. (Big Countdown Ser.). (ENG.). 32p. (gr. 3-5). 29.99 *(978-1-4109-6877-7(4),* Raintree Perspectives) Heinemann-Raintree.

Rockwell, Lizzy. The Busy Body Book: A Kid's Guide to Fitness. Rockwell, Lizzy, illus. (ENG., Illus.). 40p. (J). (gr. -1-2). 2008. pap. 7.99 *(978-0-553-11374-7(7),* Dragonfly Bks.) 2004. 15.95 *(978-0-375-82203-2(8),* Crown Books For Young Readers) Random Hse. Children's Bks.

—Busy Body Book: A Kid's Guide to Fitness. 2014. 17.00 *(978-1-63419-689-5(9))* Perfection Learning Corp.

Rogers, Simon. Information Graphics: Human Body. Grundy, Peter, illus. 2014. (ENG.). 80p. (J). (gr. 1-4). 17.99 *(978-0-7636-7123-5(1),* Big Picture Press) Candlewick Pr.

Rooney, Anne. A Math Journey Through the Human Body. 2014. (ENG.). 32p. (J). *(978-0-7787-0734-9(2))* Crabtree Publishing Co.

Rosa-Mendoza, Gladys. My Body/Mi Cuerpo. Butler, Chris, illus. 2007. (English Spanish Foundations Ser.). (ENG & SPA.). 20p. (gr. -1-2). pap. 19.95 *(978-1-931398-85-5(2))* Me+Mi Publishing.

Rosa-Mendoza, Gladys, creator. My Body. 2004. (English-Spanish Foundations Ser.: 8).Tr. of Mi Cuerpo. (SPA & ENG., Illus.). 20p. (J). bds. 6.95 *(978-1-931398-08-4(9))* Me+Mi Publishing.

Rose, Simon. Muscular System. 2014. (J). *(978-1-4896-1170-3(3))* Weigl Pubs., Inc.

Rosen Publishing Staff. Let's Find Out! the Human Body, 1 vol. 2015. (Let's Find Out! Ser.). (ENG.). 32p. (J). 187.60 *(978-1-62275-655-1(X),* Britannica Educational Publishing) Rosen Publishing Group, Inc., The.

Ross, Michael. Body Cycles. 2003. (Illus.). 32p. (J). (gr. 2-5). pap. 7.95 *(978-0-7613-1976-4(X),* First Avenue Editions) Lerner Publishing Group.

Rotner, Shelley. Body Actions. Rotner, Shelley & White, David A., illus. 2012. (ENG.). 32p. (J). 16.95 *(978-0-8234-2366-8(2))* Holiday Hse., Inc.

Royston, Angela. Bones & Muscles. 2011. (Your Body Inside & Out Ser.). (Illus.). 32p. (J). (gr. 3-6). lib. bdg. 28.50 *(978-1-59771-263-7(9))* Sea-To-Sea Pubns.

Roza, Greg. Indside the Human Body: Using Exonential & Scientific Notation. 2006. (Math Big Bookstm Ser.). (ENG.). 32p. (gr. 6-7). 47.50 *(978-1-4042-6366-6(7))* Rosen Publishing Group, Inc., The.

—Inside the Human Body: Using Scientific & Exponential Notation. (Math for the Real World Ser.). 32p. 2009. (ENG., Illus.). (gr. 6-7). pap. 10.00 *(978-1-4042-6077-1(3))* 2009. (gr. 5-5). 47.90 *(978-1-60851-359-8(9),* PowerKids Pr.) 2006. (Illus.). (YA). (gr. 5-9). lib. bdg. 25.25 *(978-1-4042-3362-1(8))* Rosen Publishing Group, Inc., The.

—The Skeletal System. 2012. (Human Body Ser.). (ENG., Illus.). 32p. (J). (gr. 4-6). pap. 10.50 *(978-1-4339-6598-2(4),* Gareth Stevens Learning Library); lib. bdg. 26.60 *(978-1-4339-6596-8(8))* Stevens, Gareth Publishing LLLP.

Rustad, Martha E. H. My Body, 1 vol. 2013. (Little Scientist Ser.). (ENG., 32p. (gr. 1-2). Illus.). 6.95 *(978-1-4765-3544-9(2));* 27.99 *(978-1-4765-0250-2(1));* pap. 6.95 *(978-1-4765-3550-0(7))* Capstone Press of Coughlan Cos.

Sachse, Dina, illus. My Body: 12 Lift-N-Learn Flashcards about the Human Body, 12 vols. 2013. (Early Start Singles Ser.). (ENG.). 12p. (J). *(978-1-77132-070-2(2))* SpiceBox Products Ltd.

Saddleback, creator. Human Body. 2008. (Factoscope Ser.). (Illus.). 64p. (YA). (gr. 8-12). per. 10.95 *(978-1-59905-234-2(2))* Saddleback Educational Publishing, Inc.

Saltz, Gail. Amazing You! Getting Smart about Your Private Parts. Cravath, Lynne Avril, illus. 2005. (ENG.). 32p. (J). (gr. -1-2). 16.99 *(978-0-525-47389-3(0),* Dutton Books for Young Readers) Penguin Young Readers Group.

Samuels, Charlie. Astonishing Bodies. 2012. (ENG.). 32p. (J). *(978-0-7787-8006-9(6));* pap. *(978-0-7787-8011-3(2))* Crabtree Publishing Co.

Sarkisian, K. You Need Your Nose: Learning the N Sound. 2009. (PowerPhonics Ser.). 24p. (gr. 1-1). 39.90 *(978-1-60851-482-3(X),* PowerKids Pr.) Rosen Publishing Group, Inc., The.

Sayer, Melissa & Naik, Anita. Too Fat? Too Thin? The Healthy Eating Handbook. 2009. (Really Useful Handbooks Ser.). (ENG., Illus.). 48p. (J). (gr. 5-11). pap. *(978-0-7787-4405-4(1));* lib. bdg. *(978-0-7787-4392-7(6))* Crabtree Publishing Co.

Scholastic, Inc. Staff, contrib. by. Where Is Your Nose? 2015. (Rookie Toddler(tm) Ser.). (ENG., Illus.). 12p. (J). bds. 6.95 *(978-0-531-21263-9(7),* Children's Pr.) Scholastic Library Publishing.

Schumacher, Bev. Body Parts / Las Partes Del Cuerpo: Partes Del Cuerpo. 2005.Tr. of Las Partes Del Cuerpo. (SPA & ENG., Illus.). 20p. (J). lib. bdg. 9.95 *(978-0-9741549-4-7(6))* Learning Props.

—Body Parts (Chinese-English) 2008. 20p. (J). lib. bdg. 9.95 *(978-1-935292-01-2(3))* Learning Props.

Schumacher, Bev, creator. Body Parts. 2005. 20p. (J). lib. bdg. 9.95 *(978-0-9768706-0-9(6))* Learning Props.

Seidlitz, Lauri. Human Body. 2007. (Life Science (Weigl Hardcover) Ser.). (Illus.). 32p. (J). (gr. 4-7). lib. bdg. 26.00 *(978-1-59036-705-6(7));* per. 9.95 *(978-1-59036-706-3(5))* Weigl Pubs., Inc.

Senior, Kathryn. The Human Body. 2016. (Wise Up Ser.). 32p. (gr. 2-6). 31.35 *(978-1-62588-340-7(4),* Smart Apple Media) Black Rabbit Bks.

Shand, Jennifer. Why Do Feet Get So Stinky? 2015. (Why Do... ? Ser.). lib. bdg. 19.65 *(978-1-4867-0623-5(1))* Turtleback Bks.

Shea, John M. Gross Things about Your Body. 2012. (That's Gross! Ser.). (Illus.). 24p. (J). (gr. 2-5). pap. 8.15 *(978-1-4339-7112-9(7));* lib. bdg. 22.60 *(978-1-4339-7111-2(9))* Stevens, Gareth Publishing LLLP.

Shufen, Li. Questions about the Human Body. 2003. 62p. pap. *(978-7-80051-850-8(7))* Dolphin Books, China.

Sian Revision Body Basics. 2004. (Science in A Nutshell Ser.). (J). *(978-1-59242-004-9(4))* Delta Education, LLC.

Sian Revision Human Machine. 2004. (J). *(978-1-59242-077-3(X))* Delta Education, LLC.

Sian revision peek inside You. 2004. (Science in A Nutshell Ser.). (Illus.). (J). *(978-1-59242-000-1(1))* Delta Education, LLC.

Sideri, Simona. Let's Look at Mouths. Noble, Sheilagh, illus. 2003. (Let's Look at Ser.). 24p. (J). *(978-1-84089-147-8(5))* Zero to Ten, Ltd.

Silver Dolphin Staff. Cuerpo humano/Human Body. 2011. 16p. *(978-607-404-318-1(3),* Silver Dolphin en Español) Advanced Marketing, S. de R. L. de C. V.

Silverman, Buffy. Body Parts: Double-Jointedness, Hitchhiker's Thumb, & More. 2012. (Lightning Bolt Books (tm) — What Traits Are in Your Genes? Ser.). (Illus.). 32p. (gr. k-2). (SPA & ENG.). pap. 7.95 *(978-1-58013-953-3(1));* (ENG., lib. bdg. 26.60 *(978-0-7613-8942-2(3),* Lerner Pubns.) Lerner Publishing Group.

Simon, Seymour & Carle, Eric. De la Cabeza a los Pies, 1 vol. Carle, Eric, illus. 2003.Tr. of From Head to Toe. (SPA., Illus.). 32p. (J). (gr. -1-3). 17.99 *(978-0-06-051302-3(0))* HarperCollins Pubs.

SMARTLAB Creative Team. Inside Out! the Human Body. 2010. 12p. mass mkt. 39.99 *(978-1-60380-052-5(2))* becker&mayer! books.

Smith, A. & Tatchell, J. How are Babies Made? How do Your Senses Work? What Happens to Your Food? rev. ed. 2004. (Flip Flaps Ser.). 48p. (J). (gr. 2-18). 14.95 *(978-0-7945-0618-6(6),* Usborne) EDC Publishing.

Solway, Andrew. Growing. 2011. (Your Body Inside & Out Ser.). (Illus.). 32p. (J). (gr. 3-6). lib. bdg. 28.50 *(978-1-59771-265-1(5))* Sea-To-Sea Pubns.

Souza, Dorothy M. Look What Mouths Can Do. 2006. (Look What Animals Can Do Ser.). (Illus.). 48p. (J). (gr. -1-3). lib. bdg. 22.60 *(978-0-7613-9462-4(1),* Lerner Pubns.) Lerner Publishing Group.

Spilsbury, Louise. Head-to-Toe Body Questions. 2010. (Crabtree Connections Ser.). (ENG.). 24p. (J). (gr. 3-6). *(978-0-7787-9954-2(9));* pap. *(978-0-7787-9976-4(X))* Crabtree Publishing Co.

—Respiration & Circulation. 2016. (Human Machine Ser.). (ENG.). 32p. pap. 8.29 *(978-1-4846-3819-4(0),* Heinemann InfoSearch) Heinemann-Raintree.

Stark, Freddy. Gray's Anatomy: A Fact-Filled Coloring Book. 2011. (ENG.). 128p. (J). (gr. -1-17). pap. 12.95 *(978-0-7624-4073-3(2))* Running Pr. Bk. Pubs.

Starry Dog Books. The Human Body. Stalio, Ivan, illus. 2007. (Back to Basics Ser.). 31p. (J). lib. bdg. *(978-88-6098-050-2(X))* McRae Bks. Srl.

Steck-Vaughn Staff. Bones! The Frame Inside Us. 2003. pap. 4.10 *(978-0-7398-7630-5(9))* Steck-Vaughn.

Steele, Philip. My Body. 2009. (Now We Know About... Ser.). (ENG., Illus.). 24p. (J). (gr. k-3). pap. *(978-0-7787-4738-3(7))* Crabtree Publishing Co.

Steele, Philip & Goldsmith, Mike. My Body. 2009. (ENG., Illus.). 24p. (J). (gr. k-4). lib. bdg. *(978-0-7787-4721-5(2))* Crabtree Publishing Co.

Stevens, Noel. In the Never-Never-Converse with an Archangel. 2008. 132p. pap. 13.95 *(978-0-595-52727-4(2))* iUniverse, Inc.

Stewart, David. How Your Body Works: A Good Look Inside You Insides. Franklin, Carolyn, illus. 2008. (Amaze Ser.). (ENG.). 32p. (J). (gr. k-3). pap. 8.95 *(978-0-531-20455-9(3),* Children's Pr.) Scholastic Library Publishing.

—How Your Body Works: A Good Look Inside Your Insides. Franklin, Carolyn, illus. 2008. (Amaze Ser.). (ENG.). 32p. (J). (gr. k-3). 27.00 *(978-0-531-20444-3(8),* Children's Pr.) Scholastic Library Publishing.

Stewart, Gregory J. The Skeletal & Muscular Systems. 2009. (Human Body: How It Works Ser.). (Illus.). 136p. (C). (gr. 9-18). 35.00 *(978-1-60413-365-3(1),* Chelsea Hse.) Facts On File, Inc.

Stewart, Melissa. The Bone Zone: The Secrets of Muscles & Bones. 2010. (Gross & Goofy Body 2 Ser.). 48p. (gr. 3). 29.93 *(978-0-7614-4166-3(2))* Marshall Cavendish Corp.

—Give Me a Hand: The Secrets of Hands, Feet, Arms, & Legs. Hamlin, Janet, illus. 2010. (Gross & Goofy Body 2 Ser.). 48p. (gr. 3). lib. bdg. 29.93 *(978-0-7614-4158-8(1))* Marshall Cavendish Corp.

—The Gross & Goofy Body, 6 vols., Set. Incl. Blasts of Gas: The Secrets of Breathing, Burping, & Farting. 29.93 *(978-0-7614-4155-7(7));* Eyes Have It: The Secrets of Eyes & Seeing. Hamlin, Janet, illus. 29.93 *(978-0-7614-4167-0(0));* It's Spit-Acular! The Secrets of Saliva. Hamlin, Janet, illus. 29.93 *(978-0-7614-4163-2(8));* Now Hear This! The Secrets of Ears & Hearing. Hamlin, Janet, illus. 29.93 *(978-0-7614-4161-8(1));* Pump It Up! The Secrets of the Heart & Blood. Hamlin, Janet, illus. 29.93 *(978-0-7614-4164-9(6));* Up Your Nose! The Secrets of Schnozes & Snouts. Hamlin, Janet, illus. 29.93 *(978-0-7614-4170-0(0));* 48p. (gr. 3-4). (Gross & Goofy Body Ser.). 2009. Set lib. bdg. 179.58 o.p. *(978-0-7614-4154-0(9))* Marshall Cavendish Corp.

—Up Your Nose! The Secrets of Schnozes & Snouts. Hamlin, Janet, illus. 2009. (Gross & Goofy Body Ser.). 48p. (gr. 3-4). 29.93 *(978-0-7614-4170-0(0))* Marshall Cavendish Corp.

Stinson, Kathy. The Bare Naked Book. Collins, Heather, illus. 20th ed. 2006. (ENG.). 32p. (J). (gr. -1-1). 19.95 *(978-1-55451-050-4(3),* 9781554510504); pap. 6.95 *(978-1-55451-049-8(X),* 9781554510498) Annick Pr., Ltd. CAN. Dist: Publishers Group West (PGW).

Stowell, Louie. Look Inside Your Body. (Look Inside Board Bks). (J). 2011. 13p. ring bd. 15.99 *(978-0-7945-2996-3(8))* 2013. 10p. ring bd. 14.99 *(978-0-7945-3311-3(6))* EDC Publishing. (Usborne).

Stoyles, Pennie & Pentland, Peter. The Human Body. 2011. (Energy in Action Ser.). (Illus.). 32p. (J). (gr. 4). 28.50 *(978-1-60870-570-2(6))* Marshall Cavendish GBR. Dist: Marshall Cavendish Corp.

Street, Pat & Brace, Eric. You're Pulling My Leg! 400 Human-Body Sayings from Head to Toe. Brace, Eric, illus. (ENG., Illus.). 48p. (J). (gr. 1-5). 2017. 8.99 *(978-0-8234-3772-6(8))* 2016. 18.95 *(978-0-8234-2135-0(X))* Holiday Hse., Inc.

Sullivan, Erin Ash. Human Body Math & Matemáticas del cuerpo Humano: 6 English, 6 Spanish Adaptations. 2011. (ENG & SPA.). (J). 89.00 net. *(978-1-4108-5682-1(8))* Benchmark Education Co.

Sundance/Newbridge LLC Staff. The Human Body. 2007. (Early Science Ser.). (gr. k-3). 18.95 *(978-1-4007-6161-6(1));* pap. 6.10 *(978-1-4007-6157-9(3))* Sundance/Newbridge Educational Publishing.

Swanson, Diane. You Are Weird: Your Body's Peculiar Parts & Funny Functions. Boake, Kathy, illus. 2009. (ENG.). 40p. (J). (gr. 3-7). 16.95 *(978-1-55453-282-7(5));* pap. 7.95 *(978-1-55453-283-4(3))* Kids Can Pr., Ltd. CAN. Dist: Hachette Bk. Group.

Taylor, Barbara. Slide & Discover: Human Body. 2015. (Slide & Discover Ser.). (ENG., Illus.). 24p. (J). (gr. 1). 19.95 *(978-1-60710-810-8(0),* Silver Dolphin Bks.) Readerlink Distribution Services, LLC.

Taylor-Butler, Christine. The Digestive System. 2008. (True Bks.). (ENG., Illus.). 48p. (J). (gr. 3-7). 29.00 *(978-0-531-16857-8(3),* Children's Pr.) Scholastic Library Publishing.

—The Respitory System. 2008. (True Book(tm), a — Health & the Human Body Ser.). (ENG., Illus.). 48p. (J). (gr. 3-7). 31.00 *(978-0-531-16862-2(X),* Children's Pr.) Scholastic Library Publishing.

—Tiny Life on Your Body. 2006. (Rookie Read-about Science Ser.). (Illus.). 31p. (J). (gr. 1-2). 12.60 *(978-0-7569-7120-5(9))* Perfection Learning Corp.

—Tiny Life on Your Body. 2005. (Rookie Read-About Science Ser.). (ENG., Illus.). 32p. (J). (gr. 1-2). lib. bdg. 20.50 *(978-0-516-25299-5(2),* Children's Pr.) Scholastic Library Publishing.

—A True Book: Health & the Human Body, 7 vols., Set. Incl. Circulatory System. (Illus.). 31.00 *(978-0-531-16856-1(5));* Digestive System. (Illus.). 29.00 *(978-0-531-16857-8(3));* Nervous System. 31.00 *(978-0-531-16861-5(1));* Respitory System. (Illus.). 31.00 *(978-0-531-16862-2(X));* 48p. (J). (gr. 3-7). (True Bks.). 2008. Set lib. bdg. 261.00 *(978-0-531-20545-7(2),* Children's Pr.) Scholastic Library Publishing.

Taylor-Butler, Christine & National Geographic Learning Staff. Tiny Life on Your Body. 2010. (Rise & Shine Ser.). (ENG., Illus.). 32p. (C). (gr. 1-2). per. 21.95 *(978-0-516-25480-7(4))* National Geographic School Publishing, Inc.

Theisen, Patricia. The Enchanting Song of the Human: Composed of Thoughts Generated by Ancient Eastern Tradition & Modern Western Science. 2005. (Illus.). 500p. *(978-0-9793076-0-7(0))* Theisen, Patricia.

—A Magical Mystery Tour of hte Senses: What Does it Mean to be a Human? All about Your Body & You, 1 CD. Theisen, Patricia, illus. l.t. ed. 2007. (Illus.). 160p. (YA). *(978-0-9793076-1-4(9))* Theisen, Patricia.

H
I

Throp, Claire. A Day Inside the Human Body: Fantasy Science Field Trips, 1 vol. 2014. (Fantasy Science Field Trips Ser.). (ENG., Illus.). 32p. (gr. 1-3). lib. bdg. 29.99 (978-1-4109-6199-0(0), Read Me!) Heinemann-Raintree.

—Fantasy Science Field Trips, 1 vol. 2014. (Fantasy Science Field Trips Ser.). (ENG.). 32p. (gr. 1-3). lib. bdg. 119.96 (978-1-4109-6201-0(6), Read Me!) Heinemann-Raintree.

Tieck, Sarah. Body Systems, 6 vols., Set. Incl. Circulatory System. lib. bdg. 27.07 (978-1-61613-497-6(6)); Digestive System. lib. bdg. 27.07 (978-1-61613-498-3(4)); Muscular System. lib. bdg. 27.07 (978-1-61613-499-0(2)); Nervous System. lib. bdg. 27.07 (978-1-61613-500-3(X)); Respiratory System. lib. bdg. 27.07 (978-1-61613-501-0(8)); Skeletal System. lib. bdg. 27.07 (978-1-61613-502-7(6)); (J). (gr. 2-5). (Body Systems Ser.). (Illus.). 32p. 2011. 162.42 (978-1-61613-496-9(8), Buddy Bks.) ABDO Publishing Co.

—Circulatory System, 1 vol. 2011. (Body Systems Ser.). (ENG., Illus.). 32p. (J). (gr. 2-5). lib. bdg. 27.07 (978-1-61613-497-6(6)) ABDO Publishing Co.

—Digestive System, 1 vol. 2011. (Body Systems Ser.). (ENG., Illus.). 32p. (J). (gr. 2-5). lib. bdg. 27.07 (978-1-61613-498-3(4)) ABDO Publishing Co.

Tilden, Thomasine E. Lewis & Lewis-Tilden, Thomasine E. Belly-Busting Worm Invasions! Parasites That Love Your Insides! 2007. (24/7: Science Behind the Scenes Ser.). (ENG., Illus.). 64p. (J). (gr. 9-12). 29.00 (978-0-531-12068-2(6)); pap. 7.95 (978-0-531-18736-4(5)) Scholastic Library Publishing. (Watts, Franklin).

Top That Publishing Staff, ed. Human Body. 2004. (Know How Know Why Ser.). (Illus.). (J). 48p. pap. (978-1-84510-027-8(1)); 24p. pap. (978-1-84510-115-2(4)); 48p. pap. (978-1-84510-046-9(8)) Top That! Publishing PLC.

Towne, Isobel & Viegas, Jennifer. The Mouth & Nose in 3D. 2015. (Human Body In 3D Ser.). (ENG., Illus.). 64p. (J). (gr. 5-6). 32.95 (978-1-4994-3609-9(2), Rosen Central) Rosen Publishing Group, Inc., The.

Townsend, John. 101 Things You Didn't Know about Your Body, 1 vol. 2011. (101 Ser.). (ENG., Illus.). 56p. (gr. 5-9). 34.65 (978-1-4109-3896-1(4), NA-r) Heinemann-Raintree.

Turnbull, Stephanie. Your Body. 2006. (Beginners Science: Level 2 Ser.). (Illus.). 32p. (J). (gr. 1-3). 4.99 (978-0-7945-1402-0(2), Usborne) EDC Publishing.

TUXWORTH NICOLA. Bodies. 2014. (ENG., Illus.). 20p. (J). (gr. k-2). bds. 6.99 (978-1-84322-860-8(2), Armadillo) Anness Publishing GBR. Dist: National Bk. Network.

Unbelievable Bodies. 2014. (Ripleys Believe It or Not! Dare to Look Ser.: 8). 36p. (J). (gr. 4-18). lib. bdg. 20.95 (978-1-4222-3146-3(1)) Mason Crest.

Understanding the Human Body, 6 vols., Set. Incl. Understanding Food & Digestion. Snedden, Robert. lib. bdg. 29.25 (978-1-4358-9687-1(4)); Understanding Muscles & the Skeleton. Snedden, Robert. lib. bdg. 29.25 (978-1-4358-9686-4(6)); Understanding Reproduction. Ballard, Carol. lib. bdg. 29.25 (978-1-4358-9682-6(3)); Understanding the Brain & the Nervous System. Snedden, Robert. lib. bdg. 29.25 (978-1-4358-9685-7(8)); Understanding the Heart, Lungs, & Blood. Levete, Sarah. lib. bdg. 29.25 (978-1-4358-9684-0(X)); Understanding the Senses. Ballard, Carol. lib. bdg. 29.25 (978-1-4358-9683-3(1)); (YA). (gr. 5-8). 2010. (Illus.). 48p. 2010. Set lib. bdg. 159.00 (978-1-4358-9706-9(4), Rosen Reference) Rosen Publishing Group, Inc., The.

Valat, Pierre-Marie & Houbre, Gilbert. Inside the Body. Valat, Pierre-Marie, illus. 2012. (ENG., Illus.). 36p. (J). (gr. -1-k). 14.99 (978-1-85103-412-3(9)) Moonlight Publishing, Ltd. GBR. Dist: Independent Pubs. Group.

Vander Klipp, Michael. God Made My Body, 1 vol. 2008. (God Made... Ser.). 14p. (J). bds. 3.99 (978-0-8254-3912-4(4)) Kregel Pubns.

Vermond, Kira. Growing Up, Inside & Out. 2013. 104p. (978-1-77147-036-0(4)) Owlkids Bks. Inc.

Waibel, Stacy Raye. Rudy's Incredible Kidney Machine. Gruebele, Michelle, illus. 2011. 32p. (J). 10.95 (978-0-9820983-3-2(2)) Purple Cow Pr.

Waldron, Melanie. Human Body. 2013. (Essential Life Science Ser.). (ENG.). 48p. (gr. 4-6). 33.32 (978-1-4329-7806-8(3), Heinemann InfoSearch) Heinemann-Raintree.

—Your Body by Numbers, 1 vol. 2014. (Your Body by Numbers Ser.). (ENG.). 48p. (gr. 3-5). lib. bdg. 130.60 (978-1-4109-5984-3(8)) Heinemann-Raintree.

Waldron, Melanie, et al. Essential Life Science, 1 vol. 2014. (Essential Life Science Ser.). (ENG.). 48p. (gr. 4-6). lib. bdg. 133.28 (978-1-4329-7814-3(4), Heinemann InfoSearch) Heinemann-Raintree.

Walker, Richard. Body: [an Amazing Tour of Human Anatomy]. 2014. (Illus.). 96p. (J). (978-1-4351-5684-5(6)) Barnes & Noble, Inc.

—Build the Human Body. Bernstein, Galia & Ruffle, Mark, illus. 2013. (Build It Ser.). (ENG.). 32p. (J). (gr. k). 19.95 (978-1-60710-413-1(X), Silver Dolphin Bks.) Readerlink Distribution Services, LLC.

—Human Body. 2006. (Kingfisher Knowledge Ser.). (Illus.). 64p. (J). (978-0-7534-1317-3(5), Kingfisher) Roaring Brook Pr.

Wanjie, Anne, ed. The Basics of the Human Body. 2013. (Core Concepts Ser.). (ENG., Illus.). 96p. (YA). (gr. 7-12). lib. bdg. 34.60 (978-1-4777-0555-1(4)) Rosen Publishing Group, Inc., The.

Waters, Sophie. The Female Reproductive System. 2009. (Girls' Health Ser.). 48p. (gr. 5-6). 53.00 (978-1-61512-732-0(1), Rosen Reference) Rosen Publishing Group, Inc., The.

Watkins, Christine. Is Selling Body Parts Ethical? 2012. (At Issue Ser.). (ENG.). 128p. (gr. 10-12). lib. bdg. 39.40 (978-0-7377-6189-4(X), Greenhaven Pr., Inc.) Cengage Gale.

Watkins, Christine, ed. Is Selling Body Parts Ethical? 2012. (At Issue Ser.). (ENG.). 128p. (gr. 10-12). pap. 24.45 (978-0-7377-6190-0(3), Greenhaven Pr., Inc.) Cengage Gale.

Weber, Rebecca. Health & Your Body. 2012. (Health & Your Body Ser.). (ENG.). 24p. (gr. k-1). pap. 333.60 (978-1-4296-8349-4(X)); pap. 43.74 (978-1-4296-8348-7(1)); lib. bdg. 79.95 (978-1-4296-6838-5(5)); lib. bdg. 213.20 (978-1-4296-8140-7(3)) Capstone Press of Coughlan Cos. (Pebble Plus).

—How Your Body Works, 1 vol. (Health & Your Body Ser.). (ENG.). 24p. (gr. k-1). 2011. pap. 7.29 (978-1-4296-7128-6(9)) 2011. pap. 41.70 (978-1-4296-7134-7(3)) 2010. lib. bdg. 26.65 (978-1-4296-6609-1(9)) Capstone Press of Coughlan Cos. (Pebble Plus).

Weber, Rebecca, et al. Health & Your Body. 2011. (Health & Your Body Ser.). (ENG.). 24p. (gr. k-1). pap. 250.20 (978-1-4296-7138-5(6)); lib. bdg. 159.90 (978-1-4296-6839-2(3)); lib. bdg. 53.30 (978-1-4296-8568-9(9)); pap. 41.70 (978-1-4296-7137-8(8)) Capstone Press of Coughlan Cos. (Pebble Plus).

Weschler, Toni. Cycle Savvy: The Smart Teen's Guide to the Mysteries of Her Body. 2006. (ENG., Illus.). 240p. pap. 15.99 (978-0-06-082964-3(8), Harper Perennial) HarperCollins Pubs.

What's Inside Me?, 5 Bks, Set. 2004. (J). 128.14 (978-0-7614-1776-7(1)) Marshall Cavendish Corp.

Whittemore, Susan. The Respiratory System. 2009. (Human Body: How It Works Ser.). (Illus.). 112p. (C). (gr. 9-18). 35.00 (978-1-60413-375-2(9), Chelsea Hse.) Facts On File, Inc.

Wicks, Maris. Human Body Theater. 2015. (ENG., Illus.). 240p. (J). (gr. 4-8). pap. 14.99 (978-1-59643-929-0(7), 9781596439290, First Second Bks.) Roaring Brook Pr.

Wilcox, Christine. Teens & Body Image. 2015. (ENG., Illus.). 80p. (J). lib. bdg. (978-1-60152-828-5(0)) ReferencePoint Pr., Inc.

Wile, Jay L. & Shannon, Marilyn. Companion CD-ROM for the Human Body: Fearfully & Wonderfully Made! on CD-ROM. 2004. cd-rom 15.00 (978-1-932012-53-8(2)) Apologia Educational Ministries, Inc.

Wilkes, Angela, contrib. by. Mi Cuerpo y Yo: Me & My Body. 2004. (Ladders Ser.). (SPA & ENG., Illus.). 32p. (J). (gr. -1-3). 12.95 (978-1-58728-443-4(X)) Cooper Square Publishing Llc.

Winston, Jeannie, illus. Head, Shoulders, Knees, & Toes. 2005. (Ready-to-Read Ser.). 24p. (J). lib. bdg. 15.00 (978-1-59054-962-9(7)) Fitzgerald Bks.

Winston, Robert. My Amazing Body Machine. Gildersleeve, Owen, illus. 2017. (ENG.). 128p. (J). (gr. 2-4). 19.99 (978-1-4654-6185-8(X), DK Children) Dorling Kindersley Publishing, Inc.

—What Makes Me, Me? 2015. (Big Questions Ser.). (ENG., Illus.). 96p. (J). (gr. 5-12). pap. 9.99 (978-1-4654-3905-5(6), DK Children) Dorling Kindersley Publishing, Inc.

Winters, Pierre. My Body. van Lindenhuizen, Eline, illus. 2013. (Want to Know Ser.). (ENG.). 32p. (J). (gr. k-2). 16.95 (978-1-60537-143-6(2)) Cobblestone Publishing Co.

Wohnoutka, Mike, illus. Head, Shoulders, Knees, & Toes. 2009. (J). (978-0-545-15604-2(1)) Scholastic, Inc.

Wood, Alix. Body Bugs. 2013. (Earth's Grossest Animals Ser.). 32p. (J). (gr. k-5). pap. 10.00 (978-1-61533-781-1(4), PowerKids Pr.) Rosen Publishing Group, Inc., The.

Woodward, John. What Lives on Your Body? 2007. (What Lives in... ? Ser.). (Illus.). 48p. (gr. 2-6). lib. bdg. 27.00 (978-0-8368-7861-5(2), Gareth Stevens Learning Library) Stevens, Gareth Publishing LLLP.

Woodward, John & Gray, Leon. Our Bodies. 2007. (Close-up Ser.). (Illus.). 32p. (J). (gr. -1-3). lib. bdg. (978-1-933834-17-7(X)) Brown Bear Books.

World Book, Inc Staff, contrib. by. The Digestive System/The Urinary System. 2006. (World Book's Human Body Works). (Illus.). 48p. (J). (978-0-7166-4429-3(0)) World Bk., Inc.

—Encyclopedia of Human Beings, 2 vols. 2014. (Illus.). (J). (978-0-7166-7520-4(X)) World Bk., Inc.

—The Endocrine & Reproductive Systems. 2013. (J). (978-0-7166-1844-7(3)) World Bk., Inc.

—Explore & Learn-Me & My Body. 2008. (J). (978-0-7166-3021-0(4)) World Bk., Inc.

—My Body. 2007. (J). (978-0-7166-7727-7(X)) World Bk., Inc.

—The Respiratory System. 2006. (World Book's Human Body Works). (Illus.). 48p. (J). (978-0-7166-4428-6(2)) World Bk., Inc.

World Book's Human Body Works, 6 vols., Set. 2007. 288p. (gr. 4-8). 149.00 (978-0-7166-4425-5(8), 40051) World Bk., Inc.

Wynne, Patricia J. & Silver, Donald M. BOOST My First Human Body Coloring Book. 2013. (BOOST Educational Ser.). (ENG.). 32p. (J). (gr. 1-2). pap. 4.99 (978-0-486-49410-4(1)) Dover Pubns., Inc.

—My First Human Body Book. 2009. (Dover Children's Science Bks.). (ENG., Illus.). 32p. (J). (gr. 1-5). pap. 3.99 (978-0-486-46821-1(6)) Dover Pubns., Inc.

Yount, Lisa. The Father of Anatomy: Galen & His Dissections. 2009. (Great Minds of Ancient Science & Math Ser.). (Illus.). 128p. (J). (gr. 4-7). lib. bdg. 33.27 (978-0-7660-3380-1(5)) Enslow Pubs., Inc.

Your Body at Its Grossest. 2017. (Your Body at Its Grossest Ser.). 24p. (gr. 1-2). pap. 48.90 (978-1-5382-0494-8(0)); lib. bdg. 135.60 (978-1-5382-0480-1(0)) Stevens, Gareth Publishing LLLP.

Zuchora-Walske, Christine. The Amazing Human Body. 2018. (ENG.). 32p. (gr. 3-6). 31.35 (978-1-63235-416-7(0), 12-Story Library) Pr. Room Editions LLC.

Zuchora-Walske, Christine. Your Head Shape Reveals Your Personality! Science's Biggest Mistakes about the Human Body. 2014. (Science Gets It Wrong Ser.). (Illus.). 32p. (gr. 4-6). pap. 7.95 (978-1-4677-4551-2(0)); (ENG., (J). lib. bdg. 26.60 (978-1-4677-3661-9(9), Lerner Pubns.) Lerner Publishing Group.

HUMAN BODY—FICTION

Aronson, Deborah. Where's My Tushy? Stevanovic, Ivica, illus. 2014. (ENG.). 24p. (J). (gr. -1-3). 17.95 (978-1-4677-1197-5(7), Carolrhoda Bks.) Lerner Publishing Group.

Camilleri, Andrea. The Story of the Nose. Sartarelli, Stephen, tr. from ITA. Celija, Maja, illus. 2016. (Save the Story Ser.). (ENG.). 104p. (J). (gr. 3-7). 19.95 (978-1-78269-017-7(4), Pushkin Press) Steerforth Pr.

Davick, Linda. I Love You, Nose! I Love You, Toes! Davick, Linda, illus. 2013. (ENG., Illus.). 32p. (J). (gr. -1-1). 17.99 (978-1-4424-6037-9(7), Beach Lane Bks.) Beach Lane Bks.

Egan, Kate & Cole, Joanna. The Magic School Bus Fights Germs. Bracken, Carolyn, illus. 2008. pap. (978-0-545-03465-4(5), Scholastic, Inc.) Scholastic, Inc.

Fromental, Jean-Luc. Bonesville. Jolivet, Joëlle, illus. 2016. (ENG.). 48p. (J). (gr. k-2). 18.95 (978-1-4197-2277-6(8), Abrams Bks. for Young Readers) Abrams, Inc.

Gleitzman, Morris. Aristotle's Nostril. 2016. (ENG.). 144p. (J). (gr. 1-3). 14.99 (978-0-14-330894-2(7)) Random Hse. Australia AUS. Dist: Independent Pubs. Group.

Greenwell, Jessica. Noisy Body Book. 2012. (Noisy Bks). 10p. (J). ring bd. 18.99 (978-0-7945-3133-1(4), Usborne) EDC Publishing.

Harrington, Tim. Nose to Toes, You Are Yummy! Harrington, Tim, illus. 2015. (ENG., Illus.). 32p. (J). (gr. -1-3). 17.99 (978-0-06-232816-8(6)) HarperCollins Pubs.

Hasany, Syed M. Where Is My Stethoscope? 2012. 24p. pap. 14.93 (978-1-4669-6888-2(5)) Trafford Publishing.

Hudson, Cheryl Willis. Hands Can. Bourke, John-Francis, photos by. 2012. (ENG., Illus.). 32p. (J). (gr. k-k). pap. 24.99 (978-0-7636-5819-9(7)) Candlewick Pr.

—Hands Can. 2013. lib. bdg. 14.75 (978-0-606-31602-6(7), Turtleback) Turtleback Bks.

Jenkins, Pete. Ears. Quintanilla, Hazel, illus. 2017. (I See, I Saw Ser.). (ENG.). (J). (gr. k-1). 28.51 (978-1-68342-152-8(3)) Rourke Educational Media.

Kitamura, Satoshi. My Hand. 2016. (ENG., Illus.). 32p. (J). (gr. -1-k). 17.99 (978-1-78344-288-1(3)) Andersen Pr. GBR. Dist: Independent Pubs. Group.

Lois, Lowry. Gooney Bird & All Her Charms. Thomas, Middy, illus. 2014. (Gooney Bird Greene Ser.). (ENG.). 160p. (J). (gr. 1-4). 16.99 (978-0-544-11354-1(3)) Houghton Mifflin Harcourt Publishing Co.

Miles, Brenda & Patterson, Colleen A. Move Your Mood! A Guide for Kids about Mind-Body Connection. Clifton-Brown, Holly, illus. 2016. 32p. (J). (978-1-4338-2112-7(5), Magination Pr.) American Psychological Assn.

Schreiber, Joe. Lenny Cyrus, School Virus. Smith, Matt, illus. 2014. (ENG.). 288p. (J). (gr. 5-7). pap. 6.99 (978-0-544-33628-5(3), HMH Books For Young Readers) Houghton Mifflin Harcourt Publishing Co.

Scieszka, Jon. The Brain Turbo. Biggs, Brian, illus. 2015. (Frank Einstein Ser.). (ENG.). 192p. (J). (gr. 3-7). 13.95 (978-1-4197-1643-0(3), Amulet Bks.) Abrams, Inc.

Tarpley, Todd. Ten Tiny Toes. 2012. (ENG., Illus.). 32p. (J). (gr. -1 — 1). 16.99 (978-0-316-12921-3(6)) Little Brown & Co.

Watson, Lauren, ed. Little Doctor. 2013. (ENG., Illus.). 16p. (J). (gr. -1-3). bds. 14.95 (978-1-61889-353-6(X)) AZ Bks. LLC.

HUMAN ECOLOGY

see also Community Life; Human Beings—Effect of Environment on; Human Geography; Nature—Effect of Human Beings on; Population; Social Psychology

Aitken, Stephen, illus. People in Trouble. 2011. (J). (978-1-61641-675-1(0)) Magic Wagon.

Baker, Stuart. In the Arctic. 2009. (Climate Change Ser.). 32p. (gr. 4). 28.50 (978-0-7614-4437-4(8)) Marshall Cavendish GBR. Dist: Marshall Cavendish Corp.

Baldwin, Christy. Care for Creation. Draven, Shelly, illus. 2010. (ENG.). 32p. (J). lib. bdg. 16.95 (978-0-9822565-6-5(6)) Tribute Bks.

Barraclough, Sue. Move & Run. 2012. (Healthy Habits Ser.). (Illus.). 24p. (gr. 1-3). lib. bdg. 24.25 (978-1-59771-308-5(2)) Sea-To-Sea Pubns.

Boothroyd, Jennifer. People & the Environment. 2008. (First Step Nonfiction - Ecology Ser.). (Illus.). 23p. (J). (gr. -1-3). lib. bdg. 18.60 (978-0-8225-8601-2(0), Lerner Pubns.); pap. 34.95 (978-0-8225-9357-7(2)) Lerner Publishing Group.

Brelsfoard, Sam. Life Inside the Arctic Circle. 2005. (Illus.). 24p. (J). (978-0-328-13638-4(7), Scott Foresman) Addison-Wesley Educational Pubs., Inc.

Caduto, Michael J. In the Beginning: The Story of Genesis & Earth Activities for Children. 2004. 48p. 16.95 (978-0-8091-6717-3(4), 6717-4) Paulist Pr.

Carroll, Michael & Carroll, Caroline. I Love God's Green Earth: Devotions for Kids Who Want to Take Care of God's Creation. 2010. (ENG.). 192p. (J). (gr. 3-7). pap. 12.99 (978-1-4143-3179-9(7), Tyndale Kids) Tyndale Hse. Pubs.

Carson, Mary Kay. Inside Biosphere 2: Earth Science under Glass. Uhlman, Tom, photos by. 2015. (Scientists in the Field Ser.). (ENG., Illus.). 80p. (J). (gr. 5-7). 18.99 (978-0-544-41664-2(3), HMH Books For Young Readers) Houghton Mifflin Harcourt Publishing Co.

Challen, Paul C. Migration in the 21st Century: How Will Globalization & Climate Change Affect Migration & Settlement? 2010. (Investigating Human Migration & Settlement Ser.). (ENG., Illus.). 48p. (J). (gr. 5-8). (978-0-7787-5181-6(3)); pap. (978-0-7787-5196-0(1)) Crabtree Publishing Co.

Champion, Neil & Ganeri, Anita. Finding Food & Water. 2011. (How the World Makes Music Ser.). 32p. (gr. 4-7). lib. bdg. 31.35 (978-1-59920-479-6(7)) Black Rabbit Bks.

Friedman, Lauri S., ed. Environmentalism. 2011. (Introducing Issues with Opposing Viewpoints Ser.). (ENG., Illus.). 144p. (gr. 7-10). lib. bdg. 36.95 (978-0-7377-6495-6(3), Greenhaven Pr., Inc.) Cengage Gale.

Gibson, Brylee. Looking after Our World. 2007. (Connectors Ser.). (gr. 2-5). pap. (978-1-877453-03-8(X)) Global Education Systems Ltd.

Greene, Carol. I Love Our People. 2012. (I Love Our Earth Ser.). (Illus.). 24p. (J). pap. 7.95 (978-1-4644-0136-7(5)); (gr. 3-4). 22.60 (978-0-7660-4041-0(0)) Enslow Pubs., Inc. (Enslow Elementary).

Hewitt, Sally. Caring for Our Earth. 2010. (Starting Geography Ser.). 32p. (J). (gr. 2-5). 28.50 (978-1-60753-124-1(0)) Amicus Publishing.

—Caring for the Earth. 2012. (Deadly & Incredible Animals Ser.). 32p. (gr. 2-6). 27.10 (978-1-59920-410-9(X)) Black Rabbit Bks.

Jakab, Cheryl. Ecological Footprints. 2010. (Environment in Focus Ser.). 32p. (gr. 4). 28.50 (978-1-60870-088-2(7)) Marshall Cavendish Corp.

Johnson, J. Angelique. The Eco-Family's Guide to Living Green, 1 vol. Poling, Kyle, illus. 2010. (Point It Out! Tips for Green Living Ser.). (ENG.). 24p. (gr. 2-3). lib. bdg. 26.65 (978-1-4048-6026-1(6)) Picture Window Bks.

—The Eco-Neighbor's Guide to a Green Community, 1 vol. Poling, Kyle, illus. 2010. (Point It Out! Tips for Green Living Ser.). (ENG.). 24p. (gr. 2-3). lib. bdg. 26.65 (978-1-4048-6028-5(2)) Picture Window Bks.

Kalman, Bobbie. The ABCs of the Environment. 2009. (ABCs of the Natural World Ser.). (ENG., Illus.). 32p. (J). (gr. 1-5). pap. (978-0-7787-3437-6(4)); (gr. 2-4). lib. bdg. (978-0-7787-3417-8(X)) Crabtree Publishing Co.

—We Are the Earth. 2009. (Our Multicultural World Ser.). (ENG., Illus.). 32p. (J). (gr. 1-4). pap. (978-0-7787-4649-2(6)) Crabtree Publishing Co.

Kelsey, Elin. Not Your Typical Book about the Environment. Hanmer, Clayton & Owlkids Books Inc. Staff, illus. 2010. (ENG.). 64p. (J). (gr. 4-7). pap. 14.95 (978-1-897349-84-7(X), Owlkids) Owlkids Bks. Inc. CAN. Dist: Publishers Group West (PGW).

—You Are Stardust. Kim, Soyeon, illus. 2012. (ENG.). 32p. (J). (gr. 1-4). 18.95 (978-1-926973-35-7(6)) Owlkids Bks. Inc. CAN. Dist: Publishers Group West (PGW).

Kirk, Ellen. Human Footprint: Everything You Will Eat, Use, Wear, Buy, & Throw Out in Your Lifetime. 2011. (ENG., Illus.). 32p. (J). (gr. 3-7). pap. 6.95 (978-1-4263-0767-6(5), National Geographic Children's Bks.) National Geographic Society.

Lehman-Wilzig, Tami. Green Bible Stories for Children. Bernhard, Durga Yael, illus. 2011. (Bible Ser.). (ENG.). 48p. (J). (gr. 3-5). pap. 7.95 (978-0-7613-5136-8(1), Kar-Ben Publishing) Lerner Publishing Group.

—Green Bible Stories for Children. Bernhard, Durga, illus. 2011. (Bible Ser.). (ENG.). 48p. (J). (gr. 3-5). lib. bdg. 17.95 (978-0-7613-5135-1(3), Kar-Ben Publishing) Lerner Publishing Group.

Love, Ann & Drake, Jane. The Kids Book of the Far North. Bouchard, Jocelyne, illus. 2009. (Kids Book Of Ser.). (ENG.). 48p. (J). (gr. 3-7). 14.95 (978-1-55453-258-2(2)) Kids Can Pr., Ltd. CAN. Dist: Hachette Bk. Group.

Maloof, Torrey. People & the Planet, 1 vol. 2015. (Science Readers: Content & Literacy Ser.). (ENG., Illus.). 32p. (gr. 3-3). pap. 8.99 (978-1-4807-4650-3(9)) Teacher Created Materials, Inc.

Porterfield, Jason. The Homestead Act Of 1862: A Primary Source History of the Settlement of the American Heartland in the Late 19th Century. 2009. (Primary Sources in American History Ser.). 64p. (gr. 5-8). 58.50 (978-1-60851-496-0(X)) Rosen Publishing Group, Inc., The.

Ring, Susan. Places We Live. 2005. (Yellow Umbrella Fluent Level Ser.). (ENG.). 16p. (gr. k-1). pap. 35.70 (978-0-7368-5316-3(2), Yellow Umbrella Bks.) Capstone Press of Coughlan Cos.

Rose, Elizabeth. Human Impact on the Environment. (Life Science Library). 24p. (gr. 3-4). 2009. 42.50 (978-1-60854-006-8(5), PowerKids Pr.) 2006. (Illus.). (YA). lib. bdg. 22.60 (978-1-4042-2822-1(5)) Rosen Publishing Group, Inc., The.

Sawyer, Ava. Human Environmental Impact: How We Affect Earth. 2017. (Humans & Our Planet Ser.). (ENG.). 32p. (gr. 3-4). lib. bdg. 27.32 (978-1-5157-7196-8(2), Fact Finders) Capstone Press of Coughlan Cos.

—Humans & Earth's Atmosphere: What's in the Air? 2017. (Humans & Our Planet Ser.). (ENG.). 32p. (gr. 3-4). lib. bdg. 27.32 (978-1-5157-7199-9(7), Fact Finders) Capstone Press of Coughlan Cos.

—Humans & Other Life on Earth: Sharing the Planet. 2017. (Humans & Our Planet Ser.). (ENG.). 32p. (gr. 3-4). lib. bdg. 27.32 (978-1-5157-7197-5(0), Fact Finders) Capstone Press of Coughlan Cos.

—Humans & the Hydrosphere: Protecting Earth's Water Sources. 2017. (Humans & Our Planet Ser.). (ENG.). 32p. (gr. 3-4). lib. bdg. 27.32 (978-1-5157-7198-2(9), Fact Finders) Capstone Press of Coughlan Cos.

Schaefer, Lola M. We are All Alike. 2011. (Early Connections Ser.). (J). (978-1-61672-654-6(7)) Benchmark Education Co.

Sirota, Lyn. People & the Planet. 2016. (Let's Explore Science Ser.). (ENG., Illus.). 48p. (gr. 5-8). 35.64 (978-1-68191-396-4(8)) Rourke Educational Media.

Smith, Paula. Be the Change for the Environment. 2014. (ENG., Illus.). 24p. (J). (978-0-7787-0620-5(6)) Crabtree Publishing Co.

—Be the Change in Your Community. 2014. (ENG., Illus.). 24p. (J). (978-0-7787-0624-3(9)) Crabtree Publishing Co.

Suzuki, David & Vanderlinden, Kathy. You Are the Earth: Know Your World So You Can Help Make It Better. Edwards, Wallace, illus. 2nd rev. ed. 2010. (ENG.). 160p. (gr. k-7). pap. 18.95 (978-1-55365-476-6(5)) Greystone Books Ltd. CAN. Dist: Publishers Group West (PGW).

Tieck, Sarah. Skeletal System, 1 vol. 2011. (Body Systems Ser.). (ENG., Illus.). 32p. (J). (gr. 2-5). lib. bdg. 27.07 (978-1-61613-502-7(6)) ABDO Publishing Co.

La Tierra en Acción (Earth in Action) 2010. (Tierra en Acción/Earth in Action Ser.). (MUL.). 24p. (gr. k-1). 53.30 (978-1-4296-6657-2(9)) Capstone Press of Coughlan Cos.

Wells, Robert E. What's So Special about Planet Earth? 2012. (J). (978-1-61913-154-5(4)) Weigl Pubs., Inc.

Weston Woods Staff, creator. Giving Thanks. 2011. 29.95 (978-0-439-73469-1(X)); 18.95 (978-0-439-72673-3(5)); 38.75 (978-0-439-72676-4(X)) Weston Woods Studios, Inc.

Whiting, Karen & White, Rebecca. The Nature Girl: A Guide to Caring for God's Creation, 1 vol. 2014. (ENG.). 176p. (J). pap. 7.99 (978-0-310-72500-8(3)) Zonderkidz.

Yasuda, Anita. Eat Green. 2010. (Being Green Ser.). (Illus.). 32p. (YA). (gr. 3-6). lib. bdg. 27.13 (978-1-61690-091-5(1)); (J). (gr. 4-6). pap. 12.95 (978-1-61690-092-2(X)) Weigl Pubs., Inc.

Young, Mary. Nos Gusta Vivir Verde: We Like to Live Green. Parker, Zachary, illus. 2010. (SPA & ENG.). 32p. (J). pap. 10.95 (978-1-935387-01-5(4)) Hohm Pr.

HUMAN EVOLUTION

see also Human Beings—Origin

Anderson, Dale. How Do We Know the Nature of Human Origins. 2009. (Great Scientific Questions & the Scientists Who Answered Them Ser.). 112p. (gr. 7-12). 63.90 (978-1-61513-202-7(3)) Rosen Publishing Group, Inc., The.

Cole, Joanna. The Human Body. 2014. (Magic School Bus Presents Ser.). lib. bdg. 17.20 (978-0-606-35815-6(3)) Turtleback Bks.

Cole, Joanna, et al. The Human Body. Degen, Bruce & Bracken, Carolyn, illus. 2014. (Magic School Bus Presents Ser.). (ENG.). 32p. (J). (gr. 1-3). pap. 6.99 (978-0-545-68364-7(5)) Scholastic, Inc.

Diagram Group Staff. Life on Earth Set, 6 vols. 2004. (Life on Earth Ser.). (Illus.). 112p. (gr. 5-8). 210.00 (978-0-8160-5044-4(9)) Facts On File, Inc.

Diagram Group Staff, contrib. by. The First Humans. 2004. (Life on Earth Ser.). (Illus.). 112p. (gr. 5-8). 35.00 *(978-0-8160-5050-5(3))* Facts On File, Inc.

Diamond, Jared. The Third Chimpanzee for Young People: On the Evolution & Future of the Human Animal. 2015. (For Young People Ser.). (ENG., Illus.). 368p. (J). (gr. 7). pap. 17.95 *(978-1-60980-611-8(5)*, Triangle Square) Seven Stories Pr.

The First Humans & Early Civilizations. 2016. (First Humans & Early Civilizations Ser.). 64p. (gr. 6-6). 172.25 *(978-1-4777-8552-2(3))*; pap. 64.75 *(978-1-4994-6423-8(1))* Rosen Publishing Group, Inc., The. (Rosen Young Adult).

Holt, Rinehart and Winston Staff. Holt Science & Technology Chapter 8: Life Science: History of Life on Earth. 5th ed. 2004. (Illus.). pap. 12.86 *(978-0-03-030196-4(3))* Holt McDougal.

Huddle, Rusty. Human Evolution. 2016. (Study of Science Ser.). 00104p. (J). (gr. 8-8). 36.25 *(978-1-5081-0429-2(8))* Rosen Publishing Group, Inc., The.

Johanson, Paula. The Paleolithic Revolution. 2016. (First Humans & Early Civilizations Ser.). (ENG.). 64p. (J). (gr. 6-6). pap. 12.95 *(978-1-4994-6314-9(6))* Rosen Publishing Group, Inc., The.

Kortemeier, Todd. Discovering the Origin of Human Life. 2017. (Science Frontiers Ser.). (ENG., Illus.). 32p. (J). (gr. 3-6). 21.95 *(978-1-63235-376-4(8))* Pr. Room Editions LLC.

Norton, James R. Looking at the Mechanisms & Patterns of Evolution with Graphic Organizers. 2005. (Using Graphic Organizers to Study the Living Environment Ser.). (Illus.). 48p. (YA). (gr. 5-9). 29.25 *(978-1-4042-0616-8(7)*, 1253990) Rosen Publishing Group, Inc., The.

Rignstad, Arnold. Discovering the Origin of Human Life. 2016. (Science Frontiers Ser.). (ENG., Illus.). 32p. (J). pap. 9.95 *(978-1-63235-393-1(8)*, 12-Story Library) Pr. Room Editions LLC.

Rushworth, Gary. What Makes a Human a Human: Text Pairs. 2008. (Bridges/Navigators Ser.). (J). (gr. 4). 89.00 *(978-1-4108-8399-5(X))* Benchmark Education Co.

Schertle, Alice. We, 1 vol. Addison, Kenneth, illus. 2013. (ENG.). 32p. (J). (gr. 1-4). 16.95 *(978-1-58430-060-1(4))* Lee & Low Bks., Inc.

Stefoff, Rebecca. Humans: An Evolutionary History, 4 vols., Set. Incl. First Humans. (YA). (gr. 8-18). lib. bdg. 37.07 *(978-0-7614-4184-7(0))*; Ice Age Neanderthals. (gr. 7-18). 37.07 *(978-0-7614-4186-1(7))*; Modern Humans. (gr. 7-18). lib. bdg. 37.07 *(978-0-7614-4187-8(5))*; Origins. (gr. 7-18). lib. bdg. 37.07 *(978-0-7614-4183-0(2))*; 112p. 2009. 2010. Set lib. bdg. 148.29 o.p. *(978-0-7614-4181-6(6))* Marshall Cavendish Corp.

Stefoff, Rebecca, adapted by. The Third Chimpanzee for Young People: On the Evolution & Future of the Human Animal. 2014. (For Young People Ser.). (ENG., Illus.). 352p. (J). (gr. 7). 22.95 *(978-1-60980-522-7(4)*, Triangle Square) Seven Stories Pr.

Weaver, Anne H. Children of Time: Evolution & the Human Story. Celeskey, Matt, illus. 2012. (ENG.). 192p. (J). 19.95 *(978-0-8263-4442-7(9))* Univ. of New Mexico Pr.

West, David. The Rise of Humans. 2014. (Prehistoric! Ser.). (Illus.). 32p. (gr. 2-5). 31.35 *(978-1-62588-087-1(1))* Black Rabbit Bks.

HUMAN FIGURE IN ART

see Anatomy; Figure Drawing

HUMAN GEOGRAPHY

see also Human Beings—Effect of Environment on

Aloian, Molly. Living Green at Home. 2013. (ENG., Illus.). 24p. (J). *(978-0-7787-0274-0(X))*; pap. *(978-0-7787-0285-6(5))* Crabtree Publishing Co.

Benchmark Education Co., LLC. Physical & Human Geography. 2014. (PRIME Ser.). (J). (gr. 6-8). pap. *(978-1-4509-9502-3(0))* Benchmark Education Co.

Benduhn, Tea. Living in Deserts. 2007. (Life on the Edge Ser.). 24p. (gr. 1-4). pap. 8.15 *(978-0-8368-8346-6(2))*; (Illus.). lib. bdg. 22.00 *(978-0-8368-8341-1(1))* Stevens, Gareth Publishing LLLP. (Weekly Reader Leveled Readers).

—Living in Mountains. 2007. (Life on the Edge Ser.). 24p. (gr. 1-4). pap. 8.15 *(978-0-8368-8347-3(0))*; (Illus.). lib. bdg. 22.00 *(978-0-8368-8342-8(X))* Stevens, Gareth Publishing LLLP. (Weekly Reader Leveled Readers).

—Living in Tropical Rain Forests. 2007. (Life on the Edge Ser.). (Illus.). 24p. (gr. 1-4). pap. 8.15 *(978-0-8368-8349-7(7))*; lib. bdg. 22.00 *(978-0-8368-8344-2(6))* Stevens, Gareth Publishing LLLP. (Weekly Reader Leveled Readers).

—La Vida en los Desiertos. 2007. (vida al límite (Spanish- Life on the Edge) Ser.). (SPA., Illus.). 24p. (gr. 1-4). pap. 8.15 *(978-0-8368-8356-5(X))*; lib. bdg. 22.00 *(978-0-8368-8351-0(9))* Stevens, Gareth Publishing LLLP. (Weekly Reader Leveled Readers).

Burton, Margie, et al. Where People Live. 2011. (Early Connections Ser.). (J). *(978-1-61672-513-6(3))* Benchmark Education Co.

Canavan, Thomas. What Makes You Hiccup? Questions & Answers about the Human Body. 2013. (Science F. A. Q. Ser.). (Illus.). 32p. (gr. 3-6). 31.35 *(978-1-78212-394-1(6))* Arcturus Publishing GBR. Dist: Black Rabbit Bks.

Cella, Clara. Earth Day, 1 vol. 2012. (Let's Celebrate Ser.). (ENG., Illus.). 24p. (gr. k-1). lib. bdg. 26.65 *(978-1-4296-8730-0(4)*, Pebble Plus) Capstone Press of Coughlan Cos.

Coleman, Miriam. Earth-Friendly Living. 2011. (How to Be Earth Friendly Ser.). (Illus.). 32p. (gr. 3-4). (J). pap. 10.00 *(978-1-4488-2773-2(6)*, PowerKids Pr.); (YA). lib. bdg. 25.25 *(978-1-4488-2592-9(X))* Rosen Publishing Group, Inc., The.

Cooke, Tim. Mapping Human Activity. 2017. (Illus.). 32p. (J). ***(978-0-7787-3222-8(3))*** Crabtree Publishing Co.

Corr, Kendra & Coletti, Sharon. The Ancient Greeks: I Think: It's Elementary! 2013. pap. 29.95 *(978-1-938275-05-0(5))* InspirEd Educators.

Country ABCs, 12 bks. Incl. Australia ABCs: A Book about the People & Places of Australia. Heiman, Sarah. Avila, Arturo, illus. 2002. 27.99 *(978-1-4048-0018-2(2))*; Egypt ABCs: A Book about the People & Places of Egypt. Heiman, Sarah. Ouren, Todd, illus. 2002. 27.99 *(978-1-4048-0019-9(0))*; Germany ABCs: A Book about the People & Places of Germany. Heiman, Sarah. Millet, Jason, illus. 2002. 27.99 *(978-1-4048-0020-5(4))*; Japan ABCs: A Book about the People & Places of Japan. Heiman, Sarah. Ouren, Todd, illus. 2002. 27.99 *(978-1-4048-0021-2(2))*; Kenya ABCs: A Book about the People & Places of Kenya. Heiman, Sarah. Avila, Arturo, illus. 2002. 27.99 *(978-1-4048-0022-9(0))*; Mexico ABCs: A Book about the People & Places of Mexico. Heiman, Sarah. Ouren, Todd, illus. 2002. 27.99 *(978-1-4048-0023-6(9))*; New Zealand ABCs: A Book about the People & Places of New Zealand. Schroeder, Holly. Wolf, Claudia, illus. 2004. 27.99 *(978-1-4048-0178-3(2)*, 1229507); United States ABCs: A Book about the People & Places of the United States. Schroeder, Holly. Yesh, Jeff, illus. 2004. 27.99 *(978-1-4048-0181-3(2)*, 1229509); (gr. k-5). (Country ABCs Ser.). (ENG.). 32p. 2004. 335.88 o.p. *(978-1-4048-0177-6(4))* Picture Window Bks.

Doherty, Gillian & Claybourne, Anna. Peoples of the World. rev. ed. 2012. (World Cultures Ser.). 96p. (J). pap. 14.99 *(978-0-7945-3280-2(2)*, Usborne) EDC Publishing.

East, Mike, et al. Global Issues No. 3: Project Organizer. Lelievre, Barclay, ed. 2010. (IB MYP Ser.). (ENG., Illus.). 80p. 19.00 *(978-0-19-918081-3(4))* Oxford Univ. Pr., Inc.

Gale Editors & Corporate Contributor Staff, eds. Junior Worldmark Encyclopedia of World Cultures, 9 vols., 9 Volume Set. 2nd ed. 2011. (ENG.). 2000p. lib. bdg. 742.00 *(978-1-4144-8671-0(5)*, UXL) Cengage Gale.

Gall, Timothy L. & Gall, Susan B. Junior Worldmark Encyclopedia of World Cultures. 2nd ed. 2011. (J). *(978-1-4144-8673-4(1))*; *(978-1-4144-8679-6(0))*; *(978-1-4144-8678-9(2))*; *(978-1-4144-8677-2(4))*; *(978-1-4144-8672-7(3))*; *(978-1-4144-8680-2(4))*; *(978-1-4144-8674-1(X))*; *(978-1-4144-8675-8(8))*; *(978-1-4144-8676-5(6))* Cengage Gale. (UXL).

Ganeri, Anita. Indian Subcontinent. 2005. (Flashpoints Ser.). (Illus.). 44p. (YA). (gr. 7-12). lib. bdg. 29.95 *(978-1-58340-602-1(6))* Black Rabbit Bks.

Giraudon, David, illus. Our Living Earth: A Story of People, Ecology, & Preservation. Arthus-Bertrand, Yann, photos by. 2008. (ENG.). 160p. (J). (gr. 3-7). 24.95 *(978-0-8109-7132-5(1)*, Abrams Bks. for Young Readers) Abrams, Inc.

Gosman, Gillian. Earth-Friendly Shopping. 2011. (How to Be Earth Friendly Ser.). (Illus.). 32p. (gr. 3-4). (J). pap. 10.00 *(978-1-4488-2771-8(X)*, PowerKids Pr.); (YA). lib. bdg. 25.25 *(978-1-4488-2591-2(1))* Rosen Publishing Group, Inc., The.

Green, Mary. Rivers in Action. 2004. (Earth's Changing Landscape Ser.). (Illus.). 46p. (YA). (gr. 7-12). lib. bdg. 28.50 *(978-1-58340-477-5(5))* Black Rabbit Bks.

Harris, P. M. G. The History of Human Populations Vol. II: Migration, Urbanization, & Structural Change, 1 vol. 2003. (Illus.). 584p. (C). 138.00 *(978-0-275-97191-5(0)*, C7191, Greenwood) ABC-CLIO, LLC.

Helgren. People, Places & Changes: Online Edition Plus. 3rd ed. 2003. 17.26 *(978-0-03-037418-0(9))* Holt McDougal.

Helgren, David M. People, Places & Change: Enhanced Online Edition. 3rd ed. 2003. 70.53 *(978-0-03-072533-3(X))* Holt McDougal.

Hewitt, Sally. Caring for Our Earth. 2010. (Starting Geography Ser.). 32p. (J). (gr. 2-5). 28.50 *(978-1-60753-124-1(0))* Amicus Publishing.

—Caring for the Earth. 2012. (Deadly & Incredible Animals Ser.). 32p. (gr. 2-6). 27.10 *(978-1-59920-410-9(X))* Black Rabbit Bks.

—Homes. 2010. (Starting Geography Ser.). 32p. (J). (gr. 2-5). 28.50 *(978-1-60753-125-8(9))* Amicus Publishing.

Jenson-Elliott, Cindy. Arctic Communities Past & Present, 1 vol. 2014. (Who Lived Here? Ser.). (ENG.). 24p. (gr. 1-2). pap. 7.95 *(978-1-4765-5142-5(1))*; lib. bdg. 25.32 *(978-1-4765-4060-3(8))* Capstone Press of Coughlan Cos. (First Facts).

Jenson-Elliott, Cindy, et al. Who Lived Here?, 1 vol. 2014. (Who Lived Here? Ser.). (ENG.). 24p. (gr. 1-2). pap. 27.80 *(978-1-4765-7406-6(5)*, First Facts) Capstone Press of Coughlan Cos.

Knight, Margy Burns. Talking Walls. O'Brien, Anne Sibley, illus. 2004. 34p. (gr. 3-8). 19.45 *(978-0-7569-4256-4(X))* Perfection Learning Corp.

—Talking Walls: Discover Your World. O'Brien, Anne Sibley, illus. 2014. (ENG.). 64p. (gr. 2-7). 18.95 *(978-0-88448-356-4(8)*, 884356) Tilbury Hse. Pubs.

Labrecque, Ellen. Living Beside a River. 2015. (Places We Live Ser.). (ENG., Illus.). 32p. (gr. 1-3). 27.32 *(978-1-4846-0801-2(1)*, Heinemann First Library) Heinemann-Raintree.

—Living in a Valley. 2015. (Places We Live Ser.). (ENG., Illus.). 32p. (gr. 1-3). 27.32 *(978-1-4846-0804-3(6)*, Heinemann First Library) Heinemann-Raintree.

—Living on a Mountain. 2015. (Places We Live Ser.). (ENG., Illus.). 32p. (gr. 1-3). 27.32 *(978-1-4846-0806-7(2)*, Heinemann First Library) Heinemann-Raintree.

—Places We Live. 2015. (Places We Live Ser.). (ENG.). 32p. (gr. 1-3). 163.92 *(978-1-4846-0807-4(0)*, Heinemann First Library) Heinemann-Raintree.

Learning Company Books Staff, ed. Carmen Sandiego USA Adventures. 2004. (Illus.). 64p. (J). pap. *(978-0-7630-7615-3(5))* Magma.

—Carmen Sandiego World Adventures. 2004. (Illus.). 64p. (J). pap. *(978-0-7630-7616-0(3))* Magma.

Lindeen, Mary. Where People Live, 1 vol. 2011. (Wonder Readers Fluent Level Ser.). (ENG.). (gr. -1-2). 32p. pap. 5.99 *(978-1-4296-7975-6(1))*; 16p. pap. 35.94 *(978-1-4296-8207-7(8))* Capstone Press of Coughlan Cos. (Wonder Readers).

Low, Robert. Peoples of the Savanna. 2009. (Peoples & Their Environments Ser.). 24p. (gr. 2-3). 42.50 *(978-1-60851-162-4(6)*, PowerKids Pr.) Rosen Publishing Group, Inc., The.

Morlock, Theresa. Ancient Inca Geography. 2016. (Spotlight on the Maya, Aztec, & Inca Civilizations Ser.). 32p. (J). (gr. 6-4). pap. 11.75 *(978-1-4994-1943-6(0)*, PowerKids Pr.) Rosen Publishing Group, Inc., The.

Naughton, Diane. Our Green Future. 2014. (ENG., Illus.). 28p. (J). pap. 9.50 *(978-1-107-67286-4(4))* Cambridge Univ. Pr.

O'Hara, Megan. Plains Communities Past & Present, 1 vol. 2014. (Who Lived Here? Ser.). (ENG.). 24p. (gr. 1-2). lib. bdg. 25.32 *(978-1-4765-4061-0(6)*, First Facts) Capstone Press of Coughlan Cos.

Richards, Jon. People on Earth. 2016. (Mapographica Ser.). (ENG., Illus.). 32p. (J). (gr. 3-6). *(978-0-7787-2656-2(8))* Crabtree Publishing Co.

Scariest Places on Earth. 2014. (Scariest Places on Earth Ser.). 24p. (J). (gr. 2-5). pap. 293.40 *(978-1-4824-1584-1(4))* Stevens, Gareth Publishing LLLP.

Schuetz, Kari. Life in a Desert. 2016. (Biomes Alive! Ser.). (ENG., Illus.). 24p. (J). (gr. k-3). lib. bdg. 25.95 *(978-1-62617-316-3(8)*, Blastoff! Readers) Bellwether Media.

Smith, David J. If America Were a Village: A Book about the People of the United States. Armstrong, Shelagh, illus. 2009. (CitizenKid Ser.). (ENG.). 32p. (J). (gr. 3-7). 18.95 *(978-1-55453-344-2(9))* Kids Can Pr., Ltd. CAN. Dist: Hachette Bk. Group.

—If the World Were a Village: A Book about the World's People. Armstrong, Shelagh, illus. 2nd ed. 2011. (CitizenKid Ser.). (ENG.). 32p. (J). (gr. 3-7). 18.95 *(978-1-55453-595-8(6))* Kids Can Pr., Ltd. CAN. Dist: Hachette Bk. Group.

Smith-Llera, Danielle. River Communities Past & Present, 1 vol. 2014. (Who Lived Here? Ser.). (ENG.). 24p. (gr. 1-2). lib. bdg. 25.32 *(978-1-4765-4058-0(6)*, First Facts) Capstone Press of Coughlan Cos.

Smith-Llera, Danielle, et al. Who Lived Here?, 1 vol. 2014. (Who Lived Here? Ser.). (ENG.). 24p. (gr. 1-2). lib. bdg. 101.28 *(978-1-4765-7404-2(9)*, First Facts) Capstone Press of Coughlan Cos.

Vermond, Kira. Why We Live Where We Live. McLaughlin, Julie, illus. 2014. (ENG.). 48p. (J). (gr. 4-6). 17.95 *(978-1-77147-011-7(9)*, Owlkids) Owlkids Bks. Inc. CAN. Dist: Publishers Group West (PGW).

Waldron, Melanie. Geography Matters in Ancient Egypt. 2015. (Geography Matters in Ancient Civilizations Ser.). (ENG., Illus.). 48p. (gr. 3-6). 33.32 *(978-1-4846-0962-0(X)*, Heinemann InfoSearch) Heinemann-Raintree.

—Geography Matters in Ancient Greece. 2015. (Geography Matters in Ancient Civilizations Ser.). (ENG., Illus.). 48p. (gr. 3-6). 33.32 *(978-1-4846-0963-7(8)*, Heinemann InfoSearch) Heinemann-Raintree.

—Geography Matters in Ancient Rome. 2015. (Geography Matters in Ancient Civilizations Ser.). (ENG., Illus.). 48p. (gr. 3-6). 33.32 *(978-1-4846-0964-4(6)*, Heinemann InfoSearch) Heinemann-Raintree.

—Geography Matters in the Inca Empire. 2015. (Geography Matters in Ancient Civilizations Ser.). (ENG., Illus.). 48p. (gr. 3-6). 33.32 *(978-1-4846-0965-1(4)*, Heinemann InfoSearch) Heinemann-Raintree.

HUMAN RACE

see Human Beings

HUMAN RELATIONS

see Interpersonal Relations

HUMAN RESOURCE DEVELOPMENT

see Manpower Policy

HUMAN RIGHTS

Here are entered works on the rights of persons regardless of their legal, socioeconomic or cultural status and as recognized by the international community. Works on citizens' rights as established by law and protected by constitution are entered under Civil rights. Some works on human rights cataloged before 1987 may be found under Civil Rights.

see also Civil Rights

Altman, Linda Jacobs. The American Civil Rights Movement: The African-American Struggle for Equality. 2004. (Issues in Focus Ser.). (Illus.). 128p. (J). lib. bdg. 26.60 *(978-0-7660-1944-7(6))* Enslow Pubs., Inc.

Amnesty International Australia Staff, told to. We Are All Born Free: The Universal Declaration of Human Rights in Pictures. 2011. (ENG., Illus.). 72p. (J). (gr. 1-4). 8.95 *(978-1-84780-151-7(X)*, Frances Lincoln) Quarto Publishing Group UK GBR. Dist: Hachette Bk. Group.

Amnesty International Staff. We Are All Born Free: The Universal Declaration of Human Rights in Pictures. 2016. (ENG., Illus.). 72p. (J). (gr. 1-4). pap. 8.99 *(978-1-84780-663-5(5)*, Frances Lincoln) Quarto Publishing Group UK GBR. Dist: Littlehampton Bk Services, Ltd.

Anastasio, Dina, et al. Who Is Malala Yousafzai? Thomson, Andrew, illus. 2015. (Who Was? Ser.). (ENG.). 112p. (J). (gr. 3-7). 5.99 *(978-0-448-48937-7(6)*, Grosset & Dunlap) Penguin Young Readers Group.

Baughan, Brian. Human Rights in Africa. Ojakorotu, Victor & Rotberg, Robert I., eds. 2013. (Africa: Progress & Problems Ser.: 13). (Illus.). 112p. (J). (gr. 7-18). 24.95 *(978-1-4222-2942-2(4))* Mason Crest.

Berlatsky, Noah. China. 2010. (Opposing Viewpoints Ser.). (Illus.). 240p. (J). 42.95 *(978-0-7377-4765-2(X)*, 1304557); pap. 29.45 *(978-0-7377-4766-9(8)*, 1304557) Cengage Gale. (Greenhaven Pr., Inc.).

Bradley, Catherine. Freedom of Movement. 2005. (What Do We Mean by Human Rights? Ser.). (Illus.). 46p. (YA). (gr. 5-9). lib. bdg. 29.95 *(978-1-932889-64-2(7))* Sea-To-Sea Pubns.

Braun, Eric. Taking Action for Civil & Political Rights. 2016. (Who's Changing the World? Ser.). (ENG., Illus.). 48p. (J). (gr. 4-6). 33.32 *(978-1-4677-9394-0(9))*; 50.65 *(978-1-4677-9665-1(4)*, Lerner Pubns.) Lerner Publishing Group.

Bryfonski, Dedria. Child Custody. 2011. (Opposing Viewpoints Ser.). 240p. pap. 29.45 *(978-0-7377-5218-2(1))*; (ENG.). 224p. (gr. 12-12). lib. bdg. 48.80 *(978-0-7377-5217-5(3))* Cengage Gale. (Greenhaven Pr., Inc.).

Cahill, Bryon. Freedom from Want. 2013. (Four Freedoms Ser.). (Illus.). 32p. (gr. 3-5). pap. 8.95 *(978-1-937529-85-7(1))* Red Chair Pr.

Catalano, Angela. Community Needs: Meeting Needs & Wants in the Community. 2009. (Communities at Work Ser.). 24p. (gr. 2-2). 42.50 *(978-1-61511-889-2(6)*, PowerKids Pr.) Rosen Publishing Group, Inc., The.

Currie, Stephen. Religious Oppression. 2003. (Great Escapes Ser.). (ENG., Illus.). 112p. (J). 30.85 *(978-1-59018-280-2(4)*, Lucent Bks.) Cengage Gale.

Downing, David. The Debate about Terrorist Tactics. 2007. (Ethical Debates Ser.). (Illus.). 48p. (YA). (gr. 5-9). lib. bdg. 29.25 *(978-1-4042-3757-5(7))* Rosen Publishing Group, Inc., The.

Farrell, Courtney. Children's Rights, 1 vol. 2010. (Essential Issues Set 1 Ser.). (ENG.). 112p. (J). (gr. 6-12). lib. bdg. 35.64 *(978-1-60453-952-3(6)*, Essential Library) ABDO Publishing Co.

Feldman, Jean R. & Karapetkova, Holly. Basic Needs (Lap Book) 2010. (ENG., Illus.). 12p. (gr. -1-k). 9.95 *(978-1-61590-212-5(0))* Rourke Educational Media.

Finucane, Brendan. Critical World Issues: Human Rights, Vol. 16. 2016. (Critical World Issues Ser.: Vol. 16). (ENG., Illus.). 112p. (J). (gr. 7-12). 25.95 *(978-1-4222-3657-4(9))* Mason Crest.

Friedman, Mark D. Human Rights, 1 vol. 2012. (Hot Topics Ser.). (ENG.). 64p. (gr. 7-8). 34.65 *(978-1-4329-6035-3(0))*; pap. 9.99 *(978-1-4329-6043-8(1))* Heinemann-Raintree. (NA-h).

Gadri, Stephen Awudi. The Revealed Myths about Trokosi Slavery: Human Rights Violations. 2010. 96p. pap. 28.99 *(978-1-4490-3702-4(X))* AuthorHouse.

Gold, Susan Dudley. Son of Sam Case: Simon & Schuster V. Members of United States Crime Victims Board. 2014. (Illus.). 143p. (J). lib. bdg. *(978-1-62712-399-0(7))* Cavendish Square Publishing.

Haugen, David M. Human Rights. 2013. (Opposing Viewpoints Ser.). (ENG., Illus.). 224p. (gr. 10-12). pap. 33.80 *(978-0-7377-4774-4(9))*; lib. bdg. 48.80 *(978-0-7377-4773-7(0))* Cengage Gale. (Greenhaven Pr., Inc.).

Haugen, David M. Human Rights in Focus: Illegal Immigrants. 2017. (ENG.). 80p. (YA). (gr. 5-12). ***(978-1-68282-229-6(X))*** ReferencePoint Pr., Inc.

Hertkorn, Michaela C. Little Cloud Upset. Ayala, Joseph, illus. 2010. 28p. pap. 14.95 *(978-1-4389-9837-4(6))* AuthorHouse.

Herumin, Wendy. Child Labor Today: A Human Rights Issue. 2007. (Issues in Focus Today Ser.). (Illus.). 112p. (J). (gr. 3-7). lib. bdg. 33.27 *(978-0-7660-2682-7(5))* Enslow Pubs., Inc.

Hinds, Maurene J. You Have the Right to Know Your Rights: What Teens Should Know. 2005. (Issues in Focus Today Ser.). (Illus.). 104p. (J). (gr. 6-12). lib. bdg. 33.27 *(978-0-7660-2358-1(3))* Enslow Pubs., Inc.

Holt, David H. Religious, Cultural, & Minority Rights, Vol. 8. Lansford, Tom, ed. 2016. (Foundations of Democracy Ser.). (Illus.). 64p. (J). (gr. 7). 23.95 *(978-1-4222-3632-1(3))* Mason Crest.

Hunt, Jilly. Human Rights for All. 2017. (Beyond the Headlines! Ser.). (ENG.). 48p. (gr. 4-6). lib. bdg. 33.32 ***(978-1-4846-4141-5(8)***, Heinemann InfoSearch) Heinemann-Raintree.

Hyde, Natalie. LGBTQ Rights. 2017. 48p. (J). ***(978-0-7787-3942-5(2))*** Crabtree Publishing Co.

Jacobs, Thomas A. What Are My Rights? Q&A about Teens & the Law. 3rd rev. ed. 2011. (ENG.). 224p. (YA). (gr. 6). pap. 15.99 *(978-1-57542-380-7(4))* Free Spirit Publishing, Inc.

Joy, Berry. Mine & Yours. 2008. 48p. 12.95 *(978-1-60577-701-6(3))* Berry, Joy Enterprises.

Kidder, Tracy. Mountains Beyond Mountains (Adapted for Young People) The Quest of Dr. Paul Farmer, a Man Who Would Cure the World. 2014. (ENG.). (YA). (gr. 7). lib. bdg. 19.60 ***(978-1-68065-029-7(7))*** Perfection Learning Corp.

Kidder, Tracy & French, Michael. Mountains Beyond Mountains (Adapted for Young People) The Quest of Dr. Paul Farmer, a Man Who Would Cure the World. 2014. (ENG.). 288p. (YA). (gr. 7). pap. 9.99 *(978-0-385-74319-8(X)*, Ember) Random Hse. Children's Bks.

McCarney, Rosemary. Every Day Is Malala Day, 1 vol. 2014. (ENG., Illus.). 32p. (J). (gr. 3-5). 18.95 *(978-1-927583-31-9(4))* Second Story Pr. CAN. Dist: Orca Bk. Pubs. USA.

Melman, Anna. Islam, Law & Human Rights. 2010. (World of Islam Ser.). (Illus.). 64p. (YA). (gr. 6-10). lib. bdg. 22.95 *(978-1-4222-1362-9(5))* Mason Crest.

Merino, Noel. Selfincrimination. Gale, ed. 2014. (Teen Rights & Freedoms Ser.). (ENG., Illus.). 176p. (gr. 10-12). lib. bdg. 42.00 *(978-0-7377-6432-1(5)*, Greenhaven Pr., Inc.) Cengage Gale.

National Geographic Editors. Every Human Has Rights: A Photographic Declaration for Kids. 2008. (ENG., Illus.). 48p. (J). (gr. 5). 26.90 *(978-1-4263-0511-5(7)*, National Geographic Children's Bks.) National Geographic Society.

—Every Human Has Rights: What You Need to Know about Your Human Rights. 2008. (ENG., Illus.). 48p. (J). (gr. 5). 17.95 *(978-1-4263-0510-8(9)*, National Geographic Children's Bks.) National Geographic Society.

O'Connor, Maureen. Equal Rights. 2005. (What Do We Mean by Human Rights? Ser.). (Illus.). 46p. (YA). (gr. 5-9). lib. bdg. 29.95 *(978-1-932889-63-5(9))* Sea-To-Sea Pubns.

Ogden, Charlie. Human Rights & Liberty. 2017. (Illus.). 32p. (J). ***(978-0-7787-3267-9(3))*** Crabtree Publishing Co.

Parry, Ann. Amnesty International. 2005. (Humanitarian Organizations Ser.). (Illus.). 32p. (gr. 5-8). lib. bdg. 25.00 *(978-0-7910-8813-5(8)*, Chelsea Hse.) Facts On File, Inc.

Pezzi, Bryan. Craig Kielburger. 2010. (Illus.). 24p. *(978-1-77071-597-4(5))*; pap. *(978-1-77071-603-2(3))* Weigl Educational Pubs. Ltd.

Phillips, Douglas A. Human Rights. 2009. (Global Connections Ser.). (Illus.). 128p. (gr. 5-8). 35.00 *(978-1-60413-286-1(8)*, Chelsea Hse.) Facts On File, Inc.

Prior, Katherine. Workers' Rights. 2005. (What Do We Mean by Human Rights? Ser.). (Illus.). 46p. (YA). (gr. 5-9). lib. bdg. 29.95 *(978-1-932889-68-0(X))* Sea-To-Sea Pubns.

Rodger, Ellen & Gleason, Carrie. Human Rights Activist. 2009. (Get Involved! Ser.). (ENG., Illus.). 32p. (J). (gr. 3-6). *(978-0-7787-4695-9(X))*; pap. *(978-0-7787-4707-9(7))* Crabtree Publishing Co.

Rosen Publishing Staff. Know Your Rights, 1 vol. 2015. (Know Your Rights Ser.). (ENG.). 64p. (YA). 232.75 *(978-1-4777-8056-5(4)*, Rosen Central) Rosen Publishing Group, Inc., The.

Scherer, Lauri S. Human Rights. Greenhaven Press Editors & Gale Editors, eds. 2014. (Introducing Issues with Opposing Viewpoints Ser.). (ENG., Illus.). 144p. (gr. 10-12). lib. bdg. 42.00 *(978-0-7377-6924-1(6)*, Greenhaven Pr., Inc.) Cengage Gale.

Serres, Alain. I Have the Right to Be a Child, 1 vol. Mixter, Helen, tr. from FRE. Fronty, Aurélia, illus. 2012. (ENG.). 48p. (J). (gr. -1-2). 18.95 *(978-1-55498-149-6(2))* Groundwood Bks. CAN. Dist: Publishers Group West (PGW).

Smith, Roger. Human Rights & Protecting Individuals, Vol. 10. Russett, Bruce, ed. 2015. (United Nations: Leadership & Challenges in a Global World Ser.). (Illus.). 88p. (J). (gr. 7). lib. bdg. 24.95 (978-1-4222-3437-2(1)) Mason Crest.

Two-Can Publishing Ltd. Staff, contrib. by. Stand up for Your Rights. 2004. (Stand Up... Ser.). (Illus.). 96p. (J). (gr. 3-6). 14.95 (978-1-58728-400-7(6)); pap. 9.95 (978-1-58728-401-4(4)) T&N Children's Publishing. (Two-Can Publishing).

Watkins, Christine & Haugen, David. Do Children Have Rights? 2010. (At Issue Ser.). (ENG.). 128p. (gr. 10-12). pap. 27.80 (978-0-7377-4877-2(X), Greenhaven Pr., Inc.) Cengage Gale.

Watkins, Christine & Haugen, David M. Do Children Have Rights? 2010. (At Issue Ser.). (ENG.). 128p. (gr. 10-12). 39.40 (978-0-7377-4876-5(1)) Cengage Gale.

HUMAN SKIN COLOR

Barnes, Brynne. Colors of Me. Nelson, Annika M., illus. 2011. (ENG.). 28p. 15.95 (978-1-58536-541-8(6)) Sleeping Bear Pr.

Ollhoff, Jim. The Roots of Humanity, 1 vol. 2011. (African American History Ser.). (ENG., Illus.). 32p. (YA). (gr. 5-9). lib. bdg. 27.07 (978-1-61714-713-5(3)) ABDO Publishing Co.

Tyler, Michael. The Skin You Live In. Csicsko, David Lee, illus. 2005. (ENG.). 32p. (J). (gr. k-2). 15.95 (978-0-9759580-0-1(3)) Chicago Children's Museum.

HUMANISM

see also Learning and Scholarship; Renaissance

Bennett, Helen. Humanism, What's That? A Book for Curious Kids. 2005. (ENG.). 77p. (J). (gr. 5). pap. 13.99 (978-1-59102-387-6(4)) Prometheus Bks., Pubs.

Rosen, Michael & Young, Annemarie. What Is Humanism? How Do You Live Without a God? And Other Big Questions for Kids. 2016. (ENG., Illus.). 48p. (J). (gr. 4-6). pap. 11.99 (978-0-7502-8842-2(6), Wayland) Hachette Children's Group GBR. Dist: Hachette Bk. Group.

HUMMINGBIRDS

Amstutz, Lisa J. Hummingbirds. 2016. (Backyard Birds Ser.). (ENG., Illus.). 24p. (gr. k-1). lib. bdg. 26.65 (978-1-4914-8513-2(2), Pebble Plus) Capstone Press of Coughlan Cos.

Amim, Aife. A Bird Watcher's Guide to Hummingbirds. 2017. (Backyard Bird Watchers Ser.). 32p. (J). (gr. 2-3). pap. 10.50 **(978-1-5382-0315-6(4))** Stevens, Gareth Publishing LLLP.

Arnold, Quinn M. Hummingbirds. (Seedlings Ser.). (Illus.). 24p. (J). (gr. k-2). 2017. (ENG.). pap. 7.99 (978-1-62832-333-7(7), Creative Paperbacks) 2016. (978-1-60818-737-9(3), Creative Education) Creative Co., The.

Bader, Bonnie & dePaola, Tomie. Hummingbirds. 2015. (ENG., Illus.). 32p. (J). (gr. -1-k). bds. 3.99 (978-0-448-48713-7(6), Grosset & Dunlap) Penguin Young Readers Group.

Berger, Bruce. A Dazzle of Hummingbirds: The Colorful Life of a Tiny Scrapper. Leon, Vicki, ed. 2nd ed. 2005. (Jean-Michel Cousteau Presents Ser.). (ENG., Illus.). 48p. (J). pap. 7.95 (978-0-9666490-7-9(9)) London Town Pr.

Berne, Emma Carlson. Hummingbirds. 2013. (Animal Superpowers Ser.). 24p. (J). (gr. k-5). pap. 8.25 (978-1-4777-0841-5(3), PowerKids Pr.) Rosen Publishing Group, Inc., The.

Berne, Emma Carlson & Carlson Berne, Emma. Hummingbirds. 2013. 24p. (J). (gr. k-5). 22.60 (978-1-4777-0750-0(6), PowerKids Pr.) Rosen Publishing Group, Inc., The.

Borgert-Spaniol, Megan. Hummingbirds. 2014. (Backyard Wildlife Ser.). (ENG., Illus.). 24p. (J). (gr. k-3). lib. bdg. 25.95 (978-1-62617-059-9(2), Blastoff! Readers) Bellwether Media.

Bowman, Chris. Ruby-Throated Hummingbirds. 2016. (North American Animals Ser.). (ENG., Illus.). 24p. (J). (gr. k-3). lib. bdg. 25.95 (978-1-62617-337-8(0), Blastoff! Readers) Bellwether Media.

Carlson Berne, Emma. Hummingbirds: Faster Than a Jet! 2013. (Animal Superpowers Ser.). 24p. (J). (gr. k-5). pap. 49.50 (978-1-4777-0842-2(1), PowerKids Pr.) Rosen Publishing Group, Inc., The.

Elliott, David. On the Wing. Stadtlander, Becca, illus. 2017. (ENG.). 32p. (J). (gr. -1-2). 6.99 (978-0-7636-9302-2(2)) Candlewick Pr.

Gish, Melissa. Hummingbirds. 2011. (Illus.). 46p. (J). 35.65 (978-1-60818-078-3(6), Creative Education) Creative Co., The.

Goddard, Jolyon. Hummingbirds. 2008. (Nature's Children Ser.). (Illus.). 52p. (J). (978-0-7172-6257-1(X)) Grolier, Ltd.

Gregory, Josh. Hummingbirds. 2016. (Nature's Children Ser.). (ENG., Illus.). 48p. (J). pap. 6.95 (978-0-531-21935-5(6), Children's Pr.) Scholastic Library Publishing.

Griff, Peter. Colibres Pequeitos / Itty Bitty Hummingbirds, Vol. 1. 2014. (Animales Pequeñitos / Itty Bitty Animals Ser.). (SPA & BYN.). 24p. (J). (gr. k-2). 22.60 (978-1-4339-9909-3(9)) Stevens, Gareth Publishing LLLP.

—Itty Bitty Hummingbirds, Vol. 1. 2014. (Itty Bitty Animals Ser.). (ENG.). 24p. (J). (gr. k-k). 22.60 (978-1-4339-9886-7(6)) Stevens, Gareth Publishing LLLP.

Hamilton, Robert M. The Amazing Hummingbird. 2013. (Rosen Readers Ser.). (ENG.). 24p. (J). (gr. 3-4). pap. 8.25 (978-1-4777-2489-7(3)); pap. 49.50 (978-1-4777-2490-3(7)) Rosen Publishing Group, Inc., The. (Rosen Classroom).

Hirsch, Rebecca E. Ruby-Throated Hummingbirds: Tiny Hovering Birds. 2016. (Comparing Animal Traits Ser.). (ENG.). 32p. (J). (gr. 2-4). 39.99 (978-1-4677-9632-3(8)) Lerner Publishing Group.

Hudak, Heather C. Hummingbirds. 2008. (Backyard Animals Ser.). (Illus.). 24p. (J). (gr. 4-7). lib. bdg. 24.45 (978-1-60596-004-3(7)) Weigl Pubs., Inc.

Hudak, Heather C., ed. Hummingbirds. 2008. (Backyard Animals Ser.). (Illus.). 24p. (J). (gr. 4-7). pap. 8.95 (978-1-60596-010-4(1)) Weigl Pubs., Inc.

Hummingbird Garden: Big Book: Level J, Group 1. (Story Box Ser.). 16p. 31.50 (978-0-322-02469-4(2)) Wright Group/McGraw-Hill.

Jango-Cohen, Judith. Hovering Hummingbirds. 2003. (Pull Ahead Bks.). (Illus.). 32p. (J). 22.60 (978-0-8225-4666-5(3), Lerner Pubns.); (ENG., pap. 7.95 (978-0-8225-3649-9(8)) Lerner Publishing Group.

Kelly, Irene. It's a Hummingbird's Life. 2003. (ENG., Illus.). 36p. (J). (gr. k-3). tchr. ed. 17.95 (978-0-8234-1658-5(5)) Holiday Hse., Inc.

Macken, JoAnn Early. The Life Cycle of a Hummingbird. 2006. (Things with Wings Ser.). (Illus.). 24p. (gr. k-3). pap. 8.15 (978-0-8368-6390-1(9)); lib. bdg. 22.00 (978-0-8368-6383-3(6)) Stevens, Gareth Publishing LLLP. (Weekly Reader Leveled Readers).

Murray, Julie. Hummingbirds, 1 vol. 2005. (Animal Kingdom Set Ii Ser.). (ENG., Illus.). 24p. (gr. k-4). 25.65 (978-1-59197-320-1(1), Buddy Bks.) ABDO Publishing Co.

Otfinoski, Steven. Hummingbirds. 2014. (Backyard Safari Ser.). 32p. (J). (gr. 3-5). 28.50 (978-1-62712-828-5(X)) Cavendish Square Publishing.

—Hummingbirds. 2008. (Animals Animals Ser.). 48p. (gr. 3-18). lib. bdg. 29.93 (978-0-7614-2932-6(8), Benchmark Bks.) Marshall Cavendish Corp.

Paige, Joy. The Hummingbird: World's Smallest Bird. 2009. (Record-Breaking Animals Ser.). 24p. (gr. 1-1). 42.50 (978-1-60852-442-6(6), PowerKids Pr.) Rosen Publishing Group, Inc., The.

Peterson, Megan Cooley. The Smallest Animals. 2012. (Extreme Animals Ser.). (ENG.). 24p. (gr. k-1). pap. 41.70 (978-1-4296-8341-8(4), Pebble Plus) Capstone Press of Coughlan Cos.

Petrie, Kristin. Hummingbirds, 1 vol. 2014. (Backyard Animals Ser.). (ENG.). 32p. (J). (gr. 3-6). 27.07 (978-1-62403-661-3(9)) ABDO Publishing Co.

Quinlivan, Ana. Hummingbirds: World's Fastest Wings. 2013. (InfoMax Readers Ser.). (ENG.). 24p. (J). (gr. 3-4). pap. 49.50 (978-1-4777-2501-6(6)); (Illus.). pap. 8.25 (978-1-4777-2500-9(8)) Rosen Publishing Group, Inc., The. (Rosen Classroom).

Read, Tracy. Exploring the World of Hummingbirds. 2017. (Exploring the World Of Ser.). (ENG., Illus.). 24p. (J). (gr. 3-7). 16.95 **(978-1-77085-946-3(2)**, 9781770859463); pap. 6.95 **(978-1-77085-947-0(0)**, 9781770859470) Firefly Bks., Ltd.

Riggs, Kate. Amazing Animals: Hummingbirds. 2014. (Amazing Animals Ser.). (ENG.). 24p. (J). (gr. 1-3). pap. 8.99 (978-0-89812-927-4(3), Creative Paperbacks) Creative Co., The.

—Hummingbirds. 2014. (J). 25.65 (978-1-60818-348-7(3), Creative Education) Creative Co., The.

Sill, Cathryn. About Hummingbirds: A Guide for Children, 1 vol. Sill, John, illus. 2015. (About... Ser.). (ENG.). 48p. (gr. -1-2). pap. 7.95 (978-1-56145-837-0(6)) Peachtree Pubs.

Sill, Cathryn P. & Sill, John. About Hummingbirds, 1 vol. Sill, Cathryn P. & Sill, John, illus. 2011. (ENG., Illus.). 48p. (J). (gr. -1-2). 16.95 (978-1-56145-588-1(1)) Peachtree Pubs.

Stout, Frankie. Hummingbirds: Hovering in Nature. 2009. (Things with Wings Ser.). 24p. (gr. 2-3). 42.50 (978-1-60854-352-6(8)); (Illus.). (J). lib. bdg. 22.60 (978-1-4042-4494-8(8)) Rosen Publishing Group, Inc., The. (PowerKids Pr.).

Waldendorf, Kurt. How Small Is a Hummingbird? 2017. (Comparison Fun Ser.). (ENG.). 24p. (J). (gr. -1-2). lib. bdg. 27.07 (978-1-5038-1680-0(X), 211515) Child's World, Inc., The.

HUMORISTS

Aykroyd, Clarissa. Savage Satire: The Story of Jonathan Swift. 2006. (World Writers Ser.). (Illus.). 160p. (J). (gr. 3-7). lib. bdg. 27.95 (978-1-59935-027-1(0)) Reynolds, Morgan Inc.

Bodden, Valerie. Mark Twain, 1 vol. 2013. (Great American Authors Ser.). (ENG.). 48p. (J). (gr. 3-6). lib. bdg. 32.79 (978-1-61783-719-7(9)) ABDO Publishing Co.

Burleigh, Robert. The Adventures of Mark Twain by Huckleberry Finn. Blitt, Barry, illus. 2011. (ENG.). 48p. (J). (gr. 2-5). 17.99 (978-0-689-83041-9(6), Atheneum Bks. for Young Readers) Simon & Schuster Children's Publishing.

Caravantes, Peggy. A Great & Sublime Fool: The Story of Mark Twain. 2010. (World Writers Ser.). (Illus.). 176p. (YA). (gr. 8-18). lib. bdg. 28.95 (978-1-59935-088-2(2)) Reynolds, Morgan Inc.

Maloof, Torrey. Stepping into Mark Twain's World. 2017. (TIME for KIDS(r) Nonfiction Readers Ser.). 48p. (J). (gr. 7-7). pap. 9.99 **(978-1-4938-3620-8(X))** Teacher Created Materials, Inc.

HUMOROUS PICTURES

see Cartoons and Comics; Comic Books, Strips, etc.

HUMOROUS POETRY

see also Limericks; Nonsense Verses

Allen, Brian. Rickety Rackety Rhymes. 2012. 102p. pap. 27.50 (978-1-62212-279-0(8), Strategic Bk. Publishing) Strategic Book Publishing & Rights Agency (SBPRA).

Andreae, Giles. ABC Animal Jamboree. Wojtowycz, David, illus. 2010. (ENG.). 32p. (J). (gr. -1-2). 16.95 (978-1-58925-092-5(3)) Tiger Tales.

Attaboy. You Might Be a Monster: And Other Stories I Made Up! 2011. (ENG., Illus.). 36p. (J). (gr. 1-3). 15.95 (978-1-59702-025-1(7)) Immedium.

Black, Baxter A. Rudolph's Night Off. Patterson, Bill, illus. 2011. (ENG.). 32p. (J). (gr. -1-3). 19.95 (978-0-939343-54-6(1)) Coyote Cowboy Co.

Brown, Hilary. Two-Liners for Kids. 2010. (Illus.). 50p. pap. (978-1-84748-707-0(6)) Athena Pr.

Burgess, Gelett. Goops & How to Be Them: A Manual of Manners for Polite Infants. 2005. (ENG., Illus.). 108p. 17.95 (978-1-55709-392-9(X)) Applewood Bks.

Carpenter, Stephen, illus. If Kids Ruled the School: More Kids' Favorite Funny School Poems. 2004. 73p. (J). 8.95 (978-0-88166-468-3(5)) Meadowbrook Pr.

—Mary Had a Little Jam, & Other Silly Rhymes. 2004. 32p. (J). (978-0-88166-470-6(7)) Meadowbrook Pr.

—What I Did on My Summer Vacation: Kids' Favorite Funny Summer Vacation Poems. 2009. (Giggle Poetry Ser.). (ENG.). 80p. (J). (gr. 1-8). pap. 8.95 (978-1-4169-7047-7(9)) Meadowbrook Pr.

Cole, Joanna & Calmenson, Stephanie. Yours till Banana Splits: 201 Autograph Rhymes. Tiegreen, Alan, illus. 2004. 64p. (J). (gr. 6-8). reprint ed. pap. 7.00 (978-0-7567-7349-6(0)) DIANE Publishing Co.

Cope, Steven R. Crow. 2010. 156p. pap. 15.00 (978-1-936138-13-5(1)) Wind Pubns.

Craven, Josh. Hayrides. Craven, Josh, illus. 2011. (Illus.). 16p. pap. 24.95 (978-1-4626-1123-2(0)) America Star Bks.

Crawley, Dave. Reading, Rhyming, & 'Rithmetic. Callen, Liz, illus. 2010. (ENG.). 32p. (J). (gr. 2-4). 17.95 (978-1-59078-565-2(7), Wordsong) Boyds Mills Pr.

Dahl, Roald. Revolting Rhymes. 2009. (ENG.). 48p. (J). (gr. 1-3). pap. 7.99 (978-0-14-241482-8(4), Puffin Books) Penguin Young Readers Group.

Dordick, Barry. Macaroni on the Moon. Amado, Defne, illus. 2003. 110p. pap. 11.95 (978-0-595-26886-3(2)) iUniverse, Inc.

Dyan, Penelope. In My Attic. Dyan, Penelope, illus. 2010. (Illus.). 34p. pap. 11.95 (978-1-935630-23-4(7)) Bellissima Publishing, LLC.

—It's Nice to Be Gone When You're in Milan, a Kid's Guide to Milan, Italy. Weigand, John D., photos by. 2010. (Illus.). 50p. pap. 11.95 (978-1-935630-03-6(2)) Bellissima Publishing, LLC.

—There Are No Ants in My Pants! for Boys Only(r). Dyan, Penelope, illus. 2010. (Illus.). 32p. pap. 11.95 (978-1-935630-16-6(4)) Bellissima Publishing, LLC.

Florian, Douglas. Laugh-Eteria. Florian, Douglas, illus. 2008. (ENG., Illus.). 160p. (J). (gr. 1-4). pap. 8.99 (978-0-15-206148-7(7)) Houghton Mifflin Harcourt Publishing Co.

Forbes, Robert L. Beast Friends Forever. Searle, Ronald, illus. 2013. (ENG.). 80p. (J). (gr. 4-13). 19.95 (978-1-59020-808-3(0), 902808) Overlook Pr., The.

Foster, John. Fantastic Football Poems. Paul, Korky, illus. 2008. (ENG.). 32p. (YA). (gr. 4-7). pap. 10.95 (978-0-19-276349-5(0)) Oxford Univ. Pr., Inc.

Foxworthy, Jeff. Dirt on My Shirt. Björkman, Steve, illus. 32p. (J). 2013. (ENG.). (gr. -1-3). 9.99 (978-0-06-223191-8(X)) 2009. (gr. -1-3). 16.99 (978-0-06-176525-4(2)) 2009. (ENG.). (gr. k-3). pap. 3.99 (978-0-06-176524-7(4)) 2008. (gr. -1-2). lib. bdg. 17.89 (978-0-06-120847-8(7)) 2008. (ENG.). (gr. -1-3). 17.99 (978-0-06-120846-1(9)) HarperCollins Pubs.

Fuertes, Gloria. Poesias, Rimas y Disparates: Pienso Mesa y Digo Silla. 2003. (SPA.). 128p. (978-84-305-8535-9(4), SU4859) Susaeta Ediciones, S.A. ESP. Dist: Lectorum Pubns., Inc.

Greenberg, David. Don't Forget Your Etiquette! The Essential Guide to Misbehavior. Westcott, Nadine Bernard, illus. 2006. (ENG.). 40p. (J). (gr. 1-4). 17.99 (978-0-374-34990-5(8), 9780374349905, Farrar, Straus & Giroux (BYR)) Farrar, Straus & Giroux.

Grimly, Gris. Gris Grimly's Wicked Nursery Rhymes II. 2006. (ENG., Illus.). 32p. (J). (gr. 4-7). 16.95 (978-0-9729388-3-9(4)) Baby Tattoo Bks.

Hannah, Tom & Hannah, Tess. The Endless String: Poems for Children (and the people who read to Them) 2007. 60p. per. 9.95 (978-1-4327-1610-3(7)) Outskirts Pr., Inc.

Hoce, Charley. Beyond Old McDonald: Funny Poems from down on the Farm. Fernandes, Eugenie, illus. 2005. (ENG.). 32p. (J). (gr. -1-2). 16.95 (978-1-59078-312-2(3)) Boyds Mills Pr.

Johns, Isabel G. I'm Happy Being Me. Stegall, Joel E., illus. 2012. 32p. pap. 14.95 (978-1-61493-093-8(7)) Peppertree Pr., The.

Kammeraad, Kevin. The Tomato Collection. 2007. (ENG., Illus.). 64p. (J). (gr. k-5). pap., stu. ed. 12.95 (978-0-9669504-3-4(7)) Cooperfly Creative Arts, Inc.

Katz, Alan. Poems from under My Bed: LOL Halloween Rhymes. LaCoste, Gary, illus. 2013. 47p. (J). pap. (978-0-545-48295-0(X)) Scholastic, Inc.

—Poems I Wrote When No One Was Looking. Koren, Edward, illus. 2011. (ENG.). 160p. (J). (gr. 2-5). 17.99 (978-1-4169-3518-6(5), McElderry, Margaret K. Bks.) McElderry, Margaret K. Bks.

Lansky, Bruce. Rolling in the Aisles: A Collection of Laugh-Out-Loud Poems. Carpenter, Stephen, illus. 2004. 116p. (J). (978-0-88166-473-7(1)) Meadowbrook Pr.

Lansky, Bruce. A Bad Case of the Giggles. Carpenter, Stephen, illus. 2013. (Giggle Poetry Ser.). (ENG.). 128p. (J). (gr. 1-6). per. 9.95 (978-1-4169-5197-1(0)) Meadowbrook Pr.

—I Hope I Don't Strike Out! & Other Funny Sports Poems. Carpenter, Stephen, illus. 2008. 30p. (978-0-88166-535-2(5)) Meadowbrook Pr.

—What I Did on My Summer Vacation: Kids' Favorite Funny Poems about Summer Vacation. Carpenter, Stephen, illus. 2009. (978-0-88166-539-0(8)) Meadowbrook Pr.

Letendre, Peter A. If I Could Be a Doughnut. 2008. 128p. 23.95 (978-0-595-50309-4(8)); (Illus.). pap. 13.95 (978-0-595-50022-2(6)) iUniverse, Inc.

Levine, Gail Carson. Forgive Me, I Meant to Do It: False Apology Poems. Schmid, Paul & Cordell, Matthew, illus. 2012. 80p. (J). (gr. 3-7). (ENG.). 16.99 (978-0-06-178725-6(6)); lib. bdg. 16.89 (978-0-06-178726-3(4)) HarperCollins Pubs.

Lewis, J. Patrick. If You Were a Chocolate Mustache. Cordell, Matthew, illus. 2012. (ENG.). 160p. (J). (gr. 3). 18.95 (978-1-59078-927-8(X), Wordsong) Boyds Mills Pr.

—Once upon a Tomb: A Collection of Gravely Humorous Verses. Bartram, Simon, illus. 2006. (ENG.). 32p. (J). (gr. 1-4). 16.99 (978-0-7636-1837-7(3)) Candlewick Pr.

Lovvorn, Ann R. Purple Frogs & Pumpkin Seeds. Ingram, Jan, illus. 2008. 44p. per. 24.95 (978-1-4241-8734-8(6)) America Star Bks.

McMahon, Jeff & Warrick, Jessica. Swimming to the Moon: A Collection of Rhymes Without Reason. 2013. (ENG., Illus.). 192p. (J). 19.98 (978-0-9890270-0-7(7)) Leisure Time Pr.

Meadowbrook Press Staff. If Kids Ruled the School. Carpenter, Stephen, illus. 2004. (ENG.). 80p. (J). (gr. 1-6). pap. 8.95 (978-0-689-03273-8(0)) Meadowbrook Pr.

Nathan, Jeff. Calling All Animals: The First Book of PunOETRY. Ball, Liz, illus. 2003. 96p. per. 9.95 (978-0-9702730-1-7(0)) Chuckleboks. Publishing.

Nesbitt, Kenn. The Aliens Have Landed at Our School! Lucas, Margeaux, illus. 2006. (Giggle Poetry Ser.). (ENG.). 87p. (J). (gr. 1-6). per. 9.95 (978-0-689-04864-7(5)) Meadowbrook Pr.

Prelutsky, Jack. Be Glad Your Nose Is on Your Face: And Other Poems - Some of the Best of Jack Prelutsky. Dorman, Brandon, illus. 2008. (ENG.). 208p. (J). (gr. 1-5). 22.99 (978-0-06-157653-9(0), Greenwillow Bks.) HarperCollins Pubs.

—I've Lost My Hippopotamus. Urbanovic, Jackie, illus. 2012. 144p. (J). (gr. k-5). (ENG.). 18.99 (978-0-06-201457-3(9)); lib. bdg. 19.89 (978-0-06-201458-0(7)) HarperCollins Pubs. (Greenwillow Bks.).

—The New Kid on the Block. Stevenson, James, illus. 2013. (ENG.). 160p. (J). (gr. k-5). pap. 9.99 (978-0-06-223950-1(3), Greenwillow Bks.) HarperCollins Pubs.

Schoff, Bill. If Life Were a Hollywood Movie: Still More Humorous Poems for Kids & Adults. 2012. (ENG.). 75p. pap. 24.95 (978-1-4787-1708-9(4)) Outskirts Pr., Inc.

Sheppard, Keith. Welcome to the Crazyverse: A Collection of Comic Poems about Famous People in History. 2012. (Illus.). 108p. pap. (978-1-904808-85-5(9)) Evertype.

Silverstein, Shel. Don't Bump the Glump! And Other Fantasies. Silverstein, Shel, illus. 2014. (ENG., Illus.). 64p. (J). (gr. -1-3). 17.99 (978-0-06-149338-6(4)) HarperCollins Pubs.

—Every Thing on It. Silverstein, Shel, illus. 2011. (Illus.). 208p. (J). (gr. -1-3). (ENG.). 19.99 (978-0-06-199816-4(8)); lib. bdg. 20.89 (978-0-06-199817-1(6)) HarperCollins Pubs.

—Falling Up: Poems & Drawings. Silverstein, Shel, illus. 2006. (ENG., Illus.). 184p. (J). (gr. -1-3). 19.99 (978-0-06-024802-4(5)) HarperCollins Pubs.

—Falling Up: Poems & Drawings. 2006. (CHI., Illus.). 171p. (J). (978-7-5442-3557-0(2)) Nanhai Publishing Co.

—Falling up Special Edition. Silverstein, Shel, illus. 2015. (ENG., Illus.). 200p. (J). (gr. -1-3). 19.99 (978-0-06-232133-6(1)) HarperCollins Pubs.

—Hay Luz en el Desvan. Alonso Blanco, Victoria, tr. 2006. (SPA & ENG.). 169p. (J). (gr. 4-7). pap. 16.95 (978-84-666-0567-0(3), EB31012) Ediciones B ESP. Dist: Independent Pubs. Group, Lectorum Pubns., Inc.

—Runny Babbit: A Billy Sook. Silverstein, Shel, illus. (ENG., Illus.). 96p. (J). (gr. -1-3). 2015. 18.99 (978-0-06-025653-1(2)) 2006. 22.99 (978-0-06-113047-2(8)) HarperCollins Pubs.

—Runny Babbit Returns. Silverstein, Shel, illus. 2017. (Illus.). 96p. (J). (gr. -1-3). 19.99 **(978-0-06-247939-6(3))**; lib. bdg. 20.89 **(978-0-06-247985-3(7))** HarperCollins Pubs.

Silverstein, Shel. Where the Sidewalk Ends: Poems & Drawings. Silverstein, Shel, illus. (Illus.). (J). (gr. -1-3). 2014. (ENG.). 176p. 19.99 (978-0-06-025667-8(2)) 30th anniv. ed. 2014. (ENG., 192p. 18.99 (978-0-06-057234-1(5)) 30th anniv. ed. 2004. 192p. lib. bdg. 19.89 (978-0-06-058653-9(2)) HarperCollins Pubs.

Spinelli, Eileen. Do You Have a Hat? Valério, Geraldo, illus. 2004. (ENG.). 40p. (J). (gr. -1-3). 17.99 (978-0-689-86253-3(9), Simon & Schuster Bks. For Young Readers) Simon & Schuster Bks. For Young Readers.

Starr, L. Lee. Huggily Buggily & the Magical Fart of Wind. 2012. 40p. pap. 14.00 (978-0-9848694-4-2(1)) Mystic Hippo Media Publishing.

Steig, Jeanne. Consider the Lemming. Steig, William, illus. 2016. (ENG.). 48p. (J). (gr. -1-3). 17.99 (978-1-4814-3963-3(4), Atheneum/Caitlyn Dlouhy Books) Simon & Schuster Children's Publishing.

—Divine Comedies: The Old Testament Made Easy & a Gift from Zeus. Steig, William, illus. 2016. (ENG.). 200p. (YA). (gr. 7). 19.99 (978-1-4814-3957-2(X)) Simon & Schuster Children's Publishing.

Stone, Tiffany. Floyd the Flamingo: And His Flock of Friends, 1 vol. Shoemaker, Kathryn, illus. 2004. (ENG.). 64p. (J). (gr. 2-5). per. 7.95 (978-1-896580-58-6(0)) Tradewind Bks. CAN. Dist: Orca Bk. Pubs. USA.

Swaim, Jessica. Scarum Fair. Ashley, Carol, illus. 2010. (ENG.). 32p. (J). (gr. 4-6). 17.95 (978-1-59078-590-4(8), Wordsong) Boyds Mills Pr.

Trillin, Calvin. No Fair! No Fair! And Other Jolly Poems of Childhood. Chast, Roz, illus. 2016. (ENG.). 40p. (J). (gr. -1-3). 17.99 (978-0-545-82578-8(4), Orchard Bks.) Scholastic, Inc.

Whiting, Jim. No Perfect People, Please! Poems & audio cd By. 2007. (Illus.). 64p. (J). 16.95 (978-0-9759276-2-5(0)) Culturelink Pr.

Wilson, Karma. What's the Weather Inside? Blitt, Barry, illus. 2009. (ENG.). 176p. (J). (gr. 1-5). 17.99 (978-1-4169-0092-4(6), McElderry, Margaret K. Bks.) McElderry, Margaret K. Bks.

HUMOROUS STORIES

see also Wit and Humor

Aakeson, Kim Fupz & Garde, Ruth. Vitello Becomes a Businessman. Bojesen, Niels Bo, illus. 2014. (ENG.). 32p. (J). (gr. k-3). pap. 9.99 (978-1-78269-001-6(8), Pushkin Press) Steerforth Pr.

—Vitello Carries a Knife. Bojesen, Niels Bo, illus. 2014. (ENG.). 32p. (J). (gr. k-3). pap. 9.99 (978-1-78269-005-4(0), Pushkin Press) Steerforth Pr.

—Vitello Gets a Yucky Girlfriend. Bojesen, Niels Bo, illus. 2014. (ENG.). 32p. (J). (gr. k-3). pap. 9.99 (978-1-78269-003-0(4), Pushkin Press) Steerforth Pr.

—Vitello Scratches a Car. Bojesen, Niels Bo, illus. 2014. (ENG.). 32p. (J). (gr. k-3). pap. 9.99 (978-1-78269-002-3(6), Pushkin Press) Steerforth Pr.

—Vitello Wants a Dad. Bojesen, Niels Bo, illus. 2014. (ENG.). 32p. (J). (gr. k-3). pap. 9.99 (978-1-78269-004-7(2), Pushkin Press) Steerforth Pr.

Abbott, Bud & Costello, Lou. Who's on First? 2013. (Pop Classics Ser.). (ENG., Illus.). 40p. (J). (gr. 1-4). 16.95 (978-1-59474-590-4(0)) Quirk Bks.

Abrefah, Nana K. My Amazing Short Stories & Questions. 2008. 60p. pap. 8.95 (978-0-595-51861-6(3)) iUniverse, Inc.

Abu-Bakr, Sandra. Tales of Lovable Spike: Spike- on the Go! 2008. 72p. pap. 8.95 (978-0-595-47326-7(1)) iUniverse, Inc.

Acher, Gabriela. El Amor en Tiempos del Colesterol.Tr. of Love in Cholesterol Times. (SPA.). (978-950-07-1540-9(6)) Editorial Sudamericana S.A.

Adam, Adam, et al. Who Is It? Two Yellow Eyes Shining in the Dark... 2012. (ENG., Illus.). 16p. (J). (gr. -1). bds. 9.95 (978-2-7338-2146-6(6)) Auzou, Philippe Editions FRA. Dist: Consortium Bk. Sales & Distribution.

Adams, Pam, illus. There Was an Old Lady Who Swallowed the Sea. 2007. (Classic Books with Holes Board Book Ser.). (ENG.). 14p. (J). (gr. -1-k). bds. (978-1-84643-073-2(9)) Child's Play International Ltd.

Adams, Richard. The Tyger Voyage. Bayley, Nicola, illus. 2013. 32p. (J). 15.95 net. (978-1-56792-491-6(3)) Godine, David R. Pub.

Adams, William J. Hate that Thunder. Stiglich, Tom, illus. 2005. 24p. (J). pap. 8.95 (978-0-9772757-0-0(1)) Mandy & Andy Bks., Inc.

Adamson, Ged, illus. I Want to Grow. 2017. (ENG.). 32p. (J). (gr. -1-3). 16.95 (978-1-62979-585-0(2)) Boyds Mills Pr.

—Meet the Mckaws. 2015. (ENG.). 32p. (J). (gr. -1-k). 16.95 (978-1-62914-618-8(8), Sky Pony Pr.) Skyhorse Publishing Co., Inc.

Adderson, Caroline. Jasper John Dooley: Not in Love. Clanton, Ben, illus. 2015. (Jasper John Dooley Ser.). (ENG.). 132p. (J). (gr. 2-5). pap. 7.95 (978-1-77138-343-1(7)) Kids Can Pr., Ltd. CAN. Dist: Hachette Bk. Group.

Adeney, Anne. Two Hungry Birds. O'Kif, illus. 2008. (Reading Corner Ser.). (ENG.). 24p. (J). (gr. k-2). pap. 6.99 (978-0-7496-7693-3(0), Franklin Watts) Hachette Children's Group GBR. Dist: Hachette Bk. Group.

—Where Are My Glasses? Vagnozzi, Barbara, illus. 2008. (Reading Corner Ser.). (ENG.). 24p. (J). (gr. k-2). pap. 6.99 (978-0-7496-7694-0(9), Franklin Watts) Hachette Children's Group GBR. Dist: Hachette Bk. Group.

Agee, Jon. It's Only Stanley. 2015. (J). 14.99 (978-1-63379-787-1(2)); 49.99 (978-1-63379-786-4(4)) Dreamscape Media, LLC.

—It's Only Stanley. 2015. (ENG., Illus.). 32p. (J). (gr. k-3). 17.99 (978-0-8037-3907-9(9), Dial Bks) Penguin Young Readers Group.

—Milo's Hat Trick. 2017. (ENG., Illus.). 40p. (J). (gr. k-3). 17.99 **(978-0-7352-2987-7(2)**, Dial Bks) Penguin Young Readers Group.

Agee, Jon. Nothing. Agee, Jon, illus. 2007. (ENG., Illus.). 32p. (gr. -1-3). 16.99 (978-0-7868-3694-9(6)) Hyperion Pr.

Ahlberg, Allan. Previously. Ingman, Bruce, illus. 2011. (ENG.). 32p. (J). (gr. -1-3). pap. 6.99 (978-0-7636-5304-0(7)) Candlewick Pr.

—Starting School. braille ed. 2004. (J). (gr. k-3). spiral bd. (978-0-616-01526-1(7)) Canadian National Institute for the Blind/Institut National Canadien pour les Aveugles.

Ahlberg, Allan & Ahlberg, Janet. Starting School. (ENG., Illus.). 32p. (J). pap. 9.95 (978-0-14-050737-9(X)) Penguin Bks., Ltd. GBR. Dist: Trafalgar Square Publishing.

Aiken, Joan. Arabel's Raven. Blake, Quentin, illus. 2007. (ENG.). 160p. (J). (gr. 2-5). pap. 11.95 (978-0-15-206094-7(4)) Houghton Mifflin Harcourt Publishing Co.

—The Serial Garden. 2012. (ENG.). 320p. (J). (gr. 4). pap. 16.00 (978-1-931520-82-9(8), Big Mouth Hse.) Small Beer Pr.

Ailes, Mark Cusco. The Tree of No Boundaries: Book One. 2009. 196p. pap. 14.95 (978-0-595-52834-9(1)) iUniverse, Inc.

Albee, Sarah. The Bunny Hop. Swanson, Maggie, illus. 2004. (Big Bird's Favorites Board Bks.). (ENG.). 24p. (J). (gr. k — 1). bds. 4.99 (978-0-375-82693-1(9), Random Hse. Bks. for Young Readers) Random Hse. Children's Bks.

—Elmo's Tricky Tongue Twisters. Swanson, Maggie, illus. 2011. (Big Bird's Favorites Board Bks.). (ENG.). 24p. (J). (gr. k — 1). bds. 4.99 (978-0-375-87249-5(3), Random Hse. Bks. for Young Readers) Random Hse. Children's Bks.

Alexander, Lori. Backhoe Joe. Cameron, Craig, illus. 2014. (ENG.). 40p. (J). (gr. -1-3). 15.99 (978-0-06-225015-5(9)) HarperCollins Pubs.

Alexander, Troas. A Cat's Tale. Roberts, Ramona, illus. 2007. 36p. per. 14.95 (978-1-59858-371-7(9)) Dog Ear Publishing, LLC.

Allan, Nicholas. Android in the Attic. 2013. (ENG., Illus.). 192p. (J). (gr. 2-4). pap. 7.99 (978-0-340-99706-2(0)) Hodder & Stoughton GBR. Dist: Hachette Bk. Group.

Allard, Harry G., Jr. Miss Nelson Is Back, 1 vol. Marshall, James, illus. 2011. (ENG.). 32p. (J). (gr. -1-3). audio compact disk 10.99 (978-0-547-57718-0(4)) Houghton Mifflin Harcourt Publishing Co.

Allen, Elanna. Itsy Mitsy Runs Away. Allen, Elanna, illus. 2011. (ENG., Illus.). 40p. (J). (gr. -1-2). 16.99 (978-1-4424-0671-1(2), Atheneum Bks. for Young Readers) Simon & Schuster Children's Publishing.

Allen, Traudi. The Squeaky Door. 2012. 40p. pap. 16.95 (978-1-4525-0826-9(7)) Balboa Pr.

Allen, Will. Swords for Hire: Two of the Most Unlikely Heroes You'll Ever Meet. Beck, David Michael, illus. 2003. 168p. (gr. 3-18). pap. 6.95 (978-0-9724882-0-4(0)) Centerpunch Pr.

Allison, Jennifer. Gilda Joyce, Psychic Investigator. 2006. (Gilda Joyce Ser.). (ENG.). 336p. (J). (gr. 5-18). reprint ed. 8.99 (978-0-14-240698-4(8), Puffin Books) Penguin Young Readers Group.

Alonso, Fernando. Sopaboba. 8th ed. 2003. (SPA., Illus.). 136p. (978-84-239-9025-2(7), EC1519) Espasa Calpe, S.A. ESP. Dist: Lectorum Pubns., Inc.

Altebrando, Tara. My Life in Dioramas. 2015. (ENG., Illus.). 256p. (J). (gr. 2-7). 14.95 (978-0-7624-5681-9(7), Running Pr. Kids) Running Pr. Bk. Pubs.

Amato, Mary. Our Teacher Is a Vampire & Other (Not) True Stories. Long, Ethan, illus. 2017. (ENG.). 256p. (J). (gr. 3-7). pap. 6.99 (978-0-8234-3769-6(8)) Holiday Hse., Inc.

—Stinky & Successful: The Riot Brothers Never Stop! Long, Ethan, illus. 2007. (ENG.). 160p. (J). (gr. 2-5). 16.95 (978-0-8234-2100-8(7)) Holiday Hse., Inc.

American Heritage Dictionary Editors. Qué Día Es? Zagarenski, Pamela, illus. 2005.Tr. of What Day Is It? (SPA & ENG.). 8p. (J). (— 1). bds. 3.95 (978-0-618-44874-6(8)) Houghton Mifflin Harcourt Publishing Co.

Andersen, Hans Christian. El Ruisenor.Tr. of Nightingale. (SPA.). 32p. (J). (gr. 2-3). 12.95 (978-84-233-1567-3(3)) Ediciones Destino ESP. Dist: Planeta Publishing Corp.

Anderson, Brian. The Adventures of Commander Zack Proton & the Red Giant. Holgate, Douglas, illus. 2006. (Adventures of Commander Zack Proton Ser.: 1). (ENG.). 128p. (J). (gr. 2-5). pap. 5.99 (978-1-4169-1364-1(5), Simon & Schuster/Paula Wiseman Bks.) Simon & Schuster/Paula Wiseman Bks.

—The Adventures of Commander Zack Proton & the Warlords of Nibblecheese. Holgate, Douglas, illus. 2006. (Adventures of Commander Zack Proton Ser.: 2). (ENG.). 112p. (J). (gr. 2-5). pap. 5.99 (978-1-4169-1365-8(3), Aladdin) Simon & Schuster Children's Publishing.

Anderson, Brian & Anderson, Liam. Monster Chefs. Anderson, Brian, illus. 2014. (ENG., Illus.). 32p. (J). (gr. -1-2). 16.99 (978-1-59643-808-8(8), 9781596438088) Roaring Brook Pr.

Anderson, Derek. Ten Hungry Pigs: An Epic Lunch Adventure. Anderson, Derek, illus. 2016. (ENG., Illus.). 40p. (J). (gr. -1-k). 16.99 (978-0-545-16848-9(1)) Scholastic, Inc.

Anderson, John David. Sidekicked. 2013. (ENG.). 384p. (J). (gr. 3-7). 16.99 (978-0-06-213314-4(4), Waldon Pond Pr.) HarperCollins Pubs.

Anderson, Laurie Halse. The Hair of Zoe Fleefenbacher Goes to School. Hoyt, Ard, illus. 2009. (ENG.). 32p. (J). (gr. 1-5). 17.99 (978-0-689-85809-3(4), Simon & Schuster Bks. For Young Readers) Simon & Schuster Bks. For Young Readers.

Anderson, M. T. Agent Q, or the Smell of Danger! Cyrus, Kurt, illus. (Pals in Peril Tale Ser.). (ENG.). (J). (gr. 5-9). 2011. 320p. pap. 6.99 (978-1-4424-2640-5(3)) 2010. 304p. 16.99 (978-1-4169-8640-9(5)) Beach Lane Bks. (Beach Lane Bks.).

—Burger Wuss. 2008. (ENG., Illus.). 192p. (YA). (gr. 9). per. 8.99 (978-0-7636-3178-9(7)) Candlewick Pr.

—The Clue of the Linoleum Lederhosen. Cyrus, Kurt, illus. 2010. (Pals in Peril Tale Ser.). (ENG.). (J). (gr. 5-9). 256p. 17.99 (978-1-4424-0697-1(6)); 272p. pap. 6.99 (978-1-4424-0702-2(6)) Beach Lane Bks. (Beach Lane Bks.).

—He Laughed with His Other Mouths. Cyrus, Kurt, illus. 2014. (Pals in Peril Tale Ser.). (ENG.). 304p. (J). (gr. 5-9). 17.99 (978-1-4424-5110-0(6), Beach Lane Bks.) Beach Lane Bks.

—Jasper Dash & the Flame-Pits of Delaware. Cyrus, Kurt, illus. (Pals in Peril Tale Ser.). (ENG.). (J). (gr. 5-9). 2010. 448p. pap. 6.99 (978-1-4424-0838-8(3)) 2009. 432p. 16.99 (978-1-4169-8639-3(1)) Beach Lane Bks. (Beach Lane Bks.).

—Zombie Mommy. Cyrus, Kurt, illus. (Pals in Peril Tale Ser.). (ENG.). 224p. (J). (gr. 5-9). 2012. pap. 6.99 (978-1-4424-5440-8(7)) 2011. 16.99 (978-1-4169-8641-6(3)) Beach Lane Bks. (Beach Lane Bks.).

—Zombie Mommy. Cyrus, Kurt, illus. 2011. (M. T. Anderson's Thrilling Tales Ser.). 240p. 16.99 (978-1-4424-3068-6(0)) Simon & Schuster Children's Publishing.

Anderson, Patricia. Tails of a Woodswoman. 2008. 72p. pap. 9.95 (978-1-4327-2615-7(3)) Outskirts Pr., Inc.

Anderson, Peggy Perry. La Niñera Dijo: "Es Hora de Ir a la Cama" 2017. (Green Light Readers Level 1 Ser.). (ENG., Illus.). 32p. (J). (gr. -1-3). pap. 3.99 (978-0-544-80895-9(9), HMH Books For Young Readers) Houghton Mifflin Harcourt Publishing Co.

Andrea, Karen. The Enchanted Library. 2008. 172p. pap. (978-1-84923-182-4(6)) YouWriteOn.

Andrews, Jesse. The Haters. (ENG.). 336p. (YA). (gr. 8-17). 2017. pap. 9.95 (978-1-4197-2370-4(7)) 2016. 18.95 (978-1-4197-2078-9(3)) Abrams, Inc. (Amulet Bks.).

—The Haters. 2017. (YA). lib. bdg. 20.80 **(978-0-606-39688-2(8))** Turtleback Bks.

Andrews, Jesse. Me & Earl & the Dying Girl. (ENG.). 304p. (YA). (gr. 9-17). 2012. 17.95 (978-1-4197-0176-4(2), Amulet Bks.) 2015. 17.95 (978-1-4197-2027-7(9)) 2015. 17.95 (978-1-4197-2013-0(9), Amulet Bks.) 2015. pap. 9.95 (978-1-4197-1960-8(2), Amulet Bks.) Abrams, Inc.

—Me & Earl & the Dying Girl. 2015. (CHI.). 320p. (YA). (gr. 9-17). pap. (978-986-344-282-0(8)) Rye Field Publishing, Co.

—Me & Earl & the Dying Girl. 2015. lib. bdg. 20.80 (978-0-606-37113-1(3)) Turtleback Bks.

Angleberger, Tom. Crankee Doodle. Bell, Cece, illus. 2013. (ENG.). 32p. (J). (gr. -1-3). 16.99 (978-0-547-81854-2(8)) Houghton Mifflin Harcourt Publishing Co.

—Emperor Pickletine Rides the Bus. (Origami Yoda Ser.). (ENG., Illus.). (J). (gr. 3-7). 2016. 240p. pap. 7.95 (978-1-4197-2201-1(8)) 2014. 224p. 13.95 (978-1-4197-0933-3(X)) Abrams, Inc. (Amulet Bks.).

—Emperor Pickletine Rides the Bus. 2014. (Origami Yoda Files Ser.: 6). (J). lib. bdg. 25.70 (978-0-606-36168-2(5)) Turtleback Bks.

—Fake Mustache: Or, How Jodie o'Rodeo & Her Wonder Horse (and Some Nerdy Kid) Saved the U. S. Presidential Election from a Mad Genius Criminal Mastermind. 2012. (ENG., Illus.). 208p. (J). (gr. 3-7). 14.95 (978-1-4197-0194-8(0), Amulet Bks.) Abrams, Inc.

—Inspector Flytrap. Bell, Cece, illus. 2016. (Inspector Flytrap Ser.). (ENG.). 112p. (J). (gr. 1-4). 14.95 (978-1-4197-0948-7(8)); 14.95 (978-1-4197-0955-5(0)); pap. 5.95 (978-1-4197-0965-4(8)) Abrams, Inc. (Amulet Bks.).

—Poop Fountain! (Qwikpick Papers). (ENG., Illus.). (J). (gr. 3-7). 2015. 160p. pap. 6.95 (978-1-4197-1636-2(0)) 2014. 144p. 12.95 (978-1-4197-0425-3(7)) Abrams, Inc. (Amulet Bks.).

—The Rat with the Human Face. 2015. (Qwikpick Papers). (ENG., Illus.). 160p. (J). (gr. 3-7). 12.95 (978-1-4197-1489-4(9), Amulet Bks.) Abrams, Inc.

—The Rat with the Human Face: The Qwikpick Papers. 2016. (Qwikpick Papers). (ENG., Illus.). 176p. (J). (gr. 3-7). pap. 6.95 (978-1-4197-1940-0(8), Amulet Bks.) Abrams, Inc.

—Rocket & Groot: Keep on Truckin'! Angleberger, Tom, illus. 2017. (Marvel Middle Grade Novel Ser.). (ENG., Illus.). 272p. (J). (gr. 3-7). 13.99 (978-1-4847-8141-8(4), Marvel Pr.) Disney Publishing Worldwide.

—To Kick a Corpse: The Qwikpick Papers. 2016. (Qwikpick Papers). (ENG., Illus.). 160p. (J). (gr. 3-7). 12.95 (978-1-4197-1906-6(8), Amulet Bks.) Abrams, Inc.

Angleberger, Tom & Dellinger, Paul. Fuzzy. 2016. (ENG.). 272p. (J). (gr. 3-7). 14.95 (978-1-4197-2122-9(4), Amulet Bks.) Abrams, Inc.

Anglemyer, Jordan, illus. Grandpa's Favorites: A collection of quotes, things to ponder, stories, bits of verse, & Humor. 2007. 77p. (YA). per. 10.95 (978-0-9796251-2-1(2)) Robertson Publishing.

Anholt, Laurence. Bendy Ben. Ross, Tony, illus. 2015. (My Freaky Family Ser.: 5). (ENG.). 48p. (J). (gr. k-2). pap. 8.99 (978-1-4083-3758-5(4)) Hodder & Stoughton GBR. Dist: Hachette Bk. Group.

—Hairy Harold. Ross, Tony, illus. 2015. (Seriously Scary Ser.: 8). (ENG.). 48p. (J). (gr. k-2). pap. 8.99 (978-1-4083-3752-3(5)) Hodder & Stoughton GBR. Dist: Hachette Bk. Group.

—Poetic Polly. Ross, Tony, illus. 2015. (My Freaky Family Ser.: 3). (ENG.). 48p. (J). (gr. k-2). pap. 8.99 (978-1-4083-3754-7(1)) Hodder & Stoughton GBR. Dist: Hachette Bk. Group.

—Rude Ruby. Ross, Tony, illus. 2015. (My Freaky Family Ser.: 1). (ENG.). 48p. (J). (gr. k-2). pap. 8.99 (978-1-4083-3639-7(1)) Hodder & Stoughton GBR. Dist: Hachette Bk. Group.

Anstee, Ashlyn. Are We There, Yeti? Anstee, Ashlyn, illus. 2015. (ENG., Illus.). 40p. (J). (gr. -1-3). 17.99 (978-1-4814-3089-0(0), Simon & Schuster Bks. For Young Readers) Simon & Schuster Bks. For Young Readers.

Appelt, Kathi. The True Blue Scouts of Sugar Man Swamp. 2014. (ENG., Illus.). 352p. (J). (gr. 3-7). pap. 8.99 (978-1-4424-2108-0(8), Atheneum Bks. for Young Readers) Simon & Schuster Children's Publishing.

—The True Blue Scouts of Sugar Man Swamp. Bricking, Jennifer, illus. 2013. (ENG.). 336p. (J). (gr. 3-7). 16.99 (978-1-4424-2105-9(3)) Simon & Schuster Children's Publishing.

—The True Blue Scouts of Sugar Man Swamp. 2014. lib. bdg. 19.65 (978-0-606-35793-7(9)) Turtleback Bks.

Applegate, Katherine. Don't Swap Your Sweater for a Dog. Biggs, Brian, illus. 2008. (Roscoe Riley Rules Ser.: 3). (ENG.). 96p. (J). (gr. 1-5). 15.99 (978-0-06-114886-6(5)); pap. 4.99 (978-0-06-114885-9(7)) HarperCollins Pubs.

—Don't Tap-Dance on Your Teacher. Biggs, Brian, illus. 2009. (Roscoe Riley Rules Ser.: 5). (ENG.). 96p. (J). (gr. 1-5). pap. 4.99 (978-0-06-114889-7(X)) HarperCollins Pubs.

—Don't Tap-Dance on Your Teacher. 2009. (Roscoe Riley Rules Ser.: 5). (J). lib. bdg. 14.75 (978-0-606-05007-4(8), Turtleback) Turtleback Bks.

—Never Glue Your Friends to Chairs. Biggs, Brian, illus. 2008. (Roscoe Riley Rules Ser.: 1). (ENG.). 96p. (J). (gr. 1-5). 15.99 (978-0-06-114882-8(2)); pap. 4.99 (978-0-06-114881-1(4)) HarperCollins Pubs.

—Never Race a Runaway Pumpkin. Biggs, Brian, illus. 2009. (Roscoe Riley Rules Ser.: 7). (ENG.). 96p. (J). (gr. 1-5). 15.99 (978-0-06-178372-2(2)); pap. 4.99 (978-0-06-178370-8(6)) HarperCollins Pubs.

—Never Race a Runaway Pumpkin. 2009. (Roscoe Riley Rules Ser.: 7). (J). lib. bdg. 14.75 (978-0-606-06090-5(1), Turtleback) Turtleback Bks.

—Never Swim in Applesauce. Biggs, Brian, illus. 2008. (Roscoe Riley Rules Ser.: 4). (ENG.). 96p. (J). (gr. 1-5). 15.99 (978-0-06-114888-0(1)); pap. 4.99 (978-0-06-114887-3(3)) HarperCollins Pubs.

—Never Swipe a Bully's Bear. Biggs, Brian, illus. 2008. (Roscoe Riley Rules Ser.: 2). (ENG.). 96p. (J). (gr. 1-5). 15.99 (978-0-06-114884-2(9)); pap. 4.99 (978-0-06-114883-5(0)) HarperCollins Pubs.

—Never Walk in Shoes That Talk. Biggs, Brian, illus. 2009. (Roscoe Riley Rules Ser.: 6). (ENG.). 96p. (J). (gr. 1-5). 14.99 (978-0-06-114892-7(X)); pap. 4.99 (978-0-06-114891-0(1)) HarperCollins Pubs.

—Never Walk in Shoes That Talk. 2009. (Roscoe Riley Rules Ser.: 06). lib. bdg. 14.75 (978-0-606-05019-7(1), Turtleback) Turtleback Bks.

Aptekar, Devan. How to Train Your Dragon - Befriending a Foe. 2010. (How to Train Your Dragon Ser.). 24p. (J). (gr. -1-2). pap. 3.99 (978-0-06-156735-3(3), HarperFestival) HarperCollins Pubs.

Archambault, Douglas J. The Adventures of Little Buddy & Grizz, 1 vol. 2009. 64p. pap. 19.95 (978-1-60836-159-5(4)) America Star Bks.

Archambault, Marc. Hal the Unwashed Dragon. 2009. 28p. pap. 18.98 (978-0-557-09894-1(7)) Lulu Pr., Inc.

—Hal the Unwashed Dragon (perfect Bound) 2009. 32p. pap. 18.97 (978-0-557-12009-3(8)) Lulu Pr., Inc.

Archer, Dosh. Big Bad Wolf. Archer, Dosh, illus. (Urgency Emergency! Ser.). (ENG., Illus.). 48p. (J). (gr. -1-3). 2015. pap. 9.99 (978-0-8075-8351-7(0)) 2013. 12.99 (978-0-8075-8352-4(9)) Whitman, Albert & Co.

—Humpty's Fall. Archer, Dosh, illus. (Urgency Emergency! Ser.). (ENG., Illus.). 48p. (J). (gr. -1-3). 2016. pap. 9.99 (978-0-8075-8362-3(6)) 2015. 12.99 (978-0-8075-8356-2(1)) Whitman, Albert & Co.

—Itsy Bitsy Spider. Archer, Dosh, illus. 2013. (Urgency Emergency! Ser.). (ENG., Illus.). 48p. (J). (gr. -1-3). 12.99 (978-0-8075-8358-6(8)) Whitman, Albert & Co.

—Little Elephant's Blocked Trunk. Archer, Dosh, illus. 2014. (Urgency Emergency! Ser.). (ENG., Illus.). 48p. (J). (gr. -1-3). 12.99 (978-0-8075-8354-8(5)) Whitman, Albert & Co.

Archer, E. Geek Fantasy Novel. 2011. (ENG.). 320p. (J). (gr. 7-7). 17.99 (978-0-545-16040-7(5), Scholastic Pr.) Scholastic, Inc.

Archer, Nick & McDonald, Megan. Rule of Three. 2010. (Sisters Club Ser.: 2). (ENG., Illus.). 240p. (J). (gr. 3-7). pap. 5.99 (978-0-7636-4830-5(2)) Candlewick Pr.

—Rule of Three. Consolazio, Pamela A., illus. 2009. (Sisters Club Ser.: 2). (ENG.). 240p. (J). (gr. 3-7). 15.99 (978-0-7636-4153-5(7)) Candlewick Pr.

Archibold, Tim, illus. Knock Knock! The Best Knock Knock Jokes Ever! 2004. (Sidesplitters Ser.). (ENG.). 64p. (YA). (gr. 1-5). pap. 6.99 (978-0-7534-5707-8(5), 9780753457078, Kingfisher) Roaring Brook Pr.

Armstrong-Ellis, Carey F. I Love You More Than Moldy Ham. 2015. (ENG., Illus.). 32p. (J). (gr. -1-3). 14.95 (978-1-4197-1646-1(8), Abrams Bks. for Young Readers) Abrams, Inc.

Armstrong-Ellis, Carey F. Ten Creepy Monsters. (ENG., Illus.). 32p. (J). (gr. k-2). 2017. pap. 4.95 **(978-1-4197-2741-2(9))** 2012. 15.95 (978-1-4197-0433-8(8)) Abrams, Inc. (Abrams Bks. for Young Readers).

Armstrong, Jennifer. Once upon a Banana. Small, David, illus. (ENG.). 48p. (J). (gr. -1-3). 2013. 6.99 (978-0-689-85951-9(1)) 2006. 17.99 (978-0-689-84251-1(1)) Simon & Schuster/Paula Wiseman Bks. (Simon & Schuster/Paula Wiseman Bks.).

Arnold, Tedd. Dirty Gert. Arnold, Tedd, illus. (ENG., Illus.). (J). (gr. 2-5). 2014. 32p. 6.99 (978-0-8234-3054-3(5)) 2013. 40p. 16.95 (978-0-8234-2404-7(9)) Holiday Hse., Inc.

—Fly Guy's Ninja Christmas. Arnold, Tedd, illus. 2016. (Fly Guy Ser.: 16). (ENG., Illus.). 32p. (J). (gr. -1-3). 6.99 (978-0-545-66277-2(X)) Scholastic, Inc.

—No Jumping on the Bed! 25th anniv. ed. 2012. (ENG., Illus.). 32p. (J). (gr. -1-1). 16.99 (978-0-8037-3563-7(4), Dial Bks) Penguin Young Readers Group.

—A Pet for Fly Guy. Arnold, Tedd, illus. 2014. (Fly Guy Ser.). (ENG., Illus.). 32p. (J). (gr. -1-3). 16.99 (978-0-545-31615-6(4), Orchard Bks.) Scholastic, Inc.

—Prince Fly Guy. 2015. (Fly Guy Ser.: 15). (ENG., Illus.). 32p. (J). (gr. -1-3). 6.99 (978-0-545-66275-8(3), Cartwheel Bks.) Scholastic, Inc.

—Prince Fly Guy. 2015. (Fly Guy Ser.: 15). lib. bdg. 17.20 (978-0-606-37831-4(6)) Turtleback Bks.

—There Was an Old Lady Who Swallowed Fly Guy. Arnold, Tedd, illus. 2007. (Fly Guy Ser.: 4). (ENG., Illus.). 32p. (J). (gr. -1-3). 6.99 (978-0-439-63906-4(9)) Scholastic, Inc.

Arnold, Tedd, et al. Noodlehead Nightmares. Arnold, Tedd, illus. 2016. (ENG., Illus.). 48p. (J). (gr. 1-5). 15.95 (978-0-8234-3566-1(0)) Holiday Hse., Inc.

—Noodleheads See the Future. Arnold, Tedd, illus. 2017. (ENG., Illus.). 48p. (J). (gr. 1-5). 15.95 (978-0-8234-3673-6(X)) Holiday Hse., Inc.

Aronson, Deborah. Where's My Tushy? Stevanovic, Ivica, illus. 2014. (ENG.). 24p. (J). (gr. -1-3). 17.95 (978-1-4677-1197-5(7), Carolrhoda Bks.) Lerner Publishing Group.

Arps, Melissa & Lagonegro, Melissa. Friends Forever. Random House Disney Staff, illus. 2009. (Step into Reading Ser.). (ENG.). 32p. (J). (gr. k-3). pap. 3.99 (978-0-7364-2597-1(7), RH/Disney) Random Hse. Children's Bks.

Asher, Sandy. Chicken Story Time. Fearing, Mark, illus. 2016. (ENG.). 40p. (J). (-k). 17.99 (978-0-8037-3944-4(3), Dial Bks) Penguin Young Readers Group.

Asquith, Ros. Letters from an Alien Schoolboy. 2013. (ENG., Illus.). 192p. (J). (gr. 1-5). 12.95 (978-1-62087-536-0(5), 620536, Sky Pony Pr.) Skyhorse Publishing Co., Inc.

—Trixie Ace Ghost Buster. 2008. (Trixie Ser.). (ENG., Illus.). 176p. (J). (gr. 3-6). pap. 7.99 (978-0-00-725909-0(3)) HarperCollins Pubs. Ltd. GBR. Dist: Independent Pubs. Group.

Athey, Victoria. No Peas, Please! Delaney, Molly, illus. 2005. (ENG.). 20p. (gr. k-2). pap. 8.95 (978-1-57874-087-1(8), Kaeden Bks.) Kaeden Corp.

Atwater, Richard. Mr. Popper's Penguins. 2009. 160p. pap. 6.99 (978-0-316-10616-0(X)) Little, Brown Bks. for Young Readers.

Atwater, Richard & Atwater, Florence. Mr. Popper's Penguins. 2009. 9.00 (978-0-7848-3295-0(1), Everbind) Marco Bk. Co.

Atwood, Megan. Ice Cream Summer. Andrewson, Natalie, illus. 2017. (Orchard Novel Ser.: 1). (ENG.). 272p. (J). (gr. 2-6). 12.99 **(978-1-4814-9047-4(8)**, Aladdin) Simon & Schuster Children's Publishing.

Auch, Mary Jane. Beauty & the Beaks: A Turkey's Cautionary Tale. Auch, Herm & Auch, Mary Jane, illus. 2007. (ENG.). 32p. (J). (gr. -1-3). 17.95 (978-0-8234-1990-6(8)) Holiday Hse., Inc.

—Chickerella. Auch, Herm, illus. 2006. (ENG.). 32p. (J). (gr. -1-3). 6.95 (978-0-8234-2015-5(9)) Holiday Hse., Inc.

—The Plot Chickens. Auch, Mary Jane & Auch, Herm, illus. (ENG.). 32p. (J). (gr. -1-3). 2010. pap. 7.99 (978-0-8234-2307-1(7)) 2009. 17.95 (978-0-8234-2087-2(6)) Holiday Hse., Inc.

—The Princess & the Pizza. Auch, Herm, illus. 2003. (ENG.). 32p. (J). (gr. k-3). 7.99 (978-0-8234-1798-8(0)) Holiday Hse., Inc.

Auch, Mary Jane & Auch, Herm. The Buk Buk Buk Festival. 2015. (ENG., Illus.). 32p. (J). (gr. -1-3). 16.95 (978-0-8234-3201-1(7)) Holiday Hse., Inc.

Auerbach, Adam. Monkey Brother. Auerbach, Adam, illus. 2017. (ENG., Illus.). 40p. (J). 17.99 (978-1-62779-600-2(2), 9781627796002, Holt, Henry & Co. Bks. For Young Readers) Holt, Henry & Co.

Auerbach, Annie. Cindy Big Hair: A Twisted (and Teased & Braided) Cinderella Story. Maxey, David, illus. 2005. 16p. (J). 12.95 (978-1-58117-387-1(3), Intervisual/Piggy Toes) Bendon, Inc.

—Hall Monitor, Vol. 3. 2004. 64p. (J). (gr. 2-5). pap. 17.00 incl. audio (978-0-8072-1988-1(6), Listening Library) Random Hse. Audio Publishing Group.

—Spongebob Superstar, Vol. 5. 2004. 64p. (J). (gr. 2-5). pap. 17.00 incl. audio (978-1-4000-8628-3(0), Listening Library) Random Hse. Audio Publishing Group.

Austen, Jane & Carbone, Courtney. Darcy Swipes Left. 2016. (OMG Classics Ser.). (ENG., Illus.). 128p. (YA). (gr. 9). 9.99 (978-1-101-94052-5(2), Random Hse. Bks. for Young Readers) Random Hse. Children's Bks.

Austin, Mike. Monsters Love School. Austin, Mike, illus. 2014. (ENG., Illus.). 40p. (J). (gr. -1-3). 15.99 (978-0-06-228618-5(8)) HarperCollins Pubs.

Averbeck, Jim. One Word from Sophia. Ismail, Yasmeen, illus. 2015. (ENG.). 40p. (J). (gr. -1-3). 17.99 (978-1-4814-0514-0(4)) Simon & Schuster Children's Publishing.

Avi. Romeo & Juliet Together (and Alive!) at Last. 2012. (ENG.). 128p. (J). (gr. 5-9). pap. 6.99 (978-0-545-43097-5(6), Scholastic Paperbacks) Scholastic, Inc.

Avi & Vail, Rachel. Never Mind! 2005. (Twin Novels Ser.). 200p. (gr. 5-9). 16.00 (978-0-7569-5667-7(6)) Perfection Learning Corp.

Awalt, Barbe. Don't Touch This Book. 2015. (ENG., Illus.). 28p. (J). (gr. -1-k). pap. 16.99 (978-1-936744-28-2(7)) LPD Pr.

Award, Anna & Biro, Val. The Bear & the Travellers & the Ducks & the Tortoise. 2014. (ENG.). 24p. (J). pap. 6.95 (978-1-84135-959-5(9)) Award Pubns. Ltd. GBR. Dist: Parkwest Pubns., Inc.

Axelrod, Amy. Pigs in the Corner: Fun with Math & Dance. McGinley-Nally, Sharon, illus. 2005. (ENG.). 40p. (J). (gr. -1-4). 8.99 (978-1-4169-0335-2(6), Simon & Schuster/Paula Wiseman Bks.) Simon & Schuster/Paula Wiseman Bks.

Axis of Weasels. 2004. pap. 12.95 (978-0-9761414-0-2(X)) MacMenamin Pr.

Azose, Elana & Amancio, Brandon. Never Insult a Killer Zucchini. Clark, David, illus. 2016. (ENG.). 32p. (J). (gr. 2-5). lib. bdg. 16.95 (978-1-58089-618-4(9)) Charlesbridge Publishing, Inc.

B. Robert Clark. The Man with Big Hair. 2009. 32p. pap. 14.49 (978-1-4389-7636-5(4)) AuthorHouse.

Bacon, Daskam Josephine. While Caroline Was Growing. 2007. 188p. 95.99 (978-1-4280-7721-8(9)); per. 89.99 (978-1-4280-7710-2(3)) IndyPublish.com.

Bagley, Jessixa. Laundry Day. 2017. (ENG., Illus.). 32p. (J). 17.99 (978-1-62672-317-7(6), 9781626723177) Roaring Brook Pr.

H
I

Bahz, Kahanni. Ants? in My Pants? An Antimated Tale. Fraser, Kevin, illus. 2005. 72p. (J). (gr. k-4). reprint ed. 22.00 (978-0-7567-8705-9(X)) DIANE Publishing Co.

Bailey, Helen. Falling Hook, Line & Sinker. 2010. (ENG.). 304p. (YA). (gr. 7-17). 9.99 (978-0-340-98923-4(8)) Hodder & Stoughton GBR. Dist: Hachette Bk. Group.

—Out of My Depth. 2010. (ENG.). 304p. (YA). (gr. 7-17). pap. 9.99 (978-0-340-95029-6(3)) Hodder & Stoughton GBR. Dist: Hachette Bk. Group.

Bailey, Linda. Stanley's Beauty Contest. Slavin, Bill, illus. 2009. (ENG.). 32p. (J). (gr. -1-2). 17.95 (978-1-55453-318-3(X)) Kids Can Pr., Ltd. CAN. Dist: Hachette Bk. Group.

—Stanleys Wild Ride. Slavin, Bill, illus. 2006. (ENG.). 32p. (J). (gr. -1-2). 16.95 (978-1-55337-960-7(8)) Kids Can Pr., Ltd. CAN. Dist: Hachette Bk. Group.

Bailey, Michael. Cartoon Nation, 6 bks., Set. Incl. Citizenship. Skog, Jason. Brown, Kelly, illus. 30.65 (978-1-4296-1331-6(9)); Political Elections. Miller, Davis Worth & Brevard, Katherine M. Barnett, Charles, III, illus. 30.65 (978-1-4296-1333-0(5)); Political Parties. Burgan, Michael & Hoena, Blake A. Barnett, Charles et al, illus. lib. bdg. 30.65 (978-1-4296-1334-7(3)); 32p. (gr. 3-4). (Cartoon Nation Ser.). (ENG.). 2008. 91.95 (978-1-4296-1675-1(X), Graphic Library) Capstone Press of Coughlan Cos.

Bailey, Tressie. Things Sammy Likes to Do. 2009. 37p. pap. 24.10 (978-0-557-04150-3(3)) Lulu Pr., Inc.

Baker, Brianna & Hastie, F. Bowman. Little White Lies. 2017. (ENG.). 272p. (YA). (gr. 9). pap. 10.99 (978-1-61695-707-0(7), Soho Teen) Soho Pr., Inc.

Baker, E. D. Dragon Kiss. 2nd ed. 2009. (Tales of the Frog Princess Ser.). (ENG.). 288p. (YA). (gr. 5-8). 16.99 (978-1-59990-348-4(2), 9781599903484, Bloomsbury USA Childrens) Bloomsbury Publishing USA.

—The Dragon Princess. 2008. (Tales of the Frog Princess Ser.). (ENG., Illus.). 224p. (YA). (gr. 4-8). 16.99 (978-1-59990-194-7(3), 9781599901947, Bloomsbury USA Childrens) Bloomsbury Publishing USA.

—Dragon's Breath: Read-Along/Homework Pack, 6 vols. unabr. ed. 2005. (Frog Princess Ser.: 2). (SPA.). (J). (gr. 5-8). 78.75 (978-1-4193-3563-1(4), 42041) Recorded Bks., Inc.

—The Perfect Match. (Fairy-Tale Matchmaker Ser.). (ENG.). 2016. 304p. (J). pap. 8.99 (978-1-68119-147-8(4), 9781681191478) 2015. 288p. (YA). (gr. 3-6). 16.99 (978-1-61963-588-3(7), 9781619635883) Bloomsbury Publishing USA. (Bloomsbury USA Childrens).

—A Prince among Frogs. 2nd ed. 2010. (Tales of the Frog Princess Ser.). (ENG.). 224p. (YA). (gr. 5-8). 16.99 (978-1-59990-349-1(0), 9781599903491, Bloomsbury USA Childrens) Bloomsbury Publishing USA.

—The Truest Heart. 2016. (Fairy-Tale Matchmaker Ser.). (ENG.). 272p. (J). 16.99 (978-1-61963-849-5(5), 9781619638495, Bloomsbury USA Childrens) Bloomsbury Publishing USA.

Baker, E. D. & Baker, E. No Place for Magic, Bk. 4. 2006. (Tales of the Frog Princess Ser.: 4). (ENG.). 256p. (YA). (gr. 4-6). 16.99 (978-1-58234-654-0(2), 9781582346540, Bloomsbury USA Childrens) Bloomsbury Publishing USA.

Baker, Keith. Cookies: A Mr. & Mrs. Green Adventure. 2012. (Green Light Readers Level 2 Ser.). (ENG., Illus.). 24p. (J). (gr. -1-3). pap. 3.99 (978-0-547-74561-9(3)) Houghton Mifflin Harcourt Publishing Co.

—Gumballs: A Mr. & Mrs. Green Adventure. 2014. (Green Light Readers Level 2 Ser.). (ENG., Illus.). 32p. (J). (gr. -1-3). 12.99 (978-0-544-23605-9(X), HMH Books For Young Readers) Houghton Mifflin Harcourt Publishing Co.

—Lucky Days with Mr. & Mrs. Green, 1 vol. Baker, Keith, illus. 2007. (Mr. & Mrs. Green Ser.). (ENG., Illus.). 72p. (gr. 2-4). 27.07 (978-1-59961-300-0(X)) Spotlight.

—On the Go with Mr. & Mrs. Green, 1 vol. Baker, Keith, illus. 2007. (Mr. & Mrs. Green Ser.). (ENG., Illus.). 72p. (gr. 2-4). 27.07 (978-1-59961-303-1(4)) Spotlight.

Bakos, Lisa M. Wrong Side of the Bed. Raff, Anna, illus. 2016. (ENG.). 40p. (J). (-k). 16.99 (978-0-399-16572-6(X), G.P. Putnam's Sons Books for Young Readers) Penguin Young Readers Group.

Balaban, Bob. Boy or Beast. Rash, Andy, illus. (Creature from the 7th Grade Ser.: 1). (ENG.). (J). (gr. 5). 2013. 272p. pap. 7.99 (978-0-14-242542-8(7), Puffin Books) 2012. 256p. 15.99 (978-0-670-01271-8(8), Viking Books for Young Readers) Penguin Young Readers Group.

Balan, Judy. How to Stop Your Grownup from Making Bad Decisions. 2016. (Nina the Philosopher Ser.). (J). 6.99 (978-93-5136-997-4(8)) HarperCollins Pubs.

Balch, Betty Neff & Poythress, Jean Hill. Tales of the Cinnamon Dragon Book I: Adventures in Farr Elvenhome. Balch, Betty Neff, illus. 2004. (Illus.). 152p. (J). lib. bdg. 16.95 (978-1-930580-46-6(0), Luminary Media Group) Pine Orchard, Inc.

Baldwin, Christopher. Little Dee & the Penguin. 2016. (ENG., Illus.). 128p. (J). (gr. 3-7). pap. 10.99 (978-0-8037-4108-9(1), Dial Bks) Penguin Young Readers Group.

Balian, Lorna. The Socksnatchers, 1 vol. 2005. (ENG., Illus.). 32p. (J). (gr. -1-3). 15.95 (978-1-59572-003-0(0)) Star Bright Bks., Inc.

Ball, Duncan. Selby Santa. Stomann, Allan, illus. 2007. 192p. (978-0-7322-8679-8(4)) HarperCollins Pubs. Australia.

Ball, Tom. The Marty Graw Book. 2003. 220p. pap. 15.95 (978-1-59113-252-3(5)) Booklocker.com, Inc.

Ballinger, Bryan. Animal Gas. 2015. (ENG., Illus.). 32p. (J). (gr. -1-2). 12.95 (978-1-4549-1616-1(8)) Sterling Publishing Co., Inc.

Baltazar, Art & Aureliani, Franco. Meet Tiny Titans East!, 1 vol. Baltazar, Art & Aureliani, Franco, illus. 2013. (Tiny Titans Ser.). (ENG., Illus.). 32p. (gr. 1-2). lib. bdg. 22.60 (978-1-4342-4696-7(5)) Stone Arch Bks.

—Report Card Pickup!, 1 vol. Baltazar, Art & Aureliani, Franco, illus. 2013. (Tiny Titans Ser.). (ENG., Illus.). 32p. (gr. 1-2). lib. bdg. 22.60 (978-1-4342-4699-8(X)) Stone Arch Bks.

—Tiny Titans. Baltazar, Art & Aureliani, Franco, illus. 2013. (Tiny Titans Ser.). (ENG., Illus.). 32p. (gr. 1-2). 90.40 (978-1-4342-4853-4(4)); 113.00 (978-1-4342-4854-1(2)) Stone Arch Bks.

—Titans in Space, 1 vol. Baltazar, Art & Aureliani, Franco, illus. 2013. (Tiny Titans Ser.). (ENG., Illus.). 32p. (gr. 1-2). lib. bdg. 22.60 (978-1-4342-4698-1(1)) Stone Arch Bks.

—Welcome to the Treehouse, 1 vol. Baltazar, Art & Aureliani, Franco, illus. 2013. (Tiny Titans Ser.). (ENG., Illus.). 32p. (gr. 1-2). lib. bdg. 22.60 (978-1-4342-4697-4(3)) Stone Arch Bks.

Balukoff, Constance. Mooky's Bad Hair Day. 2004. 21p. pap. 24.95 (978-1-4137-1480-7(3)) PublishAmerica, Inc.

Bancks, Tristan. My Life & Other Exploding Chickens. Gordon, Gus, illus. 2016. (My Life & Other Stuff... Ser.: 4). (ENG.). 192p. (J). (gr. 4-7). 9.99 (978-0-85798-531-6(0)) Random Hse. Australia AUS. Dist: Independent Pubs. Group.

Bankert, Lisa. Operation: Oddball. Meyers, Nancy, illus. 2007. 100p. per. 5.99 (978-0-9795364-0-3(5)) Chowder Bay Bks.

Banks, Steven. SpongeBob Goes to the Doctor. Saunders, Zina, illus. 2005. (SpongeBob SquarePants Ser.: 9). (ENG.). 24p. (J). pap. 3.99 (978-1-4169-0359-8(3), Simon Spotlight/Nickelodeon) Simon Spotlight/Nickelodeon.

—Spongebob Goes to the Doctor. Saunders, Zina, illus. 2005. 22p. (J). lib. bdg. 15.00 (978-1-4242-0976-7(5)) Fitzgerald Bks.

—Stop the Presses! DePorter, Vince, illus. 2005. 22p. (J). lib. bdg. 15.00 (978-1-4242-0973-6(0)) Fitzgerald Bks.

Baratz-Logsted, Lauren. Rebecca's Rashness, Bk. 7. 2011. (Sisters Eight Ser.: 7). (ENG., Illus.). 144p. (J). (gr. 1-4). pap. 5.99 (978-0-547-55434-1(6)) Houghton Mifflin Harcourt Publishing Co.

—Zinnia's Zaniness. 2011. (Sisters Eight Ser.: 8). (ENG., Illus.). 128p. (J). (gr. 1-4). pap. 5.99 (978-0-547-55439-6(7)) Houghton Mifflin Harcourt Publishing Co.

Baratz-Logsted, Lauren, et al. The Final Battle... for Now Bk. 9. 2012. (Sisters Eight Ser.: 9). (ENG., Illus.). 160p. (J). (gr. 1-4). pap. 6.99 (978-0-547-55441-9(9)) Houghton Mifflin Harcourt Publishing Co.

Barba, Ale. When Your Elephant Comes to Play. Barba, Ale, illus. 2016. (ENG., Illus.). 32p. (J). (gr. -1-2). 16.99 (978-0-399-16312-8(3), Philomel Bks.) Penguin Young Readers Group.

Barden, Stephanie. Cinderella Smith. Goode, Diane, illus. 2012. (Cinderella Smith Ser.: 1). (ENG.). 176p. (J). (gr. 3-7). pap. 5.99 (978-0-06-196425-1(5)) HarperCollins Pubs.

Bardhan-Quallen, Sudipta. Caveboy Is Bored! Wight, Eric, illus. 2017. (Caveboy Ser.). (ENG.). 80p. (J). 9.99 (978-1-68119-045-7(1), 9781681190457, Bloomsbury USA Childrens) Bloomsbury Publishing USA.

—Duck, Duck, Moose! Jones, Noah Z., illus. 2014. (ENG.). 32p. (J). (gr. -1-k). 16.99 (978-1-4231-7110-2(1)) Hyperion Bks. for Children.

—Hampire! Fine, Howard, illus. 2011. (ENG.). 32p. (J). (gr. -1-3). 16.99 (978-0-06-114239-0(5)) HarperCollins Pubs.

—Quackenstein Hatches a Family. Jones, Brian T., illus. 2010. (ENG.). 32p. (J). (gr. k-2). 15.95 (978-0-8109-8973-3(5), Abrams Bks. for Young Readers) Abrams, Inc.

—Snoring Beauty. Manning, Jane, illus. 2014. (J). (978-0-06-087405-6(8)) Harper & Row Ltd.

—Snoring Beauty. Manning, Jane, illus. 2014. (ENG.). 32p. (J). (gr. -1-3). 17.99 (978-0-06-087403-2(1)) HarperCollins Pubs.

Barensfeld, Debrae. Fox: Lost & Found. 2006. 12.95 (978-0-9776617-0-1(9)) CreoXimius Publishing Company.

Barkaw, Henriette. Don't Cry Sly: Big Book English Only. Johnson, Richard, illus. 2004. (J). (978-1-85269-999-4(X)) Mantra Lingua.

Barkow, Henriette. The Giant Turnip: Le Navet Geant. Johnson, Richard, illus. 2004. (ENG & FRE.). 32p. (J). pap. (978-1-85269-738-9(5)) Mantra Lingua.

Barnes, Jennifer Lynn. Fate. 2009. (ENG.). 368p. (YA). (gr. 7-18). pap. 8.99 (978-0-385-73537-7(5), Delacorte Bks. for Young Readers) Random Hse. Children's Bks.

—Perfect Cover. 2008. (The Squad). (ENG.). 288p. (YA). (gr. 7). mass mkt. 7.99 (978-0-385-73454-7(9), Laurel Leaf) Random Hse. Children's Bks.

—Tattoo. 2007. (ENG.). 272p. (YA). (gr. 7-12). pap. 7.99 (978-0-385-73347-2(5), Delacorte Bks. for Young Readers) Random Hse. Children's Bks.

Barnett, Mac. Billy Twitters & His Blue Whale Problem. Rex, Adam, illus. 2009. (ENG.). 48p. (J). (gr. -1-2). 16.99 (978-0-7868-4958-1(4)) Hyperion Pr.

—The Case of the Case of Mistaken Identity. Rex, Adam, illus. (Brixton Brothers Ser.: 1). (ENG.). (J). (gr. 3-7). 2010. 208p. pap. 7.99 (978-1-4169-7816-9(X)) 2009. 192p. 15.99 (978-1-4169-7815-2(1)) Simon & Schuster Bks. For Young Readers. (Simon & Schuster Bks. For Young Readers).

—Chloe & the Lion. Rex, Adam, illus. 2012. (ENG.). 48p. (J). (gr. -1-k). 16.99 (978-1-4231-1334-8(9)) Hyperion Pr.

—Danger Goes Berserk. Myers, Matthew, illus. (Brixton Brothers Ser.: 4). (ENG.). 256p. (J). (gr. 3-7). 2013. pap. 7.99 (978-1-4424-3978-8(5)) 2012. 17.99 (978-1-4424-3977-1(7)) Simon & Schuster Bks. For Young Readers. (Simon & Schuster Bks. For Young Readers).

—Extra Yarn. Klassen, Jon, illus. 2012. (ENG.). 40p. (J). (gr. -1-3). 17.99 (978-0-06-195338-5(5)) HarperCollins Pubs.

—It Happened on a Train. Rex, Adam, illus. (Brixton Brothers Ser.: 3). (ENG.). (J). (gr. 3-7). 2012. 304p. pap. 7.99 (978-1-4169-7820-6(8)) 2011. 288p. 17.99 (978-1-4169-7819-0(4)) Simon & Schuster Bks. For Young Readers. (Simon & Schuster Bks. For Young Readers).

—Mysterious Case of Cases: The Case of the Case of Mistaken Identity - The Ghostwriter Secret - It Happened on a Train - Danger Goes Berserk. Rex, Adam & Myers, Matthew, illus. 2013. (Brixton Brothers Ser.). (ENG.). 1024p. (J). (gr. 3-7). pap. 29.99 (978-1-4424-9818-1(8), Simon & Schuster Bks. For Young Readers) Simon & Schuster Bks. For Young Readers.

—Oh No! Or How My Science Project Destroyed the World. Santat, Dan, illus. 2010. (ENG.). 40p. (J). (gr. -1-2). 16.99 (978-1-4231-2312-5(3)) Hyperion Pr.

—Oh No! Not Again! Or How I Built a Time Machine to Save History - Or at Least My History Grade. Santat, Dan, illus. 2012. (Oh No! Picture Book Ser.). (ENG.). 40p. (J). (gr. -1-k). 17.99 (978-1-4231-4912-5(2)) Hyperion Pr.

—President Taft Is Stuck in the Bath. Van Dusen, Chris, illus. 2016. (ENG.). 32p. (J). (gr. -1-3). 7.99 (978-0-7636-6556-2(8)) Candlewick Pr.

—Sam & Dave Dig a Hole. 2015. (JPN.). (J). (978-4-7515-2714-6(2)) Asunaro Shobo.

—Sam & Dave Dig a Hole. Klassen, Jon, illus. 2014. (ENG.). 40p. (J). (gr. -1-3). 16.99 (978-0-7636-6229-5(1)) Candlewick Pr.

—Sam & Dave Dig a Hole. 2014. (CHI.). (J). (gr. -1-3). pap. (978-986-241-935-9(0)) Common Wealth.

—Sam & Dave Dig a Hole. 2014. (CHI.). 32p. (J). (gr. -1-3). (978-7-5332-8178-6(0)) Mingtian Chubanshe.

—The Skunk. McDonnell, Patrick, illus. 2015. (ENG.). 40p. (J). (gr. -1-3). 17.99 (978-1-59643-966-5(1), 9781596439665) Roaring Brook Pr.

—Triangle. Klassen, Jon, illus. 2017. (ENG.). 48p. (J). (gr. k-4). 15.99 (978-0-7636-9603-0(X)) Candlewick Pr.

Barnett, Mac & John, Jory. The Terrible Two. Cornell, Kevin, illus. (Terrible Two Ser.). (ENG.). (J). (gr. 3-7). 2016. 224p. 13.95 (978-1-4197-1680-5(8), Amulet Bks.) 2016. pap. 7.95 (978-1-4197-1925-7(4)) 2015. 224p. 13.95 (978-1-4197-1491-7(0), Amulet Bks.) Abrams, Inc.

—The Terrible Two. 2017. (Terrible Two Ser.: 1). lib. bdg. 18.40 **(978-0-606-40723-6(5))**; lib. bdg. 18.40 **(978-0-606-40724-3(3))** Turtleback Bks.

Barnett, Mac & Klassen, Barnett -. Sam y Leo Cavan un Hoyo. 2014.Tr. of Sam & Dave Dig a Hole. (SPA.). 44p. (gr. 1-3). 21.99 (978-84-261-4091-3(2)) Juventud, Editorial ESP. Dist: Lectorum Pubns., Inc.

Barnette, Brandon. Word Fanatics. 2012. 32p. pap. 14.50 (978-1-4669-2942-5(1)) Trafford Publishing.

Barnholdt, Lauren. Devon Delaney Should Totally Know Better. 2009. (Mix Ser.). (ENG.). 288p. (J). (gr. 4-8). pap. 6.99 (978-1-4169-8019-3(9), Aladdin) Simon & Schuster Children's Publishing.

—The Secret Identity of Devon Delaney. 2007. (Mix Ser.). (ENG.). 272p. (J). (gr. 4-8). pap. 5.99 (978-1-4169-3503-2(7), Aladdin) Simon & Schuster Children's Publishing.

—Watch Me. 2010. (ENG.). 304p. (YA). (gr. 7). pap. 9.99 (978-1-4424-0255-3(5), Simon Pulse) Simon Pulse.

Baron, Jeff. Sean Rosen Is Not for Sale. (ENG.). 384p. (J). (gr. 3-7). 2015. pap. 6.99 (978-0-06-218751-2(1)) 2014. 16.99 (978-0-06-218750-5(3)) HarperCollins Pubs. (Greenwillow Bks.).

Baron, Lindamichelle. The Lion & the Man: A Fable. Huggins, Carl, illus. 2009. 72p. pap. 15.95 (978-0-940938-25-0(1)) Harlin Jacque Pubns.

Barrett, Judi. Los Animales No Se Visten. 2004.Tr. of Animals Should Definely Not Wear Clothes. (SPA.). (gr. k-3). lib. bdg. 23.30 (978-0-8335-7297-4(0), Turtleback) Turtleback Bks.

—Cloudy with a Chance of Meatballs. Barrett, Ronald, illus. 2012. (ENG.). 32p. (J). (gr. -1-3). pap. 9.99 (978-1-4424-4337-2(5), Little Simon) Little Simon.

—Cloudy with a Chance of Meatballs. Barrett, Ron, illus. 2009. 9.00 (978-1-55744-455-4(2), Everbind) Marco Bk. Co.

Barrett, Judi & Barrett, Ron. The Marshmallow Incident. Barrett, Ron, illus. 2009. (Illus.). (J). pap. (978-0-545-04654-1(8), Scholastic Pr.) Scholastic, Inc.

Barrett, Ron. Cats Get Famous. Barrett, Ron, illus. 2015. (ENG., Illus.). 32p. (J). (gr. -1-3). 17.99 (978-1-4424-9453-4(0), Simon & Schuster Bks. For Young Readers) Simon & Schuster Bks. For Young Readers.

Barrows, Annie. Ivy + Bean Take the Case. Blackall, Sophie, illus. (ENG.). (J). (gr. 1-4). 2014. 136p. pap. 5.99 (978-1-4521-2871-9(5)) 2013. 128p. 14.99 (978-1-4521-0699-1(1)) Chronicle Bks. LLC.

Barrows, Annie & Blackall, Sophie. Ivy + Bean, Set. 2010. (ENG., Illus.). 392p. (J). (gr. 1-5). 19.99 (978-0-8118-7665-0(9)) Chronicle Bks. LLC.

Barry, Dave. The Worst Class Trip Ever. 2015. (Class Trip Ser.). (ENG.). 224p. (J). (gr. 3-7). 13.99 (978-1-4847-0849-1(0)) Disney Pr.

—The Worst Night Ever. 2016. (Class Trip Ser.). (ENG.). 256p. (J). (gr. 3-7). 13.99 (978-1-4847-0850-7(4)) Hyperion Bks. for Children.

Barry, Dave & Pearson, Ridley. Peter & the Shadow Thieves. Call, Greg & Brown, Roberta, illus. rev. ed. 2007. (Peter & the Starcatchers Ser.). (ENG.). 592p. (J). (gr. 5-9). pap. 9.99 (978-1-4231-0855-9(8), Disney Editions) Disney Pr.

—Peter & the Shadow Thieves. Call, Greg, illus. 2007. (Starcatchers Ser.: Bk. 2). 556p. (gr. 5-9). 19.00 (978-0-7569-8060-3(7)) Perfection Learning Corp.

—Peter & the Starcatchers. Call, Greg, illus. rev. ed. 2006. (Peter & the Starcatchers Ser.). (ENG.). 480p. (J). (gr. 5-9). reprint ed. pap. 9.99 (978-0-7868-4907-9(X), Disney Editions) Disney Pr.

—Peter & the Sword of Mercy. Call, Greg, illus. 2011. (Peter & the Starcatchers Ser.: Bk. 4). (ENG.). 528p. (J). (gr. 5-9). pap. 9.99 (978-1-4231-3070-3(7)) Hyperion Pr.

Bartles, Veronica. The Princess & the Frogs. Palacios, Sara, illus. 2016. 40p. (J). (gr. -1-3). 17.99 (978-0-06-236591-0(6)) HarperCollins Pubs.

Barton, Chris. That's Not Bunny! Jack, Colin, illus. 2016. (ENG.). 32p. (J). (gr. -1-k). 16.99 (978-1-4231-9086-8(6)) Disney Pr.

The Bash Street Kids Annual 2004. annuals 2003. (Illus.). 96p. (978-0-85116-815-9(9)) Thomson, D.C. & Co., Ltd. GBR. Dist: APG Sales & Distribution Services.

Basu, Jayinee. HJBRL - A Nonsense Story by Sukumar Ray. 2005. 68p. pap. 10.98 (978-1-4116-3983-6(9)) Lulu Pr., Inc.

Basye, Dale E. Blimpo Vol. 3: The Third Circle of Heck. Dob, Bob, illus. 2011. (Heck Ser.). (ENG.). 464p. (J). (gr. 3-7). pap. 7.99 (978-0-375-85677-8(3), Yearling) Random Hse. Children's Bks.

—Fibble. Dob, Bob, illus. 2012. (Heck Ser.). (ENG.). 384p. (J). (gr. 4-7). pap. 6.99 (978-0-375-85679-2(X), Yearling) Random Hse. Children's Bks.

—Precocia: the Sixth Circle of Heck. Dob, Bob, illus. 2013. (Heck Ser.). (ENG.). 432p. (J). (gr. 3-7). 6.99 (978-0-375-86807-8(0), Yearling) Random Hse. Children's Bks.

—Rapacia. Dob, Bob, illus. 2010. (Heck Ser.). (ENG.). 384p. (J). (gr. 3-7). pap. 6.99 (978-0-375-84078-4(8), Yearling) Random Hse. Children's Bks.

—Where the Bad Kids Go. Dob, Bob, illus. 2009. (Heck Ser.). (ENG.). 304p. (J). (gr. 3-7). 6.99 (978-0-375-84076-0(1), Yearling) Random Hse. Children's Bks.

—Wise Acres: the Seventh Circle of Heck. Dob, Bob, illus. 2013. (Heck Ser.). (ENG.). 448p. (J). (gr. 4-7). 16.99 (978-0-307-98185-1(1), Random Hse. Bks. for Young Readers) Random Hse. Children's Bks.

Bauer, Jutta. Madrechillona. 2nd ed. 2003. (Rosa y Manzana Ser.). (SPA., Illus.). 28p. (J). (gr. k-2). (978-84-89804-36-4(2), LC30478) Lóguez Ediciones ESP. Dist: Lectorum Pubns., Inc.

Bauer, Michael Gerard. Don't Call Me Ishmael. 2007. 255p. (YA). (gr. 9-12). lib. bdg. 17.89 (978-0-06-134835-8(X), HarperTeen) HarperCollins Pubs.

Baum, L. Frank. The Woggle-Bug Book. 2008. 52p. pap. 7.95 (978-1-60664-008-1(9)) Aegypan.

—The Woggle-Bug Book. 2011. 52p. 14.95 (978-1-4638-9578-5(X)) Rodgers, Alan Bks.

Beale, C. R. A Silly Flop-Flipping Parade. 2009. 40p. pap. 16.50 (978-1-60860-022-9(X), Strategic Bk. Publishing) Strategic Book Publishing & Rights Agency (SBPRA).

Bean, Raymond. Rippin' It Old School, 0 vols. unabr. ed. 2010. (Sweet Farts Ser.: 2). (ENG.). 184p. (J). (gr. 4-6). pap. 9.95 (978-1-935597-08-7(6), 9781935597087, Two Lions) Amazon Publishing.

—Sweet Farts, 0 vols. unabr. ed. 2012. (Sweet Farts Ser.: 1). (ENG.). 138p. (J). (gr. 4-6). pap. 9.95 (978-1-61218-250-6(X), 9781612182506, Amazon Children's Publishing) Amazon Publishing.

Beaton, Kate. The Princess & the Pony. 2015. (ENG., Illus.). 40p. (J). (gr. -1-3). 17.99 (978-0-545-63708-4(2)) Scholastic, Inc.

Beaty, Andrea. Artist Ted. Lemaître, Pascal, illus. 2012. (ENG.). 32p. (J). (gr. -1-3). 17.99 (978-1-4169-5374-6(4), McElderry, Margaret K. Bks.) McElderry, Margaret K. Bks.

—Attack of the Fluffy Bunnies. 2012. (Fluffy Bunnies Ser.). (ENG.). 192p. (YA). (gr. 2-8). pap. 7.95 (978-1-4197-0519-9(9), Amulet Bks.) Abrams, Inc.

—Dorko the Magnificent. (ENG.). (J). (gr. 3-7). 2014. 240p. pap. 7.95 (978-1-4197-1019-3(2)) 2013. (Illus.). 224p. 17.95 (978-1-4197-0638-7(1)) Abrams, Inc. (Amulet Bks.).

—Firefighter Ted. Lemaître, Pascal, illus. 2009. (ENG.). 32p. (J). (gr. -1-3). 17.99 (978-1-4169-2821-8(9), McElderry, Margaret K. Bks.) McElderry, Margaret K. Bks.

—Fluffy Bunnies 2: The Schnoz of Doom. Santat, Dan, illus. (Fluffy Bunnies Ser.). (ENG.). (J). (gr. 3-7). 2016. 208p. pap. 7.95 (978-1-4197-1942-4(4)) 2015. 192p. 12.95 (978-1-4197-1051-3(6)) Abrams, Inc. (Amulet Bks.).

Beaumont, Karen. Doggone Dogs! Catrow, David, illus. 2008. (ENG.). 40p. (J). (gr. -1-k). 16.99 (978-0-8037-3157-8(4), Dial Bks) Penguin Young Readers Group.

Beck, Barbara. Bill Every Cloud Has a Silver Lining. 2012. 108p. pap. 19.95 (978-1-4626-9718-2(6)) America Star Bks.

Beck, W. H. Malcolm at Midnight. Lies, Brian, illus. (ENG.). 272p. (J). (gr. 2-5). 2015. pap. 7.99 (978-0-544-33666-7(6), HMH Books For Young Readers) 2012. 16.99 (978-0-547-68100-9(3)) Houghton Mifflin Harcourt Publishing Co.

—Malcolm under the Stars. Lies, Brian, illus. (ENG.). 272p. (J). (gr. 2-5). 2016. pap. 7.99 (978-0-544-81312-0(X)) 2015. 16.99 (978-0-544-39267-0(1)) Houghton Mifflin Harcourt Publishing Co. (HMH Books For Young Readers).

Becker-Doyle, Eve & Doyle, Evan Brain. Evan Brain's Christmas List & Other Shenanigans: Boy Warrior Fights Evil. Doyle, Evan Brain, illus. 2008. (ENG., Illus.). 64p. pap. 15.95 (978-0-9794716-3-6(X)) BDA Publishing.

Beckhorn, Susan Williams. Moose Eggs: Or, Why Moose Has Flat Antlers. Stevens, Helen, illus. 2007. (ENG.). 32p. (J). (gr. -1-3). 15.95 (978-0-89272-689-9(X)) Down East Bks.

Beech, Sandy. Worst Class Trip Ever. Holder, Jimmy, illus. 2005. (Castaways Ser.: 1). (ENG.). 176p. (J). (gr. 3-7). pap. 9.99 (978-0-689-87596-0(7), Aladdin) Simon & Schuster Children's Publishing.

Behrens, Andy. The Fast & the Furriest. 2011. (ENG.). 256p. (J). (gr. 3-7). 7.99 (978-0-375-85900-7(4), Yearling) Random Hse. Children's Bks.

Beil, Karen Magnuson. Jack's House. Wohnoutka, Mike, illus. 2009. (ENG.). 32p. (J). (gr. -1-3). pap. 7.99 (978-0-8234-2242-5(9)) Holiday Hse., Inc.

Bell, Cece. I Yam a Donkey! Bell, Cece, illus. 2015. (ENG., Illus.). 32p. (J). (gr. -1-3). 16.99 (978-0-544-08720-0(8)) Houghton Mifflin Harcourt Publishing Co.

—Itty Bitty. Bell, Cece, illus. (ENG., Illus.). (J). (gr. -1-2). 2017. 24p. bds. 6.99 **(978-0-7636-9313-8(8))** 2009. 32p. 9.99 (978-0-7636-3615-6(9)) Candlewick Pr.

—Rabbit & Robot. 2014. (Candlewick Sparks Ser.). lib. bdg. 13.55 (978-0-606-35169-0(8)) Turtleback Bks.

—Rabbit & Robot: The Sleepover. Bell, Cece, illus. 2012. (ENG., Illus.). 56p. (J). (gr. k-4). 14.99 (978-0-7636-5475-7(2)) Candlewick Pr.

—Rabbit & Robot - The Sleepover. Bell, Cece, illus. 2014. (Candlewick Sparks Ser.). (ENG., Illus.). 56p. (J). (gr. k-4). pap. 3.99 (978-0-7636-6875-4(3)) Candlewick Pr.

—Rabbit & Robot & Ribbit. Bell, Cece, illus. 2016. (ENG., Illus.). 48p. (J). (gr. k-4). 14.99 (978-0-7636-7935-4(6)) Candlewick Pr.

Bell, Jennifer. Pony Tale. 2004. (Illus.). 50p. 7.00 (978-1-84161-011-5(9)) Ravette Publishing, Ltd. GBR. Dist: Parkwest Pubns., Inc.

Bell, Sophie. Lilac Attack! 2014. (Ultra Violets Ser.: 3). (ENG., Illus.). 304p. (J). (gr. 3-7). 12.99 (978-1-59514-648-9(2), Razorbill) Penguin Young Readers Group.

Benjamin, A. H. Wanted: Prince Charming. Fiorin, Fabiano, illus. 2014. (ENG.). 32p. (J). (978-0-7787-1313-5(X)) Crabtree Publishing Co.

Benjamin, Paul. Monsters, Inc: Laugh Factory. Mebberson, Amy, illus. 2010. (ENG.). 112p. (J). pap. 9.99 (978-1-60886-508-6(8)) Boom! Studios.

Benjamin, Paul & Rosa, Don. Monsters, Inc: Laugh Factory. Mebberson, Amy & Rosa, Don, illus. 2010. (ENG.). 112p. (J). 24.99 (978-1-60886-533-8(9)) Boom! Studios.

Bennet, Chloe. Season Three. 2017. (Boywatching Ser.). (ENG.). 288p. (J). (gr. 6-10). 10.99 (978-1-4083-4512-2(9), Orchard Bks.) Hachette Children's Group GBR. Dist: Hachette Bk. Group.

Bennett, Sandra. Gingerbread Aliens. Welsh, Hayley, illus. 2012. (ENG.). 56p. (J). pap. (978-0-9872356-4-0(8)) Australian Self Publishing Group/ Inspiring Pubs.

Bentley, Tadgh. Little Penguin Gets the Hiccups. Bentley, Tadgh, illus. 2015. (ENG., Illus.). 40p. (J). (gr. -1-3). 17.99 (978-0-06-233536-4(7)) HarperCollins Pubs.

—Little Penguin Gets the Hiccups Board Book. Bentley, Tadgh, illus. 2016. (Illus.). 34p. (J). (gr. -1 — 1). bds. 7.99 (978-0-06-265224-9(9)) HarperCollins Pubs.

Bently, Peter. The Great Balloon Hullaballoo. Matsuoka, Mei, illus. 2014. (ENG.). 32p. (J). (gr. -1-3). 16.95 (978-1-4677-3449-3(7)) Lerner Publishing Group.

Benton, Jim. Am I the Princess or the Frog? Benton, Jim, illus. 2005. (Dear Dumb Diary Ser.: 3). (ENG., Illus.). 160p. (J). (gr. 3-7). pap. 6.99 (978-0-439-62907-2(1)) Scholastic, Inc.

—Attack of the 50-Ft. Cupid. Benton, Jim, illus. (Franny K. Stein, Mad Scientist Ser.: 2). (ENG., Illus.). 112p. (J). (gr. 2-5). 2005. pap. 5.99 (978-0-689-86296-0(2)) 2004. 16.99 (978-0-689-86292-2(X)) Simon & Schuster Bks. For Young Readers. (Simon & Schuster Bks. For Young Readers).

—Attack of the 50-Ft. Cupid, 1 vol. Benton, Jim, illus. 2011. (Franny K. Stein, Mad Scientist Ser.). (ENG., Illus.). 112p. (gr. 3-6). 24.21 (978-1-59961-818-0(4)) Spotlight.

—Crate of Danger. Benton, Jim, illus. 2005. (Franny K. Stein, Mad Scientist Ser.). (ENG., Illus.). 448p. (J). (gr. 2-5). pap. 23.99 (978-1-4169-1402-0(1), Simon & Schuster Bks. For Young Readers) Simon & Schuster Bks. For Young Readers.

—The Fran That Time Forgot. Benton, Jim, illus. 4th ed. 2005. (Franny K. Stein, Mad Scientist Ser.: 4). (ENG., Illus.). 112p. (J). (gr. 2-5). mass mkt. 5.99 (978-0-689-86298-4(9)); 16.99 (978-0-689-86294-6(6)) Simon & Schuster Bks. For Young Readers. (Simon & Schuster Bks. For Young Readers).

—The Fran That Time Forgot, 1 vol. Benton, Jim, illus. 2011. (Franny K. Stein, Mad Scientist Ser.). (ENG., Illus.). 112p. (gr. 3-6). 24.21 (978-1-59961-820-3(6)) Spotlight.

—The Fran with Four Brains. Benton, Jim, illus. 2006. (Franny K. Stein, Mad Scientist Ser.: 6). (ENG., Illus.). 112p. (J). (gr. 2-5). 17.99 (978-1-4169-0231-7(7), Simon & Schuster Bks. For Young Readers) Simon & Schuster Bks. For Young Readers.

—The Fran with Four Brains, 1 vol. Benton, Jim, illus. 2011. (Franny K. Stein, Mad Scientist Ser.). (ENG., Illus.). 112p. (gr. 3-6). 24.21 (978-1-59961-822-7(2)) Spotlight.

—The Fran with Four Brains. 2007. (Franny K. Stein, Mad Scientist Ser.: 6). lib. bdg. 16.00 (978-1-4177-9038-8(5), Turtleback) Turtleback Bks.

—The Frandidate, No. 7. Benton, Jim, illus. 2008. (Franny K. Stein, Mad Scientist Ser.: 7). (ENG., Illus.). 128p. (J). (gr. 2-5). 17.99 (978-1-4169-0233-1(3), Simon & Schuster Bks. For Young Readers) Simon & Schuster Bks. For Young Readers.

—The Frandidate, 1 vol. Benton, Jim, illus. 2011. (Franny K. Stein, Mad Scientist Ser.). (ENG., Illus.). 128p. (gr. 3-6). 24.21 (978-1-59961-823-4(0)) Spotlight.

—Franny K. Stein, Mad Scientist, 7 vols., Set. Benton, Jim, illus. Incl. Attack of the 50-Ft. Cupid. 112p. 24.21 (978-1-59961-818-0(4)); Fran That Time Forgot. 112p. 24.21 (978-1-59961-820-3(6)); Fran with Four Brains. 112p. 24.21 (978-1-59961-822-7(2)); Frandidate. 128p. 24.21 (978-1-59961-823-4(0)); Frantastic Voyage. 112p. 24.21 (978-1-59961-821-0(4)); Invisible Fran. 112p. 24.21 (978-1-59961-819-7(2)); Lunch Walks among Us. 112p. 24.21 (978-1-59961-817-3(6)); (gr. 3-6). (Franny K. Stein, Mad Scientist Ser.). (Illus.). 2011. 169.47 (978-1-59961-816-6(8)) Spotlight.

—Frantastic Voyage, 1 vol. Benton, Jim, illus. 2011. (Franny K. Stein, Mad Scientist Ser.). (ENG., Illus.). 112p. (gr. 3-6). 24.21 (978-1-59961-821-0(4)) Spotlight.

—Howard Hubbins Half Hour Hero. 2008. (J). pap. 4.99 (978-0-06-059774-0(7)) HarperCollins Pubs.

—The Invisible Fran. Benton, Jim, illus. 2004. (Franny K. Stein, Mad Scientist Ser.: 3). (ENG., Illus.). 112p. (J). (gr. 2-5). 17.99 (978-0-689-86293-9(8), Simon & Schuster Bks. For Young Readers) Simon & Schuster Bks. For Young Readers.

—Let's Do a Thing! 2017. (Victor Shmud, Total Expert Ser.: 1). (ENG.). 128p. (J). (gr. 2-5). pap. 5.99 **(978-0-545-93229-5(7))**; lib. bdg. 16.99 **(978-0-545-93233-2(5))** Scholastic, Inc. (Scholastic Paperbacks).

—Let's Pretend This Never Happened. Benton, Jim, illus. 2004. (Dear Dumb Diary Ser.: 1). (Illus.). 95p. (gr. -1-2). 17.20 (978-1-4176-3050-9(7), Turtleback) Turtleback Bks.

—Lunch Walks among Us. Benton, Jim, illus. (Franny K. Stein, Mad Scientist Ser.: 1). (ENG., Illus.). 112p. (J). (gr. 2-5). 2004. mass mkt. 5.99 (978-0-689-86295-3(4)) 2003. 16.99 (978-0-689-86291-5(1)) Simon & Schuster Bks. For Young Readers. (Simon & Schuster Bks. For Young Readers).

—Lunch Walks among Us, 1 vol. Benton, Jim, illus. 2011. (Franny K. Stein, Mad Scientist Ser.). (ENG., Illus.). 112p. (gr. 3-6). 24.21 (978-1-59961-817-3(6)) Spotlight.

—Lunch Walks among Us. Benton, Jim, illus. 2004. (Franny K. Stein, Mad Scientist Ser.: 1). (Illus.). 102p. (gr. 2-5). lib. bdg. 16.00 (978-1-4176-4054-6(5), Turtleback) Turtleback Bks.

—Me (Just Like You, Only Better) Benton, Jim, illus. 2011. (Dear Dumb Diary Ser.: 12). (ENG., Illus.). 160p. (J). (gr. 3-7). pap. 6.99 (978-0-545-11616-9(3), Scholastic Paperbacks) Scholastic, Inc.

—My Pants Are Haunted! Benton, Jim, illus. 2004. (Dear Dumb Diary Ser.: 2). (ENG., Illus.). 144p. (J). (gr. 2-5). mass mkt. 6.99 (978-0-439-62905-8(5), Scholastic Paperbacks) Scholastic, Inc.

—The Problem with Here Is That It's Where I'm From. 2007. (Dear Dumb Diary Ser.: 6). (ENG., Illus.). 128p. (J). (gr. 3-7). 6.99 (978-0-439-79622-4(9), Scholastic Paperbacks) Scholastic, Inc.

—The Problem with Here Is That It's Where I'm From. 2007. (Dear Dumb Diary Ser.: 6). 17.20 (978-1-4177-8231-4(5), Turtleback) Turtleback Bks.

—The Super-Nice Are Super-Annoying. 2012. (Dear Dumb Diary: Year Two Ser.: 2). lib. bdg. 16.00 (978-0-606-26188-3(5), Turtleback) Turtleback Bks.

Benton, Jim & Kelly, Jamie. Can Adults Become Human? 2006. (Dear Dumb Diary Ser.: 5). (ENG., Illus.). 144p. (J). (gr. 3-7). 6.99 (978-0-439-79621-7(0), Scholastic Paperbacks) Scholastic, Inc.

—Never Do Anything, Ever. Benton, Jim, illus. 2005. (Dear Dumb Diary Ser.: 4). (ENG., Illus.). 144p. (J). (gr. 3-7). pap. 6.99 (978-0-439-62908-9(X), Scholastic Paperbacks) Scholastic, Inc.

—Never Underestimate Your Dumbness. Benton, Jim, illus. 2008. (Dear Dumb Diary Ser.: 7). (ENG., Illus.). 160p. (J). (gr. 3-7). 6.99 (978-0-439-82596-2(2)) Scholastic, Inc.

Berenstain, Jan & Berenstain, Mike. The Berenstain Bears' Really Big Pet Show. Berenstain, Jan & Berenstain, Mike, illus. 2008. (Berenstain Bears Ser.). (Illus.). 32p. (J). (gr. -1-2). 8.99 (978-0-06-057406-2(2)); (ENG., pap. 3.99 (978-0-06-057390-4(2)) HarperCollins Pubs. (HarperFestival).

Berenstain, Jan, et al. Berenstain Bears. 2009. (I Can Read Level 1 Ser.). (J). (gr. k-3). pap. 9.99 (978-0-06-171904-2(8)) HarperCollins Pubs.

Berger, Joe. The Pudding Problem. Berger, Joe, illus. 2017. (Lyttle Lies Ser.: 1). (ENG., Illus.). 240p. (J). (gr. 3-7). 13.99 **(978-1-4814-7083-4(3)**, McElderry, Margaret K. Bks.) McElderry, Margaret K. Bks.

Berger, Samantha. Monster's New Undies. Carpenter, Tad, illus. 2017. (ENG.). 40p. (J). (gr. -1-k). 16.99 **(978-0-545-87973-6(6)**, Orchard Bks.) Scholastic, Inc.

Bergstrom, Gunilla. Good Night, Alfie Atkins. Dyssegaard, Elisabeth Kallick, tr. from SWE. Bergström, Gunilla, illus. 2005. 32p. (J). 15.00 (978-91-29-66154-5(4)) R & S Bks. SWE. Dist: Macmillan.

Bergström, Gunilla. Very Tricky, Alfie Atkins. Dyssegaard, Elisabeth Kallick, tr. from SWE. 2005. (Illus.). 32p. (J). 15.00 (978-91-29-66152-1(8)) R & S Bks. SWE. Dist: Macmillan.

Bernstein, Jonathan. Bridget Wilder #2: Spy to the Rescue. 2017. (Bridget Wilder Ser.: 2). 320p. (J). (gr. 3-7). pap. 6.99 (978-0-06-238270-2(5), Tegen, Katherine Bks) HarperCollins Pubs.

Berresford, J. R. Gerald Giraffe's Garage. Parmelee, George, illus. 2013. (ENG.). 32p. (J). (gr. -1-3). 11.95 (978-0-9860321-0-3(7)) Tuscarora Publishing Company.

Berrow, G. M. Applejack & the Honest-To-Goodness Switcheroo. 2014. (My Little Pony Chapter Bks.). (J). lib. bdg. 16.00 (978-0-606-35301-4(1)) Turtleback Bks.

Berry, Julie. The Emperor's Ostrich. 2017. (ENG.). 288p. (J). 16.99 (978-1-59643-958-0(0), 9781596439580) Roaring Brook Pr.

—The Scandalous Sisterhood of Prickwillow Place. 2014. (ENG.). 368p. (J). (gr. 5-9). 15.99 (978-1-59643-956-6(4), 9781596439566) Roaring Brook Pr.

Berry, Julie & Gardner, Sally Faye. The Rat Brain Fiasco. 2010. (Splurch Academy Ser.: 1). (ENG.). 208p. (J). (gr. 3-7). pap. 6.99 (978-0-448-45359-0(2), Grosset & Dunlap) Penguin Young Readers Group.

Beverly, James. Seamus the Sheltie to the Rescue! 2011. 156p. pap. 14.95 (978-1-933449-88-3(8)) Nightengale Pr.

Beyers, Kathryn. Babe's Vacation. 2012. 32p. pap. 17.49 (978-1-4771-5671-1(2)) Xlibris Corp.

Bianchi, John. Can I Do It? 2015. (2G Bird, Bunny & Bear Ser.). (ENG., Illus.). 16p. (J). pap. 5.99 (978-1-63437-151-3(8)) American Reading Co.

—My Ride. Bianchi, John, illus. 2014. (2G Potato Chip Bks.). (ENG., Illus.). 12p. (J). pap. 5.99 (978-1-61406-682-8(5)) American Reading Co.

—Over & Under. Bianchi, John, illus. 2014. (2G Bird, Bunny & Bear Ser.). (ENG., Illus.). 16p. (J). pap. 5.99 (978-1-61406-686-6(8)) American Reading Co.

—The Sun. Bianchi, John, illus. 2014. (2G Bird, Bunny & Bear Ser.). (ENG., Illus.). 16p. (J). pap. 5.99 (978-1-61406-688-0(4)) American Reading Co.

—What Can You Do? Bianchi, John, illus. 2014. (2G Bird. Bunny & Bear Ser.). (ENG., Illus.). 16p. (J). pap. 5.99 (978-1-61406-681-1(7)) American Reading Co.

Biedrzycki, David. Breaking News: Bear Alert. Biedrzycki, David, illus. (Breaking News Ser.). (ENG., Illus.). 32p. (J). (gr. -1-3). 2016. lib. bdg. 17.95 (978-1-58089-624-5(3)) 2014. 17.95 (978-1-58089-663-4(4)) Charlesbridge Publishing, Inc.

—Santa Retires. Biedrzycki, David, illus. 2012. (ENG., Illus.). 32p. (J). (gr. -1-3). 16.95 (978-1-58089-293-3(0)); pap. 7.95 (978-1-58089-294-0(9)) Charlesbridge Publishing, Inc.

—Santa's New Jet. Biedrzycki, David & Bonnet, Rosalinde, illus. 2011. (ENG.). 32p. (J). (gr. -1-2). 16.95 (978-1-58089-291-9(4)); pap. 7.95 (978-1-58089-292-6(2)) Charlesbridge Publishing, Inc.

—Santa's New Jet. 2007. (Illus.). (J). pap. (978-0-545-00238-7(9)) Scholastic, Inc.

Big Idea Entertainment, LLC. LarryBoy & the Foolish Fig from Faraway. Jones, Cory, illus. 2016. (VeggieTales Ser.). (ENG.). 32p. (J). (gr. -1-3). pap. 3.99 (978-1-4336-4340-8(5), B&H Kids) B&H Publishing Group.

—LarryBoy & the Merciless Mango. Jones, Cory, illus. 2016. (VeggieTales Ser.). (ENG.). 32p. (J). (gr. -1-3). pap. 3.99 (978-1-4336-4338-5(3), B&H Kids) B&H Publishing Group.

—LarryBoy & the Prideosaurus. Jones, Cory, illus. 2016. (VeggieTales Ser.). (ENG.). 32p. (J). (gr. -1-3). pap. 3.99 (978-1-4336-4341-5(3), B&H Kids) B&H Publishing Group.

—LarryBoy & the Quitter Critter Quad Squad. Jones, Cory, illus. 2016. (VeggieTales Ser.). (ENG.). 32p. (J). (gr. -1-3). pap. 3.99 (978-1-4336-4342-2(1), B&H Kids) B&H Publishing Group.

—LarryBoy & the Reckless Ruckus. Jones, Cory, illus. 2016. (VeggieTales Ser.). (ENG.). 32p. (J). (gr. -1-3). pap. 3.99 (978-1-4336-4343-9(X), B&H Kids) B&H Publishing Group.

—LarryBoy & the Rude Beet. Jones, Cory, illus. 2016. (VeggieTales Ser.). (ENG.). 32p. (J). (gr. -1-3). pap. 3.99 (978-1-4336-4344-6(8), B&H Kids) B&H Publishing Group.

—The League of Incredible Vegetables. Jones, Cory, illus. 2016. (VeggieTales Ser.). (ENG.). 32p. (J). (gr. -1-3). pap. 3.99 (978-1-4336-4350-7(2), B&H Kids) B&H Publishing Group.

—Lyle the Kindly Viking. Jones, Cory, illus. 2016. (VeggieTales Ser.). (ENG.). 32p. (J). (gr. -1-3). pap. 3.99 (978-1-4336-4345-3(6), B&H Kids) B&H Publishing Group.

—MacLarry & the Stinky Cheese Battle. Jones, Cory, illus. 2016. (VeggieTales Ser.). (ENG.). 32p. (J). (gr. -1-3). pap. 3.99 (978-1-4336-4346-0(4), B&H Kids) B&H Publishing Group.

—Minnesota Cuke & the Search for Samson's Hairbrush. Jones, Cory, illus. 2016. (VeggieTales Ser.). (ENG.). 32p. (J). (gr. -1-3). pap. 3.99 (978-1-4336-4347-7(2), B&H Kids) B&H Publishing Group.

Bigler, Stephanie, et al. Sir Francis Bacon & the Wolves of Isle Royale: A Little Pig's Big Adventure. 2008. 24p. pap. 13.99 (978-1-4389-1524-1(1)) AuthorHouse.

Bilgrey, Marc. And Don't Forget to Rescue the Other Princess. 2009. 252p. 25.95 (978-1-59414-744-9(2), Five Star) Cengage Gale.

Billam, Rosemary. The Mud Monster. Remphry, Martin, illus. 2008. (Reading Corner Ser.). (ENG.). 24p. (J). (gr. k-2). pap. 6.99 (978-0-7496-7695-7(7), Franklin Watts) Hachette Children's Group GBR. Dist: Hachette Bk. Group.

Bingham, Kelly. Circle, Square, Moose. Zelinsky, Paul O., illus. 2014. (ENG.). 48p. (J). (gr. -1-3). 17.99 (978-0-06-229003-8(7), Greenwillow Bks.) HarperCollins Pubs.

—Z Is for Moose. Zelinsky, Paul O., illus. 2012. 32p. (J). (gr. -1-2). (ENG.). 16.99 (978-0-06-079984-7(6)); lib. bdg. 17.89 (978-0-06-079985-4(4)) HarperCollins Pubs. (Greenwillow Bks.).

Birchall, Katy. The It Girl. 2016. (It Girl Ser.: 1). (ENG., Illus.). 352p. (J). (gr. 4-8). 16.99 (978-1-4814-6362-1(4), Aladdin) Simon & Schuster Children's Publishing.

—Team Awkward. 2017. (It Girl Ser.: 2). (ENG., Illus.). 304p. (YA). (gr. 4-8). 16.99 (978-1-4814-6365-2(9), Simon & Schuster/Paula Wiseman Bks.) Simon & Schuster/Paula Wiseman Bks.

Bird, Benjamin. A Cat Is Chasing Me Through This Book!, 1 vol. Pérez, Carmen, illus. 2014. (Tom & Jerry Ser.). (ENG.). 32p. (gr. -1-2). 22.65 (978-1-4795-5229-0(1)) Picture Window Bks.

—Don't Give This Book a Bowl of Milk!, 1 vol. Pérez, Carmen, illus. 2014. (Tom & Jerry Ser.). (ENG.). 32p. (gr. -1-2). 22.65 (978-1-4795-5230-6(5)) Picture Window Bks.

—This Book Is Not a Piece of Cheese!, 1 vol. Pérez, Carmen, illus. 2014. (Tom & Jerry Ser.). (ENG.). 32p. (gr. -1-2). 22.65 (978-1-4795-5231-3(3)) Picture Window Bks.

—Tom & Jerry, 1 vol. 2014. (Tom & Jerry Ser.). (ENG.). 32p. (gr. -1-2). 90.60 (978-1-4795-5685-4(8)) Picture Window Bks.

Birdsall, Jeanne. Lucky & Squash. Dyer, Jane, illus. 2012. (ENG.). 32p. (J). (gr. -1-2). 16.99 (978-0-06-083150-9(2)) HarperCollins Pubs.

—My Favorite Pets. Bliss, Harry, illus. 2016. (ENG.). 40p. (J). (gr. -1-2). 16.99 (978-0-385-75570-2(8), Knopf Bks. for Young Readers) Random Hse. Children's Bks.

Birdseye, Tom. Attack of the Mutant Underwear. 2006. (ENG., Illus.). 208p. (J). (gr. 3-7). 7.99 (978-0-14-240734-9(8), Puffin Books) Penguin Young Readers Group.

Birney, Betty G. The Princess & the Peabodys. 2007. (ENG.). 256p. (J). (gr. 5-9). 15.99 (978-0-06-084720-3(4)) HarperCollins Pubs.

Bishop, Claire Huchet. The Man Who Lost His Head. McCloskey, Robert, illus. 2009. (ENG.). 64p. (J). (gr. -1-3). 17.95 (978-1-59017-332-9(5), NYR Children's Collection) New York Review of Bks., Inc., The.

Blabey, Aaron. The Bad Guys. (Bad Guys Ser.: bk.4). (ENG.). 144p. (J). (gr. 2-5). 2017. pap. 5.99 **(978-1-338-08753-6(3)**, Scholastic Paperbacks) 2017. pap. 5.99 (978-0-545-91241-9(5), Scholastic Pr.) 2016. pap. 5.99 (978-0-545-91240-2(7), Scholastic Pr.) Scholastic, Inc.

Black, Cassandra. Twinkle: A Chapter Book. 2003. 113p. (J). 7.99 (978-0-9742739-0-7(2)) Lavender Bks.

Black, Cuyler. The Goat of Many Colors, 1 vol. 2010. (ENG.). 32p. (J). (gr. k-3). pap. 4.99 (978-0-310-71634-1(9)) Zonderkidz.

Black, Michael Ian. Cock-a-Doodle-Doo-Bop. Myers, Matthew, illus. 2015. (ENG.). 40p. (J). (gr. -1-3). 17.99 (978-1-4424-9510-4(3), Simon & Schuster Bks. For Young Readers) Simon & Schuster Bks. For Young Readers.

—Naked! Ohi, Debbie Ridpath, illus. 2014. (ENG.). 40p. (J). (gr. -1-3). 17.99 (978-1-4424-6738-5(X), Simon & Schuster Bks. For Young Readers) Simon & Schuster Bks. For Young Readers.

—A Pig Parade Is a Terrible Idea. Hawkes, Kevin, illus. 2010. (ENG.). 40p. (J). (gr. -1-3). 17.99 (978-1-4169-7922-7(0), Simon & Schuster Bks. For Young Readers) Simon & Schuster Bks. For Young Readers.

—The Purple Kangaroo. Brown, Peter, illus. 2009. (ENG.). 32p. (J). (gr. -1-3). 16.99 (978-1-4169-5771-3(5), Simon & Schuster Bks. For Young Readers) Simon & Schuster Bks. For Young Readers.

Black, Simon. The Dog Child. Robledo, Honorio, illus. 2006. (ENG.). 32p. (J). (gr. -1-3). 17.95 (978-0-938317-42-5(3)) Cinco Puntos Pr.

Blackall, Sophie. Are You Awake? Blackall, Sophie, illus. 2011. (ENG., Illus.). 40p. (J). (gr. -1-k). 12.99 (978-0-8050-7858-9(4), 9780805078589, Holt, Henry & Co. Bks. For Young Readers) Holt, Henry & Co.

—The Baby Tree. Blackall, Sophie, illus. 2014. (ENG., Illus.). 32p. (J). (gr. k-3). 17.99 (978-0-399-25718-6(7), Nancy Paulsen Books) Penguin Young Readers Group.

Blackford, Andy. The Three Little Pigs & the New Neighbor. 2014. (ENG., Illus.). 32p. (J). (978-0-7787-0447-8(5)); pap. (978-0-7787-0482-9(3)) Crabtree Publishing Co.

Blake, Jon. Holiday Mania at the House of Fun. Roberts, David, illus. 2007. (ENG.). 128p. (J). (gr. k-2). pap. 6.95 (978-0-340-93129-5(9)) Hachette Children's Group GBR. Dist: Hachette Bk. Group.

Blankenship, LeeAnn. Mr. Tuggle's Troubles. Dugan, Karen, illus. 2005. (ENG.). 32p. (J). (gr. k-3). 15.95 (978-1-59078-196-8(1)) Boyds Mills Pr.

Blecha, Aaron. Good Morning, Grizzle Grump! Blecha, Aaron, illus. 2017. (Illus.). 32p. (J). (gr. -1-3). 17.99 (978-0-06-229749-5(X)) HarperCollins Pubs.

Bliss, Harry. Luke on the Loose. Bliss, Harry, illus. 2009. (ENG., Illus.). 32p. (J). (gr. -1-3). 12.95 (978-1-935179-00-9(4)) TOON Books / RAW Junior, LLC.

—Luke on the Loose. 2014. (Toon Books Level 2 Ser.). lib. bdg. 14.75 (978-0-606-32101-3(2), Turtleback) Turtleback Bks.

Bloch, Serge. Reach for the Stars: And Other Advice for Life's Journey. 2010. (ENG., Illus.). 32p. (J). (gr. -1). 12.95 (978-1-4027-7129-3(0)) Sterling Publishing Co., Inc.

Bloom, C. P. The Monkey & the Bee. Raymundo, Peter, illus. 2015. (Monkey Goes Bananas Ser.). (ENG.). 40p. (J). (gr. -1-2). 14.95 (978-1-4197-0886-2(4), Abrams Bks. for Young Readers) Abrams, Inc.

—The Monkey Goes Bananas. Raymundo, Peter, illus. 2014. (Monkey Goes Bananas Ser.). (ENG.). 40p. (J). (gr. k-2). 14.95 (978-1-4197-0885-5(6), Abrams Bks. for Young Readers) Abrams, Inc.

Bloom, Suzanne. Oh! What a Surprise! 2012. (Goose & Bear Stories Ser.). (ENG.). 32p. (J). (gr. -1-k). 16.95 (978-1-59078-892-9(3)) Boyds Mills Pr.

Bloomfield, Kevin. Mr. Biggs in the City. Bloomfield, Kevin, illus. 2011. (ENG & SPA., Illus.). 32p. (gr. -1-3). lib. bdg. 16.95 (978-1-936299-26-3(7), Raven Tree Pr.,Csi) Continental Sales, Inc.

Blume, Judy. Double Fudge. 2007. (ENG.). 240p. (J). (gr. 3-7). 7.99 (978-0-14-240878-0(6), Puffin Books) Penguin Young Readers Group.

—Double Fudge. 2004. (Fudge Ser.). 160p. (J). (gr. 3-7). pap. 36.00 incl. audio (978-0-8072-2036-8(1), Listening Library) Random Hse. Audio Publishing Group.

—Double Fudge. 2013. pap. (978-0-439-58549-1(X), Scholastic) Scholastic, Inc.

—Double Fudge. 2007. (Fudge Bks.: 5). lib. bdg. 18.40 (978-1-4177-8371-7(0), Turtleback) Turtleback Bks.

—Freckle Juice. 47p. (J). (gr. 1-3). pap. 4.50 (978-0-8072-1330-8(6), Listening Library) Random Hse. Audio Publishing Group.

—Freckle Juice. Lisker, Sonia & Ohi, Debbie Ridpath, illus. 2014. (ENG.). 64p. (J). (gr. 1-5). pap. 5.99 (978-1-4814-1102-8(0), Atheneum Bks. for Young Readers) Simon & Schuster Children's Publishing.

—Fudge-a-Mania. 2004. (ENG.). 176p. (J). (gr. 3-7). 6.99 (978-0-425-19382-2(9), Berkley) Penguin Publishing Group.

—Fudge-a-Mania. 2007. (ENG.). 176p. (J). (gr. 3-7). 7.99 (978-0-14-240877-3(8), Puffin Books) Penguin Young Readers Group.

—Jugo de Pecas.Tr. of Freckle Juice. (SPA.). 40p. (J). 6.95 (978-84-372-3050-4(0)) Santillana USA Publishing Co., Inc.

—The One in the Middle Is the Green Kangaroo. Ohi, Debbie Ridpath, illus. 2014. (ENG.). 48p. (J). (gr. 1-5). pap. 5.99 (978-1-4814-1131-8(4), Atheneum Bks. for Young Readers) Simon & Schuster Children's Publishing.

—Superfudge. (Fudge Ser.).Tr. of Superfudge. 166p. (J). (gr. 2-4). pap. 4.99 (978-0-8072-1457-2(4), Listening Library) Random Hse. Audio Publishing Group.

—Superfudge. 2007. (Fudge Bks.: 3).Tr. of Superfudge. lib. bdg. 18.40 (978-1-4177-8843-9(7), Turtleback) Turtleback Bks.

—Tales of a Fourth Grade Nothing. 2009. 8.32 (978-0-7848-3046-8(0)); 8.32 (978-0-7848-0332-5(3)) Marco Bk. Co. (Everbind).

—Tales of a Fourth Grade Nothing. 2007. 17.00 (978-0-7569-7937-9(4)) 2004. (ENG.). 144p. (J). (gr. 3-7). 7.99 (978-0-425-19379-2(9), Berkley) Penguin Publishing Group.

—Tales of a Fourth Grade Nothing. 2007. (ENG.). 160p. (J). (gr. 3-7). 7.99 (978-0-14-240881-0(6), Puffin Books) Penguin Young Readers Group.

—Tales of a Fourth Grade Nothing. (Fudge Ser.). 120p. (J). (gr. 3-5). pap. 4.99 (978-0-8072-1496-1(5), Listening Library) Random Hse. Audio Publishing Group.

—Tales of a Fourth Grade Nothing. 2003. pap. (978-0-439-57779-3(9), Scholastic) Scholastic, Inc.

Blyton, Enid. Mr Pink-Whistle Interferes. (ENG., Illus.). 112p. (J). pap. 7.99 (978-0-7475-3859-2(X)) Bloomsbury Publishing Plc GBR. Dist: Trafalgar Square Publishing.

Boldi, Florina, illus. Pug in Boots. 2013. 42p. pap. 9.99 (978-0-9829132-6-0(5)) Left Paw Pr.

Boldt, Mike. Colors Versus Shapes. Boldt, Mike, illus. 2014. (ENG., Illus.). 40p. (J). (gr. -1-3). 16.99 (978-0-06-210303-1(2)) HarperCollins Pubs.

Bolger, Kevin. Fun with Ed & Fred. Hodson, Ben, illus. 2016. 40p. (J). (gr. -1-3). 7.99 (978-0-06-228600-0(5)) HarperCollins Pubs.

—Gran on a Fan. Hodson, Ben, illus. 2015. (ENG.). 40p. (J). (gr. -1-3). 7.99 (978-0-06-228596-6(3)) HarperCollins Pubs.

—See Fred Run. Hodson, Ben, illus. 2017. 40p. (J). (gr. -1-3). 7.99 **(978-0-06-228602-4(1))** HarperCollins Pubs.

—Sir Fartsalot Hunts the Booger. Gilpin, Stephen, illus. 2009. (ENG.). 224p. (J). (gr. 3-7). 7.99 (978-1-59514-284-9(3), Razorbill) Penguin Young Readers Group.

—Zombiekins 2. Blecha, Aaron, illus. 2011. (J). 10.99 (978-1-59514-432-4(3), Razorbill) Penguin Publishing Group.

Bolling, Ruben. Ghostly Thief of Time: An EMU Club Adventure. 2015. (ENG., Illus.). 144p. (J). 12.99 (978-1-4494-5710-5(X)) Andrews McMeel Publishing.

Bolton, Robin. Roo-Star, the Smartest Chicken in the Coop. 2013. 28p. pap. 13.99 (978-1-4624-0585-5(1), Inspiring Voices) Author Solutions, Inc.

Bond, Clint & Clark, Andy, illus. The Great Snail Race. 2005. (SpongeBob SquarePants Ser.). (ENG.). 24p. (J). pap. 3.99 (978-0-689-87313-3(1), Simon Spotlight/Nickelodeon) Simon Spotlight/Nickelodeon.

Bondor-Stone, Annabeth & White, Connor. The Shivering. Holden, Anthony, illus. 2016. (Shivers! Ser.: 2). 208p. (J). (gr. 3-7). 12.99 (978-0-06-231389-8(4)) HarperCollins Pubs.

—Shivers! - The Pirate Who's Afraid of Everything. Holden, Anthony, illus. 2015. (Shivers! Ser.: 1). (ENG.). 192p. (J). (gr. 3-7). 12.99 (978-0-06-231387-4(8)) HarperCollins Pubs.

Boniface, William. The Extraordinary Adventures of Ordinary Boy. Gilpin, Stephen, illus. 2008. (Extraordinary Adventures of Ordinary Boy Ser.: 2). (ENG.). 368p. (J). (gr. 3-7). pap. 6.99 (978-0-06-077469-1(X)) HarperCollins Pubs.

—The Extraordinary Adventures of Ordinary Boy Bk. 3: The Great Powers Outage. Gilpin, Stephen, illus. 2010. (Extraordinary Adventures of Ordinary Boy Ser.: 3). (ENG.). 352p. (J). (gr. 3-7). pap. 7.99 (978-0-06-077472-1(X)) HarperCollins Pubs.

Bonilla, Barbara Ann. The Wacky World of Wendy White! A Whopper of a Tale. 2013. (ENG.). 47p. (J). pap. 12.95 (978-1-4787-1543-6(X)) Outskirts Pr., Inc.

Bonnett-Rampersaud, Louise. Never Ask a Bear. Barrette, Doris, illus. 2009. (ENG.). 32p. (J). (gr. -1-1). 16.99 (978-0-06-112876-9(7)) HarperCollins Pubs.

Bonwill, Ann. The Frazzle Family Finds a Way. Gammell, Stephen, illus. 2013. (ENG.). 32p. (J). (gr. -1-3). 16.95 (978-0-8234-2405-4(7)) Holiday Hse., Inc.

The Book with No Pictures. 2014. (ENG.). 48p. (J). (gr. k-3). 17.99 (978-0-8037-4171-3(5), Dial Bks) Penguin Publishing Group.

Booraem, Ellen. Texting the Underworld. 2013. (ENG.). 320p. (J). (gr. 5). 16.99 (978-0-8037-3704-4(1), Dial Bks) Penguin Young Readers Group.

Boudreau, Helene. I Dare You Not to Yawn. Bloch, Serge, illus. 2017. (ENG.). 28p. (J). (— 1). bds. 8.99 (978-0-7636-9307-7(3)) Candlewick Pr.

Bourgeois, Paulette & Clark, Brenda. Franklin's Nickname. Southern, Shelley, tr. Southern, Shelley, illus. 2004. (Franklin TV Storybook Ser.). (ENG.). 32p. (J). (gr. -1-3). 4.95

(978-1-55337-490-9(8)); 10.95 *(978-1-55337-489-3(4))* Kids Can Pr., Ltd. CAN. Dist: Hachette Bk. Group.

Bowles, Coy. When You're Feeling Sick. Elkerton, Andy, illus. 2017. (ENG.). 32p. (J). (gr. -1-2). 12.99 *(978-0-399-55286-1(3)*, Doubleday Bks. for Young Readers) Random Hse. Children's Bks.

Boyce, Frank Cottrell. The Astounding Broccoli Boy. 2015. 384p. (J). (gr. 3-7). 16.99 *(978-0-06-240017-8(7)*, Waldon Pond Pr.) HarperCollins Pubs.

—Desirable. 2012. (Stoke Books Titles Ser.). 64p. (J). (gr. 5-8). pap. 7.95 *(978-1-78112-014-9(5))*; lib. bdg. 22.60 *(978-1-78112-013-2(7))* Stoke Bks.

—Framed. Lenton, Steven, illus. unabr. ed. 2006. (ENG.). 320p. pap. 15.95 *(978-0-330-43425-6(X))* Macmillan Pubs., Ltd. GBR. Dist: Trans-Atlantic Pubns., Inc.

Boyce, Frank Cottrell & Boyce, Frank Cottrell. Millions. (J). (gr. 3-18). 2004. (Illus.). 256p. 15.99 *(978-0-06-073330-8(6))* 2004. (Illus.). 256p. lib. bdg. 16.89 *(978-0-06-073331-5(4))* 2005. 272p. reprint ed. pap. 8.99 *(978-0-06-073332-2(2))* HarperCollins Pubs.

Boyle, Keri Claiborne. Teddy the Dog: Be Your Own Dog. Sneider, Jonathan, illus. 2016. (Teddy the Dog Ser.: 1). 32p. (J). (gr. -1-3). 17.99 *(978-0-06-238283-2(7))* HarperCollins Pubs.

—Teddy the Dog: (Almost) Best in Show. Sneider, Jonathan, illus. 2017. (Teddy the Dog Ser.). 32p. (J). (gr. -1-3). 17.99 *(978-0-06-238284-9(5))* HarperCollins Pubs.

Boynton, Sandra. Big Box of Boynton. Boynton, Sandra, illus. 2005. (ENG., Illus.). 24p. (J). (gr. k — 1). bds. 21.00 *(978-0-7611-3989-8(3)*, 13989) Workman Publishing Co., Inc.

—Moo, Baa, la la La! Boynton, Sandra, illus. 2004. (ENG., Illus.). 16p. (J). (gr. -1 — 1). bds. 9.99 *(978-0-689-87027-9(2)*, Little Simon) Little Simon.

The Boys from Brooklyn: The Great Robbery. 2004. (J). mass mkt. 9.95 *(978-0-9761440-0-7(X))* Booksforboys.

Braddock, Paige. Stinky Cecil in Operation Pond Rescue. 2015. (Stinky Cecil Ser.: 1). (ENG.). 128p. (J). pap. 9.99 *(978-1-4494-5711-2(8))* Andrews McMeel Publishing.

—Stinky Cecil in Terrarium Terror. 2016. (Stinky Cecil Ser.: 2). (ENG.). 128p. (J). pap. 9.99 *(978-1-4494-7186-6(2))* Andrews McMeel Publishing.

Bradfield, Jolly Roger. Pickle-Chiffon Pie. 2004. (Illus.). 64p. (J). (gr. -1-3). 18.95 *(978-1-930900-30-1(9))* Purple Hse. Pr.

Bradfield, Roger, illus. The Pickle-Chiffon Pie Olympics. 2011. 64p. (J). (gr. -1-3). 18.95 *(978-1-930900-52-3(X))* Purple Hse. Pr.

Bradford, Arthur. Benny's Brigade. Hanawalt, Lisa, illus. 2012. (ENG.). 48p. 19.95 *(978-1-936365-61-6(8))* McSweeney's Publishing.

Bradman, Tony. Mr. Giant & the Beastly Baron, 1 vol. Warburton, Sarah, illus. 2014. (After Happily Ever After Ser.). (ENG.). 56p. (gr. 2-3). lib. bdg. 25.32 *(978-1-4342-7949-1(9)*, After Happily Ever After) Stone Arch Bks.

—Mr. Wolf Bounces Back, 1 vol. Warburton, Sarah, illus. 2013. (After Happily Ever After Ser.). (ENG.). 56p. (gr. 2-3). pap. 5.05 *(978-1-4342-6414-5(9)*, After Happily Ever After) Stone Arch Bks.

—The Mummy Family Find Fame. 2006. (Red Bananas Ser.). (ENG., Illus.). 48p. (J). (gr. -1-3). lib. bdg. *(978-0-7787-1076-9(9))* Crabtree Publishing Co.

—Red Riding Hood Takes Charge, 1 vol. Warburton, Sarah, illus. 2013. (After Happily Ever After Ser.). (ENG.). 56p. (gr. 2-3). pap. 5.05 *(978-1-4342-6413-8(0)*, After Happily Ever After) Stone Arch Bks.

—Snow White & the Magic Mirror, 1 vol. Warburton, Sarah, illus. 2014. (After Happily Ever After Ser.). (ENG.). 56p. (gr. 2-3). lib. bdg. 25.32 *(978-1-4342-7950-7(2)*, After Happily Ever After) Stone Arch Bks.

—The Three Little Pigs Go Camping, 1 vol. Warburton, Sarah, illus. 2014. (After Happily Ever After Ser.). (ENG.). 56p. (gr. 2-3). lib. bdg. 25.32 *(978-1-4342-7952-1(9)*, After Happily Ever After) Stone Arch Bks.

—The Ugly Duckling Returns, 1 vol. Warburton, Sarah, illus. 2014. (After Happily Ever After Ser.). (ENG.). 56p. (gr. 2-3). lib. bdg. 25.32 *(978-1-4342-7953-8(7)*, After Happily Ever After) Stone Arch Bks.

—Who Will Marry Prince Harry? Bitskoff, Aleksei, illus. 2016. (Reading Ladder Ser.). (ENG.). 48p. (J). (gr. k-2). pap. 7.99 *(978-1-4052-7824-9(2))* Egmont Bks., Ltd. GBR. Dist: Independent Pubs. Group.

—The Wicked Stepmother Helps Out, 1 vol. Warburton, Sarah, illus. 2014. (After Happily Ever After Ser.). (ENG.). 56p. (gr. 2-3). lib. bdg. 25.32 *(978-1-4342-7951-4(0)*, After Happily Ever After) Stone Arch Bks.

Bradman, Tony & Chatterton, Martin. The Surprise Party. 2005. (Red Bananas Ser.). (ENG., Illus.). 48p. (J). (gr. 1-3). *(978-0-7787-1084-4(X))* Crabtree Publishing Co.

Bradshaw, John. Fun campfire Stories. 2009. 132p. pap. 13.98 *(978-0-557-17897-1(5))* Lulu Pr., Inc.

Braeuner, Shellie. The Great Dog Wash. Neubecker, Robert, illus. 2009. (ENG.). 32p. (J). (gr. -1-1). 15.99 *(978-1-4169-7116-0(5)*, Simon & Schuster Bks. For Young Readers) Simon & Schuster Bks. For Young Readers.

Brallier, Max. Galactic Hot Dogs 1: Cosmoe's Wiener Getaway. Maguire, Rachel & Kelley, Nichole, illus. 2016. (Galactic Hot Dogs Ser.: 1). (ENG.). 304p. (J). (gr. 3-7). 13.99 *(978-1-4814-8098-7(7)*, Aladdin) Simon & Schuster Children's Publishing.

—The Last Kids on Earth. Holgate, Douglas, illus. (J). 2017. pap. ***(978-0-425-28872-6(2))*** 2016. (Last Kids on Earth Ser.: Vol. 2). (ENG.). 304p. (gr. 3-7). 13.99 *(978-0-670-01662-4(4))* 2015. (Last Kids on Earth Ser.: 1). (ENG.). 240p. (gr. 3-7). 13.99 *(978-0-670-01661-7(6))* Penguin Young Readers Group. (Viking Books for Young Readers).

Bramsen, Carin. Just a Duck? 2015. (ENG., Illus.). 40p. (J). (gr. -1-2). 17.99 *(978-0-385-38415-5(7)*, Random Hse. Bks. for Young Readers) Random Hse. Children's Bks.

Brandon, Demi. Princess Shakina's Locks. 2007. 48p. per. 16.95 *(978-1-4241-7195-8(4))* America Star Bks.

Brandreth, Gyles. Madcap Book of Laughs. Hawkins, Colin et al, illus. 288p. (J). pap. 6.95 *(978-0-233-99569-4(2))* Andre Deutsch GBR. Dist: Trafalgar Square Publishing.

Braun, Eric. Trust Me, Jack's Beanstalk Stinks! The Story of Jack & the Beanstalk as Told by the Giant. Bernardini, Cristian, illus. 2011. (Other Side of the Story Ser.). (ENG.). 24p. (gr. 2-3). pap. 6.95 *(978-1-4048-7050-5(4))*; lib. bdg. 27.32 *(978-1-4048-6675-1(2))* Picture Window Bks.

Brauner, Barbara & Mattson, James Iver. Oh My Godmother the Magic Mistake. Halpin, Abigail, illus. 2014. (Oh My Godmother Ser.). (ENG.). 272p. (J). (gr. 3-7). pap. 6.99 *(978-1-4231-6479-1(2))* Hyperion Bks. for Children.

Bravi, Soledad. Mommy, Pick Me Up. 2016. (ENG., Illus.). 40p. (J). 17.99 *(978-0-374-30268-9(5)*, 9780374302689, Farrar, Straus & Giroux (BYR)) Farrar, Straus & Giroux.

Bray, Libba. Beauty Queens. (ENG.). 400p. (J). (gr. 7). 2012. pap. 10.99 *(978-0-439-89598-9(7)*, Scholastic Paperbacks) 2011. 18.99 *(978-0-439-89597-2(9)*, Scholastic Pr.) Scholastic, Inc.

Breathed, Berkeley. Flawed Dogs: The Novel: the Shocking Raid on Westminster. 2017. lib. bdg. 19.65 ***(978-0-606-39787-2(6))*** Turtleback Bks.

Breathed, Berkeley. Pete & Pickles. Breathed, Berkeley, illus. 2008. (ENG., Illus.). 48p. (J). (gr. -1-k). 17.99 *(978-0-399-25082-8(4)*, Philomel Bks.) Penguin Young Readers Group.

Brecon, Connah. Paws Mcdraw. Brecon, Connah, illus. 2016. (ENG., Illus.). 32p. (J). (gr. -1-2). 16.99 *(978-1-68010-035-8(1))* Tiger Tales.

Breen, Steve. A Perfect Mess. 2016. (ENG., Illus.). 32p. (J). (-k). 16.99 *(978-0-8037-4156-0(1)*, Dial Bks) Penguin Young Readers Group.

—Stick. 2009. (ENG.). 48p. (J). (gr. -1-k). pap. 6.99 *(978-0-14-241303-6(8)*, Puffin Books) Penguin Young Readers Group.

Brennan, Herbie. Zartog's Remote. Layton, Neal, illus. 2003. (Middle Grade Fiction Ser.). 96p. (J). (gr. 3-6). 14.95 *(978-1-57505-507-7(4)*, Carolrhoda Bks.) Lerner Publishing Group.

Brewer, Elly. Jerry & the Jannans. 2006. (ENG.). 320p. (J). (gr. 4-7). pap. 11.99 *(978-0-7475-8213-7(0))* Bloomsbury Publishing Plc GBR. Dist: Independent Pubs. Group.

Brière-Haquet, Alice. ONE Very Big Bear. Philipponneau, Olivier & Enjary, Raphaële, illus. 2016. (ENG.). 32p. (J). (gr. -1-k). 14.95 *(978-1-4197-2117-5(8)*, Abrams Appleseed) Abrams, Inc.

Briggs, John. Leaping Lemmings! Slater, Nicola, illus. 2016. (ENG.). 32p. (J). (gr. -1). 14.95 *(978-1-4549-1819-6(5))* Sterling Publishing Co., Inc.

Briggs, Mark T. Jermaine Peterman & the Encounter in the Forest. 2012. 44p. pap. 16.95 *(978-1-4626-8431-1(9))* America Star Bks.

Bringsvaerd, Tor Age. When Two Are Angry at Each Other. Vetleseter, Tonje, tr. from NOR. Soli, Tina, illus. 2008. 32p. (J). (gr. -1-1). 14.95 *(978-0-9790347-8-7(7))* Mackenzie Smiles, LLC.

Britten, Adam. The Man Who Stole a Planet. Hamer, Arthur, illus. 2013. (Captain Valiant Ser.). (ENG.). 160p. (J). (gr. k-3). pap. 9.99 *(978-1-84812-347-2(7))* Bonnier Publishing GBR. Dist: Independent Pubs. Group.

Broach, Elise. Gumption! Egielski, Richard, illus. 2010. (ENG.). 40p. (J). (gr. k-3). 18.99 *(978-1-4169-1628-4(8)*, Atheneum Bks. for Young Readers) Simon & Schuster Children's Publishing.

—When Dinosaurs Came with Everything. Small, David, illus. 2007. (ENG.). 40p. (J). (gr. -1-3). 17.99 *(978-0-689-86922-8(3)*, Atheneum Bks. for Young Readers) Simon & Schuster Children's Publishing.

Broberg, Penelope Northrop. Sleuthy Gumshoe: The Remarkable Detective. 2011. 32p. (gr. -1). pap. 14.39 *(978-1-4567-6404-3(7))* AuthorHouse.

Bronstein, Christine. Starts School. Young, Karen L., illus. 2014. (Stewie BOOM! Ser.). (ENG.). 48p. (J). (gr. -1-3). 17.99 *(978-0-9904652-0-1(9))* Nothing But The Truth, LLC.

—Stewie BOOM! Starts School. Young, Karen L., illus. 2014. (Stewie BOOM! Ser.). (ENG.). 48p. (gr. -1-3). pap. 9.99 *(978-0-9883754-9-9(4))* Nothing But The Truth, LLC.

Brooks, Felicity. Max & Millie Start School. Guicciardini, Desideria, illus. 2013. (Toddler Bks.). (ENG.). 23p. (gr. -1). 7.99 *(978-0-7945-3302-1(7)*, Usborne) EDC Publishing.

Brooks, Karl. Pros & Cons of an Outdoor John. Dixon, Carol, illus. 2013. 36p. pap. 24.95 *(978-1-63000-813-0(3))* America Star Bks.

Brooks, Mel & Reiner, Carl. The 2000 Year Old Man Goes to School. Bennett, James, illus. 2006. 32p. (J). (gr. 4-8). reprint ed. 18.00 *(978-1-4223-5622-7(1))* DIANE Publishing Co.

—The 2000 Year Old Man Goes to School. Bennett, James, illus. 2005. (ENG.). 40p. (J). (gr. -1-3). 17.99 *(978-0-06-076676-4(X))* HarperCollins Pubs.

Brooks, Walter R. The Clockwork Twin: A Freddy the Pig Book on Everything. Wiese, Kurt, illus. 2013. (ENG.). 256p. (gr. 4-13). pap. 10.99 *(978-1-4683-0349-0(X)*, 460349) Overlook Pr., The.

—Freddy & Mr. Camphor. Wiese, Kurt, illus. 2013. (ENG.). 256p. (gr. 4-13). pap. 10.99 *(978-1-4683-0666-8(9)*, 460666) Overlook Pr., The.

—Freddy & the Dragon. Wiese, Kurt, tr. 2012. (ENG., Illus.). 240p. (gr. 4-13). pap. 10.99 *(978-1-59020-866-3(8)*, 902866) Overlook Pr., The,

—Freddy Plays Football. Wiese, Kurt, illus. 2013. (ENG.). 288p. (gr. 4-13). pap. 10.99 *(978-1-4683-0667-5(7)*, 460667) Overlook Pr., The.

—Freddy Rides Again. Wiese, Kurt, illus. 2013. (ENG.). 240p. (gr. 4-13). pap. 10.99 *(978-1-4683-0724-5(X)*, 460724) Overlook Pr., The.

—Freddy the Magician. Wiese, Kurt, illus. 2011. (ENG.). 224p. (gr. 4-13). pap. 10.99 *(978-1-59020-481-8(6)*, 902481) Overlook Pr., The.

—Freddy's Cousin Weedly. Wiese, Kurt, illus. 2014. (ENG.). 240p. (gr. 4-13). pap. 10.99 *(978-1-4683-0914-0(5)*, 460914) Overlook Pr., The.

Brosgol, Vera. Leave Me Alone! Brosgol, Vera, illus. 2016. (ENG., Illus.). 40p. (J). 17.99 *(978-1-62672-441-9(5)*, 9781626724419) Roaring Brook Pr.

Brouwer, Sigmund. Justine Mckeen, Queen of Green, 1 vol. Whamond, Dave, illus. 2011. (Orca Echoes Ser.). (ENG.). 64p. (J). (gr. 2-3). pap. 6.95 *(978-1-55469-927-8(4))* Orca Bk. Pubs. USA.

Brown, Benjamin Thomas. The Best Dog. 2010. 16p. 8.49 *(978-1-4520-1010-6(2))* AuthorHouse.

Brown, Calef. Boy Wonders. Brown, Calef, illus. 2011. (ENG., Illus.). 40p. (J). (gr. -1-3). 16.99 *(978-1-4169-7877-0(1)*, Atheneum Bks. for Young Readers) Simon & Schuster Children's Publishing.

Brown, Jeff. Flat Stanley. Nash, Scott, illus. 2006. (Flat Stanley Ser.). (ENG.). 40p. (J). (gr. -1-3). 17.99 *(978-0-06-112904-9(6))* HarperCollins Pubs.

—Flat Stanley: Flat Stanley, His Original Adventure; Stanley, Flat Again; Stanley & the Magic Lamp; & Stanley in Space. Pamintuan, Macky, illus. 2016. (Flat Stanley Ser.). 416p. (J). (gr. 1-5). 14.99 *(978-0-06-249670-6(0))* HarperCollins Pubs.

—Flat Stanley: Show & Tell, Flat Stanley! Pamintuan, Macky, illus. 2014. (I Can Read Level 2 Ser.). (ENG.). 32p. (J). (gr. -1-3). 16.99 *(978-0-06-218976-9(X))* HarperCollins Pubs.

—Flat Stanley & the Haunted House. Pamintuan, Macky, illus. 2010. (I Can Read Level 2 Ser.). (ENG.). 32p. (J). (gr. -1-3). pap. 3.99 *(978-0-06-143005-3(6))* HarperCollins Pubs.

—Flat Stanley & the Very Big Cookie. Pamintuan, Macky, illus. 2015. (I Can Read Level 2 Ser.). (ENG.). 32p. (J). (gr. -1-3). 16.99 *(978-0-06-218979-0(4))*; pap. 3.99 *(978-0-06-218978-3(6))* HarperCollins Pubs.

—The Flat Stanley Collection, Set. Pamintuan, Macky, illus. 2013. (Flat Stanley Ser.). 400p. (J). (gr. 1-5). pap. 14.99 *(978-0-06-180247-8(6))* HarperCollins Pubs.

—Flat Stanley Goes Camping. 2013. (J). lib. bdg. 13.55 *(978-0-606-31815-0(1)*, Turtleback) Turtleback Bks.

—Invisible Stanley. Nash, Scott & Pamintuan, Macky, illus. 2009. (Flat Stanley Ser.). (ENG.). 112p. (J). (gr. 2-5). pap. 4.99 *(978-0-06-009792-9(2))* HarperCollins Pubs.

—Invisible Stanley. 2009. (Flat Stanley Ser.: 4). (J). (gr. k-3). lib. bdg. 14.75 *(978-0-613-68434-7(6)*, Turtleback) Turtleback Bks.

—Stanley, Flat Again! Nash, Scott & Pamintuan, Macky, illus. (Flat Stanley Ser.). (ENG.). 96p. (J). (gr. 2-5). 2009. pap. 4.99 *(978-0-06-442173-7(2))* 2003. 15.99 *(978-0-06-009551-2(2))* HarperCollins Pubs.

Brown, Jeffrey. Lucy & Andy Neanderthal. 2016. (Lucy & Andy Neanderthal Ser.: 1). (ENG., Illus.). 224p. (J). (gr. 3-7). 12.99 *(978-0-385-38835-1(7)*, Crown Books For Young Readers) Random Hse. Children's Bks.

Brown, Jennifer. How Lunchbox Jones Saved Me from Robots, Traitors, & Missy the Cruel. 2017. (ENG.). 256p. (J). pap. 7.99 *(978-1-68119-441-7(4)*, 9781681194417, Bloomsbury USA Childrens) Bloomsbury Publishing USA.

—Pennybaker School Is Headed for Disaster. Kissi, Marta, illus. 2017. (ENG.). 320p. (J). 16.99 *(978-1-68119-174-4(1)*, 9781681191744, Bloomsbury USA Childrens) Bloomsbury Publishing USA.

Brown, Peter. Children Make Terrible Pets. 2010. (Starring Lucille Beatrice Bear Ser.). (ENG., Illus.). 40p. (J). (gr. -1-3). 17.99 *(978-0-316-01548-6(2))* Little, Brown Bks. for Young Readers.

—You Will Be My Friend! 2011. (Starring Lucille Beatrice Bear Ser.). (ENG., Illus.). 40p. (J). (gr. -1-3). 18.00 *(978-0-316-07030-0(0))* Little, Brown Bks. for Young Readers.

Bruel, Nick. Bad Kitty Does Not Like Candy. 2015. (Bad Kitty Ser.). (ENG., Illus.). 24p. (J). (gr. -1-k). 4.99 *(978-1-62672-230-9(7)*, 9781626722309) Square Fish.

—Bad Kitty Does Not Like Snow. 2016. (Bad Kitty Ser.). (ENG., Illus.). 24p. (J). pap. 4.99 *(978-1-62672-581-2(0)*, 9781626725812) Roaring Brook Pr.

—Bad Kitty Does Not Like Video Games. 2016. (Bad Kitty Ser.). (ENG., Illus.). 24p. (J). pap. 4.99 *(978-1-62672-582-9(9)*, 9781626725829) Roaring Brook Pr.

—Bad Kitty Drawn to Trouble. 2014. (Bad Kitty Ser.). (ENG., Illus.). 128p. (J). (gr. 2-5). 13.99 *(978-1-59643-671-8(9)*, 9781596436718) Roaring Brook Pr.

—Bad Kitty Gets a Bath. Bruel, Nick, illus. 2008. (Bad Kitty Ser.). (ENG., Illus.). 128p. (J). (gr. 2-5). 15.99 *(978-1-59643-341-0(8)*, 9781596433410) Roaring Brook Pr.

—Bad Kitty Gets a Bath. Bruel, Nick, illus. 2009. (Bad Kitty Ser.). (ENG., Illus.). 144p. (J). (gr. 2-5). pap. 6.99 *(978-0-312-58138-1(6)*, 9780312581381) Square Fish.

—Bad Kitty Goes to the Vet. 2016. (Bad Kitty Ser.). (ENG., Illus.). 144p. (J). 13.99 *(978-1-59643-977-1(7)*, 9781596439771) Roaring Brook Pr.

—Bad Kitty Meets the Baby. Bruel, Nick, illus. 2011. (Bad Kitty Ser.). (ENG., Illus.). 144p. (J). (gr. 2-5). 14.99 *(978-1-59643-597-1(6)*, 9781596435971) Roaring Brook Pr.

—Bad Kitty Meets the Baby. Bruel, Nick, illus. 2012. (Bad Kitty Ser.). (ENG., Illus.). 160p. (J). (gr. 2-5). pap. 6.99 *(978-0-312-64121-4(4)*, 9780312641214) Square Fish.

—Bad Kitty Meets the Baby. 2012. (Bad Kitty Chapter Bks.). (J). lib. bdg. 17.20 *(978-0-606-23754-3(2)*, Turtleback) Turtleback Bks.

—Bad Kitty Scaredy-Cat. 2016. (Bad Kitty Ser.). (ENG., Illus.). 32p. (J). 16.99 *(978-1-59643-978-8(5)*, 9781596439788) Roaring Brook Pr.

—Bad Kitty School Daze. 2013. (Bad Kitty Ser.). (ENG., Illus.). 160p. (J). (gr. 2-5). 13.99 *(978-1-59643-670-1(0)*, 9781596436701) Roaring Brook Pr.

—Bad Kitty School Daze. 2014. (Bad Kitty Ser.). (ENG., Illus.). 176p. (J). (gr. 2-5). pap. 6.99 *(978-1-250-03947-7(9)*, 9781250039477) Square Fish.

—Bad Kitty School Daze. 2014. (Bad Kitty Chapter Bks.). (J). lib. bdg. 17.20 *(978-0-606-34010-6(6)*, Turtleback) Turtleback Bks.

—Bad Kitty Storytime Set. unabr. ed. 2014. (ENG.). (J). 12.99 *(978-1-4272-3178-9(8)*, 9781427231789) Macmillan Audio.

—Bad Kitty Takes a Test. 2017. (Bad Kitty Ser.). (ENG., Illus.). 144p. (J). 13.99 *(978-1-62672-589-8(6)*, 9781626725898) Roaring Brook Pr.

—Bad Kitty vs. Uncle Murray. Bruel, Nick, illus. 2011. (Bad Kitty Ser.). (ENG., Illus.). 176p. (J). (gr. 2-5). pap. 6.99 *(978-0-312-67483-0(X)*, 9780312674830) Square Fish.

—Bad Kitty vs. Uncle Murray. 2011. (Bad Kitty Chapter Bks.). (J). lib. bdg. 17.20 *(978-0-606-23753-6(4)*, Turtleback) Turtleback Bks.

—Bad Kitty vs. Uncle Murray: The Uproar at the Front Door. Bruel, Nick, illus. 2010. (Bad Kitty Ser.). (ENG., Illus.). 160p. (J). (gr. 2-5). 14.99 *(978-1-59643-596-4(8)*, 9781596435964) Roaring Brook Pr.

—Does Not Like Dogs, 2 vols. 2015. (Bad Kitty Ser.). (ENG., Illus.). 24p. (J). (gr. -1-k). 4.99 *(978-1-62672-231-6(5)*, 9781626722316) Square Fish.

—Happy Birthday, Bad Kitty. Bruel, Nick, illus. 2009. (Bad Kitty Ser.). (ENG., Illus.). 160p. (J). (gr. 2-5). 15.99 *(978-1-59643-342-7(6)*, 9781596433427) Roaring Brook Pr.

—Happy Birthday, Bad Kitty. Bruel, Nick, illus. 2010. (Bad Kitty Ser.). (ENG., Illus.). 176p. (J). (gr. 2-5). pap. 6.99 *(978-0-312-62902-1(8)*, 9780312629021) Square Fish.

—Puppy's Big Day. Bruel, Nick, illus. 2015. (Bad Kitty Ser.). (ENG., Illus.). 160p. (J). (gr. 2-5). 13.99 *(978-1-59643-976-4(9)*, 9781596439764) Roaring Brook Pr.

—Who Is Melvin Bubble? Bruel, Nick, illus. 2006. (ENG., Illus.). 32p. (J). (gr. -1-3). 17.99 *(978-1-59643-116-4(4)*, 9781596431164) Roaring Brook Pr.

—A Wonderful Year. Bruel, Nick, illus. 2015. (ENG., Illus.). 40p. (J). (gr. -1-1). 17.99 *(978-1-59643-611-4(5)*, 9781596436114) Roaring Brook Pr.

Brutton, Elizabeth. Tabbies & Tigers in Provence. 2009. (Illus.). 112p. pap. 12.49 *(978-1-4490-2104-7(2))* AuthorHouse.

Bryan, Sean. A Boy & His Bunny. Murphy, Tom, illus. 2011. (ENG.). 32p. (J). (gr. -1-k). 14.95 *(978-1-61145-023-1(3)*, 611023, Arcade Publishing) Skyhorse Publishing Co., Inc.

—A Girl & Her Gator. Murphy, Tom, illus. 2011. (ENG.). 32p. (J). (gr. -1-k). 14.95 *(978-1-61145-032-3(2)*, 611032, Arcade Publishing) Skyhorse Publishing Co., Inc.

—The Juggling Pug. Murphy, Tom, illus. 2011. (ENG.). 32p. (J). (gr. -1-k). 12.95 *(978-1-61608-329-8(8)*, 608329, Sky Pony Pr.) Skyhorse Publishing Co., Inc.

Bryan, Sean & Thomas, Evan. A Bear & His Boy. Murphy, Tom, illus. 2011. (ENG.). 32p. (J). (gr. -1-k). 14.95 *(978-1-61145-027-9(6)*, 611027, Arcade Publishing) Skyhorse Publishing Co., Inc.

Buckeridge, Anthony. Jennings' Little Hut. l.t. ed. 2005. (Dales Ser.). (Illus.). 272p. (J). 23.99 *(978-1-84262-370-1(2))* Magna Large Print Bks. GBR. Dist: Ulverscroft Large Print Bks., Ltd.

Buckley, Michael. Attack of the Bullies. (Nerds Ser.). (ENG.). (gr. 3-7). 2013. 336p. (YA). 16.95 *(978-1-4197-0857-2(0))*Bk. 5. 2014. (Illus.). 352p. (J). pap. 7.95 *(978-1-4197-1222-7(5))* Abrams, Inc. (Amulet Bks.).

—The Cheerleaders of Doom, Bk. 3. 2012. (Nerds Ser.). (ENG.). 304p. (YA). (gr. 3-7). pap. 7.95 *(978-1-4197-0414-7(1)*, Amulet Bks.) Abrams, Inc.

—The Cheerleaders of Doom. 2012. (Nerds Ser.: 3). (YA). lib. bdg. 18.40 *(978-0-606-26927-8(4)*, Turtleback) Turtleback Bks.

—Kel Gilligan's Daredevil Stunt Show. Santat, Dan, illus. 2012. (ENG.). 40p. (J). (gr. k-2). 17.95 *(978-1-4197-0379-9(X)*, Abrams Bks. for Young Readers) Abrams, Inc.

—M Is for Mama's Boy. Beavers, Ethen, illus. 2010. (Nerds Ser.). (ENG.). 288p. (J). (gr. 3-7). 16.95 *(978-0-8109-8986-3(7))*; pap. 6.95 *(978-0-8109-9674-8(X))* Abrams, Inc. (Amulet Bks.).

—M Is for Mama's Boy, Bk. 2. 2011. (Nerds Ser.). (ENG., Illus.). 304p. (J). (gr. 3-7). pap. 7.95 *(978-1-4197-0023-1(5)*, Amulet Bks.) Abrams, Inc.

—NERDS: National Espionage, Rescue, & Defense Society, 5 vols. 2009. (N. E. R. D. S. Ser.: 1). (J). 86.75 *(978-1-4407-4239-2(1))*; 88.75 *(978-1-4407-4237-8(5))*; 71.75 *(978-1-4407-4235-4(9))*; 190.75 *(978-1-4407-4234-7(0))*; 1.25 *(978-1-4407-4243-9(X))*; 73.75 *(978-1-4407-4233-0(2))* Recorded Bks., Inc.

—NERDS Bk. 1: National Espionage, Rescue, & Defense Society. 2010. (Nerds Ser.). (ENG., Illus.). 352p. (J). (gr. 3-7). pap. 7.95 *(978-0-8109-8985-6(9)*, Amulet Bks.) Abrams, Inc.

—Nerds Bk. 1: National Espionage, Rescue, & Defense Society. Beavers, Ethen, illus. 2009. (Nerds Ser.). (ENG.). 336p. (J). (gr. 3-7). 16.95 *(978-0-8109-4324-7(7)*, Amulet Bks.) Abrams, Inc.

—NERDS - National Espionage, Rescue, & Defense Society. 2010. (Nerds Ser.: 1). (J). lib. bdg. 18.40 *(978-0-606-15084-2(6)*, Turtleback) Turtleback Bks.

—NERDS 2: M für Muttersöhnchen. 2011. (SPA.). 260p. (J). (gr. 6-8). pap. 10.99 *(978-987-612-335-8(1))* V&R Editoras.

—Las Porristas del Infierno. 2013. 288p. (J). pap. 11.99 *(978-987-612-627-4(X))* V&R Editoras.

—The Villain Virus. (Nerds Ser.). (ENG.). (gr. 3-7). 2013. 304p. (YA). pap. 7.95 *(978-1-4197-0975-3(5))* 2012. (Illus.). 288p. (J). 16.95 *(978-1-4197-0415-4(X))* Abrams, Inc. (Amulet Bks.).

Budde, Nadia. Bristly Hair & I Don't Care! 2015. (ENG., Illus.). 40p. (J). 15.95 *(978-0-7358-4205-2(1))* North-South Bks., Inc.

Budge, Robyn E. Whoda Thunkit: Rhyming Tales for the Young & Not So. 2013. 180p. pap. 15.95 *(978-1-4787-2097-3(2))* Outskirts Pr., Inc.

Buehner, Caralyn. Dex: The Heart of a Hero. Buehner, Mark, illus. 2007. (ENG.). 32p. (J). (gr. -1-3). pap. 6.99 *(978-0-06-443845-2(7))* HarperCollins Pubs.

Bug. Patty Cat & the Woong: An I've Got Feelings! Feel Better Book. 2010. 48p. pap. 18.49 *(978-1-4520-5270-0(0))* AuthorHouse.

The Bug Ball. 2003. (Daisy Board Books Ser.). 10p. (J). bds. 9.95 *(978-0-7525-8296-2(8))* Parragon, Inc.

Bullard, Lisa. Not Enough Beds! A Christmas Alphabet Book. Oeltjenbruns, Joni, illus. 2004. (Carolrhoda Picture Books Ser.). 32p. (J). (gr. -1-3). per. 6.95 *(978-1-57505-797-2(2))* Lerner Publishing Group.

Bumble's Sweet Surprise. 2003. (Daisy Board Books Ser.). 10p. (J). bds. 9.95 *(978-0-7525-8297-9(6))* Parragon, Inc.

Burch, Christian. Hit the Road, Manny: A Manny Files Novel. 2008. (ENG.). 240p. (J). (gr. 3-7). 16.99 *(978-1-4169-2812-6(X)*, Atheneum Bks. for Young Readers) Simon & Schuster Children's Publishing.

Burfoot, Ella, illus. Don't Kiss the Frog! Princess Stories with Attitude. 2013. (ENG.). 80p. (YA). (gr. 1-5). pap. 8.99 *(978-0-7534-6946-0(4)*, 9780753469460, Kingfisher) Roaring Brook Pr.

Burgerman, Jon. Splat! Burgerman, Jon, illus. 2017. (ENG., Illus.). 32p. (J). (-k). 16.99 *(978-0-7352-2876-4(0)*, Dial Bks) Penguin Young Readers Group.

Burghard, Marie. Captain's Best Imbecile: A Young Pirate's Story. 2008. 184p. pap. 12.99 *(978-1-4357-3807-2(1))* Lulu Pr., Inc.

—Captain's Best Imbecile: A Young Pirate's Story: Collector's Edition. 2008. 184p. 29.99 *(978-1-4357-4521-6(3))* Lulu Pr., Inc.

Burks, James. Bird & Squirrel on the Run! 2012. (Bird & Squirrel Ser.). (ENG., Illus.). 128p. (J). (gr. 2-5). pap. 8.99 *(978-0-545-31283-7(3)*, Graphix) Scholastic, Inc.

Burnette, Margarette. Counting in the Crazy Garden. Henson, Brooke, illus. 2008. (Chipper Kids Ser.). 30p. (J). (gr. -1-2). 15.95 *(978-0-9653791-3-7(2))* JenPrint Pubns., LLC.

Burnham, Molly B. Almost a Winner. Spencer, Trevor, illus. 2017. (Teddy Mars Ser.: 2). 288p. (J). (gr. 3-7). pap. 6.99 (978-0-06-227814-2(2), Tegen, Katherine Bks) HarperCollins Pubs.

—Teddy Mars: Almost a World Record Breaker. Spencer, Trevor, illus. (Teddy Mars Ser.: 2). (J). (gr. 3-7). 2016. 288p. 16.99 (978-0-06-227813-5(4), Tegen, Katherine Bks) 2015. (ENG.). 224p. 16.99 (978-0-06-227810-4(X)) HarperCollins Pubs.

Burnham, Niki. Spin Control. 2011. (Romantic Comedies Ser.). (ENG.). 256p. (YA). (gr. 9). pap. 12.99 (978-1-4424-3112-6(1), Simon Pulse) Simon Pulse.

Burns, Catherine Lloyd. The Good, the Bad & the Beagle. 2014. (ENG.). 336p. (J). (gr. 5-7). 16.99 (978-0-374-30039-5(9), 9780374300395, Farrar, Straus & Giroux (BYR)) Farrar, Straus & Giroux.

—The Half-True Lies of Cricket Cohen. 2017. (ENG.). 256p. (J). 16.99 (978-0-374-30041-8(0), 9780374300418, Farrar, Straus & Giroux (BYR)) Farrar, Straus & Giroux.

Burns, Ian. Lissie Pendle. 2006. 196p. pap. 13.04 (978-1-4116-5491-4(9)) Lulu Pr., Inc.

Burns, T. R. The Bad Apple. (Merits of Mischief Ser.: 1). (ENG.). (J). (gr. 3-7). 2013. 368p. pap. 7.99 (978-1-4424-4030-2(9)) 2012. 352p. 16.99 (978-1-4424-4029-6(5)) Simon & Schuster Children's Publishing. (Aladdin).

—Watch Your Step. (Merits of Mischief Ser.: 3). (ENG., Illus.). (J). (gr. 3-7). 2015. 464p. pap. 7.99 (978-1-4424-4036-4(8)) 2014. 480p. 16.99 (978-1-4424-4035-7(X)) Simon & Schuster Children's Publishing. (Aladdin).

—A World of Trouble. (Merits of Mischief Ser.: 2). (ENG., Illus.). (J). (gr. 3-7). 2014. 400p. pap. 7.99 (978-1-4424-4033-3(3)) 2013. 384p. 16.99 (978-1-4424-4032-6(5)) Simon & Schuster Children's Publishing. (Aladdin).

Burton M.Sc., Kathryn Mac. Diarmid. Haley Honeybee: Finds the Magic Rose. Cox, Glendyne Dewhurst, illus. 2013. 50p. pap. (978-0-9917941-0-2(9)) Burton, K. Publishing.

Busath, Isabelle & Thordsen, Isabella. Little Book of Rules. Burris, Priscilla, illus. 2013. (ENG.). 120p. (J). (gr. 3-7). 12.99 (978-1-4424-9980-5(X), Simon Spotlight) Simon Spotlight.

Bushell, Sharon. The Trouble with Bernie. 2004. (Illus.). 160p. (J). per. 6.99 (978-0-9721725-2-3(1)) Road Tunes Media.

Butler, Steven. Singin' in the Drain. 4th ed. 2015. (Wrong Pong Ser.: 4). (ENG., Illus.). 176p. (J). (gr. k-2). pap. 8.99 (978-0-14-134044-9(4)) Penguin Bks., Ltd. GBR. Dist: Independent Pubs. Group.

—The Wrong Pong. Fisher, Chris, illus. 2015. (Wrong Pong Ser.: 1). (ENG.). 160p. (J). (gr. k-2). pap. 8.99 (978-0-14-133390-8(1)) Penguin Bks., Ltd. GBR. Dist: Independent Pubs. Group.

Butterworth, Nick. Percy's Bumpy Ride. Butterworth, Nick, illus. 2011. (Tales from Percy's Park Ser.). (ENG., Illus.). 32p. (J). pap. 11.00 (978-0-00-715514-9(X), HarperCollins Children's Bks.) HarperCollins Pubs. Ltd. GBR. Dist: HarperCollins Pubs.

—Tiger. 2009. (ENG., Illus.). 32p. 10.95 (978-0-00-725772-0(4)) HarperCollins Pubs. Ltd. GBR. Dist: Independent Pubs. Group.

Buzzeo, Toni. One Cool Friend. 2014. (KOR.). 32p. (J). (gr. k-3). (978-89-7938-087-3(9)) Dasan Publishing Hse.

—One Cool Friend. Small, David, illus. 2012. (ENG.). 32p. (J). (gr. k-3). 17.99 (978-0-8037-3413-5(1), Dial Bks) Penguin Young Readers Group.

—One Cool Friend. Small, David, illus. 2015. DVD 59.95 (978-0-545-67553-6(7)) Scholastic, Inc.

Byars, Betsy. Burbujas, el Pez de una Tonelada. 2003.Tr. of Two-Thousand-Pound Goldfish. (SPA., Illus.). 160p. (YA). (gr. 5-8). pap. 11.99 (978-84-279-3191-6(3), NG3953) Noguer y Caralt Editores, S. A. ESP. Dist: Lectorum Pubns., Inc.

Byous, Shawn. Because I Stubbed My Toe, 1 vol. 2014. (ENG.). 32p. (gr. -1-3). pap. 6.95 (978-1-4795-3808-9(6), Fiction Picture Bks.) Picture Window Bks.

Byrne, Richard. This Book Is Out of Control! 2016. (ENG., Illus.). 32p. (J). 16.99 (978-1-62779-933-1(8), 9781627799331, Holt, Henry & Co. Bks. For Young Readers) Holt, Henry & Co.

—This Book Just Ate My Dog! Byrne, Richard, illus. 2014. (ENG., Illus.). 32p. (J). (gr. -1). 16.99 (978-1-62779-071-0(3), 9781627790710, Holt, Henry & Co. Bks. For Young Readers) Holt, Henry & Co.

—We're in the Wrong Book! Byrne, Richard, illus. 2015. (ENG., Illus.). 32p. (J). (gr. -1-3). 16.99 (978-1-62779-451-0(4), 9781627794510, Holt, Henry & Co. Bks. For Young Readers) Holt, Henry & Co.

Cabatingan, Erin. A Is for Musk Ox. Myers, Matthew, illus. 2012. (Musk Ox Ser.: 1). (ENG.). 40p. (J). (gr. k-2). 18.99 (978-1-59643-676-3(X), 9781596436763) Roaring Brook Pr.

—Musk Ox Counts. Myers, Matthew, illus. 2013. (Musk Ox Ser.: 2). (ENG.). 36p. (J). (gr. k-2). 16.99 (978-1-59643-798-2(7), 9781596437982) Roaring Brook Pr.

—The World According to Musk Ox. Myers, Matthew, illus. 2014. (Musk Ox Ser.: 3). (ENG.). 40p. (J). (gr. k-2). 17.99 (978-1-59643-799-9(5), 9781596437999) Roaring Brook Pr.

Cabot, Meg. All-American Girl. 2008. (All-American Girl Ser.: 1). (ENG.). 416p. (YA). (gr. 8). pap. 8.99 (978-0-06-147989-2(6), HarperTeen) HarperCollins Pubs.

—All-American Girl. 2008. (All-American Girl Ser.: Vol. 1). 398p. (YA). (gr. 7-12). 19.65 (978-1-4178-2386-4(0), Turtleback) Turtleback Bks.

—Princess in Love, Vol. 3. 2008. (Princess Diaries: 3). (ENG.). 256p. (YA). (gr. 8-12). pap. 9.99 (978-0-06-147995-3(0), HarperTeen) HarperCollins Pubs.

—Princess in Love. 2004. (Princess Diaries: Vol. 3). 288p. (J). (gr. 7-18). pap. 38.00 incl. audio (978-0-8072-2284-3(4), Listening Library) Random Hse. Audio Publishing Group.

—Princess in Pink. 2008. (Princess Diaries: 5). (ENG.). 288p. (YA). (gr. 8). pap. 9.99 (978-0-06-154363-0(2), HarperTeen) HarperCollins Pubs.

—Princess on the Brink. 2007. (Princess Diaries: 8). (ENG.). 272p. (YA). (gr. 8). pap. 9.99 (978-0-06-072460-3(9), HarperTeen) HarperCollins Pubs.

—The Princess Present. 2004. (Princess Diaries: 6.5). (ENG.). 96p. (YA). (gr. 8-18). 12.99 (978-0-06-075433-4(8), HarperTeen) HarperCollins Pubs.

—Ready or Not. 2005. (All-American Girl Ser.: Vol. 2). (ENG.). 256p. (J). (gr. 7-18). 16.99 (978-0-06-072450-4(1)) HarperCollins Pubs.

—Valentine Princess. 2006. (Princess Diaries: 7.75). (ENG.). 96p. (YA). (gr. 8-12). 12.99 (978-0-06-084718-0(2), HarperTeen) HarperCollins Pubs.

Caddy, David. Whammy! (Illus.). 120p. (YA). pap. 10.72 (978-1-86368-163-6(9)) Fremantle Pr. AUS. Dist: Independent Pubs. Group.

Calame, Don. Beat the Band. 2010. (ENG., Illus.). 400p. (YA). (gr. 9-18). 16.99 (978-0-7636-4633-2(4)) Candlewick Pr.

Cali, Davide. I Didn't Do My Homework Because... Chaud, Benjamin, illus. 2014. (ENG.). 44p. (J). (gr. 1-4). 12.99 (978-1-4521-2551-0(1)) Chronicle Bks. LLC.

Cali, Davide & Chaud, Benjamin. A Funny Thing Happened at the Museum ... 2017. (ENG., Illus.). 44p. (J). (gr. 1-4). 12.99 (978-1-4521-5593-7(3)) Chronicle Bks. LLC.

Cali, Davide & Chaud, Benjamin. A Funny Thing Happened on the Way to School... 2015. (ENG., Illus.). 44p. (J). (gr. 1-4). 12.99 (978-1-4521-3168-9(6)) Chronicle Bks. LLC.

Callahan, Charlie. Samantha Loses Her Sweet Tooth. Callahan, Charlie, illus. 2004. (Illus.). (J). (978-0-9754019-0-3(4)) Periscope Pr.

Callahan, Thera S. All Wrapped Up. 2004. (Rookie Reader Español Ser.). (ENG., Illus.). 32p. (J). (gr. k-2). pap. 4.95 (978-0-516-21949-3(9), Children's Pr.) Scholastic Library Publishing.

—All Wrapped Up. Gordon, Mike, illus. 2003. (Rookie Readers Ser.). 32p. (J). 19.50 (978-0-516-22844-0(7), Children's Pr.) Scholastic Library Publishing.

Calmenson, Stephanie. Oopsy, Teacher! Yoshikawa, Sachiko, illus. 2012. (Carolrhoda Picture Bks.). (ENG.). 32p. (J). (gr. -1-2). lib. bdg. 16.95 (978-0-7613-5894-7(3)) Lerner Publishing Group.

Calmenson, Stephanie & Cole, Joanna. Hot Diggity Dogs. Ross, Heather, illus. 2015. (Ready, Set, Dogs! Ser.: 2). (ENG.). 112p. (J). (gr. 1-4). 14.99 (978-0-8050-9649-1(3), 9780805096491, Holt, Henry & Co. Bks. For Young Readers) Holt, Henry & Co.

—No Dogs Allowed. Ross, Heather, illus. 2014. (Ready, Set, Dogs! Ser.: 1). (ENG.). 144p. (J). (gr. 1-4). pap. 5.99 (978-1-250-04414-3(6), 9781250044143) Square Fish.

—Teacher's Pets. Ross, Heather, illus. 2015. (Ready, Set, Dogs! Ser.: 2). (ENG.). 144p. (J). (gr. 1-4). pap. 5.99 (978-1-250-05705-1(1), 9781250057051) Square Fish.

Calvert, Deanna. Las Sombras: Shadows. Lester, Mike, illus. 2005. (Rookie Reader Español Ser.). (SPA.). 24p. (gr. k-2). 19.50 (978-0-516-24448-8(5), Children's Pr.) Scholastic Library Publishing.

Cammuso, Frank. Big Birthday Bash. 2014. (Misadventures of Salem Hyde Ser.). (ENG., Illus.). 96p. (J). (gr. 1-4). 14.95 (978-1-4197-1025-4(7), Amulet Bks.) Abrams, Inc.

Campbell, James. Boyface & the Power of Three & a Bit. 2015. (Boyface Ser.). (ENG., Illus.). 144p. (J). (gr. 2-4). pap. 8.99 (978-1-4449-1806-9(0)) Hodder & Stoughton GBR. Dist: Hachette Bk. Group.

Campbell, K. G. Dylan the Villain. Campbell, K. G., illus. 2016. (ENG., Illus.). 32p. (J). (gr. -1-1). 17.99 (978-0-451-47642-5(5), Viking Books for Young Readers) Penguin Young Readers Group.

Campbell, K. G., illus. Dylan the Villain. 2016. (J). (978-0-698-40517-2(X)) Penguin Bks., Ltd.

Campbell, L. A. Cartboy & the Time Capsule. (Cartboy Ser.: 1). (ENG.). 208p. (J). (gr. 3-7). 2015. pap. 6.99 (978-0-7653-7844-6(2), 9780765378446) 2013. (Illus.). 12.99 (978-0-7653-3317-9(1), 9780765333179) Doherty, Tom Assocs., LLC. (Starscape).

—Cartboy Goes to Camp. 2014. (Cartboy Ser.: 2). (ENG., Illus.). 224p. (J). (gr. 3-7). 12.99 (978-0-7653-3327-8(9), 9780765333278, Starscape) Doherty, Tom Assocs., LLC.

Candlewick Press, Candlewick. Peppa Pig & the Treasure Hunt. 2015. (Peppa Pig Ser.). (ENG.). 32p. (J). (-k). 12.99 (978-0-7636-7703-9(5), Candlewick Entertainment) Candlewick Pr.

Canfield, Andrea. Sassy the Seahag. Hallinan, Susan, illus. 2003. Orig. Title: Sassy the Seahag. (J). per. (978-0-9721327-3-2(2)) Bad Choices Media.

Cannon, A. E. Sophie's Fish. White, Lee, illus. 2012. (ENG.). 32p. (J). (gr. -1-k). 15.99 (978-0-670-01291-6(2), Viking Books for Young Readers) Penguin Young Readers Group.

Cannon, Jonathan. Greetings from Scurf Bay: Wish We Weren't Here! 2005. 178p. 23.95 (978-0-595-67010-9(5)) iUniverse, Inc.

Caple, Kathy. A Night at the Zoo. Caple, Kathy, illus. 2014. (I Like to Read(r) Ser.). (ENG., Illus.). 24p. (J). (gr. -1-3). 14.95 (978-0-8234-3044-4(8)) Holiday Hse., Inc.

Captain Underpants & the Tyrannical Retaliation of the Turbo Toilet 2000. 2014. (Captain Underpants Ser.: Bk. 11). (ENG., Illus.). 224p. (J). (gr. 2-5). 9.99 (978-0-545-50490-4(2)) Scholastic, Inc.

Carle, Eric & Mack, Jeff. The Nonsense Show. Carle, Eric, illus. 2015. (ENG., Illus.). 40p. (J). (gr. -1-2). bds. 18.99 (978-0-399-17687-6(X), Philomel Bks.) Penguin Young Readers Group.

Carlson, Bert H. The Perilous African Adventures of Sir Bert & Sir Gilbert. 2013. 106p. pap. 32.10 (978-1-4669-8744-9(8)) Trafford Publishing.

Carlson, Martin D. Rfaud Tastes Wisdom. Oketch, Alphonce Omondi, illus. 2013. 36p. pap. 11.00 (978-0-9848791-2-0(9)) BoCook Publishing.

Carman, Patrick. Floozombies! Sheesley, Brian, illus. 2016. (Fizzopolis Ser.: 2). 176p. (J). (gr. 3-7). 12.99 (978-0-06-239392-0(8), Tegen, Katherine Bks) HarperCollins Pubs.

—Snoodles! Sheesley, Brian, illus. 2017. (Fizzopolis Ser.: 3). 160p. (J). (gr. 3-7). 12.99 (978-0-06-239394-4(4), Tegen, Katherine Bks) HarperCollins Pubs.

—The Trouble with Fuzzwonker Fizz. Sheesley, Brian, illus. 2016. (Fizzopolis Ser.: 1). 160p. (J). (gr. 3-7). 12.99 (978-0-06-239390-6(1)) HarperCollins Pubs.

Carta, Karla K. Chocolate in My Pocket. 2006. 21p. (J). 10.68 (978-1-4116-9312-8(4)) Lulu Pr., Inc.

Carter, David A., creator. Glitter Critters: Dave Carter's Pop-up Book! 2005. (ENG., Illus.). 14p. (J). 14.95 (978-1-58117-199-0(4), Intervisual/Piggy Toes) Bendon, Inc.

Carter-Reed, Lorye. I Saw God in My Room. 2010. 24p. 12.99 (978-1-4520-1136-3(2)) AuthorHouse.

Caruso, Barbara, reader. Elvis the Rooster Almost Goes to Heaven, 4 bks., Set. unabr. ed. 2006. (Readalongs for Beginning Readers Ser.). (Illus.). (J). (gr. -1-3). pap. 31.95 incl. audio compact disk (978-1-59519-685-9(4)); pap. 29.95 incl. audio (978-1-59519-684-2(6)) Live Oak Media.

Carvell, Tim. Planet Tad. Holgate, Doug, illus. (Planet Tad Ser.: 1). 256p. (J). (gr. 3-7). 2014. (ENG.). pap. 6.99 (978-0-06-193438-4(0)) 2012. (ENG.). 12.99 (978-0-06-193436-0(4)) 2012. lib. bdg. 14.89 (978-0-06-193437-7(2)) HarperCollins Pubs.

—Return to Planet Tad. 2014. (Planet Tad Ser.: 2). (ENG., Illus.). 240p. (J). (gr. 3-7). 12.99 (978-0-06-226625-5(X)) HarperCollins Pubs.

Casale, Karen. Never Let a Ghost Borrow Your Library Book: Book Care Guidelines from the Library Secret Service. Rebora, Cecilia, illus. 2012. 32p. (J). 17.75 (978-1-60213-061-6(2), Upstart Bks.) Highsmith Inc.

Castle, M. E. Fakespeare: Something Stinks in Hamlet. Jennewein, Daniel, illus. 2017. (J). pap. **(978-1-250-10157-0(3))** St. Martin's Pr.

—Fakespeare: Starcrossed in Romeo & Juliet. Jennewein, Daniel, illus. 2017. (J). pap. **(978-1-250-10160-0(3))** St. Martin's Pr.

Castle, M. E. Fakespeare: Something Stinks in Hamlet. Jennewein, Daniel, illus. 2017. (Fakespeare Ser.: 1). (ENG.). 272p. (J). 13.99 (978-1-250-10159-4(X), 9781250101594) Imprint IND. Dist: Macmillan.

Catalanotto, Peter. Question Boy Meets Little Miss Know-It-All. Catalanotto, Peter, illus. 2012. (ENG., Illus.). 40p. (J). (gr. -1-3). 17.99 (978-1-4424-0670-4(4), Atheneum/Richard Jackson Bks.) Simon & Schuster Children's Publishing.

Catling, Patrick Skene. The Chocolate Touch. 2014. (ENG.). 128p. (J). (gr. 3-7). 10.24 (978-1-63245-319-8(3)) Lectorum Pubns., Inc.

—The Chocolate Touch. 2009. 8.32 (978-1-55744-369-4(6), Everbind) Marco Bk. Co.

—The Chocolate Touch. 2006. 16.00 (978-0-7569-6383-5(4)) Perfection Learning Corp.

—The Chocolate Touch. 87p. (J). (gr. 3-5). pap. 4.99 (978-0-8072-1454-1(X), Listening Library) Random Hse. Audio Publishing Group.

Catling, Patrick Skene & Catling, P. The Chocolate Touch. Apple, Margot, illus. 2006. 126p. (J). (gr. 3-7). 17.20 (978-1-4177-3437-5(X), Turtleback) Turtleback Bks.

Catling, Patrick Skene & Catling, Patrick S. The Chocolate Touch. Apple, Margot, illus. 2006. (ENG.). 128p. (J). (gr. 3-7). pap. 7.99 (978-0-688-16133-0(2)) HarperCollins Pubs.

Catlow, Nikalas & Wesson, Tim. Robots vs. Gorillas in the Desert. Catlow, Nikalas & Wesson, Tim, illus. 2011. (Mega Mash-Up Ser.). (ENG., Illus.). 96p. (J). (gr. 2-5). pap. 6.99 (978-0-7636-5873-1(1), Nosy Crow) Candlewick Pr.

—Romans vs. Dinosaurs on Mars. Catlow, Nikalas & Wesson, Tim, illus. 2011. (Mega Mash-Up Ser.). (ENG., Illus.). 96p. (J). (gr. 2-5). pap. 6.99 (978-0-7636-5872-4(3), Nosy Crow) Candlewick Pr.

Catlow, Nikalas, et al. The Funny Fingers Are Going on Holiday. 2015. (Funny Fingers Ser.: 3). (ENG., Illus.). 32p. (J). (gr. -1-k). pap. 10.99 (978-1-4052-7366-4(6)) Egmont Bks., Ltd. GBR. Dist: Independent Pubs. Group.

Catone, Gina. Homework Time with Charlie. 2011. 20p. pap. 10.99 (978-1-4567-1713-1(8)) AuthorHouse.

Catrow, David. Best in Show. 2013. (Scholastic Reader Level 1 Ser.). lib. bdg. 13.55 (978-0-606-31509-8(8), Turtleback) Turtleback Bks.

—The Fly Flew In. 2013. (I Like to Read(r) Ser.). (ENG.). 24p. (J). (gr. -1-3). pap. 6.99 (978-0-8234-2909-7(1)) Holiday Hse., Inc.

—The Fly Flew In. Catrow, David, illus. 2012. (I Like to Read(r) Ser.). (ENG., Illus.). 24p. (J). (gr. -1-3). 14.95 (978-0-8234-2418-4(9)) Holiday Hse., Inc.

Cazenave, Florencia. Tengo Fiebre. (Que Pasa Coleccion). (SPA., Illus.). (J). pap. 6.36 (978-950-24-0681-7(8)) Albatros ARG. Dist: Lectorum Pubns., Inc.

Cazet, Denys. Bob & Tom. Cazet, Denys, illus. 2017. (ENG., Illus.). 40p. (J). (gr. -1-3). 17.99 **(978-1-4814-6140-5(0)**, Atheneum/Richard Jackson Bks.) Simon & Schuster Children's Publishing.

—Minnie & Moo: Hooves of Fire. Cazet, Denys, illus. 2014. (ENG., Illus.). 208p. (J). (gr. k-6). 15.95 (978-1-939547-08-8(3)) Creston Bks.

—Minnie & Moo: The Case of the Missing Jelly Donut. Cazet, Denys, illus. 2006. (I Can Read Bks.). (ENG., Illus.). 48p. (J). (gr. k-3). pap. 3.99 (978-0-06-073009-3(9)) HarperCollins Pubs.

—Minnie & Moo: The Case of the Missing Jelly Donut. Cazet, Denys, illus. 2007. (Minnie & Moo Ser.). (Illus.). 45p. (J). (gr. -1-3). pap. 29.95 incl. audio (978-1-4301-0088-1(5)) Live Oak Media.

—Minnie & Moo: The Case of the Missing Jelly Donut, 4 bks., Set. 2007. (J). (gr. k-2). pap. 31.95 incl. audio compact disk (978-1-4301-0091-1(5)) Live Oak Media.

—Minnie & Moo: The Night Before Christmas. Cazet, Denys, illus. 2004. (Readalongs for Beginning Readers Ser.). (Illus.). 25.95 incl. audio (978-1-59112-884-7(6)) Live Oak Media.

—Minnie & Moo: The Night of the Living Bed. Cazet, Denys, illus. 2003. (I Can Read Bks.). (Illus.). 48p. (J). (gr. k-3). lib. bdg. 16.89 (978-0-06-000504-7(1)) HarperCollins Pubs.

—Minnie & Moo - The Night of the Living Bed. Cazet, Denys, illus. 2004. (I Can Read Level 3 Ser.). (ENG., Illus.). 48p. (J). (gr. k-3). pap. 3.99 (978-0-06-000505-4(X)) HarperCollins Pubs.

—Minnie & Moo & the Haunted Sweater. Cazet, Denys, illus. 2007. (I Can Read Level 3 Ser.). (ENG., Illus.). 48p. (J). (gr. k-3). 16.99 (978-0-06-073016-1(1)) HarperCollins Pubs.

—Minnie & Moo & the Seven Wonders of the World. Cazet, Denys, illus. 2003. (ENG., Illus.). 144p. (J). (gr. 2-5). 19.99 (978-0-689-85330-2(0), Atheneum/Richard Jackson Bks.) Simon & Schuster Children's Publishing.

—Minnie & Moo Meet Frankenswine. Cazet, Denys, illus. 2004. (Readalongs for Beginning Readers Ser.). (Illus.). 28.95 incl. audio compact disk (978-1-59112-876-2(5)); (J). 25.95 incl. audio (978-1-59112-262-3(7)); (J). pap. 29.95 incl. audio (978-1-59112-263-0(5)) Live Oak Media.

—Minnie & Moo Meet Frankenswine, 4 bks. 2004. (Readalongs for Beginning Readers Ser.). (Illus.). 48p. (J). (gr. -1-2). pap. 31.95 incl. audio compact disk (978-1-59112-877-9(3)) Live Oak Media.

—The Night of the Living Bed. Cazet, Denys, illus. unabr. ed. 2005. (Minnie & Moo Ser.). (Illus.). (J). (gr. k-4). 25.95 incl. audio (978-1-59519-389-6(8));Set. pap. 31.95 incl. audio compact disk (978-1-59519-394-0(4));Set. pap. 29.95 incl. audio (978-1-59519-390-2(1)) Live Oak Media.

—The Shrunken Head. 2007. (I Can Read Bks.: No. 3). (Illus.). 48p. (J). (gr. -1-3). lib. bdg. 16.89 (978-0-06-073014-7(5)) HarperCollins Pubs.

Cederborg, Else. The Naughty Peteyboy, Sonya & the Magic Word. 2011. (Illus.). 28p. pap. 13.78 (978-1-4567-7671-8(1)) AuthorHouse.

Celano, June. Dripsy the Cloud. 2008. 28p. per. 24.95 (978-1-4241-9958-7(1)) America Star Bks.

Cervantes, Angela. Allie, First at Last: a Wish Novel. 2017. (ENG.). 208p. (J). (gr. 3-7). pap. 6.99 **(978-0-545-81268-9(2)**, Scholastic Paperbacks) Scholastic, Inc.

Chalmers, Jason. Fall Nightmares 101: A Parody. 2011. 72p. pap. 19.95 (978-1-4626-2883-4(4)) America Star Bks.

Chambers, Mark, illus. Zach & Lucy & the Museum of Natural Wonders. 2016. (Zach & Lucy Ser.). (ENG.). 40p. (J). (gr. 1-3). pap. 3.99 (978-1-4814-3935-0(9), Simon Spotlight) Simon Spotlight.

—Zach & Lucy & the Yoga Zoo. 2016. (Zach & Lucy Ser.). (ENG.). 40p. (J). (gr. 1-3). pap. 3.99 (978-1-4814-3938-1(3), Simon Spotlight) Simon Spotlight.

Chan, Marty. True Story. Bennett, Lorna, illus. 2009. (ENG.). 32p. (J). 9.95 (978-0-9810449-0-3(5)) Ink Jockey, Inc. CAN. Dist: Univ. of Toronto Pr.

Chananie, Gloria. Fearful Frannie & Her Fateful Trip to Maui. 2003. 57p. 16.95 (978-1-4137-0162-3(0)) America Star Bks.

Chandler, Paul. Mouse of Commons - Mouse of Lords. 2006. 186p. pap. 14.99 (978-1-4116-8447-8(8)) Lulu Pr., Inc.

Chang, Victoria. Is Mommy... ? Frazee, Marla, illus. 2015. (ENG.). 40p. (J). (gr. -1-k). 15.99 (978-1-4814-0292-7(7), Beach Lane Bks.) Beach Lane Bks.

Chapman, Jared. Vegetables in Underwear. 2015. (ENG., Illus.). 40p. (J). (gr. -1-k). 14.95 (978-1-4197-1464-1(3)) Abrams, Inc.

Charles, Kaye Ellen. Macarthur & Martha. 2013. 56p. pap. 20.95 (978-1-4525-8512-3(1), Balboa Pr.) Author Solutions, Inc.

Charlie Bumpers vs. the Squeaking Skull, 1 vol. 2014. (Charlie Bumpers Ser.). (ENG., Illus.). (J). (gr. 2-4). 10p. 16.95 (978-1-56145-809-7(0)); 160p. 13.95 (978-1-56145-808-0(2)) Peachtree Pubs.

Charlip, Remy. Little Old Big Beard & Big Young Little Beard: A Short & Tall Tale, 1 vol. Charlip, Remy & Rettenmund, Tamara, illus. 2006. (ENG.). 300p. (J). (gr. -1-3). pap. 5.95 (978-0-7614-5288-1(5)) Marshall Cavendish Corp.

Charman, Katrina. The Ninjabread Man. 2016. (ENG., Illus.). 32p. (J). (978-0-7787-2472-8(7)) Crabtree Publishing Co.

Chast, Roz. Around the Clock. Chast, Roz, illus. 2015. (ENG., Illus.). 32p. (J). (gr. -1-3). 18.99 (978-1-4169-8476-4(3), Atheneum Bks. for Young Readers) Simon & Schuster Children's Publishing.

—Marco Goes to School. Chast, Roz, illus. 2012. (ENG., Illus.). 32p. (J). (gr. -1-3). 16.99 (978-1-4169-8475-7(5), Atheneum Bks. for Young Readers) Simon & Schuster Children's Publishing.

—Too Busy Marco. Chast, Roz, illus. 2010. (ENG., Illus.). 32p. (J). (gr. -1-3). 16.99 (978-1-4169-8474-0(7), Atheneum Bks. for Young Readers) Simon & Schuster Children's Publishing.

Chatterton, Martin. The Brain Full of Holes, 1 vol. 2010. (ENG.). 256p. (J). (gr. 5-9). 16.95 (978-1-56145-527-0(X)) Peachtree Pubs.

Chatterton, Martin & Bradman, Tony. The Surprise Party. Chatterton, Martin, illus. 2005. (Red Bananas Ser.). (ENG., Illus.). 48p. (J). lib. bdg. (978-0-7787-1068-4(8)) Crabtree Publishing Co.

Chaud, Benjamin & Cali, Davide. I Didn't Do My Homework Because Doodle Book of Excuses. 2015. (ENG., Illus.). 144p. (J). (gr. 1-5). pap. 14.99 (978-1-4521-4175-6(4)) Chronicle Bks. LLC.

—Yo No Hice Mi Tarea Porque ... 2017. (ENG & SPA., Illus.). 44p. (J). 12.99 (978-1-4521-5934-8(3)) Chronicle Bks. LLC.

Cheshire, Simon. The Treasure of Dead Man's Lane & Other Case Files: Saxby Smart, Private Detective: Book 2. Alley, R. W., illus. 2011. (Saxby Smart, Private Detective Ser.: 2). (ENG.). 224p. (J). (gr. 3-7). pap. 8.99 (978-0-312-67434-2(1), 9780312674342) Square Fish.

Chesterfield, Sadie & Universal Studios Staff. Minions: The Junior Novel. 2015. (ENG., Illus.). 144p. (J). (gr. 3-7). pap. 6.99 (978-0-316-29995-4(2)) Little, Brown Bks. for Young Readers.

Cheva, Cherry. She's So Money. 2008. 304p. (gr. 7-12). (J). lib. bdg. 17.89 (978-0-06-128852-4(7)); (ENG.). (YA). 16.99 (978-0-06-128855-5(1)) HarperCollins Pubs. (HarperTeen).

Chew, Ruth. No Such Thing as a Witch. 2013. (Matter-Of-Fact Magic Book Ser.). (ENG., Illus.). 128p. (J). (gr. 2-5). 5.99 (978-0-449-81562-5(5)); 15.99 (978-0-449-81559-5(5)) Random Hse. Children's Bks. (Random Hse. Bks. for Young Readers).

Child, Lauren. Absolutely One Thing: Featuring Charlie & Lola. Child, Lauren, illus. 2016. (ENG., Illus.). 32p. (J). (gr. -1-3). 17.99 (978-0-7636-8728-1(6)) Candlewick Pr.

—Clarice Bean Spells Trouble. Child, Lauren, illus. 2006. (Clarice Bean Ser.). (Illus.). 189p. (J). (gr. 3-6). 13.65 (978-0-7569-7919-5(6)) Perfection Learning Corp.

—I Am Not Sleepy & I Will Not Go to Bed. Child, Lauren, illus. 2008. (Charlie & Lola Ser.). (ENG., Illus.). 16p. (J). (gr. -1-2). 19.99 (978-0-7636-4098-9(0)) Candlewick Pr.

—Spells Trouble. Child, Lauren, illus. 2006. (Clarice Bean Ser.). (ENG., Illus.). 192p. (J). (gr. 3-7). pap. 6.99 (978-0-7636-2903-8(0)) Candlewick Pr.

—Utterly Me, Clarice Bean. Child, Lauren, illus. 2005. (Clarice Bean Ser.). (ENG., Illus.). 208p. (J). (gr. 3-7). reprint ed. pap. 5.99 (978-0-7636-2788-1(7)) Candlewick Pr.

—Utterly Me, Clarice Bean. Child, Lauren, illus. 2006. (Clarice Bean Ser.). (Illus.). 16.00 (978-0-7569-6567-9(5)) Perfection Learning Corp.

Chrismer, Melanie. Phoebe Clappsaddle for Sheriff, 1 vol. Roeder, Virginia M., illus. 2003. (ENG.). 32p. (J). (gr. k-3). 16.99 (978-1-58980-127-1(X)) Pelican Publishing Co., Inc.

—Phoebe Clappsaddle Has a Tumbleweed Christmas, 1 vol. Roeder, Virginia M., illus. 2004. (ENG.). 32p. (J). (gr. k-3). 16.99 (978-1-58980-241-4(1)) Pelican Publishing Co., Inc.

Christelow, Eileen. Five Little Monkeys Storybook Treasury. 2009. (Five Little Monkeys Story Ser.). (ENG., Illus.). 192p. (J). (gr. -1-3). 11.99 *(978-0-547-23873-9(8))* Houghton Mifflin Harcourt Publishing Co.

Churchill, Ginger. Carmen's Sticky Scab. Gott, Barry, illus. 2007. (ENG.). 32p. (J). (gr. -1-3). 15.95 *(978-1-933718-13-2(7))* Tanglewood Pr.

Ciencin, Scott. Attack of the Cling-Ons, 1 vol. Crowther, Jeff, illus. 2011. (Graphic Sparks Ser.). (ENG.). 40p. (gr. 1-3). pap. 5.95 *(978-1-4342-3067-6(8))*; lib. bdg. 23.99 *(978-1-4342-2637-2(9))* Stone Arch Bks. (Graphic Sparks).

Civardi, Anne. First Experiences. 2004. (First Experiences Ser.). 144p. (J). 8.95 *(978-0-7945-0341-3(1))* EDC Publishing.

Clancy, Charmaine. My Zombie Dog. 2012. 132p. pap. *(978-0-9872863-1-4(5))* Hot Doggy Digital Pr.

Clark, Henry. The Book That Proves Time Travel Happens. 2015. (ENG., Illus.). 416p. (J). (gr. 3-7). 17.00 *(978-0-316-40617-8(1))* Little Brown & Co.

—What We Found in the Sofa & How It Saved the World. 2014. (ENG., Illus.). 384p. (J). (gr. 3-7). pap. 8.00 *(978-0-316-20665-5(2))* Little, Brown Bks. for Young Readers.

Clark, Kent & Snider, Brandon. Peter Powers. Bardin, Dave, illus. 2016. (Peter Powers Ser.: 1). (ENG.). 128p. (J). (gr. 1-5). 15.99 *(978-0-316-35932-0(7))* Little, Brown Bks. for Young Readers.

Clark, Kent & Snider, Brandon T. Peter Powers & the Rowdy Robot Raiders! Bardin, Dave, illus. 2016. (Peter Powers Ser.: 2). (ENG.). 128p. (J). (gr. 1-5). 15.99 *(978-0-316-35941-2(6))* Little, Brown Bks. for Young Readers.

Clark, Platte F. Bad Unicorn. 2013. (Bad Unicorn Trilogy Ser.: 1). (ENG., Illus.). 432p. (J). (gr. 3-7). 15.99 *(978-1-4424-5012-7(6))*, Aladdin) Simon & Schuster Children's Publishing.

—Fluff Dragon. 2014. (Bad Unicorn Trilogy Ser.: 2). (ENG., Illus.). 384p. (J). (gr. 3-7). 16.99 *(978-1-4424-5015-8(0))*, Aladdin) Simon & Schuster Children's Publishing.

—Good Ogre. 2015. (Bad Unicorn Trilogy Ser.: 3). (ENG., Illus.). 384p. (J). (gr. 3-7). 17.99 *(978-1-4424-5018-9(5))*, Aladdin) Simon & Schuster Children's Publishing.

Clarke, Jane & Fuge, Charles. Gilbert the Great. 2016. (ENG., Illus.). 32p. (J). (gr. -1-2). 6.95 *(978-1-4549-1912-4(4))* Sterling Publishing Co., Inc.

Clarke, Judith. Al Capsella & Watchdogs. 164p. pap. *(978-0-7022-2294-8(1))* Univ. of Queensland Pr.

Clarkson, Stephanie. Sleeping Cinderella & Other Princess Mix-Ups. Barrager, Brigette, illus. 2015. (ENG.). 40p. (J). (gr. -1-3). 17.99 *(978-0-545-56564-6(2))*, Orchard Bks.) Scholastic, Inc.

Clary, Julian. The Bolds. Roberts, David, illus. (Bolds Ser.). (ENG.). 272p. (J). (gr. 3-6). 2017. pap. 7.99 ***(978-1-5124-8174-7(2))*** 2016. 16.99 *(978-1-5124-0440-1(3))* Lerner Publishing Group. (Carolrhoda Bks.).

Clary, Julian. The Bolds to the Rescue. Roberts, David, illus. 2017. (Bolds Ser.: 2). (ENG.). 288p. (J). (gr. 3-6). 16.99 *(978-1-5124-1022-8(5))*, Carolrhoda Bks.) Lerner Publishing Group.

Claude on the Slopes, 1 vol. 2014. (Claude Ser.). (ENG., Illus.). 96p. (J). (gr. 1-3). 12.95 *(978-1-56145-805-9(8))* Peachtree Pubs.

Claybourne, Anna. Don't Kiss the Frog! Princess Stories with Attitude. Burfoot, Ella et al, illus. 2008. (ENG.). 80p. (YA). (gr. 1-5). 14.99 *(978-0-7534-5953-9(1))*, 9780753459539, Kingfisher) Roaring Brook Pr.

Cleary, Beverly. Beezus & Ramona. Darling, Louis & Rogers, Jacqueline, illus. 2013. (Ramona Ser.: 1). (ENG.). 208p. (J). (gr. 3-7). pap. 6.99 *(978-0-380-70918-2(X))* HarperCollins Pubs.

—Beezus & Ramona. Darling, Louis et al, illus. 2013. (Ramona Ser.: 1). (ENG.). 208p. (J). (gr. 3-7). 16.99 *(978-0-688-21076-2(7))* HarperCollins Pubs.

—Beezus & Ramona. Dockray, Tracy & Rogers, Jacqueline, illus. movie tie-in ed. 2010. (Ramona Ser.: 1). (ENG.). 208p. (J). (gr. 3-7). pap. 5.99 *(978-0-06-191461-4(4))*, HarperFestival) HarperCollins Pubs.

—Beezus & Ramona. 2011. 9.01 *(978-0-7848-3570-8(5))*, Everbind) Marco Bk. Co.

—Beezus & Ramona. (Ramona Quimby Ser.). 142p. (J). (gr. 3-5). pap. 4.99 *(978-0-8072-1441-1(8))*, Listening Library) Random Hse. Audio Publishing Group.

—Beezus & Ramona. Darling, Louis, illus. (gr. 3-5). pap. *(978-0-545-24980-5(5))* Scholastic, Inc.

—Beezus & Ramona. (Ramona Quimby Ser.: 1). (J). 2013. lib. bdg. 17.20 *(978-0-88103-289-5(1))* 2010. lib. bdg. 16.00 *(978-0-606-15072-9(2))* Turtleback Bks. (Turtleback).

—Just for Me: My Ramona Quimby Journal. Rogers, Jacqueline & Parlagreco, Aurora M., illus. 2013. (ENG.). 144p. (J). (gr. 3-7). 11.99 *(978-0-06-223049-2(2))* HarperCollins Pubs.

—The Ramona Collection Vol. 1: Beezus & Ramona, Ramona & Her Father, Ramona the Brave, Ramona the Pest, Vol. 1. Dockray, Tracy & Rogers, Jacqueline, illus. 2013. (Ramona Ser.). (ENG.). (J). (gr. 3-7). pap. 22.99 *(978-0-06-124647-0(6))* HarperCollins Pubs.

—The Ramona Collection Vol. 2: Ramona & Her Mother; Ramona Quimby, Age 8; Ramona Forever; Ramona's World. Dockray, Tracy & Rogers, Jacqueline, illus. 2013. (Ramona Ser.). (ENG.). (J). (gr. 3-7). pap. 22.99 *(978-0-06-124648-7(4))* HarperCollins Pubs.

Coates, Angel J. Mommy Loves No I 2008. (Illus.). 48p. pap. 19.95 *(978-1-4343-8642-7(2))* AuthorHouse.

Coats, Vivian. Safe in His Love. 2009. 28p. pap. 12.99 *(978-1-4490-0377-7(X))* AuthorHouse.

Cobot, Meg. All-American Girl. 2004. 416p. (J). (gr. 7-18). pap. 44.00 incl. audio *(978-0-8072-2281-2(X))*, Listening Library) Random Hse. Audio Publishing Group.

Cochran, Jean M. Farmer Brown & His Little Red Truck. Enos, Daryl, illus. 2009. (ENG.). 32p. (J). (gr. -1-k). 16.95 *(978-0-9792035-0-3(3))* Pleasant St. Pr.

Codell, Esmé Raji. Fairly Fairy Tales. Chavarri, Elisa, illus. 2011. (ENG.). 32p. (J). (gr. -1-3). 18.99 *(978-1-4169-9086-4(0))*, Aladdin) Simon & Schuster Children's Publishing.

Coffelt, Nancy. Catch That Baby! Nash, Scott, illus. 2011. (ENG.). 40p. (J). (gr. -1-3). 16.99 *(978-1-4169-9148-9(4))*, Aladdin) Simon & Schuster Children's Publishing.

—Uh-Oh, Baby! Nash, Scott, illus. 2013. (ENG.). 40p. (J). (gr. -1-3). 16.99 *(978-1-4169-9149-6(2))*, Simon & Schuster/Paula Wiseman Bks.) Simon & Schuster/Paula Wiseman Bks.

Cohen, Peter. Boris's Glasses. Sandin, Joan, tr. from SWE. Landstrom, Olof, illus. 2003. 28p. (J). (gr. k-3). 15.00 *(978-91-29-65942-9(6))* R & S Bks. SWE. Dist: Macmillan.

Colandro, Lucille. There Was a Cold Lady Who Swallowed Some Snow! Lee, Jared, illus. (J). 2006. (ENG.). (gr. -1-3). 18.95 *(978-0-439-89841-6(2))* 2003. (ENG.). 32p. (gr. -1-3). pap. 6.99 *(978-0-439-56703-9(3))*, Cartwheel Bks.) 2003. 32p. (gr. k-3). pap. 5.95 *(978-0-439-47109-1(5))*, Cartwheel Bks.) 2006. (ENG.). (gr. -1-3). 9.95 *(978-0-439-89556-9(1))* Scholastic, Inc.

—There Was a Cold Lady Who Swallowed Some Snow! 2003. (There Was an Old Lady Ser.). (gr. k-3). lib. bdg. 17.20 *(978-0-613-72229-2(9))*, Turtleback) Turtleback Bks.

—There Was an Old Lady Who Swallowed a Bat! Lee, Jared D., illus. 2009. (ENG.). (J). (gr. -1-3). 9.99 *(978-0-545-16353-8(6))* Scholastic, Inc.

—There Was an Old Lady Who Swallowed a Frog! Lee, Jared D., illus. 2014. (There Was an Old Lad Ser.). (ENG.). 32p. (J). (gr. k-2). pap. 6.99 *(978-0-545-69138-3(9))*, Cartwheel Bks.) Scholastic, Inc.

—There Was an Old Lady Who Swallowed Some Books! Lee, Jared D., illus. 2012. (J). *(978-0-545-48186-1(4))* Scholastic, Inc.

—There Was an Old Lady Who Swallowed Some Leaves! Lee, Jared, illus. 2010. (ENG.). 32p. (J). (gr. -1-k). pap. 6.99 *(978-0-545-24198-4(7))*, Cartwheel Bks.) Scholastic, Inc.

Colbert, Catherine McNulty. Downsize Your Parents! Tips for Moving from a 2400 Sq Ft Home into an 800 Sq Ft Home. 2009. 34p. pap. 9.00 *(978-1-935125-48-8(6))* Robertson Publishing.

Colbert, Larry C. Insights from an Out-of-Sight Guy. 2005. 111p. per. 20.00 *(978-0-9766329-0-0(X))* Driving Vision, Inc.

Cole, Babette. El Libro de Etiqueta de Lady Lupina. 2003. (Babette Cole Ser.).Tr. of Lady Lupin's Book of Etiquett. (SPA.). (J). 18.95 *(978-84-233-3337-0(X))* Ediciones Destino ESP. Dist: Planeta Publishing Corp.

Cole, Frank. Hashbrown Winters & the Mashimoto Madness. 2010. 128p. (J). pap. 8.99 *(978-1-59955-378-8(3))* Cedar Fort, Inc./CFI Distribution.

—Hashbrown Winters & the Phantom of Pordunce. 2010. 128p. (J). pap. 7.99 *(978-1-59955-398-6(8))* Cedar Fort, Inc./CFI Distribution.

Colfer, Chris. The Land of Stories: Queen Red Riding Hood's Guide to Royalty. 2017. (ENG.). 128p. (J). (gr. 3-7). 10.99 *(978-0-316-38336-3(8))* Little Brown & Co.

—The Mother Goose Diaries. 2017. (ENG.). 128p. (J). (gr. 3-7). 10.99 *(978-0-316-38334-9(1))* Little Brown & Co.

—Struck by Lightning: The Carson Phillips Journal. (ENG.). 272p. (YA). (gr. 10-17). 2013. pap. 10.00 *(978-0-316-23293-7(9))* 2012. 17.99 *(978-0-316-23295-1(5))* Little, Brown Bks. for Young Readers.

Colleen, Marcie. Super Happy Party Bears: Knock Knock on Wood. James, Steve, illus. 2016. (Super Happy Party Bears Ser.: 2). (ENG.). 144p. (J). pap. 5.99 *(978-1-250-09808-5(4))*, 9781250098085) Imprint IND. Dist: Macmillan.

Collet-Derby, Pierre. Barnaby Never Forgets. Collet-Derby, Pierre, illus. 2017. (ENG., Illus.). 32p. (J). (gr. k-3). 16.99 ***(978-0-7636-8853-0(3))*** Candlewick Pr.

Collins, Paul. Lucy & the Red Street Boyz. Bocquée, Christian, illus. 2015. (Legends in Their Own Lunchbox Ser.). (ENG.). 56p. (gr. 2-3). pap. 7.99 *(978-1-4966-0260-2(9))*, Legends in Their Own Lunchbox) Capstone Classroom.

—Lucy in a Jam. Bocquée, Christian, illus. 2015. (Legends in Their Own Lunchbox Ser.). (ENG.). 48p. (gr. 1-2). pap. 7.99 *(978-1-4966-0248-0(X))*, Legends in Their Own Lunchbox) Capstone Classroom.

—Lucy, Kung-Fu Queen. Bocquée, Christian, illus. 2015. (Legends in Their Own Lunchbox Ser.). (ENG.). 48p. (gr. 1-2). pap. 7.99 *(978-1-4966-0242-8(0))*, Legends in Their Own Lunchbox) Capstone Classroom.

—Lucy, the Boss. Bocquée, Christian, illus. 2015. (Legends in Their Own Lunchbox Ser.). (ENG.). 56p. (gr. 2-3). pap. 7.99 *(978-1-4966-0254-1(4))*, Legends in Their Own Lunchbox) Capstone Classroom.

Collins, Ross. The Elephantom. Collins, Ross, illus. 2015. (ENG., Illus.). 40p. (J). (gr. -1-2). 16.99 *(978-0-7636-7591-2(1))*, Templar) Candlewick Pr.

Collins, Terry. Tea at the Treedome. 2004. 64p. (J). (gr. 2-5). pap. 17.00 incl. audio *(978-0-8072-1986-7(X))*, Listening Library) Random Hse. Audio Publishing Group.

Collins, Tim. Fangs a Lot: Final Notes from a Totally Lame Vampire. Pinder, Andrew, illus. 2014. (ENG.). 320p. (J). (gr. 5-9). 13.99 *(978-1-4814-2134-8(4))*, Aladdin) Simon & Schuster Children's Publishing.

—Notes from a Hairy-Not-Scary Werewolf. Pinder, Andrew, illus. 2013. (ENG.). 288p. (J). (gr. 5-9). 12.99 *(978-1-4424-8207-4(9))*, Aladdin) Simon & Schuster Children's Publishing.

—Notes from a Totally Lame Vampire: Because the Undead Have Feelings Too! Pinder, Andrew, illus. 2010. (ENG.). 336p. (J). (gr. 5-9). 12.99 *(978-1-4424-1183-8(X))*, Aladdin) Simon & Schuster Children's Publishing.

Collinson, Roger. Butterfingers. 2003. (ENG., Illus.). 80p. (J). (gr. 4-7). pap. 9.99 *(978-1-84270-290-1(4))* Andersen Pr. GBR. Dist: Independent Pubs. Group.

Coman, Carolyn. The Big House. Shepperson, Rob, illus. 2004. (ENG.). 224p. (J). (gr. 4-6). 16.95 *(978-1-932425-09-3(8))*, Lemniscaat) Boyds Mills Pr.

—Sneaking Suspicions. Shepperson, Rob, illus. 2007. (ENG.). 204p. (J). (gr. 4-6). 16.95 *(978-1-59078-491-4(X))*, Front Street) Boyds Mills Pr.

Comeau, Joey. Ninja-Rella. Lozano, Omar, illus. 2015. (Far Out Fairy Tales Ser.). (ENG.). 40p. (gr. 3-4). lib. bdg. 25.32 *(978-1-4342-9647-4(4))* Stone Arch Bks.

Condon, Bill. How to Survive in the Jungle by the Person Who Knows, 1 vol. rev. ed. 2013. (Fiction Readers Ser.). (ENG., Illus.). 28p. (J). (gr. 3-3). pap. 8.99 *(978-1-4333-5599-8(X))* Shell Educational Publishing.

—How to Survive in the Jungle by the Person Who Knows. rev. ed. 2013. (Fiction Readers Ser.). (ENG., Illus.). 28p. (J). (gr. 3-3). pap. 19.96 *(978-1-4807-1721-3(5))* Teacher Created Materials, Inc.

—The Joker. Smith, Craig, illus. 2004. iv, 36p. (J). pap. *(978-0-7608-6742-6(9))* Sundance/Newbridge Educational Publishing.

Condon, Tom. The Sandman: Stories to Read to Children. 2003. 136p. (J). pap. 11.95 *(978-0-595-27291-4(6))* iUniverse, Inc.

Conford, Ellen. Annabel the Actress Starring in Camping It Up. Andriani, Renee W., illus. 2005. (Annabel the Actress Ser.). 60p. (J). (gr. 2-5). 11.65 *(978-0-7569-5555-7(6))* Perfection Learning Corp.

—Annabel the Actress Starring in Camping It Up. Andriani, Renee W., illus. 2013. (ENG.). 64p. (J). (gr. 2-5). pap. 13.99 *(978-1-4814-0147-0(5))*, Simon & Schuster Bks. For Young Readers) Simon & Schuster Bks. For Young Readers.

—Annabel the Actress Starring in the Hound of the Barkervilles. Andriani, Renee W., illus. 2004. (Annabel the Actress Ser.). 83p. (gr. 2-5). 14.00 *(978-0-7569-2180-4(5))* Perfection Learning Corp.

—A Case for Jenny Archer. Palmisciano, Diane & Brooks, Erik, illus. 2nd ed. 2006. (ENG.). 64p. (J). (gr. 1-4). per. 13.99 *(978-0-316-01486-1(9))* Little, Brown Bks. for Young Readers.

—Jenny Archer, Author. Palmisciano, Diane & Brooks, Erik, illus. 2006. (ENG.). 64p. (J). (gr. 1-4). per. 12.99 *(978-0-316-01487-8(7))* Little, Brown Bks. for Young Readers.

—A Job for Jenny Archer. Palmisciano, Diane & Brooks, Erik, illus. 2006. (ENG.). 80p. (J). (gr. 1-4). per. 13.99 *(978-0-316-01484-7(2))* Little, Brown Bks. for Young Readers.

—What's Cooking, Jenny Archer? Palmisciano, Diane & Brooks, Erik, illus. 2006. (ENG.). 80p. (J). (gr. 1-4). per. 13.99 *(978-0-316-01488-5(5))* Little, Brown Bks. for Young Readers.

Connolly, Tina. Seriously Wicked. 2015. (ENG.). 208p. (YA). (gr. 8-12). 17.99 *(978-0-7653-7516-2(8))*, 9780765375162, Tor Teen) Doherty, Tom Assocs., LLC.

Connors, Jerrold. Now, Louie! Connors, Jerrold, illus. 2006. (Illus.). 40p. (J). 12.99 *(978-0-9721416-1-1(8))* Alligator Boogaloo.

Conway, David. The Great Fairy Tale Disaster. Williamson, Melanie, illus. 2012. (ENG.). 32p. (J). *(978-1-58925-111-3(3))* Tiger Tales.

Cook, Donna. The Silly Solar System. 2009. pap. 15.00 *(978-1-61623-557-4(8))* Independent Pub.

Cook, Julia. Personal Space Camp. Hartman, Carrie, illus. 2008. 32p. (J). (gr. -1-3). pap. 9.95 *(978-1-931636-87-2(7))* National Ctr. For Youth Issues.

Cooling, Wendy, ed. Mirrors: Anthology. 2009. (ENG., Illus.). 240p. (J). pap. 9.99 *(978-0-00-710589-2(4))*, HarperCollins Children's Bks.) HarperCollins Pubs. Ltd. GBR. Dist: HarperCollins Pubs.

Cooper, Susan. The Boggart. 2004. 196p. (gr. 3-7). 17.00 *(978-0-7569-3932-8(1))* Perfection Learning Corp.

Cooper, Wendy. My First Ride with Isaiah. Elizabeth Mobley, illus. 2006. 18p. (J). 11.95 *(978-0-9772964-8-4(2))* Kingdom Publishing Group, Inc.

Corderoy, Tracey. Beastly Feast!, 1 vol. Artful Doodlers Limited Staff, illus. 2012. (Grunt & the Grouch Ser.). (ENG.). 112p. (gr. 1-3). pap. 5.19 *(978-1-4342-4269-3(2))*; 25.32 *(978-1-4342-4603-5(5))* Stone Arch Bks.

—Big Splash!, 1 vol. Artful Doodlers Limited Staff, illus. 2012. (Grunt & the Grouch Ser.). (ENG.). 112p. (gr. 1-3). pap. 5.19 *(978-1-4342-4268-6(4))*; 25.32 *(978-1-4342-4602-8(7))* Stone Arch Bks.

—Freaky Funfair, 1 vol. 2013. (Grunt & the Grouch Ser.). (ENG.). 112p. (gr. 1-3). pap. 5.19 *(978-1-4342-4828-2(3))*; lib. bdg. 25.32 *(978-1-4342-4620-2(5))* Stone Arch Bks.

—Pick 'n' Mix, 1 vol. 2013. (Grunt & the Grouch Ser.). (ENG.). 112p. (gr. 1-3). pap. 5.19 *(978-1-4342-4829-9(1))*; lib. bdg. 25.32 *(978-1-4342-4621-9(3))* Stone Arch Bks.

Coster, Simon. My Dinosaur Is More Awesome! 2015. (ENG., Illus.). 48p. (J). (gr. -1-k). 16.99 *(978-1-63220-416-5(9))*, Sky Pony Pr.) Skyhorse Publishing Co., Inc.

Côté, Geneviève. Me & You. Côté, Geneviève, illus. 2009. (Piggy & Bunny Ser.). (ENG., Illus.). 32p. (J). (gr. -1-k). 16.95 *(978-1-55453-446-3(1))* Kids Can Pr., Ltd. CAN. Dist: Hachette Bk. Group.

Cotter, Bill. Don't Push the Button! 2015. (ENG., Illus.). 24p. (J). (-3). bds. 8.99 *(978-1-4926-0763-2(0))* Sourcebooks, Inc.

—Don't Touch This Book! (ENG.). (J). 2017. 24p. bds. 8.99 *(978-1-4926-3319-8(4))*, 9781492633198) 2016. (Illus.). 28p. bds. 6.99 *(978-1-4926-4804-8(3))*, 9781492648048) 2016. (Illus.). 32p. 16.99 *(978-1-4926-3224-5(4))*, 9781492632245) Sourcebooks, Inc. (Sourcebooks Jabberwocky).

Coudray, Jean-Luc. A Goofy Guide to Penguins: TOON Level 1. Coudray, Philippe, illus. 2016. (ENG.). 40p. (J). (gr. k). 12.95 *(978-1-935179-96-2(9))* TOON Books / RAW Junior, LLC.

Coudray, Philippe. Benjamin Bear in Brain Storms! 2015. (Benjamin Bear Ser.). (ENG., Illus.). 40p. (J). (gr. -1-3). 12.95 *(978-1-935179-82-5(9))* TOON Books / RAW Junior, LLC.

—Benjamin Bear in Bright Ideas! 2013. (Benjamin Bear Ser.). (ENG., Illus.). 32p. (J). (gr. -1-3). 12.95 *(978-1-935179-22-1(5))* TOON Books / RAW Junior, LLC.

—Benjamin Bear in Fuzzy Thinking. 2011. (Benjamin Bear Ser.). (ENG., Illus.). 32p. (J). (gr. -1-3). 12.95 *(978-1-935179-12-2(8))* TOON Books / RAW Junior, LLC.

—Benjamin Bear in Fuzzy Thinking. 2013. (Toon Books Level 2 Ser.). lib. bdg. 14.75 *(978-0-606-31596-8(9))*, Turtleback) Turtleback Bks.

Courtauld, Sarah. Buckle & Squash: the Gigantic Giant Goof-Up. 2016. (Buckle & Squash Ser.). (ENG., Illus.). 192p. (J). 14.99 *(978-1-250-05279-7(3))*, 9781250052797) Feiwel & Friends.

Courtenay, L. A. Space Penguins Cosmic Crash! Davies, James, illus. 2015. (Space Penguins Ser.). (ENG.). 112p. (gr. 2-3). lib. bdg. 22.65 *(978-1-4342-9785-3(3))* Stone Arch Bks.

—Space Penguins Galaxy Race! Davies, James, illus. 2015. (Space Penguins Ser.). (ENG.). 112p. (gr. 2-3). lib. bdg. 22.65 *(978-1-4342-9783-9(7))* Stone Arch Bks.

—Space Penguins Meteor Madness! Davies, James, illus. 2015. (Space Penguins Ser.). (ENG.). 112p. (gr. 2-3). lib. bdg. 22.65 *(978-1-4342-9782-2(9))* Stone Arch Bks.

—Space Penguins Star Attack! Davies, James, illus. 2015. (Space Penguins Ser.). (ENG.). 112p. (gr. 2-3). lib. bdg. 22.65 *(978-1-4342-9784-6(5))* Stone Arch Bks.

Coverly, Dave. Night of the Living Shadows. 2016. (Speed Bump & Slingshot Misadventure Ser.). (ENG., Illus.). 128p. (J). 13.99 *(978-0-8050-8887-8(3))*, 9780805088878, Holt, Henry & Co. Bks. For Young Readers) Holt, Henry & Co.

—Night of the Living Worms: A Speed Bump & Slingshot Misadventure. Coverly, Dave, illus. 2015. (Speed Bump & Slingshot Misadventure Ser.). (ENG., Illus.). 128p. (J). (gr. 2-5). 13.99 *(978-0-8050-8886-1(5))*, 9780805088861, Holt, Henry & Co. Bks. For Young Readers) Holt, Henry & Co.

Coville, Bruce. Diary of a Mad Brownie. 2015. (Enchanted Files Ser.). (ENG., Illus.). 256p. (J). (gr. 3-7). lib. bdg. 19.99 *(978-0-385-39248-8(6))*, Random Hse. Bks. for Young Readers) Random Hse. Children's Bks.

—Diary of a Runaway Griffin. Douglas, Allen, illus. 2016. (Enchanted Files Ser.: 2). (ENG.). 272p. (J). (gr. 3-7). 16.99 *(978-0-385-39255-6(9))*, Random Hse. Bks. for Young Readers) Random Hse. Children's Bks.

—Hatched. Kidby, Paul, illus. 2017. (Enchanted Files Ser.: 2). (ENG.). 288p. (J). (gr. 3-7). pap. 6.99 *(978-0-385-39258-7(3))*, Yearling) Random Hse. Children's Bks.

—I Lost My Grandfather's Brain. unabr. ed. 2004. (I Was a Sixth Grade Alien Ser.: Vol. 3). 160p. (J). (gr. 3-6). pap. 29.00 incl. audio *(978-0-8072-8385-1(1))*, YA180SP, Listening Library) Random Hse. Audio Publishing Group.

—I Was a Sixth Grade Alien. (I Was a Sixth Grade Alien Ser.: Vol. 1). 170p. (J). (gr. 4-6). pap. 3.99 *(978-0-8072-8202-1(2))*; 2004. (gr. 3-6). pap. 29.00 incl. audio *(978-0-8072-8201-4(4))*, S YA 138 SP) Random Hse. Audio Publishing Group. (Listening Library).

Coville, Bruce. Trolled. Kidby, Paul, illus. 2017. (Enchanted Files Ser.: 3). (ENG.). 288p. (J). (gr. 3-7). 16.99 ***(978-0-385-39259-4(1))***, Random Hse. Bks. for Young Readers) Random Hse. Children's Bks.

Cowell, Cressida. A Hero's Guide to Deadly Dragons. 2010. (ENG., Illus.). 272p. (J). *(978-0-340-99913-4(6))*, Hodder Children's Books) Hachette Children's Group GBR. Dist: Hachette Bk. Group.

—A Hero's Guide to Deadly Dragons. (How to Train Your Dragon Ser.: 6). (ENG.). (J). (gr. 3-7). 2010. 272p. pap. 8.00 *(978-0-316-08532-8(4))* 2009. 256p. 12.99 *(978-0-316-11779-1(X))* Little, Brown Bks. for Young Readers.

—How to Be a Pirate. 2010. (ENG., Illus.). 240p. (J). *(978-0-340-99908-0(X))*, Hodder Children's Books) Hachette Children's Group GBR. Dist: Hachette Bk. Group.

—How to Be a Pirate. (How to Train Your Dragon Ser.: 2). (ENG.). (J). (gr. 3-7). 2010. 240p. pap. 8.99 *(978-0-316-08528-1(6))* 2005. (Illus.). 224p. 13.99 *(978-0-316-15598-4(5))* Little, Brown Bks. for Young Readers.

—How to Break a Dragon's Heart. 2010. (ENG., Illus.). 320p. (J). *(978-0-340-99692-8(7))*, Hodder Children's Books) Hachette Children's Group GBR. Dist: Hachette Bk. Group.

—How to Cheat a Dragon's Curse. 2010. (ENG., Illus.). 256p. (J). *(978-0-340-99910-3(1))*, Hodder Children's Books) Hachette Children's Group GBR. Dist: Hachette Bk. Group.

—How to Cheat a Dragon's Curse. 2010. (How to Train Your Dragon Ser.: 4). (ENG.). 272p. (J). (gr. 3-7). pap. 8.99 *(978-0-316-08530-4(8))* Little, Brown Bks. for Young Readers.

—How to Cheat a Dragon's Curse. Cowell, Cressida, illus. 2007. (How to Train Your Dragon Ser.: 4). (ENG., Illus.). 256p. (J). (gr. 3-7). 14.99 *(978-0-316-11425-7(1))* Little, Brown Bks. for Young Readers.

—How to Ride a Dragon's Storm. 2010. (ENG., Illus.). 288p. (J). *(978-0-340-99912-7(8))*, Hodder Children's Books) Hachette Children's Group GBR. Dist: Hachette Bk. Group.

—How to Ride a Dragon's Storm. (How to Train Your Dragon Ser.: 7). (ENG.). (J). (gr. 3-7). 2011. 288p. pap. 8.99 *(978-0-316-07909-9(X))* 2010. 272p. 12.99 *(978-0-316-07916-7(2))* Little, Brown Bks. for Young Readers.

—How to Seize a Dragon's Jewel. (How to Train Your Dragon Ser.: 10). (ENG., Illus.). 416p. (J). (gr. 3-7). 2014. pap. 8.00 *(978-0-316-24408-4(2))* 2013. 12.99 *(978-0-316-24409-1(0))* Little, Brown Bks. for Young Readers.

—How to Seize a Dragon's Jewel. 2014. (How to Train Your Dragon Ser.: 10). (J). lib. bdg. 18.45 *(978-0-606-35307-6(0))* Turtleback Bks.

—How to Speak Dragonese. 2010. (ENG., Illus.). 256p. (J). *(978-0-340-99909-7(8))*, Hodder Children's Books) Hachette Children's Group GBR. Dist: Hachette Bk. Group.

—How to Speak Dragonese. (How to Train Your Dragon Ser.: 3). (ENG.). (J). (gr. 3-7). 2010. 256p. pap. 8.99 *(978-0-316-08529-8(4))* 2006. (Illus.). 240p. 12.99 *(978-0-316-15600-4(0))* Little, Brown Bks. for Young Readers.

—How to Steal a Dragon's Sword. 2013. (How to Train Your Dragon Ser.: 9). (ENG.). 384p. (J). (gr. 3-7). pap. 8.00 *(978-0-316-20570-2(2))* Little, Brown Bks. for Young Readers.

—How to Steal a Dragon's Sword. 2013. (How to Train Your Dragon Ser.: 9). (J). lib. bdg. 18.45 *(978-0-606-31742-9(2))*, Turtleback) Turtleback Bks.

—How to Train Your Dragon. 2010. (ENG., Illus.). (J). 240p. *(978-0-340-99907-3(1))*; 240p. pap. *(978-0-340-99716-1(8))*;No. 1. 304p. *(978-0-340-99717-8(6))* Hachette Children's Group GBR. (Hodder Children's Books). Dist: Hachette Bk. Group.

—How to Train Your Dragon. (How to Train Your Dragon Ser.: 1). (ENG.). (J). (gr. 3-7). 2004. Illus.). 224p. 13.99 *(978-0-316-73737-1(2))*Bk. 1. 2010. 240p. pap. 8.99 *(978-0-316-08527-4(8))* Little, Brown Bks. for Young Readers.

—How to Twist a Dragon's Tale. 2010. (ENG., Illus.). 272p. (J). *(978-0-340-99911-0(X))*, Hodder Children's Books) Hachette Children's Group GBR. Dist: Hachette Bk. Group.

—How to Twist a Dragon's Tale. (How to Train Your Dragon Ser.: 5). (ENG.). (J). (gr. 3-7). 2008. Illus.). 256p. 10.99 *(978-0-316-11774-6(9))*Bk. 5. 2010. 272p. pap. 8.99 *(978-0-316-08531-1(6))* Little, Brown Bks. for Young Readers.

Cowley, Joy. Freddy Bear & the Beach. Webb, Philip, illus. 2016. (Freddy Bear Ser.). (ENG.). 20p. (J). (gr. -1-k). bds. 12.99 *(978-1-927262-56-6(9))* Upstart Pr. NZL. Dist: Independent Pubs. Group.

—Freddy Bear & the Green Peas. Webb, Philip, illus. 2016. (Freddy Bear Ser.). (ENG.). 20p. (J). (gr. -1-k). bds. 12.99 (978-1-927262-57-3(7)) Upstart Pr. NZL. Dist: Independent Pubs. Group.
—Stories of the Wild West Gang. Pye, Trevor, illus. 2012. (Gecko Press Titles Ser.). (ENG.). 368p. (gr. -1-1). 16.95 (978-1-877579-21-9(1)) Gecko Pr. NZL. Dist: Lerner Publishing Group.
Cox, Judy. Don't Be Silly, Mrs. Millie!, 0 vols. Mathieu, Joe, illus. 2010. (ENG.). 34p. (J). (gr. k-3). pap. 6.99 (978-0-7614-5727-5(5), 9780761457275, Amazon Children's Publishing) Amazon Publishing.
—Happy Birthday, Mrs. Millie!, 0 vols. Mathieu, Joe, illus. 2012. (ENG.). 32p. (J). (gr. k-3). 16.99 (978-0-7614-6126-5(4), 9780761461265, Amazon Children's Publishing) Amazon Publishing.
—Mrs. Millie Goes to Philly!, 0 vols. Mathieu, Joe, illus. 2013. (ENG.). 32p. (J). (gr. -1-2). pap. 9.99 (978-1-4778-1680-6(1), 9781477816806, Amazon Children's Publishing) Amazon Publishing.
—Pick a Pumpkin, Mrs. Millie!, 0 vols. Mathieu, Joe, illus. 2009. (ENG.). 32p. (J). (gr. -1-3). 15.99 (978-0-7614-5573-8(6), 9780761455738, Amazon Children's Publishing) Amazon Publishing.
Coyle, Carmela Lavigna. Thank You, Aunt Tallulah! MacPherson, Bruce, illus. 2006. (ENG.). 32p. (J). (gr. -1-3). 15.95 (978-0-87358-891-1(6)) Cooper Square Publishing Llc.
Craddock, Erik. BC Mambo. Craddock, Erik, illus. 2009. (Stone Rabbit Ser.: Bk. 1). (ENG., Illus.). 96p. (J). (gr. 3-7). pap. 6.99 (978-0-375-84360-0(4), Random Hse. Bks. for Young Readers) Random Hse. Children's Bks.
—Dragon Boogie. Craddock, Erik, illus. 2012. (Stone Rabbit Ser.: Vol. 7). (ENG., Illus.). 96p. (J). (gr. 2-5). pap. 6.99 (978-0-375-86912-9(3), Random Hse. Bks. for Young Readers) Random Hse. Children's Bks.
—Dragon Boogie. 2012. (Stone Rabbit Ser.: 7). lib. bdg. 17.20 (978-0-606-23868-7(9), Turtleback) Turtleback Bks.
—Ninja Slice. Craddock, Erik, illus. 2010. (Stone Rabbit Ser.: No. 5). (ENG., Illus.). 96p. (J). (gr. 3-7). pap. 6.99 (978-0-375-86723-1(6), Random Hse. Bks. for Young Readers) Random Hse. Children's Bks.
—Pirate Palooza. Craddock, Erik, illus. 2009. (Stone Rabbit Ser.: Bk. 2). (ENG., Illus.). 96p. (J). (gr. 3-7). pap. 6.99 (978-0-375-85660-0(9), Random Hse. Bks. for Young Readers) Random Hse. Children's Bks.
—Stone Rabbit #6: Night of the Living Dust Bunnies. Craddock, Erik, illus. 2011. (Stone Rabbit Ser.: 6). (ENG., Illus.). 96p. (J). (gr. 3-7). pap. 6.99 (978-0-375-86724-8(4), Random Hse. Bks. for Young Readers) Random Hse. Children's Bks.
—Stone Rabbit #8: Robot Frenzy. Craddock, Erik, illus. 2013. (Stone Rabbit Ser.). (ENG., Illus.). 96p. (J). (gr. 2-5). pap. 6.99 (978-0-375-86913-6(1), Random Hse. Bks. for Young Readers) Random Hse. Children's Bks.
Craig, Ellen. Making a Book a Best Seller: Marketing Techniques above & Beyond the Rest. 2009. (ENG., Illus.). 130p. per. 24.97 (978-0-9779960-7-0(7), Books To Believe In) Thornton Publishing, Inc.
Craig-Gaddis, Lora. Elsie & Pooka Stories of the Sabbats & Seasons. 2008. 126p. pap. 43.18 (978-0-557-01530-6(8)) Lulu Pr., Inc.
Crimi, Carolyn. Dear Tabby. Roberts, David, illus. 2011. (ENG.). 32p. (J). (gr. -1-3). 16.99 (978-0-06-114245-1(X)) HarperCollins Pubs.
—The Louds Move In!, 1 vol. Dunnick, Regan, illus. 2006. (ENG.). 32p. (J). (gr. -1-3). 14.95 (978-0-7614-5221-8(4)) Marshall Cavendish Corp.
Croce, Warren. Opposite Day. 2007. (ENG.). 28p. per. 14.90 (978-1-4303-0659-7(9)) Lulu Pr., Inc.
Cronin, Doreen. A Barnyard Collection: Click, Clack, Moo & More. Lewin, Betsy, illus. 2010. (Click, Clack Book Ser.). (ENG.). 128p. (J). (gr. -1-3). 19.99 (978-1-4424-1263-7(1), Atheneum Bks. for Young Readers) Simon & Schuster Children's Publishing.
—A Busy Day at the Farm. Lewin, Betsy, illus. 2009. (Click, Clack Book Ser.). (ENG.). 16p. (J). (gr. -1-k). pap. 6.99 (978-1-4169-5518-4(6), Little Simon) Little Simon.
—The Case of the Weird Blue Chicken: The Next Misadventure. 2015. (Chicken Squad Ser.: 2). 35.75 (978-1-4906-4049-5(5)) Recorded Bks., Inc.
—The Chicken Squad. Cornell, Kevin, illus. 2014. 92p. (J). **(978-0-605-90609-9(2))** Simon & Schuster Children's Publishing.
—The Chicken Squad: The First Misadventure. 2014. (Chicken Squad Ser.: 1). 1.25 (978-1-4906-2066-4(4)); 35.75 (978-1-4906-2065-7(6)); 33.75 (978-1-4906-2064-0(8)) Recorded Bks., Inc.
—The Chicken Squad: The First Misadventure. Cornell, Kevin, illus. (Chicken Squad Ser.: 1). (ENG.). 112p. (J). (gr. 2-5). 2015. pap. 6.99 (978-1-4424-9677-4(0)) 2014. 12.99 (978-1-4424-9676-7(2)) Simon & Schuster Children's Publishing. (Atheneum Bks. for Young Readers).
—Click, Clack, Peep! Lewin, Betsy, illus. 2015. (Click, Clack Book Ser.). (ENG.). 40p. (J). (gr. -1-3). 17.99 (978-1-4814-2411-0(4)) Simon & Schuster Children's Publishing.
—Dooby Dooby Moo. Lewin, Betsy, illus. 2010. (Click, Clack Book Ser.). (ENG.). 40p. (J). (gr. -1-k). bds. 7.99 (978-1-4424-0890-6(1), Little Simon) Little Simon.
—Dooby Dooby Moo. Lewin, Betsy, illus. 2006. (Click, Clack Book Ser.). (ENG.). 40p. (J). (gr. -1-3). 17.99 (978-0-689-84507-9(3), Atheneum Bks. for Young Readers) Simon & Schuster Children's Publishing.
—Dooby Dooby Moo. Lewin, Betsy, illus. 2017. (Click, Clack Book Ser.). (ENG.). 40p. (J). (gr. k-2). 16.99 **(978-1-5344-0177-8(6))**; pap. 3.99 **(978-1-5344-0176-1(8))** Simon Spotlight. (Simon Spotlight).
—Dooby Dooby Moo, 1 vol. Lewin, Betsy, illus. 2008. (Doreen Cronin: Click-Clack & More Ser.). (ENG.). 40p. (gr. -1-3). lib. bdg. 24.21 (978-1-59961-423-6(5)) Spotlight.
—Dooby Dooby Moo. Lewin, Betsy, illus. 2011. (J). (gr. -1-3). 29.95 (978-0-545-04281-9(X)) Weston Woods Studios, Inc.
—Dubi Dubi Muu. Jimenez Rioja, Alberto, tr. from ENG. 2007.Tr. of Dooby Dooby Moo. (SPA., Illus.). 35p. (J). (gr. -1-1). 15.95 (978-1-933032-33-7(2)) Lectorum Pubns., Inc.
—Into the Wild: Yet Another Misadventure. Warrick, Jessica & Gilpin, Stephen, illus. 2017. (Chicken Squad Ser.: 3). (ENG.). 112p. (J). (gr. 2-5). pap. 6.99 (978-1-4814-5047-8(6)) Simon & Schuster Children's Publishing.
—Into the Wild: Yet Another Misdventure. Gilpin, Stephen, illus. 2016. (Chicken Squad Ser.: 3). (ENG.). 112p. (J). (gr. 2-5). 12.99 (978-1-4814-5046-1(8), Atheneum/Caitlyn Dlouhy Books) Simon & Schuster Children's Publishing.
—M. O. M. (Mom Operating Manual) Cornell, Laura, illus. 2011. (ENG.). 56p. (J). (gr. -1-3). 16.99 (978-1-4169-6150-5(X), Atheneum Bks. for Young Readers) Simon & Schuster Children's Publishing.
—Rescue Bunnies. Menchin, Scott, illus. 2010. (ENG.). 32p. (J). (gr. -1-3). 16.99 (978-0-06-112871-4(6)) HarperCollins Pubs.
—The Trouble with Chickens. Cornell, Kevin, illus. (J). (gr. 1-5). 2012. (ENG.). 144p. pap. 5.99 (978-0-06-121534-6(1)) 2011. (ENG.). 128p. 14.99 (978-0-06-121532-2(5)) 2011. 128p. lib. bdg. 15.89 (978-0-06-121533-9(3)) HarperCollins Pubs.
Crowe, Caroline. Pirates in Pajamas. Knight, Tim, illus. 2015. (ENG.). 32p. (J). (gr. -1-3). 16.99 (978-1-58925-190-8(3)) Tiger Tales.
Crummel, Susan Stevens & Stevens, Janet. Cook-a-Doodle-Doo! 2005. (ENG., Illus.). 48p. (J). (gr. -1-3). reprint ed. pap. 7.99 (978-0-15-205658-2(0)) Houghton Mifflin Harcourt Publishing Co.
Cruz, Kelly De La. Super Boy's Adventurous Imagination: Let your imagination Flow. 2010. 50p. pap. 26.99 (978-1-4500-3867-6(0)) Xlibris Corp.
Cuillain, Adam & Cuillain, Charlotte. The Pirates on Holiday. Van Wyk, Rupert, illus. 2014. (ENG.). 32p. (J). (978-0-7787-1311-1(3)) Crabtree Publishing Co.
Cullen, Seán. Hamish X & the Cheese Pirates. 2007. (ENG.). 304p. (J). (gr. 7-18). 9.99 (978-0-14-305311-8(6), Penguin Canada) Penguin Canada CAN. Dist: Penguin Random Hse. LLC.
Cupidity. 2014. (Romantic Comedies Ser.). (ENG., Illus.). 288p. (YA). (gr. 9). pap. 13.99 (978-1-4814-2746-3(6), Simon Pulse) Simon Pulse.
Curry, Cicero. The Tickle Man. Ledbetter, John'el, illus. 2013. 44p. pap. 24.95 (978-1-63000-015-8(9)) America Star Bks.
Curry, Don, ed. The Crate Escape No. 2. 2008. (I Can Find It Ser.). 22p. (J). 7.99 (978-0-696-23490-3(4)) Meredith Bks.
—Esape Africa. 2008. 22p. (J). 15.95 (978-0-696-23488-0(2)) Meredith Bks.
Cusick, John M. Cherry Money Baby. 2013. (ENG.). 400p. (YA). (gr. 9). 16.99 (978-0-7636-5557-0(0)) Candlewick Pr.
Cutler, Betty Jackson. The Flight of SaraJane, 1 vol. 2010. 30p. 24.95 (978-1-4512-1018-7(3)) PublishAmerica, Inc.
Cyrus, Kurt. Shake a Leg, Egg! Cyrus, Kurt, illus. 2017. (ENG., Illus.). 32p. (J). (gr. -1-3). 17.99 (978-1-4814-5848-1(5), Beach Lane Bks.) Beach Lane Bks.
Czekaj, Jef. A Call for a New Alphabet. Czekaj, Jef, illus. 2011. (ENG., Illus.). 48p. (J). (gr. 1-4). pap. 5.95 (978-1-58089-229-2(9)) Charlesbridge Publishing, Inc.
—Dog Rules. Czekaj, Jef, illus. 2016. (Illus.). 32p. (J). (gr. -1-3). 17.99 (978-0-06-228018-3(X)) HarperCollins Pubs.
—Oink-a-Doodle-Moo. Czekaj, Jef, illus. 2012. (ENG., Illus.). 32p. (J). (gr. -1-1). 16.99 (978-0-06-206011-2(2)) HarperCollins Pubs.
D C Thomson Staff, ed. The Broons 2004. 2003. (Illus.). 96p. (J). 9.95 (978-0-85116-835-7(3)) Thomson, D.C. & Co., Ltd. GBR. Dist: APG Sales & Distribution Services.
—The Broons & Oor Wullie 2004: More Classics from the Fifties. 2003. (Illus.). 144p. (J). 12.95 (978-0-85116-836-4(1)) Thomson, D.C. & Co., Ltd. GBR. Dist: APG Sales & Distribution Services.
Dahl, Roald. The BFG. 2016. (CHI.). 112p. (J). (gr. 3-6). pap. **(978-986-479-012-8(9))** Commonwealth Publishing Co., Ltd.
—The BFG. 30th rev. ed. 2014. (ENG.). 208p. (J). (gr. 2-12). 11.24 (978-1-63245-341-9(X)) Lectorum Pubns., Inc.
—The BFG. 2009. 9.00 (978-0-7848-2054-4(6), Everbind) Marco Bk. Co.
—The BFG. Dahl, Roald & Blake, Quentin, illus. 2007. 17.00 (978-0-7569-8233-1(2)) Penguin Publishing Group.
—The BFG. movie tie-in ed. 2016. (ENG., Illus.). 224p. (J). (gr. 3-7). 7.99 (978-1-101-99769-7(9), Puffin Books) Penguin Young Readers Group.
—The BFG. Blake, Quentin, illus. 30th anniv. ed. 2007. (ENG.). 224p. (J). (gr. 3-7). 7.99 (978-0-14-241038-7(1), Puffin Books) Penguin Young Readers Group.
—The BFG. 2005. (J). 1.25 (978-1-4193-5995-8(9)) Recorded Bks., Inc.
—The BFG. 2007. 18.40 (978-1-4177-8612-1(4), Turtleback) Turtleback Bks.
—Charlie & the Chocolate Factory. movie tie-in ed. Date not set. 174p. (J). 19.95 (978-0-8488-2241-5(2)) Amereon Ltd.
—Charlie & the Chocolate Factory. 2009. 9.00 (978-0-88483-905-7(2), Everbind) Marco Bk. Co.
—Charlie & the Chocolate Factory. Brunetti, Ivan & Schindelman, Joseph, illus. 2011. (Penguin Classics Deluxe Edition Ser.). (ENG.). 176p. (gr. 5). 16.00 (978-0-14-310633-3(3), Penguin Classics) Penguin Publishing Group.
—Charlie & the Chocolate Factory. Blake, Quentin, illus. 2007. 17.00 (978-0-7569-8213-3(8)) Penguin Publishing Group.
—Charlie & the Chocolate Factory. Blake, Quentin, illus. (ENG.). (J). (gr. 3-7). 2011. 160p. 15.99 (978-0-14-241821-5(8)) 2007. 192p. 7.99 (978-0-14-241031-8(4)) 2004. 176p. pap. 7.99 (978-0-14-240108-8(0)) Penguin Young Readers Group. (Puffin Books).
—Charlie & the Chocolate Factory. Blake, Quentin, illus. 40th anniv. movie tie-in ed. 2014. (ENG.). 160p. (J). (gr. k-4). 27.99 (978-0-375-83197-3(5), Knopf Bks. for Young Readers) Random Hse. Children's Bks.
—Charlie & the Chocolate Factory. 2008. (J). 1.25 (978-1-4193-5983-5(5)) Recorded Bks., Inc.
—Charlie & the Chocolate Factory. 2007. 18.40 (978-1-4177-8609-1(4)) 2004. 18.40 (978-1-4177-0487-3(X)) Turtleback Bks. (Turtleback).
—Charlie & the Great Glass Elevator. Blake, Quentin, illus. 2007. (ENG.). 192p. (J). (gr. 3-7). 7.99 (978-0-14-241032-5(2), Puffin Books) Penguin Young Readers Group.
—Charlie & the Great Glass Elevator. Blake, Quentin, illus. 2005. (Puffin Modern Classics Ser.). (ENG.). 176p. (J). (gr. 3-7). pap. 7.99 (978-0-14-240412-6(8), Puffin Books) Penguin Young Readers Group.
—Charlie & the Great Glass Elevator. 2007. 18.40 (978-1-4177-8610-7(8), Turtleback) Turtleback Bks.
—Le Doigt Magique.Tr. of Magic Finger. pap. 16.95 (978-2-07-053723-5(4)) Gallimard, Editions FRA. Dist: Distribooks, Inc.
—The Giraffe & the Pelly & Me. Blake, Quentin, illus. 2009. (ENG.). 96p. (Orig.). (J). (gr. 3-7). 7.99 (978-0-14-241384-5(4), Puffin Books) Penguin Young Readers Group.
—Matilda.Tr. of Matilda. (FRE.). (J). pap. 19.95 (978-2-07-051254-6(1)) Gallimard, Editions FRA. Dist: Distribooks, Inc.
—Matilda. Blake, Quentin & Terrazzini, Daniela Jaglenka, illus. 2013.Tr. of Matilda. (ENG.). 240p. (J). (gr. 3-7). 16.99 (978-0-14-242427-8(7), Puffin Books) Penguin Young Readers Group.
—Matilda. Blake, Quentin, illus.Tr. of Matilda. (ENG.). (J). (gr. 3-7). 2007. 256p. 7.99 (978-0-14-241037-0(3)) 2004. 240p. pap. 7.99 (978-0-14-240253-5(2)) 2013. 256p. pap. 7.99 (978-0-14-242538-1(9)) Penguin Young Readers Group. (Puffin Books).
—MATILDA. 46th ed. 2006. (Alfaguara Juvenil Ser.). (SPA., Illus.). 230p. (J). (gr. 5-8). pap. 12.95 (978-84-204-6454-1(6)) Ediciones Alfaguara ESP. Dist: Santillana USA Publishing Co., Inc.
—The Missing Golden Ticket & Other Splendiferous Secrets. Blake, Quentin, illus. 2010. (ENG.). 128p. (J). (gr. 3-7). 7.99 (978-0-14-241742-3(4), Puffin Books) Penguin Young Readers Group.
—The Twits. 2009. 8.32 (978-1-55744-311-3(4), Everbind) Marco Bk. Co.
—The Twits. Blake, Quentin, illus. 2007. (ENG.). 112p. (J). (gr. 3-7). 7.99 (978-0-14-241039-4(X), Puffin Books) Penguin Young Readers Group.
—The Twits. Blake, Quentin, illus. 2007. 76p. (gr. 4-7). 18.00 (978-0-7569-8234-8(0)) Perfection Learning Corp.
—The Twits. 2007. 18.40 (978-1-4177-8618-3(3), Turtleback) Turtleback Bks.
Dairman, Tara. Stars So Sweet. 2016. (All Four Stars Ser.: Bk. 3). (ENG.). 288p. (J). (gr. 3-7). 16.99 (978-1-101-99648-5(X), G.P. Putnam's Sons Books for Young Readers) Penguin Young Readers Group.
Dale, Elizabeth. Little Red Hen's Great Escape. 2016. (ENG., Illus.). 32p. (J). (978-0-7787-2461-2(1)) Crabtree Publishing Co.
Damico, Gina. Hellhole. (ENG.). (YA). (gr. 9). 2016. 384p. pap. 9.99 (978-0-544-54117-7(0)) 2015. 368p. 17.99 (978-0-544-30710-0(0)) Houghton Mifflin Harcourt Publishing Co. (HMH Books For Young Readers).
—Rogue. 2013. (ENG.). 336p. (YA). (gr. 7). pap. 8.99 (978-0-544-10884-4(1)) Houghton Mifflin Harcourt Publishing Co.
—Scorch. 2012. (ENG.). 352p. (YA). (gr. 7). pap. 8.99 (978-0-547-62457-0(3)) Houghton Mifflin Harcourt Publishing Co.
—Scorch. 2012. (Croak Ser.: 2). lib. bdg. 19.65 (978-0-606-26627-7(5), Turtleback) Turtleback Bks.
—Wax. 2016. (ENG.). 368p. (J). (gr. 7). 17.99 (978-0-544-63315-5(6), HMH Books For Young Readers) Houghton Mifflin Harcourt Publishing Co.
Daneshvari, Gitty. Ghoulfriends Just Want to Have Fun. 2013. (ENG., Illus.). 272p. (J). (gr. 3-7). 12.99 (978-0-316-22253-2(4)) Little, Brown Bks. for Young Readers.
—The League of Unexceptional Children. 2015. (League of Unexceptional Children Ser.: 1). (ENG., Illus.). 240p. (J). (gr. 3-7). 17.00 (978-0-316-40570-6(1)) Little Brown & Co.
—The League of Unexceptional Children. 2016. (League of Unexceptional Children Ser.: 1). (ENG., Illus.). 256p. (J). (gr. 3-7). pap. 6.99 (978-0-316-40568-3(X)) Little, Brown Bks. for Young Readers.
—Monster High: Ghoulfriends the Ghoul-It-Yourself Book. 2014. (Monster High Ghoulfriends Ser.: 4.5). (ENG., Illus.). 240p. (J). (gr. 3-7). 13.99 (978-0-316-28222-2(7)) Little, Brown Bks. for Young Readers.
—Who's That Ghoulfriend? 2013. Bk. 3. (ENG., Illus.). 272p. (J). (gr. 3-7). 13.00 (978-0-316-22254-9(2)) Little, Brown Bks. for Young Readers.
Daneshvari, Gitty, ed. Get Smart-Ish. 2016. (League of Unexceptional Children Ser.: 2). (ENG., Illus.). 240p. (J). (gr. 3-7). 16.99 (978-0-316-40574-4(4)) Little, Brown Bks. for Young Readers.
Daniell, G. Dusty & Albert's Beaver Tales. 2009. 50p. pap. 24.00 (978-0-557-08541-5(1)) Lulu Pr., Inc.
Danziger, Paula. There's a Bat in Bunk Five. 2006. (ENG.). 208p. (J). (gr. 5-18). 8.99 (978-0-14-240681-6(3), Puffin Books) Penguin Young Readers Group.
Darling, Nina. Pet Shop Talk: A Grooming for Max, 1 vol. 2009. 27p. pap. 24.95 (978-1-60813-646-9(9)) America Star Bks.
Darrows, Eva. Dead Little Mean Girl. 2017. (ENG.). 256p. 18.99 (978-0-373-21241-5(0), Harlequin Teen) Harlequin Enterprises, Ltd. CAN. Dist: HarperCollins Pubs.
Daudet, Alphonse. The Siege of Berlin & Other Stories. 2004. reprint ed. pap. 1.99 (978-1-4192-8248-5(4)); pap. 15.95 (978-1-4191-8248-8(X)) Kessinger Publishing, LLC.
Dave & Matt. Yuck's Fart Club. Baines, Nigel, illus. 2013. (Yuck Ser.). (ENG.). 112p. (J). (gr. 2-5). pap. 6.99 (978-1-4424-8152-7(8), Simon & Schuster/Paula Wiseman Bks.) Simon & Schuster/Paula Wiseman Bks.
David, Keren. Lia's Guide to Winning the Lottery. 2011. (ENG.). 352p. (J). (gr. 7-10). pap. 8.99 (978-1-84780-191-3(9), Frances Lincoln) Quarto Publishing Group UK GBR. Dist: Littlehampton Bk Services, Ltd.
David, Lawrence. The Invasion of the Shag Carpet Creature. Gott, Barry, illus. 2004. (Horace Splattly Ser.). 151p. (J). (gr. 4-7). 12.65 (978-0-7569-2818-6(4)) Perfection Learning Corp.
—The Terror of the Pink Dodo Balloons. Gott, Barry, illus. 2003. (Horace Splattly Ser.). 153p. (J). (gr. 4-7). 12.65 (978-0-7569-2816-2(8)) Perfection Learning Corp.
David, Stuart. My Brilliant Idea (and How It Caused My Downfall) (ENG.). 240p. (YA). (gr. 7). 2017. pap. 9.99 (978-0-544-93886-1(0)) 2016. 17.99 (978-0-544-69961-8(0)) Houghton Mifflin Harcourt Publishing Co. (HMH Books For Young Readers).
David, Yvonne. Out of the Apple Orchard. 2005. (Illus.). 72p. (J). 18.95 (978-0-9621385-4-6(1)) Arbiter Pr.
Davidowitz, Stacy. Camp Rolling Hills. (Camp Rolling Hills Ser.: 3). (ENG., Illus.). (J). (gr. 3-7). 2017. 240p. pap. 8.95 (978-1-4197-2291-2(3))Bk. 1. 2016. 256p. pap. 8.95 (978-1-4197-1885-4(1)) Abrams, Inc. (Amulet Bks.).
—Crossing Over, Bk. 2. 2016. (Camp Rolling Hills Ser.: 2). (ENG., Illus.). 240p. (J). (gr. 3-7). pap. 8.95 (978-1-4197-1880-9(0), Amulet Bks.) Abrams, Inc.
Davies, Christie. Dewi the Dragon. 2006. (ENG.). 96p. (J). pap. 9.95 (978-0-86243-770-1(9)) Y Lolfa GBR. Dist: Dufour Editions, Inc.
Davies, Jacqueline. Nothing but Trouble. 2016. (Nothing but Trouble Ser.: 1). 320p. (J). (gr. 3-7). 16.99 (978-0-06-236988-8(1), Tegen, Katherine Bks) HarperCollins Pubs.
Davies, Katie. The Great Cat Conspiracy. Shaw, Hannah, illus. 2012. (Great Critter Capers Ser.). (ENG.). 224p. (J). (gr. 3-7). 12.99 (978-1-4424-4513-0(0), Beach Lane Bks.) Beach Lane Bks.
—The Great Dog Disaster. Shaw, Hannah, illus. 2013. (Great Critter Capers Ser.). (ENG.). 208p. (J). (gr. 3-7). 12.99 (978-1-4424-4517-8(3), Beach Lane Bks.) Beach Lane Bks.
—The Great Hamster Massacre. Shaw, Hannah, illus. 2011. (Great Critter Capers Ser.). (ENG.). 208p. (J). (gr. 3-7). 12.99 (978-1-4424-2062-5(6), Beach Lane Bks.) Beach Lane Bks.
Davis, Alexus. Juke Joint. 2010. 169p. pap. 9.76 (978-0-557-23687-9(8)) Lulu Pr., Inc.
Davis, Brian. My Shoes Got the Blues Wheeler, Ron, illus. 2003. (Book of Matt Ser.: 2). 80p. (J). pap. 4.99 (978-1-59269-057-2(2)) Mcruffy Pr.
Davis, Danielle. Zinnia & the Bees. Horton, Laura K., illus. 2017. (Middle-Grade Novels Ser.). (ENG.). 240p. (gr. 4-7). lib. bdg. 26.65 **(978-1-4965-4661-6(X))** Stone Arch Bks.
Davis, David. Rock 'n' Roll Dogs, 1 vol. Galey, Chuck, illus. 2006. (ENG.). 32p. (J). (gr. k-3). 16.99 (978-1-58980-349-7(3)) Pelican Publishing Co., Inc.
Davis, Donald. Mama Learns to Drive: Stories That Celebrate Mothers. 2006. (ENG., Illus.). 128p. (J). (gr. -1-17). 17.95 (978-0-87483-745-2(6), 1235376) August Hse. Pubs., Inc.
Davis, Eleanor. Flop to the Top! TOON Level 3. Weing, Drew, illus. 2015. (ENG.). 40p. (J). (gr. k). 12.95 (978-1-935179-89-4(6)) TOON Books / RAW Junior, LLC.
Davis, Jim. Fat Cat, No.1. 2003. (Garfield Ser.). (gr. 5-8). lib. bdg. 29.40 (978-0-613-68581-8(4), Turtleback) Turtleback Bks.
—Garfield Caution - Wide Load. 2013. (Garfield Ser.: 56). (ENG., Illus.). 96p. pap. 14.00 (978-0-345-52596-3(5), Ballantine Bks.) Random House Publishing Group.
—Garfield Gets in a Pickle. 2012. (Garfield Ser.: 54). lib. bdg. 25.75 (978-0-606-26835-6(9), Turtleback) Turtleback Bks.
Davis, Regina & Spencer, Carolyn Royer. Señor Smarty Pantaloons & the Mystery of the Missing Teachers. 2011. 32p. (gr. 1-2). pap. 17.59 (978-1-4567-4557-8(3)) AuthorHouse.
Day, Alexandra. The Fairy Dogfather. Day, Alexandra, illus. 2012. (ENG., Illus.). 32p. (J). 8.95 (978-1-59583-455-3(9), Green Tiger Pr.) Laughing Elephant.
Daywalt, Drew. The Legend of Rock, Paper, Scissors. Rex, Adam, illus. 2017. 48p. (J). (gr. -1-3). 17.99 (978-0-06-243889-8(1)) HarperCollins Pubs.
de Moraes, Ana. The Zoomers' Handbook. de Moraes, Thiago, illus. 2016. (ENG.). 32p. (J). (gr. -1-3). 17.99 (978-1-5124-0424-1(1)) Lerner Publishing Group.
Deacon, Alexis. Cheese Belongs to You! Schwarz, Viviane, illus. 2013. (ENG.). 32p. (J). (gr. -1-1). 15.99 (978-0-7636-6608-8(4)) Candlewick Pr.
—A Place to Call Home. Schwarz, Viviane, illus. 2011. (ENG.). 40p. (J). (gr. -1-2). 16.99 (978-0-7636-5360-6(8)) Candlewick Pr.
Deacon, Melissa. Chicken Pox? 2011. 20p. pap. 24.95 (978-1-4626-0528-6(1)) America Star Bks.
Deàk, Erzsi. Pumpkin Time! Cushman, Doug, illus. 2014. (ENG.). 32p. (J). (-3). 14.99 (978-1-4022-9526-3(X), 9781402295263, Sourcebooks Jabberwocky) Sourcebooks, Inc.
Debose, Alison. Lenny & Di in the Frog & the Fly. 2011. 28p. pap. 24.95 (978-1-4626-0394-7(7)) PublishAmerica, Inc.
DeCamp, Alison. My Near-Death Adventures: I Almost Died. Again. 2016. (ENG., Illus.). 288p. (J). (gr. 3-7). 16.99 (978-0-385-39048-4(3), Crown Books For Young Readers) Random Hse. Children's Bks.
Degman, Lori. Cock-A-Doodle-Oops! Zemke, Deborah, illus. 2014. (ENG.). 36p. (J). (gr. -1-4). 16.95 (978-1-939547-07-1(5)) Creston Bks.
deGroat, Diane. No More Pencils, No More Books, No More Teacher's Dirty Looks! deGroat, Diane, illus. 2009. (Gilbert Ser.). (ENG., Illus.). 32p. (J). (gr. -1-3). pap. 6.99 (978-0-06-079116-2(0)) HarperCollins Pubs.
Dempsey, Kristy. Superhero Instruction Manual. Fearing, Mark, illus. 2016. (ENG.). 40p. (J). (gr. k-3). 16.99 (978-0-385-75534-4(1), Knopf Bks. for Young Readers) Random Hse. Children's Bks.
Dennard, Susan. Strange & Ever After. 2014. (Something Strange & Deadly Trilogy Ser.: 3). (ENG.). 400p. (YA). (gr. 9). 17.99 (978-0-06-208332-6(5)) HarperCollins Pubs.
Denton, Terry. The Minotaur's Maze. 2004. (Storymaze Ser.). (ENG., Illus.). 144p. (J). (gr. 4-8). pap. 24.99 (978-1-74114-088-0(9)) Allen & Unwin AUS. Dist: Independent Pubs. Group.
—The Obelisk of Eeeno. 2004. (Storymaze Ser.). (ENG., Illus.). 144p. (J). (gr. 4-8). pap. 11.99 (978-1-74114-089-7(7)) Allen & Unwin AUS. Dist: Independent Pubs. Group.
Deogratias Simba. The Mystery Door. 2005. (Illus.). 22p. pap. (978-9987-417-21-6(3)) Mkuki na Nyoka Pubs. TZA. Dist: Michigan State Univ. Pr.
DePalma, Mary Newell. Uh-Oh! 2011. (ENG., Illus.). 32p. (YA). 14.00 (978-0-8028-5372-1(2)) Eerdmans, William B. Publishing Co.
dePaola, Tomie. Strega Nona's Gift. dePaola, Tomie, illus. 2011. (ENG., Illus.). 32p. (J). (gr. -1-3). 17.99 (978-0-399-25649-3(0), Nancy Paulsen Books) Penguin Young Readers Group.
DePrisco, Dorothea. Pig-a-Boo! A Farmyard Peekaboo Book. Runnells, Patricia & Runnells, Treesha, illus. 2009. (ENG.). 14p. (J). (gr. -1-k). 9.99 (978-1-4169-7226-6(9), Little Simon) Little Simon.

Derby, Kenneth. The Top Ten Ways to Ruin the First Day of 5th Grade. 2004. (ENG.). 176p. (J). (gr. 4-6). tchr. ed. 16.95 (978-0-8234-1851-0(0)) Holiday Hse., Inc.

Derek the Ghost Staff. Monsters on the March. Fischer, Scott M., illus. 2013. (Scary School Ser.: 2). (ENG.). 272p. (J). (gr. 3-7). pap. 6.99 (978-0-06-196097-0(7)) HarperCollins Pubs.

—The Northern Frights. Fischer, Scott M., illus. 2013. (Scary School Ser.: 3). (ENG.). 272p. (J). (gr. 3-7). 16.99 (978-0-06-196098-7(5)) HarperCollins Pubs.

—Scary School. Fischer, Scott M., illus. (Scary School Ser.: 1). (ENG.). (J). (gr. 3-7). 2012. 272p. pap. 6.99 (978-0-06-196094-9(2)) 2011. 256p. 16.99 (978-0-06-196092-5(6)) HarperCollins Pubs.

Derkez, Linda. Chip's Sharing Day. Doehring, Phoebe, illus. 2012. 16p. pap. 9.95 (978-1-61633-245-7(X)) Guardian Angel Publishing, Inc.

deRubertis, Barbara. Alexander Anteater's Amazing Act. Alley, R. W., illus. 2010. (Animal Antics A to Z Ser.). 32p. (J). (ENG.). (gr. -1-3). pap. 7.95 (978-1-57565-300-6(1)); (gr. k-1). lib. bdg. 22.60 (978-1-57565-304-4(4)) Kane Press, Inc.

—Bobby Baboon's Banana Be-Bop. Alley, R. W., illus. 2010. (Animal Antics A to Z Ser.). 32p. (J). lib. bdg. 22.60 (978-1-57565-305-1(2)); (ENG.). (gr. -1-3). pap. 7.95 (978-1-57565-301-3(X)) Kane Press, Inc.

—Corky Cub's Crazy Caps. Alley, R. W., illus. 2010. (Animal Antics A to Z Ser.). 32p. (J). lib. bdg. 22.60 (978-1-57565-306-8(0)); (ENG.). (gr. -1-3). pap. 7.95 (978-1-57565-302-0(8)) Kane Press, Inc.

—Dilly Dog's Dizzy Dancing. Alley, R. W., illus. 2010. (Animal Antics A to Z Ser.). 32p. (J). lib. bdg. 22.60 (978-1-57565-307-5(9)); (ENG.). (gr. -1-3). pap. 7.95 (978-1-57565-303-7(6)) Kane Press, Inc.

—Eddie Elephant's Exciting Egg-Sitting. Alley, R. W., illus. 2010. (Animal Antics A to Z Ser.). 32p. (J). (gr. -1-3). pap. 7.95 (978-1-57565-309-9(5)); lib. bdg. 22.60 (978-1-57565-316-7(8)) Kane Press, Inc.

—Frances Frog's Forever Friend. Alley, R. W., illus. 2010. (Animal Antics A to Z Ser.). 32p. (J). (gr. -1-3). (ENG.). pap. 7.95 (978-1-57565-310-5(9)); lib. bdg. 22.60 (978-1-57565-317-4(6)) Kane Press, Inc.

—Gertie Gorilla's Glorious Gift. Alley, R. W., illus. 2010. (Animal Antics A to Z Ser.). 32p. (J). (gr. -1-3). pap. 7.95 (978-1-57565-311-2(7)); lib. bdg. 22.60 (978-1-57565-318-1(4)) Kane Press, Inc.

—Hanna Hippo's Horrible Hiccups. Alley, R. W., illus. 2010. (Animal Antics A to Z Ser.). 32p. (J). (gr. -1-3). pap. 7.95 (978-1-57565-312-9(5)); lib. bdg. 22.60 (978-1-57565-319-8(2)) Kane Press, Inc.

—Izzy Impala's Imaginary Illnesses. Alley, R. W., illus. 2010. (Animal Antics A to Z Ser.). 32p. (J). (gr. -1-3). pap. 7.95 (978-1-57565-313-6(3)); lib. bdg. 22.60 (978-1-57565-320-4(6)) Kane Press, Inc.

—Jeremy Jackrabbit's Jumping Journey. Alley, R. W., illus. 2010. (Animal Antics A to Z Ser.). 32p. (J). (gr. -1-3). pap. 7.95 (978-1-57565-314-3(1)); lib. bdg. 22.60 (978-1-57565-321-1(4)) Kane Press, Inc.

Derubertis, Barbara. Sammy Skunk's Super Sniffer. Alley, R. W., illus. 2011. (Animal Antics A to Z Set III Ser.). pap. 45.32 (978-0-7613-8428-1(6)) Kane Press, Inc.

deRubertis, Barbara. Sammy Skunk's Super Sniffer. Alley, R. W., illus. 2011. (Animal Antics A to Z Ser.). pap. 7.95 (978-1-57565-344-0(3)); lib. bdg. 22.60 (978-1-57565-352-5(4)) Kane Press, Inc.

deRubertis, Barbara & DeRubertis, Barbara. Alexander Anteater's Amazing Act. Alley, R. W., illus. 2012. (Animal Antics A to Z Ser.). 32p. (J). (gr. 2 — 1). cd-rom 7.95 (978-1-57565-394-5(X)) Kane Press, Inc.

—Bobby Baboon's Banana Be-Bop. Alley, R. W., illus. 2012. (Animal Antics A to Z Ser.). 32p. (J). (gr. 2 — 1). cd-rom 7.95 (978-1-57565-395-2(8)) Kane Press, Inc.

—Corky Cub's Crazy Caps. Alley, R. W., illus. 2012. (Animal Antics A to Z Ser.). 32p. (J). (gr. 2 — 1). cd-rom 7.95 (978-1-57565-396-9(6)) Kane Press, Inc.

—Dilly Dog's Dizzy Dancing. Alley, R. W., illus. 2012. (Animal Antics A to Z Ser.). 32p. (J). (gr. 2 — 1). cd-rom 7.95 (978-1-57565-397-6(4)) Kane Press, Inc.

—Eddie Elephant's Exciting Egg-Sitting. Alley, R. W., illus. 2012. (Animal Antics A to Z Ser.). 32p. (J). (gr. 2 — 1). cd-rom 7.95 (978-1-57565-398-3(2)) Kane Press, Inc.

—Frances Frog's Forever Friend. Alley, R. W., illus. 2012. (Animal Antics A to Z Ser.). 32p. (J). (gr. 2 — 1). cd-rom 7.95 (978-1-57565-399-0(0)) Kane Press, Inc.

—Gertie Gorilla's Glorious Gift. Alley, R. W., illus. 2012. (Animal Antics A to Z Ser.). 32p. (J). (gr. 2 — 1). cd-rom 7.95 (978-1-57565-400-3(8)) Kane Press, Inc.

—Hanna Hippo's Horrible Hiccups. Alley, R. W., illus. 2012. (Animal Antics A to Z Ser.). 32p. (J). (gr. 2 — 1). cd-rom 7.95 (978-1-57565-401-0(6)) Kane Press, Inc.

—Izzy Impala's Imaginary Illnesses. Alley, R. W., illus. 2012. (Animal Antics A to Z Ser.). 32p. (J). (gr. 2 — 1). cd-rom 7.95 (978-1-57565-402-7(4)) Kane Press, Inc.

—Jeremy Jackrabbit's Jumping Journey. Alley, R. W., illus. 2012. (Animal Antics A to Z Ser.). 32p. (J). (gr. 2 — 1). cd-rom 7.95 (978-1-57565-403-4(2)) Kane Press, Inc.

—Sammy Skunk's Super Sniffer. Alley, R. W., illus. 2012. (Animal Antics A to Z Ser.). 32p. (J). (gr. 2 — 1). cd-rom 7.95 (978-1-57565-412-6(1)) Kane Press, Inc.

Desjardins, Margaret M. Murky, Quirky, Beserky Math. Bohart, Lisa, illus. 2013. 24p. pap. 13.95 (978-1-61493-210-9(7)) Peppertree Pr., The.

Desrosiers, Sylvie. Hocus Pocus. Simard, Rémy, illus. 2011. (Hocus Pocus Ser.). (ENG.). 32p. (J). (gr. -1-2). 16.95 (978-1-55453-577-4(8)) Kids Can Pr., Ltd. CAN. Dist: Hachette Bk. Group.

Deutsch, Stacia, adapted by. Cloudy with a Chance of Meatballs 2 Movie Novelization. 2013. (Cloudy with a Chance of Meatballs Movie Ser.). (ENG., Illus.). 128p. (J). (gr. 3-7). pap. 5.99 (978-1-4424-9551-7(0), Simon Spotlight) Simon Spotlight.

DeVillers, Julia & Roy, Jennifer Rozines. Trading Faces. Smith, Alison, illus. 2009. (Mix Ser.). (ENG.). 320p. (J). (gr. 4-8). pap. 7.99 (978-1-4169-6168-0(2), Aladdin) Simon & Schuster Children's Publishing.

DiCamillo, Kate. Mercy Watson: Princess in Disguise. Van Dusen, Chris, illus. 2010. (Mercy Watson Ser.: 4). (ENG.). 80p. (J). (gr. 1-4). pap. 5.99 (978-0-7636-4951-7(1)) Candlewick Pr.

—Mercy Watson: Something Wonky This Way Comes. Van Dusen, Chris, illus. 2011. (Mercy Watson Ser.: 6). (ENG.). 96p. (J). (gr. 1-4). pap. 5.99 (978-0-7636-5232-6(6)) Candlewick Pr.

—Mercy Watson: Something Wonky This Way Comes. 2011. 16.00 (978-1-61383-049-9(1)) Perfection Learning Corp.

—Mercy Watson Boxed Set: Adventures of a Porcine Wonder, 6 vols. Van Dusen, Chris, illus. 2011. (Mercy Watson Ser.). (ENG.). (J). (gr. k-3). pap. 29.99 (978-0-7636-5709-3(3)) Candlewick Pr.

—Mercy Watson Fights Crime. Van Dusen, Chris, illus. 2010. (Mercy Watson Ser.: 3). (ENG.). 80p. (J). (gr. 1-4). pap. 5.99 (978-0-7636-4952-4(X)) Candlewick Pr.

—Mercy Watson Fights Crime. DiCamillo, Kate & Van Dusen, Chris, illus. 2006. (Mercy Watson Ser.: 3). (ENG.). 80p. (J). (gr. k-3). 14.99 (978-0-7636-2590-0(6)) Candlewick Pr.

—Mercy Watson Fights Crime. 2010. (Mercy Watson Ser.: Bk. 3). lib. bdg. 16.00 (978-0-606-14927-3(9), Turtleback) Turtleback Bks.

—Mercy Watson Goes for a Ride. Van Dusen, Chris, illus. 2006. (Mercy Watson Ser.: 2). (ENG.). 80p. (J). (gr. k-4). 14.99 (978-0-7636-2332-6(6)) Candlewick Pr.

—Mercy Watson Goes for a Ride. 2012. 16.00 (978-1-61383-702-3(X)) Perfection Learning Corp.

—Mercy Watson Goes for a Ride. Van Dusen, Chris, illus. 2009. (Mercy Watson Ser.: 2). (ENG.). 80p. (J). (gr. 1-4). pap. 5.99 (978-0-7636-4505-2(2)) Candlewick Pr.

—Mercy Watson Goes for a Ride. 2009. (Mercy Watson Ser.: Bk. 2). lib. bdg. 16.00 (978-0-606-06699-0(3), Turtleback) Turtleback Bks.

—Mercy Watson Thinks Like a Pig. Van Dusen, Chris, illus. (Mercy Watson Ser.: 5). (ENG.). 80p. (J). (gr. 1-4). 2011. pap. 5.99 (978-0-7636-5231-9(8)) 2008. 12.99 (978-0-7636-3265-6(1)) Candlewick Pr.

—Mercy Watson to the Rescue. DiCamillo, Kate & Van Dusen, Chris, illus. 2009. (Mercy Watson Ser.: 1). (ENG.). 80p. (J). (gr. 1-4). pap. 5.99 (978-0-7636-4504-5(4)) Candlewick Pr.

—Mercy Watson to the Rescue. Van Dusen, Chris, illus. 2005. (Mercy Watson Ser.: 1). (ENG.). 80p. (J). (gr. k-4). 14.99 (978-0-7636-2270-1(2)) Candlewick Pr.

—Mercy Watson to the Rescue. 2009. (Mercy Watson Ser.: Bk. 1). lib. bdg. 16.00 (978-0-606-06704-1(3), Turtleback) Turtleback Bks.

DiCamillo, Kate & Mcghee, Alison. Best Friends Forever. Fucile, Tony, illus. (Bink & Gollie Ser.). (ENG.). (J). (gr. 1-4). 2014. 88p. pap. 6.99 (978-0-7636-7092-4(8)) 2013. 96p. 15.99 (978-0-7636-3497-1(2)) Candlewick Pr.

—Bink & Gollie. Fucile, Tony, illus. (Bink & Gollie Ser.). (ENG.). (J). (gr. 1-4). 2012. 88p. pap. 6.99 (978-0-7636-5954-7(1)) 2010. 96p. 15.99 (978-0-7636-3266-3(X)) Candlewick Pr.

—Bink & Gollie. 2012. (Bink & Gollie Ser.: 1). lib. bdg. 17.20 (978-0-606-23813-7(1), Turtleback) Turtleback Bks.

—Bink & Gollie - The Completely Marvelous Collection. Fucile, Tony, illus. 2014. (Bink & Gollie Ser.). (ENG.). (J). (gr. 1-4). pap. 19.99 (978-0-7636-7536-3(9)) Candlewick Pr.

—Two for One. Fucile, Tony, illus. (Bink & Gollie Ser.). (ENG.). 96p. (J). (gr. 1-4). 2013. pap. 6.99 (978-0-7636-6445-9(6)) 2012. 15.99 (978-0-7636-3361-5(5)) Candlewick Pr.

—Two for One. 2013. (Bink & Gollie Ser.: 2). lib. bdg. 17.20 (978-0-606-31607-1(8), Turtleback) Turtleback Bks.

DiCamillo, Kate & Van Dusen, Chris. Mercy Watson: Princess in Disguise. Van Dusen, Chris, illus. 2007. (Mercy Watson Ser.: 4). (ENG., Illus.). 80p. (J). (gr. 1-4). 14.99 (978-0-7636-3014-0(4)) Candlewick Pr.

Dickinson, Donald J. A Bird's Eye View of the Civil War in Loudon County & Campbell's Station, TN: A Book for Children. 2003. (Illus.). 251p. (J). per. (978-0-9637951-3-7(9)) Hart-Whitlow Pubs.

Dillard, Sarah. Extraordinary Warren: A Super Chicken. Dillard, Sarah, illus. 2014. (Pix Ser.). (ENG., Illus.). 64p. (J). (gr. 1-4). 12.99 (978-1-4424-5340-1(0), Aladdin) Simon & Schuster Children's Publishing.

Dillman, Shanley Chris. The Black Pond. 2004. 126p. pap. 19.95 (978-1-4137-3861-2(3)) America Star Bks.

Dinosaurs Offside. 2014. (Downtown Dinosaurs Ser.). (ENG., Illus.). 176p. (J). (gr. k-3). pap. 9.99 (978-1-84812-362-5(0)) Bonnier Publishing GBR. Dist: Independent Pubs. Group.

Dipucchio, Kelly. Dog Days of School. Biggs, Brian, illus. 2014. (ENG.). 40p. (J). (gr. 1-3). 16.99 (978-0-7868-5493-6(6)) Hyperion Bks. for Children.

—Dog Days of School [8x8 with Stickers]. Biggs, Brian, illus. 2017. (ENG.). 40p. (J). (gr. -1-k). pap. 5.99 **(978-1-368-00297-4(8))** Hyperion Bks. for Children.

—Everyone Loves Cupcake. Wight, Eric, illus. 2016. (ENG.). 40p. (J). 17.99 (978-0-374-30293-1(6), 9780374302931, Farrar, Straus & Giroux (BYR)) Farrar, Straus & Giroux.

—Gilbert Goldfish Wants a Pet. Shea, Bob, illus. 2011. (ENG.). 32p. (J). (gr. -1-k). 16.99 (978-0-8037-3394-7(1), Dial Bks) Penguin Young Readers Group.

—Zombie in Love. Joseph, Robin & Campbell, Scott, illus. 2011. (ENG.). 32p. (J). (gr. -1-3). 15.99 (978-1-4424-0270-6(9), Atheneum Bks. for Young Readers) Simon & Schuster Children's Publishing.

—Zombie in Love 2 + 1. Campbell, Scott, illus. 2014. (ENG.). 32p. (J). (gr. -1-3). 14.99 (978-1-4424-5937-3(9), Atheneum Bks. for Young Readers) Simon & Schuster Children's Publishing.

DiSalvo-Ryan, DyAnne. The Sloppy Copy Slipup. 2005. (ENG., Illus.). 128p. (J). (gr. 2-6). 16.95 (978-0-8234-1947-0(9)) Holiday Hse., Inc.

Disney. Inside Out #2. 2015. (Step into Reading Level 3 Ser.). lib. bdg. 14.75 (978-0-606-36388-4(2)) Turtleback Bks.

—Inside Out Junior Novel. 2015. lib. bdg. 16.00 (978-0-606-37272-5(5)) Turtleback Bks.

—Journey into the Mind. 2015. (Step into Reading Level 3 Ser.). lib. bdg. 14.75 (978-0-606-36387-7(4)) Turtleback Bks.

Disney Book Group. Finding Dory (Picture Book) 2016. (ENG.). 40p. (J). (gr. 1-3). 16.99 (978-1-4847-2585-6(9)) Disney Pr.

Disney Book Group Staff. Inside Out - Driven by Emotions. Disney Storybook Art Team, illus. 2015. (ENG.). 240p. (J). (gr. 3-7). 10.99 (978-1-4847-2203-9(5)) Disney Pr.

—Inside Out - Sadly Ever After? Purchase Includes Disney Ebook! 2015. (ENG., Illus.). 40p. (J). (gr. 1-3). 17.99 (978-1-4847-1280-1(3)) Disney Pr.

—Inside Out Box of Mixed Emotions. 2015. (ENG.). 120p. (J). (gr. -1-k). 12.99 (978-1-4847-1671-7(X)) Disney Pr.

Disney Book Group Staff & Bergen, Lara. Tangled Ever After. Disney Storybook Artists Staff, illus. 2012. (Read-Along Storybook & CD Ser.). (ENG.). 32p. (J). (gr. -1 — 1). pap. 6.99 (978-1-4231-6582-8(9)) Disney Pr.

Disney Book Group Staff & Ryals, Lexi. Jessie Livin' the Life. 2014. (Jessie Junior Novel Ser.). (ENG.). 128p. (J). (gr. 3-7). pap. 5.99 (978-1-4231-8411-9(4)) Disney Pr.

Disney Editors. Anna's Act of Love. 2013. (Frozen 8X8 Ser.). lib. bdg. 14.75 (978-0-606-32204-1(3), Turtleback) Turtleback Bks.

—Finding Dory Junior Novelization. 2016. lib. bdg. 17.20 (978-0-606-38893-1(1)) Turtleback Bks.

Disney Staff & Glumm, Felicity. Inside Out 8x8 Pictureback. 2015. lib. bdg. 14.75 (978-0-606-36386-0(6)) Turtleback Bks.

Disney Storybook Art Team, illus. Finding Dory (Read-Along Storybook & CD) 2016. (Disney Storybook & CD Ser.). (ENG.). 32p. (J). (gr. 1-3). pap. 6.99 (978-1-4847-2586-3(7)) Disney Pr.

DiTerlizzi, Tony. Jimmy Zangwow's Out-of-This-World Moon-Pie Adventure. DiTerlizzi, Tony, illus. 2003. (ENG., Illus.). 40p. (J). (gr. k-3). 7.99 (978-0-689-85563-4(X), Simon & Schuster Bks. For Young Readers) Simon & Schuster Bks. For Young Readers.

Doan, Lisa. Jack & the Wild Life. Stevanovic, Ivica, illus. (Berenson Schemes Ser.: 2). (ENG.). 144p. (J). (gr. 4-6). 2015. pap. 6.95 (978-1-4677-2476-0(9), Darby Creek) 2014. 17.95 (978-1-4677-1077-0(6)) Lerner Publishing Group.

—Jack at the Helm. Stevanovic, Ivica, illus. 2015. (J). 9.99 (978-1-4677-7787-2(0)); (Berenson Schemes Ser.: 3). (ENG.). 152p. (gr. 4-6). 17.95 (978-1-4677-1078-7(4)) Lerner Publishing Group.

—Jack the Castaway. Stevanovic, Ivica, illus. 2014. (Berenson Schemes Ser.: 1). (ENG.). 152p. (J). (gr. 4-6). 17.95 (978-1-4677-1076-3(8), Darby Creek) Lerner Publishing Group.

Dobkin, Bonnie. Crazy Pizza Day. Dey, Romi, illus. 2010. (J). (978-1-60617-150-9(X)) Teaching Strategies, LLC.

Doerrfeld, Cori. Little Bunny Foo Foo: The Real Story. 2012. (ENG., Illus.). 32p. (J). (gr. -1-k). 16.99 (978-0-8037-3470-8(0), Dial Bks) Penguin Young Readers Group.

Doherty, Berlie. Coconut Comes to School. Bates, Ivan, illus. 2004. (ENG.). 32p. (J). (gr. k-2). 18.00 (978-0-00-710433-8(2), HarperCollins Children's Bks.) HarperCollins Pubs. Ltd. GBR. Dist: Independent Pubs. Group.

Dokey, Cameron. How Not to Spend Your Senior Year. 2012. (Romantic Comedies Ser.). (ENG.). 304p. (YA). (gr. 9). pap. 14.99 (978-1-4424-6056-0(3), Simon Pulse) Simon Pulse.

Dolan, Penny. The Lovely Duckling. 2014. (ENG., Illus.). 32p. (J). (978-0-7787-0445-4(9)); pap. (978-0-7787-0480-5(7)) Crabtree Publishing Co.

Dominguez, Ramon Garcia. Una Pirana en mi Banera. (SPA.). (J). 7.95 (978-958-04-6022-0(1)) Norma S.A. COL. Dist: Distribuidora Norma, Inc.

Donahue, Peter & Coloring Books Staff. Robot Buddies Stained Glass Coloring Book. 2012. (Dover Stained Glass Coloring Book Ser.). (ENG., Illus.). 32p. (J). (gr. k-5). pap. 6.99 (978-0-486-48673-4(7)) Dover Pubns., Inc.

Donaldson, Julia. El Grufalo. Scheffler, Axel, illus. 2003. (SPA.). 32p. (J). (gr. k-2). 7.96 (978-84-233-3145-1(8), DS4478) Ediciones Destino ESP. Dist: Lectorum Pubns., Inc.

—The Spiffiest Giant in Town. Scheffler, Axel, illus. 2005. (ENG.). 32p. (J). (gr. -1-2). reprint ed. pap. 6.99 (978-0-14-240275-7(3), Puffin Books) Penguin Young Readers Group.

—A Squash & a Squeeze. Scheffler, Axel, illus. 2016. (ENG.). 32p. (J). (gr. -1-k). 16.99 (978-1-338-05220-6(9)) Scholastic, Inc.

Donbavand, Tommy. Duck! (EDGE: Tommy Donbavand's Funny Shorts Ser.). (ENG., Illus.). 64p. (J). 2017. (gr. 2-4). pap. 7.99 **(978-1-4451-4677-5(0))** 2016. (gr. 1-3). 12.99 (978-1-4451-4676-8(2)) Hachette Children's Group GBR. (Franklin Watts). Dist: Hachette Bk. Group.

—Granny Bit My Bum! 2017. (EDGE: Tommy Donbavand's Funny Shorts Ser.). (ENG., Illus.). 64p. (J). (gr. 2-4). pap. 7.99 **(978-1-4451-4633-1(9)**, Franklin Watts) Hachette Children's Group GBR. Dist: Hachette Bk. Group.

—My Granny Bit My Bum. 2016. (EDGE: Tommy Donbavand's Funny Shorts Ser.). (ENG., Illus.). 64p. (J). (gr. 1-3). 12.99 (978-1-4451-4617-1(7), Franklin Watts) Hachette Children's Group GBR. Dist: Hachette Bk. Group.

—Night of the Toddlers. 2016. (EDGE: Tommy Donbavand's Funny Shorts Ser.). (ENG., Illus.). 64p. (J). (gr. 2-4). 12.99 (978-1-4451-4685-0(1), Franklin Watts) Hachette Children's Group GBR. Dist: Hachette Bk. Group.

—Viking Kong. 2016. (EDGE: Tommy Donbavand's Funny Shorts Ser.). (ENG., Illus.). 64p. (J). (gr. 2-4). 12.99 (978-1-4451-4673-7(8), Franklin Watts) Hachette Children's Group GBR. Dist: Hachette Bk. Group.

Donbavand, Tommy & Harpercollins Staff. Our Head Teacher Is a Super-Villain. Mosedale, Julian, illus. 2015. (Collins Big Cat Ser.). (ENG.). 32p. (J). (gr. 2-2). pap. 7.95 (978-0-00-759122-0(5)) HarperCollins Pubs. Ltd. GBR. Dist: Independent Pubs. Group.

Donnelly, Rebecca. How to Stage a Catastrophe. 2017. (ENG.). 256p. (gr. 4-7). 12.95 (978-1-62370-807-8(9)) Capstone Young Readers of Coughlan Cos.

Dooby Dooby Moo. 2014. (Click, Clack Book Ser.). (ENG., Illus.). 40p. (J). (gr. -1-3). pap. 9.99 (978-1-4814-1456-2(9), Little Simon) Little Simon.

Doodler, Todd H. Super Fly 4: Rise of the Evil Army. 2017. (Super Fly Ser.). (ENG., Illus.). 128p. (J). pap. 6.99 (978-1-61963-387-2(6), 9781619633872, Bloomsbury USA Childrens) Bloomsbury Publishing USA.

—Super Fly vs. Furious Flea! 2016. (Super Fly Ser.). (ENG., Illus.). 128p. (J). pap. 6.99 (978-1-61963-384-1(1), 9781619633841, Bloomsbury USA Childrens) Bloomsbury Publishing USA.

—Veggies with Wedgies. Doodler, Todd H., illus. 2014. (ENG., Illus.). 32p. (J). (gr. -1-k). 14.99 (978-1-4424-9340-7(2), Little Simon) Little Simon.

—The Zoo I Drew. 2009. (ENG., Illus.). 56p. (J). (gr. -1-k). 14.99 (978-0-375-85201-5(8), Random Hse. Bks. for Young Readers) Random Hse. Children's Bks.

Doremus, Gaetan, creator. Coyote Run. 2014. (Stories Without Words Ser.). (ENG., Illus.). 32p. (J). (gr. -1-3). 14.95 (978-1-59270-147-6(7)) Enchanted Lion Bks., LLC.

Dorenda W. Madkins. Sammy's Battle with the L-I-E Word. 2011. 48p. pap. 24.95 (978-1-4626-2650-2(5)) America Star Bks.

Dorion, Betty F. & Dorion, Betty. Whose Side Are You On?, 1 vol. 2005. (ENG., Illus.). 216p. (J). (gr. 6-18). pap. 7.95 (978-1-55050-179-7(8)) Coteau Bks. CAN. Dist: Fitzhenry & Whiteside, Ltd.

Dormer, Frank W. Click! Dormer, Frank W., illus. 2016. (ENG., Illus.). 38p. (J). (-k). 17.99 (978-0-451-47644-9(1), Viking Books for Young Readers) Penguin Young Readers Group.

—Firefighter Duckies! Dormer, Frank W., illus. 2017. (ENG., Illus.). 40p. (J). (gr. -1-3). 17.99 (978-1-4814-6090-3(0), Atheneum Bks. for Young Readers) Simon & Schuster Children's Publishing.

—The Sword in the Stove. Dormer, Frank W., illus. 2016. (ENG., Illus.). 40p. (J). (gr. -1-3). 17.99 (978-1-4814-3167-5(6)) Simon & Schuster, Inc.

Dotlich, Rebecca Kai. Digger the Dinosaur. 2013. (Digger the Dinosaur I Can Read Ser.). (J). lib. bdg. 13.55 (978-0-606-31828-0(3), Turtleback) Turtleback Bks.

Dougherty, John. Stinkbomb & Ketchup-Face & the Badness of Badgers. Ricks, Sam, illus. 2017. (Stinkbomb & Ketchup-Face Ser.). (ENG.). 144p. (J). (gr. 3-7). 15.99 (978-1-101-99662-1(5), G.P. Putnam's Sons Books for Young Readers) Penguin Young Readers Group.

Dougherty, Meghan. Rise of the Undead Redhead. Birnbach, Alece, illus. 2014. (Dorothy's Derby Chronicles Ser.: 1). (ENG.). 256p. (J). (gr. 3-6). pap. 6.99 (978-1-4022-9535-5(9), Sourcebooks Jabberwocky) Sourcebooks, Inc.

—Woe of Jade Doe. Birnbach, Alece, illus. 2015. (Dorothy's Derby Chronicles Ser.: 2). (ENG.). 288p. (J). (gr. 4-7). pap. 6.99 (978-1-4926-0147-0(0), Sourcebooks Jabberwocky) Sourcebooks, Inc.

Dowd, Tara. No More Boogers Book. 2009. 16p. 11.50 (978-0-615-26122-5(1)) Pick It Publishing.

Dowell, Frances O'Roark. Phineas L. Macguire... Blasts Off! McDaniels, Preston, illus. 2008. (From the Highly Scientific Notebooks of Phineas L. MacGuire Ser.). (ENG.). 208p. (J). (gr. 3-7). 16.99 (978-1-4169-2689-4(5), Atheneum Bks. for Young Readers) Simon & Schuster Children's Publishing.

Downard, Barry. The Race of the Century. Downard, Barry, illus. 2008. (ENG., Illus.). 40p. (J). (gr. -1-3). 17.99 (978-1-4169-2509-5(0), Simon & Schuster Bks. For Young Readers) Simon & Schuster Bks. For Young Readers.

Downing, Erin. Dancing Queen. 2006. (Romantic Comedies Ser.). (ENG.). 272p. (YA). (gr. 9-12). mass mkt. 6.99 (978-1-4169-2510-1(4), Simon Pulse) Simon Pulse.

Doyle, Bill. The Prizewinners of Piedmont Place. Jack, Colin, illus. 2016. (Prizewinners of Piedmont Place Ser.: 1). (ENG.). 192p. (J). (gr. 3-7). 15.99 (978-0-553-52177-1(2), Random Hse. Bks. for Young Readers) Random Hse. Children's Bks.

Doyle, Bill H. Extreme Home Takeover/C by Bill Doyle; Illustrated by Colin Jack. Jack, Colin, illus. 2017. (Prizewinners of Piedmont Place Ser.). (ENG.). 208p. (J). (gr. 3-7). 15.99 (978-0-553-52181-8(0), Random Hse. Bks. for Young Readers) Random Hse. Children's Bks.

Dr. Seuss Enterprises Staff. Hop on Pop. 2004. (Bright & Early Board Books Ser.). (ENG., Illus.). 24p. (J). (gr. k-1). bds. 4.99 (978-0-375-82837-9(0), Random Hse. Bks. for Young Readers) Random Hse. Children's Bks.

Drachman, Eric. It's Me! Isabelle, Decenciere, illus. 2005. (ENG.). 32p. (J). (gr. -1-2). 18.95 incl. audio compact disk (978-0-9703809-2-0(5)) Kidwick Bks.

Dudley, Marie Luther. Tennessee Ocean Frogs. Primm. Patricia, illus. 2008. 24p. pap. 24.95 (978-1-60474-261-9(5)) America Star Bks.

Dumbleton, Mike. Muddled-Up Farm, 1 vol. Murphy, Jobi, illus. 2013. (ENG.). 32p. (J). 16.99 (978-1-59572-630-8(6)); pap. 6.99 (978-1-59572-631-5(4)) Star Bright Bks., Inc.

Dunklee, Annika. My Name Is Elizabeth! Forsythe, Matthew, illus. 2011. (ENG.). 24p. (J). (gr. -1-2). 14.95 (978-1-55453-560-6(3)) Kids Can Pr., Ltd. CAN. Dist: Hachette Bk. Group.

Dunrea, Olivier. Me & Annie McPhee. Hillenbrand, Will, illus. 2016. (ENG.). 32p. (J). (gr. -1-2). 16.99 (978-0-399-16808-6(7), Philomel Bks.) Penguin Young Readers Group.

Dupuy, W. The Story of Poppy's Frankentoe, 1 vol. 2010. 24p. 24.95 (978-1-4489-7585-3(9)) PublishAmerica, Inc.

Durand, Delphine. Bob & Co. 2007. (ENG., Illus.). 64p. (J). (gr. -1-3). pap. 9.95 (978-1-85437-723-4(X)) Tate Publishing, Ltd. GBR. Dist: Hachette Bk. Group.

—My House. Adams, Sarah, tr. from FRE. 2007. (ENG., Illus.). 44p. (J). (gr. k-2). 12.95 (978-1-905341-09-2(1)) WingedChariot Pr. GBR. Dist: Independent Pubs. Group.

Durango, Julia. Cha-Cha Chimps. Taylor, Eleanor, illus. 2006. (ENG.). 32p. (J). (gr. -1-3). 17.99 (978-0-689-86456-8(6), Simon & Schuster Bks. For Young Readers) Simon & Schuster Bks. For Young Readers.

Durk, Jim, illus. Rabbid of the Sea. 2015. (Rabbids Invasion Ser.). (ENG.). 40p. (J). (gr. 1-3). pap. 3.99 (978-1-4814-3545-1(0), Simon Spotlight) Simon Spotlight.

Durrant, Sabine. Cross Your Heart, Connie Pickles. 2007. 263p. (YA). (gr. 7-12). lib. bdg. 17.89 (978-0-06-085480-5(4), HarperTeen) HarperCollins Pubs.

Dyan, Penelope. Bake a Cake, Make Two — -and Let Them Eat Cake. Dyan, Penelope, illus. 2008. (Illus.). 44p. pap. 11.95 (978-1-935118-18-3(8)) Bellissima Publishing, LLC.

—Bubble Trouble — -for Boys Only (r). Dyan, Penelope, illus. 2011. (Illus.). 34p. pap. 11.95 (978-1-935630-92-0(X)) Bellissima Publishing, LLC.

—The Carousel. Dyan, Penelope, illus. 2010. (Illus.). 34p. pap. 11.95 (978-1-935630-26-5(1)) Bellissima Publishing, LLC.

—Go Far Star Car — Even Though Cars Are Not People. Dyan, Penelope, illus. 2008. (Illus.). 44p. pap. 11.95 (978-1-935118-12-1(9)) Bellissima Publishing, LLC.

—Go Run, Have Fun — -Because Everyone Likes Fun. Dyan, Penelope, illus. 2008. (Illus.). 44p. pap. 11.95 (978-1-935118-15-2(3)) Bellissima Publishing, LLC.

—A Lot of Snot, a for Boys Only Book. Dyan, Penelope, illus. 2008. (Illus.). 44p. pap. 11.95 (978-1-935118-23-7(4)) Bellissima Publishing, LLC.

—Tony Pickleloni, a Boy Full of Baloney. Dyan, Penelope, illus. 2009. (Illus.). 44p. pap. 11.95 *(978-1-935118-52-7(8))* Bellissima Publishing, LLC.
Dyckman, Ame. You Don't Want a Unicorn! Climo, Liz, illus. 2017. (ENG.). 40p. (J). (gr. -1-3). 16.99 *(978-0-316-34347-3(1))* Little Brown & Co.
Dyer, Jonah Lisa & Dyer, Stephen. The Season. 2016. (ENG.). 352p. (YA). (gr. 9). 17.99 *(978-0-451-47634-0(4),* Viking Books for Young Readers) Penguin Young Readers Group.
Earls, Nick. 48 Shades of Brown. 2004. (ENG.). 288p. (YA). (gr. 7-18). pap. 16.99 *(978-0-618-45295-8(8))* Houghton Mifflin Harcourt Publishing Co.
Eastman, P. D. Aaron Has a Lazy Day. 2015. (Step into Reading Ser.). (ENG., Illus.). 32p. (J). (gr. -1-1). lib. bdg. 12.99 *(978-0-375-97411-3(3),* Random Hse. Bks. for Young Readers) Random Hse. Children's Bks.
—Aaron Is Cool. 2015. (Step into Reading Ser.). (ENG., Illus.). 32p. (J). (gr. -1-1). 12.99 *(978-0-553-51238-0(2),* Random Hse. Bks. for Young Readers) Random Hse. Children's Bks.
—Aaron Loves Apples & Pumpkins. 2015. (Step into Reading Ser.). (ENG., Illus.). 32p. (J). (gr. -1-1). 12.99 *(978-0-553-51235-9(8),* Random Hse. Bks. for Young Readers) Random Hse. Children's Bks.
—Big Blue Book of Beginner Books. 2008. (Beginner Books(R) Ser.). (ENG., Illus.). 368p. (J). (gr. -1-2). 16.99 *(978-0-375-85552-8(1),* Random Hse. Bks. for Young Readers) Random Hse. Children's Bks.
Eastman, P. D., et al. The Big Red Book of Beginner Books. 2010. (Beginner Books(R) Ser.). (ENG., Illus.). 344p. (J). (gr. -1-2). 16.99 *(978-0-375-86531-2(4),* Random Hse. for Young Readers) Random Hse. Children's Bks.
Easton, T. S. Boys Don't Knit. 2015. (ENG.). 272p. (YA). (gr. 8). 16.99 *(978-1-250-05331-2(5),* 9781250053312) Feiwel & Friends.
—Boys Don't Knit. 2016. (ENG.). 272p. (YA). pap. 9.99 *(978-1-250-07354-9(5),* 9781250073549) Square Fish.
Ecton, Emily. Boots & Pieces. 2008. (ENG.). 240p. (J). (gr. 3-7). pap. 11.99 *(978-1-4169-6167-3(4),* Aladdin) Simon & Schuster Children's Publishing.
—The Curse of Cuddles McGee. 2008. (ENG.). 272p. (J). (gr. 3-7). pap. 12.99 *(978-1-4169-6450-6(9),* Simon & Schuster/Paula Wiseman Bks.) Simon & Schuster/Paula Wiseman Bks.
Edwards, Gareth. Never Ask a Dinosaur to Dinner. Parker-Rees, Guy, illus. 2015. (ENG.). 32p. (J). (gr. -1-k). 17.99 *(978-0-545-81296-2(8),* Scholastic Pr.) Scholastic, Inc.
Eglington, Tara. How to Keep a Boy from Kissing You. 2016. (ENG.). 320p. (YA). 18.99 *(978-1-250-04953-7(9),* 9781250049537) St. Martin's Pr.
Ehlert, Lois. RRRalph. Ehlert, Lois, illus. 2011. (ENG., Illus.). 40p. (J). (gr. -1-1). 17.99 *(978-1-4424-1305-4(0),* Beach Lane Bks.) Beach Lane Bks.
Ehrenhaft, Daniel. Friend Is Not a Verb. 2010. (ENG.). 256p. (YA). (gr. 8-18). 16.99 *(978-0-06-113106-6(7),* HarperTeen) HarperCollins Pubs.
Einstein, James Allan. Gross & Disgusting Jokes for Kids, 1 vol. 2014. (ENG.). 120p. (J). pap. 9.95 *(978-1-926700-45-8(7),* 9781926700458) Blue Bike Bks. CAN. Dist: Lone Pine Publishing USA.
—Hockey Jokes for Kids, 1 vol. 2014. (ENG.). 120p. (J). pap. 9.95 *(978-1-926700-47-2(3),* 9781926700472) Blue Bike Bks. CAN. Dist: Lone Pine Publishing USA.
—Kids Only Jokes, 1 vol. 2014. (ENG.). 120p. (J). pap. 9.95 *(978-1-926700-48-9(1),* 9781926700489) Blue Bike Bks. CAN. Dist: Lone Pine Publishing USA.
Eland, Lindsay. Scones & Sensibility. 2010. (ENG.). 320p. (J). (gr. 4-7). 6.99 *(978-1-60684-158-7(0),* Carolrhoda Bks.) Lerner Publishing Group.
Elfakir, Mahamad Ali. Blueberry Bubble Gum. 2013. 44p. 16.95 *(978-0-578-10978-7(6))* Elfa Bks.
Eliot, Jan. The First Collection of the Syndicated Cartoon Strip, No. 1. 2004. 128p. pap. 10.95 *(978-0-9674102-2-7(3))* Four Panel Pr.
Elish, Dan. The Attack of the Frozen Woodchucks. Call, Greg, illus. 2008. (ENG.). 256p. (J). (gr. 3-7). 16.99 *(978-0-06-113870-6(3),* Geringer, Laura Book) HarperCollins Pubs.
Ellen, Raskin. The Westing Game. 2014. (Puffin Modern Classics Ser.). (ENG.). 192p. (J). (gr. 5-12). 12.24 *(978-1-63245-142-2(5))* Lectorum Pubns., Inc.
Elliott, David. This Orq. (He Cave Boy.) Nichols, Lori, illus. 2014. (ENG.). 40p. (J). (gr. -1-2). 15.95 *(978-1-62091-521-9(9))* Boyds Mills Pr.
—Wuv Bunnies from Outers Pace. Long, Ethan, illus. 2008. (ENG.). (J). 108p. (gr. 4-7). pap. 6.95 *(978-0-8234-2183-1(X));* 112p. (gr. 2-4). 16.95 *(978-0-8234-1902-9(9))* Holiday Hse., Inc.
Elliott, R. Kenley. Stories from a Kentucky Boy. 2012. 74p. pap. 12.95 *(978-1-4772-5429-5(3))* AuthorHouse.
Ellis, Kathy. Mrs. Upside down & Her House. 2013. 32p. pap. 16.99 *(978-1-4525-8283-2(1),* Balboa Pr.) Author Solutions, Inc.
Ellison, Joy D. Carol & Connie. 2008. 28p. per. 24.95 *(978-1-4241-9276-2(5))* America Star Bks.
Emberley, Ed & Emberley, Rebecca. Red Hen. Emberley, Ed, illus. 2010. (ENG., Illus.). 32p. (J). (gr. -1-2). 18.99 *(978-1-59643-492-9(9),* 9781596434929) Roaring Brook Pr.
Emily, Katelyn. The Treasure-Trove Tales at the Gazebo. 2009. 120p. 18.95 *(978-1-59858-940-5(7));* pap. 8.95 *(978-1-59858-855-2(9))* Dog Ear Publishing, LLC.
Emmett, Jonathan. The Santa Trap, 1 vol. Bernatene, Poly, illus. 2012. (ENG.). 32p. (J). 15.95 *(978-1-56145-670-3(5))* Peachtree Pubs.
Emmett, Jonathan & Dunn, David H. The Princess & the Pig. Bernatene, Poly, illus. 2011. (ENG.). 32p. (J). (gr. k-8). 17.99 *(978-0-8027-2334-5(9),* 9780802723345, Bloomsbury USA Childrens) Bloomsbury Publishing USA.
Emzer, Counselor. Duane, You Must be Insane. 2005. 20p. 7.97 *(978-1-4116-3091-8(2))* Lulu Pr., Inc.
Enderle, Dotti. Book 13: Yo Ho No!, 1 vol. 2014. (Ghost Detectors Set 3 Ser.). (ENG., Illus.). 80p. (J). (gr. 2-5). lib. bdg. 27.07 *(978-1-62402-001-8(1),* Calico Chapter Bks) Magic Wagon.
—Book 14: Plop!, 1 vol. 2014. (Ghost Detectors Set 3 Ser.). (ENG., Illus.). 80p. (J). (gr. 2-5). lib. bdg. 27.07 *(978-1-62402-002-5(X),* Calico Chapter Bks) Magic Wagon.
—Book 15: Rock & Roll!, 1 vol. 2014. (Ghost Detectors Set 3 Ser.). (ENG., Illus.). 80p. (J). (gr. 2-5). lib. bdg. 27.07 *(978-1-62402-003-2(8),* Calico Chapter Bks) Magic Wagon.
—Book 16: Abracadabra!, 1 vol. 2014. (Ghost Detectors Set 3 Ser.). (ENG., Illus.). 80p. (J). (gr. 2-5). lib. bdg. 27.07 *(978-1-62402-004-9(6),* Calico Chapter Bks) Magic Wagon.
—Book 17: Grow a Ghost! 2014. (Ghost Detectors Set 3 Ser.). 80p. (J). (gr. 2-5). lib. bdg. 27.07 *(978-1-62402-005-6(4),* Calico Chapter Bks) Magic Wagon.
—Book 18: Spaced Out! 2014. (Ghost Detectors Set 3 Ser.). 80p. (J). (gr. 2-5). lib. bdg. 27.07 *(978-1-62402-006-3(2),* Calico Chapter Bks) Magic Wagon.
—Gingerbread Man Superhero!, 1 vol. Kulka, Joe, illus. 2009. (ENG.). 32p. (J). (gr. k-3). 16.99 *(978-1-58980-521-7(6))* Pelican Publishing Co., Inc.
—Grow a Ghost!, 1 vol. McWilliam, Howard, illus. 2016. (ENG.). 80p. (J). *(978-1-62402-100-8(X))* Magic Wagon.
—Spaced Out!, 1 vol. McWilliam, Howard, illus. 2016. (ENG.). 80p. (J). *(978-1-62402-101-5(8))* Magic Wagon.
—Tell No One!, 1 vol. McWilliam, Howard, illus. 2010. (Ghost Detectors Ser.: No. 1). (ENG.). 80p. (J). (gr. 2-5). 27.07 *(978-1-60270-692-7(1))* Magic Wagon.
Enderle, Dotti & McWilliam, Howard. Ghost Detectors Book 12: Monsters!, 1 vol. 2012. (Ghost Detectors Ser.). (ENG., Illus.). 80p. (J). (gr. 2-5). 27.07 *(978-1-61641-628-7(9))* Magic Wagon.
—Ghost Detectors Book 7: Pop!, 1 vol. 2012. (Ghost Detectors Ser.). (ENG., Illus.). 80p. (J). (gr. 2-5). 27.07 *(978-1-61641-623-2(8))* Magic Wagon.
—Ghost Detectors Book 9: Never! Never! Never!, 1 vol. 2012. (Ghost Detectors Ser.). (ENG., Illus.). 80p. (J). (gr. 2-5). 27.07 *(978-1-61641-625-6(4))* Magic Wagon.
English, David. Confessions of a Dedicated Englishman, 1. unabr. ed. 2006. (ENG., Illus.). 352p. 44.50 *(978-1-4050-5361-7(5))* Macmillan Pubs., Ltd. GBR. Dist: Trans-Atlantic Pubns., Inc.
Enriquez, Jose. Saving the Mango Farm. 2006. 23p. (J). 10.98 *(978-1-4116-5917-9(1))* Lulu Pr., Inc.
Erickson, John R. The Case of the Black-Hooded Hangmans. Holmes, Gerald L., illus. 2011. (Hank the Cowdog Ser.). (ENG.). 113p. (J). (gr. 3-6). pap. 5.99 *(978-1-59188-124-7(2))* Maverick Bks., Inc.
—The Case of the Blazing Sky. Holmes, Gerald L., illus. 2011. (Hank the Cowdog Ser.). (ENG.). 129p. (J). (gr. 3-6). pap. 5.99 *(978-1-59188-151-3(X))* Maverick Bks., Inc.
—The Case of the Booby-Trapped Pickup. Holmes, Gerald L., illus. 2011. (Hank the Cowdog Ser.). (ENG.). 129p. (J). (gr. 3-6). pap. 5.99 *(978-1-59188-149-0(8))* Maverick Bks., Inc.
—The Case of the Burrowing Robot. Holmes, Gerald L., illus. 2011. (Hank the Cowdog Ser.). (ENG.). 125p. (J). (gr. 3-6). pap. 5.99 *(978-1-59188-142-1(0))* Maverick Bks., Inc.
—The Case of the Car-Barkaholic Dog. Holmes, Gerald L., illus. 2011. (Hank the Cowdog Ser.). (ENG.). 115p. (J). (gr. 3-6). pap. 5.99 *(978-1-59188-117-9(X))* Maverick Bks., Inc.
—The Case of the Coyote Invasion. Holmes, Gerald L., illus. 2011. (Hank the Cowdog Ser.: No. 56). (ENG.). 132p. (J). (gr. 3-6). pap. 5.99 *(978-1-59188-156-8(0))* Maverick Bks., Inc.
—The Case of the Deadly Ha-Ha Game. Holmes, Gerald L., illus. 2011. (Hank the Cowdog Ser.). (ENG.). 128p. (J). (gr. 3-6). pap. 5.99 *(978-1-59188-137-7(4))* Maverick Bks., Inc.
—The Case of the Dinosaur Birds. Holmes, Gerald L., illus. 2011. (Hank the Cowdog Ser.). (ENG.). 125p. (J). (gr. 3-6). pap. 5.99 *(978-1-59188-154-4(4))* Maverick Bks., Inc.
—The Case of the Double Bumblebee Sting. Holmes, Gerald L., illus. 2011. (Hank the Cowdog Ser.: No. 22). (ENG.). 114p. (J). (gr. 3-6). pap. 5.99 *(978-1-59188-122-3(6))* Maverick Bks., Inc.
—The Case of the Falling Sky. Holmes, Gerald L., illus. 2011. (Hank the Cowdog Ser.: No. 45). (ENG.). 129p. (J). (gr. 3-6). pap. 5.99 *(978-1-59188-145-2(5))* Maverick Bks., Inc.
—The Case of the Fiddle-Playing Fox. Holmes, Gerald L., illus. 2011. (Hank the Cowdog Ser.: No. 12). (ENG.). 118p. (J). (gr. 3-6). pap. 5.99 *(978-1-59188-112-4(9))* Maverick Bks., Inc.
—The Case of the Halloween Ghost. Holmes, Gerald L., illus. 2011. (Hank the Cowdog Ser.). (ENG.). 123p. (J). (gr. 3-6). pap. 5.99 *(978-1-59188-109-4(9))* Maverick Bks., Inc.
—The Case of the Haystack Kitties. Holmes, Gerald L., illus. 2011. (Hank the Cowdog Ser.). (ENG.). 123p. (J). (gr. 3-6). pap. 5.99 *(978-1-59188-130-8(7))* Maverick Bks., Inc.
—The Case of the Hooking Bull. Holmes, Gerald L., illus. 2011. (Hank the Cowdog Ser.). (ENG.). 119p. (J). (gr. 3-6). pap. 5.99 *(978-1-59188-118-6(8))* Maverick Bks., Inc.
—The Case of the Kidnapped Collie. Holmes, Gerald L., illus. 2011. (Hank the Cowdog Ser.). (ENG.). 113p. (J). (gr. 3-6). pap. 5.99 *(978-1-59188-126-1(9))* Maverick Bks., Inc.
—The Case of the Measled Cowboy. Holmes, Gerald L., illus. 2011. (Hank the Cowdog Ser.: No. 33). (ENG.). 126p. (J). (gr. 3-6). pap. 5.99 *(978-1-59188-133-9(1))* Maverick Bks., Inc.
—The Case of the Midnight Rustler. Holmes, Gerald L., illus. 2011. (Hank the Cowdog Ser.: No. 19). (ENG.). 113p. (J). (gr. 3-6). pap. 5.99 *(978-1-59188-119-3(6))* Maverick Bks., Inc.
—The Case of the Missing Bird Dog. Holmes, Gerald L., illus. 2011. (Hank the Cowdog Ser.: No. 40). (ENG.). 126p. (J). (gr. 3-6). pap. 5.99 *(978-1-59188-140-7(4))* Maverick Bks., Inc.
—The Case of the Missing Cat. Holmes, Gerald L., illus. 2011. (Hank the Cowdog Ser.: No. 15). (ENG.). 114p. (J). (gr. 3-6). pap. 5.99 *(978-1-59188-115-5(3))* Maverick Bks., Inc.
—The Case of the Monkey Burglar. Holmes, Gerald L., illus. 2011. (Hank the Cowdog Ser.: No. 48). (ENG.). 129p. (J). (gr. 3-6). pap. 5.99 *(978-1-59188-148-3(X))* Maverick Bks., Inc.
—The Case of the Most Ancient Bone. Holmes, Gerald L., illus. 2011. (Hank the Cowdog Ser.). (ENG.). 239p. (J). (gr. 3-6). pap. 5.99 *(978-1-59188-150-6(1))* Maverick Bks., Inc.
—The Case of the Mysterious Voice. Holmes, Gerald L., illus. 2012. (Hank the Cowdog (Quality) Ser.: Vol. 58). (ENG.). 123p. (J). (gr. 3-6). pap. 5.99 *(978-1-59188-158-2(7))* Maverick Bks., Inc.
—The Case of the Night-Stalking Bone Monster. Holmes, Gerald L., illus. 2011. (Hank the Cowdog Ser.). (ENG.). 115p. (J). (gr. 3-6). pap. 5.99 *(978-1-59188-127-8(7))* Maverick Bks., Inc.
—The Case of the One-Eyed Killer Stud Horse. Holmes, Gerald L., illus. 2011. (Hank the Cowdog Ser.: No. 8). (ENG.). 120p. (J). (gr. 3-6). pap. 5.99 *(978-1-59188-108-7(0))* Maverick Bks., Inc.
—The Case of the Perfect Dog. Holmes, Gerald L., illus. 2012. 127p. (J). *(978-1-59188-259-6(1))* Maverick Bks.
—The Case of the Perfect Dog. Holmes, Gerald L., illus. 2012. (Hank the Cowdog (Quality) Ser.). (ENG.). 127p. (J). (gr. 3-6). pap. 5.99 *(978-1-59188-159-9(5))* Maverick Bks., Inc.
—The Case of the Raging Rottweiler. Holmes, Gerald L., illus. 2011. (Hank the Cowdog Ser.). (ENG.). 131p. (J). (gr. 3-6). pap. 5.99 *(978-1-59188-136-0(6))* Maverick Bks., Inc.
—The Case of the Saddle House Robbery. Holmes, Gerald L., illus. 2011. (Hank the Cowdog Ser.: No. 35). (ENG.). 125p. (J). (gr. 3-6). pap. 5.99 *(978-1-59188-135-3(8))* Maverick Bks., Inc.
—The Case of the Secret Weapon. Holmes, Gerald L., illus. 2011. (Hank the Cowdog Ser.). (ENG.). 125p. (J). (gr. 3-6). pap. 5.99 *(978-1-59188-155-1(2))* Maverick Bks., Inc.
—The Case of the Shipwrecked Tree. Holmes, Gerald L., illus. 2011. (Hank the Cowdog Ser.: No. 41). (ENG.). 119p. (J). (gr. 3-6). pap. 5.99 *(978-1-59188-141-4(2))* Maverick Bks., Inc.
—The Case of the Swirling Killer Tornado. Holmes, Gerald L., illus. 2011. (Hank the Cowdog Ser.). (ENG.). 112p. (J). (gr. 3-6). pap. 5.99 *(978-1-59188-125-4(0))* Maverick Bks., Inc.
—The Case of the Tender Cheeping Chickies. Holmes, Gerald L., illus. 2011. (Hank the Cowdog Ser.). (ENG.). 129p. (J). (gr. 3-6). pap. 5.99 *(978-1-59188-147-6(1))* Maverick Bks., Inc.
—The Case of the Three Rings. Holmes, Gerald L., illus. 2014. 124p. (J). pap. *(978-1-59188-164-3(1))* Maverick Bks., Inc.
—The Case of the Tricky Trap. Holmes, Gerald L., illus. 2011. (Hank the Cowdog Ser.). (ENG.). 126p. (J). (gr. 3-6). pap. 5.99 *(978-1-59188-146-9(3))* Maverick Bks., Inc.
—The Case of the Twisted Kitty. Holmes, Gerald L., illus. 2004. (Hank the Cowdog Ser.: No. 43). 131p. (J). lib. bdg. 17.00 *(978-1-4242-1600-0(1))* Fitzgerald Bks.
—The Case of the Twisted Kitty. Holmes, Gerald L., illus. 2011. (Hank the Cowdog Ser.). (ENG.). 131p. (J). (gr. 3-6). pap. 5.99 *(978-1-59188-143-8(9))* Maverick Bks., Inc.
—The Case of the Vampire Cat. Holmes, Gerald L., illus. 2011. (Hank the Cowdog Ser.). (ENG.). 115p. (J). (gr. 3-6). pap. 5.99 *(978-1-59188-121-6(8))* Maverick Bks., Inc.
—The Case of the Vampire Vacuum Sweeper. Holmes, Gerald L., illus. 2011. (Hank the Cowdog Ser.). (ENG.). 119p. (J). (gr. 3-6). pap. 5.99 *(978-1-59188-129-2(3))* Maverick Bks., Inc.
—The Case of the Vanishing Fishhook. Holmes, Gerald L., illus. 2011. (Hank the Cowdog Ser.: No. 31). (ENG.). 124p. (J). (gr. 3-6). pap. 5.99 *(978-1-59188-131-5(5))* Maverick Bks., Inc.
—The Curse of the Incredible Priceless Corncob. Holmes, Gerald L., illus. 2011. (Hank the Cowdog Ser.: No. 7). (ENG.). 127p. (J). (gr. 3-6). pap. 5.99 *(978-1-59188-107-0(2))* Maverick Bks., Inc.
—The Disappearance of Drover. Holmes, Gerald L., illus. 2011. (Hank the Cowdog Ser.). (ENG.). 122p. (J). (gr. 3-6). pap. 5.99 *(978-1-59188-157-5(9))* Maverick Bks., Inc.
—The Dungeon of Doom. Holmes, Gerald L., illus. 2004. (Hank the Cowdog Ser.: No. 44). 122p. (J). lib. bdg. 17.00 *(978-1-4242-1601-7(X))* Fitzgerald Bks.
—The Dungeon of Doom. Holmes, Gerald L., illus. 2011. (Hank the Cowdog Ser.). (ENG.). 122p. (J). (gr. 3-6). pap. 5.99 *(978-1-59188-144-5(7))* Maverick Bks., Inc.
—Every Dog Has His Day. Holmes, Gerald L., illus. 2011. (Hank the Cowdog Ser.). (ENG.). 118p. (J). (gr. 3-6). pap. 5.99 *(978-1-59188-110-0(2))* Maverick Bks., Inc.
—Faded Love. Holmes, Gerald L., illus. 2011. (Hank the Cowdog Ser.: No. 5). (ENG.). 125p. (J). (gr. 3-6). pap. 5.99 *(978-1-59188-105-6(6))* Maverick Bks., Inc.
—The Fling. Holmes, Gerald L., illus. 2011. (Hank the Cowdog Ser.). (ENG.). 126p. (J). (gr. 3-6). pap. 5.99 *(978-1-59188-138-4(2))* Maverick Bks., Inc.
—The Garbage Monster from Outer Space. Holmes, Gerald L., illus. 2011. (Hank the Cowdog Ser.). (ENG.). 126p. (J). (gr. 3-6). pap. 5.99 *(978-1-59188-132-2(3))* Maverick Bks., Inc.
—Hank Cowdog 50. Holmes, Gerald L., illus. 2007. 256p. 16.99 *(978-0-670-62249-8(4),* Viking Adult) Penguin Publishing Group.
—Hank the Cowdog & Monkey Business. Holmes, Gerald L., illus. 2011. (Hank the Cowdog Ser.). (ENG.). 110p. (J). (gr. 3-6). pap. 5.99 *(978-1-59188-114-8(5))* Maverick Bks., Inc.
—It's a Dog's Life. Holmes, Gerald L., illus. (Hank the Cowdog Ser.: No. 3). (J). 100p. (gr. 2-5). 9.95 *(978-0-916941-04-8(3));* 2011. (ENG.). 127p. (gr. 3-6). pap. 5.99 *(978-1-59188-103-2(X))* Maverick Bks., Inc.
—Let Sleeping Dogs Lie. Holmes, Gerald L., illus. 2011. (Hank the Cowdog Ser.: No. 6). (ENG.). 129p. (J). (gr. 3-6). pap. 5.99 *(978-1-59188-106-3(4))* Maverick Bks., Inc.
—Lost in the Blinded Blizzard. Holmes, Gerald L., illus. 2011. (Hank the Cowdog Ser.). (ENG.). 115p. (J). (gr. 3-6). pap. 5.99 *(978-1-59188-116-2(1))* Maverick Bks., Inc.
—Lost in the Dark Unchanted Forest. Holmes, Gerald L., illus. 2011. (Hank the Cowdog Ser.). (ENG.). 124p. (J). (gr. 3-6). pap. 5.99 *(978-1-59188-111-7(0))* Maverick Bks., Inc.
—Moonlight Madness. Holmes, Gerald L., illus. 2011. (Hank the Cowdog Ser.: No. 23). (ENG.). 114p. (J). (gr. 3-6). pap. 5.99 *(978-1-59188-123-0(4))* Maverick Bks., Inc.
—The Mopwater Files. Holmes, Gerald L., illus. 2011. (Hank the Cowdog Ser.). (ENG.). 111p. (J). (gr. 3-6). pap. 5.99 *(978-1-59188-128-5(5))* Maverick Bks., Inc.
—Murder in the Middle Pasture. Holmes, Gerald L., illus. 2011. (Hank the Cowdog Ser.). (ENG.). 120p. (J). (gr. 3-6). pap. 5.99 *(978-1-59188-104-9(8))* Maverick Bks., Inc.
—The Original Adventures of Hank the Cowdog. Holmes, Gerald L., illus. (ENG.). 127p. (J). (gr. 3-6). 2012. (Hank the Cowdog Ser.: Vol. 1). 15.99 *(978-1-59188-201-5(X))* 2011. (Hank the Cowdog Ser.: No. 1). pap. 5.99 *(978-1-59188-101-8(3))* Maverick Bks., Inc.
—The Phantom in the Mirror. Holmes, Gerald L., illus. 2011. (Hank the Cowdog Ser.: No. 20). (ENG.). 114p. (J). (gr. 3-6). pap. 5.99 *(978-1-59188-120-9(X))* Maverick Bks., Inc.
—The Quest for the Great White Quail. Holmes, Gerald L., illus. 2011. (Hank the Cowdog Ser.). (ENG.). 123p. (J). (gr. 3-6). pap. 5.99 *(978-1-59188-152-0(8))* Maverick Bks., Inc.
—The Return of the Charlie Monsters. Holmes, Gerald L., illus. 2014. 128p. (J). pap. *(978-1-59188-163-6(3))* Maverick Bks., Inc.
—The Secret Laundry Monster Files. Holmes, Gerald L., illus. 2011. (Hank the Cowdog Ser.). (ENG.). 128p. (J). (gr. 3-6). pap. 5.99 *(978-1-59188-139-1(0))* Maverick Bks., Inc.
—Slim's Good-Bye. Holmes, Gerald L., illus. 2011. (Hank the Cowdog Ser.). (ENG.). 132p. (J). (gr. 3-6). pap. 5.99 *(978-1-59188-134-6(X))* Maverick Bks., Inc.
—The Wounded Buzzard on Christmas Eve. Holmes, Gerald L., illus. 2011. (Hank the Cowdog Ser.: No. 13). (ENG.). 112p. (J). (gr. 3-6). pap. 5.99 *(978-1-59188-113-1(7))* Maverick Bks., Inc.
Erickson, John R. & Holmes, Gerald L., illus. The Case of the Prowling Bear. 2013. 126p. (J). *(978-1-59188-261-9(3));* pap. *(978-1-59188-161-2(7))* Maverick Bks.
Ericson, Nora. Dill & Bizzy: An Odd Duck & a Strange Bird. Ericson, Lisa, illus. 2016. 40p. (J). (gr. -1-3). 17.99 *(978-0-06-230452-0(6))* HarperCollins Pubs.
Ernst, Lisa Campbell. The Gingerbread Girl. Ernst, Lisa Campbell, illus. 2009. (Illus.). 32p. (J). (gr. -1-k). pap. 6.99 *(978-0-14-241448-4(4),* Puffin) Penguin Publishing Group.
—The Gingerbread Girl. Ernst, Lisa Campbell, illus. 2006. (ENG., Illus.). 32p. (J). (gr. -1-k). 16.99 *(978-0-525-47667-2(9),* Dutton Books for Young Readers) Penguin Young Readers Group.
Escoffier, Michaël. A Mammoth in the Fridge. 2013. (ENG.). 36p. 16.95 *(978-1-877579-50-9(5))* 21st Century Publishing.
Essence, Angel. The Amazing Adventures of Callie the Cat: The Long Night. 2012. 28p. pap. 19.99 *(978-1-4772-9907-4(6))* AuthorHouse.
Everett Hale, Edward. Last of the Peterkins with Others of the. 2006. pap. *(978-1-4068-1087-5(8))* Echo Library.
Facey, La-Toya S. Brielle-Elaine Tries to Fit In! 2011. 24p. pap. 14.99 *(978-1-4634-2353-7(5))* AuthorHouse.
Fagan, Cary. Directed by Kaspar Snit. 2007. (ENG.). 160p. (J). (gr. 3-7). per. 9.95 *(978-0-88776-753-1(2),* Tundra Bks.) Tundra Bks. CAN. Dist: Penguin Random Hse. LLC.
—I Wish I Could Draw, 1 vol. 2014. (ENG., Illus.). 32p. (J). (gr. k-3). 12.95 *(978-1-55498-318-6(5))* Groundwood Bks. CAN. Dist: Publishers Group West (PGW).
—Jacob Two-Two on the High Seas. Petricic, Dusan, illus. 2009. (Jacob Two-Two Ser.). (ENG.). 112p. (J). (gr. 4-7). 10.95 *(978-0-88776-895-8(4),* Tundra Bks.) Tundra Bks. CAN. Dist: Penguin Random Hse. LLC.
—Oy, Feh, So?, 1 vol. Clement, Gary, illus. 2013. (ENG.). 40p. (J). (gr. -1-3). 17.95 *(978-1-55498-148-9(4))* Groundwood Bks. CAN. Dist: Publishers Group West (PGW).
—Thing-Thing. Debon, Nicolas, illus. 2008. (ENG.). 32p. (J). (gr. -1-1). 18.95 *(978-0-88776-839-2(3),* Tundra Bks.) Tundra Bks. CAN. Dist: Penguin Random Hse. LLC.
Fairgray, Richard & Jones, Terry. Gorillas in Our Midst. 2015. (ENG., Illus.). 32p. (J). (gr. -1-k). 16.99 *(978-1-63220-607-7(2),* Sky Pony Pr.) Skyhorse Publishing Co., Inc.
Fairgray, Richard & Jones, Terry, illus. My Grandpa Is a Dinosaur. 2016. (ENG.). 32p. (J). (gr. -1-k). 16.99 *(978-1-63450-632-8(4),* Sky Pony Pr.) Skyhorse Publishing Co., Inc.
Falatko, Julie. Snappsy the Alligator (Did Not Ask to Be in This Book) Miller, Tim J., illus. 2016. (ENG.). 40p. (J). (gr. -1-3). 16.99 *(978-0-451-46945-8(3),* Viking Books for Young Readers) Penguin Young Readers Group.
Falconer, Ian. Olivia fait son Cirque. (Olivia Ser.). 29.95 *(978-2-02-051642-6(X))* Editions du Seuil FRA. Dist: Distribooks, Inc.
Fallon, Joe & Scarborough, Ken. Halfway Hank. Davis, Jack E., illus. 2005. 40p. (J). 15.99 *(978-0-06-623636-0(3))* HarperCollins Pubs.
Farley, Donna. The Ravens of Farne: A Tale of Saint Cuthbert. 2010. 32p. pap. 14.95 *(978-0-9822770-5-8(9))* Ancient Faith Publishing.
Farley, Jan. Griffin & Griseld: Book 3 in the Fleur Series. 2011. 84p. pap. 19.95 *(978-1-4626-3592-4(X))* America Star Bks.
Farrell, Darren. Thank You, Octopus. 2014. (ENG.). 40p. (J). (gr. -1-k). 16.99 *(978-0-8037-3438-8(7),* Dial Bks) Penguin Young Readers Group.
Farrelly, Linda. Elliot's Amazing Adventures Number 1. Farrelly, Linda & Hopkins, Simon, illus. 2013. 52p. pap. *(978-0-9560331-5-4(6))* Childrens' Story Pubs.
Farrey, Brian. The Shadowhand Covenant. Helquist, Brett, illus. 2013. (Vengekeep Prophecies Ser.: 2). (ENG.). 384p. (J). (gr. 3-7). 16.99 *(978-0-06-204931-5(3))* HarperCollins Pubs.
Farrington Wilson, Lynda. Squirmy Wormy: How I Learned to Help Myself. 2009. (ENG., Illus.). 32p. (gr. 1). pap. 14.95 *(978-1-935567-18-9(7),* 9781935567189) Sensory Resources.
Fearing, Mark. Dilly Dally Daisy. 2015. (ENG., Illus.). 32p. (J). (gr. -1-k). 16.99 *(978-0-8037-4065-5(4),* Dial Bks) Penguin Young Readers Group.
—The Great Thanksgiving Escape. Fearing, Mark, illus. 2014. (ENG., Illus.). 32p. (J). (gr. k-3). 15.99 *(978-0-7636-6306-3(9))* Candlewick Pr.
Fearnley, Jan. Mr Wolf's Pancakes. 2008. (ENG., Illus.). 32p. (J). (gr. -1-2). 12.95 *(978-1-4052-3872-4(0))* Egmont Bks., Ltd. GBR. Dist: Independent Pubs. Group.
Federle, Tim. Better Nate Than Ever. 2014. lib. bdg. 18.40 *(978-0-606-35430-1(1))* Turtleback Bks.
Feierabend, John M. & Poulin, Ashley. Risseldy, Rosseldy. 2012. (First Steps in Music Ser.). (ENG., Illus.). 32p. (J). (gr. k-2). 16.95 *(978-1-57999-902-5(6))* G I A Pubns., Inc.
Feiffer, Jules. Bark, George. 2004. 29.95 *(978-1-55592-700-4(9))* Weston Woods Studios, Inc.
—By the Side of the Road. 2005. (Illus.). 59p. (J). (gr. k-4). reprint ed. 16.00 *(978-0-7567-9371-5(8))* DIANE Publishing Co.
—A Room with a Zoo. Feiffer, Jules, illus. 2007. (ENG., Illus.). 192p. (gr. 2-7). per. 7.99 *(978-0-7868-3703-8(9),* di Capua, Michael Bks.) Hyperion Bks. for Children.
Feiffer, Kate. But I Wanted a Baby Brother! Goode, Diane, illus. 2010. (ENG.). 32p. (J). (gr. -1-3). 16.99 *(978-1-4169-3941-2(5),* Simon & Schuster/Paula Wiseman Bks.) Simon & Schuster/Paula Wiseman Bks.
—Henry the Dog with No Tail. Feiffer, Jules, illus. 2007. (ENG.). 32p. (J). (gr. -1-3). 18.99 *(978-1-4169-1614-7(8),* Simon &

Schuster/Paula Wiseman Bks.) Simon & Schuster/Paula Wiseman Bks.

—My Mom Is Trying to Ruin My Life. Goode, Diane, illus. 2009. (ENG.). 32p. (J). (gr. -1-3). 18.99 (978-1-4169-4100-2(2), Simon & Schuster/Paula Wiseman Bks.) Simon & Schuster/Paula Wiseman Bks.

—President Pennybaker. Goode, Diane, illus. 2012. (ENG.). 32p. (J). (gr. -1-3). 7.99 (978-1-4169-1355-9(6), Simon & Schuster/Paula Wiseman Bks.) Simon & Schuster/Paula Wiseman Bks.

—President Pennybaker. Glasser, Robin Preiss & Goode, Diane, illus. 2008. (ENG.). 32p. (J). (gr. -1-3). 16.99 (978-1-4169-1354-2(8), Simon & Schuster/Paula Wiseman Bks.) Simon & Schuster/Paula Wiseman Bks.

—The Problem with the Puddles. Tusa, Tricia, illus. 2009. (ENG.). 208p. (J). (gr. 3-7). 16.99 (978-1-4169-4961-9(5), Simon & Schuster/Paula Wiseman Bks.) Simon & Schuster/Paula Wiseman Bks.

—Which Puppy? Feiffer, Kate & Feiffer, Jules, illus. 2009. (ENG.). 32p. (J). (gr. -1-3). 16.99 (978-1-4169-9147-2(6), Simon & Schuster/Paula Wiseman Bks.) Simon & Schuster/Paula Wiseman Bks.

—The Wild, Wild Inside: A View from Mommy's Tummy! Huliska-Beith, Laura, illus. 2010. (ENG.). 32p. (J). (gr. -1-3). 15.99 (978-1-4169-4099-9(5), Simon & Schuster/Paula Wiseman Bks.) Simon & Schuster/Paula Wiseman Bks.

Feit, Maureen. Letters & Laughs from a to Z. 2009. (Illus.). 52p. pap. 22.50 (978-1-4490-2527-4(7)) AuthorHouse.

Fell, Amy. Two Terrible Eaters. 2012. 72p. pap. (978-1-105-43640-6(3)) Lulu.com.

Fenske, Jonathan. Guppy Up! Fenske, Jonathan, illus. 2013. (Penguin Young Readers, Level 1 Ser.). (ENG., Illus.). 32p. (J). (gr. k-1). mass mkt. 3.99 (978-0-448-49646-7(1), Penguin Young Readers) Penguin Young Readers Group.

—Guppy Up! 2013. (Penguin Young Readers Level 1 Ser.). lib. bdg. 13.55 (978-0-606-28736-4(1), Turtleback) Turtleback Bks.

Fenske, Jonathan & Bader, Bonnie. A Pig, a Fox, & a Box. Fenske, Jonathan, illus. 2015. (Penguin Young Readers, Level 2 Ser.). (ENG., Illus.). 32p. (J). (gr. 1-2). 3.99 (978-0-448-48510-2(9), Penguin Young Readers) Penguin Young Readers Group.

Ferraiolo, Jack D. The Big Splash. 2008. (ENG.). 288p. (YA). (gr. 5-9). 16.95 (978-0-8109-7067-0(8), Amulet Bks.) Abrams, Inc.

Ferriell, Phil. Bernie Bocks Makes the Team. 2007. 86p. 16.95 (978-1-4241-4991-9(6)) PublishAmerica, Inc.

Ferris, Jean. Once upon a Marigold. 2004. 275p. (gr. 5). 17.00 (978-0-7569-3613-6(6)) Perfection Learning Corp.

—Once upon a Marigold: Part Comedy, Part Love Story, Part Everything-but-the-kitchen-Sink. 2013. (ENG.). 288p. (J). (gr. 2-5). pap. 7.99 (978-0-544-05400-4(8)) Houghton Mifflin Harcourt Publishing Co.

—Thrice upon a Marigold: A Royal Kidnapping Caper. 2014. (ENG.). 256p. (J). (gr. 2-5). pap. 6.99 (978-0-544-30262-4(1), HMH Books For Young Readers) Houghton Mifflin Harcourt Publishing Co.

—Twice upon a Marigold. 2013. (ENG.). 304p. (J). (gr. 2-5). pap. 7.99 (978-0-544-05098-3(3)) Houghton Mifflin Harcourt Publishing Co.

Fields, Bryan W. Lunchbox & the Aliens. Atteberry, Kevan, illus. 2009. (Froonga Ser.). (ENG.). 208p. (J). (gr. 4-7). pap. 11.99 (978-0-312-56115-4(6), 9780312561154) Square Fish.

Fine, Anne. Countdown. 2006. (Yellow Bananas Ser.). (ENG., Illus.). 48p. (J). (gr. -1-3). (978-0-7787-1004-2(1)) Crabtree Publishing Co.

—Hole in the Road. 2014. (Read On Ser.). (ENG., Illus.). 48p. (J). (gr. 5). 9.99 (978-0-00-746481-4(9)) HarperCollins Pubs. Ltd. GBR. Dist: Independent Pubs. Group.

Finney, Patricia. I, Jack. Bailey, Peter, illus. 2004. 192p. (J). 15.99 (978-0-06-052207-0(0)); lib. bdg. 16.89 (978-0-06-052208-7(9)) HarperCollins Pubs.

Finzo. It So Happens. 2016. (ENG., Illus.). 68p. (J). (gr. k-3). 17.99 (978-0-9942895-0-6(2)) Berbay Publishing AUS. Dist: Independent Pubs. Group.

Fischer, Debbie Reed. This Is Not the Abby Show. 2016. (ENG.). 320p. (J). (gr. 4-7). 16.99 (978-0-553-53634-8(6), Delacorte Bks. for Young Readers) Random Hse. Children's Bks.

Fischer, Ellen. If an Armadillo Went to a Restaurant. Wood, Laura, illus. 2014. (ENG.). 32p. (J). (-2). 14.95 (978-1-938063-39-8(2), Mighty Media Kids) Mighty Media Pr.

—If an Elephant Went to School. Wood, Laura, illus. 2015. (ENG.). 32p. (J). (-2). 14.95 (978-1-938063-61-9(9), Mighty Media Kids) Mighty Media Pr.

Fishbone, Greg. The Penguins of Doom. 2007. (From the Desk of Septina Nash Ser.). (ENG., Illus.). 182p. (J). (gr. 2-7). 13.95 (978-1-933831-03-9(0)) Blooming Tree Pr.

Fishel, Dennis. Russell's Revenge, 1. 2005. (YA). 17.95 (978-0-9763398-2-3(X)) Dragonon, Inc.

Fisher, Carolyn. A Twisted Tale. 2004. (Illus.). 33p. (J). (gr. k-4). reprint ed. 16.00 (978-0-7567-8412-6(3)) DIANE Publishing Co.

Fisher, Isla. Why Follow the Rules When You Cam Invent Your Own? Ceulemans, Eglantine, illus. 2017. (Marge in Charge Ser.: 1). 176p. (J). (gr. 3-7). 15.99 **(978-0-06-266218-7(X))** HarperCollins Pubs.

Fitzgerald, John. Great Brain. 2006. 20.75 (978-0-8446-7293-9(9)) Smith, Peter Pub., Inc.

Fitzgerald, John D. The Great Brain. Mayer, Mercer, illus. 2004. (Great Brain Ser.). (ENG.). 208p. (J). (gr. 3-7). 6.99 (978-0-14-240058-6(0), Puffin Books) Penguin Young Readers Group.

—The Great Brain. 175p. (J). (gr. 4-6). pap. 4.50 (978-0-8072-1422-0(1), Listening Library) Random Hse. Audio Publishing Group.

—Me & My Little Brain. Mayer, Mercer, illus. 2004. (Great Brain Ser.). (ENG.). 160p. (J). (gr. 3-7). 6.99 (978-0-14-240064-7(5), Puffin Books) Penguin Young Readers Group.

—Me & My Little Brain. Mayer, Mercer, illus. 2004. (Great Brain Ser.). 137p. (gr. 3-7). 16.00 (978-0-7569-2541-3(X)) Perfection Learning Corp.

Fitzgerald, Sarah Moore. Back to Blackbrick. 2013. (ENG., Illus.). 208p. (J). (gr. 5-9). 15.99 (978-1-4424-8155-8(2), McElderry, Margaret K. Bks.) McElderry, Margaret K. Bks.

Flanagan, James. Stories Heard Around the Lunchroom. 2010. 96p. pap. 11.49 (978-1-4490-8443-1(5)) AuthorHouse.

Flannery, John. Beard Boy. Weinberg, Steven, illus. 2016. (ENG.). 32p. (J). (-k). 16.99 (978-0-399-17336-3(6), G.P. Putnam's Sons Books for Young Readers) Penguin Young Readers Group.

Fleischman, Paul. The Dunderheads. Roberts, David, illus. 2012. (ENG.). 56p. (J). (gr. 1-4). pap. 6.99 (978-0-7636-5239-5(3)) Candlewick Pr.

—The Dunderheads. 2012. lib. bdg. 17.20 (978-0-606-23804-5(2), Turtleback) Turtleback Bks.

—The Dunderheads Behind Bars. Roberts, David, illus. 2012. (ENG.). 48p. (J). (gr. 1-4). 16.99 (978-0-7636-4543-4(5)) Candlewick Pr.

Fleming, Candace. Muncha! Muncha! Muncha! 2004. (Illus.). (J). 28.95 incl. audio compact disk (978-1-59112-924-0(9)) Live Oak Media.

—Westward Ho, Carlotta! Catrow, David, illus. 2009. (ENG.). 36p. (J). (gr. -1-2). 10.99 (978-1-4424-0218-8(0), Atheneum Bks. for Young Readers) Simon & Schuster Children's Publishing.

Fletcher, Melinda. The Dancing Pyjamas. 2012. 20p. pap. 17.99 (978-1-4685-0006-6(6)) AuthorHouse.

Flor Ada, Alma. Bajo las Palmas Reales. (SPA., Illus.). 96p. (J). (gr. 5-8). 15.95 (978-1-58105-656-3(7)) Santillana USA Publishing Co., Inc.

Flora, James, creator. Kangaroo for Christmas. 2011. (ENG., Illus.). 40p. (J). (gr. -1-3). 16.95 (978-1-59270-113-1(2)) Enchanted Lion Bks., LLC.

Florence, Debbi Michiko. Jasmine Toguchi, Mochi Queen. Vukovic, Elizabet, illus. 2017. (Jasmine Toguchi Ser.: 1). (ENG.). 128p. (J). pap. 5.99 **(978-0-374-30834-6(9)**, 9780374308346, Farrar, Straus & Giroux (BYR)) Farrar, Straus & Giroux.

—Jasmine Toguchi, Super Sleuth. Vukovic, Elizabet, illus. 2017. (Jasmine Toguchi Ser.: 2). (ENG.). 128p. (J). pap. 5.99 **(978-0-374-30835-3(7)**, 9780374308353, Farrar, Straus & Giroux (BYR)) Farrar, Straus & Giroux.

Florian, Douglas. How to Draw a Dragon. Florian, Douglas, illus. 2015. (ENG., Illus.). 42p. (J). (gr. -1-3). 17.99 (978-1-4424-7399-7(1), Beach Lane Bks.) Beach Lane Bks.

Florido, Lorraine. Hugo the Punk. Shami, Susan, ed. Ewing, John, illus. 2013. 106p. (YA). pap. 9.98 (978-0-9818449-6-1(0)) Thinkus Pubs.

Flowers, Luke. Ninja on the Farm (Scholastic Reader, Level 1: Moby Shinobi) 2016. (Scholastic Reader, Level 1 Ser.). (ENG.). 32p. (J). (gr. -1-1). pap. 3.99 (978-0-545-93537-1(7)) Scholastic, Inc.

Flynn, Tatum. Hell's Belles. 2017. (d'Evil Diaries). (ENG., Illus.). 256p. (J). (gr. 4-6). pap. 7.99 (978-1-4083-3578-9(6), Orchard Bks.) Hachette Children's Group GBR. Dist: Hachette Bk. Group.

Foley, Lizzie K. & Foley, Elizabeth. Remarkable. 2012. (ENG.). 336p. (J). (gr. 3-7). 16.99 (978-0-8037-3706-8(8), Dial Bks) Penguin Young Readers Group.

Folk Tale Staff. Gingerbread Man. Rodriguez, Beatrix, illus. 2012. (ENG.). 32p. (J). (gr. -1-3). 17.95 (978-0-7358-4086-7(5)) North-South Bks., Inc.

Ford, Bernette. No More Diapers for Ducky! Williams, Sam, illus. 2007. (Ducky & Piggy Ser.). (ENG.). 26p. (J). (gr. -1 — 1). bds. 7.95 (978-1-905417-38-4(1)) Boxer Bks., Ltd. GBR. Dist: Sterling Publishing Co., Inc.

Ford, Christopher. An Epic Doodle, Bk. 1. Ford, Christopher, illus. 2011. (Stickman Odyssey Ser.: 1). (ENG., Illus.). 208p. (J). (gr. 3-7). 12.99 (978-0-399-25426-0(9), Philomel Bks.) Penguin Young Readers Group.

—The Wrath of Zozimos, 2 vols., Bk. 2. Ford, Christopher, illus. 2012. (Stickman Odyssey Ser.: 2). (ENG., Illus.). 224p. (J). (gr. 3-7). 12.99 (978-0-399-25427-7(7), Philomel Bks.) Penguin Young Readers Group.

Ford, Lorry. Goodnight Red: A Lesson in Courage, 1 vol. 2009. 15p. pap. 24.95 (978-1-61582-421-2(9)) PublishAmerica, Inc.

Foreman, Michael. Oh! If Only... Foreman, Michael, illus. 2013. (Illus.). 32p. (gr. -1-3). 16.95 (978-1-4677-1213-2(2)) Andersen Pr. GBR. Dist: Lerner Publishing Group.

Forey, Martin. Maurice Minor's Incredible Adventure: A Children's Book for Grown-Ups. 2010. (Illus.). 256p. pap. 14.49 (978-1-4490-6875-2(8)) AuthorHouse.

Forsythe, Matthew, illus. Please, Open This Book! 2015. (ENG.). 40p. (J). (gr. -1-3). 17.99 (978-1-4424-5071-4(1), Simon & Schuster/Paula Wiseman Bks.) Simon & Schuster/Paula Wiseman Bks.

Forward, Toby. The Wolf's Story: What Really Happened to Little Red Riding Hood. Cohen, Izhar, illus. 2005. (ENG.). 32p. (J). (gr. -1-3). 17.99 (978-0-7636-2785-0(2)) Candlewick Pr.

Fox, Diane. The Cat, the Dog, Little Red, the Exploding Eggs, the Wolf, & Grandma. Fox, Christyan, illus. 2014. (ENG.). 32p. (J). (gr. -1-3). 16.99 (978-0-545-69481-0(7), Scholastic Pr.) Scholastic, Inc.

France, Richard. Joshua Stories: Book 1 - New School, New Friends. 2011. (Illus.). 104p. (gr. 4-6). pap. 14.09 (978-1-4567-7732-6(7)) AuthorHouse.

Frank, Lucy. Just Ask Iris. 2003. (ENG., Illus.). 224p. (J). (gr. 5-9). pap. 10.99 (978-0-689-84454-6(9), Atheneum Bks. for Young Readers) Simon & Schuster Children's Publishing.

Franklin, Jo. I'm an Alien & I Want to Go Home. Kelley, Marty, illus. 2015. (ENG.). 192p. (J). (gr. 5-7). 16.99 (978-0-544-44295-5(4)) Houghton Mifflin Harcourt Publishing Co.

—I'M an Alien & I Want to Go Home! Kelley, Marty, illus. 2017. (ENG.). 192p. (J). (gr. 5-7). pap. 6.99 (978-0-544-93824-3(0), HMH Books For Young Readers) Houghton Mifflin Harcourt Publishing Co.

Franklin Watts, contrib. by. Wait Skates! & Other Funny Stories. 2009. (Rookie Reader Treasury Ser.). (ENG., Illus.). 128p. (J). 11.95 (978-0-531-20849-6(4), Children's Pr.) Scholastic Library Publishing.

Frazee, Marla. The Boss Baby. Frazee, Marla, illus. 2010. (ENG., Illus.). 40p. (J). (gr. -1-3). 17.99 (978-1-4424-0167-9(2), Beach Lane Bks.) Beach Lane Bks.

—The Boss Baby. Frazee, Marla, illus. 2013. (Classic Board Bks.). (ENG., Illus.). 36p. (J). (gr. -1 — 1). bds. 7.99 (978-1-4424-8779-6(8), Little Simon) Little Simon.

—The Bossier Baby. Frazee, Marla, illus. 2016. (ENG., Illus.). 40p. (J). (gr. -1-3). 17.99 (978-1-4814-7162-6(7), Beach Lane Bks.) Beach Lane Bks.

—Roller Coaster. 2006. (ENG., Illus.). 32p. (J). (gr. -1-3). reprint ed. pap. 7.99 (978-0-15-205744-2(7)) Houghton Mifflin Harcourt Publishing Co.

Frederick, Heather Vogel. Dear Pen Pal. 2009. (Mother-Daughter Book Club Ser.). (ENG.). 416p. (J). (gr. 4-7). 16.99 (978-1-4169-7430-7(X), Simon & Schuster Bks. For Young Readers) Simon & Schuster Bks. For Young Readers.

Freedman, Claire. Aliens in Underpants Save the World. Cort, Ben, illus. 2012. (Underpants Bks.). (ENG.). 32p. (J). (gr. -1-2). 17.99 (978-1-4424-2768-6(X), Simon & Schuster/Paula Wiseman Bks.) Simon & Schuster/Paula Wiseman Bks.

—Aliens Love Dinopants. Cort, Ben, illus. 2016. (Underpants Bks.). (ENG.). 32p. (J). (gr. -1-2). 17.99 (978-1-4814-6736-0(0), Aladdin) Simon & Schuster Children's Publishing.

—Dragon Jelly. Hendra, Sue, illus. 2015. (ENG.). 32p. (J). (gr. k-3). 14.99 (978-1-61963-682-8(4), 9781619636828, Bloomsbury USA Childrens) Bloomsbury Publishing USA.

—Spider Sandwiches. Hendra, Sue, illus. 2014. (ENG.). 32p. (J). (gr. k-3). 14.99 (978-1-61963-364-3(7), 9781619633643, Bloomsbury USA Childrens) Bloomsbury Publishing USA.

French, Mary B. Bear-Ly There with Compass. Coffey, Kevin, illus. 2012. 122p. pap. 6.00 (978-0-9852821-0-3(X)) Mary B./French.

French, Vivian. Mountain Mona: Band 09/Gold. Fisher, Chris, illus. 2006. (Collins Big Cat Ser.). (ENG.). 24p. (J). (gr. 2-2). pap. 7.99 (978-0-00-718700-3(9)) HarperCollins Pubs. Ltd. GBR. Dist: Independent Pubs. Group.

—Polly's Pink Pajamas. Heap, Sue, illus. 2010. (ENG.). 32p. (J). (gr. -1-2). 14.99 (978-0-7636-4807-7(8)) Candlewick Pr.

Fretz, Denette. Conrad & the Cowgirl Next Door, 1 vol. Barretta, Gene, illus. 2014. (Next Door Ser.). (ENG.). 40p. (J). 12.99 (978-0-310-72349-3(3)) Zonderkidz.

freysinger, karen. Adventures of Countess Pigula up, up & Away. freysinger, karen, illus. 2009. (Illus.). 32p. (J). 16.99 (978-0-9786729-1-1(7)) Aha! Elora Danan Productions.

Fridman, Sashi. The Great Friday Clean-up (French Flap) Salem, Iosi, illus. 2009. 32p. 12.95 (978-1-934440-77-3(9), Pitspopany Pr.) Simcha Media Group.

—The Great Friday Clean-up (Hard Cover) Salem, Iosi, illus. 2009. 32p. 17.95 (978-1-934440-93-3(0), Pitspopany Pr.) Simcha Media Group.

Friedman, Aimee. A Novel Idea. 2006. (Romantic Comedies Ser.). (ENG., Illus.). 256p. (YA). (gr. 9-12). mass mkt. 7.99 (978-1-4169-0785-5(8), Simon Pulse) Simon Pulse.

Friedman, Kinky. Curse of the Missing Puppet Head. 2003. lib. bdg. 29.95 (978-0-9702383-6-8(3), CMPH01) Vandam Pr., Inc.

Friesen, Ray. Lookit!, Vol. 2. 2004. (YA). per. 4.95 (978-0-9728177-3-8(5)) Don't Eat Any Bugs Prodns.

—RQW, Vol. 3. 2003. (YA). 2.95 (978-0-9728177-2-1(7)) Don't Eat Any Bugs Prodns.

Fromental, Jean-Luc. Oops! Connors, Thomas, tr. from FRE. Jolivet, Joëlle, illus. 2010. (ENG.). 42p. (J). (gr. -1-k). 17.95 (978-0-8109-8749-4(X)) Abrams, Inc.

Frost, C. Amethyst. Dismal Thoughts. 2012. 132p. pap. 6.99 (978-0-9847236-0-7(9)) Frost, C. A.

Fry, Michael. How to Be a Supervillain. 2017. (How to Be a Supervillain Ser.). (ENG., Illus.). 320p. (J). (gr. 3-9). 13.99 (978-0-316-31869-3(8), Jimmy Patterson) Little Brown & Co.

Fry, Michael & Jackson, Bradley. The Naughty List. Fry, Michael, illus. 2015. (ENG., Illus.). 240p. (J). (gr. 3-7). 12.99 (978-0-06-235475-4(2)) HarperCollins Pubs.

Fucile, Tony. Let's Do Nothing! Fucile, Tony, illus. 2012. (ENG., Illus.). 40p. (J). (gr. -1-3). pap. 6.99 (978-0-7636-5269-2(5)) Candlewick Pr.

Fuertes, Gloria. Cuentos de Humor: Un Pulpo en un Garaje. 2003. (SPA.). 128p. 15.16 (978-84-305-7987-7(7), SU5205) Susaeta Ediciones, S.A. ESP. Dist: Lectorum Pubns., Inc.

Funny School Stories: Learning to Read Box Set. 2016. (I Can Read Level 1 Ser.). 192p. (J). (gr. -1-3). pap. 16.99 (978-0-06-231336-2(3)) HarperCollins Pubs.

Gág, Wanda. The Funny Thing. 2003. (Fesler-Lampert Minnesota Heritage Ser.). (ENG., Illus.). 32p. 14.95 (978-0-8166-4241-0(9)) Univ. of Minnesota Pr.

Gage, Wilson. A Wild Goose Tale. Rounds, Glen, illus. 2012. 114p. 39.95 (978-1-258-25188-8(4)); pap. 24.95 (978-1-258-25729-3(7)) Literary Licensing, LLC.

Gaiman, NEil. Crazy Hair. McKean, Dave, illus. (ENG.). 40p. (J). (gr. -1-3). 2015. pap. 6.99 (978-0-06-057910-4(2)) 2009. 18.99 (978-0-06-057908-1(0)) HarperCollins Pubs.

—Crazy Hair. 2015. (J). lib. bdg. 17.20 (978-0-606-36478-2(1)) Turtleback Bks.

—The Day I Swapped My Dad for Two Goldfish. McKean, Dave, illus. 64p. (J). (gr. k-3). 2006. (ENG.). pap. 7.99 (978-0-06-058703-1(2)) 2004. lib. bdg. 17.89 (978-0-06-058702-4(4)) 2004. (ENG.). 17.99 (978-0-06-058701-7(6)) HarperCollins Pubs.

—Fortunately, the Milk. Young, Skottie, illus. (ENG.). 128p. (J). (gr. 3-7). 2014. pap. 5.99 (978-0-06-222408-8(5)) 2013. 14.99 (978-0-06-222407-1(7)) HarperCollins Pubs.

—Fortunately, the Milk. 2014. (J). lib. bdg. 16.00 (978-0-606-35965-8(6)) Turtleback Bks.

Gall, Chris. Awesome Dawson. 2013. (ENG., Illus.). 40p. (J). (gr. -1-3). 17.99 (978-0-316-21330-1(6)) Little, Brown Bks. for Young Readers.

Gallagher, Diana G. Pool Problem: The Complicated Life of Claudia Cristina Cortez, 1 vol. Garvey, Brann, illus. 2009. (Claudia Cristina Cortez Ser.). (ENG.). 88p. (gr. 2-3). pap. 6.10 (978-1-4342-1758-5(2), Claudia Cristina Cortez) Stone Arch Bks.

Gallagher, Toni. Twist My Charm: Love Potion #11. 2016. (Twist My Charm Ser.). (ENG.). 272p. (J). (gr. 3-7). 16.99 (978-0-553-51119-2(X), Random Hse. Bks. for Young Readers) Random Hse. Children's Bks.

Gallo, Tina. Po's Awesomely Perfect Present. 2015. (Kung Fu Panda 8x8 Ser.). lib. bdg. 13.55 (978-0-606-37870-3(7)) Turtleback Bks.

Galveston, Louise. By the Grace of Todd. 2015. (ENG., Illus.). 272p. (J). (gr. 3-7). pap. 8.99 (978-1-59514-678-6(4), Razorbill) Penguin Young Readers Group.

Gamble, Paul. The Monster's Daughter. 2017. (Ministry of SUITs Ser.: 2). (ENG.). 384p. (J). 16.99 (978-1-250-07683-0(8), 9781250076830) Feiwel & Friends.

Ganeri, Anita. Funny Stories: Writing Stories, 1 vol. 2013. (Writing Stories Ser.). (ENG.). 32p. (gr. 1-3). 27.32 (978-1-4329-7534-0(X)); pap. 8.95 (978-1-4329-7541-8(2)) Heinemann-Raintree. (Heinemann First Library).

Gangsei, Jan. The Wild Bunch. 2017. (Max Ser.). (ENG., Illus.). 192p. (J). (gr. 4-8). pap. 7.99 **(978-1-4814-6828-2(6)**, Aladdin) Simon & Schuster Children's Publishing.

Gannon, Nicholas. The Doldrums. 368p. (J). (gr. 3-7). 2017. pap. 7.99 **(978-0-06-232095-7(5))** 2015. (ENG., Illus.). 17.99 (978-0-06-232094-0(7)) HarperCollins Pubs. (Greenwillow Bks.).

Gantos, Jack. The Follower. 2015. (ENG.). 224p. (YA). (gr. 7-10). 17.99 (978-0-374-37995-7(5), 9780374379957, Farrar, Straus & Giroux (BYR)) Farrar, Straus & Giroux.

—From Norvelt to Nowhere. 2015. (J). lib. bdg. 18.40 (978-0-606-37280-0(6)) Turtleback Bks.

Garant, Andre J. The Circus Kids. 2008. 140p. pap. 11.99 (978-1-4389-2833-3(5)) AuthorHouse.

—The Elite Eight. 2011. 120p. (gr. 4-6). pap. 10.99 (978-1-4567-4302-4(3)) AuthorHouse.

—Jake's Tree House. 2010. 128p. pap. 10.99 (978-1-4490-8369-4(2)) AuthorHouse.

Gardner, Lyn & Asquith, Ros. The Ghastly McNastys Bk. 2: Raiders of the Lost Shark. 2014. (Ghastly Mcnastys Ser.). (ENG., Illus.). 192p. (J). (gr. k-3). pap. 9.99 (978-1-84812-363-2(9)) Bonnier Publishing GBR. Dist: Independent Pubs. Group.

Gardner, Sally. El Niño Invisible. Tapia, Sonia, tr. 2005. (Niños Mágicos Ser.). (SPA & ENG., Illus.). 112p. (J). (gr. 2-4). per. 7.95 (978-84-666-1342-2(0)) Ediciones B ESP. Dist: Independent Pubs. Group.

Garfield, Leon. The Complete Bostock & Harris. 2014. (ENG.). 336p. (J). (gr. 3-7). 17.95 (978-1-59017-783-9(5), NYR Children's Collection) New York Review of Bks., Inc., The.

Garland, Michael. Oh, What a Christmas! Garland, Michael, illus. 2011. (ENG., Illus.). 40p. (J). (gr. -1-3). 16.99 (978-0-545-24210-3(X), Scholastic Pr.) Scholastic, Inc.

—Where's My Homework? Garland, Michael, illus. 2014. (ENG., Illus.). 32p. (J). (gr. -1-k). pap. 6.99 (978-0-545-43655-7(9), Cartwheel Bks.) Scholastic, Inc.

Garriel, Barbara. I Know a Shy Fellow Who Swallowed a Cello. O'brien, John, illus. 2012. (ENG.). 32p. (J). (gr. k-2). pap. 6.95 (978-1-59078-946-9(6)) Boyds Mills Pr.

Garriel, Barbara S. I Know a Shy Fellow Who Swallowed a Cello. O'brien, John, illus. 2004. (ENG.). 32p. (J). (gr. k-3). 17.95 (978-1-59078-043-5(4)) Boyds Mills Pr.

Garza, Xavier. Charro Claus & the Tejas Kid. 2008. (SPA & ENG., Illus.). 40p. (J). (gr. k-6). 17.95 (978-1-933693-24-8(X)) Cinco Puntos Pr.

Gaston, Sharon D. Who's Laughing Now? & Don't Burn Your Bridge. 2009. 48p. pap. 19.50 (978-1-4389-7832-1(4)) AuthorHouse.

Gates, Susan & Ceredigion, Cymdeithas Lyfrau. Babi Bag Siwgwr. Williams, Dylan, tr. from ENG. Braun, Sebastien, illus. 2005. (WEL.). 80p. pap. (978-1-902416-96-0(1)) Cymdeithas Lyfrau Ceredigion.

Gatou, Shouji. Full Metal Panic - Overload!, Vol. 5. Nagai, Tomohiro, illus. 2006. (Full Metal Panic: Overload! Ser.). 200p. (YA). pap. 9.99 (978-1-4139-0342-3(8)) ADV Manga.

Gauthier, Gilles. Le Beau Valentino Sort Ses Crocs. Derome, Pierre-Andre, tr. 2003. (Premier Roman Ser.). (FRE., Illus.). 64p. (J). (gr. 1-4). pap. (978-2-89021-636-5(5)) Diffusion du livre Mirabel (DLM).

Gay, Homel D. On the Road Again! More Travels with My Family. Gay, Marie-Louise, illus. 2008. (ENG.). 120p. (J). (gr. 1-5). 15.95 (978-0-88899-846-0(5)) Groundwood Bks. CAN. Dist: Publishers Group West (PGW).

Gaydos, Nora. My World. Sams, B. B., illus. 2004. (NIR! Leveled Readers Ser.). (ENG.). 128p. (J). (gr. -1-2). 16.99 (978-1-58476-263-8(2), Now I'm Reading!) Random Hse. Children's Bks.

—Snack Attack, Level 2. Sams, B. B., illus. 2004. (NIR! Leveled Readers Ser.). (ENG.). 128p. (J). (gr. -1-3). 16.99 (978-1-58476-264-5(0), Now I'm Reading!) Random Hse. Children's Bks.

Gayton, Sam. Hercufleas. 2016. (ENG.). 272p. (J). (gr. 5-7). 16.99 (978-0-544-63620-0(1)) Houghton Mifflin Harcourt Publishing Co.

Gehl, Laura. Peep & Egg: I'm Not Hatching. Wan, Joyce, illus. 2017. (Peep & Egg Ser.). (ENG.). 32p. (J). bds. 7.99 (978-0-374-30542-0(0), 9780374305420, Farrar, Straus & Giroux (BYR)) Farrar, Straus & Giroux.

Gehrmann, Katja, illus. Goose the Bear. 2014. (ENG.). 40p. (J). (gr. -1-3). 16.95 (978-1-62636-384-7(6), Sky Pony Pr.) Skyhorse Publishing Co., Inc.

Gent, Ron. A Tale of Two Hamsters. 2008. 52p. pap. 12.99 (978-1-4343-2319-4(6)) AuthorHouse.

Gerhardt, Jake. Me & Miranda Mullaly. 2016. (ENG.). 256p. (J). (gr. 5). 16.99 (978-0-451-47540-4(2), Viking Books for Young Readers) Penguin Young Readers Group.

—My Future Ex-Girlfriend. 2017. (ENG.). 240p. (J). (gr. 5). 16.99 (978-0-451-47541-1(0), Viking Books for Young Readers) Penguin Young Readers Group.

Germein, Katrina. My Dad Thinks He's Funny. Jellett, Tom, illus. 2013. (ENG.). 32p. (J). (gr. k-3). 14.99 (978-0-7636-6522-7(3)) Candlewick Pr.

Gerstein, Mordicai. You Can't Have Too Many Friends! Gerstein, Mordicai, illus. 2014. (ENG., Illus.). 32p. (J). (gr. -1-2). 16.95 (978-0-8234-2393-4(X)) Holiday Hse., Inc.

Ghigna, Charles & Ghigna, Debra. Barn Storm. Greenseid, Diane, illus. 2010. (Step into Reading Ser.). (ENG.). 32p. (J). (gr. -1-1). pap. 3.99 (978-0-375-86114-7(9), Random Hse. Bks. for Young Readers) Random Hse. Children's Bks.

Giarrusso, Chris. The G-Man Super Journal: Awesome Origins. 2015. (ENG.). 240p. (J). 13.99 (978-1-4494-5844-7(0)) Andrews McMeel Publishing.

Gibert, Bruno. A King Seen from the Sky. 2015. (ENG., Illus.). 32p. (J). 16.95 (978-1-60606-460-3(6), J. Paul Getty Museum) Getty Pubns.

Giddens, Martha Anne. The Unluckiest Kid in the Universe. 2006. 56p. pap. 9.95 (978-1-4120-7935-8(7)) Trafford Publishing.

Gidwitz, Adam. The Grimm Conclusion. 2014. (Grimm Ser.: 3). lib. bdg. 18.40 (978-0-606-36187-3(1)) Turtleback Bks.

—In a Glass Grimmly. Santat, Dan, illus. 2013. (ENG.). 352p. (J). (gr. 5). pap. 7.99 *(978-0-14-242506-0(0),* Puffin Books) Penguin Young Readers Group.
—In a Glass Grimmly. D'Andrade, Hugh, illus. 2012. (ENG.). 336p. (J). (gr. 5). 16.99 *(978-0-525-42581-6(0),* Dutton Books for Young Readers) Penguin Young Readers Group.
—In a Glass Grimmly. 2013. (Grimm Ser.: 2). lib. bdg. 18.40 *(978-0-606-32135-8(7),* Turtleback) Turtleback Bks.
Giff, Patricia Reilly. Hunter Moran Digs Deep. Sheban, Chris, illus. 2014. (ENG.). 160p. (J). (gr. 3-7). 16.95 *(978-0-8234-3165-6(7))* Holiday Hse., Inc.
—Hunter Moran Hangs Out. (ENG.). 144p. (J). (gr. 3-7). 2014. pap. 6.99 *(978-0-8234-3189-2(4))* 2013. (Illus.). 16.95 *(978-0-8234-2859-5(1))* Holiday Hse., Inc.
—Hunter Moran Saves the Universe. (ENG.). 128p. (J). (gr. 2-7). 2013. pap. 6.99 *(978-0-8234-2917-2(2))* 2012. 16.95 *(978-0-8234-1949-4(5))* Holiday Hse., Inc.
Gifford, Peggy. Moxy Maxwell Does Not Love Stuart Little. Fisher, Valorie, photos by. 2008. (Moxy Maxwell Ser.). (ENG., Illus.). 112p. (J). (gr. 2-5). 5.99 *(978-0-440-42230-3(2),* Yearling) Random Hse. Children's Bks.
—Moxy Maxwell Does Not Love Writing Thank-You Notes. Fisher, Valorie, illus. 2009. (Moxy Maxwell Ser.). (ENG.). 192p. (J). (gr. 2-5). 6.99 *(978-0-375-84343-3(4),* Yearling) Random Hse. Children's Bks.
Gilbert, Paul T. Bertram & His Funny Animals. Rousseff, Minnie H., illus. 2016. (ENG.). 140p. (J). 24.95 *(978-0-7649-7372-7(X),* POMEGRANATE KIDS) Pomegranate Communications, Inc.
Gilfillan, Ross. Losing It: The Growing Pains of a Teenage Vampire. 2014. (ENG.). 257p. (YA). (gr. 8-17). pap. 12.95 *(978-1-78279-366-3(6),* Lodestone Bks.) Hunt, John Publishing Ltd. GBR. Dist: National Bk. Network.
Gillam, David. Gingertown. Gilliam, David, illus. 2012. 216p. (J). 29.99 *(978-1-60131-122-1(2))* Big Tent Bks.
Gilson, Jamie. My Teacher Is an Idiom. Tilley, Debbie, illus. 2015. (ENG.). 144p. (J). (gr. 1-4). 16.99 *(978-0-544-05680-0(9))* Houghton Mifflin Harcourt Publishing Co.
Ginkel, Anne. I've Got an Elephant, 1 vol. Bynum, Janie, illus. (ENG.). 32p. (J). 2013. (gr. -1-3). 7.95 *(978-1-56145-685-7(3))* 2006. (gr. k-3). 16.95 *(978-1-56145-373-3(0))* Peachtree Pubs.
Girard, Franck. Toby Goes Bananas. Bloch, Serge, illus. 2017. (ENG.). 96p. (J). (gr. 2-5). 19.99 ***(978-0-545-85284-5(6))***; pap. 9.99 ***(978-0-545-85283-8(8))*** Scholastic, Inc. (Graphix).
Glaser, Shirley. If Apples Had Teeth. Bedrick, Muriel, illus. 2017. (ENG.). 40p. (J). (-3). 16.95 *(978-1-59270-226-8(0))* Enchanted Lion Bks., LLC.
Glass, Susan. The Great Eggscape, 1 vol. Van Wright, Cornelius, illus. 2011. 32p. (J). (gr. k-5). (ENG.). 16.95 *(978-1-59572-261-4(0));* pap. 6.95 *(978-1-59572-253-9(X))* Star Bright Bks., Inc.
Gleitzman, Morris. Aristotle's Nostril. 2016. (ENG.). 144p. (J). (gr. 1-3). 14.99 ***(978-0-14-330894-2(7))*** Random Hse. Australia AUS. Dist: Independent Pubs. Group.
—Other Facts of Life. 2016. (ENG.). 144p. (J). (gr. 4-6). 14.99 ***(978-0-14-330878-2(5))*** Random Hse. Australia AUS. Dist: Independent Pubs. Group.
Glock-Cooper, Allison. Changers Book Three: Kim. 2016. (Changers Ser.). (ENG.). 240p. (J). (gr. 6). pap. 11.95 *(978-1-61775-489-0(7),* Black Sheep) Akashic Bks.
Glover, Rosanne Harper. Chloe, the Very Special Goat. Sites, Jennifer, illus. 2012. (ENG.). 48p. (J). 16.95 *(978-0-938467-53-3(0))* Headline Bks., Inc.
Gold, Gina. Minnie: A Walk in the Park. 2014. (Mickey & Friends World of Reading Ser.). (J). lib. bdg. 13.55 *(978-0-606-35902-3(8))* Turtleback Bks.
—Minnie: Hocus Bow-Cus! 2014. (Mickey & Friends World of Reading Ser.). (J). lib. bdg. 13.55 *(978-0-606-35270-3(8))* Turtleback Bks.
Goldberg, Barry, illus. Bubble Blowers, Beware! 2004. (SpongeBob SquarePants Ser.). (ENG.). 24p. (J). pap. 3.99 *(978-0-689-86862-7(6),* Simon Spotlight/Nickelodeon) Simon Spotlight/Nickelodeon.
Goldberg, Mara J. Issavich's Unruly Nest. 2009. 20p. pap. 12.49 *(978-1-4343-7992-4(2))* AuthorHouse.
Golden Books Staff. Little Golden Book Favorites. Scarry, Richard & Golden Books Staff, illus. 2008. (Little Golden Book Favorites Ser.). (ENG.). 80p. (J). (gr. -1-2). 7.99 *(978-0-375-84580-2(1),* Golden Bks.) Random Hse. Children's Bks.
Golden Books Staff & Miryam. The Happy Man & His Dump Truck. Gergely, Tibor, illus. 2005. (Little Golden Book Ser.). (ENG.). 24p. (J). (gr. -1-k). 4.99 *(978-0-375-83207-9(6),* Golden Bks.) Random Hse. Children's Bks.
Goldman, Leslie & Trenc, Milan. Night at the Museum. 2006. (ENG., Illus.). 144p. (J). (gr. 3-7). per. 4.99 *(978-0-7641-3576-7(7))* Barron's Educational Series, Inc.
Gonick, Larry. Kokopelli & Company in Attack of the Smart Pies. 2005. (ENG., Illus.). 192p. (J). 15.95 *(978-0-8126-2740-4(7))* Cricket Bks.
Goniwicha, William. Spike a Relli: A Week at the Lake. 2009. 28p. pap. 13.99 *(978-1-4389-2902-6(1))* AuthorHouse.
—Spike a Relli: The Mini Doberman. 2009. 28p. pap. 13.99 *(978-1-4389-5678-7(9))* AuthorHouse.
Gonzalez, L. M. R. Gifts Lucy. The Terrible Monster. 2008. 52p. pap. 24.93 *(978-1-4357-5500-0(6))* Lulu Pr., Inc.
Good, Jason. Must. Push. Buttons! Krosoczka, Jarrett J., illus. 2015. (ENG.). 32p. (J). (gr. -1-1). 16.99 *(978-1-61963-095-6(8),* 9781619630956, Bloomsbury USA Childrens) Bloomsbury Publishing USA.
Goodhart, Pippa. Little Nelly's Big Book. Rowland, Andy, illus. 2012. (ENG.). 32p. (J). (gr. -1-3). 16.99 *(978-1-59990-779-6(8),* 9781599907796, Bloomsbury USA Childrens) Bloomsbury Publishing USA.
Goodrich, Carter. The Hermit Crab. Goodrich, Carter, illus. 2009. (ENG., Illus.). 40p. (J). (gr. 1-5). 16.99 *(978-1-4169-3892-7(3),* Simon & Schuster Bks. For Young Readers) Simon & Schuster Bks. For Young Readers.
Gorbachev, Valeri. Catty Jane Who Hated the Rain. Gorbachev, Valeri, illus. 2012. (ENG., Illus.). 32p. (J). (gr. -1-3). 16.95 *(978-1-59078-700-7(5))* Boyds Mills Pr.
—Pizza-Pie Snowman. 2016. (ENG., Illus.). 32p. (J). 16.95 *(978-0-8234-3654-5(3))* Holiday Hse., Inc.
Gordon, Domenica More. Archie. 2012. (ENG., Illus.). 48p. (J). (gr. -1-1). 17.99 *(978-1-59990-936-3(7),* 9781599909363, Bloomsbury USA Childrens) Bloomsbury Publishing USA.
—Archie's Vacation. 2014. (ENG., Illus.). 32p. (J). (gr. -1-1). 17.99 *(978-1-61963-190-8(3),* 9781619631908, Bloomsbury USA Childrens) Bloomsbury Publishing USA.
Gore, Jim. Witch Snatchit & Mr Grabbit. 2005. (Illus.). 80p. pap. *(978-1-84401-486-6(X))* Athena Pr.
Gorey, Edward. Thoughtful Alphabets: The Just Dessert / The Deadly Blotter. 2012. 64p. 14.95 *(978-0-7649-6336-0(8))* Pomegranate Communications, Inc.
Goscinny, René. Asterix Chez les Belges. (FRE.). (J). pap. 21.95 *(978-2-01-210156-2(9))* Hachette Groupe Livre FRA. Dist: Distribooks, Inc.
—Asterix en Hispanie. (FRE.). (J). pap. 21.95 *(978-2-01-210146-3(1))* Hachette Groupe Livre FRA. Dist: Distribooks, Inc.
—Nicholas Again. Bell, Anthea, tr. from FRE. Sempé, Jean-Jacques, illus. rev. ed. 2006. (ENG.). 120p. (gr. 8-17). 19.95 *(978-0-7148-4564-7(7))* Phaidon Pr., Inc.
—Nicholas on Vacation. Bell, Anthea, tr. Sempé, Jean-Jacques, illus. 2013. (ENG.). 136p. (J). (gr. 1-4). pap. 9.95 *(978-0-7148-6224-8(X))* Phaidon Pr., Inc.
—Where's Asterix? Uderzo, Albert, illus. 2012. (ENG.). 32p. (J). (gr. 4-6). pap. 9.99 *(978-1-4440-0554-7(5),* Orion) Orion Publishing Group, Ltd. GBR. Dist: Hachette Bk. Group.
Goscinny, René, text. Asterix Chez les Belges. (FRE.). pap. 21.95 *(978-2-01-210024-4(4),* DR24E) Hachette Groupe Livre FRA. Dist: Distribooks, Inc.
Goscinny, René & Uderzo, Albert. Asterix Chez les Helvetes. (FRE.). (J). pap. 21.95 *(978-2-01-210016-9(3))* Hachette Groupe Livre FRA. Dist: Distribooks, Inc.
—Asterix en Corse. (FRE.). 21.95 *(978-2-01-210020-6(1))* Hachette Groupe Livre FRA. Dist: Distribooks, Inc.
—Asterix en Hispanie. (FRE.). 21.95 *(978-2-01-210014-5(7))* Hachette Groupe Livre FRA. Dist: Distribooks, Inc.
—Asterix et le Bombe. (FRE.). 21.95 *(978-2-01-210008-4(2))* Hachette Groupe Livre FRA. Dist: Distribooks, Inc.
—Asterix French. 21.95 *(978-2-01-210009-1(0));* 21.95 *(978-2-01-210022-0(8))* Hachette Groupe Livre FRA. Dist: Distribooks, Inc.
—Le Tour de Gaule d'Asterix. (FRE.). 21.95 *(978-2-01-210005-3(8))* Hachette Groupe Livre FRA. Dist: Distribooks, Inc.
Goslee, S. J. Whatever. 2016. (ENG.). 272p. (YA). 17.99 *(978-1-62672-399-3(0),* 9781626723993) Roaring Brook Pr.
Gosselink, John. The Defense of Thaddeus A. Ledbetter. 2010. (ENG., Illus.). 240p. (J). (gr. 3-7). 14.95 *(978-0-8109-8977-1(8),* Amulet Bks.) Abrams, Inc.
Grabenstein, Chris. I Funny: A Middle School Story. Patterson, James, ed. Park, Laura, illus. 2012. 303p. (J). 11.99 *(978-0-316-22638-7(6),* 1351607) Little Brown & Co.
Graff, Lisa. The Great Treehouse War. 2017. (ENG.). 288p. (J). (gr. 3-7). 16.99 *(978-0-399-17500-8(8),* Philomel Bks.) Penguin Young Readers Group.
—Sophie Simon Solves Them All. Beene, Jason, illus. 2012. (ENG.). 112p. (J). (gr. 3-5). pap. 6.99 *(978-1-250-02898-3(1),* 9781250028983) Square Fish.
Grambling, Lois G. T. Rex & the Mother's Day Hug. Davis, Jack E., illus. 2011. (ENG.). 32p. (J). (gr. -1-1). pap. 6.99 *(978-0-06-053128-7(2),* Tegen, Katherine Bks) HarperCollins Pubs.
Grandits, John. Seven Rules You Absolutely Must Not Break If You Want to Survive the Cafeteria. Austin, Michael Allen, illus. 2017. (ENG.). 32p. (J). (gr. 1-4). 16.99 *(978-0-544-69951-9(3),* Clarion Bks.) Houghton Mifflin Harcourt Trade & Reference Pubs.
—Ten Rules You Absolutely Must Not Break If You Want to Survive the School Bus. Austin, Michael Allen, illus. 2011. (ENG.). 32p. (J). (gr. 1-4). 16.99 *(978-0-618-78822-4(0))* Houghton Mifflin Harcourt Publishing Co.
Grant, Holly. The Dastardly Deed. Portillo, Josie, illus. 2016. (League of Beastly Dreadfuls Ser.: Bk. 2). (ENG.). 368p. (J). (gr. 3-7). 16.99 *(978-0-385-37025-7(3),* Random Hse. Bks. for Young Readers) Random Hse. Children's Bks.
—The League of Beastly Dreadfuls. 2015. (League of Beastly Dreadfuls Ser.: Bk. 1). (ENG., Illus.). 320p. (J). (gr. 3-7). 16.99 *(978-0-385-37007-3(5),* Random Hse. Bks. for Young Readers) Random Hse. Children's Bks.
Grant, Michael. The Call. (Magnificent 12 Ser.: 1). (ENG.). (J). (gr. 3-7). 2011. 272p. pap. 6.99 *(978-0-06-183367-0(3))* 2010. (Illus.). 256p. 16.99 *(978-0-06-183366-3(5))* HarperCollins Pubs. (Tegen, Katherine Bks).
—The Key. (Magnificent 12 Ser.: 3). (ENG.). (J). (gr. 3-7). 2013. 304p. pap. 5.99 *(978-0-06-183371-7(1))* 2012. (Illus.). 288p. 16.99 *(978-0-06-183370-0(3))* HarperCollins Pubs. (Tegen, Katherine Bks).
—The Power. 2013. (Magnificent 12 Ser.: 4). (ENG.). 288p. (J). (gr. 3-7). 16.99 *(978-0-06-183372-4(X),* Tegen, Katherine Bks) HarperCollins Pubs.
—The Trap. (Magnificent 12 Ser.: 2). (ENG.). (J). (gr. 3-7). 2012. 320p. pap. 5.99 *(978-0-06-183369-4(X))* 2011. 304p. 16.99 *(978-0-06-183368-7(1))* HarperCollins Pubs. (Tegen, Katherine Bks).
Grant, Vicki. Dead-End Job, 1 vol. 2005. (Orca Soundings Ser.). (ENG.). 128p. (YA). (gr. 8-12). per. 9.95 *(978-1-55143-378-3(8))* Orca Bk. Pubs. USA.
—Pigboy. 2007. (Orca Currents Ser.). 101p. (gr. 5). 19.95 *(978-0-7569-8067-2(4))* Perfection Learning Corp.
—Quid Pro Quo, 1 vol. 2005. (ENG.). 176p. (J). (gr. 4-9). per. 7.95 *(978-1-55143-370-7(2))* Orca Bk. Pubs. USA.
Gravel, Elise. The Cranky Ballerina. Gravel, Elise, illus. 2016. (Illus.). 32p. (J). (gr. -1-3). 17.99 *(978-0-06-235124-1(9),* Tegen, Katherine Bks) HarperCollins Pubs.
Gravel, Élise. Olga & the Smelly Thing from Nowhere. 2017. (Illus.). 176p. (J). ***(978-0-06-267180-6(4))*** Harper & Row Ltd.
—Olga & the Smelly Thing from Nowhere. Gravel, Élise, illus. 2017. (Olga Ser.: 1). (Illus.). 176p. (J). (gr. 3-7). 12.99 *(978-0-06-235126-5(5))* HarperCollins Pubs.
Graves, Keith. Chicken Big. 2010. (ENG., Illus.). 40p. (J). (gr. -1-3). 16.99 *(978-0-8118-7237-9(8))* Chronicle Bks. LLC.
—Puppy! 2016. (ENG., Illus.). 32p. (J). 16.99 *(978-1-62672-225-5(0),* 9781626722255) Roaring Brook Pr.
—Second Banana. 2015. (ENG., Illus.). 32p. (J). (gr. 2-5). 17.99 *(978-1-59643-883-5(5),* 9781596438835) Roaring Brook Pr.
Graves, Sue. Harry's Hat. Worsley, Belinda, illus. 2008. (Reading Corner Ser.). (ENG.). 24p. (J). (gr. k-2). pap. 6.99 *(978-0-7496-7692-6(2),* Franklin Watts) Hachette Children's Group GBR. Dist: Hachette Bk. Group.
Gravett, Emily. Dogs. Gravett, Emily, illus. 2010. (ENG., Illus.). 32p. (J). (gr. -1-1). 15.99 *(978-1-4169-8703-1(7),* Simon & Schuster Bks. For Young Readers) Simon & Schuster Bks. For Young Readers.
—Wolves. Gravett, Emily, illus. 2006. (ENG., Illus.). 40p. (J). (gr. k-3). 17.99 *(978-1-4169-1491-4(9),* Simon & Schuster Bks. For Young Readers) Simon & Schuster Bks. For Young Readers.
Gray, Kes. Daisy & the Trouble with Giants. Sharratt, Nick & Parsons, Garry, illus. 2010. (Daisy Ser.: 10). (ENG.). 256p. (J). (gr. 2-4). pap. 11.99 *(978-1-86230-495-6(5),* Red Fox) Random House Children's Books GBR. Dist: Independent Pubs. Group.
—Nuddy Ned. Parsons, Garry, illus. 2014. (ENG.). 32p. (J). (gr. -1-k). 13.99 *(978-1-4088-3659-0(9),* 9781408836590, Bloomsbury USA Childrens) Bloomsbury Publishing USA.
Green, Andi. The Monster Who Couldn't Decide. 2010. (WorryWoo Monsters Ser.). 98p. (J). 14.99 *(978-0-9792860-3-2(4))* Monsters in My Head, LLC, The.
Green, Brandon. This Wriggler Is a Giggler a Review of Diary of a Worm. 2017. (Text Connections Guided Close Reading Ser.). (J). (gr. 2). *(978-1-4900-1836-2(0))* Benchmark Education Co.
Green, D. L. Zeke Meeks. Alves, Josh, illus. 2013. (Zeke Meeks Ser.). (ENG.). 128p. (gr. 2-2). 90.60 *(978-1-4048-8053-5(4));* 181.20 *(978-1-4048-8052-8(6))* Picture Window Bks. (Zeke Meeks).
—Zeke Meeks vs His Big Phony Cousin, 1 vol. Alves, Josh, illus. 2014. (Zeke Meeks Ser.). (ENG.). 128p. (gr. 2-2). pap. 5.95 *(978-1-4795-3810-2(8));* 22.65 *(978-1-4795-2167-8(1))* Picture Window Bks. (Zeke Meeks).
—Zeke Meeks vs the Annoying Princess Sing-Along, 1 vol. Alves, Josh, illus. 2014. (Zeke Meeks Ser.). (ENG.). 128p. (gr. 2-2). 22.65 *(978-1-4795-4828-6(6),* Zeke Meeks) Picture Window Bks.
—Zeke Meeks vs the Big Blah-Rific Birthday, 1 vol. Alves, Josh, illus. 2013. (Zeke Meeks Ser.). (ENG.). 128p. (gr. 2-2). 8.95 *(978-1-4048-8105-1(0));* lib. bdg. 22.65 *(978-1-4048-7637-8(5))* Picture Window Bks. (Zeke Meeks).
—Zeke Meeks vs the Crummy Class Play, 1 vol. Alves, Josh, illus. 2014. (Zeke Meeks Ser.). (ENG.). 128p. (gr. 2-2). 22.65 *(978-1-4795-4827-9(8),* Zeke Meeks) Picture Window Bks.
—Zeke Meeks vs the Gruesome Girls, 1 vol. Alves, Josh, illus. 2012. (Zeke Meeks Ser.). (ENG.). 128p. (gr. 2-2). pap. 5.95 *(978-1-4048-7221-9(3));* lib. bdg. 22.65 *(978-1-4048-6805-2(4))* Picture Window Bks. (Zeke Meeks).
—Zeke Meeks vs the Horrendous Halloween, 1 vol. Alves, Josh, illus. 2013. (Zeke Meeks Ser.). (ENG.). 128p. (gr. 2-2). lib. bdg. 22.65 *(978-1-4048-7638-5(3),* Zeke Meeks) Picture Window Bks.
—Zeke Meeks vs the Horrifying TV-Turnoff Week, 1 vol. Alves, Josh, illus. 2012. (Zeke Meeks Ser.). (ENG.). 128p. (gr. 2-2). pap. 5.95 *(978-1-4048-7220-2(5));* lib. bdg. 22.65 *(978-1-4048-6804-5(6))* Picture Window Bks. (Zeke Meeks).
—Zeke Meeks vs the Mother's Day Meltdown. Alves, Josh, illus. 2015. (Zeke Meeks Ser.). (ENG.). 128p. (gr. 2-2). 22.65 *(978-1-4795-2168-5(X),* Zeke Meeks) Picture Window Bks.
—Zeke Meeks vs the No-Fun Fund-Raiser, 1 vol. Alves, Josh, illus. 2013. (Zeke Meeks Ser.). (ENG.). 128p. (gr. 2-2). lib. bdg. 22.65 *(978-1-4048-7640-8(5),* Zeke Meeks) Picture Window Bks.
—Zeke Meeks vs the Pain-In-the-Neck Pets, 1 vol. Alves, Josh, illus. 2014. (Zeke Meeks Ser.). (ENG.). 128p. (gr. 2-2). 22.65 *(978-1-4795-2166-1(3),* Zeke Meeks) Picture Window Bks.
—Zeke Meeks vs the Putrid Puppet Pals, 1 vol. Alves, Josh, illus. 2012. (Zeke Meeks Ser.). (ENG.). 128p. (gr. 2-2). pap. 5.95 *(978-1-4048-7223-3(X));* lib. bdg. 22.65 *(978-1-4048-6803-8(8))* Picture Window Bks. (Zeke Meeks).
—Zeke Meeks vs the Stinkin' Science Fair, 1 vol. Alves, Josh, illus. 2012. (Zeke Meeks Ser.). (ENG.). 128p. (gr. 2-2). pap. 5.95 *(978-1-4048-7222-6(1));* lib. bdg. 22.65 *(978-1-4048-6802-1(X))* Picture Window Bks. (Zeke Meeks).
—Zeke Meeks vs the Stinky Soccer Team. Alves, Josh, illus. 2015. (Zeke Meeks Ser.). (ENG.). 128p. (gr. 2-2). 22.65 *(978-1-4795-5768-4(4),* Zeke Meeks) Picture Window Bks.
—Zeke Meeks vs the Super Stressful Talent Show, 1 vol. Alves, Josh, illus. 2013. (Zeke Meeks Ser.). (ENG.). 128p. (gr. 2-2). 8.95 *(978-1-4048-8106-8(9));* lib. bdg. 22.65 *(978-1-4048-7639-2(1))* Picture Window Bks. (Zeke Meeks).
Green, Jack. The Microchip Kid. 2011. 52p. pap. 16.95 *(978-1-4560-8494-3(1))* America Star Bks.
Green, John. Terdellaline: A Free-Spirited, Energeti. 2005. 48p. pap. 16.95 *(978-1-4137-9528-8(5))* PublishAmerica, Inc.
Greenburg, Dan. How I Went from Bad to Verse. Davis, Jack E., illus. 2004. (Zack Files Ser.). 59p. lib. bdg. 15.00 *(978-0-7569-2235-1(6))* Perfection Learning Corp.
—Just Add Water... & Scream! Davis, Jack E., illus. 2004. (Zack Files Ser.). 56p. lib. bdg. 15.00 *(978-0-7569-2239-9(9))* Perfection Learning Corp.
Greenburg, Dan & National Geographic Learning Staff. Just Add Water... & Scream!, 29 vols. Davis, Jack E., illus. 2003. (Zack Files Ser.: 29). (ENG.). 64p. (J). (gr. 2-5). mass mkt. 4.99 *(978-0-448-42867-1(3),* Grosset & Dunlap) Penguin Young Readers Group.
Greene, Stephanie. Owen Foote, Super Spy. Weston, Martha, illus. 2005. (ENG.). 96p. (J). (gr. 1-4). pap. 8.95 *(978-0-618-55159-0(X))* Houghton Mifflin Harcourt Publishing Co.
—Pig Pickin', 0 vols. Mathieu, Joe, illus. 2013. (Moose & Hildy Ser.). (ENG.). 68p. (J). (gr. -1-3). pap. 9.99 *(978-1-4778-1684-4(4),* 9781477816844, Amazon Children's Publishing) Amazon Publishing.
—The Show-Off, 0 vols. Mathieu, Joe, illus. 2007. (Moose & Hildy Ser.: 0). (ENG.). 64p. (J). (gr. 1-4). lib. bdg. 14.99 *(978-0-7614-5374-1(1),* 9780761453741, Amazon Children's Publishing) Amazon Publishing.
Greenwald, Tom. My Dog Is Better Than Your Dog. Stower, Adam, illus. 2015. 198p. (J). pap. *(978-0-545-91669-1(0),* Scholastic Pr.) Scholastic, Inc.
Greenwald, Tommy. Charlie Joe Jackson's Guide to Extra Credit. Coovert, J. P., illus. 2012. (Charlie Joe Jackson Ser.: 2). (ENG.). 272p. (J). (gr. 4-7). 15.99 *(978-1-59643-692-3(1),* 9781596436923) Roaring Brook Pr.
—Charlie Joe Jackson's Guide to Extra Credit. Coovert, J. P., illus. 2013. (Charlie Joe Jackson Ser.: 2). (ENG.). 288p. (J). (gr. 4-7). pap. 7.99 *(978-1-250-01670-6(3),* 9781250016706) Square Fish.
—Charlie Joe Jackson's Guide to Extra Credit. 2013. (Charlie Joe Jackson's Guide Ser.: 2). (J). lib. bdg. 18.40 *(978-0-606-28461-5(3),* Turtleback) Turtleback Bks.
—Charlie Joe Jackson's Guide to Making Money. Coovert, J. P., illus. 2014. (Charlie Joe Jackson Ser.: 4). (ENG.). 208p. (J). (gr. 4-7). 13.99 *(978-1-59643-840-8(1),* 9781596438408) Roaring Brook Pr.
—Charlie Joe Jackson's Guide to Not Growing Up. Burniac, Lauren, ed. Coovert, J. P., illus. 2016. (Charlie Joe Jackson Ser.: 6). (ENG.). 192p. (J). 13.99 *(978-1-62672-169-2(6),* 9781626721692) Roaring Brook Pr.
—Charlie Joe Jackson's Guide to Not Reading. Coovert, J. P., illus. 2011. (Charlie Joe Jackson Ser.: 1). (ENG.). 224p. (J). (gr. 4-7). 15.99 *(978-1-59643-691-6(3),* 9781596436916) Roaring Brook Pr.
—Charlie Joe Jackson's Guide to Not Reading. 2012. (Charlie Joe Jackson's Guide Ser.: 1). (J). lib. bdg. 17.20 *(978-0-606-26127-2(3),* Turtleback) Turtleback Bks.
—Charlie Joe Jackson's Guide to Planet Girl. Coovert, J. P., illus. 2015. (Charlie Joe Jackson Ser.: 5). (ENG.). 208p. (J). (gr. 4-7). 13.99 *(978-1-59643-841-5(X),* 9781596438415) Roaring Brook Pr.
—Charlie Joe Jackson's Guide to Summer Vacation. Coovert, J. P., illus. (Charlie Joe Jackson Ser.: 3). (ENG.). 240p. (J). (gr. 5-7). 2014. 13.99 *(978-1-62672-031-2(2),* 9781626720312) 2013. 14.99 *(978-1-59643-757-9(X),* 9781596437579) Roaring Brook Pr.
—It's a Doggy Dog World. Stower, Adam, illus. 2016. (Crimebiters Ser.: 2). (ENG.). 240p. (J). (gr. 3-7). 12.99 *(978-0-545-78397-2(6),* Scholastic Pr.) Scholastic, Inc.
—Jack Strong Takes a Stand. Mendes, Melissa, illus. 2013. (ENG.). 240p. (J). (gr. 4-7). 15.99 *(978-1-59643-836-1(3),* 9781596438361) Roaring Brook Pr.
—Katie Friedman Gives up Texting! And Lives to Tell about It. Coovert, J. P., illus. 2015. (ENG.). 240p. (J). (gr. 4-7). 13.99 *(978-1-59643-837-8(1),* 9781596438378) Roaring Brook Pr.
—My Dog Is Better Than Your Dog (Crimebiters! #1) Stower, Adam, illus. 2015. (Crimebiters Ser.: 1). (ENG.). 208p. (J). (gr. 3-7). 12.99 *(978-0-545-77332-4(6),* Scholastic Pr.) Scholastic, Inc.
—The Real Us. Burniac, Lauren, ed. Coovert, J. P., illus. 2017. (ENG.). 256p. (J). 16.99 *(978-1-62672-171-5(8),* 9781626721715) Roaring Brook Pr.
Griffiths, Andy. The Big Fat Cow That Goes Kapow. Denton, Terry, illus. 2010. (ENG.). 144p. (J). (gr. -1-3). pap. 7.99 *(978-0-312-65301-9(8),* 9780312653019) Square Fish.
—The Cat on the Mat Is Flat. Denton, Terry, illus. 2009. (ENG.). 192p. (J). (gr. -1-3). pap. 7.99 *(978-0-312-53584-1(8),* 9780312535841) Square Fish.
—The Day My Butt Went Psycho! 2003. (Andy Griffiths' Butt Ser.). (ENG.). 240p. (J). (gr. 3-7). pap. 6.99 *(978-0-439-42469-1(0))* Scholastic, Inc.
—The Day My Butt Went Psycho! 2003. (gr. 5-8). lib. bdg. 17.20 *(978-0-613-62939-3(6),* Turtleback) Turtleback Bks.
—Ed & Ted & Ted's Dog Fred. Denton, Terry, illus. 2014. (My Readers Ser.). (ENG.). 32p. (J). (gr. -1-1). 15.99 *(978-1-250-04447-1(2),* 9781250044471) Square Fish.
—Ed & Ted & Ted's Dog Fred. 2014. (My Readers: Level 2 Ser.). (J). lib. bdg. 13.55 *(978-0-606-35525-4(1))* Turtleback Bks.
—Killer Koalas from Outer Space: And Lots of Other Very Bad Stuff That Will Make Your Brain Explode! Denton, Terry, illus. 2011. (ENG.). 176p. (J). (gr. 3-7). 12.99 *(978-0-312-36789-3(9),* 9780312367893) Feiwel & Friends.
—Killer Koalas from Outer Space & Lots of Other Very Bad Stuff That Will Make Your Brain Explode! Denton, Terry, illus. 2012. (ENG.). 192p. (J). (gr. 3-7). pap. 7.99 *(978-1-250-01017-9(9),* 9781250010179) Square Fish.
—The 13-Story Treehouse. Denton, Terry, illus. 2013. (Treehouse Bks.: 1). (ENG.). 256p. (J). (gr. 1-5). 13.99 *(978-1-250-02690-3(3),* 9781250026903) Feiwel & Friends.
—The 13-Story Treehouse. Denton, Terry, illus. 2015. (Treehouse Bks.: 1). (ENG.). 272p. (J). (gr. 1-5). pap. 6.99 *(978-1-250-07065-4(1),* 9781250070654) Square Fish.
—The 26-Story Treehouse. Denton, Terry, illus. 2014. (Treehouse Bks.: 2). (ENG.). 352p. (J). (gr. 1-5). 13.99 *(978-1-250-02691-0(1),* 9781250026910) Feiwel & Friends.
—The 39-Story Treehouse. Denton, Terry, illus. 2015. (Treehouse Bks.). (ENG.). 352p. (J). (gr. 1-5). 13.99 *(978-1-250-02692-7(X),* 9781250026927) Feiwel & Friends.
—The 39-Story Treehouse. Barcellona, Christine, ed. Denton, Terry, illus. 2016. (Treehouse Bks.: 3). (ENG.). 368p. (J). pap. 6.99 *(978-1-250-07511-6(4),* 9781250075116) Square Fish.
Groening, Matt. Simpsons Comics Colossal Compendium Volume 3. 2015. (ENG., Illus.). 176p. pap. 17.99 *(978-0-06-236059-5(0),* Collins Design) HarperCollins Pubs.
Grogan, John. Marley & the Kittens. Cowdrey, Richard, illus. 2010. (Marley Ser.). 40p. (J). (gr. -1-3). (ENG.). 17.99 *(978-0-06-171486-3(0));* lib. bdg. 18.89 *(978-0-06-171487-0(9))* HarperCollins Pubs.
—Marley Goes to School. Cowdrey, Richard, illus. (Marley Ser.). 40p. (J). (gr. -1-3). 2012. (ENG.). 9.99 *(978-0-06-211366-5(6))* 2009. (ENG.). 17.99 *(978-0-06-156151-1(7))* 2009. lib. bdg. 18.89 *(978-0-06-156152-8(5))* HarperCollins Pubs.
—Marley Storybook Treasury. Cowdrey, Richard, illus. 2012. (I Can Read Level 2 Ser.). (ENG.). 192p. (J). (gr. k-3). 11.99 *(978-0-06-212331-2(9))* HarperCollins Pubs.
—Snow Dog Marley. Cowdrey, Richard, illus. 2010. (I Can Read Level 2 Ser.). (ENG.). 32p. (J). (gr. k-3). 16.99 *(978-0-06-185393-7(3));* pap. 3.99 *(978-0-06-185392-0(5))* HarperCollins Pubs.
Grosgebauer, Clare Ham. Snickerdoodle! a Tall Tale about a Powerful Pee-Wee! Rissing, Karen, illus. 3rd ed. 2005. 40p. (J). (gr. -1-3). 12.99 *(978-0-9741888-2-9(4))* Small Wonders Enterprises.
Grubman, Bonnie. How Do You Get a Mouse to Smile?, 1 vol. Van Wright, Cornelius, illus. 2009. (ENG.). 32p. (J). (gr. -1-3). pap. 6.50 *(978-1-59572-167-9(3))* Star Bright Bks., Inc.

Guardo, Attilio. A Special Time in Clear Creek. 2004. 184p. pap. 24.95 *(978-1-4137-2872-9(3))* America Star Bks.

Guerra, S. F. Billy the Kid Is Not Crazy, 0 vols. 2013. (ENG.). 224p. (J). (gr. 4-6). 16.99 *(978-1-4778-1732-2(8),* 9781477817322, Amazon Children's Publishing) Amazon Publishing.

Guillain, Adam & Guillain, Charlotte. The Pirate Pie Ship. Van Wyk, Rupert, illus. 2014. (ENG.). 32p. (J). *(978-0-7787-1309-8(1));* pap. *(978-0-7787-1368-5(7))* Crabtree Publishing Co.

Guillian, Adam & Guillain, Charlotte. Emma Peror's New Clothes. Waters, Erica-Jane, illus. 2015. (Fairy Tales Today Ser.). (ENG.). 24p. (gr. 1-2). 23.99 *(978-1-4795-8617-2(X))* Picture Window Bks.

Gunderson, Jessica. Really, Rapunzel Needed a Haircut! The Story of Rapunzel, as Told by Dame Gothel. Alonso, Denis, illus. 2013. (Other Side of the Story Ser.). (ENG.). 24p. (gr. 2-3). 27.32 *(978-1-4048-7941-6(2))* Picture Window Bks.

—Really, Rapunzel Needed a Haircut! The Story of Rapunzel As Told by Dame Gothel. Alonso, Denis, illus. 2013. (Other Side of the Story Ser.). (ENG.). 24p. (gr. 2-3). 9.95 *(978-1-4795-1946-0(4))* Picture Window Bks.

Gunderson, Jessica & Loewen, Nancy. Really, Rapunzel Needed a Haircut! The Story of Rapunzel As Told by Dame Gothel. Alonso, Denis & Tayal, Amit, illus. 2013. (Other Side of the Story Ser.). (ENG.). 24p. (gr. 2-3). pap. 6.95 *(978-1-4795-1950-7(2))* Picture Window Bks.

Gundert, Margaret. D. Q. & the SOOYOO, 1 vol. Gundert, Marjorie, illus. 2010. 20p. 24.95 *(978-1-4512-1226-6(7))* PublishAmerica, Inc.

Gutch, Michael. Sticky, Sticky, Stuck! Björkman, Steve, illus. 2013. (ENG.). 32p. (J). (gr. -1-3). 17.99 *(978-0-06-199818-8(4))* HarperCollins Pubs.

Gutierrez, Debbi Miller. Cactus Factory. 2007. (J). pap. 5.99 *(978-0-9740173-4-1(5))* Prints By Mail.

Gutman, Dan. Back to School, Weird Kids Rule! Paillot, Jim, illus. 2014. (My Weird School Special Ser.). (ENG.). 144p. (J). (gr. 1-5). pap. 5.99 *(978-0-06-220685-5(0))* HarperCollins Pubs.

—Back to School, Weird Kids Rule! 2014. (My Weird School Ser.). (J). lib. bdg. 16.00 *(978-0-606-35502-5(2))* Turtleback Bks.

—Bunny Double, We're in Trouble! Paillot, Jim, illus. 2014. (My Weird School Special Ser.). 144p. (J). (gr. 1-5). (ENG.). pap. 5.99 *(978-0-06-228400-6(2));* lib. bdg. 16.89 *(978-0-06-228401-3(0))* HarperCollins Pubs.

—Bunny Double, We're in Trouble! 2014. (My Weird School Ser.). (J). lib. bdg. 16.00 *(978-0-606-35055-6(1),* Turtleback) Turtleback Bks.

—The Christmas Genie. Santat, Dan, illus. 2009. (ENG.). 160p. (J). (gr. 3-7). 16.99 *(978-1-4169-9001-7(1),* Simon & Schuster Bks. For Young Readers) Simon & Schuster Bks. For Young Readers.

—Coach Hyatt Is a Riot! Paillot, Jim, illus. 2008. (My Weird School Daze Ser.: 4). 112p. (J). (gr. 1-5). lib. bdg. 15.89 *(978-0-06-155408-7(1));* 4th ed. (ENG.). pap. 4.99 *(978-0-06-155406-3(5))* HarperCollins Pubs.

—Deck the Halls, We're off the Walls! Paillot, Jim, illus. 2013. (My Weird School Special Ser.). 144p. (J). (gr. 1-5). (ENG.). pap. 5.99 *(978-0-06-220682-4(6));* lib. bdg. 16.89 *(978-0-06-220683-1(4))* HarperCollins Pubs.

—Dr. Brad Has Gone Mad! Paillot, Jim, illus. 2009. (My Weird School Daze Ser.: 7). 112p. (J). (gr. 1-5). lib. bdg. 15.89 *(978-0-06-155414-8(6))* HarperCollins Pubs.

—Dr. Brad Has Gone Mad! 2009. (My Weird School Daze Ser.: 7). (J). lib. bdg. 14.75 *(978-0-606-06969-4(0),* Turtleback) Turtleback Bks.

—Dr. Carbles Is Losing His Marbles! Paillot, Jim, illus. 2007. (My Weird School Ser.: 19). 112p. (J). (ENG.). (gr. 1-5). pap. 4.99 *(978-0-06-123477-4(X));* (gr. 2-5). lib. bdg. 15.89 *(978-0-06-123478-1(8))* HarperCollins Pubs.

—Dr. Carbles Is Losing His Marbles! Paillot, Jim, illus. 2007. (My Weird School Ser.: No. 19). 99p. (J). (gr. 2-5). 11.65 *(978-0-7569-8810-4(1))* Perfection Learning Corp.

—Dr. Nicholas Is Ridiculous! Paillot, Jim, illus. 2013. (My Weirder School Ser.: 8). 112p. (J). (gr. 1-5). 15.89 *(978-0-06-204219-4(X));* (ENG.). pap. 4.99 *(978-0-06-204218-7(1))* HarperCollins Pubs.

—Funny Boy Meets the Airsick Alien from Andromeda. Dykes, John S., illus. 2012. (Funny Boy Ser.). (ENG.). 136p. (J). (gr. 2-5). pap. 10.99 *(978-1-4532-9527-4(5))* Open Road Integrated Media, Inc.

—Funny Boy Meets the Dumbbell Dentist from Deimos (with Dangerous Dental Decay) Dietz, Mike, illus. 2012. (Funny Boy Ser.). (ENG.). 120p. (J). (gr. 2-5). pap. 6.99 *(978-1-4532-7070-7(1))* Open Road Integrated Media, Inc.

—Funny Boy Takes on the Chit-Chatting Cheeses from Chattanooga. Dietz, Mike, illus. 2012. (Funny Boy Ser.). (ENG.). 138p. (J). (gr. 2-5). pap. 10.99 *(978-1-4532-9530-4(5))* Open Road Integrated Media, Inc.

—Funny Boy Versus the Bubble-Brained Barbers from the Big Bang. Dietz, Mike, illus. 2012. (Funny Boy Ser.). (ENG.). 144p. (J). (gr. 2-5). pap. 6.99 *(978-1-4532-9532-8(1))* Open Road Integrated Media, Inc.

—The Homework Machine. 2007. (ENG.). 176p. (J). (gr. 3-7). pap. 6.99 *(978-0-689-87679-0(3),* Simon & Schuster Bks. For Young Readers) Simon & Schuster Bks. For Young Readers.

—It's Halloween, I'm Turning Green! 2013. (My Weird School Ser.). (J). lib. bdg. 16.00 *(978-0-606-32560-8(3),* Turtleback) Turtleback Bks.

—Mayor Hubble Is in Trouble! Paillot, Jim, illus. 2012. (My Weirder School Ser.: 6). 112p. (J). (gr. 1-5). (ENG.). pap. 4.99 *(978-0-06-204212-5(2));* lib. bdg. 15.89 *(978-0-06-204213-2(0))* HarperCollins Pubs.

—Mayor Hubble Is in Trouble! 2012. (My Weirder School Ser.: 6). (J). lib. bdg. 14.75 *(978-0-606-26525-6(2),* Turtleback) Turtleback Bks.

—The Million Dollar Strike. 2004. 176p. (J). lib. bdg. 18.46 *(978-1-4242-2107-3(2))* Fitzgerald Bks.

—The Million Dollar Strike. 2006. 176p. (J). (gr. 3-7). 13.65 *(978-0-7569-7023-9(7))* Perfection Learning Corp.

—Miss Brown Is Upside Down! Paillot, Jim, illus. 2015. (My Weirdest School Ser.: 3). (ENG.). 112p. (J). (gr. 1-5). pap. 4.99 *(978-0-06-228427-3(4))* HarperCollins Pubs.

—Miss Child Has Gone Wild! Paillot, Jim, illus. 2011. (My Weirder School Ser.: 1). 112p. (J). (gr. 1-5). (ENG.). pap. 4.99 *(978-0-06-196916-4(8));* lib. bdg. 15.89 *(978-0-06-196917-1(6))* HarperCollins Pubs.

—Miss Daisy Is Crazy! Paillot, Jim, illus. 2004. (My Weird School Ser.: 1). (ENG.). 96p. (J). (gr. 1-5). pap. 4.99 *(978-0-06-050700-8(4))* HarperCollins Pubs.

—Miss Klute Is a Hoot! Paillot, Jim, illus. 2014. (My Weirder School Ser.: 11). 112p. (J). (gr. 1-5). 15.89 *(978-0-06-219845-7(9));* (ENG.). pap. 4.99 *(978-0-06-219844-0(0))* HarperCollins Pubs.

—Miss Klute Is a Hoot! 2014. (My Weirder School Ser.: 11). (J). lib. bdg. 14.75 *(978-0-606-35503-2(0))* Turtleback Bks.

—Miss Kraft Is Daft! Paillot, Jim, illus. 2012. (My Weirder School Ser.: 7). 112p. (J). (gr. 1-5). (ENG.). pap. 4.99 *(978-0-06-204215-6(7));* lib. bdg. 15.89 *(978-0-06-204216-3(5))* HarperCollins Pubs.

—Miss Kraft Is Daft! Paillot, Jim, illus. 2012. (My Weirder School Ser.: 7). (J). lib. bdg. 14.75 *(978-0-606-27125-7(2),* Turtleback) Turtleback Bks.

—Miss Laney Is Zany! Paillot, Jim, illus. 2010. (My Weird School Daze Ser.: 8). 112p. (J). (gr. 1-5). (ENG.). pap. 4.99 *(978-0-06-155415-5(4));* lib. bdg. 15.89 *(978-0-06-155417-9(0))* HarperCollins Pubs.

—Miss Laney Is Zany! 2010. (My Weird School Daze Ser.: 8). (J). lib. bdg. 14.75 *(978-0-606-10112-7(8),* Turtleback) Turtleback Bks.

—Miss Mary Is Scary! Paillot, Jim, illus. 2010. (My Weird School Daze Ser.: 10). 112p. (J). (gr. 1-5). (ENG.). pap. 4.99 *(978-0-06-170397-3(4));* lib. bdg. 15.89 *(978-0-06-170398-0(2))* HarperCollins Pubs.

—Miss Small Is off the Wall! Paillot, Jim, illus. 2005. (My Weird School Ser.: 5). (ENG.). 112p. (J). (gr. 1-5). pap. 4.99 *(978-0-06-074518-9(5))* HarperCollins Pubs.

—Miss Suki Is Kooky! Paillot, Jim, illus. 2007. (My Weird School Ser.: 17). (J). 14.75 *(978-1-4177-7430-2(4),* Turtleback) Turtleback Bks.

—Mr. Burke Is Berserk! Paillot, Jim, illus. 2012. (My Weirder School Ser.: 4). 112p. (J). (gr. 1-5). (ENG.). pap. 4.99 *(978-0-06-196922-5(2));* lib. bdg. 15.89 *(978-0-06-196923-2(0))* HarperCollins Pubs.

—Mr. Burke Is Berserk! 2012. (My Weirder School Ser.: 4). (J). lib. bdg. 14.75 *(978-0-606-23571-6(X),* Turtleback) Turtleback Bks.

—Mr. Cooper Is Super! Paillot, Jim, illus. 2015. (My Weirdest School Ser.: 1). (ENG.). 112p. (J). (gr. 1-5). pap. 4.99 *(978-0-06-228421-1(5))* HarperCollins Pubs.

—Mr. Cooper Is Super! Paillot, Jim, illus. 2015. (My Weirdest School Ser.: 1). (J). lib. bdg. 14.75 *(978-0-606-36482-9(X))* Turtleback Bks.

—Mr. Docker Is off His Rocker! Paillot, Jim, illus. 2006. (My Weird School Ser.: 10). (ENG.). 112p. (J). (gr. 1-5). pap. 4.99 *(978-0-06-082227-9(9))* HarperCollins Pubs.

—Mr. Granite Is from Another Planet!, No. 3. Paillot, Jim, illus. 2008. (My Weird School Daze Ser.: 3). (ENG.). 112p. (J). (gr. 1-5). pap. 4.99 *(978-0-06-134611-8(X))* HarperCollins Pubs.

—Mr. Harrison Is Embarrassin'! Paillot, Jim, illus. 2011. (My Weirder School Ser.: 2). (ENG.). 112p. (J). (gr. 1-5). pap. 4.99 *(978-0-06-196918-8(4))* HarperCollins Pubs.

—Mr. Hynde Is Out of His Mind! Paillot, Jim, illus. 2005. (My Weird School Ser.: 6). (ENG.). 112p. (J). (gr. 1-5). pap. 4.99 *(978-0-06-074520-2(7))* HarperCollins Pubs.

—Mr. Jack Is a Maniac! Paillot, Jim, illus. 2014. (My Weirder School Ser.: 10). 112p. (J). (gr. 1-5). (ENG.). pap. 4.99 *(978-0-06-219841-9(6));* lib. bdg. 15.89 *(978-0-06-219842-6(4))* HarperCollins Pubs.

—Mr. Jack Is a Maniac! 2014. (My Weirder School Ser.: 10). (J). lib. bdg. 13.55 *(978-0-606-35066-2(7),* Turtleback) Turtleback Bks.

—Mr. Louie Is Screwy! Paillot, Jim, illus. 2007. (My Weird School Ser.: 20). (ENG.). 112p. (J). (gr. 1-5). pap. 4.99 *(978-0-06-123479-8(6))* HarperCollins Pubs.

—Mr. Macky Is Wacky! Paillot, Jim, illus. 2006. (My Weird School Ser.: 15). (ENG.). 112p. (J). (gr. 1-5). pap. 4.99 *(978-0-06-114151-5(8))* HarperCollins Pubs.

—Mr. Macky Is Wacky! Paillot, Jim, illus. 2006. (My Weird School Ser.: 15). (J). lib. bdg. 14.75 *(978-1-4177-7429-6(0),* Turtleback) Turtleback Bks.

—Mr. Sunny Is Funny! Paillot, Jim, illus. 2008. (My Weird School Daze Ser.: 2). 112p. (J). (gr. 1-5). (ENG.). pap. 4.99 *(978-0-06-134609-5(8));*No. 2. lib. bdg. 15.89 *(978-0-06-134610-1(1))* HarperCollins Pubs.

—Mr. Tony Is Full of Baloney! Paillot, Jim, illus. 2010. (My Weird School Daze Ser.: 11). 112p. (J). (gr. 1-5). (ENG.). pap. 4.99 *(978-0-06-170399-7(0));* lib. bdg. 15.89 *(978-0-06-170400-0(8))* HarperCollins Pubs.

—Mrs. Cooney Is Loony! Paillot, Jim, illus. 2005. (My Weird School Ser.: 7). (ENG.). 112p. (J). (gr. 1-5). pap. 4.99 *(978-0-06-074522-6(3))* HarperCollins Pubs.

—Mrs. Dole Is Out of Control! Paillot, Jim, illus. 2008. (My Weird School Daze Ser.: 1). (ENG.). 112p. (J). (gr. 1-5). pap. 4.99 *(978-0-06-134607-1(1))* HarperCollins Pubs.

—Mrs. Jafee Is Daffy! Paillot, Jim, illus. 2009. (My Weird School Daze Ser.: 6). (ENG.). 128p. (J). (gr. 1-5). pap. 4.99 *(978-0-06-155411-7(1))* HarperCollins Pubs.

—Mrs. Jafee Is Daffy! 2009. (My Weird School Daze Ser.: 6). (J). lib. bdg. 14.75 *(978-0-606-05035-7(3),* Turtleback) Turtleback Bks.

—Mrs. Kormel Is Not Normal! Paillot, Jim, illus. 2006. (My Weird School Ser.: 11). (ENG.). 96p. (J). (gr. 1-5). pap. 4.99 *(978-0-06-082229-3(5))* HarperCollins Pubs.

—Mrs. Lane Is a Pain! Paillot, Jim, illus. 2014. (My Weirder School Ser.: 12). 112p. (J). (gr. 1-5). (ENG.). pap. 4.99 *(978-0-06-219847-1(5));* lib. bdg. 15.89 *(978-0-06-219848-8(3))* HarperCollins Pubs.

—Mrs. Lane Is a Pain! 2014. (My Weirder School Ser.: 12). (J). lib. bdg. 14.75 *(978-0-606-35964-1(8))* Turtleback Bks.

—Mrs. Lilly Is Silly! Paillot, Jim, illus. 2011. (My Weirder School Ser.: 3). (ENG.). 112p. (J). (gr. 1-5). pap. 4.99 *(978-0-06-196920-1(6))* HarperCollins Pubs.

—Mrs. Lizzy Is Dizzy! Paillot, Jim, illus. 2010. (My Weird School Daze Ser.: 9). 112p. (J). (gr. 1-5). (ENG.). pap. 4.99 *(978-0-06-155416-2(2));* lib. bdg. 15.89 *(978-0-06-155418-6(9))* HarperCollins Pubs.

—Mrs. Lizzy Is Dizzy! 2010. (My Weird School Daze Ser.: 9). (J). lib. bdg. 14.75 *(978-0-606-10113-4(6),* Turtleback) Turtleback Bks.

—Mrs. Master Is a Disaster! 2017. (My Weirdest School Ser.: 8). lib. bdg. 14.75 ***(978-0-606-40078-7(8))*** Turtleback Bks.

—Mrs. Meyer Is on Fire! Paillot, Jim, illus. 2016. 105p. (J). ***(978-1-4806-9926-7(8))*** Harper & Row Ltd.

—Mrs. Patty Is Batty! Paillot, Jim, illus. 2006. (My Weird School Ser.: 13). (ENG.). 112p. (J). (gr. 1-5). pap. 4.99 *(978-0-06-085380-8(8))* HarperCollins Pubs.

—Mrs. Yonkers Is Bonkers! Paillot, Jim, illus. 2007. (My Weird School Ser.: 18). (J). 14.75 *(978-1-4177-8222-2(6),* Turtleback) Turtleback Bks.

—Ms. Beard Is Weird! Paillot, Jim, illus. 2012. (My Weirder School Ser.: 5). (ENG.). 112p. (J). (gr. 1-5). pap. 4.99 *(978-0-06-204209-5(2))* HarperCollins Pubs.

—Ms. Coco Is Loco! Paillot, Jim, illus. 2007. (My Weird School Ser.: 16). (ENG.). 112p. (J). (gr. 1-5). pap. 4.99 *(978-0-06-114153-9(4))* HarperCollins Pubs.

—Ms. Coco Is Loco! Paillot, Jim, illus. 2007. (My Weird School Ser.: 16). (J). 14.75 *(978-1-4177-7428-9(2),* Turtleback) Turtleback Bks.

—Ms. Hannah Is Bananas! Paillot, Jim, illus. 2004. (My Weird School Ser.: 4). (ENG.). 96p. (J). (gr. 1-5). pap. 4.99 *(978-0-06-050706-0(3))* HarperCollins Pubs.

—Ms. Leakey Is Freaky! Paillot, Jim, illus. 2011. (My Weird School Daze Ser.: 12). 112p. (J). (gr. 1-5). lib. bdg. 15.89 *(978-0-06-170403-1(2))* HarperCollins Pubs.

—Ms. Sue Has No Clue! Paillot, Jim, illus. 2013. (My Weirder School Ser.: 9). 112p. (J). (gr. 1-5). (ENG.). pap. 4.99 *(978-0-06-219838-9(6));* lib. bdg. 15.89 *(978-0-06-219839-6(4))* HarperCollins Pubs.

—Ms. Sue Has No Clue! 2013. (My Weirder School Ser.: 9). (J). lib. bdg. 14.75 *(978-0-606-32173-0(X),* Turtleback) Turtleback Bks.

—Ms. Todd Is Odd! Paillot, Jim, illus. 2006. (My Weird School Ser.: 12). (ENG.). 112p. (J). (gr. 1-5). pap. 4.99 *(978-0-06-082231-6(7))* HarperCollins Pubs.

—My Weird School: Class Pet Mess! Paillot, Jim, illus. 2017. (I Can Read Level 2 Ser.). 32p. (J). (gr. -1-3). pap. 3.99 *(978-0-06-236746-4(3))* HarperCollins Pubs.

—My Weird School Daze! Paillot, Jim, illus. 2007. (J). *(978-1-4287-4814-9(8))* HarperCollins Pubs.

—My Weird School Daze 12-Book Box Set, 12 vols. Paillot, Jim, illus. 2013. (My Weird School Daze Ser.). (ENG.). 500p. (J). (gr. 1-5). pap. 45.00 *(978-0-06-228891-2(1))* HarperCollins Pubs.

—My Weirdest School #8: Mrs. Master Is a Disaster! Paillot, Jim, illus. 2017. (My Weirdest School Ser.: 8). 112p. (J). (gr. 1-5). pap. 4.99 *(978-0-06-242933-9(7))* HarperCollins Pubs.

—My Weirdest School #9: Miss Tracy Is Spacey! Paillot, Jim, illus. 2017. (My Weirdest School Ser.: 9). 112p. (J). (gr. 1-5). pap. 4.99 ***(978-0-06-242936-0(1))*** HarperCollins Pubs.

—Officer Spence Makes No Sense! Paillot, Jim, illus. 2009. (My Weird School Daze Ser.: 5). 112p. (J). (gr. 1-5). (ENG.). pap. 4.99 *(978-0-06-155409-4(X));* lib. bdg. 15.89 *(978-0-06-155410-0(3))* HarperCollins Pubs.

—Oh, Valentine, We've Lost Our Minds! Paillot, Jim, illus. 2014. (My Weird School Special Ser.). (ENG.). 144p. (J). (gr. 1-5). pap. 5.99 *(978-0-06-228403-7(7))* HarperCollins Pubs.

—Oh, Valentine, We've Lost Our Minds! 2014. (My Weird School Ser.). (J). lib. bdg. 16.00 *(978-0-606-36460-7(9))* Turtleback Bks.

Habek, Wendy. Good Boy, Troy! 2009. 20p. (J). pap. 13.95 *(978-1-4327-3192-2(0))* Outskirts Pr., Inc.

Hafer, Tom. The Lemonade Crash. Terry, Brian, illus. 2010. 24p. 16.95 *(978-1-4520-1439-5(6))* AuthorHouse.

Hagen, George. Gabriel Finley & the Raven's Riddle. 2016. (ENG.). 384p. (J). (gr. 4-7). 18.40 *(978-0-606-39345-4(5))* Turtleback Bks.

Haggis-On-Whey, Doris & Haggis-On-Whey, Benny. Giraffes? Giraffes! 2008. (How Ser.: 1). (ENG., Illus.). 64p. (gr. 4-7). 20.00 *(978-1-932416-97-8(8))* McSweeney's Publishing.

Hahn, Phil. Henrietta: The Homely Duckling. Coker, Paul, Jr., illus. 2004. (Weewisdom Bks.). 47p. (J). 16.95 *(978-0-87159-293-4(2),* 168, Unity Hse.) Unity Schl. of Christianity.

Haight, Travis. 2:30 AM: Wired on Coffee; Six Premium Blended (Not So) Shorts. 2007. 203p. pap. 13.95 *(978-1-4303-1004-4(9))* Lulu Pr., Inc.

Hale, Bruce. The Big Nap. Hale, Bruce, illus. 2008. (Chet Gecko Mystery Ser.: No. 4). (ENG., Illus.). 128p. (gr. 1-5). 24.21 *(978-1-59961-461-8(8))* Spotlight.

—Dial M for Mongoose: A Chet Gecko Mystery. 2010. (Chet Gecko Ser.: 15). (ENG., Illus.). 128p. (J). (gr. 2-5). pap. 5.99 *(978-0-547-48079-4(2))* Houghton Mifflin Harcourt Publishing Co.

—Fat Cat of Underwhere. Hillman, Shane, illus. 2009. (Underwhere Ser.). 176p. (J). pap. 5.99 *(978-0-06-085135-4(X))* HarperCollins Pubs.

—From Russia with Lunch: A Chet Gecko Mystery. 2010. (Chet Gecko Ser.: 14). (ENG., Illus.). 128p. (J). (gr. 2-5). pap. 6.99 *(978-0-547-32882-9(6))* Houghton Mifflin Harcourt Publishing Co.

—Give My Regrets to Broadway. 2005. (Chet Gecko Mystery Ser.). (Illus.). 115p. (gr. 3-7). 16.00 *(978-0-7569-5247-1(6))* Perfection Learning Corp.

—The Hamster of the Baskervilles. 2003. (Chet Gecko Ser.: 5). (ENG., Illus.). 144p. (J). (gr. 2-5). pap. 6.99 *(978-0-15-202509-0(X))* Houghton Mifflin Harcourt Publishing Co.

—Hiss Me Deadly. Hale, Bruce, illus. 2009. (Chet Gecko Ser.: 13). (ENG., Illus.). 128p. (J). (gr. 2-5). pap. 5.99 *(978-0-15-206424-2(9))* Houghton Mifflin Harcourt Publishing Co.

—Key Lardo: A Chet Gecko Mystery. Hale, Bruce, illus. 2007. (Chet Gecko Ser.: 12). (ENG., Illus.). 128p. (J). (gr. 2-5). pap. 5.99 *(978-0-15-205235-5(6))* Houghton Mifflin Harcourt Publishing Co.

—The Malted Falcon. 2007. (Chet Gecko Mystery Ser.). (Illus.). 107p. (J). (gr. 4-7). pap. 6.60 *(978-1-4189-5239-6(7))* Harcourt Trade Pubs.

—The Malted Falcon. 2008. (Chet Gecko Ser.: 7). (ENG., Illus.). 128p. (J). (gr. 2-5). pap. 5.99 *(978-0-15-216712-7(9))* Houghton Mifflin Harcourt Publishing Co.

—The Malted Falcon. Hale, Bruce, illus. 2008. (Chet Gecko Mystery Ser.: No. 7). (ENG., Illus.). 128p. (gr. 1-5). 24.21 *(978-1-59961-467-0(7))* Spotlight.

—Mole Men of Underwhere. Hillman, Shane, illus. 2009. (Underwhere Ser.). 160p. (J). 15.99 *(978-0-06-085136-1(8))* HarperCollins Pubs.

—Murder, My Tweet. 2005. (Chet Gecko Mystery Ser.). (Illus.). 117p. (gr. 3-7). 16.00 *(978-0-7569-5248-8(4))* Perfection Learning Corp.

—Murder, My Tweet. Hale, Bruce, illus. 2008. (Chet Gecko Mystery Ser.: No. 10). (ENG., Illus.). 136p. (gr. 1-5). 24.21 *(978-1-59961-468-7(5))* Spotlight.

—The Mystery of Mr. Nice. Hale, Bruce, illus. 2008. (Chet Gecko Mystery Ser.: No. 2). (ENG., Illus.). 112p. (gr. 1-5). 24.21 *(978-1-59961-469-4(3))* Spotlight.

—Pirates of Underwhere. Hillman, Shane, illus. (Underwhere Ser.: 2). (J). (gr. 3-7). 2009. (ENG.). 176p. pap. 6.99 *(978-0-06-085129-3(5))* 2008. 164p. lib. bdg. 16.89 *(978-0-06-085128-6(7))* HarperCollins Pubs.

—The Possum Always Rings Twice. Hale, Bruce, illus. 2007. (Chet Gecko Ser.: 11). (ENG., Illus.). 128p. (J). (gr. 2-5). pap. 5.99 *(978-0-15-205233-1(X))* Houghton Mifflin Harcourt Publishing Co.

—Prince of Underwhere. Hillman, Shane, illus. 2009. (Underwhere Ser.: 1). (ENG.). 176p. (J). (gr. 3-7). pap. 5.99 *(978-0-06-085126-2(0))* HarperCollins Pubs.

—School for SPIES Book 2 Thicker Than Water. Dorman, Brandon, illus. 2014. (School for Spies Novel Ser.). (ENG.). 352p. (J). (gr. 3-7). 16.99 *(978-1-4231-6851-5(8))* Hyperion Bks. for Children.

—This Gum for Hire. 2003. (Chet Gecko Ser.: 6). (ENG., Illus.). 144p. (J). (gr. 2-5). pap. 5.99 *(978-0-15-202497-0(2))* Houghton Mifflin Harcourt Publishing Co.

—This Gum for Hire. 2007. (Chet Gecko Mystery Ser.). (Illus.). 115p. (J). (gr. 4-7). pap. 6.60 *(978-1-4189-5216-7(8))* Houghton Mifflin Harcourt Supplemental Pubs.

—This Gum for Hire. Hale, Bruce, illus. 2008. (Chet Gecko Mystery Ser.: No. 6). (ENG., Illus.). 128p. (gr. 1-5). 24.21 *(978-1-59961-471-7(5))* Spotlight.

—Trouble Is My Beeswax. 2004. (Chet Gecko Mystery Ser.). (Illus.). 111p. (gr. 3-7). 16.00 *(978-0-7569-3488-0(5))* Perfection Learning Corp.

—Trouble Is My Beeswax. Hale, Bruce, illus. 2008. (Chet Gecko Mystery Ser.: No. 8). (ENG., Illus.). 128p. (gr. 1-5). 24.21 *(978-1-59961-472-4(3))* Spotlight.

—Trouble Is My Beeswax: A Chet Gecko Mystery. 2004. (Chet Gecko Ser.: 8). (ENG., Illus.). 144p. (J). (gr. 2-5). pap. 6.99 *(978-0-15-216724-0(2))* Houghton Mifflin Harcourt Publishing Co.

Hale, Dean. Scapegoat: The Story of a Goat Named Oat & a Chewed-Up Coat. Slack, Michael, illus. 2011. (ENG.). 32p. (J). (gr. -1-3). 16.99 *(978-1-59990-468-9(3),* 9781599904689, Bloomsbury USA Childrens) Bloomsbury Publishing USA.

Hale, Lucretia. The Peterkin Papers. Brett, Harold M., illus. 2005. reprint ed. pap. 24.95 *(978-1-4179-3265-8(1))* Kessinger Publishing, LLC.

Hale, Lucretia P. The Peterkin Papers. 2009. (Dover Children's Classics Ser.). (ENG., Illus.). 224p. (J). (gr. k-6). pap. 7.99 *(978-0-486-47170-9(5))* Dover Pubns., Inc.

—The Peterkin Papers. 2004. reprint ed. pap. 1.99 *(978-1-4192-7709-2(X));* pap. 20.95 *(978-1-4191-7709-5(5))* Kessinger Publishing, LLC.

—The Peterkin Papers. 2006. (New York Review Children's Collection). (ENG., Illus.). 324p. (J). (gr. 4-7). 18.95 *(978-1-59017-212-4(4),* NYR Children's Collection) New York Review of Bks., Inc., The.

Hall / Waltz. Mortimer Jones: The Bubble Gum Nerd, 1. l.t. ed. 2003. (Illus.). 32p. 19.95 *(978-0-9741774-2-7(3))* D. W. Publishing.

Hall, John. Is He or Isn't He? 2006. (ENG.). 304p. (YA). (gr. 9). pap. 8.99 *(978-0-06-078747-9(3),* HarperTeen) HarperCollins Pubs.

Hall, Michael. Frankencrayon. Hall, Michael, illus. 2016. (Illus.). 40p. (J). (gr. -1-3). 17.99 *(978-0-06-225211-1(9));* lib. bdg. 18.89 *(978-0-06-225212-8(7))* HarperCollins Pubs. (Greenwillow Bks.).

Hall, Shirley. Buggy Buggy. Ledger, Faye, illus. 2010. 20p. 12.00 *(978-1-4520-6787-2(2))* AuthorHouse.

Hamburg, Jennifer. Hazy Bloom & the Tomorrow Power. Mourning, Tuesday & Hamie, Jenn, illus. 2017. (Hazy Bloom Ser.). (ENG.). 176p. (J). 15.99 *(978-0-374-30494-2(7),* 9780374304942, Farrar, Straus & Giroux (BYR)) Farrar, Straus & Giroux.

—Monkey & Duck Quack Up! Fotheringham, Edwin, illus. 2015. (ENG.). 32p. (J). (gr. -1-3). 17.99 *(978-0-545-64514-0(X),* Scholastic Pr.) Scholastic, Inc.

—A Moose That Says Moo. Truesdell, Sue, illus. 2013. (ENG.). 32p. (J). (gr. -1 — 1). 16.99 *(978-0-374-35058-1(2),* 9780374350581, Farrar, Straus & Giroux (BYR)) Farrar, Straus & Giroux.

Hamilton, Kersten. The Ire of Iron Claw. Hamilton, James, illus. (Gadgets & Gears Ser.: 2). (ENG.). (J). (gr. 2-5). 2016. 192p. pap. 6.99 *(978-0-544-66854-6(5),* HMH Books For Young Readers) 2015. 176p. 16.99 *(978-0-544-22502-2(3))* Houghton Mifflin Harcourt Publishing Co.

—The Tick-Tock Man. Hamilton, James, illus. 2016. (Gadgets & Gears Ser.: 3). (ENG.). 144p. (J). (gr. 2-5). 16.99 *(978-0-544-43300-7(9))* Houghton Mifflin Harcourt Publishing Co.

Handford, Martin. The Fantastic Journey. Handford, Martin, illus. deluxe ed. 2013. (Where's Waldo? Ser.). (ENG., Illus.). 32p. (J). (gr. k-12). 16.99 *(978-0-7636-4528-1(1))* Candlewick Pr.

—Where's Waldo? Handford, Martin, illus. (Where's Waldo? Ser.). (ENG., Illus.). (J). (gr. k-4). 2011. 64p. pap. 9.99 *(978-0-7636-5416-0(7))* 2nd ed. 2007. 32p. pap. 7.99 *(978-0-7636-3498-8(0))* 25th anniv. deluxe ed. 2012. 32p. 16.99 *(978-0-7636-4525-0(7))* Candlewick Pr.

—Where's Waldo? 2007. (Where's Waldo? Ser.). (Illus.). 24p. (gr. 4-7). lib. bdg. 18.40 *(978-1-4178-2424-3(7),* Turtleback) Turtleback Bks.

—Where's Waldo? in Hollywood. Handford, Martin, illus. (Where's Waldo? Ser.). (ENG., Illus.). 32p. (J). (gr. k-4). 2007. pap. 7.99 *(978-0-7636-3501-5(4))* 2013. 16.99 *(978-0-7636-4527-4(3))* Candlewick Pr.

—Where's Waldo? in Hollywood. 2007. (Where's Waldo? Ser.). (Illus.). 24p. (gr. 4-7). lib. bdg. 18.40 *(978-1-4178-2425-0(5),* Turtleback) Turtleback Bks.

—Where's Waldo? the Fantastic Journey. Handford, Martin, illus. 2007. (Where's Waldo? Ser.). (ENG., Illus.). 32p. (J). (gr. k-4). pap. 7.99 *(978-0-7636-3500-8(6))* Candlewick Pr.

—Where's Waldo? the Great Picture Hunt. Handford, Martin, illus. (Where's Waldo? Ser.). (ENG., Illus.). 24p. (J). (gr. k-4). 2010. pap. 7.99 (978-0-7636-4215-0(0)) 2006. 14.99 (978-0-7636-3043-0(8)) Candlewick Pr.

—Where's Waldo? the Wonder Book. Handford, Martin, illus. (Where's Waldo? Ser.). (ENG., Illus.). 32p. (J). (gr. k-12). 2014. 16.99 (978-0-7636-4530-4(3)) 2007. pap. 7.99 (978-0-7636-3502-2(2)) Candlewick Pr.

—Where's Waldo Now? Handford, Martin, illus. (Where's Waldo? Ser.). (ENG., Illus.). 32p. (J). (gr. k-4). 2007. pap. 7.99 (978-0-7636-3499-5(9)) 25th anniv. deluxe ed. 2012. 16.99 (978-0-7636-4526-7(5)) Candlewick Pr.

—The Wow Collection: Six Amazing Books & a Puzzle. Handford, Martin, illus. 2012. (Where's Waldo? Ser.). (ENG., Illus.). (J). (gr. k-4). 49.99 (978-0-7636-6179-3(1)) Candlewick Pr.

Handy Manny Pop-up Tool Book. 2009. 6p. 12.99 (978-1-4231-2114-5(7)) Disney Pr.

Hanna, James Milton, Sr. Once upon a Time in the South. l.t. ed. 2004. (Illus.). 235p. per. 12.95 (978-1-930052-15-4(4)) Cherokee Bks.

Hannah Lane, illus. A Frog Named Dude. 2007. 16p. (J). (978-0-9800870-0-0(7)) Robillard, Kristy.

Hannan, Peter. Freddy! Deep-Space Food Fighter. Hannan, Peter, illus. 2011. (Freddy! Ser.: 2). (ENG., Illus.). 144p. (J). (gr. 2-6). pap. 5.99 (978-0-06-128468-7(8)) HarperCollins Pubs.

—Freddy! King of Flurb. Hannan, Peter, illus. 2011. (Freddy! Ser.: 1). (ENG., Illus.). 160p. (J). (gr. 2-6). pap. 5.99 (978-0-06-128466-3(1)) HarperCollins Pubs.

—Freddy! Locked in Space. Hannan, Peter, illus. 2011. (Freddy! Ser.: 3). (ENG., Illus.). 160p. (J). (gr. 2-6). pap. 5.99 (978-0-06-128470-0(X)) HarperCollins Pubs.

—Petlandia. Hannan, Peter, illus. 2015. (ENG., Illus.). 144p. (J). (gr. 2-5). 8.99 (978-0-545-16211-1(4), Scholastic Pr.) Scholastic, Inc.

Hansen, Tevin. Hole in the Wall. Cochran, Shaun, illus. 2017. 300p. (J). 14.99 **(978-1-941429-54-9(8))** Handersen Publishing.

Hansen, Tevin. Hole in the Wall: (humorous Action & Adventure - Ages 8+) Cochran, Shaun, illus. l.t. ed. 2014. (ENG.). 300p. (J). (gr. 2-7). pap. 11.99 (978-1-941429-00-6(9)) Handersen Publishing.

Hanson, Warren. It's Monday, Mrs. Jolly Bones! Tusa, Tricia, illus. 2013. (ENG.). 32p. (J). (gr. -1-1). 16.99 (978-1-4424-1229-3(1), Beach Lane Bks.) Beach Lane Bks.

Hapka, Catherine, pseud. How to Train Your Dragon: Meet the Dragons. Grosvenor, Charles & Gerard, Justin, illus. 2010. (I Can Read Book 1 Ser.). 32p. (J). (gr. k-3). pap. 3.99 (978-0-06-156733-9(7)) HarperCollins Pubs.

—Love on Cue. 2009. (Romantic Comedies Ser.). (ENG.). 288p. (YA). (gr. 7-18). mass mkt. 6.99 (978-1-4169-6857-3(1), Simon Pulse) Simon Pulse.

—Something Borrowed. 2008. (Romantic Comedies Ser.). (ENG.). 272p. (YA). (gr. 7-18). mass mkt. 6.99 (978-1-4169-5441-5(4), Simon Pulse) Simon Pulse.

—The Twelve Dates of Christmas. 2008. (Romantic Comedies Ser.). (ENG.). 272p. (YA). (gr. 7-18). mass mkt. 6.99 (978-1-4169-6412-4(6), Simon Pulse) Simon Pulse.

Harder, Christopher. It's Tough to Nap on a Turtle. Harder, Rolf, illus. 2008. (ENG.). 11p. (J). (gr. -1). bds. 5.95 (978-0-9726614-9-2(2)) Shenanigan Bks.

Hardin, Becky. Shug E Bear. 2008. 24p. pap. 19.99 (978-1-4389-3247-7(2)) AuthorHouse.

Hargreaves, Adam. Little Miss Princess. 2011. (Mr. Men & Little Miss Ser.). (ENG.). 32p. (J). (gr. -1-2). mass mkt. 4.99 (978-0-8431-9834-8(6), Price Stern Sloan) Penguin Young Readers Group.

Hargreaves, Adam & Hargreaves, Roger. Little Miss Birthday. Hargreaves, Adam, illus. 2007. (Mr. Men & Little Miss Ser.). (ENG., Illus.). 32p. (J). (gr. -1-2). mass mkt. 4.99 (978-0-8431-2131-5(9), Price Stern Sloan) Penguin Young Readers Group.

Hargreaves, Roger. Little Miss Bad. 2010. (Mr. Men & Little Miss Ser.). (ENG.). 32p. (J). (gr. -1-2). mass mkt. 3.99 (978-0-8431-3333-2(3), Price Stern Sloan) Penguin Young Readers Group.

—Little Miss Late. 2008. (Mr. Men & Little Miss Ser.). (ENG.). 32p. (J). (gr. -1-2). mass mkt. 4.99 (978-0-8431-3349-3(X), Price Stern Sloan) Penguin Young Readers Group.

—Little Miss Scary. 2009. (Mr. Men & Little Miss Ser.). (ENG.). 32p. (J). (gr. -1-2). mass mkt. 4.99 (978-0-8431-3568-8(9), Price Stern Sloan) Penguin Young Readers Group.

—Mr. Cool. 2008. (Mr. Men & Little Miss Ser.). (ENG.). 32p. (J). (gr. -1-2). mass mkt. 4.99 (978-0-8431-3351-6(1), Price Stern Sloan) Penguin Young Readers Group.

—Mr. Fussy. 2010. (Mr. Men & Little Miss Ser.). (ENG.). 32p. (J). (gr. -1-2). mass mkt. 4.99 (978-0-8431-9957-4(1), Price Stern Sloan) Penguin Young Readers Group.

—Mr. Good. 2010. (Mr. Men & Little Miss Ser.). (ENG.). 32p. (J). (gr. -1-2). mass mkt. 3.99 (978-0-8431-3334-9(1), Price Stern Sloan) Penguin Young Readers Group.

—Mr. Happy. 2011. (Mr. Men & Little Miss Ser.). (ENG.). 32p. (J). (gr. -1-2). mass mkt. 4.99 (978-0-8431-9894-2(X), Price Stern Sloan) Penguin Young Readers Group.

—Mr. Nobody. Hargreaves, Adam, illus. 2011. (Mr. Men & Little Miss Ser.). (ENG.). 32p. (J). (gr. -1-2). mass mkt. 4.99 (978-0-8431-9876-8(1), Price Stern Sloan) Penguin Young Readers Group.

—Mr. Rude. 2009. (Mr. Men & Little Miss Ser.). (ENG.). 32p. (J). (gr. -1-2). mass mkt. 4.99 (978-0-8431-3569-5(7), Price Stern Sloan) Penguin Young Readers Group.

—Mr. Silly. 2008. (Mr. Men & Little Miss Ser.). (ENG.). 32p. (J). (gr. -1-2). mass mkt. 4.99 (978-0-8431-3352-3(X), Price Stern Sloan) Penguin Young Readers Group.

—Mr. Stingy. 2011. (Mr. Men & Little Miss Ser.). (ENG.). 32p. (J). (gr. -1-2). mass mkt. 4.99 (978-0-8431-9959-8(8), Price Stern Sloan) Penguin Young Readers Group.

—Mr. Tickle. 2011. (Mr. Men & Little Miss Ser.). (ENG.). 32p. (J). (gr. -1-2). mass mkt. 4.99 (978-0-8431-9896-6(6), Price Stern Sloan) Penguin Young Readers Group.

—Mr. Worry. 2011. (Mr. Men & Little Miss Ser.). (ENG.). 32p. (J). (gr. -1-2). mass mkt. 3.99 (978-0-8431-9961-1(X), Price Stern Sloan) Penguin Young Readers Group.

Hargreaves, Roger & Hargreaves, Adam. Little Miss Sunshine & the Wicked Witch. Hargreaves, Adam, illus. 2007. (Mr. Men & Little Miss Ser.). (ENG., Illus.). 32p. (J). (gr. -1-2). mass mkt. 4.99 (978-0-8431-2490-3(3), Price Stern Sloan) Penguin Young Readers Group.

Harkrader, Lisa. No Place Like Space: Kindness. Warrick, Jessica, illus. 2017. (How to Be an Earthling (r) Ser.: 5). (ENG.). 64p. (J). (gr. 1-3). lib. bdg. 22.65 (978-1-57565-843-8(7)) Kane Press, Inc.

Harley, Bill. Charlie Bumpers vs. His Big Blabby Mouth, 1 vol. Gustavson, Adam, illus. 2017. (Charlie Bumpers Ser.). (ENG.). 186p. (J). (gr. 2-4). 14.95 **(978-1-56145-940-7(2))** Peachtree Pubs.

—Charlie Bumpers vs. the Perfect Little Turkey, 1 vol. Gustavson, Adam, illus. 2015. (Charlie Bumpers Ser.). (ENG.). 164p. (J). (gr. 2-4). 13.95 (978-1-56145-835-6(X)) Peachtree Pubs.

—Charlie Bumpers vs. the Really Nice Gnome, 1 vol. Gustavson, Adam, illus. (Charlie Bumpers Ser.). (ENG.). 160p. (J). (gr. 2-4). 2015. pap. 6.95 (978-1-56145-831-8(7)) 2014. 13.95 (978-1-56145-740-3(X)) Peachtree Pubs.

—Charlie Bumpers vs. the Teacher of the Year, 1 vol. Gustavson, Adam, illus. (Charlie Bumpers Ser.). (ENG.). 160p. (J). 2014. pap. 6.95 (978-1-56145-824-0(4)) 2013. (gr. 2-4). 14.95 (978-1-56145-732-8(9)) Peachtree Pubs.

—Dirty Joe the Pirate: A True Story. Davis, Jack E., illus. 2008. (ENG.). 32p. (J). (gr. k-3). 17.99 (978-0-06-623780-0(7)) HarperCollins Pubs.

Harper, Benjamin. Far Out Fairy Tales. Cano, Fern, illus. 2016. (Far Out Fairy Tales Ser.). (ENG.). 40p. (gr. 3-4). pap. 11.90 (978-1-4965-3135-3(3), Far Out Fairy Tales) Stone Arch Bks.

Harper, Charise Mericle. Alien Encounter. Harper, Charise Mericle, illus. 2014. (Sasquatch & Aliens Ser.: 1). (ENG., Illus.). 208p. (J). (gr. 2-5). 12.99 (978-0-8050-9621-7(3), 9780805096217, Holt, Henry & Co. Bks. For Young Readers) Holt, Henry & Co.

—The Ball. 2013. (Bean Dog & Nugget Ser.). lib. bdg. 14.75 (978-0-606-31944-7(1), Turtleback) Turtleback Bks.

—The Cookie. 2013. (Bean Dog & Nugget Ser.). lib. bdg. 14.75 (978-0-606-31945-4(X), Turtleback) Turtleback Bks.

—Crafty Cat. 2017. (Crafty Cat Ser.: 1). (ENG., Illus.). 128p. (J). 13.99 (978-1-62672-486-0(5), 9781626724860, First Second Bks.) Roaring Brook Pr.

—Just Grace & the Snack Attack. 2009. (Just Grace Ser.: 5). (ENG., Illus.). 176p. (J). (gr. 1-4). 15.00 (978-0-547-15223-3(X)) Houghton Mifflin Harcourt Publishing Co.

—Super Sasquatch Showdown. Harper, Charise Mericle, illus. 2015. (Sasquatch & Aliens Ser.: 2). (ENG., Illus.). 176p. (J). (gr. 2-5). 13.99 (978-0-8050-9622-4(1), 9780805096224, Holt, Henry & Co. Bks. For Young Readers) Holt, Henry & Co.

—Wedgieman & the Big Bunny Trouble. Shea, Bob, illus. 2014. (Step into Reading Ser.). (ENG.). 48p. (J). (gr. k-3). 3.99 (978-0-307-93073-6(4), Random Hse. Bks. for Young Readers) Random Hse. Children's Bks.

Harrell, Rob. Life of Zarf: The Trouble with Weasels. 2016. (Life of Zarf Ser.: 3). (ENG., Illus.). 272p. (J). (gr. 3-7). 15.99 (978-0-8037-4105-8(7), Dial Bks) Penguin Young Readers Group.

—The Troll Who Cried Wolf. 2015. (Life of Zarf Ser.: 2). (ENG., Illus.). 272p. (J). (gr. 3-7). 14.99 (978-0-8037-4104-1(9), Dial Bks) Penguin Young Readers Group.

—The Trouble with Weasels. 2014. (Life of Zarf Ser.: 1). (ENG.). 288p. (J). (gr. 3-7). 14.99 (978-0-8037-4103-4(0), Dial Bks) Penguin Young Readers Group.

Harrington, Tim. This Little Piggy. Harrington, Tim, illus. 2013. (ENG., Illus.). 32p. (J). (gr. -1-3). 15.99 (978-0-06-221808-7(5)) HarperCollins Pubs.

Harris, Joel Chandler. Nights with Uncle Remus. 2008. 288p. 29.95 (978-1-60664-915-2(9)) Aegypan.

Harris, Marian. Ten Little Kittens. Harris, Jim, illus. 2010. (ENG.). 28p. (J). (gr. k). 15.99 (978-0-7407-9197-0(4)) Andrews McMeel Publishing.

Harris, Patrick. Where the Day Takes You volume One. 2010. 172p. pap. 10.00 (978-0-557-04401-6(4)) Lulu Pr., Inc.

Harrison, David L. Paul Bunyan: My Story. Kanzler, John, illus. 2008. (Step into Reading Ser.). (ENG.). 48p. (J). (gr. k-3). 4.99 (978-0-375-84688-5(3), Random Hse. Bks. for Young Readers) Random Hse. Children's Bks.

Hartley, Steve. Attack of the Alien Brain. Lum, Bernice, illus. unabr. ed. 2015. (Oliver Fibbs Ser.: 1). (ENG.). 192p. (J). (gr. 2-5). pap. 10.99 (978-1-4472-2023-7(4)) Pan Macmillan GBR. Dist: Independent Pubs. Group.

—The World's Biggest Bogey. unabr. ed. 2010. (Danny Baker Record Breaker Ser.: 1). (ENG., Illus.). 128p. (J). (gr. 1). pap. 9.99 (978-0-330-50916-9(0)) Pan Macmillan GBR. Dist: Independent Pubs. Group.

Hartman, Bob. The Wolf Who Cried Boy. Raglin, Tim, illus. 2004. (Picture Puffins Ser.). (gr. k-3). 17.00 (978-0-7569-2950-3(4)) Perfection Learning Corp.

Harvey, Alex. Dancing with the Star. 2013. (Spongebob Squarepants Step into Reading Ser.). lib. bdg. 13.55 (978-0-606-23687-4(2), Turtleback) Turtleback Bks.

Harvey, Damian. Whizzy Witch. Dumortier, Marjorie, illus. 2008. (Reading Corner Ser.). (ENG.). 24p. (J). (gr. k-2). pap. 6.99 (978-0-7496-7699-5(X), Franklin Watts) Hachette Children's Group GBR. Dist: Hachette Bk. Group.

Harvey, Matt. Shopping with Dad. Latimer, Miriam, illus. 2008. (ENG.). 32p. (J). (gr. -1-3). 16.99 (978-1-84686-172-7(1)) Barefoot Bks., Inc.

Haseley, Dennis. The Invisible Moose. Kellogg, Steven, illus. 2008. (ENG.). 40p. (J). (gr. -1-3). pap. 6.99 (978-0-14-241066-0(7), Puffin Books) Penguin Young Readers Group.

Haughton, Chris. Oh No, George! Haughton, Chris, illus. 2015. (ENG., Illus.). 32p. (J). (-k). bds. 7.99 (978-0-7636-7652-0(7)) Candlewick Pr.

—Shh! We Have a Plan. Haughton, Chris, illus. 2014. (ENG., Illus.). 40p. (J). (gr. -1-2). 16.99 (978-0-7636-7293-5(9)) Candlewick Pr.

Hautman, Pete. The Flinkwater Factor: A Novel in Five Thrilling Episodes. 2015. (Flinkwater Chronicles Ser.: 1). (ENG.). 256p. (J). (gr. 4-8). 16.99 (978-1-4814-3251-1(6), Simon & Schuster Bks. For Young Readers) Simon & Schuster Bks. For Young Readers.

Hautman, Pete & Logue, Mary. Snatched. 2007. (Bloodwater Mysteries Ser.). (ENG.). 224p. (J). (gr. 5-7). 7.99 (978-0-14-240795-0(X), Puffin Books) Penguin Young Readers Group.

Haven, Paul. Two Hot Dogs with Everything. Jessell, Tim, illus. 2007. (ENG.). 320p. (J). (gr. 3-7). per. 7.99 (978-0-375-83349-6(8), Yearling) Random Hse. Children's Bks.

Hawkins, Colin. Mr Wolf's Week. 2004. (ENG., Illus.). 32p. (J). pap. 9.99 (978-1-4052-0683-9(7)) Egmont Bks., Ltd. GBR. Dist: Trafalgar Square Publishing.

Hawley, Richard And Elizabeth. There's a Monster in My Nose. Hawley, R. Spencer, illus. 2009. 36p. pap. 24.95 (978-1-61546-177-6(9)) America Star Bks.

Hay, Sam. Gasp of the Ghoulish Guinea Pig #7. Cooper, Simon, illus. 2016. (Undead Pets Ser.: 7). (ENG.). 112p. (J). (gr. 1-3). 5.99 (978-0-448-49003-8(X), Grosset & Dunlap) Penguin Young Readers Group.

—Hour of the Doomed Dog. 2016. (Undead Pets Ser.: 8). lib. bdg. 16.00 (978-0-606-38839-9(7)) Turtleback Bks.

—Hour of the Doomed Dog #8. Cooper, Simon, illus. 2016. (Undead Pets Ser.: 8). (ENG.). 112p. (J). (gr. 1-3). 5.99 (978-0-448-49004-5(8), Grosset & Dunlap) Penguin Young Readers Group.

—Night of the Howling Hound, No. 3. Cooper, Simon, illus. 2014. (Undead Pets Ser.: 3). (ENG.). 112p. (J). (gr. 1-3). 5.99 (978-0-448-47797-8(1), Grosset & Dunlap) Penguin Young Readers Group.

—Revenge of the Phantom Furball. 2014. (Undead Pets Ser.: 2). lib. bdg. 16.00 (978-0-606-35706-7(8)) Turtleback Bks.

Hayes, Joe. The Recycled Hambone. Castro L., Antonio, illus. 2016. (ENG.). 32p. (J). (gr. -1-2). 16.95 (978-1-941026-54-0(0)) Cinco Puntos Pr.

—Recycled Hambone. Castro L., Antonio, illus. 2016. (ENG.). 32p. (J). (gr. -1-2). pap. 7.95 (978-1-941026-55-7(9)) Cinco Puntos Pr.

Hayles, Marsha. Bunion Burt. Davis, Jack E., illus. 2009. (ENG.). 32p. (J). (gr. -1-3). 16.99 (978-1-4169-4132-3(0), McElderry, Margaret K. Bks.) McElderry, Margaret K. Bks.

Haynes, Martha Sue. The Ladies of Color. 2011. (Illus.). 16p. (gr. 1-2). pap. 9.49 (978-1-4520-9877-7(8)) AuthorHouse.

Haywood, Ebony. There Was Once a Potato. 2009. 42p. (J). pap. 21.95 (978-1-4327-3871-6(2)) Outskirts Pr., Inc.

Hazell, Mark. Flight of the Cloud Sailor. 2004. 172p. pap. (978-1-84401-137-7(2)) Athena Pr.

Head, Mat. Warduff & the Corn Cob Caper. Head, Mat, illus. 2011. (Andersen Press Picture Books Ser.). (Illus.). 16.95 (978-0-7613-8095-5(7)) Andersen Pr. GBR. Dist: Lerner Publishing Group.

Healy, Christopher. The Hero's Guide to Being an Outlaw. Harris, Todd, illus. 2014. (Hero's Guide Ser.: 3). (ENG.). 528p. (J). (gr. 3-7). 16.99 (978-0-06-211848-6(X), Waldon Pond Pr.) HarperCollins Pubs.

—The Hero's Guide to Saving Your Kingdom. Harris, Todd, illus. 2012. (Hero's Guide Ser.: 1). (ENG.). 448p. (J). (gr. 3-7). 16.99 (978-0-06-211743-4(2), Waldon Pond Pr.) HarperCollins Pubs.

Helakoski, Leslie. Big Chickens. Cole, Henry, illus. 2008. (J). (gr. -1-3). lib. bdg. 14.65 (978-0-7569-8913-2(2)) Perfection Learning Corp.

—Big Chickens Fly the Coop. Cole, Henry, illus. 2010. (ENG.). 32p. (J). (gr. -1-k). pap. 6.99 (978-0-14-241464-4(6), Puffin Books) Penguin Young Readers Group.

Heling, Kathryn & Hembrook, Deborah. I Wish I Had Freckles Like Abby. Adamson, Bonnie, illus. 2009. (ENG.). 32p. (J). (gr. -1-3). 16.95 (978-1-934960-46-2(2), Raven Tree Pr.,Csi) Continental Sales, Inc.

—I Wish I Had Freckles Like Abby/Quisiera Tener Pecas Como Abby. Adamson, Bonnie, illus. 2007. (SPA & ENG.). 32p. (J). (gr. -1-3). pap. 7.95 (978-0-9770906-6-2(3), Raven Tree Pr.,Csi) Continental Sales, Inc.

—I Wish I Had Glasses Like Rosa. Adamson, Bonnie, illus. 2009. (ENG.). 32p. (J). (gr. 4-7). 16.95 (978-1-934960-48-6(9), Raven Tree Pr.,Csi) Continental Sales, Inc.

—I Wish I Was Strong Like Manuel. Adamson, Bonnie, illus. 2009. (ENG.). 32p. (J). (gr. -1-3). 16.95 (978-1-934960-52-3(7), Raven Tree Pr.,Csi) Continental Sales, Inc.

—I Wish I Was Tall Like Willie. Adamson, Bonnie, illus. (I Wish Ser.). (ENG.). 32p. (J). (gr. 4-7). 2010. pap. 7.95 (978-1-934960-51-6(9)) 2009. 16.95 (978-1-934960-50-9(0)) Continental Sales, Inc. (Raven Tree Pr.,Csi).

Heling, Kathryn, et al. I Wish I Had Freckles Like Abby/Quisiera Tener Pecas Como Abby. de La Vega, Eida, tr. Adamson, Bonnie, illus. 2007. (I Wish Ser.). (SPA & ENG.). 32p. (J). (gr. -1-3). 16.95 (978-0-9724973-8-1(2), 626999, Raven Tree Pr.,Csi) Continental Sales, Inc.

Heller, Linda. The Castle on Hester Street. Kulikov, Boris, illus. 25th ed. 2007. (ENG.). 40p. (J). (gr. -1-3). 18.99 (978-0-689-87434-5(0), Simon & Schuster Bks. For Young Readers) Simon & Schuster Bks. For Young Readers.

Helliwell, Sheila. Gammy. Hawthorn, Paul & Hopkins, Simon, illus. 2nd ed. 2013. 70p. pap. (978-0-9560331-4-7(8)) Children' Story Pubs.

Hellman, Charles. Fun Is... 2005. 124p. (gr. 4-7). per. 9.95 (978-0-935938-16-6(8)) LuckySports.

Helmore, Jim. Letterbox Lil: A Cautionary Tale. 2006. (Illus.). (J). (978-1-4156-4110-1(2)) Book Wholesalers, Inc.

Helquist, Brett & Helquist. Roger: The Jolly Pirate. Helquist, Brett, illus. 2004. (ENG., Illus.). 40p. (J). (gr. -1-3). 16.99 (978-0-06-623805-0(6)) HarperCollins Pubs.

—Roger, the Jolly Pirate. Helquist, Brett, illus. 2007. (ENG., Illus.). 40p. (J). (gr. -1-2). pap. 6.99 (978-0-06-443851-3(1)) HarperCollins Pubs.

Hemingway, Edward. Field Guide to the Grumpasaurus. 2016. (ENG., Illus.). 32p. (J). (gr. -1-3). 16.99 (978-0-544-54665-3(2)) Houghton Mifflin Harcourt Publishing Co.

Henkes, Kevin. A Box Full of Lilly: Lilly's Big Day. Henkes, Kevin, illus. 2006. (Illus.). (J). (gr. -1-4). 27.99 (978-0-06-112852-3(X), Greenwillow Bks.) HarperCollins Pubs.

—A Box of Treats: Five Little Picture Books about Lilly & Her Friends. Henkes, Kevin, illus. 2004. (ENG., Illus.). (J). (gr. -1-k). pap. 14.99 (978-0-06-073211-0(3), Greenwillow Bks.) HarperCollins Pubs.

—The Year of Billy Miller. Henkes, Kevin, illus. 2013. (Illus.). 240p. (J). (gr. 3-7). (ENG.). 16.99 (978-0-06-226812-9(0)); lib. bdg. 17.89 (978-0-06-226813-6(9)) HarperCollins Pubs. (Greenwillow Bks.).

—The Year of Billy Miller. Henkes, Kevin, illus. 2015. (ENG., Illus.). (J). (gr. 3-7). lib. bdg. 17.60 **(978-1-62765-762-4(2))** Perfection Learning Corp.

—The Year of Billy Miller. 2015. (J). lib. bdg. 17.20 (978-0-606-36977-0(5)) Turtleback Bks.

Henry, William. Growing up Country: Life on the Farm. 2003. 108p. pap. 11.95 (978-0-595-26864-1(1), Writers Club Pr.) iUniverse, Inc.

Heos, Bridget. Mustache Baby. Ang, Joy, illus. 2016. (ENG.). 36p. (J). (— 1). bds. 7.99 (978-0-544-78984-5(9), HMH Books For Young Readers) Houghton Mifflin Harcourt Publishing Co.

—Mustache Baby. Ang, Joy, illus. (Mustache Baby Ser.). (ENG.). 40p. (J). (gr. -1-3). 2015. 16.99 (978-0-544-36375-5(2)) 2013. 17.99 (978-0-547-77357-5(9)) Houghton Mifflin Harcourt Trade & Reference Pubs. (Clarion Bks.).

Herbach, Geoff. Hair-Pocalypse. Gilpin, Stephen, illus. 2017. (Fiction Picture Bks.). (ENG.). 32p. (gr. 1-3). lib. bdg. 23.32 **(978-1-5158-1411-5(4)**, Fiction Picture Bks.) Picture Window Bks.

Hergé. Aventures de Tintin au Pays des Soviets. (FRE.). 21.95 (978-2-203-00100-8(3)) Casterman, Editions FRA. Dist: Distribooks, Inc.

Herzog, Kenny. Phil Pickle. Canby, Kelly, illus. 2016. (J). (978-1-4413-1933-3(6)) Peter Pauper Pr. Inc.

Hetherington, Lisa. Oscar & Willie: Silly Oscar's Days of the Week. Lawrey, Derek, illus. 2012. (ENG.). 26p. (J). pap. 9.99 (978-0-9839963-0-9(X)) Hetherington Hall.

Hietpas, Polly. Rosie Cat's Bad Fur Day. 2009. 20p. pap. 10.49 (978-1-4490-0777-5(5)) AuthorHouse.

Higgins, Nadia. Blimey, That's Slimy!, 1 vol. Holder, Jimmy, illus. 2008. (Barnacle Barb & Her Pirate Crew Ser.). (ENG.). 32p. (gr. -1-3). 28.50 (978-1-60270-091-8(5), Looking Glass Library) ABDO Publishing Co.

Higgins, Ryan T. Be Quiet! Higgins, Ryan T., illus. 2017. (ENG., Illus.). 40p. (J). (gr. -1-k). 17.99 (978-1-4847-3162-8(X)) Hyperion Bks. for Children.

—Hotel Bruce. Higgins, Ryan T., illus. 2016. (Mother Bruce Ser.). (ENG., Illus.). 48p. (J). (gr. -1-k). 17.99 (978-1-4847-4362-1(8)) Hyperion Bks. for Children.

Hileman, Jane. Will You Go? Bianchi, John, illus. 2014. (2G Potato Chip Bks.). (ENG.). 12p. (J). pap. 5.99 (978-1-61406-684-2(1)) American Reading Co.

Hill, Susanna Leonard. No Sword Fighting in the House. Kelley, True, illus. (Holiday House Reader Ser.: Level 2). (ENG.). 32p. (J). (gr. k-3). 14.95 (978-0-8234-1916-6(9)) Holiday Hse., Inc.

Hillenburg, Steven, creator. SpongeBob SquarePants Vol. 1: Krusty Krab Adventures, 2 vols. 2003. (Illus.). 96p. (J). pap. 14.99 (978-1-59182-398-8(6), Tokyopop Kids) TOKYOPOP, Inc.

—SpongeBob SquarePantsTM: Friends Forever. 2003. (Illus.). 96p. pap. 14.99 (978-1-59182-399-5(4), Tokyopop Kids) TOKYOPOP, Inc.

Himmelman, John. Bunjitsu Bunny Jumps to the Moon. Himmelman, John, illus. 2016. (Bunjitsu Bunny Ser.). (ENG., Illus.). 128p. (J). 13.99 (978-1-62779-732-0(7), 9781627797320, Holt, Henry & Co. Bks. For Young Readers) Holt, Henry & Co.

—Bunjitsu Bunny's Best Move. Himmelman, John, illus. 2016. (Bunjitsu Bunny Ser.: 2). (ENG., Illus.). 128p. (J). (gr. 1-3). 16.00 (978-0-606-39298-3(X)) Turtleback Bks.

—Chickens to the Rescue. Himmelman, John, illus. 2006. (Barnyard Rescue Ser.). (ENG., Illus.). 32p. (J). (gr. -1-3). 17.99 (978-0-8050-7951-7(3), 9780805079517, Holt, Henry & Co. Bks. For Young Readers) Holt, Henry & Co.

—Cows to the Rescue. Himmelman, John, illus. 2011. (Barnyard Rescue Ser.). (ENG., Illus.). 32p. (J). (gr. -1-3). 17.99 (978-0-8050-9249-3(8), 9780805092493, Holt, Henry & Co. Bks. For Young Readers) Holt, Henry & Co.

—Duck to the Rescue. Himmelman, John, illus. 2014. (Barnyard Rescue Ser.). (ENG., Illus.). 32p. (J). (gr. -1-3). 16.99 (978-0-8050-9485-5(7), 9780805094855, Holt, Henry & Co. Bks. For Young Readers) Holt, Henry & Co.

Hirsch, Andy. Varmints. 2016. (ENG., Illus.). 224p. (J). pap. 16.99 (978-1-62672-279-8(X), 9781626722798, First Second Bks.) Roaring Brook Pr.

Hoban, Russell. Bread & Jam for Frances. Hoban, Lillian, illus. 2015. (ENG.). 32p. (J). (gr. -1-3). pap. 5.99 (978-0-06-239237-4(9), HarperFestival) HarperCollins Pubs.

—The Marzipan Pig. Blake, Quentin, illus. 2016. (ENG.). 48p. (J). (gr. 1-4). 15.95 (978-1-59017-999-4(4), NYR Children's Collection) New York Review of Bks., Inc., The.

Hobbs, Brice Edward. Beth's Woodpecker. 2004. 108p. 26.45 (978-1-4208-0135-4(X)) AuthorHouse.

Hobbs, Leigh. Mr Chicken Arriva a Roma. 2017. (Mr Chicken Ser.). (ENG.). 32p. (J). (gr. -1-3). 17.99 **(978-1-925266-77-1(X))** Allen & Unwin AUS. Dist: Independent Pubs. Group.

Hodges, Jean A. Drinking Dragon Sam Learns Drinking Doesn't Pay. 2011. 40p. pap. 24.95 (978-1-4560-5507-3(0)) America Star Bks.

Hodgkinson, Leigh. Boris & the Wrong Shadow. 2012. (ENG.). 32p. (J). pap. (978-1-58925-434-3(1)) Tiger Tales.

—Limelight Larry. Hodgkinson, Leigh, illus. 2011. (ENG., Illus.). 32p. (J). (978-1-58925-102-1(4)) Tiger Tales.

Hodgman, Ann. Uh-Oh! Oh No! Barnard, Lucy, illus. 2012. (Into-Everything Baby Stages Ser.). (ENG.). 18p. (gr. -1). bds. 7.95 (978-1-58925-866-2(5)) Tiger Tales.

Hoena, Blake A. Swamp Sting!, 1 vol. Facio, Sebastian, illus. 2011. (Graphic Sparks Ser.). (ENG.). 40p. (gr. 1-3). pap. 5.95 (978-1-4342-3065-2(1)); lib. bdg. 23.99 (978-1-4342-2960-1(2)) Stone Arch Bks. (Graphic Sparks).

Hoffman, Beth Greiner. Animal Gym. Gergely, Tibor, illus. 2009. (Little Golden Book Ser.). (ENG.). 24p. (J). (gr. -1-2). 4.99 (978-0-375-84751-6(0), Golden Bks.) Random Hse. Children's Bks.

Hoffman, Terri. Sly Fly & the Gray Mare. BURNS, Theresa, illus. 2013. 26p. 15.95 (978-1-940224-15-2(2)) Taylor and Seale Publishing, LLC.

Hoffmann, Heinrich. Slovenly Kate & Other Stories: From the Struwwelpeter Library. Hosemann, Theodor, illus. 2012. (Dover Children's Classics Ser.). (ENG.). 96p. (J). (gr. 3-5). pap. 12.99 (978-0-486-49032-8(7)) Dover Pubns., Inc.

Hoffmire, Baird, illus. The Big Wide-Mouth Frog. 2009. (J). pap. *(978-0-87483-890-9(8)*, August House Story Cove) August Hse. Pubs., Inc.

Holechek, Max. Edsel Mcfarlan's New Car. Toland, Darrell, illus. 2010. 52p. (J). *(978-1-935359-40-1(1))* Book Pubs. Network.

Holly, Julia. Mrs Winkler's Cure. Holly, Julia, illus. 2010. (Illus.). 214p. pap. 19.99 *(978-1-883376-45-1(9))* Stellium Pr.

Holm, Jennifer L. I'm Grumpy (My First Comics) Holm, Matthew, illus. 2016. (ENG.). 24p. (J). (— 1). 7.99 *(978-0-553-53344-6(4)*, Random Hse. Bks. for Young Readers) Random Hse. Children's Bks.

—Middle School Is Worse Than Meatloaf: A Year Told Through Stuff. Castaldi, Elicia, illus. 2007. (ENG.). 128p. (J). (gr. 3-7). 12.99 *(978-0-689-85281-7(9)*, Atheneum Bks. for Young Readers) Simon & Schuster Children's Publishing.

Holm, Jennifer L. & Holm, Matthew. Babymouse Goes for the Gold. Holm, Jennifer L. & Holm, Matthew, illus. 2016. (Babymouse Ser.: 20). (ENG., Illus.). 96p. (J). (gr. 2-5). pap. 6.99 *(978-0-307-93163-4(3)*, Random Hse. Bks. for Young Readers) Random Hse. Children's Bks.

—Babymouse Tales from the Locker Presents Lights, Camera, Messy Whiskers. 2017. (Babymouse Tales from the Locker Ser.: 1). (ENG., Illus.). 208p. (J). (gr. 3-7). 13.99 *(978-0-399-55438-4(6)*, Random Hse. Bks. for Young Readers) Random Hse. Children's Bks.

—Bad Babysitter. Holm, Jennifer L. & Holm, Matthew, illus. 2015. (Babymouse Ser.: 19). (ENG., Illus.). 96p. (J). (gr. 2-5). pap. 6.99 *(978-0-307-93162-7(5)*, Random Hse. Bks. for Young Readers) Random Hse. Children's Bks.

—Burns Rubber. 2010. (Babymouse Ser.: 12). lib. bdg. 17.20 *(978-0-606-07025-6(7)*, Turtleback) Turtleback Bks.

—A Very Babymouse Christmas. Holm, Jennifer L. & Holm, Matthew, illus. 2011. (Babymouse Ser.: 15). (ENG., Illus.). 96p. (J). (gr. 2-5). 12.99 *(978-0-375-96779-5(6))*; pap. 6.99 *(978-0-375-86779-8(1))* Random Hse. Children's Bks. (Random Hse. Bks. for Young Readers).

Holm, Jennifer L., et al. Comics Squad: Recess! 2014. (Comics Squad Ser.). (ENG., Illus.). 144p. (J). (gr. 2-5). pap. 7.99 *(978-0-385-37003-5(2)*, Random Hse. Bks. for Young Readers) Random Hse. Children's Bks.

Holm, Jennifer L., et al. Comics Squad #3: Detention! 2017. (Comics Squad Ser.: 3). (ENG., Illus.). 160p. (J). (gr. 2-5). lib. bdg. 12.99 ***(978-0-553-51268-7(4)***, Random Hse. Bks. for Young Readers) Random Hse. Children's Bks.

Holm, Matthew, et al. Comics Squad #2: Lunch! 2016. (Comics Squad Ser.). (ENG., Illus.). 144p. (J). (gr. 2-5). pap. 7.99 *(978-0-553-51264-9(1)*, Random Hse. Bks. for Young Readers) Random Hse. Children's Bks.

Holmes, Andy. If You Give a Boy a Bible. 2004. 32p. (J). 10.99 *(978-0-8254-5513-1(8))* Kregel Pubns.

Holt, K. A. Rhyme Schemer. 2014. (ENG., Illus.). 176p. (J). (gr. 5-9). 15.99 *(978-1-4521-2700-2(X))* Chronicle Bks. LLC.

Holt, Kimberly Willis. Dinner with the Highbrows. Brooker, Kyrsten, illus. 2014. (ENG.). 36p. (J). (gr. -1-2). 17.99 *(978-0-8050-8088-9(0)*, 9780805080889, Holt, Henry & Co. Bks. For Young Readers) Holt, Henry & Co.

Holub, Joan. Itty Bitty Kitty. Burks, James, illus. 2015. (ENG.). 32p. (J). (gr. -1-3). 17.99 *(978-0-06-232219-7(2))* HarperCollins Pubs.

—Itty Bitty Kitty & the Rainy Play Day. Burks, James, illus. 2016. 32p. (J). (gr. -1-3). 17.99 *(978-0-06-232220-3(6))* HarperCollins Pubs.

—Little Red Writing. Sweet, Melissa, illus. (ENG.). 36p. (J). (gr. k-3). 2016. pap. 7.99 *(978-1-4521-5209-7(8))* 2013. 16.99 *(978-0-8118-7869-2(4))* Chronicle Bks. LLC.

—Zero the Hero. Lichtenheld, Tom, illus. 2012. (ENG.). 40p. (J). (gr. 1-5). 17.99 *(978-0-8050-9384-1(2)*, 9780805093841, Holt, Henry & Co. Bks. For Young Readers) Holt, Henry & Co.

Holzhauser-Peters, Leslie & Grizinski, Yolande. Thinking Through Problems at School: Social Problem Solving Scenarios to Enhance Communication, Thinking, & Decision Making Skills. 2008. 96p. pap. 13.95 *(978-1-4327-2573-0(4))* Outskirts Pr., Inc.

Holzwarth, Werner & Erlbruch, Wolf. The Story of the Little Mole Who Went in Search of Whodunit. 2007. (ENG., Illus.). (J). (gr. -1-5). 24p. 15.95 *(978-0-8109-1641-8(X)*, Abrams Bks. for Young Readers); 22p. 10.95 *(978-0-8109-4457-2(X)*, Abrams Image) Abrams, Inc.

Honey, Elizabeth. Hop up! Wriggle Over! 2017. (ENG., Illus.). 40p. (J). (gr. -1-3). 16.99 *(978-0-544-79084-1(7)*, Clarion Bks.) Houghton Mifflin Harcourt Trade & Reference Pubs.

Hopman, Philip. Valentine & His Violin. 2012. (ENG., Illus.). 32p. (J). (gr. -1). 17.95 *(978-1-935954-17-0(2)*, 9781935954170) Lemniscaat USA.

Horowitz, Anthony. Public Enemy Number Two. 2004. (Diamond Brothers Ser.). (ENG.). 208p. (J). (gr. 3-7). 16.99 *(978-0-399-24154-3(X)*, Philomel Bks.); pap. 6.99 *(978-0-14-240218-4(4)*, Puffin Books) Penguin Young Readers Group.

—South by Southeast. 2005. (Diamond Brothers Ser.). (ENG.). 160p. (J). (gr. 3-7). 6.99 *(978-0-14-240374-7(1)*, Puffin Books) Penguin Young Readers Group.

—Three of Diamonds. 2005. (Diamond Brothers Ser.). (ENG.). 240p. (J). (gr. 3-7). 6.99 *(978-0-14-240298-6(2)*, Puffin Books) Penguin Young Readers Group.

Horowitz, Dave. Five Little Gefiltes. Horowitz, Dave, illus. 2007. (ENG., Illus.). 32p. (J). (gr. -1-3). 15.99 *(978-0-399-24608-1(8)*, G.P. Putnam's Sons Books for Young Readers) Penguin Young Readers Group.

—Humpty Dumpty Climbs Again. Horowitz, Dave, illus. 2011. (ENG., Illus.). 32p. (J). (gr. -1-k). pap. 6.99 *(978-0-14-241932-8(X)*, Puffin Books) Penguin Young Readers Group.

—Twenty-Six Pirates: An Alphabet Book. Horowitz, Dave, illus. 2013. (ENG., Illus.). 32p. (J). (gr. -1-k). 16.99 *(978-0-399-25777-3(2)*, Nancy Paulsen Books) Penguin Young Readers Group.

Horse, Harry. The Last Cowboys. Horse, Harry, illus. 2008. (ENG., Illus.). 128p. (J). (gr. 1-5). 12.95 *(978-1-56145-451-8(6)*, Peachtree Junior) Peachtree Pubs.

Horvath, Polly. The Pepins & Their Problems, 1 vol. Hafner, Marylin, illus. (ENG.). 192p. pap. 13.95 *(978-0-88899-633-6(0))* Groundwood Bks. CAN. Dist: Publishers Group West (PGW).

—The Pepins & Their Problems. Hafner, Marylin, illus. 2008. (ENG.). 208p. (J). (gr. 3-7). per. 9.99 *(978-0-312-37751-9(7)*, 9780312377519) Square Fish.

Houghton Mifflin Harcourt Children's Group Staff & Rey, H. A. Family Storybook Treasury: Tales of Laughter, Curiosity, & Fun. 2011. (ENG., Illus.). 304p. (J). (gr. -1-3). 18.99 *(978-0-547-61221-8(4))* Houghton Mifflin Harcourt Publishing Co.

Houran, Lori Haskins. Alien in the Outfield: Perseverance. Warrick, Jessica, illus. 2017. (How to Be an Earthling (r) Ser.: 6). (ENG.). 64p. (J). (gr. 1-3). lib. bdg. 22.65 *(978-1-57565-844-5(5))* Kane Press, Inc.

—Alien in the Outfield: Perseverance. Warrick, Jessica, illus. 2017. (How to Be an Earthling (r) Ser.: 6). (ENG.). 64p. (J). (gr. 1-3). 6.99 *(978-1-57565-848-3(8))* Kane Press, Inc.

—Earth's Got Talent! Warrick, Jessica, illus. 2016. (How to Be an Earthling (r) Ser.: 4). (ENG.). 64p. (gr. 1-3). lib. bdg. 22.65 *(978-1-57565-827-8(5))* Kane Press, Inc.

—Earth's Got Talent! Courage. Warrick, Jessica, illus. 2016. (How to Be an Earthling (r) Ser.: 4). (ENG.). 64p. (gr. 1-3). 34.65 *(978-1-57565-829-2(1))* Kane Press, Inc.

—Greetings, Sharkling! Warrick, Jessica, illus. 2016. (How to Be an Earthling (r) Ser.: 2). (ENG.). 64p. (gr. 1-3). 22.65 *(978-1-57565-821-6(6))* Kane Press, Inc.

—Greetings, Sharkling! Honesty. Warrick, Jessica, illus. 2016. (How to Be an Earthling (r) Ser.: 2). (ENG.). 64p. (gr. 1-3). 34.65 *(978-1-57565-823-0(2))* Kane Press, Inc.

—Money Doesn't Grow on Mars: Self-Control. Warrick, Jessica, illus. 2017. (How to Be an Earthling (r) Ser.: 8). (ENG.). 64p. (gr. 1-3). 34.65 ***(978-1-57565-854-4(2))***; (J). lib. bdg. 22.65 *(978-1-57565-846-9(1))* Kane Press, Inc.

Houran, Lori Haskins. Money Doesn't Grow on Mars: Self-Control. Warrick, Jessica, illus. 2017. (How to Be an Earthling (r) Ser.: 8). (ENG.). 64p. (J). (gr. 1-3). 6.99 *(978-1-57565-850-6(X))* Kane Press, Inc.

Howard, Kate. The Duck Vinci Code & Other Tales. 2013. (ENG.). 112p. (J). (gr. 2-5). pap. 4.99 *(978-0-545-49291-1(2))* Scholastic, Inc.

Howard, Martin. Shaun the Sheep: Pranks a Lot! Janes, Andy, illus. 2016. (Tales from Mossy Bottom Farm Ser.). (ENG.). 96p. (J). (gr. k-3). pap. 4.99 *(978-0-7636-8742-7(1)*, Candlewick Entertainment) Candlewick Pr.

Howe, James. Bud Barkin, Private Eye. Helquist, Brett, illus. (Tales from the House of Bunnicula Ser.: 5). (ENG.). (J). (gr. 2-5). 2004. 112p. pap. 5.99 *(978-0-689-86989-1(4))* 2003. 96p. 13.99 *(978-0-689-85632-7(6))* Simon & Schuster Children's Publishing. (Atheneum Bks. for Young Readers).

—Bunnicula Meets Edgar Allan Crow. Fortune, Eric, illus. (Bunnicula & Friends Ser.). (ENG.). 160p. (J). (gr. 3-7). 2008. pap. 6.99 *(978-1-4169-1473-0(0))* 2006. 15.95 *(978-1-4169-1458-7(7))* Simon & Schuster Children's Publishing. (Atheneum Bks. for Young Readers).

—Howie Monroe & the Doghouse of Doom. 2004. (Tales from the House of Bunnicula Ser.). 85p. (J). (gr. 3-6). pap. 17.00 incl. audio *(978-1-4000-8634-4(5)*, Listening Library) Random Hse. Audio Publishing Group.

—Invasion of the Mind Swappers from Asteroid 6! 2004. (Tales from the House of Bunnicula Ser.). 112p. (J). (gr. 3-6). pap. 17.00 incl. audio *(978-1-4000-8633-7(7)*, Listening Library) Random Hse. Audio Publishing Group.

—Invasion of the Mind Swappers from Asteroid 6! Helquist, Brett, illus. 2003. (Tales from the House of Bunnicula Ser.). 89p. (J). (gr. 2-5). 11.65 *(978-0-7569-2814-8(1))* Perfection Learning Corp.

—Invasion of the Mind Swappers from Asteroid 6! Helquist, Brett, illus. 2003. (Tales from the House of Bunnicula Ser.: 2). (ENG.). 112p. (J). (gr. 2-5). pap. 5.99 *(978-0-689-83950-4(2)*, Simon & Schuster/Paula Wiseman Bks.) Simon & Schuster/Paula Wiseman Bks.

—It Came from Beneath the Bed! 2004. (Tales from the House of Bunnicula Ser.). 112p. (J). (gr. 3-6). pap. 17.00 incl. audio *(978-1-4000-8632-0(9)*, Listening Library) Random Hse. Audio Publishing Group.

—The Odorous Adventures of Stinky Dog. Helquist, Brett, illus. 2003. (Tales from the House of Bunnicula Ser.: 6). (ENG.). 112p. (J). (gr. 2-5). 13.99 *(978-0-689-85633-4(4)*, Atheneum Bks. for Young Readers) Simon & Schuster Children's Publishing.

—Screaming Mummies of the Pharaoh's Tomb II. Helquist, Brett, illus. 2003. (Tales from the House of Bunnicula Ser.: 4). (ENG.). 112p. (J). (gr. 2-4). 13.99 *(978-0-689-83953-5(7)*, Atheneum Bks. for Young Readers) Simon & Schuster Children's Publishing.

Hoylie, Gerry. Byron Unleashed. 2005. 60p. pap. 14.95 *(978-1-59113-670-5(9))* Booklocker.com, Inc.

Hub, Ulrich & Ragg-Kirkby, Helena. Becoming the Wolf. Mühle, Jörg, illus. 2012. (ENG.). 64p. (YA). 12.00 *(978-0-8028-5409-4(5)*, Eerdmans Bks For Young Readers) Eerdmans, William B. Publishing Co.

Hughes, Alison. Poser, 1 vol. 2013. (ENG.). 168p. (J). (gr. 4-7). pap. 9.95 *(978-1-4598-0147-9(4))* Orca Bk. Pubs. USA.

Hughes, Langston. Simple Speaks His Mind. (J). (gr. 5-6). reprint ed. lib. bdg. 22.95 *(978-0-88411-061-3(3))* Amereon Ltd.

Hurwitz, Johanna. Ethan Out & about Big Book: Brand New Readers. Fioca, Brian, illus. 2010. (Brand New Readers Ser.). (ENG.). 48p. (J). (gr. -1-3). pap. 24.99 *(978-0-7636-4811-4(6))* Candlewick Pr.

—Fourth-Grade Fuss. Hammond, Andy, illus. 2004. 144p. (J). lib. bdg. 16.89 *(978-0-06-052344-2(1))*; (ENG.). (gr. 3-7). 16.99 *(978-0-06-052343-5(3))* HarperCollins Pubs.

—Magical Monty. McGrory, Anik, illus. 2013. (Monty Ser.). (ENG.). 112p. (J). (gr. k-4). pap. 5.99 *(978-0-7636-6457-2(X))* Candlewick Pr.

Hurwitz, Johanna, ed. I Fooled You: Ten Stories of Tricks, Jokes & Switcheroos. Nihoff, Tim, illus. 2010. (ENG.). 192p. (J). (gr. 4-7). 16.99 *(978-0-7636-3789-7(0))* Candlewick Pr.

Hutchins, Hazel. Robyn's Party-in-the-Park. Cathcart, Yvonne, illus. 2005. (Formac First Novels Ser.: 31). (ENG.). 64p. (J). (gr. 2-5). 14.95 *(978-0-88780-663-6(5)*, 9780887806636) Formac Publishing Co., Ltd. CAN. Dist: Casemate Pubs. & Bk. Distributors, LLC.

—Robyn's Party in the Park, 1 vol. Cathcart, Yvonne, illus. 2005. (Formac First Novels Ser.: 31). (ENG.). 64p. (J). (gr. 2-5). 4.95 *(978-0-88780-662-9(7)*, 9780887806629) Formac Publishing Co., Ltd. CAN. Dist: Casemate Pubs. & Bk. Distributors, LLC.

I Thought This Was a Bear Book. 2015. (ENG., Illus.). 32p. (J). (gr. -1-2). 17.99 *(978-1-4424-6307-3(4)*, Aladdin) Simon & Schuster Children's Publishing.

Ianieri, Tom. Polar Pals. 2011. 28p. pap. 15.99 *(978-1-4628-5403-5(6))* Xlibris Corp.

Ibbotson, Eva. The Haunting of Granite Falls. Hawkes, Kevin, illus. 2005. (ENG.). 224p. (J). (gr. 3-7). 6.99 *(978-0-14-240371-6(7)*, Puffin Books) Penguin Young Readers Group.

—Not Just a Witch. Hawkes, Kevin, illus. 2004. (ENG.). 192p. (J). (gr. 3-7). pap. 5.99 *(978-0-14-240232-0(X)*, Puffin Books) Penguin Young Readers Group.

—The Ogre of Oglefort. 2012. (ENG.). 272p. (J). (gr. 3-7). pap. 6.99 *(978-0-14-242135-2(9)*, Puffin Books) Penguin Young Readers Group.

Idle, Molly. Camp Rex. Idle, Molly, illus. 2014. (ENG., Illus.). 40p. (J). (gr. -1-k). 16.99 *(978-0-670-78573-5(3)*, Viking Books for Young Readers) Penguin Young Readers Group.

—Tea Rex. 2013. (ENG., Illus.). 36p. (J). (gr. -1-k). 16.99 *(978-0-670-01430-9(3)*, Viking Books for Young Readers) Penguin Young Readers Group.

Iggulden, Conn & Duncan, Lizzy. Tollins 2: Dynamite Tales, Vol. 2. 2012. (Tollins Ser.: 2). (Illus.). 192p. (J). 16.99 *(978-0-06-173101-3(3))* HarperCollins Pubs.

Incomprehensible, Vordak T. & Seegert, Scott. Double Trouble. Martin, John, illus. 2012. (Vordak the Incomprehensible Ser.: No. 3). (ENG.). 192p. (J). (gr. 5). 13.99 *(978-1-60684-372-7(9)*, Darby Creek) Lerner Publishing Group.

—How to Grow up & Rule the World. Martin, John, illus. 2010. (Vordak the Incomprehensible Ser.: No. 1). (ENG.). 208p. (gr. 5-18). 13.99 *(978-1-60684-013-9(4)*, Darby Creek) Lerner Publishing Group.

Ingram, Catherine. Arnold's Extraordinary Art Museum. Stoten, Jim, illus. 2016. (ENG.). 64p. (J). (gr. 2-6). 19.95 *(978-1-78067-863-4(0))* King, Laurence Publishing GBR. Dist: Hachette Bk. Group.

Inoue, Kazurou. Midori Days. Inoue, Kazurou, illus. 2006. (Midori Days Ser.). (ENG., Illus.). 208p. Vol. 6. pap. 9.99 *(978-1-4215-0495-7(2))* Vol. 7. pap. 9.99 *(978-1-4215-0496-4(0))* Viz Media.

Irwin, Kate. Alfie's Great Escape. Elsom, Clare, illus. 2016. (Reading Ladder Ser.). (ENG.). 48p. (J). (gr. k-2). 7.99 *(978-1-4052-8217-8(7))* Egmont Bks., Ltd. GBR. Dist: Independent Pubs. Group.

Is That Funny? 2004. (J). per. 15.95 *(978-0-9741319-2-4(X))* 4N Publishing LLC.

Isaacs, Anne. Meanwhile, Back at the Ranch. Hawkes, Kevin, illus. 2014. (ENG.). 56p. (J). (gr. k-4). 17.99 *(978-0-375-86745-3(7)*, Schwartz & Wade Bks.) Random Hse. Children's Bks.

Iserson, David. Firecracker. 2014. (ENG.). 336p. (YA). (gr. 7). pap. 9.99 *(978-1-59514-681-6(4)*, Razorbill) Penguin Young Readers Group.

The J-Files: Individual Title, 6 Packs. (Bookweb Ser.). 32p. (gr. 3-18). 34.00 *(978-0-7635-3941-2(4))* Rigby Education.

Jackson, A. Isaiah J. Jiffy: You, You, You. Bully! 2005. 50p. pap. 16.95 *(978-1-4137-8524-1(7))* PublishAmerica, Inc.

Jaffe, Michele. Bad Kitty. 2006. (Bad Kitty Ser.: Bk. 1). (ENG., Illus.). 288p. (YA). (gr. 7-12). 16.99 *(978-0-06-078108-8(4))* HarperCollins Pubs.

—Kitty Kitty. 2008. (Bad Kitty Ser.: Bk. 2). 320p. (YA). (gr. 7-18). lib. bdg. 17.89 *(978-0-06-078114-9(9)*, HarperTeen) HarperCollins Pubs.

James, Dalton. The Sneakiest Pirates. 2008. 20p. pap. 10.95 *(978-1-4327-2477-1(0))* Outskirts Pr., Inc.

James, Eric. A Halloween Scare in Connecticut. Le Ray, Marina, illus. 2015. (ENG.). 32p. (J). (-5). 9.99 *(978-1-4926-2370-0(9)*, 9781492623700, Sourcebooks Jabberwocky) Sourcebooks, Inc.

—A Halloween Scare in Edmonton. Le Ray, Marina, illus. 2015. (ENG.). 32p. (J). (-5). 11.99 *(978-1-4926-2372-4(5)*, 9781492623724, Sourcebooks Jabberwocky) Sourcebooks, Inc.

—A Halloween Scare in Hawaii. Le Ray, Marina, illus. 2015. (ENG.). 32p. (J). (-5). 9.99 *(978-1-4926-2373-1(3)*, 9781492623731, Sourcebooks Jabberwocky) Sourcebooks, Inc.

—A Halloween Scare in Idaho. Le Ray, Marina, illus. 2015. (ENG.). 32p. (J). (-5). 9.99 *(978-1-4926-2374-8(1)*, 9781492623748, Sourcebooks Jabberwocky) Sourcebooks, Inc.

—A Halloween Scare in Kansas. Le Ray, Marina, illus. 2015. (ENG.). 32p. (J). (-5). 9.99 *(978-1-4926-2376-2(8)*, 9781492623762, Sourcebooks Jabberwocky) Sourcebooks, Inc.

—A Halloween Scare in Kansas City. Le Ray, Marina, illus. 2015. (ENG.). 32p. (J). (-5). 9.99 *(978-1-4926-2377-9(6)*, 9781492623779, Sourcebooks Jabberwocky) Sourcebooks, Inc.

—A Halloween Scare in Las Vegas. Le Ray, Marina, illus. 2015. (ENG.). 32p. (J). (-5). 9.99 *(978-1-4926-2378-6(4)*, 9781492623786, Sourcebooks Jabberwocky) Sourcebooks, Inc.

—A Halloween Scare in Los Angeles. Le Ray, Marina, illus. 2015. (ENG.). 32p. (J). (-5). 9.99 *(978-1-4926-2379-3(2)*, 9781492623793, Sourcebooks Jabberwocky) Sourcebooks, Inc.

—A Halloween Scare in Maine. Le Ray, Marina, illus. 2015. (ENG.). 32p. (J). (-5). 9.99 *(978-1-4926-2380-9(6)*, 9781492623809, Sourcebooks Jabberwocky) Sourcebooks, Inc.

—A Halloween Scare in Massachusetts. Le Ray, Marina, illus. 2015. (ENG.). 32p. (J). (-5). 9.99 *(978-1-4926-2381-6(4)*, 9781492623816, Sourcebooks Jabberwocky) Sourcebooks, Inc.

—A Halloween Scare in Mississippi. Le Ray, Marina, illus. 2015. (ENG.). 32p. (J). (-5). 9.99 *(978-1-4926-2382-3(2)*, 9781492623823, Sourcebooks Jabberwocky) Sourcebooks, Inc.

—A Halloween Scare in Missouri. Le Ray, Marina, illus. 2015. (ENG.). 32p. (J). (-5). 9.99 *(978-1-4926-2383-0(0)*, 9781492623830, Sourcebooks Jabberwocky) Sourcebooks, Inc.

—A Halloween Scare in Montana. Le Ray, Marina, illus. 2015. (ENG.). 32p. (J). (-5). 9.99 *(978-1-4926-2384-7(9)*, 9781492623847, Sourcebooks Jabberwocky) Sourcebooks, Inc.

—A Halloween Scare in Nebraska. Le Ray, Marina, illus. 2015. (ENG.). 32p. (J). (-5). 9.99 *(978-1-4926-2385-4(7)*, 9781492623854, Sourcebooks Jabberwocky) Sourcebooks, Inc.

—A Halloween Scare in Nevada. Le Ray, Marina, illus. 2015. (ENG.). 32p. (J). (-5). 9.99 *(978-1-4926-2386-1(5)*, 9781492623861, Sourcebooks Jabberwocky) Sourcebooks, Inc.

—A Halloween Scare in New Hampshire. Le Ray, Marina, illus. 2015. (ENG.). 32p. (J). (-5). 9.99 *(978-1-4926-2387-8(3)*, 9781492623878, Sourcebooks Jabberwocky) Sourcebooks, Inc.

—A Halloween Scare in New Mexico. Le Ray, Marina, illus. 2015. (ENG.). 32p. (J). (-5). 9.99 *(978-1-4926-2388-5(1)*, 9781492623885, Sourcebooks Jabberwocky) Sourcebooks, Inc.

—A Halloween Scare in New York City. Le Ray, Marina, illus. 2015. (ENG.). 32p. (J). (-5). 9.99 *(978-1-4926-2389-2(X)*, 9781492623892, Sourcebooks Jabberwocky) Sourcebooks, Inc.

—A Halloween Scare in North Carolina. Le Ray, Marina, illus. 2015. (ENG.). 32p. (J). (-5). 9.99 *(978-1-4926-2855-2(7)*, 9781492628552, Sourcebooks Jabberwocky) Sourcebooks, Inc.

—A Halloween Scare in North Dakota. Le Ray, Marina, illus. 2015. (ENG.). 32p. (J). (-5). 9.99 *(978-1-4926-2390-8(3)*, 9781492623908, Sourcebooks Jabberwocky) Sourcebooks, Inc.

—A Halloween Scare in Oklahoma. Le Ray, Marina, illus. 2015. (ENG.). 32p. (J). (-5). 9.99 *(978-1-4926-2391-5(1)*, 9781492623915, Sourcebooks Jabberwocky) Sourcebooks, Inc.

—A Halloween Scare in Omaha. Le Ray, Marina, illus. 2015. (ENG.). 32p. (J). (-5). 9.99 *(978-1-4926-2392-2(X)*, 9781492623922, Sourcebooks Jabberwocky) Sourcebooks, Inc.

—A Halloween Scare in Oregon. Le Ray, Marina, illus. 2015. (ENG.). 32p. (J). (-5). 9.99 *(978-1-4926-2393-9(8)*, 9781492623939, Sourcebooks Jabberwocky) Sourcebooks, Inc.

—A Halloween Scare in Ottawa. Le Ray, Marina, illus. 2015. (ENG.). 32p. (J). (-5). 11.99 *(978-1-4926-2394-6(6)*, 9781492623946, Sourcebooks Jabberwocky) Sourcebooks, Inc.

—A Halloween Scare in Pittsburgh. Le Ray, Marina, illus. 2015. (ENG.). 32p. (J). (-5). 9.99 *(978-1-4926-2396-0(2)*, 9781492623960, Sourcebooks Jabberwocky) Sourcebooks, Inc.

—A Halloween Scare in Portland. Le Ray, Marina, illus. 2015. (ENG.). 32p. (J). (-5). 9.99 *(978-1-4926-2397-7(0)*, 9781492623977, Sourcebooks Jabberwocky) Sourcebooks, Inc.

—A Halloween Scare in Rhode Island. Le Ray, Marina, illus. 2015. (ENG.). 32p. (J). (-5). 9.99 *(978-1-4926-2398-4(9)*, 9781492623984, Sourcebooks Jabberwocky) Sourcebooks, Inc.

—A Halloween Scare in San Francisco. Le Ray, Marina, illus. 2015. (ENG.). 32p. (J). (-5). 9.99 *(978-1-4926-2399-1(7)*, 9781492623991, Sourcebooks Jabberwocky) Sourcebooks, Inc.

—A Halloween Scare in South Carolina. Le Ray, Marina, illus. 2015. (ENG.). 32p. (J). (-5). 9.99 *(978-1-4926-2860-6(3)*, 9781492628606, Sourcebooks Jabberwocky) Sourcebooks, Inc.

—A Halloween Scare in South Dakota. Le Ray, Marina, illus. 2015. (ENG.). 32p. (J). (-5). 9.99 *(978-1-4926-2400-4(4)*, 9781492624004, Sourcebooks Jabberwocky) Sourcebooks, Inc.

—A Halloween Scare in St. Louis. Le Ray, Marina, illus. 2015. (ENG.). 32p. (J). (-5). 9.99 *(978-1-4926-2401-1(2)*, 9781492624011, Sourcebooks Jabberwocky) Sourcebooks, Inc.

—A Halloween Scare in Tampa Bay. Le Ray, Marina, illus. 2015. (ENG.). 32p. (J). (-5). 9.99 *(978-1-4926-2402-8(0)*, 9781492624028, Sourcebooks Jabberwocky) Sourcebooks, Inc.

—A Halloween Scare in the Carolinas. Le Ray, Marina, illus. 2014. (ENG.). 32p. (J). (-5). 9.99 *(978-1-4926-0576-8(X)*, 9781492605768, Sourcebooks Jabberwocky) Sourcebooks, Inc.

—A Halloween Scare in Toronto. Le Ray, Marina, illus. 2015. (ENG.). 32p. (J). (-5). 11.99 *(978-1-4926-2403-5(9)*, 9781492624035, Sourcebooks Jabberwocky) Sourcebooks, Inc.

—A Halloween Scare in Tulsa. Le Ray, Marina, illus. 2015. (ENG.). 32p. (J). (-5). 9.99 *(978-1-4926-2404-2(7)*, 9781492624042, Sourcebooks Jabberwocky) Sourcebooks, Inc.

—A Halloween Scare in Utah. La Ray, Marina, illus. 2015. (ENG.). 32p. (J). (-5). 9.99 *(978-1-4926-2405-9(5)*, 9781492624059, Sourcebooks Jabberwocky) Sourcebooks, Inc.

—A Halloween Scare in Vancouver. Le Ray, Marina, illus. 2015. (ENG.). 32p. (J). (-5). 11.99 *(978-1-4926-2406-6(3)*, 9781492624066, Sourcebooks Jabberwocky) Sourcebooks, Inc.

—A Halloween Scare in Vermont. Le Ray, Marina, illus. 2015. (ENG.). 32p. (J). (-5). 9.99 *(978-1-4926-2407-3(1)*, 9781492624073, Sourcebooks Jabberwocky) Sourcebooks, Inc.

—A Halloween Scare in Virginia. Le Ray, Marina, illus. 2014. (ENG.). 32p. (J). (-5). 9.99 *(978-1-4926-0636-9(7)*, 9781492606369, Sourcebooks Jabberwocky) Sourcebooks, Inc.

—A Halloween Scare in Washington. Le Ray, Marina, illus. 2014. (ENG.). 32p. (J). (-5). 9.99 *(978-1-4926-0639-0(1)*, 9781492606390, Sourcebooks Jabberwocky) Sourcebooks, Inc.

—A Halloween Scare in Washington, DC. Le Ray, Marina, illus. 2015. (ENG.). 32p. (J). (-5). 9.99 *(978-1-4926-2408-0(X)*, 9781492624080, Sourcebooks Jabberwocky) Sourcebooks, Inc.

—A Halloween Scare in West Virginia. Le Ray, Marina, illus. 2015. (ENG.). 32p. (J). (-5). 9.99 *(978-1-4926-2409-7(8)*,

9781492624097, Sourcebooks Jabberwocky) Sourcebooks, Inc.

—A Halloween Scare in Wisconsin. Le Ray, Marina, illus. 2014. (ENG.). 32p. (J). (-5). 9.99 *(978-1-4926-0642-0(1)*, 9781492606420, Sourcebooks Jabberwocky) Sourcebooks, Inc.

—A Halloween Scare in Wyoming. Le Ray, Marina, illus. 2015. (ENG.). 32p. (J). (-5). 9.99 *(978-1-4926-2410-3(1)*, 9781492624103, Sourcebooks Jabberwocky) Sourcebooks, Inc.

James, Simon. Baby Brains. James, Simon, illus. 2016. (ENG., Illus.). 32p. (J). (gr. -1-3). 9.99 *(978-0-7636-8177-7(6))* Candlewick Pr.

Jamieson, Victoria. The Great Pet Escape. Jamieson, Victoria, illus. 2016. (Pets on the Loose! Ser.). (ENG., Illus.). 64p. (J). 15.99 *(978-1-62779-105-2(1)*, 9781627791052, Holt, Henry & Co. Bks. For Young Readers) Holt, Henry & Co.

Janese, Julie. The Little Booger Book. 2009. 24p. pap. 11.49 *(978-1-4490-0310-4(9))* AuthorHouse.

Janisch, Heinz. The Fantastic Adventures of Baron Munchausen. Cooper, Belinda, tr. from GER. Blau, Aljoscha, illus. 2010. (ENG.). 32p. (J). (gr. -1-3). 17.95 *(978-1-59270-091-2(8))* Enchanted Lion Bks., LLC.

Jardine, Alan. Sloop John B: A Pirate's Tale. Pickering, Jimmy, illus. 2005. (ENG.). 32p. (J). (gr. 4-7). 17.95 *(978-1-59687-181-6(4))* IBks., Inc.

Jarman, Julia. Class Three at Sea. Chapman, Lynne, illus. 2008. (ENG.). 32p. (J). (gr. k-3). 16.95 *(978-0-8225-7617-4(1)*, Carolrhoda Bks.) Lerner Publishing Group.

—Class Two at the Zoo. Chapman, Lynne, illus. 2007. (Carolrhoda Picture Bks.). (ENG.). 32p. (J). (gr. k-2). 16.95 *(978-0-8225-7132-2(3)*, Carolrhoda Bks.) Lerner Publishing Group.

—Little Bad Riding Hood. 2014. (ENG., Illus.). 32p. (J). *(978-0-7787-0442-3(4))*; pap. *(978-0-7787-0450-8(5))* Crabtree Publishing Co.

Jeff, Brown. Flat Stanley - His Original Adventure! 40th rev. ed. 2014. (Flat Stanley Ser.). (ENG.). 96p. (J). (gr. 3-7). 9.24 *(978-1-63245-236-8(7))* Lectorum Pubns., Inc.

Jeffers, Oliver. It Wasn't Me: A Hueys Book. Jeffers, Oliver, illus. 2014. (Hueys Ser.: 2). (ENG., Illus.). 32p. (J). (gr. -1-k). 17.99 *(978-0-399-25768-1(3)*, Philomel Bks.) Penguin Young Readers Group.

—Stuck. Jeffers, Oliver, illus. 2011. (ENG., Illus.). 32p. (J). (gr. -1-2). 17.99 *(978-0-399-25737-7(3)*, Philomel Bks.) Penguin Young Readers Group.

Jeffrey, Gary. Autopsies: Pathologists at Work. Riley, Terry, illus. 2008. (Graphic Forensic Science Ser.). (ENG.). 48p. (gr. 5-8). per. 14.05 *(978-1-4042-1447-7(X))*; (YA). lib. bdg. 31.95 *(978-1-4042-1446-0(1))* Rosen Publishing Group, Inc., The.

Jenkins, Alan & N. Ray. Jokes for Kids 2. 2012. 32p. pap. 19.99 *(978-1-4772-7575-7(4))* AuthorHouse.

Jenkins, N. Ray. Jokes for Kids. 2012. (Illus.). 32p. pap. 19.99 *(978-1-4772-5590-2(7))* AuthorHouse.

Jennewein, James & Parker, Tom S. RuneWarriors. 2008. (RuneWarriors Ser.). 320p. (J). (gr. 3-7). lib. bdg. 17.89 *(978-0-06-144937-6(7)*, Geringer, Laura Book) HarperCollins Pubs.

—Shield of Odin. 2009. (RuneWarriors Ser.: 1). (ENG.). 336p. (J). (gr. 3-7). pap. 6.99 *(978-0-06-144938-3(5))* HarperCollins Pubs.

—Ship of the Dead. 2010. (RuneWarriors Ser.: 3). (ENG.). 304p. (J). (gr. 3-7). 17.99 *(978-0-06-144942-0(3))* HarperCollins Pubs.

—Sword of Doom. 2009. (RuneWarriors Ser.: 2). (ENG.). 432p. (J). (gr. 3-7). 17.99 *(978-0-06-144939-0(3))* HarperCollins Pubs.

Jennings, Patrick. Lucky Cap. 2012. (ENG.). 224p. (J). (gr. 4-7). 6.99 *(978-1-60684-306-2(0)*, Carolrhoda Bks.) Lerner Publishing Group.

—My Homework Ate My Homework. 2013. (ENG.). 224p. (J). (gr. 4-7). 15.99 *(978-1-60684-286-7(2)*, Carolrhoda Bks.) Lerner Publishing Group.

—Odd, Weird & Little. 2015. (ENG.). 160p. (gr. 3-7). pap. 6.99 *(978-1-60684-568-4(3))* Lerner Publishing Group.

—We Can't All Be Rattlesnakes. (J). 2011. (ENG.). 144p. (gr. 3-7). pap. 5.99 *(978-0-06-082117-3(5))* 2009. 121p. lib. bdg. 16.89 *(978-0-06-082116-6(7))* HarperCollins Pubs.

Jensen, Joel, et al. Tiny Hamster Is a Giant Monster. 2015. (ENG., Illus.). 32p. (J). (gr. -1-3). 17.99 *(978-1-4814-5110-9(3)*, Simon & Schuster Bks. For Young Readers) Simon & Schuster Bks. For Young Readers.

Jethani, Rita. Baby has a Burp. 2006. (Illus.). 24p. (J). 12.00 *(978-0-9774147-0-3(1))* Laasya Design.

Jin, Chris & Trimmer, Christian. Simon's New Bed. Van der Paardt, Melissa, illus. 2015. (ENG.). 32p. (J). (gr. -1-3). 17.99 *(978-1-4814-3019-7(X))* Simon & Schuster Children's Publishing.

Jin, Susie Lee. Mine! Jin, Susie Lee, illus. 2016. (ENG., Illus.). 40p. (J). (gr. -1-3). 16.99 *(978-1-4814-2772-2(5)*, Simon & Schuster Bks. For Young Readers) Simon & Schuster Bks. For Young Readers.

Jinks, Catherine. The Reformed Vampire Support Group. 2010. (ENG.). 384p. (YA). (gr. 7). pap. 8.99 *(978-0-547-41166-8(9))* Houghton Mifflin Harcourt Publishing Co.

Johannes, Shelley. Beatrice Zinker, Upside down Thinker. Johannes, Shelley, illus. 2017. (Beatrice Zinker, Upside down Thinker Ser.). (ENG., Illus.). 160p. (J). (gr. 2-5). 14.99 ***(978-1-4847-6738-2(1))*** Hyperion Bks. for Children.

John, Jory. The Bad Seed. Oswald, Pete, illus. 2017. 40p. (J). (gr. -1-3). 17.99 ***(978-0-06-246776-8(X))*** HarperCollins Pubs.

—Goodnight Already! Davies, Benji, illus. 2014. (ENG.). 32p. (J). (gr. -1-3). 17.99 *(978-0-06-228620-8(X))* HarperCollins Pubs.

—I Love You Already! Davies, Benji, illus. 2015. 32p. (J). (gr. -1-3). 17.99 *(978-0-06-237095-2(2))* HarperCollins Pubs.

—Penguin Problems. Smith, Lane, illus. 2016. (ENG.). 32p. (J). (gr. -1-2). lib. bdg. 20.99 *(978-0-375-97465-6(2)*, Random Hse. Bks. for Young Readers) Random Hse. Children's Bks.

Johns, Phillip. Little Levi & Uncle Donut. 2012. 34p. pap. 9.49 *(978-0-615-47658-2(9))* BrotherBiz Publishing.

Johnson, Gillian. Thora. Johnson, Gillian, illus. 2003. (Illus.). 128p. *(978-0-207-19815-1(2))* HarperCollins Pubs. Australia.

Johnson, Lafayette, Jr. & Liberty, Dendron. Tyler's Wise Old Tree. 2012. (Illus.). 65p. (J). pap. 12.99 *(978-0-9817448-1-0(8))* MaMbabooks.com.

Johnson, Linda & Hodges, Quae. 21st Century Parables: A Child's Book. 2006. 48p. pap. 14.95 *(978-1-60145-071-5(0))* Booklocker.com, Inc.

Johnson, Shane L. illus. Attack of the Zombie Rabbids. 2016. (Rabbids Invasion Ser.). (ENG.). 40p. (J). (gr. 1-3). pap. 3.99 *(978-1-4814-6066-8(8)*, Simon Spotlight) Simon Spotlight.

—The Chickens & the Eggs. 2014. (Rabbids Invasion Ser.). (ENG.). 40p. (J). (gr. 1-3). pap. 3.99 *(978-1-4814-0042-8(8)*, Simon Spotlight) Simon Spotlight.

Jonell, Lynne. Emmy & the Home for Troubled Girls. Bean, Jonathan, illus. 2010. (Emmy & the Rat Ser.: 2). (ENG.). 384p. (J). (gr. 4-7). pap. 12.99 *(978-0-312-60873-6(X)*, 9780312608736) Square Fish.

—Emmy & the Incredible Shrinking Rat. Bean, Jonathan, illus. 2008. (Emmy & the Rat Ser.: 1). (ENG.). 368p. (J). (gr. 4-7). pap. 8.99 *(978-0-312-38460-9(2)*, 9780312384609) Square Fish.

—Emmy & the Incredible Shrinking Rat. l.t. ed. 2008. 426p. (YA). 23.95 *(978-1-4104-0778-8(0))* Thorndike Pr.

—Emmy & the Rats in the Belfry. Bean, Jonathan, illus. 2011. (Emmy & the Rat Ser.: 3). (ENG.). 384p. (J). (gr. 4-7). 17.99 *(978-0-8050-9183-0(1)*, 9780805091830, Holt, Henry & Co. Bks. For Young Readers) Holt, Henry & Co.

Jones, A. Responsibility. 2011. 32p. pap. 24.95 *(978-1-4626-2167-5(8))* America Star Bks.

Jones, Brian and Brad. The Righteous Heroes. 2005. 36p. pap. 13.99 *(978-1-4116-5423-5(4))* Lulu Pr., Inc.

Jones, Bryan E. Somebody Stole My Yawn! Embry, Stacey, illus. 2009. 28p. pap. 24.95 *(978-1-60749-877-3(4))* America Star Bks.

Jones, Carrie. Quest for the Golden Arrow. 2017. (Time Stoppers Ser.). (ENG.). 464p. (J). 16.99 *(978-1-61963-863-1(0)*, 9781619638631, Bloomsbury USA Childrens) Bloomsbury Publishing USA.

Jones, Christianne C. Miles Mchale, Tattletale. Ellis, Elina, illus. 2017. (Little Boost Ser.). (ENG.). 32p. (gr. k-2). lib. bdg. 23.99 *(978-1-5158-0752-0(5)*, Little Boost) Picture Window Bks.

Jones, Harmony. The High Note. 2017. (ENG.). 240p. (J). 16.99 *(978-1-61963-949-2(1)*, 9781619639492, Bloomsbury USA Childrens) Bloomsbury Publishing USA.

Jones, Marcia Thornton & Dadey, Debbie. Dragons Do Eat Homework. Dreidemy, Joëlle, illus. 2007. 64p. (J). *(978-0-545-00234-9(6))* Scholastic, Inc.

Jones, Noah Z. Jack & the Snackstalk. Jones, Noah Z., illus. 2016. (ENG., Illus.). 80p. (J). (gr. k-2). 15.99 *(978-0-545-84862-6(8))* Scholastic, Inc.

—Little Red Quacking Hood. 2014. (Princess Pink & the Land of Fake-Believe Ser.: 2). (ENG.). 80p. (J). (gr. k-2). 15.99 *(978-0-545-63842-5(9))* Scholastic, Inc.

—Little Red Quacking Hood. Jones, Noah Z., illus. 2014. (Princess Pink & the Land of Fake-Believe Ser.: 2). (ENG., Illus.). 80p. (J). (gr. k-2). pap. 4.99 *(978-0-545-63841-8(0))* Scholastic, Inc.

—Little Red Quacking Hood. 2014. (Princess Pink & the Land of Fake-Believe Ser.: 2). lib. bdg. 14.75 *(978-0-606-36048-7(4))* Turtleback Bks.

—Moldylocks & the Three Beards. Jones, Noah Z., illus. 2014. (Princess Pink & the Land of Fake-Believe Ser.: 1). (ENG., Illus.). 80p. (J). (gr. k-2). pap. 4.99 *(978-0-545-63839-5(9))* Scholastic, Inc.

—The Three Little Pugs. 2015. (ENG., Illus.). 80p. (J). (gr. k-2). pap. 4.99 *(978-0-545-84857-2(1))* Scholastic, Inc.

Jones, Sam. Yolo. 2014. (ENG., Illus.). 224p. (YA). (gr. 9). pap. 9.99 *(978-1-4814-1548-4(4)*, Simon Pulse) Simon Pulse.

Jordan, Mary Ellen & Weldon, Andrew. Lazy Daisy, Cranky Frankie: Bedtime on the Farm. Weldon, Andrew, illus. 2013. (ENG., Illus.). 24p. (J). (gr. -1-3). 15.99 *(978-0-8075-4400-6(0))* Whitman, Albert & Co.

Joy, Angelica. My Cat Merigold. Bolle, Frank, illus. 2008. 56p. pap. 19.95 *(978-1-59858-591-9(6))* Dog Ear Publishing, LLC.

Joy, Susan. My 1st Wacky ABCs. 2008. 32p. pap. 24.95 *(978-1-4241-9955-6(7))* America Star Bks.

Joyce, William. A Day with Wilbur Robinson. Joyce, William, illus. 2006. (ENG., Illus.). 40p. (J). (gr. -1-3). 16.99 *(978-0-06-089098-8(3))* HarperCollins Pubs.

—The Mischievians. Joyce, William, illus. 2013. (ENG., Illus.). 56p. (J). (gr. k-3). 17.99 *(978-1-4424-7347-8(9)*, Atheneum Bks. for Young Readers) Simon & Schuster Children's Publishing.

Juby, Susan. Alice MacLeod, Realist at Last. 2005. 320p. (J). (ENG.). 15.99 *(978-0-06-051549-2(X))*; lib. bdg. 16.89 *(978-0-06-051550-8(3))* HarperCollins Pubs. (HarperTeen).

Judge, Malcolm. Jonny Jakes Investigates the Old School Ghoul. Brown, Alan, illus. 2016. (Middle-Grade Novels Ser.). (ENG.). 240p. (gr. 4-7). lib. bdg. 25.99 *(978-1-4965-2829-2(8))* Stone Arch Bks.

Jules, Jacqueline. My Vida Loca. Smith, Kim, illus. 2016. (Sofia Martinez Ser.). (ENG.). 96p. (gr. k-2). pap. 4.95 *(978-1-4795-8720-9(6)*, Sofia Martinez) Picture Window Bks.

Julius, Nicholas. The Mythfitz: Unee the Unicorn. 2012. (ENG., Illus.). 62p. 28.95 *(978-1-4327-9868-0(5))*; pap. 23.95 *(978-1-4327-9365-4(9))* Outskirts Pr., Inc.

Jung, Mike. Geeks, Girls, & Secret Identities. Maihack, Mike, illus. 2012. (J). (ENG.). 320p. (gr. 3-7). 16.99 *(978-0-545-33548-5(5))*; pap. *(978-0-545-33549-2(3))* Scholastic, Inc. (Levine, Arthur A. Bks.).

Justice, Joseph. Lawyer's Week Before Christmas, 1 vol. Alikhan, Salima, illus. 2010. (Night Before Christmas Ser.). (ENG.). 32p. (J). (gr. 4-8). 16.99 *(978-1-58980-739-6(1))* Pelican Publishing Co., Inc.

Kain, P. G. The Social Experiments of Dorie Dilts: Dumped by Popular Demand. 2007. (Mix Ser.). (ENG., Illus.). 272p. (J). (gr. 4-8). pap. 5.99 *(978-1-4169-3519-3(3)*, Simon & Schuster/Paula Wiseman Bks.) Simon & Schuster/Paula Wiseman Bks.

—The Social Experiments of Dorie Dilts: The School for Cool. 2008. (Mix Ser.). (ENG.). 288p. (J). (gr. 4-8). pap. 13.99 *(978-1-4169-3520-9(7)*, Simon & Schuster/Paula Wiseman Bks.) Simon & Schuster/Paula Wiseman Bks.

Kai's Cake. 2004. (Illus.). 23p. (J). pap. 29.99 *(978-0-9749469-0-0(7))* Crunchpeep Media.

Kamateros, Litsa & Morfonios, Nia. Sarah's Socks: My World of Autism. 2010. 24p. pap. 10.95 *(978-1-61633-023-1(6))* Guardian Angel Publishing, Inc.

Kang, A. N. The Very Fluffy Kitty, Papillon. Kang, A. N., illus. 2016. (Papillon Ser.). (ENG., Illus.). 40p. (J). (gr. -1-k). 16.99 *(978-1-4847-1798-1(8))* Disney Pr.

Kann, Victoria. Peterrific. Kann, Victoria, illus. 2017. (Pinkalicious Ser.). (Illus.). 40p. (J). (gr. -1-3). 17.99 *(978-0-06-256356-9(4))* HarperCollins Pubs.

—Pinkalicious: Pink Around the Rink. Kann, Victoria, illus. 2010. (I Can Read Level 1 Ser.). (ENG., Illus.). 32p. (J). (gr. -1-3). 16.99 *(978-0-06-192880-2(1))*; pap. 3.99 *(978-0-06-192879-6(8))* HarperCollins Pubs.

—The Pinkatastic. Kann, Victoria, illus. 2011. (Pinkalicious Ser.). (ENG., Illus.). 100p. (J). (gr. -1-2). pap. 12.99 *(978-0-06-192889-5(5)*, HarperFestival) HarperCollins Pubs.

—Teeny Tiny Pinky Library, 4 vols. 2012. (Pinkalicious Ser.). (ENG., Illus.). 36p. (J). (gr. -1-3). 14.99 *(978-0-06-222724-9(6))* HarperCollins Pubs.

—Tickled Pink. Kann, Victoria, illus. 2010. (Pinkalicious Ser.). (ENG., Illus.). 24p. (J). (gr. -1-3). pap. 3.99 *(978-0-06-192877-2(1)*, HarperFestival) HarperCollins Pubs.

—Tickled Pink. Kann, Victoria, illus. 2010. (Pinkalicious Ser.). (Illus.). (J). lib. bdg. 13.55 *(978-0-606-14869-6(8)*, Turtleback) Turtleback Bks.

Kaplan, Bruce Eric. Cousin Irv from Mars. Kaplan, Bruce Eric, illus. 2013. (ENG., Illus.). 40p. (J). (gr. -1-3). 16.99 *(978-1-4424-4923-7(3)*, Simon & Schuster Bks. For Young Readers) Simon & Schuster Bks. For Young Readers.

Kaputa, Christine C. Bad Kitty! 2007. 16p. per. 9.95 *(978-1-59858-478-3(2))* Dog Ear Publishing, LLC.

Kasdan, Mallory. Ella. Chin, Marcos, illus. 2015. (ENG.). 56p. (J). (gr. k-3). bds. 17.99 *(978-0-670-01675-4(6)*, Viking Books for Young Readers) Penguin Young Readers Group.

Kasza, Keiko. No Te Rias, Pepe. (Buenas Noches Ser.). (SPA.). (J). (gr. k-3). *(978-958-04-3623-2(1))* Norma S.A.

Kasza, Keiko & McPike, Elizabeth. Finders Keepers. Kasza, Keiko, illus. 2015. (ENG., Illus.). 32p. (J). (gr. -1-k). bds. 16.99 *(978-0-399-16898-7(2)*, G.P. Putnam's Sons Books for Young Readers) Penguin Young Readers Group.

Katz, Alan. The Day the Mustache Came Back. Easler, Kris, illus. 2016. (Mustache Ser.: 2). (ENG.). 224p. (J). 13.99 *(978-1-61963-560-9(7)*, 9781619635609, Bloomsbury USA Childrens) Bloomsbury Publishing USA.

—The Day the Mustache Took Over. Easler, Kris, illus. (Mustache Ser.: 1). (ENG.). 208p. 2016. (J). pap. 6.99 *(978-1-68119-148-5(2)*, 9781681191485) 2015. (YA). (gr. 2-4). 13.99 *(978-1-61963-558-6(5)*, 9781619635586) Bloomsbury Publishing USA. (Bloomsbury USA Childrens).

—That Stinks! A Punny Show-and-Tell. Gilpin, Stephen, illus. 2016. (ENG.). 32p. (J). (gr. -1-3). 17.99 *(978-1-4169-7880-0(1)*, Simon & Schuster Bks. For Young Readers) Simon & Schuster Bks. For Young Readers.

Katzwinkle, William, et al. Walter the Farting Dog Goes on a Cruise. Colman, Audrey, illus. 2008. (J). 13.99 *(978-1-59319-939-5(2))* LeapFrog Enterprises, Inc.

Kaupp, Rosemarie. The Amberella Tales: Amberella & Double Double Trouble. 2013. 144p. (gr. 2-4). 20.77 *(978-1-4669-9233-7(6))*; pap. 10.77 *(978-1-4669-9234-4(4))* Trafford Publishing.

Kay, Cassandra. A Week in the Life of Mertyle. 2009. 96p. pap. 10.49 *(978-1-4389-4049-6(1))* AuthorHouse.

Keeble, Helen. Fang Girl. 2012. (ENG.). 352p. (YA). (gr. 8). pap. 9.99 *(978-0-06-208225-1(6)*, HarperTeen) HarperCollins Pubs.

Keillor, Garrison. The Old Man Who Loved Cheese. braille ed. 2004. (Illus.). (J). (gr. k-3). spiral bd. *(978-0-616-01687-9(5))* Canadian National Institute for the Blind/Institut National Canadien pour les Aveugles.

Keller, Laurie. Arnie the Doughnut. Keller, Laurie, illus. rev. ed. 2003. (Adventures of Arnie the Doughnut Ser.: 1). (ENG., Illus.). 40p. (J). (gr. -1-3). 18.99 *(978-0-8050-6283-0(1)*, 9780805062830, Holt, Henry & Co. Bks. For Young Readers) Holt, Henry & Co.

—Arnie the Doughnut. Keller, Laurie, illus. 2005. (Illus.). (J). (gr. k-4). 29.95 *(978-0-439-76641-8(9)*, WHCD649) Weston Woods Studios, Inc.

—Bowling Alley Bandit. Keller, Laurie, illus. 2013. (Adventures of Arnie the Doughnut Ser.: 1). (ENG., Illus.). 128p. (J). (gr. 2-5). 13.99 *(978-0-8050-9076-5(2)*, 9780805090765, Holt, Henry & Co. Bks. For Young Readers) Holt, Henry & Co.

—Invasion of the Ufonuts. Keller, Laurie, illus. 2014. (Adventures of Arnie the Doughnut Ser.: 2). (ENG., Illus.). 128p. (J). (gr. 2-5). 13.99 *(978-0-8050-9075-8(4)*, 9780805090758, Holt, Henry & Co. Bks. For Young Readers) Holt, Henry & Co.

—The Spinny Icky Showdown. Keller, Laurie, illus. 2015. (Adventures of Arnie the Doughnut Ser.: 3). (ENG., Illus.). 128p. (J). (gr. 2-5). 13.99 *(978-0-8050-9074-1(6)*, 9780805090741, Holt, Henry & Co. Bks. For Young Readers) Holt, Henry & Co.

Kelley, Jane. Sol-Ray Man & the Freaky Flood. 2017. (Escapades of Clint Mccool Ser.: 2). lib. bdg. 16.00 ***(978-0-606-40112-8(1))*** Turtleback Bks.

Kelley, Marty. The Best Friend Bandit. Kelley, Marty, illus. 2017. (Molly Mac Ser.). (ENG., Illus.). 56p. (gr. k-2). lib. bdg. 22.65 *(978-1-5158-0836-7(X))* Picture Window Bks.

—Fame, Fortune, & the Bran Muffins of Doom. Kelley, Marty, illus. 2012. (ENG., Illus.). 144p. (J). 16.95 *(978-0-8234-2606-5(8))* Holiday Hse., Inc.

—The Messiest Desk. 2009. (J). *(978-1-55933-319-1(7))* Zino Pr. Children's Bks.

—Sammy's Great Escape. Kelley, Marty, illus. 2017. (Molly Mac Ser.). (ENG., Illus.). 56p. (gr. k-2). lib. bdg. 22.65 *(978-1-5158-0835-0(1))* Picture Window Bks.

—Tooth Fairy Trouble. Kelley, Marty, illus. 2017. (Molly Mac Ser.). (ENG., Illus.). 56p. (gr. k-2). lib. bdg. 22.65 *(978-1-5158-0838-1(6))* Picture Window Bks.

Kelley, Marty, illus. Spring Goes Squish: A Vibrant Volume of Vociferous Vernal Verse. 2008. (J). (gr. k-2). 14.95 *(978-1-55933-315-3(4))* Zino Pr. Children's Bks.

Kelley, True. The Dog Who Saved Santa. Kelley, True, illus. 2008. (ENG., Illus.). 32p. (J). (gr. -1-3). 16.95 *(978-0-8234-2120-6(1))* Holiday Hse., Inc.

Kelly, Bernadette & Ward, Krista. Naughty Norton, 1 vol. Alger, Liz, illus. 2009. (Pony Tales Ser.). (ENG.). 56p. (gr. 2-2). lib. bdg. 21.32 *(978-1-4048-5504-5(1)*, Chapter Readers) Picture Window Bks.

—Norton Saves the Day, 1 vol. Alger, Liz, illus. 2009. (Pony Tales Ser.). (ENG.). 56p. (gr. 2-2). lib. bdg. 21.32 *(978-1-4048-5505-2(X)*, Chapter Readers) Picture Window Bks.

—Norton's First Show, 1 vol. Alger, Liz, illus. 2009. (Pony Tales Ser.). (ENG.). 56p. (gr. 2-2). lib. bdg. 21.32 *(978-1-4048-5506-9(8)*, Chapter Readers) Picture Window Bks.

—Who Stole Norton?, 1 vol. Alger, Liz, illus. 2009. (Pony Tales Ser.). (ENG.). 56p. (gr. 2-2). lib. bdg. 21.32 *(978-1-4048-5503-8(3)*, Chapter Readers) Picture Window Bks.

Kelly, Jamie & Benton, Jim. Never Underestimate Your Dumbness. 2008. (Dear Dumb Diary Ser.). (Illus.). 150p. (gr. 4-7). 16.00 *(978-0-7569-8814-2(4))* Perfection Learning Corp.

Kelly, Katy. Melonhead. Johnson, Gillian, illus. 2010. (Melonhead Ser.). (ENG.). 240p. (J). (gr. 3-7). 6.99 *(978-0-440-42187-0(X)*, Yearling) Random Hse. Children's Bks.

—Melonhead & the Undercover Operation. Johnson, Gillian, illus. 2012. (Melonhead Ser.). (ENG.). 256p. (J). (gr. 3-7). 7.99 *(978-0-375-84528-4(3)*, Yearling) Random Hse. Children's Bks.

Kelly, Mij. One More Sheep. Ayto, Russell, illus. 2006. (ENG.). 32p. (J). (gr. k-3). 16.95 *(978-1-56145-378-8(1))* Peachtree Pubs.

Keltz, Karen. Sally Jo Survives Sixth Grade: A Journal. Carrigg, Susan, illus. 2013. 180p. pap. 9.99 *(978-0-9857281-1-3(6))* HAPPY HOUSE PR.

Kennedy, J. Aday. Stella, the Fire Farting Dragon. Foster, Jack, illus. 2011. 20p. pap. 10.95 *(978-1-61633-149-8(6))* Guardian Angel Publishing, Inc.

Kennedy, J. Aday & Foster, Jack. Klutzy Kantor. 2010. 24p. pap. 10.95 *(978-1-61633-051-4(1))* Guardian Angel Publishing, Inc.

Kenney, Cindy. Veggie Tales I Can! And So Can You!, 1 vol. 2004. (Big Idea Books / VeggieTales Ser.). (ENG., Illus.). (J). bds. 12.99 *(978-0-310-70893-3(1))* Zonderkidz.

Kent, Jaden. #1: the Cave of Aaaaah! Doom! Bodnaruk, Iryna, illus. 2017. (Ella & Owen Ser.: 1). (ENG.). 112p. (J). (gr. 1-3). pap. 5.99 *(978-1-4998-0368-6(0))* Little Bee Books Inc.

—#2: Attack of the Stinky Fish Monster! Bodnaruk, Iryna, illus. 2017. (Ella & Owen Ser.: 2). (ENG.). 112p. (J). (gr. 1-3). pap. 5.99 *(978-1-4998-0369-3(9))* Little Bee Books Inc.

Kerr, Judith. Twinkles, Arthur & Puss. Kerr, Judith, illus. 2008. (ENG., Illus.). 40p. (J). (gr. k-2). pap. 9.95 *(978-0-00-725447-7(4))* HarperCollins Pubs. Ltd. GBR. Dist: Independent Pubs. Group.

Kerr, Philip. The Most Frightening Story Ever Told. 2016. (ENG.). 320p. (J). (gr. 3-7). 16.99 *(978-0-553-52209-9(4)*, Knopf Bks. for Young Readers) Random Hse. Children's Bks.

Kessler, Leonard P. Mrs. Pine Takes a Trip. Kessler, Leonard P., illus. 2005. (Illus.). (J). 16.00 *(978-1-930900-25-7(2))* Purple Hse. Pr.

Kiker, Jean. Jumping Lizard Tales. 2005. pap. 12.95 *(978-1-932196-51-1(X))* WordWright.biz, Inc.

Kilpatrick, Irene. Welcome to Gabba Land! 2009. (Yo Gabba Gabba! Ser.). (ENG.). 14p. (J). (gr. -1-k). 8.99 *(978-1-4169-7096-5(7)*, Simon Spotlight) Simon Spotlight.

Kilpatrick, Leanne. One Night on Earth: The Story of Christmas. 2013. 28p. pap. *(978-0-906672-82-2(1))* Oleander Pr., The.

Kim, Derek Kirk. Vanishing Point. Kim, Derek Kirk, illus. 2012. (Tune Ser.: 1). (ENG., Illus.). 160p. pap. 17.99 *(978-1-59643-516-2(X)*, 9781596435162, First Second Bks.) Roaring Brook Pr.

Kimmel, Elizabeth Cody. My Penguin Osbert. Lewis, H. B., illus. 2005. 40p. pap. *(978-1-84428-565-5(0))* Walker Bks., Ltd.

Kimmel, Eric A. Bernal & Florinda: A Spanish Tale. Rayevsky, Robert, illus. 2004. 29p. (J). (gr. k-4). reprint ed. 16.00 *(978-0-7567-7906-1(5))* DIANE Publishing Co.

—Hayyim's Ghost. 2005. (Illus.). 40p. (J). pap. 9.95 *(978-1-932687-03-3(3)*, Devora Publishing) Simcha Media Group.

—Hayyim's Ghost. Binus, Ari, illus. 2005. 40p. (J). 16.95 *(978-1-932687-02-6(5)*, Devora Publishing) Simcha Media Group.

—Little Red Hot, 0 vols. Huliska-Beith, Laura, illus. 2013. (ENG.). 32p. (J). (gr. -1-3). 17.99 *(978-1-4778-1638-7(0)*, 9781477816387, Amazon Children's Publishing) Amazon Publishing.

Kinard, Kami. The Boy Prediction: Notes & Observations of Tabitha Reddy. 2014. (ENG., Illus.). 272p. (J). (gr. 3-7). 12.99 *(978-0-545-57586-7(9)*, Scholastic Pr.) Scholastic, Inc.

King, Emily. Mrs. Twiggenbotham Goes to Town. 2003. (Twiggenbotham Adventure Ser.). (Illus.). 32p. (J). 12.99 *(978-0-8254-3064-0(X))* Kregel Pubns.

King, Jane. Welcome to Chillsville Elementary. 2013. (Ghoul School Ser.: 1). (ENG.). 80p. (J). (gr. 1-4). pap. 13.99 *(978-1-4814-2162-1(X)*, Simon & Schuster/Paula Wiseman Bks.) Simon & Schuster/Paula Wiseman Bks.

King-smith, Dick. Funny Frank. Eastwood, John, illus. 2003. (ENG.). 112p. (J). (gr. 1-4). 5.99 *(978-0-440-41880-1(1)*, Yearling) Random Hse. Children's Bks.

King, Trey. Mystery on the Lego Express. Wang, Sean, illus. 2014. (Lego City Ser.). (ENG.). 24p. (J). (gr. -1-3). 3.99 *(978-0-545-60366-9(8))* Scholastic, Inc.

King, Wesley. The Incredible Space Raiders from Space! 2015. (ENG., Illus.). 304p. (J). (gr. 3-7). 16.99 *(978-1-4814-2319-9(3)*, Simon & Schuster Bks. For Young Readers) Simon & Schuster Bks. For Young Readers.

The Kingfisher Book of Funny Stories. 2003. 80p. (J). 17.95 *(978-0-7534-5558-6(7))* Kingfisher Bks.

Kinney, Jeff. Cabin Fever. 2011. (Diary of a Wimpy Kid Ser.). (ENG., Illus.). 224p. (J). (gr. 3-7). 13.95 *(978-1-4197-0223-5(8)*, Amulet Bks.) Abrams, Inc.

—Cabin Fever, 2 vols. 2011. (Diary of a Wimpy Kid Ser.: 6). (J). 46.75 *(978-1-4640-2148-0(1))*; 1.25 *(978-1-4640-4524-0(0))*; 44.75 *(978-1-4640-2151-0(1))*; *(978-1-4640-2149-7(X))*; 44.75 *(978-1-4640-2152-7(X))* Recorded Bks., Inc.

—Cabin Fever. 2011. (Diary of a Wimpy Kid Ser.: 6). (J). lib. bdg. 25.70 *(978-0-606-23667-6(8)*, Turtleback) Turtleback Bks.

—El Diario de Greg, un Renacuajo. Morán, Esteban, tr. 2008. (SPA.). 218p. (J). (gr. 3-6). 17.99 *(978-1-933032-52-8(9))* Lectorum Pubns., Inc.

—Diary of a Wimpy Kid. 2014. pap. *(978-1-4197-1499-3(6))* 2013. pap. *(978-1-4197-1176-3(8))* 2009. pap. *(978-0-8109-8888-0(7))* 2007. (Diary of a Wimpy Kid Ser.). (ENG., Illus.). 224p. (J). (gr. 2-8). 13.95 *(978-0-8109-9313-6(9))* 2007. pap. *(978-0-8109-8893-4(3))* 2007. pap. *(978-0-8109-8292-5(7))* 2007. (Diary of a Wimpy Kid Ser.: Bk. 1). 217p. pap. *(978-0-8109-9455-3(0))*Bks. 1-4. 2014. (ENG.). 896p. (J). (gr. 3-7). 56.00 *(978-1-4197-1669-0(7))* Abrams, Inc. (Amulet Bks.).

—Diary of a Wimpy Kid. (Diary of a Wimpy Kid Ser.). (CHI., Illus.). (J). 2009. (gr. 4-8). ***(978-986-84847-4-0(X))*** 2008. (gr. 3-7). ***(978-986-84847-0-2(7))*** DaskoviK, Izdatel'sko-torgovaja korporacija.

—Diary of a Wimpy Kid. 2013. (Diary of a Wimpy Kid Ser.: 16). (CHI.). (J). pap. 13.95 *(978-7-5405-7891-6(2))* Guangdong New Era Publishing Hse. CHN. Dist: Chinasprout, Inc.

—Diary of a Wimpy Kid. 2009. (Diary of a Wimpy Kid Ser.: Bk. 1). 1.00 *(978-1-4074-4434-5(4))* 2008. (Diary of a Wimpy Kid Ser.: 1). (J). 75.75 *(978-1-4361-3290-9(8))* 2008. (Diary of a Wimpy Kid Ser.: 1). (J). 44.75 *(978-1-4281-8196-0(2))* 2008. (Diary of a Wimpy Kid Ser.: 1). (J). 46.75 *(978-1-4281-8194-6(6))* 2008. (Diary of a Wimpy Kid Ser.: 1). (J). 46.75 *(978-1-4281-8198-4(9))* 2008. (Diary of a Wimpy Kid Ser.: 1). (J). 44.75 *(978-1-4281-8200-4(4))* 2008. (Diary of a Wimpy Kid Ser.: 1). (J). 1.25 *(978-1-4281-8191-5(1))* 2008. (Diary of a Wimpy Kid Ser.: 1). (J). 173.75 *(978-1-4281-8195-3(4))* Recorded Bks., Inc.

—Diary of a Wimpy Kid. 2007. (Diary of a Wimpy Kid Ser.: 1). (Illus.). 217p. (J). lib. bdg. 25.70 *(978-0-606-23662-1(7)*, Turtleback) Turtleback Bks.

—Dog Days. 2009. (Diary of a Wimpy Kid Ser.: 4). (ENG., Illus.). 224p. (J). (gr. 3-7). 13.95 *(978-0-8109-8391-5(5)*, Amulet Bks.) Abrams, Inc.

—Dog Days. (Diary of a Wimpy Kid Ser.: 4). (J). 2011. 75.75 *(978-1-4407-7756-1(X))* 2010. (SPA.). 181.75 *(978-1-4407-7748-6(9))* 2010. 54.75 *(978-1-4407-7747-9(0))* 2010. 46.75 *(978-1-4407-7751-6(9))* 2010. 44.75 *(978-1-4407-7753-0(5))* 2009. 52.75 *(978-1-4407-7749-3(7))* 2009. 1.25 *(978-1-4407-7755-4(1))* Recorded Bks., Inc.

—Dog Days. 2009. (Diary of a Wimpy Kid Ser.: 4). (J). lib. bdg. 25.70 *(978-0-606-23665-2(1)*, Turtleback) Turtleback Bks.

—Double Down. 2016. (Diary of a Wimpy Kid Ser.: Bk. 11). (ENG., Illus.). 224p. (J). (gr. 3-7). 13.95 *(978-1-4197-2344-5(8))*; E-Book 12.56 *(978-1-61312-992-0(0))* Abrams, Inc. (Amulet Bks.).

—Double Down. 2016. (Diary of a Wimpy Kid Ser.: 11). (J). lib. bdg. 25.70 *(978-0-606-38998-3(9))* Turtleback Bks.

—Hard Luck. 2013. (Diary of a Wimpy Kid Ser.: Bk. 8). (ENG., Illus.). 224p. (J). (gr. 3-7). 13.95 *(978-1-4197-1132-9(6)*, Amulet Bks.) Abrams, Inc.

—Hard Luck. 2013. (Diary of a Wimpy Kid Ser.: 8). (J). lib. bdg. 25.70 *(978-0-606-32062-7(8)*, Turtleback) Turtleback Bks.

—The Last Straw. 2009. (Diary of a Wimpy Kid Ser.). (Illus.). (J). (gr. 3-7). (ENG.). 224p. 13.95 *(978-0-8109-7068-7(6)*, Amulet Bks.); 218p. pap. *(978-0-8109-7108-0(9))* Abrams, Inc.

—The Last Straw. 2009. (Diary of a Wimpy Kid Ser.: 3). (ENG.). 224p. (J). (gr. 4-6). pap. 17.95 *(978-1-4395-8262-6(9))*, 0008062297, Paw Prints) Baker & Taylor, CATS.

—The Last Straw. 2009. (Diary of a Wimpy Kid Ser.: Bk. 3). (JPN., Illus.). 221p. (J). *(978-4-591-10910-6(0))* Poplar Publishing.

—The Last Straw. 2010. (Diary of a Wimpy Kid Ser.: 3). (J). 1.25 *(978-1-4407-2984-3(0))* 2010. (Diary of a Wimpy Kid Ser.: 3). (J). 46.75 *(978-1-4407-2976-8(X))* 2009. (Diary of a Wimpy Kid Ser.: 3). (J). 75.75 *(978-1-4407-2986-7(7))* 2009. (Diary of a Wimpy Kid Ser.: 3). (J). 44.75 *(978-1-4407-2982-9(4))* 2009. (Diary of a Wimpy Kid Ser.: 3). (J). 173.75 *(978-1-4407-2977-5(8))* 2009. (Diary of a Wimpy Kid Ser.: 3). (J). 45.75 *(978-1-4407-2980-5(8))* 2009. (Diary of a Wimpy Kid Ser.: 3). (J). 44.75 *(978-1-4407-2978-2(6))* 2009. (Diary of a Wimpy Kid Ser.: Bk. 3). 1.00 *(978-1-4416-1788-0(4))* Recorded Bks., Inc.

—The Last Straw. 2009. (Diary of a Wimpy Kid Ser.: 3). (Illus.). 217p. (J). lib. bdg. 25.70 *(978-0-606-23664-5(3)*, Turtleback) Turtleback Bks.

—The Long Haul. Kinney, Jeff, illus. 2014. (Diary of a Wimpy Kid Ser.: Bk. 9). (ENG., Illus.). 224p. (J). (gr. 3-7). 13.95 *(978-1-4197-1189-3(X)*, Amulet Bks.) Abrams, Inc.

—The Long Haul. (CHI.). (J). 2015. 368p. (gr. 4-8). pap. *(978-986-6104-59-6(1))* 2014. *(978-986-6104-52-7(4))* DaskoviK, Izdatel'sko-torgovaja korporacija.

—The Long Haul. 2014. (JPN.). 221p. (J). *(978-4-591-14196-0(9))* Poplar Publishing.

—The Long Haul. 2013. (Diary of a Wimpy Kid Ser.: 9). (J). 40.75 *(978-1-4906-4383-0(4))*; 43.75 *(978-1-4906-4058-7(4))* Recorded Bks., Inc.

—The Long Haul. 2014. (Diary of a Wimpy Kid Ser.: 9). (J). lib. bdg. 25.70 *(978-0-606-36074-6(3))* Turtleback Bks.

—Old School. 2015. (Diary of a Wimpy Kid Ser.: Bk. 10). (ENG., Illus.). 224p. (J). (gr. 3-7). 13.95 *(978-1-4197-1701-7(4)*, Amulet Bks.) Abrams, Inc.

—Old School. 2015. (Diary of a Wimpy Kid Ser.: 10). (J). lib. bdg. 25.70 *(978-0-606-37422-4(1))* Turtleback Bks.

—Rodrick Rules. 2008. (Diary of a Wimpy Kid Ser.). (Illus.). (J). (ENG.). 224p. (gr. 3-7). 13.95 *(978-0-8109-9473-7(9)*, Amulet Bks.); 216p. pap. 4.99 *(978-0-8109-9552-9(2))* Abrams, Inc.

—Rodrick Rules. 2008. (Diary of a Wimpy Kid Ser.: Bk. 2). (JPN., Illus.). 220p. (J). *(978-4-591-10464-4(8))* Poplar Publishing.

—Rodrick Rules, 2 vols. (Diary of a Wimpy Kid Ser.: 2). (J). 2010. 173.75 *(978-1-4361-3864-2(7))* 2010. 75.75 *(978-1-4407-0420-8(1))* 2009. 1.25 *(978-1-4361-3860-4(4))* 2009. 46.75 *(978-1-4361-3863-5(9))* 2009. 44.75 *(978-1-4361-3869-7(8))* 2009. 44.75 *(978-1-4361-3865-9(5))* 2009. (gr. 4-8). 46.75 *(978-1-4361-3867-3(1))* Recorded Bks., Inc.

—Rodrick Rules. 2008. (Diary of a Wimpy Kid Ser.: 2). (J). lib. bdg. 25.70 *(978-0-606-23663-8(5)*, Turtleback) Turtleback Bks.

—The Third Wheel. 2012. (ENG.). (J). (gr. 3-7). pap. 8.49 *(978-1-4197-0729-2(9))*; (Illus.). 224p. 13.95 *(978-1-4197-0584-7(9)*, Amulet Bks.) Abrams, Inc.

—The Third Wheel. 2012. (Diary of a Wimpy Kid Ser.: 7). (Illus.). 217p. (YA). lib. bdg. 25.70 *(978-0-606-26514-0(7)*, Turtleback) Turtleback Bks.

—The Ugly Truth. 2010. (Diary of a Wimpy Kid Ser.). (ENG.). 224p. (J). (gr. 3-7). 13.95 *(978-0-8109-8491-2(1)*, Amulet Bks.) Abrams, Inc.

—The Ugly Truth. 2010. (Diary of a Wimpy Kid Ser.: Bk. 5). (JPN., Illus.). 221p. (J). (gr. 4-7). *(978-4-591-12117-7(8))* Poplar Publishing.

—The Ugly Truth, 2 vols. 2010. (Diary of a Wimpy Kid Ser.: 5). (J). 44.75 *(978-1-4498-4534-6(7))*; 46.75 *(978-1-4498-4532-2(0))*; 173.75 *(978-1-4498-4530-8(4))*; 1.25 *(978-1-4498-4535-3(5))*; 44.75 *(978-1-4498-4531-5(2))* Recorded Bks., Inc.

—The Ugly Truth. 2010. (Diary of a Wimpy Kid Ser.: 5). (J). lib. bdg. 25.70 *(978-0-606-23666-9(X)*, Turtleback) Turtleback Bks.

Kirkman, Rick & Scott, Jerry. Gross! A Baby Blues Collection. 2016. (Baby Blues Ser.: 40). (ENG., Illus.). 208p. pap. 18.99 *(978-1-4494-7781-3(X))* Andrews McMeel Publishing.

Kisseloff, Jeff & Wells, Rosemary. Ruby's Tea for Two. 2003. (Max & Ruby Ser.). (ENG.). 12p. (J). (gr. -1 — 1). bds. 6.99 *(978-0-670-03652-3(8)*, Viking Books for Young Readers) Penguin Young Readers Group.

Klassen, Jon. This Is Not My Hat. Klassen, Jon, illus. 2012. (ENG., Illus.). 40p. (J). (gr. -1-3). 16.99 *(978-0-7636-5599-0(6))* Candlewick Pr.

Klimo, Kate. Dog Diaries #10: Rolf. Jessell, Tim, illus. 2017. (Dog Diaries). (ENG.). 160p. (J). (gr. 2-5). pap. 7.99 *(978-0-399-55128-4(X)*, Random Hse. Bks. for Young Readers) Random Hse. Children's Bks.

Kline, Suzy. Horrible Harry Goes to Sea: Puffine Chapters. Remkiewicz, Frank, illus. 2003. (Horrible Harry Ser.). (ENG.). 64p. (J). (gr. 2-4). 4.99 *(978-0-14-250002-6(X)*, Puffin Books) Penguin Young Readers Group.

—Horrible Harry Goes to Sea: Puffine Chapters. 2003. (Horrible Harry Ser.: 13). (gr. 3-6). lib. bdg. 14.75 *(978-0-613-61629-4(4)*, Turtleback) Turtleback Bks.

—Horrible Harry Takes the Cake. Remkiewicz, Frank, illus. 2007. (Horrible Harry Ser.). (ENG.). 64p. (J). (gr. 2-4). 4.99 *(978-0-14-240939-8(1)*, Puffin Books) Penguin Young Readers Group.

Klise, Kate. Dying to Meet You. Klise, M. Sarah, illus. (43 Old Cemetery Road Ser.: Bk. 1). (ENG.). 160p. (J). (gr. 2-5). 2010. pap. 6.99 *(978-0-547-39848-8(4))* 2009. 16.99 *(978-0-15-205727-5(7))* Houghton Mifflin Harcourt Publishing Co.

—Greetings from the Graveyard. Klise, M. Sarah, illus. (43 Old Cemetery Road Ser.). (ENG.). 160p. (J). (gr. 2-5). 2015. pap. 6.99 *(978-0-544-54010-1(7))* 2014. 15.99 *(978-0-544-10567-6(2))* Houghton Mifflin Harcourt Publishing Co. (HMH Books For Young Readers).

—Hollywood, Dead Ahead. Klise, M. Sarah, illus. (43 Old Cemetery Road Ser.: 5). (ENG.). 144p. (J). (gr. 2-5). 2014. pap. 6.99 *(978-0-544-33661-2(5)*, HMH Books For Young Readers) 2013. 15.99 *(978-0-547-85283-6(5))* Houghton Mifflin Harcourt Publishing Co.

—The Loch Ness Punster. Klise, M. Sarah, illus. 2016. (43 Old Cemetery Road Ser.: 7). (ENG.). 144p. (J). (gr. 2-5). pap. 6.99 *(978-0-544-81085-3(6)*, HMH Books For Young Readers) Houghton Mifflin Harcourt Publishing Co.

—Over My Dead Body. Klise, M. Sarah, illus. (43 Old Cemetery Road Ser.: Bk. 2). (ENG.). 128p. (J). (gr. 2-5). 2011. pap. 6.99 *(978-0-547-57713-5(3))* 2009. 15.99 *(978-0-15-205734-3(X))* Houghton Mifflin Harcourt Publishing Co.

—The Phantom of the Post Office. Klise, M. Sarah, illus. (43 Old Cemetery Road Ser.: 4). (ENG.). 160p. (J). (gr. 2-5). 2013. pap. 6.99 *(978-0-544-02281-2(5))* 2012. 16.99 *(978-0-547-51974-6(5))* Houghton Mifflin Harcourt Publishing Co.

—The Phantom of the Post Office. 2013. (43 Old Cemetery Road Ser.: 4). lib. bdg. 17.20 *(978-0-606-31668-2(X)*, Turtleback) Turtleback Bks.

—Regarding the Bathrooms: A Privy to the Past. Klise, Kate & Klise, M. Sarah, illus. 2008. (Regarding The ... Ser.: Bk. 4). (ENG.). 160p. (J). (gr. 2-5). pap. 6.99 *(978-0-15-206261-3(0))* Houghton Mifflin Harcourt Publishing Co.

—Till Death Do Us Bark. Klise, M. Sarah, illus. 2012. (43 Old Cemetery Road Ser.: 3). (ENG.). 144p. (J). (gr. 2-5). pap. 6.99 *(978-0-547-85081-8(6))* Houghton Mifflin Harcourt Publishing Co.

—Till Death Do Us Bark. 2012. (43 Old Cemetery Road Ser.: 3). lib. bdg. 17.20 *(978-0-606-26543-0(0)*, Turtleback) Turtleback Bks.

Klise, Kate & Klise, Kate. Regarding the Bees: A Lesson, in Letters, on Honey, Dating, & Other Sticky Subjects. Klise, M. Sarah, illus. 2009. (Regarding The ... Ser.: Bk. 5). (ENG.). 144p. (J). (gr. 2-5). pap. 6.99 *(978-0-15-206668-0(3))* Houghton Mifflin Harcourt Publishing Co.

Klise, Kate & Klise, M. Sarah. Regarding the Trees: A Splintered Saga Rooted in Secrets. 2007. (Regarding The ... Ser.: Bk. 3). (ENG., Illus.). 160p. (J). (gr. 2-5). pap. 7.99 *(978-0-15-206090-9(1))* Houghton Mifflin Harcourt Publishing Co.

—Till Death Do Us Bark. Klise, Kate & Klise, M. Sarah, illus. 2011. (43 Old Cemetery Road Ser.: 3). (ENG., Illus.). 144p. (J). (gr. 2-5). 16.99 *(978-0-547-40036-5(5))* Houghton Mifflin Harcourt Publishing Co.

Kloepfer, John. Galaxy's Most Wanted. Edwards, Nick, illus. 2014. (Galaxy's Most Wanted Ser.: 1). (ENG.). 224p. (J). (gr. 3-7). 12.99 *(978-0-06-223101-7(4))* HarperCollins Pubs.

—Galaxy's Most Wanted #2: into the Dorkness. Edwards, Nick, illus. 2016. (Galaxy's Most Wanted Ser.: 2). 272p. (J). (gr. 3-7). pap. 6.99 *(978-0-06-223109-3(X))* HarperCollins Pubs.

—Galaxy's Most Wanted #3: Starship Bloopers. Edwards, Nick, illus. 2016. (Galaxy's Most Wanted Ser.: 3). 240p. (J). (gr. 3-7). 12.99 *(978-0-06-223106-2(5))* HarperCollins Pubs.

—Into the Dorkness. Edwards, Nick, illus. 2015. (Galaxy's Most Wanted Ser.: 2). (ENG.). 256p. (J). (gr. 3-7). 12.99 *(978-0-06-223104-8(9))* HarperCollins Pubs.

—Nothing Left to Ooze. DeGrand, David, illus. 2014. (Zombie Chasers Ser.: 5). (ENG.). 240p. (J). (gr. 3-7). pap. 6.99 *(978-0-06-223099-7(9))* HarperCollins Pubs.

—Sludgment Day. Wolfhard, Steve, illus. 2012. (Zombie Chasers Ser.: 3). (ENG.). 224p. (J). (gr. 3-7). pap. 5.99 *(978-0-06-185311-1(9))*; 16.99 *(978-0-06-185310-4(0))* HarperCollins Pubs.

—Sludgment Day. 2012. (Zombie Chasers Ser.: 3). (J). lib. bdg. 16.00 *(978-0-606-26867-7(7)*, Turtleback) Turtleback Bks.

—Undead Ahead. Wolfhard, Steve, illus. 2011. (Zombie Chasers Ser.: 2). (ENG.). 224p. (J). (gr. 3-7). pap. 6.99 *(978-0-06-185308-1(9))*; 16.99 *(978-0-06-185307-4(0))* HarperCollins Pubs.

Klug, Eric. The Monster in My Closet. Klug, Eric, illus. 2007. (Illus.). 32p. (J). (gr. -1-3). 15.95 *(978-1-60108-007-3(7))* Red Cygnet Pr.

Kluger, Steve. My Most Excellent Year: A Novel of Love, Mary Poppins, & Fenway Park. 2009. (ENG.). 416p. (YA). (gr. 7-18). 9.99 *(978-0-14-241343-2(7)*, Speak) Penguin Young Readers Group.

Knapman, Timothy. Superhero Dad. Berger, Joe, illus. 2016. (ENG.). (J). (gr. -1-2). 15.99 *(978-0-7636-8657-4(3)*, Nosy Crow) Candlewick Pr.

Knickerbocker, S. J. King of the Ball. 2008. 24p. pap. 13.50 *(978-1-60693-215-5(2)*, Eloquent Bks.) Strategic Book Publishing & Rights Agency (SBPRA).

Knotoff, Karenann. The Island of Rouge. 2007. 96p. per. 19.95 *(978-1-4241-7575-8(5))* America Star Bks.

Knowlton, Laurie. I Know a Librarian Who Chewed on a Word, 1 vol. Leonhard, Herb, illus. 2012. (ENG.). 32p. (J). (gr. k-3). 16.99 *(978-1-58980-892-8(4))* Pelican Publishing Co., Inc.

Kochalka, James. The Glorkian Warrior & the Mustache of Destiny. 2016. (Glorkian Warrior Ser.: 3). (ENG., Illus.). 128p. (J). pap. 14.99 *(978-1-62672-022-0(3)*, 9781626720220, First Second Bks.) Roaring Brook Pr.

—The Glorkian Warrior Delivers a Pizza. Kochalka, James, illus. 2014. (Glorkian Warrior Ser.: 1). (ENG., Illus.). 112p. (J). (gr. k-4). pap. 12.99 *(978-1-59643-917-7(3)*, 9781596439177, First Second Bks.) Roaring Brook Pr.

Kogler, Jennifer Anne. Ruby Tuesday. 2005. 256p. (J). (gr. 7-18). lib. bdg. 16.89 *(978-0-06-073957-7(6))* HarperCollins Pubs.

Kohake, Beverly. The Funny Bunny. 2008. 32p. pap. 16.95 *(978-1-4303-2736-3(7))* Lulu Pr., Inc.

Könnecke, Ole. Anton & the Battle. Chidgey, Catherine, tr. from GER. 2013.Tr. of Anton und der grosse Streit. (ENG., Illus.). 32p. (gr. -1-3). 17.95 *(978-1-877579-26-4(2))* Gecko Pr. NZL. Dist: Lerner Publishing Group.

Kontis, Alethea. Alpha Oops! The Day Z Went First. Kolar, Bob, illus. 2012. (ENG.). 48p. (J). (gr. -1-3). pap. 6.99 *(978-0-7636-6084-0(1))* Candlewick Pr.

—AlphaOops! H Is for Halloween. Kolar, Bob, illus. 2010. (ENG.). 40p. (J). (gr. -1-3). 15.99 *(978-0-7636-3966-2(4))* Candlewick Pr.

—Alphaoops! H Is for Halloween. Kolar, Bob, illus. 2011. (ENG.). 40p. (J). (gr. -1-3). 7.99 *(978-0-7636-5686-7(0))* Candlewick Pr.

Kopley, Richard. The Remarkable David Wordsworth. Fazio, Michael, illus. 2013. 30p. (J). pap. *(978-1-936172-67-2(4))* Eifrig Publishing.

Korda, Lerryn. So Cozy. Korda, Lerryn, illus. 2015. (ENG., Illus.). 32p. (J). (— 1). 15.99 *(978-0-7636-7373-4(0))* Candlewick Pr.

Koren, Edward. Very Hairy Harry. Koren, Edward, illus. 2003. (Illus.). *(978-0-06-057744-5(4))*; (J). *(978-0-06-056868-9(2))* HarperCollins Pubs.

Korman, Gordon. The Dragonfly Effect (the Hypnotists #3) 2015. (Hypnotists Ser.: 3). (ENG.). 256p. (J). (gr. 3-7). 16.99 *(978-0-545-50336-5(1)*, Scholastic Pr.) Scholastic, Inc.

—No More Dead Dogs. 2017. Orig. Title: Touchdown Stage Left. (J). lib. bdg. 17.20 ***(978-0-606-40570-6(4))*** Turtleback Bks.

—No More Dead Dogs (repackage) 2017. (ENG.). 240p. (J). (gr. 5-9). pap. 6.99 *(978-1-4847-9844-7(9))* Hyperion Bks. for Children.

—Ungifted. 288p. (J). (gr. 5). 2014. pap. 7.99 *(978-0-06-174267-5(8))* 2012. 16.99 *(978-0-06-174266-8(X))* 2012. lib. bdg. 17.89 *(978-0-06-174268-2(6))* HarperCollins Pubs.

Kotecki, Jason. Stupid Swimming Lessons: Kim & Jason Annual #3. 2004. 134p. per. 13.95 *(978-0-9715253-2-0(3))* JBIRD iNK, Ltd.

Kotzwinkle, William & Murray, Glenn. Walter the Farting Dog: Trouble at the Yard Sale. Coleman, Audrey & Audrey, Colman, illus. 2006. (ENG.). 32p. (J). (gr. k-3). reprint ed. pap. 6.99 *(978-0-14-240626-7(0)*, Puffin Books) Penguin Young Readers Group.

Kotzwinkle, William, et al. Walter the Farting Dog: Banned from the Beach. Coleman, Audrey, illus. 2009. (ENG.). 32p. (J). (gr. k-3). pap. 7.99 *(978-0-14-241394-4(1)*, Puffin Books) Penguin Young Readers Group.

—Walter the Farting Dog Goes on a Cruise. Coleman, Audrey, illus. 2006. (ENG.). 32p. (J). (gr. k-3). 16.99 *(978-0-525-47714-3(4)*, Dutton Books for Young Readers) Penguin Young Readers Group.

Kowitt, Holly. Dracula's De-Composition Book. 2007. (Illus.). 170p. (J). *(978-0-545-00307-0(5))* Scholastic, Inc.

—The Principal's Bra Is Missing. Kowitt, Holly, illus. 2017. (ENG., Illus.). 224p. (J). 16.99 *(978-1-250-09132-1(2)*, 9781250091321) Feiwel & Friends.

Kraft, Erik P. Lenny & Mel. Kraft, Erik P., illus. 2012. (Ready-for-Chapters Ser.). (ENG., Illus.). 64p. (J). (gr. 2-5). pap. 6.99 *(978-0-689-85891-8(4)*, Aladdin) Simon & Schuster Children's Publishing.

Krall, Dan. The Great Lollipop Caper. Krall, Dan, illus. 2013. (ENG., Illus.). 48p. (J). (gr. -1-3). 16.99 *(978-1-4424-4460-7(6)*, Simon & Schuster Bks. For Young Readers) Simon & Schuster Bks. For Young Readers.

Krause, Ute. Oscar & the Very Hungry Dragon. 2010. (ENG., Illus.). 40p. (gr. -1-3). 16.95 *(978-0-7358-2306-8(5))* North-South Bks., Inc.

Krauss, Ruth. The Backward Day. Simont, Marc, illus. 2007. (ENG.). 40p. (J). (gr. -1-2). 14.95 *(978-1-59017-237-7(X)*, NYR Children's Collection) New York Review of Bks., Inc., The.

Krensky, Stephen. Dinosaurs in Disguise. Munsinger, Lynn, illus. 2016. (ENG.). 32p. (J). (gr. -1-3). 17.99 *(978-0-544-47271-6(3)*, HMH Books For Young Readers) Houghton Mifflin Harcourt Publishing Co.

—Noah's Bark. Girard, Roger, illus. 2010. (ENG.). 32p. (J). (gr. -1-2). lib. bdg. 16.95 *(978-0-8225-7645-7(7))* Lerner Publishing Group.

—Open Wide! Burks, James, illus. 2014. (ENG.). 14p. (J). (— 1). bds. 6.99 *(978-0-545-53368-3(6)*, Cartwheel Bks.) Scholastic, Inc.

—Trucks. Lola & Ivanke, illus. 2009. (Ready-To-Reads Ser.). (ENG.). 32p. (J). (gr. -1-1). pap. 3.99 *(978-1-4169-0236-2(8)*, Simon Spotlight) Simon Spotlight.

Kroll, Virginia. Mosquito, 1 vol. LePlatt, Betsy, illus. 2011. (ENG.). 32p. (J). (gr. k-3). 16.99 *(978-1-58980-883-6(5))* Pelican Publishing Co., Inc.

Krosoczka, Jarrett J. Baghead. Krosoczka, Jarrett J., illus. 2004. (ENG., Illus.). 40p. (J). (gr. -1-2). reprint ed. pap. 7.99 *(978-0-553-11172-9(8)*, Dragonfly Bks.) Random Hse. Children's Bks.

Krpata, Mitch. The Lost Expedition. Merritt, Kory, illus. 2016. (Poptropica Ser.). (ENG.). 112p. (J). (gr. 1-4). 9.95 *(978-1-4197-2129-8(1)*, Amulet Bks.) Abrams, Inc.

Krulik, Nancy. Burp or Treat ... Smell My Feet! Super Special. Blecha, Aaron, illus. 2014. (George Brown, Class Clown Ser.: No. 3). (ENG.). 208p. (J). (gr. 2-4). 5.99 *(978-0-448-46115-1(3)*, Grosset & Dunlap) Penguin Young Readers Group.

—Eww! What's on My Shoe? 2013. (George Brown, Class Clown Ser.: 11). lib. bdg. 14.75 *(978-0-606-32126-6(8)*, Turtleback) Turtleback Bks.

—How Do You Pee in Space? Blecha, Aaron, illus. 2014. (George Brown, Class Clown Ser.: 13). (ENG.). 128p. (J). (gr. 2-4). pap. 4.99 *(978-0-448-46113-7(7)*, Grosset & Dunlap) Penguin Young Readers Group.

—Ice-Cream Dreams. Martinez, Heather, illus. 2004. 22p. (J). lib. bdg. 15.00 *(978-1-4242-0975-0(7))* Fitzgerald Bks.

—Lice Check, No. 12. Blecha, Aaron, illus. 2014. (George Brown, Class Clown Ser.: 12). (ENG.). 128p. (J). (gr. 2-4). 4.99 *(978-0-448-46112-0(9)*, Grosset & Dunlap) Penguin Young Readers Group.

—Lice Check. 2014. (George Brown, Class Clown Ser.: 12). lib. bdg. 14.75 *(978-0-606-34144-8(7)*, Turtleback) Turtleback Bks.

—Return to the Scene of the Burp. 2017. (George Brown, Class Clown Ser.: 19). lib. bdg. 16.00 ***(978-0-606-39773-5(6))*** Turtleback Bks.

Krulik, Nancy. She's Got the Beat. 2010. (Romantic Comedies Ser.). (ENG.). 320p. (YA). (gr. 9). pap. 14.99 *(978-1-4424-1419-8(7)*, Simon Pulse) Simon Pulse.

Krulik, Nancy & Burwasser, Amanda Elizabeth. Science No Fair! Project Droid #1. Moran, Mike, illus. 2016. (Project Droid Ser.). (ENG.). 112p. (J). (gr. 1-4). 13.99 *(978-1-5107-1018-4(3)*, Sky Pony Pr.) Skyhorse Publishing Co., Inc.

Krulik, Nancy & dePaola, Tomie. A Royal Pain in the Burp, No. 15A. Blecha, Aaron, illus. 2015. (George Brown, Class Clown Ser.: 15). (ENG.). 128p. (J). (gr. 1-3). bds. 4.99 *(978-0-448-48283-5(5)*, Grosset & Dunlap) Penguin Young Readers Group.

—'Snot Funny! Blecha, Aaron, illus. 2015. (George Brown, Class Clown Ser.: 14). (ENG.). 128p. (J). (gr. 2-4). bds. 4.99 *(978-0-448-48282-8(7)*, Grosset & Dunlap) Penguin Young Readers Group.

Krull, Kathleen & Brewer, Paul. Fartiste. Kulikov, Boris, illus. 2008. (ENG.). 40p. (J). (gr. -1-3). 17.99 *(978-1-4169-2828-7(6)*, Simon & Schuster Bks. For Young Readers) Simon & Schuster Bks. For Young Readers.

Kruse, Donald W. Fleas, Please. Crank, Donny, illus. 2012. 48p. pap. 12.95 *(978-1-59663-858-7(3)*, Castle Keep Pr.) Rock, James A. & Co. Pubs.

Kuefler, Joseph. Rulers of the Playground. Kuefler, Joseph, illus. 2017. (Illus.). 48p. (J). (gr. -1-3). 17.99 *(978-0-06-242432-7(7))* HarperCollins Pubs.

Kuenzler, Lou. Eat Your People! Wojtowycz, David, illus. (ENG.). 32p. (J). (gr. -1-k). 2017. pap. 7.99 *(978-1-4083-3034-0(2))* 2016. 17.99 *(978-1-4083-3033-3(4))* Hachette Children's Group GBR. (Orchard Bks.). Dist: Hachette Bk. Group.

—Princess DisGrace: a Royal Disaster. 2016. (Princess DisGrace Ser.). (ENG., Illus.). 240p. (J). (gr. 3-7). 12.99 *(978-0-553-53775-8(X)*, Random Hse. Bks. for Young Readers) Random Hse. Children's Bks.

Kuhn, Camilla. Samira & the Skeletons. 2016. (ENG., Illus.). 34p. (J). 16.00 *(978-0-8028-5463-6(X)*, Eerdmans Bks For Young Readers) Eerdmans, William B. Publishing Co.

Kuipers, Alice. Violet & Victor Write the Most Fabulous Fairy Tale. 2016. (ENG., Illus.). 40p. (J). (gr. -1-3). 17.00 *(978-0-316-21202-1(4))* Little Brown & Co.

Kulka, Joe. The Rope, 1 vol. 2008. (ENG., Illus.). 32p. (J). (gr. k-3). 16.99 *(978-1-58980-487-6(2))* Pelican Publishing Co., Inc.

—Vacation's Over! Return of the Dinosaurs. Kulka, Joe, illus. 2010. (Carolrhoda Picture Bks.). (ENG., Illus.). 32p. (J). (gr. k-3). lib. bdg. 17.95 *(978-0-7613-5212-9(0))* Lerner Publishing Group.

Kulka, Joe, illus. My Crocodile Does Not Bite. 2013. (ENG.). 32p. (J). (gr. k-3). lib. bdg. 16.95 *(978-0-7613-8937-8(7)*, Carolrhoda Bks.) Lerner Publishing Group.

Kunhardt, Dorothy. Junket Is Nice. Kunhardt, Dorothy, illus. 2013. (ENG., Illus.). 72p. (J). (gr. -1-2). 16.95 *(978-1-59017-628-3(6)*, NYR Children's Collection) New York Review of Bks., Inc., The.

Kurtz, Chris. The Pup Who Cried Wolf. Francis, Guy, illus. 2010. (ENG.). 144p. (YA). (gr. 2-4). 15.99 *(978-1-59990-497-9(7)*, 9781599904979); pap. 5.99 *(978-1-59990-492-4(6)*, 9781599904924) Bloomsbury Publishing USA. (Bloomsbury USA Childrens).

Kurzweil, Allen. Leon & the Champion Chip. Bertholf, Bret, illus. 2005. 352p. (J). 15.99 *(978-0-06-053933-7(X))*; lib. bdg. 16.89 *(978-0-06-053934-4(8))* HarperCollins Pubs.

—Leon & the Spitting Image. Bertholf, Bret, illus. (ENG.). 320p. (J). (gr. 3-18). 2005. pap. 7.99 *(978-0-06-053932-0(1)*, Greenwillow Bks.) 2003. 16.99 *(978-0-06-053930-6(5))* HarperCollins Pubs.

Kusaka, Hidenori & Harukaze, Santa. Pokémon Pocket Comics Vol. 1: Black & White. 2013. (ENG., Illus.). 320p. (J). pap. 9.99 *(978-1-4215-5910-0(2))* Viz Media.

Kwan, James. Dear Yeti. 2015. (ENG., Illus.). 40p. (J). (gr. -1-2). 17.99 *(978-0-374-30045-6(3)*, 9780374300456, Farrar, Straus & Giroux (BYR)) Farrar, Straus & Giroux.

La Rue, Coco. A New Pig in Town. May, Kyla, illus. 2013. 127p. (J). pap. *(978-0-545-46607-3(5))* Scholastic, Inc.

Laden, Nina. Are We There Yet? McCauley, Adam, illus. 2016. (ENG.). 36p. (J). (gr. -1-k). 16.99 *(978-1-4521-3155-9(4))* Chronicle Bks. LLC.

LaFer, Jenni. Ben Dhere! Don Dhat! Tall Tales from the Island of Gullah. Weitzel, Erica, illus. 2007. 96p. (J). per. 18.95 *(978-0-9800816-0-2(2))* Bread & Butter Bks.

Lagonegro, Melissa. A Tale of Two Sisters. Random House Disney Staff, illus. 2013. (Step into Reading Ser.). (ENG.). 32p. (J). (gr. -1-1). 3.99 *(978-0-7364-3120-0(9)*, RH/Disney) Random Hse. Children's Bks.

Lampman, Evelyn Sibley. The Shy Stegosaurus of Cricket Creek. Buel, Hubert, illus. 2007. 218p. (J). (gr. 4-7). per. 12.00 *(978-1-930900-37-0(6))* Purple Hse. Pr.

Landers, Ace. Yoda's Secret Missions, Bk. 1. Ameet Studio Staff, illus. 2014. (Lego Star Wars Ser.). (ENG.). 64p. (J). (gr. 2-5). pap. 4.99 *(978-0-545-65700-6(8))* Scholastic, Inc.

Landstrom, Olof, et al. Boo & Baa Have Company. Sandin, Joan, tr. from SWE. 2006. (Illus.). 40p. (J). (gr. -1-1). 15.00 *(978-91-29-66546-8(9))* R & S Bks. SWE. Dist: Macmillan.

Landy, Derek. Scepter of the Ancients. Percival, Tom, illus. 2009. (Skulduggery Pleasant Ser.: Bk. 1). (ENG.). 416p. (J). pap. 3.99 *(978-0-06-173155-6(2)*, Harper Trophy) HarperCollins Pubs.

Lane, Jessica E. Fletcher: The Quickest Chicken Catcher. 2009. 52p. pap. 31.99 *(978-1-4415-3461-3(X))* Xlibris Corp.

Lane, Nathan & Elliott, Devlin. Naughty Mabel. Krall, Dan, illus. 2015. (Naughty Mabel Ser.). (ENG.). 48p. (J). (gr. -1-3). 17.99 *(978-1-4814-3022-7(X)*, Simon & Schuster Bks. For Young Readers) Simon & Schuster Bks. For Young Readers.

—Naughty Mabel Sees It All. Krall, Dan, illus. 2016. (Naughty Mabel Ser.). (ENG.). 48p. (J). (gr. -1-3). 17.99 *(978-1-4814-3024-1(6)*, Simon & Schuster Bks. For Young Readers) Simon & Schuster Bks. For Young Readers.

Langridge, Roger, text. The Muppets Omnibus. 2014. (ENG., Illus.). 600p. (J). (gr. -1-17). 59.99 *(978-0-7851-8792-9(8))* Marvel Worldwide, Inc.

Langteau, Scott. Sofa Boy. Vernon, Rion, illus. 2008. (ENG.). 40p. 14.95 *(978-0-615-25125-7(0))* Shake the Moon Bks.

Lapuss, Stephane & Ah-Koon, Didier. Minions - Evil Panic, Vol. 2. 2015. (ENG., Illus.). 48p. (gr. 1-4). pap. 6.99 *(978-1-78276-555-4(7))* Titan Bks. Ltd. GBR. Dist: Penguin Random Hse. LLC.

LaReau, Kara. The Infamous Ratsos. Myers, Matt, illus. 2016. (Infamous Ratsos Ser.). (ENG.). 64p. (J). (gr. k-3). 14.99 *(978-0-7636-7636-0(5))* Candlewick Pr.

—Unintentional Adventures of the Bland Sisters. Hill, Jen, illus. 2017. (ENG.). 176p. (J). (gr. 3-7). 14.95 *(978-1-4197-2136-6(4)*, Amulet Bks.) Abrams, Inc.

Lariviere, Sarah. The Bad Kid. 2016. (ENG., Illus.). 304p. (J). (gr. 3-7). 16.99 *(978-1-4814-3581-9(7)*, Simon & Schuster Bks. For Young Readers) Simon & Schuster Bks. For Young Readers.

LaRochelle, David. Moo! Wohnoutka, Mike, illus. (ENG.). (J). (gr. -1-3). 2014. 32p. bds. 7.99 *(978-0-8027-3802-8(8)*, 9780802738028) 2013. 40p. 16.99 *(978-0-8027-3409-9(X)*, 9780802734099) Bloomsbury Publishing USA. (Bloomsbury USA Childrens).

Larsen, Mylisa. How to Put Your Parents to Bed. Cole, Babette, illus. 2016. 32p. (J). (gr. -1-3). 17.99 *(978-0-06-232064-3(5))* HarperCollins Pubs.

Latimer, Àlex. The Boy Who Cried Ninja. 1 vol. Latimer, Àlex, illus. 2011. (ENG., Illus.). 32p. (J). (gr. -1-3). 15.95 *(978-1-56145-579-9(2))* Peachtree Pubs.

—The Boy Who Cried Ninja. 2014. lib. bdg. 18.40 *(978-0-606-35511-7(1))* Turtleback Bks.

—Stay! a Top Dog Story. 1 vol. Latimer, Àlex, illus. 2015. (ENG., Illus.). 32p. (J). (gr. -1-3). 16.95 *(978-1-56145-884-4(8))* Peachtree Pubs.

Lavender, Todd. Farmer Fred & His Hen So Red. Lavender, Todd, illus. 2012. (Illus.). 48p. pap. 9.99 *(978-0-9850410-0-7(5))* Akmaeon Publishing, LLC.

Lawrence, Michael. The Curse of the Poltergoose. 2012. (ENG.). 176p. (J). (gr. 4-6). pap. 8.99 *(978-1-4083-0400-6(7))* Hodder & Stoughton GBR. Dist: Hachette Bk. Group.

—The Iron, the Switch & the Broom Cupboard. 2012. (ENG.). 352p. (J). (gr. 4-6). pap. 10.99 *(978-1-4083-0405-1(8))* Hodder & Stoughton GBR. Dist: Hachette Bk. Group.

—Jiggy the Vampire Slayer: A Bloodcurdling Caper! 2011. (ENG.). 224p. (J). (gr. 4-6). pap. 7.99 *(978-1-4083-0804-2(5))* Hodder & Stoughton GBR. Dist: Hachette Bk. Group.

—Jiggy's Magic Balls: A Medieval Mess! 2010. (ENG.). 176p. (J). (gr. k-2). pap. 7.99 *(978-1-4083-0803-5(7))* Hodder & Stoughton GBR. Dist: Hachette Bk. Group.

—Kid Swap. Nadler, Ellis, illus. 2009. (ENG.). 256p. (J). (gr. 4-6). pap. 8.99 *(978-1-4083-0402-0(3))* Hodder & Stoughton GBR. Dist: Hachette Bk. Group.

—The Killer Underpants. abr. ed. 2014. (Jiggy Mccue Ser.). (ENG., Illus.). 208p. (J). (gr. 4-6). pap. 9.99 *(978-1-4083-2425-7(3))* Hodder & Stoughton GBR. Dist: Hachette Bk. Group.

—The Meanest Genie. 2009. (ENG.). 288p. (J). (gr. 4-6). pap. 8.99 *(978-1-4083-0403-7(1))* Hodder & Stoughton GBR. Dist: Hachette Bk. Group.

—Nudie Dudie. 2012. (ENG.). 144p. (J). (gr. 4-6). pap. 8.99 *(978-1-4083-0406-8(6))* Hodder & Stoughton GBR. Dist: Hachette Bk. Group.

—Rudie Dudie. 2010. (ENG.). 160p. (J). (gr. k-2). pap. 8.99 *(978-1-4083-0483-9(X))* Hodder & Stoughton GBR. Dist: Hachette Bk. Group.

—Ryan's Brain. 2012. (ENG.). 320p. (J). (gr. 4-6). pap. 8.99 *(978-1-4083-0409-9(0))* Hodder & Stoughton GBR. Dist: Hachette Bk. Group.

—The Snottle. 2012. (ENG.). 224p. (J). (gr. 4-6). pap. 8.99 *(978-1-4083-0408-2(2))* Hodder & Stoughton GBR. Dist: Hachette Bk. Group.

Lawrence, Michael & Nadler, Ellis. One for All & All for Lunch. 2009. (ENG.). 256p. (J). (gr. 4-6). pap. 8.99 *(978-1-84616-956-4(9))* Hodder & Stoughton GBR. Dist: Hachette Bk. Group.

Layne, Steven L. Thomas's Sheep & the Spectacular Science Project, 1 vol. Board, Perry, illus. 2004. (ENG.). 32p. (J). (gr. k-3). 16.99 *(978-1-58980-210-0(1))* Pelican Publishing Co., Inc.

Lê, Minh. Let Me Finish! Roxas, Isabel, illus. 2016. (ENG.). 20p. (J). (gr. -1-k). 16.99 *(978-1-4847-2173-5(X))* Disney Pr.

Leavitt, Lindsey. The Big Move. Ford, A. G., illus. 2016. (Commander in Cheese Ser.: 1). (ENG.). 112p. (J). (gr. 2-5). 4.99 *(978-1-101-93112-7(4)*, Random Hse. Bks. for Young Readers) Random Hse. Children's Bks.

—Have a Mice Flight! Ford, A. G., illus. 2016. (Commander in Cheese Ser.: 3). (ENG.). 112p. (J). (gr. 2-5). 4.99 *(978-1-101-93118-9(3)*, Random Hse. Bks. for Young Readers) Random Hse. Children's Bks.

Leblanc, Louise. Le Tombeau en Peril, Vol. 56. Brochard, Philippe, illus. 2003. (Premier Roman Ser.). (FRE.). 64p. (J). (gr. 2-5). pap. *(978-2-89021-282-4(3))* Diffusion du livre Mirabel (DLM).

Lebost, Diana. Mr. Kite & the Perilous Flight: Izzy & Daisy. Ersoz, Sahin, illus. 2013. 88p. pap. 18.95 *(978-0-9912023-5-5(X))* Pep & Olie Publishing.

Lechner, John. Sticky Burr: Adventures in Burrwood Forest. Lechner, John, illus. 2008. (ENG., Illus.). 56p. (J). (gr. 1-4). pap. 7.99 *(978-0-7636-3567-1(7))* Candlewick Pr.

Lee, Honest & Gilbert, Matthew J. The Disastrous Magical Wishes of Classroom 13. Dreidemy, Joëlle, illus. 2017. (Classroom 13 Ser.: 2). (ENG.). 128p. (J). (gr. 1-5). 15.99 ***(978-0-316-46454-3(6))***; pap. 5.99 ***(978-0-316-46456-7(2))*** Little, Brown Bks. for Young Readers.

—The Disastrous Magical Wishes of Classroom 13. 2017. (Classroom 13 Ser.: 2). (J). lib. bdg. 16.00 ***(978-0-606-40638-3(7))*** Turtleback Bks.

—The Fantastic & Terrible Fame of Classroom 13. 2018. (Classroom 13 Ser.: 3). (J). lib. bdg. 16.00 ***(978-0-606-40639-0(5))*** Turtleback Bks.

—The Unlucky Lottery Winners of Classroom 13. Dreidemy, Joëlle, illus. 2017. (Classroom 13 Ser.: 1). (ENG.). 128p. (J). (gr. 1-5). 15.99 ***(978-0-316-46465-9(1))***; pap. 5.99 ***(978-0-316-46462-8(7))*** Little, Brown Bks. for Young Readers.

Lee, Jared D., illus. The Dentist from the Black Lagoon, 1 vol. 2014. (ENG.). 32p. (J). 24.21 *(978-1-61479-197-3(X))* Spotlight.

Lee, Newman. Creepy Kitchen. Elizabeth, Neering, ed. Dan, Houser, illus. 2012. 40p. (J). pap. 10.00 *(978-1-62314-873-7(1))* Fisticuff Publishing.

Lee, Patty. Three Dogs & a Horse Named Blue. Lee, Jack, illus. 2009. 80p. pap. 10.49 *(978-1-4389-9685-1(3))* AuthorHouse.

Lee, Quinlan B. Valentine Surprise. Haefele, Steve, illus. 2008. (Clifford the Big Red Dog Ser.). (J). *(978-0-545-02845-5(0))* Scholastic, Inc.

Leeds, Robert X. HOW to Almost MAKE A MILLION DOLLARS: I Almost Did it. You Can Almost Do it Too! 2005. 246p. pap. 16.95 *(978-0-9674025-5-0(7))* EPIC Publishing Co.

—HOW to almost MAKE A MILLION DOLLARS: I almost did it. You can almost do it Too! 2005. (CHI.). 246p. 21.95 *(978-0-9674025-6-7(5))* EPIC Publishing Co.

Lehrhaupt, Adam. Chicken in Space. Kober, Shahar, illus. 2016. 40p. (J). (gr. -1-3). 17.99 *(978-0-06-236412-8(X))* HarperCollins Pubs.

—Warning: Do Not Open This Book! Forsythe, Matthew, illus. 2013. (ENG.). 40p. (J). (gr. -1-3). 17.99 *(978-1-4424-3582-7(8)*, Simon & Schuster Bks. For Young Readers) Simon & Schuster Bks. For Young Readers.

Lemke, Donald B. Spokes on the Water, 1 vol. Holgate, Douglas, illus. 2011. (Bike Rider Ser.). (ENG.). 40p. (gr. 1-3). lib. bdg. 23.99 *(978-1-4342-2537-5(2)*, Graphic Sparks) Stone Arch Bks.

—Wheelies of Justice, 1 vol. Holgate, Douglas, illus. 2010. (Bike Rider Ser.). (ENG.). 40p. (gr. 1-3). lib. bdg. 23.99 *(978-1-4342-1892-6(9)*, Graphic Sparks) Stone Arch Bks.

Lenahan, John. The Sons of Macha. 2013. (Shadowmagic Ser.: 3). (ENG., Illus.). 288p. (J). 6.99 *(978-0-00-745674-1(3)*, Friday Project) HarperCollins Pubs. Ltd. GBR. Dist: HarperCollins Pubs.

Lendler, Ian. An Undone Fairy Tale. Martin, Whitney, illus. 2005. (ENG.). 32p. (J). (gr. 1-5). 18.99 *(978-0-689-86677-7(1)*, Simon & Schuster Bks. For Young Readers) Simon & Schuster Bks. For Young Readers.

Lennon, Maria T. Watch Out, Hollywood! More Confessions of a So-Called Middle Child. 2014. (ENG.). 224p. (J). (gr. 3-7). 16.99 *(978-0-06-212693-1(8))* HarperCollins Pubs.

Leno, Jay. If Roast Beef Could Fly. Whitehead, S. B., illus. 2005. 30p. (J). (gr. k-4). 18.00 *(978-0-7567-9365-4(3))* DIANE Publishing Co.

Lester, Helen. The Loch Mess Monster. Munsinger, Lynn, illus. 2014. (ENG.). 32p. (J). (gr. -1-3). 16.99 *(978-0-544-09990-6(7)*, HMH Books For Young Readers) Houghton Mifflin Harcourt Publishing Co.

—The Sheep in Wolf's Clothing. Munsinger, Lynn, illus. 2014. (Laugh-Along Lessons Ser.). (ENG.). 32p. (J). (gr. -1-3). 8.99 *(978-0-544-23300-3(X)*, HMH Books For Young Readers) Houghton Mifflin Harcourt Publishing Co.

Lester, Sharon. The Boy Who Wouldn't Sit Still!, Vol. 2. Smith, Jeff, illus. 2nd ed. 2011. 40p. (J). 15.95 *(978-0-9802302-2-2(5))* Privileged Communications, LLC.

Levine, Martha Peaslee. Stop That Nose!, 1 vol. White, Lee, illus. 2006. (ENG.). 32p. (J). (gr. -1-3). 14.95 *(978-0-7614-5280-5(X))* Marshall Cavendish Corp.

Levine, Rhoda. Harrison Loved His Umbrella. Kuskin, Karla, illus. 2016. (ENG.). 56p. (J). (-k). 14.95 *(978-1-59017-991-8(9)*, NYR Children's Collection) New York Review of Bks., Inc., The.

Levinthal, David. Who Pushed Humpty Dumpty? And Other Notorious Nursery Tale Mysteries. Nickle, John, illus. 2012. (ENG.). 40p. (J). (gr. -1-3). 17.99 *(978-0-375-84195-8(4))*; 20.99 *(978-0-375-94595-3(4))* Random Hse. Children's Bks. (Schwartz & Wade Bks.).

Levy, Dana Alison. The Family Fletcher Takes Rock Island. (ENG.). 272p. (J). (gr. 4-7). 2017. 6.99 ***(978-0-553-52133-7(0)***, Yearling) 2016. 16.99 *(978-0-553-52130-6(6)*, Delacorte Bks. for Young Readers) Random Hse. Children's Bks.

Levy, Elizabeth. A Hare-Raising Tale. Gerstein, Mordicai, illus. unabr. ed. 2006. (First Chapter Bks.). (J). (gr. 2-4). pap. 20.95 incl. audio compact disk *(978-1-59519-705-4(2))*; pap. 17.95 incl. audio *(978-1-59519-704-7(4))* Live Oak Media.

—The Mixed-Up Mask Mystery: A Fletcher Mystery. Gerstein, Mordicai, illus. unabr. ed. 2006. (First Chapter Bks.). (J). (gr. 2-4). pap. 17.95 incl. audio *(978-1-59519-710-8(9))*; pap. 20.95 incl. audio compact disk *(978-1-59519-711-5(7))* Live Oak Media.

Lewis, Gill. Pip & the Paw of Friendship. Home, Sarah, illus. 2017. (Puppy Academy Ser.). (ENG.). 128p. (J). pap. 5.99 *(978-1-250-09285-4(X)*, 9781250092854, Holt, Henry & Co. Bks. For Young Readers) Holt, Henry & Co.

Lewis, Jill. A Mom in a Million. Gulbis, Stephen, illus. 2005. 32p. (J). *(978-1-84458-368-3(6)*, Pavilion Children's Books) Pavilion Bks.

Lewis, L. W. Poodles Tigers Monsters & You. Harris, Lorrayne R., illus. 2004. 64p. kivar 12.95 *(978-0-9711572-1-7(9))* Red Pumpkin Pr.

Lewis, Steve, Sr. The Course of a Horse. 2006. (J). 65.00 *(978-1-59971-897-2(9))* Aardvark Global Publishing.

Lewman, David. Branch & the Cooking Catastrophe (DreamWorks Trolls Chapter Book #2) Random House, illus. 2017. (ENG.). 128p. (J). (gr. 1-4). 6.99 ***(978-1-5247-1708-7(8))***; lib. bdg. 12.99 ***(978-1-5247-1709-4(6))*** Random Hse. Children's Bks. (Random Hse. Bks. for Young Readers).

—Case File #4 Rabbids Go Viral. Spaziante, Patrick, illus. 2015. (Rabbids Invasion Ser.). (ENG.). 96p. (J). (gr. 2-5). 16.99 *(978-1-4814-2766-1(0)*, Simon Spotlight) Simon Spotlight.

—Case File #7 Red Carpet Rabbids. Johnson, Shane L., illus. 2016. (Rabbids Invasion Ser.). (ENG.). 96p. (J). (gr. 2-5). 16.99 *(978-1-4814-5253-3(3)*, Simon Spotlight) Simon Spotlight.

—The Case of the Vanished Squirrel. Moore, Harry, illus. 2008. (SpongeBob SquarePants Ser.). (ENG.). 16p. (J). (gr. -1-3). pap. 5.99 *(978-1-4169-4939-8(9)*, Simon Spotlight/Nickelodeon) Simon Spotlight/Nickelodeon.

—New Developments, No. 2. Spaziante, Patrick, illus. 2014. (Rabbids Invasion Ser.). (ENG.). 96p. (J). (gr. 2-5). pap. 4.99 *(978-1-4814-0204-0(8)*, Simon Spotlight) Simon Spotlight.

—Red Carpet Rabbids. Johnson, Shane L., illus. 2016. (Rabbids Invasion Ser.). (ENG.). 96p. (J). (gr. 2-5). pap. 5.99 *(978-1-4814-5252-6(5)*, Simon Spotlight) Simon Spotlight.

—SpongeBob, Soccer Star! Reed, Stephen, illus. 2010. (SpongeBob SquarePants Ser.). (ENG.). 24p. (J). (gr. -1-3). pap. 3.99 *(978-1-4169-9445-9(9)*, Simon Spotlight/Nickelodeon) Simon Spotlight/Nickelodeon.

Liberty, Anita. The Center of the Universe: Yep, That Would Be Me. 2008. (ENG.). 304p. (YA). (gr. 7-18). pap. 9.99 *(978-1-4169-5789-8(8)*, Simon Pulse) Simon Pulse.

Lichtenheld, Tom. What Mess? 2012. (ENG., Illus.). 40p. (J). (gr. -1-3). pap. 7.00 *(978-0-316-20123-0(5))* Little, Brown Bks. for Young Readers.

—What Mess? 2012. (J). lib. bdg. 17.20 *(978-0-606-26686-4(0)*, Turtleback) Turtleback Bks.

Lieb, Josh. I Am a Genius of Unspeakable Evil & I Want to Be Your Class President. 2010. (ENG.). 304p. (J). (gr. 5-7). 8.99 *(978-1-59514-354-9(8)*, Razorbill) Penguin Young Readers Group.

Light, Steve. Lucky Lazlo. Light, Steve, illus. 2016. (ENG., Illus.). 32p. (J). (gr. -1-2). 16.99 *(978-0-7636-8825-7(8))* Candlewick Pr.

The Lil Dudes. 2006. (YA). per. *(978-1-59872-308-3(1))* Instant Pub.

Lin, Grace. Ling & Ting: Twice As Silly. 2014. (ENG., Illus.). 48p. (J). (gr. 1-4). 16.00 *(978-0-316-18402-1(0))* Little, Brown Bks. for Young Readers.

Lindaman, Jane. Zip It! Carlson, Nancy, illus. 2012. (Carolrhoda Picture Bks.). (ENG.). 32p. (J). (gr. k-4). lib. bdg. 16.95 *(978-0-7613-5592-2(8))* Lerner Publishing Group.

Lindenbaum, Pija. When Owen's Mom Breathed Fire. Dyssegaard, Elisabeth Kallick, tr. 2006. (Illus.). 32p. (J). (gr. -1-3). 16.00 *(978-91-29-66548-2(5))* R & S Bks. SWE. Dist: Macmillan.

Lindgren, Astrid. Happy Times in Noisy Village. Wikland, Ilon, illus. 2003. Orig. Title: Bullerby Boken. 119p. (J). pap. 10.95 *(978-1-883937-66-9(3))* Bethlehem Bks.

—Pippi in the South Seas. Turner, Marianne, tr. from SWE. Ross, Tony, illus. 2006. 128p. pap. *(978-0-19-275481-3(5))* Oxford Univ. Pr.

—Pippi Longstocking. Nunally, Tina, tr. Child, Lauren, illus. 2011. (Pippi Longstocking Ser.). (ENG.). 208p. (J). (gr. 2-5). pap. 15.99 *(978-0-670-01404-0(4)*, Viking Books for Young Readers) Penguin Young Readers Group.

Lindgren, Barbro. Benny's Had Enough! Dyssegaard, Elisabeth Kallick, tr. from SWE. Landstrom, Olof, illus. 2005. 28p. (J). (gr. -1-1). reprint ed. 6.95 *(978-91-29-66338-9(5))* R & S Bks. SWE. Dist: Macmillan.

Lindgren, Barbro. Soda Pop. Adbage, Lisen, illus. 2017. (ENG.). 112p. (J). (gr. 3-5). 16.99 ***(978-1-77657-010-2(3))*** Gecko Pr. NZL. Dist: Lerner Publishing Group.

Lindsay, Norman. The Magic Pudding. 2012. (Dover Children's Classics Ser.). (ENG., Illus.). 144p. (J). (gr. 3-8). per. 8.95 *(978-0-486-45281-4(6))* Dover Pubns., Inc.

—The Magic Pudding. deluxe ed. (Illus.). 180p. 20.00 *(978-0-207-18355-3(4))* HarperCollins Pubs.

—The Magic Pudding. 2004. reprint ed. pap. 15.95 *(978-1-4191-7119-2(4))*; pap. 1.99 *(978-1-4192-7119-9(9))* Kessinger Publishing, LLC.

—The Magic Pudding: The Adventures of Bunyip Bluegum. 2008. 208p. *(978-0-7322-8432-9(5))* HarperCollins Pubs. Australia.

Link, Amy. My Mommy Wears a Wig. 2009. 16p. pap. 17.95 *(978-1-4490-0218-3(8))* AuthorHouse.

Linklater, Eric. The Wind on the Moon. Bentley, Nicolas, illus. 2017. (New York Review Children's Collection). (ENG.). 376p. (J). (gr. 7). pap. 12.99 *(978-1-68137-103-0(0)*, NYRB Kids) New York Review of Bks., Inc., The.

Liput, Andrew L. Who Put the Snarfdoodle in My Lunch Box? 2nd ed. 2003. 108p. per. *(978-1-932077-62-9(6))* Athena Pr.

Lithgow, John. Carnival of the Animals. Kulikov, Boris, illus. 2007. (ENG.). 40p. (J). (gr. -1-3). 7.99 *(978-0-689-87343-0(3)*, Simon & Schuster Bks. For Young Readers) Simon & Schuster Bks. For Young Readers.

Little, Jean. I Know an Old Laddie. 2004. (Illus.). (J). (gr. k-3). spiral bd. *(978-0-616-01703-6(0))* Canadian National Institute for the Blind/Institut National Canadien pour les Aveugles.

Little, Jean & de Vries, Maggie. Once upon a Golden Apple: 25th Anniversary Edition. Gilman, Phoebe, illus. 25th ed. 2016. (ENG.). 26p. (J). (— 1). bds. 7.99 *(978-0-670-07007-7(6)*, Puffin Canada) Penguin Random House Canada Young Readers CAN. Dist: Penguin Random Hse. LLC.

Litwin, Eric. The Nuts: Bedtime at the Nut House. Magoon, Scott, illus. 2014. (ENG.). 32p. (J). (gr. -1-3). 18.00 *(978-0-316-32244-7(X))* Little, Brown Bks. for Young Readers.

Lively, Deborah Dreher. Hateya Sam. 2009. 32p. pap. 13.75 *(978-1-60860-029-8(7)*, Eloquent Bks.) Strategic Book Publishing & Rights Agency (SBPRA).

Lobel, Anita. Playful Pigs from A to Z. 2015. (ENG., Illus.). 40p. (J). (gr. -1-2). lib. bdg. 19.99 *(978-0-553-50833-8(4)*, Knopf Bks. for Young Readers) Random Hse. Children's Bks.

Lobel, Arnold. The Arnold Lobel Treasury. 2014. (ENG., Illus.). 160p. (J). (gr. 1-4). pap. 14.99 *(978-0-486-78078-8(3))* Dover Pubns., Inc.

Lockhart, E., et al. How to Be Bad. 2008. 325p. (YA). (gr. 9-12). lib. bdg. 17.89 *(978-0-06-128423-6(8)*, HarperTeen) HarperCollins Pubs.

Loehr, Patrick. Mucumber McGee & the Half-Eaten Hot Dog. Loehr, Patrick, illus. 2007. (Illus.). 32p. (J). (gr. -1-3). lib. bdg. 16.89 *(978-0-06-082328-3(3)*, Tegen, Katherine Bks) HarperCollins Pubs.

Loewen, Nancy. Believe Me, Goldilocks Rocks! The Story of the Three Bears As Told by Baby Bear. Avakyan, Tatevik, illus. 2011. (Other Side of the Story Ser.). (ENG.). 24p. (gr. 2-3). pap. 6.95 *(978-1-4048-7044-4(X))* Picture Window Bks.

—Believe Me, Goldilocks Rocks! The Story of the Three Bears as Told by Baby Bear. Avakyan, Tatevik, illus. 2011. (Other Side of the Story Ser.). (ENG.). 24p. (gr. 2-3). lib. bdg. 27.32 *(978-1-4048-6672-0(8))* Picture Window Bks.

—Believe Me, I Never Felt a Pea! The Story of the Princess & the Pea As Told by the Princess. Bernardini, Cristian, illus. 2016. (Other Side of the Story Ser.). (ENG.). 24p. (gr. 2-3). lib. bdg. 27.32 *(978-1-4795-8622-6(6))* Picture Window Bks.

—Frankly, I Never Wanted to Kiss Anybody! The Story of the Frog Prince As Told by the Frog. Alonso, Denis, illus. 2013. (Other Side of the Story Ser.). (ENG.). 24p. (gr. 2-3). 27.32 *(978-1-4048-8304-8(5))* Picture Window Bks.

—Frankly, I Never Wanted to Kiss Anybody! The Story of the Frog Prince, As Told by the Frog. Alonso, Denis, illus. 2013. (Other Side of the Story Ser.). (ENG.). 24p. (gr. 2-3). 9.95 *(978-1-4795-1948-4(0))* Picture Window Bks.

—Frankly, I Never Wanted to Kiss Anybody! The Story of the Frog Prince, As Told by the Frog. Alonso, Denis & Tayal, Amit, illus. 2013. (Other Side of the Story Ser.). (ENG.). 24p. (gr. 2-3). pap. 6.95 *(978-1-4795-1952-1(9))* Picture Window Bks.

—Make Me Giggle: Writing Your Own Silly Story, 1 vol. Doerrfeld, Cori & Lyles, Christopher, illus. 2009. (Writer's Toolbox Ser.). (ENG.). 32p. (gr. 2-4). pap. 8.95 *(978-1-4048-5704-9(4))* Picture Window Bks.

—No Kidding, Mermaids Are a Joke! The Story of the Little Mermaid, As Told by the Prince. Tayal, Amit & Alonso, Denis, illus. 2013. (Other Side of the Story Ser.). (ENG.). 24p. (gr. 2-3). pap. 6.95 *(978-1-4795-1951-4(0))* Picture Window Bks.

—No Kidding, Mermaids Are a Joke! The Story of the Little Mermaid As Told by the Prince. Tayal, Amit, illus. 2013. (Other Side of the Story Ser.). (ENG.). 24p. (gr. 2-3). 9.95 *(978-1-4795-1947-7(2))* Picture Window Bks.

—No Kidding, Mermaids Are a Joke! The Story of the Little Mermaid as Told by the Prince. Tayal, Amit, illus. 2013. (Other Side of the Story Ser.). (ENG.). 24p. (gr. 2-3). 27.32 *(978-1-4048-8303-1(7))* Picture Window Bks.

—No Lie, I Acted Like a Beast! The Story of Beauty & the Beast As Told by the Beast, 1 vol. Bernardini, Cristian, illus. 2013. (Other Side of the Story Ser.). (ENG.). 24p. (gr. 2-3). pap. 6.95 *(978-1-4048-8083-2(6))*; lib. bdg. 27.32 *(978-1-4048-7938-6(2))* Picture Window Bks.

—No Lie, I Acted Like a Beast: The Story of Beauty & the Beast as Told by the Beast. Bernardini, Cristian, illus. 2013. (Other Side of the Story Ser.). (ENG.). 24p. (gr. 2-3). 9.95 *(978-1-4795-1944-6(8))* Picture Window Bks.

—Seriously, Snow White Was So Forgetful! The Story of Snow White as Told by the Dwarves. Guerlais, Gérald, illus. 2013. (Other Side of the Story Ser.). (ENG.). 24p. (gr. 2-3). pap. 6.95 *(978-1-4048-8085-6(2))*; lib. bdg. 27.32 *(978-1-4048-7937-9(4))* Picture Window Bks.

—Seriously, Snow White Was SO Forgetful! The Story of Snow White As Told by the Dwarves, 1 vol. Guerlais, Gérald, illus. 2013. (Other Side of the Story Ser.). (ENG.). 24p. (gr. 2-3). 9.95 *(978-1-4795-1943-9(X))* Picture Window Bks.

Loewen, Nancy & Braun, Eric. Trust Me, Jack's Beanstalk Stinks! The Story of Jack & the Beanstalk as Told by the Giant. Guerlais, Gérald & Bernardini, Cristian, illus. 2013. (Other Side of the Story Ser.). (ENG.). 24p. (gr. 2-3). 9.95 *(978-1-4795-1942-2(1))* Picture Window Bks.

Logan, Erika. The Tick Tribe. 2012. 188p. pap. 13.99 *(978-1-4525-0712-5(0)*, Balboa Pr.) Author Solutions, Inc.

Logelin, Matthew & Jensen, Sara Bee. Be Glad Your Dad. Chapman, Jared, illus. 2016. (ENG.). 40p. (J). (gr. -1-3). 16.99 *(978-0-316-25438-0(X))* Little Brown & Co.

Logue, Stephanie. Mango's Revenge. Murphy, Chris, illus. 2006. (J). pap. *(978-1-59336-769-5(4))* Mondo Publishing.

Lois, Lowry. Anastasia Tiene las Respuestas. Bustelo, Ana, tr. Alonso Díaz-Toledo, Juan Ramón, illus. 2003. (Anastasia Krupnik Ser.).Tr. of Anastasia Has the Answers. (SPA.). 160p. (J). 9.95 *(978-84-239-6334-8(9))* Espasa Calpe, S.A. ESP. Dist: Planeta Publishing Corp., Lectorum Pubns., Inc.

—Gooney Bird & the Room Mother. Thomas, Middy, illus. 2006. (Gooney Bird Ser.: No. 2). (ENG.). 80p. (J). (gr. 3-7). 5.99 *(978-0-440-42133-7(0)*, Yearling) Random Hse. Children's Bks.

—Gooney Bird Greene. Middy Chilman, Thomas, illus. 2004. (Gooney Bird Ser.: No. 1). 88p. (gr. 2-5). 16.00 *(978-0-7569-2583-3(5))* Perfection Learning Corp.

H
I

—Gooney the Fabulous. 2009. (Gooney Bird Ser.: No. 3). (ENG.). 96p. (J). (gr. 3-7). 5.99 *(978-0-440-42253-2(1),* Yearling) Random Hse. Children's Bks.

—The Willoughbys. Lois, Lowry, illus. 2008. (ENG., Illus.). 176p. (J). (gr. 1-4). 17.99 *(978-0-618-97974-5(3))* Houghton Mifflin Harcourt Publishing Co.

—The Willoughbys. 2010. (ENG.). 176p. (J). (gr. 3-7). 6.99 *(978-0-385-73776-0(9),* Yearling) Random Hse. Children's Bks.

Lombardi, Tom. My Summer on Earth. 2008. (ENG.). 256p. (YA). (gr. 9-12). pap. 12.99 *(978-1-4169-5563-4(1),* Simon Pulse) Simon Pulse.

London, Jonathan. Froggy Goes to the Doctor. 2004. (Illus.). (J). (gr. k-3). spiral bd. *(978-0-616-14586-9(1));* spiral bd. *(978-0-616-14585-2(3))* Canadian National Institute for the Blind/Institut National Canadien pour les Aveugles.

—Froggy Goes to the Doctor. Remkiewicz, Frank, illus. 2004. (Froggy Ser.). (ENG.). 32p. (J). (gr. -1-k). pap. 6.99 *(978-0-14-240193-4(5),* Puffin Books) Penguin Young Readers Group.

—Froggy Goes to the Doctor. 2004. (Froggy Ser.). (J). (gr. -1-18). 1.25 *(978-1-4025-3420-1(5))* Recorded Bks., Inc.

—Froggy's Sleepover. Remkiewicz, Frank, illus. 2007. (Froggy Ser.). (ENG.). 32p. (J). (gr. -1-k). pap. 6.99 *(978-0-14-240750-9(X),* Puffin Books) Penguin Young Readers Group.

—Froggy's Worst Playdate. Remkiewicz, Frank, illus. 2013. (Froggy Ser.). (ENG.). 32p. (J). (gr. -1-k). 16.99 *(978-0-670-01427-9(3),* Viking Books for Young Readers) Penguin Young Readers Group.

Long, Ethan & McPike, Elizabeth. In, over & on the Farm. Long, Ethan, illus. 2015. (ENG., Illus.). 40p. (J). (gr. -1-k). bds. 15.99 *(978-0-399-16907-6(5),* G.P. Putnam's Sons Books for Young Readers) Penguin Young Readers Group.

Long, Heather & Long, Ethan. Max & Milo Go to Sleep! Long, Ethan, illus. 2013. (ENG., Illus.). 32p. (J). (gr. -1-3). 14.99 *(978-1-4424-5143-8(2),* Aladdin) Simon & Schuster Children's Publishing.

—Max & Milo the Mixed-Up Message. Long, Ethan, illus. 2013. (ENG., Illus.). 32p. (J). (gr. -1-3). 14.99 *(978-1-4424-5140-7(8),* Simon & Schuster/Paula Wiseman Bks.) Simon & Schuster/Paula Wiseman Bks.

Long, Kathy. Christopher SAT Straight up in Bed. Cantor, Patricia, illus. 2013. (ENG.). 40p. (J). 16.00 *(978-0-8028-5359-2(5),* Eerdmans Bks For Young Readers) Eerdmans, William B. Publishing Co.

Long, Matty. Super Happy Magic Forest. Long, Matty, illus. 2016. (ENG., Illus.). 32p. (J). (gr. -1-3). 17.99 *(978-0-545-86059-8(8),* Scholastic Pr.) Scholastic, Inc.

Look, Lenore. Alvin Ho: Allergic to Girls, School, & Other Scary Things. Pham, LeUyen, illus. 2009. (Alvin Ho Ser.). (ENG.). 192p. (J). (gr. 1-4). 6.99 *(978-0-375-84930-5(0),* Yearling) Random Hse. Children's Bks.

Lopez, David Mark. Walk Like an Egyptian. 2006. (J). (gr. 3-7). *(978-0-9744097-0-2(7))* Lopez, David.

Lorraine, Florido. Dezzer the Gasser. Shami, Susan & Crossman, Keith, eds. Ewing, John, illus. 2009. 32p. (J). 15.99 *(978-0-9818449-0-9(1))* Thinkus Pubs.

Lorton, Barbara. Sidney Seagull Marks Lighthouses & Buoys of the Chesapeake. 2013. (Illus.). 28p. pap. 16.99 *(978-1-4582-1055-5(3),* Abbott Pr.) Author Solutions, Inc.

Loser, Barry & Smith, Jim. I Am Not a Loser. 3rd ed. 2013. (Barry Loser Ser.: 1). (ENG., Illus.). 240p. (J). (gr. 2-4). pap. 11.99 *(978-1-4052-6031-2(9))* Egmont Bks., Ltd. GBR. Dist: Independent Pubs. Group.

Love, Mary. Mama's House. 2005. 44p. per. 23.99 *(978-1-4257-0254-0(6))* Xlibris Corp.

Lovelace, Victoria. Animal Crackers & Alphabet Soup. 2014. (ENG.). 84p. pap. 19.95 *(978-1-4670-3532-3(7),* b9230d6d-2918-4b50-9842-302a1082f149) AuthorHouse.

Loves, June. Mi Ángel de la Guarda. (Torre de Papel Ser.). (SPA., Illus.). (J). (gr. 2). 7.95 *(978-958-04-5048-1(X))* Norma S.A. COL. Dist: Distribuidora Norma, Inc.

Lowery, Mark. Attack of the Woolly Jumper. 2017. (Roman Garstang Disaster Ser.). (ENG., Illus.). 224p. (J). (gr. 4-7). pap. 8.99 ***(978-1-84812-582-7(8))*** Bonnier Publishing GBR. Dist: Independent Pubs. Group.

Lubar, David. The Battle of the Red Hot Pepper Weenies: And Other Warped & Creepy Tales. 2010. (Weenies Stories Ser.). (ENG.). 192p. (J). (gr. 4-7). mass mkt. 5.99 *(978-0-7653-6075-5(6),* 9780765360755, Starscape) Doherty, Tom Assocs., LLC.

—The Bully Bug: A Monsterrific Tale. 2014. (Monsterrific Tales Ser.). (ENG., Illus.). 144p. (J). (gr. 3-7). 24.99 *(978-0-7653-3082-6(2),* 9780765330826, Starscape) Doherty, Tom Assocs., LLC.

Lubner, Susan. The Upside of Ordinary. 2012. (ENG.). 128p. (J). 16.95 *(978-0-8234-2417-7(0))* Holiday Hse., Inc.

Luper, Eric. Jeremy Bender vs. the Cupcake Cadets. 2011. (ENG.). 240p. (J). (gr. 3-7). 16.99 *(978-0-06-201512-9(5))* HarperCollins Pubs.

Luurtsema, Nat. Goldfish. 2016. (ENG.). 240p. (YA). 17.99 *(978-1-250-08918-2(2),* 9781250089182) Feiwel & Friends.

Luzzatto, Caroline. Interplanetary Avenger. 2005. (ENG., Illus.). 128p. (J). (gr. 3-7). 16.95 *(978-0-8234-1933-3(9))* Holiday Hse., Inc.

Lyle-Soffe, Shari. Nothing Stops Noah. Collier, Kevin Scott, illus. 2008. 24p. pap. 10.95 *(978-1-935137-19-1(0))* Guardian Angel Publishing, Inc.

Lyles, Whitney. Love Off-Limits. 2009. (Romantic Comedies Ser.). (ENG.). 304p. (YA). (gr. 7-18). mass mkt. 6.99 *(978-1-4169-7508-3(X),* Simon Pulse) Simon Pulse.

—Party Games. 2012. (Romantic Comedies Ser.). (ENG.). 304p. (YA). (gr. 7). pap. 14.99 *(978-1-4424-6060-7(1),* Simon Pulse) Simon Pulse.

Lynch, Brian. Minions: The Junior Novel. 2015. (J). lib. bdg. 17.20 *(978-0-606-37222-0(9))* Turtleback Bks.

Lynch, Jay. Otto's Backwards Day. Cammuso, Frank, illus. 2013. (ENG.). 32p. (J). (gr. -1-3). 12.95 *(978-1-935179-33-7(0))* TOON Books / RAW Junior, LLC.

Lyons, Jayne. 100% Wolf. Rivas, Victor, illus. 2009. (ENG.). 256p. (J). (gr. 2-7). 16.99 *(978-1-4169-7474-1(1),* Atheneum Bks. for Young Readers) Simon & Schuster Children's Publishing.

MacDonald, Alan. Alien Attack! Baines, Nigel, illus. 2015. (ENG.). 192p. (YA). (gr. 2-4). pap. 9.99 *(978-1-4088-2524-2(4),* 9781408825242, Bloomsbury USA Childrens) Bloomsbury Publishing USA.

—Curse of the Evil Custard. 2015. (ENG., Illus.). 192p. (J). (gr. 2-4). pap. 9.99 *(978-1-4088-2525-9(2),* 9781408825259, Bloomsbury USA Childrens) Bloomsbury Publishing USA.

Macdonald, Alan. Dirty Bertie: Burp! Roberts, David, illus. 2008. 96p. (J). (gr. 1-5). 3.99 *(978-1-56148-644-1(2),* Good Bks.) Skyhorse Publishing Co., Inc.

MacDonald, Alan. Fangs!, 1 vol. Roberts, David, illus. 2012. (Dirty Bertie Ser.). (ENG.). 112p. (gr. 1-3). pap. 4.95 *(978-1-4342-4267-9(6));* 25.32 *(978-1-4342-4601-1(9))* Stone Arch Bks.

—Fleas!, 1 vol. Roberts, David, illus. 2013. (Dirty Bertie Ser.). (ENG.). 112p. (gr. 1-3). pap. 4.95 *(978-1-4342-4822-0(4));* lib. bdg. 25.32 *(978-1-4342-4618-9(3))* Stone Arch Bks.

—Germs!, 1 vol. Roberts, David, illus. 2012. (Dirty Bertie Ser.). (ENG.). 112p. (gr. 1-3). pap. 4.95 *(978-1-4342-4266-2(8));* 25.32 *(978-1-4342-4600-4(0))* Stone Arch Bks.

—Superhero School: The Revenge of the Green Meanie. Baines, Nigel, illus. 2015. (ENG.). 176p. (YA). (gr. 2-4). pap. 9.99 *(978-1-4088-2523-5(6),* 9781408825235, Bloomsbury USA Childrens) Bloomsbury Publishing USA.

—Thunderbot's Day of Doom. Baines, Nigel, illus. 2017. (ENG.). 160p. (J). pap. 9.99 *(978-1-4088-2526-6(0),* 9781408825266, Bloomsbury USA Childrens) Bloomsbury Publishing USA.

—Worms!, 1 vol. Roberts, David, illus. 2013. (Dirty Bertie Ser.). (ENG.). 112p. (gr. 1-3). pap. 4.95 *(978-1-4342-4823-7(2));* lib. bdg. 25.32 *(978-1-4342-4619-6(1))* Stone Arch Bks.

MacDonald, Betty Bard. Hello, Mrs Piggle Wiggle. unabr. ed. 2004. 125p. (J). (gr. 2-5). pap. 29.00 incl. audio *(978-0-8072-1184-7(2),* S YA 1018 SP, Listening Library) Random Hse. Audio Publishing Group.

—Mrs. Piggle-Wiggle. unabr. ed. 2004. (Illus.). 119p. (J). (gr. 2-5). pap. 29.00 incl. audio *(978-0-8072-1180-9(X),* S YA 1022 SP, Listening Library) Random Hse. Audio Publishing Group.

MacDonald, Betty Bard & Canham, Anne MacDonald. Happy Birthday, Mrs. Piggle-Wiggle. Boiger, Alexandra, illus. (ENG.). 208p. (J). (gr. 3-7). 2008. pap. 6.99 *(978-0-06-072814-4(0))* 2007. 16.99 *(978-0-06-072812-0(4))* HarperCollins Pubs.

Maciejewski, Mark. I Am Fartacus. 2017. (Max Ser.). (ENG., Illus.). 336p. (J). (gr. 4-8). pap. 7.99 *(978-1-4814-6419-2(1),* Simon & Schuster/Paula Wiseman Bks.) Simon & Schuster/Paula Wiseman Bks.

—I Am Fartacus. 2017. lib. bdg. 18.40 ***(978-0-606-40158-6(X))*** Turtleback Bks.

Mack, Jeff. Clueless Mcgee. Mack, Jeff, illus. 2012. (Clueless Mcgee Ser.: 1). (ENG., Illus.). 240p. (J). (gr. 3-7). 12.99 *(978-0-399-25749-0(7),* Philomel Bks.) Penguin Young Readers Group.

—Clueless McGee & the Inflatable Pants, Bk. 2. Mack, Jeff, illus. 2013. (Clueless Mcgee Ser.: 2). (ENG., Illus.). 256p. (J). (gr. 3-7). 12.99 *(978-0-399-25750-6(0),* Philomel Bks.) Penguin Young Readers Group.

—Clueless Mcgee Gets Famous. Mack, Jeff, illus. 2014. (Clueless Mcgee Ser.: 3). (ENG., Illus.). 288p. (J). (gr. 3-7). 12.99 *(978-0-399-25751-3(9),* Philomel Bks.) Penguin Young Readers Group.

—Look! Mack, Jeff, illus. 2015. (ENG., Illus.). 32p. (J). (gr. -1-k). 16.99 *(978-0-399-16205-3(4),* Philomel Bks.) Penguin Young Readers Group.

—Playtime? Mack, Jeff, illus. 2016. (ENG., Illus.). 32p. (J). (-k). 16.99 *(978-0-399-17598-5(9),* Philomel Bks.) Penguin Young Readers Group.

—Who Wants a Hug? Mack, Jeff, illus. 2015. (ENG., Illus.). 40p. (J). (gr. -1-3). 17.99 *(978-0-06-222026-4(8))* HarperCollins Pubs.

Mackerel, Seymour & RH Disney Staff. Fish School. Home, Philip & Loter, John, illus. 2003. (Pictureback(R) Ser.). (ENG.). 24p. (J). (gr. -1-2). pap. 3.99 *(978-0-7364-2127-0(0),* RH/Disney) Random Hse. Children's Bks.

MacKey, Cindy. A Curious Abc's: An Alphabet for Non Linear Thinkers. 2013. 32p. pap. 12.99 *(978-0-9892699-8-8(1))* Cyrano Bks.

Mackintosh, David. Marshall Armstrong Is New to Our School. 2011. (ENG., Illus.). 32p. (J). (gr. k-2). 17.95 *(978-1-4197-0036-1(7),* Abrams Bks. for Young Readers) Abrams, Inc.

—Standing in for Lincoln Green. 2013. (ENG., Illus.). 32p. (J). (gr. k-2). 16.95 *(978-1-4197-0787-2(6),* Abrams Bks. for Young Readers) Abrams, Inc.

Maclear, Kyo. Spork. Arsenault, Isabelle, illus. 2017. (ENG.). 21p. (J). (gr. -1-2). pap. 8.95 *(978-1-77138-805-4(6))* Kids Can Pr., Ltd. CAN. Dist: Hachette Bk. Group.

MacLellan, Erin. Run from the Nun! 2003. (ENG.). 128p. (J). (gr. 4-6). tchr. ed. 16.95 *(978-0-8234-1796-4(4))* Holiday Hse., Inc.

MacRae, Tom. The Opposite, 1 vol. Odriozola, Elena, illus. 2006. (ENG.). 32p. (J). (gr. k-3). 15.95 *(978-1-56145-371-9(4))* Peachtree Pubs.

Maddox, Jake & McMullan, Kate. Stop That Bull, Theseus!, 1 vol. Zilber, Denis, illus. 2010. (Myth-O-Mania Ser.: Bk. 5). (ENG.). 192p. (gr. 4-8). 25.32 *(978-1-4342-3034-8(1),* Myth-O-Mania) Stone Arch Bks.

Madison, Alan. Pecorino Plays Ball. Cantone, AnnaLaura, illus. 2006. (ENG.). 40p. (J). (gr. -1-3). 15.95 *(978-0-689-86522-0(8),* Atheneum Bks. for Young Readers) Simon & Schuster Children's Publishing.

—Pecorino's First Concert. Cantone, AnnaLaura, illus. 2010. (ENG.). 40p. (J). (gr. -1-3). 16.99 *(978-1-4424-2191-2(6),* Atheneum Bks. for Young Readers) Simon & Schuster Children's Publishing.

Magaziner, Lauren. Pilfer Academy: A School So Bad It's Criminal. 2016. (ENG.). 272p. (J). (gr. 3-7). 16.99 *(978-0-8037-3919-2(2),* Dial Bks) Penguin Young Readers Group.

Magusin, Matthew. Diary of a Nerd. the Start of Middle School. 2012. 72p. pap. 8.25 *(978-1-61170-103-6(1))* Robertson Publishing.

Maher, Mickle Brandt. Master Stitchum & the Moon. Dousias, Spiro, illus. 2003. (J). 19.99 *(978-1-932188-01-1(0))* Bollix Bks.

Mahy, Margaret. Aunt Nasty. Mould, Chris, illus. 2016. (Early Reader Ser.). (ENG.). 80p. (J). (gr. k-2). 6.99 *(978-1-4440-1442-6(0),* Orion Children's Bks.) Hachette Children's Group GBR. Dist: Hachette Bk. Group.

—Bubble Trouble. Dunbar, Polly, illus. (ENG.). (J). (gr. -1-3). 2013. 40p. pap. 6.99 *(978-0-547-99483-3(4))* 2011. 32p. bds. 7.99 *(978-0-547-50725-5(9))* 2009. 40p. 16.00 *(978-0-547-07421-4(2))* Houghton Mifflin Harcourt Publishing Co.

—The Great Piratical Rumbustification & the Librarian & the Robbers. Blake, Quentin, illus. 2012. (ENG.). 64p. (J). pap. 6.95 *(978-1-56792-169-4(8))* Godine, David R. Pub.

—Stop That Stew! Rigby, Deborah, illus. 2009. (Treasure Chest Readers Ser.). 24p. (J). (gr. -1-2). pap. 8.15 *(978-1-60754-683-2(3));* lib. bdg. 22.60 *(978-1-60754-682-5(5))* Windmill Bks.

Maki-Griffis, Linda R. In the Berry Patch. 2012. (ENG.). (YA). pap. *(978-1-4675-3814-5(0))* Independent Pub.

Malak, Annabel, illus. Goldilocks & the Three Bears. (Classic Stories Ser.). 48p. (J). audio, audio compact disk *(978-2-921997-84-3(3))* Coffragants.

Maloney, Brenna. Philomena's New Glasses. 2017. (ENG., Illus.). 40p. (J). (gr. -1-1). 16.99 ***(978-0-425-28814-6(5),*** Viking Books for Young Readers) Penguin Young Readers Group.

Mamah, Michael. Imp. 2013. 76p. pap. 10.85 *(978-1-61933-865-4(3))* FastPencil, Inc.

Mamakas, Stavroula & Lagoutaris, Maria Mamakas. Mama Lagoo: Bath Time Battle. 2011. 28p. pap. 14.95 *(978-1-4634-1524-2(9))* AuthorHouse.

Mansbach, Adam & Zweibel, Alan. Benjamin Franklin: Huge Pain in My... 2015. (Benjamin Franklin Ser.). (ENG., Illus.). 208p. (J). (gr. 5-9). 12.99 *(978-1-4847-1304-4(4))* Hyperion Bks. for Children.

Marciano, John Bemelmans. The Nine Lives of Alexander Baddenfield. Blackall, Sophie, illus. (ENG.). 144p. (J). (gr. 5). 2014. pap. 7.99 *(978-0-14-751233-8(6),* Puffin Books) 2013. 16.99 *(978-0-670-01406-4(0),* Viking Books for Young Readers) Penguin Young Readers Group.

Marcionette, Jake. Just Jake. Villa, Victor Rivas, illus. 2014. (Just Jake Ser.: No. 1). (ENG.). 160p. (J). (gr. 3-7). 11.99 *(978-0-448-46692-7(9),* Grosset & Dunlap) Penguin Young Readers Group.

—Just Jake: Dog Eat Dog. Villa, Victor Rivas, illus. 2015. (Just Jake Ser.: No. 2). (ENG.). 196p. (J). (gr. 3-7). 11.99 *(978-0-448-46693-4(7),* Grosset & Dunlap) Penguin Young Readers Group.

Marcus, Leonard S., ed. Funny Business: Conversations with Writers of Comedy. 2009. (ENG., Illus.). 224p. (J). (gr. 5-18). 24.99 *(978-0-7636-3254-0(6))* Candlewick Pr.

Marino, Peter. Dough Boy. 2007. (ENG.). 176p. (YA). (gr. 7-12). pap. 6.95 *(978-0-8234-2096-4(5))* Holiday Hse., Inc.

Marion, L. K. Summer Holiday with Funny Bunny. 2012. 32p. pap. 17.25 *(978-1-4669-6475-4(8))* Trafford Publishing.

Markell, Denis. Hush, Little Monster. Iwai, Melissa, illus. 2012. (ENG.). 32p. (J). (gr. -1-1). 9.99 *(978-1-4424-4195-8(X),* Little Simon) Little Simon.

Marko, Cyndi. The Birdy Snatchers. 2014. (Kung Pow Chicken Ser.: 3). (ENG.). 80p. (J). (gr. k-2). 15.99 *(978-0-545-61072-8(9))* Scholastic, Inc.

—The Birdy Snatchers. Marko, Cyndi, illus. 2014. (Kung Pow Chicken Ser.: 3). (ENG., Illus.). 80p. (J). (gr. k-2). pap. 4.99 *(978-0-545-61068-1(0))* Scholastic, Inc.

—The Birdy Snatchers. 2014. (Kung Pow Chicken Ser.: 3). lib. bdg. 14.75 *(978-0-606-35358-8(5))* Turtleback Bks.

—Bok! Bok! Boom! Marko, Cyndi, illus. 2014. (Kung Pow Chicken Ser.: 2). (ENG., Illus.). 80p. (J). (gr. k-2). 15.99 *(978-0-545-61064-3(8));* pap. 4.99 *(978-0-545-61063-6(X))* Scholastic, Inc.

—Heroes on the Side. Marko, Cyndi, illus. 2014. (Kung Pow Chicken Ser.: 4). (ENG., Illus.). 80p. (J). (gr. k-2). 15.99 *(978-0-545-61077-3(X));* pap. 4.99 *(978-0-545-61074-2(5))* Scholastic, Inc.

—Heroes on the Side. 2014. (Kung Pow Chicken Ser.: 4). lib. bdg. 14.75 *(978-0-606-36049-4(2))* Turtleback Bks.

—Let's Get Cracking! Marko, Cyndi, illus. 2014. (Kung Pow Chicken Ser.: 1). (ENG., Illus.). 80p. (J). (gr. k-2). 15.99 *(978-0-545-61062-9(1));* pap. 4.99 *(978-0-545-61061-2(3))* Scholastic, Inc.

Marois, André. Avis de Recherche. Lemardele, Stephane, tr. 2003. (Roman Jeunesse Ser.). (FRE.). 96p. (J). (gr. 4-7). pap. *(978-2-89021-646-4(2))* Diffusion du livre Mirabel (DLM).

Marsh, Richard Phillip. Mattress People Go to Bear Park. 2009. 44p. pap. 10.95 *(978-1-935125-39-6(7))* Robertson Publishing.

Martin, Andreu & Ribero, J. No Pidas Sardinas Fuera de Temporada. 35th ed. 2003. (SPA., Illus.). 178p. (J). (gr. 8-12). pap. 11.95 *(978-84-204-4796-4(X))* Santillana USA Publishing Co., Inc.

Martin, Ann M. & Parnell, Annie. Missy Piggle-Wiggle & the Whatever Cure. Hatke, Ben, illus. 2016. (Missy Piggle-Wiggle Ser.). (ENG.). 256p. (J). 16.99 *(978-1-250-07169-9(0),* 9781250071699) Feiwel & Friends.

—Missy Piggle-Wiggle & the Whatever Cure. Hatke, Ben, illus. 2017. (Missy Piggle-Wiggle Ser.). (ENG.). 272p. (J). pap. 7.99 ***(978-1-250-12953-6(2),*** 9781250129536) Square Fish.

—Missy Piggle-Wiggle & the Whatever Cure. 2017. (Missy Piggle-Wiggle Ser.). (J). lib. bdg. 18.40 ***(978-0-606-40585-0(2))*** Turtleback Bks.

—Missy Piggle-Wiggle & the Won't-Walk-The-Dog Cure. Hatke, Ben, illus. 2017. (Missy Piggle-Wiggle Ser.). (ENG.). 240p. (J). 16.99 ***(978-1-250-07170-5(4),*** 9781250071705) Feiwel & Friends.

Martin, Harvey. The Shaggy Dog Story Book. 2009. 108p. pap. 10.00 *(978-1-59858-932-0(6))* Dog Ear Publishing, LLC.

Martin, J. P. Uncle. Blake, Quentin, illus. 2017. (ENG.). 176p. (J). (gr. 4-7). pap. 9.99 ***(978-1-68137-185-6(5),*** NYRB Kids) New York Review of Bks., Inc., The.

Martin, J. P. Uncle Cleans Up. Blake, Quentin, illus. 2008. (ENG.). 184p. (J). (gr. 4-7). 17.95 *(978-1-59017-276-6(0),* NYR Children's Collection) New York Review of Bks., Inc., The.

Martin, Steve & Chast, Roz. The Alphabet from A to Y with Bonus Letter Z! 2007. (ENG., Illus.). 64p. (J). (gr. k-k). 17.95 *(978-0-385-51662-4(2),* Flying Dolphin Pr.) Knopf Doubleday Publishing Group.

Martin, Timothy. Wimps Like Me, 1 vol. 2010. 112p. pap. 19.95 *(978-1-4489-7004-9(0))* America Star Bks.

Martinez, Heather, illus. Ice-Cream Dreams. 2004. (SpongeBob SquarePants Ser.). (ENG.). 24p. (J). pap. 3.99 *(978-0-689-86861-0(8),* Simon Spotlight/Nickelodeon) Simon Spotlight/Nickelodeon.

Martins, Isabel Minhós & Carvalho, Bernardo. Don't Cross the Line! 2016. (ENG., Illus.). 40p. (gr. k-3). 16.99 *(978-1-77657-074-4(X))* Gecko Pr. NZL. Dist: Lerner Publishing Group.

Marunowski, Barbara L. My Cow Book. 2009. 56p. pap. 21.99 *(978-1-4490-0254-1(4))* AuthorHouse.

Marusak, Elaine. Truly Tales & Girl Fish Stories. 2006. 93p. pap. 16.95 *(978-1-4241-3244-7(4))* PublishAmerica, Inc.

Maslen, Bobby Lynn & Maslen. Beginning Readers, Set. 2006. (Bob Bks.). (ENG., Illus.). 12p. (J). (gr. -1-3). pap. 16.99 *(978-0-439-84500-7(9),* Scholastic Paperbacks) Scholastic, Inc.

Maslen, Bobby Lynn & Maslen, John R. Long Vowels, Set. 2006. (Bob Bks.: No. 5). (ENG.). 16p. (J). (gr. -1-3). pap. 16.99 *(978-0-439-86541-8(7),* Scholastic Paperbacks) Scholastic, Inc.

Maslen, John R. & Maslen, Bobby Lynn. Advancing Beginners, Set. 2006. (Bob Bks.). (ENG., Illus.). 16p. (J). (gr. -1-3). pap. 16.99 *(978-0-439-84502-1(5),* Scholastic Paperbacks) Scholastic, Inc.

—Compound Words, Set. Maslen, John R., illus. 2006. (Bob Bks.). (ENG., Illus.). 16p. (J). (gr. -1-3). pap. 16.99 *(978-0-439-84506-9(8),* Scholastic Paperbacks) Scholastic, Inc.

Massicotte, Sylvie & Sottolichio, Rafael. Tu Rêves, Pitchounette? 2004. (Premier Roman Ser.). (FRE., Illus.). 64p. (J). (gr. 1-4). pap. *(978-2-89021-581-8(4))* Diffusion du livre Mirabel (DLM).

Masters, Jane E. Indy. 2013. 40p. pap. 9.99 *(978-1-62839-260-9(6))* Salem Author Services.

Mather, Daniel, illus. Case File #3 the Accidental Accomplice. 2014. (Rabbids Invasion Ser.: 3). (ENG.). 96p. (J). (gr. 2-5). pap. 4.99 *(978-1-4814-1720-4(7),* Simon Spotlight) Simon Spotlight.

Matheron, Annaliese. Ninja Nan Strikes Again. 2013. 132p. pap. *(978-1-909411-21-0(3))* Mauve Square Publishing.

Matison, Jimbo. I'm Going to Catch My Tail! 2014. (ENG., Illus.). 40p. (J). (gr. k-2). 14.95 *(978-1-4197-1382-8(5),* Abrams Bks. for Young Readers) Abrams, Inc.

Matt & Dave. Yuck's Big Booger Challenge. Baines, Nigel, illus. 2013. (Yuck Ser.). (ENG.). 112p. (J). (gr. 2-5). 15.99 *(978-1-4424-8311-8(3));* pap. 4.99 *(978-1-4424-8312-5(1))* Simon & Schuster/Paula Wiseman Bks. (Simon & Schuster/Paula Wiseman Bks.).

—Yuck's Pet Worm. Baines, Nigel, illus. 2013. (Yuck Ser.). (ENG.). 112p. (J). (gr. 2-5). 15.99 *(978-1-4424-8150-3(1));* pap. 6.99 *(978-1-4424-8149-7(8))* Simon & Schuster/Paula Wiseman Bks. (Simon & Schuster/Paula Wiseman Bks.).

—Yuck's Robotic Butt Blast. Baines, Nigel, illus. 2013. (Yuck Ser.). (ENG.). 112p. (J). (gr. 2-5). pap. 4.99 *(978-1-4424-8309-5(1),* Simon & Schuster/Paula Wiseman Bks.) Simon & Schuster/Paula Wiseman Bks.

Mattel. Monster High: the Skultimate Sticker Book. 2014. (ENG., Illus.). 96p. (J). (gr. k-17). pap. 12.99 *(978-0-316-27706-8(1))* Little, Brown Bks. for Young Readers.

Matthews, Morgan & Sinden, David. Yuck's Robotic Butt Blast. Baines, Nigel, illus. 2013. (Yuck Ser.). (ENG.). 112p. (J). (gr. 2-5). 15.99 *(978-1-4424-8308-8(3),* Simon & Schuster/Paula Wiseman Bks.) Simon & Schuster/Paula Wiseman Bks.

Matulewicz, Elisabeth Ann. Benny & Marshmallow. Sponaugle, Kim, illus. 2008. 31p. (J). pap. 15.00 *(978-0-9786211-7-9(4),* Ithaca Pr.) Authors & Artists Publishers of New York, Inc.

Maxwell-Hyslop, Miranda. Fish Go Woof! 2005. (Illus.). 36p. (J). *(978-0-340-87338-0(8))* Hodder & Stoughton.

Maxwell, Katie. The Taming of the Dru. 2004. (YA). mass mkt. 5.99 *(978-0-8439-5298-8(9))* Dorchester Publishing Co., Inc.

Mayberry, Michael. Kid Donut: How to Handle Strangers. 2011. 28p. pap. 13.99 *(978-1-4634-3555-4(X))* AuthorHouse.

Mayer, Kirsten. Despicable Me 2 - Undercover Super Spies. 2013. (ENG.). 24p. (J). (gr. -1-3). 4.99 *(978-0-316-23446-7(X))* Little, Brown Bks. for Young Readers.

Mayer, Mercer. Just a Little Critter Collection. Mayer, Mercer, illus. 2005. (ENG., Illus.). 176p. (J). (gr. -1-2). 9.99 *(978-0-375-83255-0(6),* Golden Bks.) Random Hse. Children's Bks.

—Just Me & My Mom. 2014. (Little Critter Ser.). lib. bdg. 14.75 *(978-0-606-35555-1(3))* Turtleback Bks.

—Professor Wormbog in Search for the Zipperump-a-Zoo. 2011. (Classic Collectible Ser.: 1). (ENG.). 42p. (J). (gr. -1-3). pap. 12.95 *(978-1-60746-765-6(8),* Premiere) FastPencil, Inc.

Maynor, Megan. Ella & Penguin Stick Together. Bonnet, Rosalinde, illus. 2016. (ENG.). (J). (gr. -1-3). 17.99 *(978-0-06-233088-8(8))* HarperCollins Pubs.

McAnulty, Stacy. Dear Santasaurus. Kaminsky, Jef, illus. 2013. (ENG.). 32p. (J). (gr. k-3). 15.95 *(978-1-59078-876-9(1))* Boyds Mills Pr.

—Excellent Ed. Sarcone-Roach, Julia, illus. 2016. (ENG.). 32p. (J). (gr. -1-3). 16.99 *(978-0-553-51023-2(1),* Knopf Bks. for Young Readers) Random Hse. Children's Bks.

—101 Reasons Why I'm Not Taking a Bath. Ang, Joy, illus. 2016. (ENG.). 40p. (J). (gr. -1-2). lib. bdg. 20.99 *(978-0-375-97365-9(6),* Random Hse. Bks. for Young Readers) Random Hse. Children's Bks.

McCarroll, Barbara. Tongue Turning Tales for the Classroom. Godfrey, Arthur Dwayne, illus. 2008. 36p. pap. 24.95 *(978-1-60703-254-0(6))* America Star Bks.

McCarthy, Jenna. Lola Knows a Lot. Palacios, Sara, illus. 2016. 32p. (J). (gr. -1-3). 17.99 *(978-0-06-225017-9(5))* HarperCollins Pubs.

McCleery, Peter. Bob & Joss Get Lost! Vogel, Vin, illus. 2017. 32p. (J). (gr. -1-3). 17.99 *(978-0-06-241531-8(X))* HarperCollins Pubs.

McCleery, William. Wolf Story. Chappell, Warren, illus. 2012. (ENG.). 88p. (J). (gr. k-4). 15.95 *(978-1-59017-589-7(1),* NYR Children's Collection) New York Review of Bks., Inc., The.

McClements, George. Night of the Veggie Monster. McClements, George, illus. (ENG., Illus.). 32p. (J). (gr. -1-1). 2014. 7.99 *(978-1-61963-180-9(6),* 9781619631809) 2008. 16.99 *(978-1-59990-061-2(0),* 9781599900612) Bloomsbury Publishing USA. (Bloomsbury USA Childrens).

McCloskey, Robert. Homer Price. l.t. ed. 2004. (Beeler Mystery Ser.). 158p. 29.95 (978-1-58118-123-4(X)) LRS.

—Homer Price. l.t. ed. (J). (gr. 4-6). reprint ed. 10.00 (978-0-89064-072-2(6)) National Assn. for Visually Handicapped.

—Homer Price. McCloskey, Robert, illus. 2005. (Puffin Modern Classics Ser.). (ENG., Illus.). 160p. (J). (gr. 3-7). 6.99 (978-0-14-240415-7(2), Puffin Books) Penguin Young Readers Group.

McClymer, Kelly. Getting to Third Date. 2006. (Romantic Comedies Ser.). (ENG., Illus.). 304p. (YA). (gr. 9-18). mass mkt. 6.99 (978-1-4169-1479-2(X), Simon Pulse) Simon Pulse.

McCombie, Karen. Candy Girl. 2012. (Stoke Books Titles Ser.). 64p. (J). (gr. 5-8). pap. 7.95 (978-1-78112-012-5(9)); lib. bdg. 22.60 (978-1-78112-011-8(0)) Stoke Bks.

Mccormick, Scott. Camping Catastrophe! Lazzell, R. H., illus. 2016. (Mr. Pants Ser.: 4). (ENG.). 128p. (J). (gr. k-3). 12.99 (978-0-525-42812-1(7), Dial Bks) Penguin Young Readers Group.

McCourt, Lisa. Merry Christmas, Stinky Face. Moore, Cyd, illus. 2008. (ENG.). 32p. (J). (gr. k — 1). bds. 6.99 (978-0-439-73123-2(2), Cartwheel Bks.) Scholastic, Inc.

McCreely, Havelock. My Zombie Hamster. 2014. (ENG.). 200p. (J). (gr. 3-7). 15.99 (978-1-60684-491-5(1), Carolrhoda Bks.) Lerner Publishing Group.

McCurdy, Steve. Keeper at the Inn. Lohmann, Stephanie, illus. 2007. 36p. 17.95 (978-0-9761179-2-6(4)) StoryMaster Pr.

McDonald, Megan. Cloudy with a Chance of Boys. (Sisters Club Ser.: 3). (ENG., Illus.). 272p. (J). (gr. 3-7). 2012. pap. 5.99 (978-0-7636-5577-8(5)) 2011. 15.99 (978-0-7636-4615-8(6)) Candlewick Pr.

—The Doctor Is In! Reynolds, Peter H., illus. 2010. (Judy Moody Ser.: 5). (ENG.). 176p. (J). (gr. 1-4). 15.99 (978-0-7636-4862-6(0)); pap. 5.99 (978-0-7636-4861-9(2)) Candlewick Pr.

—The Doctor Is In! 2010. (Judy Moody Ser.: 5). lib. bdg. 16.00 (978-0-606-12343-3(1), Turtleback) Turtleback Bks.

—Judy Moody Declares Independence. Reynolds, Peter H., illus. 2010. (Judy Moody Ser.: 6). (ENG.). 160p. (J). (gr. 1-4). 15.99 (978-0-7636-4852-7(3)); pap. 5.99 (978-0-7636-4851-0(5)) Candlewick Pr.

—Judy Moody Declares Independence. (Judy Moody Ser.: 6). 2010. lib. bdg. 16.00 (978-0-606-12345-7(8)) 2007. 16.00 (978-1-4177-6896-7(7)) Turtleback Bks. (Turtleback).

—Judy Moody Gets Famous! Reynolds, Peter H., illus. 2010. (Judy Moody Ser.: 2). (ENG.). 144p. (J). (gr. 1-4). 15.99 (978-0-7636-4854-1(X)); pap. 5.99 (978-0-7636-4853-4(1)) Candlewick Pr.

—Judy Moody Goes to College. (Judy Moody Ser.: 8). 2010. lib. bdg. 16.00 (978-0-606-12352-5(0)) 2009. lib. bdg. 16.00 (978-0-606-01313-0(X)) Turtleback Bks. (Turtleback).

—Judy Moody Goes to College, Bk. 8. Reynolds, Peter H., illus. 2010. (Judy Moody Ser.: 8). (ENG.). (J). (gr. 1-4). 144p. 15.99 (978-0-7636-4856-5(6)); 160p. pap. 5.99 (978-0-7636-4855-8(8)) Candlewick Pr.

—Judy Moody Predicts the Future. Reynolds, Peter H., illus. 2010. (Judy Moody Ser.: 4). (ENG.). 160p. (J). (gr. 1-4). 15.99 (978-0-7636-4858-9(2)); pap. 5.99 (978-0-7636-4857-2(4)) Candlewick Pr.

—Judy Moody Saves the World! Reynolds, Peter H., illus. 2004. (Judy Moody Ser.: Bk. 3). 144p. (J). (gr. 1-5). 13.65 (978-0-7569-2588-8(6)) Perfection Learning Corp.

—Judy Moody Saves the World! Reynolds, Peter H., illus. 2010. (Judy Moody Ser.: 3). (ENG.). 160p. (J). (gr. 1-4). 15.99 (978-0-7636-4860-2(4)) Candlewick Pr.

—Judy Moody Saves the World! 2010. (Judy Moody Ser.: 3). lib. bdg. 16.00 (978-0-606-12340-2(7), Turtleback) Turtleback Bks.

—Judy Moody Saves the World!, Bk. 3. Reynolds, Peter H., illus. 2010. (Judy Moody Ser.: 3). (ENG.). 160p. (J). (gr. 1-4). pap. 5.99 (978-0-7636-4859-6(0)) Candlewick Pr.

—The Sisters Club. 2008. (Sisters Club Ser.: 1). (ENG., Illus.). 208p. (J). (gr. 3-7). pap. 5.99 (978-0-7636-3251-9(1)) Candlewick Pr.

—The Sisters Club. 2008. (Sisters Club Ser.: 1). lib. bdg. 16.00 (978-1-4178-1785-6(2), Turtleback) Turtleback Bks.

—Solar System Superhero, Bk. 5. Reynolds, Peter H., illus. 2013. (Stink Ser.: 5). (ENG.). 128p. (J). (gr. 1-4). 12.99 (978-0-7636-6392-6(1)) Candlewick Pr.

—Solar System Superhero, 1 vol. Reynolds, Peter H., illus. 2012. (Stink Ser.: No. 2). (ENG.). 144p. (J). (gr. 2-5). 24.21 (978-1-59961-197-6(X)) Spotlight.

—Solar System Superhero. 2013. (Stink Ser.: 5). lib. bdg. 14.75 (978-0-606-31591-3(8), Turtleback) Turtleback Bks.

—Stink: The Incredible Shrinking Kid. Reynolds, Peter H., illus. 2010. (Stink Ser.: No. 1). 112p. (J). (gr. k-4). 24.21 (978-1-59961-686-5(6)) Spotlight.

—Stink: Twice As Incredible. Reynolds, Peter H., illus. 2016. (Stink Ser.). (ENG.). (J). (gr. 1-4). pap. 7.99 (978-0-7636-8829-5(0)) Candlewick Pr.

—Stink - The Super-Incredible Collection, Bks. 1-3. Reynolds, Peter H., illus. 2013. (Stink Ser.). (ENG.). 352p. (J). (gr. k-3). pap. 14.97 (978-0-7636-6831-0(1)) Candlewick Pr.

—Stink & the Freaky Frog Freakout. Reynolds, Peter H., illus. 2013. (Stink Ser.: 8). (ENG.). 160p. (J). (gr. 1-4). 12.99 (978-0-7636-6140-3(6)) Candlewick Pr.

—Stink & the Great Guinea Pig Express, Bk. 4. Reynolds, Peter H., illus. 2013. (Stink Ser.: 4). (ENG.). (J). (gr. 1-4). 128p. 12.99 (978-0-7636-6391-9(3)); 144p. pap. 4.99 (978-0-7636-6421-3(9)) Candlewick Pr.

—Stink & the Great Guinea Pig Express. Reynolds, Peter H., illus. 2010. (Stink Ser.: No. 4). 128p. (J). (gr. k-4). 24.21 (978-1-59961-683-4(1)) Spotlight.

—Stink & the Great Guinea Pig Express. 2013. (Stink Ser.: 4). lib. bdg. 14.75 (978-0-606-31590-6(X), Turtleback) Turtleback Bks.

—Stink & the Incredible Super-Galactic Jawbreaker. Reynolds, Peter H., illus. 2013. (Stink Ser.: 2). (ENG.). (J). (gr. 1-4). 144p. pap. 4.99 (978-0-7636-6420-6(0));Bk. 2. 128p. 12.99 (978-0-7636-6389-6(1)) Candlewick Pr.

—Stink & the Incredible Super-Galactic Jawbreaker. Reynolds, Peter H., illus. 2010. (Stink Ser.: No. 2). 128p. (J). (gr. k-4). 24.21 (978-1-59961-684-1(X)) Spotlight.

—Stink & the Incredible Super-Galactic Jawbreaker. 2013. (Stink Ser.: 2). lib. bdg. 14.75 (978-0-606-31588-3(8), Turtleback) Turtleback Bks.

—Stink & the Midnight Zombie Walk. Reynolds, Peter H., illus. 2013. (Stink Ser.: 7). (ENG.). 160p. (J). (gr. 1-4). 12.99 (978-0-7636-6394-0(8)); pap. 4.99 (978-0-7636-6422-0(7)) Candlewick Pr.

—Stink & the Midnight Zombie Walk. 2013. (Stink Ser.: 7). lib. bdg. 14.75 (978-0-606-31586-9(1), Turtleback) Turtleback Bks.

—Stink & the Ultimate Thumb-Wrestling Smackdown. Reynolds, Peter H., illus. 2013. (Stink Ser.: 6). (ENG.). 144p. (J). (gr. 1-4). pap. 4.99 (978-0-7636-6423-7(5));Bk. 6. 12.99 (978-0-7636-6393-3(X)) Candlewick Pr.

—Stink & the Ultimate Thumb-Wrestling Smackdown, 1 vol. Reynolds, Peter H., illus. 2012. (Stink Ser.: No. 2). (ENG.). 144p. (J). (gr. 2-5). 24.21 (978-1-59961-194-5(5)) Spotlight.

—Stink & the World's Worst Super-Stinky Sneakers, Bk. 3. Reynolds, Peter H., illus. 2013. (Stink Ser.: 3). (ENG.). 144p. (J). (gr. 1-4). pap. 4.99 (978-0-7636-6424-4(3));Bk. 3. 12.99 (978-0-7636-6390-2(5)) Candlewick Pr.

—Stink & the World's Worst Super-Stinky Sneakers. Reynolds, Peter H., illus. 2010. (Stink Ser.: No. 3). 144p. (J). (gr. k-4). 24.21 (978-1-59961-685-8(8)) Spotlight.

—Stink & the World's Worst Super-Stinky Sneakers. 2013. (Stink Ser.: 3). lib. bdg. 14.75 (978-0-606-31589-0(6), Turtleback) Turtleback Bks.

—Stink It Up! A Guide to the Gross, the Bad, & the Smelly. Reynolds, Peter H., illus. 2013. (Stink Ser.). (ENG.). 128p. (J). (gr. 1-4). pap. 5.99 (978-0-7636-5942-4(8)) Candlewick Pr.

—Stink Moody in Master of Disaster. Madrid, Erwin, illus. 2015. (Judy Moody Ser.: 5). (ENG.). 64p. (J). (gr. -1-1). 12.99 (978-0-7636-7218-8(1)) Candlewick Pr.

—Stink y el increíble Rompemuelas Supergaláctico. 2008. (SPA.). 207p. (J). (gr. 3-5). pap. 7.95 (978-1-60396-194-3(1)) Ediciones Alfaguara ESP. Dist: Two Rivers Distribution.

—Stink y los Tenis Más Apestosos del Mundo. 2008. (SPA.). 208p. (J). (gr. 3-5). pap. 7.95 (978-1-60396-195-0(X), Alfaguara) Santillana USA Publishing Co., Inc.

—Was in a Mood. Reynolds, Peter H., illus. 2010. (Judy Moody Ser.: 1). (ENG.). 176p. (J). (gr. 1-4). pap. 5.99 (978-0-7636-4849-7(3)) Candlewick Pr.

McDonnell, Patrick. A Perfectly Messed-Up Story. 2014. (ENG., Illus.). 40p. (J). (gr. -1-3). 17.99 (978-0-316-22258-7(5)) Little, Brown Bks. for Young Readers.

McElligott, Matthew. Even Aliens Need Snacks. McElligott, Matthew, illus. 2014. (ENG., Illus.). 40p. (J). (gr. k-3). pap. 7.99 (978-0-8027-3652-9(1), 9780802736529, Bloomsbury USA Childrens) Bloomsbury Publishing USA.

—Even Monsters Need Haircuts. McElligott, Matthew, illus. 2012. (ENG., Illus.). 40p. (J). (gr. k-8). pap. 8.99 (978-0-8027-2801-2(4), 9780802728012, Bloomsbury USA Childrens) Bloomsbury Publishing USA.

McElligott, Matthew & Tuxbury, Larry David. Benjamin Franklinstein Lives! McElligott, Matthew, illus. 2011. (Benjamin Franklinstein Ser.: 1). (ENG., Illus.). 144p. (J). (gr. 3-7). 7.99 (978-0-14-241935-9(4), Puffin Books) Penguin Young Readers Group.

McGeddon, R. Aliens! McGeddon, R. & Littler, Jamie, illus. 2016. (Disaster Diaries). (ENG.). 208p. (J). 9.99 (978-1-250-09088-1(1), 9781250090881) Imprint IND. Dist: Macmillan.

—Brainwashed! McGeddon, R., illus. 2016. (Disaster Diaries). (ENG., Illus.). 208p. (J). 9.99 (978-1-250-09091-1(1), 9781250090911) Imprint IND. Dist: Macmillan.

—Disaster Diaries: Brainwashed! Littler, Jamie, illus. 2016. (J). pap. (978-1-250-09093-5(8)) ETT Imprint.

—Robots! 2017. (Disaster Diaries: 4). (ENG., Illus.). 192p. (J). 9.99 (978-1-250-13562-9(1), 9781250135629) Imprint IND. Dist: Macmillan.

—Zombies! McGeddon, R. & Littler, Jamie, illus. 2016. (Disaster Diaries: 2). (ENG.). 192p. (J). 9.99 (978-1-250-09084-3(9), 9781250090843) Imprint IND. Dist: Macmillan.

McGeddon, R., illus. Zombies! 2016. (Disaster Diaries). 178p. (J). pap. (978-1-250-09086-7(5)) ETT Imprint.

McGee, Joe. Peanut Butter & Aliens: A Zombie Culinary Tale. Santoso, Charles, illus. 2017. (ENG.). 32p. (J). (gr. -1-2). 16.95 (978-1-4197-2530-2(0), Abrams Bks. for Young Readers) Abrams, Inc.

McGee, Joe. Peanut Butter & Brains. Santoso, Charles, illus. 2015. (ENG.). 32p. (J). (gr. -1-3). 16.95 (978-1-4197-1247-0(0), Abrams Bks. for Young Readers) Abrams, Inc.

McGee, Pamela M. Keri: Dandelions. Miller, Dawn Ellen, illus. 2012. 24p. pap. 24.95 (978-1-4626-9977-3(4)) America Star Bks.

—Keri: The Wedding. Miller, Dawn Ellen, illus. 2013. 20p. pap. 24.95 (978-1-63004-171-7(8)) America Star Bks.

Mcghee, Alison. Mrs. Watson Wants Your Teeth. Bliss, Harry, illus. unabr. ed. 2007. (Picture Book Readalong Ser.). (J). (gr. -1-2). 28.95 incl. audio compact disk (978-1-59519-902-7(0)) Live Oak Media.

—Song of Middle C. Menchin, Scott, illus. 2009. (ENG.). 32p. (J). (gr. k-3). 16.99 (978-0-7636-3013-3(6)) Candlewick Pr.

McGill, Erin. I Do Not Like Al's Hat. McGill, Erin, illus. 2017. (Illus.). 32p. (J). (gr. -1-3). 17.99 (978-0-06-245576-5(1), Greenwillow Bks.) HarperCollins Pubs.

McGraw, Royal, et al. Grumpy Cat & Pokey. 2016. (ENG., Illus.). 104p. (J). 12.99 (978-1-5241-0004-9(8), 9781524100049, Dynamite Entertainment) Dynamic Forces, Inc.

McHeffey, Adam. Rudy & Claude Splash into Art, 0 vols. 2014. (ENG., Illus.). 32p. (J). (gr. -1-2). 16.99 (978-1-4778-4777-0(4), 9781477847770, Amazon Children's Publishing) Amazon Publishing.

Mcintyre, Gary P. Jake Fall & Winter. 2011. 198p. pap. 24.95 (978-1-4560-4085-7(5)) America Star Bks.

McKay, Hilary. The Exiles at Home. 2007. (ENG.). 208p. (J). (gr. 3-7). pap. 12.95 (978-1-4169-6729-3(X), McElderry, Margaret K. Bks.) McElderry, Margaret K. Bks.

—Lulu & the Duck in the Park. Lamont, Priscilla, illus. (Lulu Ser.: Book 1). (ENG.). (J). (gr. 1-5). 2012. 104p. 13.99 (978-0-8075-4808-0(1))Bk. 1. 2014. 112p. 4.99 (978-0-8075-4809-7(X)) Whitman, Albert & Co.

—The Terrible Time Without Tilly. Scott, Kimberley, illus. 2016. (Reading Ladder Ser.). (ENG.). 48p. (J). (gr. k-2). 7.99 (978-1-4052-8248-2(7)) Egmont Bks., Ltd. GBR. Dist: Independent Pubs. Group.

McKee, David. Gladiator. McKee, David, illus. 2005. (ENG., Illus.). 32p. (J). (gr. k-2). pap. 12.99 (978-1-84270-372-4(2)) Trafalgar Square Publishing.

McKendry, Sam. Are You Ticklish? Mitchell, Melanie, illus. 2006. (ENG.). 12p. (J). (gr. -1-18). bds. 10.95 (978-1-58117-376-5(8), Intervisual/Piggy Toes) Bendon, Inc.

McKenzie, Heath. My Rules for Being a Pretty Princess. 2015. (ENG., Illus.). 32p. (J). (-3). 16.99 (978-1-4926-1520-0(X)) Sourcebooks, Inc.

McKenzie, Tim A. Baxter Barret Brown's Bass Fiddle. Shaw, Charles, illus. 2004. (ENG.). 24p. (J). (gr. 2-4). 19.95 (978-1-931721-06-6(8)) Bright Sky Pr.

McKnight, Marty. Jim Nasium Is a Strikeout King. Jones, Chris, illus. 2016. (Jim Nasium Ser.). (ENG.). 88p. (gr. 2-3). lib. bdg. 25.32 (978-1-4965-3025-7(X)) Stone Arch Bks.

—Jim Nasium Is a Tennis Mismatch. Jones, Chris, illus. 2016. (Jim Nasium Ser.). (ENG.). 88p. (gr. 2-3). lib. bdg. 25.32 (978-1-4965-3026-4(8)) Stone Arch Bks.

McKown, Hunter. Meet Jack Truck! Shannon, David et al, illus. 2008. (Jon Scieszka's Trucktown Ser.). (ENG.). 14p. (J). (gr. -1-1). bds. 5.99 (978-1-4169-4173-6(8), Little Simon) Little Simon.

McKy, Katie. It All Began with a Bean: The True Story of the World's Biggest Fart. Hill, Tracy, illus. 2011. (ENG.). 32p. (J). (gr. -1-3). pap. 8.95 (978-1-933718-23-1(4)) Tanglewood Pr.

McLean, Michael & McLean, Scott. Fairy Tale Christmas. 2014. (ENG., Illus.). 176p. (J). (gr. 3-9). 15.99 (978-1-60907-930-7(2), Shadow Mountain) Shadow Mountain Publishing.

McMahon, Michael. The Zoo & You: A Guidebook, 1 vol. rev. ed. 2013. (Fiction Readers Ser.). (ENG., Illus.). 28p. (J). (gr. 3-3). pap. 8.99 (978-1-4333-5606-3(6)) Shell Educational Publishing.

—The Zoo & You: A Guidebook. rev. ed. 2013. (Fiction Readers Ser.). (ENG., Illus.). 28p. (gr. 3-3). pap. 19.96 (978-1-4807-1728-2(2)) Teacher Created Materials, Inc.

McMullan, Kate. Get Lost, Odysseus!, 1 vol. 2014. (Myth-O-Mania Ser.). (ENG., Illus.). 240p. (gr. 4-8). 25.32 (978-1-4342-6016-1(X)) Stone Arch Bks.

—Get to Work, Hercules!, 1 vol. Zilber, Denis, illus. (Myth-O-Mania Ser.: Bk. 7). (ENG.). 208p. (gr. 4-8). 2011. pap. 5.95 (978-1-4342-3440-7(1)) 2010. lib. bdg. 25.32 (978-1-4342-3196-3(8)) Stone Arch Bks. (Myth-O-Mania).

—Go for the Gold, Atalanta!, 1 vol. Zilber, Denis, illus. (Myth-O-Mania Ser.: Bk. 8). (ENG.). 192p. (gr. 4-8). 2011. pap. 5.95 (978-1-4342-3441-4(X)) 2010. lib. bdg. 25.32 (978-1-4342-3197-0(6)) Stone Arch Bks. (Myth-O-Mania).

—Have a Hot Time, Hades!, 1 vol. Zilber, Denis, illus. 2011. (Myth-O-Mania Ser.: Bk. 1). (ENG.). 176p. (gr. 4-8). pap. 5.95 (978-1-4342-3437-7(1)); lib. bdg. 25.32 (978-1-4342-2136-0(9)) Stone Arch Bks. (Myth-O-Mania).

—Hit the Road, Helen! (Myth-O-Mania Ser.: Bk. 9). (ENG.). 240p. (gr. 4-8). 2015. pap. 5.95 (978-1-4342-9304-6(1), Myth-O-Mania) 2013. 10.95 (978-1-4342-6219-6(7)) 2013. lib. bdg. 25.32 (978-1-4342-4990-6(5)) Stone Arch Bks.

—Keep a Lid on It, Pandora! 2003. (Myth-o-Mania Ser.: No. 6). (Illus.). 160p. (J). 9.99 (978-0-7868-0862-5(4)) Hyperion Bks. for Children.

—Keep a Lid on It, Pandora!, 1 vol. Zilber, Denis, illus. (Myth-O-Mania Ser.: Bk. 6). (ENG.). 192p. (gr. 4-8). 2011. pap. 5.95 (978-1-4342-3439-1(8)) 2010. lib. bdg. 25.32 (978-1-4342-3195-6(X)) Stone Arch Bks. (Myth-O-Mania).

—Myth-O-Mania. (Myth-O-Mania Ser.). (ENG.). (gr. 4-8). 2014. 253.20 (978-1-4342-9467-8(6)) 2013. 227.88 (978-1-4342-6061-1(5)) Stone Arch Bks. (Myth-O-Mania).

—Nice Shot, Cupid!, 1 vol. Zilber, Denis, illus. 2011. (Myth-O-Mania Ser.: Bk. 4). (ENG.). 208p. (gr. 4-8). pap. 5.95 (978-1-4342-3435-3(5)); lib. bdg. 25.32 (978-1-4342-1985-5(2)) Stone Arch Bks. (Myth-O-Mania).

—Phone Home, Persephone!, 1 vol. Zilber, Denis, illus. 2011. (Myth-O-Mania Ser.: Bk. 2). (ENG.). 176p. (gr. 4-8). pap. 5.95 (978-1-4342-3436-0(3)); lib. bdg. 25.32 (978-1-4342-2135-3(0)) Stone Arch Bks. (Myth-O-Mania).

—Say Cheese, Medusa!, 1 vol. Zilber, Denis, illus. 2011. (Myth-O-Mania Ser.: Bk. 3). (ENG.). 208p. (gr. 4-8). pap. 5.95 (978-1-4342-3442-1(8)); lib. bdg. 25.32 (978-1-4342-2998-4(X)) Stone Arch Bks. (Myth-O-Mania).

—School! Adventures at the Harvey N. Trouble Elementary School. Booth, George, illus. 2012. (ENG.). 176p. (J). (gr. 1-4). pap. 8.99 (978-0-312-55595-5(4), 9780312555955) Square Fish.

—School's Out... Forever! Basso, Bill & Gilpin, Stephen, illus. 2012. (Dragon Slayers' Academy Ser.: 20). (ENG.). 112p. (J). (gr. 2-5). pap. 4.99 (978-0-448-44571-7(9), Grosset & Dunlap) Penguin Young Readers Group.

—Stop That Bull, Theseus!, 1 vol. Zilber, Denis, illus. 2011. (Myth-O-Mania Ser.: Bk. 5). (ENG.). 192p. (gr. 4-8). pap. 5.95 (978-1-4342-3438-4(X), Myth-O-Mania) Stone Arch Bks.

McNeill, Audrey. From the Desk of a Three-Year-Old. Grondel, April, illus. 2009. 20p. pap. 24.95 (978-1-60749-476-8(0)) America Star Bks.

McPhail, David. Big Pig & Little Pig. 2003. (Green Light Readers Level 1 Ser.). (ENG., Illus.). 24p. (J). (gr. -1-3). pap. 3.95 (978-0-15-204857-0(X)) Houghton Mifflin Harcourt Publishing Co.

McQueen, Todd. Bob & Rob & Corn on the Cob. McQueen, Todd, illus. 2014. (ENG., Illus.). 32p. (J). (gr. -1-k). 16.95 (978-1-62873-591-8(0), Sky Pony Pr.) Skyhorse Publishing Co., Inc.

McVoy, Terra Elan. This Is All Your Fault, Cassie Parker. 2016. 272p. (J). (gr. 3-7). 16.99 (978-0-06-241449-6(6), Tegen, Katherine Bks) HarperCollins Pubs.

Meacham, Margaret. A Fairy's Guide to Understanding Humans. 2007. (ENG.). 160p. (J). (gr. 5-18). 16.95 (978-0-8234-2078-0(7)) Holiday Hse., Inc.

—A Mid-Semester Night's Dream. 2004. (ENG.). 144p. (J). (gr. 4-6). tchr. ed. 16.95 (978-0-8234-1815-2(4)) Holiday Hse., Inc.

Mead, David & Berry, Ron. Can You Make the Monster Giggle? A Halloween Self-Scare Book! Sharp, Chris, illus. 2011. 16p. (J). 10.99 (978-0-8249-1526-1(7), Ideal Pubns.) Worthy Publishing.

Mead, Purnima. Bibia Meets Gripper. 2013. 24p. pap. 12.45 (978-1-4497-9751-5(2), WestBow Pr.) Author Solutions, Inc.

Meadows, Thomas. The Tales of Tommy Tucker: The Thought That Out Thunk the Thinker! 2012. 24p. pap. 14.93 (978-1-4669-5789-3(1)) Trafford Publishing.

Meddaugh, Susan. Campfire Stories. 2013. (Martha Speaks Ser.). (ENG., Illus.). 96p. (J). (gr. 1-4). pap. 5.99 (978-0-547-97021-9(8)) Houghton Mifflin Harcourt Publishing Co.

—Funny Bone Jokes & Riddles. 2013. (Martha Speaks Ser.). (ENG., Illus.). 24p. (J). (gr. -1-3). pap. 3.99 (978-0-547-86579-9(1)) Houghton Mifflin Harcourt Publishing Co.

—Martha Speaks: Campfire Stories (Chapter Book) 2013. (Martha Speaks Ser.). (ENG., Illus.). 96p. (J). (gr. 1-4). 14.99 (978-0-547-97024-0(2)) Houghton Mifflin Harcourt Publishing Co.

—Martha Speaks: Funny Bone Jokes & Riddles. 2013. (Martha Speaks Ser.). (ENG., Illus.). 24p. (J). (gr. -1-3). 12.99 (978-0-547-86577-5(5)) Houghton Mifflin Harcourt Publishing Co.

Meddour, Wendy. The Black Cat Detectives. 2012. (Cinnamon Grove Ser.). (Illus.). 176p. (J). pap. (978-1-84780-226-2(5), Frances Lincoln) Quarto Publishing Group UK.

Meisel, Peter. Stinky Spike & the Royal Rescue. Meisel, Paul, illus. 2017. (ENG.). 80p. (J). 9.99 (978-1-61963-883-9(5), 9781619638839, Bloomsbury USA Childrens) Bloomsbury Publishing USA.

—Stinky Spike the Pirate Dog. Meisel, Paul, illus. 2017. (ENG.). 80p. (J). 9.99 (978-1-61963-778-8(2), 9781619637788, Bloomsbury USA Childrens) Bloomsbury Publishing USA.

Meister, Cari. Tiny on the Farm. Davis, Rich, illus. 2008. (Tiny Ser.). (ENG.). 32p. (J). (gr. -1-1). 16.99 (978-0-670-06246-1(4), Viking Books for Young Readers) Penguin Young Readers Group.

Mejias, John & Mejias, John, illus. The Hungry Brothers. 2009. (ENG.). 32p. (J). (gr. -1-2). 15.95 (978-0-9798841-1-5(X)) 4N Publishing LLC.

Melling, David. Dont Worry Douglas. Melling, David, illus. 2011. (ENG., Illus.). 32p. 12.95 (978-1-58925-106-9(7)) Tiger Tales.

Menges, Thais D. Granny & the Tractor. King, Joseph, illus. 2012. 36p. pap. 10.95 (978-1-60920-047-3(0)) Ajoyin Publishing, Inc.

Meres, Jonathan. Includes Delivery. 2016. (World of Norm Ser.). (ENG., Illus.). 288p. (J). (gr. 3-17). pap. 7.99 (978-1-4083-4193-3(X), Orchard Bks.) Hachette Children's Group GBR. Dist: Hachette Bk. Group.

—May Be Recycled, Bk. 11. 2016. (World of Norm Ser.). (ENG., Illus.). 288p. (J). (gr. 2-4). pap. 9.99 (978-1-4083-4484-2(X), Orchard Bks.) Hachette Children's Group GBR. Dist: Hachette Bk. Group.

—May Contain Buts. 2015. (World of Norm Ser.: 8). (ENG., Illus.). 288p. (J). (gr. 4-6). pap. 9.99 (978-1-4083-3406-5(2)) Hodder & Stoughton GBR. Dist: Hachette Bk. Group.

—Must End Soon. 2017. (World of Norm Ser.). (ENG., Illus.). 288p. (J). (gr. 2-4). 7.99 (978-1-4083-4603-7(6), Orchard Bks.) Hachette Children's Group GBR. Dist: Hachette Bk. Group.

Meres, Jonathan. The World of Norm: May Still Be Charged. 2015. (Tales from Schwartzgarten Ser.: 9). (ENG.). 288p. (J). (gr. 4-6). pap. 9.99 (978-1-4083-3411-9(9)) Hodder & Stoughton GBR. Dist: Hachette Bk. Group.

Merola, Caroline. La Trahison de Laurent Lareau. Merola, Caroline, illus. 2003. (Premier Roman Ser.). (FRE., Illus.). 64p. (J). (gr. 1-4). pap. (978-2-89021-645-7(4)) Diffusion du livre Mirabel (DLM).

Meschenmoser, Sebastian. Pug Man's 3 Wishes. 2016. (ENG., Illus.). 48p. (J). (gr. -1-3). 16.95 (978-0-7358-4261-8(2)) North-South Bks., Inc.

Metzger, Steve. Princess Kitty. Okstad, Ella, illus. 2017. 32p. (J). (gr. -1-3). 17.99 (978-0-06-230662-3(6)) HarperCollins Pubs.

Metzler, Chris & Kim, Sunyoung. Me & 10 Babies. (Illus.). 36p. (978-0-9688338-4-1(5)) Cadence Publishing.

Meyer, Franklyn. More Me & Caleb Again. 2008. (Illus.). 191p. (J). 16.95 (978-0-9789388-2-6(8)) Hester Publishing.

Meyer, Franklyn E. Me & Caleb. Smith, Lawrence Beall, illus. 2006. (J). kivar 16.95 (978-0-9789388-0-2(1)) Hester Publishing.

—Me & Caleb Again. Liese, Charles, illus. 2006. (J). kivar 16.95 (978-0-9789388-1-9(X)) Hester Publishing.

Meyer, Ken, Jr., illus. Lucky Lionel. 2009. (J). (978-1-60108-020-2(4)) Red Cygnet Pr.

Meyerhoff, Jenny. The Barftastic Life of Louie Burger. Week, Jason, illus. 2013. (Barftastic Life of Louie Burger Ser.: 1). (ENG.). 240p. (J). (gr. 3-6). 13.99 (978-0-374-30518-5(8), 9780374305185, Farrar, Straus & Giroux (BYR)) Farrar, Straus & Giroux.

—Class B. U. R. P. Week, Jason, illus. 2014. (Barftastic Life of Louie Burger Ser.: 2). (ENG.). 288p. (J). (gr. 3-6). 13.99 (978-0-374-30521-5(8), 9780374305215, Farrar, Straus & Giroux (BYR)) Farrar, Straus & Giroux.

Miceli, Mary Anne. Confessor's Animal Wartime Blues. 2009. 56p. pap. 31.99 (978-1-4415-2867-4(9)) Xlibris Corp.

—How 'Pilly-Pine', the Alpaca, Lost His Quills. Terry, Roger, illus. 2012. 44p. pap. 20.00 (978-0-578-10145-3(9)) Miceli, Mary Anne.

Michalak, Jamie. Joe & Sparky Get New Wheels. Remkiewicz, Frank, illus. 2013. (Candlewick Sparks Ser.). (ENG.). 48p. (J). (gr. k-4). pap. 3.99 (978-0-7636-6641-5(6)) Candlewick Pr.

Michiko Florence, Debbi. Jasmine Toguchi, Super Sleuth. Vukovic, Elizabet, illus. 2017. (Jasmine Toguchi Ser.). (ENG.). 128p. (J). 15.99 (978-0-374-30413-3(0), 9780374304133, Farrar, Straus & Giroux (BYR)) Farrar, Straus & Giroux.

Miéville, China. Worst Breakfast. Smith, Zak, illus. 2016. (ENG.). 32p. (J). (gr. -1-2). 16.95 (978-1-61775-486-9(2), Black Sheep) Akashic Bks.

Miglis, Jenny. And the Winner Is... Meurer, Caleb, illus. 2004. (SpongeBob SquarePants Ser.). (ENG.). 24p. (J). pap. 3.99 (978-0-689-86327-1(6), Simon Spotlight/Nickelodeon) Simon Spotlight/Nickelodeon.

Mihaley, James. You Can't Have My Planet: But Take My Brother, Please. 2013. (ENG.). 272p. (J). (gr. 4-7). pap. 8.99 (978-1-250-01667-6(3), 9781250016676) Square Fish.

Miles, Chris. Spurt. 2017. (ENG., Illus.). 272p. (J). (gr. 6-9). 16.99 *(978-1-4814-7972-1(5),* Simon & Schuster Bks. For Young Readers) Simon & Schuster Bks. For Young Readers.

Miller, Andrew. Arthur Dudley Dunstan. 2009. 47p. pap. 12.03 *(978-0-557-07115-9(1))* Lulu Pr., Inc.

Miller, Tim. Moo Moo in a Tutu. Miller, Tim, illus. 2017. (Moo Moo & Mr. Quackers Book Ser.). (Illus.). 32p. (J). (gr. -1-3). 17.99 *(978-0-06-241440-3(2))* HarperCollins Pubs.

Mills, Nancy Libbey. Never Eat Cabbage on Thursday. Wells, Shan, illus. ltd. ed. 2005. 32p. (J). 12.95 *(978-1-893815-08-7(0))* Pie in the Sky Publishing, LLC.

Milway, Alex. Pigsticks & Harold & the Incredible Journey. Milway, Alex, illus. 2014. (ENG., Illus.). 84p. (J). (gr. k-4). 12.99 *(978-0-7636-6615-6(7))* Candlewick Pr.

Minhós Martins, Isabel. At Our House. Matoso, Madalena, illus. 2013. (ENG.). 28p. 12.95 *(978-1-84976-049-2(7))* Tate Publishing, Ltd. GBR. Dist: Abrams, Inc.

Miss Gomez's Third Grade Class Staff. Wacky Stories from Wisdom Academy for Young Scientists. 2013. (ENG.). 63p. (YA). pap. 16.95 *(978-1-4787-1103-2(5))* Outskirts Pr., Inc.

Mistretta, Jay. Joe E, 1 vol. Gallet, Karl, illus. 2009. 19p. pap. 24.95 *(978-1-60749-850-6(2))* America Star Bks.

Mitchell, Marie & Smith, Mason. Squatch Watch & Other Stories. 2013. 130p. pap. 9.95 *(978-0-692-02010-4(1))* Smith, Mason.

Miyares, Daniel. Bring Me a Rock! Miyares, Daniel, illus. 2016. (ENG., Illus.). 40p. (J). (gr. -1-3). 17.99 *(978-1-4814-4602-0(9),* Simon & Schuster Bks. For Young Readers) Simon & Schuster Bks. For Young Readers.

Mlynowski, Sarah. Frogs & French Kisses. 2007. (Magic in Manhattan Ser.: No. 2). (ENG.). 304p. (YA). (gr. 7). pap. 8.99 *(978-0-385-73185-0(X),* Delacorte Pr.) Random Hse. Children's Bks.

—Parties & Potions. 2010. (Magic in Manhattan Ser.: No. 4). (ENG., Illus.). 368p. (YA). (gr. 7). pap. 10.99 *(978-0-385-73646-6(0),* Ember) Random Hse. Children's Bks.

—Spells & Sleeping Bags. 2008. (Magic in Manhattan Ser.: No. 3). (ENG.). 320p. (YA). (gr. 7-12). pap. 8.99 *(978-0-385-73388-5(7),* Delacorte Pr.) Random Hse. Children's Bks.

Modan, Rutu. Maya Makes a Mess. Modan, Rutu, illus. 2012. (ENG., Illus.). 32p. (J). (gr. -1-3). 12.95 *(978-1-935179-17-7(9))* TOON Books / RAW Junior, LLC.

Mogk, Matt. That's Not Your Mommy Anymore: A Zombie Tale. Wells, Aja, illus. 2011. (ENG.). 32p. pap. 10.00 *(978-1-56975-926-4(X))* Ulysses Pr.

Moisher, Phil. Long Before I Knew Better. 2011. 70p. pap. 19.95 *(978-1-4560-4007-9(3))* America Star Bks.

Molski, Carol. Swimming Sal. DePalma, Mary Newell, illus. 2009. 36p. (J). (gr. -1-3). 17.00 *(978-0-8028-5327-1(7),* Eerdmans Bks For Young Readers) Eerdmans, William B. Publishing Co.

Montanari, Susan McElroy. Who's the Grossest of Them All? Parker, Jake, illus. 2016. (ENG.). 40p. (J). (gr. -1-3). 17.99 *(978-0-553-51190-1(4),* Schwartz & Wade Bks.) Random Hse. Children's Bks.

Montes, Marisa. Juan Bobo Busca Trabajo, 1 vol. Cepeda, Joe, illus. 2006. (SPA.). 32p. (J). (gr. -1-4). pap. 6.99 *(978-0-06-113681-8(6),* Rayo) HarperCollins Pubs.

Moore, P. B. The Day the Buffalo Ran. 2008. 48p. pap. 16.95 *(978-1-60563-461-6(1))* America Star Bks.

Moore, S. D. The Adventures of PJ & Split Pea Vol. II: Nothing but the Tooth. 2010. 37p. (J). pap. 12.95 *(978-1-4327-1289-1(6))* Outskirts Pr., Inc.

More Gordon, Domenica. Archie. More Gordon, Domenica, illus. 2012. (ENG., Illus.). 48p. (J). (gr. -1-1). 18.89 *(978-1-59990-947-9(2),* 9781599909479, Bloomsbury USA Childrens) Bloomsbury Publishing USA.

Morgan, Angie. Shouty Arthur at the Seaside. 2016. (Shouty Arthur Ser.: 2). (ENG., Illus.). 32p. (J). (gr. -1-k). pap. 9.99 *(978-1-4052-6678-9(3))* Egmont Bks., Ltd. GBR. Dist: Independent Pubs. Group.

Morgan, Kerry. Lickety Lick. 2012. 32p. pap. 16.49 *(978-1-4685-5510-3(3))* AuthorHouse.

—Smile Rhymes. 2011. (Illus.). 32p. (gr. 1-2). pap. 13.99 *(978-1-4567-6339-8(3))* AuthorHouse.

Morgan, Matthew, et al. Yuck's Fart Club. Baines, Nigel, illus. 2013. (Yuck Ser.). (ENG.). 112p. (J). (gr. 2-5). 15.99 *(978-1-4424-8153-4(6),* Simon & Schuster/Paula Wiseman Bks.) Simon & Schuster/Paula Wiseman Bks.

Morris, Gerald. The Lioness & Her Knight. 2008. (Squire's Tales Ser.: 7). (ENG.). 352p. (J). (gr. 5-7). pap. 7.99 *(978-0-547-01485-2(6))* Houghton Mifflin Harcourt Publishing Co.

Morris, Jennifer E. Scholastic Reader Level 1: the Sea Monster: A Steve & Wessley Reader. 2014. (Scholastic Reader Level 1 Ser.). (ENG., Illus.). 32p. (J). (gr. -1-2). pap. 3.99 *(978-0-545-61482-5(1))* Scholastic, Inc.

Morris, Kimberly. Take Me to Your Weeder. Warrick, Jessica, illus. 2016. (How to Be an Earthling (r) Ser.: 3). (ENG.). 64p. (gr. 1-3). lib. bdg. 22.65 *(978-1-57565-824-7(0))* Kane Press, Inc.

—Take Me to Your Weeder: Responsibility. Warrick, Jessica, illus. 2016. (How to Be an Earthling (r) Ser.: 3). (ENG.). 64p. (gr. 1-3). 34.65 *(978-1-57565-826-1(7))* Kane Press, Inc.

Morris, Richard T. Piggypine. Jarvis, Peter, illus. 2017. (J). *(978-0-525-43000-1(8),* Dial Bks) Penguin Young Readers Group.

Morrison, Kevin. Frank Is a Chihuahua. De La Cruz, Erin Harris, illus. 2007. 32p. (J). (gr. 1-4). *(978-1-929039-43-2(3))* Ambassador Bks., Inc.

Mosel, Arlene. Tikki Tikki Tembo Book & CD Storytime Set. Lent, Blair, illus. unabr. ed. 2012. (ENG.). (J). 12.99 *(978-1-4272-3211-3(3),* 9781427232113) Macmillan Audio.

Moseley, Steven. The Trailer Park King. 2013. (ENG.). 48p. (J). pap. 8.95 *(978-1-4787-1765-2(3))* Outskirts Pr., Inc.

Moser, Lisa. Squirrel's Fun Day. Gorbachev, Valeri, illus. 2015. (Candlewick Sparks Ser.). (ENG.). 48p. (J). (gr. k-4). pap. 3.99 *(978-0-7636-7789-3(2))* Candlewick Pr.

—Squirrel's World. Gorbachev, Valeri, illus. 2013. (Candlewick Sparks Ser.). (ENG.). 48p. (J). (gr. k-4). pap. 3.99 *(978-0-7636-6644-6(0))* Candlewick Pr.

Moses, Will. Raining Cats & Dogs: A Collection of Irresistible Idioms & Illustrations to Tickle the Funny Bones. Moses, Will, illus. 2008. (ENG., Illus.). 40p. (J). (gr. k-3). 17.99 *(978-0-399-24233-5(3),* Philomel Bks.) Penguin Young Readers Group.

Mosesson, Connie. Lovey Dovey & the Makeover Mistake. 2008. 40p. pap. 16.50 *(978-1-60693-275-9(6),* Eloquent Bks.) Strategic Book Publishing & Rights Agency (SBPRA).

Moss, Marissa. Amelia's Boy Survival Guide. Moss, Marissa, illus. 2012. (Amelia Ser.). (ENG., Illus.). 80p. (J). (gr. 4-8). 9.99 *(978-1-4424-4084-5(8),* Simon & Schuster/Paula Wiseman Bks.) Simon & Schuster/Paula Wiseman Bks.

—Amelia's Guide to Babysitting. Moss, Marissa, illus. 2008. (Amelia Ser.). (ENG., Illus.). 80p. (J). (gr. 5-8). 9.99 *(978-1-4169-5051-6(6),* Simon & Schuster/Paula Wiseman Bks.) Simon & Schuster/Paula Wiseman Bks.

—Amelia's Itchy-Twitchy, Lovey-Dovey Summer at Camp Mosquito. Moss, Marissa, illus. 2008. (Amelia Ser.). (ENG., Illus.). 80p. (J). (gr. 5-8). 12.99 *(978-1-4169-4722-6(1),* Simon & Schuster/Paula Wiseman Bks.) Simon & Schuster/Paula Wiseman Bks.

—Amelia's Middle School Survival Guide: Amelia's Most Unforgettable Embarrassing Moments, Amelia's Guide to Gossip. Moss, Marissa, illus. 2009. (Amelia Ser.). (ENG., Illus.). 160p. (J). (gr. 5-8). 14.99 *(978-1-4169-7987-6(5),* Simon & Schuster/Paula Wiseman Bks.) Simon & Schuster/Paula Wiseman Bks.

—Amelia's Must-Keep Resolutions for the Best Year Ever! Moss, Marissa, illus. 2006. (Amelia Ser.). (ENG., Illus.). 40p. (J). (gr. 4-7). 12.99 *(978-1-4169-3361-8(1),* Simon & Schuster/Paula Wiseman Bks.) Simon & Schuster/Paula Wiseman Bks.

—Blood Diaries: Tales of a 6th-Grade Vampire. Moss, Marissa, illus. 2014. (ENG., Illus.). 136p. (J). (gr. 2-7). 13.00 *(978-1-939547-05-7(9))* Creston Bks.

—The Fake Friend! Moss, Marissa, illus. 2012. (Daphne's Diary of Daily Disasters Ser.). (ENG., Illus.). 96p. (J). (gr. 2-5). 9.99 *(978-1-4424-4014-2(7));* pap. 5.99 *(978-1-4424-4015-9(5))* Simon & Schuster/Paula Wiseman Bks. (Simon & Schuster/Paula Wiseman Bks.).

Moulton, Mark Kimball. Twisted Sistahs. Good, Karen H., illus. 2006. (ENG.). 32p. (J). (gr. 2-3). 14.95 *(978-0-8249-8676-6(8),* Ideal Pubns.) Worthy Publishing.

Mudaly, Jessica. And That's Just the Trouble with Cats! 2011. 116p. pap. 10.95 *(978-1-61204-186-5(8),* Eloquent Bks.) Strategic Book Publishing & Rights Agency (SBPRA).

Muir, Sabine. Meeting Wolfie: A Story about Mozart. 2006. 129p. pap. 19.95 *(978-1-4241-3968-2(6))* PublishAmerica, Inc.

Muldrow, Diane. Everything I Need to Know about Family I Learned from a Little Golden Book. 2017. (ENG., Illus.). 96p. (gr. 7-12). 9.99 *(978-0-553-53851-9(9),* Golden Bks.) Random Hse. Children's Bks.

Mule Days: Stories about Survivors of the Great Depression. 2004. (YA). lib. bdg. 22.50 net. *(978-0-9755117-0-1(X))* Hidden Forest Pubs.

Mulligan, Andy. Return to Ribblestrop. 2016. (Ribblestrop Ser.). (ENG., Illus.). 352p. (J). (gr. 3-7). 17.99 *(978-1-4424-9907-2(9),* Beach Lane Bks.) Beach Lane Bks.

—Ribblestrop. (Ribblestrop Ser.). (ENG., Illus.). (J). (gr. 3-7). 2016. 400p. pap. 7.99 *(978-1-4424-9905-8(2))* 2014. 384p. 16.99 *(978-1-4424-9904-1(4))* Beach Lane Bks. (Beach Lane Bks.).

—Ribblestrop Forever! 2016. (Ribblestrop Ser.). (ENG., Illus.). 320p. (J). (gr. 3-7). 16.99 *(978-1-4424-9910-2(9),* Beach Lane Bks.) Beach Lane Bks.

Munro, Marija. Mardi Loves Lipstick. 2009. 24p. pap. 11.49 *(978-1-60693-754-9(5),* Eloquent Bks.) Strategic Book Publishing & Rights Agency (SBPRA).

Munsch, Robert. Alligator Baby. 2004. (Illus.). (J). (gr. k-3). spiral bd. *(978-0-616-01730-2(8));* spiral bd. *(978-0-616-01731-9(6))* Canadian National Institute for the Blind/Institut National Canadien pour les Aveugles.

—Espera y Verás. Aguirre, Rigo, tr. from ENG. Martchenko, Michael, illus. 2004. (SPA.). 24p. (J). (gr. -1-2). pap. 5.95 *(978-1-55037-872-6(4),* 9781550378726) Annick Pr., Ltd. CAN. Dist: Publishers Group West (PGW).

—Get Out of Bed! 2004. (Illus.). (J). (gr. k-3). spiral bd. *(978-0-616-04557-2(3));* spiral bd. *(978-0-616-03049-3(5))* Canadian National Institute for the Blind/Institut National Canadien pour les Aveugles.

—I'm So Embarrassed! 2007. (J). 12.65 *(978-0-7569-7624-8(3))* Perfection Learning Corp.

—Makeup Mess. 2004. (Illus.). (J). (gr. k-3). spiral bd. *(978-0-616-11125-3(8))* Canadian National Institute for the Blind/Institut National Canadien pour les Aveugles.

—Makeup Mess. Martchenko, Michael, illus. 2004. (J). (gr. k-3). spiral bd. *(978-0-616-11124-6(X))* Canadian National Institute for the Blind/Institut National Canadien pour les Aveugles.

—More Pies! 2004. (Illus.). (J). (gr. k-3). spiral bd. *(978-0-616-14589-0(6))* Canadian National Institute for the Blind/Institut National Canadien pour les Aveugles.

—Mud Puddle. Petricic, Dusan, illus. 3rd ed. 2012. (Munsch for Kids Ser.). (ENG.). 32p. (J). (gr. -1-2). 19.95 *(978-1-55451-427-4(4),* 9781554514274) Annick Pr., Ltd. CAN. Dist: Publishers Group West (PGW).

—Smelly Socks. Martchenko, Michael, illus. 2005. (ENG.). 32p. (J). (gr. -1-3). pap. 4.99 *(978-0-439-64948-3(X),* Cartwheel Bks.) Scholastic, Inc.

—El Traje de Nieve de Tomás. Aguirre, Rigo, tr. from ENG. Martchenko, Michael, illus. 2004. (Munsch for Kids Ser.). (SPA.). 24p. (J). (gr. -1-2). pap. 7.95 *(978-1-55037-854-2(6),* 9781550378542) Annick Pr., Ltd. CAN. Dist: Publishers Group West (PGW).

Murakami, Jon & BeachHouse Publishing. Geckos Surf. 2007. (ENG.). 16p. (J). (gr. -1-5). bds. 7.95 *(978-1-933067-22-3(5))* Beachhouse Publishing, LLC.

Murphy, Brendán. Ready for School, Murphy? Murphy, Brendán, illus. 2015. (ENG., Illus.). 40p. (J). (gr. -1-k). 16.99 *(978-1-4847-0740-1(0))* Disney Publishing Worldwide.

Murphy, Jill. Five Minutes' Peace. Murphy, Jill, illus. 2012. (ENG., Illus.). 24p. (J). (gr. -1 — 1). bds. 7.99 *(978-0-399-25707-0(1),* G.P. Putnam's Sons Books for Young Readers) Penguin Young Readers Group.

—The Worst Witch Saves the Day. Murphy, Jill, illus. 2014. (Worst Witch Ser.). (ENG., Illus.). 160p. (J). (gr. 3-7). pap. 5.99 *(978-0-7636-7255-3(6))* Candlewick Pr.

—The Worst Witch to the Rescue. Murphy, Jill, illus. 2014. (Worst Witch Ser.). (ENG., Illus.). 176p. (J). (gr. 3-7). 14.99 *(978-0-7636-6999-7(7))* Candlewick Pr.

Murphy, Jim. Revenge of the Green Banana. 2017. (ENG.). 224p. (J). (gr. 5-7). 16.99 *(978-0-544-78677-6(7),* Clarion Bks.) Houghton Mifflin Harcourt Trade & Reference Pubs.

Murray, Alison. Hickory Dickory Dog. Murray, Alison, illus. 2014. (ENG., Illus.). 32p. (J). (-k). 16.99 *(978-0-7636-6826-6(5))* Candlewick Pr.

Murtagh, Ciaran. Prom King. Wesson, Tim, illus. 2017. (Fincredible Diary of Fin Spencer Ser.: 4). (ENG.). 224p. (J). (gr. 4-7). pap. 8.99 ***(978-1-84812-558-2(5))*** Bonnier Publishing GBR. Dist: Independent Pubs. Group.

Myer, Andy. Delia's Dull Day: An Incredibly Boring Story. 2012. (ENG., Illus.). 32p. (J). 16.95 *(978-1-58536-804-4(0))* Sleeping Bear Pr.

Myers, Bill. My Life as a Haunted Hamburger, Hold the Pickles, 1 vol. 2006. (Incredible Worlds of Wally Mcdoogle Ser.: 27). (ENG., Illus.). 128p. (gr. 3-7). per. 6.99 *(978-1-4003-0636-7(1))* Nelson, Thomas Inc.

—My Life as a Stupendously Stomped Soccer Star, 1 vol. 2006. (Incredible Worlds of Wally Mcdoogle Ser.: 26). (ENG.). 128p. (gr. 3-7). per. 6.99 *(978-1-4003-0635-0(3))* Nelson, Thomas Inc.

—My Life as a Supersized Superhero... with Slobber, 1 vol. 2007. (Incredible Worlds of Wally Mcdoogle Ser.: 28). (ENG.). 128p. (gr. 3-7). per. 6.99 *(978-1-4003-0637-4(X))* Nelson, Thomas Inc.

—My Life As a Tarantula Toe Tickler, 1 vol., Vol. 22. 2003. (Incredible Worlds of Wally Mcdoogle Ser.: 22). (ENG., Illus.). 128p. pap. 6.99 *(978-0-8499-5993-6(4))* Nelson, Thomas Inc.

Nadin, Joanna. Ordinary George. Serrano, Lucia, illus. 2016. (Reading Ladder Ser.). (ENG.). 48p. (J). (gr. k-2). pap. 7.99 *(978-1-4052-7542-2(1))* Egmont Bks., Ltd. GBR. Dist: Independent Pubs. Group.

Napoli, Donna Jo & Johnston, Shelagh. Hotel Jungle. Spengler, Kenneth, tr. Spengler, Kenneth, illus. 2004. 33p. (J). 15.95 *(978-1-59336-002-3(9));* pap. *(978-1-59336-003-0(7))* Mondo Publishing.

Naughton, Bill. Pony Boy. 2012. (ENG.). 256p. (YA). pap. 15.99 *(978-1-4482-0327-7(9),* 9781448203277, Bloomsbury Reader) Bloomsbury Publishing Plc GBR. Dist: Macmillan.

Nayeri, Daniel and Dina. Another Faust. 2010. (ENG., Illus.). 400p. (YA). (gr. 9). pap. 8.99 *(978-0-7636-4834-3(5))* Candlewick Pr.

Naylor, Phyllis Reynolds. The Boys Return. 2003. (Boys Against Girls Ser.: No. 7). 132p. (gr. 4-7). 16.00 *(978-0-7569-1381-6(0))* Perfection Learning Corp.

Nefflen, Marjorie E. My Big Sister Knows... 2012. 30p. (-18). 24.95 *(978-1-62709-509-9(8))* America Star Bks.

Nelson, Peter. Creature Keepers & the Swindled Soil-Soles. Rao, Rohitash, illus. 2015. (Creature Keepers Ser.: 2). (ENG.). 384p. (J). (gr. 3-7). 12.99 *(978-0-06-223645-6(8))* HarperCollins Pubs.

Nesbitt, Kenn. More Bears! Cummings, Troy, illus. 2017. (ENG.). 28p. (J). bds. 7.99 ***(978-1-4926-5467-4(1),*** Sourcebooks Jabberwocky) Sourcebooks, Inc.

Nesbitt, Kenn. The Ultimate Top Secret Guide to Taking over the World. Long, Ethan, illus. 2011. (ENG.). 208p. (J). (gr. 4-8). pap. 10.99 *(978-1-4022-3834-5(7),* Sourcebooks Jabberwocky) Sourcebooks, Inc.

Nesbø, Jo. Bubble in the Bathtub. Chace, Tara F., tr. Lowery, Mike, illus. 2011. (Doctor Proctor's Fart Powder Ser.). (ENG.). 448p. (J). (gr. 3-7). pap. 7.99 *(978-1-4169-7975-3(1),* Aladdin) Simon & Schuster Children's Publishing.

—Bubble in the Bathtub. Chace, Tara, tr. from NOR. Lowery, Mike, illus. 2011. (Doctor Proctor's Fart Powder Ser.). (ENG.). 432p. (J). (gr. 3-7). 17.99 *(978-1-4169-7974-6(3),* Aladdin) Simon & Schuster Children's Publishing.

—Doctor Proctor's Fart Powder. Chace, Tara F., tr. Lowery, Mike, illus. 2010. (Doctor Proctor's Fart Powder Ser.). (ENG.). 288p. (J). (gr. 3-7). pap. 7.99 *(978-1-4169-7973-9(5),* Aladdin) Simon & Schuster Children's Publishing.

—Doctor Proctor's Fart Powder. Chace, Tara, tr. from GER. Lowery, Mike, illus. 2009. (Doctor Proctor's Fart Powder Ser.). (ENG.). 272p. (J). (gr. 3-7). 17.99 *(978-1-4169-7972-2(7),* Aladdin) Simon & Schuster Children's Publishing.

—Doctor Proctor's Fart Powder. 2010. (Dr. Proctor's Fart Powder Ser.: 1). lib. bdg. 18.40 *(978-0-606-15419-2(1),* Turtleback) Turtleback Bks.

—The Magical Fruit. 2014. (Doctor Proctor's Fart Powder Ser.). (ENG., Illus.). 320p. (J). (gr. 3-7). pap. 7.99 *(978-1-4424-9343-8(7),* Aladdin) Simon & Schuster Children's Publishing.

—The Magical Fruit. Chace, Tara F., tr. from NOR. Lowery, Mike, illus. 2013. (Doctor Proctor's Fart Powder Ser.). (ENG.). 320p. (J). (gr. 3-7). 17.99 *(978-1-4424-9342-1(9),* Aladdin) Simon & Schuster Children's Publishing.

—Silent (but Deadly) Night. Lowery, Mike, illus. 2017. (J). pap. ***(978-1-5344-1000-8(7),*** Simon & Schuster/Paula Wiseman Bks.) Simon & Schuster/Paula Wiseman Bks.

Nesbø, Jo. Who Cut the Cheese? Chace, Tara F., tr. Lowery, Mike, illus. 2012. (Doctor Proctor's Fart Powder Ser.). (ENG.). 464p. (J). (gr. 3-7). pap. 7.99 *(978-1-4424-3308-3(6),* Aladdin) Simon & Schuster Children's Publishing.

—Who Cut the Cheese? Chace, Tara, tr. from NOR. Lowery, Mike, illus. 2012. (Doctor Proctor's Fart Powder Ser.). (ENG.). 464p. (J). (gr. 3-7). 17.99 *(978-1-4424-3307-6(8),* Aladdin) Simon & Schuster Children's Publishing.

Neville, Emily. It's Like This, Cat. Weiss, Emil, illus. 2017. (ENG.). 192p. (J). (gr. 2-6). pap. 5.95 *(978-0-486-81478-0(5))* Dover Pubns., Inc.

New Players Club LLC Staff, New Players Club L. L. C. Coco Boom Boom. 2006. 32p. 12.99 *(978-1-4116-8191-0(6))* Lulu Pr., Inc.

New York City High School Staff, ed. Sonny Paine. 2007. (ENG.). 86p. (J). (gr. 9-12). per. 8.00 *(978-0-9790073-5-4(6))* 826 Valencia.

Newell, Stephanie Jordy. Nite, Nite Farm. 2009. 24p. pap. 12.98 *(978-1-4490-0170-4(X))* AuthorHouse.

Newman, Barbara Johansen. Glamorous Glasses. 2012. (ENG.). 40p. (J). (gr. k-3). 16.95 *(978-1-59078-878-3(8))* Boyds Mills Pr.

Newman, Patrice Tomasetti. Where Oh Where? It's in My Hair! 2012. 26p. 24.95 *(978-1-4626-6284-5(6))* America Star Bks.

Nichols, Travis. Fowl Play. 2015. (ENG., Illus.). 40p. (J). (gr. k-3). 14.99 *(978-1-4521-3182-5(1))* Chronicle Bks. LLC.

Nichols, Tucker & Nichols, Jon, illus. Crabtree. 2013. (ENG.). 32p. (J). (gr. -1-3). 17.95 *(978-1-936365-82-1(0))* McSweeney's Publishing.

Nickel, Scott. Curse of the Red Scorpion, 1 vol. Harpster, Steve, illus. 2006. (Graphic Sparks Ser.). (ENG.). 40p. (gr. 1-3). 23.99 *(978-1-59889-034-1(4),* Graphic Sparks) Stone Arch Bks.

Nickelodeon. SpongeBob SquarePants: Goodnight Lagoon. 2014. (ENG.). 32p. (J). (-3). 15.99 *(978-1-4926-1669-6(9),* Sourcebooks Jabberwocky) Sourcebooks, Inc.

Nield, Joan. Children's Story Book. 2008. (Illus.). 24p. 11.04 *(978-1-4251-2449-6(6))* Trafford Publishing.

Nielsen, Jennifer A. Elliot & the Last Underworld War. Kendall, Gideon, illus. 2012. (ENG.). 208p. (J). (gr. 3-8). 12.99 *(978-1-4022-4021-8(X),* Sourcebooks Jabberwocky) Sourcebooks, Inc.

Nishimura, Kae. Dinah! 2004. 32p. 14.00 *(978-0-618-33613-5(3),* Clarion Bks.) Houghton Mifflin Harcourt Trade & Reference Pubs.

Nix, Jonathan J. Egghead: The Story of One Small Trout. 2008. 24p. pap. 24.95 *(978-1-60474-955-7(5))* America Star Bks.

Nobisso, Josephine. En Ingles, por Supuesto. Ziborova, Dasha, illus. 2003. Orig. Title: In English, of Course. (SPA & ENG.). 32p. (J). (gr. k-2). 16.95 *(978-0-940112-14-8(0))* Gingerbread Hse.

—En ingles, por Supuesto. Ziborova, Dasha, illus. 2003. Orig. Title: In English, of Course. (SPA & ENG.). 32p. (J). (gr. k-2). pap. 8.95 *(978-0-940112-16-2(7))* Gingerbread Hse.

—In English, of Course. Ziborova, Dasha, illus. 2003.Tr. of En Ingles, Por Supuesto. 32p. (J). (gr. -1). (SPA & ENG.). 16.95 *(978-0-940112-07-0(8));* (ENG.). pap. 8.95 *(978-0-940112-08-7(6))* Gingerbread Hse.

Nobleman, Marc Tyler. The Chupacabra Ate the Candelabra. Aranda, Ana, illus. 2017. (ENG.). 32p. (J). (gr. k-3). 17.99 *(978-0-399-17443-8(5),* Nancy Paulsen Books) Penguin Young Readers Group.

Nolan, Lucy. Bad to the Bone, 0 vols. Reed, Mike, illus. 2011. (Down Girl & Sit Ser.: 3). (ENG.). 64p. (J). (gr. 1-4). pap. 9.99 *(978-0-7614-5834-0(4),* 9780761458340, Amazon Children's Publishing) Amazon Publishing.

—A Fairy in a Dairy, 0 vols. Bryant, Laura J., illus. 2013. (ENG.). 33p. (J). (gr. -1-2). pap. 9.99 *(978-1-4778-1678-3(X),* 9781477816783, Amazon Children's Publishing) Amazon Publishing.

—Home on the Range, 0 vols. Reed, Mike, illus. 2010. (Down Girl & Sit Ser.: 4). (ENG.). 64p. (J). (gr. 1-4). 14.99 *(978-0-7614-5649-0(X),* 9780761456490, Amazon Children's Publishing) Amazon Publishing.

—On the Road, 0 vols. Reed, Mike, illus. unabr. ed. 2009. (Down Girl & Sit Ser.: 2). (ENG.). 68p. (J). (gr. 1-4). pap. 9.99 *(978-0-7614-5572-1(8),* 9780761455721, Amazon Children's Publishing) Amazon Publishing.

—Smarter Than Squirrels, 0 vols. Reed, Mike, illus. unabr. ed. 2009. (Down Girl & Sit Ser.: 1). (ENG.). 68p. (J). (gr. 1-4). pap. 9.99 *(978-0-7614-5571-4(X),* 9780761455714, Amazon Children's Publishing) Amazon Publishing.

Nolen, Jerdine. Plantzilla Goes to Camp. Catrow, David, illus. 2006. (ENG.). 32p. (J). (gr. k-3). 17.99 *(978-0-689-86803-0(0),* Simon & Schuster/Paula Wiseman Bks.) Simon & Schuster/Paula Wiseman Bks.

Nolen, Jerdine & Keliher, Brian. Plantzilla. Catrow, David, illus. 2005. (ENG.). 32p. (J). (gr. -1-3). reprint ed. pap. 7.99 *(978-0-15-205392-5(1))* Houghton Mifflin Harcourt Publishing Co.

Norsgaard, E. Jaediker. How Krokken & Poppen Made Peace. 2008. 31p. pap. 24.95 *(978-1-60672-426-2(6))* America Star Bks.

North, Laura. The Big Bad Wolf & the Robot Pig. 2014. (ENG., Illus.). 32p. (J). *(978-0-7787-1291-6(5))* Crabtree Publishing Co.

—Cinderella's Big Foot. 2014. (ENG., Illus.). 32p. (J). *(978-0-7787-0440-9(8));* pap. *(978-0-7787-0448-5(3))* Crabtree Publishing Co.

—Jack & the Bean Pie. 2014. (ENG., Illus.). 32p. (J). *(978-0-7787-0441-6(6));* pap. *(978-0-7787-0449-2(1))* Crabtree Publishing Co.

—The Princess & the Frozen Peas. 2014. (ENG., Illus.). 32p. (J). *(978-0-7787-0446-1(7));* pap. *(978-0-7787-0481-2(5))* Crabtree Publishing Co.

—Sleeping Beauty — 100 Years Later. 2014. (ENG., Illus.). 32p. (J). *(978-0-7787-0444-7(0));* pap. *(978-0-7787-0479-9(3))* Crabtree Publishing Co.

North, Lynne. Gerties Gets It Right. 2008. 204p. pap. *(978-1-84923-231-9(8))* YouWriteOn.

Norton, Tamra. Comfortable in My Own Genes: A Novel. 2004. 175p. pap. 15.95 *(978-1-55517-772-0(7))* Cedar Fort, Inc./CFI Distribution.

Nthemuka, Patty Froese. Hyacinth Doesn't Go to Jail: And, Hyacinth Doesn't Miss Christmas. 2009. (J). pap. 10.99 *(978-0-8163-2372-2(0))* Pacific Pr. Publishing Assn.

Numeroff, Laura Joffe. If You Give a Cat a Cupcake. Bond, Felicia, illus. 2008. (If You Give... Ser.). 32p. (J). (gr. -1-3). lib. bdg. 17.89 *(978-0-06-028325-4(4))* HarperCollins Pubs.

—If You Give a Cat a Cupcake. Bond, Felicia, illus. 2008. (If You Give... Ser.). (ENG.). 32p. (J). (gr. -1-3). 17.99 *(978-0-06-028324-7(6))* HarperCollins Pubs.

—If You Give a Dog a Donut. Bond, Felicia, illus. 2011. (If You Give... Ser.). 40p. (J). (gr. -1-3). 17.89 *(978-0-06-026684-4(8));* (ENG.). 17.99 *(978-0-06-026683-7(X))* HarperCollins Pubs.

—A Mouse Cookie First Library: If You Give a Mouse a Cookie; If You Take a Mouse to School. Bond, Felicia, illus. 2007. (If You Give... Ser.). (ENG.). 100p. (J). (gr. -1-2). bds. 15.99 *(978-0-06-117479-7(3),* HarperFestival) HarperCollins Pubs.

Nunez, Alonso. El Invencible y Malvado Dragon Curiambro. (SPA.). (J). (gr. 2-4). 18.95 *(978-968-494-096-3(3),* CI30452) Centro de Informacion y Desarrollo de la Comunicacion y la Literatura MEX. Dist: AIMS International Bks., Inc., Lectorum Pubns., Inc.

Nuttbucket, Oliver S., III. A Boy Scout's Handbook of Madcap Tales. Glover, Robert, illus. 2003. 48p. (YA). per. 7.95 *(978-0-9741310-0-9(8)*, 0-9741310-0-8) Lost Scout Pr.

Nybo, B. J. Elmo Jackson Great Yellow Ball. 2005. *(978-0-9742322-0-1(3))* New Art & Vision, LLC.

Nyikos, Stacy. Waggers. Anegon, Tamara, illus. 2014. (ENG.). 32p. (J). (gr. -1-k). 16.95 *(978-1-62914-629-4(3)*, Sky Pony Pr.) Skyhorse Publishing Co., Inc.

Oaklee, Mammy. My Keyboard Was Hi~Jacked! 2013. 40p. pap. *(978-1-4602-2616-2(X))* FriesenPress.

O'brien, John. Look ... Look Again! 2012. (ENG.). 64p. (J). (gr. 3). 18.95 *(978-1-59078-894-3(X))* Boyds Mills Pr.

Oceanak, Karla. Egghead. Spanjer, Kendra, illus. 2012. (Aldo Zelnick Comic Novel Ser.: 5). (ENG.). 160p. (gr. 1-8). 12.95 *(978-1-934649-17-6(1))* Bailiwick Pr.

—Finicky. Spanjer, Kendra, illus. 2012. (Aldo Zelnick Comic Novel Ser.: 6). (ENG.). 160p. (J). (gr. 3-7). 12.95 *(978-1-934649-24-4(4))* Bailiwick Pr.

—Glitch. Spanjer, Kendra, illus. 2012. (Aldo Zelnick Comic Novel Ser.: 7). (ENG.). 160p. (J). (gr. 3-7). 12.95 *(978-1-934649-25-1(2))* Bailiwick Pr.

—Kerfuffle. Spanjer, Kendra, illus. 2015. (Aldo Zelnick Comic Novel Ser.: 11). (ENG.). 160p. (gr. 1-8). 12.95 *(978-1-934649-53-4(8))* Bailiwick Pr.

O'connell, Tyne. A Royal Match. 2011. (Calypso Chronicles Ser.). (ENG.). 512p. (YA). pap. 9.99 *(978-1-59990-751-2(8)*, 9781599907512, Bloomsbury USA Childrens) Bloomsbury Publishing USA.

O'Connor, Jane. Fancy Nancy: Tea for Two. Glasser, Robin Preiss, illus. 2012. (Fancy Nancy Ser.). (ENG.). 24p. (J). (gr. -1-3). pap. 3.99 *(978-0-06-123597-9(0)*, HarperFestival) HarperCollins Pubs.

—Fancy Nancy - Nancy Clancy Chapter. Glasser, Robin Preiss, illus. 2017. (Nancy Clancy Ser.: 8). 144p. (J). (gr. 1-5). 9.99 *(978-0-06-226973-7(9))* HarperCollins Pubs.

—Fancy Nancy & the Missing Easter Bunny. Glasser, Robin Preiss, illus. 2017. (Fancy Nancy Ser.). 24p. (J). (gr. -1-3). pap. 4.99 *(978-0-06-237792-0(2)*, HarperFestival) HarperCollins Pubs.

—Fancy Nancy & the Sensational Babysitter. Glasser, Robin Preiss et al, illus. 2010. (Fancy Nancy Ser.). (ENG.). 24p. (J). (gr. -1-3). pap. 3.99 *(978-0-06-170378-2(8)*, HarperFestival) HarperCollins Pubs.

—Fancy Nancy & the Sensational Babysitter. 2010. (Fancy Nancy Picture Bks.). (J). lib. bdg. 13.55 *(978-0-606-14840-5(X)*, Turtleback) Turtleback Bks.

—Fancy Nancy & the Wedding of the Century. Glasser, Robin Preiss, illus. 2014. (Fancy Nancy Ser.). 32p. (J). (gr. -1-3). (ENG.). 17.99 *(978-0-06-208319-7(8))*; lib. bdg. 18.89 *(978-0-06-208320-3(1))* HarperCollins Pubs.

—Fancy Nancy: It's Backward Day! Glasser, Robin Preiss, illus. 2016. (I Can Read Level 1 Ser.). 32p. (J). (gr. -1-3). pap. 3.99 *(978-0-06-226981-2(X))* HarperCollins Pubs.

—Fancy Nancy: Jojo & the Big Mess. Glasser, Robin Preiss, illus. 2017. (My First I Can Read Ser.). 32p. (J). (gr. -1-3). pap. 3.99 *(978-0-06-237798-2(1))* HarperCollins Pubs.

—Fancy Nancy Petite Library. Glasser, Robin Preiss, illus. 2010. (Fancy Nancy Ser.). (ENG.). 32p. (J). (gr. k-3). 14.99 *(978-0-06-191527-7(0)*, HarperFestival) HarperCollins Pubs.

—Halloween... or Bust! Glasser, Robin Preiss & Bracken, Carolyn, illus. 2009. (Fancy Nancy Ser.). (ENG.). 24p. (J). (gr. -1-3). pap. 4.99 *(978-0-06-123595-5(4)*, HarperFestival) HarperCollins Pubs.

—Heart to Heart. Glasser, Robin Preiss & Bracken, Carolyn, illus. 2009. (Fancy Nancy Ser.). (ENG.). 24p. (J). (gr. -1-3). pap. 4.99 *(978-0-06-123596-2(2)*, HarperFestival) HarperCollins Pubs.

—Nancy Clancy - Secret of the Silver Key. Glasser, Robin Preiss, illus. 2015. (Nancy Clancy Ser.: 4). (ENG.). 144p. (J). (gr. 1-5). pap. 4.99 *(978-0-06-208422-4(4))* HarperCollins Pubs.

—Nancy Clancy, Star of Stage & Screen. Glasser, Robin Preiss, illus. 2015. (Nancy Clancy Ser.: Bk. 5). (ENG.). 128p. (J). (gr. 1-5). 9.99 *(978-0-06-226964-5(X))* HarperCollins Pubs.

—Nancy la Elegante, 1 vol. Valenzuela, Liliana, tr. from ENG. Glasser, Robin Preiss, illus. 2008. (Fancy Nancy Ser.). (SPA.). 32p. (J). (gr. -1-2). 17.99 *(978-0-06-143528-7(7))* HarperCollins Pubs.

—Tea for Two. Glasser, Robin Preiss, illus. 2012. (Fancy Nancy Picture Bks.). (J). lib. bdg. 13.55 *(978-0-606-23577-8(9)*, Turtleback) Turtleback Bks.

O'Connor, Jane & Preiss-Glasser, Robin. It's Backward Day! Enik, Ted, illus. 2016. 32p. (J). *(978-1-4806-9929-8(2))* Harper & Row Ltd.

Odanaka, Barbara. A Crazy Day at the Critter Café. White, Lee, illus. 2009. (ENG.). 32p. (J). (gr. -1-3). 17.99 *(978-1-4169-3914-6(8)*, McElderry, Margaret K. Bks.) McElderry, Margaret K. Bks.

Ode, Eric. Bigfoot Does Not Like Birthday Parties. Temairik, Jaime, illus. 2015. (ENG.). 40p. (J). (gr. -1-3). 16.99 *(978-1-63217-004-0(3)*, Little Bigfoot) Sasquatch Bks.

O'Doherty, David. Danger Is Everywhere: A Handbook for Avoiding Danger. Judge, Chris, illus. 2017. (Danger Is Everywhere Ser.: 1). (ENG.). 272p. (J). (gr. 3-7). pap. 6.99 *(978-0-316-50183-5(2))* Little, Brown Bks. for Young Readers.

—Danger Is Still Everywhere: Beware of the Dog! Judge, Chris, illus. 2015. (Danger Is Everywhere Ser.: 2). (ENG.). 224p. (J). (gr. 3-7). 12.99 *(978-0-316-29934-3(0))* Little, Brown Bks. for Young Readers.

Odom, Rebecca. Grandpa & the Raccoon. Tebbit, Jake, illus. 2009. 36p. pap. 24.95 *(978-1-60749-912-1(6))* America Star Bks.

O'Donnell, Barbara. Mrs Mumble, Bumble, Grumble. 2003. (Illus.). (J). pap. 5.98 *(978-0-89914-503-7(5)*, 503-5) 3rd Party Publishing Co.

O'Donnell, Tom. Hamstersaurus Rex. Miller, Tim, illus. 2016. (Hamstersaurus Rex Ser.: 1). 272p. (J). (gr. 3-7). 12.99 *(978-0-06-237754-8(X))* HarperCollins Pubs.

O'Donnell, Tom. Hamstersaurus Rex vs. Squirrel Kong. Miller, Tim, illus. 2017. (Hamstersaurus Rex Ser.: 2). 304p. (J). (gr. 3-7). 12.99 ***(978-0-06-237756-2(6))*** HarperCollins Pubs.

Offill, Jenny. While You Were Napping. Blitt, Barry, illus. 2014. (ENG.). 40p. (J). (gr. -1-3). 16.99 *(978-0-375-86572-5(1)*, Schwartz & Wade Bks.) Random Hse. Children's Bks.

—11 Experiments That Failed. Carpenter, Nancy, illus. 2011. (ENG.). 40p. (J). (gr. -1-3). 17.99 *(978-0-375-84762-2(6)*, Schwartz & Wade Bks.) Random Hse. Children's Bks.

Ogden, Charles. Frost Bites. Carton, Rick, illus. 2008. (Edgar & Ellen Nodyssey Ser.: 2). (ENG.). 192p. (J). (gr. 3-7). 23.99 *(978-1-4169-5464-4(3)*, Simon & Schuster/Paula Wiseman Bks.) Simon & Schuster/Paula Wiseman Bks.

—Hot Air. Carton, Rick, illus. 2008. (Edgar & Ellen Nodyssey Ser.: 1). (ENG.). 192p. (J). (gr. 3-7). 9.99 *(978-1-4169-5465-1(1)*, Aladdin) Simon & Schuster Children's Publishing.

—Nod's Limbs. Carton, Rick, illus. 2007. (Edgar & Ellen Ser.: 6). (ENG.). 224p. (J). (gr. 3-7). 24.99 *(978-1-4169-1501-0(X)*, Simon & Schuster/Paula Wiseman Bks.) Simon & Schuster/Paula Wiseman Bks.

—Pet's Revenge. Carton, Rick, illus. 2006. (Edgar & Ellen Ser.: 4). (ENG.). 192p. (J). (gr. 3-7). 23.99 *(978-1-4169-1408-2(0)*, Simon & Schuster/Paula Wiseman Bks.) Simon & Schuster/Paula Wiseman Bks.

—Rare Beasts. Carton, Rick, illus. 2006. (Edgar & Ellen Ser.: 1). (ENG.). 144p. (J). (gr. 3-7). 22.99 *(978-1-4169-1409-9(9)*, Aladdin) Simon & Schuster Children's Publishing.

—Tourist Trap. Carton, Rick, illus. 2006. (Edgar & Ellen Ser.: 2). (ENG.). 176p. (J). (gr. 3-7). 23.99 *(978-1-4169-1411-2(0)*, Simon & Schuster/Paula Wiseman Bks.) Simon & Schuster/Paula Wiseman Bks.

—Under Town. Carton, Rick, illus. 2006. (Edgar & Ellen Ser.: 3). (ENG.). 160p. (J). (gr. 3-7). 22.99 *(978-1-4169-1412-9(9)*, Simon & Schuster/Paula Wiseman Bks.) Simon & Schuster/Paula Wiseman Bks.

Ogden, Charles, ed. Edgar & Ellen Graphic Novelty: A Comics Collection. 2009. (Edgar & Ellen Ser.). (ENG.). 112p. (J). (gr. 3-7). pap. 7.99 *(978-1-4169-5004-2(4)*, Simon & Schuster/Paula Wiseman Bks.) Simon & Schuster/Paula Wiseman Bks.

Ogilvy, Ian. Measle & the Dragodon. 2006. 344p. (J). (gr. 3-8). per. 6.99 *(978-0-06-058690-4(7)*, Harper Trophy) HarperCollins Pubs.

O'Hara, Mo. Jurassic Carp. Jagucki, Marek, illus. 2017. (My Big Fat Zombie Goldfish Ser.: 6). (ENG.). 224p. (J). pap. 6.99 ***(978-1-250-10260-7(X)***, 9781250102607) Square Fish.

O'Hely, Eileen. Penny the Pencil. Phelan, Nicky, illus. 2005. (ENG.). 200p. (J). pap. 13.95 *(978-1-85635-475-2(X))* Mercier Pr., Ltd., The IRL. Dist: Dufour Editions, Inc.

Oirich, Alan. The Amnesia Countdown. Randall, Ron, illus. 2003. (Jewish Hero Corps. Ser.: 1). 24p. (J). pap. 3.95 *(978-1-932443-06-6(1)*, JHC1, Shayach Comics) Judaica Pr., Inc., The.

Oldfield, Jenny. Don't Make Me Laugh, Liam. Layton, Neal, illus. (ENG.). 128p. (J). pap. 8.99 *(978-0-340-85107-4(4))* Macmillan Pubs., Ltd. GBR. Dist: Trafalgar Square Publishing.

Oliver, Ilanit. Are You My Daddy? Parker-Rees, Guy, illus. 2015. (ENG.). 16p. (J). (gr. -1-k). bds. 8.99 *(978-0-545-77558-8(2)*, Cartwheel Bks.) Scholastic, Inc.

Oliver, Lin. Attack of the Growling Eyeballs. Gilpin, Stephen, illus. 2009. (Who Shrunk Daniel Funk? Ser.: 1). (ENG.). 160p. (J). (gr. 3-7). pap. 6.99 *(978-1-4169-0958-3(3)*, Simon & Schuster Bks. For Young Readers) Simon & Schuster Bks. For Young Readers.

—Escape of the Mini-Mummy. Gilpin, Stephen, illus. 2009. (Who Shrunk Daniel Funk? Ser.: 2). (ENG.). 160p. (J). (gr. 3-7). pap. 8.99 *(978-1-4169-0960-6(5)*, Simon & Schuster Bks. For Young Readers) Simon & Schuster Bks. For Young Readers.

—Revenge of the Itty-Bitty Brothers. Gilpin, Stephen, illus. (Who Shrunk Daniel Funk? Ser.: 3). (ENG.). 176p. (J). (gr. 3-7). 2010. pap. 6.99 *(978-1-4169-0962-0(1))* 2009. 14.99 *(978-1-4169-0961-3(3))* Simon & Schuster Bks. For Young Readers. (Simon & Schuster Bks. For Young Readers).

—Secret of the Super-Small Superstar. Gilpin, Stephen, illus. 2010. (Who Shrunk Daniel Funk? Ser.: 4). (ENG.). 160p. (J). (gr. 3-7). 14.99 *(978-1-4169-0963-7(X)*, Simon & Schuster Bks. For Young Readers) Simon & Schuster Bks. For Young Readers.

Oliver, Lin & Winkler, Henry. My Book of Pickles... Oops, I Mean Lists. Heitz, Tim, illus. 2014. (Hank Zipzer Ser.). (ENG.). 144p. (J). (gr. 3-7). 5.99 *(978-0-448-48361-0(0)*, Grosset & Dunlap) Penguin Young Readers Group.

Oliver, Lin, et al. There's a Zombie in My Bathtub #5. Garrett, Scott, illus. 2015. (Here's Hank Ser.: 5). (ENG.). 128p. (J). (gr. 1-3). bds. 5.99 *(978-0-448-48512-6(5)*, Grosset & Dunlap) Penguin Young Readers Group.

Olker, Constance. The Punctuation Pals Go Snow Skiing. Guzman, Minerva, illus. 2005. 22p. (J). (gr. -1-3). per. 18.95 *(978-1-933449-14-2(4))* Nightengale Pr.

—The Punctuation Pals Go Snow Skiing. l.t. ed. 2005. (Illus.). (J). per. 17.95 *(978-0-9761289-7-7(7))* Nightengale Pr.

Olson, Tod. How to Get Rich on the Oregon Trail. Proch, Gregory & Allred, Scott, illus. 2009. (How to Get Rich Ser.). (ENG.). 48p. (J). (gr. 5-9). lib. bdg. 27.90 *(978-1-4263-0413-2(7)*, National Geographic Children's Bks.) National Geographic Society.

Olswanger, Anna. Shlemiel Crooks. Goodman Koz, Paula, illus. 2008. 36p. (J). pap. 11.95 *(978-1-58838-236-8(2)*, Junebug Bks.) NewSouth, Inc.

O'Malley, Kevin. Backpack Stories. O'Malley, Kevin, illus. 2009. (ENG., Illus.). 32p. (J). (gr. 2-3). 16.99 *(978-0-8075-0504-5(8))* Whitman, Albert & Co.

—Herbert Fieldmouse, Secret Agent. 2003. (Illus.). 32p. (J). pap. *(978-1-59336-043-6(6))*; (gr. 1-6). 15.95 *(978-1-59336-042-9(8))* Mondo Publishing.

—Mount Olympus Basketball. 2004. (Illus.). 32p. (J). (gr. 2-6). 16.85 *(978-0-8027-8845-0(9))* Walker & Co.

—Once upon a Cool Motorcycle Dude. O'Malley, Kevin et al, illus. 2005. (ENG.). 32p. (J). (gr. 1-5). 16.99 *(978-0-8027-8947-1(1)*, 9780802789471, Bloomsbury USA Childrens) Bloomsbury Publishing USA.

One Cool Friend. 2014. pap. 16.99 *(978-0-545-67554-3(5))* Scholastic, Inc.

O'Neil, Dave. Lies Your Parents Tell You. Morris, Kiran, illus. 2005. 160p. pap. *(978-0-7344-0292-9(9)*, Lothian Children's Bks.) Hachette Australia.

Oram, Hiawyn. My Unwilling Witch Gets a Makeover. Warburton, Sarah, illus. 2010. (Rumblewick's Diary Ser.: 4). (ENG.). 112p. (J). (gr. 1-4). 7.99 *(978-0-316-03462-3(2))* Little, Brown Bks. for Young Readers.

Orloff, Karen Kaufman. I Wanna Go Home. Catrow, David, illus. 2014. (ENG.). 32p. (J). (gr. k-3). 16.99 *(978-0-399-25407-9(2)*, G.P. Putnam's Sons Books for Young Readers) Penguin Young Readers Group.

—I Wanna New Room. Catrow, David, III, illus. 2010. (ENG.). 32p. (J). (gr. k-3). 16.99 *(978-0-399-25405-5(6)*, G.P. Putnam's Sons Books for Young Readers) Penguin Young Readers Group.

Ormondroyd, Edward. David & the Phoenix. Raysor, Joan, illus. 2012. (ENG.). 191p. (J). (gr. 3-6). pap. 2.99 *(978-1-930900-58-5(9))* Purple Hse. Pr.

—David & the Phoenix. 2009. 76p. (gr. 4-7). pap. 4.75 *(978-1-60459-691-5(0))* Wilder Pubns., Corp.

Orr, Leah. Messy Tessy. 2009. 36p. pap. 17.99 *(978-1-4389-9398-0(6))* AuthorHouse.

Orr, Wendy. Mokie & Bik Go to Sea. Bean, Jonathan, illus. 2010. (ENG.). 80p. (J). (gr. 2-5). 15.99 *(978-0-8050-8174-9(7)*, 9780805081749, Holt, Henry & Co. Bks. For Young Readers) Holt, Henry & Co.

Orshoski, Paul. We Both Read Bilingual Edition-The Mouse in My House/un Raton en Mi Casa. Canetti, Yanitzia, tr. from ENG. Ebbeler, Jeffrey, illus. 2014. (We Both Read - Level 1 (Quality) Ser.). (ENG & SPA.). 44p. (J). (gr. 1). pap. 4.99 *(978-1-60115-056-1(3))* Treasure Bay, Inc.

—We Both Read-The Mouse in My House. Ebbeler, Jeffrey, illus. 2012. 44p. (J). 9.95 *(978-1-60115-257-2(4))*; pap. 4.99 *(978-1-60115-258-9(2))* Treasure Bay, Inc.

—We Read Phonics-Who Took the Cookbook? Light, Kelly, illus. 2012. 32p. (J). 9.95 *(978-1-60115-347-0(3))*; pap. 4.99 *(978-1-60115-348-7(1))* Treasure Bay, Inc.

Osterweil, Adam. The Amulet of Komondor. Thorpe, Peter, illus. 2003. (ENG.). 112p. (J). (gr. 4-6). 15.95 *(978-1-886910-81-2(2)*, Lemniscaat) Boyds Mills Pr.

Ostow, Micol. Gettin' Lucky. (Romantic Comedies Ser.). (ENG.). 256p. (YA). (gr. 9). 2012. pap. 12.99 *(978-1-4424-8568-6(X))* 2007. mass mkt. 6.99 *(978-1-4169-3536-0(3))* Simon Pulse. (Simon Pulse).

—Louise Trapeze Can SO Save the Day. Barrager, Brigette, illus. 2016. (Louise Trapeze Ser.). (ENG.). 112p. (J). (gr. 1-4). 5.99 *(978-0-553-49750-2(2))*; 14.99 *(978-0-553-49747-2(2))* Random Hse. Children's Bks. (Random Hse. Bks. for Young Readers).

—30 Guys in 30 Days. 2005. (Romantic Comedies Ser.). (ENG.). 304p. (YA). pap. 6.99 *(978-1-4169-0278-2(3)*, Simon Pulse) Simon Pulse.

Ostrovski, Emil. The Paradox of Vertical Flight. 2013. (ENG.). 272p. (YA). (gr. 9). 17.99 *(978-0-06-223852-8(3)*, Greenwillow Bks.) HarperCollins Pubs.

Overstreet, Tommy & Vest, Dale G. The Graham Cracker Kid & the Calico Girl. Anderson, Jesse, illus. 2012. 46p. 12.95 *(978-1-62016-014-5(5))* AWOC.COM.

Owen, Anna. A Day Out. Hammond, Andy, illus. 2005. (Collins Big Cat Ser.). (ENG.). 80p. (J). (gr. -1-k). pap. 5.99 *(978-0-00-718555-9(3))* HarperCollins Pubs. Ltd. GBR. Dist: Independent Pubs. Group.

Owens, Greg. Rupert the Wrong-Word Pirate. Beaky, Suzanne, illus. 2006. (J). *(978-1-58987-143-4(X))* Kindermusik International.

Oxenbury, Helen, illus. We're Going on a Bear Hunt. 2004. 33p. (J). *(978-1-85269-719-8(9))*; *(978-1-85269-713-6(X))*; (ENG & ARA.). pap. *(978-1-85269-707-5(5))* Mantra Lingua.

Page, Louise. Furballs' Fables. 2008. 100p. pap. 17.50 *(978-1-4092-1068-9(5))* Lulu Pr., Inc.

Paiba, Helen, ed. Funny Stories for 5 Year Olds. 2016. (ENG., Illus.). 224p. (J). (gr. k-2). 8.99 *(978-1-5098-0493-1(5))* Pan Macmillan GBR. Dist: Independent Pubs. Group.

—Funny Stories for 6 Year Olds. 2016. (ENG., Illus.). 272p. (J). (gr. k-2). 8.99 *(978-1-5098-0495-5(1))* Pan Macmillan GBR. Dist: Independent Pubs. Group.

Palahicky, Sophia. Kid's Reading Craze - a Collection of 20 Short Stories. 2013. 64p. pap. *(978-1-4602-1576-0(1))* FriesenPress.

Palatini, Margie. Bad Boys Get Cookie! 2007. (J). (gr. k-3). 27.95 incl. audio compact disk *(978-0-8045-6957-6(6))*; 29.95 incl. audio compact disk *(978-0-8045-4180-0(9))* Spoken Arts, Inc.

—Bad Boys Get Henpecked! Cole, Henry, illus. 2009. (ENG.). 32p. (J). (gr. -1-2). 17.99 *(978-0-06-074433-5(2)*, Tegen, Katherine Bks) HarperCollins Pubs.

—Boo-Hoo Moo. Graves, Keith, illus. 2009. 32p. (J). (gr. -1-3). lib. bdg. 18.89 *(978-0-06-114376-2(6))* HarperCollins Pubs.

—The Cheese. Johnson, Steve & Fancher, Lou, illus. 2007. (ENG.). 32p. (J). (gr. -1-2). 17.99 *(978-0-06-052630-6(0)*, Tegen, Katherine Bks) HarperCollins Pubs.

—Earthquack! Moser, Barry, illus. 2005. (ENG.). 32p. (J). (gr. -1-3). 7.99 *(978-1-4169-0260-7(0)*, Simon & Schuster Bks. For Young Readers) Simon & Schuster Bks. For Young Readers.

—Goldie & the Three Hares. Davis, Jack E., illus. 2011. (ENG.). 32p. (J). (gr. -1-2). 16.99 *(978-0-06-125314-0(6)*, Tegen, Katherine Bks) HarperCollins Pubs.

—Moosestache. 32p. pap. *(978-0-7868-1497-8(7))* Hyperion Bks. for Children.

—Oink? Cole, Henry, illus. 2006. (ENG.). 40p. (J). (gr. -1-3). 17.99 *(978-0-689-86258-8(X)*, Simon & Schuster Bks. For Young Readers) Simon & Schuster Bks. For Young Readers.

—Piggie Pie!, 1 vol. Fine, Howard, illus. 2008. (Read along Book & CD Ser.). (ENG.). 32p. (J). (gr. -1-3). audio compact disk 10.99 *(978-0-547-18178-3(7))* Houghton Mifflin Harcourt Publishing Co.

—The Three Silly Billies. Moser, Barry, illus. 2005. (ENG.). 32p. (J). (gr. -1-3). 17.99 *(978-0-689-85862-8(0)*, Simon & Schuster Bks. For Young Readers) Simon & Schuster Bks. For Young Readers.

—Under a Pig Tree: A History of the Noble Fruit. Groenink, Chuck, illus. 2015. (ENG.). 40p. (J). (gr. -1-3). 16.95 *(978-1-4197-1488-7(0)*, Abrams Bks. for Young Readers) Abrams, Inc.

—The Zoey Zone. Palatini, Margie, illus. (ENG., Illus.). 192p. (J). (gr. 3-6). 2010. pap. 6.99 *(978-0-06-113900-0(9))* 2008. 10.99 *(978-0-06-113898-0(3))* HarperCollins Pubs. (Tegen, Katherine Bks).

Palatini, Margie & Davis, Jack E. Sweet Tooth. Davis, Jack E., illus. 2004. (ENG., Illus.). 40p. (J). (gr. -1-3). 18.99 *(978-0-689-85159-9(6)*, Simon & Schuster Bks. For Young Readers) Simon & Schuster Bks. For Young Readers.

Pallotta, Jerry. Santa Pups. Terry, Will, illus. 2016. (ENG.). 32p. (J). (gr. -1-k). 6.99 *(978-0-545-48479-4(0))* Scholastic, Inc.

—What I Saw in the Teachers' Lounge. McWilliam, Howard, illus. 2012. (J). *(978-0-545-38472-8(9))* Scholastic, Inc.

Papa Rolly. Sam the Semi Goes to Chicago. 2012. (Illus.). 36p. pap. 18.40 *(978-1-4669-1137-6(9))* Trafford Publishing.

Parachini, Jodie. This Is a Serious Book. Rieley, Daniel, illus. 2016. 32p. (J). (gr. -1-3). 17.99 *(978-0-06-247052-2(3)*, Greenwillow Bks.) HarperCollins Pubs.

Paranuzzi, Fred. Babak. Prigent, Andrée, illus. 2016. (ENG.). 32p. (J). 17.95 *(978-0-7358-4251-9(5))* North-South Bks., Inc.

Paretzky, Leah. Doda Golda Comes for Pesach. David, Racheli, illus. 2012. 24p. 10.95 *(978-1-60091-195-8(1))* Israel Bookshop Pubns.

Parish, Herman. Amelia Bedelia. Avril, Lynne, illus. 2013. (Amelia Bedelia Ser.: No. 2). (ENG.). 160p. (J). (gr. 1-5). pap. 5.99 *(978-0-06-209499-5(8)*, Greenwillow Bks.) HarperCollins Pubs.

—Amelia Bedelia & the Cat. Sweat, Lynn, illus. (I Can Read Level 2 Ser.). (ENG.). 48p. (J). (gr. k-3). 2009. pap. 3.99 *(978-0-06-084351-9(9))* 2008. 16.99 *(978-0-06-084349-6(7))* HarperCollins Pubs. (Greenwillow Bks.).

—Amelia Bedelia Bakes Off. Sweat, Lynn, illus. 2010. (I Can Read Level 2 Ser.). 64p. (J). (gr. k-3). (ENG.). pap. 3.99 *(978-0-06-084360-1(8))*; (ENG.). 17.99 *(978-0-06-084358-8(6))*; lib. bdg. 18.89 *(978-0-06-084359-5(4))* HarperCollins Pubs. (Greenwillow Bks.).

—Amelia Bedelia, Bookworm. Sweat, Lynn, illus. (I Can Read Level 2 Ser.). (ENG.). 64p. (J). (gr. k-3). 2005. pap. 3.99 *(978-0-06-051892-9(8))* 2003. 17.99 *(978-0-06-051890-5(1))* HarperCollins Pubs. (Greenwillow Bks.).

—Amelia Bedelia, Bookworm. Sweat, Lynn, illus. 2005. (I Can Read Bks.). 63p. (gr. -1-3). 14.00 *(978-0-7569-5766-7(4))* Perfection Learning Corp.

—Amelia Bedelia by the Yard. Avril, Lynne, illus. 2016. (I Can Read Level 1 Ser.). 32p. (J). (gr. -1-3). pap. 3.99 *(978-0-06-233427-5(1)*, Greenwillow Bks.) HarperCollins Pubs.

—Amelia Bedelia Chalks It Up! Avril, Lynne, illus. 2014. (I Can Read Level 1 Ser.). (ENG.). 32p. (J). (gr. -1-3). 16.99 *(978-0-06-233422-0(0)*, Greenwillow Bks.) HarperCollins Pubs.

—Amelia Bedelia Chalks One Up. Avril, Lynne, illus. 2014. (I Can Read Level 1 Ser.). (ENG.). 32p. (J). (gr. -1-3). pap. 3.99 *(978-0-06-233421-3(2)*, Greenwillow Bks.) HarperCollins Pubs.

—Amelia Bedelia Chalks One Up. 2014. (Amelia Bedelia: I Can Read! Ser.). (J). lib. bdg. 13.55 *(978-0-606-35947-4(8))* Turtleback Bks.

—Amelia Bedelia Chapter Book #10: Amelia Bedelia Ties the Knot. Avril, Lynne, illus. 2016. (Amelia Bedelia Ser.). 160p. (J). (gr. 1-5). pap. 4.99 *(978-0-06-233416-9(6)*, Greenwillow Bks.) HarperCollins Pubs.

—Amelia Bedelia Chapter Book #2: Amelia Bedelia Unleashed (Special Edition) 2013. (ENG., Illus.). 160p. (J). *(978-0-06-227056-6(7)*, Collins Design) HarperCollins Pubs.

—Amelia Bedelia Chapter Book #3: Amelia Bedelia Road Trip! (Special Edition) 2013. (ENG., Illus.). 160p. (J). *(978-0-06-227057-3(5)*, Collins Design) HarperCollins Pubs.

—Amelia Bedelia Chapter Book #4: Amelia Bedelia Goes Wild! (Special Edition) 2014. (ENG.). 160p. (J). *(978-0-06-227058-0(3)*, Collins Design) HarperCollins Pubs.

—Amelia Bedelia Chapter Book #5. Avril, Lynne, illus. 2014. (Amelia Bedelia Ser.). (ENG.). 160p. (J). (gr. 1-5). 9.99 *(978-0-06-233399-5(2)*, Greenwillow Bks.) HarperCollins Pubs.

—Amelia Bedelia Chapter Book #6: Amelia Bedelia Cleans Up (POB) Avril, Lynne, illus. 2015. (Amelia Bedelia Ser.). (ENG.). 160p. (J). (gr. 1-5). 9.99 *(978-0-06-233403-9(4)*, Greenwillow Bks.) HarperCollins Pubs.

—Amelia Bedelia Chapter Book #8: Amelia Bedelia Dances Off. Avril, Lynne, illus. 2015. (Amelia Bedelia Ser.). (ENG.). 160p. (J). (gr. 1-5). 15.99 *(978-0-06-233409-1(3)*, Greenwillow Bks.) HarperCollins Pubs.

—Amelia Bedelia Chapter Book #9: Amelia Bedelia on the Job. Avril, Lynne, illus. 2016. (Amelia Bedelia Ser.). 160p. (J). (gr. 1-5). pap. 4.99 *(978-0-06-233412-1(3)*, Greenwillow Bks.) HarperCollins Pubs.

—Amelia Bedelia Cleans Up. Avril, Lynne, illus. 2015. (Amelia Bedelia Ser.). (ENG.). 160p. (J). (gr. 1-5). pap. 4.99 *(978-0-06-233400-8(X)*, Greenwillow Bks.) HarperCollins Pubs.

—Amelia Bedelia, Cub Reporter. Sweat, Lynn, illus. 2012. (I Can Read Level 2 Ser.). (ENG.). 64p. (J). (gr. -1-3). 16.99 *(978-0-06-209510-7(2))*; pap. 3.99 *(978-0-06-209509-1(9))* HarperCollins Pubs. (Greenwillow Bks.).

—Amelia Bedelia Goes Wild! Avril, Lynne, illus. 2014. (Amelia Bedelia Ser.: No. 4). (ENG.). 160p. (J). (gr. 1-5). 15.99 *(978-0-06-209507-7(2)*, Greenwillow Bks.) HarperCollins Pubs.

—Amelia Bedelia Goes Wild! 2014. (Amelia Bedelia Chapter Book Ser.: 4). (J). lib. bdg. 14.75 *(978-0-606-35077-8(2)*, Turtleback) Turtleback Bks.

—Amelia Bedelia Hits the Trail. Avril, Lynne, illus. 2013. (I Can Read Level 1 Ser.). (ENG.). 32p. (J). (gr. -1-3). 16.99 *(978-0-06-209527-5(7)*, Greenwillow Bks.) HarperCollins Pubs.

—Amelia Bedelia Hits the Trail. 2013. (Amelia Bedelia: I Can Read! Ser.). (J). lib. bdg. 13.55 *(978-0-606-27135-6(X)*, Turtleback) Turtleback Bks.

—Amelia Bedelia Is for the Birds. Avril, Lynne, illus. 2015. (I Can Read Level 1 Ser.). (ENG.). 32p. (J). (gr. -1-3). pap. 3.99 *(978-0-06-233424-4(7)*, Greenwillow Bks.) HarperCollins Pubs.

—Amelia Bedelia Joins the Club. Avril, Lynne, illus. 2014. (I Can Read Level 1 Ser.). (ENG.). 32p. (J). (gr. -1-3). 16.99 *(978-0-06-222131-5(0))*; pap. 3.99 *(978-0-06-222130-8(2))* HarperCollins Pubs. (Greenwillow Bks.).

—Amelia Bedelia Joins the Club. 2014. (Amelia Bedelia: I Can Read! Ser.). (J). lib. bdg. 13.55 *(978-0-606-35051-8(9)*, Turtleback) Turtleback Bks.

—Amelia Bedelia Makes a Splash. Avril, Lynne, illus. 2017. (Amelia Bedelia Ser.). 160p. (J). (gr. 1-5). pap. 4.99 *(978-0-06-265839-5(5)*, Greenwillow Bks.) HarperCollins Pubs.

H
I

—Amelia Bedelia Means Business. Avril, Lynne, illus. (Amelia Bedelia Ser.). (ENG.). (J). (gr. 1-5). 2015. 320p. 12.99 (978-0-06-240367-4(2)) 2013. 160p. 15.99 (978-0-06-209497-1(1)) 2013. 149p. pap. 5.99 (978-0-06-209496-4(3)) HarperCollins Pubs. (Greenwillow Bks.).

—Amelia Bedelia Means Business. Avril, Lynne, illus. 2013. (Amelia Bedelia Chapter Book Ser.: 1). (J). lib. bdg. 14.75 (978-0-606-27137-0(6), Turtleback) Turtleback Bks.

—Amelia Bedelia Road Trip! 2013. (Amelia Bedelia Chapter Book Ser.: 3). (J). lib. bdg. 14.75 (978-0-606-32453-3(4), Turtleback) Turtleback Bks.

—Amelia Bedelia, Rocket Scientist? Sweat, Lynn, illus. (I Can Read Level 2 Ser.). 64p. (J). 2007. (ENG.). (gr. k-3). pap. 3.99 (978-0-06-051889-9(8), Greenwillow Bks.) 2005. (gr. 1-18). 15.99 (978-0-06-051887-5(1)) 2005. (gr. k-4). lib. bdg. 17.89 (978-0-06-051888-2(X), Greenwillow Bks.) HarperCollins Pubs.

—Amelia Bedelia, Rocket Scientist? Sweat, Lynn, illus. 2007. (I Can Read Ser.). 64p. 14.00 (978-0-7569-8058-0(5)) Perfection Learning Corp.

—Amelia Bedelia, Rocket Scientist? Sweat, Lynn, illus. 2007. (Amelia Bedelia: I Can Read! Ser.: 19). (J). lib. bdg. 13.55 (978-1-4177-8068-6(1), Turtleback) Turtleback Bks.

—Amelia Bedelia Sets Sail. Avril, Lynne, illus. 2015. (Amelia Bedelia Ser.). (ENG.). 160p. (J). (gr. 1-5). pap. 4.99 (978-0-06-233404-6(2), Greenwillow Bks.) HarperCollins Pubs.

—Amelia Bedelia Shapes Up! Avril, Lynne, illus. 2014. (Amelia Bedelia Ser.). (ENG.). 160p. (J). (gr. 1-5). pap. 4.99 (978-0-06-233396-4(8), Greenwillow Bks.) HarperCollins Pubs.

—Amelia Bedelia Sleeps Over. Avril, Lynne, illus. 2012. (I Can Read Level 1 Ser.). (ENG.). 32p. (J). (gr. -1-3). 16.99 (978-0-06-209524-4(2)); pap. 3.99 (978-0-06-209523-7(4)) HarperCollins Pubs. (Greenwillow Bks.).

—Amelia Bedelia Sleeps Over. 2012. (Amelia Bedelia: I Can Read! Ser.). (J). lib. bdg. 13.55 (978-0-606-26849-3(9), Turtleback) Turtleback Bks.

—Amelia Bedelia Talks Turkey. Sweat, Lynn, illus. (I Can Read Level 2 Ser.). (ENG.). 64p. (J). (gr. k-3). 2009. pap. 3.99 (978-0-06-084354-0(3)) 2008. 16.99 (978-0-06-084352-6(7)) HarperCollins Pubs. (Greenwillow Bks.).

—Amelia Bedelia Talks Turkey. Parish, Herman & Sweat, Lynn, illus. 2008. (Amelia Bedelia Ser.). 64p. (J). (gr. k-4). lib. bdg. 17.89 (978-0-06-084353-3(5), Greenwillow Bks.) HarperCollins Pubs.

—Amelia Bedelia Ties the Knot. 2016. (Amelia Bedelia Chapter Book Ser.: 10). (J). lib. bdg. 14.75 (978-0-606-38762-0(5)) Turtleback Bks.

—Amelia Bedelia under Construction. Sweat, Lynn, illus. (I Can Read Level 2 Ser.). 64p. (J). (gr. k-3). 2007. (ENG.). pap. 3.99 (978-0-06-084346-5(2)) 2006. (ENG.). 15.99 (978-0-06-084344-1(6)) 2006. lib. bdg. 16.89 (978-0-06-084345-8(4)) HarperCollins Pubs. (Greenwillow Bks.).

—Amelia Bedelia under Construction. Sweat, Lynn, illus. 2007. (I Can Read Bks.). 64p. (gr. k-3). 14.00 (978-0-7569-8054-2(2)) Perfection Learning Corp.

—Amelia Bedelia Unleashed. Avril, Lynne, illus. 2013. (Amelia Bedelia Ser.: No. 2). (ENG.). 160p. (J). (gr. 1-5). 15.99 (978-0-06-209500-8(5), Greenwillow Bks.) HarperCollins Pubs.

—Amelia Bedelia Unleashed. Avril, Lynne, illus. 2013. (Amelia Bedelia Chapter Book Ser.: 2). (J). lib. bdg. 14.75 (978-0-606-27138-7(4), Turtleback) Turtleback Bks.

—Amelia Bedelia's Backpack Bundle. Sweat, Lynn, illus. 2012. 192p. (J). (978-1-4351-4392-0(2), Greenwillow Bks.) HarperCollins Pubs.

—Amelia Bedelia's First Apple Pie. Avril, Lynne, illus. 2012. (Amelia Bedelia Ser.). (ENG.). 32p. (J). (gr. -1-3). pap. 6.99 (978-0-06-196411-4(5), Greenwillow Bks.) HarperCollins Pubs.

—Amelia Bedelia's First Day of School. Avril, Lynne, illus. (Amelia Bedelia Ser.). (ENG.). 32p. (J). (gr. -1-3). 2015. pap. 6.99 (978-0-06-154457-6(4)) 2011. 9.99 (978-0-06-203274-4(7)) 2009. 16.99 (978-0-06-154455-2(8)) HarperCollins Pubs. (Greenwillow Bks.).

—Amelia Bedelia's First Field Trip. Avril, Lynne, illus. 2011. (Amelia Bedelia Ser.). (ENG.). 32p. (J). (gr. -1-3). 16.99 (978-0-06-196413-8(1), Greenwillow Bks.) HarperCollins Pubs.

—Amelia Bedelia's First Field Trip. 2013. (Amelia Bedelia Picture Bks.). (J). lib. bdg. 17.20 (978-0-606-31818-1(6), Turtleback) Turtleback Bks.

—Amelia Bedelia's First Library Card. Avril, Lynne, illus. 2013. (Amelia Bedelia Ser.). 32p. (J). (gr. -1-3). (ENG.). 17.99 (978-0-06-209512-1(9)); lib. bdg. 18.89 (978-0-06-209513-8(7)) HarperCollins Pubs. (Greenwillow Bks.).

—Amelia Bedelia's First Valentine. Avril, Lynne, illus. (Amelia Bedelia Ser.). (ENG.). 32p. (J). (gr. -1-3). 2014. pap. 6.99 (978-0-06-154460-6(4)) 2011. 9.99 (978-0-06-203275-1(5)) 2009. 16.99 (978-0-06-154458-3(2)) HarperCollins Pubs. (Greenwillow Bks.).

—Amelia Bedelia's First Valentine. 2014. (Amelia Bedelia Picture Bks.). (J). lib. bdg. 17.20 (978-0-606-35971-9(0)) Turtleback Bks.

—Amelia Bedelia's Masterpiece. Sweat, Lynn, illus. (I Can Read Level 2 Ser.). (ENG.). 64p. (J). (gr. k-3). 2008. pap. 3.99 (978-0-06-084357-1(8)) 2007. 16.99 (978-0-06-084355-7(1)) HarperCollins Pubs. (Greenwillow Bks.).

—Be My Valentine, Amelia Bedelia. Sweat, Lynn, illus. 2004. (Amelia Bedelia Ser.). (ENG.). 20p. (J). (gr. -1-3). pap. 6.99 (978-0-06-051886-8(3), Greenwillow Bks.) HarperCollins Pubs.

—Calling Doctor Amelia Bedelia. Sweat, Lynn, illus. 2004. (I Can Read Level 2 Ser.). (ENG.). 64p. (J). (gr. k-3). pap. 3.99 (978-0-06-008780-7(3), Greenwillow Bks.) HarperCollins Pubs.

—Calling Doctor Amelia Bedelia. Sweat, Lynn, illus. 2004. (Amelia Bedelia Ser.). 64p. (gr. -1-2). 14.00 (978-0-7569-3209-1(2)) Perfection Learning Corp.

—Go West, Amelia Bedelia! Sweat, Lynn, illus. (I Can Read Level 2 Ser.). 64p. (J). (gr. k-4). 2012. (ENG.). pap. 3.99 (978-0-06-084363-2(2)) 2011. (ENG.). 17.99 (978-0-06-084361-8(6)) 2011. lib. bdg. 18.89 (978-0-06-084362-5(4)) HarperCollins Pubs. (Greenwillow Bks.).

—Goes Wild! Avril, Lynne, illus. 2014. (Amelia Bedelia Ser.: No. 4). (ENG.). 160p. (J). (gr. 1-5). pap. 5.99 (978-0-06-209506-0(4), Greenwillow Bks.) HarperCollins Pubs.

—Happy Haunting, Amelia Bedelia. Sweat, Lynn, illus. (I Can Read Level 2 Ser.). 64p. (J). (gr. k-3). 2006. (ENG.). pap. 3.99 (978-0-06-051895-0(2)) 2004. (ENG.). 16.99 (978-0-06-051893-6(6)) 2004. lib. bdg. 16.89 (978-0-06-051894-3(4)) HarperCollins Pubs. (Greenwillow Bks.).

—Sets Sail. Avril, Lynne, illus. 2015. (Amelia Bedelia Ser.). (ENG.). 160p. (J). (gr. 1-5). 15.99 (978-0-06-233405-3(0), Greenwillow Bks.) HarperCollins Pubs.

Parish, Peggy. Amelia Bedelia. Siebel, Fritz, illus. 50th ed. 2012. (I Can Read Level 2 Ser.). (ENG.). 64p. (J). (gr. k-3). pap. 3.99 (978-0-06-444155-1(5), Greenwillow Bks.) HarperCollins Pubs.

—Amelia Bedelia. Siebel, Fritz, illus. 2012. (Amelia Bedelia: I Can Read! Ser.: 1). (J). (gr. 1-3). lib. bdg. 13.55 (978-0-88103-916-0(0), Turtleback) Turtleback Bks.

—Amelia Bedelia & the Baby. Sweat, Lynn, illus. 2004. (I Can Read Level 2 Ser.). (ENG.). 64p. (J). (gr. k-3). pap. 3.99 (978-0-06-051105-0(2), Greenwillow Bks.) HarperCollins Pubs.

—Amelia Bedelia Goes Camping. Sweat, Lynn, illus. 2003. (I Can Read Level 2 Ser.). (ENG.). 64p. (J). (gr. k-3). pap. 3.99 (978-0-06-051106-7(0), Greenwillow Bks.) HarperCollins Pubs.

—Amelia Bedelia Goes Camping. 2003. (Amelia Bedelia: I Can Read! Ser.: 10). (J). (gr. k-3). lib. bdg. 13.55 (978-0-613-62664-4(8), Turtleback) Turtleback Bks.

—Amelia Bedelia's Family Album. Sweat, Lynn, illus. 2003. (I Can Read Level 2 Ser.). (ENG.). 48p. (J). (gr. k-3). pap. 3.99 (978-0-06-051116-6(8), Greenwillow Bks.) HarperCollins Pubs.

—Amelia Bedelia's Family Album. 2003. (Amelia Bedelia: I Can Read! Ser.: 12). (J). (gr. k-3). lib. bdg. 13.55 (978-0-613-62129-8(8), Turtleback) Turtleback Bks.

—Teach Us, Amelia Bedelia. Sweat, Lynn, illus. 2005. (Amelia Bedelia Ser.). 58p. (gr. -1-3). 14.00 (978-0-7569-4804-7(5)) Perfection Learning Corp.

Parish, Peggy & Parish, Herman. An Amelia Bedelia Celebration: Four Stories Tall. Sweat, Lynn & Siebel, Fritz, illus. 2009. (Amelia Bedelia Ser.). (ENG.). 224p. (J). (gr. -1-3). 19.99 (978-0-06-171030-8(X), Greenwillow Bks.) HarperCollins Pubs.

Park, Barbara. Aloha-Ha-Ha! Brunkus, Denise, illus. 2006. (Junie B. Jones Ser.: No. 9). (ENG.). 128p. (J). (gr. 1-4). lib. bdg. 13.95 (978-0-375-93403-2(0), Random Hse. Bks. for Young Readers) Random Hse. Children's Bks.

—Boo... & I Mean It! Brunkus, Denise, illus. 2004. (Junie B. Jones Ser.: No. 7). (ENG.). 96p. (J). (gr. 1-4). lib. bdg. 13.99 (978-0-375-92806-2(5), Random Hse. Bks. for Young Readers) Random Hse. Children's Bks.

—Boss of Lunch. 2003. (Junie B. Jones Ser.: 19). (gr. k-3). lib. bdg. 14.75 (978-0-613-63168-6(4), Turtleback) Turtleback Bks.

—Cheater Pants. Brunkus, Denise, tr. Brunkus, Denise, illus. 2004. (Junie B. Jones Ser.: No. 4). (ENG.). 96p. (J). (gr. 1-4). 4.99 (978-0-375-82302-2(6), Random Hse. Bks. for Young Readers) Random Hse. Children's Bks.

—Cheater Pants. Brunkus, Denise, illus. 2003. (Junie B. Jones Ser.: No. 4). (ENG.). 96p. (J). (gr. 1-4). lib. bdg. 13.99 (978-0-375-92301-2(2), Random Hse. Bks. for Young Readers) Random Hse. Children's Bks.

—Dumb Bunny. Brunkus, Denise, illus. 2009. (Junie B. Jones Ser.). (ENG.). 128p. (J). (gr. 1-4). 4.99 (978-0-375-83810-1(4), Random Hse. Bks. for Young Readers) Random Hse. Children's Bks.

—Junie B., First Grader - Boss of Lunch. unabr. ed. 2004. (Junie B., First Grader Ser.: No. 2). 70p. (J). (gr. k-3). pap. 17.00 incl. audio (978-0-8072-1021-5(8), S FTR 259 SP, Listening Library) Random Hse. Audio Publishing Group.

—Junie B., First Grader (At Last!) unabr. ed. 2004. (Junie B., First Grader Ser.: No. 1). 70p. (J). (gr. k-3). pap. 17.00 incl. audio (978-0-8072-1020-8(X), S FTR 258 SP, Listening Library) Random Hse. Audio Publishing Group.

—Junie B. Jones & a Little Monkey Business, Vol. 2. unabr. ed. 2004. (Junie B. Jones Ser.: Vol. 2). 68p. (J). (gr. k-3). pap. 17.00 incl. audio (978-0-8072-0779-6(9), LFTR 238 SP, Listening Library) Random Hse. Audio Publishing Group.

—Junie B. Jones & Her Big Fat Mouth. unabr. ed. 2004. (Junie B. Jones Ser.: No. 3). 69p. (J). (gr. k-3). pap. 17.00 incl. audio (978-0-8072-0780-2(2), LFTR 239 SP, Listening Library) Random Hse. Audio Publishing Group.

—Junie B. Jones & Some Sneaky Peeky Spying. unabr. ed. 2004. (Junie B. Jones Ser.: No. 4). 66p. (J). (gr. k-3). pap. 17.00 incl. audio (978-0-8072-0781-9(0), LFTR 240 SP, Listening Library) Random Hse. Audio Publishing Group.

—Junie B. Jones & the Mushy Gushy Valentine. unabr. ed. 2004. (Junie B. Jones Ser.: No. 14). 69p. (J). (gr. k-3). pap. 17.00 incl. audio (978-0-8072-0335-4(1), Listening Library) Random Hse. Audio Publishing Group.

—Junie B. Jones & the Stupid Smelly Bus. unabr. ed. 2004. (Junie B. Jones Ser.: Vol. 1). 69p. (J). (gr. k-3). pap. 17.00 incl. audio (978-0-8072-0778-9(0), LFTR 237 SP, Listening Library) Random Hse. Audio Publishing Group.

—Junie B. Jones Is a Graduation Girl. unabr. ed. 2004. (Junie B. Jones Ser.: No. 17). 69p. (J). (gr. k-3). pap. 17.00 incl. audio (978-0-8072-1019-2(6), S FTR 257 SP, Listening Library) Random Hse. Audio Publishing Group.

—Junie B.'s Essential Survival Guide to School. Brunkus, Denise, illus. 2013. (Junie B. Jones Ser.). (ENG.). 144p. (J). (gr. 1-4). 12.99 (978-0-449-81783-4(0), Random Hse. Bks. for Young Readers) Random Hse. Children's Bks.

—One-Man Band. Brunkus, Denise, tr. Brunkus, Denise, illus. 2004. (Junie B. Jones Ser.: No. 5). (ENG.). 96p. (J). (gr. 1-4). 4.99 (978-0-375-82536-1(3), Random Hse. Bks. for Young Readers) Random Hse. Children's Bks.

—One-Man Band. Brunkus, Denise, illus. 2003. (Junie B. Jones Ser.: No. 5). (ENG.). 96p. (J). (gr. 1-4). lib. bdg. 13.99 (978-0-375-92522-1(8), Random Hse. Bks. for Young Readers) Random Hse. Children's Bks.

—Skinnybones. 2016. (ENG.). 160p. (J). (gr. 3-7). 12.99 (978-0-394-94988-8(9), Yearling) Random Hse. Children's Bks.

—Toothless Wonder. Brunkus, Denise, illus. 2003. (Junie B. Jones Ser.: Bk. 3). 80p. (gr. 1-4). 15.00 (978-0-7569-1621-3(6)) Perfection Learning Corp.

—Turkeys We Have Loved & Eaten, No. 28. Brunkus, Denise, illus. 2012. (Junie B. Jones Ser.: 28). (ENG.). 144p. (J). (gr. 1-4). lib. bdg. 14.99 (978-0-375-97063-4(0), Random Hse. Bks. for Young Readers) Random Hse. Children's Bks.

—Turkeys We Have Loved & Eaten (and Other Thankful Stuff), No. 28. Brunkus, Denise, illus. 2012. (Junie B. Jones Ser.). (ENG.). 144p. (J). (gr. 1-4). 11.99 (978-0-375-87063-7(6), Random Hse. Bks. for Young Readers) Random Hse. Children's Bks.

—Turkeys We Have Loved & Eaten (and Other Thankful Stuff) 2014. (Junie B. Jones Ser.: 28). lib. bdg. 14.75 (978-0-606-36015-9(8)) Turtleback Bks.

Park, Linda Sue. Yaks Yak: Animal Word Pairs. Reinhardt, Jennifer Black, illus. 2016. (ENG.). 40p. (J). (gr. -1-3). 16.99 (978-0-544-39101-7(2), Clarion Bks.) Houghton Mifflin Harcourt Trade & Reference Pubs.

Parker, Vic, compiled by. Down the Rabbit Hole & Other Silly Stories. 2016. (Silly Stories Ser.). (ENG.). 40p. (J). (gr. 2-3). pap. 14.05 (978-1-4824-4179-6(9)) Stevens, Gareth Publishing LLLP.

—How the Cow Jumped over the Moon & Other Silly Stories. 2016. (Silly Stories Ser.). (ENG.). 40p. (J). (gr. 2-3). pap. 14.05 (978-1-4824-4183-3(7)) Stevens, Gareth Publishing LLLP.

—How the Dragon Was Tricked & Other Silly Stories. 2016. (Silly Stories Ser.). (ENG.). 40p. (J). (gr. 2-3). pap. 14.05 (978-1-4824-4187-1(X)) Stevens, Gareth Publishing LLLP.

—How the Leopard Got His Spots & Other Silly Stories. 2016. (Silly Stories Ser.). (ENG.). 40p. (J). (gr. 2-3). pap. 14.05 (978-1-4824-4191-8(8)) Stevens, Gareth Publishing LLLP.

—The Open Road & Other Silly Stories. 2016. (Silly Stories Ser.). (ENG.). 40p. (J). (gr. 2-3). pap. 14.05 (978-1-4824-4211-3(6)) Stevens, Gareth Publishing LLLP.

—The Remarkable Rocket & Other Silly Stories. 2016. (Silly Stories Ser.). (ENG.). 40p. (J). (gr. 2-3). pap. 14.05 (978-1-4824-4215-1(9)) Stevens, Gareth Publishing LLLP.

Parkinson, Ethelyn. Good Old Archibald. Stevens, Mary, illus. 2014. 145p. (J). pap. 14.95 (978-1-932350-42-5(X)) Bethlehem Bks.

Parkinson, Rebecca. Look Out! 2015. (Archie Ser.: Vol. 2). (ENG., Illus.). 92p. (J). (gr. 4-7). pap. (978-1-84625-423-9(X)) DayOne Pubns.

Parrish, Edith E. It's Not Easy Being a Purple Goose. Odom, Kelly, illus. 2011. 44p. pap. 24.95 (978-1-4626-4207-6(1)) America Star Bks.

Parsley, Elise. If You Ever Want to Bring a Circus to the Library, Don't! 2017. (Magnolia Says DON'T! Ser.). (ENG., Illus.). 40p. (J). (gr. -1-3). 17.99 (978-0-316-37661-7(2)) Little Brown & Co.

—If You Ever Want to Bring a Piano to the Beach, Don't! 2016. (Magnolia Says DON'T! Ser.). (ENG., Illus.). 40p. (J). (gr. -1-3). 16.99 (978-0-316-37659-4(0)) Little, Brown Bks. for Young Readers.

—If You Ever Want to Bring an Alligator to School, Don't! Parsley, Elise, illus. 2015. (ENG., Illus.). 40p. (J). (gr. -1-1). 17.00 (978-0-316-37657-0(4)) Little Brown & Co.

Parsons, Wendelin Van Draanen. The Secret Life of Lincoln Jones. 2016. (ENG.). 272p. (J). (gr. 3-7). 16.99 (978-1-101-94040-2(9), Knopf Bks. for Young Readers) Random Hse. Children's Bks.

Particular, Nowen N. Boomtown, 1 vol. 2010. (ENG.). 320p. pap. 9.99 (978-1-4003-1553-6(0)) Nelson, Thomas Inc.

Pascal, Francine. My First Love & Other Disasters. 2011. (ENG.). 256p. (YA). (gr. 4-9). pap. 11.99 (978-1-4424-5234-3(X), Simon Pulse) Simon Pulse.

Pass, Erica. Hooray for Dads! 2014. (SpongeBob Squarepants 8X8 Ser.). lib. bdg. 14.75 (978-0-606-35560-5(X)) Turtleback Bks.

Pass, Erica & Artifact Group Staff. Hooray for Dads! 2007. (SpongeBob SquarePants Ser.: 14). (ENG., Illus.). 24p. (J). (gr. k-2). pap. 3.99 (978-1-4169-2782-2(4), Simon Spotlight/Nickelodeon) Simon Spotlight/Nickelodeon.

Passey, Marion. Sneezles & Wheezles. Harston, Jerry, illus. 2006. 32p. (J). (gr. -1-3). 15.99 (978-1-55517-912-0(6)) Cedar Fort, Inc./CFI Distribution.

Pastis, Stephan. Mistakes Were Made. Pastis, Stephan, illus. 2013. (Timmy Failure Ser.: No. 1). (ENG., Illus.). 304p. (J). (gr. 3-7). 14.99 (978-0-7636-6050-5(7)); 100.00 (978-0-7636-6689-7(0)) Candlewick Pr.

—Now Look What You've Done. 2016. (Timmy Failure Ser.: 2). lib. bdg. 18.40 (978-0-606-37947-2(9)) Turtleback Bks.

—Sanitized for Your Protection. Pastis, Stephan, illus. 2015. (Timmy Failure Ser.: 4). (ENG., Illus.). 288p. (J). (gr. 3-7). 14.99 (978-0-7636-8092-3(3)) Candlewick Pr.

—Stephan's Web: A Pearls Before Swine Collection. 2016. (Pearls Before Swine Ser.: 26). (ENG.). 128p. pap. 14.99 (978-1-4494-8202-2(3)) Andrews McMeel Publishing.

—Timmy Failure: the Cat Stole My Pants. Pastis, Stephan, illus. 2017. (Timmy Failure Ser.: 6). (ENG., Illus.). 288p. (J). (gr. 3-7). 14.99 (978-0-7636-9733-4(8)) Candlewick Pr.

—Timmy Failure: We Meet Again. Pastis, Stephan, illus. 2016. (Timmy Failure Ser.). (ENG., Illus.). 288p. (J). (gr. 3-7). pap. 7.99 (978-0-7636-9106-6(2)) Candlewick Pr.

Patricelli, Leslie. Nighty-Night. Patricelli, Leslie, illus. 2017. (Leslie Patricelli Board Bks.). (ENG., Illus.). 26p. (J). (— 1). bds. 6.99 (978-0-7636-7932-3(1)) Candlewick Pr.

—The Patterson Puppies & the Rainy Day. Patricelli, Leslie, illus. 2009. (ENG., Illus.). 40p. (J). (gr. -1-k). 14.99 (978-0-7636-3242-7(2)) Candlewick Pr.

—Potty. Patricelli, Leslie, illus. 2010. (Leslie Patricelli Board Bks.). (ENG., Illus.). 28p. (J). (gr. k — 1). bds. 6.99 (978-0-7636-4476-5(5)) Candlewick Pr.

—Potty/Bacinica. Patricelli, Leslie, illus. 2016. (Leslie Patricelli Board Bks.). (ENG & SPA., Illus.). (J). (— 1). bds. 6.99 (978-0-7636-8777-9(4)) Candlewick Pr.

Patterson, James. House of Robots: Robot Revolution. Neufeld, Juliana, illus. 2017. (House of Robots Ser.: 3). (ENG.). 336p. (J). (gr. 3-7). 13.99 (978-0-316-34958-1(5), Jimmy Patterson) Little Brown & Co.

—Public School Superhero. 2015. (ENG., Illus.). 304p. (J). (gr. 3-7). 13.99 (978-0-316-32214-0(8), Jimmy Patterson) Little Brown & Co.

—The Worst Years of My Life. 2014. lthr. 79.00 (978-1-62715-524-3(4)) Leatherbound Bestsellers.

—The Worst Years of My Life. 2012. 18.00 (978-1-61383-331-5(8)) Perfection Learning Corp.

Patterson, James & Grabenstein, Chris. House of Robots. Neufeld, Juliana, illus. (House of Robots Ser.: 1). (ENG.). (J). (gr. 3-7). 2015. 336p. pap. 7.99 (978-0-316-34679-5(9)) 2014. 352p. 13.99 (978-0-316-40591-1(4)) Little Brown & Co. (Jimmy Patterson).

—House of Robots. 2015. (J). lib. bdg. 18.40 (978-0-606-37527-6(9)) Turtleback Bks.

—I Even Funnier: A Middle School Story. Park, Laura, illus. 2013. (I Funny Ser.: 2). (ENG.). 368p. (J). (gr. 3-7). 13.99 (978-0-316-20697-6(0), Jimmy Patterson) Little Brown & Co.

—I Funny: A Middle School Story. Park, Laura, illus. (I Funny Ser.: 1). (ENG.). 320p. (J). (gr. 3-7). 2015. pap. 8.00 (978-0-316-20692-1(X)) 2013. 13.99 (978-0-316-32200-3(8)) Little Brown & Co. (Jimmy Patterson).

—I Funny TV: A Middle School Story. Park, Laura, illus. 2015. (I Funny Ser.: 4). (ENG.). 336p. (J). (gr. 3-7). 13.99 (978-0-316-30109-1(4), Jimmy Patterson) Little Brown & Co.

—I Totally Funniest: A Middle School Story. Park, Laura, illus. 2015. (J). 320p. (978-0-316-26161-6(0)); (ENG.). 336p. (gr. 3-7). 13.99 (978-0-316-40593-5(0), Jimmy Patterson) Little Brown & Co.

—Jacky Ha-Ha. Kerascoët, illus. 2016. (ENG.). 384p. (J). (gr. 3-7). 13.99 (978-0-316-26249-1(8), Jimmy Patterson) Little Brown & Co.

—Jacky Ha-Ha. 2017. (Jacky Ha-Ha Ser.). (J). lib. bdg. 18.40 **(978-0-606-40732-8(4))** Turtleback Bks.

—Laugh Out Loud. Ebbeler, Jeff, illus. 2017. (ENG.). 304p. (J). (gr. 3-7). 13.99 **(978-0-316-43146-0(X)**, Jimmy Patterson) Little Brown & Co.

—Pottymouth & Stoopid. Gilpin, Stephen, illus. 2017. (ENG.). 336p. (J). (gr. 3-7). 13.99 (978-0-316-34963-5(1)) Little Brown & Co.

—Robots Go Wild. Neufeld, Juliana, illus. 2015. (House of Robots Ser.: 2). (ENG.). 336p. (J). (gr. 3-7). 13.99 (978-0-316-28479-0(3), Jimmy Patterson) Little Brown & Co.

Patterson, James & Papademetriou, Lisa. Big Fat Liar. Swaab, Neil, illus. 2014. (Middle School Ser.: Bk. 3). (ENG.). 304p. (J). (gr. 3-7). 13.99 (978-0-316-32203-4(2), Jimmy Patterson) Little Brown & Co.

Patterson, James & Tebbetts, Chris. How I Survived Bullies, Broccoli, & Snake Hill. Park, Laura, illus. 2013. (Middle School Ser.: 4). (ENG.). 336p. (J). (gr. 3-7). 14.00 (978-0-316-23175-6(4), Jimmy Patterson) Little Brown & Co.

—Just My Rotten Luck. Park, Laura, illus. 2015. (Middle School Ser.: 7). (ENG.). 320p. (J). (gr. 3-7). 13.99 (978-0-316-28477-6(7), Jimmy Patterson) Little Brown & Co.

—Middle School: Dog's Best Friend. Tejido, Jomike, illus. 2016. (Middle School: Book 8 Ser.: 8). (ENG.). 256p. (J). (gr. 3-7). 13.99 (978-0-316-34954-3(2), Jimmy Patterson) Little Brown & Co.

—Public School Superhero. Thomas, Cory, illus. 2016. (ENG.). 304p. (J). (gr. 3-7). pap. 7.99 (978-0-316-26598-0(5), Jimmy Patterson) Little Brown & Co.

—Save Rafe! Park, Laura, illus. 2014. (Middle School Ser.: 6). (ENG.). 288p. (J). (gr. 3-7). 13.99 (978-0-316-32212-6(1), Jimmy Patterson) Little Brown & Co.

—The Worst Years of My Life. Park, Laura, illus. (Middle School Ser.: Bk. 1). (ENG.). (J). (gr. 3-7). 2014. 320p. 13.99 (978-0-316-32202-7(4), Jimmy Patterson) 2013. pap. 0.01 (978-0-316-25251-5(4)) 2012. 336p. pap. 8.00 (978-0-316-10169-1(9), Jimmy Patterson) Little Brown & Co.

—The Worst Years of My Life. Park, Laura, illus. 2012. (Middle School Ser.: 1). (J). lib. bdg. 18.45 (978-0-606-26164-7(8), Turtleback) Turtleback Bks.

Patterson, James & Tebbetts, Christopher. From Hero to Zero. Park, Laura, illus. 2017. (J). pap. **(978-0-316-35756-2(1))** Little Brown & Co.

Patterson, James & Tebbetts, Christopher. Save Rafe! Park, Laura, illus. 2014. 269p. (J). (978-0-316-28629-9(X)) Little Brown & Co.

Patterson, James, et al. Public School Superhero. 2015. (978-0-316-34231-5(9)) Little, Brown Bks. for Young Readers.

Patterson, Lagene E. What a Peculiar Day. 2009. 16p. pap. 8.49 (978-1-4490-1859-7(9)) AuthorHouse.

Patterson, Matthew. Shake Them up, Mrs Nut. 2008. 104p. per. 9.95 (978-1-4327-2008-7(2)) Outskirts Pr., Inc.

Paul, Miranda. Are We Pears Yet? Berger, Carin, illus. 2017. (ENG.). 40p. (J). 17.99 **(978-1-62672-351-1(6)**, 9781626723511) Roaring Brook Pr.

—Blobfish Throws a Party. Caton, Maggie, illus. 2017. (ENG.). 32p. (J). (gr. -1-3). 16.99 **(978-1-4998-0422-5(9))** Little Bee Books Inc.

—The Great Pasta Escape. Joaquin, Javier, illus. 2017. (ENG.). 40p. (J). (gr. -1-3). 17.99 **(978-1-4998-0480-5(6))** Little Bee Books Inc.

Paul, Ruth. Stomp! 2013. pap. (978-0-545-52940-2(9)) Scholastic, Inc.

Paul, Ruth & Lombana, J. P. Stomp! la Marchar! 2013. (SPA & ENG., Illus.). (978-0-545-52795-8(3)) Scholastic, Inc.

Pauline Roberts & Donnie Obina. Promises! Promises! Who Can I Trust. 2013. 28p. pap. 16.09 (978-1-4669-7959-8(3)) Trafford Publishing.

Paulsen, Gary. Crush: The Theory, Practice & Destructive Properties of Love. (ENG.). 144p. (J). (gr. 4-7). 2013. pap. 6.99 (978-0-385-74231-3(2), Yearling) 2012. 12.99 (978-0-385-74230-6(4), Lamb, Wendy Bks.) Random Hse. Children's Bks.

—Family Ties. 2014. (ENG.). 144p. (J). (gr. 4-7). 12.99 (978-0-385-37380-7(5), Lamb, Wendy Bks.) Random Hse. Children's Bks.

—Flat Broke: The Theory, Practice & Destructive Properties of Greed. (ENG.). 128p. (J). (gr. 3-7). 2012. pap. 6.99 (978-0-375-86612-8(4), Yearling) 2011. 12.99 (978-0-385-74002-9(6), Lamb, Wendy Bks.) Random Hse. Children's Bks.

—Lawn Boy Returns. 2011. (ENG.). 112p. (J). (gr. 3-7). pap. 5.99 (978-0-553-49430-3(9), Yearling) Random Hse. Children's Bks.

—Masters of Disaster. 2011. (ENG.). 112p. (J). (gr. 3-7). 5.99 (978-0-375-86610-4(8), Yearling) Random Hse. Children's Bks.

—Molly Mcginty Has a Really Good Day. 2006. (Illus.). 105p. (J). (gr. 3-7). 13.15 (978-0-7569-6621-8(3)) Perfection Learning Corp.

—Mudshark. 2010. (ENG.). 96p. (J). (gr. 3-7). 6.99 (978-0-553-49464-8(3), Yearling) Random Hse. Children's Bks.

—Six Kids & a Stuffed Cat. 2016. (ENG., Illus.). 144p. (J). (gr. 3-7). 16.99 (978-1-4814-5223-6(1), Simon & Schuster Bks. For Young Readers) Simon & Schuster Bks. For Young Readers.

—Vote. 2013. (ENG.). 144p. (J). (gr. 4-7). 12.99 (978-0-385-74228-3(2), Lamb, Wendy Bks.) Random Hse. Children's Bks.

—Vote: The Theory, Practice, & Destructive Properties of Politics. 2014. (ENG.). 144p. (J). (gr. 4-7). pap. 6.99 (978-0-385-74229-0(0), Yearling) Random Hse. Children's Bks.

Paye, Won-Ldy & Lippert, Margaret H. Head, Body, Legs: A Story from Liberia. Paschkis, Julie, illus. 2006. (gr. -1-3). lib. bdg. 18.00 (978-0-7569-6925-7(5)) Perfection Learning Corp.

Pearlman, Robb. Groundhog's Day Off. Helquist, Brett, illus. 2015. (ENG.). 40p. (J). (gr. -1-1). 16.99 (978-1-61963-289-9(6), 9781619632899, Bloomsbury USA Childrens) Bloomsbury Publishing USA.

Pearson, Mary E. Generous Me. Krejca, Gary, illus. 2011. (Rookie Ready to Learn — All about Me! Ser.). 40p. (J). (gr. -1-k). lib. bdg. 25.00 (978-0-531-26427-0(0)); (ENG.). pap. 5.95 (978-0-531-26652-6(4)) Scholastic Library Publishing. (Children's Pr.).

Pearson, Peter. How to Eat an Airplane. Catusanu, Mircea, illus. 2016. (Bad Idea Book Club Ser.). 40p. (J). (gr. -1-3). 17.99 (978-0-06-232062-9(9)) HarperCollins Pubs.

Pearson, Ridley & Barry, Dave. Peter & the Secret of Rundoon. Call, Greg, illus. rev. ed. 2009. (Peter & the Starcatchers Ser.: Bk. 3). (ENG.). 496p. (J). (gr. 5-9). pap. 9.99 (978-1-4231-2326-2(3)) Hyperion Pr.

Pearson, Tracey Campbell. Bob. Pearson, Tracey Campbell, illus. 2006. (ENG., Illus.). 32p. (J). (gr. -1-1). reprint ed. 8.99 (978-0-374-40871-8(8), 9780374408718) Square Fish.

Peck, Richard. Fair Weather. 2003. (ENG., Illus.). 160p. (J). (gr. 3-7). pap. 7.99 (978-0-14-250034-7(8), Puffin Books) Penguin Young Readers Group.

—Fair Weather. 2003. (Illus.). 146p. (gr. 4-7). 17.00 (978-0-7569-1376-2(4)) Perfection Learning Corp.

—Fair Weather. 2004. 146p. (J). (gr. 5-9). pap. 36.00 incl. audio (978-0-8072-2038-2(8), Listening Library) Random Hse. Audio Publishing Group.

—A Season of Gifts. 2010. (ENG.). 208p. (J). (gr. 5-18). 7.99 (978-0-14-241729-4(7), Puffin Books) Penguin Young Readers Group.

—The Teacher's Funeral. 2006. (ENG.). 224p. (J). (gr. 3-7). reprint ed. 7.99 (978-0-14-240507-9(8), Puffin Books) Penguin Young Readers Group.

Peckham, Lori, ed. Guide's Greatest Funny Stories. 2014. (ENG.). 160p. pap. 11.99 (978-0-8280-2778-6(1)) Review & Herald Publishing Assn.

Peirce, Lincoln. Big Nate. 2012. (ENG.). 224p. pap. 12.99 (978-1-4494-1144-2(4)) Andrews McMeel Publishing.

—Big Nate: From the Top. 2010. (Big Nate Ser.: 1). (ENG., Illus.). 224p. (J). (gr. 2-7). pap. 9.99 (978-1-4494-0232-7(1)) Andrews McMeel Publishing.

—Big Nate: I Can't Take It! 2013. (ENG., Illus.). 224p. pap. 9.99 (978-1-4494-2937-9(8)) Andrews McMeel Publishing.

—Big Nate — Genius Mode. Peirce, Lincoln, illus. 2013. (Big Nate Ser.). (ENG., Illus.). 224p. (J). (gr. 3-7). pap. 9.99 (978-0-06-208698-3(7)) HarperCollins Pubs.

—Big Nate — In a Class by Himself. Peirce, Lincoln, illus. 2015. (Big Nate Ser.: 1). (ENG., Illus.). 224p. (J). (gr. 3-7). pap. 6.99 (978-0-06-228359-7(6)) HarperCollins Pubs.

—Big Nate — In a Class by Himself. 2010. pap. (978-0-06-199287-2(9)) HarperCollins Pubs.

—Big Nate — In a Class by Himself. 2015. (Big Nate Ser.: 1). (J). lib. bdg. 17.20 (978-0-606-36505-5(2)) Turtleback Bks.

—Big Nate — In the Zone. Peirce, Lincoln, illus. 2014. (Big Nate Ser.: 6). (Illus.). 224p. (J). (gr. 3-7). (ENG.). 13.99 (978-0-06-199665-8(3)); lib. bdg. 14.89 (978-0-06-199666-5(1)) HarperCollins Pubs.

—Big Nate Blasts Off. Peirce, Lincoln, illus. 2016. (Big Nate Ser.: 8). (ENG., Illus.). 224p. (J). (gr. 3-7). 13.99 (978-0-06-211111-1(6)) HarperCollins Pubs.

—Big Nate Flips Out. Peirce, Lincoln, illus. 2013. (Big Nate Ser.). (Illus.). 224p. (J). (gr. 3-7). (ENG.). 13.99 (978-0-06-199663-4(7)); lib. bdg. 14.89 (978-0-06-199664-1(5)) HarperCollins Pubs.

—Big Nate Goes for Broke. Peirce, Lincoln, illus. (Big Nate Ser.: 4). (Illus.). 224p. (J). (gr. 3-7). 2016. pap. 6.99 (978-0-06-236753-2(6)) 2012. (ENG., 12.99 (978-0-06-199661-0(0)) 2012. lib. bdg. 14.89 (978-0-06-199662-7(9)) HarperCollins Pubs.

—Big Nate Goes for Broke. 2016. (Big Nate Ser.: 4). 224p. (J). lib. bdg. 17.20 (978-0-606-38137-6(6)) Turtleback Bks.

—Big Nate Lives It Up. Peirce, Lincoln, illus. 2015. (Big Nate Ser.: 7). (Illus.). 224p. (J). (gr. 3-7). lib. bdg. 13.89 (978-0-06-211109-8(4)) HarperCollins Pubs.

—Big Nate on a Roll. Peirce, Lincoln, illus. (Big Nate Ser.: 3). (Illus.). 224p. (J). (gr. 3-7). 2015. (ENG.). pap. 6.99 (978-0-06-228357-3(X)) 2011. (ENG., 12.99 (978-0-06-194438-3(6)) 2011. lib. bdg. 14.89 (978-0-06-194439-0(4)) HarperCollins Pubs.

—Big Nate Strikes Again. Peirce, Lincoln, illus. 2010. (Big Nate Ser.: 2). (Illus.). 224p. (J). (gr. 3-7). (ENG.). 12.99 (978-0-06-194436-9(X)); lib. bdg. 14.89 (978-0-06-194437-6(8)) HarperCollins Pubs.

—Game On! 2013. (Big Nate Graphic Novels Ser.). lib. bdg. 20.85 (978-0-606-27021-2(3), Turtleback) Turtleback Bks.

—A Good Old-Fashioned Wedgie. 2017. (Big Nate Ser.: bk.17). (ENG.). 176p. (J). pap. 9.99 **(978-1-4494-6230-7(8))** Andrews McMeel Publishing.

—Here Goes Nothing. Peirce, Lincoln, illus. 2012. (Big Nate Comix Ser.: 2). (ENG., Illus.). 224p. (J). (gr. 3-7). pap. 9.99 (978-0-06-208696-9(0)) HarperCollins Pubs.

—I Can't Take It! 2013. (Big Nate Graphic Novels Ser.). lib. bdg. 20.85 (978-0-606-32313-0(9), Turtleback) Turtleback Bks.

—In a Class by Himself. Peirce, Lincoln, illus. (Big Nate Ser.: 1). (Illus.). (J). (gr. 3-7). 2010. (ENG.). 224p. 12.99 (978-0-06-194434-5(3)) 2010. 224p. lib. bdg. 14.89 (978-0-06-194435-2(1)) 2012. (ENG., 240p. 12.99 (978-0-06-220773-9(3)) HarperCollins Pubs.

—Nate el Grande: ¡Hola! 2014. (Big Nate Ser.: 10). (ENG & SPA.). 224p. (J). pap. 9.99 (978-1-4494-6443-1(2)) Andrews McMeel Publishing.

—Nate el Grande Ataca de Nuevo. 2015.Tr. of Big Nate Strikes Again. (SPA.). 216p. (J). (gr. 3-5). 17.99 (978-1-933032-79-5(0)) Lectorum Pubns., Inc.

—What Could Possibly Go Wrong? Peirce, Lincoln, illus. 2012. (Big Nate Comix Ser.: 1). (ENG., Illus.). 224p. (J). (gr. 3-7). pap. 9.99 (978-0-06-208694-5(4)) HarperCollins Pubs.

—What Could Possibly Go Wrong? 2012. (Big Nate Ser.). (J). lib. bdg. 20.85 (978-0-606-23589-1(2), Turtleback) Turtleback Bks.

Peirce, Lincoln, illus. Big Nate Flips Out. 2013. 216p. (J). (978-0-06-224637-0(2)) Harper & Row Ltd.

Peirce, Lincoln, et al. Big Nate Makes the Grade. Peirce, Lincoln, illus. 2012. (Big Nate Ser.: 4). (ENG., Illus.). 224p. (J). 9.99 (978-1-4494-2566-1(6)) Andrews McMeel Publishing.

Pelletier, Marthe. Leo a la Mer. Cote, Genevieve, tr. 2003. (Premier Roman Ser.). (FRE., Illus.). 64p. (J). (gr. 1-4). pap. (978-2-89021-637-2(3)) Diffusion du livre Mirabel (DLM).

Penner, Evelyn. The Kid Who Ate Dog Food. Chullabrahm, T. M., illus. 2008. 32p. (J). 15.99 (978-0-9796500-0-0(3)) Peppernut Publishing.

Pennypacker, Sara. Clementine. Frazee, Marla, illus. (ENG.). (J). 2008. 160p. (gr. 2-5). pap. 5.99 (978-0-7868-3883-7(3)) 2006. 144p. (gr. 1-3). 14.99 (978-0-7868-3882-0(5)) Hyperion Pr.

—Clementine & the Family Meeting. Frazee, Marla, illus. (ENG.). 176p. (J). (gr. 2-5). 2012. pap. 5.99 (978-1-4231-2436-8(7)) 2011. 14.99 (978-1-4231-2356-9(5)) Hyperion Pr.

—Clementine & the Family Meeting. 2012. (Clementine Ser.: 5). (J). lib. bdg. 16.00 (978-0-606-26093-0(5), Turtleback) Turtleback Bks.

—Clementine, Friend of the Week. Frazee, Marla, illus. (Clementine Book Ser.). (ENG.). 176p. (J). 2011. (gr. 1-3). pap. 5.99 (978-1-4231-1560-1(0)) 2010. (gr. 2-5). 14.99 (978-1-4231-1355-3(1)) Hyperion Pr.

—Completely Clementine. Frazee, Marla, illus. 2015. (Clementine Book Ser.). (ENG.). 192p. (J). (gr. 1-3). 14.99 (978-1-4231-2358-3(1)) Disney Pr.

—Completely Clementine. Frazee, Marla, illus. 2016. (Clementine Book Ser.). (ENG.). 208p. (J). (gr. 1-3). pap. 5.99 (978-1-4231-2438-2(3)) Hyperion Bks. for Children.

—Meet the Dullards. Salmieri, Daniel, illus. 2015. (ENG.). 32p. (J). (gr. -1-3). 17.99 (978-0-06-219856-3(4)) HarperCollins Pubs.

Perkins, Lynne Rae. Frank & Lucky Get Schooled. Perkins, Lynne Rae, illus. 2016. (Illus.). 32p. (J). (gr. -1-3). 17.99 (978-0-06-237345-8(5), Greenwillow Bks.) HarperCollins Pubs.

Perl, Erica S. The Capybara Conspiracy: A Novel in Three Acts. 2016. (ENG.). 192p. (J). (gr. 5). 16.99 (978-0-399-55171-0(9), Knopf Bks. for Young Readers) Random Hse. Children's Bks.

—Chicken Butt! Cole, Henry, illus. 2009. (ENG.). 32p. (J). (gr. -1-k). 13.95 (978-0-8109-8325-0(7), Abrams Bks. for Young Readers) Abrams, Inc.

—Ferocious Fluffity: A Mighty Bite-Y Class Pet. Cole, Henry, illus. 2016. (ENG.). 32p. (J). (gr. k-2). 16.95 (978-1-4197-2182-3(8), Abrams Bks. for Young Readers) Abrams, Inc.

Perlman, Rhea. Born to Drive. Santat, Dan, illus. 2006. (Otto Undercover Ser.). 127p. (J). (gr. 4-7). 14.99 (978-0-06-075496-9(6), Tegen, Katherine Bks) HarperCollins Pubs.

—Canyon Catastrophe. Santat, Dan, illus. 2006. (Otto Undercover Ser.). 128p. (J). (gr. 4-7). 14.99 (978-0-06-075498-3(2)) HarperCollins Pubs.

Perret, Delphine. Pedro & George. Perret, Delphine, illus. 2015. (ENG., Illus.). 32p. (J). (gr. -1-3). 17.99 (978-1-4814-2925-2(6)) Simon & Schuster Children's Publishing.

Perry, Andrea. The Bicklebys' Birdbath. Angaramo, Roberta, illus. 2010. (ENG.). 40p. (J). (gr. -1-1). 16.99 (978-1-4169-0624-7(X), Atheneum Bks. for Young Readers) Simon & Schuster Children's Publishing.

Perry, Fred. Grossery Games. 2012. (ENG., Illus.). 128p. (J). (gr. 4-7). pap. 10.99 (978-0-9850925-5-9(6), 9780985092559) Antarctic Pr., Inc.

—Playing Dead. 2012. (ENG., Illus.). 128p. (J). pap. 10.99 (978-0-9850925-4-2(8), 9780985092542) Antarctic Pr., Inc.

Perry, John. The Book That Eats People. Fearing, Mark, illus. 2009. (ENG.). 38p. (J). (gr. -1-2). 15.99 (978-1-58246-268-4(2), Tricycle Pr.) Random Hse. Children's Bks.

Petrone, Catherine. Moon Worms. 2010. 27p. (J). pap. 12.95 (978-1-4327-1477-2(5)) Outskirts Pr., Inc.

Petrucha, Stefan. Breaking Down, No. 2. Parker, Rick, illus. 2011. (Papercutz Slices Ser.: 2). (ENG.). 64p. (J). (gr. 5-12). 10.99 (978-1-59707-245-8(1), 9781597072458) Papercutz.

Petrucha, Stefan & Kinney-Petrucha, Margo. Percy Jackson & the Ovolactovegetarians, No. 3. 2011. (Papercutz Slices Ser.). (ENG., Illus.). 64p. (J). (gr. 5-12). pap. 6.99 (978-1-59707-264-9(8), 9781597072649) Papercutz.

Pett, Mark, illus. This Is My Book. 2016. (ENG.). 40p. (J). (gr. -1-2). 17.99 (978-1-101-93790-7(4), Knopf Bks. for Young Readers) Random Hse. Children's Bks.

Petty, J. T. Fairy Killer. Davis, Will, illus. 2011. (ENG.). 128p. (J). (gr. 3-7). pap. 7.99 (978-1-4424-3097-6(4), Simon & Schuster Bks. For Young Readers) Simon & Schuster Bks. For Young Readers.

Pham, LeUyen. The Bear Who Wasn't There. Pham, LeUyen, illus. 2016. (ENG., Illus.). 40p. (J). 16.99 (978-1-59643-970-2(X), 9781596439702) Roaring Brook Pr.

—A Piece of Cake. Pham, LeUyen, illus. 2014. (ENG., Illus.). 40p. (J). (gr. -1-3). 16.99 (978-0-06-199264-3(X)) HarperCollins Pubs.

Philip, Simon. I Don't Know What to Call My Cat. Bailey, Ella, illus. 2017. (ENG.). 32p. (J). (gr. -1-3). 16.99 (978-0-544-97143-1(4), HMH Books For Young Readers) Houghton Mifflin Harcourt Publishing Co.

Phillipps, J. C. Monkey Ono. 2013. (ENG., Illus.). 40p. (J). (gr. -1-k). 16.99 (978-0-670-78505-6(9), Viking Books for Young Readers) Penguin Young Readers Group.

—The Simples Love a Picnic. 2014. (ENG., Illus.). 32p. (J). (gr. -1-3). 16.99 (978-0-544-16667-7(1), HMH Books For Young Readers) Houghton Mifflin Harcourt Publishing Co.

Phillips, Dee & Ticktock Media, Ltd. Staff. What Do Cats Do? 2009. (What Do Animals Do? Ser.). (ENG.). 5p. (J). (gr. k — 1). bds. 4.95 (978-1-84696-958-4(1), TickTock Books) Octopus Publishing Group GBR. Dist: Independent Pubs. Group.

—What Do Monkeys Do? 2009. (What Do Animals Do? Ser.). (ENG.). 5p. (J). (gr. k — 1). bds. 4.95 (978-1-84696-960-7(3), TickTock Books) Octopus Publishing Group GBR. Dist: Independent Pubs. Group.

—What Do Rabbits Do? 2009. (What Do Animals Do? Ser.). (ENG.). 5p. (J). (gr. k — 1). bds. 4.95 (978-1-84696-961-4(1), TickTock Books) Octopus Publishing Group GBR. Dist: Independent Pubs. Group.

Phillips, Sparkle. How to Meet the Man (or Woman) of your Dreams: Or at least, how I met Mine. 2009. (ENG., Illus.). 88p. per. 9.99 (978-0-9779960-3-2(4), Books To Believe In) Thornton Publishing, Inc.

Picayo, Mario & Picayo, Pablo, illus. Four Wishes for Robbie. 2012. (J). (978-1-934370-19-3(3), Campanita Bks.) Editorial Campana.

Pichon, Liz. The Brilliant World of Tom Gates: Read It & Go Ha! Ha! Ha! Pichon, Liz, illus. 2014. (Tom Gates Ser.: 1). (ENG., Illus.). 256p. (J). (gr. 3-7). 12.99 (978-0-7636-7472-4(9)) Candlewick Pr.

—Penguins. 2008. (J). (978-0-545-08292-1(7), Orchard Bks.) Scholastic, Inc.

—TOM GATES: FESTIVAL DE GENIALIDADES (MÁS O MENOS) 2013. (SPA.). 410p. (J). pap. 21.99 (978-84-216-8814-4(6)) Lectorum Pubns., Inc.

—Tom Gates That's Me! (Books One, Two, Three) Pichon, Liz, illus. 2016. (Tom Gates Ser.). (ENG., Illus.). (J). (gr. 3-7). pap. 23.97 (978-0-7636-9216-2(6)) Candlewick Pr.

Pierce, Angelica. Wizard in Blue Jeans. 2007. 184p. pap. 10.95 (978-1-4303-0647-4(5)) Lulu Pr., Inc.

Pilger, Seamus. Fart Squad. Gilpin, Stephen, illus. 2015. (Fart Squad Ser.: 1). (ENG.). 112p. (J). (gr. 1-5). pap. 4.99 (978-0-06-229045-8(2), HarperFestival) HarperCollins Pubs.

—Fartasaurus Rex. Gilpin, Stephen, illus. 2015. (Fart Squad Ser.: 2). (ENG.). 112p. (J). (gr. 1-5). 15.99 (978-0-06-236632-0(7)); pap. 4.99 (978-0-06-229047-2(9)) HarperCollins Pubs.

Pilkey, Dav. The Adventures of Captain Underpants. Pilkey, Dav, illus. 2013. (Captain Underpants Ser.: 1). (ENG., Illus.). 144p. (J). (gr. 2-5). 9.99 (978-0-545-49908-8(9)) Scholastic, Inc.

—The Adventures of Captain Underpants. 2004. (Captain Underpants Ser.: No. 1). (J). lib. bdg. 19.95 (978-0-439-68434-7(X), Scholastic, Inc.) Scholastic, Inc.

—The Adventures of Captain Underpants. 2013. (Captain Underpants Color Edition Ser.: 1). lib. bdg. 20.85 (978-0-606-32441-0(0), Turtleback) Turtleback Bks.

—The Adventures of Super Diaper Baby. Pilkey, Dav, illus. 2014. (ENG., Illus.). 144p. (J). (gr. 3-7). 9.99 (978-0-545-66544-5(2)) Scholastic, Inc.

—The Adventures of Super Diaper Baby. 2004. (J). lib. bdg. 19.95 (978-0-439-68435-4(8), Scholastic, Inc.) Scholastic, Inc.

—The Adventures of Super Diaper Baby. 2014. (Super Diaper Baby Ser.: 1). lib. bdg. 20.85 (978-0-606-36273-3(8)) Turtleback Bks.

—Big, Bad Battle of the Bionic Booger Boy: The Night of the Nasty Nostril Nuggets. 2003. (Captain Underpants Ser.: 6). (gr. 3-6). lib. bdg. 16.00 (978-0-613-68836-9(8), Turtleback) Turtleback Bks.

—El Capitan Calzoncillos y la Furia de la Supermujer Macroelastica. 2003. (Captain Underpants Ser.: 5). (SPA & ENG., Illus.). 176p. (J). (gr. 2-5). pap. 5.99 (978-0-439-53820-6(3), Scholastic en Espanol) Scholastic, Inc.

—El Capitan Calzoncillos y la Ridicula Historia de los Seres del Inodoro Morado. 2008. (Captain Underpants Ser.). (SPA., Illus.). 176p. (J). (gr. 2-5). pap. 5.99 (978-0-545-02583-6(4), Scholastic en Espanol) Scholastic, Inc.

—Captain Underpants & the Attack of the Talking Toilets. 2004. (Captain Underpants Ser.: No. 2). (J). lib. bdg. 19.95 (978-0-439-68436-1(6), Scholastic, Inc.) Scholastic, Inc.

—Captain Underpants & the Big, Bad Battle of the Bionic Booger Boy Part 1: The Night of the Nasty Nostril Nuggets. (Captain Underpants Ser.: Bk. 6). (J). 2004. lib. bdg. 19.95 (978-0-439-68438-5(2), Scholastic, Inc.) 2003. (ENG., Illus.). 176p. (gr. 2-5). 18.99 (978-0-439-37609-9(2)) Scholastic, Inc.

—Captain Underpants & the Big, Bad Battle of the Bionic Booger Boy Part 1: The Night of the Nasty Nostril Nuggets. Pilkey, Dav, illus. 2003. (Captain Underpants Ser.: 6). (ENG., Illus.). 176p. (J). (gr. 2-5). pap. 5.99 (978-0-439-37610-5(6)) Scholastic, Inc.

—Captain Underpants & the Big, Bad Battle of the Bionic Booger Boy Part 2: The Revenge of the Ridiculous Robo-Boogers. 2004. (Captain Underpants Ser.: Bk. 7). (J). lib. bdg. 19.95 (978-0-439-68437-8(4), Scholastic, Inc.) Scholastic, Inc.

—Captain Underpants & the Big, Bad Battle of the Bionic Booger Boy Part 2: The Revenge of the Ridiculous Robo-Boogers. Pilkey, Dav, illus. 2003. (Captain Underpants Ser.: 7). (ENG., Illus.). 176p. (J). (gr. 2-5). 18.99 (978-0-439-37611-2(4)); pap. 5.99 (978-0-439-37612-9(2)) Scholastic, Inc.

—Captain Underpants & the Big, Bad Battle of the Bionic Booger Boy Part 2: The Revenge of the Ridiculous Robo-Boogers. 2003. (Captain Underpants Ser.: 7). lib. bdg. 16.00 (978-0-613-68837-6(6), Turtleback) Turtleback Bks.

—Captain Underpants & the Invasion of the Incredibly Naughty Cafeteria Ladies from Outer Space: (and the Subsequent Assault of the Equally Evil Lunchroom Zombie Nerds) 2004. (Captain Underpants Ser.: No. 3). (J). lib. bdg. 19.95 (978-0-439-68439-2(0), Scholastic, Inc.) Scholastic, Inc.

—Captain Underpants & the Perilous Plot of Professor Poopypants. 2004. (Captain Underpants Ser.: No. 4). (J). lib. bdg. 19.95 (978-0-439-68440-8(4), Scholastic, Inc.) Scholastic, Inc.

—Captain Underpants & the Revolting Revenge of the Radioactive Robo-Boxers. Pilkey, Dav, illus. 2013. (Captain Underpants Ser.: 10). (ENG., Illus.). 192p. (J). (gr. 2-5). 9.99 (978-0-545-17536-4(4)) Scholastic, Inc.

—Captain Underpants & the Revolting Revenge of the Radioactive Robo-Boxers. 2013. (Captain Underpants Ser.: 10). lib. bdg. 20.85 (978-0-606-31563-0(2), Turtleback) Turtleback Bks.

—Captain Underpants & the Sensational Saga of Sir Stinks-a-Lot. Pilkey, Dav, illus. 2015. (Captain Underpants Ser.: 12). (ENG., Illus.). 208p. (J). (gr. 2). 9.99 (978-0-545-50492-8(9)) Scholastic, Inc.

—Captain Underpants & the Sensational Saga of Sir Stinks-a-Lot. Pilkey, Dav, illus. 2015. (Captain Underpants Ser.: 12). (ENG., Illus.). 208p. (J). (gr. 2). lib. bdg. 20.85 (978-0-606-37924-3(X)) Turtleback Bks.

—Captain Underpants & the Terrifying Return of Tippy Tinkletrousers. Pilkey, Dav, illus. 2012. (Captain Underpants Ser.: 9). (ENG., Illus.). 304p. (J). (gr. 2-5). 9.99 (978-0-545-17534-0(8)) Scholastic, Inc.

—Captain Underpants & the Terrifying Return of Tippy Tinkletrousers. 2012. (Captain Underpants Ser.: 9). lib. bdg. 20.85 (978-0-606-26523-2(6), Turtleback) Turtleback Bks.

—Captain Underpants & the Wrath of the Wicked Wedgie Woman. 2004. (Captain Underpants Ser.: No. 5). (J). lib. bdg. 19.95 (978-0-439-68441-5(2), Scholastic, Inc.) Scholastic, Inc.

—Dog Breath! The Horrible Trouble with Hally Tosis. 2004. (Scholastic Bookshelf Ser.). (Illus.). 32p. (gr. -1-3). 17.00 (978-0-7569-3189-6(4)) Perfection Learning Corp.

—Dog Breath! The Horrible Trouble with Hally Tosis. Pilkey, Dav, illus. 3rd ed. 2004. (Scholastic Bookshelf Ser.). (ENG., Illus.). 32p. (J). (gr. -1-3). pap. 6.99 (978-0-439-59839-2(7), Scholastic Paperbacks) Scholastic, Inc.

—Dog Man. Pilkey, Dav, illus. 2016. (Dog Man Ser.: 1). (ENG., Illus.). 240p. (J). (gr. 2). 9.99 (978-0-545-58160-8(5), Graphix) Scholastic, Inc.

—Dog Man Unleashed. 2016. (Dog Man Ser.: 2). (ENG., Illus.). 224p. (J). (gr. 2-7). 9.99 (978-0-545-93520-3(2), Graphix) Scholastic, Inc.

—Dog Man Unleashed. 2016. (Dog Man Ser.: 2). (ENG.). (J). (gr. 2). lib. bdg. 20.85 **(978-0-606-39709-4(4))**; 240p. 20.85 (978-0-606-39115-3(0)) Turtleback Bks.

—The Dumb Bunnies. 2007. (Dumb Bunnies Ser.). (ENG., Illus.). 32p. (J). (gr. -1-3). 12.99 (978-0-545-03938-3(X), Levine, Arthur A. Bks.) Scholastic, Inc.

—The Dumb Bunnies' Easter. 2008. (Dumb Bunnies Ser.). (ENG., Illus.). 32p. (J). (gr. -1-3). pap. 6.99 (978-0-545-00880-8(8), Scholastic Paperbacks) Scholastic, Inc.

—Dumb Bunnies' Easter. Pilkey, Dav, illus. 2009. (Dumb Bunnies Ser.). (ENG., Illus.). 32p. (J). (gr. -1-3). 16.99 (978-0-545-03946-8(0)) Scholastic, Inc.

—The Dumb Bunnies Go to the Zoo. (Dumb Bunnies Ser.). (ENG.). 32p. 2009. (J). (gr. -1-3). 16.99 (978-0-545-03937-6(1)) 2007. pap. 5.99 (978-0-439-93049-9(9)) Scholastic, Inc.

—The Invasion of the Potty Snatchers. 2011. (Super Diaper Baby Ser.: 2). lib. bdg. 20.85 (978-0-606-23331-6(8), Turtleback) Turtleback Bks.

—Make Way for Dumb Bunnies. 2007. (Dumb Bunnies Ser.). (ENG., Illus.). 32p. (J). (gr. -1-3). 10.99 (978-0-545-03939-0(8), Levine, Arthur A. Bks.) Scholastic, Inc.

—Mighty Robot vs. the Mecha-Monkeys from Mars. Santat, Dan, illus. 2014. (Ricky Ricotta Ser.: 4). (ENG.). 144p. (J). (gr. -1-3). pap. 5.99 (978-0-545-63012-2(6)) Scholastic, Inc.

—Mighty Robot vs. the Mutant Mosquitoes from Mercury. Santat, Dan, illus. 2014. (Ricky Ricotta Ser.: 2). (ENG.). 128p. (J). (gr. -1-3). pap. 5.99 (978-0-545-63010-8(X)) Scholastic, Inc.

—Ricky Ricotta's Mighty Robot vs. the Jurassic Jackrabbits from Jupiter. Santat, Dan, illus. 2014. (Ricky Ricotta Ser.: 5). (ENG.). 128p. (J). (gr. -1-3). pap. 5.99 (978-0-545-63013-9(4)) Scholastic, Inc.

—A Tale of Two Kitties. 2017. (Dog Man Ser.: bk.3). (ENG., Illus.). 256p. (J). (gr. 2-5). 9.99 **(978-0-545-93521-0(0),** Graphix) Scholastic, Inc.

—A Tale of Two Kitties. 2017. (Dog Man Ser.: 3). lib. bdg. 20.85 **(978-0-606-40547-8(X))** Turtleback Bks.

Pilkey, Dav. The Voodoo Vultures from Venus. Santat, Dan, illus. 2014. (Ricky Ricotta Ser.: 3). (ENG.). 128p. (J). (gr. -1-3). pap. 5.99 (978-0-545-63011-5(8)) Scholastic, Inc.

Pilkey, Dav & Scholastic Canada Ltd. Staff. The Invasion of the Potty Snatchers. Pilkey, Dav, illus. 2011. (Captain Underpants Ser.: 2). (ENG., Illus.). 192p. (J). (gr. 2-5). 9.99 (978-0-545-17532-6(1)) Scholastic, Inc.

Pilutti, Deb. Bear & Squirrel Are Friends ... Yes, Really! Pilutti, Deb, illus. 2015. (ENG., Illus.). 40p. (J). (gr. -1-3). 17.99 (978-1-4814-2913-9(2), Simon & Schuster Bks. For Young Readers) Simon & Schuster Bks. For Young Readers.

—Ten Rules of Being a Superhero. Pilutti, Deb, illus. 2014. (ENG., Illus.). 32p. (J). (gr. -1-2). 17.99 (978-0-8050-9759-7(7), 9780805097597, Holt, Henry & Co. Bks. For Young Readers) Holt, Henry & Co.

Pinkwater, Daniel M. Adventures of a Cat-Whiskered Girl. 2011. (ENG., Illus.). 288p. (J). (gr. 5-7). pap. 16.95 (978-0-547-55002-2(2)) Houghton Mifflin Harcourt Publishing Co.

—Bear in Love. Hillenbrand, Will, illus. 2012. (ENG.). 40p. (J). (gr. k-k). 15.99 (978-0-7636-4569-4(9)) Candlewick Pr.

—Dancing Larry, 1 vol. Pinkwater, Jill, illus. 2006. (ENG.). 32p. (J). (gr. -1-3). 16.95 (978-0-7614-5220-1(6)) Marshall Cavendish Corp.

—Four Hoboken Stories. 2017. (ENG.). 224p. (J). pap. 16.95 **(978-0-486-81571-8(4))** Dover Pubns., Inc.

—The Hoboken Chicken Emergency. Auth, Tony, illus. 2007. (ENG.). 112p. (J). (gr. 1-4). pap. 5.99 (978-1-4169-2810-2(3), Aladdin) Simon & Schuster Children's Publishing.

—Irving & Muktuk: Two Bad Bears. 2004. (Illus.). (J). (gr. k-3). spiral bd. (978-0-616-11136-9(3)); spiral bd.

(978-0-616-11137-6(1)) Canadian National Institute for the Blind/Institut National Canadien pour les Aveugles.

—Mrs. Noodlekugel. Stower, Adam, illus. (Mrs. Noodlekugel Ser.). (ENG.). 80p. (J). (gr. k-4). 2013. pap. 5.99 (978-0-7636-6452-7(9)) 2012. 14.99 (978-0-7636-5053-7(6)) Candlewick Pr.

—Mrs. Noodlekugel & Four Blind Mice. Stower, Adam, illus. (Mrs. Noodlekugel Ser.). (ENG.). 96p. (J). (gr. k-4). 2015. pap. 5.99 (978-0-7636-7658-2(6)) 2013. 14.99 (978-0-7636-5054-4(4)) Candlewick Pr.

—The Neddiad: How Neddie Took the Train, Went to Hollywood, & Saved Civilization. Brown, Calef, illus. 2009. (ENG.). 320p. (J). (gr. 5-7). pap. 8.99 (978-0-547-13367-6(7)) Houghton Mifflin Harcourt Publishing Co.

—The Yggyssey: How Iggy Wondered What Happened to All the Ghosts, Found Out Where They Went, & Went There. 2010. (ENG., Illus.). 256p. (J). (gr. 5-7). pap. 6.99 (978-0-547-32865-2(6)) Houghton Mifflin Harcourt Publishing Co.

Pirc, Jerri J. Kate & Caboodle. Smith, Jane, illus. 2015. pap. (978-0-473-32583-1(7)) Pirc, Jerri J.

Pitcock, Tiffany. Just Friends. 2017. (ENG.). 320p. (YA). pap. 10.99 (978-1-250-08405-7(9), 9781250084057) Feiwel & Friends.

Pitt, Marilyn. Run Away. 2015. (1B Potato Chip Bks.). (ENG., Illus.). 16p. (J). pap. 5.99 (978-1-63437-090-5(2)) American Reading Co.

—Smelling Good. Bianchi, John, illus. 2014. (1B Potato Chip Bks.). (ENG.). 16p. (J). pap. 5.99 (978-1-61406-685-9(X)) American Reading Co.

—What Are You Thinking? 2015. (1B Potato Chip Bks.). (ENG., Illus.). 16p. (J). pap. 5.99 (978-1-63437-056-1(2)) American Reading Co.

Pittar, Gill. Milly, Molly & Aunt Maude (book W/dolls) 2006. 28p. pap. (978-1-86972-101-5(2)) Milly Molly Bks.

—Milly, Molly & Taffy Bogle (book W/dolls) 2006. 28p. pap. (978-1-86972-092-6(X)) Milly Molly Bks.

Pittau, Francesco & Gervais, Bernadette. That's Dangerous! 2004. (ENG., Illus.). 80p. 9.99 (978-1-57912-350-5(3), 81350, Black Dog & Leventhal Pubs. Inc.) Hachette Bks.

Pizzoli, Greg. The Watermelon Seed. Pizzoli, Greg, illus. 2013. (ENG., Illus.). 40p. (J). (gr. -1-k). 16.99 (978-1-4231-7101-0(2)) Disney Pr.

Plante, Raymond. Le Grand Role de Marilou Polaire. Favreau, Marie-Claude, illus. 2003. (Premier Roman Ser.). (FRE.). 64p. (J). (gr. 2-5). pap. (978-2-89021-288-6(2)) Diffusion du livre Mirabel (DLM).

Plourde, Josee. La Promesse des iles. Lemelin, Linda, tr. 2003. (Premier Roman Ser.). (FRE., Illus.). 64p. (J). (gr. 1-4). pap. (978-2-89021-630-3(6)) Diffusion du livre Mirabel (DLM).

Plourde, Lynn. Book Fair Day. Wickstrom, Thor, illus. 2006. (J). (978-1-4156-8095-7(7), Dutton Juvenile) Penguin Publishing Group.

Pluta, K. There's a Yak in my Bed. Stallop, Christy, illus. 2007. (ENG.). 32p. (J). (gr. -1 — 1). 16.95 (978-0-9769417-4-3(0)) Blooming Tree Pr.

Pochenko. Conspiracy Prophecy II: WWIII & Rumors of WWIV in Revelation. 2003. 230p. (YA). pap. 14.95 (978-0-595-26419-3(0), Writer's Showcase Pr.) iUniverse, Inc.

Poer, Karla R. The Busy-Body Book of Fun-Atomy Tunes. 2008. (ENG.). 56p. pap. 21.99 (978-1-4389-3296-5(0)) AuthorHouse.

Polacco, Patricia. Ginger & Petunia. Polacco, Patricia, illus. 2007. (ENG., Illus.). 40p. (J). (gr. -1-3). 17.99 (978-0-399-24539-8(1), Philomel Bks.) Penguin Young Readers Group.

—Oh, Look! Polacco, Patricia, illus. 2004. (ENG., Illus.). 32p. (J). (gr. -1-3). 16.99 (978-0-399-24223-6(6), Philomel Bks.) Penguin Young Readers Group.

Polette, Keith. Moon over the Mountain. 2009. (ENG.). 32p. (J). (gr. -1-3). 16.95 (978-1-934960-07-3(1), Raven Tree Pr.,Csi) Continental Sales, Inc.

—Moon over the Mountain/Luna Sobre la Montana. 2009. (ENG & SPA.). 32p. (J). (gr. -1-3). 16.95 (978-1-932748-85-7(7)); pap. 7.95 (978-1-932748-84-0(9)) Continental Sales, Inc. (Raven Tree Pr.,Csi).

—Paco & the Giant Chile Plant/Paco y la Planta de Chile Gigante. Dulemba, Elizabeth, illus. 2008. (ENG & SPA.). 32p. (J). (gr. -1-3). pap. 7.95 (978-0-9794462-3-8(6), Raven Tree Pr.,Csi) Continental Sales, Inc.

Polhemus, Coleman. The Crocodile Blues. Polhemus, Coleman, illus. 2007. (ENG., Illus.). 48p. (J). (gr. -1-2). 16.99 (978-0-7636-3543-5(X)) Candlewick Pr.

Pollard, Mary Jean. Octrina the Octopus. 2011. 28p. pap. 15.99 (978-1-4568-4778-4(3)) Xlibris Corp.

Ponti, Jamie. Sea of Love. 2008. (Romantic Comedies Ser.). (ENG.). 272p. (YA). (gr. 7-18). mass mkt. 6.99 (978-1-4169-6791-0(5), Simon Pulse) Simon Pulse.

Poole, Vera. The Adventures of Natsoodatle: The Stolen Blankets. 2013. 24p. pap. 14.93 (978-1-4669-8719-7(7)) Trafford Publishing.

Port, Cynthia. Kibble Talk. Port, Cynthia, illus. 2013. (Illus.). 214p. pap. 9.99 (978-0-9912278-0-8(8)) Port, Cynthia L.

Portis, Antoinette. Best Frints in the Whole Universe. 2016. (ENG., Illus.). 40p. (J). 16.99 (978-1-62672-136-4(X), 9781626721364) Roaring Brook Pr.

Poskitt, Kjartan. Agatha Parrot & the Heart of Mud. Hargis, Wes, illus. 2016. (Agatha Parrot Ser.). (ENG.). 160p. (J). (gr. 2-5). 16.99 (978-0-544-50876-7(9)) Houghton Mifflin Harcourt Publishing Co.

—Agatha Parrot & the Odd Street School Ghost. Hargis, Wes, illus. (ENG.). 160p. (J). (gr. 2-5). 2017. pap. 6.99 (978-0-544-93530-3(6), HMH Books For Young Readers) 2016. 16.99 (978-0-544-50672-5(3)) Houghton Mifflin Harcourt Publishing Co.

Poskitt, Kjartan & Hargis, Wes. Agatha Parrot & the Thirteenth Chicken. 2017. (Agatha Parrot Ser.). (ENG., Illus.). 160p. (J). (gr. 2-5). 16.99 (978-0-544-50909-2(9)) Houghton Mifflin Harcourt Publishing Co.

Postgate, Daniel. Love Stinks. 2012. (J). (978-1-61913-132-3(3)) Weigl Pubs., Inc.

Potter, Beatrix. Mystery Thief! 2013. (Peter Rabbit Animation Ser.). (ENG.). 32p. (J). (gr. -1-k). 3.99 (978-0-7232-8041-5(X), Warne) Penguin Young Readers Group.

Potter, Ellen. Otis Dooda: Strange but True. Heatley, David, illus. 2013. (Otis Dooda Ser.: 1). (ENG.). 240p. (J). (gr. 2-5). 13.99 (978-1-250-01176-3(0), 9781250011763) Feiwel & Friends.

—Otis Dooda: Downright Dangerous. Heatley, David, illus. 2014. (Otis Dooda Ser.: 2). (ENG.). 240p. (J). (gr. 2-5). 13.99 (978-1-250-01177-0(9), 9781250011770) Feiwel & Friends.

Pounder, Sibéal. Witch Switch. Anderson, Laura Ellen, illus. 2017. (Witch Wars Ser.). (ENG.). 272p. (J). 16.99 (978-1-61963-984-3(X), 9781619639843, Bloomsbury USA Childrens) Bloomsbury Publishing USA.

—Witch Wars. Anderson, Laura Ellen, illus. 2016. (Witch Wars Ser.). (ENG.). 272p. (J). 16.99 (978-1-61963-925-6(4), 9781619639256, Bloomsbury USA Childrens) Bloomsbury Publishing USA.

Powell, Joyce. The Greatest Marriage Ever. Schacher, Tracey, illus. 2011. 26p. pap. 11.95 (978-1-4575-0215-6(1)) Dog Ear Publishing, LLC.

Powell, Randy. Three Clams & an Oyster. 2007. 216p. (gr. 7-12). 16.95 (978-0-7569-8184-6(0)) Perfection Learning Corp.

Power, Timothy. The Boy Who Howled. 2012. (ENG.). 272p. (YA). (gr. 3-12). pap. 7.99 (978-1-59990-852-6(2), 9781599908526, Bloomsbury USA Childrens) Bloomsbury Publishing USA.

Pratchett, Terry. The Amazing Maurice & His Educated Rodents. 2008. (Discworld Novels Ser.). 368p. (YA). (gr. 8-18). pap. 8.99 (978-0-06-001235-9(8)) HarperCollins Pubs.

—The Amazing Maurice & His Educated Rodents. 2003. (ENG.). 340p. (gr. 7). 19.00 (978-0-7569-1458-5(2)) Perfection Learning Corp.

—The Amazing Maurice & His Educated Rodents. 2008. (Discworld Ser.: 33). (YA). (gr. 5-8). 19.65 (978-0-613-65757-0(8), Turtleback) Turtleback Bks.

—Dodger. 368p. (YA). (gr. 8). 2013. pap. 9.99 (978-0-06-200951-7(6)) 2012. 17.99 (978-0-06-200949-4(4)) 2012. lib. bdg. 18.89 (978-0-06-200950-0(8)) HarperCollins Pubs.

—Dragons at Crumbling Castle: And Other Tales. Beech, Mark, illus. (ENG.). 352p. (J). 2016. (gr. 5-7). pap. 7.99 (978-0-544-81313-7(8), HMH Books For Young Readers) 2015. (gr. 4-7). 16.99 (978-0-544-46659-3(4)) Houghton Mifflin Harcourt Publishing Co.

—A Hat Full of Sky. 2004. (Tiffany Aching Ser.: 2). 288p. (YA). (gr. 8-18). 17.99 (978-0-06-058660-7(5)) HarperCollins Pubs.

—A Hat Full of Sky. 2005. 407p. (gr. 7). 19.00 (978-0-7569-5126-9(7)) Perfection Learning Corp.

—A Hat Full of Sky. 2005. (Discworld Ser.: 32). 407p. (YA). 19.65 (978-1-4177-2658-5(X), Turtleback) Turtleback Bks.

—Johnny & the Dead. 2006. (Johnny Maxwell Trilogy). 213p. (J). (gr. 3-7). 15.99 (978-0-06-054188-0(1)); lib. bdg. 16.89 (978-0-06-054189-7(X)) HarperCollins Pubs.

—Sourcery. 2013. (Discworld Ser.: 5). (gr. 5-8). 20.85 (978-0-613-57278-1(5), Turtleback) Turtleback Bks.

—The Wee Free Men. (Tiffany Aching Ser.). (YA). (gr. 8). 2010. 576p. pap. 9.99 (978-0-06-201217-3(7)) 2006. 400p. reprint ed. pap. 8.99 (978-0-06-001238-0(2)) HarperCollins Pubs.

—The Wee Free Men. 2004. 19.00 (978-0-7569-3252-7(1)) Perfection Learning Corp.

—The Wee Free Men. 2006. (Discworld Ser.: 28). (YA). 19.65 (978-1-4176-2764-6(6), Turtleback) Turtleback Bks.

Press, J. Robots Don't Clean Toilets. Kline, Michael, illus. 2013. (Doodles of Sam Dibble Ser.: 3). (ENG.). 128p. (J). (gr. 1-3). pap. 4.99 (978-0-448-46109-0(9), Grosset & Dunlap) Penguin Young Readers Group.

Preussler, Otfried. The Robber Hotzenplotz. Bell, Anthea, tr. Tripp, F. J., illus. 2016. (ENG.). 128p. (J). (gr. k-4). 15.95 (978-1-59017-961-1(7), NYR Children's Collection) New York Review of Bks., Inc., The.

Price, Olivia. All Aboard Noah's Ark: A Touch & Feel Book. Mitchell, Melanie, illus. 2008. (ENG.). 12p. (J). (gr. -1). 12.95 (978-1-58117-778-7(X), Intervisual/Piggy Toes) Bendon, Inc.

Price, Roger & Stern, Leonard. Spy Mad Libs. 2012. (Mad Libs Ser.). (ENG.). 48p. (J). (gr. 3-7). 4.99 (978-0-8431-7297-3(5), Mad Libs) Penguin Young Readers Group.

Price, Roger & Stern, Leonard, creators. Adventure Time Mad Libs. 2012. (Adventure Time Ser.). (ENG.). 48p. (J). (gr. 3-7). 4.99 (978-0-8431-7221-8(5), Mad Libs) Penguin Young Readers Group.

—Mr. Men Little Miss Mad Libs. 2012. (Mr. Men & Little Miss Ser.). (ENG.). 48p. (J). (gr. 3-7). pap. 3.99 (978-0-8431-6712-2(2), Mad Libs) Penguin Young Readers Group.

—Penguin Classics Mad Libs. 2012. (Mad Libs Ser.). (ENG.). 48p. (J). (gr. 3-7). pap. 4.99 (978-0-8431-7196-9(0), Mad Libs) Penguin Young Readers Group.

—Totally Pink Mad Libs. 2010. (Mad Libs Ser.). (ENG.). 48p. (J). (gr. 3-7). 4.99 (978-0-8431-9898-0(2), Mad Libs) Penguin Young Readers Group.

—Undead Mad Libs. 2011. (Mad Libs Ser.). (ENG.). 48p. (J). (gr. 3-7). 4.99 (978-0-8431-9863-8(X), Mad Libs) Penguin Young Readers Group.

Priceman, Marjorie. How to Make a Cherry Pie & See the U. S. A. 2013. lib. bdg. 18.40 (978-0-606-32190-7(X), Turtleback) Turtleback Bks.

Primavera, Elise. Louise the Big Cheese & the Back-To-School Smarty-Pants. Goode, Diane, illus. 2011. (ENG.). 40p. (J). (gr. k-3). 16.99 (978-1-4424-0600-1(3), Simon & Schuster/Paula Wiseman Bks.) Simon & Schuster/Paula Wiseman Bks.

—Louise the Big Cheese & the La-Di-Da Shoes. Goode, Diane, illus. 2010. (ENG.). 40p. (J). (gr. k-3). 16.99 (978-1-4169-7181-8(5), Simon & Schuster/Paula Wiseman Bks.) Simon & Schuster/Paula Wiseman Bks.

—Secret Order Gumm Street Girl, No. 2. 2006. (978-0-06-056950-1(6)); (978-0-06-056949-5(2)) HarperCollins Canada, Ltd.

Pringle, Cindy & Pringle, Kirby. Happy Tails: Earl & Pearl on the Farm. l.t. ed. 2006. (ENG., Illus.). 32p. (J). (gr. k-2). (978-0-9777126-0-1(5)) Dogtown Artworks.

Prinz, Yvonne. Still There, Clare. 2005. (ENG.). 4p. (J). pap., tchr. ed. (978-1-55192-821-0(3)) Raincoast Bk. Distribution CAN. Dist: Publishers Group West (PGW).

Prioleau, J. N. Clyde & His Messy Room. 2009. 24p. 13.95 (978-0-578-00427-3(5)) Prioleau, Jivonne.

Pritchett, Georgia. Wilf the Mighty Worrier: Battles a Pirate. 2016. (Wilf the Mighty Worrier Ser.: 2). (ENG., Illus.). 208p. (J). 16.99 (978-1-68144-320-1(1)) Quercus NA.

Proimos, James, Jr. Apocalypse Meow Meow. Proimos, James, Jr., illus. 2015. (ENG., Illus.). 224p. (J). (gr. 3-6). 13.99 (978-1-61963-472-5(4), 9781619634725, Bloomsbury USA Childrens) Bloomsbury Publishing USA.

Proimos, James. The Complete Adventures of Johnny Mutton. 2014. (ENG., Illus.). 160p. (J). (gr. 1-4). 12.99 (978-0-544-32404-6(8), HMH Books For Young Readers) Houghton Mifflin Harcourt Publishing Co.

Proimos, James, III & Proimos, James, Jr. Apocalypse Bow Wow. Proimos, James, Jr., illus. 2015. (ENG., Illus.). 224p. (J). (gr. 3-6). 13.99 (978-1-61963-442-8(2), 9781619634428, Bloomsbury USA Childrens) Bloomsbury Publishing USA.

Prom Crashers. 2014. (Romantic Comedies Ser.). (ENG., Illus.). 256p. (YA). (gr. 9). pap. 12.99 (978-1-4814-2747-0(4), Simon Pulse) Simon Pulse.

Publications International Ltd. Staff, ed. Spooky Stories. 2008. (J). 12.98 (978-1-4127-9384-1(X)) Publications International, Ltd.

Pullman, Philip. The Scarecrow & His Servant. Bailey, Peter, illus. (ENG.). 240p. (J). (gr. 3-7). 2007. 7.99 (978-0-440-42130-6(6), Yearling) 2005. 15.95 (978-0-375-81531-7(7), Knopf Bks. for Young Readers) Random Hse. Children's Bks.

—Spring-Heeled Jack. Mostyn, David, illus. 2004. (ENG.). 112p. (J). (gr. 3-7). pap. 5.99 (978-0-440-41881-8(X), Yearling) Random Hse. Children's Bks.

—Two Crafty Criminals! And How They Were Captured by the Daring Detectives of the New Cut Gang. (ENG.). 288p. (J). (gr. 3-7). 2013. 7.99 (978-0-307-93035-4(1), Yearling) 2012. (Illus.). 16.99 (978-0-375-87029-3(6), Knopf Bks. for Young Readers) Random Hse. Children's Bks.

Pulver, Robin. Persuading Miss Doover. Sisson, Stéphanie Roth, illus. 2015. (J). (978-0-8234-3426-8(5)) Holiday Hse., Inc.

—Thank You, Miss Doover. Sisson, Stéphanie Roth, illus. 2010. (ENG.). 32p. (J). (gr. k-3). 17.95 (978-0-8234-2046-9(9)) Holiday Hse., Inc.

Punter, Russell & MacKinnon, Mairi. Snail Brings the Mail. Blunt, Fred, illus. 2014. (Usborne Phonics Readers Ser.). (ENG.). (J). pap. 6.99 (978-0-7945-3369-4(8), Usborne) EDC Publishing.

Quartey, Esme. Life with My Sister ChanSadiefay Thompso. 2006. 64p. per. 8.95 (978-0-595-39224-7(5)) iUniverse, Inc.

Quillen, Carl. Dragon Girl Myra. 2009. 53p. pap. 5.56 (978-0-557-08268-1(4)) Lulu Pr., Inc.

Quinn, Spencer, pseud. Paw & Order: A Chet & Bernie Mystery. 2015. (Chet & Bernie Mystery Ser.: 7). (ENG.). 336p. pap. 16.00 (978-1-4767-0340-4(X)) Simon & Schuster, Inc.

Rabe, Tish. Big Snowman, Little Snowman. Random House Disney Staff, illus. 2013. (Step into Reading Ser.). (ENG.). 32p. (J). (gr. -1-1). 3.99 (978-0-7364-3119-4(5), RH/Disney) Random Hse. Children's Bks.

—Innovative Kids Readers: Milly's Silly Suitcase - Level 1. Janovitz, Marilyn, illus. 2006. (J). (gr. -1-1). 6.99 (978-1-58476-493-9(7)) Innovative Kids.

Raczka, Bob. Fall Mixed Up. Cameron, Chad, illus. 2011. (Carolrhoda Picture Books Ser.). (ENG.). 40p. (J). (gr. -1-3). lib. bdg. 17.95 (978-0-7613-4606-7(6), Carolrhoda Bks.) Lerner Publishing Group.

Raf, Mindy. The Symptoms of My Insanity. 2014. (ENG.). 384p. (YA). (gr. 7). pap. 9.99 (978-0-14-242264-9(9), Speak) Penguin Young Readers Group.

Rains, Deborah Jane. A Spooky Happy Halloween with Cuddles & Snuggles. 2011. 20p. pap. 24.95 (978-1-4489-4423-1(6)) America Star Bks.

Ramsnips, Tunder. The Hardly Boys. 2010. 196p. pap. 15.95 (978-0-557-38767-0(1)) Lulu Pr., Inc.

Randles, Slim & Montoya, Jerry, illus. Ol' Jimmy Dollar. 2015. 42p. (J). (978-1-936744-40-4(6)) LPD Pr.

Random House Disney. Moana Junior Novelization. Random House Disney, illus. 2016. (Junior Novel Ser.). (ENG., Illus.). 144p. (J). (gr. 2-5). 17.20 (978-0-606-39357-7(9)) Turtleback Bks.

Random House Disney Staff. Anna's Act of Love - Elsa's Icy Magic, 2 bks. in 1. Random House Disney Staff, illus. 2013. (Pictureback(R) Ser.). (ENG., Illus.). 24p. (J). (gr. -1-2). 4.99 (978-0-7364-3061-6(X), RH/Disney) Random Hse. Children's Bks.

—Frozen Junior Novelization (Disney Frozen) Random House Disney Staff, illus. 2013. (Junior Novel Ser.). (ENG., Illus.). 128p. (J). (gr. 3-7). 4.99 (978-0-7364-3118-7(7), RH/Disney) Random Hse. Children's Bks.

—Frozen Little Golden Book (Disney Frozen) Random House Disney Staff, illus. 2013. (Little Golden Book Ser.). (ENG., Illus.). 24p. (J). (-k). 3.99 (978-0-7364-3051-7(2), Golden/Disney) Random Hse. Children's Bks.

—Up. Random House Disney Staff, illus. 2009. (Little Golden Book Ser.). (ENG., Illus.). 24p. (J). (gr. -1-2). 4.99 (978-0-7364-2581-0(0), Golden/Disney) Random Hse. Children's Bks.

—Walt Disney's Mary Poppins (Disney Classics) Random House Disney Staff, illus. 2016. (Little Golden Book Ser.). (ENG., Illus.). 24p. (J). (gr. -1-k). 4.99 (978-0-7364-3468-3(2), Golden/Disney) Random Hse. Children's Bks.

—Zootopia Big Golden Book (Disney Zootopia) Random House Disney Staff, illus. 2016. (Big Golden Book Ser.). (ENG., Illus.). 64p. (J). (gr. -1-2). 9.99 (978-0-7364-3384-6(8), Golden/Disney) Random Hse. Children's Bks.

—Zootopia Junior Novelization (Disney Zootopia) Random House Disney Staff, illus. 2016. (Junior Novel Ser.). (ENG., Illus.). 128p. (J). (gr. 4-7). 5.99 (978-0-7364-3394-5(5), RH/Disney) Random Hse. Children's Bks.

—Zootopia: the Official Handbook (Disney Zootopia) Random House Disney Staff, illus. 2016. (Official Guide Ser.). (ENG., Illus.). 64p. (J). (gr. 4-7). 7.99 (978-0-7364-3395-2(3), RH/Disney) Random Hse. Children's Bks.

Random House Disney Staff & Knowles, Heather. Zootopia Little Golden Book (Disney Zootopia) Random House Disney Staff, illus. 2016. (Little Golden Book Ser.). (ENG., Illus.). 24p. (J). (gr. -1-k). 4.99 (978-0-7364-3389-1(9), Golden/Disney) Random Hse. Children's Bks.

Ransom, Jeanie Franz. The Crown Affair. Axelsen, Stephen, illus. 2015. (Nursery-Rhyme Mysteries Ser.). (ENG.). 40p. (J). (gr. 1-4). lib. bdg. 16.95 (978-1-58089-552-1(2)) Charlesbridge Publishing, Inc.

—What Do Parents Do? (When You're Not Home), 1 vol. Moore, Cyd, illus. 2007. (ENG.). 32p. (J). (gr. k-3). 16.95 (978-1-56145-409-9(5)) Peachtree Pubs.

—What Really Happened to Humpty? From the Files of a Hard-Boiled Detective. Axelsen, Stephen, illus. 2010. (Nursery-Rhyme Mysteries Ser.). (ENG.). 40p. (J). (gr. 1-4). pap. 7.95 (978-1-58089-391-6(0)) Charlesbridge Publishing, Inc.

Rao, Lisa. Don't Bite Your Friends! 2009. (Yo Gabba Gabba! Ser.). (ENG.). 10p. (J). (gr. -1-2). 8.99 (978-1-4169-9014-7(3), Simon Spotlight) Simon Spotlight.

Raschka, Chris. Clammy Clam. Raschka, Chris, illus. 2014. (Thingy Things Ser.). (ENG., Illus.). 24p. (J). (gr. -1-k). 6.95 (978-1-4197-1201-2(2), Abrams Appleseed) Abrams, Inc.

—Cowy Cow. 2014. (Thingy Things Ser.). (ENG., Illus.). 24p. (J). (gr. -1-k). 6.95 (978-1-4197-1055-1(9), Abrams Appleseed) Abrams, Inc.

—The Doorman's Repose. 2017. (ENG., Illus.). 184p. (J). (gr. 5-7). 17.95 (978-1-68137-100-9(6), NYR Children's Collection) New York Review of Bks., Inc., The.

Rash, Andy. Archie the Daredevil Penguin. Rash, Andy, illus. 2015. (ENG., Illus.). 34p. (J). (gr. -1-3). 16.99 (978-0-451-47123-9(7), Viking Books for Young Readers) Penguin Young Readers Group.

Rasheed, Winnona. Itchy Scratchy Spots. 2012. 56p. pap. 8.99 (978-1-60820-727-5(7)) MLR Pr., LLC.

Raskin, Ellen. The Mysterious Disappearence of Leon. Raskin, Ellen, illus. 2011. (ENG., Illus.). 176p. (J). (gr. 3-7). 6.99 (978-0-14-241700-3(9), Puffin Books) Penguin Young Readers Group.

—The Westing Game. 2003. 182p. (J). lib. bdg. 15.00 (978-1-4242-2271-1(0)) Fitzgerald Bks.

Rateau, Loy. David's Prayers: A Boy's Perseverance of Conquering the Enemy. 2005. 17.00 (978-0-8059-9834-4(9)) Dorrance Publishing Co., Inc.

Rayburn, Tricia. Ruby's Slippers. 2010. (ENG.). 352p. (J). (gr. 4-8). pap. 7.99 (978-1-4169-8701-7(0), Aladdin) Simon & Schuster Children's Publishing.

Rayner, Robert. Miss Little's Losers, 1 vol. 2003. (Lorimer Sports Stories Ser.). (ENG.). 128p. (J). (gr. 4-8). 16.95 (978-1-55028-811-7(3), 9781550288117) Lorimer, James & Co., Ltd., Pubs. CAN. Dist: Casemate Pubs. & Bk. Distributors, LLC.

Reader's Digest Staff. Tractor Trouble Drive Through Storybook. Pitt, Sarah, illus. 2011. (Drive-Through Storybooks Ser.). (ENG.). 10p. (J). (gr. -1-1). bds. 12.99 (978-0-7944-2169-4(5)) Reader's Digest Assn., Inc., The.

Ready Set Laugh. 2004. (J). per. (978-1-57657-458-4(X)) Paradise Pr., Inc.

Reagan, Jean. How to Babysit a Grandpa. Wildish, Lee, illus. 2012. (ENG.). 32p. (J). (gr. k-3). 16.99 (978-0-375-86713-2(9), Knopf Bks. for Young Readers) Knopf, Alfred A. Inc.

Real, Stuart. The Cone Stories. 2007. 140p. per. 11.95 (978-0-9556755-0-8(2)) Lulu Pr., Inc.

Redeker, Kent. Don't Splash the Sasquatch! Staake, Bob, illus. 2016. (Sasquatch Picture Book Ser.). (ENG.). 40p. (J). (gr. -1-k). 16.99 (978-1-4231-5233-0(6)) Hyperion Bks. for Children.

Reed, Lynn Rowe. Bear's Big Breakfast. Helquist, Brett, illus. 2016. 32p. (J). (gr. -1-3). 17.99 (978-0-06-226455-8(9)) HarperCollins Pubs.

Reeder, Marilou. The Daring Prince Dashing. West, Karl, illus. 2015. (ENG.). 32p. (J). (gr. -1-k). 16.99 (978-1-63450-161-3(6), Sky Pony Pr.) Skyhorse Publishing Co., Inc.

Rees, Douglas. Jeannette Claus Saves Christmas. Latyk, Olivier, illus. 2010. (ENG.). 40p. (J). (gr. k-3). 16.99 (978-1-4169-2686-3(0), McElderry, Margaret K. Bks.) McElderry, Margaret K. Bks.

—Tyrannosaurus Rex vs. Edna, the Very First Chicken. Henry, Jed, illus. 2017. (ENG.). 40p. (J). 17.99 **(978-1-62779-510-4(3)**, 9781627795104, Holt, Henry & Co. Bks. For Young Readers) Holt, Henry & Co.

—Uncle Pirate. Auth, Tony, illus. (ENG.). 112p. (J). (gr. 2-5). 2009. pap. 6.99 (978-1-4169-4763-9(9)) 2008. 15.99 (978-1-4169-4762-2(0)) McElderry, Margaret K. Bks. (McElderry, Margaret K. Bks.).

—Uncle Pirate to the Rescue. Auth, Tony, illus. 2010. (ENG.). 112p. (J). (gr. 2-5). pap. 6.99 (978-1-4169-7505-2(5), McElderry, Margaret K. Bks.) McElderry, Margaret K. Bks.

Reeve, Philip. Oliver & the Sea Monkeys. Mcintyre, Sarah, illus. 2016. (Not-So-Impossible Tale Ser.). (ENG.). 224p. (J). (gr. 2-5). pap. 6.99 (978-0-385-38789-7(X), Yearling) Random Hse. Children's Bks.

—Oliver & the Seawigs. Mcintyre, Sarah, illus. 2014. (Not-So-Impossible Tale Ser.). (ENG.). 208p. (J). (gr. 2-5). 12.99 (978-0-385-38788-0(1), Random Hse. Bks. for Young Readers) Random Hse. Children's Bks.

Regan, Dian. Barnyard Slam. Meisel, Paul, illus. 2009. (ENG.). 32p. (J). (gr. -1-3). 16.95 (978-0-8234-1907-4(X)) Holiday Hse., Inc.

—The World According to Kaley. 2005. (ENG., Illus.). 112p. (J). (gr. 2-5). 14.99 (978-1-58196-039-6(5), Darby Creek) Lerner Publishing Group.

Reger, Rob. Emily the Strange, Vol. 1. Reger, Rob & Brooks, Brian, illus. 2006. (Emily the Strange (Spanish) Ser.). (SPA.). 64p. 19.95 (978-1-59497-188-4(9)) Public Square Bks.

Reichert, Amy. Take Your Mama to Work Today. Boiger, Alexandra, illus. 2012. (ENG.). 40p. (J). (gr. -1-8). 16.99 (978-1-4169-7095-8(9), Atheneum Bks. for Young Readers) Simon & Schuster Children's Publishing.

Reid, Alastair. Supposing. Gill, Bob, illus. 2010. (ENG.). 48p. (J). (gr. -1-3). 15.95 (978-1-59017-369-5(4), NYR Children's Collection) New York Review of Bks., Inc., The.

Reilly, Michael. Monster Sandwich. 2009. 50p. (J). pap. 31.99 (978-1-4415-0056-4(1)) Xlibris Corp.

Reiner, Carl. Tell Me a Silly Story. Bennett, James, illus. 2010. 32p. (J). (gr. -1). 16.95 (978-1-60747-713-6(0), Pickwick Pr.) Phoenix Bks., Inc.

Reiss, Mike. City of Hamburgers. Feinberg, Xeth, illus. 2008. 32p. (J). 14.95 *(978-1-59299-346-8(X))* Inkwater Pr.
—Santa's Eleven Months Off, 1 vol. Montgomery, Michael G., illus. (ENG.). (J). 2016. 28p. (gr. -1-3). pap. 7.95 *(978-1-56145-962-9(3))* 2007. 32p. (gr. k-3). 16.95 *(978-1-56145-421-1(4))* Peachtree Pubs.
Reiss, Mike & Reiss, Mike. Late for School, 1 vol. Austin, Michael, illus. 2003. (ENG.). 32p. (J). (gr. k-3). 16.95 *(978-1-56145-286-6(6),* Q35957) Peachtree Pubs.
Remphry, Martin. Pirates Are Stealing Our Cows. 2014. (ENG., Illus.). 32p. (J). *(978-0-7787-1330-2(X))* Crabtree Publishing Co.
Rennison, Louise. Angus, Thongs & Full-Frontal Snogging. 2006. (Confessions of Georgia Nicolson Ser.: 1). (ENG.). 272p. (YA). (gr. 8-18). pap. 9.99 *(978-0-06-447227-2(2),* HarperTeen) HarperCollins Pubs.
—Angus, Thongs & Full-Frontal Snogging. 2009. (Confessions of Georgia Nicolson Ser.: No. 1). 10.36 *(978-0-7848-1994-4(7),* Everbind) Marco Bk. Co.
—Angus, Thongs & Full-Frontal Snogging. (Confessions of Georgia Nicolson Ser.: 1). (J). 2008. 70.49 *(978-1-4281-7895-3(3))* 2005. 1.25 *(978-1-4193-4293-6(2))* 2004. 68.75 *(978-1-4025-9087-0(3))* Recorded Bks., Inc.
—Are These My Basoomas I See Before Me? Final Confessions of Georgia Nicolson. (Confessions of Georgia Nicolson Ser.: 10). (ENG.). 2010. 336p. (YA). (gr. 8-9). pap. 8.99 *(978-0-06-145937-5(2))* 2009. 256p. (J). (gr. 7-18). 16.99 *(978-0-06-145935-1(6))* HarperCollins Pubs. (HarperTeen).
—Dancing in My Nuddy-Pants. 2006. (Confessions of Georgia Nicolson Ser.: 4). (ENG.). 240p. (YA). (gr. 8). reprint ed. pap. 8.99 *(978-0-06-009748-6(5),* HarperTeen) HarperCollins Pubs.
—Fabbity-Fab! A Big Box of Georgia: Angus, Thongs & Full-frontal Snogging; On the Bright Side I'm Now the Girlfriend of a Sex God; Knocked Out by My Nunga-Nungas. 2005. (Confessions of Georgia Nicolson Ser.: Nos. 1-3). (J). pap. 19.99 *(978-0-06-079724-9(X),* HarperTeen) HarperCollins Pubs.
—Knocked Out by My Nunga-Nungas. 2004. (Confessions of Georgia Nicolson Ser.: No. 3). (ENG., Illus.). 208p. (J). (gr. 8-18). reprint ed. pap. 6.99 *(978-0-06-058991-2(4))* HarperCollins Pubs.
—Knocked Out by My Nunga-Nungas. 2006. (Confessions of Georgia Nicolson Ser.: No. 3). 183p. (gr. 7-12). 19.00 *(978-0-7569-6729-1(5))* Perfection Learning Corp.
—Love Is a Many Trousered Thing. (Confessions of Georgia Nicolson Ser.: 8). (YA). 2008. (ENG.). 304p. (gr. 8). pap. 9.99 *(978-0-06-085389-1(1))* 2007. 256p. (gr. 7-12). 16.99 *(978-0-06-085387-7(5))* HarperCollins Pubs. (HarperTeen).
—A Midsummer Tights Dream. 2013. (Misadventures of Tallulah Casey Ser.: 2). (ENG.). 272p. (YA). (gr. 8). pap. 9.99 *(978-0-06-179938-9(6),* HarperTeen) HarperCollins Pubs.
—On the Bright Side, I'm Now the Girlfriend of a Sex God: Further Confessions of Georgia Nicolson. (Confessions of Georgia Nicolson Ser.: 2). (ENG.). 2006. 272p. (YA). (gr. 8). pap. 8.99 *(978-0-06-447226-5(4),* HarperTeen) 2003. 256p. (J). pap. 6.99 *(978-0-06-052185-1(6))* HarperCollins Pubs.
—Startled by His Furry Shorts. (Confessions of Georgia Nicolson Ser.: 7). (YA). 2007. (ENG.). 304p. (gr. 8-12). pap. 9.99 *(978-0-06-085386-0(7))* 2006. 288p. (gr. 7-12). 16.99 *(978-0-06-085384-6(0))* 2006. 278p. (gr. 7-12). lib. bdg. 17.89 *(978-0-06-085385-3(9))* HarperCollins Pubs. (HarperTeen).
—Stop in the Name of Pants! (Confessions of Georgia Nicolson Ser.: 9). (YA). 2009. (ENG.). 336p. (gr. 8). pap. 9.99 *(978-0-06-145934-4(8))* 2008. 256p. (gr. 7-18). 16.99 *(978-0-06-145932-0(1))* 2008. 320p. (gr. 7-18). lib. bdg. 17.89 *(978-0-06-145933-7(X))* HarperCollins Pubs. (HarperTeen).
—Stop in the Name of Pants!, 6 vols. 2010. (Confessions of Georgia Nicolson Ser.: 9). (YA). 82.75 *(978-1-4407-7777-6(2));* 85.75 *(978-1-4407-7775-2(6));* 1.25 *(978-1-4407-7779-0(9));* 70.75 *(978-1-4407-7771-4(3));* 67.75 *(978-1-4407-7773-8(X));* 172.75 *(978-1-4407-7772-1(1))* Recorded Bks., Inc.
—The Taming of the Tights. 2013. (Misadventures of Tallulah Casey Ser.: 3). (ENG.). 320p. (YA). (gr. 8). 17.99 *(978-0-06-222620-4(7),* HarperTeen) HarperCollins Pubs.
—Then He Ate My Boy Entrancers: More Mad, Marvy Confessions of Georgia Nicolson. (Confessions of Georgia Nicolson Ser.: 6). 2006. (ENG.). 336p. (YA). (gr. 8-12). pap. 9.99 *(978-0-06-058939-4(6))* 2005. 320p. (J). lib. bdg. 16.89 *(978-0-06-058938-7(8))* HarperCollins Pubs. (HarperTeen).
—Withering Tights. (Misadventures of Tallulah Casey Ser.: 1). (ENG.). (YA). (gr. 8). 2012. 304p. pap. 8.99 *(978-0-06-179933-4(5))* 2011. 288p. 16.99 *(978-0-06-179931-0(9))* HarperCollins Pubs. (HarperTeen).
Resnikoff, Irene & Valas, Claudia. OG in Jerusalem. 2003. (OG the Terrible Ser.: Vol. 3). (HEB & ENG., Illus.). 24p. (J). pap. 4.50 *(978-0-939144-43-3(3))* EKS Publishing Co.
Rettig, Liz. Jumping to Confusions. 2010. (ENG.). 320p. (YA). (gr. 7-18). pap. 8.99 *(978-0-552-55757-3(9))* Transworld Publishers Ltd. GBR. Dist: Independent Pubs. Group.
Revenge of the Bully. 2014. (How to Beat the Bully Ser.). (ENG., Illus.). 288p. (J). (gr. 3-7). 17.99 *(978-1-4424-5677-8(9),* Simon & Schuster/Paula Wiseman Bks.) Simon & Schuster/Paula Wiseman Bks.
Rex, Adam. Fat Vampire: A Never Coming of Age Story. 2011. (ENG.). 336p. (YA). (gr. 9). pap. 8.99 *(978-0-06-192092-9(4))* HarperCollins Pubs.
—Smek for President! Rex, Adam, illus. (Smek Smeries Ser.). (ENG., Illus.). 272p. (J). (gr. 3-7). 2016. pap. 7.99 *(978-1-4847-0969-6(1))* 2015. 16.99 *(978-1-4847-0951-1(9))* Hyperion Bks. for Children.
—The True Meaning of Smekday. Rex, Adam, illus. 2015. (ENG., Illus.). 432p. (J). (gr. 3-7). pap. 7.99 *(978-1-4847-2946-5(3))* Hyperion Bks. for Children.
—The True Meaning of Smekday. Rex, Adam, illus. 2009. (Smek Smeries Ser.). (ENG., Illus.). 432p. (J). (gr. 3-7). pap. 7.99 *(978-0-7868-4901-7(0))* Hyperion Pr.
—The True Meaning of Smekday. 2009. (Illus.). 423p. 18.00 *(978-1-60686-525-5(0))* Perfection Learning Corp.
—XO, OX: A Love Story. Campbell, Scott, illus. 2017. (ENG.). 40p. (J). 17.99 *(978-1-62672-288-0(9),* 9781626722880) Roaring Brook Pr.
Rex, Michael. The Egg of Misery. Rex, Michael, illus. 2012. (Fangbone! Third Grade Barbarian Ser.). (ENG., Illus.). 128p. (J). (gr. 2-4). E-Book *(978-1-101-55043-4(0),* G.P. Putnam's Sons Books for Young Readers) Penguin Young Readers Group.
—The Egg of Misery: Fangbone, Third Grade Barbarian. Rex, Michael, illus. 2012. (Fangbone! Third Grade Barbarian Ser.: 2). (ENG., Illus.). 128p. (J). (gr. 2-4). 7.99 *(978-0-399-25522-9(2),* G.P. Putnam's Sons Books for Young Readers) Penguin Young Readers Group.
—The End of the World. Rex, Michael, illus. 2013. (Icky Ricky Ser.: 2). (ENG., Illus.). 128p. (J). (gr. 1-4). 4.99 *(978-0-307-93169-6(2),* Random Hse. Bks. for Young Readers) Random Hse. Children's Bks.
—Fangbone! Third-Grade Barbarian. 2012. (Illus.). 120p. (J). *(978-0-545-44042-4(4),* Putnam Juvenile) Penguin Publishing Group.
—The Hole to China. 2014. (Icky Ricky Ser.: 4). (ENG., Illus.). 128p. (J). (gr. 1-4). 4.99 *(978-0-385-37556-6(5),* Random Hse. Bks. for Young Readers) Random Hse. Children's Bks.
—Icky Ricky #3: the Dead Disco Raccoon. Rex, Michael, illus. 2014. (Icky Ricky Ser.: 3). (ENG., Illus.). 128p. (J). (gr. 1-4). 4.99 *(978-0-307-93171-9(4),* Random Hse. Bks. for Young Readers) Random Hse. Children's Bks.
—Icky Ricky #6: the Backpack Aquarium. 2015. (Icky Ricky Ser.: 6). (ENG., Illus.). 128p. (J). (gr. 1-4). 4.99 *(978-0-385-37562-7(X),* Random Hse. Bks. for Young Readers) Random Hse. Children's Bks.
—Toilet Paper Mummy. Rex, Michael, illus. 2013. (Icky Ricky Ser.: 1). (ENG., Illus.). 128p. (J). (gr. 1-4). pap. 4.99 *(978-0-307-93167-2(6),* Random Hse. Bks. for Young Readers) Random Hse. Children's Bks.
—The Two-Dollar Dirt Shirt. 2015. (Icky Ricky Ser.: 5). (ENG., Illus.). 128p. (J). (gr. 1-4). pap. 4.99 *(978-0-385-37559-7(X),* Random Hse. Bks. for Young Readers) Random Hse. Children's Bks.
Reynolds, Aaron. Creepy Carrots! Brown, Peter, illus. 2012. (ENG.). 40p. (J). (gr. -1-3). 17.99 *(978-1-4424-0297-3(0),* Simon & Schuster Bks. For Young Readers) Simon & Schuster Bks. For Young Readers.
—Pirates vs. Cowboys. Barneda, David, illus. 2013. (ENG.). 40p. (J). (gr. k-3). 16.99 *(978-0-375-85874-1(1),* Knopf Bks. for Young Readers) Random Hse. Children's Bks.
—President Squid. Varon, Sara, illus. 2016. (ENG.). 44p. (J). (gr. k-3). 16.99 *(978-1-4521-3647-9(5))* Chronicle Bks. LLC.
—Las Zanahorias Maléficas. 2015.Tr. of Creepy Carrots. (SPA.). 40p. (J). (gr. k-3). 24.95 *(978-84-16117-13-0(6))* Ediciones Obelisco ESP. Dist: Spanish Pubs., LLC.
Reynolds, Aaron & Wells, Rosemary. Caveboy Dave: More Scrawny Than Brawny. McAndrew, Phil, illus. 2016. (Caveboy Dave Ser.: 1). (ENG.). 256p. (J). (gr. 3-7). bds. 12.99 *(978-0-14-751658-9(7),* Viking Books for Young Readers) Penguin Young Readers Group.
RH Disney. Finding Dory Deluxe Step into Reading (Disney/Pixar Finding Dory) RH Disney, illus. 2016. (Step into Reading Ser.). (ENG., Illus.). 24p. (J). (gr. -1-1). pap. 4.99 *(978-0-7364-3704-2(5));* lib. bdg. 12.99 *(978-0-7364-8188-5(5))* Random Hse. Children's Bks. (RH/Disney).
RH Disney Staff. Anna's Icy Adventure. RH Disney Staff, illus. 2013. (Golden First Chapters Ser.). (ENG., Illus.). 80p. (J). (gr. 1-4). 4.99 *(978-0-7364-8132-8(X),* Golden/Disney) Random Hse. Children's Bks.
—Frozen Big Golden Book (Disney Frozen) RH Disney Staff, illus. 2013. (Big Golden Book Ser.). (ENG., Illus.). 64p. (J). (gr. -1-2). 9.99 *(978-0-7364-3065-4(2),* Golden/Disney) Random Hse. Children's Bks.
—Inside Out Big Golden Book (Disney/Pixar Inside Out) RH Disney Staff, illus. 2015. (Big Golden Book Ser.). (ENG., Illus.). 64p. (J). (gr. -1-2). 9.99 *(978-0-7364-3313-6(9),* RH/Disney) Random Hse. Children's Bks.
—Olaf's 1-2-3. RH Disney Staff, illus. 2013. (Glitter Board Book Ser.). (ENG., Illus.). 12p. (J). (— 1). bds. 6.99 *(978-0-7364-3064-7(4),* Golden/Disney) Random Hse. Children's Bks.
—Rainbow of Emotions. RH Disney Staff, illus. 2015. (Color Plus Rainbow Pencil Ser.). (ENG., Illus.). 128p. (J). (gr. -1-2). pap. 7.99 *(978-0-7364-3287-0(6),* Golden/Disney) Random Hse. Children's Bks.
RH Disney Staff & Rabe, Tish. Frozen - Big Snowman, Little Snowman. RH Disney Staff, illus. 2013. (Step into Reading Ser.). (ENG., Illus.). 32p. (J). (gr. -1-1). lib. bdg. 12.99 *(978-0-7364-8130-4(3),* RH/Disney) Random Hse. Children's Bks.
Ricard, Anouk. I Dunno, What Do You Want to Do? Dascher, Helge, tr. from FRE. 2013. (Anna & Froga Ser.). (ENG., Illus.). 40p. (J). (gr. k-4). 14.95 *(978-1-77046-120-8(5),* 9781770461208) Drawn & Quarterly Pubns. CAN. Dist: Macmillan.
Ricci, Laura. Dr. Mike's Adventures. 2006. 63p. pap. 16.95 *(978-1-4241-2653-8(3))* PublishAmerica, Inc.
Riccobono, Michael P. Billy Balonie & the Belly Buttonie. 2010. (Illus.). 28p. pap. 19.00 *(978-1-4490-3119-0(6))* AuthorHouse.
Richards, Pat. Bardolph Bedivere Wolf Returns. Richards, Charles, illus. 2007. 42p. (J). *(978-0-9790796-4-1(0))* PJR Assocs., Ltd.
Richardson, Lin Douglas. The Meaning of Me. 2011. 28p. pap. 24.95 *(978-1-4626-2891-9(5))* America Star Bks.
Richemont, Enid. Brownilocks & the Three Bowls of Cornflakes. 2016. (ENG., Illus.). 32p. (J). *(978-0-7787-2459-9(X))* Crabtree Publishing Co.
—Princess Frog. 2014. (ENG., Illus.). 32p. (J). *(978-0-7787-0443-0(2));* pap. *(978-0-7787-0452-2(1))* Crabtree Publishing Co.
Richler, Mordecai. Jacob Two-Two & the Dinosaur. Eyolfson, Norman, illus. 2004. (Jacob Two-Two Ser.). (ENG.). 96p. (J). (gr. 3-7). pap. 6.95 *(978-0-88776-712-8(5))* Tundra Bks. CAN. Dist: Random Hse., Inc.
Richmond, Jacob. Polly Perfect & the Tragic Fart. Pine, Hank, illus. 2012. (ENG.). 64p. (J). pap. 9.95 *(978-1-897411-36-0(7))* Bayeux Arts, Inc. CAN. Dist: Chicago Distribution Ctr.
Richmond, Marianne. Dear Grandson. 2008. (ENG., Illus.). 40p. (gr. -1-3). 5.95 *(978-1-934082-43-0(0),* Marianne Richmond Studios, Inc.) Sourcebooks, Inc.
Richter, Danny. The Big Gozonga. 2006. 16.95 *(978-0-9786107-0-8(9))* Arbor Bks.
Ridell, Chris. Ottoline va al colegio/ Ottolina Goes To School. 2008. (SPA.). 172p. (J). 13.95 *(978-84-263-6833-1(6))* Vives, Luis Editorial (Edelvives) ESP. Dist: Baker & Taylor Bks.
Riffe, Ruth. Survival Guide for the Teenage Life. Smith, Geoff & Aretha, David, eds. 2016. (ENG., Illus.). 124p. (J). pap. 12.49 *(978-1-61984-511-4(3))* Price World Publishing.
Riker, Richard K. School Days Daze. l.t. ed. 2005. (Illus.). 168p. (J). 15.95 *(978-0-9760416-0-3(X))* Safe Harbor Pubns.
Riley, Andy. King Flashypants & the Evil Emperor. Riley, Andy, illus. 2017. (King Flashypants Ser.). (ENG., Illus.). 224p. (J). 13.99 *(978-1-62779-809-9(9),* 9781627798099, Holt, Henry & Co. Bks. For Young Readers) Holt, Henry & Co.
Rissi, Anica Mrose. The Teacher's Pet. OHora, Zachariah, illus. 2017. (ENG.). 40p. (J). (gr. -1-k). 17.99 *(978-1-4847-4364-5(4))* Disney Pr.
Rix, Jamie. Tough Turkey. 2003. (ENG., Illus.). 240p. pap. *(978-0-440-86479-0(8),* Yearling) Random Hse. Children's Bks.
Roberts, A. A. Bobo World. 2003. (Illus.). 190p. (J). (gr. 5-7). pap. 14.95 *(978-0-9718544-0-6(8))* AntHill Publishing.
Roberts, Daniel. The Dragon, the Princess & the Peanut Butter Sandwiches. 2009. 36p. pap. 16.99 *(978-1-4389-8277-9(1))* AuthorHouse.
—Harrison & His Dinosaur Robot & the Purple Spotted Sea Monster. 2012. 36p. pap. 20.99 *(978-1-4772-6979-4(7))* AuthorHouse.
Robertson, Si, et al. Everything's Better with a Beard. 2014. (ENG., Illus.). 48p. (J). (gr. -1-3). 14.99 *(978-1-4814-1817-1(3),* Simon & Schuster Bks. For Young Readers) Simon & Schuster Bks. For Young Readers.
Robins, Eleanor. A Very Good Year. 2005. (Carter High Chronicles Senior Year Ser.). (Illus.). 48p. (J). per. 3.95 *(978-1-56254-784-4(4),* SP7844) Saddleback Educational Publishing, Inc.
Robinson, Barbara. The Best Christmas Pageant Ever. Cornell, Laura, illus. 2011. (ENG.). 40p. (J). (gr. -1-3). 16.99 *(978-0-06-089074-2(6))* HarperCollins Pubs.
—The Best Christmas Pageant Ever. 2005. (ENG., Illus.). 128p. (J). (gr. 3-7). pap. 5.99 *(978-0-06-440275-0(4))* HarperCollins Pubs.
—The Best Christmas Pageant Ever. 2009. 8.32 *(978-0-7848-1246-4(2),* Everbind) Marco Bk. Co.
—The Best Christmas Pageant Ever. 2005. (Illus.). 108p. (gr. 3-7). 16.00 *(978-0-7569-6531-0(4))* Perfection Learning Corp.
—The Best Christmas Pageant Ever. 2005. (J). 16.00 *(978-0-88103-998-6(5),* Turtleback) Turtleback Bks.
—The Best Halloween Ever. 2006. (Illus.). 117p. (J). (gr. 3-7). 13.65 *(978-0-7569-6985-1(9))* Perfection Learning Corp.
Robinson, Craig & Mansbach, Adam. Jake the Fake Keeps It Real. Knight, Keith, illus. 2017. (Jake the Fake Ser.: 1). (ENG.). 144p. (J). (gr. 3-7). 13.99 *(978-0-553-52351-5(1),* Crown Books For Young Readers) Random Hse. Children's Bks.
Robinson, Fiona. The Useful Moose: A Truthful, Moose-Full Tale. 2004. (ENG., Illus.). 32p. (J). (gr. -1-3). 15.95 *(978-0-8109-4925-6(3))* Abrams, Inc.
—What Animals Really Like. 2011. (ENG., Illus.). 24p. (J). (gr. k-2). 15.95 *(978-0-8109-8976-4(X),* Abrams Bks. for Young Readers) Abrams, Inc.
Robinson, Hilary. The Elves & the Emperor. Sanfilippo, Simona, illus. 2012. (ENG.). 32p. (J). *(978-0-7787-8025-0(2));* pap. *(978-0-7787-8036-6(8))* Crabtree Publishing Co.
—Goldilocks & the Wolf. Sanfilippo, Simona, illus. 2012. (ENG.). 32p. (J). *(978-0-7787-8023-6(6));* pap. *(978-0-7787-8034-2(1))* Crabtree Publishing Co.
—Snow White & the Enormous Turnip. Sanfilippo, Simona, illus. 2012. (ENG.). 32p. (J). pap. *(978-0-7787-8035-9(X))* Crabtree Publishing Co.
—Three Pigs & a Gingerbread Man. Sanfilippo, Simona, illus. 2012. (ENG.). 32p. (J). *(978-0-7787-8026-7(0));* pap. *(978-0-7787-8037-3(6))* Crabtree Publishing Co.
Robinson, Michelle. A Beginner's Guide to Bear Spotting. Roberts, David, illus. 2016. (ENG.). 32p. (J). 16.99 *(978-1-68119-026-6(5),* 9781681190266, Bloomsbury USA Childrens) Bloomsbury Publishing USA.
—Ding Dong! Gorilla!, 1 vol. Lord, Leonie, illus. 2013. (ENG.). 32p. (J). (gr. -1-3). 15.95 *(978-1-56145-730-4(2))* Peachtree Pubs.
—The Forgetful Knight. Blunt, Fred, illus. 2016. (ENG.). 40p. (J). (gr. -1-3). 16.99 *(978-0-8037-4067-9(0),* Dial Bks) Penguin Young Readers Group.
—How to Wash a Woolly Mammoth. Hindley, Kate, illus. 2014. (ENG.). 32p. (J). (gr. -1-3). 16.99 *(978-0-8050-9966-9(2),* 9780805099669, Holt, Henry & Co. Bks. For Young Readers) Holt, Henry & Co.
—There's a Lion in My Cornflakes. Field, Jim, illus. 2015. (ENG.). 32p. (J). (gr. -1-1). 16.99 *(978-0-8027-3836-3(2),* 9780802738363, Bloomsbury USA Childrens) Bloomsbury Publishing USA.
—What to Do If an Elephant Stands on Your Foot. Reynolds, Peter H., illus. 2012. (ENG.). 32p. (J). (gr. -1-k). 16.99 *(978-0-8037-3398-5(4),* Dial Bks) Penguin Young Readers Group.
Rodkey, Geoff. The Tapper Twins Go to War (with Each Other) 2015. (Tapper Twins Ser.: 1). (ENG., Illus.). 240p. (J). (gr. 3-7). 13.99 *(978-0-316-29779-0(8))* Little Brown & Co.
—The Tapper Twins Go Viral. 2017. (Tapper Twins Ser.: 4). (ENG., Illus.). 256p. (J). (gr. 3-7). 13.99 *(978-0-316-29784-4(4))* Little Brown & Co.
—The Tapper Twins Run for President. 2016. (Tapper Twins Ser.: 3). (ENG., Illus.). 304p. (J). (gr. 3-7). 13.99 *(978-0-316-29785-1(2))* Little, Brown Bks. for Young Readers.
—The Tapper Twins Tear up New York. 2015. (Tapper Twins Ser.: 2). (ENG., Illus.). 288p. (J). (gr. 3-7). 13.99 *(978-0-316-29783-7(6))* Little Brown & Co.
—The Tapper Twins Tear up New York. 2016. (Tapper Twins Ser.: 2). (ENG., Illus.). 288p. (J). (gr. 3-7). pap. 5.99 *(978-0-316-31601-9(6))* Little, Brown Bks. for Young Readers.
Rodriguez, Béatrice. The Chicken Thief. 2010. (Stories Without Words Ser.).Tr. of Voleur de Poule. (ENG., Illus.). 32p. (J). (gr. -1-2). 14.95 *(978-1-59270-092-9(6))* Enchanted Lion Bks., LLC.
Romig, Hilary. Meet Ruby & Louise. 2009. 16p. pap. 8.49 *(978-1-4389-4609-2(0))* AuthorHouse.
Romney, J. P. The Monster on the Road Is Me. 2016. (ENG.). 336p. (YA). 17.99 *(978-0-374-31654-9(6),* 9780374316549, Farrar, Straus & Giroux (BYR)) Farrar, Straus & Giroux.
Rompella, Natalie. Edgar, Allan, & Poe, & the Tell-Tale Beets. l.t. ed. 2012. 63p. (J). pap. *(978-1-4596-3447-3(0))* ReadHowYouWant.com, Ltd.
Rooks, Elizabeth. Where Does Santa Go on Vacation after Christmas? 2012. 24p. pap. 17.99 *(978-1-4772-6535-2(X))* AuthorHouse.
Root, Phyllis. Aunt Nancy & the Bothersome Visitors. Parkinson, David, illus. 2007. (ENG.). 64p. (J). (gr. 2-5). 16.99 *(978-0-7636-3074-4(8))* Candlewick Pr.
—Toot Toot Zoom! Cordell, Matthew, illus. 2009. (ENG.). 40p. (J). (gr. -1-2). 15.99 *(978-0-7636-3452-0(2))* Candlewick Pr.
Rose, Deborah Lee. The Spelling Bee Before Recess. Armstrong-Ellis, Carey F., illus. 2013. (ENG.). 32p. (J). (gr. 1-4). 16.95 *(978-1-4197-0847-3(3),* Abrams Bks. for Young Readers) Abrams, Inc.
Rosen, Lucy. Long Live King Bob! 2015. (Minions 8X8 Ser.). (J). lib. bdg. 13.55 *(978-0-606-37220-6(2))* Turtleback Bks.
—Minions: Who's the Boss? 2015. (Passport to Reading Level 2 Ser.). (J). lib. bdg. 13.55 *(978-0-606-37221-3(0))* Turtleback Bks.
Rosen, Michael. Bilal's Brilliant Bee. Ross, Tony, illus. 2016. (ENG.). 96p. (J). (gr. k-2). pap. 10.99 *(978-1-78344-395-6(2))* Andersen Pr. GBR. Dist: Independent Pubs. Group.
—Don't Forget Tiggs! Ross, Tony, illus. 2015. (ENG.). 96p. (J). (gr. k-2). pap. 8.99 *(978-1-78344-269-0(7))* Andersen Pr. GBR. Dist: Independent Pubs. Group.
—Happy Harry's Cafe. Holland, Richard, illus. 2012. (ENG.). 32p. (J). (gr. -1-2). 16.99 *(978-0-7636-6239-4(9))* Candlewick Pr.
—Ronquidos! Langley, Jonathan, illus.Tr. of Snore! (SPA.). (J). (gr. 1-3). *(978-958-04-4646-0(6))* Norma S.A.
—We're Going on a Bear Hunt. Oxenbury, Helen, illus. 2004. (J). 32p. *(978-1-85269-710-5(5));* 32p. *(978-1-85269-711-2(3));* 32p. *(978-1-85269-716-7(4));* 32p. *(978-1-85269-718-1(0));* 32p. *(978-1-85269-720-4(2));* 32p. *(978-1-85269-706-8(7));* (ENG & BEN.). 33p. pap. *(978-1-85269-708-2(3));* (ENG & PAN.). 33p. pap. *(978-1-85269-714-3(8));* (ENG & URD.). 33p. pap. *(978-1-85269-721-1(0))* Mantra Lingua.
—We're Going on a Bear Hunt. Oxenbury, Helen, illus. 2003. (ENG.). 36p. (J). (gr. -1-3). pap. 7.99 *(978-0-689-85349-4(1),* McElderry, Margaret K. Bks.) McElderry, Margaret K. Bks.
Rosenberg, Madelyn. How to Behave at a Dog Show. Ross, Heather, illus. 2015. (ENG.). 32p. (J). (gr. -1-3). 17.99 *(978-0-06-227927-9(0))* HarperCollins Pubs.
Rosenberg, Madelyn & Shang, Wendy Wan-Long. This Is Just a Test: A Novel. 2017. (ENG.). 256p. (J). (gr. 3-7). 17.99 ***(978-1-338-03772-2(2),*** Scholastic Pr.) Scholastic, Inc.
Rosenthal, Amy Krouse. Bedtime for Mommy. Pham, LeUyen, illus. 2010. (ENG.). 32p. (J). (gr. -1-k). 16.99 *(978-1-59990-341-5(5),* 9781599903415, Bloomsbury USA Childrens) Bloomsbury Publishing USA.
—Chopsticks. Magoon, Scott, illus. 2012. (ENG.). 40p. (J). (gr. -1-k). 16.99 *(978-1-4231-0796-5(9))* Hyperion Pr.
Rosenthal, Amy Krouse & Redmond, Lea. On the Spot. te Loo, Sanne, illus. 2017. (ENG.). 32p. (J). (gr. -1-2). 16.99 *(978-1-101-93230-8(9),* Random Hse. Bks. for Young Readers) Random Hse. Children's Bks.
Rosenthal, Betsy R. It's Not Worth Making a Tzimmes Over! Rivers, Ruth, illus. 2006. 32p. (J). (gr. k-3). lib. bdg. 16.99 *(978-0-8075-3677-3(6))* Whitman, Albert & Co.
Rosenthal, Marc. Phooey! Rosenthal, Marc, illus. 2007. (Illus.). 40p. (J). (gr. -1-3). lib. bdg. 17.89 *(978-0-06-075249-1(1),* Cotler, Joanna Books) HarperCollins Pubs.
Rosoff, Meg. Meet Wild Boars. Blackall, Sophie, illus. 2008. (Wild Boars Ser.). (ENG.). 40p. (J). (gr. k-3). pap. 7.99 *(978-0-312-37963-6(3),* 9780312379636) Square Fish.
—There Is No Dog. 2012. (ENG.). 288p. (YA). (gr. 7-18). 17.99 *(978-0-399-25764-3(0),* G.P. Putnam's Sons Books for Young Readers) Penguin Young Readers Group.
Ross, Jay. Bungalow 29. Klimko, Andrew, illus. 2015. 92p. pap. 5.99 *(978-0-9771994-0-2(1))* Visor Bks.
Ross, Tony. Super Dooper Jezebel. (ENG., Illus.). 32p. (J). pap. 9.99 *(978-1-84270-096-9(0))* Andersen Pr. GBR. Dist: Trafalgar Square Publishing.
Rossbacher, John R. T. O. A. D. Trombone Ollie & Dyslexia. 2011. 124p. (gr. 4-6). 21.49 *(978-1-4567-3941-6(7));* pap. 12.49 *(978-1-4567-3942-3(5))* AuthorHouse.
Rostoker-Gruber, Karen & Isaacs, Ronald H. Farmer Kobi's Hanukkah Match. Decker, C. B., illus. 2015. (J). *(978-1-68115-501-2(X));* pap. *(978-0-87441-924-5(7))* Behrman Hse., Inc.
Rothstein, Nancy H. & Gilpin, Stephen. My Daddy Snores. 2006. (Illus.). (J). pap. *(978-0-439-87142-6(5))* Scholastic, Inc.
Rovetch, L. Bob. And the Surprisingly Slobbery Attack of the Dog-Wash Doggies. Whamond, Dave, illus. 2007. (Hot Dog & Bob Ser.: HOTD). (ENG.). 96p. (J). (gr. 1-5). per. 4.95 *(978-0-8118-5746-8(8))* Chronicle Bks. LLC.
—Hot Dog & Bob: And the Dangerously Dizzy Attack of the Hypno Hamsters. Whamond, Dave, illus. 2007. (Hot Dog & Bob Ser.: HOTD). (ENG.). 96p. (J). (gr. 1-5). per. 4.95 *(978-0-8118-5602-7(X))* Chronicle Bks. LLC.
Rowe, W. W. The Wand Goes Wild. 2011. 120p. (gr. 3-7). pap. 12.95 *(978-0-9843754-4-8(9))* Sanctuary Publishing, Inc.
Roy, James. Chaz & the Missing Mayo. Gorissen, Dean, illus. 2015. (J). pap. *(978-1-4966-0245-9(5))* Capstone Classroom.
—Chaz at the Fish Market. Gorissen, Dean, illus. 2015. (J). pap. *(978-1-4966-0251-0(X))* Capstone Classroom.
—Chaz, Superbarf Surprise. Gorissen, Dean, illus. 2015. (J). pap. *(978-1-4966-0239-8(0))* Capstone Classroom.
—Chaz, TV Superstar? Gorissen, Dean, illus. 2015. (J). pap. *(978-1-4966-0257-2(9))* Capstone Classroom.
Roy, Ron. Fireworks at the FBI. Bush, Timothy, illus. 2006. (Capital Mysteries Ser.: No. 6). (ENG.). 96p. (J). (gr. 1-4). per. 4.99 *(978-0-375-87527-4(1),* Random Hse. Bks. for Young Readers) Random Hse. Children's Bks.

H
I

Rubi, Nicholas. My Mom's Not Cool. Maia, Chavez Larkin, illus. 2008. 24p. (J). per. 12.95 *(978-0-9776906-4-0(4))* Blueline Publishing.

Rubin, Adam. Big Bad Bubble. Salmieri, Daniel, illus. 2014. (ENG.). 40p. (J). (gr. -1-3). 16.99 *(978-0-544-04549-1(1))* Houghton Mifflin Harcourt Publishing Co.

—Dragons Love Tacos. Salmieri, Daniel, illus. 2012. (ENG.). 40p. (J). (gr. -1-2). 16.99 *(978-0-8037-3680-1(0),* Dial Bks) Penguin Young Readers Group.

—Dragons Love Tacos 2: The Sequel. Salmieri, Daniel, illus. 2017. (ENG.). 48p. (J). (-k). 18.99 *(978-0-525-42888-6(7),* Dial Bks) Penguin Young Readers Group.

—Secret Pizza Party. Salmieri, Daniel, illus. 2013. (ENG.). 36p. (J). (gr. -1-2). 17.99 *(978-0-8037-3947-5(8),* Dial Bks) Penguin Young Readers Group.

—Those Darn Squirrels! Salmieri, Daniel, illus. (ENG.). 32p. (J). (gr. -1-3). 2011. pap. 7.99 *(978-0-547-57681-7(1))* 2008. 17.99 *(978-0-547-00703-8(5))* Houghton Mifflin Harcourt Publishing Co.

—Those Darn Squirrels & the Cat Next Door. Salmieri, Daniel, illus. 2011. (ENG.). 32p. (J). (gr. -1-3). 17.99 *(978-0-547-42922-9(3))* Houghton Mifflin Harcourt Publishing Co.

—Those Darn Squirrels Fly South. Salmieri, Daniel, illus. 2012. (ENG.). 32p. (J). (gr. -1-3). 17.99 *(978-0-547-67823-8(1))* Houghton Mifflin Harcourt Publishing Co.

Rubin, Adam & Salmieri, Daniel. Dragons Love Tacos. 2016. (ENG., Illus.). 40p. (J). (gr. -1-2). 17.99 *(978-0-7352-2823-8(X),* Dial Bks) Penguin Young Readers Group.

Ruditis, Paul. Entrances & Exits. 2008. (Drama! Ser.). (ENG.). 256p. (YA). (gr. 9). pap. 12.99 *(978-1-4169-5906-9(8),* Simon Pulse) Simon Pulse.

Rudnick, Paul. It's All Your Fault. (ENG.). 304p. (J). (gr. 9). 2017. pap. 10.99 *(978-0-545-46429-1(3))* 2016. 19.99 *(978-0-545-46428-4(5),* Scholastic Pr.) Scholastic, Inc.

Rue, Ginger. Aleca Zamm Is a Wonder. Persico, Zoe, illus. 2017. (Aleca Zamm Ser.: 1). (ENG.). 160p. (J). (gr. 2-5). 16.99 ***(978-1-4814-7061-2(2),*** Aladdin) Simon & Schuster Children's Publishing.

Ruelle, Karen Gray. Mother's Day Mess. 2003. (ENG., Illus.). 32p. (J). (gr. k-3). tchr. ed. 14.95 *(978-0-8234-1773-5(5))* Holiday Hse., Inc.

Rundstrom, T. S. Baribold Jones & Big Big Booger Grabber. 2004. (Illus.). per. *(978-1-932062-43-4(2))* Hability Solution Services, Inc.

Running Press Staff. Berenstain Bears Light-Up Tree House. 2016. (Miniature Editions Ser.). (ENG., Illus.). 32p. pap. 12.95 *(978-0-7624-6083-0(0),* Running Pr. Minature Editions) Running Pr. Bk. Pubs.

Running Press Staff, ed. Adventure Time Bowling. 2016. (Miniature Editions Ser.). (ENG., Illus.). 32p. pap. 12.95 *(978-0-7624-5798-4(8),* Running Pr. Minature Editions) Running Pr. Bk. Pubs.

Rushton, Rosie. How Could You Do This to Me, Mum? 2005. 224p. (J). pap. 5.99 *(978-0-7868-5187-4(2))* Hyperion Bks. for Children.

—I Think I'll Just Curl up & Die. 2005. 176p. (J). pap. 5.99 *(978-0-7868-5188-1(0))* Hyperion Bks. for Children.

—Just Don't Make a Scene, Mum! 2005. 224p. (J). pap. 5.99 *(978-0-7868-5186-7(4))* Hyperion Bks. for Children.

—Where Do We Go from Here? 2005. 224p. (J). pap. 5.99 *(978-0-7868-5189-8(9))* Hyperion Bks. for Children.

Russel, Mary. Flickertail & Paint, Barnyard Sleuths, 1 vol. 2010. 96p. pap. 19.95 *(978-1-4489-7248-7(5))* America Star Bks.

Russell, David O. & Auseon, Andrew. Alienated. 2010. (ENG.). 352p. (J). (gr. 3-7). pap. 5.99 *(978-1-4169-8299-9(X),* Aladdin) Simon & Schuster Children's Publishing.

Russell, Rachel Renée. Locker Hero. Russell, Rachel Renée, illus. 2016. (Misadventures of Max Crumbly Ser.: 1). (ENG., Illus.). 320p. (J). (gr. 4-8). 13.99 *(978-1-4814-6001-9(3),* Aladdin) Simon & Schuster Children's Publishing.

—Tales from a Not-So-Dorky Drama Queen, 3 vols. unabr. ed. 2015. (Dork Diaries: 8). (ENG.). 320p. (gr. 4-8). audio compact disk 14.99 *(978-1-4423-7023-4(8))* Simon & Schuster Audio.

—Tales from a Not-So-Dorky Drama Queen. Russell, Rachel Renée, illus. 2015. (Dork Diaries: Bk. 9). (ENG., Illus.). 352p. (J). (gr. 4-8). 13.99 *(978-1-4424-8769-7(0),* Aladdin Paperbacks) Simon & Schuster Children's Publishing.

—Tales from a Not-So-Graceful Ice Princess. Russell, Rachel Renée, illus. 2012. (Dork Diaries: 4). (ENG., Illus.). 368p. (J). (gr. 4-8). 13.99 *(978-1-4424-1192-0(9),* Aladdin) Simon & Schuster Children's Publishing.

—Tales from a Not-So-Happy Heartbreaker. Russell, Rachel Renée, illus. 2013. (Dork Diaries: 6). (ENG., Illus.). 352p. (J). (gr. 4-8). 13.99 *(978-1-4424-4963-3(2),* Aladdin) Simon & Schuster Children's Publishing.

—Tales from a Not-So-Perfect Pet Sitter. Russell, Rachel Renée, illus. 2015. (Dork Diaries: 10). (ENG., Illus.). 320p. (J). (gr. 4-8). 13.99 *(978-1-4814-5704-0(7),* Aladdin) Simon & Schuster Children's Publishing.

Rylander, Chris. Codename Zero. 2014. (Codename Conspiracy Ser.: 1). (ENG.). 368p. (J). (gr. 3-7). 16.99 *(978-0-06-212008-3(5),* Waldon Pond Pr.) HarperCollins Pubs.

—Countdown Zero. 2015. (Codename Conspiracy Ser.: 2). (ENG.). 368p. (J). (gr. 3-7). 16.99 *(978-0-06-212011-3(5),* Waldon Pond Pr.) HarperCollins Pubs.

Rylant, Cynthia. Puppy Mudge Finds a Friend. Stevenson, Suçie, illus. 2004. (Puppy Mudge Ser.). (ENG.). 32p. (J). (gr. -1-k). 16.99 *(978-0-689-83982-5(0),* Simon Spotlight) Simon Spotlight.

—Puppy Mudge Has a Snack. Mones, Isidre, illus. 2004. (Puppy Mudge Ser.). (ENG.). 32p. (J). (gr. -1-k). pap. 3.99 *(978-0-689-86995-2(9),* Simon Spotlight) Simon Spotlight.

—Puppy Mudge Loves His Blanket. Mones, Isidre, illus. 2005. (Puppy Mudge Ser.). (ENG.). 32p. (J). (gr. -1-k). pap. 3.99 *(978-1-4169-0336-9(4),* Simon Spotlight) Simon Spotlight.

—Puppy Mudge Wants to Play. Stevenson, Suçie, illus. 2005. (Puppy Mudge Ser.). (ENG.). 32p. (J). (gr. -1-k). 16.99 *(978-0-689-83984-9(7),* Simon Spotlight) Simon Spotlight.

Sachar, Louis. Marvin Redpost #1: Kidnapped at Birth? Record, Adam, illus. 2015. (Marvin Redpost Ser.: 1). (ENG.). 96p. (J). (gr. 1-4). lib. bdg. 12.99 *(978-0-553-53540-2(4),* Random Hse. Bks. for Young Readers) Random Hse. Children's Bks.

—Sideways Stories from Wayside School. McCauley, Adam, illus. 2003. (Wayside School Ser.). (ENG.). 128p. (J). (gr. 3-7). pap. 6.99 *(978-0-380-69871-4(4))* HarperCollins Pubs.

Sadler, Marilyn & Comstock, Eric. Charlie Piechart & the Case of the Missing Pizza Slice. Comstock, Eric, illus. 2015. (Charlie Piechart Ser.). (ENG., Illus.). 40p. (J). (gr. -1-3). 17.99 *(978-0-06-237054-9(5),* Tegen, Katherine Bks) HarperCollins Pubs.

Sage, Angie. TodHunter Moon, Book Three: StarChaser. Zug, Mark, illus. 2017. (World of Septimus Heap Ser.: 3). 496p. (J). (gr. 3-7). pap. 7.99 ***(978-0-06-227252-2(7),*** Tegen, Katherine Bks) HarperCollins Pubs.

Salisbury, Linda G. Mudd Saves the Earth: Booger Glue, Cow Diapers & Other Good Ideas. 2009. (Illus.). 96p. (J). pap. 8.95 *(978-1-881539-47-6(4))* Tabby Hse. Bks.

Salm, Arthur. Anyway: A Story about Me with 138 Footnotes, 27 Exaggerations, & 1 Plate of Spaghetti. 2012. (ENG., Illus.). 192p. (J). (gr. 3-7). 15.99 *(978-1-4424-2930-7(5),* Simon & Schuster Bks. For Young Readers) Simon & Schuster Bks. For Young Readers.

Salsi, Lynn. Jack & the Giants. Young, James, illus. 2012. (ENG.). 32p. (J). 16.95 *(978-0-938467-52-6(2))* Headline Bks., Inc.

Sandburg, Carl. The Huckabuck Family: And How They Raised Popcorn in Nebraska & Quit & Came Back. Small, David, illus. 2006. 30p. (J). (gr. k-4). reprint ed. 16.00 *(978-1-4223-5854-2(2))* DIANE Publishing Co.

Sanderson, Brandon. Alcatraz Versus the Evil Librarians. Lazo, Hayley, illus. 2016. (Alcatraz Versus the Evil Librarians Ser.: 1). (ENG.). 320p. (J). 16.99 *(978-0-7653-7894-1(9),* 9780765378941, Starscape) Doherty, Tom Assocs., LLC.

—Alcatraz Versus the Shattered Lens. 2016. (Alcatraz Versus the Evil Librarians Ser.: 4). (ENG.). 336p. (J). 16.99 *(978-0-7653-7900-9(7),* 9780765379009, Starscape) Doherty, Tom Assocs., LLC.

—The Scrivener's Bones. 2016. (Alcatraz Versus the Evil Librarians Ser.: 2). (ENG.). 368p. (J). 16.99 *(978-0-7653-7896-5(5),* 9780765378965, Starscape) Doherty, Tom Assocs., LLC.

Santat, Dan, illus. Mighty Robot vs. the Stupid Stinkbugs from Saturn. 2015. (Ricky Ricotta Ser.: 6). (ENG.). 128p. (J). (gr. -1-3). 15.99 *(978-0-545-63121-1(1))* Scholastic, Inc.

Santat, Dan & Willems, Mo. The Cookie Fiasco. Santat, Dan & Willems, Mo, illus. 2016. (Elephant & Piggie Like Reading! Ser.). (ENG., Illus.). 64p. (J). (gr. 1-3). 9.99 *(978-1-4847-2636-5(7))* Hyperion Bks. for Children.

Santos, Antonio. El Viaje de Pancho. 2006. (Coleccion Libros para Sonar Ser.). (Illus.). (J). (gr. -1-3). *(978-84-96388-08-6(5))* Kalandraka Editora, S.L.

Sarcone-Roach, Julia. The Bear Ate Your Sandwich. 2015. (ENG., Illus.). 40p. (J). (gr. -1-2). 16.99 *(978-0-375-85860-4(1));* lib. bdg. 19.99 *(978-0-375-95860-1(6))* Random Hse. Children's Bks. (Knopf Bks. for Young Readers).

Sargant, Pam. Mother's Survival Kit. 2007. 68p. pap. 34.50 *(978-1-4303-2786-8(3))* Lulu Pr., Inc.

Sasa, Fungisayi. Search for the Perfect Head. 2009. 28p. pap. 16.50 *(978-1-60693-255-1(1),* Eloquent Bks.) Strategic Book Publishing & Rights Agency (SBPRA).

Sastrias, Marta. Cuentos de Todo y de Nada. Martinez y Luis San Vicente, Enrique, illus. 2003. (SPA.). 82p. (J). (gr. 3-5). *(978-968-19-0551-4(2))* Aguilar, Altea, Taurus, Alfaguara, S.A. de C.V.

Sattler, Jennifer. A Chick 'n' Pug Christmas. 2014. (ENG., Illus.). 32p. (J). (gr. -1-1). 16.99 *(978-1-59990-602-7(3),* 9781599906027, Bloomsbury USA Childrens) Bloomsbury Publishing USA.

—Chick 'n' Pug: the Love Pug. 2015. (ENG., Illus.). 32p. (J). (gr. -1-1). 16.99 *(978-1-61963-672-9(7),* 9781619636729, Bloomsbury USA Childrens) Bloomsbury Publishing USA.

Sattler, Jennifer Gordon, illus. A Chick 'n' Pug Christmas. 2014. (J). *(978-1-61963-463-3(5))* Bloomsbury Pr.

Sauer, Tammi. Chicken Dance. Santat, Dan, illus. (ENG.). 40p. (J). (gr. -1-2). 2015. pap. 6.95 *(978-1-4549-1477-8(7))* 2009. 14.95 *(978-1-4027-5366-4(7))* Sterling Publishing Co., Inc.

—Mr. Duck Means Business. Mack, Jeff, illus. 2011. (ENG.). 32p. (J). (gr. -1-3). 15.99 *(978-1-4169-8522-8(0),* Simon & Schuster/Paula Wiseman Bks.) Simon & Schuster/Paula Wiseman Bks.

—Nugget & Fang. 2015. lib. bdg. 17.20 *(978-0-606-36825-4(6))* Turtleback Bks.

—Nugget & Fang: Friends Forever - Or Snack Time? Slack, Michael, illus. 2013. (ENG.). 40p. (J). (gr. -1-3). 16.99 *(978-0-547-85285-0(1))* Houghton Mifflin Harcourt Publishing Co.

—Nugget & Fang: Friends Forever — Or Snack Time? Slack, Michael, illus. 2015. (ENG.). 40p. (J). (gr. -1-3). 6.99 *(978-0-544-48171-8(2),* HMH Books For Young Readers) Houghton Mifflin Harcourt Publishing Co.

—Princess in Training. Berger, Joe, illus. (ENG.). 40p. (J). (gr. -1-3). 2015. 6.99 *(978-0-544-45609-9(2),* HMH Books For Young Readers) 2012. 16.99 *(978-0-15-206599-7(7))* Houghton Mifflin Harcourt Publishing Co.

Saunders, Louise. The Knave of Hearts. Parrish, Maxfield, illus. 2008. (Calla Editions Ser.). (ENG.). 40p. (gr. 3). 30.00 *(978-1-60660-001-6(X))* Dover Pubns., Inc.

Saunders, Zina, illus. Trouble at the Krusty Krab! 2004. (SpongeBob SquarePants Ser.). (ENG.). 32p. (J). pap. 3.99 *(978-0-689-86838-2(3),* Simon Spotlight/Nickelodeon) Simon Spotlight/Nickelodeon.

Savage, J. Scott. Case File 13 #4: Curse of the Mummy's Uncle. Holgate, Doug, illus. 2016. (Case File 13 Ser.: 4). 272p. (J). (gr. 3-7). pap. 6.99 *(978-0-06-232407-8(1))* HarperCollins Pubs.

—Zombie Kid. Holgate, Doug, illus. 2012. (Case File 13 Ser.: 1). (ENG.). 288p. (J). (gr. 3-7). 14.99 *(978-0-06-213325-0(X))* HarperCollins Pubs.

Sawyer-Aitch, Anne. Nalah & the Pink Tiger. Sawyer-Aitch, Anne, illus. 2013. (ENG., Illus.). 40p. pap. 13.95 *(978-1-938063-00-8(7),* Mighty Media Kids) Mighty Media Pr.

Say Please, Says Squeeze. 2009. (ENG.). 32p. pap. 3.99 *(978-1-4231-1755-1(7))* Disney Pr.

Sazaklis, John. Billy Burger, Model Citizen. Robinson, Lee, illus. 2016. (Billy Burger, Model Citizen Ser.). (ENG.). 96p. (gr. 2-3). 90.60 *(978-1-4965-2733-2(X))* Stone Arch Bks.

Scarry, Richard. Biggest, Busiest Storybook Ever. Scarry, Richard, illus. 2009. (Picture Book Ser.). (ENG., Illus.). 184p. (J). (gr. -1-2). 27.99 *(978-0-375-85483-5(5),* Golden Bks.) Random Hse. Children's Bks.

—The Night Before the Night Before Christmas! Scarry, Richard, illus. 2014. (ENG., Illus.). 48p. (J). (gr. -1-2). 14.99 *(978-0-385-38804-7(7),* Golden Bks.) Random Hse. Children's Bks.

—Richard Scarry's Funniest Storybook Ever! 2016. (ENG., Illus.). 64p. (J). (gr. -1-2). 15.99 *(978-0-385-38297-7(9),* Golden Bks.) Random Hse. Children's Bks.

Scarsbrook, Richard. Cheeseburger Subversive. 2006. (ENG.). 204p. pap. 15.95 *(978-1-894345-54-5(1))* Thistledown Pr., Ltd. CAN. Dist: Univ. of Toronto Pr.

Schachner, Judy. Skippyjon Jones. Schachner, Judy, illus. 2003. (Skippyjon Jones Ser.). (ENG., Illus.). 32p. (J). (gr. -1-k). 17.99 *(978-0-525-47134-9(0),* Dutton Books for Young Readers) Penguin Young Readers Group.

—Skippyjon Jones Snow What. 2014. (Skippyjon Jones Ser.). (ENG., Illus.). 32p. (J). (gr. -1-k). 17.99 *(978-0-8037-3789-1(0),* Dial Bks) Penguin Publishing Group.

Schaedler, Kimberly. My Freaky Family. 2007. 24p. per. 15.95 *(978-1-4327-0617-3(9))* Outskirts Pr., Inc.

Schafer, Milton. I'm Big! Lew-Vriethoff, Joanne, illus. 2006. (J). *(978-1-4156-8150-3(3),* Dial) Penguin Publishing Group.

Schanen, Adriana Brad. Partners in Slime. Santoso, Charles, illus. (Quinny & Hopper Ser.). (ENG.). 272p. (J). (gr. 3-7). 2017. pap. 6.99 ***(978-1-4847-7822-7(7))*** 2016. 15.99 *(978-1-4847-7506-6(6))* Hyperion Bks. for Children.

Schanen, Adriana Brad. Quinny & Hopper. Swearingen, Greg, illus. 2014. (ENG.). 240p. (J). (gr. 3-7). 15.99 *(978-1-4231-7829-3(7))* Hyperion Bks. for Children.

Scharer, Niko. Emily's House, 1 vol. Fitzgerald, Joanne, illus. 2010. (ENG.). 22p. (J). (gr. k — 1). bds. 7.95 *(978-0-88899-831-6(7))* Groundwood Bks. CAN. Dist: Publishers Group West (PGW).

Schlaht, Kim. Ronnie's Rotten Recipes. Tijerina, Arnold G., III, ed. 2006. (Illus.). 70p. (J). (gr. -1). per. 18.95 *(978-0-9777688-1-3(3))* TICO Publishing.

Schlunke, Eva & Fitzgerald, Paul. Little Worm's Big Question, 1 vol. 2016. (ENG., Illus.). 36p. (J). (gr. -1-3). pap. 9.95 *(978-1-78026-261-1(2))* New Internationalist Pubns., Ltd. GBR. Dist: Consortium Bk. Sales & Distribution.

Schmid, Paul. A Pet for Petunia. 2011. (J). lib. bdg. 14.89 *(978-0-06-196332-2(1))* HarperCollins Pubs.

—A Pet for Petunia. Schmid, Paul, illus. 2011. (ENG., Illus.). 40p. (J). (gr. -1-2). 12.99 *(978-0-06-196331-5(3))* HarperCollins Pubs.

—Petunia Goes Wild. Schmid, Paul, illus. 2012. (ENG., Illus.). 40p. (J). (gr. -1-2). 12.99 *(978-0-06-196334-6(8))* HarperCollins Pubs.

Schmid, Susan Maupin. Ghost of a Chance. Marlin, Lissy, illus. 2017. (100 Dresses Ser.: 2). (ENG.). 320p. (J). (gr. 3-7). 16.99 *(978-0-553-53373-6(8),* Random Hse. Bks. for Young Readers) Random Hse. Children's Bks.

Schmid, Susan Maupin. If the Magic Fits. (100 Dresses Ser.: 1). (ENG.). (J). (gr. 3-7). 2017. 320p. 7.99 ***(978-0-553-53369-9(X),*** Yearling) 2016. (Illus.). 304p. 16.99 *(978-0-553-53366-8(5),* Random Hse. Bks. for Young Readers) Random Hse. Children's Bks.

Schneider, Robyn. Extraordinary Means. 2016. 352p. (YA). (gr. 8). pap. 9.99 *(978-0-06-221717-2(8),* Tegen, Katherine Bks) HarperCollins Pubs.

Schnetzler, Pattie L. Widdermaker. Sealock, Rick, illus. 2005. 32p. (gr. k-2). 15.95 *(978-0-87614-647-7(7))* Lerner Publishing Group.

Schnitzlein, Danny. The Monster Who Did My Math, 1 vol. Mayer, Bill, illus. (ENG.). 32p. (J). 2012. pap. 7.95 *(978-1-56145-668-0(3))* 2007. 16.95 *(978-1-56145-420-4(6))* Peachtree Pubs.

Scholastic, Inc. Staff. Dear Mrs. Larue. 2005. (ENG.). (J). pap. 550.00 *(978-0-439-70787-9(0),* Sidekicks TM) Scholastic, Inc.

Schrefer, Eliot. Geek Fantasy Novel. 2016. (ENG.). 320p. (J). (gr. 7). pap. 9.99 *(978-0-545-16041-4(3))* Scholastic, Inc.

Schreiber, Joe. Game over, Pete Watson. Rash, Andy, illus. 2014. (ENG.). 224p. (J). (gr. 5-7). 16.99 *(978-0-544-15756-9(7),* HMH Books For Young Readers) Houghton Mifflin Harcourt Publishing Co.

Schulz, Charles. Love Is Walking Hand in Hand. 2012. (ENG.). 72p. 7.95 *(978-1-60433-302-2(2))* Cider Mill Pr. Bk. Pubs., LLC.

—Peanuts Movie Novelization. 2015. (Peanuts Movie Ser.). (ENG., Illus.). 144p. (J). (gr. 3-7). 17.99 *(978-1-4814-6044-6(7));* pap. 6.99 *(978-1-4814-4136-0(1))* Simon Spotlight. (Simon Spotlight).

Schulz, Charles & Scott, Vicki. It's Tokyo, Charlie Brown! Braddock, Paige, illus. 2012. (Peanuts Ser.). (ENG.). 96p. (J). (gr. 2). pap. 9.99 *(978-1-60886-270-2(4))* Boom! Studios.

Schulz, Charles M. Batter up, Charlie Brown! 2014. (ENG., Illus.). 64p. 9.99 *(978-1-60699-725-3(4),* 699725) Fantagraphics Bks.

Schulz, Heidi. Giraffes Ruin Everything. Robertson, Chris, illus. 2016. (ENG.). 40p. (J). 16.99 *(978-1-61963-475-6(9),* 9781619634756, Bloomsbury USA Childrens) Bloomsbury Publishing USA.

Schwarz, Viviane. Is There a Dog in This Book? Schwarz, Viviane, illus. 2014. (ENG., Illus.). 32p. (J). (gr. -1-2). 16.99 *(978-0-7636-6991-1(1))* Candlewick Pr.

—Shark & Lobster's Amazing Undersea Adventure. Stewart, Joel, illus. 2006. 34p. (J). *(978-1-4156-8140-4(6))* Candlewick Pr.

Scieszka, Jon. The Brain Turbo. Biggs, Brian, illus. 2015. (Frank Einstein Ser.). (ENG.). 192p. (J). (gr. 3-7). 13.95 *(978-1-4197-1643-0(3),* Amulet Bks.) Abrams, Inc.

—Da Wild, Da Crazy, Da Vinci, No. 14. McCauley, Adam & Adam, Mccauley, illus. 2006. (Time Warp Trio Ser.: 14). (ENG.). 96p. (J). (gr. 2-4). 5.99 *(978-0-14-240465-2(9),* Puffin Books) Penguin Young Readers Group.

—Da Wild, Da Crazy, Da Vinci. McCauley, Adam, illus. 2006. (Time Warp Trio Ser.: No. 14). 72p. (gr. 4-7). 15.00 *(978-0-7569-6677-5(9))* Perfection Learning Corp.

—Frank Einstein & the Antimatter Motor. Biggs, Brian, illus. 2014. (Frank Einstein Ser.: 1). (ENG.). 192p. (J). (gr. 2-6). 13.95 *(978-1-4197-1218-0(7),* Amulet Bks.) Abrams, Inc.

—Frank Einstein & the Antimatter Motor. 2017. (Frank Einstein Ser.: 1). (J). lib. bdg. 18.40 ***(978-0-606-39683-7(7))*** Turtleback Bks.

—Frank Einstein & the Electro-Finger. Biggs, Brian, illus. 2015. (Frank Einstein Ser.: 2). (ENG.). 176p. (J). (gr. 3-7). 13.95 *(978-1-4197-1483-2(X),* Amulet Bks.) Abrams, Inc.

—Frank Einstein & the Evoblaster Belt. Bk. 4. Biggs, Brian, illus. 2016. (Frank Einstein Ser.). (ENG.). 208p. (J). (gr. 3-7). pap. 7.95 *(978-1-4197-2379-7(0))* Abrams, Inc.

—Frank Einstein & the EvoBlaster Belt (Frank Einstein Series #4) Book Four. Biggs, Brian, illus. 2016. (Frank Einstein Ser.). (ENG.). 208p. (J). (gr. 3-7). 13.95 *(978-1-4197-1887-8(8),* Amulet Bks.) Abrams, Inc.

—Frank Einstein & the EvoBlaster Belt (Frank Einstein Series #4) Book Four. Biggs, Brian, illus. 2017. (Frank Einstein Ser.). (ENG.). 224p. (J). (gr. 3-7). pap. 7.99 ***(978-1-4197-2736-8(2),*** Amulet Bks.) Abrams, Inc.

—Hey Kid, Want to Buy a Bridge? McCauley, Adam, illus. 2005. (Time Warp Trio Ser.: No. 11). 74p. (gr. 4-7). 15.00 *(978-0-7569-5988-3(8))* Perfection Learning Corp.

—It's All Greek to Me. Smith, Lane, illus. 2006. (Time Warp Trio Ser.: No. 8). 71p. (gr. 4-7). 15.00 *(978-0-7569-6780-2(5))* Perfection Learning Corp.

—Marco? Polo!, No. 16. McCauley, Adam, illus. 2008. (Time Warp Trio Ser.: 16). (ENG.). 96p. (J). (gr. 2-4). 5.99 *(978-0-14-241177-3(9),* Puffin Books) Penguin Young Readers Group.

—Marco? Polo! McCauley, Adam, illus. 2008. (Time Warp Trio Ser.: No. 16). 90p. (J). (gr. 4-6). 12.65 *(978-0-7569-8923-1(X))* Perfection Learning Corp.

—Me Oh Maya. McCauley, Adam, illus. 2005. (Time Warp Trio Ser.: 13). (ENG.). 96p. (J). (gr. 2-4). 5.99 *(978-0-14-240300-6(8),* Puffin Books) Penguin Young Readers Group.

—Me Oh Maya. McCauley, Adam, illus. 2005. (Time Warp Trio Ser.: No. 13). 69p. (gr. 2-6). 15.00 *(978-0-7569-5060-6(0))* Perfection Learning Corp.

—Oh Say, I Can't See, No. 15. McCauley, Adam, illus. 2007. (Time Warp Trio Ser.: 15). (ENG.). 80p. (J). (gr. 2-4). 5.99 *(978-0-14-240808-7(5),* Puffin Books) Penguin Young Readers Group.

—El Pirata Barbanegra. Smith, Lane, illus. (SPA.). (J). (gr. 5-8). 7.95 *(978-958-04-3401-6(8),* NR8584) Norma S.A. COL. Dist: Distribuidora Norma, Inc., Lectorum Pubns., Inc.

—Robot Zot! Shannon, David, illus. 2009. (ENG.). 40p. (J). (gr. -1-2). 17.99 *(978-1-4169-6394-3(4),* Simon & Schuster Bks. For Young Readers) Simon & Schuster Bks. For Young Readers.

—Robot Zot! Shannon, David, illus. 2011. (J). (gr. -1-2). 29.95 *(978-0-545-32739-8(3))* Weston Woods Studios, Inc.

—Sam Samurai. McCauley, Adam, illus. 2004. (Time Warp Trio Ser.: 10). (ENG.). 96p. (J). (gr. 2-4). pap. 5.99 *(978-0-14-240088-3(2),* Puffin Books) Penguin Young Readers Group.

—Sam Samurai. McCauley, Adam, illus. 2006. (Time Warp Trio Ser.: No. 10). 85p. (gr. 4-7). 15.00 *(978-0-7569-6779-6(1))* Perfection Learning Corp.

—See You Later, Gladiator. McCauley, Adam, illus. 2004. (Time Warp Trio Ser.: 9). (ENG.). 96p. (J). (gr. 2-4). pap. 5.99 *(978-0-14-240117-0(X),* Puffin Books) Penguin Young Readers Group.

—See You Later, Gladiator. McCauley, Adam, illus. 2004. (Time Warp Trio Ser.: No. 9). 87p. (J). (gr. 4-7). 12.65 *(978-0-7569-5986-9(1))* Perfection Learning Corp.

—Squids Will Be Squids: Fresh Morals, Beastly Fables. Smith, Lane, illus. 2003. (ENG.). 48p. (J). (gr. 3-7). pap. 7.99 *(978-0-14-250040-8(2),* Puffin Books) Penguin Young Readers Group.

—The True Story of the 3 Little Pigs! Smith, Lane, illus. 25th anniv. ed. 2014. (ENG.). 32p. (J). (gr. k-3). 17.99 *(978-0-451-47195-6(4),* Viking Books for Young Readers) Penguin Young Readers Group.

—Tut, Tut. Smith, Lane, illus. 2004. (Time Warp Trio Ser.: No. 6). 74p. (gr. 4-7). 15.00 *(978-0-7569-4050-8(8))* Perfection Learning Corp.

—Viking It & Liking It. McCauley, Adam, illus. 2004. (Time Warp Trio Ser.: No. 12). 73p. (gr. 2-6). 15.00 *(978-0-7569-2589-5(4))* Perfection Learning Corp.

—Your Mother Was a Neanderthal. Smith, Lane, illus. 2006. (Time Warp Trio Ser.: No. 4). 78p. (gr. 4-7). 15.00 *(978-0-7569-6782-6(1))* Perfection Learning Corp.

—Your Mother Was a Neanderthal. Smith, Lane, illus. 2004. (Time Warp Trio Ser.: 4). 78p. (J). 16.00 *(978-1-4176-3603-7(3))* Turtleback Bks.

Scieszka, Jon & Barnett, Mac. Battle Bunny. Myers, Matthew, illus. 2013. (ENG.). 32p. (J). (gr. k-4). 14.99 *(978-1-4424-4673-1(0),* Simon & Schuster Bks. For Young Readers) Simon & Schuster Bks. For Young Readers.

Scieszka, Jon & Brian Biggs. Frank Einstein & the Electro-Finger. 2017. (Frank Einstein Ser.: 2). (J). lib. bdg. 18.40 ***(978-0-606-39684-4(5))*** Turtleback Bks.

Scieszka, Jon, et al. Funny Business. Rex, Adam, illus. 2010. (Guys Read Ser.: 1). (ENG.). 288p. (J). (gr. 3-7). 16.99 *(978-0-06-196374-2(7));* pap. 6.99 *(978-0-06-196373-5(9))* HarperCollins Pubs. (Waldon Pond Pr.).

Scott, Janine. Café Cosmos. Wood, Hannah, illus. 2009. (Treasure Chest Readers Ser.). 24p. (J). (gr. -1-2). pap. 8.15 *(978-1-60754-674-0(4));* lib. bdg. 22.60 *(978-1-60754-673-3(6))* Windmill Bks.

—Mars Mouse. Wood, Hannah, illus. 2009. (Treasure Chest Readers Ser.). 24p. (J). (gr. -1-2). pap. 8.15 *(978-1-60754-677-1(9));* lib. bdg. 22.60 *(978-1-60754-676-4(0))* Windmill Bks.

—The Noisy Parrot. Rigby, Deborah, illus. 2009. (Treasure Chest Readers Ser.). 24p. (J). (gr. -1-2). pap. 8.15 *(978-1-60754-680-1(9));* lib. bdg. 22.60 *(978-1-60754-679-5(5))* Windmill Bks.

Scott, Jerry. Chillax. Borgman, Jim, illus. 2013. (Zits Ser.: 1). (ENG.). 256p. (YA). (gr. 8). pap. 9.99 *(978-0-06-222851-2(X),* HarperTeen) HarperCollins Pubs.

—Zits Vol. 7: Carretera y Manta. 2007. (SPA., Illus.). 128p. reprint ed. pap. 19.95 *(978-1-59497-337-6(7))* Public Square Bks.

Scott, Kate. Spies in Disguise: Boy in Tights. 2016. (ENG., Illus.). 192p. (J). (gr. 1-5). pap. 7.99 *(978-1-63450-689-2(8),* Sky Pony Pr.) Skyhorse Publishing Co., Inc.

Scott, Kieran. A Non-Blonde Cheerleader in Love. 2008. (ENG.). 272p. (YA). (gr. 7-18). 8.99 *(978-0-14-241186-5(8),* Speak) Penguin Young Readers Group.

Scott, Ron. Latte's Counting Book, 1 vol. 2009. 24p. pap. 24.95 *(978-1-60813-992-7(1))* America Star Bks.
Scotton, Rob. Fishy Tales. 2012. (Splat the Cat 8X8 Ser.). (J). lib. bdg. 13.55 *(978-0-606-26858-5(8),* Turtleback) Turtleback Bks.
—I Scream for Ice Cream. Scotton, Rob, illus. 2015. (I Can Read Level 1 Ser.). (ENG., Illus.). 32p. (J). (gr. -1-3). 16.99 *(978-0-06-229419-7(9))* HarperCollins Pubs.
—Secret Agent Splat! Scotton, Rob, illus. 2012. (Splat the Cat Ser.). (Illus.). 40p. (J). (gr. -1-2). (ENG.). 16.99 *(978-0-06-197871-5(X))*; lib. bdg. 17.89 *(978-0-06-197872-2(8))* HarperCollins Pubs.
—Sings Flat. Scotton, Rob, illus. 2011. (I Can Read Level 1 Ser.). (ENG., Illus.). 32p. (J). (gr. -1-3). 16.99 *(978-0-06-197854-8(X))* HarperCollins Pubs.
—Splat the Cat. Scotton, Rob, illus. 2008. (Splat the Cat Ser.). (Illus.). 40p. (J). (gr. -1-3). (ENG.). 17.99 *(978-0-06-083154-7(5))*; lib. bdg. 17.89 *(978-0-06-083155-4(3))* HarperCollins Pubs.
—Splat the Cat. 2011. (J). (gr. -1-2). 29.95 *(978-0-545-23794-9(7))* Weston Woods Studios, Inc.
—Splat the Cat - I Scream for Ice Cream. Scotton, Rob, illus. 2015. (I Can Read Level 1 Ser.). (ENG., Illus.). 32p. (J). (gr. -1-3). pap. 3.99 *(978-0-06-229418-0(0))* HarperCollins Pubs.
—Splat the Cat & the Big Secret. Farley, Rick & Eberz, Robert, illus. 2016. (J). ***(978-1-4844-8600-9(5))*** Publishers Quality Library Service.
—Splat the Cat & the Pumpkin-Picking Plan. Scotton, Rob, illus. 2014. (Splat the Cat Ser.). (ENG., Illus.). 24p. (J). (gr. -1-3). pap. 4.99 *(978-0-06-211586-7(3))* HarperCollins Pubs.
—Splat the Cat for President. 2016. (Splat the Cat 8X8 Ser.). (J). lib. bdg. 13.55 ***(978-0-606-40003-9(6))*** Turtleback Bks.
—Splat the Cat Goes to the Doctor. Scotton, Rob, illus. 2014. (Splat the Cat Ser.). (ENG., Illus.). 24p. (J). (gr. -1-3). pap. 4.99 *(978-0-06-211588-1(X),* HarperFestival) HarperCollins Pubs.
—Splat the Cat Makes Dad Glad. Scotton, Rob, illus. 2014. (I Can Read Level 1 Ser.). (ENG., Illus.). 32p. (J). (gr. -1-3). 16.99 *(978-0-06-211599-7(5))*; pap. 3.99 *(978-0-06-211597-3(9))* HarperCollins Pubs.
—Splat the Cat Makes Dad Glad. 2014. (Splat the Cat: I Can Read Ser.). (J). lib. bdg. 13.55 *(978-0-606-35475-2(1))* Turtleback Bks.
—Splat the Cat Sings Flat. Scotton, Rob, illus. 2011. (I Can Read Level 1 Ser.). (ENG., Illus.). 32p. (J). (gr. -1-3). pap. 3.99 *(978-0-06-197853-1(1))* HarperCollins Pubs.
—Splat the Cat Storybook Collection. Scotton, Rob, illus. 2013. (Splat the Cat Ser.). (ENG., Illus.). 192p. (J). (gr. -1-3). 11.99 *(978-0-06-213383-0(7))* HarperCollins Pubs.
Scotton, Rob & Driscoll, Laura. I Scream for Ice Cream. 2015. (Splat the Cat: I Can Read Ser.). (J). lib. bdg. 13.55 *(978-0-606-36948-0(1))* Turtleback Bks.
Scrimger, Richard. The Boy from Earth. 2004. (ENG.). 168p. (J). (gr. 3-7). pap. 7.95 *(978-0-88776-591-9(2),* Tundra Bks.) Tundra Bks. CAN. Dist: Penguin Random Hse. LLC.
—Into the Ravine. 2007. (ENG.). 264p. (YA). (gr. 5-12). per. 9.95 *(978-0-88776-822-4(9),* Tundra Bks.) Tundra Bks. CAN. Dist: Penguin Random Hse. LLC.
Scroggs, Kirk. Snoop Troop - Sloppy Joe Stink-O-Rama. 2015. (Snoop Troop Ser.: 3). (ENG., Illus.). 192p. (J). (gr. 3-7). 13.99 *(978-0-316-24278-3(0))* Little, Brown Bks. for Young Readers.
—Snoop Troop: Attack of the Ninja Potato Clones. 2015. (Snoop Troop Ser.: 2). (ENG., Illus.). 192p. (J). (gr. 1-4). 13.99 *(978-0-316-24277-6(2))* Little, Brown Bks. for Young Readers.
See, Ee Lin. My Kiasu Teenage Life in Singapore. 2005. (ENG., Illus.). 1p. per. 12.95 *(978-981-05-3016-7(1))* Monsoon Bks. Pte. Ltd. SGP. Dist: Tuttle Publishing.
Seegert, Scott. Vordak the Incomprehensible: Time Travel Trouble. Martin, John, illus. 2013. (Vordak the Incomprehensible Ser.). (ENG.). 192p. (J). (gr. 5). 13.99 *(978-1-60684-461-8(X),* Darby Creek) Lerner Publishing Group.
Seegert, Scott & Martin, John. Sci-Fi Junior High. 2017. (Sci-Fi Junior High Ser.: 1). (ENG., Illus.). 320p. (J). (gr. 3-7). 13.99 *(978-0-316-31516-6(8),* Jimmy Patterson) Little Brown & Co.
Seghetti, Nancy & Esseveld, Nelson. The Day Mom Quit. 2009. 36p. pap. 16.99 *(978-1-4389-2168-6(3))* AuthorHouse.
Seif Simpson, Martha. What NOT to Give Your Mom on Mother's Day, 0 vols. 2013. (ENG.). 24p. (J). (gr. -1-2). 12.99 *(978-1-4778-1647-9(X),* 9781477816479, Amazon Children's Publishing) Amazon Publishing.
Sellers, Sandra. Gran's Story III: The Long Awaited Trip to the Haunted House. 2010. 28p. pap. 17.99 *(978-1-4269-3244-1(8))* Trafford Publishing.
Service, Pamela F. Alien Expedition. 2010. pap. 33.92 *(978-0-7613-6958-5(9))* Lerner Publishing Group.
—Alien Expedition. Gorman, Mike, illus. (Alien Agent Ser.: 3). (ENG.). 160p. (J). (gr. 4-6). 2009. 16.95 *(978-0-8225-8870-2(6))*No. 3. 2010. pap. 5.95 *(978-0-7613-5249-5(X))* Lerner Publishing Group. (Carolrhoda Bks.).
—Camp Alien. 2010. pap. 33.92 *(978-0-7613-6955-4(4))* Lerner Publishing Group.
—Camp Alien. Gorman, Mike, illus. (Alien Agent Ser.: 2). (ENG.). 160p. (J). (gr. 4-6). 2010. pap. 5.95 *(978-0-7613-5247-1(3))* 2009. 16.95 *(978-0-8225-8656-2(8),* Carolrhoda Bks.) Lerner Publishing Group.
—My Cousin, the Alien. Gorman, Mike, illus. (Alien Agent Ser.: 1). (ENG.). 160p. (J). (gr. 4-6). 2009. pap. 5.95 *(978-0-7613-4964-8(2),* First Avenue Editions) 2008. 16.95 *(978-0-8225-7627-3(9),* Carolrhoda Bks.) Lerner Publishing Group.
Serwacki, Kevin & Pallace, Chris. Joey & Johnny - The Ninjas - Get Mooned. Serwacki, Kevin & Pallace, Chris, illus. 2015. (Joey & Johnny, the Ninjas Ser.: 1). (ENG., Illus.). 320p. (J). (gr. 3-7). 12.99 *(978-0-06-229933-8(6))* HarperCollins Pubs.
—Joey & Johnny, the Ninjas: Epic Fail. Serwacki, Kevin & Pallace, Chris, illus. 2016. (Joey & Johnny, the Ninjas Ser.: 2). (Illus.). 384p. (J). (gr. 3-7). 12.99 *(978-0-06-229935-2(2))* HarperCollins Pubs.
Seuling, Barbara. Robert & the Practical Jokes. Brewer, Paul, illus. 2006. (Robert Bks.). (ENG.). 150p. (J). (gr. k-4). 16.95 *(978-0-8126-2741-1(5))* Cricket Bks.
Seuss. Gerald Mcboing Boing. Crawford, Mel, illus. 2017. (Classic Seuss Ser.). (ENG.). 40p. (J). (gr. k-4). 16.99 ***(978-1-5247-1635-6(9))***; lib. bdg. 19.99 ***(978-1-5247-1757-5(6))*** Random Hse. Children's Bks. (Random Hse. Bks. for Young Readers).
Seuss, Dr. Battaglia dell Burro. pap. 24.95 *(978-88-09-02449-6(4))* Giunti Gruppo Editoriale ITA. Dist: Distribooks, Inc.
—Daisy-Head Mayzie. 2016. (Classic Seuss Ser.). (ENG., Illus.). 64p. (J). (gr. k-4). 17.99 *(978-0-553-53900-4(0))*; lib. bdg. 20.99 *(978-0-553-53906-6(X))* Random Hse. Children's Bks. (Random Hse. Bks. for Young Readers).
—Gerald McBoing Boing. Seuss, Dr., illus. 2004. (Little Golden Book Ser.). (ENG., Illus.). 24p. (J). (gr. -1-2). 4.99 *(978-0-375-82721-1(8),* Golden Bks.) Random Hse. Children's Bks.
—Hop on Pop, 1 vol. 2005. (Book & CD Ser.). (ENG., Illus.). 64p. (J). (gr. -1-2). 9.95 *(978-0-375-83493-6(1),* Random Hse. Bks. for Young Readers) Random Hse. Children's Bks.
—There's a Zamp in My Lamp! 2006. (Bright & Early Playtime Bks.). (ENG., Illus.). 14p. (J). (gr. k-k). 8.99 *(978-0-375-83632-9(2),* Random Hse. Bks. for Young Readers) Random Hse. Children's Bks.
—What Pet Should I Get? 2015. (Classic Seuss Ser.). (ENG., Illus.). 48p. (J). (gr. -1-2). 17.99 *(978-0-553-52426-0(7))*; lib. bdg. 20.99 *(978-0-553-52427-7(5))* Random Hse. Children's Bks. (Random Hse. Bks. for Young Readers).
—What Pet Should I Get? 2015. 48p. (J). lib. bdg. 30.60 *(978-0-606-37381-4(0))* Turtleback Bks.
—Your Favorite Seuss: A Baker's Dozen by the One & Only Dr. Seuss. 2004. (Classic Seuss Ser.). (ENG., Illus.). 368p. (J). (gr. k-4). 34.99 *(978-0-375-81061-9(7),* Random Hse. Bks. for Young Readers) Random Hse. Children's Bks.
Sewell, Byron W. Alix's Adventures in Wonderland: Lewis Carroll's Nightmare. 2011. (Illus.). 130p. pap. *(978-1-904808-72-5(7))* Evertype.
Shannon, David. Bugs in My Hair! Shannon, David, illus. 2013. (ENG., Illus.). 32p. (J). (gr. -1-3). 17.99 *(978-0-545-14313-4(6),* Blue Sky Pr., The) Scholastic, Inc.
—Uh-Oh, David! A David Sticker Book. Shannon, David, illus. 2013. (ENG., Illus.). 16p. (J). (gr. -1-k). 6.99 *(978-0-545-43768-4(7),* Cartwheel Bks.) Scholastic, Inc.
Shannon, George. Wise Acres. Zemke, Deborah, illus. 2004. (ENG.). 40p. (J). (gr. -1-7). 15.95 *(978-1-59354-041-8(8),* Handprint Bks.) Chronicle Bks. LLC.
Shannon, Molly. Tilly the Trickster. Hoyt, Ard, illus. 2011. (ENG.). 32p. (J). (gr. k-2). 16.95 *(978-1-4197-0030-9(8),* Abrams Bks. for Young Readers) Abrams, Inc.
Shaskan, Stephen. Toad on the Road: A Cautionary Tale. Shaskan, Stephen, illus. 2017. (Illus.). 32p. (J). (gr. -1-3). 17.99 *(978-0-06-239347-0(2))* HarperCollins Pubs.
Shaskan, Trisha Speed. Honestly, Red Riding Hood Was Rotten! The Story of Little Red Riding Hood As Told by the Wolf, 1 vol. Guerlais, Gérald, illus. 2013. (Other Side of the Story Ser.). (ENG.). 24p. (gr. 2-3). 9.95 *(978-1-4795-1940-8(5))* Picture Window Bks.
—Honestly, Red Riding Hood Was Rotten! The Story of Little Red Riding Hood as Told by the Wolf. Guerlais, Gérald, illus. 2011. (Other Side of the Story Ser.). (ENG.). 24p. (gr. 2-3). pap. 6.95 *(978-1-4048-7046-8(6))*; lib. bdg. 27.32 *(978-1-4048-6673-7(6))* Picture Window Bks.
—Seriously, Cinderella Is So Annoying! The Story of Cinderella as Told by the Wicked Stepmother. Guerlais, Gérald, illus. (Other Side of the Story Ser.). (ENG.). 24p. (gr. 2-3). 2013. 9.95 *(978-1-4795-1941-5(3))* 2011. pap. 6.95 *(978-1-4048-7048-2(2))* 2011. lib. bdg. 27.32 *(978-1-4048-6674-4(4))* Picture Window Bks.
—Truly, We Both Loved Beauty Dearly! The Story of Sleeping Beauty as Told by the Good & Bad Fairies. Tayal, Amit, illus. 2013. (Other Side of the Story Ser.). (ENG.). 24p. (gr. 2-3). 27.32 *(978-1-4048-7940-9(4))* Picture Window Bks.
—Truly, We Both Loved Beauty Dearly! The Story of Sleeping Beauty As Told by the Good & Bad Fairies. Tayal, Amit, illus. 2013. (Other Side of the Story Ser.). (ENG.). 24p. (gr. 2-3). 9.95 *(978-1-4795-1945-3(6))* Picture Window Bks.
Shaskan, Trisha Speed & Loewen, Nancy. Truly, We Both Loved Beauty Dearly! The Story of Sleeping Beauty, As Told by the Good & Bad Fairies. Tayal, Amit & Alsonso, Denis, illus. 2013. (Other Side of the Story Ser.). (ENG.). 24p. (gr. 2-3). pap. 6.95 *(978-1-4795-1949-1(9))* Picture Window Bks.
Shaw, Natalie. I Can Do Anything! 2016. (Olivia 8x8 Ser.). lib. bdg. 13.55 *(978-0-606-38242-7(9))* Turtleback Bks.
—I'M Feeling Silly. Fruchter, Jason, illus. 2016. (Daniel Tiger's Neighborhood Ser.). (ENG.). 14p. (J). (gr. -1 — 1). bds. 5.99 *(978-1-4814-6815-2(4),* Simon Spotlight) Simon Spotlight.
Shea, Bob. Cheetah Can't Lose. Shea, Bob, illus. 2013. (ENG., Illus.). 40p. (J). (gr. -1-3). 17.99 *(978-0-06-173083-2(1))* HarperCollins Pubs.
—Dinosaur vs. Mommy. Shea, Bob, illus. 2015. (Dinosaur vs. Book Ser.). (ENG., Illus.). 40p. (J). (gr. -1-k). 16.99 *(978-1-4231-6086-1(X))* Hyperion Bks. for Children.
—Dinosaur vs. Santa. Shea, Bob, illus. 2014. (Dinosaur vs. Book Ser.). (ENG., Illus.). 30p. (J). (gr. -1-k). bds. 7.99 *(978-1-4231-6824-9(0))* Hyperion Bks. for Children.
—Dinosaur vs. School. Shea, Bob, illus. (Dinosaur vs. Book Ser.). (ENG., Illus.). (J). (gr. -1-k). 2016. 32p. bds. 7.99 *(978-1-4231-6094-6(0))* 2014. 40p. 16.99 *(978-1-4231-6087-8(8))* Hyperion Bks. for Children.
—Dinosaur vs. the Potty. Shea, Bob, illus. 2012. (ENG., Illus.). 30p. (J). (gr. -1-1). bds. 6.99 *(978-1-4231-5179-1(8))* Hyperion Pr.
—The Happiest Book Ever. Shea, Bob, illus. 2016. (ENG., Illus.). 40p. (J). (gr. 1-3). 16.99 *(978-1-4847-3045-4(3))* Hyperion Bks. for Children.
—I'm a Shark. Shea, Bob, illus. 2011. (ENG., Illus.). 40p. (J). (gr. -1-1). 16.99 *(978-0-06-199846-1(X))* HarperCollins Pubs.
—Kid Sheriff & the Terrible Toads. Smith, Lane, illus. 2014. (ENG.). 32p. (J). (gr. -1-3). 17.99 *(978-1-59643-975-7(0),* 9781596439757) Roaring Brook Pr.
Shea, Bob. The Scariest Book Ever. Shea, Bob, illus. 2017. (ENG., Illus.). 40p. (J). (gr. 1-3). 16.99 ***(978-1-4847-3046-1(1))*** Hyperion Bks. for Children.
Shealy, Dennis. I'm a T. Rex! Biggs, Brian, illus. 2010. (Little Golden Book Ser.). (ENG.). 24p. (J). (gr. -1-2). 4.99 *(978-0-375-85806-2(7),* Golden Bks.) Random Hse. Children's Bks.
Shekunov, Vladimir. Nature & Us: Whether Ants Can Think. 2011. 24p. pap. 14.00 *(978-1-4520-5863-4(6))* AuthorHouse.
Sheldon, Dyan. Deep & Meaningful Diaries from Planet Janet. 2007. (ENG.). 464p. (YA). (gr. 9). per. 8.99 *(978-0-7636-3216-8(3))* Candlewick Pr.
—The Truth about My Success. 2015. (ENG.). 352p. (J). (gr. 7). 16.99 *(978-0-7636-7272-0(6))* Candlewick Pr.
Shepherd, Donna J. Chizzy's Topsy Tale. Collier, Kevin Scott, illus. 2008. 20p. pap. 10.95 *(978-1-935137-10-8(7))* Guardian Angel Publishing, Inc.
Shepherd, Donna J. & Foster, Jack. Where Is Salami. 2011. (Illus.). 16p. pap. 9.95 *(978-1-61633-147-4(X))* Guardian Angel Publishing, Inc.
Sherman, Caroline. A Dog's Life, 0 vols. Wu, Donald, illus. 2012. (ENG.). 24p. (J). (gr. -1-2). 12.99 *(978-0-7614-6200-2(7),* 9780761462002, Amazon Children's Publishing) Amazon Publishing.
Sherrard, Valerie. There's a Goldfish in My Shoe!, 1 vol. Jardine, David, illus. 2009. (ENG.). 32p. (J). (gr. 1-7). 12.95 *(978-1-897174-47-0(0),* Tuckamore Bks) Creative Bk. Publishing CAN. Dist: Orca Bk. Pubs. USA.
Sherry, Kevin. I'm the Best Artist in the Ocean! 2008. (ENG.). 24p. (J). (gr. -1-3). 16.99 *(978-0-8037-3255-1(4),* Dial Bks) Penguin Young Readers Group.
—Meet the Bigfeet. 2014. (Yeti Files Ser.: 1). (ENG.). 128p. (J). (gr. 2-5). 8.99 *(978-0-545-55617-0(1),* Scholastic Pr.) Scholastic, Inc.
—Monsters on the Run. 2015. (Yeti Files Ser.: 2). (ENG., Illus.). 128p. (J). (gr. 2-5). 8.99 *(978-0-545-55619-4(8),* Scholastic Pr.) Scholastic, Inc.
Sherry, Kevin. Remy Sneakers vs. the Robo-Rats. Sherry, Kevin, illus. 2017. (Remy Sneakers Ser.: 1). (ENG., Illus.). 128p. (J). (gr. 2-5). 9.99 ***(978-1-338-03460-8(X),*** Scholastic Pr.) Scholastic, Inc.
Shore, Diane Z. How to Drive Your Sister Crazy. Rankin, Laura, illus. (I Can Read Level 2 Ser.). (ENG.). 48p. (J). (gr. k-3). 2012. pap. 3.99 *(978-0-06-052764-8(1))* 2008. 16.99 *(978-0-06-052762-4(5))* HarperCollins Pubs.
—How to Drive Your Sister Crazy. Rankin, Laura, illus. 2012. (I Can Read! Level 2 Ser.). (J). lib. bdg. 13.55 *(978-0-606-26869-1(3),* Turtleback) Turtleback Bks.
Shreve, Steve. Stan & the Toilet Monster, 0 vols. 2011. (ENG.). 164p. (J). (gr. 2-6). 12.99 *(978-0-7614-5977-4(4),* 9780761459774, Amazon Children's Publishing) Amazon Publishing.
Shull, Megan. Bounce. 2016. 384p. (J). (gr. 5-7). 16.99 *(978-0-06-231172-6(7),* Tegen, Katherine Bks) HarperCollins Pubs.
Shults, Sylvia. Double Double Love & Trouble. 2013. 150p. pap. 12.99 *(978-0-9848931-3-3(X))* Dark Continents Publishing.
Shurtliff, Liesl. Jack: The True Story of Jack & the Beanstalk. 2015. (ENG.). 304p. (J). (gr. 3-7). 16.99 *(978-0-385-75579-5(1),* Knopf Bks. for Young Readers) Random Hse. Children's Bks.
—Rump: The True Story of Rumpelstiltskin. (ENG.). 272p. (J). (gr. 3-7). 2014. pap. 7.99 *(978-0-307-97796-0(X),* Yearling) 2013. 16.99 *(978-0-307-97793-9(5),* Knopf Bks. for Young Readers) 2013. lib. bdg. 19.99 *(978-0-307-97794-6(3),* Knopf Bks. for Young Readers) Random Hse. Children's Bks.
Silberberg, Alan. The Awesome, Almost 100% True Adventures of Matt & Craz. Silberberg, Alan, illus. (ENG., Illus.). 336p. (J). (gr. 4-8). 2014. pap. 7.99 *(978-1-4169-9433-6(5))* 2013. 16.99 *(978-1-4169-9432-9(7))* Simon & Schuster Children's Publishing. (Aladdin).
Silverhardt, Lauryn. SpongeBob SpookyPants. Style Guide Staff, illus. 2004. (SpongeBob SquarePants Ser.). (ENG.). 16p. (J). bds. 5.99 *(978-0-689-87320-1(4),* Simon Spotlight/Nickelodeon) Simon Spotlight/Nickelodeon.
Silverstein, Shel. Who Wants a Cheap Rhinoceros? Silverstein, Shel, illus. 50th anniv. ed. 2014. (ENG., Illus.). 64p. (J). (gr. -1-3). 17.99 *(978-1-4814-1593-4(X),* Simon & Schuster Bks. For Young Readers) Simon & Schuster Bks. For Young Readers.
Simee. Giggles Feel Good, 1 vol. 2010. 18p. pap. 24.95 *(978-1-4489-4878-9(9))* PublishAmerica, Inc.
Simendinger, Ted. Jurassic Trout: A Flyfishing Comedy. 2004. per. 9.95 *(978-0-9702405-5-2(4))* Airplane Reader Publishing.
—12 Miles to Paradise: A People Story about Horses & Horseracing. 2nd ed. 2004. 364p. per. 12.95 *(978-0-9702405-4-5(6))* Airplane Reader Publishing.
Simon, Annette. Mocking Birdies. 2005. (ENG., Illus.). 32p. (J). (gr. -1-3). 16.95 *(978-1-894965-29-3(9))* Simply Read Bks. CAN. Dist: Ingram Publisher Services.
Simon, Coco. Emma on Thin Icing. 2011. (Cupcake Diaries: 3). (ENG.). 160p. (J). (gr. 3-7). pap. 6.99 *(978-1-4424-2279-7(3),* Simon Spotlight) Simon Spotlight.
Simon, Francesca. Horrid Henry, 1 vol. Ross, Tony, illus. 2012. (Horrid Henry Ser.). (ENG.). 112p. (J). (gr. 2-5). lib. bdg. 24.21 *(978-1-59961-185-3(6))* Spotlight.
—Horrid Henry & the Mummy's Curse. 2009. (Horrid Henry Ser.). lib. bdg. 17.20 *(978-0-606-06805-5(8),* Turtleback) Turtleback Bks.
—Horrid Henry & the Scary Sitter. Ross, Tony, illus. 2009. (Horrid Henry Ser.: 0). (ENG.). 112p. (J). (gr. 2-5). pap. 6.99 *(978-1-4022-1781-4(1),* 9781402217814, Sourcebooks Jabberwocky) Sourcebooks, Inc.
—Horrid Henry & the Scary Sitter, 1 vol. Ross, Tony, illus. 2012. (Horrid Henry Ser.). (ENG.). 112p. (J). (gr. 2-5). lib. bdg. 24.21 *(978-1-59961-188-4(0))* Spotlight.
—Horrid Henry & the Soccer Fiend. Ross, Tony, illus. 2009. (Horrid Henry Ser.: 0). (ENG.). 112p. (J). (gr. 2-5). pap. 6.99 *(978-1-4022-1778-4(1),* Sourcebooks Jabberwocky) Sourcebooks, Inc.
—Horrid Henry & the Soccer Fiend, 1 vol. Ross, Tony, illus. 2012. (Horrid Henry Ser.). (ENG.). 112p. (J). (gr. 2-5). lib. bdg. 24.21 *(978-1-59961-189-1(9))* Spotlight.
—Horrid Henry & the Soccer Fiend. 2009. (Horrid Henry Ser.). lib. bdg. 17.20 *(978-0-606-06798-0(1),* Turtleback) Turtleback Bks.
—Horrid Henry Robs the Bank. Ross, Tony, illus. 2013. (Horrid Henry Ser.: 0). (ENG.). 112p. (J). (gr. 2-5). pap. 6.99 *(978-1-4022-7995-9(7),* 9781402279959, Sourcebooks Jabberwocky) Sourcebooks, Inc.
—Horrid Henry's Christmas. Ross, Tony, illus. 2009. (Horrid Henry Ser.: 0). (ENG.). 112p. (J). (gr. 2-5). pap. 5.99 *(978-1-4022-1782-1(X),* Sourcebooks Jabberwocky) Sourcebooks, Inc.
—The Mega-Mean Time Machine. Ross, Tony, illus. 2009. (Horrid Henry Ser.: 0). (ENG.). 112p. (J). (gr. 2-5). pap. 6.99 *(978-1-4022-1780-7(3),* 9781402217807, Sourcebooks Jabberwocky) Sourcebooks, Inc.
—The Mega-Mean Time Machine, 1 vol. Ross, Tony, illus. 2012. (Horrid Henry Ser.). (ENG.). 112p. (J). (gr. 2-5). lib. bdg. 24.21 *(978-1-59961-187-7(2))* Spotlight.
—The Mega-Mean Time Machine. 2009. (Horrid Henry Ser.). lib. bdg. 17.20 *(978-0-606-06776-8(0),* Turtleback) Turtleback Bks.
—Monster Movie. Ross, Tony, illus. 2012. (Horrid Henry Ser.: 0). (ENG.). 112p. (J). (gr. 2-5). pap. 4.99 *(978-1-4022-7737-5(7),* Sourcebooks Jabberwocky) Sourcebooks, Inc.
—Stinkbomb. Ross, Tony, illus. 2009. (Horrid Henry Ser.: 0). (ENG.). 112p. (J). (gr. 2-5). pap. 6.99 *(978-1-4022-1779-1(X),* 9781402217791, Sourcebooks Jabberwocky) Sourcebooks, Inc.
—Stinkbomb. 2009. (Horrid Henry Ser.). lib. bdg. 17.20 *(978-0-606-06795-9(7),* Turtleback) Turtleback Bks.
—Tricks the Tooth Fairy, 1 vol. Ross, Tony, illus. 2012. (Horrid Henry Ser.). (ENG.). 112p. (J). (gr. 2-5). lib. bdg. 24.21 *(978-1-59961-191-4(0))* Spotlight.
—Tricks the Tooth Fairy. 2009. (Horrid Henry Ser.). lib. bdg. 17.20 *(978-0-606-06769-0(8),* Turtleback) Turtleback Bks.
—Underpants. Ross, Tony, illus. 2009. 112p. (J). (gr. 2-5). (Horrid Henry Ser.: 0). (ENG.). pap. 6.99 *(978-1-4022-3825-3(8))*; pap. 4.99 *(978-1-4022-1777-7(3))* Sourcebooks, Inc. (Sourcebooks Jabberwocky).
—Underpants. 2009. (Horrid Henry Ser.). lib. bdg. 17.20 *(978-0-606-06766-9(3),* Turtleback) Turtleback Bks.
—Wakes the Dead. Ross, Tony, illus. 2011. (Horrid Henry Ser.: 0). (ENG.). 112p. (J). (gr. 2-5). pap. 4.99 *(978-1-4022-5934-0(4),* Sourcebooks Jabberwocky) Sourcebooks, Inc.
—Wakes the Dead, 1 vol. Ross, Tony, illus. 2012. (Horrid Henry Ser.). (ENG.). 112p. (J). (gr. 2-5). lib. bdg. 24.21 *(978-1-59961-192-1(9))* Spotlight.
Simonson, Louise. Snow White & the Seven Robots. Sanchez, Jimena, illus. 2015. (Far Out Fairy Tales Ser.). (ENG.). 40p. (gr. 3-4). lib. bdg. 25.32 *(978-1-4342-9648-1(2))* Stone Arch Bks.
Simonson, Louise, et al. Far Out Fairy Tales. Frampton, Otis et al, illus. 2016. (Far Out Fairy Tales Ser.). (ENG.). 176p. (gr. 3-4). pap. 12.95 *(978-1-4965-2511-6(6),* Far Out Fairy Tales) Stone Arch Bks.
Singhose, Rose. Granny's GIGGLES BOOK FIVE. 2010. 35p. pap. 16.95 *(978-0-557-61001-3(X))* Lulu Pr., Inc.
—Granny's GIGGLES BOOK SEVEN. 2010. 33p. pap. 16.95 *(978-0-557-61004-4(4))* Lulu Pr., Inc.
—Granny's giggles book Three. 2010. 33p. pap. 16.95 *(978-0-557-59768-0(4))* Lulu Pr., Inc.
Sitomer, Alan Lawrence. Daddy's Back-To-School Shopping Adventure. Carter, Abby, illus. 2015. (ENG.). 40p. (J). (gr. -1-k). 16.99 *(978-1-4231-8421-8(1))* Hyperion Bks. for Children.
Skandle, D. L. Little Duckie's Day. 2010. 28p. pap. 15.49 *(978-1-4490-9705-9(7))* AuthorHouse.
Skye, obert. Batneezer. Skye, obert, illus. 2016. (Creature from My Closet Ser.: 6). (ENG., Illus.). 208p. (J). 13.99 *(978-1-62779-163-2(9),* 9781627791632, Holt, Henry & Co. Bks. For Young Readers) Holt, Henry & Co.
—Katfish. Skye, obert, illus. 2014. (Creature from My Closet Ser.: 4). (ENG., Illus.). 256p. (J). (gr. 4-7). 13.99 *(978-0-8050-9690-3(6),* 9780805096903, Holt, Henry & Co. Bks. For Young Readers) Holt, Henry & Co.
—Lord of the Hat. Skye, obert, illus. 2015. (Creature from My Closet Ser.: 5). (ENG., Illus.). 256p. (J). (gr. 4-7). 13.99 *(978-1-62779-162-5(0),* 9781627791625, Holt, Henry & Co. Bks. For Young Readers) Holt, Henry & Co.
—Pinocula. Skye, obert, illus. 2013. (Creature from My Closet Ser.: 3). (ENG., Illus.). 256p. (J). (gr. 4-7). 12.99 *(978-0-8050-9689-7(2),* 9780805096897, Holt, Henry & Co. Bks. For Young Readers) Holt, Henry & Co.
—Potterwookiee. Skye, obert, illus. 2012. (Creature from My Closet Ser.: 2). (ENG., Illus.). 256p. (J). (gr. 4-7). 13.99 *(978-0-8050-9451-0(2),* 9780805094510, Holt, Henry & Co. Bks. For Young Readers) Holt, Henry & Co.
—Wonkenstein. Skye, obert, illus. 2011. (Creature from My Closet Ser.: 1). (ENG., Illus.). 240p. (J). (gr. 4-7). 12.99 *(978-0-8050-9268-4(4),* 9780805092684, Holt, Henry & Co. Bks. For Young Readers) Holt, Henry & Co.
—Wonkenstein. Skye, obert, illus. 2015. (Creature from My Closet Ser.: 1). (ENG., Illus.). 256p. (J). (gr. 4-7). pap. 6.99 *(978-1-250-01022-3(5),* 9781250010223) Square Fish.
Slack, Michael. Wazdot? 2014. (ENG., Illus.). 48p. (J). (gr. -1 — 1). 16.99 *(978-1-4231-8347-1(9))* Hyperion Bks. for Children.
Slate, Jenny & Fleischer-Camp, Dean. Marcel the Shell with Shoes On: Things about Me, 1 vol. 2011. (Marcel the Shell Ser.: 1). (ENG.). 42p. (J). (gr. k-3). 18.99 *(978-1-59514-455-3(2),* Razorbill) Penguin Young Readers Group.
—The Most Surprised I've Ever Been. 2014. (Marcel the Shell Ser.: 2). (ENG.). 42p. (J). (gr. k-3). 18.99 *(978-1-59514-456-0(0),* Razorbill) Penguin Young Readers Group.
Slater, Dashka. Dangerously Ever After. Docampo, Valeria, illus. 2012. (ENG.). 40p. (J). (gr. k-3). 16.99 *(978-0-8037-3374-9(7),* Dial Bks) Penguin Young Readers Group.
—Escargot. Hanson, Sydney, illus. 2017. (ENG.). 40p. (J). 16.99 *(978-0-374-30281-8(2),* 9780374302818, Farrar, Straus & Giroux (BYR)) Farrar, Straus & Giroux.
Slater, David Michael. Ned Loses His Head, 1 vol. 2007. (Missy Swiss & More Ser.). (ENG., Illus.). 32p. (gr. -1-4). 28.50 *(978-1-60270-011-6(7),* Looking Glass Library) ABDO Publishing Co.
Sloan, Price Stern & Mad Libs Staff. Doctor Who Mad Libs. 2014. (Mad Libs Ser.). (ENG.). 48p. (J). (gr. 3-7). 4.99 *(978-0-8431-8246-0(6),* Mad Libs) Penguin Young Readers Group.

H I

Slonim, David. I Loathe You. Slonim, David, illus. 2012. (ENG., Illus.). 24p. (J). (gr. -1-2). 15.99 *(978-1-4424-2244-5(0), Aladdin)* Simon & Schuster Children's Publishing.
Small, Wylie J. The Great Prune Caper. 2009. 94p. pap. 9.98 *(978-1-84728-350-4(0))* Lulu Pr., Inc.
Smart, Jamie. Bunny vs. Monkey. Smart, Jamie, illus. 2016. (ENG., Illus.). 64p. (J). (gr. 2-5). pap. 7.99 *(978-0-545-86184-7(5), Graphix)* Scholastic, Inc.
Smileyworld Ltd. Staff. Where's Smiley? Smileyworld Ltd. Staff, illus. 2010. (SmileyWorld Ser.). (ENG., Illus.). 34p. (J). (gr. k-3). 9.99 *(978-1-4424-0756-5(5), Little Simon)* Little Simon.
Smith, Alex T. Claude at the Beach, 1 vol. Smith, Alex T., illus. (Claude Ser.). (ENG., Illus.). 96p. (J). (gr. 1-3). 2016. pap. 7.95 *(978-1-56145-919-3(4))* 2014. 12.95 *(978-1-56145-703-8(5))* Peachtree Pubs.
—Claude at the Circus, 1 vol. Smith, Alex T., illus. 2013. (Claude Ser.). (ENG., Illus.). 96p. (J). (gr. 2-4). 12.95 *(978-1-56145-702-1(7))* Peachtree Pubs.
—Claude in the City, 1 vol. Smith, Alex T., illus. (Claude Ser.). (ENG., Illus.). 96p. (J). (gr. 2-4). 2015. pap. 7.95 *(978-1-56145-843-1(0))* 2013. 12.95 *(978-1-56145-697-0(7))* Peachtree Pubs.
—Claude in the Country, 1 vol. Smith, Alex T., illus. 2016. (Claude Ser.). (ENG., Illus.). 96p. (J). (gr. 1-3). 12.95 *(978-1-56145-918-6(6))* Peachtree Pubs.
—Claude in the Spotlight, 1 vol. Smith, Alex T., illus. 2015. (Claude Ser.). (ENG., Illus.). 96p. (J). (gr. 1-3). 12.95 *(978-1-56145-895-0(3))* Peachtree Pubs.
—Claude on the Slopes, 1 vol. Smith, Alex T., illus. 2016. (Claude Ser.). (ENG., Illus.). 96p. (J). (gr. 1-3). pap. 7.95 *(978-1-56145-923-0(2))* Peachtree Pubs.
—Foxy & Egg: Starring Vivien Vixen As Foxy Dubois - Introducing Edward l'Ouef As Egg. Smith, Alex T., illus. 2011. (Illus.). 32p. (J). (gr. -1-3). 17.95 *(978-0-8234-2330-9(1))* Holiday Hse., Inc.
—Little Red & the Very Hungry Lion. 2016. (ENG., Illus.). 32p. (J). (gr. -1-k). 17.99 *(978-0-545-91438-3(8), Scholastic Pr.)* Scholastic, Inc.
Smith, Andrew. Grasshopper Jungle. 2015. (ENG.). 416p. (YA). (gr. 9). pap. 10.99 *(978-0-14-242500-8(1), Speak)* Penguin Young Readers Group.
Smith, Ben Bailey. I Am Bear. Akyüz, Sav, illus. 2016. (ENG.). (J). (-k). 15.99 *(978-0-7636-7743-5(4), Candlewick Entertainment)* Candlewick Pr.
Smith, E. K. Alien Dude! & the Attack of Wormzilla!! Grosshauser, Peter, illus. 2014. (Alien Dude! Ser.). (ENG.). 64p. (J). (gr. 2-4). pap. 4.99 *(978-0-9883792-0-6(1))* Zip Line Publishing.
—Alien Dude! Mr. Evil Potato Man & the Food Fight. Grosshauser, Peter, illus. 2014. (Alien Dude! Ser.). (ENG.). 64p. (J). (gr. 2-4). pap. 4.99 *(978-0-9883792-1-3(X))* Zip Line Publishing.
Smith, Elwood. I'm Not a Pig in Underpants. Smith, Elwood, illus. 2013. (ENG., Illus.). 40p. (J). (gr. 1-3). 18.99 *(978-1-56846-229-5(8), Creative Editions)* Creative Co., The.
Smith, J. E. Complex City: All in a Day's Work. 2003. 120p. per. 12.95 *(978-0-9728070-0-5(4))* Better Comics.
Smith, Jeff. Bone Vol. 2: La Gran Carrera de Vacas. 2007. (SPA., Illus.). 144p. reprint ed. 24.95 *(978-1-59497-347-5(4))* Public Square Bks.
—Bone Vol. 3: Los Ojos de la Tormenta. 2007. (SPA., Illus.). 144p. reprint ed. 24.95 *(978-1-59497-348-2(2))* Public Square Bks.
—Out from Boneville. Smith, Jeff & Hamaker, Steve, illus. 2005. (Bone Ser.: 1). (ENG.). 144p. (J). pap. 12.99 *(978-0-439-70640-7(8), Graphix)* Scholastic, Inc.
Smith, Jennifer E. This Is What Happy Looks Like. 2013. (ENG.). 432p. (YA). (gr. 7-17). pap. 10.99 *(978-0-316-21281-6(4), Poppy)* Little, Brown Bks. for Young Readers.
Smith, Jim. Barry Loser & the Holiday of Doom. 2015. (Barry Loser Ser.: 5). (ENG., Illus.). 240p. (J). (gr. 2-4). pap. 10.99 *(978-1-4052-6802-8(6))* Egmont Bks., Ltd. GBR. Dist: Independent Pubs. Group.
—Barry Loser Hates Half Term! 2016. (Barry Loser Ser.: 7). (ENG., Illus.). 256p. (J). (gr. 2-6). pap. 8.99 *(978-1-4052-6914-8(6))* Egmont Bks., Ltd. GBR. Dist: Independent Pubs. Group.
—I Am So over Being a Loser. 2014. (Barry Loser Ser.). (ENG., Illus.). 240p. (J). (gr. 2-4). pap. 10.99 *(978-1-4052-6033-6(5))* Egmont Bks., Ltd. GBR. Dist: Independent Pubs. Group.
—I Am Sort of a Loser. 2014. (Barry Loser Ser.: 4). (ENG., Illus.). 240p. (J). (gr. 2-4). pap. 11.99 *(978-1-4052-6801-1(8))* Egmont Bks., Ltd. GBR. Dist: Independent Pubs. Group.
Smith, Joseph K. The Substitute Kid. 2008. 54p. pap. 16.95 *(978-1-60672-272-5(7))* America Star Bks.
Smith, Lane. It's a Book. Smith, Lane, illus. 2010. (ENG., Illus.). 32p. (J). (gr. 1-5). 15.99 *(978-1-59643-606-0(9), 9781596436060)* Roaring Brook Pr.
—It's a Little Book. 2011. (ENG., Illus.). 24p. (J). (— 1). bds. 7.99 *(978-1-59643-758-6(8), 9781596437586)* Roaring Brook Pr.
—John, Paul, George & Ben. Smith, Lane, illus. 2006. (ENG., Illus.). 40p. (J). (gr. -1 — 1). 17.99 *(978-0-7868-4893-5(6))* Hyperion Pr.
—John, Paul, George & Ben. 2011. (J). (gr. 2-5). 29.95 *(978-0-439-02754-0(3), WHCD807)* Weston Woods Studios, Inc.
—Madam President. Smith, Lane, illus. 2008. (ENG., Illus.). 40p. (J). (gr. -1-k). 16.99 *(978-1-4231-0846-7(9))* Hyperion Pr.
—Madam President. 2011. (J). (gr. 1-4). 29.95 *(978-0-545-10688-7(5))* Weston Woods Studios, Inc.
Smith, Linda. The Inside Tree. Brown, Kathryn, illus. Date not set. 32p. (J). (gr. -1-3). 5.99 *(978-0-06-443542-0(3))* HarperCollins Pubs.
Smith, Robert Kimmel. Chocolate Fever. Fiammenghi, Gioia, illus. 2006. (ENG.). 96p. (J). (gr. 3-7). 5.99 *(978-0-14-240595-6(7), Puffin Books)* Penguin Young Readers Group.
Smith, Shoham. An after Bedtime Story. Tsarfati, Einat, illus. 2016. (ENG.). 48p. (J). (gr. k-2). 16.95 *(978-1-4197-1873-1(8), Abrams Bks. for Young Readers)* Abrams, Inc.
Snicket, Lemony, pseud. The Austere Academy. Helquist, Brett, illus. 2008. (Series of Unfortunate Events Ser.: Bk. 5). (ENG.). 240p. (J). (gr. 5-18). pap. 6.99 *(978-0-06-114634-3(X), Harper Trophy)* HarperCollins Pubs.
—The Bad Beginning. 2007. (Ser. of Unfortunate Events Ser.: 1). (J). lib. bdg. 17.20 *(978-1-4177-8840-8(2), Turtleback)* Turtleback Bks.
—The Bad Beginning No. 1: Or, Orphans! Helquist, Brett & Kupperman, Michael, illus. 2007. (Series of Unfortunate Events Ser.: 1). (ENG.). 176p. (J). (gr. 5-9). pap. 7.99 *(978-0-06-114630-5(7))* HarperCollins Pubs.
—The Beatrice Letters. Helquist, Brett, illus. 2006. (Series of Unfortunate Events Ser.). (ENG.). 72p. (J). (gr. 5-7). 22.99 *(978-0-06-058658-4(3))* HarperCollins Pubs.
—The Complete Wreck, Bks. 1-13. Helquist, Brett, illus. 2006. (Series of Unfortunate Events Ser.: Bks. 1-13). (J). (gr. 5). 180.00 *(978-0-06-111906-4(7))* HarperCollins Pubs.
—The Dilemma Deepens, 3 vols. Helquist, Brett, illus. 2003. (Series of Unfortunate Events Ser.: Bks. 7-9). (J). (gr. 5-6). 41.99 *(978-0-06-055620-4(X))* HarperCollins Pubs.
—The End. Helquist, Brett & Kupperman, Michael, illus. 2006. (Series of Unfortunate Events Ser.: 13). (ENG.). 368p. (J). (gr. 5-18). 13.99 *(978-0-06-441016-8(1))* HarperCollins Pubs.
—The End. Helquist, Brett, illus. 2006. (Series of Unfortunate Events Ser.: Bk. 13). 368p. (J). lib. bdg. 15.89 *(978-0-06-029644-5(5))* HarperCollins Pubs.
—File Under - 13 Suspicious Incidents. Seth, illus. 2014. (ENG.). 272p. (J). (gr. 3-17). 12.00 *(978-0-316-28403-5(3))* Little, Brown Bks. for Young Readers.
—The Gloom Looms, Bks. 10-12. Helquist, Brett, illus. 2005. (Series of Unfortunate Events Ser.: Bks. 10-12). (J). (gr. 5). 41.99 *(978-0-06-083909-3(0))* HarperCollins Pubs.
—The Grim Grotto. Helquist, Brett, illus. 2004. (Series of Unfortunate Events Ser.: Bk. 11). 352p. (J). (gr. 3-6). lib. bdg. 15.89 *(978-0-06-029642-1(9))* HarperCollins Pubs.
—The Grim Grotto. Helquist, Brett & Kupperman, Michael, illus. 2004. (Series of Unfortunate Events Ser.: 11). (ENG.). 352p. (J). (gr. 5-6). 13.99 *(978-0-06-441014-4(5))* HarperCollins Pubs.
—Un Infausto Inizio. pap. 23.95 *(978-88-7782-951-1(6))* Salani ITA. Dist: Distribooks, Inc.
—Lemony Snicket: The Unauthorized Autobiography. Helquist, Brett, illus. 2003. (Series of Unfortunate Events Ser.). (ENG.). 240p. (J). (gr. 5-6). pap. 7.99 *(978-0-06-056225-0(0))* HarperCollins Pubs.
—Lemony Snicket: The Unauthorized Autobiography. 2003. (Ser. of Unfortunate Events Ser.). (J). (gr. 5-8). lib. bdg. 17.20 *(978-0-613-67209-2(7), Turtleback)* Turtleback Bks.
—The Loathsome Library, Bks. 1-6. Helquist, Brett, illus. 2005. (Series of Unfortunate Events Ser.: Bks. 1-6). (J). (gr. 5). 65.00 *(978-0-06-083353-4(X))* HarperCollins Pubs.
—The Miserable Mill, 13 vols. Helquist, Brett, illus. 2008. (Series of Unfortunate Events Ser.: Bk. 4). (ENG.). 208p. (J). (gr. 5-18). pap. 6.99 *(978-0-06-114632-9(3), Harper Trophy)* HarperCollins Pubs.
—Ouragan sur le Lac. pap. 24.95 *(978-2-09-282356-9(6))* Nathan, Fernand FRA. Dist: Distribooks, Inc.
—The Reptile Room: Or, Murder! Helquist, Brett & Kupperman, Michael, illus. 2007. (Series of Unfortunate Events Ser.: 2). (ENG.). 192p. (J). (gr. 5-9). pap. 6.99 *(978-0-06-114631-2(5))* HarperCollins Pubs.
—Der Schlimme Anfang. *(978-3-407-79815-2(6))* Beltz, Julius GmbH & Company KG.
—Shouldn't You Be in School? Seth, illus. (All the Wrong Questions Ser.: 3). (ENG.). (J). (gr. 3-17). 2015. 352p. pap. 7.99 *(978-0-316-38060-7(1))* 2014. 336p. 16.00 *(978-0-316-12306-8(4))* 2014. 352p. 18.00 *(978-0-316-40968-1(5))* Little, Brown Bks. for Young Readers.
—The Slippery Slope. Helquist, Brett, illus. 2003. (Series of Unfortunate Events Ser.: Bk. 10). (YA). (gr. 5-18). 197.82 *(978-0-06-057743-8(6))*; 352p. (J). (gr. 3-6). lib. bdg. 15.89 *(978-0-06-029641-4(0))* HarperCollins Pubs.
—The Slippery Slope. Helquist, Brett & Kupperman, Michael, illus. 2003. (Series of Unfortunate Events Ser.: 10). (ENG.). 352p. (J). (gr. 5-6). 13.99 *(978-0-06-441013-7(7))* HarperCollins Pubs.
—The Trouble Begins. Helquist, Brett, illus. movie tie-in ed. 2004. (Series of Unfortunate Events Ser.: Bks. 1-3). (J). 35.99 *(978-0-06-075773-1(6))* HarperCollins Pubs.
—When Did You See Her Last? Seth, illus. (All the Wrong Questions Ser.: 2). (ENG.). (J). (gr. 3-17). 2014. 304p. pap. 7.99 *(978-0-316-33684-0(X))* 2013. 288p. 16.00 *(978-0-316-12305-1(6))* 2013. 304p. 29.99 *(978-0-316-23993-6(3))* Little, Brown Bks. for Young Readers.
—Who Could That Be at This Hour? Seth, illus. (All the Wrong Questions Ser.: 1). (ENG.). (J). (gr. 3-17). 2014. 288p. pap. 7.99 *(978-0-316-33547-8(9))* 2012. 272p. 15.99 *(978-0-316-12308-2(0))* Little, Brown Bks. for Young Readers.
—Why Is This Night Different from All Other Nights? Seth, illus. 2015. (ENG.). 304p. (J). (gr. 3-17). 16.00 *(978-0-316-12304-4(8))* Little, Brown Bks. for Young Readers.
—The Wide Window - Or, Disappearance! Helquist, Brett & Kupperman, Michael, illus. 2007. (Series of Unfortunate Events Ser.: 3). (ENG.). 208p. (J). (gr. 5). pap. 6.99 *(978-0-06-114633-6(1))* HarperCollins Pubs.
Snicket, Lemony, pseud & Seth. Who Could That Be at This Hour? 2012. *(978-0-316-24771-9(5))* Little Brown & Co.
Sniegoski, Tom. Quest for the Spark. Smith, Jeff, illus. 2012. (Bone Ser.). (ENG.). 240p. (J). (gr. 3-7). pap. 10.99 *(978-0-545-14104-8(4))*; Bk. 2. 26.99 *(978-0-545-14103-1(6))* Scholastic, Inc. (Graphix).
—Quest for the Spark. 2012. (Bone: Quest for the Spark Ser.: 2). lib. bdg. 22.10 *(978-0-606-23947-9(2), Turtleback)* Turtleback Bks.
Sniegoski, Tom & Smith, Jeff. Quest for the Spark, Bk. 1. Smith, Jeff, illus. 2011. (BONE: Quest for the Spark Ser.: 1). (ENG., Illus.). 224p. (J). (gr. 3-7). 26.99 *(978-0-545-14101-7(X), Graphix)* Scholastic, Inc.
Snyder, Laurel. Baxter, the Pig Who Wanted to Be Kosher. Goldin, David, illus. 2010. (ENG.). 32p. (J). (gr. -1-2). 15.99 *(978-1-58246-315-5(8), Tricycle Pr.)* Random Hse. Children's Bks.
—Baxter, the Pig Who Wanted to Be Kosher. 2010. (J). pap. 2.46 *(978-1-58246-373-5(5), Tricycle Pr.)* Ten Speed Pr.
Soffer, Gilad. Duck's Vacation. 2015. (ENG., Illus.). 48p. (J). (gr. -1-k). 17.99 *(978-1-250-05647-4(0), 9781250056474)* Feiwel & Friends.
Solomon, Martha. Christmas in Da Hood. 2012. 28p. pap. 12.50 *(978-0-9883126-3-0(8))* iScribe Pubns. LLC.
Solomon, Michelle & Pereira, Lavinia. Uh - Oh! Faust, Laurie A., illus. 2009. 24p. pap. 10.96 *(978-1-4251-8950-1(4))* Trafford Publishing.
Solomons, David. My Brother Is a Superhero. (ENG.). (J). (gr. 3-7). 2017. 320p. 7.99 *(978-0-14-751605-3(6), Puffin Books)* 2015. 304p. 16.99 *(978-0-451-47477-3(5), Viking Books for Young Readers)* Penguin Young Readers Group.
Soltis, Sue. Nothing Like a Puffin. Kolar, Bob, illus. 2011. (ENG.). 40p. (J). (gr. -1-1). 15.99 *(978-0-7636-3617-3(7))* Candlewick Pr.
Sommer, Carl. The Ant & the Grasshopper. Noé, Ignacio, illus. 2016. (ENG.). 32p. (J). (gr. k-4). lib. bdg. 16.95 *(978-1-57537-925-8(2), Another Sommer-Time Story)* Advance Publishing, Inc.
—Your Job Is Easy Read-along 2003. (Another Sommer-Time Story Ser.). (Illus.). 48p. (J). lib. bdg. 23.95 incl. audio *(978-1-57537-767-4(5))* Advance Publishing, Inc.
—Your Job Is Easy Read-along. James, Kennon, illus. 2003. (Another Sommer-Time Story Ser.). (ENG.). 48p. (J). lib. bdg. 23.95 incl. audio compact disk *(978-1-57537-717-9(9))* Advance Publishing, Inc.
Sommerset, Mark. Baa Baa Smart Sheep. Sommerset, Rowan, illus. 2016. (ENG.). 32p. (J). (gr. k-3). 14.00 *(978-0-7636-8066-4(4))* Candlewick Pr.
Song, Mika. Tea with Oliver. Song, Mika, illus. 2017. (Illus.). 40p. (J). (gr. -1-3). 17.99 ***(978-0-06-242948-3(5))*** HarperCollins Pubs.
Sonnenblick, Jordan. Dodger for President. 2010. (Dodger & Me Ser.: 2). (ENG.). 192p. (J). (gr. 3-7). pap. 8.99 *(978-0-312-61112-5(9), 9780312611125)* Square Fish.
Sorenson, Margo. Spaghetti Smiles, 1 vol. Harrington, David, illus. 2014. (ENG.). 32p. (J). (gr. k-3). 16.99 *(978-1-4556-1922-1(1))* Pelican Publishing Co., Inc.
Soto, Gary. Chato Goes Cruisin' Guevara, Susan, illus. 2008. (Chato Ser.). (J). pap. 16.95 *(978-1-59519-905-8(5))* Live Oak Media.
Soule, Jean Conder. Never Tease a Weasel. Booth, George, illus. 2011. (ENG.). 40p. (J). (gr. -1-2). pap. 6.99 *(978-0-375-87285-3(X), Dragonfly Bks.)* Random Hse. Children's Bks.
Souliere, Lisa. Guess What? I Have Diabetes. 2008. 36p. pap. 14.95 *(978-1-60693-287-2(X), Eloquent Bks.)* Strategic Book Publishing & Rights Agency (SBPRA).
Soup, Cuthbert. Another Whole Nother Story. Timmins, Jeffrey Stewart, illus. (Whole Nother Story Ser.). (ENG.). (YA). (gr. 3-6). 2012. 320p. pap. 7.99 *(978-1-59990-737-6(2), 9781599907376)* 2010. 304p. 16.99 *(978-1-59990-436-8(5), 9781599904368)* Bloomsbury Publishing USA. (Bloomsbury USA Childrens).
—No Other Story. (Whole Nother Story Ser.). (ENG., Illus.). 256p. (YA). (gr. 3-6). 2013. pap. 7.99 *(978-1-61963-120-5(2), 9781619631205)* 2012. 16.99 *(978-1-59990-824-3(7), 9781599908243)* Bloomsbury Publishing USA. (Bloomsbury USA Childrens).
—A Whole Nother Story. Timmins, Jeffrey Stewart, illus. 2010. (Whole Nother Story Ser.). (ENG.). 288p. (YA). (gr. 3-6). pap. 7.99 *(978-1-59990-518-1(3), 9781599905181*, Bloomsbury USA Childrens) Bloomsbury Publishing USA.
Sowa, Elizabeth. The Hexagon . 2004. 24p. (J). pap. 24.95 *(978-1-4137-2130-0(3))* PublishAmerica, Inc.
Spafford-Fitz, Karen. Dog Walker, 1 vol. 2006. (Orca Currents Ser.). (ENG.). 136p. (J). (gr. 5-9). per. 9.95 *(978-1-55143-522-0(5))* Orca Bk. Pubs. USA.
Spalding, Amy. The Reece Malcolm List. 2013. (ENG.). 352p. (YA). (gr. 8). pap. 9.99 *(978-1-62061-240-8(2), 9781620612408)* Entangled Publishing, LLC.
Sparks, Kerry. Frost Bites. 2009. 92p. pap. 11.49 *(978-1-4389-5414-1(X))* AuthorHouse.
Spear, Lisa D. Thunderburps. Baker, David, illus. 2012. 26p. 24.95 *(978-1-4626-0793-8(4))* America Star Bks.
Speck, Katie. Maybelle Goes to School. Tagyos, Paul Rátz de, illus. 2015. (Maybelle Ser.). (ENG.). 64p. (J). (gr. 2-5). 16.99 *(978-0-8050-9158-8(0), 9780805091588*, Holt, Henry & Co. Bks. For Young Readers) Holt, Henry & Co.
Spellman, David & Lutz, Lisa. How to Negotiate Everything. Temairik, Jaime, illus. 2013. (ENG.). 32p. (J). (gr. -1-3). 16.99 *(978-1-4424-5119-3(X), Simon & Schuster Bks. For Young Readers)* Simon & Schuster Bks. For Young Readers.
Spinelli, Eileen. Silly Tilly, 0 vols. Slonim, David, illus. 2012. (ENG.). 32p. (J). (gr. -1-2). pap. 9.99 *(978-0-7614-5990-3(1), 9780761459903*, Amazon Children's Publishing) Amazon Publishing.
—Thanksgiving at the Tappletons' Cocca-Leffler, Maryann, illus. 2015. (ENG.). 32p. (J). (gr. -1-3). pap. 6.99 *(978-0-06-236397-8(2))* HarperCollins Pubs.
—Thanksgiving at the Tappletons' Lloyd, Megan, illus. 2005. (gr. -1-3). 17.00 *(978-0-7569-5762-9(1))* Perfection Learning Corp.
Spires, Ashley. Edie's Ensembles. 2014. (ENG., Illus.). 32p. (J). (gr. -1-3). 17.99 *(978-1-77049-490-9(1), Tundra Bks.)* Tundra Bks. CAN. Dist: Penguin Random Hse. LLC.
—Small Saul. Spires, Ashley, illus. 2011. (ENG., Illus.). 32p. (J). (gr. -1-2). 16.95 *(978-1-55453-503-3(4))* Kids Can Pr., Ltd. CAN. Dist: Hachette Bk. Group.
Spooner, Joe. The Elephant Walk. McCann, Michelle, ed. Spooner, Joe, illus. 2005. (ENG., Illus.). 36p. (J). (gr. -1-3). 15.00 *(978-0-9745686-3-8(5))* ACS, LLC Amica Creative Services.
A Spoonful of Melancholy in a Bucketful of Laughs at a House Called Awful End. 2003. (Eddie Dickens Trilogy: Bk. 1). (J). pap. *(978-0-439-41268-1(4))* Scholastic, Inc.
Spratt, R. A. The Adventures of Nanny Piggins. Santat, Dan, illus. 2012. (Nanny Piggins Ser.: 1). (ENG.). 272p. (J). (gr. 3-7). pap. 7.00 *(978-0-316-06818-5(7))* Little, Brown Bks. for Young Readers.
—Nanny Piggins & the Runaway Lion. 2014. (Nanny Piggins Ser.: 3). (ENG., Illus.). 320p. (J). (gr. 3-7). 17.00 *(978-0-316-25453-3(3))* Little, Brown Bks. for Young Readers.
—Nanny Piggins & the Wicked Plan. 2013. (Nanny Piggins Ser.: 2). (ENG.). 320p. (J). (gr. 3-7). pap. 7.99 *(978-0-316-19922-3(2))* Little, Brown Bks. for Young Readers.
Spurr, Elizabeth. Monsters, Mind Your Manners! Scales, Simon, illus. 2012. (J). 34.28 *(978-1-61913-124-8(2))* Weigl Pubs., Inc.
Staake, Bob. The Donut Chef. Staake, Bob, illus. 2008. (Golden Classic Ser.). (ENG., Illus.). 40p. (J). (gr. -1-2). 14.99 *(978-0-375-84403-4(1), Golden Bks.)* Random Hse. Children's Bks.
Stadler, Alexander. Invasion of the Relatives. 2009. (Julian Rodriguez Ser.: 2). (ENG.). 144p. (J). (gr. 2-5). pap. 5.99 *(978-0-439-91971-5(1), Scholastic Pr.)* Scholastic, Inc.
Stadler, John. The Cats of Mrs. Calamari, 1 vol. 2011. (ENG., Illus.). 32p. (J). pap. 6.95 *(978-1-59572-257-7(2))* Star Bright Bks., Inc.
Stahnke, Rich. Furious Fist of the Drunken Monkey: Origin of the Species #3. 2007. (Illus.). 2.95 *(978-0-9791192-4-8(3))* Silent Devil Productions.
Stanek, Linda. The Pig & Miss Prudence, 1 vol. Castillo, Lauren, illus. 2008. (ENG.). 32p. (J). (gr. -1-3). 15.95 *(978-1-59572-125-9(8))* Star Bright Bks., Inc.
Stanek, Robert, pseud. The Bugville Critters Too Much Sweets: Buster Bee's School Days #1. 2008. (ENG., Illus.). 60p. (J). per. 18.95 *(978-1-57545-167-1(0))* RP Media.
—The Bugville Critters Vacation Surprise: Buster Bee's School Days #3. 2008. (ENG., Illus.). 68p. (J). per. 18.95 *(978-1-57545-172-5(7))* RP Media.
Staniszewski, Anna. Dogosaurus Rex. Hawkes, Kevin, illus. 2017. (ENG.). 40p. (J). 17.99 *(978-0-8050-9706-1(6), 9780805097061*, Holt, Henry & Co. Bks. For Young Readers) Holt, Henry & Co.
—The Truth Game. 2016. (Dirt Diary Ser.: 4). (ENG., Illus.). 224p. (J). (gr. 5-9). pap. 7.99 *(978-1-4926-3272-6(4), 9781492632726*, Sourcebooks Jabberwocky) Sourcebooks, Inc.
Stanley, Lesa, told to. You Have That in Your Purse, Mrs. Connor? 2004. (J). pap. 16.00 *(978-0-8059-6466-0(5))* Dorrance Publishing Co., Inc.
Stanton, Andy. Danny Mcgee Drinks the Sea. Layton, Neal, illus. 2017. (ENG.). 32p. (J). (gr. -1-3). 17.99 ***(978-1-5247-1736-0(3))***; lib. bdg. 20.99 ***(978-1-5247-1737-7(1))*** Random Hse. Children's Bks. (Schwartz & Wade Bks.).
Stanton, Andy. Mr. Gum & the Biscuit Billionaire. Tazzyman, David, illus. 2013. (Mr Gum Ser.: 2). (ENG.). 144p. (J). (gr. 2-5). pap. 7.99 *(978-1-4052-2815-2(6))* Egmont Bks., Ltd. GBR. Dist: Independent Pubs. Group.
Stanton, Beck & Stanton, Matt. This Is a Ball. 2017. (Books That Drive Kids CRAZY! Ser.: 2). (ENG., Illus.). 32p. (J). (gr. -1-3). 14.99 *(978-0-316-43437-9(X))* Little, Brown Bks. for Young Readers.
Stanton, Elizabeth Rose. Henny. Stanton, Elizabeth Rose, illus. 2014. (ENG., Illus.). 40p. (J). (gr. -1-3). 17.99 *(978-1-4424-8436-8(5), Simon & Schuster/Paula Wiseman Bks.)* Simon & Schuster/Paula Wiseman Bks.
Stanton, Matt. Funny Kid for President. Stanton, Matt, illus. 2018. (Funny Kid for President Ser.: 1). (Illus.). 240p. (J). (gr. 3-7). 12.99 ***(978-0-06-257291-2(1))*** HarperCollins Pubs.
Starkey, Scott. The Call of the Bully. 2013. (How to Beat the Bully Ser.). (ENG.). 272p. (J). (gr. 3-7). 15.99 *(978-1-4424-5674-7(4), Simon & Schuster/Paula Wiseman Bks.)* Simon & Schuster/Paula Wiseman Bks.
—The Call of the Bully: A Rodney Rathbone Novel. 2014. (How to Beat the Bully Ser.). (ENG., Illus.). 272p. (J). (gr. 3-7). pap. 6.99 *(978-1-4424-5675-4(2), Simon & Schuster/Paula Wiseman Bks.)* Simon & Schuster/Paula Wiseman Bks.
—How to Beat the Bully Without Really Trying. (How to Beat the Bully Ser.). (ENG.). 272p. (J). (gr. 3-7). 2013. pap. 7.99 *(978-1-4424-8473-3(X))* 2012. 15.99 *(978-1-4424-1685-7(8))* Simon & Schuster/Paula Wiseman Bks. (Simon & Schuster/Paula Wiseman Bks.).
Staunton, Ted. Great Play, Morgan. Slavin, Bill, illus. 2008. (First Novel Ser.). (ENG.). 64p. (J). (gr. 2-6). *(978-0-88780-772-5(0))* Formac Publishing Co., Ltd. CAN. Dist: Casemate Pubs. & Bk. Distributors, LLC.
—Morgan Makes a Deal. Slavin, Bill, illus. 2005. (Formac First Novels Ser.: 33). (ENG.). 64p. (J). (gr. 2-5). 14.95 *(978-0-88780-667-4(8), 9780887806674)* Formac Publishing Co., Ltd. CAN. Dist: Casemate Pubs. & Bk. Distributors, LLC.
—Morgan Makes a Deal, 1 vol. Slavin, Bill & Shannon, Ben, illus. 2005. (Formac First Novels Ser.: 33). (ENG.). 64p. (J). (gr. 2-5). 4.95 *(978-0-88780-666-7(X), 9780887806667)* Formac Publishing Co., Ltd. CAN. Dist: Casemate Pubs. & Bk. Distributors, LLC.
Steadman, Ralph. Little. com. 2014. (Illus.). 32p. (J). 16.95 *(978-1-56792-520-3(0))* Godine, David R. Pub.
Steele, Michael Anthony. Night at the Museum: Secret of the Tomb. 3rd ed. 2014. (ENG.). 176p. (J). (gr. 3-7). pap. 5.99 *(978-1-4380-0524-9(5))* Barron's Educational Series, Inc.
Steig, William. Farmer Palmer's Wagon Ride. Steig, William, illus. 2014. (ENG., Illus.). 32p. (J). (gr. -1-3). 6.99 *(978-1-250-05791-4(4), 9781250057914)* Square Fish.
—Shrek! Steig, William, illus. 20th anniv. ed. 2010. (ENG., Illus.). 40p. (J). (gr. -1-3). 18.99 *(978-0-374-36879-1(1), 9780374368791*, Farrar, Straus & Giroux (BYR)) Farrar, Straus & Giroux.
—Shrek! Steig, William, illus. 2003. (Illus.). (J). (gr. -1-2). pap. 35.95 incl. audio compact disk *(978-1-59112-551-8(0))* Live Oak Media.
—Shrek!. Set. Steig, William, illus. unabr. ed. 2009. (ENG., Illus.). (J). (gr. -1-3). 9.99 *(978-1-4272-0827-9(1), 9781427208279)* Macmillan Audio.
—Shrek! 2008. (Illus.). (gr. -1-3). 17.00 *(978-1-60686-207-0(3))* Perfection Learning Corp.
—Shrek! Steig, William, illus. 2008. (ENG., Illus.). 32p. (J). (gr. -1-3). pap. 7.99 *(978-0-312-38449-4(1), 9780312384494)* Square Fish.
—Shrek! 2008. (J). (gr. -1-2). 18.40 *(978-0-7857-2221-2(1), Turtleback)* Turtleback Bks.
—Spinky Sulks. Steig, William, illus. 2011. (ENG., Illus.). 32p. (J). (gr. -1-3). pap. 7.99 *(978-0-312-67246-1(2), 9780312672461)* Square Fish.
Stein, David Ezra. I'm My Own Dog. Stein, David Ezra, illus. 2014. (ENG., Illus.). 32p. (J). (gr. -1-3). 15.99 *(978-0-7636-6139-7(2))* Candlewick Pr.

—I'm My Own Dog. 2014. 36.75 (978-1-4906-4378-6(8)); 38.75 (978-1-4906-4052-5(5)) Recorded Bks., Inc.
—Interrupting Chicken. Stein, David Ezra, illus. (ENG., Illus.). 40p. (J). (gr. -1-3). 2016. 7.99 (978-0-7636-8903-2(3)) 2010. 16.99 (978-0-7636-4168-9(5)) Candlewick Pr.
—Interrupting Chicken. (J). 1.25 (978-1-4498-6832-1(0)); 2011. 37.75 (978-1-4498-6828-4(2)); 2011. 37.75 (978-1-4498-6831-4(2)); 2011. 39.75 (978-1-4498-6829-1(0)) Recorded Bks., Inc.
—Interrupting Chicken. Stein, David Ezra, illus. 2016. (ENG., Illus.). 40p. (J). (gr. -1-3). 18.40 (978-0-606-39099-6(5)) Turtleback Bks.
—Ol' Mama Squirrel. Stein, David Ezra, illus. 2013. (ENG., Illus.). 32p. (J). (gr. -1-k). 16.99 (978-0-399-25672-1(5), Nancy Paulsen Books) Penguin Young Readers Group.
Steinberg, Laya. Thesaurus Rex Finds a Friend. Harter, Debbie, illus. 2006. (J). (978-1-905236-48-0(4)) Barefoot Bks., Inc.
Steinsiek, Sabra Brown. The Tale of the Pronghorned Cantaloupe. Chilton, Noel Dora, illus. 2013. 48p. 24.95 (978-1-936744-11-4(2), Rio Grande Bks.) LPD Pr.
—The Tale of the Pronghorned Cantaloupe. Chilton, Noel, illus. 2009. (SPA & ENG.). 48p. (J). (gr. -1-3). pap. 17.95 (978-1-890689-85-8(8), Rio Grande Bks.) LPD Pr.
Stephens, Ann Marie. Cy Makes a Friend. Subisak, Tracy, illus. 2017. (ENG.). 32p. (J). (gr. -1-3). 16.95 (978-1-62979-578-2(X)) Boyds Mills Pr.
Stephens, Evelyn. Five Little Yaks. 2007. (Illus.). 56p. (J). per. 15.00 (978-0-9716039-2-9(8)) Lawrence Publishing.
Stephens, Sarah Hines. Pranks for Nothing! 2006. (Zoey 101 Ser.). 109p. (J). (978-1-4156-5292-3(9)) Scholastic, Inc.
Steps To Literacy Staff, compiled by. Mercy Watson Collection: Class Pack (4 Titles, 6 Each) 2010. (ENG., Illus.). (J). pap. 136.75 (978-1-60923-560-4(6)) Steps To Literacy, LLC.
—Mercy Watson Collection: Variety Pack (4 Titles, 1 Each) 2010. (ENG., Illus.). (J). pap. 23.95 (978-1-60923-559-8(2)) Steps To Literacy, LLC.
Stern, Ricki. Mission Impossible. Date not set. (Beryl E. Bean Ser.: Vol. 3). (Illus.). (J). lib. bdg. 15.89 (978-0-06-028773-3(X), Harper Trophy) HarperCollins Pubs.
Stern, Ricki & Worcester, Heidi P. Adventure: Lonely Leader. Bates, Amy, illus. 2003. (Beryl E. Bean Ser.: No. 3). 64p. (J). lib. bdg. 16.89 (978-0-06-028774-0(8)) HarperCollins Pubs.
Sternberg, Julie. Friendship Over, Bk. 1. Wright, Johanna, illus. 2015. (Top-Secret Diary of Celie Valentine Ser.). (ENG.). 160p. (J). (gr. 2-6). pap. 6.95 (978-1-62979-405-1(8)) Boyds Mills Pr.
—Secrets Out!, Bk. 2. Wright, Johanna, illus. 2015. (Top-Secret Diary of Celie Valentine Ser.). (ENG.). 176p. (J). (gr. 2-6). 15.95 (978-1-62091-777-0(7)) Boyds Mills Pr.
Stevens, Eric. Finn Reeder, Flu Fighter: How I Survived a Worldwide Pandemic, the School Bully, & the Craziest Game of Dodge Ball Ever. Fraser, Kay, illus. 2009. (Finn Reeder Ser.). (ENG.). 80p. (gr. 2-3). lib. bdg. 26.65 (978-1-4342-2450-7(3)) Capstone Digital.
—Flu Fighter: How I Survived a Worldwide Pandemic, the School Bully, & the Craziest Game of Dodge Ball Ever. Fraser, Kay, illus. 2010. (Finn Reeder Ser.). (ENG.). 80p. (gr. 3-4). 9.99 (978-1-4342-2562-7(3)) Capstone Digital.
Stevens, Janet & Crummel, Susan Stevens. The Great Fuzz Frenzy. (ENG., Illus.). 56p. (J). (gr. -1-3). 2017. pap. 7.99 (978-0-544-94391-9(0), HMH Books For Young Readers) 2005. 17.99 (978-0-15-204626-2(7)) Houghton Mifflin Harcourt Publishing Co.
—The Great Fuzz Frenzy. unabr. ed. 2006. (J). (gr. k-3). 27.99 incl. audio (978-0-8045-6940-8(1), SAC6941) Spoken Arts, Inc.
—The Great Fuzz Frenzy. 2017. (ENG.). (J). (gr. -1-3). lib. bdg. 18.40 **(978-0-606-39816-9(3))** Turtleback Bks.
—Help Me, Mr. Mutt! Expert Answers for Dogs with People Problems. 2008. (ENG., Illus.). 56p. (J). (gr. -1-3). 17.99 (978-0-15-204628-6(3)) Houghton Mifflin Harcourt Publishing Co.
—Help Me, Mr. Mutt! Expert Answers for Dogs with People Problems. 2010. (J). (gr. 1-4). 29.95 incl. audio compact disk (978-0-8045-4217-3(1)) Spoken Arts, Inc.
—Jackalope. 2003. (ENG., Illus.). 56p. (J). (gr. -1-3). 17.00 (978-0-15-216736-3(6)) Houghton Mifflin Harcourt Publishing Co.
—The Little Red Pen. Stevens, Janet, illus. 2011. (ENG., Illus.). 56p. (J). (gr. 1-4). 17.99 (978-0-15-206432-7(X)) Houghton Mifflin Harcourt Publishing Co.
Stevens, Jon Ellis. Old Softy & Angel, 1 vol. 2017. (Old Softy & Angel Ser.). (ENG.). 40p. (J). 34.99 (978-1-4512-0551-0(1)) America Star Bks.
Stevens, Roger & Quarto Generic Staff. The Comic Café. 2012. (ENG.). 288p. (J). (gr. 4-7). pap. 8.99 (978-1-84780-270-5(2), Frances Lincoln) Quarto Publishing Group UK GBR. Dist: Hachette Bk. Group.
Stewart, Joel. Dexter Bexley & the Big Blue Beastie on the Road. 2010. (ENG., Illus.). 32p. (J). (gr. -1-3). pap. 16.95 (978-0-8234-2292-0(5)) Holiday Hse., Inc.
Stewart, Kiera. How to Break a Heart. 2015. (ENG., Illus.). 316p. (J). (gr. 5-9). 16.99 (978-1-4231-7181-2(0)) Hyperion Bks. for Children.
Stilton, Geronimo. Christmas Catastrophe. 2007. (Geronimo Stilton Ser.). (Illus.). 93p. (J). (gr. 2-5). 14.65 (978-0-7569-8804-3(7)) Perfection Learning Corp.
—Christmas Catastrophe. 2007. (Geronimo Stilton Special Edition Ser.). (ENG., Illus.). 128p. (J). (gr. 2-5). pap. 8.99 (978-0-545-00902-7(2), Scholastic Paperbacks) Scholastic, Inc.
—Don't Wake the Dinosaur! 2014. (Geronimo Stilton Cavemice Ser.: 6). (ENG.). 128p. (J). (gr. 2-5). pap. 7.99 (978-0-545-65603-0(6), Scholastic Paperbacks) Scholastic, Inc.
—Don't Wake the Dinosaur! 2014. (Geronimo Stilton Cavemice Ser.: 6). lib. bdg. 18.40 (978-0-606-36057-9(3)) Turtleback Bks.
—The Enormouse Pearl Heist. 2012. (Geronimo Stilton Ser.: 51). lib. bdg. 18.40 (978-0-606-26756-4(5), Turtleback) Turtleback Bks.
—A Fabumouse Vacation for Geronimo. Keys, Larry, illus. 2004. (Geronimo Stilton Ser.: 9). (ENG.). 128p. (J). (gr. 2-5). pap. 7.99 (978-0-439-55971-3(5), Scholastic Paperbacks) Scholastic, Inc.
—The Fast & the Frozen. 2014. (Geronimo Stilton Cavemice Ser.: 4). (ENG., Illus.). 128p. (J). (gr. 2-5). pap. 7.99 (978-0-545-64291-0(4), Scholastic Paperbacks) Scholastic, Inc.
—Flight of the Red Bandit. 2014. (ENG., Illus.). 128p. (J). (gr. 2-5). pap. 7.99 (978-0-545-55630-9(9), Scholastic Paperbacks) Scholastic, Inc.
—The Galactic Goal. 2015. (Geronimo Stilton Spacemice Ser.: 4). (ENG., Illus.). 128p. (J). (gr. 2-5). pap. 7.99 (978-0-545-74620-5(5), Scholastic Paperbacks) Scholastic, Inc.
—Geronimo & the Gold Medal Mystery. 2008. (Geronimo Stilton Ser.). (Illus.). 87p. (J). (gr. 2-5). lib. bdg. 14.65 (978-0-7569-8803-6(9)) Perfection Learning Corp.
—Geronimo Stilton Bk. 59: Welcome to Moldy Manor. 2014. (ENG., Illus.). 128p. (J). (gr. 2-5). pap. 7.99 (978-0-545-74613-7(2), Scholastic Paperbacks) Scholastic, Inc.
—Geronimo's Valentine. 2009. (Geronimo Stilton Ser.: 36). (Illus.). 103p. (J). 18.40 (978-1-4364-5051-5(9), Turtleback) Turtleback Bks.
—Get the Scoop, Geronimo! 2015. (Geronimo Stilton Cavemice Ser.: 9). 128p. (J). lib. bdg. 17.20 (978-0-606-37779-9(4)) Turtleback Bks.
—The Haunted Castle. 2011. (ENG.). 128p. (J). (gr. 2-5). pap. 7.99 (978-0-545-10374-9(6), Scholastic Paperbacks) Scholastic, Inc.
—The Hunt for the Curious Cheese. 2015. (Geronimo Stilton Special Edition Ser.). (ENG., Illus.). 224p. (J). (gr. 2-5). 14.99 (978-0-545-79151-9(0), Scholastic Paperbacks) Scholastic, Inc.
—I'm Too Fond of My Fur! Wolf, Matt, illus. 2004. (Geronimo Stilton Ser.: No. 4). 116p. (J). lib. bdg. 10.00 (978-1-4242-0698-8(7)) Fitzgerald Bks.
—It's Halloween, You 'Fraidy Mouse! Wolf, Matt, illus. 2004. 113p. (J). lib. bdg. 10.00 (978-1-4242-0280-5(9)) Fitzgerald Bks.
—The Karate Mouse. 2010. (Geronimo Stilton Ser.: 40). (ENG., Illus.). 128p. (J). (gr. 2-5). 7.99 (978-0-545-10369-5(X), Scholastic Paperbacks) Scholastic, Inc.
—Lost Treasure of the Emerald Eye. Wolf, Matt, illus. 2004. (Geronimo Stilton Ser.: No. 1). 116p. (J). lib. bdg. 10.00 (978-1-4242-0695-7(2)) Fitzgerald Bks.
—Lost Treasure of the Emerald Eye. Wolf, Matt & Keys, Larry, illus. 2004. (Geronimo Stilton Ser.: 1). (ENG.). 128p. (J). (gr. 2-5). pap. 7.99 (978-0-439-55963-8(4), Scholastic Paperbacks) Scholastic, Inc.
—Meet Me in Horrorwood. 2011. (Geronimo Stilton — Creepella Von Cacklefur Ser.: 2). (Illus.). 112p. (J). lib. bdg. 18.40 (978-0-606-22947-0(7), Turtleback) Turtleback Bks.
—The Mona Mousa Code. Wolf, Matt, illus. 2005. (Geronimo Stilton Ser.: No. 15). 113p. (J). lib. bdg. 10.00 (978-1-4242-0284-3(1)) Fitzgerald Bks.
—The Mouse Island Marathon. 2007. (Geronimo Stilton Ser.: 30). lib. bdg. 18.40 (978-1-4177-7839-3(3), Turtleback) Turtleback Bks.
—The Mysterious Cheese Thief. 2007. (Geronimo Stilton Ser.). (Illus.). 111p. (J). (gr. 2-5). 14.65 (978-0-7569-8303-1(7)) Perfection Learning Corp.
—The Mysterious Cheese Thief. 2007. (Geronimo Stilton Ser.: 31). (Illus.). 111p. (J). (gr. 4-7). 18.40 (978-1-4177-9646-5(4), Turtleback) Turtleback Bks.
—The Phantom of the Subway. Wolf, Matt, illus. 2004. (Geronimo Stilton Ser.: No. 13). 112p. (J). lib. bdg. 10.00 (978-1-4242-0282-9(5)) Fitzgerald Bks.
—The Race Across America. 2009. (Geronimo Stilton Ser.: 37). lib. bdg. 18.40 (978-0-606-00228-8(6), Turtleback) Turtleback Bks.
—Rescue Rebellion. 2015. (Geronimo Stilton Spacemice Ser.: 5). lib. bdg. 17.20 (978-0-606-37775-1(1)) Turtleback Bks.
—Singing Sensation. 2009. (Geronimo Stilton Ser.: 39). lib. bdg. 18.40 (978-0-606-00230-1(8), Turtleback) Turtleback Bks.
—The Stinky Cheese Vacation. 2014. (Geronimo Stilton Ser.: 57). lib. bdg. 18.40 (978-0-606-35843-9(9)) Turtleback Bks.
—The Stone of Fire. 2013. (Geronimo Stilton Cavemice Ser.: 1). lib. bdg. 18.40 (978-0-606-31526-5(8), Turtleback) Turtleback Bks.
—The Temple of the Ruby of Fire. Wolf, Matt, illus. 2004. (Geronimo Stilton Ser.: No. 14). 109p. (J). lib. bdg. 10.00 (978-1-4242-0283-6(3)) Fitzgerald Bks.
—This Hotel Is Haunted! 2012. (Geronimo Stilton Ser.: 50). lib. bdg. 18.40 (978-0-606-26182-1(6), Turtleback) Turtleback Bks.
—The Underwater Planet. 2016. (Geronimo Stilton Spacemice Ser.: 6). (ENG., Illus.). 128p. (J). (gr. 2-5). pap. 7.99 (978-0-545-87243-0(X), Scholastic Paperbacks) Scholastic, Inc.
—Valentine's Day Disaster. Keys, Larry et al, illus. 2006. (Geronimo Stilton Ser.: No. 23). 122p. (J). lib. bdg. 18.46 (978-1-4242-0292-8(2)) Fitzgerald Bks.
—Valley of the Giant Skeletons. 2008. (Illus.). 111p. (J). lib. bdg. 15.38 (978-1-4242-4303-7(3)) Fitzgerald Bks.
—Valley of the Giant Skeletons. 2008. (Geronimo Stilton Ser.). (Illus.). 110p. (gr. 2-5). 17.00 (978-0-7569-8805-0(5)) Perfection Learning Corp.
—Valley of the Giant Skeletons. 2008. (Geronimo Stilton Ser.: 32). (ENG., Illus.). 128p. (J). (gr. 2-5). pap. 7.99 (978-0-545-02132-6(4), Scholastic Paperbacks) Scholastic, Inc.
—Valley of the Giant Skeletons. 2008. (Geronimo Stilton Ser.: 32). lib. bdg. 18.40 (978-1-4364-2713-5(4)) Turtleback Bks.
—The Way of the Samurai. 2012. (Geronimo Stilton Ser.: No. 49). (ENG.). 128p. (J). (gr. 2-5). pap. 7.99 (978-0-545-34101-1(9), Scholastic Paperbacks) Scholastic, Inc.
—Welcome to Moldy Manor. 2014. (Geronimo Stilton Ser.: 59). lib. bdg. 18.40 (978-0-606-36351-8(3)) Turtleback Bks.
—You're Mine, Captain! 2014. (Geronimo Stilton Spacemice Ser.: 2). lib. bdg. 18.40 (978-0-606-35845-3(5)) Turtleback Bks.
Stilton, Geronimo & Pizzelli, Anna. The Underwater Planet. Facciotto, Giuseppe & Verzini, Daniele, illus. 2016. 113p. (J). **(978-1-5182-0303-9(5))** Scholastic, Inc.
Stilton, Geronimo & Stilton, Thea. Thea Stilton & the Mystery in Paris. 2010. (Thea Stilton Ser.: 5). (ENG.). 176p. (J). (gr. 2-5). pap. 8.99 (978-0-545-22773-5(9), Scholastic Paperbacks) Scholastic, Inc.
Stilton, Geronimo & Tramontozzi, Lidia Morson. The Treasure of Easter Island. Ferrario, Giuseppe & Fausone, Flavio, illus. 2015. 106p. (J). (978-1-4844-5770-2(6)) Scholastic, Inc.
Stilton, Geronimo & Wolf, Matt. All Because of a Cup of Coffee. 2004. (Geronimo Stilton Ser.: No. 10). (Illus.). 112p. (J). lib. bdg. 10.00 (978-1-4242-0279-9(5)) Fitzgerald Bks.
Stilton, Thea. Thea Stilton & the Mystery on the Orient Express. 2012. (Thea Stilton Ser.: 13). lib. bdg. 19.65 (978-0-606-26757-1(3), Turtleback) Turtleback Bks.
—Thea Stilton & the Prince's Emerald. 2012. (Thea Stilton Ser.: 12). lib. bdg. 19.65 (978-0-606-26534-8(1), Turtleback) Turtleback Bks.
Stine, R. L. Dr. Maniac vs. Robby Schwartz. 2008. (Goosebumps HorrorLand Ser.: No. 5). (J). 34.99 (978-1-60640-953-4(0)) Findaway World, LLC.
—The Great Smelling Bee. Park, Trip, illus. 2008. (Rotten School Ser.: 2). (ENG.). 128p. (J). (gr. 3-7). pap. 5.99 (978-0-06-078591-8(8)) HarperCollins Pubs.
—Help! We Have Strange Powers! 2009. (Goosebumps Horrorland Ser.: 10). (ENG.). 160p. (J). (gr. 3-7). 6.99 (978-0-439-91878-7(2), Scholastic Paperbacks) Scholastic, Inc.
—Punk'd & Skunked, 1 vol. Park, Trip, illus. 2011. (Rotten School Ser.: No. 11). (ENG.). 128p. (gr. 2-5). 24.21 (978-1-59961-835-7(4)) Spotlight.
—Punk'd & Skunked. Park, Trip, illus. 2007. (Rotten School Ser.: 11). (ENG.). 128p. (J). (gr. 3-7). 6.99 (978-0-06-078830-8(5)) HarperCollins Pubs.
—The Rottenest Angel. Park, Trip, illus. 2006. (Rotten School Ser.: 10). (ENG.). 128p. (J). (gr. 3-7). 6.99 (978-0-06-078827-8(5)) HarperCollins Pubs.
—The Teacher from Heck, 1 vol. Park, Trip, illus. 2011. (Rotten School Ser.: No. 8). (ENG.). 128p. (gr. 2-5). 24.21 (978-1-59961-832-6(X)) Spotlight.
—Terror Trips. Thompson, Jill et al, illus. 2007. (Goosebumps Graphix Ser.: 2). (ENG.). 144p. (J). (gr. 3-7). pap. 9.99 (978-0-439-85780-2(5), Graphix) Scholastic, Inc.
Stinkorb, Patricia. Stranger Danger: The reluctantly written but absolutly necessary book for todays boys & Girls. 2005. (Illus.). 32p. (J). 12.99 (978-0-9758709-9-0(8)) Journey Stone Creations, LLC.
Stoeke, Janet Morgan. Snow Hens. 2016. (Loopy Coop Hens Ser.). (ENG., Illus.). 32p. (J). (gr. 1-2). pap. 3.99 (978-0-448-48843-1(4), Penguin Young Readers) Penguin Young Readers Group.
Stoeke, Janet Morgan & Bader, Bonnie. Letting Go. Stoeke, Janet Morgan, illus. 2015. (Loopy Coop Hens Ser.). (ENG., Illus.). 32p. (J). (gr. 1-2). 3.99 (978-0-448-48458-7(7), Penguin Young Readers) Penguin Young Readers Group.
Stohl, Margaret. Royce Rolls. 2017. (ENG.). 400p. (YA). (gr. 9-17). 18.99 (978-1-4847-3233-5(2)) Disney Publishing Worldwide.
Stokholm, Susan Mary. Between a Shadow & the Moon. 2010. 252p. pap. 14.49 (978-1-4520-1752-5(2)) AuthorHouse.
Storck, Patrick & Rik Hoskin. Dreamworks Madagascar Comics Collection. 2017. (J). lib. bdg. 20.85 (978-0-606-39426-0(5)) Turtleback Bks.
Storm, Falcon. The Persnickety Princess (Tales from upon A. Time - Book 1) l.t. ed. 2013. (ENG.). 94p. pap. 9.95 (978-1-62253-047-2(0)) Evolved Publishing.
Storr, Catherine. The Complete Polly & the Wolf. Watts, Marjorie Anne & Bennett, Jill, illus. 2016. (ENG.). 304p. (J). (gr. 3-7). 17.95 (978-1-68137-001-9(8), NYR Children's Collection) New York Review of Bks., Inc., The.
Stout, Shawn K. & Docampo, Valeria. Penelope Crumb Finds Her Luck. 2014. (Penelope Crumb Ser.: 3). (ENG., Illus.). 240p. (J). (gr. 2-5). pap. 6.99 (978-0-14-242637-1(7), Puffin Books) Penguin Young Readers Group.
Stram, Dawn. Fat Ladies Shouldn't Have Orange Hair! 2011. 56p. pap. 31.99 (978-1-4568-5804-9(1)) Xlibris Corp.
Strand, Jeff. Elrod McBugle on the Loose. 2006. (ENG.). 136p. (YA). per. 9.25 (978-0-7599-4325-4(7)) Hard Shell Word Factory.
—The Greatest Zombie Movie Ever. 2016. (ENG.). 272p. (YA). (gr. 6-12). pap. 10.99 (978-1-4926-2814-9(X), 9781492628149) Sourcebooks, Inc.
Stratton, Erin. There's Nothing Wrong with Boys. Gregeory, Vicki, illus. 2010. 26p. pap. 12.00 (978-1-60911-021-5(8), Eloquent Bks.) Strategic Book Publishing & Rights Agency (SBPRA).
Stripland, Rubye Weldon. Lucy Bell, Queen of the Pasture. 2008. 92p. pap. 10.95 (978-1-4357-1472-4(5)) Lulu Pr., Inc.
—Lucy Bell, Queen of the Pasture, Book Three. 2008. 90p. pap. 10.95 (978-1-4357-3418-0(1)) Lulu Pr., Inc.
—Lucy Bell, Queen of the Pasture Book Two. 2008. 100p. pap. 10.95 (978-1-4357-1895-1(X)) Lulu Pr., Inc.
Strong, Jeremy. Dinosaur Pox. Sharratt, Nick, illus. (ENG.). 128p. (J). 7.95 (978-0-14-038979-1(2)) Penguin Bks., Ltd. GBR. Dist: Trafalgar Square Publishing.
—The Sneezles. Blundell, Tony, illus. 2005. (Collins Big Cat Ser.). (ENG.). 32p. (J). (gr. 1-3). pap. 7.99 (978-0-00-718628-0(2)) HarperCollins Pubs. Ltd. GBR. Dist: Independent Pubs. Group.
Stroud, Scott. Baby Kong. Hunt, Jim, illus. 2006. (J). 8.95 (978-1-60131-001-9(3), Castlebridge Bks.) Big Tent Bks.
Stubben, Michael. Clark vs. the Rainforest. 2012. 110p. pap. 9.99 (978-1-105-54615-0(2)) Lulu Pr., Inc.
Stuchner, Joan Betty. Can Hens Give Milk?, 1 vol. Weissmann, Joe, illus. 2013. (ENG.). 32p. (J). (gr. -1-3). 9.95 (978-1-4598-0427-2(9)) Orca Bk. Pubs. USA.
Sturgis, Brenda Reeves. 10 Turkeys in the Road, 0 vols. Slonim, David, illus. 2011. (ENG.). 32p. (J). (gr. -1-1). 16.99 (978-0-7614-5847-0(6), 9780761458470, Amazon Children's Publishing) Amazon Publishing.
StVil, Lola. Girls Like Me. 2016. (ENG.). 320p. (YA). (gr. 7). 17.99 (978-0-544-70674-3(9), HMH Books For Young Readers) Houghton Mifflin Harcourt Publishing Co.
Sue. The Whinermans. 2010. 72p. (gr. 1-2). pap. 8.95 (978-1-4502-4998-0(1)) iUniverse, Inc.
Sullivan, Michael. Escapade Johnson & Mayhem at Mount Moosilauke. Kolitsky, Joy, illus. 2007. (Escapade Johnson Ser.). (ENG.). 96p. (J). (gr. 2-4). per. 3.95 (978-1-929945-70-2(1)) Big Guy Bks., Inc.
—Escapade Johnson & the Witches of Belknap County. Kolitsky, Joy, illus. 2008. (Escapade Johnson Ser.). (ENG.). 99p. (J). (gr. 2-4). pap. 3.95 (978-1-929945-90-0(6)) Big Guy Bks., Inc.
Susan A. McCoy. The Christmas That Saved Pie Town. 2009. 56p. pap. 23.99 (978-1-4389-4027-4(0)) AuthorHouse.
Swaab, Neil. Class Election. 2016. (Secrets to Ruling School Ser.: 2). (ENG., Illus.). 240p. (YA). (gr. 5-9). 13.95 (978-1-4197-2126-7(7), Amulet Bks.) Abrams, Inc.
—Without Even Trying, Bk. 1. 2015. (Secrets to Ruling School Ser.). (ENG., Illus.). 240p. (J). (gr. 5-9). 13.95 (978-1-4197-1221-0(7), Amulet Bks.) Abrams, Inc.
Swallow, Gerry. Blue in the Face: A Story of Risk, Rhyme, & Rebellion. Fabretti, Valerio, illus. 2016. (Magnificent Tales of Misadventure Ser.). (ENG.). 320p. (J). 16.99 (978-1-61963-487-9(2), 9781619634879, Bloomsbury USA Childrens) Bloomsbury Publishing USA.
—Long Live the Queen: A Blue in the Face Novel. Fabretti, Valerio, illus. 2017. (Magnificent Tales of Misadventure Ser.). (ENG.). 288p. (J). 16.99 (978-1-61963-490-9(2), 9781619634909, Bloomsbury USA Childrens) Bloomsbury Publishing USA.
Swallow, Pamela Curtis & Swallow, Pamela C. Groundhog Gets a Say. Bunkus, Denise, illus. 2007. (ENG.). 40p. (J). (gr. k-3). pap. 6.99 (978-0-14-240896-4(4), Puffin Books) Penguin Young Readers Group.
Swanson, Matthew. Babies Ruin Everything. Behr, Robbi, illus. 2016. (ENG.). 40p. (J). 16.99 (978-1-250-08057-8(6), 9781250080578) Imprint IND. Dist: Macmillan.
Swenson, Jamie. Woof & Quack in Winter (reader) Sias, Ryan, illus. 2017. (Green Light Readers Level 1 Ser.). (ENG.). 32p. (J). (gr. -1-3). 12.99 **(978-0-544-95949-1(3)**, HMH Books For Young Readers) Houghton Mifflin Harcourt Publishing Co.
Swift, John. Tea with a Vampire. 2007. pap. 9.00 (978-0-8059-8963-2(3)) Dorrance Publishing Co., Inc.
Sydor, Colleen. Raising a Little Stink. Constantin, Pascale, illus. 2006. (ENG.). 32p. (J). (gr. -1-2). 16.95 (978-1-55337-896-9(2)) Kids Can Pr., Ltd. CAN. Dist: Hachette Bk. Group.
Sylvander, Matthieu. The Battle of the Vegetables. Barrier, Perceval, illus. 2016. (ENG.). 48p. (J). (gr. 1-4). 15.99 (978-0-544-35942-0(9), Clarion Bks.) Houghton Mifflin Harcourt Trade & Reference Pubs.
Tabby, Abigail. The KnitWits Make a Move! Wildish, Lee, illus. Frost, Michael, photos by. 2013. (ENG.). 32p. (J). (gr. -1-1). 14.99 (978-1-4424-5342-5(7), Little Simon) Little Simon.
Tabor, Corey R. Fox & the Bike Ride. Tabor, Corey R., illus. 2017. (Illus.). 32p. (J). (gr. -1-3). 17.99 **(978-0-06-239875-8(X))** HarperCollins Pubs.
Tacang, Brian. Bully-Be-Gone: The Misadventures of Millicent Madding #1. 2006. (Illus.). 216p. (J). (gr. 3-7). 17.89 (978-0-06-073912-6(6)) HarperCollins Pubs.
Talbott, Hudson. It's All about Me-Ow. Talbott, Hudson, illus. 2012. (ENG., Illus.). 32p. (J). (gr. -1-2). 16.99 (978-0-399-25403-1(X), Nancy Paulsen Books) Penguin Young Readers Group.
Talty, Caryn. Cilie Yack Is under Attack: This Is the story of how one boy turned his problems into a Triumph, 1 nos., no. 1. l.t. ed. 2010. (Illus.). 144p. (J). pap. 8.99 (978-0-9828173-0-8(4)) Leni Bks.
Tarter, Mildred. Alexis Sets up Search Groups. 2013. 26p. pap. 16.49 (978-1-4389-6881-0(7)) AuthorHouse.
Tashjian, Janet. Einstein the Class Hamster & the Very Real Game Show. Tashjian, Jake, illus. 2014. (Einstein the Class Hamster Ser.: 2). (ENG.). 176p. (J). (gr. 2-5). 12.99 (978-1-62779-026-0(8), 9781627790260, Holt, Henry & Co. Bks. For Young Readers) Holt, Henry & Co.
—Einstein the Class Hamster Saves the Library. Tashjian, Jake, illus. 2015. (Einstein the Class Hamster Ser.: 3). (ENG.). 192p. (J). (gr. 2-5). 13.99 (978-1-62779-061-1(6), 9781627790611, Holt, Henry & Co. Bks. For Young Readers) Holt, Henry & Co.
—Sticker Girl. Wilmink, Inga, illus. 2016. (Sticker Girl Ser.). (ENG.). 176p. (J). 13.99 (978-1-62779-335-3(6), 9781627793353, Holt, Henry & Co. Bks. For Young Readers) Holt, Henry & Co.
Tashlin, Frank. The Possum That Didn't. 2016. (ENG., Illus.). 64p. (gr. 5-5). pap. 3.99 (978-0-486-80080-6(6)) Dover Pubns., Inc.
Tatulli, Mark, et al. Lio: Making Friends. 2013. (Lio Ser.: 8). (ENG., Illus.). 224p. (J). pap. 9.99 (978-1-4494-2558-6(5)) Andrews McMeel Publishing.
Taxali, Gary. This Is Silly! 2010. (J). (978-0-439-71837-0(6), Scholastic Pr.) Scholastic, Inc.
Tayler, Amber. What Do Monsters Look Like? Birth, Ryan, illus. 2009. 36p. pap. 11.25 (978-1-935125-51-8(6)) Robertson Publishing.
Tayleur, Karen. Excuses! Survive & Succeed with David Mortimore Baxter. Garvey, Brann, illus. 2007. (David Mortimore Baxter Ser.). (ENG.). 88p. (gr. 2-3). per. 6.05 (978-1-59889-205-5(3), David Mortimore Baxter) Stone Arch Bks.
—Liar! The True Story of David Mortimore Baxter. Garvey, Brann, illus. 2007. (David Mortimore Baxter Ser.). (ENG.). 80p. (gr. 2-3). per. 6.05 (978-1-59889-206-2(1), David Mortimore Baxter) Stone Arch Bks.
—Manners! Staying Out of Trouble with David Mortimore Baxter. Garvey, Brann, illus. 2007. (David Mortimore Baxter Ser.). (ENG.). 88p. (gr. 2-3). per. 6.05 (978-1-59889-207-9(X), David Mortimore Baxter) Stone Arch Bks.
—Promises! Vote for David Mortimore Baxter. Garvey, Brann, illus. 2007. (David Mortimore Baxter Ser.). (ENG.). 96p. (gr. 2-3). per. 6.05 (978-1-59889-208-6(8), David Mortimore Baxter) Stone Arch Bks.
—The Truth! David Mortimore Baxter Comes Clean, 1 vol. Garvey, Brann, illus. 2006. (David Mortimore Baxter Ser.). (ENG.). 96p. (gr. 2-3). lib. bdg. 26.65 (978-1-59889-078-5(6), David Mortimore Baxter) Stone Arch Bks.
Taylor, Billy. Thieving Weasels. 2016. (ENG.). 256p. (YA). (gr. 7). 17.99 (978-0-525-42924-1(7), Dial Bks) Penguin Young Readers Group.
Taylor, Sean. Hoot Owl, Master of Disguise. Jullien, Jean, illus. 2015. (ENG.). 48p. (J). (gr. -1-2). 15.99 (978-0-7636-7578-3(4)) Candlewick Pr.
—Huck Runs Amuck! Reynolds, Peter, illus. 2011. (ENG.). 48p. (J). (gr. k-3). 16.99 (978-0-8037-3261-2(9), Dial Bks) Penguin Young Readers Group.

H
I

—When a Monster Is Born. Sharratt, Nick, illus. 2011. (ENG.). 32p. (J). (gr. -1-1). pap. 6.99 (978-0-312-55348-7(X), 9780312553487) Square Fish.

Teague, Mark. Dear Mrs. LaRue: Letters from Obedience School. Teague, Mark, illus. 2003. (LaRue Bks.). (ENG., Illus.). 32p. (J). (gr. -1-3). 17.99 (978-0-439-20663-1(4), Scholastic Pr.) Scholastic, Inc.

—Detective LaRue: Letters from the Investigation. Teague, Mark, illus. 2004. (LaRue Bks.). (ENG., Illus.). 32p. (J). (gr. -1-3). 17.99 (978-0-439-45868-9(4), Scholastic Pr.) Scholastic, Inc.

—The Sky Is Falling! 2015. (ENG., Illus.). 32p. (J). (gr. -1-k). 16.99 (978-0-545-63217-1(X)) Scholastic, Inc.

Teague, Mark & Scholastic, Inc. Staff. The Doom Machine. Teague, Mark, illus. 2009. (ENG., Illus.). 384p. (J). (gr. 3-7). 17.99 (978-0-545-15142-9(2), Blue Sky Pr., The) Scholastic, Inc.

Teitelbaum, Michael. Halloween Howlers: Frightfully Funny Knock-Knock Jokes. Ho, Jannie, illus. 2011. (ENG.). 16p. (J). (gr. k-3). pap. 6.99 (978-0-06-180891-3(1), HarperFestival) HarperCollins Pubs.

Temple, Bob. The Day Mom Finally Snapped, 1 vol. Harpster, Steve, illus. 2006. (Graphic Sparks Ser.). (ENG.). 40p. (gr. 1-3). 23.99 (978-1-59889-038-9(7), Graphic Sparks) Stone Arch Bks.

Tenney, Shawna J. C., illus. Brunhilda's Backwards Day. 2016. (ENG.). 32p. (J). (gr. -1-k). 16.99 (978-1-63450-691-5(X), Sky Pony Pr.) Skyhorse Publishing Co., Inc.

Terasaki, Stanley Todd. Ghosts for Breakfast. Shinjo, Shelly, illus. 2013. (ENG.). 32p. (J). (gr. k-4). 16.95 (978-1-58430-046-5(9)) Lee & Low Bks., Inc.

Terwilliger, Kelly. Barnyard Purim. Newman, Barbara Johansen, illus. 2012. (Purim Ser.). (ENG.). 32p. (J). (gr. k-3). pap. 7.95 (978-0-7613-4514-5(0)); lib. bdg. 17.95 (978-0-7613-4513-8(2)) Lerner Publishing Group. (Kar-Ben Publishing).

Thaler, Mike. The Art Teacher from the Black Lagoon, 1 vol. Lee, Jared, illus. 2012. (Black Lagoon Set 2 Ser.: No. 2). (ENG.). 32p. (J). (gr. 1-4). lib. bdg. 24.21 (978-1-59961-952-1(0)) Spotlight.

—The Big Game from the Black Lagoon. Lee, Jared D., illus. 2013. 63p. (J). pap. (978-0-545-61639-3(5)) Scholastic, Inc.

—The Book Fair from the Black Lagoon. Lee, Jared, illus. 2006. pap. (978-0-439-88348-1(2)) Scholastic, Inc.

—The Cafeteria Lady from the Black Lagoon, 1 vol. Lee, Jared, illus. 2012. (Black Lagoon Set 2 Ser.: No. 2). (ENG.). 32p. (J). (gr. 1-4). lib. bdg. 24.21 (978-1-59961-954-5(7)) Spotlight.

—Church Summer Cramp, 1 vol. Lee, Jared, illus. 2009. (Tales from the Back Pew Ser.). (ENG.). 32p. (J). (gr. 1-4). pap. 3.99 (978-0-310-71592-4(X)) Zonderkidz.

—The Class Picture Day from the Black Lagoon. Lee, Jared D., illus. 2012. 64p. (J). pap. (978-0-545-47666-9(6)) Scholastic, Inc.

—The Computer Teacher from the Black Lagoon. Lee, Jared, illus. 2007. (J). (978-0-439-87133-4(6)) Scholastic, Inc.

—The Computer Teacher from the Black Lagoon, 1 vol. Lee, Jared, illus. 2012. (Black Lagoon Set 2 Ser.: No. 2). (ENG.). 32p. (J). (gr. 1-4). lib. bdg. 24.21 (978-1-59961-955-2(5)) Spotlight.

—Easter Egg Haunt, 1 vol. Lee, Jared, illus. 2009. (Tales from the Back Pew Ser.). (ENG.). 32p. (J). (gr. 1-4). pap. 3.99 (978-0-310-71591-7(1)) Zonderkidz.

—The Field Day from the Black Lagoon. Lee, Jared, illus. 2008. (From the Black Lagoon Ser.). 64p. (gr. 2-5). 14.00 (978-0-7569-8801-2(2)) Perfection Learning Corp.

—The Field Day from the Black Lagoon. Lee, Jared, illus. 2008. (Black Lagoon Adventures Ser.: 6). (ENG.). 64p. (J). (gr. 2-5). pap. 4.99 (978-0-439-68076-9(X)) Scholastic, Inc.

—The Field Day from the Black Lagoon, 1 vol. Lee, Jared, illus. 2011. (Black Lagoon Adventures Ser.: No. 1). (ENG.). 64p. (gr. 3-6). 24.21 (978-1-59961-812-8(5)) Spotlight.

—The Gym Teacher from the Black Lagoon, 1 vol. Lee, Jared, illus. 2011. (Black Lagoon Set 1 Ser.: No. 1). (ENG.). 32p. (gr. -1-2). lib. bdg. 24.21 (978-1-59961-794-7(3)) Spotlight.

—The Gym Teacher from the Black Lagoon. 2008. (Black Lagoon Ser.). (gr. -1-2). lib. bdg. 13.55 (978-0-613-37714-0(1), Turtleback) Turtleback Bks.

—The Gym Teacher from the Black Lagoon. Lee, Jared, illus. (J). (gr. -1-3). 2009. pap. 18.95 incl. audio compact disk (978-0-545-19706-9(6)) 2008. (ENG.). 32p. pap. 3.99 (978-0-545-06931-1(9)) Weston Woods Studios, Inc.

—Hubie Cool: Vampire Hunter. Lee, Jared D., illus. 2015. 64p. (J). pap. **(978-0-545-85075-9(4))** Scholastic, Inc.

—The Librarian from the Black Lagoon. Lee, Jared, illus. unabr. ed. 2007. (J). (gr. k-2). pap. 14.95 incl. audio (978-0-439-02773-1(X)) Scholastic, Inc.

—The Music Teacher from the Black Lagoon, 1 vol. Lee, Jared, illus. 2011. (Black Lagoon Set 1 Ser.: No. 1). (ENG.). 32p. (gr. -1-2). lib. bdg. 24.21 (978-1-59961-796-1(X)) Spotlight.

—The New Kid from the Black Lagoon. 2004. (Black Lagoon Ser.). (Illus.). 32p. (978-0-439-55719-1(4)) Scholastic, Inc.

—The Principal from the Black Lagoon. Lee, Jared, illus. 2009. (From the Black Lagoon Ser.). 14.00 (978-1-60686-507-1(2)) Perfection Learning Corp.

—The Principal from the Black Lagoon, 1 vol. Lee, Jared, illus. 2011. (Black Lagoon Set 1 Ser.: No. 1). (ENG.). 32p. (gr. -1-2). lib. bdg. 24.21 (978-1-59961-797-8(8)) Spotlight.

—The Principal from the Black Lagoon. 2008. (Black Lagoon Ser.). (gr. k-3). lib. bdg. 13.55 (978-0-7857-0430-0(2), Turtleback) Turtleback Bks.

—The School Carnival from the Black Lagoon. Lee, Jared, illus. 2005. 64p. (J). pap. (978-0-439-80075-4(7)) Scholastic, Inc.

—The School Carnival from the Black Lagoon, 1 vol. Lee, Jared, illus. 2012. (Black Lagoon Adventures Ser.: No. 2). (ENG.). 64p. (J). (gr. 2-5). 24.21 (978-1-59961-962-0(8)) Spotlight.

—School Play from the Black Lagoon, 1 vol. 2014. (Black Lagoon Adventures Set 3 Ser.). (ENG.). 64p. (J). (gr. 3-6). lib. bdg. 24.21 (978-1-61479-205-5(4)) Spotlight.

—The School Secretary from the Black Lagoon. Lee, Jared, illus. 2006. (J). (978-0-439-80077-8(3)) Scholastic, Inc.

—The Talent Show from the Black Lagoon, 1 vol. Lee, Jared, illus. 2011. (Black Lagoon Adventures Ser.: No. 1). (ENG.). 64p. (gr. 3-6). 24.21 (978-1-59961-815-9(X)) Spotlight.

—The Teacher from the Black Lagoon. Lee, Jared, illus. 2008. (From the Black Lagoon Ser.). (gr. -1-3). 14.00 (978-0-7569-8779-4(2)) Perfection Learning Corp.

—The Teacher from the Black Lagoon. Lee, Jared D., illus. 2008. (Black Lagoon Adventures Ser.). (ENG.). 32p. (J). (gr. -1-3). pap. 3.99 (978-0-545-06522-1(4), Cartwheel Bks.) Scholastic, Inc.

—The Teacher from the Black Lagoon, 1 vol. Lee, Jared, illus. 2011. (Black Lagoon Set 1 Ser.: No. 1). (ENG.). 32p. (gr. -1-2). lib. bdg. 24.21 (978-1-59961-799-2(4)) Spotlight.

—The Teacher from the Black Lagoon. Lee, Jared, illus. 2004. (J). (gr. k-3). 18.95 (978-1-55592-495-9(6)) Weston Woods Studios, Inc.

—The Three Wise Guys, 1 vol. Lee, Jared, illus. 2010. (Tales from the Back Pew Ser.). (ENG.). 32p. (J). (gr. 1-4). pap. 3.99 (978-0-310-71593-1(8)) Zonderkidz.

—Vacation Bible Snooze, 1 vol. Lee, Jared, illus. 2010. (Tales from the Back Pew Ser.). (ENG.). 32p. (J). (gr. 1-4). pap. 3.99 (978-0-310-71596-2(2)) Zonderkidz.

—The Vice Principal from the Black Lagoon. Lee, Jared, illus. 2007. (J). pap. (978-0-439-87132-7(8)) Scholastic, Inc.

Thomas, Cameron. The Utt Jungle Airline: The Jungle of Utt. Krystoforski, Andrej, illus. 2004. (Jungle of Utt Ser.). 48p. (J). 16.95 (978-0-921800-03-3(7)) MGT Developments, Ltd. CAN. Dist: Independent Pubs. Group.

Thomas, Chandler Turner. Fundays with the Crime Fighters for Justice. 2011. 36p. pap. 24.95 (978-1-4560-8419-6(4)) America Star Bks.

Thomas, Isabel. Cindy-Ella & the Incredible Techno-Slippers. Moor, Becka, illus. 2015. (Fairy Tales Today Ser.). (ENG.). 24p. (gr. 1-2). 23.99 (978-1-4795-8616-5(1)) Picture Window Bks.

—Hansel, Gretel, & the Pudding Plot. Carretero-Suarez, Mónica, illus. 2015. (Fairy Tales Today Ser.). (ENG.). 24p. (gr. 1-2). 23.99 (978-1-4795-8614-1(5)) Picture Window Bks.

Thomas, Jan. Here Comes the Big, Mean Dust Bunny! Thomas, Jan, illus. 2009. (ENG., Illus.). 40p. (J). (gr. -1-3). 15.99 (978-1-4169-9150-2(6), Beach Lane Bks.) Beach Lane Bks.

—Is Everyone Ready for Fun? Thomas, Jan, illus. 2011. (ENG., Illus.). 40p. (J). (gr. -1-3). 14.99 (978-1-4424-2364-0(1), Beach Lane Bks.) Beach Lane Bks.

—Is That Wise, Pig? Thomas, Jan, illus. 2016. (ENG., Illus.). 40p. (J). (gr. -1-3). 15.99 (978-1-4169-8582-2(4), Beach Lane Bks.) Beach Lane Bks.

—Let's Sing a Lullaby with the Brave Cowboy. Thomas, Jan, illus. 2012. (ENG., Illus.). 40p. (J). (gr. -1-3). 12.99 (978-1-4424-4276-4(X), Beach Lane Bks.) Beach Lane Bks.

—Rhyming Dust Bunnies. Thomas, Jan, illus. 2009. (ENG., Illus.). 40p. (J). (gr. -1-3). 14.99 (978-1-4169-7976-0(X), Beach Lane Bks.) Beach Lane Bks.

Thomas, Rockwell. How to Eat Fried Worms. 2014. (ENG.). 128p. (gr. 3-7). 10.24 (978-1-63245-295-5(2)) Lectorum Pubns., Inc.

Thomas, Shelley Moore. This Book Is Not about Dragons. Koehler, Fred, illus. 2016. (ENG.). 32p. (J). (gr. -1-2). 16.95 (978-1-62979-168-5(7)) Boyds Mills Pr.

Thompson, Colin. The Floods #2: School Plot. Scrambly, Crab, illus. 2008. (Floods Ser.). (J). (ENG.). 224p. 15.99 (978-0-06-113861-4(4)); 256p. lib. bdg. 16.89 (978-0-06-113855-3(X)) HarperCollins Pubs.

—Good Neighbors. Scrambly, Crab, illus. 2008. (Floods Ser.: No. 1). 214p. (J). (gr. 3-7). 15.99 (978-0-06-113196-7(2)) HarperCollins Pubs.

—The Great Montefiasco. Redlich, Ben, illus. 2004. 40p. (J). (gr. -1 — 1). 16.95 (978-1-59572-008-5(1)) Star Bright Bks., Inc.

—Out to Launch. 2015. (Watch This Space Ser.: 1). (ENG.). 224p. (J). (gr. 4-7). pap. 9.99 (978-1-74275-620-2(4)) Random Hse. Australia AUS. Dist: Independent Pubs. Group.

Thompson, Debra. The Crumb Snatchers. Dennis, Tammy D., illus. 2012. 24p. pap. 12.95 (978-1-61493-037-2(6)) Peppertree Pr., The.

Thompson, Joan. Lucy Russell: Lucy in the Wings. 2003. 129p. (YA). pap. 10.95 (978-0-595-26906-8(0), Writers Club Pr.) iUniverse, Inc.

—Lucy Russell: The Starstruck Summer. 2003. 129p. (YA). pap. 10.95 (978-0-595-26903-7(6), Writers Advantage Pr.) iUniverse, Inc.

Thompson, Joan R. Terrible Turnoff & Me. 2006. pap. 11.95 (978-0-595-39902-4(9), Backinprint.com) iUniverse, Inc.

Thompson, Kay. Eloise at the Wedding. Lyon, Tammie Speer, illus. 2006. (Eloise Ser.). (ENG.). 32p. (J). (gr. -1-1). pap. 3.99 (978-0-689-87449-9(9), Simon Spotlight) Simon Spotlight.

Thompson, Kay & Knight, Hilary. Eloise Ready-To-Read Value Pack #2: Eloise Breaks Some Eggs; Eloise & the Dinosaurs; Eloise at the Ball Game; Eloise Has a Lesson; Eloise Skates!; Eloise's New Bonnet. 2013. (Eloise Ser.). (ENG.). 192p. (J). (gr. -1-1). pap. 15.96 (978-1-4424-9439-8(5), Simon Spotlight) Simon Spotlight.

Thomson, Jamie. Headmaster of Doom. 2017. (Dark Lord Ser.). (ENG., Illus.). 288p. (J). (gr. 4-6). 7.99 **(978-1-4083-4142-1(5)**, Orchard Bks.) Hachette Children's Group GBR. Dist: Hachette Bk. Group.

Thottam, Meena. The Last Dancer. 2006. (J). 3.95 (978-0-9776917-7-7(2), Curcumin Bks.) Davlaw Press.

Thottam, Meena, adapted by. Brothers of the Jungle. 2006. (J). 3.95 (978-0-9776917-4-6(8), Curcumin Bks.) Davlaw Press.

—Chameil's Choice. 2006. (J). 3.95 (978-0-9776917-6-0(4), Curcumin Bks.) Davlaw Press.

—Death, Where are You? 2006. (J). 3.95 (978-0-9776917-5-3(6), Curcumin Bks.) Davlaw Press.

—Maybe I am, Maybe I am Not. 2006. (J). 3.95 (978-0-9776917-8-4(0), Curcumin Bks.) Davlaw Press.

—The Pretender. 2006. (J). 3.95 (978-0-9776917-3-9(X), Curcumin Bks.) Davlaw Press.

—Road to Riches. 2006. (J). 3.95 (978-0-9776917-9-1(9), Curcumin Bks.) Davlaw Press.

—The Sage's Daughter. 2006. (J). 3.95 (978-0-9776917-2-2(1), Curcumin Bks.) Davlaw Press.

Thurber, James. The Wonderful O. Simont, Marc, illus. 2017. (Penguin Classics Deluxe Edition Ser.). (ENG.). 96p. pap. 17.00 **(978-0-14-313042-0(0)**, Penguin Classics) Penguin Publishing Group.

Tibo, Gilles. Corre, Nicolas, Corre! Rioja, Alberto Jimenez, tr. from FRE. St. Aubin, Bruno, illus. 2009. (SPA & ENG.). 32p. (J). (gr. 2-4). pap. 6.99 (978-1-933032-57-3(X)) Lectorum Pubns., Inc.

Tillworth, Mary. Cupcake Challenge! (Barbie: Life in the Dreamhouse) 2015. (Step into Reading Ser.). (ENG., Illus.). 48p. (J). (gr. k-3). 3.99 (978-0-553-50745-4(1), Random Hse. Bks. for Young Readers) Random Hse. Children's Bks.

Tim, Fireball. Big Book of Wacky Rides! 2013. (ENG.). 32p. (J). (gr. -1). 17.95 (978-1-933492-81-0(3)) Design Studio Pr.

Tipton, Annie. Diary of a Real Payne Book 3: Oh Baby! 2014. (ENG.). 192p. (J). pap. 5.99 (978-1-62836-864-2(0), Barbour Bks.) Barbour Publishing, Inc.

Tobin, Paul. The Genius Factor - How to Capture an Invisible Cat. Lafontaine, Thierry, illus. 2016. (ENG.). 272p. (J). 16.99 (978-1-61963-840-2(1), 9781619638402, Bloomsbury USA Childrens) Bloomsbury Publishing USA.

—How to Outsmart a Billion Robot Bees. Lafontaine, Thierry & Abey, Katie, illus. 2017. (ENG.). 320p. (J). 16.99 (978-1-61963-897-6(5), 9781619638976, Bloomsbury USA Childrens) Bloomsbury Publishing USA.

Togden, Ra Chel. The Legendary Rabbit of Death - Volume One [Paperback]. 2013. 108p. pap. (978-1-898185-27-7(1)) Aro Bks. worldwide.

Toliver, Wendy. Miss Match. 2009. (Romantic Comedies Ser.). (ENG.). 304p. (YA). (gr. 7-18). mass mkt. 6.99 (978-1-4169-6413-1(4), Simon Pulse) Simon Pulse.

—The Secret Life of a Teenage Siren. (Romantic Comedies Ser.). (ENG.). 304p. (YA). (gr. 7). 2012. pap. 14.99 (978-1-4424-7494-9(7)) 2007. mass mkt. 6.99 (978-1-4169-5065-3(6)) Simon Pulse. (Simon Pulse).

Tommasi, Michael Richard. Stinky Mcgee. 2008. 16p. pap. 9.95 (978-1-4343-6004-5(0)) AuthorHouse.

Torrey, Richard. My Dog, Bob. Torrey, Richard, illus. 2016. (ENG., Illus.). 32p. (J). (gr. -1-3). 6.99 (978-0-8234-3691-0(8)) Holiday Hse., Inc.

—My Dog, Bob. 2015. (ENG., Illus.). 32p. (J). (gr. -1-3). 16.95 (978-0-8234-3386-5(2)) Holiday Hse., Inc.

Tort, Pep & Josep, Tort. El Rey Ignacio. Duran, Teresa, illus. 2006. (Montana Encantada Ser.). (SPA.). 47p. (J). per. (978-84-241-8558-9(7)) Everest Editora.

Toybox Innovations, creator. Meet the Robinson's. 2007. (Disney's Read Along Ser.). (ENG.). 24p. (J). (gr. -1-3). pap. (978-0-7634-2187-8(1)) Walt Disney Records.

Trabert, John. Gnome Chronicles. 2007. 172p. pap. 4.99 (978-1-4343-1950-0(4)) AuthorHouse.

Tracy, Kristen. Crimes of the Sarahs. 2008. (ENG.). 368p. (YA). (gr. 9). pap. 7.99 (978-1-4169-5519-1(4), Simon Pulse) Simon Pulse.

Tracy, Roseann. Whose Toes Are Those? 2008. 24p. pap. 12.99 (978-1-4343-9291-6(0)) AuthorHouse.

Tremblay, Alain Ulysse. L' Héritage de Julien. Malépart, Céline, illus. 2004. (Roman Jeunesse Ser.). (FRE.). 96p. (J). (gr. 4-7). pap. (978-2-89021-682-2(9)) Diffusion du livre Mirabel (DLM).

Trenchard, Robert. The Famous Frog Fiasco. 2008. 265p. (J). pap. 13.99 (978-0-615-20974-6(2)) Soxwings Publishing.

Trine, Greg. Attack of the Valley Girls. Montijo, Rhode, illus. 6th ed. 2008. (Melvin Beederman, Superhero Ser.: 6). (ENG.). 144p. (J). (gr. 2-5). pap. 8.99 (978-0-8050-8161-9(5), 9780805081619) Square Fish.

—The Brotherhood of the Traveling Underpants. 2009. (Melvin Beederman Superhero Ser.: 7). (J). lib. bdg. 19.65 (978-0-606-01751-0(8), Turtleback) Turtleback Bks.

—The Curse of the Bologna Sandwich. Montijo, Rhode, illus. 2006. (Melvin Beederman, Superhero Ser.: 1). (ENG.). 144p. (J). (gr. 2-5). pap. 8.99 (978-0-8050-7836-7(3), 9780805078367) Square Fish.

—Dinos Are Forever. Dormer, Frank W., illus. 2012. (Adventures of Jo Schmo Ser.: 1). (ENG.). 112p. (J). (gr. 1-4). 12.99 (978-0-547-76341-5(7)) Houghton Mifflin Harcourt Publishing Co.

—The Fake Cape Caper. Montijo, Rhode, illus. 5th rev. ed. 2007. (Melvin Beederman, Superhero Ser.: 5). (ENG.). 144p. (J). (gr. 2-5). pap. 8.99 (978-0-8050-8159-6(3), 9780805081596) Square Fish.

—The Grateful Fred. Montijo, Rhode, illus. 3rd rev. ed. 2006. (Melvin Beederman, Superhero Ser.: 3). (ENG.). 144p. (J). (gr. 2-5). pap. 8.99 (978-0-8050-7922-7(X), 9780805079227) Square Fish.

—Invasion from Planet Dork. Montijo, Rhode, illus. 2010. (Melvin Beederman, Superhero Ser.: 8). (ENG.). 144p. (J). (gr. 2-7). pap. 8.99 (978-0-8050-8167-1(4), 9780805081671) Square Fish.

—Pinkbeard's Revenge. Dormer, Frank W., illus. 2013. (Adventures of Jo Schmo Ser.: 4). (ENG.). 128p. (J). (gr. 1-4). 12.99 (978-0-547-80797-3(X)) Houghton Mifflin Harcourt Publishing Co.

—The Revenge of the McNasty Brothers. Montijo, Rhode, illus. 2nd rev. ed. 2006. (Melvin Beederman, Superhero Ser.: 2). (ENG.). 144p. (J). (gr. 2-5). pap. 8.99 (978-0-8050-7837-4(1), 9780805078374) Square Fish.

—Shifty Business. Dormer, Frank W., illus. (Adventures of Jo Schmo Ser.: 3). (ENG.). 112p. (J). (gr. 1-4). 2014. pap. 5.99 (978-0-544-33911-8(8), HMH Books For Young Readers) 2013. 12.99 (978-0-547-80796-6(1)) Houghton Mifflin Harcourt Publishing Co.

—Terror in Tights. Montijo, Rhode, illus. 4th rev. ed. 2007. (Melvin Beederman, Superhero Ser.: 4). (ENG.). 144p. (J). (gr. 2-5). pap. 8.99 (978-0-8050-7924-1(6), 9780805079241) Square Fish.

—Willy Maykit in Space. Burks, James, illus. (ENG.). 208p. (J). (gr. 2-5). 2016. pap. 7.99 (978-0-544-66848-5(0)) 2015. 13.99 (978-0-544-31351-4(8)) Houghton Mifflin Harcourt Publishing Co. (HMH Books For Young Readers).

—Wyatt Burp Rides Again. Dormer, Frank W., illus. 2014. (Adventures of Jo Schmo Ser.: 2). (ENG.). 112p. (J). (gr. 1-4). pap. 5.99 (978-0-544-01899-0(0), HMH Books For Young Readers) Houghton Mifflin Harcourt Publishing Co.

Tripp, Valerie. Very Funny, Elizabeth! England, Tamara, ed. Andreasen, Dan, illus. 2005. (ENG.). 96p. (gr. 3). pap. 6.95 (978-1-59369-061-8(4), American Girl) American Girl Publishing, Inc.

Tritt, Adam Byrn. Bud the Spud. Goldacker, "Java John", illus. 2012. (ENG.). 52p. (J). (gr. 3-7). 16.95 (978-1-60419-062-5(0)) Axios Pr.

Tubb, Kristin O'Donnell. A Dog Like Daisy. 2017. 192p. (J). (gr. 3-7). 16.99 (978-0-06-246324-1(1), Tegen, Katherine Bks) HarperCollins Pubs.

Tuell, Todd. Ninja, Ninja, Never Stop! Carpenter, Tad, illus. 2014. (ENG.). 32p. (J). (gr. -1-k). 14.95 (978-1-4197-1027-8(3), Abrams Appleseed) Abrams, Inc.

Tulien, Sean. The Not-So-Deadly Dragon. Cunyat, Pol, illus. 2016. (Thud & Blunder Ser.). (ENG.). 56p. (gr. 2-4). pap. 4.95 (978-1-4965-3224-4(4)); lib. bdg. 23.99 (978-1-4965-3220-6(1)) Stone Arch Bks.

—The Not-So-Evil Wizard. Cunyat, Pol, illus. 2016. (Thud & Blunder Ser.). (ENG.). 56p. (gr. 2-4). pap. 4.95 (978-1-4965-3225-1(2)); lib. bdg. 23.99 (978-1-4965-3221-3(X)) Stone Arch Bks.

—Super Billy Goats Gruff. Cano, Fernando, illus. 2015. (Far Out Fairy Tales Ser.). (ENG.). 40p. (gr. 3-4). lib. bdg. 25.32 (978-1-4342-9649-8(0)) Stone Arch Bks.

Tulien, Sean & Hoena, Blake. The Not-So-Helpless Princess. Cunyat, Pol, illus. 2016. (Thud & Blunder Ser.). (ENG.). 56p. (gr. 2-4). pap. 4.95 (978-1-4965-3222-0(8)); lib. bdg. 23.99 (978-1-4965-3218-3(X)) Stone Arch Bks.

—The Not-So-Heroic Knight. Cunyat, Pol, illus. 2016. (Thud & Blunder Ser.). (ENG.). 56p. (gr. 2-4). pap. 4.95 (978-1-4965-3223-7(6)); lib. bdg. 23.99 (978-1-4965-3219-0(8)) Stone Arch Bks.

Tulien, Sean & Simonson, Louise. Far Out Fairy Tales. Cano, Fern & Sanchez S., Jimena, illus. 2016. (Far Out Fairy Tales Ser.). (ENG.). 40p. (gr. 3-4). 151.92 (978-1-4965-2515-4(9), Far Out Fairy Tales) Stone Arch Bks.

Tulloch, Scott. Willy's Mum. 2008. (Illus.). 32p. pap. (978-1-86950-682-7(0)) HarperCollins Pubs. Australia.

Tully, Justin. Lost from the Christmas Mansion. 2008. 141p. pap. 16.95 (978-1-4092-5106-4(3)) Lulu Pr., Inc.

Tuma, Refe & Tuma, Susan. What the Dinosaurs Did Last Night: A Very Messy Adventure. 2015. (What the Dinosaurs Did Ser.: 1). (ENG., Illus.). 40p. (J). (gr. -1-1). 17.00 (978-0-316-33562-1(2)) Little Brown & Co.

Turnbull-Kennedy, Tiffany. No School for Evil Eraser! 2011. (Illus.). 48p. pap. 16.59 (978-1-4634-3965-1(2)) AuthorHouse.

Twain, Mark, pseud. The Adventures of Tom Sawyer. Ingpen, Robert R., illus. 2010. (Sterling Illustrated Classics Ser.). (ENG.). 240p. (J). (gr. 5-18). 19.95 (978-1-4027-6762-3(5)) Sterling Publishing Co., Inc.

—Advice to Little Girls. Radunsky, Vladimir, illus. 2013. (ENG.). 24p. (gr. k). 14.95 (978-1-59270-129-2(9)) Enchanted Lion Bks., LLC.

—Tom Sawyer, 1 vol. Mullarkey, Lisa, illus. 2010. (Calico Illustrated Classics Ser.: No. 1). (ENG.). 112p. (J). (gr. 3-6). 27.07 (978-1-60270-704-7(9)) Magic Wagon.

—Tom Sawyer. 2009. 196p. (gr. 4-7). pap. 12.99 (978-1-934941-63-8(8)) Red & Black Pubs.

Twinkle Books. Terrible Tommy. 2006. (J). 14.98 (978-0-9792992-6-1(8)) Twinkle Bks.

Twohy, Mike. Outfoxed. Twohy, Mike, illus. 2013. (ENG., Illus.). 40p. (J). (gr. -1-3). 16.99 (978-1-4424-7392-8(4), Simon & Schuster Bks. For Young Readers) Simon & Schuster Bks. For Young Readers.

Tym, Kate. Be Nice. 2008. (Manners Ser.). (Illus.). 24p. (J). (gr. -1-1). lib. bdg. 16.95 (978-1-59566-590-4(0)) QEB Publishing Inc.

Tyner, Christopher. I'll Do It Tommarra Laura. 2004. 37p. (J). pap. 24.95 (978-1-4137-2753-1(0)) PublishAmerica, Inc.

Uderzo, Albert & Goscinny, René. Asterix & the Falling Sky. Bell, Anthea & Hockridge, Derek, trs. from FRE. Uderzo, Albert, illus. 2006. (ENG., Illus.). 48p. pap. 12.99 (978-0-7528-7548-4(5), Orion) Orion Publishing Group, Ltd. GBR. Dist: Hachette Bk. Group.

Underwood, Deborah. Here Comes Teacher Cat. Rueda, Claudia, illus. 2017. (ENG.). 88p. (J). (-k). 16.99 **(978-0-399-53905-3(0)**, Dial Bks) Penguin Young Readers Group.

—Here Comes the Tooth Fairy Cat. Rueda, Claudia, illus. 2015. (ENG.). 96p. (J). (gr. -1-k). 16.99 (978-0-525-42774-2(0), Dial Bks) Penguin Young Readers Group.

—Here Comes Valentine Cat. Rueda, Claudia, illus. 2015. (ENG.). 88p. (J). (-k). 16.99 (978-0-525-42915-9(8), Dial Bks) Penguin Young Readers Group.

—Pirate Mom. Gilpin, Stephen, illus. 2006. (Step into Reading Ser.: Vol. 3). (ENG.). 48p. (J). (gr. k-3). per. 3.99 (978-0-375-83323-6(4), Random Hse. Bks. for Young Readers) Random Hse. Children's Bks.

Ungerer, Tomi. The Beast of Monsieur Racine. 2014. (ENG., Illus.). 32p. (gr. -1-3). 16.95 (978-0-7148-6081-7(6)) Phaidon Pr., Inc.

Universal. Minions. 2015. (ENG., Illus.). 96p. (J). (gr. k-17). pap. 12.99 (978-0-316-30001-8(2)) Little, Brown Bks. for Young Readers.

Universal & Rosen, Lucy. Minions: Long Live King Bob! 2015. (ENG., Illus.). 24p. (J). (gr. -1-3). pap. 3.99 (978-0-316-29993-0(6)) Little, Brown Bks. for Young Readers.

Universal & Snider, Brandon T. Minions. Miller, Ed, illus. 2015. (ENG.). 32p. (J). (gr. -1-3). 12.99 (978-0-316-30000-1(4)) Little, Brown Bks. for Young Readers.

Universal Books Staff & King, Trey. Minions: Seek & Find. Fractured Pixels, illus. 2015. (ENG.). 24p. (J). (gr. 1-4). 8.99 (978-0-316-29997-8(9)) Little, Brown Bks. for Young Readers.

Universal Dreamworks Pictures Staff & Greenberg, James. Cat in the Hat. 2003. (ENG., Illus.). 128p. pap. 12.95 (978-1-57243-609-1(3), 53846352) Triumph Bks.

Urban, Linda. A Crooked Kind of Perfect. (ENG., Illus.). 224p. (J). (gr. 5-7). 2009. pap. 7.99 (978-0-15-206608-6(X)) 2007. 16.00 (978-0-15-206007-7(3)) Houghton Mifflin Harcourt Publishing Co.

Urey, Gary. Super Schnoz & the Booger Blaster Breakdown. Frawley, Keith, illus. 2015. (Super Schnoz Ser.: 3). (ENG.). 192p. (J). (gr. 3-7). 14.99 (978-0-8075-7562-8(3)) Whitman, Albert & Co.

—Super Schnoz & the Gates of Smell. Long, Ethan, illus. (Super Schnoz Ser.: 1). (ENG.). 160p. (J). (gr. 3-7). 2015. pap. 6.99 (978-0-8075-7560-4(7)) 2013. 14.99 (978-0-8075-7555-0(0)) Whitman, Albert & Co.

—Super Schnoz & the Invasion of the Snore Snatchers. Frawley, Keith, illus. 2014. (Super Schnoz Ser.: 2). (ENG.). 160p. (J). (gr. 3-7). 14.99 (978-0-8075-7557-4(7)) Whitman, Albert & Co.

Uribe Urbieta, Kirmen & Lete, Nere. Garmendia & the Black Rider. 2015. (Illus.). 93p. (J). pap. (978-1-935709-64-0(X)) Ctr. for Basque Studies.
Ustinov, Pavla. Peggy Pots. 2008. 76p. pap. 33.32 (978-1-4257-1347-8(5)) Xlibris Corp.
Vail, Rachel & Avi. Never Mind! 2005. (ENG.). 208p. (J). (gr. 5-18). reprint ed. pap. 6.99 (978-0-06-054316-7(7)) HarperCollins Pubs.
van de Ruit, John. Spud. 2005. 300p. pap. (978-0-14-302484-2(1)) Penguin Publishing Group.
—Spud. 2008. (ENG.). 336p. (YA). (gr. 7-18). 9.99 (978-1-59514-187-3(1), Razorbill) Penguin Young Readers Group.
Van De Ruit, John. Spud - The Madness Continues. 2009. (ENG.). 352p. (YA). (gr. 7-18). 9.99 (978-1-59514-245-0(2), Razorbill) Penguin Young Readers Group.
Van Draanen, Wendelin. The Gecko & Sticky: the Power Potion. Gilpin, Stephen, illus. 2011. (Gecko & Sticky Ser.). (ENG.). 240p. (J). (gr. 3-7). 6.99 (978-0-440-42245-7(0), Yearling) Random Hse. Children's Bks.
—The Greatest Power. Gilpin, Stephen, illus. 2011. (Gecko & Sticky Ser.: Bk. 1). (ENG.). 208p. (J). (gr. 3-7). 7.99 (978-0-440-42243-3(4), Yearling) Random Hse. Children's Bks.
—Sinister Substitute. Gilpin, Stephen, illus. 2011. (Gecko & Sticky Ser.: Bk. 3). (ENG.). 224p. (J). (gr. 3-7). 7.99 (978-0-440-42244-0(2), Yearling) Random Hse. Children's Bks.
Van Duzen, Fisher. Searching for Sand Dollars. 2013. 416p. 19.99 (978-0-9896335-0-5(0)) PoorHse. Publishing LLC.
Van Fleet, Matthew. Munch! Van Fleet, Matthew, illus. 2013. (ENG., Illus.). 14p. (J). (gr. -1-1). 9.99 (978-1-4424-9425-1(5), Simon & Schuster/Paula Wiseman Bks.) Simon & Schuster/Paula Wiseman Bks.
van Genechten, Guido. No Ghost under My Bed. 2010. (ENG.). 30p. (J). (gr. -1-k). 17.95 (978-1-60537-069-9(X)) Cobblestone Publishing Co.
Van Leeuwen, Jean. The Great Cheese Conspiracy, 0 vols. 2011. (ENG.). 96p. (J). (gr. 1-4). 15.99 (978-0-7614-5972-9(3), 9780761459729, Amazon Children's Publishing) Amazon Publishing.
Van Lemon, M. Champions of the Garden Games: Winter Fun for Everyone. 2009. 48p. pap. 20.95 (978-1-4490-3580-8(9)) AuthorHouse.
Van Patter, Bruce. Tucker Took It! 2010. (ENG., Illus.). 32p. (J). (gr. k-2). 16.95 (978-1-59078-698-7(X)) Boyds Mills Pr.
Van Slyke, Rebecca. Lexie the Word Wrangler. Hartland, Jessie, illus. 2017. (ENG.). 40p. (J). (gr. k-3). 17.99 (978-0-399-16957-1(1), Nancy Paulsen Books) Penguin Young Readers Group.
—Where Do Pants Go? Robertson, Chris, illus. 2016. (ENG.). 40p. (J). (gr. -1). 9.95 (978-1-4549-1592-8(7)) Sterling Publishing Co., Inc.
Vande Velde, Vivian. Frogged. 2013. (ENG., Illus.). 208p. (J). (gr. 5-7). 16.99 (978-0-547-94215-5(X)) Houghton Mifflin Harcourt Publishing Co.
—Squirrel in the House. Björkman, Steve, illus. 2016. (ENG.). 80p. (J). 15.95 (978-0-8234-3633-0(0)) Holiday Hse., Inc.
—Tales from the Brothers Grimm & the Sisters Weird. Weinman, Brad, illus. 2005. (ENG.). 144p. (J). (gr. 5-7). reprint ed. pap. 6.99 (978-0-15-205572-1(X)) Houghton Mifflin Harcourt Publishing Co.
—Wizard at Work. 2004. (ENG., Illus.). 144p. (J). (gr. 5-7). pap. 10.95 (978-0-15-205309-3(3)) Houghton Mifflin Harcourt Publishing Co.
—8 Class Pets + 1 Squirrel ÷ 1 Dog = Chaos. Björkman, Steve, illus. (ENG.). 80p. (J). 2012. pap. 6.99 (978-0-8234-2594-5(0)) 2011. 15.95 (978-0-8234-2364-4(6)) Holiday Hse., Inc.
Vandereyken, Leen. Loulou in Love. 2008. (Girls Only Ser.). (ENG.). 155p. (YA). (gr. 4-18). 16.95 (978-1-60537-025-5(8)) Clavis Publishing.
Vatcher-Martin M.A., Cheryl A. The Cornstalks Are Whispering. 2009. 20p. pap. 17.99 (978-1-4490-1206-9(X)) AuthorHouse.
Vega, Denise. If Your Monster Won't Go to Bed. OHora, Zachariah, illus. 2017. (ENG.). 40p. (J). (gr. -1-2). 17.99 (978-0-553-49655-0(7), Knopf Bks. for Young Readers) Random Hse. Children's Bks.
Venable, Colleen A. F. And Then There Were Gnomes. Yue, Stephanie, illus. 2010. (Guinea Pig, Pet Shop Private Eye Ser.: 2). (ENG.). 48p. (J). (gr. 2-5). pap. 6.95 (978-0-7613-5480-2(8)); lib. bdg. 27.93 (978-0-7613-4599-2(X)) Lerner Publishing Group.
—The Ferret's a Foot, 3 vols. Yue, Stephanie, illus. 2011. (Guinea Pig, Pet Shop Private Eye Ser.: 3). (ENG.). 48p. (J). (gr. 2-5). 27.93 (978-0-7613-5223-5(6)); pap. 6.95 (978-0-7613-5629-5(0)) Lerner Publishing Group.
—Fish You Were Here, No. 4. Yue, Stephanie, illus. 2011. (Guinea Pig, Pet Shop Private Eye Ser.: 4). (ENG.). 48p. (J). (gr. 2-5). pap. 6.95 (978-0-7613-5630-1(4)); lib. bdg. 27.93 (978-0-7613-5224-2(4)) Lerner Publishing Group.
—Going, Going, Dragon! 2013. 48p. pap. 14.95 (978-1-4677-0973-6(5)) Lerner Publishing Group.
—Going, Going, Dragon! Yue, Stephanie, illus. 2013. (Guinea Pig, Pet Shop Private Eye Ser.: 6). (ENG.). 48p. (J). (gr. 2-5). pap. 6.95 (978-1-4677-0726-8(0)); lib. bdg. 27.93 (978-0-7613-6009-4(3)) Lerner Publishing Group.
—Hamster & Cheese. Yue, Stephanie, illus. 2010. (Guinea Pig, Pet Shop Private Eye Ser.: 1). (ENG.). 48p. (J). (gr. 2-5). pap. 6.95 (978-0-7613-5479-6(4)); lib. bdg. 27.93 (978-0-7613-4598-5(1)) Lerner Publishing Group.
—Raining Cats & Detectives. Yue, Stephanie, illus. 2012. (Guinea Pig, Pet Shop Private Eye Ser.: 5). (ENG.). 48p. (J). (gr. 2-5). lib. bdg. 27.93 (978-0-7613-6008-7(5)) Lerner Publishing Group.
Venable, Colleen Af. Mervin the Sloth Is about to Do the Best Thing in the World. Chan, Ruth, illus. 2016. 40p. (J). (gr. -1-3). 17.99 (978-0-06-233847-1(1), Greenwillow Bks.) HarperCollins Pubs.
Vere, Ed. Max el Valiente. 2014. (SPA.). 36p. (gr. k-2). 20.99 (978-84-261-4071-5(8)) Juventud, Editorial ESP. Dist: Lectorum Pubns., Inc.
—Max the Brave. 2015. (Max Ser.: 1). (ENG.). 32p. (J). (-2). 16.99 (978-1-4926-1651-1(6), 9781492616511, Sourcebooks Jabberwocky) Sourcebooks, Inc.
Vernick, Audrey. First Grade Dropout. Cordell, Matthew, illus. 2015. (ENG.). 32p. (J). (gr. -1-3). 16.99 (978-0-544-12985-6(7), Clarion Bks.) Houghton Mifflin Harcourt Trade & Reference Pubs.
—I Won a What? Neubecker, Robert, illus. 2016. (ENG.). 40p. (J). (gr. -1-2). 17.99 (978-0-553-50993-9(4), Knopf Bks. for Young Readers) Random Hse. Children's Bks.
—Teach Your Buffalo to Play Drums. Jennewein, Daniel, illus. 2011. (ENG.). 32p. (J). (gr. -1-3). 16.99 (978-0-06-176253-6(9)) HarperCollins Pubs.
Vernick, Audrey & Scanlon, Liz Garton. Bob, Not Bob! Cordell, Matthew, illus. 2017. (ENG.). 40p. (J). (gr. -1-k). 17.99 (978-1-4847-2302-9(3)) Disney Pr.
Vernon, Ursula. Castle Hangnail. 2015. (ENG., Illus.). 384p. (J). (gr. 3-7). 16.99 (978-0-8037-4129-4(4), Dial Bks) Penguin Young Readers Group.
—Curse of the Were-Wiener. 3rd ed. 2010. (Dragonbreath Ser.: 3). (ENG.). 208p. (J). (gr. 3-7). 12.99 (978-0-8037-3469-2(7), Dial Bks) Penguin Young Readers Group.
—The Frozen Menace. 2016. (Dragonbreath Ser.: 11). (ENG., Illus.). 208p. (J). (gr. 3-7). 12.99 (978-0-8037-3986-4(9), Dial Bks) Penguin Young Readers Group.
—Harriet the Invincible. 2015. (Hamster Princess Ser.: 1). (ENG., Illus.). 208p. (J). (gr. 3-7). 12.99 (978-0-8037-3983-3(4), Dial Bks) Penguin Young Readers Group.
—No Such Thing as Ghosts. 5th ed. 2011. (Dragonbreath Ser.: 5). (ENG.). 208p. (J). (gr. 3-7). 12.99 (978-0-8037-3527-9(8), Dial Bks) Penguin Young Readers Group.
—Of Mice & Magic. 2016. (Hamster Princess Ser.: 2). (ENG., Illus.). 240p. (J). (gr. 3-7). 12.99 (978-0-8037-3984-0(2), Dial Bks) Penguin Young Readers Group.
—Ratpunzel. 2016. (Hamster Princess Ser.: 3). (ENG., Illus.). 240p. (J). (gr. 3-7). 12.99 (978-0-8037-3985-7(0), Dial Bks) Penguin Young Readers Group.
—Revenge of the Horned Bunnies, No. 6. 6th ed. 2012. (Dragonbreath Ser.: 6). (ENG.). 208p. (J). (gr. 3-7). 12.99 (978-0-8037-3677-1(0), Dial Bks) Penguin Young Readers Group.
—When Fairies Go Bad, No. 7. 7th ed. 2012. (Dragonbreath Ser.: 7). (ENG.). 208p. (J). (gr. 3-7). 12.99 (978-0-8037-3678-8(9), Dial Bks) Penguin Young Readers Group.
Vick-E & Random House Disney Staff. Wall-E. Orpinas, Jean-Paul et al, illus. 2008. (Little Golden Book Ser.). (ENG.). 24p. (J). (gr. -1-2). 3.99 (978-0-7364-2422-6(9), RH/Disney) Random Hse. Children's Bks.
Vick, Jacqueline. Logical Larry. 2009. 66p. pap. 9.95 (978-0-557-01341-8(0)) Lulu Pr., Inc.
Viky Toma Unas Vacaciones Divetidas. 2003. (SPA.). 62p. (J). (gr. -1-1). (978-968-5308-80-9(2), Silver Dolphin en Español) Advanced Marketing, S. de R. L. de C. V.
Villiers, Alan. Joey Goes to Sea. Dowling, Victor J., illus. 2005. (Maritime Ser.). (ENG.). 70p. (J). (gr. 4-7). pap. 9.95 (978-0-939511-10-5(X)) Mystic Seaport Museum, Inc.
Viorst, Judith. Alexander & the Terrible, Horrible, No Good, Very Bad Day. Cruz, Ray, illus. 2009. (ENG.). 32p. (J). (gr. -1-2). 17.99 (978-1-4169-8595-2(6), Atheneum Bks. for Young Readers) Simon & Schuster Children's Publishing.
—Alexander, Who's Trying His Best to Be the Best Boy Ever. 2014. (ENG., Illus.). 40p. (J). (gr. -1-3). 17.99 (978-1-4814-2353-3(3), Atheneum Bks. for Young Readers) Simon & Schuster Children's Publishing.
Virján, Emma J. What This Story Needs Is a Pig in a Wig. Virján, Emma J., illus. 2015. (Pig in a Wig Book Ser.). (ENG., Illus.). 40p. (J). (gr. -1-3). 9.99 (978-0-06-232724-6(0)) HarperCollins Pubs.
Vivat, Booki. Frazzled: Everyday Disasters & Impending Doom. Vivat, Booki, illus. 2016. (Illus.). 240p. (J). (gr. 3-7). 12.99 (978-0-06-239879-6(2)) HarperCollins Pubs.
Vrettos, Adrienne Maria. The Exile of Gigi Lane. (ENG.). (YA). (gr. 7). 2011. 368p. pap. 8.99 (978-1-4424-2121-9(5)) 2010. 352p. 16.99 (978-1-4169-2433-3(7)) McElderry, Margaret K. Bks. (McElderry, Margaret K. Bks.).
Waber, Bernard. Ira Sleeps Over, 1 vol. 2008. (Read along Book & CD Ser.). (ENG., Illus.). 48p. (J). (gr. -1-3). audio compact disk 10.99 (978-0-618-85282-6(4)) Houghton Mifflin Harcourt Publishing Co.
Wagner, Brian. 10 Things Not to Do with Your Eyeball. 2005. 20p. 9.99 (978-1-4116-5977-3(5)) Lulu Pr., Inc.
Waguespack, Michael. The Deer Hunting Book. 2013. 104p. pap. 7.95 (978-0-9754624-6-1(6)) Country Kid Publishing LLC.
Waldron, Kevin. Mr. Peek & the Misunderstanding at the Zoo. Waldron, Kevin, illus. 2010. (ENG., Illus.). 48p. (J). (gr. k-12). 15.99 (978-0-7636-4549-6(4), Templar) Candlewick Pr.
Walker, Anna. Hurry up, Alfie! 2016. (ENG., Illus.). 24p. (J). (gr. -1-3). 14.99 (978-0-544-58654-3(9)) Houghton Mifflin Harcourt Publishing Co.
Walker, Nan. Spork Out of Orbit. Warrick, Jessica, illus. 2016. (How to Be an Earthling (r) Ser.: 1). (ENG.). 64p. (J). (gr. 1-3). 22.65 (978-1-57565-818-6(6)) Kane Press, Inc.
—Spork Out of Orbit: Respect. Warrick, Jessica, illus. 2016. (How to Be an Earthling (r) Ser.: 1). (ENG.). 64p. (J). (gr. 1-3). 34.65 (978-1-57565-820-9(8)) Kane Press, Inc.
Walker, Rhonda. Willie Out West. 2013. 24p. pap. 12.95 (978-1-4497-9848-2(9), WestBow Pr.) Author Solutions, Inc.
Walker, Sally M. The Vowel Family: A Tale of Lost Letters. Luthardt, Kevin, illus. 2008. (ENG.). 32p. (J). (gr. k-3). lib. bdg. 16.95 (978-0-8225-7982-3(0)) Lerner Publishing Group.
Wall, Jean Jones. I Can Stand by a Rase. 2004. (Illus.). 60p. (J). (gr. 3-5). pap. 12.00 (978-0-9760518-0-0(X)) JWall Publishing.
Wallace, Bill. No Dogs Allowed! 2005. (ENG.). 224p. (J). (gr. 3-7). pap. 6.99 (978-1-4169-0381-9(X), Aladdin) Simon & Schuster Children's Publishing.
Wallace, Bill & Wallace, Carol. That Doggone Calf. 2009. (ENG.). 160p. (J). (gr. 3-7). 16.95 (978-0-8234-2228-9(3)) Holiday Hse., Inc.
Wallace, Karen. Flash Harriet & the Loch Ness Monster. Nayler, Sarah, illus. 2007. (Collins Big Cat Ser.). (ENG.). 160p. (J). (gr. 2-4). pap. 8.99 (978-0-00-723082-2(6)) HarperCollins Pubs. Ltd. GBR. Dist: Independent Pubs. Group.
Walliams, David. Billionaire Bairn: Billionaire Boy in Scots. Fitt, Matthew, tr. from ENG. Ross, Tony, illus. 2015. (ENG.). 288p. (J). (gr. 1-7). pap. 10.99 (978-1-84502-995-1(X)) Black and White Publishing Ltd. GBR. Dist: Independent Pubs. Group.
—Demon Dentist. Ross, Tony, illus. 2016. (J). (gr. 3-7). 464p. pap. 7.99 (978-0-06-241705-3(3)); (ENG.). 448p. 16.99 (978-0-06-241704-6(5)) HarperCollins Pubs.
—Grandpa's Great Escape. Ross, Tony, illus. 2017. 464p. (J). (gr. 3-7). 16.99 (978-0-06-256089-6(1)) HarperCollins Pubs.
—The World's Worst Children 2. Ross, Tony, illus. 2016. (ENG.). 272p. (J). (978-0-00-819703-2(2), HarperCollins Children's Bks.) HarperCollins Pubs. Ltd. GBR. Dist: HarperCollins Pubs.
Walsh, Ann. Flower Power, 1 vol. 2005. (Orca Currents Ser.). (ENG.). 128p. (J). (gr. 5-9). per. 9.95 (978-1-55143-386-8(9)) Orca Bk. Pubs. USA.
Walsh, Maria Elena. Cuentopos de Gulubu. Lavandeira, Sandra, illus. 2003. (SPA.). 120p. (J). (gr. 3-5). 14.95 (978-950-511-630-0(6)) Alfaguara S.A. de Ediciones ARG. Dist: Santillana USA Publishing Co., Inc.
Walter, Judy S. The Grey & White Stranger. 2012. 96p. pap. 9.95 (978-0-578-10299-3(4)) Sluser Publishing.
Walton, Rick. Bullfrog Pops!, 1 vol. McAllister, Chris, illus. 2005. (ENG.). 32p. (J). (gr. 3-3). pap. 7.99 (978-1-58685-840-7(8)) Gibbs Smith, Publisher.
—Girl & Gorilla. Berger, Joe, illus. 2016. 32p. (J). (gr. -1-3). 17.99 (978-0-06-227891-3(6)) HarperCollins Pubs.
—I Need My Own Country! Hargis, Wes, illus. 2012. (ENG.). 40p. (J). (gr. -1-3). 17.89 (978-1-59990-560-0(4), 9781599905600, Bloomsbury USA Childrens) Bloomsbury Publishing USA.
—Mr. President Goes to School, 1 vol. Sneed, Brad, illus. 2010. (ENG.). 32p. (J). (gr. -1-3). 15.95 (978-1-56145-538-6(5)) Peachtree Pubs.
Walton, Rick & Kraus, Franz. I Need My Own Country! Hargis, Wes, illus. 2012. (ENG.). 40p. (J). (gr. -1-8). 16.99 (978-1-59990-559-4(0), 9781599905594, Bloomsbury USA Childrens) Bloomsbury Publishing USA.
Wang, Margaret. Who Stole the Cookie from the Cookie Jar? Schneider, Christine, illus. 2006. (ENG.). 22p. (J). bds. 10.95 (978-1-58117-383-3(0), Intervisual/Piggy Toes) Bendon, Inc.
Ward, B. J. Farty Marty. Kellogg, Steven, illus. 2013. (ENG.). 32p. (J). (gr. -1-3). 16.99 (978-1-4424-3901-6(7), Simon & Schuster Bks. For Young Readers) Simon & Schuster Bks. For Young Readers.
Ward, Lindsay. Rosco vs. the Baby. Ward, Lindsay, illus. 2016. (ENG., Illus.). 32p. (J). (gr. -1-3). 17.99 (978-1-4814-3657-1(0), Simon & Schuster Bks. For Young Readers) Simon & Schuster Bks. For Young Readers.
Wardlaw, Lee. Won Ton & Chopstick. Yelchin, Eugene, illus. 2015. (ENG.). 40p. (J). (gr. -1-3). 17.99 (978-0-8050-9987-4(5), 9780805099874, Holt, Henry & Co. Bks. For Young Readers) Holt, Henry & Co.
—101 Ways to Bug Your Teacher. 2005. (ENG.). 256p. (J). (gr. 3-7). pap. 6.99 (978-0-14-240331-0(8), Puffin Books) Penguin Young Readers Group.
Wargin, Kathy-jo. Moose on the Loose. Bendall-Brunello, John, illus. 2009. (ENG.). 32p. (J). (gr. k-6). 15.95 (978-1-58536-427-5(4)) Sleeping Bear Pr.
Warnasuriya, Chandrani. Children's Stories of Wit & Humor: Stories from Sri Lanka (The Grand-Old-Man & The Big Five) 2008. 50p. pap. 16.95 (978-1-60672-624-2(2)) America Star Bks.
Watase, Yuu. Alice 19th, Vol. 6, 7 vols. Watase, Yuu, illus. 2004. (ENG., Illus.). 200p. pap. 9.99 (978-1-59116-243-8(2)) Viz Media.
Watase, Yuu & Caselman, Lance. The Lost Word, 7 vols. Watase, Yuu, illus. 2004. (Alice 19th Ser.). (ENG., Illus.). 200p. pap. 9.99 (978-1-59116-244-5(0)) Viz Media.
Waterton, Betty. A Bumblebee Sweater, 1 vol. LaFave, Kim, illus. 2007. (ENG.). 32p. (J). (gr. -1-3). (978-1-55455-028-9(9)) Fitzhenry & Whiteside, Ltd.
Watson, J. D. My Socks Don't Match. 2004. 41p. pap. 24.95 (978-1-4137-1935-2(X)) PublishAmerica, Inc.
Watson, J. R. Wizard down Under. 2009. 160p. 23.50 (978-1-60860-138-7(2), Eloquent Bks.) Strategic Book Publishing & Rights Agency (SBPRA).
Watson, Tom. Cats in the City. 2017. (Stick Cat Ser.: 2). 224p. (J). (gr. 3-7). 12.99 (978-0-06-241102-0(0)) HarperCollins Pubs.
—Stick Dog. Long, Ethan, illus. 2013. (Stick Dog Ser.: 1). (ENG.). 192p. (J). (gr. 3-7). 12.99 (978-0-06-211078-7(0)) HarperCollins Pubs.
—Stick Dog Chases a Pizza. 2014. (Stick Dog Ser.: 3). (ENG.). 208p. (J). (gr. 3-7). 12.99 (978-0-06-227805-0(3)) HarperCollins Pubs.
—Stick Dog Dreams of Ice Cream. 2015. (Stick Dog Ser.: 4). (ENG., Illus.). 224p. (J). (gr. 3-7). 12.99 (978-0-06-227807-4(X)) HarperCollins Pubs.
—Stick Dog Slurps Spaghetti. Long, Ethan, illus. 2016. (Stick Dog Ser.: 6). 240p. (J). (gr. 3-7). 12.99 (978-0-06-234322-2(X)) HarperCollins Pubs.
—Stick Dog Tries to Take the Donuts. 2016. (Stick Dog Ser.: 5). (Illus.). 224p. (J). (gr. 3-7). 12.99 (978-0-06-234320-8(3)) HarperCollins Pubs.
—Stick Dog Wants a Hot Dog. Long, Ethan, illus. 2013. 200p. (J). (978-0-06-229593-4(4)) Harper & Row Ltd.
Watson, Tom & Long, Ethan, illus. Stick Dog Dreams of Ice Cream. 2015. 216p. (J). (978-0-06-238092-0(3)) Harper & Row Ltd.
Watts, Frances. Extraordinary Ernie & Marvelous Maud. Watson, Judy, illus. 2010. (ENG.). 80p. (J). (gr. 2-5). pap. 6.00 (978-0-8028-5363-9(3), Eerdmans Bks For Young Readers) Eerdmans, William B. Publishing Co.
Waxman, Mark. The Mcventures of Me, Morgan Mcfactoid: Hair Today, Gone Tomorrow. 2016. (ENG.). 192p. (J). (gr. 2-7). 15.99 (978-1-63450-148-4(9), Sky Pony Pr.) Skyhorse Publishing Co., Inc.
We Meet Again. 2014. (Timmy Failure Ser.: No. 3). (ENG., Illus.). 272p. (J). (gr. 3-7). 14.99 (978-0-7636-7375-8(7)) Candlewick Pr.
Weathers, Regina Lorick. Safety Sam, I Am: How to Avoid A Sticky Jelly Jam. Short, Gregory T., illus. 2004. (J). per. 7.95 (978-0-9665909-6-8(1)) Kalawantis Publishing Services, Inc.
Webb, Mack H., Jr. Webb's Wondrous Tales Book 2. Webb, Celia, illus. 2007. 156p. (J). per. 14.95 (978-0-9779576-3-7(2)) Pilinut Pr., Inc.
Weeks, Sarah. Sophie Peterman Tells the Truth! Neubecker, Robert, illus. 2009. (ENG.). 32p. (J). (gr. -1-3). 17.99 (978-1-4169-8686-7(3), Beach Lane Bks.) Beach Lane Bks.
Wegman, William. Dress up Batty. Wegman, William, illus. 2004. (ENG., Illus.). 18p. (gr. -1-17). 19.99 (978-0-7868-1849-5(2)) Hyperion Bks. for Children.
Wegwerth, A. L. Little Bo Peep & Her Bad, Bad Sheep: A Mother Goose Hullabaloo. Flowers, Luke, illus. 2016. (Fiction Picture Bks.). (ENG.). 40p. (gr. -1-2). lib. bdg. 22.65 (978-1-4795-6483-5(4), Fiction Picture Bks.) Picture Window Bks.
Wehner, Adrienna. Elephants & Roses. 2003. (Illus.). (YA). (gr. 2-18). 22.00 (978-0-9653866-3-0(5)) Wehner, Adrienna.
Weidt, Maryann. Mama Loved to Worry. Balsaitis, Rachael, illus. 2016. (ENG.). 32p. (J). (gr. -1-1). 16.95 (978-0-87351-994-6(9)) Minnesota Historical Society Pr.
Weiner, Ellis. The Templeton Twins Have an Idea. Holmes, Jeremy, illus. 2012. (ENG.). 232p. (J). (gr. 4-7). 16.99 (978-0-8118-6679-8(3)) Chronicle Bks. LLC.
—The Templeton Twins Have an Idea: Book 1. Holmes, Jeremy, illus. 2013. (Templeton Twins Ser.). (ENG.). 240p. (J). (gr. 3-7). pap. 6.99 (978-1-4521-2704-0(2)) Chronicle Bks. LLC.
—The Templeton Twins Make a Scene: Book 2. Holmes, Jeremy, illus. 2014. (ENG.). 272p. (J). (gr. 3-7). pap. 6.99 (978-1-4521-2872-6(3)) Chronicle Bks. LLC.
Weiner, Jennifer. The Littlest Bigfoot. 2017. (Littlest Bigfoot Ser.: 1). (ENG.). 352p. (J). (gr. 3-7). pap. 7.99 **(978-1-4814-7075-9(2)**, Aladdin) Simon & Schuster Children's Publishing.
—The Littlest Bigfoot. Mulvanny, Sara, illus. 2016. (Littlest Bigfoot Ser.: 1). (ENG.). 304p. (J). (gr. 3-7). 16.99 (978-1-4814-7074-2(4), Aladdin) Simon & Schuster Children's Publishing.
—The Littlest Bigfoot. 2017. lib. bdg. 18.40 **(978-0-606-40206-4(3))** Turtleback Bks.
Weis, Carol. When the Cows Got Loose. Hoyt, Ard, illus. 2006. (ENG.). 40p. (J). (gr. -1-1). 17.99 (978-0-689-85166-7(9), Simon & Schuster Bks. For Young Readers) Simon & Schuster Bks. For Young Readers.
Weiss, Ellen. Eloise & the Very Secret Room. Lyon, Tammie Speer & Lyon, Tammie, illus. 2006. (Eloise Ser.). (ENG.). 32p. (J). (gr. -1-1). pap. 3.99 (978-0-689-87450-5(2), Simon Spotlight) Simon Spotlight.
—Eloise & the Very Secret Room, 1 vol. Lyon, Tammie, illus. 2016. (ENG.). 32p. (J). **(978-1-61479-403-5(0))** Spotlight.
—I Love You, Little Monster. Arnold, Ali, illus. 2012. (ENG.). 16p. (J). (gr. -1 — 1). bds. 7.99 (978-1-4424-2850-8(3), Little Simon) Little Simon.
—Whatever You Do, I Love You. Williams, Sam, illus. 2010. (ENG.). 16p. (J). (gr. -1 — 1). bds. 7.99 (978-1-4424-0809-8(X), Little Simon) Little Simon.
Weldon, Andrew. Kid with the Amazing Head. 2016. (ENG.). 96p. (J). (gr. 2-4). 8.99 **(978-0-14-330916-1(1))** Random Hse. Australia AUS. Dist: Independent Pubs. Group.
Welling, Peter. Joe Van der Katt & the Great Picket Fence, 1 vol. Welling, Peter, illus. 2005. (ENG., Illus.). 32p. (J). (gr. k-3). 16.99 (978-1-58980-281-0(0)) Pelican Publishing Co., Inc.
Welling, Peter J. Michael le Soufflé & the April Fool, 1 vol. Welling, Peter J., illus. 2003. (ENG., Illus.). 32p. (J). (gr. k-3). 16.99 (978-1-58980-105-9(9)) Pelican Publishing Co., Inc.
Wells, Rosemary. Miracle Melts Down. Wells, Rosemary, illus. 2012. (ENG., Illus.). 40p. (J). (gr. -1-3). 14.99 (978-0-06-192115-5(7), Tegen, Katherine Bks) HarperCollins Pubs.
Welsh, Joey. The Gekkleberry Tree: A Humorous Tail about the Gekkards & One Legendary Tree. Welsh, Joey, illus. 2005. (Illus.). (J). (gr. -1-3). 17.95 (978-1-59247-244-4(3)) Scholargy Publishing, Inc.
West, Abby. The Adventures of Penny Ann & Alexa Jane. 2013. (ENG., Illus.). 28p. (gr. -1-4). pap. 13.95 (978-1-936205-33-2(5)) Austin, Stephen F. State Univ. Pr.
West, Tracey, adapted by. The Boss Baby Junior Novelization. 2017. (Boss Baby Movie Ser.). (ENG., Illus.). 112p. (J). (gr. 2-5). 17.99 (978-1-4814-9170-9(9)); pap. 6.99 (978-1-4814-7006-3(X)) Simon Spotlight. (Simon Spotlight).
Westaway, Kylie. A Whale in the Bathtub. Jellett, Tom, illus. 2016. (ENG.). 40p. (J). (gr. -1-3). 16.99 (978-0-544-53535-0(9)) Houghton Mifflin Harcourt Publishing Co.
Weston Woods Staff, creator. Caps for Sale. 2011. 38.75 (978-0-439-72925-3(4)); 18.95 (978-0-439-72924-6(6)) Weston Woods Studios, Inc.
—Children Make Terrible Pets. 2011. 29.95 (978-0-545-40221-7(2)) Weston Woods Studios, Inc.
—Dem Bones. 2004. 29.95 (978-1-55592-702-8(5)) Weston Woods Studios, Inc.
—Goldilocks & the Three Bears. 2011. 29.95 (978-0-439-73471-4(1)); 18.95 (978-0-439-72679-5(4)); 38.75 (978-0-439-72682-5(4)) Weston Woods Studios, Inc.
—The Gym Teacher from the Black Lagoon. 2011. 38.75 (978-0-545-19711-3(2)) Weston Woods Studios, Inc.
—Millions of Cats Weston Woods. 2011. 18.95 (978-0-439-72840-9(1)); 29.95 (978-0-439-73496-7(7)); 38.75 (978-0-439-72842-3(8)) Weston Woods Studios, Inc.
—This Is the House That Jack Built. 2011. 38.75 (978-0-439-78426-9(3)); 18.95 (978-0-439-78424-5(7)) Weston Woods Studios, Inc.
Whamhower, Shogun. Nerdy Ninjas vs the Really Really Bad Guys. McKenzie, Heath, illus. 2012. 137p. (J). (978-0-545-53736-0(3)) Scholastic, Inc.
Wharton, Ellie. Fairy Magic! Lee, Maxine & Enright, Amanda, illus. 2014. (ENG.). 10p. (J). (gr. -1-k). 9.99 (978-1-78244-827-3(6)) Top That! Publishing PLC GBR. Dist: Independent Pubs. Group.
What Is Fun? Individual Title Six-Packs. (gr. 1-2). 22.00 (978-0-7635-9094-9(0)) Rigby Education.
Wheeler, Ron. Stinky Stevens: Escape from Aunt Smoochie-Kiss (Book 4) 2012. 114p. pap. 6.95 (978-0-9829377-7-8(6)) Written World Communications.
—Stinky Stevens: The Missing Soggy Soccer Shoe (Book 3) 2012. 114p. pap. 6.95 (978-0-9829377-6-1(8)) Written World Communications.
Where's Waldo: the Complete Set. 2006. (J). 82.94 (978-0-7636-3510-7(3)) Candlewick Pr.

H
I

Whint, Ana Lee. Espalemit. 2003. (ENG.). 112p. pap. 9.95 *(978-0-595-26259-5(7),* Writers Club Pr.) iUniverse, Inc.

White, Kathy. Little Green Riding Hood. 2006. (J). pap. *(978-1-4108-6182-5(1))* Benchmark Education Co.

White, Wade Albert. The Adventurer's Guide to Dragons (and Why They Keep Biting Me) 2017. (Adventurer's Guide Ser.: 2). (ENG.). 384p. (J). (gr. 3-7). 16.99 ***(978-0-316-30531-0(6))*** Little, Brown Bks. for Young Readers.

Whitehouse, Howard. The Faceless Fiend: Being the Tale of a Criminal Mastermind, His Masked Minions & a Princess with a Butter Knife, Involving Explosives & a Certain Amount of Pushing & Shoving. Slavin, Bill, illus. 2007. (Mad Misadventures of Emmaline & Rubberbones Ser.). (ENG.). 272p. (J). (gr. 4-7). 7.95 *(978-1-55453-180-6(2))* Kids Can Pr., Ltd. CAN. Dist: Hachette Bk. Group.

—The Island of Mad Scientists: Being an Excursion to the Wilds of Scotland, Involving Many Marvels of Experimental Invention, Pirates, a Heroic Cat, a Mechanical Man & a Monkey. Slavin, Bill, illus. 2008. (Mad Misadventures of Emmaline & Rubberbones Ser.). (ENG.). 264p. (J). (gr. 4-7). pap. 7.95 *(978-1-55453-237-7(X))* Kids Can Pr., Ltd. CAN. Dist: Hachette Bk. Group.

Whiting, Sue & Martin, Stuart. That's Funny! 2003. (Illus.). 14p. 12.95 *(978-1-74047-272-2(1))* Book Co. Publishing Pty, Ltd., The AUS. Dist: Penton Overseas, Inc.

Whitlock, Matt. Punk's Christmas Carol: A Punk 'n Patch Book. Whitlock, Matt, illus. 2006. (Illus.). 32p. (J). (gr. -1-3). 16.95 *(978-0-9769057-1-4(X))* Little Hero.

Whittemore, Jo. Brooke's Bad Luck. 2017. (Confidentially Yours Ser.: 5). 288p. (J). (gr. 3-7). pap. 6.99 *(978-0-06-235901-8(0))* HarperCollins Pubs.

Whybrow, Ian. Ella the Superstar. McCullen, Sam, illus. 2007. (Collins Big Cat Ser.). (ENG.). 32p. (J). (gr. 1-2). pap. 6.99 *(978-0-00-718681-5(9))* HarperCollins Pubs. Ltd. GBR. Dist: Independent Pubs. Group.

—That Naughty Meerkat! Parsons, Garry, illus. 2016. (ENG.). 32p. (J). 17.99 *(978-0-00-813945-2(8),* HarperCollins Children's Bks.) HarperCollins Pubs. Ltd. GBR. Dist: HarperCollins Pubs.

Whyman, Matt. Bad Apple. 2016. (ENG.). 352p. (YA). (gr. 7). pap. 9.99 ***(978-1-4714-0420-7(X))*** Bonnier Publishing GBR. Dist: Independent Pubs. Group.

Whytock, Cherry. My Cup Runneth Over: The Life of Angelica Cookson Potts. Whytock, Cherry, illus. 2012. (ENG., Illus.). 192p. (YA). (gr. 7). pap. 9.99 *(978-1-4424-6055-3(5),* Simon Pulse) Simon Pulse.

—My Scrumptious Scottish Dumplings: The Life of Angelica Cookson Potts. Whytock, Cherry, illus. 2006. (ENG., Illus.). 192p. (YA). mass mkt. 5.99 *(978-0-689-86552-7(X),* Simon Pulse) Simon Pulse.

Wicke, Ed. Wicked Tales. 2006. (ENG., Illus.). 156p. (J). per. 9.99 *(978-0-9677652-7-3(7),* BlacknBlue Pr. UK) Blacknblue Pr.

Wilcox, Leah. Falling for Rapunzel. Monks, Lydia, illus. (ENG.). 32p. (J). (gr. -1-3). 2005. pap. 6.99 *(978-0-14-240399-0(7),* Puffin Books) 2003. 15.99 *(978-0-399-23794-2(1),* G.P. Putnam's Sons Books for Young Readers) Penguin Young Readers Group.

—Waking Beauty. Monks, Lydia, illus. 2011. (ENG.). 32p. (J). (gr. -1-k). pap. 6.99 *(978-0-14-241538-2(3),* Puffin Books) Penguin Young Readers Group.

Wilhelm, Hans. Buddy for President. Wilhelm, Hans, illus. 2016. (Illus.). 32p. (J). (gr. -1-3). 17.99 *(978-0-06-240366-7(4))* HarperCollins Pubs.

Wilkinson, Lili. Green Valentine. 2016. (ENG.). 288p. (YA). (gr. 9-12). 12.99 *(978-1-76011-027-7(2))* Allen & Unwin AUS. Dist: Independent Pubs. Group.

Wilkinson, Thomas M. A Forest Through the Trees. 2009. 87p. pap. 12.99 *(978-0-557-17693-9(X))* Lulu Pr., Inc.

Willems, Mo. Don't Let the Pigeon Drive the Bus! Willems, Mo, illus. 2012. (Pigeon Ser.). (ENG., Illus.). 40p. (J). (gr. -1-k). pap. 19.99 *(978-1-4231-4514-1(3))* Hyperion Pr.

—The Duckling Gets a Cookie!? Willems, Mo, illus. 2012. (ENG., Illus.). 40p. (J). (gr. -1-k). 16.99 *(978-1-4231-5128-9(3))* Hyperion Pr.

—An Elephant & Piggie Biggie! Willems, Mo, illus. 2017. (Elephant & Piggie Book Ser.). (ENG., Illus.). 320p. (J). (gr. 1-3). 16.99 ***(978-1-4847-9967-3(4))*** Hyperion Bks. for Children.

—Elephants Cannot Dance! 2012. (Elephant & Piggie Bks.). (CHI & ENG.). (J). pap. ***(978-986-189-325-9(3))*** Grimm Cultural Ent., Co., Ltd.

—Elephants Cannot Dance! Willems, Mo, illus. 2009. (Elephant & Piggie Book Ser.). (ENG., Illus.). 64p. (J). (gr. -1-k). 9.99 *(978-1-4231-1410-9(8))* Hyperion Pr.

—Elephants Cannot Dance! 2011. (ENG & KOR.). (J). ***(978-89-7184-930-9(4))*** Pu-Reun-Sup Publishing Co., Ltd.

—¡Esperar No Es Fácil! Willems, Mo, illus. 2017. (Elephant & Piggie Book Ser.). (ENG & SPA., Illus.). 64p. (J). (gr. 1-3). 9.99 *(978-1-4847-8698-7(X))* Hyperion Bks. for Children.

—I Am Going! Willems, Mo, illus. 2010. (Elephant & Piggie Book Ser.). (ENG., Illus.). 64p. (J). (gr. -1-k). 9.99 *(978-1-4231-1990-6(8))* Hyperion Pr.

—I'm a Frog! Willems, Mo, illus. 2013. (Elephant & Piggie Ser.). (ENG., Illus.). 64p. (J). (gr. 1-3). 9.99 *(978-1-4231-8305-1(3))* Hyperion Pr.

—Knuffle Bunny: A Cautionary Tale. Willems, Mo, illus. 2004. (Knuffle Bunny Ser.). (ENG., Illus.). 40p. (J). (gr. -1-k). 17.99 *(978-0-7868-1870-9(0))* Hyperion Pr.

—Let's Go for a Drive! Willems, Mo, illus. 2012. (Elephant & Piggie Book Ser.). (ENG., Illus.). 64p. (J). (gr. -1-k). 9.99 *(978-1-4231-6482-1(2))* Hyperion Pr.

—My New Friend Is So Fun! Willems, Mo, illus. 2014. (Elephant & Piggie Ser.). (ENG., Illus.). 64p. (J). (gr. 1-3). 9.99 *(978-1-4231-7958-0(7))* Hyperion Bks. for Children.

—¡No Dejes Que la Paloma Conduzca el Autobús! Willems, Mo, illus. 2011.Tr. of Don't Let the Pigeon Drive the Bus. (SPA & ENG., Illus.). 40p. (J). (gr. -1-k). pap. 7.99 *(978-1-4231-4052-8(4))* Hyperion Pr.

—Sam, the Most Scaredy-Cat Kid in the Whole World. Willems, Mo, illus. 2017. (ENG., Illus.). 48p. (J). (gr. -1-k). 17.99 ***(978-1-368-00214-1(5))*** Hyperion Bks. for Children.

—That Is Not a Good Idea! Willems, Mo, illus. 2013. (ENG., Illus.). 48p. (J). (gr. k-3). 17.99 *(978-0-06-220309-0(6))* HarperCollins Pubs.

—Waiting Is Not Easy! Willems, Mo, illus. 2014. (Elephant & Piggie Ser.). (ENG., Illus.). 64p. (J). (gr. 1-3). 9.99 *(978-1-4231-9957-1(X))* Hyperion Bks. for Children.

Willems, Mo & Campoy, F. Isabel. !Estamos en un Libro! Willems, Mo, illus. 2015. (Elephant & Piggie Book Ser.). (SPA., Illus.). 64p. (J). (gr. 1-3). 9.99 *(978-1-4847-2288-6(4))* Hyperion Bks. for Children.

—¡La Paloma Encuentra un Perro Caliente! Willems, Mo, illus. 2011. (SPA & ENG., Illus.). 40p. (J). (gr. -1-k). pap. 9.99 *(978-1-4231-4051-1(6))* Hyperion Pr.

Willems, Mo & Harper, Charise Mericle. The Good for Nothing Button! Willems, Mo & Harper, Charise Mericle, illus. 2017. (Elephant & Piggie Like Reading! Ser.). (ENG., Illus.). 64p. (J). (gr. 1-3). 9.99 *(978-1-4847-2646-4(4))* Disney Pr.

Willems, Mo & Keller, Laurie. We Are Growing! Willems, Mo & Keller, Laurie, illus. 2016. (Elephant & Piggie Like Reading! Ser.). (ENG., Illus.). 64p. (J). (gr. 1-3). 9.99 *(978-1-4847-2635-8(9))* Hyperion Bks. for Children.

Willems, Mo & Scieszka, Jon, narrated by. Don't Let the Pigeon Drive the Bus! 2011. (J). (gr. -1-1). 29.95 *(978-0-545-13453-8(6))* Weston Woods Studios, Inc.

Williams, Maiya. Kaboom Academy. 2016. (ENG.). 240p. (J). (gr. 5). 6.99 *(978-0-449-81615-8(X),* Yearling) Random Hse. Children's Bks.

Williams, Vera B. A Chair for My Mother. 2007. (Reading Rainbow Bks.). (Illus.). 32p. (J). (gr. -1-3). 18.40 *(978-0-8085-3385-6(1),* Turtleback) Turtleback Bks.

Willis, Jeanne. I'M Sure I Saw a Dinosaur. Reynolds, Adrian, illus. 2011. (Andersen Press Picture Books Ser.). 16.95 *(978-0-7613-8093-1(0))* Andersen Pr. GBR. Dist: Lerner Publishing Group.

—Never Too Little to Love. Fearnley, Jan, illus. 2013. (ENG.). 32p. (J). (gr. -1-2). 8.99 *(978-0-7636-6656-9(4))* Candlewick Pr.

—Supercat vs the Pesky Pirate (Supercat, Book 3) 2015. (Supercat Ser.: 3). (ENG., Illus.). 224p. (J). pap. 5.99 *(978-0-00-812470-0(1),* HarperCollins Children's Bks.) HarperCollins Pubs. Ltd. GBR. Dist: HarperCollins Pubs.

Willis, Jeanne & Ross, Tony. Como Era Yo Cuando Era un Bebe? (Buenas Noches Ser.). (SPA., Illus.). (J). (gr. k-3). 8.95 *(978-958-04-6031-2(0))* Norma S.A. COL. Dist: Distribuidora Norma, Inc., Lectorum Pubns., Inc.

Willis, Jeanne, et al. The Best Bear in All the World. Burgess, Mark, illus. 2016. (Winnie-The-Pooh Ser.). (ENG.). 128p. (J). (gr. 3-7). 21.99 *(978-0-399-18747-6(2),* Dutton Books for Young Readers) Penguin Young Readers Group.

Willson, Sarah. Class Confusion. Dress, Robert, illus. 2006. (SpongeBob SquarePants Ser.: 11). (ENG.). 24p. (J). (gr. -1-3). pap. 3.99 *(978-1-4169-1239-2(8),* Simon Spotlight/Nickelodeon) Simon Spotlight/Nickelodeon.

—Just Say Please! Moore, Harry, illus. 2007. (SpongeBob SquarePants Ser.). (ENG.). 32p. (J). (gr. k-2). pap. 3.99 *(978-1-4169-4129-3(0),* Simon Spotlight/Nickelodeon) Simon Spotlight/Nickelodeon.

Wilson, Anna. Kitten Catastrophe. 2016. (Kitten Chaos Ser.: 3). (ENG., Illus.). 304p. (J). (gr. 4-7). pap. 9.99 *(978-1-5098-0466-5(8))* Pan Macmillan GBR. Dist: Independent Pubs. Group.

Wilson, Bryan M. Benjamin's Report Card Blues. 2011. 28p. pap. 12.95 *(978-1-4567-3530-2(6))* AuthorHouse.

Wilson, Karma. The Cow Loves Cookies. Hall, Marcellus, illus. 2010. (ENG.). 40p. (J). (gr. -1-3). 17.99 *(978-1-4169-4206-1(8),* McElderry, Margaret K. Bks.) McElderry, Margaret K. Bks.

—Duddle Puck: The Puddle Duck. Hall, Marcellus, illus. 2015. (ENG.). 40p. (J). (gr. -1-3). 17.99 *(978-1-4424-4927-5(6),* McElderry, Margaret K. Bks.) McElderry, Margaret K. Bks.

—Horseplay! McMullan, Jim, illus. 2012. (ENG.). 40p. (gr. -1-3). 16.99 *(978-0-316-93842-6(4))* Little Brown & Co.

Wilson, Rachel M. Don't Touch. 2014. (ENG.). 432p. (YA). (gr. 9). 17.99 *(978-0-06-222093-6(4),* HarperTeen) HarperCollins Pubs.

Winkler, Henry & Oliver, Lin. Barfing in the Backseat: How I Survived My Family Road Trip. Watson, Jesse Joshua, illus. 2007. (Hank Zipzer Ser.: No. 12). 152p. (gr. 4-7). 15.00 *(978-0-7569-8162-4(X))* Perfection Learning Corp.

—Bookmarks Are People Too! Garrett, Scott, illus. 2014. (Here's Hank Ser.: 1). (ENG.). 128p. (J). (gr. 1-3). 14.99 *(978-0-448-48239-2(8))*;No. 1. 5.99 *(978-0-448-47997-2(4))* Penguin Young Readers Group. (Grosset & Dunlap).

—Bookmarks Are People Too! 2014. (Here's Hank Ser.: 1). lib. bdg. 16.00 *(978-0-606-34142-4(0),* Turtleback) Turtleback Bks.

—A Brand-New Me! Watson, Jesse Joshua & Heitz, Tim, illus. 2010. (Hank Zipzer Ser.: 17). (ENG.). 160p. (J). (gr. 3-7). pap. 5.99 *(978-0-448-45210-4(3),* Grosset & Dunlap) Penguin Young Readers Group.

—The Curtain Went Up, My Pants Fell Down. Watson, Jesse Joshua, illus. 2007. (Hank Zipzer Ser.: 11). (ENG.). 160p. (J). (gr. 3-7). pap. 5.99 *(978-0-448-44267-9(1),* Grosset & Dunlap) Penguin Young Readers Group.

—Fake Snakes & Weird Wizards. Garrett, Scott, illus. 2015. (Here's Hank Ser.: No. 4). (ENG.). 128p. (J). (gr. 1-3). 5.99 *(978-0-448-48252-1(5),* Grosset & Dunlap) Penguin Young Readers Group.

—Help! Somebody Get Me Out of Fourth Grade! Watson, Jesse Joshua & Heitz, Tim, illus. 2004. (Hank Zipzer Ser.: 7). (ENG.). 160p, (J). (gr. 3-7). mass mkt. 5.99 *(978-0-448-43619-7(1),* Grosset & Dunlap) Penguin Young Readers Group.

—Holy Enchilada! Heyer, Carol et al, illus. 2004. (Hank Zipzer Ser.: 6). (ENG.). 160p. (J). (gr. 3-7). pap. 5.99 *(978-0-448-43353-0(2),* Grosset & Dunlap) Penguin Young Readers Group.

—I Got a D in Salami. Watson, Jesse Joshua et al, illus. 2004. (Hank Zipzer Ser.: 6). (ENG.). 176p. (J). (gr. 3-7). mass mkt. 5.99 *(978-0-448-43163-5(7),* Grosset & Dunlap) Penguin Young Readers Group.

—I Got a D in Salami. 2004. (Hank Zipzer Ser.: No. 2). 128p. (J). (gr. 2-6). pap. 29.00 incl. audio *(978-1-4000-9007-5(5),* Listening Library) Random Hse. Audio Publishing Group.

—The Life of Me (Enter at Your Own Risk) 2008. (Hank Zipzer Ser.: No. 14). (Illus.). 186p. (gr. 3-7). 16.00 *(978-0-7569-8819-7(5))* Perfection Learning Corp.

—My Dog's a Scaredy-Cat, 10 vols. Watson, Jesse Joshua, illus. 2006. (Hank Zipzer Ser.: 10). (ENG.). 160p. (J). (gr. 3-7). pap. 5.99 *(978-0-448-43878-8(X),* Grosset & Dunlap) Penguin Young Readers Group.

—Niagara Falls, or Does It? Watson, Jesse Joshua et al, illus. 2004. (Hank Zipzer Ser.: 1). (ENG.). 144p. (J). (gr. 3-7). pap. 5.99 *(978-0-448-43162-8(9),* Grosset & Dunlap) Penguin Young Readers Group.

—Niagara Falls, or Does It? 2004. (Hank Zipzer Ser.: No. 1). 128p. (J). (gr. 2-6). pap. 29.00 incl. audio *(978-1-4000-9006-8(7),* Listening Library) Random Hse. Audio Publishing Group.

—A Short Tale about a Long Dog. Garrett, Scott, illus. 2014. (Here's Hank Ser.: 2). (ENG.). 128p. (J). (gr. 1-3). 14.99 *(978-0-448-48240-8(1))*;No. 2. 5.99 *(978-0-448-47998-9(2))* Penguin Young Readers Group. (Grosset & Dunlap).

—A Short Tale about a Long Dog. 2014. (Here's Hank Ser.: 2). lib. bdg. 16.00 *(978-0-606-34143-1(9),* Turtleback) Turtleback Bks.

—Stop That Frog! Garrett, Scott, illus. 2014. (Here's Hank Ser.: 3). (ENG.). 128p. (J). (gr. 1-3). 5.99 *(978-0-448-48152-4(9))*; 14.99 *(978-0-448-48241-5(X))* Penguin Young Readers Group. (Grosset & Dunlap).

—Stop That Frog! 2014. (Here's Hank Ser.: 3). lib. bdg. 16.00 *(978-0-606-36161-3(8))* Turtleback Bks.

—Summer School! What Genius Thought That Up? Heyer, Carol, illus. 2005. (Hank Zipzer Ser.: 8). (ENG.). 160p. (J). (gr. 3-7). 14.99 *(978-0-448-43740-8(6),* Grosset & Dunlap) Penguin Young Readers Group.

—Summer School! What Genius Thought That Up?, 8 vols. Heyer, Carol et al, illus. 2005. (Hank Zipzer Ser.: 8). (ENG.). 160p. (J). (gr. 3-7). mass mkt. 5.99 *(978-0-448-43739-2(2),* Grosset & Dunlap) Penguin Young Readers Group.

—Summer School! What Genius Thought That Up? 2006. (Hank Zipzer Ser.: No. 8). (Illus.). 157p. (J). (gr. 3-9). lib. bdg. 24.21 *(978-1-59961-107-5(4))* Spotlight.

—Who Ordered This Baby? Definitely Not Me! 2007. (Hank Zipzer Ser.: No. 13). (Illus.). 152p. (gr. 4-7). 15.00 *(978-0-7569-8163-1(8))* Perfection Learning Corp.

—The Zippity Zinger, 4 vols. Heitz, Tim, illus. 2004. (Hank Zipzer Ser.: 4). (ENG.). 160p. (J). (gr. 3-7). mass mkt. 5.99 *(978-0-448-43193-2(9),* Grosset & Dunlap) Penguin Young Readers Group.

Winkler, Henry, et al. How to Hug an Elephant #6. Garrett, Scott, illus. 2015. (Here's Hank Ser.: 6). (ENG.). 128p. (J). (gr. 1-3). bds. 5.99 *(978-0-448-48656-7(3))*; bds. 14.99 *(978-0-448-48657-4(1))* Penguin Young Readers Group. (Grosset & Dunlap).

Wishinsky, Frieda. A Bee in Your Ear, 1 vol. Laliberté, Louise-Andrée, illus. 2004. (Orca Echoes Ser.). (ENG.). 64p. (J). (gr. 2-3). pap. 6.95 *(978-1-55143-324-0(9))* Orca Bk. Pubs. USA.

Wittlinger, Ellen. Hard Love. unabr. ed. 2004. 240p. (J). (gr. 7-18). pap. 38.00 incl. audio *(978-0-8072-0865-6(5),* LYA 283 SP, Listening Library) Random Hse. Audio Publishing Group.

Wohnoutka, Mike. Dad's First Day. Wohnoutka, Mike, illus. 2015. (ENG., Illus.). 40p. (J). (gr. -1-3). 16.99 *(978-1-61963-473-2(2),* 9781619634732, Bloomsbury USA Childrens) Bloomsbury Publishing USA.

Wojciechowski, Susan. Beany Goes to Camp. Natti, Susanna, illus. 2005. (Beany Adventures Ser.). 104p. (J). (gr. 4-7). 13.65 *(978-0-7569-6499-3(7))* Perfection Learning Corp.

Wolff, Kathy. What George Forgot. Byrne, Richard, illus. 2017. (ENG.). 32p. (J). 16.99 *(978-1-61963-871-6(1),* 9781619638716, Bloomsbury USA Childrens) Bloomsbury Publishing USA.

Wollman, Jessica. The Chipster's Sister. MacNeil, Chris, illus. 2005. (Penelope Fritter: Super-Sitter Ser.: 1). (ENG.). 128p. (J). (gr. 3-7). pap. 7.99 *(978-1-4169-0089-4(6),* Simon & Schuster/Paula Wiseman Bks.) Simon & Schuster/Paula Wiseman Bks.

—Meet the Phonees. MacNeil, Chris, illus. 2005. (Penelope Fritter: Super-Sitter Ser.: 2). (ENG.). 144p. (J). (gr. 3-7). pap. 4.99 *(978-1-4169-0090-0(X),* Aladdin) Simon & Schuster Children's Publishing.

Wood, Audrey. The Napping House. Wood, Don, illus. 2005. (ENG.). 16p. (J). (gr. k — 1). bds. 11.99 *(978-0-15-205620-9(3))* Houghton Mifflin Harcourt Publishing Co.

—Silly Sally. braille ed. 2004. (J). (gr. 1). spiral bd., bds. *(978-0-616-01864-4(9))* Canadian National Institute for the Blind/Institut National Canadien pour les Aveugles.

—Silly Sally: Lap-Sized Board Book. 2007. (ENG., Illus.). 30p. (J). (gr. -1-3). bds. 11.99 *(978-0-15-205902-6(4))* Houghton Mifflin Harcourt Publishing Co.

Wood, Douglas. When Mama Mirabelle Comes Home. Wagner, Andy, illus. 2007. (ENG.). 32p. (J). (gr. -1-2). 16.95 *(978-1-4263-0194-0(4))*; 24.90 *(978-1-4263-0195-7(2))* National Geographic Society. (National Geographic Children's Bks.).

Wood, Maryrose. The Incorrigible Children of Ashton Place Bk. IV: The Interrupted Tale. Wheeler, Eliza, illus. 2013. (Incorrigible Children of Ashton Place Ser.: 4). (ENG.). 400p. (J). (gr. 3-7). 16.99 *(978-0-06-179122-2(9))* HarperCollins Pubs.

—The Unmapped Sea Bk. 5. Wheeler, Eliza, illus. 2015. (Incorrigible Children of Ashton Place Ser.: 5). (ENG.). 416p. (J). (gr. 3-7). 15.99 *(978-0-06-211041-1(1))* HarperCollins Pubs.

Wood, Nancy. Mr. & Mrs. God in the Creation Kitchen. Ering, Timothy Basil, illus. 2006. (ENG.). 32p. (J). (gr. k-4). 16.99 *(978-0-7636-1258-0(8))* Candlewick Pr.

Woodard, Amy. The Day the Teacher Rode a Horse to School. 2008. 24p. pap. 24.95 *(978-1-60441-736-4(6))* America Star Bks.

Woodrow, Allan. Class Dismissed. 2017. (ENG.). 272p. (J). (gr. 3-7). pap. 6.99 ***(978-0-545-80072-3(2),*** Scholastic Paperbacks) Scholastic, Inc.

Woodward, Kay. Sleeping Handsome & the Princess Engineer. de Ruiter, Jo, illus. 2015. (Fairy Tales Today Ser.). (ENG.). 24p. (gr. 1-2). 23.99 *(978-1-4795-8615-8(3))* Picture Window Bks.

Worm, Piet. Three Little Horses. 2007. (Illus.). 61p. (J). (gr. -1-3). 18.95 *(978-1-930900-36-3(8))* Purple Hse. Pr.

Worthington, Lisa & Moon, Susan. People Do Silly Things. Totire, Valerie, illus. 2003. (ENG.). 16p. (gr. k-2). pap. 7.95 *(978-1-57874-037-6(1),* Kaeden Bks.) Kaeden Corp.

Wright, Bud. My Momma Raised Ugly Children Not Stupid Ones: The Ruminations & Reminiscences of a Gentle Southern Man. 2008. 332p. pap. 22.95 *(978-1-4327-2880-9(6))* Outskirts Pr., Inc.

Wright, Joshua. Hapless, Hopeless, Horrible. 2004. (ENG., Illus.). 192p. (J). (gr. 3-8). pap. 11.99 *(978-1-74114-082-8(X))* Allen & Unwin AUS. Dist: Independent Pubs. Group.

Wright, Maureen. Sleep, Big Bear, Sleep!, 0 vols. Hillenbrand, Will, illus. 2009. (ENG.). 32p. (J). (gr. -1-3). 16.99 *(978-0-7614-5560-8(4),* 9780761455608, Amazon Children's Publishing) Amazon Publishing.

Wronski, Gareth. Holly Farb & the Princess of the Galaxy. 2017. (ENG., Illus.). 320p. (J). (gr. 3-7). 16.99 ***(978-1-4814-7177-0(5),*** Aladdin) Simon & Schuster Children's Publishing.

Yankovic, Al, pseud. My New Teacher & Me! Hargis, Wes, illus. 2013. (ENG.). 40p. (J). (gr. -1-3). 17.99 *(978-0-06-219203-5(5))* HarperCollins Pubs.

—When I Grow Up. Hargis, Wes, illus. 2011. (ENG.). 32p. (J). (gr. -1-3). 17.99 *(978-0-06-192691-4(4))* HarperCollins Pubs.

Yeoman, John. The Wild Washerwomen. Blake, Quentin, illus. 2009. (Andersen Press Picture Bks). (ENG.). 32p. (J). (gr. k-3). 16.95 *(978-0-7613-5152-8(3))* Lerner Publishing Group.

Yolen, Jane. ¿Cómo Comen los Dinosaurios? Teague, Mark, illus. 2006. (How Do Dinosaurs... Ser.). (SPA.). 40p. (J). (gr. -1-k). pap. 6.99 *(978-0-439-76404-9(1),* Scholastic en Espanol) Scholastic, Inc.

Yorinks, Arthur. Company's Going. (J). pap. 14.99 *(978-0-06-205125-7(3))* HarperCollins Pubs.

—The Invisible Man. Cushman, Doug, illus. 2011. (ENG.). 32p. (J). (gr. -1-3). 16.99 *(978-0-06-156148-1(7))* HarperCollins Pubs.

Yorinks, Arthur, et al. Company's Going. Date not set. (J). lib. bdg. 15.89 *(978-0-06-205126-4(1))* HarperCollins Pubs.

Yost-Filgate, Susan. Rip Squeak & His Friends. Filgate, Leonard, illus. 2004. 32p. (J). 16.95 *(978-1-59384-058-7(6))* Parklane Publishing.

Young, Jessica. Original Recipe. Secheret, Jessica, illus. 2015. (Finley Flowers Ser.). (ENG.). 128p. (gr. 2-3). 8.95 *(978-1-4795-5878-0(8),* Finley Flowers) Picture Window Bks.

—Spy Guy: The Not-So-Secret Agent. Santoso, Charles, illus. 2015. (ENG.). 40p. (J). (gr. -1-3). 16.99 *(978-0-544-20859-9(5),* HMH Books For Young Readers) Houghton Mifflin Harcourt Publishing Co.

Young, Kirk. The Chronicles of His Excellency: Almost-an-Eighth-of-a-Memoir. 2003. 120p. (YA). pap. 12.95 *(978-0-595-27583-0(4),* Writers Advantage Pr.) iUniverse, Inc.

Young, Steve. Winchell Mink: The Misadventure Begins. 2004. 144p. (J). 16.89 *(978-0-06-053500-1(8))* HarperCollins Pubs.

Young, Timothy. I Hate Picture Books!, 1 vol. 2013. (ENG., Illus.). 32p. (J). 16.99 *(978-0-7643-4387-2(4),* 9780764343872) Schiffer Publishing, Ltd.

Yourgrau, Barry. Another Nastybook: The Curse of the Tweeties. DeJesus, Robert, illus. 2006. 171p. (J). (gr. 5-9). lib. bdg. 13.89 *(978-0-06-057982-1(X),* Cotler, Joanna Books) HarperCollins Pubs.

—Nasty Book. 2005. (ENG.). 192p. (J). (gr. 5-9). 11.99 *(978-0-06-057978-4(1))* HarperCollins Pubs.

—NASTYbook. 2005. 192p. (J). (gr. k-9). lib. bdg. 13.89 *(978-0-06-057979-1(X))* HarperCollins Pubs.

—Nastybook. 2007. (ENG.). 192p. (J). (gr. 5-9). pap. 5.99 *(978-0-06-057980-7(3),* Harper Trophy) HarperCollins Pubs.

Zann, Tara. Wild Child: Forest's First Home. Ermos, George & Widdowson, Dan, illus. 2017. (Wild Child Ser.: 1). (ENG.). 144p. (J). pap. 5.99 *(978-1-250-10383-3(5),* 9781250103833) Imprint IND. Dist: Macmillan.

Zeitlin, Meredith. Freshman Year & Other Unnatural Disasters. 2013. (ENG.). 288p. (YA). (gr. 7). pap. 8.99 *(978-0-14-242421-6(8),* Speak) Penguin Young Readers Group.

Zellerhoff, Christi. Princesses Can Be Pirates Too! Davis, Amy, illus. 2012. 38p. 17.99 *(978-1-935961-68-0(3))*; pap. 8.99 *(978-1-935961-95-6(0))* Booktrope. (Booktrope Editions).

Zeltser, David. Ninja Baby. Goode, Diane, illus. 2015. (ENG.). 32p. (J). (gr. -1-k). 16.99 *(978-1-4521-3542-7(8))* Chronicle Bks. LLC.

Zenz, Aaron. The Hiccupotamus, 0 vols. 2009. (ENG.). 32p. (J). (gr. -1-2). 12.99 *(978-0-7614-5622-3(8),* 9780761456223, Amazon Children's Publishing) Amazon Publishing.

Zepf, Máire. Don't Go to School! Krüse, Tarsila, illus. 2017. (ENG.). 40p. (J). (gr. -1). 14.95 ***(978-1-4549-2359-6(8))*** Sterling Publishing Co., Inc.

Zettler, Andrew. The Teeniest Tiniest Yawn. Zettler, Andrew, illus. l.t. ed. 2014. (ENG., Illus.). 36p. (J). 17.99 *(978-0-9912370-0-5(5))* Royal Penny Pr., The.

Ziegler, Jennifer. Revenge of the Angels. 2015. (ENG.). 256p. (J). (gr. 3-7). 16.99 *(978-0-545-83899-3(1),* Scholastic Pr.) Scholastic, Inc.

Ziegler, Jennifer. Revenge of the Happy Campers. 2017. (Brewster Triplets Ser.). (ENG.). 272p. (J). (gr. 3-7). 16.99 ***(978-1-338-09119-9(0),*** Scholastic Pr.) Scholastic, Inc.

Zimet, Sara Goodman. Hannah & the Perfect Picture Pony: A Story of the Great Depression. Fuller, Sandy Ferguson, illus. 2005. 24p. (J). lib. bdg. 16.95 *(978-0-9645159-2-5(X))* Discovery Pr. Pubns., Inc.

Zimmer, Elizabeth & Zimmer, Eric. The Turtle & the Deep Blue Sky. 2007. (ENG., Illus.). 32p. (J). (gr. -1-3). 12.95 *(978-1-55591-597-1(3))* Fulcrum Publishing.

Zion, Gene. Harry the Dirty Dog. Graham, Margaret Bloy, illus. 50th ed. 2006. (ENG.). 34p. (J). (gr. -1-3). bds. 7.99 *(978-0-06-084244-4(X),* HarperFestival) HarperCollins Pubs.

Zondervan Staff & Poth, Karen. Junior Comes Clean, 1 vol. 2013. (I Can Read! / Big Idea Books / VeggieTales Ser.). (ENG.). 32p. (J). pap. 3.99 *(978-0-310-73208-2(5))* Zonderkidz.

—LarryBoy & the Mudslingers, 1 vol. 2013. (I Can Read! / Big Idea Books / VeggieTales Ser.). (ENG.). 32p. (J). pap. 3.99 *(978-0-310-73214-3(X))* Zonderkidz.

HUMPHREY, HUBERT H. (HUBERT HORATIO), 1911-1978

Birney, Betty G. Humphrey's Creepy-Crawly Camping Adventure. Burris, Priscilla, illus. 2015. (Humphrey's Tiny Tales Ser.: 3). (ENG.). 96p. (J). (gr. k-3). 4.99 *(978-0-14-751459-2(2),* Puffin Books) Penguin Young Readers Group.

HUNDRED YEARS' WAR, 1339-1453

Lace, William W. Joan of Arc & the Hundred Years' War in World History. 2003. (In World History Ser.). (Illus.). 128p. (J). (gr. 5-12). lib. bdg. 27.94 *(978-0-7660-1938-6(1))* Enslow Pubs., Inc.

Whiting, Jim. The Life & Times of Joan of Arc. 2005. (Biography from Ancient Civilizations Ser.). (Illus.). 48p. (J). (gr. 4-8). lib. bdg. 29.95 *(978-1-58415-345-0(8))* Mitchell Lane Pubs., Inc.

HUNDRED YEARS' WAR, 1339-1453—FICTION

Russell, Christopher. Dogboy. 2006. 272p. (J). (gr. 5). 15.99 *(978-0-06-084116-4(8),* Greenwillow Bks.) HarperCollins Pubs.

HUNGARIANS—UNITED STATES—FICTION

Konigsburg, E. L. The Outcasts of 19 Schuyler Place. 2004. (ENG.). 304p. (J). (gr. 5-9). 16.95 *(978-0-689-86636-4(4),* Atheneum Bks. for Young Readers) Simon & Schuster Children's Publishing.

HUNGARY

Bisson, Michelle. Hedy's Journey The True Story of a Hungarian Girl Fleeing the Holocaust. Ramon, El Primo, illus. 2017. (Encounter: Narrative Nonfiction Picture Bks.). (ENG.). 40p. (gr. 5-6). 15.95 ***(978-1-5157-8222-3(0))*** Encounter Bks.

Bjorklund, Ruth. Hungary. 2016. (Enchantment of the World Ser.). (ENG., Illus.). 144p. (J). lib. bdg. 40.00 *(978-0-531-23295-8(6),* Children's Pr.) Scholastic Library Publishing.

Brimson, Samuel. Hungary-Kiribati, 8 vols., Vol. 4. 2003. (Nations of the World Ser.: Vol. 4). (Illus.). 64p. (gr. 5-12). lib. bdg. 31.00 *(978-0-8368-5488-6(8),* Gareth Stevens Secondary Library) Stevens, Gareth Publishing LLLP.

Docalavich, Heather. Hungary. 2007. (European Union Ser.). (Illus.). 88p. (YA). (gr. 3-7). lib. bdg. 21.95 *(978-1-4222-0050-6(7),* 1248003) Mason Crest.

Stalcup, Ann. Hungary. 2005. (Enchantment of the World Ser.). (ENG., Illus.). 144p. (YA). (gr. 5-9). 39.00 *(978-0-516-23683-4(0))* Scholastic Library Publishing.

Tresco, Betsy Dru. How to Draw Hungary's Sights & Symbols. 2009. (Kid's Guide to Drawing the Countries of the World Ser.). 48p. (gr. 4-4). 53.00 *(978-1-61511-112-1(3),* PowerKids Pr.) Rosen Publishing Group, Inc., The.

HUNGARY—FICTION

Bentley, Dawn & Studio Mouse Staff. Tyrannosaurus Rex. Carr, Karen, illus. 2008. (ENG.). 24p. (J). (gr. 3-7). 4.99 *(978-1-59069-621-7(2))* Studio Mouse LLC.

Cheng, Andrea. The Bear Makers. 2008. (ENG., Illus.). 176p. (J). (gr. 6-9). 16.95 *(978-1-59078-518-8(5),* Front Street) Boyds Mills Pr.

—The Lace Dowry. 2005. (ENG.). 115p. (J). (gr. 6-9). 16.95 *(978-1-932425-20-8(9),* Lemniscaat) Boyds Mills Pr.

Clark, Kathy. Guardian Angel House, 1 vol. 2009. (Holocaust Remembrance Ser.). (ENG., Illus.). 180p. (J). (gr. 4-8). pap. 14.95 *(978-1-897187-58-6(0))* Second Story Pr. CAN. Dist: Orca Bk. Pubs. USA.

Hippely, Hilary Horder. A Song for Lena. Baker, Leslie, illus. 2011. (ENG.). 40p. (J). (gr. -1-3). 19.99 *(978-1-4424-2946-8(1),* Simon & Schuster Bks. For Young Readers) Simon & Schuster Bks. For Young Readers.

Lobel, Anita. 10 Hungry Rabbits: Counting & Color Concepts. Bowers, Tim, illus. 2012. (ENG.). 24p. (J). (gr. k-k). 9.99 *(978-0-375-86864-1(X),* Knopf Bks. for Young Readers) Random Hse. Children's Bks.

Seredy, Kate. The Chestry Oak. 2015. (Illus.). 253p. (J). pap. 12.95 *(978-1-930900-81-3(3))* Purple Hse. Pr.

Watkins, Dawn L. Zoli's Legacy (Christian Fiction) 2003. (Illus.). 297p. (J). pap. 9.95 *(978-1-57924-763-8(6))* BJU Pr.

Wiseman, Eva. Kanada. 2006. (ENG., Illus.). 264p. (YA). (gr. 5). pap. 9.95 *(978-0-88776-729-6(X),* Tundra Bks.) Tundra Bks. CAN. Dist: Penguin Random Hse. LLC.

—Puppet. 2012. (ENG., Illus.). 248p. (YA). (gr. 5). pap. 9.95 *(978-1-77049-296-7(8),* Tundra Bks.) Tundra Bks. CAN. Dist: Penguin Random Hse. LLC.

HUNGARY—HISTORY

Docalavich, Heather & Indovino, Shaina Carmel. Hungary. 2012. (J). *(978-1-4222-2245-4(4));* pap. *(978-1-4222-2276-8(4))* Mason Crest.

Dyan, Penelope. Over a Bridge! a Kid's Guide to Budapest, Hungary. Weigand, John D., photos by. 2013. (Illus.). 38p. pap. 11.95 *(978-1-61477-071-8(9))* Bellissima Publishing, LLC.

Esbenshade, Richard S. & Nevins, Debbie. Hungary. 2015. (Cultures of the World (r) Ser.). (ENG., Illus.). 144p. (J). (gr. 5-5). 47.07 *(978-1-5026-0338-8(1))* Cavendish Square Publishing.

Guillain, Charlotte. Hungary, 1 vol. 2011. (Countries Around the World Ser.). (ENG.). 48p. (gr. 3-6). pap. 9.95 *(978-1-4329-5231-0(5));* 33.32 *(978-1-4329-5206-8(4))* Heinemann-Raintree. (NA-h).

Idzikowski, Lisa. Raoul Wallenberg: Rescuer of Hungarian Jews During the Holocaust. 2017. (J). ***(978-1-5383-8118-2(4));*** pap. ***(978-1-5383-8117-5(6))*** Rosen Publishing Group, Inc., The.

Kor, Eva Mozes & Buccieri, Lisa Rojany. Surviving the Angel of Death: The True Story of a Mengele Twin in Auschwitz. 2012. (ENG.). 175p. (J). (gr. 6). pap. 8.95 *(978-1-933718-57-6(9))* Tanglewood Pr.

—Surviving the Angel of Death: The True Story of a Mengele Twin in Auschwitz. 2012. lib. bdg. 19.60 *(978-0-606-23838-0(7),* Turtleback) Turtleback Bks.

Kor, Eva Mozes, et al. Surviving the Angel of Death: The Story of a Mengele Twin in Auschwitz. 2009. (ENG., Illus.). 141p. (J). (gr. 6-18). 14.95 *(978-1-933718-28-6(5))* Tanglewood Pr.

Owings, Lisa. Hungary. 2015. (Exploring Countries Ser.). (ENG., Illus.). 32p. (J). (gr. 3-7). lib. bdg. 26.95 *(978-1-62617-175-6(0),* Blastoff! Readers) Bellwether Media.

HUNGARY—HISTORY—REVOLUTION, 1956

Kalman, Bobbie. Refugee Child: My Memories of the 1956 Hungarian Revolution. Bedell, Barbara, illus. 2006. (ENG.). 224p. (J). (gr. 3-7). lib. bdg. *(978-0-7787-2760-6(2))* Crabtree Publishing Co.

—Refugee Child Activity Guide. 2006. (ENG., Illus.). 32p. (J). (gr. 3-7). bds. *(978-0-7787-2759-0(9))* Crabtree Publishing Co.

HUNS

Britton, Arthur K. Attila the Hun. 2016. (History's Most Murderous Villains Ser.). (Illus.). 32p. (J). (gr. 5-4). pap. 10.50 *(978-1-4824-4780-4(0))* Stevens, Gareth Publishing LLLP.

Hinds, Kathryn. Huns. 2009. (Barbarians! Ser.). 80p. (gr. 6). 35.64 *(978-0-7614-4066-6(6))* Marshall Cavendish GBR. Dist: Marshall Cavendish Corp.

Price, Sean Stewart & Price, Sean. Attila the Hun: Leader of the Barbarian Hordes. 2009. (Wicked History Ser.). (ENG.). 128p. (J). (gr. 6-12). pap. 5.95 *(978-0-531-20737-6(4),* Watts, Franklin) Scholastic Library Publishing.

Rice, Earle. The Life & Times of Attila the Hun. 2009. (Biography from Ancient Civilizations Ser.). 48p. (J). (gr. 4-8). 29.95 *(978-1-58415-741-0(0))* Mitchell Lane Pubs., Inc.

HUNS—FICTION

Griffin, Philip. Ursula's Maiden Army. 2006. 287p. per. 14.95 *(978-0-9749610-1-9(9))* Beagle Bay Bks.

Slade, Arthur. Villainology: Fabulous Lives of the Big, the Bad, & the Wicked. Mah, Derek, illus. 2007. (ENG.). 96p. (J). (gr. 4-7). per. 9.95 *(978-0-88776-809-5(1),* Tundra Bks.) Tundra Bks. CAN. Dist: Penguin Random Hse. LLC.

HUNTING

see also Falconry; Game and Game Birds; Game Protection; Tracking and Trailing; Trapping

Adamson, Thomas K. Bowhunting, 1 vol. 2010. (Wild Outdoors Ser.). (ENG.). 32p. (gr. 1-2). lib. bdg. 26.65 *(978-1-4296-4808-0(2),* Blazers) Capstone Press of Coughlan Cos.

The Advantage Max-4 HD Waterfowl Coloring & Activity Book. 2003. (J). pap. *(978-0-9745863-0-4(7))* Cypress Knees Publishing.

Arnosky, Jim. Wild Tracks! A Guide to Nature's Footprints. 2015. (ENG., Illus.). 32p. (J). (gr. 1-5). pap. 6.95 *(978-1-4549-1472-3(6))* Sterling Publishing Co., Inc.

Bear Hunting in Alaska: The Brown & Grizzly Bear Hunter's Guide. 2004. (Illus.). 280p. bds. 30.00 *(978-0-9741684-0-1(8))* Northern Publishing.

Bestful, Scott & Hurteau, Dave. Field & Stream's Guide to Hunting Whitetail. The Editors of Field & Stream, ed. 2015. (Field & Stream's Guide to the Outdoors Ser.). (ENG., Illus.). 96p. (J). (gr. 6-8). lib. bdg. 35.95 *(978-1-4824-3187-2(4),* 1390565) Stevens, Gareth Publishing LLLP.

Boddington, Craig. Buffalo! 2010. (ENG.). 248p. 39.95 *(978-1-57157-354-4(2))* Safari Pr., Inc.

Bowen, Betsy. Tracks in the Wild. 2015. (Fesler-Lampert Minnesota Heritage Ser.). (ENG., Illus.). 32p. (J). 19.95 *(978-0-8166-9883-7(X))* Univ. of Minnesota Pr.

Bringle, Jennifer. Wing Shooting. 2011. (Hunting: Pursuing Wild Game! Ser.). 64p. (YA). (ENG.). pap. 12.95 *(978-1-4488-2271-3(8),* Rosen Reference); (Illus.). (gr. 5-9). lib. bdg. 31.95 *(978-1-4488-1241-7(0))* Rosen Publishing Group, Inc., The.

Browne, Bellmore H. Hunting & Shooting: A Vintage Classic. Beard, Daniel, ed. 2017. (ENG.). 112p. (J). pap. 8.95 *(978-0-486-81327-1(4))* Dover Pubns., Inc.

Bruce, Julia. Hunt! Can You Survive the Stone Age? Dennis, Peter, illus. 2009. (Step into History Ser.). 32p. (J). (gr. 2-5). lib. bdg. 23.94 *(978-0-7660-3476-1(3))* Enslow Pubs., Inc.

Canino, Kate. Turkey Hunting. 2011. (Hunting: Pursuing Wild Game! Ser.). 64p. (YA). (ENG.). pap. 12.95 *(978-1-4488-2274-4(2),* Rosen Reference); (Illus.). (gr. 5-9). lib. bdg. 31.95 *(978-1-4488-1244-8(5))* Rosen Publishing Group, Inc., The.

Carpenter, Tom. Bear Hunting, 1 vol. 2016. (ENG., Illus.). 48p. (J). *(978-1-62403-831-0(X),* 1391416, SportsZone) ABDO Publishing Co.

—Big Game Hunting: Bear, Deer, Elk, Sheep, & More. 2012. (Great Outdoors Sports Zone Ser.). (ENG., Illus.). 32p. (gr. 4-8). lib. bdg. 26.60 *(978-1-4677-0222-5(6),* Lerner Pubns.) Lerner Publishing Group.

—Bowhunting, 1 vol. 2016. (ENG., Illus.). 48p. (J). *(978-1-62403-832-7(8),* 1391417, SportsZone) ABDO Publishing Co.

—Pheasant Hunting, 1 vol. 2016. (ENG., Illus.). 48p. *(978-1-62403-835-8(2))* ABDO Publishing Co.

—Small-Game Hunting, 1 vol. 2016. (ENG., Illus.). 48p. (J). *(978-1-62403-836-5(0),* 1391423, SportsZone) ABDO Publishing Co.

—Small Game Hunting: Rabbit, Raccoon, Squirrel, Opossum, & More. 2012. (Great Outdoors Sports Zone Ser.). (ENG., Illus.). 32p. (gr. 4-8). lib. bdg. 26.60 *(978-1-4677-0224-9(2),* Lerner Pubns.) Lerner Publishing Group.

—Upland Bird Hunting: Wild Turkey, Pheasant, Grouse, Quail, & More. 2012. (Great Outdoors Sports Zone Ser.). (ENG., Illus.). 32p. (gr. 4-8). lib. bdg. 26.60 *(978-1-4677-0223-2(4),* Lerner Pubns.) Lerner Publishing Group.

—Waterfowl Hunting: Duck, Goose, & More. 2012. (Great Outdoors Sports Zone Ser.). (ENG., Illus.). 32p. (gr. 4-8). lib. bdg. 26.60 *(978-1-4677-0221-8(8),* Lerner Pubns.) Lerner Publishing Group.

Chandler, Matt. Bear Hunting for Kids, 1 vol. 2013. (Into the Great Outdoors Ser.). (ENG.). 32p. (gr. 3-4). pap. 7.95 *(978-1-62065-693-8(0));* lib. bdg. 27.99 *(978-1-4296-9901-3(9))* Capstone Press of Coughlan Cos.

—Deer Hunting for Kids, 1 vol. 2012. (Into the Great Outdoors Ser.). (ENG., Illus.). 32p. (gr. 3-4). lib. bdg. 27.99 *(978-1-4296-8425-5(9),* Edge Bks.) Capstone Press of Coughlan Cos.

Chandler, Matthew Allan. Deer Hunting for Kids, 1 vol. 2012. (Into the Great Outdoors Ser.). (ENG., Illus.). 32p. (gr. 3-4). pap. 7.95 *(978-1-4296-9267-0(7),* Edge Bks.) Capstone Press of Coughlan Cos.

Clarke, Nadine. Get Bushwise: on Safari Desert, River, Bushveld: A Young Explorer's Guide. 2013. 192p. pap. 23.00 *(978-1-4317-0206-0(4))* Penguin Random House Grupo Editorial ESP. Dist: Casemate Pubs. & Bk. Distributors, LLC.

Complete Guide to Hunting, 3 vols., Set. (Illus.). 96,112p. (YA). (gr. 7-18). lib. bdg. *(978-1-59084-499-1(8))* Mason Crest.

DiLorenzo, Michael A. Bows, Does & Bucks! An Introduction to Archery Deer Hunting. Julich, Jenniffer, illus. 2010. 88p. (J). 19.95 *(978-0-9777210-2-3(7))* Running Moose Publications.

Doeden, Matt. Duck Hunting. 2017. (Great Outdoors Ser.). (ENG., Illus.). 32p. (J). (gr. 1-3). pap. 9.99 *(978-1-68152-077-3(X))* Amicus.

—Duck Hunting. 2016. (Great Outdoors Ser.). (ENG., Illus.). 32p. (J). (gr. 1-4). 20.95 *(978-1-60753-798-4(2))* Amicus Publishing.

Editors of Kingfisher. Extreme Hunters: Come Face to Face with Nature's Deadliest Killers. 2016. (Fast Facts Ser.). (ENG., Illus.). 32p. (J). pap. 6.99 *(978-0-7534-7246-0(5),* 9780753472460, Kingfisher) Roaring Brook Pr.

Frazel, Ellen. Bow Hunting. 2013. (Outdoor Adventures Ser.). (ENG., Illus.). 24p. (J). (gr. 3-8). lib. bdg. 25.95 *(978-1-60014-889-7(1),* Pilot Bks.) Bellwether Media.

Ganeri, Anita. How to Live Like a Stone-Age Hunter. Epelbaum, Mariano, illus. 2015. (How to Live Like... Ser.). (ENG.). 32p. (J). (gr. 3-6). pap. 7.99 *(978-1-4677-7207-5(0));* lib. bdg. 26.65 *(978-1-4677-6352-3(7))* Lerner Publishing Group.

Gaspar, Joe & Weaver, Jack. Hunting, 01 vols., 1. 2016. (Outdoor Life Ser.). (ENG., Illus.). 64p. (J). 32.95 *(978-1-4994-6237-1(9),* Rosen Young Adult) Rosen Publishing Group, Inc., The.

Gilmore, Kaylee. We're Going Small-Game Hunting. 2016. (Hunting & Fishing: a Kid's Guide Ser.). 00032p. (J). (gr. 3-3). pap. 10.00 *(978-1-4994-2747-9(6),* PowerKids Pr.) Rosen Publishing Group, Inc., The.

Green, Sara. Turkey Hunting. 2014. (Outdoor Adventures Ser.). (ENG., Illus.). 24p. (J). (gr. 3-8). lib. bdg. 25.95 *(978-1-62617-086-5(X),* Pilot Bks.) Bellwether Media.

Gurtler, Janet. Small Game. (J). 2016. ***(978-1-4896-5722-0(3))*** 2012. *(978-1-61913-504-8(3))* 2012. pap. *(978-1-61913-508-6(6))* Weigl Pubs., Inc.

Hackenberg, Richard. Moose Hunting in Alaska: The Secrets to Success. Russ, Tony & O'Loughlin, Diane, eds. 2003. (Illus.). 280p. per. 22.95 *(978-0-9639869-9-3(6))* Northern Publishing.

Hahn, Michael T. Dad's Deer Tactics 1000: Tom Hahn's Hunting Secrets Revealed by His Son. Hahn, Michael T., photos by. unabr. ed. 2003. (Illus.). 295p. (YA). pap. 19.95 *(978-0-9721716-0-1(6),* 1) In Cider Pr.

Hardyman, Robyn. Hunting. 2013. (Adventures in the Great Outdoors Ser.). (ENG., Illus.). 32p. (J). (gr. 3-6). pap. 11.75 *(978-1-61533-813-9(6),* PowerKids Pr.) Rosen Publishing Group, Inc., The.

—Hunting. 2013. (Adventures in the Great Outdoors Ser.). 32p. (J). (gr. 3-6). 26.50 *(978-1-61533-748-4(2));* pap. 70.50 *(978-1-61533-814-6(4))* Windmill Bks.

Hemstock, Annie Wendt. Bow Hunting. 2014. (Open Season Ser.). 32p. (J). (gr. 4-6). lib. bdg. 26.25 *(978-1-4777-6715-3(0),* PowerKids Pr.) Rosen Publishing Group, Inc., The.

—Hunting Gear. 2014. (Open Season Ser.). 32p. (J). (gr. 4-6). lib. bdg. 26.25 *(978-1-4777-6730-6(4),* PowerKids Pr.) Rosen Publishing Group, Inc., The.

—Hunting Laws & Safety. 2014. (Open Season Ser.). 32p. (J). (gr. 4-6). lib. bdg. 26.25 *(978-1-4777-6725-2(8),* PowerKids Pr.) Rosen Publishing Group, Inc., The.

—Hunting with Rifles. 2014. (Open Season Ser.). 32p. (J). (gr. 4-6). lib. bdg. 26.25 *(978-1-4777-6710-8(X),* PowerKids Pr.) Rosen Publishing Group, Inc., The.

—Hunting with Shotguns. 2014. (Open Season Ser.). (Illus.). 32p. (J). (gr. 4-6). lib. bdg. 26.25 *(978-1-4777-6705-4(3),* PowerKids Pr.) Rosen Publishing Group, Inc., The.

—Know Your Quarry. 2014. (Open Season Ser.). 32p. (J). (gr. 4-6). lib. bdg. 26.25 *(978-1-4777-6720-7(7),* PowerKids Pr.) Rosen Publishing Group, Inc., The.

Hester, Beth Landis. Hunting, Vol. 10. 2016. (Great Outdoors! Ser.: Vol. 10). (ENG., Illus.). 48p. (J). (gr. 5-8). 20.95 *(978-1-4222-3571-3(8))* Mason Crest.

Howard, Melanie A. Bowhunting for Kids, 1 vol. 2012. (Into the Great Outdoors Ser.). (ENG., Illus.). 32p. (gr. 3-4). pap. 7.95 *(978-1-4296-9265-6(0));* lib. bdg. 27.99 *(978-1-4296-8424-8(0))* Capstone Press of Coughlan Cos.

Hunters. (Amazing Animals Ser.). 32p. (J). (gr. 1). pap. *(978-1-882210-78-7(6))* Action Publishing, Inc.

Hunting: Pursuing Wild Game!, 6 vols., Set. Incl. Big Game Hunting. Peterson, Judy Monroe. lib. bdg. 31.95 *(978-1-4488-1240-0(2));* Small Game Hunting. Peterson, Judy Monroe. lib. bdg. 31.95 *(978-1-4488-1242-4(9));* Turkey Hunting. Canino, Kate. lib. bdg. 31.95 *(978-1-4488-1244-8(5));* Varmint Hunting. Peterson, Judy Monroe. lib. bdg. 31.95 *(978-1-4488-1245-5(3));* Water Fowl. Wolny, Philip. lib. bdg. 31.95 *(978-1-4488-1243-1(7));* Wing Shooting. Bringle, Jennifer. lib. bdg. 31.95 *(978-1-4488-1241-7(0));* (YA). (gr. 5-9). 2011. (Hunting: Pursuing Wild Game! Ser.). (Illus.). 64p. 2011. Set lib. bdg. 175.50 *(978-1-4488-1389-6(1),* Rosen Reference) Rosen Publishing Group, Inc., The.

Hunting & Fishing: A Kid's Guide. 2016. (Hunting & Fishing: a Kid's Guide Ser.). 00032p. (J). (gr. 3-3). 157.50 *(978-1-4994-2648-9(8),* PowerKids Pr.) Rosen Publishing Group, Inc., The.

Keoke, Emory Dean & Porterfield, Kay Marie. Food, Farming, & Hunting. 2005. (American Indian Contributions to the World Ser.). (Illus.). 160p. (gr. 5-8). 35.00 *(978-0-8160-5393-3(6))* Facts On File, Inc.

Klein, Adam G. Hunting, 1 vol. 2008. (Outdoor Adventure! Ser.). (ENG., Illus.). 32p. (gr. k-6). 27.07 *(978-1-59928-960-1(1),* Checkerboard Library) ABDO Publishing Co.

Lambert, Hines. Hunting Deer. 2013. (Let's Go Hunting Ser.). (ENG., Illus.). 32p. (J). (gr. 4-6). pap. 10.00 *(978-1-4488-9776-6(9));* lib. bdg. 25.25 *(978-1-4488-9659-2(2))* Rosen Publishing Group, Inc., The. (PowerKids Pr.).

—Hunting Moose & Elk. 2013. (Let's Go Hunting Ser.). (ENG., Illus.). 32p. (J). (gr. 4-6). pap. 10.00 *(978-1-4488-9784-1(X));* lib. bdg. 25.25 *(978-1-4488-9663-9(0))* Rosen Publishing Group, Inc., The. (PowerKids Pr.).

—Hunting Quail & Pheasants. 2013. (Let's Go Hunting Ser.). (ENG., Illus.). 32p. (J). (gr. 4-6). 25.25 *(978-1-4488-9664-6(9));* pap. 10.00 *(978-1-4488-9786-5(6))* Rosen Publishing Group, Inc., The. (PowerKids Pr.).

—Hunting Rabbits. 2013. (Let's Go Hunting Ser.). (ENG., Illus.). 32p. (J). (gr. 4-6). 25.25 *(978-1-4488-9662-2(2));* pap. 10.00 *(978-1-4488-9782-7(3))* Rosen Publishing Group, Inc., The. (PowerKids Pr.).

—Hunting Turkeys. 2013. (Let's Go Hunting Ser.). (ENG., Illus.). 32p. (J). (gr. 4-6). pap. 10.00 *(978-1-4488-9778-0(5));* lib. bdg. 25.25 *(978-1-4488-9660-8(6))* Rosen Publishing Group, Inc., The. (PowerKids Pr.).

Laney, Dawn. Hunting. 2007. (Opposing Viewpoints Ser.). (ENG., Illus.). 200p. (YA). (gr. 10-12). 29.45 *(978-0-7377-3897-1(9),* LML02109-238367, Greenhaven Pr., Inc.) Cengage Gale.

Law, Andrew. We're Going Big-Game Hunting. 2016. (Hunting & Fishing: a Kid's Guide Ser.). 00032p. (J). (gr. 3-3). 26.25 *(978-1-4994-2874-2(X));* pap. 10.00 *(978-1-4994-2751-6(4))* Rosen Publishing Group, Inc., The. (PowerKids Pr.).

Loh-Hagan, Virginia. Bounty Hunter. 2016. (Odd Jobs Ser.). (ENG., Illus.). 32p. (J). (gr. 4-8). 29.93 *(978-1-63471-094-7(0,* 208487, 45th Parallel Press) Cherry Lake Publishing.

Low, Vicki. Cave of Secrets. Rooth, Mike, illus. 2007. (Timeline Ser.). 48p. pap. 8.99 *(978-1-4190-4391-8(9))* Steck-Vaughn.

MacRae, Sloan. Big-Game Hunting: Bears, Elk, & Other Large Animals. 2010. (Open Season Ser.). (ENG.). 32p. (J). pap. 10.00 *(978-1-4488-1371-1(9));* lib. bdg. 25.25 *(978-1-4488-0705-5(0))* Rosen Publishing Group, Inc., The. (PowerKids Pr.).

—Deer Hunting. 2010. (Open Season Ser.). (ENG.). 32p. (J). pap. 10.00 *(978-1-4488-1381-0(6));* lib. bdg. 25.25 *(978-1-4488-0710-9(7))* Rosen Publishing Group, Inc., The. (PowerKids Pr.).

—Small-Game Hunting: Squirrels, Rabbits, & Other Small Animals. 2010. (Open Season Ser.). (ENG.). 32p. (J). pap. 10.00 *(978-1-4488-1375-9(1));* lib. bdg. 25.25 *(978-1-4488-0707-9(7))* Rosen Publishing Group, Inc., The. (PowerKids Pr.).

—Turkey Hunting. 2010. (Open Season Ser.). (ENG.). 32p. (J). pap. 10.00 *(978-1-4488-1379-7(4));* lib. bdg. 25.25 *(978-1-4488-0709-3(3))* Rosen Publishing Group, Inc., The. (PowerKids Pr.).

—Upland Hunting: Pheasant, Quail, & Other Game Birds. 2010. (Open Season Ser.). (ENG.). 32p. (J). pap. 10.00 *(978-1-4488-1373-5(5));* lib. bdg. 25.25 *(978-1-4488-0706-2(9))* Rosen Publishing Group, Inc., The. (PowerKids Pr.).

—Waterfowl Hunting. 2010. (Open Season Ser.). (ENG.). 32p. (J). pap. 10.00 *(978-1-4488-1377-3(8));* lib. bdg. 25.25 *(978-1-4488-0708-6(5))* Rosen Publishing Group, Inc., The. (PowerKids Pr.).

Markle, Sandra. Animal Prey. 2008. pap. 280.95 *(978-0-8225-9243-3(6));* pap. 46.95 *(978-0-8225-9048-4(4))* Lerner Publishing Group.

McDowell, Pamela. Birds. 2016. (J). ***(978-1-4896-5716-9(9))*** Weigl Pubs., Inc.

McNeice, Connie-Lee. Big Game. (J). 2016. ***(978-1-4896-5713-8(4))*** 2012. *(978-1-61913-502-4(7))* 2012. pap. *(978-1-61913-506-2(X))* Weigl Pubs., Inc.

Moran, Shelby. We're Going Deer Hunting. 2016. (Hunting & Fishing: a Kid's Guide Ser.). 00032p. (J). (gr. 3-3). pap. 10.00 *(978-1-4994-2750-9(6),* PowerKids Pr.) Rosen Publishing Group, Inc., The.

Nickens, T. Eward. Field & Stream's Guide to Hunting. 2015. (Field & Stream's Guide to the Outdoors Ser.). (ENG., Illus.). 96p. (J). (gr. 6-8). 35.95 *(978-1-4824-2302-0(2))* Stevens, Gareth Publishing LLLP.

O'DellKathryn. SHOOT TO KILL: WHY WE HUNT HIGH BEGINNING BOOK WITH ONLINE ACCESS. 2014. (ENG., Illus.). 24p. (J). pap. 9.50 *(978-1-107-62253-1(0))* Cambridge Univ. Pr.

Omoth, Tyler. Turkey Hunting for Kids, 1 vol. 2012. (Into the Great Outdoors Ser.). (ENG., Illus.). 32p. (gr. 3-4). pap. 7.95 *(978-1-4296-9270-0(7));* lib. bdg. 27.99 *(978-1-4296-8615-0(4))* Capstone Press of Coughlan Cos.

Open Season: Set 2. 2014. (Open Season Ser.). 32p. (J). (gr. 4-6). 157.50 *(978-1-4777-6655-2(3),* PowerKids Pr.) Rosen Publishing Group, Inc., The.

Open Season: Sets 1-2. 2014. (Open Season Ser.). 32p. (J). (gr. 4-6). pap. 720.00 *(978-1-4777-7265-2(0));* pap. 120.00 *(978-1-4777-7264-5(2))* Rosen Publishing Group, Inc., The. (PowerKids Pr.).

Outdoor Adventure. 2014. (Outdoor Adventure Ser.). 32p. (J). (gr. 3-6). pap. 63.00 *(978-1-4824-1579-7(8))* Stevens, Gareth Publishing LLLP.

The Outdoor Youth Adventures Young Hunter's Colorinig Book. 2004. (J). pap. *(978-0-9745863-6-6(6))* Cypress Knees Publishing.

Patterson, John Henry. The Man-Eaters of Tsavo. 2011. 148p. pap. 7.49 *(978-1-61382-001-8(1))* Simon & Brown.

Pendergast, George. Deer Hunting. 2014. (Outdoor Adventure Ser.). 32p. (J). (gr. 3-6). pap. 63.00 *(978-1-4824-0932-1(1))* Stevens, Gareth Publishing LLLP.

—Duck Hunting. 2014. (Outdoor Adventure Ser.). 32p. (J). (gr. 3-6). pap. 63.00 *(978-1-4824-0966-6(6))* Stevens, Gareth Publishing LLLP.

—Turkey Hunting. 2014. (Outdoor Adventure Ser.). 32p. (J). (gr. 3-6). pap. 63.00 *(978-1-4824-1238-3(1))* Stevens, Gareth Publishing LLLP.

Peterson, Judy Monroe. Big Game Hunting. 2011. (Hunting: Pursuing Wild Game! Ser.). 64p. (YA). (ENG.). pap. 12.95 *(978-1-4488-2270-6(X));* (Illus.). (gr. 5-9). lib. bdg. 31.95 *(978-1-4488-1240-0(2))* Rosen Publishing Group, Inc., The.

—Small Game Hunting. 2011. (Hunting: Pursuing Wild Game! Ser.). 64p. (YA). (ENG.). pap. 12.95 *(978-1-4488-2272-0(6),* Rosen Reference); (Illus.). (gr. 5-9). lib. bdg. 31.95 *(978-1-4488-1242-4(9))* Rosen Publishing Group, Inc., The.

—Varmint Hunting. 2011. (Hunting: Pursuing Wild Game! Ser.). 64p. (YA). (ENG.). pap. 12.95 *(978-1-4488-2275-1(0),* Rosen Reference); (Illus.). (gr. 5-9). lib. bdg. 31.95 *(978-1-4488-1245-5(3))* Rosen Publishing Group, Inc., The.

Potter, Jonathan. We're Going Turkey Hunting. 2016. (Hunting & Fishing: a Kid's Guide Ser.). 00032p. (J). (gr. 3-3). pap. 10.00 *(978-1-4994-2746-2(8),* PowerKids Pr.) Rosen Publishing Group, Inc., The.

Pound, Blake. Deer Hunting. 2012. (Outdoor Adventures Ser.). (ENG., Illus.). 24p. (J). (gr. 3-8). lib. bdg. 25.95 *(978-1-60014-796-8(8),* Pilot Bks.) Bellwether Media.

Prohibited! Individual Title Six-Packs. (Bookweb Ser.). 32p. (gr. 6-18). 34.00 *(978-0-7578-0908-8(1))* Rigby Education.

Randolph, Ryan P. Following the Great Herds: The Plains Indians & the American Buffalo. 2009. (Library of the Westward Expansion Ser.). 24p. (gr. 3-4). 42.50 *(978-1-60853-934-5(2),* PowerKids Pr.) Rosen Publishing Group, Inc., The.

H
I

The Realtree Deer Hunting Activity & Coloring Book. 2003. (J). pap. (978-0-9745863-1-1(5)) Cypress Knees Publishing.

The Realtree Hunting Coloring Book. 2003. (J). pap. (978-0-9745863-3-5(1)) Cypress Knees Publishing.

Ringstad, Arnold. Hunting. 2014. (Great Outdoors Ser.). (ENG.). 24p. (J). (gr. 2-5). 28.50 (978-1-62687-331-5(3), 207171) Child's World, Inc., The.

Russ, Tony. Bear Hunting in Alaska: How to Hunt Brown & Grizzly Bears. O'Loughlin, Diane, ed. 2004. (Illus.). 296p. per. 22.95 (978-0-9639869-8-6(8)) Northern Publishing.

Shea, Nicole. Poaching & Illegal Trade. 2013. (Animal 911: Environmental Threats Ser.). 48p. (J). (gr. 3-5). pap. 84.30 (978-1-4339-9720-4(7)); (ENG., Illus.). lib. bdg. 31.95 (978-1-4339-9718-1(5)) Stevens, Gareth Publishing LLLP.

Shea, Robert Kennedy. Hunting. 2012. (Great Outdoors Ser.). (Illus.). 24p. (J). (gr. 2-5). pap. 8.15 (978-1-4339-7100-6(3)); lib. bdg. 22.60 (978-1-4339-7099-3(6)) Stevens, Gareth Publishing LLLP.

Staeger, Rob. Hunting with the Native Americans. Johnson, Troy, ed. 2013. (Native American Life Ser.: 15). 64p. (J). (gr. 5-18). 19.95 (978-1-4222-2966-8(1)) Mason Crest.

Strom, Laura Layton. Caught with a Catch: Poaching in Africa. 2007. (Shockwave: Economics & Geography Ser.). (ENG., Illus.). 36p. (J). (gr. 3-5). 25.00 (978-0-531-17798-3(X), Children's Pr.) Scholastic Library Publishing.

Swope, Bob. Teach'n Beginning Hunting & Hunter Safety Free Flow Handbook. 2013. 128p. pap. 19.95 (978-0-9911151-3-6(9)) Jacobob Pr., LLC.

Trout, John, Jr. Hunting Rutting Bucks: Secrets for Tagging the Biggest Buck of Your Life! 2004. (Illus.). 224p. 24.95 net. (978-0-9722804-6-4(4)) Woods N' Water Pr., Inc.

Tuchman, Gail. Safari. 2010. (Readers Ser.). (ENG., Illus.). 24p. (J). (gr. -1-k). pap. 3.99 (978-1-4263-0614-3(8)); lib. bdg. 13.90 (978-1-4263-0615-0(6)) National Geographic Society. (National Geographic Children's Bks.).

Watkins, Sue. Getting Involved! A Guide to Hunting & Conservation for Kids. 2011. (ENG.). 128p. pap. 12.95 (978-1-57157-377-3(1)) Safari Pr., Inc.

Weakland, Mark. Yogi Bear's Guide to Animal Tracks. Cornia, Christian, illus. 2015. (Yogi Bear's Guide to the Great Outdoors Ser.). (ENG.). 32p. (gr. 1-2). lib. bdg. 27.99 (978-1-4914-6545-5(X)) Capstone Press of Coughlan Cos.

Wolny, Philip. Avoiding Danger on the Hunt. 2012. (Hunting: Pursuing Wild Game! Ser.). (ENG., Illus.). 64p. (YA). (gr. 5-8). pap. 12.95 (978-1-4488-8283-0(4)); lib. bdg. 31.95 (978-1-4488-8278-6(8)) Rosen Publishing Group, Inc., The. (Rosen Reference).

Wood, Alix. Hunting on the Map. 2014. (Fun with Map Skills Ser.). (Illus.). 32p. (J). (gr. 3-6). lib. bdg. 26.25 (978-1-4777-6980-5(3), PowerKids Pr.) Rosen Publishing Group, Inc., The.

Young, Jeff C. Pheasant Hunting for Kids, 1 vol. 2013. (Into the Great Outdoors Ser.). (ENG.). 32p. (gr. 3-4). pap. 7.95 (978-1-62065-696-9(5)); lib. bdg. 27.99 (978-1-4296-9900-6(0)) Capstone Press of Coughlan Cos.

HUNTING—FICTION

Allende, Isabel. Forest of the Pygmies. 2009. (City of the Beasts Ser.: Bk. 3).Tr. of Bosque de los Pigmeos. (ENG.). 320p. pap. 14.99 (978-0-06-182510-1(7), Harper Perennial) HarperCollins Pubs.

—Forest of the Pygmies. Peden, Margaret Sayers, tr. from SPA. (City of the Beasts Ser.: Bk. 3).Tr. of Bosque de los Pigmeos. 304p. (J). (gr. 5-12). 2006. (ENG.). pap. 10.99 (978-0-06-076198-1(9)) 2005. 19.99 (978-0-06-076196-7(2)) HarperCollins Pubs. (Rayo).

—Forest of the Pygmies. l.t. ed. 2005. (City of the Beasts Ser.: Bk. 3).Tr. of Bosque de los Pigmeos. 304p. (J). (gr. 5-18). pap. 19.99 (978-0-06-076200-1(4), Rayo) HarperCollins Pubs.

Auger, Dale. Mwâkwa Talks to the Loon: A Cree Story for Children, 1 vol. Auger, Dale, illus. 2007. (ENG., Illus.). 32p. (J). (gr. k-3). pap. 12.95 (978-1-894974-32-5(8)) Heritage Hse. CAN. Dist: Orca Bk. Pubs. USA.

Avi. Old Wolf. Floca, Brian, illus. 2015. (ENG.). 160p. (J). (gr. 3-7). 16.99 (978-1-4424-9921-8(4)) Simon & Schuster Children's Publishing.

Ballantyne, R. M. Blown to Bits; or, the Lonely Man of Rak. 2006. pap. (978-1-4065-0515-3(3)) Dodo Pr.

—Gorilla Hunters A Tale of the Wilds of A. 2006. pap. 36.95 (978-1-4286-5952-0(8)) Kessinger Publishing, LLC.

Ballantyne, Robert Michael. The Rover of the Andes: A Tale of Adventure in South America. 2007. (ENG.). 266p. pap. 21.99 (978-1-4346-3753-6(0)); 296p. pap. 23.99 (978-1-4346-3767-3(0)) Creative Media Partners, LLC.

Ballard, Lisa. A Moose for Mackenzie. Doucette, Constance, illus. 2008. 32p. pap. 24.95 (978-1-60610-123-0(4)) America Star Bks.

Barnum, P. T. Dick Broadhead: A Story of Perilous Adve. 2006. pap. 30.95 (978-1-4286-1959-3(3)) Kessinger Publishing, LLC.

Bartlett, Susan & Wrenn, Luanne. Opening Day, 1 vol. 2007. (ENG., Illus.). 32p. (gr. 1-4). 16.95 (978-0-88448-288-8(X), 884288) Tilbury Hse. Pubs.

Beckman, Dean A. The Making of a Deer Hunter. 2006. 83p. pap. 19.95 (978-1-4241-1403-0(9)) America Star Bks.

Bonehill, Ralph. Four Boy Hunters. 2006. (ENG., Illus.). 242p. (J). (gr. 4-7). per. 14.95 (978-1-55753-390-6(3), 15ceff12-ce02-4f4f-a000-6f497a07dadd) Purdue Univ. Pr.

—Guns & Snowshoes. 2006. 27.95 (978-1-4218-3002-5(7)); pap. 12.95 (978-1-4218-3102-2(3)) 1st World Publishing, Inc.

—Guns & Snowshoes: Or, the Winter Outing of the Young Hunters. 2006. 160p. pap. 19.99 (978-1-4264-3173-9(2)) 2007. (ENG.). 174p. pap. 21.99 (978-1-4264-3208-8(9)) Creative Media Partners, LLC.

—Out with Gun & Camera. 2006. (ENG., Illus.). 264p. (J). (gr. 4-7). per. 14.95 (978-1-55753-392-0(X), bd49c68d-0f66-4e9a-aa91-d982014892eb) Purdue Univ. Pr.

—Young Hunters of the Lake. rev. ed. 2006. 212p. 27.95 (978-1-4218-1805-4(1)); pap. 12.95 (978-1-4218-1905-1(8)) 1st World Publishing, Inc. (1st World Library - Literary Society).

Brenning, Juli. Maggi & Milo. Burris, Priscilla, illus. 2014. (ENG.). 32p. (J). (gr. -1-k). 16.99 (978-0-8037-3795-2(5), Dial Bks) Penguin Young Readers Group.

Bruchac, Joseph. Killer of Enemies, 1 vol. 2013. (Killer of Enemies Ser.). (ENG.). 400p. (YA). 19.95 (978-1-62014-143-4(4), Tu Bks.) Lee & Low Bks., Inc.

—Trail of the Dead, 1 vol. 2015. (Killer of Enemies Ser.). (ENG.). 400p. (YA). 19.95 (978-1-62014-261-5(9)) Lee & Low Bks., Inc.

Burgess, Thornton W. The Adventures of Poor Mrs Quack. 2007. 124p. 23.95 (978-1-60312-595-6(7)) Aegypan.

—The Adventures of Poor Mrs Quack. 2011. 124p. 24.95 (978-1-4638-9562-4(3)) Rodgers, Alan Bks.

—The Adventures of Poor Mrs. Quack. 2004. reprint ed. pap. 15.95 (978-1-4191-5160-6(6)); pap. 1.99 (978-1-4192-5160-3(0)) Kessinger Publishing, LLC.

Busteed, Kerri J. Will's Bow Hunting Adventure. Byers, Leon, illus. 2012. 108p. pap. 30.00 (978-1-61897-207-1(3), Strategic Bk. Publishing) Strategic Book Publishing & Rights Agency (SBPRA).

—Will's First Hunt. Byers, Leon, illus. 2010. 80p. pap. 21.50 (978-1-60911-483-1(3), Eloquent Bks.) Strategic Book Publishing & Rights Agency (SBPRA).

Butler, Matthew. Billy Goes Hunting: A boy's journey to discover the values & traditions of Hunting. 2007. (Illus.). 28p. (J). pap. 9.95 (978-0-9800643-0-8(9)) Antlers & Fins LLC.

Calhoun, Bonnie S. Thunder: A Novel. 2015. (Stone Braide Chronicles Ser.: 1). (ENG.). 432p. (YA). pap. 13.00 (978-0-8007-2445-0(3)) Revell.

Callsen, Terri. The Outdoor Adventures of Charlie & Kaylee: Hunting Fear (book 1) Lignor, Amy, ed. Blondahl, Samuel, illus. 2012. 156p. pap. 9.85 (978-1-938634-10-9(1)) Freedom of Speech Publishing, Inc.

Carter, Herbert. The Boy Scouts on the Trail or Scouting. 2005. pap. 27.95 (978-1-885529-56-5(2)) Stevens Publishing.

Casanova, Mary. Wolf Shadows. 2nd ed. 2009. (J). (978-0-9793444-1-1(7)) Quercus Press.

Clark, Patricia Nikolina. In the Shadow of the Mammoth. LeTourneau, Anthony Alex, illus. (J). 2005. 14.99 (978-0-9674602-8-4(X)) 2003. 190p. pap. 6.99 (978-0-9674602-4-6(7)) Blue Marlin Pubns.

Climer, Steven Lee. Young of Heart. 2006. (YA). pap. (978-0-9790649-5-1(3)) Mardi Gras Publishing, LLC.

Cole, Molly. Joe & His Strong Purr. 2012. 26p. 24.95 (978-1-4626-6149-7(1)) America Star Bks.

Connell, Richard. The Most Dangerous Game. 2006. pap. 9.99 (978-1-59986-969-8(1)) Filiquarian Publishing, LLC.

—The Most Dangerous Game. 2004. reprint ed. pap. 1.99 (978-1-4192-7460-2(0)) Kessinger Publishing, LLC.

Connell, Richard Edward. The Most Dangerous Game. 2010. (Creative Short Stories Ser.). (Illus.). 48p. (J). (gr. 5-18). 19.95 (978-1-58341-920-5(9), Creative Education) Creative Co., The.

Dahl, Roald. The Magic Finger. Blake, Quentin, illus. 2009. (ENG.). 96p. (J). (gr. 3-7). 7.99 (978-0-14-241385-2(2), Puffin Books) Penguin Young Readers Group.

—The Magic Finger. Blake, Quentin, illus. 2003. (CHI.). 133p. (J). pap. 11.70 (978-957-574-476-2(4)) Youth Cultural Publishing Co. CHN. Dist: Chinasprout, Inc.

Dahlstrom, S. J. The Elk Hunt: The Adventure Begins. 2013. (Adventures of Wilder Good Ser.). (ENG., Illus.). 110p. (J). (gr. 3). pap. 8.95 (978-1-58988-087-0(0)) Dry, Paul Bks., Inc.

Dharma Publishing. The Hunter & the Quail: The Story about the Power of Cooperation. 2010. (ENG.). 36p. (gr. -1-7). pap. 8.95 (978-0-89800-602-5(3)) Dharma Publishing.

Dharma Publishing Staff. Golden Foot: A Story about Unselfish Love. 3rd ed. 2013. (ENG.). 36p. (gr. -1-7). pap. 8.95 (978-0-89800-517-2(5)) Dharma Publishing.

—The Monkey King: A Story about Compassion & Leadership. 2nd ed. 2013. (ENG.). 36p. (gr. -1-7). pap. 8.95 (978-0-89800-495-3(0)) Dharma Publishing.

Don, Lari. Never Trust a Tiger: A Story from Korea. Williamson, Melanie, illus. 2012. (Animal Stories Ser.). (ENG.). 48p. (J). (gr. 1-4). pap. 8.99 (978-1-84686-776-7(2)) Barefoot Bks., Inc.

Dorsey, Angela. Autumn of Angels. 2013. 128p. pap. (978-1-927100-30-1(5)) Enchanted Pony Bks.

Duvoisin, Roger, illus. Happy Hunter. 2016. (ENG.). 40p. (J). (gr. -1-3). 16.95 (978-1-59270-205-3(8)) Enchanted Lion Bks., LLC.

Eaton, Gordon J. Piebald & the Parade of Small Animals. 2009. 184p. pap. 14.99 (978-1-60791-991-9(5)) Salem Author Services.

Eichler, Ken. Swift Eagle's Dangerous Journey, 1 vol. 2009. 80p. pap. 16.95 (978-1-61582-289-8(5)) PublishAmerica, Inc.

Engelhardt. Efficient Use of School Build. 2013. (Fesler-Lampert Minnesota Heritage Ser.). (ENG.). 128p. pap. 9.95 (978-0-8166-9019-0(7)) Univ. of Minnesota Pr.

Ferguson, Chad. Stuff for the Hunt. 2007. 44p. per. 24.95 (978-1-4241-8850-5(4)) America Star Bks.

Fukuda, Andrew. The Hunt. 2012. (Hunt Trilogy Ser.: 1). (ENG.). 304p. (YA). (gr. 7). pap. 11.99 (978-1-250-00529-8(9), 9781250005298); 17.99 (978-1-250-00514-4(0), 9781250005144) St. Martin's Pr. (St. Martin's Griffin).

Fyne, Olga. Squirrel Race. 2009. 28p. pap. 13.99 (978-1-4389-3676-5(1)) AuthorHouse.

Gebhart, Ryan. There Will Be Bears. (ENG.). 224p. (J). (gr. 5). 2016. pap. 8.99 (978-0-7636-8765-6(0)) 2014. 16.99 (978-0-7636-6521-0(5)) Candlewick Pr.

Geraghty, Paul. The Hunter. Geraghty, Paul, illus. 2012. (ENG., Illus.). 32p. (J). (gr. k-2). pap. 12.99 (978-1-84939-376-8(1)) Andersen Pr. GBR. Dist: Independent Pubs. Group.

Green, Julia. Hunter's Heart. 2007. 264p. (YA). (gr. 7-12). 16.95 (978-0-7613-9493-8(1), Carolrhoda Bks.) Lerner Publishing Group.

Henry, Marguerite. Cinnabar, the One O'Clock Fox. Dennis, Wesley, illus. (ENG.). 144p. (J). (gr. 3-7). 2015. 19.99 (978-1-4814-0401-3(6)) 2014. pap. 6.99 (978-1-4814-0400-6(8)) Simon & Schuster Children's Publishing. (Aladdin).

Herrold. City & Village Planning & Zon. 2013. (Fesler-Lampert Minnesota Heritage Ser.). (ENG.). 136p. pap. 9.95 (978-0-8166-9031-2(6)) Univ. of Minnesota Pr.

Higgins, Wendy. The Great Hunt. (YA). (gr. 8). 2017. 448p. pap. 9.99 (978-0-06-238134-7(2)) 2016. 432p. 17.99 (978-0-06-238133-0(4)) HarperCollins Pubs. (HarperTeen).

Hodder, Beth. Stealing the Wild. 2010. 166p. (J). pap. 11.95 (978-0-9793963-1-1(X)) Grizzly Ridge Publishing.

Jordan, Sophie. Firelight. (Firelight Ser.: 1). (ENG.). (YA). (gr. 8). 2011. 352p. pap. 9.99 (978-0-06-193509-1(3)) 2010. 336p. 16.99 (978-0-06-193508-4(5)) HarperCollins Pubs.

Kazenbroot, Nelly. Down the Chimney with Googal & Googolplex. 2004. 63p. (J). lib. bdg. 20.00 (978-1-4242-1257-6(X)) Fitzgerald Bks.

Khanna, Balraj. Rajah: King of the Jungle. 2011. (ENG.). 112p. 16.95 (978-1-935677-03-1(9)) Mapin Publishing Pvt. Ltd IND. Dist: National Bk. Network.

Laswell, Wendy Jo. Gone Hunting. 2004. (Illus.). (J). lib. bdg. (978-1-932252-42-2(8)) Creative Continuum, Inc.

Leslie, Lawrence J. With Trapper Jim in the North Woods. 2004. reprint ed. pap. 1.99 (978-1-4192-9451-8(2)); pap. 19.95 (978-1-4191-9451-1(8)) Kessinger Publishing, LLC.

Lo, Malinda. Ash. 2010. (ENG.). 272p. (gr. 10-17). pap. 10.99 (978-0-316-04010-5(X)) Little, Brown Bks. for Young Readers.

—Huntress. 2012. (ENG.). 416p. (YA). (gr. 10-17). pap. 11.99 (978-0-316-03999-4(3)) Little, Brown Bks. for Young Readers.

Lois, Lowry. Crow Call. Ibatoulline, Bagram, illus. 2009. (ENG.). 32p. (J). (gr. 3-7). 19.99 (978-0-545-03035-9(8), Scholastic Pr.) Scholastic, Inc.

—Crow Call. 2011. (J). (gr. -1-2). 29.95 incl. audio compact disk (978-0-545-29674-8(9)) Weston Woods Studios, Inc.

London, Jack. Faith of Men. 2006. 116p. per. 9.95 (978-1-59818-074-9(6)) Aegypan.

Maberry, Jonathan. Flesh & Bone. 2013. (Rot & Ruin Ser.: 3). (ENG., Illus.). 496p. (YA). (gr. 7). pap. 11.99 (978-1-4424-3990-0(4), Simon & Schuster Bks. For Young Readers) Simon & Schuster Bks. For Young Readers.

Maddox, Jake. The Hunter's Code. Tiffany, Sean, illus. 2008. (Jake Maddox Sports Stories Ser.). (ENG.). 72p. (gr. 2-3). 25.32 (978-1-4342-0782-1(X)); pap. 5.95 (978-1-4342-0878-1(8)) Stone Arch Bks.

Margaret Bruce Clarke. Hunter's Marjory: A Story for Girls. 2007. (ENG.). 200p. pap. 19.99 (978-1-4264-8118-5(7)); 224p. pap. 22.99 (978-1-4346-3052-0(8)) Creative Media Partners, LLC.

Markle, Sandra. Family Pack. Marks, Alan, illus. 2011. (ENG.). 32p. (J). (gr. -1-3). 15.95 (978-1-58089-217-9(5)) Charlesbridge Publishing, Inc.

Marrone, Amanda. Slayed. 2010. (ENG., Illus.). 272p. (YA). (gr. 9-18). pap. 9.99 (978-1-4169-9487-9(4), Simon Pulse) Simon Pulse.

Martin, Francesca. Los Cazadores de Miel. (SPA., Illus.). 27p. (J). pap. 11.95 (978-980-257-175-8(X), EK2944) Ekare, Ediciones VEN. Dist: Kane Miller, Lectorum Pubns., Inc.

Mary-Todd, Jonathan. Shot Down. 2012. (After the Dust Settled Ser.). (ENG.). 104p. (YA). (gr. 6-12). pap. 7.95 (978-0-7613-9399-3(4), Darby Creek); lib. bdg. 27.93 (978-0-7613-8329-1(8)) Lerner Publishing Group.

Mason, Charlene. Landon's Backyard Adventures. 2012. 24p. pap. 24.95 (978-1-4626-7470-1(4)) America Star Bks.

Meierhenry, Mark & Volk, David. The Mystery of the Pheasants. Turnbull, Susan, illus. 2012. 44p. (J). 14.95 (978-0-9845041-9-0(2)) South Dakota State Historical Society Pr.

Milani, Mino. El Ultimo Lobo. (Barco de Vapor).Tr. of Last Wolf. (SPA.). 144p. (YA). (gr. 5-8). (978-84-348-4520-6(2)) SM Ediciones.

Myers, Tim J. The Outfoxed Fox: Based on a Japanese Kyogen, 0 vols. 2013. (ENG.). 32p. (J). (gr. k-3). pap. 9.99 (978-1-4778-1681-3(X), 9781477816813, Amazon Children's Publishing) Amazon Publishing.

Nichols, Walter H. The Measure of a Boy. 2005. (Illus.). pap. 28.95 (978-1-885529-73-2(2)) Stevens Publishing.

Nolan, Dennis. Hunters of the Great Forest. Nolan, Dennis, illus. 2014. (ENG., Illus.). 40p. (J). (gr. -1-2). 17.99 (978-1-59643-896-5(7), 9781596438965) Roaring Brook Pr.

O'Dell, Scott. Black Star, Bright Dawn. 2008. (ENG., Illus.). 144p. (J). (gr. 5-7). pap. 6.99 (978-0-547-05319-6(3)) Houghton Mifflin Harcourt Publishing Co.

Olaizola, José Luis. El Cazador Urbano.Tr. of Urban Hunter. (SPA.). 160p. (J). 6.50 (978-84-355-0814-8(5)) Minon, S.A. ESP. Dist: AIMS International Bks., Inc.

Oxenbury, Helen, illus. We're Going on a Bear Hunt. 2004. 33p. (J). (978-1-85269-719-8(9)); (978-1-85269-713-6(X)); (ENG & ARA.). pap. (978-1-85269-707-5(5)) Mantra Lingua.

Oxley, J. Mcdonald. The Young Woodsman: Life in the Forests of Canada. 2007. 90p. pap. 16.99 (978-1-4346-4267-7(4)); 100p. pap. 18.99 (978-1-4346-4268-4(2)) Creative Media Partners, LLC.

Paulsen, Gary. Brian's Hunt. 2005. 103p. (YA). (gr. 4-8). reprint ed. 15.00 (978-0-7567-9570-2(2)) DIANE Publishing Co.

—Tracker. 2007. (ENG.). 96p. (J). (gr. 5-9). pap. 6.99 (978-1-4169-3940-5(7), Simon & Schuster Bks. For Young Readers) Simon & Schuster Bks. For Young Readers.

Penner, Lucille Recht. Osos en la Mente; Bears on the Brain. 2008. pap. 34.95 (978-1-58013-769-0(5)) Kane Press, Inc.

Peterfreund, Diana. Ascendant. (ENG.). (YA). (gr. 9). 2012. 416p. pap. 8.99 (978-0-06-149005-7(9)) 2010. 400p. 17.99 (978-0-06-149002-6(4)) HarperCollins Pubs. (HarperTeen).

—Rampant. 2010. (ENG.). 432p. (YA). (gr. 9). pap. 8.99 (978-0-06-149004-0(0), HarperTeen) HarperCollins Pubs.

Reich, J. J. Snort, Wheeze, Rattle & Grunt. Hillmann, Joe & Cox, Chad, illus. 2006. (J). 8.99 (978-0-9762971-1-6(6)) Outdoor Originals LLC.

—Snort, Wheeze, Rattle & Grunt: Kampp Tales Outdoor Adventures. Johnathan, Kuehl, illus. 2006. 64p. (J). (978-0-9762971-2-3(4)) Outdoor Originals LLC.

Reid, Mayne. Young Yagers or A Narrative of Hunting A. 2006. (Illus.). pap. 31.95 (978-1-4286-2205-0(5)) Kessinger Publishing, LLC.

Remolina, Tere. Un Cambio de Piel. Martinez, Enrique, illus. (Barril Sin Fondo Ser.). (SPA.). (J). (gr. 3-5). pap. (978-968-6465-20-4(0)) Casa de Estudios de Literatura y Talleres Artisticos Amaquemecan A.C. MEX. Dist: Lectorum Pubns., Inc.

Robinson, Sharon. Under the Same Sun. Ford, A. G., illus. 2014. (ENG.). 40p. (J). (gr. -1-3). 17.99 (978-0-545-16672-0(1), Scholastic Pr.) Scholastic, Inc.

Rockwell, Carey. The Revolt on Venus. 2007. 120p. per. (978-1-4068-3961-6(2)) Echo Library.

Roddy, Lee. The Hair-Pulling Bear Dog. 2008. (D. J. Dillon Adventure Ser.: No. 1). (J). 7.99 (978-0-88062-265-3(2)) Mott Media.

Rosen, Michael. Vamos a Caca de Um Urso. Oxenbury, Helen, illus. 2004. Orig. Title: We're Going on a Bear Hunt. (ENG & POR.). 33p. (J). pap. (978-1-85269-715-0(6)) Mantra Lingua.

—We're Going on a Bear Hunt. Oxenbury, Helen, illus. 2004. (J). 32p. (978-1-85269-706-8(7)); 32p. (978-1-85269-710-5(5)); 32p. (978-1-85269-711-2(3)); 32p. (978-1-85269-716-7(4)); 32p. (978-1-85269-718-1(0)); 32p. (978-1-85269-720-4(2)); (ENG & FRE.). 33p. pap. (978-1-85269-712-9(1)); (ENG & URD.). 33p. pap. (978-1-85269-721-1(0)); (ENG & PAN.). 33p. pap. (978-1-85269-714-3(8)); (ENG & BEN.). 33p. pap. (978-1-85269-708-2(3)) Mantra Lingua.

—We're Going on a Bear Hunt. Oxenbury, Helen, illus. 2003. (ENG.). 36p. (J). (gr. -1-3). pap. 7.99 (978-0-689-85349-4(1), McElderry, Margaret K. Bks.) McElderry, Margaret K. Bks.

—We're Going on a Bear Hunt. Oxenbury, Helen, illus. 2003. (gr. k-3). 18.40 (978-0-613-61665-2(0), Turtleback) Turtleback Bks.

—We're Going on a Bear Hunt: Anniversary Edition of a Modern Classic. Oxenbury, Helen, illus. 2009. (Classic Board Bks.). (ENG.). 36p. (J). (gr. -1-k). bds. 9.99 (978-1-4169-8712-3(6), Little Simon) Little Simon.

—We're Going on a Bear Hunt: Anniversary Edition of a Modern Classic. Oxenbury, Helen, illus. 2009. (ENG.). 40p. (J). (gr. -1-3). 18.99 (978-1-4169-8711-6(8), McElderry, Margaret K. Bks.) McElderry, Margaret K. Bks.

—We're Going on a Bear Hunt: Sound Book. Oxenbury, Helen, illus. 2014. (ENG.). 40p. (J). (gr. -1-2). 19.99 (978-0-7636-7702-2(7)) Candlewick Pr.

Rosen, Michael & Oxenbury, Helen, illus. Chung Ta Di Sian Gau. 2004. Orig. Title: We're Going on a Bear Hunt. (VIE & ENG.). 33p. (J). (978-1-85269-722-8(9)) Mantra Lingua.

Ruark, Robert C. I Didn't Know It Was Loaded. (J). 22.95 (978-0-89190-958-3(3)) Amereon Ltd.

Sam, Joe, illus. The Invisible Hunters (Los Cazadores Invisibles) (YA). (gr. 1-18). 25.95 incl. audio (978-0-89239-036-6(0)) Lee & Low Bks., Inc.

Santillo, LuAnn. The Big Hunt. Santillo, LuAnn, ed. 2003. (Half-Pint Kids Readers Ser.). (Illus.). 7p. (J). (gr. -1-1). pap. 1.00 (978-1-59256-076-9(8)) Half-Pint Kids, Inc.

Sargent, Pat. The Bobcat, 8 vols., Vol. 5. Lenoir, Jane, illus. 2003. (Barney the Bear Killer Ser.: Vol. 5). 136p. (J). lib. bdg. 26.25 (978-1-56763-971-1(2)) Ozark Publishing.

Scollon, William & Disney Book Group Staff. The Great Treasure Hunt. Disney Storybook Art Team, illus. 2013. (ENG.). 10p. (J). (gr. -1-k). bds. 8.99 (978-1-4231-6396-1(6)) Disney Pr.

—The Key to Skull Rock, Level 1. Disney Storybook Art Team, illus. 2013. (World of Reading Ser.). (ENG.). 32p. (J). (gr. -1-k). pap. 3.99 (978-1-4231-6397-8(4)) Disney Pr.

Searcher Hunter. 2004. (Caravan Ser.). 80p. pap. 9.50 (978-0-8341-2124-9(7)) Beacon Hill Pr. of Kansas City.

Skipper, Cecil. The Deer Lick. 2004. 166p. (YA). pap. 12.95 (978-0-595-30949-8(6)) iUniverse, Inc.

Standish, Burt L. Frank Merriwell's Hunting Tour. Rudman, Jack, ed. (Frank Merriwell Ser.). (YA). (gr. 9-18). 29.95 (978-0-8373-9307-0(8)); 2003. pap. 9.95 (978-0-8373-9007-9(9), FM-007) Merriwell, Frank Inc.

Stilton, Geronimo & Stilton, Thea. Thea Stilton & the Ghost of the Shipwreck. 2010. (Thea Stilton Ser.: 3). lib. bdg. 19.65 (978-0-606-06843-7(0), Turtleback) Turtleback Bks.

Stowell, Louie. Brer Rabbit down the Well. Muszynski, Eva, illus. 2010. (First Reading Level 2 Ser.). 32p. (J). 6.99 (978-0-7945-2674-0(8), Usborne) EDC Publishing.

Stratemeyer, Edward. The Rover Boys on a Hunt: Or the Mysterious House in the Woods. 2007. 194p. pap. 19.99 (978-1-4346-4363-6(8)); (ENG.). 214p. pap. 22.99 (978-1-4346-4364-3(6)) Creative Media Partners, LLC.

Suen, Anastasia. We're Going on a Dinosaur Dig. Myer, Ed, illus. 2012. (ENG.). 24p. (gr. k-1). pap. 8.95 (978-1-61810-299-7(0)) Rourke Educational Media.

Sutherland, E. B. Tallie's in a Sea of Trouble. 2013. 44p. pap. 21.99 (978-1-4797-3988-2(X)) Xlibris Corp.

Taitano, Janice G. The Legend of Lutung. 2006. 260p. pap. 29.00 (978-1-59752-482-7(4), Resource Pubns.(OR)) Wipf & Stock Pubs.

Talbot, Amy. Deer & His Dear Friends: A Tale from India. 2006. (J). pap. (978-1-4108-6173-3(2)) Benchmark Education Co.

VanDerpool, Jessie. Little Rose Becomes a Hunter. 2013. 24p. pap. 24.95 (978-1-4626-9554-6(X)) America Star Bks.

Waguespack, Michael. The Deer Hunting Book. 2013. 104p. pap. 7.95 (978-0-9754624-6-1(6)) Country Kid Publishing LLC.

Walker, Lane. The Day It Rained Ducks. 2014. (Hometown Hunters Collection: Vol. 5). (ENG.). 151p. (J). (gr. 4-7). pap. 9.99 (978-1-58169-564-9(0), Evergreen Pr.) Genesis Communications, Inc.

—The Hunt for Scarface. 2014. (ENG.). 161p. (YA). (gr. 7-13). pap. 9.99 (978-1-58169-518-2(7), Evergreen Pr.) Genesis Communications, Inc.

—Legend of the Ghost Buck. 2014. (ENG.). 135p. (YA). (gr. 7-13). pap. 9.99 (978-1-58169-517-5(9), Evergreen Pr.) Genesis Communications, Inc.

—Terror at Deadwood Lake. 2014. (Hometown Hunters Collection: Vol. 3). (ENG.). 137p. (YA). (gr. 7-13). pap. 9.99 (978-1-58169-519-9(5), Evergreen Pr.) Genesis Communications, Inc.

Warren, George A. Bob Chase after Grizzly Bears. 2005. (Illus.). pap. 24.95 (978-1-885529-40-4(6)) Stevens Publishing.

We're Going on a Bear Hunt: Lap Edition. 2014. (ENG., Illus.). 36p. (J). (gr. -1-k). bds. 12.99 (978-1-4814-1924-6(2), Little Simon) Little Simon.

Weston Woods Staff, creator. Crow Call. 2011. 18.95 (978-0-545-37493-4(6)); 38.75 (978-0-545-37494-1(4)) Weston Woods Studios, Inc.

Whitney, Elliott. The Blind Lion of the Congo. 2011. 128p. pap. 9.99 (978-1-61203-066-1(1)) Bottom of the Hill Publishing.

Wildsmith, Brian. Hunter & His Dog, 1 vol. Wildsmith, Brian, illus. 2008. (ENG., Illus.). 32p. (J). 16.95 (978-1-59572-123-5(1)) Star Bright Bks., Inc.

Zerbe, Tim. The King of Pumpkin Ridge. 2012. 28p. pap. 9.95 (978-1-937600-80-8(7)) Salem Author Services.

HURON, LAKE (MICH. AND ONT.)—FICTION

Beveridge, Cathy. Stormstruck. 2006. (ENG., Illus.). 214p. (J). pap. (978-1-55380-041-5(9)) Ronsdale Pr.

HURRICANES

Aboff, Marcie. Hurricanes!, 1 vol. Sotirovski, Aleksandar, illus. 2012. (First Graphics: Wild Earth Ser.). (ENG.). 24p. (gr. 1-2). pap. 6.29 (978-1-4296-7951-0(4)); pap. 35.70 (978-1-4296-8371-5(6)); lib. bdg. 23.99 (978-1-4296-7607-6(8)) Capstone Press of Coughlan Cos.

Allberti, Frances C. Finding Rover. Gremillion, Barry, illus. 2006. (J). per. (978-0-9785937-1-1(5)) Open Pages Publishing.

Armentrout, David & Armentrout, Patricia. Hurricanes. 2006. (ENG., Illus.). 32p. (gr. 2-5). pap. 9.95 (978-1-60694-918-4(7)) Rourke Educational Media.

Armour, Cy. Tornadoes & Hurricanes!, 1 vol. 2nd rev. ed. 2014. (TIME for KIDS(r) Nonfiction Readers Ser.). (ENG., Illus.). 24p. (J). (gr. 2-2). pap. 23.96 (978-1-4807-1041-2(5)) Shell Educational Publishing.

—Tornadoes & Hurricanes!, 1 vol. 2nd rev. ed. 2011. (Nonfiction Readers Ser.). (ENG.). 24p. (J). (gr. 2-2). pap. 6.99 (978-1-4333-3614-0(6)) Teacher Created Materials, Inc.

Aronin, Miriam. Mangled by a Hurricane! 2010. (Disaster Survivors Ser.). (Illus.). 32p. (YA). (gr. 4-7). lib. bdg. 25.27 (978-1-936087-49-5(9)) Bearport Publishing Co., Inc.

Bailey, Rachel. Superstorm Sandy, 1 vol. 2013. (History's Greatest Disasters Ser.). (ENG., Illus.). 48p. (J). (gr. 3-6). lib. bdg. 32.79 (978-1-61783-961-0(2), 1360926) ABDO Publishing Co.

—Superstorm Sandy Paperback. 2013. (Illus.). 48p. (J). pap. 15.64 (978-1-62403-026-0(2), 1360926, Core Library) ABDO Publishing Co.

Baker, John R. The World's Worst Hurricanes. 2016. (World's Worst Natural Disasters Ser.). (ENG., Illus.). 32p. (gr. 1-2). lib. bdg. 26.65 (978-1-5157-1789-8(5)) Capstone Press of Coughlan Cos.

Baltzer, Rochelle. Hurricanes, 1 vol. 2011. (Natural Disasters Ser.). (ENG., Illus.). 32p. (J). (gr. 2-5). 28.50 (978-1-61783-032-7(1)) ABDO Publishing Co.

Bell, Samantha S. Detecting Hurricanes. 2017. (Detecting Disasters (hardcover) Ser.). (ENG., Illus.). 32p. (J). (gr. 4-7). lib. bdg. 28.50 **(978-1-63517-003-0(6)**, Focus Readers) North Star Editions.

Benoit, Peter. Hurricane Katrina. 2011. (True Bk Ser.). (ENG., Illus.). 48p. (J). pap. 6.95 (978-0-531-26626-7(5)); (gr. 3-5). lib. bdg. 29.00 (978-0-531-25421-9(6)) Scholastic Library Publishing. (Children's Pr.).

Berger, Melvin & Berger, Gilda. Hurricanes Have Eyes but Can't See: And Other Amazing Facts about Wild Weather. 2003. (Illus.). 48p. (J). (978-0-439-54980-6(9)) Scholastic, Inc.

Blaisdell, Molly. Hurricane Fury. 2008. (Discovering & Exploring Science Ser.). (Illus.). 16p. (J). (gr. -1-3). lib. bdg. 12.95 (978-0-7569-8258-4(8)) Perfection Learning Corp.

Bodden, Valerie. Hurricanes. 2012. (Illus.). 24p. (J). 25.65 (978-1-60818-147-6(2), Creative Education) Creative Co., The.

—Our Wonderful Weather: Hurricanes. 2014. (Our Wonderful Weather Ser.). (ENG., Illus.). 24p. (J). (gr. 4-7). pap. 9.99 (978-0-89812-920-5(6), Creative Paperbacks) Creative Co., The.

Boothroyd, Jennifer. What Is Severe Weather? 2014. (First Step Nonfiction - Let's Watch the Weather Ser.). 24p. (gr. k-2). (Illus.). pap. 6.95 (978-1-4677-4499-7(9)); (ENG.). lib. bdg. 23.93 (978-1-4677-3919-1(7), Lerner Pubns.) Lerner Publishing Group.

Brown, Don. Drowned City: Hurricane Katrina & New Orleans. 2015. (ENG., Illus.). 96p. (YA). (gr. 7). 18.99 (978-0-544-15777-4(X), HMH Books For Young Readers) Houghton Mifflin Harcourt Publishing Co.

—Drowned City: Hurricane Katrina & New Orleans. 2017. (ENG.). (YA). (gr. 7). lib. bdg. 20.85 **(978-0-606-39819-0(8))** Turtleback Bks.

Burgan, Michael. Total Devastation: The Story of Hurricane Katrina. 2016. (Tangled History Ser.). (ENG., Illus.). 112p. (gr. 3-4). lib. bdg. 31.99 (978-1-4914-8452-4(7)) Capstone Press of Coughlan Cos.

Caravantes, Peggy. Hurricane Katrina, 1 vol. 2013. (History's Greatest Disasters Ser.). (ENG.). 48p. (J). (gr. 3-6). lib. bdg. 32.79 (978-1-61783-958-0(2)) ABDO Publishing Co.

—Hurricane Katrina Paperback. 2013. (J). pap. 15.64 (978-1-62403-023-9(8), Core Library) ABDO Publishing Co.

Challen, Paul. Hurricane & Typhoon Alert! 3rd rev. ed. 2011. (Disaster Alert! Ser.: No. 17). (ENG., Illus.). 32p. (J). (gr. 3-6). pap. (978-0-7787-1626-6(0)) Crabtree Publishing Co.

Close, Edward. Extreme Weather, 1 vol., 1. 2014. (Discovery Education: Earth & Space Science Ser.). (ENG.). 32p. (gr. 3-6). 26.25 (978-1-4777-6194-6(2), PowerKids Pr.) Rosen Publishing Group, Inc., The.

Cox Cannons, Helen. Wind, 1 vol. 2014. (Weather Wise Ser.). (ENG., Illus.). 24p. (gr. -1-1). pap. 5.99 (978-1-4846-0559-2(4), Acorn) Heinemann-Raintree.

Demarest, Chris L. Hurricane Hunters! Riders on the Storm. Demarest, Chris L., illus. 2006. (ENG., Illus.). 40p. (J). (gr. -1-5). 19.99 (978-0-689-86168-0(0), McElderry, Margaret K. Bks.) McElderry, Margaret K. Bks.

Dill, Pamela Wescovich. Katrina's Rainbow: The Miracle of the Storm Crosses. 2006. (Illus.). 42p. (J). 17.99 (978-1-59879-302-4(0)) Lifevest Publishing, Inc.

Doeden, Matt. Hurricanes. 2008. pap. 40.95 (978-0-8225-9443-7(9)); (ENG.). 32p. pap. 7.95 (978-0-8225-9017-0(4)); (ENG., Illus.). 32p. lib. bdg. 22.60 (978-0-8225-7906-9(5), Lerner Pubns.) Lerner Publishing Group.

Donnelly, Karen. Storms of the Past & the Future. 2009. (Earth's Changing Weather & Climate Ser.). 24p. (gr. 4-4). 42.50 (978-1-61512-250-9(8), PowerKids Pr.) Rosen Publishing Group, Inc., The.

Donnelly, Karen J. Storms of the Past & the Future. 2003. (Earth's Changing Weather & Climate Ser.). (Illus.). 24p. (J). lib. bdg. 22.60 (978-0-8239-6216-7(4), PowerKids Pr.) Rosen Publishing Group, Inc., The.

Dougherty, Terri. Anatomy of a Hurricane. (Disasters Ser.). (ENG.). 48p. (gr. 3-4). 2011. pap. 59.70 (978-1-4296-7366-2(4)) 2010. lib. bdg. 31.99 (978-1-4296-4795-3(7)) Capstone Press of Coughlan Cos.

—The Worst Hurricanes of All Time. 2012. (Epic Disasters Ser.). (ENG.). 32p. (gr. 3-4). pap. 47.70 (978-1-4296-8508-5(5), Edge Bks.) Capstone Press of Coughlan Cos.

Espejo, Roman. Hurricane Katrina. 2006. (At Issue Ser.). (ENG.). 91p. (J). (gr. 6-10). pap. 31.80 (978-0-7377-3551-2(1), Greenhaven Pr., Inc.) Cengage Gale.

Fleisher, Paul. Lightning, Hurricanes, & Blizzards: The Science of Storms. 2010. (Weatherwise Ser.). (ENG.). 48p. (gr. 4-8). lib. bdg. 29.27 (978-0-8225-7536-8(1)) Lerner Publishing Group.

Fradin, Dennis Brindell & Fradin, Judith Bloom. Hurricane Katrina. 2009. (Turning Points in U. S. History Ser.). 48p. (gr. 3-6). 31.36 (978-0-7614-4261-5(8)) Marshall Cavendish Corp.

Fradin, Judith Bloom & Fradin, Dennis Brindell. Hurricanes. 2007. (Witness to Disaster Ser.). (ENG., Illus.). 48p. (J). (gr. 4-7). 16.95 (978-1-4262-0111-0(7)); 26.90 (978-1-4262-0112-7(5)) National Geographic Society. (National Geographic Children's Bks.).

Freed, Kira. Surviving Hurricane Katrina. 2015. (Surviving Disaster Ser.). (ENG., Illus.). 48p. (J). (gr. 5-6). 30.25 (978-1-4994-3665-5(3), Rosen Central) Rosen Publishing Group, Inc., The.

Gibbons, Gail. Hurricanes! Gibbons, Gail, illus. (ENG., Illus.). 32p. (J). (gr. -1-3). 2010. pap. 7.99 (978-0-8234-2297-5(6)) 2009. 17.95 (978-0-8234-2233-3(X)) Holiday Hse., Inc.

Gibson, Karen Bush. The Fury of Hurricane Andrew 1992. 2005. (Natural Disasters Ser.). (Illus.). 32p. (J). (gr. 1-4). lib. bdg. 25.70 (978-1-58415-416-7(0)) Mitchell Lane Pubs., Inc.

Gifford, Clive. Chasing the World's Most Dangerous Storms. 2010. (Extreme! Ser.). (ENG.). 32p. (gr. 3-4). pap. 47.70 (978-1-4296-5123-3(7), Fact Finders) Capstone Press of Coughlan Cos.

Gigliotti, Jim. Hurricanes. 2006. (Reading Rocks! Ser.). (ENG., Illus.). 32p. (J). (gr. 2-5). 28.50 (978-1-59296-731-5(0), 200717) Child's World, Inc., The.

Gonzales, Doreen. Hurricanes. 2012. (Killer Disasters Ser.). (ENG., Illus.). 24p. (J). (gr. 3-6). pap. 8.25 (978-1-4488-7513-9(7)); lib. bdg. 22.60 (978-1-4488-7440-8(8)) Rosen Publishing Group, Inc., The. (PowerKids Pr.).

Gray-Wilburn, Renée & Kalz, Jill. Hurricanes: Be Aware & Prepare, 1 vol. 2014. (Weather Aware Ser.). (ENG.). 32p. (gr. 1-2). lib. bdg. 27.32 (978-1-4765-9903-8(3)) Capstone Press of Coughlan Cos.

Green, Jen. Hurricane Andrew. 2005. (Disasters Ser.). (Illus.). 32p. (gr. 2-6). lib. bdg. 26.00 (978-0-8368-4497-9(1), Gareth Stevens Learning Library) Stevens, Gareth Publishing LLLP.

Gregory, Josh. If You Were a Kid Surviving a Hurricane. Kennedy, Kelly, illus. 2017. (If You Were a Kid Ser.). (ENG.). 32p. (J). lib. bdg. 26.00 **(978-0-531-23745-8(1)**, Children's Pr.) Scholastic Library Publishing.

Gregory, Josh. The Superstorm Hurricane Sandy. 2013. (True Book(tm), A — Disasters Ser.). (J). 31.00 (978-0-531-23750-2(8)); (ENG.). 48p. pap. 6.95 (978-0-531-23751-9(6)) Scholastic Library Publishing. (Children's Pr.).

Group/McGraw-Hill, Wright. Savage Storms: Tornadoes & Hurricanes, 6 vols. (Book2WebTM Ser.). (gr. 4-8). 36.50 (978-0-322-04424-1(3)) Wright Group/McGraw-Hill.

Hamilton, S. L. Hurricanes. 2012. 32p. 27.07 (978-1-61783-261-1(8), Abdo & Daughters) ABDO Publishing Co.

Harper, Kristine. Hurricane Andrew. 2005. (Environmental Disasters Ser.). (Illus.). 112p. (gr. 6-12). 35.00 (978-0-8160-5759-7(1)) Facts On File, Inc.

Hawkins, John. Hurricane Disasters. 2011. (Catastrophe! Ser.). (ENG., Illus.). 48p. (J). (gr. 5-9). lib. bdg. 29.25 (978-1-4488-6004-3(0)) Rosen Publishing Group, Inc., The.

Henningfeld, Diane Andrews & Haugen, David. Hurricane Katrina. 2010. (At Issue Ser.). (ENG.). 128p. (gr. 10-12). 39.40 (978-0-7377-4882-6(6)); pap. 27.80 (978-0-7377-4883-3(4)) Cengage Gale. (Greenhaven Pr., Inc.).

Hirschmann, Kris. Hurricane!, 1 vol. 2008. (What's It Like Out? Ser.). (ENG.). 32p. (gr. k-6). 27.07 (978-1-59928-942-7(3), Checkerboard Library) ABDO Publishing Co.

Hoena, Blake. Hurricane Katrina: An Interactive Modern History Adventure, 1 vol. 2014. (You Choose: Modern History Ser.). (ENG.). 112p. (gr. 3-4). 31.99 (978-1-4765-4189-1(2), You Choose Bks.) Capstone Press of Coughlan Cos.

Hoffman, Mary Ann. Hurricane Katrina. 2007. (Nature in the News Ser.). (Illus.). 32p. (YA). (gr. 2-5). lib. bdg. 21.25 (978-1-4042-3537-3(X)) Rosen Publishing Group, Inc., The.

Huracan a la Vista! 6 Small Books. (Saludos Ser.: Vol. 2). (SPA.). (gr. 3-5). 31.00 (978-0-7635-2069-4(1)) Rigby Education.

Hurricane on Its Way!, 6 Packs. (Greetings Ser.: Vol. 2). (gr. 3-5). 31.00 (978-0-7635-2063-2(2)) Rigby Education.

Hurricanes, Typhoons, & Other Tropical Cyclones. 2nd ed. 2009. (Illus.). 47p. (J). (978-0-7166-9824-1(2)) World Bk., Inc.

Jensen, Belinda. Spinning Wind & Water: Hurricanes. Kurilla, Renee, illus. 2016. (Bel the Weather Girl Ser.). (ENG.). 24p. (J). (gr. -1-3). 25.32 (978-1-4677-7962-3(8), Millbrook Pr.) Lerner Publishing Group.

Johnson, Robin. What Is a Hurricane? 2016. (ENG., Illus.). 24p. (J). (978-0-7787-2398-1(4)) Crabtree Publishing Co.

Jones, Lynda. Hurricane Disaster. 2011. (Illus.). 32p. (J). (978-0-545-34539-2(1)) Scholastic, Inc.

Kallio, Jamie. 12 Things to Know about Wild Weather. 2015. (ENG., Illus.). 32p. (J). (978-1-63235-035-0(1)) Pr. Room Editions LLC.

Kidd, Sabrina. Examining Hurricanes. 2015. (ENG., Illus.). 48p. (J). lib. bdg. 24.95 net. (978-1-934545-64-5(3)) Oliver Pr., Inc.

Kliman, Gilbert. My Personal Story about Hurricanes Katrina & Rita: A Guided Activity Workbook for Middle & High School Students. 2005. (YA). spiral bd. 19.00 (978-0-9790846-9-0(5)) Children's Psychological Health Ctr., Inc., The.

Koontz, Robin. What Was Hurricane Katrina? 2015. (What Was... ? Ser.). lib. bdg. 16.00 (978-0-606-36762-2(4)) Turtleback Bks.

Koontz, Robin & dePaola, Tomie. What Was Hurricane Katrina? Hinderliter, John & McVeigh, Kevin, illus. 2015. (What Was? Ser.). (ENG.). 112p. (J). (gr. 3-7). 5.99 (978-0-448-48662-8(8), Penguin Workshop) Penguin Young Readers Group.

Krohn, Katherine & Milgrom, Al. The Whirlwind World of Hurricanes with Max Axiom, Super Scientist. 2010. (Graphic Science Ser.). (ENG., Illus.). 32p. (gr. 3-4). pap. 8.10 (978-1-4296-5636-8(0), Graphic Library) Capstone Press of Coughlan Cos.

Krohn, Katherine E., et al. The Whirlwind World of Hurricanes with Max Axiom, Super Scientist, 1 vol. 2010. (Graphic Science Ser.). (ENG.). 32p. (gr. 3-4). lib. bdg. 30.65 (978-1-4296-4773-1(6), Graphic Library) Capstone Press of Coughlan Cos.

Langley, Andrew. Hurricane: Perspectives on Storm Disasters, 1 vol. 2014. (Disaster Dossiers Ser.). (ENG., Illus.). 56p. (gr. 7-8). 34.65 (978-1-4846-0181-5(5)) Heinemann-Raintree.

Latham, Donna. Hurricane! The 1900 Galveston Night of Terror. 2005. (X-Treme Disasters That Changed America Ser.). (Illus.). 32p. (J). (gr. 3-7). lib. bdg. 25.27 (978-1-59716-071-1(7)) Bearport Publishing Co., Inc.

Lay, Kathryn. Hurricane Harry, 1 vol., Vol. 6. Wolff, Jason, illus. 2011. (Wendy's Weather Warriors Ser.). (ENG.). 80p. (gr. 2-5). 27.07 (978-1-60270-759-7(6), Calico Chapter Bks) Magic Wagon.

Levy, Janey. World's Worst Hurricanes. 2009. (Deadly Disasters Ser.). 24p. (gr. 2-6). pap. 9.40 (978-1-4042-4535-8(9), Rosen Classroom); (gr. 2-3). 42.50 (978-1-61512-141-0(2), PowerKids Pr.); (Illus.). (J). lib. bdg. 22.60 (978-1-4042-4511-2(1), PowerKids Pr.) Rosen Publishing Group, Inc., The.

Lewis, Suzanne. A Penguin Named Patience: A Hurricane Katrina Rescue Story. Anchin, Lisa, illus. 2015. (ENG.). 24p. (J). (gr. 1-4). 15.95 (978-1-58536-840-2(7), 203732) Sleeping Bear Pr.

Linde, Barbara M. When Hurricanes Howl. 2015. (Eye on the Sky Ser.). (ENG., Illus.). 32p. (J). (gr. 3-4). pap. 10.50 (978-1-4824-2888-9(1)) Stevens, Gareth Publishing LLLP.

Lusted, Marcia Amidon & Elkins, Elizabeth. Investigating Hurricanes. 2017. (Investigating Natural Disasters Ser.). (ENG., Illus.). 32p. (gr. 3-4). lib. bdg. 27.99 (978-1-5157-4039-1(0), Edge Bks.) Capstone Press of Coughlan Cos.

Manolis, Kay. Hurricanes. 2008. (Extreme Weather Ser.). (ENG., Illus.). 24p. (J). (gr. 2-5). lib. bdg. 25.95 (978-1-60014-185-0(4)) Bellwether Media.

Mattern, Joanne. Hurricanes. 2013. (Illus.). 48p. (J). pap. 15.64 (978-1-62403-004-8(1)); (ENG., (gr. 3-6). lib. bdg. 32.79 (978-1-61783-939-9(6)) ABDO Publishing Co.

McAuliffe, Bill. Hurricanes. 2017. (J). **(978-1-60818-825-3(6)**, Creative Education) 2010. 47p. (YA). (gr. 4-7). lib. bdg. 23.95 (978-1-58341-928-1(4)) Creative Co., The.

Meister, Cari. Hurricanes. 2015. (Illus.). 24p. (J). lib. bdg. 25.65 (978-1-62031-221-6(2)) Jump! Inc.

Mezzanotte, Jim. Huracanes. 2007. (Tormentas (Storms) Ser.). (ENG & SPA., Illus.). 24p. (J). (gr. 1-4). pap. 8.15 (978-0-8368-8078-6(1)); lib. bdg. 22.00 (978-0-8368-8071-7(4)) Stevens, Gareth Publishing LLLP. (Weekly Reader Leveled Readers).

—Huracanes (Hurricanes) 2009. (Tiempo extremo Ser.). (SPA.). 24p. (J). (gr. k-3). pap. 8.15 (978-1-4339-2368-5(8)); lib. bdg. 22.00 (978-1-4339-2354-8(8)) Stevens, Gareth Publishing LLLP. (Weekly Reader Leveled Readers).

—Hurricanes. (Wild Weather Ser.). 24p. 2009. (ENG.). (J). (gr. k-3). pap. 8.15 (978-1-4339-2362-3(9)) 2009. (ENG.). (J). (gr. k-3). lib. bdg. 22.00 (978-1-4339-2348-7(3)) 2007. (Illus.). (gr. 1-4). pap. 8.15 (978-0-8368-7920-9(1)) 2007. (Illus.). (gr. 1-4). lib. bdg. 22.00 (978-0-8368-7913-1(9)) Stevens, Gareth Publishing LLLP. (Weekly Reader Leveled Readers).

Miller, Mara. Hurricane Katrina Strikes the Gulf Coast: Disaster & Survival. 2006. (Deadly Disasters Ser.). (Illus.). 48p. (J). (gr. 4-10). lib. bdg. 25.27 (978-0-7660-2803-6(8), 1251895) Enslow Pubs., Inc.

Miller, Petra. Hurricanes. 2015. (J). lib. bdg. (978-1-62713-521-4(9)) Cavendish Square Publishing.

Morris, Neil & Steele, Philip. Inside Hurricanes & Tornadoes. 2006. (Inside Nature's Disasters Ser.). (Illus.). 36p. (gr. 3-7). lib. bdg. 26.00 (978-0-8368-7249-1(5), Gareth Stevens Learning Library) Stevens, Gareth Publishing LLLP.

Murray, Peter. Hurricanes. 2015. (Forces of Nature Ser.). (ENG.). 24p. (J). (gr. 2-5). 27.07 (978-1-63143-767-0(4), 208607) Child's World, Inc., The.

Orr, Tamra B. We Have Hurricanes. 2015. (Tell Me Why Library). (ENG., Illus.). 24p. (J). (gr. 2-5). 27.07 (978-1-63362-619-5(9), 206660) Cherry Lake Publishing.

Ouellette, Jeannine. Hurricane Katrina, 1 vol. 2007. (Essential Events Set 1 Ser.). (ENG., Illus.). 112p. (J). (gr. 6-12). lib. bdg. 35.64 (978-1-59928-852-9(4)) ABDO Publishing Co.

Oxlade, Chris. Hurricanes. 2013. (Kingfisher Readers Ser.). (ENG., Illus.). 32p. (J). (gr. k-3). 12.99 (978-0-7534-6963-7(4), 9780753469637); pap. 3.99 (978-0-7534-6933-0(2), 9780753469330) Roaring Brook Pr. (Kingfisher).

Peppas, Lynn. Superstorm Sandy. 2013. (ENG., Illus.). 48p. (J). (978-0-7787-1193-3(5)); pap. (978-0-7787-1195-7(1)) Crabtree Publishing Co.

Perish, Patrick. Survive a Hurricane. 2016. (Survival Zone Ser.). (ENG., Illus.). 24p. (J). (gr. 3-7). 25.95 (978-1-62617-443-6(1), Torque Bks.) Bellwether Media.

Person, Stephen. Saving Animals from Hurricanes. 2011. (Rescuing Animals from Disasters Ser.). 32p. (YA). (gr. 2-5). lib. bdg. 25.27 (978-1-61772-290-5(1)) Bearport Publishing Co., Inc.

Phelan, Glen. Extreme Weather. 2007. (Reading Expeditions Ser.). (ENG., Illus.). 32p. (J). pap. 17.95 (978-0-7922-4575-9(X)) CENGAGE Learning.

Pietras, Jamie. Hurricane Katrina. 2008. (Great Historic Disasters Ser.). (Illus.). 128p. (gr. 5-8). lib. bdg. 35.00 (978-0-7910-9639-0(4), Chelsea Hse.) Facts On File, Inc.

Pitt, Steve. Rain Tonight: A Story of Hurricane Hazel. Collins, Heather, illus. 2004. (ENG.). 48p. (J). (gr. 3-7). pap. 6.95 (978-0-88776-641-1(2), Tundra Bks.) Tundra Bks. CAN. Dist: Penguin Random Hse. LLC.

Plattner, Josh & Craig, Diane. Hurricane or Waterspout?, 1 vol. 2016. (This or That? Weather Ser.). (ENG., Illus.). 24p. (J). (gr. k-4). 25.65 (978-1-62403-955-3(3)) ABDO Publishing Co.

Portman, Michael. Destructive Hurricanes. 2012. (Angry Earth Ser.). (ENG.). 32p. (gr. 3-6). (J). pap. 10.50 (978-1-4339-6539-5(9), Gareth Stevens Learning Library); (YA). lib. bdg. 26.60 (978-1-4339-6537-1(2)) Stevens, Gareth Publishing LLLP.

Pratt, Mary K. Hurricane Katrina & the Flooding of New Orleans: A Cause-And-Effect Investigation. 2016. (Cause-And-Effect Disasters Ser.). (ENG., Illus.). 40p. (J). (gr. 4-6). lib. bdg. 30.65 (978-1-5124-1117-1(5)) Lerner Publishing Group.

Randolph, Joanne, ed. Hurricane Warning! 2017. (Weather Report). 32p. (gr. 3-3). pap. 10.52 **(978-0-7660-9013-2(2))** Enslow Pubs., Inc.

Raum, Elizabeth. Hurricane! 2016. (Natural Disasters Ser.). (ENG., Illus.). 32p. (J). (gr. k-3). 20.95 (978-1-60753-991-9(8)) Amicus Publishing.

—Surviving Hurricanes, 1 vol. 2011. (Children's True Stories: Natural Disasters Ser.). (ENG.). 32p. (gr. 3-3). pap. 8.29 (978-1-4109-4100-8(0)); 30.65 (978-1-4109-4093-3(4)) Heinemann-Raintree. (Raintree Perspectives).

Reher, Matt. Hurricane Survival Guide. 2016. (2R Science Ser.). (ENG., Illus.). 32p. (J). pap. 5.99 **(978-1-63437-692-1(7))** American Reading Co.

Reina, Mary. The Science of a Hurricane. 2014. (21st Century Skills Library: Disaster Science Ser.). (ENG.). 32p. (J). (gr. 4-8). pap. 14.21 (978-1-63137-669-6(1), 205280) Cherry Lake Publishing.

Rice, William B. Los Huracanes, 1 vol. rev. ed. 2010. (Science Readers: a Closer Look Ser.). (SPA., Illus.). 32p. (J). (gr. 2-3). pap. 8.99 (978-1-4333-2156-6(4)) Shell Educational Publishing.

Rodger, Ellen. Hurricane Katrina. 2006. (Disaster Alert! Ser.). (ENG., Illus.). 32p. (J). (gr. 4). pap. (978-0-7787-1618-1(X)) Crabtree Publishing Co.

Royston, Angela. Hurricanes! 2010. (Eyewitness Disaster Ser.). 32p. (J). (gr. 2-5). 28.50 (978-1-60870-003-5(8)) Marshall Cavendish Corp.

—The Science of Hurricanes. 2013. (Nature's Wrath: the Science Behind Natural Disasters Ser.). (Illus.). 48p. (J). (gr. 4-6). 31.95 (978-1-4339-8659-8(0)); pap. 14.05 (978-1-4339-8660-4(4)) Stevens, Gareth Publishing LLLP. (Gareth Stevens Learning Library).

Rudolph, Jessica. Huracan. 2014. (Pedacitos Primeros Lectores: Que Desastre! Ser.). (SPA., Illus.). 24p. (J). (gr. -1-2). lib. bdg. 23.93 (978-1-62724-249-3(X)) Bearport Publishing Co., Inc.

—Hurricane. 2014. (It's a Disaster! Ser.). 24p. (J). (gr. -1-3). lib. bdg. 23.93 (978-1-62724-127-4(2)) Bearport Publishing Co., Inc.

Rustad, Martha E. H. Hurricanes, 1 vol. 2014. (Little Scientist Ser.). (ENG., Illus.). 32p. (gr. 1-2). 6.95 (978-1-4765-5268-2(1)) Capstone Press of Coughlan Cos.

—When Will It Rain? Noticing Weather Patterns. Conger, Holli, illus. 2015. (ENG.). 24p. (J). (gr. k-2). 25.32 (978-1-4677-8557-0(1), Millbrook Pr.) Lerner Publishing Group.

Ryback, Carol. Hurricanes. 2008. (Ultimate 10 Ser.). 48p. (YA). (gr. 5-9). lib. bdg. 31.00 (978-0-8368-9152-2(X)) Stevens, Gareth Publishing LLLP.

Sanders, Doug. Superstorm Sandy. 2013. (Code Red Ser.). 32p. (J). (gr. 2-7). lib. bdg. 25.27 (978-1-61772-898-3(5)) Bearport Publishing Co., Inc.

Schuh, Mari C. Hurricanes. 2016. (Earth in Action Ser.). (ENG.). 24p. pap. 6.95 (978-1-5157-6209-6(2), Pebble Plus) Capstone Press of Coughlan Cos.

—Hurricanes [Scholastic]. 2010. (Earth in Action Ser.). (ENG.). 24p. pap. 0.49 (978-1-4296-5800-3(2), Pebble Plus) Capstone Press of Coughlan Cos.

Shulman, Mark. Super Storms That Rocked the World: Hurricanes, Tsunamis, & Other Disasters. 2007. (Illus.). 40p. (J). (978-0-696-23702-7(4)) Meredith Bks.

Silverstein, Alvin, et al. Hurricanes: The Science Behind Killer Storms. 2009. (Science Behind Natural Disasters Ser.). (Illus.). 48p. (J). (gr. 5-9). lib. bdg. 25.27 (978-0-7660-2971-2(9)) Enslow Pubs., Inc.

Simon, Seymour. Hurricanes. 2015. 32p. pap. 7.00 (978-1-61003-608-5(5)) Center for the Collaborative Classroom.

—Hurricanes. (Illus.). 32p. (J). 2007. (ENG.). (gr. k-4). 17.99 (978-0-06-117072-0(0), Collins) 2007. (ENG., (gr. k-4). pap. 6.99 (978-0-06-117071-3(2), Collins) 2003. (gr. -1-3). lib. bdg. 17.89 (978-0-688-16292-4(4)) HarperCollins Pubs.

Somervill, Barbara A. Hurricanes. 2012. (21st Century Skills Library: Real World Math Ser.). (ENG., Illus.). 32p. (J). (gr. 4-8). pap. 14.21 (978-1-61080-408-0(2), 201340); lib. bdg. 28.50 (978-1-61080-325-0(6), 201302) Cherry Lake Publishing.

Sood, Malini. Hurricanes & Tornadoes. (Wild Nature Ser.). 48p. 2009. (gr. 4-5). 53.00 (978-1-60854-794-4(9), PowerKids Pr.) 2007. (Illus.). (YA). (gr. 3-6). lib. bdg. 29.25 (978-1-4042-3900-5(6)) Rosen Publishing Group, Inc., The.

Sorenson, Margo. Hurricane! Nature's Most Destructive Force. 2005. (Cover-to-Cover Informational Ser.). (Illus.). 56p. (gr. 4-7). lib. bdg. 17.95 (978-0-7569-4751-4(0)) Perfection Learning Corp.

Spilsbury, Louise & Spilsbury, Richard. Howling Hurricanes, 1 vol. 2nd ed. 2010. (Awesome Forces of Nature Ser.). (ENG., Illus.). 32p. (gr. 3-6). 33.32 (978-1-4329-3781-2(2)); pap. 8.29 (978-1-4329-3788-1(X)) Heinemann-Raintree. (Heinemann InfoSearch).

—Hurricanes & Tornadoes in Action. 2009. (Natural Disasters in Action Ser.). (ENG., Illus.). 48p. (J). (gr. 5-8). pap. 11.75 (978-1-4358-5133-7(1), 1284479, Rosen Reference) Rosen Publishing Group, Inc., The.

—Top 10 Worst Hurricanes. 2016. (Nature's Ultimate Disasters Ser.). 00032p. (J). (gr. 3-4). pap. 10.00 (978-1-4994-3077-6(9), PowerKids Pr.) Rosen Publishing Group, Inc., The.

Steele, Philip, et al. Extreme Planet. 2014. (Illus.). 128p. (J). (978-1-4351-5523-7(8)) Barnes & Noble, Inc.

Stewart, Melissa. Hurricane Watch. Morley, Taia, illus. 2015. (Let's-Read-And-Find-Out Science 2 Ser.). (ENG.). 40p. (J). (gr. -1-3). pap. 6.99 (978-0-06-232775-8(5)) HarperCollins Pubs.

Strom, Laura Layton. Built below Sea Level: New Orleans. 2007. (Shockwave: People & Communities Ser.). (ENG., Illus.). 36p. (J). (gr. 3-5). 25.00 *(978-0-531-17746-4(7),* Children's Pr.) Scholastic Library Publishing.

Thomas, Rick & Picture Window Books Staff. El Ojo de la Tormenta: Un Libro Sobre Huracanes, 1 vol. Robledo, Sol, tr. from ENG. Shea, Denise, illus. 2007. (Ciencia Asombrosa: el Tiempo Ser.). (SPA.). 24p. (gr. -1-3). 26.65 *(978-1-4048-3214-5(9))* Picture Window Bks.

Thoron, Joe. Hurricanes. 2006. (Kaleidoscope Natural Disasters Ser.). (Illus.). 48p. (gr. 3-7). lib. bdg. 20.95 *(978-0-7614-2103-0(3),* Benchmark Bks.) Marshall Cavendish Corp.

Torres, John. Hurricane Katrina 2005. 2006. (Natural Disasters Ser.). (Illus.). 32p. (J). (gr. 1-4). lib. bdg. 25.70 *(978-1-58415-498-3(5))* Mitchell Lane Pubs., Inc.

Torres, John Albert. Hurricane Katrina & the Devastation of New Orleans 2005. 2006. (Monumental Milestones Ser.). (Illus.). 48p. (YA). (gr. 4-7). lib. bdg. 29.95 *(978-1-58415-473-0(X))* Mitchell Lane Pubs., Inc.

Wall, Suzy. Hurricanes. 2004. (Shared Connections Ser.). (J). pap. *(978-1-4108-1643-6(5));* instr.'s gde. ed. 27.00 *(978-1-4108-1619-1(2))* Benchmark Education Co.

Why the Wild Winds Blow: Six-Pack. (Greetings Ser.: Vol. 1). (gr. 3-5). 31.00 *(978-0-7635-1838-7(7))* Rigby Education.

Wilson, Cristi. Just Because. Wilson, Cristi, illus. l.t. ed. 2006. (Illus.). 24p. (J). (gr. -1-3). per. 10.99 *(978-1-59879-251-5(2))* Lifevest Publishing, Inc.

Wolny, Philip. Hurricane: True Stories of Survival. 2009. (Survivor Stories Ser.). 48p. (gr. 5-5). 53.00 *(978-1-60853-254-4(2),* Rosen Reference) Rosen Publishing Group, Inc., The.

Woods, Matt. The Hurricane. 2017. (Text Connections Guided Close Reading Ser.). (J). (gr. 1). *(978-1-4900-1809-6(3))* Benchmark Education Co.

Woods, Michael & Woods, Mary B. Hurricanes. 2006. (Disasters up Close Ser.). (Illus.). 64p. (J). (gr. 3-7). lib. bdg. 27.93 *(978-0-8225-4710-5(4),* Lerner Pubns.) Lerner Publishing Group.

World Book, Inc. Staff, contrib. by. Hurricanes, Typhoons, & Other Tropical Cyclones. 2007. (J). *(978-0-7166-9808-1(0))* World Bk., Inc.

Zullo, Allan. Heroes of Hurricane Katrina. 2015. xii, 180p. (J). *(978-1-4806-8729-5(4))* Scholastic, Inc.

HURRICANES—FICTION

Abrams, Penny. The Calabash Tales. Mikki, illus. 2011. 66p. 28.00 *(978-1-4349-1169-8(1))* Dorrance Publishing Co., Inc.

Anastasia School, Amerigo. Powerful Hands. l.t. ed. 2006. (Illus.). 16p. (J). 19.95 *(978-1-59879-120-4(6));* per. 10.99 *(978-1-59879-096-2(X))* Lifevest Publishing, Inc.

Anderson, Laurie Halse. Storm Rescue. 2008. (Vet Volunteers Ser.: 6). (ENG.). 144p. (J). (gr. 3-7). 6.99 *(978-0-14-241101-8(9),* Puffin Books) Penguin Young Readers Group.

Anderson, T. Neill. City of the Dead: Galveston Hurricane 1900. 2013. (J). pap. 16.95 *(978-1-58089-515-6(8));* (ENG., Illus.). 144p. (YA). (gr. 7). 16.95 *(978-1-58089-514-9(X))* Charlesbridge Publishing, Inc.

Barret, Marie. Ms. Irene Is so Demanding. Guiza, Victor, illus. 2012. 26p. (J). 14.95 *(978-1-60131-110-8(9))* Big Tent Bks.

Beserra, Donna. Twirly Shirley In Hurricane Shirley. 2005. 22p. (J). 8.00 *(978-0-9729484-4-9(9))* Seventh Street Pr.

Brown, Joe. Race to the Rescue. Marchesi, Stephen, illus. 2009. (J). *(978-0-545-13473-6(0))* Scholastic, Inc.

Burk, Rachelle. Tree House in a Storm. Schneider, Rex, illus. 2009. 42p. (J). (gr. k-4). 16.95 *(978-0-916144-23-4(2))* Stemmer Hse. Pubs.

Candy, Wolf. The Tree, the House & the Hurricane. l.t. ed. 2005. (Illus.). 24p. (J). 7.00 *(978-0-9762292-3-0(4))* New Global Publishing.

Carter, Denzel T. Hannah & the Hurricane. 2015. (Rosen REAL Readers: STEM & STEAM Collection). (ENG.). 12p. (gr. 1-2). pap. 6.33 *(978-1-4994-9527-0(7),* Rosen Classroom) Rosen Publishing Group, Inc., The.

Cohen, Pamela. Ashie: Lost in a Hurricane, 1 vol. 2010. 40p. 24.95 *(978-1-4512-1169-6(4))* PublishAmerica, Inc.

Collard, Sneed B., III. Double Eagle, 1 vol. 2011. (ENG.). 256p. pap. 7.95 *(978-1-56145-599-7(7),* Peachtree Junior) Peachtree Pubs.

Connelly, Neil. Into the Hurricane. 2017. (ENG.). 240p. (J). (gr. 9). 17.99 ***(978-0-545-85381-1(8),*** Levine, Arthur A. Bks.) Scholastic, Inc.

Cronin, Carol Newman. Cape Cod Surprise: Oliver Matches Wits with Hurricane Carol. Cronin, Laurie Ann, illus. 2010. (ENG.). 150p. (J). pap. 9.95 *(978-1-934848-47-0(6))* GemmaMedia.

—Oliver's Surprise: A Boy, a Schooner, & the Great Hurricane of 1938. Cronin, Laurie, illus. rev. ed. 2009. (ENG.). 150p. (J). (gr. 4-7). pap. 9.95 *(978-1-934848-62-3(X))* GemmaMedia.

Davis, Mike. Land of the Lost Mammoths: A Science Adventure. 2003. (Illus.). 174p. (J). 15.95 *(978-0-9747078-0-8(5))* Perceval Pr.

Day, Jan. Kissimmee Pete & the Hurricane, 1 vol. Mason, Janeen, illus. 2008. (ENG.). 32p. (J). (gr. 1-3). 16.99 *(978-1-58980-544-6(5))* Pelican Publishing Co., Inc.

Dean, Janice. Freddy the Frogcaster & the Huge Hurricane. 2015. (Freddy the Frogcaster Ser.). (ENG., Illus.). 40p. (J). (gr. -1-3). 16.99 *(978-1-62157-260-2(9),* Regnery Kids) Regnery Publishing, Inc., An Eagle Publishing Co.

Donald, Margaret. Tipsy: The Hurricane Hero. 2007. (ENG.). 26p. (J). (gr. k-2). *(978-81-8386-050-5(8))* India Research Pr. IND. Dist: Independent Pubs. Group.

Dragon, Laura. Hurricane Boy, 1 vol. 2014. (ENG., Illus.). 160p. (J). (gr. 3-7). pap. 8.95 *(978-1-4556-1916-0(7))* Pelican Publishing Co., Inc.

Eleanor, Coalson. Simon Says Run. 2006. (Illus.). (J). 8.95 *(978-1-56167-944-7(5))* American Literary Pr.

Ely, Scott. The Elephant Mountains, 1 vol. 2011. (ENG.). 216p. (J). (gr. 8-12). lib. bdg. 19.95 *(978-1-55469-406-8(X))* Orca Bk. Pubs. USA.

Escott, John & Pearson Longman Staff. Hannah & the Hurricane. 2nd ed. 2009. (ENG., Illus.). 20p. pap. 11.99 *(978-1-4058-6947-8(X))* Pearson Education.

Ford, Sandy Lee, illus. Guilah, the Nawleans Cat Meets Katrina. 2007. 32p. (J). *(978-0-9793637-0-2(5))* Hart Street Pubs.

Freeman, Shannon. Traumatized. 2014. (Port City High Ser.: 7). (YA). lib. bdg. 20.80 *(978-0-606-36619-9(9))* Turtleback Bks.

Gilbert, Julie. Into the Storm: A Mermaid's Journey. Fagan, Kirbi, illus. 2017. (Dark Waters Ser.). (ENG.). 160p. (gr. 2-4). pap. 6.95 *(978-1-4965-4175-8(8));* lib. bdg. 26.65 *(978-1-4965-4171-0(5))* Stone Arch Bks.

Gildea, Kathy. The Adventures of Baylee Beagle — Hurricane Hound. Larson, Amanda, illus. 2005. 28p. (J). 7.95 *(978-0-9767096-2-6(7))* Maxim Pr.

Gott, Robert. Jinxed. 2007. 96p. (YA). pap. *(978-1-4207-0732-8(9))* Sundance/Newbridge Educational Publishing.

Greene, Janice. The Eye of the Hurricane, 1 vol. unabr. ed. 2010. (Q Reads Ser.). (ENG.). 32p. (YA). (gr. 9-12). pap. 6.95 *(978-1-61651-191-3(5))* Saddleback Educational Publishing, Inc.

Hale, Marian. Dark Water Rising. 2010. (ENG.). 256p. (J). (gr. 5-9). pap. 7.99 *(978-0-312-62908-3(7),* 9780312629083) Square Fish.

Hanson, Ed. Hurricane. 2005. (Barclay Family Adventures 2 Ser.). 64p. (J). per. 3.95 *(978-1-56254-805-6(0),* SP8050) Saddleback Educational Publishing, Inc.

Harlow, Joan Hiatt. Blown Away! (ENG.). 272p. (J). (gr. 4-7). 2008. pap. 7.99 *(978-1-4169-0782-4(3))* 2007. 16.99 *(978-1-4169-0781-7(5))* McElderry, Margaret K. Bks. (McElderry, Margaret K. Bks.).

Haydel, Catherine. Uno the Cat & Hurricane Katrina. 2006. 18.00 *(978-0-8059-7341-9(9))* Dorrance Publishing Co., Inc.

Jackson, Nellie O. The Worst Day of My Life. 2008. 24p. pap. 24.95 *(978-1-60474-524-5(X))* America Star Bks.

Kapica, Dan. Mangrove Seed Chronicles: Learning to Trust. 2007. (Illus.). 64p. 24.95 *(978-0-9797158-0-8(6),* Mangrove Seed Expressions) Mangrove Seed, Inc.

Kephart, Beth. This Is the Story of You. 2016. (ENG., Illus.). 264p. (YA). (gr. 7-12). 17.99 *(978-1-4521-4284-5(X))* Chronicle Bks. LLC.

Key, Watt. Terror at Bottle Creek. 2016. (ENG.). 224p. (J). 16.99 *(978-0-374-37430-3(9),* 9780374374303, Farrar, Straus & Giroux (BYR)) Farrar, Straus & Giroux.

Lake, Julie. Galveston's Summer of the Storm. 2003. (Chaparral Bks.). (ENG.). 158p. pap. 17.95 *(978-0-87565-272-6(7))* Texas Christian Univ. Pr.

Lamana, Julie T. Upside down in the Middle of Nowhere. 2015. (ENG.). 328p. (J). (gr. 4-7). pap. 7.99 *(978-1-4521-2880-1(4))* Chronicle Bks. LLC.

Lance, Scott. Pourman's Library. 2003. 108p. (YA). pap. 10.95 *(978-0-595-30148-5(7))* iUniverse, Inc.

Laurie, Peter. Mauby & the Hurricane. 2007. (Illus.). 56p. pap. 16.00 *(978-1-4050-7718-7(2))* Macmillan Caribbean GBR. Dist: Interlink Publishing Group, Inc.

Maguire, Gregory. What-the-Dickens: The Story of a Rogue Tooth Fairy. 2008. (ENG., Illus.). 304p. (gr. 4-7). pap. 8.99 *(978-0-7636-4147-4(2))* Candlewick Pr.

Mann's Miracles, creator. When the Hurricane Blew. 2005. (Illus.). 34p. (J). (gr. 3-7). per. *(978-0-9773569-0-4(6))* Clear Horizon.

Marsh, Carole. The Horrendous Hurricane Mystery. 2007. (Masters of Disasters Ser.). (Illus.). 118p. (J). (gr. 2-9). 14.95 *(978-0-635-06396-0(4))* Gallopade International.

Mason, Dianne. Danny's Ghost. 2007. 156p. pap. 9.39 *(978-1-4116-4937-8(0))* Lulu Pr., Inc.

Mau, Connie. Catch me if you Can. Lemus, Kristina, illus. l.t. ed. 2006. 28p. (J). 14.95 *(978-0-9778843-0-8(9))* Mau, C. Publishing Co.

McDonald, Megan. Judy Moody & Stink: the Big Bad Blackout. Reynolds, Peter H., illus. 2015. (Judy Moody Ser.). (ENG.). 144p. (J). (gr. 1-4). pap. 6.99 *(978-0-7636-7665-0(9))* Candlewick Pr.

Mercier, Deirdre McLaughlin. Yesterday We Had a Hurricane. 2006. (Illus.). 40p. (J). (gr. -1-3). 17.95 *(978-0-9754342-5-3(X))* Bumble Bee Publishing.

—Yesterday We Had a Hurricane/Ayer Tuvimos un Huracan. 2006. (SPA & ENG., Illus.). 40p. (J). (gr. -1-3). lib. bdg. 17.95 *(978-0-9754342-9-1(2))* Bumble Bee Publishing.

Miller, D. C. Hurricane Hunters: A Craig Hancock Adventure. 2005. (YA). pap. 12.95 *(978-1-59088-646-5(1))* Wings ePress, Inc.

Navarro-Talavera, Carmen. The Ant Lucy & the Hurricane. 2009. 48p. pap. 17.49 *(978-1-4389-7788-1(3))* AuthorHouse.

—La Hormiguita Lucy y el Huracán. 2009. 48p. pap. 17.49 *(978-1-4389-7787-4(5))* AuthorHouse.

Nicholls, Dee. Hurricane Day. 2013. 26p. pap. 8.99 *(978-1-60820-862-3(1))* MLR Pr., LLC.

Paley, Jane. Hooper Finds a Family: A Hurricane Katrina Dog's Survival Tale. 2011. (ENG.). 144p. (J). (gr. 3-7). 16.99 *(978-0-06-201103-9(0))* HarperCollins Pubs.

Paterson, Diane. Hurricane Wolf. Paterson, Diane, illus. 2006. (ENG., Illus.). 32p. (J). (gr. k-3). lib. bdg. 16.99 *(978-0-8075-3438-0(2))* Whitman, Albert & Co.

Patrick, Denise Lewis. Finding Someplace. 2015. (ENG.). 224p. (J). (gr. 3-7). 16.99 *(978-0-8050-4716-5(6),* 9780805047165, Holt, Henry & Co. Bks. For Young Readers) Holt, Henry & Co.

—Finding Someplace. 2016. (ENG.). 224p. (J). pap. 7.99 *(978-1-250-07982-4(9),* 9781250079824) Square Fish.

—Finding Someplace. 2016. (J). lib. bdg. 17.20 *(978-0-606-38560-2(6))* Turtleback Bks.

Philbrick, Rodman. Zane & the Hurricane: A Story of Katrina. 2015. (ENG.). 192p. (J). (gr. 5-9). 18.00 *(978-1-68065-202-4(8))* Perfection Learning Corp.

—Zane & the Hurricane: A Story of Katrina. 2014. (ENG., Illus.). 192p. (J). (gr. 5-9). 16.99 *(978-0-545-34238-4(4),* Blue Sky Pr., The) Scholastic, Inc.

Pippin, Sheila C. Katrina: Through Mango's Eyes. Pippin, Kristin A. & Pippin, Sheila C., illus. 2007. (J). (gr. -1-5). pap. 12.95 *(978-1-56167-956-0(9))* American Literary Pr.

Powell, GinaMarie. Ayiana & the Hurricane Katrina Classmate. Bray, Pamela, illus. 2008. 28p. pap. 24.95 *(978-1-60441-965-8(2))* America Star Bks.

Ransom, Candice. The Night of the Hurricane's Fury. Tong, Paul, illus. (On My Own History Ser.). 48p. 2011. (J). pap. 39.62 *(978-0-7613-7621-7(6),* First Avenue Editions) 2011. (ENG.). (gr. 2-4). pap. 6.95 *(978-0-7613-3940-3(X),* First Avenue Editions) 2009. (ENG.). (gr. 2-4). 25.26 *(978-0-8225-7893-2(X))* Lerner Publishing Group.

Raver-Lampman, Greg. Adrift: Lost in Life, Marooned at Sea. 2006. 132p. 14.95 *(978-1-888842-32-6(6))* Absey & Co.

Rhodes, Jewell Parker. Ninth Ward. 2010. (ENG.). 224p. (J). (gr. 5-17). 15.99 *(978-0-316-04307-6(9))* Little, Brown Bks. for Young Readers.

Rivers, Phoebe. A Perfect Storm. 2013. (Saranormal Ser.: 10). (ENG., Illus.). 160p. (J). (gr. 3-7). 15.99 *(978-1-4424-8959-2(6));* pap. 5.99 *(978-1-4424-8958-5(8))* Simon Spotlight. (Simon Spotlight).

Robison, Peggy. Prince Cody Runs Ahead of the Hurricane. Clay, Doris, illus. 2005. 64p. per. 9.95 *(978-0-9764982-7-8(8))* Legacy Publishing Services, Inc.

Roddy, Lee. Eye of the Hurricane. 2007. (Ladd Family Adventure Ser.: Vol. 9). (Illus.). 161p. (J). (gr. 3-7). per. 7.99 *(978-0-88062-258-5(X))* Mott Media.

Rose, Caroline Starr. Over in the Wetlands: A Hurricane on the Bayou Story. Dunlavey, Rob, illus. 2015. (ENG.). 40p. (J). (gr. -1-3). 17.99 *(978-0-449-81016-3(X),* Schwartz & Wade Bks.) Random Hse. Children's Bks.

Ryherd, Tim. My Hurricane Book. 2006. (Illus.). (J). 12.95 *(978-0-9749974-1-4(2))* Ryherd, Tim Publishing.

Saddleback Educational Publishing, ed. Shelter, 1 vol. 2013. (Heights Ser.). (ENG.). 52p. (gr. 5-8). 7.95 *(978-1-62250-046-8(6))* Saddleback Educational Publishing, Inc.

Salisbury, Graham. Hero of Hawaii. Rogers, Jacqueline, illus. 2012. (Calvin Coconut Ser.). (ENG.). 160p. (J). (gr. 2-5). pap. 6.99 *(978-0-375-86505-3(5),* Yearling) Random Hse. Children's Bks.

Salkey, Andrew. Hurricane. 2011. (Caribbean Modern Classics Ser.). (ENG., Illus.). 104p. (J). (gr. 7-7). pap. 13.95 *(978-1-84523-180-4(5))* Peepal Tree Pr., Ltd. GBR. Dist: Independent Pubs. Group.

Sanchez, Kevin & Sanchez, Laura. Nikki's Hurricane Adventure. 2011. 24p. pap. 11.32 *(978-1-4567-1452-9(X))* AuthorHouse.

Shah, Meera. And, Then Came Katrina. l.t. ed. 2005. (Illus.). 32p. (YA). pap. 12.99 *(978-0-9774219-0-9(2))* Shah, Meera.

Shotz, Jennifer Li. Hurricane Rescue. 2017. (Hero Ser.: 2). lib. bdg. 18.40 ***(978-0-606-40134-0(2))*** Turtleback Bks.

Smith, Roland. Storm Runners. (Storm Runners Ser.: Bk. 1). (ENG.). 160p. (J). (gr. 3-7). 2012. pap. 5.99 *(978-0-545-08177-1(7),* Scholastic Pr.) 2011. 16.99 *(978-0-545-08175-7(0))* Scholastic, Inc.

—The Surge. 2011. (Storm Runners Ser.: 2). (J). (ENG.). 144p. (gr. 3-7). 16.99 *(978-0-545-08179-5(3));* 133p. pap. *(978-0-545-39462-8(7))* Scholastic, Inc. (Scholastic Pr.).

Smith, Tamara Ellis. Another Kind of Hurricane. 2015. (ENG.). 336p. (J). (gr. 4-7). 19.99 *(978-0-553-51194-9(7));* 16.99 *(978-0-553-51193-2(9))* Random Hse. Children's Bks. (Schwartz & Wade Bks.).

Sniegoski, Thomas E. Savage. (Savage Ser.). (ENG.). (YA). (gr. 9). 2017. 432p. pap. 9.99 *(978-1-4814-4374-6(7))* 2016. (Illus.). 416p. 17.99 *(978-1-4814-4373-9(9))* Simon Pulse. (Simon Pulse).

Snyder, Sandy. New Orleans Dogs Allowed. 2008. 60p. pap. 19.95 *(978-1-60672-781-2(8))* America Star Bks.

Strong, Jeremy. Giant Jim & the Hurricane. (Illus.). 96p. (J). pap. 7.95 *(978-0-14-038248-8(8))* Penguin Bks., Ltd. GBR. Dist: Trafalgar Square Publishing.

Tarshis, Lauren. I Survived Hurricane Katrina 2005. 2011. (I Survived Ser.: 3). (ENG.). 112p. (J). (gr. 3-7). pap. 4.99 *(978-0-545-20696-9(0),* Scholastic Paperbacks) Scholastic, Inc.

—I Survived Hurricane Katrina 2005. 2011. (I Survived ... Ser.: No. 3). lib. bdg. 14.75 *(978-0-606-23743-7(7),* Turtleback) Turtleback Bks.

Trueman, Terry. Hurricane. 2008. (ENG.). 144p. (J). (gr. 5-9). 16.99 *(978-0-06-000018-9(X))* HarperCollins Pubs.

Uhlberg, Myron. A Storm Called Katrina, 1 vol. Bootman, Colin, illus. 2011. (ENG.). 40p. (J). (gr. 2-6). 17.95 *(978-1-56145-591-1(1))* Peachtree Pubs.

Wallner, Alexandra. Sergio & the Hurricane. 2006. (Illus.). (J). (gr. 1-3). 14.60 *(978-0-7569-6800-7(3))* Perfection Learning Corp.

Watson, Renée. A Place Where Hurricanes Happen. Strickland, Shadra, illus. 2014. (ENG.). 40p. (J). (gr. k-4). 7.99 *(978-0-385-37668-6(5),* Dragonfly Bks.) Random Hse. Children's Bks.

—A Place Where Hurricanes Happen. Strickland, Shadra, illus. 2010. (ENG.). 40p. (J). (gr. k-4). 17.99 *(978-0-375-85609-9(9),* Random Hse. Bks. for Young Readers) Random Hse. Children's Bks.

What Young Hearts Whisper. 2006. (Illus.). (J). per. 23.00 *(978-0-9785269-0-0(2))* Phi Sigma Omega, Alpha Kappa Alpha Sorority, Inc.

What Young Hearts Whisper - Stories of Survival - Hurricanes Katrina & Rita Special Edition. 2006. per. 27.50 *(978-0-9785269-1-7(0))* Phi Sigma Omega, Alpha Kappa Alpha Sorority, Inc.

Wiesner, David. Hurricane, 1 vol. Wiesner, David, illus. 2008. (Read along Book & CD Ser.). (ENG., Illus.). 32p. (J). (gr. -1-3). 10.99 *(978-0-547-06433-8(0))* Houghton Mifflin Harcourt Publishing Co.

Woods, Brenda. Saint Louis Armstrong Beach. 2012. (ENG.). 160p. (J). (gr. 5). pap. 5.99 *(978-0-14-242186-4(3),* Puffin Books) Penguin Young Readers Group.

—Saint Louis Armstrong Beach. 2012. lib. bdg. 16.00 *(978-0-606-26661-1(5),* Turtleback) Turtleback Bks.

Woodson, Jacqueline. Beneath a Meth Moon: An Elegy. (ENG.). (YA). (gr. 7). 2013. 240p. pap. 8.99 *(978-0-14-242392-9(0),* Speak) 2012. 144p. 16.99 *(978-0-399-25250-1(9),* Nancy Paulsen Books) Penguin Young Readers Group.

HUSSEIN, SADDAM, 1937-2006

Anderson, Dale. Saddam Hussein. 2004. (A&E Biography Ser.). (Illus.). 112p. (J). 29.27 *(978-0-8225-5005-1(9),* Lerner Pubns.) Lerner Publishing Group.

Payment, Simone. Finding & Capturing Saddam Hussein: A Successful Military Manhunt. 2009. (Frontline Coverage of Current Events Ser.). 48p. (gr. 5-5). 53.00 *(978-1-61512-654-5(6))* Rosen Publishing Group, Inc., The.

Richie, Jason. Iraq & the Fall of Saddam Hussein. 2003. (Illus.). 112p. (J). (gr. 5-18). lib. bdg. 24.95 *(978-1-881508-63-2(3))* Oliver Pr., Inc.

Shields, Charles J. & Koestler-Grack, Rachel A. Saddam Hussein. 2nd rev. ed. 2005. (Major World Leaders Ser.). (Illus.). 112p. (gr. 6-12). 30.00 *(978-0-7910-8576-9(7),* Chelsea Hse.) Facts On File, Inc.

Wheeler, Jill C. Saddam Hussein. 2004. (War in Iraq Ser.). 48p. (gr. 4-8). 27.07 *(978-1-59197-499-4(2),* Abdo & Daughters) ABDO Publishing Co.

Wingate, Brian. Saddam Hussein. 2009. (Middle East Leaders Ser.). 112p. (gr. 5-8). 66.50 *(978-1-61514-648-2(2),* Rosen Reference) Rosen Publishing Group, Inc., The.

—Saddam Hussein: The Rise & Fall of a Dictator. 2004. (Middle East Leaders Ser.). (Illus.). 112p. (J). (gr. 5-8). lib. bdg. 34.60 *(978-0-8239-4468-2(9),* Rosen Reference) Rosen Publishing Group, Inc., The.

HUTCHINSON, ANNE MARBURY, 1591-1643

Aller, Susan Bivin. Anne Hutchinson. 2010. (History Maker Biographies Ser.). (ENG.). 48p. (gr. 3-6). lib. bdg. 27.93 *(978-0-7613-5208-2(2),* Lerner Pubns.) Lerner Publishing Group.

Marsh, Carole. Anne Hutchinson. 2004. 12p. (gr. k-4). 2.95 *(978-0-635-02370-4(9))* Gallopade International.

Miller, Barbara Kiely. Anne Hutchinson. 2007. (Great Americans Ser.). 24p. (gr. 1-4). pap. 8.15 *(978-0-8368-8324-4(1));* (SPA.). pap. 8.15 *(978-0-8368-8337-4(3));* (Illus.). lib. bdg. 22.00 *(978-0-8368-8317-6(9));* (SPA., Illus.). lib. bdg. 22.00 *(978-0-8368-8330-5(6))* Stevens, Gareth Publishing LLLP. (Weekly Reader Leveled Readers).

Nichols, Joan K. A Matter of Conscience: The Trial of Anne Hutchinson. Krovatin, Dan, illus. 2009. (Steck-Vaughn Stories of America Ser.). (ENG.). 112p. (gr. 3-8). pap. 14.20 *(978-0-8114-8073-4(9))* Houghton Mifflin Harcourt Publishing Co.

Slavicek, Louise Chipley. Anne Hutchinson. 2010. (Leaders of the Colonial Era Ser.). 120p. (gr. 5-8). 35.00 *(978-1-60413-741-5(X),* Chelsea Hse.) Facts On File, Inc.

HYBRIDIZATION

see Plant Breeding

HYDRAULIC ENGINEERING

see also Hydrostatics; Irrigation; Reclamation of Land; Rivers; Water; Water-Supply Engineering; Wells

Bjorklund, Ruth. The Pros & Cons of Natural Gas & Fracking. 2014. (Economics of Energy Ser.). 80p. (YA). (gr. 7-10). lib. bdg. 35.64 *(978-1-62712-921-3(9))* Cavendish Square Publishing.

Dickmann, Nancy. Fracking: Fracturing Rock to Reach Oil & Gas Underground. 2015. (Next Generation Energy Ser.). (ENG., Illus.). 32p. (J). *(978-0-7787-1984-7(7));* pap. *(978-0-7787-2007-2(1))* Crabtree Publishing Co.

Felix, Rebecca. 12 Things to Know about Fracking. 2015. (ENG., Illus.). 32p. (J). *(978-1-63235-029-9(7))* Pr. Room Editions LLC.

—12 Things to Know about Fracking. 2015. (Today's News Ser.). lib. bdg. 20.80 *(978-0-606-37378-4(0))* Turtleback Bks.

Loh-Hagan, Virginia. Water Parks. 2017. (21st Century Junior Library: Extraordinary Engineering Ser.). (ENG., Illus.). 24p. (J). (gr. 2-5). lib. bdg. 27.07 *(978-1-63472-168-4(3),* 209244) Cherry Lake Publishing.

Nagelhout, Ryan. Fracking. 2014. (Habitat Havoc Ser.). (Illus.). 32p. (J). (gr. 2-5). pap. 10.50 *(978-1-4339-9855-3(6))* Stevens, Gareth Publishing LLLP.

—FRACKING. 2014. (Illus.). 32p. (J). *(978-1-4339-9856-0(4));* lib. bdg. *(978-1-4339-9919-2(6))* Stevens, Gareth Publishing LLLP.

—How Do Dams Work? 2016. (STEM Waterworks Ser.). 32p. (J). (gr. 5-5). pap. 11.75 *(978-1-4994-1999-3(6),* PowerKids Pr.) Rosen Publishing Group, Inc., The.

Parker, Steve. Natural Gas, Vol. 12. 2015. (North American Natural Resources Ser.). (Illus.). 64p. (J). (gr. 7). 23.95 *(978-1-4222-3385-6(5))* Mason Crest.

Phillips, Cynthia & Priwer, Shana. Dams & Waterways. 2009. (ENG., Illus.). 112p. (C). (gr. 6-18). lib. bdg. 158.00 *(978-0-7656-8122-5(6),* Y181910) Routledge.

Spilsbury, Richard & Spilsbury, Louise. Water, Waves, & Tidal Power. 2012. (Let's Discuss Energy Resources Ser.). (Illus.). 32p. (YA). (gr. 4-7). lib. bdg. 26.50 *(978-1-4488-5263-5(3))* Rosen Publishing Group, Inc., The.

Squire, Ann O. Hydrofracking. 2013. (Cornerstones of Freedom™, Third Ser.). (ENG.). 64p. (J). 30.00 *(978-0-531-23604-8(8));* pap. 8.95 *(978-0-531-21962-1(3))* Scholastic Library Publishing. (Children's Pr.).

HYDROELECTRIC POWER

see Water Power

HYDROFOIL BOATS

Tieck, Sarah. Hovercraft, 1 vol. 2011. (Amazing Vehicles Set 2 Ser.). (ENG., Illus.). 32p. (J). (gr. 2-5). 28.50 *(978-1-61714-698-5(6))* ABDO Publishing Co.

HYDROLOGY

see Water

HYDROSTATICS

Adler, David A. Things That Float & Things That Don't. Raff, Anna, illus. (ENG.). 32p. (J). (gr. -1-2). 2014. 7.99 *(978-0-8234-3176-2(2))* 2013. 16.95 *(978-0-8234-2862-5(1))* Holiday Hse., Inc.

Boothroyd, Jennifer. What Floats? What Sinks? A Look at Density. 2010. (Lightning Bolt Books (tm) — Exploring Physical Science Ser.). (ENG.). 32p. (gr. k-2). pap. 7.95 *(978-0-7613-6055-1(7));* (Illus.). lib. bdg. 26.60 *(978-0-7613-5433-8(6))* Lerner Publishing Group.

Famighetti, Robert, et al. Why Do Ships Float? 2009. (Science in the Real World Ser.). (Illus.). 32p. (gr. 4-6). 28.00 *(978-1-60413-466-7(6),* Chelsea Clubhouse) Facts On File, Inc.

Guillain, Charlotte. Flota o Se Hunde, 1 vol. 2010. (Las Propiedades de Los Materiales Ser.). (SPA.). 24p. (gr. -1-1). 22.65 *(978-1-4329-4243-4(3));* pap. 6.29 *(978-1-4329-4251-9(4))* Heinemann-Raintree. (Bellota).

Murray, Julie. Floating & Sinking, 1 vol. 2006. (First Science Ser.). (ENG.). 24p. (gr. k-4). 25.65 *(978-1-59679-823-6(8),* Buddy Bks.) ABDO Publishing Co.

Nelson, Robin. Flotar y Hundirse. Translations.com Staff, tr. from ENG. 2007. (Mi Primer Paso Al Mundo Real - Fuerzas y Movimiento (First Step Nonfiction - Forces & Motion) Ser.). (SPA., Illus.). 24p. (gr. k-2). lib. bdg. 23.93 *(978-0-8225-7808-6(5),* Ediciones Lerner) Lerner Publishing Group.

—Flotar Y Hundirse; Float & Sink. 2008. pap. 34.95 (978-0-8225-9896-1(5)) Lerner Publishing Group.

Weakland, Mark. Captain Kidd's Crew Experiments with Sinking & Floating, 1 vol. Cummings, Troy, illus. 2012. (In the Science Lab Ser.). (ENG.). 24p. (gr. 2-3). pap. 9.95 (978-1-4048-7236-3(1)); lib. bdg. 26.65 (978-1-4048-7144-1(6)) Picture Window Bks.

HYENAS

Carr, Aaron. Hyena. 2014. (J). (978-1-4896-2629-5(8)) Weigl Pubs., Inc.

Gagne, Tammy. Hyenas: Built for the Hunt. 2016. (Predator Profiles Ser.). (ENG., Illus.). 24p. (gr. 1-2). lib. bdg. 25.32 (978-1-4914-8259-9(1)) Capstone Press of Coughlan Cos.

Gibbs, Maddie. Hyenas. 2011. (Safari Animals Ser.). (ENG.). 24p. (J). pap. 8.25 (978-1-4488-2598-1(9)); lib. bdg. 22.60 (978-1-4488-2506-6(7)) Rosen Publishing Group, Inc., The. (PowerKids Pr.).

—Hyenas: Hienas. 2011. (Safari Animals / Animales de Safari Ser.). (ENG & SPA.). 24p. (J). (gr. -1-2). lib. bdg. 22.60 (978-1-4488-3120-3(2)) Rosen Publishing Group, Inc., The.

Grucella, Ethan. Hyenas. 2010. (Animals That Live in the Grasslands Ser.). (ENG.). 24p. (J). (gr. -1-3). pap. 8.15 (978-1-4339-3870-2(7)); lib. bdg. 22.60 (978-1-4339-3869-6(3)) Stevens, Gareth Publishing LLLP.

Lunis, Natalie. Hyena: Who's Laughing? 2011. (Animal Loudmouths: Noisy Animals Ser.). 24p. (J). (gr. k-3). lib. bdg. 22.61 (978-1-61772-278-3(2)) Bearport Publishing Co., Inc.

Malam, John. Hyenas - Scary Creatures. 2008. (Scary Creatures Ser.). (ENG., Illus.). 32p. (J). (gr. 2-4). 27.00 (978-0-531-21746-7(9), Watts, Franklin) Scholastic Library Publishing.

Markle, Sandra. Hyenas. (Animal Scavengers Ser.). (ENG., Illus.). 40p. (gr. 3-6). 2006. pap. 7.95 (978-0-8225-3468-6(1), First Avenue Editions) 2005. lib. bdg. 25.26 (978-0-8225-3194-4(1), Lerner Pubns.) Lerner Publishing Group.

O'Mara, Kennon. Hunting with Hyenas, Vol. 1. 2014. (Animal Attack! Ser.). (Illus.). 32p. (J). (gr. 2-5). pap. 48.90 (978-1-4824-0492-0(3), 1368252) Stevens, Gareth Publishing LLLP.

Owens, Henry. How to Track a Hyena, 1. 2014. (Scatalog: a Kid's Field Guide to Animal Poop Ser.). (ENG.). 24p. (J). (gr. k-5). 23.60 (978-1-61533-889-4(6), Windmill Bks.) Rosen Publishing Group, Inc., The.

Pearl, Norman. Hyenas: Fierce Hunters. 2009. (Powerful Predators Ser.). 24p. (gr. 2-3). 42.50 (978-1-60851-347-5(5)); (Illus.). (J). lib. bdg. 22.60 (978-1-4042-4508-2(1)) Rosen Publishing Group, Inc., The. (PowerKids Pr.).

Quinlan, Julia J. Hyenas. 2013. (Ferocious Fighting Animals Ser.). (ENG., Illus.). 24p. (J). (gr. k-5). pap. 8.25 (978-1-4488-9804-6(8), PowerKids Pr.) Rosen Publishing Group, Inc., The.

Rake, Jody Sullivan. Hyenas: On the Hunt, 1 vol. 2010. (Killer Animals Ser.). (ENG.). 32p. (gr. 1-2). lib. bdg. 26.65 (978-1-4296-3926-2(1), Blazers) Capstone Press of Coughlan Cos.

Roza, Greg. Tasmanian Devil vs. Hyena. 2015. (Bizarre Beast Battles Ser.). (ENG.). 24p. (J). (gr. 2-3). 22.60 (978-1-4824-2798-1(2)) Stevens, Gareth Publishing LLLP.

Rudolph, Jessica. Mi Melena Es Corta e Hirsuta (Hyena) 2016. (Pistas de Animales 2 Ser.). (SPA.). 24p. (J). (gr. -1-3). 17.95 (978-1-944102-76-0(0)) Bearport Publishing Co., Inc.

—My Mane Is Short & Spiky (Hyena) 2016. (Zoo Clues 2 Ser.). (ENG.). 24p. (J). (gr. -1-3). 17.95 (978-1-944102-58-6(2)) Bearport Publishing Co., Inc.

Schlaepfer, Gloria G. Hyenas. 2010. (Animals, Animals Ser.). 48p. (gr. 3-6). 23.95 (978-0-7614-4838-9(1)) Marshall Cavendish GBR. Dist: Marshall Cavendish Corp.

Schuetz, Kari. Hyenas. 2012. (Animal Safari Ser.). (ENG., Illus.). 24p. (J). (gr. k-3). lib. bdg. 25.95 (978-1-60014-717-3(8), Blastoff! Readers) Bellwether Media.

Spilsbury, Louise. Hyena, 1 vol. 2011. (Day in the Life: Grassland Animals Ser.). (ENG., Illus.). 24p. (J). (gr. k-2). pap. 6.79 (978-1-4329-4742-2(7), Heinemann Read & Learn) Heinemann-Raintree.

HYENAS—FICTION

Bloch, Carole. The Hyena & the Seven Little Kids. Morris, Hannah, illus. 2012. (Best Loved Tales for Africa Ser.). (ENG.). 32p. (J). (gr. k-2). pap. 9.95 (978-1-77009-820-6(8)) Jacana Media ZAF. Dist: Independent Pubs. Group.

Cannon, Janell. Pinduli. Cannon, Janell, illus. 2004. (ENG., Illus.). 48p. (J). (gr. -1-3). 17.99 (978-0-15-204668-2(2)) Houghton Mifflin Harcourt Publishing Co.

Clary, Julian. The Bolds. Roberts, David, illus. (Bolds Ser.). (ENG.). 272p. (J). (gr. 3-6). 2017. pap. 7.99 **(978-1-5124-8174-7(2))** 2016. 16.99 (978-1-5124-0440-1(3)) Lerner Publishing Group. (Carolrhoda Bks.).

Clary, Julian. The Bolds to the Rescue. Roberts, David, illus. 2017. (Bolds Ser.: 2). (ENG.). 288p. (J). (gr. 3-6). 16.99 (978-1-5124-1022-8(5), Carolrhoda Bks.) Lerner Publishing Group.

Forsythe, Amanda J. The Contabulous Adventures of M E. 2012. 28p. 24.95 (978-1-4626-6531-0(4)) America Star Bks.

Jantzen, Doug. Henry Hyena, Why Won't You Laugh? Claude, Jean, illus. 2015. (ENG.). 32p. (J). (gr. -1-2). 17.99 (978-1-4814-2822-4(5), Aladdin) Simon & Schuster Children's Publishing.

Liv‡n, Paco. THE THING THAT HURTS MOST IN THE WORLD. 2007. (ENG., Illus.). 36p. (J). 17.95 (978-84-96788-89-3(X)) OQO, Editora ESP. Dist: Baker & Taylor Bks.

McGowan, Steve. The Adventures of Keke & the Golden Coconut. 2012. 48p. pap. 21.92 (978-1-4251-4407-4(1)) Trafford Publishing.

Renert, Gerry. Nathan & the Really Big Bully. Bradshaw, Carrie, illus. 2012. (ENG.). 32p. 16.95 (978-1-62167-072-8(4), Raven Tree Pr.,Csi) Continental Sales, Inc.

Ringbom, Antonia & Wiklund, Alison. The Hiding Hyena (Chichewa) 2005. (J). (978-0-9753285-5-2(7)) H.B.P., Inc.

Wiklund, Alison & Ringbom, Antonia. The Hiding Hyena. 2004. (Illus.). 48p. (J). (978-0-9753285-3-8(0)) H.B.P., Inc.

Williams, Dawn. How Hooper the Hyaena Lost His Laugh. Chou, Joey, illus. 2008. 56p. (J). (gr. -1-3). 15.00 (978-0-9770783-4-9(5)) SunriseHouse Pubs.

Willis, Jeanne. That's Not Funny! Reynolds, Adrian, illus. 2010. (Andersen Press Picture Bks). (ENG.). 32p. (J). (gr. -1-3). 16.95 (978-0-7613-6445-0(5)) Lerner Publishing Group.

Zubeyr Mohamed. The Fox & the Hyen. 2013. 32p. pap. 17.25 (978-1-4669-7232-2(7)) Trafford Publishing.

HYGIENE

see Health

HYGIENE—FICTION

Akubue, Chira. Azuka. 2012. (Illus.). 16p. pap. 18.30 (978-1-4670-0796-2(X)) AuthorHouse.

Anderson, Peggy Perry. Let's Clean Up! 2012. (Green Light Readers — Level 1 Ser.). lib. bdg. 13.55 (978-0-606-24024-6(1), Turtleback) Turtleback Bks.

Bain, Michelle. Las aventuras de Juanito el Pulgarcito Liborio el Microbio y el apretón de Manos: Liborio el Microbio y el apretón de Manos. Lizana, Lorenzo, illus. 2007.Tr. of Jimmy Jam Germ & the Happy Handshake! (SPA.). (J). pap. 16.95 (978-0-9795832-1-6(7)) Pixie Stuff LLC.

Balukoff, Constance. Mooky's Bad Hair Day . 2004. 21p. pap. 24.95 (978-1-4137-1480-7(3)) PublishAmerica, Inc.

Barchers, Suzanne I. A Big Job, 1 vol. 2011. (Targeted Phonics Ser.). (ENG., Illus.). 16p. (J). (gr. k-2). pap. 5.99 (978-1-4333-2413-0(X)) Teacher Created Materials, Inc.

—Ren in a Mess, 1 vol. 2011. (Targeted Phonics Ser.). (ENG.). 16p. (J). (gr. k-2). pap. 5.99 (978-1-4333-2418-5(0)) Teacher Created Materials, Inc.

Bell, Cece. Sock Monkey Takes a Bath. Bell, Cece, illus. 2015. (ENG., Illus.). 32p. (J). (gr. -1-3). 14.00 (978-0-7636-7759-6(0)) Candlewick Pr.

Berenstain, Jan & Berenstain, Mike. The Berenstain Bears & a Job Well Done, 1 vol. Berenstain, Stan, illus. 2010. (Berenstain Bears/Living Lights Ser.). (ENG.). 32p. (J). (gr. -1-2). pap. 3.99 (978-0-310-71254-1(8)) Zonderkidz.

Berenstain, Stan & Berenstain, Jan. The Berenstain Bears & the Trouble with Chores. Berenstain, Jan, illus. 2005. (Berenstain Bears Ser.). (ENG., Illus.). 32p. (J). (gr. -1-3). pap. 3.99 (978-0-06-057382-9(1), HarperFestival) HarperCollins Pubs.

—The Berenstain Bears Clean House. 2005. (I Can Read Bks.). (Illus.). (gr. -1-3). 14.00 (978-0-7569-5227-3(1)) Perfection Learning Corp.

Bernheimer, Kate. The Girl Who Wouldn't Brush Her Hair. Parker, Jake, illus. 2013. (ENG.). 40p. (J). (gr. -1-3). 17.99 (978-0-375-86878-8(X), Schwartz & Wade Bks.) Random Hse. Children's Bks.

Bester, Marco. Johnny & the Thingamajigs. 2011. 16p. pap. 9.98 (978-0-557-12911-9(7)) Lulu Pr., Inc.

Booth-Alberstadt, Sheila. Maggie Mcnair Has Sugar Bugs in There. Hall, Norris, illus. 2013. (ENG.). 36p. (J). (gr. -1-1). 14.95 (978-0-9711404-6-2(4)) SBA Bks., LLC.

Breen, Steve. A Perfect Mess. 2016. (ENG., Illus.). 32p. (J). (-k). 16.99 (978-0-8037-4156-0(1), Dial Bks) Penguin Young Readers Group.

Brenner, Martha F. Montones de Problemas. Woodruff, Liza, illus. 2007. (Math Matters en Espanol Ser.). (SPA.). 32p. (J). (gr. 1-3). pap. 5.95 (978-1-57565-252-8(8)) Kane Press, Inc.

Brouwer, Sigmund. Justine Mckeen, Pooper Scooper, 1 vol. Whamond, Dave, illus. 2012. (Orca Echoes Ser.). (ENG.). 64p. (J). (gr. 2-3). pap. 6.95 (978-1-55469-931-5(2)) Orca Bk. Pubs. USA.

Brown, Margaret Wise. The Dirty Little Boy, 1 vol. Salerno, Steven, illus. 2005. (ENG.). 32p. (J). (gr. -1-1). pap. 5.95 (978-0-7614-5180-8(3)) Marshall Cavendish Corp.

Chatman, Dudley D. I Brush My Teeth & I Smile, 1 vol. 2009. 48p. pap. 16.95 (978-1-4489-2179-9(1)) America Star Bks.

Cocca-Leffler, Maryann. Dog Wash Day. Cocca-Leffler, Maryann, illus. 2004. (All Aboard Picture Reader Ser.). (ENG., Illus.). 32p. (J). (gr. -1-k). mass mkt. 3.99 (978-0-448-43370-7(2), Grosset & Dunlap) Penguin Young Readers Group.

Cook, Julia. I'm a Booger... Treat Me with Respect! 2007. (J). pap. 9.95 (978-1-934073-11-7(3)) National Ctr. For Youth Issues.

Cordwell, Mary Hebert. The Dirty-Foot Fairy. 2010. 28p. 13.99 (978-1-4490-9153-8(9)) AuthorHouse.

Cowley, Joy. Mrs. WishyWashy & the Big Wash Big Book. 2010. 48.25 (978-1-60559-247-3(1)) Hameray Publishing Group, Inc.

Dahl, Michael. Pig Takes a Bath, 1 vol. Vidal, Oriol, illus. 2010. (Hello Genius Ser.). (ENG.). 20p. (gr. 1-2). bds. 7.99 (978-1-4048-5729-2(X)) Picture Window Bks.

Dale, Jenny. Bubble & Squeak. Heliard, Susan, illus. 2005. 60p. (J). (978-0-439-79122-9(7)) Scholastic, Inc.

deRubertis, Barbara. Polly Porcupine's Painting Prize. Alley, R. W., illus. 2011. (Animal Antics A to Z Ser.). 32p. (J). lib. bdg. 22.60 (978-1-57565-337-2(0)) Kane Press, Inc.

—Polly Porcupine's Painting Prizes. Alley, R. W., illus. 2011. (Animal Antics A to Z Ser.). (ENG.). 32p. (J). (gr. -1-3). pap. 7.95 (978-1-57565-328-0(1)) Kane Press, Inc.

Diggle, David Mark. Samantha: One Finger, One Nose, A Whole Lot of Bugs. Preuss, Sarah Louise, illus. 2011. 24p. (J). pap. (978-0-9871658-0-0(1)) Diggle de Doo Productions Pty, Ltd.

Dyan, Penelope. Frugal Frannie — and the Big Room Cleaning Day. Dyan, Penelope, illus. 2009. (Illus.). 44p. pap. 11.95 (978-1-935118-47-3(1)) Bellissima Publishing, LLC.

Edwards, W M, illus. Booger Boogie. 2007. (Playdate Kids Musical Ser.). 27p. (J). (gr. -1-3). 14.95 incl. audio compact disk (978-1-933721-13-2(8)) Playdate Kids Publishing.

ETA/Cuisenaire Staff. Ben's Bath. 2003. (SunSprouts Big Bk Ser.). (ENG.). (gr. -1-3). pap. 33.50 (978-0-7406-2018-8(5), SunSprouts) ETA hand2mind.

Fenwick, Margaret. Stella's Hair. 2009. 36p. pap. 14.75 (978-1-60693-857-7(6), Eloquent Bks.) Strategic Book Publishing & Rights Agency (SBPRA).

Fulton, T. C. Jan the Cleaning Lady. 2009. 20p. pap. 10.95 (978-1-60860-447-0(0), Strategic Bk. Publishing) Strategic Book Publishing & Rights Agency (SBPRA).

Galveston, Louise. By the Grace of Todd. 2015. (ENG., Illus.). 272p. (J). (gr. 3-7). pap. 8.99 (978-1-59514-678-6(4), Razorbill) Penguin Young Readers Group.

Gaspard, Helen. Doctor Dan the Bandage Man. 2004. (Little Golden Book Ser.). (ENG., Illus.). 24p. (J). (gr. -1-2). 4.99 (978-0-375-82880-5(X), Golden Bks.) Random Hse. Children's Bks.

Grimshaw, Luke. Sniffle, Sneeze, Cough... Back Off!, 1 vol. Brzozowski, Christina, illus. 2010. 22p. 24.95 (978-1-4512-1034-7(5)) America Star Bks.

Hallinan, P. K. Let's Be Helpful. Hallinan, P. K., illus. 2009. (ENG., Illus.). 24p. (J). (gr. -1-2). 8.99 (978-0-8249-5611-0(7), Ideal Pubns.) Worthy Publishing.

Hammond, Tasha. Boogey Monster. 2013. 12p. pap. 15.99 (978-1-4817-0513-4(X)) AuthorHouse.

Hansen, Justin LaRocca. Monster Hunter. 2012. (ENG., Illus.). 32p. (J). (gr. -1-k). 16.95 (978-1-61608-968-9(7), 608968, Sky Pony Pr.) Skyhorse Publishing Co., Inc.

Hargreaves, Roger. Mr. Messy. 2011. (Mr. Men & Little Miss Ser.). (ENG.). 32p. (J). (gr. -1-2). mass mkt. 4.99 (978-0-8431-9895-9(8), Price Stern Sloan) Penguin Young Readers Group.

Harris, Missy. I'm Allergic: Imma Lurgic's Story. 2009. 24p. pap. 12.99 (978-1-4490-1071-3(7)) AuthorHouse.

Hart, Caryl. Whiffy Wilson: The Wolf Who Wouldn't Wash. Lord, Leonie, illus. 2012. (ENG.). 32p. (J). (gr. -1-k). pap. 10.99 (978-1-4083-0919-3(X)) Hodder & Stoughton GBR. Dist: Hachette Bk. Group.

Headley, Justina Chen & Chen, Justina. North of Beautiful. 2010. (Justina Chen Novel Ser.). (ENG.). 384p. (YA). (gr. 7-17). pap. 11.99 (978-0-316-02506-5(2)) Little, Brown Bks. for Young Readers.

Heller, Andrew. No Bones about It. Rene, Perez, illus. l.t. ed. 2003. 12p. (J). 7.99 (978-0-9722038-5-2(0)) Mr Do It All, Inc.

Heller, Donna & Payne, James. The Enchanted Tree. Zamboni, David, illus. 2007. 44p. per. 14.95 (978-1-934246-72-6(7)) Peppertree Pr., The.

Herbach, Geoff. Hair-Pocalypse. Gilpin, Stephen, illus. 2017. (Fiction Picture Bks.). (ENG.). 32p. (gr. 1-3). lib. bdg. 23.32 **(978-1-5158-1411-5(4)**, Fiction Picture Bks.) Picture Window Bks.

I'm a Booger... Treat Me with Respect! 2007. (J). 15.95 (978-1-934073-12-4(1)) National Ctr. For Youth Issues.

Jensen, Patricia. The Mess. 2004. (My First Reader Ser.). (ENG., Illus.). 32p. (J). (gr. k-1). pap. 3.95 (978-0-516-24634-5(8), Children's Pr.) Scholastic Library Publishing.

Jones, Christianne C. The Messy One, 1 vol. Martinez-Neal, Juana, illus. 2012. (Little Boost Ser.). (ENG.). 32p. (J). (gr. k-3). 7.95 (978-1-4048-7417-6(8), Little Boost) Picture Window Bks.

Keane, Dave. Sloppy Joe. Brunkus, Denise, illus. 2009. (ENG.). 32p. (J). (gr. -1-2). 16.99 (978-0-06-171020-9(2)) HarperCollins Pubs.

Kristen, Mantooth. Danny Goes to the Doctor. Kristen, Mantooth, illus. 2007. (Illus.). 24p. (J). 10.00 (978-0-9800580-0-0(7)) Ballyhoo Printing.

Kulling, Monica & Walker, Nan. The Messiest Room on the Planet. Smath, Jerry, illus. 2009. (Social Studies Connects Ser.). 32p. (J). (gr. k-2). pap. 5.95 (978-1-57565-282-5(X)) Kane Press, Inc.

Leonard, Marcia. Me Gusta el Desorden; I Like Mess. 2008. pap. 34.95 (978-0-8225-9495-6(1)) Lerner Publishing Group.

Llewellyn, Claire. A Banarse! Aprender Sobre Higiene Personal.Tr. of Who Wash! Learning about Personal Hygiene. (SPA.). (J). (gr. k-2). pap. 6.36 (978-950-24-0947-4(7)) Albatros ARG. Dist: Lectorum Pubns., Inc.

MacHado, Cj & Jones, Gareth P. Even Cowgirls Brush Their Teeth. 2012. 26p. pap. 13.99 (978-1-4624-0463-6(4), Inspiring Voices) Author Solutions, Inc.

Markels, Bobby. How to Be a Human Bean. Leek, Kenny, illus. Date not set. 24p. (J). (gr. 3-18). reprint ed. pap. 4.50 (978-1-880991-01-5(2)) Stone Publishing Co.

Matt & Dave. Yuck's Big Booger Challenge. Baines, Nigel, illus. 2013. (Yuck Ser.). (ENG.). 112p. (J). (gr. 2-5). 15.99 (978-1-4424-8311-8(3)); pap. 4.99 (978-1-4424-8312-5(1)) Simon & Schuster/Paula Wiseman Bks. (Simon & Schuster/Paula Wiseman Bks.).

McElroy, Jean. Let's Get Cleany-Clean! Zdanowicz, Paul, illus. 2009. (Yo Gabba Gabba! Ser.). (ENG.). 24p. (J). (gr. -1-2). pap. 3.99 (978-1-4169-9099-4(2), Simon Spotlight) Simon Spotlight.

McKissack, Patricia C. & McKissack, Fredrick L. Messy Bessey Vol. 2: Messy Bessey's Closet; Messy Bessey's Family Reunion; Messy Bessey's Garden. Regan, Dana, illus. 2008. (Rookie Reader Ser.). (ENG.). 96p. (J). (gr. k-2). pap. 9.95 (978-0-516-25301-5(8), Children's Pr.) Scholastic Library Publishing.

McMullan, Kate. I'm Dirty! McMullan, Jim, illus. 2015. (ENG.). 40p. (J). (gr. -1-3). pap. 6.99 (978-0-06-009295-5(5)) HarperCollins Pubs.

—I'm Dirty! Board Book. McMullan, Jim, illus. 2015. (ENG.). 34p. (J). (gr. -1 — 1). bds. 7.99 (978-0-06-234318-5(1)) HarperCollins Pubs.

McNamara, Margaret. Wash Your Hands! Gordon, Mike, illus. 2010. (Robin Hill School Ser.). (ENG.). 32p. (J). (gr. -1-1). pap. 3.99 (978-1-4169-9172-4(7), Simon Spotlight) Simon Spotlight.

McOmber, Rachel B., ed. McOmber Phonics Storybooks: The Haircut. rev. ed. (Illus.). (J). (978-0-944991-53-4(X)) Swift Learning Resources.

—McOmber Phonics Storybooks: The Tub. rev. ed. (Illus.). (J). (978-0-944991-24-4(6)) Swift Learning Resources.

Mitter, Matt & Rudko, Che. Ready, Set, Brush! Brannon, Tom, illus. 2008. (Pop-Up Book Ser.). (ENG.). 12p. (J). (gr. -1-k). bds. 12.99 (978-0-7944-1445-0(1), Reader's Digest Children's Bks.) Studio Fun International.

Muñoz, Mercedes. Boogie the Booger. 2008. 20p. pap. 12.95 (978-1-4327-2211-1(5)) Outskirts Pr., Inc.

Munsch, Robert. Smelly Socks. 2005. 15.00 (978-0-7569-5139-9(9)) Perfection Learning Corp.

Murphy, Stuart J. Scrubba Dub, Carlos. Jones, Tim, illus. 2013. (I See I Learn Ser.). (ENG.). 32p. (J). (-k). 14.95 (978-1-58089-478-4(X)); pap. 6.95 (978-1-58089-479-1(8)) Charlesbridge Publishing, Inc.

O'connor, Jane. JoJo & the Big Mess. 2017. (Fancy Nancy - I Can Read! Ser.). (J). lib. bdg. 13.55 **(978-0-606-39639-4(X))** Turtleback Bks.

Oltchick, Peter. Clean Clara. Jasuna, Aija, illus. 2012. 34p. (J). (-18). 16.95 (978-1-60131-127-6(3), Castlebridge Bks.) Big Tent Bks.

Overland, Sarah. Pamela la Impaciente y los Microbios. Arroyo Seppa, Carmen, tr. Conway, Aaron, illus. 2006. (SPA & ENG.). 32p. (J). (gr. k-2). per. 7.95 (978-1-930650-39-8(6)) mTrellis Publishing, Inc.

Peck, Michael. The Booger Train, 1 vol. 2009. 31p. pap. 24.95 (978-1-60813-939-2(5)) America Star Bks.

Prioleau, J. N. Clyde & His Messy Room. 2009. 24p. 13.95 (978-0-578-00427-3(5)) Prioleau, Jivonne.

Rayburn, Tricia. Maggie Bean Stays Afloat. 2008. (ENG.). 320p. (J). (gr. 4-8). pap. 6.99 (978-1-4169-3347-2(6), Aladdin) Simon & Schuster Children's Publishing.

Rey, H. A. Curious George Colors Eggs. 2012. (Curious George Ser.). (ENG., Illus.). 24p. (J). (gr. -1-3). pap. 3.99 (978-0-547-31585-0(6)) Houghton Mifflin Harcourt Publishing Co.

—Curious George Colors Eggs (CGTV Reader) 2012. (Curious George Ser.). (ENG., Illus.). 24p. (J). (gr. -1-3). 12.99 (978-0-547-55904-9(6)) Houghton Mifflin Harcourt Publishing Co.

Roberts Edd, Catherine L. That's the Second Time This Has Happened to Me, but It Was Only 57¢. 2012. 36p. pap. 20.99 (978-1-4772-1306-3(6)) AuthorHouse.

Rome, Jacqueline Thomas. Do I Have to Clean My Room? 2011. 36p. 14.95 (978-1-936513-26-0(9)) PearlStone Publishing, Inc.

—Do I Have to Clean My Room? Brown, Lillie Wyatt, illus. 2011. 36p. pap. 9.95 (978-1-936513-24-6(2)) PearlStone Publishing, Inc.

Santopolo, Jill. Purple Nails & Puppy Tails. 2014. (Sparkle Spa Ser.: 2). (ENG., Illus.). 128p. (J). (gr. 2-5). pap. 5.99 (978-1-4424-7383-6(5), Aladdin) Simon & Schuster Children's Publishing.

Scott, Kimberly Ann. Mommy! There's a Snot Man Standing Next to You! 2009. 44p. pap. 18.49 (978-1-4389-9996-8(8)) AuthorHouse.

Smart Kidz, creator. This Is the Way We Take a Bath. 2013. (Sing N Play Songs Ser.). (ENG., Illus.). (gr. -1). bds. 12.99 (978-1-891100-08-6(4), Smart Kids) Penton Overseas, Inc.

Speakes, Leslie. The Hygiene Mystery. 2004. 31p. pap. 24.95 (978-1-4137-1860-7(4)) PublishAmerica, Inc.

Spinelli, Eileen. How to Clean Your Room. Leonard, David, illus. 2009. (ENG.). 20p. (J). (gr. k-3). 18.99 (978-0-8249-5551-9(X), Ideal Pubns.) Worthy Publishing.

Stewart, Amber & Rankin, Laura. Rabbit Ears. Rankin, Laura, illus. 2012. (ENG., Illus.). 32p. (J). (gr. -1-1). pap. 8.99 (978-1-59990-740-6(2), 9781599907406, Bloomsbury USA Childrens) Bloomsbury Publishing USA.

Thorold, Jade Melissa. The Dirty Dinosaur. 2010. 28p. pap. 15.99 (978-1-4500-6483-5(3)) Xlibris Corp.

Tremblay, Carole. Floop Does the Laundry. Beshwaty, Steve, illus. 2009. (Floop Ser.). 24p. (J). (gr. -1-k). 22.60 (978-1-60754-333-6(8)); pap. 8.15 (978-1-60754-334-3(6)) Windmill Bks.

Valderrama, Linda N. Brush Barry Brush. Memarzadeh, Sudabeh, illus. 2011. 32p. (J). pap. 11.95 (978-0-578-06605-9(X)) Shirley's Girl Pubns.

Vogel, Elizabeth. Al Agua Patos. 2004. (Limpieza y Salud Todo el Dia Ser.). (SPA & ENG., Illus.). 24p. (J). (gr. -1-2). lib. bdg. 18.75 (978-0-8239-6616-5(X)) Rosen Publishing Group, Inc., The.

—Taking My Bath: Al Agua Patos. 2004. (Limpieza y Salud Todo el Dia Ser.). (SPA & ENG., Illus.). 24p. (J). lib. bdg. 18.75 (978-0-8239-6617-2(8), Editorial Buenas Letras) Rosen Publishing Group, Inc., The.

Watt, F. Al Agua Patos! 2004. (Mundo del Pequenin Ser.). (SPA., Illus.). 16p. (J). (gr. -1-18). 4.95 (978-0-7460-3867-3(4)) EDC Publishing.

Watt, Fiona & Wells, Rachel, eds. Potty Time. 2004. (Baby's World Ser.). (ENG., Illus.). 1p. (J). (gr. -1-18). pap. 4.95 (978-0-7460-3839-0(9)) EDC Publishing.

Wilkerson, L. Kobie, 3rd, reader. Fred & Mary. 2008. (Illus.). 32p. (J). 24.95 incl. DVD, audio compact disk (978-0-9796679-0-9(9)) Love II Learn Bks.

HYGIENE, MENTAL

see Mental Health

HYGIENE, PUBLIC

see Public Health

HYGIENE, SOCIAL

see Public Health; Sexually Transmitted Diseases

HYMENOPTERA

see Ants; Bees; Wasps

HYMNOLOGY

see Hymns

HYMNS

see also Carols; Church Music

Alexander, Cecil Frances & Hudson, Katy, illus. All Things Bright & Beautiful. 2016. (J). (978-0-8249-5676-9(1), Ideal Pubns.) Worthy Publishing.

Andrews, Pam. We Can Praise! An Easy-to-Sing, Easy-to-Stage Mini-Musical for Children. 2007. (ENG.). 64p. pap. 5.99 (978-0-8341-7594-5(0), 0834175940) Lillenas Publishing Co.

Bartlett, E. M., contrib. by. Victory in Jesus. 7.50 (978-0-8054-5926-5(X)) B&H Publishing Group.

Bond, Douglas. Mr. Pipes & the British Hymn Makers. 2008. (Illus.). 256p. (J). (gr. 6-9). pap. 9.95 (978-1-930092-12-9(1), CLP29760) Christian Liberty Pr.

Brown, Jean. My Treasure Book of Nursery Rhymes & Hymns. 2007. (Illus.). 56p. per. (978-1-84748-087-3(X)) Athena Pr.

Bryan, Ashley. Let It Shine: Three Favorite Spirituals. Bryan, Ashley, illus. 2007. (ENG., Illus.). 40p. (J). (gr. -1-3). 18.99 (978-0-689-84732-5(7), Atheneum Bks. for Young Readers) Simon & Schuster Children's Publishing.

Cross, Elsa. El Himno de las Ranas. Zacchi, Lucia, illus. 2005. (SPA.). (J). (gr. k-2). pap. 10.95 (978-968-494-052-9(1), CI2003) Centro de Informacion y Desarrollo de la Comunicacion y la Literatura MEX. Dist: Iaconi, Mariuccia Bk. Imports, Lectorum Pubns., Inc.

Cunningham, Edie. One Day. McInturff, Linda & Brownlie, Ian, illus. 2004. 28p. (J). pap. (978-1-932381-09-2(0), 6340) Bible Visuals International, Inc.

Davis, Rebecca Henry. Fanny Crosby: Queen of Gospel Songs. 2003. (Illus.). 107p. (J). 6.49 (978-1-57924-970-0(1)) BJU Pr.

Elkins, Stephen. The Word & Song Songbook Vol. 2: The New Testament. 2004. (Illus.). 64p. (J). 12.99 (978-0-8054-1695-4(1)) B&H Publishing Group.

Elkins, Stephen. 5-Minute Bible: 100 Stories & Songs, 1 vol. 2017. (ENG., Illus.). 208p. (J). 12.99 *(978-0-7180-9764-6(5))* Nelson, Thomas Inc.
Feldstein, Sandy & Clark, Larry. Festival Chorale & March. 2004. (YA). pap. 40.00 *(978-1-932895-02-5(7))* PlayinTime Productions, Inc.
Granfield, Linda. Amazing Grace: The Story of the Hymn. braille ed. 2004. (Illus.). (J). (gr. 2-4). spiral bd. *(978-0-616-01661-9(1))* Canadian National Institute for the Blind/Institut National Canadien pour les Aveugles.
—Out of Slavery: The Journey to Amazing Grace. Wilson, Janet, illus. 2009. (ENG.). 40p. (J). (gr. k-12). 15.95 *(978-0-88776-915-3(2))*, Tundra Bks.) Tundra Bks. CAN. Dist: Penguin Random Hse. LLC.
Gynux, illus. Jesus Loves Me, 1 vol. 2017. (Sing-Along Book Ser.). (ENG.). 20p. (J). bds. 8.99 *(978-0-310-75894-5(7))* Zonderkidz.
Horrobin, Peter. Complete Junior Praise Words. 2008. (ENG.). 176p. (J). 11.95 *(978-0-00-725978-6(6))* HarperCollins Pubs. Ltd. GBR. Dist: Independent Pubs. Group.
Jesus Wants Me for a Sunbeam: A Sing-along Book of Songs about the Savior. 2006. 14p. (J). bds. 15.95 *(978-1-59038-634-7(5)*, Shadow Mountain) Shadow Mountain Publishing.
Living Stream Ministry Staff. Hymns: #1-1348. 1311p. (J). (gr. 6). per. 22.50 *(978-0-7363-1122-9(X)*, 02-003-001); per. 20.00 *(978-0-7363-1123-6(8)*, 02-004-001) Living Stream Ministry.
—Hymns: 100 Selected. 150p. (J). (gr. 6). per. 6.25 *(978-0-87083-234-5(4)*, 02-007-001) Living Stream Ministry.
—Hymns #1-1348. 1311p. (J). (gr. 6). per. 25.00 *(978-0-7363-1121-2(1)*, 02-017-001) Living Stream Ministry.
McInturff, Linda & Tweed, Sean, illus. The Light of the World Is Jesus. 2004. 16p. (J). pap. *(978-1-932381-08-5(2))* Bible Visuals International, Inc.
McKay, Graham. A Hymn a Day. 2003. 99p. pap. *(978-0-9717444-1-7(6))* O'More Publishing.
Pierpoint, Folliott Sandford & Kocher, Conrad. For the Beauty of the Earth. Fleming, Lucy, illus. 2017. (J). 16.99 ***(978-1-5064-2183-4(0)***, Sparkhouse Family) Augsburg Fortress, Pubs.
Pinkney, Gloria Jean. Music from Our Lord's Holy Heaven. Pinkney, Jerry et al, illus. 2005. 48p. (J). (gr. -1-18). lib. bdg. 18.89 incl. audio compact disk *(978-0-06-000769-0(9))* HarperCollins Pubs.
Raschka, Chris. Simple Gifts. Raschka, Chris, illus. 2003. (Illus.). pap. 43.95 incl. audio compact disk *(978-1-59112-604-1(5))*; pap. 41.95 incl. audio *(978-0-87499-642-5(2))* Live Oak Media.
Sas, Alfredo C., ed. Reformation Hymnal. 2003.Tr. of No Temáls, Manada Pequeña. (ENG.). 14.95 *(978-0-9745295-0-9(8))* Reformation Herald Publishing Assn.
Schram, Ruth Elaine, et al. Sing & Celebrate 2! Sacred Songs for Young Voices. 2013. (ENG.). 56p. pap. 39.99 incl. audio compact disk *(978-1-4803-0859-6(5)*, 1480308595) Shawnee Pr., Inc.
Shea, John. Canticle: Biblical Songs Illuminated. Mullan, G. E., illus. 2009. (J). 29.95 *(978-1-58459-427-7(6))* World Library Pubns.
Spring Psalm. 7.50 *(978-0-8054-5939-5(1))* B&H Publishing Group.
Stoop, Naoko, illus. All Creatures Great & Small. 2012. (ENG.). 22p. (J). (gr. k — 1). bds. 6.95 *(978-1-4027-8581-8(X))* Sterling Publishing Co., Inc.
Summer Psalm. 7.50 *(978-0-8054-5922-7(7))* B&H Publishing Group.
Warnes, Tim. Jesus Loves Me! Warnes, Tim, illus. 2006. (ENG., Illus.). 32p. (J). (gr. -1-3). 15.99 *(978-1-4169-0065-8(9)*, Simon & Schuster Bks. For Young Readers) Simon & Schuster Bks. For Young Readers.
Warnes, Tim, illus. Jesus Loves Me! 2008. (ENG.). 26p. (J). (gr. -1-k). bds. 7.99 *(978-1-4169-5367-8(1)*, Little Simon) Little Simon.
Watts, I. Divine Songs. 2006. 52p. pap. *(978-1-84702-997-3(3))* Echo Library.
Wezeman, Phyllis Vos & Liechty, Anna L. Hymn Stories for Children: The Apostles' Creed. 2004. (Illus.). 64p. (J). 10.95 *(978-0-9752605-8-6(8))* LOGOS System Assocs.
Wilger, Jennifer Root. Wiggle Worms Learn the Psalms. 2003. (Godprints Bible Funstuff Ser.). 112p. pap., pap. 16.99 *(978-0-7814-3960-2(4)*, 0781439604) Cook, David C.

HYPNOTISM

see also Mind and Body; Psychoanalysis

Gale Editor, ed. Hypnosis. 2011. (Mysterious Encounters Ser.). (Illus.). 48p. lib. bdg. 27.50 *(978-0-7377-5867-2(8)*, Kidhaven) Cengage Gale.
Rosen, Marvin. Meditation & Hypnosis. 2005. (Gray Matter Ser.). (Illus.). 128p. (J). (gr. 9-12). lib. bdg. 35.00 *(978-0-7910-8515-8(5))* Facts On File, Inc.

I

ICE

see also Glaciers; Icebergs

Baker, Amber. The Ice Cube Experiment. 2009. (Real Life Readers Ser.). 12p. (gr. 1-2). pap. 5.90 *(978-1-4042-7901-8(6)*, Rosen Classroom) Rosen Publishing Group, Inc., The.
Berger, Melvin & Berger, Gilda. Ice Is Nice. 2010. (Illus.). 16p. (J). *(978-0-545-16083-4(9))* Scholastic, Inc.
Bundey, Nikki. Ice & People. 2005. (Science of Weather Ser.). (Illus.). 32p. (gr. 4-6). lib. bdg. 21.27 *(978-1-57505-497-1(3))* Lerner Publishing Group.
Fowler, Leona. Making Ice: Checking Your Work. 2017. (Computer Science for the Real World Ser.). 8p. (gr. 5-6). pap. 6.20 ***(978-1-5383-5076-8(9)***, Rosen Classroom) Rosen Publishing Group, Inc., The.
Galla, Nicole. Water & Ice. 2009. (Real Life Readers Ser.). 8p. (gr. k-1). pap. 5.15 *(978-1-4042-7979-7(2)*, Rosen Classroom) Rosen Publishing Group, Inc., The.
Hopwood, James. Cool Dry Ice Devices: Fun Science Projects with Dry Ice, 1 vol. 2008. (Cool Science Ser.). (ENG.). 32p. (YA). (gr. 2-5). 28.50 *(978-1-59928-907-6(5))* ABDO Publishing Co.
Lilly, Melinda. Water & Ice. (Read & Do Science Ser.). (Illus.). (J). 20.64 *(978-1-58952-639-6(2))* Rourke Educational Media.
Maurer, Daniel D. Do You Really Want to Skate on Thin Ice? A Book about States of Matter. Alberini, Teresa, illus. 2016. (Adventures in Science Ser.). (ENG.). 24p. (J). (gr. k-3). 20.95 *(978-1-60753-958-2(6))* Amicus Publishing.
Norquist, Lara & Spalding, Frank. The Truth about Methamphetamine & Crystal Meth. 2011. (Drugs & Consequences Ser.). (Illus.). 64p. (YA). (gr. 7-12). lib. bdg. 31.95 *(978-1-4488-4641-2(2))* Rosen Publishing Group, Inc., The.
Ollhoff, Jim. Water & Ice, 1 vol. 2010. (ABDO & Daughters Ser.). (ENG.). 32p. 27.07 *(978-1-61613-458-7(5)*, Abdo & Daughters) ABDO Publishing Co.
Pringle, Laurence. Ice! The Amazing History of the Ice Business. 2012. (ENG.). 80p. (J). (gr. 4-6). 17.95 *(978-1-59078-801-1(X)*, Calkins Creek) Boyds Mills Pr.
Proudfit, Benjamin. Why Do Ice Cubes Float? 2016. (Everyday Mysteries Ser.). (ENG.). 24p. (J). (gr. 1-2). pap. 8.15 *(978-1-4824-3852-9(6))* Stevens, Gareth Publishing LLLP.
Selwyn, Josephine. When Does Water Turn into Ice? 2014. (Little Books of Answers: Level F Ser.). (Illus.). 16p. (gr. k-2). pap. 7.95 *(978-1-927136-59-1(8))* Three Crows Media NZL. Dist: RiverStream Publishing.
Wells, Robert E. Polar Bear, Why Is Your World Melting? Wells, Robert E., illus. 2008. (Wells of Knowledge Science Ser.). (ENG., Illus.). 32p. (J). (gr. 2-3). 16.99 *(978-0-8075-6598-8(9))* Whitman, Albert & Co.
Wendorff, Anne. Ice Storms. 2008. (Extreme Weather Ser.). (ENG., Illus.). 24p. (J). (gr. 2-5). lib. bdg. 25.95 *(978-1-60014-186-7(2))* Bellwether Media.
Wood, Ira. Water, Ice, & Steam. (Rosen Real Readers Big Bookstm Ser.). (ENG., Illus.). 12p. (gr. 1-2). 2006. 33.50 *(978-1-4042-6215-7(6))* 2003. pap. 5.90 *(978-0-8239-6353-9(5))* Rosen Publishing Group, Inc., The.
World Book, Inc Staff, contrib. by. Icy Worlds. 2011. (J). *(978-0-7166-1788-4(9))* World Bk., Inc.

ICE AGE

see Glacial Epoch

ICE CREAM, ICES, ETC.

Bernard, Jan. Ice Cream. 2016. (J). *(978-1-4896-4533-3(0))* Weigl Pubs., Inc.
—Ice Cream Before the Store. McGeehan, Dan, illus. 2012. (Before the Store Ser.). (ENG.). 32p. (J). (gr. 2-5). lib. bdg. 29.93 *(978-1-60973-677-4(X)*, 201252) Child's World, Inc., The.
Boekhoff, P. M. Ben & Jerry. 2004. (Inventors & Creators Ser.). (ENG., Illus.). 48p. (J). (gr. 4-7). 27.50 *(978-0-7377-2611-4(3)*, Greenhaven Pr., Inc.) Cengage Gale.
Gibbons, Gail. Ice Cream: The Full Scoop. (ENG., Illus.). 32p. (J). (gr. 4-8). 2008. 7.99 *(978-0-8234-2155-8(4))* 2006. 17.95 *(978-0-8234-2000-1(0))* Holiday Hse., Inc.
Greve, Tom. How to Make Ice Cream. 2015. (ENG.). 24p. (gr. k-3). 28.50 *(978-1-63430-353-8(9))* Rourke Educational Media.
Heos, Bridget. From Milk to Ice Cream. Coleman, Stephanie Fizer, illus. 2017. (Who Made My Lunch? Ser.). (ENG.). 24p. (gr. 1-4). 20.95 ***(978-1-68151-121-4(5))*** Amicus Publishing.
Herrington, Lisa M. Milk to Ice Cream. 2013. (Rookie Read-About(r) Science Ser.). (ENG.). 32p. (J). 23.00 *(978-0-531-24742-6(2))*; pap. 5.95 *(978-0-531-24708-2(2))* Scholastic Library Publishing. (Children's Pr.).
Lunis, Natalie. Making Ice Cream. 2011. (Early Connections Ser.). (J). *(978-1-61672-562-4(1))* Benchmark Education Co.
Marks, Ed. Ice Cream Collectibles, 1 vol. 2003. (ENG., Illus.). 160p. (gr. 10-13). pap. 29.95 *(978-0-7643-1856-6(X)*, 9780764318566) Schiffer Publishing, Ltd.
Mattern, Joanne. Ben & Jerry: Ice Cream Manufacturers, 1 vol. 2011. (Food Dudes Ser.). (ENG., Illus.). 32p. (YA). (gr. 3-6). 27.07 *(978-1-61613-554-6(9))* ABDO Publishing Co.
Meachen Rau, Dana. Helado. 2008. (Qué Preparamos Hoy? Ser.). (SPA.). 24p. (gr. k-1). lib. bdg. 15.95 *(978-0-7614-3439-9(9)*, Benchmark Bks.) Marshall Cavendish Corp.
—Ice Cream. 2008. (What's Cooking? Ser.). 24p. (gr. k-1). lib. bdg. 15.95 *(978-0-7614-2893-0(3)*, Benchmark Bks.) Marshall Cavendish Corp.
Murray, Julie. Milk to Ice Cream, 1 vol. 2006. (Beginning to End Ser.). (ENG., Illus.). 24p. (gr. k-4). 25.65 *(978-1-59679-838-0(6)*, Buddy Bks.) ABDO Publishing Co.
Olmstead, Lucinda. But Not on My Ice Cream, Please. 2008. (Illus.). 20p. pap. 13.99 *(978-1-4389-0917-2(9))* AuthorHouse.
Rosenberg, Pam. How Did That Get to My Table? Ice Cream. 2009. (Community Connections: How Did That Get to My Table? Ser.). (ENG.). 24p. (gr. 2-5). lib. bdg. 25.64 *(978-1-60279-467-2(7)*, 200263) Cherry Lake Publishing.
Shofner, Shawndra. How it Happens: At the Ice Cream Factory. 2008. (How It Happens Ser.). (YA). (gr. 2-5). lib. bdg. 21.95 *(978-1-934545-06-5(6))* Oliver Pr., Inc.
Snyder, Inez. Milk to Ice Cream. 2003. (How Things Are Made Ser.). (ENG., Illus.). 24p. (J). 19.00 *(978-0-516-24268-2(7)*, Children's Pr.) Scholastic Library Publishing.
Sundance/Newbridge LLC Staff. Make Mine Ice Cream. 2007. (Early Science Ser.). (gr. k-3). 18.95 *(978-1-4007-6522-5(6))* Sundance/Newbridge Educational Publishing.
Taus-Bolstad, Stacy. From Milk to Ice Cream. (Illus.). 24p. (gr. k-3). 2012. (Start to Finish, Second Series: Food Ser.: No. 2). (ENG.). (J). lib. bdg. 23.93 *(978-0-7613-9177-7(0)*, Lerner Pubns.) 2012. (Start to Finish, Second Series: Food Ser.: No. 2). (ENG., pap. 6.95 *(978-1-58013-968-7(X))* 2003. (From Start to Finish Ser.). (J). 18.60 *(978-0-8225-0714-7(5)*, Lerner Pubns.) Lerner Publishing Group.

ICE HOCKEY

see Hockey

ICE SKATING

see Skating

ICE SPORTS

see Winter Sports

ICEBERGS

Prokos, Anna. Ice Queen: Exploring Icebergs & Glaciers. Tablason, Jamie, illus. 2017. (Imagine That! Ser.). (ENG.). 32p. (J). (gr. 2-4). lib. bdg. 26.65 *(978-1-63440-149-4(2))*; 39.99 ***(978-1-63440-161-6(1))*** Red Chair Pr.

ICEBOXES

see Refrigeration and Refrigerating Machinery

ICELAND

Deady, Kathleen W. Iceland. 2005. (True Bks.). (ENG., Illus.). 48p. (J). (gr. 3-5). pap. 6.95 *(978-0-516-25832-4(X)*, Children's Pr.) Scholastic Library Publishing.
Harper, Judith E. Unique Places. 2005. (Real Deal Ser.). (Illus.). 32p. (J). pap. *(978-0-7608-9635-8(6))* Sundance/Newbridge Educational Publishing.
Indovino, Shaina Carmel. Iceland. 2012. (J). *(978-1-4222-2277-5(2))*; *(978-1-4222-2246-1(2))* Mason Crest.
Miller, Jennifer A. Iceland. 2010. pap. 51.02 *(978-0-7613-6975-2(9))*; (ENG.). 48p. (gr. 2-4). pap. 9.95 *(978-0-7613-6035-3(2))*; (ENG.). 48p. (gr. 2-4). lib. bdg. 29.27 *(978-0-7613-5314-0(3))* Lerner Publishing Group.
Moore, David. Expl on Your Own the Island /Formed in 1 Day. 2009. (Explore on Your Own Ser.). (ENG., Illus.). 12p. (J). pap. 7.95 *(978-0-7362-5522-6(2))* National Geographic School Publishing, Inc.
Nevins, Debbie & Latif, Zawiah Abdul. Iceland. 3rd enl. ed. 2016. (Cultures of the World (Third Edition) (r) Ser.). 144p. (J). lib. bdg. 47.07 *(978-1-5026-2218-1(1))* Cavendish Square Publishing.
O'Brien, Cynthia. Cultural Traditions in Iceland. 2017. 32p. (J). ***(978-0-7787-8097-7(X))*** Crabtree Publishing Co.
Owings, Lisa. Iceland. 2012. (Exploring Countries Ser.). (ENG., Illus.). 32p. (J). (gr. 3-7). lib. bdg. 26.95 *(978-1-60014-762-3(3)*, Blastoff! Readers) Bellwether Media.
Somervill, Barbara A. Iceland. (Enchantment of the World™, Second Ser.). (ENG.). 144p. (J). 2013. 40.00 *(978-0-531-25602-2(2))* 2003. (Illus.). (gr. 5-9). 37.00 *(978-0-516-22694-1(0))* Scholastic Library Publishing. (Children's Pr.).
Waldron, Melanie. Iceland, 1 vol. 2012. (Countries Around the World Ser.). (ENG.). 48p. (gr. 3-6). lib. bdg. 33.32 *(978-1-4329-6099-5(7)*, NA-h) Heinemann-Raintree.
Wilcox, Jonathan & Latif, Zawiah Abdul. Iceland. 2nd rev. ed. 2006. (Cultures of the World Ser.). (Illus.). 144p. (gr. 6-7). lib. bdg. 42.79 *(978-0-7614-2074-3(6)*, Benchmark Bks.) Marshall Cavendish Corp.

ICELAND—FICTION

Bear, F. T. Connor Finn: The Secret of Snow. 2013. 258p. pap. *(978-0-646-91485-5(5))* F. T. Bear.
Cabell, Robert W. The Mermaid Adventures of Princess Miranda: Volume One. Cabell, Robert W., illus. 2013. (Illus.). 128p. pap. 7.95 *(978-0-9890974-3-7(9)*, Oceanus Bks.) Warrington Pubns.
Clark, Hannah L. Uncovering Cobbogoth. 2014. pap. 17.99 *(978-1-4621-1426-9(1))* Cedar Fort, Inc./CFI Distribution.
Dahl, Michael. The Viking Claw. 2011. (Finnegan Zwake Ser.: 4). (ENG.). 192p. (YA). (gr. 7). pap. 9.99 *(978-1-4424-3101-0(6)*, Simon Pulse) Simon Pulse.
Erich, James. Seidman. 2016. (ENG., Illus.). (YA). 24.99 ***(978-1-63533-071-7(8)***, Harmony Ink Pr.) Dreamspinner Pr.
Erich, James. Seidman [Library Edition]. 2012. 210p. pap. 14.99 *(978-1-62380-904-1(5)*, Harmony Ink Pr.) Dreamspinner Pr.
Erlings, Fridrik. Boy on the Edge. 2014. (ENG.). 240p. (YA). (gr. 9). 16.99 *(978-0-7636-6680-4(7))* Candlewick Pr.
French, Allen. The Story of Rolf & the Viking Bow. 2008. 148p. (gr. 7-12). pap. 8.15 *(978-1-60459-522-2(1))* Wilder Pubns., Corp.
Hall, Jennie. The Viking Tales. 2008. 88p. pap. 8.15 *(978-1-60459-529-1(9))* Wilder Pubns., Corp.
Hapka, Catherine, pseud & Hapka, Cathy. Elska. Griffin-Scott, Janet & Sanderson, Ruth, illus. 2009. (Horse Diaries: No. 1). (ENG.). 144p. (J). (gr. 3-7). pap. 7.99 *(978-0-375-84732-5(4)*, Random Hse. Bks. for Young Readers) Random Hse. Children's Bks.
Kane, Doug. Ariel's Journey. 2008. 256p. pap. 8.95 *(978-0-9817234-0-2(3))* Blue Ink Pr.
McClintock, Norah. Close to the Heel, 1 vol. 2012. (Seven (the Series) Ser.). (ENG., Illus.). 272p. (J). (gr. 5-10). pap. 9.95 *(978-1-55469-950-6(9))* Orca Bk. Pubs. USA.
Messner, Kate. Land of Fire & Ice. McMorris, Kelley, illus. 2017. (Ranger in Time Ser.: 5). (ENG.). 160p. (J). (gr. 2-5). pap. 5.99 *(978-0-545-90978-5(3))* Scholastic, Inc.
Stilton, Thea. Thea Stilton & the Frozen Fiasco. 2017. (Thea Stilton Ser.: 25). lib. bdg. 19.65 ***(978-0-606-40181-4(4))*** Turtleback Bks.
—Thea Stilton & the Frozen Fiasco: a Geronimo Stilton Adventure (Thea Stilton #25) 2017. (Thea Stilton Ser.: 25). (ENG.). 176p. (J). (gr. 2-5). pap. 8.99 ***(978-1-338-08786-4(X)***, Scholastic Paperbacks) Scholastic, Inc.
Verne, Jules. A Journey to the Interior of the Earth. 2006. 196p. per. 13.95 *(978-1-59818-461-7(X))* Aegypan.
—Journey to the Interior of the Earth. 2006. 196p. 26.95 *(978-1-59818-557-7(8))* Aegypan.

ICHTHYOLOGY

see Fishes

ICONOGRAPHY

see Art; Christian Art and Symbolism; Portraits

IDAHO

Brown, Jonatha A. Idaho. 2006. (Portraits of the States Ser.). 32p. (gr. 2-6). pap. 10.50 *(978-0-8368-4717-8(2))*; (Illus.). lib. bdg. 26.00 *(978-0-8368-4700-0(8))* Stevens, Gareth Publishing LLLP. (Gareth Stevens Learning Library).
Brown, Vanessa. Idaho. 2009. (Bilingual Library of the United States of America Ser.). (SPA.). 32p. (gr. 2-2). 47.90 *(978-1-60853-357-2(3)*, Editorial Buenas Letras) Rosen Publishing Group, Inc., The.
—Idaho. Brusca, Maria Cristina, tr. 2005. (Bilingual Library of the United States of America Ser.: Set 1). (ENG & SPA., Illus.). 32p. (J). (gr. 3-6). lib. bdg. 25.25 *(978-1-4042-3077-4(7))* Rosen Publishing Group, Inc., The.
Crutcher, Chris. King of the Mild Frontier: An Ill-Advised Autobiography. 2004. (ENG.). 272p. (YA). (gr. 9). reprint ed. pap. 9.99 *(978-0-06-050251-5(7)*, Greenwillow Bks.) HarperCollins Pubs.
Durrie, Karen. Idaho: The Gem State. 2012. (J). *(978-1-61913-343-3(1))*; pap. *(978-1-61913-344-0(X))* Weigl Pubs., Inc.
Edwards, Karen. Idaho. 2003. (World Almanac Library of the States). (Illus.). 48p. (gr. 4-9). pap. 14.05 *(978-0-8368-5321-6(0)*, Gareth Stevens Learning Library) Stevens, Gareth Publishing LLLP.
—Idaho: The Gem State. 2003. (World Almanac Library of the States). (Illus.). 48p. (gr. 4-9). lib. bdg. 31.00 *(978-0-8368-5150-2(1)*, Gareth Stevens Learning Library) Stevens, Gareth Publishing LLLP.
Foran, Jill. Idaho. 2011. (Guide to American States Ser.). (Illus.). 48p. (YA). (gr. 3-6). 29.99 *(978-1-61690-784-6(3))*; (J). *(978-1-61690-460-9(7))* Weigl Pubs., Inc.
Marsh, Carole. Idaho Current Events Projects: 30 Cool, Activities, Crafts, Experiments & More for Kids to Do to Learn about Your State! 2003. (Idaho Experience Ser.). 32p. (gr. k-5). pap. 5.95 *(978-0-635-02031-4(9)*, Marsh, Carole Bks.) Gallopade International.
—Idaho Geography Projects: 30 Cool, Activities, Crafts, Experiments & More for Kids to Do to Learn about Your State! 2003. (Idaho Experience Ser.). 32p. (gr. k-5). pap. 5.95 *(978-0-635-01831-1(4)*, Marsh, Carole Bks.) Gallopade International.
—Idaho Government Projects: 30 Cool, Activities, Crafts, Experiments & More for Kids to Do to Learn about Your State! 2003. (Idaho Experience Ser.). 32p. (gr. k-5). pap. 5.95 *(978-0-635-01931-8(0)*, Marsh, Carole Bks.) Gallopade International.
—Idaho People Projects: 30 Cool, Activities, Crafts, Experiments & More for Kids to Do to Learn about Your State! 2003. (Idaho Experience Ser.). 32p. (gr. k-5). pap. 5.95 *(978-0-635-01981-3(7)*, Marsh, Carole Bks.) Gallopade International.
—Idaho Symbols & Facts Projects: 30 Cool, Activities, Crafts, Experiments & More for Kids to Do to Learn about Your State! 2003. (Idaho Experience Ser.). 32p. (gr. k-5). pap. 5.95 *(978-0-635-01881-6(0)*, Marsh, Carole Bks.) Gallopade International.
Ollhoff, Jim. Idaho, 1 vol. 2009. (United States Ser.). (ENG., Illus.). 48p. (YA). (gr. 2-5). 27.07 *(978-1-60453-647-8(0))* ABDO Publishing Co.
Pelta, Kathy. Idaho. 2012. (J). lib. bdg. 25.26 *(978-0-7613-4187-1(0)*, Lerner Pubns.) Lerner Publishing Group.
Peterson, Sheryl. Idaho. 2008. (This Land Called America Ser.). 32p. (YA). (gr. 3-6). 22.95 *(978-1-58341-637-2(4))* Creative Co., The.
Quasha, Jennifer. How to Draw Idaho's Sights & Symbols. 2009. (Kid's Guide to Drawing America Ser.). 32p. (gr. k-k). 50.50 *(978-1-61511-059-9(3)*, PowerKids Pr.) Rosen Publishing Group, Inc., The.
Sanders, Doug. Idaho. 2013. (It's My State 2nd Ed 5 Ser.). 80p. (J). (gr. 4-8). pap. 17.64 *(978-1-62712-099-9(8))* Cavendish Square Publishing.
—Idaho. 2004. (It's My State! Ser.). (Illus.). 80p. (J). (gr. 3-7). lib. bdg. 27.07 *(978-0-7614-1824-5(5))* Marshall Cavendish Corp.
Schaffer, David. Idaho: A MyReportLinks. Com Book. 2003. (States Ser.). (Illus.). 48p. (J). lib. bdg. 25.26 *(978-0-7660-5134-8(X)*, MyReportLinks.com Bks.) Enslow Pubs., Inc.
Stanley, John. Idaho: Past & Present. 2010. (United States: Past & Present Ser.). (ENG.). 48p. (YA). pap. 11.75 *(978-1-4358-9507-2(X))*; lib. bdg. 29.25 *(978-1-4358-9480-8(4))* Rosen Publishing Group, Inc., The. (Rosen Reference).
Stefoff, Rebecca. Idaho. 2nd rev. ed. 2008. (Celebrate the States Ser.). 144p. (gr. 6-18). lib. bdg. 42.79 *(978-0-7614-3003-2(2)*, Benchmark Bks.) Marshall Cavendish Corp.
Steiner, Stan, et al. P Is for Potato: An Idaho Alphabet. Slack, Jocelyn, illus. 2005. (Discover America State by State Ser.). (ENG.). 40p. (J). 17.95 *(978-1-58536-155-7(0))* Sleeping Bear Pr.
Swanson, Angie. Idaho. 2016. (States Ser.). (ENG., Illus.). 32p. (gr. 3-4). lib. bdg. 27.32 *(978-1-5157-0398-3(3))* Next Page Pr., The.
Taylor, Gwen. Exploring Idaho from A to Z. Harvey, Robin, illus. 2003. (J). pap. *(978-1-930043-35-0(X))* Scott Publishing Co.
Zollman, Pam. Idaho. 2006. (Rookie Read-About Geography Ser.). (ENG., Illus.). 32p. (J). (gr. 1-2). lib. bdg. 20.50 *(978-0-516-24965-0(7)*, Children's Pr.) Scholastic Library Publishing.

IDAHO—FICTION

Balch, Glenn. White Ruff: Famous Dog Stories. Priest, Dick, illus. 2011. 240p. 46.95 *(978-1-258-09962-6(4))* Literary Licensing, LLC.
Blake, Stephanie J. The Marble Queen, 0 vols. 2012. (ENG.). 192p. (YA). (gr. 5-9). 16.99 *(978-0-7614-6227-9(9)*, 9780761462279, Amazon Children's Publishing) Amazon Publishing.
Creech, Sharon. Walk Two Moons. 2003. (Walk Two Moons Ser.: 1). 304p. (J). (gr. 3-7). pap. 7.99 *(978-0-06-056013-3(4)*, HarperTeen) HarperCollins Pubs.
—Walk Two Moons. (J). 2011. (gr. 5-8). lib. bdg. 18.40 *(978-0-613-00204-2(0))* 2003. (gr. 7-12). 18.40 *(978-0-613-81971-8(3))* Turtleback Bks. (Turtleback).
Crutcher, Chris. The Sledding Hill. 2006. (ENG.). 256p. (YA). (gr. 8-12). pap. 9.99 *(978-0-06-050245-4(2)*, Greenwillow Bks.) HarperCollins Pubs.
Dorie & Me. 2003. (YA). per. *(978-1-59431-071-3(8)*, Ebks. On The Net) Write Words, Inc.
Forever Lost. 2011. (Hardy Boys (All New) Undercover Brothers Ser.: 36). (ENG.). 160p. (J). (gr. 3-7). pap. 6.99 *(978-1-4424-0264-5(4)*, Aladdin) Simon & Schuster Children's Publishing.
Gebhart, Ryan. There Will Be Bears. 2016. (ENG.). 224p. (J). (gr. 5). pap. 8.99 *(978-0-7636-8765-6(0))* Candlewick Pr.
George, Jean Craighead. Snowboard Twist. Minor, Wendell, illus. 2004. (Outdoor Adventures Ser.). (ENG.). 32p. (J). 15.99 *(978-0-06-050595-0(8))* HarperCollins Pubs.
Gregory, Kristiana. My Darlin' Clementine. 2009. (ENG.). 192p. (J). (gr. 5-18). 16.95 *(978-0-8234-2198-5(8))* Holiday Hse., Inc.
Hansen, Tevin. Life in Yarn Hill. 2016. (ENG.). 208p. (YA). pap. 7.99 *(978-1-941429-45-7(9))* Handersen Publishing.

Heimbuch, Carol. Shadow Stallion. 2011. 170p. pap. 11.50 *(978-1-59330-693-9(8))* Aventine Pr.

Heimbuch, Carol Jo. Twilight Tracks. 2007. 112p. per. 10.95 *(978-1-59330-466-9(8))* Aventine Pr.

Hoffman, Joey. The Greedy Courier. 2013. 280p. (gr. -1). pap. 17.48 *(978-1-4907-1362-5(X))* Trafford Publishing.

Hutchens, Calvin. The Adventures of Otis Possum. 2007. 52p. per. 16.95 *(978-1-4241-7065-4(6))* America Star Bks.

Ingold, Jeanette. The Big Burn: Teddy Roosevelt & the Fire That Saved America. 2003. (Illus.). 301p. (YA). (gr. 8-12). 14.60 *(978-0-7569-4283-0(7))* Perfection Learning Corp.

Ingold, Jeanette & Egan, Timothy. The Big Burn: Teddy Roosevelt & the Fire That Saved America. 2003. (ENG., Illus.). 320p. (YA). (gr. 7-12). pap. 6.95 *(978-0-15-204924-9(X))* Houghton Mifflin Harcourt Publishing Co.

Jacobs, Lily. The Littlest Bunny in Idaho: An Easter Adventure. 2015. (ENG.). 32p. (J). (-3). 9.99 *(978-1-4926-1078-6(X)*, Sourcebooks Jabberwocky) Sourcebooks, Inc.

James, Eric. A Halloween Scare in Boise. Le Ray, Marina, illus. 2015. (ENG.). 32p. (J). (-5). 9.99 *(978-1-4926-2365-6(2)*, 9781492623656, Sourcebooks Jabberwocky) Sourcebooks, Inc.

—A Halloween Scare in Idaho. Le Ray, Marina, illus. 2015. (ENG.). 32p. (J). (-5). 9.99 *(978-1-4926-2374-8(1)*, 9781492623748, Sourcebooks Jabberwocky) Sourcebooks, Inc.

—Santa's Sleigh Is on Its Way to Idaho: A Christmas Adventure. Dunn, Robert, illus. 2016. (ENG.). 32p. (J). (-2). 12.99 *(978-1-4926-4329-6(7)*, 9781492643296, Sourcebooks Jabberwocky) Sourcebooks, Inc.

Littke, Lael. Searching for Selene. 2003. 203p. (J). pap. 13.95 *(978-1-59038-179-3(3))* Deseret Bk. Co.

Norton, Tamra. Make Me a Home. 2008. 159p. (J). (gr. 3-7). pap. 12.99 *(978-1-59955-113-5(6))* Cedar Fort, Inc./CFI Distribution.

Oblich, Kathleen. Jake & the Scarecrow. 2007. 48p. pap. 16.95 *(978-1-4241-3101-3(4))* PublishAmerica, Inc.

Pileggi, Leah. Prisoner 88. 2013. (J). 16.95 *(978-1-60734-611-1(7))*; (ENG., Illus.). 144p. (gr. 5). 16.95 *(978-1-58089-560-6(3))* Charlesbridge Publishing, Inc.

Reedy, Trent. Burning Nation. 2015. 417p. (YA). *(978-0-545-75282-4(5))*; (Divided We Fall Ser.: 2). (ENG.). 432p. (J). (gr. 9). 17.99 *(978-0-545-54873-1(X)*, Levine, Arthur A. Bks.) Scholastic, Inc.

—Divided We Fall. 2014. (Divided We Fall Ser.: 1). (ENG.). 384p. (J). (gr. 9). pap. 9.99 *(978-0-545-54368-2(1))*; 17.99 *(978-0-545-54367-5(3))* Scholastic, Inc. (Levine, Arthur A. Bks.).

Reedy, Trent. The Last Full Measure. (Divided We Fall Ser.: 3). (ENG.). 464p. (gr. 9-9). 2017. (J). pap. 9.99 ***(978-0-545-54878-6(0))*** 2016. (YA). 17.99 *(978-0-545-54877-9(2)*, Levine, Arthur A. Bks.) Scholastic, Inc.

Romano, Elaine. The Magic Potato - la Papa Magica: Story & coloring book in English & Spanish, 1. Nielsen, Emily, tr. Winchel, Heidi, illus. 2nd ed. 2004. (SPA.). 20p. (J). 3.00 *(978-0-9728225-3-4(4))* Mill Park Publishing.

Saldin, Erin. The Girls of No Return. 2012. (YA). pap. *(978-0-545-31027-7(X))*; (ENG.). 352p. (J). (gr. 9-9). 17.99 *(978-0-545-31026-0(1))* Scholastic, Inc. (Levine, Arthur A. Bks.).

Shay, Michael K. A Flash in Time: A Novel. 2016. (J). pap. *(978-1-63293-141-2(9))* Sunstone Pr.

Silvano, Wendi. Love Is All Around Boise. Czernichowska, Joanna, illus. 2016. (ENG.). 32p. (J). (-6). 12.99 *(978-1-4926-2906-1(5)*, Sourcebooks Jabberwocky) Sourcebooks, Inc.

—Love Is All Around Idaho. Czernichowska, Joanna, illus. 2016. (ENG.). 32p. (J). (-6). 12.99 *(978-1-4926-2921-4(9)*, Sourcebooks Jabberwocky) Sourcebooks, Inc.

Smallman, Steve. Santa Is Coming to Boise. Dunn, Robert, illus. 2013. (ENG.). 32p. (J). (-3). 9.99 *(978-1-4022-9118-0(3)*, Sourcebooks Jabberwocky) Sourcebooks, Inc.

—Santa Is Coming to Idaho. Dunn, Robert, illus. 2013. (ENG.). 32p. (J). (-3). 9.99 *(978-1-4022-9511-9(1)*, Sourcebooks Jabberwocky) Sourcebooks, Inc.

Thurber, Ginny. My Nanny Comes Today. 2009. 16p. pap. 10.95 *(978-1-60693-386-2(8)*, Eloquent Bks.) Strategic Book Publishing & Rights Agency (SBPRA).

Tracy, Kristen. Camille McPhee Fell under the Bus. 2010. (ENG.). 304p. (J). (gr. 3-7). 7.99 *(978-0-375-84546-8(1)*, Yearling) Random Hse. Children's Bks.

—The Reinvention of Bessica Lefter. 2012. (ENG.). 320p. (J). (gr. 5). 7.99 *(978-0-375-84547-5(X)*, Yearling) Random Hse. Children's Bks.

Tregay, Sarah. Love & Leftovers. 2014. (ENG.). 464p. (YA). (gr. 8). pap. 9.99 *(978-0-06-202360-5(8)*, Tegen, Katherine Bks) HarperCollins Pubs.

IDAHO—HISTORY

Edgar, Sherra G. What's Great about Idaho? 2015. (ENG., Illus.). 32p. (J). (gr. 2-5). 26.65 *(978-1-4677-3881-1(6))* Lerner Publishing Group.

Foran, Jill. Idaho: The Gem State. 2016. (J). *(978-1-4896-4851-8(8))* Weigl Pubs., Inc.

Hall, Carol S. & Hansen, T. J. This Is Idaho. 342p. (J). (gr. 1-6). pap. 49.95 *(978-1-56861-051-1(3))* Swift Learning Resources.

Jerome, Kate B. Lucky to Live in Idaho. 2017. (Arcadia Kids Ser.). (ENG., Illus.). 32p. (J). 16.99 ***(978-0-7385-2805-2(6))*** Arcadia Publishing.

Kent, Deborah. Idaho (Revised Edition) 2014. (America the Beautiful, Third Ser. (Revised Edition) Ser.). (ENG.). 144p. (J). lib. bdg. 40.00 *(978-0-531-28278-6(3))* Scholastic Library Publishing.

Lusted, Marcia Amidon. Idaho: The Gem State. 2010. (Our Amazing States Ser.). (ENG.). 24p. (J). pap. 8.25 *(978-1-4488-0755-0(7))*; lib. bdg. 22.60 *(978-1-4488-0661-4(5))* Rosen Publishing Group, Inc., The. (PowerKids Pr.).

Marsh, Carole. Exploring Idaho Through Project-Based Learning. 2016. (Idaho Experience Ser.). (ENG.). (J). pap. 9.99 *(978-0-635-12336-7(3))* Gallopade International.

—Idaho History Projects: 30 Cool, Activities, Crafts, Experiments & More for Kids to Do to Learn about Your State! 2003. (Idaho Experience Ser.). 32p. (gr. k-5). pap. 5.95 *(978-0-635-01781-9(4)*, Marsh, Carole Bks.) Gallopade International.

Miller, Amy. Idaho. 2009. (From Sea to Shining Sea, Second Ser.). (ENG.). 80p. (J). pap. 7.95 *(978-0-531-21128-1(2)*, Children's Pr.) Scholastic Library Publishing.

O'Neill, Elizabeth. Alfred Visits Idaho. 2009. 24p. (J). pap. 12.00 *(978-0-9822288-8-3(0))* Global Business Information Strategies, Inc.

Sanders, Doug & Gorman, Jacqueline Laks. Idaho. 2nd ed. 2013. 80p. (J). (gr. 4-8). 31.36 *(978-0-7614-7998-7(8))* Cavendish Square Publishing.

Sanders, Doug, et al. Idaho. 2016. (ENG., Illus.). 80p. (J). 34.21 *(978-1-62713-195-7(7))* Cavendish Square Publishing.

Tieck, Sarah. Idaho, 1 vol. 2012. (Explore the United States Ser.). (ENG., Illus.). 32p. (J). (gr. 2-5). 28.50 *(978-1-61783-350-2(9))* ABDO Publishing Co.

Ziff, John. Northwest: Idaho, Oregon, Washington, Vol. 19. 2015. (Let's Explore the States Ser.). (Illus.). 64p. (J). (gr. 5). 23.95 *(978-1-4222-3331-3(6))* Mason Crest.

IDENTITY (PSYCHOLOGY)

see also Individuality

Cronn-Mills, Kirstin. Transgender Lives: Complex Stories, Complex Voices. 2014. 88p. (J). (gr. 6-12). lib. bdg. 34.60 *(978-0-7613-9022-0(7)*, Twenty-First Century Bks.) Lerner Publishing Group.

Evans, Barbara Greene. Oscar, the Inquisitive Spider. Greene, Kelly Evelyn, illus. 2013. (ENG.). 45p. (J). pap. 24.95 *(978-1-4787-1779-9(3))* Outskirts Pr., Inc.

Hachler, Bruno. I Am Who I Am. Wolferman, Iris, illus. 2010. (ENG.). 16p. (J). (gr. -1 — 1). bds. 8.95 *(978-0-7358-2299-3(9))* North-South Bks., Inc.

McGillian, Jamie Kyle. Quiz Me! 2017. (ENG., Illus.). 96p. (J). (gr. 3-7). pap. 6.95 ***(978-1-4549-2336-7(9))*** Sterling Publishing Co., Inc.

Orr, Tamra. Home & Family Relationships. 2010. (Teens: Being Gay, Lesbian, Bisexual, or Transgender Ser.). (Illus.). 80p. (YA). (gr. 7-12). lib. bdg. 33.25 *(978-1-4358-3579-5(4))* Rosen Publishing Group, Inc., The.

Payment, Simone. Friendship, Dating, & Relationships. 2010. (Teens: Being Gay, Lesbian, Bisexual, or Transgender Ser.). (Illus.). 80p. (YA). (gr. 7-12). lib. bdg. 33.25 *(978-1-4358-3578-8(6))* Rosen Publishing Group, Inc., The.

Rosen, Michael J. Girls vs. Guys: Surprising Differences Between the Sexes. 2014. (Illus.). 72p. (J). (gr. 6-12). lib. bdg. 33.27 *(978-1-4677-1610-9(3)*, Twenty-First Century Bks.) Lerner Publishing Group.

Scowen, Kate. I. D. Stuff That Happens to Define Us. Mitchell, Peter, illus. 2010. (ENG.). 160p. (YA). (gr. 7-18). 24.95 *(978-1-55451-225-6(5)*, 9781554512256); pap. 12.95 *(978-1-55451-224-9(7)*, 9781554512249) Annick Pr., Ltd. CAN. Dist: Publishers Group West (PGW).

Seba, Jaime A. Feeling Wrong in Your Own Body: Understanding What It Means to Be Transgender. 2009. (Gallup's Guide to Modern Gay, Lesbian, & Transgender Lifestyle Ser.). 64p. (YA). (gr. 7-18). lib. bdg. 22.95 *(978-1-4222-1746-7(9))* Mason Crest.

skelton, J. wallace. Transphobia: Deal with It & Be a Gender Transcender. Johnson, Nick, illus. 2017. (Lorimer Deal with It Ser.). (ENG.). 32p. (J). (gr. 4-9). 22.65 ***(978-1-4594-0766-4(0)***, 9781459407664) Lorimer, James & Co., Ltd., Pubs. CAN. Dist: Casemate Pubs. & Bk. Distributors, LLC.

Smith, Grace. Granddaughter of the Heart: Search for Identity. 2011. pap. 14.95 *(978-0-7414-6541-2(8))* Infinity Publishing.

Solomon, Andrew. Far from the Tree. 2017. (J). pap. *(978-1-4814-4091-2(8)*, Simon & Schuster Bks. For Young Readers) Simon & Schuster Bks. For Young Readers.

—Far from the Tree: Young Adult Edition. 2017. (ENG., Illus.). 464p. (YA). (gr. 9). 18.99 *(978-1-4814-4090-5(X)*, Simon & Schuster Bks. For Young Readers) Simon & Schuster Bks. For Young Readers.

Tebow, Tim. Shaken: Young Reader's Edition: Fighting to Stand Strong No Matter What Comes Your Way. 2017. (ENG.). 208p. (J). (gr. 5). 17.99 ***(978-0-7352-8996-3(4)***, WaterBrook Pr.) Crown Publishing Group.

IDENTITY—FICTION

Alegria, Malin. Sofi Mendoza's Guide to Getting Lost in Mexico. 2008. (ENG.). 304p. (YA). (gr. 7). pap. 10.99 *(978-0-689-87812-1(5)*, Simon & Schuster Bks. For Young Readers) Simon & Schuster Bks. For Young Readers.

Alexie, Sherman. Thunder Boy Jr. Morales, Yuyi, illus. 2016. (ENG.). 40p. (J). (gr. -1-3). 17.99 *(978-0-316-01372-7(2))* Little, Brown Bks. for Young Readers.

Alger, Horatio. Hector's Inheritance: Or, The Boys of Smith Institute. 2006. pap. *(978-1-4065-0708-9(3))* Dodo Pr.

—Hector's Inheritance: Or: the Boys of Smith Institute. 2007. (ENG.). 186p. pap. 19.99 *(978-1-4346-5065-8(0))*; 192p. pap. 21.99 *(978-1-4346-5066-5(9))* Creative Media Partners, LLC.

Alger, Horatio & Stratemeyer, Edward. Young Captain Jack: The Son of a Soldier. 2007. (ENG.). 180p. pap. 19.99 *(978-1-4346-5115-0(0))*; 192p. pap. 21.99 *(978-1-4346-5116-7(9))* Creative Media Partners, LLC.

Alger Jr. Horatio Staff. Hector's Inheritance. rev. ed. 2006. 276p. 28.95 *(978-1-4218-1758-3(6))*; pap. 13.95 *(978-1-4218-1858-0(2))* 1st World Publishing, Inc. (1st World Library - Literary Society).

Ali, S. K. Saints, Misfits, Monsters, & Mayhem. 2017. (ENG., Illus.). 336p. (YA). (gr. 9). 18.99 ***(978-1-4814-9924-8(6)***, Salaam Reads) Simon & Schuster Bks. For Young Readers.

Allen, M. E. Gotta Get Some Bish Bash Bosh. 2005. (Illus.). 208p. (J). 15.99 *(978-0-06-073198-4(2)*, HarperTeen) HarperCollins Pubs.

Alphin, Elaine Marie. Counterfeit Son. 2010. (ENG., Illus.). 192p. (YA). (gr. 9). pap. 7.99 *(978-0-547-25853-9(4))* Houghton Mifflin Harcourt Publishing Co.

—Simon Says. 2005. (ENG.). 264p. (YA). (gr. 9-12). pap. 14.95 *(978-0-15-204678-1(X))* Houghton Mifflin Harcourt Publishing Co.

Altebrando, Tara. The Leaving. 2016. (ENG.). 432p. (YA). 17.99 *(978-1-61963-803-7(7)*, 9781619638037, Bloomsbury USA Childrens) Bloomsbury Publishing USA.

Anderson, Jodi Lynn. Midnight at the Electric. 2017. 272p. (YA). (gr. 9). 17.99 *(978-0-06-239354-8(5)*, HarperTeen) HarperCollins Pubs.

Anderson, John David. Sidekicked. 2013. (ENG.). 384p. (J). (gr. 3-7). 16.99 *(978-0-06-213314-4(4)*, Waldon Pond Pr.) HarperCollins Pubs.

Anderson, R. J. Quicksilver. 2013. (ENG.). 328p. (YA). (gr. 7-12). 17.95 *(978-0-7613-8799-2(4)*, Carolrhoda Lab™) Lerner Publishing Group.

Arbuthnott, Gill. The Keepers' Tattoo. 2010. (ENG.). 432p. (J). (gr. 3-7). 17.99 *(978-0-545-17166-3(0)*, Chicken Hse., The) Scholastic, Inc.

Archer, Jennifer. The Shadow Girl. 2013. (ENG.). 336p. (YA). (gr. 8). pap. 9.99 *(978-0-06-183460-8(2)*, HarperTeen) HarperCollins Pubs.

Armentrout, Jennifer L. Don't Look Back. 2014. (Novel Ser.: 1). (ENG.). 384p. (YA). (gr. 9-17). 16.99 *(978-1-4231-7512-4(3))* Hyperion Bks. for Children.

Avi. Crispin: La Cruz de Plomo. 2004.Tr. of Crispin: The Cross of Lead. (SPA., Illus.). (YA). pap. 7.99 *(978-84-348-9601-7(X))* SM Ediciones ESP. Dist: Lectorum Pubns., Inc.

—Crispin: The Cross of Lead. 2004. (Crispin Ser.). (ENG.). 320p. (J). (gr. 3-7). reprint ed. pap. 7.99 *(978-0-7868-1658-3(9))* Hyperion Pr.

Aviation Book Company Staff. Crispin: The Cross of Lead. 2004. (J). (gr. 3-6). 18.40 *(978-0-613-74965-7(0)*, Turtleback) Turtleback Bks.

Bachorz, Pam. Candor. 2010. (ENG.). 272p. (gr. 7). pap. 8.99 *(978-1-60684-135-8(1))* Lerner Publishing Group.

Bacon, Lee. Joshua Dread. 2013. (Joshua Dread Ser.: 1). (ENG.). 272p. (J). (gr. 4-7). 6.99 *(978-0-307-92998-3(1)*, Yearling) Random Hse. Children's Bks.

—Joshua Dread: the Dominion Key. 2015. (Joshua Dread Ser.: 3). (ENG.). 256p. (J). (gr. 4-7). 6.99 *(978-0-385-37126-1(8)*, Yearling) Random Hse. Children's Bks.

Banash, Jennifer. The Elite. 2008. (ENG.). 256p. (YA). (gr. 9-18). 9.99 *(978-0-425-22157-0(1)*, Berkley) Penguin Publishing Group.

—In Too Deep. 2009. (ENG.). 256p. (YA). (gr. 9-18). 9.99 *(978-0-425-22353-6(1)*, Berkley) Penguin Publishing Group.

—Simply Irresistible. 2009. (ENG.). 256p. (YA). (gr. 9-18). 9.99 *(978-0-425-22783-1(9)*, Berkley) Penguin Publishing Group.

Banks, Kate. Dillon Dillon. 2005. 149p. (gr. 3-7). 18.00 *(978-0-7569-5767-4(2))* Perfection Learning Corp.

Bansch, Helga. Odd Bird Out. 2011. (Gecko Press Titles Ser.). (ENG., Illus.). 32p. pap. 17.95 *(978-1-877467-08-0(1))* Gecko Pr. NZL. Dist: Lerner Publishing Group.

Baptiste, Tracey. Angel's Grace. 2009. (ENG.). 176p. (YA). (gr. 7). pap. 9.99 *(978-1-4169-9537-1(4)*, Simon & Schuster/Paula Wiseman Bks.) Simon & Schuster/Paula Wiseman Bks.

Barnes, Jennifer Lynn. Every Other Day. 2013. (ENG.). 352p. (J). (gr. 7). pap. 9.99 *(978-1-60684-415-1(6)*, Carolrhoda Lab™) Lerner Publishing Group.

Barnett, Mac. The Case of the Case of Mistaken Identity. Rex, Adam, illus. 2010. (Brixton Brothers Ser.: 1). (ENG.). 208p. (J). (gr. 3-7). pap. 7.99 *(978-1-4169-7816-9(X)*, Simon & Schuster Bks. For Young Readers) Simon & Schuster Bks. For Young Readers.

—Mysterious Case of Cases: The Case of the Case of Mistaken Identity - The Ghostwriter Secret - It Happened on a Train - Danger Goes Berserk. Rex, Adam & Myers, Matthew, illus. 2013. (Brixton Brothers Ser.). (ENG.). 1024p. (J). (gr. 3-7). pap. 29.99 *(978-1-4424-9818-1(8)*, Simon & Schuster Bks. For Young Readers) Simon & Schuster Bks. For Young Readers.

Barrett, Tracy. The Missing Heir. 2012. (Sherlock Files Ser.: 4). (ENG., Illus.). 192p. (J). (gr. 3-7). pap. 8.99 *(978-1-250-00480-2(2)*, 9781250004802) Square Fish.

—The Missing Heir. 2012. (Sherlock Files Ser.: 4). (J). lib. bdg. 19.65 *(978-0-606-26131-9(1)*, Turtleback) Turtleback Bks.

Barrow, Rebecca. You Don't Know Me but I Know You. 2017. 336p. (YA). (gr. 9). 17.99 ***(978-0-06-249419-1(8)***, HarperTeen) HarperCollins Pubs.

Baskin, Nora Raleigh. The Truth about My Bat Mitzvah. 2009. (Mix Ser.). (ENG.). 144p. (J). (gr. 4-8). pap. 7.99 *(978-1-4169-7469-7(5)*, Aladdin) Simon & Schuster Children's Publishing.

Bateson, Catherine. The Boyfriend Rules of Good Behavior. 2006. (ENG.). 192p. (YA). (gr. 8-12). 16.95 *(978-0-8234-2026-1(4))* Holiday Hse., Inc.

Bath, K. P. The Secret of Castle Cant. 2005. 1.00 *(978-1-4237-3189-4(1))* Recorded Bks., Inc.

Batson, Wayne Thomas. Isle of Swords, 1 vol. 2008. (ENG.). 352p. pap. 9.99 *(978-1-4003-1363-1(5))* Nelson, Thomas Inc.

Beale, Fleur. I Am Not Esther. 2013. 246p. pap. *(978-1-4596-5748-9(9))* ReadHowYouWant.com, Ltd.

Beam, Cris. I Am J. 2012. (ENG.). 352p. (YA). (gr. 10-17). pap. 10.99 *(978-0-316-05360-0(0))* Little, Brown Bks. for Young Readers.

Beatty, Robert. Serafina & the Black Cloak. (Serafina Ser.). (ENG.). (J). (gr. 3-7). 2016. 320p. pap. 7.99 *(978-1-4847-1187-3(4))* 2015. 304p. 16.99 *(978-1-4847-0901-6(2))* Hyperion Bks. for Children.

—Serafina & the Black Cloak. 2016. (J). lib. bdg. 18.40 *(978-0-606-38336-3(0))* Turtleback Bks.

—Serafina & the Splintered Heart. 2017. (Serafina Ser.: bk.3). (ENG.). 368p. (J). (gr. 3-7). 16.99 ***(978-1-4847-7504-2(X))*** Hyperion Bks. for Children.

Beatty, Robert. Serafina & the Twisted Staff. (Serafina Ser.). (ENG.). (J). (gr. 3-7). 2017. 400p. pap. 7.99 ***(978-1-4847-7806-7(5))*** 2016. 384p. 16.99 *(978-1-4847-7503-5(1))* Hyperion Bks. for Children.

—Serafina & the Twisted Staff. 2017. (J). lib. bdg. 18.40 ***(978-0-606-39977-7(1))*** Turtleback Bks.

Beaumont, Karen. I Like Myself! Catrow, David, illus. (ENG.). 32p. (J). (gr. -1 — 1). 2010. bds. 11.99 *(978-0-547-40163-8(9))* 2004. 17.99 *(978-0-15-202013-2(6))* Houghton Mifflin Harcourt Publishing Co.

—I Like Myself! (board Book) Catrow, David, illus. 2016. (ENG.). 32p. (J). (— 1). bds. 7.99 *(978-0-544-64101-3(9)*, HMH Books For Young Readers) Houghton Mifflin Harcourt Publishing Co.

Bedford, Martyn. The Flip. 2012. (ENG.). 272p. (YA). (gr. 7). pap. 8.99 *(978-0-375-86552-7(7)*, Ember) Random Hse. Children's Bks.

Bendinger, Jessica. The Seven Rays. 2010. (ENG.). 336p. (YA). (gr. 9). pap. 9.99 *(978-1-4169-3840-8(0)*, Simon & Schuster Bks. For Young Readers) Simon & Schuster Bks. For Young Readers.

Bennett, Jenn. Alex, Approximately. 2017. (ENG., Illus.). 400p. (YA). (gr. 9). 17.99 *(978-1-4814-7877-9(X)*, Simon Pulse) Simon Pulse.

Benton, Jim. The Fran with Four Brains, 1 vol. Benton, Jim, illus. 2011. (Franny K. Stein, Mad Scientist Ser.). (ENG., Illus.). 112p. (gr. 3-6). 24.21 *(978-1-59961-822-7(2))* Spotlight.

—Lunch Walks among Us. Benton, Jim, illus. (Franny K. Stein, Mad Scientist Ser.: 1). (ENG., Illus.). 112p. (J). (gr. 2-5). 2004. mass mkt. 5.99 *(978-0-689-86295-3(4))* 2003. 16.99 *(978-0-689-86291-5(1))* Simon & Schuster Bks. For Young Readers. (Simon & Schuster Bks. For Young Readers).

—Lunch Walks among Us, 1 vol. Benton, Jim, illus. 2011. (Franny K. Stein, Mad Scientist Ser.). (ENG., Illus.). 112p. (gr. 3-6). 24.21 *(978-1-59961-817-3(6))* Spotlight.

—Lunch Walks among Us. Benton, Jim, illus. 2004. (Franny K. Stein, Mad Scientist Ser.: 1). (Illus.). 102p. (gr. 2-5). lib. bdg. 16.00 *(978-1-4176-4054-6(5)*, Turtleback) Turtleback Bks.

Bergstrom, Scott. The Cruelty. 2017. (Cruelty Ser.). (ENG.). 384p. (YA). 18.99 *(978-1-250-10818-0(7)*, 9781250108180) Feiwel & Friends.

Berry, Nina. Othersphere. 2013. (Otherkin Ser.). (ENG.). 320p. (YA). (gr. 9). pap. 9.95 *(978-0-7582-9238-4(4)*, K-Teen) Kensington Publishing Corp.

Besser, Kenneth/R. Arnie Carver & the Plague of Demeverde. 2007. (Illus.). x, 338p. (J). *(978-1-934316-02-3(4))* RTMC Organization, LLC.

Bingham, Kelly. Formerly Shark Girl. 2015. (ENG.). 352p. (YA). (gr. 7). pap. 8.99 *(978-0-7636-7673-5(X))* Candlewick Pr.

Bjorkman, Lauren. My Invented Life. 2009. (ENG.). 240p. (YA). (gr. 9-13). 27.99 *(978-0-8050-8950-9(0)*, Holt, Henry & Co. Bks. For Young Readers) Holt, Henry & Co.

Blackburne, Livia. Daughter of Dusk. 2015. (Midnight Thief Ser.). (ENG., Illus.). 380p. (YA). (gr. 7-12). 17.99 *(978-1-4847-2208-4(6))* Hyperion Bks. for Children.

Blackwell, Paul E. Undercurrent. 2013. 320p. (YA). (gr. 9). 17.99 *(978-0-06-212350-3(5)*, HarperTeen) HarperCollins Pubs.

Blevins, Wiley. Rice & Beans. Cerato, Mattia, illus. 2014. (Family Snaps Ser.). (ENG.). 32p. (J). (gr. k-2). pap. 6.95 *(978-1-939656-63-6(X))* Red Chair Pr.

Blumenthal, Deborah. A Different Me. 2014. (ENG.). 272p. (YA). (gr. 8-12). 16.99 *(978-0-8075-1573-0(6))* Whitman, Albert & Co.

—Mafia Girl. 2014. (ENG.). 272p. (YA). (gr. 8-12). 16.99 *(978-0-8075-4911-7(8))* Whitman, Albert & Co.

Bode, N. E. The Anybodies. Ferguson, Peter, illus. 2005. (ENG.). 288p. (J). (gr. 5-8). reprint ed. pap. 6.99 *(978-0-06-055737-9(0))* HarperCollins Pubs.

Bow, Erin. Sorrow's Knot. 2013. (ENG.). 352p. (J). (gr. 7). 17.99 *(978-0-545-16666-9(7)*, Levine, Arthur A. Bks.) Scholastic, Inc.

Boylan, Jennifer Finney. Falcon Quinn & the Black Mirror. Dorman, Brandon, illus. (Falcon Quinn Ser.: 1). (ENG.). (J). (gr. 5-9). 2011. 512p. pap. 7.99 *(978-0-06-172834-1(9))* 2010. 496p. 16.99 *(978-0-06-172832-7(2))* HarperCollins Pubs. (Tegen, Katherine Bks).

—Falcon Quinn & the Crimson Vapor. 2011. (Falcon Quinn Ser.: 2). (ENG.). 384p. (J). (gr. 5-9). 16.99 *(978-0-06-172835-8(7)*, Tegen, Katherine Bks) HarperCollins Pubs.

Boynton, Sandra. Are You a Cow? Boynton, Sandra, illus. 2012. (ENG., Illus.). 16p. (J). (gr. -1-k). bds. 5.99 *(978-1-4424-1733-5(1)*, Little Simon) Little Simon.

Bracken, Beth & Fraser, Kay. The Willow Queen's Gate, 1 vol. Sawyer, Odessa, illus. 2012. (Faerieground Ser.). (ENG.). 96p. (gr. 1-3). lib. bdg. 23.99 *(978-1-4342-3304-2(9)*, Faerieground) Stone Arch Bks.

—Wish, 1 vol. Sawyer, Odessa, illus. 2013. (Faerieground Ser.). (ENG.). 304p. (gr. 4-8). 12.95 *(978-1-62370-003-4(5))* Stone Arch Bks.

Brian, Kate, pseud. The Princess & the Pauper. 2004. (ENG., Illus.). 272p. (YA). reprint ed. mass mkt. 6.99 *(978-0-689-87042-2(6)*, Simon Pulse) Simon Pulse.

Brissenden, Constance & Loyie, Larry. Goodbye Buffalo Bay, 1 vol. 2008. (ENG.). 160p. pap. 14.95 *(978-1-894778-62-6(6))* Theytus Bks., Ltd. CAN. Dist: Univ. of Toronto Pr.

Britt, Paige. Why Am I Me? Qualls, Sean & Alko, Selina, illus. 2017. (ENG.). 40p. (J). (gr. -1-3). 17.99 ***(978-1-338-05314-2(0)***, Scholastic Pr.) Scholastic, Inc.

Brooks, Kevin. Being. 2008. (ENG.). 352p. (J). (gr. 9). pap. 9.99 *(978-0-439-90342-4(4)*, PUSH) Scholastic, Inc.

Brown, Teri. Born of Illusion. 2013. (ENG.). 384p. (YA). (Born of Illusion Ser.: 1). (gr. 8). 17.99 *(978-0-06-218754-3(6))*; pap. 9.99 *(978-0-06-227720-6(0))* HarperCollins Pubs.

Brugman, Alyssa. Alex As Well. 2015. (ENG.). 224p. (YA). (gr. 9). 16.99 *(978-1-62779-014-7(4)*, Holt, Henry & Co. Bks. For Young Readers) Holt, Henry & Co.

Buckley-Archer, Linda. The Many Lives of John Stone. 2015. (ENG., Illus.). 544p. (YA). (gr. 7). 17.99 *(978-1-4814-2637-4(0))* Simon & Schuster Children's Publishing.

Bullen, Alexandra. Wishful Thinking. 2011. (ENG.). 256p. (J). (gr. 9-9). 17.99 *(978-0-545-13907-6(4))* Scholastic, Inc.

Burgess, Melvin. Sara's Face. 2007. (ENG., Illus.). 272p. (YA). (gr. 9-12). 16.99 *(978-1-4169-3617-6(3)*, Simon & Schuster Bks. For Young Readers) Simon & Schuster Bks. For Young Readers.

—Sara's Face. 2007. 272p. 16.99 *(978-1-4169-3295-6(X))* Simon & Schuster Children's Publishing.

—Sara's Face. 2008. (ENG.). 288p. (YA). (gr. 9-12). pap. 7.99 *(978-1-4169-5815-4(0)*, Simon Pulse) Simon Pulse.

Burkinshaw, Kathleen. The Last Cherry Blossom. 2016. (J). ***(978-1-63450-618-2(9))*** Skyhorse Publishing Co., Inc.

Burns, Joanne. Pamela Platypus' Problem. 2005. 21p. (J). 8.99 *(978-1-4116-5226-2(6))* Lulu Pr., Inc.

Burns, Laura J. & Metz, Melinda. Sacrifice. 2011. (ENG.). 272p. (YA). (gr. 9). 17.99 *(978-1-4424-3900-9(9))*; pap. 9.99 *(978-1-4424-0818-0(9))* Simon & Schuster Bks. For Young Readers. (Simon & Schuster Bks. For Young Readers).

Butcher, Kristin. Chat Room, 1 vol. 2006. (Orca Currents Ser.). (ENG.). 128p. (J). (gr. 5-9). per. 9.95 *(978-1-55143-485-8(7))* Orca Bk. Pubs. USA.

—Chat Room. 2006. (Orca Currents Ser.). 102p. (gr. 4-7). 19.95 *(978-0-7569-6873-1(9))* Perfection Learning Corp.
Butler, Dori Hillestad. The Case of the Mixed-Up Mutts, Bk. 2. Tugeau, Jeremy, illus. 2010. (Buddy Files Ser.: 2). (ENG.). 128p. (J). (gr. 1-5). 14.99 *(978-0-8075-0911-1(6))* Whitman, Albert & Co.
—The Case of the Mixed-Up Mutts Bk. 2, 1 vol., Bk. 2. Tugeau, Jeremy, illus. 2010. (Buddy Files Ser.: 2). (ENG.). 128p. (J). (gr. 1-5). pap. 5.99 *(978-0-8075-0933-3(7))* Whitman, Albert & Co.
—Yes, I Know Monkey Man, 1 vol. 2009. (ENG.). 224p. (YA). (gr. 5-9). 16.95 *(978-1-56145-479-2(6))* Peachtree Pubs.
Byng, Georgia. Molly Moon & the Morphing Mystery. 2011. (Molly Moon Ser.: 5). (ENG.). 416p. (J). (gr. 3-7). pap. 7.99 *(978-0-06-166162-4(7))* HarperCollins Pubs.
Cabot, Meg. Airhead. (Airhead Ser.: 1). (ENG.). 352p. (J). (gr. 7). 2009. pap. 9.99 *(978-0-545-04054-9(X))* 2008. 16.99 *(978-0-545-04052-5(3))* Scholastic, Inc.
—Avalon High. 2007. (Avalon High Coronation Ser.: Bk. 1). (ENG.). 320p. (YA). (gr. 8-12). pap. 8.99 *(978-0-06-075588-1(1)*, HarperTeen) HarperCollins Pubs.
—Being Nikki. (Airhead Ser.: 2). (ENG.). 352p. (J). 2010. (gr. 3-7). pap. 9.99 *(978-0-545-04058-7(2))* 2009. (gr. 7-18). 16.99 *(978-0-545-04056-3(6))* Scholastic, Inc.
—Homecoming. Coronado, Jinky, illus. 2008. (Avalon High Coronation Ser.: Bk. 2). (ENG.). 192p. (YA). (gr. 8-18). pap. 9.99 *(978-0-06-117709-5(1))* HarperCollins Pubs.
—The Merlin Prophecy. (Avalon High Coronation Ser.: Bk. 1). 304p. (YA). 2006. (ENG.). (gr. 7-12). 16.99 *(978-0-06-075586-7(5))* 2005. (gr. 8-12). lib. bdg. 17.89 *(978-0-06-075587-4(3)*, HarperTeen) HarperCollins Pubs.
—The Princess Diaries. 2008. (Princess Diaries: 1). (ENG.). 256p. (YA). (gr. 8). pap. 9.99 *(978-0-06-147993-9(4))*Vols. 1-3, Set. 2006. (Princess Diaries: Vol. I). (J). pap., pap. 19.99 *(978-0-06-115389-1(3))* HarperCollins Pubs. (HarperTeen).
—The Princess Diaries. 2008. 20.00 *(978-0-7569-8793-0(8))* Perfection Learning Corp.
—The Princess Diaries. unabr. ed. 2004. (Princess Diaries: Vol. I). 240p. (J). (gr. 7-18). pap. 38.00 incl. audio *(978-0-8072-0669-0(5)*, Listening Library) Random Hse. Audio Publishing Group.
—The Princess Diaries. 2008. (Princess Diaries: 1). (YA). lib. bdg. 20.85 *(978-1-4178-2328-4(3)*, Turtleback) Turtleback Bks.
—The Princess Diaries Box Set: The Princess Diaries; Princess in the Spotlight; Princess in Love. 2003. (Princess Diaries). 304p. (gr. 7-18). pap. 19.99 *(978-0-06-058745-1(8))* HarperCollins Pubs.
—Princess in Love, Vol. 3. 2008. (Princess Diaries: 3). (ENG.). 256p. (YA). (gr. 8-12). pap. 9.99 *(978-0-06-147995-3(0)*, HarperTeen) HarperCollins Pubs.
—Princess in Love. 2004. (Princess Diaries: Vol. 3). 288p. (J). (gr. 7-18). pap. 38.00 incl. audio *(978-0-8072-2284-3(4)*, Listening Library) Random Hse. Audio Publishing Group.
—Princess in the Spotlight. 2008. (Princess Diaries). 222p. (gr. 7-12). 19.00 *(978-0-7569-8794-7(6))* Perfection Learning Corp.
—Princess in the Spotlight, unabr. ed. 2004. (Princess Diaries: Vol. 2). 272p. (J). (gr. 7-18). pap. 38.00 incl. audio *(978-0-8072-1197-7(4)*, S YA 332 SP, Listening Library) Random Hse. Audio Publishing Group.
—Princess in the Spotlight Vol. 2. 2008. (Princess Diaries: 2). (ENG.). 256p. (YA). (gr. 8-12). pap. 9.99 *(978-0-06-147994-6(2)*, HarperTeen) HarperCollins Pubs.
Calhoun, Dia. Firegold. 2003. (Sunburst Bks.). 284p. (YA). 16.60 *(978-0-7569-2809-4(5))* Perfection Learning Corp.
—Firegold. l.t. ed. 2005. (Thorndike Literacy Bridge Ser.). 415p. (YA). (gr. 7-12). per. 21.95 *(978-0-7862-7696-7(7)*, Large Print Pr.) Thorndike Pr.
Calonita, Jen. Secrets of My Hollywood Life. 2007. (Secrets of My Hollywood Life Ser.: 1). (ENG.). 256p. (J). (gr. 7-17). per. 19.99 *(978-0-316-15443-7(1)*, Poppy) Little, Brown Bks. for Young Readers.
Cannon, A. E. The Loser's Guide to Life & Love. 2008. 272p. (J). (gr. 7-18). lib. bdg. 17.89 *(978-0-06-112847-9(3))*; (ENG.). (YA). (gr. 8-18). 16.99 *(978-0-06-112846-2(5))* HarperCollins Pubs. (HarperTeen).
Card, Orson Scott. Pathfinder. (ENG.). 672p. (YA). (gr. 7). 2011. pap. 12.99 *(978-1-4169-9179-3(4))* 2010. 19.99 *(978-1-4169-9176-2(X))* Simon Pulse. (Simon Pulse).
—Pathfinder. l.t. ed. 2011. (Pathfinder Ser.). (ENG.). 802p. 23.99 *(978-1-4104-3681-8(0))* Thorndike Pr.
Carey, Anna. Blackbird. (Blackbird Ser.: 1). (ENG.). (YA). (gr. 9). 2015. 272p. pap. 9.99 *(978-0-06-229974-1(3))* 2014. 256p. 17.99 *(978-0-06-229973-4(5))* HarperCollins Pubs. (HarperTeen).
—Blackbird. 2015. (SPA.). 240p. (YA). (gr. 9-12). pap. 17.99 *(978-987-612-909-1(0))* Lectorum Pubns., Inc.
—Deadfall. 2015. 256p. (J). pap. *(978-0-06-242788-5(1))* HarperCollins Pubs.
—Once. 2013. (Eve Ser.: 2). (ENG.). 384p. (YA). (gr. 8). pap. 9.99 *(978-0-06-204855-4(4))* HarperCollins Pubs.
Carlson, Melody. Mixed Bags, 1 vol. 2014. (Carter House Girls Ser.). (ENG.). 224p. (YA). pap. 9.99 *(978-0-310-74756-7(2))* Zondervan.
Carmichael, Clay. Brother, Brother. 2013. (ENG.). 320p. (YA). (gr. 7). 17.99 *(978-1-59643-743-2(X))* Roaring Brook Pr.
Cart, Michael, et al. How Beautiful the Ordinary. 2009. (ENG.). 368p. (YA). (gr. 9-18). 17.99 *(978-0-06-115498-0(9)*, HarperTeen) HarperCollins Pubs.
Carvell, Marlene. Sweetgrass Basket. 2005. (ENG.). 256p. (J). (gr. 5-6). 16.99 *(978-0-525-47547-7(8)*, Dutton Books for Young Readers) Penguin Young Readers Group.
Casanova, Mary. Frozen. 2013. (Fesler-Lampert Minnesota Heritage Ser.). (ENG.). 256p. pap. 11.95 *(978-0-8166-8057-3(4))* Univ. of Minnesota Pr.
Cassidy, Anne. Looking for JJ. 2009. (ENG., Illus.). 336p. (J). (gr. 7). pap. 20.95 *(978-0-15-206638-3(1))* Houghton Mifflin Harcourt Publishing Co.
Cassidy, Yvonne. How Many Letters Are in Goodbye? 2016. (ENG.). 432p. (YA). pap. 11.99 *(978-0-7387-4745-3(9)*, Flux) North Star Editions.
Castellucci, Cecil. Boy Proof. (ENG.). 208p. (YA). (gr. 9-18). 2005. 15.99 *(978-0-7636-2333-3(4))* 2006. reprint ed. per. 8.99 *(978-0-7636-2796-6(8))* Candlewick Pr.
—Boy Proof, 4 vols. 2005. (YA). 62.75 *(978-1-4193-5131-0(1))* Recorded Bks., Inc.
Catmull, Katherine. The Radiant Road. 2016. (ENG.). 368p. (YA). (gr. 7). 17.99 *(978-0-525-95347-0(7)*, Dutton Books for Young Readers) Penguin Young Readers Group.
Cavanaugh, Nancy. Just Like Me. 2016. (ENG.). 256p. (J). (gr. 3-7). 16.99 *(978-1-4926-0427-3(5)*, 9781492604273, Sourcebooks Jabberwocky) Sourcebooks, Inc.
Cerrito, Angela. The Safest Lie. 2015. (ENG.). 192p. (J). (gr. 3-7). 16.95 *(978-0-8234-3310-0(2))* Holiday Hse., Inc.
Cheng, Andrea. The Year of the Fortune Cookie. Barton, Patrice, illus. 2014. (Anna Wang Novel Ser.: 3). (ENG.). 176p. (J). (gr. 1-4). 15.99 *(978-0-544-10519-5(2)*, HMH Books For Young Readers) Houghton Mifflin Harcourt Publishing Co.
Chima, Cinda Williams. The Warrior Heir. 2007. (Heir Chronicles Ser.). (ENG.). 448p. (J). (gr. 5-9). pap. 9.99 *(978-0-7868-3917-9(1))* Hyperion Pr.
—The Warrior Heir. 2006. (Heir Chronicles: No. 1). 1.00 *(978-1-4294-0323-8(3))* Recorded Bks., Inc.
—The Wizard Heir. 2008. (Heir Chronicles Ser.). (ENG.). 480p. (J). (gr. 5-9). pap. 9.99 *(978-1-4231-0488-9(9))* Hyperion Pr.
Choyce, Lesley. Deconstructing Dylan. 2006. (ENG.). 180p. (J). (gr. 7). pap. 12.99 *(978-1-55002-603-0(8)*, Boardwalk Bks.) Dundurn CAN. Dist: Ingram Publisher Services.
Clanton, Ben. Mo's Mustache. 2013. (ENG., Illus.). 32p. (J). (gr. -1-2). 16.99 *(978-1-77049-538-8(X)*, Tundra Bks.) Tundra Bks. CAN. Dist: Penguin Random Hse. LLC.
Clare, Cassandra. Clockwork Prince. (Infernal Devices Ser.: Bk. 2). (YA). 2015. (ENG., Illus.). 560p. (gr. 9). pap. 13.99 *(978-1-4814-5601-2(6))* 2011. (ENG., Illus.). 528p. (gr. 9-18). 24.99 *(978-1-4169-7588-5(8))* 2011. 502p. *(978-1-4424-5174-2(2))* McElderry, Margaret K. Bks. (McElderry, Margaret K. Bks.).
—Clockwork Prince. 2013. (Infernal Devices Ser.: 2). (ENG., Illus.). 256p. (gr. 8-17). pap. 13.00 *(978-0-316-20096-7(4)*, Yen Pr.) Orbit.
—Clockwork Prince. 2015. (Infernal Devices Ser.: Bk. 2). 560p. (YA). lib. bdg. 25.75 *(978-0-606-37895-6(2))* 2013. (Infernal Devices Graphic Novel Ser.: 2). lib. bdg. 24.55 *(978-0-606-32258-4(2)*, Turtleback) Turtleback Bks.
—Clockwork Princess. 2013. (Infernal Devices Ser.: 3). (ENG., Illus.). 592p. (YA). (gr. 9). 24.99 *(978-1-4169-7590-8(X)*, McElderry, Margaret K. Bks.) McElderry, Margaret K. Bks.
Clark, Hannah L. Uncovering Cobbogoth. 2014. pap. 17.99 *(978-1-4621-1426-9(1))* Cedar Fort, Inc./CFI Distribution.
Clarke, Cat. The Lost & the Found. 2016. (ENG.). 368p. (YA). (gr. 9). 17.99 *(978-1-101-93204-9(X)*, Crown Books For Young Readers) Random Hse. Children's Bks.
Clements, Andrew. Lost & Found. Elliott, Mark, illus. 2010. (ENG.). 192p. (J). (gr. 3-7). pap. 7.99 *(978-1-4169-0986-6(9)*, Atheneum Bks. for Young Readers) Simon & Schuster Children's Publishing.
—Things Hoped For. 2008. (ENG.). 176p. (J). (gr. 5-18). 7.99 *(978-0-14-241073-8(X)*, Puffin Books) Penguin Young Readers Group.
—Things Hoped For. 2008. 167p. (gr. 5-9). 17.00 *(978-0-7569-8933-0(7))* Perfection Learning Corp.
—Things Hoped For. l.t. ed. 2008. (Thorndike Literacy Bridge Ser.). 207p. 23.95 *(978-1-4104-0500-5(1))* Thorndike Pr.
Cobb, Amy. First Chair, 1 vol. Cattish, Anna, illus. 2015. (ENG.). 112p. (J). *(978-1-62402-074-2(7))* Magic Wagon.
—Snaring the Trumpet, 1 vol. Cattish, Anna, illus. 2015. (ENG.). 112p. (J). *(978-1-62402-077-3(1))* Magic Wagon.
Cobb, Nyelah. True Identity. 2003. 104p. pap. 9.95 *(978-0-595-28227-2(X))* iUniverse, Inc.
Cofer, Judith Ortiz. Call Me Maria. 2011. 8.44 *(978-0-7848-3341-4(9)*, Everbind) Marco Bk. Co.
—Call Me Maria. 2006. (First Person Fiction Ser.). (ENG.). 176p. (J). (gr. 3-7). per. 6.99 *(978-0-439-38578-7(4)*, Scholastic Paperbacks) Scholastic, Inc.
Cohn, Rachel & Levithan, David. Dash & Lily's Book of Dares. 2011. (ENG.). 288p. (YA). (gr. 7). pap. 9.99 *(978-0-375-85955-7(1)*, Ember) Random Hse. Children's Bks.
Collins, Janet Ann. The Peril of the Sinister Scientist. 2009. 98p. pap. 7.95 *(978-1-935137-79-5(4))* Guardian Angel Publishing, Inc.
Collins, Pat Lowery. Daughter of Winter. 2010. (ENG., Illus.). 352p. (YA). (gr. 5-18). 16.99 *(978-0-7636-4500-7(1))* Candlewick Pr.
Comrie, Margaret S. The Heroes of Castle Bretten. 2003. (Illus.). 229p. (J). *(978-1-894666-65-7(8))* Inheritance Pubns.
Connolly, MarcyKate. Monstrous. Young, Skottie, illus. (J). (gr. 3-7). 2016. 448p. pap. 7.99 *(978-0-06-227272-0(1))* 2015. (ENG.). 432p. 16.99 *(978-0-06-227271-3(3))* HarperCollins Pubs.
—Monstrous. 2016. (J). lib. bdg. 18.40 *(978-0-606-38136-9(8))* Turtleback Bks.
Cooney, Caroline B. The Face on the Milk Carton. 2009. 9.14 *(978-0-7848-0397-4(8)*, Everbind) Marco Bk. Co.
—The Face on the Milk Carton. 2012. (ENG.). 208p. (YA). (gr. 7). pap. 9.99 *(978-0-385-74238-2(X)*, Ember) Random Hse. Children's Bks.
—The Face on the Milk Carton. 2012. (Janie Bks.: 1). lib. bdg. 20.85 *(978-0-606-26368-9(3)*, Turtleback) Turtleback Bks.
—Janie Face to Face. 2013. (ENG.). 352p. (YA). (gr. 7). 17.99 *(978-0-385-74206-1(1)*, Delacorte Bks. for Young Readers) Random Hse. Children's Bks.
—They Never Came Back. 2011. (ENG., Illus.). 208p. (YA). (gr. 7). pap. 7.99 *(978-0-385-73809-5(9)*, Ember) Random Hse. Children's Bks.
—What Janie Found. 2012. (ENG.). 208p. (YA). (gr. 7). pap. 9.99 *(978-0-385-74241-2(X)*, Ember) Random Hse. Children's Bks.
—What Janie Found. 2012. (Janie Bks.: 4). lib. bdg. 20.85 *(978-0-606-26370-2(5)*, Turtleback) Turtleback Bks.
—Whatever Happened to Janie? 2012. (ENG.). 224p. (YA). (gr. 7). pap. 9.99 *(978-0-385-74239-9(8)*, Ember) Random Hse. Children's Bks.
Cooper, T. & Glock-Cooper, Allison. Drew. 2014. (Changers Ser.). (ENG., Illus.). 288p. (gr. 6). pap. 11.95 *(978-1-61775-195-0(2)*, Black Sheep) Akashic Bks.
Cory, Kim Delmar. Home to Mackinac: The Tale of Young Jack Murphy's Discovery of Loyalty, Family, & Forgiveness. Evans, Laura, illus. 2007. (ENG.). 175p. (J). (gr. 3-7). per. 9.95 *(978-0-911872-87-3(6))* Mackinac State Historic Parks.
Cremer, Andrea. Nightshade. (Nightshade Ser.: 1). (ENG.). (YA). (gr. 9-18). 2011. 496p. pap. 9.99 *(978-0-14-241980-9(X)*, Speak) 2010. 464p. 17.99 *(978-0-399-25482-6(X)*, Philomel Bks.) Penguin Young Readers Group.
Cross, Shauna. Whip It. 2009. (ENG.). 272p. (YA). (gr. 9-12). pap. 9.99 *(978-0-312-53599-5(6)*, 9780312535995) Square Fish.
Crossley-Holland, Kevin. At the Crossing-Places. 2004. (Arthur Trilogy). (Illus.). 394p. (YA). (gr. 7-12). 15.65 *(978-0-7569-3182-7(7))* Perfection Learning Corp.
Cruz, Maria Colleen. Border Crossing. 2003. 128p. (J). pap. 9.95 *(978-1-55885-405-5(3)*, Piñata Books) Arte Publico Pr.
—Border Crossing. 2006. 122p. (gr. 8-12). 19.95 *(978-0-7569-6587-7(X))* Perfection Learning Corp.
Cummings, Troy. March of the Vanderpants - A Branches Book. Cummings, Troy, illus. 2017. (Notebook of Doom Ser.: 12). (ENG., Illus.). 96p. (J). (gr. 1-3). pap. 4.99 ***(978-1-338-03452-3(9))***; lib. bdg. 15.99 ***(978-1-338-03453-0(7))*** Scholastic, Inc.
Curtis, Jamie Lee. This Is Me: A Story of Who We Are & Where We Came From. Cornell, Laura, illus. 2016. (ENG.). 32p. (J). (gr. -1-3). 17.89 *(978-1-5235-0005-5(0))*; 16.95 *(978-0-7611-8011-1(7))* Workman Publishing Co., Inc.
Davies, Jocelyn. A Beautiful Dark. 2012. (ENG.). 416p. (YA). (gr. 8). pap. 9.99 *(978-0-06-199066-3(3)*, HarperTeen) HarperCollins Pubs.
—A Fractured Light. 2013. (ENG.). 368p. (YA). (gr. 8). pap. 9.99 *(978-0-06-199068-7(X)*, HarperTeen) HarperCollins Pubs.
Davis, Terry. If Rock & Roll Were a Machine. 2015. (ENG., Illus.). 256p. (YA). (gr. 7). pap. 10.99 *(978-1-4814-5632-6(6)*, Simon & Schuster Bks. For Young Readers) Simon & Schuster Bks. For Young Readers.
Dawe, Ted. Into the River. 2016. (ENG.). 304p. (J). (gr. 7). 17.99 *(978-1-943818-19-8(3))* Polis Bks.
Dawn, Sasha. Splinter. 2017. (ENG.). 304p. (YA). (gr. 8-12). 18.99 *(978-1-5124-1151-5(5))*; 9.99 ***(978-1-5124-3434-7(5)***, Carolrhoda Lab™); 38.65 ***(978-1-5124-3435-4(3)***, Carolrhoda Lab™); 38.65 ***(978-1-5124-2695-3(4)***, Carolrhoda Lab™) Lerner Publishing Group.
De la Peña, Matt. Mexican WhiteBoy. 2010. (ENG.). 256p. (YA). (gr. 9). pap. 9.99 *(978-0-440-23938-3(9)*, Ember) Random Hse. Children's Bks.
—Mexican WhiteBoy. 2010. lib. bdg. 20.85 *(978-0-606-12316-7(4)*, Turtleback) Turtleback Bks.
DeLuca, Laura. Destiny. 2011. (ENG.). 276p. (YA). pap. 12.95 *(978-0-9826747-2-7(4))* Free Focus Publishing.
Dessen, Sarah. What Happened to Goodbye. 2013. (ENG.). 432p. (YA). (gr. 7). pap. 9.99 *(978-0-14-242383-7(1)*, Speak) Penguin Young Readers Group.
—What Happened to Goodbye. 2013. lib. bdg. 20.85 *(978-0-606-30864-9(4)*, Turtleback) Turtleback Bks.
Detweiler, Katelyn. Transcendent. 2016. (ENG.). 448p. (YA). (gr. 9). 17.99 *(978-0-451-46963-2(1)*, Viking Books for Young Readers) Penguin Young Readers Group.
DeVillers, Julia & Roy, Jennifer Rozines. Trading Faces. 2008. (ENG.). 304p. (J). (gr. 4-8). 16.99 *(978-1-4169-7531-1(4)*, Simon & Schuster/Paula Wiseman Bks.) Simon & Schuster/Paula Wiseman Bks.
Dickerson, Melanie. The Noble Servant, 1 vol. 2017. (ENG.). 336p. (J). 14.99 *(978-0-7180-2660-8(8))* Nelson, Thomas Inc.
—The Princess Spy, 1 vol. 2014. (Fairy Tale Romance Ser.). (ENG.). 304p. (YA). pap. 12.99 *(978-0-310-73098-9(8))* Zondervan.
Diggs, Taye. Mixed Me! Evans, Shane W., illus. 2015. (ENG.). 40p. (J). (gr. -1-3). 17.99 *(978-1-250-04719-9(6)*, 9781250047199) Feiwel & Friends.
Disney Book Group. World of Reading: Elena of Avalor Isabel's School Adventure: Journey to Crystal Caverns: Level 1. Disney Storybook Art Team, illus. 2017. (World of Reading Ser.). (ENG.). 32p. (J). (gr. 1-3). pap. 4.99 *(978-1-4847-4798-8(4))* Disney Pr.
DiTerlizzi, Tony. A Hero for WondLa, 13 vols. 2012. (Search for Wondra Ser.: 2). (J). 110.75 *(978-1-4640-3934-8(8))* Recorded Bks., Inc.
—A Hero for WondLa. DiTerlizzi, Tony, illus. (Search for WondLa Ser.: 2). (ENG., Illus.). (J). (gr. 5). 2013. 480p. pap. 8.99 *(978-1-4169-8313-2(9))* 2012. 464p. 17.99 *(978-1-4169-8312-5(0))* Simon & Schuster Bks. For Young Readers. (Simon & Schuster Bks. For Young Readers).
—The Search for WondLa. DiTerlizzi, Tony, illus. (Search for WondLa Ser.: 1). (ENG., Illus.). (J). (gr. 5). 2012. 512p. pap. 12.99 *(978-1-4169-8311-8(2))* 2010. 496p. 17.99 *(978-1-4169-8310-1(4))* Simon & Schuster Bks. For Young Readers. (Simon & Schuster Bks. For Young Readers).
Doller, Trish. Where the Stars Still Shine. 2013. (ENG.). 352p. (YA). (gr. 9). 17.99 *(978-1-61963-144-1(X)*, 9781619631441, Bloomsbury USA Childrens); 256p. 17.99 *(978-1-61963-145-8(8))* Bloomsbury Publishing USA.
Downer, Ann. Shark Baby, 1 vol. Bersani, Shennen, illus. 2013. (SPA & ENG.). 32p. (J). (gr. -1-3). 17.95 *(978-1-60718-622-9(5))*; pap. 9.95 *(978-1-62855-351-2(0))*; pap. 9.95 *(978-1-60718-634-2(9))* Arbordale Publishing.
—Tiburoncito, 1 vol. Bersani, Shennen, illus. 2013. (SPA.). 32p. (J). (gr. -1-3). 17.95 *(978-1-60718-709-7(4))* Arbordale Publishing.
Downing, Erin. Moon Shadow. 2017. (ENG., Illus.). 256p. (J). (gr. 3-7). 17.99 ***(978-1-4814-7521-1(5)***, Aladdin) Simon & Schuster Children's Publishing.
Driza, Debra. Mila 2.0. 2013. (Mila 2. 0 Ser.: 1). (ENG.). 480p. (YA). (gr. 8). 17.99 *(978-0-06-209036-2(4)*, Tegen, Katherine Bks) HarperCollins Pubs.
—Mila 2.0: Redemption. 2016. (Mila 2. 0 Ser.: 3). (ENG.). 416p. (YA). (gr. 8). 17.99 *(978-0-06-209042-3(9)*, Tegen, Katherine Bks) HarperCollins Pubs.
Duane, Diane. Games Wizards Play. 2016. (Young Wizards Ser.: 10). (ENG.). 640p. (YA). (gr. 7). 17.99 *(978-0-547-41806-3(X)*, HMH Books For Young Readers) Houghton Mifflin Harcourt Publishing Co.
Dunbar, Joyce. A Chick Called Saturday. Granström, Brita, illus. 2004. 32p. (J). 16.00 *(978-0-8028-5260-1(2))* Eerdmans, William B. Publishing Co.
Dunnington, Gwenyth. Second Chance: Girl with the Heart of a Dragon. 2003. 422p. (YA). pap. 22.95 *(978-0-595-29525-8(8))* iUniverse, Inc.
Durst, Sarah Beth. Conjured. 2014. (ENG.). 384p. (YA). (gr. 9). pap. 9.99 *(978-0-8027-3749-6(8)*, 9780802737496, Bloomsbury USA Childrens) Bloomsbury Publishing USA.
Eames, Brian. The Dagger Quick. (Dagger Chronicles Ser.). (ENG., (J). (gr. 3-7). 2013. Illus.). 352p. pap. 6.99 *(978-1-4424-8368-2(7))* 2011. 336p. 15.99 *(978-1-4424-2311-4(0))* Simon & Schuster/Paula Wiseman Bks. (Simon & Schuster/Paula Wiseman Bks.).
—The Dagger X. 2013. (Dagger Chronicles Ser.). (ENG.). 368p. (J). (gr. 3-7). 15.99 *(978-1-4424-6855-9(6)*, Simon & Schuster Bks. For Young Readers) Simon & Schuster Bks. For Young Readers.
—The Dagger X. 2013. (Dagger Chronicles Ser.). (ENG., Illus.). 368p. (J). (gr. 3-7). pap. 6.99 *(978-1-4424-6856-6(4)*, Simon & Schuster/Paula Wiseman Bks.) Simon & Schuster/Paula Wiseman Bks.
Easton, Kelly. To Be Mona. (ENG.). 224p. (YA). (gr. 7). 2009. pap. 7.99 *(978-1-4169-0055-9(1))* 2008. 16.99 *(978-1-4169-0054-2(3))* McElderry, Margaret K. Bks. (McElderry, Margaret K. Bks.).
—Walking on Air. 2010. (ENG.). 240p. (YA). (gr. 7). pap. 11.99 *(978-1-4424-1437-2(5)*, McElderry, Margaret K. Bks.) McElderry, Margaret K. Bks.
Ehrlich, Amy. Joyride. 2008. (ENG., Illus.). 256p. (YA). (gr. 7). pap. 8.99 *(978-0-7636-2321-0(0))* Candlewick Pr.
Elkeles, Simone. How to Ruin a Summer Vacation. 2006. (How to Ruin a Summer Vacation Novel Ser.: 1). (ENG.). 240p. (YA). (gr. 8-12). per. 9.95 *(978-0-7387-0961-1(1)*, Flux) North Star Editions.
—How to Ruin My Teenage Life. 2007. (How to Ruin a Summer Vacation Novel Ser.: 2). (ENG.). 288p. (YA). (gr. 7-12). per. 11.99 *(978-0-7387-1019-8(9)*, Flux) North Star Editions.
Emerson, Carl. What Are You, Patty? A Platypus Tale, 1 vol. Trover, Zachary, illus. 2007. (Animal Underdogs Ser.). (ENG.). 32p. (gr. -1-4). 28.50 *(978-1-60270-020-8(6)*, Looking Glass Library) ABDO Publishing Co.
Emerson, Kevin. The Dark Shore. 2013. (Atlanteans Ser.: 2). (ENG.). 480p. (YA). (gr. 8). 17.99 *(978-0-06-206282-6(4))* HarperCollins Pubs.
—The Lost Code. 2012. (Atlanteans Ser.: 1). (ENG.). 448p. (YA). (gr. 8). 17.99 *(978-0-06-206279-6(4)*, Tegen, Katherine Bks) HarperCollins Pubs.
Everblaze. 2014. (Keeper of the Lost Cities Ser.: 3). (ENG., Illus.). 624p. (J). (gr. 3-7). 18.99 *(978-1-4424-4599-4(8)*, Aladdin) Simon & Schuster Children's Publishing.
Fantaskey, Beth. Jessica's Guide to Dating on the Dark Side. 2010. (ENG., Illus.). 384p. (YA). (gr. 9-18). pap. 8.99 *(978-0-547-25940-6(9))* Houghton Mifflin Harcourt Publishing Co.
Feiffer, Kate. Henry the Dog with No Tail. Feiffer, Jules, illus. 2007. (ENG.). 32p. (J). (gr. -1-3). 18.99 *(978-1-4169-1614-7(8)*, Simon & Schuster/Paula Wiseman Bks.) Simon & Schuster/Paula Wiseman Bks.
Fernandez, Eugenia. Astria & the Missing Prince. 2009. (Illus.). 39p. (J). 31.99 *(978-1-4363-7543-6(6))* Xlibris Corp.
Fischer, Hans. Pitschi. 2010. (ENG., Illus.). 32p. (J). (gr. -1-3). 16.95 *(978-0-7358-2278-8(6))* North-South Bks., Inc.
Fisher, Catherine. Sapphique. (ENG.). (YA). (gr. 7-18). 2011. 480p. 10.99 *(978-0-14-241979-3(6)*, Firebird) 2010. 464p. 17.99 *(978-0-8037-3397-8(6)*, Dial Bks) Penguin Young Readers Group.
Fleischman, Paul. The Animal Hedge. Ibatoulline, Bagram, illus. 2008. (ENG.). 48p. (J). (gr. 1-4). pap. 8.99 *(978-0-7636-3842-9(0))* Candlewick Pr.
Flor Ada, Alma. The Unicorn of the West. 2007.Tr. of El Unicornio del Oeste. (ENG.). 32p. (J). (gr. -1-3). 11.99 *(978-1-4169-6843-6(1)*, Simon & Schuster/Paula Wiseman Bks.) Simon & Schuster/Paula Wiseman Bks.
—Unicorn of the West (Spanish Edition) 2007. (ENG.). 32p. (J). (gr. -1-3). 11.99 *(978-1-4169-6844-3(X)*, Simon & Schuster/Paula Wiseman Bks.) Simon & Schuster/Paula Wiseman Bks.
Fosberry, Jennifer. My Name Is Not Alexander. Litwin, Mike, illus. 2011. (ENG.). 32p. (J). (gr. k-3). 16.99 *(978-1-4022-5433-8(4)*, Sourcebooks Jabberwocky) Sourcebooks, Inc.
—My Name Is Not Isabella. Litwin, Mike, illus. 2008. 32p. (J). (gr. -1-3). lib. bdg. 19.99 *(978-0-9802000-7-2(5))* Monkey Barrel Pr.
—My Name Is Not Isabella: Just How Big Can a Little Girl Dream? Litwin, Mike, illus. 2010. (ENG.). 32p. (J). (gr. k-3). 16.99 *(978-1-4022-4395-0(2)*, Sourcebooks Jabberwocky) Sourcebooks, Inc.
Frazier, Sundee T. The Other Half of My Heart. 2011. (ENG.). 304p. (J). (gr. 3-7). 7.99 *(978-0-440-24006-8(9)*, Yearling) Random Hse. Children's Bks.
Friend, Natasha. The Other F-Word. 2017. (ENG.). 336p. (YA). 17.99 *(978-0-374-30234-4(0)*, 9780374302344, Farrar, Straus & Giroux (BYR)) Farrar, Straus & Giroux.
Fry, Michael. How to Be a Supervillain. 2017. (How to Be a Supervillain Ser.). (ENG., Illus.). 320p. (J). (gr. 3-9). 13.99 *(978-0-316-31869-3(8)*, Jimmy Patterson) Little Brown & Co.
Fusco, Kimberly Newton. Beholding Bee. 2015. (ENG.). 336p. (J). (gr. 3-7). 7.99 *(978-0-375-86808-5(9)*, Yearling) Random Hse. Children's Bks.
Gaither, Stefanie. Into the Abyss. 2016. (ENG., Illus.). 352p. (YA). (gr. 7). 18.99 *(978-1-4814-4995-3(8)*, Simon & Schuster Bks. For Young Readers) Simon & Schuster Bks. For Young Readers.
Gansworth, Eric L. If I Ever Get Out of Here. (ENG.). 368p. (J). (gr. 7). 2015. pap. 10.99 *(978-0-545-41731-0(7))* 2013. 17.99 *(978-0-545-41730-3(9))* Scholastic, Inc. (Levine, Arthur A. Bks.).
García, Cristina. I Wanna Be Your Shoebox. 2009. (ENG.). 208p. (J). (gr. 3-7). pap. 6.99 *(978-1-4169-7904-3(2)*, Simon & Schuster Bks. For Young Readers) Simon & Schuster Bks. For Young Readers.
Gardner, Sally. The Silver Blade. 2010. (ENG.). 384p. (YA). (gr. 7-18). 8.99 *(978-0-14-241731-7(9)*, Speak) Penguin Young Readers Group.
Garvin, Jeff. Symptoms of Being Human. 2016. 352p. (YA). (gr. 9). 17.99 *(978-0-06-238286-3(1))* HarperCollins Pubs.
Gatewood, June S. Mandy Miller & the Brownie Troop. Connors, Mary, illus. 2009. 48p. pap. 17.49 *(978-1-4389-1727-6(9))* AuthorHouse.

Gerber, Linda. Now & Zen. 2006. (S. A. S. S. Ser.). (ENG., Illus.). 224p. (YA). (gr. 7-18). 7.99 *(978-0-14-240657-1(0),* Speak) Penguin Young Readers Group.

Gibney, Shannon. See No Color. 2015. (ENG.). 192p. (YA). (gr. 7-12). 18.99 *(978-1-4677-8814-4(7),* Carolrhoda Lab™); 18.99 *(978-1-4677-7682-0(3))* Lerner Publishing Group.

Gibson, Marley. The Discovery. 2011. (ENG.). 264p. (YA). (gr. 7-18). pap. 8.99 *(978-0-547-39308-7(3))* Houghton Mifflin Harcourt Publishing Co.

Giles, Gail. Right Behind You. 2008. (ENG.). 320p. (J). (gr. 10-17). pap. 10.99 *(978-0-316-16637-9(5))* Little, Brown Bks. for Young Readers.

Gill, Nav K. Under the Moonlit Sky. 2010. (ENG.). 352p. (YA). pap. 15.95 *(978-1-894917-99-5(5),* Napoleon & Co.) Dundurn CAN. Dist: Ingram Publisher Services.

Girard, M-E. Girl Mans Up. 2016. 384p. (YA). (gr. 9). 17.99 *(978-0-06-240417-6(2),* HarperTeen) HarperCollins Pubs.

Gold, Rachel. Being Emily. 2012. (ENG.). 264p. (gr. 9). pap. 15.95 *(978-1-59493-283-0(2))* Bella Bks., Inc.

Golding, Theresa Martin. Niner. 2008. (ENG.). 208p. (J). (gr. 6-9). 16.95 *(978-1-59078-549-2(5),* Front Street) Boyds Mills Pr.

Goodhart, Pippa. Little Nelly's Big Book. Rowland, Andy, illus. 2012. (ENG.). 32p. (J). (gr. -1-3). 16.99 *(978-1-59990-779-6(8),* 9781599907796, Bloomsbury USA Childrens) Bloomsbury Publishing USA.

Goodman, Carol. Blythewood. 2014. (Blythewood Novel Ser.). (ENG.). 512p. (YA). (gr. 7). pap. 9.99 *(978-0-14-242251-9(7),* Speak) Penguin Young Readers Group.

—Ravencliffe. 2015. (Blythewood Novel Ser.). (ENG.). 432p. (YA). (gr. 7). pap. 10.99 *(978-0-14-242252-6(5),* Speak) Penguin Young Readers Group.

Graff, Lisa. A Tangle of Knots. 2013. (ENG.). 240p. (J). (gr. 3-7). 16.99 *(978-0-399-25517-5(6),* Philomel Bks.) Penguin Young Readers Group.

Grant, Vicki. I. D., 1 vol. 2007. (Orca Soundings Ser.). (ENG.). 112p. (YA). (gr. 8-12). per. 9.95 *(978-1-55143-694-4(9))* Orca Bk. Pubs. USA.

—Identificación, 1 vol. 2009. (Spanish Soundings Ser.). (SPA.). 112p. (YA). (gr. 8-12). pap. 9.95 *(978-1-55469-134-0(6))* Orca Bk. Pubs. USA.

Green, Tim. Lost Boy. 2015. (ENG.). 304p. (J). (gr. 3-7). 16.99 *(978-0-06-231708-7(3))* HarperCollins Pubs.

—Pinch Hit. (ENG.). (J). (gr. 3-7). 2013. 336p. pap. 6.99 *(978-0-06-201247-0(9))* 2012. 320p. 16.99 *(978-0-06-201246-3(0))* HarperCollins Pubs.

Gribben, Valerie. The Fairytale Trilogy: Fairytale, the Emperor's Realm, & the Three Crowns. 2010. (ENG.). 320p. (YA). (gr. 5-10). 24.95 *(978-1-58838-251-1(6),* NewSouth Bks.) NewSouth, Inc.

Grimes, Nikki. Bronx Masquerade. 2003. (ENG.). 176p. (YA). (gr. 7-11). 6.99 *(978-0-14-250189-4(1),* Speak) Penguin Young Readers Group.

—Bronx Masquerade. 2003. (gr. 7-12). lib. bdg. 17.20 *(978-0-613-81701-1(X),* Turtleback) Turtleback Bks.

Grund, Carol A. Anna Mei, Blessing in Disguise. 2011. 181p. (J). pap. *(978-0-8198-0796-0(6))* Pauline Bks. & Media.

Guerra, Elisa Puricelli. The Order of the Owls, 1 vol. Bernstein, Gabo León, illus. 2014. (Minerva Mint Ser.). (ENG.). 160p. (gr. 2-4). 9.95 *(978-1-62370-038-6(8))* Capstone Young Readers of Coughlan Cos.

Guest, Jacqueline. Dream Racer, 1 vol. 2006. (Lorimer SideStreets Ser.). (ENG.). 136p. (YA). (gr. 9-12). 16.95 *(978-1-55028-945-9(4),* 9781550289459); 9.95 *(978-1-55028-942-8(X),* 9781550289428) Lorimer, James & Co., Ltd., Pubs. CAN. Dist: Casemate Pubs. & Bk. Distributors, LLC.

Guinan, Jack. I'm a Lot of Sometimes: A Growing-Up Story of Identity. Rudebjer, Lars, illus. 2017. (Growing Up Ser.). (ENG.). 24p. (gr. -1-1). lib. bdg. 19.99 *(978-1-63440-177-7(8));* 30.65 ***(978-1-63440-181-4(6))*** Red Chair Pr.

Gurtler, Janet. I'M Not Her. 2011. (ENG.). 304p. (YA). (gr. 7-12). pap. 12.99 *(978-1-4022-5636-3(1),* 9781402256363) Sourcebooks, Inc.

Guzman, Lila & Guzman, Rick. Lorenzo's Secret Mission. 2005. 153p. (gr. 4-7). 19.95 *(978-0-7569-5599-1(8))* Perfection Learning Corp.

Haddix, Margaret Peterson. Double Identity. 2007. 218p. (gr. 5-9). 17.00 *(978-0-7569-8190-7(5))* Perfection Learning Corp.

—Double Identity. (ENG.). (J). (gr. 5-9). 2007. 192p. pap. 7.99 *(978-0-689-87379-9(4))* 2005. 224p. 16.99 *(978-0-689-87374-4(3))* Simon & Schuster Bks. For Young Readers. (Simon & Schuster Bks. For Young Readers).

—Double Identity. rev. l.t. ed. 2007. (Literacy Bridge Young Adult Ser.). 299p. (J). (gr. 5-9). 22.95 *(978-0-7862-9702-3(6))* Thorndike Pr.

—Palace of Mirrors. 2010. (Palace Chronicles Ser.: 2). (ENG.). 320p. (J). (gr. 5-9). pap. 7.99 *(978-1-4424-0667-4(4),* Simon & Schuster Bks. For Young Readers) Simon & Schuster Bks. For Young Readers.

Hahn, Rebecca. A Creature of Moonlight. 2014. (ENG.). 224p. (YA). (gr. 7-12). 17.99 *(978-0-544-10935-3(X),* HMH Books For Young Readers) Houghton Mifflin Harcourt Publishing Co.

Hale, Bruce. School for SPIES Book 2 Thicker Than Water. Dorman, Brandon, illus. 2014. (School for Spies Novel Ser.). (ENG.). 352p. (J). (gr. 3-7). 16.99 *(978-1-4231-6851-5(8))* Hyperion Bks. for Children.

—School for SPIES Book One Playing with Fire. Dorman, Brandon, illus. 2014. (School for Spies Novel Ser.). (ENG.). 336p. (J). (gr. 3-7). pap. 6.99 *(978-1-4231-7105-8(5))* Hyperion Bks. for Children.

—School for SPIES Thicker Than Water. Dorman, Brandon, illus. 2015. (ENG.). 368p. (J). (gr. 3-7). pap. 6.99 *(978-1-4231-7106-5(3))* Hyperion Bks. for Children.

Hall, Maggie. The Conspiracy of Us. 2015. (Conspiracy of Us Ser.). (ENG.). (YA). 336p. (gr. 7). 17.99 *(978-0-399-16650-1(5));*Pack. 161.91 *(978-0-399-17404-9(4))* Penguin Young Readers Group. (G.P. Putnam's Sons Books for Young Readers).

Hall, Michael. Red: A Crayon's Story. Hall, Michael, illus. 2015. (ENG., Illus.). 40p. (J). (gr. -1-3). 17.99 *(978-0-06-225207-4(0),* Greenwillow Bks.) HarperCollins Pubs.

Hamilton, Virginia, et al. Plain City. (Barco de Vapor). (SPA.). 176p. (YA). (gr. 5-8). 6.95 *(978-84-348-4686-9(1),* LEC6861) SM Ediciones ESP. Dist: Continental Bk. Co., Inc.

Hancock, R. C. An Uncommon Blue. 2014. (Illus.). xi, 275p. (YA). pap. 16.99 *(978-1-4621-1488-7(1))* Cedar Fort, Inc./CFI Distribution.

Hardinge, Frances. Cuckoo Song. (ENG.). (YA). (gr. 7-12). 2016. 432p. pap. 9.95 *(978-1-4197-1939-4(4))* 2015. 416p. 17.95 *(978-1-4197-1480-1(5))* Abrams, Inc. (Amulet Bks.).

—Cuckoo Song. 2016. lib. bdg. 20.80 *(978-0-606-38211-3(9))* Turtleback Bks.

Hargreaves, Roger. Mr. Nobody. Hargreaves, Adam, illus. 2011. (Mr. Men & Little Miss Ser.). (ENG.). 32p. (J). (gr. -1-2). mass mkt. 4.99 *(978-0-8431-9876-8(1),* Price Stern Sloan) Penguin Young Readers Group.

Harlow, Joan Hiatt. The Watcher. 2015. (ENG.). 304p. (J). (gr. 3-7). pap. 6.99 *(978-1-4424-2912-3(7),* McElderry, Margaret K. Bks.) McElderry, Margaret K. Bks.

Harrison, Emma. Escaping Perfect. 2016. (ENG., Illus.). 336p. (YA). (gr. 9). 17.99 *(978-1-4814-4212-1(0),* Simon Pulse) Simon Pulse.

Harrison, Troon. The Twilight Box. 2007. (Tales of Terre Ser.: No. 2). (Illus.). 362p. (gr. 7-18). per. 10.95 *(978-0-9768126-7-8(3))* Brown Barn Bks.

Hartman, Rachel. Seraphina. (ENG.). (YA). (gr. 7). 2014. 528p. pap. 10.99 *(978-0-375-86622-7(1),* Ember) 2012. 512p. lib. bdg. 20.99 *(978-0-375-96656-9(0),* Random Hse. Bks. for Young Readers) Random Hse. Children's Bks.

Harvey, Sarah N. El Blanco, 1 vol. 2010. (Spanish Soundings Ser.). (SPA.). 128p. (YA). (gr. 8-12). pap. 9.95 *(978-1-55469-317-7(9))* Orca Bk. Pubs. USA.

Hasiuk, Brenda. Where the Rocks Say Your Name. 2006. (ENG.). 296p. per. 19.95 *(978-1-897235-11-9(9))* Thistledown Pr., Ltd. CAN. Dist: Univ. of Toronto Pr.

Hawthorne, Rachel. Shadow of the Moon. 2010. (Dark Guardian Ser.: 4). (ENG.). 256p. (YA). (gr. 9-18). pap. 8.99 *(978-0-06-196290-5(2),* HarperTeen) HarperCollins Pubs.

Headley, Maria Dahvana. Magonia. (Magonia Ser.: 1). (YA). (gr. 8). 2016. 336p. pap. 9.99 *(978-0-06-232053-7(X))* 2015. (ENG.). 320p. 17.99 *(978-0-06-232052-0(1),* HarperTeen) HarperCollins Pubs.

Helmetag Murdock, Kita. Future Flash. 2014. (ENG.). 208p. (J). (gr. 2-7). 12.95 *(978-1-62873-822-3(7),* Sky Pony Pr.) Skyhorse Publishing Co., Inc.

Heltzel, Anne. Circle Nine. 2011. (ENG.). 272p. (YA). (gr. 9). 16.99 *(978-0-7636-5333-0(0))* Candlewick Pr.

Henry, April. The Girl I Used to Be. 2016. (ENG., Illus.). 240p. (YA). 17.99 *(978-1-62779-332-2(1),* 9781627793322, Holt, Henry & Co. Bks. For Young Readers) Holt, Henry & Co.

Henry, James. The Cabinet of Curiosities. 2010. 240p. pap. 21.50 *(978-0-9559851-0-2(2))* Blue Cat GBR. Dist: Lulu Pr., Inc.

Hicks, Deron R. The Van Gogh Deception. 2017. (ENG.). 320p. (J). (gr. 5-7). 16.99 *(978-0-544-75927-5(3),* HMH Books For Young Readers) Houghton Mifflin Harcourt Publishing Co.

Hidier, Tanuja Desai. Born Confused. 2014. (ENG.). 512p. (J). (gr. 9). pap. 10.99 *(978-0-545-66451-6(9),* PUSH) Scholastic, Inc.

Hilton, Marilyn. Found Things. (ENG.). 240p. (J). (gr. 4-7). 2015. pap. 7.99 *(978-1-4424-6088-1(1))* 2014. 16.99 *(978-1-4424-6087-4(3))* Simon & Schuster Children's Publishing.

Hoban, Russell. A Birthday for Frances. Hoban, Lillian, illus. 2012. (I Can Read Level 2 Ser.). (ENG.). 48p. (J). (gr. k-3). pap. 3.99 *(978-0-06-083797-6(7))* HarperCollins Pubs.

Hobbs, Valerie. Carolina Crow Girl. 2013. 146p. pap. 12.95 *(978-1-62352-008-3(8))* IntoPrint Publishing LLC.

Hoffman, Alice. Incantation. rev. ed. 2007. (ENG., Illus.). 192p. (YA). (gr. 7-17). per. 10.00 *(978-0-316-15428-4(8))* Little, Brown Bks. for Young Readers.

Hoffman, Mary. Amazing Grace. (Illus.). 32p. (J). (ARA & ENG.). *(978-1-85430-334-9(1),* 93433); (ENG & VIE., *(978-1-85430-340-0(6),* 93435) Little Tiger Pr. Group.

Hooks, Bell. Skin Again. Raschka, Chris, illus. 2017. (ENG.). 40p. (J). (gr. -1-k). 12.99 ***(978-1-4847-9923-9(2),*** Jump at the Sun) Hyperion Bks. for Children.

Hoover, P. J. Solstice. 2013. (ENG.). 384p. (YA). (gr. 8). 17.99 *(978-0-7653-3469-5(0),* Tor Teen) Doherty, Tom Assocs., LLC.

Hopkins, Ellen. Burned. 2013. (ENG., Illus.). 560p. (YA). (gr. 9). pap. 12.99 *(978-1-4424-9461-9(1),* McElderry, Margaret K. Bks.) McElderry, Margaret K. Bks.

—The You I've Never Known. 2017. (ENG., Illus.). 608p. (YA). (gr. 9). 18.99 *(978-1-4814-4290-9(2),* McElderry, Margaret K. Bks.) McElderry, Margaret K. Bks.

Hopkinson, Nalo. The Chaos. 2012. (ENG.). 256p. (YA). (gr. 9). 16.99 *(978-1-4169-5488-0(0),* McElderry, Margaret K. Bks.) McElderry, Margaret K. Bks.

Horowitz, Anthony. Raven's Gate. 2006. (Gatekeepers Ser.: 1). (ENG.). 272p. (J). (gr. 3-7). pap. 8.99 *(978-0-439-68009-7(3),* Scholastic Paperbacks) Scholastic, Inc.

—Raven's Gate. 2005. 288p. pap. *(978-1-84428-619-5(3))* Walker Bks., Ltd.

—The Switch. 2010. (ENG.). 192p. (J). (gr. 5-18). 7.99 *(978-0-14-241547-4(2),* Puffin Books) Penguin Young Readers Group.

Horowitz, Dave. The Ugly Pumpkin. Horowitz, Dave, illus. 2008. (ENG., Illus.). 40p. (J). (gr. -1-k). pap. 6.99 *(978-0-14-241145-2(0),* Puffin Books) Penguin Young Readers Group.

Horrocks, Anita. What They Don't Know. braille ed. 2003. (J). (gr. 2). spiral bd. *(978-0-616-15267-6(1))* Canadian National Institute for the Blind/Institut National Canadien pour les Aveugles.

Houghton Mifflin Harcourt Publishing Company Staff. Girl Power 5-Minute Stories. 2015. (5-Minute Stories Ser.). (ENG., Illus.). 224p. (J). (gr. -1-3). 12.99 *(978-0-544-33925-5(8),* HMH Books For Young Readers) Houghton Mifflin Harcourt Publishing Co.

Hourihan, Kelly. 4 to 16 Characters. 2013. 376p. pap. 11.50 *(978-0-9897411-0-1(9))* Lemon Sherbet Pr.

Howard, Arthur. When I Was Five. 2014. 40p. pap. 7.00 *(978-1-61003-185-1(7))* Center for the Collaborative Classroom.

Howe, James. Addie on the Inside. (Misfits Ser.). (ENG., Illus.). (J). (gr. 5-9). 2012. 240p. pap. 8.99 *(978-1-4169-1385-6(8))* 2011. 224p. 16.99 *(978-1-4169-1384-9(X))* Simon & Schuster Children's Publishing. (Atheneum Bks. for Young Readers).

Hru, Dakari. Joshua's Masai Mask. Rich, Anna, illus. 2013. (ENG.). 32p. (J). (gr. -1-5). pap. 9.95 *(978-1-880000-32-8(6))* Lee & Low Bks., Inc.

Hudson, Wade. The Two Tyrones. Page, Mark, illus. 2004. 32p. (J). lib. bdg. 15.00 *(978-1-4242-0239-3(6))* Fitzgerald Bks.

—The Two Tyrones. Page, Mark, illus. 2004. (Just for You Ser.). (ENG.). 32p. (gr. 2-3). pap. 3.99 *(978-0-439-56866-1(8),* Teaching Resources) Scholastic, Inc.

Hunter, Erin. Sunrise. (Warriors: Power of Three Ser.: 6). (ENG.). (J). (gr. 3-7). 2010. 368p. pap. 7.99 *(978-0-06-089219-7(6))* 6th ed. 2009. 352p. 16.99 *(978-0-06-089217-3(X))* HarperCollins Pubs.

Hurley, Tonya. The Blessed. Watkins, Abbey, illus. 2012. (Blessed Ser.). (ENG.). 416p. (YA). (gr. 9). 17.99 *(978-1-4424-2951-2(8),* Simon & Schuster Bks. For Young Readers) Simon & Schuster Bks. For Young Readers.

—Precious Blood. Watkins, Abbey, illus. 2013. (Blessed Ser.). (ENG.). 432p. (YA). (gr. 9). pap. 9.99 *(978-1-4424-2952-9(6),* Simon & Schuster Bks. For Young Readers) Simon & Schuster Bks. For Young Readers.

Ibbotson, Eva. The Star of Kazan. Hawkes, Kevin, illus. 2006. (ENG.). 416p. (J). (gr. 3-7). reprint ed. 8.99 *(978-0-14-240582-6(5),* Puffin Books) Penguin Young Readers Group.

Ingold, Jeanette. Paper Daughter. 2013. (ENG.). 224p. (YA). (gr. 7). pap. 7.99 *(978-0-544-10484-6(6))* Houghton Mifflin Harcourt Publishing Co.

Jacobson, Jennifer Richard. The Complete History of Why I Hate Her. 2010. (ENG.). 192p. (YA). (gr. 7-18). 16.99 *(978-0-689-87800-8(1),* Atheneum/Richard Jackson Bks.) Simon & Schuster Children's Publishing.

Jahn-Clough, Lisa. Country Girl, City Girl. 2009. (ENG.). 192p. (YA). (gr. 7). pap. 12.95 *(978-0-547-22322-3(6))* Houghton Mifflin Harcourt Publishing Co.

James, Howe. Pinky & Rex & the Bully. 2014. (Pinky & Rex Ser.). (ENG.). 48p. (J). (gr. 1-3). 8.24 *(978-1-63245-347-1(9))* Lectorum Pubns., Inc.

Jefferson, Joanne K. Lightning & Blackberries, 1 vol. 2008. (ENG.). 192p. (YA). (gr. 7-12). pap. 10.95 *(978-1-55109-654-4(4))* Nimbus Publishing, Ltd. CAN. Dist: Orca Bk. Pubs. USA.

Jenkins, Jerry B. & Fabry, Chris. The Minions of Time. 2008. (Wormling Ser.: 4). (ENG.). 336p. (J). (gr. 5-9). per. 7.99 *(978-1-4143-0158-7(8))* Tyndale Hse. Pubs.

Jennings, Sharon. Dancing on the Edge. Doherty, Catherine, illus. 2007. (HIP Edge Ser.). 112p. (YA). (gr. 7-18). pap. *(978-1-897039-27-4(1))* High Interest Publishing (HIP).

Jensen, Brandi Ann & Courtright, Jordan K. The Hilarious & Brave Adventures of Hog & Dog. 2011. 40p. pap. 16.95 *(978-1-4560-3955-4(5))* America Star Bks.

Jesus, Opal De. The Golden Apple Kingdom, 1 vol. 2009. 48p. pap. 16.95 *(978-1-60749-414-0(0))* America Star Bks.

Jinks, Catherine. Evil Genius. 2007. 486p. (J). *(978-1-4287-3510-1(0))* Harcourt Trade Pubs.

—Evil Genius. 2008. (ENG., Illus.). 496p. (YA). (gr. 7). pap. 9.99 *(978-0-15-206185-2(1))* Houghton Mifflin Harcourt Publishing Co.

—Genius Squad. 2009. (ENG., Illus.). 448p. (J). (gr. 7). pap. 8.99 *(978-0-15-206650-5(0))* Houghton Mifflin Harcourt Publishing Co.

—The Genius Wars. 2011. (ENG.). 384p. (YA). (gr. 7). pap. 8.99 *(978-0-547-57727-2(3))* Houghton Mifflin Harcourt Publishing Co.

Johansson, J. R. Cut Me Free. 2015. (ENG.). 304p. (YA). (gr. 9-16). 17.99 *(978-0-374-30023-4(2),* 9780374300234, Farrar, Straus & Giroux (BYR)) Farrar, Straus & Giroux.

Johnson, Angela. Sweet, Hereafter. 2011. (ENG.). 128p. (YA). (gr. 7). pap. 8.99 *(978-0-689-87386-7(7),* Simon & Schuster Bks. For Young Readers) Simon & Schuster Bks. For Young Readers.

—Sweet, Hereafter, Bk. 3. 2010. 128p. (YA). (gr. 9-18). pap. 16.99 *(978-1-4169-9995-9(7))* Simon & Schuster Children's Publishing.

Johnson, Christine. Nocturne. (ENG.). (YA). (gr. 7). 2012. 384p. pap. 9.99 *(978-1-4424-0777-0(8))* 2011. 368p. 16.99 *(978-1-4424-0776-3(X))* Simon Pulse. (Simon Pulse).

Jonell, Lynne. The Sign of the Cat. 2015. (ENG., Illus.). 368p. (J). (gr. 3-7). 16.99 *(978-0-8050-9683-5(3),* 9780805096835, Holt, Henry & Co. Bks. For Young Readers) Holt, Henry & Co.

Jones, Frewin. The Enchanted Quest. 2011. (Faerie Path Ser.: 5). (ENG.). 368p. (YA). (gr. 8). pap. 9.99 *(978-0-06-087160-4(1),* HarperTeen) HarperCollins Pubs.

—The Faerie Path. 2008. (Faerie Path Ser.: 1). (ENG., Illus.). 336p. (YA). (gr. 8-12). pap. 8.99 *(978-0-06-087104-8(0),* HarperTeen) HarperCollins Pubs.

—The Lost Queen. (Faerie Path Ser.: 2). (YA). 2008. (ENG.). 352p. (gr. 8). pap. 8.99 *(978-0-06-087107-9(5),* HarperTeen) 2007. 335p. (gr. 7). lib. bdg. 17.89 *(978-0-06-087106-2(7),* Eos) 2007. (ENG.). 352p. (gr. 7-12). 16.99 *(978-0-06-087105-5(9),* Eos) HarperCollins Pubs.

—The Seventh Daughter. 2009. (Faerie Path Ser.: 3). (ENG.). 352p. (YA). (gr. 8). pap. 9.99 *(978-0-06-087110-9(5),* HarperTeen) HarperCollins Pubs.

Jordan, Jesse. This Is Not the End. 2016. (ENG.). 450p. (gr. 6). pap. 9.99 *(978-1-942546-30-6(0))* Nodin Pr.

Jules, Jacqueline. Picture Perfect. Smith, Kim, illus. 2015. (Sofia Martinez Ser.). (ENG.). 32p. (gr. k-2). lib. bdg. 21.32 *(978-1-4795-5773-8(0),* Sofia Martinez) Picture Window Bks.

Jung, Mike. Unidentified Suburban Object. (ENG.). 272p. (J). (gr. 3-7). 2017. pap. 6.99 ***(978-0-545-78227-2(9))*** 2016. 16.99 *(978-0-545-78226-5(0),* Levine, Arthur A. Bks.) Scholastic, Inc.

Katcher, Brian. Almost Perfect. 2010. (ENG.). 368p. (YA). (gr. 9). pap. 9.99 *(978-0-385-73665-7(7),* Delacorte Bks. for Young Readers) Random Hse. Children's Bks.

Kaufman, Sashi. Wired Man & Other Freaks of Nature. 2016. (ENG.). 264p. (YA). (gr. 9-12). 17.99 *(978-1-4677-8563-1(6),* Carolrhoda Bks.); 35.99 *(978-1-4677-9564-7(X),* Carolrhoda Lab™) Lerner Publishing Group.

Keene, Carolyn. Identity Revealed. 2009. (Nancy Drew (All New) Girl Detective Ser.: 35). (ENG.). 208p. (J). (gr. 3-7). pap. 5.99 *(978-1-4169-6828-3(8),* Aladdin) Simon & Schuster Children's Publishing.

Keeney, Stephen S. Spencer the Adventurer & the Castle of Bran. 2009. (ENG.). 256p. (J). pap. 14.99 *(978-1-934135-31-0(3),* Zumaya Thresholds) Zumaya Pubns. LLC.

Kelly, Nikki. Gabriel. 2015. (Styclar Saga Ser.: 2). (ENG.). 384p. (YA). (gr. 7). 17.99 *(978-1-250-05153-0(3),* 9781250051530) Feiwel & Friends.

King-smith, Dick. Funny Frank. Eastwood, John, illus. 2003. (ENG.). 112p. (J). (gr. 1-4). 5.99 *(978-0-440-41880-1(1),* Yearling) Random Hse. Children's Bks.

Knox, Elizabeth. Mortal Fire. 2013. (ENG.). 448p. (YA). (gr. 7). 17.99 *(978-0-374-38829-4(6),* 9780374388294, Farrar, Straus & Giroux (BYR)) Farrar, Straus & Giroux.

Konigsberg, Bill. Honestly Ben. 2017. (ENG.). 336p. (J). (gr. 9). 17.99 *(978-0-545-85826-7(7))* Scholastic, Inc.

—Openly Straight. 2013. (ENG.). 336p. (J). (gr. 9). 17.99 *(978-0-545-50989-3(0),* Levine, Arthur A. Bks.) Scholastic, Inc.

Konigsburg, E. L. Throwing Shadows. 2007. (ENG.). 176p. (J). (gr. 3-7). pap. 7.99 *(978-1-4169-4959-6(3),* Atheneum Bks. for Young Readers) Simon & Schuster Children's Publishing.

Korman, Gordon. Born to Rock. 2008. (ENG.). 272p. (J). (gr. 7-17). per. 8.99 *(978-0-7868-0921-9(3))* Hyperion Pr.

—Born to Rock. 2011. 10.36 *(978-0-7848-3479-4(2),* Everbind) Marco Bk. Co.

—Born to Rock (repackage) 2017. (ENG.). 240p. (J). (gr. 5-9). pap. 8.99 ***(978-1-4847-9841-6(4))*** Hyperion Bks. for Children.

—The Hypnotists. 2015. (Hypnotists Ser.). (ENG.). 240p. (J). (gr. 3-7). pap. 6.99 *(978-0-545-50332-7(9),* Scholastic Pr.) Scholastic, Inc.

—Memory Maze. 2014. (Hypnotists Ser.: 2). (ENG.). 240p. (J). (gr. 3-7). 16.99 *(978-0-545-50329-7(9),* Scholastic Pr.) Scholastic, Inc.

—Memory Maze. 2015. (Hypnotists Ser.: 2). lib. bdg. 17.20 *(978-0-606-37016-5(1))* Turtleback Bks.

Krensky, Stephen. Big Bad Wolves at School. 2008. (J). (gr. k-3). 27.95 incl. audio *(978-0-8045-6966-8(5))* Spoken Arts, Inc.

Lake, Nick. Blood Ninja. 2010. (Blood Ninja Ser.: Bk. 1). (ENG., Illus.). 400p. (YA). (gr. 7). pap. 9.99 *(978-1-4169-8628-7(6),* Simon & Schuster Bks. For Young Readers) Simon & Schuster Bks. For Young Readers.

Lasky, Kathryn. Hannah. 2011. (Daughters of the Sea Ser.: 1). (ENG.). 320p. (J). (gr. 7-7). pap. 9.99 *(978-0-545-23803-8(X))* Scholastic, Inc.

—May. (Daughters of the Sea Ser.). (ENG.). 336p. (J). (gr. 7-7). 2012. pap. 9.99 *(978-0-545-24331-5(9))* 2011. 17.99 *(978-0-439-78311-8(9))* Scholastic, Inc. (Scholastic Pr.).

Lawson, Jessica. Nooks & Crannies. Andrewson, Natalie, illus. 2015. (ENG.). 336p. (J). (gr. 3-7). 16.99 *(978-1-4814-1921-5(8),* Simon & Schuster Bks. For Young Readers) Simon & Schuster Bks. For Young Readers.

Leaver, Trisha. The Secrets We Keep. 2015. (ENG.). 304p. (YA). (gr. 7). 17.99 *(978-0-374-30046-3(1),* Farrar, Straus & Giroux (BYR)) Farrar, Straus & Giroux.

Lee, Kathy. Hall of Mirrors. 2011. 144p. pap. *(978-1-84427-506-9(X))* Scripture Union.

Levine, Gail Carson. Fairest. 2006. 326p. (J). (gr. 3-7). lib. bdg. 18.89 *(978-0-06-073409-1(4))* HarperCollins Pubs.

—Fairest. l.t. rev. ed. 2007. (Literacy Bridge Young Adult Ser.). 349p. (J). (gr. 3-7). 23.95 *(978-0-7862-9270-7(9))* Thorndike Pr.

Levine, Gail Carson & Levine, Gail C. Fairest. 2012. (ENG.). 352p. (J). (gr. 3-7). pap. 6.99 *(978-0-06-073410-7(8))* HarperCollins Pubs.

Levithan, David. Another Day. 2015. (ENG.). 336p. (YA). (gr. 7). lib. bdg. 20.99 *(978-0-385-75621-1(6));* 17.99 *(978-0-385-75620-4(8))* Random Hse. Children's Bks. (Knopf Bks. for Young Readers).

—Every Day. 2015. (KOR.). 424p. (J). pap. *(978-89-374-3204-0(8))* Min-eumsa Publishing Co., Ltd.

—Every Day. (ENG.). (YA). (gr. 7). 2013. 400p. pap. 9.99 *(978-0-307-93189-4(7),* Ember) 2012. 336p. 17.99 *(978-0-307-93188-7(9),* Knopf Bks. for Young Readers) Random Hse. Children's Bks.

—Every Day. 2013. lib. bdg. 20.85 *(978-0-606-32238-6(8),* Turtleback) Turtleback Bks.

Levy, Debbie. Underwater. 2007. (Darby Creek Exceptional Titles Ser.). 155p. (J). (gr. 4-7). 16.95 *(978-1-58196-053-2(0),* Darby Creek) Lerner Publishing Group.

Lewis, Ellen Parry. An Unremarkable Girl. 2011. 434p. (YA). pap. 19.99 *(978-0-9843437-8-2(4))* Metal Lunchbox Publishing.

Lewis, R. C. Stitching Snow. 2014. (ENG., Illus.). 332p. (YA). (gr. 9-17). 17.99 *(978-1-4231-8507-9(2))* Hyperion Bks. for Children.

Lewis, T. I am who I say I Am. 2011. 32p. (gr. -1). pap. 12.77 *(978-1-4567-6269-8(9))* AuthorHouse.

Lieb, Josh. I Am a Genius of Unspeakable Evil & I Want to Be Your Class President. 2010. (ENG.). 304p. (J). (gr. 5-7). 8.99 *(978-1-59514-354-9(8),* Razorbill) Penguin Young Readers Group.

Lionni, Leo. Pezzettino. 2012. (ENG., Illus.). 40p. (J). (gr. -1-3). pap. 6.99 *(978-0-307-92999-0(X),* Dragonfly Bks.) Random Hse. Children's Bks.

—Pezzettino. 2012. lib. bdg. 17.20 *(978-0-606-23846-5(8),* Turtleback) Turtleback Bks.

Lipsyte, Robert. Center Field. 2010. (ENG.). 288p. (YA). (gr. 8-18). 17.99 *(978-0-06-055704-1(4),* HarperTeen) HarperCollins Pubs.

Lisle, Janet Taylor. The Crying Rocks. 2005. 281p. (YA). (gr. 7-12). 14.65 *(978-0-7569-5507-6(6))* Perfection Learning Corp.

Littman, Sarah Darer. Confessions of a Closet Catholic. 2006. (ENG.). 208p. (J). (gr. 5-18). reprint ed. 7.99 *(978-0-14-240597-0(3),* Puffin Books) Penguin Young Readers Group.

Longshore, Katherine. Manor of Secrets. 2014. (ENG.). 336p. (J). (gr. 7). 17.99 *(978-0-545-56758-9(0))* Scholastic, Inc.

Love, D. Anne. Defying the Diva. 2008. (ENG., Illus.). 272p. (YA). (gr. 7-12). 17.99 *(978-1-4169-3481-3(2),* McElderry, Margaret K. Bks.) McElderry, Margaret K. Bks.

Ludwig, Elisa. Pretty Sly. 2014. (Pretty Crooked Trilogy Ser.: 2). (ENG.). 336p. (YA). (gr. 8). 17.99 *(978-0-06-206609-1(9)*, Tegen, Katherine Bks) HarperCollins Pubs.

Lundquist, Jenny. The Princess in the Opal Mask. 2013. (ENG.). 352p. (YA). (gr. 2-17). pap. 9.95 *(978-0-7624-5109-8(2)*, Running Pr. Kids) Running Pr. Bk. Pubs.

Lynch, Chris. Slot Machine. 2003. 23.00 *(978-0-8446-7249-6(1))* Smith, Peter Pub., Inc.

Lyon, Annabel. All-Season Edie, 1 vol. 2008. (ENG., Illus.). 192p. (J). (gr. 5-10). pap. 13.00 *(978-1-55143-713-2(9))* Orca Bk. Pubs. USA.

Maas, Sarah J. Heir of Fire. 2014. (Throne of Glass Ser.: Bk. 3). (ENG., Illus.). 576p. (YA). (gr. 9). 18.99 *(978-1-61963-065-9(6)*, 9781619630659, Bloomsbury USA Childrens) Bloomsbury Publishing USA.

—Queen of Shadows. 2015. (Throne of Glass Ser.: Vol. 4). (ENG., Illus.). 656p. (YA). (gr. 9). 18.99 *(978-1-61963-604-0(2)*, 9781619636040, Bloomsbury USA Childrens) Bloomsbury Publishing USA.

MacCullough, Carolyn. Once a Witch. 2010. (ENG.). 320p. (YA). (gr. 7). pap. 8.99 *(978-0-547-41730-1(6))* Houghton Mifflin Harcourt Publishing Co.

MacDonald, Maryann. Odette's Secrets. 2013. (ENG., Illus.). 240p. (YA). (gr. 5-8). 16.99 *(978-1-59990-750-5(X)*, 9781599907505, Bloomsbury USA Childrens) Bloomsbury Publishing USA.

Maggi, Nicole. The Forgetting. 2015. (ENG.). 352p. (YA). (gr. 8-12). pap. 9.99 *(978-1-4926-0356-6(2)*, 9781492603566) Sourcebooks, Inc.

Magnus, Kellie. Little Lion Goes to School. Robinson, Michael, illus. l.t. ed. 2003. 16p. (J). 9.99 *(978-0-9744211-0-0(3))* Media Magic New York.

Maguire, Gregory. Egg & Spoon. 2015. (ENG.). 496p. (YA). (gr. 7). pap. 11.99 *(978-0-7636-8016-9(8))* Candlewick Pr.

Mahoney, Daniel J. Monstergarten. Kaminsky, Jef, illus. 2013. (ENG.). 40p. (J). (gr. -1-k). 16.99 *(978-1-250-01441-2(7)*, 9781250014412) Feiwel & Friends.

Mahy, Margaret. The Magician of Hoad. 2010. (ENG.). 432p. (YA). (gr. 9). pap. 9.99 *(978-1-4169-7808-4(9)*, McElderry, Margaret K. Bks.) McElderry, Margaret K. Bks.

Manning, Jane. Cat Nights. Manning, Jane, illus. 2008. (Illus.). 32p. (J). lib. bdg. 17.89 *(978-0-06-113889-8(4)*, Greenwillow Bks.) HarperCollins Pubs.

Mantchev, Lisa. Eyes Like Stars. 2010. (Theatre Illuminata Ser.: 1). (ENG.). 384p. (YA). (gr. 7-12). pap. 11.99 *(978-0-312-60866-8(7)*, 9780312608668) Square Fish.

Manzano, Sonia. The Revolution of Evelyn Serrano. 2012. (ENG.). 224p. (J). (gr. 7-9). 17.99 *(978-0-545-32505-9(6)*, Scholastic Pr.) Scholastic, Inc.

Marchetta, Melina. Jellicoe Road. 2010. (ENG.). 432p. (YA). (gr. 9). pap. 9.99 *(978-0-06-143185-2(0)*, HarperTeen) HarperCollins Pubs.

Margolis, Leslie. If I Were You. 2015. (ENG.). 224p. (YA). (gr. 5-9). 15.99 *(978-0-374-30068-5(2)*, 9780374300685, Farrar, Straus & Giroux (BYR)) Farrar, Straus & Giroux.

Mariz, Rae. The Unidentified. (ENG.). 304p. (YA). (gr. 8). 2012. pap. 8.99 *(978-0-06-180209-6(3))* 2010. 16.99 *(978-0-06-180208-9(5))* HarperCollins Pubs.

Marrone, Amanda. The Shape-Shifter's Curse. 2010. (Magic Repair Shop Ser.: 2). (ENG.). 240p. (J). (gr. 3-7). pap. 5.99 *(978-1-4169-9034-5(8)*, Aladdin) Simon & Schuster Children's Publishing.

Marsden, Carolyn. The Gold-Threaded Dress. 2006. (ENG.). 80p. (J). (gr. 2-4). reprint ed. per. 6.99 *(978-0-7636-2993-9(6))* Candlewick Pr.

—The Gold-Threaded Dress. 2006. 73p. (gr. 2-4). 17.00 *(978-0-7569-6574-7(8))* Perfection Learning Corp.

Martin, Ann M. Here Today. 2005. 308p. (gr. 5-9). 18.00 *(978-0-7569-5104-7(6))* Perfection Learning Corp.

—Here Today. 2005. (ENG.). 336p. (J). (gr. 3-7). pap. 7.99 *(978-0-439-57945-2(7)*, Scholastic Paperbacks) Scholastic, Inc.

—Home Is the Place. 2014. (Family Tree Ser.: 4). (ENG.). 224p. (J). (gr. 3-7). 16.99 *(978-0-545-35945-0(7)*, Scholastic Pr.) Scholastic, Inc.

Martinez, Kathleen. Identity in the Mirror. 2009. 52p. pap. 15.99 *(978-1-4415-0213-1(0))* Xlibris Corp.

Martinusen-Coloma, Cindy. Ruby Unscripted, 1 vol. 2009. (ENG.). 272p. (YA). (gr. 7-18). pap. 12.99 *(978-1-59554-356-1(2))* Nelson, Thomas Inc.

Mason, Ashley. Everybody Is Somebody Special. 2004. 33p. pap. 24.95 *(978-1-4137-3044-9(2))* PublishAmerica, Inc.

Mason, Jane B. Without Annette. 2016. (ENG.). 336p. (YA). (gr. 7). 18.99 *(978-0-545-81995-4(4)*, Scholastic Pr.) Scholastic, Inc.

May, Eleanor. The Bay School Blogger. 2008. pap. 34.95 *(978-1-58013-772-0(5))* Kane Press, Inc.

—The Real Me. Gott, Barry, illus. 2006. (Social Studies Connects). 32p. (J). (gr. k-2). pap. 5.95 *(978-1-57565-186-6(6))* Kane Press, Inc.

McBride, Lish. Hold Me Closer, Necromancer. 2010. (Necromancer Ser.: 1). (ENG.). 352p. (YA). (gr. 9-13). 16.99 *(978-0-8050-9098-7(3)*, 9780805090987, Holt, Henry & Co. Bks. For Young Readers) Holt, Henry & Co.

McCartney, Tania. Peas in a Pod. Snerling, Tina, illus. 2015. (ENG.). 32p. (J). (gr. -1-2). 17.95 *(978-1-921966-71-2(8))* Exisle Publishing Pty Ltd. AUS. Dist: Hachette Bk. Group.

McCarty, Peter. T Is for Terrible. McCarty, Peter, illus. 2008. (ENG., Illus.). 32p. (J). (gr. -1-1). pap. 7.99 *(978-0-312-38423-4(8)*, 9780312384234) Square Fish.

McGee, Krista. Revolutionary, 1 vol. 2014. (Anomaly Ser.: 3). (ENG.). 320p. (YA). pap. 9.99 *(978-1-4016-8876-9(4))* Nelson, Thomas Inc.

Mcghee, Alison. Pablo & Birdy. Juan, Ana, illus. 2017. (ENG.). 304p. (J). (gr. 3-7). 17.99 ***(978-1-4814-7026-1(4)***, Atheneum/Caitlyn Dlouhy Books) Simon & Schuster Children's Publishing.

McGraw, Eloise. The Moorchild. 2006. 241p. (gr. 4-7). 17.00 *(978-0-7569-6823-6(2))* Perfection Learning Corp.

—The Moorchild. 2006. (ENG.). 256p. (J). (gr. 4-7). pap. 8.99 *(978-1-4169-2768-6(9)*, Aladdin) Simon & Schuster Children's Publishing.

McMann, Lisa. Dead to You. 2012. (ENG.). (YA). (gr. 9). 272p. pap. 10.99 *(978-1-4424-0389-5(6))*; 256p. 16.99 *(978-1-4424-0388-8(8))* Simon Pulse. (Simon Pulse).

McMullan, Kate. School's Out... Forever! Basso, Bill & Gilpin, Stephen, illus. 2012. (Dragon Slayers' Academy Ser.: 20). (ENG.). 112p. (J). (gr. 2-5). pap. 4.99 *(978-0-448-44571-7(9)*, Grosset & Dunlap) Penguin Young Readers Group.

McNamee, Barbara Oakley. Kelsey & Seattle. 2007. (J). pap. 15.00 *(978-0-8059-7428-7(8))* Dorrance Publishing Co., Inc.

McNaughton, Janet. To Dance at the Palais Royale. 2006. (ENG.). 252p. (J). mass mkt. 6.99 *(978-0-00-639541-6(4)*, Harper Trophy) HarperCollins Pubs.

McQuerry, Maureen Doyle. The Peculiars. 2014. (ENG.). 384p. (YA). (gr. 7-17). pap. 8.95 *(978-1-4197-1206-7(3)*, Amulet Bks.) Abrams, Inc.

Meadows, Jodi. Asunder. 2013. (Incarnate Trilogy Ser.: 2). (ENG.). (YA). (gr. 8). 432p. pap. 9.99 *(978-0-06-206079-2(1))*; 416p. 17.99 *(978-0-06-206078-5(3))* HarperCollins Pubs. (Tegen, Katherine Bks).

—Incarnate. 2013. (Incarnate Trilogy Ser.: 1). (ENG.). 400p. (YA). (gr. 8). pap. 9.99 *(978-0-06-206076-1(7)*, Tegen, Katherine Bks) HarperCollins Pubs.

—Infinite. (Incarnate Trilogy Ser.: 3). (ENG.). (YA). (gr. 8). 2015. 448p. pap. 9.99 *(978-0-06-206082-2(1))* 2014. 432p. 17.99 *(978-0-06-206081-5(3))* HarperCollins Pubs. (Tegen, Katherine Bks).

Medina, Meg. The Girl Who Could Silence the Wind. (ENG.). 256p. (YA). (gr. 9). 2013. pap. 8.99 *(978-0-7636-6419-0(7))* 2012. (Illus.). 17.99 *(978-0-7636-4602-8(4))* Candlewick Pr.

Meehl, Brian. Suck It Up. 2009. (ENG.). 336p. (YA). (gr. 7). pap. 8.99 *(978-0-440-42091-0(1)*, Delacorte Bks. for Young Readers) Random Hse. Children's Bks.

Meister, Cari. What Can I Be? Phillips, Matt, illus. 2003. (Rookie Readers Ser.). 24p. (J). 19.50 *(978-0-516-22876-1(5)*, Children's Pr.) Scholastic Library Publishing.

Messenger, Shannon. Keeper of the Lost Cities. (Keeper of the Lost Cities Ser.: 1). (ENG., Illus.). (J). (gr. 3-7). 2013. 512p. pap. 8.99 *(978-1-4424-4594-9(7))* 2012. 496p. 16.99 *(978-1-4424-4593-2(9))* 2015. 1744p. pap. 26.99 *(978-1-4814-5112-3(X))* Simon & Schuster Children's Publishing. (Aladdin).

—Lodestar. 2016. (Keeper of the Lost Cities Ser.: 5). (ENG., Illus.). 688p. (J). (gr. 3-7). 18.99 *(978-1-4814-7495-5(2)*, Aladdin) Simon & Schuster Children's Publishing.

Meyer, Carolyn. Jubilee Journey. 2007. (ENG., Illus.). 288p. (J). (gr. 5-7). pap. 17.95 *(978-0-15-205845-6(1))* Houghton Mifflin Harcourt Publishing Co.

—Jubilee Journey. 2007. 271p. (J). (gr. 5-9). 14.60 *(978-0-7569-6682-9(5))* Perfection Learning Corp.

Michaels, Rune. Nobel Genes. (ENG., (YA). (gr. 7). 2011. Illus.). 208p. pap. 8.99 *(978-1-4424-2401-2(X))* 2010. 192p. 16.99 *(978-1-4169-1259-0(2))* Simon & Schuster Children's Publishing. (Atheneum Bks. for Young Readers).

Miklowitz, Gloria D. Secrets in the House of Delgado. 2004. 192p. (J). (gr. 4-18). pap. 8.00 *(978-0-8028-5210-6(6))* Eerdmans, William B. Publishing Co.

Milford, Kate. Ghosts of Greenglass House. 2017. (ENG., Illus.). 464p. (J). (gr. 5-7). 17.99 ***(978-0-544-99146-0(X)***, Clarion Bks.) Houghton Mifflin Harcourt Trade & Reference Pubs.

Miller, Kirsten. The Darkness Dwellers. 2013. (Kiki Strike Ser.). (ENG., Illus.). 416p. (YA). (gr. 7-12). 17.99 *(978-1-59990-736-9(4)*, 9781599907369, Bloomsbury USA Childrens) Bloomsbury Publishing USA.

—The Empress's Tomb. 2013. (Kiki Strike Ser.). (ENG.). 384p. (YA). (gr. 7-12). pap. 9.99 *(978-1-59990-921-9(9)*, 9781599909219, Bloomsbury USA Childrens) Bloomsbury Publishing USA.

—Inside the Shadow City. (Kiki Strike Ser.). (ENG.). 400p. (YA). 2013. (gr. 7-12). pap. 9.99 *(978-1-59990-920-2(0)*, 9781599909202) 2006. (gr. 4-8). 16.95 *(978-1-58234-960-2(6)*, 9781582349602) Bloomsbury Publishing USA. (Bloomsbury USA Childrens).

Milligan, Joe. I Bee the Bee, 1 vol. Raymond, Alejandro, illus. 2016. (ENG.). 32p. (J). 9.95 *(978-1-4556-2201-6(X))* Pelican Publishing Co., Inc.

Miranda, Megan. The Safest Lies. (ENG.). 368p. (YA). (gr. 9). 2017. pap. 9.99 ***(978-0-553-53754-3(7)***, Ember) 2016. 17.99 *(978-0-553-53751-2(2)*, Crown Books For Young Readers) Random Hse. Children's Bks.

Mitchell, Susan K. Kersplatypus, 1 vol. Rogers, Sherry, illus. 2008. (ENG.). 32p. (J). (gr. -1-2). 16.95 *(978-1-934359-07-5(6))*; pap. 8.95 *(978-1-934359-23-5(8))* Arbordale Publishing.

Moore, Meredith. Fiona. 2016. (ENG.). 384p. (YA). (gr. 7). 17.99 *(978-1-59514-784-4(5)*, Razorbill) Penguin Young Readers Group.

Moran, Katy. Bloodline. 2009. (ENG., Illus.). 320p. (YA). (gr. 7). 16.99 *(978-0-7636-4083-5(2))* Candlewick Pr.

Mullarkey, Lisa. A Filming Fiasco, 1 vol. Franco, Paula, illus. 2016. (ENG.). 112p. (J). lib. bdg. *(978-1-62402-164-0(6))* Magic Wagon.

—Hopes in Hiding, 1 vol. Franco, Paula, illus. 2016. (ENG.). 112p. (J). lib. bdg. *(978-1-62402-165-7(4))* Magic Wagon.

Myers, Suzanne. I'm from Nowhere. 2017. (ENG.). 304p. (YA). (gr. 9). pap. 10.99 *(978-1-61695-706-3(9)*, Soho Teen) Soho Pr., Inc.

Myklusch, Matt. The Accidental Hero. 2011. (Jack Blank Adventure Ser.: 1). (ENG., Illus.). 496p. (J). (gr. 3-7). pap. 7.99 *(978-1-4169-9562-3(5)*, Aladdin) Simon & Schuster Children's Publishing.

—The End of Infinity. 2013. (Jack Blank Adventure Ser.: 3). (ENG., Illus.). 416p. (J). (gr. 3-7). pap. 8.99 *(978-1-4169-9568-5(4)*, Aladdin) Simon & Schuster Children's Publishing.

—The End of Infinity. 2012. (Jack Blank Adventure Ser.: 3). (ENG., Illus.). 416p. (J). (gr. 3-7). 16.99 *(978-1-4169-9567-8(6)*, Simon & Schuster/Paula Wiseman Bks.) Simon & Schuster/Paula Wiseman Bks.

—Jack Blank & the Imagine Nation. 2010. (Jack Blank Adventure Ser.: Bk. 1). (ENG., Illus.). 480p. (J). (gr. 3-7). 16.99 *(978-1-4169-9561-6(7)*, Aladdin) Simon & Schuster Children's Publishing.

Myracle, Lauren. Kissing Kate. 2007. (ENG.). 208p. (YA). (gr. 7-18). 7.99 *(978-0-14-240869-8(7)*, Speak) Penguin Young Readers Group.

Namioka, Lensey. Half & Half. 2005. 136p. (gr. 3-7). 16.00 *(978-0-7569-5680-6(3))* Perfection Learning Corp.

—Half & Half. 2004. (ENG.). 144p. (J). (gr. 3-7). 5.99 *(978-0-440-41890-0(9)*, Yearling) Random Hse. Children's Bks.

Naylor, Phyllis Reynolds. Almost Alice. 2008. (Alice Ser.: 20). (ENG.). 288p. (YA). (gr. 9-18). 16.99 *(978-0-689-87096-5(5)*, Atheneum Bks. for Young Readers) Simon & Schuster Children's Publishing.

—Almost Alice. 2009. (Alice Ser.: 20). (ENG.). 288p. (YA). (gr. 9). mass mkt. 6.99 *(978-0-689-87097-2(3)*, Simon Pulse) Simon Pulse.

—Outrageously Alice. 2011. (Alice Ser.: 9). (ENG., Illus.). 176p. (J). (gr. 5-9). pap. 6.99 *(978-1-4424-2853-9(8)*, Atheneum Bks. for Young Readers) Simon & Schuster Children's Publishing.

—Please Don't Be True: Dangerously Alice; Almost Alice; Intensely Alice. 2011. (Alice Ser.). (ENG., Illus.). 768p. (YA). (gr. 9). pap. 12.99 *(978-1-4424-1721-2(8)*, Atheneum Bks. for Young Readers) Simon & Schuster Children's Publishing.

—Sang Spell. 224p. (YA). (gr. 5-18). pap. 4.99 *(978-0-8072-8294-6(4)*, Listening Library) Random Hse. Audio Publishing Group.

—Sang Spell. 2013. (ENG., Illus.). 224p. (YA). (gr. 7). pap. 13.99 *(978-1-4814-1589-7(1)*, Atheneum Bks. for Young Readers) Simon & Schuster Children's Publishing.

Nazemian, Abdi. The Authentics. 2017. 288p. (YA). (gr. 8). 17.99 *(978-0-06-248646-2(2))* HarperCollins Pubs.

Neasi, Barbara J. So Many Me's. Ochoa, Ana, illus. (Rookie Ready to Learn Ser.). (J). 2011. (ENG.). 40p. pap. 5.95 *(978-0-531-26677-9(X))* 2011. 40p. (gr. -1-k). lib. bdg. 23.00 *(978-0-531-26372-3(X))* 2003. 32p. 19.50 *(978-0-516-22883-9(8))* Scholastic Library Publishing. (Children's Pr.).

Neasi, Barbara J. & Ochoa, Ana. Muchas Veces Yo. Ochoa, Ana, illus. 2011. (Rookie Ready to Learn Español Ser.). (SPA., Illus.). 40p. (J). pap. 5.95 *(978-0-531-26789-9(X))*; lib. bdg. 23.00 *(978-0-531-26121-7(2))* Scholastic Library Publishing. (Children's Pr.).

Nelson, Marilyn. American Ace. 2016. (ENG.). 128p. (YA). (gr. 7). 17.99 *(978-0-8037-3305-3(4)*, Dial Bks) Penguin Young Readers Group.

Nelson-Schmidt, Michelle. Bob Is a Unicorn. Nelson-Schmidt, Michelle, illus. 2014. (ENG., Illus.). 28p. (J). 14.99 *(978-1-61067-155-2(4))* Kane Miller.

Nichols, Amy K. Now That You're Here. (Duplexity Ser.). (ENG.). (YA). (gr. 7). 2016. 608p. pap. 12.99 *(978-0-385-75396-8(9)*, Ember) 2014. 304p. 16.99 *(978-0-385-75389-0(6)*, Knopf Bks. for Young Readers) Random Hse. Children's Bks.

—While You Were Gone (Duplexity, Part II) 2015. (Duplexity Ser.). (ENG.). 304p. (YA). (gr. 7). 17.99 *(978-0-385-75392-0(6)*, Knopf Bks. for Young Readers) Random Hse. Children's Bks.

Norriss, Andrew. Friends for Life. 2015. (ENG.). 240p. (J). (gr. 3-7). 17.99 *(978-0-545-85186-2(6))* Scholastic, Inc.

Nuri, Amanda. Emerald Butterfly. 2013. 284p. (J). 31.32 *(978-1-105-66481-6(3))* Lulu Pr., Inc.

Oakes, Stephanie. The Arsonist. 2017. (ENG.). 496p. (YA). (gr. 7). 17.99 ***(978-0-8037-4071-6(9)***, Dial Bks) Penguin Young Readers Group.

Oates, Joyce Carol. Where Is Little Reynard? Graham, Mark, illus. 2003. 32p. (J). 16.89 *(978-0-06-029583-7(X))* HarperCollins Pubs.

O'Brien, Caragh M. The Rule of Mirrors. 2016. (Vault of Dreamers Trilogy Ser.: 2). (ENG., Illus.). 432p. (YA). (gr. 7). 17.99 *(978-1-59643-940-5(8)*, 9781596439405) Roaring Brook Pr.

O'Connor, Jane. Fancy Nancy & the Posh Puppy (Nancy la Elegante y la Perrita Popoff), 1 vol. Glasser, Robin Preiss, illus. 2011. (Fancy Nancy Ser.). (SPA & ENG.). 32p. (J). (gr. -1-3). 16.99 *(978-0-06-179961-7(0))* HarperCollins Pubs.

Omololu, C. J. The Third Twin. 2015. (ENG.). 336p. (YA). (gr. 7). 20.99 *(978-0-375-99171-4(9)*, Delacorte Pr.) Random Hse. Children's Bks.

O'Neal, Eilis. The False Princess. 2012. (ENG.). 336p. (J). (gr. 7). pap. 8.99 *(978-1-60684-392-5(3)*, Carolrhoda Lab™) Lerner Publishing Group.

Orona-Ramirez, Kristy. Kiki's Journey. Warm Day, Jonathan, illus. (ENG.). 32p. (J). 2017. pap. 9.95 ***(978-0-89239-410-4(2)***, Children's Book Press) 2013. 16.95 *(978-0-89239-214-8(2))* Lee & Low Bks., Inc.

Ostow, Micol. Emily Goldberg Learns to Salsa. 2007. (ENG.). 208p. (YA). (gr. 7-18). 8.99 *(978-1-59514-144-6(8)*, Razorbill) Penguin Young Readers Group.

Owen, Karen. I Could Be- Barroux, illus. 2009. (J). *(978-1-84686-289-2(2))* Barefoot Bks., Inc.

—I Could Be, You Could Be. Barroux, illus. 2010. (ENG.). 32p. (J). (gr. 1-3). 16.99 *(978-1-84686-405-6(4))* Barefoot Bks., Inc.

Owen, Karen & Barroux. I Could Be, You Could Be. 2012. (ENG., Illus.). 32p. (J). (gr. -1-1). pap. 7.99 *(978-1-84686-763-7(0))* Barefoot Bks., Inc.

Paige, D. M. Chart Topper. 2015. (Opportunity Ser.). (ENG.). 112p. (YA). (gr. 6-12). 34.65 *(978-1-4677-6014-0(5)*, Lerner Digital) Lerner Publishing Group.

Parker, Emma. What Will JoJo Be? 2010. (Illus.). pap. *(978-1-877561-06-1(1))* First Edition Ltd.

Pashley, Hilton. Gabriel's Clock. 2014. (ENG.). 304p. (J). (gr. 5-7). 16.99 *(978-0-544-30176-4(5)*, HMH Books For Young Readers) Houghton Mifflin Harcourt Publishing Co.

Paterson, Katherine. Jacob Have I Loved. 2003. (Trophy Bk.). (ENG.). 272p. (YA). (gr. 8-18). pap. 6.99 *(978-0-06-440368-9(8))* HarperCollins Pubs.

—Jip: His Story. 2005. (Puffin Modern Classics Ser.). (ENG.). 192p. (J). (gr. 3-7). pap. 6.99 *(978-0-14-240411-9(X)*, Puffin Books) Penguin Young Readers Group.

Patten, E. J. Return to Exile. Rocco, John, illus. (Hunter Chronicles Ser.: 1). (ENG.). 512p. (J). (gr. 3-7). 2013. pap. 7.99 *(978-1-4424-2033-5(2))* 2011. 16.99 *(978-1-4424-2032-8(4))* Simon & Schuster Bks. For Young Readers. (Simon & Schuster Bks. For Young Readers).

Paulsen, Gary. The Island. 2006. (Point Ser.). 202p. (gr. 7-12). 16.00 *(978-0-7569-6382-8(6))* Perfection Learning Corp.

Pearl, Alexa. The #1: Big Secret. Sordo, Paco, illus. 2017. (Tales of Sasha Ser.: 1). (ENG.). 112p. (J). (gr. 1-3). pap. 5.99 *(978-1-4998-0389-1(3))* Little Bee Books Inc.

—#2: Journey Beyond the Trees. Sordo, Paco, illus. 2017. (Tales of Sasha Ser.: 2). (ENG.). 112p. (J). (gr. 1-3). pap. 5.99 *(978-1-4998-0391-4(5))* Little Bee Books Inc.

Pearson, Mary E. The Fox Inheritance. 2011. (Jenna Fox Chronicles Ser.: 2). (ENG.). 304p. (YA). (gr. 7-12). 16.99 *(978-0-8050-8829-8(6)*, Holt, Henry & Co. Bks. For Young Readers) Holt, Henry & Co.

—The Fox Inheritance. 2013. (Jenna Fox Chronicles Ser.: 2). (ENG.). 320p. (YA). (gr. 7-12). pap. 11.99 *(978-1-250-01032-2(2)*, 9781250010322) Square Fish.

Peck, Richard. The Mouse with the Question Mark Tail. Murphy, Kelly, illus. 2013. (ENG.). 240p. (J). (gr. 3-7). 16.99 *(978-0-8037-3838-6(2)*, Dial Bks) Penguin Young Readers Group.

Perkins, Lynne Rae. Criss Cross. (ENG., Illus.). (J). (gr. 5-9). 2007. 368p. pap. 6.99 *(978-0-06-009274-0(2))* 2005. 352p. 16.99 *(978-0-06-009272-6(6))* HarperCollins Pubs. (Greenwillow Bks.).

Perritano, John. The Snickerblooms & the Age Bug, 1 vol. Laughead, Mike, illus. 2014. (Kid Squad Saves the World Ser.). (ENG.). 112p. (J). (gr. 8-12). 27.07 *(978-1-62402-041-4(0))* Magic Wagon.

Peters, Julie Anne. Luna. 2006. (ENG.). 256p. (YA). (gr. 10-17). reprint ed. pap. 10.99 *(978-0-316-01127-3(4)*, Tingley, Megan Bks.) Little, Brown Bks. for Young Readers.

Pike, Christopher, pseud. The Secret of Ka. 2011. (ENG.). 416p. (YA). (gr. 7). pap. 8.99 *(978-0-547-57729-6(X))* Houghton Mifflin Harcourt Publishing Co.

Pixley, Marcella. Freak. 2013. (ENG.). 160p. (YA). (gr. 7-10). pap. 10.99 *(978-1-250-02742-9(X)*, 9781250027429) Square Fish.

Portman, Frank. King Dork. 2007. 344p. 19.00 *(978-0-7569-7950-8(1))* Perfection Learning Corp.

—King Dork. 2008. (ENG.). 368p. (YA). (gr. 9-12). pap. 9.99 *(978-0-385-73450-9(6)*, Delacorte Bks. for Young Readers) Random Hse. Children's Bks.

Powell, Huw. Spacejackers. 2015. (Spacejackers Ser.). (ENG.). 336p. (YA). (gr. 3-6). 16.99 *(978-1-61963-515-9(1)*, 9781619635159, Bloomsbury USA Childrens) Bloomsbury Publishing USA.

Prineas, Sarah. Summerkin. 2013. (Summerlands Ser.: 2). (ENG.). (J). (gr. 3-7). 288p. pap. 6.99 *(978-0-06-192108-7(4))*; 272p. 16.99 *(978-0-06-192106-3(8))* HarperCollins Pubs.

—Winterling. (J). (gr. 5-7). 2013. (Summerlands Ser.: 1). (ENG.). 272p. pap. 6.99 *(978-0-06-192105-6(X))* 2012. 256p. lib. bdg. 17.89 *(978-0-06-192104-9(1))* 2012. (Summerlands Ser.: 1). (ENG.). 256p. 16.99 *(978-0-06-192103-2(3))* HarperCollins Pubs.

—Winterling, 5 vols. 2012. (Winterling Ser.: 1). (J). 75.75 *(978-1-4640-1032-3(3))*; 230.75 *(978-1-4640-1034-7(X))*; 73.75 *(978-1-4640-1036-1(6))*; 73.75 *(978-1-4640-1037-8(4))* Recorded Bks., Inc.

Quinn, Kate Karyus. Another Little Piece. 2013. (ENG.). 432p. (YA). (gr. 9). 17.99 *(978-0-06-213595-7(3)*, HarperTeen) HarperCollins Pubs.

Quintana, Adrienne. Eruption. 2015. 282p. (YA). pap. 16.99 *(978-1-4621-1536-5(5))* Cedar Fort, Inc./CFI Distribution.

Randall, Barbara. Jacob Daddy. Randall, Barbara & Newman, J. Heidi, eds. 2010. (Little Lily Mays Ser.: vol. 3). (Illus.). 300p. pap. 14.95 *(978-0-9712383-3-6(2))* Culturatti Ink.

Razi, Michaele. Frank the Seven-Legged Spider. 2017. (ENG.). 32p. (J). (gr. -1-3). 16.99 ***(978-1-63217-128-3(7)***, Little Bigfoot) Sasquatch Bks.

Rech, Lindsay Faith. It Started with a Dare. 2010. (ENG.). 312p. (YA). (gr. 7-18). pap. 17.99 *(978-0-547-23558-5(5))* Houghton Mifflin Harcourt Publishing Co.

Reeve, Philip. Fever Crumb. 2011. (Fever Crumb Ser.). (ENG.). 336p. (J). (gr. 7-7). pap. 9.99 *(978-0-545-22215-0(X)*, Scholastic Pr.) Scholastic, Inc.

—Scrivener's Moon. 2012. (ENG.). 352p. (J). (gr. 7). 17.99 *(978-0-545-22218-1(4)*, Scholastic Pr.) Scholastic, Inc.

Regan, Dian. Cam's Quest: The Continuing Story of Princess Nevermore & the Wizard's Apprentice. 2007. (Junior Library Guild Selection Ser.). 334p. (J). (gr. 4-8). 17.95 *(978-1-58196-056-3(5)*, Darby Creek) Lerner Publishing Group.

Reisz, Kristopher. Unleashed. 2010. (ENG.). 352p. (YA). (gr. 9). pap. 9.99 *(978-1-4424-0637-7(2)*, Simon Pulse) Simon Pulse.

Richter, Conrad. The Light in the Forest. Chappell, Warren, illus. 2005. (Everyman's Library Children's Classics Ser.). (ENG.). 176p. (J). (gr. 5-7). 15.95 *(978-1-4000-4426-9(X)*, Everyman's Library) Knopf Doubleday Publishing Group.

Robinson, Nikki Slade. Muddle & Mo. 2017. (ENG., Illus.). 32p. (J). (gr. -1-3). 14.99 *(978-0-544-71612-4(4))* Houghton Mifflin Harcourt Publishing Co.

Rossell, Judith. Withering-By-Sea. Rossell, Judith, illus. 2017. (ENG., Illus.). 288p. (J). (gr. 3-7). pap. 7.99 *(978-1-4814-4368-5(2))* Simon & Schuster Children's Publishing.

Rossell, Judith. Wormwood Mire. Rossell, Judith, illus. 2017. (ENG., Illus.). 288p. (J). (gr. 3-7). 16.99 ***(978-1-4814-4370-8(4)***, Atheneum Bks. for Young Readers) Simon & Schuster Children's Publishing.

Roth, Veronica. Allegiant. (Divergent Ser.: 3). (YA). (gr. 9). 2016. 592p. pap. 12.99 *(978-0-06-242009-1(7))* 2016. 592p. pap. 12.99 *(978-0-06-202407-7(8))* 2013. (ENG.). 544p. 19.99 *(978-0-06-202406-0(X))* 2016. 592p. 19.99 *(978-0-06-242008-4(9))* HarperCollins Pubs. (Tegen, Katherine Bks).

—Allegiant. l.t. ed. 2016. (Divergent Ser.: 3). (ENG.). 580p. pap. 12.99 *(978-1-59413-960-4(1)*, Large Print Pr.) Thorndike Pr.

—Allegiant. 2016. (Divergent Ser.: 3). lib. bdg. 24.50 *(978-0-606-38141-3(4))*; lib. bdg. 24.50 *(978-0-606-38182-6(1))* Turtleback Bks.

—Divergent. 2013. (KOR.). ***(978-89-5660-710-8(9))*** Eunhaeng Namu Publishing Co.

—Divergent. Delort, Nicolas, photos by. 2014. (Divergent Ser.: 1). (ENG., Illus.). 576p. (YA). (gr. 9). pap. 12.99 *(978-0-06-238724-0(3)*, Tegen, Katherine Bks) HarperCollins Pubs.

—Divergent. 2012. (ENG.). 512p. pap. *(978-0-06-219406-0(2))* HarperCollins Pubs.

—Divergent, 3 vols. Delort, Nicolas, photos by. (Divergent Ser.: 1). (ENG., Illus.). (YA). (gr. 9-18). 2011. 496p. 17.99

(978-0-06-202402-2(7)) 2014. 576p. 19.99 (978-0-06-235217-0(2)) HarperCollins Pubs. (Tegen, Katherine Bks).

—Divergent. movie tie-in ed. 2014. (Divergent Ser.: Bk. 1). (ENG.). 496p. (YA). (gr. 9). 17.99 (978-0-06-228984-1(5), Tegen, Katherine Bks) HarperCollins Pubs.

—Divergent, 1. 2012. (ENG.). 496p. (978-0-00-742042-1(0)) HarperCollins Pubs. Ltd.

—Divergent. 2014. (Divergent Ser.). (ENG.). 496p. (J). 14.24 (978-1-63245-208-5(1)) Lectorum Pubns., Inc.

—Divergent. 2009. (Divergent Ser.: Bk. 1). 11.04 (978-0-7848-3786-3(4), Everbind) Marco Bk. Co.

—Divergent. 2014. (Divergent Trilogy Ser.). (ENG.). (YA). (gr. 9). lib. bdg. 23.60 **(978-1-62765-593-4(X))** Perfection Learning Corp.

—Divergent. l.t. ed. 2014. (Divergent Ser.: Bk. 1). (ENG.). 530p. pap. 12.99 (978-1-59413-745-7(5), Large Print Pr.) Thorndike Pr.

—Divergent. 2014. (Divergent Ser.: 1). (YA). lib. bdg. 24.50 (978-0-606-36515-4(X)) Turtleback Bks.

—Divergent; Insurgent; Allegiant, 3 vols., Set. 2013. (Divergent Ser.: Bks. 1-3). (ENG.). (YA). (gr. 9). 55.97 (978-0-06-227878-4(9), Tegen, Katherine Bks) HarperCollins Pubs.

—Divergente. 2013. (Divergent Ser.: Bk. 1).Tr. of Divergent. (SPA.). 464p. (YA). pap. 21.99 (978-84-272-0118-7(4)) Molino, Editorial ESP. Dist: Lectorum Pubns., Inc.

—Four: A Divergent Collection: The Transfer; The Initiate; The Son; The Traitor. 2014. (Divergent Ser.). (ENG.). 304p. (J). (gr. 9). 17.99 (978-0-06-234521-9(4)) HarperCollins Pubs.

—Insurgent. 2014. (KOR.). **(978-89-5660-758-0(3))** Eunhaeng Namu Publishing Co.

—Insurgent. 2015. pap. (978-0-06-238845-2(2)) 2015. (Divergent Ser.: 2). (ENG.). 592p. (J). (gr. 9). pap. 12.99 (978-0-06-202405-3(1)) 2012. (Divergent Ser.: 2). (ENG.). 544p. (YA). (gr. 9). 17.99 (978-0-06-202404-6(3)) 2012. (Divergent Ser.: 2). 544p. (YA). (gr. 9). pap. 12.00 (978-0-06-212784-6(5)) 2012. (Divergent Ser.: 2). (ENG.). 592p. (YA). (gr. 9). 19.99 (978-0-06-223493-3(5)) 2015. (Divergent Ser.: 2). (ENG.). 544p. (YA). (gr. 9). 17.99 (978-0-06-237284-0(X)) 2015. (Divergent Ser.: Bk. 2). (ENG.). 592p. (YA). (gr. 9). pap. 12.99 (978-0-06-237285-7(8)) HarperCollins Pubs. (Tegen, Katherine Bks).

—Insurgent. 2015. (Divergent Trilogy Ser.). (ENG.). (YA). (gr. 9). lib. bdg. 23.60 **(978-1-62765-988-8(9))** Perfection Learning Corp.

—Insurgent. 2015. (Divergent Ser.: 2). (YA). lib. bdg. 24.50 (978-0-606-36475-1(7)) Turtleback Bks.

Rubin, Lance. Denton Little's Deathdate. 2015. (ENG.). 352p. (YA). (gr. 9). 17.99 (978-0-553-49696-3(4), Knopf Bks. for Young Readers) Random Hse. Children's Bks.

Rudnick, Paul. Gorgeous. (ENG.). 336p. (J). (gr. 9). 2014. pap. 9.99 (978-0-545-46427-7(7)) 2013. 18.99 (978-0-545-46426-0(9)) Scholastic, Inc. (Scholastic Pr.).

Rush, Jennifer. Altered. 2013. (Altered Ser.: 1). (ENG.). (YA). (gr. 7-17). 352p. pap. 10.00 (978-0-316-19709-0(2)); 336p. 18.00 (978-0-316-19708-3(4)) Little, Brown Bks. for Young Readers.

Rutkoski, Marie. The Shadow Society. 2013. (ENG.). 448p. (YA). (gr. 7-12). pap. 9.99 (978-1-250-03424-3(8)) Square Fish.

Ryan, Carrie. Daughter of Deep Silence. 2015. (ENG.). 384p. (YA). (gr. 9). 17.99 (978-0-525-42650-9(7), Dutton Books for Young Readers) Penguin Young Readers Group.

Ryan, Patrick. Gemini Bites. 2011. (ENG.). 240p. (J). (gr. 7-8). 17.99 (978-0-545-22128-3(5), Scholastic Pr.) Scholastic, Inc.

Sáenz, Benjamin Alire. The Inexplicable Logic of My Life. 2017. (ENG.). 464p. (gr. 7). 17.99 (978-0-544-58650-5(6)) Houghton Mifflin Harcourt Publishing Co.

Saldana, Rene, Jr. A Mystery Bigger Than Big / un Misterio Mas Grande Que Grandisimo: A Mickey Rangel Mystery / Colección Mickey Rangel, Detective Privado. 2016. (Mickey Rangel Mystery / Coleccion Mickey Rangel, Detective P Ser.). (MUL, ENG & SPA., Illus.). 64p. (J). (gr. 3-6). pap. 9.95 (978-1-55885-824-4(5), Piñata Books) Arte Publico Pr.

Sanchez, Alex. Boyfriends with Girlfriends. (ENG.). 224p. (YA). (gr. 7). 2012. pap. 10.99 (978-1-4169-3775-3(7)) 2011. 16.99 (978-1-4169-3773-9(0)) Simon & Schuster Bks. For Young Readers. (Simon & Schuster Bks. For Young Readers).

Schmatz, Pat. Mousetraps. Hauser, Bill, illus. 2008. (ENG.). 192p. (YA). (gr. 7-12). 17.95 (978-0-8225-8657-9(6), Carolrhoda Bks.) Lerner Publishing Group.

Schmid, Susan Maupin. If the Magic Fits. (100 Dresses Ser.: 1). (ENG.). (J). (gr. 3-7). 2017. 320p. 7.99 **(978-0-553-53369-9(X)**, Yearling) 2016. (Illus.). 304p. 16.99 (978-0-553-53366-8(5), Random Hse. Bks. for Young Readers) Random Hse. Children's Bks.

Schmidt, Gary D. Anson's Way. 2009. (ENG.). 224p. (J). (gr. 2-5). pap. 15.95 (978-0-547-23761-9(8)) Houghton Mifflin Harcourt Publishing Co.

Schraff, Anne. One of Us. 2010. (Urban Underground — Harriet Tubman High School Ser.). (YA). lib. bdg. 20.80 (978-0-606-14267-0(3), Turtleback) Turtleback Bks.

Scott, Elizabeth. Stealing Heaven. 2009. (ENG.). 336p. (YA). (gr. 8). pap. 8.99 (978-0-06-112282-8(3), HarperTeen) HarperCollins Pubs.

Scott, Kieran. I Was a Non-Blonde Cheerleader. 2007. (ENG.). 272p. (YA). (gr. 7-18). 8.99 (978-0-14-240910-7(3), Speak) Penguin Young Readers Group.

Scraper, Katherine. Remember the Rules. 2006. (Early Explorers Ser.). (J). pap. (978-1-4108-6031-6(0)) Benchmark Education Co.

Sensel, Joni. The Farwalker's Quest. (ENG.). 384p. (YA). (gr. 3-6). 2010. pap. 7.99 (978-1-59990-450-4(0), 9781599904504) 2009. 16.99 (978-1-59990-272-2(9), 9781599902722) Bloomsbury Publishing USA. (Bloomsbury USA Childrens).

Service, Pamela F. My Cousin, the Alien. 2010. pap. 33.92 (978-0-7613-6952-3(X)) Lerner Publishing Group.

—My Cousin, the Alien. Gorman, Mike, illus. (Alien Agent Ser.: 1). (ENG.). 160p. (J). (gr. 4-6). 2009. pap. 5.95 (978-0-7613-4964-8(2), First Avenue Editions) 2008. 16.95 (978-0-8225-7627-3(9), Carolrhoda Bks.) Lerner Publishing Group.

Sheinmel, Alyssa. Faceless. 2015. (ENG.). 352p. (J). (gr. 7). 18.99 (978-0-545-67601-4(0), Scholastic Pr.) Scholastic, Inc.

Sheinmel, Courtney. My So-Called Family. 2008. (ENG.). 208p. (J). (gr. 4-7). 15.99 (978-1-4169-5785-0(5), Simon & Schuster Bks. For Young Readers) Simon & Schuster Bks. For Young Readers.

Sheldon, Dyan. Confessions of a Teenage Drama Queen. braille ed. 2003. (J). (gr. 2). spiral bd. (978-0-616-15873-9(4)) Canadian National Institute for the Blind/Institut National Canadien pour les Aveugles.

Sher, Emil. Young Man with Camera. Wyman, David, photos by. 2015. (ENG., Illus.). 240p. (J). (gr. 7). 17.99 (978-0-545-54131-2(X), Levine, Arthur A. Bks.) Scholastic, Inc.

Sheridan, Sara. I'm Me! Chamberlain, Margaret, illus. 2011. (ENG.). 32p. (J). (gr. -1-k). 17.99 (978-0-545-28222-2(5), Chicken Hse., The) Scholastic, Inc.

Shin, Sun Yung. Cooper's Lesson. Cogan, Kim & Paek, Min, trs. from ENG. Cogan, Kim, illus. 2004. (ENG & KOR.). 32p. (J). 16.95 (978-0-89239-193-6(6)) Lee & Low Bks., Inc.

—Cooper's Lesson. Cogan, Kim, illus. 2015. (ENG & KOR.). 32p. (J). (gr. k-3). pap. 9.95 (978-0-89239-361-9(0), Children's Book Press) Lee & Low Bks., Inc.

Shirtliffe, Leanne. The Change Your Name Store. Kügler, Tina, illus. 2014. (ENG.). 32p. (J). (gr. -1-k). 16.95 (978-1-62873-608-3(9), Sky Pony Pr.) Skyhorse Publishing Co., Inc.

Shirvington, Jessica. One Past Midnight. (ENG.). 352p. (YA). (gr. 9). 2015. pap. 9.99 (978-0-8027-3707-6(2), 9780802737076) 2014. 17.99 (978-0-8027-3702-1(1), 9780802737021) Bloomsbury Publishing USA. (Bloomsbury USA Childrens).

Shoup, Barbara. Wish You Were Here. 2008. (ENG.). 336p. (YA). (gr. 7). pap. 9.95 (978-0-7387-1355-7(4), Flux) North Star Editions.

Shusterman, Neal. The Dark Side of Nowhere. 2012. (ENG.). (YA). (gr. 7). 240p. 17.99 (978-1-4424-5812-3(7)); 256p. pap. 9.99 (978-1-4424-2281-0(5)) Simon & Schuster Bks. For Young Readers. (Simon & Schuster Bks. For Young Readers).

—UnSouled. (Unwind Dystology Ser.: 3). (ENG., Illus.). (YA). (gr. 7). 2014. 432p. pap. 11.99 (978-1-4424-2370-1(6)) 2013. 416p. 17.99 (978-1-4424-2369-5(2)) Simon & Schuster Bks. For Young Readers. (Simon & Schuster Bks. For Young Readers).

—Unsouled. 2014. (Unwind Dystology Ser.: 3). lib. bdg. 23.30 (978-0-606-36107-1(3)) Turtleback Bks.

—UnWholly. (Unwind Dystology Ser.: 2). (ENG.). 416p. (YA). (gr. 7). 2013. pap. 11.99 (978-1-4424-2367-1(6), Simon & Schuster Bks. For Young Readers) 2012. 19.99 (978-1-4424-2366-4(8)) Simon & Schuster Bks. For Young Readers.

—UnWholly. 2013. (Unwind Dystology Ser.: 2). lib. bdg. 23.30 (978-0-606-32336-9(8), Turtleback) Turtleback Bks.

—Unwind. 2011. 10.36 (978-0-7848-3496-1(2), Everbind) Marco Bk. Co.

—Unwind. (Unwind Dystology Ser.: 1). (ENG., Illus.). (YA). 2009. 384p. (gr. 8). pap. 11.99 (978-1-4169-1205-7(3)) 2007. 352p. (gr. 7-12). 19.99 (978-1-4169-1204-0(5)) Simon & Schuster Bks. For Young Readers. (Simon & Schuster Bks. For Young Readers).

—Unwind. 2009. (Unwind Dystology Ser.: 1). lib. bdg. 23.30 (978-0-606-10700-6(2), Turtleback) Turtleback Bks.

Sima, Jessie. Not Quite Narwhal. Sima, Jessie, illus. 2017. (ENG., Illus.). 40p. (J). (gr. -1-3). 17.99 (978-1-4814-6909-8(6), Simon & Schuster Bks. For Young Readers) Simon & Schuster Bks. For Young Readers.

Singleton, Linda Joy. Dead Girl Walking. 2008. (Dead Girl Ser.: 1). (ENG.). 312p. (YA). (gr. 8-18). pap. 9.95 (978-0-7387-1405-9(4), Flux) North Star Editions.

Skye, obert. Pillage. (YA). 2010. (Pillage Ser.: 1). (ENG.). 320p. (gr. 7). mass mkt. 7.99 (978-1-60641-680-8(4)) 2008. (Illus.). 352p. 17.95 (978-1-59038-922-5(0)) Shadow Mountain Publishing. (Shadow Mountain).

Smith, Ronald L. The Mesmerist. 2017. (ENG.). 272p. (J). (gr. 5-7). 16.99 (978-0-544-44528-4(7), Clarion Bks.) Houghton Mifflin Harcourt Trade & Reference Pubs.

Smolik, Jane Petrlik. Currents. 2015. (ENG., Illus.). 336p. (YA). (gr. 4-7). lib. bdg. 16.95 (978-1-58089-648-1(0)) Charlesbridge Publishing, Inc.

Snow, Carol. Switch. 2009. (ENG.). 240p. (YA). (gr. 8). pap. 8.99 (978-0-06-145210-9(6), HarperTeen) HarperCollins Pubs.

Sobat, Gail Sidonie. Gravity Journal. 2008. (ENG.). 162p. (YA). (gr. 15-18). pap. 14.95 (978-1-894283-78-6(3)) Great Plains Pubns. CAN. Dist: Publishers Group Canada.

Sobel, Sheila. Color Blind. 2016. (ENG.). 253p. (YA). 17.99 (978-1-4405-9746-6(4), Simon Pulse) Simon Pulse.

Sommer, Carl. I Am a Lion! Budwine, Greg, illus. 2014. (J). (978-1-57537-403-1(X)) Advance Publishing, Inc.

—I Am a Lion!(Yo Soy un León!) Budwine, Greg, illus. 2009. (Another Sommer-Time Story Bilingual Ser.). (SPA & ENG.). 48p. (J). lib. bdg. 16.95 (978-1-57537-153-5(7)) Advance Publishing, Inc.

—The Roar. Budwine, Greg, illus. 2009. (Quest for Success Ser.). (ENG.). 56p. (YA). pap. 4.95 (978-1-57537-284-6(3)); lib. bdg. 12.95 (978-1-57537-259-4(2)) Advance Publishing, Inc.

—The Roar(El Rugido) Budwine, Greg, illus. 2009. (Quest for Success Bilingual Ser.). (SPA & ENG.). 96p. (YA). lib. bdg. 14.95 (978-1-57537-233-4(9)) Advance Publishing, Inc.

Sonnenblick, Jordan. Zen & the Art of Faking It. 2007. (ENG.). 272p. (J). (gr. 7-12). 16.99 (978-0-439-83707-1(3), Scholastic Pr.) Scholastic, Inc.

Sorrells, Walter. Fake ID. 2007. (Hunted Ser.). (ENG.). 336p. (YA). (gr. 7-18). 9.99 (978-0-14-240762-2(3), Puffin Books) Penguin Young Readers Group.

Sourcebooks. Twisted. 2016. (ENG.). 320p. (YA). (gr. 8-12). pap. 10.99 (978-1-4926-3179-8(5), 9781492631798) Sourcebooks, Inc.

Sparks, Megan. Falling Hard, 1 vol. 2013. (Roller Girls Ser.). (ENG.). 256p. (gr. 8-10). 12.95 (978-1-62370-023-2(X)) Capstone Young Readers of Coughlan Cos.

—Hell's Belles, 1 vol. 2013. (Roller Girls Ser.). (ENG.). 256p. (gr. 8-10). 12.95 (978-1-62370-024-9(8)) Capstone Young Readers of Coughlan Cos.

—Hell's Belles/By Megan Sparks. 2013. 255p. (YA). (978-1-62370-022-5(1)) Capstone Young Readers of Coughlan Cos.

Spooner, M. Entr@pment: A High School Comedy in Chat. 2009. (ENG.). 320p. (YA). (gr. 8-18). 16.99 (978-1-4169-5889-5(4), McElderry, Margaret K. Bks.) McElderry, Margaret K. Bks.

Springer, Nancy. Possessing Jessie. 2010. (ENG.). 128p. (YA). (gr. 7-18). pap. 16.95 (978-0-8234-2259-3(3)) Holiday Hse., Inc.

—Somebody. 2009. (ENG.). 128p. (YA). (gr. 7-18). 16.95 (978-0-8234-2099-5(X)) Holiday Hse., Inc.

St. Crow, Lili. Jealousy. 2010. (Strange Angels Ser.: 3). (ENG.). 320p. (YA). (gr. 7-18). 9.99 (978-1-59514-290-0(8), Razorbill) Penguin Young Readers Group.

—Jealousy, 10 vols. 2010. (Strange Angels Ser.: 3). (J). 86.75 (978-1-4498-2774-8(8)); 68.75 (978-1-4498-2773-1(X)); 83.75 (978-1-4498-2776-2(4)); 1.25 (978-1-4498-2777-9(2)); 209.75 (978-1-4498-2772-4(1)) Recorded Bks., Inc.

—Jealousy. 2010. (Strange Angels Ser.: 3). lib. bdg. 20.85 (978-0-606-14566-4(4), Turtleback) Turtleback Bks.

—Strange Angels. 2009. (Strange Angels Ser.: 1). (ENG., Illus.). 304p. (YA). (gr. 7-18). pap. 9.99 (978-1-59514-251-1(7), Razorbill) Penguin Young Readers Group.

—Strange Angels, 9 vols. 2009. (Strange Angels Ser.: 1). (J). 84.75 (978-1-4407-6195-9(7)); 181.75 (978-1-4407-6194-2(9)); 117.75 (978-1-4407-6197-3(3)); 114.75 (978-1-4407-6199-7(X)); 87.75 (978-1-4407-6193-5(0)) Recorded Bks., Inc.

—Strange Angels. 2009. (Strange Angels Ser.: 1). lib. bdg. 20.85 (978-0-606-08957-9(8), Turtleback) Turtleback Bks.

Stanley, Diane. The Cup & the Crown. 2013. (Silver Bowl Ser.: 2). (ENG.). 368p. (J). (gr. 3-7). pap. 6.99 (978-0-06-196323-0(2)) HarperCollins Pubs.

Stanwood, Jane. Squeak's Bus Company. 2008. 28p. per. 11.95 (978-1-4327-1964-7(5)) Outskirts Pr., Inc.

Stein, Gertrude & Hurd, Thacher. The World Is Round. Hurd, Clement, illus. 75th ed. 2013. (ENG.). 128p. 19.99 (978-0-06-220307-6(X), Collins Design) HarperCollins Pubs.

Stephens, John. The Black Reckoning. 2015. (Books of Beginning Ser.). (ENG.). 432p. (J). (gr. 3-7). 17.99 (978-0-375-86872-6(0), Knopf Bks. for Young Readers) Random Hse. Children's Bks.

—The Emerald Atlas. (Books of Beginning Ser.). (ENG.). (J). (gr. 3-7). 2012. 448p. 7.99 (978-0-375-87271-6(X), Yearling) 2011. 432p. 17.99 (978-0-375-86870-2(4), Knopf Bks. for Young Readers) Random Hse. Children's Bks.

—The Emerald Atlas. l.t. ed. 2012. (Books of Beginning Ser.). (ENG.). 548p. (J). (gr. 4-7). 23.99 (978-1-4104-4234-5(9)) Thorndike Pr.

—The Fire Chronicle. 2012. (Illus.). 437p. (J). (978-0-449-81015-6(1)) Knopf, Alfred A. Inc.

—The Fire Chronicle. (Books of Beginning Ser.). (ENG.). 448p. (J). (gr. 3-7). 2013. 7.99 (978-0-375-87272-3(8), Yearling) 2012. (Illus.). 17.99 (978-0-375-86871-9(2), Knopf Bks. for Young Readers) Random Hse. Children's Bks.

Stevenson, Robin. Out of Order, 1 vol. 2007. (ENG.). 232p. (YA). (gr. 7-12). per. 9.95 (978-1-55143-693-7(0)) Orca Bk. Pubs. USA.

Stewart, Paul & Riddell, Chris. Beyond the Deepwoods. 2008. (Edge Chronicles Ser.: Bk. 1). (ENG.). 288p. (J). (gr. 3-7). 8.99 (978-0-440-42087-3(3), Bluefire) Random Hse. Children's Bks.

Stone, Phoebe. The Romeo & Juliet Code. 2012. (ENG.). 320p. (J). (gr. 3-7). pap. 7.99 (978-0-545-21827-6(6), Levine, Arthur A. Bks.) Scholastic, Inc.

—Romeo Blue. (ENG.). 352p. (J). (gr. 3-7). 2015. pap. 7.99 (978-0-545-44361-6(X)) 2013. 16.99 (978-0-545-44360-9(1)) Scholastic, Inc. (Levine, Arthur A. Bks.).

Stork, Francisco X. Irises. 2012. (YA). pap. (978-0-545-15136-8(8)); (ENG.). 304p. (J). (gr. 9). 17.99 (978-0-545-15135-1(X)) Scholastic, Inc. (Levine, Arthur A. Bks.).

The Strange & Beautiful Sorrows of Ava Lavender. 2014. 320p. (J). (gr. 9). E-Book 8.99 (978-0-7636-7034-4(0)) Candlewick Pr.

Stratton, Allan. Borderline. (ENG.). (YA). (gr. 8). 2012. 320p. pap. 9.99 (978-0-06-145113-3(4)) 2010. (Illus.). 304p. 16.99 (978-0-06-145111-9(8)) HarperCollins Pubs. (HarperTeen).

—The Grave Robber's Apprentice. 2012. 288p. (J). (gr. 5). 16.99 (978-0-06-197608-7(3)) HarperCollins Pubs.

Sullivan, Kiki. Midnight Dolls. 2015. (Dolls Ser.: 2). (ENG.). 336p. (YA). (gr. 8). pap. 9.99 (978-0-06-228150-0(X)) HarperCollins Pubs.

Sullivan, Maureen. Cabbages & Queens. Ferrando, Carol, illus. 2010. 57p. (J). pap. (978-0-9820381-3-0(5)) MoJo InkWorks.

Sussman, Elissa. Stray. 2014. (Stray Ser.: 1). (ENG., Illus.). 384p. (YA). (gr. 8). 17.99 (978-0-06-227455-7(4), Greenwillow Bks.) HarperCollins Pubs.

Sutherland, Tui T. The Brightest Night. 2015. (Wings of Fire Ser.: Bk. 5). (ENG.). 336p. (J). (gr. 3-7). pap. 6.99 (978-0-545-34927-7(3), Scholastic Paperbacks) Scholastic, Inc.

—The Dark Secret. (Wings of Fire Ser.: 4). (ENG.). 336p. (J). (gr. 3-7). 2014. pap. 6.99 (978-0-545-34926-0(5)) 2013. (Illus.). 16.99 (978-0-545-34921-5(4)) Scholastic, Inc. (Scholastic Pr.).

—The Dark Secret. 2014. (Wings of Fire Ser.: 4). lib. bdg. 17.20 (978-0-606-36033-3(6)) Turtleback Bks.

—Darkstalker. 2016. (Wings of Fire Ser.). (ENG., Illus.). 400p. (J). (gr. 3-7). 17.99 (978-1-338-05361-6(2), Scholastic Pr.) Scholastic, Inc.

—Escaping Peril. 2015. (Wings of Fire Ser.: Bk. 8). (ENG., Illus.). 336p. (J). (gr. 3-7). 16.99 (978-0-545-68544-3(3), Scholastic Pr.) Scholastic, Inc.

—The Hidden Kingdom. 2013. (Wings of Fire Ser.: 3). (ENG., Illus.). 336p. (J). (gr. 3-7). 16.99 (978-0-545-34920-8(6), Scholastic Pr.) Scholastic, Inc.

—Moon Rising. (Wings of Fire Ser.: 6). (ENG.). 336p. (J). (gr. 3-7). 2016. pap. 6.99 (978-0-545-68536-8(2)) 2014. 16.99 (978-0-545-68534-4(6), Scholastic Pr.) Scholastic, Inc.

Tashiro, Chisato. Chameleon's Colors. Martens, Marianne, tr. from JPN. 2007. (Michael Neugebauer Books Ser.). (ENG., Illus.). 32p. (J). (gr. -1-3). pap. 7.95 (978-0-7358-2111-8(9)) North-South Bks., Inc.

Tashjian, Janet. The Gospel According to Larry. 2003. (Illus.). 227p. 17.00 (978-0-7569-1451-6(5)) Perfection Learning Corp.

—Larry & the Meaning of Life. 2014. (Larry Ser.: 3). (ENG., Illus.). 240p. (YA). (gr. 7-12). pap. 9.99 (978-1-250-05035-9(9), 9781250050359) Square Fish.

Tashlin, Frank. The Bear That Wasn't. 2010. (ENG., Illus.). 64p. (J). (gr. -1-3). 16.95 (978-1-59017-344-2(9), NYR Children's Collection) New York Review of Bks., Inc., The.

—The Possum That Didn't. 2016. (ENG., Illus.). 64p. (gr. 5-5). pap. 3.99 (978-0-486-80080-6(6)) Dover Pubns., Inc.

Taylor, Billy. Thieving Weasels. 2016. (ENG.). 256p. (YA). (gr. 7). 17.99 (978-0-525-42924-1(7), Dial Bks) Penguin Young Readers Group.

Terry, Teri. Fractured. 2014. (Slated Ser.: 2). (ENG.). 352p. (YA). (gr. 7). pap. 9.99 (978-0-14-242504-6(4), Speak) Penguin Young Readers Group.

—Shattered. (Slated Ser.: 3). (ENG.). (YA). (gr. 7). 2015. 336p. pap. 9.99 (978-0-14-242507-7(9), Speak) 2014. 320p. 17.99 (978-0-399-16174-2(0), Nancy Paulsen Books) Penguin Young Readers Group.

—Slated. 2013. (Slated Ser.: 1). (ENG.). 368p. (YA). (gr. 7). pap. 9.99 (978-0-14-242503-9(6), Speak) Penguin Young Readers Group.

Tewkesbury, Alexa. Paul's Potty Pages. 2008. (ENG., Illus.). 128p. (J). (978-1-85345-456-1(7)) Crusade for World Revival.

Tharp, Tim. Knights of the Hill Country. 2008. 233p. 17.00 (978-1-60686-365-7(7)) Perfection Learning Corp.

—Knights of the Hill Country. 2013. (ENG.). 240p. (YA). (gr. 7). pap. 8.99 (978-0-449-81287-7(1), Ember) Random Hse. Children's Bks.

Thomas, Lois Jean. Me & You — We Are Who? 2006. (J). pap. (978-0-9785969-2-7(7)) Sambodh Society, Inc., The.

Thompson, Kay. Eloise's What I Absolutely Love Love Love. 2005. (Eloise Ser.). (ENG., Illus.). 32p. (J). 12.99 (978-0-689-84965-7(6), Simon & Schuster Bks. For Young Readers) Simon & Schuster Bks. For Young Readers.

Todd, Ilima. Remake. 2014. (Remake Ser.: 1). (ENG.). 304p. (YA). (gr. 7). 17.99 (978-1-60907-924-6(8), Shadow Mountain) Shadow Mountain Publishing.

Tomlinson, Heather. The Swan Maiden. 2008. (ENG.). 320p. (YA). (gr. 7-12). pap. 22.99 (978-0-312-38447-0(5), 9780312384470) Square Fish.

Traver., N. K. & Traver, N. K. Duplicity. 2015. (ENG.). 256p. (YA). (gr. 9-12). 18.99 (978-1-250-05914-7(3), 9781250059147, Dunne, Thomas Bks.) St. Martin's Pr.

Trevayne, Emma. The Accidental Afterlife of Thomas Marsden. 2016. (ENG.). 272p. (J). (gr. 3-7). pap. 7.99 (978-1-4424-9884-6(6), Simon & Schuster Bks. For Young Readers) Simon & Schuster Bks. For Young Readers.

Triana, Gaby. Cubanita. 2005. 195p. (YA). (gr. 7-17). 15.99 (978-0-06-056020-1(7), Rayo) HarperCollins Pubs.

Turnage, Sheila. The Ghosts of Tupelo Landing. 2015. (ENG.). 368p. (J). (gr. 5). 7.99 (978-0-14-242571-8(0), Puffin Books) Penguin Young Readers Group.

—The Ghosts of Tupelo Landing. 2015. lib. bdg. 18.40 (978-0-606-36773-8(X)) Turtleback Bks.

—Three Times Lucky. (ENG.). (J). (gr. 5). 2013. 336p. pap. 7.99 (978-0-14-242605-0(9), Puffin Books) 2012. 314p. 16.99 (978-0-8037-3670-2(3), Dial Bks) Penguin Young Readers Group.

—Three Times Lucky. 2013. lib. bdg. 18.40 (978-0-606-34168-4(4), Turtleback) Turtleback Bks.

Turner, Sadie & Freedman, Colette. Anomalies. 2016. (ENG.). 336p. (J). (gr. 9-12). 17.95 (978-1-59079-361-9(7)) Select Bks., Inc.

Twain, Mark, pseud. The Prince & the Pauper. Pamment, Katie, illus. 2008. (Young Reading Series 2 Gift Books Ser.). 63p. (J). 8.99 (978-0-7945-1818-9(4), Usborne) EDC Publishing.

Umansky, Kaye. Solomon Snow & the Silver Spoon. Nash, Scott, illus. 2007. (ENG.). 304p. (J). (gr. 2-5). 12.99 (978-0-7636-3218-2(X)) Candlewick Pr.

Updale, Eleanor. Montmorency's Revenge. 2007. 289p. (J). 25.66 (978-1-4287-3312-1(4), Follettbound) Follett School Solutions.

—Thief, Liar, Gentleman? 2005. (Montmorency Ser.). 232p. (J). (gr. 4-7). 14.65 (978-0-7569-6316-3(8)) Perfection Learning Corp.

Vail, Rachel. Please, Please, Please. 2014. (Friendship Ring Ser.: 2). (ENG.). 176p. (J). (gr. 5). pap. 7.99 (978-0-14-751119-5(4), Puffin Books) Penguin Young Readers Group.

—Well, That Was Awkward. 2017. (ENG.). 320p. (J). (gr. 5). 16.99 (978-0-670-01308-1(0), Viking Books for Young Readers) Penguin Young Readers Group.

—You, Maybe: The Profound Asymmetry of Love in High School. (YA). 2007. (ENG.). 224p. (gr. 8-12). pap. 7.99 (978-0-06-056919-8(0)) 2006. (ENG.). 208p. (gr. 7-12). 15.99 (978-0-06-056917-4(4)) 2006. 199p. (gr. 7-12). lib. bdg. 16.89 (978-0-06-056918-1(2)) HarperCollins Pubs.

Van Draanen, Wendelin. Sammy Keyes & the Showdown in Sin City. 2013. (Sammy Keyes Ser.: Bk. 16). (ENG.). 304p. (J). (gr. 5). pap. 7.99 (978-0-307-93061-3(0), Yearling) Random Hse. Children's Bks.

Vanasse, Patricia. Resilient. Shalaby, Asharaf, illus. 2013. (ENG.). 328p. (YA). pap. 13.99 (978-0-9860373-2-0(X)) Pants On Fire Pr.

Vander Zee, Ruth. Erika's Story. Innocenti, Roberto, illus. 2013. (ENG.). 24p. (J). (gr. 1-3). pap. 10.99 (978-0-89812-891-8(9), Creative Paperbacks) Creative Co., The.

Vivian, Siobhan. The List. (ENG.). 336p. (J). (gr. 9). 2014. pap. 9.99 (978-0-545-16918-9(6), Scholastic Paperbacks) 2012. 17.99 (978-0-545-16917-2(8), PUSH) Scholastic, Inc.

Wagman, Diana. Extraordinary October. 2016. (ENG.). 264p. (YA). (gr. 6). 18.95 (978-1-63246-036-3(X)) Ig Publishing, Inc.

Waid, Mark & Walker, Landry. Revenge from Below. Takara, Marcio, illus. 2010. (Incredibles Ser.). (ENG.). 112p. (J). (gr. 3-6). pap. 9.99 (978-1-60886-518-5(5)) Boom! Studios.

Walker, Brian F. Black Boy White School. 2012. (ENG.). 256p. (YA). (gr. 9). 17.99 (978-0-06-191483-6(5), HarperTeen) HarperCollins Pubs.

Walker, Nan. The Bay School Blogger. Wummer, Amy, illus. 2008. (Social Studies Connects Ser.). 32p. (J). (gr. -1-3). pap. 5.95 (978-1-57565-258-0(7)) Kane Press, Inc.

Wallace, Becky. The Storyspinner. 2015. (Keepers' Chronicles Ser.). (ENG., Illus.). 432p. (YA). (gr. 9). 17.99

(978-1-4814-0565-2(9), McElderry, Margaret K. Bks.) McElderry, Margaret K. Bks.

Walsh, Pat. The Crowfield Demon. (J). 2013. 360p. *(978-0-545-37350-0(6))* 2012. (ENG.). 368p. (gr. 3-7). 16.99 *(978-0-545-31769-6(X)*, Chicken Hse., The) Scholastic, Inc.

Walsh, Sara. The Dark Light. (ENG., (YA). (gr. 9). 2013. Illus.). 512p. pap. 9.99 *(978-1-4424-3458-5(9))* 2012. 496p. 16.99 *(978-1-4424-3455-4(4))* Simon Pulse. (Simon Pulse).

Walton, Leslye. The Strange & Beautiful Sorrows of Ava Lavender. (ENG.). 320p. (YA). (gr. 9). 2015. pap. 8.99 *(978-0-7636-8027-5(3))* 2014. 17.99 *(978-0-7636-6566-1(5))* Candlewick Pr.

—The Strange & Beautiful Sorrows of Ava Lavender. 2015. lib. bdg. 19.65 *(978-0-606-36879-7(5))* Turtleback Bks.

Weatherly, Lee. Child X. 2004. 211p. 16.00 *(978-0-7569-3211-4(4))* Perfection Learning Corp.

Webb, Holly. Rose & the Silver Ghost. 2015. (Rose Ser.: 4). (ENG.). 224p. (J). (gr. 3-6). pap. 6.99 *(978-1-4926-0433-4(X)*, Sourcebooks Jabberwocky) Sourcebooks, Inc.

Weeks, Sarah. As Simple as It Seems. (ENG.). 192p. (J). (gr. 3-7). 2011. pap. 5.99 *(978-0-06-084665-7(8))* 2010. 15.99 *(978-0-06-084663-3(1))* HarperCollins Pubs.

—I'm a Pig. Berry, Holly, illus. 2005. 32p. (J). (gr. -1-2). lib. bdg. 16.89 *(978-0-06-074344-4(1)*, Geringer, Laura Book) HarperCollins Pubs.

—So B. It. 2009. 9.00 *(978-0-7848-3326-1(5)*, Everbind) Marco Bk. Co.

—So B. It. 2005. 17.00 *(978-0-7569-5112-2(7))* Perfection Learning Corp.

—So B. It. 2007. (J). 1.25 *(978-1-4193-7988-8(7))* Recorded Bks., Inc.

Weeks, Sarah & Weeks. So B. It. (ENG.). (J). (gr. 5). 2005. 288p. pap. 7.99 *(978-0-06-441047-2(1))* 2004. 256p. 16.99 *(978-0-06-623622-3(3))* HarperCollins Pubs.

Weil, Sylvie. My Guardian Angel. Rosner, Gillian, tr. from FRE. 2014. (ENG., Illus.). 208p. (J). pap. 14.95 *(978-0-8276-1211-2(7))* Jewish Pubn. Society.

Welch, Jenna Evans. Love & Gelato. (ENG., Illus.). 400p. (YA). (gr. 7). 2017. pap. 10.99 ***(978-1-4814-3255-9(9))*** 2016. 17.99 *(978-1-4814-3254-2(0))* Simon Pulse. (Simon Pulse).

Wells, Dan. Fragments. 2013. (Partials Sequence Ser.: 2). (ENG.). 576p. (YA). (gr. 9). 17.99 *(978-0-06-207107-1(6))* HarperCollins Pubs.

Wenzel, Brendan. They All Saw a Cat. Wenzel, Brendan, illus. 2016. (Illus.). 44p. pap. 16.99 *(978-1-4521-8805-8(X))*; (ENG., (J). (gr. -1-k). 16.99 *(978-1-4521-5013-0(3))* Chronicle Bks. LLC.

West, Hannah. Kingdom of Ash & Briars. 2016. (ENG., Illus.). 368p. (YA). 17.95 *(978-0-8234-3651-4(9))* Holiday Hse., Inc.

Weston Woods Staff, creator. T Is for Terrible. 2011. 18.95 *(978-0-545-11791-3(7))*; 38.75 *(978-0-545-11793-7(3))* Weston Woods Studios, Inc.

Weyn, Suzanne. The Bar Code Tattoo. 2012. (ENG.). 256p. (J). (gr. 7). pap. 9.99 *(978-0-545-47054-4(4)*, Scholastic Paperbacks) Scholastic, Inc.

Whaley, John Corey. Noggin. (ENG., Illus.). (YA). (gr. 9). 2015. 368p. pap. 12.99 *(978-1-4424-5873-4(9))* 2014. 352p. 18.99 *(978-1-4424-5872-7(0))* Simon & Schuster Children's Publishing. (Atheneum Bks. for Young Readers).

White, Kiersten. Endlessly. (Paranormalcy Ser.: 3). (ENG.). (YA). (gr. 8). 2013. 416p. pap. 9.99 *(978-0-06-198589-8(9))* 2012. 400p. 17.99 *(978-0-06-198588-1(0))* HarperCollins Pubs. (HarperTeen).

—Paranormalcy. (Paranormalcy Ser.: 1). (ENG.). (YA). (gr. 8). 2011. 368p. pap. 9.99 *(978-0-06-198585-0(6))* 2010. 352p. 16.99 *(978-0-06-198584-3(8))* HarperCollins Pubs. (HarperTeen).

—Supernaturally. (Paranormalcy Ser.: 2). (ENG.). (YA). (gr. 8). 2012. 368p. pap. 9.99 *(978-0-06-198587-4(2))* 2011. 352p. 17.99 *(978-0-06-198586-7(4))* HarperCollins Pubs. (HarperTeen).

White, Kiersten & Di Bartolo, Jim. In the Shadows. Di Bartolo, Jim, illus. 2014. (ENG., Illus.). 384p. (J). (gr. 7). 21.99 *(978-0-545-56144-0(2)*, Scholastic Pr.) Scholastic, Inc.

White, Ruth. Belle Prater's Boy. unabr. ed. 2004. 196p. (J). (gr. 5-9). pap. 38.00 incl. audio *(978-0-8072-8682-1(6)*, YA234SP, Listening Library) Random Hse. Audio Publishing Group.

—Way down Deep. 2011. (ENG.). 224p. (J). (gr. 5-8). pap. 7.99 *(978-0-312-66096-3(0)*, 9780312660963) Square Fish.

White, Tara. I Like Who I Am, 1 vol. 2010. (ENG., Illus.). 44p. pap. 12.95 *(978-1-894778-63-3(4))* Theytus Bks., Ltd. CAN. Dist: Univ. of Toronto Pr.

Whitman, Emily. Wildwing. 2010. (ENG.). 368p. (YA). (gr. 8-18). 16.99 *(978-0-06-172452-7(1)*, Greenwillow Bks.) HarperCollins Pubs.

Wilke, Daria & Schwartz, Marian. Playing a Part. 2015. (ENG.). 176p. (J). (gr. 7). 18.99 *(978-0-545-72607-8(7))* Scholastic, Inc.

Wilkinson, Lili. Pink. (ENG.). 320p. (YA). (gr. 8). 2012. pap. 9.99 *(978-0-06-192654-9(X))* 2011. 16.99 *(978-0-06-192653-2(1))* HarperCollins Pubs. (HarperTeen).

Willems, Mo. Knuffle Bunny Too: A Case of Mistaken Identity. Willems, Mo, illus. rev. ed. 2007. (Knuffle Bunny Ser.). (ENG., Illus.). 48p. (J). (gr. -1-k). 17.99 *(978-1-4231-0299-1(1))* Hyperion Pr.

Wilson, Diane Lee. Black Storm Comin' 2006. (ENG.). 240p. (J). (gr. 5-9). pap. 7.99 *(978-0-689-87138-2(4)*, McElderry, Margaret K. Bks.) McElderry, Margaret K. Bks.

—Black Storm Comin' 2006. (Illus.). 291p. (gr. 5-9). 17.00 *(978-0-7569-6908-0(5))* Perfection Learning Corp.

Winick, Judd. The Boy Who Crashed to Earth. 2015. (Hilo Ser.: 1). (ENG., Illus.). 208p. (J). (gr. 3-7). 16.99 *(978-0-385-38618-0(4)*, Random Hse. Bks. for Young Readers) Random Hse. Children's Bks.

Winters, Kari-Lynn. French Toast. Thisdale, François, illus. 2016. (ENG.). 32p. (J). (gr. k-2). 17.95 *(978-1-77278-006-2(5))* Pajama Pr. CAN. Dist: Ingram Publisher Services.

Winthrop, Elizabeth. Squashed in the Middle. Cummins, Pat, illus. 2008. (J). (gr. k-4). 25.95 incl. audio *(978-1-4301-0440-7(6))*; 28.95 incl. audio compact disk *(978-1-4301-0443-8(0))* Live Oak Media.

Wittlinger, Ellen. Parrotfish. 2007. (ENG., Illus.). 304p. (YA). (gr. 7-12). 19.99 *(978-1-4169-1622-2(9)*, Simon & Schuster Bks. For Young Readers) Simon & Schuster Bks. For Young Readers.

Wong, Benedict Norbert. Lo & Behold. Wong, Benedict Norbert, illus. l.t. ed. 2003. (Illus.). 38p. (gr. 1-18). 16.95 *(978-0-9728192-0-6(7)*, LOBE) Taiji Arts Publishing.

—Lo & Behold: Good Enough to Eat. Wong, Benedict Norbert, illus. l.t. ed. 2003. (Illus.). 40p. (J). (gr. 1-12). 16.95 *(978-0-9728192-1-3(5)*, 1002LB) Taiji Arts Publishing.

Wong, Liz. Quackers. 2016. (ENG.). 40p. (J). (gr. -1-2). 15.99 *(978-0-553-51154-3(8)*, Knopf Bks. for Young Readers) Random Hse. Children's Bks.

Wright, Bill & Wright, Bil. When the Black Girl Sings. 2008. (ENG.). 272p. (YA). (gr. 7-12). 16.99 *(978-1-4169-3995-5(4)*, Simon & Schuster Bks. For Young Readers) Simon & Schuster Bks. For Young Readers.

—When the Black Girl Sings. 2009. (ENG.). 272p. (YA). (gr. 7). mass mkt. 6.99 *(978-1-4169-4003-6(0)*, Simon Pulse) Simon Pulse.

Wunsch, Emma. The Movie Version. 2016. (ENG.). 368p. (YA). (gr. 9-17). 18.95 *(978-1-4197-1900-4(9)*, Amulet Bks.) Abrams, Inc.

Yang, Gene Luen. American Born Chinese. 2011. 10.04 *(978-0-7848-3435-0(0)*, Everbind) Marco Bk. Co.

—American Born Chinese. 2011. 20.00 *(978-1-60686-920-8(5))* 2007. 29.00 *(978-0-7569-7745-0(2))* Perfection Learning Corp.

—American Born Chinese. Yang, Gene Luen & Pien, Lark, illus. 2007. (ENG.). 240p. (YA). (gr. 7-18). 23.99 *(978-1-59643-373-1(6)*, 9781596433731, First Second Bks.) Roaring Brook Pr.

—American Born Chinese. Yang, Gene Luen, illus. rev. ed. 2006. (ENG., Illus.). 240p. (YA). (gr. 7-12). pap. 18.99 *(978-1-59643-152-2(0)*, 9781596431522, First Second Bks.) Roaring Brook Pr.

—American Born Chinese. Yang, Gene Luen, illus. 2008. (ENG., Illus.). 240p. (YA). (gr. 7-12). pap. 10.99 *(978-0-312-38448-7(3)*, 9780312384487) Square Fish.

—American Born Chinese. 2008. (YA). lib. bdg. 22.10 *(978-0-606-14484-1(6)*, Turtleback) Turtleback Bks.

Yangsook, Choi. The Name Jar. 2014. (ENG.). 40p. (J). (gr. k-2). 11.24 *(978-1-63245-313-6(4))* Lectorum Pubns., Inc.

Young, Suzanne. The Epidemic. 2016. (Program Ser.: 4). (ENG., Illus.). 384p. (YA). (gr. 9). 17.99 *(978-1-4814-4470-5(0)*, Simon Pulse) Simon Pulse.

—The Remedy. 2015. (Program Ser.: 3). (ENG., Illus.). 416p. (YA). (gr. 9). 17.99 *(978-1-4814-3765-3(8)*, Simon Pulse) Simon Pulse.

Zahler, Diane. A True Princess. (ENG.). (J). (gr. 3-7). 2012. 208p. pap. 6.99 *(978-0-06-182503-4(3))* 2011. 192p. 15.99 *(978-0-06-182501-9(8))* HarperCollins Pubs.

Zemke, Deborah. The Curse of Einstein's Pencil. 2017. (Bea Garcia Ser.: 2). (ENG., Illus.). 144p. (J). (gr. 1-4). 15.99 *(978-0-8037-4155-3(3)*, Dial Bks) Penguin Young Readers Group.

Zhang, Kat. Echoes of Us: The Hybrid Chronicles, Book 3. 2015. (Hybrid Chronicles Ser.: 3). (ENG.). 368p. (YA). (gr. 8). pap. 9.99 *(978-0-06-211494-5(8))* HarperCollins Pubs.

—Once We Were: The Hybrid Chronicles, Book 2. 2014. (Hybrid Chronicles Ser.: 2). (ENG.). 384p. (YA). (gr. 8). pap. 9.99 *(978-0-06-211491-4(3))* HarperCollins Pubs.

IDENTITY, PERSONAL

see Identity (Psychology); Personality

IDIOMS

see names of languages with the subdivision Idioms, e.g. English Language—Idioms

Berne, Emma Carlson. What Is an Idiom When It's at Home? 2017. (Why Do We Say That? Ser.). (ENG.). 32p. (gr. 3-4). lib. bdg. 27.32 ***(978-1-5157-6388-8(9)***, Fact Finders) Capstone Press of Coughlan Cos.

Johnson, Robin. Understanding Sayings. 2015. (Figuratively Speaking Ser.). (ENG., Illus.). 32p. (J). *(978-0-7787-1778-2(X))* Crabtree Publishing Co.

Just the Bee's Knees: Individual Title Six-Packs. (Story Steps Ser.). (gr. k-2). 32.00 *(978-0-7635-9844-0(5))* Rigby Education.

Oelschlager, Vanita. Birds of a Feather. Hegan, Robin, illus. 2011. (ENG.). 32p. (J). (gr. -1-3). pap. 8.95 *(978-0-9826366-1-9(X))* VanitaBooks.

—Life Is a Bowl Full of Cherries. 2011. (ENG., Illus.). 40p. (J). (gr. -1-3). 15.95 *(978-0-9826366-3-3(6))*; pap. 8.95 *(978-0-9826366-2-6(8))* VanitaBooks.

Sebastiani, Laura, creator. Penny & Drew's Penciltips: Idioms. 2006. 80p. (J). 4.95 *(978-0-9766793-2-5(9))* ThoughtRockets, Inc.

IGNATIUS, OF LOYOLA, SAINT, 1491-1556

Matas, Toni. St. Ignatius of Loyola, Leading the Way. Picanyol, illus. 2013. (J). 8.95 *(978-0-8198-7298-2(9))* Pauline Bks. & Media.

ILLEGAL ALIENS

Byers, Ann. Immigration: Interpreting the Constitution. 2014. (Understanding the United States Constitution Ser.). 112p. (YA). (gr. 7-12). 35.60 *(978-1-4777-7512-7(9))* Rosen Publishing Group, Inc., The.

Currie, Stephen. Undocumented Immigrant Youth. 2016. (ENG.). 80p. (J). (gr. 5-12). lib. bdg. *(978-1-60152-960-0(5))* ReferencePoint Pr., Inc.

DiConsiglio, John. Reporting Live. 2011. (J). *(978-0-531-22552-3(6))* Scholastic, Inc.

Haerens, Margaret. Illegal Immigration. 2006. (Opposing Viewpoints Ser.). (ENG.). 212p. (J). (gr. 7-18). pap. 39.70 *(978-0-7377-3356-3(X))*; (Illus.). 27.50 *(978-0-7377-3357-0(8))* Cengage Gale. (Greenhaven Pr., Inc.).

Haugen, David. What Should Be Done about Illegal Immigration? 2016. (ENG.). 80p. (J). (gr. 5-12). lib. bdg. *(978-1-68282-099-5(8))* ReferencePoint Pr., Inc.

Haugen, David M. Human Rights in Focus: Illegal Immigrants. 2017. (ENG.). 80p. (YA). (gr. 5-12). ***(978-1-68282-229-6(X))*** ReferencePoint Pr., Inc.

Howell, Sara. Los Inmigrantes Indocumentados. 2014. (Mosaico Americano: la Inmigración Hoy en día (the American Mosaic: Immigration Today) Ser.). (SPA., Illus.). 24p. (J). (gr. 3-6). pap. 49.50 *(978-1-4777-6811-2(4)*, PowerKids Pr.) Rosen Publishing Group, Inc., The.

—Undocumented Immigrants. 2014. (American Mosaic: Immigration Today Ser.). (Illus.). 24p. (J). (gr. 3-6). pap. 8.25 *(978-1-4777-6745-0(2))*; pap. 49.50 *(978-1-4777-6650-7(2))*; lib. bdg. 23.60 *(978-1-4777-6744-3(4))* Rosen Publishing Group, Inc., The. (PowerKids Pr.).

Kenney, Karen. Illegal Immigration, 1 vol. 2007. (Essential Viewpoints Set 1 Ser.). (ENG., Illus.). 112p. (J). (gr. 6-12). lib. bdg. 35.64 *(978-1-59928-861-1(3))* ABDO Publishing Co.

Levy, Janey. Illegal Immigration & Amnesty: Open Borders & National Security. 2010. (In the News Ser.). (Illus.). 64p. (YA). (gr. 7-12). lib. bdg. 31.95 *(978-1-4358-3583-2(2))* Rosen Publishing Group, Inc., The.

McCormick, Lisa Wade. Frequently Asked Questions about Growing up As an Undocumented Immigrant. 2012. (FAQ: Teen Life Ser.). (ENG., Illus.). 64p. (YA). (gr. 7-12). lib. bdg. 31.95 *(978-1-4488-8329-5(6))* Rosen Publishing Group, Inc., The.

Merino, Noël. Illegal Immigration. Greenhaven Press Staff, ed. 2015. (Opposing Viewpoints Ser.). (ENG., Illus.). 224p. (gr. 10-12). pap. 33.80 *(978-0-7377-7273-9(5))*; lib. bdg. 48.80 *(978-0-7377-7272-2(7))* Cengage Gale. (Greenhaven Pr., Inc.).

—What Rights Should Illegal Immigrants Have? 2010. (At Issue Ser.). (ENG.). 128p. (gr. 10-12). 39.40 *(978-0-7377-4902-1(4))*; pap. 27.80 *(978-0-7377-4903-8(2))* Cengage Gale. (Greenhaven Pr., Inc.).

Miller, Debra A. Illegal Immigration. 2007. (Compact Research Ser.). (Illus.). 110p. (YA). (gr. 7-12). lib. bdg. 25.95 *(978-1-60152-009-6(3))* ReferencePoint Pr., Inc.

Miller, Debra A., ed. Illegal Immigration. 2007. (Current Controversies Ser.). (ENG., Illus.). (YA). 222p. (gr. 8-12). 27.50 *(978-0-7377-3724-0(7)*, Greenhaven Pr., Inc.); 240p. (gr. 9-12). pap. 39.70 *(978-0-7377-3723-3(9))* Cengage Gale.

Nazario, Sonia. Enrique's Journey: The True Story of a Boys Determined to Reunite with His Mother. 2013. (ENG.). 288p. (YA). (gr. 7). 16.99 *(978-0-385-74327-3(0)*, Delacorte Bks. for Young Readers) Random Hse. Children's Bks.

Newman, Lori M. What Rights Should Illegal Immigrants Have? 2006. (At Issue Ser.). (ENG., Illus.). 90p. (YA). (gr. 8-12). 22.50 *(978-0-7377-3481-2(7))*; lib. bdg. 31.80 *(978-0-7377-3480-5(9))* Cengage Gale. (Greenhaven Pr., Inc.).

Oeppen, Ceri. Hopes, Needs, Rights, & Laws: How Do Governments & Citizens Manage Migration & Settlement? 2010. (Investigating Human Migration & Settlement Ser.). (ENG., Illus.). 48p. (J). (gr. 5-8). *(978-0-7787-5180-9(5))*; pap. *(978-0-7787-5195-3(3))* Crabtree Publishing Co.

Staley, Erin. I'm an Undocumented Immigrant, Now What? 2016. (Teen Life 411 Ser.). 00112p. (J). (gr. 7-7). 37.10 *(978-1-5081-7193-5(9))* Rosen Publishing Group, Inc., The.

ILLEGAL ALIENS—FICTION

Alexander, William. Ambassador. 2015. (ENG.). 256p. (J). (gr. 3-7). pap. 7.99 *(978-1-4424-9765-8(3)*, McElderry, Margaret K. Bks.) McElderry, Margaret K. Bks.

—Nomad. 2015. (ENG., Illus.). 272p. (J). (gr. 3-7). 16.99 *(978-1-4424-9767-2(X)*, McElderry, Margaret K. Bks.) McElderry, Margaret K. Bks.

Alvarez, Julia. Devolver Al Remitente. 2010.Tr. of Return to Sender. (SPA & ENG.). 368p. (J). (gr. 3-7). 7.99 *(978-0-375-85124-7(0)*, Yearling) Random Hse. Children's Bks.

—Return to Sender. 2010. (ENG.). 352p. (J). (gr. 3-7). 6.99 *(978-0-375-85123-0(2)*, Yearling) Random Hse. Children's Bks.

Ambassador. 2014. (ENG., Illus.). 240p. (J). (gr. 3-7). 16.99 *(978-1-4424-9764-1(5)*, McElderry, Margaret K. Bks.) McElderry, Margaret K. Bks.

Belford, Bibi. Canned & Crushed. 2015. (ENG.). 192p. (J). (gr. 2-7). 14.99 *(978-1-63220-435-6(5)*, Sky Pony Pr.) Skyhorse Publishing Co., Inc.

Budhos, Marina. Ask Me No Questions. 2007. 159p. (gr. 7-12). 20.00 *(978-0-7569-8114-3(X))* Perfection Learning Corp.

Cannella, Marco & Marron, Jose Luis, illus. Tattoo of Death. 2007. (Choose Your Own Adventure Ser.: No. 22). 113p. (J). (gr. 4-7). pap. 6.99 *(978-1-933390-22-2(0))* Chooseco LLC.

Giff, Patricia Reilly. Until I Find Julian. 2015. (ENG.). 160p. (J). (gr. 3-7). 16.99 *(978-0-385-74482-9(X)*, Lamb, Wendy Bks.) Random Hse. Children's Bks.

Hobbs, Will. Crossing the Wire. 2007. (ENG.). 224p. (J). (gr. 5-9). pap. 7.99 *(978-0-06-074140-2(6))* HarperCollins Pubs.

—Crossing the Wire. 2007. (Illus.). 216p. (gr. 5-9). 17.00 *(978-0-7569-8053-5(4))* Perfection Learning Corp.

Jones, Patrick. Bridge. 2014. (Alternative Ser.). (ENG.). 96p. (YA). (gr. 6-12). lib. bdg. 27.93 *(978-1-4677-3903-0(0))* Lerner Publishing Group.

Lupica, Mike. Heat. 2007. (ENG.). 256p. (J). (gr. 5-18). 7.99 *(978-0-14-240757-8(7)*, Puffin Books) Penguin Young Readers Group.

—Heat. 2007. 220p. (gr. 5-9). 18.00 *(978-0-7569-8131-0(X))* Perfection Learning Corp.

—Heat. 2007. 18.40 *(978-1-4177-7264-3(6)*, Turtleback) Turtleback Bks.

Lupita Manana. 3rd ed. (J). pap., stu. ed. *(978-0-13-772500-7(0))* Prentice Hall (Schl. Div.).

Marina, Budhos. Ask Me No Questions. 2014. (ENG.). 176p. (YA). (gr. 7-12). 14.24 *(978-1-63245-300-6(2))* Lectorum Pubns., Inc.

McClintock, Norah. Nothing to Lose. 2012. (Robyn Hunter Mysteries Ser.: 3). (ENG.). 200p. (YA). (gr. 6-12). pap. 8.95 *(978-0-7613-8531-8(2)*, Darby Creek); lib. bdg. 27.93 *(978-0-7613-8513-4(1))* Lerner Publishing Group.

McNeal, Laura. Dark Water. 2011. (ENG.). 324p. (YA). (gr. 7). pap. 9.99 *(978-0-375-84330-3(2)*, Ember) Random Hse. Children's Bks.

Prinz, Yvonne. All You Get Is Me. 2010. (ENG.). 288p. (YA). (gr. 9-18). 16.99 *(978-0-06-171580-8(8))* HarperCollins Pubs.

Resau, Laura. Estrella en el Bosque (Star in the Forest) 2016. (ENG & SPA.). 160p. (J). (gr. 2-5). 18.40 *(978-0-606-39132-0(0))* Turtleback Bks.

—Red Glass. 2009. (ENG.). 304p. (YA). (gr. 7). pap. 8.99 *(978-0-440-24025-9(5)*, Delacorte Bks. for Young Readers) Random Hse. Children's Bks.

—Star in the Forest. 2012. (ENG.). 160p. (J). (gr. 2-5). 6.99 *(978-0-375-85410-1(X)*, Yearling) Random Hse. Children's Bks.

Restrepo, Bettina. Illegal. 2011. (ENG.). 272p. (YA). (gr. 8-18). 17.99 *(978-0-06-195342-2(3)*, Tegen, Katherine Bks) HarperCollins Pubs.

Rushford, Patricia H. Secrets of Ghost Island. 2007. (J). *(978-88-02-46255-4(0))* Moody Pubs.

Saldana, Rene, Jr. A Mystery Bigger Than Big / un Misterio Mas Grande Que Grandisimo: A Mickey Rangel Mystery / Colección Mickey Rangel, Detective Privado. 2016. (Mickey Rangel Mystery / Coleccion Mickey Rangel, Detective P Ser.). (MUL, ENG & SPA., Illus.). 64p. (J). (gr. 3-6). pap. 9.95 *(978-1-55885-824-4(5)*, Piñata Books) Arte Publico Pr.

Simmons, Ted. Diablo Creek. 2007. (ENG.). 168p. (YA). pap. *(978-0-9776958-7-4(5))* CyPress Pubns.

Vanished. 64p. (YA). (gr. 6-12). pap. *(978-0-8224-2367-6(7))* Globe Fearon Educational Publishing.

ILLINOIS

Alter, Judy. Illinois: A MyReportLinks.com Book. 2003. (States Ser.). (Illus.). 48p. (J). (gr. 4-10). lib. bdg. 25.26 *(978-0-7660-5111-9(0)*, MyReportLinks.com Bks.) Enslow Pubs., Inc.

Anderson, Kathy P. Illinois. 2012. (J). lib. bdg. 25.26 *(978-0-7613-4530-5(2)*, Lerner Pubns.) Lerner Publishing Group.

Bodden, Valerie. Illinois. 2010. (Let's Explore America Ser.). 24p. (J). (gr. k-2). 19.95 *(978-1-58341-834-5(2))* Creative Co., The.

Boekhoff, P. M. Illinois. 2005. (Portraits of the States Ser.). (Illus.). 32p. (gr. 2-6). pap. 10.50 *(978-0-8368-4643-0(5))*; lib. bdg. 26.00 *(978-0-8368-4624-9(9))* Stevens, Gareth Publishing LLLP. (Gareth Stevens Learning Library).

Brill, Marlene Targ. Illinois. 2nd rev. ed. 2005. (Celebrate the States Ser.). (Illus.). 144p. (gr. 6-7). lib. bdg. 42.79 *(978-0-7614-1735-4(4)*, Benchmark Bks.) Marshall Cavendish Corp.

Brown, Vanessa. Illinois. (Bilingual Library of the United States of America Ser.). 32p. 2009. (SPA.). (gr. 2-2). 47.90 *(978-1-60853-358-9(1)*, Editorial Buenas Letras) 2005. (ENG & SPA., Illus.). (J). (gr. 3-6). lib. bdg. 25.25 *(978-1-4042-3078-1(5))* Rosen Publishing Group, Inc., The.

Burgan, Michael. Illinois. 144p. (J). 2014. (America the Beautiful Ser.: 3). (ENG.). lib. bdg. 40.00 *(978-0-531-24883-6(6))* 2011. (America the Beautiful, Third Ser.). pap. 12.95 *(978-0-531-22923-1(8)*, Children's Pr.) Scholastic Library Publishing.

Craats, Rennay. Illinois. 2011. (Guide to American States Ser.). (Illus.). 48p. (YA). (gr. 3-6). 29.99 *(978-1-61690-785-3(1))*; (J). *(978-1-61690-461-6(5))* Weigl Pubs., Inc.

Deinard, Jenny. How to Draw Illinois's Sights & Symbols. 2009. (Kid's Guide to Drawing America Ser.). 32p. (gr. k-k). 50.50 *(978-1-61511-060-5(7)*, PowerKids Pr.) Rosen Publishing Group, Inc., The.

Elias, Megan & Feeley, Kathleen. Illinois. 2003. (World Almanac Biblioteca de los Estados). (SPA., Illus.). 48p. (gr. 4-9). pap. 14.05 *(978-0-8368-5551-7(5)*, Gareth Stevens Learning Library) Stevens, Gareth Publishing LLLP.

Feeley, Kathleen. Illinois. Porras, Carlos & D'Andrea, Patricia, trs. from ENG. 2003. (World Almanac Biblioteca de los Estados). (SPA., Illus.). 48p. (gr. 4-9). lib. bdg. 31.00 *(978-0-8368-5544-9(2)*, Gareth Stevens Learning Library) Stevens, Gareth Publishing LLLP.

Lewis, Anne Margaret. What Am I? Illinois. Mills, Tom, illus. 2011. (ENG.). 24p. (J). (gr. -1 — 1). bds. 9.99 *(978-0-8075-8960-1(8))* Whitman, Albert & Co.

Lusted, Marcia Amidon. Illinois: The Prairie State. (Illus.). 24p. (J). 2010. pap. 8.25 *(978-1-4358-3368-5(6))* 2009. lib. bdg. 22.60 *(978-1-4042-8121-9(5))* Rosen Publishing Group, Inc., The. (PowerKids Pr.).

Marciniak, Kristin. What's Great about Illinois? 2015. (Our Great States Ser.). (ENG.). 32p. (J). (gr. 2-5). pap. 7.95 *(978-1-4677-6091-1(9)*, Lerner Pubns.) Lerner Publishing Group.

Marsh, Carole. The Big Illinois Reproducible Activity Book. 2004. (Carole Marsh Illinois Bks.). (Illus.). 96p. (J). (gr. 2-6). pap. 9.95 *(978-0-7933-9460-9(0))* Gallopade International.

—Illinois Current Events Projects: 30 Cool, Activities, Crafts, Experiments & More for Kids to Do to Learn about Your State! 2003. (Illinois Experience Ser.). 32p. (gr. k-5). pap. 5.95 *(978-0-635-02032-1(7)*, Marsh, Carole Bks.) Gallopade International.

—Illinois Geography Projects: 30 Cool, Activities, Crafts, Experiments & More for Kids to Do to Learn about Your State! 2003. (Illinois Experience Ser.). 32p. (gr. k-5). pap. 5.95 *(978-0-635-01832-8(2)*, Marsh, Carole Bks.) Gallopade International.

—Illinois Government Projects: 30 Cool, Activities, Crafts, Experiments & More for Kids to Do to Learn about Your State! 2003. (Illinois Experience Ser.). 32p. (gr. k-5). pap. 5.95 *(978-0-635-01932-5(9)*, Marsh, Carole Bks.) Gallopade International.

—Illinois People Projects: 30 Cool, Activities, Crafts, Experiments & More for Kids to Do to Learn about Your State! 2003. (Illinois Experience Ser.). 32p. (gr. k-5). pap. 5.95 *(978-0-635-01982-0(5)*, Marsh, Carole Bks.) Gallopade International.

—Illinois Symbols & Facts Projects: 30 Cool, Activities, Crafts, Experiments & More for Kids to Do to Learn about Your State! 2003. (Illinois Experience Ser.). 32p. (gr. k-5). pap. 5.95 *(978-0-635-01882-3(9)*, Marsh, Carole Bks.) Gallopade International.

Mattern, Joanne. Illinois: Past & Present. 2009. (Illus.). 48p. (J). 70.50 *(978-1-4358-5567-0(1))*; pap. 11.75 *(978-1-4358-5566-3(3))*; (ENG., lib. bdg. 29.25 *(978-1-4358-5284-6(2))* Rosen Publishing Group, Inc., The. (Rosen Reference).

Shofner, Shawndra. Illinois. 2008. (This Land Called America Ser.). (Illus.). 32p. (YA). (gr. 3-6). 22.95 *(978-1-58341-638-9(2))* Creative Co., The.

Smith, Rich. Illinois, 1 vol. 2009. (United States Ser.). (ENG., Illus.). 48p. (YA). (gr. 2-5). 27.07 *(978-1-60453-648-5(9))* ABDO Publishing Co.

Wargin, Kathy-jo. L Is for Lincoln: An Illinois Alphabet. van Frankenhuyzen, Gijsbert, illus. 2004. (Discover America State by State Ser.). (ENG.). 40p. (J). (gr. 1-3). pap. 7.95 *(978-1-58536-250-9(6)*, 202283) Sleeping Bear Pr.

—Prairie Numbers: An Illinois Number Book. O'Malley, Kathy, illus. 2006. (Count Your Way Across the U. S. A. Ser.).

(ENG.). 40p. (J). (gr. -1-3). 17.95 *(978-1-58536-180-9(1))* Sleeping Bear Pr.

ILLINOIS—FICTION

Alegre, Mari. Destiny. 2011. 174p. 29.99 *(978-1-4568-2040-4(0))*; pap. 19.99 *(978-1-4568-2039-8(7))* Xlibris Corp.

Amato, Anne McCoy. Moving Shelly: A Novel. 2010. 148p. (gr. 4-6). 22.95 *(978-1-4502-2586-1(1))* iUniverse, Inc.

Aryal, Aimee. Lets Go Illini! Shrestha, Anuj, illus. 2004. 24p. (J). lib. bdg. 19.95 *(978-1-932888-21-8(7))* Mascot Bks., Inc.

Balaban, Bob. Boy or Beast. Rash, Andy, illus. (Creature from the 7th Grade Ser.: 1). (ENG.). (J). (gr. 5). 2013. 272p. pap. 7.99 *(978-0-14-242542-8(7)*, Puffin Books) 2012. 256p. 15.99 *(978-0-670-01271-8(8)*, Viking Books for Young Readers) Penguin Young Readers Group.

Bates, Susan Welch. The Rag Picker's Christmas. 2008. 17p. pap. 24.95 *(978-1-60672-967-0(5))* America Star Bks.

Bauer, Marion Dane. Killing Miss Kitty & Other Sins. 2008. (ENG.). 176p. (YA). (gr. 7). pap. 12.95 *(978-0-547-07614-0(2))* Houghton Mifflin Harcourt Publishing Co.

Beaty, Andrea. Secrets of the Cicada Summer. (ENG.). 176p. (gr. 3-7). 2010. (YA). pap. 6.95 *(978-0-8109-8419-6(9))* 2008. (J). 16.95 *(978-0-8109-9472-0(0))* Abrams, Inc. (Amulet Bks.).

Bellisario, Gina. The Twelve Days of Christmas in Illinois. Ebbeler, Jeffrey, illus. 2012. (Twelve Days of Christmas in America Ser.). (ENG.). 40p. (J). (gr. k-3). 12.95 *(978-1-4027-9733-0(8))* Sterling Publishing Co., Inc.

Brandeis, Gayle. My Life with the Lincolns. 2010. (ENG.). 256p. (J). (gr. 5-9). 34.99 *(978-0-8050-9013-0(4)*, 9780805090130, Holt, Henry & Co. Bks. For Young Readers) Holt, Henry & Co.

Clements, Andrew. Extra Credit. Elliott, Mark, illus. (ENG.). (J). (gr. 3-7). 2011. 224p. pap. 7.99 *(978-1-4169-4931-2(3))* 2009. 192p. 16.99 *(978-1-4169-4929-9(1))* Simon & Schuster Children's Publishing. (Atheneum Bks. for Young Readers).

Clifton, Lutricia. Freaky Fast Frankie Joe. (ENG.). 272p. (J). 2013. pap. 7.99 *(978-0-8234-2867-0(2))* 2012. 16.95 *(978-0-8234-2367-5(0))* Holiday Hse., Inc.

Colbert, Brandy. Pointe. (ENG.). 352p. (YA). (gr. 9). 2015. pap. 9.99 *(978-0-14-751441-7(X)*, Speak) 2014. 17.99 *(978-0-399-16034-9(5)*, G.P. Putnam's Sons Books for Young Readers) Penguin Young Readers Group.

Cowing, Sue. Call Me Drog. 2014. (ENG.). 320p. (J). 13.99 *(978-0-00-757804-7(0))* HarperCollins Pubs. Ltd. GBR. Dist: Independent Pubs. Group.

—You Will Call Me Drog. 2011. (Exceptional Reading & Language Arts Titles for Intermediate Grades Ser.). (ENG.). 288p. (J). (gr. 4-7). 16.95 *(978-0-7613-6076-6(X)*, Carolrhoda Bks.) Lerner Publishing Group.

Dalton, Sherry A. Do Indians Eat Soup? 2011. 32p. pap. 24.95 *(978-1-4560-7463-0(6))* America Star Bks.

Dohr, Robert. The Pumpkin Se. Dewyea, Glenn, illus. 2012. 32p. pap. 13.50 *(978-1-61204-337-1(2)*, Strategic Bk. Publishing) Strategic Book Publishing & Rights Agency (SBPRA).

Elkeles, Simone. Better Than Perfect. 2014. (Wild Cards Ser.). (ENG.). 352p. (YA). (gr. 9). pap. 9.99 *(978-0-8027-3725-0(0)*, 9780802737250, Bloomsbury USA Childrens) Bloomsbury Publishing USA.

Ervin, Randy. Maycroft From 232nd. 2010. 150p. (YA). pap. 10.00 *(978-0-578-05732-3(8))* Ervin, Randy.

Fenner, Carol. Yolonda's Genius. unabr. ed. 2004. 211p. (J). (gr. 4-6). pap. 38.00 incl. audio *(978-0-8072-0462-7(5)*, Listening Library) Random Hse. Audio Publishing Group.

Fleming, Candace. Lowji Discovers America. 2008. (ENG.). 160p. (J). (gr. 2-6). pap. 7.99 *(978-1-4169-5832-1(0)*, Aladdin) Simon & Schuster Children's Publishing.

—On the Day I Died: Stories from the Grave. 2012. (ENG.). 208p. (J). (gr. 5-9). 16.99 *(978-0-375-86781-1(3)*, Schwartz & Wade Bks.) Random Hse. Children's Bks.

Greenlee, Don. This Countryboy Guardian Was Heaven Sent. 2007. (Illus.). 114p. (YA). per. 14.95 net. *(978-0-9795574-0-8(2))* Country Boy Publishing Co.

Gunderson, Jessica A. How to Keep a Secret for Detectives. 2008. 206p. pap. 15.50 *(978-0-557-01369-2(0))* Lulu Pr., Inc.

Haddix, Margaret Peterson. Claim to Fame. (ENG.). 272p. (YA). (gr. 7). 2010. pap. 9.99 *(978-1-4169-3918-4(0))* 2009. 16.99 *(978-1-4169-3917-7(2))* Simon & Schuster Bks. For Young Readers. (Simon & Schuster Bks. For Young Readers).

Henity, Kristi. Kimi's Grand Adventures, Vol. 1. 2004. 55p. pap. 16.95 *(978-1-4137-2869-9(3))* America Star Bks.

Henne, R. J. & Wilson, Marlys. Harley Boogle & His Bulldog Buster, 1 vol. 2009. 77p. pap. 19.95 *(978-1-60672-955-7(1))* America Star Bks.

Hurwitz, Michele Weber. The Summer I Saved the World ... in 65 Days. 2015. (ENG.). 272p. (J). (gr. 5). pap. 9.99 *(978-0-385-37109-4(8)*, Ember) Random Hse. Children's Bks.

Jacobs, Lily. The Littlest Bunny in Illinois: An Easter Adventure. Dunn, Robert, illus. 2015. (ENG.). 32p. (J). (-3). 9.99 *(978-1-4926-1081-6(X)*, Sourcebooks Jabberwocky) Sourcebooks, Inc.

James, Eric. A Halloween Scare in Illinois. Le Ray, Marina, illus. 2015. (ENG.). 32p. (J). (-5). 9.99 *(978-1-4926-2375-5(X)*, 9781492623755, Sourcebooks Jabberwocky) Sourcebooks, Inc.

—Santa's Sleigh Is on Its Way to Illinois. Dunn, Robert, illus. 2015. (ENG.). 32p. (J). (-2). 12.99 *(978-1-4926-2746-3(1)*, Sourcebooks Jabberwocky) Sourcebooks, Inc.

Keplinger, Kody. A Midsummer's Nightmare. 2013. (ENG.). 304p. (YA). (gr. 10-17). pap. 9.99 *(978-0-316-08421-5(2)*, Poppy) Little, Brown Bks. for Young Readers.

Kirk, Donald. Hinsdale: The Summer Of '58. 2003. (ENG., Illus.). 252p. (YA). pap. 12.95 *(978-0-9654341-4-0(1)*, Sweetwater Stagelines) Old West Co., The.

Leitch, Will. Catch. 2005. (ENG.). 304p. (YA). (gr. 9-12). 8.99 *(978-1-59514-069-2(7)*, Razorbill) Penguin Young Readers Group.

Levine, Kristin. The Paper Cowboy. 2016. (ENG.). 368p. (J). (gr. 5). 8.99 *(978-0-14-242715-6(2)*, Puffin Books) Penguin Young Readers Group.

Lo, Ginnie & Lo, Beth. Auntie Yang's Great Soybean Picnic. 2012. (ENG., Illus.). 32p. (J). 18.95 *(978-1-60060-442-3(0))* Lee & Low Bks., Inc.

Madormo, John V. The Homemade Stuffing Caper, Bk. 1. 2013. (Charlie Collier, Snoop for Hire Ser.: 1). (ENG.). 272p. (J). (gr. 5). pap. 7.99 *(978-0-14-242380-6(7)*, Puffin Books) Penguin Young Readers Group.

Martin, Amy. In Your Dreams. 2012. 254p. pap. 9.99 *(978-0-9882051-0-9(6))* Martin, Amy.

Minton, Ross. Baseball, from the Street to the Diamond, 1 vol. 2010. 94p. pap. 19.95 *(978-1-4489-4918-2(1))* America Star Bks.

Monroe, Mary A. Tagger: Graffiti Was His Life - & Soul. 2011. 176p. 29.99 *(978-1-4567-5028-2(3))*; pap. 19.99 *(978-1-4567-5029-9(1))* AuthorHouse.

O'Dell, Kathryn L. From Wagon to Train. Chalk, Chris, illus. 2017. (Text Connections Guided Close Reading Ser.). (J). (gr. 2). *(978-1-4900-1854-6(9))* Benchmark Education Co.

Park, Linda Sue. Project Mulberry. 2007. 225p. (gr. 4-7). 17.00 *(978-0-7569-7921-8(8))* Perfection Learning Corp.

—Project Mulberry. 2007. (ENG.). 240p. (J). (gr. 3-7). 6.99 *(978-0-440-42163-4(2)*, Yearling) Random Hse. Children's Bks.

Peck, Richard. A Long Way from Chicago. 2004. (Puffin Modern Classics Ser.). (ENG.). 160p. (J). (gr. 5-7). pap. 7.99 *(978-0-14-240110-1(2)*, Puffin Books) Penguin Young Readers Group.

—On the Wings of Heroes. 2008. (ENG.). 160p. (J). (gr. 3-7). 7.99 *(978-0-14-241204-6(X)*, Puffin Books) Penguin Young Readers Group.

—On the Wings of Heroes. rev. l.t. ed. 2007. (Literacy Bridge Middle Reader Ser.). 171p. (J). (gr. 4-7). 23.95 *(978-0-7862-9703-0(4))* Thorndike Pr.

—A Season of Gifts. 2010. (ENG.). 208p. (J). (gr. 5-18). 7.99 *(978-0-14-241729-4(7)*, Puffin Books) Penguin Young Readers Group.

—A Year down Yonder. unabr. ed. 2004. (Middle Grade Cassette Librariestm Ser.). 144p. (J). (gr. 5-9). pap. 29.00 incl. audio *(978-0-8072-0991-2(0)*, S YA 256 SP, Listening Library) Random Hse. Audio Publishing Group.

Rapp, Adam. The Children & the Wolves. Ering, Timothy Basil, illus. 2012. (ENG.). 160p. (YA). (gr. 9). 16.99 *(978-0-7636-5337-8(3))* Candlewick Pr.

Rutkoski, Marie. The Shadow Society. 2013. (ENG.). 448p. (YA). (gr. 7-12). pap. 9.99 *(978-1-250-03424-3(8))* Square Fish.

Schraff, Anne. Freedom Knows No Color. 2008. (Passages to History Ser.). 118p. (J). lib. bdg. 13.95 *(978-0-7569-8392-5(4))*; (YA). (gr. 7-12). pap. 8.50 *(978-0-7891-7567-0(3))* Perfection Learning Corp.

Sherman, M. Zachary. Unchained, Vol. 4. Majado, Caio & Emery, Thomas J., illus. 2011. (Tony Hawk's 900 Revolution Ser.). (ENG.). 128p. (gr. 3-4). pap. 7.19 *(978-1-4342-3454-4(1))*; lib. bdg. 26.65 *(978-1-4342-3215-1(8))* Stone Arch Bks. (Tony Hawk's 900 Revolution).

Silvano, Wendi. Love Is All Around Illinois. Czernichowska, Joanna, illus. 2016. (ENG.). 32p. (J). (-6). 12.99 *(978-1-4926-2922-1(7)*, Sourcebooks Jabberwocky) Sourcebooks, Inc.

Smallman, Steve. Santa Is Coming to Illinois. Dunn, Robert, illus. 2013. (ENG.). 32p. (J). (-3). 9.99 *(978-1-4022-9103-6(5)*, Sourcebooks Jabberwocky) Sourcebooks, Inc.

Sparks, Megan. Falling Hard, 1 vol. 2013. (Roller Girls Ser.). (ENG.). 256p. (gr. 8-10). 12.95 *(978-1-62370-023-2(X))* Capstone Young Readers of Coughlan Cos.

—Hell's Belles, 1 vol. 2013. (Roller Girls Ser.). (ENG.). 256p. (gr. 8-10). 12.95 *(978-1-62370-024-9(8))* Capstone Young Readers of Coughlan Cos.

—Hell's Belles/By Megan Sparks. 2013. 255p. (YA). *(978-1-62370-022-5(1))* Capstone Young Readers of Coughlan Cos.

Stone, Tamara Ireland. Time after Time. 2014. (ENG.). 368p. (YA). (gr. 7-12). pap. 9.99 *(978-1-4231-5981-0(0))* Hyperion Bks. for Children.

Strow, Lorie. The Shimmers. 2011. 32p. pap. 21.99 *(978-1-4568-8133-7(7))* Xlibris Corp.

Trumbo, Stephen. Friends of the Forest. 2008. 39p. pap. 24.95 *(978-1-60563-781-5(5))* America Star Bks.

Vaughn, Royce, illus. Seymour Bluffs & Robert Wadlow, the Tallest Man in the World: A Story about Diversity & Tolerance. 2007. 28p. (J). 12.95 *(978-0-9728538-4-2(7))* Amica Publishing.

Wartik, David J. The VonNesta Project: Camp Fingerlake. 2007. 148p. per. 13.95 *(978-1-60145-394-5(9))* Booklocker.com, Inc.

Wells, Rosemary. On the Blue Comet. Ibatoulline, Bagram, illus. (ENG.). 336p. (J). (gr. 5). 2012. pap. 8.99 *(978-0-7636-5815-1(4))* 2010. 16.99 *(978-0-7636-3722-4(X))* Candlewick Pr.

ILLINOIS—HISTORY

Alexander, Carol. The Big Squeal: A True Story about a Homeless Pig's Search for Life, Liberty & the Pursuit of Happiness. 2013. (ENG., Illus.). 32p. (J). pap. 16.00 *(978-1-61009-112-1(4)*, Acorn) Oak Tree Publishing.

—The Big Squeal: A True Story about a Homeless Pig's Search for Life, Liberty & the Pursuit of Happiness. Kalpart Designs, illus. 2012. (ENG.). 24p. (J). 24.00 *(978-1-61009-036-0(5)*, Acorn) Oak Tree Publishing.

Bechtold, Phyliss. Seymour Bluffs & the Legend of the Piasa Bird. 2007. 26p. 9.95 *(978-0-9728532-8-6(6))* New Horizons Christian Ctr.

Bechtold, Phyllis. Seymour Bluffs Activities Coloring Book. 2006. 32p. spiral bd. 5.95 *(978-0-9728538-3-5(9))* Amica Publishing.

Brill, Marlene Targ. Annie Shapiro & the Clothing Workers' Strike. 2010. pap. 56.72 *(978-0-7613-6924-0(4))* Lerner Publishing Group.

Capstone Press Geography Department Staff. Illinois. 2012. (One Nation (Revised & Updated) Ser.). (ENG.). 48p. (gr. 3-4). pap. 8.95 *(978-1-4765-0067-6(3)*, Social Studies Collections) Capstone Press of Coughlan Cos.

Craats, Rennay. Illinois: The Prairie State. 2016. (J). *(978-1-4896-4854-9(2))* Weigl Pubs., Inc.

Durrie, Karen. Illinois: The Prairie State. 2012. (J). *(978-1-61913-345-7(8))*; pap. *(978-1-61913-346-4(6))* Weigl Pubs., Inc.

Epstein, Brad M. Barack Obama 101. l.t. ed. 2009. (My First Presidential Board Book Ser.). (Illus.). 28p. (J). (gr. -1-1). bds. *(978-1-60730-044-1(3)*, 101 Bk.) Michaelson Entertainment.

Gregory, Josh. Illinois. 2017. (True Book — My United States Ser.). (ENG.). 48p. (J). pap. 7.95 ***(978-0-531-23286-6(7)***, Children's Pr.) Scholastic Library Publishing.

Hershenhorn, Esther. Little Illinois. Monroe, Michael Glenn, illus. 2011. (My Little State Ser.). (ENG.). 22p. (J). 9.95 *(978-1-58536-537-1(8))* Sleeping Bear Pr.

Jerome, Kate B. Lucky to Live in Illinois. 2017. (Arcadia Kids Ser.). (ENG., Illus.). 32p. (J). 16.99 ***(978-0-7385-2776-5(9))*** Arcadia Publishing.

Joyce, Jaime. Going Ballistic: Who Pulled the Trigger in a Gangland Massacre? 2011. (J). pap. *(978-0-545-32801-2(2))* Scholastic, Inc.

Kenney, Karen Latchana. Pizza Pie in the Sky: A Story about Illinois, 1 vol. 2008. (Fact & Fable: State Stories Ser.). (ENG., Illus.). 24p. (J). (gr. -1-2). 25.65 *(978-1-60453-186-2(X))* ABDO Publishing Co.

Marciniak, Kristin. What's Great about Illinois? 2015. (Our Great States Ser.). (ENG., Illus.). 32p. (J). (gr. 2-5). lib. bdg. 26.60 *(978-1-4677-3867-5(0)*, Lerner Pubns.) Lerner Publishing Group.

Marsh, Carole. Exploring Illinois Through Project-Based Learning. 2016. (Illinois Experience Ser.). (ENG.). (J). pap. 9.99 *(978-0-635-12337-4(1))* Gallopade International.

—Illinois History Projects: 30 Cool, Activities, Crafts, Experiments & More for Kids to Do to Learn about Your State! 2003. (Illinois Experience Ser.). 32p. (gr. k-5). pap. 5.95 *(978-0-635-01782-6(2)*, Marsh, Carole Bks.) Gallopade International.

Murray, Julie. Illinois, 1 vol. 2012. (Explore the United States Ser.). (ENG.). 32p. (J). (gr. 2-5). lib. bdg. 28.50 *(978-1-61783-351-9(7)*, Big Buddy Bks.) ABDO Publishing Co.

Price-Groff, Claire & Kaplan, Elizabeth. Illinois. 2nd rev. ed. 2010. (It's My State! Ser.). 80p. (gr. 3-18). lib. bdg. 31.36 *(978-1-60870-050-9(X))* Marshall Cavendish Corp.

Price-Groff, Claire, et al. Illinois. 2015. (J). lib. bdg. *(978-1-62712-491-1(8))*; (ENG., Illus.). 80p. (gr. 4-4). 34.21 *(978-1-5026-0011-0(0))* Cavendish Square Publishing.

Sheinkin, Steve. Lincoln's Grave Robbers. 2013. (ENG.). 224p. (J). (gr. 5-9). 16.99 *(978-0-545-40572-0(6)*, Scholastic Pr.) Scholastic, Inc.

Vaughn, Royce, illus. Seymour Bluffs & the Legend of the Piasa Bird. 2006. 24p. (J). pap. 9.95 *(978-0-9728538-2-8(0))* Amica Publishing.

Wessel, Nancy Davis. The People of Friendlyville. 2012. 52p. pap. 10.95 *(978-1-936688-41-8(7))* AKA:yoLa.

Ziff, John. Western Great Lakes: Illinois, Minnesota, Wisconsin, Vol. 19. 2015. (Let's Explore the States Ser.). (Illus.). 64p. (J). (gr. 5). 23.95 *(978-1-4222-3338-2(3))* Mason Crest.

ILLITERACY

see Literacy

ILLUMINATION

see Lighting

ILLUSIONS

see Optical Illusions

ILLUSTRATION OF BOOKS

see also Caldecott Medal; Drawing

Bankston, John. Randolph J. Caldecott & the Story of the Caldecott Medal. 2003. (Great Achiever Awards Ser.). (Illus.). 48p. (J). (gr. 4-8). lib. bdg. 29.95 *(978-1-58415-200-2(1))* Mitchell Lane Pubs., Inc.

Ford, Carin T. Dr. Seuss: Best-Loved Author. 2003. (People to Know Ser.). (Illus.). 112p. (J). (gr. 6-12). lib. bdg. 27.94 *(978-0-7660-2106-8(8))* Enslow Pubs., Inc.

Frank, Vivien & Jaffe, Deborah. Make a Book: Six Different Books to Make, Write, & Illustrate. 2004. (Illus.). 32p. (J). (gr. 2-8). reprint ed. pap. 15.00 *(978-0-7567-7703-6(8))* DIANE Publishing Co.

Leedy, Loreen. Look at My Book! How Kids Can Write & Illustrate Terrific Books. 2005. (ENG., Illus.). 32p. (J). 8.99 *(978-0-8234-1959-3(2))* Holiday Hse., Inc.

—Look at My Book! How Kids Can Write & Illustrate Terrific Books. Leedy, Loreen, tr. 2005. (ENG., Illus.). 32p. (J). (gr. -1-3). tchr. ed. 17.95 *(978-0-8234-1590-8(2))* Holiday Hse., Inc.

McSweeney's Editors, creator. The Author-Illustrator Starter Kit. 2011. (ENG.). 96p. 15.95 *(978-1-936365-45-6(6))* McSweeney's Publishing.

Stalcup, Ann & Politi, Leo. Leo Politi: Artist of the Angels. 2004. (gr. 4). 24.95 *(978-1-893110-38-0(9))* Silver Moon Pr.

Walker, Rachel. Book Art. 2015. (ENG., Illus.). 16p. (-2). pap. *(978-1-77654-136-2(7)*, Red Rocket Readers) Flying Start Bks.

ILLUSTRATIONS, HUMOROUS

see Cartoons and Comics

IMAGINARY ANIMALS

see Animals, Mythical

IMAGINARY VOYAGES

see Voyages, Imaginary

IMAGINATION

see also Creation (Literary, Artistic, etc.)

Acampora, Courtney. Eyes & Ears. Kushnir, Hilli, illus. 2016. (ENG.). 22p. (J). (gr. -1). bds. 12.99 *(978-1-62686-749-0(6)*, Silver Dolphin Bks.) Readerlink Distribution Services, LLC.

—Heads & Tails. Tinarelli, Beatrice, illus. 2016. (ENG.). 22p. (J). (gr. -1). bds. 12.99 *(978-1-62686-748-2(8)*, Silver Dolphin Bks.) Readerlink Distribution Services, LLC.

Canetti, Yanitzia. Casos y cosas que dan Risa. 2010. (SPA.). 32p. (J). pap. *(978-1-59835-252-8(0)*, BrickHouse Education) Cambridge BrickHouse, Inc.

—Could It Be? 2010. 32p. (J). pap. 8.99 *(978-1-59835-253-5(9)*, BrickHouse Education) Cambridge BrickHouse, Inc.

—Que le Dijo? Bate, bate, Disparates. 2010. (J). pap. 8.99 *(978-1-59835-254-2(7)*, BrickHouse Education) Cambridge BrickHouse, Inc.

—Say What? 2010. 32p. 8.99 *(978-1-59835-255-9(5)*, BrickHouse Education) Cambridge BrickHouse, Inc.

Collins, Meg. Twinkle, Twinkle Starry Sky. 2010. 36p. 15.49 *(978-1-4520-4453-8(8))* AuthorHouse.

Dalmatian Press Staff. My Race into Space! 2008. (ENG.). 9p. bds. 4.95 *(978-1-58117-717-6(8)*, Intervisual/Piggy Toes) Bendon, Inc.

Edgar, Kathleen J., et al. Imagination. 2003. (J). *(978-1-59203-058-3(0))* Learning Challenge, Inc.

Hahn, Beverly. Twenty Acres of Love: Irrigation Time. Hahn, Beverly, illus. 2003. (Illus.). v, 65p. (J). (gr. -1-6). spiral bd. 12.95 *(978-0-9722494-0-9(0))* Hahn, Beverly.

Mariolle, Mathieu. Even for A Dreamer Like Me. 3rd rev. ed. 2010. pap. 56.72 *(978-0-7613-6960-8(0))* Lerner Publishing Group.

Matthews, Caitlin & Matthews, John. Legends of the Sea: Create-A-Story Kit. 2011. (Storyworld Ser.). (ENG., Illus.). 22p. (J). (gr. 4-7). 9.99 *(978-0-7636-5320-0(9)*, Templar) Candlewick Pr.

Matthews, John & Matthews, Caitlin. Storyworld: Create a Story Kit. 2010. (Illus.). *(978-0-7636-5319-4(5))* Templar Publishing.

McNulty John. I Am Your Imagination. Gilmour, Karen, illus. 2006. 32p. *(978-0-9769580-3-1(1))* I Am Your Playground LLC.

Rinaldo, Denise. Leonardo Da Vinci: With a Discussion of Imagination. 2003. (Values in Action Ser.). (J). *(978-1-59203-066-8(1))* Learning Challenge, Inc.

Sorensen, "Miss Nancy". Alexa's Rainbow. 2008. 16p. pap. 8.49 *(978-1-4343-9342-5(9))* AuthorHouse.

Taylor, Jeremy. Strength of Love. 2012. 32p. pap. 24.95 *(978-1-4626-7083-3(0))* America Star Bks.

Tsin, Justin. What Would You Imagine? 2008. (Illus.). 32p. (gr. k-3). per. 19.95 *(978-1-60396-039-7(2))* Santillana USA Publishing Co., Inc.

IMAGINATION—FICTION

Abdo Publishing. Monster on the Loose, 1 vol. 2013. (Monster on the Loose Ser.: 4). (ENG.). 32p. (J). (gr. -1-4). lib. bdg. 114.00 *(978-1-61641-930-1(X)*, Looking Glass Library) Magic Wagon.

Abercrombie, Barbara. The Show-and-Tell Lion. Cravath, Lynne Avril & Avril, Lynne, illus. 2006. (ENG.). 32p. (J). (gr. -1-2). 17.99 *(978-0-689-86408-7(6)*, McElderry, Margaret K. Bks.) McElderry, Margaret K. Bks.

Abraham, Ametta. Miss Robbie's House. 2009. 64p. pap. 23.49 *(978-1-4490-4571-5(5))* AuthorHouse.

Abrahams, Alayne. Dreams & Daydreams. 2010. 26p. 14.95 *(978-1-4269-4173-3(0))* Trafford Publishing.

Accord Publishing Staff. What Do You See? A Lift-The-Flap Book. 2014. (ENG.). 12p. (J). (-k). bds. 6.99 *(978-1-4494-4385-6(0))* Andrews McMeel Publishing.

Achatz, Eric. The Adventures of Ryan Alexander: The Great Space Chase. 2010. 52p. pap. 23.50 *(978-1-4269-3763-7(6))* Trafford Publishing.

Acopiado, Ginger. Over the Rainbow with Joey. Fuglestad, R. A., illus. l.t. ed. 2004. 22p. (J). bds. 8.99 *(978-0-9729093-0-3(3))* Tike Time, Inc.

Adams, Lacole Sessions. Maggie & Her Tree. 2011. 28p. (gr. -1). pap. 15.29 *(978-1-4567-2416-0(9))* AuthorHouse.

Agaoglu, Basak. The Almost Impossible Thing. Green, Michael, ed. 2017. (ENG., Illus.). 32p. (J). (gr. -1-2). 16.99 *(978-0-399-54827-7(0)*, Philomel Bks.) Penguin Young Readers Group.

Ahlberg, Jessica. Fairy Tales for Mr. Barker: A Peek-Through Story. Ahlberg, Jessica, illus. 2016. (ENG., Illus.). 32p. (J). (-k). 15.99 *(978-0-7636-8124-1(5))* Candlewick Pr.

Ahmdt, Paula D. Toof Fairy Tales. 2011. 24p. (gr. 1-2). pap. 12.74 *(978-1-4567-6028-1(9))* AuthorHouse.

Alcántara, Ricardo. El Hijo Del Viento. 2003. (SPA., Illus.). 64p. *(978-84-207-6971-4(1)*, GS2762) Grupo Anaya, S.A. ESP. Dist: Lectorum Pubns., Inc.

Alda, Arlene. Here a Face, There a Face. 2008. (ENG., Illus.). 32p. (J). (gr. k-k). 14.95 *(978-0-88776-845-3(8)*, Tundra Bks.) Tundra Bks. CAN. Dist: Penguin Random Hse. LLC.

Aldis, Dorothy & Collins, Heather. Hiding. (FRE.). (J). pap. 7.99 *(978-0-590-24195-3(8))* Scholastic, Inc.

Aliaga, Roberto. A Night Time Story. 2012. (ENG., Illus.). 24p. (J). (gr. k-2). *(978-84-15241-98-0(4))* D P & G Military Pubs.

Allan, Delores. Magical Moments with Roy & Toni: Do You Ever Wonder. 2012. 24p. pap. 17.99 *(978-1-4772-8910-5(0))* AuthorHouse.

Alley, R. W. Clark in the Deep Sea. 2016. (ENG., Illus.). 32p. (J). (gr. -1-3). 14.99 *(978-0-547-90692-8(7))* Houghton Mifflin Harcourt Publishing Co.

—Gretchen over the Beach. 2016. (ENG., Illus.). 32p. (J). (gr. -1-3). 14.99 *(978-0-547-90708-6(7))* Houghton Mifflin Harcourt Publishing Co.

—Mitchell on the Moon. 2016. (ENG., Illus.). 32p. (J). (gr. -1-3). 14.99 *(978-0-547-90703-1(6))* Houghton Mifflin Harcourt Publishing Co.

Alsenas, Linas. The Princess of 8th Street. 2012. (ENG., Illus.). 32p. (J). (gr. k-2). 16.95 *(978-0-8109-8972-6(7)*, Abrams Bks. for Young Readers) Abrams, Inc.

Amelia Asks Why... Book of Fun. 2007. (J). 1.09 *(978-0-9726075-7-5(9))* EPI Bks.

Amestoy, Jennifer. Junkyard Junction: The Story of the Magic Microwave. 2008. 32p. pap. 14.75 *(978-1-4389-1755-9(4))* AuthorHouse.

Anbinder, Adrienne. Clarence Blooms in Winter. Pickman, Marian, illus. 2009. 40p. pap. 16.99 *(978-1-4389-7028-8(5))* AuthorHouse.

Andersen, David W. Tell Us a Story about Flying. 2012. 28p. pap. 24.95 *(978-1-4626-8081-8(X))* America Star Bks.

Anderson, Carolyn. No Counting Sheep, 1 vol. 2010. 34p. 24.95 *(978-1-4489-9078-8(5))* PublishAmerica, Inc.

Anderson, David. Emily's Imaginary Airplane. 2013. 24p. pap. 10.99 *(978-1-4808-0347-3(2))* Archway Publishing.

Anderson, Eric B. Alena & the Favorite Thing. Kuzma, Jakub, illus. 2008. 36p. (J). (ENG.). 18.95 *(978-0-9798659-2-3(1))*; pap. 13.95 *(978-0-9798659-3-0(X))* Edgecliff Pr. LLC.

Andreae, Giles. Captain Flinn & the Pirate Dinosaurs. Ayto, Russell, illus. 2005. (Captain Flinn & the Pirate Dinosaurs Ser.). (ENG.). 32p. (J). (gr. -1-1). 17.99 *(978-1-4169-0713-8(0)*, McElderry, Margaret K. Bks.) McElderry, Margaret K. Bks.

—Missing Treasure! Ayto, Russell, illus. 2008. (Captain Flinn & the Pirate Dinosaurs Ser.). (ENG.). 32p. (J). (gr. -1-3). 17.99 *(978-1-4169-6745-3(1)*, McElderry, Margaret K. Bks.) McElderry, Margaret K. Bks.

Anita D Martinez. Worm Imposters. 2009. 32p. pap. 14.49 (978-1-4389-2605-6(7)) AuthorHouse.

Anna, Holly. Daisy Dreamer & the Totally True Imaginary Friend. Santos, Genevieve, illus. 2017. (Daisy Dreamer Ser.: 1). (ENG.). 128p. (J). (gr. k-4). pap. 5.99 (978-1-4814-8630-9(6), Little Simon) Little Simon.

—Daisy Dreamer & the World of Make Believe. Santos, Genevieve, illus. 2017. (Daisy Dreamer Ser.: 2). (ENG.). 128p. (J). (gr. k-4). pap. 5.99 (978-1-4814-8633-0(0), Little Simon) Little Simon.

Anna, Holly. Sparkle Fairies & the Imaginaries. Santos, Genevieve, illus. 2017. (Daisy Dreamer Ser.: 3). (ENG.). 128p. (J). (gr. k-4). pap. 5.99 **(978-1-4814-9185-3(7)**, Little Simon) Little Simon.

Arkangel, Brian. Cow Story. Moffat, Ross, illus. 2009. 24p. pap. 24.95 (978-1-60703-272-4(4)) America Star Bks.

Armstrong, Ashley Sage-Taylor. The Adventures of Starlight & Sunny: Book Four in the Adventures of Starlight & Sunny Series, ?Princesses Don't Need a Job !? How to Be an Indepen. 2013. 52p. pap. (978-1-927863-02-2(3)) Armstrong, Ashley.

—The Adventures of Starlight & Sunny: I Am Me ! Who Are You?, How to Find Good Quality Friends & Stand up for One Another, with Positive Morals, Pi. 2013. 52p. pap. (978-1-927863-00-8(7)) Armstrong, Ashley.

Armstrong, Kim. Petunia in Manhattan. 2009. 50p. pap. 12.99 (978-1-935436-97-3(X)) Rodaian Pr.

Arnold, Tedd. Prince Fly Guy. 2015. (Fly Guy Ser.: 15). (ENG., Illus.). 32p. (J). (gr. -1-3). 6.99 (978-0-545-66275-8(3), Cartwheel Bks.) Scholastic, Inc.

—Prince Fly Guy. 2015. (Fly Guy Ser.: 15). lib. bdg. 17.20 (978-0-606-37831-4(6)) Turtleback Bks.

Arteaga, Marta. Inside My Imagination. 2013. (ENG., Illus.). 24p. (J). (gr. k-2). 15.95 (978-84-15503-59-0(8)) Eastern National.

Asch, Frank. Monsieur Saguette & His Baguette. Asch, Frank, illus. 2006. (ENG., Illus.). 32p. (J). (gr. -1-2). 6.95 (978-1-55337-978-2(0)) Kids Can Pr., Ltd. CAN. Dist: Hachette Bk. Group.

Ashman, Linda. Sailing off to Sleep. Winter, Susan, illus. 2010. (ENG.). 32p. (J). (gr. -1-1). pap. 9.99 (978-1-4424-1435-8(9), Simon & Schuster Bks. For Young Readers) Simon & Schuster Bks. For Young Readers.

Ashta, Lucia. The Perfect Fuzzy-Wuzz. 2010. 48p. pap. 17.45 (978-1-4525-0041-6(X)) Get Published.

Austin, Rikey. Tilly & the Magic Wand: Alice's Bear Shop. 2012. 28p. pap. (978-1-78092-146-4(2)) MX Publishing, Ltd.

Avi. Who Was That Masked Man, Anyway? 2014. (ENG.). 176p. (J). (gr. 3-7). pap. 6.99 (978-0-439-52355-4(9), Scholastic Paperbacks) Scholastic, Inc.

AZ Books Staff. Our Faraway Jungle. Zayceva, Irina, ed. 2012. (Hook-And-Loop-Pictures Ser.). (ENG.). 12p. (J). (-k). bds. 11.95 (978-1-61889-158-7(8)) AZ Bks. LLC.

Babin, Claire. Gus Is a Fish. Bedrick, Claudia Z., tr. from FRE. Tallec, Olivier & Sorman, Joy, illus. 2008. (ENG.). 32p. (J). (gr. -1-2). 14.95 (978-1-59270-101-8(9)) Enchanted Lion Bks., LLC.

Bahk, Jane. Juna's Jar. Hoshino, Felicia, illus. 2015. (ENG.). 32p. (J). 17.95 (978-1-60060-853-7(1), 9781600000000) Lee & Low Bks., Inc.

Bancks, Tristan. Noob, the Boy Who Could Fly. Gorissen, Dean, illus. 2015. (Legends in Their Own Lunchbox Ser.). (ENG.). 56p. (gr. 2-3). pap. 7.99 (978-1-4966-0259-6(5), Legends in Their Own Lunchbox) Capstone Classroom.

Bandsuh, Jim. Helmet Hank. 2007. (Illus.). (J). per. 15.99 (978-1-933156-19-4(8), Visikid Bks.) GSVQ Publishing.

Banks, Kate. Max's Castle. Kulikov, Boris, illus. 2011. (Max's Words Ser.: 3). (ENG.). 40p. (J). (gr. -1-3). 18.99 (978-0-374-39919-1(0), 9780374399191, Farrar, Straus & Giroux (BYR)) Farrar, Straus & Giroux.

—Max's Dragon. Kulikov, Boris, illus. 2008. (Max's Words Ser.: 2). (ENG.). 32p. (J). (gr. -1-3). 17.99 (978-0-374-39921-4(2), 9780374399214, Farrar, Straus & Giroux (BYR)) Farrar, Straus & Giroux.

Barba, Ale. Time Out! Barba, Ale, illus. 2017. (ENG., Illus.). 32p. (J). (gr. -1-2). 16.99 **(978-0-399-16304-3(2)**, Philomel Bks.) Penguin Young Readers Group.

Barcelo, François. My Daddy's Footsteps. Mongeau, Marc, illus. 2009. (My First Stories Ser.). 24p. (J). (gr. -1-3). 22.60 (978-1-60754-359-6(1)); pap. 8.15 (978-1-60754-360-2(5)) Windmill Bks.

—My Mommy's Hands. Mongeau, Marc, illus. 2009. (My First Stories Ser.). 24p. (J). (gr. -1-3). 22.60 (978-1-60754-362-6(1)); pap. 8.15 (978-1-60754-365-7(6)) Windmill Bks.

Barnett, Brandi. Glamour. 2008. 231p. 19.95 (978-1-930709-68-3(4)) HAWK Publishing Group.

Barnett, Mac. Sam & Dave Dig a Hole. 2015. (JPN.). (J). (978-4-7515-2714-6(2)) Asunaro Shobo.

—Sam & Dave Dig a Hole. Klassen, Jon, illus. 2014. (ENG.). 40p. (J). (gr. -1-3). 16.99 (978-0-7636-6229-5(1)) Candlewick Pr.

—Sam & Dave Dig a Hole. 2014. (CHI.). (J). (gr. -1-3). pap. (978-986-241-935-9(0)) Common Wealth.

—Sam & Dave Dig a Hole. 2014. (CHI.). 32p. (J). (gr. -1-3). (978-7-5332-8178-6(0)) Mingtian Chubanshe.

Barrett, Nana. A Terrible Case of the Collywobbles! 2008. 16p. pap. 24.95 (978-1-4241-9603-6(5)) America Star Bks.

Barulich-Liederbach, Terri & Liederbach, Tom. The Memory Chair. 2010. 48p. pap. 19.49 (978-1-4520-5672-2(2)) AuthorHouse.

Base, Graeme. Eye to Eye. Base, Graeme, illus. 2015. (ENG., Illus.). 42p. (J). (gr. -1-1). 24.99 **(978-0-670-07859-2(X))** Random Hse. Australia AUS. Dist: Independent Pubs. Group.

Base, Graeme. The Legend of the Golden Snail. 2010. (ENG., Illus.). 48p. (J). (gr. k-2). 21.95 (978-0-8109-8965-8(4), Abrams Bks. for Young Readers) Abrams, Inc.

Bassett, Alisa Cuthbertson. Threads of Time. 2013. 24p. pap. 24.95 (978-1-63000-063-9(9)) America Star Bks.

Bazile, Lanetta R. Painted Shapes What Will They Make? 2009. 24p. pap. 12.50 (978-0-557-09217-8(5)) Lulu Pr., Inc.

Beaty, Andrea. Artist Ted. Lemaître, Pascal, illus. 2012. (ENG.). 32p. (J). (gr. -1-3). 17.99 (978-1-4169-5374-6(4), McElderry, Margaret K. Bks.) McElderry, Margaret K. Bks.

—Doctor Ted. Lemaître, Pascal, illus. 2008. (ENG.). 32p. (J). (gr. -1-3). 17.99 (978-1-4169-2820-1(0), McElderry, Margaret K. Bks.) McElderry, Margaret K. Bks.

—Firefighter Ted. Lemaître, Pascal, illus. 2009. (ENG.). 32p. (J). (gr. -1-3). 17.99 (978-1-4169-2821-8(9), McElderry, Margaret K. Bks.) McElderry, Margaret K. Bks.

Becker, Michele Joy. What If Marshmallows Fell from the Sky. Joslin, Irene, illus. 2009. 32p. pap. 12.99 (978-1-4389-0152-7(6)) AuthorHouse.

Becker, Savan. Starry Night (2nd Edition) 2008. 60p. pap. 25.95 (978-0-615-23554-7(9)) Becker, Savan C.

Beddor, Frank. ArchEnemy: The Looking Glass Wars, Book Three, 3 vols. 2010. (Looking Glass Wars Ser.: 3). (ENG.). 384p. (YA). (gr. 7-18). 9.99 (978-0-14-241689-1(4), Speak) Penguin Young Readers Group.

—Seeing Redd. (Looking Glass Wars Ser.: 2). (ENG.). (YA). (gr. 7-18). 2008. 400p. 9.99 (978-0-14-241209-1(0), Speak) 2007. (Illus.). 384p. 17.99 (978-0-8037-3155-4(8), Dial Bks) Penguin Young Readers Group.

Bedford, David. The Copy Crocs, 1 vol. Bolam, Emily, illus. 2015. (ENG.). 32p. (J). (gr. -1-3). pap. 7.95 (978-1-56145-885-1(6)) Peachtree Pubs.

Behind My Eyelids. 2005. (J). 15.00 (978-0-9773608-0-2(6)) Shiny Red Ball Publishing.

Beiko, S. M. The Lake & the Library. l.t. ed. 2013. 542p. pap. (978-1-4596-6871-3(5)) ReadHowYouWant.com, Ltd.

Beletic, Kittie Nesius. What Color Is Your Dream? 2007. (Illus.). 44p. (J). 16.95 (978-1-933285-56-6(7)) Brown Books Publishing Group.

Bell, Holly. Ethan Goes Green. Sidwell, Kathy, illus. 2009. 32p. pap. 12.99 (978-1-4389-0115-2(1)) AuthorHouse.

Bell, Lucy J. Rufus Loses His Cape. Garton, Michael, illus. 2017. (J). 12.99 **(978-1-5064-1788-2(4)**, Sparkhouse Family) Augsburg Fortress, Pubs.

Bell, Wade. No Place Fit for a Child. 2009. (Prose Ser.: 80). (ENG.). 144p. 18.00 (978-1-55071-266-7(7)) Guernica Editions, Inc. CAN. Dist: Univ. of Toronto Pr.

Benavides, Desiree. Little Henry's Adventures: Henry's Trip to the Supermarket. 2008. 24p. pap. 24.95 (978-1-60563-011-3(X)) America Star Bks.

Benchmark Education Co., LLC. Look at Me! Big Book. 2014. (Shared Reading Foundations Ser.). (J). (gr. -1). (978-1-4509-9421-7(0)) Benchmark Education Co.

Bencomo, Martin. Paloma Padilla. 2010. 32p. (J). (978-0-9790350-3-6(1)) Star Fire.

Benedetto, K. & Barlow, J. I See the World. 2009. pap. (978-1-61584-125-7(3)) Independent Pub.

Bennett, Kelly. One Day I Went Rambling. Murphy, Terri, illus. 2012. (ENG.). 24p. (J). (gr. k-3). 17.95 (978-1-936474-06-6(9)) Bright Sky Pr.

Bentley, Jonathan, illus. Little Big. 2015. (ENG.). 32p. (J). 16.00 (978-0-8028-5462-9(1), Eerdmans Bks For Young Readers) Eerdmans, William B. Publishing Co.

Bently, Peter. King Jack & the Dragon. Oxenbury, Helen, illus. 2011. (ENG.). 32p. (J). (gr. -1-k). 17.99 (978-0-8037-3698-6(3), Dial Bks) Penguin Young Readers Group.

—King Jack & the Dragon Board Book. Oxenbury, Helen, illus. 2013. (ENG.). 14p. (J). (gr. -1 — 1). bds. 7.99 (978-0-8037-3987-1(7), Dial Bks) Penguin Young Readers Group.

Berenstain, Mike. The Berenstain Bears Are SuperBears! Berenstain, Mike, illus. 2015. (I Can Read Level 1 Ser.). (ENG., Illus.). 32p. (J). (gr. -1-3). pap. 3.99 (978-0-06-235006-4(0)) HarperCollins Pubs.

Berger, Susan J. Growing up Dreams. Bell, Samantha, illus. 2010. 24p. pap. 10.95 (978-1-61633-029-3(5)) Guardian Angel Publishing, Inc.

Bernabe, Victor. What to Be When I Grow Up. Bernabe, Tabitha Victoria, illus. 2008. 28p. pap. 24.95 (978-1-60703-696-8(7)) America Star Bks.

Best, Cari. If I Could Drive, Mama. Shin, Simone, illus. 2016. (ENG.). 40p. (J). 17.99 (978-0-374-30205-4(7), 9780374302054, Farrar, Straus & Giroux (BYR)) Farrar, Straus & Giroux.

Bill Henry Edge. Blip & the Seat of Arthur. 2009. 500p. pap. 24.99 (978-1-4389-5971-9(0)) AuthorHouse.

Bishop, Sherry & Bishop, Meghan. Leopold the Leprechaun: A Story of Imagination. 2012. 36p. pap. 20.99 (978-1-4389-3119-7(0)) AuthorHouse.

Blabey, Aaron. The Dreadful Fluff. 2017. (ENG.). 32p. (J). (gr. -1-k). pap. 9.99 **(978-0-14-350700-0(1))** Random Hse. Australia AUS. Dist: Independent Pubs. Group.

Black, Michael Ian. I'm Bored. Ohi, Debbie Ridpath, illus. 2012. (ENG.). 40p. (J). (gr. -1-3). 17.99 (978-1-4424-1403-7(0), Simon & Schuster Bks. For Young Readers) Simon & Schuster Bks. For Young Readers.

—The Purple Kangaroo. Brown, Peter, illus. 2009. (ENG.). 32p. (J). (gr. -1-3). 16.99 (978-1-4169-5771-3(5), Simon & Schuster Bks. For Young Readers) Simon & Schuster Bks. For Young Readers.

—Qué Aburrido! 2014. (SPA.). 36p. (J). (gr. k-1). pap. 16.95 (978-1-933032-90-0(1)) Lectorum Pubns., Inc.

Blackburn, Sheila M. Stewie Scraps & the Star Rocket. 2008. 76p. pap. (978-1-903853-87-0(7)) Brilliant Pubns.

Blake, Christine & Lopez, Jill. Signs, Signs, Everywhere Signs. 2008. 32p. pap. 15.95 (978-1-4327-2523-5(8)) Outskirts Pr., Inc.

Blanc, Katherine & Ebbeler, Jeffrey. Melvin the Mouth. Mottram, Dave, illus. 2017. (ENG.). 32p. (J). (gr. -1-3). lib. bdg. 16.99 (978-1-58089-714-3(2)) Charlesbridge Publishing, Inc.

Blevins-Counts, Charlotte. A Pot Full of Te. 2009. 24p. pap. 12.95 (978-1-59858-962-7(8)) Dog Ear Publishing, LLC.

Blevins, Wiley. Big Box of Shapes. Kreloff, Elliott, illus. 2016. (Basic Concepts Ser.). (ENG.). 24p. (J). (gr. -1-1). lib. bdg. 14.99 (978-1-63440-082-4(8)) Red Chair Pr.

Blexbolex, creator. Ballad. 2013. (ENG., Illus.). 280p. (J). (gr. -1). 22.95 (978-1-59270-137-7(X)) Enchanted Lion Bks., LLC.

Bliss, Barbara. Abigail Elliot & the Dollhouse Family. 2008. (ENG.). 258p. pap. 9.99 (978-1-4196-7615-4(6)) CreateSpace Independent Publishing Platform.

Bloom, Suzanne. A Mighty Fine Time Machine. Bloom, Suzanne, illus. 2014. (ENG., Illus.). 32p. (J). (gr. k-2). pap. 6.95 (978-1-62091-605-6(3)) Boyds Mills Pr.

—A Mighty Fine Time Machine. 2009. (ENG., Illus.). 32p. (J). (gr. -1-2). 16.95 (978-1-59078-527-0(4)) Boyds Mills Pr.

Blume, Judy. Starring Sally J. Freedman As Herself. 2014. (ENG., Illus.). (J). (gr. 3-7). 384p. 17.99 (978-1-4814-1437-1(2)); 400p. pap. 7.99 (978-1-4814-1355-8(4)) Simon & Schuster Children's Publishing. (Atheneum Bks. for Young Readers).

Boiger, Alexandra, Max & Marla. Boiger, Alexandra, illus. 2015. (ENG., Illus.). 32p. (J). (-k). 17.99 (978-0-399-17504-6(0), G.P. Putnam's Sons Books for Young Readers) Penguin Young Readers Group.

Bond, Tammy. I Wish of Things That I Could Be. 2003. 32p. pap. 9.00 (978-0-8059-5919-2(X)) Dorrance Publishing Co., Inc.

Bowater, Alan. A Pig Called Pete. Pascoe, Pete, illus. 2009. (Pig Called Pete Ser.). 32p. (J). (gr. -1-2). 22.60 (978-1-60754-558-3(6)); pap. 10.55 (978-1-60754-559-0(4)) Windmill Bks.

Bowman, Patty. The Amazing Hamweenie Escapes! Bowman, Patty, illus. 2015. (Amazing Hamweenie Ser.: 2). (ENG., Illus.). 32p. (J). (gr. k-3). 16.99 (978-0-399-25689-9(X), Philomel Bks.) Penguin Young Readers Group.

Bowser, Kimberly M. The Circus Dogs. 2012. 20p. pap. 24.95 (978-1-4626-6524-2(1)) America Star Bks.

The Box. 2012. (ENG.). 30p. (J). (gr. -1-k). 16.95 (978-1-60537-134-4(3)) Cobblestone Publishing Co.

Boyce, Frank Cottrell. The Astounding Broccoli Boy. 2015. 384p. (J). (gr. 3-7). 16.99 (978-0-06-240017-8(7), Walden Pond Pr.) HarperCollins Pubs.

Boyd, G. A. Alchemy Jones & the Source of Magic. 2011. 324p. (gr. -1). 29.95 (978-1-4620-2234-2(0)); pap. 19.95 (978-1-4620-2232-8(4)) iUniverse, Inc.

Bradfield, Roger. Hello, Rock. 2012. (ENG., Illus.). 28p. (J). 9.95 (978-1-930900-64-6(3)) Purple Hse. Pr.

—¡Hola, Piedrita!/Hello, Rock. 2012. (SPA., Illus.). 25p. (J). (gr. -1-3). 9.95 (978-1-930900-65-3(1)) Purple Hse. Pr.

Bradford, Danette J. Eric & Wrinkles Meet the Snacker Sneakers. 2013. 24p. pap. 24.95 (978-1-4626-9990-2(1)) America Star Bks.

Bradley, A. M. Finnegan's Magic Sunglasses. 2013. 24p. pap. 24.95 (978-1-62709-814-4(3)) America Star Bks.

Branchaud, R. Gary. Toasty Town! 2011. 64p. pap. 19.50 (978-1-60976-039-7(5), Eloquent Bks.) Strategic Book Publishing & Rights Agency (SBPRA).

Brand, Brandon. Lily Is... Wide Awake. 2008. 32p. (J). 16.00 (978-0-9802329-0-5(2)) Upside Down Tree Publishing.

Branda, Barnabus. Myself, I & Me. Villella, Jessica, illus. 2013. 28p. pap. 24.95 (978-1-63004-064-2(9)) America Star Bks.

Branford, Anna. Violet Mackerel's Brilliant Plot. Allen, Elanna, illus. 2012. (Violet Mackerel Ser.). (ENG.). 112p. (J). (gr. 1-5). 15.99 (978-1-4424-3585-8(2)); pap. 5.99 (978-1-4424-3586-5(0)) Simon & Schuster Children's Publishing. (Atheneum Bks. for Young Readers).

Brennan-Nelson, Denise & Brennan, Rosemarie. Willow. Moore, Cyd, illus. 2008. (ENG.). 32p. (J). (gr. k-6). 16.95 (978-1-58536-342-1(1)) Sleeping Bear Pr.

Brewer, Michelle. Sunrise in My Cup. 2011. 28p. (gr. -1). pap. 13.99 (978-1-4567-3995-9(6)) AuthorHouse.

Briscoe, Holly. The Boy in the Shower. 2008. 25p. 16.50 (978-1-4357-1506-6(3)) Lulu Pr., Inc.

Britt, Paige. The Lost Track of Time. 2016. (ENG.). 320p. (J). (gr. 3-7). pap. 9.99 (978-0-545-53813-8(0), Scholastic Pr.) Scholastic, Inc.

—The Lost Track of Time. White, Lee, illus. 2015. (ENG.). 320p. (J). (gr. 3-7). 17.99 (978-0-545-53812-1(2), Scholastic Pr.) Scholastic, Inc.

Brittany's Books, illus. & creator. I Can Too! African American Girls. Brittany's Books, creator. 2006. 44p. (J). lib. bdg. 9.95 (978-0-9778796-8-7(2)) Brittany's Bks.

The Broken Plant. 2007. pap. 8.00 (978-0-9769152-2-5(7)) Feed My Sheep Bks.

Brooks, Donna. The Amazing Apple Tree. 2011. 40p. pap. 16.95 (978-1-61204-563-4(4), Strategic Bk. Publishing) Strategic Book Publishing & Rights Agency (SBPRA).

Brooks, Elizabeth. Montefiore's Goddaughter. 2012. (ENG.). 304p. (YA). (gr. 4-6). 15.95 (978-1-84982-099-8(6)) MP Publishing Ltd. GBR. Dist: Midpoint Trade Bks., Inc.

Brooks-Scrivanich, Olivia. Fiscal Pear & Shimmer in the Call of River Whale. 2008. (ENG.). 92p. pap. 14.99 (978-1-4196-9589-6(4)) CreateSpace Independent Publishing Platform.

Brown. The Wondrous Worlds of the Wishing Well, 1 vol. 2009. 46p. pap. 24.95 (978-1-60749-779-0(4)) America Star Bks.

Browne, Anthony. What If... ? Browne, Anthony, illus. 2014. (ENG., Illus.). 32p. (J). (gr. k-3). 16.99 (978-0-7636-7419-9(2)) Candlewick Pr.

Bruss, Deborah. Big Box for Ben, 1 vol. Bogacki, Tomek, illus. 2011. (ENG.). 16p. (J). (gr. -1-k). bds. 6.95 (978-1-59572-265-2(3)) Star Bright Bks., Inc.

Bulkowski, James. O'Briah: A Bedtime Story. 2011. 64p. pap. 8.95 (978-1-4620-1333-3(3)) iUniverse, Inc.

Bunce, Margaret. Adventures with Nature: A Story about Olivia & Her Little Dog, Jake. 2011. 24p. pap. 12.95 (978-1-4567-2497-9(5)) AuthorHouse.

Bunting, Eve. Pirate Boy. Fortenberry, Julie, illus. (ENG.). 32p. (J). (gr. -1-2). 2012. pap. 7.99 (978-0-8234-2546-4(0)) 2011. 16.95 (978-0-8234-2321-7(2)) Holiday Hse., Inc.

Burbank, Vivian. My Grandma's Playhouse. 2010. 29p. (J). pap. 17.95 (978-1-4327-5112-8(3)) Outskirts Pr., Inc.

Burks II, Tony Lamair. The Tale of Imani the Bunny. 2013. 24p. pap. 14.95 (978-1-62646-460-5(X)) Booklocker.com, Inc.

Burlinson, J. Imagination Goodnight. Perron, Debra, illus. 2005. 24p. (J). 14.95 (978-1-59879-068-9(4)) Lifevest Publishing, Inc.

Burningham, John. There's Going to Be a Baby. Oxenbury, Helen, illus. 48p. (J). 2014. (ENG.). (-k). 7.99 (978-0-7636-7265-2(3)) 2010. (978-0-7445-4996-6(5)) 2010. (ENG.). (gr. -1-k). 16.99 (978-0-7636-4907-4(4)) Candlewick Pr.

Burns, Catherine Lloyd. The Half-True Lies of Cricket Cohen. 2017. (ENG.). 256p. (J). 16.99 (978-0-374-30041-8(0), 9780374300418, Farrar, Straus & Giroux (BYR)) Farrar, Straus & Giroux.

Burwitz, Patrick. Mia's Dogcow. 2009. 28p. pap. 13.00 (978-1-4343-8580-2(9)) AuthorHouse.

Busch, Jean. Colleen & the Willow Fairy. 2008. 48p. pap. 16.95 (978-1-60672-212-1(3)) America Star Bks.

Bush, Laura & Hager, Jenna Bush. Read All about It! Brunkus, Denise, illus. 2008. 32p. (J). (gr. -1-3). (ENG.). 17.99 (978-0-06-156075-0(8)); lib. bdg. 18.89 (978-0-06-156076-7(6)) HarperCollins Pubs.

Calhoun, Dia. Eva of the Farm. Slater, Kate, illus. 2012. (ENG.). 256p. (J). (gr. 4-7). 16.99 (978-1-4424-1700-7(5), Atheneum Bks. for Young Readers) Simon & Schuster Children's Publishing.

Cali, Davide & Chaud, Benjamin. A Funny Thing Happened at the Museum ... 2017. (ENG., Illus.). 44p. (J). (gr. 1-4). 12.99 (978-1-4521-5593-7(3)) Chronicle Bks. LLC.

Cali, Davide & Chaud, Benjamin. A Funny Thing Happened on the Way to School... 2015. (ENG., Illus.). 44p. (J). (gr. 1-4). 12.99 (978-1-4521-3168-9(6)) Chronicle Bks. LLC.

Callahan, Michael P. Daddy Daddy, It's Time for Bed! 2009. 24p. pap. 12.99 (978-1-4389-1288-2(9)) AuthorHouse.

Callahan, Sean. A Wild Day with Dad. Howarth, Daniel, illus. 2012. (ENG.). 18p. (J). (gr. -1 — 1). bds. 7.99 (978-0-8075-2295-0(3)) Whitman, Albert & Co.

Camacho, Celi C. Bedtime for Meaghan. 2008. 33p. pap. 24.95 (978-1-60563-527-9(8)) America Star Bks.

Capucilli, Alyssa Satin. Ralph & the Rocket Ship. Cole, Henry, illus. 2016. (Ready-To-Reads Ser.). (ENG.). 24p. (J). (gr. -1-1). pap. 3.99 (978-1-4814-5866-5(3), Simon Spotlight) Simon Spotlight.

Cardwell, Michelle. Seeing the World Through Different Eyes. 2009. 32p. pap. 12.99 (978-1-4389-9776-6(0)) AuthorHouse.

Carle, Eric & Mack, Jeff. The Nonsense Show. Carle, Eric, illus. 2015. (ENG., Illus.). 40p. (J). (gr. -1-2). bds. 18.99 (978-0-399-17687-6(X), Philomel Bks.) Penguin Young Readers Group.

Carlson, Nancy. Henry's Amazing Imagination. 2010. (ENG.). 32p. (J). (gr. -1-1). pap. 6.99 (978-0-14-241605-1(3), Puffin Books) Penguin Young Readers Group.

—This Morning Sam Went to Mars: A Book about Paying Attention. 2013. (ENG., Illus.). 32p. (J). (gr. -1-3). 12.99 (978-1-57542-433-0(9)) Free Spirit Publishing, Inc.

Carmony, Crystal. Ima Gene's Imagination. 2008. 24p. pap. 14.49 (978-1-4389-0557-0(2)) AuthorHouse.

Carpenter, Lynette Stutzman. My Brother, the Senator. 2010. 40p. pap. 16.95 (978-1-4497-0629-6(0), WestBow Pr.) Author Solutions, Inc.

Carroll, Claudia. Shmadiggle & the Imagination Asteroid. 2008. 68p. pap. 9.95 (978-0-557-01566-5(9)) Lulu Pr., Inc.

Carroll, Lewis, pseud. Alice's Adventures in Wonderland: With a Discussion of Imagination. Schneider, Rex, tr. Schneider, Rex, illus. 2003. (J). (978-1-59203-046-0(7)) Learning Challenge, Inc.

Carter, Brei. Delia Goes to Dreamland. 2011. 36p. pap. 18.99 (978-1-4520-5001-0(5)) AuthorHouse.

Casagrande, Jerry. The Birthday Train. 2012. 24p. pap. 14.49 (978-1-4772-1050-5(4)) AuthorHouse.

Caviezel, Giovanni. Ballerina. Mesturini, C., illus. 2011. (Mini People Shape Bks.). (ENG.). 10p. (J). bds. 5.99 (978-0-7641-6436-1(8)) Barron's Educational Series, Inc.

—Builder. Mesturini, C., illus. 2011. (Mini People Shape Bks.). (ENG.). 10p. (J). bds. 5.99 (978-0-7641-6437-8(6)) Barron's Educational Series, Inc.

—Cowboy. Mesturini, C., illus. (Mini People Shape Bks.). (ENG.). (J). 2011. 10p. bds. 5.99 (978-0-7641-6438-5(4)) 2009. 12p. (gr. -1-2). bds. 10.99 (978-0-7641-6191-9(1)) Barron's Educational Series, Inc.

—Farmer. Mesturini, C., illus. 2011. (Mini People Shape Bks.). (ENG.). 10p. (J). bds. 5.99 (978-0-7641-6439-2(2)) Barron's Educational Series, Inc.

Cervi, Isaac. Pockets. 2008. 20p. pap. 12.50 (978-1-4389-0368-2(5)) AuthorHouse.

Chabon, Michael. The Astonishing Secret of Awesome Man. Parker, Jake, illus. 2011. (ENG.). 40p. (J). (gr. -1-3). 17.99 (978-0-06-191462-1(2)) HarperCollins Pubs.

Chabot, Jacob. Hello Kitty: Work of Art. 2014. lib. bdg. 18.40 (978-0-606-36123-1(5)) Turtleback Bks.

—Hello Kitty: Work of Art. McGinty, Ian et al, illus. 2014. (ENG.). 64p. (J). pap. 7.99 (978-1-4215-7542-1(6)) Viz Media.

Chast, Roz. Around the Clock. Chast, Roz, illus. 2015. (ENG., Illus.). 32p. (J). (gr. -1-3). 18.99 (978-1-4169-8476-4(3), Atheneum Bks. for Young Readers) Simon & Schuster Children's Publishing.

Chatterton, Martin. The Brain Finds a Leg. 2007. 207p. (978-1-921049-79-8(0)) Little Hare Bks. AUS. Dist: HarperCollins Pubs. Australia.

—The Brain Finds a Leg, 1 vol. 2009. (ENG.). 224p. (YA). (gr. 5-9). 16.95 (978-1-56145-503-4(2)) Peachtree Pubs.

Child, Lauren. Slightly Invisible. Child, Lauren, illus. 2011. (Charlie & Lola Ser.). (ENG., Illus.). 40p. (J). (gr. -1-2). 16.99 (978-0-7636-5347-7(0)) Candlewick Pr.

Chisholm, Donneisha Dee. The Baby Patch. 2012. 28p. pap. 24.95 (978-1-4626-8885-2(3)) America Star Bks.

Choo, Missy. What Color Is Monday. 2010. 32p. pap. 17.25 (978-1-4269-3070-6(4)) Trafford Publishing.

Christian, Lmh. Stories from the Red Glass. 2008. 48p. pap. 14.95 (978-0-9798154-9-2(5)) Living Waters Publishing Co.

Christian Mauricio Constante. What a Catch! 2009. 24p. pap. 11.49 (978-1-4389-6423-2(4)) AuthorHouse.

Chronicle Books Staff & Leuck, Laura. For Just One Day. Boutavant, Marc, illus. 2009. (ENG.). 32p. (J). (gr. -1 — 1). 16.99 (978-0-8118-5610-2(0)) Chronicle Bks. LLC.

Church, Caroline Jayne. Here Comes Christmas! Church, Caroline Jayne, illus. 2010. (ENG., Illus.). 14p. (J). (gr. k — 1). bds. 7.99 (978-0-545-11817-0(4), Cartwheel Bks.) Scholastic, Inc.

Clanton, Ben. Something Extraordinary. Clanton, Ben, illus. 2015. (ENG., Illus.). 40p. (J). (gr. -1-3). 17.99 (978-1-4814-0358-0(3), Simon & Schuster Bks. For Young Readers) Simon & Schuster Bks. For Young Readers.

Clark, M. H. I Can Fly? 2013. (Story Lines Ser.). (ENG.). 32p. (J). (gr. -1-3). 9.95 (978-1-935414-95-7(X)) Compendium, Inc., Publishing & Communications.

—No Birthday Cake for Me. Riedler, Amelia, ed. 2013. (Story Lines Ser.). (ENG.). 24p. (J). (gr. -1-3). 9.95 (978-1-935414-96-4(8)) Compendium, Inc., Publishing & Communications.

Cleary, Beverly. Emily's Runaway Imagination. Krush, Beth et al, illus. 2008. (Cleary Reissue Ser.). (ENG.). 288p. (J). (gr. 3-7). pap. 6.99 (978-0-380-70923-6(6)) HarperCollins Pubs.

—Emily's Runaway Imagination. 221p. (J). (gr. 2-4). pap. 4.95 *(978-0-8072-1416-9(7)*, Listening Library) Random Hse. Audio Publishing Group.
Clegg, Maryanne & Bester, Maryanne. Why Dog Is Afraid of Storms. Bester, Shayle, illus. 2012. (ENG.). 32p. (J). (gr. -1-k). pap. 12.95 *(978-1-4314-0219-9(2))* Jacana Media ZAF. Dist: Independent Pubs. Group.
Clemesha, David & Zimmerman, Andrea. Fire Engine Man. Clemesha, David & Zimmerman, Andrea, illus. 2007. (ENG., Illus.). 32p. (J). (gr. -1-k). 17.99 *(978-0-8050-7905-0(X)*, 9780805079050, Holt, Henry & Co. Bks. For Young Readers) Holt, Henry & Co.
Clemson, C. J. Charlie Mcbly & the Long Walk Home. 2010. 24p. pap. 14.93 *(978-1-4269-4771-1(2))* Trafford Publishing.
Coakley, Lena. Worlds of Ink & Shadow. 2016. (ENG.). 352p. (YA). (gr. 8-17). 17.95 *(978-1-4197-1034-6(6)*, Amulet Bks.) Abrams, Inc.
Cofer, Judith Ortiz. The Poet Upstairs. Ortiz, Oscar, illus. 2012. (J). (gr. 5-9). 16.95 *(978-1-55885-704-9(4)*, Piñata Books) Arte Publico Pr.
—La Poeta Del Piso de Arriba. Baeza Ventura, Gabriela, tr. from ENG. Ortiz, Oscar, illus. 2014. (SPA.). (J). 17.95 *(978-1-55885-788-9(5)*, Piñata Books) Arte Publico Pr.
Coiner, Tea Railene. Hear the Song of the Fairies. 2009. 74p. pap. 19.95 *(978-1-61582-833-3(8))* America Star Bks.
Colbert, Cory. Sammy the Sea Otter Makes New Friends: Adventures of Sammy the Sea Otter. 2011. 18p. pap. 11.95 *(978-1-4327-7648-0(7))* Outskirts Pr., Inc.
Cole, Gina, illus. Adapt. 2005. 40p. (J). 17.00 *(978-0-9659538-3-2(1))* Soul Vision Works Publishing.
Colfer, Chris. The Land of Stories: an Author's Odyssey. 2017. (Land of Stories Ser.: 5). (ENG., Illus.). 464p. (J). (gr. 3-7). pap. 9.99 ***(978-0-316-38321-9(X))*** Little, Brown Bks. for Young Readers.
Colfer, Eoin. Imaginary Fred. Jeffers, Oliver, illus. 2015. (ENG.). 48p. (J). (gr. -1-3). 18.99 *(978-0-06-237955-9(0))* HarperCollins Pubs.
Collingridge, Richard. Lionheart. 2016. (ENG., Illus.). 32p. (J). (gr. -1-k). 17.99 *(978-0-545-83321-9(3))* Scholastic, Inc.
Collins, Michael. Anu & the Blue. 2009. 166p. pap. 16.68 *(978-0-557-20316-1(3))* Lulu Pr., Inc.
Colón, Raúl. Draw! Colón, Raúl, illus. 2014. (ENG., Illus.). 40p. (J). (gr. -1-3). 17.99 *(978-1-4424-9492-3(1)*, Simon & Schuster/Paula Wiseman Bks.) Simon & Schuster/Paula Wiseman Bks.
Condon, Bill. Race to the Moon, 1 vol. rev. ed. 2013. (Fiction Readers Ser.). (ENG., Illus.). 28p. (J). (gr. 3-3). pap. 8.99 *(978-1-4333-5605-6(8))* Shell Educational Publishing.
—Race to the Moon. rev. ed. 2013. (Fiction Readers Ser.). (ENG., Illus.). 28p. (gr. 3-3). pap. 19.96 *(978-1-4807-1727-5(4))* Teacher Created Materials, Inc.
Conford, Ellen. Jenny Archer, Author. Palmisciano, Diane & Brooks, Erik, illus. 2006. (ENG.). 64p. (J). (gr. 1-4). per. 12.99 *(978-0-316-01487-8(7))* Little, Brown Bks. for Young Readers.
Connell, Julie. The Adventures of Cutie Pie & Mr. Squishy. 2008. 12p. pap. 24.95 *(978-1-60703-826-9(9))* America Star Bks.
Conner, Sharon Landsberg. The Magnetizing Princess: A children's story that uses some of the most powerful tools available, to get more of what you Want. 2007. 56p. per. 8.95 *(978-0-595-44229-4(3))* iUniverse, Inc.
Connor, David. Archie & Billy in Monster Cave. 2011. (Illus.). 40p. 18.68 *(978-1-4567-7308-3(9))* AuthorHouse.
Cook, Gary. The Best Saturday Ever! Sward, Adam, illus. 2013. (Robbie's Big Adventures Ser.). (ENG.). 40p. (J). (gr. k-3). 15.95 *(978-1-938063-25-1(2)*, Mighty Media Kids) Mighty Media Pr.
Cooley, Judy. Mom Says I Can. 2008. (Illus.). 32p. (J). (gr. -1-3). lib. bdg. 17.95 *(978-1-59038-872-3(0)*, Shadow Mountain) Shadow Mountain Publishing.
Cordell, Matthew. Dream. Cordell, Matthew, illus. 2017. (Wish Ser.). (ENG., Illus.). 48p. (J). (gr. -1-k). 16.99 *(978-1-4847-7340-6(3))* Hyperion Bks. for Children.
Coro, Edys. Edys' Collection of Short Tales. 2008. 64p. pap. 19.95 *(978-1-60672-856-7(3))* America Star Bks.
Cosgrove, Stephen. Snugg N. Flitter: Facing Your Fears. Arroyo, Fian, illus. 2004. (J). *(978-1-58804-377-1(0))* P C I Education.
Coster, Simon. My Dinosaur Is More Awesome! 2015. (ENG., Illus.). 48p. (J). (gr. -1-k). 16.99 *(978-1-63220-416-5(9)*, Sky Pony Pr.) Skyhorse Publishing Co., Inc.
Cotter, Bill. Don't Touch This Book! 2016. (ENG., Illus.). (J). 28p. bds. 6.99 *(978-1-4926-4804-8(3)*, 9781492648048); 32p. 16.99 *(978-1-4926-3224-5(4)*, 9781492632245) Sourcebooks, Inc. (Sourcebooks Jabberwocky).
Cowan, Catherine. My Life with the Wave. 2004. (Illus.). (J). (gr. k-3). spiral bd. *(978-0-616-01621-3(2))* Canadian National Institute for the Blind/Institut National Canadien pour les Aveugles.
—My Life with the Wave. Buehner, Mark, illus. 2004. (ENG.). 32p. (J). (gr. -1-3). reprint ed. pap. 7.99 *(978-0-06-056200-7(5))* HarperCollins Pubs.
Cowen-Fletcher, Jane. Nell's Elf. Cowen-Fletcher, Jane, illus. 2006. (ENG., Illus.). 32p. (J). (gr. -1-3). 14.99 *(978-0-7636-2391-3(1))* Candlewick Pr.
Cowley, Joy. Little Dan. 2009. pap. 8.25 *(978-1-60559-225-1(0))* Hameray Publishing Group, Inc.
Coyle, Carmela Lavigna. Do Superheroes Have Teddy Bears? Gordon, Mike, illus. 2012. (ENG.). 32p. (J). (gr. -1-2). 15.95 *(978-1-58979-693-5(4))* Taylor Trade Publishing.
Crabtree, Sally. Magic Train Ride. Esplugas, Sonia & Esplugas, Sonia, illus. 2007. (ENG.). 32p. (J). (gr. -1-k). 6.99 *(978-1-84686-132-1(2))* Barefoot Bks., Inc.
—Magic Train Ride. Esplugas, Sonia, illus. (Barefoot Singalongs Ser.). (J). 2007. (ENG.). 32p. (gr. -1-k). pap. 9.99 *(978-1-905236-91-6(3))* 2006. 0032p. 16.99 *(978-1-905236-52-7(2))* Barefoot Bks., Inc.
Crawford-Haynes, Debra. Bedtime with Julian. 2010. 32p. 16.99 *(978-1-4520-6943-2(3))* AuthorHouse.
Crayon, Paula. Mittens in the Attic. 2010. 40p. pap. 18.99 *(978-1-4520-9218-8(4))* AuthorHouse.
Creech, Sharon. Fishing in the Air. Raschka, Chris, illus. 2003. (ENG.). 32p. (J). (gr. -1-3). pap. 6.99 *(978-0-06-051606-2(2))* HarperCollins Pubs.
—Fishing in the Air. Raschka, Chris, illus. 2003. pap. 9.95 incl. audio *(978-1-59112-223-4(6))* Live Oak Media.
—Fishing in the Air. 2003. (J). (gr. k-3). 17.20 *(978-0-613-66967-2(3)*, Turtleback) Turtleback Bks.
Crespo, Ana. JP & the Bossy Dinosaur: Feeling Unhappy. Sirotich, Erica, illus. 2016. (My Emotions & Me Ser.). (ENG.). 32p. (J). (gr. -1-3). 16.99 *(978-0-8075-3981-1(3))* Whitman, Albert & Co.
—JP & the Giant Octopus: Feeling Afraid. Sirotich, Erica, illus. 2015. (My Emotions & Me Ser.). (ENG.). 32p. (J). (gr. -1-3). 16.99 *(978-0-8075-3975-0(9))* Whitman, Albert & Co.
—JP & the Polka-Dotted Aliens: Feeling Angry. Sirotich, Erica, illus. 2015. (My Emotions & Me Ser.). (ENG.). 32p. (J). (gr. -1-3). 16.99 *(978-0-8075-3977-4(5))* Whitman, Albert & Co.
—JP & the Stinky Monster: Feeling Jealous. Sirotich, Erica, illus. 2016. (My Emotions & Me Ser.). (ENG.). 32p. (J). (gr. -1-3). 16.99 *(978-0-8075-3979-8(1))* Whitman, Albert & Co.
Cresse, Peter. The Bloody Hand. 2009. (Illus.). 40p. pap. 18.95 *(978-1-4389-2161-7(6))* AuthorHouse.
Criscuolo, Jill. I Want To... Coloring Book. 2013. 48p. (gr. -1). pap. 9.89 *(978-1-4669-7625-2(X))*; 40p. (gr. 4-6). pap. 16.46 *(978-1-4669-7629-0(2))* Trafford Publishing.
Crockett, Johns. Harold et le crayon Rose. pap. 13.95 *(978-2-266-09592-1(7))* Presses Pocket FRA. Dist: Distribooks, Inc.
Cruz, Kelly De La. Super Boy's Adventurous Imagination: Let your imagination Flow. 2010. 50p. pap. 26.99 *(978-1-4500-3867-6(0))* Xlibris Corp.
Cua, Marcus Loo. How the Hungry T-Rex Got Fixed. 2012. 24p. pap. 28.03 *(978-1-4653-9643-3(8))* Xlibris Corp.
Cuartas, Jennifer M. So Many Things. 2012. 28p. 24.95 *(978-1-4626-6328-6(1))* America Star Bks.
Cushenberry, Lisa. No Tears for Teary. 2009. 84p. pap. 9.99 *(978-1-60860-556-9(6)*, Strategic Bk. Publishing) Strategic Book Publishing & Rights Agency (SBPRA).
Custer, Jason. Everyday Monsters. 2005. (J). lib. bdg. 19.95 *(978-0-9754728-3-5(6))* Big Ransom Studio.
DaCosta, Barbara. Nighttime Ninja. 2012. (ENG., Illus.). 32p. (J). (gr. -1-3). 16.99 *(978-0-316-20384-5(X))* Little, Brown Bks. for Young Readers.
Daddo, Andrew. When I Grow Up. Bentley, Jonathan, illus. 2017. 32p. 17.99 *(978-0-7333-3341-5(9))* ABC Bks. AUS. Dist: HarperCollins Pubs.
Dahl, Michael. Bedtime for Batman. Beavers, Ethen, illus. 2016. (DC Super Heroes Ser.). (ENG.). 32p. (gr. -1-2). 15.95 *(978-1-62370-732-3(3))*; lib. bdg. 22.65 *(978-1-5158-0652-3(9))* Stone Arch Bks. (DC Super Heroes).
Damiron, Anya. Dreamboy. Pino, Pablo, illus. 2010. (SPA.). 26p. (J). *(978-9945-421-42-2(5))* Lucia Stories.
—Inventor Boy. Pino, Pablo, illus. 2010. (SPA.). 26p. (J). *(978-9945-00-157-0(4))* Lucia Stories.
—Nino Inventor. Pino, Pablo, illus. 2010. 26p. (J). *(978-9945-00-153-2(1))* Lucia Stories.
Daniels, Kristine. Floyd & the Irresistible Cookie. 2009. 32p. pap. 18.00 *(978-1-60844-276-8(4))* Dog Ear Publishing, LLC.
Danowski, Edwin K. The Green Turkey & Other Holiday Classics: (for Kids of All Ages & All Seasons Plus Reflections from the Heart -for Those a Little Older) 2007. 284p. per. 27.95 *(978-1-4241-8271-8(9))* America Star Bks.
Davenport, Kelly. Do Hotdogs Grow on Trees? 2010. 32p. pap. 17.99 *(978-1-4520-6636-3(1))* AuthorHouse.
David, Kate. Murphy & the Magical Hat. 2012. (ENG.). 26p. (J). 18.95 *(978-1-4327-8582-6(6))* Outskirts Pr., Inc.
Davidson, Susanna. Princess Handbook. Gordon, Mike, illus. 2006. 80p. (J). (gr. 3-7). 12.99 *(978-0-7945-1329-0(8)*, Usborne) EDC Publishing.
Davis, Helen J. Good Times with Gregory: Airplanes: A Visit to A 747. Davis, Robyn L., illus. 2008. (Good Times with Gregory Ser.). 37p. (J). (gr. -1-4). 12.95 *(978-1-935122-11-1(8))* K&B Products.
Davis, Jacky. The Amazing Adventures of Bumblebee Boy. Soman, David, illus. 2011. (Ladybug Girl Ser.). (ENG.). 40p. (J). (gr. -1-k). 16.99 *(978-0-8037-3418-0(2)*, Dial Bks) Penguin Young Readers Group.
—Ladybug Girl. Soman, David, illus. 2015. (Ladybug Girl Ser.). (ENG.). 40p. (J). (-k). 18.99 *(978-1-101-99433-7(9)*, Dial Bks) Penguin Young Readers Group.
—Ladybug Girl & the Best Ever Playdate. Soman, David, illus. 2015. (Ladybug Girl Ser.). (ENG.). 40p. (J). (gr. -1-k). 17.99 *(978-0-8037-4030-3(1)*, Dial Bks) Penguin Young Readers Group.
Davis, Jacky & Soman, David. Ladybug Girl. Soman, David, illus. 2008. (Ladybug Girl Ser.). (ENG., Illus.). 40p. (J). (gr. -1-k). 17.99 *(978-0-8037-3195-0(7)*, Dial Bks) Penguin Young Readers Group.
—Ladybug Girl & Bumblebee Boy. Soman, David, illus. 2009. (Ladybug Girl Ser.). (ENG., Illus.). 40p. (J). (gr. -1-k). 17.99 *(978-0-8037-3339-8(9)*, Dial Bks) Penguin Young Readers Group.
—Ladybug Girl & the Big Snow. Soman, David, illus. 2013. (Ladybug Girl Ser.). (ENG., Illus.). 40p. (J). (gr. -1-k). 17.99 *(978-0-8037-3583-5(9)*, Dial Bks) Penguin Young Readers Group.
—Ladybug Girl Loves... Soman, David, illus. 2010. (Ladybug Girl Ser.). (ENG., Illus.). 12p. (J). (gr. -1 — 1). bds. 5.99 *(978-0-448-45374-3(6)*, Grosset & Dunlap) Penguin Young Readers Group.
—Ladybug Girl Makes Friends. Soman, David, illus. 2012. (Ladybug Girl Ser.). (ENG., Illus.). 12p. (J). (gr. -1 — 1). bds. 5.99 *(978-0-448-45764-2(4)*, Grosset & Dunlap) Penguin Young Readers Group.
—Ladybug Girl Plays. Soman, David, illus. 2013. (Ladybug Girl Ser.). (ENG., Illus.). 14p. (J). (gr. -1 — 1). bds. 5.99 *(978-0-8037-3892-8(7)*, Dial Bks) Penguin Young Readers Group.
—Super Catarina y los Super Insectos. Soman, David, illus. 2012. (Ladybug Girl Ser.).Tr. of Ladybug Girl & the Bug Squad. (ENG & SPA., Illus.). 40p. (J). (gr. -1-k). mass mkt. 6.99 *(978-0-14-242582-4(6)*, Puffin Books) Penguin Young Readers Group.
Dean, Lani. One Misty Morning. Cassidy, Al, illus. 2004. 36p. (J). 14.95 *(978-0-9645844-9-5(2))* Manor Hse. Publishing Co., Inc.
DeFelice, Cynthia C. The Ghost of Fossil Glen. 2010. (Ghost Mysteries Ser.: 1). (ENG.). 192p. (J). (gr. 3-7). pap. 7.99 *(978-0-312-60213-0(8)*, 9780312602130) Square Fish.
Degen, Bruce. I Said, Bed! Degen, Bruce, illus. (I Like to Read(r) Ser.). (ENG., Illus.). 24p. (J). (gr. -1-2). 2015. 6.99 *(978-0-8234-3311-7(0))* 2014. 14.95 *(978-0-8234-2938-7(5))* Holiday Hse., Inc.
Delcoglin, Gwen. Bella's Umbrella. Delcoglin, Nathan, illus. 2007. 28p. (J). (gr. -1-3). per. 10.99 *(978-1-59879-315-4(2))* Lifevest Publishing, Inc.
Demarest, Chris L. My Blue Boat. 20th ed. 2014. (J). 18.95 *(978-1-930900-76-9(7))* Purple Hse. Pr.
DeMatteis, J. M. Imaginalis. 2010. (ENG.). 256p. (J). (gr. 3-7). 16.99 *(978-0-06-173286-7(9)*, Tegen, Katherine Bks) HarperCollins Pubs.
Denman, K. L. Stuff We All Get, 1 vol. 2011. (Orca Currents Ser.). (ENG.). 128p. (J). (gr. 5-9). pap. 9.95 *(978-1-55469-820-2(0))*; lib. bdg. 16.95 *(978-1-55469-821-9(9))* Orca Bk. Pubs. USA.
DePalma, Johnny. The Raindrop Keeper. Crabapple, Molly, illus. 2006. (J). per. 8.50 *(978-0-9791127-1-3(0))* Umbrelly Bks.
—The Raindrop Keeper: (Limited Edition Hardcover) Crabapple, Molly, illus. 2006. 50p. (J). 16.50 *(978-0-9791127-2-8(8))* Umbrelly Bks.
Derby, Sally. Sunday Shopping, 1 vol. Strickland, Shadra, illus. 2015. (ENG.). 32p. (J). 17.95 *(978-1-60060-438-6(2)*, 9781600000000) Lee & Low Bks., Inc.
Derrick, David G., Jr. Animals Don't, So I Won't! 2012. (ENG., Illus.). 36p. (J). (gr. -1-3). 15.95 *(978-1-59702-029-9(X))* Immedium.
Devol, Laura. To Be a Frog. Boone, Patti, illus. 2010. 20p. pap. 12.95 *(978-1-60910-278-4(9))* Booklocker.com, Inc.
Dewane, Patrick Ryan. What If the Rain Were Bugs? Konecny, John, illus. 2013. 24p. 14.99 *(978-1-937165-39-0(6))* Orange Hat Publishing.
Dipucchio, Kelly. Super Manny Stands Up! Graegin, Stephanie, illus. 2017. (Super Manny Ser.). (ENG.). 40p. (J). (gr. -1-3). 17.99 *(978-1-4814-5960-0(0))* Simon & Schuster Children's Publishing.
Dixon, Amy. Sophie's Animal Parade. Wish, Katia, illus. 2015. (ENG.). 32p. (J). (gr. -1-k). 16.99 *(978-1-63220-403-5(7)*, Sky Pony Pr.) Skyhorse Publishing Co., Inc.
Docherty, Thomas. To the Beach. Docherty, Thomas, illus. 2009. (ENG., Illus.). 40p. (J). (gr. -1-2). 15.99 *(978-0-7636-4429-1(3)*, Templar) Candlewick Pr.
Doerrfeld, Cori. Maggie & Wendel: Imagine Everything! Doerrfeld, Cori, illus. 2016. (ENG., Illus.). 48p. (J). (gr. -1-3). 17.99 *(978-1-4814-3974-9(X)*, Simon & Schuster Bks. For Young Readers) Simon & Schuster Bks. For Young Readers.
Donahue, Bill. Grandma Wentworth's Children's Storybooks, Volume One. 2007. 56p. per. 16.95 *(978-1-4241-3269-0(X))* PublishAmerica, Inc.
Doodler, Todd H. Super Rawr! Doodler, Todd H., illus. 2016. (ENG., Illus.). 40p. (J). (gr. -1-k). 12.99 *(978-0-545-79969-0(4)*, Scholastic Pr.) Scholastic, Inc.
Doors, Mason. The I T I P. 2012. 36p. pap. 20.99 *(978-1-4772-2046-7(1))* AuthorHouse.
Dorling Kindersley Publishing Staff. Playtime. 2016. (Skills for Starting School Ser.). (ENG.). 18p. (J). (-k). 13.99 *(978-1-4654-5132-3(3)*, DK Children) Dorling Kindersley Publishing, Inc.
Dorman, Brandon, illus. The Slippery Map. 2007. 288p. (J). (gr. 3-7). lib. bdg. 17.89 *(978-0-06-079109-4(8))* HarperCollins Pubs.
Dormer, Frank W. The Sword in the Stove. Dormer, Frank W., illus. 2016. (ENG., Illus.). 40p. (J). (gr. -1-3). 17.99 *(978-1-4814-3167-5(6))* Simon & Schuster, Inc.
Douglas, Atom. Mathew's Space Ship. Douglas, Atom, . 2007. (Illus.). 32p. (J). 6.50 *(978-0-9798316-0-7(1))* JaxPublishing.net.
Dove, S. R. Gabriel the First Christmas Dragon, 1 vol. 2009. 39p. pap. 24.95 *(978-1-60836-855-6(6))* America Star Bks.
Doyle, Teresa J. The Dream Box: Big Dreams for Little Sleepers. 2008. 84p. pap. 26.95 *(978-1-4343-9086-8(1))* AuthorHouse.
Dream Catchers - Evaluation Guide: Evaluation Guide. 2006. (J). *(978-1-55942-403-5(6))* Witcher Productions.
Duerr, Doug. The Adventures of Jazz & Elliott: Danielle goes to the Magical Land of Roop-E-Doo. 2010. 29p. (J). pap. 17.95 *(978-1-4327-5405-1(X))* Outskirts Pr., Inc.
Duley, Wayla C. Strawberry Soup & Other Crazy Things. 2013. 28p. pap. 24.95 *(978-1-63000-952-6(0))* America Star Bks.
Durst, Sarah Beth. Roar & Sparkles Go to School. Whitehouse, Ben, illus. 2017. (ENG.). 40p. (J). (gr. -1-1). 16.99 ***(978-0-7624-5986-5(7)***, Running Pr.) Running Pr. Bk. Pubs.
Duty, William. Boomtown: Darkpit Mountain & the Princess Three, 1 vol. 2010. 76p. pap. 19.95 *(978-1-4489-5971-6(3))* America Star Bks.
Duvall, Sheila Marie. I See Fun. 2009. 16p. pap. 8.75 *(978-1-4389-4963-5(4))* AuthorHouse.
Dyan, Penelope. Ben's Adventures — -Proof Positive That Boys Will Be Boys. Dyan, Penelope. 2008. (Illus.). 44p. pap. 11.95 *(978-1-935118-40-4(4))* Bellissima Publishing, LLC.
—The Day an Elephant Flies! Dyan, Penelope, illus. 2013. (Illus.). 34p. pap. 11.95 *(978-1-61477-113-5(8))* Bellissima Publishing, LLC.
—Did You Call? 2011. 34p. pap. 11.95 *(978-1-935630-78-4(4))* Bellissima Publishing, LLC.
—The Hatchling, the Story of Stegi Stegosaurus. Dyan, Penelope, illus. 2010. (Illus.). 42p. pap. 11.95 *(978-1-935630-08-1(3))* Bellissima Publishing, LLC.
Dyan, Peneope. Bunny Ears. Dyan, Penelope, illus. 2011. 34p. pap. 11.95 *(978-1-935630-68-5(7))* Bellissima Publishing, LLC.
D'yans, Masha. Razzle-Dazzle Ruby. D'yans, Masha, illus. 2011. (ENG., Illus.). 20p. (J). (— 1). bds. 17.99 *(978-0-545-22500-7(0))* Scholastic, Inc.
E. O., Monalisa. Dan & Derrick's Prayer to the Troops. 2007. 36p. per. 16.95 *(978-1-4327-0753-8(1))* Outskirts Pr., Inc.
Eaton, Deborah J. My Wild Woolly. Karas, G. Brian, illus. 2005. (Green Light Readers Level 2 Ser.). (ENG.). 24p. (J). (gr. -1-3). pap. 3.95 *(978-0-15-205147-1(3))* Houghton Mifflin Harcourt Publishing Co.
—My Wild Woolly. Karas, G. Brian, illus. 2005. (Green Light Readers Level 2 Ser.). (gr. k-2). 13.95 *(978-0-7569-5445-1(2))* Perfection Learning Corp.
Ebbers, Susan M. Jamie's Journey: The Savannah. Godbey, Cory, illus. 2012. 38p. 17.99 *(978-0-9833971-8-2(X))*; pap. 9.99 *(978-0-9833971-9-9(8))* Rowe Publishing and Design.
Ebeltoft, Christine. Koo & Jay in the Rainforest. 2004. 34p. pap. 24.95 *(978-1-4137-3698-4(X))* PublishAmerica, Inc.
Eddy, Catherine J. Sandbox Sandshoes. Krupnek, Joann J., illus. 2009. 38p. pap. 10.95 *(978-0-9818488-5-3(0))* Ajoyin Publishing, Inc.
Eddy, Olympia. Mysterious View. 2010. 20p. pap. 13.99 *(978-1-60844-423-6(6))* Dog Ear Publishing, LLC.
Edwards, Cindi. Imagination Rocks. Bruner, Justine, illus. 2009. 28p. pap. 13.99 *(978-1-4490-0386-9(9))* AuthorHouse.
Ehlert, Lois. Rain Fish. Ehlert, Lois, illus. 2016. (ENG., Illus.). 40p. (J). (gr. -1-3). 17.99 *(978-1-4814-6152-8(4)*, Beach Lane Bks.) Beach Lane Bks.
Ehrlich, Amy, ed. When I Was Your Age Vols. I & II: Original Stories about Growing Up. 2012. (ENG., Illus.). 352p. (J). (gr. 4-7). pap. 14.99 *(978-0-7636-5892-2(8))* Candlewick Pr.
Einhorn, Kama. Olivia Imagines: A Carryalong Treasury. 2011. (Olivia TV Tie-In Ser.). (ENG.). 22p. (J). (gr. -1-1). 14.99 *(978-1-4424-2048-9(0)*, Simon Spotlight) Simon Spotlight.
Eisen, Laura. Clouds for Breakfast. Cissna, Kent, illus. 2013. 60p. pap. 14.95 *(978-0-9882113-4-6(3))*; pap. 14.95 *(978-0-9882113-7-7(8))* StarryBks.
—Nubes para Desayunar. Cissna, Kent, illus. 2013. 60p. pap. 14.95 *(978-0-9882113-2-2(7))* StarryBks.
Ellery, Amanda. If I Were a Jungle Animal. Ellery, Tom, illus. 2009. (ENG.). 40p. (J). (gr. -1-3). 17.99 *(978-1-4169-3778-4(1)*, Simon & Schuster Bks. For Young Readers) Simon & Schuster Bks. For Young Readers.
Elzina, Philda. Purple Is the Magic Colour. 2008. 36p. pap. 12.95 *(978-1-4327-1805-3(3))* Outskirts Pr., Inc.
Eman, Leisa M. Pugsley's Imagination. 2007. 52p. per. 8.95 *(978-0-595-44247-8(1))* iUniverse, Inc.
Emily Reed-Guldin, Reed-Guldin & Emily Reed-Guldin. Sarah & Sammi's Playhouse Bedroom. 2009. 32p. pap. 14.49 *(978-1-4389-5881-1(1))* AuthorHouse.
Empson, Jo. Never Ever. Empson, Jo, illus. 2013. (Child's Play Library). (ENG., Illus.). 32p. (J). *(978-1-84643-552-2(8))* Child's Play International Ltd.
Escoffier, Michaël. The Day I Lost My Superpowers. Di Giacomo, Kris, illus. 2014. (ENG.). 32p. (J). (gr. -1-3). 16.95 *(978-1-59270-144-5(2))* Enchanted Lion Bks., LLC.
—A Mammoth in the Fridge. 2013. (ENG.). 36p. 16.95 *(978-1-877579-50-9(5))* 21st Century Publishing.
Espinosa, Marta Catalina Vanni. Testigos 25 D - Y Mas. 2010. 56p. pap. 23.95 *(978-1-61764-285-2(1))* AuthorHouse.
Espluga, Maria. I Am a Ballerina. 2009. (I Am A... (Alphabet Soup) Ser.). (Illus.). 24p. (J). (gr. k-1). pap. 8.15 *(978-1-60754-252-0(8))*; lib. bdg. 22.60 *(978-1-60754-251-3(X))* Windmill Bks.
Estes-Hill, Katrina. My Imagination. Kwong, Alvina, illus. 2007. 32p. (J). (gr. -1-2). 15.95 *(978-0-9745715-6-0(3))* KRBY Creations, LLC.
Eulate, Ana. Life Is Beautiful! 2013. (ENG., Illus.). 28p. (J). (gr. -1-k). 16.95 *(978-84-15619-26-0(X))* Eastern National.
—The Sky of Afghanistan. 2012. (ENG., Illus.). 24p. (J). (gr. k-2). *(978-84-15503-04-0(0))* D P & G Military Pubs.
Evans, Dustin, illus. Costume Craziness, 1 vol. 2013. (Mystical Pencil Ser.). (ENG.). 32p. (J). (gr. 3-6). 28.50 *(978-1-61641-926-4(1))* Magic Wagon.
—Dinosaur Drama, 1 vol. 2013. (Mystical Pencil Ser.). (ENG.). 32p. (J). (gr. 3-6). 28.50 *(978-1-61641-927-1(X))* Magic Wagon.
—A Medieval Mess, 1 vol. 2013. (Mystical Pencil Ser.). (ENG.). 32p. (J). (gr. 3-6). 28.50 *(978-1-61641-928-8(8))* Magic Wagon.
—Raging Robots, 1 vol. 2013. (Mystical Pencil Ser.). (ENG.). 32p. (J). (gr. 3-6). 28.50 *(978-1-61641-929-5(6))* Magic Wagon.
Evans, Yvette Kemp. If I Take a Shower. 2008. 32p. pap. 24.95 *(978-1-4241-9953-2(0))* America Star Bks.
Fabrizio, T. L. Natalie Bean. 2011. 28p. pap. 24.95 *(978-1-4626-0645-0(8))* America Star Bks.
Fagan, Cary. Ella May & the Wishing Stone. Cote, Genevieve, illus. 2011. (ENG.). 32p. (J). (gr. -1-1). 17.95 *(978-1-77049-225-7(9)*, Tundra Bks.) Tundra Bks. CAN. Dist: Penguin Random Hse. LLC.
—I Wish I Could Draw, 1 vol. 2014. (ENG., Illus.). 32p. (J). (gr. k-3). 12.95 *(978-1-55498-318-6(5))* Groundwood Bks. CAN. Dist: Publishers Group West (PGW).
Falwell, Cathryn. Word Wizard. 2006. (ENG., Illus.). 32p. (J). (gr. -1-3). pap. 7.99 *(978-0-618-68924-8(9))* Houghton Mifflin Harcourt Publishing Co.
Fardell, John. The Day Louis Got Eaten. Fardell, John, illus. 2012. (Andersen Press Picture Bks). (ENG., Illus.). 32p. (J). (gr. -1-3). 16.95 *(978-1-4677-0315-4(X))* Lerner Publishing Group.
Farkle, Sandy. The Day the Gummies Wrecked: Square Bears Race the Fakers. 2011. 88p. pap. 19.95 *(978-1-4560-4242-4(4))* America Star Bks.
Fearnley, Jan. A Special Something. 2004. (Illus.). 32p. 7.95 *(978-0-7497-4639-1(4))* Egmont Bks., Ltd. GBR. Dist: Trafalgar Square Publishing.
Feiffer, Jules. I'm Not Bobby! Feiffer, Jules, illus. 2006. (Illus.). 28p. (J). (gr. k-4). reprint ed. 16.00 *(978-0-7567-9853-6(1))* DIANE Publishing Co.
Fenton, Joe. What's under the Bed? Fenton, Joe, illus. 2008. (ENG., Illus.). 32p. (J). (gr. -1-2). 15.99 *(978-1-4169-4943-5(7)*, Simon & Schuster Bks. For Young Readers) Simon & Schuster Bks. For Young Readers.
Fenwick, Carol. Jenell & the Berry Thicket Village. 2011. 36p. pap. 15.75 *(978-1-4634-5016-8(8))* AuthorHouse.
—Jennell & the Horse in the Enchanted Valley. 2011. 32p. pap. 12.95 *(978-1-4634-4445-7(1))* AuthorHouse.
Fernandes, Eugenie. Waves in the Bathtub. 2015. (ENG., Illus.). 32p. (J). (gr. -1-k). 16.99 *(978-1-63220-429-5(0)*, Sky Pony Pr.) Skyhorse Publishing Co., Inc.
Filoche, Eric. Hey ! We're Talking about Ourselves ! 2013. 68p. pap. *(978-2-9538737-4-0(0))* Koshkindom.
Fine, Anne. Countdown. 2006. (Yellow Bananas Ser.). (ENG., Illus.). 48p. (J). (gr. -1-3). lib. bdg. *(978-0-7787-0958-9(2))* Crabtree Publishing Co.
Finney, Jefferson. Clever Dog. Hopper, Pegge, illus. 2007. 32p. (J). pap. 15.95 *(978-1-56647-845-8(6))* Mutual Publishing LLC.

H
I

Fleming, Geronda. Among the Fairies. 2008. 149p. pap. 14.00 *(978-0-615-16737-4(3))* Faye Bks.

Fleming, K. C. What If? 2011. 36p. (gr. -1). pap. 15.50 *(978-1-4634-0756-8(4))* AuthorHouse.

Flesher, Brandon. Shattered Dreams in Light. 2014. (J). *(978-1-938237-10-2(2))* Skywater Publishing Co.

Flyte, Min. Box. Beardshaw, Rosalind, illus. 2016. (ENG.). 26p. (J). (gr. -1-2). 15.99 *(978-0-7636-8939-1(4),* Nosy Crow) Candlewick Pr.

Fontaine, Renee. Boy in the Hoodie. Margolis, Al, illus. 2012. 34p. (J). 19.95 *(978-1-61863-105-3(5))* Bookstand Publishing.

Fontes, Justine. Jordan's Silly Sick Day. Lee, Jared, tr. Lee, Jared, illus. 2004. (Rookie Readers Ser.). 31p. (J). 19.50 *(978-0-516-25897-3(4),* Children's Pr.) Scholastic Library Publishing.

Ford, Martyn. The Imagination Box. 2016. (ENG.). 240p. (J). (gr. 4-7). 16.99 *(978-1-101-93627-6(4),* Delacorte Pr.) Random Hse. Children's Bks.

Fosberry, Jennifer. My Name Is Not Alexander. Litwin, Mike, illus. 2011. (ENG.). 32p. (J). (gr. k-3). 16.99 *(978-1-4022-5433-8(4),* Sourcebooks Jabberwocky) Sourcebooks, Inc.

—My Name Is Not Isabella. Litwin, Mike, illus. 2008. 32p. (J). (gr. -1-3). lib. bdg. 19.99 *(978-0-9802000-7-2(5))* Monkey Barrel Pr.

—My Name Is Not Isabella: Just How Big Can a Little Girl Dream? Litwin, Mike, illus. 2010. (ENG.). 32p. (J). (gr. k-3). 16.99 *(978-1-4022-4395-0(2),* Sourcebooks Jabberwocky) Sourcebooks, Inc.

Fox, Mem. Tell Me about Your Day Today. Stringer, Lauren, illus. 2012. (ENG.). 40p. (J). (gr. -1-3). 17.99 *(978-1-4169-9006-2(2),* Beach Lane Bks.) Beach Lane Bks.

Fraley, Patty. One Day I Will Grow Up. Worrell, Nicole, illus. 2013. 18p. pap. 7.75 *(978-1-4575-2142-3(3))* Dog Ear Publishing, LLC.

Francis, Jamaine. The Adventures of Pb & Brown Bear: Lost & Found. 2009. 28p. pap. 12.88 *(978-1-4490-1817-7(3))* AuthorHouse.

Frank, Connie. Sadie & the Night Sky, 1 vol. 2009. 24p. pap. 24.95 *(978-1-60703-911-2(7))* America Star Bks.

Frank, Hannah. The Train to Baker Street. 2008. 44p. pap. 19.49 *(978-1-4389-1026-0(6))* AuthorHouse.

Franklin, Teii L. Ameelia's Adventures: Ameelia's First Play. 2010. 32p. pap. 16.49 *(978-1-4520-3613-7(6))* AuthorHouse.

French, Cindy. A Loud Roar. 2012. 24p. pap. 11.50 *(978-1-61897-626-0(5),* Strategic Bk. Publishing) Strategic Book Publishing & Rights Agency (SBPRA).

Friend, David. With Any Luck, I'll Drive a Truck. Rex, Michael, illus. 2016. (ENG.). 32p. (J). (-k). 16.99 *(978-0-399-16956-4(3),* Nancy Paulsen Books) Penguin Young Readers Group.

Frisch, Aaron. A Night on the Range. Sheban, Chris, illus. (ENG.). 32p. (J). 2013. (gr. -1-17). pap. 7.99 *(978-0-89812-829-1(3),* Creative Paperbacks) 2010. (gr. 1-3). 19.99 *(978-1-56846-205-9(0),* Creative Editions) Creative Co., The.

—Pirates at the Plate. Summers, Mark, illus. 2012. (ENG.). 32p. (J). (gr. 1-3). 17.99 *(978-1-56846-210-3(7),* Creative Editions) Creative Co., The.

Fuchs, Menucha. Just a Pinch. 2004. (Illus.). 20p. (J). 6.95 *(978-1-932443-22-6(3),* JAPH) Judaica Pr., Inc., The.

Fulmer, Jeffrey. My Imagination Kit. Pickering, Jimmy, tr. Pickering, Jimmy, illus. 2003. (J). 24p. 15.95 *(978-1-59336-008-5(8));* 23p. pap. *(978-1-59336-009-2(6))* Mondo Publishing.

Galasso, Marina. I Wish. 2009. (Illus.). 24p. pap. 12.95 *(978-1-4269-1087-6(8))* Trafford Publishing.

Gall, Chris. Awesome Dawson. 2013. (ENG., Illus.). 40p. (J). (gr. -1-3). 17.99 *(978-0-316-21330-1(6))* Little, Brown Bks. for Young Readers.

Gammell, Stephen. Mudkin. Gammell, Stephen, illus. 2011. (Carolrhoda Picture Bks.). (ENG., Illus.). 32p. (J). (gr. k-3). 16.95 *(978-0-7613-5790-2(4))* Lerner Publishing Group.

Gan, Jessie Low. How Giraffe Got Spots. 2012. 24p. pap. 15.99 *(978-1-4797-1203-8(5))* Xlibris Corp.

Ganz-Schmitt, Sue. Planet Kindergarten. Prigmore, Shane, illus. (ENG.). (J). (gr. -1-k). 2016. 36p. 7.99 *(978-1-4521-5644-6(1))* 2014. 40p. 16.99 *(978-1-4521-1893-2(0))* Chronicle Bks. LLC.

—Planet Kindergarten. Prigmore, Shane, illus. 2014. 1.25 *(978-1-4906-3415-9(0));* 37.75 *(978-1-4906-3417-3(7));* 39.75 *(978-1-4906-3418-0(5))* Recorded Bks., Inc.

—Planet Kindergarten: 100 Days in Orbit. Prigmore, Shane, illus. 2016. (ENG.). 36p. (J). (gr. -1-k). 16.99 *(978-1-4521-3776-6(5))* Chronicle Bks. LLC.

Garcia, Victoria. I Imagine Things Because I Picture Myself There: Imagino Cosas... Porque Pienso Que Estoy Ah. 2012. 52p. pap. 24.99 *(978-1-4685-3697-3(4));* 64p. pap. 24.99 *(978-1-4685-3698-0(2))* AuthorHouse.

Garey, Barbara J. The Adventures of Princess Naomia, 1 vol. 2009. 32p. pap. 24.95 *(978-1-61546-090-8(X))* America Star Bks.

Garfein, Stanley Joe. Tales of the Temple Mice. 2006. (Illus.). 92p. (J). 14.95 *(978-0-9787422-0-1(6))* Garfein, Stanley.

Garrett, Christine. Dream Bunny's Tales - Saving the Land of Dreams. 2009. (Illus.). 48p. pap. 13.95 *(978-1-60860-451-7(9),* Eloquent Bks.) Strategic Book Publishing & Rights Agency (SBPRA).

Garrett, Diane Marie. Buger the Butterfly & the Lion Kitties' First Adventure. Gulley, Hardrick M., illus. 2008. 16p. pap. 24.95 *(978-1-60672-237-4(9))* America Star Bks.

Garton, Carol. The Land of Carin. 2007. 108p. 19.95 *(978-1-4327-1027-9(3));* 104p. per. 10.95 *(978-1-4327-1634-9(4))* Outskirts Pr., Inc.

Garton, Sam. Otter in Space. Garton, Sam, illus. 2015. (ENG., Illus.). 32p. (J). (gr. -1-3). 16.99 *(978-0-06-224776-6(X))* HarperCollins Pubs.

Gauch, Patricia Lee. Christina Katerina & the Box. 2012. (ENG.). 32p. (J). (gr. -1-3). 7.95 *(978-1-59078-915-5(6))* Boyds Mills Pr.

Gauthier, Pamela. The Adventures of Bernie the Moose: Bernie Meets Maria. 2009. 20p. pap. 10.49 *(978-1-4490-3019-3(X))* AuthorHouse.

Gay, Marie-Louise. Princess Pistachio, 1 vol. Homel, Jacob, tr. from FRE. Gay, Marie-Louise, illus. 2015. Orig. Title: Princesse Pistache. (ENG., Illus.). 48p. (J). (gr. k-3). 10.95 *(978-1-927485-69-9(X))* Pajama Pr. CAN. Dist: Ingram Publisher Services.

Geisert, Arthur, creator. The Giant Seed. 2012. (Stories Without Words Ser.). (ENG., Illus.). 32p. (J). (gr. -1-3). 14.95 *(978-1-59270-115-5(9))* Enchanted Lion Bks., LLC.

Geist, Christina. Buddy's Bedtime Battery. Bowers, Tim, illus. 2016. (ENG.). 40p. (J). (gr. -1-2). lib. bdg. 19.99 *(978-0-375-97468-7(7),* Random Hse. Bks. for Young Readers) Random Hse. Children's Bks.

Gemmen, Heather. But It's True. Lagares, Luciano, illus. 2004. (Tough Stuff for Kids Ser.). 36p. (J). (gr. 4-7). pap., pap. 5.99 *(978-0-7814-4033-2(5),* 0781440335) Cook, David C.

Gentry, Jennifer Mills. Maria the Cat, 1 vol. 2010. 24p. pap. 24.95 *(978-1-4489-7748-2(7))* PublishAmerica, Inc.

George, Audra. Vagabonding. George, Audra, illus. 2006. (Illus.). 32p. (J). (gr. -1-3). 17.95 *(978-1-60108-010-3(7))* Red Cygnet Pr.

Geraldine Anderson. Bev's Amazing Adventures: The Kitten. 2012. 28p. pap. 24.95 *(978-1-4626-7386-5(4))* America Star Bks.

Gerlach, Carolyn. Robert Lee. 2012. 24p. 24.95 *(978-1-4626-6031-5(2))* America Star Bks.

Gerstein, Mordicai. The First Drawing. 2013. (ENG., Illus.). 40p. (J). (gr. -1-3). 18.99 *(978-0-316-20478-1(1))* Little, Brown Bks. for Young Readers.

Giff, Patricia Reilly. The Big Something. Palmisciano, Diane, illus. 2012. (Fiercely & Friends Ser.). (ENG.). 40p. (J). (gr. -1-3). 16.99 *(978-0-545-43369-3(X))* Scholastic, Inc.

—Fiercely & Friends: the Sneaky Snow Fox. Palmisciano, Diane, illus. 2012. (Fiercely & Friends Ser.). (ENG.). 40p. (J). (gr. k-2). 16.99 *(978-0-545-43378-5(9),* Orchard Bks.) Scholastic, Inc.

Gilbert, Heather. Skyler the Pirate, 1 vol. 2009. 25p. pap. 24.95 *(978-1-60813-820-3(8))* America Star Bks.

Giorgio, Marg. Maxi's Magical Dream. 2011. 24p. pap. 12.79 *(978-1-4634-4491-4(5))* AuthorHouse.

Girnay, Aracelis. Changing, Changing: Story & Collages. Girmay, Aracelis, illus. 2005. (ENG., Illus.). 48p. (gr. 1-17). 19.95 *(978-0-8076-1553-9(6),* 761553) Braziller, George Inc.

Gittemeier, Tausha. Hmmm, I was Thinking... What If? 2004. 20p. pap. 24.95 *(978-1-4137-3429-4(4))* PublishAmerica, Inc.

Glavin, Kevin. All the Things You'll Do! Grepo, Sarah, illus. 2012. 80p. 17.95 *(978-0-9825466-3-5(7))* Glavin, Kevin.

Goddard, Mary Beth. How Would It Feel? Mycek-Wodecki, Anna, illus. 2005. (ENG.). 32p. (J). (gr. -1-6). 15.95 *(978-1-59143-050-6(X),* Bear Cub Bks.) Bear & Co.

Godin, Thelma Lynne. How to Dress a Dragon. Barclay, Eric, illus. 2016. (ENG.). 40p. (J). (gr. -1-k). 16.99 *(978-0-545-67846-9(3),* Scholastic Pr.) Scholastic, Inc.

Gomi, Taro. Over the Ocean. 2016. (ENG., Illus.). 36p. (J). (gr. -1 — 1). 16.99 *(978-1-4521-4515-0(6))* Chronicle Bks. LLC.

Gonsalves, Rob. Imagine a World. Gonsalves, Rob, illus. 2015. (Imagine A... Ser.). (ENG., Illus.). 48p. (J). (gr. -1-3). 17.99 *(978-1-4814-4973-1(7))* Simon & Schuster Canada CAN. Dist: Simon & Schuster, Inc.

Gonyea, Maria. Princess Maria. 2013. 28p. pap. 13.95 *(978-1-4525-8189-7(4),* Balboa Pr.) Author Solutions, Inc.

Gonzalez, Ada Acosta. Mayte & the Bogeyman/Mayte y el Cuco. Rodriguez, Christina, illus. 2006. (ENG & SPA.). 32p. (J). (gr. -1-2). 16.95 *(978-1-55885-442-0(8),* Piñata Books) Arte Publico Pr.

Gonzalez, Rigoberto & González, Rigoberto. Soledad Sigh-Sighs. Ibarra, Rosa, illus. 2014.Tr. of Soledad Suspiros. (ENG & SPA.). 32p. (J). pap. 8.95 *(978-0-89239-309-1(2),* Children's Book Press) Lee & Low Bks., Inc.

Goodhart, Pippa. Just Imagine. Sharratt, Nick, illus. 2014. 32p. (J). 12.99 *(978-1-61067-343-3(3))* Kane Miller.

Goodhart, Pippa & Sharratt, Nick. You Choose! (ENG., Illus.). 32p. (J). 19.99 *(978-0-385-60176-4(X),* Doubleday Children's) Random House Children's Books GBR. Dist: Trafalgar Square Publishing.

Goodman, Katie & Kisiel, Soren. The Night Our Parents Went Out. 2015. (ENG., Illus.). 32p. (J). (gr. -1-2). 16.95 *(978-1-57687-747-0(7),* powerHouse Bks.) powerHouse Cultural Entertainment, Inc.

Goodrich, Carter. We Forgot Brock! Goodrich, Carter, illus. 2015. (ENG., Illus.). 48p. (J). (gr. -1-3). 17.99 *(978-1-4424-8090-2(4),* Simon & Schuster Bks. For Young Readers) Simon & Schuster Bks. For Young Readers.

Goodrich, Murleen. Think! Pete. 2012. 16p. pap. 15.99 *(978-1-4685-8110-2(4))* AuthorHouse.

Goodwin, Aimee. A Fish Named Luke. 2011. 24p. 11.32 *(978-1-4567-3497-8(0))* AuthorHouse.

Gorbachev, Valeri. Doctor Nice. (ENG.). 32p. (J). (gr. -1-3). 2016. 6.99 *(978-0-8234-3690-3(X))* 2015. (Illus.). 16.95 *(978-0-8234-3203-5(3))* Holiday Hse., Inc.

Gore, Leonid. Danny's First Snow. Gore, Leonid, illus. 2007. (ENG., Illus.). 40p. (J). (gr. -1-2). 16.99 *(978-1-4169-1330-6(0),* Atheneum Bks. for Young Readers) Simon & Schuster Children's Publishing.

Gorey, Edward. The West Wing. 2009. (ENG., Illus.). 64p. 12.00 *(978-1-60819-064-5(1),* 9781608190645) Bloomsbury Publishing USA.

Goss, Leon. In Your Seat, Mr. Pete! Velez, Jill Ondercin, illus. 2005. (J). pap. *(978-1-933156-11-8(2));* per. 16.99 *(978-1-933156-04-0(X))* GSVQ Publishing. (VisionQuest Kids).

Gossett, Susan. A True Superhero. 2009. 28p. pap. 16.50 *(978-1-4490-3147-3(1))* AuthorHouse.

Gottschalk, Bre. The Lucky Necklace. 2011. 24p. pap. 11.99 *(978-1-4389-8725-5(0))* AuthorHouse.

Gould, Susan Lynn. A Gift from Grandma. Verkruysse, Toni, illus. 2013. 56p. pap. 20.50 *(978-1-61897-230-9(8),* Strategic Bk. Publishing) Strategic Book Publishing & Rights Agency (SBPRA).

Gownley, Jimmy. Amelia in Fireflies & Time, 1 vol. 2013. (Amelia Rules! Set 2 Ser.). (ENG.). 36p. (J). (gr. 3-6). 24.21 *(978-1-61479-069-3(8))* Spotlight.

Graham, Cheryl. A Special Project. 2010. (Illus.). 24p. (J). pap. 13.95 *(978-1-4327-4037-5(7))* Outskirts Pr., Inc.

Gray, Kes & Parsons, Garry. Billy's Bucket. 2003. (ENG., Illus.). 32p. (J). 24.95 *(978-0-370-32596-5(6))* Random Hse. GBR. Dist: Random Hse. of Canada.

Graziani, Mary. Fat Pigs Fly! 2007. 24p. per. 24.95 *(978-1-4241-8344-9(8))* America Star Bks.

Green, M. L. Underneath My Favorite Tree. 2008. 20p. pap. 24.95 *(978-1-60474-858-1(3))* America Star Bks.

Greer, Hannah. The Velvet Bag Memoirs, Bk. 1. 2008. 132p. pap. 24.95 *(978-1-60672-190-2(9))* America Star Bks.

Griffiths, Andy. The 13-Story Treehouse. Denton, Terry, illus. 2013. (Treehouse Bks.: 1). (ENG.). 256p. (J). (gr. 1-5). 13.99 *(978-1-250-02690-3(3),* 9781250026903) Feiwel & Friends.

—The 13-Story Treehouse. Denton, Terry, illus. 2015. (Treehouse Bks.: 1). (ENG.). 272p. (J). (gr. 1-5). pap. 6.99 *(978-1-250-07065-4(1),* 9781250070654) Square Fish.

—The 26-Story Treehouse. Denton, Terry, illus. 2014. (Treehouse Bks.: 2). (ENG.). 352p. (J). (gr. 1-5). 13.99 *(978-1-250-02691-0(1),* 9781250026910) Feiwel & Friends.

—The 39-Story Treehouse. Denton, Terry, illus. 2015. (Treehouse Bks.). (ENG.). 352p. (J). (gr. 1-5). 13.99 *(978-1-250-02692-7(X),* 9781250026927) Feiwel & Friends.

—The 39-Story Treehouse. Barcellona, Christine, ed. Denton, Terry, illus. 2016. (Treehouse Bks.: 3). (ENG.). 368p. (J). pap. 6.99 *(978-1-250-07511-6(4),* 9781250075116) Square Fish.

Griswold, Elaine. The Fairy Walk: A True Story of Imagination. 2013. 34p. pap. 14.95 *(978-1-4575-2394-6(9))* Dog Ear Publishing, LLC.

Groenewald, Catherine. I Could Be Anywhere. 2011. (ENG.). 16p. (J). (gr. 2-4). pap. 6.99 *(978-1-77009-833-6(X))* Jacana Media ZAF. Dist: Independent Pubs. Group.

Gross, S. D. Mugallumps. 2007. (Illus.). 32p. (J). per. 13.99 *(978-1-59879-303-1(9))* Lifevest Publishing, Inc.

Gurney, Stella. Sally Sets Sail. Worsley, Belinda, illus. 2009. (Get Ready (Windmill Books) Ser.). 32p. (J). (gr. k-2). lib. bdg. 22.60 *(978-1-60754-261-2(7))* Windmill Bks.

Guy, Ginger Foglesong. Go Back to Bed! Bernardin, James, illus. 2006. (ENG.). 32p. (J). (gr. k-3). 16.95 *(978-1-57505-750-7(6),* Carolrhoda Bks.) Lerner Publishing Group.

H & T Imaginations Unlimited, Inc. Kid's Sand Box Fun with Professor Woodpecker: Good Old Fashion Wholesome Fun Children's Story. 2008. 12p. pap. 8.49 *(978-1-4389-1116-8(5))* AuthorHouse.

—Sand Castles with Professor Woodpecker. 2009. 12p. pap. 8.49 *(978-1-4389-7262-6(8))* AuthorHouse.

Haesche, Richard Paul, Sr. My Pet Dinosaur. 2007. (ENG.). 60p. (J). 6.99 *(978-0-9800552-0-7(2))* Kreative X-Pressions Pubns.

Haft, Sheryl. I Love You, Blankie. Massey, Jane, illus. 2015. (ENG.). 22p. (J). (gr. -1 — 1). bds. 8.99 *(978-0-316-28356-4(8))* Little, Brown Bks. for Young Readers.

Hagin, Karen. If I Could Reach the Sky. 2005. (J). lib. bdg. 19.95 *(978-0-9754728-7-3(9))* Big Ransom Studio.

Hall, Michael. Cat Tale. Hall, Michael, illus. 2012. (ENG., Illus.). 40p. (J). (gr. -1-k). 16.99 *(978-0-06-191516-1(5),* Greenwillow Bks.) HarperCollins Pubs.

—It's an Orange Aardvark! Hall, Michael, illus. 2014. (ENG., Illus.). 40p. (J). (gr. -1-3). 17.99 *(978-0-06-225206-7(2),* Greenwillow Bks.) HarperCollins Pubs.

Hall, Tara. Good Girls Do. Raluca, Cristina Cirti, illus. 2013. 36p. pap. 9.99 *(978-1-61286-192-0(X))* Avid Readers Publishing Group.

Hamilton, Tim. The Big Fib. Hamilton, Tim, illus. (I Like to Read(r) Ser.). (ENG., Illus.). 24p. (J). (gr. -1-3). 2015. 6.99 *(978-0-8234-3312-4(9))* 2014. 14.95 *(978-0-8234-2939-4(3))* Holiday Hse., Inc.

Hamlin, Robyn Maria. Polly Dactyl's Magic Castle Missions. 2011. 64p. pap. 31.99 *(978-1-4628-5146-1(0))* Xlibris Corp.

Hammer. Willy's Wild Weekend: Friday. 2007. 30p. pap. 24.95 *(978-1-4241-8875-8(X))* America Star Bks.

Hampton, Patrick. Down by the Mulberry Tree, 1 vol. 2009. 15p. pap. 24.95 *(978-1-60703-672-2(X))* America Star Bks.

Hanlon, Abby. Dory & the Real True Friend. 2016. (Dory Ser.: 2). lib. bdg. 18.40 *(978-0-606-38846-7(X))* Turtleback Bks.

—Dory Fantasmagory. (Dory Fantasmagory Ser.: 1). (ENG.). (J). (gr. 1-3). 2015. Illus.). 176p. 7.99 *(978-0-14-751067-9(8),* Puffin Books) 2014. 160p. 14.99 *(978-0-8037-4088-4(3),* Dial Bks) Penguin Young Readers Group.

—Dory Fantasmagory. 2015. (Dory Ser.: 1). lib. bdg. 18.40 *(978-0-606-36746-2(2))* Turtleback Bks.

—The Real True Friend. 2015. (Dory Fantasmagory Ser.: 2). (ENG., Illus.). 160p. (J). (gr. 1-3). 14.99 *(978-0-525-42866-4(6),* Dial Bks) Penguin Young Readers Group.

Hanlon, Abigail & Hanlon, Abby. Dory Dory Black Sheep. 2016. (Dory Fantasmagory Ser.). (ENG., Illus.). 160p. (J). (gr. 1-3). 14.99 *(978-1-101-99426-9(6),* Dial Bks) Penguin Young Readers Group.

Hannigan, Katherine. Dirt + Water = Mud. Hannigan, Katherine, illus. 2016. (Illus.). 40p. (J). (gr. -1-3). 17.99 *(978-0-06-234517-2(6),* Greenwillow Bks.) HarperCollins Pubs.

Hannigan, Paula & Accord Publishing Staff. Music Star. Slade, Christian, illus. 2011. (ENG.). 16p. (J). (gr. -1-3). 14.99 *(978-1-4494-0173-3(2))* Andrews McMeel Publishing.

Hansen, Justin LaRocca. Monster Hunter. 2012. (ENG., Illus.). 32p. (J). (gr. -1-k). 16.95 *(978-1-61608-968-9(7),* 608968, Sky Pony Pr.) Skyhorse Publishing Co., Inc.

Hansen, Tevin. Hole in the Wall. Cochran, Shaun, illus. 2017. 300p. (J). 14.99 ***(978-1-941429-54-9(8))*** Handersen Publishing.

Hanson, Faye. The Wonder. Hanson, Faye, illus. 2015. (ENG., Illus.). 40p. (J). (gr. -1-2). 16.99 *(978-0-7636-7957-6(7),* Templar) Candlewick Pr.

Harger, Teresa. Nicky & the Princess. 2010. 20p. pap. 12.79 *(978-1-4520-6035-4(5))* AuthorHouse.

Harper, Charise Mericle. If Waffles Were Like Boys. Magoon, Scott, illus. 2011. (ENG.). 40p. (J). (gr. -1-1). 14.99 *(978-0-06-177998-5(9))* HarperCollins Pubs.

—Mae & June & the Wonder Wheel. Spires, Ashley, illus. 2017. (ENG.). 128p. (J). (gr. 1-4). 15.99 *(978-0-544-63063-5(7),* HMH Books For Young Readers) Houghton Mifflin Harcourt Publishing Co.

Harris, Angela L. Mommy What Is a Ceo? Chapman, Debbie, illus. 2013. 32p. pap. 10.00 *(978-0-615-62527-0(4))* ALHsicceeslines.

Harris, Dorothy Joan. Un Perro Muy Diferente. Rioja, Alberto Jimenez, tr. from ENG. LaFave, Kim, illus. 2006. (SPA.). 28p. (J). (gr. 5-6). pap. 7.99 *(978-1-933032-04-7(9))* Lectorum Pubns., Inc.

Harris, Shelly J. A Snowman's Love, 1 vol. 2009. 19p. pap. 24.95 *(978-1-60836-708-5(8))* America Star Bks.

Hartley, Steve. Oliver Fibbs & the Giant Boy-Munching Bugs. Lum, Bernice, illus. unabr. ed. 2015. (Oliver Fibbs Ser.: 2). (ENG.). 192p. (J). (gr. 2-5). pap. 8.99 *(978-1-4472-2024-4(2))* Pan Macmillan GBR. Dist: Independent Pubs. Group.

Hartnett, Edmond. Dreams. 2010. 28p. 16.09 *(978-1-4269-3812-2(8))* Trafford Publishing.

Hartnett, Sonya. Sadie & Ratz. James, Ann, illus. 2012. (ENG.). 64p. (J). (gr. k-3). 14.99 *(978-0-7636-5315-6(2))* Candlewick Pr.

Harvey, Matthea. The Little General & the Giant Snowflake. Zechel, Elizabeth, illus. 2009. (ENG.). 64p. (gr. 3-5). 10.95 *(978-0-9820539-1-1(6),* 982391) Tin Hse. Bks., LLC.

Haseley, Dennis. My Father Doesn't Know about the Woods & Me. 2013. (ENG., Illus.). 32p. (J). (gr. -1-3). 16.99 *(978-1-4814-0159-3(9),* Atheneum Bks. for Young Readers) Simon & Schuster Children's Publishing.

Hauser, Dana. Imagination's Amazing Planet, 1 vol. 2009. 24p. pap. 24.95 *(978-1-60703-873-3(0))* America Star Bks.

Hawk, J. L. If I Were a Creature under the Seaà. 2008. 12p. pap. 24.95 *(978-1-60703-378-3(X))* America Star Bks.

Hawthorn, Libby. Incredibilia. 2017. (ENG.). 40p. (J). (gr. -1-k). 17.99 ***(978-1-76012-525-7(3))*** Little Hare Bks. AUS. Dist: Independent Pubs. Group.

Hayes, Angela. Just an Existence, 1 vol. 2010. 50p. pap. 16.95 *(978-1-60749-035-7(8))* PublishAmerica, Inc.

Hayes, Geoffrey. Benny & Penny in Just Pretend, 1 vol. 2013. (Toon Bks). (ENG.). 36p. (J). (gr. 1-2). lib. bdg. 27.07 *(978-1-61479-148-5(1))* Spotlight.

Hearn, Jeff. Cutting Yards on Mars: Writer's Block. 2007. 172p. per. 15.95 *(978-1-4327-1688-2(3))* Outskirts Pr., Inc.

Heiman, Laura. My Favorite Michael. Keen, Sophie, illus. 2009. (J). (gr. -1-2). 32p. 15.95 *(978-1-58925-086-4(9));* 24p. pap. 7.95 *(978-1-58925-419-0(8))* Tiger Tales.

Heller, Alyson. Raggedy Ann's Beach Bag. Thomas, Laura, illus. 2009. (Raggedy Ann & Me! Ser.). (ENG.). 10p. (J). (gr. -1-k). bds. 5.99 *(978-1-4169-5546-7(1),* Little Simon) Little Simon.

Helliwell, Sheila. Gammy. Hawthorn, Paul & Hopkins, Simon, illus. 2nd ed. 2013. 70p. pap. *(978-0-9560331-4-7(8))* Children' Story Pubs.

Henkes, Kevin. My Garden. Henkes, Kevin, illus. 2010. (Illus.). 40p. (J). (gr. -1-2). (ENG.). 17.99 *(978-0-06-171517-4(4));* lib. bdg. 18.89 *(978-0-06-171518-1(2))* HarperCollins Pubs. (Greenwillow Bks.).

Hermanson, Tammy. Did You Ever Wonder? 2009. 28p. pap. 12.49 *(978-1-4389-4167-7(6))* AuthorHouse.

Herzog, Pearl. The Pink Dollhouse. 2008. 112p. 29.99 *(978-1-58330-797-7(4))* Feldheim Pubs.

Hesselberth, Joyce. Shape Shift. Hesselberth, Joyce, illus. 2016. (ENG., Illus.). 32p. (J). 16.99 *(978-1-62779-057-4(8),* 9781627790574, Holt, Henry & Co. Bks. For Young Readers) Holt, Henry & Co.

Hicks, Barbara Jean. Monsters Don't Eat Broccoli. Hendra, Sue, illus. (ENG.). 40p. (J). (gr. -1-2). 2014. 7.99 *(978-0-385-75521-4(X),* Dragonfly Bks.) 2009. 16.99 *(978-0-375-85686-0(2),* Knopf Bks. for Young Readers) Random Hse. Children's Bks.

Hill, Susanna Leonard. Not yet, Rose. Rutten, Nicole, illus. 2009. (ENG.). 34p. (J). (gr. -1-3). 16.50 *(978-0-8028-5326-4(9),* Eerdmans Bks For Young Readers) Eerdmans, William B. Publishing Co.

Hillert, Margaret. Away Go the Boats. Kelleher, Kathie, illus. 2016. (BeginningtoRead Ser.). (ENG.). 32p. (J). (gr. 1-2). 22.60 *(978-1-59953-792-4(3))* Norwood Hse. Pr.

Hinckley, Betts. Mr Bumble. 2011. 24p. pap. 15.99 *(978-1-4568-9714-7(4))* Xlibris Corp.

Hines, Anna Grossnickle. I Am a Tyrannosaurus. Hines, Anna Grossnickle, illus. 2011. (ENG., Illus.). 40p. (J). (gr. -1-2). 12.99 *(978-1-58246-413-8(8),* Tricycle Pr.) Random Hse. Children's Bks.

Hinton, Stephanie, illus. Muddle & Match: Adventure. 2014. 16p. (J). bds. 8.99 *(978-1-61067-288-7(7))* Kane Miller.

—Muddle & Match: Imagine. 2014. 16p. (J). bds. 8.99 *(978-1-61067-289-4(5))* Kane Miller.

—Muddle & Match Jungle Animals. 2015. (ENG.). 16p. (J). bds. 8.00 *(978-1-61067-401-0(4))* Kane Miller.

—Muddle & Match Monsters. 2015. (ENG.). 16p. (J). bds. *(978-1-61067-423-2(5))* Kane Miller.

Hochman, Marisa. A Walk in Pirate's Cove. Woodland, Bette, illus. 2012. (ENG.). 32p. (J). *(978-0-9865679-0-2(6))* Fitzhenry & Whiteside, Ltd.

Hoffman, C. J. Hiss: A Story about Love, Trust & Growing Up. 2008. 24p. pap. 11.49 *(978-1-4389-3842-4(X))* AuthorHouse.

Hoffman, Eric. A Dark, Dark Cave. Tabor, Corey R., illus. 2016. (ENG.). 40p. (J). (gr. -1-1). 17.99 *(978-0-670-01636-5(5),* Viking Books for Young Readers) Penguin Young Readers Group.

Hoffman, Michael. I'm Only Three. 2010. 24p. 12.99 *(978-1-4490-9805-6(3))* AuthorHouse.

Hoffman, Robert M. The Adventures of Mia & Squeaky: Tails of Imagination. 2011. 32p. pap. 14.99 *(978-1-257-37254-6(8))* Lulu Pr., Inc.

Hohmeier, Maria. Amazingly Wonderful Things. Weber, Penny, illus. 2011. (ENG & SPA.). 32p. (J). (gr. -1-3). lib. bdg. 16.95 *(978-1-936299-10-2(0),* Raven Tree Pr.,Csi) Continental Sales, Inc.

Hole, Stian. Anna's Heaven. 2014. (ENG., Illus.). 42p. (J). 17.00 *(978-0-8028-5441-4(9),* Eerdmans Bks For Young Readers) Eerdmans, William B. Publishing Co.

Hollands, Judith. Mrs. Mudgie & Mr. James. 2013. (ENG., Illus.). 32p. (J). (gr. -1-3). 16.99 *(978-1-4814-2139-3(5),* Atheneum Bks. for Young Readers) Simon & Schuster Children's Publishing.

Holm, Jennifer L. Little Babymouse & the Christmas Cupcakes. Holm, Matthew, illus. 2016. (ENG.). 40p. (J). (gr. -1-2). 17.99 *(978-1-101-93743-3(2),* Random Hse. Bks. for Young Readers) Random Hse. Children's Bks.

Holm, Jennifer L. & Holm, Matthew. Burns Rubber. 2010. (Babymouse Ser.: 12). lib. bdg. 17.20 *(978-0-606-07025-6(7),* Turtleback) Turtleback Bks.

—Dragonslayer. Holm, Jennifer L. & Holm, Matthew, illus. 2009. (Babymouse Ser.: 11). (ENG., Illus.). 96p. (J). (gr. 2-5). pap. 6.99 *(978-0-375-85712-6(5));* lib. bdg. 12.99

(978-0-375-95712-3(X)) Random Hse. Children's Bks. (Random Hse. Bks. for Young Readers).

—Extreme Babymouse. Holm, Jennifer L. & Holm, Matthew, illus. 2013. (Babymouse Ser.: 17). (ENG., Illus.). 96p. (J). (gr. 2-5). pap. 6.99 *(978-0-307-93160-3(9))*; lib. bdg. 12.99 *(978-0-375-97096-2(7))* Random Hse. Children's Bks. (Random Hse. Bks. for Young Readers).

—Extreme Babymouse. 2013. (Babymouse Ser.: 17). lib. bdg. 17.20 *(978-0-606-26999-5(1)*, Turtleback) Turtleback Bks.

—Happy Birthday, Babymouse! Holm, Jennifer L. & Holm, Matthew, illus. 2014. (Babymouse Ser.: 18). (ENG., Illus.). 96p. (J). (gr. 2-5). 12.99 *(978-0-375-97097-9(5)*, Random Hse. Bks. for Young Readers) Random Hse. Children's Bks.

—Happy Birthday, Babymouse. Holm, Jennifer L. & Holm, Matthew, illus. 2014. (Babymouse Ser.: 18). (ENG., Illus.). 96p. (J). (gr. 2-5). pap. 6.99 *(978-0-307-93161-0(7)*, Random Hse. Bks. for Young Readers) Random Hse. Children's Bks.

—Happy Birthday, Babymouse. 2014. (Babymouse Ser.: 18). lib. bdg. 17.20 *(978-0-606-35567-4(7))* Turtleback Bks.

—The Musical. Holm, Jennifer L. & Holm, Matthew, illus. 2009. (Babymouse Ser.: 10). (ENG., Illus.). 96p. (J). (gr. 2-5). pap. 6.99 *(978-0-375-84388-4(4))*; lib. bdg. 12.99 *(978-0-375-93791-0(9))* Random Hse. Children's Bks. (Random Hse. Bks. for Young Readers).

—Queen of the World! 2005. (Babymouse Ser.: 1). (ENG., Illus.). 96p. (J). (gr. 2-5). pap. 6.99 *(978-0-375-83229-1(7))*; lib. bdg. 12.99 *(978-0-375-93229-8(1))* Random Hse. Children's Bks. (Random Hse. Bks. for Young Readers).

—A Very Babymouse Christmas. Holm, Jennifer L. & Holm, Matthew, illus. 2011. (Babymouse Ser.: 15). (ENG., Illus.). 96p. (J). (gr. 2-5). 12.99 *(978-0-375-96779-5(6))*; pap. 6.99 *(978-0-375-86779-8(1))* Random Hse. Children's Bks. (Random Hse. Bks. for Young Readers).

Holt, Cija. Zwarkowski & the Show & Tell Collection. 2010. 48p. pap. 11.49 *(978-1-4520-4173-5(3))* AuthorHouse.

Honey, Elizabeth. That's Not a Daffodil! Honey, Elizabeth, illus. 2011. (ENG., Illus.). 32p. (J). (gr. -1-k). 19.99 *(978-1-74237-248-8(1))* Allen & Unwin AUS. Dist: Independent Pubs. Group.

Hooper, Leta. The Dream That Saved Grizzly Forest. 2010. 16p. pap. 9.00 *(978-1-4490-5087-0(5))* AuthorHouse.

Hoover, Paulette. What's That Lump in Your Bed? 2011. 28p. pap. 21.95 *(978-1-4567-1859-6(2))* AuthorHouse.

Hoppe, Bethany A. Molly B. Golly's Wonderful Dancing Debut. Ayotte, Andie C., illus. 2013. 32p. 28.00 *(978-1-937763-85-5(4))* Published by Westview, Inc.

Hoppe, Paul. Hat. Hoppe, Paul, illus. 2009. (ENG., Illus.). 32p. (J). (gr. -1-1). 14.99 *(978-1-59990-247-0(8)*, 9781599902470, Bloomsbury USA Childrens) Bloomsbury Publishing USA.

Hopper, Bobby E. Bleep the Purple Bear. Hopper, Andy Lee, illus. 2009. 36p. pap. 18.99 *(978-1-4389-1908-9(5))* AuthorHouse.

Horton, Susan. Inside Lily's World. 2012. 56p. (gr. 4-6). pap. 11.95 *(978-1-4772-7627-3(0))* AuthorHouse.

House, Brandy. Under a Toadstool, 1 vol. 2009. 12p. pap. 24.95 *(978-1-60836-290-5(6))* America Star Bks.

Howell, Lauren. If I Was the Mayor. Dawson, Sheldon, illus. 2005. 32p. (J). per. *(978-0-9735798-1-9(1))* Three Bears Publishing.

Howie, Betsy. Unscripted by Lainey McBride. Lowery, Mike, illus. 2012. 183p. (J). *(978-0-545-39705-6(7))* Scholastic, Inc.

Huber, Mike. The Amazing Erik. Cowman, Joseph, illus. 2014. (ENG.). 32p. (gr. -1). 15.95 *(978-1-60554-209-6(1))* Redleaf Pr.

Hueller, Andy. Dizzy Fantastic & Her Flying Bicycle. 2010. (Illus.). 155p. (J). pap. 8.99 *(978-1-59955-395-5(3))* Cedar Fort, Inc./CFI Distribution.

Hughes, Melissa. Myles & Otis: A Story of Friendship. 2009. (Illus.). 30p. (J). pap. 14.95 *(978-1-4327-5182-1(4))* Outskirts Pr., Inc.

Hughes, Stephen B. The Adventures of Bruno a Dogg & Bowser T Houn' 2009. 80p. pap. 14.98 *(978-1-4389-8677-7(7))* AuthorHouse.

Hughes, Susan. Earth to Audrey. Poulin, Stéphane, illus. 2007. (ENG.). 32p. (J). (gr. k-3). 6.95 *(978-1-55453-165-3(9))* Kids Can Pr., Ltd. CAN. Dist: Hachette Bk. Group.

Hull, Bunny. The Friendship Seed. Fleming, Kye, illus. 2007. (Young Masters Ser.). 28p. (J). (gr. -1-2). per. 13.95 incl. audio compact disk *(978-0-9721478-6-6(1)*, Dream A World) BrassHeart Music.

—Young Masters: The Magic Eye. Fleming, Kye, illus. 2007. (Young Masters Ser.). (J). (gr. -1). 13.95 incl. audio compact disk *(978-0-9721478-7-3(X))* BrassHeart Music.

Hull, Claudia. Procrastimonsters! They're Everywhere. Mikle, Toby, illus. 2012. 44p. pap. 15.95 *(978-1-257-64007-2(0))* Shalako Pr.

Hull, Maureen. Rainy Days with Bear. l.t. ed. 2012. 51p. (J). pap. *(978-1-4596-3453-4(5))* ReadHowYouWant.com, Ltd.

Hulme, John & Wexler, Michael. The Lost Train of Thought, Bk. 3. 2009. (Seems Ser.). (ENG., Illus.). 304p. (YA). (gr. 3-6). 16.99 *(978-1-59990-131-2(5)*, 9781599901312, Bloomsbury USA Childrens) Bloomsbury Publishing USA.

Hulst, W. G. van de & Hulst, Willem G. van de, illus. The Secret Hiding Place. 2014. (J). *(978-1-928136-16-3(8))* Inheritance Pubns.

Hummel, Jim. Imagination: On Planet Hic-Cup. 2013. 36p. pap. 15.49 *(978-1-4669-8903-0(3))* Trafford Publishing.

Huneke, Amanda. A Monster at School, 1 vol. Wolek, Guy, illus. 2013. (Monster on the Loose Ser.). (ENG.). 32p. (J). (gr. -1-4). 28.50 *(978-1-61641-931-8(8))* Magic Wagon.

—A Monster in the Park, 1 vol. Wolek, Guy, illus. 2013. (Monster on the Loose Ser.). (ENG.). 32p. (J). (gr. -1-4). 28.50 *(978-1-61641-932-5(6))* Magic Wagon.

—A Monster on the Bus, 1 vol. Wolek, Guy, illus. 2013. (Monster on the Loose Ser.). (ENG.). 32p. (J). (gr. -1-4). 28.50 *(978-1-61641-933-2(4))* Magic Wagon.

—A Monster on the Loose, 1 vol. Wolek, Guy, illus. 2013. (Monster on the Loose Ser.). (ENG.). 32p. (J). (gr. -1-4). 28.50 *(978-1-61641-934-9(2))* Magic Wagon.

Hurst, Christine. Symphony Smythe Wants a Pet. 2013. (Illus.). 50p. pap. *(978-0-473-26322-5(X))* Prickly Cat Publishing.

Hurst, Elise. Imagine a City. 2016. (ENG., Illus.). 32p. (J). (gr. -1-2). 16.99 *(978-1-101-93457-9(3)*, Doubleday Bks. for Young Readers) Random Hse. Children's Bks.

Husband, Amy. Dear Teacher. 2010. (ENG.). 24p. (J). (gr. 1-3). pap. 9.99 *(978-1-4022-4268-7(9)*, Sourcebooks Jabberwocky) Sourcebooks, Inc.

Hutchins, Hazel J. I'd Know You Anywhere. 2004. (Illus.). (J). (gr. -1-18). spiral bd. *(978-0-616-14577-7(2))*; spiral bd. *(978-0-616-14578-4(0))* Canadian National Institute for the Blind/Institut National Canadien pour les Aveugles.

I Want a Friend. 2017. (ENG., Illus.). 32p. (J). (gr. -1-k). 16.99 ***(978-0-7459-7707-2(3))*** Lion Hudson PLC GBR. Dist: Independent Pubs. Group.

The Imaginary Zoo. 2007. (J). 16.95 *(978-0-9789880-0-5(0))* Wild About Learning, Inc.

Imagination Movers Who's Afraid of the Dark. 2010. bds. 4.99 *(978-1-4231-3137-3(1))* Disney Pr.

Ismail, Yasmeen. Imagine That! 2017. (ENG., Illus.). 32p. (J). 16.99 *(978-1-68119-362-5(0)*, 9781681193625, Bloomsbury USA Childrens) Bloomsbury Publishing USA.

Jackson, Bridgett. The Bobos Save the Day: Book One of Tales from the Creek. 2008. 36p. pap. 14.49 *(978-1-4389-2034-4(2))* AuthorHouse.

Jakubowski, Michele. Outside Surprise. Waters, Erica-Jane, illus. 2015. (Perfectly Poppy Ser.). (ENG.). 32p. (gr. k-2). 22.65 *(978-1-4795-5802-5(8))* Picture Window Bks.

James, Dalton. The Heroes of Googley Woogley. 2009. 22p. (J). pap. 10.95 *(978-1-4327-2782-6(6))* Outskirts Pr., Inc.

Janni, Rebecca. Every Cowgirl Loves a Rodeo. Avril, Lynne, illus. 2012. (Every Cowgirl Ser.). (ENG.). 32p. (J). (gr. -1-k). 16.99 *(978-0-8037-3734-1(3)*, Dial Bks) Penguin Young Readers Group.

—Every Cowgirl Needs a Horse. Avril, Lynne, illus. 2010. (Every Cowgirl Ser.). (ENG.). 32p. (J). (gr. -1-k). 16.99 *(978-0-525-42164-1(5)*, Dutton Books for Young Readers) Penguin Young Readers Group.

—Every Cowgirl Needs Dancing Boots. Avril, Lynne, illus. 2011. (Every Cowgirl Ser.). (ENG.). 32p. (J). (gr. -1-k). 16.99 *(978-0-525-42341-6(9)*, Dutton Books for Young Readers) Penguin Young Readers Group.

Jeffers, Oliver & Winston, Sam. A Child of Books. Jeffers, Oliver & Winston, Sam, illus. 2016. (ENG., Illus.). 40p. (J). (gr. k-12). 17.99 *(978-0-7636-9077-9(5))* Candlewick Pr.

Jeffers, Susan. My Pony. Jeffers, Susan, illus. 2008. (ENG., Illus.). 32p. (J). (gr. -1-3). 6.99 *(978-1-4231-1295-2(4))* Hyperion Pr.

Jefferson Elementary Art Club, illus. Domino. 2007. 32p. (J). 15.00 *(978-0-9767244-2-1(1))* SkyMacSyd Publishing.

Jennerich, Douglas Todd. My Little Half-Moon. Berube, Kate, illus. 2017. (ENG.). 32p. (J). (gr. k-3). 16.99 *(978-0-399-16901-4(6)*, G.P. Putnam's Sons Books for Young Readers) Penguin Young Readers Group.

Jens, Charlene. Ookie Gets a New Best Friend. 2008. 39p. pap. 24.95 *(978-1-60474-475-0(8))* America Star Bks.

JiSeung, Kook. Ouch! It Stings! JiSeung, Kook, illus. rev. ed. 2014. (MySELF Bookshelf Ser.). (ENG., Illus.). 32p. (J). (gr. k-2). pap. 11.94 *(978-1-60357-653-6(3))*; lib. bdg. 25.27 *(978-1-59953-644-6(7))* Norwood Hse. Pr.

Johnson, Crockett. Harold & the Purple Crayon Board Book. Johnson, Crockett, illus. 2015. (ENG., Illus.). 34p. (J). (gr. -1-3). bds. 7.99 *(978-0-06-208652-5(9)*, HarperFestival) HarperCollins Pubs.

—Harold & the Purple Crayon Lap Edition. Johnson, Crockett, illus. 2016. (Illus.). 34p. (J). (gr. -1 — 1). pap. 12.99 *(978-0-06-242730-4(X)*, HarperFestival) HarperCollins Pubs.

—Harold's ABC Board Book. Johnson, Crockett, illus. 2015. (ENG., Illus.). 34p. (J). (gr. -1 — 1). bds. 7.99 *(978-0-06-242731-1(8)*, HarperFestival) HarperCollins Pubs.

Johnson, Crockett, illus. Harold et le Crayon Violet: The French Edition of Harold & the Purple Crayon. 2013. (FRE & ENG.). 64p. (J). (gr. -1-3). 10.00 *(978-1-61243-164-2(X))* Ulysses Pr.

Johnson, Donnie. The Little Flying Boy. 2012. 36p. pap. 17.95 *(978-1-4685-4750-4(X))* AuthorHouse.

Johnson, Joshua C. The Raccoon in My Room. 2010. 20p. 10.49 *(978-1-4520-7273-9(6))* AuthorHouse.

Johnson, Kevin D. Around Every Corner. 2011. 24p. (gr. 1-2). pap. 11.32 *(978-1-4567-4869-2(6))* AuthorHouse.

Johnson, Sonia M. Tyler's Third Grade Science Project. 2009. (Illus.). 20p. pap. 12.49 *(978-1-4343-5553-9(5))* AuthorHouse.

Johnson, Terry David. As I Sat on My Grandpa's Knee. 2009. 32p. pap. 16.50 *(978-1-60860-202-5(8)*, Eloquent Bks.) Strategic Book Publishing & Rights Agency (SBPRA).

Johnston, Kayla & Johnston, David. Butterflies in My Belly. 2010. 16p. pap. 10.99 *(978-1-4490-5339-0(4))* AuthorHouse.

Johnston, Tamra L. Libby the Little Leprechaun. 2012. 42p. pap. 20.99 *(978-1-4772-0750-5(3))* AuthorHouse.

Jones, Lee. Whimper. 2011. 142p. pap. 12.00 *(978-0-557-57961-7(9))* Lulu Pr., Inc.

Jones, V. C. Anna Banana Goes to Louisiana. 2010. 16p. 8.49 *(978-1-4490-8390-8(0))* AuthorHouse.

—Anna Banana Goes to Montana. 2010. 16p. 8.49 *(978-1-4490-8386-1(2))* AuthorHouse.

Joyce, William. Billy's Booger. Joyce, William, illus. 2015. (ENG., Illus.). 40p. (J). (gr. -1-3). 17.99 *(978-1-4424-7351-5(7))* Simon & Schuster Children's Publishing.

Jules. Bubble's World: Book Four Enchanted England. 2010. 40p. 16.99 *(978-1-4520-5407-0(X))* AuthorHouse.

Kann, Victoria. Goldilicious. Kann, Victoria, illus. 2009. (Illus.). 40p. (J). (gr. k-3). (ENG.). 17.99 *(978-0-06-124408-7(2))*; lib. bdg. 18.89 *(978-0-06-124409-4(0))* HarperCollins Pubs.

—Peterrific. Kann, Victoria, illus. 2017. (Pinkalicious Ser.). (Illus.). 40p. (J). (gr. -1-3). 17.99 *(978-0-06-256356-9(4))* HarperCollins Pubs.

Kares, P. S. Hole-in-the-Wall with the Prairie Orphans. 2009. 32p. pap. 24.95 *(978-1-60813-521-9(7))* America Star Bks.

Karlik, Danielle. The Kaylee Chronicles: First Day Fright. 2007. 20p. per. 24.95 *(978-1-4241-8346-3(4))* America Star Bks.

Kasdepke, Grzegorz. The Beast in My Belly. Kozlowski, Tomasz, illus. 2015. (ENG.). 48p. (J). (gr. k-4). 16.95 *(978-1-59270-160-5(4))* Enchanted Lion Bks., LLC.

Katz, Karen. ¡Cu-Cú, Bebé! Katz, Karen, illus. 2009. (SPA., Illus.). 14p. (J). (gr. -1 — 1). bds. 7.99 *(978-1-4169-7938-8(7)*, Libros Para Ninos) Libros Para Ninos.

Keane, Claire. Once upon a Cloud. 2015. (ENG., Illus.). 34p. (J). (gr. -1-k). 17.99 *(978-0-8037-3911-6(7)*, Dial Bks) Penguin Young Readers Group.

Keats, Ezra Jack. Regards to the Man in the Moon. 2009. (ENG.). 40p. (J). (gr. -1-2). 15.99 *(978-0-670-01137-7(1)*, Viking Books for Young Readers) Penguin Young Readers Group.

Kellenbarger, Sandy Hurst. Magic Gnomes. 2012. 24p. (gr. 2-4). pap. 14.93 *(978-1-4669-6526-3(6))* Trafford Publishing.

Kelly, Kevin Vincent. Hattie Mcdimple Makes a Wish. 2012. 20p. pap. 24.95 *(978-1-4626-8310-9(X))* America Star Bks.

Kelsey, Annie. Love & Chicken Nuggets. 2016. (Pippa Morgan's Diary Ser.: 2). (ENG.). 176p. (J). (gr. 3-7). 12.99 *(978-1-4926-3141-5(8)*, 9781492631415, Sourcebooks Jabberwocky) Sourcebooks, Inc.

Kelty, Colleen Alyce. I Guess I'll Be, 1 vol. Swope, Brenda, illus. 2010. 24p. 24.95 *(978-1-4489-4937-3(8))* PublishAmerica, Inc.

Kendall, Bridget. Bond & the Big Green Hill. 2009. 28p. pap. 13.99 *(978-1-4490-1458-2(5))* AuthorHouse.

Kennemore, Tim. Alice's Shooting Star. 2009. 100p. (J). (gr. 2-6). 12.00 *(978-0-8028-5337-0(4)*, Eerdmans Bks For Young Readers) Eerdmans, William B. Publishing Co.

Kern, Dale & Katic, Marija. Imagine. 2013. 40p. pap. *(978-1-4602-1168-7(5))* FriesenPress.

Kerr, Valerie. My World Within: Fun with Animals. 2013. 28p. pap. 13.54 *(978-1-4669-8612-1(3))* Trafford Publishing.

—My World Within: Up in the Clouds. 2012. 48p. pap. 18.41 *(978-1-4669-7012-0(X))* Trafford Publishing.

Keys, Dalen. Just a Quilt? Sponaugle, Kim, illus. 2nd ed. 2012. (ENG.). 32p. (J). 16.00 *(978-1-886068-56-8(9))* Fruitbearer Publishing, LLC.

Khan, Nicholai. Nicho the Tiger - Create Your World. 2011. (Illus.). 28p. (J). 14.95 *(978-0-9820801-2-2(3))* Nicho The Tiger LLC.

Kibbe, Pat. Mrs. Kiddy & the Moonbooms. 2010. 112p. pap. 9.95 *(978-1-4401-9968-4(X))* iUniverse, Inc.

Kilpatrick, Irene. Let's Use Our Imaginations! Giles, Mike, illus. 2009. (Yo Gabba Gabba! Ser.). (ENG.). 24p. (J). (gr. -1-2). pap. 3.99 *(978-1-4169-7854-1(2)*, Simon Spotlight) Simon Spotlight.

Kimball, Angela. Of All the Silly Things. 2011. 52p. (gr. -1 — 1). pap. 25.49 *(978-1-4567-2259-3(X))* AuthorHouse.

Kimmel, Haven. Kaline Klattermaster's Tree House. Brown, Peter, illus. 2010. (ENG.). 160p. (J). (gr. 2-7). pap. 5.99 *(978-0-689-87403-1(0)*, Atheneum Bks. for Young Readers) Simon & Schuster Children's Publishing.

King Iii, Dudley Allen. Skye's High Fly'n Adventures: How Skye Gets His Name. 2012. 28p. pap. 10.95 *(978-1-4626-7445-9(3))* America Star Bks.

Kintz, Elizabeth. The Magic Hose. 2012. 30p. 16.95 *(978-1-4575-1087-8(1))*; pap. 14.00 *(978-1-4575-0948-3(2))* Dog Ear Publishing, LLC.

Kirby, Matthew J. Spell Robbers. 2014. (Quantum League Ser.: No. 1). (ENG.). 272p. (J). (gr. 3-7). 16.99 *(978-0-545-50226-9(8)*, Scholastic Pr.) Scholastic, Inc.

Kisko, Stephen. Sailing the Puddles. 2013. 36p. pap. 12.95 *(978-1-62838-002-6(0))* Page Publishing Inc.

Kitamura, Satoshi. Millie's Marvellous Hat. 2009. (Andersen Press Picture Bks). (ENG., Illus.). 32p. (J). (gr. -1-3). 16.95 *(978-0-7613-5153-5(1))* Lerner Publishing Group.

Klein, Pamela. Swing! Tanis, Joel E., illus. 2006. (ENG.). (J). 15.95 *(978-1-932514-05-6(8))* College of DuPage Pr.

Knapman, Timothy. Dinosaurs Don't Have Bedtimes! Dyson, Nikki, illus. 2016. (ENG.). 32p. (J). (gr. -1-2). 15.99 *(978-0-7636-8927-8(0))* Candlewick Pr.

Knight-Mudie, Karen. Yarns from Yandilla. 2013. 344p. pap. *(978-0-9875697-0-7(8))* Davey, Mary Stella.

Knowlton, Laurie Lazzaro. Pirates Don't Say Please!, 1 vol. Tans, Adrian, illus. 2012. (ENG.). 32p. (J). (gr. k-3). 16.99 *(978-1-58980-982-6(3))* Pelican Publishing Co., Inc.

Kohake, Beverly. The Red Dragon Kite. 2008. (Illus.). 48p. pap. 9.95 *(978-1-4357-1568-4(3))* Lulu Pr., Inc.

Kopley, Richard. The Remarkable David Wordsworth. Fazio, Michael, illus. 2013. 30p. (J). pap. *(978-1-936172-67-2(4))* Elfrig Publishing.

Korda, Lerryn. It's Vacation Time. Korda, Lerryn, illus. 2010. (Playtime with Little Nye Ser.). (ENG., Illus.). 26p. (J). (— 1). 8.99 *(978-0-7636-4813-8(2))* Candlewick Pr.

Kovalkova-McKenna, Svetlana & McKenna, Alexandra. The Fairy Book. 2009. 52p. pap. 7.58 *(978-0-557-06160-0(1))* Lulu Pr., Inc.

Kramer, Jackie Azúa. The Green Umbrella. Sassouni, Maral, illus. 2017. (ENG.). 32p. (J). (gr. -1-3). 17.95 *(978-0-7358-4218-2(3))* North-South Bks., Inc.

Krensky, Stephen. What Do You See? A Lift-the-Flap Book about Endangered Animals. Schimler, Amy, illus. 2009. (Little Green Bks.). (ENG.). 16p. (J). (gr. -1-k). 6.99 *(978-1-4169-7123-8(8)*, Little Simon) Little Simon.

Kroll, Steven. The Tyrannosaurus Game, 0 vols. Schindler, S. D., illus. 2010. (ENG.). 32p. (J). (gr. -1-3). 17.99 *(978-0-7614-5603-2(1)*, 9780761456032, Amazon Children's Publishing) Amazon Publishing.

Kwarta, Darlene. Walking with King Tut. 2008. 48p. pap. 9.95 *(978-1-60693-040-3(0)*, Eloquent Bks.) Strategic Book Publishing & Rights Agency (SBPRA).

La Coccinella. Guess Who? 2014. (Look & See! Ser.). (ENG., Illus.). 24p. (J). (gr. -1 — 1). bds. 6.95 *(978-1-4549-0852-4(1))* Sterling Publishing Co., Inc.

Lam, Fiona Tinwei. Rainbow Rocket. 2013. (ENG., Illus.). 32p. 19.95 *(978-0-88982-282-5(4))* Oolichan Bks. CAN. Dist: Univ. of Toronto Pr.

Lambert, Megan Dowd & Daniels, Peter. Real Sisters Pretend, 1 vol. Carmb, Sara Lynn & Tadgell, Nicole, illus. 2016. (ENG.). 32p. (J). (gr. k-5). 17.95 *(978-0-88448-441-7(6)*, 884441) Tilbury Hse. Pubs.

Lammle, Leslie. Once upon a Saturday. Lammle, Leslie, illus. 2009. (Illus.). 32p. (J). (gr. k-2). lib. bdg. 18.89 *(978-0-06-125191-7(7))*; (ENG., 17.99 *(978-0-06-125190-0(9))* HarperCollins Pubs.

Lamotte, Kathleen. The Horsetrailer Mystery. 2008. 49p. pap. 16.95 *(978-1-60474-449-1(9))* America Star Bks.

Lampkins, Antonia. Favorite Things. 2009. 20p. pap. 24.95 *(978-1-61546-420-3(4))* America Star Bks.

Lancaster, Cindy Clark. Flowers in the Desert. 2012. 24p. 24.95 *(978-1-4626-5755-1(9))* America Star Bks.

Lane, Jessica E. The Secret of the Swans. 2009. 52p. pap. 31.99 *(978-1-4415-5517-5(X))* Xlibris Corp.

LaRochelle, David. It's a Tiger! Tankard, Jeremy, illus. 2012. (ENG.). 36p. (J). (gr. -1-k). 16.99 *(978-0-8118-6925-6(3))* Chronicle Bks. LLC.

Larsen, Andrew. The Imaginary Garden. Luxbacher, Irene, illus. 2009. (ENG.). 32p. (J). (gr. -1-2). 16.95 *(978-1-55453-279-7(5))* Kids Can Pr., Ltd. CAN. Dist: Hachette Bk. Group.

Lasswell, Barbara. Different Ways, 1 vol. 2009. 29p. pap. 24.95 *(978-1-60749-328-0(4))* America Star Bks.

Lathrop, Brandy. Jalen Goes to Mars. 2008. 22p. pap. 24.95 *(978-1-4241-9010-2(X))* America Star Bks.

Laurie, Cook, illus. Amelia Asks Why. 2007. (J). 3.99 *(978-0-9726075-4-4(4))* EPI Bks.

Leavitt, Martine. Heck Superhero. 2014. (ENG.). 144p. (gr. 6-9). pap. 7.95 *(978-1-62979-109-8(1))* Boyds Mills Pr.

LeBreton, Heather. Rhyming with the Little Ones, 1 vol. LeBreton, Zachary, illus. 2009. 31p. pap. 24.95 *(978-1-60749-114-9(1))* America Star Bks.

Lee, Carolyn A. My World & Me: The & Me Collection. 2010. 28p. 18.00 *(978-1-4269-4054-5(8))* Trafford Publishing.

Lee, Ingrid. Dragon Tide, 1 vol. Meister, Soizick, illus. 2006. (ENG.). 32p. (J). (gr. -1-3). 17.95 *(978-1-55143-352-3(4))* Orca Bk. Pubs. USA.

Lee, Suzy. Shadow. 2010. (ENG., Illus.). 44p. (J). (gr. -1-3). 15.99 *(978-0-8118-7280-5(7))* Chronicle Bks. LLC.

Lehrer, Damon, illus. Rocket Boy. 2016. (J). ***(978-1-56792-587-6(1))*** Godine, David R. Pub.

Lehrhaupt, Adam. Chicken in Space. Kober, Shahar, illus. 2016. 40p. (J). (gr. -1-3). 17.99 *(978-0-06-236412-8(X))* HarperCollins Pubs.

—I Don't Draw, I Color! Sala, Felicita, illus. 2017. (ENG.). 32p. (J). (gr. -1-3). 17.99 *(978-1-4814-6275-4(X)*, Simon & Schuster/Paula Wiseman Bks.) Simon & Schuster/Paula Wiseman Bks.

Leigh-Anna Tehan. Beyond All Imagination: The First Souvenir. Paul Reising, illus. 2009. 44p. pap. 18.49 *(978-1-4389-6452-2(8))* AuthorHouse.

Leiter, Richard & Kober, Shahar. The Flying Hand of Marco B. 2015. (ENG., Illus.). 24p. (J). (gr. k-2). 15.99 *(978-1-58536-888-4(1)*, 203813) Sleeping Bear Pr.

Leon, Loni. Can you Imagine..., 1. Leon, Loni & Huston, Kyle, illus. 2006. 49p. (J). 21.95 *(978-0-9728556-0-0(2))* Sullivan, Kelley Enterprises.

Leoni, Gail. Chalk Dust. 2008. 36p. pap. 24.95 *(978-1-60474-881-9(8))* America Star Bks.

Lethem, Mara. The Highest Mountain of Books in the World. Bonilla, Rocio, illus. 2016. (J). *(978-1-4413-1999-9(9))* Peter Pauper Pr. Inc.

Letria, José Jorge. If I Were a Book. Letria, Andre, illus. 2014. (ENG.). 64p. 12.95 *(978-1-4521-2144-4(3))* Chronicle Bks. LLC.

Leung, Erika. The Dinosaur Hunt. 2010. 28p. pap. 12.99 *(978-1-4490-9584-0(4))* AuthorHouse.

Levy, Carol L. Elphy Grey. 2012. 24p. pap. 17.99 *(978-1-4772-6687-8(9))* AuthorHouse.

Lewis, Anne Margaret. Puddle Jumpers. Cote, Nancy, illus. 2016. (ENG.). 32p. (J). (gr. -1-k). 16.99 *(978-1-63450-185-9(3)*, Sky Pony Pr.) Skyhorse Publishing Co., Inc.

Lewis, T. Caroline's Beautiful Pictures. 2012. 16p. pap. 15.99 *(978-1-4772-6195-8(8))* AuthorHouse.

Liberto, Lorenzo. Matt the Rat & His Magic Cloud / Raton Mateo y Su Nube Magica: A Day at School / un Dia de Escuela. Gomez, Rocio, ed. Torres, Irving, illus. 2003. (Matt the Rat Ser. / La Serie de Ratón Mateo). (ENG & SPA.). 32p. (J). lib. bdg. 20.00 *(978-0-9743668-0-7(3))* Harvest Sun Pr., LLC.

Liberto, Lorenzo, et al. Matt the Rat's Incredible Creations / Las Creaciones Increíbles de Ratón Mateo. Torres, Irving, illus. 2004. (ENG & SPA.). 32p. (J). lib. bdg. 20.00 *(978-0-9743668-3-8(8))* Harvest Sun Pr., LLC.

Liguori, Tara. Silly Milly Is a Princess. 2008. 28p. pap. 24.95 *(978-1-60703-349-3(6))* America Star Bks.

Lithgow, John. The Carnival of the Animals. Kulikov, Boris, illus. 2004. (ENG.). 40p. (J). (gr. -1-3). 19.99 *(978-0-689-86721-7(2)*, Simon & Schuster Bks. For Young Readers) Simon & Schuster Bks. For Young Readers.

—I'm a Manatee. Hoyt, Ard, illus. 2007. (ENG.). 32p. (J). (gr. -1-3). pap. 9.99 *(978-0-689-85452-1(8)*, Little Simon) Little Simon.

—I'M a Manatee. Hoyt, Ard, illus. 2003. (ENG.). 32p. (J). (gr. -1-3). 18.99 *(978-0-689-85427-9(7)*, Simon & Schuster Bks. For Young Readers) Simon & Schuster Bks. For Young Readers.

Little, Cynthia. Mom's Imaginary Child. 2008. pap. *(978-0-9747707-2-7(8))* Sleepless Warrior Publishing.

Liwska, Renata. Red Wagon. Liwska, Renata, illus. 2013. (ENG., Illus.). 32p. (J). (gr. -1 — 1). 6.99 *(978-0-399-16239-8(9)*, Philomel Bks.) Penguin Young Readers Group.

Lock, Brian. Chicken Lips & Rocket Ships, 1 vol. 2009. 56p. pap. 16.95 *(978-1-61582-205-8(4))* America Star Bks.

Lockhart, Kendra. Favorite Hat. 2010. (Illus.). 24p. (J). pap. 14.95 *(978-0-9843883-3-2(8)*, Green Lady Pr., The) RealityIsBooks.com, Inc.

Lockley, Belinda. Sometimes I Think of the Fish in the Sea. 2008. 16p. pap. 24.95 *(978-1-60474-844-4(3))* America Star Bks.

Lodding, Linda Ravin. Little Red Riding Sheep. Atkinson, Cale, illus. 2017. (ENG.). 40p. (J). (gr. -1-3). 17.99 *(978-1-4814-5748-4(9))* Simon & Schuster Children's Publishing.

London, Jonathan. The Lion Who Had Asthma. Westcott, Nadine Bernard, illus. 2012. (J). *(978-1-61913-119-4(6))* Weigl Pubs., Inc.

—My Big Rig, 0 vols. Garofoli, Viviana, illus. 2013. (ENG.). 32p. (J). (gr. -1-3). pap. 9.99 *(978-1-4778-1673-8(9)*, 9781477816738, Amazon Children's Publishing) Amazon Publishing.

Long, Ethan. Clara & Clem Take a Ride. Long, Ethan, illus. 2012. (Penguin Young Readers, Level 1 Ser.). (ENG., Illus.). 32p. (J). (gr. k-1). mass mkt. 3.99 *(978-0-448-46264-6(8)*, Penguin Young Readers) Penguin Young Readers Group.

—Clara & Clem Take a Ride. 2012. (Penguin Young Readers Level 1 Ser.). lib. bdg. 13.55 *(978-0-606-26639-0(9)*, Turtleback) Turtleback Bks.

H
I

Long, Loren & Bader, Bonnie. What Does Otis See? Long, Loren, illus. 2015. (Otis Ser.). (ENG., Illus.). 32p. (J). (gr. k-1). 3.99 *(978-0-448-48758-8(6)*, Penguin Young Readers) Penguin Young Readers Group.

Lopez, Cheyene Montana. Blue Sky Rainbows: A Series of Children's Stories of the World of Dreams & Imaginations, 1 vol. 2009. 82p. pap. 16.95 *(978-1-61582-290-4(9))* PublishAmerica, Inc.

Lopez, Denise M. If God Was a Superhero. 2013. 16p. pap. 7.95 *(978-1-4497-9707-2(5)*, WestBow Pr.) Author Solutions, Inc.

Lopez, Sixto. Snarloff Duwaki's Adventures. 2011. 24p. pap. 24.95 *(978-1-4626-2557-4(6))* America Star Bks.

Lorenz, Albert. The Exceptionally, Extraordinarily Ordinary First Day of School. 2010. (ENG., Illus.). 32p. (J). (gr. 1-4). 15.95 *(978-0-8109-8960-3(3)*, Abrams Bks. for Young Readers) Abrams, Inc.

Lotz, Dana R. Kids' Tales. 2008. 85p. pap. 19.95 *(978-1-60672-179-7(8))* America Star Bks.

Lovell, Patty. Have Fun, Molly Lou Melon. Lovell, Patty & Catrow, David, illus. 2012. (ENG.). 32p. (J). (gr. k-3). 16.99 *(978-0-399-25406-2(4)*, G.P. Putnam's Sons Books for Young Readers) Penguin Young Readers Group.

Lowenstein, Sallie, illus. Sir Kyle & Lady Madeline. Lowenstein, Sallie, . 2007. 32p. (J). 18.95 *(978-0-9658486-6-4(3))* Lion Stone Bks.

Lucas & His Long Loopy Laces. 2013. (Illus.). 48p. 16.99 *(978-0-9823519-4-9(1))* Tall Tails Publishing Hse.

Lynch, Kendra. Sweet Dreams Little. 2011. 24p. pap. 12.74 *(978-1-4520-8295-0(2))* AuthorHouse.

Lynn, Michelle. Fall Leaves. 2008. 17p. pap. 24.95 *(978-1-60672-027-1(9))* America Star Bks.

Lynn, Sarah. 1-2-3 Va-Va-Vroom! A Counting Book, 0 vols. Griffo, Daniel, illus. 2012. (ENG.). 32p. (J). (gr. -1-3). 16.99 *(978-0-7614-6162-3(0)*, 9780761461623, Amazon Children's Publishing) Amazon Publishing.

Lytton, Deborah. Ruby Starr. 2017. (Ruby Starr Ser.: 1). (ENG.). 272p. (J). (gr. 3-7). pap. 7.99 ***(978-1-4926-4577-1(X)***, Sourcebooks Jabberwocky) Sourcebooks, Inc.

M. F Feierabend, J. Olivia Ponty & Friends to the Rescue. 2012. 32p. pap. 32.70 *(978-1-4771-1081-2(X))* Xlibris Corp.

Maar, Paul. El Viaje de Lisa. Kasparavicius, Kestutis, illus. 2008. (la Orilla del Viento Ser.). (SPA.). 28p. (J). (gr. -1-3). 12.99 *(978-968-16-7452-6(9))* Fondo de Cultura Economica USA.

MacDonald, Alysha. Noodles - a Lunchtime Adventure. Swaim, Mike, illus. 2012. 28p. pap. *(978-0-9735526-8-3(9))* Cold Rock Publishing.

Mackall, Dandi Daley. Natalie & the One-of-a-Kind Wonderful Day!, 1 vol. Blakeslee, Lys, illus. 2009. (That's Nat! Ser.). (ENG.). 96p. (J). (gr. 1-4). pap. 4.99 *(978-0-310-71566-5(0))* Zonderkidz.

MacMillan, Lesley. What Would You Be? Holcomb, Michele, illus. 2006. 21p. (J). (gr. -1-3). per. 12.99 *(978-1-59879-228-7(8))* Lifevest Publishing, Inc.

MacNeil, Ben. The Farmer & His Animals. Smith, Charlie E. T., illus. 2013. 26p. pap. *(978-1-927625-02-6(5))* Quarter Castle Publishing.

MacRae, Tom. When I Woke up I Was a Hippopotamus. Collins, Ross, illus. 2011. (Andersen Press Picture Books Ser.). (J). 16.95 *(978-0-7613-8099-3(X))* Andersen Pr. GBR. Dist: Lerner Publishing Group.

Maddock, Lisa. A Tale of Two Guinea Pigs. 2009. 184p. pap. 11.95 *(978-1-59858-960-3(1))* Dog Ear Publishing, LLC.

Madlener, Michael & Reeves, Patrick. Feed Your Fish. 2012. 40p. 24.95 *(978-1-4626-6707-9(4))* PublishAmerica, Inc.

Magic Wagon Staff. A Flip-Flop Adventure, 1 vol. 2011. (Flip-Flop Adventure Ser.). (ENG., Illus.). 32p. 114.00 *(978-1-61641-650-8(5)*, Looking Glass Library) Magic Wagon.

Magoo, Flossy. Upside down & Backwards. 2011. 24p. pap. 11.32 *(978-1-4520-6789-6(9))* AuthorHouse.

Mahy, Margaret. A Lion in the Meadow. 2013. (ENG., Illus.). 32p. (gr. 4-13). 17.95 *(978-1-4683-0665-1(0)*, 460665) Overlook Pr., The.

—The Man from the Land of Fandango. Dunbar, Polly, illus. 2012. (ENG.). 32p. (J). (gr. -1-3). 16.99 *(978-0-547-81988-4(9))* Houghton Mifflin Harcourt Publishing Co.

Maier, Inger M. When Fuzzy Was Afraid of Big & Loud Things. Candon, Jennifer, illus. 2005. (Fuzzy the Little Sheep Ser.). (J). (gr. -1-3). 32p. 14.95 *(978-1-59147-322-0(5))*; 30p. per. 9.95 *(978-1-59147-323-7(3))* American Psychological Assn. (Magination Pr.).

Malik, Katherine. Giselle's Magical World, 1 vol. 2009. 150p. pap. 24.95 *(978-1-4489-1902-4(9))* America Star Bks.

Maloney, Brenna. Ready Rabbit Gets Ready! 2015. *(978-0-698-15065-2(1))* Penguin Publishing Group.

Mangskau, Monica. My Grandpa the Super Hero. 2010. 16p. 9.49 *(978-1-4343-8088-3(2))* AuthorHouse.

Manley, Curtis. Shawn Loves Sharks. Subisak, Tracy, illus. 2017. (ENG.). 32p. (J). 17.99 *(978-1-62672-134-0(3)*, 9781626721340) Roaring Brook Pr.

Manushkin, Fran. Make-Believe Class, 1 vol. Lyon, Tammie, illus. 2010. (Katie Woo Ser.). (ENG.). 32p. (gr. k-2). lib. bdg. 21.32 *(978-1-4048-5732-2(X))* Picture Window Bks.

Manzak, Bonnie. Lairame's Birthday Surprise. 2011. 28p. pap. 15.99 *(978-1-4568-5815-5(7))* Xlibris Corp.

Mariolle, Mathieu. Even for a Dreamer Like Me. MiniKim et al, illus. 2010. (Nola's Worlds Ser.: 3). (ENG.). 128p. (J). (gr. 6-9). 30.60 *(978-0-7613-6505-1(2))* Lerner Publishing Group.

—Even for a Dreamer Like Me. Jeffrey, Erica Olson, tr. from FRE. MiniKim et al, illus. 2010. (Nola's Worlds Ser.: 3). (ENG.). 136p. (J). (gr. 6-9). pap. 9.95 *(978-0-7613-6541-9(9)*, Graphic Universe™) Lerner Publishing Group.

—Nola's Worlds, 3 vols., Set. MiniKim et al, illus. Incl. Changing Moon. 136p. 30.60 *(978-0-7613-6502-0(8))*; Even for a Dreamer Like Me. 128p. 30.60 *(978-0-7613-6505-1(2))*; Ferrets & Ferreting Out. 136p. 30.60 *(978-0-7613-6504-4(4))*; (Illus.). (J). (gr. 6-9). 2010. Set lib. bdg. 91.80 *(978-0-7613-6500-6(1)*, Graphic Universe™) Lerner Publishing Group.

Marshland, Brad. The Imagicators & the Wind Between the Worlds. 2008. 184p. pap. 13.95 *(978-0-595-53370-1(1))* iUniverse, Inc.

Martella, Liz. Izabella & her Wardrobe. 2007. 18p. 12.95 *(978-0-615-14941-7(3))* Martella, Liz.

Martin, Amy. Symphony City. 2011. (ENG., Illus.). 48p. (J). (gr. -1-4). 17.95 *(978-1-936365-39-5(1))* McSweeney's Publishing.

Martin, Bob. James' Night of Terror. Salinas, Alex, illus. 2010. 120p. (gr. 4-6). 20.95 *(978-1-4502-6500-3(6))*; pap. 10.95 *(978-1-4502-6498-3(0))* iUniverse, Inc.

Martin, Emily Winfield. Day Dreamers: A Journey of Imagination. (ENG., Illus.). 32p. (J). 2016. (— 1). bds. 8.99 *(978-1-101-93522-4(7))* 2014. (gr. -1-2). 17.99 *(978-0-385-37670-9(7))* 2014. (gr. -1-2). lib. bdg. 20.99 *(978-0-375-97326-0(5))* Random Hse. Children's Bks. (Random Hse. Bks. for Young Readers).

Martin, Marc. A River. 2017. (ENG., Illus.). 44p. (J). 17.99 *(978-1-4521-5423-7(6))* Chronicle Bks. LLC.

Marzollo, Jean & Scholastic / LeapFrog. I Spy Imagine That! Wick, Walter, illus. 2008. (J). 13.99 *(978-1-59319-933-3(3))* LeapFrog Enterprises, Inc.

Maskell, Philip Mo. King Milo & His Royal Court. 2011. 36p. pap. 19.95 *(978-1-4634-1792-5(6))* AuthorHouse.

Mason, Jane B. & Hines-Stephens, Sarah. Disguised & Dangerous. Phillips, Craig, illus. 2011. 92p. (J). *(978-0-545-37469-9(3))* Scholastic, Inc.

Mathes, Charles. In Every Moon There Is a Face. Graston, Arlene, illus. 2003. 32p. 15.95 *(978-0-9701907-4-1(3))* Illumination Arts Publishing Co., Inc.

Mathews, David George. We Can Do Anything! 2009. (Illus.). 28p. pap. 12.49 *(978-1-4490-5014-6(X))* AuthorHouse.

Mathews, Madge. Amelia Asks May I Have A Pet. Cook, Laurie, illus. 2008. 24p. (J). 3.99 *(978-0-9796536-1-2(4)*, EPI Kid Bks.) EPI Bks.

Mattern, Carrie. Papa, Why Does the Wind Blow? 2009. 24p. pap. 15.95 *(978-1-4490-0809-3(7))* AuthorHouse.

Mayo, Jason. Do Witches Make Fishes? 2010. 36p. pap. 16.99 *(978-1-4520-6944-9(1))* AuthorHouse.

Mcaleney, Kimberly. The Mouse & the Music Box: A Bedtime Story. 2008. 16p. pap. 8.49 *(978-1-4389-3134-0(4))* AuthorHouse.

McCardell, Ken. BibleRhymes' Christmas Story, bk. 3. Chirco, Antonella, illus. ed. 2008. (BibleRhymes Ser.: 3). 28p. (J). 17.95 *(978-0-9790605-2-6(4)*, BibleRhymes) BibleRhymes Publishing, L.L.C.

—BibleRhymes' Creation. Chirco, Antonella, illus. 2007. (BibleRhymes Ser.). 32p. (J). 17.95 *(978-0-9790605-0-2(8)*, BibleRhymes) BibleRhymes Publishing, L.L.C.

McCarty, Bryan. Devyn's Gold. 2008. pap. 17.00 *(978-0-8059-8640-2(5))* Dorrance Publishing Co., Inc.

McClain, Jennie. Monday I Was a Monkey: A "Tale" of Reverence. Eichelberger, Jennifer, illus. 2011. (J). *(978-1-60861-243-7(0))* Covenant Communications.

McCourt, Lisa. Happy Halloween, Stinky Face. Moore, Cyd, illus. 2011. (ENG.). 32p. (J). (gr. k — 1). bds. 6.99 *(978-0-545-28542-1(9)*, Cartwheel Bks.) Scholastic, Inc.

—I Love You, Stinky Face. Moore, Cyd, illus. 2009. (ENG.). (J). (gr. -1-3). 9.99 *(978-0-545-11757-9(7))* Scholastic, Inc.

—I Miss You, Stinky Face. Moore, Cyd, illus. 2009. (ENG.). (J). (gr. -1-3). 9.95 *(978-0-545-13849-9(3))* Scholastic, Inc.

McCoy, Sharon. What If? 2013. 28p. pap. 16.95 *(978-1-4908-1754-5(9)*, WestBow Pr.) Author Solutions, Inc.

McCullough, Angela. Night Nite. 2008. 24p. pap. 10.00 *(978-1-934925-10-2(1)*, Eloquent Bks.) Strategic Book Publishing & Rights Agency (SBPRA).

McCullough, Jerletha. Fairies of the Lilies. 2009. 20p. pap. 16.49 *(978-1-4389-2286-7(8))* AuthorHouse.

McDonald, Regina. Friday Night at the Zoo, 1 vol. McDonald, Amanda, illus. 2010. 16p. 24.95 *(978-1-4489-4090-5(7))* PublishAmerica, Inc.

McDonnell, Kathleen. The Songweavers, 1 vol. 2008. (Notherland Journeys Ser.: 3). (ENG.). 232p. (YA). (gr. 4-8). pap. 9.95 *(978-1-897187-42-5(4))* Second Story Pr. CAN. Dist: Orca Bk. Pubs. USA.

Mcdoogle, Farrah. Olivia Says Good Night. 2016. (Olivia 8x8 Ser.). lib. bdg. 13.55 *(978-0-606-39244-0(0))* Turtleback Bks.

McEwan, Ian. The Daydreamer, 2 vols. 2004. (J). 33.75 *(978-1-4025-9960-6(9))*; 36.75 *(978-1-4025-8430-5(X))* Recorded Bks., Inc.

Mcghee, Alison. Someday. Reynolds, Peter H., illus. 2015. (ENG.). 42p. (J). bds. 9.99 *(978-1-4814-6012-5(9)*, Little Simon) Little Simon.

—Someday. 2014. pap. 29.95 *(978-0-545-79756-6(X))* Scholastic, Inc.

—Someday. Reynolds, Peter H., illus. 2007. (ENG.). 40p. (J). (gr. -1-3). 16.99 *(978-1-4169-2811-9(1)*, Atheneum Bks. for Young Readers) Simon & Schuster Children's Publishing.

—Someday. Reynolds, Peter H., illus. 2008. (J). (gr. -1-2). 27.95 incl. audio *(978-0-8045-6975-0(4))*; 29.95 incl. audio compact disk *(978-0-8045-4200-5(7))* Spoken Arts, Inc.

—Song of Middle C. Menchin, Scott, illus. 2009. (ENG.). 32p. (J). (gr. k-3). 16.99 *(978-0-7636-3013-3(6))* Candlewick Pr.

Mcgranahan, Patrick D. Imaginary Jerry: And the Tale of His Daring Escape from Imaginaria. 2011. 292p. (gr. -1). 27.99 *(978-1-4389-4728-0(3))*; pap. 17.99 *(978-1-4389-4727-3(5))* AuthorHouse.

McKinney, Frank & Mason, Kate. Dead Fred, Flying Lunchboxes & the Good Luck Circle. 2009. (ENG.). 336p. (J). (gr. 4-8). 18.95 *(978-0-7573-1382-0(5))* Health Communications, Inc.

McLachlan, Edward. Simon in the Land of Chalk Drawings: Four Stories That Inspired the TV Series! 2016. (ENG.). 128p. (J). (gr. 2-4). pap. 14.99 *(978-0-486-80103-2(9))* Dover Pubns., Inc.

McLaughlin, Tom. The Cloudspotter. McLaughlin, Tom, illus. 2015. (ENG., Illus.). 32p. (J). (gr. -1-1). 18.99 *(978-1-4088-5496-9(1)*, 9781408854969, Bloomsbury USA Childrens) Bloomsbury Publishing USA.

—The Story Machine. 2015. (ENG., Illus.). 32p. (J). (gr. -1-1). 12.99 *(978-1-4088-3934-8(2)*, 9781408839348, Bloomsbury USA Childrens) Bloomsbury Publishing USA.

McLellan, Cortney. The Woodoodyots. 2008. 16p. per. 24.95 *(978-1-4241-8834-5(2))* America Star Bks.

McLerran, Alice & Mclerran, Alice. Roxaboxen. Cooney, Barbara, illus. 2004. (ENG.). 32p. (J). (gr. -1-3). pap. 6.99 *(978-0-06-052633-7(5))* HarperCollins Pubs.

McMahon, Kim. My Dog, Buddy, 1 vol. 2010. 16p. pap. 24.95 *(978-1-4489-6624-0(8))* PublishAmerica, Inc.

McMahon, V. Karen. I Saw a White Horse Today. Bailey, Loretta Dovell, illus. Black, Janet, photos by. 2011. 28p. pap. 24.95 *(978-1-4626-0282-7(7))* America Star Bks.

McMasters, Anne. Anne's Stories for Children of All Ages. 2008. 24p. pap. 12.50 *(978-1-4343-9204-6(X))* AuthorHouse.

McMullen, Brian & Jägel, Jason. Hang Glider & Mud Mask. 2012. (ENG., Illus.). 32p. (J). (gr. -1-3). 14.95 *(978-1-936365-83-8(9))* McSweeney's Publishing.

McMullin, Perry. The Boy Who Could Fly. 2009. 44p. pap. 18.95 *(978-1-4490-0904-5(2))* AuthorHouse.

McNamee, Kevin. My Brother the Frog. Morris, Alexander, illus. 2011. 24p. 19.95 *(978-1-61633-167-2(4))*; pap. 10.95 *(978-1-61633-159-7(3))* Guardian Angel Publishing, Inc.

—What Is That Thing? Snider, K. C., illus. 2011. 16p. pap. 9.95 *(978-1-61633-141-2(0))* Guardian Angel Publishing, Inc.

McNaughton, Colin. Lemmy Was a Diver. (ENG., Illus.). 32p. (J). 17.99 *(978-1-84270-301-4(3))* Andersen Pr. GBR. Dist: Trafalgar Square Publishing.

McPhail, David. Olivia Loves Owl. 2016. (ENG., Illus.). 20p. (J). (gr. -1 — 1). bds. 8.95 *(978-1-4197-2127-4(5)*, Abrams Appleseed) Abrams, Inc.

McQuinn, Anna. Lola Loves Stories. Beardshaw, Rosalind, illus. 2010. (ENG.). 28p. (J). (gr. k-3). pap. 6.95 *(978-1-58089-259-9(0))* Charlesbridge Publishing, Inc.

McQuinn, Anna & Beardshaw, Rosalind. A Lola le Encantan Los Cuentos. Canetti, Yanitzia, tr. from ENG. Beardshaw, Rosalind, illus. 2012. (SPA., Illus.). 28p. (J). (-k). pap. 7.95 *(978-1-58089-444-9(5))* Charlesbridge Publishing, Inc.

McRee Turner, Amber. Sway. 2013. (ENG.). 320p. (J). (gr. 4-7). pap. 6.99 *(978-1-4231-3784-9(1))* Hyperion Pr.

Menchin, Scott. What If Everything Had Legs? Menchin, Scott, illus. 2011. (ENG., Illus.). 32p. (J). (gr. -1-3). 15.99 *(978-0-7636-4220-4(7))* Candlewick Pr.

Mercado-López, Larissa. Esteban de Luna, Baby Rescuer / Esteban de Luna, ¡rescatador de Bebés! Pardo DeLange, Alex, illus. 2017. (ENG & SPA.). 32p. (J). (gr. k-3). 17.95 *(978-1-55885-847-3(4)*, Piñata Books) Arte Publico Pr.

Miles, David. The Book. Hoopes, Natalie, illus. 2015. (ENG.). 32p. (J). 16.95 *(978-1-939629-65-4(9))* Familius LLC.

Militzer, Jill. Kizzy's Castle. 2005. 35p. 13.24 *(978-1-4116-5538-6(9))* Lulu Pr., Inc.

Miller, Janet. DuckDumB. 2010. 32p. pap. 21.95 *(978-0-557-57669-2(5))* Lulu Pr., Inc.

Miller, Joanne Fairchild & Logsdon, Clara Isabel. What If It Were Possible? 2016. (ENG., Illus.). 40p. (J). pap. 9.95 *(978-1-63047-638-0(2))* Morgan James Publishing.

Miller, Paula K. Amy, Louise & Me. 2008. 24p. pap. 24.95 *(978-1-4241-9757-6(0))* America Star Bks.

Mills, Tessa L. The Adventures of Avery & Cali. 2007. 60p. per. 16.95 *(978-1-4241-7982-4(3))* America Star Bks.

Molesworth & Molesworth, Mary Louisa S. Peterkin. 2009. 128p. 23.95 *(978-1-60664-659-5(1))* Rodgers, Alan Bks.

Molesworth, Mary Louisa S. & Molesworth. Peterkin. 2009. 128p. pap. 10.95 *(978-1-60664-287-0(1))* Rodgers, Alan Bks.

Moll, Amanda. Liam's Lost It. 2013. 24p. 15.99 *(978-0-9886409-4-8(5))* Mindstir Media.

Mon, S. Aka - the Wonder Girl. 2011. (Illus.). 40p. pap. 18.79 *(978-1-4567-8047-0(6))* AuthorHouse.

Mongredien, Sue. Be My Valentine. 2010. (Sleepover Club Ser.). (ENG.). 128p. (J). (gr. 2-6). pap. 6.99 *(978-0-00-727705-6(9))* Lion Hudson PLC GBR. Dist: Independent Pubs. Group.

Montgomery, L. M. Anne of Green Gables. Fiona Fox Staff, ed. 2012. (ENG., Illus.). 416p. (J). 15.00 *(978-1-84135-842-0(8))* Award Pubns. Ltd. GBR. Dist: Parkwest Pubns., Inc.

Moodey, Mary. Christopher Counts the Constellation, bks. 500, bk. 500. Shingle, Jude, illus. 500th l.t. ed. 2012. (ENG.). 37p. 16.99 *(978-0-9853579-0-0(8))* MarMooWorks,LLC.

Moore, Jodi. When a Dragon Moves In. McWilliam, Howard, illus. 2011. (When a Dragon Moves In Ser.). (ENG.). 32p. (J). (gr. k-2). 16.95 *(978-0-9799746-7-0(4))* Flashlight Pr.

Moore, Lonnette. The Misplaced Splatter. 2011. 20p. pap. 24.95 *(978-1-4560-8891-0(2))* America Star Bks.

Moore, Natascha. Lost Verloren. 2013. 28p. pap. 19.99 *(978-1-4817-0664-3(0))* AuthorHouse.

Moore, Rosey. Dreams. 2010. 228p. pap. 14.49 *(978-1-4520-7485-6(2))* AuthorHouse.

Morales, Yuyi. Niño: Wrestles the World. Morales, Yuyi, illus. 2013. (ENG., Illus.). 40p. (J). (gr. -1-3). 17.99 *(978-1-59643-604-6(2)*, 9781596436046) Roaring Brook Pr.

Moree, Katie. Jesse's Peekaboo Safari. 2008. 20p. pap. 24.95 *(978-1-60672-473-6(8))* America Star Bks.

Morgan, Michelle. Colorsaurus. 2009. 32p. pap. 18.00 *(978-0-557-06120-4(2))* Lulu Pr., Inc.

Moritzky, Kayla. The Great I Don't Know. 2009. 28p. pap. 15.49 *(978-1-4389-8651-7(3))* AuthorHouse.

Moroni, Lisa. Watch Out for the Crocodile. 2014. (Illus.). 32p. (J). (gr. -1-3). 17.95 *(978-1-877579-89-9(0))* Gecko Pr. NZL. Dist: Lerner Publishing Group.

Morris, Jennifer E. The Sea Monster. 2014. (Scholastic Reader Level 1 Ser.). (Illus.). (J). lib. bdg. 13.55 *(978-0-606-36046-3(8))* Turtleback Bks.

Muha, Christina. Porchville. 2009. 16p. pap. 8.52 *(978-1-4389-8139-0(2))* AuthorHouse.

Murguia, Bethanie Deeney. The Too-Scary Story. 2017. (ENG., Illus.). 40p. (J). (gr. -1-k). 16.99 *(978-0-545-73242-0(5))* Scholastic, Inc.

—Zoe's Jungle. 2014. (ENG.). 40p. (J). (gr. -1-k). 16.99 *(978-0-545-55869-3(7)*, Levine, Arthur A. Bks.) Scholastic, Inc.

Murphy, Jill. On the Way Home. Murphy, Jill, illus. 2nd rev. ed. 2007. (ENG., Illus.). 32p. (J). (gr. k-2). pap. 11.95 *(978-0-230-01584-5(0))* Pan Macmillan GBR. Dist: Independent Pubs. Group.

Musgrave, Susan. Dreams Are More Real Than Bathtubs. braille ed. 2004. (Illus.). (J). (gr. k-3). spiral bd. *(978-0-616-01748-7(0))* Canadian National Institute for the Blind/Institut National Canadien pour les Aveugles.

Muten, Burleigh. Miss Emily. Phelan, Matt, illus. 2014. (ENG.). 144p. (J). (gr. 2-5). 15.99 *(978-0-7636-5734-5(4))* Candlewick Pr.

Myers, Christopher. My Pen. Myers, Christopher, illus. 2015. (ENG., Illus.). 32p. (J). (gr. -1-k). 16.99 *(978-1-4231-0371-4(8))* Hyperion Bks. for Children.

Nagy, Jim. Daniel the Spaniel- Let's Go Home! 2010. 36p. (J). pap. 15.95 *(978-1-4327-5310-8(X))* Outskirts Pr., Inc.

Namm, Diane. Guess Who? Sheldon, David, illus. 2004. (My First Reader Ser.). (ENG.). 32p. (J). (gr. k-1). pap. 3.95 *(978-0-516-25503-3(7)*, Children's Pr.) Scholastic Library Publishing.

Naumann, Jen. Cheating Death. 2013. 370p. pap. 13.99 *(978-0-9883902-0-1(5))* Naumann, Jennifer.

Nayar, Nandini. What Could It Be? Manetti, Francesco, illus. 2013. (ENG.). 28p. (J). (gr. -1). 11.95 *(978-81-8190-285-6(8))* Karadi Tales Co. Pvt. Ltd. IND. Dist: Consortium Bk. Sales & Distribution.

Neffen, Marjorie E. My Big Sister Knows... 2012. 30p. (-18). 24.95 *(978-1-62709-509-9(8))* America Star Bks.

Nelson-Schmidt, Michelle. Bob Is a Unicorn. Nelson-Schmidt, Michelle, illus. 2014. (ENG., Illus.). 28p. (J). 14.99 *(978-1-61067-155-2(4))* Kane Miller.

Nesbit, E. Story of the Treasure Seekers. 2006. pap. *(978-1-4068-3507-6(2))* Echo Library.

—The Story of the Treasure Seekers: Being the Adventures of the Bastable Children in Search of a Fortune. 2007. (ENG.). 150p. pap. 18.99 *(978-1-4346-5163-1(0))*; 170p. pap. 21.99 *(978-1-4346-5164-8(9))* Creative Media Partners, LLC.

—The Story of the Treasure Seekers: Being the Adventures of the Bastable Children in Search of A Fortune. l.t. ed. 2005. 288p. pap. *(978-1-84637-207-0(0))* Echo Library.

Neubecker, Robert. What Little Boys Are Made Of. Neubecker, Robert, illus. 2012. (ENG., Illus.). 32p. (J). (gr. -1-3). 14.99 *(978-0-06-202355-1(1))* HarperCollins Pubs.

Newland, James P. A Smile Says It All. 2009. 48p. pap. 17.49 *(978-1-4490-3438-2(1))* AuthorHouse.

Nichols, Tucker & Nichols, Jon, illus. Crabtree. 2013. (ENG.). 32p. (J). (gr. -1-3). 17.95 *(978-1-936365-82-1(0))* McSweeney's Publishing.

Nielsen-Fernlund, Susin. The Magic Beads. Cote, Genevieve, illus. 2007. (ENG.). 32p. (J). (gr. -1-3). 16.95 *(978-1-894965-47-7(7))* Simply Read Bks. CAN. Dist: Ingram Publisher Services.

Niemann, Christoph. That's How! Niemann, Christoph, illus. 2011. (ENG., Illus.). 32p. (J). (gr. -1-k). 16.99 *(978-0-06-201963-9(5)*, Greenwillow Bks.) HarperCollins Pubs.

Nimmo, Jenny. The Beasties. Millward, Gwen, illus. 2012. (ENG.). 32p. (J). (gr. -1-k). pap. 8.99 *(978-1-4052-4335-3(X))* Egmont Bks., Ltd. GBR. Dist: Independent Pubs. Group.

NorthSouth Editors. Doodletastic! You Complete the Pictures! 2011. (ENG., Illus.). 164p. (J). (gr. k-k). pap. 12.95 *(978-0-7358-4047-8(4))* North-South Bks., Inc.

Not Every Princess. 2014. (Illus.). (J). *(978-1-4338-1647-5(4)*, Magination Pr.) American Psychological Assn.

November, Deborah, et al. Let's Visit Sesame Street. Mathieu, Joe, illus. 2010. (ENG.). 24p. (J). bds. 14.99 *(978-0-7944-2101-4(6))* Reader's Digest Assn., Inc., The.

Numeroff, Laura Joffe. Dogs Don't Wear Sneakers. Mathieu, Joe, illus. 2014. 40p. pap. 8.00 *(978-1-61003-344-2(2))* Center for the Collaborative Classroom.

Obiols, Anna. Stegosaurus: the Friendliest Dinosaur. Subi, illus. 2012. (Dinosaur Bks.). (ENG.). 36p. (J). (gr. -1-1). pap. 6.99 *(978-1-4380-0107-4(X))* Barron's Educational Series, Inc.

—Triceratops: the Strongest Dinosaur. Subi, illus. 2012. (Dinosaur Bks.). (ENG.). 36p. (J). (gr. -1-1). pap. 6.99 *(978-1-4380-0108-1(8))* Barron's Educational Series, Inc.

O'Brien, Thomas E. The Magic of Finbar. 2011. 68p. pap. 19.95 *(978-1-4560-4235-6(1))* America Star Bks.

O'Byrne, Nicola. Use Your Imagination. O'Byrne, Nicola, illus. 2015. (ENG., Illus.). 36p. (J). (gr. -1-2). 15.99 *(978-0-7636-8001-5(X)*, Nosy Crow) Candlewick Pr.

O'Connell, S. L. Short Stories to Tickle the Imagination. 2009. 48p. pap. 16.50 *(978-1-60693-670-2(0)*, Eloquent Bks.) Strategic Book Publishing & Rights Agency (SBPRA).

O'Connor, Jane. Express Yourself! A Doodle & Draw Book. Glasser, Robin Preiss, illus. 2011. (Fancy Nancy Ser.). (ENG.). 64p. (J). (gr. -1-3). pap. 6.99 *(978-0-06-188281-4(X)*, HarperFestival) HarperCollins Pubs.

—Sand Castles & Sand Palaces. Glasser, Robin Preiss, illus. 2014. (Fancy Nancy Ser.). (ENG.). 24p. (J). (gr. -1-3). pap. 4.99 *(978-0-06-226954-6(2)*, HarperFestival) HarperCollins Pubs.

O'Dowd, Chris & Murphy, Nick V. The Blunder Years. 2015. (Moone Boy Ser.). (ENG., Illus.). 400p. (J). (gr. 4-7). 14.99 *(978-1-250-05707-5(8)*, 9781250057075) Feiwel & Friends.

Oelschlager, Vanita. Francesca. Blanc, Mike, illus. 2008. (ENG.). 32p. (J). (gr. -1-3). 17.95 *(978-0-9800162-4-6(X))* VanitaBooks.

Offen, Hilda. There Might Be Giants. (Illus.). 25p. (J). pap. *(978-0-340-68149-7(7))* Hodder & Stoughton.

Oppenheim, Joanne. Wake up, Baby! Lynn, Sweat, illus. 2015. (ENG.). 34p. (J). pap. 11.95 *(978-1-899694-56-3(0)*, ipicturebooks) ibooks, Inc.

Oram, Hiawyn. In the Attic. Kitamura, Satoshi, illus. 2012. (ENG.). 32p. (J). (gr. -1-k). pap. 13.99 *(978-1-84939-298-3(6))* Andersen Pr. GBR. Dist: Independent Pubs. Group.

Orion, Cody. Do You Believe? 2008. 24p. pap. 12.99 *(978-1-4363-2434-2(3))* Xlibris Corp.

Ormerod, Jan. Lizzie Nonsense. Ormerod, Jan, illus. 2004. (Illus.). 40p. (J). *(978-1-877003-59-2(X))* Little Hare Bks. AUS. Dist: HarperCollins Pubs. Australia.

Osborne, Mary Pope. The Brave Little Seamstress. Potter, Giselle, illus. 2006. 32p. (gr. -1-3). 17.00 *(978-0-7569-6613-3(2))* Perfection Learning Corp.

Osteen, Victoria. Unexpected Treasures. Palmisciano, Diane, illus. 2009. (ENG.). 32p. (J). (gr. -1-3). 17.99 *(978-1-4169-5550-4(X)*, Little Simon Inspirations) Little Simon Inspirations.

Osterhold, Jared, illus. OLIVIA Takes a Trip. 2010. (Olivia TV Tie-In Ser.). (ENG.). 24p. (J). (gr. -1-1). 16.99 *(978-1-4424-1381-8(6)*, Simon Spotlight) Simon Spotlight.

O'Toole-Freel, Judy. Aardvark, Aardvark, How Do You Do!, 1 vol. 2008. (ENG.). 31p. 24.95 *(978-1-4241-6618-3(7))* America Star Bks.

Owen, Karen. I Could Be- Barroux, illus. 2009. (J). *(978-1-84686-289-2(2))* Barefoot Bks., Inc.

—I Could Be, You Could Be. Barroux, illus. 2010. (ENG.). 32p. (J). (gr. 1-3). 16.99 *(978-1-84686-405-6(4))* Barefoot Bks., Inc.

Owen, Karen & Barroux. I Could Be, You Could Be. 2012. (ENG., Illus.). 32p. (J). (gr. -1-1). pap. 7.99 *(978-1-84686-763-7(0))* Barefoot Bks., Inc.

Page, Nick. Do You Do a Didgeridoo. Baker, Sara, illus. 2008. 40p. (J). (gr. -1-3). bds. 15.99 *(978-1-84610-571-5(4))* Make Believe Ideas GBR. Dist: Nelson, Thomas Inc.

Paquette, Ammi-Joan. The Tiptoe Guide to Tracking Fairies. Unzner, Christa, illus. 2009. (ENG.). 32p. (J). (gr. -1-3). 15.95 *(978-1-933718-20-0(X))* Tanglewood Pr.

Paquette, Ammi-Joan & Unzner, Christa. The Tiptoe Guide to Tracking Fairies. 2010. (ENG., Illus.). 32p. (J). (gr. -1-3). pap. 8.95 *(978-1-933718-50-7(1))* Tanglewood Pr.

Park, Devin & Lee, Claudia. Howl Michigan. 2011. 138p. pap. 24.95 *(978-1-4560-8895-8(5))* America Star Bks.

Parker, Emma. All Aboard! 2010. (Illus.). 20p. pap. *(978-1-877561-74-0(6))* First Edition Ltd.

—Billy & the Deep Sea Monster. 2010. (Illus.). 20p. pap. *(978-1-877561-57-3(6))* First Edition Ltd.

Parlato, Stephen. The World That Loved Books. rev. ed. 2008. (ENG., Illus.). 32p. (J). (gr. -1-3). 16.95 *(978-1-894965-98-9(1))* Simply Read Bks. CAN. Dist: Ingram Publisher Services.

Patricelli, Leslie. The Birthday Box. Patricelli, Leslie, illus. 2009. (Leslie Patricelli Board Bks.). (ENG., Illus.). 26p. (J). (gr. k — 1). bds. 6.99 *(978-0-7636-4449-9(8))* Candlewick Pr.

—Faster! Faster! Patricelli, Leslie, illus. (Leslie Patricelli Board Bks.). (ENG., Illus.). (J). (-k). 2013. 30p. bds. 6.99 *(978-0-7636-6222-6(4))* 2012. 32p. 15.99 *(978-0-7636-5473-3(6))* Candlewick Pr.

—Faster! Faster!/Mas Rapido! Mas Rapido! Patricelli, Leslie, illus. 2013. (Leslie Patricelli Board Bks.). (ENG., Illus.). 30p. (J). (-k). bds. 6.99 *(978-0-7636-6611-8(4))* Candlewick Pr.

—Higher! Higher! Patricelli, Leslie, illus. 2010. (Leslie Patricelli Board Bks.). (ENG., Illus.). 30p. (J). (-k). bds. 6.99 *(978-0-7636-4433-8(1))* Candlewick Pr.

Patrick.J.Jardine. S r b U: Sir. Robert, Belmont, Uberdon the Third. 2011. 16p. pap. 13.99 *(978-1-4490-4336-0(4))* AuthorHouse.

Pavón, Mar. Zaira & the Dolphins. 2012. (ENG., Illus.). 32p. (J). (gr. k-2). *(978-84-15241-07-2(0))* D P & G Military Pubs.

—Zaira y los Delfines. 2012. (SPA & ENG., Illus.). 32p. (J). (gr. k-2). *(978-84-15241-02-7(X))* D P & G Military Pubs.

Payne, Gaynell. I Go Exploring. Buffinet, Jacqueline, illus. 2012. 34p. 21.99 *(978-0-9884657-0-1(1))* DreamLand Mediaworks LLC.

Payne, Laurie. Mush & the Big Blue Flower. Campbell, Ruth, illus. 2007. (ENG.). 104p. (J). (gr. -1). pap. 12.95 *(978-0-88982-242-9(5))* Oolichan Bks. CAN. Dist: Univ. of Toronto Pr.

Paz, Veronica. Play Pretend with Muno. 2009. (Yo Gabba Gabba! Ser.). (ENG.). 12p. (J). (gr. -1-1). bds. 6.99 *(978-1-4169-8508-2(5),* Simon Spotlight) Simon Spotlight.

Peaty, Mary Alice. The Girl Who Lived on the Moon. 2008. 44p. pap. 26.95 *(978-0-557-02225-0(8))* Lulu Pr., Inc.

A Pebble Story. 2014. (ENG., Illus.). 26p. (J). (gr. -1 — 1). bds. 6.95 *(978-1-55451-654-4(4),* 9781554516544) Annick Pr., Ltd. CAN. Dist: Publishers Group West (PGW).

Peck, Jan. Pirate Treasure Hunt!, 1 vol. Tans, Adrian, illus. 2008. (ENG.). 32p. (J). (gr. k-3). 16.99 *(978-1-58980-549-1(6))* Pelican Publishing Co., Inc.

Peck, Michael. The Booger Train, 1 vol. 2009. 31p. pap. 24.95 *(978-1-60813-939-2(5))* America Star Bks.

Pedersen, Laura & Weber, Penny. Ava's Adventure, 1 vol. 2014. (ENG., Illus.). 32p. (gr. 1-6). 16.95 *(978-0-88448-388-5(6),* 884388) Tilbury Hse. Pubs.

Pedersen, Peggy A. Jasmine & the Magic Squirrel. 2008. 12p. pap. 24.95 *(978-1-60474-052-3(3))* America Star Bks.

Pedlar, David Stewart. The Emu Who Knew He Could Fly! 2013. 32p. pap. 16.95 *(978-1-4525-7612-1(2),* Balboa Pr.) Author Solutions, Inc.

Pennypacker, Sara. Sparrow Girl. Tanaka, Yoko, illus. 2009. (ENG.). 40p. (J). (gr. k-4). 16.99 *(978-1-4231-1187-0(7))* Hyperion Pr.

Perrault, Charles. OXFORD WORLD'S CLASSICS: THE COMPLETE FAIRY TALES. 2010. (Oxford World's Classics Ser.). (ENG., Illus.). 256p. pap. 13.95 *(978-0-19-958580-9(6))* Oxford Univ. Pr., Inc.

Perry, Gina. Small. 2017. (ENG.). 40p. (J). (gr. -1-3). 17.99 ***(978-1-4998-0401-0(6))*** Little Bee Books Inc.

Peruzzo, Nicolas. Safari Dreams. Peruzzo, Nicolas, illus. 2012. (Illus.). 26p. pap. 9.99 *(978-1-61225-162-2(5))* Mirror Publishing.

Petrella, Angela, et al. Recipe. Althea, Erin & Bertino, Mike, illus. 2013. (ENG.). 48p. (J). (gr. -1-3). 17.95 *(978-1-936365-84-5(7))* McSweeney's Publishing.

Petreman, Gwen. A Weird Week. 2012. 20p. (-18). pap. 11.59 *(978-1-4669-5495-3(7))* Trafford Publishing.

Petty, Dev. Claymates. 2017. (ENG., Illus.). 40p. (J). (gr. -1-3). 16.99 *(978-0-316-30311-8(9))* Little Brown & Co.

Philips, Lyn D. Curiosity. Gadeselli, Natalie, illus. 2013. 32p. pap. *(978-1-904928-27-0(7))* Copeland & Wickson.

Phillips, Beth Ann. Crystal Kingdom, 1 vol. 2009. 63p. pap. 19.95 *(978-1-60813-003-0(7))* America Star Bks.

Phillips, Dee. What Can I Be? 2010. (Look at Me! Ser.). (ENG.). 5p. (J). (gr. -1-k). bds. 6.95 *(978-1-84696-199-1(8),* TickTock Books) Octopus Publishing Group GBR. Dist: Independent Pubs. Group.

—Who Can I Be? 2010. (Look at Me! Ser.). (ENG.). 5p. (J). (gr. -1-k). bds. 6.95 *(978-1-84696-200-4(5),* TickTock Books) Octopus Publishing Group GBR. Dist: Independent Pubs. Group.

Picado, Gail. Magical Bandages. 2008. 32p. per. 24.95 *(978-1-4241-8851-2(2))* America Star Bks.

Pinette, Melanie. Looking Up. 2008. 17p. pap. 24.95 *(978-1-60610-905-2(7))* America Star Bks.

Pipal, Michele. Lines. 2012. 20p. pap. 15.10 *(978-1-4772-4887-4(0))* AuthorHouse.

Pirnot, Karen Hutchins. The Door in the Floor. Ross, Julie, illus. 2009. 24p. pap. 12.95 *(978-0-9823002-6-8(3))* Peppertree Pr., The.

Pizzoli, Greg. The Watermelon Seed. Pizzoli, Greg, illus. 2013. (ENG., Illus.). 40p. (J). (gr. -1-k). 16.99 *(978-1-4231-7101-0(2))* Disney Pr.

Poblocki, Dan. The Haunting of Gabriel Ashe. (ENG.). 288p. (J). (gr. 5-9). 2015. pap. 7.99 *(978-0-545-40271-2(9))* 2013. 16.99 *(978-0-545-40270-5(0))* Scholastic, Inc. (Scholastic Pr.).

Polacco, Patricia. Emma Kate. Polacco, Patricia, illus. (ENG., Illus.). (J). (gr. -1-k). 2008. 32p. pap. 6.99 *(978-0-14-241196-4(5),* Puffin Books) 2005. 40p. 17.99 *(978-0-399-24452-0(2),* Philomel Bks.) Penguin Young Readers Group.

Pollock, Jim. A Whole Different Animal. Pollock, Mary Ellen, illus. 2007. 89p. (J). 17.00 net. *(978-0-9763675-2-9(1))* First Flight Bks.

Portis, Antoinette. Not a Stick. Portis, Antoinette, illus. 2007. (ENG., Illus.). 32p. (J). (gr. -1-1). 14.99 *(978-0-06-112325-2(0))* HarperCollins Pubs.

—Princess Super Kitty. Portis, Antoinette, illus. 2011. (ENG., Illus.). 40p. (J). (gr. -1-3). 14.99 *(978-0-06-182725-9(8))* HarperCollins Pubs.

Posner-Sanchez, Andrea. A Knight in Sticky Armor (Disney Junior: Doc Mcstuffins) Random House Disney Staff, illus. 2012. (Little Golden Book Ser.). (ENG.). 24p. (J). (-k). 4.99 *(978-0-7364-3030-2(X),* Golden/Disney) Random Hse. Children's Bks.

Potter, Giselle. Tell Me What to Dream About. 2015. (ENG., Illus.). 40p. (J). (gr. -1-2). 17.99 *(978-0-385-37423-1(2),* Schwartz & Wade Bks.) Random Hse. Children's Bks.

—This Is My Dollhouse. 2016. (ENG., Illus.). 40p. (J). (gr. -1-3). 17.99 *(978-0-553-52153-5(5),* Schwartz & Wade Bks.) Random Hse. Children's Bks.

Povandra, Shirley. My Imaginary Friend. 2007. 44p. pap. 17.95 *(978-1-59526-669-9(0))* Aeon Publishing Inc.

Press, Applesauce. 3-D Disgusting Doodles Book & Kit: Where Your Gross-Out Imagination Jumps off the Page! 2012. (ENG.). 128p. (J). 12.95 *(978-1-60433-225-4(5),* Applesauce Pr.) Cider Mill Pr. Bk. Pubs., LLC.

Preston-Gannon, Frann. Sloth Slept On. 2015. (ENG., Illus.). 32p. (J). (gr. -1 — 1). 14.95 *(978-1-4549-1611-6(7))* Sterling Publishing Co., Inc.

Pynn, Susan. Jelly Bean Row, 1 vol. Pratt, Liz, illus. 2011. (ENG.). 32p. (J). (gr. k-5). pap. 9.95 *(978-1-897174-80-7(2),* Tuckamore Bks) Creative Bk. Publishing CAN. Dist: Orca Bk. Pubs. USA.

Quinton, Sasha. Florabelle. Barrager, Brigette & Tcherevkoff, Michel, illus. 2015. (ENG.). 40p. (J). (gr. -1-3). 15.99 *(978-0-06-229182-0(3))* HarperCollins Pubs.

Ragin, M. K. Mildred Row & Improper Bounds. 2006. 185p. pap. 24.95 *(978-1-4137-9724-4(5))* America Star Bks.

Raine, Ame. A Ray of Light: Key Keepers Book #3. 2008. 180p. pap. 13.95 *(978-0-595-53464-7(3))* iUniverse, Inc.

Rancourt, Cheryle. The Puff Family: Volume 1. 2009. 28p. pap. 12.99 *(978-1-4389-4442-5(X))* AuthorHouse.

Randolph, Tammy. Cricket's Starry Night. 2011. 28p. pap. 15.99 *(978-1-4568-4506-3(3))* Xlibris Corp.

Rash, Ron. The Shark's Tooth. Martin, Cecile L. K., illus. 2015. (Young Palmetto Bks.). (ENG.). 40p. (J). pap. 12.95 *(978-1-61117-527-1(5))* Univ. of South Carolina Pr.

Rasheed, Winona. Smiles & Frowns Through Animal Town's Storybook. 2008. 55p. pap. 13.70 *(978-1-4357-4617-6(1))* Lulu Pr., Inc.

—Sugar & Spice Fairy Tales for Girls. 2008. 69p. pap. 20.51 *(978-1-4357-4619-0(8))* Lulu Pr., Inc.

Rath, Tom H. Donkey Oatie's Fashion Statement. MacAdam, Ian Paul, illus. 2012. 32p. pap. *(978-0-9866065-7-1(X))* Wood Islands Prints.

Rau, Dana. Moon Walk. Buchs, Thomas, illus. 3rd ed. 2003. (Soundprints' Read-and-Discover Ser.). (ENG.). 48p. (J). (gr. -1-3). pap. 4.35 *(978-1-59249-015-8(8),* S2006) Soundprints.

Ray, Ann. Just Imagine What You Can Do! 2008. 20p. pap. 12.99 *(978-1-4343-8874-2(3))* AuthorHouse.

Raymond, Jeanpaul. The Kids That Could. 2009. 40p. pap. 17.99 *(978-1-4389-5585-8(5))* AuthorHouse.

Reed-Guldin, Emily. Sarah & Sammi's Playhouse: Mermaid Adventure. 2009. 36p. pap. 16.99 *(978-1-4389-9342-3(0))* AuthorHouse.

Regan, Dian. Space Boy & His Dog. Neubecker, Robert, illus. 2015. (Space Boy Ser.). (ENG.). 32p. (J). (gr. k-5). 16.95 *(978-1-59078-955-1(5))* Boyds Mills Pr.

—Space Boy & the Space Pirate. Neubecker, Robert, illus. 2016. (Space Boy Ser.). (ENG.). 40p. (J). (gr. k-5). 16.95 *(978-1-59078-956-8(3))* Boyds Mills Pr.

Reid, Alastair. Supposing. Gill, Bob, illus. 2010. (ENG.). 48p. (J). (gr. -1-3). 15.95 *(978-1-59017-369-5(4),* NYR Children's Collection) New York Review of Bks., Inc., The.

Reilly, Michael. Monster Sandwich. 2009. 50p. (J). pap. 31.99 *(978-1-4415-0056-4(1))* Xlibris Corp.

Reizer, Edwina & Licata, Rosemarie. The Magic Mountain. 2010. 48p. pap. 20.00 *(978-0-557-39884-3(3))* Lulu Pr., Inc.

Renfroe, Marjorie. The Doll Safari. 2009. 28p. pap. 15.49 *(978-1-4389-5130-0(2))* AuthorHouse.

Reschke, Kathleen. Monsters in My Basement. 2009. 72p. pap. 24.99 *(978-1-4389-5793-7(9))* AuthorHouse.

Rexing, Debbie. The Writing Traits... My Perilous Journey, & I'm Only A 3rd Grader! 2010. 20p. 12.00 *(978-0-557-51197-6(6))* Lulu Pr., Inc.

Reynolds, Luke. Bedtime Blast-Off! Yamada, Mike, illus. 2016. (ENG.). 40p. (J). (gr. -1-1). 16.99 *(978-0-545-77855-8(7),* Orchard Bks.) Scholastic, Inc.

Reynolds, Peter H. Happy Dreamer. 2017. (ENG., Illus.). 32p. (J). (gr. -1-3). 17.99 *(978-0-545-86501-2(8))* Scholastic, Inc.

RH Disney & Posner-Sanchez, Andrea. Olaf Loves ... Everything! (Disney Frozen) RH Disney, illus. 2016. (Pictureback(R) Ser.). (ENG., Illus.). 16p. (J). (gr. -1-1). pap. 4.99 *(978-0-7364-3590-1(5),* RH/Disney) Random Hse. Children's Bks.

Ricchi, Brenda. The Grandchildren's Bible Journeys - the Creation Story. 2010. 35p. pap. 17.00 *(978-0-557-14903-2(7))* Lulu Pr., Inc.

Rice, Clay. The Stick. Rice, Clay, illus. 2014. (ENG., Illus.). 32p. (J). 16.95 *(978-1-939629-28-9(4),* 9781939629289) Familius LLC.

Rice, Dona Herweck. I Can Be Anything, 1 vol. 2009. (Early Childhood Themes Ser.). (ENG., Illus.). 16p. (J). (gr. -1-2). pap. 6.99 *(978-1-4333-1475-9(4))* Shell Educational Publishing.

Rice, Donna Herweck. I Can Be Anything, 1 vol. 2009. (Early Childhood Themes Ser.). (ENG., Illus.). 16p. (J). (gr. -1-2). pap. 19.99 *(978-1-4333-1476-6(2))* Shell Educational Publishing.

Richard Bellingham Edd. The Fables of Boris: Invitations to Meaningful Conversations. 2009. 280p. 27.95 *(978-1-4401-6247-3(6));* pap. 17.95 *(978-1-4401-6245-9(X))* iUniverse, Inc.

Riley, Christine. Chester's Field O'Brien, Laurel, illus. 2004. 296p. (J). per. 17.50 *(978-0-9740683-6-7(5))* Authors & Artists Publishers of New York, Inc.

Rinck, Maranke & van der Linden, Martijn. I Feel a Foot. 2008. (ENG., Illus.). 32p. (J). (gr. -1-1). 16.95 *(978-1-59078-638-3(6),* Lemniscaat) Boyds Mills Pr.

Rinker, Sherri Duskey. Silly Wonderful You. McDonnell, Patrick, illus. 2016. 40p. (J). (gr. -1-3). 17.99 *(978-0-06-227105-1(9))* HarperCollins Pubs.

Riordan, Betty J. The Imaginary Journeys of Bj & Dobbin. 2008. 108p. pap. 11.99 *(978-1-60647-432-7(4))* Salem Author Services.

Rivera, Rafael, et al. Baseball on Mars/Béisbol en Marte. Rivera, Rafael et al, illus. 2009.Tr. of Béisbol en Marte. (SPA & ENG.). 32p. (J). (gr. -1-3). 16.95 *(978-1-55885-521-2(1))* Arte Publico Pr.

Robaard, Jedda. If My Mom Were a Bird. 2015. (ENG., Illus.). 40p. (J). (gr. -1-2). 14.99 *(978-1-4998-0021-0(5))* Little Bee Books Inc.

Robert, Bulla Clyde. The Chalk Box Kid. 10th rev. ed. 2014. (Stepping Stone Book Ser.). (ENG.). 64p. (J). (gr. 12-12). 8.24 *(978-1-63245-220-7(0))* Lectorum Pubns., Inc.

Robert, Nadine. Joseph Fipps. Godbout, Geneviève, illus. 2014. (ENG.). 64p. (J). (gr. -1-2). 16.95 *(978-1-59270-117-9(5))* Enchanted Lion Bks., LLC.

Roberts, Victoria. Best Pet Ever. Allwright, Deborah, illus. 2011. (ENG.). 32p. pap. 7.95 *(978-1-58925-432-9(5))* Tiger Tales.

Robinson, Hilary. Croc by the Rock. Gordon, Mike, illus. 2005. 32p. (J). lib. bdg. 9.00 *(978-1-4242-0885-2(8))* Fitzgerald Bks.

Robinson, Timberly. Masterpiece Creation. 2009. 16p. pap. 8.99 *(978-1-4343-5462-4(8))* AuthorHouse.

Robinson, Vickie J. Use Your Imagination. Long, Corey, illus. 2008. 24p. pap. 24.95 *(978-1-60703-825-2(0))* America Star Bks.

Rodriguez, Angelica. Mia y Primos/Mia & Cousins: Yo grito,corro y grito / I scream, run & Scream. 2009. 24p. pap. 12.49 *(978-1-4389-7095-0(1))* AuthorHouse.

Rodriguez, Susan R. The Meadow of Mine. 2009. 52p. pap. 22.49 *(978-1-4389-9979-1(8))* AuthorHouse.

Rogers, Suzanne J. Cody Meets A Butterfly. 2008. 72p. pap. 19.95 *(978-1-4327-2069-8(4))* Outskirts Pr., Inc.

Roorda, Julie. Wings of a Bee, 1 vol. 2008. (ENG., Illus.). 224p. (YA). (gr. 7-11). pap. *(978-1-894549-68-4(6),* Sumach Pr.) Canadian Scholars.

Roscoe, Lily. The Night Parade. Walker, David, illus. 2014. (ENG.). 32p. (J). (— 1). 16.99 *(978-0-545-39623-3(9),* Orchard Bks.) Scholastic, Inc.

Rose, Jeremy. If I Could Fly... 2013. 36p. pap. 15.99 *(978-1-4624-0665-4(3),* Inspiring Voices) Author Solutions, Inc.

Rosenbaum, Andria Warmflash. Meg Goldberg on Parade. Lyles, Christopher, illus. 2015. (ENG.). 32p. (J). (gr. -1-3). 17.99 *(978-1-4677-3906-1(5),* Kar-Ben Publishing) Lerner Publishing Group.

Ross, Marlene. The Adventures of Donny the Doorknob. Hallam, Colleen and Peggy, illus. 2009. 32p. pap. 24.95 *(978-1-61546-539-2(1))* America Star Bks.

Rossell, Judith. Oliver. Rossell, Judith, illus. 2012. (ENG., Illus.). 32p. (J). (gr. -1-2). 16.99 *(978-0-06-202210-3(5))* HarperCollins Pubs.

Roth, David. The Adventures of the Magnificent Seven. 2009. 347p. pap. 26.88 *(978-0-557-09999-3(4))* Lulu Pr., Inc.

Rothman, Seymour. Tales from the Imagi Nation. 2010. 80p. pap. 17.99 *(978-1-4490-7088-5(4))* AuthorHouse.

Rudd, Bill. Broken Circle: The Black-footed Ferrets. 2010. (Illus.). (J). 19.99 *(978-1-60507-066-7(1))* Lunchbox Lessons.

Rudge, Glen. The Sun Rose & the Wind Blue. 2009. 16p. pap. 12.95 *(978-1-4389-5735-7(1))* AuthorHouse.

Rudolph, Miriam. A Frozen Dream. 2009. 28p. pap. 12.00 *(978-1-60693-962-8(9),* Eloquent Bks.) Strategic Book Publishing & Rights Agency (SBPRA).

Rue, Nancy N. Sophie Steps Up, 1 vol. 2009. (Faithgirlz! Ser.: No. 4). (ENG.). 128p. (J). pap. 6.99 *(978-0-310-71841-3(4))* Zonderkidz.

—Sophie's Friendship Fiasco. 2009. (Faithgirlz! Ser.: No. 7). (ENG.). 128p. (J). pap. 6.99 *(978-0-310-71842-0(2))* Zonderkidz.

Ruiz, Rachel. When Penny Met POTUS. Manwill, Melissa A., illus. 2016. (Fiction Picture Bks.). (ENG.). 32p. (gr. 2-3). lib. bdg. 27.99 *(978-1-5158-0218-1(3),* Fiction Picture Bks.) Picture Window Bks.

Russell, Katherine. Imagine the Butterfly Within Me. 2008. 52p. pap. 26.95 *(978-1-4327-2642-3(0))* Outskirts Pr., Inc.

Ryan, Muriel Drake. The Innkeeper's Wife. 2012. 34p. pap. 16.95 *(978-1-4497-6244-5(1),* WestBow Pr.) Author Solutions, Inc.

S, Peter. 12 Minutes: So Short Stories. 2011. 28p. pap. 15.99 *(978-1-4568-8841-1(2))* Xlibris Corp.

Saccheri, Josephine. Magic on the Wall, 1 vol. Carrescia, Reid, illus. 2009. 11p. pap. 24.95 *(978-1-61546-374-9(7))* America Star Bks.

Safer, Catherine Hogan. What If Your Mom Made Raisin Buns?, 1 vol. Rose, Hilda, illus. 2007. (ENG.). 32p. (J). (gr. -1-2). pap. 8.95 *(978-1-897174-03-6(9),* Tuckamore Bks) Creative Bk. Publishing CAN. Dist: Orca Bk. Pubs. USA.

Sajewel, Jamie. Do Watermelons Grow on Trees? 2011. 51p. pap. 23.95 *(978-1-4327-5859-2(4))* Outskirts Pr., Inc.

Salesman, Awel P. Jo-Dene's Little Feet. 2009. 16p. pap. 8.49 *(978-1-4389-4529-3(9))* AuthorHouse.

Salisbury, Linda G. Mudd Saves the Earth: Booger Glue, Cow Diapers & Other Good Ideas. 2009. (Illus.). 96p. (J). pap. 8.95 *(978-1-881539-47-6(4))* Tabby Hse. Bks.

Salyer, Jennifer Marie. My Shadow. Salyer, Adam Ernest, illus. 2011. 32p. pap. *(978-1-77067-642-8(2))* FriesenPress.

Sande, Hans. Snake in the Grass. Vetleseter, Tonje, tr. from NOR. Moursund, Gry, illus. 2008. 40p. (J). (gr. -1-1). 16.95 *(978-0-9815761-0-7(9))* Mackenzie Smiles, LLC.

Sanders, Gaye Lynn. Chameleon Girl. 2008. 60p. pap. 16.95 *(978-1-60703-643-2(6))* America Star Bks.

Sanders, Rob. Rodzilla. Santat, Dan, illus. 2017. (ENG.). 48p. (J). (gr. -1-3). 17.99 ***(978-1-4814-5779-8(9),*** McElderry, Margaret K. Bks.) McElderry, Margaret K. Bks.

Sanders-Wells, Linda. Maggie's Monkeys. Carter, Abby, illus. 2009. (ENG.). 32p. (J). (gr. -1-2). 16.99 *(978-0-7636-3326-4(7))* Candlewick Pr.

Sanrio Company, LTD. Hello Kitty Presents the Storybook Collection: Alice's Adventures in Wonderland. 2017. (Hello Kitty Storybook Ser.). (ENG., Illus.). 32p. (J). (gr. -1-k). pap. 6.95 *(978-1-4197-2488-6(6),* Abrams Appleseed) Abrams, Inc.

Santat, Dan. The Adventures of Beekle: The Unimaginary Friend. 2014. (ENG., Illus.). 40p. (J). (gr. -1-3). 17.99 *(978-0-316-19998-8(2))* Little, Brown Bks. for Young Readers.

Saphin, Wendy. Rosie's Box: A Box Full of Surprises. Saphin, Wendy, illus. 2012. (Illus.). 20p. pap. 10.95 *(978-1-62212-457-2(X),* Strategic Bk. Publishing) Strategic Book Publishing & Rights Agency (SBPRA).

Sarah, Linda. Big Friends. Davies, Benji, illus. 2016. (ENG.). 32p. (J). 16.99 *(978-1-62779-330-8(5),* 9781627793308, Holt, Henry & Co. Bks. For Young Readers) Holt, Henry & Co.

Sargent, Dave & Sargent, Pat. Bo Bo's Big Imagination, 10 vols., Vol. 13. Robinson, Laura, illus. 2004. (Learn to Read Ser.: 10).Tr. of Gran Imaginacion de Bo Bo. 18p. (J). pap. 10.95 *(978-1-56763-822-6(8))* Ozark Publishing.

Sauer, Cat. Flip Flop & Hoot. Jankowski, Daniel, illus. l.t. ed. 2006. (Brown Bag Bedtime Bks.: 1). 35p. (J). (gr. -1-2). 16.95 incl. audio compact disk *(978-0-9704460-6-0(3))* Writer's Ink. Studios, Inc.

—A Possum in the Roses. Jankowski, Daniel, illus. l.t. ed. 2006. (Brown Bag Bedtime Bks.: 1). 27p. (J). (gr. -1-2). 16.95 incl. audio compact disk *(978-0-9704460-7-7(1))* Writer's Ink. Studios, Inc.

—What's a Jaybird to Do? Jankowski, Dan, illus. l.t. ed. 2003. (Brown Bag Bedtime Bks.: 1). 31p. (YA). spiral bd. 16.95 *(978-0-9704460-8-4(X))* Writer's Ink. Studios, Inc.

Sawyer-Aitch, Anne. Nalah & the Pink Tiger. Sawyer-Aitch, Anne, illus. 2013. (ENG., Illus.). 40p. pap. 13.95 *(978-1-938063-00-8(7),* Mighty Media Kids) Mighty Media Pr.

Scanlon, Liz Garton. Another Way to Climb a Tree. Hooper, Hadley, illus. 2017. (ENG.). 40p. (J). 17.99 *(978-1-62672-352-8(4),* 9781626723528) Roaring Brook Pr.

Schachner, Judy. Skippyjon Jones. Schachner, Judy, illus. 2005. (Skippyjon Jones Ser.). (ENG., Illus.). 32p. (J). (gr. k-k). reprint ed. pap. 6.99 *(978-0-14-240403-4(9),* Puffin Books) Penguin Young Readers Group.

—Skippyjon Jones. 2009. (Illus.). 32p. 17.00 *(978-1-60686-417-3(3))* Perfection Learning Corp.

—Skippyjon Jones in the Doghouse. 2009. (Illus.). 32p. 17.00 *(978-1-60686-419-7(X))* Perfection Learning Corp.

—Skippyjon Jones Presto-Change-O. 2010. (Skippyjon Jones Ser.). (ENG.). 32p. (J). (gr. -1-k). 17.99 *(978-0-525-42358-4(3),* Dutton Books for Young Readers) Penguin Young Readers Group.

—Up & Down. Schachner, Judy, illus. 2007. (Skippyjon Jones Ser.). (ENG., Illus.). 12p. (J). (gr. -1 — 1). bds. 6.99 *(978-0-525-47807-2(8),* Dutton Books for Young Readers) Penguin Young Readers Group.

Schaefer, Lola M. One Busy Day: A Story for Big Brothers & Sisters. Meserve, Jessica, illus. 2014. (ENG.). 40p. (J). (gr. -1-k). 16.99 *(978-1-4231-7112-6(8))* Hyperion Bks. for Children.

Scheel, Morgan Lee. The Fabulous Glitter Girl. Sbandelli, Angela, illus. 2017. (ENG.). 54p. (J). pap. 9.95 *(978-1-63047-998-5(5))* Morgan James Publishing.

Schmatjen, Marc. My Giraffe Makes Me Laugh. 2010. 24p. 12.95 *(978-1-4520-0941-4(4))* AuthorHouse.

Schoene, Kerstin & Gunetsreiner, Nina. Milo Is Not a Dog Today. 2015. (Illus.). 32p. (J). *(978-1-4896-3867-0(9))* Weigl Pubs., Inc.

—Milo Is Not a Dog Today. Schoene, Kerstin & Gunetsreiner, Nina, illus. 2014. (ENG., Illus.). 32p. (J). (gr. -1-3). 16.99 *(978-0-8075-4793-9(X))* Whitman, Albert & Co.

Scholastic, Inc. Staff. Friends Forever. 2012. (Lalaloopsy Ser.). (ENG.). 10p. (J). (gr. -1-k). bds. 12.99 *(978-0-545-46223-5(1))* Scholastic, Inc.

Schrader, Margaret. Green Knee-High Farm. Schrader, Kimberly, illus. 2009. 28p. pap. 12.95 *(978-1-60844-000-9(1))* Dog Ear Publishing, LLC.

Schuepbach, Lynnette. Cat Time. 2006. 28p. pap. 12.95 *(978-0-9759613-2-2(2))* Creative Sources.

Schwartz, Joanne. Pinny in Summer, 1 vol. Malenfant, Isabelle, illus. 2016. (ENG.). 32p. (J). (gr. -1-2). 16.95 *(978-1-55498-782-5(2))* Groundwood Bks. CAN. Dist: Publishers Group West (PGW).

Schwarz, Viviane. How to Find Gold. Schwarz, Viviane, illus. 2016. (ENG., Illus.). 32p. (J). (-k). 16.99 *(978-0-7636-8104-3(0))* Candlewick Pr.

Scott, Brandon James, illus. The Pancake Express. 2012. (Justin Time Ser.). (ENG.). 36p. (J). (gr. -1-3). 15.95 *(978-1-59702-035-0(4))* Immedium.

Scott, Lucy. Busy Busy! Scott, Lucy, illus. 2016. (ENG., Illus.). 32p. (J). (gr. -1-k). 15.99 *(978-1-939547-25-5(3))* Creston Bks.

Scott, Molly. Broken Bones Are No Fun, but Broken Bones Won't Stop My Play! Baker, David, illus. 2012. 32p. pap. 24.95 *(978-1-4626-7424-4(0))* America Star Bks.

Scotton, Rob. The Big Helper. Scotton, Rob, illus. 2015. (Splat the Cat Ser.). (ENG., Illus.). 24p. (J). (gr. -1-3). pap. 3.99 *(978-0-06-229427-2(X),* HarperFestival) HarperCollins Pubs.

—The Big Helper. 2015. (Splat the Cat 8X8 Ser.). (J). lib. bdg. 13.55 *(978-0-606-36491-1(9))* Turtleback Bks.

Scrivanich, Kerry Ann. My Gifted & Talented Adventure. 2010. 28p. pap. 14.99 *(978-1-4490-8502-5(4))* AuthorHouse.

Seiss, Ellie, adapted by. It's Okay, Try Again! 2011. (Yo Gabba Gabba! Ser.). (ENG.). 14p. (J). (gr. -1-k). bds. 5.99 *(978-1-4424-2900-0(3),* Simon Spotlight) Simon Spotlight.

Seuss, Dr. Oh, the Thinks You Can Think! 2014. (Big Bright & Early Board Book Ser.). (ENG., Illus.). 24p. (J). (-k). bds. 6.99 *(978-0-385-38713-2(X),* Random Hse. Bks. for Young Readers) Random Hse. Children's Bks.

—Y Pensar Que lo Vi Por la Calle Porvenir, 1. Canetti, Yanitzia James, tr. from ENG. 2006.Tr. of And to Think That I Saw It on Mulberry Street. (SPA., Illus.). (J). (gr. -1-3). 14.99 *(978-1-933032-07-8(3))* Lectorum Pubns., Inc.

H I

Sewell, Kele. Beewee & Meager to the Rescue! the Underbed Entertainment Network. 2008. 28p. pap. 12.50 (978-1-60693-326-8(4), Eloquent Bks.) Strategic Book Publishing & Rights Agency (SBPRA).
Shanahan, Lisa. My Mom Tarzan. Guthridge, Bettina, illus. 2008. (ENG.). 32p. (J). (gr. -1-3). (978-1-59692-239-6(7)) MacAdam/Cage Publishing, Inc.
Shannon, David. Alice the Fairy. Shannon, David, illus. (ENG., Illus.). (J). (gr. -1-k). 2009. pap. 9.95 incl. audio compact disk (978-0-545-11758-6(5)) 2004. 40p. 17.99 (978-0-439-49025-2(1), Blue Sky Pr., The) Scholastic, Inc.
—Alice the Fairy. 2004. (J). pap. (978-0-439-79165-6(0)) Scholastic, Inc.
Sharp, Euan. Diggedy Dozer in Ned at Night. 2009. 32p. pap. 13.90 (978-0-557-04447-4(2)) Lulu Pr., Inc.
Shaskan, Stephen. Max Speed. 2016. (ENG., Illus.). 32p. (J). (gr. -1-3). 17.99 (978-1-4814-4590-0(1), Simon & Schuster Bks. For Young Readers) Simon & Schuster Bks. For Young Readers.
Shea, John. If I Wasn't Me. 2009. 18p. 19.40 (978-0-557-05950-8(X)) Lulu Pr., Inc.
Sheridan, Luke. Luke & His Amazing Space Bed. McCartney, Jen, illus. 2010. (ENG.). 32p. (J). (gr. -1-3). 17.95 (978-0-9814536-6-8(X), Cambridge House Pr.) Sterling & Ross Pubs.
Sheridan, Sara. I'm Me! Chamberlain, Margaret, illus. 2011. (ENG.). 32p. (J). (gr. -1-k). 17.99 (978-0-545-28222-2(5), Chicken Hse., The) Scholastic, Inc.
Sheth, Kashmira. Tiger in My Soup, 1 vol. Ebbeler, Jefferey, illus. 2015. (ENG.). 32p. (J). (gr. -1-3). pap. 7.95 (978-1-56145-890-5(2)) Peachtree Pubs.
Shevah, Emma. Dream on, Amber. Crawford-White, Helen, illus. 2015. (ENG.). 272p. (J). (gr. 3-7). 12.99 (978-1-4926-2250-5(8), 9781492622505, Sourcebooks Jabberwocky) Sourcebooks, Inc.
Shield ARP, Peter J. Don Quixote & the Windmills, 1 vol. 2010. 30p. 24.95 (978-1-4512-9032-5(2)) PublishAmerica, Inc.
Shock, Tanya & Thomson, Roger. Walking in Courage: Stories of Virtue's Forest. 2012. 24p. pap. 12.95 (978-1-4497-3443-5(X), WestBow Pr.) Author Solutions, Inc.
Siewart, Pauline, illus. Look What I Can Do! 2009. (Watch This! Ser.). 32p. (J). (gr. -1-k). 22.60 (978-1-60754-452-4(0)); pap. 10.55 (978-1-60754-453-1(9)) Windmill Bks.
—Look What I Can Make! 2009. (Watch This! Ser.). 32p. (J). (gr. -1-k). 22.60 (978-1-60754-446-3(6)); pap. 10.55 (978-1-60754-447-0(4)) Windmill Bks.
—Look What I Can Play! 2009. (Watch This! Ser.). 32p. (J). (gr. -1-k). 22.60 (978-1-60754-458-6(X)); pap. 10.55 (978-1-60754-586-6(1)) Windmill Bks.
—See What I Can Do! 2009. (Watch This! Ser.). 32p. (J). (gr. -1-k). 22.60 (978-1-60754-455-5(5)); pap. 10.55 (978-1-60754-456-2(3)) Windmill Bks.
—See What I Can Make! 2009. (Watch This! Ser.). 32p. (J). (gr. -1-k). 22.60 (978-1-60754-449-4(0)); pap. 10.55 (978-1-60754-450-0(4)) Windmill Bks.
—See What I Can Play! 2009. (Watch This! Ser.). 32p. (J). (gr. -1-k). 22.60 (978-1-60754-461-6(X)); pap. 10.55 (978-1-60754-462-3(8)) Windmill Bks.
Siewart, Pauline. Look What I Can Play! 2009. (YA). pap. 10.55 (978-1-80754-586-4(5)) Windmill Bks.
Sif, Birgitta. Swish & Squeak's Noisy Day. 2017. (ENG.). 32p. (J). (-k). 16.99 **(978-0-399-55622-7(2))**; lib. bdg. 19.99 **(978-0-399-55623-4(0))** Random Hse. Children's Bks. (Knopf Bks. for Young Readers).
Sif, Birgitta. Where My Feet Go. 2016. (ENG., Illus.). 32p. (J). (-k). 16.99 (978-0-553-51164-2(5), Knopf Bks. for Young Readers) Random Hse. Children's Bks.
Silas, Steve. Where Do Bubbles Go? 2010. 24p. pap. 12.93 (978-1-4251-0964-6(0)) Trafford Publishing.
Silver, Connie. A Story Book for Beginning Readers. 2007. 124p. 20.95 (978-0-595-70501-6(4)); per. 10.95 (978-0-595-46524-8(2)) iUniverse, Inc.
Silverman, Erica. Let's Go to the Moon. Golden, Jess, illus. 2017. (Green Light Readers Level 2 Ser.). (ENG.). 32p. (J). (gr. -1-3). 12.99 (978-0-544-86760-4(2), HMH Books For Young Readers) Houghton Mifflin Harcourt Publishing Co.
Simplicity, Barberella. Uh-Oh, My Foogle Flopped! 2008. 20p. pap. 18.50 (978-1-60693-088-5(5), Eloquent Bks.) Strategic Book Publishing & Rights Agency (SBPRA).
Singer, Marilyn. What's a Banana? Pizzoli, Greg, illus. 2016. (ENG.). 24p. (J). (gr. -1-k). 12.95 (978-1-4197-2139-7(9), Abrams Appleseed) Abrams, Inc.
—What's an Apple? Pizzoli, Greg, illus. 2016. (ENG.). 24p. (J). (gr. -1-k). 12.95 (978-1-4197-2140-3(2), Abrams Appleseed) Abrams, Inc.
Sís, Peter. Dinosaur! Sís, Peter, illus. 2005. (ENG., Illus.). 28p. (J). (gr. -1-1). bds. 7.99 (978-0-06-075967-4(4), Greenwillow Bks.) HarperCollins Pubs.
—Madlenka. Sís, Peter, illus. 2010. (ENG., Illus.). 48p. (J). (gr. -1-3). pap. 8.99 (978-0-312-65912-7(1), 9780312659127) Square Fish.
Sisler, Stephanie. Matthews Monsters, a Creative Comprehensive Exercise. Grzelak, Kyle, illus. 2011. 32p. pap. 12.95 (978-1-61493-015-0(5)) Peppertree Pr., The.
Skyberg, Andrea, creator. Snickeyfritz. 2009. (ENG., Illus.). 48p. (J). 17.99 (978-0-615-25177-6(3)) Wooden Nickel Pr.
Smith-Armand, Kristie. Diamond in the Rough: More Fun Adventures with Abby Diamond. 2010. 256p. pap. 16.95 (978-1-4502-4618-7(4)) iUniverse, Inc.
Smith, Danna. Pirate Nap: A Book of Colors. Petrone, Valeria, illus. 2011. (ENG.). 40p. (J). lib. bdg. 14.99 (978-0-547-57531-5(9)) Houghton Mifflin Harcourt Publishing Co.
Smith, Darshiel & Haddi, Javon. Introducing the Rollies. 2013. 28p. pap. 24.95 (978-1-63000-582-5(7)) America Star Bks.
Smith, Gail. The Journey. 2008. 33p. pap. 19.95 (978-0-557-02065-2(4)) Lulu Pr., Inc.
Smith, Jennifer Dawn Deconinck. If I Could Float on A Cloud, Where Would I Go? 2010. 64p. pap. 12.99 (978-1-4520-3628-1(4)) AuthorHouse.
Smith, Jennifer Lynne. Things I Wonder. Perez, Angela J., ed. Gray, Angela M., illus. 2007. 36p. (J). 14.95 (978-0-9778328-5-9(6)) His Work Christian Publishing.
Smith, John C. Popee the Purple Pig-a-Saurus. 2010. 40p. pap. 16.99 (978-1-4490-9285-6(3)) AuthorHouse.
Smith, Linda. Kelly's Cabin, 1 vol. Krasulja, Zorica, illus. 2006. (Orca Echoes Ser.). (ENG.). 64p. (J). (gr. 2-3). per. 6.95 (978-1-55143-408-7(3)) Orca Bk. Pubs. USA.
Smith, Sr. Every Time I Look Up. 2011. 20p. pap. 24.95 (978-1-4626-1191-1(5)) America Star Bks.
Snider, Jesse Blaze. Toy Story: Some Assembly Required. Watson, Nathan, illus. 2010. (Toy Story Ser.). 112p. (J). pap. 9.99 (978-1-60886-570-3(3)) Boom! Studios.
Snyder, Donna. Rose & Rosey. 2008. 16p. pap. 24.95 (978-1-60441-618-3(1)) America Star Bks.
Snyder, Zilpha Keatley. The Egypt Game. 2011. 9.00 (978-0-7848-3470-1(9), Everbind) Marco Bk. Co.
—The Egypt Game. Raible, Alton, illus. 2007. (ENG.). 224p. (J). (gr. 3-7). 17.99 (978-1-4169-6065-2(1), Atheneum Bks. for Young Readers) Simon & Schuster Children's Publishing.
Sohmer, Ryan. Least I Could Do Beginnings Volume 1: Look at Me: Look at Me. 2010. 32p. 19.95 (978-0-9812163-3-1(1)) Blind Ferret Entertainment CAN. Dist: Diamond Bk. Distributors.
Soman, David & Davis, Jacky. Play All Day with Ladybug Girl. Soman, David, illus. 2013. (Ladybug Girl Ser.). (ENG., Illus.). 16p. (J). (gr. -1-k). 6.99 (978-0-448-46686-6(4), Grosset & Dunlap) Penguin Young Readers Group.
Spanabel, H. A. Skyler & the Skunks. 2009. 48p. pap. (978-1-84923-954-7(1)) YouWriteOn.
Spangler, Jon. The Sky Princess Moves to the Land of Peaches. 2009. 24p. pap. 11.95 (978-1-4490-0015-8(0)) AuthorHouse.
Spinelli, Eileen. Someday. Winstead, Rosie, illus. 2007. (ENG.). 32p. (J). (gr. -1-3). 17.99 (978-0-8037-2941-4(3), Dial Bks) Penguin Young Readers Group.
Spires, Ashley. Binky Takes Charge. Spires, Ashley, illus. 2012. (Binky Adventure Ser.: 4). (ENG., Illus.). 64p. (J). (gr. 2-5). 7.95 (978-1-55453-768-6(1)); 16.95 (978-1-55453-703-7(7)) Kids Can Pr., Ltd. CAN. Dist: Hachette Bk. Group.
Springer, Kristina. My Fake Boyfriend Is Better Than Yours. 2013. (ENG.). 208p. (YA). (gr. 6-9). pap. 6.99 (978-0-312-64159-7(1), 9780312641597) Square Fish.
Stadler, Alexander. Invasion of the Relatives. 2009. (Julian Rodriguez Ser.: 2). (ENG.). 144p. (J). (gr. 2-5). pap. 5.99 (978-0-439-91971-5(1), Scholastic Pr.) Scholastic, Inc.
—Trash Crisis on Earth, No. 1. 2009. (Julian Rodriguez Ser.: 1). (ENG.). 128p. (J). (gr. 2-5). 5.99 (978-0-439-91970-8(3), Scholastic Paperbacks) Scholastic, Inc.
Stanek, Robert, pseud. Explore the Solar System. 2010. 42p. pap. 11.99 (978-1-57545-179-4(4), Reagent Pr. Bks. for Young Readers) RP Media.
Stasio, M. L. Imagine If. 2011. 238p. pap. 24.95 (978-1-4626-4842-9(8)) America Star Bks.
Stein, Mathilde. The Child Cruncher. Van Hout, Mies, illus. 2008. (ENG.). 32p. (J). (gr. -1-3). 16.95 (978-1-59078-635-2(1)) Lemniscaat USA.
—Dear Daisy Dunnington. Groeninik, Chuck, illus. 2012. (ENG.). 32p. (J). (gr. 1). 17.95 (978-1-935954-18-7(0), 9781935954187) Lemniscaat USA.
Steiner, Dawn. The Silver Squirrel & Friends: The Original Book. 2009. 16p. pap. 8.99 (978-1-4389-2944-6(7)) AuthorHouse.
Steinke, Misty. Who Hung the Moon. 2013. 20p. pap. 6.99 (978-1-938768-17-0(5)) Gypsy Pubns.
Steinkraus, Kyla. La Casita Del Arbol. 2012. (SPA & ENG.). 24p. (gr. 2-3). pap. 8.95 (978-1-61810-539-4(6)) Rourke Educational Media.
Stephane, Nelly. Roland. François, André, illus. 2016. (ENG.). 36p. (J). (gr. -1-3). 17.95 (978-1-59270-204-6(X)) Enchanted Lion Bks., LLC.
Sterer, Gideon. Skyfishing. Bernatene, Poly, illus. 2017. (ENG.). 40p. (J). (gr. -1-3). 17.95 (978-1-4197-1911-0(4), Abrams Bks. for Young Readers) Abrams, Inc.
Stern, A. J. Funny Business, 4 vols. Marts, Doreen Mulryan, illus. 2011. (Frankly, Frannie Ser.: 4). (ENG.). 128p. (J). (gr. 1-3). pap. 5.99 (978-0-448-45540-2(4), Grosset & Dunlap) Penguin Young Readers Group.
Stewart, Joel. Dexter Bexley & the Big Blue Beastie. Stewart, Joel, illus. 2007. (ENG., Illus.). 32p. (J). (gr. -1-3). 16.95 (978-0-8234-2068-1(X)) Holiday Hse., Inc.
Stimpson, Aaron & Stimpson, Sarah. The Story Builders. 2010. 107p. pap. 12.95 (978-0-557-61011-2(7)) Lulu Pr., Inc.
Stockdale, Sean & Strick, Alex. Max the Champion. Asquith, Ros, illus. 2014. 32p. (J). pap. 8.99 (978-1-84780-519-5(1), Frances Lincoln) Quarto Publishing Group UK GBR. Dist: Littlehampton Bk Services, Ltd.
Stuart, Tara. Tara's Tales: Dream. 2012. 50p. pap. 16.99 (978-1-4575-0742-7(0)) Dog Ear Publishing, LLC.
Stussy, Virginia. Wishes & Wonder. 2007. (ENG.). 52p. per. 16.95 (978-1-4241-6086-0(3)) America Star Bks.
Suen, Anastasia. We're Going on a Dinosaur Dig. Myer, Ed, illus. 2012. (ENG.). 24p. (gr. k-1). pap. 8.95 (978-1-61810-299-7(0)) Rourke Educational Media.
Sullivan, Tom. I Used to Be a Fish. Sullivan, Tom, illus. 2016. (Illus.). 48p. (J). (gr. -1-3). 17.99 (978-0-06-245198-9(7)) HarperCollins Pubs.
Sundaram, Siddhartha & Raghuraman, Renuka S. Horace Leclaire & His Bottles of Air. Raghuraman, Savitri, illus. 2008. 36p. pap. 9.99 (978-1-935105-03-9(5)) Avid Readers Publishing Group.
Sutherland, Marc. The Waiting Place. Sutherland, Marc, illus. 2004. (Illus.). 24p. (J). (gr. k-4). reprint ed. 15.00 (978-0-7567-8382-2(8)) DIANE Publishing Co.
Sutton, Kelsey. The Lonely Ones. 2016. (ENG.). 240p. (J). (gr. 5). 16.99 (978-0-399-17289-2(0), Philomel Bks.) Penguin Young Readers Group.
Swann, Linda. The Land of Watermelon Mountains: Destinations Thru Imaginations. 2008. 24p. 12.99 (978-1-4389-2570-7(0)) AuthorHouse.
Sweetland, Nancy & Sweetland, Robert. If I Could/Si Yo Pudiera. 2008. (ENG & SPA.). 32p. (J). (gr. 4-7). pap. 7.95 (978-0-9794462-2-1(8)); 16.95 (978-0-9770906-9-3(8)) Continental Sales, Inc. (Raven Tree Pr.,Csi).
Swenson, Jamie A. If You Were a Dog. Raschka, Chris, illus. 2014. (ENG.). 40p. (J). (gr. -1-1). 17.99 (978-0-374-33530-4(3), 9780374335304, Farrar, Straus & Giroux (BYR)) Farrar, Straus & Giroux.
Sylvester, Sr. Talking Memories. Morrison, Nancy, illus. 2011. 36p. pap. 24.95 (978-1-4489-4967-0(X)) America Star Bks.
Tandi's World. 2006. (J). (978-0-9772634-0-0(1)) Hall, Monique P. Productions.
Tanksley, David. Michael Waylon & His Dinosaur Crew. 2012. 24p. pap. 24.95 (978-1-62709-763-5(5)) America Star Bks.
Tarver, Monroe S. Tales from the Mapmaker: Imagia & the Magic Pearls. 2015. (ENG.). 100p. (J). (gr. k-4). pap. 6.99 (978-0-9723936-5-2(X)) Wizarding World Pr.
Tashjian, Janet. Sticker Girl. Wilmink, Inga, illus. 2016. (Sticker Girl Ser.). (ENG.). 176p. (J). 13.99 (978-1-62779-335-3(6), 9781627793353, Holt, Henry & Co. Bks. For Young Readers) Holt, Henry & Co.
Tate, Bernice & Andy. Funspell. 2009. 20p. pap. 14.95 (978-1-4343-7103-4(4)) AuthorHouse.
Teague, Mark. The Pirate Jamboree. 2016. (ENG., Illus.). 40p. (J). (gr. -1-k). 17.99 (978-0-545-63221-8(8)) Scholastic, Inc.
Thaler, Mike. The Vice Principal from the Black Lagoon. Lee, Jared, illus. 2007. (J). pap. (978-0-439-87132-7(8)) Scholastic, Inc.
The Ciletti Publishing Group. Story Time Cafe Maisy's Blue Bath Set. The Ciletti Publishing Group, illus. 2010. (Illus.). (J). 24.95 (978-0-917665-71-4(6)) Ciletti Publishing Group, Inc., The.
Theroux, Phyllis. Serefina under the Circumstances. Priceman, Marjorie, illus. 2004. 30p. (J). (gr. k-4). reprint ed. (978-0-7567-7756-2(9)) DIANE Publishing Co.
Thomas, Jan. Can You Make a Scary Face? Thomas, Jan, illus. 2009. (ENG., Illus.). 40p. (J). (gr. -1-3). 15.99 (978-1-4169-8581-5(6), Beach Lane Bks.) Beach Lane Bks.
Thomas, Joan G. If Jesus Came to My House. McElrath-Eslick, Lori, illus. 2008. (HarperBlessings Ser.). (ENG.). 40p. (J). (gr. -1-3). 16.99 (978-0-06-083942-0(2)) HarperCollins Pubs.
Thomas, Maribel. Party in the Sky. 2009. 20p. pap. 13.50 (978-1-60693-364-0(7), Eloquent Bks.) Strategic Book Publishing & Rights Agency (SBPRA).
Thomas, Rob. Boom! Boom! Boom! There's a Dinosaur in My Room! 2013. 26p. pap. 9.99 (978-0-9910560-1-9(9)) Lincoln Bks.
Thompson, Heather M. If the World Were Made of Chocolate, 1 vol. 2009. 36p. pap. 24.95 (978-1-61546-965-9(6)) America Star Bks.
Thompson, John. Daniel & the Amazing Tickling Keefro. 2011. (Illus.). 32p. pap. 14.73 (978-1-4567-7630-5(4)) AuthorHouse.
Thompson, John M. & Schultz, George M. Just Imagine. Wodin, illus. 2006. 32p. (J). (gr. -1-3). 16.95 (978-0-9740190-6-2(2)) Illumination Arts Publishing Co., Inc.
Thompson, Kate. Switchers. 220p. (J). (gr. 4-7). pap. 5.99 (978-0-8072-1553-1(8)); 2004. (Switchers Ser.: Vol. 1). (gr. 5-9). pap. 38.00 incl. audio (978-0-8072-8138-3(7), YA115SP) Random Hse. Audio Publishing Group. (Listening Library).
Thomson, Sarah L. Imagine a Day. Gonsalves, Rob, illus. 2005. (Imagine A... Ser.). (ENG.). 40p. (J). (gr. -1-3). 19.99 (978-0-689-85219-0(3), Atheneum Bks. for Young Readers) Simon & Schuster Children's Publishing.
—Imagine a Night. Gonsalves, Rob, illus. 2003. (Imagine A... Ser.). (ENG.). 40p. (J). (gr. -1-3). 19.99 (978-0-689-85218-3(5), Atheneum Bks. for Young Readers) Simon & Schuster Children's Publishing.
—Imagine a Place. Gonsalves, Rob, illus. 2008. (Imagine A... Ser.). (ENG.). 40p. (J). (gr. -1-6). 19.99 (978-1-4169-6802-3(4), Atheneum Bks. for Young Readers) Simon & Schuster Children's Publishing.
Thurston, Alecia Frances. Shumalady's Butterfly Tree. 2010. 40p. pap. 18.49 (978-1-4490-5609-4(1)) AuthorHouse.
Tibo, Gilles. Simon's Disguise. 2004. (J). (gr. -1-2). spiral bd. (978-0-616-01790-6(1)); spiral bd. (978-0-616-01791-3(X)) Canadian National Institute for the Blind/Institut National Canadien pour les Aveugles.
Tidwell, Mae B. & Hancock, Vicki. Kyle Wants to Be a Monkey, 1 vol. 2009. 24p. pap. 24.95 (978-1-60749-751-6(4)) America Star Bks.
Tillman, Nancy. I'd Know You Anywhere, My Love. Tillman, Nancy, illus. (ENG., Illus.). (J). 2015. 34p. bds. 7.99 (978-1-250-07292-4(1), 9781250072924) 2013. 32p. (gr. -1-3). 17.99 (978-0-312-55368-5(4), 9780312553685) Feiwel & Friends.
Time for Your Mind. l.t. ed. 2006. (Illus.). 35p. (J). (978-0-9785480-1-8(9)) Mielcarek, David.
Timmers, Leo. Franky. Timmers, Leo, illus. 2016. (ENG., Illus.). 40p. (gr. -1-2). 16.99 (978-1-927271-93-3(2)); 33.32 (978-1-77657-053-9(7)); 33.32 (978-1-77657-054-6(5)) Gecko Pr. NZL. Dist: Lerner Publishing Group.
Tolan, Stephanie S. Wishworks, Inc. Bates, Amy June, illus. 2011. (ENG.). 160p. (J). (gr. 2-5). pap. 5.99 (978-0-545-03155-4(9), Levine, Arthur A. Bks.) Scholastic, Inc.
Tompert, Ann & Lister, Ralph. Little Fox Goes to the End of the World, 0 vols. Bryant, Laura J., illus. 2010. (ENG.). 32p. (J). (gr. -1-2). 16.99 (978-0-7614-5703-9(8), 9780761457039, Amazon Children's Publishing) Amazon Publishing.
Tone, Satoe. The Very Big Carrot. 2013. (ENG., Illus.). 26p. (J). 12.00 (978-0-8028-5426-1(5), Eerdmans Bks For Young Readers) Eerdmans, William B. Publishing Co.
Tong, Kevin. The Earth Machine. Tong, Kevin, illus. 2007. (Illus.). 32p. (J). (gr. -1-3). 15.95 (978-1-60108-001-1(8)) Red Cygnet Pr.
Tomio, Stacy. Cathy's Animal Garden: Enter at Your Own Risk. Bell, Samantha, illus. 2010. (J). (978-1-934617-04-5(0), Alma Little) Elva Resa Publishing, LLC.
Torrey, Richard. The Almost Terrible Playdate. Torrey, Rich, illus. 2016. (ENG.). 40p. (J). (gr. -1-2). 19.99 (978-0-375-97430-4(X), Doubleday Bks. for Young Readers) Random Hse. Children's Bks.
Toshiley. The Sponge & the River of Sleepiness. 2009. 24p. pap. 13.50 (978-1-60860-562-0(0), Eloquent Bks.) Strategic Book Publishing & Rights Agency (SBPRA).
Tracy, Joe. Arnie the Imagination Boy. 2011. 24p. pap. 15.99 (978-1-4568-9135-0(9)) Xlibris Corp.
Travitzky, Paul Joseph & Travitzky, Brianna Marie. Brianna Marie Wants to Be: A Cowgirl. 2009. 20p. pap. 11.95 (978-1-4490-2110-8(7)) AuthorHouse.
—Brianna Marie Wants to Be... A Veterinarian. 2010. 20p. 11.00 (978-1-4490-7701-3(3)) AuthorHouse.
Trevino, Ruby. Chocolate Feet, 1 vol. 2009. 16p. pap. 24.95 (978-1-61546-402-9(6)) America Star Bks.
Troyer, Gloria Irene. Beatrice & the Snow People. 2013. 114p. pap. 14.95 (978-1-62646-481-0(2)) Booklocker.com, Inc.
True, J. J. Billy Brite: Africa & Beyond. 2011. (Illus.). 112p. pap. 14.03 (978-1-4567-7281-9(3)) AuthorHouse.
Tullet, Hervé. The Game of Let's Go! Edicare Staff, ed. 2011. (ENG., Illus.). 14p. (gr. -1 — 1). 9.95 (978-0-7148-6075-6(1)) Phaidon Pr., Inc.
—iMezclalo Bien! 2017.Tr. of Couleurs. (ENG & SPA., Illus.). 64p. (J). 15.99 (978-1-4521-5933-1(5)) Chronicle Bks. LLC.
—Let's Play! 2016. (ENG., Illus.). 68p. (J). (gr. -1-k). 15.99 (978-1-4521-5477-0(5)) Chronicle Bks. LLC.
—Mix It Up! 2014.Tr. of Couleurs. (ENG., Illus.). 56p. (J). (gr. -1-k). 15.99 (978-1-4521-3735-3(8)) Chronicle Bks. LLC.
—Press Here. 2011. (ENG., Illus.). 56p. (J). (gr. -1-17). 15.99 (978-0-8118-7954-5(2)) Chronicle Bks. LLC.
—Press Here: The Big Book. 2016. (ENG., Illus.). 56p. (J). (gr. -1-k). 24.99 (978-1-4521-5480-0(5)) Chronicle Bks. LLC.
Tullet, Hervé & Perez, Peter L. Presiona Aqui. Perez, Peter L., illus. 2012. (SPA & ENG., Illus.). 56p. (J). (gr. -1-3). 15.99 (978-1-4521-1287-9(8)) Chronicle Bks. LLC.
Turcotte, Michael. Colours Made in Heaven, 1 vol. Turcotte, Derek, illus. 2009. 13p. pap. 24.95 (978-1-60836-316-2(3)) America Star Bks.
Tusa, Tricia. Follow Me. 2011. (ENG., Illus.). 40p. (J). (gr. -1-3). 16.99 (978-0-547-27201-6(4)) Houghton Mifflin Harcourt Publishing Co.
Tuvu. Tiny & Flat: Two Bestfriends. 2012. 32p. pap. 17.25 (978-1-4669-3651-5(7)) Trafford Publishing.
Twain, Mark, pseud. The Adventures of Tom Sawyer: With a Discussion of Imagination. Butterfield, Ned, illus. 2003. (Values in Action Illustrated Classics Ser.). 190p. (J). (978-1-59203-027-9(0)) Learning Challenge, Inc.
Uhlberg, Myron. Flying over Brooklyn, 1 vol. Fitzgerald, Gerald, illus. 2003. (ENG.). 32p. (J). (gr. k-3). pap. 7.95 (978-1-56145-294-1(7)) Peachtree Pubs.
Uhlig, Elizabeth. I Want to Be. Uhlig, Elizabeth, illus. 2008. (ENG., Illus.). (J). pap. 12.95 (978-0-9815345-1-0(1)) Marble Hse. Editions.
Underwood, Deborah. Super Saurus Saves Kindergarten. Young, Ned, illus. 2017. (ENG.). 40p. (J). (gr. -1-k). 16.99 (978-1-4231-7568-1(9)) Disney Pr.
Valentino, Carla. When Can We Run, Play & Dance Again? An Enchanting Story about Family, Learning & Imagination. 2011. 32p. (gr. 2-4). pap. 17.95 (978-1-4567-5495-2(5)) AuthorHouse.
Van Allsburg, Chris. The Wreck of the Zephyr. 2014. 32p. pap. 9.00 (978-1-61003-222-3(5)) Center for the Collaborative Classroom.
—The Wreck of the Zephyr. 30th anniv. ed. 2013. (ENG., Illus.). 32p. (J). (gr. -1-3). 18.99 (978-0-544-05005-1(3)) Houghton Mifflin Harcourt Publishing Co.
van de Vendel, Edward. The Dog That Nino Didn't Have. Van Hertbruggen, Anton, illus. 2015. (ENG.). 34p. (J). 17.00 (978-0-8028-5451-3(6), Eerdmans Bks For Young Readers) Eerdmans, William B. Publishing Co.
Van Dusen, Chris. If I Built a House. 2012. (ENG.). 32p. (J). (-k). 17.99 (978-0-8037-3751-8(3), Dial Bks) Penguin Young Readers Group.
van Genechten, Guido. Knight Ricky. van Genechten, Guido, illus. 2010. (Ricky Ser.). (ENG., Illus.). 30p. (J). (gr. -1-k). 16.95 (978-1-60537-059-0(2)) Cobblestone Publishing Co.
Vasquez, Paula. Lili Wool, 1 vol. 2017. (ENG.). 40p. (J). (gr. k-3). 14.99 **(978-1-4236-4728-7(9))** Gibbs Smith, Publisher.
Verde, Susan. I Am Yoga. Reynolds, Peter H., illus. 2015. (ENG.). 32p. (J). (gr. -1-3). 14.95 (978-1-4197-1664-5(6), Abrams Bks. for Young Readers) Abrams, Inc.
Victoria, Roberts. The Best Pet Ever. Deborah, Allwright, illus. 2010. (ENG.). 32p. (J). (gr. -1-2). 15.95 (978-1-58925-089-5(3)) Tiger Tales.
Villani, Donna. The Capture of Art. 2008. 244p. pap. 14.95 (978-1-60693-104-2(0), Eloquent Bks.) Strategic Book Publishing & Rights Agency (SBPRA).
Villeneuve, Anne. Loula Is Leaving for Africa. Villeneuve, Anne, illus. 2013. (Loula Ser.). (ENG., Illus.). 32p. (J). (gr. -1-2). 16.95 (978-1-55453-941-3(2)) Kids Can Pr., Ltd. CAN. Dist: Hachette Bk. Group.
Villoldo, Alberto. Skeleton Woman. 2008. (ENG.). 36p. (J). (gr. -1-3). 12.99 (978-1-4169-8962-2(5), Simon & Schuster Bks. For Young Readers) Simon & Schuster Bks. For Young Readers.
Vivian, Bart. Imagine. Vivian, Bart, illus. 2013. (ENG., Illus.). 32p. (J). (gr. -1-3). 14.99 (978-1-58270-329-9(9)) Aladdin/Beyond Words.
Wack, Nancy. Puddle Pirate. 2007. 40p. 20.50 (978-0-615-16634-6(2)) Wack, Nancy.
Wadham, Tim. The Queen of France. Denton, Kady MacDonald, illus. 2011. (ENG.). 32p. (J). (gr. -1-3). 16.99 (978-0-7636-4102-3(2)) Candlewick Pr.
Wadsworth, Wallace. The Modern Story Book. Eger, Caroline Ruth, illus. 2010. (Dover Read & Listen Ser.). (ENG.). 112p. (J). (gr. 1-5). pap. 14.99 incl. audio compact disk (978-0-486-47844-9(0)) Dover Pubns., Inc.
Wahl, Jan. I Met a Dinosaur. Sheban, Chris, illus. 2015. (ENG.). 32p. (J). (gr. 1-3). 17.99 (978-1-56846-233-2(6), Creative Editions) Creative Co., The.
Waldman, Neil. Al & Teddy. 2013. 48p. 17.95 (978-0-615-72969-5(X)) Dream Yard Pr.
Walker, Rachael. Angel Starlight & the Wish Book. 2006. 204p. per. (978-1-905529-52-0(X)) Grosvenor Hse. Publishing Ltd.
Wallace, Karen & Bostock, Mike. Imagine You Are a Dolphin. (Illus.). 25p. (J). pap. (978-0-340-67833-6(X)) Hodder & Stoughton.
Walter-Sereg, D. Bonnie Catches Lights in the Night Sky. 2012. 28p. pap. 24.95 (978-1-4626-5856-5(3)) America Star Bks.
—Bonnie, the Trapeze Artist. 2012. 32p. pap. 24.95 (978-1-4626-5858-9(X)) America Star Bks.
—Bonnie Tracks a Jungle Animal. 2012. 24p. 24.95 (978-1-4626-5857-2(1)) America Star Bks.
Wan Aisyah, Aisyah & Wan Aisyah. The Potty Monster. 2010. 32p. pap. (978-1-4269-3019-5(4)) Trafford Publishing (UK) Ltd.
Wand, Dana. Shanie June Jumped over the Moon. Tinling, Molly, illus. 2013. 32p. pap. (978-1-4602-0466-5(2)) FriesenPress.
Wasson, Dave. The Big Ideas of Buster Bickles. Wasson, Dave, illus. 2015. (ENG., Illus.). 40p. (J). (gr. -1-3). 17.99 (978-0-06-229178-3(5)) HarperCollins Pubs.

Waters, Lilly. Hurry Harry! Hurry! Quinn, Valerie, illus. 2014. (ENG.). 32p. (J). 14.99 *(978-0-9888610-0-8(3))* Jade Tree Bks.

Waters, Terrance D. I f I Y: A Novel Based on a True Story. 2008. 148p. 26.00 *(978-1-4251-3496-9(3))* Trafford Publishing.

Watkins, Rowboat. Pete with No Pants. 2017. (ENG., Illus.). 40p. (J). 16.99 *(978-1-4521-4401-6(X))* Chronicle Bks. LLC.

Watson, M. Desmond & the Challenge on Mudwig Mountain. 2005. 109p. pap. *(978-1-84401-010-3(4))* Athena Pr.

Watson, Vicki. Bob & the Alien Escapade. 2013. 226p. pap. *(978-0-9574062-2-3(3))* Green, Callisto.

Weale, David. Doors in the Air, 1 vol. Pratt, Pierre, illus. 2012. (ENG.). 32p. (J). (gr. -1-3). 19.95 *(978-1-55469-250-7(4))* Orca Bk. Pubs. USA.

Weeks, Sarah. If I Were a Lion. Solomon, Heather M., illus. 2004. (ENG.). 40p. (J). (gr. -1-3). 17.99 *(978-0-689-84836-0(6)*, Atheneum Bks. for Young Readers) Simon & Schuster Children's Publishing.

Weitzman, Jacqueline Preiss. Superhero Joe. Barrett, Ron, illus. 2011. (ENG.). 32p. (J). (gr. -1-3). 16.99 *(978-1-4169-9157-1(3)*, Simon & Schuster/Paula Wiseman Bks.) Simon & Schuster/Paula Wiseman Bks.

—Superhero Joe & the Creature Next Door. Barrett, Ron, illus. 2013. (ENG.). 32p. (J). (gr. -1-3). 16.99 *(978-1-4424-1268-2(2)*, Simon & Schuster Bks. For Young Readers) Simon & Schuster Bks. For Young Readers.

Welborn, Kathleen. The Cacklebeans, 1 vol. 2009. 33p. pap. 24.95 *(978-1-4489-1933-8(9))* America Star Bks.

Wells, Misty. Hank the Horse. 2012. 20p. pap. 15.99 *(978-1-4685-7968-0(1))* AuthorHouse.

Wells, Shannon Nicole. Gold! A Tall Tale. 2009. (J). pap. 7.00 *(978-1-61623-111-8(4))* Independent Pub.

Wendling, Peter. Caterpillars Never Lie, 1 vol. 2010. 26p. pap. 24.95 *(978-1-4489-4676-1(X))* PublishAmerica, Inc.

—Matthew Leads the Animal Parade, 1 vol. 2010. 30p. 24.95 *(978-1-4512-1836-7(2))* PublishAmerica, Inc.

Wenz, Graham D. The Day a Cockroach Crawled under My Door: This Book Won't Be a Bore! 2012. 44p. pap. 21.99 *(978-1-4797-0761-4(9))* Xlibris Corp.

Weston Woods Staff, creator. Crictor. 2011. 38.75 *(978-0-545-23361-3(5))*; 18.95 *(978-0-545-23360-6(7))* Weston Woods Studios, Inc.

—Harold & the Purple Crayon. 2011. 18.95 *(978-0-439-72691-7(3))*; 29.95 *(978-0-439-73474-5(6))*; 38.75 *(978-0-439-72693-1(X))* Weston Woods Studios, Inc.

—Harold's Fairy Tale. 2011. 38.75 *(978-0-439-72706-8(5))*; 18.95 *(978-0-439-72704-4(9))* Weston Woods Studios, Inc.

—A Picture for Harold's Room. 2011. 38.75 *(978-0-439-72872-0(X))*; 18.95 *(978-0-439-72871-3(1))* Weston Woods Studios, Inc.

Wheeler, Mary A. The Secret Stone: Book One. 2010. 72p. pap. 9.95 *(978-1-60844-398-7(1))* Dog Ear Publishing, LLC.

White, Amanda. Sand Sister. 2016. (ENG.). 32p. (J). (gr. -1-2). pap. 8.99 *(978-1-78285-279-7(4))* Barefoot Bks., Inc.

White, Kathryn. Ruby's School Walk. Latimer, Miriam, illus. 2010. (ENG.). 32p. (J). (gr. -1-2). 16.99 *(978-1-84686-275-5(2))* Barefoot Bks., Inc.

—Ruby's Sleepover. Latimer, Miriam, illus. 2012. (ENG.). 32p. (J). 16.99 *(978-1-84686-593-0(X))* Barefoot Bks., Inc.

White, Melissa. Purple Frogs, Imagine High. 2009. 131p. pap. 13.24 *(978-0-557-02960-0(0))* Lulu Pr., Inc.

Wick, Kimberly. Katie's First Day of School: The Adventures of Mrs. Swirlie. 2009. 36p. pap. 15.49 *(978-1-4389-2257-7(4))* AuthorHouse.

Wiesner, David. Hurricane, 1 vol. Wiesner, David, illus. 2008. (Read along Book & CD Ser.). (ENG., Illus.). 32p. (J). (gr. -1-3). 10.99 *(978-0-547-06433-8(0))* Houghton Mifflin Harcourt Publishing Co.

Wiesner, Karen Sue. Cody Knows. Hardy, Candace J., illus. 2012. 16p. pap. 9.95 *(978-1-61633-260-0(3))* Guardian Angel Publishing, Inc.

Wigden, Susan. Silly Rhymes for Fun Times. Columbin, Corey, illus. 2011. 20p. pap. 11.95 *(978-1-60888-107-9(5))* Nimble Bks. LLC.

Wight, Eric. Frankie Pickle & the Closet of Doom. Wight, Eric, illus. (Frankie Pickle Ser.). (ENG., Illus.). 96p. (J). (gr. 2-5). 2010. pap. 5.99 *(978-1-4424-1304-7(2))* 2009. 9.99 *(978-1-4169-6484-1(3))* Simon & Schuster Bks. For Young Readers. (Simon & Schuster Bks. For Young Readers).

—Frankie Pickle & the Pine Run 3000. Wight, Eric, illus. 2010. (Frankie Pickle Ser.). (ENG., Illus.). 96p. (J). (gr. 2-5). 9.99 *(978-1-4169-6485-8(1)*, Simon & Schuster Bks. For Young Readers) Simon & Schuster Bks. For Young Readers.

Willard, Nancy. The Three Mouths of Little Tom Drum. Hawkes, Kevin, illus. 2015. (ENG.). 48p. (J). (gr. -1-3). 16.99 *(978-0-7636-5476-4(0))* Candlewick Pr.

Willems, Mo. I'm a Frog! Willems, Mo, illus. 2013. (Elephant & Piggie Ser.). (ENG., Illus.). 64p. (J). (gr. 1-3). 9.99 *(978-1-4231-8305-1(3))* Hyperion Pr.

Willems, Mo, narrated by. Leonardo, the Terrible Monster. 2011. (Illus.). (J). (gr. -1-3). 29.95 *(978-0-439-02766-3(7)*, WHCD801) Weston Woods Studios, Inc.

Williams, Allen. Claude the Backward Jumping Bullfrog - Firefighter: Buster's Great Adventure. 2009. 36p. pap. 16.99 *(978-1-4389-7817-8(0))* AuthorHouse.

Williams, Darnell Denzel. One in a Million. 2013. 32p. pap. 17.25 *(978-1-4669-7913-0(5))* Trafford Publishing.

Williams, Suzanne. Master of Minds? Carter, Abby, illus. 2004. 58p. (J). lib. bdg. 15.00 *(978-1-4242-0911-8(0))* Fitzgerald Bks.

—Master of Minds? Carter, Abby, illus. 2004. (Marvelous Mind of Matthew Mcghee Age 8 Ser.). 58p. (J). 11.65 *(978-0-7569-5530-4(0))* Perfection Learning Corp.

Wilson, A. c. & Wilson, A. C. Ambersil - the Legacy of Mr Harrison. 2011. 496p. pap. *(978-1-908105-45-5(3))* Grosvenor Hse. Publishing Ltd.

Wilson, Anna. The Smug Pug, 1. unabr. ed. 2014. (Pooch Parlour Ser.: 3). (ENG., Illus.). 256p. (J). (gr. 2-4). pap. 7.99 *(978-1-4472-0075-8(6))* Pan Macmillan GBR. Dist: Independent Pubs. Group.

Wilson, Karma. Princess Me. Unzner, Christa, illus. 2007. (ENG.). 32p. (J). (gr. -1-3). 16.99 *(978-1-4169-4098-2(7)*, McElderry, Margaret K. Bks.) McElderry, Margaret K. Bks.

Wilson, N. D. Ninja Boy Goes to School. 2014. (ENG., Illus.). 32p. (J). (gr. -1-3). 16.99 *(978-0-375-86584-8(5)*, Random Hse. Bks. for Young Readers) Random Hse. Children's Bks.

Wilson, Rock. If I Had My Way — /By Rock S. Wilson; Illustrated by Carol Dixon. Dixon, Carol, illus. 2010. 32p. (J). *(978-0-929915-44-9(5))* Headline Bks., Inc.

Windt, Zelna Banks. Blow, Wind, Blow! 2010. 24p. 11.49 *(978-1-4520-3851-3(1))* AuthorHouse.

Wise-Douglas, Terri. The Wonderful World of Cupcakes. Duckworth, Jeffrey, illus. 2011. 28p. pap. 24.95 *(978-1-4626-3570-2(9))* America Star Bks.

Wise, Keith. Isabella's Playmate. 2011. 278p. pap. 27.95 *(978-1-4560-7320-6(6))* America Star Bks.

Wise, Linda. Pearl's Gems. 2010. 96p. pap. 28.99 *(978-1-4520-1129-5(X))* AuthorHouse.

Witek, Jo. In My Room: A Book of Creativity & Imagination. Roussey, Christine, illus. 2017. (Growing Hearts Ser.). (ENG.). 32p. (J). (gr. -1 — 1). 16.95 ***(978-1-4197-2644-6(7)***, Abrams Appleseed) Abrams, Inc.

Wlodarski, Loran. If a Dolphin Were a Fish, 1 vol. Klein, Laurie Allen, illus. 2006. (ENG.). 32p. (J). (gr. -1-2). 15.95 *(978-0-9768823-2-9(9))* Arbordale Publishing.

Wood, Douglas. A Quiet Place. Andreasen, Dan, illus. 2005. (ENG.). 32p. (J). (gr. -1-3). reprint ed. 8.99 *(978-0-689-87609-7(2)*, Simon & Schuster Bks. For Young Readers) Simon & Schuster Bks. For Young Readers.

Woods, Brenda. Zoe in Wonderland. 2017. (ENG.). 224p. (J). (gr. 3-7). 8.99 ***(978-0-425-28891-7(9)***, Puffin Books) Penguin Young Readers Group.

Woods, Brenda & Airgood, Ellen. Zoe in Wonderland. 2016. (ENG.). 208p. (J). (gr. 3-7). 16.99 *(978-0-399-17097-3(9)*, Nancy Paulsen Books) Penguin Young Readers Group.

Woods-Whitaker, Kim. Elijah's Big Imagination: A Ball of an Adventure. 2010. 20p. 11.49 *(978-1-4490-1518-3(2))* AuthorHouse.

Written By Tori Velle; Illustrated By Al. Tia Tot Rules! Aguila, Alicia del, illus. 2011. 44p. pap. 24.95 *(978-1-4241-7833-9(9))* America Star Bks.

Wyss, Tyan. Night Flyer. Immelman, Sarita, illus. 2006. 40p. (J). per. 14.95 *(978-1-58939-916-7(1))* Virtualbookworm.com Publishing, Inc.

Yakola, Carrie. Full Moon Maxi. 2008. 36p. pap. 19.99 *(978-1-4343-3966-9(1))* AuthorHouse.

Yamamoto, Lani. Albert. Yamamoto, Lani, illus. 2004. (ENG., Illus.). 32p. (J). 10.95 *(978-1-58536-251-6(4))* Sleeping Bear Pr.

Yang, James. Joey & Jet: Book 1 of Their Adventures. Yang, James, illus. 2012. (ENG., Illus.). 32p. (J). (gr. -1-k). pap. 16.99 *(978-1-4424-5930-4(1)*, Atheneum Bks. for Young Readers) Simon & Schuster Children's Publishing.

—Joey & Jet in Space. Yang, James, illus. 2006. (ENG., Illus.). 32p. (J). (gr. -1-k). 17.99 *(978-0-689-86927-3(4)*, Atheneum/Richard Jackson Bks.) Simon & Schuster Children's Publishing.

Yankovic, Al, pseud. My New Teacher & Me! Hargis, Wes, illus. 2013. (ENG.). 40p. (J). (gr. -1-3). 17.99 *(978-0-06-219203-5(5))* HarperCollins Pubs.

Yasuda, Anita. The Swim Race, 1 vol. Harpster, Steve, illus. 2012. (My First Graphic Novel Ser.). (ENG.). 32p. (gr. k-2). pap. 6.25 *(978-1-4342-3864-1(4))*; lib. bdg. 24.65 *(978-1-4342-3280-9(8))* Stone Arch Bks. (My First Graphic Novel).

Yellowknife, Jessica. Spring Break Adventure. 2011. 84p. pap. 11.11 *(978-1-4269-6952-2(X))* Trafford Publishing.

Ying, Jonathan. Not Quite Black & White Board Book. Ying, Victoria, illus. 2017. 28p. (J). (gr. -1 — 1). bds. 7.99 ***(978-0-06-238067-8(2)***, HarperFestival) HarperCollins Pubs.

Yolen, Jane. What to Do with a Box. Sheban, Chris, illus. 2016. (ENG.). 32p. (J). (gr. 1-3). 18.99 *(978-1-56846-289-9(1)*, Creative Editions) Creative Co., The.

Yoo, Taeeun. You Are a Lion! And Other Fun Yoga Poses. Yoo, Taeeun, illus. 2012. (ENG., Illus.). 40p. (J). (gr. -1-k). 17.99 *(978-0-399-25602-8(4)*, Nancy Paulsen Books) Penguin Young Readers Group.

Yoon, Salina. Be a Friend. 2016. (ENG.). 40p. (J). 17.99 *(978-1-61963-951-5(3)*, 9781619639515, Bloomsbury USA Childrens) Bloomsbury Publishing USA.

—Tap to Play! 2014. (ENG.). 40p. (J). (gr. -1-3). 15.99 *(978-0-06-228684-0(6))* HarperCollins Pubs.

Young, Jessica. All Paws on Deck. Burks, James, illus. 2016. (Haggis & Tank Unleashed Ser.: 1). (ENG.). 80p. (J). (gr. k-2). pap. 4.99 *(978-0-545-81886-5(9))* Scholastic, Inc.

—Digging for Dinos. Burks, James, illus. 2016. (Haggis & Tank Unleashed Ser.: 2). (ENG.). 80p. (J). (gr. k-2). 15.99 *(978-0-545-81889-6(3))* Scholastic, Inc.

—Howl at the Moon. 2017. (Haggis & Tank Unleashed — Branches Ser.: 3). lib. bdg. 14.75 ***(978-0-606-40190-6(3))*** Turtleback Bks.

—Howl at the Moon: a Branches Book (Haggis & Tank Unleashed #3) Burks, James, illus. 2017. (Haggis & Tank Unleashed Ser.: 3). (ENG.). 80p. (J). (gr. k-2). pap. 4.99 ***(978-1-338-04525-3(3))*** Scholastic, Inc.

Young, Ned. Zoomer. Young, Ned, illus. 2010. (ENG., Illus.). 32p. (J). (gr. -1-2). 16.99 *(978-0-06-170088-0(6))* HarperCollins Pubs.

—Zoomer's Summer Snowstorm. Young, Ned, illus. 2011. (ENG., Illus.). 32p. (J). (gr. -1-2). 16.99 *(978-0-06-170092-7(4))* HarperCollins Pubs.

Yum, Hyewon. Puddle. 2016. (ENG., Illus.). 40p. (J). 16.99 *(978-0-374-31695-2(3)*, 9780374316952, Farrar, Straus & Giroux (BYR)) Farrar, Straus & Giroux.

Zagarenski, Pamela. The Whisper. 2015. (ENG., Illus.). 40p. (J). (gr. -1-3). 17.99 *(978-0-544-41686-4(4)*, HMH Books For Young Readers) Houghton Mifflin Harcourt Publishing Co.

Zaring, Laurie. Who Could You Be at the Zoo? Barlup, Jessica, illus. 2013. 24p. pap. 12.95 *(978-1-61244-175-7(0))* Halo Publishing International.

Zimmerman, Andrea & Clemesha, David. Digger Man. Zimmerman, Andrea & Clemesha, David, illus. 2007. (ENG., Illus.). 32p. (J). (gr. -1-k). pap. 7.99 *(978-0-8050-8203-6(4)*, 9780805082036) Square Fish.

—Fire Engine Man. Zimmerman, Andrea & Clemesha, David, illus. 2016. (ENG., Illus.). 30p. (J). bds. 7.99 *(978-1-62779-503-6(0)*, 9781627795036, Holt, Henry & Co. Bks. For Young Readers) Holt, Henry & Co.

—Train Man. Zimmerman, Andrea & Clemesha, David, illus. 2012. (ENG., Illus.). 32p. (J). (gr. -1-k). 14.99 *(978-0-8050-7991-3(2)*, 9780805079913, Holt, Henry & Co. Bks. For Young Readers) Holt, Henry & Co.

Zimmerman, Andrea Griffing & Clemesha, David. Digger Man. Zimmerman, Andrea Griffing & Clemesha, David, illus. rev. ed. 2003. (ENG., Illus.). 32p. (J). (gr. -1-k). 17.95 *(978-0-8050-6628-9(4)*, 9780805066289, Holt, Henry & Co. Bks. For Young Readers) Holt, Henry & Co.

Zolotow, Charlotte. The Seashore Book. Minor, Wendell, illus. 2004. (Reading Rainbow Bks.). (gr. -1-3). 17.00 *(978-0-7569-4234-2(9))* Perfection Learning Corp.

Zolotow, Charlotte & Minor, Wendell. The Seashore Book. 2017. (ENG., Illus.). 32p. (J). (-k). lib. bdg. 16.99 *(978-1-58089-787-7(8))* Charlesbridge Publishing, Inc.

Zuppardi, Sam. The Nowhere Box. Zuppardi, Sam, illus. 2013. (ENG., Illus.). 40p. (J). (gr. -1-3). 15.99 *(978-0-7636-6367-4(0))* Candlewick Pr.

123 Sesame Street, ed. When Zoe Grows Up. 2009. (ENG.). 20p. 9.99 *(978-1-59069-820-4(7))* Studio Mouse LLC.

IMBECILITY

see People with Mental Disabilities

IMMERSION, BAPTISMAL

see Baptism

IMMIGRANTS

Here are entered works on foreign-born persons who enter a country intending to become permanent residents or citizens.

see also Illegal Aliens

Alvarez, Pilar. New Jobs, New Opportunities: British Immigrants Arrive in America (1830s-1890s), 01 vols., 1. 2016. (Spotlight on Immigration & Migration Ser.). (ENG., Illus.). 24p. (J). pap. 10.00 *(978-1-5081-4090-0(1)*, PowerKids Pr.) Rosen Publishing Group, Inc., The.

Ambrosek, Renee. America Debates United States Policy on Immigration. 2007. (America Debates Ser.). (Illus.). 64p. (YA). (gr. 5-9). lib. bdg. 31.95 *(978-1-4042-1924-3(2))* Rosen Publishing Group, Inc., The.

Bausum, Ann. Denied, Detained, Deported: Stories from the Dark Side of American Immigration. 2009. (ENG., Illus.). 112p. (J). (gr. 5). lib. bdg. 32.90 *(978-1-4263-0333-3(5)*, National Geographic Children's Bks.) National Geographic Society.

Behnke, Alison. Chinese in America. 2004. (In America Ser.). (ENG., Illus.). 80p. (gr. 5-8). lib. bdg. 27.93 *(978-0-8225-4695-5(7))* Lerner Publishing Group.

Benson, Sonia. U. S. Immigration & Migration: Almanac, 2.0. 2004. (US Immigration & Migration Reference Library). (ENG., Illus.). 685p. (J). 191.00 *(978-0-7876-7732-9(9)*, UXL) Cengage Gale.

Bozzone, Donna M. Famous Immigrant Computer Scientists. 2017. (YA). ***(978-0-7660-9246-4(1))*** Enslow Pubs., Inc.

Bryan, Nichol. Filipino Americans, 1 vol. 2004. (One Nation Set 1 Ser.). (ENG.). 32p. (gr. k-6). 27.07 *(978-1-57765-988-4(0)*, Checkerboard Library) ABDO Publishing Co.

—German Americans, 1 vol. 2004. (One Nation Set 1 Ser.). (ENG.). 32p. (gr. k-6). 27.07 *(978-1-57765-981-5(3)*, Checkerboard Library) ABDO Publishing Co.

—Indian Americans, 1 vol. 2004. (One Nation Set 1 Ser.). (ENG.). 32p. (gr. k-6). 27.07 *(978-1-57765-984-6(8)*, Checkerboard Library) ABDO Publishing Co.

Burgan, Michael. Exposing Hidden Worlds: How Jacob Riis' Photos Became Tools for Social Reform. 2017. (Captured History Ser.). (ENG.). 64p. (gr. 5-7). lib. bdg. 34.65 ***(978-0-7565-5618-1(X)***, CPB Grades 4-8) Compass Point Bks.

Byers, Ann. Immigration: Interpreting the Constitution. 2014. (Understanding the United States Constitution Ser.). 112p. (YA). (gr. 7-12). 35.60 *(978-1-4777-7512-7(9))* Rosen Publishing Group, Inc., The.

Ciongoli, A. Kenneth & Parini, Jay. Passage to Liberty: The Story of Italian Immigration & the Rebirth of America. 2003. (Illus.). 32p. (YA). (gr. 9-12). 30.00 *(978-0-7567-6841-6(1))* DIANE Publishing Co.

Coy, John. Their Great Gift: Courage, Sacrifice, & Hope in a New Land. Huie, Wing Young, photos by. 2016. (ENG., Illus.). 32p. (J). (gr. k-3). 19.99 *(978-1-4677-8054-4(5))*; 38.65 *(978-1-4677-9756-6(1))* Lerner Publishing Group. (Carolrhoda Bks.).

Currie, Stephen. Undocumented Immigrant Youth. 2016. (ENG.). 80p. (J). (gr. 5-12). lib. bdg. *(978-1-60152-980-0(5))* ReferencePoint Pr., Inc.

DiConsiglio, John. Reporting Live. 2011. (J). *(978-0-531-22552-3(6))* Scholastic, Inc.

Flores, Mina. The Growth of the American City: Immigrants & Migrants Travel for Work, 01 vols., 1. 2016. (Spotlight on Immigration & Migration Ser.). (ENG., Illus.). 24p. (J). pap. 10.00 *(978-1-5081-4076-4(6)*, PowerKids Pr.) Rosen Publishing Group, Inc., The.

Furgang, Adam. Famous Immigrant Artists. 2017. (J). ***(978-0-7660-9245-7(3))*** Enslow Pubs., Inc.

Girod, Christina M. Indian Americans. 2003. (Immigrants in America Ser.). (ENG., Illus.). 112p. (J). 30.85 *(978-1-59018-270-3(7)*, Lucent Bks.) Cengage Gale.

Grande, Reyna. The Distance Between Us: A Memoir. 2017. (ENG., Illus.). 336p. (J). (gr. 5-9). pap. 7.99 ***(978-1-4814-6370-6(5)***, Aladdin) Simon & Schuster Children's Publishing.

—The Distance Between Us: A Memoir. 2016. (ENG., Illus.). 336p. (J). (gr. 5-9). 17.99 *(978-1-4814-6371-3(3)*, Simon & Schuster/Paula Wiseman Bks.) Simon & Schuster/Paula Wiseman Bks.

Hall, Margaret C. Irish Americans. 2003. (We Are America Ser.). (Illus.). 32p. (J). (gr. 2-4). lib. bdg. 24.22 *(978-1-4034-0734-4(7))* Heinemann-Raintree.

Heaney, Shane. The Scotch-Irish Immigration to America: Economic Hardship in Ireland (1603-1775), 01 vols., 1. 2016. (Spotlight on Immigration & Migration Ser.). (ENG., Illus.). 24p. (J). pap. 10.00 *(978-1-5081-4095-5(2)*, PowerKids Pr.) Rosen Publishing Group, Inc., The.

Heckt, Jackie. Immigration to Colonial America, 01 vols., 1. 2016. (Spotlight on Immigration & Migration Ser.). (ENG., Illus.). 24p. (J). pap. 10.00 *(978-1-5081-4081-8(2)*, PowerKids Pr.) Rosen Publishing Group, Inc., The.

Hill, Christina. Lue Gim Gong: The Citrus Wizard (Florida) 2016. (Primary Source Readers Ser.). (Illus.). 32p. (J). (gr. 4-4). pap. 8.99 *(978-1-4938-3549-2(1))* Teacher Created Materials, Inc.

Hossell, Karen Price. The Irish Americans. 2003. (Immigrants in America Ser.). (ENG., Illus.). 112p. (J). 30.85 *(978-1-56006-752-8(7)*, Lucent Bks.) Cengage Gale.

Lo Bosco, Maryellen. Famous Immigrant Scientists. 2017. (J). ***(978-0-7660-9244-0(5))*** Enslow Pubs., Inc.

Lüsted, Marcia Amidon. What You Need to Know about Your Status As an Immigrant under the Law. 2015. (Know Your Rights Ser.). (ENG., Illus.). 64p. (J). (gr. 6-6). 33.25 *(978-1-4777-8102-9(1)*, Rosen Young Adult) Rosen Publishing Group, Inc., The.

Lusted, Marcia Amidon. Your Legal Rights As an Immigrant. 2015. (Know Your Rights Ser.). (ENG., Illus.). 64p. (J). (gr. 6-6). pap. 12.95 *(978-1-4777-8618-5(X)*, Rosen Young Adult) Rosen Publishing Group, Inc., The.

McCormick, Lisa Wade. Frequently Asked Questions about Growing up As an Undocumented Immigrant. 2012. (FAQ: Teen Life Ser.). (ENG., Illus.). 64p. (YA). (gr. 7-12). lib. bdg. 31.95 *(978-1-4488-8329-5(6))* Rosen Publishing Group, Inc., The.

Metz, Lorijo. A Nation of Immigrants, 1 vol., 1. 2014. (Let's Celebrate Freedom! Ser.). (ENG.). 24p. (J). (gr. 3-6). 23.60 *(978-1-4777-2899-4(6)*, PowerKids Pr.) Rosen Publishing Group, Inc., The.

Mooney, Carla. Confronting Discrimination Against Immigrants. 2017. (J). pap. ***(978-1-5383-8164-9(8)***, Rosen Young Adult) Rosen Publishing Group, Inc., The.

Nazario, Sonia. Enrique's Journey: The True Story of a Boys Determined to Reunite with His Mother. 2013. (ENG.). 288p. (YA). (gr. 7). 16.99 *(978-0-385-74327-3(0)*, Delacorte Bks. for Young Readers) Random Hse. Children's Bks.

Newman, Lori M. What Rights Should Illegal Immigrants Have? 2006. (At Issue Ser.). (ENG., Illus.). 90p. (YA). (gr. 8-12). 22.50 *(978-0-7377-3481-2(7))*; lib. bdg. 31.80 *(978-0-7377-3480-5(9))* Cengage Gale. (Greenhaven Pr., Inc.).

O'Donoghue, Sean. The Disaster of the Irish Potato Famine: Irish Immigrants Arrive in America (1845-1850), 01 vols., 1. 2016. (Spotlight on Immigration & Migration Ser.). (ENG., Illus.). 24p. (J). pap. 10.00 *(978-1-5081-4066-5(9)*, PowerKids Pr.) Rosen Publishing Group, Inc., The.

Oeppen, Ceri. Hopes, Needs, Rights, & Laws: How Do Governments & Citizens Manage Migration & Settlement? 2010. (Investigating Human Migration & Settlement Ser.). (ENG., Illus.). 48p. (J). (gr. 5-8). *(978-0-7787-5180-9(5))*; pap. *(978-0-7787-5195-3(3))* Crabtree Publishing Co.

Parker, Lewis K. Why Mexican Immigrants Came to America. (Coming to America Ser.). 24p. 2009. (gr. 2-3). 42.50 *(978-1-61511-887-8(X))* 2003. (Illus.). (J). lib. bdg. 22.60 *(978-0-8239-6459-8(0))* Rosen Publishing Group, Inc., The. (PowerKids Pr.).

Perritano, John. The Making of the Modern World: 1945 to the Present: Migration & Refugees, Vol. 9. van Dijk, Ruud, ed. 2016. (Making of the Modern World: 1945 to the Present Ser.: Vol. 9). (ENG.). 64p. (J). (gr. 7-12). 23.95 *(978-1-4222-3640-6(4))* Mason Crest.

Poole, H. W. Immigrant Families, Vol. 12. 2016. (Families Today Ser.). (Illus.). 48p. (J). (gr. 5). 20.95 *(978-1-4222-3617-8(X))* Mason Crest.

Roberts, Ceri. Refugees & Migrants. Kai, Hanane, illus. 2017. (Children in Our World Ser.). (ENG.). 32p. (J). (gr. 1-4). 9.99 ***(978-1-4380-5020-1(8))*** Barron's Educational Series, Inc.

Ruiz, José. Mexican Immigrants. 2017. (Illus.). 112p. (J). ***(978-1-4222-3679-6(X))*** Mason Crest.

Sánchez, Sonia, illus. Here I Am. 2014. (J). ***(978-1-4795-1932-3(4))*** Picture Window Bks.

Sandler, Martin W. Immigrants. 2014. (Library of Congress Classics). (ENG., Illus.). 96p. (J). (gr. 3-18). pap. 12.99 *(978-0-06-446744-5(9))* HarperCollins Pubs.

Scheppler, Bill. Guantánamo Bay & Military Tribunals: The Detention & Trial of Suspected Terrorists. 2009. (Frontline Coverage of Current Events Ser.). 48p. (gr. 5-5). 53.00 *(978-1-61512-655-2(4))* Rosen Publishing Group, Inc., The.

Schmermund, Elizabeth. Immigration Bans. 2017. (J). pap. ***(978-1-5345-0057-0(X))*** Greenhaven Publishing LLC.

Shane, C. J. The Mexicans. 2005. pap. 22.45 *(978-0-7377-2157-7(X)*, Greenhaven Pr., Inc.) Cengage Gale.

Shea, Therese. Immigration to America: Identifying Different Points of View About an Issue. 2005. (Critical Thinking in American History Ser.). (Illus.). 48p. (J). (gr. k-3). lib. bdg. 29.25 *(978-1-4042-0414-0(8))* Rosen Publishing Group, Inc., The.

Sioux, Tracee. Immigrants in Colonial America. (Primary Sources of Immigration & Migration in America Ser.). 24p. 2009. (gr. 3-4). 42.50 *(978-1-60851-777-0(2))* 2004. (ENG., Illus.). (gr. 4-8). pap. 9.40 *(978-0-8239-8949-2(6))* 2004. (Illus.). (J). lib. bdg. 22.60 *(978-0-8239-6823-7(5))* Rosen Publishing Group, Inc., The. (PowerKids Pr.).

Thornton, Jeremy. The Gold Rush: Chinese Immigrants Come to America (1848-1882) (Primary Sources of Immigration & Migration in America Ser.). 24p. 2009. (gr. 3-4). 42.50 *(978-1-60851-784-8(5))* 2004. (Illus.). (J). lib. bdg. 22.60 *(978-0-8239-6833-6(2))* Rosen Publishing Group, Inc., The. (PowerKids Pr.).

—The Gold Rush: Chinese Immigrants Come to America, 1848-1882. 2004. (Primary Sources of Immigration & Migration in America Ser.). (ENG., Illus.). 24p. (gr. 4-8). pap. 9.40 *(978-0-8239-8959-1(3)*, PowerKids Pr.) Rosen Publishing Group, Inc., The.

—Hard Times in Ireland: The Scotch-Irish Come to America (1603-1775) (Primary Sources of Immigration & Migration in America Ser.). 24p. 2009. (gr. 3-4). 42.50 *(978-1-60851-775-6(6))* 2004. (Illus.). (J). lib. bdg. 22.60 *(978-0-8239-6830-5(8))* Rosen Publishing Group, Inc., The. (PowerKids Pr.).

—Hard Times in Ireland: The Scotch-Irish Come to America, 1603-1775. 2004. (Primary Sources of Immigration & Migration in America Ser.). (ENG., Illus.). 24p. (gr. 4-8). pap. 9.40 *(978-0-8239-8956-0(9)*, PowerKids Pr.) Rosen Publishing Group, Inc., The.

—New Industries, New Jobs: British Immigrants Come to America (1830s-1890s) 2004. (Primary Sources of Immigration & Migration Ser.). (Illus.). 24p. (ENG.). (gr. 4-8). pap. 9.40 *(978-0-8239-8958-4(5)*, Rosen Classroom); (J). lib. bdg. 22.60 *(978-0-8239-6832-9(4)*, PowerKids Pr.) Rosen Publishing Group, Inc., The.

H
I

Torres, John Albert. Famous Immigrant Athletes. 2017. (J). **(978-0-7660-9243-3(7))** Enslow Pubs., Inc.
Whitman, Sylvia. Immigrant Children. 2005. (Picture the American Past Ser.). (Illus.). 48p. (gr. 2-5). lib. bdg. 22.60 *(978-1-57505-395-0(0))* Lerner Publishing Group.
Worth, Richard & Asher, Robert. Jewish Immigrants. 2004. (Immigration to the United States Ser.). (Illus.). 96p. (gr. 4-9). 35.00 *(978-0-8160-5684-2(6))* Facts On File, Inc.

IMMIGRANTS—FICTION

Behar, Ruth. Lucky Broken Girl. 2017. (ENG.). 256p. (J). (gr. 5). 16.99 *(978-0-399-54644-0(8),* Nancy Paulsen Books) Penguin Young Readers Group.
Chambers, Veronica. The Go-Between. 2017. (ENG.). 208p. (YA). (gr. 7). 16.99 **(978-1-101-93095-3(0),** Delacorte Pr.) Random Hse. Children's Bks.
Crowder, Melanie. Audacity. 2016. (ENG.). 400p. (YA). (gr. 7). pap. 10.99 *(978-0-14-751249-9(2),* Speak) Penguin Young Readers Group.
Fleischman, Paul. The Matchbox Diary. Ibatoulline, Bagram, illus. 2016. (ENG.). 40p. (J). (gr. 1-4). 7.99 *(978-0-7636-7638-4(1))* Candlewick Pr.
—The Matchbox Diary. Ibatoulline, Bagram, illus. 2016. (ENG.). 40p. (J). (gr. 1-4). 18.40 *(978-0-606-39097-2(9))* Turtleback Bks.
Freeman, Ruth. One Good Thing about America. Honesta, Kathrin, illus. 2017. (ENG.). 160p. (J). (gr. 3-6). 16.95 *(978-0-8234-3695-8(0))* Holiday Hse., Inc.
Girard, M-E. Girl Mans Up. 2016. 384p. (YA). (gr. 9). 17.99 *(978-0-06-240417-6(2),* HarperTeen) HarperCollins Pubs.
Goring, Ruth & Meza, Erika. Los Angeles de Adriana (Spanish Edition) Meza, Erika, illus. 2017. (SPA., Illus.). (J). 16.99 **(978-1-5064-2507-8(0),** Sparkhouse Family) Augsburg Fortress, Pubs.
Halahmy, Miriam. Hidden. 2016. (ENG.). 224p. (J). 16.95 *(978-0-8234-3694-1(2))* Holiday Hse., Inc.
Herman, Michael. Under the Sabbath Lamp. Massari, Alida, illus. 2017. (ENG.). 32p. (J). (gr. -1-2). 17.99 *(978-1-5124-0841-6(7),* Kar-Ben Publishing) Lerner Publishing Group.
Honeyman, Kay. The Fire Horse Girl. 2016. (ENG.). 336p. (J). (gr. 7). pap. 9.99 *(978-0-545-40311-5(1),* Levine, Arthur A. Bks.) Scholastic, Inc.
Joseph, Lynn. Flowers in the Sky. 2013. (ENG.). 240p. (YA). (gr. 8). 17.99 *(978-0-06-029794-7(8),* HarperTeen) HarperCollins Pubs.
Kelly, Erin Entrada. The Land of Forgotten Girls. 2016. 304p. (J). (gr. 3-7). 16.99 *(978-0-06-223864-1(7),* Greenwillow Bks.) HarperCollins Pubs.
Laínez, René Colato. Mamá the Alien: Mamá la Extraterrestre. Lacámara, Laura, illus. 2016. (ENG & SPA.). 32p. (J). (gr. -1-4). 17.95 *(978-0-89239-298-8(3))* Lee & Low Bks., Inc.
Martinez, Jessica. The Vow. 2013. (ENG.). 432p. (YA). (gr. 9). 17.99 *(978-1-4424-5864-2(X),* Simon Pulse) Simon Pulse.
Patel, Sonia. Rani Patel in Full Effect. 2016. (ENG.). 224p. (J). (gr. 6). 16.95 *(978-1-941026-49-6(4))* Cinco Puntos Pr.
Perkins, Mitali. You Bring the Distant Near. 2017. (ENG.). 320p. (YA). 17.99 **(978-0-374-30490-4(4),** 9780374304904, Farrar, Straus & Giroux (BYR)) Farrar, Straus & Giroux.
Powell, Maud Macrory. City of Grit & Gold. 2017. (ENG.). 164p. (J). (gr. 4-6). pap. 16.99 **(978-0-9967558-5-6(3))** Allium Pr. of Chicago.
Pung, Alice. Lucy & Linh. 2016. (ENG.). 352p. (YA). (gr. 7). 17.99 *(978-0-399-55048-5(8),* Knopf Bks. for Young Readers) Random Hse. Children's Bks.
Redding, LaTisha. Calling the Water Drum. 1 vol. Boyd, Aaron, illus. 2016. (ENG.). 32p. (J). (gr. 1-4). 17.95 *(978-1-62014-194-6(9))* Lee & Low Bks., Inc.
Rippin, Sally. The Copycat Kid. Fukuoka, Aki, illus. 2015. 42p. (J). *(978-1-61067-449-2(9))* Kane Miller.
Steinberg, Jessica. Not This Turkey! Pike, Amanda, illus. 2016. (ENG.). 32p. (J). (gr. -1-3). 16.99 *(978-0-8075-7908-4(4))* Whitman, Albert & Co.
Weeks, Sarah & Varadarajan, Gita. Save Me a Seat. 2016. (ENG.). 240p. (J). (gr. 3-7). 16.99 *(978-0-545-84660-8(9),* Scholastic Pr.) Scholastic, Inc.

IMMIGRATION AND EMIGRATION

see Emigration and Immigration

IMMUNITY

see also Allergy; Communicable Diseases; Vaccination

Benchmark Education Company. Fighting Disease (Teacher Guide) 2005. *(978-1-4108-4657-0(1))* Benchmark Education Co.
Defenses. (Amazing Animals Ser.). 32p. (J). (gr. 1). pap. *(978-1-882210-79-4(4))* Action Publishing, Inc.
Jerome, Kate Boehm & National Geographic Learning Staff. Fighting Disease. 2007. (Rise & Shine Ser.). (ENG., Illus.). 32p. (J). pap. 17.95 *(978-0-7922-8865-7(3))* CENGAGE Learning.
Klosterman, Lorrie. Immune System. 2008. (Amazing Human Body Ser.). 80p. (gr. 5-18). lib. bdg. 34.21 *(978-0-7614-3054-4(7),* Benchmark Bks.) Marshall Cavendish Corp.
Lew, Kristi. The Exterminator: Wiping Out the World's Most Infectious Diseases. 2009. (Current Science Ser.). 48p. (YA). (gr. 4-7). lib. bdg. 31.00 *(978-1-4339-2061-5(1))* Stevens, Gareth Publishing LLLP.
Parsons, Michelle Hyde. Fighting Disease. 2005. (J). pap. *(978-1-4108-4609-9(1))* Benchmark Education Co.
Ribke, Simone T. I Have Allergies. 2016. (Rookie Read-About Health Ser.). (ENG., Illus.). 32p. (J). pap. 5.95 *(978-0-531-22580-6(1),* Children's Pr.) Scholastic Library Publishing.
Sherman, Josepha. The War Against Germs. (Germs: the Library of Disease-Causing Organisms Ser.). 48p. 2009. (gr. 5-5). 53.00 *(978-1-61512-718-4(6))* 2004. (Illus.). (gr. 7-12). lib. bdg. 29.25 *(978-0-8239-4495-8(6))* Rosen Publishing Group, Inc., The.
Stewart, Melissa. Germ Wars! The Secrets of the Immune System. 2010. (Gross & Goofy Body 2 Ser.). 48p. (gr. 3). 29.93 *(978-0-7614-4165-6(4))* Marshall Cavendish Corp.
Thames, Susan. Our Immune System. 2007. (ENG., Illus.). 24p. (gr. k-1). per. 8.95 *(978-1-60044-672-6(8))* Rourke Educational Media.

IMPERIAL TRANS-ANTARCTIC EXPEDITION, 1914-1917

Ganeri, Anita. Endurance: Shackleton's Incredible Antarctic Expedition. 2016. (ENG., Illus.). 48p. (J). (gr. 4-6). pap. 12.99 *(978-0-7502-9709-7(3),* Wayland) Hachette Children's Group GBR. Dist: Hachette Bk. Group.
Hoena, Blake A. & Hoena, B. A. Shackleton & the Lost Antarctic Expedition, 1 vol. Hoover, Dave et al, illus. 2006. (Disasters in History Ser.). (ENG.). 32p. (gr. 3-4). 30.65 *(978-0-7368-5482-5(7),* Graphic Library) Capstone Press of Coughlan Cos.
Johnson, Kristin. The Endurance Expedition, 1 vol. 2011. (Essential Events Set 6 Ser.). (ENG., Illus.). 112p. (J). (gr. 6-12). lib. bdg. 35.64 *(978-1-61714-764-7(8))* ABDO Publishing Co.

IMPLEMENTS, UTENSILS, ETC.

see Agricultural Machinery; Household Equipment and Supplies; Tools

IMPORTS

see Commerce

IMPOSTORS AND IMPOSTURE

see also Fraud

Acer, David. Gotcha! 18 Amazing Ways to Freak Out Your Friends. MacEachern, Stephen, illus. 2008. (ENG.). 48p. (J). (gr. 3-7). 16.95 *(978-1-55453-194-3(2));* pap. 8.95 *(978-1-55453-195-0(0))* Kids Can Pr., Ltd. CAN. Dist: Hachette Bk. Group.
Blackwood, Gary L. Perplexing People. 2005. (Unsolved History Ser.). (Illus.). 80p. (gr. 6-7). lib. bdg. 23.95 *(978-0-7614-1890-0(3),* Benchmark Bks.) Marshall Cavendish Corp.
Blackwood, Gary L. & Miller, Susan Martins. Perplexing People. 2009. (Benchmark Rockets: History's Mysteries Ser.). 32p. (gr. 3). 28.50 *(978-0-7614-4360-5(6))* Marshall Cavendish Corp.
Herbst, Judith. Hoaxes. 2004. (Unexplained Ser.). (Illus.). 48p. (J). pap. 7.95 *(978-0-8225-2406-9(6),* Lerner Pubns.); (ENG., (gr. 5-12). lib. bdg. 26.60 *(978-0-8225-1629-3(2))* Lerner Publishing Group.
Jones, Carrie. Sarah Emma Edmonds Was a Great Pretender: The True Story of a Civil War Spy. Oldroyd, Mark, illus. 2011. (Carolrhoda Picture Bks.). (ENG.). 32p. (J). (gr. 2-5). 17.95 *(978-0-7613-5399-7(2))* Lerner Publishing Group.
Levete, Sarah. Fakes & Hoaxes. 2016. (Mystery Hunters Ser.). 00048p. (J). pap. 14.05 **(978-1-4824-6004-9(1))** Stevens, Gareth Publishing LLLP.

IMPRESSIONISM (ART)

see also Post-Impressionism (Art)

Boutan, Mila. Renoir & Me. 2010. (ENG., Illus.). 48p. (J). (gr. 3-7). pap. 17.95 *(978-1-4081-2384-3(3),* 9781408123843, A&C Black) Bloomsbury Publishing Plc GBR. Dist: Macmillan.
Cernak, Linda. Edgar Degas. Morrow, J. T., illus. 2014. (World's Greatest Artists Ser.). (ENG.). 24p. (J). (gr. 2-5). 28.50 *(978-1-62687-349-0(6),* 207189) Child's World, Inc., The.
Gunderson, Jessica. Impressionism. 2008. (Movements in Art Ser.). 48p. (YA). (gr. 5-9). 22.95 *(978-1-58341-611-2(0))* Creative Co., The.
—Impressionism: Odysseys in Art. 2016. (Odysseys in Art Ser.). (ENG.). 80p. (J). (gr. 7-10). pap. 14.99 *(978-1-62832-134-0(2),* Creative Paperbacks) Creative Co., The.
Harris, Lois V. Mary Cassatt: Impressionist Painter, 1 vol. Cassatt, Mary, illus. 2007. (ENG.). 32p. (J). (gr. k-3). 16.99 *(978-1-58980-452-4(X))* Pelican Publishing Co., Inc.
Haynes, Sara. Gauguin, Vol. 7. 2015. (Great Artists Collection). (Illus.). 64p. (J). (gr. 7). lib. bdg. 23.95 *(978-1-4222-3259-0(X))* Mason Crest.
Heine, Florian. Impressionism: 13 Artists Children Should Know. 2015. (ENG., Illus.). 48p. (J). (gr. 3-7). 14.95 *(978-3-7913-7206-8(8))* Prestel Verlag GmbH & Co KG. DEU. Dist: Penguin Random Hse. LLC.
Hirshmann, Kris. Impressionism. 2014. (Discovering Art). (ENG., Illus.). 80p. (J). lib. bdg. *(978-1-60152-700-4(4))* ReferencePoint Pr., Inc.
Hyde, Margaret E., ed. Impressionists for Kids. 2004. (Great Art for Kids Ser.). (Illus.). (J). 12p. pap. 8.95 *(978-1-58980-203-2(9));* 2nd ed. (ENG., 14p. (gr. -1-k). bds. 8.95 *(978-1-58980-265-0(9))* Pelican Publishing Co., Inc.
Klein, Adam G. Claude Monet, 1 vol. 2007. (Great Artists Set 2 Ser.). (ENG., Illus.). 32p. (gr. -1-3). 27.07 *(978-1-59679-732-1(0),* Checkerboard Library) ABDO Publishing Co.
—Pierre-Auguste Renoir, 1 vol. 2007. (Great Artists Set 2 Ser.). (ENG., Illus.). 32p. (gr. -1-3). 27.07 *(978-1-59679-736-9(3),* Checkerboard Library) ABDO Publishing Co.
Mason, Antony. El Arte Impresionista: En Los Tiempos de Renoir. 2005. (Arte Alrededor del Mundo Ser.). (Illus.). 48p. (J). (gr. 4-7). pap. 9.95 *(978-85-7416-229-4(9))* Callis Editora Ltda BRA. Dist: Independent Pubs. Group.
Nichols, Catherine. Pierre-Auguste Renoir. 2009. (Primary Source Library of Famous Artists Ser.). 32p. (gr. 3-4). 42.50 *(978-1-60854-104-1(5),* PowerKids Pr.) Rosen Publishing Group, Inc., The.
Noble, Marty & Dover, A. T. Impressionist Art Masterpieces to Color: 60 Great Paintings from Renoir to Gauguin. 2007. (Dover Art Coloring Book Ser.). (ENG., Illus.). 128p. (gr. 6-8). per. 9.95 *(978-0-486-45135-0(6))* Dover Pubns., Inc.
Parks, Peggy J. Impressionism. 2006. (Eye on Art Ser.). (ENG., Illus.). 112p. (YA). (gr. 6-9). lib. bdg. 34.80 *(978-1-59018-958-0(2),* LML02109-228005, Lucent Bks.) Cengage Gale.
Riggs, Kate. What Is Impressionism? 2016. (Artworld Ser.). 24p. (J). (ENG.). (gr. 2-4). pap. 9.99 *(978-1-62832-224-8(1),* Creative Paperbacks); (Illus.). *(978-1-60818-626-6(1),* Creative Education) Creative Co., The.
Salvi, Francesco. The Impressionists. 2008. (Art Masters Ser.). 64p. (YA). (gr. 6-18). lib. bdg. 24.95 net. *(978-1-934545-03-4(1))* Oliver Pr., Inc.
Sellier, Marie. Renoir's Colors. 2010. (ENG., Illus.). 40p. (J). (gr. -1-k). 16.95 *(978-1-60606-003-2(1))* Getty Pubns.
Sorbier, Frederic. The Impressionists. Chabot, Jean-Phillipe, illus. 2012. (ENG.). 32p. (J). (gr. 2-6). pap. 11.99 *(978-1-85103-296-9(7))* Moonlight Publishing, Ltd. GBR. Dist: Independent Pubs. Group.
Spence, David. The Impressionists: Monet, Cezanne, Renoir, Degas. 2010. (ENG.). 128p. (J). (gr. 4-7). pap. 12.95 *(978-1-84696-217-2(X),* TickTock Books) Octopus Publishing Group GBR. Dist: Independent Pubs. Group.
—Renoir. 2010. (Great Artists & Their World Ser.). 48p. 32.80 *(978-1-84898-317-5(4))* Black Rabbit Bks.
—Renoir: Color y Naturaleza. (Coleccion Grandes Artistas).Tr. of Renoir: Colot & Nature. (SPA.). (YA). (gr. 5-8). 12.76 *(978-84-8211-137-7(X))* Celeste Ediciones, S.A. ESP. Dist: Lectorum Pubns., Inc.
Stephens, Pamela Geiger. Dropping in on Impressionists. McNeill, Jim, illus. 2009. (ENG.). 32p. (J). 15.95 *(978-1-56290-633-7(X))* Crystal Productions.
Waldron, Ann. Who Was Claude Monet? Harrison, Nancy & Marchesi, Stephen, illus. 2009. (Who Was? Ser.). (ENG.). 112p. (J). (gr. 3-7). pap. 5.99 *(978-0-448-44985-2(4),* Grosset & Dunlap) Penguin Young Readers Group.
—Who Was Claude Monet? 2009. (Who Was... ? Ser.). lib. bdg. 16.00 *(978-0-606-04028-0(5),* Turtleback) Turtleback Bks.
Zaczek, Iain. Georges Seurat. 2014. (Great Artists Ser.). 32p. (J). (gr. 3-6). pap. 63.00 *(978-1-4824-1248-2(9))* Stevens, Gareth Publishing LLLP.

IMPRISONMENT

see Prisons

IN-LINE SKATING

Blomquist, Christopher. In-Line Skating in the X Games. (Kid's Guide to the X Games Ser.). 24p. 2009. (gr. 3-3). 42.50 *(978-1-61511-208-1(1))* 2003. (Illus.). (J). lib. bdg. 22.60 *(978-0-8239-6302-7(0))* Rosen Publishing Group, Inc., The. (PowerKids Pr.).
Crossingham, John & Kalman, Bobbie. Extreme in-Line Skating. 2003. (Extreme Sports - No Limits Ser.). (ENG., Illus.). 32p. (J). (gr. 3). pap. *(978-0-7787-1713-3(5))* Crabtree Publishing Co.
David, Jack. In-Line Skating. 2008. (Action Sports Ser.). (ENG., Illus.). 24p. (J). (gr. 3-7). lib. bdg. 25.95 *(978-1-60014-137-9(4))* Bellwether Media.
Glidewell, Steve. Inline Skating. 2003. (Extreme Sports Ser.). (ENG., Illus.). 32p. (gr. 3-6). lib. bdg. 22.60 *(978-0-8225-1244-8(0))* Lerner Publishing Group.
In-Line Skating. 2004. (I-Quest Ser.). (Illus.). 48p. (J). per. *(978-1-84229-755-1(4))* Top That! Publishing PLC.
Mahaney, Ian F. Taig Khris: In-Line Skate Champion. 2005. (Extreme Sports Biographies Ser.). (Illus.). 24p. (J). 22.60 *(978-1-4042-2746-0(6),* PowerKids Pr.) Rosen Publishing Group, Inc., The.
—Taig Khris: In-Line Skating Champion. 2009. (Extreme Sports Biographies Ser.). 24p. (gr. 3-4). 42.50 *(978-1-61512-471-8(3),* PowerKids Pr.) Rosen Publishing Group, Inc., The.
Murdico, Suzanne J. In-Line Skating: Techniques & Tricks. (Rad Sports: Techniques & Tricks Ser.). 48p. (gr. 5-8). 2009. 53.00 *(978-1-60851-933-0(3),* Rosen Reference) 2005. (Illus.). (YA). lib. bdg. 29.25 *(978-0-8239-3844-5(1))* Rosen Publishing Group, Inc., The.
Orr, Tamra. Extreme In-Line Skating. 2011. (Sports on the Edge Ser.). (Illus.). 48p. (J). (gr. 6). 29.93 *(978-1-60870-225-1(1))* Marshall Cavendish Corp.
Rosenberg, Aaron. Taig Khris: In-Line Skating Superstar. 2009. (Extreme Sports Biographies Ser.). 24p. (gr. 3-4). 58.50 *(978-1-61512-470-1(5),* Rosen Reference) Rosen Publishing Group, Inc., The.
—Taig Khris:In-Line Skating. 2005. (Extreme Sports Biographies Ser.). (Illus.). 64p. (J). (gr. 5-8). lib. bdg. 31.95 *(978-1-4042-0069-2(X))* Rosen Publishing Group, Inc., The.
Shafran, Michael. Skate! Your Guide to Inline, Aggressive, Vert, Street, Roller Hockey, Speed Skating, Dance, Fitness Training, & More. 2003. (Extreme Sports Ser.). (ENG., Illus.). 64p. (J). (gr. 4-7). pap. 8.95 *(978-0-7922-5107-1(5),* National Geographic Children's Bks.) National Geographic Society.
Smith, Martin. In-Line Skating. 2012. (To the Limit Ser.). (ENG., Illus.). 32p. (J). (gr. 5-8). pap. 10.00 *(978-1-4488-7060-8(7));* lib. bdg. 25.25 *(978-1-4488-7026-4(7))* Rosen Publishing Group, Inc., The. (PowerKids Pr.).
Woods, Bob. In-Line Skating. 2003. (Extreme Sports Ser.). (Illus.). 24p. (gr. 2-5). lib. bdg. 23.00 *(978-0-8368-3722-3(3),* Gareth Stevens Learning Library) Stevens, Gareth Publishing LLLP.

INCANDESCENT LAMPS

see Electric Lamps

INCAS

Alexander, Mark. The Incredible Incas. 2009. (Real Life Readers Ser.). 24p. (gr. 3-5). pap. 8.25 *(978-1-4358-0229-2(2),* Rosen Classroom) Rosen Publishing Group, Inc., The.
Apte, Sunita. The Inca: Set Of 6. 2011. (Navigators Ser.). (J). pap. 48.00 net. *(978-1-4108-5100-0(1))* Benchmark Education Co.
—The Inca: Text Pairs. 2008. (Bridges/Navigators Ser.). (J). (gr. 4). 89.00 *(978-1-4108-8385-8(X))* Benchmark Education Co.
Benchmark Education Company. The Inca World (Teacher Guide) 2005. *(978-1-4108-4673-0(3))* Benchmark Education Co.
Brannon, Barbara. Discover the Inca. 2005. (J). pap. *(978-1-4108-5148-2(6))* Benchmark Education Co.
Burgan, Michael. Ancient Incas. 2012. (Ancient World Ser.). (ENG., Illus.). 112p. (J). pap. 9.95 *(978-0-531-25979-5(X));* (gr. 6-9). lib. bdg. 34.00 *(978-0-531-25179-9(9))* Scholastic Library Publishing.
Burling, Alexis. The Destruction of the Inca Civilization. 2017. (J). **(978-1-5081-7738-8(4),** Rosen Young Adult) Rosen Publishing Group, Inc., The.
Byers, Helen. Peru. 2007. (Nonfiction Reading & Writing Workshops Ser.). (ENG., Illus.). 24p. (J). pap. 14.95 *(978-0-7922-4538-4(5))* CENGAGE Learning.
Callery, Sean. The Dark History of the Aztec Empire. 2010. (Dark Histories Ser.). 64p. (gr. 5). 32.79 *(978-1-60870-085-1(2))* Marshall Cavendish Corp.
Conklin, Wendy. Mayas, Aztecs, Incas: All-in-One Resource with Background Information, Map Activities, Simulations & Games, & a Read-Aloud Play to Support Comprehension & Critical Thinking in Social Studies. 2006. (ENG., Illus.). 80p. (gr. 5-12). per. 12.99 *(978-0-439-53994-4(3),* Teaching Resources) Scholastic, Inc.
—Mayas, Incas, & Aztecs, 1 vol. 2007. (Primary Source Readers Ser.). (ENG., Illus.). 32p. (J). (gr. 5-5). pap. 8.99 *(978-0-7439-0456-8(7))* Shell Educational Publishing.
Croy, Anita. Solving the Mysteries of Machu Picchu. 2008. (Digging into History Ser.). 32p. (gr. 4-18). lib. bdg. 29.93 *(978-0-7614-3103-9(9),* Benchmark Bks.) Marshall Cavendish Corp.
Dorling Kindersley Publishing Staff. Aztec, Inca & Maya. 2011. (DK Eyewitness Bks.). (ENG.). 72p. (J). (gr. 3-7). 16.99 *(978-0-7566-7320-8(8),* DK Children) Dorling Kindersley Publishing, Inc.
Grant, Neil. Everyday Life of the Aztecs, Incas & Mayans. Cappon, Manuela et al, illus. 2003. (Uncovering History Ser.). 46p. (J). lib. bdg. 28.50 *(978-1-58340-253-5(5))* Black Rabbit Bks.
Gruber, Beth, et al. Ancient Inca: Archaeology Unlocks the Secrets of the Inca's Past. 2006. (National Geographic Investigates Ser.). (ENG., Illus.). 64p. (J). (gr. 3-7). 17.95 *(978-0-7922-7827-6(5));* (gr. 4-7). 27.90 *(978-0-7922-7873-3(9))* National Geographic Society. (National Geographic Children's Bks.).
Hayes, Amy. Ancient Inca Government. 2016. (Spotlight on the Maya, Aztec, & Inca Civilizations Ser.). (Illus.). 32p. (J). (gr. 6-4). pap. 11.75 *(978-1-4994-1948-1(1),* PowerKids Pr.) Rosen Publishing Group, Inc., The.
Hiram Bingham & the Dream of Gold. 2014. (ENG.). 192p. (J). (gr. 3-7). pap. 13.95 *(978-1-59077-350-5(0))* Evans, M. & Co., Inc.
Hoogenboom, Lynn. Francisco Pizarro. 2009. (Primary Source Library of Famous Explorers Ser.). 24p. (gr. 4-4). 42.50 *(978-1-60854-121-8(5),* PowerKids Pr.) Rosen Publishing Group, Inc., The.
—Francisco Pizarro: A Primary Source Biography. 2006. (Primary Source Library of Famous Explorers Ser.). (Illus.). 24p. (YA). (gr. 2-5). lib. bdg. 22.60 *(978-1-4042-3038-5(6))* Rosen Publishing Group, Inc., The.
Kachurek, Sandra J. Francisco Pizarro: Explorer of South America. 2004. (Explorers! Ser.). (Illus.). 48p. (J). lib. bdg. 23.93 *(978-0-7660-2178-5(5))* Enslow Pubs., Inc.
Kops, Deborah. Machu Picchu. 2008. (Unearthing Ancient Worlds Ser.). (ENG.). 80p. (gr. 5-8). lib. bdg. 30.60 *(978-0-8225-7584-9(1))* Lerner Publishing Group.
Kovacs, Lawrence & Rizvi, Farah. Inca: Discover the Culture & Geography of a Lost Civilization with 25 Projects. 2013. (Build It Yourself Ser.). (ENG., Illus.). 128p. (J). (gr. 3-7). 21.95 *(978-1-61930-141-2(5));* pap. 15.95 *(978-1-61930-140-5(7))* Open City Bks.
Meltzer, Milton. Francisco Pizarro: The Conquest of Peru. 2003. (Great Explorations Ser.). (J). 29.93 *(978-0-7614-1607-4(2),* Benchmark Bks.) Marshall Cavendish Corp.
Morlock, Theresa. Ancient Inca Geography. 2016. (Spotlight on the Maya, Aztec, & Inca Civilizations Ser.). 32p. (J). (gr. 6-4). pap. 11.75 *(978-1-4994-1943-6(0),* PowerKids Pr.) Rosen Publishing Group, Inc., The.
Mountjoy, Shane. Francisco Pizarro & the Conquest of the Inca. Goetzmann, William H., ed. 2005. (Explorers of New Lands Ser.). (Illus.). 100p. (gr. 5-8). 30.00 *(978-0-7910-8614-8(3),* Chelsea Hse.) Facts On File, Inc.
Nagelhout, Ryan. Ancient Inca Technology. 2016. (Spotlight on the Maya, Aztec, & Inca Civilizations Ser.). (Illus.). 32p. (J). (gr. 6-4). pap. 11.75 *(978-1-4994-1953-5(8),* PowerKids Pr.) Rosen Publishing Group, Inc., The.
Nelson, Kristen Rajczak. Ancient Inca Culture. 2016. (Spotlight on the Maya, Aztec, & Inca Civilizations Ser.). (Illus.). 32p. (J). (gr. 6-4). pap. 11.75 *(978-1-4994-1928-3(7),* PowerKids Pr.) Rosen Publishing Group, Inc., The.
Newman, Sandra. The Inca Empire. (True Book(tm), a — Ancient Civilizations Ser.). (ENG.). 48p. (J). 2009. (gr. 2-5). 31.00 *(978-0-531-25228-4(0))* 2010. (Illus.). (gr. 3-5). pap. 6.95 *(978-0-531-24109-7(2))* Scholastic Library Publishing.
Niver, Heather Moore. Ancient Inca Daily Life. 2016. (Spotlight on the Maya, Aztec, & Inca Civilizations Ser.). (Illus.). 32p. (J). (gr. 6-4). pap. 11.75 *(978-1-4994-1933-7(3),* PowerKids Pr.) Rosen Publishing Group, Inc., The.
Peterson, Sheryl. Machu Picchu. 2005. (Ancient Wonders of the World Ser.). (Illus.). 32p. (J). (gr. 4-7). lib. bdg. 18.95 *(978-1-58341-357-9(X),* Creative Education) Creative Co., The.
Ramen, Fred. Francisco Pizarro: The Exploration of Peru & the Conquest of the Inca. (Library of Explorers & Exploration Ser.). 112p. (gr. 5-8). 2009. 66.50 *(978-1-60853-603-0(3))* 2004. (Illus.). lib. bdg. 34.60 *(978-0-8239-3618-2(X))* Rosen Publishing Group, Inc., The. (Rosen Reference).
Richardson, Hazel. Life in Ancient South America. 2005. (Peoples of the Ancient World Ser.). (ENG., Illus.). 32p. (J). (gr. -1-9). pap. *(978-0-7787-2072-0(1));* lib. bdg. *(978-0-7787-2042-3(X))* Crabtree Publishing Co.
Riggs, Kate. Machu Picchu. 2009. (Places of Old Ser.). 24p. (J). (gr. 1-5). lib. bdg. 24.25 *(978-1-58341-709-6(5),* Creative Education) Creative Co., The.
Saunders, Nicholas J. & Saunders, Nick. The Inca City of Cuzco. 2005. (Places in History Ser.). (Illus.). 48p. (gr. 5-12). lib. bdg. 31.00 *(978-0-8368-5812-9(3),* World Almanac Library) Stevens, Gareth Publishing LLLP.
Sayer, Chloe. The Incan Empire. 2010. (Exploring the Ancient World Ser.). (Illus.). 64p. (YA). (gr. 6-8). lib. bdg. 34.60 *(978-1-4339-4187-0(2),* Gareth Stevens Secondary Library) Stevens, Gareth Publishing LLLP.
Snedden, Robert. Aztec, Inca & Maya. 2009. (Technology in Times Past Ser.). (J). 32.80 *(978-1-59920-299-0(9))* Black Rabbit Bks.
—Aztec, Inca, & Maya. 2009. (Technology in Times Past Ser.). (Illus.). 46p. (J). (gr. 4-7). pap. *(978-1-897563-64-9(7))* Saunders Bk. Co.
Somervill, Barbara A. Empire of the Incas, Revised Edition. 2nd rev. ed. 2009. (Great Empires of the Past Ser.). (Illus.). 152p. (gr. 6-12). 35.00 *(978-1-60413-158-1(6),* Chelsea Hse.) Facts On File, Inc.
Steele, Philip. Incas: Step into the Spectacular World of Ancient South America, with 340 Exciting Pictures & 15 Step-by-Step Projects. 2014. (ENG., Illus.). 64p. (J). (gr. -1-12). pap. 12.99 *(978-1-84322-731-1(2),* Armadillo) Anness Publishing GBR. Dist: National Bk. Network.
Thomas, Emma. The Inca Tomb. 2011. (History Detectives Ser.). (ENG.). 32p. (J). (gr. 4-7). spiral bd. 9.95

(978-1-84898-187-4(2), TickTock Books) Octopus Publishing Group GBR. Dist: Independent Pubs. Group.
Trumbauer, Lisa. The Inca World. 2005. (J). pap. (978-1-4108-4625-9(3)) Benchmark Education Co.
Von Hagen, Victor Wolfgang. The Incas: People of the Sun. 2003. 127p. pap. 29.00 (978-0-7581-0248-5(8)) Textbook Pubs.
Waldron, Melanie. Geography Matters in the Inca Empire. 2015. (Geography Matters in Ancient Civilizations Ser.). (ENG., Illus.). 48p. (gr. 3-6). 33.32 (978-1-4846-0965-1(4), Heinemann InfoSearch) Heinemann-Raintree.
Weitzman, Elizabeth. Mysteries of Machu Picchu. 2017. (Ancient Mysteries Ser.). (ENG.). 32p. (J). (gr. 3-6). 27.99 **(978-1-5124-4018-8(3))** Lerner Publishing Group.
West, David. The Incas. 2016. (Discovering Ancient Civilizations Ser.). 32p. (gr. 3-3). pap. 10.50 (978-1-4824-5051-4(8)) Stevens, Gareth Publishing LLLP.
World Book, Inc Staff, contrib. by. The Enduring Mystery of Machu Picchu. 2015. (Illus.). 48p. (J). (978-0-7166-2675-6(6)) World Bk., Inc.
—The Inca. 2009. (J). (978-0-7166-2135-5(5)) World Bk., Inc.
Zronik, John Paul & Zronik, John. Francisco Pizarro: Journeys Through Peru & South America. 2005. (In the Footsteps of Explorers Ser.). (ENG., Illus.). 32p. (J). (gr. -1-9). pap. (978-0-7787-2447-6(6)) Crabtree Publishing Co.

INCAS—FICTION

Becket, Jim. Inca Gold: Choose Your Own Adventure #20. 2007. (Choose Your Own Adventure Ser.: 20). (Illus.). 144p. (J). per. 6.99 (978-1-933390-20-8(4), CHCL20) Chooseco LLC.
Ellis, Leanne Statland. The Ugly One. 2015. (ENG.). 256p. (J). (gr. 5-7). pap. 7.99 (978-0-544-43917-7(1), HMH Books For Young Readers) Houghton Mifflin Harcourt Publishing Co.
Ficklin, Jonene H. Orinoco Intrigue. 2005. (YA). 14.95 (978-0-9761188-1-7(5)) Victor's Crown Publishing.
Horowitz, Anthony. Evil Star. 2007. (Gatekeepers Ser.: 2). 318p. lib. bdg. 19.65 (978-1-4177-7663-4(3), Turtleback) Turtleback Bks.
Jendresen, Erik & Villoldo, Alberto. The First Story Ever Told. Yoshi, illus. 2008. (ENG.). 36p. (J). (gr. -1-2). 12.99 (978-1-4169-8961-5(7), Simon & Schuster Bks. For Young Readers) Simon & Schuster Bks. For Young Readers.
Kerr, P. B., pseud. The Eye of the Forest. 2009. (Children of the Lamp Ser.: 5). (ENG.). 432p. (J). (gr. 3-7). 17.99 (978-0-439-93215-8(7), Orchard Bks.) Scholastic, Inc.
O'Dell, Scott. The Seven Serpents Trilogy. 2009. (ENG.). 560p. (J). (gr. 4-6). pap. 19.99 (978-1-4022-1836-1(2), Sourcebooks Jabberwocky) Sourcebooks, Inc.
Paris, Harper. The Mystery Across the Secret Bridge. Calo, Marcos, illus. 2015. (Greetings from Somewhere Ser.: 7). (ENG.). 128p. (J). (gr. k-4). pap. 5.99 (978-1-4814-2367-0(3), Little Simon) Little Simon.
Stokes, Jonathan W. Addison Cooke & the Treasure of the Incas. 2016. (Addison Cooke Ser.). (ENG., Illus.). 336p. (J). (gr. 3-7). 16.99 (978-0-399-17377-6(3), Philomel Bks.) Penguin Young Readers Group.
Vajda, Tibor Timothy. The End of the World. 2008. 96p. pap. 9.95 (978-0-595-52914-8(3)) iUniverse, Inc.

INCEST

McKinnon, Margie & McKinnon, Tom W. Repair for Kids: A Children's Program for Recovery from Incest & Childhood Sexual Abuse. McKinnon, Margie & McKinnon, Tom W., illus. 2008. (Illus.). 92p. (J). pap. 34.95 (978-1-932690-57-6(3)) Loving Healing Pr., Inc.
Terpstra, Marcia J. Splinters from My Rocking Chair: A Journey Through Incest Survival. 2011. 128p. pap. 14.99 (978-1-4634-3928-6(8)) AuthorHouse.

INCEST—FICTION

Amateau, Gigi. Claiming Georgia Tate. (ENG.). 208p. (YA). (gr. 9-12). 2007. per. 7.99 (978-0-7636-3311-0(9)) 2005. 15.99 (978-0-7636-2339-5(3)) Candlewick Pr.
Block, Francesca Lia. Wasteland. 2003. (Illus.). 160p. (J). 16.89 (978-0-06-028645-3(8), Cotler, Joanna Books) HarperCollins Pubs.
Brooks, Kevin. Dawn. 2010. (ENG.). 272p. (J). (gr. 9). pap. 8.99 (978-0-545-06092-9(3), PUSH) Scholastic, Inc.
Michaels, Rune. Nobel Genes. (ENG., (YA). (gr. 7). 2011. Illus.). 208p. pap. 8.99 (978-1-4424-2401-2(X)) 2010. 192p. 16.99 (978-1-4169-1259-0(2)) Simon & Schuster Children's Publishing. (Atheneum Bks. for Young Readers).
Scott, Mindi. Live Through This. 2012. (ENG.). 304p. (YA). (gr. 9). 17.99 (978-1-4424-4059-3(7)); pap. 9.99 (978-1-4424-4060-9(0)) Simon Pulse. (Simon Pulse).
Suzuma, Tabitha. Forbidden. (ENG.). 464p. (YA). (gr. 11). 2012. pap. 11.99 (978-1-4424-1996-4(2)) 2011. 17.99 (978-1-4424-1995-7(4)) Simon Pulse. (Simon Pulse).
Woodson, Jacqueline. I Hadn't Meant to Tell You This. 2006. 114p. (YA). (gr. 7-12). 13.65 (978-0-7569-6730-7(9)) Perfection Learning Corp.

INCINERATION

see Refuse and Refuse Disposal

INCOME

Beaton, Kathryn. Payday! 2015. (21st Century Skills Library: Real World Math Ser.). (ENG., Illus.). 32p. (J). (gr. 4-7). 29.93 (978-1-63362-573-0(7), 206476) Cherry Lake Publishing.
Brezina, Corona. Understanding the Gross Domestic Product & the Gross National Product. 2011. (Real World Economics Ser.). (ENG.). 80p. (YA). (gr. 7-12). lib. bdg. 33.25 (978-1-4488-5569-8(1)) Rosen Publishing Group, Inc., The.
Cunningham, Anne C. Critical Perspectives on the Minimum Wage. 2016. (Analyzing the Issues Ser.). 208p. (J). (gr. 8-8). 47.93 (978-0-7660-7675-4(X)) Enslow Pubs., Inc.
Dakers, Diane. It Doesn't Grow on Trees: Sources of Income. 2017. (Financial Literacy for Life Ser.). (ENG.). 48p. (J). **(978-0-7787-3096-5(4))**; pap. **(978-0-7787-3105-4(7))** Crabtree Publishing Co.
Eagen, Rachel. Learning about Earning. 2016. (Money Sense: an Introduction to Financial Literacy Ser.). (ENG., Illus.). 24p. (J). (gr. 1-4). (978-0-7787-2665-4(7)) Crabtree Publishing Co.
Fradin, Dennis Brindell & Fradin, Judith Bloom. Earning. 2010. (Money Smart Ser.). 64p. (gr. 4). 32.79 (978-1-60870-123-0(9)) Marshall Cavendish Corp.
Kemper, Bitsy. Earning Income. 2015. (Searchlight Books (tm) — How Do We Use Money? Ser.). (ENG., Illus.). 40p. (gr. 3-5). 39.99 (978-1-4677-8915-8(1), Lerner Digital); (J). pap. 8.99 (978-1-4677-6107-9(9), Lerner Pubns.); (J). lib. bdg. 27.99 (978-1-4677-5227-5(4), Lerner Pubns.) Lerner Publishing Group.
Kukathas, Uma. The Minimum Wage. 2009. (EXAMINING ISS COURT DECSNS Ser.). (ENG., Illus.). 240p. (J). 42.15 (978-0-7377-4491-0(X), Greenhaven Pr., Inc.) Cengage Gale.
Larson, Jennifer S. What Can You Do with Money? Earning, Spending, & Saving. 2010. (Lightning Bolt Books — Exploring Economics Ser.). (ENG., Illus.). 32p. (gr. k-2). pap. 7.95 (978-0-7613-5666-0(5)); lib. bdg. 26.60 (978-0-7613-3910-6(8)) Lerner Publishing Group.
Whitehead, William. Family Money. Beech, Mark, illus. 2015. (How Money Works). (ENG.). 64p. (J). (gr. 4-6). lib. bdg. 29.27 (978-1-59953-717-7(6)) Norwood Hse. Pr.

INDEPENDENCE DAY (U.S.)

see Fourth of July

INDEPENDENCE HALL (PHILADELPHIA, PA.)

Anderson, T. Neill. Horrors of History: People of the Plague: Philadelphia Flu Epidemic 1918. 2014. (ENG., Illus.). 160p. (YA). (gr. 7). 16.95 (978-1-58089-518-7(2)) Charlesbridge Publishing, Inc.
Hepburn, Greg. Liam Goes to Independence Hall. 2013. (InfoMax Readers Ser.). (ENG.). 24p. (J). (gr. 2-3). pap. 8.25 (978-1-4777-2419-4(2)); pap. 49.50 (978-1-4777-2420-0(6)) Rosen Publishing Group, Inc., The. (Rosen Classroom).
Marcovitz, Hal. Independence Hall: Birthplace of Freedom. Moreno, Barry, ed. 2014. (Patriotic Symbols of America Ser.: 20). 48p. (J). (gr. 4-18). lib. bdg. 20.95 (978-1-4222-3124-1(0)) Mason Crest.
Potter, Becky Ann. Have You Been to Independence Hall? 2013. (Rosen Readers Ser.). (ENG.). 24p. (J). (gr. 2-3). pap. 8.25 (978-1-4777-2265-7(3)); pap. 49.50 (978-1-4777-2266-4(1)) Rosen Publishing Group, Inc., The. (Rosen Classroom).
RJF Publishing Staff & Staton, Hilarie. Independence Hall. 2009. (Symbols of American Freedom Ser.). 48p. (gr. 4-6). 30.00 (978-1-60413-521-3(2), Chelsea Clubhouse) Facts On File, Inc.
Wood, Alexander. Visit Independence Hall. 2012. (Landmarks of Liberty Ser.). (ENG.). 24p. (gr. 2-5). pap. 8.15 (978-1-4339-6386-5(8), Gareth Stevens Learning Library); (J). lib. bdg. 22.60 (978-1-4339-6384-1(1)) Stevens, Gareth Publishing LLLP.

INDIA

Abdul Kalam, A. P. J. Children Ask Kalam. Kathuria, Rohit, illus. 2006. 109p. (J). (978-81-7758-245-1(3)) Pearson Education.
Aboff, Marcie. India ABCs: A Book about the People & Places of India, 1 vol. Moore, Frances, illus. 2006. (Country ABCs Ser.). (ENG.). 32p. (gr. k-5). 27.99 (978-1-4048-1571-1(6)) Picture Window Bks.
Apte, Sunita. India. 2009. (True Book(tm), A — Countries Ser.). (ENG., 48p. (J). Illus.). (gr. 2-5). 31.00 (978-0-531-16890-5(5)); (gr. 3-5). pap. 6.95 (978-0-531-21357-5(9), Children's Pr.) Scholastic Library Publishing.
Arnold, Caroline & Comora, Madeleine. Taj Mahal. Bhushan, Rahul, illus. 2007. (ENG.). 32p. (J). (gr. k-12). lib. bdg. 17.95 (978-0-7613-2609-0(X), Millbrook Pr.) Lerner Publishing Group.
Atkinson, Tim. Discover India. 2012. (Discover Countries Ser.). (Illus.). 32p. (YA). (gr. 4-7). lib. bdg. 26.50 (978-1-4488-5268-0(4)) Rosen Publishing Group, Inc., The.
Barker, Amanda. India. (World Focus Ser.). (Illus.). 32p. (J). (gr. 3-7). 3.99 (978-0-431-07258-6(2)) Oxfam Publishing GBR. Dist: Stylus Publishing, LLC.
Brooks, Susie. India. 2006. (Our Lives, Our World Ser.). (Illus.). (J). (978-1-59389-288-3(8)) Chrysalis Education.
Brownlie Bojang, Ali & Barber, Nicola. Focus on India. 2006. (World in Focus Ser.). (Illus.). 64p. (gr. 5-12). pap. 14.05 (978-0-8368-6728-2(9)); lib. bdg. 34.00 (978-0-8368-6721-3(1)) Stevens, Gareth Publishing LLLP. (Gareth Stevens Secondary Library).
Caper, William. India & China: Set Of 6. 2010. (Navigators Ser.). (J). pap. 50.00 net. (978-1-4108-5112-3(5)) Benchmark Education Co.
Centore, Michael. My Teenage Life in India. 2017. (Custom & Cultures of the World Ser.). (ENG.). (YA). (gr. 7-12). 23.95 **(978-1-4222-3905-6(5))** Mason Crest.
Chambers, Catherine. A Day at an Indian Market. 2011. (Big Picture: Food Ser.). (ENG.). 24p. (gr. 1-2). pap. 41.70 (978-1-4296-6725-8(7), First Facts) Capstone Press of Coughlan Cos.
Doak, Robin Santos. Indian Americans. 2007. (American Immigrants Ser.). (Illus.). 48p. (J). (gr. 4-6). lib. bdg. (978-1-60044-612-2(4)) Rourke Educational Media.
Draper, Allison Stark. India: A Primary Source Cultural Guide. 2009. (Primary Sources of World Cultures Ser.). 128p. (gr. 4-5). 79.90 (978-1-60851-923-1(6)) Rosen Publishing Group, Inc., The.
Elgin, Kathy. India. 2008. (Costume Around the World Ser.). (Illus.). 32p. (gr. 4-6). 28.00 (978-0-7910-9768-7(4), Chelsea Clubhouse) Facts On File, Inc.
Engfer, LeeAnne. India in Pictures. 2nd rev. ed. 2003. (Visual Geography Ser.). (Illus.). 80p. (J). (gr. 5-12). 27.93 (978-0-8225-0371-2(9)) Lerner Publishing Group.
Ganeri, Anita. India. 2007. (Countries in the News/Watts Ser.). (Illus.). 32p. (YA). (gr. 4-7). lib. bdg. 28.50 (978-1-59920-017-0(1)) Black Rabbit Bks.
—India. 2010. (World of Food Ser.). 32p. (YA). (gr. 4-7). lib. bdg. 24.95 (978-1-934545-11-9(2)) Oliver Pr., Inc.
—India: A Benjamin Blog & His Inquisitive Dog Guide, 1 vol. Isik, Semur, illus. 2014. (Country Guides, with Benjamin Blog & His Inquisitive Dog Ser.). (ENG.). 32p. (gr. 1-3). pap. 7.99 (978-1-4109-6671-1(2), Read Me!) Heinemann-Raintree.
Goodman, Susan E. & National Geographic Learning Staff. India in the Past & Present. 2007. (Language, Literacy, & Vocabulary - Reading Expeditions Ser.). (ENG., Illus.). 36p. pap. 18.95 (978-0-7922-5466-9(X)) CENGAGE Learning.
Green, Jen. Mumbai. Fairclough, Chris, photos by. 2007. (Global Cities Ser.). (Illus.). 61p. (gr. 5-8). lib. bdg. 30.00 (978-0-7910-8851-7(0), Chelsea Hse.) Facts On File, Inc.
Hardyman, Robyn. Celebrate: India. 2009. (Celebrate Country Ser.). 32p. (gr. 4-6). 28.00 (978-1-60413-265-6(5), Chelsea Clubhouse) Facts On File, Inc.
Harkrader, Lisa. India: A MyReportLinks. com Book. 2004. (Top Ten Countries of Recent Immigrants Ser.). (Illus.). 48p. (J). lib. bdg. 26.60 (978-0-7660-5180-5(3), MyReportLinks.com Bks.) Enslow Pubs., Inc.
Helfand, Lewis. Mother Teresa: Saint of the Slums. Banerjee, Sankha & Nagar, Sachin, illus. 2013. (Campfire Graphic Novels Ser.). (ENG.). 88p. (YA). (gr. 5). pap. 11.99 (978-93-80028-70-5(9), Campfire) Steerforth Pr.
Humble, Darryl. India. 2010. (Countries in Our World Ser.). 32p. (gr. 4-7). lib. bdg. 31.35 (978-1-59920-439-0(8)) Black Rabbit Bks.
Jackson, Elaine. India. 2004. (QEB Travel Through Ser.). (Illus.). 32p. (J). lib. bdg. 18.95 (978-1-59566-060-2(7)) QEB Publishing Inc.
Johnson, Robin & Kalman, Bobbie. Spotlight on India. 2008. (Spotlight on my Country Ser.). (ENG., Illus.). 32p. (J). (gr. 3-7). pap. (978-0-7787-3481-9(1)) Crabtree Publishing Co.
Kissock, Heather. Taj Mahal. 2011. (J). (978-1-61690-436-4(4)) Weigl Pubs., Inc.
Kissock, Heather, ed. Taj Mahal. 2011. (J). (gr. 4-6). pap. 12.95 (978-1-61690-769-3(X), AV2 by Weigl); (Illus.). 24p. (gr. 2-5). 27.13 (978-1-61690-765-5(7)) Weigl Pubs., Inc.
Leigh, Autumn. A Primary Source Guide to India. 2009. (Countries of the World). 24p. (gr. 2-3). 42.50 (978-1-61512-033-8(5), PowerKids Pr.) Rosen Publishing Group, Inc., The.
Lewin, Ted & Lewin, Betsy. Balarama: A Royal Elephant, 1 vol. 2014. (Adventures Around the World Ser.). (ENG.). 48p. (J). pap. 11.95 (978-1-62014-186-1(8)) Lee & Low Bks., Inc.
—Balarama: A Royal Elephant. Lewin, Ted & Lewin, Betsy, illus. 2009. (Adventures Around the World Ser.). (ENG., Illus.). 56p. (J). (gr. 1-6). 19.95 (978-1-60060-265-8(7)) Lee & Low Bks., Inc.
Littlefield, Holly. Colors of India. Porter, Janice Lee, illus. 2003. (Colors of the World Ser.). 24p. (J). (gr. 1-4). 5.95 (978-1-57505-368-4(3)) Lerner Publishing Group.
Mahadevan, Madhavi S. Hanuman's Adventures in the Nether World: A 600 Year Old Classic Retold. Srivi, illus. 2005. (J). (978-81-89020-30-9(7)) Katha.
Marsh, Carole. India: Land of Six Senses & Intriguing Mystery! 2009. (It's Your World Ser.). 48p. (J). (gr. 2-9). pap. 7.99 (978-0-635-06813-2(3)) Gallopade International.
McNeil, Niki, et al. HOCPP 1114 Ancient India. 2006. spiral bd. 20.00 (978-1-60308-114-6(3)) In the Hands of a Child.
Mehta, Anurag & Prajapati, Rajesh. India after Independence: For Children. 2004. (Illus.). 216p. (J). (978-81-7676-036-2(6)) Nita Mehta Publications.
Mis, Melody S. How to Draw India's Sights & Symbols. 2009. (Kid's Guide to Drawing the Countries of the World Ser.). 48p. (gr. 4-4). 53.00 (978-1-61511-113-8(1), PowerKids Pr.) Rosen Publishing Group, Inc., The.
Moon, Walt K. Let's Explore India. 2017. (Bumba Books (tm) — Let's Explore Countries Ser.). (ENG.). 24p. (J). (gr. -1-1). 12.99 **(978-1-5124-3735-5(2)**, Lerner Pubns.); 38.65 **(978-1-5124-3018-9(8)**, Lerner Pubns.); 38.65 **(978-1-5124-3734-8(4)**, Lerner Pubns.); (Illus.). 25.32 (978-1-5124-3006-6(4)) Lerner Publishing Group.
Oachs, Emily Rose. India. 2017. (Country Profiles Ser.). (ENG., Illus.). 32p. (J). (gr. 3-8). lib. bdg. 26.95 **(978-1-62617-681-2(7)**, Blastoff! Discovery) Bellwether Media.
Oliver Optic. Across India: Or - Live Boys in the Far East. I.t. ed. 2007. (ENG.). 294p. pap. 23.99 (978-1-4264-8745-3(2)) Creative Media Partners, LLC.
Popper, Garry. Mina in India. Johnson, Andi, illus. 2004. 36p. (gr. -1-7). 4.00 (978-1-84161-079-5(8)) Ravette Publishing, Ltd. GBR. Dist: Parkwest Pubns., Inc.
Powell, Jillian. Descubramos India. 2007. (Descubramos paises del mundo (Looking at Countries) Ser.). (SPA., Illus.). 32p. (gr. 1-5). lib. bdg. 26.00 (978-0-8368-7954-4(6), Gareth Stevens Learning Library) Stevens, Gareth Publishing LLLP.
—Looking at India. 2007. (Looking at Countries Ser.). (Illus.). 32p. (gr. 1-5). pap. 10.50 (978-0-8368-7676-5(8)); lib. bdg. 26.00 (978-0-8368-7669-7(5)) Stevens, Gareth Publishing LLLP. (Gareth Stevens Learning Library).
Raatma, Lucia. India. 2010. (Explorer Library: Social Studies Explorer Ser.). (ENG.). 48p. (gr. 4-8). lib. bdg. 31.36 (978-1-60279-824-3(9), 200514) Cherry Lake Publishing.
Roza, Greg. A Primary Source Guide to India. 2003. (Countries of the World). (Illus.). 24p. (J). lib. bdg. 22.60 (978-0-8239-6596-0(1), PowerKids Pr.) Rosen Publishing Group, Inc., The.
Roza, Greg & Leigh, Autumn. A Primary Source Guide to India. 2003. (Countries of the World). (ENG., Illus.). 24p. (gr. 3-6). pap. 8.25 (978-0-8239-8080-2(4), PowerKids Pr.) Rosen Publishing Group, Inc., The.
Stefoff, Rebecca. Asian Empires. 2004. (Illus.). 48p. (J). 31.36 (978-0-7614-1643-2(9), Benchmark Bks.) Marshall Cavendish Corp.
Streissguth, Tom. India. 2008. pap. 40.95 (978-0-8225-9302-7(5)); (ENG., Illus.). 48p. (gr. 2-4). lib. bdg. 29.27 (978-0-8225-8662-3(2)) Lerner Publishing Group.
Tagliaferro, Linda. Taj Mahal: India's Majestic Tomb. 2005. (Castles, Palaces, & Tombs Ser.). (Illus.). 32p. (J). lib. bdg. 25.27 (978-1-59716-004-9(0)) Bearport Publishing Co., Inc.
Thomson, Ruth. Living in India. Hampton, David, illus. 2006. (Living In- Ser.). 32p. (J). (gr. 4-7). lib. bdg. 27.10 (978-1-59771-046-6(6)) Sea-To-Sea Pubns.
Tierney, Tom. Fashions from India. 2013. (Dover Fashion Coloring Book Ser.). (ENG., Illus.). 48p. (J). (gr. 3-12). pap. 4.99 (978-0-486-43040-9(5)) Dover Pubns., Inc.
Vaughan, Jenny. India. 2015. (Emerging Nations Ser.). (ENG., Illus.). 48p. (J). (gr. 4-9). 37.10 (978-1-59920-986-9(1)) Black Rabbit Bks.
Weber, Valerie J. I Come from India. 2006. (This Is My Story Ser.). (Illus.). 24p. (gr. 1-4). pap. 8.15 (978-0-8368-7242-2(8)); lib. bdg. 22.00 (978-0-8368-7235-4(5)) Stevens, Gareth Publishing LLLP. (Weekly Reader Leveled Readers).
Worth, Richard. Vasco da Gama. 2009. (Great Explorers Ser.). (Illus.). 104p. (gr. 6-12). 30.00 (978-1-60413-423-0(2), Chelsea Hse.) Facts On File, Inc.

INDIA—BIOGRAPHY

Benge, Janet & Benge, Geoff. Christian Heroes - Then & Now - Sundar Singh: Footprints over the Mountains. 2005. (Christian Heroes Ser.). (ENG., Illus.). 181p. (YA). pap. 9.99 (978-1-57658-318-0(X)) YWAM Publishing.
—Paul Brand: Helping Hands. 2011. (ENG.). (YA). pap. 9.99 (978-1-57658-536-8(0)) YWAM Publishing.
Bridges, Shirin Yim & Yim Bridges, Shirin. Nur Jahan of India. Nguyen, Albert, illus. 2010. (Thinking Girl's Treasury of Real Princesses Ser.). (ENG.). 24p. (J). (gr. 3-8). 18.95 (978-0-9845098-5-0(2)) Goosebottom Bks. LLC.
Brierley, Saroo. Lion: A Long Way Home Young Readers' Edition. 2017. (ENG.). 272p. (J). (gr. 5). 8.99 **(978-0-425-29176-4(6)**, Puffin Books) Penguin Young Readers Group.
Burleigh, Robert. Tiger of the Snows: Tenzing Norgay: the Boy Whose Dream Was Everest. Young, Ed, illus. 2010. (ENG.). 40p. (J). (gr. 2-5). 16.99 (978-1-4424-2192-9(4), Atheneum Bks. for Young Readers) Simon & Schuster Children's Publishing.
Cook, Diane. Mohandas Gandhi: Spiritual Leader. 2013. (People of Importance Ser.: 21). (Illus.). 32p. (J). (gr. 4-18). 19.95 (978-1-4222-2852-4(5)) Mason Crest.
Devi, Dulari, illus. Following My Paint Brush. 2011. (ENG.). 32p. (J). (gr. 2-18). (978-93-80340-11-1(7)) Tara Publishing.
Doeden, Matt. Darkness Everywhere: The Assassination of Mohandas Gandhi. 2013. 80p. pap. 31.93 (978-1-4677-1659-8(6)) Lerner Publishing Group.
—Mohandas Gandhi. 2011. (J). lib. bdg. (978-0-7613-5483-3(2)) Twenty First Century Bks.
Gandhi, Arun & Hegedus, Bethany. Be the Change: A Grandfather Gandhi Story. Turk, Evan, illus. 2016. (ENG.). 48p. (J). (gr. -1-3). 18.99 (978-1-4814-4265-7(1)) Simon & Schuster Children's Publishing.
Ganeri, Anita. Mother Teresa's Alms Bowl. Radford, Karen & Noyes, Leighton, illus. 2008. (Stories of Great People Ser.). (ENG.). 40p. (J). (gr. 3-8). pap. (978-0-7787-3712-4(8)) Crabtree Publishing Co.
Ganeri, Anita & Bailey, Gerry. Mother Teresa's Alms Bowl. 2008. (Stories of Great People Ser.). (ENG., Illus.). 40p. (J). (gr. 3-8). lib. bdg. (978-0-7787-3690-5(3)) Crabtree Publishing Co.
Haldy, Emma E. Mother Teresa. Bane, Jeff, illus. 2017. (My Early Library: My Itty-Bitty Bio Ser.). (ENG.). 24p. (J). (gr. k-1). lib. bdg. 28.50 (978-1-63472-154-7(3), 209188) Cherry Lake Publishing.
Jones, Brenn. Learning about Love from the Life of Mother Teresa. 2009. (Character Building Book Ser.). 24p. (gr. 2-3). 42.50 (978-1-61511-001-8(1), PowerKids Pr.) Rosen Publishing Group, Inc., The.
Kuhn, Betsy. The Force Born of Truth: Mohandas Gandhi & the Salt March, India, 1930. 2010. (Civil Rights Struggles around the World Ser.). (ENG., Illus.). 160p. (gr. 9-12). lib. bdg. 38.60 (978-0-8225-8968-6(0)) Lerner Publishing Group.
Lucas, Eileen. Mahatma Gandhi: Fighting for Indian Independence. 2017. (Rebels with a Cause Ser.). 128p. (J). (gr. 8-8). lib. bdg. 37.27 **(978-0-7660-8513-8(9))** Enslow Pubs., Inc.
MacKenzie, Catherine. Amy Carmichael - Can Brown Eyes Be Made Blue? Ammassari, Rita, illus. 2011. (Little Lights Ser.). (ENG.). 24p. (J). (gr. -1-2). 7.99 (978-1-84550-108-2(X), 91ca3a79-be4d-488e-9c3f-283c9f77bf68) Christian Focus Pubns. GBR. Dist: Bookmasters Distribution.
Mahoney, Ellen. Gandhi for Kids: His Life & Ideas, with 21 Activities. 2016. (For Kids Ser.). (ENG., Illus.). 144p. (J). (gr. 9). pap. 17.99 (978-1-61373-122-2(1)) Chicago Review Pr., Inc.
Miller, Jennifer A. Mother Teresa. 2009. (History Maker Biographies Ser.). (Illus.). 48p. (J). (gr. 3-6). 26.60 (978-1-58013-702-7(4), Lerner Pubns.) Lerner Publishing Group.
Nelson, Robin. Mother Teresa: A Life of Caring. (Pull Ahead Books-Biographies Ser.). (Illus.). 32p. 2007. (ENG.). (gr. k-3). pap. 7.95 (978-0-8225-6433-1(5)) 2006. (J). (gr. 3-7). lib. bdg. 22.60 (978-0-8225-6384-6(3), Lerner Pubns.) Lerner Publishing Group.
Rau, Dana Meachen. Who Was Gandhi? Hoare, Jerry & Harrison, Nancy, illus. 2014. (Who Was? Ser.). (ENG.). 112p. (J). (gr. 3-7). pap. 5.99 (978-0-448-48235-4(5), Grosset & Dunlap) Penguin Young Readers Group.
Rivera, Sheila. Mohandas Gandhi: A Life of Integrity. 2006. (Pull Ahead Bks.). (Illus.). 32p. (J). (gr. 3-7). lib. bdg. 22.60 (978-0-8225-6383-9(5), Lerner Pubns.) Lerner Publishing Group.
Shaw, Maura D. Gandhi: India's Great Soul. Marchesi, Stephen, illus. 2003. (ENG.). 32p. (J). (gr. 1-3). 12.95 (978-1-893361-91-1(8), 9781893361911, Skylight Paths Publishing) LongHill Partners, Inc.
Slavicek, Louise Chipley. Mother Teresa: Caring for the World's Poor. 2007. (Modern Peacemakers Ser.). (Illus.). 113p. (YA). (gr. 9-12). lib. bdg. 30.00 (978-0-7910-9433-4(2)) Facts On File, Inc.
Sullivan, Anne Marie. Mother Teresa: Religious Humanitarian. 2013. (People of Importance Ser.: 21). (Illus.). 32p. (J). (gr. 4-18). 19.95 (978-1-4222-2853-1(3)) Mason Crest.
Trussell-Cullen, Alan. Mahatma Gandhi. 2009. pap. 13.25 (978-1-60559-064-6(9)) Hameray Publishing Group, Inc.
—Mother Teresa. 2009. pap. 13.25 (978-1-60559-066-0(5)) Hameray Publishing Group, Inc.
Vander Hook, Sue. Mahatma Gandhi: Proponent of Peace, 1 vol. 2010. (Essential Lives Set 5 Ser.). (ENG.). 112p. (J). (gr. 6-12). lib. bdg. 35.64 (978-1-61613-515-7(8)) ABDO Publishing Co.
Vescia, Monique & Nicholson, Michael. Mahatma Gandhi: Champion of the Indian Independence Movement. 2017. (J). **(978-1-5383-8084-0(6)**, Rosen Young Adult) Rosen Publishing Group, Inc., The.
Wheeler, Jill C. Gandhi. 2003. (Breaking Barriers Ser.). 64p. (gr. 3-8). 27.07 (978-1-57765-906-8(6), Abdo & Daughters) ABDO Publishing Co.
Wilkinson, Philip. Gandhi: The Young Protester Who Founded a Nation. 2007. (National Geographic World History Biographies Ser.). (ENG., Illus.). 64p. (J). (gr. 3-7). pap. 7.99 (978-1-4263-0132-2(4), National Geographic Children's Bks.) National Geographic Society.
Woog, Adam. Jyotirmayee Mohapatra, Advocate for India's Young Women. 2006. (Young Heroes Ser.). (ENG., Illus.). 64p. (gr. 3-7). lib. bdg. 35.70 (978-0-7377-3611-3(9), Kidhaven) Cengage Gale.

INDIA—DESCRIPTION AND TRAVEL

A Yusuf, Ali. Three Travellers to India. 2006. 108p. per. (978-1-4067-3192-7(7), Hesperides Pr.) Read Bks.

H
I

Ganeri, Anita. Indian Subcontinent. 2005. (Flashpoints Ser.). (Illus.). 44p. (YA). (gr. 7-12). lib. bdg. 29.95 *(978-1-58340-602-1(6))* Black Rabbit Bks.

Hartley, Jill, photos by. Fruits of India. 2010. (ENG., Illus.). 24p. (J). (gr. k — 1). bds. 7.95 *(978-81-907546-8-2(8))* Tara Books Agency IND. Dist: Publishers Group West (PGW).

—Vegetables of India. 2010. (ENG., Illus.). 24p. (J). (gr. k — 1). bds. 7.95 *(978-81-907546-9-9(6))* Tara Books Agency IND. Dist: Publishers Group West (PGW).

Henzel, Cynthia Kennedy. Taj Mahal, 1 vol. 2011. (Troubled Treasures: World Heritage Sites Ser.). (ENG., Illus.). 32p. (J). (gr. 3-6). 27.07 *(978-1-61613-568-3(9))* ABDO Publishing Co.

Kalman, Bobbie. India: The Land. 3rd rev. ed. 2009. (ENG., Illus.). 32p. (J). (gr. 4-6). *(978-0-7787-9285-7(4))* Crabtree Publishing Co.

Kumar, Monica & Kumar, Asha. The Great Desert Adventure. 2008. (HIN & ENG., Illus.). 32p. (J). *(978-0-9797191-1-0(9))* MeeraMasi, Inc.

Schorr, Titus. Asra Is from India, 01 vols., 1. 2016. (Rosen REAL Readers: Social Studies Nonfiction / Fiction: Family, Community, & the World Ser.). (ENG.). 12p. (J). pap. 6.33 *(978-1-5081-1743-8(8)*, Rosen Classroom) Rosen Publishing Group, Inc., The.

Shofner, Shawndra. Taj Mahal. 2005. (Ancient Wonders of the World Ser.). (Illus.). 32p. (J). (gr. 4-7). lib. bdg. 18.95 *(978-1-58341-361-6(8)*, Creative Education) Creative Co., The.

Teacher Created Resources Staff. India: Come on a Journey of Discovery. 2008. (Qeb Travel Through Ser.). (ENG., Illus.). 32p. (gr. 4-7). pap. 7.99 *(978-1-4206-8283-0(0))* Teacher Created Resources, Inc.

Webster, Christine. Taj Mahal. 2007. (Structural Wonders Ser.). (Illus.). 32p. (J). (gr. 4-7). lib. bdg. 26.00 *(978-1-59036-729-2(4))*; per. 9.95 *(978-1-59036-730-8(8))* Weigl Pubs., Inc.

Wolf, Helmut, photos by. Flowers of India. 2010. (ENG., Illus.). 24p. (J). (gr. k — 1). bds. *(978-81-907546-7-5(X))* Tara Publishing.

INDIA—FICTION

Adams, Andy. Mystery of the Ambush in Indi: A Biff Brewster Mystery. 2011. 180p. 42.95 *(978-1-258-09701-1(X))* Literary Licensing, LLC.

All My Noble Dreams & Then What Happens. 2013. (ENG.). 272p. (J). (gr. 4-7). 15.99 *(978-1-4424-4976-3(4)*, Simon & Schuster/Paula Wiseman Bks.) Simon & Schuster/Paula Wiseman Bks.

Alsius, Lourdes. Unos Padres Para Aruna. 2005. (SPA.). 32p. (J). 18.95 *(978-84-8418-096-8(4))* Zendrera Zariquiey, Editorial ESP. Dist: Iaconi, Mariuccia Bk. Imports.

Amazing Mallika - Evaluation Guide: Evaluation Guide. 2006. (J). *(978-1-55942-398-4(6))* Witcher Productions.

Angel, Ido. Vipo in India: The Elephant with Bad Memory. 2015. (AV2 Animated Storytime Ser.). (ENG.). (J). lib. bdg. 29.99 *(978-1-4896-3899-1(7)*, AV2 by Weigl) Weigl Pubs., Inc.

Atwarie, Rossi. The Adventures of Fox Brown. Bachan, Krystal Ann, illus. 2011. 62p. pap. 19.00 *(978-1-60911-845-7(6)*, Eloquent Bks.) Strategic Book Publishing & Rights Agency (SBPRA).

Bajaj, Varsha. Abby Spencer Goes to Bollywood. 2014. (ENG.). 256p. (J). (gr. 3-7). 16.99 *(978-0-8075-6363-2(3))* Whitman, Albert & Co.

Banerjee, Anjali. Looking for Bapu. 2008. (ENG.). 176p. (J). (gr. 3-7). 6.50 *(978-0-553-49425-9(2)*, Yearling) Random Hse. Children's Bks.

Bannerman, Helen. Little Black Sambo. 2006. (Illus.). pap. *(978-1-4065-0179-0(5))* Dodo Pr.

—Little Black Sambo. 2007. (Illus.). 72p. per. 11.45 *(978-1-59462-581-7(6)*, Book Jungle) Standard Pubns., Inc.

—Short Works of Helen Bannerman. I.t. ed. 2007. (ENG.). 54p. pap. 18.99 *(978-1-4346-4066-6(3))* Creative Media Partners, LLC.

—The Story of Little Babaji. 2004. (Illus.). (J). (gr. -1-18). spiral bd. *(978-0-616-14615-6(9))* Canadian National Institute for the Blind/Institut National Canadien pour les Aveugles.

—The Story of Little Black Mingo & the Story of Little Black Sambo. 2010. 92p. pap. 34.50 *(978-1-4452-8667-9(X))* Lulu Pr., Inc.

—The Story of Little Black Sambo. 2007. pap. 7.99 *(978-1-59986-912-4(8)*, FQ Classics) Filiquarian Publishing, LLC.

Benchimol, Brigitte. Jadyn & the Magic Bubble: Discovering India. Benchimol, Brigitte & Zima, Siegfried, illus. 2007. 58p. (J). (gr. 3-4). 19.95 *(978-0-9701654-9-7(8))* East West Discovery Pr.

Bodger, Holly. 5 to 1. 2015. (ENG.). 256p. (YA). (gr. 7). 17.99 *(978-0-385-39153-5(6)*, Knopf Bks. for Young Readers) Random Hse. Children's Bks.

Bradbury, Jennifer. A Moment Comes. 2013. (ENG., Illus.). 288p. (YA). (gr. 7). 17.99 *(978-1-4169-7876-3(3))* Simon & Schuster Children's Publishing.

Bradbury, Jennifer. Outside In. 2017. (ENG., Illus.). 288p. (J). (gr. 3-7). 16.99 ***(978-1-4424-6827-6(0)**, Atheneum/Caitlyn Dlouhy Books)* Simon & Schuster Children's Publishing.

Brahmachari, Sita. Jasmine Skies. 2014. (ENG.). 336p. (J). (gr. 3-7). 16.99 *(978-0-8075-3782-4(9))* Whitman, Albert & Co.

Brian, Kate, pseud. Lucky T. 2007. (ENG.). 304p. (YA). (gr. 9-12). pap. 9.99 *(978-1-4169-3545-2(2)*, Simon & Schuster Bks. For Young Readers) Simon & Schuster Bks. For Young Readers.

Brooks, John. The Sundarbans Tiger. 2006. 115p. (J). pap. 13.58 *(978-0-9661789-4-4(7))* Canis Lupus Productions.

Broutin, Christian. In the Jungle. Broutin, Christian, illus. 2013. (ENG., Illus.). 36p. (J). (gr. -1-k). 12.99 *(978-1-85103-417-8(X))* Moonlight Publishing, Ltd. GBR. Dist: Independent Pubs. Group.

Burnett, Frances Hodgson. Sara Crewe. 2011. 66p. 16.95 *(978-1-4638-9633-1(6))* Rodgers, Alan Bks.

Byng, Georgia. Molly Moon Viaja a Traes del Tiempo. Crispin, Maria Dolores, tr. 2005. (SPA.). 350p. *(978-84-675-0570-2(2))* SM Ediciones.

—Molly Moon's Hypnotic Time Travel Adventure. (ENG.). 400p. (J). 2006. (Molly Moon Ser.: 3). (gr. 3-7). pap. 7.99 *(978-0-06-075034-3(0))* 2005. (Illus.). 16.99 *(978-0-06-075032-9(4))* HarperCollins Pubs.

—Molly Moon's Hypnotic Time Travel Adventure. 2007. (Molly Moon Ser.). (Illus.). 392p. (gr. 3-7). 18.00 *(978-0-7569-7761-0(4))* Perfection Learning Corp.

—Molly Moon's Hypnotic Time-Travel Adventure. 2005. (Illus.). 400p. (J). lib. bdg. 18.89 *(978-0-06-075033-6(2))* HarperCollins Pubs.

Capucilli, Alyssa Satin. Monkey Play. 2012. (Step into Reading Ser.). (ENG., Illus.). 32p. (J). (gr. -1-1). pap. 3.99 *(978-0-375-86993-8(X)*, Random Hse. Bks. for Young Readers) Random Hse. Children's Bks.

Caravan. 2007. (Choose Your Own Adventure - Dragonlarks Ser.). (Illus.). 64p. (J). (gr. 4-7). pap. 7.99 *(978-1-933390-54-3(9))* Chooseco LLC.

Carter, David. The Nutters of Pendle Forest - Part 1 the Enchanted Valley. 2012. (Illus.). 222p. pap. *(978-1-908098-54-2(6))* 2QT, Ltd. (Publishing).

Chadda, Sarwat. The City of Death. 2013. (J). pap. *(978-0-545-38519-0(9))*; (ENG.). 336p. (gr. 4-7). 16.99 *(978-0-545-38518-3(0)*, Levine, Arthur A. Bks.) Scholastic, Inc.

—The Savage Fortress. 2012. (ENG.). 304p. (J). (gr. 4-7). 16.99 *(978-0-545-38516-9(4)*, Levine, Arthur A. Bks.) Scholastic, Inc.

Chadha, Radhika. Basava & the Dots of Fire. Phatak, Bhakti, illus. 2005. 24p. (J). *(978-81-8146-165-0(7))* Tulika Pubs.

Chadha, Radhika & Kuriyan, Priya. I'm So Sleepy. 2004. (Illus.). 24p. (J). *(978-81-8146-033-2(2))* Tulika Pubs.

Charles, Veronika Martenova. The Birdman. Galouchko, Annouchka Gravel & Daigle, Stephan, illus. 2006. (ENG.). 32p. (J). (gr. k-3). 17.95 *(978-0-88776-740-1(0)*, Tundra Bks.) Tundra Bks. CAN. Dist: Penguin Random Hse. LLC.

C.M.M. A Life of Many Forms. 2012. 52p. pap. 16.95 *(978-1-62709-318-7(4))* America Star Bks.

Cyr, Joe. Shadi, the Shadow Who Wanted to Be Free. Owen, Ramon, illus. 2010. 40p. pap. 14.95 *(978-1-936343-08-9(8))* Peppertree Pr., The.

Dalton, Annie. Feeling the Vibes: Babysit a Buddha! 2008. (Mel Beeby Agent Angel Ser.). (ENG.). 208p. (J). (gr. 4-7). pap. 6.95 *(978-0-00-716140-9(9))* HarperCollins Pubs. Ltd. GBR. Dist: Independent Pubs. Group.

Daswani, Kavita. Indie Girl. 2007. (ENG.). 208p. (YA). (gr. 7-12). pap. 10.99 *(978-1-4169-4892-6(9)*, Simon Pulse) Simon Pulse.

Deshpande, Sanjay. In Defense of the Realm: Graphic Novel. Sharma, Lalit Kumar, illus. 2011. (Campfire Graphic Novels Ser.). (ENG.). 104p. (YA). (gr. 3-7). pap. 12.99 *(978-93-80028-64-4(4)*, Campfire) Steerforth Pr.

Dharma Publishing Staff. Great Gift & the Wish-Fulfilling Gem: A Story about the Wish to Help Others. 2010. (ENG.). 36p. (gr. -1-7). pap. 8.95 *(978-0-89800-600-1(7))* Dharma Publishing.

Dharmarajan, Geeta. The Magic Raindrop. Thapar, Bindia, illus. 2005. (J). *(978-81-89020-28-6(5))* Katha.

Di Gregorio, Robert & Schauer, S. Ava the Adventurer: Ava in India. 2014. 36p. pap. 22.50 *(978-1-4828-9662-6(1))* Partridge Pub.

Dinerstein, Eric. What Elephants Know. 2016. (ENG.). 288p. (J). (gr. 3-7). 16.99 *(978-1-4847-2854-3(8))* Disney Publishing Worldwide.

Divakaruni, Chitra Banerjee. The Conch Bearer. 2005. (ENG.). 272p. (J). (gr. 3-7). reprint ed. pap. 8.99 *(978-0-689-87242-6(9)*, Aladdin) Simon & Schuster Children's Publishing.

—The Mirror of Fire & Dreaming. 2007. (ENG.). 336p. (J). (gr. 3-7). pap. 14.99 *(978-1-4169-1768-7(3)*, Aladdin) Simon & Schuster Children's Publishing.

Doder, Joshua. Grk Smells a Rat. 2009. (J). *(978-0-385-90654-8(4)*, Delacorte Pr) Random House Publishing Group.

D'souza, Nadine. Revenge of the Puppets. Rajvanshi, Ayush, illus. 2013. (ENG.). 32p. (J). (gr. -1). pap. 9.95 *(978-81-8190-197-2(5))* Karadi Tales Co. Pvt, Ltd. IND. Dist: Consortium Bk. Sales & Distribution.

Dutta, Arup Kumar. The Boy Who Became King. Arya, Viki, illus. 2004. 122p. (J). *(978-81-291-0405-2(9))* Rupa & Co.

Ellis, Deborah. No Ordinary Day, 1 vol. (ENG.). (J). (gr. 3-7). 2014. 160p. pap. 9.95 *(978-1-55498-108-3(5))* 2011. 144p. 16.95 *(978-1-55498-134-2(4))* Groundwood Bks. CAN. Dist: Publishers Group West (PGW).

—No Ordinary Day. 2013. 164p. pap. *(978-1-4596-6451-7(5))* ReadHowYouWant.com, Ltd.

Ely, Kosa. The Peaceable Forest: India's Tale of Kindness to Animals. Johansson, Anna, illus. 2012. (ENG.). 32p. (gr. k). 16.99 *(978-1-60887-115-5(0))* Mandala Publishing.

Gaffney, Ellen. Wings for a Flower. Gaffney, Ellen, illus. 2013. (Illus.). 32p. 16.95 *(978-0-9882212-6-0(8))* Three Bean Pr.

Gavin, Jamila. Three Indian Princesses: The Stories of Savitri, Damayanti & Sita. 2004. (Illus.). 112p. (Orig.). (J). pap. 7.50 *(978-0-7497-4613-1(0))* Egmont Bks., Ltd. GBR. Dist: Trafalgar Square Publishing.

Ghosh, Premola, illus. Ten Timeless Tales. 2005. 38p. (J). *(978-81-89013-35-6(1))* Zubaan.

Gill, Heidi. 2 Kurious Kids: India. Carter, Kris, illus. 2012. 38p. (J). 14.95 *(978-1-936319-92-3(6))* Mascot Bks., Inc.

Gill, Nav K. Under the Moonlit Sky. 2010. (ENG.). 352p. (YA). pap. 15.95 *(978-1-894917-99-5(5)*, Napoleon & Co.) Dundurn CAN. Dist: Ingram Publisher Services.

Gosling, Sharon. The Sapphire Cutlass. 2016. (Diamond Thief Ser.). (ENG.). 336p. (gr. 9-12). 16.95 *(978-1-63079-041-7(9))* Switch Pr.

Graham, Bob. Vanilla Ice Cream. Graham, Bob, illus. 2014. (ENG., Illus.). 40p. (J). (gr. -1-1). 16.99 *(978-0-7636-7377-2(3))* Candlewick Pr.

Graydon, William Murray. The Jungle Boy; or, Sexton Blake's Adventures in India. 2007. 120p. per. 14.99 *(978-1-4344-0189-2(8))* Wildside Pr., LLC.

Greene, Joshua M. Kaliya, Serpent King. Wire, Patrick, illus. rev. ed. 2012. (ENG.). 24p. (gr. -1). 14.99 *(978-1-60887-148-3(7))* Mandala Publishing.

Guignard, Lars. The Yogi's Curse. 2013. 342p. pap. *(978-0-9877753-9-9(1))* Guignard, Lars.

Guillain, Adam. Bella Balistica & the Indian Summer. 2005. (Bella Balistica Ser.). (ENG., Illus.). 350p. (J). (gr. 4-7). pap. 9.95 *(978-1-84059-407-2(1))* Milet Publishing.

Gunderson, Jessica. The Elephant Dancer: A Story of Ancient India, 1 vol. Hu, Caroline, illus. 2009. (Read-It! Chapter Books: Historical Tales Ser.). (ENG.). 64p. (gr. 2-4). 22.65 *(978-1-4048-5219-8(0)*, Chapter Readers) Picture Window Bks.

—The Horse on the Hill: A Story of Ancient India, 1 vol. Hu, Caroline, illus. 2009. (Read-It! Chapter Books: Historical Tales Ser.). (ENG.). 64p. (gr. 2-4). 22.65 *(978-1-4048-5222-8(0)*, Chapter Readers) Picture Window Bks.

—The King's Warrior: A Story of Ancient India, 1 vol. Hu, Caroline, illus. 2009. (Read-It! Chapter Books: Historical Tales Ser.). (ENG.). 64p. (gr. 2-4). 22.65 *(978-1-4048-5228-0(X)*, Chapter Readers) Picture Window Bks.

—The Servant & the Water Princess: A Story of Ancient India, 1 vol. Hu, Caroline, illus. 2009. (Read-It! Chapter Books: Historical Tales Ser.). (ENG.). 64p. (gr. 2-4). 22.65 *(978-1-4048-5225-9(5)*, Chapter Readers) Picture Window Bks.

Hall, Amanda, illus. In Andal's House. 2013. (Tales of the World Ser.). (ENG.). 40p. (J). (gr. 2-5). 17.95 *(978-1-58536-603-3(X)*, 202358) Sleeping Bear Pr.

Hamilton, Martha & Weiss, Mitch. The Ghost Catcher: A Bengali Folktale. Balouch, Kristen, illus. 2007. (ENG.). 32p. (J). (gr. -1-3). 16.95 *(978-0-87483-835-0(5))* August Hse. Pubs., Inc.

Hammersiough, Jane. Langur Monkey's Day. Buelt, Laura, illus. 2005. (Wild Reading Adventures! Ser.). (ENG.). 36p. (J). (gr. -1-2). 2.95 *(978-1-59249-143-8(X)*, S7156); 9.95 *(978-1-59249-144-5(8)*, PS7156) Soundprints.

—Langur Monkey's Day. Buelt, Laura, tr. Buelt, Laura, illus. 2005. (Wild Reading Adventures! Ser.). (ENG.). 36p. (J). (gr. -1-2). 15.95 *(978-1-59249-141-4(3)*, B7106); pap. 6.95 *(978-1-59249-142-1(1)*, S7106) Soundprints.

—Langur Monkey's Day. Buelt, Laura, illus. 2005. (Wild Reading Adventures! Ser.). (ENG.). 32p. (J). (gr. -1-2). 19.95 *(978-1-59249-221-3(5)*, BC7106); 8.95 *(978-1-59249-222-0(3)*, SC7106) Soundprints.

Hammersiough, Jane & Smithsonian Institution Staff. Langur Monkey's Day. Buelt, Laura, illus. rev. ed. 2008. (ENG.). 24p. (J). (gr. -1-3). 4.99 *(978-1-59249-706-5(3)*, Little Soundprints) Soundprints.

Hausman, Gerald. The Otter, the Spotted Frog & the Great Flood: A Creek Indian Story. Shiloh, Ramon, illus. 2013. (ENG.). 36p. (J). (gr. k-3). 17.95 *(978-1-937786-12-0(9)*, Wisdom Tales) World Wisdom, Inc.

Heine, Teresa & Heine, Theresa. Elephant Dance: Memories of India. Moxley, Sheila, illus. 2004. (ENG.). 40p. (J). 16.99 *(978-1-84148-917-9(4))* Barefoot Bks., Inc.

Heine, Theresa. El Baile del Elefante: Recuerdos de la India. Moxley, Sheila, illus. 2005. (SPA.). 44p. (gr. 2-3). 22.99 *(978-84-8452-356-7(X))* Fundacion Intermon ESP. Dist: Lectorum Pubns., Inc.

—Elephant Dance: A Journey to India. Moxley, Sheila, illus. 2006. (ENG.). 40p. (J). (gr. -1-2). 8.99 *(978-1-905236-79-4(4))* Barefoot Bks., Inc.

Henty, George Alfred. Through Three Campaigns: A Story of Chitral Tirah & Ashanti. 2007. (ENG.). 318p. pap. 23.99 *(978-1-4346-4617-0(3))*; 356p. pap. 26.99 *(978-1-4346-4618-7(1))* Creative Media Partners, LLC.

—With Clive in India. 2006. pap. *(978-1-4068-1316-6(8))* Echo Library.

—With Clive in India: Or the Beginnings of an Empire. 2007. (ENG.). 324p. pap. 23.99 *(978-1-4264-9462-8(9))*; 358p. pap. 26.99 *(978-1-4264-9843-5(8))* Creative Media Partners, LLC.

Hergé. The Blue Lotus. 2011. (Adventures of Tintin: Young Readers Edition Ser.). (ENG., Illus.). 96p. (J). (gr. 3-17). pap. 9.99 *(978-0-316-13382-1(5))* Little, Brown Bks. for Young Readers.

Hidier, Tanuja Desai. Bombay Blues. 2014. (ENG.). 560p. (J). (gr. 9). 18.99 *(978-0-545-38478-0(8)*, PUSH) Scholastic, Inc.

Hildahl, Violetta R. Peacock of Taj Mahal. 2011. 28p. (gr. -1). pap. 13.59 *(978-1-4520-0259-0(2))* AuthorHouse.

Houck, Colleen. Tiger's Curse, Bk. 1. 2012. (Tiger's Curse Ser.: Bk. 1). (ENG.). 456p. (J). (gr. 7). pap. 9.95 *(978-1-4549-0249-2(3))* Sterling Publishing Co., Inc.

—Tiger's Curse. 2012. (Tiger's Curse Ser.: Bk. 1). lib. bdg. 20.80 *(978-0-606-23822-9(0)*, Turtleback) Turtleback Bks.

—Tiger's Destiny. 2015. (Tiger's Curse Ser.: Bk. 4). (ENG.). 464p. (J). (gr. 7). pap. 9.95 *(978-1-4549-0356-7(2))* Sterling Publishing Co., Inc.

—Tiger's Quest. (Tiger's Curse Ser.: Bk. 2). (ENG.). (J). (gr. 7). 2013. 512p. pap. 9.95 *(978-1-4549-0358-1(9))* 2011. 496p. 17.95 *(978-1-4027-8404-0(X))* Sterling Publishing Co., Inc.

—Tiger's Voyage. (Tiger's Curse Ser.: Bk. 3). (ENG.). (J). (gr. 7). 2014. 568p. pap. 9.95 *(978-1-4549-0357-4(0))*Bk. 3. 2011. 560p. 17.95 *(978-1-4027-8405-7(8))* Sterling Publishing Co., Inc.

Hudson, Bonnie Rose. The Hidden Village. 2017. (J). ***(978-1-62856-311-5(7))*** BJU Pr.

Husain, Aliya. Neither This nor That. 2010. 260p. pap. 19.99 *(978-0-557-22302-2(4))* Lulu Pr., Inc.

Husain, Zakir & Mishra, Samina. Sunshine for Amma. Pottenkulam, Pooja, illus. 2004. 16p. (J). *(978-81-89013-41-7(6))* Zubaan.

Infante, Begona. Minu Yo Soy de India (I'm from India) (SPA.). 32p. (J). 12.95 *(978-84-246-9401-2(5))* La Galera, S.A. Editorial ESP. Dist: AIMS International Bks., Inc.

Jacober, Virginia. Trail Followers in India. 2013. pap. 12.95 *(978-0-7414-8181-8(2))* Infinity Publishing.

Javaherbin, Mina & Jalal al-Din Rumi. Elephant in the Dark. Yelchin, Eugene, illus. 2015. (ENG.). 40p. (J). (gr. -1-3). 17.99 *(978-0-545-63670-4(1)*, Scholastic Pr.) Scholastic, Inc.

Jeeva Raghunath & Nayar, Deeya. Malli. Nancy Raj, illus. 2005. (HIN & ENG.). 16p. (J). *(978-81-8146-089-9(8))* Tulika Pubs.

Jenisch, Betty. Rennie. 2007. 9.00 *(978-0-8059-8947-2(1))* Dorrance Publishing Co., Inc.

Jones, Thomas Rumsey. Boris: The Bengal Tiger. Eguiguren, India J. & Eguiguren, A. R., illus. 2013. 46p. pap. 5.99 *(978-1-883378-81-3(8))* Sun on Earth Bks.

Kato, Etsuo. The King Who Saved the Dove. Yasui, Koji, illus. 2014. (J). 8.95 *(978-1-935523-68-0(6))* World Tribune Pr.

Keen, Karl D. They Call Me Chief. 2004. (YA). per. 10.95 *(978-0-9742791-3-8(7))* Litho Tech, LLC.

Keith, David. Hands Across Time. 2010. 129p. pap. 10.98 *(978-0-557-27121-4(5))* Lulu Pr., Inc.

Kelly, Lynne. Chained, 1 vol. 2012. (ENG.). 256p. (J). (gr. 5-9). 17.99 *(978-0-374-31237-4(0)*, 9780374312374, Farrar, Straus & Giroux (BYR)) Farrar, Straus & Giroux.

Khanna, Balraj. Rajah: King of the Jungle. 2011. (ENG.). 112p. 16.95 *(978-1-935677-03-1(9))* Mapin Publishing Pvt. Ltd IND. Dist: National Bk. Network.

Kipling, Rudyard. The Jungle Book. Thorne, Jenny, illus. 2014. (ENG.). 48p. (J). (gr. k-5). pap. 7.99 *(978-1-84322-882-0(3)*, Armadillo) Anness Publishing GBR. Dist: National Bk. Network.

—The Jungle Book. Daily, Don, illus. 2014. (ENG.). 68p. (J). (gr. -1). 18.95 *(978-1-60433-475-3(4))* Cider Mill Pr. Bk. Pubs., LLC.

—The Jungle Book. 2010. 318p. (gr. 3-7). pap. 30.75 *(978-1-142-79715-7(5))* Creative Media Partners, LLC.

—The Jungle Book. Detmold, Edward J. & Detmold, Maurice, illus. 2010. (Calla Editions Ser.). (ENG.). 192p. 30.00 *(978-0-60660-009-2(5))* Dover Pubns., Inc.

—The Jungle Book. 2008. (Bring the Classics to Life Ser.). (ENG., Illus.). 72p. (gr. 1-12). pap., act. bk. ed. 10.95 *(978-1-55576-355-8(3)*, EDCTR-109B) EDCON Publishing Group.

—The Jungle Book. 2009. 122p. (gr. 3-7). pap. 19.99 *(978-1-4589-2084-3(4))* General Bks. LLC.

—The Jungle Book. Drake, W. H., Jr., illus. 2015. (Macmillan Classics Ser.). (ENG.). 320p. (J). (gr. 2-4). 17.99 *(978-1-4472-7307-3(9))* Pan Macmillan GBR. Dist: Independent Pubs. Group.

—The Jungle Book. Basford, Johanna, illus. 2013. (ENG.). 256p. (J). (gr. 4-7). pap. 10.99 *(978-0-09-957302-9(4))* Random Hse. GBR. Dist: Independent Pubs. Group.

—The Jungle Book. 2014. (Word Cloud Classics Ser.). (ENG., Illus.). 320p. pap. 14.99 *(978-1-62686-258-6(3)*, Thunder Bay Pr.) Readerlink Distribution Services, LLC.

—The Jungle Book. Corvino, Lucy, illus. 2008. (Classic Starts(tm) Ser.). (ENG.). 160p. (J). (gr. 2-4). 6.95 *(978-1-4027-4576-8(1))* Sterling Publishing Co., Inc.

—The Jungle Book. Ingpen, Robert R., illus. 2012. (Sterling Illustrated Classics Ser.). (ENG.). 192p. (J). (gr. 5-8). 19.95 *(978-1-4027-8284-8(5))* Sterling Publishing Co., Inc.

—The Jungle Book: Rikki-Tikki-Tavi Moves In. Madsen, Jim, illus. 2008. (Easy Reader Classics Ser.). (ENG.). 32p. (gr. 4-7). lib. bdg. 24.21 *(978-1-59961-336-9(0))* Spotlight.

—The Jungle Books. 2004. (Barnes & Noble Classics Ser.). (ENG., Illus.). 432p. pap. 7.95 *(978-1-59308-109-6(X))* Barnes & Noble, Inc.

—The Jungle Books. 2013. (ENG.). 384p. (gr. 12). mass mkt. 5.95 *(978-0-451-41918-7(9)*, Signet) Penguin Publishing Group.

—Kim. 2013. (Cambridge Library Collection - Fiction & Poetry Ser.). (ENG., Illus.). 444p. pap. 45.99 *(978-1-108-05712-7(8))* Cambridge Univ. Pr.

—Kim. 2008. (Bring the Classics to Life Ser.). (ENG., Illus.). 72p. (gr. 5-12). pap., act. bk. ed. 10.95 *(978-0-931334-69-6(1)*, EDCTR-503B) EDCON Publishing Group.

—Kim. Trivedi, Harish & Montefiore, Jan, eds. 2011. (ENG., Illus.). 432p. (gr. 12). 10.00 *(978-0-14-144237-2(9)*, Penguin Classics) Penguin Publishing Group.

—Kim. 2011. (Puffin Classics Ser.). (ENG.). 400p. (J). (gr. 5-7). 5.99 *(978-0-14-133250-5(6)*, Puffin Books) Penguin Young Readers Group.

—Kim. 2017. (ENG., Illus.). (J). (gr. 5). pap. 12.99 ***(978-1-366-58963-7(7))*** Blurb, Inc.

—Mowgli of the Jungle Book: The Complete Stories. 2016. (ENG.). 224p. (gr. 1). pap. 6.99 *(978-1-944686-32-1(0)*, Racehorse Publishing) Skyhorse Publishing Co., Inc.

—Rikki-Tikki-Tavi & Toomai of the Elephants. 2008. (Unabridged Classics (in Audio) Ser.). (J). pap. 36.00 incl. audio compact disk *(978-1-58472-431-5(5)*, In Audio) Sound Room Pubs., Inc.

Kipling, Rudyard & Kipling, John Lockwood, illus. The Jungle Book. 2014. (J). 13.32 *(978-1-4677-5836-9(1)*, First Avenue Editions) Lerner Publishing Group.

Kipling, Rudyard & Landolf, Diane Wright. The Jungle Book. Rowe, John, illus. 2008. (Stepping Stone Book(TM) Ser.). (ENG.). 112p. (J). (gr. 1-4). per. 3.99 *(978-0-375-84276-4(4)*, Random Hse. Bks. for Young Readers) Random Hse. Children's Bks.

Kipling, Rudyard & Pinkney, Jerry. Rikki-Tikki-Tavi. Pinkney, Jerry, illus. 2004. (ENG., Illus.). 48p. (J). (gr. -1-3). reprint ed. pap. 6.99 *(978-0-06-058785-7(7))* HarperCollins Pubs.

—Rikki-Tikki-Tavi. 2004. (Illus.). (gr. -1-3). 17.00 *(978-0-7569-3250-3(5))* Perfection Learning Corp.

Kipling, Rudyard & Wolek, Guy. The Jungle Book, 1 vol. 2012. (Calico Illustrated Classics Ser.: No. 4). (ENG., Illus.). 112p. (J). (gr. 3-6). 27.07 *(978-1-61641-616-4(5))* Magic Wagon.

Kirk B. Gradin. Jadhu Ram & the Thirsty Forest. 2012. 36p. 17.95 *(978-1-105-04735-0(0))*; pap. 10.95 *(978-0-9855683-0-6(5))* Banyan Bks.

Kong, Anja & Sunkara, Naveena. The Battle Of: Secret of the Taj. 2010. 172p. 23.95 *(978-1-4502-0954-0(8))*; pap. 13.95 *(978-1-4502-0952-6(1))* iUniverse, Inc.

Krishnaswami, Uma. Chachaji's Cup. Sitaraman, Soumya, illus. 2013. (ENG.). 32p. (J). (gr. 1-18). 16.95 *(978-0-89239-178-3(2))* Lee & Low Bks., Inc.

—The Grand Plan to Fix Everything. Halpin, Abigail, illus. (ENG.). (J). (gr. 3-7). 2013. 288p. pap. 8.99 *(978-1-4169-9590-6(0))* 2011. 272p. 16.99 *(978-1-4169-9589-0(7))* Simon & Schuster Children's Publishing. (Atheneum Bks. for Young Readers).

—Out of the Way! Out of the Way!, 1 vol. Krishnaswamy, Uma, illus. 2012. (ENG.). 28p. (J). (gr. -1-2). 17.95 *(978-1-55498-130-4(1))* Groundwood Bks. CAN. Dist: Publishers Group West (PGW).

Kroll, Virginia. Selvakumar Knew Better. Li, Xiaojun, illus. 2009. (Selvakumar Knew Better Ser.). 32p. (J). (gr. -1-3). pap. 8.95 *(978-1-885008-36-7(8)*, Shen's Bks.) Lee & Low Bks., Inc.

Krulik, Nancy. Magic Bone: Two Tales, One Dog. Braun, Sebastien, illus. 2016. (Magic Bone Ser.: 12). (ENG.). 192p. (J). (gr. 1-3). 6.99 *(978-0-448-48877-6(9)*, Grosset & Dunlap) Penguin Young Readers Group.

Kureishy, Simala. Lore of Love Series: Bismi & the Secret of the Kohinoor. 2010. 60p. pap. 12.99 *(978-1-4490-7340-4(9))* AuthorHouse.

Lacey, Josh. The Sultan's Tigers. 2014. (ENG.). 304p. (J). (gr. 5-7). pap. 6.99 (978-0-544-33629-2(1), HMH Books For Young Readers) Houghton Mifflin Harcourt Publishing Co.

Laidlaw, S. J. Fifteen Lanes. 2016. (ENG., Illus.). 302p. (YA). (gr. 9). 17.99 (978-1-101-91780-0(6), Tundra Bks.) Tundra Bks. CAN. Dist: Penguin Random Hse. LLC.

Laird, Elizabeth. Dindy & the Elephant. 2015. (ENG., Illus.). 128p. (J). (gr. 2-4). 13.99 **(978-1-4472-8604-2(9))** Pan Macmillan GBR. Dist: Independent Pubs. Group.

Lal, Anupa, tr. Premchand Selected Stories. 2012. (ENG.). 168p. (J). (gr. 3-4). pap. 9.95 (978-93-5036-122-1(1)) Ratna, Sagar Pvt. Ltd. IND. Dist: Midpoint Trade Bks., Inc.

Lewis, Lisa. Tsunaxen's Journey. 2013. (ENG.). 23p. (J). pap. 14.95 (978-1-4787-1979-3(6)) Outskirts Pr., Inc.

Limon, Helen. Om Shanti Babe. 2012. (Illus.). 192p. (J). pap. (978-1-84780-357-3(1), Frances Lincoln) Quarto Publishing Group UK.

Majumdar, Debu. Viku & the Elephant: A Story from the Forests of India. Wolfe, Lynn, illus. 2011. (ENG.). 54p. (J). pap. 12.99 (978-0-9832227-0-5(3)) Bo-Tree Hse.

Marsh, Laura. Toot's Tour of India. 2009. (Toot & Puddle Ser.). (ENG., Illus.). 24p. (J). (gr. -1-2). pap. 3.99 (978-1-4263-0418-7(8)); lib. bdg. 11.90 (978-1-4263-0419-4(6)) National Geographic Society. (National Geographic Children's Bks.).

McCormick, Patricia. Sold. 2011. 10.36 (978-0-7848-3420-6(2), Everbind) Marco Bk. Co.

—Sold. 2008. 263p. (J). (gr. 7-12). 19.65 (978-1-4178-1810-5(7), Turtleback) Turtleback Bks.

McDonald, Megan. Baya, Baya, Lulla-By-a. Rosenberry, Vera, illus. 2014. (ENG.). 32p. (J). (gr. -1-1). 16.99 (978-1-4814-2533-9(1), Atheneum Bks. for Young Readers) Simon & Schuster Children's Publishing.

McMiller, Theresa R. Bessie Goes All over the World. 2012. 28p. pap. 24.95 (978-1-4626-9464-8(0)) America Star Bks.

Medina, Sylvia M. & Ballock-Dixon, Saige J. Jade Elephant. Eagle, Joy, illus. 2012. 36p. pap. 11.49 (978-0-9836602-4-8(7)) Green Kids Club, Inc.

Mehta, Lila. Anklet for a Princess: A Cinderella Story from India. Tang, Youshan, illus. 2014. (ENG.). 32p. (J). pap. 9.95 (978-1-885008-46-6(5), Shen's Bks.) Lee & Low Bks., Inc.

Michaelis, Antonia. Tiger Moon. 2009. (ENG.). 480p. (YA). (gr. 7-11). pap. 9.95 (978-0-8109-4499-2(5), Amulet Bks.) Abrams, Inc.

Milan, D. S. A Year of Starless Nights. 2013. 154p. pap. 14.95 (978-1-62432-012-5(0)) Loose Leaves Publishing.

Mills, Samuel. The Demon Slayer. 2009. 192p. (YA). pap. 15.00 (978-0-88010-701-3(4)) SteinerBooks, Inc.

Molesworth & Molesworth, Mary Louisa S. Grandmother Dear. 2008. 128p. pap. 10.95 (978-1-60664-225-2(1)) Aegypan.

—Robin Redbreast. 2011. 190p. 26.95 (978-1-4638-9847-2(9)); pap. 14.95 (978-1-4638-0123-6(8)) Rodgers, Alan Bks.

Molesworth, Mary Louisa S. & Molesworth. Grandmother Dear. 2008. 128p. 23.95 (978-1-60664-726-4(1)) Rodgers, Alan Bks.

Moorthy, Anita. Monkey's Drum. Sarkar, Soumitro, illus. 2003. (ENG.). 24p. pap. 3.99 (978-81-86211-15-1(2)) Penguin Publishing Group.

Moverley, Richard. The Reluctant Rajput. Dean, David, illus. 2005. (Yellow Go Bananas Ser.). (ENG.). 48p. (J). (gr. 3-4). (978-0-7787-2745-3(9)); lib. bdg. (978-0-7787-2723-1(8)) Crabtree Publishing Co.

The Mystery of the Tiny Key. 2008. 32p. pap. 4.99 (978-0-8341-2351-9(7), 083-412-3517) Beacon Hill Pr. of Kansas City.

Namjoshi, Suniti & Jain, Shefalee. Aditi & the Marine Sage. 2004. (Simply a Story Ser.). (Illus.). 80p. (J). (978-81-8146-040-0(5)) Tulika Pubs.

Nanji, Shenaaz & Corr, Christopher. Indian Tales: A Barefoot Collection. Corr, Christopher, illus. 2007. (ENG., Illus.). 96p. (J). (gr. 2-18). 19.99 (978-1-84686-083-6(0)) Barefoot Bks., Inc.

Narsimhan, Mahtab. Mission Mumbai. 2016. (ENG.). 272p. (J). (gr. 4-7). 16.99 (978-0-545-74651-9(5), Scholastic Pr.) Scholastic, Inc.

Newsome, Richard. The Emerald Casket. Duddle, Jonny, illus. 2012. (Archer Legacy Ser.). 384p. (J). (gr. 3-7). pap. 6.99 (978-0-06-194493-2(9), Waldon Pond Pr.) HarperCollins Pubs.

Ojha, Siva Gopal. Twilight Days. 2008. 122p. pap. 11.08 (978-1-4357-1899-9(2)) Lulu Pr., Inc.

Orrell, Brenda M. Eliza Blackbird. 2010. 256p. pap. 14.49 (978-1-4520-8359-9(2)) AuthorHouse.

Osborne, Mary Pope. A Crazy Day with Cobras. Murdocca, Sal, illus. (ENG.). (J). 2012. (Magic Tree House Merlin Missions Ser.: No. 17). 144p. (gr. 1-4). 5.99 (978-0-375-86795-8(3)) 2011. (Magic Tree House Merlin Mission Ser.: 45). 128p. (gr. 2-5). 12.99 (978-0-375-86823-8(2)) Random Hse. Children's Bks. (Random Hse. Bks. for Young Readers).

—A Crazy Day with Cobras. 2012. (Magic Tree House Merlin Missions Ser.: 17). lib. bdg. 16.00 (978-0-606-26997-1(5), Turtleback) Turtleback Bks.

—The Mystery of the Enchanted Dog, 4 vols., Set. Murdocca, Sal, illus. 2009. (ENG.). 96p. (J). (gr. 1-4). 23.96 (978-0-375-85811-6(3), Random Hse. Bks. for Young Readers) Random Hse. Children's Bks.

—Tigers at Twilight. unabr. ed. 2004. (Magic Tree House Ser.: No. 19). 72p. (J). (gr. k-3). pap. 17.00 incl. audio (978-0-8072-0928-8(7), S FTR 251 SP, Listening Library) Random Hse. Audio Publishing Group.

Ostlere, Cathy. Karma. 2012. (ENG.). 544p. (YA). (gr. 7-18). 9.99 (978-1-59514-384-6(X), Razorbill) Penguin Young Readers Group.

Padma, T. V. The Forbidden Temple: Stories from the Past. Vyas, Bhavana, illus. 2004. 95p. (J). (978-81-8146-041-7(3)) Tulika Pubs.

Padma, T. V., et al. Growing Gold. 2007. (Story Cove Ser.). (ENG., Illus.). 32p. (J). (gr. -1-3). pap. 4.95 (978-0-87483-860-2(6)) August Hse. Pubs., Inc.

Panamkat, Matthew. Karan Quma & the Meluha Tree. 2007. 348p. per. 19.95 (978-0-595-41816-9(3)) iUniverse, Inc.

Pandya, Mamata. The Hare Scare: Based on the Original Gujarati Story by Gijubhai Badheka. 2004. (Illus.). 24p. (J). (978-81-291-0441-0(5)) Rupa & Co.

Paris, Harper. The Mystery of the Suspicious Spices. Calo, Marcos, illus. 2014. (Greetings from Somewhere Ser.: 6). (ENG.). 128p. (J). (gr. k-4). pap. 5.99 (978-1-4814-1467-8(4), Little Simon) Little Simon.

Parmar, Tavisha, illus. The Class Photograph. 2005. (J). (978-81-902492-1-8(5)) Vivera Bks.

Patel, Sanjay & Haynes, Emily. Ganesha's Sweet Tooth. 2015. (ENG., Illus.). 40p. (J). (gr. -1-3). 7.99 (978-1-4521-4556-3(3)) Chronicle Bks. LLC.

Perkins, Mitali. Secret Keeper. 2010. (ENG.). 240p. (YA). (gr. 7). pap. 8.99 (978-0-440-23955-0(9), Ember) Random Hse. Children's Bks.

—Tiger Boy. 2017. (ENG.). 144p. (J). (gr. 2-5). pap. 6.99 (978-1-58089-661-0(8)) Charlesbridge Publishing, Inc.

Perritano, John. Warlock Stone, 1 vol. 2014. (Kid Squad Saves the World Ser.). (ENG.). 112p. (J). (gr. 8-12). lib. bdg. 27.07 (978-1-62402-042-1(9), Calico Chapter Bks) Magic Wagon.

Rae, Kimberly. Buying Samir. 2014. (YA). (978-1-60682-952-3(1)) BJU Pr.

—Capturing Jasmina. 2014. (YA). (978-1-60682-853-3(3)) BJU Pr.

—Seeking Mother. 2015. 168p. (YA). (978-1-62856-028-2(2)) BJU Pr.

Raghbeer, Anjali. A Jar of Sound: Bhil Art. Kundu, Kunal, illus. 2012. (Art Tales from India Ser.). (ENG.). 24p. 14.95 (978-81-8328-188-1(5)) Wisdom Tree IND. Dist: SCB Distributors.

—A Poster Boy: Indian Cinema Poster Art. 2012. (Art Tales from India Ser.). (ENG., Illus.). 24p. 14.95 (978-81-8328-193-5(1)) Wisdom Tree IND. Dist: SCB Distributors.

—A Royal Deck: Ganjifa Art. Modak, Tejas, illus. 2012. (Art Tales from India Ser.). (ENG.). 23p. 14.95 (978-81-8328-187-4(7)) Wisdom Tree IND. Dist: SCB Distributors.

Raju, P. V. Ramaswami. Indian Fables. 2009. 178p. pap. 9.95 (978-1-59915-374-2(2)) Yesterday's Classics.

Ranade, Soumitra. Tak-Tak! Suleman, Shilo Shiv, illus. 2013. (ENG.). 32p. (J). (gr. k). pap. 9.95 (978-81-8190-183-5(5)) Karadi Tales Co. Pvt. Ltd. IND. Dist: Consortium Bk. Sales & Distribution.

Raote, Komilla. The Princess with the Longest Hair. Bist, Vandana, illus. 26p. (J). (978-81-85586-78-6(0)) Katha.

Ravishankar, Anushka. Excuse Me, Is This India? Leutwiler, Anita, illus. 2003. 24p. (J). 14.95 (978-81-86211-56-4(X)) Tara Publishing IND. Dist: Consortium Bk. Sales & Distribution.

—Excuses Excuses. Manglou, Gabrielle, illus. 2012. (ENG.). 48p. (J). (gr. k). 17.95 (978-93-80340-12-8(5)) Tara Books Agency IND. Dist: Publishers Group West (PGW).

—The Rumor. Kini, Kanyika, illus. 2012. (ENG.). 32p. (J). (gr. -1-1). 17.95 (978-1-77049-280-6(1), Tundra Bks.) Tundra Bks. CAN. Dist: Penguin Random Hse. LLC.

Ray, Satyajit. Unicorn Expedition & Other Stories: The Exploits of Professor Shonku. 2004. (Illus.). x, 237p. (J). pap. (978-0-14-333584-9(7), Puffin) Penguin Publishing Group.

Reeve, Penny. The Back Leg of a Goat: A Tania Abbey Adventure. Apps, Fred, illus. 2008. (Tania Abbey Adventure Ser.). (ENG.). 96p. (J). pap. 6.99 (978-1-84550-340-6(6), c8e23bb3-9904-4201-971e-e57faa66b8f3) Christian Focus Pubns. GBR. Dist: Bookmasters Distribution.

—Water or Goo? Apps, Fred, illus. 2008. (Tania Abbey Adventure Ser.). (ENG.). 96p. (J). pap. 6.99 (978-1-84550-341-3(4), 748295d7-9d18-4862-90d7-b454340bafc1) Christian Focus Pubns. GBR. Dist: Bookmasters Distribution.

Rhatigan, Joe & Numberg, Charles. The Jungle Book: Mowgli's Adventures. Dacey, Bob & Bandelin, Debra, illus. 2016. (Modern Retelling Ser.). (ENG.). 28p. (J). (gr. -1-1). 17.95 (978-1-63322-113-0(X), Moondance) Quarto Publishing Group USA.

Rowe, John, ed. The Jungle Book. (J). reprint ed. lib. bdg. 24.95 (978-0-88411-819-0(3)) Amereon Ltd.

—The Jungle Book. 2007. (Illustrated Classics Ser.). (Illus.). 40p. (gr. 3-6). lib. bdg. 26.00 (978-0-8368-7663-5(6), Gareth Stevens Learning Library) Stevens, Gareth Publishing LLLP.

Schomer-Wendel, Gretchen & Schomer, Adam Anthony. Becka Goes to India. 2009. (Becka & the Big Bubble Ser.). (Illus.). 32p. (J). (gr. -1-3). pap. 10.55 (978-1-60754-111-0(4)) Windmill Bks.

Senzai, N. H. Ticket to India. 2015. (ENG., Illus.). 288p. (J). (gr. 3-7). 16.99 (978-1-4814-2258-1(8), Simon & Schuster/Paula Wiseman Bks.) Simon & Schuster/Paula Wiseman Bks.

Sheth, Kashmira. Boys Without Names. (ENG.). 320p. (J). (gr. 4-7). 2011. pap. 6.99 (978-0-06-185762-1(9)) 2010. 16.99 (978-0-06-185760-7(2)) HarperCollins Pubs.

—Keeping Corner. 2009. (ENG.). 304p. (J). (gr. 7-17). pap. 7.99 (978-0-7868-3860-8(4)) Hyperion Pr.

—Koyal Dark, Mango Sweet. (ENG.). 224p. (gr. 7-17). 2006. 15.99 (978-0-7868-3857-8(4)) 2007. pap. 7.99 (978-0-7868-3858-5(2)) Hyperion Pr.

—Monsoon Afternoon, 1 vol. Jaeggi, Yoshiko, illus. 2008. (ENG.). 32p. (J). (gr. k-3). 16.95 (978-1-56145-455-6(9), Peachtree Junior) Peachtree Pubs.

Siegel, Elizabeth. Taj. Toye, Derek, illus. 2007. 48p. (J). lib. bdg. 23.08 (978-1-4242-1632-1(X)) Fitzgerald Bks.

Small Acts of Amazing Courage. 2013. (ENG., Illus.). 240p. (J). (gr. 4-7). pap. 6.99 (978-1-4424-9495-4(6), Simon & Schuster/Paula Wiseman Bks.) Simon & Schuster/Paula Wiseman Bks.

Somaiah, Ranjan & Somaiah, Rosemarie. Indian Children's Favorite Stories. 2006. (ENG., Illus.). 80p. (J). (gr. k-8). 18.95 (978-0-8048-3687-6(6)) Tuttle Publishing.

Souhami, Jessica. Rama & the de Mon King: An Ancient Tale from India. 2006. (Illus.). 30p. (J). (gr. k-4). reprint ed. 15.00 (978-0-7567-9813-0(2)) DIANE Publishing Co.

Spreng, Robert C. The Tahoe Tiger & the Lahontan Lion. 2008. 38p. pap. 14.50 (978-0-557-02370-7(X)) Lulu Pr., Inc.

Steel, Flora. The Adventures of Akbar. 2007. 116p. per. 9.95 (978-1-60312-207-8(9)) Aegypan.

Stevenson, Steve. The Pearl of Bengal. Turconi, Stefano, illus. 2013. (Agatha: Girl of Mystery Ser.: 2). (ENG.). 144p. (J). (gr. 2-5). pap. 6.99 (978-0-448-46219-6(2), Grosset & Dunlap) Penguin Young Readers Group.

—The Pearl of Bengal. 2013. (Agatha Girl of Mystery Ser.: 2). lib. bdg. 17.20 (978-0-606-30016-2(3), Turtleback) Turtleback Bks.

Stewart, Angela. The Curious Adventures of India Sophia. Stuart, Mitchell, illus. 2004. (Juvenile Novel Ser.). 176p. (J). (gr. 4-6). pap. 9.95 (978-1-895836-78-3(6)) River Bks. CAN. Dist: Fitzhenry & Whiteside, Ltd.

Stilton, Thea. Thea Stilton & the Prince's Emerald. 2012. (Thea Stilton Ser.: 12). lib. bdg. 19.65 (978-0-606-26534-8(1), Turtleback) Turtleback Bks.

Thorne, Jenny, illus. The Jungle Book. 2016. (ENG.). 24p. pap. 7.99 (978-1-86147-814-6(3), Armadillo) Anness Publishing GBR. Dist: National Bk. Network.

Thottam, Meena. The Last Dancer. 2006. (J). 3.95 (978-0-9776917-7-7(2), Curcumin Bks.) Davlaw Press.

Thottam, Meena, adapted by. Brothers of the Jungle. 2006. (J). 3.95 (978-0-9776917-4-6(8), Curcumin Bks.) Davlaw Press.

—Chameli's Choice. 2006. (J). 3.95 (978-0-9776917-6-0(4), Curcumin Bks.) Davlaw Press.

—Death, Where are You? 2006. (J). 3.95 (978-0-9776917-5-3(6), Curcumin Bks.) Davlaw Press.

—Maybe I am, Maybe I am Not. 2006. (J). 3.95 (978-0-9776917-8-4(0), Curcumin Bks.) Davlaw Press.

—The Pretender. 2006. (J). 3.95 (978-0-9776917-3-9(X), Curcumin Bks.) Davlaw Press.

—Road to Riches. 2006. (J). 3.95 (978-0-9776917-9-1(9), Curcumin Bks.) Davlaw Press.

—The Sage's Daughter. 2006. (J). 3.95 (978-0-9776917-2-2(1), Curcumin Bks.) Davlaw Press.

Venkatraman, Padma. Climbing the Stairs. 2010. (ENG., Illus.). 272p. (YA). (gr. 7-18). 9.99 (978-0-14-241490-3(5), Speak) Penguin Young Readers Group.

—A Time to Dance. (ENG.). (YA). (gr. 7). 2015. 336p. pap. 9.99 (978-0-14-751440-0(1), Speak) 2014. 320p. 17.99 (978-0-399-25710-0(1), Nancy Paulsen Books) Penguin Young Readers Group.

Vishpriya. Tales from Indi: Character Counts! RESPECT. Ruble, Eugene, illus. 2009. 24p. pap. 10.95 (978-1-933090-57-3(X)) Guardian Angel Publishing, Inc.

Viswanath, Shobha. An Elephant in My Backyard. Jawa, Sadhvi, illus. 2013. (ENG.). 28p. (J). (gr. -1). 11.95 (978-81-8190-240-5(8)) Karadi Tales Co. Pvt. Ltd. IND. Dist: Consortium Bk. Sales & Distribution.

Wendel, Gretchen Schomel, et al. Becka Goes to India. Renthrope, Damon, illus. 2007. (ENG.). 32p. (J). 11.99 (978-1-933754-13-0(3)) Waterside Publishing.

Wendel, Gretchen Schomer & Schomer, Adam Anthony. Becka Goes to India. Renthrope, Damon, illus. 2009. (Becka & the Big Bubble Ser.). 32p. (J). (gr. -1-2). lib. bdg. 22.60 (978-1-60754-110-3(6)) Windmill Bks.

Weston Woods Staff, creator. Rikki-Tikki-Tavi. 2011. 18.95 (978-0-439-72977-2(7)); 38.75 (978-0-439-72979-6(3)) Weston Woods Studios, Inc.

—Seven Blind Mice. 2011. 38.75 (978-0-439-02777-9(2)) Weston Woods Studios, Inc.

Whelan, Gloria. All My Noble Dreams & Then What Happens. 2014. (ENG., Illus.). 272p. (J). (gr. 4-7). pap. 6.99 (978-1-4424-5157-5(2), Simon & Schuster/Paula Wiseman Bks.) Simon & Schuster/Paula Wiseman Bks.

—Homeless Bird. unabr. ed. 2004. 240p. (J). (gr. 5-9). pap. 29.00 incl. audio (978-0-8072-8859-7(4), Listening Library) Random Hse. Audio Publishing Group.

—Small Acts of Amazing Courage. 2011. (ENG.). 224p. (J). (gr. 4-7). 15.99 (978-1-4424-0931-6(2), Simon & Schuster/Paula Wiseman Bks.) Simon & Schuster/Paula Wiseman Bks.

Williams, Marcia. The Elephant's Friend & Other Tales from Ancient India. Williams, Marcia, illus. 2014. (ENG., Illus.). 40p. (J). (gr. 1-4). 6.99 (978-0-7636-7055-9(3)) Candlewick Pr.

Williston, Teresa Peirce. Hindu Stories. Squire, Maud Hunt, illus. 2011. 110p. 39.95 (978-1-258-02581-6(7)) Literary Licensing, LLC.

Wilson, John. Where Soldiers Lie. rev. ed. 2007. (ENG., Illus.). 192p. (YA). (gr. 7-18). 12.95 (978-1-55263-790-6(5)) Leaf Storm Pr.

Wilson-Timmons, Karen & Dubois, Marie Thérèse. Agha the Eight-Mile Monster. rev. ed. 2012. (ENG., Illus.). 32p. (J). (gr. -1). 16.99 (978-1-60887-124-7(X)) Mandala Publishing.

Winskill, John. Jungle Friends. Disney Global Artists Staff & Random House Disney Staff, illus. 2003. (Step into Reading Ser.). (ENG.). 32p. (J). (gr. -1-1). pap. 3.99 (978-0-7364-2089-1(4), RH/Disney) Random Hse. Children's Bks.

Wolf, Gita. The Very Hungry Lion: A Folktale. Roy, Indrapramit, illus. 2006. (ENG.). 24p. 20.95 (978-81-86211-02-1(0)) Tara Publishing IND. Dist: Consortium Bk. Sales & Distribution.

Young, Beryl. Follow the Elephant. 2010. (ENG., Illus.). 248p. pap. 10.95 (978-1-55380-098-9(2)) Ronsdale Pr. CAN. Dist: SPD-Small Pr. Distribution.

Zacharias, Ravi. The Merchant & the Thief: A Folktale from India, 1 vol. Fournier, Laure, illus. 2012. (ENG.). 32p. (J). 15.99 (978-0-310-71636-5(5)) Zonderkidz.

Zafón, Carlos Ruiz. The Midnight Palace. 2012. (ENG.). 320p. (YA). (gr. 7-17). pap. 10.00 (978-0-316-04474-5(1)) Little, Brown Bks. for Young Readers.

Zia, F. Hot, Hot Roti for Dada-Ji. Min, Ken, illus. 2011. (ENG.). 32p. (J). (gr. k-5). 17.95 (978-1-60060-443-0(9)) Lee & Low Bks., Inc.

Zia, F. & Min, Ken. Hot Hot Roti for Dada-Ji. 2016. (ENG.). 32p. (J). (gr. k-3). pap. 9.95 **(978-1-62014-352-0(6))** Lee & Low Bks., Inc.

Zia, Farhana. Child of Spring, 1 vol. 2016. (ENG., Illus.). 192p. (J). (gr. 3-6). 16.95 (978-1-56145-904-9(6)) Peachtree Pubs.

INDIA—HISTORY

Ali, Daud. Ancient India. 2009. (Passport to the Past Ser.). (Illus.). 64p. (YA). (gr. 4-7). lib. bdg. 31.95 (978-1-4358-5169-6(2)) Rosen Publishing Group, Inc., The.

—Hands-On History! Ancient India: Discover the Rich Heritage of the Indus Valley & the Mughal Empire, with 15 Step-By-Step Projects & 340 Pictures. 2014. (ENG., Illus.). 64p. (J). (gr. k-8). 12.99 (978-1-84322-823-3(8), Armadillo) Anness Publishing GBR. Dist: National Bk. Network.

Ancient India DBA. 2003. spiral bd. 16.95 (978-1-56004-153-6(6)) Social Studies Schl. Service.

Ancient Mesopotamia/India. 2003. (Mr. Donn & Maxie's Always Something You Can Use Ser.). spiral bd. 19.95 (978-1-56004-166-5(8)) Social Studies Schl. Service.

Bailer, Darice. India. 2015. (One World, Many Countries Ser.). (ENG.). 32p. (J). (gr. 1-4). 28.50 (978-1-63407-047-8(X), 208875) Child's World, Inc., The.

Bailey, Katharine. Vasco Da Gama: Quest for the Spice Trade. 2007. (In the Footsteps of Explorers Ser.). (ENG., Illus.). 32p. (J). (gr. 3-7). lib. bdg. (978-0-7787-2421-6(2)); pap. (978-0-7787-2457-5(3)) Crabtree Publishing Co.

Bajaj, Varsha. T Is for Taj Mahal: An India Alphabet. Crawford, Robert, illus. 2011. (Discover the World Ser.). (ENG.). 40p. (J). (gr. k-6). 17.95 (978-1-58536-504-3(1)) Sleeping Bear Pr.

—T Is for Taj Mahal: An India Alphabet. 2016. (Av2 Fiction Readalong 2017 Ser.). (ENG.). (J). (gr. k-6). 34.28 **(978-1-4896-5227-0(2)**, AV2 by Weigl) Weigl Pubs., Inc.

Bankston, John. Ancient India: Maurya Empire. 2012. (Explore Ancient Worlds Ser.). (J). (gr. 3-6). lib. bdg. 29.95 (978-1-61228-280-0(6)) Mitchell Lane Pubs., Inc.

Barr, Marilynn G. India. 2003. (Illus.). 48p. (J). pap. 7.95 (978-1-57310-413-5(2)) Teaching & Learning Co.

Bridges, Shirin Yim & Yim Bridges, Shirin. Nur Jahan of India. Nguyen, Albert, illus. 2010. (Thinking Girl's Treasury of Real Princesses Ser.). (ENG.). 24p. (J). (gr. 3-8). 18.95 (978-0-9845098-5-0(2)) Goosebottom Bks. LLC.

Brownlie Bojang, Ali. India, 1 vol. 2011. (Countries Around the World Ser.). (ENG.). 48p. (gr. 3-6). pap. 9.95 (978-1-4329-5232-7(3)); 33.32 (978-1-4329-5207-5(2)) Heinemann-Raintree. (NA-h).

Buckley, A. M. India, 1 vol. 2011. (Countries of the World Set 1 Ser.). (ENG., Illus.). 144p. (J). (gr. 6-12). lib. bdg. 37.07 (978-1-61783-111-9(5)) ABDO Publishing Co.

Caper, William. India & China: Text Pairs. 2008. (Bridges/Navigators Ser.). (J). (gr. 6). 94.00 (978-1-4108-8441-1(4)) Benchmark Education Co.

Carroll, Jamuna. India. 2009. (Opposing Viewpoints Ser.). (ENG.). (J). (gr. 10-12). 224p. 48.80 (978-0-7377-4370-8(0)); 240p. pap. 29.45 (978-0-7377-4369-2(7)) Cengage Gale. (Greenhaven Pr., Inc.).

Centore, Michael. India, Vol. 12. 2015. (Major Nations in a Global World: Tradition, Culture, & Daily Life Ser.). (Illus.). 64p. (J). (gr. 7). 23.95 (978-1-4222-3345-0(6)) Mason Crest.

Chambers, Jo. Discovering India. 2007. (Trackers-Math Ser.). (gr. 2-5). pap. 5.00 (978-1-59055-926-0(6)) Pacific Learning, Inc.

Coleman, Miriam. The Culture & Crafts of India. 2015. (Cultural Crafts Ser.). (ENG., Illus.). 32p. (J). (gr. 4-6). pap. 11.75 (978-1-4994-1121-8(9), PowerKids Pr.) Rosen Publishing Group, Inc., The.

Conklin, Wendy. Ancient Civilizations - China - India - Africa - Mesopotamia: All-in-One Resource with Background Information, Map Activities, Simulations & Games, & a Read-Aloud Play to Support Comprehension & Critical Thinking in Social Studies, Grades 5 & Up. 2006. (Ancient Civilizations Ser.). (ENG., Illus.). 96p. (gr. 5). per. 14.99 (978-0-439-53993-7(5), Teaching Resources) Scholastic, Inc.

Crabtree Staff & Hynson, Colin. Understanding Indian Myths. 2012. (ENG., Illus.). 48p. (J). pap. (978-0-7787-4529-7(5)) Crabtree Publishing Co.

Dalal, A. Kamala & National Geographic Kids Staff. India. 2007. (Countries of the World Ser.). (ENG., Illus.). 64p. (J). (gr. 5-9). lib. bdg. 27.90 (978-1-4263-0127-8(8), National Geographic Children's Bks.) National Geographic Society.

Dalal, Anita. Ancient India: Archaelogy Unlocks the Secrets of India's Past. 2007. (National Geographic Investigates Ser.). (ENG., Illus.). 64p. (J). (gr. 5-9). lib. bdg. 27.90 (978-1-4263-0071-4(9), National Geographic Children's Bks.) National Geographic Society.

—Ancient India: Archaeology Unlocks the Secrets of India's Past. 2007. (National Geographic Investigates Ser.). (ENG., Illus.). 64p. (J). (gr. 5-7). 17.95 (978-1-4263-0070-7(0), National Geographic Children's Bks.) National Geographic Society.

Darraj, Susan Muaddi. The Indian Independence Act Of 1947. 2011. (Milestones in Modern World History Ser.). (Illus.). 120p. (J). (gr. 9). 35.00 (978-1-60413-496-4(8), Chelsea Hse.) Facts On File, Inc.

Dunn, John M. Birth of Modern India. Greenhaven Press Editors, ed. 2014. (World History Ser.). (ENG., Illus.). 128p. (gr. 7-10). lib. bdg. 39.90 (978-1-4205-0897-0(0), Lucent Bks.) Cengage Gale.

Ejaz, Khadija. Meet Our New Student from India. 2009. (Meet Our New Student Ser.). (Illus.). 48p. (J). (gr. 2-5). lib. bdg. 25.70 (978-1-58415-779-3(8)) Mitchell Lane Pubs., Inc.

Fine, Jil. Writing in Ancient India. 2003. (Writing in the Ancient World Ser.). (Illus.). 24p. (J). lib. bdg. 22.60 (978-0-8239-6508-3(2), PowerKids Pr.) Rosen Publishing Group, Inc., The.

Flatt, Lizann. India. 2009. (Facts about Countries Ser.). (Illus.). 32p. (J). (gr. 3-5). lib. bdg. 27.10 (978-1-59771-117-3(9)) Sea-To-Sea Pubns.

Friesen, Helen Lepp. India. 2013. (J). (978-1-62127-253-3(2)); pap. (978-1-62127-259-5(1)) Weigl Pubs., Inc.

Gandhi, Arun & Hegedus, Bethany. Grandfather Gandhi. Turk, Evan, illus. 2014. (ENG.). 48p. (J). (gr. -1-3). 17.99 (978-1-4424-2365-7(X)) Simon & Schuster Children's Publishing.

Gandhi, Mahatma. My Experiments with Truth. Chougule, Shailja Jain, illus. 2016. (ENG.). 64p. pap. 6.95 (978-1-906230-88-3(9)) Real Reads Ltd. GBR. Dist: Casemate Pubs. & Bk. Distributors, LLC.

Ganeri, Anita. India. 2016. (Journey Through Ser.). (ENG., Illus.). 32p. (J). (gr. 4-6). 16.99 (978-1-4451-3678-3(3), Franklin Watts) Hachette Children's Group GBR. Dist: Hachette Bk. Group.

Goldish, Meish. Poisoned Air: Bhopal, India. 2017. (Eco-Disasters Ser.). (ENG.). 32p. (J). (gr. 2-7). 19.95 **(978-1-68402-221-2(5))** Bearport Publishing Co., Inc.

Gray, Kim. I'm from India. 2013. (Rosen Readers Ser.). (ENG.). 24p. (J). (gr. 2-3). pap. 49.50 (978-1-4777-2392-0(7)); pap. 8.25 (978-1-4777-2391-3(9)) Rosen Publishing Group, Inc., The. (Rosen Classroom).

Greeley, August. Writing in Ancient India. 2009. (Writing in the Ancient World Ser.). 24p. (gr. 3-3). 42.50 (978-1-60854-906-1(2), PowerKids Pr.) Rosen Publishing Group, Inc., The.

Green, Jen. Gandhi & the Quit India Movement: Days of Decision, 1 vol. 2013. (Days of Decision Ser.). (ENG.). 64p.

H
I

(gr. 7-8). 35.99 *(978-1-4329-7635-4(4))*; pap. 10.95 *(978-1-4329-7642-2(7))* Heinemann-Raintree.
—Living in India. 2016. (Living In Ser.). (ENG., Illus.). 24p. (J). (gr. 1-3). 16.99 *(978-1-4451-4862-5(5)*, Franklin Watts) Hachette Children's Group GBR. Dist: Hachette Bk. Group.
Hankin, Rosemary. An Indian Cookbook for Kids. 2013. (Cooking Around the World Ser.). 32p. (J). (gr. 3-6). pap. 70.50 *(978-1-4777-1525-3(8))*; pap. 11.75 *(978-1-4777-1524-6(X))*; lib. bdg. 26.50 *(978-1-4777-1338-9(7))* Rosen Publishing Group, Inc., The. (PowerKids Pr.).
Harmon, Daniel E. Ayatollah Ruhollah Khomeini. 2004. (Spiritual Leaders & Thinkers Ser.). (Illus.). 120p. (J). (gr. 9-13). 30.00 *(978-0-7910-7865-5(5)*, Chelsea Hse.) Facts On File, Inc.
Hawker, Frances & Bhatia, Mohini. Sikhism in India. Campbell, Bruce, photos by. 2009. (ENG., Illus.). 32p. (J). (gr. 3-6). *(978-0-7787-5011-6(6))*; pap. *(978-0-7787-5028-4(0))* Crabtree Publishing Co.
Heing, Bridey. Trade Routes to India. 2017. (J). ***(978-1-5026-2694-3(2))*** Cavendish Square Publishing.
Henneberg, Susan. The Religion & Beliefs of Ancient India. 2016. (Spotlight on the Rise & Fall of Ancient Civilizations Ser.). 48p. (J). (gr. 6-6). pap. 11.75 *(978-1-4777-8938-4(3))* Rosen Publishing Group, Inc., The.
Hickman, Pamela & Taraschi-Carr, Gola. Righting Canada's Wrongs: the Komagata Maru & Canada's Anti-Indian Immigration Policies in the Twentieth Century. 2014. (Righting Canada's Wrongs Ser.). (ENG., Illus.). 104p. (YA). (gr. 8-12). 34.95 *(978-1-4594-0437-3(8)*, 9781459404373) Lorimer, James & Co., Ltd., Pubs. CAN. Dist: Casemate Pubs. & Bk. Distributors, LLC.
Hirsch, E. D., Jr., ed. Ancient India. 2003. tchr. ed. 9.95 *(978-0-7690-5045-4(X))*; stu. ed. 49.95 *(978-0-7690-2949-8(3))* Pearson Learning.
Holm, Kirsten C. Everyday Life in Ancient India. 2012. (Jr. Graphic Ancient Civilizations Ser.). (ENG.). 24p. (J). (gr. 3-6). pap. 10.60 *(978-1-4488-6397-6(X))*; lib. bdg. 25.25 *(978-1-4488-6219-1(1))* Rosen Publishing Group, Inc., The. (PowerKids Pr.).
Hynson, Colin. Understanding Indian Myths. 2012. (ENG.). 48p. (J). *(978-0-7787-4524-2(4))* Crabtree Publishing Co.
India, 1835-1952, Vol. IV, Pt. II. (J). (gr. k). 95.00 *(978-0-932106-63-6(3))* Durst, Sanford J.
Johnson, Anne E. Exploring Ancient India. 2018. (ENG.). 32p. (gr. 3-6). ***(978-1-63235-464-8(0)***, 12-Story Library) Pr. Room Editions LLC.
Johnson, Robin & Kalman, Bobbie. Conoce India. 2009. (SPA.). 32p. (J). *(978-0-7787-8193-6(3))*; (gr. 2-5). pap. *(978-0-7787-8213-1(1))* Crabtree Publishing Co.
Juarez, Christine. Egypt, 1 vol. 2014. (Countries Ser.). (ENG.). 24p. (gr. k-1). lib. bdg. 26.65 *(978-1-4765-4226-3(0)*, Pebble Plus) Capstone Press of Coughlan Cos.
—India, 1 vol. 2014. (Countries Ser.). (ENG.). 24p. (gr. k-1). lib. bdg. 26.65 *(978-1-4765-4227-0(9)*, Pebble Plus) Capstone Press of Coughlan Cos.
Kagda, Falaq. India. 2010. (Festivals of the World Ser.). 32p. (gr. 3). 28.50 *(978-1-60870-101-8(8))* Marshall Cavendish Corp.
Kalman, Bobbie. India: The Culture. 3rd rev. ed. 2009. (Lands, Peoples, & Cultures Ser.). (ENG., Illus.). 32p. (J). (gr. 4-5). pap. *(978-0-7787-9657-2(4))*; *(978-0-7787-9287-1(0))* Crabtree Publishing Co.
—India: The Land. 3rd rev. ed. 2009. (Lands, Peoples, & Cultures Ser.). (ENG., Illus.). 32p. (J). (gr. 4-5). pap. *(978-0-7787-9655-8(8))* Crabtree Publishing Co.
—India: The People. 3rd rev. ed. 2009. (Lands, Peoples, & Cultures Ser.). (ENG., Illus.). 32p. (J). (gr. 4-5). pap. *(978-0-7787-9656-5(6))* Crabtree Publishing Co.
—India - The People. 3rd rev. ed. 2009. (ENG., Illus.). 32p. (J). (gr. 4-6). *(978-0-7787-9286-4(2))* Crabtree Publishing Co.
Khan, Aisha. A Historical Atlas of India. 2009. (Historical Atlases of South Asia, Central Asia, & the Middle East Ser.). 64p. (gr. 6-6). 61.20 *(978-1-61513-318-5(6))* Rosen Publishing Group, Inc., The.
Kuhn, Betsy. The Force Born of Truth: Mohandas Gandhi & the Salt March, India, 1930. 2010. (Civil Rights Struggles around the World Ser.). (ENG., Illus.). 160p. (gr. 9-12). lib. bdg. 38.60 *(978-0-8225-8968-6(0))* Lerner Publishing Group.
Kumar, Monica. Jay & Juhi: Taj Mahal Kee Saahsik Khoj. Aggarwal, Madhu, tr. Sona & Jacob, illus. 2008.Tr. of Jay & Juhi: the Taj Mahal Adventure. (HIN & ENG.). 32p. (J). pap. 14.99 *(978-0-9797191-4-1(3))* MeeraMasi, Inc.
Kuskowski, Alex. Super Simple Indian Art: Fun & Easy Art from Around the World, 1 vol. 2014. (Super Simple Cultural Art Set 2 Ser.). (ENG.). 32p. (gr. 5-10). lib. bdg. 27.07 *(978-1-62403-280-6(X)*, Super SandCastle) ABDO Publishing Co.
Landau, Jennifer. Vasco Da Gama. 2016. (Spotlight on Explorers & Colonization Ser.). 48p. (J). (gr. 6-6). pap. 11.75 *(978-1-4777-8825-7(5))* Rosen Publishing Group, Inc., The.
Lassieur, Allison. Ancient India. 2012. (Ancient World Ser.). (ENG.). 112p. (J). pap. 9.95 *(978-0-531-25980-1(3))*; lib. bdg. 34.00 *(978-0-531-25180-5(2))* Scholastic Library Publishing.
Lewis, Adam. Life in India. 2013. (InfoMax Readers Ser.). (ENG.). 24p. (J). (gr. 2-3). pap. 49.50 *(978-1-4777-2388-3(9))*; (Illus.). pap. 8.25 *(978-1-4777-2387-6(0))* Rosen Publishing Group, Inc., The. (Rosen Classroom).
Markovics, Joyce L. India. 2015. (Countries We Come From Ser.). (ENG., Illus.). 32p. (J). (gr. k-3). lib. bdg. 26.60 *(978-1-62724-857-0(9))* Bearport Publishing Co., Inc.
Marsico, Katie. The Wettest & the Driest. 2015. (True Book(tm), a — Extreme Places Ser.). (ENG., Illus.). 48p. (J). lib. bdg. 31.00 *(978-0-531-21847-1(3)*, Children's Pr.) Scholastic Library Publishing.
McDaniel, Jan. Indian Immigration. 2005. (Changing Face of North America Ser.). (Illus.). 112p. (YA). lib. bdg. 24.95 *(978-1-59084-683-4(4))* Mason Crest.
McGinty, Alice B. Gandhi: The March to the Sea, 0 vols. González, Thomas, illus. 2013. (ENG.). 40p. (J). (gr. 4-7). 17.99 *(978-1-4778-1644-8(5)*, 9781477816448, Amazon Children's Publishing) Amazon Publishing.
Montgomery, Sy. The Man-Eating Tigers of Sundarbans. Briggs, Eleanor, photos by. 2004. (Illus.). 57p. (J). 14.60 *(978-0-7569-5180-1(1))* Perfection Learning Corp.
Moon, Walt K. Exploremos India. 2017. (Bumba Books (tm) en Español — Exploremos Países (Let's Explore Countries) Ser.). (SPA.). 24p. (J). (gr. -1-1). 25.32 ***(978-1-5124-4122-2(8))*** Lerner Publishing Group.
Murray, Julie. India, 1 vol. 2013. (Explore the Countries Ser.). (ENG.). 40p. (J). (gr. 2-5). lib. bdg. 29.93 *(978-1-61783-812-5(8)*, Big Buddy Bks.) ABDO Publishing Co.
Napoli, Tony. Vasco Da Gama: Discovering the Sea Route to India. 2010. (Great Explorers of the World Ser.). (Illus.). 112p. (J). (gr. 7-12). 33.27 *(978-1-59845-127-6(8))* Enslow Pubs., Inc.
Nardo, Don. India. 2012. (Enchantment of the World, Second Ser.). (ENG., Illus.). 144p. (J). (gr. 5-9). lib. bdg. 40.00 *(978-0-531-25310-6(4)*, Children's Pr.) Scholastic Library Publishing.
Nichols, Susan. The Culture of Ancient India. 2016. (Spotlight on the Rise & Fall of Ancient Civilizations Ser.). 48p. (J). (gr. 6-6). pap. 11.75 *(978-1-4777-8918-6(9))* Rosen Publishing Group, Inc., The.
Perkins, Chloe. Living in ... India. Woolley, Tom, illus. 2016. (Living In... Ser.). (ENG.). 32p. (J). (gr. k-2). pap. 3.99 *(978-1-4814-7089-6(2))* Simon & Schuster.
Perritano, John. Australia. 2015. (Illus.). 64p. (J). *(978-1-4222-3339-9(1))* Mason Crest.
Powell, Jillian. Descubramos la India. 2007. (Descubramos países del mundo (Looking at Countries) Ser.). (ENG & SPA.). 32p. (gr. 1-5). pap. 10.50 *(978-0-8368-7961-2(9)*, Gareth Stevens Learning Library) Stevens, Gareth Publishing LLLP.
—India. 2014. (My Country Ser.). 24p. (gr. k-3). lib. bdg. 28.50 *(978-1-59920-906-7(3))* Black Rabbit Bks.
Price, Nigel, et al. Cambridge IGCSE India Studies. 2013. (Cambridge International IGCSE Ser.). (ENG.). 176p. pap. 17.44 *(978-0-521-14923-5(1))* Cambridge Univ. Pr.
Ram-Prasad, Chakravarthi. Exploring the Life, Myth, & Art of India. 2009. (Civilizations of the World Ser.). (YA). (gr. 7-12). lib. bdg. 42.60 *(978-1-4358-5615-8(5))* Rosen Publishing Group, Inc., The.
Ranganathan, Murali. Govind Narayan's Mumbai: An Urban Biography From 1863. 2009. (Anthem South Asian Studies). (ENG., Illus.). 416p. pap. 35.00 *(978-1-84331-305-2(7))* Anthem Pr. GBR. Dist: Books International, Inc.
Rice, Dona. Mohandas Gandhi, 1 vol. 2nd rev. ed. 2014. (TIME for KIDS(r) Nonfiction Readers Ser.). (ENG., Illus.). 32p. (J). (gr. 3-3). pap. 25.96 *(978-1-4807-1091-7(1))* Shell Educational Publishing.
Rice, William & Rice, Dona. Mohandas Gandhi. 2017. (TIME for Kids en Español - Level 3 Ser.). (SPA.). 32p. (gr. 3-3). lib. bdg. 31.99 ***(978-1-5157-5189-2(9))*** Time for Kids Inc AUS. Dist: Capstone Pub.
Richardson, Hazel. Life in the Ancient Indus River Valley. 2005. (Peoples of the Ancient World Ser.). (ENG., Illus.). 32p. (J). (gr. -1-9). pap. *(978-0-7787-2070-6(5))* Crabtree Publishing Co.
Riggs, Kate. Taj Mahal. 2009. (Places of Old Ser.). 24p. (J). (gr. 1-5). lib. bdg. 24.25 *(978-1-58341-712-6(5)*, Creative Education) Creative Co., The.
Rose, Simon. Sri Harmandir Sahib. 2014. (J). *(978-1-4896-2609-7(3))* Weigl Pubs., Inc.
Rossi, Ann. India. 2007. (Reading Expeditions Ser.). (ENG., Illus.). 24p. (J). pap. 14.95 *(978-0-7922-4537-7(7))* CENGAGE Learning.
Rowell, Rebecca. Ancient India, 1 vol. 2014. (Ancient Civilizations Ser.). (ENG., Illus.). 112p. (J). (gr. 6-12). lib. bdg. 35.64 *(978-1-62403-539-5(6)*, Essential Library) ABDO Publishing Co.
Roxburgh, Ellis. The Mauryan Empire of India. 2015. (Great Empires Ser.). (ENG., Illus.). 48p. (J). (gr. 7-7). lib. bdg. 31.36 *(978-1-5026-0640-2(2))* Cavendish Square Publishing.
SargentBrian. LIFE IN MUMBAI HIGH BEGINNING BOOK WITH ONLINE ACCESS. 2014. (ENG., Illus.). 24p. pap. 9.50 *(978-1-107-62167-1(4))* Cambridge Univ. Pr.
Sen Gupta, Subhadra & Gupta, Priyankar, illus. A Children's History of India. 2015. 442p. (J). ***(978-81-291-3697-8(X))*** Rupa & Co.
Sexton, Colleen & Bartell, Jim. India. 2010. (Exploring Countries Ser.). (ENG., Illus.). 32p. (J). (gr. 3-7). lib. bdg. 26.95 *(978-1-60014-482-0(9)*, Blastoff! Readers) Bellwether Media.
Shea, Mary Molly. Foods of India. 2011. (Culture in the Kitchen Ser.). 24p. (J). (gr. 2-5). pap. 8.15 *(978-1-4339-5708-6(6))*; lib. bdg. 22.60 *(978-1-4339-5706-2(X))* Stevens, Gareth Publishing LLLP. (Gareth Stevens Learning Library).
Sheehan, Patricia & Ong, Jacqueline. Côte D'Ivoire. 2nd rev. ed. 2009. (Cultures of the World 19 Ser.). 144p. (gr. 6). 42.79 *(978-0-7614-4854-9(3))* Marshall Cavendish GBR. Dist: Marshall Cavendish Corp.
Shoup, Kate. India. 2015. (Illus.). 32p. (J). *(978-1-5026-0579-5(1))* Musa Publishing.
Spotlight on the Rise & Fall of Ancient Civilizations: India. 2016. (Spotlight on the Rise & Fall of Ancient Civilizations Ser.). 48p. (gr. 6-6). pap. 70.50 *(978-1-4994-6417-7(7)*, Rosen Young Adult) Rosen Publishing Group, Inc., The.
Srinivasan, Radhika, et al. India. 3rd rev. ed. 2011. (Cultures of the World: 3rd Edition 1 Ser.). (Illus.). 144p. (J). (gr. 6). 47.07 *(978-1-60870-782-9(2))* Marshall Cavendish Corp.
Taylor, Trace. India. 2010. pap. 39.62 *(978-1-61541-092-7(9))* American Reading Co.
Taylor, Trace & Sánchez, Lucía M. India. 2010. (1Y Nuestro Mundo Ser.). (SPA.). 16p. (J). (gr. k-1). pap. 6.99 *(978-1-61541-120-7(8))* American Reading Co.
Taylor, Trace & SáNchez, LucíA M. India. 2010. pap. 39.62 *(978-1-61541-121-4(6))* American Reading Co.
Thomson, Ruth. India. 2011. (Countries Ser.). (Illus.). 24p. (J). (gr. k-3). lib. bdg. 22.60 *(978-1-4488-3276-7(4))* Rosen Publishing Group, Inc., The.
Todd, Anne M. Mohandas Gandhi. 2004. (Spiritual Leaders & Thinkers Ser.). (Illus.). 120p. (C). (gr. 9-13). 30.00 *(978-0-7910-7864-8(7)*, Chelsea Hse.) Facts On File, Inc.
Walsh, Judith E. India. 2nd rev. ed. 2011. (Brief History Ser.). 432p. (C). (gr. 9). 49.50 *(978-0-8160-8143-1(3))* Facts On File, Inc.
Wells, Robert E. Can We Share the World with Tigers? Wells, Robert E., illus. 2012. (Wells of Knowledge Science Ser.). (ENG., Illus.). 32p. (J). (gr. 1-3). 16.99 *(978-0-8075-1055-1(6))* Whitman, Albert & Co.
Wheeler, Jill C. Gandhi. 2003. (Breaking Barriers Ser.). 64p. (gr. 3-8). 27.07 *(978-1-57765-906-8(6)*, Abdo & Daughters) ABDO Publishing Co.
Wood, Alix. Uncovering the Culture of Ancient India, 01 vols., 1. 2016. (Archaeology & Ancient Cultures Ser.). (ENG.). 32p. (J). pap. 10.00 *(978-1-5081-4659-9(4)*, PowerKids Pr.) Rosen Publishing Group, Inc., The.
World Book, Inc Staff, contrib. by. Independence of India & Pakistan. 2010. (J). *(978-0-7166-1506-4(1))* World Bk., Inc.
Zamosky, Lisa. India, 1 vol. 2007. (Primary Source Readers Ser.). (ENG.). 32p. (J). (gr. 5-5). pap. 8.99 *(978-0-7439-0430-8(3))* Shell Educational Publishing.

INDIA—POLITICS AND GOVERNMENT

Darraj, Susan Muaddi. The Indian Independence Act Of 1947. 2011. (Milestones in Modern World History Ser.). (Illus.). 120p. (J). (gr. 9). 35.00 *(978-1-60413-496-4(8)*, Chelsea Hse.) Facts On File, Inc.
Doeden, Matt. Darkness Everywhere: The Assassination of Mohandas Gandhi. 2013. 80p. pap. 31.93 *(978-1-4677-1659-8(6))* Lerner Publishing Group.
—Mohandas Gandhi. 2011. (J). lib. bdg. *(978-0-7613-5483-3(2))* Twenty First Century Bks.
Green, Jen. Gandhi & the Quit India Movement: Days of Decision, 1 vol. 2013. (Days of Decision Ser.). (ENG.). 64p. (gr. 7-8). 35.99 *(978-1-4329-7635-4(4))*; pap. 10.95 *(978-1-4329-7642-2(7))* Heinemann-Raintree.
Kuhn, Betsy. The Force Born of Truth: Mohandas Gandhi & the Salt March, India, 1930. 2010. (Civil Rights Struggles around the World Ser.). (ENG., Illus.). 160p. (gr. 9-12). lib. bdg. 38.60 *(978-0-8225-8968-6(0))* Lerner Publishing Group.
Lucas, Eileen. Mahatma Gandhi: Fighting for Indian Independence. 2017. (Rebels with a Cause Ser.). 128p. (J). (gr. 8-8). lib. bdg. 37.27 ***(978-0-7660-8513-8(9))*** Enslow Pubs., Inc.
Malaspina, Ann. Mahatma Gandhi & India's Independence. 2016. (People & Events That Changed the World Ser.). (ENG., Illus.). 128p. (J). (gr. 7-8). lib. bdg. 37.27 *(978-0-7660-7262-6(2))* Enslow Pubs., Inc.
Schupack, Sara. Indira Gandhi. 2013. (Leading Women 2 Ser.). 96p. (gr. 7-12). (YA). pap. 19.99 *(978-1-62712-113-2(7))*; (Illus.). (J). 39.93 *(978-0-7614-4955-3(8))* Cavendish Square Publishing.
Vander Hook, Sue. Mahatma Gandhi: Proponent of Peace, 1 vol. 2010. (Essential Lives Set 5 Ser.). (ENG.). 112p. (J). (gr. 6-12). lib. bdg. 35.64 *(978-1-61613-515-7(8))* ABDO Publishing Co.
World Book, Inc Staff, contrib. by. Independence of India & Pakistan. 2010. (J). *(978-0-7166-1506-4(1))* World Bk., Inc.

INDIA RUBBER

see Rubber

INDIAN CAPTIVITIES

Aller, Susan Bivin. Living with the Senecas: A Story about Mary Jemison. Harden, Laurie, illus. 2007. (Creative Minds Biographies Ser.). 64p. (J). (gr. 3-7). lib. bdg. 22.60 *(978-0-8225-5989-4(7))* Lerner Publishing Group.
Egan, Tracie. Cynthia Ann Parker: Cautiva de los comanches (Cynthia Ann Parker: Comanche Captive) 2009. (Grandes personajes en la historia de los Estados Unidos (Famous People in American History) Ser.). (SPA.). 32p. (gr. 2-3). 47.90 *(978-1-61512-796-2(8)*, Editorial Buenas Letras) Rosen Publishing Group, Inc., The.
—Cynthia Ann Parker: Comanche Captive. 2009. (Primary Sources of Famous People in American History Ser.). 32p. (gr. 2-3). 47.90 *(978-1-60851-667-4(9))* Rosen Publishing Group, Inc., The.
—Cynthia Ann Parker: Comanche Captive / Cautiva de los Comanches. 2009. (Famous People in American History/Grandes personajes en la historia de los Estados Unidos Ser.). (ENG & SPA.). 32p. (gr. 2-3). 47.90 *(978-1-61512-542-5(6)*, Editorial Buenas Letras) Rosen Publishing Group, Inc., The.
Gonzalez, Catherine Troxell. Cynthia Ann Parker: Indian Captive. 2005. (Illus.). 78p. (J). pap. 9.95 *(978-1-940130-37-8(9))* Eakin Pr.

INDIAN CAPTIVITIES—FICTION

Abbott, E. F. Mary Jemison: Native American Captive. 2016. (Based on a True Story Ser.). (ENG., Illus.). 224p. (J). 15.99 *(978-1-250-06838-5(X)*, 9781250068385) Feiwel & Friends.
Cooney, Caroline B. The Ransom of Mercy Carter. 2011. (ENG.). 256p. (YA). (gr. 7). pap. 8.99 *(978-0-385-74046-3(8)*, Ember) Random Hse. Children's Bks.
Harvey, Gwen. Esperanza Means Hope. Porfirio, Guy, illus. 2010. (J). *(978-0-910037-51-8(5))*; pap. *(978-0-910037-52-5(3))* Arizona Historical Society.
Leet, Karen M. Sarah's Courage: A Kentucky Frontier Kidnapping. 2014. (ENG., Illus.). 144p. (gr. 4-7). 14.99 *(978-1-62619-477-9(7)*, History Pr., The) Arcadia Publishing.
Osborne, Mary Pope. Standing in the Light: The Diary of Catharine Carey Logan, Delaware Valley, Pennsylvania, 1763. 2011. (Dear America Ser.). (ENG.). 176p. (J). (gr. 5-9). 12.99 *(978-0-545-26687-1(4))* Scholastic, Inc.
Smith, Mary P. Boy Captive of Old Deerfield. (Illus.). (J). (gr. 5-6). reprint ed. lib. bdg. 22.95 *(978-0-89190-961-3(3)*, Rivercity Pr.) Amereon Ltd.
Wheeler, Arville. White Squaw: The True Story of Jennie Wiley. Bengtz, Ture, illus. 2011. 178p. (gr. 4-7). 42.95 *(978-1-258-05911-8(8))* Literary Licensing, LLC.

INDIAN MYTHOLOGY

Brown, Virginia Pounds & Owens, Laurella, eds. Southern Indian Myths & Legends. Glick, Nathan, illus. 2014. (ENG.). 160p. pap. 19.95 *(978-1-58838-253-5(2)*, NewSouth Bks.) NewSouth, Inc.
Collinson, Clare. Arts, Society, & Religion. 2010. (CC: Native North Americans Ser.). (Illus.). 112p. (gr. 6-12). 42.80 *(978-1-933834-79-5(X))* Brown Bear Bks.
Crabtree Staff & Hyde, Natalie. Understanding Mesoamerican Myths. 2012. (ENG., Illus.). 48p. (J). pap. *(978-0-7787-4530-3(9))* Crabtree Publishing Co.
Crabtree Staff & Kopp, Megan. Understanding Native American Myths. 2012. (ENG., Illus.). 48p. (J). pap. *(978-0-7787-4531-0(7))* Crabtree Publishing Co.
Croy, Anita. Myths & Legends of Central & South America. 2015. (Illus.). 64p. (J). *(978-0-7166-2628-2(4))* World Bk., Inc.
Dalal, Anita. Native American Myths. 2010. (Myths from Around the World Ser.). 48p. (gr. 6-8). (YA). lib. bdg. 31.00 *(978-1-4339-3530-5(9))*; (Illus.). (J). pap. 14.05 *(978-1-4339-3531-2(7))* Stevens, Gareth Publishing LLLP. (Gareth Stevens Secondary Library).
Daning, Tom. Mesoamerican Mythology: Quetzalcoatl. 2009. (Jr. Graphic Mythologies Ser.). (Illus.). 24p. (J). (gr. 2-3). 47.90 *(978-1-61513-867-8(6)*, PowerKids Pr.) Rosen Publishing Group, Inc., The.
—Mitología Mesoamericana: Quetzalcóatl. Obregón, José María, illus. 2009. (Historietas Juveniles: Mitologías (Jr. Graphic Mythologies) Ser.). (SPA.). 24p. (J). (gr. 3-6). lib. bdg. 25.25 *(978-1-4358-8569-1(4))* Rosen Publishing Group, Inc., The.
Daning, Tom & Obregón, José María. Mitología Mesoamericana: Quetzalcóatl. 2009. (Historietas Juveniles: Mitologías (Jr. Graphic Mythologies) Ser.). (Illus.). 24p. (gr. 3-8). pap. 10.60 *(978-1-4358-3332-6(5))* Rosen Publishing Group, Inc., The.
Hibbert, Clare. Terrible Tales of Native America, Vol. 1. 2014. (Monstrous Myths Ser.). (ENG.). 32p. (J). (gr. 4-5). 26.60 *(978-1-4824-0190-5(8))* Stevens, Gareth Publishing LLLP.
Hyde, Natalie. Understanding Mesoamerican Myths. 2012. (ENG.). 48p. (J). *(978-0-7787-4525-9(2))* Crabtree Publishing Co.
Kessler, Tim. When God Made the Dakotas. Morin, Paul, illus. 2006. 32p. (J). (gr. k). 17.00 *(978-0-8028-5275-5(0)*, Eerdmans Bks For Young Readers) Eerdmans, William B. Publishing Co.
Kopp, Megan. Understanding Native American Myths. 2012. (ENG.). 48p. (J). *(978-0-7787-4526-6(0))* Crabtree Publishing Co.
McKinley, Herald. Myths of the Native Americans. 2016. (World Mythologies Ser.). (ENG., Illus.). 96p. (J). (gr. 6-6). 42.79 *(978-1-5026-0990-8(8))* Cavendish Square Publishing.
Montejo, Victor. Popol Vuh: A Sacred Book of the Maya, 1 vol. Unger, David, tr. from SPA. Garay, Luis, illus. 2009. (ENG.). 88p. (J). (gr. 3-4). pap. 14.95 *(978-0-88899-921-4(6))* Groundwood Bks. CAN. Dist: Publishers Group West (PGW).
Nagle, Jeanne, ed. Native American Spirit Beings. 2014. (Gods & Goddesses of Mythology Ser.). 160p. (YA). (gr. 9-12). 32.90 *(978-1-62275-399-4(2))* Rosen Publishing Group, Inc., The.
Native American. 2nd rev. ed. 2010. (Mythology A to Z Ser.). (Illus.). 160p. (gr. 5-8). 45.00 *(978-1-60413-894-8(7)*, Chelsea Hse.) Facts On File, Inc.
O'Brien, Cynthia. Myths & Legends of North America: Canada & the Northern United States. 2015. (Illus.). 64p. (J). *(978-0-7166-2626-8(8))* World Bk., Inc.
Olhoff, Jim. Native American Mythology, 1 vol. 2011. (World of Mythology Ser.). (ENG., Illus.). 32p. (YA). (gr. 5-9). 27.07 *(978-1-61714-717-3(6))* ABDO Publishing Co.
Peacock, Thomas Love & Wisuri, Marlene. The Good Path: Ojibwe Learning & Activity Book for Kids. 2009. (ENG., Illus.). 128p. (J). (gr. 5-8). pap. 19.95 *(978-0-87351-783-6(0))* Minnesota Historical Society Pr.
Schomp, Virginia. The Native Americans. 2007. (Myths of the World Ser.). (Illus.). 96p. (J). (gr. 3-7). lib. bdg. 32.79 *(978-0-7614-2550-2(0)*, Benchmark Bks.) Marshall Cavendish Corp.
Wolfson, Evelyn. Mythology of the American Indians. 2014. (Mythology, Myths, & Legends Ser.). 96p. (J). (gr. 6-12). pap. 10.95 *(978-0-7660-6163-7(9))*; (Illus.). 27.94 *(978-0-7660-6162-0(0))* Enslow Pubs., Inc.
Zimmerman, Larry J. Exploring the Life, Myth, & Art of Native Americans. 2009. (Civilizations of the World Ser.). (YA). (gr. 7-12). lib. bdg. 42.60 *(978-1-4358-5614-1(7))* Rosen Publishing Group, Inc., The.

INDIAN SIGN LANGUAGE

Coulter, Lavrie. Secrets in Stone: All about Maya Hieroglyphs. English, Sarah Jane, illus. 2003. 48p. (gr. 4-8). 18.00 *(978-0-7567-9000-4(X))* DIANE Publishing Co.

INDIANA

Brezina, Corona. Indiana: Past & Present. 2010. (United States: Past & Present Ser.). (ENG., Illus.). 48p. (J). pap. 11.75 *(978-1-4358-8492-2(2))*; lib. bdg. 29.25 *(978-1-4358-3521-4(2))* Rosen Publishing Group, Inc., The. (Rosen Reference).
Brill, Marlene Targ. Indiana. 2nd rev. ed. 2005. (Celebrate the States Ser.). (Illus.). 144p. (gr. 6-7). lib. bdg. 42.79 *(978-0-7614-2020-0(7)*, Benchmark Bks.) Marshall Cavendish Corp.
Brown, Jonatha A. & Orr, Tamra. Indiana. 2005. (Portraits of the States Ser.). (Illus.). 32p. (gr. 2-6). pap. 10.50 *(978-0-8368-4644-7(3)*, Gareth Stevens Learning Library) Stevens, Gareth Publishing LLLP.
Brown, Jonatha A. & Orr, Tamra B. Indiana. 2005. (Portraits of the States Ser.). (Illus.). 32p. (gr. 2-6). lib. bdg. 26.00 *(978-0-8368-4625-6(7)*, Gareth Stevens Learning Library) Stevens, Gareth Publishing LLLP.
Brown, Vanessa. Indiana. (Bilingual Library of the United States of America Ser.). 32p. 2009. (SPA.). (gr. 2-2). 47.90 *(978-1-60853-359-6(X)*, Editorial Buenas Letras) 2005. (ENG & SPA., Illus.). (J). (gr. 3-6). lib. bdg. 25.25 *(978-1-4042-3079-8(3))* Rosen Publishing Group, Inc., The.
Craats, Rennay. Indiana. 2011. (Guide to American States Ser.). (Illus.). 48p. (YA). (gr. 3-6). 29.99 *(978-1-61690-786-0(X))*; (J). *(978-1-61690-462-3(3))* Weigl Pubs., Inc.
Deinard, Jenny. How to Draw Indiana's Sights & Symbols. 2009. (Kid's Guide to Drawing America Ser.). 32p. (gr. k-k). 50.50 *(978-1-61511-063-6(1)*, PowerKids Pr.) Rosen Publishing Group, Inc., The.
Derzipilski, Kathleen. Indiana. 2007. (Its My State! Ser.). (Illus.). 80p. (J). (gr. 4-7). lib. bdg. 29.93 *(978-0-7614-1927-3(6)*, Benchmark Bks.) Marshall Cavendish Corp.
Derzipilski, Kathleen & Hantula, Richard. Indiana. 2nd rev. ed. 2011. (It's My State! 2 Ser.). 80p. (gr. 3). 31.36 *(978-1-60870-522-1(6))* Marshall Cavendish GBR. Dist: Marshall Cavendish Corp.
Dhilawala, Sakina. Armenia. 2nd rev. ed. 2007. (Celebrate the States Ser.). (Illus.). 144p. (gr. 6). lib. bdg. 42.79 *(978-0-7614-2029-3(0))* Marshall Cavendish Corp.
Downey, Tika. Indiana: The Hoosier State. 2010. (Our Amazing States Ser.). (ENG.). 24p. (J). pap. 8.25 *(978-1-4358-9798-4(6))*; lib. bdg. 22.60 *(978-1-4358-9397-9(2))* Rosen Publishing Group, Inc., The. (PowerKids Pr.).

Hyde, Judith Jensen. Indiana. 2007. (Rookie Read-About Geography Ser.). (Illus.). 31p. (J). (gr. 1-2). 20.50 (978-0-516-21846-5(8), Children's Pr.) Scholastic Library Publishing.

Knapp, Ron. Indiana: A MyReportLinks.com Book. 2003. (States Ser.). (Illus.). 48p. (J). (gr. 4-10). lib. bdg. 25.26 (978-0-7660-5118-8(8), MyReportLinks.com Bks.) Enslow Pubs., Inc.

Marsh, Carole. Indiana Current Events Projects: 30 Cool, Activities, Crafts, Experiments & More for Kids to Do to Learn about Your State! 2003. (Indiana Experience Ser.). 32p. (gr. k-5). pap. 5.95 (978-0-635-02033-8(5), Marsh, Carole Bks.) Gallopade International.

—Indiana Geography Projects: 30 Cool, Activities, Crafts, Experiments & More for Kids to Do to Learn about Your State! 2003. (Indiana Experience Ser.). 32p. (gr. k-5). pap. 5.95 (978-0-635-01833-5(0), Marsh, Carole Bks.) Gallopade International.

—Indiana Government Projects: 30 Cool, Activities, Crafts, Experiments & More for Kids to Do to Learn about Your State! 2003. (Indiana Experience Ser.). 32p. (gr. k-5). pap. 5.95 (978-0-635-01933-2(7), Marsh, Carole Bks.) Gallopade International.

—Indiana Jeopardy! Answers & Questions about Our State! 2004. (Illus.). 32p. (J). (gr. 3-8). pap., act. bk. ed. 7.95 (978-0-7933-9796-9(0)) Gallopade International.

—Indiana "Jography" A Fun Run Through Our State! 2004. (Illus.). 32p. (J). (gr. 3-8). pap., act. bk. ed. 7.95 (978-0-7933-9825-6(8)) Gallopade International.

—Indiana People Projects: 30 Cool, Activities, Crafts, Experiments & More for Kids to Do to Learn about Your State! 2003. (Indiana Experience Ser.). 32p. (gr. k-5). pap. 5.95 (978-0-635-01983-7(3), Marsh, Carole Bks.) Gallopade International.

—Indiana Symbols & Facts Projects: 30 Cool, Activities, Crafts, Experiments & More for Kids to Do to Learn about Your State! 2003. (Indiana Experience Ser.). 32p. (gr. k-5). pap. 5.95 (978-0-635-01883-0(7), Marsh, Carole Bks.) Gallopade International.

—My First Book about Indiana. 2004. (Illus.). 32p. (J). (gr. k-4). pap. 7.95 (978-0-7933-9883-6(5)) Gallopade International.

McNamara, Connie. My First Purdue University Words. 2004. (J). bds. 11.95 (978-0-9743244-9-4(3)) Shamrock Publishing, Inc.

Messer, Luke. Hoosier Heart. Messer, Jennifer K., illus. 2006. 32p. (J). 16.95 (978-0-9786799-1-0(1)) Eva Publishing, LLC.

Mitschelen, Katie. Central till Plain. 2015. (Illus.). 32p. (J). lib. bdg. (978-1-938813-22-1(7)) State Standards Publishing, LLC.

Murray, Julie. Indiana, 1 vol. 2006. (Buddy Book Ser.). (ENG., Illus.). 32p. (gr. 2-4). 27.07 (978-1-59197-673-8(1), Buddy Bks.) ABDO Publishing Co.

Shofner, Shawndra. Indiana. 2008. (This Land Called America Ser.). (Illus.). 32p. (YA). (gr. 3-6). 22.95 (978-1-58341-639-6(0)) Creative Co., The.

Smith, Rich. Indiana, 1 vol. 2009. (United States Ser.). (ENG., Illus.). 48p. (YA). (gr. 2-5). 27.07 (978-1-60453-649-2(7)) ABDO Publishing Co.

Stille, Darlene R. Indiana. 2014. (America the Beautiful Ser.: 3). (ENG.). 144p. (J). lib. bdg. 40.00 (978-0-531-24884-3(4)) Scholastic Library Publishing.

Swain, Gwenyth. Indiana. 2012. (J). lib. bdg. 25.26 (978-0-7613-4531-2(0), Lerner Pubns.) Lerner Publishing Group.

INDIANA—FICTION

Ailes, Mark Cusco. The Tree of No Boundaries: Book One. 2009. 196p. 24.95 (978-0-595-63594-8(6)); pap. 14.95 (978-0-595-52834-9(1)) iUniverse, Inc.

Aryal, Aimee. Let's Go Hoosiers! Shrestha, Anuj, illus. 2004. 24p. (J). 19.95 (978-1-932888-32-4(2)) Mascot Bks., Inc.

Baldwin, James. In My Youth. 2010. 568p. pap. 18.95 (978-1-59915-314-8(9)) Yesterday's Classics.

Barnett, Wm. Billy's Wish. Kiste, Tori Lynn, illus. 2008. 28p. pap. 24.95 (978-1-60563-330-5(5)) America Star Bks.

The Bears of Blue River. 2008. 100p. pap. 10.95 (978-1-60459-531-4(0)) Wilder Pubns., Corp.

Benedict, Norma. Grammy Hits the Road. 2009. 40p. pap. 16.99 (978-1-4490-0905-2(0)) AuthorHouse.

Cabot, Meg. Teen Idol. 2005. 291p. (YA). 16.65 (978-0-7569-5735-3(4)) Perfection Learning Corp.

Cohen-Spence, Susan. An Amazing Adventure Back in Time. Scott, Susan, illus. 2013. 32p. pap. 14.99 (978-0-9886360-4-0(2)) Kids At Heart Publishing, LLC.

Cullen, Lynn. Diary of Nelly Vandorn. Date not set. 128p. (gr. 3-18). mass mkt. 4.99 (978-0-06-440926-1(0)) HarperCollins Pubs.

Curtis, Christopher Paul. The Mighty Miss Malone. (ENG.). 320p. (J). (gr. 4-7). 2013. pap. 7.99 (978-0-440-42214-3(0), Yearling) 2012. 15.99 (978-0-385-73491-2(3), Lamb, Wendy Bks.) Random Hse. Children's Bks.

—The Mighty Miss Malone. 2013. lib. bdg. 18.40 (978-0-606-27007-6(8), Turtleback) Turtleback Bks.

Doutrive, Kaleb D. The Funny Chaps. 2012. 24p. pap. 11.00 (978-0-9851574-1-8(0)) Bran Nue Productions.

Doyle, Mary K. Saint Theodora & Her Promise to God. Velikan, Phil, illus. 2013. 34p. 16.99 (978-0-9897397-0-2(8)) Sisters of Providence.

Faces of War. 2004. (Illus.). 210p. per. 10.97 (978-0-9754291-1-2(6)) Booth, John Harvey.

Frost, Helen. Salt: A Story of Friendship in a Time of War. 2013. (ENG.). 160p. (J). (gr. 5-9). 17.99 (978-0-374-36387-1(0), 9780374363871, Farrar, Straus & Giroux (BYR)) Farrar, Straus & Giroux.

Gamble, Adam & Jasper, Mark. Good Night Indiana. 2013. (Good Night Our World Ser.). (ENG., Illus.). 20p. (J). (— 1). bds. 9.95 (978-1-60219-075-7(5)) Good Night Bks.

Garinger, Alan K. Alone: The Journey of the Boy Sims. 2008. (J). 15.95 (978-0-87195-266-0(1)); pap. 7.95 (978-0-87195-267-7(X)) Indiana Historical Society.

Giles, Gail. Right Behind You. 2008. (ENG.). 320p. (J). (gr. 10-17). pap. 10.99 (978-0-316-16637-9(5)) Little, Brown Bks. for Young Readers.

Griffin, Donna. The Twelve Days of Christmas in Indiana. Cummings, Troy, illus. 2014. (Twelve Days of Christmas in America Ser.). (ENG.). 40p. (J). (gr. k). 12.95 (978-1-4549-0888-3(2)) Sterling Publishing Co., Inc.

Guerra, Stephanie. Torn, 0 vols. 2012. (ENG.). 272p. (YA). (gr. 10-12). 17.99 (978-0-7614-6272-9(4), 9780761462729, Amazon Children's Publishing) Amazon Publishing.

Harp, Susan. Evie Goes Clean & Green. Siau, Jon, illus. 2013. 24p. (J). lib. bdg. 14.95 (978-1-938730-09-2(7)) M.T. Publishing Co., Inc.

—Retrieving with Evie. Siau, John, illus. 2007. (ENG.). 24p. (J). lib. bdg. 12.95 (978-1-932439-67-0(6)) M.T. Publishing Co., Inc.

Houts, Michelle. The Beef Princess of Practical County. 2010. (ENG.). 240p. (J). (gr. 3-7). 7.99 (978-0-440-42270-9(1), Yearling) Random Hse. Children's Bks.

Immel, Mary Blair. Giant Steps: Suffragettes & Soldiers. 2016. (J). pap. **(978-0-87195-406-0(0))** Indiana Historical Society.

Jacobs, Lily. The Littlest Bunny in Indiana: An Easter Adventure. Dunn, Robert, illus. 2015. (ENG.). 32p. (J). (-3). 9.99 (978-1-4926-1084-7(4), Sourcebooks Jabberwocky) Sourcebooks, Inc.

James, Eric. A Halloween Scare in Indiana. Le Ray, Marina, illus. 2014. (ENG.). 32p. (J). (-5). 9.99 (978-1-4926-0591-1(3), 9781492605911, Sourcebooks Jabberwocky) Sourcebooks, Inc.

—Santa's Sleigh Is on Its Way to Indiana. Dunn, Robert, illus. 2015. (ENG.). 32p. (J). (-2). 12.99 (978-1-4926-2753-1(4), Sourcebooks Jabberwocky) Sourcebooks, Inc.

Johnson, Virginia. Officer Rick & the Raccoon — a True Story. 2011. 24p. pap. 11.50 (978-1-60976-114-1(6), Eloquent Bks.) Strategic Book Publishing & Rights Agency (SBPRA).

Kimpton, Paul & Kimpton, Ann Kaczkowski. Stepping Up: The Bully in the Band. 2015. (Adventures with Music Ser.: 4). (ENG.). 288p. (J). (gr. 4-7). pap. 8.95 (978-1-62277-141-7(9)) G I A Pubns., Inc.

Kipling, Rudyard. Rikki-Tikki-Tavi. Jones, Chuck, illus. 2006. (ENG.). 32p. (J). (gr. -1-3). 8.95 (978-0-8249-6597-6(3), Ideal Pubns.) Worthy Publishing.

Kjellberg, B. Apple Acres: The Farm. 2006. (J). per. 7.95 (978-0-912868-10-3(4)) Kjellberg, Inc.

Kjellberg Publishers. Courtnee: A Farm Girl, 6 vols., bk. 1. 2nd ed. 2005. (ENG., Illus.). 84p. (J). 7.95 (978-0-912868-06-6(6), Kjellberg Pubs.) Kjellberg, Inc.

—Sandy: A City Girl, 6 bks., bk. 1. 2nd ed. 2005. (ENG., Illus.). 94p. (J). 7.95 (978-0-912868-08-0(2), 8080, Kjellberg Pubs.) Kjellberg, Inc.

Kjellberg Publishing. Abe: A Farm Boy, 6 vols., vol. 1. 2nd l.t. ed. 2006. (Illus.). 96p. (J). 7.95 (978-0-912868-07-3(4), Kjellberg Pubs.) Kjellberg, Inc.

Lambert, Janet. Just Jenifer. 2011. 184p. 42.95 (978-1-258-09133-0(X)) Literary Licensing, LLC.

Lasky, Kathryn. Chasing Orion. 2010. (ENG., Illus.). 368p. (J). (gr. 5-18). 17.99 (978-0-7636-3982-2(6)) Candlewick Pr.

—Christmas after All. 2012. (Dear America Ser.). (ENG.). 192p. (J). (gr. 3-7). 12.99 (978-0-545-38177-2(0)) Scholastic, Inc.

Lewis, Calvin, Jr. & Wilhite, Susan L. It Comes in the Night: Speaking Eagle, Book One. 2006. pap. 9.95 (978-1-934130-03-2(6), 3002) Flood Crest Pr.

Lord, Emery. The Start of Me & You. 2015. (ENG.). 384p. (YA). (gr. 7). 17.99 (978-1-61963-359-9(0), 9781619633599, Bloomsbury USA Childrens) Bloomsbury Publishing USA.

Macenski, Geraldine. Healthy, Happy Gigi! 2009. 28p. pap. 15.99 (978-1-4415-3644-0(2)) Xlibris Corp.

Martin, Rebecca. Blossoms on the Roof. 2015. (Amish Frontier Ser.). (ENG.). 160p. (J). (gr. 2-7). pap. 8.99 (978-0-7369-6367-1(7)) Harvest Hse. Pubs.

May, Sophie. Dotty Dimple Out West. 2005. reprint ed. pap. 22.95 (978-1-4179-8845-7(2)) Kessinger Publishing, LLC.

Mazer, Harry. My Brother Abe: Sally Lincoln's Story. 2009. (ENG.). 208p. (J). (gr. 3-7). pap. 5.99 (978-1-4169-3894-1(X)); 15.99 (978-1-4169-3884-2(2)) Simon & Schuster Bks. For Young Readers. (Simon & Schuster Bks. For Young Readers).

McCormick, Wilfred. Flying Tackle: A Bronc Burnett Story. 2011. 192p. 42.95 (978-1-258-07557-6(1)) Literary Licensing, LLC.

McPherson, Missie & O'Neill, Elizabeth. Alfred Visits Indiana. 2003. (ENG.). 24p. (J). pap. 12.00 (978-0-9771836-0-9(2)) Lipp, G. Douglas & Assocs.

Myers, Byrona. Turn Here for Strawberry Roam. Jauss, Anne Marie, illus. 2011. 134p. 40.95 (978-1-258-08195-9(4)) Literary Licensing, LLC.

Newsome, Richard. The Emerald Casket. Duddle, Jonny, illus. 2011. (Archer Legacy Ser.). 368p. (J). (gr. 3-7). 16.99 (978-0-06-194492-5(0), Waldon Pond Pr.) HarperCollins Pubs.

Niven, Jennifer. All the Bright Places. 2015. (ENG.). 400p. pap. (978-0-14-135703-4(7)) Penguin Bks., Ltd.

—All the Bright Places. (ENG.). (YA). (gr. 9). 2016. 416p. pap. 10.99 (978-0-385-75591-7(0), Ember) 2015. 400p. lib. bdg. 20.99 (978-0-385-75589-4(9), Knopf Bks. for Young Readers) 2015. 400p. 17.99 (978-0-385-75588-7(0), Knopf Bks. for Young Readers) Random Hse. Children's Bks.

—All the Bright Places. 2016. lib. bdg. 22.10 (978-0-606-38876-4(1)) Turtleback Bks.

O'Maley, Elizabeth. By Freedom's Light. 2009. 188p. (J). 15.95 (978-0-87195-273-8(4)); pap. 7.95 (978-0-87195-274-5(2)) Indiana Historical Society.

Parrish, Harry. Kate & Alice. 2009. 28p. pap. 13.40 (978-1-4389-3120-3(4)) AuthorHouse.

Peck, Richard. Here Lies the Librarian. 2007. (ENG.). 160p. (J). (gr. 5-18). 7.99 (978-0-14-240908-4(1), Puffin Books) Penguin Young Readers Group.

—Here Lies the Librarian. 2007. 145p. (J). (gr. 4-7). 14.65 (978-0-7569-8193-8(X)) Perfection Learning Corp.

—Here Lies the Librarian. rev. l.t. ed. 2007. (Thorndike Literacy Bridge Ser.). 173p. (J). (gr. 5-9). 23.95 (978-0-7862-9183-0(4)) Thorndike Pr.

—The Teacher's Funeral. 2006. (ENG.). 224p. (J). (gr. 3-7). reprint ed. 7.99 (978-0-14-240507-9(8), Puffin Books) Penguin Young Readers Group.

Penrose, Margaret. The Motor Girls on Cedar Lake: Or the Hermit of Fern Island. 2007. (ENG.). 156p. pap. 19.99 (978-1-4346-5783-1(3)); 178p. pap. 21.99 (978-1-4346-5784-8(1)) Creative Media Partners, LLC.

Porter, Gene Stratton-. A Girl of the Limberlost. 2011. 266p. pap. 17.99 (978-1-61279-071-8(2)) Publishing in Motion.

Rochea, Vanessa. Kamlyn's Journal, 1 vol. 2009. 48p. pap. 16.95 (978-1-4489-1937-6(1)) America Star Bks.

Rosenberg, Meira. Indiana Bamboo: A Novel. 2017. (J). pap. **(978-1-60454-245-5(4)**, Iris Pr.) Iris Publishing Group, Inc., The.

Runkle, Toni & Webb, Stephen. Glitter Girl. 2013. (ENG.). 256p. (J). (gr. 4-7). pap. 7.99 (978-1-4022-8557-8(4), Sourcebooks Jabberwocky) Sourcebooks, Inc.

Sanders, Scott Russell. Bad Man Ballad. 2004. (Library of Indiana Classics Ser.). (ENG.). 256p. reprint ed. pap. 14.95 (978-0-253-21688-5(5), 0253216885) Indiana Univ. Pr.

Savage, Bridgette Z. Fly Like the Wind. Savage, Charles J., ed. Savage, Bridgette Z., illus. Savage, Charles J., photos by. 2005. (ENG., Illus.). 112p. (YA). (gr. 5). per. 16.99 (978-0-9771494-0-7(4)) Buckbeech Studios.

Silvano, Wendi. Love Is All Around Indiana. Czernichowska, Joanna, illus. 2016. (ENG.). 32p. (J). (-6). 12.99 (978-1-4926-2923-8(5), Sourcebooks Jabberwocky) Sourcebooks, Inc.

Smallman, Steve. Santa Is Coming to Indiana. Dunn, Robert, illus. 2013. (ENG.). 32p. (J). (-3). 9.99 (978-1-4022-8803-6(4), Sourcebooks Jabberwocky) Sourcebooks, Inc.

—Santa Is Coming to Indianapolis. Dunn, Robert, illus. 2015. (ENG.). 32p. (J). (-3). 9.99 (978-1-4926-2636-7(8), Sourcebooks Jabberwocky) Sourcebooks, Inc.

Smith, Jane. Adventure on White High Island. 2006. (YA). per. (978-0-9777074-0-9(7)) Beverly Hills Publishing.

Stratton-Porter, Gene. At the Foot of the Rainbow. 2007. 180p. 18.95 (978-1-934169-52-0(8)); pap. 7.95 (978-1-934169-53-7(6)) Norilana Bks.

—A Daughter of the Land. 2008. pap. (978-1-84830-034-7(4), Wildhern Pr.) Echo Library.

—A Daughter of the Land. 2007. 340p. 22.95 (978-1-934169-46-9(3)); pap. 11.95 (978-1-934169-47-6(1)) Norilana Bks.

—Freckles. (J). reprint ed. lib. bdg. 24.95 (978-0-89190-949-1(4), Rivercity Pr.) Amereon Ltd.

—Freckles. (ENG., 2015. Illus.). (J). 27.95 **(978-1-297-66159-4(1))** 2015. (Illus.). (J). 27.95 **(978-1-297-91217-7(9))** 2007. 248p. pap. 22.99 (978-1-4264-5654-1(9)) Creative Media Partners, LLC.

—Freckles. 2006. 236p. (YA). 19.95 (978-1-934169-32-2(3)); pap. 8.95 (978-1-934169-33-9(1)) Norilana Bks.

—A Girl of the Limberlost. (J). reprint ed. lib. bdg. 33.95 (978-0-89190-948-4(6), Rivercity Pr.) Amereon Ltd.

—A Girl of the Limberlost. Benda, Wladyslaw T., illus. 2005. reprint ed. pap. 38.95 (978-0-7661-9424-3(8)) Kessinger Publishing, LLC.

—A Girl of the Limberlost. 2006. 336p. (YA). 21.95 (978-1-934169-30-8(7)); pap. 10.95 (978-1-934169-31-5(5)) Norilana Bks.

—A Girl of the Limberlost. (Twelve-Point Ser.). 2003. (J). lib. bdg. 25.00 (978-1-58287-232-2(5)) 2004. 463p. 26.00 (978-1-58287-716-7(5)) North Bks.

—The Harvester. 2006. pap. (978-1-4068-3133-7(6)) Echo Library.

—The Strike at Shane's. 2006. 92p. per. (978-1-4067-9583-7(6), Pierides Pr.) Read Bks.

—Wonder, Hope, Love, & Loss: The Selected Novels of Gene Stratton-Porter. 2015. (ENG.). 784p. (gr. 6). pap. 17.99 (978-1-63220-320-5(0), Sky Pony Pr.) Skyhorse Publishing Co., Inc.

Thompson, Emily Weisner & Hussey, Mandy. But What If There's No Chimney? Lampe, Kate, illus. 2016. (ENG.). 24p. 12.00 (978-0-253-02392-6(0)) Indiana Univ. Pr.

Thrasher, Crystal. The Dark Didn't Catch Me. 2004. (Library of Indiana Classics Ser.). (ENG.). 192p. reprint ed. pap. 14.95 (978-0-253-21685-4(0), 0253216850) Indiana Univ. Pr.

Trigiani, Adriana. Viola in Reel Life. (Viola Ser.: 1). (ENG.). (YA). (gr. 8). 2011. 304p. pap. 8.99 (978-0-06-145104-1(5)) 2009. 288p. 17.99 (978-0-06-145102-7(9)) HarperCollins Pubs. (HarperTeen).

Walker, Cheryl. The Little Black & White Pony. 2003. 28p. (J). pap. 2.50 (978-0-9726326-1-4(1)) TechArts International LLC.

Weeks, Sarah. Honey. 2015. (ENG.). 160p. (J). (gr. 4-7). 16.99 (978-0-545-46557-1(5), Scholastic Pr.) Scholastic, Inc.

Wertheim, L. Jon & Moskowitz, Tobias J. The Rookie Bookie. (ENG., Illus.). 272p. (J). (gr. 3-7). 2015. pap. 7.00 (978-0-316-24979-9(3)) 2014. 17.00 (978-0-316-24981-2(5)) Little, Brown Bks. for Young Readers.

INDIANA—HISTORY

Baer, M. Teresa. Indianapolis: A City of Immigrants. 2012. (J). pap. (978-0-87195-299-8(8)) Indiana Historical Society.

Barnes, Kenneth Edward. Life on Pigeon Creek. 2011. 204p. (gr. -1). 24.59 (978-1-4634-0897-8(8)); pap. 15.95 (978-1-4634-0901-2(X)) AuthorHouse.

Bissonette, Aimee. Miss Colfax's Light. Ewen, Eileen Ryan, illus. 2016. (ENG.). 32p. (J). (gr. 1-4). 16.99 (978-1-58536-955-3(1), 204029) Sleeping Bear Pr.

Cameron, Merilee Ann. The Violet-Covered Teacup. 2013. (ENG.). 28p. (J). 14.95 (978-1-4525-7810-1(9), Balboa Pr.) Author Solutions, Inc.

Craats, Rennay. Indiana: The Hoosier State. 2016. (J). (978-1-4896-4857-0(7)) Weigl Pubs., Inc.

Harcourt School Publishers Staff. Horizons: Indiana Edition. 3rd ed. 2003. (Illus.). 69.80 (978-0-15-321348-9(5)) Harcourt Schl. Pubs.

Helweg, Laura. Eastern Great Lakes: Indiana, Michigan, Ohio, Vol. 19. 2015. (Let's Explore the States Ser.). 64p. (J). (gr. 5). 23.95 (978-1-4222-3323-8(5)) Mason Crest.

Hillery, Louise. Bold Women in Indiana History. 2016. (Illus.). 212p. (J). pap. (978-0-87842-655-3(8)) Mountain Pr. Publishing Co., Inc.

Jerome, Kate B. Lucky to Live in Indiana. 2017. (Arcadia Kids Ser.). (ENG., Illus.). 32p. (J). 16.99 **(978-0-7385-2784-0(X))** Arcadia Publishing.

Karcher, Angie. Where the River Grins: The History of Evansville, Indiana. 2012. (ENG., Illus.). 48p. lib. bdg. 17.95 (978-1-934729-99-1(X)) M.T. Publishing Co., Inc.

Ling, Bettina. Indiana. 2009. (From Sea to Shining Sea, Second Ser.). (ENG.). 80p. (J). pap. 7.95 (978-0-531-21129-8(0), Children's Pr.) Scholastic Library Publishing.

Madison, James H., et al. Hoosiers & the American Story: A Student Guide. 2014. (J). (978-0-87195-363-6(3)) Indiana Historical Society.

Marsh, Carole. Exploring Indiana Through Project-Based Learning. 2016. (Indiana Experience Ser.). (ENG.). (J). pap. 9.99 (978-0-635-12338-1(X)) Gallopade International.

—Indiana History Projects: 30 Cool, Activities, Crafts, Experiments & More for Kids to Do to Learn about Your State! 2003. (Indiana Experience Ser.). 32p. (gr. k-5). pap. 5.95 (978-0-635-01783-3(0), Marsh, Carole Bks.) Gallopade International.

—Let's Discover Indiana! 2003. (J). (gr. 2-8). cd-rom 14.95 (978-0-7933-9970-3(X)) Gallopade International.

Mitschelen, Katie. Maumee Lake Plain. 2015. (Illus.). 32p. (J). (978-1-938813-23-8(5)) State Standards Publishing, LLC.

—Northern Moraine & Lake. 2015. (Illus.). 32p. (J). (978-1-938813-24-5(3)) State Standards Publishing, LLC.

—Southern Hills & Lowlands. 2015. (Illus.). 32p. (J). lib. bdg. (978-1-938813-25-2(1)) State Standards Publishing, LLC.

Murray, Julie. Indiana, 1 vol. 2012. (Explore the United States Ser.). (ENG., Illus.). 32p. (J). (gr. 2-5). 28.50 (978-1-61783-352-6(5)) ABDO Publishing Co.

Phipps, Shane. The Carter Journals: Time Travels in Early U.S. History. 2015. (Illus.). xii, 189p. (J). pap. (978-0-87195-364-3(1)) Indiana Historical Society.

Pohlen, Jerome. Oddball Indiana: A Guide to 350 Really Strange Places. 2nd ed. 2017. (Oddball Ser.). (ENG., Illus.). 288p. pap. 16.99 **(978-1-61373-849-8(8))** Chicago Review Pr., Inc.

Ransom, Candice. What's Great about Indiana? 2015. (Our Great States Ser.). (ENG.). 32p. (J). (gr. 2-5). pap. 7.95 (978-1-4677-6095-9(1)); (Illus.). lib. bdg. 26.60 (978-1-4677-3871-2(9)) Lerner Publishing Group. (Lerner Pubns.).

Swanson, Angie. Indiana. 2016. (States Ser.). (ENG., Illus.). 32p. (gr. 3-4). lib. bdg. 27.32 (978-1-5157-0401-0(7)) Next Page Pr., The.

Vescia, Monique & Nicholson, Michael. Mahatma Gandhi: Champion of the Indian Independence Movement. 2017. (J). pap. **(978-1-5383-8083-3(8)**, Rosen Young Adult) Rosen Publishing Group, Inc., The.

Wyner, Zach. Indiana Pacers. 2013. (On the Hardwood Ser.). (ENG., Illus.). 48p. (gr. 3-8). pap. 8.95 (978-1-61570-836-9(7)) Scobre Pr. Corp.

Yasuda, Anita. Indiana: The Hoosier State. 2012. (J). (978-1-61913-347-1(4)); pap. (978-1-61913-348-8(2)) Weigl Pubs., Inc.

INDIANAPOLIS COLTS (FOOTBALL TEAM)

Adamson, Thomas K. The Indianapolis Colts Story. 2016. (NFL Teams Ser.). (ENG., Illus.). 32p. (J). (gr. 3-7). lib. bdg. 26.95 (978-1-62617-368-2(0), Torque Bks.) Bellwether Media.

Burgess, Zack. Meet the Indianapolis Colts. 2016. (Big Picture Sports Ser.). (ENG., Illus.). 24p. (J). (gr. k-3). lib. bdg. 22.60 (978-1-59953-731-3(1)) Norwood Hse. Pr.

Epstein, Brad M. Indianapolis Colts 101. 2010. (ENG., Illus.). 24p. (J). bds. (978-1-60730-113-4(X), 101 Bk.) Michaelson Entertainment.

Frisch, Aaron. Indianapolis Colts. 2011. (Super Bowl Champions Ser.). (J). (gr. 1-3). 24.25 (978-1-60818-019-6(0)) Creative Co., The.

—Indianapolis Colts. 2014. (Illus.). 24p. (J). (978-1-60818-377-7(7), Creative Education) Creative Co., The.

Gilbert, Sara. NFL Today: Indianapolis Colts. 2013. (NFL Today Ser.). (ENG., Illus.). 48p. (J). (gr. 4-7). pap. 12.00 (978-0-89812-858-1(7), Creative Paperbacks) Creative Co., The.

—The Story of the Indianapolis Colts. 2013. (Illus.). 48p. (J). 35.65 (978-1-60818-305-0(X), Creative Education) Creative Co., The.

Glave, Tom. Indianapolis Colts. 2015. (Insider's Guide to Pro Football Ser.). (ENG.). 32p. (J). (gr. k-3). 28.50 (978-1-63143-996-4(0), 208831) Child's World, Inc., The.

Hawkes, Brian. The History of the Indianapolis Colts. 2004. (NFL Today Ser.). (Illus.). 32p. (YA). (gr. 5-9). 18.95 (978-1-58341-299-2(9)) Creative Co., The.

Hoblin, Paul. Andrew Luck: Rising NFL Star, 1 vol. 2013. (Playmakers Set 4 Ser.). (ENG.). 32p. (gr. 2-6). lib. bdg. 27.07 (978-1-61783-702-9(4), SportsZone) ABDO Publishing Co.

MacRae, Sloan. The Indianapolis Colts. 2011. (America's Greatest Teams Ser.). (Illus.). 24p. (J). pap. 8.25 (978-1-4488-2743-5(4)); lib. bdg. 22.60 (978-1-4488-2577-6(6)) Rosen Publishing Group, Inc., The. (PowerKids Pr.).

Omoth, Tyler. The Story of the Indianapolis Colts. 2009. (NFL Today Ser.). 48p. (YA). (gr. 5-9). 22.95 (978-1-58341-758-4(3)) Creative Co., The.

Peloza, Brian. Indianapolis Colts, 1 vol. 2010. (Inside the NFL Ser.). (ENG.). 48p. (YA). (gr. 3-6). lib. bdg. 32.79 (978-1-61714-014-3(7)) ABDO Publishing Co.

Wyner, Zach. Indianapolis Colts. 2014. (Inside the NFL Ser.). (ENG., Illus.). 32p. (J). lib. bdg. 28.55 (978-1-4896-0834-5(6), AV2 by Weigl) Weigl Pubs., Inc.

Zappa, Marcia. Indianapolis Colts, 1 vol. 2014. (NFL's Greatest Teams Set 2 Ser.). (ENG.). 32p. (gr. 2-5). 28.50 (978-1-62403-586-9(8)) ABDO Publishing Co.

INDIANAPOLIS SPEEDWAY RACE

Daniel, P. K. IndyCar Racing, 1 vol. 2014. (Inside the Speedway Ser.). (ENG., Illus.). 48p. (J). (gr. 3-6). lib. bdg. 32.79 (978-1-62403-404-6(7), SportsZone) ABDO Publishing Co.

King, Mike. I Is for Indy. Rodgers, John, illus. 2006. 48p. (J). (gr. 4-18). 18.95 (978-1-891390-21-0(X)) Witness Productions.

Polydoros, Lori. Indy Car Racing, 1 vol. 2013. (Super Speed Ser.). (ENG.). 32p. (gr. 1-2). lib. bdg. 26.65 (978-1-4296-9995-2(7)) Capstone Press of Coughlan Cos.

Riggs, Kate. Indy Cars. 2010. (Now That's Fast! Ser.). 24p. (J). (gr. -1-3). 16.95 (978-1-58341-912-0(8), Creative Education) Creative Co., The.

INDIANS

see also Indians of Central America; Indians of Mexico; Indians of North America; Indians of South America

Ancient Americas. 2016. (Ancient Americas Ser.). 32p. (gr. 5-5). 157.50 (978-1-4994-2246-7(6)); pap. 60.00

(978-1-5081-5245-3(4)) Rosen Publishing Group, Inc., The. (PowerKids Pr.).

Anderson, Michael. Early Civilizations of the Americas. 2011. (J). lib. bdg. 31.70 *(978-1-61530-525-4(4))* Rosen Publishing Group, Inc., The.

Benson, Sonia & Baker, Deborah J. Almanac, Early Civilizations, 2 vols. 2005. (Early Civilizations in the Americas Ser.). (ENG., Illus.). 336p. (J). lib. bdg. 106.00 *(978-0-7876-7679-7(9),* UXL) Cengage Gale.

—Early Civilizations in the, 2.0. 2005. (Early Civilizations in the Americas Ser.). (ENG., Illus.). xii, 551p. (J). 191.00 *(978-0-7876-9252-0(2),* UXL) Cengage Gale.

—Primary Sources, Early Americas, 2 vols. 2005. (Early Civilizations in the Americas Ser.). (ENG., Illus.). 368p. (J). lib. bdg. 106.00 *(978-0-7876-7681-0(0),* UXL) Cengage Gale.

Harrison, David L. Mammoth Bones & Broken Stones: The Mystery of North America's First People. Hilliard, Richard, illus. 2010. (ENG.). 48p. (J). (gr. 4-6). 18.95 *(978-1-59078-561-4(4))* Boyds Mills Pr.

Joseph, Frank. Legends & Lore of Ancient America, 1 vol., 1. 2014. (Discovering Ancient America Ser.). (ENG.). 296p. (YA). (gr. 7-12). lib. bdg. 38.25 *(978-1-4777-2807-9(4))* Rosen Publishing Group, Inc., The.

Nextext Staff, contrib. by. The Ancient Americas: 30,000 B.C.-A.D.1600. 2004. (Stories in History Ser.). (Illus.). 192p. (gr. 6-12). tchr. ed. *(978-0-618-25525-2(7),* 2-00331) Holt McDougal.

Nolan, Frederick W. Native Peoples. 2015. (Wild West Ser.). (Illus.). 64p. (J). (gr. 9-12). 39.95 *(978-1-78404-079-6(7))* Arcturus Publishing GBR. Dist: Black Rabbit Bks.

Randolph, Joanne, ed. Living & Working in the Pre-Columbian Americas. 2017. (Back in Time Ser.). 48p. (J). (gr. 5-6). pap. 11.70 ***(978-0-7660-8977-8(0))***; lib. bdg. 27.93 ***(978-0-7660-8979-2(7))*** Enslow Pubs., Inc.

Ward, Jill. Georgia's First People. 2010. (J). *(978-1-935077-74-9(0))*; pap. *(978-1-935077-81-7(3))* State Standards Publishing, LLC.

Wirkner, Linda. Learning about the Settlement of the Americas with Graphic Organizers. 2006. (Graphic Organizers in Science & Social Studies Ser.). (ENG.). 24p. (gr. 4-6). pap. 8.25 *(978-1-4042-5057-4(3),* Rosen Classroom) Rosen Publishing Group, Inc., The.

INDIANS, TREATMENT OF

Bauman, Amy & Durman, Laura. History. 2010. (CC: Native North Americans Ser.). 112p. (gr. 6-12). 42.80 *(978-1-933834-82-5(X))* Brown Bear Bks.

Blomquist, Katie. American Indians in The 1800s: Right & Resistance (America in The 1800s) 2017. (Primary Source Readers Ser.). (Illus.). 32p. (J). (gr. 4-5). pap. 8.99 ***(978-1-4938-3799-1(0))*** Teacher Created Materials, Inc.

Callery, Sean. The Dark History of America's Old West. 2010. (Dark Histories Ser.). 64p. (gr. 5). 32.79 *(978-1-60870-086-8(0))* Marshall Cavendish Corp.

Ditchfield, Christin. Spanish Missions. 2006. (True Bks.). (Illus.). 48p. (J). (gr. 3-7). pap. 6.95 *(978-0-516-21746-8(1),* Children's Pr.) Scholastic Library Publishing.

Gendell, Megan. The Spanish Missions of Texas. 2010. (True Book(tm), a — Spanish Missions Ser.). (ENG.). 48p. (J). (gr. 2-5). 31.00 *(978-0-531-20580-8(0))*; (Illus.). pap. 6.95 *(978-0-531-21243-1(2))* Scholastic Library Publishing.

Green, Mary. Sarah Winnemucca: The Inspiring Life Story of the Activist & Educator. 2016. (Inspiring Stories Ser.). (ENG., Illus.). 112p. (gr. 5-7). lib. bdg. 35.99 *(978-0-7565-5167-4(6),* CPB Grades 4-8) Compass Point Bks.

Machajewski, Sarah. American Indian Rights Movement. 2016. (Civic Participation: Working for Civil Rights Ser.). 00032p. (J). (gr. 5-5). pap. 10.00 *(978-1-4994-2675-5(5),* PowerKids Pr.) Rosen Publishing Group, Inc., The.

O'Brien, Cynthia. Go West: First Contact with Native Nations. 2016. (ENG.). 32p. (J). *(978-0-7787-2331-8(3))* Crabtree Publishing Co.

O'Maley, Elizabeth. Bones on the Ground. 2014. (J). *(978-0-87195-362-9(5))* Indiana Historical Society.

Stout, Mary A. Native American Boarding Schools, 1 vol. 2012. (Landmarks of the American Mosaic Ser.). (Illus.). 214p. (C). 64.00 *(978-0-313-38676-3(5),* A3118C, Greenwood) ABC-CLIO, LLC.

Waldman, Stuart. We Asked for Nothing. McNally, Tom, illus. 2014. (ENG.). 208p. (J). (gr. 5-7). pap. 8.95 *(978-1-931414-50-0(5),* 9781931414500) Mikaya Pr.

INDIANS OF CANADA

see Indians of North America—Canada

INDIANS OF CENTRAL AMERICA

Coulter, Laurie. Ballplayers & Bonesetters: One Hundred Ancient Aztec & Maya Jobs You Might Have Adored or Abhorred. Newbigging, Martha, illus. 2008. (Jobs in History Ser.). (ENG.). 96p. (J). (gr. 4-7). 25.95 *(978-1-55451-141-9(0),* 9781554511419); pap. 16.95 *(978-1-55451-140-2(2),* 9781554511402) Annick Pr., Ltd. CAN. Dist: Publishers Group West (PGW).

Dawson, Patricia A. First Peoples of the Americas & the European Age of Exploration. 2015. (Exploring the Ancient & Medieval Worlds Ser.). (ENG., Illus.). 160p. (J). (gr. 8-8). lib. bdg. 45.64 *(978-1-5026-0685-3(2))* Cavendish Square Publishing.

Fine, Jil. Mayan Writing in Mesoamerica. 2003. (Writing in the Ancient World Ser.). (Illus.). 24p. (J). lib. bdg. 22.60 *(978-0-8239-6511-3(2),* PowerKids Pr.) Rosen Publishing Group, Inc., The.

Fourstar, Jerome & Blue Talk, Richard. How the Morning & Evening Stars Came to Be: And Other Assiniboine Indian Stories. 2003. (Indian Reading Ser.). (ENG., Illus.). 48p. pap. 9.95 *(978-0-917298-96-7(9))* Montana Historical Society Pr.

Greeley, August. Mayan Writing in Mesoamerica. 2009. (Writing in the Ancient World Ser.). 24p. (gr. 3-3). 42.50 *(978-1-60854-903-0(8),* PowerKids Pr.) Rosen Publishing Group, Inc., The.

Mercer, Abbie. The Totally Gross History of Ancient Mesoamerica, 01 vols., 1. 2016. (Totally Gross History Ser.). (ENG.). 48p. (J). 30.25 *(978-1-4994-3762-1(5))*; pap. 11.75 *(978-1-4994-3760-7(9))* Rosen Publishing Group, Inc., The. (Rosen Central).

Montejo, Victor. Popol Vuh: A Sacred Book of the Maya, 1 vol. Unger, David, tr. from SPA. Garay, Luis, illus. 2009. (ENG.). 88p. (J). (gr. 3-4). pap. 14.95 *(978-0-88899-921-4(6))* Groundwood Bks. CAN. Dist: Publishers Group West (PGW).

Spinden, Herbert Joseph. Ancient Civilizations of Mexico & Central America. 2011. (Native American Ser.). (ENG., Illus.). 270p. pap. 19.95 *(978-0-486-40902-3(3))* Dover Pubns., Inc.

Swanton, John R. Indian Tribes of Mexico, Central America & the West Indies. (Shorey Indian Ser.). 40p. (J). reprint ed. pap. 10.00 *(978-0-8466-0087-9(0),* S87) Shorey's Bookstore.

Woods, Michael & Woods, Mary B. Seven Wonders of Ancient Central & South America. 2008. (Seven Wonders Ser.). (ENG., Illus.). 80p. (gr. 5-8). lib. bdg. 33.26 *(978-0-8225-7570-2(1))* Lerner Publishing Group.

INDIANS OF CENTRAL AMERICA—FICTION

Albert, Burton. Journey of the Nightly Jaguar. Roth, Robert, illus. 2007. (ENG.). 32p. (J). (gr. k-3). 10.99 *(978-1-4169-7092-7(4),* Simon & Schuster/Paula Wiseman Bks.) Simon & Schuster/Paula Wiseman Bks.

Cameron, Ann. Colibrí. 2005. (Readers Circle Ser.). (ENG.). 256p. (YA). (gr. 7). mass mkt. 5.99 *(978-0-440-42052-1(0),* Laurel Leaf) Random Hse. Children's Bks.

Grant, Joan Marshall. Redskin Morning & Other Stories. Lavers, Ralph, illus. 2010. (J). pap. *(978-1-59731-555-5(9))* Perennis, Sophia.

Guzman, Lila. Kichi in Jungle Jeopardy. Johnson, Regan, illus. (J). 2007. (ENG.). 135p. (gr. 2-7). pap. 8.95 *(978-0-9769417-2-9(4))* 2006. 144p. 13.95 *(978-0-9769417-1-2(6))* Blooming Tree Pr.

La Farge, Oliver. Cochise of Arizona. 2014. 222p. pap. 24.95 *(978-0-86534-675-8(5))* Sunstone Pr.

Marshall, Linda Elovitz. Rainbow Weaver/Tejedora del Arcoíris. Chavarri, Elisa, illus. 2016. (ENG & SPA.). 40p. (J). (gr. 1-4). 18.95 *(978-0-89239-374-9(2))* Lee & Low Bks., Inc.

Mikaelsen, Ben. Tree Girl. 2005. (ENG.). 240p. (YA). (gr. 8). pap. 9.99 *(978-0-06-009006-7(5),* HarperTeen) HarperCollins Pubs.

Osborne, Mary Pope. Shadow of the Shark. 2017. (Magic Tree House Merlin Mission Ser.: 25). (ENG., Illus.). 144p. (J). (gr. 2-5). 5.99 ***(978-0-553-51084-3(3),*** Random Hse. Bks. for Young Readers) Random Hse. Children's Bks.

—Shadow of the Shark. Murdocca, Sal, illus. 2015. (Magic Tree House Merlin Mission Ser.: No. 25). (ENG.). 144p. (J). (gr. 2-5). lib. bdg. 15.99 *(978-0-553-51082-9(7),* Random Hse. Bks. for Young Readers) Random Hse. Children's Bks.

Trout, Richard. Eclipse of the Jaguar, 1 vol. 2011. (ENG., Illus.). 224p. (YA). (gr. 8-12). 16.99 *(978-1-58980-872-0(X))* Pelican Publishing Co., Inc.

Voelkel, Jon & Voelkel, Pamela. The River of No Return, Bk. 3. 2012. (Jaguar Stones Ser.: Bk. 3). (ENG.). 352p. (J). (gr. 5). 16.99 *(978-1-60684-073-3(8),* Darby Creek) Lerner Publishing Group.

INDIANS OF CENTRAL AMERICA—MAYAS

see Indians of Mexico—Mayas

INDIANS OF MEXICO

Fine, Jil. Mayan Writing in Mesoamerica. 2003. (Writing in the Ancient World Ser.). (Illus.). 24p. (J). lib. bdg. 22.60 *(978-0-8239-6511-3(2),* PowerKids Pr.) Rosen Publishing Group, Inc., The.

Greeley, August. Mayan Writing in Mesoamerica. 2009. (Writing in the Ancient World Ser.). 24p. (gr. 3-3). 42.50 *(978-1-60854-903-0(8),* PowerKids Pr.) Rosen Publishing Group, Inc., The.

Mercer, Abbie. The Totally Gross History of Ancient Mesoamerica, 01 vols., 1. 2016. (Totally Gross History Ser.). (ENG.). 48p. (J). 30.25 *(978-1-4994-3762-1(5))*; pap. 11.75 *(978-1-4994-3760-7(9))* Rosen Publishing Group, Inc., The. (Rosen Central).

Quezada, Juan. Juan Quezada. Dale, Shelley, illus. 2003. (SPA.). 40p. (J). pap. 9.95 *(978-0-9708617-1-9(0))*; (gr. -1-8). 16.95 *(978-0-9708617-0-2(2))* Norman Bks.

—Juan Quezada. Mlawer, Teresa, tr. Dale, Shelley, illus. 2003. 40p. (J). (gr. k-6). 16.95 *(978-0-9708617-4-0(5))*; pap. 9.95 *(978-0-9708617-5-7(3))* Norman Bks.

Rose, Simon. Zapotecs. 2014. (Illus.). 32p. (J). *(978-1-62127-510-7(8))* Weigl Pubs., Inc.

Stein, R. Conrad. Ancient Mexico. 2011. (Story of Mexico Ser.). (Illus.). 144p. (gr. 7-12). 28.95 *(978-1-59935-161-2(7))* Reynolds, Morgan Inc.

Swanton, John R. Indian Tribes of Mexico, Central America & the West Indies. (Shorey Indian Ser.). 40p. (J). reprint ed. pap. 10.00 *(978-0-8466-0087-9(0),* S87) Shorey's Bookstore.

Williams, Colleen Madonna Flood. The People of Mexico. (Mexico: Beautiful Land, Diverse People Ser.). 64p. (YA). (gr. 7-12). 2009. (Illus.). 21.95 *(978-1-4222-0663-8(7))* 2007. pap. 9.95 *(978-1-4222-0730-7(7))* Mason Crest.

Woods, Mary B. & Woods, Michael. Seven Wonders of Ancient North America. 2008. (Seven Wonders Ser.). (ENG., Illus.). 80p. (gr. 5-8). lib. bdg. 33.26 *(978-0-8225-7572-6(8))* Lerner Publishing Group.

INDIANS OF MEXICO—AZTECS

Anton, Ferdinand. The Secret World of the Aztecs. Wynne, Christopher, ed. Aston, Paul, tr. from GER. 2006. (Illus.). 28p. (J). (gr. 4-8). reprint ed. 17.00 *(978-1-4223-5338-7(9))* DIANE Publishing Co.

Apte, Sunita. The Aztec Empire. (True Book(tm), a — Ancient Civilizations Ser.). (ENG.). 48p. (J). 2009. (gr. 2-5). 31.00 *(978-0-531-25227-7(2))* 2010. (Illus.). (gr. 3-5). pap. 6.95 *(978-0-531-24108-0(4))* Scholastic Library Publishing.

Barghoorn, Linda. Xiuhtezcatl Martinez: Protecting the Environment & Indigenous Rights. 2017. (Illus.). 32p. (J). ***(978-0-7787-3421-5(8))*** Crabtree Publishing Co.

Benchmark Education Company. The Aztec World (Teacher Guide) 2005. *(978-1-4108-4666-2(0))* Benchmark Education Co.

Bezanilla, Clara. A Pocket Dictionary of Aztec & Mayan Gods & Goddesses. 2010. (ENG., Illus.). 48p. (gr. 4-7). 9.95 *(978-1-60606-008-7(2))* Getty Pubns.

Bingham, Jane. Aztec Empire (Freestyle Express) 2014. 22.50 *(978-1-63419-686-4(4))* Perfection Learning Corp.

Bodden, Valerie. Ancient Civilization: Aztec Empire. 2015. (Ancient Civilization Ser.). (ENG.). 48p. (J). (gr. 5-8). pap. 12.00 *(978-0-89812-977-9(X),* Creative Paperbacks) Creative Co., The.

—Aztec Empire. 2014. (J). *(978-1-60818-390-6(4),* Creative Education) Creative Co., The.

—Aztec Warriors. 2015. (Ancient Warriors Ser.). (ENG.). 32p. (J). (gr. 2-5). 28.50 *(978-1-63143-754-0(2),* 208586) Child's World, Inc., The.

Brannon, Barbara. Discover the Aztec. 2005. (J). pap. *(978-1-4108-5147-5(8))* Benchmark Education Co.

Burgan, Michael. Ancient Aztecs. 2012. (Ancient World Ser.). (ENG., Illus.). 112p. (J). pap. 9.95 *(978-0-531-25975-7(7))*; (gr. 6-9). lib. bdg. 34.00 *(978-0-531-25175-1(6))* Scholastic Library Publishing.

Callery, Sean. The Dark History of the Aztec Empire. 2010. (Dark Histories Ser.). 64p. (gr. 5). 32.79 *(978-1-60870-085-1(2))* Marshall Cavendish Corp.

Caper, William. The Aztec: Set Of 6. 2011. (Navigators Ser.). (J). pap. 48.00 net. *(978-1-4108-5099-7(4))* Benchmark Education Co.

—The Aztec: Text Pairs. 2008. (Bridges/Navigators Ser.). (J). (gr. 4). 81.00 *(978-1-4108-8381-0(7))* Benchmark Education Co.

Clarke, Catriona. Aztecs - Internet Referenced (Level 2) 2007. 32p. (J). 4.99 *(978-0-7945-1579-9(7),* Usborne) EDC Publishing.

Clint, Marc. Aztec Warriors. 2011. (History's Greatest Warriors Ser.). (ENG., Illus.). 24p. (J). (gr. 3-7). lib. bdg. 25.95 *(978-1-60014-626-8(0),* Torque Bks.) Bellwether Media.

Cohn, Jessica. The Aztecs. 2012. (Crafts from the Past Ser.). (Illus.). 48p. (J). (gr. 4-6). pap. 14.05 *(978-1-4339-7714-5(1))*; lib. bdg. 31.95 *(978-1-4339-7713-8(3))* Stevens, Gareth Publishing LLLP.

Conklin, Wendy. Mayas, Aztecs, Incas: All-in-One Resource with Background Information, Map Activities, Simulations & Games, & a Read-Aloud Play to Support Comprehension & Critical Thinking in Social Studies. 2006. (ENG., Illus.). 80p. (gr. 5-12). per. 12.99 *(978-0-439-53994-4(3),* Teaching Resources) Scholastic, Inc.

—Mayas, Incas, & Aztecs, 1 vol. 2007. (Primary Source Readers Ser.). (ENG., Illus.). 32p. (J). (gr. 5-5). pap. 8.99 *(978-0-7439-0456-8(7))* Shell Educational Publishing.

—Moctezuma: Aztec Ruler, 1 vol. 2007. (Primary Source Readers Ser.). (ENG.). 32p. (J). (gr. 4-4). pap. 8.99 *(978-0-7439-0457-5(5))* Shell Educational Publishing.

Cooke, Tim. Ancient Aztec: Archaeology Unlocks the Secrets of Mexico's Past. 2007. (National Geographic Investigates Ser.). (ENG., Illus.). 64p. (J). (gr. 5-9). lib. bdg. 27.90 *(978-1-4263-0073-8(5),* National Geographic Children's Bks.) National Geographic Society.

—The Aztecs. 2015. (At Home With... Ser.). (Illus.). 32p. (gr. 5-9). lib. bdg. 31.35 *(978-1-78121-086-4(1),* Brown Bear Bks.) Windmill Bks. Ltd. GBR. Dist: Black Rabbit Bks.

Coulter, Laurie. Ballplayers & Bonesetters: One Hundred Ancient Aztec & Maya Jobs You Might Have Adored or Abhorred. Newbigging, Martha, illus. 2008. (Jobs in History Ser.). (ENG.). 96p. (J). (gr. 4-7). 25.95 *(978-1-55451-141-9(0),* 9781554511419); pap. 16.95 *(978-1-55451-140-2(2),* 9781554511402) Annick Pr., Ltd. CAN. Dist: Publishers Group West (PGW).

Crabtree Staff & Hyde, Natalie. Understanding Mesoamerican Myths. 2012. (ENG., Illus.). 48p. (J). pap. *(978-0-7787-4530-3(9))* Crabtree Publishing Co.

Croy, Anita. Ancient Aztec & Maya. 2010. (Facts at Your Fingertips Ser.). (YA). (gr. 7-12). 35.65 *(978-1-933834-58-0(7))* Brown Bear Books.

—Myths & Legends of Central & South America. 2015. (Illus.). 64p. (J). *(978-0-7166-2628-2(4))* World Bk., Inc.

—Solving the Mysteries of Aztec Cities. 2008. (Digging into History Ser.). 32p. (gr. 4-18). lib. bdg. 29.93 *(978-0-7614-3102-2(0),* Benchmark Bks.) Marshall Cavendish Corp.

Daning, Tom. Mesoamerican Mythology: Quetzalcoatl. 2007. (Jr. Graphic Mythologies Ser.). (ENG., Illus.). 24p. (J). (gr. 2-5). lib. bdg. 25.25 *(978-1-4042-3401-7(2))*; (gr. 3-8). pap. 10.60 *(978-1-4042-2154-3(9),* PowerKids Pr.) Rosen Publishing Group, Inc., The.

—Mitología Mesoamericana: Quetzalcóatl. Obregón, José María, illus. 2009. (Historietas Juveniles: Mitologías (Jr. Graphic Mythologies) Ser.). (SPA.). 24p. (J). (gr. 3-6). lib. bdg. 25.25 *(978-1-4358-8569-1(4))* Rosen Publishing Group, Inc., The.

Daning, Tom & Obregón, José María. Mitología Mesoamericana: Quetzalcóatl. 2009. (Historietas Juveniles: Mitologías (Jr. Graphic Mythologies) Ser.). (Illus.). 24p. (gr. 3-8). pap. 10.60 *(978-1-4358-3332-6(5))* Rosen Publishing Group, Inc., The.

Dawson, Imogen. Food & Feasts with the Aztecs. 2004. (Illus.). 32p. (J). (gr. 4-8). reprint ed. 14.00 *(978-0-7567-7143-0(9))* DIANE Publishing Co.

de Las Casas, Dianne. Blue Frog: The Legend of Chocolate, 1 vol. Stone-Barker, Holly, illus. 2011. (ENG.). 32p. (J). (gr. k-3). 16.99 *(978-1-4556-1459-2(9))* Pelican Publishing Co., Inc.

DeMocker, Michael. Long Ago & Far Away the Aztecs: The Aztecs. 2015. (ENG., Illus.). 32p. (J). 26.50 *(978-1-62469-132-4(3))* Purple Toad Publishing, Inc.

Doeden, Matt. The Aztecs: Life in Tenochtitlan. Hiti, Samuel, illus. 2009. (Life in Ancient Civilizations Ser.). (ENG.). 48p. (gr. 3-6). lib. bdg. 29.27 *(978-0-8225-8684-5(3),* Millbrook Pr.) Lerner Publishing Group.

Dorling Kindersley Publishing Staff. Aztec, Inca & Maya. 2011. (DK Eyewitness Bks.). (ENG.). 72p. (J). (gr. 3-7). 16.99 *(978-0-7566-7320-8(8),* DK Children) Dorling Kindersley Publishing, Inc.

Dwyer, Helen & Stout, Mary. Aztec History & Culture. 2012. (Native American Library). (Illus.). 48p. (J). (gr. 3-6). pap. 14.05 *(978-1-4339-7410-6(X))*; lib. bdg. 31.95 *(978-1-4339-7409-0(6))* Stevens, Gareth Publishing LLLP.

Farndon, John. How to Live Like an Aztec Priest. Aloisi, Giuliano, illus. 2016. (How to Live Like... Ser.). (ENG.). 32p. (J). (gr. 3-6). 26.65 *(978-1-5124-0628-3(7))* Lerner Publishing Group.

Ganeri, Anita. How the Aztecs Lived. 2010. (Life in Ancient Times Ser.). (ENG.). 32p. (J). (gr. 3-6). lib. bdg. 26.60 *(978-1-4339-4097-2(3),* Gareth Stevens Learning Library) Stevens, Gareth Publishing LLLP.

Grant, Neil. Everyday Life of the Aztecs, Incas & Mayans. Cappon, Manuela et al, illus. 2003. (Uncovering History Ser.). 46p. (J). lib. bdg. 28.50 *(978-1-58340-253-5(5))* Black Rabbit Bks.

Green, Carl R. Cortés: Conquering the Powerful Aztec Empire. 2010. (Great Explorers of the World Ser.). (Illus.). 112p. (J). (gr. 7-12). 33.27 *(978-1-59845-099-6(9))* Enslow Pubs., Inc.

Green, Jen. Aztecs. 2009. (Flashback History Ser.). (Illus.). 48p. (YA). (gr. 3-6). lib. bdg. 29.25 *(978-1-4358-5498-7(5))*; (ENG., (J). (gr. 4-6). pap. 11.75 *(978-1-4358-5499-4(3),* PowerKids Pr.) Rosen Publishing Group, Inc., The.

—Hail! Aztecs. 2010. (ENG.). 32p. (J). *(978-0-7787-6625-4(X))*; pap. *(978-0-7787-6632-2(2))* Crabtree Publishing Co.

Greenberg, Imogen. The Aztec Empire. Greenberg, Isabel, illus. 2017. (Discover... Ser.). (ENG.). 32p. (J). (gr. 3-6). 14.99 ***(978-1-84780-950-6(2),*** Frances Lincoln Children's Bks.) Quarto Publishing Group UK GBR. Dist: Hachette Bk. Group.

Haberstroh, Marilyn, et al. Tale of Chocolate. 2014. (Quetzalcóatl Tales Ser.). (ENG., Illus.). 48p. (gr. k-5). pap., tchr. ed. 9.95 *(978-1-60732-322-8(2))* Univ. Pr. of Colorado.

Heinrichs, Ann. The Aztecs. 2011. (Technology of the Ancients Ser.). 64p. (gr. 5). 32.79 *(978-1-60870-765-2(2))* Marshall Cavendish Corp.

Honders, Christine. Ancient Aztec Government. 2016. (Spotlight on the Maya, Aztec, & Inca Civilizations Ser.). (Illus.). 32p. (J). (gr. 6-4). pap. 11.75 *(978-1-4994-1914-6(7),* PowerKids Pr.) Rosen Publishing Group, Inc., The.

Howell, Izzi. Aztecs. 2017. (Explore! Ser.). (ENG., Illus.). 32p. (J). (gr. 4-6). 16.99 *(978-1-5263-0059-1(1),* Wayland) Hachette Children's Group GBR. Dist: Hachette Bk. Group.

Hull, Robert. The Aztec Empire. 2010. (Exploring the Ancient World Ser.). (Illus.). 64p. (YA). (gr. 6-8). lib. bdg. 34.60 *(978-1-4339-4161-0(9),* Gareth Stevens Secondary Library) Stevens, Gareth Publishing LLLP.

Hyde, Natalie. Understanding Mesoamerican Myths. 2012. (ENG.). 48p. (J). *(978-0-7787-4525-9(2))* Crabtree Publishing Co.

Jacob, E. Como Leer un Codice. (SPA., Illus.). 20p. (J). pap. 4.95 *(978-968-24-2354-3(6),* TRM546) Trillas Editorial, S. A. MEX. Dist: Continental Bk. Co., Inc.

Jovinelly, Joann. The Crafts & Culture of the Aztecs. 2009. (Crafts of the Ancient World Ser.). 48p. (gr. 5-8). 58.50 *(978-1-61512-064-2(5),* Rosen Reference) Rosen Publishing Group, Inc., The.

Kenney, Karen Latchana. Ancient Aztecs, 1 vol. 2014. (Ancient Civilizations Ser.). (ENG., Illus.). 112p. (J). (gr. 6-12). lib. bdg. 35.64 *(978-1-62403-535-7(3),* Essential Library) ABDO Publishing Co.

King, David C. Projects about the Ancient Aztecs. 2006. (Hands-On History Ser.). (Illus.). 48p. (gr. 3-7). lib. bdg. 21.95 *(978-0-7614-2256-3(0),* Benchmark Bks.) Marshall Cavendish Corp.

Landau, Elaine. Exploring the World of the Aztecs with Elaine Landau. 2005. (Exploring Ancient Civilizations with Elaine Landau Ser.). (Illus.). 48p. (J). (gr. 4-7). lib. bdg. 23.93 *(978-0-7660-2341-3(9),* Enslow Elementary) Enslow Pubs., Inc.

Lee, Adrienne. Aztec Warriors, 1 vol. 2013. (Legendary Warriors Ser.). (ENG.). 32p. (gr. 1-2). lib. bdg. 26.65 *(978-1-4765-3117-5(X))* Capstone Press of Coughlan Cos.

Linde, Barbara M. Ancient Aztec Geography. 2016. (Spotlight on the Maya, Aztec, & Inca Civilizations Ser.). (Illus.). 32p. (J). (gr. 6-4). pap. 11.75 *(978-1-4994-1909-2(0),* PowerKids Pr.) Rosen Publishing Group, Inc., The.

Long, Erin. Aztec, 01 vols., 1. 2016. (Spotlight on Native Americans Ser.). (ENG., Illus.). 32p. (J). pap. 11.75 *(978-1-5081-4135-8(5),* PowerKids Pr.) Rosen Publishing Group, Inc., The.

Loria, Laura. Malinche: Indigenous Translator for Hernán Cortés in Mexico. 2017. (Women Who Changed History Ser.). 48p. (gr. 10-12). pap. 14.05 ***(978-1-68048-649-0(7),*** Britannica Educational Publishing) Rosen Publishing Group, Inc., The.

MacDonald, Fiona. Aztec & Maya: Rediscover The Lost World Of Ancient Central America, With 450 Exciting Pictures & Is Step-by-Step Projects. 2014. (ENG., Illus.). 64p. (J). (gr. -1-12). pap. 12.99 *(978-1-84322-730-4(4),* Armadillo) Anness Publishing GBR. Dist: National Bk. Network.

—The Aztec & Maya Worlds. 2009. (Passport to the Past Ser.). (Illus.). 64p. (J). (gr. 4-7). lib. bdg. 31.95 *(978-1-4358-5170-2(6))* Rosen Publishing Group, Inc., The.

—Aztecs: Dress, Eat, Write & Play Just Like the Aztecs. 2008. (Hands-on History Ser.). (ENG., Illus.). 32p. (J). (gr. 3-7). pap. *(978-0-7787-4070-4(6))* Crabtree Publishing Co.

Macdonald, Fiona. Do You Want to Be an Aztec Warrior? 2015. (Do You Want to Be... Ser.). (Illus.). 32p. (gr. 3-6). 28.50 *(978-1-909645-32-5(X))* Book Hse. GBR. Dist: Black Rabbit Bks.

MacDonald, Fiona. How to Be an Aztec Warrior. Antram, Dave & Bergin, Mark, illus. 2008. (How to Be Ser.). (ENG.). 32p. (J). (gr. 3-7). pap. 5.95 *(978-1-4263-0168-1(5),* National Geographic Children's Bks.) National Geographic Society.

—How to Be an Aztec Warrior. Bergin, Mark & Antram, David, illus. 2005. (How to Be Ser.). (ENG.). 32p. (J). (gr. 3-7). 14.95 *(978-0-7922-3617-7(3),* National Geographic Children's Bks.) National Geographic Society.

—How to Be an Aztec Warrior. Bergin, Mark & Antram, Dave, illus. 2005. (How to Be Ser.). (ENG.). 32p. (J). (gr. 3-7). lib. bdg. 21.90 *(978-0-7922-3632-0(7),* National Geographic Children's Bks.) National Geographic Society.

Macdonald, Fiona. You Wouldn't Want to Be an Aztec Sacrifice: Gruesome Things You'd Rather Not Know. Antram, David, illus. rev. ed. 2013. (ENG.). (J). 32p. 29.00 *(978-0-531-27104-9(8))*; 40p. pap. 9.95 *(978-0-531-23855-4(5))* Scholastic Library Publishing. (Watts, Franklin).

Mahoney, Emily Jankowski. Ancient Aztec Culture. 2016. (Spotlight on the Maya, Aztec, & Inca Civilizations Ser.). (Illus.). 32p. (J). (gr. 6-4). pap. 11.75 *(978-1-4994-1895-8(7),* PowerKids Pr.) Rosen Publishing Group, Inc., The.

—Ancient Aztec Technology. 2016. (Spotlight on the Maya, Aztec, & Inca Civilizations Ser.). (Illus.). 32p. (J). (gr. 6-4). pap. 11.75 *(978-1-4994-1923-8(6),* PowerKids Pr.) Rosen Publishing Group, Inc., The.

McCullough, Naomi V. The Technology of the Aztecs. 2016. (Ancient Innovations Ser.). 64p. (J). 34.21 *(978-1-5026-2239-6(4))* Cavendish Square Publishing.

McKinley, Herald P. Myths of the Aztecs. 2016. (World Mythologies Ser.). (ENG., Illus.). 96p. (J). (gr. 6-6). lib. bdg.

42.79 *(978-1-5026-0996-0(7))* Cavendish Square Publishing.
Mitchell, Peter. Ancient Maya & Aztec Civilization. 3rd rev. ed. 2007. (Cultural Atlas for Young People Ser.). (Illus.). 96p. (YA). (gr. 5-9). 35.00 *(978-0-8160-6820-3(8))* Facts On File, Inc.
Morris, Ting. Arts & Crafts of the Aztecs & Maya. Young, Emma, illus. 2006. (Arts & Crafts of the Ancient World Ser.). 32p. (J). lib. bdg. 28.50 *(978-1-58340-915-2(7)*, 1262694) Black Rabbit Bks.
Murray, Laura K. Exploring the Aztec Empire. 2018. (ENG.). 32p. (gr. 3-6). ***(978-1-63235-467-9(5)***, 12-Story Library) Pr. Room Editions LLC.
Naden, Corinne J. & Blue, Rose. The Aztecs & Tenochtitlan. 2003. (J). pap. *(978-1-58417-321-2(1))*; lib. bdg. *(978-1-58417-320-5(3))* Lake Street Pubs.
Nardo, Don. Aztec Civilization. 2010. (World History Ser.). (Illus.). 128p. (J). 34.95 *(978-1-4205-0242-8(5)*, Lucent Bks.) Cengage Gale.
—Aztec Mythology. Currie, Stephen, ed. 2014. (Mythology & Culture Worldwide Ser.). (ENG., Illus.). 128p. (gr. 7-10). lib. bdg. 39.40 *(978-1-4205-0922-9(5)*, Lucent Bks.) Cengage Gale.
Niver, Heather Moore. Ancient Aztec Daily Life. 2016. (Spotlight on the Maya, Aztec, & Inca Civilizations Ser.). (Illus.). 32p. (J). (gr. 6-4). pap. 11.75 *(978-1-4994-1900-9(7)*, PowerKids Pr.) Rosen Publishing Group, Inc., The.
Noble, William. The Aztec Empire. 2009. (How'd They Do That? Ser.). (Illus.). 64p. (J). (gr. 4-8). lib. bdg. 33.95 *(978-1-58415-824-0(7))* Mitchell Lane Pubs., Inc.
Orr, Tamra. The Aztecs. 2012. (Explore Ancient Worlds Ser.). (Illus.). 48p. (J). (gr. 3-6). lib. bdg. 29.95 *(978-1-61228-284-8(9))* Mitchell Lane Pubs., Inc.
Powell, Jillian. The Aztecs. 2010. (Gruesome Truth about Ser.). (ENG., Illus.). 32p. (gr. 4-6). 22.60 *(978-1-61533-216-8(2))* Windmill Bks.
Raum, Elizabeth. The Aztec Empire: An Interactive History Adventure, 1 vol. 2012. (You Choose: Historical Eras Ser.). (ENG., 112p. (gr. 3-4). Illus.). pap. 6.95 *(978-1-4296-9474-2(2))*; pap. 41.70 *(978-1-4296-9475-9(0))*; (Illus.). 31.99 *(978-1-4296-4779-3(5))* Capstone Press of Coughlan Cos. (You Choose Bks.).
—What Did the Aztecs Do for Me?, 1 vol. 2010. (Linking the Past & Present Ser.). (ENG.). 32p. (gr. 3-6). 33.32 *(978-1-4329-3744-7(8))*; pap. 8.29 *(978-1-4329-3751-5(0))* Heinemann-Raintree. (Heinemann InfoSearch).
Roxburgh, Ellis. The Aztec Empire. 2015. (Great Empires Ser.). (ENG., Illus.). 48p. (J). (gr. 7-7). lib. bdg. 31.36 *(978-1-5026-0638-9(0))* Cavendish Square Publishing.
Russell, Henry & Cooke, Tim. Ancient Aztec: Archaeology Unlocks the Secrets of Mexico's Past. 2007. (National Geographic Investigates Ser.). (ENG., Illus.). 64p. (J). (gr. 5-18). 17.95 *(978-1-4263-0072-1(7)*, National Geographic Children's Bks.) National Geographic Society.
Santella, Andrew. The Aztec. 2006. (True Bks.). (Illus.). 47p. (gr. 3-5). 16.95 *(978-0-7569-7135-9(7))* Perfection Learning Corp.
—The Aztec. 2003. (True Bks.). (ENG., Illus.). 48p. (J). (gr. 3-5). pap. 6.95 *(978-0-516-26973-3(9)*, Children's Pr.) Scholastic Library Publishing.
Schomp, Virginia. The Aztecs. 2008. (Myths of the World Ser.). 96p. (gr. 6-18). lib. bdg. 34.21 *(978-0-7614-3096-4(2)*, Benchmark Bks.) Marshall Cavendish Corp.
Schulz, Elizabeth. Montezuma II. 2017. (J). ***(978-1-5026-2789-6(2))*** Cavendish Square Publishing.
Smalley, Roger. The Aztecs: Rise & Fall of a Great Empire, 6 vols. 2003. (High Five Reading - Red Ser.). (ENG.). 48p. (gr. 2-3). pap. 54.00 *(978-0-7368-2838-3(9))*; (Illus.). per. 9.00 *(978-0-7368-2828-4(1))* Capstone Press of Coughlan Cos. (High Five Reading (RBL)).
Snedden, Robert. Aztec, Inca & Maya. 2009. (Technology in Times Past Ser.). (J). 32.80 *(978-1-59920-299-0(9))* Black Rabbit Bks.
—Aztec, Inca, & Maya. 2009. (Technology in Times Past Ser.). (Illus.). 46p. (J). (gr. 4-7). pap. *(978-1-897563-64-9(7))* Saunders Bk. Co.
Somervill, Barbara A. Empire of the Aztecs. 2009. (Great Empires of the Past Ser.). (Illus.). 144p. (gr. 6-12). 35.00 *(978-1-60413-149-9(7)*, Chelsea Hse.) Facts On File, Inc.
Spotlight on the Maya, Aztec, & Inca Civilizations. 2016. (Spotlight on the Maya, Aztec, & Inca Civilizations Ser.). 32p. (gr. 6-4). 472.50 *(978-1-4994-1893-4(0)*, PowerKids Pr.) Rosen Publishing Group, Inc., The.
Steele, Philip & Rosso, Norma. History News: the Aztec News. 2009. (History News Ser.). (ENG., Illus.). 32p. (J). (gr. 4-7). pap. 7.99 *(978-0-7636-4200-6(2))* Candlewick Pr.
Stout, Mary A. Aztec. 2003. (Native American Peoples Ser.). (Illus.). 32p. (gr. 3-7). lib. bdg. 26.00 *(978-0-8368-3699-8(5)*, Gareth Stevens Learning Library) Stevens, Gareth Publishing LLLP.
Tieck, Sarah. Aztec, 1 vol. 2014. (Native Americans Set 2 Ser.). (ENG.). 32p. (gr. 2-5). 28.50 *(978-1-62403-576-0(0))* ABDO Publishing Co.
Top That Publishing Staff, ed. Aztec Madness. 2004. (Wicked Tattoos Ser.). (Illus.). 16p. (J). pap. *(978-1-84510-109-1(X))* Top That! Publishing PLC.
Trumbauer, Lisa. The Aztec World. 2005. (J). pap. *(978-1-4108-4618-1(0))* Benchmark Education Co.
West, David. The Aztecs. 2016. (Discovering Ancient Civilizations Ser.). 32p. (gr. 3-3). pap. 10.50 *(978-1-4824-5055-2(0))* Stevens, Gareth Publishing LLLP.
Wiseman, Blaine & Kissock, Heather. Aztecs. 2016. (Illus.). 32p. (J). *(978-1-5105-1094-4(X))* SmartBook Media, Inc.
World Book, Inc Staff, contrib. by. The Aztec. 2009. (J). *(978-0-7166-2133-1(9))* World Bk., Inc.

INDIANS OF MEXICO—AZTECS—FICTION

Blake, Chris. Aztec Attack. 2014. (Time Hunters Ser.: 12). (ENG., Illus.). 176p. (J). 5.99 *(978-0-00-755004-3(9)*, HarperCollins Children's Bks.) HarperCollins Pubs. Ltd. GBR. Dist: HarperCollins Pubs.
Camper, Cathy. Lowriders to the Center of the Earth. 2016. (ENG., Illus.). 128p. (J). (gr. 3-7). 22.99 *(978-1-4521-2343-1(8))* Chronicle Bks. LLC.
Lopez, Victoria. The Little King: An Aztec Tale. 2011. (Illus.). 84p. (YA). 14.95 *(978-1-890379-21-6(2))* Randall, Charles Inc.
O'Dell, Scott. The Seven Serpents Trilogy. 2009. (ENG.). 560p. (J). (gr. 4-6). pap. 19.99 *(978-1-4022-1836-1(2)*, Sourcebooks Jabberwocky) Sourcebooks, Inc.
Robins, Eleanor. The Aztec Ring Mystery. 2006. (Walker High Mysteries Ser.). (Illus.). 48p. (J). per. *(978-1-59905-028-7(5))* Saddleback Educational Publishing, Inc.

INDIANS OF MEXICO—FICTION

Aimard, Gustave. The Indian Scout: a Story of the Aster City. 2006. (ENG.). 464p. per. 37.95 *(978-1-4286-1776-6(0))* Kessinger Publishing, LLC.
Anaya, Rudolfo A. How Chile Came to New Mexico. Nasario, Garcia, tr. from ENG. Nicolas, Otero, illus. 2014. (SPA & ENG.). 48p. (J). (gr. -1-3). 24.95 *(978-1-936744-20-6(1)*, Rio Grande Bks.) LPD Pr.
Bronson, Wilfrid S., illus. Stooping Hawk & Stranded Whale, Sons of Liberty. 2009. 236p. (J). pap. 22.95 *(978-0-86534-715-1(8))* Sunstone Pr.
Crum, Sally. Race to Moonrise Rev. Carlson, Eric S., illus. 2006. 12.95 *(978-1-932738-31-5(2))* Western Reflections Publishing Co.
—Race to the River: The Ancient Journey Continues. 2009. (YA). pap. 12.95 *(978-1-932738-72-8(X))* Western Reflections Publishing Co.
Donploypetch, Jintanan & Montgomery, R. A. Mystery of the Maya. Pornkerd, Vorrarit & Yaweera, Sasiprapa, illus. 2006. (Choose Your Own Adventure Ser.: No. 5). 144p. (J). (gr. 4-8). per. 6.99 *(978-1-933390-05-5(0)*, CHCL05) Chooseco LLC.
MacColl, Michaela. Lost Ones. 2016. (Hidden Histories Ser.). (ENG.). 256p. (J). (gr. 3-7). 17.95 *(978-1-62091-625-4(8)*, Calkins Creek) Boyds Mills Pr.
Mora, Pat, et al. La Hermosa Señora: Nuestra Señora de Guadalupe. Johnson, Steve & Fancher, Lou, illus. 2012. (SPA & ENG.). 40p. (J). (gr. k-3). pap. 8.99 *(978-0-375-86840-5(2)*, Dragonfly Bks.) Random Hse. Children's Bks.
Price, Mara & Ventura, Gabriela Baeza. Grandma's Chocolate/El Chocolate de Abuelita. Fields, Lisa, illus. 2010. (SPA.). 32p. (J). (gr. -1-3). 16.95 *(978-1-55885-587-8(4)*, Piñata Books) Arte Publico Pr.
Ramírez, Antonio. Napí, 1 vol. Domi, illus. 2004. (SPA.). 40p. (J). 15.95 *(978-0-88899-611-4(X))* Groundwood Bks. CAN. Dist: Publishers Group West (PGW).
Scieszka, Jon. Me Oh Maya. McCauley, Adam, illus. 2005. (Time Warp Trio Ser.: 13). (ENG.). 96p. (J). (gr. 2-4). 5.99 *(978-0-14-240300-6(8)*, Puffin Books) Penguin Young Readers Group.
—Me Oh Maya. McCauley, Adam, illus. 2005. (Time Warp Trio Ser.: No. 13). 69p. (gr. 2-6). 15.00 *(978-0-7569-5060-6(0))* Perfection Learning Corp.
Sutton, Laurie S. The Mystery of the Aztec Tomb, 1 vol. Neely, Scott, illus. 2014. (You Choose Stories: Scooby-Doo Ser.). (ENG.). 112p. (gr. 2-3). 32.65 *(978-1-4342-9127-1(8)*, You Choose Bks.) Capstone Press of Coughlan Cos.
Wells, Marcia. Mystery in Mayan Mexico. Calo, Marcos, illus. 2016. (Eddie Red Undercover Ser.: 2). (ENG.). 224p. (J). (gr. 5-7). pap. 7.99 *(978-0-544-66850-8(2)*, HMH Books For Young Readers) Houghton Mifflin Harcourt Publishing Co.

INDIANS OF MEXICO—FOLKLORE

Haberstroh, Marilyn, et al. Tale of Chocolate. 2014. (Quetzalcóatl Tales Ser.). (ENG., Illus.). 48p. (gr. k-5). pap., tchr. ed. 9.95 *(978-1-60732-322-8(2))* Univ. Pr. of Colorado.
Lopez, Victoria. The Little King: An Aztec Tale. 2011. (Illus.). 84p. (YA). 14.95 *(978-1-890379-21-6(2))* Randall, Charles Inc.
Tonatiuh, Duncan. The Princess & the Warrior: A Tale of Two Volcanoes. 2016. (ENG., Illus.). 40p. (J). (gr. 1-4). 16.95 *(978-1-4197-2130-4(5)*, Abrams Bks. for Young Readers) Abrams, Inc.
World Book, Inc Staff, contrib. by. Myths & Legends of Central & South America. 2015. (Illus.). 64p. (J). *(978-0-7166-2625-1(X))* World Bk., Inc.
—Myths & Legends of North America: The Southwestern United States & Mexico. 2015. (Illus.). 64p. (J). *(978-0-7166-2627-5(6))* World Bk., Inc.

INDIANS OF MEXICO—LEGENDS

see Indians of Mexico—Folklore

INDIANS OF MEXICO—MAYAS

Bell-Rehwoldt, Sheri. Maya: Amazing Inventions You Can Build Yourself. Casteel, Tom, illus. 2nd ed. 2011. (Build It Yourself Ser.). (ENG.). 128p. (J). (gr. 3-7). 21.95 *(978-1-936749-61-4(0))*; pap. 15.95 *(978-1-936749-60-7(2))* Open City Bks.
—Maya: Inventos Increibles Que Puedes Construir Tu Mismo. Casteel, Tom, illus. 2011. (Build It Yourself Ser.). (SPA & ENG.). 128p. (J). (gr. 3-7). pap. 15.95 *(978-1-936749-62-1(9))* Open City Bks.
Benchmark Education Company. The Maya World (Teacher Guide) 2005. *(978-1-4108-4680-8(6))* Benchmark Education Co.
Bezanilla, Clara. A Pocket Dictionary of Aztec & Mayan Gods & Goddesses. 2010. (ENG., Illus.). 48p. (gr. 4-7). 9.95 *(978-1-60606-008-7(2))* Getty Pubns.
Brannon, Barbara. Discover the Maya. 2005. (J). pap. *(978-1-4108-5149-9(4))* Benchmark Education Co.
Callery, Sean. The Dark History of the Aztec Empire. 2010. (Dark Histories Ser.). 64p. (gr. 5). 32.79 *(978-1-60870-085-1(2))* Marshall Cavendish Corp.
Conklin, Wendy. Mayas, Aztecs, Incas: All-in-One Resource with Background Information, Map Activities, Simulations & Games, & a Read-Aloud Play to Support Comprehension & Critical Thinking in Social Studies. 2006. (ENG., Illus.). 80p. (gr. 5-12). per. 12.99 *(978-0-439-53994-4(3)*, Teaching Resources) Scholastic, Inc.
—Mayas, Incas, & Aztecs, 1 vol. 2007. (Primary Source Readers Ser.). (ENG., Illus.). 32p. (J). (gr. 5-5). pap. 8.99 *(978-0-7439-0456-8(7))* Shell Educational Publishing.
Cooper, Debbie, illus. Ancient Maya: Cultures of the Caribbean & Central America, 2 bks. l.t. ed. 2005. 32p. (J). per. 9.99 *(978-0-9760406-1-3(1)*, A Kidz World) ABUAA, Inc.
Coulter, Laurie. Ballplayers & Bonesetters: One Hundred Ancient Aztec & Maya Jobs You Might Have Adored or Abhorred. Newbigging, Martha, illus. 2008. (Jobs in History Ser.). (ENG.). 96p. (J). (gr. 4-7). 25.95 *(978-1-55451-141-9(0)*, 9781554511419); pap. 16.95 *(978-1-55451-140-2(2)*, 9781554511402) Annick Pr., Ltd. CAN. Dist: Publishers Group West (PGW).
Coulter, Lavrie. Secrets in Stone: All about Maya Hieroglyphs. English, Sarah Jane, illus. 2003. 48p. (gr. 4-8). 18.00 *(978-0-7567-9000-4(X))* DIANE Publishing Co.
Croy, Anita. Ancient Aztec & Maya. 2010. (Facts at Your Fingertips Ser.). (YA). (gr. 7-12). 35.65 *(978-1-933834-58-0(7))* Brown Bear Books.
Day, Nancy. Your Travel Guide to the Ancient Mayan Civilization. 2005. (Passport to History Ser.). (Illus.). 96p. (gr. 5-8). lib. bdg. 26.50 *(978-0-8225-3077-0(5))* Lerner Publishing Group.
Doeden, Matt. Tools & Treasures of the Ancient Maya. 2014. (Searchlight Books: What Can We Learn from Early Civilizations? Ser.). (ENG., Illus.). 40p. (gr. 3-5). lib. bdg. 27.93 *(978-1-4677-1431-0(3)*, Lerner Pubns.) Lerner Publishing Group.
Dorling Kindersley Publishing Staff. Aztec, Inca & Maya. 2011. (DK Eyewitness Bks.). (ENG.). 72p. (J). (gr. 3-7). 16.99 *(978-0-7566-7320-8(8)*, DK Children) Dorling Kindersley Publishing, Inc.
Edwards, Sue Bradford. Ancient Maya, 1 vol. 2014. (Ancient Civilizations Ser.). (ENG.). 112p. (J). (gr. 6-12). lib. bdg. 35.64 *(978-1-62403-540-1(X)*, Essential Library) ABDO Publishing Co.
Empires of the Maya. 2009. (Great Empires of the Past Ser.). (Illus.). 160p. (gr. 6-12). 35.00 *(978-1-60413-155-0(1)*, Chelsea Hse.) Facts On File, Inc.
Gassós, Dolors. MAYAS. 2006. (SPA.). 32p. (J). (gr. 6-8). 10.40 *(978-84-342-2738-5(X)*, PR33933) Parramon Ediciones S.A. ESP. Dist: Lectorum Pubns., Inc.
George, Charles & George, Linda. Mayan Civilization. 2010. (World History Ser.). (Illus.). 128p. (J). 34.95 *(978-1-4205-0240-4(9)*, Lucent Bks.) Cengage Gale.
Grant, Neil. Everyday Life of the Aztecs, Incas & Mayans. Cappon, Manuela et al, illus. 2003. (Uncovering History Ser.). 46p. (J). lib. bdg. 28.50 *(978-1-58340-253-5(5))* Black Rabbit Bks.
Harvey, Stephanie, et al. Ladders Social Studies 5: the Maya (on-Level) 2014. (Ladders Social Studies). (ENG.). 32p. 8.95 *(978-1-285-34924-4(5))* National Geographic School Publishing, Inc.
Hayes, Amy. Ancient Maya Geography. 2016. (Spotlight on the Maya, Aztec, & Inca Civilizations Ser.). 32p. (J). (gr. 6-4). pap. 11.75 *(978-1-4994-1971-9(6)*, PowerKids Pr.) Rosen Publishing Group, Inc., The.
Hofer, Charles. Ancient Maya Technology. 2016. (Spotlight on the Maya, Aztec, & Inca Civilizations Ser.). (Illus.). 32p. (J). (gr. 6-4). 26.25 *(978-1-4994-1983-2(X)*, PowerKids Pr.) Rosen Publishing Group, Inc., The.
Hoffman, Mary Ann. The History of the Maya: Using Computational Skills in Problem Solving. (Powermath Ser.). 32p. 2009. (ENG., Illus.). (gr. 5-6). pap. 10.00 *(978-1-4042-5148-9(0))* 2009. (gr. 4-5). 47.90 *(978-1-60851-421-2(8))* 2005. (Illus.). (J). (gr. 3-6). lib. bdg. 25.25 *(978-1-4042-2942-6(6))* Rosen Publishing Group, Inc., The. (PowerKids Pr.).
Holm, Kirsten C. Everyday Life in the Maya Civilization. 2012. (Jr. Graphic Ancient Civilizations Ser.). (ENG.). 24p. (J). (gr. 3-6). pap. 10.60 *(978-1-4488-6393-8(7))*; lib. bdg. 25.25 *(978-1-4488-6217-7(5))* Rosen Publishing Group, Inc., The.
Honders, Christine. Ancient Maya Culture. 2016. (Spotlight on the Maya, Aztec, & Inca Civilizations Ser.). (Illus.). 32p. (J). (gr. 6-4). pap. 11.75 *(978-1-4994-1958-0(9)*, PowerKids Pr.) Rosen Publishing Group, Inc., The.
Howell, Izzi. Mayan Civilisation. 2016. (Explore! Ser.). (ENG., Illus.). 32p. (J). (gr. 4-6). 16.99 *(978-1-5263-0018-8(4)*, Wayland) Hachette Children's Group GBR. Dist: Hachette Bk. Group.
Hunter, Nick. Daily Life in the Maya Civilization. 2015. (Daily Life in Ancient Civilizations Ser.). (ENG., Illus.). 48p. (gr. 3-6). pap. 8.99 *(978-1-4846-2581-1(1))* Heinemann-Raintree.
Jolley, Dan. The Hero Twins: Against the Lords of Death. 2009. pap. 52.95 *(978-0-7613-4755-2(0))* Lerner Publishing Group.
—The Hero Twins: Against the Lords of Death: A Mayan Myth. Witt, David, illus. 2008. (Graphic Myths & Legends Ser.). 48p. (J). (gr. 3-7). lib. bdg. 26.60 *(978-0-8225-7495-8(0))* Lerner Publishing Group.
Keppeler, Jill. Ancient Maya Government. 2016. (Spotlight on the Maya, Aztec, & Inca Civilizations Ser.). (Illus.). 32p. (J). (gr. 6-4). pap. 11.75 *(978-1-4994-1976-4(7)*, PowerKids Pr.) Rosen Publishing Group, Inc., The.
Kops, Deborah. Palenque. 2008. (Unearthing Ancient Worlds Ser.). (ENG., Illus.). 80p. (J). (gr. 5-8). lib. bdg. 30.60 *(978-0-8225-7504-7(3))* Lerner Publishing Group.
Kule, Elaine A. Exploring the Ancient Maya. 2018. (ENG.). 32p. (gr. 3-6). ***(978-1-63235-465-5(9)***, 12-Story Library) Pr. Room Editions LLC.
Lechner, Judith. The Maya: Set Of 6. 2011. (Navigators Ser.). (J). pap. 48.00 net. *(978-1-4108-5101-7(X))* Benchmark Education Co.
—The Maya: Text Pairs. 2008. (Bridges/Navigators Ser.). (J). (gr. 4). 89.00 *(978-1-4108-8389-6(2))* Benchmark Education Co.
Levy, Janey. The Ancient Maya Economy. 2016. (Spotlight on the Maya, Aztec, & Inca Civilizations Ser.). (Illus.). 32p. (J). (gr. 6-4). pap. 11.75 *(978-1-4994-1966-5(X)*, PowerKids Pr.) Rosen Publishing Group, Inc., The.
MacDonald, Fiona. Aztec & Maya: Rediscover The Lost World Of Ancient Central America, With 450 Exciting Pictures & Is Step-by-Step Projects. 2014. (ENG., Illus.). 64p. (J). (gr. -1-12). pap. 12.99 *(978-1-84322-730-4(4)*, Armadillo) Anness Publishing GBR. Dist: National Bk. Network.
—The Aztec & Maya Worlds. 2009. (Passport to the Past Ser.). (Illus.). 64p. (J). (gr. 4-7). lib. bdg. 31.95 *(978-1-4358-5170-2(6))* Rosen Publishing Group, Inc., The.
Maloy, Jackie. The Ancient Maya. (True Book(tm), a — Ancient Civilizations Ser.). (ENG.). 48p. (J). 2009. (gr. 2-5). 31.00 *(978-0-531-25229-1(9))* 2010. (Illus.). (gr. 3-5). pap. 6.95 *(978-0-531-24110-3(6))* Scholastic Library Publishing.
Matthews, Rupert. Be a Mayan Soothsayer! Fortunes You'd Rather Not Tell. Antram, David, illus. 2007. (You Wouldn't Want to...: Ancient Civilization Ser.). (ENG.). 32p. (J). (gr. 2-5). 29.00 *(978-0-531-18746-3(2)*, Watts, Franklin) Scholastic Library Publishing.
—Mayan Soothsayer! Fortunes You'D Rather Not Tell. Antram, David, illus. 2007. (You Wouldn't Want to...: Ancient Civilization Ser.). (ENG.). 32p. (J). (gr. 2-5). pap. 9.95 *(978-0-531-13925-7(5)*, Watts, Franklin) Scholastic Library Publishing.
Menchú, Rigoberta & Liano, Dante. The Girl from Chimel, 1 vol. Unger, David, tr. from SPA. Domi, Carlos, illus. 2005. (ENG.). 56p. (J). (gr. 4-7). 18.95 *(978-0-88899-666-4(7))* Groundwood Bks. CAN. Dist: Publishers Group West (PGW).
Mitchell, Peter. Ancient Maya & Aztec Civilization. 3rd rev. ed. 2007. (Cultural Atlas for Young People Ser.). (Illus.). 96p. (YA). (gr. 5-9). 35.00 *(978-0-8160-6820-3(8))* Facts On File, Inc.
Moore, Elizabeth & Couvillon, Alice. How the Gods Created the Finger People, 1 vol. Lopez, Luz-Maria, illus. 2011. (ENG & SPA.). 32p. (J). (gr. k-3). 18.99 *(978-1-58980-889-8(4))* Pelican Publishing Co., Inc.
Mora, Pat. The Night the Moon Fell: A Maya Myth, 1 vol. Domi, Carlos, illus. 2009. (ENG.). 32p. (J). (gr. k-k). pap. 6.95 *(978-0-88899-938-2(0))* Groundwood Bks. CAN. Dist: Publishers Group West (PGW).
—La Noche Que Se Cayó la Luna. Domi, illus. 2009. (SPA.). 32p. (J). (gr. k-k). pap. 6.95 *(978-0-88899-963-4(1))* Groundwood Bks. CAN. Dist: Publishers Group West (PGW).
Morris, Ting. Arts & Crafts of the Aztecs & Maya. Young, Emma, illus. 2006. (Arts & Crafts of the Ancient World Ser.). 32p. (J). lib. bdg. 28.50 *(978-1-58340-915-2(7)*, 1262694) Black Rabbit Bks.
Naden, Corinne J. & Blue, Rose. Ancient Maya & Tikal. 2003. (J). pap. *(978-1-58417-319-9(X))*; lib. bdg. *(978-1-58417-318-2(1))* Lake Street Pubs.
Niver, Heather Moore. Ancient Maya Daily Life. 2016. (Spotlight on the Maya, Aztec, & Inca Civilizations Ser.). (Illus.). 32p. (J). (gr. 6-4). pap. 11.75 *(978-1-4994-1963-4(5)*, PowerKids Pr.) Rosen Publishing Group, Inc., The.
Pipe, Jim. Mysteries of the Mayan Calendar. 2012. (ENG.). 48p. (J). *(978-0-7787-7923-0(8))*; pap. *(978-0-7787-7932-2(7))* Crabtree Publishing Co.
Platt, Richard. The Maya. 2015. (Collins Big Cat Ser.). (ENG., Illus.). 80p. (J). (gr. 5). pap. 9.95 *(978-0-00-812797-8(2))* HarperCollins Pubs. Ltd. GBR. Dist: Independent Pubs. Group.
Scholl, Elizabeth J. The Mayan Civilization. 2009. (How'd They Do That? Ser.). (Illus.). 64p. (J). (gr. 4-8). lib. bdg. 33.95 *(978-1-58415-822-6(0))* Mitchell Lane Pubs., Inc.
Schuman, Michael A. Maya & Aztec Mythology Rocks! Bock, William Sauts, illus. 2011. (Mythology Rocks! Ser.). 128p. (J). (gr. 6-18). lib. bdg. 33.27 *(978-0-7660-3899-8(8))* Enslow Pubs., Inc.
Snedden, Robert. Aztec, Inca & Maya. 2009. (Technology in Times Past Ser.). (J). 32.80 *(978-1-59920-299-0(9))* Black Rabbit Bks.
—Aztec, Inca, & Maya. 2009. (Technology in Times Past Ser.). (Illus.). 46p. (J). (gr. 4-7). pap. *(978-1-897563-64-9(7))* Saunders Bk. Co.
Somervill, Barbara A. Ancient Maya. 2012. (Ancient World Ser.). (ENG.). 112p. (J). pap. 9.95 *(978-0-531-25981-8(1))*; (gr. 6-9). lib. bdg. 34.00 *(978-0-531-25181-2(0))* Scholastic Library Publishing.
Spilsbury, Louise. The Mayans. 2016. (History Hunters Ser.). (ENG.). 32p. (gr. 3-4). lib. bdg. 27.99 *(978-1-5157-2551-0(0)*, Edge Bks.) Capstone Press of Coughlan Cos.
Spotlight on the Maya, Aztec, & Inca Civilizations. 2016. (Spotlight on the Maya, Aztec, & Inca Civilizations Ser.). 32p. (gr. 6-4). 472.50 *(978-1-4994-1893-4(0)*, PowerKids Pr.) Rosen Publishing Group, Inc., The.
Stuckey, Rachel. Ancient Maya Inside Out. 2017. (Ancient Worlds Inside Out Ser.). (ENG.). 32p. (J). ***(978-0-7787-2878-8(1))***; (Illus.). pap. ***(978-0-7787-2892-4(7))*** Crabtree Publishing Co.
Tieck, Sarah. Maya, 1 vol. 2014. (Native Americans Set 2 Ser.). (ENG.). 32p. (gr. 2-5). 28.50 *(978-1-62403-581-4(7))* ABDO Publishing Co.
Torres, John Albert. The Guatemalan Genocide of the Maya People. 2017. (J). ***(978-1-5081-7736-4(8))*** Rosen Publishing Group, Inc., The.
Trumbauer, Lisa. The Maya World. 2005. (J). pap. *(978-1-4108-4632-7(6))* Benchmark Education Co.
VanVoorst, Jennifer Fretland. The Ancient Maya, 1 vol. 2012. (Exploring the Ancient World Ser.). (ENG., Illus.). 48p. (gr. 5-6). 29.32 *(978-0-7565-4564-2(1))* Compass Point Bks.
—The Ancient Maya, 1 vol. 2012. (Exploring the Ancient World Ser.). (ENG., Illus.). 48p. (gr. 5-6). pap. 9.10 *(978-0-7565-4584-0(6))* Compass Point Bks.
Wagner, Heather Lehr. Rigoberta Menchu Tum: Activist for Indigenous Rights in Guatemala. 2007. (Modern Peacemakers Ser.). (Illus.). 114p. (YA). (gr. 9-12). lib. bdg. 30.00 *(978-0-7910-8998-9(3))* Facts On File, Inc.
Where Did the Maya Go? Individual Title Six-Packs. (Action Packs Ser.). 104p. (gr. 3-5). 44.00 *(978-0-7635-8416-0(9))* Rigby Education.
World Book, Inc Staff, contrib. by. The Maya. 2009. (J). *(978-0-7166-2136-2(3))* World Bk., Inc.
—The Mysteries of the Maya. 2014. (J). *(978-0-7166-2663-3(2))* World Bk., Inc.

INDIANS OF MEXICO—MAYAS—ANTIQUITIES

Goldsworthy, Kaite. Chichen Itza. 2014. (Illus.). 24p. (J). *(978-1-62127-461-2(6))* Weigl Pubs., Inc.

INDIANS OF MEXICO—MAYAS—FICTION

Albert, Burton. Journey of the Nightly Jaguar. Roth, Robert, illus. 2007. (ENG.). 32p. (J). (gr. k-3). 10.99 *(978-1-4169-7092-7(4)*, Simon & Schuster/Paula Wiseman Bks.) Simon & Schuster/Paula Wiseman Bks.
Marsden, Carolyn. Starfields. 2011. (ENG., Illus.). 224p. (J). (gr. 5). 15.99 *(978-0-7636-4820-6(5))* Candlewick Pr.
Mystery of the Maya: Choose Your Own Adventure. 2004. per. 5.95 *(978-0-9745356-3-0(X))* Chooseco LLC.
O'Dell, Scott. The Seven Serpents Trilogy. 2009. (ENG.). 560p. (J). (gr. 4-6). pap. 19.99 *(978-1-4022-1836-1(2)*, Sourcebooks Jabberwocky) Sourcebooks, Inc.
Thompson, Susan Conklin, et al, eds. Mayan Folktales: Cuentos Folklóricos Mayas, 1 vol. 2007. (World Folklore Ser.). (SPA & ENG., Illus.). 236p. (C). 40.00 *(978-1-59158-138-3(9)*, LU1389, Libraries Unlimited) ABC-CLIO, LLC.
Voelkel, Jon & Voelkel, Pamela. The River of No Return, Bk. 3. 2012. (Jaguar Stones Ser.: Bk. 3). (ENG.). 352p. (J). (gr. 5).

H
I

16.99 *(978-1-60684-073-3(8)*, Darby Creek) Lerner Publishing Group.

INDIANS OF NORTH AMERICA

see also Cliff Dwellers and Cliff Dwellings; Indians of North America—Canada; Mounds and Mound Builders

Akyroyd, Clarrissa. Native American Horsemanship. Johnson, Troy, ed. 2013. (Native American Life Ser.: 15). 64p. (J). (gr. 5-18). 19.95 *(978-1-4222-2971-2(8))* Mason Crest.

Alarcon, Roben. Sitting Bull, 1 vol. 2005. (Primary Source Readers Ser.). (ENG.). 24p. (J). (gr. 4-4). pap. 8.99 *(978-0-7439-8914-5(7))* Shell Educational Publishing.

Alexander, Richard. Broken Treaties: Native American Migrations, 01 vols., 1. 2016. (Spotlight on Immigration & Migration Ser.). (ENG., Illus.). 24p. (J). pap. 10.00 *(978-1-5081-4056-6(1)*, PowerKids Pr.) Rosen Publishing Group, Inc., The.

Alfrey, Eunice, et al. The Turtle Who Went to War: And Other Sioux Stories. 2003. (Indian Reading Ser.). (ENG., Illus.). 48p. pap. 9.95 *(978-0-917298-95-0(0))* Montana Historical Society Pr.

Alvarez, Juan. Chocolate, Chipmunks, & Canoes: An American Indian Words Coloring Book. Alvarez, Juan, illus. 2004. (ENG., Illus.). 32p. (gr. -1-3). pap. 3.95 *(978-1-878610-03-4(1))* Red Crane Bks., Inc.

American Indians. (J). (gr. -1-12). 2.95 *(978-0-936672-83-0(8))* Aerial Photography Services, Inc.

Anderson, Zachary. Discovering Mission La Purísima Concepción. 2014. (California Missions Ser.). (Illus.). 48p. (J). (gr. 4-6). lib. bdg. 31.36 *(978-1-62713-094-3(2))* Cavendish Square Publishing.

—Discovering Mission Nuestra Señora de la Soledad. 2014. (California Missions Ser.). 48p. (J). (gr. 4-6). 31.36 *(978-1-62713-079-0(9))* Cavendish Square Publishing.

Bailey, Gerry & Foster, Karen. Sitting Bull's Tomahawk. Radford, Karen & Noyes, Leighton, illus. 2008. (Stories of Great People Ser.). (ENG.). 40p. (J). (gr. 3-8). pap. *(978-0-7787-3714-8(4))*; lib. bdg. *(978-0-7787-3692-9(X))* Crabtree Publishing Co.

Baker, Brynn. Navajo Code Talkers: Secret American Indian Heroes of World War II. 2015. (Military Heroes Ser.). (ENG., Illus.). 32p. (gr. 3-4). lib. bdg. 27.32 *(978-1-4914-4837-3(7))* Capstone Press of Coughlan Cos.

Beckett, Leslie. Native American Recipes. 2017. (J). (gr. 3-3). 24p. 27.25 ***(978-1-5345-2094-3(5))***; pap. 63.60 ***(978-1-5345-2093-6(7))***; 24p. pap. 10.60 ***(978-1-5345-2092-9(9))*** Greenhaven Publishing LLC. (KidHaven Publishing).

Benchmark Education Company, LLC Staff, compiled by. Native AMER. 2006. spiral bd. 119.00 *(978-1-4108-7112-1(6))* Benchmark Education Co.

Bennett, Doraine. The Kwakiutl. 2013. (Illus.). 32p. (J). pap. *(978-1-935884-96-5(4))*; lib. bdg. *(978-1-935884-90-3(5))* State Standards Publishing, LLC.

Benoit, Peter. A True Book: American Indians, 12 vols., Set. Incl. Apache. Friedman, Mark. 29.00 *(978-0-531-20769-7(2))*; Cheyenne. Cunningham, Kevin. 31.00 *(978-0-531-20759-8(5))*; Comanche. Cunningham, Kevin. 31.00 *(978-0-531-20770-3(6))*; Inuit. Cunningham, Kevin. 29.00 *(978-0-531-20760-4(9))*; Iroquois. Dolbear, Emily J. 29.00 *(978-0-531-20771-0(4))*; Navajo. Cunningham, Kevin. 31.00 *(978-0-531-20762-8(5))*; Pueblo. Cunningham, Kevin. 29.00 *(978-0-531-20763-5(3))*; Sioux. Cunningham, Kevin. 31.00 *(978-0-531-20768-0(4))*; Timucua. Dolbear, Emily J. 31.00 *(978-0-531-20767-3(6))*; Ute. Cunningham, Kevin. 29.00 *(978-0-531-20765-9(X))*; Wampanoag. Cunningham, Kevin. 29.00 *(978-0-531-20766-6(8))*; Zuni. Cunningham, Kevin. 31.00 *(978-0-531-20761-1(7))*; 48p. (J). (gr. 3-5). 2011. Set lib. bdg. 348.00 *(978-0-531-27625-9(2)*, Children's Pr.) Scholastic Library Publishing.

Bial, Raymond. Lifeways, 4 bks., Group 7. Incl. Cree. 128p. 2006. lib. bdg. *(978-0-7614-1902-0(0))*; Crow. 124p. 2005. lib. bdg. *(978-0-7614-1901-3(2))*; Menominee. 127p. 2006. lib. bdg. *(978-0-7614-1903-7(9))*; (Illus.). (J). (gr. 3-7). 2005. *(978-0-7614-1900-6(4)*, Benchmark Bks.) Marshall Cavendish Corp.

Bishop, Amanda & Kalman, Bobbie. Life of the Navajo. 2003. (Native Nations of North America Ser.). (ENG., Illus.). 32p. (J). (gr. 5). pap. *(978-0-7787-0468-3(8))*; lib. bdg. *(978-0-7787-0376-1(2))* Crabtree Publishing Co.

Bishop, Celeste. Native American Art of the Northwest Coast. 2013. (InfoMax Readers Ser.). (ENG.). 24p. (J). (gr. 3-4). pap. 8.25 *(978-1-4777-2652-5(7))*; pap. 49.50 *(978-1-4777-2653-2(5))* Rosen Publishing Group, Inc., The. (Rosen Classroom).

Bodden, Valerie. Apache: Peoples of North America. 2016. (Peoples of North America Ser.). (ENG.). 48p. (J). (gr. 5-9). pap. 12.00 *(978-1-62832-151-7(2)*, Creative Paperbacks) Creative Co., The.

—Cherokee: Peoples of North America. 2016. (Peoples of North America Ser.). (ENG.). 48p. (J). (gr. 5-9). pap. 12.00 *(978-1-62832-152-4(0)*, Creative Paperbacks) Creative Co., The.

—Navajo: Peoples of North America. 2016. (Peoples of North America Ser.). (ENG.). 48p. (J). (gr. 5-9). pap. 12.00 *(978-1-62832-154-8(7)*, Creative Paperbacks) Creative Co., The.

—Nez Perce: Peoples of North America. 2016. (Peoples of North America Ser.). (ENG.). 48p. (J). (gr. 5-9). pap. 12.00 *(978-1-62832-155-5(5)*, Creative Paperbacks) Creative Co., The.

—Sioux: Peoples of North America. 2016. (Peoples of North America Ser.). (ENG.). 48p. (J). (gr. 5-9). pap. 12.00 *(978-1-62832-156-2(3)*, Creative Paperbacks) Creative Co., The.

Bonvillain, Nancy & Rosier, Paul C. The Zuni. 2011. (History & Culture of Native Americans Ser.). (Illus.). 156p. (gr. 6-12). 35.00 *(978-1-60413-799-6(1)*, Chelsea Hse.) Facts On File, Inc.

Bowman, Donna Janell. The Sioux: The Past & Present of the Dakota, Lakota, & Nakota. 2015. (American Indian Life Ser.). (ENG.). 32p. (gr. 3-4). pap. 7.95 *(978-1-4914-5002-4(9)*, Fact Finders) Capstone Press of Coughlan Cos.

Brown, Robin C. The Crafts of Florida's First People. 2003. (ENG., Illus.). 63p. (J). pap. 9.95 *(978-1-56164-282-3(7))* Pineapple Pr., Inc.

Brown, Virginia Pounds & Owens, Laurella. The World of the Southern Indians: Tribes, Leaders, & Customs from Prehistoric Times to the Present. Glick, Nathan H., illus. 2010. (ENG.). 176p. pap. 19.95 *(978-1-58838-252-8(4)*, NewSouth Bks.) NewSouth, Inc.

Brown, Virginia Pounds & Owens, Laurella, eds. Southern Indian Myths & Legends. Glick, Nathan, illus. 2014. (ENG.). 160p. pap. 19.95 *(978-1-58838-253-5(2)*, NewSouth Bks.) NewSouth, Inc.

Bruchac, Joseph. Many Nations. Goetzl, Robert F., illus. 2004. (ENG.). 32p. (J). (gr. 5-9). pap. 6.99 *(978-0-439-63590-5(X))* Scholastic, Inc.

Buckley, Jeannette. Discovering Mission San Luis Obispo de Tolosa. 2014. (California Missions Ser.). (Illus.). 48p. (J). (gr. 4-6). lib. bdg. 31.36 *(978-1-62713-091-2(8))* Cavendish Square Publishing.

Burgan, Michael. The Arapaho. 2008. (First Americans Ser.). 48p. (gr. 3-7). lib. bdg. 31.36 *(978-0-7614-3017-9(2)*, Benchmark Bks.) Marshall Cavendish Corp.

Cantillo, Oscar. Discovering Mission San Fernando Rey de España. 2014. (California Missions Ser.). 48p. (J). (gr. 4-6). lib. bdg. 31.36 *(978-1-62713-106-3(X))* Cavendish Square Publishing.

—Discovering Mission San Francisco de Asís. 2014. (J). lib. bdg. *(978-1-62713-061-5(6))* Musa Publishing.

Carew-Miller, Anna. Native American Confederacies. Johnson, Troy, ed. 2013. (Native American Life Ser.: 15). 64p. (J). (gr. 5-18). 19.95 *(978-1-4222-2967-5(X))* Mason Crest.

—Native American Cooking. Johnson, Troy, ed. 2013. (Native American Life Ser.: 15). 64p. (J). (gr. 5-18). 19.95 *(978-1-4222-2968-2(8))* Mason Crest.

Carole Marsh. Alabama Indians. 2004. (Alabama Experience Ser.). 36p. (gr. 3-8). pap. 7.95 *(978-0-635-02246-2(X))* Gallopade International.

—Alaska Indians. 2004. (Alaska Experience Ser.). 36p. (gr. 3-8). pap. 7.95 *(978-0-635-02248-6(6))*; lib. bdg. 29.95 *(978-0-635-02249-3(4))* Gallopade International.

—Arizona Indians. 2004. (Arizona Experience Ser.). lib. bdg. 29.95 *(978-0-635-02251-6(6))*; 36p. (gr. 3-8). pap. 7.95 *(978-0-635-02250-9(8))* Gallopade International.

—Arkansas Indians. 2004. (Arkansas Experience Ser.). lib. bdg. 29.95 *(978-0-635-02253-0(2))*; 36p. (gr. 3-8). pap. 7.95 *(978-0-635-02252-3(4))* Gallopade International.

—Big Book of Native American Activities. 2004. (Native American Heri Ser.). 48p. (gr. 2-6). pap. 9.95 *(978-0-635-02397-1(0))* Gallopade International.

—California Indians. 2004. (California Experienc Ser.). 36p. (gr. 3-8). 29.95 *(978-0-635-02255-4(9))* Gallopade International.

—Celebrating Native American Heritage. 2004. (Native American Heri Ser.). 24p. (gr. 3-8). pap. 5.95 *(978-0-635-02399-5(7))* Gallopade International.

—Colorado Indians. 2004. (Colorado Experience Ser.). 36p. (gr. 3-8). 29.95 *(978-0-635-02257-8(5))*; pap. 7.95 *(978-0-635-02256-1(7))* Gallopade International.

—Florida Indians. 2004. (Florida Experience Ser.). lib. bdg. 29.95 *(978-0-635-02263-9(X))*; 36p. (gr. 3-8). pap. 7.95 *(978-0-635-02262-2(1))* Gallopade International.

—Georgia Indians. 2004. (Georgia Experience Ser.). 36p. (gr. 3-8). pap. 7.95 *(978-0-635-02264-6(8))* Gallopade International.

—Hawaii Indians. 2004. (Hawaii Experience Ser.). 36p. (gr. 3-8). pap. 7.95 *(978-0-635-02266-0(4))*; lib. bdg. 29.95 *(978-0-635-02267-7(2))* Gallopade International.

—Idaho Indians. 2004. (Idaho Experience Ser.). 36p. (gr. 3-8). pap. 7.95 *(978-0-635-02268-4(0))*; lib. bdg. 29.95 *(978-0-635-02269-1(9))* Gallopade International.

—Illinois Indians. 2004. (Illinois Experience Ser.). 36p. (gr. 3-8). pap. 7.95 *(978-0-635-02270-7(2))* Gallopade International.

—Indiana Indians. 2004. (Indiana Experience Ser.). 36p. (gr. 3-8). 29.95 *(978-0-635-02273-8(7))*; pap. 7.95 *(978-0-635-02272-1(9))* Gallopade International.

—Iowa Indians. 2004. (Iowa Experience Ser.). 36p. (gr. 3-8). pap. 7.95 *(978-0-635-02274-5(5))*; 29.95 *(978-0-635-02275-2(3))* Gallopade International.

—Kansas Indians. 2004. (Kansas Experience Ser.). 36p. (gr. 3-8). 29.95 *(978-0-635-02277-6(X))*; pap. 7.95 *(978-0-635-02276-9(1))* Gallopade International.

—Kentucky Indians. 2004. (Kentucky Experience Ser.). 36p. (gr. 3-8). pap. 7.95 *(978-0-635-02278-3(8))*; lib. bdg. 29.95 *(978-0-635-02279-0(6))* Gallopade International.

—Louisiana Indians. 2004. (Louisiana Experience Ser.). 36p. (gr. 3-8). pap. 7.95 *(978-0-635-02280-6(X))* Gallopade International.

—Maine Indians. 2004. (Maine Experience Ser.). lib. bdg. 29.95 *(978-0-635-02283-7(4))*; 36p. (gr. 3-8). pap. 7.95 *(978-0-635-02282-0(6))* Gallopade International.

—Maryland Indians. 2004. (Maryland Experience Ser.). lib. bdg. 29.95 *(978-0-635-02285-1(0))*; 36p. (gr. 3-8). pap. 7.95 *(978-0-635-02284-4(2))* Gallopade International.

—Massachusetts Indians. 2004. (Massachusetts Experi Ser.). 36p. (gr. 3-8). 29.95 *(978-0-635-02287-5(7))*; pap. 7.95 *(978-0-635-02286-8(9))* Gallopade International.

—Michigan Indians. 2004. (Michigan Experience Ser.). lib. bdg. 29.95 *(978-0-635-02289-9(3))*; 36p. (gr. 3-8). pap. 7.95 *(978-0-635-02288-2(5))* Gallopade International.

—Minnesota Indians. 2004. (Minnesota Experience Ser.). lib. bdg. 29.95 *(978-0-635-02291-2(5))*; 36p. (gr. 3-8). pap. 7.95 *(978-0-635-02290-5(7))* Gallopade International.

—Mississippi Indians. 2004. (Mississippi Experien Ser.). 36p. (gr. 3-8). pap. 7.95 *(978-0-635-02292-9(3))*; lib. bdg. 29.95 *(978-0-635-02293-6(1))* Gallopade International.

—Missouri Indians. 2004. (Missouri Experience Ser.). 36p. (gr. 3-8). pap. 7.95 *(978-0-635-02294-3(X))* Gallopade International.

—Montana Indians. 2004. (Montana Experience Ser.). 36p. (gr. 3-8). pap. 7.95 *(978-0-635-02296-7(6))*; lib. bdg. 29.95 *(978-0-635-02297-4(4))* Gallopade International.

—Nebraska Indians. 2004. (Nebraska Experience Ser.). 36p. (gr. 3-8). pap. 7.95 *(978-0-635-02298-1(2))*; lib. bdg. 29.95 *(978-0-635-02299-8(0))* Gallopade International.

—Nevada Indians. 2004. (Nevada Experience Ser.). 36p. (gr. 3-8). pap. 7.95 *(978-0-635-02300-1(8))*; lib. bdg. 29.95 *(978-0-635-02301-8(6))* Gallopade International.

—New Hampshire Indians. 2004. (New Hampshire Experi Ser.). lib. bdg. 29.95 *(978-0-635-02303-2(2))*; 36p. (gr. 3-8). pap. 7.95 *(978-0-635-02302-5(4))* Gallopade International.

—New Jersey Indians. 2004. (New Jersey Experienc Ser.). 36p. (gr. 3-8). 29.95 *(978-0-635-02305-6(9))*; pap. 7.95 *(978-0-635-02304-9(0))* Gallopade International.

—New Mexico Indians. 2004. (New Mexico Experienc Ser.). 36p. (gr. 3-8). pap. 7.95 *(978-0-635-02306-3(7))*; lib. bdg. 29.95 *(978-0-635-02307-0(5))* Gallopade International.

—New York Indians. 2004. (New York Experience Ser.). lib. bdg. 29.95 *(978-0-635-02309-4(1))*; 36p. (gr. 3-8). pap. 7.95 *(978-0-635-02308-7(3))* Gallopade International.

—North Carolina Indians. 2004. (North Carolina Exper Ser.). 36p. (gr. 3-8). 29.95 *(978-0-635-02311-7(3))*; pap. 7.95 *(978-0-635-02310-0(5))* Gallopade International.

—North Dakota Indians. 2004. (North Dakota Experie Ser.). 36p. (gr. 3-8). pap. 7.95 *(978-0-635-02312-4(1))*; lib. bdg. 29.95 *(978-0-635-02313-1(X))* Gallopade International.

—Ohio Indians. 2004. (Ohio Experience Ser.). 36p. (gr. 3-8). pap. 7.95 *(978-0-635-02314-8(8))* Gallopade International.

—Oklahoma Indians. 2004. (Oklahoma Experience Ser.). 36p. (gr. 3-8). 29.95 *(978-0-635-02317-9(2))*; pap. 7.95 *(978-0-635-02316-2(4))* Gallopade International.

—Oregon Indians. 2004. (Oregon Experience Ser.). lib. bdg. 29.95 *(978-0-635-02319-3(9))*; 36p. (gr. 3-8). pap. 7.95 *(978-0-635-02318-6(0))* Gallopade International.

—Pennsylvania Indians. 2004. (Pennsylvania Experie Ser.). 36p. (gr. 3-8). 29.95 *(978-0-635-02321-6(0))*; pap. 7.95 *(978-0-635-02320-9(2))* Gallopade International.

—Rhode Island Indians. 2004. (Rhode Island Experie Ser.). 36p. (gr. 3-8). pap. 7.95 *(978-0-635-02322-3(9))*; lib. bdg. 29.95 *(978-0-635-02323-0(7))* Gallopade International.

—South Carolina Indians. 2004. (South Carolina Exper Ser.). 36p. (gr. 3-8). 29.95 *(978-0-635-02325-4(3))*; pap. 7.95 *(978-0-635-02324-7(5))* Gallopade International.

—South Dakota Indians. 2004. (South Dakota Experie Ser.). 36p. (gr. 3-8). pap. 7.95 *(978-0-635-02326-1(1))*; 29.95 *(978-0-635-02327-8(X))* Gallopade International.

—Tennessee Indians. 2004. (Tennessee Experience Ser.). 36p. (gr. 3-8). pap. 7.95 *(978-0-635-02328-5(8))*; lib. bdg. 29.95 *(978-0-635-02329-2(6))* Gallopade International.

—Texas Indians. 2004. (Texas Experience Ser.). 36p. (gr. 3-8). pap. 7.95 *(978-0-635-02330-8(X))* Gallopade International.

Charleyboy, Lisa. Urban Tribes: Native Americans in the City. Leatherdale, Mary Beth, ed. 2015. (ENG., Illus.). 136p. (YA). (gr. 6-12). pap. 14.95 *(978-1-55451-750-3(8)*, 9781554517503) Annick Pr., Ltd. CAN. Dist: Publishers Group West (PGW).

Cherrington, Janelle. Native American Baskets, 6 vols., Set. 2003. (Phonics Readers 1-36 Ser.). (ENG.). 8p. (gr. k-1). pap. 29.70 *(978-0-7368-3220-5(3)*, Phonics Readers) Capstone Press of Coughlan Cos.

Ching, Jacqueline. Mission San Rafael Arcangel. 2003. (Missions of California Ser.). 64p. (J). 26.50 *(978-0-8239-5886-3(8)*, PowerKids Pr.) Rosen Publishing Group, Inc., The.

Ching, Jacqueline & Connelly, Jack. Discovering Mission San Rafael Arcángel. 2014. (California Missions Ser.). (Illus.). 48p. (J). (gr. 4-6). lib. bdg. 31.36 *(978-1-62713-058-5(6))* Cavendish Square Publishing.

Coates, Julia. Trail of Tears, 1 vol. 2014. (Landmarks of the American Mosaic Ser.). (Illus.). 235p. (C). 58.00 *(978-0-313-38448-6(7)*, A2916C, Greenwood) ABC-CLIO, LLC.

Collard, Sneed B., III. Sitting Bull: Tatanka-Iyotake. 2009. (American Heroes Ser.). 48p. (gr. 3-18). 29.93 *(978-0-7614-4059-8(3))* Marshall Cavendish Corp.

Corrigan, Jim. Europeans & Native Americans. Johnson, Troy, ed. 2013. (Native American Life Ser.: 15). 64p. (J). (gr. 5-18). 19.95 *(978-1-4222-2964-4(5))* Mason Crest.

Crompton, Samuel. Native American Cultures of Georgia. 2017. (Spotlight on Georgia Ser.). 32p. (gr. 9-10). 26.25 ***(978-1-5081-6029-8(5)***, PowerKids Pr.) Rosen Publishing Group, Inc., The.

Cunningham, Kevin & Benoit, Peter. The Zuni. 2011. (True Book(tm), a — American Indians Ser.). 48p. (J). (gr. 3-5). 31.00 *(978-0-531-20761-1(7))*; pap. 6.95 *(978-0-531-29303-4(3))* Scholastic Library Publishing. (Children's Pr.).

Dalton, Anne. The Lenape of Pennsylvania, New Jersey, New York, Delaware, Wisconsin, Oklahoma, & Ontario. 2005. (Library of Native Americans). (Illus.). 64p. (J). (gr. k-5). lib. bdg. 26.50 *(978-1-4042-2872-6(1)*, PowerKids Pr.) Rosen Publishing Group, Inc., The.

Davies, Gill. Native America 900 BC - the Present. Aronson, Marc, ed. 2005. (National Geographic Timelines Ser.). (Illus.). 64p. (J). 17.95 *(978-0-7922-6456-9(8))*; 27.90 *(978-0-7922-7078-2(9))* CENGAGE Learning.

Davis, Kenneth C. Don't Know Much about the Pioneers & Indians. 48p. (J). Date not set. (gr. 1-4). pap. 5.99 *(978-0-06-446232-7(3))* 2003. (Picture Bks.: No. 6). (Illus.). (gr. -1-1). 16.89 *(978-0-06-028618-7(0))* HarperCollins Pubs.

Davis, Lucile. The Caddo of Texas. (Library of Native Americans Ser.). 64p. 2009. (gr. 4-4). 58.50 *(978-1-60853-743-3(9)*, PowerKids Pr.) 2003. (Illus.). (YA). (gr. 3-6). lib. bdg. 26.50 *(978-0-8239-6435-2(3))* Rosen Publishing Group, Inc., The.

Dawson, Patricia A. First Peoples of the Americas & the European Age of Exploration. 2015. (Exploring the Ancient & Medieval Worlds Ser.). (ENG., Illus.). 160p. (J). (gr. 8-8). lib. bdg. 45.64 *(978-1-5026-0685-3(2))* Cavendish Square Publishing.

De Capua, Sarah. The Menominee. 2009. (First Americans 5 Ser.). 48p. (gr. 3). 31.36 *(978-0-7614-4131-1(X))* Marshall Cavendish Corp.

—The Shoshone. 2007. (First Americans Ser.). (Illus.). 48p. (J). (gr. 4-7). lib. bdg. 31.36 *(978-0-7614-2683-7(3)*, Benchmark Bks.) Marshall Cavendish Corp.

—The Tlingit. 2009. (First Americans 5 Ser.). 48p. (gr. 3). 31.36 *(978-0-7614-4135-9(2))* Marshall Cavendish Corp.

DeKeyser, Stacy. The Wampanoag. 2005. (Watts Library). (ENG., Illus.). 64p. (J). (gr. 5-7). 25.50 *(978-0-531-12298-3(0))* Scholastic Library Publishing.

Dimartino, Catherine. Early American Alliances. 2005. (ENG., Illus.). 16p. (J). (gr. 5-5). pap. 7.47 net. *(978-0-328-14893-6(8)*, Scott Foresman) Pearson Schl.

Dinsdale, Christopher. Betrayed: The Legend of Oak Island. 2009. (Stories of Canada Ser.). (ENG., Illus.). 304p. (J). (gr. 6-8). pap. 10.95 *(978-1-894917-91-9(X)*, Napoleon & Co.) Dundurn CAN. Dist: Ingram Publisher Services.

Ditchfield, Christin. Northeast Indians, 1 vol. 2011. (First Nations of North America Ser.). (ENG.). 48p. (J). (gr. 3-3). pap. 9.95 *(978-1-4329-4959-4(4))*; 33.32 *(978-1-4329-4948-8(9))* Heinemann-Raintree. (Heinemann InfoSearch).

Doherty, Craig A. Northwest Coast Indians. Facts on File, Inc. Staff, ed. 2010. (Native America Ser.). 136p. (J). (gr. 5-8). 35.00 *(978-0-8160-5977-5(2))* Facts On File, Inc.

—Subarctic Peoples. Facts on File, Inc. Staff, ed. 2010. (Native America Ser.). (Illus.). 136p. (J). (gr. 5-8). 35.00 *(978-0-8160-5978-2(0))* Facts On File, Inc.

Dolbear, Emily J. & Benoit, Peter. The Timucua. 2011. (True Book(tm), a — American Indians Ser.). 48p. (J). (gr. 3-5). 31.00 *(978-0-531-20767-3(6))*; pap. 6.95 *(978-0-531-29309-6(2))* Scholastic Library Publishing. (Children's Pr.).

Dorling Kindersley Publishing Staff & Murdoch, David S. North American Indian. 2005. (DK Eyewitness Bks.). (ENG.). 72p. (J). (gr. 3-7). 16.99 *(978-0-7566-1081-4(8)*, DK Children) Dorling Kindersley Publishing, Inc.

Draper, Allison Stark. Mission San Francisco de Solano. 2003. (Missions of Californiatm Ser.). (Illus.). 64p. (J). (gr. 4-18). 26.50 *(978-0-8239-5884-9(1))* Rosen Publishing Group, Inc., The.

Edgar, Kathleen J. & Edgar, Susan E. Mission San Carlos Borromeo Del Rio Carmelo. 2003. (Missions of Californiatm Ser.). (Illus.). 64p. (YA). (gr. 4-7). 26.50 *(978-0-8239-5890-0(6))* Rosen Publishing Group, Inc., The.

—Mission San Francisco de Asis. 2003. (Missions of Californiatm Ser.). (Illus.). 64p. (J). (gr. 4-18). 26.50 *(978-0-8239-5887-0(6))* Rosen Publishing Group, Inc., The.

Edgar, Kathleen J., et al. Discovering Mission San Miguel Arcángel. 2014. (California Missions Ser.). 48p. (J). (gr. 4-6). lib. bdg. 31.36 *(978-1-62713-088-2(8))* Cavendish Square Publishing.

Edwards, Laurie J., et al. U*X*L Encyclopedia of Native American Tribes, 5 vols. 3rd ed. 2012. (J). *(978-1-4144-9096-0(8))*; *(978-1-4144-9095-3(X))*; *(978-1-4144-9094-6(1))*; *(978-1-4144-9097-7(6))*; *(978-1-4144-9093-9(3))* Cengage Gale. (UXL).

First North Americans Kid Kit. 2003. (Illus.). 32p. 14.95 *(978-1-58086-532-6(1))*; 15.95 *(978-1-58086-533-3(X))* EDC Publishing.

Flood, Nancy Bo. The Navajo Year, Walk Through Many Seasons: Activities for Learning & Exploring. Ruffenach, Jessie E., ed. Whitethorne, Billy & Whitethorne, Bahe, Jr., illus. 2006. (ENG.). 48p. (J). (gr. 4-7). pap. 7.95 *(978-1-893354-98-2(9))* Salina Bookshelf Inc.

Fourstar, Jerome & Blue Talk, Richard. How the Morning & Evening Stars Came to Be: And Other Assiniboine Indian Stories. 2003. (Indian Reading Ser.). (ENG., Illus.). 48p. pap. 9.95 *(978-0-917298-96-7(9))* Montana Historical Society Pr.

Fourstar, Jerome, et al. How the Summer Season Came: And Other Assiniboine Indian Stories. 2003. (Indian Reading Ser.). (ENG., Illus.). 104p. pap. 9.95 *(978-0-917298-94-3(2))* Montana Historical Society Pr.

Gachot, Lynn. June-Ah-Vee's Blessing. 2010. 24p. 14.50 *(978-1-4520-7747-5(9))* AuthorHouse.

Gale. U-X-L Encyclopedia of Native American Tribes, 5 vols. 3rd ed. 2012. (U-X-L Encyclopedia of Native American Tribes Ser.). (ENG., Illus.). 1200p. lib. bdg. 458.00 *(978-1-4144-9092-2(5)*, UXL) Cengage Gale.

Gendell, Megan. Spanish Missions of California. 2010. (True Book(tm), a — Spanish Missions Ser.). (Illus.). 48p. (J). (gr. 2-5). 31.00 *(978-0-531-20577-8(0))* Scholastic Library Publishing.

—The Spanish Missions of California. 2010. (True Book Ser.). (ENG.). 48p. (J). (gr. 3-5). pap. 6.95 *(978-0-531-21240-0(8)*, Children's Pr.) Scholastic Library Publishing.

—The Spanish Missions of Texas. 2010. (True Book(tm), a — Spanish Missions Ser.). (ENG.). 48p. (J). (gr. 2-5). 31.00 *(978-0-531-20580-8(0))*; (Illus.). pap. 6.95 *(978-0-531-21243-1(2))* Scholastic Library Publishing.

George, Lynn. Calendars of Native Americans: Timekeeping Methods of Ancient North America. 2009. (PowerMath Ser.). (ENG., Illus.). 32p. (gr. 4-5). pap. 10.00 *(978-0-8239-8918-6(6)*, PowerKids Pr.) Rosen Publishing Group, Inc., The.

Glatzer, Jenna. Native American Festivals & Ceremonies. Johnson, Troy, ed. 2013. (Native American Life Ser.: 15). 64p. (J). (gr. 5-18). 19.95 *(978-1-4222-2970-5(X))* Mason Crest.

Goddu, Krystyna Poray. Native Peoples of the Great Basin. 2016. (North American Indian Nations Ser.). (ENG., Illus.). 48p. (J). (gr. 3-5). 33.32 *(978-1-4677-8310-1(2))* Lerner Publishing Group.

—Native Peoples of the Northwest. 2016. (North American Indian Nations Ser.). (ENG., Illus.). 48p. (J). (gr. 3-5). 33.32 *(978-1-4677-7939-5(3))* Lerner Publishing Group.

—Native Peoples of the Plateau. 2016. (North American Indian Nations Ser.). (ENG., Illus.). 48p. (J). (gr. 3-5). lib. bdg. 33.32 *(978-1-4677-8309-5(9))* Lerner Publishing Group.

Goldstein, Margaret J. You Are Now on Indian Land: The American Indian Occupation of Alcatraz Island, California, 1969. 2011. (Civil Rights Struggles around the World Ser.). (ENG.). 160p. (gr. 9-12). lib. bdg. 38.60 *(978-0-7613-5769-8(6))* Lerner Publishing Group.

Gonzalez, Catherine Troxell. Cynthia Ann Parker: Indian Captive. 2005. (Illus.). 78p. (J). pap. 9.95 *(978-1-940130-37-8(9))* Eakin Pr.

Gray-Kanatiiosh, Barbara A. Modoc, 1 vol. 2007. (Native Americans Set 4 Ser.). (ENG., Illus.). 32p. (gr. -1-3). 27.07 *(978-1-59197-656-1(1)*, Checkerboard Library) ABDO Publishing Co.

Greathouse, Lisa E. California's Spanish Missions. 2017. (Primary Source Readers Ser.). (Illus.). 32p. (gr. 4-4). 9.99 ***(978-1-4258-3234-6(2))*** Teacher Created Materials, Inc.

Green, Rayna & Fernandez, Melanie. The Encyclopedia of the First Peoples of North America. 35.00 *(978-0-88899-380-9(3))* Groundwood Bks. CAN. Dist: Publishers Group West (PGW).

Griggs, Howard. The Native American Mound Builders. 2013. (InfoMax Readers Ser.). (ENG.). 24p. (J). (gr. 3-4). pap. 49.50 *(978-1-4777-2659-4(4))*; pap. 8.25 *(978-1-4777-2658-7(6))* Rosen Publishing Group, Inc., The. (Rosen Classroom).

Gutner, Howard. America's Secret Weapon: The Navajo Code Talkers of World War II. 2003. (ENG., Illus.). 32p. (J). (gr.

6-8). pap. 7.97 net. *(978-0-7652-3266-3(9)*, Celebration Pr.) Pearson Schl.

Hamilton, Sam. Discovering Mission San Buenaventura. 2014. (California Missions Ser.). 48p. (J). (gr. 4-6). lib. bdg. 31.36 *(978-1-62713-103-2(5))* Cavendish Square Publishing.

—Discovering Mission San Diego de Alcalá. 2014. (California Missions Ser.). 48p. (J). (gr. 4-6). lib. bdg. 31.36 *(978-1-62713-109-4(4))* Cavendish Square Publishing.

Hansen-Krening, Nancy, et al, eds. Kaleidoscope: A Multicultural Booklist for Grades K-8. 4th ed. 2003. (NCTE Bibliography Ser.). (Illus.). 118p. (J). pap. 30.95 *(978-0-8141-2539-7(5)*, 25395) National Council of Teachers of English.

Hayes, Amy. Native Peoples of the Southwest. 2016. (Native Peoples of North America Ser.). (Illus.). 32p. (J). (gr. 3-2). 25.25 *(978-1-4824-4820-7(3))* Stevens, Gareth Publishing LLLP.

Helbrough, Emma. A Day in the Life of a Native American. 2009. (Day in the Life Ser.). 32p. (gr. 4-5). 47.90 *(978-1-61511-005-6(4)*, PowerKids Pr.) Rosen Publishing Group, Inc., The.

Hicks, Terry Allan. The Mandan. 2009. (First Americans 5 Ser.). 48p. (gr. 3). 31.36 *(978-0-7614-4130-4(1))* Marshall Cavendish Corp.

—The Zuni. 2009. (First Americans 5 Ser.). 48p. (gr. 3). 31.36 *(978-0-7614-4137-3(9))* Marshall Cavendish Corp.

Higgins, Nadia. Spanish Missions of the Old West. 2006. (Events in American History Ser.). (Illus.). 48p. (YA). (gr. 3-6). lib. bdg. 31.36 *(978-1-60044-128-8(9))* Rourke Educational Media.

Hughes, Michael A., ed. Indian War's Civil War. 2006. (Journal of the Indian Wars Ser.: Vol. 1, No. 3). (ENG., Illus.). 188p. pap. 12.99 *(978-1-882810-81-9(3))* Savas Beatie.

James, Lincoln. Native American Homes. 2009. (Real Life Readers Ser.). 24p. (gr. 3-4). pap. 8.25 *(978-1-4358-0127-1(X)*, Rosen Classroom) Rosen Publishing Group, Inc., The.

James, Soloman & Salt, Allan. Little Book of Animals. 2010. (OJI & ENG., Illus.). 43p. *(978-0-9745168-6-8(4))* Cotsen Occasional Pr.

Jenner, Caryn. Pocahontas, Level 2. 2009. (DK Readers Ser.). (ENG.). 32p. (J). (gr. 1-3). 3.99 *(978-0-7566-5611-9(7)*, DK Children) Dorling Kindersley Publishing, Inc.

Johnson, Michael. Native Tribes of North America, 6 bks. Incl. Native Tribes of California & the Southwest. Yenne, Bill. lib. bdg. 34.00 *(978-0-8368-5609-5(0))*; Native Tribes of the Great Basin & Plateau. Clarke, Duncan. lib. bdg. 34.00 *(978-0-8368-5610-1(4))*; Native Tribes of the North & Northwest Coast. Burkinshaw, Jane. lib. bdg. 34.00 *(978-0-8368-5611-8(2))*; Native Tribes of the Plains & Prairie. lib. bdg. 34.00 *(978-0-8368-5613-2(9))*; Native Tribes of the Southeast. Clarke, Duncan. lib. bdg. 34.00 *(978-0-8368-5614-9(7))*; (gr. 5-12)., Gareth Stevens Secondary Library (Native Tribes of North America Ser.). (Illus.). 64p. 2004. 199.62 o.p. *(978-0-8368-5608-8(2)*, World Almanac Library) Stevens, Gareth Publishing LLLP.

Jones, Donald M., photos by. Buffalo Country: America's National Bison Range. 2005. (Illus.). 72p. per. 14.95 *(978-1-931832-56-4(0)*, 8667872363) Riverbend Publishing.

Joseph, Frank. Legends & Lore of Ancient America, 1 vol., 1. 2014. (Discovering Ancient America Ser.). (ENG.). 296p. (YA). (gr. 7-12). lib. bdg. 38.25 *(978-1-4777-2807-9(4))* Rosen Publishing Group, Inc., The.

Junior Library of American Indians. 2005. (Junior Library of American Indians Ser.). 80p. (gr. 4-6). 225.00 *(978-0-7910-8471-7(X)*, Chelsea Hse.) Facts On File, Inc.

The Kalapuyans: A Sourcebook on the Indians of the Willamette Valley. 2nd exp. ed. 2004. pap. 12.95 *(978-0-9753484-0-6(X))* Mission Mill Museum.

Kallio, Jamie. Mayflower Compact, 1 vol. 2013. (Foundations of Our Nation Ser.). (ENG.). 48p. (J). (gr. 3-6). lib. bdg. 32.79 *(978-1-61783-711-1(3))*; (Illus.). pap. 15.64 *(978-1-61783-761-6(X)*, Core Library) ABDO Publishing Co.

Kalman, Bobbie. Nations of the Plains. 2003. (Native Nations of North America Ser.). (ENG., Illus.). 32p. (J). (gr. 5). pap. *(978-0-7787-0460-7(2))*; lib. bdg. *(978-0-7787-0368-6(1))* Crabtree Publishing Co.

Kalman, Bobbie & Bishop, Amanda. Nations of the Southwest. 2003. (Native Nations of North America Ser.). (ENG., Illus.). 32p. (J). (gr. 3-9). pap. *(978-0-7787-0466-9(1))*; lib. bdg. *(978-0-7787-0374-7(6))* Crabtree Publishing Co.

Katz, William Loren. Black Indians: A Hidden Heritage. 2012. (ENG.). 272p. (YA). (gr. 7). 21.99 *(978-1-4424-4636-6(6))*; (Illus.). pap. 12.99 *(978-1-4424-4637-3(4))* Simon & Schuster Children's Publishing. (Atheneum Bks. for Young Readers).

Kavin, Kim & Hetland, Beth. Native Americans: Discover the History & Cultures of the First Americans with 15 Projects. 2013. (Build It Yourself Ser.). (ENG., Illus.). 128p. (J). (gr. 3-7). 21.95 *(978-1-61930-175-7(X))*; pap. 16.95 *(978-1-61930-170-2(9))* Open City Bks.

Keating, Susan. Native American Rivalries. Johnson, Troy, ed. 2013. (Native American Life Ser.: 15). 64p. (J). (gr. 5-18). 19.95 *(978-1-4222-2975-0(0))* Mason Crest.

Kessel, Joyce K. Squanto y el Primer Dia de Accion de Gracias. Donze, Lisa, illus. 2007. (Yo Solo - Festividades (on My Own - Holidays) Ser.). 48p. (J). (gr. 4-7). per. 6.95 *(978-0-8225-7795-9(X))* Lerner Publishing Group.

—Squanto y el Primer Día de Acción de Gracias. Translations.com Staff, tr. from ENG. Donze, Lisa, illus. 2007. (Yo Solo - Festividades (on My Own - Holidays) Ser.). (SPA.). 48p. (gr. 2-4). lib. bdg. 25.26 *(978-0-8225-7792-8(5))* Lerner Publishing Group.

Kessler, Tim. When God Made the Dakotas. Morin, Paul, illus. 2006. 32p. (J). (gr. k). 17.00 *(978-0-8028-5275-5(0)*, Eerdmans Bks For Young Readers) Eerdmans, William B. Publishing Co.

King, David C. The Blackfeet. 2009. (First Americans 5 Ser.). 48p. (gr. 3). 31.36 *(978-0-7614-4129-8(8))* Marshall Cavendish Corp.

—First People: An Illustrated History of American Indians. 2008. (ENG.). 192p. (J). (gr. 3-7). 19.99 *(978-0-7566-4092-7(X)*, DK Children) Dorling Kindersley Publishing, Inc.

—The Mohawk. 2009. (J). 31.36 *(978-0-7614-4132-8(8))* Marshall Cavendish GBR. Dist: Marshall Cavendish Corp.

—The Powhatan. 2007. (First Americans Ser.). (Illus.). 48p. (J). lib. bdg. 31.36 *(978-0-7614-2681-3(7)*, Benchmark Bks.) Marshall Cavendish Corp.

King, Margaret. The Legacy & Legend of Sacagawea. 2017. (Primary Source Readers Ser.). (Illus.). 32p. (J). (gr. 4-5). pap. 8.99 *(978-1-4938-3793-9(1))* Teacher Created Materials, Inc.

Kirkman, Marissa. The Life & Times of the First Americans. 2016. (Life & Times Ser.). (ENG., Illus.). 24p. (gr. 1-2). lib. bdg. 25.32 *(978-1-5157-2475-9(1)*, First Facts) Capstone Press of Coughlan Cos.

Kjelgaard, Jim. The Story of Geronimo. Meadowcroft, Enid Lamonte, ed. Wilson, Charles Banks, illus. 2011. 192p. 42.95 *(978-1-258-05298-0(9))* Literary Licensing, LLC.

Knott, Marie, ed. Why Waabooz Has Long Ears. 2007. (Illus.). 27p. (J). pap. 8.95 net. *(978-0-9779895-2-2(6))* Knott, Joan.

Kolich, Heather N. The Pawnee. 2013. (Illus.). 32p. (J). lib. bdg. *(978-1-935884-92-7(1))* State Standards Publishing, LLC.

Kukathas, Uma. Native American Rights. 2008. (Issues on Trial Ser.). (ENG., Illus.). 240p. (gr. 10-12). 48.30 *(978-0-7377-4076-9(0)*, Greenhaven Pr., Inc.) Cengage Gale.

Kuskowski, Alex. Super Simple Native American Art: Fun & Easy Art from Around the World, 1 vol. 2012. (ENG.). 32p. 27.07 *(978-1-61783-214-7(6)*, Super SandCastle) ABDO Publishing Co.

Labastida, Roberta. My Ancestor's Village. 2003. (Illus.). 32p. (J). 9.95 *(978-0-932653-61-1(8))* Sunbelt Pubns., Inc.

Lacey, Theresa Jensen & Rosier, Paul C. The Blackfeet. 2nd rev. ed. 2011. (History & Culture of Native Americans Ser.). (Illus.). 122p. (gr. 6-12). 35.00 *(978-1-60413-795-8(9)*, Chelsea Hse.) Facts On File, Inc.

Lajiness, Katie. Chickasaw, 1 vol. 2016. (ENG., Illus.). 32p. (J). *(978-1-68078-197-7(9))* ABDO Publishing Co.

Landau, Elaine. Celebrate the First Thanksgiving with Elaine Landau. 2006. (Explore Colonial America with Elaine Landau Ser.). (Illus.). 48p. (J). (gr. 3-7). lib. bdg. 25.27 *(978-0-7660-2556-1(X)*, Enslow Elementary) Enslow Pubs., Inc.

Landon, Rocky. A Native American Thought of It: Amazing Inventions & Innovations. (We Thought of It Ser.). (ENG., Illus.). 48p. (J). (gr. 5-7). 2nd ed. 2008. 19.95 *(978-1-55451-155-6(0)*, 9781554511556) 3rd ed. 2013. pap. 9.95 *(978-1-55451-154-9(2)*, 9781554511549) Annick Pr., Ltd. CAN. Dist: Publishers Group West (PGW).

Lange, Karen. 1607: A New Look at Jamestown. Block, Ira, photos by. 2007. (ENG., Illus.). 48p. (J). (gr. 4-7). 17.95 *(978-1-4263-0012-7(3)*, National Geographic Children's Bks.) National Geographic Society.

Lawton, Cassie M. & Bial, Raymond. The People & Culture of the Shawnee. 2016. (Illus.). 128p. (J). *(978-1-5026-1892-4(3))* Hudson Hills Pr. LLC.

Legay, Gilbert. Atlas de los Indios Norteamericanos. (SPA., Illus.). 96p. (YA). (gr. 5-8). *(978-84-261-2924-6(2)*, IV1599) Juventud, Editorial ESP. Dist: Lectorum Pubns., Inc.

The Library of Native Americans: Set 4. (J). (gr. k-5). 159.00 *(978-1-4042-2961-7(2))* Rosen Publishing Group, Inc., The.

Liddell, Daniel & Basta, Mary, illus. Native Americans of North America, Set, 11. 2003. (Native Americans of North America). 48p. (J). (gr. 3-6). pap. 6.45 *(978-1-877599-61-3(1))* Merryant Pubs.

Lilly, Melinda. Misiones Espanolas (Spanish Missions) Capaldi, Gina, illus. 2005. (Lecturas Historicas Norteamericanas (Reading American Histor Ser.). 24p. (J). (gr. 3-7). lib. bdg. 22.79 *(978-1-59515-638-9(0))* Rourke Educational Media.

Linde, Barbara M. Native Peoples of the Southeast. 2016. (Native Peoples of North America Ser.). (Illus.). 32p. (J). (gr. 3-2). 25.25 *(978-1-4824-4818-4(1))* Stevens, Gareth Publishing LLLP.

Lindeen, Carol K. Native American Powwows, 6 vols., Set. 2004. (Phonics Readers Books 37-72 Ser.). (ENG.). 16p. (gr. k-1). pap. 35.70 *(978-0-7368-4082-8(6)*, Phonics Readers) Capstone Press of Coughlan Cos.

Lowery, Linda. Native Peoples of California. 2016. (North American Indian Nations Ser.). (ENG., Illus.). 48p. (J). (gr. 3-5). 33.32 *(978-1-4677-7932-6(6))* Lerner Publishing Group.

—Native Peoples of the Plains. 2016. (North American Indian Nations Ser.). (ENG., Illus.). 48p. (J). (gr. 3-5). 33.32 *(978-1-4677-7934-0(2))* Lerner Publishing Group.

—Native Peoples of the Southwest. 2016. (North American Indian Nations Ser.). (ENG., Illus.). 48p. (J). (gr. 3-5). 33.32 *(978-1-4677-7936-4(9))* Lerner Publishing Group.

Lyon, Robin. The Spanish Missions of Arizona. 2010. (True Book(tm), a — Spanish Missions Ser.). 48p. (J). (gr. 2-5). 31.00 *(978-0-531-20576-1(2))*; (ENG.). pap. 6.95 *(978-0-531-21239-4(4))* Scholastic Library Publishing.

—Spanish Missions of New Mexico. 2010. (True Book(tm), a — Spanish Missions Ser.). (ENG.). 48p. (J). (gr. 2-5). 31.00 *(978-0-531-20579-2(7))* Scholastic Library Publishing.

—The Spanish Missions of New Mexico. 2010. (True Book Ser.). (ENG.). 48p. (J). pap. 6.95 *(978-0-531-21242-4(4)*, Children's Pr.) Scholastic Library Publishing.

Machajewski, Sarah. American Indian Rights Movement. 2016. (Civic Participation: Working for Civil Rights Ser.). 00032p. (J). (gr. 5-5). pap. 10.00 *(978-1-4994-2675-5(5)*, PowerKids Pr.) Rosen Publishing Group, Inc., The.

Manning, Jack. Pueblos, 1 vol. 2014. (American Indian Homes Ser.). (ENG.). 24p. (gr. 1-2). lib. bdg. 25.32 *(978-1-4914-0315-0(2))* Capstone Press of Coughlan Cos.

Margaret, Amy. Mission San Buenaventura. 2003. (Missions of Californiatm Ser.). (Illus.). 64p. (J). (gr. 4-18). 26.50 *(978-0-8239-5888-7(4))* Rosen Publishing Group, Inc., The.

—Mission Santa Barbara. 2003. (Missions of Californiatm Ser.). (Illus.). 64p. (J). (gr. 4-18). 26.50 *(978-0-8239-5880-1(9))* Rosen Publishing Group, Inc., The.

—Mission Santa Clara de Asis. 2003. (Missions of Californiatm Ser.). (Illus.). 64p. (J). (gr. 4-18). 26.50 *(978-0-8239-5883-2(3))* Rosen Publishing Group, Inc., The.

Marsh, Carole. Alabama Native Americans: A Kid's Look at Our State's Chiefs, Tribes, Reservations, Powwows, Lore, & More from the Past & the Present. 2004. (Alabama Experience Ser.). (Illus.). 36p. (J). (gr. 3-8). 29.95 *(978-0-635-02247-9(8))* Gallopade International.

—The Best Book of Native American Biographies. Corsey, Jenny, ed. 2004. (Native American Heri Ser.). (Illus.). 32p. (J). (gr. 3-8). pap. 7.95 *(978-0-635-02400-8(4))* Gallopade International.

—Georgia Native Americans: A Kid's Look at Our State's Chiefs, Tribes, Reservations, Powwows, Lore & More from the Past & the Present. 2004. (Georgia Experience Ser.). (Illus.). 36p. (J). (gr. 3-8). 29.95 *(978-0-635-02265-3(6))* Gallopade International.

—Illinois Native Americans: A Kid's Look at Our State's Chiefs, Tribes, Reservations, Powwows, Lore, & More from the Past & the Present. 2004. (Illinois Experience Ser.). (Illus.). 36p. (J). (gr. 3-8). 29.95 *(978-0-635-02271-4(0))* Gallopade International.

—Louisiana Native Americans: A Kid's Look at Our State's Chiefs, Tribes, Reservations, Powwows, Lore, & More from the Past & the Present. 2004. (Louisiana Experience Ser.). (Illus.). 36p. (J). (gr. 3-8). 29.95 *(978-0-635-02281-3(8))* Gallopade International.

—Missouri Native Americans: A Kid's Look at Our State's Chiefs, Tribes, Reservations, Powwows, Lore, & More from the Past & the Present. 2004. (Missouri Experience Ser.). (Illus.). 36p. (J). (gr. 3-8). 29.95 *(978-0-635-02295-0(8))* Gallopade International.

—Native American Coloring Book. Corsey, Jenny, ed. 2004. (Native American Heri Ser.). (Illus.). 24p. (J). (gr. k-2). 3.95 *(978-0-635-02398-8(9))* Gallopade International.

—Ohio Native Americans: A Kid's Look at Our State's Chiefs, Tribes, Reservations, Powwows, Lore, & More from the Past & the Present. 2004. (Ohio Experience Ser.). (Illus.). 36p. (J). (gr. 3-8). 29.95 *(978-0-635-02315-5(6))* Gallopade International.

—Texas Native Americans: A Kid's Look at Our State's Chiefs, Tribes, Reservations, Powwows, Lore, & More from the Past & the Present. Corsey, Jenny & Valentine, Teresa, eds. 2004. (Texas Experience Ser.). (Illus.). 36p. (J). (gr. 3-8). 29.95 *(978-0-635-02331-5(8))* Gallopade International.

Martini, Teri. The True Book of Indians. Heston, Charles, illus. 2011. 48p. 35.95 *(978-1-258-05468-7(X))* Literary Licensing, LLC.

Massie, Elizabeth. The Powhatan. 2016. (Spring Forward Ser.). (J). (gr. 2). *(978-1-4900-6030-9(8))* Benchmark Education Co.

Mayrl, Damon. The Potawatomi of Wisconsin. 2003. (Library of Native Americans). (Illus.). 64p. (J). lib. bdg. 26.50 *(978-0-8239-6428-4(0)*, PowerKids Pr.) Rosen Publishing Group, Inc., The.

McCay, William. Pueblos del Mundo. 2011. (SPA.). 32p. (J). pap. 49.00 net. *(978-1-4108-2346-5(6)*, A23466) Benchmark Education Co.

McDaniel, Melissa. Great Basin Indians, 1 vol. 2011. (First Nations of North America Ser.). (ENG.). 48p. (gr. 3-3). pap. 9.95 *(978-1-4329-4958-7(6))*; 33.32 *(978-1-4329-4947-1(0))* Heinemann-Raintree. (Heinemann InfoSearch).

McGinty, Alice B. Mission San Gabriel Arcangel. 2003. (Missions of Californiatm Ser.). (Illus.). 64p. (J). (gr. 4-18). 26.50 *(978-0-8239-5892-4(2))* Rosen Publishing Group, Inc., The.

McGinty, Alice B. & Stevens, Madeline. Discovering Mission San Gabriel Arcángel. 2014. (California Missions Ser.). 48p. (J). (gr. 4-6). lib. bdg. 31.36 *(978-1-62713-115-5(9))* Cavendish Square Publishing.

McLeese, Tex. Monta en Silla y a Pelo. Palacios, Argentina, tr.Tr. of Bronc & Bareback Riding. (SPA., Illus.). 24p. (J). (gr. 1-3). lib. bdg. 19.27 *(978-1-57103-386-4(6))* Rourke Educational Media.

McNeil, Niki, et al. HOCPP 1090 Native Americans of California. 2006. spiral bd. 19.50 *(978-1-60308-090-3(2))* In the Hands of a Child.

Miller, Helen Markley. Thunder Rolling: The Story of Chief Joseph. Orbaan, Albert, illus. 2011. 190p. 42.95 *(978-1-258-06189-0(9))* Literary Licensing, LLC.

Moreno, Barry. The Native Americans. (Major American Immigration Ser.). 2010. (Illus.). 64p. (gr. 9-12). 22.95 *(978-1-4222-0615-7(7))* 2007. pap. 9.95 *(978-1-4222-0682-9(3))* Mason Crest.

Morris, Ting. Arts & Crafts of the Native Americans. Young, Emma, illus. 2006. (Arts & Crafts of the Ancient World Ser.). 32p. (J). lib. bdg. 28.50 *(978-1-58340-916-9(5))* Black Rabbit Bks.

Moskal, Greg. An Apache Indian Community. 2009. (Reading Room Collection 2 Ser.). 24p. (gr. 3-4). 42.50 *(978-1-60851-956-9(2)*, PowerKids Pr.) Rosen Publishing Group, Inc., The.

Munz, Casey "Naanaage Binesik", illus. Sshtaa taa Haa! Oh No! 2004. (OJI & ENG.). 16p. (J). per. *(978-0-9758801-0-4(1))* Bay Mills Indian Community.

Murdoch, David & Dorling Kindersley Publishing Staff. North American Indian. 2005. (DK Eyewitness Bks.). (ENG., Illus.). 72p. (J). (gr. 3-7). 16.99 *(978-0-7566-1082-1(6)*, DK Children) Dorling Kindersley Publishing, Inc.

Native America, 4 vols., Set. 2008. (Native America Ser.). 152p. (gr. 5-8). 105.00 *(978-0-8160-6813-5(5))* Facts On File, Inc.

Native Americans. 2004. (Illus.). lib. bdg. 7.95 *(978-0-8225-4276-6(5))* Lerner Publishing Group.

Native Americans. Date not set. (Mini Question & Answers America Ser.). 32p. (J). 3.98 *(978-0-7525-9873-4(2))* Parragon, Inc.

Native Americans I. (YA). tchr. ed. 41.95 *(978-0-382-40674-4(5))* Cobblestone Publishing Co.

Native Americans II. (J). tchr. ed. 41.95 *(978-0-382-40675-1(3))* Cobblestone Publishing Co.

Los Nativos Americanos: El Pueblo Indígena de Norteamerica.Tr. of Native Americans: The Native People of North America. (SPA.). 256p. (YA). (gr. 5-8). 36.00 *(978-84-7630-201-9(0))* Editorial Libsa, S.A. ESP. Dist: Lectorum Pubns., Inc.

Nelson, Kadir. Heart & Soul: The Story of America & African Americans. 2013. (J). lib. bdg. 19.65 *(978-0-606-35050-1(0)*, Turtleback) Turtleback Bks.

The New World: Prehistory To 1542. 2010. (Discovering U. S. History Ser.). (Illus.). 128p. (gr. 5-8). 35.00 *(978-1-60413-348-6(1)*, Chelsea Hse.) Facts On File, Inc.

Noble, Trinka Hakes. People of Ten Thousand Winters. 2012. (Tales of the World Ser.). (ENG., Illus.). 32p. (J). (gr. k-5). 16.95 *(978-1-58536-529-6(7))* Sleeping Bear Pr.

Nuñes, Sofia. Discovering Mission Santa Inés. 2014. (California Missions Ser.). (Illus.). 48p. (J). (gr. 4-6). lib. bdg. 31.36 *(978-1-62713-097-4(7))* Cavendish Square Publishing.

Nussbaum, Ben. California's Indian Nations. 2017. (Primary Source Readers Ser.). 32p. (gr. 4-4). 9.99 ***(978-1-4258-3232-2(6))*** Teacher Created Materials, Inc.

—Junipero Serra: A Spanish Missionary. 2017. (Primary Source Readers Ser.). (Illus.). 32p. (gr. 4-4). 9.99 ***(978-1-4258-3235-3(0))*** Teacher Created Materials, Inc.

O'Brien, Cynthia. Go West: First Contact with Native Nations. 2016. (ENG.). 32p. (J). *(978-0-7787-2331-8(3))* Crabtree Publishing Co.

O'Dell, Kathryn L. Oklahoma Fame! Jim Thorpe, Will Rogers, Maria Tallchief. 2017. (Text Connections Guided Close Reading Ser.). (J). (gr. 2). *(978-1-4900-1855-3(7))* Benchmark Education Co.

Orr, Tamra. Native American Medicine. Johnson, Troy, ed. 2013. (Native American Life Ser.: 15). 64p. (J). (gr. 5-18). 19.95 *(978-1-4222-2973-6(4))* Mason Crest.

—Native American Medicine. 2004. (Native American Life Ser.). (Illus.). 64p. (YA). (gr. 5-18). lib. bdg. 19.95 *(978-1-59084-119-8(0))* Mason Crest.

Ostrow, Kim. Mission Nuestra Senora de la Soledad. 2003. (Missions of Californiatm Ser.). (Illus.). 64p. (J). (gr. 4-18). 26.50 *(978-0-8239-5882-5(5))* Rosen Publishing Group, Inc., The.

—Mission Santa Cruz. 2009. (Missions of California Ser.). 64p. (gr. 4-4). 58.50 *(978-1-60854-041-9(3)*, PowerKids Pr.) Rosen Publishing Group, Inc., The.

Otfinoski, Steven. Native Americans at the Time of the Explorers: Set Of 6. 2011. (Navigators Ser.). (J). pap. 48.00 net. *(978-1-4108-5106-2(0))* Benchmark Education Co.

Paleja, S. N. Native Americans: A Visual Exploration. 2013. (ENG., Illus.). 48p. (J). (gr. 5-9). 19.95 *(978-1-55451-485-4(1)*, 9781554514854) Annick Pr., Ltd. CAN. Dist: Publishers Group West (PGW).

Parker-Rock, Michelle. Joseph Bruchac: An Author Kids Love. 2009. (Authors Kids Love Ser.). (Illus.). 48p. (J). (gr. 3-4). lib. bdg. 25.27 *(978-0-7660-3160-9(8)*, Enslow Elementary) Enslow Pubs., Inc.

Patent, Dorothy Hinshaw. The Horse & the Plains Indians: A Powerful Partnership. Munoz, William, photos by. 2012. (ENG., Illus.). 112p. (J). (gr. 5-7). 17.99 *(978-0-547-12551-0(8))* Houghton Mifflin Harcourt Publishing Co.

Patrick, Bethanne. Native American Languages. Johnson, Troy, ed. 2013. (Native American Life Ser.: 15). 64p. (J). (gr. 5-18). 19.95 *(978-1-4222-2972-9(6))* Mason Crest.

People of the California Missions. (Illus.). (J). (gr. k-5). 151.50 *(978-0-8239-7263-0(1))* Rosen Publishing Group, Inc., The.

Peppas, Lynn. Trail of Tears. 2013. (ENG., Illus.). 48p. (J). *(978-0-7787-1174-2(9))*; pap. *(978-0-7787-1187-2(0))* Crabtree Publishing Co.

Perritano, John. Spanish Missions. 2010. (True Book(tm), a — Spanish Missions Ser.). (Illus.). 48p. (J). (gr. 2-5). 31.00 *(978-0-531-20575-4(4))*; pap. 6.95 *(978-0-531-21238-7(6))* Scholastic Library Publishing.

Phan, Sandy. Los Caddo y los Comanche. 2013. (Primary Source Readers Ser.). (SPA.). lib. bdg. 19.65 *(978-0-606-31861-7(5)*, Turtleback) Turtleback Bks.

—Los Indigenas Americanos de Texas (American Indians in Texas) 2013. (Primary Source Readers Ser.). (SPA.). lib. bdg. 19.65 *(978-0-606-31860-0(7)*, Turtleback) Turtleback Bks.

Potts, Steve. Iroquois: Peoples of North America. 2016. (Peoples of North America Ser.). (ENG.). 48p. (J). (gr. 5-9). pap. 12.00 *(978-1-62832-153-1(9)*, Creative Paperbacks) Creative Co., The.

Randolph, Joanne. The Iroquois League. 2009. (Reading Room Collection 2 Ser.). 24p. (gr. 3-4). 42.50 *(978-1-60851-995-8(3)*, PowerKids Pr.) Rosen Publishing Group, Inc., The.

Randolph, Ryan P. Following the Great Herds: The Plains Indians & the American Buffalo. 2009. (Library of the Westward Expansion Ser.). 24p. (gr. 3-4). 42.50 *(978-1-60853-934-5(2)*, PowerKids Pr.) Rosen Publishing Group, Inc., The.

Rice, Dona Herwick & Bradley, Kathleen. Chief Joseph & the Nez Perce, 1 vol. 2009. (Building Fluency Through Reader's Theater Ser.). (ENG., Illus.). 32p. (J). (gr. 3-5). pap. 7.99 *(978-1-4333-0543-6(7))* Teacher Created Materials, Inc.

Robbins, Trina & Hess, Debra. Native Princess: Sarah Winnemucca. 2007. (Read on! Special Edition: Level AA Ser.). (Illus.). 23p. pap. 4.84 *(978-1-4190-3515-9(0))* Steck-Vaughn.

Robertson, David Alexander. The Pact. Henderson, Scott B., illus. 2011. (7 Generations Ser.: 4). (ENG.). 32p. (YA). pap. *(978-1-55379-230-7(0)*, 9781553792307, HighWater Pr.) Portage & Main Pr.

Rodgers, Kelly. The Creek & the Cherokee. 2016. (Primary Source Readers Ser.). (Illus.). 32p. (gr. 2-2). 8.99 *(978-1-4938-2553-0(4))* Teacher Created Materials, Inc.

Ruffenach, Jessie, ed. Baby Learns to Count. Thomas, Peter, tr. Blacksheep, Beverly, illus. I.t. ed. 2003. (NAV & ENG.). 16p. (J). (gr. -1-12). 7.95 *(978-1-893354-47-0(4))* Salina Bookshelf Inc.

Ryckman, Tatiana & Bial, Raymond. The People & Culture of the Mandan. 2016. (First Peoples of North America Ser.). 128p. (J). 45.64 *(978-1-5026-2249-5(1))* Cavendish Square Publishing.

Rzeczkowski, Frank & Rosier, Paul C. The Lakota Sioux. 2011. (History & Culture of Native Americans Ser.). (Illus.). 144p. (gr. 6-12). 35.00 *(978-1-60413-800-9(9)*, Chelsea Hse.) Facts On File, Inc.

Sanford, William R. Comanche Chief Quanah Parker. 2013. (Native American Chiefs & Warriors Ser.). 48p. (J). (gr. 5-18). lib. bdg. 22.60 *(978-0-7660-4095-3(X))*; pap. 8.95 *(978-1-4644-0255-5(8))* Enslow Pubs., Inc.

—Oglala Lakota Chief Red Cloud. 2013. (Native American Chiefs & Warriors Ser.). 48p. (J). (gr. 5-18). 22.60 *(978-0-7660-4096-0(8))* Enslow Pubs., Inc.

Santella, Andrew. The First Thanksgiving. 2003. (Cornerstones of Freedom Ser.). (ENG., Illus.). 48p. (YA). (gr. 4-7). 26.00 *(978-0-516-24204-0(0))* Scholastic Library Publishing.

—Southeast Indians, 1 vol. 2011. (First Nations of North America Ser.). (ENG.). 48p. (gr. 3-3). pap. 9.95 *(978-1-4329-4963-1(2))*; 33.32 *(978-1-4329-4952-5(7))* Heinemann-Raintree. (Heinemann InfoSearch).

Scholastic Library Publishing. A True Book-the Thirteen Colonies. 2011. (True Book-the Thirteen Colonies Ser.). (J). (gr. 3-5). 377.00 (978-0-531-22149-5(0), Children's Pr.) Scholastic Library Publishing.

Serafin, Kim. Mission San Antonio de Padua. 2003. (Missions of Californiatm Ser.). (Illus.). 64p. (J). (gr. 4-18). 26.50 (978-0-8239-5891-7(4)) Rosen Publishing Group, Inc., The.

Serrano, Francisco. The Poet King of Tezcoco: A Great Leader of Ancient Mexico, 1 vol. Balch, Trudy & Engelbert, Jo Anne, trs. from SPA. Serrano, Pablo, illus. 2007. (ENG.). 48p. (J). (gr. 3-6). 18.95 (978-0-88899-787-6(6)) Groundwood Bks. CAN. Dist: Publishers Group West (PGW).

Silver, Donald M. & Wynne, Patricia J. Northeast Indians: Reproducible Models That Help Students Build Content Area Knowledge & Vocabulary & Learn about the Traditional Life of Native American Peoples. 2005. (Easy Make & Learn Projects Ser.). (ENG., Illus.). 80p. (gr. 3-5). per. 12.99 (978-0-439-24116-8(2), Teaching Resources) Scholastic, Inc.

Sioux, Tracee. Native American Migration. 2009. (Primary Sources of Immigration & Migration in America Ser.). 24p. (gr. 3-4). 42.50 (978-1-60851-781-7(0), PowerKids Pr.) Rosen Publishing Group, Inc., The.

Sjonger, Rebecca & Kalman, Bobbie. Nations of the Eastern Great Lakes. 2004. (Native Nations of North America Ser.). (ENG., Illus.). 32p. (J). pap. (978-0-7787-0473-7(4)) Crabtree Publishing Co.

Smithyman, Kathryn & Kalman, Bobbie. Native North American Foods & Recipes. 2005. (Native Nations of North America Ser.). (ENG., Illus.). 32p. (J). (gr. 4-7). lib. bdg. (978-0-7787-0383-9(5)) Crabtree Publishing Co.

Smithyman, Kathryn, et al. Nations of the Northwest Coast. 2003. (Native Nations of North America Ser.). (ENG., Illus.). 32p. (J). (gr. 5). lib. bdg. (978-0-7787-0378-5(9)) Crabtree Publishing Co.

Sneve, Virginia Driving Hawk. Standing Bear of the Ponca. (ENG.). 2017. (YA). (gr. 8-12). 14.95 **(978-1-4962-0410-3(7))** 2013. (Illus.). 56p. (J). pap. 14.95 (978-0-8032-2826-9(0)) Univ. of Nebraska Pr. (Bison Bks.).

Solomon, Sharon. Lewis Tewanima: Born to Run, 1 vol. Fields, Lisa, illus. 2014. (ENG.). 32p. (J). (gr. k-3). 16.99 (978-1-4556-1941-2(8)) Pelican Publishing Co., Inc.

Sonneborn, Liz. The American Indian Experience. 2010. (USA TODAY Cultural Mosaic Ser.). (ENG.). 80p. (gr. 6-8). lib. bdg. 33.26 (978-0-7613-4086-7(6)) Lerner Publishing Group.

—California Indians, 1 vol. 2011. (First Nations of North America Ser.). (ENG.). 48p. (gr. 3-3). pap. 9.95 (978-1-4329-4957-0(8)); 33.32 (978-1-4329-4946-4(2)) Heinemann-Raintree. (Heinemann InfoSearch).

—Native Peoples of the Northeast. 2016. (North American Indian Nations Ser.). (ENG., Illus.). 48p. (J). (gr. 3-5). 33.32 (978-1-4677-7933-3(4)) Lerner Publishing Group.

—Northwest Coast Indians, 1 vol. 2011. (First Nations of North America Ser.). (ENG.). 48p. (gr. 3-3). pap. 9.95 (978-1-4329-4960-0(8)); 33.32 (978-1-4329-4949-5(7)) Heinemann-Raintree. (Heinemann InfoSearch).

—Wilma Mankiller. 2010. (Leading Women Ser.). 96p. (YA). (gr. 7-12). 39.93 (978-0-7614-4959-1(0)) Marshall Cavendish Corp.

Staeger, Rob. Hunting with the Native Americans. Johnson, Troy, ed. 2013. (Native American Life Ser.: 15). 64p. (J). (gr. 5-18). 19.95 (978-1-4222-2966-8(1)) Mason Crest.

—Native American Religions. Johnson, Troy, ed. 2013. (Native American Life Ser.: 15). 64p. (J). (gr. 5-18). 19.95 (978-1-4222-2974-3(2)) Mason Crest.

—Native American Sports & Games. Johnson, Troy, ed. 2013. (Native American Life Ser.: 15). 64p. (J). (gr. 5-18). 19.95 (978-1-4222-2976-7(9)) Mason Crest.

—Native American Tools & Weapons. Johnson, Troy, ed. 2013. (Native American Life Ser.: 15). 64p. (J). (gr. 5-18). 19.95 (978-1-4222-2977-4(7)) Mason Crest.

Stein, R. Conrad. Spanish Missionaries: Bringing Spanish Culture to the Americas. 2005. (Proud Heritage: the Hispanic Library). (ENG., Illus.). 40p. (J). (gr. 3-6). 29.93 (978-1-59296-387-4(0), 200014) Child's World, Inc., The.

Sterngass, Jon. Crazy Horse: The Wild West for Kids. 2014. (ENG., Illus.). 160p. (J). (gr. 2-7). pap. 12.95 (978-1-62636-159-1(2), 263159, Sky Pony Pr.) Skyhorse Publishing Co., Inc.

Stevens, Madeline. Discovering Mission San José. 2014. (California Missions Ser.). (Illus.). 48p. (J). (gr. 4-6). lib. bdg. 31.36 (978-1-62713-064-6(0)) Cavendish Square Publishing.

—Discovering Mission San Juan Bautista. 2014. (California Missions Ser.). (Illus.). 48p. (J). (gr. 4-6). lib. bdg. 31.36 (978-1-62713-073-8(X)) Cavendish Square Publishing.

Stone, Omar. Chickasaw, 01 vols., 1. 2016. (Spotlight on Native Americans Ser.). (ENG., Illus.). 32p. (J). pap. 11.75 (978-1-5081-4105-1(3), PowerKids Pr.) Rosen Publishing Group, Inc., The.

Stout, Mary. Blackfoot History & Culture. 2011. (Native American Library). (Illus.). 48p. (J). (gr. 3-6). pap. 14.05 (978-1-4339-5956-1(9)); lib. bdg. 31.95 (978-1-4339-5954-7(2)) Stevens, Gareth Publishing LLLP. (Gareth Stevens Learning Library).

Suben, Eric. The Spanish Missions of Florida. 2010. (True Book(tm), a — Spanish Missions Ser.). 48p. (J). (gr. 2-5). 31.00 (978-0-531-20578-5(9)); (gr. 3-5). pap. 6.95 (978-0-531-21241-7(6)) Scholastic Library Publishing.

Takacs, Stefanie. The Seminole. 2004. (True Books Ser.). (Illus.). 47p. (J). 14.60 (978-0-7569-7159-5(4)) Perfection Learning Corp.

Tan, Richard. The Native American Peoples of New York City. 2011. (My Community Ser.). (ENG., Illus.). 12p. (gr. 2-2). pap. 6.95 (978-1-4488-5724-1(4), Rosen Classroom) Rosen Publishing Group, Inc., The.

Taylor, Colin, et al. Plains Indians. 2010. (Native America Ser.). 136p. (J). (gr. 5-8). 35.00 (978-0-8160-5976-8(4)) Facts On File, Inc.

Thomas, Marjorie & Ruffenach, Jessie. What Does 'died' Mean? Haíshá óolyé Daaztsâa? Begay, Patrick, illus. 2005. (ENG & NAV.). 32p. (J). (gr. 4-7). pap. 9.00 (978-1-893354-56-2(3)) Salina Bookshelf Inc.

Thomas, Penny. Powwow Counting in Cree. Josie, Melinda, illus. 2013. (CRE & ENG.). 24p. (978-1-55379-392-2(7), 9781553793922, HighWater Pr.) Portage & Main Pr.

Tieck, Sarah. Sacagawea, 1 vol. 2006. (Buddy Book Ser.). (ENG., Illus.). 32p. (gr. -1-3). 27.07 (978-1-59679-789-5(4), Buddy Bks.) ABDO Publishing Co.

Torr, James D., ed. Westward Expansion. 2003. (Interpreting American History Through Primary Documents Ser.x). (Illus.). 208p. (J). 32.45 (978-0-7377-1134-9(5), Greenhaven Pr., Inc.) Cengage Gale.

Tousey, Sanford. Indians & Cowboys: A One Volume Edition of Indians of the Plains & Cowboys of America. 2011. 78p. 37.95 (978-1-258-10130-5(0)) Literary Licensing, LLC.

Waldman, Carl. Encyclopedia of Native American Tribes. 3rd rev. ed. 2006. (Facts on File Library of American History). (Illus.). 368p. (gr. 3-7). pap. 21.95 (978-0-8160-6274-4(9), Checkmark Bks.); (C). 75.00 (978-0-8160-6273-7(0)) Facts On File, Inc.

Walker, Paul Robert. Remember Little Bighorn: Indians, Soldiers, & Scouts Tell Their Stories. (ENG., Illus.). 64p. (J). (gr. 5). 2015. pap. 7.99 (978-1-4263-2246-4(1)) 2006. 17.95 (978-0-7922-5521-5(6)) 2006. lib. bdg. 27.90 (978-0-7922-5522-2(4)) National Geographic Society. (National Geographic Children's Bks.).

Wallace, Ian. The Huron Carol, 1 vol. 2013. (ENG., Illus.). 32p. (J). (gr. -1). 14.95 (978-1-55498-394-0(0)) Groundwood Bks. CAN. Dist: Publishers Group West (PGW).

Wallace, Mary. The Inuksuk Book. Wallace, Mary & Owlkids Books Inc. Staff, illus. 2004. (Wow Canada! Ser.). (ENG.). 64p. (J). (gr. 3-6). pap. 13.95 (978-1-897066-13-3(9), Owlkids) Owlkids Bks. Inc. CAN. Dist: Publishers Group West (PGW).

Webster, Christine & Kissock, Heather. Salish. 2010. (Illus.). 24p. (978-1-55388-646-4(1)); pap. (978-1-55388-652-5(6)) Weigl Educational Pubs. Ltd.

Welch, Deborah. Economic Issues & Development. 2005. (Contemporary Native American Issues Ser.). (Illus.). 160p. (YA). (gr. 9-12). lib. bdg. 30.00 (978-0-7910-7973-7(2)) Facts On File, Inc.

West, David. Lots of Things You Want to Know about Plains Indians... & Some You Don't! 2015. (Lots of Things You Want to Know About Ser.). (Illus.). 24p. (J). 28.50 (978-1-62588-093-2(6)) Black Rabbit Bks.

Whitcraft, Melissa. The Mayflower Compact. 2003. (Cornerstones of Freedom Ser.). (ENG., Illus.). 48p. (YA). (gr. 4-7). 26.00 (978-0-516-24203-3(2)) Scholastic Library Publishing.

White, Tekla. San Francisco Bay Area Missions. 2007. (Exploring California Missions Ser.). (ENG., Illus.). 64p. (gr. 4-7). lib. bdg. 27.93 (978-0-8225-0900-4(8), Lerner Pubns.) Lerner Publishing Group.

Williams, Colleen. Native American Family Life. Johnson, Troy, ed. 2013. (Native American Life Ser.: 15). 64p. (J). (gr. 5-18). 19.95 (978-1-4222-2969-9(6)) Mason Crest.

Williams, Colleen Madonna Flood. Homes of the Native Americans. 2004. (Native American Life Ser.). (Illus.). 64p. (YA). (gr. 5-18). lib. bdg. 19.95 (978-1-59084-120-4(4)) Mason Crest.

—What the Native Americans Wore. 2004. (Native American Life Ser.). (Illus.). 64p. (YA). (gr. 5-18). lib. bdg. 19.95 (978-1-59084-125-9(5)) Mason Crest.

Williams, Jack S. The Chumash of California. 2009. (Library of Native Americans Ser.). 64p. (gr. 4-4). 58.50 (978-1-60853-744-0(7), PowerKids Pr.) Rosen Publishing Group, Inc., The.

—The Esselen of California. (Library of Native Americans Ser.). 64p. 2009. (gr. 4-4). 58.50 (978-1-60853-745-7(5), PowerKids Pr.) 2003. (Illus.). (J). lib. bdg. 26.50 (978-0-8239-6433-8(7)) Rosen Publishing Group, Inc., The.

—Indians of the California Mission Frontier. 2009. (People of the California Missions Ser.). 64p. (gr. 4-4). 58.50 (978-1-60851-157-0(X), PowerKids Pr.) Rosen Publishing Group, Inc., The.

—The Luiseano of California. 2003. (Library of Native Americans). (Illus.). 64p. (J). lib. bdg. 26.50 (978-0-8239-6431-4(0), PowerKids Pr.) Rosen Publishing Group, Inc., The.

—The Luiseno of California. 2009. (Library of Native Americans Ser.). 64p. (gr. 4-4). 58.50 (978-1-60853-752-5(8), PowerKids Pr.) Rosen Publishing Group, Inc., The.

—The Modoc of California. 2004. (Library of Native Americans). (Illus.). 64p. (J). lib. bdg. 26.50 (978-1-4042-2660-9(5)) Rosen Publishing Group, Inc., The.

—The Mojavo of California. 2004. (Library of Native Americans). (Illus.). 64p. (J). lib. bdg. 26.50 (978-1-4042-2661-6(3)) Rosen Publishing Group, Inc., The.

—The Mono of California. 2004. (Library of Native Americans). (Illus.). 64p. (J). lib. bdg. 26.50 (978-1-4042-2662-3(1)) Rosen Publishing Group, Inc., The.

—The Ohlone of California. 2009. (Library of Native Americans Ser.). 64p. (gr. 4-4). 58.50 (978-1-60853-757-0(9), PowerKids Pr.) Rosen Publishing Group, Inc., The.

—The Pomo of California. (Library of Native Americans Ser.). 64p. 2009. (gr. 4-4). 58.50 (978-1-60853-760-0(9)) 2003. (Illus.). (J). lib. bdg. 26.50 (978-0-8239-6436-9(1)) Rosen Publishing Group, Inc., The. (PowerKids Pr.).

—The Shasta of California. 2004. (Library of Native Americans of California). (Illus.). 64p. (J). lib. bdg. 26.50 (978-1-4042-2663-0(X)) Rosen Publishing Group, Inc., The.

—The Shoshone of California. 2004. (Library of Native Americans of California). (Illus.). 64p. (J). lib. bdg. 26.50 (978-1-4042-2664-7(8)) Rosen Publishing Group, Inc., The.

—The Tongva of California. (Library of Native Americans Ser.). 64p. 2009. (gr. 4-4). 58.50 (978-1-60853-764-8(1)) 2003. (Illus.). (J). lib. bdg. 26.50 (978-0-8239-6429-1(9)) Rosen Publishing Group, Inc., The. (PowerKids Pr.).

Williams, Jack S. & Davis, Thomas L. Indians of the California Mission Frontier. 2004. (People of the California Missions Ser.). (Illus.). 64p. (J). lib. bdg. 26.50 (978-0-8239-6281-5(4), PowerKids Pr.) Rosen Publishing Group, Inc., The.

Willis, Michelle "Osawazhinkwaa-Ikwe. Kwezenhs Bimose. Willis, Michelle "Osawazhinkwaa-Ikwe, illus. 2004. (OJI., Illus.). 8p. (J). per. (978-0-9758801-1-1(X)) Bay Mills Indian Community.

Wolf, Linda Little. Visions of the Buffalo People, 1 vol. 2nd ed. 2003. (ENG., Illus.). 128p. (J). (gr. 3-6). pap., act. bk. ed. 15.95 (978-1-58980-124-0(5)) Pelican Publishing Co., Inc.

Wolfson, Evelyn. Native Americans. 2009. (History Explorers Ser.). (ENG.). 24p. (J). (gr. k-2). pap. 5.95 (978-1-84696-214-1(5), TickTock Books) Octopus Publishing Group GBR. Dist: Independent Pubs. Group.

World Book, Inc Staff, contrib. by. Indians of the Northwest Coast & Plateau. 2009. (J). (978-0-7166-2137-9(1)) World Bk., Inc.

—Myths & Legends of Central & South America. 2015. (Illus.). 64p. (J). (978-0-7166-2625-1(X)) World Bk., Inc.

Yasuda, Anita. Explore Native American Cultures! With 25 Great Projects. Keller, Jennifer K., illus. 2013. (Explore Your World Ser.). (ENG.). 96p. (J). (gr. k-4). pap. 12.95 (978-1-61930-160-3(1)) Open City Bks.

Zappler, Georg. Texas Indians. Ivy, Elena T., illus. 2007. (ENG.). 48p. (J). (gr. 1-7). pap. 10.95 (978-0-292-71684-1(2)) Univ. of Texas Pr.

INDIANS OF NORTH AMERICA—ABENAKI INDIANS—FICTION

Bruchac, Joseph. Night Wings. Comport, Sally Wern, illus. 2009. (ENG.). 208p. (J). (gr. 3-7). 15.99 (978-0-06-112318-4(8)) HarperCollins Pubs.

—The Way. 2007. (Darby Creek Exceptional Titles Ser.). 156p. (J). (gr. 4-7). 16.95 (978-1-58196-062-4(X), Darby Creek) Lerner Publishing Group.

—The Winter People. 2004. (ENG., Illus.). 176p. (J). (gr. 3-7). 7.99 (978-0-14-240229-0(X), Puffin Books) Penguin Young Readers Group.

INDIANS OF NORTH AMERICA—ACOMA INDIANS—FICTION

Little, Kimberley Griffiths. The Last Snake Runner. 2006. 201p. (YA). (gr. 7-10). reprint ed. 16.00 (978-1-4223-5838-2(0)) DIANE Publishing Co.

Ortiz, Simon J. The Good Rainbow Road. Lacapa, Michael, illus. 2010. (ENG.). 80p. pap. 9.95 (978-0-8165-2935-3(3)) University of Arizona Pr.

INDIANS OF NORTH AMERICA—AGRICULTURE

Keoke, Emory Dean & Porterfield, Kay Marie. Food, Farming, & Hunting. 2005. (American Indian Contributions to the World Ser.). (Illus.). 160p. (gr. 5-8). 35.00 (978-0-8160-5393-3(6)) Facts On File, Inc.

INDIANS OF NORTH AMERICA—ALGONKIN INDIANS

see Indians Of North America—Algonquian Indians

INDIANS OF NORTH AMERICA—ALGONQUIAN INDIANS

Banting, Erinn & Kissock, Heather. Cree. 2010. (Illus.). 24p. (978-1-55388-645-7(3)); pap. (978-1-55388-651-8(8)) Weigl Educational Pubs. Ltd.

Bjorklund, Ruth. The Cree. 2008. (First Americans Ser.). 48p. (gr. 3-7). lib. bdg. 31.36 (978-0-7614-3020-9(2), Benchmark Bks.) Marshall Cavendish Corp.

First Americans, 6 bks., Set. Incl. Arapaho. Burgan, Michael. lib. bdg. 31.36 (978-0-7614-3017-9(2)); Choctaw. De Capua, Sarah. lib. bdg. 31.36 (978-0-7614-3018-6(0)); Cree. Bjorklund, Ruth. lib. bdg. 31.36 (978-0-7614-3020-9(2)); Hopi. Bjorklund, Ruth. lib. bdg. 31.36 (978-0-7614-3021-6(0)); Lakota. Burgan, Michael. lib. bdg. 31.36 (978-0-7614-3023-0(7)); 48p. (gr. 3-7). (First Americans 4 Ser.). 2008. Set lib. bdg. 188.16 (978-0-7614-3016-2(4), Benchmark Bks.) Marshall Cavendish Corp.

Kissock, Heather. Algonquin. 2010. (Illus.). 24p. (978-1-55388-647-1(X)); pap. (978-1-55388-653-2(4)) Weigl Educational Pubs. Ltd.

McLeese, Tex. Monta deToro y Toreo. Palacios, Argentina, tr. (SPA., Illus.). 24p. (J). (gr. 1-3). lib. bdg. 19.27 (978-1-57103-388-8(2)) Rourke Educational Media.

Pearce, Q. L. Wendigo. 2009. (Monsters Ser.). (ENG., Illus.). 48p. (gr. 4-8). 35.20 (978-0-7377-4409-5(X), Kidhaven) Cengage Gale.

The Puritans, Algonkians & Roger Williams (NCHS) (J). (gr. 5-8). spiral bd., tchr.'s planning gde. ed. 13.50 (978-0-382-44447-0(7)) Cobblestone Publishing Co.

The Puritans, Algonkians & Roger Williams (NCHS) Grades 5-8. (J). tchr. ed. 18.00 (978-0-382-44537-8(6)) Cobblestone Publishing Co.

Rivkin, Jennifer. Searching for the Wendigo. 2014. (Mysterious Monsters Ser.). (Illus.). 32p. (J). (gr. 3-6). lib. bdg. 26.25 (978-1-4777-7117-4(4), PowerKids Pr.) Rosen Publishing Group, Inc., The.

Tieck, Sarah. Algonquin, 1 vol. 2014. (Native Americans Ser.). (ENG.). 32p. (gr. 7-11). 28.50 (978-1-62403-350-6(4)) ABDO Publishing Co.

INDIANS OF NORTH AMERICA—ALGONQUIAN INDIANS—FICTION

Bruchac, Joseph. The Heart of a Chief. 2007. 153p. (gr. 4-7). 17.00 (978-0-7569-7805-1(X)) Perfection Learning Corp.

Lowden, Stephanie. Time of the Eagle: A Story of an Ojibwe Winter. 2004. 128p. (J). pap. 12.00 (978-1-883953-34-8(0)) Great Lakes Literary, LLC.

INDIANS OF NORTH AMERICA—AMUSEMENTS

see Indians of North America—Games; Indians of North America—Social Life and Customs

INDIANS OF NORTH AMERICA—ANTIQUITIES

see also Mounds and Mound Builders

Alexander, Suzanna M., et al. Prehistoric People of Moccasin Bend, Chattanooga, Tennessee: An Educational Coloring Book. 2006. (J). (978-0-9779189-3-5(9)) Waldenhouse Pubs., Inc.

Aveni, Anthony. Buried Beneath Us: Discovering the Ancient Cities of the Americas. Roy, Katherine, illus. 2013. (ENG.). 96p. (J). (gr. 4-8). 18.99 (978-1-59643-567-4(4), 9781596435674) Roaring Brook Pr.

Bauman, Amy & Durman, Laura. Personalities & Places. 2010. (CC: Native North Americans Ser.). 112p. (gr. 6-12). 42.80 (978-1-933834-81-8(1)) Brown Bear Bks.

Boule, Mary Null. Navajo People: SW Region, Set. Liddell, Daniel & Basta, Mary, illus. (Native Americans of North America Ser.). 50-60p. (J). (gr. 3-6). pap. 7.95 (978-1-877599-59-0(X)) Merryant Pubs.

Collins, Terry, et al. The Mesa Verde Cliff Dwellers: An Isabel Soto Archaeology Adventure, 1 vol. 2010. (Graphic Expeditions Ser.). (ENG.). 32p. (gr. 3-4). pap. 8.10 (978-1-4296-4861-5(9)); pap. 47.70 (978-1-4296-5144-8(X)) Capstone Press of Coughlan Cos. (Graphic Library).

—The Mesa Verde Cliff Dwellers: An Isabel Soto Archaeology Adventure, 1 vol. Anderson, Bill, illus. 2010. (Graphic Expeditions Ser.). (ENG.). 32p. (gr. 3-4). lib. bdg. 30.65 (978-1-4296-3971-2(7), Graphic Library) Capstone Press of Coughlan Cos.

Fay, Gail. Secrets of Mesa Verde: Cliff Dwellings of the Pueblo, 1 vol. 2014. (Archaeological Mysteries Ser.). (ENG.). 32p. (gr. 3-4). lib. bdg. 27.99 (978-1-4765-9918-2(1)) Capstone Press of Coughlan Cos.

Holliday, Diane & Malone, Bobbie. Digging & Discovery, Teachers Guide & Student Materials, 2nd Edition, on CD: Wisconsin Archaeology. 2011. (New Badger History Ser.). (ENG.). (J). cd-rom 49.95 (978-0-87020-480-7(7)) Wisconsin Historical Society.

Holliday, Diane Young & Malone, Bobbie. Digging & Discovery: Wisconsin Archaeology. 2nd ed. 2006. (New Badger History Ser.). (Illus.). 120p. (gr. 2-7). pap. 15.95 (978-0-87020-376-3(2)) Wisconsin Historical Society.

Levy, Janey. Hidden History: North America's First People. 2016. (Hidden History Ser.). 00032p. (J). pap. 10.50 (978-1-4824-5790-2(3)) Stevens, Gareth Publishing LLLP.

Mann, Charles C. Before Columbus: The Americas of 1491. 2009. (ENG., Illus.). 128p. (J). (gr. 3-7). 24.99 (978-1-4169-4900-8(3), Atheneum Bks. for Young Readers) Simon & Schuster Children's Publishing.

Miller, Connie R. The Lakota. 2003. (Digging up Native American History Ser.). (J). pap. (978-1-58417-109-6(X)); lib. bdg. (978-1-58417-046-4(8)) Lake Street Pubs.

Rosebrough, Amy & Malone, Bobbie. Water Panthers, Bears, & Thunderbirds: Exploring Wisconsin's Effigy Mounds. 2003. (New Badger History Ser.). (ENG., Illus.). 48p. (J). (gr. 4-7). pap. 9.95 (978-0-87020-357-2(6)) Wisconsin Historical Society.

Steele, Kris. Journey to Cahokia. Steele, Kris, illus. (Illus.). 32p. (Orig.). (J). (gr. 4-6). pap. 4.95 (978-1-881563-02-0(2)) Cahokia Mounds Museum Society.

Ward, Jill. Mississippian Indians. 2010. (J). (978-1-935077-77-0(5)); pap. (978-1-935077-84-8(8)) State Standards Publishing, LLC.

—Shell Mound Builders. 2010. (J). (978-1-935077-75-6(9)); pap. (978-1-935077-82-4(1)) State Standards Publishing, LLC.

—Woodland Indians. 2010. (J). (978-1-935077-76-3(7)); pap. (978-1-935077-83-1(X)) State Standards Publishing, LLC.

Woods, Mary B. & Woods, Michael. Seven Wonders of Ancient North America. 2008. (Seven Wonders Ser.). (ENG., Illus.). 80p. (gr. 5-8). lib. bdg. 33.26 (978-0-8225-7572-6(8)) Lerner Publishing Group.

INDIANS OF NORTH AMERICA—APACHE INDIANS

Bial, Raymond. The People & Culture of the Apache. 2016. (First Peoples of North America Ser.). (ENG., Illus.). 128p. (J). (gr. 6-6). 45.70 (978-1-5026-1010-2(8)) Cavendish Square Publishing.

Bodden, Valerie. Apache. 2015. (Illus.). 48p. (J). (978-1-60818-550-4(8), Creative Education) Creative Co., The.

Dean, Arlan. With All My Might: Cochise & the Indian Wars. 2004. (Great Moments in American History Ser.). (Illus.). 32p. (J). (gr. 3-7). lib. bdg. 22.50 (978-0-8239-4338-8(0), Rosen Reference) Rosen Publishing Group, Inc., The.

Friedman, Mark & Benoit, Peter. The Apache. 2011. (True Bk Ser.). 48p. (J). (ENG.). pap. 6.95 (978-0-531-29311-9(4)); (gr. 3-5). 29.00 (978-0-531-20769-7(2)) Scholastic Library Publishing. (Children's Pr.).

Haugen, Brenda. Geronimo: The Inspiring Life Story of an Apache Warrior. 2016. (Inspiring Stories Ser.). (ENG., Illus.). 112p. (gr. 5-7). lib. bdg. 35.99 (978-0-7565-5162-9(5), CPB Grades 4-8) Compass Point Bks.

Jastrzembski, Joseph C. The Apache Wars: The Final Resistance. 2007. (Landmark Events in Native American History Ser.). (Illus.). 133p. (YA). (gr. 9-12). pap. 35.00 (978-0-7910-9343-6(3)) Facts On File, Inc.

Kissock, Heather & McGill, Jordan. Apache. 2010. (American Indian Art & Culture Ser.). 24p. (J). (gr. 3-6). lib. bdg. 25.70 (978-1-60596-991-6(5)) Weigl Pubs., Inc.

—Apache: American Indian Art & Culture. 2010. pap. 9.95 (978-1-60596-992-3(3)) Weigl Pubs., Inc.

McIntosh, Kenneth. Apache. 2005. (North American Indians Today Ser.). (Illus.). 96p. (YA). (gr. 7-9). lib. bdg. 22.95 (978-1-59084-664-3(8)) Mason Crest.

McLeese, Tex. Enlace en el Rodeo. Palacios, Argentina, tr.Tr. of Rodeo Roping. (SPA., Illus.). 24p. (J). (gr. 1-3). lib. bdg. 19.27 (978-1-57103-384-0(X)) Rourke Educational Media.

Miller, Connie R. The Apache. 2003. (Uncovering Native American History Ser.). (J). pap. (978-1-58417-113-3(8)); lib. bdg. (978-1-58417-050-1(6)) Lake Street Pubs.

Roberts, Russell. The Apache of the Southwest: Apache. 2014. (ENG.). 47p. (J). 29.95 (978-1-62469-005-1(X)) Purple Toad Publishing, Inc.

Sanford, William R. Apache Chief Geronimo. 2013. (Native American Chiefs & Warriors Ser.). 48p. (J). (gr. 5-18). lib. bdg. 22.60 (978-0-7660-4093-9(3)); pap. 8.95 (978-1-4644-0253-1(1)) Enslow Pubs., Inc.

Spilsbury, Richard. Geronimo, 1 vol. Faure, Florence, illus. 2013. (Hero Journals). (ENG.). 48p. (gr. 4-6). pap. 9.95 (978-1-4109-5367-4(X), NA-r) Heinemann-Raintree.

—Geronimo, 1 vol. 2013. (Hero Journals). (ENG., Illus.). 48p. (gr. 4-6). 33.32 (978-1-4109-5360-5(2), NA-r) Heinemann-Raintree.

Tayac, Gabrielle. Meet Naiche: A Native Boy from the Chesapeake Bay Area. Harrington, John, photos by. 2007. (My World: Young Native Americans Today Ser.). (ENG., Illus.). 48p. (J). (gr. 4-7). 15.95 (978-1-57178-146-8(3)) Council Oak Bks.

Tieck, Sarah. Apache, 1 vol. 2014. (Native Americans Ser.). (ENG.). 32p. (gr. 7-11). 28.50 (978-1-62403-351-3(2)) ABDO Publishing Co.

INDIANS OF NORTH AMERICA—APACHE INDIANS—FICTION

Cohen, Rafael. Makoy, the Apache Boy. Balkovek, James, illus. 2013. (ENG.). (J). 14.95 (978-1-62086-340-4(5)) Mascot Bks., Inc.

Paulsen, Gary. Canyons. 2011. 184p. (gr. 4-7). lib. bdg. 18.40 (978-0-8335-6467-2(6), Turtleback) Turtleback Bks.

Sandoval, John. The Witches of Ruidoso. 2013. (ENG.). 120p. (YA). pap. 12.95 (978-1-55885-766-7(4), Piñata Books) Arte Publico Pr.

Taschek, Karen. Horse of Seven Moons. 2005. (ENG., Illus.). 192p. (YA). pap. 14.95 (978-0-8263-3215-8(3)) Univ. of New Mexico Pr.

Wood, Elizabeth Lamb. There Go the Apaches. 2005. pap. 26.95 *(978-1-4191-5979-4(8))* Kessinger Publishing, LLC.

INDIANS OF NORTH AMERICA—ARAWAK INDIANS

Swanton, John R. Indian Tribes of Mexico, Central America & the West Indies. (Shorey Indian Ser.). 40p. (J). reprint ed. pap. 10.00 *(978-0-8466-0087-9(0),* S87) Shorey's Bookstore.

INDIANS OF NORTH AMERICA—ART

American Indian Crafts. 2005. (Book Treks Ser.). (J). (gr. 3-18). stu. ed. 34.95 *(978-0-673-62838-1(8))* Celebration Pr.

Bishop, Celeste. Native American Art of the Northwest Coast. 2013. (InfoMax Readers Ser.). (ENG.). 24p. (J). (gr. 3-4). pap. 8.25 *(978-1-4777-2652-5(7));* pap. 49.50 *(978-1-4777-2653-2(5))* Rosen Publishing Group, Inc., The. (Rosen Classroom).

Collinson, Clare. Arts, Society, & Religion. 2010. (CC: Native North Americans Ser.). (Illus.). 112p. (gr. 6-12). 42.80 *(978-1-933834-79-5(X))* Brown Bear Bks.

Downs, Dorothy. Patchwork: Seminole & Miccosukee Art & Activities. 2005. (ENG., Illus.). 55p. (J). (gr. 3-7). per. 12.95 *(978-1-56164-332-5(7))* Pineapple Pr., Inc.

Falconer, Shelley & White, Shawna. Stones, Bones & Stitches: Storytelling Through Inuit Art. 2007. (Lord Museum Book Ser.). (ENG., Illus.). 48p. (J). (gr. k-12). 22.95 *(978-0-88776-854-5(7),* Tundra Bks.) Tundra Bks. CAN. Dist: Penguin Random Hse. LLC.

Gaspas, Dianne. Southwest Indian Designs Coloring Book. 2003. (Dover Design Coloring Bks.). (ENG., Illus.). 32p. (gr. 3-8). pap. 3.99 *(978-0-486-43042-3(1))* Dover Pubns., Inc.

Gnojewski, Carol. American Indian Crafts Kids Can Do! 2006. (Multicultural Crafts Kids Can Do! Ser.). (Illus.). 32p. (J). (gr. 3-4). lib. bdg. 23.94 *(978-0-7660-2458-8(X),* Enslow Elementary) Enslow Pubs., Inc.

Hall, Margaret C. & Hall, Margaret. Venom & Visions: Art of the Southwest. 2007. (Shockwave: Arts & Culture Ser.). (ENG., Illus.). 36p. (J). (gr. 4-8). 25.00 *(978-0-531-17788-4(2),* Children's Pr.) Scholastic Library Publishing.

Ketchum, Jr. Native American Art. 2017. (Art Collections: Vol. 7). (ENG., Illus.). (YA). (gr. 9-12). 26.95 ***(978-1-4222-3937-7(3))*** Mason Crest.

Kissock, Heather. Comanche. 2010. (American Indian Art & Culture Ser.). 24p. (J). (gr. 3-6). lib. bdg. 25.70 *(978-1-60596-988-6(5))* Weigl Pubs., Inc.

—Comanche: American Indian Art & Culture. 2010. pap. 9.95 *(978-1-60596-989-3(3))* Weigl Pubs., Inc.

Kissock, Heather & McGill, Jordan. Apache. 2010. (American Indian Art & Culture Ser.). 24p. (J). (gr. 3-6). lib. bdg. 25.70 *(978-1-60596-991-6(5))* Weigl Pubs., Inc.

—Apache: American Indian Art & Culture. 2010. pap. 9.95 *(978-1-60596-992-3(3))* Weigl Pubs., Inc.

Kissock, Heather & Small, Rachel. Caddo. 2010. (American Indian Art & Culture Ser.). 24p. (J). (gr. 3-6). lib. bdg. 25.70 *(978-1-60596-979-4(6))* Weigl Pubs., Inc.

—Caddo: American Indian Art & Culture. 2010. pap. 9.95 *(978-1-60596-980-0(X))* Weigl Pubs., Inc.

—Cherokee. 2010. (American Indian Art & Culture Ser.). 24p. (J). (gr. 3-6). lib. bdg. 25.70 *(978-1-60596-994-7(X))* Weigl Pubs., Inc.

—Cherokee: American Indian Art & Culture. 2010. pap. 9.95 *(978-1-60596-995-4(8))* Weigl Pubs., Inc.

Levy, Janey. Native American Art from the Pueblos. (Reading Room Collection 2 Ser.). 24p. 2009. (gr. 3-4). 42.50 *(978-1-60851-981-1(3),* PowerKids Pr.) 2003. (Illus.). (J). lib. bdg. 22.60 *(978-0-8239-3702-8(X))* Rosen Publishing Group, Inc., The.

Native American Art & Artists, 6 vols. (Book2WebTM Ser.). (gr. 4-8). 36.50 *(978-0-322-02981-1(3))* Wright Group/McGraw-Hill.

Nolan, Mary. Totem Poles & Masks: Art of Northwest Coast Tribes. 2013. (Rosen Readers Ser.). (ENG.). 24p. (J). (gr. 3-4). pap. 8.25 *(978-1-4777-2611-2(X));* pap. 49.50 *(978-1-4777-2612-9(8))* Rosen Publishing Group, Inc., The. (Rosen Classroom).

Worth, Richard. George Catlin: Painter of Indian Life. 2009. (ENG., Illus.). 80p. (C). (gr. 6-18). lib. bdg. 158.00 *(978-0-7656-8152-2(8),* Y182314) Routledge.

Zimmerman, Larry J. Exploring the Life, Myth, & Art of Native Americans. 2009. (Civilizations of the World Ser.). (YA). (gr. 7-12). lib. bdg. 42.60 *(978-1-4358-5614-1(7))* Rosen Publishing Group, Inc., The.

INDIANS OF NORTH AMERICA—BIOGRAPHY

Adams, Colleen. Pocahontas. 2009. (Reading Room Collection 1 Ser.). 16p. (gr. 2-3). 37.50 *(978-1-60851-949-1(X),* PowerKids Pr.) Rosen Publishing Group, Inc., The.

Annino, J. G. She Sang Promise: The Story of Betty Mae Jumper, Seminole Tribal Leader. Desimini, Lisa, illus. 2010. (ENG.). 48p. (J). (gr. 1-4). 17.95 *(978-1-4263-0592-4(3),* National Geographic Children's Bks.) National Geographic Society.

Annino, J G. She Sang Promise: The Story of Betty Mae Jumper, Seminole Tribal Leader. Desimini, Lisa, illus. 2010. (ENG.). 48p. (J). (gr. 1-4). 26.90 *(978-1-4263-0593-1(1),* National Geographic Children's Bks.) National Geographic Society.

Bailey, Tom. Red Eagle: Legendary Creek Warrior. 2009. (Illus.). 104p. (J). pap. *(978-1-59421-047-1(0))* Seacoast Publishing, Inc.

Banks, Sara Harrell. Tomo-Chi-Chi: Gentle Warrior. (J). pap. 12.95 *(978-0-913720-79-0(8))* Beil, Frederic C. Pub., Inc.

Bauman, Amy & Durman, Laura. Personalities & Places. 2010. (CC: Native North Americans Ser.). 112p. (gr. 6-12). 42.80 *(978-1-933834-81-8(1))* Brown Bear Bks.

Becker, Sandra. Pocahontas. 2003. (Folk Heroes Ser.). (Illus.). 24p. (J). lib. bdg. 24.45 *(978-1-59036-074-3(5))* Weigl Pubs., Inc.

Belarde-Lewis, Miranda. Meet Lydia: A Native Girl from Southeast Alaska. Harrington, John, photos by. 2004. (My World: Young Native Americans Today Ser.). (ENG., Illus.). 48p. (J). 15.95 *(978-1-57178-147-5(1))* Council Oak Bks.

Benjamin, Andrew. Pocahontas. 2014. (Illus.). 32p. (J). lib. bdg. *(978-1-62712-292-4(3))* Cavendish Square Publishing.

Bennett, Doraine. Sequoyah. 2008. *(978-1-935077-05-3(8));* pap. *(978-1-935077-12-1(0))* State Standards Publishing, LLC.

—Tomochichi. 2008. (J). *(978-1-935077-06-0(6));* pap. *(978-1-935077-13-8(9))* State Standards Publishing, LLC.

Biskup, Agnieszka. Thunder Rolling down the Mountain: The Story of Chief Joseph & the Nez Perce, 1 vol. Zimmerman, Rusty, illus. 2011. (American Graphic Ser.). (ENG.). 32p. (gr. 3-4). pap. 8.10 *(978-1-4296-6270-3(0));* pap. 47.70 *(978-1-4296-6437-0(1))* Capstone Press of Coughlan Cos. (Graphic Library).

Bolden, Tonya. Searching for Sarah Rector: The Richest Black Girl in America. 2014. (ENG., Illus.). 80p. (J). (gr. 3-7). 21.95 *(978-1-4197-0846-6(5),* Abrams Bks. for Young Readers) Abrams, Inc.

Brennan, Kristine. Native Americans. (Successful Americans Ser.). 64p. (YA). 2009. (Illus.). (gr. 9-12). 22.95 *(978-1-4222-0517-4(7))* 2007. (gr. 7-18). pap. 9.95 *(978-1-4222-0866-3(4))* Mason Crest.

Brimner, Larry Dane. Chief Crazy Horse: Following a Vision. 2008. (American Heroes Ser.). 48p. (gr. 3-18). lib. bdg. 29.93 *(978-0-7614-3061-2(X),* Benchmark Bks.) Marshall Cavendish Corp.

—Pocahontas: Bridging Two Worlds. 2008. (American Heroes Ser.). 48p. (gr. 3-18). lib. bdg. 29.93 *(978-0-7614-3065-0(2),* Benchmark Bks.) Marshall Cavendish Corp.

Bruchac, Joseph. Buffalo Song. Farnsworth, Bill, illus. 2008. (J). Lee & Low Bks., Inc.

—Buffalo Song. Farnsworth, Bill, illus. 2013. (ENG.). 40p. (C). pap. 15.95 *(978-1-60060-990-9(2))* National Geographic School Publishing, Inc.

—Jim Thorpe, Original All-American. 2008. (ENG.). 288p. (YA). (gr. 7-18). 9.99 *(978-0-14-241233-6(3),* Speak) Penguin Young Readers Group.

Buffalohead, Julie & Erdrich, Liselotte. Sacagawea. Buffalohead, Julie, illus. 2003. (ENG., Illus.). 40p. (J). (gr. 3-6). 17.95 *(978-0-87614-646-0(9),* Carolrhoda Bks.) Lerner Publishing Group.

Capaldi, Gina. A Boy Named Beckoning: The True Story of Dr. Carlos Montezuma, Native American Hero. Capaldi, Gina, illus. 2008. (Exceptional Social Studies Titles for Intermediate Grades). (ENG., Illus.). 32p. (J). (gr. 3-6). lib. bdg. 16.95 *(978-0-8225-7644-0(9))* Lerner Publishing Group.

Carole Marsh. California Indians. 2004. (California Experience Ser.). 36p. (gr. 3-8). pap. 7.95 *(978-0-635-02254-7(0))* Gallopade International.

Charleyboy, Lisa. Urban Tribes: Native Americans in the City. Leatherdale, Mary Beth, ed. 2015. (ENG., Illus.). 136p. (YA). (gr. 6-12). pap. 14.95 *(978-1-55451-750-3(8),* 9781554517503) Annick Pr., Ltd. CAN. Dist: Publishers Group West (PGW).

Chatlien, Ruth Hull. Modern American Indian Chiefs. 2009. (Sharing the American Dream Ser.). (Illus.). 64p. (YA). (gr. 7-12). 22.95 *(978-1-4222-0592-1(4))* Mason Crest.

Chatlien, Ruth Hull & Cohon, Rhody. Modern American Indian Chiefs. 2007. (Sharing the American Dream Ser.). 64p. (YA). (gr. 7-18). pap. 9.95 *(978-1-4222-0757-4(9))* Mason Crest.

Coleman, Miriam. The Life of Black Elk. 2016. (Native American Biographies Ser.). (Illus.). 32p. (J). (gr. 5-4). 26.25 *(978-1-5081-4814-2(7),* PowerKids Pr.) Rosen Publishing Group, Inc., The.

Colich, Abby. Wilma Mankiller, 1 vol. 2014. (Great Women in History Ser.). (ENG., Illus.). 24p. (gr. k-1). pap. 6.29 *(978-1-4914-0543-7(0),* Pebble Bks.) Capstone Press of Coughlan Cos.

Collard, Sneed B., III. Sacagawea: Brave Shoshone Girl. 2006. (American Heroes Ser.). (Illus.). 48p. (gr. 3-7). lib. bdg. 29.93 *(978-0-7614-2166-5(1),* Benchmark Bks.) Marshall Cavendish Corp.

Collier, James Lincoln. The Tecumseh You Never Knew. Copeland, Greg, illus. 2004. (You Never Knew Ser.). (ENG.). (J). 25.50 *(978-0-516-24426-6(4),* Children's Pr.) Scholastic Library Publishing.

Collins, David R., et al. Ishi: The Last of His People. Welch, Kelly, illus. 2004. (Notable Americans Ser.). 96p. (YA). (gr. 6-12). 23.95 *(978-1-883846-54-1(4),* First Biographies) Reynolds, Morgan Inc.

Cosson, Jody. Sacagawea: Indian Guide, 1 vol. Soud, illus. 2008. (Beginner Biographies Ser.). (ENG.). 32p. (gr. -1-3). 28.50 *(978-1-60270-252-3(7),* Looking Glass Library-Nonfiction) Magic Wagon.

Crazy Horse. 2010. (Legends of the Wild West Ser.). (Illus.). 144p. (gr. 6-12). 35.00 *(978-1-60413-526-8(3),* Chelsea Hse.) Facts On File, Inc.

Crosby, Michael T. Sacagawea: Lewis & Clark's Pathfinder. 2007. 144p. (J). (gr. 6-18). 25.95 *(978-1-59556-026-1(2))* OTTN Publishing.

Davis, Kenneth C. Don't Know Much about Sitting Bull Sitting Bull, Vol. 2. 2003. (Don't Know Much About Ser.). (Illus.). 144p. (J). (gr. 3-7). 16.89 *(978-0-06-028818-1(3))* HarperCollins Pubs.

Dean, Arlan. With All My Might: Cochise & the Indian Wars. 2009. (Great Moments in American History Ser.). 32p. (gr. 3-3). 47.90 *(978-1-61513-137-2(X))* Rosen Publishing Group, Inc., The.

DeFord, Diane. Chief Sitting Bull. 2009. pap. 13.25 *(978-1-60559-070-7(3))* Hameray Publishing Group, Inc.

—Sacagawea. 2009. pap. 13.25 *(978-1-60559-069-1(X))* Hameray Publishing Group, Inc.

Dell, Pamela. Apache Resistance: Causes & Effects of Geronimo's Campaign. 2015. (Cause & Effect: American Indian History Ser.). (ENG., Illus.). 32p. (gr. 3-4). pap. 7.95 *(978-1-4914-4904-2(7))* Capstone Press of Coughlan Cos.

Deutsch, Stacia & Cohon, Rhody. John B. Herrington. (Sharing the American Dream Ser.). 64p. (YA). (gr. 7-12). 2009. 22.95 *(978-1-4222-0579-2(7))* 2007. pap. 9.95 *(978-1-4222-0747-5(1))* Mason Crest.

Doremus, Robert, illus. Sacagawea. 2014. (History's All-Stars Ser.). (ENG.). 208p. (J). (gr. 3-7). pap. 6.99 *(978-1-4814-1499-9(2),* Simon & Schuster/Paula Wiseman Bks.) Simon & Schuster/Paula Wiseman Bks.

Dunn, Joeming W. Sacagawea, 1 vol. Espinosa, Rod, illus. 2008. (Bio-Graphics Ser.). (ENG.). 32p. 28.50 *(978-1-60270-176-2(8),* Graphic Planet- Nonfiction) ABDO Publishing Co.

Eastman, Charles Alexander. Indian Boyhood: The True Story of a Sioux Upbringing. Fitzgerald, Michael Oren, ed. Rasch, Heidi M., illus. 2016. (ENG.). 40p. (J). (gr. k-3). 17.95 *(978-1-937786-56-4(0),* Wisdom Tales) World Wisdom, Inc.

Egan, Tracie. Cynthia Ann Parker: Cautiva de los Comanches. Gonzalez, Tomas, tr. 2004. (Grandes Personajes en la Historia de Los Estados Unidos Ser.). (ENG & SPA.). 32p. (gr. 3-6). pap. 10.00 *(978-0-8239-4225-1(2))* Rosen Publishing Group, Inc., The.

—Cynthia Ann Parker: Cautiva de los comanches (Cynthia Ann Parker: Comanche Captive) 2009. (Grandes personajes en la historia de los Estados Unidos (Famous People in American History) Ser.). (SPA.). 32p. (gr. 2-3). 47.90 *(978-1-61512-796-2(8),* Editorial Buenas Letras) Rosen Publishing Group, Inc., The.

—Cynthia Ann Parker: Comanche Captive. 2009. (Primary Sources of Famous People in American History Ser.). 32p. (gr. 2-3). 47.90 *(978-1-60851-667-4(9))* Rosen Publishing Group, Inc., The.

—Cynthia Ann Parker: Comanche Captive / Cautiva de los Comanches. 2009. (Famous People in American History/Grandes personajes en la historia de los Estados Unidos Ser.). (ENG & SPA.). 32p. (gr. 2-3). 47.90 *(978-1-61512-542-5(6),* Editorial Buenas Letras) Rosen Publishing Group, Inc., The.

Feinstein, Stephen. Lee Sobre Sacagawea/Read about Sacagawea. 2006. (I Like Biographies! Bilingual Ser.). (ENG & SPA., Illus.). 24p. (J). (gr. 1-3). lib. bdg. 22.60 *(978-0-7660-2674-2(4),* Enslow Elementary) Enslow Pubs., Inc.

—Read about Sacagawea. 2004. (I Like Biographies! Ser.). (Illus.). 24p. (J). lib. bdg. 22.60 *(978-0-7660-2297-3(8))* Enslow Pubs., Inc.

First Americans Group 2, 6 bks., Set. Incl. Cheyenne. De Capua, Sarah. 47p. (J). lib. bdg. 31.36 *(978-0-7614-2248-8(X));* Comanche. De Capua, Sarah. 48p. lib. bdg. 31.36 *(978-0-7614-2249-5(8));* Haida. King, David C. 48p. (J). lib. bdg. 31.36 *(978-0-7614-2250-1(1));* Huron. King, David C. 48p. lib. bdg. 31.36 *(978-0-7614-2251-8(X));* Ojibwe. King, David C. 48p. lib. bdg. 31.36 *(978-0-7614-2252-5(8));* Seminole. King, David C. 48p. (J). lib. bdg. 31.36 *(978-0-7614-2253-2(6));* (Illus.). (gr. 3-7). 2006. 2007. Set lib. bdg. 188.14 *(978-0-7614-2247-1(1),* Benchmark Bks.) Marshall Cavendish Corp.

Ford, Carin T. Sacagawea: Meet an American Legend. 2003. (Meeting Famous People Ser.). (Illus.). 32p. (J). lib. bdg. 22.60 *(978-0-7660-2004-7(5))* Enslow Pubs., Inc.

Franklin, Virgil. The Story of Sacagawea. 2009. (Reading Room Collection 2 Ser.). 24p. (gr. 3-4). 42.50 *(978-1-60851-997-2(X),* PowerKids Pr.) Rosen Publishing Group, Inc., The.

Frazier, Neta. Path to the Pacific: The Story of Sacagawea. 2017. (Great Leaders & Events Ser.). (ENG.). (J). (gr. 4-8). lib. bdg. 35.99 ***(978-1-942875-44-4(4))*** Quarto Publishing Group USA.

Frazier, Neta Lohnes. Path to the Pacific: The Story of Sacagawea. 2016. (Young Voyageur Ser.). (ENG., Illus.). 208p. (J). (gr. 4-9). pap. 12.99 *(978-0-7603-5227-4(5),* Voyageur Pr.) Quarto Publishing Group USA.

Furbee, Mary Rodd. Wild Rose: Nancy Ward & the Cherokee Nation. 2004. (Women of the Frontier Ser.). (Illus.). 112p. (YA). (gr. 6-12). 23.95 *(978-1-883846-71-8(4),* First Biographies) Reynolds, Morgan Inc.

Gourley, Catherine. Who Is Maria Tallchief? Taylor, Val Paul, illus. 2003. (Who Was... ? Ser.). 103p. 15.00 *(978-0-7569-1592-6(9))* Perfection Learning Corp.

Griffiths, Katie. Sacagawea. 2017. (J). ***(978-1-5026-2747-6(7))*** Cavendish Square Publishing.

Gunderson, Jessica Sarah. Sacagawea: Journey into the West, 1 vol. Martin, Cynthia & Schulz, Barbara, illus. 2006. (Graphic Biographies Ser.). (ENG.). 32p. (gr. 3-4). per. 8.10 *(978-0-7368-9663-4(5),* Graphic Library) Capstone Press of Coughlan Cos.

Gunther, Vanessa. Chief Joseph: A Biography, 1 vol. 2010. (Greenwood Biographies Ser.). (Illus.). 178p. (C). 39.00 *(978-0-313-37920-8(3),* GR7920, Greenwood) ABC-CLIO, LLC.

Haldy, Emma E. Sacagawea. Bane, Jeff, illus. 2016. (My Early Library: My Itty-Bitty Bio Ser.). (ENG.). 24p. (J). (gr. k-1). 28.50 *(978-1-63470-482-3(7),* 207659) Cherry Lake Publishing.

Harkins, Susan Sales & Harkins, William H. Pochantas. 2008. (What's So Great About... ? Ser.). (Illus.). 32p. (J). (gr. 2-4). lib. bdg. 25.70 *(978-1-58415-682-6(1))* Mitchell Lane Pubs., Inc.

Harrington, John, illus. & photos by. Meet Mindy: A Native Girl from the Southwest. Harrington, John, photos by. Secakuku, Susan, photos by. 2013. 48p. (J). *(978-1-933565-20-0(9))* Smithsonian National Museum of the American Indian.

Hayhurst, Chris. Sitting Bull: Sioux War Chief. 2009. (Primary Sources of Famous People in American History Ser.). 32p. (gr. 2-3). 47.90 *(978-1-60851-724-4(1))* Rosen Publishing Group, Inc., The.

—Sitting Bull / Toro Sentado: Sioux War Chief / Jefe Sioux. 2009. (Famous People in American History/Grandes personajes en la historia de los Estados Unidos Ser.). (SPA.). 32p. (gr. 2-3). 47.90 *(978-1-61512-555-5(8),* Editorial Buenas Letras) Rosen Publishing Group, Inc., The.

—Toro Sentado: Jefe Sioux. 2004. (Grandes personajes en la historia de los Estados Unidos Ser.). (ENG & SPA.). 32p. (gr. 3-6). pap. 10.00 *(978-0-8239-4238-1(4))* Rosen Publishing Group, Inc., The.

—Toro Sentado: Jefe sioux (Sitting Bull: Sioux War Chief) 2009. (Grandes personajes en la historia de los Estados Unidos (Famous People in American History) Ser.). (SPA.). 32p. (gr. 2-3). 47.90 *(978-1-61512-809-9(3),* Editorial Buenas Letras) Rosen Publishing Group, Inc., The.

Heiderstadt, Dorothy. Indian Friends & Foes: A Baker's Dozen Portraits from Pocahontas to Geronimo. Miller, David Humphreys, illus. 2011. 144p. 40.95 *(978-1-258-08676-3(X))* Literary Licensing, LLC.

Hemingway, Al. Chuck Norris. 2007. (Sharing the American Dream Ser.). 64p. (YA). (gr. 7-18). pap. 9.95 *(978-1-4222-0758-1(7))* Mason Crest.

Holliday, Diane Young. Mountain Wolf Woman: A Ho-Chunk Girlhood. 2007. (Badger Biographies Ser.). (ENG., Illus.). 88p. (J). (gr. 3-7). per. 12.95 *(978-0-87020-381-7(9))* Wisconsin Historical Society.

Hopping, Lorraine Jean. Chief Joseph: The Voice for Peace. 2010. (Sterling Biographies(r) Ser.). (ENG., Illus.). 128p. (J). (gr. 5-18). pap. 5.95 *(978-1-4027-6004-4(3))* Sterling Publishing Co., Inc.

Howard, Annabelle. Cry Out Liberty: Sarah Winnemucca, Indian Princess. 2005. (J). pap. *(978-1-4108-4204-6(5))* Benchmark Education Co.

Hunt, Santana. Geronimo. 2015. (Native American Heroes Ser.). (ENG., Illus.). 24p. (J). (gr. 1-2). pap. 8.15 *(978-1-4824-2685-4(4))* Stevens, Gareth Publishing LLLP.

—Osceola. 2015. (Native American Heroes Ser.). (ENG., Illus.). 24p. (J). (gr. 1-2). pap. 8.15 *(978-1-4824-2689-2(7))* Stevens, Gareth Publishing LLLP.

Jazynka, Kitson. Sacagawea. 2015. (Readers Bios Ser.). (ENG., Illus.). 32p. (J). (gr. 1-4). pap. 3.99 *(978-1-4263-1963-1(0),* National Geographic Children's Bks.) National Geographic Society.

Jeffrey, Gary. Sitting Bull: The Life of a Lakota Chief. 2009. (Graphic Nonfiction Biographies Ser.). (ENG.). 48p. (YA). (gr. 4-5). 58.50 *(978-1-61513-027-6(6),* Rosen Reference) Rosen Publishing Group, Inc., The.

Jeffrey, Gary & Petty, Kate. Sitting Bull: The Life of a Lakota Sioux Chief. 2005. (Graphic Nonfiction Biographies Ser.). (ENG., Illus.). 48p. (YA). (gr. 4-7). lib. bdg. 31.95 *(978-1-4042-0247-4(1))* Rosen Publishing Group, Inc., The.

Jones, Victoria Garrett. Pocahontas: A Life in Two Worlds. 2010. (Sterling Biographies(r) Ser.). (ENG., Illus.). 128p. (J). (gr. 5-18). pap. 5.95 *(978-1-4027-5158-5(3))* Sterling Publishing Co., Inc.

Juettner, Bonnie. 100 Native-Americans Who Shaped American History. 2015. (ENG., Illus.). 100p. (J). pap. 7.95 *(978-0-912517-51-3(4))* Bluewood Bks.

Kalman, Bobbie & Aloian, Molly. Famous Native North Americans. 2003. (Native Nations of North America Ser.). (ENG., Illus.). 32p. (J). (gr. 5). pap. *(978-0-7787-0471-3(8));* lib. bdg. *(978-0-7787-0379-2(7))* Crabtree Publishing Co.

Kessel, Joyce K. Squanto Y el Primer Dia de Accion de Gracias; Squanto & the First Thanksgiving. 2008. pap. 40.95 *(978-0-8225-9678-3(4))* Lerner Publishing Group.

Krull, Kathleen. Sacajawea. Collins, Matt, illus. 2015. (Women Who Broke the Rules Ser.). (ENG.). 48p. (J). (gr. 1-4). 16.99 *(978-0-8027-3799-1(4),* 9780802737991, Bloomsbury USA Childrens) Bloomsbury Publishing USA.

Labrecque, Ellen. What's Your Story, Sacagawea? 2015. (ENG., Illus.). 32p. (J). (gr. k-3). 26.65 *(978-1-4677-7966-1(0))* Lerner Publishing Group.

Laplante, Walter. Sitting Bull. 2015. (Native American Heroes Ser.). (ENG., Illus.). 24p. (J). (gr. 1-2). 22.60 *(978-1-4824-2702-8(8))* Stevens, Gareth Publishing LLLP.

Littlechild, George. This Land Is My Land, 1 vol. Littlechild, George, illus. 2014. (ENG., Illus.). 32p. (J). pap. 10.95 *(978-0-89239-184-4(7),* Children's Book Press) Lee & Low Bks., Inc.

Lobb, Nancy. 16 Extraordinary Native Americans. 2nd ed. 2007. (Illus.). 132p. (YA). (gr. 6-12). tchr. ed., per. 25.00 *(978-0-8251-6282-4(3))* Walch Education.

Lynette, Rachel. Sacagawea. 2013. (Pioneer Spirit: the Westward Expansion Ser.). 24p. (J). (gr. 3-6). 22.60 *(978-1-4777-0782-1(4));* pap. 49.50 *(978-1-4777-0898-9(7));* (ENG., Illus.). pap. 8.25 *(978-1-4777-0897-2(9))* Rosen Publishing Group, Inc., The. (PowerKids Pr.).

Mapua, Jeff. Sitting Bull, 01 vols., 1. 2016. (Britannica Beginner Bios Ser.). (ENG., Illus.). 32p. (J). pap. 12.90 *(978-1-5081-0062-1(4),* Britannica Educational Publishing) Rosen Publishing Group, Inc., The.

Marcovitz, Hal. Sacagawea: Guide for the Lewis & Clark Expedition. 2007. (Illus.). 63p. (J). pap. 12.00 *(978-1-4223-6712-4(6))* DIANE Publishing Co.

Marsh, Carole. Ben Nighthorse Campbell. 2003. 12p. (gr. k-4). 2.95 *(978-0-635-02383-4(0))* Gallopade International.

—Crazy Horse. 2003. 12p. (gr. k-4). 2.95 *(978-0-635-02382-7(2))* Gallopade International.

—Father Junipero Serra: California Missions Founder: California Missions Founder. 2003. 12p. (gr. k-4). 2.95 *(978-0-635-02136-6(6))* Gallopade International.

—Geronimo. 2003. 12p. (gr. k-4). 2.95 *(978-0-635-02381-0(4))* Gallopade International.

—Sequoyah. 2003. 12p. (gr. k-4). 2.95 *(978-0-635-02363-6(6))* Gallopade International.

—Sitting Bull. 2003. 12p. (gr. k-4). 2.95 *(978-0-635-02378-0(4))* Gallopade International.

McAneney, Caitie. The Life of Sacagawea. 2016. (Native American Biographies Ser.). (Illus.). 32p. (J). (gr. 5-4). 26.25 *(978-1-5081-4819-7(8),* PowerKids Pr.) Rosen Publishing Group, Inc., The.

McGovern, Ann. Native American Heroes: Osceola, Tecumseh & Cochise. 2014. (ENG.). 128p. (J). (gr. 3-7). pap. 4.99 *(978-0-545-46720-9(9),* Scholastic Nonfiction) Scholastic, Inc.

Metaxas, Eric. Squanto & the First Thanksgiving: The Legendary American Tale. Donato, Michael A., illus. 2004. 36p. (J). (gr. 3-8). reprint ed. 19.00 *(978-0-7567-7123-2(4))* DIANE Publishing Co.

Miller, Barbara Kiely. Chief Joseph. 2007. (Great Americans Ser.). 24p. (gr. 1-4). pap. 8.15 *(978-0-8368-8321-3(7));* lib. bdg. 22.00 *(978-0-8368-8314-5(4))* Stevens, Gareth Publishing LLLP. (Weekly Reader Leveled Readers).

Monceaux, Morgan & Katcher, Ruth. My Heroes, My People: African Americans & Native Americans in Thewest. Monceaux, Morgan, illus. 2004. (Illus.). 63p. (J). (gr. k-4). reprint ed. 18.00 *(978-0-7567-7868-2(9))* DIANE Publishing Co.

Moskal, Greg. Un pueblo apache (an Apache Indian Community) 2009. (Reading Room Collection: Spanish Ser.). (SPA.). 24p. (gr. 3-4). 42.50 *(978-1-60854-180-5(0),* Editorial Buenas Letras) Rosen Publishing Group, Inc., The.

Naquin, Roy. Tales of Little Bear & Little Buffalo. 2011. 80p. pap. 9.95 *(978-1-4327-6627-6(9))* Outskirts Pr., Inc.

Native American Biographies, 6 bks., Set. (Illus.). (YA). (gr. 6-12). lib. bdg. 125.70 *(978-0-89490-965-8(7))* Enslow Pubs., Inc.

Native American Biographies. 2016. (Native American Biographies Ser.). 32p. (gr. 5-4). 157.50 *(978-1-4994-1868-2(X));* pap. 70.50 *(978-1-4994-1889-7(2))* Rosen Publishing Group, Inc., The. (PowerKids Pr.).

Native American Writers. 2010. (Multicultural Voices Ser.). (Illus.). 126p. (gr. 6-12). 35.00 *(978-1-60413-314-1(7),* Chelsea Hse.) Facts On File, Inc.

H
I

Nelson, Maria. The Life of Sacagawea. 2012. (Famous Lives Ser.). (ENG., Illus.). 24p. (J). (gr. k-3). lib. bdg. 22.60 *(978-1-4339-6357-5(4))*; (gr. 1-4). pap. 8.15 *(978-1-4339-6359-9(0))* Stevens, Gareth Publishing LLLP.

—Red Cloud. 2015. (Native American Heroes Ser.). (ENG., Illus.). 24p. (J). (gr. 1-2). pap. 8.15 *(978-1-4824-2692-2(7))* Stevens, Gareth Publishing LLLP.

—Red Jacket. 2015. (Native American Heroes Ser.). (ENG., Illus.). 24p. (J). (gr. 1-2). pap. 8.15 *(978-1-4824-2696-0(X))* Stevens, Gareth Publishing LLLP.

Nelson, S. D. Black Elk's Vision: A Lakota Story. 2010. (ENG., Illus.). 56p. (J). (gr. 3-7). 21.95 *(978-0-8109-8399-1(0),* Abrams Bks. for Young Readers) Abrams, Inc.

—Buffalo Bird Girl: A Hidatsa Story. 2015. (ENG., Illus.). 56p. (J). (gr. 1-4). 9.95 *(978-1-4197-1838-0(X),* Abrams Bks. for Young Readers) Abrams, Inc.

—Quiet Hero: The Ira Hayes Story. 2006. (ENG., Illus.). 32p. (J). 16.95 *(978-1-58430-263-6(1))* Lee & Low Bks., Inc.

—Red Cloud: A Lakota Story of War & Surrender. 2017. (ENG., Illus.). 64p. (J). (gr. 3-7). 19.95 *(978-1-4197-2313-1(8),* Abrams Bks. for Young Readers) Abrams, Inc.

—Sitting Bull: Lakota Warrior & Defender of His People. 2015. (ENG., Illus.). 64p. (J). (gr. 3-7). 19.95 *(978-1-4197-0731-5(0),* Abrams Bks. for Young Readers) Abrams, Inc.

Niethammer, Carolyn J. Keeping the Rope Straight: Annie Dodge Wauneka's Life of Service to the Navajo. 2006. (ENG., Illus.). 128p. (J). (gr. 4-7). 22.95 *(978-1-893354-72-2(5))* Salina Bookshelf Inc.

Olson, Greg. Great Walker: Ioway Leader. Hare, John, illus. 2014. (ENG.). 48p. (J). lib. bdg. 24.00 *(978-1-61248-112-8(4))* Truman State Univ. Pr.

O'Maley, Elizabeth. Bones on the Ground. 2014. (J). *(978-0-87195-362-9(5))* Indiana Historical Society.

Petrie, Kristin. Sacagawea, 1 vol. 2007. (Explorers Set 2 Ser.). (ENG., Illus.). 32p. (gr. 4-7). 27.07 *(978-1-59679-749-9(5),* Checkerboard Library) ABDO Publishing Co.

Phillips, Larissa. Cochise: Apache Chief. 2009. (Primary Sources of Famous People in American History Ser.). 32p. (gr. 2-3). 47.90 *(978-1-60851-660-5(1))* Rosen Publishing Group, Inc., The.

—Cochise: Apache Chief / Cochise: Jefe Apache. 2009. (Famous People in American History/Grandes personajes en la historia de los Estados Unidos Ser.). (ENG & SPA.). 32p. (gr. 2-3). 47.90 *(978-1-61512-540-1(X),* Editorial Buenas Letras) Rosen Publishing Group, Inc., The.

—Cochise: Jefe Apache. de la Vega, Eida, tr. from ENG. 2004. (Grandes Personajes en la Historia de Los Estados Unidos Ser.). (ENG & SPA., Illus.). 32p. (gr. 3-6). pap. 10.00 *(978-0-8239-4223-7(6))* Rosen Publishing Group, Inc., The.

—Cochise: Jefe apache (Cochise: Apache Chief) 2009. (Grandes personajes en la historia de los Estados Unidos (Famous People in American History) Ser.). (SPA.). 32p. (gr. 2-3). 47.90 *(978-1-61512-792-4(5),* Editorial Buenas Letras) Rosen Publishing Group, Inc., The.

Pohl, Amelia E. Mary Musgrove: Georgia, My State Biographies. l.t. ed. 2008. (ENG., Illus.). 24p. (J). (gr. k-2). 22.60 *(978-1-935077-02-2(3),* Everett Pr.) State Standards Publishing, LLC.

Poulakidas, Georgene. Black Hawk's War. 2009. (Primary Sources of American Wars Ser.). 24p. (gr. 3-4). 42.50 *(978-1-60851-518-9(4),* PowerKids Pr.) Rosen Publishing Group, Inc., The.

Rausch, Monica. Sacagawea. 2007. (Grandes personajes (Spanish- Great Americans) Ser.). 24p. (gr. 1-4). (SPA.). pap. 8.15 *(978-0-8368-7991-9(0))*; (Illus.). pap. 8.15 *(978-0-8368-7692-5(X))*; (Illus.). lib. bdg. 22.00 *(978-0-8368-7685-7(7))* Stevens, Gareth Publishing LLLP. (Weekly Reader Leveled Readers).

Rausch, Monica L. Sacagawea. 2007. (Grandes personajes (Great Americans) Ser.). (SPA., Illus.). 24p. (gr. 1-4). lib. bdg. 22.00 *(978-0-8368-7984-1(8),* Weekly Reader Leveled Readers) Stevens, Gareth Publishing LLLP.

Ray, Deborah Kogan. Paiute Princess: The Story of Sarah Winnemucca, 1 vol. Ray, Deborah Kogan, illus. 2012. (ENG., Illus.). 48p. (J). (gr. 3-7). 17.99 *(978-0-374-39897-2(6),* 9780374398972, Farrar, Straus & Giroux (BYR)) Farrar, Straus & Giroux.

Rickard, Kris A. & Bial, Raymond. The People & Culture of the Arapaho. 2016. (First Peoples of North America Ser.). 128p. (J). 45.64 *(978-1-5026-2253-2(X))* Cavendish Square Publishing.

Robertson, David. The Ballad of Nancy April: Shawnadithit. Henderson, Scott B., illus. 2014. (Tales from Big Spirit Ser.: 6). (ENG.). 32p. (J). (gr. 4-6). pap. *(978-1-55379-477-6(X),* 7a5bbbca-e620-446e-8c13-29bf73a0b984, HighWater Pr.) Portage & Main Pr.

—The Land of Os: John Ramsay. Tien, Wai, illus. 2014. (Tales from Big Spirit Ser.: 6). (ENG.). 32p. (J). (gr. 4-6). pap. *(978-1-55379-491-2(5),* 71d193fb-9d6f-4711-9ca7-63e7716b3ed2, HighWater Pr.) Portage & Main Pr.

—The Scout: Tommy Prince. Henderson, Scott B., illus. 2014. (Tales from Big Spirit Ser.: 6). (ENG.). 32p. (J). (gr. 4-6). pap. *(978-1-55379-478-3(8),* 78912685-2d85-4153-9f88-b7d8feb31ffe, HighWater Pr.) Portage & Main Pr.

—The Slave Woman: Thanadelthur. Tien, Wai, illus. 2014. (Tales from Big Spirit Ser.: 6). (ENG.). 32p. (J). (gr. 4-6). pap. *(978-1-55379-479-0(6),* 51f7764c-c947-4547-8ce4-63887e0f4e03, HighWater Pr.) Portage & Main Pr.

Rucker, Jeffrey A. La historia de Toro Sentado (the Story of Sitting Bull) 2009. (Reading Room Collection: Spanish Ser.). (SPA.). 24p. (gr. 3-4). 42.50 *(978-1-60854-178-2(9),* Editorial Buenas Letras) Rosen Publishing Group, Inc., The.

—The Story of Sitting Bull. 2003. (Rosen Real Readers Big Bookstm Ser.). (ENG.). 24p. (gr. 3-4). 43.95 *(978-0-8239-8731-3(0))* Rosen Publishing Group, Inc., The.

Sacajawea, Traductora Y Guia. 2003. (Notas Biograficas Ser.). (YA). pap. 48.95 *(978-0-8136-5915-2(9))* Modern Curriculum Pr.

Sanford, William R. Hunkpapa Lakota Chief Sitting Bull. 2013. (Native American Chiefs & Warriors Ser.). 48p. (J). (gr. 5-18). lib. bdg. 22.60 *(978-0-7660-4097-7(6))* Enslow Pubs., Inc.

—Nez Percé Chief Joseph. 2013. (Native American Chiefs & Warriors Ser.). 48p. (J). (gr. 5-18). 22.60 *(978-0-7660-4092-2(5))* Enslow Pubs., Inc.

—Oglala Sioux Chief Crazy Horse. 2013. (Native American Chiefs & Warriors Ser.). 48p. (J). (gr. 5-18). 22.60 *(978-0-7660-4094-6(1))* Enslow Pubs., Inc.

Sanford, William R. & Green, Carl R. Sacagawea: Courageous American Indian Guide. 2012. (Courageous Heroes of the American West Ser.). (Illus.). 48p. (J). (gr. 5-18). 22.60 *(978-0-7660-4006-9(2))* Enslow Pubs., Inc.

Schilling, Vincent. Native Athletes in Action. 2016. (Illus.). x, 107p. (J). pap. *(978-1-939053-14-5(5))* Book Publishing Co.

—Native Athletes in Action: Sports Stars Past & Present. Peterson, Gary, illus. 2007. (Native Trailblazers Ser.). (ENG.). 128p. (YA). (gr. 3-11). pap. 9.95 *(978-0-9779183-0-0(0),* 7th Generation) Book Publishing Co.

—Native Men of Courage. 2016. (Illus.). x, 117p. (J). pap. 9.95 *(978-1-939053-16-9(1))* Book Publishing Co.

—Native Musicians in the Groove, 1 vol. 2009. (Native Trailblazers Ser.). (ENG.). 132p. (YA). (gr. 5-10). pap. 9.95 *(978-0-9779183-4-8(3),* 7th Generation) Book Publishing Co.

Schilling, Vincent & Benjamin, Michelle. Native Men of Courage, 1 vol. 2008. (Native Trailblazers Ser.). (ENG.). 128p. (YA). (gr. 5-11). pap. 9.95 *(978-0-9779183-3-1(5),* 7th Generation) Book Publishing Co.

Schomp, Virginia. Hiawatha & the Great Peace. 2013. 32p. (J). (gr. 6-9). 28.50 *(978-1-60870-440-8(8))* Cavendish Square Publishing.

Schwartz, Heather E. Pocahontas: Her Life & Legend. 2016. (Primary Source Readers Ser.). (Illus.). 32p. (J). (gr. 4-5). pap. 8.99 *(978-1-4938-3072-5(4))* Teacher Created Materials, Inc.

Shaffer, Jody Jensen. What's Your Story, Sequoyah? 2016. (Cub Reporter Meets Famous Americans Ser.). (ENG., Illus.). 32p. (J). (gr. k-3). 26.65 *(978-1-4677-8786-4(8))* Lerner Publishing Group.

Shea, John. Outsiders. 2011. (J). *(978-0-531-22556-1(9))* Scholastic, Inc.

Shepherd, Jodie. Sacagawea. 2015. (Rookie Biographies(tm) Ser.). (ENG., Illus.). 32p. (J). lib. bdg. 25.00 *(978-0-531-21414-5(1),* Children's Pr.) Scholastic Library Publishing.

Shull, Jodie A. Voice of the Paiutes: A Story about Sarah Winnemucca. Birdsong, Keith, illus. 2007. (Creative Minds Biography Ser.). 64p. (J). (gr. 3-7). lib. bdg. 22.60 *(978-0-8225-5990-0(0))* Lerner Publishing Group.

Silate, Jennifer. Seeing the Future: The Final Vision of Sitting Bull. 2009. (Great Moments in American History Ser.). 32p. (gr. 3-3). 47.90 *(978-1-61513-150-1(7))* Rosen Publishing Group, Inc., The.

Simermeyer, Genevieve. Meet Christopher: An Osage Indian Boy from Oklahoma. Fogden, Katherine, photos by. 2008. (My World — Young Native Americans Today Ser.). (ENG., Illus.). 48p. (J). 15.95 *(978-1-57178-217-5(6))* Council Oak Bks.

Sita, Lisa. Pocahontas: The Powhatan Culture & the Jamestown Colony. 2009. (Library of American Lives & Times Ser.). 112p. (gr. 5-5). 69.20 *(978-1-60853-500-2(2))* Rosen Publishing Group, Inc., The.

Sitting Bull. 2010. (Legends of the Wild West Ser.). (Illus.). 128p. (gr. 6-12). 35.00 *(978-1-60413-527-5(1),* Chelsea Hse.) Facts On File, Inc.

Sonneborn, Liz. Sherman Alexie. 2012. (All about the Author Ser.). (ENG.). 112p. (YA). (gr. 7-12). lib. bdg. 34.60 *(978-1-4488-6941-1(2))* Rosen Publishing Group, Inc., The.

Spinner, Stephanie. Who Was Sitting Bull? Eldridge, Jim & Harrison, Nancy, illus. 2014. (Who Was? Ser.). (ENG.). 112p. (J). (gr. 3-7). 5.99 *(978-0-448-47965-1(6),* Grosset & Dunlap) Penguin Young Readers Group.

—Who Was Sitting Bull? 2014. (Who Was... ? Ser.). lib. bdg. 16.00 *(978-0-606-36179-8(0))* Turtleback Bks.

St. George, Judith. Sacagawea. 2006. pap. 8.75 *(978-0-15-365175-5(X))* Harcourt Schl. Pubs.

Stanley, George E. Crazy Horse: Young War Chief. Henderson, Meryl, illus. 2005. (Childhood of Famous Americans Ser.). (ENG.). 208p. (J). (gr. 3-7). pap. 7.99 *(978-0-689-85746-1(2),* Aladdin) Simon & Schuster Children's Publishing.

Summitt, April R. Sequoyah & the Invention of the Cherokee Alphabet, 1 vol. 2012. (Landmarks of the American Mosaic Ser.). (Illus.). 164p. (C). 41.00 *(978-0-313-39177-4(7),* A3212C, Greenwood) ABC-CLIO, LLC.

Sutcliffe, Jane. Chief Joseph. 2004. (History Maker Bios Ser.). (J). pap. 6.95 *(978-0-8225-2068-9(0))* Lerner Publishing Group.

—Chief Joseph. Parlin, Tim, tr. Parlin, Tim, illus. 2004. (History Maker Bios Ser.). 48p. (J). (gr. 3-5). lib. bdg. 26.60 *(978-0-8225-0696-6(3))* Lerner Publishing Group.

—Sacagawea. 2009. (History Maker Biographies Ser.). (ENG.). 48p. (gr. 3-6). 27.93 *(978-0-7613-4222-9(2),* Lerner Pubns.) Lerner Publishing Group.

Tayac, Gabrielle. Meet Naiche: A Native Boy from the Chesapeake Bay Area. Harrington, John, photos by. 2007. (My World: Young Native Americans Today Ser.). (ENG., Illus.). 48p. (J). (gr. 4-7). 15.95 *(978-1-57178-146-8(3))* Council Oak Bks.

Tieck, Sarah. Sacagawea, 1 vol. 2006. (Buddy Book Ser.). (ENG., Illus.). 32p. (gr. -1-3). 27.07 *(978-1-59679-789-5(4),* Buddy Bks.) ABDO Publishing Co.

Townsend, Dana E. Sequoyah & the Cherokee Alphabet. Gabriel, Andrea, illus. 2006. (Voices Reading Ser.). 32p. (J). *(978-0-7367-2953-6(4))* Zaner-Bloser, Inc.

Vegetarians of Washington Staff. Vegetarian Pacific Northwest: A Guide to Restaurants & Shopping. 2008. (ENG., Illus.). 128p. (gr. 4-7). pap. 14.95 *(978-1-57067-211-8(3))* Book Publishing Co.

Wade, Mary Dodson. Amazing Cherokee Writer Sequoyah. (Amazing Americans Ser.). (Illus.). 24p. (J). 2013. (gr. k-3). pap. 7.95 *(978-0-7660-5976-4(6),* Enslow Elementary) 2009. (gr. 1-3). lib. bdg. 22.60 *(978-0-7660-3285-9(X))* Enslow Pubs., Inc.

Walsh, Steve. Chief Ouray: Ute Chief & Man of Peace. 2011. (ENG & SPA., Illus.). 54p. (J). pap. 8.95 *(978-0-86541-121-0(2))* Filter Pr., LLC.

Weil, Ann. Geronimo, 1 vol. 2012. (American Biographies Ser.). (ENG.). 48p. (gr. 4-6). pap. 9.95 *(978-1-4329-6458-0(5))*; lib. bdg. 32.65 *(978-1-4329-6447-4(X))* Heinemann-Raintree. (NA-h).

Zemlicka, Shannon. Quanah Parker. 2004. (History Maker Bios Ser.). (J). pap. 6.95 *(978-0-8225-2070-2(2))*; (ENG., Illus.). 48p. (gr. 3-6). 27.93 *(978-0-8225-0724-6(2),* Carolrhoda Bks.) Lerner Publishing Group.

INDIANS OF NORTH AMERICA—CANADA

Bailey, Katharine. Radisson & des Groseilliers: Fur Traders of the North. 2006. (In the Footsteps of Explorers Ser.). (ENG., Illus.). 32p. (J). (gr. 3-7). lib. bdg. *(978-0-7787-2422-3(0),* 1253444); (gr. 4-7). pap. *(978-0-7787-2458-2(1),* 1253444) Crabtree Publishing Co.

Bruchac, Joseph. The Hunter's Promise: An Abenaki Tale. Farnsworth, Bill, illus. 2015. (ENG.). 32p. (J). (gr. k-3). 16.95 *(978-1-937786-43-4(9),* Wisdom Tales) World Wisdom, Inc.

Collinson, Clare. Peoples of the East, Southeast, & Plains. 2010. (CC: Native North Americans Ser.). 112p. (gr. 6-12). 42.80 *(978-1-933834-77-1(3))* Brown Bear Bks.

Corrigan, Kathleen. Building a Nation. 2016. (Canada Through Time Ser.). (ENG., Illus.). 32p. (gr. 1-4). lib. bdg. 29.99 *(978-1-4109-8120-2(7),* Read Me!) Heinemann-Raintree.

Doak, Robin S. Subarctic Peoples, 1 vol. 2011. (First Nations of North America Ser.). (ENG.). 48p. (gr. 3-3). pap. 9.95 *(978-1-4329-4965-5(9),* Heinemann InfoSearch) Heinemann-Raintree.

Dwyer, Helen. Peoples of the Southwest, West, & North. 2010. (CC: Native North Americans Ser.). 112p. (gr. 6-12). 42.80 *(978-1-933834-78-8(1))* Brown Bear Bks.

Hayes, Amy. Native Peoples of the Subarctic. 2016. (Native Peoples of North America Ser.). (Illus.). 32p. (J). (gr. 3-2). 25.25 *(978-1-4824-4821-4(1))* Stevens, Gareth Publishing LLLP.

Howse, Jennifer. Les Métis: Les Autochtones du Canada. Karvonen, Tanjah, tr. from ENG. 2011. (FRE.). 24p. (YA). (gr. 2-4). *(978-1-77071-406-9(5))* Weigl Educational Pubs. Ltd.

Howse, Jennifer & Kissock, Heather. Métis. 2010. (Illus.). 24p. *(978-1-55388-644-0(5))*; pap. *(978-1-55388-650-1(X))* Weigl Educational Pubs. Ltd.

Johnson, Michael & Burkinshaw, Jane. Native Tribes of the North & Northwest Coast. 2004. (Native Tribes of North America Ser.). (Illus.). 64p. (gr. 5-12). lib. bdg. 34.00 *(978-0-8368-5611-8(2),* Gareth Stevens Secondary Library) Stevens, Gareth Publishing LLLP.

Koopmans, Carol & Kissock, Heather. Aboriginal Peoples. 2010. (Illus.). 24p. *(978-1-55388-649-5(6))* Weigl Educational Pubs. Ltd.

Littlechild, George. This Land Is My Land, 1 vol. Littlechild, George, illus. 2014. (ENG., Illus.). 32p. (J). pap. 10.95 *(978-0-89239-184-4(7),* Children's Book Press) Lee & Low Bks., Inc.

McIntyre, Sandra. Canoes: Canadian Icons. 2010. (Illus.). 24p. *(978-1-77071-575-2(4))*; pap. *(978-1-77071-582-0(7))* Weigl Educational Pubs. Ltd.

Meuse, Theresa. The Sharing Circle: Stories about First Nations Culture, 1 vol. Stevens, Arthur A., illus. 2003. (ENG.). 52p. (J). (gr. k-3). pap. 12.95 *(978-1-55109-450-2(9))* Nimbus Publishing, Ltd. CAN. Dist: Orca Bk. Pubs. USA.

Meuse, Theresa & Labrador, Bonnie. L' nuk: the Mi'kmaq of Atlantic Canada, 1 vol. 2017. (ENG., Illus.). 80p. (J). (gr. 1-5). pap. 17.95 *(978-1-77108-452-9(9))* Nimbus Publishing, Ltd. CAN. Dist: Orca Bk. Pubs. USA.

Robertson, David Alexander. Ends/Begins. Henderson, Scott B., illus. 2010. (7 Generations Ser.: 3). (ENG.). 32p. (YA). (gr. 9-12). pap. *(978-1-55379-262-8(9),* 72bc3568-4f12-4574-9f82-146597fa1b3a, HighWater Pr.) Portage & Main Pr.

Samuels, Barbara. Multiculturalism in Early Canada: Multiculturalism in Canada. 2011. 32p. (gr. 5-8). *(978-1-77071-704-6(8))* Weigl Educational Pubs. Ltd.

Schilling, Vincent. Native Athletes in Action: Sports Stars Past & Present. Peterson, Gary, illus. 2007. (Native Trailblazers Ser.). (ENG.). 128p. (YA). (gr. 3-11). pap. 9.95 *(978-0-9779183-0-0(0),* 7th Generation) Book Publishing Co.

Stout, Mary A. Cree. 2003. (Native American Peoples Ser.). (Illus.). 32p. (gr. 3-7). lib. bdg. 26.00 *(978-0-8368-3703-2(7),* Gareth Stevens Learning Library) Stevens, Gareth Publishing LLLP.

Turner, Patrenia. A Christmas Carol For Keeng Troyius. 2016. (Illus.). pap. *(978-0-578-18261-2(0))* Royalty Patrenia Turner Publications.

Vickers, Roy Henry & Budd, Robert. Cloudwalker. Vickers, Roy Henry, illus. 2014. (ENG., Illus.). 40p. (J). 19.95 *(978-1-55017-619-3(6))* Harbour Publishing Co., Ltd. CAN. Dist: Midpoint Trade Bks., Inc.

Ward, Jill. Woodland Indians. 2010. (J). *(978-1-935077-76-3(7))*; pap. *(978-1-935077-83-1(X))* State Standards Publishing, LLC.

Webster, Christine. Les Mi'kmaq: Les Autochtones du Canada. Karvonen, Tanjah, tr. from ENG. 2011. (FRE.). 24p. (YA). (gr. 2-4). *(978-1-77071-405-2(7))* Weigl Educational Pubs. Ltd.

World Book, Inc Staff, contrib. by. Indians of Eastern Canada & the United States. 2009. (J). *(978-0-7166-2138-6(X))* World Bk., Inc.

INDIANS OF NORTH AMERICA—CANADA—FICTION

Bell, Aaron. Jak's Story. 2010. (ENG., Illus.). 96p. (YA). (gr. 4). pap. 10.99 *(978-1-55488-710-1(0))* Dundurn CAN. Dist: Ingram Publisher Services.

Brissenden, Constance & Loyie, Larry. Goodbye Buffalo Bay, 1 vol. 2008. (ENG.). 160p. pap. 14.95 *(978-1-894778-62-6(6))* Theytus Bks., Ltd. CAN. Dist: Univ. of Toronto Pr.

Bruchac, Joseph. The Way. 2013. (ENG.). 160p. (YA). (gr. 6-12). pap. 9.95 *(978-1-4677-0862-3(3),* Darby Creek) Lerner Publishing Group.

Buffie, Margaret. Winter Shadows. (ENG., (YA). (gr. 5). 2012. Illus.). 330p. pap. 11.95 *(978-1-77049-358-2(1))* 2010. 336p. 19.95 *(978-0-88776-968-9(3))* Tundra Bks. CAN. (Tundra Bks.). Dist: Penguin Random Hse. LLC.

Campbell, Nicola. Shi-Shi-Etko, 1 vol. LaFave, Kim, illus. 2005. (ENG.). 32p. (J). (gr. -1-2). 18.95 *(978-0-88899-659-6(4))* Groundwood Bks. CAN. Dist: Publishers Group West (PGW).

Cooney, Caroline B. The Ransom of Mercy Carter. 2011. (ENG.). 256p. (YA). (gr. 7). pap. 8.99 *(978-0-385-74046-3(8),* Ember) Random Hse. Children's Bks.

Downie, Mary Alice & Downie, John. Alison's Ghosts, 1 vol. 2008. (Lorimer Streetlights Ser.). (ENG.). 104p. (J). (gr. 2-4). 8.95 *(978-1-55277-013-9(3),* 9781552770139) Lorimer, James & Co., Ltd., Pubs. CAN. Dist: Casemate Pubs. & Bk. Distributors, LLC.

Dumas, William. Pisim Finds Her Miskinow. Paul, Leonard, illus. 2013. (ENG & CRE.). 48p. (gr. 5-12). *(978-1-55379-394-6(3),* 9781553793946, HighWater Pr.) Portage & Main Pr.

Gunderson, Jessica. Passage to Fortune: Searching for Saguenay. Kurtz, Rory, illus. 2016. (Discovering the New World Ser.). (ENG.). 96p. (gr. 3-4). pap. 7.95 *(978-1-4965-3482-8(4),* Connect) Stone Arch Bks.

Hartson. Willa's New World: The Novel Study. 124p. stu. ed. 29.95 *(978-1-55378-058-8(2))* Edmonton Public Schls. Centre for Education CAN. Dist: Coteau Bks.

Howse, Jennifer. Les Totems: Les Emblèmes Canadiens. McMann, Julie, tr. from ENG. 2011. (FRE.). 24p. (YA). (gr. 2-4). *(978-1-77071-412-0(X))* Weigl Educational Pubs. Ltd.

Kissock, Heather. Les Algonquins: Les Autochtones du Canada. Karvonen, Tanjah, tr. from ENG. 2011. (FRE.). 24p. (YA). (gr. 2-4). *(978-1-77071-401-4(4))* Weigl Educational Pubs. Ltd.

Langrish, Katherine. Troll Blood. Stevens, Tim & Wyatt, David, illus. 2008. 352p. (gr. 5-8). (ENG.). (J). 16.99 *(978-0-06-111674-2(2))*; (YA). lib. bdg. 17.89 *(978-0-06-111675-9(0),* Eos) HarperCollins Pubs.

Lomberg, Michelle. Les Ojibwés: Les Autochtones du Canada. Karvonen, Tanjah, tr. from ENG. 2011. (FRE.). 24p. (YA). (gr. 2-4). *(978-1-77071-404-5(9))* Weigl Educational Pubs. Ltd.

Maracle, Lee. Will's Garden. 2nd rev. ed. 2008. (ENG.). 194p. pap. 16.95 *(978-1-894778-59-6(6))* Theytus Bks., Ltd. CAN. Dist: Univ. of Toronto Pr.

Melling, O. R. The Book of Dreams. 2009. (Chronicles of Faerie Ser.). (ENG.). 720p. (J). (gr. 2-8). 19.95 *(978-0-8109-8346-5(X),* Amulet Bks.) Abrams, Inc.

Messner, Kate. Champlain & the Silent One. Gulley, Martha, illus. 2008. (J). *(978-1-59531-050-7(9))* North Country Bks., Inc.

Nerveille, Rosemarie. The Witch of Beaver Creek Mine. 2007. (ENG.). 160p. (J). (gr. 3-7). 14.95 *(978-0-89272-741-4(1))*; 2nd ed. pap. 9.95 *(978-0-89272-763-6(2))* Down East Bks.

Oborowsky, S. L. S. Ivy: The Blossoming of a Rose. 2012. (ENG.). 112p. (YA). pap. 10.95 *(978-1-59299-769-5(4))* Inkwater Pr.

Olsen, Sylvia. Counting on Hope, 1 vol. 2010. (ENG.). 304p. (YA). (gr. 6-12). pap. 14.95 *(978-1-55039-173-2(9))* Sono Nis Pr. CAN. Dist: Orca Bk. Pubs. USA.

Rebus, Anna. Les PiedsNoirs: Les Autochtones du Canada. Karvonen, Tanjah, tr. from ENG. 2011. (FRE.). 24p. (YA). (gr. 2-4). *(978-1-77071-402-1(2))* Weigl Educational Pubs. Ltd.

Revelle, Rick. Algonquin Spring: An Algonquin Quest Novel. 2015. (Algonquin Quest Novel Ser.: 2). (ENG., Illus.). 296p. (YA). pap. 12.99 *(978-1-4597-3063-2(1))* Dundurn CAN. Dist: Ingram Publisher Services.

Richardson, Faith. Tree Root & River Rat. 2003. (Illus.). 248p. (J). 21.95 *(978-0-9744989-4-2(7))*; pap. 12.95 *(978-0-9744989-5-9(5))* Fox Song Bks.

Robertson, David. Will I See, 1 vol. Chomichuk, G. M. B., illus. 2017. (ENG.). 56p. (YA). (gr. 10-12). pap. 18.95 *(978-1-55379-674-9(8),* HighWater Pr.) Portage & Main Pr. CAN. Dist: Orca Bk. Pubs. USA.

Robertson, David A. When We Were Alone, 1 vol. Flett, Julie, illus. 2017. (ENG.). 24p. (J). (gr. k-3). 18.95 *(978-1-55379-673-2(X),* HighWater Pr.) Portage & Main Pr. CAN. Dist: Orca Bk. Pubs. USA.

Schultz Nicholson, Lorna. Northern Star, 1 vol. 2006. (Lorimer Sports Stories Ser.). (ENG.). 112p. (J). (gr. 4-8). 16.95 *(978-1-55028-911-4(X),* 9781550289114); 9.95 *(978-1-55028-910-7(1),* 9781550289107) Lorimer, James & Co., Ltd., Pubs. CAN. Dist: Casemate Pubs. & Bk. Distributors, LLC.

Sellars, Willie. Dipnetting with Dad. Easthope, Kevin, illus. 2014. (ENG.). 48p. (J). (gr. 1-2). bds. 16.95 *(978-1-927575-53-6(2))* Caitlin Pr., Inc. CAN. Dist: Midpoint Trade Bks., Inc.

Trottier, Maxine. The Death of My Country: The Plains of Abraham Diary of Geneviève Aubuchon. 2005. (Dear Canada Ser.). (ENG., Illus.). 216p. *(978-0-439-96762-4(7))* Scholastic Canada, Ltd.

Watson, Krista M. Pépère's Fiddle. 2008. (J). *(978-0-9717214-5-6(9))* Sunnyside Pr.

White, Tara. I Like Who I Am, 1 vol. 2010. (ENG., Illus.). 44p. pap. 12.95 *(978-1-894778-63-3(4))* Theytus Bks., Ltd. CAN. Dist: Univ. of Toronto Pr.

Yee, Paul. Learning to Fly, 1 vol. 2008. (Orca Soundings Ser.). (ENG.). (YA). (gr. 8-12). 112p. 16.95 *(978-1-55143-955-6(7))*; 136p. pap. 9.95 *(978-1-55143-953-2(0))* Orca Bk. Pubs. USA.

INDIANS OF NORTH AMERICA—CAPTIVITIES

see Indian Captivities

INDIANS OF NORTH AMERICA—CHEROKEE INDIANS

Behnke, Alison. A Timeline History of the Trail of Tears. 2015. (ENG., Illus.). 48p. (J). (gr. 5-8). 30.65 *(978-1-4677-8582-2(2))* Lerner Publishing Group.

Birchfield, D. L. Cherokee. 2003. (Native American Peoples Ser.). (Illus.). 32p. (gr. 3-7). lib. bdg. 26.00 *(978-0-8368-3700-1(2),* Gareth Stevens Learning Library) Stevens, Gareth Publishing LLLP.

Bodden, Valerie. Cherokee. 2015. (Illus.). 48p. (J). *(978-1-60818-551-1(6),* Creative Education) Creative Co., The.

Byers, Ann. The Trail of Tears: A Primary Source History of the Forced Relocation of the Cherokee Nation. (Primary Sources in American History Ser.). 64p. (gr. 5-8). 2009. 58.50 *(978-1-60851-504-2(4))* 2004. (Illus.). (J). lib. bdg. 31.95 *(978-0-8239-4007-3(1),* Rosen Reference) Rosen Publishing Group, Inc., The.

Caswell, Max. My Life on the Trail of Tears. 2017. (My Place in History Ser.). 24p. (J). (gr. 2-3). pap. 8.15 *(978-1-5382-0309-5(X))* Stevens, Gareth Publishing LLLP.

Cloud Tapper, Suzanne & Tapper, Suzanne Cloud. The Cherokee: A Proud People. 2005. (American Indians Ser.). (Illus.). 48p. (J). (gr. 4-7). lib. bdg. 25.27

(978-0-7660-2454-0(7), Enslow Elementary) Enslow Pubs., Inc.

Griffis, Molly Levite. Great American Bunion Derby. 2003. (Illus.). viii, 87p. (J). 15.95 (978-1-57168-801-9(3), Eakin Pr.) Eakin Pr.

Josephson, Judith Pinkerton. Why Did Cherokees Move West? And Other Questions about the Trail of Tears. 2010. (Six Questions of American History Ser.). (ENG.). (gr. 4-6). pap. 56.72 (978-0-7613-6950-9(3)) Lerner Publishing Group.

Kissock, Heather & Small, Rachel. Cherokee. 2010. (American Indian Art & Culture Ser.). 24p. (J). (gr. 3-6). lib. bdg. 25.70 (978-1-60596-994-7(X)) Weigl Pubs., Inc.

—Cherokee: American Indian Art & Culture. 2010. pap. 9.95 (978-1-60596-995-4(8)) Weigl Pubs., Inc.

Klar, Jeremy & Byers, Ann. A Primary Source Investigation of the Trail of Tears. 2015. (Uncovering American History Ser.). (ENG., Illus.). 64p. (J). (gr. 5-6). 32.95 (978-1-4994-3515-3(0), Rosen Central) Rosen Publishing Group, Inc., The.

Lawton, Cassie M. & Bial, Raymond. The People & Culture of the Cherokee. 2016. (First Peoples of North America Ser.). (Illus.). 128p. (J). (gr. 6-6). 45.64 (978-1-5026-1886-3(9)) Cavendish Square Publishing.

Machajewski, Sarah. The Cherokee People. 2015. (Native American Cultures Ser.). (ENG., Illus.). 32p. (J). (gr. 2-3). pap. 10.50 (978-1-4824-1977-1(7)) Stevens, Gareth Publishing LLLP.

McLaughlin, Kari Massie. My Adventure with the Cherokee. 2007. 44p. (J). 8.99 (978-1-59092-446-4(0)) Blue Forge Pr.

Miller, Connie R. The Cherokee. 2003. (Uncovering Native American History Ser.). (J). pap. (978-1-58417-111-9(1)); lib. bdg. (978-1-58417-048-8(4)) Lake Street Pubs.

Petrini, Catherine M., tr. The Cherokee. 2003. (North American Indians Ser.). (ENG., Illus.). 48p. (J). 27.50 (978-0-7377-1511-8(1), Greenhaven Pr., Inc.) Cengage Gale.

Rumford, James. Sequoyah: The Cherokee Man Who Gave His People Writing. Huckaby, Anna Sixkiller, tr. 2010. (ENG & CHR., Illus.). 32p. (C). (gr. -1-3). tchr. ed. 26.95 (978-0-618-36947-8(3)) National Geographic School Publishing, Inc.

Smith-Llera, Danielle. The Cherokee: The Past & Present of a Proud Nation. 2015. (American Indian Life Ser.). (ENG., Illus.). 32p. (gr. 3-4). pap. 7.95 (978-1-4914-5003-1(7)) Capstone Press of Coughlan Cos.

Tieck, Sarah. Cherokee, 1 vol. 2014. (Native Americans Ser.). (ENG.). 32p. (gr. 7-11). 28.50 (978-1-62403-352-0(0)) ABDO Publishing Co.

Ward, Jill. The Cherokees. 2010. (J). (978-1-935077-79-4(1)); pap. (978-1-935077-86-2(4)) State Standards Publishing, LLC.

—Creeks & Cherokees Today. 2010. (J). (978-1-935077-80-0(5)); pap. (978-1-935077-87-9(2)) State Standards Publishing, LLC.

Waxman, Laura Hamilton. Sequoyah. 2004. (History Maker Biographies Ser.). (ENG., Illus.). 48p. (gr. 3-6). 27.93 (978-0-8225-0697-3(1), Carolrhoda Bks.) Lerner Publishing Group.

Zardes, Cassandra. Cherokee. 2015. (Spotlight on Native Americans Ser.). (ENG., Illus.). 32p. (J). (gr. 4-6). 26.25 (978-1-4994-1658-9(X), PowerKids Pr.) Rosen Publishing Group, Inc., The.

INDIANS OF NORTH AMERICA—CHEROKEE INDIANS—FICTION

Anderson, Dee, retold by. Otter Gets Tricked! A Cherokee Trickster Story. l.t. ed. 2004. (Illus.). 32p. (J). pap. 6.00 (978-0-9755934-1-7(2)) Colonel Davenport Historical Foundation.

Cahill, Byron. The Legend of Skywoman. 2005. (J). pap. (978-1-4108-4232-9(0)) Benchmark Education Co.

Cartwright, Stan & Dixon, Edna. Strong Fox: How Fox Came to Help a Village Grow Stronger. 2010. 28p. pap. 12.49 (978-1-4490-4376-6(3)) AuthorHouse.

Ellington, Charlotte Jane. Dancing Leaf. 2007. 183p. (J). (gr. 4-7). 15.95 (978-1-57072-311-7(7)) Overmountain Pr.

Hanington, John G. The Adventures of Quick Fox. 2006. (ENG.). 92p. per. 9.95 (978-0-7414-3223-0(4)) Infinity Publishing.

Jeb. Destinations in Time. 2008. 101p. pap. 19.95 (978-1-60672-653-2(6)) America Star Bks.

Martone, Ginny. Trouble at Big Bear Falls. 2011. 90p. pap. 19.95 (978-1-4626-2558-1(4)) America Star Bks.

McKinney-Whitaker, Courtney. The Last Sister: A Novel. 2014. (Young Palmetto Bks.). (ENG.). 232p. (YA). 39.95 (978-1-61117-429-8(5)) Univ. of South Carolina Pr.

Paquette, Lenny & Willis, Dan. Everett the Evergreen. 2012. 44p. pap. 21.99 (978-1-4797-2711-7(3)) Xlibris Corp.

Penn, Audrey. The Whistling Tree. Gibson, Barbara Leonard, illus. 2006. (ENG.). 32p. (J). (gr. -1-3). 16.95 (978-0-9749303-9-8(3)) Tanglewood Pr.

Robinson, Gary. Paranormal: A Billy Buckhorn Supernatural Adventure. 2014. (PathFinders Ser.). (ENG.). 147p. (J). pap. (978-1-939053-08-4(0)) Book Publishing Co.

—Supranormal. 2015. (ENG.). 128p. (J). pap. (978-1-939053-12-1(9)) Book Publishing Co.

Stewart, Dianne C. Season of the Cold Moon. 2011. (ENG.). 108p. (J). (gr. 2). pap. 8.95 (978-0-9831032-0-2(8), BeanPole Bks.) Harren Communications, LLC.

Tanner, Miriam. A Rose after Midnight. 2006. 100p. pap. 16.95 (978-1-4241-0693-6(1)) PublishAmerica, Inc.

Wood, D. K. Nightmare at Indian Cave. 2006. pap. 10.00 (978-1-4257-1640-0(7)) Xlibris Corp.

Yasuda, Anita. How the World Was Made: A Cherokee Creation Myth. Pennington, Mark, illus. 2012. (Short Tales Native American Myths Ser.). 32p. (J). (gr. 3-6). lib. bdg. 24.21 (978-1-61641-881-6(8)) Magic Wagon.

INDIANS OF NORTH AMERICA—CHEYENNE INDIANS

Birchfield, D. L. Cheyenne. 2003. (Native American Peoples Ser.). (Illus.). 32p. (gr. 3-7). lib. bdg. 26.00 (978-0-8368-3701-8(0), Gareth Stevens Learning Library) Stevens, Gareth Publishing LLLP.

Cheyenne, 1 vol. 2014. (Native Americans Ser.). (ENG.). 32p. (gr. 7-11). 28.50 (978-1-62403-353-7(9)) ABDO Publishing Co.

Cunningham, Kevin & Benoit, Peter. The Cheyenne. 2011. (True Book(tm), a — American Indians Ser.). 48p. (J). (gr. 3-5). 31.00 (978-0-531-20759-8(5)); pap. 6.95 (978-0-531-29301-0(7)) Scholastic Library Publishing. (Children's Pr.).

Lawton, Cassie M. & Bial, Raymond. The People & Culture of the Cheyenne. 2016. (First Peoples of North America Ser.). (Illus.). 128p. (J). (gr. 6-6). 45.64 (978-1-5026-1888-7(5)) Cavendish Square Publishing.

Maron, Terra Rose. Cheyenne. 2015. (Spotlight on Native Americans Ser.). (ENG., Illus.). 32p. (J). (gr. 4-6). 26.25 (978-1-4994-1678-7(4), PowerKids Pr.) Rosen Publishing Group, Inc., The.

McIntosh, Kenneth & McIntosh, Marsha. Cheyenne. 2005. (North American Indians Today Ser.). (Illus.). 96p. (YA). lib. bdg. 22.95 (978-1-59084-666-7(4)) Mason Crest.

—Seminoles, 15 vols., Set. 2004. (North American Indians Today Ser.). (Illus.). 96p. (J). lib. bdg. (978-1-59084-663-6(X)) Mason Crest.

McLeese, Tex. Carrera de Barril. Palacios, Argentina, tr. (Rodeo (Spanish) Ser.).Tr. of Rodeo Barrel Racing. (SPA., Illus.). 24p. (YA). (gr. 1-4). lib. bdg. 19.27 (978-1-57103-387-1(4)) Rourke Educational Media.

INDIANS OF NORTH AMERICA—CHEYENNE INDIANS—FICTION

Eichler, Ken. Swift Eagle's Dangerous Journey, 1 vol. 2009. 80p. pap. 16.95 (978-1-61582-289-8(5)) PublishAmerica, Inc.

—Swift Eagle's Vision Quest, 1 vol. 2009. 95p. pap. 19.95 (978-1-60703-649-4(5)) America Star Bks.

Gilliland, Hap. Alone in the Wilderness. 2003. (Illus.). 160p. (YA). (gr. 6-10). pap. 14.95 (978-0-87961-257-3(6)) Naturegraph Pubs., Inc.

Robinson, Gary. Thunder on the Plains. 2013. (PathFinders Ser.). (ENG.). 128p. (J). pap. 9.95 (978-1-939053-00-8(5), 7th Generation) Book Publishing Co.

INDIANS OF NORTH AMERICA—CHILDREN

Ajmera, Maya & Hirschfelder, Arlene. Children of Native America Today. 2014. (ENG.). 64p. (J). (gr. 3-7). pap. 9.95 (978-1-57091-965-7(8)) Charlesbridge Publishing, Inc.

Littlefield, Holly. Children of the Indian Boarding Schools. 2005. (Picture the American Past Ser.). (Illus.). 48p. (J). (gr. 2-5). lib. bdg. 22.60 (978-1-57505-467-4(1)) Lerner Publishing Group.

Simermeyer, Genevieve. Meet Christopher: An Osage Indian Boy from Oklahoma. Fogden, Katherine, photos by. 2008. (My World — Young Native Americans Today Ser.). (ENG., Illus.). 48p. (J). 15.95 (978-1-57178-217-5(6)) Council Oak Bks.

INDIANS OF NORTH AMERICA—CHIPPEWA INDIANS—FICTION

Sargent, Dave, et al. Knocking the Rice Vol. 9: (Chippewa) Be Powerful, 20 vols. Lenoir, Jane, illus. l.t. ed. 2003. (Story Keeper Ser.: 9). 42p. (J). pap. 10.95 (978-1-56763-920-9(8)) Ozark Publishing.

INDIANS OF NORTH AMERICA—CHOCTAW INDIANS

Nephew, Samantha & Bial, Raymond. The People & Culture of the Choctaw. 2016. (First Peoples of North America Ser.). 128p. (J). 45.64 (978-1-5026-2245-7(9)) Cavendish Square Publishing.

Quinlivan, Ada. Choctaw, 01 vols., 1. 2016. (Spotlight on Native Americans Ser.). (ENG., Illus.). 32p. (J). pap. 11.75 (978-1-5081-4110-5(X), PowerKids Pr.) Rosen Publishing Group, Inc., The.

Tingle, Tim. Saltypie: A Choctaw Journey from Darkness into Light. Clarkson, Karen, illus. 2010. (ENG.). 40p. (J). (gr. 2-6). 17.95 (978-1-933693-67-5(3)) Cinco Puntos Pr.

INDIANS OF NORTH AMERICA—CHUMASHAN INDIANS

Ching, Jacqueline. Mission Santa Ines. 2009. (Missions of California Ser.). 64p. (gr. 4-4). 58.50 (978-1-60854-042-6(1), PowerKids Pr.) Rosen Publishing Group, Inc., The.

Gray-Kanatiiosh, Barbara A. Chumash, 1 vol. 2004. (Native Americans Set 3 Ser.). (ENG.). 32p. (gr. k-6). 27.07 (978-1-57765-933-4(3), Checkerboard Library) ABDO Publishing Co.

Hicks, Terry Allan. The Chumash. 2007. (First Americans Ser.). (Illus.). 48p. (gr. 3-7). lib. bdg. 31.36 (978-0-7614-2678-3(7), Benchmark Bks.) Marshall Cavendish Corp.

Margaret, Amy. Mission San Buenaventura. 2009. (Missions of California Ser.). 64p. (gr. 4-4). 58.50 (978-1-60854-026-6(X), PowerKids Pr.) Rosen Publishing Group, Inc., The.

—Mission Santa Barbara. 2009. (Missions of California Ser.). 64p. (gr. 4-4). 58.50 (978-1-60854-037-2(5), PowerKids Pr.) Rosen Publishing Group, Inc., The.

McGinty, Alice B. Mission San Gabriel Arcangel. 2009. (Missions of California Ser.). 64p. (gr. 4-4). 58.50 (978-1-60854-030-3(8), PowerKids Pr.) Rosen Publishing Group, Inc., The.

Miller, Connie R. The Chumash. 2003. (Uncovering Native American History Ser.). (J). pap. (978-1-58417-112-6(X)); lib. bdg. (978-1-58417-049-5(2)) Lake Street Pubs.

Newsome, Joel, et al. The People & Culture of the Chumash. 2016. (First Peoples of North America Ser.). 128p. (J). 45.64 (978-1-5026-2255-6(6)) Cavendish Square Publishing.

Skelton, Renee. Time for Kids Readers: the Chumash. 2003. (Illus.). pap. 33.07 (978-0-15-340560-0(0)) Harcourt Schl. Pubs.

Smith-Llera, Danielle. The Chumash: The Past & Present of California's Seashell People. 2016. (American Indian Life Ser.). (ENG., Illus.). 32p. (gr. 3-4). lib. bdg. 27.32 (978-1-5157-0237-5(5)) Capstone Press of Coughlan Cos.

Tieck, Sarah. Chumash, 1 vol. 2014. (Native Americans Set 2 Ser.). (ENG.). 32p. (gr. 2-5). 28.50 (978-1-62403-578-4(7)) ABDO Publishing Co.

Williams, Jack S. The Chumash of California. 2003. (Library of Native Americans). (Illus.). 64p. (J). lib. bdg. 26.50 (978-0-8239-6426-0(4), PowerKids Pr.) Rosen Publishing Group, Inc., The.

INDIANS OF NORTH AMERICA—CLOTHING

Krohn, Katherine E. Calico Dresses & Buffalo Robes: American West Fashions from the 1840s to the 1890s. 2011. (Dressing a Nation: the History of U. S. Fashion Ser.). (ENG., Illus.). 64p. (gr. 5-12). lib. bdg. 31.93 (978-0-7613-5890-9(0), Twenty-First Century Bks.) Lerner Publishing Group.

Williams, Colleen Madonna Flood. What the Native Americans Wore. Johnson, Troy, ed. 2013. (Native American Life Ser.: 15). 64p. (J). (gr. 5-18). 19.95 (978-1-4222-2978-1(5)) Mason Crest.

INDIANS OF NORTH AMERICA—COMANCHE INDIANS

Birchfield, D. L. Comanche. 2003. (Native American Peoples Ser.). (Illus.). 32p. (gr. 3-7). lib. bdg. 26.00 (978-0-8368-3702-5(9), Gareth Stevens Learning Library) Stevens, Gareth Publishing LLLP.

Cunningham, Kevin & Benoit, Peter. The Comanche. 2011. (True Book(tm), a — American Indians Ser.). 48p. (J). (gr. 3-5). 31.00 (978-0-531-20770-3(6)); pap. 6.95 (978-0-531-29312-6(2)) Scholastic Library Publishing. (Children's Pr.).

Egan, Tracie. Cynthia Ann Parker: Comanche Captive. 2004. (Primary Sources of Famous People in American History Ser.). (ENG., Illus.). 32p. (gr. 4-8). pap. 10.00 (978-0-8239-4179-7(5)) Rosen Publishing Group, Inc., The.

Golden, Nancy. Life with the Comanches: The Kidnapping of Cynthia Ann Parker. 2009. (Great Moments in American History Ser.). 32p. (gr. 3-3). 47.90 (978-1-61513-146-4(9)) Rosen Publishing Group, Inc., The.

Kissock, Heather. Comanche. 2010. (American Indian Art & Culture Ser.). 24p. (J). (gr. 3-6). lib. bdg. 25.70 (978-1-60596-988-6(5)) Weigl Pubs., Inc.

—Comanche: American Indian Art & Culture. 2010. pap. 9.95 (978-1-60596-989-3(3)) Weigl Pubs., Inc.

Phan, Sandy. The Caddo & Comanche: American Indians Tribes in Texas, 1 vol. 2012. (Primary Source Readers Ser.). (ENG.). 32p. (J). (gr. 3-3). pap. 8.99 (978-1-4333-5041-2(6)) Teacher Created Materials, Inc.

Zemlicka, Shannon. Quanah Parker. 2004. (History Maker Bios Ser.). (J). pap. 6.95 (978-0-8225-2070-2(2)); (ENG., Illus.). 48p. (gr. 3-6). 27.93 (978-0-8225-0724-6(2), Carolrhoda Bks.) Lerner Publishing Group.

INDIANS OF NORTH AMERICA—COMANCHE INDIANS—FICTION

Finotti, M. C. Paintbrushes & Arrows. 2016. 113p. (J). **(978-1-56164-968-6(6))** Pineapple Pr., Inc.

Gephart, Donna. As If Being 12 3/4 Isn't Bad Enough, My Mother Is Running for President! Kocsis, J. C., illus. 2010. (ENG.). 240p. (J). (gr. 3-7). pap. 7.99 (978-0-440-42211-2(6), Yearling) Random Hse. Children's Bks.

INDIANS OF NORTH AMERICA—CREE INDIANS—FICTION

Flett, Julie. Wild Berries. Cook, Earl N., tr. Flett, Julie, illus. 2013. (ENG., Illus.). 32p. (J). (gr. -1-3). pap. 16.95 (978-1-897476-89-5(2)) Simply Read Bks. CAN. Dist: Ingram Publisher Services.

Nicholson, Caitlin Dale. Niwechihaw / I Help, 1 vol. Morin-Neilson, Leona, tr. 2008. (CRE, ENG, HRV & SCR., Illus.). 24p. (J). (gr. k-k). 18.95 (978-0-88899-812-5(0)) Groundwood Bks. CAN. Dist: Publishers Group West (PGW).

Wheeler, Jordan & Jackson, Dennis. Christmas at Wapos Bay, 1 vol. 2005. (From Many Peoples Ser.). (ENG.). 152p. (J). (gr. 4-7). per. 7.95 (978-1-55050-324-1(3)) Coteau Bks. CAN. Dist: Orca Bk. Pubs. USA.

INDIANS OF NORTH AMERICA—CREEK INDIANS

Grailey, Trevor. Cree. 2015. (Spotlight on Native Americans Ser.). (ENG., Illus.). 32p. (J). (gr. 4-6). 26.25 (978-1-4994-1709-8(8), PowerKids Pr.) Rosen Publishing Group, Inc., The.

Maloof, Torrey. Mary Musgrove: Bringing People Together. 2016. (Primary Source Readers Ser.). (Illus.). 32p. (gr. 2-2). 8.99 (978-1-4938-2557-8(7)) Teacher Created Materials, Inc.

Smith-Llera, Danielle. The Creek: The Past & Present of the Muscogee. 2016. (American Indian Life Ser.). (ENG., Illus.). 32p. (gr. 3-4). lib. bdg. 27.32 (978-1-5157-0238-2(3)) Capstone Press of Coughlan Cos.

Tieck, Sarah. Creek, 1 vol. 2014. (Native Americans Set 2 Ser.). (ENG.). 32p. (gr. 2-5). 28.50 (978-1-62403-579-1(5)) ABDO Publishing Co.

Ward, Jill. The Creeks. 2010. (J). (978-1-935077-78-7(3)); pap. (978-1-935077-85-5(6)) State Standards Publishing, LLC.

—Creeks & Cherokees Today. 2010. (J). (978-1-935077-80-0(5)); pap. (978-1-935077-87-9(2)) State Standards Publishing, LLC.

INDIANS OF NORTH AMERICA—CROW INDIANS

Bial, Raymond. The People & Culture of the Crow. 2016. (First Peoples of North America Ser.). (ENG., Illus.). 128p. (J). (gr. 6-6). 45.70 (978-1-5026-1000-3(0)) Cavendish Square Publishing.

Ditchfield, Christin. The Crow. 2006. (True Bks.). (ENG., Illus.). 48p. (J). (gr. 3-7). per. 6.95 (978-0-516-25591-0(6), Children's Pr.) Scholastic Library Publishing.

INDIANS OF NORTH AMERICA—CUSTOMS

see Indians of North America—Social Life and Customs

INDIANS OF NORTH AMERICA—DAKOTA INDIANS

Aller, Susan Bivin. Sitting Bull. 2004. (History Maker Bios Ser.). (J). pap. 6.95 (978-0-8225-2072-6(9)) Lerner Publishing Group.

—Sitting Bull. Parlin, Tim, tr. Parlin, Tim, illus. 2004. (History Maker Bios Ser.). 47p. (J). 26.60 (978-0-8225-0700-0(5), Carolrhoda Bks.) Lerner Publishing Group.

Bodden, Valerie. Sioux. 2015. (Illus.). 48p. (J). (978-1-60818-555-9(9), Creative Education) Creative Co., The.

Bowman, Donna Janell. The Sioux: The Past & Present of the Dakota, Lakota, & Nakota. 2015. (American Indian Life Ser.). (ENG., Illus.). 32p. (gr. 3-4). lib. bdg. 27.32 (978-1-4914-4990-5(X)) Capstone Press of Coughlan Cos.

Cunningham, Kevin & Benoit, Peter. The Lakota Sioux. 2011. (True Bk Ser.). (ENG.). 48p. (J). pap. 6.95 (978-0-531-29310-2(6), Children's Pr.) Scholastic Library Publishing.

—The Sioux. 2011. (True Book(tm), a — American Indians Ser.). 48p. (J). (gr. 3-5). 31.00 (978-0-531-20768-0(4), Children's Pr.) Scholastic Library Publishing.

Laplante, Walter. Sitting Bull. 2015. (Native American Heroes Ser.). (ENG., Illus.). 24p. (J). (gr. 1-2). 22.60 (978-1-4824-2702-8(8)) Stevens, Gareth Publishing LLLP.

Lawton, Cassie M. & Bial, Raymond. The People & Culture of the Sioux. 2016. (First Peoples of North America Ser.). (Illus.). 128p. (J). (gr. 6-6). 45.64 (978-1-5026-1894-8(X)) Cavendish Square Publishing.

McDonnell, Julia. Sitting Bull in His Own Words. 2014. (Eyewitness to History Ser.). 32p. (J). (gr. 4-6). pap. 63.00 (978-1-4824-1223-9(3)) Stevens, Gareth Publishing LLLP.

Nelson, S. D., illus. Greet the Dawn: The Lakota Way. 2012. (J). 18.95 (978-0-9845041-6-9(8), South Dakota State Historical Society Pr.) South Dakota State Historical Society Pr.

Rucker, Jeffrey A. The Story of Sitting Bull. 2009. (Reading Room Collection 2 Ser.). 24p. (gr. 3-4). 42.50 (978-1-60851-998-9(8), PowerKids Pr.) Rosen Publishing Group, Inc., The.

Shaffer, Jody Jensen. Sitting Bull: Eagles Cannot Be Crows. 2017. (Primary Source Readers Ser.). 32p. (J). (gr. 4-5). pap. 8.99 (978-1-4938-3800-4(8)) Teacher Created Materials, Inc.

Stein, R. Conrad. The Sioux: A Proud People. 2005. (American Indians Ser.). (Illus.). 48p. (J). lib. bdg. 25.27 (978-0-7660-2452-6(0), Enslow Elementary) Enslow Pubs., Inc.

Swain, Gwenyth. Little Crow: Leader of the Dakota. 2004. (ENG., Illus.). 112p. (J). pap. 12.95 (978-0-87351-503-0(X), Borealis Bk.) Minnesota Historical Society Pr.

Weil, Ann. Sitting Bull, 1 vol. 2012. (American Biographies Ser.). (ENG.). 48p. (gr. 4-6). pap. 9.95 (978-1-4329-6460-3(7)); lib. bdg. 32.65 (978-1-4329-6449-8(6)) Heinemann-Raintree. (NA-h).

INDIANS OF NORTH AMERICA—DAKOTA INDIANS—FICTION

Nelson, S. D. Gift Horse: A Lakota Story. 2016. (ENG., Illus.). 40p. (gr. -1-3). pap. 9.95 (978-1-4197-2064-2(3), Abrams Bks. for Young Readers) Abrams, Inc.

Osborne, Mary Pope. Buffalo Before Breakfast. 2004. (Magic Tree House Ser.: No. 18). 72p. (J). (gr. k-3). pap. 17.00 incl. audio (978-0-8072-0927-1(9), Listening Library) Random Hse. Audio Publishing Group.

Schultz, Jan Neubert. Battle Cry. Allen, Rick, illus. 2006. (ENG.). 240p. (YA). (gr. 6-12). 15.95 (978-1-57505-928-0(2), Carolrhoda Bks.) Lerner Publishing Group.

Wood, Gail. Lizzie, Light Feather & the Quarry Bluff Storm. 2015. (Illus.). viii, 88p. (J). pap. (978-1-57249-415-2(8), White Mane Kids) White Mane Publishing Co., Inc.

INDIANS OF NORTH AMERICA—DELAWARE INDIANS

Bial, Raymond. The People & Culture of the Delaware. 2016. (First Peoples of North America Ser.). (ENG., Illus.). 128p. (J). (gr. 6-6). 45.70 (978-1-5026-1004-1(3)) Cavendish Square Publishing.

Carole Marsh. Delaware Indians. 2004. (Delaware Experience Ser.). 36p. (gr. 3-8). pap. 7.95 (978-0-635-02260-8(5)); lib. bdg. 29.95 (978-0-635-02261-5(3)) Gallopade International.

Myers, Albert Cook, ed. William Penn's Own Account of the Lenni Lenape or Delaware Indians. 2005. (Illus.). 96p. (YA). (gr. 7). per. (978-0-912608-13-6(7)) Middle Atlantic Pr.

Spizzirri, Linda, ed. Northeast Indians. (Illus.). 32p. (J). (gr. 1-8). pap. 4.98 incl. audio (978-0-86545-040-0(4)) Spizzirri Pr., Inc.

Stanley, Joseph. Delaware (Lenape), 01 vols., 1. 2016. (Spotlight on Native Americans Ser.). (ENG., Illus.). 32p. (J). pap. 11.75 (978-1-5081-4115-0(0), PowerKids Pr.) Rosen Publishing Group, Inc., The.

INDIANS OF NORTH AMERICA—DELAWARE INDIANS—FICTION

Richter, Conrad. The Light in the Forest. (YA). (gr. 7-18). 21.95 (978-0-89190-333-8(X)) Amereon Ltd.

INDIANS OF NORTH AMERICA—DWELLINGS

Aveni, Anthony. Buried Beneath Us: Discovering the Ancient Cities of the Americas. Roy, Katherine, illus. 2013. (ENG.). 96p. (J). (gr. 4-8). 18.99 (978-1-59643-567-4(4), 9781596435674) Roaring Brook Pr.

Flynn, Riley. Plank Houses. 2015. (American Indian Homes Ser.). (ENG.). 24p. (gr. 1-2). lib. bdg. 25.32 (978-1-4914-2055-3(3)) Capstone Press of Coughlan Cos.

—Wickiups. 2015. (American Indian Homes Ser.). (ENG.). 24p. (gr. 1-2). pap. 6.95 (978-1-4914-2242-7(4)) Capstone Press of Coughlan Cos.

Manning, Jack. Tepees, 1 vol. 2014. (American Indian Homes Ser.). (ENG.). 24p. (gr. 1-2). lib. bdg. 25.32 (978-1-4914-0316-7(0)) Capstone Press of Coughlan Cos.

Meachen Rau, Dana. Bookworms: The Inside Story, 6 bks., Set. Incl. Castle. 32p. (gr. k-2). lib. bdg. 15.95 (978-0-7614-2272-3(2)); Igloo. 32p. (gr. k-2). lib. bdg. 15.95 (978-0-7614-2273-0(0)); Log Cabin. 31p. (J). (gr. -1-3). lib. bdg. 22.79 (978-0-7614-2274-7(9)); Pyramid. 32p. (gr. k-2). lib. bdg. 15.95 (978-0-7614-2275-4(7)); Skyscraper. 32p. (gr. k-2). lib. bdg. 15.95 (978-0-7614-2276-1(5)); Tepee. 31p. (J). (gr. -1-3). lib. bdg. 22.79 (978-0-7614-2277-8(3)); (Illus.). 2006. 2006. Set lib. bdg. 136.71 (978-0-7614-2271-6(4), Benchmark Bks.) Marshall Cavendish Corp.

—Tepee. 2006. (Bookworms Ser.). (Illus.). 31p. (J). (gr. -1-3). lib. bdg. 22.79 (978-0-7614-2277-8(3), Benchmark Bks.) Marshall Cavendish Corp.

Rau, Dana Meachen. Tepee. 2007. (J). pap. 6.99 (978-0-7614-3304-0(X)) Marshall Cavendish Corp.

Williams, Colleen. Homes of the Native Americans. Johnson, Troy, ed. 2013. (Native American Life Ser.: 15). 64p. (J). (gr. 5-18). 19.95 (978-1-4222-2965-1(3)) Mason Crest.

INDIANS OF NORTH AMERICA—EDUCATION

Littlefield, Holly. Children of the Indian Boarding Schools. 2005. (Picture the American Past Ser.). (Illus.). 48p. (J). (gr. 2-5). lib. bdg. 22.60 (978-1-57505-467-4(1)) Lerner Publishing Group.

INDIANS OF NORTH AMERICA—EDUCATION—FICTION

Brissenden, Constance & Loyie, Larry. Goodbye Buffalo Bay, 1 vol. 2008. (ENG.). 160p. pap. 14.95 (978-1-894778-62-6(6)) Theytus Bks., Ltd. CAN. Dist: Univ. of Toronto Pr.

Henty, George Alfred. True to the Old Flag. 2007. 286p. pap. 21.99 (978-1-4264-4288-9(2)) Creative Media Partners, LLC.

Hobbs, Will & Hobbs, William. Far North. 2004. (ENG., Illus.). 304p. (J). (gr. 3-7). pap. 8.99 (978-0-06-054096-8(6), HarperTeen) HarperCollins Pubs.

INDIANS OF NORTH AMERICA—FICTION

Abbott, E. F. Mary Jemison: Native American Captive. 2016. (Based on a True Story Ser.). (ENG., Illus.). 224p. (J). 15.99 (978-1-250-06838-5(X), 9781250068385) Feiwel & Friends.

Aland, Carilyn & Markel, Marilyn. Hits With His Fist Gives a Helping Hand: Mimbres Children Learn about Caring. 2012. (Illus.). 113p. (J). pap. 16.95 (978-0-86534-508-9(2)) Sunstone Pr.

H
I

—Old Grandfather Teaches a Lesson: Mimbres Children Learn Respect. Alarid, Carilyn & Markel, Marilyn, illus. 2004. (Illus.). 116p. (J). pap. 16.95 (978-0-86534-418-1(3)) Sunstone Pr.

—Talks All Day Has the Courage to Speak: Mimbres Children Learn Citizenship. Alarid, Carilyn & Markel, Marilyn, illus. 2006. (Illus.). 125p. (J). pap. 16.95 (978-0-86534-470-9(1)) Sunstone Pr.

Alarid, Carilyn & Markel, Marilyn, illus. Runs Like the Wind Stops in Her Tracks: Mimbres Children Learn about Trustworthiness. 2016. (J). pap. (978-1-63293-099-6(4)) Sunstone Pr.

Alexie, Sherman. The Absolutely True Diary of a Part-Time Indian. Forney, Ellen, illus. (ENG.). (YA). (gr. 7-17). 2009. 288p. pap. 15.99 (978-0-316-01369-7(2)) 2007. 240p. 20.00 (978-0-316-01368-0(4)) Little, Brown Bks. for Young Readers.

—The Absolutely True Diary of a Part-Time Indian. 10th anniv. ed. 2017. (ENG., Illus.). 320p. (YA). (gr. 7-17). 20.99 (978-0-316-50404-1(1)) Little, Brown Bks. for Young Readers.

—The Absolutely True Diary of a Part-Time Indian. 2011. 10.36 (978-0-7848-3391-9(5)) 2009. 14.44 (978-0-7848-3800-6(3)) Marco Bk. Co. (Everbind).

—The Absolutely True Diary of a Part-Time Indian. Forney, Ellen, illus. 2008. 230p. 25.00 (978-1-60686-072-4(0)) Perfection Learning Corp.

—The Absolutely True Diary of a Part-Time Indian. 2008. (YA). 1.25 (978-1-4281-8291-2(8)); 78.49 (978-1-4361-0259-9(6)); 57.75 (978-1-4281-8294-3(2)); 68.75 (978-1-4281-8300-1(0)); 212.75 (978-1-4281-8295-0(0)); 55.75 (978-1-4281-8296-7(9)); 70.75 (978-1-4281-8298-1(5)) Recorded Bks., Inc.

—The Absolutely True Diary of a Part-Time Indian. Forney, Ellen, illus. l.t. ed. 2008. (Thorndike Literacy Bridge Ser.). (ENG.). 302p. (YA). (gr. 7-12). 23.95 (978-1-4104-0499-2(4)) Thorndike Pr.

—The Absolutely True Diary of a Part-Time Indian. 2009. (YA). lib. bdg. 28.15 (978-0-606-07296-0(9), Turtleback) Turtleback Bks.

—Thunder Boy Jr. Morales, Yuyi, illus. 2016. (ENG.). 40p. (J). (gr. -1-3). 17.99 (978-0-316-01372-7(2)) Little, Brown Bks. for Young Readers.

Alice, Dalgliesh. The Courage of Sarah Noble. 2nd rev. ed. 2014. (ENG.). 64p. (J). (gr. 2-5). 9.24 (978-1-63245-307-5(X)) Lectorum Pubns., Inc.

Altsheler, Joseph A. The Young Trailers. 2007. (Young Trailers Ser.: Vol. 1). 248p. reprint ed. per. 12.45 (978-1-60424-031-3(8), Book Jungle) Standard Pubns., Inc.

—The Young Trailers: A Story of Early Kentucky. 2006. (Young Trailers Ser.: Vol. 1). (J). 27.95 (978-1-4218-2970-8(3)); reprint ed. pap. 12.95 (978-1-4218-3070-4(1)) 1st World Publishing, Inc.

—The Young Trailers: A Story of Early Kentucky. (Young Trailers Ser.: Vol. 1). (J). reprint ed. 25.95 (978-0-89190-824-1(2)) Amereon Ltd.

—The Young Trailers: A Story of Early Kentucky. l.t. ed. (Young Trailers Ser.: Vol. 1). (J). reprint ed. 2007. 222p. pap. 22.99 (978-1-4346-3289-0(X)) 2008. 224p. 24.99 (978-0-554-36772-9(6)) 2008. 224p. 27.99 (978-0-554-27469-0(8)) 2007. (ENG.). 202p. pap. 20.99 (978-1-4346-3288-3(1)) Creative Media Partners, LLC.

—The Young Trailers: A Story of Early Kentucky. 2007. (Young Trailers Ser.: Vol. 1). 228p. (J). reprint ed. per. (978-1-4065-6553-9(9)) Dodo Pr.

—The Young Trailers: A Story of Early Kentucky. 2007. (Young Trailers Ser.: Vol. 1). 144p. (J). reprint ed. per. (978-1-4068-1694-5(9)) Echo Library.

—The Young Trailers: A Story of Early Kentucky. 2004. (Young Trailers Ser.: Vol. 1). (J). reprint ed. pap. 22.95 (978-1-4191-8924-1(7)); pap. 1.99 (978-1-4192-8924-8(1)) Kessinger Publishing, LLC.

—The Young Trailers: A Story of Early Kentucky. 2012. (Young Trailers Ser.: Vol. 1). 200p. (J). (gr. 4-7). reprint ed. pap. (978-3-8472-3210-0(X)) Tredition GmbH.

—The Young Trailers - A Story of Early Kentucky. 2008. (Young Trailers Ser.: Vol. 1). 244p. reprint ed. pap. 14.45 (978-1-60597-191-9(X), Book Jungle) Standard Pubns., Inc.

Anastasio, Dina. How Raven Became Black & Owl Got Its Spots & Por qué el cuervo es negro y el búho tiene Manchitas: 6 English, 6 Spanish Adaptations. 2011. (ENG & SPA.). (J). 75.00 net. (978-1-4108-5626-5(7)) Benchmark Education Co.

Anaya, Rudolfo A. How Chile Came to New Mexico. Nasario, Garcia, tr. from ENG. Nicolas, Otero, illus. 2014. (SPA & ENG.). 48p. (J). (gr. -1-3). 24.95 (978-1-936744-20-6(1), Rio Grande Bks.) LPD Pr.

Anderson, Jane. Iktomi Takes to the Sky: A Native American Folktale. 2006. (J). pap. (978-1-4108-7164-0(9)) Benchmark Education Co.

Armer, Laura Adams. Waterless Mountain. Armer, Sidney, illus. 2014. (ENG.). 256p. (J). (gr. 5-9). pap. 5.99 (978-0-486-49288-9(5)) Dover Pubns., Inc.

Armstrong, Alan. Raleigh's Page. Jessell, Tim, illus. 2009. (ENG.). 336p. (J). (gr. 3-7). 7.99 (978-0-375-83320-5(X), Yearling) Random Hse. Children's Bks.

Armstrong, Jeannette C. Dancing with the Cranes. Hall, Ron, illus. 2nd rev. ed. 2009. (ENG.). 24p. pap. 10.95 (978-1-894778-70-1(7)) Theytus Bks., Ltd. CAN. Dist: Univ. of Toronto Pr.

Arrathoon, Leigh A. Summer of the Bear: An Historical Novel about the Anishinabeg & the Fur Traders in Michigan. 2005. (Journals of Kevin Murphy Ser.: Bk. 1). (J). (978-1-893047-07-5(5)) Archus Pr., LLC.

Ashley-Hollinger, Mika. Precious Bones. 2013. (ENG.). 352p. (J). (gr. 4-7). 8.99 (978-0-307-93070-5(X), Yearling) Random Hse. Children's Bks.

Auger, Daniel. Watishka Warriors, 1 vol. 2009. (ENG.). 168p. (J). pap. 14.95 **(978-0-9810942-2-9(8)**, 0981094228) Eschia Bks. CAN. Dist: Lone Pine Publishing USA.

Awiakta, Marilou. Rising Fawn & the Fire Mystery. Bringle, Beverly, illus. 2007. (ENG.). 96p. (J). (gr. 4-7). pap. 14.95 (978-1-55591-600-8(7)) Fulcrum Publishing.

Ball, Jeff. Son Who Returns. 2014. (ENG.). (YA). pap. 9.95 (978-1-939053-04-6(8), 7th Generation) Book Publishing Co.

Ballantyne, R. M. The Norsemen in the West or America Before Columbus. 2004. reprint ed. pap. 1.99 (978-1-4192-7571-5(2)) Kessinger Publishing, LLC.

—Silver Lake. 2004. reprint ed. pap. 19.95 (978-1-4191-4729-6(3)); pap. 1.99 (978-1-4192-4729-3(8)) Kessinger Publishing, LLC.

Ballantyne, Robert Michael. Fort Desolation: Red Indians & Fur Traders of Rupert's Land. 2007. (ENG.). 60p. pap. 16.99 (978-1-4346-3669-0(0)); 64p. pap. 18.99 (978-1-4346-3717-8(4)) Creative Media Partners, LLC.

Ballard, George Anne. White Fire, the Indian Boy. James, Melody, illus. 2012. 24p. pap. 12.00 (978-0-9855312-3-2(1)) Bolton Publishing LLC.

Banks, Lynne Reid. The Indian in the Cupboard. 2011. 9.14 (978-0-7848-3449-7(0), Everbind) Marco Bk. Co.

—The Indian in the Cupboard. 181p. (J). (Indian in the Cupboard Ser.: No. 1). (gr. 4-7). pap. 4.99 (978-0-8072-1433-6(7)); 2004. (Indian in the Cupboard Ser.). (gr. 3-7). pap. 36.00 incl. audio (978-0-8072-7308-1(2), YA809SP) Random Hse. Audio Publishing Group. (Listening Library).

—The Key to the Indian. Watling, James, illus. 2004. (Indian in the Cupboard Ser.: No. 5). (ENG.). 288p. (J). (gr. 4-18). pap. 6.99 (978-0-380-80373-6(9)) HarperCollins Pubs.

—The Key to the Indian. (Indian in the Cupboard Ser.: No. 5). 240p. (J). (gr. 4-7). pap. 4.99 (978-0-8072-1551-7(1), Listening Library) Random Hse. Audio Publishing Group.

—The Key to the Indian. 2004. (Indian in the Cupboard Ser.: 5). (J). (gr. 3-6). lib. bdg. 17.20 (978-0-613-23006-3(X), Turtleback) Turtleback Bks.

—The Return of the Indian. (Indian in the Cupboard Ser.: No. 2). 189p. (J). (gr. 4-7). pap. 4.99 (978-0-8072-1434-3(5), Listening Library) Random Hse. Audio Publishing Group.

—The Return of the Indian. 2010. (Indian in the Cupboard Ser.). (ENG.). 208p. (J). (gr. 3-7). 6.99 (978-0-375-85523-8(8), Yearling) Random Hse. Children's Bks.

—Return of the Indian. 2003. (ENG., Illus.). 192p. pap. (978-0-00-714899-8(2)) HarperCollins Pubs. Ltd.

Banks, Lynne Reid & Banks, L. The Return of the Indian. 2010. (Indian in the Cupboard Ser.: 2). (gr. 3-6). lib. bdg. 17.20 (978-0-8335-0902-4(0), Turtleback) Turtleback Bks.

Banks, Sara Harrell. Remember My Name. 2nd ed. 2003. (YA). pap. 10.95 (978-0-89992-158-7(2)) Council for Indian Education.

Batdorf, Carol. Tinka Coloring Book: A Day in a Little Girl's Life. 2005. (Illus.). 24p. (Orig.). (J). (gr. 1-6). pap. 5.95 (978-0-88839-249-7(4)) Hancock Hse. Pubs.

Bauer Mueller, Pamela. An Angry Drum Echoed: Mary Musgrove, Queen of the Creeks. 2007. (ENG., Illus.). 296p. (YA). (gr. 6-7). per. 13.95 (978-0-9685097-8-4(9)); 18.95 (978-0-9685097-7-7(0)) Pinata Publishing CAN. Dist: Midpoint Trade Bks., Inc.

Baxter, Jean Rae. The Way Lies North. 2007. (ENG., Illus.). 342p. (J). per. (978-1-55380-048-4(6)) Ronsdale Pr.

Ben, Mikaelsen. Touching Spirit Bear. 2014. (ENG.). 256p. (J). 11.24 (978-1-63245-157-6(3)) Lectorum Pubns., Inc.

Besson, Sam. Coyote: A Trickster Tale, 1 vol. rev. ed. 2013. (Fiction Readers Ser.). (ENG., Illus.). 28p. (J). (gr. 3-3). pap. 8.99 (978-1-4333-5608-7(2)) Shell Educational Publishing.

Bickel, Karla. Handmade Necklace. Bickel, Karla, illus. l.t. ed. 2004. (Illus.). 16p. (J). (gr. -1-6). pap. 5.00 (978-1-891452-11-6(8), 1) Heart Arbor Bks.

Bjornson, Nancy. Llamas, Ponies & Pyrite. 2007. (J). (978-1-930596-82-5(0)) Amherst Pr.

—Mustangs, Fires & Snakes. 2007. (J). (978-1-930596-84-9(7)) Amherst Pr.

Blondin, John. The Old Man with the Otter Medicine. Sundberg, Mary Rose, tr. Beaverho, Archie, illus. 2007. (Old Man with the Otter Medicine Ser.). (ENG, DOI & DGR.). 40p. 22.95 (978-1-894778-49-7(9)) Theytus Bks., Ltd. CAN. Dist: Univ. of Toronto Pr.

Blos, Joan W. Brothers of the Heart: A Story of the Old Northwest, 1837-1838. 2008. (ENG.), 176p. (J). (gr. 3-7). pap. 5.99 (978-1-4169-7561-8(6), Simon & Schuster/Paula Wiseman Bks.) Simon & Schuster/Paula Wiseman Bks.

Blue, Martha. Little Prankster Girl: At'Eed Adilahi Yazhi. Ruffenach, Jessie, ed. Thomas, Peter, tr. from NAV. Smith, Keith, illus. 2008. (NAV & ENG.). 32p. (J). (gr. -1-3). 17.95 (978-1-893354-36-4(9)) Salina Bookshelf Inc.

BlueWolf, James Don. Speaking for Fire. Greenlee, Carolyn Wing, illus. 2007. (ENG.). 44p. (gr. 2-7). per. 12.95 (978-1-887400-31-2(1)) Earthen Vessel Production, Inc.

Bly, Stephen A. The Lost Wagon Train. 2005. (Retta Barre's Oregon Trail Ser.: Vol. 1). 110p. pap. 5.99 (978-1-58134-391-5(4), Crossway Bibles) Crossway.

Bombay, Cal & Sharpe, Margaret. Slave, Brave & Free, 10 bks. 2003. 256p. (J). per. 12.99 (978-1-929125-41-8(0), Multnomah) Doubleday Religious Publishing Group, The.

Bond, Douglas. Guns of Thunder. 2007. (Faith & Freedom Ser.). (Illus.). 261p. (J). (gr. 4-7). per. 11.99 (978-1-59638-013-4(6)) P & R Publishing.

Bostick, B. k. Huber Hill & the Dead Man's Treasure. 2011. (J). (978-1-59955-911-7(0), Bonneville Bks.) Cedar Fort, Inc./CFI Distribution.

Bowlby, Linda S. Is That So. Helms, Dana, illus. 2008. 29p. (J). pap. 9.95 (978-0-9779993-5-4(1)) Red Earth Publishing.

Bowman, Andy. Indian Slim. Travis, Stephanie, illus. 29p. (J). (gr. 1-6). pap. 6.95 (978-1-931650-06-9(3)); lib. bdg. 14.95 (978-1-931650-07-6(1)) Coastal Publishing Carolina, Inc.

Brezenoff, Steve. Burning Secrets, 1 vol. Vue, Tou, illus. (Vortex Bks.). (ENG.). 112p. (gr. 2-3). 2008. pap. 7.19 (978-1-59889-920-7(1)) 2007. 26.65 (978-1-59889-854-5(X)) Stone Arch Bks. (Vortex Bks.).

Brezenoff, Steven. The Case of the Portrait Vandal. Weber, Lisa K., illus. 2015. (Museum Mysteries Ser.). (ENG.). 128p. (gr. 2-3). lib. bdg. 26.65 (978-1-4342-9685-6(7)) Stone Arch Bks.

Brooks, Martha. Bone Dance, 1 vol. 2005. (ENG.). 184p. (J). (gr. 6-16). pap. 8.95 (978-0-88899-336-6(6)) Groundwood Bks. CAN. Dist: Publishers Group West (PGW).

Bruchac, Joseph. Arrow of Lightning. 2017. (Killer of Enemies Ser.). (ENG.). 400p. (YA). 19.95 **(978-1-62014-330-8(5)**, Tu Bks.) Lee & Low Bks., Inc.

—Code Talker: A Novel about the Navajo Marines of World War Two. 2006. (ENG.). 240p. (YA). (gr. 7-18). 8.99 (978-0-14-240596-3(5), Speak) Penguin Young Readers Group.

—Crazy Horse's Vision. 2004. (Illus.). (J). (gr. 1-3). spiral bd. (978-0-616-07251-6(1)) Canadian National Institute for the Blind/Institut National Canadien pour les Aveugles.

—Crazy Horse's Vision. 2005. (J). 28.95 incl. audio compact disk (978-1-59112-912-7(5)) Live Oak Media.

—Crazy Horse's Vision. Nelson, S. D., illus. 2006. (gr. 1-4). 20.45 (978-0-7569-6691-1(4)) Perfection Learning Corp.

—Flying with the Eagle, Racing the Great Bear: Tales from Native North America. 2011. (ENG., Illus.). 128p. (J). (gr. 3-9). pap. 12.95 (978-1-55591-693-0(7)) Fulcrum Publishing.

—Killer of Enemies. (Killer of Enemies Ser.). (ENG.). 400p. (YA). 2016. pap. 11.99 (978-1-62014-276-9(7)) 2013. 19.95 (978-1-62014-143-4(4)) Lee & Low Bks., Inc. (Tu Bks.).

—March Toward the Thunder. 2009. (ENG.). 320p. (YA). (gr. 7-18). 9.99 (978-0-14-241446-0(8), Speak) Penguin Young Readers Group.

—On This Long Journey, the Journal of Jesse Smoke, a Cherokee Boy, the Trail of Tears 1838. 2014. (My Name Is America Ser.). (ENG.). 208p. (J). (gr. 3-7). pap. 6.99 (978-0-545-53086-6(5), Scholastic Paperbacks) Scholastic, Inc.

—Sacajawea. 2008. (ENG., Illus.). 208p. (YA). (gr. 7). pap. 7.99 (978-0-15-206455-6(9)) Houghton Mifflin Harcourt Publishing Co.

—Sacajawea: The Story of Bird Woman & the Lewis & Clark Expedition. 2003. (Illus.). 199p. (J). (gr. 4-7). 12.65 (978-0-7569-0732-7(2)) Perfection Learning Corp.

—Talking Leaves. (ENG.). (J). (gr. 5). 2017. 288p. pap. 8.99 **(978-0-14-242298-4(3)**, Puffin Books) 2016. 256p. 16.99 (978-0-8037-3508-8(1), Dial Bks) Penguin Young Readers Group.

—Trail of the Dead, 1 vol. 2015. (Killer of Enemies Ser.). (ENG.). 400p. (YA). 19.95 (978-1-62014-261-5(9)) Lee & Low Bks., Inc.

—Wabi: A Hero's Tale. 2007. (ENG.). 208p. (YA). (gr. 7-18). pap. 7.99 (978-0-14-240947-3(2), Speak) Penguin Young Readers Group.

—The Warriors. 2004. (Junior Library Guild Selection Ser.). (J). (gr. 4-18). 120p. 15.95 (978-1-58196-002-0(6)); (ENG.). 128p. per. 4.99 (978-1-58196-022-8(0)) Lerner Publishing Group. (Darby Creek).

—Whisper in the Dark. Comport, Sally Wern, illus. 2009. (ENG.). 192p. (J). (gr. 5). pap. 6.99 (978-0-06-058089-6(5)) HarperCollins Pubs.

—Wolf Mark, 1 vol. 2013. (ENG.). 392p. (J). 17.95 (978-1-60060-661-8(X), Tu Bks.) Lee & Low Bks., Inc.

Bryson, Jamie S. The War Canoe. 2nd ed. 2009. (ENG., Illus.). 180p. (YA). (gr. 8-12). pap. 9.95 (978-0-88240-758-6(9), Alaska Northwest Bks.) Graphic Arts Ctr. Publishing Co.

Calahasen, Stella. Dream Catcher. 2009. (Dream Catcher Ser.). (ENG.). 96p. (gr. 7-9). pap. 12.95 (978-1-894778-92-3(8)) Theytus Bks., Ltd. CAN. Dist: Univ. of Toronto Pr.

Cameron, Anne. Dreamspeaker. unabr. ed. 2005. (ENG.). 128p. pap. 9.95 (978-1-55017-364-2(2)) Harbour Publishing Co., Ltd. CAN. Dist: Midpoint Trade Bks., Inc.

Campbell, Nicola I. Grandpa's Girls, 1 vol. LaFave, Kim, illus. 2011. (ENG & SAL.). 32p. (J). (gr. -1-2). 16.95 (978-1-55498-084-0(4)) Groundwood Bks. CAN. Dist: Publishers Group West (PGW).

Carbone, Elisa. Blood on the River: James Town 1607. 2007. (ENG.). 256p. (J). (gr. 5-18). 7.99 (978-0-14-240932-9(4), Puffin Books) Penguin Young Readers Group.

—Blood on the River: James Town 1607. 2009. (Illus.). 237p. 17.00 (978-1-60686-385-5(1)) Perfection Learning Corp.

Carlson, Lori Marie & Carlson, Lori M. Moccasin Thunder: American Indian Stories for Today. 2005. (ENG.). 176p. (YA). (gr. 8-18). 17.99 (978-0-06-623957-6(5), HarperTeen) HarperCollins Pubs.

Carvell, Marlene. Sweetgrass Basket. 2005. (ENG.). 256p. (J). (gr. 5-6). 16.99 (978-0-525-47547-7(8), Dutton Books for Young Readers) Penguin Young Readers Group.

Chappell, Crissa-Jean. More Than Good Enough. 2014. (ENG.). 216p. (YA). pap. 9.99 (978-0-7387-3644-0(9), Flux) North Star Editions.

Chickasaw Adventures: More than Warriors. 2005. (J). (978-1-4265-0002-2(5)) Layne Morgan Media, Inc.

Chickasaw Adventures: Tears at Fort Coffee. 2004. (J). (978-0-9762904-2-1(1)) Layne Morgan Media, Inc.

Chickasaw Adventures: The Civil War. 2005. (J). (978-1-4265-0000-8(9)) Layne Morgan Media, Inc.

Chickasaw Adventures: War with the Creeks. 2005. (J). (978-1-4265-0001-5(7)) Layne Morgan Media, Inc.

Chickasaw Adventures No. 1: The Journey Begins. 2004. (J). (978-0-9762904-0-7(5)) Layne Morgan Media, Inc.

Chief & the Storyteller: Not All Wanderers Are Lost. 2004. (Illus.). 150p. (YA). per. 16.95 (978-0-9747972-0-5(0)) Great Adventures Publishing.

Christie, Caroline. Silver Heels: A Story of Blackfeet Indians at Glacier National Park. Wilde, George, illus. 2011. 162p. 41.95 (978-1-258-00441-5(0)) Literary Licensing, LLC.

Clark, Electa. Wildcat, the Seminole: The Florida War. Nicholas, Frank, illus. 2011. 194p. 42.95 (978-1-258-06128-9(7)) Literary Licensing, LLC.

Cooper, James Fenimore. The Last of the Mohicans. Wyeth, N. C., illus. 2013. (Scribner Classics Ser.). (ENG.). 368p. (J). (gr. 5). 24.99 (978-1-4424-8130-5(7), Atheneum Bks. for Young Readers) Simon & Schuster Children's Publishing.

—The Last of the Mohicans. Howell, Troy, illus. 2008. (Classic Starts(tm) Ser.). (ENG.). 160p. (J). (gr. 2-4). 6.95 (978-1-4027-4577-5(X)) Sterling Publishing Co., Inc.

—Last of the Mohicans, 1 vol. Fields, Jan, illus. 2010. (Calico Illustrated Classics Ser.: No. 1). (ENG.). 112p. (J). (gr. 3-6). 27.07 (978-1-60270-708-5(1)) Magic Wagon.

Cooper, Susan. Ghost Hawk. 2013. (ENG.). 336p. (J). (gr. 5-9). 16.99 (978-1-4424-8141-1(2), McElderry, Margaret K. Bks.) McElderry, Margaret K. Bks.

Coulson, Art. The Creator's Game: A Story of Baaga'adowe/Lacrosse. Desjarlait, Robert, illus. 2013. (ENG.). 48p. (J). (gr. 3-6). pap. 6.95 (978-0-87351-909-0(4)) Minnesota Historical Society Pr.

Crawford, Ann Fears. Keechee: The Witch of the Woods. 2005. (J). (978-1-931823-21-0(9)) Halcyon Pr.

Crazy Horse's Vision. pap. incl. audio (978-1-59112-453-5(0)); pap. 18.95 incl. audio compact disk (978-1-59112-911-0(7)); pap. 52.95 incl. audio compact disk (978-1-59112-913-4(3)); pap. 16.95 incl. audio (978-1-59112-451-1(4)) Live Oak Media.

Creel, Ann Howard. Under a Stand Still Moon. 2005. 183p. (YA). (gr. 7-12). per. 8.95 (978-0-9746481-8-7(3)) Brown Barn Bks.

Crum, Sally. Race to Moonrise Rev. Carlson, Eric S., illus. 2006. 12.95 (978-1-932738-31-5(2)) Western Reflections Publishing Co.

—Race to the River: The Ancient Journey Continues. 2009. (YA). pap. 12.95 (978-1-932738-72-8(X)) Western Reflections Publishing Co.

Cuate, Melodie A. Journey to la Salle's Settlement. 2010. (Mr. Barrington's Mysterious Trunk Ser.). (ENG., Illus.). 184p. (J). lib. bdg. 18.95 (978-0-89672-704-5(1)) Texas Tech Univ. Pr.

Curtin, Ann. Dreamcatcher. 2015. 201p. (YA). (978-1-61271-246-8(0)) Zumaya Pubns. LLC.

Cuthand, Beth. Sikihpsis. Cuthand, Stan, tr. Longman, Mary, illus. ed. 2007. (Little Duck Ser.). (CRE & ENG.). 28p. 17.00 (978-1-894778-44-2(8)) Theytus Bks., Ltd. CAN. Dist: Univ. of Toronto Pr.

Daher, Anita. On the Trail of the Bushman, 1 vol. 2009. (Orca Young Readers Ser.). (ENG.). 128p. (J). (gr. 3-6). pap. 7.95 (978-1-55469-013-8(7)) Orca Bk. Pubs. USA.

Dance, Jennifer. Red Wolf. 2014. (ENG., Illus.). 256p. (YA). pap. 12.99 (978-1-4597-0810-5(5), 9781459708105) Dundurn CAN. Dist: Ingram Publisher Services.

Davis, Russell G. & Ashabranner, Brent. The Choctaw Code. 2006. 121p. (J). (gr. 3-7). per. 8.99 (978-1-59166-621-9(X)) BJU Pr.

De Leeuw, Cateau. Fear in the Forest. Vosburgh, Leonard, illus. 2014. (ENG.). 123p. (J). pap. 14.95 (978-1-932350-43-2(8)) Bethlehem Bks.

Dérib & Jeffrey, Erica. Yakari & Great Eagle. 2007. (Yakari Ser.: 1). (ENG., Illus.). 48p. (J). (gr. 4-7). per. 11.95 (978-1-905460-04-5(X)) CineBook GBR. Dist: National Bk. Network.

Desoto, Ernestine. Sugar Bear Story. 2004. (NAI & ENG.). 32p. pap. 9.95 (978-0-932653-70-3(7)) Sunbelt Pubns., Inc.

Dodge, Mary Mapes. Po No Kah an Indian Tale of Long Ago. 2004. reprint ed. pap. 15.95 (978-1-4191-4185-0(6)) Kessinger Publishing, LLC.

—PoNoKah an Indian Tale of Long Ago. 2006. pap. 21.95 (978-1-4286-5828-8(9)) Kessinger Publishing, LLC.

Domiteaux, Diane & Wallis, Karen. Washoe Seasons of Life: A Native American Story. 2004. (Illus.). 44p. (J). lib. bdg. 19.95 (978-0-9749610-3-3(5), 1234960) Beagle Bay Bks.

Dorris, Michael. Sees Behind Trees. 104p. (J). (gr. 4-6). pap. 4.95 (978-0-8072-1516-6(3), Listening Library) Random Hse. Audio Publishing Group.

Down, Heather. A Deadly Distance. 2007. (ENG.). 136p. (J). (gr. 6-8). pap. 9.99 (978-1-55002-637-5(2), Sandcastle Bks.) Dundurn CAN. Dist: Ingram Publisher Services.

Downing, Johnette. Why the Possum Has a Large Grin, 1 vol. Wald, Christina, illus. 2012. (ENG.). 32p. (J). (gr. k-3). 16.99 (978-1-4556-1639-8(7)) Pelican Publishing Co., Inc.

Downing, Sybil & Barker, Jane Valentine. Mesas to Mountains. (Colorado Heritage Ser.). (Illus.). 47p. (J). (gr. -1-8). reprint ed. pap. 7.95 (978-1-878611-04-8(6)) Silver Rim Pr.

Dugger, Elizabeth L. & Kanell, Beth. The Darkness under the Water. 2008. (ENG., Illus.). 320p. (YA). (gr. 7). 16.99 (978-0-7636-3719-4(X)) Candlewick Pr.

Duvall, Deborah L. Rabbit & the Fingerbone Necklace. Jacob, Murv, illus. 2009. (ENG.). 32p. (J). (gr. 1). 19.95 (978-0-8263-4723-7(1)) Univ. of New Mexico Pr.

Dyer, K. C. Facing Fire. 2010. (ENG.). 224p. pap. 12.95 (978-0-385-66638-1(1), Doubleday Can) Doubleday Canada, Ltd. CAN. Dist: Random Hse., Inc.

Ecton, Anne Massey. Passing Through Camelot. 2006. (J). (978-0-88092-620-1(1)) Royal Fireworks Publishing Co.

Editorial El Antillano. Tai Juega Pelota. Editorial El Antillano, ed. 2008. (Illus.). (J). 4.00 (978-0-9793026-2-6(5)) Editorial El Antillano, Inc.

Edwardson, Debby Dahl. My Name Is Not Easy, 0 vols. 2013. (ENG.). 256p. (YA). (gr. 7-9). pap. 9.99 (978-1-4778-1629-5(1), 9781477816295, Amazon Children's Publishing) Amazon Publishing.

Eggleston, George Cary. The Big Brother: A Story of Indian War. 2007. (Illus.). 104p. per. (978-1-4065-2541-0(3)) Dodo Pr.

Eichler, Ken. Swift Eagle's Odyssey with the Buffalo. 2007. 59p. pap. 16.95 (978-1-60474-199-5(6)) America Star Bks.

Elliott, Eric. Dear Miss Karana. 2016. 117p. (J). pap. (978-1-59714-323-3(5)) Heyday.

Ellis, Edward Sylvester & Coghlan, John. The Camp in the Mountains. 2004. (Illus.). 200p. (J). pap. 19.95 (978-0-9713470-8-3(5)) Phoenix International, Inc.

—The Hunters of the Ozark. 2004. (Illus.). 224p. (J). pap. 19.95 (978-0-9713470-2-1(6)) Phoenix International, Inc.

Erdrich, Louise. Chickadee. Erdrich, Louise, illus. (Birchbark House Ser.: 4). (Illus.). (J). (gr. 3-7). 2013. (ENG.). 224p. pap. 6.99 (978-0-06-057792-6(4)) 2012. (ENG., 208p. 16.99 (978-0-06-057790-2(8)) 2012. 208p. lib. bdg. 17.89 (978-0-06-057791-9(6)) HarperCollins Pubs.

—The Porcupine Year. Erdrich, Louise, illus. 2010. (Birchbark House Ser.: 3). (Illus.). 224p. (J). (gr. 3-7). pap. 6.99 (978-0-06-441030-4(7)) HarperCollins Pubs.

Ernst, Kathleen. Trouble at Fort la Pointe. 2009. (Mysteries Through Time Ser.). 144 - 176p. (YA). (gr. 4-8). 31.95 (978-1-60754-426-5(1)); pap. 15.25 (978-1-60754-427-2(X)) Windmill Bks.

Eustache, Harold. Shuswap Journey. 2004. (Shuswap Journey Ser.). (ENG.). 176p. pap. 15.95 (978-1-894778-15-2(4)) Theytus Bks., Ltd. CAN. Dist: Univ. of Toronto Pr.

Farley, Walter. Little Black, a Pony: Liishzhiin Yazhi. Carr, Elsie, tr. Whitethorne, Baje, illus. 2006. (ENG & NAV.). 64p. (J). (gr. 4-7). 21.95 (978-1-893354-90-6(3)) Salina Bookshelf Inc.

Feagan, Robert. Mystery at Shildii Rock. 2007. (Mysteries & Secrets Ser.: 3). (ENG.). 168p. (J). (gr. 7). pap. 9.99 (978-1-55002-668-9(2), Sandcastle Bks.) Dundurn CAN. Dist: Ingram Publisher Services.

—Napachee. 2005. 128p. (YA). (gr. 3-8). pap., tchr. ed. (978-0-88878-403-2(1), Sandcastle Bks.) Dundurn.

Fifield, Lisa. Bears Make Rock Soup. Erdrich, Lise, illus. 2013. (ENG.). 32p. (J). pap. 9.95 (978-0-89239-300-8(9), Children's Book Press) Lee & Low Bks., Inc.

Finotti, M. C. Paintbrushes & Arrows: A Story of St. Augustine. 2016. (ENG.). 112p. (J). pap. 9.95 *(978-1-56164-963-1(5))* Pineapple Pr., Inc.

A First Clay Gathering (Review Multiple Meanings), Level C. 2003. ("Plaid" Phonics & Stories Libraries). 43.50 *(978-0-8136-9234-0(2))* Modern Curriculum Pr.

Flood, Nancy Bo. Soldier Sister, Fly Home. Begay, Shonto, illus. 2016. (ENG.). 176p. (YA). (gr. 5). lib. bdg. 16.95 *(978-1-58089-702-0(9))* Charlesbridge Publishing, Inc.

Flor Ada, Alma. Celebrate a Powwow with Sandy Starbright. Alvarez, Maria Jesus, illus. 2007. (Cuentos para Celebrar / Stories to Celebrate Ser.). 30p. (gr. k-6). per. 11.95 *(978-1-59820-127-7(1))* Santillana USA Publishing Co., Inc.

Football, Virginia. How the Fox Saved the People. Wedzin, James, illus. 2009. (Fox Ser.). (ENG & DGR.). 56p. (gr. k-6). 26.95 *(978-1-894778-75-6(8))* Theytus Bks., Ltd. CAN. Dist: Univ. of Toronto Pr.

Football, Virginia & Mantla, Rosa. How the Fox Got His Crossed Legs. Siemens, Mary, tr. Wedzin, James, illus. 2009. (Fox Ser.). (ENG & DGR.). 32p. (gr. 2-3). 20.95 *(978-1-894778-74-9(X))* Theytus Bks., Ltd. CAN. Dist: Univ. of Toronto Pr.

Forester, MaMa Eagle. Young Eagle, Pretty Flower. Spears, Ashley E., illus. 2004. 16p. (J). 7.95 *(978-0-9762389-4-2(2))* Trent's Prints.

Fox, Lee White. Toby Erdrich & the Golden Eclipse. Selyov, Trebor E., ed. 2005. 170p. (YA). (gr. 7-12). pap. 11.95 *(978-0-9665055-7-3(3),* 5) Hallmark Emporium.

Francis, Lee DeCora. Kunu's Basket: A Story of Indian Island, 1 vol. Drucker, Susan, illus. 2012. (ENG.). 32p. (J). 16.95 *(978-0-88448-330-4(4))* Tilbury Hse. Pubs.

Frost, Helen. Diamond Willow. 2011. (ENG.). 144p. (J). (gr. 5-9). pap. 7.99 *(978-0-312-60383-0(5),* 9780312603830) Square Fish.

—Salt: A Story of Friendship in a Time of War. 2013. (ENG.). 160p. (J). (gr. 5-9). 17.99 *(978-0-374-36387-1(0),* 9780374363871, Farrar, Straus & Giroux (BYR)) Farrar, Straus & Giroux.

Furman, A. L., ed. Indian Stories. Geer, Charles, illus. 2011. 190p. 42.95 *(978-1-258-09304-4(9))* Literary Licensing, LLC.

Gansworth, Eric L. If I Ever Get Out of Here. (ENG.). 368p. (J). (gr. 7). 2015. pap. 10.99 *(978-0-545-41731-0(7))* 2013. 17.99 *(978-0-545-41730-3(9))* Scholastic, Inc. (Levine, Arthur A. Bks.).

Garcia, Emmett Shkeme. Sister Rabbit's Tricks. Pringle, Victoria, illus. 2013. (ENG.). 40p. (J). pap. 18.95 *(978-0-8263-5268-2(5))* Univ. of New Mexico Pr.

García, Nasario. Grandpa Lolo's Navajo Saddle Blanket: La Tilma de Abuelito Lolo. Moeller, Richard, illus. Moeller, Richard, photos by. 2012. (J). *(978-0-8263-5078-7(X));* 61p. pap. *(978-0-8263-5080-0(1));* (SPA.). 72p. pap. *(978-0-8263-5079-4(8))* Univ. of New Mexico Pr.

Gensler, Sonia. The Revenant. 2013. (ENG.). 354p. (YA). (gr. 7). pap. 9.99 *(978-0-375-86139-0(4),* Ember) Random Hse. Children's Bks.

George, Jean Craighead. Julie of the Wolves. Schoenherr, John, illus. (Julie of the Wolves Ser.: 1). (ENG.). (J). (gr. 8-18). 2016. 224p. pap. 6.99 *(978-0-06-440058-9(1))* 2003. 208p. pap. 8.99 *(978-0-06-054095-1(8),* HarperTeen) HarperCollins Pubs.

Goble, Paul. The Girl Who Loved Wild Horses. 2015. 32p. pap. 8.00 *(978-1-61003-619-1(0))* Center for the Collaborative Classroom.

—Horse Raid: The Making of a Warrior. 2014. (ENG., Illus.). 44p. (J). (gr. 2-4). 16.95 *(978-1-937786-25-0(0),* Wisdom Tales) World Wisdom, Inc.

—Walking Along: Plains Indian Trickster Stories. Goble, Paul, illus. 2011. (Illus.). (J). 19.95 *(978-0-9845041-5-2(X),* South Dakota State Historical Society Pr.) South Dakota State Historical Society Pr.

Golio, Janet & Golio, Mike. Present from the Past. 2nd ed. 2009. (ENG.). 120p. (YA). pap. 14.99 *(978-1-59092-145-6(3))* Blue Forge Pr.

—Puzzle from the Past. 2nd ed. 2009. (ENG.). 120p. (YA). pap. 14.99 *(978-1-59092-146-3(1))* Blue Forge Pr.

Gould, Carol. My Native American School. Drzewiecki, Paul, illus. I.t. ed. 2003. (ENG.). 16p. (gr. k-2). pap. 7.95 *(978-1-879835-77-1(0),* Kaeden Bks.) Kaeden Corp.

Grace & the Guiltless. 2014. (Wanted Ser.). (ENG.). 272p. 16.95 *(978-1-63079-001-1(X))* Switch Pr.

Green, Timothy. Mystery of Coyote Canyon, 1 vol. Green, Timothy, illus. 2008. (ENG., Illus.). 137p. (gr. 8-12). pap. 12.95 *(978-0-941270-83-0(1))* Gibbs Smith, Publisher.

Grinnell, George Bird. Jack among the Indians. 2006. (Illus.). pap. 30.95 *(978-1-4286-3276-9(X))* Kessinger Publishing, LLC.

Gromosiak, Paul. Owahonton: Maid of the Mist. 2012. (ENG.). (J). pap. 12.95 *(978-1-4675-4107-7(9))* Independent Pub.

Guillain, Charlotte. The Foolish, Timid Rabbit: An Indian Folk Tale, 1 vol. Dorado, Steve, illus. 2014. (Folk Tales from Around the World Ser.). (ENG.). 24p. (gr. 1-3). pap. 6.95 *(978-1-4109-6700-8(X),* NA-r) Heinemann-Raintree.

Gunderson, Jessica. Passage to Fortune: Searching for Saguenay. Kurtz, Rory, illus. 2016. (Discovering the New World Ser.). (ENG.). 96p. (gr. 3-4). lib. bdg. 26.65 *(978-1-4965-3481-1(6),* Connect) Stone Arch Bks.

Gutman, Dan. Jim & Me. 2010. (Baseball Card Adventures Ser.). (ENG.). 224p. (J). (gr. 5-9). pap. 6.99 *(978-0-06-059496-1(9))* HarperCollins Pubs.

—Jim & Me. 2010. (Baseball Card Adventures Ser.). (J). lib. bdg. 17.20 *(978-0-606-09536-5(5),* Turtleback) Turtleback Bks.

Haig-Brown, Roderick L. & Haig-Brown, Roderick. The Whale People. unabr. ed. 2003. (ENG., Illus.). 206p. (YA). pap. 14.95 *(978-1-55017-277-5(8))* Harbour Publishing Co., Ltd. CAN. Dist: Midpoint Trade Bks., Inc.

Halter, Loretta. A Voice for the Redwoods. du Houx, Emily, illus. 2003. 64p. pap. 14.00 *(978-1-882190-66-9(1))* Polar Bear & Co.

Harvey, Gwen. Esperanza Means Hope. Porfirio, Guy, illus. 2010. (J). *(978-0-910037-51-8(5));* pap. *(978-0-910037-52-5(3))* Arizona Historical Society.

Hawke, Jay Jordan. Pukawiss the Outcast. 2016. (ENG., Illus.). (J). 24.99 ***(978-1-63533-066-3(1))*** 2014. 204p. pap. 14.99 *(978-1-62798-646-5(4))* Dreamspinner Pr. (Harmony Ink Pr.).

—A Scout Is Brave. 2nd ed. 2016. (ENG., Illus.). (J). 24.99 ***(978-1-63477-929-6(0),*** Harmony Ink Pr.) Dreamspinner Pr.

Hay, Barbara. Lesson of the White Eagle. Hay, Peter, illus. 2012. (ENG.). 144p. (YA). pap. 11.99 *(978-1-937054-01-4(2))* RoadRunner Pr.

Henty, George Alfred. In the Heart of the Rockies. I.t. ed. 2006. 322p. pap. 24.99 *(978-1-4264-3253-8(4))* Creative Media Partners, LLC.

—In the Heart of the Rockies. 2004. reprint ed. pap. 1.99 *(978-1-4192-2600-7(2));* pap. 27.95 *(978-1-4191-2600-0(8))* Kessinger Publishing, LLC.

—True to the Old Flag. I.t. ed. 2007. (ENG.). 318p. pap. 24.99 *(978-1-4264-4352-7(8))* Creative Media Partners, LLC.

Herr, Melody & Darnell, Regna. Edward Sapir: Linguist, Anthropologist, Humanist. 2010. (ENG., Illus.). 520p. pap. 35.00 *(978-0-8032-2437-7(0))* Univ. of Nebraska Pr.

Hill, Janet Muirhead. The Horse & the Crow: A Miranda & Starlight Story. 2015. (ENG.). 268p. (J). pap. 13.00 *(978-1-937849-27-6(9))* Raven Publishing Inc. of Montana.

Hill, Kirkpatrick. Winter Camp. 2007. (ENG.). 192p. (J). (gr. 3-7). pap. 10.99 *(978-1-4169-6455-1(X),* Simon & Schuster/Paula Wiseman Bks.) Simon & Schuster/Paula Wiseman Bks.

—The Year of Miss Agnes. 2003. (Aladdin Historical Fiction Ser.). 115p. (gr. 3-7). 17.00 *(978-0-7569-1407-3(8))* Perfection Learning Corp.

hines, j. Finding Raven. 2007. 101p. pap. 8.95 *(978-0-615-17723-6(9))* Hines, Jerry.

Hobbs, Will. Beardream. Kastner, Jill, illus. 2014. 32p. pap. 8.00 *(978-1-61003-340-4(X))* Center for the Collaborative Classroom.

—The Big Wander. 2004. (Illus.). 181p. (J). (gr. 5-9). 13.65 *(978-0-7569-4970-9(X))* Perfection Learning Corp.

—Kokopelli's Flute. 2005. 148p. (gr. 5-9). 17.00 *(978-0-7569-5503-8(3))* Perfection Learning Corp.

—Kokopelli's Flute. 2005. (ENG.). 160p. (J). (gr. 5-9). pap. 7.99 *(978-1-4169-0250-8(3),* Simon & Schuster/Paula Wiseman Bks.) Simon & Schuster/Paula Wiseman Bks.

Hobbs, Will & Hobbs, William. Far North. 2004. (ENG., Illus.). 304p. (J). (gr. 3-7). pap. 8.99 *(978-0-06-054096-8(6),* HarperTeen) HarperCollins Pubs.

Holler, Sue Farrell. Lacey & the African Grandmothers, 1 vol. 2009. (Kid's Power Ser.). (ENG.). 118p. (J). (gr. 4-8). pap. 14.95 *(978-1-897187-61-6(0))* Second Story Pr. CAN. Dist: Orca Bk. Pubs. USA.

Holm, Jennifer L. An Adventure. 2010. (Boston Jane Ser.: No. 1). (ENG.). 272p. (J). (gr. 3-7). 7.99 *(978-0-375-86204-5(8),* Yearling) Random Hse. Children's Bks.

—The Claim. 2010. (Boston Jane Ser.: No. 2). (ENG.). 224p. (J). (gr. 3-7). pap. 7.99 *(978-0-375-86206-9(4),* Yearling) Random Hse. Children's Bks.

—Wilderness Days. 2004. (Boston Jane Ser.: No. 2). 256p. (J). (gr. 5-18). pap. 5.99 *(978-0-06-440881-3(7),* Harper Trophy) HarperCollins Pubs.

—Wilderness Days. unabr. ed. 2004. (Boston Jane Ser.: No. 2). 288p. (J). (gr. 5-9). pap. 38.00 incl. audio *(978-0-8072-0787-1(X),* S YA 307 SP, Listening Library) Random Hse. Audio Publishing Group.

—Wilderness Days. 2010. (Boston Jane Ser.: No. 2). (ENG.). 256p. (J). (gr. 3-7). pap. 7.99 *(978-0-375-86205-2(6),* Yearling) Random Hse. Children's Bks.

Hood, Ann. Crazy Horse: Brave Warrior. Altmann, Scott & Zilber, Denis, illus. 2013. (Treasure Chest Ser.: 5). (ENG.). 192p. (J). (gr. 3-7). pap. 6.99 *(978-0-448-45728-4(8),* Grosset & Dunlap) Penguin Young Readers Group.

Hopkins, K. C. The Night the Spirits Danced. 2008. 115p. pap. 15.00 *(978-0-615-23929-3(3))* Hopkins, KC.

Hopkins, Suzette. Little Wolf's Christmas. Taylor, Jill, illus. 2004. (Little Wolf & Friends Ser.). 19p. (J). 12.95 *(978-1-932133-72-1(0))* Writers' Collective, The.

House, Silas & Vaswani, Neela. Same Sun Here. Schenker, Hilary, illus. 2013. (ENG.). 304p. (J). (gr. 4-7). pap. 7.99 *(978-0-7636-6451-0(0))* Candlewick Pr.

Hyde, Heidi Smith. Elan, Son of Two Peoples. Prevost, Mikela, illus. 2014. (Life Cycle Ser.). (ENG.). 32p. (J). (gr. k-3). 17.95 *(978-0-7613-9051-0(0),* Kar-Ben Publishing) Lerner Publishing Group.

The Indian in the Cupboard. 2004. (J). *(978-1-59564-280-6(3))* Steps To Literacy, LLC.

Inglis, Lucy. Crow Mountain. 2016. (ENG.). 368p. (YA). (gr. 9). 17.99 *(978-0-545-90407-0(2),* Chicken Hse., The) Scholastic, Inc.

Irbinskas, Heather. The Lost Kachina. Albert, Robert & Anthis, Brian, illus. 2004. 32p. (J). 15.95 *(978-1-885772-33-6(5))* Kiva Publishing, Inc.

Jaffe, Nina. La Flor de Oro: Un Mito Taino de Puerto Rico. Ventura, Gabriela Baeza, tr. from ENG. Sanchez, Enrique O., illus. 2006. (SPA.). 32p. (J). (gr. -1-3). 16.95 *(978-1-55885-463-5(0),* Piñata Books) Arte Publico Pr.

James, J. Alison. Sing for a Gentle Rain. 2012. (ENG.). 224p. (J). (gr. 3-7). pap. 10.99 *(978-1-4424-7483-3(1),* Atheneum Bks. for Young Readers) Simon & Schuster Children's Publishing.

Jameson, Catherine. Zoe & the Fawn. Flett, Julie, illus. 2006. (ENG.). 32p. pap. 11.95 *(978-1-894778-43-5(X))* Theytus Bks., Ltd. CAN. Dist: Univ. of Toronto Pr.

Jennings, Paulla. Strawberry Thanksgiving. Peters, Ramona, illus. 2005. (Multicultural Celebrations Ser.). 32p. (J). 4.95 *(978-1-59373-010-9(1))* Bunker Hill Publishing, Inc.

Job. The River of Forgetfulness. Dérib, illus. 2013. (Yakari Ser.: 10). (ENG.). 48p. pap. 11.95 *(978-1-84918-140-2(3))* CineBook GBR. Dist: National Bk. Network.

—Yakari & Nanabozo. Derib, illus. 2014. (Yakari Ser.: 11). (ENG.). 48p. pap. 11.95 *(978-1-84918-177-8(2))* CineBook GBR. Dist: National Bk. Network.

—Yakari & the Coyote. Dérib, illus. 2012. (Yakari Ser.: 9). (ENG.). 48p. (J). (gr. 1-6). pap. 11.95 *(978-1-84918-101-3(2))* CineBook GBR. Dist: National Bk. Network.

—Yakari in the Land of Wolves. 2009. (Yakari Ser.: 6). (ENG., Illus.). 46p. pap. 11.95 *(978-1-905460-29-8(5))* CineBook GBR. Dist: National Bk. Network.

Job & Dérib. Yakari & the White Fleece. 2011. (Yakari Ser.: 8). (ENG., Illus.). 48p. pap. 11.95 *(978-1-84918-055-9(5))* CineBook GBR. Dist: National Bk. Network.

John, Roberta. Dibe Lizhini Jiliigo Bee Shanah IDLI/Proud to Be a Blacksheep. Thomas, Peter A., tr. from ENG. Smith, Keith, illus. 2007. (NAV & ENG.). 32p. (J). (gr. 4-7). 17.95 *(978-1-893354-05-0(9))* Salina Bookshelf Inc.

Johnson, E. Pauline. The Lost Island. Atanas, illus. 2010. (ENG.). 40p. (J). (gr. -1-3). pap. 9.95 *(978-1-897476-44-4(2))* Simply Read Bks. CAN. Dist: Ingram Publisher Services.

Johnson, Erin. Her Cold Revenge. 2015. (Wanted Ser.). (ENG.). 272p. 16.95 *(978-1-63079-007-3(9))* Switch Pr.

Johnson, Lois Walfrid. Trouble at Wild River. 2009. (J). 8.99 *(978-0-88062-279-0(2))* Mott Media.

Jones, Carrie, et al. After Obsession. 2012. (ENG.). 336p. (YA). (gr. 7-12). pap. 9.99 *(978-1-59990-913-4(8),* 9781599909134, Bloomsbury USA Childrens) Bloomsbury Publishing USA.

Jones, Kimberly K. Sand Dollar Summer. 2008. (ENG., Illus.). 224p. (J). (gr. 4-8). pap. 5.99 *(978-1-4169-5834-5(7),* McElderry, Margaret K. Bks.) McElderry, Margaret K. Bks.

Jones, Patrick. Target. 2014. (Alternative Ser.). (ENG.). 128p. (YA). (gr. 6-12). pap. 7.95 *(978-1-4677-4485-0(9),* Darby Creek); lib. bdg. 27.93 *(978-1-4677-3900-9(6))* Lerner Publishing Group.

Kadohata, Cynthia. Weedflower. (ENG.). 272p. (J). (gr. 5-9). 2009. pap. 7.99 *(978-1-4169-7566-3(7))* 2006. (Illus.). 19.99 *(978-0-689-86574-9(0))* Simon & Schuster Children's Publishing. (Atheneum Bks. for Young Readers).

Karr, Kathleen. Worlds Apart, 0 vols. unabr. ed. 2013. (ENG.). 208p. (J). (gr. 5-7). pap. 9.99 *(978-1-4778-1710-0(7),* 9781477817100, Amazon Children's Publishing) Amazon Publishing.

Kastner, Janet. The Snake Fence: A Novel. 2012. (J). pap. 14.95 *(978-1-937768-13-3(9))* QuakerPress.

Kimmel, Eric A. The Lady in the Blue Cloak: Legends from the Texas Missions. Guevara, Susan, illus. 2006. (ENG.). 40p. (J). (gr. 6-10). 16.95 *(978-0-8234-1738-4(7))* Holiday Hse., Inc.

Kirk, Connie Ann. Sky Dancers, 1 vol. Hale, Christy, illus. 2013. (ENG.). 32p. (J). (gr. 2-4). pap. 8.95 *(978-1-62014-147-2(7))* Lee & Low Bks., Inc.

Klein, Lisa. Cate of the Lost Colony. 2012. (ENG.). 336p. (YA). (gr. 9-12). pap. 9.99 *(978-1-59990-739-0(9),* 9781599907390, Bloomsbury USA Childrens) Bloomsbury Publishing USA.

Knife, Ivan M. Uses the. Black Thursday. 2010. 108p. pap. 15.99 *(978-1-4500-6311-1(X))* Xlibris Corp.

Knutsson, Catherine. Shadows Cast by Stars. (ENG., Illus.). 464p. (YA). (gr. 7). 2013. pap. 11.99 *(978-1-4424-0192-1(3))* 2012. 17.99 *(978-1-4424-0191-4(5))* Simon & Schuster Children's Publishing. (Atheneum Bks. for Young Readers).

Krensky, Stephen. How Coyote Stole the Summer: [A Native American Folktale]. Dupre, Kelly, illus. 2009. (On My Own Folklore Ser.). (ENG.). 48p. (gr. 2-4). pap. 6.95 *(978-1-58013-848-2(9),* First Avenue Editions) Lerner Publishing Group.

Kroll, Francis Lynde. Young Crow Raider: Young Heroes Library. Geer, Charles H., illus. 2011. 186p. 42.95 *(978-1-258-09906-0(3))* Literary Licensing, LLC.

—Young Sioux Warrior. Geer, Charles H., illus. 2011. 188p. 42.95 *(978-1-258-10209-8(9))* Literary Licensing, LLC.

Kudlinski, Kathleen V. My Lady Pocahontas, 0 vols. unabr. ed. 2013. (ENG.). 288p. (gr. 5-9). pap. 9.99 *(978-1-4778-1711-7(5),* 9781477817117, Amazon Children's Publishing) Amazon Publishing.

Lackey, Mercedes & Edghill, Rosemary. Dead Reckoning. 2012. (ENG.). 336p. (YA). (gr. 7-12). 16.99 *(978-1-59990-684-3(8),* 9781599906843, Bloomsbury USA Childrens) Bloomsbury Publishing USA.

L'Allier, Peter Wesley Thomas. Rotten Robbie & the Legend of Wanabinoo. 2006. (Illus.). 215p. 18.95 *(978-0-9724022-8-6(4))* TangleTown Media Inc.

Lapallo, Connie. Dark Enough to See the Stars in a Jamestown Sky. 2006. (YA). (gr. 7-18). pap. 19.95 *(978-1-59526-421-3(3))* Aeon Publishing Inc.

Lasky, Kathryn. A Voice in the Wind. 2008. (ENG., Illus.). 272p. (J). (gr. 2-5). pap. 15.95 *(978-0-15-205875-3(3))* Houghton Mifflin Harcourt Publishing Co.

Lawlor, Laurie. Wind on the River. 2004. 156p. (J). lib. bdg. 16.92 *(978-1-4242-0771-8(1))* Fitzgerald Bks.

Lawton, Wendy G. The Captive Princess: A Story Based on the Life of Young Pocahontas. 2008. (Daughters of the Faith Ser.). (ENG.). 144p. (gr. 3-7). per. 7.99 *(978-0-8024-7640-1(6))* Moody Pubs.

Lee, Melicent Humason & Lee, Leslie W., illus. Indians of the Oaks. 2nd ed. 2007. xiv, 244p. (J). pap. *(978-0-937808-50-4(4))* San Diego Museum of Man.

Leet, Karen M. Sarah's Courage: A Kentucky Frontier Kidnapping. 2014. (ENG., Illus.). 144p. (gr. 4-7). 14.99 *(978-1-62619-477-9(7),* History Pr., The) Arcadia Publishing.

Levitt, Steve. Journey to the MountainA Roots Tale. 2007. 144p. pap. 19.95 *(978-1-84728-086-2(2))* Lulu Pr., Inc.

Lewis, Floyd. The Foundered Mule. 2006. (YA). 9.95 *(978-0-9788283-2-5(1))* Acacia Publishing, Inc.

Lewis, Paul Owen. Frog Girl. 2004. (Illus.). 38p. (J). tchr. ed., tchr.'s planning gde. ed. 2.95 *(978-1-58246-009-3(4),* Tricycle Pr.) Ten Speed Pr.

—Frog Girl. (ENG., Illus.). 32p. (J). (gr. -1-5). 18.95 *(978-1-55110-658-8(2))* Whitecap Bks., Ltd. CAN. Dist: Graphic Arts Ctr. Publishing Co.

—Storm Boy. 2004. (Illus.). (J). tchr. ed. 2.95 *(978-1-58246-008-6(6),* Tricycle Pr.) Ten Speed Pr.

—Storm Boy, 1 vol. Lewis, Paul Owen, illus. 2008. (ENG., Illus.). 32p. (J). (gr. -1-3). pap. 8.95 *(978-1-55285-268-2(7))* Whitecap Bks., Ltd. CAN. Dist: Graphic Arts Ctr. Publishing Co.

Lincoln Collier, James. The Corn Raid. 2004. 142p. (J). lib. bdg. 16.92 *(978-1-4242-0768-8(1))* Fitzgerald Bks.

Lipsyte, Robert. The Brave. 2003. (Charlotte Zolotow Bk.). (ENG.). 240p. (J). (gr. 8-18). pap. 6.99 *(978-0-06-447079-7(2))* HarperCollins Pubs.

Lisle, Janet Taylor. The Crying Rocks. 2005. 281p. (YA). (gr. 7-12). 14.65 *(978-0-7569-5507-6(6))* Perfection Learning Corp.

Loendorf, Lawrence L. & Stone, Nancy Medaris. Two Hawk Dreams. 2014. (ENG., Illus.). 88p. (J). pap. 16.95 *(978-0-8032-6488-5(7),* Bison Bks.) Univ. of Nebraska Pr.

London, Jonathan. Giving Thanks. Manchess, Gregory, illus. 2011. (ENG.). 32p. (J). (gr. -1-2). pap. 6.99 *(978-0-7636-5594-5(5))* Candlewick Pr.

Long, Olivia. Thunderbirds & Thunderbeings. Long, Olivia, illus. Date not set. (Our Precious Planet Ser.). (Illus.). 32p. (J). (gr. -1-4). *(978-1-880042-10-6(X))* Shelf-Life Bks.

Lopez, David Mark. Maddie's Magic Markers: Ride Like an Indian. 2006. (J). (gr. 3-7). *(978-0-9744097-1-9(5))* Lopez, David.

Loyie, Larry & Brissenden, Constance. The Gathering Tree. 2nd ed. 2006. (Larry Loyie Ser.). (ENG., Illus.). 48p. pap. 18.95 *(978-1-894778-42-8(1))* Theytus Bks., Ltd. CAN. Dist: Univ. of Toronto Pr.

MacPhee, Bill. Stella, Nothing Has Changed. 2008. 312p. 28.50 *(978-1-60693-230-8(6),* Strategic Bk. Publishing) Strategic Book Publishing & Rights Agency (SBPRA).

Magpie, Lance White, reader. The Girl Who Loved Wild Horses. 2003. (Richard Jackson Books (Atheneum Hardcover) Ser.). (Illus.). (J). (gr. -1-2). 28.95 incl. audio compact disk *(978-1-59112-752-9(1))* Live Oak Media.

Markle, Sandra. The Fledglings. 2003. (ENG.). 144p. (YA). (gr. 4-6). pap. 9.95 *(978-1-56397-696-4(X))* Boyds Mills Pr.

Marsh, Carole. Pocahontas. (Read-Along Ser.). (J). 7.99 incl. audio *(978-1-55723-739-2(5))* Walt Disney Records.

—The Puzzle of the Indian Arrowhead. 2006. (Three Amigos Ser.). (Illus.). 54p. (J). (gr. 1-3). 14.95 *(978-0-635-06201-7(1))* Gallopade International.

Marshall, Joseph. In the Footsteps of Crazy Horse. Yellowhawk, James Mark, illus. 2015. (ENG.). 176p. (J). (gr. 5-9). 16.95 *(978-1-4197-0785-8(X),* Amulet Bks.) Abrams, Inc.

Martone, Ginny. Trapped in Dead Man's Cave. 2007. 61p. pap. 19.95 *(978-1-60474-227-5(5))* America Star Bks.

Matthews, Kay. An Anasazi Welcome. Belknap, Barbara, illus. 2004. 40p. (gr. 4-7). pap. 6.95 *(978-1-878610-27-0(9))* Red Crane Bks., Inc.

Max, Jill, compiled by. Spider Spins a Story: Fourteen Legends from Native America. 2007. (ENG.). 72p. (J). (gr. 3-7). pap. 8.95 *(978-0-87358-936-9(X))* Cooper Square Publishing Llc.

Mayaprua, Alejandro Taish. Nantu & Auju: How the Moon & the Potoo Bird Came to Be. Youth of the Achuar Tribe of Ecuador, illus. 2005. (J). 15.95 *(978-0-9745477-0-1(0))* Arutam Pr.

McCabe, James Dabney, Jr. Planting the Wilderness or, the Pioneer Boys: a Story of Frontier Life. 2007. pap. 27.95 *(978-1-4304-8187-4(0))* Kessinger Publishing, LLC.

McDaris, Terry. Black Fox Tribe: The Beginning. 2007. 372p. per. 29.95 *(978-1-4241-6733-3(7))* America Star Bks.

McGaa, Ed. Spirit Horse: An Adventure in Crazy Horse Country. 2007. 80p. (YA). pap. *(978-1-57579-360-3(1))* Pine Hill Pr.

McGaa Tonemah, Paula & McGaa, Ed. The Animals Talk. 2009. 72p. (J). pap. *(978-1-57579-373-3(3))* Pine Hill Pr.

McGovern, Ann. Little Wolf. 2011. 48p. (gr. 2-4). pap. 8.95 *(978-1-4620-2711-8(3))* iUniverse, Inc.

McIntosh, Kenneth. The Trickster's Image: Forensic Art. 2009. (J). pap. 24.95 *(978-1-4222-1452-7(4))* 2007. (Illus.). 144p. (YA). (gr. 8-12). pap. 9.95 *(978-1-4222-0873-1(7))* Mason Crest.

—The Trickster's Image: Forensic Art, 3 vols. Miller, Justin, illus. 2007. (Crime Scene Club Ser.). 144p. (YA). (gr. 9-12). lib. bdg. 24.95 *(978-1-4222-0249-4(6))* Mason Crest.

McLeod, Elaine. Lessons from Mother Earth, 1 vol. Wood, Colleen, illus. 2010. (ENG.). 24p. (J). (gr. k-k). pap. 7.95 *(978-0-88899-832-3(5))* Groundwood Bks. CAN. Dist: Publishers Group West (PGW).

McMurtry, Robby, tr. Song of Moon Pony. 2003. (Illus.). 17.95 *(978-1-57168-740-1(8))* Eakin Pr.

Mead, Alice. Crossing the Starlight Bridge. 2008. (ENG.). 132p. (J). (gr. 4-6). pap. 7.99 *(978-1-4169-8964-6(1),* Simon & Schuster Bks. For Young Readers) Simon & Schuster Bks. For Young Readers.

Meierhenry, Mark V. & Volk, David. The Mystery of the Maize. Two Bulls, Marty Grant, illus. 2010. (J). *(978-0-9822749-1-0(2),* South Dakota State Historical Society Pr.) South Dakota State Historical Society Pr.

Metaxas, Eric. Princess Scargo & the Birthday Pumpkin, 1 vol. Barbour, Karen, illus. 2004. (Rabbit Ears-A Classic Tale Ser.). (ENG.). 40p. (gr. k-5). 25.65 *(978-1-59197-769-8(X))* Spotlight.

Minnema, Cheryl. Hungry Johnny. Ballinger, Wesley, illus. 2014. (ENG.). 32p. (J). 17.95 *(978-0-87351-926-7(4))* Minnesota Historical Society Pr.

Mitchard, Jacquelyn. Look Both Ways. 2010. (Midnight Twins Ser.: No. 2). (ENG.). 304p. (YA). (gr. 7-18). 8.99 *(978-1-59514-281-8(9),* Razorbill) Penguin Young Readers Group.

Molloy, Anne Stearns Baker. Captain Waymouth's Indians. Gorsline, Douglas, illus. 2011. 204p. 44.95 *(978-1-258-06802-8(8))* Literary Licensing, LLC.

Monroe, George. The Secret Cave on the Hill. 2012. 50p. pap. 21.99 *(978-1-4772-8840-5(6))* AuthorHouse.

Montgomery, Tamara & Belknap, Jodi. TiQri the Little Snow Fox. 2008. 32p. 14.95 incl. cd-rom *(978-0-9723420-0-1(1),* Calabash Bks.) Belknap Publishing & Design.

Moonshower, Candie. The Legend of Zoey. 2007. (ENG.). 224p. (J). (gr. 3-7). 6.99 *(978-0-440-23924-6(9),* Yearling) Random Hse. Children's Bks.

Moore, Billy Loran. Little Brother Real Snake. 2004. (ENG.). 144p. (J). pap. 10.95 *(978-1-58838-147-7(1),* NewSouth Bks.) NewSouth, Inc.

Moore, Elizabeth & Couvillon, Alice. Ancient Mounds of Watson Brake: Oldest Earthworks in North America, 1 vol. Anderson, Rick, illus. 2010. (ENG.). 32p. (J). (gr. k-3). 16.99 *(978-1-58980-656-6(5))* Pelican Publishing Co., Inc.

Mulcahy, Lucille. Magic Fingers. Lambo, Don, illus. 2012. 124p. 40.95 *(978-1-258-23435-5(1));* pap. 25.95 *(978-1-258-24669-3(4))* Literary Licensing, LLC.

Muldoon, Kathleen M. The Runaway Skeleton. Hilliker, Phillip, illus. 2008. (Vortex Bks.). (ENG.). 112p. (gr. 2-3). 26.65 *(978-1-4342-0800-2(1),* Vortex Bks.) Stone Arch Bks.

Muller, Seth. Keepers of the WindClaw Chronicles: The Mockingbird's Manual. Tayloe, McConnell Dubay, ed. Whitethorne, Bahe, Jr., illus. 2009. (ENG.). 128p. (J). (gr. 4-7). pap. 12.95 *(978-1-893354-04-3(0))* Salina Bookshelf Inc.

Munro, Ken. The Cross Keys Caper. 2006. (Sammy & Brian Mystery Ser.: 18). 154p. pap. 5.95 *(978-1-932864-94-6(6))* Masthof Pr.

Munsch, Robert. Ribbon Rescue. 2007. (J). 12.65 *(978-0-7569-7466-4(6))* Perfection Learning Corp.

Murphy, Barbara Beasley. Ace Flies Like an Eagle. 2003. (Can't Stop Ace Ser.: No. 3). 180p. (J). pap. 16.95 *(978-0-86534-409-9(4))* Sunstone Pr.

Myers, Tim J. The Thunder Egg. Coleman, Winfield, illus. 2015. (ENG.). 28p. (J). (gr. k-4). 15.95 *(978-1-937786-39-7(0),* Wisdom Tales) World Wisdom, Inc.

Napoli, Donna Jo. The Crossing. Madsen, Jim, illus. 2011. (ENG.). 40p. (J). (gr. -1-3). 16.99 *(978-1-4169-9474-9(2),* Atheneum Bks. for Young Readers) Simon & Schuster Children's Publishing.

Nawashani. Stepping Stones to the Sun. Wiles, Pat, illus. 2013. 68p. pap. 11.95 *(978-1-4787-0445-4(4))* Outskirts Pr., Inc.

Nelson, S. D. The Star People: A Lakota Story. 2003. (ENG., Illus.). 36p. (J). (gr. -1-3). 18.95 *(978-0-8109-4584-5(3))* Abrams, Inc.

Nesbit, Troy. The Indian Mummy Mystery, Vol. 2013. (Wilderness Mystery Ser.). (ENG., Illus.). 276p. (J). (gr. 3-7). pap. 12.95 *(978-1-58979-813-7(9))* Taylor Trade Publishing.

Nielsen, Gwyn English. Serendipity & the Dream Catcher. Nielsen, Gwyn English, ed. Colby, Devon English, illus. 2003. 176p. (gr. 3-7). pap. 5.95 *(978-0-9660726-2-4(6))* C.G.S. Pr.

Noble, Trinka Hakes. The Legend of Michigan. Van Frankenhuyzen, Gijsbert, illus. 2006. (Legend (Sleeping Bear) Ser.). (ENG.). 40p. (J). (gr. -1-3). 17.95 *(978-1-58536-278-3(6))* Sleeping Bear Pr.

—The Legend of the Cape May Diamond. Lewis, E. B., illus. rev. ed. 2007. (Legend (Sleeping Bear) Ser.). (ENG.). 40p. (J). (gr. 3-7). 17.95 *(978-1-58536-279-0(4))* Sleeping Bear Pr.

Noe, Katherine Schlick. Something to Hold. 2011. (ENG., Illus.). 256p. (J). (gr. 5-7). 17.99 *(978-0-547-55813-4(9))* Houghton Mifflin Harcourt Publishing Co.

Noël, Alyson. Mystic. 2013. (Soul Seekers Ser.: 3). (ENG.). 320p. (YA). (gr. 7). mass mkt. 9.99 *(978-1-250-04818-9(4),* 9781250048189, St. Martin's Paperbacks); pap. 9.99 *(978-0-312-57567-0(X),* 9780312575670, St. Martin's Griffin) St. Martin's Pr.

Nogar, Anna M. & Lamadrid, Enrique R. Sisters in Blue: Sor María de Ágreda Comes to New Mexico = Hermanas de Azul: Sor María de Ágreda Viene a Nuevo México. Córdova, Amy, illus. 2017. (SPA & ENG.). 88p. (J). ***(978-0-8263-5821-9(7))*** Univ. of New Mexico Pr.

O'Dell, Scott. Island of the Blue Dolphins. Lewin, Ted, illus. gif. ed. 2010. (ENG.). 192p. (J). (gr. 2-5). 22.00 *(978-0-547-42483-5(3))* Houghton Mifflin Harcourt Publishing Co.

—Island of the Blue Dolphins. 184p. (J). (gr. 3-5). pap. 5.99 *(978-0-8072-8327-1(4));* 2004. (gr. 5-9). pap. 36.00 incl. audio *(978-0-8072-8326-4(6),* YA163SP) Random Hse. Audio Publishing Group. (Listening Library).

—Island of the Blue Dolphins. l.t. ed. 2005. (ENG.). 223p. pap. 10.95 *(978-0-7862-7254-9(6),* Large Print Pr.) Thorndike Pr.

—Island of the Blue Dolphins. 2010. lib. bdg. 18.40 *(978-0-606-10724-2(X),* Turtleback) Turtleback Bks.

—Island of the Blue Dolphins. Schwebel, Sara L., ed. 2016. (ENG., Illus.). 256p. 29.95 *(978-0-520-28937-6(4))* Univ. of California Pr.

—Island of the Blue Dolphins: And Related Readings. 2006. (McDougal Littell Literature Connections Ser.). (ENG., Illus.). 208p. (gr. 6-8). 18.50 *(978-0-395-87473-8(4),* 2-70833) Great Source Education Group, Inc.

—Sing down the Moon. 2010. (ENG.). 144p. (J). (gr. 2-5). pap. 7.99 *(978-0-547-40632-9(0))* Houghton Mifflin Harcourt Publishing Co.

—Sing Down the Moon. 2006. 21.75 *(978-0-8446-7288-5(2))* Smith, Peter Pub., Inc.

—Sing down the Moon. 2011. 9.00 *(978-0-7848-3596-8(9),* Everbind) Marco Bk. Co.

—Streams to the River, River to the Sea. 2008. (ENG.). 208p. (J). (gr. 5-7). pap. 6.99 *(978-0-618-96642-4(0));* (Illus.). pap. 7.99 *(978-0-547-05316-5(9))* Houghton Mifflin Harcourt Publishing Co.

—Thunder Rolling in the Mountains. 2010. (ENG.). 144p. (J). (gr. 2-5). pap. 7.99 *(978-0-547-40628-2(2))* Houghton Mifflin Harcourt Publishing Co.

—Zia. 2011. (ENG.). 192p. (J). (gr. 2-5). pap. 7.99 *(978-0-547-40633-6(9))* Houghton Mifflin Harcourt Publishing Co.

—Zia. 2011. 9.00 *(978-0-7848-3593-7(4),* Everbind) Marco Bk. Co.

Olsen, Sylvia. The Girl with a Baby, 1 vol. 2003. (ENG.). 208p. (YA). (gr. 7-12). pap. 9.95 *(978-1-55039-142-8(9))* Sono Nis Pr. CAN. Dist: Orca Bk. Pubs. USA.

—Yellow Line, 1 vol. 2005. (Orca Soundings Ser.). (ENG.). 128p. (YA). (gr. 8-12). per. 9.95 *(978-1-55143-462-9(8))* Orca Bk. Pubs. USA.

—Yetsa's Sweater, 1 vol. Larson, Joan, illus. 2007. (ENG.). 40p. (J). (gr. -1-5). 19.95 *(978-1-55039-155-8(0))* Sono Nis Pr. CAN. Dist: Orca Bk. Pubs. USA.

Olsen, Sylvia & Martin, Ron. Which Way Should I Go?, 1 vol. Charko, Kasia, illus. 2008. (ENG.). 40p. (J). (gr. 1-5). 19.95 *(978-1-55039-161-9(5))* Sono Nis Pr. CAN. Dist: Orca Bk. Pubs. USA.

Orona-Ramirez, Kristy. Kiki's Journey. Warm Day, Jonathan, illus. (ENG.). 32p. (J). 2017. pap. 9.95 ***(978-0-89239-410-4(2),*** Children's Book Press) 2013. 16.95 *(978-0-89239-214-8(2))* Lee & Low Bks., Inc.

Ortakales, Denise. The Legend of the Old Man of the Mountain. Crawford, Robert, illus. 2004. (Legends Ser.). (ENG.). 40p. (J). 17.95 *(978-1-58536-236-3(0))* Sleeping Bear Pr.

Osborne, Mary Pope. Adaline Falling Star. unabr. ed. 2004. (Middle Grade Cassette Librariestm Ser.). 176p. (J). (gr. 3-7). pap. 29.00 incl. audio *(978-0-8072-1195-3(8),* S YA 319 SP, Listening Library) Random Hse. Audio Publishing Group.

—Standing in the Light: The Diary of Catharine Carey Logan, Delaware Valley, Pennsylvania, 1763. 2011. (Dear America Ser.). (ENG.). 176p. (J). (gr. 5-9). 12.99 *(978-0-545-26687-1(4))* Scholastic, Inc.

Osborne, Mary Pope, et al. Búfalos Antes Del Desayuno. Murdocca, Sal, illus. 2008. (Casa del Arbol Ser.: 18).Tr. of Buffalo Before Breakfast. (SPA.). (J). (gr. 2-4). pap. 5.99 *(978-1-933032-48-1(0))* Lectorum Pubns., Inc.

Otten, Charlotte F. Home in a Wilderness Fort: Copper Harbor 1844. 2006. (Illus.). 232p. (J). (gr. 2-7). per. 14.95 *(978-0-9766104-5-8(0))* Arbutus Pr.

Owens, Robert. Indian Ways. 2008. 76p. pap. 14.54 *(978-1-4357-3702-0(4))* Lulu Pr., Inc.

Panagopoulos, Janie Lynn. Little Ship under Full Sail: An Adventure in History. 2006. 160p. (J). pap. 8.95 *(978-0-938682-82-0(2))* River Road Pubns., Inc.

Parry, Rosanne. Written in Stone. 2014. (ENG., Illus.). 208p. (J). (gr. 4-7). pap. 6.99 *(978-0-375-87135-1(7),* Yearling) Random Hse. Children's Bks.

Paulsen, Gary. Canyons. 2011. (ENG.). 192p. (YA). (gr. 7). pap. 7.99 *(978-0-385-74234-4(7),* Ember) Random Hse. Children's Bks.

—The Night the White Deer Died. 2011. (ENG.). 114p. (YA). (gr. 7). pap. 6.99 *(978-0-385-74235-1(5),* Ember) Random Hse. Children's Bks.

—Woods Runner. 2011. (ENG.). 176p. (YA). (gr. 7). pap. 7.99 *(978-0-375-85908-3(X),* Lamb, Wendy Bks.) Random Hse. Children's Bks.

Pearsall, Shelley. Crooked River. 2007. 249p. (gr. 5-9). 17.00 *(978-0-7569-7771-9(1))* Perfection Learning Corp.

Peck, James E. Meet Mr. Chair Bear. 2008. 52p. pap. 16.95 *(978-1-4241-7959-6(9))* America Star Bks.

Penn, Audrey. The Whistling Tree. Gibson, Barbara, illus. 2003. 32p. 16.95 *(978-0-87868-852-4(8),* 8528, Child & Family Pr.) Child Welfare League of America, Inc.

Peralta, Joaquin. Emma Snow: At the Edge of the World. 2009. 206p. (J). pap. 17.00 *(978-1-934376-19-5(1))* Balona Bks.

Peratrovich, Roy A., Jr. Little Whale: A Story of the Last Tlingit War Canoe. 2016. (ENG., Illus.). 64p. (J). pap. 16.95 *(978-1-60223-295-2(4))* Univ. of Alaska Pr.

Perkins, Mitali. You Bring the Distant Near. 2017. (ENG.). 320p. (YA). 17.99 ***(978-0-374-30490-4(4),*** 9780374304904, Farrar, Straus & Giroux (BYR)) Farrar, Straus & Giroux.

Perrow, Angeli. Many Hands: A Penobscot Indian Story. Austin, Heather, illus. 2011. (ENG.). 32p. (J). (gr. -1-3). pap. 10.95 *(978-1-60893-014-2(9))* Down East Bks.

Peschke, Marci. Dead Man's Map, 1 vol. Smith, Tod G., illus. 2008. (Vortex Bks.). (ENG.). 112p. (gr. 2-3). pap. 7.19 *(978-1-59889-921-4(X),* 1271328, Vortex Bks.) Stone Arch Bks.

Pugliano-Martin, Carol. The Earth on Turtles Back. 2011. (Early Connections Ser.). (J). *(978-1-61672-674-4(1))* Benchmark Education Co.

Raffa, Edwina & Rigsby, Annelle. Escape to the Everglades. 2013. (Florida Historical Fiction for Youth Ser.). (ENG.). 112p. (J). pap. 9.95 *(978-1-56164-619-7(9))* Pineapple Pr., Inc.

—Escape to the Everglades Teacher's Activity Guide. 2006. (ENG., Illus.). 31p. pap., tchr. ed., act. bk. ed. 6.00 *(978-1-56164-362-2(9))* Pineapple Pr., Inc.

Ramirez, Antonio. Napí Goes to the Mountain, 1 vol. Amado, Elisa, tr. from SPA. Domi & Domi, illus. 2006. (ENG.). 48p. (J). (gr. k-3). 18.95 *(978-0-88899-713-5(2))* Groundwood Bks. CAN. Dist: Publishers Group West (PGW).

—Napí Va a la Montaña, 1 vol. Domi, illus. 2006. (SPA.). 48p. (J). (gr. k-3). 18.95 *(978-0-88899-715-9(9))* Groundwood Bks. CAN. Dist: Publishers Group West (PGW).

Reeve, Kirk. Sun Father, Corn Mother: A Novel. 2015. 168p. (YA). pap. *(978-1-63293-091-0(9))* Sunstone Pr.

Revelle, Rick. Algonquin Sunset: An Algonquin Quest Novel. 2017. (Algonquin Quest Novel Ser.: 3). (ENG.). 304p. (YA). pap. 12.99 *(978-1-4597-3702-0(4))* Dundurn CAN. Dist: Ingram Publisher Services.

—I Am Algonquin: An Algonquin Quest Novel. 2013. (Algonquin Quest Novel Ser.: 1). (ENG., Illus.). 280p. (YA). pap. 12.99 *(978-1-4597-0718-4(4),* 9781459707184) Dundurn CAN. Dist: Ingram Publisher Services.

Rice, Dona Herwick & Bradley, Kathleen. Lewis & Clark, 1 vol. 2009. (Building Fluency Through Reader's Theater Ser.). (ENG., Illus.). 32p. (J). (gr. 3-5). pap. 7.99 *(978-1-4333-0540-5(2))* Teacher Created Materials, Inc.

Richardson, Tracy. Indian Summer. 2010. (ENG.). 198p. (YA). (gr. 7). pap. 11.95 *(978-1-935462-25-5(3))* Luminis Bks., Inc.

Richter, Conrad. The Light in the Forest. Chappell, Warren, illus. 2005. (Everyman's Library Children's Classics Ser.). (ENG.). 176p. (J). (gr. 5-7). 15.95 *(978-1-4000-4426-9(X),* Everyman's Library) Knopf Doubleday Publishing Group.

Riley, Zach. Sacred Stick. Ricci, Andrés, illus. 2012. (Zach Riley Ser.). 80p. (J). (gr. 3-6). lib. bdg. 27.07 *(978-1-61783-535-3(8))* Magic Wagon.

Robertson, David. 7 Generations: A Plains Cree Saga, 1 vol. Henderson, Scott B., illus. 2016. (7 Generations Ser.). (ENG.). 136p. (YA). (gr. 9-12). pap. 34.00 *(978-1-55379-355-7(2),* 9781553793557, HighWater Pr.) Portage & Main Pr. CAN. Dist: Orca Bk. Pubs. USA.

Robertson, David Alexander. Stone. Henderson, Scott B., illus. 2010. (7 Generations Ser.: 1). (ENG.). 32p. (YA). pap. *(978-1-55379-227-7(0),* 4ae83eb9-baca-4c13-a381-ea5771ba95b7, HighWater Pr.) Portage & Main Pr.

Robertson, Robbie. Hiawatha & the Peacemaker. Shannon, David, illus. 2015. (ENG.). 48p. (J). (gr. -1-3). 19.95 *(978-1-4197-1220-3(9),* Abrams Bks. for Young Readers) Abrams, Inc.

Robinson, Gary. Little Brother of War. 2013. (PathFinders Ser.). (ENG.). 113p. (YA). pap. 9.95 *(978-1-939053-02-2(1),* 7th Generation) Book Publishing Co.

—Tribal Journey. 2013. (YA). 111p. *(978-1-939053-87-9(0));* (ENG.). 120p. pap. 9.95 *(978-1-939053-01-5(3),* 7th Generation) Book Publishing Co.

Robison, C. Dan, Jr. Wind Seer: The Story of One Boy's Contribution to the Anasazi Culture. 2005. 132p. (J). per. 18.95 *(978-0-922993-27-7(0))* Marquette Bks., LLC.

Rodgers, Greg, as told by. Chukfi Rabbit's Big, Bad Bellyache: A Trickster Tale. 2014. (ENG., Illus.). 40p. (J). pap. 7.95 *(978-1-935955-27-6(6))* Cinco Puntos Pr.

Rose, Caroline Starr & McPike, Elizabeth. Blue Birds. 2015. (ENG., Illus.). 400p. (J). (gr. 5). bds. 16.99 *(978-0-399-16810-9(9),* G.P. Putnam's Sons Books for Young Readers) Penguin Young Readers Group.

Ross, Sylvia. Blue Jay Girl. 2010. 48p. (J). (gr. 3-7). 12.95 *(978-1-59714-127-7(5))* Heyday.

—Lion Singer. Ross, Sylvia, illus. 2005. (Illus.). 33p. (J). (gr. 3-7). 12.95 *(978-1-59714-009-6(0),* Great Valley Bks.) Heyday.

Rubcic, Michael. Native Soul. 2004. 216p. (Orig.). (J). pap. 14.95 *(978-0-9746848-0-2(5))* Native Sun Pr.

Ruffenach, Jessie, ed. Baby Learns about Animals. Thomas, Peter, tr. from NAV. Blackshep, Beverly, illus. 2004. (ENG & NAV.). 16p. (J). (gr. -1-12). 7.95 *(978-1-893354-49-4(0))* Salina Bookshelf Inc.

Rylant, Cynthia & Siegel, Mark. Long Night Moon. Siegel, Mark, illus. 2004. (ENG., Illus.). 32p. (J). (gr. -1-3). 17.99 *(978-0-689-85426-2(9),* Simon & Schuster Bks. For Young Readers) Simon & Schuster Bks. For Young Readers.

Saigeon, Lori. Fight for Justice, 1 vol. 2009. (ENG.). 128p. (J). (gr. 3-6). pap. 7.95 *(978-1-55050-405-7(3))* Coteau Bks. CAN. Dist: Orca Bk. Pubs. USA.

Sanderson, Nancy. Summer of the Painted Horse. 2009. 188p. pap. 14.49 *(978-1-4490-2312-6(6))* AuthorHouse.

Sanderson, Whitney. Golden Sun. Sanderson, Ruth, illus. 2010. (Horse Diaries). (ENG.). 160p. (J). (gr. 3-7). pap. 7.99 *(978-0-375-86194-9(7),* Random Hse. Bks. for Young Readers) Random Hse. Children's Bks.

Santiago, Chiori. Home to Medicine Mountain. 2014. 18.45 *(978-1-63419-705-2(4))* Perfection Learning Corp.

Sargent, Dave & Sargent, Pat. Hoot: (Grullo) Be Creative, 30. Lenoir, Jane, illus. 2003. (Saddle up Ser.: Vol. 35). 42p. (J). 35. pap. 6.95 *(978-1-56763-696-3(9))* Vol. 35. lib. bdg. 23.60 *(978-1-56763-695-6(0))* Ozark Publishing.

—Mack: (Medicine Hat Paint) Be a Leader, 30 vols., Vol. 39. Lenoir, Jane, illus. 2003. (Saddle up Ser.: Vol. 39). 42p. (J). pap. 10.95 *(978-1-56763-700-7(0))* Ozark Publishing.

—Whiskers: (Roan) Pride & Peace, 30 vols., Vol. 59. Lenoir, Jane, illus. 2003. (Saddle up Ser.: Vol. 59). 42p. (J). pap. 10.95 *(978-1-56763-806-6(6))* Ozark Publishing.

Sargent, Dave, et al. Counting Coup Vol. 4: (Cheyenee) Be Proud, 20 vols. Lenoir, Jane, illus. l.t. ed. 2003. (Story Keeper Ser.). 42p. (J). lib. bdg. 23.60 *(978-1-56763-909-4(7))* Ozark Publishing.

Savageau, Cheryl & Hynes, Robert. Muskrat Will Be Swimming, 1 vol. 2006. (ENG., Illus.). 32p. (gr. 3-7). 7.95 *(978-0-88448-280-2(4),* 884280) Tilbury Hse. Pubs.

Sayles, Carol L. Turn the Turtle Rightside. 2007. (ENG.). 156p. (J). (gr. 4-7). per. *(978-1-933255-25-5(0))* DNA Pr.

Scaletta, Kurtis. Mudville. 2010. (ENG.). 272p. (J). (gr. 3-7). 8.99 *(978-0-375-84472-0(4),* Yearling) Random Hse. Children's Bks.

Scieszka, Jon. The Good, the Bad, & the Goofy. Smith, Lane, illus. 2004. (Time Warp Trio Ser.: 3). (ENG.). 80p. (J). (gr. 2-4). pap. 5.99 *(978-0-14-240046-3(7),* Puffin Books) Penguin Young Readers Group.

—The Good, the Bad, & the Goofy. Smith, Lane, illus. 2005. (Time Warp Trio Ser.: No. 3). 70p. (gr. 4-7). 15.00 *(978-0-7569-5876-3(8))* Perfection Learning Corp.

Shaw, Carol Anne. Hannah & the Spindle Whorl. 2010. (ENG., Illus.). 244p. pap. 10.95 *(978-1-55380-103-0(2))* Ronsdale Pr. CAN. Dist: SPD-Small Pr. Distribution.

Shay, Michael K. A Flash in Time: A Novel. 2016. (J). pap. *(978-1-63293-141-2(9))* Sunstone Pr.

Sheely, Robert. In the Hands of the Enemy. Killcoyne, Hope L., ed. Martin, John F., illus. 2003. (Adventures in America Ser.: Vol. 8). 75p. (gr. 4). 14.95 *(978-1-893110-31-1(1))* Silver Moon Pr.

Shefelman, Janice J. & Shefelman, Tom, illus. Son of Spirit Horse. 2004. 74p. (J). *(978-1-57168-833-0(1),* Eakin Pr.) Eakin Pr.

Sherman, Alexie. Flight. 2014. (ENG.). 208p. 18.25 *(978-1-63245-148-4(4))* Lectorum Pubns., Inc.

Simpson, Caroll. The First Beaver, 1 vol. rev. ed. 2009. (ENG., Illus.). 32p. (J). *(978-1-894974-50-9(6))* Heritage Hse.

—The First Beaver, 1 vol. Simpson, Caroll, illus. 2015. (Coastal Spirit Tales Ser.). (ENG., Illus.). 32p. (J). (gr. k-3). pap. 12.95 ***(978-1-77203-062-4(7))*** Heritage Hse. CAN. Dist: Orca Bk. Pubs. USA.

—The First Mosquito, 1 vol. 2010. (ENG., Illus.). 32p. (J). *(978-1-926613-67-3(8))* Heritage Hse.

—The First Mosquito, 1 vol. Simpson, Caroll, illus. 2015. (Coastal Spirit Tales Ser.). (ENG., Illus.). 32p. (J). (gr. k-3). pap. 12.95 ***(978-1-77203-063-1(5))*** Heritage Hse. CAN. Dist: Orca Bk. Pubs. USA.

Slier, Debby. Cradle Me, 1 vol. 2012. (ENG., Illus.). 32p. (J). bds. 6.95 *(978-1-59572-274-4(2))* Star Bright Bks., Inc.

Smelcer, John. The Great Death. 2009. (ENG.). 176p. (YA). (gr. 5-9). 17.99 *(978-0-8050-8100-8(3),* 9780805081008, Holt, Henry & Co. Bks. For Young Readers) Holt, Henry & Co.

—The Trap. 2007. (ENG.). 176p. (YA). (gr. 7-9). per. 9.99 *(978-0-312-37755-7(X),* 9780312377557) Square Fish.

Smith, Mary P. Wells. The Young Puritans in King Philip's War. Bridgman, L. J., illus. 2011. 396p. 54.95 *(978-1-258-05550-9(3))* Literary Licensing, LLC.

Snedden, Genevra Sis. Docas the Indian Boy of Santa Clara. 2005. pap. 21.95 *(978-1-4179-2695-4(3))* Kessinger Publishing, LLC.

Sneve, Virginia Driving Hawk. Bad River Boys. Farnsworth, Bill, illus. 2005. (ENG.). 32p. (YA). 16.95 *(978-0-8234-1856-5(1))* Holiday Hse., Inc.

—The Chichi Hoohoo Bogeyman. Agard, Nadema, illus. 2nd ed. 2008. (ENG.). 64p. (J). (gr. -1). pap. 9.95 *(978-0-8032-1745-4(5),* Bison Bks.) Univ. of Nebraska Pr.

Sneve, Virginia Driving Hawk & Sneve, Virginia. Lana's Lakota Moons. 2007. (ENG., Illus.). 127p. (gr. 3-7). pap. 14.95 *(978-0-8032-6028-3(8),* Bison Bks.) Univ. of Nebraska Pr.

Sockabasin, Allen & Raye, Rebekah. Thanks to the Animals, 1 vol. 2nd ed. 2014. (ENG., Illus.). 36p. (gr. 1-6). 17.95 *(978-0-88448-414-1(9),* 884414) Tilbury Hse. Pubs.

Soggie, Neil. The Young-Dogs of Elbow. 2007. (ENG.). 112p. per. 32.99 *(978-0-7618-3813-5(9))* Hamilton Bks.

Spalding, Andrea & Scow, Alfred. Secret of the Dance, 1 vol. Gait, Darlene, illus. 2009. (ENG.). 32p. (J). (gr. -1-3). 9.95 *(978-1-55469-129-6(X))* Orca Bk. Pubs. USA.

Speare, Elizabeth George. The Sign of the Beaver. 2011. (ENG.). 144p. (J). (gr. 5-7). pap. 7.99 *(978-0-547-57711-1(7))* Houghton Mifflin Harcourt Publishing Co.

—The Sign of the Beaver. 135p. (J). (gr. 4-6). pap. 4.99 *(978-0-8072-1517-3(1),* Listening Library) Random Hse. Audio Publishing Group.

Stanley, Brenda. I Am Nuchu. 2010. 334p. (YA). (gr. 9-18). 16.95 *(978-1-934813-47-8(8))* Westside Bks.

Stiegemeyer, Julie. Thanksgiving: A Harvest Celebration. Benoit, Renne, illus. 2006. 32p. (J). (gr. -1-3). per. 7.49 *(978-0-7586-0916-8(7))* Concordia Publishing Hse.

Stilwell, Norma. It Was Powwow Time in Plymouth. 2004. 43p. pap. 24.95 *(978-1-4137-3534-5(7))* PublishAmerica, Inc.

Stokes, Malcolm, illus. The Legend of the Blue Bonnets: A Native American Legend. 2004. (ENG.). 20p. (J). (gr. 3-3). pap. 6.47 net. *(978-0-7685-2129-0(7),* Dominie Elementary) Pearson Schl.

Stoltzfus, Sherman Matthew. Little Bear Builds a Wigwam. Zimmerman, Edith Fay Martin & Kanagy, Audrey Ann Zimmerman, illus. 2010. 32p. (J). *(978-0-9646590-2-5(6))* J&M Publishing.

Stone, Marie. On Their Own: A Journey to Jamestown. 2006. (Illus.). 166p. (J). (gr. 3-7). per. 8.95 *(978-1-57249-385-8(2),* White Mane Kids) White Mane Publishing Co., Inc.

Strelkoff, Tatiana. Jeremy & the Crow Nation. Martin, Bobi, ed. 2003. (Changer Ser.: Vol. 2). (Illus.). 128p. (Orig.). (J). (gr. 7-12). pap. 6.95 *(978-0-945522-04-1(5),* 2204-5) Rebecca Hse.

Sutherland, Margaret Bradt. The Life of Mary Jemison, Indian Captive. 2011. 36p. 35.95 *(978-1-258-00912-0(9))* Literary Licensing, LLC.

Swanson, Bruce & Swanson, Bill. Gray Wolf's Search, 1 vol. Peterson, Gary, illus. 2007. (ENG.). 24p. (J). (gr. -1-2). 14.95 *(978-0-9779183-1-7(9),* 7th Generation) Book Publishing Co.

Sweeney, Joyce. Waiting for June, 0 vols. 2006. (ENG.). 158p. (YA). (gr. 10-12). pap. 7.99 *(978-0-7614-5329-1(6),* 9780761453291, Amazon Children's Publishing) Amazon Publishing.

Sylliboy, Alan. The Thunder Maker, 1 vol. 2016. (ENG., Illus.). 32p. (J). (gr. -1-3). 19.95 *(978-1-77108-329-4(8))* Nimbus Publishing, Ltd. CAN. Dist: Orca Bk. Pubs. USA.

Taschek, Karen. The Risen Horse. 2010. (ENG.). 248p. (YA). (gr. 7-18). pap. 15.95 *(978-0-8263-4837-1(8))* Univ. of New Mexico Pr.

Taylor, C. J. Peace Walker: The Legend of Hiawatha & Tekanawita. 2014. (ENG., Illus.). 48p. (J). (gr. 2-4). pap. 8.99 *(978-1-77049-778-8(1),* Tundra Bks.) Tundra Bks. CAN. Dist: Penguin Random Hse. LLC.

—Spirits, Fairies, & Merpeople: Native Stories of Other Worlds. 2009. (ENG., Illus.). 40p. (J). (gr. 2-4). 19.95 *(978-0-88776-872-9(5),* Tundra Bks.) Tundra Bks. CAN. Dist: Penguin Random Hse. LLC.

Tingle, Tim. Crossing Bok Chitto: A Choctaw Tale of Friendship & Freedom. Bridges, Jeanne Rorex, illus. 2006. (ENG.). 40p. (J). (gr. 1-8). 17.95 *(978-0-938317-77-7(6))* Cinco Puntos Pr.

—Danny Blackgoat, Navajo Prisoner. 2013. (PathFinders Ser.). (ENG.). 151p. (YA). pap. 9.95 *(978-1-939053-03-9(X),* 7th Generation) Book Publishing Co.

—How I Became a Ghost: A Choctaw Trail of Tears Story, 1 vol. l.t. ed. 2013. (ENG., Illus.). 160p. (J). 18.95 *(978-1-937054-53-3(5))* RoadRunner Pr.

Tolson, Aaron J. Washington Putter. 2005. 248p. (YA). per. 22.00 *(978-1-58982-243-6(9),* Bedside Bks.) American Bk. Publishing Group.

Trotter, Deborah W. A Summer's Trade/Shiigo Na'iini' Toddy, Irving, illus. 2007. (ENG & NAV.). 32p. (J). (gr. -1-3). 17.95 *(978-1-893354-71-5(7))* Salina Bookshelf Inc.

Tsinajinnie, Veronica. Johonaa'ei: Bringer of Dawn. Thomas, Peter A., tr. from NAV. Singer, Ryan, illus. 2007. (ENG & NAV.). 32p. (J). (gr. -1-3). 17.95 *(978-1-893354-54-8(7))* Salina Bookshelf Inc.

Ts'o, Pauline. Whispers of the Wolf. 2015. (ENG., Illus.). 40p. (J). (gr. k-3). 16.95 *(978-1-937786-45-8(5),* Wisdom Tales) World Wisdom, Inc.

Turner, Ginger. Gold Mine! The California Gold Rush Story. 2004. (Illus.). 46p. (J). per. 15.95 *(978-0-9742502-2-9(8))* Gossamer Bks., LLC.

Turner, Ginger & Shimpi, Shekhar. Gold Mine! The California Gold Rush Story. 2004. (Illus.). 44p. (J). pap. 15.95 *(978-0-9742502-3-6(6))* Gossamer Bks., LLC.

Van Camp, Richard. Little You, 1 vol. Flett, Julie, illus. 2013. (ENG.). 24p. (J). (gr. -1-k). bds. 9.95 *(978-1-4598-0248-3(9))* Orca Bk. Pubs. USA.

—What's the Most Beautiful Thing You Know about Horses? Littlechild, George, illus. 2013. (ENG.). 32p. (J). pap. 9.95 *(978-0-89239-185-1(5))* Lee & Low Bks., Inc.

Vandever, Daniel W. Fall in Line, Holden. Frank, LaFrenda, ed. Vandever, Daniel W., illus. 2017. (Illus.). 32p. (J). ***(978-1-893354-50-0(4))*** Salina Bookshelf Inc.

Vaughan, Richard Lee. Eagle Boy: A Pacific Northwest Native Tale. Christiansen, Lee, illus. 2008. (ENG.). 32p. (J). (gr. -1-3). pap. 10.99 *(978-1-57061-592-4(6),* Little Bigfoot) Sasquatch Bks.

Wallace, Bill. The Final Freedom. 2009. (ENG.). 176p. (J). (gr. 3-7). pap. 9.99 *(978-1-4169-9421-3(1),* Simon & Schuster/Paula Wiseman Bks.) Simon & Schuster/Paula Wiseman Bks.

—The Legend of Thunderfoot. 2007. (ENG.). 160p. (J). (gr. 3-7). pap. 5.99 *(978-1-4169-0692-6(4),* Simon & Schuster/Paula Wiseman Bks.) Simon & Schuster/Paula Wiseman Bks.

Walsh, Alice. Buried Truth, 1 vol. 2013. (ENG.). 100p. (J). (gr. 4-8). pap. 11.95 *(978-1-77103-009-0(7),* Tuckamore Bks) Creative Bk. Publishing CAN. Dist: Orca Bk. Pubs. USA.

Walt Disney Company Staff. Pocahontas. 2005. (WEL., Illus.). 24p. *(978-1-899877-04-1(5))* Y Ddraig Fach.

Walters, Scott. Woman Too Young of Panther Cave. 2007. 20.95 *(978-1-934248-14-0(2))* Salem Author Services.

Warren, Wilda. Tejan: A Story of Life with the Comanche Indians. 2011. 102p. 39.95 *(978-1-258-03989-9(3))* Literary Licensing, LLC.

Washington, Kathy. Three Colors of Katie. Farina, Kathy, illus. 2010. (J). (gr. k-2). pap. 9.95 *(978-1-932514-18-6(X))* College of DuPage Pr.

Weller, Sadie Bedoka. Tsa Ch'ayah/How the Turtle Got Its Squares: A Traditional Caddo Indian Children's Story. Chafe, Wallace, tr. Montoya, Robin Michelle, illus. 2005. (CAD & ENG.). 40p. (J). (gr. 3-7). per. 16.99 *(978-1-4134-8836-4(6))* Xlibris Corp.

Westover, Steve. Crater Lake: Battle for Wizard Island. 2012. pap. 14.99 *(978-1-59955-960-5(9))* Cedar Fort, Inc./CFI Distribution.

—Return of the Mystic Gray. 2013. 15.99 *(978-1-4621-1187-9(4))* Cedar Fort, Inc./CFI Distribution.

Widener, Leslie Stall, illus. Chukfi Rabbit's Big, Bad Bellyache: A Trickster Tale. 2014. (ENG.). 40p. (J). (gr. k-5). 16.95 *(978-1-935955-26-9(8))* Cinco Puntos Pr.

Willard F. Baker. The Boy Ranchers among the Indians. 2007. 180p. per. 11.95 *(978-1-4218-4020-8(0)*, 1st World Library - Literary Society) 1st World Publishing, Inc.

Williams Hall, Kathy. Kay Kay's Adventures on Ojo Caliente: The Old Aspen Tree & the Posi Ouinge. 2012. 32p. pap. 19.99 *(978-1-4772-7667-9(X))* AuthorHouse.

Williams, Jack R. Be Brave, Tah-Hy! The Journey of Chief Joseph's Daughter. Proferes, Jo, illus. 2012. (ENG.). 134p. (J). (gr. 3-7). pap. 29.95 *(978-0-87422-313-2(X))* Washington State Univ. Pr.

Williamson, Denise J. River of Danger. 2008. (J). 8.99 *(978-1-59166-854-1(9))* BJU Pr.

Williamson, Ray A. & Monroe, Jean Guard. They Dance in the Sky: Native American Star Myths. Stewart, Edgar, illus. 2007. (ENG.). 144p. (J). (gr. 5-7). pap. 8.95 *(978-0-618-80912-7(0))* Houghton Mifflin Harcourt Publishing Co.

Wilson, John. Victorio's War, 1 vol. 2012. (Desert Legend Trilogy Ser.: 3). (ENG.). 176p. (YA). (gr. 8-12). pap. 12.95 *(978-1-55469-882-0(0))* Orca Bk. Pubs. USA.

Wolfel, Ursula. Fliegender Stern. pap. 14.95 *(978-3-570-26064-7(X))* Bertelsman, Verlagsgruppe C. GmbH DEU. Dist: Distribooks, Inc.

Wooden, Walter. Little Bear's Journey. 2011. 32p. pap. 21.99 *(978-1-4628-4440-1(5))* Xlibris Corp.

Woods, Brenda. My Name Is Sally Little Song. 2007. (ENG.). 192p. (J). (gr. 3-7). 7.99 *(978-0-14-240943-5(X)*, Puffin Books) Penguin Young Readers Group.

—My Name Is Sally Little Song. 2007. (Illus.). 182p. (gr. 2-7). 17.00 *(978-0-7569-8156-3(5))* Perfection Learning Corp.

Woolley, Barbara B. Freedom West. 2006. 22.99 *(978-1-4257-0124-6(8))*; pap. 15.99 *(978-1-4257-0123-9(X))* Xlibris Corp.

Wright, Caleb E. Marcus Blair A Story of Provincial Times. 2006. pap. 22.95 *(978-1-4286-6303-9(7))* Kessinger Publishing, LLC.

Yazzie, Seraphine G. The Three Little Sheep/Dibe Yazhi Taa'go Baa Hane' Thomas, Peter A., tr. Huna Smith, Ryan, illus. 2006. (ENG & NAV.). 32p. (J). (gr. 4-7). 12.95 *(978-1-893354-09-8(1))* Salina Bookshelf Inc.

Yeahpau, Thomas M. X-Indian Chronicles: The Book of Mausape. 2006. (ENG.). 240p. (YA). (gr. 9). 16.99 *(978-0-7636-2706-5(2))* Candlewick Pr.

Young, Judy. Minnow & Rose: An Oregon Trail Story. Farnsworth, Bill, illus. 2009. (Tales of Young Americans Ser.). (ENG.). 32p. (J). (gr. 1-5). 17.95 *(978-1-58536-421-3(5))* Sleeping Bear Pr.

Zima, Gordon. Sunbirds & Evergreens. 2006. (J). 16.00 *(978-0-9742894-5-8(0))* Hutton Electronic Publishing.

Zima, Gordon & Zima, Paula, illus. Sun Birds & Evergreens: The Nuk-Chuk Stories. 2005. (J). *(978-0-9742894-3-4(4))* Hutton Electronic Publishing.

INDIANS OF NORTH AMERICA—FOLKLORE

Benton-Banai, Edward. The Mishomis Book: The Voice of the Ojibway. 2010. (ENG., Illus.). 114p. pap. 21.95 *(978-0-8166-7382-7(9))* Univ. of Minnesota Pr.

Bruchac, Joseph. The Boy Who Lived with the Bears: And Other Iroquois Stories. Jacob, Murv, illus. 2003. (Storytime Ser.). 63p. (J). (gr. k-5). pap. 11.95 *(978-0-930407-61-2(X))* Parabola Bks.

Bruchac, Joseph & Bruchac, James. How Chipmunk Got His Stripes. Aruego, Jose & Dewey, Ariane, illus. 2003. (ENG.). 32p. (J). (gr. k-3). 6.99 *(978-0-14-250021-7(6)*, Puffin Books) Penguin Young Readers Group.

Bruchac, Joseph, III & Ross, Gayle. The Girl Who Married the Moon: Tales from Native North America. 2006. (ENG.). 128p. (J). (gr. 3-8). pap. 12.95 *(978-1-55591-566-7(3)*, 800.992.2908) Fulcrum Publishing.

Clark, Ann Nolan. Little Boy with Three Names: Stories of Taos Pueblo. Lujan, Tonita, illus. 2005. 75p. (J). (gr. 2-6). reprint ed. pap. 15.00 *(978-0-7567-9717-1(9))* DIANE Publishing Co.

Confederated Salish and Kootenai Tribes Staff. Bull Trout's Gift: By the Confederated Salish & Kootenai Tribes. 2011. (ENG., Illus.). 70p. 21.95 *(978-0-8032-3491-8(0))* Univ. of Nebraska Pr.

Curry, Jane Louise. Hold up the Sky: And Other Native American Tales from Texas & The. Watts, James, illus. 2010. (ENG.). 176p. (J). (gr. 3-7). pap. 9.99 *(978-1-4424-2155-4(X)*, McElderry, Margaret K. Bks.) McElderry, Margaret K. Bks.

Dewey, Jennifer Owings. The Shaman & the Water Serpent. Yazzie, Benton, illus. 2007. (ENG.). 40p. (J). 19.95 *(978-0-8263-4211-9(6))* Univ. of New Mexico Pr.

Duncan, Barbara, ed. The Origin of the Milky Way & Other Living Stories of the Cherokee. Standingdeer, John, Jr. & Goshorn, Shan, illus. 2008. (ENG.). 144p. (gr. 4-18). pap. 17.00 *(978-0-8078-5930-8(3))* Univ. of North Carolina Pr.

Duvall, Deborah L. How Medicine Came to the People: A Tale of the Ancient Cherokees. Jacob, Murv, illus. 2012. (Grandmother Stories Ser.). (ENG.). 32p. (J). pap. 18.95 *(978-0-8263-3008-6(8))* Univ. of New Mexico Pr.

Duvall, Deborah L., text. Rabbit & the Bears. 2004. (Grandmother Stories Ser.). (ENG., Illus.). 32p. (J). 16.95 *(978-0-8263-3131-1(9))* Univ. of New Mexico Pr.

Dwyer, Mindy. Coyote in Love: The Story of Crater Lake. 2014. (ENG., Illus.). 32p. (J). (gr. -1-3). pap. 10.99 *(978-0-88240-997-9(2)*, 9780882409979, West Winds Pr.) Graphic Arts Ctr. Publishing Co.

Endredy, James. The Journey of Tunuri & the Blue Deer: A Huichol Indian Story. Cruz, María Hernández de la & López, Casimiro de la Cruz, trs. Cruz, María Hernández de la & López, Casimiro de la Cruz, illus. 2003. (ENG.). 32p. (J). (gr. -1-6). 15.95 *(978-1-59143-016-2(X))* Bear & Co.

Gary, Ken, tr. & illus. The Fire Stealers: A Hopi Story. Gary, Ken, illus. 2003. (J). 15.95 *(978-1-885772-13-8(0))* Kiva Publishing, Inc.

Goble, Paul. All Our Relatives: Traditional Native American Thoughts about Nature. 2005. (ENG., Illus.). 36p. (J). (gr. 4-7). 15.95 *(978-0-941532-77-8(1))* World Wisdom, Inc.

—The Boy & His Mud Horses: And Other Stories from the Tipi. 2010. (ENG.). 48p. (J). (gr. 3-7). 14.95 *(978-1-935493-11-2(6))* World Wisdom, Inc.

—The Earth Made New: Plains Indian Stories of Creation. 2009. (ENG.). 40p. (J). (gr. 4-7). 17.95 *(978-1-933316-67-3(5))* World Wisdom, Inc.

—Mystic Horse. Goble, Paul, illus. 2003. (ENG., Illus.). 40p. (J). (gr. k-5). 17.99 *(978-0-06-029813-5(8))* HarperCollins Pubs.

Grinnell, George Bird. Blackfeet Indian Stories. 2005. 144p. per. 14.95 *(978-1-931832-57-1(9)*, 8667872363) Riverbend Publishing.

Haberstroh, Marilyn & Panik, Sharon. A Quetzalcóatl Tale of Corn. Castle, Lynn, illus. 2014. (Quetzalcóatl Tales Ser.). (ENG.). 48p. (J). (gr. k-5). pap. 9.95 *(978-1-60732-345-7(1))* Univ. Pr. of Colorado.

Haley, Gail E., tr. & illus. Kokopelli, Drum in Belly. Haley, Gail E., illus. 2003. (J). pap. 12.95 *(978-0-86541-069-5(0))* Filter Pr., LLC.

Hibbert, Clare. Terrible Tales of Native America, Vol. 1. 2014. (Monstrous Myths Ser.). (ENG.). 32p. (J). (gr. 4-5). 26.60 *(978-1-4824-0190-5(8))* Stevens, Gareth Publishing LLLP.

Jaffe, Nina. The Golden Flower: A Taino Myth from Puerto Rico. Sanchez, Enrique O., illus. 2005. 32p. (J). (gr. -1-3). 16.95 *(978-1-55885-452-9(5)*, Piñata Books) Arte Publico Pr.

Lind, Jenny, illus. Navajo Coyote Tales, 1 vol. 2007. (ENG.). 50p. (gr. 2-2). reprint ed. pap. 9.99 *(978-0-941270-52-6(1))* Gibbs Smith, Publisher.

Martin, Rafe. The World Before This One: A Novel Told in Legend. Nicholls, Calvin, illus. 2005. (ENG.). 208p. (J). (gr. 3-7). per. 6.99 *(978-0-590-37980-9(1)*, Levine, Arthur A. Bks.) Scholastic, Inc.

McDermott, Gerald. Arrow to the Sun: A Pueblo Indian Tale. McDermott, Gerald, illus. 2004. (Illus.). 37p. (J). (gr. k-3). reprint ed. pap. 14.00 *(978-0-7567-7103-4(X))* DIANE Publishing Co.

O'Brien, Cynthia. Myths & Legends of North America: Canada & the Northern United States. 2015. (Illus.). 64p. (J). *(978-0-7166-2626-8(8))* World Bk., Inc.

Pearce, Q. L. Wendigo. 2009. (Monsters Ser.). (ENG., Illus.). 48p. (gr. 4-8). 35.20 *(978-0-7377-4409-5(X)*, Kidhaven) Cengage Gale.

Powell, Patricia Hruby. Zinnia: How the Corn Was Saved. Ruffenach, Jessie, ed. Thomas, Peter, tr. from NAV. Benally, Kendrick, illus. 2004. (ENG & NAV.). 32p. (J). (gr. -1-3). 17.95 *(978-1-893354-38-8(5))* Salina Bookshelf Inc.

Rodanas, Kristina, illus. Yonder Mountain: A Cherokee Legend, 1 vol. 2005. (ENG.). 32p. (J). (gr. k-3). 16.95 *(978-0-7614-5113-6(7))* Marshall Cavendish Corp.

Ross, Gayle. How Rabbit Tricked Otter: And Other Cherokee Trickster Stories. Jacob, Murv, illus. 2003. (Storytime Ser.). 78p. (J). (gr. k-6). per. 12.95 *(978-0-930407-60-5(1))* Parabola Bks.

Rudolph, Nancy Lyn. Paper Animal Masks from Northwest Tribal Tales. 2004. (Illus.). 80p. (J). (gr. 4-8). reprint ed. 20.00 *(978-0-7567-7073-0(4))* DIANE Publishing Co.

Segundo, Sondra Simone & Segundo, Sondra Simone. Killer Whale Eyes. 2014. (Illus.). 42p. (J). pap. 15.00 *(978-0-9853129-5-4(5))* Sealaska Heritage Institute.

St. Romain, Rose Anne. Moon's Cloud Blanket. Waites, Joan C., illus. 2003. 32p. (J). 15.95 *(978-1-56554-922-7(8))* Pelican Publishing Co., Inc.

Taylor, C. J. Peace Walker: The Legend of Hiawatha & Tekanawita. 2004. (ENG., Illus.). 48p. (J). (gr. 2-4). 15.95 *(978-0-88776-547-6(5)*, Tundra Bks.) Tundra Bks. CAN. Dist: Penguin Random Hse. LLC.

Vanasse, Deb. Totem Tale: A Tall Story from Alaska. Brooks, Erik, illus. 2006. (Paws IV Ser.). (ENG.). 32p. (J). (gr. -1-2). pap. 10.99 *(978-1-57061-439-2(3)*, Little Bigfoot) Sasquatch Bks.

Vickers, Roy Henry & Budd, Robert. Orca Chief. Vickers, Roy Henry, illus. 2015. (ENG., Illus.). 40p. (J). 19.95 *(978-1-55017-693-5(3))* Harbour Publishing Co., Ltd. CAN. Dist: Midpoint Trade Bks., Inc.

—Peace Dancer. 2016. (ENG., Illus.). 40p. (J). 19.95 *(978-1-55017-739-8(7))* Harbour Publishing Co., Ltd. CAN. Dist: Midpoint Trade Bks., Inc.

Wade, Mary Hazelton. Indian Fairy Tales As Told to Little Chi. 2006. (Illus.). pap. 27.95 *(978-1-4254-9031-7(X))* Kessinger Publishing, LLC.

Wargin, Kathy-jo. The Legend of Leelanau. van Frankenhuyzen, Gijsbert, illus. 2003. (Great Lakes Legend Ser.). (ENG.). 40p. (J). 17.95 *(978-1-58536-150-2(X))* Sleeping Bear Pr.

Webb, Shirley G. Tales from the Keeper of the Myths: Cherokee Stories for Children. 2003. 104p. (J). pap. 9.95 *(978-0-595-27264-8(9))* iUniverse, Inc.

Welykochy, Dawn. The Legend of the Buffalo Stone, 1 vol. Bullshields, Charles, illus. 2015. (ENG.). 32p. (J). (gr. k-3). 19.95 ***(978-1-927527-41-2(4))*** Heritage Hse. CAN. Dist: Orca Bk. Pubs. USA.

Wolf, Linda Little. The Great Spirit Horse, 1 vol. 2nd ed. 2003. (ENG., Illus.). 152p. (J). (gr. 3-6). pap. 10.95 *(978-1-58980-123-3(7))* Pelican Publishing Co., Inc.

World Book, Inc Staff, contrib. by. Myths & Legends of North America: The Southwestern United States & Mexico. 2015. (Illus.). 64p. (J). *(978-0-7166-2627-5(6))* World Bk., Inc.

Yasuda, Anita. The Colors of a Sunset: An Algonquin Nature Myth. Estudio Haus, illus. 2012. (Short Tales Native American Myths Ser.). 32p. (J). (gr. 3-6). lib. bdg. 24.21 *(978-1-61641-879-3(6))* Magic Wagon.

—The Warrior Twins: A Navajo Hero Myth. Pennington, Mark, illus. 2012. (Short Tales Native American Myths Ser.). 32p. (J). (gr. 3-6). lib. bdg. 24.21 *(978-1-61641-884-7(2))* Magic Wagon.

INDIANS OF NORTH AMERICA—GAMES

Miller, Jay. American Indian Games. 2006. (True Bks). (Illus.). 47p. (gr. 3-5). 16.95 *(978-0-7569-7133-5(0))* Perfection Learning Corp.

Titus, David. Native Alaskan String Figures. 2007. (Illus.). 32p. (J). 5.99 *(978-0-9744562-7-0(6))* WRDSMTH Productions.

INDIANS OF NORTH AMERICA—GOVERNMENT RELATIONS

Bauman, Amy & Durman, Laura. History. 2010. (CC: Native North Americans Ser.). 112p. (gr. 6-12). 42.80 *(978-1-933834-82-5(X))* Brown Bear Bks.

Becker, Cynthia S. Chipeta: Ute Peacemaker. 2008. (Now You Know Bio Ser.: 11). (Illus.). 98p. (J). pap. 8.95 *(978-0-86541-091-6(7))* Filter Pr., LLC.

Blomquist, Katie. American Indians in The 1800s: Right & Resistance (America in The 1800s) 2017. (Primary Source Readers Ser.). (Illus.). 32p. (J). (gr. 4-5). pap. 8.99 ***(978-1-4938-3799-1(0))*** Teacher Created Materials, Inc.

Byers, Ann. The Trail of Tears: A Primary Source History of the Forced Relocation of the Cherokee Nation. 2004. (Primary Sources in American History Ser.). (Illus.). 64p. (J). (gr. 5-8). lib. bdg. 31.95 *(978-0-8239-4007-3(1)*, Rosen Reference) Rosen Publishing Group, Inc., The.

Chatlien, Ruth Hull. Modern American Indian Chiefs. 2009. (Sharing the American Dream Ser.). (Illus.). 64p. (YA). (gr. 7-12). 22.95 *(978-1-4222-0592-1(4))* Mason Crest.

Chatlien, Ruth Hull & Cohon, Rhody. Modern American Indian Chiefs. 2007. (Sharing the American Dream Ser.). 64p. (YA). (gr. 7-18). pap. 9.95 *(978-1-4222-0757-4(9))* Mason Crest.

Deibel, Zachary. Native American Resistance. 2017. ***(978-1-5026-2644-8(6))*** Cavendish Square Publishing.

Dell, Pamela. Apache Resistance: Causes & Effects of Geronimo's Campaign. 2015. (Cause & Effect: American Indian History Ser.). (ENG., Illus.). 32p. (gr. 3-4). pap. 7.95 *(978-1-4914-4904-2(7))* Capstone Press of Coughlan Cos.

Deloria, Vine, Jr. Indians of the Pacific Northwest: From the Coming of the White Man to the Present Day. 2012. (ENG., Illus.). 176p. (J). pap. 19.95 *(978-1-55591-688-6(0))* Fulcrum Publishing.

Domnauer, Teresa. Westward Expansion. 2010. (True Book Ser.). (ENG., Illus.). 48p. (J). pap. 6.95 *(978-0-531-21249-3(1))* Scholastic Library Publishing.

Edwards, Judith. The History of the American Indians & the Reservation. 2008. (From Many Cultures, One History Ser.). (Illus.). 128p. (J). (gr. 3-7). lib. bdg. 33.27 *(978-0-7660-2798-5(8))* Enslow Pubs., Inc.

Funk, Jack. Outside, the Women Cried: The Story of the Surrender by Chief Thunderchild's Band of Their Reserve near Delmas, Saskatchewan 1908. 2007. 108p. per. 12.95 *(978-0-595-43557-9(2))* iUniverse, Inc.

Hemingway, Al. Chuck Norris. 2007. (Sharing the American Dream Ser.). 64p. (YA). (gr. 7-18). pap. 9.95 *(978-1-4222-0758-1(7))* Mason Crest.

Johnson, Susan. Government to Government: Models of Cooperation Between States & Tribes. 2009. viii, 84p. spiral bd. *(978-1-58024-566-1(8))* National Conference of State Legislatures.

Mateusz, M. G. The Treaty of Canandaigua 1794: A Primary Source Examination of the Treaty Between the United States & the Tribes of Indians called the Six Nations. 2009. (Primary Sources of American Treaties Ser.). 64p. (gr. 5-8). 58.50 *(978-1-60851-515-8(X))* Rosen Publishing Group, Inc., The.

McCormick, Anita Louise. The Native American Struggle in United States History. 2015. (In United States History Ser.). 96p. (J). (gr. 5-12). 27.94 *(978-0-7660-6325-9(9))*; pap. 10.95 *(978-0-7660-6326-6(7))* Enslow Pubs., Inc.

Peppas, Lynn. The Displacement of Native Peoples. 2016. (ENG., Illus.). 48p. (J). *(978-0-7787-2571-8(5))* Crabtree Publishing Co.

Ramsey, Torren. Ojibwe. 2015. (Spotlight on Native Americans Ser.). (ENG., Illus.). 32p. (J). (gr. 4-6). 26.25 *(978-1-4994-1703-6(9)*, PowerKids Pr.) Rosen Publishing Group, Inc., The.

Roza, Greg. The Karankawa of Texas. (Library of Native Americans Ser.). 64p. 2009. (gr. 4-4). 58.50 *(978-1-60853-748-8(X))* 2005. (Illus.). (J). (gr. k-5). lib. bdg. 26.50 *(978-1-4042-2870-2(5))* Rosen Publishing Group, Inc., The. (PowerKids Pr.).

Schwartz, Heather E. Seeking Freedom: Causes & Effects of the Flight of the Nez Perce. 2015. (Cause & Effect: American Indian History Ser.). (ENG.). 32p. (gr. 3-4). lib. bdg. 27.32 *(978-1-4914-2034-8(0))* Capstone Press of Coughlan Cos.

Torr, James D., ed. Westward Expansion. 2003. (Interpreting American History Through Primary Documents Ser.x). (Illus.). 208p. (J). 32.45 *(978-0-7377-1134-9(5)*, Greenhaven Pr., Inc.) Cengage Gale.

INDIANS OF NORTH AMERICA—HAIDA INDIANS

Beck, Mary Giraudo. Heroes & Heroines in Tlingit-Haida Legend. DeWitt, Nancy, illus. 2003. (ENG.). 128p. (Orig.). (gr. 8-18). pap. 12.99 *(978-0-88240-334-2(6))* Graphic Arts Ctr. Publishing Co.

INDIANS OF NORTH AMERICA—HISTORY

see also Indians of North America—Wars

Abbink, Emily. Monterey Bay Area Missions. 2007. (Exploring California Missions Ser.). (ENG., Illus.). 64p. (gr. 4-7). lib. bdg. 27.93 *(978-0-8225-0887-8(7)*, Lerner Pubns.) Lerner Publishing Group.

ABDO Publishing Company Staff. Native Americans. 2014. (Native Americans Ser.: 8). (ENG.). 32p. (gr. 7-11). lib. bdg. 228.00 *(978-1-62403-349-0(0)*, Big Buddy Bks.) ABDO Publishing Co.

Alarcon, Roben. American Indians in the 1800s, 1 vol. 2005. (Primary Source Readers Ser.). (ENG., Illus.). 24p. (J). (gr. 5-5). pap. 8.99 *(978-0-7439-8913-8(9))* Shell Educational Publishing.

Aloian, Molly & Kalman, Bobbie. Life of the California Coast Nations. 2004. (Native Nations of North America Ser.). (ENG., Illus.). 32p. (J). pap. *(978-0-7787-0474-4(2))*; lib. bdg. *(978-0-7787-0382-2(7))* Crabtree Publishing Co.

—Nations of the Northeast Coast. 2005. (Native Nations of North America Ser.). (ENG., Illus.). 32p. (J). (gr. 4-7). pap. *(978-0-7787-0478-2(5))*; lib. bdg. *(978-0-7787-0386-0(X))* Crabtree Publishing Co.

—Nations of the Southeast. 2005. (Native Nations of North America Ser.). (ENG., Illus.). 32p. (J). (gr. 4-7). pap. *(978-0-7787-0477-5(7))*; lib. bdg. *(978-0-7787-0385-3(1))* Crabtree Publishing Co.

American Indian Art & Culture. 2005. (American Indian Art & Culture Ser.). (Illus.). 32p. (gr. 4-6). 153.00 *(978-0-7910-7959-1(7)*, Chelsea Hse.) Facts On File, Inc.

Annino, J. G. She Sang Promise: The Story of Betty Mae Jumper, Seminole Tribal Leader. Desimini, Lisa, illus. 2010. (ENG.). 48p. (J). (gr. 1-4). 17.95 *(978-1-4263-0592-4(3)*, National Geographic Children's Bks.) National Geographic Society.

Annino, J G. She Sang Promise: The Story of Betty Mae Jumper, Seminole Tribal Leader. Desimini, Lisa, illus. 2010. (ENG.). 48p. (J). (gr. 1-4). 26.90 *(978-1-4263-0593-1(1)*, National Geographic Children's Bks.) National Geographic Society.

Arnéz, Lynda. Native Peoples of the Arctic. 2016. (Native Peoples of North America Ser.). (Illus.). 32p. (J). (gr. 3-2). 25.25 *(978-1-4824-4807-8(6))* Stevens, Gareth Publishing LLLP.

Bailey, Katharine. Radisson & des Groseilliers: Fur Traders of the North. 2006. (In the Footsteps of Explorers Ser.). (ENG., Illus.). 32p. (J). (gr. 4-7). pap. *(978-0-7787-2458-2(1)*, 1253444) Crabtree Publishing Co.

Bauman, Amy & Durman, Laura. History. 2010. (CC: Native North Americans Ser.). 112p. (gr. 6-12). 42.80 *(978-1-933834-82-5(X))* Brown Bear Bks.

Bedry, Christa. The Pueblo. (J). 2014. *(978-1-4896-2922-7(X))* 2003. (Illus.). 32p. pap. 9.95 *(978-1-59036-179-5(2))* Weigl Pubs., Inc.

Behnke, Alison. The Apaches. 2006. (Native American Histories Ser.). (Illus.). 56p. (J). (gr. 4-7). lib. bdg. 27.93 *(978-0-8225-5915-3(3)*, Lerner Pubns.) Lerner Publishing Group.

Behrens, June. Central Coast Missions in California. 2007. (Exploring California Missions Ser.). (Illus.). 64p. (J). lib. bdg. 27.93 *(978-0-8225-0897-7(4)*, Lerner Pubns.) Lerner Publishing Group.

Benchmark Education Company, LLC Staff, compiled by. Native Land & Native AMER HIST. 2005. spiral bd. 225.00 *(978-1-4108-5810-8(3))* Benchmark Education Co.

Benjamin, Lisa. People of the Wetlands. 2005. (Voices Reading Ser.). (Illus.). 32p. (J). *(978-0-7367-2947-5(X))* Zaner-Bloser, Inc.

Bennett, Doraine. Tomochichi. 2008. (J). *(978-1-935077-06-0(6))*; pap. *(978-1-935077-13-8(9))* State Standards Publishing, LLC.

Benoit, Peter. Cornerstones of Freedom, Third Series: the Trail of Tears. 2012. (ENG.). 64p. (J). lib. bdg. 30.00 *(978-0-531-23067-1(8)*, Children's Pr.) Scholastic Library Publishing.

—The Trail of Tears. 2012. (Cornerstones of Freedom, Third Ser.). (ENG.). 64p. (J). pap. 8.95 *(978-0-531-28167-3(1))* Scholastic Library Publishing.

Bial, Raymond. The Cree. 2006. (Lifeways Ser.). (Illus.). 128p. (J). (gr. 3-7). lib. bdg. *(978-0-7614-1902-0(0)*, Benchmark Bks.) Marshall Cavendish Corp.

—The Crow. 2005. (Lifeways Ser.). (Illus.). 124p. (J). (gr. 3-7). lib. bdg. *(978-0-7614-1901-3(2)*, Benchmark Bks.) Marshall Cavendish Corp.

—The Menominee. 2006. (Lifeways Ser.). (Illus.). 127p. (J). (gr. 3-7). lib. bdg. *(978-0-7614-1903-7(9)*, Benchmark Bks.) Marshall Cavendish Corp.

Birchfield, D. L. Cherokee History & Culture. 2011. (Native American Library). 48p. (J). (gr. 3-6). pap. 14.05 *(978-1-4339-5960-8(7))*; lib. bdg. 31.95 *(978-1-4339-5958-5(5))* Stevens, Gareth Publishing LLLP. (Gareth Stevens Learning Library).

Bishop, Amanda & Kalman, Bobbie. Life of the Navajo. 2003. (Native Nations of North America Ser.). (ENG., Illus.). 32p. (J). (gr. 5). lib. bdg. *(978-0-7787-0376-1(2))* Crabtree Publishing Co.

Bishop, Amanda, et al. Nations of the Northwest Coast. 2003. (Native Nations of North America Ser.). (ENG., Illus.). 32p. (J). (gr. 5). pap. *(978-0-7787-0470-6(X))* Crabtree Publishing Co.

Bjornlund, Lydia D. Trail of Tears: The Relocation of American Indians. 2010. (American History Ser.). (Illus.). 128p. (J). 34.80 *(978-1-4205-0211-4(5)*, Lucent Bks.) Cengage Gale.

Blomquist, Katie. American Indians in The 1800s: Right & Resistance (America in The 1800s) 2017. (Primary Source Readers Ser.). (Illus.). 32p. (J). (gr. 4-5). pap. 8.99 ***(978-1-4938-3799-1(0))*** Teacher Created Materials, Inc.

Bonvillain, Nancy. The Nez Perce. 2010. (History & Culture of Native Americans Ser.). 144p. (gr. 6-12). 35.00 *(978-1-60413-791-0(6)*, Chelsea Hse.) Facts On File, Inc.

Boule, Mary Null. California Native American Tribes: Mohave Tribe, 28 booklets. Liddell, Daniel & Basta, Mary, illus. (California Native American Tribes). 52p. (J). (gr. 3-6). pap. 7.95 *(978-1-877599-73-6(5))* Merryant Pubs.

Bowes, John P. Black Hawk & the War of 1832: Removal in the North. 2007. (Landmark Events in Native American History Ser.). (Illus.). 131p. (YA). (gr. 9-12). pap. 35.00 *(978-0-7910-9342-9(5))* Facts On File, Inc.

—The Choctaw. 2010. (History & Culture of Native Americans Ser.). (Illus.). 133p. (gr. 6-12). 35.00 *(978-1-60413-788-0(6)*, Chelsea Hse.) Facts On File, Inc.

Bowman, David. Native Americans of the Eastern Woodlands: Text Pairs. 2008. (Bridges/Navigators Ser.). (J). (gr. 4). 89.00 *(978-1-4108-8391-9(4))* Benchmark Education Co.

Bowman, Donna Janell. The Sioux: The Past & Present of the Dakota, Lakota, & Nakota. 2015. (American Indian Life Ser.). (ENG., Illus.). 32p. (gr. 3-4). lib. bdg. 27.32 *(978-1-4914-4990-5(X))* Capstone Press of Coughlan Cos.

Brennan, Kristine. Native Americans. (Successful Americans Ser.). 64p. (YA). 2009. (Illus.). (gr. 9-12). 22.95 *(978-1-4222-0517-4(7))* 2007. (gr. 7-18). pap. 9.95 *(978-1-4222-0866-3(4))* Mason Crest.

Broida, Marian. The Pueblo. 2005. (First Americans Ser.). (Illus.). 48p. (J). (gr. 3-7). lib. bdg. *(978-0-7614-1898-6(9)*, Benchmark Bks.) Marshall Cavendish Corp.

Brooks, Susie. Plains Indians. 2009. (Flashback History Ser.). (Illus.). 48p. (J). pap. 11.75 *(978-1-4358-5520-5(5)*, PowerKids Pr.); (YA). (gr. 3-6). 29.25 *(978-1-4358-5519-9(1))* Rosen Publishing Group, Inc., The.

Brower, Pauline. Inland Valleys Missions in California. 2007. (Exploring California Missions Ser.). (ENG., Illus.). 64p. (gr. 4-7). lib. bdg. 27.93 *(978-0-8225-0899-1(0)*, Lerner Pubns.) Lerner Publishing Group.

Buckley, Jeannette. Discovering Mission San Luis Rey de Francia. 2014. (California Missions Ser.). 48p. (J). (gr. 4-6). 31.36 *(978-1-62713-112-4(4))* Cavendish Square Publishing.

Burgan, Michael. Shadow Catcher: How Edward S. Curtis Documented American Indian Dignity & Beauty. 2015. (Captured History Ser.). (ENG., Illus.). 64p. (gr. 5-7). pap. 9.10 *(978-0-7565-4998-5(1))* Compass Point Bks.

Capaccio, George. The Countryside. 2014. (Life in Colonial America Ser.). (Illus.). 80p. (J). (gr. 6-8). lib. bdg. 35.64 *(978-1-62712-885-8(9))* Cavendish Square Publishing.

Carole Marsh. Connecticut Indians. 2004. (Connecticut Experien Ser.). 36p. (gr. 3-8). 29.95 *(978-0-635-02259-2(1))*; pap. 7.95 *(978-0-635-02258-5(3))* Gallopade International.

H
I

—Vermont Indians. 2004. (Vermont Experience Ser.). 36p. (gr. 3-8). pap. 7.95 (978-0-635-02334-6(2)); lib. bdg. 29.95 (978-0-635-02335-3(0)) Gallopade International.

—Virginia Indians. 2004. (Virginia Experience Ser.). 36p. (gr. 3-8). 29.95 (978-0-635-02337-7(7)); pap. 7.95 (978-0-635-02336-0(9)) Gallopade International.

—Washington Indians. 2004. (Washington Experienc Ser.). lib. bdg. 29.95 (978-0-635-02339-1(3)); 36p. (gr. 3-8). pap. 7.95 (978-0-635-02338-4(5)) Gallopade International.

—West Virginia Indians. 2004. (West Virginia Experi Ser.). 36p. (gr. 3-8). pap. 7.95 (978-0-635-02340-7(7)) Gallopade International.

—Wisconsin Indians. 2004. (Wisconsin Experience Ser.). 36p. (gr. 3-8). 29.95 (978-0-635-02343-8(1)); pap. 7.95 (978-0-635-02342-1(3)) Gallopade International.

—Wyoming Indians. 2004. (Wyoming Experience Ser.). 36p. (gr. 3-8). pap. 7.95 (978-0-635-02344-5(X)) Gallopade International.

Caron, Mona, illus. Many Worlds: Native Life along the Anza Trail. 2012. (ENG.). 24p. (J). pap. 7.95 (978-1-59714-167-3(4)) Heyday.

Carr, Margaret. Colorado Settlers & Native Americans, 01 vols., 1. 2016. (Spotlight on Colorado Ser.). (ENG.). 48p. (J). (gr. 4-5). pap. 11.75 (978-1-4994-1462-2(5), PowerKids Pr.) Rosen Publishing Group, Inc., The.

Casey, Carolyn. The Apache. 2005. (First Americans Ser.). (Illus.). 48p. (J). (gr. 3-7). lib. bdg. (978-0-7614-1894-8(6), Benchmark Bks.) Marshall Cavendish Corp.

Caswell, Max. My Life in a Chinook Village. 2017. (My Place in History Ser.). 24p. (J). (gr. 2-3). pap. 8.15 **(978-1-5382-0301-9(4))** Stevens, Gareth Publishing LLLP.

—My Life on the Trail of Tears. 2017. (My Place in History Ser.). 24p. (J). (gr. 2-3). pap. 48.90 **(978-1-5382-0310-1(3))** Stevens, Gareth Publishing LLLP.

Cherry, Lynne. A River Ran Wild. 2015. 40p. pap. 7.00 (978-1-61003-490-6(2)) Center for the Collaborative Classroom.

Ching, Jacqueline. Mission San Fernando Rey de Espana. 2009. (Missions of California Ser.). 64p. (gr. 4-4). 58.50 (978-1-60854-028-0(6), PowerKids Pr.) Rosen Publishing Group, Inc., The.

—Mission San Rafael Arcangel. 2009. (Missions of California Ser.). 64p. (gr. 4-4). 58.50 (978-1-60854-036-5(7), PowerKids Pr.) Rosen Publishing Group, Inc., The.

Christian, Betsy & Christian, George. For the Love of Texas: Tell Me about the Colonists! Gruszka, Chris A., illus. 2013. Orig. Title: For the Love of Texas: Tell Me about the Colonists! (ENG.). 112p. (J). (gr. 4-7). 14.99 (978-1-62619-159-4(X), History Pr., The) Arcadia Publishing.

Cipriano, Jeri. Three Historical Communities of North America: Set Of 6. 2010. (Navigators Ser.). (J). pap. 44.00 net. (978-1-4108-5095-9(1)) Benchmark Education Co.

Cohen, Robert Z. Hernando de Soto. 2016. (Spotlight on Explorers & Colonization Ser.). 00048p. (J). (gr. 6-6). pap. 11.75 (978-1-5081-7210-9(2)) Rosen Publishing Group, Inc., The.

Collins, James. The Trail of Tears with Buffalo Bill & Farley's Raiders. 2006. (Time Traveler's Adventure Ser.). (Illus.). 56p. (J). 13.50 incl. audio compact disk (978-1-932332-31-5(6)) Toy Box Productions.

Collins, Terry, et al. The Mesa Verde Cliff Dwellers: An Isabel Soto Archaeology Adventure, 1 vol. 2010. (Graphic Expeditions Ser.). (ENG.). 32p. (gr. 3-4). pap. 8.10 (978-1-4296-4861-5(9)); pap. 47.70 (978-1-4296-5144-8(X)) Capstone Press of Coughlan Cos. (Graphic Library).

Collinson, Clare. Peoples of the East, Southeast, & Plains. 2010. (CC: Native North Americans Ser.). 112p. (gr. 6-12). 42.80 (978-1-933834-77-1(3)) Brown Bear Bks.

Conklin, Wendy. The Seminoles of Florida: Culture, Customs, & Conflict. 2016. (Primary Source Readers Ser.). 32p. (gr. 4-4). pap. 8.99 (978-1-4938-3535-5(1)) Teacher Created Materials, Inc.

Conley, Robert J. The Cherokee. 2011. (History & Culture of Native Americans Ser.). (Illus.). 112p. (gr. 6-12). 35.00 (978-1-60413-796-5(7), Chelsea Hse.) Facts On File, Inc.

Connelly, Jack. Discovering Mission Santa Bárbara. 2014. (California Missions Ser.). 48p. (J). (gr. 4-6). lib. bdg. 31.36 (978-1-62713-100-1(0)) Cavendish Square Publishing.

Costain, Meredith. Native Americans of the Great Plains. 2013. (Discovery Education: Ancient Civilizations Ser.). (ENG., Illus.). 32p. (J). (gr. 3-6). pap. 10.00 (978-1-4777-0089-1(7)); lib. bdg. 25.25 (978-1-4777-0052-5(8)) Rosen Publishing Group, Inc., The. (PowerKids Pr.).

Craats, Rennay. The Cherokee. (J). 2014. (978-1-4896-2906-7(8)) 2003. (Illus.). 32p. pap. 9.95 (978-1-59036-180-1(6)) Weigl Pubs., Inc.

—The Navajo. (J). 2014. (978-1-4896-2914-2(9)) 2003. (Illus.). 32p. pap. 9.95 (978-1-59036-182-5(2)) Weigl Pubs., Inc.

Crewe, Sabrina & Birchfield, D. L. The Trail of Tears. 2004. (Events That Shaped America Ser.). (Illus.). 32p. (gr. 3-6). lib. bdg. 26.00 (978-0-8368-3400-0(3), Gareth Stevens Learning Library) Stevens, Gareth Publishing LLLP.

Crompton, Samuel Willard. The Mohawk. 2010. (History & Culture of Native Americans Ser.). (Illus.). 136p. (gr. 6-12). 35.00 (978-1-60413-787-3(8), Chelsea Hse.) Facts On File, Inc.

Croy, Anita. Ancient Pueblo: Archaeology Unlocks the Secrets of America's Past. 2007. (National Geographic Investigates Ser.). (ENG., Illus.). 64p. (J). (gr. 5-18). 17.95 (978-1-4263-0130-8(8)); lib. bdg. 27.90 (978-1-4263-0131-5(6)) National Geographic Society. (National Geographic Children's Bks.).

Cunningham, Laura. The Bay Area Through Time. 2015. (Illus.). (J). (978-1-59714-301-1(4)) Heyday.

Dalton, Anne. The Lenape of Pennsylvania, New Jersey, New York, Delaware, Wisconsin, Oklahoma, & Ontario. 2009. (Library of Native Americans Ser.). 64p. (gr. 4-4). 58.50 (978-1-60853-749-5(8), PowerKids Pr.) Rosen Publishing Group, Inc., The.

De Capua, Sarah. The Cherokee. 2005. (First Americans Ser.). (Illus.). 48p. (J). (gr. 3-7). lib. bdg. (978-0-7614-1895-5(4), Benchmark Bks.) Marshall Cavendish Corp.

—The Cheyenne. 2006. (First Americans Ser.). (Illus.). 47p. (J). (gr. 3-7). lib. bdg. 31.36 (978-0-7614-2248-8(X), Benchmark Bks.) Marshall Cavendish Corp.

—The Comanche. 2006. (First Americans Ser.). (Illus.). 48p. (gr. 3-7). lib. bdg. 31.36 (978-0-7614-2249-5(8), Benchmark Bks.) Marshall Cavendish Corp.

—The Iroquois. 2005. (First Americans Ser.). (Illus.). 48p. (J). (gr. 3-7). lib. bdg. (978-0-7614-1896-2(2), Benchmark Bks.) Marshall Cavendish Corp.

Deer, Ada E., intro. Indians of North America. (Illus.). (gr. 9-13). pap. 59.70 (978-0-7910-8399-4(3)); lib. bdg. 137.70 (978-0-7910-8417-5(5)) Facts On File, Inc. (Chelsea Hse.).

Dell, Pamela. Cause & Effect: American Indian History, 2 vols. 2015. (Cause & Effect: American Indian History Ser.). (ENG.). 32p. (gr. 3-4). 54.64 (978-1-4914-6692-6(8)) Capstone Press of Coughlan Cos.

Denetdale, Jennifer. The Long Walk: The Forced Navajo Exile. 2007. (Landmark Events in Native American History Ser.). (Illus.). 143p. (YA). (gr. 9-12). lib. bdg. 35.00 (978-0-7910-9344-3(1)) Facts On File, Inc.

Dennis, Yvonne Wakim & Hirschfelder, Arlene. A Kid's Guide to Native American History: More Than 50 Activities. 2009. (Kid's Guide Ser.). (ENG.). 256p. (J). (gr. 2-4). pap. 16.95 (978-1-55652-802-6(7)) Chicago Review Pr., Inc.

Ditchfield, Christin. Plateau Indians, 1 vol. 2011. (First Nations of North America Ser.). (ENG.). 48p. (gr. 3-3). pap. 9.95 (978-1-4329-4962-4(4), Heinemann InfoSearch) Heinemann-Raintree.

—Spanish Missions. 2006. (True Bks.). (Illus.). 48p. (J). (gr. 3-7). pap. 6.95 (978-0-516-21746-8(1), Children's Pr.) Scholastic Library Publishing.

Doherty, Craig A. California Indians. Facts on File, Inc. Staff, ed. 2010. (Native America Ser.). (Illus.). 136p. (J). (gr. 5-8). 35.00 (978-0-8160-5973-7(X)) Facts On File, Inc.

Doherty, Craig A. & Doherty, Katherine M. Arctic Peoples. 2008. (Native America Ser.). (Illus.). 152p. (gr. 5-8). 35.00 (978-0-8160-5970-6(5)) Facts On File, Inc.

—Plateau Indians. 2008. (Native America Ser.). 152p. (gr. 5-8). 35.00 (978-0-8160-5971-3(3)) Facts On File, Inc.

—Southeast Indians. 2010. (Native America Ser.). (Illus.). 136p. (J). (gr. 5-8). 35.00 (978-0-8160-5969-0(1)) Facts On File, Inc.

Domnauer, Teresa. Westward Expansion. 2010. (True Book Ser.). (ENG., Illus.). 48p. (J). pap. 6.95 (978-0-531-21249-3(1)); (gr. 2-5). 29.00 (978-0-531-20586-0(X)) Scholastic Library Publishing.

Draper, Allison Stark. Mission San Fransisco de Solano. 2009. (Missions of California Ser.). 64p. (gr. 4-4). 58.50 (978-1-60854-029-7(4), PowerKids Pr.) Rosen Publishing Group, Inc., The.

—Mission San Juan Bautista. 2009. (Missions of California Ser.). 64p. (gr. 4-4). 58.50 (978-1-60854-032-7(4), PowerKids Pr.) Rosen Publishing Group, Inc., The.

Dwyer, Helen. Peoples of the Southwest, West, & North. 2010. (CC: Native North Americans Ser.). 112p. (gr. 6-12). 42.80 (978-1-933834-78-8(1)) Brown Bear Bks.

Dwyer, Helen & Birchfield, D. L. Ojibwe History & Culture. 2012. (Native American Library). (Illus.). 48p. (gr. 3-6). pap. 14.05 (978-1-4339-7422-9(3)); lib. bdg. 31.95 (978-1-4339-7421-2(5)) Stevens, Gareth Publishing LLLP.

Dwyer, Helen & Stone, Amy M. Creek History & Culture. 2011. (Native American Library). (Illus.). 48p. (J). (gr. 3-6). 31.95 (978-1-4339-5962-2(3)); pap. 14.05 (978-1-4339-5964-6(X)) Stevens, Gareth Publishing LLLP. (Gareth Stevens Learning Library).

—Oneida History & Culture. 2012. (Native American Library). (Illus.). 48p. (gr. 3-6). pap. 14.05 (978-1-4339-7426-7(6)); lib. bdg. 31.95 (978-1-4339-7425-0(8)) Stevens, Gareth Publishing LLLP.

Dwyer, Helen & Stout, Mary. Cree History & Culture. 2012. (Native American Library). (Illus.). 48p. (J). (gr. 3-6). pap. 14.05 (978-1-4339-7418-2(5)); lib. bdg. 31.95 (978-1-4339-7417-5(7)) Stevens, Gareth Publishing LLLP.

Dwyer, Helen & Stout, Mary A. Hopi History & Culture. 2011. (Native American Library). (Illus.). 48p. (J). (gr. 3-6). 31.95 (978-1-4339-5966-0(6)); pap. 14.05 (978-1-4339-5968-4(2)) Stevens, Gareth Publishing LLLP. (Gareth Stevens Learning Library).

Edgar, Kathleen J. Mission San Diego de Alcala. 2009. (Missions of California Ser.). 64p. (gr. 4-4). 58.50 (978-1-60854-027-3(8), PowerKids Pr.) Rosen Publishing Group, Inc., The.

—Mission San Francisco de Asis. 2009. (Missions of California Ser.). 64p. (gr. 4-4). 58.50 (978-1-60854-024-2(3), PowerKids Pr.) Rosen Publishing Group, Inc., The.

—Mission San Miguel Arcangel. 2009. (Missions of California Ser.). 64p. (gr. 4-4). 58.50 (978-1-60854-035-8(9), PowerKids Pr.) Rosen Publishing Group, Inc., The.

Flanagan, Alice K. The Pueblos. 2006. (True Bks). (Illus.). 48p. (gr. 2-4). 16.95 (978-0-7569-7158-8(6)) Perfection Learning Corp.

Flood, Nancy Bo. Cowboy Up! Ride the Navajo Rodeo. Sonnemair, Jan, illus. 2013. (ENG.). 48p. (J). (gr. 3-7). 17.95 (978-1-59078-893-6(1), Wordsong) Boyds Mills Pr.

Foran, Jill. Native-American Life. 2003. (Real Life Stories Ser.). (Illus.). 24p. (J). lib. bdg. 24.45 (978-1-59036-080-4(X)) Weigl Pubs., Inc.

Frank, Andrew K. The Seminole. 2010. (History & Culture of Native Americans Ser.). 128p. (gr. 6-12). 35.00 (978-1-60413-790-3(8), Chelsea Hse.) Facts On File, Inc.

Fullman, Joe. Native North Americans: Dress, Eat, Write, & Play Just Like the Americans. 2011. (ENG., Illus.). 32p. (J). pap. 10.95 (978-1-926853-94-9(6)) Saunders Bk. Co. CAN. Dist: RiverStream Publishing.

Furbee, Mary Rodd. Shawnee Captive: The Story of Mary Draper Ingles. 2003. (Illus.). 112p. (YA). per. 9.95 (978-1-891852-29-9(9)) Quarrier Pr.

—Shawnee Captive: The Story of Mary Draper Ingles. 2004. (Women of the Frontier Ser.). (Illus.). 112p. (J). (gr. 6-12). 23.95 (978-1-883846-69-5(2), First Biographies) Reynolds, Morgan Inc.

George, Lynn & Schimel, Kate. New York's Early Explorers. 2012. (Illus.). 24p. (J). 60.00 (978-1-4488-5772-2(4)); pap. 10.00 (978-1-4488-5771-5(6)); lib. bdg. 22.60 (978-1-4488-5749-4(X)) Rosen Publishing Group, Inc., The. (PowerKids Pr.).

Gibson, Karen Bush. Native American History for Kids: With 21 Activities. 2010. (For Kids Ser.). (ENG., Illus.). 144p. (J). (gr. 4-18). pap. 17.95 (978-1-56976-280-6(5)) Chicago Review Pr., Inc.

Gray-Kanatiiosh, Barbara A. Cahuilla, 1 vol. 2007. (Native Americans Set 4 Ser.). (ENG., Illus.). 32p. (gr. k-5). 27.07 (978-1-59197-651-6(0), Checkerboard Library) ABDO Publishing Co.

—Chickasaw, 1 vol. 2007. (Native Americans Set 4 Ser.). (ENG., Illus.). 32p. (gr. k-5). 27.07 (978-1-59197-652-3(9), Checkerboard Library) ABDO Publishing Co.

—Kiowa, 1 vol. 2007. (Native Americans Set 4 Ser.). (ENG., Illus.). 32p. (gr. 4). 27.07 (978-1-59197-654-7(5), Checkerboard Library) ABDO Publishing Co.

—Paiute, 1 vol. 2007. (Native Americans Set 4 Ser.). (ENG., Illus.). 32p. (gr. 4). 27.07 (978-1-59197-657-8(X), Checkerboard Library) ABDO Publishing Co.

—Yurok, 1 vol. 2007. (Native Americans Set 4 Ser.). (ENG., Illus.). 32p. (gr. -1-3). 27.07 (978-1-59197-658-5(8), Checkerboard Library) ABDO Publishing Co.

Green, John. Indian Life in Pre-Columbian North America Coloring Book. 2013. (Dover History Coloring Book Ser.). (ENG., Illus.). 48p. (gr. 3-12). pap. 4.99 (978-0-486-28047-9(0)) Dover Pubns., Inc.

Greenhaven Press Editors. Native Americans. 2012. (Opposing Viewpoints Ser.). (ENG., Illus.). 240p. (J). (gr. 10-12). pap. 29.45 (978-0-7377-5445-2(1), Greenhaven Pr., Inc.); (YA). (gr. 9-12). lib. bdg. 42.95 (978-0-7377-5444-5(3)) Cengage Gale.

Grudzina, Joanne, Rebecca and Tangorra & Benchmark Education Co. Staff. Opinions about the Trail of Tears. 2014. (Text Connections Ser.). (J). (gr. 5). (978-1-4900-1376-3(8)) Benchmark Education Co.

Hakim, Joy. The First Americans: Prehistory-1600. 2nd rev. ed. 2007. (History of US Ser.: 1). (ENG., Illus.). 192p. (gr. 4-7). per. 15.95 (978-0-19-532715-1(2)) Oxford Univ. Pr., Inc.

—The First Americans Prehistory 1600. 3rd rev. ed. 2006. (History of US Ser.: 1). (ENG., Illus.). 192p. (gr. 4-7). 24.95 (978-0-19-518894-3(2)) Oxford Univ. Pr., Inc.

Halvorson, Alesha. The Ojibwe: The Past & Present of the Anishinaabe. 2016. (American Indian Life Ser.). (ENG., Illus.). 32p. (gr. 3-4). lib. bdg. 27.32 (978-1-5157-0240-5(5)) Capstone Press of Coughlan Cos.

Hansson, Martina & Benchmark Education Co. Staff. Great Native American Leaders. 2014. (Text Connections Ser.). (J). (gr. 5). (978-1-4900-1373-2(3)) Benchmark Education Co.

Harasymiw, Mark & Harasymiw, Therese. Native Americans in Early America. 2011. (Story of America Ser.). (Illus.). 32p. (J). (gr. 4-6). pap. 10.50 (978-1-4339-4773-5(0)); lib. bdg. 26.60 (978-1-4339-4772-8(2)) Stevens, Gareth Publishing LLLP. (Gareth Stevens Learning Library).

Harrison, Lorraine. Sioux, 01 vols., 1. 2016. (Spotlight on Native Americans Ser.). (ENG., Illus.). 32p. (J). pap. 11.75 (978-1-5081-4160-0(6), PowerKids Pr.) Rosen Publishing Group, Inc., The.

Higgins, Nadia. Defending the Land: Causes & Effects of Red Cloud's War. 2015. (Cause & Effect: American Indian History Ser.). (ENG.). 32p. (gr. 3-4). pap. 7.95 (978-1-4914-2210-6(6)) Capstone Press of Coughlan Cos.

Houghton, Gillian. The Oneida of Wisconsin. 2009. (Library of Native Americans Ser.). 64p. (gr. 4-4). 58.50 (978-1-60853-759-4(5), PowerKids Pr.) Rosen Publishing Group, Inc., The.

Johansen, Bruce E. The Iroquois. 2010. (History & Culture of Native Americans Ser.). (Illus.). 128p. (gr. 6-12). 35.00 (978-1-60413-794-1(0), Chelsea Hse.) Facts On File, Inc.

Johnson, Michael. Native Tribes of the Plains & Prairie. 2004. (Native Tribes of North America Ser.). (Illus.). 64p. (gr. 5-12). lib. bdg. 34.00 (978-0-8368-5613-2(9), Gareth Stevens Secondary Library) Stevens, Gareth Publishing LLLP.

Johnson, Michael & Burkinshaw, Jane. Native Tribes of the North & Northwest Coast. 2004. (Native Tribes of North America Ser.). (Illus.). 64p. (gr. 5-12). lib. bdg. 34.00 (978-0-8368-5611-8(2), Gareth Stevens Secondary Library) Stevens, Gareth Publishing LLLP.

Johnson, Michael & Clarke, Duncan. Native Tribes of the Great Basin & Plateau. 2004. (Native Tribes of North America Ser.). (Illus.). 64p. (gr. 5-12). lib. bdg. 34.00 (978-0-8368-5610-1(4), Gareth Stevens Secondary Library) Stevens, Gareth Publishing LLLP.

—Native Tribes of the Southeast. 2004. (Native Tribes of North America Ser.). (Illus.). 64p. (gr. 5-12). lib. bdg. 34.00 (978-0-8368-5614-9(7), Gareth Stevens Secondary Library) Stevens, Gareth Publishing LLLP.

Johnson, Michael & Yenne, Bill. Native Tribes of California & the Southwest. 2004. (Native Tribes of North America Ser.). (Illus.). 64p. (gr. 5-12). lib. bdg. 34.00 (978-0-8368-5609-5(0), Gareth Stevens Secondary Library) Stevens, Gareth Publishing LLLP.

Josephson, Judith Pinkerton. Why Did Cherokees Move West? And Other Questions about the Trail of Tears. 2010. (Six Questions of American History Ser.). (ENG.). 48p. (gr. 4-6). pap. 9.95 (978-0-7613-6125-1(1)) Lerner Publishing Group.

—Why Did Cherokees Walk West? And Other Questions about the Trail of Tears. 2010. (Six Questions of American History Ser.). (ENG.). 48p. (gr. 4-6). lib. bdg. 30.60 (978-1-58013-668-6(0)) Lerner Publishing Group.

Kalman, Bobbie. A Visual Dictionary of Native Communities. 2007. (Visual Dictionaries Ser.). (ENG., Illus.). 32p. (J). (gr. 4-7). pap. (978-0-7787-3525-0(7)) Crabtree Publishing Co.

Kamma, Anne. If You Lived with the Hopi. 2014. 17.00 (978-1-63419-709-0(7)) Perfection Learning Corp.

—If You Lived with the Indians of the Northwest Coast. 2014. 17.00 (978-1-63419-710-6(0)) Perfection Learning Corp.

Keoke, Emory Dean. American Indian Contributions to the World, 5 Vols., Set. 2005. (American Indian Contributions to the World Ser.). 160p. (gr. 5-8). 140.00 (978-0-8160-5392-6(8)) Facts On File, Inc.

Keoke, Emory Dean & Porterfield, Kay Marie. American Indian Contributions to the World, 5 vols. 2005. (American Indian Contributions to the World Ser.). (Illus.). 160p. (gr. 5-8). 35.00 (978-0-8160-5397-1(9)); 35.00 (978-0-8160-5395-7(2)) Facts On File, Inc.

King, David C. The Haida. 2006. (First Americans Ser.). (Illus.). 48p. (J). (gr. 3-7). lib. bdg. 31.36 (978-0-7614-2250-1(1), Benchmark Bks.) Marshall Cavendish Corp.

—Huron. 2006. (First Americans Ser.). (Illus.). 48p. (gr. 3-7). lib. bdg. 31.36 (978-0-7614-2251-8(X), Benchmark Bks.) Marshall Cavendish Corp.

—The Navajo. 2005. (First Americans Ser.). (Illus.). 48p. (J). (gr. 3-7). lib. bdg. (978-0-7614-1897-9(0), Benchmark Bks.) Marshall Cavendish Corp.

—The Ojibwe. 2006. (First Americans Ser.). (Illus.). 48p. (gr. 3-7). lib. bdg. 31.36 (978-0-7614-2252-5(8), Benchmark Bks.) Marshall Cavendish Corp.

—The Seminole. 2006. (First Americans Ser.). (Illus.). 48p. (J). (gr. 3-7). lib. bdg. 31.36 (978-0-7614-2253-2(6), Benchmark Bks.) Marshall Cavendish Corp.

—The Sioux. 2005. (First Americans Ser.). (Illus.). 48p. (J). (gr. 3-7). lib. bdg. (978-0-7614-1899-3(7), Benchmark Bks.) Marshall Cavendish Corp.

Kjelle, Marylou Morano. Pre-Columbian America. 2009. (How'd They Do That? Ser.). (Illus.). 64p. (J). (gr. 4-8). lib. bdg. 33.95 (978-1-58415-826-4(3)) Mitchell Lane Pubs., Inc.

Koopmans, Anna. The Sioux. (Illus.). 32p. (J). 2014. (978-1-4896-2926-5(2)) 2003. pap. 9.95 (978-1-59036-184-9(9)) Weigl Pubs., Inc.

Kovacs, Vic. Native Americans in the West. 2015. (True History of the Wild West Ser.). (ENG., Illus.). 32p. (J). (gr. 5-5). pap. 10.00 (978-1-4994-1173-7(1), PowerKids Pr.) Rosen Publishing Group, Inc., The.

Krasner, Barbara. Native Nations of the Great Basin & Plateau. 2015. (Native Nations of North America Ser.). (ENG.). 40p. (J). (gr. 3-6). 32.79 (978-1-63407-031-7(3), 208866) Child's World, Inc., The.

—Native Nations of the Northeast. 2015. (Native Nations of North America Ser.). (ENG.). 40p. (J). (gr. 3-6). 32.79 (978-1-63407-032-4(1), 208867) Child's World, Inc., The.

—Native Nations of the Southwest. 2015. (Native Nations of North America Ser.). (ENG.). 40p. (J). (gr. 3-6). 32.79 (978-1-63407-036-2(4), 208871) Child's World, Inc., The.

Lacey, T. Jensen. The Comanche. 2010. (History & Culture of Native Americans Ser.). 136p. (gr. 6-12). 35.00 (978-1-60413-789-7(4), Chelsea Hse.) Facts On File, Inc.

Lajiness, Katie. Shoshone, 1 vol. 2016. (ENG., Illus.). 32p. (J). (978-1-68078-202-8(9)) ABDO Publishing Co.

—Yokuts, 1 vol. 2016. (ENG., Illus.). 32p. (J). (978-1-68078-204-2(5)) ABDO Publishing Co.

Lange, Karen. 1607: A New Look at Jamestown. Block, Ira, photos by. 2007. (ENG., Illus.). 48p. (J). (gr. 4-7). 27.90 (978-1-4263-0013-4(1), National Geographic Children's Bks.) National Geographic Society.

Lawton, Cassie M. & Bial, Raymond. The People & Culture of the Cherokee. 2016. (First Peoples of North America Ser.). (Illus.). 128p. (J). (gr. 6-6). 45.64 (978-1-5026-1886-3(9)) Cavendish Square Publishing.

—The People & Culture of the Cheyenne. 2016. (First Peoples of North America Ser.). (Illus.). 128p. (J). (gr. 6-6). 45.64 (978-1-5026-1888-7(5)) Cavendish Square Publishing.

—The People & Culture of the Iroquois. 2016. (First Peoples of North America Ser.). (Illus.). 128p. (J). (gr. 6-6). 45.64 (978-1-5026-1890-0(7)) Cavendish Square Publishing.

—The People & Culture of the Shoshone. 2016. (First Peoples of North America Ser.). (Illus.). 128p. (J). (gr. 6-6). 45.64 (978-1-5026-1896-2(6)) Cavendish Square Publishing.

—The People & Culture of the Sioux. 2016. (First Peoples of North America Ser.). (Illus.). 128p. (J). (gr. 6-6). 45.64 (978-1-5026-1894-8(X)) Cavendish Square Publishing.

—The People & Culture of the Wampanoag. 2016. (First Peoples of North America Ser.). (Illus.). 128p. (J). (gr. 6-6). 45.64 (978-1-5026-1898-6(2)) Cavendish Square Publishing.

Lemke, Nancy. Southern Coast Missions in California. 2007. (Exploring California Missions Ser.). (ENG., Illus.). 64p. (gr. 4-7). lib. bdg. 27.93 (978-0-8225-1935-5(6), Lerner Pubns.) Lerner Publishing Group.

Levine, Michelle. The Sioux. 2006. (Native American Histories Ser.). (Illus.). 56p. (J). (gr. 4-7). lib. bdg. 27.93 (978-0-8225-2864-7(9), Lerner Pubns.) Lerner Publishing Group.

Levy, Janey. Native Americans in Texas. 2010. (Spotlight on Texas Ser.). (ENG., Illus.). 32p. (J). (gr. 3-4). 26.25 (978-1-61532-488-0(7)); pap. 11.75 (978-1-61532-451-4(8)) Rosen Publishing Group, Inc., The.

—The Wampanoag of Massachusetts & Rhode Island. 2005. (Library of Native Americans). (Illus.). 64p. (J). (gr. k-5). lib. bdg. 26.50 (978-1-4042-2871-9(3), PowerKids Pr.) Rosen Publishing Group, Inc., The.

Lewis, J. Patrick. The Navajo Code Talkers. Kelley, Gary, illus. 2016. (ENG.). 32p. (J). (gr. 2-4). 18.99 (978-1-56846-295-0(6), Creative Editions) Creative Co., The.

The Library of Native Americans: Set 3. (J). (gr. k-5). 159.00 (978-1-4042-2657-9(5)) Rosen Publishing Group, Inc., The.

Linde, Barbara M. & Nardo, Don. Native Americans in Early North America. 2017. (American History Ser.). 104p. (YA). (gr. 7-7). lib. bdg. 39.40 **(978-1-5345-6037-6(8)**, Lucent Pr.) Greenhaven Publishing LLC.

Loew, Patty. Native People of Wisconsin, Revised Edition. 2015. (New Badger History Ser.). (ENG., Illus.). 208p. (J). (gr. 4-6). pap. 15.95 (978-0-87020-748-8(2)) Wisconsin Historical Society.

Loew, Patty, et al. Native People of Wisconsin. 2003. (New Badger History Ser.). (Illus.). 224p. (J). pap., tchr. ed., stu. ed. 59.95 (978-0-87020-349-7(5)) Wisconsin Historical Society.

—Native People of Wisconsin, Rev. TG & Student Materials. 2016. (New Badger History Ser.). (ENG.). (J). (gr. 4-6). cd-rom 49.95 (978-0-87020-749-5(0)) Wisconsin Historical Society.

Lomberg, Michelle. The Iroquois. (Illus.). 32p. (J). 2014. (978-1-4896-2910-4(6)) 2003. pap. 9.95 (978-1-59036-181-8(4)) Weigl Pubs., Inc.

—The Ojibwa. (J). 2014. (978-1-4896-2918-0(1)) 2003. (Illus.). 32p. pap. 9.95 (978-1-59036-183-2(0)) Weigl Pubs., Inc.

Lonewolf, S. William. Thunder Fox's Long Hair: (a True Story) 2012. 40p. pap. 18.50 (978-1-4685-8095-2(7)) AuthorHouse.

Lowery, Linda. Native Peoples of the Southeast. 2016. (North American Indian Nations Ser.). (ENG., Illus.). 48p. (J). (gr. 3-5). 50.65 (978-1-4677-8328-6(5), Lerner Pubns.) Lerner Publishing Group.

MacMillan, Dianne M. Los Angeles Area Missions. 2007. (Exploring California Missions Ser.). (Illus.). 64p. (J). lib. bdg. 27.93 (978-0-8225-0898-4(2), Lerner Pubns.) Lerner Publishing Group.

Mann, Charles C. Before Columbus: The Americas of 1491. 2009. (ENG., Illus.). 128p. (J). (gr. 3-7). 24.99

(978-1-4169-4900-8(3), Atheneum Bks. for Young Readers) Simon & Schuster Children's Publishing.

Margaret, Amy. Mission San Jose de Guadalupe. 2009. (Missions of California Ser.). 64p. (gr. 4-4). 58.50 *(978-1-60854-031-0(6),* PowerKids Pr.) Rosen Publishing Group, Inc., The.

Marsh, Carole. Sacagawea: Native American Heroine: Native American Heroine. 2003. 12p. (gr. k-4). 2.95 *(978-0-635-02143-4(9))* Gallopade International.

—Sitting Bull. 2003. 12p. (gr. k-4). 2.95 *(978-0-635-02378-0(4))* Gallopade International.

—West Virginia Native Americans: A Kid's Look at Our State's Chiefs, Tribes, Reservations, Powwows, Lore & More from the Past & the Present. 2004. (West Virginia Experi Ser.). (Illus.). 36p. (J). (gr. 3-8). 29.95 *(978-0-635-02341-4(5))* Gallopade International.

—Wyoming Native Americans: A Kid's Look at Our State's Chiefs, Tribes, Reservations, Powwows, Lore & More from the Past to the Present. 2004. (Wyoming Experience Ser.). (Illus.). 36p. (J). (gr. 3-8). 29.95 *(978-0-635-02345-2(8))* Gallopade International.

Mathias, Adeline. How a Young Brave Survived. Hamilton, Penny, ed. Auld, Francis & Joseph, Debbie, illus. 2009. (ENG.). 30p. (J). pap. 5.95 *(978-1-934594-04-9(0))* Salish Kootenia College Pr.

Mayrl, Damon. The Potawatamie of Wisconsin. 2009. (Library of Native Americans Ser.). 64p. (gr. 4-4). 58.50 *(978-1-60853-761-7(7),* PowerKids Pr.) Rosen Publishing Group, Inc., The.

McDaniel, Melissa. Southwest Indians, 1 vol. 2011. (First Nations of North America Ser.). (ENG.). 48p. (gr. 3-3). pap. 9.95 *(978-1-4329-4964-8(0));* 33.32 *(978-1-4329-4953-2(5))* Heinemann-Raintree. (Heinemann InfoSearch).

McNamara, Margaret. Discover the Iroquois. 2006. (J). pap. *(978-1-4108-6443-7(X))* Benchmark Education Co.

—Discover the Lakota. 2006. (J). pap. *(978-1-4108-6442-0(1))* Benchmark Education Co.

—Discover the Navajo. 2006. (J). pap. *(978-1-4108-6441-3(3))* Benchmark Education Co.

Mead, James R., et al. Hunting & Trading in Kansas, 1859-1875. 2015. (J). *(978-1-929731-25-1(6))* Rowfant Pr.

Media Projects, Inc., Staff. Student Almanac of Native American History, 2 vols., Vol. 1. 2003. (Middle School Reference Ser.). (Illus.). 144p. (C). (gr. 6-8). 101.00 *(978-0-313-32599-1(5),* MS2599, Greenwood) ABC-CLIO, LLC.

Micklos, John, Jr. A Wilderness of Experiences: Explorers & American Indians on the Frontier. 2016. (Discovering the New World Ser.). (ENG.). 48p. (gr. 3-4). pap. 8.95 *(978-1-5157-1869-7(7),* Connect) Stone Arch Bks.

—A Wilderness of Experiences - Explorers & American Indians on the Frontier. 2016. (Discovering the New World Ser.). (ENG., Illus.). 48p. (gr. 3-4). lib. bdg. 29.32 *(978-1-5157-1866-6(2))* Capstone Press of Coughlan Cos.

Minor, Wendell. Sitting Bull Remembers. Date not set. 32p. (J). (gr. -1-3). 15.99 *(978-0-06-029153-2(2));* pap. 5.99 *(978-0-06-443725-7(6));* lib. bdg. 16.89 *(978-0-06-029154-9(0))* HarperCollins Pubs.

Mullins, Terry. Melungeons Out of the Dungeon. 2010. (ENG., Illus.). 32p. pap. 9.95 *(978-1-891852-70-1(1))* Quarrier Pr.

Musolf, Nell. The Split History of Westward Expansion in the United States: A Perspectives Flip Book, 1 vol. 2012. (Perspectives Flip Bks.). (ENG.). 64p. (gr. 5-6). pap. 8.95 *(978-0-7565-4596-3(X));* lib. bdg. 33.99 *(978-0-7565-4571-0(4))* Compass Point Bks.

Naber, Therese. Native Nations of California. 2015. (Native Nations of North America Ser.). (ENG.). 40p. (J). (gr. 3-6). 32.79 *(978-1-63407-029-4(1),* 208864) Child's World, Inc., The.

—Native Nations of the Southeast. 2015. (Native Nations of North America Ser.). (ENG.). 40p. (J). (gr. 3-6). 32.79 *(978-1-63407-035-5(6),* 208870) Child's World, Inc., The.

Nagelhout, Ryan. People of the Great Lakes. 2014. (Exploring the Great Lakes Ser.). 32p. (J). (gr. 3-6). pap. 63.00 *(978-1-4824-1192-8(X))* Stevens, Gareth Publishing LLLP.

Nash, Alice & Strobel, Christoph. Daily Life of Native Americans from Post-Columbian Through Nineteenth-Century America, 1 vol. 2006. (Daily Life Ser.). (Illus.). 312p. (C). 75.00 *(978-0-313-33515-0(X),* GR3515, Greenwood) ABC-CLIO, LLC.

Native American Cultures. 2015. (Native American Cultures Ser.). (ENG.). 32p. (J). (gr. 2-3). 151.50 *(978-1-4824-1642-8(5))* Stevens, Gareth Publishing LLLP.

Native American Heroes. 2015. (Native American Heroes Ser.). (ENG.). 24p. (J). (gr. 1-2). pap., pap., pap. 293.40 *(978-1-4824-3485-9(7))* Stevens, Gareth Publishing LLLP.

Native Peoples of North America. 2016. (Native Peoples of North America Ser.). 32p. (gr. 3-2). pap. 84.00 *(978-1-4824-5294-5(4));* lib. bdg. 202.00 *(978-1-4824-4590-9(5))* Stevens, Gareth Publishing LLLP.

Nelson, S. D. Sitting Bull: Lakota Warrior & Defender of His People. 2015. (ENG., Illus.). 64p. (J). (gr. 3-7). 19.95 *(978-1-4197-0731-5(0),* Abrams Bks. for Young Readers) Abrams, Inc.

Oestreicher, David M. The Algonquian of New York. 2009. (Library of Native Americans Ser.). 64p. (gr. 4-4). 58.50 *(978-1-60853-742-6(0),* PowerKids Pr.) Rosen Publishing Group, Inc., The.

Ostrow, Kim. Mission Nuestra Senora de la Soledad. 2009. (Missions of California Ser.). 64p. (gr. 4-4). 58.50 *(978-1-60854-021-1(9),* PowerKids Pr.) Rosen Publishing Group, Inc., The.

Ostrow, Kim & Nuñes, Sofia. Discovering Mission Santa Cruz. 2014. (California Missions Ser.). (Illus.). 48p. (J). (gr. 4-6). lib. bdg. 31.36 *(978-1-62713-070-7(5))* Cavendish Square Publishing.

Otfinoski, Steven. Native Americans at the Time of the Explorers: Text Pairs. 2008. (Bridges/Navigators Ser.). (J). (gr. 5). 89.00 *(978-1-4108-8420-6(1))* Benchmark Education Co.

Otis, James. True Indian Tales from American History: In the Stirring Days of the Early Colonists. 2011. 448p. 56.95 *(978-1-258-05802-9(2))* Literary Licensing, LLC.

Page, Andrea. The Sioux Code Talkers of World War II, 1 vol. 2017. (Illus.). 136p. (J). (gr. 3-7). 14.95 *(978-1-4556-2243-6(5))* Pelican Publishing Co., Inc.

Palazzo-Craig, Janet. The Ojibwe of Michigan, Wisconsin, Minnesota, & North Dakota. (Library of Native Americans Ser.). 64p. 2009. (gr. 4-4). 58.50 *(978-1-60853-758-7(7))* 2005. (Illus.). (J). (gr. k-5). lib. bdg. 26.50 *(978-1-4042-2873-3(X))* Rosen Publishing Group, Inc., The. (PowerKids Pr.).

Parsons Yazzie, Evangeline. Little Woman Warrior Who Came Home. Ruffenach, Jessie, ed. Toddy, Irving, illus. 2005. (NAV & ENG.). 32p. (J). (gr. 4-7). 17.95 *(978-1-893354-55-5(5))* Salina Bookshelf Inc.

Patterson, Marie. Early American Indian Tribes, 1 vol. 2004. (Primary Source Readers Ser.). (ENG.). 24p. (J). (gr. 5-5). pap. 8.99 *(978-0-7439-8744-8(6))* Shell Educational Publishing.

Peterson, Cris. Birchbark Brigade: A Fur Trade History. 2009. (ENG.). 136p. (J). (gr. 4-18). 18.95 *(978-1-59078-426-6(X),* Calkins Creek) Boyds Mills Pr.

Petrikowski, Nicki Peter & Edwards, Judith. The Relocation of Native Peoples of North America. 2015. (Our Shared History Ser.). (ENG., Illus.). 128p. (J). (gr. 7-7). lib. bdg. 37.27 *(978-0-7660-7012-7(3))* Enslow Pubs., Inc.

Phan, Sandy. American Indians in Texas: Conflict & Survival, 1 vol. 2012. (Primary Source Readers Ser.). (ENG.). 32p. (J). (gr. 4-4). pap. 8.99 *(978-1-4333-5040-5(8))* Teacher Created Materials, Inc.

—The Caddo & Comanche: American Indians Tribes in Texas, 1 vol. 2012. (Primary Source Readers Ser.). (ENG.). 32p. (J). (gr. 3-3). pap. 8.99 *(978-1-4333-5041-2(6))* Teacher Created Materials, Inc.

Powell, Marie. Native Nations of the Arctic & Subarctic. 2015. (Native Nations of North America Ser.). (ENG.). 40p. (J). (gr. 3-6). 32.79 *(978-1-63407-030-0(5),* 208865) Child's World, Inc., The.

Prior, Jennifer Overend. American Indians of the Plains: Surviving the Great Expanse. 2016. (Primary Source Readers Ser.). (Illus.). 32p. (J). (gr. 4-5). pap. 8.99 *(978-1-4938-3070-1(8))* Teacher Created Materials, Inc.

—Florida's American Indians Through History. 2016. (Primary Source Readers Ser.). 32p. (gr. 4-4). pap. 8.99 *(978-1-4938-3534-8(3))* Teacher Created Materials, Inc.

Quasha, Jennifer. Mission San Luis Rey de Francia. 2009. (Missions of California Ser.). 64p. (gr. 4-4). 58.50 *(978-1-60854-034-1(0),* PowerKids Pr.) Rosen Publishing Group, Inc., The.

Rice, Katelyn. American Indians of the West: Battling the Elements. 2016. (Primary Source Readers Ser.). (Illus.). 32p. (J). (gr. 4-5). pap. 8.99 *(978-1-4938-3069-5(4))* Teacher Created Materials, Inc.

Rosier, Paul C. & Crompton, Samuel Willard. The Cheyenne. 2011. (History & Culture of Native Americans Ser.). (Illus.). 136p. (J). (gr. 6-12). 35.00 *(978-1-60413-797-2(5),* Chelsea Hse.) Facts On File, Inc.

Rossi, Ann. Cultures Collide: Native American & Europenas 1492-1700. 2004. (Crossroads America Ser.). (ENG., Illus.). 40p. (J). (gr. 5-9). 21.90 *(978-0-7922-7198-7(X),* National Geographic Children's Bks.) National Geographic Society.

Roza, Greg. The Karankawa of Texas. 2009. (Library of Native Americans Ser.). 64p. (gr. 4-4). 58.50 *(978-1-60853-748-8(X),* PowerKids Pr.) Rosen Publishing Group, Inc., The.

Ruppel, Maxine. Vostaas: White Buffalo's Story of the Plains Indians. (Indian Culture Ser.). (J). (gr. 4-10). pap. 4.95 *(978-0-89992-001-6(2))* Council for Indian Education.

Sanford, William R. Nez Percé Chief Joseph. 2013. (Native American Chiefs & Warriors Ser.). 48p. (J). (gr. 5-9). pap. 8.95 *(978-1-4644-0251-7(5))* Enslow Pubs., Inc.

Santella, Andrew. The Navajo. 2003. (True Bks). (Illus.). 47p. (J). (gr. 3-5). 14.60 *(978-0-7569-7156-4(X))* Perfection Learning Corp.

—Plains Indians, 1 vol. 2011. (First Nations of North America Ser.). (ENG.). 48p. (gr. 3-3). pap. 9.95 *(978-1-4329-4961-7(6));* 33.32 *(978-1-4329-4950-1(0))* Heinemann-Raintree. (Heinemann InfoSearch).

Schimel, Kate & Goldberg, Lynn. Native Americans: The First Peoples of New York. 2012. (Illus.). 24p. (J). 60.00 *(978-1-4488-5752-4(X));* pap. 10.00 *(978-1-4488-5751-7(1));* lib. bdg. 22.60 *(978-1-4488-5739-5(2))* Rosen Publishing Group, Inc., The. (PowerKids Pr.).

Schomp, Virginia. The Native Americans. 2007. (Myths of the World Ser.). (Illus.). 96p. (J). (gr. 3-7). lib. bdg. 32.79 *(978-0-7614-2550-2(0),* Benchmark Bks.) Marshall Cavendish Corp.

Schwartz, Heather E. American Indians of the East: Woodland People. 2016. (Primary Source Readers Ser.). (Illus.). 32p. (J). (gr. 4-5). pap. 8.99 *(978-1-4938-3071-8(6))* Teacher Created Materials, Inc.

Serafin, Kim. Mission San Antonio de Padua. 2009. (Missions of California Ser.). 64p. (gr. 4-4). 58.50 *(978-1-60854-025-9(1),* PowerKids Pr.) Rosen Publishing Group, Inc., The.

Shaffer, Jody Jensen. Sitting Bull: Eagles Cannot Be Crows. 2017. (Primary Source Readers Ser.). 32p. (J). (gr. 4-5). pap. 8.99 *(978-1-4938-3800-4(8))* Teacher Created Materials, Inc.

Sheinkin, Steve. Undefeated: Jim Thorpe & the Carlisle Indian School Football Team. Hsu, Connie, ed. 2017. (ENG., Illus.). 288p. (J). 19.99 *(978-1-59643-954-2(8),* 9781596439542) Roaring Brook Pr.

Shull, Jodie A. Voice of the Paiutes: A Story about Sarah Winnemucca. Birdsong, Keith, illus. 2007. (Creative Minds Biography Ser.). 64p. (J). (gr. 3-7). lib. bdg. 22.60 *(978-0-8225-5990-0(0))* Lerner Publishing Group.

Sjonger, Rebecca & Kalman, Bobbie. Life of the Powhatan. 2004. (Native Nations of North America Ser.). (ENG., Illus.). 32p. (J). (gr. 2-5). pap. *(978-0-7787-0472-0(6));* (gr. 5). lib. bdg. *(978-0-7787-0380-8(0))* Crabtree Publishing Co.

Smith-Llera, Danielle. The Chumash: The Past & Present of California's Seashell People. 2016. (American Indian Life Ser.). (ENG., Illus.). 32p. (gr. 3-4). lib. bdg. 27.32 *(978-1-5157-0237-5(5))* Capstone Press of Coughlan Cos.

—The Creek: The Past & Present of the Muscogee. 2016. (American Indian Life Ser.). (ENG., Illus.). 32p. (gr. 3-4). lib. bdg. 27.32 *(978-1-5157-0238-2(3))* Capstone Press of Coughlan Cos.

—The Iroquois: The Past & Present of the Haudenosaunee. 2015. (American Indian Life Ser.). (ENG., Illus.). 32p. (gr. 3-4). pap. 7.95 *(978-1-4914-5005-5(3))* Capstone Press of Coughlan Cos.

—The Powhatan: The Past & Present of Virginia's First Tribes. 2016. (American Indian Life Ser.). (ENG., Illus.). 32p. (gr. 3-4). lib. bdg. 27.32 *(978-1-5157-0239-9(1))* Capstone Press of Coughlan Cos.

Smith-Llera, Danielle & Bowman, Donna Janell. The Navajo: The Past & Present of the Dine. 2015. (American Indian Life Ser.). (ENG., Illus.). 32p. (gr. 3-4). pap. 7.95 *(978-1-4914-5004-8(5))* Capstone Press of Coughlan Cos.

Sneve, Virginia Driving Hawk. Enduring Wisdom: Sayings from American Indians. Saint James, Synthia, illus. 2003. (ENG.). 32p. (J). (gr. k-3). tchr. ed. 16.95 *(978-0-8234-1455-0(8))* Holiday Hse., Inc.

Sonneborn, Liz. The Choctaws. 2006. (Native American Histories Ser.). (ENG., Illus.). 56p. (gr. 3-6). lib. bdg. 27.93 *(978-0-8225-5911-5(0),* Lerner Pubns.) Lerner Publishing Group.

—The Chumash. 2006. (Native American Histories Ser.). (ENG., Illus.). 56p. (gr. 3-6). lib. bdg. 27.93 *(978-0-8225-5912-2(9),* Lerner Pubns.) Lerner Publishing Group.

—The Shoshones. 2006. (Native American Histories Ser.). (Illus.). 56p. (J). (gr. 4-7). lib. bdg. 27.93 *(978-0-8225-2849-4(5),* Lerner Pubns.) Lerner Publishing Group.

Spotlight on Native Americans. 2015. (Spotlight on Native Americans Ser.). (ENG.). 32p. (J). (gr. 4-4). pap., pap., pap. 720.00 *(978-1-4994-1838-5(8),* PowerKids Pr.) Rosen Publishing Group, Inc., The.

Stalcup, Ann. America's Secret Weapon: Navajo Code Talkers of World War II. 2017. (J). pap. ***(978-1-63293-176-4(1))*** Sunstone Pr.

Stone, Amy. Creek. 2004. (Native American Peoples Ser.). (Illus.). 32p. (gr. 3-7). lib. bdg. 26.00 *(978-0-8368-4217-3(0),* Gareth Stevens Learning Library) Stevens, Gareth Publishing LLLP.

—Oneida. 2004. (Native American Peoples Ser.). (Illus.). 32p. (gr. 3-7). lib. bdg. 26.00 *(978-0-8368-4220-3(0),* Gareth Stevens Learning Library) Stevens, Gareth Publishing LLLP.

Stotter, Michael. Native Americans: Find Out about the World of North American Indians, with 400 Exciting Pictures & 15 Step-by-Step Projects. 2013. (ENG., Illus.). 64p. (J). (gr. -1-3). pap. 12.99 *(978-1-84322-975-9(7),* Armadillo) Anness Publishing GBR. Dist: National Bk. Network.

Stotter, Mike. The World of North American Indians. 2009. (Passport to the Past Ser.). (Illus.). 64p. (YA). (gr. 4-7). lib. bdg. 31.95 *(978-1-4358-5171-9(4))* Rosen Publishing Group, Inc., The.

Stout, Mary. Blackfoot. 2004. (Native American Peoples Ser.). (Illus.). 32p. (gr. 3-7). lib. bdg. 26.00 *(978-0-8368-4216-6(2),* Gareth Stevens Learning Library) Stevens, Gareth Publishing LLLP.

—Shoshone History & Culture. 2011. (Native American Library). 48p. (J). (gr. 3-6). pap. 14.05 *(978-1-4339-5976-9(3));* lib. bdg. 31.95 *(978-1-4339-5974-5(7))* Stevens, Gareth Publishing LLLP. (Gareth Stevens Learning Library).

Stout, Mary & Stout, Mary A. Hopi. 2004. (Native American Peoples Ser.). (Illus.). 32p. (gr. 3-7). lib. bdg. 26.00 *(978-0-8368-4218-0(9),* Gareth Stevens Learning Library) Stevens, Gareth Publishing LLLP.

—Shoshone. 2004. (Native American Peoples Ser.). (Illus.). 32p. (gr. 3-7). lib. bdg. 26.00 *(978-0-8368-4221-0(9),* Gareth Stevens Learning Library) Stevens, Gareth Publishing LLLP.

Sullivan, Sonja. I Am A Kumeyaay. Stanley, Barbara, ed. Sullivan, Sonja, illus. 2007. (Illus.). 29p. (J). *(978-0-9790951-1-5(5))* Sycuan Pr.

Tieck, Sarah. Sioux, 1 vol. 2014. (Native Americans Ser.). (ENG.). 32p. (gr. 7-11). 28.50 *(978-1-62403-357-5(1))* ABDO Publishing Co.

Traylor, Waverley. Indian Legends of the Great Dismal Swamp. Traylor, Margaret, ed. Hancock, Stefanie, illus. 2004. 72p. (gr. 8-18). pap. 9.95 *(978-0-9715068-3-1(3))* Traylor, Waverley Publishing.

Tripp, Analisa. A Is for Acorn: A California Indian ABC. Risling, Lyn, illus. 2015. (J). *(978-1-59714-316-5(2))* Heyday.

Trumbauer, Lisa. The First Americans. 2016. (Life in the Time Of Ser.). (ENG.). 32p. pap. 8.29 *(978-1-4846-4013-5(6),* Heinemann First Library) Heinemann-Raintree.

Vander Hook, Sue. Trail of Tears, 1 vol. 2010. (Essential Events Set 4 Ser.). (ENG.). 112p. (J). (gr. 6-12). lib. bdg. 35.64 *(978-1-60453-946-2(1))* ABDO Publishing Co.

Waldman, Stuart. We Asked for Nothing. McNally, Tom, illus. 2014. (ENG.). 208p. (J). (gr. 5-7). pap. 8.95 *(978-1-931414-50-0(5),* 9781931414500) Mikaya Pr.

Walker, Niki & Kalman, Bobbie. Native North American Wisdom & Gifts. 2005. (Native Nations of North America Ser.). (ENG., Illus.). 32p. (J). (gr. 4-7). pap. *(978-0-7787-0476-8(9));* lib. bdg. *(978-0-7787-0384-6(3))* Crabtree Publishing Co.

Walsh, Steve. Chief Ouray: Ute Chief & Man of Peace. 2011. (ENG & SPA., Illus.). 54p. (J). pap. 8.95 *(978-0-86541-121-0(2))* Filter Pr., LLC.

Weil, Ann & Guillain, Charlotte. American Indian Cultures, 1 vol. 2012. (Global Cultures Ser.). (ENG.). 48p. (gr. 4-6). pap. 9.95 *(978-1-4329-6790-1(8));* 32.65 *(978-1-4329-6781-9(9))* Heinemann-Raintree. (NA-h).

Whitehurst, Susan. Plymouth Partnership: Pilgrims & Native Americans. 2009. (Library of the Pilgrims Ser.). 24p. (gr. 3-4). 42.50 *(978-1-60853-912-3(1),* PowerKids Pr.) Rosen Publishing Group, Inc., The.

Wilcox, Charlotte. The Seminoles. 2006. (Native American Histories Ser.). (Illus.). 56p. (J). (gr. 4-7). lib. bdg. 27.93 *(978-0-8225-2848-7(7),* Lerner Pubns.) Lerner Publishing Group.

Williams, Jack. The Miwok of California. 2009. (Library of Native Americans Ser.). 64p. (gr. 4-4). 58.50 *(978-1-60853-753-2(6),* PowerKids Pr.) Rosen Publishing Group, Inc., The.

—The Mojave of California. 2009. (Library of Native Americans Ser.). 64p. (gr. 4-4). 58.50 *(978-1-60853-755-6(2),* PowerKids Pr.) Rosen Publishing Group, Inc., The.

—The Mono of California. 2009. (Library of Native Americans Ser.). 64p. (gr. 4-4). 58.50 *(978-1-60853-756-3(0),* PowerKids Pr.) Rosen Publishing Group, Inc., The.

Williams, Jack S. Padres of the California Mission Frontier. 2009. (People of the California Missions Ser.). 64p. (gr. 4-4). 58.50 *(978-1-60851-158-7(8),* PowerKids Pr.) Rosen Publishing Group, Inc., The.

Wingate, Philippa & Reid, Struan. Who Were the First North Americans? 2004. (Starting Point History Ser.). (Illus.). 32p. (J). pap. 4.99 *(978-0-7945-0397-0(7),* Usborne); lib. bdg. 12.95 *(978-1-58086-512-8(7))* EDC Publishing.

Wirkner, Linda. Learning about the Settlement of the Americas with Graphic Organizers. 2006. (Graphic Organizers in Science & Social Studies Ser.). (ENG.). 24p. (gr. 4-6). pap. 8.25 *(978-1-4042-5057-4(3),* Rosen Classroom) Rosen Publishing Group, Inc., The.

Wolfe, James, et al. Understanding the Iroquois Constitution. 2015. (Primary Sources of American Political Documents Ser.). (ENG., Illus.). 160p. (J). (gr. 7-7). 37.27 *(978-0-7660-6878-0(1))* Enslow Pubs., Inc.

World Book, Inc Staff, contrib. by. Indians of the Great Plains & Great Basin. 2009. (J). *(978-0-7166-2139-3(8))* World Bk., Inc.

—Indians of the Southwest. 2009. (J). *(978-0-7166-2142-3(8))* World Bk., Inc.

—Peoples of the Arctic & Subarctic. 2009. (J). *(978-0-7166-2132-4(0))* World Bk., Inc.

Yasuda, Anita. Native Nations of the Northwest Coast. 2015. (Native Nations of North America Ser.). (ENG.). 40p. (J). (gr. 3-6). 32.79 *(978-1-63407-033-1(X),* 208868) Child's World, Inc., The.

—Native Nations of the Plains. 2015. (Native Nations of North America Ser.). (ENG.). 40p. (J). (gr. 3-6). 32.79 *(978-1-63407-034-8(8),* 208869) Child's World, Inc., The.

INDIANS OF NORTH AMERICA—HISTORY—FICTION

Banting, Erinn. Les Cris: Les Autochtones du Canada. Karvonen, Tanjah, tr. from ENG. 2011. (FRE.). 24p. (YA). (gr. 2-4). *(978-1-77071-403-8(0))* Weigl Educational Pubs. Ltd.

Dumas, William. Pisim Finds Her Miskinow. Paul, Leonard, illus. 2013. (ENG & CRE.). 48p. (gr. 5-12). *(978-1-55379-394-6(3),* 9781553793946, HighWater Pr.) Portage & Main Pr.

Hamilton, Elizabeth L. Mystery at Lake Cachuma. 2003. (Character Mystery Ser.: No. 1). (Illus.). 114p. (J). (gr. 3-6). per. 9.95 *(978-0-9713749-4-2(5),* Character-in-Action) Quiet Impact, Inc.

Lowden, Stephanie Golightly. Time of the Eagle: A Story of an Ojibwe Winter. 2006. 127p. (J). (gr. 3-7). 18.95 *(978-1-883953-38-6(3),* Blue Horse Books) Great Lakes Literary, LLC.

Parton, Paula. Room 17 Where History Comes Alive Book I—Indians. Parton, Paula, illus. 2007. (Illus.). 128p. per. 8.95 *(978-0-9794815-0-5(3))* Bellissima Publishing, LLC.

—Room 17 Where History Comes Alive! Book I-Indians. Parton, Paua, illus. 2007. 128p. 19.95 *(978-0-9794815-2-9(X))* Bellissima Publishing, LLC.

INDIANS OF NORTH AMERICA—HOPI INDIANS

Kamma, Anne. If You Lived with the Hopi. 2014. 17.00 *(978-1-63419-709-0(7))* Perfection Learning Corp.

Kuszewski, Ivy. Hopi. 2015. (Spotlight on Native Americans Ser.). (ENG., Illus.). 32p. (J). (gr. 4-6). 26.25 *(978-1-4994-1663-3(6),* PowerKids Pr.) Rosen Publishing Group, Inc., The.

Secakuku, Susan. Meet Mindy: A Native Girl from the Southwest. Harrington, John, photos by. 2006. (ENG., Illus.). 48p. (J). 15.95 *(978-1-57178-148-2(X))* Council Oak Bks.

St. Lawrence, Genevieve. The Hopi. 2003. (Uncovering Native American History Ser.). (J). pap. *(978-1-58417-115-7(4));* lib. bdg. *(978-1-58417-052-5(2))* Lake Street Pubs.

Tieck, Sarah. Hopi, 1 vol. 2014. (Native Americans Set 2 Ser.). (ENG.). 32p. (gr. 2-5). 28.50 *(978-1-62403-580-7(9))* ABDO Publishing Co.

INDIANS OF NORTH AMERICA—HOPI INDIANS—FICTION

Poleahla, Anita. Celebrate My Hopi Name. James, Eric, illus. 2013. (CAI & ENG.). (J). *(978-1-893354-65-4(2))* Salina Bookshelf Inc.

INDIANS OF NORTH AMERICA—HURON INDIANS

Gray-Kanatiiosh, Barbara A. Huron, 1 vol. 2004. (Native Americans Set 3 Ser.). (ENG., Illus.). 32p. (gr. k-6). 27.07 *(978-1-57765-935-8(X),* Checkerboard Library) ABDO Publishing Co.

INDIANS OF NORTH AMERICA—INDUSTRIES

Corwin, Judith Hoffman. Native American Crafts of the Northeast & Southeast. Corwin, Judith Hoffman, illus. 2003. (Native American Crafts Ser.). (ENG., Illus.). 48p. (J). (gr. 3-6). pap. 7.95 *(978-0-531-15593-6(5),* Watts, Franklin) Scholastic Library Publishing.

—Native American Crafts of the Plains & Plateau. Corwin, Judith Hoffman, illus. 2003. (Native American Crafts Ser.). (ENG., Illus.). 48p. (J). (gr. 3-6). pap. 7.95 *(978-0-531-15595-0(1),* Watts, Franklin) Scholastic Library Publishing.

Gnojewski, Carol. American Indian Crafts Kids Can Do! 2006. (Multicultural Crafts Kids Can Do! Ser.). (Illus.). 32p. (J). (gr. 3-4). lib. bdg. 23.94 *(978-0-7660-2458-8(X),* Enslow Elementary) Enslow Pubs., Inc.

Schiffer, Nancy N. Contemporary Hopi Kachina Dolls, 1 vol. 2003. (ENG., Illus.). 208p. (gr. 10-13). 39.95 *(978-0-7643-1848-1(9),* 9780764318481) Schiffer Publishing, Ltd.

INDIANS OF NORTH AMERICA—IROQUOIS INDIANS

Anderson, Tanya. The Maid of the Mist. 2014. (Jr. Graphic Ghost Stories Ser.). 24p. (J). (gr. 3-6). lib. bdg. 26.25 *(978-1-4777-7129-7(8),* PowerKids Pr.) Rosen Publishing Group, Inc., The.

Bowman, David. Native Americans of the Eastern Woodlands: Set Of 6. 2010. (Navigators Ser.). (J). pap. 48.00 net. *(978-1-4108-6252-5(6))* Benchmark Education Co.

Bruchac, Joseph. The Boy Who Lived with the Bears: And Other Iroquois Stories. Jacob, Murv, illus. 2003. (Storytime Ser.). 63p. (J). (gr. k-5). pap. 11.95 *(978-0-930407-61-2(X))* Parabola Bks.

Dolbear, Emily J. & Benoit, Peter. The Iroquois. 2011. (True Bks.). 48p. (J). (gr. 3-5). 29.00 *(978-0-531-20771-0(4));* pap. 6.95 *(978-0-531-29313-3(0))* Scholastic Library Publishing. (Children's Pr.).

Englar, Mary. The Iroquois: The Six Nations Confederacy. 2016. (American Indian Nations Ser.). (ENG.). 48p. (gr. 3-4). pap. 8.19 *(978-1-5157-3873-2(6),* Social Studies Collections) Capstone Press of Coughlan Cos.

H I

Idee, Ari. Great Peacemaker. 2013. 38p. pap. 9.49 *(978-0-9798991-3-3(3))* Technology & Imagination Pr.

Lawton, Cassie M. & Bial, Raymond. The People & Culture of the Iroquois. 2016. (First Peoples of North America Ser.). (Illus.). 128p. (J). (gr. 6-6). 45.64 *(978-1-5026-1890-0(7))* Cavendish Square Publishing.

Mateusz, M. G. The Treaty of Canandaigua 1794: A Primary Source Examination of the Treaty Between the United States & the Tribes of Indians called the Six Nations. 2009. (Primary Sources of American Treaties Ser.). 64p. (gr. 5-8). 58.50 *(978-1-60851-515-8(X))* Rosen Publishing Group, Inc., The.

McNamara, Margaret. Native Americans of the Eastern Woodlands: The Iroquois. 2006. (J). pap. *(978-1-4108-6440-6(5))* Benchmark Education Co.

Miller, Connie R. The Iroquois. 2003. (Digging up Native American History Ser.). (J). *(978-1-58417-045-7(X))*; pap. *(978-1-58417-108-9(1))* Lake Street Pubs.

Potts, Steve. Iroquois. 2015. (Illus.). 48p. (J). *(978-1-60818-552-8(4)*, Creative Education) Creative Co., The.

Randolph, Joanne. The Iroquois League. 2003. (Reading Room Collection 2 Ser.). (Illus.). 24p. (J). lib. bdg. 22.60 *(978-0-8239-3703-5(8))* Rosen Publishing Group, Inc., The.

Rhodes, Wendell. Iroquois (Haudenosaunee), 01 vols., 1. 2016. (Spotlight on Native Americans Ser.). (ENG., Illus.). 32p. (J). pap. 11.75 *(978-1-5081-4150-1(9)*, PowerKids Pr.) Rosen Publishing Group, Inc., The.

Schomp, Virginia. Hiawatha & the Great Peace. 2013. (American Legends & Folktales 2 Ser.). 32p. (J). (gr. 6-9). pap. 10.58 *(978-1-62712-015-9(7))* Cavendish Square Publishing.

Smith-Llera, Danielle. The Iroquois: The Past & Present of the Haudenosaunee. 2015. (American Indian Life Ser.). (ENG., Illus.). 32p. (gr. 3-4). pap. 7.95 *(978-1-4914-5005-5(3))* Capstone Press of Coughlan Cos.

Takacs, Stefanie. The Iroquois. 2003. (True Bks.). (ENG., Illus.). 48p. (J). 25.00 *(978-0-516-22777-1(7)*, Children's Pr.) Scholastic Library Publishing.

Tieck, Sarah. Iroquois, 1 vol. 2014. (Native Americans Ser.). (ENG.). 32p. (gr. 7-11). 28.50 *(978-1-62403-354-4(7))* ABDO Publishing Co.

INDIANS OF NORTH AMERICA—IROQUOIS INDIANS—FICTION

Kelsey, Avonelle. Iroquois Medicine Woman. Kelsey, Avonelle, illus. (Illus.). 300p. (Orig.). (YA). *(978-0-9640610-5-7(8))* Cheval International.

McCann, Shawn, illus. Why the Owl Has Big Ears. 2005. 32p. (J). (gr. -1-3). 8.75 *(978-0-9771466-0-4(X))* Goulasche Pr.

Schraff, Anne. And We Will Be No More. 2008. (Passages to History Ser.). 127p. (J). (gr. 4-6). lib. bdg. 13.95 *(978-0-7569-8395-6(9))* Perfection Learning Corp.

Yasuda, Anita. Sky Woman & the Big Turtle: An Iroquois Creation Myth. Pennington, Mark, illus. 2012. (Short Tales Native American Myths Ser.). 32p. (J). (gr. 3-6). lib. bdg. 24.21 *(978-1-61641-882-3(6))* Magic Wagon.

INDIANS OF NORTH AMERICA—KARANKAWA

Roza, Greg. The Karankawa of Texas. 2005. (Library of Native Americans). (Illus.). 64p. (J). (gr. k-5). lib. bdg. 26.50 *(978-1-4042-2870-2(5)*, PowerKids Pr.) Rosen Publishing Group, Inc., The.

INDIANS OF NORTH AMERICA—KIOWA INDIANS—FICTION

Momaday, N. Scott. Four Arrows & Magpie: A Kiowa Story. Momaday, N. Scott, illus. 2006. (Illus.). 35p. (J). (gr. -1-3). pap. 9.95 *(978-1-930709-63-8(3))* HAWK Publishing Group.

INDIANS OF NORTH AMERICA—LEGENDS

see Indians of North America—Folklore

INDIANS OF NORTH AMERICA—MIWOK INDIANS

Williams, Jack S. The Miwok of California. 2004. (Library of Native Americans). (Illus.). 64p. (J). lib. bdg. 26.50 *(978-1-4042-2659-3(1))* Rosen Publishing Group, Inc., The.

INDIANS OF NORTH AMERICA—MOHAVE INDIANS

Boule, Mary Null. California Native American Tribes: Mohave Tribe, 28 booklets. Liddell, Daniel & Basta, Mary, illus. (California Native American Tribes). 52p. (J). (gr. 3-6). pap. 7.95 *(978-1-877599-73-6(5))* Merryant Pubs.

Gray-Kanatiiosh, Barbara A. Mohave, 1 vol. 2004. (Native Americans Set 3 Ser.). (ENG., Illus.). 32p. (gr. k-6). 27.07 *(978-1-57765-936-5(8)*, Checkerboard Library) ABDO Publishing Co.

INDIANS OF NORTH AMERICA—MOHAWK INDIANS

Weitzman, David. Skywalkers: Mohawks Ironworkers Build the City. 2010. (ENG., Illus.). 128p. (J). (gr. 5-9). 24.99 *(978-1-59643-162-1(8)*, 9781596431621) Roaring Brook Pr.

Weston Woods Staff, creator. Giving Thanks. 2011. 18.95 *(978-0-439-72673-3(5))*; 38.75 *(978-0-439-72676-4(X))*; 29.95 *(978-0-439-73469-1(X))* Weston Woods Studios, Inc.

INDIANS OF NORTH AMERICA—MOHAWK INDIANS—BIOGRAPHY

Lewis, Wendy A. & Lewis, Wendy. Lacrosse Warrior: The Life of Mohawk Lacrosse Champion Gaylord Powless, 1 vol. 3rd ed. 2008. (Lorimer Recordbooks Ser.). (ENG., Illus.). 120p. (J). (gr. 7-12). 8.95 *(978-1-55277-001-6(X)*, 9781552770016) Lorimer, James & Co., Ltd., Pubs. CAN. Dist: Casemate Pubs. & Bk. Distributors, LLC.

Robertson, David. The Poet: Pauline Johnson. Henderson, Scott B., illus. 2014. (Tales from Big Spirit Ser.: 6). (ENG.). 32p. (J). (gr. 4-6). pap. *(978-1-55379-481-3(8)*, ab04cc8e-58f6-479c-9f04-879c4a722ff3, HighWater Pr.) Portage & Main Pr.

INDIANS OF NORTH AMERICA—MOHAWK INDIANS—FICTION

Bruchac, Joseph. Bearwalker. Comport, Sally Wern, illus. 2010. (ENG.). 240p. (J). (gr. 5). pap. 6.99 *(978-0-06-112315-3(3))* HarperCollins Pubs.

—The Return of Skeleton Man. Comport, Sally Wern, illus. 144p. (J). (gr. 5). 2008. (Skeleton Man Ser.: 2). (ENG.). pap. 7.99 *(978-0-06-058092-6(5))* 2006. lib. bdg. 16.89 *(978-0-06-058091-9(7))* HarperCollins Pubs.

—Skeleton Man. Comport, Sally Wern, illus. 2003. (Skeleton Man Ser.: 1). (ENG.). 128p. (J). (gr. 5-18). pap. 5.99 *(978-0-06-440888-2(4))* HarperCollins Pubs.

—Skeleton Man. Comport, Sally Wern, illus. 2003. 114p. (J). (gr. 5). 12.65 *(978-0-7569-3399-9(4))* Perfection Learning Corp.

Joseph, Bruchac. Eagle Song. 2014. (ENG.). 80p. (J). (gr. 12-12). 9.24 *(978-1-63245-103-3(4))* Lectorum Pubns., Inc.

INDIANS OF NORTH AMERICA—MUSIC

Schilling, Vincent. Native Musicians in the Groove, 1 vol. 2009. (Native Trailblazers Ser.). (ENG.). 132p. (YA). (gr. 5-10). pap. 9.95 *(978-0-9779183-4-8(3)*, 7th Generation) Book Publishing Co.

Tyrrell, Frances, illus. The Huron Carol. 2004. 32p. 16.00 *(978-0-8028-5263-2(7))* Eerdmans, William B. Publishing Co.

INDIANS OF NORTH AMERICA—NAVAJO INDIANS

Birchfield, D. L. Navajo. 2003. (Native American Peoples Ser.). (Illus.). 32p. (gr. 3-7). lib. bdg. 26.00 *(978-0-8368-3704-9(5)*, Gareth Stevens Learning Library) Stevens, Gareth Publishing LLLP.

Bodden, Valerie. Navajo. 2015. (Illus.). 48p. (J). *(978-1-60818-553-5(2)*, Creative Education) Creative Co., The.

Boekhoff, P. M. & Kallen, Stuart A. The Navajo. 2003. (North American Indians Ser.). (ENG.). (J). 27.50 *(978-0-7377-1512-5(X)*, Greenhaven Pr., Inc.) Cengage Gale.

Boule, Mary Null. Navajo People: SW Region, Set. Liddell, Daniel & Basta, Mary, illus. (Native Americans of North America Ser.). 50-60p. (J). (gr. 3-6). pap. 7.95 *(978-1-877599-59-0(X))* Merryant Pubs.

Cunningham, Kevin & Benoit, Peter. The Navajo. 2011. (True Book(tm), a — American Indians Ser.). 48p. (J). (gr. 3-5). 31.00 *(978-0-531-20762-8(5))*; (ENG.). pap. 6.95 *(978-0-531-29304-1(1))* Scholastic Library Publishing. (Children's Pr.).

Knowles, Gerald M. The Navajo of North America. 2005. (First Peoples Ser.). (Illus.). 48p. (gr. 4-8). lib. bdg. 23.95 *(978-0-8225-0662-1(9))* Lerner Publishing Group.

McIntosh, Kenneth. Navajo. 2005. (North American Indians Today Ser.). (Illus.). 96p. (YA). lib. bdg. 22.95 *(978-1-59084-672-8(9))* Mason Crest.

McNamara, Margaret. Native Americans of the Southwest: The Navajo. 2006. (J). pap. *(978-1-4108-6438-3(3))* Benchmark Education Co.

Rossi, Ann. Native Americans of the Southwest: Set Of 6. 2011. (Navigators Ser.). (J). pap. 48.00 net. *(978-1-4108-6251-8(8))* Benchmark Education Co.

Smith-Llera, Danielle & Bowman, Donna Janell. The Navajo: The Past & Present of the Dine. 2015. (American Indian Life Ser.). (ENG., Illus.). 32p. (gr. 3-4). pap. 7.95 *(978-1-4914-5004-8(5))* Capstone Press of Coughlan Cos.

Tieck, Sarah. Navajo, 1 vol. 2014. (Native Americans Ser.). (ENG.). 32p. (gr. 7-11). 28.50 *(978-1-62403-355-1(5))* ABDO Publishing Co.

Yasuda, Anita. The Warrior Twins: A Navajo Hero Myth. Pennington, Mark, illus. 2012. (Short Tales Native American Myths Ser.). 32p. (J). (gr. 3-6). lib. bdg. 24.21 *(978-1-61641-884-7(2))* Magic Wagon.

Yazzie, Serphine G. Beauty Beside Me: Stories of My Grandmother's Skirts. 2011. (ENG & NAV., Illus.). 32p. (J). (gr. -1-3). 21.95 *(978-1-893354-07-4(5))* Salina Bookshelf Inc.

INDIANS OF NORTH AMERICA—NAVAJO INDIANS—FICTION

Browne, Vee. The Stone Cutter & the Navajo Maiden. Manavi, Lorraine Begay, tr. from ENG. Brycelea, Clifford & Yazzie, Johnson, illus. 2008. (NAV & ENG.). 32p. (J). (gr. -1-3). 17.95 *(978-1-893354-92-0(X))* Salina Bookshelf Inc.

Crowder, Jack L., et al. Stephanie & the Coyote. Morgan, William, tr. 3rd rev. ed. (ENG & NAV., Illus.). 32p. (J). (gr. 3-18). reprint ed. pap. 4.95 *(978-0-9616589-0-8(8))* Crowder, Jack L.

Flood, Nancy Bo. The Hogan That Great-Grandfather Built. Yazzie, Peterson, illus. 2012. (ENG & NAV.). 32p. (J). (gr. -1-3). 17.95 *(978-1-893354-97-5(0))* Salina Bookshelf Inc.

Grammer, Maurine. The Navajo Brothers & the Stolen Herd. Cleveland, Fred, illus. 2004. 120p. (gr. 4-7). pap. 9.95 *(978-1-878610-23-2(6))* Red Crane Bks., Inc.

Guest, Jacqueline. Fire Fight. 2015. (ENG.). 128p. (J). pap. *(978-1-939053-11-4(0))* Book Publishing Co.

Johnson, Jann A. Wisdom Weaver/Bina'nitin Bidziilgo Atl'ohl. Manavi, Lorraine Begay, tr. from ENG. Taylor, Linda, illus. 2006. (ENG.). 32p. (J). (gr. -1-3). 17.95 *(978-1-893354-82-1(2))* Salina Bookshelf Inc.

Kent, Renee Holmes. J. J. Navajo Princess, Vol. 3. 2004. (Adventures in Misty Falls Ser.: Vol. 3). (Illus.). 100p. (gr. 4-7). pap. 4.99 *(978-1-56309-763-8(X)*, N007105) New Hope Pubs.

Robinson, Gary. Danny Blackgoat, Rugged Road to Freedom. 2014. (ENG.). (YA). pap. 9.95 *(978-1-939053-05-3(6)*, 7th Generation) Book Publishing Co.

INDIANS OF NORTH AMERICA—NEZ PERCE INDIANS

Bodden, Valerie. Nez Perce. 2015. (Illus.). 48p. (J). *(978-1-60818-554-2(0)*, Creative Education) Creative Co., The.

King, David C. The Nez Perce. 2007. (First Americans Ser.). (Illus.). 48p. (gr. 3-7). lib. bdg. 31.36 *(978-0-7614-2680-6(9)*, Benchmark Bks.) Marshall Cavendish Corp.

Miller, Connie R. The Nez Perce. 2003. (Digging up Native American History Ser.). (J). pap. *(978-1-58417-110-2(3))*; lib. bdg. *(978-1-58417-047-1(6))* Lake Street Pubs.

Nelson, Ted W. & Nelson, Sharlene P. The Nez Perce. 2003. (Watts Library). (Illus.). 64p. (J). 25.50 *(978-0-531-12169-6(0)*, Watts, Franklin) Scholastic Library Publishing.

Schwartz, Heather E. Seeking Freedom: Causes & Effects of the Flight of the Nez Perce. 2015. (Cause & Effect: American Indian History Ser.). (ENG.). 32p. (gr. 3-4). lib. bdg. 27.32 *(978-1-4914-2034-8(0))* Capstone Press of Coughlan Cos.

Tieck, Sarah. Nez Perce, 1 vol. 2014. (Native Americans Set 2 Ser.). (ENG.). 32p. (gr. 2-5). 28.50 *(978-1-62403-582-1(5))* ABDO Publishing Co.

INDIANS OF NORTH AMERICA—OGLALA INDIANS

Brimner, Larry Dane. Chief Crazy Horse: Following a Vision. 2008. (American Heroes Ser.). 48p. (gr. 3-18). lib. bdg. 29.93 *(978-0-7614-3061-2(X)*, Benchmark Bks.) Marshall Cavendish Corp.

Cunningham, Chet. Chief Crazy Horse. 2005. (Biography Ser.). (Illus.). 112p. (gr. 6-12). lib. bdg. 27.93 *(978-0-8225-4978-9(6))* Lerner Publishing Group.

Nelson, S. D. Black Elk's Vision: A Lakota Story. 2015. (ENG., Illus.). 56p. (J). (gr. 3-7). pap. 9.99 *(978-1-4197-1528-0(3)*, Abrams Bks. for Young Readers) Abrams, Inc.

Sanford, William R. Oglala Lakota Chief Red Cloud. 2013. (Native American Chiefs & Warriors Ser.). 48p. (J). (gr. 5-9). pap. 8.95 *(978-1-4644-0259-3(0))* Enslow Pubs., Inc.

—Oglala Sioux Chief Crazy Horse. 2013. (Native American Chiefs & Warriors Ser.). 48p. (J). (gr. 5-9). pap. 8.95 *(978-1-4644-0261-6(2))* Enslow Pubs., Inc.

INDIANS OF NORTH AMERICA—OJIBWAY INDIANS—FICTION

Erdrich, Louise. Makoons. Erdrich, Louise, illus. 2016. (Birchbark House Ser.: 5). (Illus.). 176p. (J). (gr. 3-7). 16.99 *(978-0-06-057793-3(2))* HarperCollins Pubs.

Erdrich, Louise & Erdrich. The Game of Silence. 2006. (Birchbark House Ser.: 2). (ENG., Illus.). 288p. (J). (gr. 3-7). reprint ed. pap. 6.99 *(978-0-06-441029-8(3))* HarperCollins Pubs.

Pearsall, Shelley. Crooked River. 2007. (ENG.). 272p. (J). (gr. 3-7). 7.99 *(978-0-440-42101-6(2)*, Yearling) Random Hse. Children's Bks.

Wagner, Elaine J. & Wagner, Elaine. Meshom & the Little One. Hamelin, Marie-Micheline et al, illus. 2006. (Meshom & the Little One Ser.). (ENG.). 58p. pap. 12.95 *(978-1-894778-35-0(9))* Theytus Bks., Ltd. CAN. Dist: Univ. of Toronto Pr.

INDIANS OF NORTH AMERICA—ORIGIN

Mann, Charles C. Before Columbus: The Americas of 1491. 2009. (ENG., Illus.). 128p. (J). (gr. 3-7). 24.99 *(978-1-4169-4900-8(3)*, Atheneum Bks. for Young Readers) Simon & Schuster Children's Publishing.

McNeese, Tim. The Fascinating History of American Indians: The Age Before Columbus. 2008. (America's Living History Ser.). (Illus.). 128p. (J). (gr. 5-9). lib. bdg. 33.27 *(978-0-7660-2938-5(7))* Enslow Pubs., Inc.

INDIANS OF NORTH AMERICA—PAIUTE INDIANS

Green, Mary. Sarah Winnemucca: The Inspiring Life Story of the Activist & Educator. 2016. (Inspiring Stories Ser.). (ENG., Illus.). 112p. (gr. 5-7). lib. bdg. 35.99 *(978-0-7565-5167-4(6)*, CPB Grades 4-8) Compass Point Bks.

INDIANS OF NORTH AMERICA—PAIUTE INDIANS—FICTION

Jennings, Terry Catasús. Vivian & the Legend of the Hoodoos. Saroff, Phyllis, illus. 2017. (ENG & SPA.). 32p. (J). (gr. k-3). 17.95 *(978-1-62855-957-6(8))* Arbordale Publishing.

—Viviana y la Leyenda de Los Hoodoos. Saroff, Phyllis, illus. 2017. (SPA.). 32p. (J). (gr. k-3). pap. 9.95 *(978-1-62855-959-0(4))* Arbordale Publishing.

INDIANS OF NORTH AMERICA—PIEGAN INDIANS

Rickard, Kris A. & Bial, Raymond. The People & Culture of the Blackfeet. 2016. (First Peoples of North America Ser.). 128p. (J). 45.64 *(978-1-5026-2247-1(5))* Cavendish Square Publishing.

INDIANS OF NORTH AMERICA—POETRY

Clark, Ann Nolan. In My Mother's House. Herrera, Velino, illus. 2004. 56p. (J). (gr. k-3). reprint ed. pap. 14.00 *(978-0-7567-7104-1(8))* DIANE Publishing Co.

Clark, Ann Nolan & Harrington, John P. Little Herder in Winter: Haigo Na'nilkaadi Ya'zhi Denetsosie, Hoke, illus. 2011. 116p. 39.95 *(978-1-258-03041-4(1))* Literary Licensing, LLC.

Harjo, Joy. For a Girl Becoming. McDonald, Mercedes, illus. 2009. (Sun Tracks Ser.: 66). (ENG.). 36p. (gr. -1). 17.95 *(978-0-8165-2797-7(0))* University of Arizona Pr.

Longfellow, Henry Wadsworth & Remington, Frederic. The Song of Hiawatha. 2004. (Nonpareil Book Ser.). (ENG., Illus.). 304p. pap. 14.95 *(978-1-56792-258-5(9))*; 23.95 *(978-1-56792-273-8(2))* Godine, David R. Pub.

Lopez, Cheyene Montana. Celebration America, 1 vol. 2009. 240p. pap. 24.95 *(978-1-61546-715-0(7))* PublishAmerica, Inc.

McCauley, Marlene. Song of Kateri: Princess of the Eucharist. McCauley, R. Allan, ed. McCauley, Marlene & Children's Art-Friends of Kateri, illus. unabr. ed. 2005. 300p. (YA). (gr. 4-7). per. 14.95 *(978-0-9633633-2-9(8))* Grace Hse. Publishing.

National Museum of the American Indian (U.S.) Staff, contrib. by. When the Rain Sings: Poems by Young Native Americans. 2008. (J). *(978-1-933565-11-8(X))* Smithsonian National Museum of the American Indian.

Robinson, Gary. Native American Twelve Days of Christmas. Hummingbird, Jesse T., illus. 2011. (ENG.). 32p. (J). 19.95 *(978-1-57416-105-2(9))* Clear Light Pubs.

Shore, Diane Z. This Is the Feast. Lloyd, Megan, illus. 2008. (ENG.). 32p. (J). (gr. -1-3). 16.99 *(978-0-06-623794-7(7))* HarperCollins Pubs.

Walking Bull, Gilbert & Moore, Sally. Rocks Not Happy in Sack. 2008. (ENG., Illus.). 40p. (J). pap. *(978-1-57579-375-7(X))* Pine Hill Pr.

Weston Woods Staff, creator. Hiawatha. 2011. 18.95 *(978-0-439-72712-9(X))* Weston Woods Studios, Inc.

—Hiawatha Weston Woods. 2011. 38.75 *(978-0-439-72714-3(6))* Weston Woods Studios, Inc.

INDIANS OF NORTH AMERICA—PUEBLO INDIANS

Cunningham, Kevin & Benoit, Peter. The Pueblo. 2011. (True Bk Ser.). 48p. (J). (ENG.). pap. 6.95 *(978-0-531-29305-8(X))*; (gr. 3-5). 29.00 *(978-0-531-20763-5(3))* Scholastic Library Publishing. (Children's Pr.).

Folsom, Franklin. Red Power on the Rio Grande. 2003. (YA). pap. 13.95 *(978-0-89992-156-3(6))* Council for Indian Education.

Kalman, Bobbie & Bishop, Amanda. Life in a Pueblo. 2003. (Native Nations of North America Ser.). (ENG., Illus.). 32p. (J). (gr. 3-9). pap. *(978-0-7787-0467-6(X))*; (gr. 5-9). lib. bdg. *(978-0-7787-0375-4(4))* Crabtree Publishing Co.

Levy, Janey. Native American Art from the Pueblos. (Reading Room Collection 2 Ser.). 24p. 2009. (gr. 3-4). 42.50 *(978-1-60851-981-1(3)*, PowerKids Pr.) 2003. (Illus.). (J). lib. bdg. 22.60 *(978-0-8239-3702-8(X))* Rosen Publishing Group, Inc., The.

McIntosh, Kenneth. Pueblo. 2005. (North American Indians Today Ser.). (Illus.). 96p. (YA). lib. bdg. 22.95 *(978-1-59084-676-6(1))* Mason Crest.

McLeese, Tex. Lucha con Novillos. Palacios, Argentina, tr.Tr. of Steer Wrestling. (SPA., Illus.). 24p. (J). (gr. 1-3). lib. bdg. 19.27 *(978-1-57103-385-7(8))* Rourke Educational Media.

INDIANS OF NORTH AMERICA—PUEBLO INDIANS—ANTIQUITIES

Anderson, Dale. The Anasazi Culture at Mesa Verde. 2003. (Landmark Events in American History Ser.). (Illus.). 48p. (gr. 5-12). lib. bdg. 31.00 *(978-0-8368-5371-1(7)*, Gareth Stevens Secondary Library) Stevens, Gareth Publishing LLLP.

Blake, Kevin & Yates, Martha. Cliff Dwellings: Empty Windows. 2015. (Abandoned: Towns Without People Ser.). (ENG.). 32p. (J). (gr. 2-7). lib. bdg. 26.60 *(978-1-62724-522-7(7))* Bearport Publishing Co., Inc.

Buchanan, Ken & National Geographic Learning Staff. This House Is Made of Mud (Esta Casa Esta Hecha de Lodo) Tracy, Libba, illus. 2010. (Rise & Shine Ser.). (ENG, SPA & MUL.). 32p. (C). (gr. -1-1). pap. 13.95 *(978-0-87358-580-4(1)*, NP801) National Geographic School Publishing, Inc.

Cipriano, Jeri. Three Historical Communities of North America: Text Pairs. 2008. (Bridges/Navigators Ser.). (J). (gr. 3). 89.00 *(978-1-4108-8375-9(2))* Benchmark Education Co.

INDIANS OF NORTH AMERICA—PUEBLO INDIANS—FICTION

Bronson, Wilfrid S. Pinto's Journey. 2007. (ENG.). 64p. (J). per. 14.95 *(978-0-86534-557-7(0))* Sunstone Pr.

Indian Trail. 2007. (Choose Your Own Adventure - Dragonlarks Ser.). (Illus.). 64p. (J). (gr. 4-7). pap. 7.99 *(978-1-933390-53-6(0))* Chooseco LLC.

INDIANS OF NORTH AMERICA—QUILEUTE INDIANS

Harrison, Lorraine. Ute, 01 vols., 1. 2016. (Spotlight on Native Americans Ser.). (ENG., Illus.). 32p. (J). pap. 11.75 *(978-1-5081-4129-7(0)*, PowerKids Pr.) Rosen Publishing Group, Inc., The.

INDIANS OF NORTH AMERICA—RECREATIONS

see Indians of North America—Games

INDIANS OF NORTH AMERICA—RELIGION

see also Totems and Totemism

Collinson, Clare. Arts, Society, & Religion. 2010. (CC: Native North Americans Ser.). (Illus.). 112p. (gr. 6-12). 42.80 *(978-1-933834-79-5(X))* Brown Bear Bks.

Crabtree Staff & Kopp, Megan. Understanding Native American Myths. 2012. (ENG., Illus.). 48p. (J). pap. *(978-0-7787-4531-0(7))* Crabtree Publishing Co.

Dalal, Anita. Native American Myths. 2010. (Myths from Around the World Ser.). 48p. (gr. 6-8). (YA). lib. bdg. 31.00 *(978-1-4339-3530-5(9))*; (Illus.). (J). pap. 14.05 *(978-1-4339-3531-2(7))* Stevens, Gareth Publishing LLLP. (Gareth Stevens Secondary Library).

Kopp, Megan. Understanding Native American Myths. 2012. (ENG.). 48p. (J). *(978-0-7787-4526-6(0))* Crabtree Publishing Co.

Nagle, Jeanne, ed. Native American Spirit Beings. 2014. (Gods & Goddesses of Mythology Ser.). 160p. (YA). (gr. 9-12). 32.90 *(978-1-62275-399-4(2))* Rosen Publishing Group, Inc., The.

O'Brien, Cynthia. Myths & Legends of North America: Canada & the Northern United States. 2015. (Illus.). 64p. (J). *(978-0-7166-2626-8(8))* World Bk., Inc.

Peacock, Thomas Love & Wisuri, Marlene. The Good Path: Ojibwe Learning & Activity Book for Kids. 2009. (ENG., Illus.). 128p. (J). (gr. 5-8). pap. 19.95 *(978-0-87351-763-6(0))* Minnesota Historical Society Pr.

Sonneborn, Liz. The Chumash. (Native American Histories Ser.). (ENG., Illus.). 56p. (gr. 3-6). 2007. pap. 8.95 *(978-0-8225-6698-4(2))* 2006. lib. bdg. 27.93 *(978-0-8225-5912-2(9)*, Lerner Pubns.) Lerner Publishing Group.

Weaver, Lisa & Weaver, J. Denny. Living the Anabaptist Story: A Guide to Early Beginnings with Questions for Today. 2015. (ENG., Illus.). 112p. (J). (gr. 7-12). pap. 19.95 *(978-1-68027-004-4(4))* Cascadia Publishing Hse., LLC.

White, Bender Richardson, et al. Native American Religions. 3rd rev. ed. 2009. (World Religions Ser.). (Illus.). 144p. (gr. 6-12). 40.00 *(978-1-60413-111-6(X)*, Chelsea Hse.) Facts On File, Inc.

Zimmerman, Larry J. Exploring the Life, Myth, & Art of Native Americans. 2009. (Civilizations of the World Ser.). (YA). (gr. 7-12). lib. bdg. 42.60 *(978-1-4358-5614-1(7))* Rosen Publishing Group, Inc., The.

INDIANS OF NORTH AMERICA—SALISH INDIANS—FICTION

Silvey, Diane. Spirit Quest. 2009. (ENG., Illus.). 64p. (J). (gr. 6). pap. 11.99 *(978-1-55002-831-7(6)*, Sandcastle Bks.) Dundurn CAN. Dist: Ingram Publisher Services.

INDIANS OF NORTH AMERICA—SAUK INDIANS

Poulakidas, Georgene. Black Hawk's War. 2006. (Primary Sources of American Wars Ser.). (Illus.). 24p. (YA). (gr. 4-7). lib. bdg. 22.60 *(978-1-4042-2682-1(6))* Rosen Publishing Group, Inc., The.

INDIANS OF NORTH AMERICA—SCHOOLS

see Indians of North America—Education

INDIANS OF NORTH AMERICA—SEMINOLE INDIANS

Conklin, Wendy. The Seminoles of Florida: Culture, Customs, & Conflict. 2016. (Primary Source Readers Ser.). 32p. (gr. 4-4). pap. 8.99 *(978-1-4938-3535-5(1))* Teacher Created Materials, Inc.

Sanford, William R. Seminole Chief Osceola. 2013. (Native American Chiefs & Warriors Ser.). 48p. (J). (gr. 5-18). lib. bdg. 22.60 *(978-0-7660-4117-2(4))*; pap. 8.95 *(978-1-4644-0263-0(9))* Enslow Pubs., Inc.

Tieck, Sarah. Seminole, 1 vol. 2014. (Native Americans Ser.). (ENG.). 32p. (gr. 7-11). 28.50 *(978-1-62403-356-8(3))* ABDO Publishing Co.

INDIANS OF NORTH AMERICA—SEMINOLE INDIANS—FICTION

Yasuda, Anita. Stolen Fire: A Seminole Trickster Myth. Estudio Haus, illus. 2012. (Short Tales Native American Myths Ser.). 32p. (J). (gr. 3-6). lib. bdg. 24.21 *(978-1-61641-883-0(4))* Magic Wagon.

INDIANS OF NORTH AMERICA—SENECA INDIANS

Aller, Susan Bivin. Living with the Senecas: A Story about Mary Jemison. Harden, Laurie, illus. 2007. (Creative Minds

Biographies Ser.). 64p. (J). (gr. 3-7). lib. bdg. 22.60 *(978-0-8225-5989-4(7))* Lerner Publishing Group.

INDIANS OF NORTH AMERICA—SENECA INDIANS—FICTION

Bruchac, Joseph. Walking Two Worlds. 2015. (ENG.). 152p. (YA). pap. *(978-1-939053-10-7(2))* Book Publishing Co.

INDIANS OF NORTH AMERICA—SHAWNEE INDIANS

De Capua, Sarah. The Shawnee. 2007. (First Americans Ser.). (Illus.). 48p. (gr. 3). lib. bdg. 31.36 *(978-0-7614-2682-0(5),* Benchmark Bks.) Marshall Cavendish Corp.

Jones, Kadeem. Shawnee, 01 vols., 1. 2016. (Spotlight on Native Americans Ser.). (ENG., Illus.). 32p. (J). pap. 11.75 *(978-1-5081-4124-2(X),* PowerKids Pr.) Rosen Publishing Group, Inc., The.

Tieck, Sarah. Shawnee, 1 vol. 2014. (Native Americans Set 2 Ser.). (ENG.). 32p. (gr. 2-5). 28.50 *(978-1-62403-583-8(3))* ABDO Publishing Co.

INDIANS OF NORTH AMERICA—SHAWNEE INDIANS—BIOGRAPHY

Aller, Susan Bivin. Tecumseh. 2004. (History Maker Bios Ser.). (J). pap. 6.95 *(978-0-8225-2073-3(7));* (ENG., Illus.). 48p. (gr. 3-6). 27.93 *(978-0-8225-0699-7(8),* Carolrhoda Bks.) Lerner Publishing Group.

Gordon, Irene Ternier. Tecumseh: Diplomat & Warrior in the War of 1812. 2009. (Amazing Stories Ser.). (ENG., Illus.). 128p. (J). (gr. 6-12). pap. 9.95 *(978-1-55277-430-4(9),* 9781552774304) Lorimer, James & Co., Ltd., Pubs. CAN. Dist: Casemate Pubs. & Bk. Distributors, LLC.

Laplante, Walter. Tecumseh. 2015. (Native American Heroes Ser.). (ENG., Illus.). 24p. (J). (gr. 1-2). 22.60 *(978-1-4824-2706-6(0))* Stevens, Gareth Publishing LLLP.

INDIANS OF NORTH AMERICA—SHAWNEE INDIANS—FICTION

Bruchac, Joseph. The Dark Pond. Comport, Sally Wern, illus. 2005. 142p. (gr. 5-9). 17.00 *(978-0-7569-5436-9(3))* Perfection Learning Corp.

—Dark Pond. Comport, Sally Wern, illus. 2005. (ENG.). 160p. (J). (gr. 5-18). pap. 6.99 *(978-0-06-052998-7(9))* HarperCollins Pubs.

INDIANS OF NORTH AMERICA—SIGN LANGUAGE

see Indian Sign Language

INDIANS OF NORTH AMERICA—SIKSIKA INDIANS

Rebus, Anna & Kissock, Heather. Blackfoot. 2010. (Illus.). 24p. *(978-1-55388-648-8(8));* pap. *(978-1-55388-654-9(2))* Weigl Educational Pubs. Ltd.

Tieck, Sarah. Blackfoot, 1 vol. 2014. (Native Americans Set 2 Ser.). (ENG.). 32p. (gr. 2-5). 28.50 *(978-1-62403-577-7(9))* ABDO Publishing Co.

INDIANS OF NORTH AMERICA—SIOUX INDIANS

Kops, Deborah. Native Americans of the Plains: Set Of 6. 2011. (Navigators Ser.). (J). pap. 48.00 net. *(978-1-4108-6250-1(X))* Benchmark Education Co.

Lawton, Cassie M. & Bial, Raymond. The People & Culture of the Sioux. 2016. (First Peoples of North America Ser.). (Illus.). 128p. (J). (gr. 6-6). 45.64 *(978-1-5026-1894-8(X))* Cavendish Square Publishing.

McNamara, Margaret. Native Americans of the Plains: The Lakota. 2006. (J). pap. *(978-1-4108-6439-0(1))* Benchmark Education Co.

Miller, Connie R. The Lakota. 2003. (Digging up Native American History Ser.). (J). lib. bdg. *(978-1-58417-046-4(8))* Lake Street Pubs.

INDIANS OF NORTH AMERICA—SIOUX INDIANS—FICTION

Altsheler, Joseph A. The Great Sioux Trail: A Story of Mountain & Plain. (Great West Ser.: Vol. 1). (J). reprint ed. 25.95 *(978-0-89190-825-8(0))* Amereon Ltd.

—The Great Sioux Trail: A Story of Mountain & Plain. 2008. 360p. 29.99 *(978-0-554-43254-0(4))* 2008. 360p. 31.99 *(978-0-554-43244-1(7))* 2010. (Great West Ser.: Vol. 1). 366p. (J). (gr. 4-7). reprint ed. pap. 32.75 *(978-1-177-69490-2(5))* 2008. 360p. reprint ed. pap. 31.75 *(978-0-554-43253-3(6))* 2008. (Great West Ser.: Vol. 1). 360p. (J). reprint ed. pap. 32.75 *(978-0-554-43247-2(1))* Creative Media Partners, LLC.

—The Great Sioux Trail: A Story of Mountain & Plain. Wrenn, Charles L., illus. 2009. 258p. (YA). pap. *(978-1-4099-7085-9(X))* Dodo Pr.

—The Great Sioux Trail: A Story of Mountain & Plain. 2009. 176p. (J). reprint ed. pap. *(978-1-4068-9445-5(1))* Echo Library.

—The Great Sioux Trail: A Story of Mountain & Plain. reprint ed. 2010. 160p. pap. 19.99 *(978-1-153-81003-6(4))* 2009. (Great West Ser.: Vol. 1). 182p. (J). pap. 26.81 *(978-1-150-71981-3(8))* General Bks. LLC.

—The Great Sioux Trail: A Story of Mountain & Plain. 2012. (Great West Ser.: Vol. 1). 370p. (J). (gr. 4-7). reprint ed. pap. *(978-1-290-67583-3(X))* HardPr.

—The Great Sioux Trail: A Story of Mountain & Plain. (Great West Ser.: Vol. 1). (J). reprint ed. 2011. (gr. 4-7). *(978-1-164-37592-0(X))* 2010. 362p. (gr. 4-7). pap. 25.56 *(978-1-164-19051-6(2))* 2008. 360p. 46.95 *(978-1-4366-5490-6(4))* 2008. 360p. pap. 31.95 *(978-0-548-90653-8(X))* Kessinger Publishing, LLC.

—The Great Sioux Trail: A Story of Mountain & Plain. 2012. (Great West Ser.: Vol. 1). 258p. (J). pap. *(978-3-8472-2260-6(0))* Tredition GmbH.

—The Lost Hunters: A Story of Wild Man & Great Beasts. (Great West Ser.: Vol. 2). 311p. (J). reprint ed. lib. bdg. 27.95 *(978-0-88411-949-4(1))* Amereon Ltd.

Nichele, Neika. Tayance, a Young Sioux Indian. Bright, Phyllis, illus. 2008. 47p. pap. 24.95 *(978-1-60703-606-7(1))* America Star Bks.

INDIANS OF NORTH AMERICA—SOCIAL CONDITIONS

Bruchac, Joseph. Buffalo Song. Farnsworth, Bill, illus. 2008. (J). Lee & Low Bks., Inc.

Fond du Lac Head Start. The Story of Manoomin. 2012. (ENG & OJI.). (J). bds. 7.95 *(978-0-615-69899-1(9))* Fond du Lac Head Start.

Halvorson, Alesha & Smith-Llera, Danielle. American Indian Life. 2016. (American Indian Life Ser.). (ENG.). 32p. (gr. 3-4). pap. 31.80 *(978-1-5157-0264-1(2),* Fact Finders) Capstone Press of Coughlan Cos.

Keoke, Emory Dean. American Indian Contributions to the World, 5 Vols., Set. 2005. (American Indian Contributions to the World Ser.). 160p. (gr. 5-8). 140.00 *(978-0-8160-5392-6(8))* Facts On File, Inc.

Keoke, Emory Dean & Porterfield, Kay Marie. American Indian Contributions to the World. 2005. (American Indian Contributions to the World Ser.). (Illus.). 160p. (gr. 5-8). 35.00 *(978-0-8160-5395-7(2));* 35.00 *(978-0-8160-5397-1(9))* Facts On File, Inc.

Ramsey, Torren. Ojibwe. 2015. (Spotlight on Native Americans Ser.). (ENG., Illus.). 32p. (J). (gr. 4-6). 26.25 *(978-1-4994-1703-6(9),* PowerKids Pr.) Rosen Publishing Group, Inc., The.

Sanna, Ellyn. Native North American Indians. 2012. (Gallup Guides for Youth Facing Persistent Prejudice Ser.). 64p. (J). (gr. 7-8). 22.95 *(978-1-4222-2469-4(4));* pap. 9.95 *(978-1-4222-2478-6(3))* Mason Crest.

Seba, Jaime. Gallup Guides for Youth Facing Persistent Prejudice. 2012. (J). *(978-1-4222-2462-5(7))* Mason Crest.

—Gallup Guides for Youth Facing Persistent Prejudice - The LGBT Community. 2012. (Gallup Guides for Youth Facing Persistent Prejudice Ser.). 64p. (J). (gr. 7-8). 22.95 *(978-1-4222-2467-0(8))* Mason Crest.

Seba, Jaime & Sanna, Ellyn. Gallup Guides for Youth Facing Persistent Prejudice. 2012. (Gallup Guides for Youth Facing Persistent Prejudice Ser.). 64p. (J). (gr. 7-8). 22.95 *(978-1-4222-2465-6(1))* Mason Crest.

Sioux, Tracee. Native American Migration. 2004. (Primary Sources of Immigration & Migration in America Ser.). (Illus.). 24p. (ENG.). (gr. 4-8). pap. 9.40 *(978-0-8239-8951-5(8));* (J). lib. bdg. 22.60 *(978-0-8239-6825-1(1))* Rosen Publishing Group, Inc., The. (PowerKids Pr.).

Smith-Llera, Danielle & Halvorson, Alesha. American Indian Life. 2016. (American Indian Life Ser.). (ENG.). 32p. (gr. 3-4). 218.56 *(978-1-5157-0259-7(6),* Fact Finders) Capstone Press of Coughlan Cos.

INDIANS OF NORTH AMERICA—SOCIAL LIFE AND CUSTOMS

see also Indians of North America—Games

Ajmera, Maya & Hirschfelder, Arlene. Children of Native America Today. 2014. (ENG.). 64p. (J). (gr. 3-7). pap. 9.95 *(978-1-57091-965-7(8))* Charlesbridge Publishing, Inc.

Aloian, Molly & Kalman, Bobbie. Life of the California Coast Nations. 2004. (Native Nations of North America Ser.). (ENG., Illus.). 32p. (J). pap. *(978-0-7787-0474-4(2));* lib. bdg. *(978-0-7787-0382-2(7))* Crabtree Publishing Co.

American Indian Art & Culture. 2005. (American Indian Art & Culture Ser.). (Illus.). 32p. (gr. 4-6). 153.00 *(978-0-7910-7959-1(7),* Chelsea Hse.) Facts On File, Inc.

Bailey, Diane. Our Teenage Life in the Navajo Nation. 2017. (Illus.). 128p. (J). ***(978-1-4222-3908-7(X))*** Mason Crest.

Barnes, Wiley. C is for Chickasaw. 2014. (Illus.). 40p. (J). 19.95 *(978-1-935684-19-0(1))* White Dog Pr., Ltd.

Bedry, Christa. The Pueblo. (J). 2014. *(978-1-4896-2922-7(X))* 2003. (Illus.). 32p. pap. 9.95 *(978-1-59036-179-5(2))* Weigl Pubs., Inc.

Behnke, Alison. The Apaches. 2006. (Native American Histories Ser.). (Illus.). 56p. (J). (gr. 4-7). lib. bdg. 27.93 *(978-0-8225-5915-3(3),* Lerner Pubns.) Lerner Publishing Group.

Belarde-Lewis, Miranda. Meet Lydia: A Native Girl from Southeast Alaska. Harrington, John, photos by. 2004. (My World: Young Native Americans Today Ser.). (ENG., Illus.). 48p. (J). 15.95 *(978-1-57178-147-5(1))* Council Oak Bks.

Benjamin, Lisa. People of the Wetlands. 2005. (Voices Reading Ser.). (Illus.). 32p. (J). *(978-0-7367-2947-5(X))* Zaner-Bloser, Inc.

Bial, Raymond. The People & Culture of the Apache. 2016. (First Peoples of North America Ser.). (ENG., Illus.). 128p. (J). (gr. 6-6). 45.70 *(978-1-5026-1010-2(8))* Cavendish Square Publishing.

—The People & Culture of the Cree. 2016. (First Peoples of North America Ser.). (ENG., Illus.). 128p. (J). (gr. 6-6). 45.70 *(978-1-5026-0998-4(3))* Cavendish Square Publishing.

—The People & Culture of the Crow. 2016. (First Peoples of North America Ser.). (ENG., Illus.). 128p. (J). (gr. 6-6). 45.70 *(978-1-5026-1000-3(0))* Cavendish Square Publishing.

—The People & Culture of the Delaware. 2016. (First Peoples of North America Ser.). (ENG., Illus.). 128p. (J). (gr. 6-6). 45.70 *(978-1-5026-1004-1(3))* Cavendish Square Publishing.

—The People & Culture of the Huron. 2016. (First Peoples of North America Ser.). (ENG., Illus.). 128p. (J). (gr. 6-6). 45.70 *(978-1-5026-1008-9(6))* Cavendish Square Publishing.

—The People & Culture of the Menominee. 2016. (First Peoples of North America Ser.). (ENG., Illus.). 128p. (J). (gr. 6-6). 45.70 *(978-1-5026-1002-7(7))* Cavendish Square Publishing.

Birchfield, D. L. Cherokee History & Culture. 2011. (Native American Library). 48p. (J). (gr. 3-6). pap. 14.05 *(978-1-4339-5960-8(7));* lib. bdg. 31.95 *(978-1-4339-5958-5(5))* Stevens, Gareth Publishing LLLP. (Gareth Stevens Learning Library).

Bishop, Amanda & Kalman, Bobbie. Life of the Navajo. 2003. (Native Nations of North America Ser.). (ENG., Illus.). 32p. (J). (gr. 5). lib. bdg. *(978-0-7787-0376-1(2))* Crabtree Publishing Co.

Bjorklund, Ruth. The Hopi. 2008. (First Americans Ser.). 48p. (gr. 3-7). lib. bdg. 31.36 *(978-0-7614-3021-6(0),* Benchmark Bks.) Marshall Cavendish Corp.

Bodden, Valerie. Nez Perce. 2015. (Illus.). 48p. (J). *(978-1-60818-554-2(0),* Creative Education) Creative Co., The.

—Sioux. 2015. (Illus.). 48p. (J). *(978-1-60818-555-9(9),* Creative Education) Creative Co., The.

Bonvillain, Nancy. The Nez Perce. 2010. (History & Culture of Native Americans Ser.). 144p. (gr. 6-12). 35.00 *(978-1-60413-791-0(6),* Chelsea Hse.) Facts On File, Inc.

Boule, Mary Null. California Native American Tribes: Mohave Tribe, 28 booklets. Liddell, Daniel & Basta, Mary, illus. (California Native American Tribes). 52p. (J). (gr. 3-6). pap. 7.95 *(978-1-877599-73-6(5))* Merryant Pubs.

Bowman, Donna Janell. American Indian Life. 2015. (American Indian Life Ser.). (ENG.). 32p. (gr. 3-4). pap. 31.80 *(978-1-4914-7299-6(5),* Fact Finders) Capstone Press of Coughlan Cos.

Boyden, Linda. Powwow's Coming. 2007. (ENG., Illus.). 32p. (J). (gr. -1-3). 19.95 *(978-0-8263-4265-2(5))* Univ. of New Mexico Pr.

Brown, Chris, illus. Chief Hawah's Book of Native American Indians. 2006. (ENG.). 32p. (J). (gr. -1-3). 14.99 *(978-0-7145-3308-7(4))* Boyars, Marion Pubs., Inc.

Buellis, Linda. Pueblo, 01 vols., 1. 2016. (Spotlight on Native Americans Ser.). (ENG., Illus.). 32p. (J). pap. 11.75 *(978-1-5081-4120-4(7),* PowerKids Pr.) Rosen Publishing Group, Inc., The.

Burgan, Michael. The Arapaho. 2008. (First Americans Ser.). 48p. (gr. 3-7). lib. bdg. 31.36 *(978-0-7614-3017-9(2),* Benchmark Bks.) Marshall Cavendish Corp.

—Inuit. 2004. (Native American Peoples Ser.). (Illus.). 32p. (gr. 3-7). lib. bdg. 26.00 *(978-0-8368-4219-7(7),* Gareth Stevens Learning Library) Stevens, Gareth Publishing LLLP.

—The Lakota. 2008. (First Americans Ser.). 48p. (gr. 3-7). lib. bdg. 31.36 *(978-0-7614-3023-0(7),* Benchmark Bks.) Marshall Cavendish Corp.

Caswell, Max. My Life in a Chinook Village. 2017. (My Place in History Ser.). 24p. (J). (gr. 2-3). pap. 8.15 ***(978-1-5382-0301-9(4))*** Stevens, Gareth Publishing LLLP.

Cloud Tapper, Suzanne & Tapper, Suzanne Cloud. The Cherokee: A Proud People. 2005. (American Indians Ser.). (Illus.). 48p. (J). (gr. 4-7). lib. bdg. 25.27 *(978-0-7660-2454-0(7),* Enslow Elementary) Enslow Pubs., Inc.

Collinson, Clare. Arts, Society, & Religion. 2010. (CC: Native North Americans Ser.). (Illus.). 112p. (gr. 6-12). 42.80 *(978-1-933834-79-5(X))* Brown Bear Bks.

—Peoples of the East, Southeast, & Plains. 2010. (CC: Native North Americans Ser.). 112p. (gr. 6-12). 42.80 *(978-1-933834-77-1(3))* Brown Bear Bks.

Conklin, Wendy. The Seminoles of Florida: Culture, Customs, & Conflict. 2016. (Primary Source Readers Ser.). 32p. (gr. 4-4). pap. 8.99 *(978-1-4938-3535-5(1))* Teacher Created Materials, Inc.

Cornell, George & Henry, Gordon. Ojibwa. 2005. (North American Indians Today Ser.). (Illus.). 96p. (YA). lib. bdg. 22.95 *(978-1-59084-673-5(7))* Mason Crest.

Craats, Rennay. The Cherokee. (J). 2014. *(978-1-4896-2906-7(8))* 2003. (Illus.). 32p. pap. 9.95 *(978-1-59036-180-1(6))* Weigl Pubs., Inc.

—The Navajo. (J). 2014. *(978-1-4896-2914-2(9))* 2003. (Illus.). 32p. pap. 9.95 *(978-1-59036-182-5(2))* Weigl Pubs., Inc.

Dalton, Anne. The Lenape of Pennsylvania, New Jersey, New York, Delaware, Wisconsin, Oklahoma, & Ontario. 2009. (Library of Native Americans Ser.). 64p. (gr. 4-4). 58.50 *(978-1-60853-749-5(8),* PowerKids Pr.) Rosen Publishing Group, Inc., The.

De Capua, Sarah. The Cheyenne. 2006. (First Americans Ser.). (Illus.). 47p. (J). (gr. 3-7). lib. bdg. 31.36 *(978-0-7614-2248-8(X),* Benchmark Bks.) Marshall Cavendish Corp.

—The Choctaw. 2008. (First Americans Ser.). 48p. (gr. 3-7). lib. bdg. 31.36 *(978-0-7614-3018-6(0),* Benchmark Bks.) Marshall Cavendish Corp.

—The Comanche. 2006. (First Americans Ser.). (Illus.). 48p. (gr. 3-7). lib. bdg. 31.36 *(978-0-7614-2249-5(8),* Benchmark Bks.) Marshall Cavendish Corp.

—The Menominee. 2009. (First Americans 5 Ser.). 48p. (gr. 3). 31.36 *(978-0-7614-4131-1(X))* Marshall Cavendish Corp.

Ditchfield, Christin. The Crow. 2006. (True Bks.). (ENG., Illus.). 48p. (J). (gr. 3-7). per. 6.95 *(978-0-516-25591-0(6),* Children's Pr.) Scholastic Library Publishing.

Dwyer, Chelly. Blackfoot. 2015. (Spotlight on Native Americans Ser.). (ENG., Illus.). 32p. (J). (gr. 4-6). 26.25 *(978-1-4994-1688-6(1),* PowerKids Pr.) Rosen Publishing Group, Inc., The.

Dwyer, Helen. Peoples of the Southwest, West, & North. 2010. (CC: Native North Americans Ser.). 112p. (gr. 6-12). 42.80 *(978-1-933834-78-8(1))* Brown Bear Bks.

Dwyer, Helen & Birchfield, D. L. Ojibwe History & Culture. 2012. (Native American Library). (Illus.). 48p. (gr. 3-6). pap. 14.05 *(978-1-4339-7422-9(3));* lib. bdg. 31.95 *(978-1-4339-7421-2(5))* Stevens, Gareth Publishing LLLP.

Dwyer, Helen & Stone, Amy M. Creek History & Culture. 2011. (Native American Library). (Illus.). 48p. (J). (gr. 3-6). 31.95 *(978-1-4339-5962-2(3));* pap. 14.05 *(978-1-4339-5964-6(X))* Stevens, Gareth Publishing LLLP. (Gareth Stevens Learning Library).

—Oneida History & Culture. 2012. (Native American Library). (Illus.). 48p. (gr. 3-6). pap. 14.05 *(978-1-4339-7426-7(6));* lib. bdg. 31.95 *(978-1-4339-7425-0(8))* Stevens, Gareth Publishing LLLP.

Dwyer, Helen & Stout, Mary. Cree History & Culture. 2012. (Native American Library). (Illus.). 48p. (J). (gr. 3-6). pap. 14.05 *(978-1-4339-7418-2(5));* lib. bdg. 31.95 *(978-1-4339-7417-5(7))* Stevens, Gareth Publishing LLLP.

Dwyer, Helen & Stout, Mary A. Hopi History & Culture. 2011. (Native American Library). (Illus.). 48p. (J). (gr. 3-6). 31.95 *(978-1-4339-5966-0(6));* pap. 14.05 *(978-1-4339-5968-4(2))* Stevens, Gareth Publishing LLLP. (Gareth Stevens Learning Library).

Eastman, Charles Alexander. Indian Boyhood: The True Story of a Sioux Upbringing. Fitzgerald, Michael Oren, ed. Rasch, Heidi M., illus. 2016. (ENG.). 40p. (J). (gr. k-3). 17.95 *(978-1-937786-56-4(0),* Wisdom Tales) World Wisdom, Inc.

Edwards, Erika, et al. The People & Culture of the Tlingit. 2016. (First Peoples of North America Ser.). 128p. (J). 45.64 *(978-1-5026-2251-8(3))* Cavendish Square Publishing.

First Americans, 6 bks., Set. Incl. Arapaho. Burgan, Michael. lib. bdg. 31.36 *(978-0-7614-3017-9(2));* Choctaw. De Capua, Sarah. lib. bdg. 31.36 *(978-0-7614-3018-6(0));* Cree. Bjorklund, Ruth. lib. bdg. 31.36 *(978-0-7614-3020-9(2));* Hopi. Bjorklund, Ruth. lib. bdg. 31.36 *(978-0-7614-3021-6(0));* Lakota. Burgan, Michael. lib. bdg. 31.36 *(978-0-7614-3023-0(7));* 48p. (gr. 3-7). (First Americans 4 Ser.). 2008. Set lib. bdg. 188.16 *(978-0-7614-3016-2(4),* Benchmark Bks.) Marshall Cavendish Corp.

Fitzgerald, Michael Oren, ed. Children of the Tipi: Life in the Buffalo Days. 2013. (ENG., Illus.). 40p. (J). (gr. -1-3). 15.95 *(978-1-937786-09-0(9),* Wisdom Tales) World Wisdom, Inc.

Flanagan, Alice K. The Pueblos. 2006. (True Bks). (Illus.). 48p. (gr. 2-4). 16.95 *(978-0-7569-7158-8(6))* Perfection Learning Corp.

—The Shawnee. 2006. (True Bks). (Illus.). 47p. (gr. 2-4). 16.95 *(978-0-7569-7160-1(8))* Perfection Learning Corp.

Flood, Nancy Bo. The Navajo Year, Walk Through Many Seasons. Whitethorne, Billy, illus. 2006. (ENG.). 32p. (J). (gr. 4-7). 17.95 *(978-1-893354-06-7(7))* Salina Bookshelf Inc.

—The Navajo Year, Walk Through Many Seasons: Activities for Learning & Exploring. Ruffenach, Jessie E., ed. Whitethorne, Billy & Whitethorne, Bahe, Jr., illus. 2006. (ENG.). 48p. (J). (gr. 4-7). pap. 7.95 *(978-1-893354-98-2(9))* Salina Bookshelf Inc.

Flynn, Riley. American Indian Homes. 2015. (American Indian Homes Ser.). (ENG.). 24p. (gr. 1-2). lib. bdg. 50.64 *(978-1-4914-2498-8(2),* First Facts) Capstone Press of Coughlan Cos.

Foran, Jill. Native-American Life. 2003. (Real Life Stories Ser.). (Illus.). 24p. (J). lib. bdg. 24.45 *(978-1-59036-080-4(X))* Weigl Pubs., Inc.

Gagne, Tammy. Life on Reservations. 2013. (ENG.). 48p. (J). (gr. 4-8). lib. bdg. 29.95 *(978-1-61228-444-6(2))* Mitchell Lane Pubs., Inc.

George, Gale. Seminole, 01 vols., 1. 2016. (Spotlight on Native Americans Ser.). (ENG., Illus.). 32p. (J). pap. 11.75 *(978-1-5081-4155-6(X),* PowerKids Pr.) Rosen Publishing Group, Inc., The.

Gibson, Karen Bush. Native American History for Kids: With 21 Activities. 2010. (For Kids Ser.). (ENG., Illus.). 144p. (J). (gr. 4-18). pap. 17.95 *(978-1-56976-280-6(5))* Chicago Review Pr., Inc.

Grailey, Trevor. Cree. 2015. (Spotlight on Native Americans Ser.). (ENG., Illus.). 32p. (J). (gr. 4-6). 26.25 *(978-1-4994-1709-8(8),* PowerKids Pr.) Rosen Publishing Group, Inc., The.

Gray-Kanatiiosh, Barbara A. Caddo, 1 vol. 2007. (Native Americans Set 4 Ser.). (ENG., Illus.). 32p. (gr. k-5). 27.07 *(978-1-59197-650-9(2),* Checkerboard Library) ABDO Publishing Co.

—Cahuilla, 1 vol. 2007. (Native Americans Set 4 Ser.). (ENG., Illus.). 32p. (gr. k-5). 27.07 *(978-1-59197-651-6(0),* Checkerboard Library) ABDO Publishing Co.

—Chickasaw, 1 vol. 2007. (Native Americans Set 4 Ser.). (ENG., Illus.). 32p. (gr. k-5). 27.07 *(978-1-59197-652-3(9),* Checkerboard Library) ABDO Publishing Co.

—Choctaw, 1 vol. 2007. (Native Americans Set 4 Ser.). (ENG., Illus.). 32p. (gr. k-5). 27.07 *(978-1-59197-653-0(7),* Checkerboard Library) ABDO Publishing Co.

—Gabrielino, 1 vol. 2004. (Native Americans Set 3 Ser.). (ENG., Illus.). 32p. (gr. k-6). 27.07 *(978-1-57765-934-1(1),* Checkerboard Library) ABDO Publishing Co.

—Kiowa, 1 vol. 2007. (Native Americans Set 4 Ser.). (ENG., Illus.). 32p. (gr. 4). 27.07 *(978-1-59197-654-7(5),* Checkerboard Library) ABDO Publishing Co.

—Kumeyaay, 1 vol. 2007. (Native Americans Set 4 Ser.). (ENG., Illus.). 32p. (gr. -1-3). 27.07 *(978-1-59197-655-4(3),* Checkerboard Library) ABDO Publishing Co.

—Paiute, 1 vol. 2007. (Native Americans Set 4 Ser.). (ENG., Illus.). 32p. (gr. 4). 27.07 *(978-1-59197-657-8(X),* Checkerboard Library) ABDO Publishing Co.

—Shoshone, 1 vol. 2004. (Native Americans Set 3 Ser.). (ENG.). 32p. (gr. k-6). 27.07 *(978-1-57765-939-6(2),* Checkerboard Library) ABDO Publishing Co.

—Ute, 1 vol. 2004. (Native Americans Set 3 Ser.). (ENG.). 32p. (gr. k-6). 27.07 *(978-1-57765-940-2(6),* Checkerboard Library) ABDO Publishing Co.

—Yokut, 1 vol. 2004. (Native Americans Set 3 Ser.). (ENG.). 32p. (gr. k-6). 27.07 *(978-1-57765-942-6(2),* Checkerboard Library) ABDO Publishing Co.

—Yurok, 1 vol. 2007. (Native Americans Set 4 Ser.). (ENG., Illus.). 32p. (gr. -1-3). 27.07 *(978-1-59197-658-5(8),* Checkerboard Library) ABDO Publishing Co.

Hall, Margaret C. & Hall, Margaret. Venom & Visions: Art of the Southwest. 2007. (Shockwave: Arts & Culture Ser.). (ENG., Illus.). 36p. (J). (gr. 4-8). 25.00 *(978-0-531-17788-4(2),* Children's Pr.) Scholastic Library Publishing.

Halvorson, Alesha. The Ojibwe: The Past & Present of the Anishinaabe. 2016. (American Indian Life Ser.). (ENG., Illus.). 32p. (gr. 3-4). lib. bdg. 27.32 *(978-1-5157-0240-5(5))* Capstone Press of Coughlan Cos.

Hicks, Terry Allan. The Zuni. 2009. (First Americans 5 Ser.). 48p. (gr. 3). 31.36 *(978-0-7614-4137-3(9))* Marshall Cavendish Corp.

Hirsch, E. D., Jr., ed. Native Americans: Cultures & Conflicts, Level 5. tchr. ed. 9.95 *(978-0-7690-5083-6(2));* stu. ed. 49.95 *(978-0-7690-2854-5(3))* Pearson Learning.

Holliday, Diane Young. Mountain Wolf Woman: A Ho-Chunk Girlhood. 2007. (Badger Biographies Ser.). (ENG., Illus.). 88p. (J). (gr. 3-7). per. 12.95 *(978-0-87020-381-7(9))* Wisconsin Historical Society.

Houghton, Gillian. The Oneida of Wisconsin. (Library of Native Americans Ser.). 64p. 2009. (gr. 4-4). 58.50 *(978-1-60853-759-4(5))* 2003. (Illus.). (J). lib. bdg. 26.50 *(978-0-8239-6432-1(9))* Rosen Publishing Group, Inc., The. (PowerKids Pr.).

Hummingbird, Sandy & Hummingbird, Jesse T. Cherokee Clothing Activity Book. 2006. (Illus.). 31p. (J). (gr. -1-3). pap., act. bk. ed. 4.95 *(978-1-57067-180-7(X),* Native Voices) Book Publishing Co.

Indians of North America Heritage Edition. 2005. (Indians of North America: Heritage Edition Ser.). (gr. 6-12). 240.00 *(978-0-7910-9186-9(4),* Chelsea Hse.) Facts On File, Inc.

Issues in Native American Life, 7 bks. (Indians of North America Ser.). (YA). (gr. 5-18). 139.65 *(978-0-7910-3828-4(9),* Chelsea Hse.) Facts On File, Inc.

Jastrzembski, Joseph C. & Rosier, Paul C. The Apache. 2nd rev. ed. 2011. (History & Culture of Native Americans Ser.). (Illus.). 130p. (gr. 6-12). 35.00 *(978-1-60413-793-4(2),* Chelsea Hse.) Facts On File, Inc.

Johnson, Michael. Native Tribes of the Plains & Prairie. 2004. (Native Tribes of North America Ser.). (Illus.). 64p. (gr. 5-12). lib. bdg. 34.00 *(978-0-8368-5613-2(9),* Gareth Stevens Secondary Library) Stevens, Gareth Publishing LLLP.

Johnson, Michael & Burkinshaw, Jane. Native Tribes of the North & Northwest Coast. 2004. (Native Tribes of North America Ser.). (Illus.). 64p. (gr. 5-12). lib. bdg. 34.00 *(978-0-8368-5611-8(2),* Gareth Stevens Secondary Library) Stevens, Gareth Publishing LLLP.

Johnson, Michael & Clarke, Duncan. Native Tribes of the Great Basin & Plateau. 2004. (Native Tribes of North America Ser.). (Illus.). 64p. (gr. 5-12). lib. bdg. 34.00

H I

(978-0-8368-5610-1(4), Gareth Stevens Secondary Library) Stevens, Gareth Publishing LLLP.

—Native Tribes of the Southeast. 2004. (Native Tribes of North America Ser.). (Illus.). 64p. (gr. 5-12). lib. bdg. 34.00 (978-0-8368-5614-9(7), Gareth Stevens Secondary Library) Stevens, Gareth Publishing LLLP.

Johnson, Michael & Yenne, Bill. Native Tribes of California & the Southwest. 2004. (Native Tribes of North America Ser.). (Illus.). 64p. (gr. 5-12). lib. bdg. 34.00 (978-0-8368-5609-5(0), Gareth Stevens Secondary Library) Stevens, Gareth Publishing LLLP.

Kallen, Stuart A. Native Peoples of the Arctic. 2016. (North American Indian Nations Ser.). (ENG., Illus.). 48p. (J). (gr. 3-5). 33.32 (978-1-4677-7937-1(7)) Lerner Publishing Group.

—Native Peoples of the Subarctic. 2016. (North American Indian Nations Ser.). (ENG., Illus.). 48p. (J). (gr. 3-5). 33.32 (978-1-4677-7938-8(5)) Lerner Publishing Group.

Kamma, Anne. If You Lived with the Hopi. 2014. 17.00 (978-1-63419-709-0(7)) Perfection Learning Corp.

Keoke, Emory Dean & Porterfield, Kay Marie. Food, Farming, & Hunting. 2005. (American Indian Contributions to the World Ser.). (Illus.). 160p. (gr. 5-8). 35.00 (978-0-8160-5393-3(6)) Facts On File, Inc.

King, David C. The Haida. 2006. (First Americans Ser.). (Illus.). 48p. (J). (gr. 3-7). lib. bdg. 31.36 (978-0-7614-2250-1(1), Benchmark Bks.) Marshall Cavendish Corp.

—Huron. 2006. (First Americans Ser.). (Illus.). 48p. (gr. 3-7). lib. bdg. 31.36 (978-0-7614-2251-8(X), Benchmark Bks.) Marshall Cavendish Corp.

—The Mohawk. 2009. (J). 31.36 (978-0-7614-4132-8(8)) Marshall Cavendish GBR. Dist: Marshall Cavendish Corp.

—The Navajo. 2005. (First Americans Ser.). (Illus.). 48p. (J). (gr. 3-7). lib. bdg. (978-0-7614-1897-9(0), Benchmark Bks.) Marshall Cavendish Corp.

—The Ojibwe. 2006. (First Americans Ser.). (Illus.). 48p. (gr. 3-7). lib. bdg. 31.36 (978-0-7614-2252-5(8), Benchmark Bks.) Marshall Cavendish Corp.

—The Seminole. 2006. (First Americans Ser.). (Illus.). 48p. (J). (gr. 3-7). lib. bdg. 31.36 (978-0-7614-2253-2(6), Benchmark Bks.) Marshall Cavendish Corp.

—The Sioux. 2005. (First Americans Ser.). (Illus.). 48p. (J). (gr. 3-7). lib. bdg. (978-0-7614-1899-3(7), Benchmark Bks.) Marshall Cavendish Corp.

Kissock, Heather. Comanche. 2010. (American Indian Art & Culture Ser.). 24p. (J). (gr. 3-6). lib. bdg. 25.70 (978-1-60596-988-6(5)) Weigl Pubs., Inc.

—Comanche: American Indian Art & Culture. 2010. pap. 9.95 (978-1-60596-989-3(3)) Weigl Pubs., Inc.

Kissock, Heather & McGill, Jordan. Tigua. 2010. (American Indian Art & Culture Ser.). 24p. (J). (gr. 3-6). lib. bdg. 25.70 (978-1-60596-982-4(6)) Weigl Pubs., Inc.

—Tigua: American Indian Art & Culture. 2010. pap. 9.95 (978-1-60596-983-1(4)) Weigl Pubs., Inc.

Kissock, Heather & Small, Rachel. Caddo. 2010. (American Indian Art & Culture Ser.). 24p. (J). (gr. 3-6). lib. bdg. 25.70 (978-1-60596-979-4(6)) Weigl Pubs., Inc.

—Caddo: American Indian Art & Culture. 2010. pap. 9.95 (978-1-60596-980-0(X)) Weigl Pubs., Inc.

—Cherokee. 2010. (American Indian Art & Culture Ser.). 24p. (J). (gr. 3-6). lib. bdg. 25.70 (978-1-60596-994-7(X)) Weigl Pubs., Inc.

—Cherokee: American Indian Art & Culture. 2010. pap. 9.95 (978-1-60596-995-4(8)) Weigl Pubs., Inc.

Kleid, Rodney. Shoshone. 2015. (Spotlight on Native Americans Ser.). (ENG., Illus.). 32p. (J). (gr. 4-6). 26.25 (978-1-4994-1683-1(0), PowerKids Pr.) Rosen Publishing Group, Inc., The.

Knowles, Gerald M. The Navajo of North America. 2005. (First Peoples Ser.). (Illus.). 48p. (gr. 4-8). lib. bdg. 23.95 (978-0-8225-0662-1(9)) Lerner Publishing Group.

Koopmans, Anna. The Sioux. (Illus.). 32p. (J). 2014. (978-1-4896-2926-5(2)) 2003. pap. 9.95 (978-1-59036-184-9(9)) Weigl Pubs., Inc.

Kops, Deborah. Native Americans of the Plains: Text Pairs. 2008. (Bridges/Navigators Ser.). (J). (gr. 4). 89.00 (978-1-4108-8392-6(2)) Benchmark Education Co.

Kuszewski, Ivy. Hopi. 2015. (Spotlight on Native Americans Ser.). (ENG., Illus.). 32p. (J). (gr. 4-6). 26.25 (978-1-4994-1663-3(6), PowerKids Pr.) Rosen Publishing Group, Inc., The.

Kyle, Amarie. Navajo. 2015. (Spotlight on Native Americans Ser.). (ENG., Illus.). 32p. (J). (gr. 4-6). 26.25 (978-1-4994-1693-0(8), PowerKids Pr.) Rosen Publishing Group, Inc., The.

Lacey, T. Jensen. The Comanche. 2010. (History & Culture of Native Americans Ser.). 136p. (gr. 6-12). 35.00 (978-1-60413-789-7(4), Chelsea Hse.) Facts On File, Inc.

Lajiness, Katie. Shoshone, 1 vol. 2016. (ENG., Illus.). 32p. (J). (978-1-68078-202-8(9)) ABDO Publishing Co.

—Yokuts, 1 vol. 2016. (ENG., Illus.). 32p. (J). (978-1-68078-204-2(5)) ABDO Publishing Co.

Lawton, Cassie M. & Bial, Raymond. The People & Culture of the Cherokee. 2016. (First Peoples of North America Ser.). (Illus.). 128p. (J). (gr. 6-6). 45.64 (978-1-5026-1886-3(9)) Cavendish Square Publishing.

—The People & Culture of the Cheyenne. 2016. (First Peoples of North America Ser.). (Illus.). 128p. (J). (gr. 6-6). 45.64 (978-1-5026-1888-7(5)) Cavendish Square Publishing.

—The People & Culture of the Iroquois. 2016. (First Peoples of North America Ser.). (Illus.). 128p. (J). (gr. 6-6). 45.64 (978-1-5026-1890-0(7)) Cavendish Square Publishing.

—The People & Culture of the Shoshone. 2016. (First Peoples of North America Ser.). (Illus.). 128p. (J). (gr. 6-6). 45.64 (978-1-5026-1896-2(6)) Cavendish Square Publishing.

—The People & Culture of the Wampanoag. 2016. (First Peoples of North America Ser.). (Illus.). 128p. (J). (gr. 6-6). 45.64 (978-1-5026-1898-6(2)) Cavendish Square Publishing.

Lee, David. Comanche, 01 vols., 1. 2016. (Spotlight on Native Americans Ser.). (ENG., Illus.). 32p. (J). pap. 11.75 (978-1-5081-4140-2(1), PowerKids Pr.) Rosen Publishing Group, Inc., The.

Levy, Janey. Native American Art from the Pueblos. 2009. (Reading Room Collection 2 Ser.). 24p. (gr. 3-4). 42.50 (978-1-60851-981-1(3), PowerKids Pr.) Rosen Publishing Group, Inc., The.

—Native Americans in Texas. 2010. (Spotlight on Texas Ser.). (ENG., Illus.). 32p. (J). (gr. 3-4). 26.25 (978-1-61532-488-0(7)); pap. 11.75 (978-1-61532-451-4(8)) Rosen Publishing Group, Inc., The.

—The Wampanoag of Massachusetts & Rhode Island. 2005. (Library of Native Americans). (Illus.). 64p. (J). (gr. k-5). lib. bdg. 26.50 (978-1-4042-2871-9(3), PowerKids Pr.) Rosen Publishing Group, Inc., The.

Loew, Patty. Native People of Wisconsin, Revised Edition. 2015. (New Badger History Ser.). (ENG., Illus.). 208p. (J). (gr. 4-6). pap. 15.95 (978-0-87020-748-8(2)) Wisconsin Historical Society.

Loew, Patty, et al. Native People of Wisconsin. 2003. (New Badger History Ser.). (Illus.). 224p. (J). pap., tchr. ed., stu. ed. 59.95 (978-0-87020-349-7(5)) Wisconsin Historical Society.

Lomberg, Michelle. The Iroquois. (Illus.). 32p. (J). 2014. (978-1-4896-2910-4(6)) 2003. pap. 9.95 (978-1-59036-181-8(4)) Weigl Pubs., Inc.

—The Ojibwa. (J). 2014. (978-1-4896-2918-0(1)) 2003. (Illus.). 32p. pap. 9.95 (978-1-59036-183-2(0)) Weigl Pubs., Inc.

Lowery, Linda. Native Peoples of the Southeast. 2016. (North American Indian Nations Ser.). (ENG., Illus.). 48p. (J). (gr. 3-5). 50.65 (978-1-4677-8328-6(5), Lerner Pubns.) Lerner Publishing Group.

Maher, Erin. Traditions of the Crow People. 2009. (Reading Room Collection 2 Ser.). 24p. (gr. 3-4). 42.50 (978-1-60851-999-6(6), PowerKids Pr.) Rosen Publishing Group, Inc., The.

Mangieri, Catherine. Powwow. 2006. (Neighborhood Readers Ser.). (ENG.). 12p. (gr. -1-3). pap. 5.90 (978-1-4042-6742-8(5), Rosen Classroom) Rosen Publishing Group, Inc., The.

Maron, Terra Rose. Cheyenne. 2015. (Spotlight on Native Americans Ser.). (ENG., Illus.). 32p. (J). (gr. 4-6). 26.25 (978-1-4994-1678-7(4), PowerKids Pr.) Rosen Publishing Group, Inc., The.

Matzke, Ann H. My Life As a Native American. 2012. (ENG.). 24p. (gr. k-2). pap. 8.95 (978-1-61810-274-4(5)) Rourke Educational Media.

McIntosh, Marsha. Teen Life on Reservations & in First Nation Communities: Growing up Native. 2009. (Youth in Rural North America Ser.). (Illus.). 96p. (YA). (gr. 3-7). lib. bdg. 22.95 (978-1-4222-0018-6(3)) Mason Crest.

Meachen Rau, Dana. Tepee. 2006. (Bookworms Ser.). (Illus.). 31p. (J). (gr. -1-3). lib. bdg. 22.79 (978-0-7614-2277-8(3), Benchmark Bks.) Marshall Cavendish Corp.

Meuse, Theresa. The Sharing Circle: Stories about First Nations Culture, 1 vol. Stevens, Arthur A., illus. 2003. (ENG.). 52p. (J). (gr. k-3). pap. 12.95 (978-1-55109-450-2(9)) Nimbus Publishing, Ltd. CAN. Dist: Orca Bk. Pubs. USA.

Miller, Connie R. The Lakota. 2003. (Digging up Native American History Ser.). (J). pap. (978-1-58417-109-6(X)); lib. bdg. (978-1-58417-046-4(8)) Lake Street Pubs.

Miller, Jay. American Indian Families. 2006. (True Bks). (Illus.). 47p. (gr. 3-5). 16.95 (978-0-7569-7130-4(6)) Perfection Learning Corp.

—American Indian Foods. 2006. (True Bks). (Illus.). 47p. (gr. 3-4). 16.95 (978-0-7569-7132-8(2)) Perfection Learning Corp.

—American Indian Games. 2006. (True Bks). (Illus.). 47p. (gr. 3-5). 16.95 (978-0-7569-7133-5(0)) Perfection Learning Corp.

Moore, Sharon. Native American Foods & Recipes. 2009. (Reading Room Collection 2 Ser.). 24p. (gr. 3-4). 42.50 (978-1-60851-982-8(1), PowerKids Pr.) Rosen Publishing Group, Inc., The.

Nash, Alice & Strobel, Christoph. Daily Life of Native Americans from Post-Columbian Through Nineteenth-Century America, 1 vol. 2006. (Daily Life Ser.). (Illus.). 312p. (C). 75.00 (978-0-313-33515-0(X), GR3515, Greenwood) ABC-CLIO, LLC.

Nelson, S. D. Buffalo Bird Girl: A Hidatsa Story. (ENG., Illus.). 56p. (J). (gr. 1-4). 2015. 9.95 (978-1-4197-1838-0(X)) 2012. 21.95 (978-1-4197-0355-3(2)) Abrams, Inc. (Abrams Bks. for Young Readers).

Nephew, Samantha & Bial, Raymond. The People & Culture of the Choctaw. 2016. (First Peoples of North America Ser.). 128p. (J). 45.64 (978-1-5026-2245-7(9)) Cavendish Square Publishing.

Newsome, Joel, et al. The People & Culture of the Chumash. 2016. (First Peoples of North America Ser.). 128p. (J). 45.64 (978-1-5026-2255-6(6)) Cavendish Square Publishing.

Oestreicher, David M. The Algonquian of New York. 2009. (Library of Native Americans Ser.). 64p. (gr. 4-4). 58.50 (978-1-60853-742-6(0), PowerKids Pr.) Rosen Publishing Group, Inc., The.

—The Algonquin of New York. 2003. (Library of Native Americans). (Illus.). 64p. (YA). (gr. 3-6). lib. bdg. 26.50 (978-0-8239-6427-7(2)) Rosen Publishing Group, Inc., The.

Palazzo-Craig, Janet. The Ojibwe of Michigan, Wisconsin, Minnesota, & North Dakota. 2005. (Library of Native Americans). (Illus.). 64p. (J). (gr. k-5). lib. bdg. 26.50 (978-1-4042-2873-3(X), PowerKids Pr.) Rosen Publishing Group, Inc., The.

Peacock, Thomas Love & Wisuri, Marlene. The Good Path: Ojibwe Learning & Activity Book for Kids. 2009. (ENG., Illus.). 128p. (J). (gr. 5-8). pap. 19.95 (978-0-87351-783-6(0)) Minnesota Historical Society Pr.

Potts, Steve. Iroquois. 2015. (Illus.). 48p. (J). (978-1-60818-552-8(4), Creative Education) Creative Co., The.

Prior, Jennifer Overend. Florida's American Indians Through History. 2016. (Primary Source Readers Ser.). 32p. (gr. 4-4). pap. 8.99 (978-1-4938-3534-8(3)) Teacher Created Materials, Inc.

Pritzker, Barry M. & Rosier, Paul C. The Hopi. 2011. (History & Culture of Native Americans Ser.). (Illus.). 122p. (gr. 6-12). 35.00 (978-1-60413-798-9(3), Chelsea Hse.) Facts On File, Inc.

Quinlivan, Ada. Choctaw, 01 vols., 1. 2016. (Spotlight on Native Americans Ser.). (ENG., Illus.). 32p. (J). pap. 11.75 (978-1-5081-4110-5(X), PowerKids Pr.) Rosen Publishing Group, Inc., The.

Rau, Dana Meachen. Tepee. 2007. (J). pap. 6.99 (978-0-7614-3304-0(X)) Marshall Cavendish Corp.

Rendon, Marcie R. Powwow Summer: A Family Celebrates the Circle of Life. Walsh Bellville, Cheryl, photos by. 2013. (ENG., Illus.). 48p. (J). (gr. 3-6). pap. 7.95 (978-0-87351-910-6(8)) Minnesota Historical Society Pr.

Richmond, Wren. Apache. 2015. (Spotlight on Native Americans Ser.). (ENG., Illus.). 32p. (J). (gr. 4-6). 26.25 (978-1-4994-1668-8(7), PowerKids Pr.) Rosen Publishing Group, Inc., The.

Rickard, Kris A. & Bial, Raymond. The People & Culture of the Arapaho. 2016. (First Peoples of North America Ser.). 128p. (J). 45.64 (978-1-5026-2253-2(X)) Cavendish Square Publishing.

Ritchie, Scot. P'ésk'a & the First Salmon Ceremony, 1 vol. 2015. (ENG., Illus.). 32p. (J). (gr. -1-2). 18.95 (978-1-55498-718-4(0)) Groundwood Bks. CAN. Dist: Publishers Group West (PGW).

Roberts, Russell. The Apache of the Southwest: Apache. 2014. (ENG.). 47p. (J). 29.95 (978-1-62469-005-1(X)) Purple Toad Publishing, Inc.

Rossi, Ann. Cultures Collide: Native American & Europeans 1492-1700. 2004. (Crossroads America Ser.). (ENG., Illus.). 40p. (J). (gr. 5-9). 21.90 (978-0-7922-7198-7(X), National Geographic Children's Bks.) National Geographic Society.

—Native Americans of the Southwest: Text Pairs. 2008. (Bridges/Navigators Ser.). (J). (gr. 4). 89.00 (978-1-4108-8393-3(0)) Benchmark Education Co.

—Two Cultures Meet - Native American & European. 2006. (Language, Literacy, & Vocabulary - Reading Expeditions Ser.). (ENG., Illus.). 40p. (J). pap. 19.95 (978-0-7922-8679-0(0)) CENGAGE Learning.

Royce, Topher. Nez Perce. 2015. (Spotlight on Native Americans Ser.). (ENG., Illus.). 32p. (J). (gr. 4-6). 26.25 (978-1-4994-1698-5(9), PowerKids Pr.) Rosen Publishing Group, Inc., The.

Roza, Greg. The Karankawa of Texas. (Library of Native Americans Ser.). 64p. 2009. (gr. 4-4). 58.50 (978-1-60853-748-8(X)) 2005. (Illus.). (J). (gr. k-5). lib. bdg. 26.50 (978-1-4042-2870-2(5)) Rosen Publishing Group, Inc., The. (PowerKids Pr.).

Ryan, Marla Felkins & Schmittroth, Linda, eds. Abenaki. 2003. (Tribes of Native America Ser.). (Illus.). 32p. (J). 23.70 (978-1-56711-574-1(8), Blackbirch Pr., Inc.) Cengage Gale.

—Chinook. 2003. (Tribes of Native America Ser.). (Illus.). 32p. (J). 23.70 (978-1-56711-685-4(X), Blackbirch Pr., Inc.) Cengage Gale.

Sanna, Ellyn. Potawatomi. 2005. (North American Indians Today Ser.). (Illus.). 96p. (YA). lib. bdg. 22.95 (978-1-59084-675-9(3)) Mason Crest.

Santella, Andrew. The Navajo. 2003. (True Bks). (Illus.). 47p. (J). (gr. 3-5). 14.60 (978-0-7569-7156-4(X)) Perfection Learning Corp.

Savage, Leah, et al. POW Wow: Niimiwin Everyone Dance. 2009. (J). (978-0-9820870-6-0(3)) IGI Pr.

Schomp, Virginia. The Native Americans. 2007. (Myths of the World Ser.). (Illus.). 96p. (J). (gr. 3-7). lib. bdg. 32.79 (978-0-7614-2550-2(0), Benchmark Bks.) Marshall Cavendish Corp.

Shoulders, Michael & Shoulders, Debbie. D Is for Drum: A Native American Alphabet. Toddy, Irving, illus. rev. ed. 2006. (ENG.). 40p. (J). (gr. k-6). 16.95 (978-1-58536-274-5(3)) Sleeping Bear Pr.

Simermeyer, Genevieve. Meet Christopher: An Osage Indian Boy from Oklahoma. Fogden, Katherine, photos by. 2008. (My World — Young Native Americans Today Ser.). (ENG., Illus.). 48p. (J). 15.95 (978-1-57178-217-5(6)) Council Oak Bks.

Sjonger, Rebecca & Kalman, Bobbie. Life of the Powhatan. 2004. (Native Nations of North America Ser.). (ENG., Illus.). 32p. (J). (gr. 2-5). pap. (978-0-7787-0472-0(6)); (gr. 5). lib. bdg. (978-0-7787-0380-8(0)) Crabtree Publishing Co.

—Nations of the Eastern Great Lakes. 2004. (Native Nations of North America Ser.). (ENG., Illus.). 32p. (J). pap. (978-0-7787-0473-7(4)) Crabtree Publishing Co.

Smith-Llera, Danielle. The Chumash: The Past & Present of California's Seashell People. 2016. (American Indian Life Ser.). (ENG., Illus.). 32p. (gr. 3-4). lib. bdg. 27.32 (978-1-5157-0237-5(5)) Capstone Press of Coughlan Cos.

—The Creek: The Past & Present of the Muscogee. 2016. (American Indian Life Ser.). (ENG., Illus.). 32p. (gr. 3-4). lib. bdg. 27.32 (978-1-5157-0238-2(3)) Capstone Press of Coughlan Cos.

—The Iroquois: The Past & Present of the Haudenosaunee. 2015. (American Indian Life Ser.). (ENG., Illus.). 32p. (gr. 3-4). pap. 7.95 (978-1-4914-5005-5(3)) Capstone Press of Coughlan Cos.

—The Powhatan: The Past & Present of Virginia's First Tribes. 2016. (American Indian Life Ser.). (ENG., Illus.). 32p. (gr. 3-4). lib. bdg. 27.32 (978-1-5157-0239-9(1)) Capstone Press of Coughlan Cos.

Smith-Llera, Danielle & Bowman, Donna Janell. American Indian Life. 2015. (American Indian Life Ser.). (ENG.). 32p. (gr. 3-4). 109.28 (978-1-4914-6691-9(X), Fact Finders) Capstone Press of Coughlan Cos.

—The Navajo: The Past & Present of the Dine. 2015. (American Indian Life Ser.). (ENG., Illus.). 32p. (gr. 3-4). pap. 7.95 (978-1-4914-5004-8(5)) Capstone Press of Coughlan Cos.

Smithyman, Kathryn, et al. Nations of the Northwest Coast. 2003. (Native Nations of North America Ser.). (ENG., Illus.). 32p. (J). (gr. 5). lib. bdg. (978-0-7787-0378-5(9)) Crabtree Publishing Co.

Sonneborn, Liz. The Choctaws. 2006. (Native American Histories Ser.). (ENG., Illus.). 56p. (gr. 3-6). lib. bdg. 27.93 (978-0-8225-5911-5(0), Lerner Pubns.) Lerner Publishing Group.

—The Chumash. (Native American Histories Ser.). (ENG., Illus.). 56p. (gr. 3-6). 2007. pap. 8.95 (978-0-8225-6698-4(2)) 2006. lib. bdg. 27.93 (978-0-8225-5912-2(9), Lerner Pubns.) Lerner Publishing Group.

—The Shoshones. 2006. (Native American Histories Ser.). (Illus.). 56p. (J). (gr. 4-7). lib. bdg. 27.93 (978-0-8225-2849-4(5), Lerner Pubns.) Lerner Publishing Group.

Stilwell, Norma Minturn. A Thought for Thanksgiving. Bingham, Pamela E., illus. 2011. 24p. pap. 14.95 (978-1-936343-93-5(2)) Peppertree Pr., The.

Stone, Amy. Creek. 2004. (Native American Peoples Ser.). (Illus.). 32p. (gr. 3-7). lib. bdg. 26.00 (978-0-8368-4217-3(0), Gareth Stevens Learning Library) Stevens, Gareth Publishing LLLP.

—Oneida. 2004. (Native American Peoples Ser.). (Illus.). 32p. (gr. 3-7). lib. bdg. 26.00 (978-0-8368-4220-3(0), Gareth Stevens Learning Library) Stevens, Gareth Publishing LLLP.

Stotter, Michael. Native Americans: Find Out about the World of North American Indians, with 400 Exciting Pictures & 15 Step-by-Step Projects. 2013. (ENG., Illus.). 64p. (J). (gr. -1-3). pap. 12.99 (978-1-84322-975-9(7), Armadillo) Anness Publishing GBR. Dist: National Bk. Network.

Stotter, Mike. The World of North American Indians. 2009. (Passport to the Past Ser.). (Illus.). 64p. (YA). (gr. 4-7). lib. bdg. 31.95 (978-1-4358-5171-9(4)) Rosen Publishing Group, Inc., The.

Stout, Mary. Blackfoot. 2004. (Native American Peoples Ser.). (Illus.). 32p. (gr. 3-7). lib. bdg. 26.00 (978-0-8368-4216-6(2), Gareth Stevens Learning Library) Stevens, Gareth Publishing LLLP.

—Shoshone History & Culture. 2011. (Native American Library). 48p. (J). (gr. 3-6). pap. 14.05 (978-1-4339-5976-9(3)); lib. bdg. 31.95 (978-1-4339-5974-5(7)) Stevens, Gareth Publishing LLLP. (Gareth Stevens Learning Library).

Stout, Mary & Stout, Mary A. Hopi. 2004. (Native American Peoples Ser.). (Illus.). 32p. (gr. 3-7). lib. bdg. 26.00 (978-0-8368-4218-0(9), Gareth Stevens Learning Library) Stevens, Gareth Publishing LLLP.

—Shoshone. 2004. (Native American Peoples Ser.). (Illus.). 32p. (gr. 3-7). lib. bdg. 26.00 (978-0-8368-4221-0(9), Gareth Stevens Learning Library) Stevens, Gareth Publishing LLLP.

Sugobono, Nahuel. Leyendas, Mitos, Cuentos y Otros Relatos de las Praderas Norteamericanas. Huadi, illus. 2003. (SPA.). 96p. pap. 11.95 (978-987-550-278-9(2)) Longseller S.A. ARG. Dist: Bilingual Pubns. Co., The.

Swamp, Jake. Giving Thanks: A Native American Good Morning Message. braille ed. 2004. (Illus.). (J). (gr. k-3). spiral bd. (978-0-616-03096-7(7)) Canadian National Institute for the Blind/Institut National Canadien pour les Aveugles.

Trumbauer, Lisa. The First Americans. 2016. (Life in the Time Of Ser.). (ENG.). 32p. pap. 8.29 (978-1-4846-4013-5(6), Heinemann First Library) Heinemann-Raintree.

Wade, Mary Dodson. Texas Native Peoples. 2003. (Heinemann State Studies). (Illus.). 48p. (J). lib. bdg. 27.07 (978-1-4034-0688-0(X)) Heinemann-Raintree.

Waterby, Ralph. Muscogee (Creek) 2015. (Spotlight on Native Americans Ser.). (ENG., Illus.). 32p. (J). (gr. 4-6). 26.25 (978-1-4994-1653-4(9), PowerKids Pr.) Rosen Publishing Group, Inc., The.

Webster, Christine. Les Mi'kmaq: Les Autochtones du Canada. Karvonen, Tanjah, tr. from ENG. 2011. (FRE.). 24p. (YA). (gr. 2-4). (978-1-77071-405-2(7)) Weigl Educational Pubs. Ltd.

Weil, Ann & Guillain, Charlotte. American Indian Cultures, 1 vol. 2012. (Global Cultures Ser.). (ENG.). 48p. (gr. 4-6). pap. 9.95 (978-1-4329-6790-1(8)); 32.65 (978-1-4329-6781-9(9)) Heinemann-Raintree. (NA-h).

Weinberger, Kimberly. Let's Read About — Pocahontas. Marchesi, Stephen, illus. 2003. (Scholastic First Biographies Ser.). (J). pap. (978-0-439-56148-8(5)) Scholastic, Inc.

White, Bender Richardson, et al. Native American Religions. 3rd rev. ed. 2009. (World Religions Ser.). (Illus.). 144p. (gr. 6-12). 40.00 (978-1-60413-111-6(X), Chelsea Hse.) Facts On File, Inc.

Wilcox, Charlotte. The Seminoles. 2006. (Native American Histories Ser.). (Illus.). 56p. (J). (gr. 4-7). lib. bdg. 27.93 (978-0-8225-2848-7(7), Lerner Pubns.) Lerner Publishing Group.

Williams, Jack. The Miwok of California. 2009. (Library of Native Americans Ser.). 64p. (gr. 4-4). 58.50 (978-1-60853-753-2(6), PowerKids Pr.) Rosen Publishing Group, Inc., The.

—The Modoc of California. 2009. (Library of Native Americans Ser.). 64p. (gr. 4-4). 58.50 (978-1-60853-754-9(4), PowerKids Pr.) Rosen Publishing Group, Inc., The.

—The Mojave of California. 2009. (Library of Native Americans Ser.). 64p. (gr. 4-4). 58.50 (978-1-60853-755-6(2), PowerKids Pr.) Rosen Publishing Group, Inc., The.

—The Mono of California. 2009. (Library of Native Americans Ser.). 64p. (gr. 4-4). 58.50 (978-1-60853-756-3(0), PowerKids Pr.) Rosen Publishing Group, Inc., The.

—The Shasta of California. 2009. (Library of Native Americans Ser.). 64p. (gr. 4-4). 58.50 (978-1-60853-762-4(5), PowerKids Pr.) Rosen Publishing Group, Inc., The.

Williams, Jack S. The Miwok of California. 2004. (Library of Native Americans). (Illus.). 64p. (J). lib. bdg. 26.50 (978-1-4042-2659-3(1)) Rosen Publishing Group, Inc., The.

—The Ohlone of California. 2003. (Library of Native Americans). (Illus.). 64p. (J). lib. bdg. 26.50 (978-0-8239-6430-7(2), PowerKids Pr.) Rosen Publishing Group, Inc., The.

World Book, Inc Staff, contrib. by. Indians of the Great Plains & Great Basin. 2009. (J). (978-0-7166-2139-3(8)) World Bk., Inc.

—Indians of the Southwest. 2009. (J). (978-0-7166-2142-3(8)) World Bk., Inc.

—Peoples of the Arctic & Subarctic. 2009. (J). (978-0-7166-2132-4(0)) World Bk., Inc.

Yasuda, Anita. Explore Native American Cultures! With 25 Great Projects. Keller, Jennifer K., illus. 2013. (Explore Your World Ser.). (ENG.). 96p. (J). (gr. k-4). pap. 12.95 (978-1-61930-160-3(1)) Open City Bks.

Yazzie, Serphine G. Beauty Beside Me: Stories of My Grandmother's Skirts. 2011. (ENG & NAV., Illus.). 32p. (J). (gr. -1-3). 21.95 (978-1-893354-07-4(5)) Salina Bookshelf Inc.

Zardes, Cassandra. Cherokee. 2015. (Spotlight on Native Americans Ser.). (ENG., Illus.). 32p. (J). (gr. 4-6). 26.25 (978-1-4994-1658-9(X), PowerKids Pr.) Rosen Publishing Group, Inc., The.

Zimmerman, Larry J. Exploring the Life, Myth, & Art of Native Americans. 2009. (Civilizations of the World Ser.). (YA). (gr. 7-12). lib. bdg. 42.60 (978-1-4358-5614-1(7)) Rosen Publishing Group, Inc., The.

INDIANS OF NORTH AMERICA—SPORTS

see Indians of North America—Games

INDIANS OF NORTH AMERICA—TAOS INDIANS

Warm Day, Jonathan. Taos Pueblo. 2003. (Illus.). 55p. (J). 16.95 *(978-1-57416-080-2(X))* Clear Light Pubs.

INDIANS OF NORTH AMERICA—UTE INDIANS

Cunningham, Kevin & Benoit, Peter. The Ute. 2011. (True Bk Ser.). 48p. (J). pap. 6.95 *(978-0-531-29307-2(6))*; (gr. 3-5). 29.00 *(978-0-531-20765-9(X))* Scholastic Library Publishing. (Children's Pr.).

INDIANS OF NORTH AMERICA—UTE INDIANS—FICTION

Hobbs, William & Hobbs, Will. Bearstone. 2004. (ENG.). 160p. (J). (gr. 5-9). pap. 6.99 *(978-0-689-87071-2(X),* Simon & Schuster/Paula Wiseman Bks.) Simon & Schuster/Paula Wiseman Bks.

INDIANS OF NORTH AMERICA—WAMPANOAG INDIANS

Cunningham, Kevin & Benoit, Peter. The Wampanoag. 2011. (True Bk Ser.). 48p. (J). (ENG.). pap. 6.95 *(978-0-531-29308-9(4))*; (gr. 3-5). 29.00 *(978-0-531-20766-6(8))* Scholastic Library Publishing. (Children's Pr.).

Gray-Kanatiiosh, Barbara A. Wampanoag, 1 vol. 2004. (Native Americans Set 3 Ser.). (ENG.). 32p. (gr. k-6). 27.07 *(978-1-57765-941-9(4),* Checkerboard Library) ABDO Publishing Co.

Kamma, Anne. If You Lived at the Time of Squanto. Johnson, Pamela Ford, illus. 2006. 63p. (J). pap. *(978-0-439-87628-5(1))* Scholastic, Inc.

Lawton, Cassie M. & Bial, Raymond. The People & Culture of the Wampanoag. 2016. (First Peoples of North America Ser.). (Illus.). 128p. (J). (gr. 6-6). 45.64 *(978-1-5026-1898-6(2))* Cavendish Square Publishing.

Levy, Janey. The Wampanoag of Massachusetts & Rhode Island. (Library of Native Americans Ser.). 64p. 2009. (gr. 4-4). 58.50 *(978-1-60853-765-5(X))* 2005. (Illus.). (J). (gr. k-5). lib. bdg. 26.50 *(978-1-4042-2871-9(3))* Rosen Publishing Group, Inc., The. (PowerKids Pr.).

Metaxas, Eric. Squanto & the First Thanksgiving: The Legendary American Tale. Donato, Michael A., illus. 2004. 36p. (J). (gr. 3-8). reprint ed. 19.00 *(978-0-7567-7123-2(4))* DIANE Publishing Co.

Sewall, Marcia. People of the Breaking Day. 2014. 16.00 *(978-1-63419-676-5(7))* Perfection Learning Corp.

Stanley, Joseph. Wampanoag, 01 vols., 1. 2016. (Spotlight on Native Americans Ser.). (ENG., Illus.). 32p. (J). pap. 11.75 *(978-1-5081-4145-7(2),* PowerKids Pr.) Rosen Publishing Group, Inc., The.

INDIANS OF NORTH AMERICA—WAMPANOAG INDIANS—FICTION

Bruchac, Joseph. Squanto's Journey: The Story of the First Thanksgiving. Shed, Greg, illus. 2007. (ENG.). 32p. (J). (gr. -1-3). pap. 7.99 *(978-0-15-206044-2(8),* HMH Books For Young Readers) Houghton Mifflin Harcourt Publishing Co.

—Squanto's Journey: The Story of the First Thanksgiving. 2014. 17.00 *(978-1-63419-743-4(7))* Perfection Learning Corp.

Collins, Pat Lowery. Daughter of Winter. 2010. (ENG., Illus.). 352p. (YA). (gr. 5-18). 16.99 *(978-0-7636-4500-7(1))* Candlewick Pr.

Cooper, Susan. Ghost Hawk. 2014. (ENG., Illus.). 352p. (J). (gr. 5-9). pap. 7.99 *(978-1-4424-8142-8(0),* McElderry, Margaret K. Bks.) McElderry, Margaret K. Bks.

INDIANS OF NORTH AMERICA—WARS

see also Little Bighorn, Battle of the, Mont., 1876; United States—History—French and Indian War, 1755-1763

Anderson, Paul C. George Armstrong Custer: The Indian Wars & the Battle of the Little Bighorn. 2009. (Library of American Lives & Times Ser.). 112p. (gr. 5-5). 69.20 *(978-1-60853-483-8(9))* Rosen Publishing Group, Inc., The.

Baker, Brynn. Buffalo Soldiers: Heroes of the American West. 2015. (Military Heroes Ser.). (ENG., Illus.). 32p. (gr. 3-4). lib. bdg. 27.32 *(978-1-4914-4838-0(5))* Capstone Press of Coughlan Cos.

Behrman, Carol H. The Indian Wars. 2005. (Chronicle of America's Wars Ser.). (Illus.). 96p. (J). (gr. 5-12). 27.93 *(978-0-8225-0847-2(8))* Lerner Publishing Group.

Biskup, Agnieszka. Thunder Rolling down the Mountain: The Story of Chief Joseph & the Nez Perce, 1 vol. Zimmerman, Rusty, illus. 2011. (American Graphic Ser.). (ENG.). 32p. (gr. 3-4). pap. 8.10 *(978-1-4296-6270-3(0))*; pap. 47.70 *(978-1-4296-6437-0(1))* Capstone Press of Coughlan Cos. (Graphic Library).

Blomquist, Katie. American Indians in The 1800s: Right & Resistance (America in The 1800s) 2017. (Primary Source Readers Ser.). (Illus.). 32p. (J). (gr. 4-5). pap. 8.99 ***(978-1-4938-3799-1(0))*** Teacher Created Materials, Inc.

Brown, Dee. Saga of the Sioux: An Adaptation from Dee Brown's Bury My Heart at Wounded Knee. 2014. (ENG., Illus.). 224p. (J). (gr. 5-9). pap. 12.99 *(978-1-250-05067-0(7),* 9781250050670) Square Fish.

Callery, Sean. The Dark History of America's Old West. 2010. (Dark Histories Ser.). 64p. (gr. 5). 32.79 *(978-1-60870-086-8(0))* Marshall Cavendish Corp.

Crazy Horse. 2010. (Legends of the Wild West Ser.). (Illus.). 144p. (gr. 6-12). 35.00 *(978-1-60413-526-8(3),* Chelsea Hse.) Facts On File, Inc.

Dean, Arlan. With All My Might: Cochise & the Indian Wars. 2009. (Great Moments in American History Ser.). 32p. (gr. 3-3). 47.90 *(978-1-61513-137-2(X))* Rosen Publishing Group, Inc., The.

Dolan, Edward F., Jr. The American Indian Wars. 2003. (Single Titles Ser.). 112p. (gr. 5-8). lib. bdg. 29.90 *(978-0-7613-1968-9(9),* Twenty-First Century Bks.) Lerner Publishing Group.

Drury, Bob & Clavin, Tom. The Heart of Everything That Is: Young Readers Edition. 2017. (ENG., Illus.). 320p. (J). (gr. 5). 16.99 *(978-1-4814-6460-4(4),* McElderry, Margaret K. Bks.) McElderry, Margaret K. Bks.

Dwyer, Helen. Warfare, Economy, & Technology. 2010. (CC: Native North Americans Ser.). 112p. (gr. 6-12). 42.80 *(978-1-933834-80-1(3))* Brown Bear Bks.

Feinstein, Stephen. Read about Geronimo. 2006. (I Like Biographies! Ser.). (Illus.). 24p. (J). (gr. 1-3). lib. bdg. 21.26 *(978-0-7660-2598-1(5),* Enslow Elementary) Enslow Pubs., Inc.

Galliker, Leslie. Native American Wars on the Western Frontier (1866-1890), Vol. 11. Musteen, Jason R., ed. 2015. (Major U. S. Historical Wars Ser.). (Illus.). 64p. (J). (gr. 7). lib. bdg. 23.95 *(978-1-4222-3357-3(X))* Mason Crest.

Geronimo. 2010. (Legends of the Wild West Ser.). (Illus.). 128p. (gr. 6-12). 35.00 *(978-1-60413-525-1(5),* Chelsea Hse.) Facts On File, Inc.

Gitlin, Martin. The Battle of the Little Bighorn, 1 vol. 2008. (Essential Events Set 2 Ser.). (ENG., Illus.). 112p. (J). (gr. 6-12). lib. bdg. 35.64 *(978-1-60453-045-2(6))* ABDO Publishing Co.

Glaser, Jason. The Buffalo Soldiers & the American West. Smith, Tod G. et al, illus. 2005. (Graphic History Ser.). (ENG.). 32p. (gr. 3-4). 30.65 *(978-0-7368-4966-1(1),* Graphic Library) Capstone Press of Coughlan Cos.

Goble, Paul. Red Cloud's War: Brave Eagle's Account of the Fetterman Fight. 2015. (ENG., Illus.). 48p. (J). (gr. 3-7). 16.95 *(978-1-937786-38-0(2),* Wisdom Tales) World Wisdom, Inc.

Gunther, Vanessa. Chief Joseph: A Biography, 1 vol. 2010. (Greenwood Biographies Ser.). (Illus.). 178p. (C). 39.00 *(978-0-313-37920-8(3),* GR7920, Greenwood) ABC-CLIO, LLC.

Haugen, Brenda. Geronimo: The Inspiring Life Story of an Apache Warrior. 2016. (Inspiring Stories Ser.). (ENG., Illus.). 112p. (gr. 5-7). lib. bdg. 35.99 *(978-0-7565-5162-9(5),* CPB Grades 4-8) Compass Point Bks.

Higgins, Nadia. Last Stand: Causes & Effects of the Battle of the Little Bighorn. 2015. (Cause & Effect: American Indian History Ser.). (ENG.). 32p. (gr. 3-4). pap. 7.95 *(978-1-4914-2208-3(4))* Capstone Press of Coughlan Cos.

Higgins, Nadia & Schwartz, Heather E. Cause & Effect: American Indian History. 2015. (Cause & Effect: American Indian History Ser.). (ENG.). 32p. (gr. 3-4). lib. bdg. 109.28 *(978-1-4914-2444-5(3),* Fact Finders) Capstone Press of Coughlan Cos.

Hooker, Forrestine Cooper. Child of the Fighting Tenth: On the Frontier with the Buffalo Soldiers. Wilson, Steve, ed. 2011. (ENG., Illus.). 296p. pap. 19.95 *(978-0-8061-4080-3(1))* Univ. of Oklahoma Pr.

Hopping, Lorraine Jean. Chief Joseph: The Voice for Peace. 2010. (Sterling Biographies(r) Ser.). (ENG., Illus.). 128p. (J). (gr. 5-18). pap. 5.95 *(978-1-4027-6004-4(3))* Sterling Publishing Co., Inc.

Hunt, Santana. Geronimo. 2015. (Native American Heroes Ser.). (ENG., Illus.). 24p. (J). (gr. 1-2). pap. 8.15 *(978-1-4824-2685-4(4))* Stevens, Gareth Publishing LLLP.

—Osceola. 2015. (Native American Heroes Ser.). (ENG., Illus.). 24p. (J). (gr. 1-2). pap. 8.15 *(978-1-4824-2689-2(7))* Stevens, Gareth Publishing LLLP.

January, Brendan. Little Bighorn: June 25, 1876. 2004. (ENG., Illus.). 32p. (J). (gr. 3-8). 14.95 *(978-1-59270-028-8(4))* Enchanted Lion Bks., LLC.

Jastrzembski, Joseph C. The Apache Wars: The Final Resistance. 2007. (Landmark Events in Native American History Ser.). (Illus.). 133p. (YA). (gr. 9-12). pap. 35.00 *(978-0-7910-9343-6(3))* Facts On File, Inc.

Jeffrey, Gary. The Battle of the Little Bighorn. Spender, Nick, illus. 2012. (Graphic History of the American West Ser.). (ENG.). 24p. (J). (gr. 3-8). pap. 8.15 *(978-1-4339-6733-7(2),* Gareth Stevens Learning Library); (gr. 4-7). lib. bdg. 23.95 *(978-1-4339-6731-3(6))* Stevens, Gareth Publishing LLLP.

Landau, Elaine. The Wounded Knee Massacre. 2004. (Cornerstones of Freedom Ser.). (ENG., Illus.). 48p. (YA). (gr. 4-7). 26.00 *(978-0-516-24244-6(X))* Scholastic Library Publishing.

Laxer, James. Tecumseh, 1 vol. Rudnicki, Richard, illus. 2012. (ENG.). 56p. (J). (gr. 3). 19.95 *(978-1-55498-123-6(9))* Groundwood Bks. CAN. Dist: Publishers Group West (PGW).

Link, Theodore. George Armstrong Custer: General de la caballería Estadounidense. 2004. (Grandes personajes en la historia de los Estados Unidos Ser.). (SPA.). 32p. (gr. 3-6). pap. 10.00 *(978-0-8239-4228-2(7),* Rosen Classroom) Rosen Publishing Group, Inc., The.

—George Armstrong Custer: General de la caballería estadounidense (George Armstrong Custer: General of the U. S. Cavalry) 2009. (Grandes personajes en la historia de los Estados Unidos (Famous People in American History) Ser.). (SPA.). 32p. (gr. 2-3). 47.90 *(978-1-61512-799-3(2),* Editorial Buenas Letras) Rosen Publishing Group, Inc., The.

—George Armstrong Custer: General of the U. S. Cavalry. 2009. (Primary Sources of Famous People in American History Ser.).Tr. of George Armstrong Custer: General de la Caballería Estadounidense. 32p. (gr. 2-3). 47.90 *(978-1-60851-680-3(6))* Rosen Publishing Group, Inc., The.

—George Armstrong Custer: General of the U. S. Cavalry / General de la caballería Estadounidense. 2009. (Famous People in American History/Grandes personajes en la historia de los Estados Unidos Ser.). (ENG & SPA.). 32p. (gr. 2-3). 47.90 *(978-1-61512-545-6(0),* Editorial Buenas Letras) Rosen Publishing Group, Inc., The.

Marker, Sherry. Plains Indian Wars. 3rd rev. ed. 2010. (America at War Ser.). (Illus.). 200p. (gr. 6-12). 45.00 *(978-0-8160-8184-4(0),* Chelsea Hse.) Facts On File, Inc.

Miller, Barbara Kiely. Chief Joseph. 2007. (Great Americans Ser.). 24p. (gr. 1-4). pap. 8.15 *(978-0-8368-8321-3(7))*; lib. bdg. 22.00 *(978-0-8368-8314-5(4))* Stevens, Gareth Publishing LLLP. (Weekly Reader Leveled Readers).

—Jefe Joseph. 2007. (Grandes Personajes (Great Americans) Ser.). (SPA.). 24p. (gr. 1-4). lib. bdg. 22.00 *(978-0-8368-8331-2(4),* Weekly Reader Leveled Readers) Stevens, Gareth Publishing LLLP.

—Jefe Joseph (Chief Joseph) 2007. (Grandes Personajes (Great Americans) Ser.). (SPA.). 24p. (gr. 1-4). pap. 8.15 *(978-0-8368-8338-1(1),* Weekly Reader Leveled Readers) Stevens, Gareth Publishing LLLP.

Morris, Richard B. The First Book of the Indian Wars. Fisher, Leonard Everett & Waltrip, Mildred, illus. 2011. 94p. 38.95 *(978-1-258-01128-4(X))* Literary Licensing, LLC.

The New South & the Old West, 1866-1890. 2010. (Discovering U. S. History Ser.). (Illus.). 136p. (gr. 5-8). 35.00 *(978-1-60413-354-7(6),* Chelsea Hse.) Facts On File, Inc.

O'Brien, Cynthia. Go West: First Contact with Native Nations. 2016. (ENG.). 32p. (J). *(978-0-7787-2331-8(3))* Crabtree Publishing Co.

Philbrick, Nathaniel. The Mayflower & the Pilgrims' New World. 2009. (ENG.). 368p. (J). (gr. 5-18). 8.99 *(978-0-14-241458-3(1),* Puffin Books) Penguin Young Readers Group.

Raabe, Emily. Buffalo Soldiers & the Western Frontier. (Westward Ho! Ser.). 24p. 2009. (gr. 2-3). 42.50 *(978-1-60854-759-3(0))* 2003. (Illus.). (J). lib. bdg. 22.60 *(978-0-8239-6495-6(7))* Rosen Publishing Group, Inc., The. (PowerKids Pr.).

—The U. S. Cavalry & the Indian Wars. (Westward Ho! Ser.). 24p. 2009. (gr. 2-3). 42.50 *(978-1-60854-764-7(7))* 2003. (Illus.). (J). lib. bdg. 22.60 *(978-0-8239-6496-3(5))* Rosen Publishing Group, Inc., The. (PowerKids Pr.).

Rice, Earle. The Life & Times of the Brothers Custer: Galloping to Glory. 2008. (Profiles in American History Ser.). (Illus.). 48p. (J). (gr. 4-8). lib. bdg. 29.95 *(978-1-58415-665-9(1))* Mitchell Lane Pubs., Inc.

Roxburgh, Ellis. The Seminole Wars. 2017. (Rebellions, Revolts, & Uprisings Ser.). 48p. (gr. 5-5). pap. 84.30 ***(978-1-5382-0755-0(9))*** Stevens, Gareth Publishing LLLP.

Sabin, Edwin L. Boys' Book of Border Battles. 2013. (ENG., Illus.). 352p. pap. 14.95 *(978-1-62087-158-4(0),* 620158) Skyhorse Publishing Co., Inc.

Sanford, William R. Apache Chief Geronimo. 2013. (Native American Chiefs & Warriors Ser.). 48p. (J). (gr. 5-18). lib. bdg. 22.60 *(978-0-7660-4093-9(3))* Enslow Pubs., Inc.

Schach, David. Comanche Warriors. 2011. (History's Greatest Warriors Ser.). (ENG., Illus.). 24p. (J). (gr. 3-7). lib. bdg. 25.95 *(978-1-60014-628-2(7),* Torque Bks.) Bellwether Media.

Silate, Jennifer. The Last Stand: The Final Military Campaign of General George Armstrong Custer. 2009. (Great Moments in American History Ser.). 32p. (gr. 3-3). 47.90 *(978-1-61513-154-9(X))* Rosen Publishing Group, Inc., The.

Swain, Gwenyth. Little Crow: Leader of the Dakota. 2004. (ENG., Illus.). 112p. (J). pap. 12.95 *(978-0-87351-503-0(X),* Borealis Bk.) Minnesota Historical Society Pr.

Weil, Ann. Geronimo, 1 vol. 2012. (American Biographies Ser.). (ENG.). 48p. (gr. 4-6). pap. 9.95 *(978-1-4329-6458-0(5))*; lib. bdg. 32.65 *(978-1-4329-6447-4(X))* Heinemann-Raintree. (NA-h).

—Sitting Bull, 1 vol. 2012. (American Biographies Ser.). (ENG.). 48p. (gr. 4-6). pap. 9.95 *(978-1-4329-6460-3(7))*; lib. bdg. 32.65 *(978-1-4329-6449-8(6))* Heinemann-Raintree. (NA-h).

INDIANS OF NORTH AMERICA—WARS—FICTION

Panagopoulos, Janie Lynn. Mark of the Bear Claw. 2007. 224p. (J). pap. 8.95 *(978-0-938682-83-7(0))* River Road Pubns., Inc.

Raffa, Edwina & Rigsby, Annelle. Escape to the Everglades Teacher's Activity Guide. 2006. (ENG., Illus.). 31p. pap., tchr. ed., act. bk. ed. 6.00 *(978-1-56164-362-2(9))* Pineapple Pr., Inc.

INDIANS OF SOUTH AMERICA

Brooks, Susie. Amazonian Indians. 2009. (Flashback History Ser.). (Illus.). 48p. (ENG.). (J). pap. 11.75 *(978-1-4358-5514-4(0),* PowerKids Pr.); (YA). (gr. 3-6). lib. bdg. 29.25 *(978-1-4358-5513-7(2))* Rosen Publishing Group, Inc., The.

Byers, Helen. Peru. 2007. (Nonfiction Reading & Writing Workshops Ser.). (ENG., Illus.). 24p. (J). pap. 14.95 *(978-0-7922-4538-4(5))* CENGAGE Learning.

Davies, Gill. Native America 900 BC - the Present. Aronson, Marc, ed. 2005. (National Geographic Timelines Ser.). (Illus.). 64p. (J). 27.90 *(978-0-7922-7078-2(9))*; 17.95 *(978-0-7922-6456-9(8))* CENGAGE Learning.

Dawson, Mike. Growing up Yanomamö: Missionary Adventures in the Amazon Rainforest. Pintor, Ruben, illus. 2009. (ENG.). 336p. (J). pap. 19.95 *(978-0-60265-009-1(8))* Grace Acres Pr.

Dawson, Patricia A. First Peoples of the Americas & the European Age of Exploration. 2015. (Exploring the Ancient & Medieval Worlds Ser.). (ENG., Illus.). 160p. (J). (gr. 8-8). lib. bdg. 45.64 *(978-1-5026-0685-3(2))* Cavendish Square Publishing.

Kachurek, Sandra J. Francisco Pizarro: Explorer of South America. 2004. (Explorers! Ser.). (Illus.). 48p. (J). lib. bdg. 23.93 *(978-0-7660-2178-5(5))* Enslow Pubs., Inc.

Krebs, Laurie. Sube y Baja Por Los Andes: Un Cuento de un Festival Peruano. Fronty, Aurélia, illus. 2011. (SPA.). 32p. (J). (gr. 1-6). pap. 7.99 *(978-1-84686-548-0(4))* Barefoot Bks., Inc.

—Up & down the Andes. Fronty, Aurélia, illus. 2011. (ENG.). 32p. (J). (gr. k-1). pap. 8.99 *(978-1-84686-468-1(2))* Barefoot Bks., Inc.

—Up & down the Andes: A Peruvian Festival Tale. Fronty, Aurélia, illus. 2008. (ENG.). 32p. (J). (gr. -1-5). 16.99 *(978-1-84686-203-8(5))* Barefoot Bks., Inc.

Reynolds, Jan. Amazon Basin. 2007. (Vanishing Cultures Ser.). (ENG., Illus.). 32p. (J). (gr. 4-7). 8.95 *(978-1-60060-125-5(1))*; 16.95 *(978-1-60060-140-8(5))* Lee & Low Bks., Inc.

Sayer, Chloe. The Incan Empire. 2010. (Exploring the Ancient World Ser.). (Illus.). 64p. (YA). (gr. 6-8). lib. bdg. 34.60 *(978-1-4339-4187-0(2),* Gareth Stevens Secondary Library) Stevens, Gareth Publishing LLLP.

Webster, Christine. Yanomami. (J). 2013. 28.55 *(978-1-62127-508-4(2))* 2013. pap. 13.95 *(978-1-62127-512-1(4))* 2004. pap. 9.95 *(978-1-59036-159-7(8))* 2004. (Illus.). 32p. lib. bdg. 26.00 *(978-1-59036-124-5(5))* Weigl Pubs., Inc.

Woods, Michael & Woods, Mary B. Seven Wonders of Ancient Central & South America. 2008. (Seven Wonders Ser.). (ENG., Illus.). 80p. (gr. 5-8). lib. bdg. 33.26 *(978-0-8225-7570-2(1))* Lerner Publishing Group.

Yacowitz, Caryn. Inuit Indians. 2016. (Native Americans Ser.). (ENG.). 32p. (gr. 2-4). pap. 7.99 *(978-1-4846-3650-3(3),* NA-h) Heinemann-Raintree.

INDIANS OF SOUTH AMERICA—FICTION

Allende, Isabel. A Cidade das Feras. 2006.Tr. of Ciudad de las Bestias. (POR.). 280p. (YA). pap. 26.95 *(978-85-286-0977-6(4))* Bertrand Brasil Editora SA BRA. Dist: Distribooks, Inc.

—City of the Beasts. 2009. (P. S. Ser.: Bk. 1). (ENG.). 448p. pap. 14.99 *(978-0-06-182511-8(5),* Harper Perennial) 2005. 464p. (J). (gr. 7-17). pap. 7.99 *(978-0-06-077645-9(5),* Rayo) HarperCollins Pubs.

—City of the Beasts. Peden, Margaret Sayers, tr. from SPA. 2004. (City of the Beasts Ser.: Bk. 1). (ENG.). 432p. (J). (gr. 5-18). reprint ed. pap. 7.99 *(978-0-06-053503-2(2),* Rayo) HarperCollins Pubs.

Arrieta, Maria Luz. El Ultimo Cacique de la Sabana. 2003. (SPA.). 208p. *(978-958-30-0581-7(9),* PV30149) Centro de Informacion y Desarrollo de la Comunicacion y la Literatura MEX. Dist: Lectorum Pubns., Inc.

Ballantyne, Robert Michael. The Rover of the Andes: A Tale of Adventure in South America. 2007. (ENG.). 266p. pap. 21.99 *(978-1-4346-3753-6(0))*; 296p. pap. 23.99 *(978-1-4346-3767-3(0))* Creative Media Partners, LLC.

Barron, T. A. Ghost Hands. Low, William, illus. 2011. (ENG.). 40p. (J). (gr. k-3). 18.99 *(978-0-399-25083-5(2),* Philomel Bks.) Penguin Young Readers Group.

Brown, Virginia Pounds. The Gold Disc of Coosa. 2007. 112p. (J). pap. 11.95 *(978-1-60306-018-9(9))* NewSouth, Inc.

Coulson, Art. The Creator's Game: A Story of Baaga'adowe/Lacrosse. Desjarlait, Robert, illus. 2013. (ENG.). 48p. (J). (gr. 3-6). pap. 6.95 *(978-0-87351-909-0(4))* Minnesota Historical Society Pr.

Crowder, Melanie. An Uninterrupted View of the Sky. 2017. (ENG.). 304p. (YA). (gr. 7). 17.99 *(978-0-399-16900-7(8),* Philomel Bks.) Penguin Young Readers Group.

Ellis, Leanne Statland. The Ugly One. 2015. (ENG.). 256p. (J). (gr. 5-7). pap. 7.99 *(978-0-544-43917-7(1),* HMH Books For Young Readers) Houghton Mifflin Harcourt Publishing Co.

Farinango, Maria Virginia & Resau, Laura. The Queen of Water. 2012. (ENG.). 368p. (YA). (gr. 7). pap. 9.99 *(978-0-375-85963-2(2),* Ember) Random Hse. Children's Bks.

Garcia, Alfredo. Erase una Vez Entre los Chibchas. 2003. (SPA.). 116p. *(978-958-30-0298-4(4),* PV30144) Centro de Informacion y Desarrollo de la Comunicacion y la Literatura MEX. Dist: Lectorum Pubns., Inc.

Guillain, Charlotte. The Tree of Life: An Amazonian Folk Tale, 1 vol. Dorado, Steve, illus. 2014. (Folk Tales from Around the World Ser.). (ENG.). 24p. (gr. 1-3). pap. 6.95 *(978-1-4109-6698-8(4),* NA-r) Heinemann-Raintree.

Horowitz, Anthony. Evil Star. 2007. (Gatekeepers Ser.: 2). 318p. lib. bdg. 19.65 *(978-1-4177-7663-4(3),* Turtleback) Turtleback Bks.

Jendresen, Erik & Villoldo, Alberto. The First Story Ever Told. Yoshi, illus. 2008. (ENG.). 36p. (J). (gr. -1-2). 12.99 *(978-1-4169-8961-5(7),* Simon & Schuster Bks. For Young Readers) Simon & Schuster Bks. For Young Readers.

Kerr, P. B., pseud. The Eye of the Forest. 2009. (Children of the Lamp Ser.: 5). (ENG.). 432p. (J). (gr. 3-7). 17.99 *(978-0-439-93215-8(7),* Orchard Bks.) Scholastic, Inc.

McDermott, Gerald. Jabutí the Tortoise: A Trickster Tale from the Amazon. 2005. (ENG., Illus.). 32p. (J). (gr. -1-3). pap. 7.99 *(978-0-15-205374-1(3))* Houghton Mifflin Harcourt Publishing Co.

Muller, Seth. Keepers of the WindClaw Chronicles: The Day of Storms, 3 vols., Vol. 2. Dubay, Tayloe, ed. Whitethorne, Bahe, Jr., illus. 2nd ed. 2010. 224p. (J). pap. 12.95 *(978-1-893354-10-4(5))* Salina Bookshelf Inc.

Nelson, N. A. Bringing the Boy Home. 2008. (ENG.). 224p. (J). (gr. 3-7). 16.99 *(978-0-06-088698-1(6))* HarperCollins Pubs.

O'Dell, Scott. The Seven Serpents Trilogy. 2009. (ENG.). 560p. (J). (gr. 4-6). pap. 19.99 *(978-1-4022-1836-1(2),* Sourcebooks Jabberwocky) Sourcebooks, Inc.

Parker, Vic. Traditional Tales from South America. 2006. 48p. (J). (gr. -1-4). reprint ed. 20.00 *(978-1-4223-5596-1(9))* DIANE Publishing Co.

Platt, Richard. The Vanishing Rainforest. van Wyk, Rupert, illus. 2007. (ENG.). 32p. (J). pap. *(978-0-7112-2170-3(7),* Frances Lincoln) Quarto Publishing Group UK.

—The Vanishing Rainforest. van Wyk, Rupert, illus. 2003. 32p. (YA). *(978-0-7112-1960-1(5))* ReiseArt Buchhandlung GmbH.

Vidali, Valerio & Uman, Jennifer. Jemmy Button. Vidali, Valerio & Uman, Jennifer, illus. 2013. (ENG., Illus.). 48p. (J). (gr. k-12). 16.99 *(978-0-7636-6487-9(1),* Templar) Candlewick Pr.

INDIANS OF SOUTH AMERICA—FOLKLORE

Jaekel, Susan M., illus. Tug of War: A Tale about Being Resourceful. 2006. (J). *(978-1-59939-091-8(4),* Reader's Digest Young Families, Inc.) Studio Fun International.

Knutson, Barbara. Love & Roast Chicken: A Trickster Tale from the Andes Mountains. Knutson, Barbara, illus. 2004. (Carolrhoda Picture Books Ser.). (ENG., Illus.). 40p. (J). (gr. k-3). 17.95 *(978-1-57505-657-9(7))* Lerner Publishing Group.

Patterson, Irania & McElvane, Catherine. Wings & Dreams (Alas y Suenos) The Legend of Angel Falls (La Leyenda del Salto Angel) 2010. (ENG & SPA.). 40p. (J). (gr. 1-3). 19.95 *(978-0-9815192-4-1(5))* Novello Festival Pr.

Springer, Jane, tr. from POR. Amazonia: Indigenous Tales from Brazil, 1 vol. Popov, Nikolai, illus. 2013. (ENG.). 128p. (J). (gr. 4). 24.95 *(978-1-55498-185-4(9))* Groundwood Bks. CAN. Dist: Publishers Group West (PGW).

INDIANS OF SOUTH AMERICA—LEGENDS

see Indians of South America—Folklore

INDIANS OF SOUTH AMERICA—PERU

Jepson-Gilbert, Anita. Maria & the Stars of Nazca (Maria y las Estrellas de Nazca) Casis, Carmen A., tr. Osban, Rodger, illus. 2004.Tr. of Maria y las Estrellas de Nazca. (SPA & ENG.). 32p. (J). pap. incl. audio compact disk *(978-0-9749745-0-7(1))* TAE Nazca Resources.

—Maria & the Stars of Nazca (Maria y las Estrellas de Nazca), without audio CD. Osban, Rodger, illus. 2004.Tr. of Maria y las Estrellas de Nazca. (ENG & SPA.). pap. 14.95 *(978-0-9749745-1-4(X))* TAE Nazca Resources.

INDIGENOUS PEOPLES

Barghoorn, Linda. Xiuhtezcatl Martinez: Protecting the Environment & Indigenous Rights. 2017. (Illus.). 32p. (J). ***(978-0-7787-3421-5(8))*** Crabtree Publishing Co.

Barrington, Richard. Bands, Tribes & First Peoples & Nations. Wolff, Ariana, ed. 2014. (Political & Economic Systems Ser.). 312p. (YA). (gr. 9-12). 45.00 *(978-1-62275-362-8(3))* Rosen Publishing Group, Inc., The.

Boyden, Linda. Giveaways: An ABC Book of Loanwords from the Americas. 2010. (ENG., Illus.). 74p. (J). (gr. 3-6). 19.95 *(978-0-8263-4726-8(6))* Univ. of New Mexico Pr.

Doudna, Kelly. People Around the World, 1 vol. 2004. (Around the World Ser.). (ENG., Illus.). 24p. (J). (gr. k-3). lib. bdg.

H I

24.21 (978-1-59197-567-0(0), SandCastle) ABDO Publishing Co.
Einarson, Earl. The Moccasins. Einarson, Earl, illus. 2004. (Moccasins Ser.). (ENG., Illus.). 16p. pap. 7.95 (978-1-894778-14-5(6)) Theytus Bks., Ltd. CAN. Dist: Univ. of Toronto Pr.
Florence, Melanie. Righting Canada's Wrongs - Residential Schools. 2015. (Righting Canada's Wrongs Ser.). (ENG., Illus.). 128p. (YA). (gr. 8-12). 34.95 (978-1-4594-0866-1(7), 9781459408661) Lorimer, James & Co., Ltd., Pubs. CAN. Dist: Casemate Pubs. & Bk. Distributors, LLC.
Gray, Carolyn. Aboriginal Treaties. 2010. (Illus.). 48p. (978-1-55388-692-1(5)); pap. (978-1-55388-697-6(6)) Weigl Educational Pubs. Ltd.
Gray Smith, Monique. Speaking Our Truth: A Journey of Reconciliation, 1 vol. 2017. (ENG.). 160p. (J). (gr. 3-7). 29.95 **(978-1-4598-1583-4(1))** Orca Bk. Pubs. USA.
Levin, Judith. Tattoos & Indigenous Peoples. (Tattooing Ser.). 64p. 2009. (gr. 5-6). 58.50 (978-1-60853-263-6(1)) 2008. (Illus.). (YA). (gr. 9-12). lib. bdg. 31.95 (978-1-4042-1828-4(9)) Rosen Publishing Group, Inc., The.
Loughran, Donna. Living in the Tundra. 2004. (Rookie Read-About Geography Ser.). (ENG., Illus.). 32p. (J). (gr. 1-2). pap. 5.95 (978-0-516-27331-0(0), Children's Pr.) Scholastic Library Publishing.
Marshall, Diana. Aboriginal Australians. 2012. (J). (978-1-61913-093-7(9)); (978-1-61913-435-5(7)) Weigl Pubs., Inc.
Marshall, James Vance. Stories from the Billabong. Firebrace, Francis, illus. 2010. (ENG.). 64p. (J). (gr. k-3). pap. 12.99 (978-1-84780-124-1(2), Frances Lincoln) Quarto Publishing Group UK GBR. Dist: Hachette Bk. Group.
Reynolds, Jan. Far North. 2007. (Vanishing Cultures Ser.). (ENG., Illus.). 32p. (J). (gr. 4-7). 8.95 (978-1-60060-127-9(8)); 16.95 (978-1-60060-142-2(1)) Lee & Low Bks., Inc.
Robertson, David Alexander. Sugar Falls: A Residential School Story. Henderson, Scott B., illus. 2012. (ENG.). 40p. (YA). (gr. 9-12). pap. (978-1-55379-334-2(X), 9781553793342, HighWater Pr.) Portage & Main Pr.
Robertson, Joanne. The Water Walker, 1 vol. 2017. (ENG., Illus.). 36p. (J). (gr. 2-6). 16.95 **(978-1-77260-038-4(5))** Second Story Pr. CAN. Dist: Orca Bk. Pubs. USA.
Rohr, Ian. Indigenous Celebrations. 2011. (Celebrations Ser.). (Illus.). 32p. (J). lib. bdg. 28.50 (978-1-59920-537-3(8)) Black Rabbit Bks.
Russell, Elaine. The Shack That Dad Built. Russell, Elaine, illus. 2005. (ENG., Illus.). 32p. (J). (gr. k-2). 10.95 (978-1-877003-94-3(8)) Little Hare Bks. AUS. Dist: Independent Pubs. Group.
Silvey, Diane. The Kids Book of Aboriginal Peoples in Canada. Mantha, John, illus. 2012. (Kids Book Of Ser.). (ENG.). 64p. (J). (gr. 3-7). 14.95 (978-1-55453-930-7(7)) Kids Can Pr., Ltd. CAN. Dist: Hachette Bk. Group.
Strudwick, Leslie & Webster, Christine. Indigenous Peoples Series, 4 vols. 2003. (J). lib. bdg. 208.00 (978-1-59036-149-8(0)) Weigl Pubs., Inc.
Wheatley, Nadia. Playground: Listening to Stories from Country & from Inside the Heart. Searle, Ken, illus. 2010. (ENG.). 72p. (J). (gr. 3-7). 34.95 (978-1-74237-097-2(7)) Allen & Unwin AUS. Dist: Independent Pubs. Group.

INDIVIDUALITY

Here are entered works on the sum total of characteristics which distinguish an individual from all others.
see also Identity (Psychology); Personality

Box, Su. You Are Very Special. Poole, Susie, illus. 2003. 32p. (J). pap. 6.95 (978-0-8198-8807-5(9), 332-417) Pauline Bks. & Media.
Danzig, Robert J. There Is Only One You: You Are Unique in the Universe. 2003. (Illus.). 72p. 9.95 (978-0-87868-884-5(6), 8846, Child & Family Pr.) Child Welfare League of America, Inc.
Dwyer, Helen, ed. The Individual & Society. 2011. (CC: Psychology Ser.). (Illus.). 112p. (gr. 6-12). lib. bdg. 42.80 (978-1-936333-19-6(8)) Brown Bear Bks.
Farrington Wilson, Lynda. Autistic? How Silly Is That! I Don't Need Any Labels at All. 2012. (ENG., Illus.). 32p. pap. 9.95 (978-1-935274-59-9(7), 9781935274599) Future Horizons, Inc.
Fox, Mem. Whoever You Are. Staub, Leslie, illus. 2007.Tr. of Sé de¿it Mak Ó. (ENG.). 28p. (J). (gr. -1 — 1). bds. 6.95 (978-0-15-206066-4(9)) Houghton Mifflin Harcourt Publishing Co.
Fritz, Greg. God Made You Special! Reed, Lisa, illus. 2015. (J). (978-0-8249-1947-4(5), Ideal Pubns.) Worthy Publishing.
Gainer, Cindy. I'm Like You, You're Like Me: A Book about Understanding & Appreciating Each Other. Sakamoto, Miki, illus. 2013. (ENG.). 48p. (J). (gr. -1-3). pap. 9.99 (978-1-57542-436-1(3)) Free Spirit Publishing, Inc.
Hachler, Bruno. I Am Who I Am. Wolferman, Iris, illus. 2010. (ENG.). 16p. (J). (gr. -1 — 1). bds. 8.95 (978-0-7358-2299-3(9)) North-South Bks., Inc.
Kalman, Bobbie. How Are We the Same & Different? 2009. (Our Multicultural World Ser.). (ENG., Illus.). 32p. (J). (gr. 1-4). pap. (978-0-7787-4648-5(8)) Crabtree Publishing Co.
Larson, Elaine M., et al. I Am Utterly Unique: Celebrating the Strengths of Children with Asperger Syndrome & High-Functioning Autism. Strand, Vivian, illus. 2006. 56p. (J). (gr. -1-3). 18.95 (978-1-931282-89-5(7)) Autism Asperger Publishing Co.
Lionni, Leo. Pezzettino. Lionni, Leo, illus. 2006. (Illus.). 40p. (J). (gr. -1-3). lib. bdg. 17.99 (978-0-394-93156-2(4), Pantheon) Knopf Doubleday Publishing Group.
Mills, Andy & Osborn, Becky. Shapesville. Neitz, Erica, illus. 2003. (ENG.). 32p. (J). 15.95 (978-0-936077-47-5(6)) Shelter Pubns., Inc.
—Shapesville. Neitz, Erica, tr. Neitz, Erica, illus. 2003. (ENG.). 32p. (J). pap. 12.95 (978-0-936077-44-4(1)) Shelter Pubns., Inc.
O'Keefe, Susan Heyboer. Be the Star That You Are: A Book for Kids Who Feel Different. Alley, R. W., illus. 2005. (Elf-Help Books for Kids). (J). per. 7.95 (978-0-87029-391-7(5)) Abbey Pr.
Onuoha-Ezemma, Glory. Don't Make Fun of My Name: My Name Is Special to My Parents & Me. unabr. ed. 2003. (Illus.). 47p. (J). (gr. k-6). pap. 9.95 (978-0-9661598-6-8(1)) Ekwike Bks. & Publishing.
Reynolds, Luke, ed. Break These Rules: 35 YA Authors on Speaking up, Standing Out, & Being Yourself. 2013. (ENG.). 224p. (YA). (gr. 7). pap. 12.95 (978-1-61374-784-1(5)) Chicago Review Pr., Inc.
Scott, Foresman and Company Staff. Work & Play, Big & Little, You & Me. (J). 18.82 (978-0-673-21373-0(0), Scott Foresman) Addison Wesley Schl.
Shulman, Mark. Are You Normal ? 2: More Than 100 Questions That Will Test Your Weirdness. 2013. (ENG., Illus.). 176p. (J). (gr. 3-7). pap. 12.95 (978-1-4263-1370-7(5)); lib. bdg. 21.95 (978-1-4263-1680-7(1)) National Geographic Society. (National Geographic Children's Bks.).
Tabor, Nancy Maria Grande. Somos un Arco Iris (We Are a Rainbow) Tabor, Nancy Maria Grande, illus. 2006. (ENG & SPA., Illus.). 28p. (gr. -1-3). 17.95 (978-0-7569-7027-7(X)) Perfection Learning Corp.

INDIVIDUALITY—FICTION

Abdullah, Shaila & Abdullah, Aanyah. My Friend Suhana: A Story of Friendship & Cerebral Palsy. 2014. 30p. pap. 14.95 (978-1-61599-211-9(1)) Loving Healing Pr., Inc.
Al-Ghani, K. I. Baby Blue Has the Blues, 1 vol. Al-Ghani, Haitham, illus. 2011. (ENG.). 32p. (J). 16.99 (978-0-7643-3732-1(7), 9780764337321, Schiffer Publishing Ltd) Schiffer Publishing, Ltd.
Anastasiu, Heather. Glitch. 2012. (Glitch Novel Ser.: 1). (ENG.). 336p. (YA). (gr. 7-12). pap. 12.99 (978-1-250-00299-0(0), 9781250002990, St. Martin's Griffin) St. Martin's Pr.
—Override. 2013. (Glitch Novel Ser.: 2). (ENG.). 320p. (YA). (gr. 7-12). pap. 9.99 (978-1-250-00300-3(8), 9781250003003, St. Martin's Griffin) St. Martin's Pr.
—Shutdown. 2013. (Glitch Novel Ser.: 3). (ENG.). 320p. (YA). (gr. 7-12). pap. 9.99 (978-1-250-00301-0(6), 9781250003010, St. Martin's Griffin) St. Martin's Pr.
Andreae, Giles. Giraffes Can't Dance. Parker-Rees, Guy, illus. (J). (gr. -1-3). 2012. (ENG.). 32p. bds. 6.99 (978-0-545-39255-6(1), Cartwheel Bks.) 2008. (ENG.). 9.99 (978-0-545-09738-3(X)) 2007. 24.95 incl. audio (978-0-439-02733-5(0)) Scholastic, Inc.
—Giraffes Can't Dance. Parker-Rees, Guy, illus. unabr. ed. 2011. (J). (gr. -1-1). 29.95 (978-0-439-02734-2(9)) Weston Woods Studios, Inc.
Appelt, Kathi. Incredible Me! Karas, G. Brian, illus. 2003. (ENG.). 32p. (J). (gr. -1-3). 16.99 (978-0-06-028622-4(9)) HarperCollins Pubs.
Arnold, Tedd. Dirty Gert. Arnold, Tedd, illus. 2014. (ENG., Illus.). 32p. (J). (gr. 2-5). 6.99 (978-0-8234-3054-3(5)) Holiday Hse., Inc.
Aucoin, Lee. Todo Sobre Mí, 1 vol. rev. ed. 2010. (Early Childhood Themes Ser.). (SPA., Illus.). 16p. (J). (gr. -1-2). pap. 19.99 (978-1-4333-1943-3(8)) Shell Educational Publishing.
—Todo Sobre Mí, 1 vol. rev. ed. 2010. (Early Childhood Themes Ser.). (SPA., Illus.). 16p. (J). (gr. -1-2). pap. 6.99 (978-1-4333-1942-6(X)) Shell Educational Publishing.
Auerbach, Adam. Edda: A Little Valkyrie's First Day of School. Auerbach, Adam, illus. 2014. (ENG., Illus.). 40p. (J). (gr. -1-3). 16.99 (978-0-8050-9703-0(1), 9780805097030, Holt, Henry & Co. Bks. For Young Readers) Holt, Henry & Co.
Baker, Keith. No Two Alike. Baker, Keith, illus. 2011. (ENG., Illus.). 40p. (J). (gr. -1-2). 16.99 (978-1-4424-1742-7(0), Beach Lane Bks.) Beach Lane Bks.
Banana-Tail. 2003. lib. bdg. 13.95 (978-0-9727681-0-8(6)) Active Media Publishing, LLC.
Bar-el, Dan. Not Your Typical Dragon. Bowers, Tim, illus. 2013. (ENG.). 40p. (J). (gr. -1-k). 16.99 (978-0-670-01402-6(8), Viking Books for Young Readers) Penguin Young Readers Group.
Barton, Suzanne. The Sleepy Songbird. 2016. (ENG., Illus.). 32p. (J). 16.99 (978-0-8027-3648-2(3), 9780802736482, Bloomsbury USA Childrens) Bloomsbury Publishing USA.
Battut, Éric. The Little Pea. Battut, Éric, illus. 2011. (ENG., Illus.). 28p. (J). (gr. -1-k). 16.95 (978-1-61608-482-0(0), 608482, Sky Pony Pr.) Skyhorse Publishing Co., Inc.
Bauer, Joan. Stand Tall. 2005. (ENG.). 192p. (YA). (gr. 7-5). pap. 8.99 (978-0-14-240427-0(6), Speak) Penguin Young Readers Group.
Bauman, Amy. Everyone Is Special! 2010. 12p. (J). (gr. -1). 9.95 (978-1-60747-719-8(X), Pickwick Pr.) Phoenix Bks., Inc.
Bea, Holly. Lucy Goose Goes to Texas. Boddy, Joe, illus. 2005. (ENG.). 32p. (J). (gr. -1-5). 15.95 (978-1-932073-15-7(9)) New World Library.
Beaumont, Karen. Wild about Us! Stevens, Janet, illus. 2015. (ENG.). 40p. (J). (gr. -1-3). 17.99 (978-0-15-206294-1(7), HMH Books For Young Readers) Houghton Mifflin Harcourt Publishing Co.
Bell, Juliet Clare. The Kite Princess. Chapman, Laura-Kate, illus. 2012. (ENG.). 32p. (J). pap. 9.99 (978-1-84686-830-6(0)) Barefoot Bks., Inc.
Bell, Juliet Clare & Chapman, Laura Kate. The Kite Princess. 2012. (ENG., Illus.). (J). 16.99 (978-1-84686-803-0(3)) Barefoot Bks., Inc.
Benton, Jim. The Invisible Fran, 1 vol. Benton, Jim, illus. 2011. (Franny K. Stein, Mad Scientist Ser.). (ENG., Illus.). 112p. (gr. 3-6). 24.21 (978-1-59961-819-7(2)) Spotlight.
Berenstain, Mike. God Made You Special, 1 vol. 2014. (Berenstain Bears/Living Lights Ser.). (ENG.). 24p. (J). pap. 3.99 (978-0-310-73483-3(5)) Zonderkidz.
Bergen, Lara. Sophie the Awesome. Tallardy, Laura, illus. 2010. 99p. (J). (978-0-545-24231-8(2)) Scholastic, Inc.
Berk, Sheryl & Berk, Carrie. Fashion Academy. 2015. (Fashion Academy Ser.: 1). (ENG.). 160p. (J). (gr. 5-8). pap. 6.99 (978-1-4926-0162-3(4), Sourcebooks Jabberwocky) Sourcebooks, Inc.
Bidelman, Jeff. The Adventures of Mr. Chicken Butt. Mozi, Jennifer, illus. 2013. (ENG.). (J). 14.95 (978-1-62086-354-1(5)) Mascot Bks., Inc.
Blabey, Aaron. Pearl Barley & Charlie Parsley. 2008. (ENG., Illus.). 32p. (J). (gr. -1-3). 16.95 (978-1-59078-596-6(7), Front Street) Boyds Mills Pr.
—Sunday Chutney. Blabey, Aaron, illus. 2009. (ENG., Illus.). 32p. (J). (gr. -1-k). 16.95 (978-1-59078-597-3(5), Front Street) Boyds Mills Pr.
Block, Francesca Lia. Pink Smog: Becoming Weetzie Bat. 2012. (Weetzie Bat Ser.: 6). (ENG.). 208p. (YA). (gr. 9). 17.99 (978-0-06-156598-4(9), HarperTeen) HarperCollins Pubs.
Bloom, Denise. More Than a Spoonful. 2007. 28p. (J). (gr. -1-2). pap. 5.95 (978-0-9778113-2-8(8)) HeartFelt Stories LLC.
Bloom, Denise, et al. More Than a Spoonful. 2007. (Heartfelt Stories Ser.). (Illus.). 28p. (J). 12.95 (978-0-9778113-0-4(1)) HeartFelt Stories LLC.
Bloom, Suzanne. A Splendid Friend, Indeed. 2005. (Goose & Bear Stories Ser.). (ENG., Illus.). 32p. (J). (gr. -1-k). 16.95 (978-1-59078-286-6(0)) Boyds Mills Pr.
Bloom, Suzanne, illus. A Splendid Friend, Indeed. 2015. (Goose & Bear Stories Ser.). (ENG.). 32p. (J). (— 1). bds. 7.99 (978-1-62979-408-2(2)) Boyds Mills Pr.
Bradley, Sandra. Henry Holton Takes the Ice. Palacios, Sara, illus. 2015. (ENG.). 40p. (J). (gr. k-3). 16.99 (978-0-8037-3856-0(0), Dial Bks) Penguin Young Readers Group.
Bradman, Tony. Goldilocks & the Just Right Club, 1 vol. Warburton, Sarah, illus. 2009. (After Happily Ever After Ser.). (ENG.). 56p. (gr. 2-3). 25.32 (978-1-4342-1304-4(8), After Happily Ever After) Stone Arch Bks.
—Michael. Ross, Tony, illus. 2009. (ENG.). 32p. (J). (gr. k-2). pap. 11.99 (978-1-84270-911-5(9)) Andersen Pr. GBR. Dist: Independent Pubs. Group.
Bramsen, Kirsten. The Yellow Tutu. Bramsen, Carin, illus. 2013. (ENG.). 40p. (J). (-k). pap. 7.99 (978-0-375-84393-8(0), Dragonfly Bks.) Random Hse. Children's Bks.
Branford, Anna. Violet Mackerel's Brilliant Plot. Allen, Elanna, illus. 2012. (Violet Mackerel Ser.). (ENG.). 112p. (J). (gr. 1-5). 15.99 (978-1-4424-3585-8(2)); pap. 5.99 (978-1-4424-3586-5(0)) Simon & Schuster Children's Publishing. (Atheneum Bks. for Young Readers).
Brashares, Ann. The Second Summer of the Sisterhood. 2004. (Sisterhood of the Traveling Pants Ser.: Bk. 2). (ENG.). 416p. (YA). (gr. 7-18). pap. 9.99 (978-0-385-73105-8(1), Ember) Random Hse. Children's Bks.
Brennan-Nelson, Denise & Hartung, Susan Kathleen. Tallulah: Mermaid of the Great Lakes. 2015. (ENG., Illus.). 40p. (J). (gr. 1-4). 16.99 (978-1-58536-909-6(8), 203812) Sleeping Bear Pr.
Bridges, Shirin Yim. The Umbrella Queen. Yoo, Taeeun, illus. 2008. (ENG.). 40p. (J). (gr. k-3). 16.99 (978-0-06-075040-4(5), Greenwillow Bks.) HarperCollins Pubs.
Briggs, Mayke Beckmann. Here You Are. Briggs, Mayke Beckmann, illus. 2007. (Illus.). 44p. (J). 16.95 (978-0-9776469-1-3(2)) BoathouseBooks.
Brignull, Irena. The Hawkweed Prophecy. 2017. (Hawkweed Ser.: 1). (ENG.). 384p. (gr. 7-17). pap. 10.99 **(978-1-60286-313-2(X)**, Weinstein Bks.) Perseus Bks. Group.
Brooks, Erik. Polar Opposites, 0 vols. 2010. (ENG., Illus.). 32p. (J). (gr. -1-3). 16.99 (978-0-7614-5685-8(6), 9780761456858, Amazon Children's Publishing) Amazon Publishing.
Brown, Derrick. Valentine the Porcupine Dances Funny. Lewis, Jenn, illus. 2011. (ENG.). 44p. 20.00 (978-1-935904-18-2(3)) Write Bloody Publishing.
Brown, Monica. Marisol McDonald & the Clash Bash/Marisol Mcdonald y la Fiesta Sin Igual. Palacios, Sara, illus. 2013. (Marisol Mcdonald Ser.). (ENG & SPA.). 40p. (J). 18.95 (978-0-89239-273-5(8)) Lee & Low Bks., Inc.
—Marisol Mcdonald Doesn't Match / Marisol Mcdonald no Combina. Palacios, Sara, illus. 2013. (Marisol Mcdonald Ser.). (SPA & ENG.). 32p. (J). (gr. -1-3). 17.95 (978-0-89239-235-3(5)) Lee & Low Bks., Inc.
Bunting, Eve. Girls A to Z. Bloom, Suzanne, illus. 2013. (ENG.). 32p. (J). (gr. k-2). pap. 6.95 (978-1-62091-028-3(4)) Boyds Mills Pr.
Butler, Dori Hillestad. The Case of the Mixed-Up Mutts, Bk. 2. Tugeau, Jeremy, illus. 2010. (Buddy Files Ser.: 2). (ENG.). 128p. (J). (gr. 1-5). 14.99 (978-0-8075-0911-1(6)) Whitman, Albert & Co.
Cabot, Meg. Princess in Love, Vol. 3. 2008. (Princess Diaries: 3). (ENG.). 256p. (YA). (gr. 8-12). pap. 9.99 (978-0-06-147995-3(0), HarperTeen) HarperCollins Pubs.
Carle, Eric. The Artist Who Painted a Blue Horse. Carle, Eric, illus. (ENG., Illus.). (J). (gr. -1 — 1). 2013. 22p. bds. 7.99 (978-0-399-16402-6(2)) 2011. 32p. 17.99 (978-0-399-25713-1(6)) Penguin Young Readers Group. (Philomel Bks.).
Carretero, Mónica. ROLY-POLIES. 2011. (Mini-Animalist Ser.). (ENG., Illus.). 32p. (J). (gr. k-2). (978-84-938240-1-3(1)) D P & G Military Pubs.
Cazet, Denys. Will You Read to Me? Cazet, Denys, illus. 2007. (ENG., Illus.). 32p. (J). (gr. -1-1). 16.99 (978-1-4169-0935-4(4), Atheneum/Richard Jackson Bks.) Simon & Schuster Children's Publishing.
Chandler, Susan. Welcome to Cuckooville. Durand, Delphine, illus. 2012. (ENG.). 24p. (J). (gr. k-3). 16.95 (978-1-61608-665-7(3), 608665, Sky Pony Pr.) Skyhorse Publishing Co., Inc.
Chapman, Jared. Steve, Raised by Wolves. 2015. (ENG., Illus.). 40p. (J). (gr. -1-3). 17.00 (978-0-316-25390-1(1)) Little Brown & Co.
Chodos-Irvine, Margaret. Ella Sarah Gets Dressed. 2003. (ENG., Illus.). 40p. (J). (gr. -1-3). 17.99 (978-0-15-216413-3(8)) Houghton Mifflin Harcourt Publishing Co.
Clarke, Jane. Plodney Creeper, Supersloth. 2006. (Blue Bananas Ser.). (ENG., Illus.). 48p. (J). (gr. -1-3). lib. bdg. (978-0-7787-0850-6(0)) Crabtree Publishing Co.
Clements, Andrew. About Average. Elliott, Mark, illus. (ENG.). (J). (gr. 3-7). 2014. 144p. pap. 7.99 (978-1-4169-9725-2(3)) 2012. 128p. 16.99 (978-1-4169-9724-5(5)) Simon & Schuster Children's Publishing. (Atheneum Bks. for Young Readers).
—Lost & Found. Elliott, Mark, illus. 2010. (ENG.). 192p. (J). (gr. 3-7). pap. 7.99 (978-1-4169-0986-6(9), Atheneum Bks. for Young Readers) Simon & Schuster Children's Publishing.
Cocca-Leffler, Maryann. Janine. Cocca-Leffler, Maryann, illus. 2015. (ENG., Illus.). 32p. (J). (gr. -1-3). 16.99 (978-0-8075-3754-1(3)) Whitman, Albert & Co.
Cochran, Bill. My Parents Are Divorced My Elbows Have Nicknames & Other Fact. Björkman, Steve, illus. 2009. (ENG.). 32p. (J). (gr. -1-3). 17.99 (978-0-06-053942-9(9)) HarperCollins Pubs.
Colfer, Chris. The Curvy Tree. Dorman, Brandon, illus. 2015. (ENG.). 32p. (J). (gr. -1-3). 17.00 (978-0-316-40685-7(6)) Little Brown & Co.
Conford, Ellen. And This Is Laura. 2014. (ENG.). 228p. (J). (gr. 3). pap. 12.95 (978-1-939601-18-6(5)) Ig Publishing, Inc.
Corderoy, Tracey. Hubble Bubble, Granny Trouble. Berger, Joe, illus. 2012. (ENG.). 32p. (J). (gr. -1-2). 14.99 (978-0-7636-5904-2(5), Nosy Crow) Candlewick Pr.
Cosgrove, Stephen. Cricket Clickett: Finding Your Talents. Arroyo, Fian, illus. 2004. (J). (978-1-58804-382-5(7)) P C I Education.
Cuevas, Michelle. Beyond the Laughing Sky. Morstad, Julie, illus. 2014. (ENG.). 160p. (J). (gr. 3-7). 16.99 (978-0-8037-3867-6(6), Dial Bks) Penguin Young Readers Group.
Czajak, Paul & Brothers Hilts Staff. Seaver the Weaver. Hilts, Ben, illus. 2015. (ENG.). 32p. (J). (-k). 15.95 (978-1-938063-57-2(0), Mighty Media Kids) Mighty Media Pr.
Dahl, Michael. Two Heads Are Better Than One, 1 vol. Ornia-Blanco, Miguel, illus. 2010. (Monster Street Ser.). (ENG.). 32p. (gr. 1-2). lib. bdg. 23.99 (978-1-4048-6067-4(3), Monster Street) Picture Window Bks.
Dakos, Kalli. Why Am I Blue? A Story about Being Yourself. Garófoli, Viviana, illus. 2017. 32p. (J). 15.95 **(978-1-4338-2734-1(4)**, Magination Pr.) American Psychological Assn.
Damjan, Mischa. The Clown Said No. 2004. (Illus.). (J). (gr. k-3). spiral bd. (978-0-616-14569-2(1)) Canadian National Institute for the Blind/Institut National Canadien pour les Aveugles.
Danielles Show & Tell Lesson. 2005. (YA). per. (978-1-59872-256-7(5)) Instant Pub.
Danziger, Paula. Can You Sue Your Parents for Malpractice? (gr. 5-6). 144p. (J). pap. 3.99 (978-0-8072-1375-9(6)); 152p. (YA). pap. 3.99 (978-0-8072-1540-1(6)) Random Hse. Audio Publishing Group. (Listening Library).
Darnton, Kate. Chloe in India. 2016. (ENG.). 224p. (J). (gr. 4-7). 16.99 (978-0-553-53504-4(8), Delacorte Bks. for Young Readers) Random Hse. Children's Bks.
Davis, Eleanor. Secret Science Alliance. 2010. (J). (978-1-59990-143-5(9)) Bloomsbury Publishing USA.
—The Secret Science Alliance. Davis, Eleanor, illus. 2009. (ENG., Illus.). 160p. (YA). (gr. 3-6). pap. 16.99 (978-1-59990-396-5(2), 9781599903965, Bloomsbury USA Childrens) Bloomsbury Publishing USA.
—The Secret Science Alliance & the Copycat Crook. Davis, Eleanor, illus. 2009. (ENG., Illus.). 160p. (J). (gr. 3-6). 18.99 (978-1-59990-142-8(0), 9781599901428, Bloomsbury USA Childrens) Bloomsbury Publishing USA.
Dean, James. Too Cool for School. 2014. (Pete the Cat I Can Read Ser.). (J). lib. bdg. 13.55 (978-0-606-35062-4(4), Turtleback) Turtleback Bks.
Dean, James & Dean, Kimberly. Pete the Cat & the New Guy. Dean, James, illus. 2014. (Pete the Cat Ser.). (ENG., Illus.). 40p. (J). (gr. -1-3). 17.99 (978-0-06-227560-8(7)); lib. bdg. 18.89 (978-0-06-227561-5(5)) HarperCollins Pubs.
deGennaro, Sue. The Pros & Cons of Being a Frog. deGennaro, Sue, illus. 2016. (ENG., Illus.). 40p. (J). (gr. -1-3). 17.99 (978-1-4814-7130-5(9), Simon & Schuster/Paula Wiseman Bks.) Simon & Schuster/Paula Wiseman Bks.
Derrick, David G., Jr. Sid the Squid: And the Search for the Perfect Job. 2010. (ENG., Illus.). 36p. (J). (gr. -1-3). 15.95 (978-1-59702-021-3(4)) Immedium.
Desbordes, Astrid. Edmond, the Moonlit Party. Boutavant, Marc, illus. 2015. (ENG.). 32p. (J). (gr. -1-3). 17.95 (978-1-59270-174-2(4)) Enchanted Lion Bks., LLC.
DeVillers, Julia & Roy, Jennifer Rozines. Take Two. 2010. (Mix Ser.). (ENG.). 304p. (J). (gr. 4-8). pap. 7.99 (978-1-4169-6731-6(1), Aladdin) Simon & Schuster Children's Publishing.
—Take Two. 2010. (ENG.). 240p. (J). (gr. 4-8). 16.99 (978-1-4169-7533-5(0), Simon & Schuster/Paula Wiseman Bks.) Simon & Schuster/Paula Wiseman Bks.
—Times Squared. 2011. (Mix Ser.). (ENG.). (J). (gr. 4-8). 272p. pap. 7.99 (978-1-4169-6732-3(X)); 240p. 16.99 (978-1-4169-7532-8(2)) Simon & Schuster Children's Publishing. (Aladdin).
Dickey, R. A. Knuckleball Ned. Bowers, Tim, illus. 2014. (ENG.). 32p. (J). (gr. -1-k). 17.99 (978-0-8037-4038-9(7), Dial Bks) Penguin Young Readers Group.
Dillard, Sarah. First Day at Zoo School. Dillard, Sarah, illus. 2014. (ENG., Illus.). 40p. (J). (gr. k-2). 14.99 (978-1-58536-890-7(3), 203670) Sleeping Bear Pr.
Dinardo, Jeff. Klink & Klank: Accepting Differences. Paillot, Jim, illus. 2014. (Funny Bone Readers: Being a Friend Ser.). 24p. (gr. -1-1). pap. 4.99 (978-1-939656-04-9(4)) Red Chair Pr.
Dipucchio, Kelly. Gaston. Robinson, Christian, illus. 2014. (Gaston & Friends Ser.). (ENG.). 40p. (J). (gr. -1-3). 17.99 (978-1-4424-5102-5(5), Atheneum Bks. for Young Readers) Simon & Schuster Children's Publishing.
—Gastón. 2016. (SPA.). 32p. (J). (gr. k-2). 23.99 **(978-607-96900-0-7(4))** Editorial Leetra MEX. Dist: Lectorum Pubns., Inc.
Dipucchio, Kelly. Gaston. Robinson, Christian, illus. 2017. (Gaston & Friends Ser.). (ENG.). 80p. (J). (gr. -1-3). 35.99 (978-1-5344-0002-3(8), Atheneum Bks. for Young Readers) Simon & Schuster Children's Publishing.
Dolan, Penny. The Lovely Duckling. 2014. (ENG., Illus.). 32p. (J). (978-0-7787-0445-4(9)); pap. (978-0-7787-0480-5(7)) Crabtree Publishing Co.
Dolenz, Micky. Gakky Two-Feet. Clark, David, illus. 2006. (J). (978-1-4156-8089-6(2), Putnam Juvenile) Penguin Publishing Group.
Donahue, Laurie. Mr. Blue a Job for You. Bryan, Hintz, illus. 2010. 32p. (J). 15.95 (978-0-9799116-2-0(1)) LifeSong Pubs.
Doudna, Kelly. Goat Cheese, 1 vol. Haberstroh, Anne, illus. 2006. (Animal Tales Ser.). 24p. (J). (gr. k-3). (ENG.). lib. bdg. 24.21 (978-1-59679-937-0(4), SandCastle); pap. 48.42 (978-1-59679-938-7(2)) ABDO Publishing Co.
Downey, Joni J. Will You Be My Friend? — We Really Are No Different. Brudos, Susan E., illus. 2004. (J). pap. (978-0-932991-34-8(3)) Place In The Woods, The.

Driscoll, Laura. We Are Twins. Campion, Pascal, illus. 2012. (Penguin Young Readers, Level 1 Ser.). (ENG.). 32p. (J). (gr. k-1). mass mkt. 3.99 *(978-0-448-46157-1(9)*, Penguin Young Readers) Penguin Young Readers Group.
—We Are Twins. 2012. (Penguin Young Readers Level 1 Ser.). lib. bdg. 13.55 *(978-0-606-26641-3(0)*, Turtleback) Turtleback Bks.
Dube, Pierrette. How to Become a Perfect Knight in Five Days. Hamel, Caroline, illus. 2009. (Rainy Day Readers Ser.). 32p. (J). (gr. -1-3). 22.60 *(978-1-60754-373-2(7))*; pap. 10.55 *(978-1-60754-374-9(5))* Windmill Bks.
—How to Become a Perfect Princess in Five Days. Melanson, Luc, illus. 2009. (Rainy Day Readers Ser.). 32p. (J). (gr. -1-3). 22.60 *(978-1-60754-376-3(1))* Windmill Bks.
Dubner, Stephen J. The Boy with Two Belly Buttons. Niemann, Christoph, illus. 2007. 32p. (J). (gr. -1-1). 17.89 *(978-0-06-113403-6(1))* HarperCollins Pubs.
Dupuy, Diane. The Little Girl Who Did... What?!!! Stockelbach, Ed, illus. 2004. 32p. 12.95 *(978-0-9730736-0-7(8))* Beyond Light CAN. Dist: Hushion Hse. Publishing, Ltd.
Earhardt, Ainsley & Cristaldi, Kathryn. Take Heart, My Child: A Mother's Dream. Kim, Jaime, illus. 2016. (ENG.). 32p. (J). (gr. -1-3). 18.99 *(978-1-4814-6622-6(4)*, Aladdin) Simon & Schuster Children's Publishing.
Eastman, Peter. Fred & Ted Go Camping. 2005. (Beginner Books(R) Ser.). (ENG., Illus.). 48p. (J). (gr. -1-2). 9.99 *(978-0-375-82965-9(2)*, Random Hse. Bks. for Young Readers) Random Hse. Children's Bks.
—Fred & Ted Like to Fly. Eastman, Peter, illus. 2007. (Beginner Books Ser.). (ENG., Illus.). 48p. (J). (gr. -1-2). 8.99 *(978-0-375-84064-7(8)*, Random Hse. Bks. for Young Readers) Random Hse. Children's Bks.
—Fred & Ted's Road Trip. 2011. (Beginner Books(R) Ser.). (ENG., Illus.). 48p. (J). (gr. -1-2). 9.99 *(978-0-375-86764-4(3)*, Random Hse. Bks. for Young Readers) Random Hse. Children's Bks.
Eaton, Jason Carter. The Catawampus Cat. Gordon, Gus, illus. 2017. (ENG.). 32p. (J). (gr. -1-3). 16.99 *(978-0-553-50971-7(3)*, Crown Books For Young Readers) Random Hse. Children's Bks.
Ebbitt, Carolyn Q. The Extra-Ordinary Princess. 2010. (ENG.). 336p. (YA). (gr. 3-6). pap. 7.99 *(978-1-59990-484-9(5)*, 9781599904849, Bloomsbury USA Childrens) Bloomsbury Publishing USA.
Ehlert, Lois. Oodles of Animals. 2008. (ENG., Illus.). 56p. (J). (gr. -1-2). 18.99 *(978-0-15-206274-3(2))* Houghton Mifflin Harcourt Publishing Co.
Emerson, Carl. Speed up, Sammy the Tree Sloth!, 1 vol. Trover, Zachary, illus. 2007. (Animal Underdogs Ser.). (ENG.). 32p. (J). (gr. -1-3). 28.50 *(978-1-60270-019-2(2)*, Looking Glass Library) ABDO Publishing Co.
Ering, Timothy Basil. Necks Out for Adventure! Ering, Timothy Basil, illus. 2008. (ENG., Illus.). 48p. (J). (gr. -1-3). 16.99 *(978-0-7636-2355-5(5))* Candlewick Pr.
Erskine, Kathryn. The Absolute Value of Mike. 2012. (ENG.). 272p. (J). (gr. 5-18). pap. 7.99 *(978-0-14-242101-7(4)*, Puffin Books) Penguin Young Readers Group.
Falconer, Ian. Olivia & the Fairy Princesses. Falconer, Ian, illus. 2012. (ENG., Illus.). 40p. (J). (gr. -1-3). 18.99 *(978-1-4424-5027-1(4)*, Atheneum Bks. for Young Readers) Simon & Schuster Children's Publishing.
—Olivia y Las Princesas. 2012. (SPA., Illus.). 32p. (J). (gr. -1-1). 17.99 *(978-1-933032-82-5(0))* Lectorum Pubns., Inc.
Falligant, Erin. Into the Spotlight. Studios, Arcana, illus. 2011. (ENG.). 120p. (YA). (gr. 3-18). pap. 8.95 *(978-1-59369-835-5(6))* American Girl Publishing, Inc.
Farley, Robin. Mia & the Girl with a Twirl. 2013. (Mia I Can Read Bks.). (J). lib. bdg. 13.55 *(978-0-606-31811-2(9)*, Turtleback) Turtleback Bks.
Fleischman, Paul. The Dunderheads. Roberts, David, illus. 2012. (ENG.). 56p. (J). (gr. 1-4). pap. 6.99 *(978-0-7636-5239-5(3))* Candlewick Pr.
—The Dunderheads. 2012. lib. bdg. 17.20 *(978-0-606-23804-5(2)*, Turtleback) Turtleback Bks.
—The Dunderheads Behind Bars. Roberts, David, illus. 2012. (ENG.). 48p. (J). (gr. 1-4). 16.99 *(978-0-7636-4543-4(5))* Candlewick Pr.
Fogg, K. L. Serpent Tide. 2006. 16.95 *(978-1-59156-861-2(7))* Covenant Communications, Inc.
Forester, Victoria. The Girl Who Could Fly. 2008. (ENG.). 336p. (J). (gr. 4-7). 16.95 *(978-0-312-37462-4(3)*, 9780312374624) Feiwel & Friends.
—The Girl Who Could Fly. Barcellona, Christine, ed. 2015. (ENG.). 352p. (J). (gr. 4-7). pap. 7.99 *(978-1-250-07246-7(8)*, 9781250072467) Square Fish.
Fox, Mem. The Straight Line Wonder. *(978-1-57255-567-9(X))* Mondo Publishing.
Friedman, J. S. The Micetro of Moscow. Beatrice, Chris, illus. 2013. (Maurice's Valises: Moral Tails in an Immoral World Ser.: Vol. 2). (ENG.). 37p. (J). (gr. k-4). pap. *(978-94-91613-06-7(5))* Mouse Prints Pr.
Friedman, Laurie. A Style All Her Own. Watts, Sharon, illus. 2005. 32p. (J). (gr. -1-3). lib. bdg. 15.95 *(978-1-57505-599-2(6))* Lerner Publishing Group.
Galante, Cecilia. The One & Only Willa Bean. Valiant, Kristi, illus. 2012. (Little Wings Ser.: 4). (ENG.). 112p. (J). (gr. 1-4). pap. 4.99 *(978-0-375-86950-1(6)*, Random Hse. Bks. for Young Readers) Random Hse. Children's Bks.
Gall, Chris. Dog vs. Cat. 2014. (ENG., Illus.). 32p. (J). (gr. -1-3). 17.99 *(978-0-316-23801-4(5))* Little, Brown Bks. for Young Readers.
Ganges, Montse. Meet Cooper. Urberuaga, Emilio, illus. 2009. (Cooper Ser.). 24p. (J). (gr. -1-3). pap. 8.15 *(978-1-60754-234-6(X))* Windmill Bks.
Ganges, Montse & Urberuaga, Emilio. Meet Cooper. 2009. (Cooper Ser.). (Illus.). 24p. (J). (gr. -1-3). lib. bdg. 22.60 *(978-1-60754-233-9(1))* Windmill Bks.
Garton, Sam. Otter Goes to School. Garton, Sam, illus. 2016. (Illus.). 32p. (J). (gr. -1-3). 17.99 *(978-0-06-235225-5(3))* HarperCollins Pubs.
—Otter: Hello, Sea Friends! Garton, Sam, illus. 2016. (My First I Can Read Ser.). (Illus.). 32p. (J). (gr. -1-3). pap. 3.99 *(978-0-06-236660-3(2))* HarperCollins Pubs.
Gateley, Edwina, illus. & text. God Goes to School. Gateley, Edwina, text. 2009. 32p. (J). pap. 9.95 *(978-0-8091-6748-7(4))* Paulist Pr.
Genhart, Michael. So Many Smarts! Clifton-Brown, Holly, illus. 2017. (J). ***(978-1-4338-2722-8(0)***, Magination Pr.) American Psychological Assn.
Giff, Patricia Reilly. Soccer Song. Sims, Blanche, illus. 2008. (Green Light Readers Level 2 Ser.). (ENG.). 24p. (J). (gr. k-2). pap. 3.95 *(978-0-15-206565-2(2))* Houghton Mifflin Harcourt Publishing Co.
Gliori, Debi. Dragon's Extraordinary Egg. 2014. (ENG., Illus.). 32p. (J). (gr. -1-3). 17.99 *(978-0-8027-3759-5(5)*, 9780802737595, Bloomsbury USA Childrens) Bloomsbury Publishing USA.
Gore, Emily. And Nick. Gore, Leonid, illus. 2015. (ENG.). 40p. (J). (gr. -1-3). 17.99 *(978-1-4169-5506-1(2))* Simon & Schuster Children's Publishing.
Goss, Leon. I'm Good, I'm Beautiful, I'm Smart. Mailey, Maria C. & Neuburger, Jenny, illus. 2005. (J). per. *(978-1-933156-02-6(3)*, VisionQuest Kids) GSVQ Publishing.
Grab, Daphne. Halftime. 2010. (J). *(978-0-385-90693-7(5))*; *(978-0-385-73783-8(1))* Random House Publishing Group. (Delacorte Pr).
Gray, Libba Moore. Miss Tizzy. Rowland, Jada, illus. 2014. 40p. pap. 8.00 *(978-1-61003-356-5(6))* Center for the Collaborative Classroom.
Green, George & Brooke, Amy/ J. George Green's, the Lion Who Couldn't Roar. 2008. (Illus.). (J). per. 16.99 *(978-1-933156-14-9(7)*, Visikid Bks.) GSVQ Publishing.
Griffin, Martha & Griffin, Grant. Sam's Birthmark. Smiley, Mary Anne, illus. 2013. (ENG.). 24p. (J). (gr. -1-3). 18.95 *(978-0-692-01920-7(0))* Griffin Group Publishing LLC.
Gudeon, Adam. Ping Wants to Play. Gudeon, Adam, illus. 2014. (I Like to Read(r) Ser.). (ENG., Illus.). 24p. (J). (gr. -1-3). 14.95 *(978-0-8234-2854-0(0))* Holiday Hse., Inc.
Gudeon, Adam & Gudeon, Adam. Ping Wants to Play. 2015. (I Like to Read(r) Ser.). (ENG.). 24p. (J). (gr. -1-3). 6.99 *(978-0-8234-3313-1(7))* Holiday Hse., Inc.
Guinan, Jack. I'm a Lot of Sometimes: A Growing-Up Story of Identity. Rudebjer, Lars, illus. 2017. (Growing Up Ser.). (ENG.). 24p. (gr. -1-1). lib. bdg. 19.99 *(978-1-63440-177-7(8))*; 30.65 ***(978-1-63440-181-4(6))*** Red Chair Pr.
Hallowell, Edward M. & Mayer, Bill. A Walk in the Rain with a Brain. 2004. (ENG., Illus.). 32p. (J). (gr. 1-3). 16.95 *(978-0-06-000731-7(1))* HarperCollins Pubs.
Hannigan, Katherine. Emmaline & the Bunny. Hannigan, Katherine, illus. 2009. (ENG., Illus.). 112p. (J). (gr. 2-7). 16.99 *(978-0-06-162654-8(6)*, Greenwillow Bks.) HarperCollins Pubs.
Hardy, Sarah Frances. Puzzled by Pink. 2012. (ENG.). 32p. (J). (gr. -1-k). 16.99 *(978-0-670-01320-3(X)*, Viking Books for Young Readers) Penguin Young Readers Group.
Harris, Robie H. Who We Are! All about Being the Same & Being Different. Westcott, Nadine Bernard, illus. 2016. (Let's Talk about You & Me Ser.). (ENG.). 40p. (J). (-k). 15.99 *(978-0-7636-6903-4(2))* Candlewick Pr.
Hautman, Pete. Rash. 2007. (ENG., Illus.). 272p. (YA). (gr. 7-12). pap. 10.99 *(978-0-689-86904-4(5)*, Simon & Schuster Bks. For Young Readers) Simon & Schuster Bks. For Young Readers.
Helakoski, Leslie. Woolbur. Harper, Lee, illus. 2008. (ENG.). 32p. (J). (gr. -1-3). 17.99 *(978-0-06-084726-5(3))* HarperCollins Pubs.
—Woolbur. 2008. (J). (gr. -1-2). 29.95 incl. audio *(978-0-8045-6971-2(1))* Spoken Arts, Inc.
Heling, Kathryn & Hembrook, Deborah. I Wish I Had Freckles Like Abby. Adamson, Bonnie, illus. 2009. (ENG.). 32p. (J). (gr. -1-3). 16.95 *(978-1-934960-46-2(2)*, Raven Tree Pr.,Csi) Continental Sales, Inc.
—I Wish I Had Freckles Like Abby/Quisiera Tener Pecas Como Abby. Adamson, Bonnie, illus. 2007. (SPA & ENG.). 32p. (J). (gr. -1-3). pap. 7.95 *(978-0-9770906-6-2(3)*, Raven Tree Pr.,Csi) Continental Sales, Inc.
—I Wish I Had Glasses Like Rosa. Adamson, Bonnie, illus. (I Wish Ser.). (ENG.). 32p. (J). (gr. 4-7). 2010. pap. 7.95 *(978-1-934960-49-3(7))* 2009. 16.95 *(978-1-934960-48-6(9))* Continental Sales, Inc. (Raven Tree Pr.,Csi).
—I Wish I Was Strong Like Manuel. Adamson, Bonnie, illus. (I Wish Ser.). (ENG.). 32p. (J). 2010. (gr. 4-7). pap. 7.95 *(978-1-934960-53-0(5))* 2009. (gr. -1-3). 16.95 *(978-1-934960-52-3(7))* Continental Sales, Inc. (Raven Tree Pr.,Csi).
—I Wish I Was Tall Like Willie. Adamson, Bonnie, illus. (I Wish Ser.). (ENG.). 32p. (J). (gr. 4-7). 2010. pap. 7.95 *(978-1-934960-51-6(9))* 2009. 16.95 *(978-1-934960-50-9(0))* Continental Sales, Inc. (Raven Tree Pr.,Csi).
Heling, Kathryn, et al. I Wish I Had Freckles Like Abby/Quisiera Tener Pecas Como Abby. de La Vega, Eida, tr. Adamson, Bonnie, illus. 2007. (I Wish Ser.). (SPA & ENG.). 32p. (J). (gr. -1-3). 16.95 *(978-0-9724973-8-1(2)*, 626999, Raven Tree Pr.,Csi) Continental Sales, Inc.
Henshon, Suzanna E. Spiders on the Ceiling. 2006. (J). *(978-0-88092-614-0(7))* Royal Fireworks Publishing Co.
Hilton, Perez. The Boy with Pink Hair. Hill, Jenn, illus. 2011. (ENG.). 32p. (J). (gr. -1-k). 17.99 *(978-0-451-23420-9(0)*, Celebra Young Readers) Penguin Publishing Group.
Holder, Jennifer. God Made You Special. Nobens, C. A., illus. 2015. (Happy Day Ser.). (ENG.). 16p. (J). pap. 2.49 *(978-1-4964-1110-5(2)*, Happy Day) Tyndale Hse. Pubs.
Holmes, Elizabeth. The Normal Kid. 2012. (Exceptional Reading & Language Arts Titles for Intermediate Grades Ser.). (ENG.). 248p. (J). (gr. 4-9). 17.95 *(978-0-7613-8085-6(X)*, Carolrhoda Bks.) Lerner Publishing Group.
Hong, Jess. Lovely. Hong, Jess, illus. 2017. (ENG., Illus.). 32p. (J). (gr. -1-2). 16.99 ***(978-1-939547-37-8(7))*** Creston Bks.
Hood, Morag. Carrot & Pea. 2017. (ENG., Illus.). 32p. (J). (gr. -1-3). 16.99 *(978-0-544-86842-7(0)*, HMH Books For Young Readers) Houghton Mifflin Harcourt Publishing Co.
Horácek, Petr. Silly Suzy Goose. Horácek, Petr, illus. 2009. (ENG., Illus.). 32p. (J). (— 1). bds. 7.99 *(978-0-7636-4141-2(3))* Candlewick Pr.
Hosford, Kate. Big Birthday. Clifton-Brown, Holly, illus. 2012. (Carolrhoda Picture Bks.). (ENG.). 32p. (J). (gr. k-2). lib. bdg. 16.95 *(978-0-7613-5410-9(7))* Lerner Publishing Group.
—Big Bouffant. Clifton-Brown, Holly, illus. 2011. (ENG.). 32p. (J). (gr. k-2). 16.95 *(978-0-7613-5409-3(3)*, Carolrhoda Bks.) Lerner Publishing Group.
Hovland, Henrik & Bartlett, Don. John Jensen Feels Different. Kove, Torill, illus. 2011. (ENG.). 40p. (J). 16.00 *(978-0-8028-5399-8(4)*, Eerdmans Bks For Young Readers) Eerdmans, William B. Publishing Co.
Hughes, Susan. Earth to Audrey. Poulin, Stéphane, illus. 2007. (ENG.). 32p. (J). (gr. k-3). 6.95 *(978-1-55453-165-3(9))* Kids Can Pr., Ltd. CAN. Dist: Hachette Bk. Group.
Hurst, Carol Otis. Terrible Storm. 2007. (Illus.). 32p. (J). (gr. k-3). lib. bdg. 17.89 *(978-0-06-009002-9(2))* HarperCollins Pubs.
Hurwitz, Michele Weber. Calli Be Gold. 2012. (ENG.). 208p. (J). (gr. 3-7). 6.99 *(978-0-375-86528-2(4)*, Yearling) Random Hse. Children's Bks.
Hwang, Sun-mi. The Hen Who Dreamed She Could Fly. 2013. lib. bdg. 28.20 *(978-0-606-35094-5(2)*, Turtleback) Turtleback Bks.
Iyengar, Malathi Michelle. Romina's Rangoli. Wanardi, Jennifer, illus. 2007. (Romina's Rangoli Ser.). 32p. (J). (gr. -1-3). 16.95 *(978-1-885008-32-9(5)*, Shen's Bks.) Lee & Low Bks., Inc.
Jeffers, Oliver. The New Sweater. Jeffers, Oliver, illus. (Hueys Ser.: 1). (ENG., Illus.). (J). (gr. -1-k). 2015. 24p. bds. 6.99 *(978-0-399-17391-2(9))* 2012. 32p. 17.99 *(978-0-399-25767-4(5))* Penguin Young Readers Group. (Philomel Bks.).
Jerry, Spinelli. Stargirl. 2014. (ENG.). 208p. (YA). 11.24 *(978-1-63245-152-1(2))* Lectorum Pubns., Inc.
John, Jory. I Love You Already! Davies, Benji, illus. 2015. 32p. (J). (gr. -1-3). 17.99 *(978-0-06-237095-2(2))* HarperCollins Pubs.
Johnson, J. J. This Girl Is Different, 1 vol. 2011. (ENG.). 288p. (YA). (gr. 7-11). 16.95 *(978-1-56145-578-2(4))* Peachtree Pubs.
Joyce, Melanie. Fly, Freddy, Fly. Seal, Julia, illus. 2014. (J). *(978-1-4351-5806-1(7))* Barnes & Noble, Inc.
Judge, Lita. Hoot & Peep. 2016. (Hoot & Peep Ser.). (ENG., Illus.). 40p. (J). (-k). 17.99 *(978-0-525-42837-4(2)*, Dial Bks) Penguin Young Readers Group.
Jungle Crossing. 2011. (ENG.). 228p. (J). (gr. 5-7). pap. 13.99 *(978-0-547-55009-1(X))* Houghton Mifflin Harcourt Publishing Co.
Kann, Victoria. Tickled Pink. Kann, Victoria, illus. 2010. (Pinkalicious Ser.). (ENG., Illus.). 24p. (J). (gr. -1-3). pap. 3.99 *(978-0-06-192877-2(1)*, HarperFestival) HarperCollins Pubs.
—Tickled Pink. Kann, Victoria, illus. 2010. (Pinkalicious Ser.). (Illus.). (J). lib. bdg. 13.55 *(978-0-606-14869-6(8)*, Turtleback) Turtleback Bks.
Kann, Victoria & Kann, Elizabeth. Purplicious. Kann, Victoria, illus. 2007. (Illus.). 40p. (J). (gr. k-3). (ENG.). 17.99 *(978-0-06-124405-6(8))*; lib. bdg. 17.89 *(978-0-06-124406-3(6))* HarperCollins Pubs.
Karpes, H. R. Morris... the Downside-Up Bat. 2013. (ENG., Illus.). 32p. (J). (gr. -1-k). 11.95 *(978-1-62087-987-0(5)*, 620987, Sky Pony Pr.) Skyhorse Publishing Co., Inc.
Kashyap, Keshni. Tina's Mouth: An Existential Comic Diary. Araki, Mari, illus. 10th ed. 2012. (ENG.). 256p. 18.95 *(978-0-618-94519-1(9))* Houghton Mifflin Harcourt Publishing Co.
Keane, Dave. First Day Frights. Keane, Dave, illus. 2012. (I Can Read Level 2 Ser.). (ENG., Illus.). 32p. (J). (gr. -1-3). pap. 3.99 *(978-0-06-085475-1(8))* HarperCollins Pubs.
—Monster School: First Day Frights. Keane, Dave, illus. 2012. (I Can Read Level 2 Ser.). (ENG., Illus.). 32p. (J). (gr. -1-3). 16.99 *(978-0-06-085476-8(6))* HarperCollins Pubs.
—Sloppy Joe. Brunkus, Denise, illus. 2009. (ENG.). 32p. (J). (gr. -1-2). 16.99 *(978-0-06-171020-9(2))* HarperCollins Pubs.
Keith, Donna. I Love You All the Same, 1 vol. Edgson, Allison, illus. 2014. (ENG.). 20p. (J). bds. 9.99 *(978-0-529-10204-1(8))* Nelson, Thomas Inc.
Kenah, Katharine. The Best Chef in Second Grade. Carter, Abby, illus. (I Can Read Level 2 Ser.). 48p. (J). 2008. (ENG.). (gr. k-3). pap. 3.99 *(978-0-06-053563-6(6))* 2007. (gr. -1-3). lib. bdg. 16.89 *(978-0-06-053562-9(8))* HarperCollins Pubs.
Kimmel, Elizabeth Cody. Suddenly Supernatural: Scaredy Kat. 2010. (Suddenly Supernatural Ser.: 2). (ENG.). 272p. (J). (gr. 3-7). pap. 5.99 *(978-0-316-08745-2(9))* Little, Brown Bks. for Young Readers.
King-Chai, Sharon. Lucy Ladybug. 2016. (ENG., Illus.). 32p. (J). (gr. -1-2). 16.99 *(978-0-553-51005-8(3)*, Random Hse. Bks. for Young Readers) Random Hse. Children's Bks.
King-smith, Dick. Funny Frank. Eastwood, John, illus. 2003. (ENG.). 112p. (J). (gr. 1-4). 5.99 *(978-0-440-41880-1(1)*, Yearling) Random Hse. Children's Bks.
Klass, David. Losers Take All. 2015. (ENG.). 320p. (YA). (gr. 7). 17.99 *(978-0-374-30136-1(0)*, 9780374301361, Farrar, Straus & Giroux (BYR)) Farrar, Straus & Giroux.
—Losers Take All. 2016. (YA). lib. bdg. 20.85 *(978-0-606-39480-2(X))* Turtleback Bks.
Koch, Miriam. Digby Differs. Garlid, Ann, tr. from GER. Koch, Miriam, illus. 2013. (Illus.). 40p. 17.99 *(978-1-4413-1306-5(0))* Peter Pauper Pr. Inc.
Kochan, Vera. What If Your Best Friend Were Blue?, 0 vols. Garófoli, Viviana, illus. 2011. (ENG.). 24p. (J). (gr. -1-2). 12.99 *(978-0-7614-5897-5(2)*, 9780761458975, Amazon Children's Publishing) Amazon Publishing.
Koja, Kathe. Straydog. 2004. (ENG.). 128p. (YA). (gr. 7-18). reprint ed. 7.99 *(978-0-14-240071-5(8)*, Speak) Penguin Young Readers Group.
Konigsburg, E. L. The Outcasts of 19 Schuyler Place. 2005. 296p. (J). (gr. 5). 13.65 *(978-0-7569-6307-1(9))* Perfection Learning Corp.
—The Outcasts of 19 Schuyler Place. (ENG.). 304p. (J). (gr. 5-9). 2004. 16.95 *(978-0-689-86636-4(4))* 2006. reprint ed. pap. 7.99 *(978-0-689-86637-1(2))* Simon & Schuster Children's Publishing. (Atheneum Bks. for Young Readers).
Kostecki-Shaw, Jenny Sue. My Travelin' Eye. Kostecki-Shaw, Jenny Sue, illus. 2008. (ENG., Illus.). 40p. (J). (gr. -1-2). 18.99 *(978-0-8050-8169-5(0)*, 9780805081695, Holt, Henry & Co. Bks. For Young Readers) Holt, Henry & Co.
Kousky, Vern. Otto the Owl Who Loved Poetry. Kousky, Vern, illus. 2015. (ENG., Illus.). 32p. (J). (gr. k-3). 16.99 *(978-0-399-16440-8(5)*, Nancy Paulsen Books) Penguin Young Readers Group.
Kranz, Linda. You Be You. Mlawer, Teresa, tr. from ENG. 2014. (ENG & SPA., Illus.). 32p. (J). (gr. -1-1). 12.95 *(978-1-63076-021-2(8))* Taylor Trade Publishing.
—You Be You. (J). 2011. *(978-1-58979-667-6(5))* 2011. (ENG., Illus.). 32p. (gr. -1-1). 12.95 *(978-1-58979-666-9(7))* Vol. 2013. (ENG., Illus.). 32p. (gr. -1 — 1). 7.95 *(978-1-58979-747-5(7))* Taylor Trade Publishing.
Kreloff, Elliot. Worth the Wait: A Growing-Up Story of Self-Esteem. Kreloff, Elliot, illus. 2017. (Growing Up Ser.). (ENG., Illus.). 32p. (gr. -1-1). lib. bdg. 19.99 ***(978-1-63440-180-7(8))***; 30.65 ***(978-1-63440-184-5(0))*** Red Chair Pr.
Krensky, Stephen. Milo the Really Big Bunny. Suber, Melissa, illus. 2010. (ENG.). 32p. (J). (gr. -1-1). 11.99 *(978-1-4424-1434-1(0)*, Simon & Schuster Bks. For Young Readers) Simon & Schuster Bks. For Young Readers.
Krulik, Nancy. Horsing Around. John and Wendy Staff, illus. 2009. (Katie Kazoo, Switcheroo Ser.: 30). (ENG.). 80p. (J). (gr. 2-4). pap. 3.99 *(978-0-448-44677-6(4)*, Grosset & Dunlap) Penguin Young Readers Group.
Kupchella, Rick. Girls Can! Make It Happen. Brown, Marilyn, illus. 2004. (ENG.). 40p. (J). 16.95 *(978-0-9726504-3-4(1))* TRISTAN Publishing, Inc.
Lang, Suzanne. Hooray for Kids! Lang, Max, illus. 2016. (ENG.). 40p. (J). (gr. -1-2). 17.99 *(978-0-553-53783-3(0)*, Random Hse. Bks. for Young Readers) Random Hse. Children's Bks.
Laughing Elephant Staff, ed. The Truth about Snow People. 2005. (ENG., Illus.). 32p. (J). (gr. -1-3). 9.95 *(978-1-59583-052-4(9)*, 9781595830524) Laughing Elephant.
Law, Felicia. Zanzibar the Zebra: A Tale of Individuality. Messina, Lilli, illus. 2010. (Animal Fair Values Ser.). 32p. (J). (gr. -1-3). pap. 10.55 *(978-1-60754-807-2(0))*; lib. bdg. 22.60 *(978-1-60754-803-4(8))* Windmill Bks.
Lechelt, Karen. What Do You Love about You? 2016. (ENG., Illus.). 32p. (J). 16.99 *(978-1-68119-093-8(1)*, 9781681190938, Bloomsbury USA Childrens) Bloomsbury Publishing USA.
Lester, Helen. Tacky the Penguin. Munsinger, Lynn, illus. (Tacky the Penguin Ser.). (ENG.). 32p. (J). (gr. -1-3). 2008. bds. 7.99 *(978-0-547-13344-7(8))* 2006. audio compact disk 10.99 *(978-0-618-73754-3(5))* Houghton Mifflin Harcourt Publishing Co.
Lewison, Wendy Cheyette. Silly Milly. Westcott, Nadine Bernard, illus. 2010. (Scholastic Reader Level 1 Ser.). (ENG.). 32p. (J). (gr. -1-3). pap. 3.99 *(978-0-545-06859-8(2))* Scholastic, Inc.
—Silly Milly. 2010. (Scholastic Reader Level 1 Ser.). lib. bdg. 13.55 *(978-0-606-10556-9(5)*, Turtleback) Turtleback Bks.
Lin, Grace. Ling & Ting: Not Exactly the Same! (Passport to Reading Level 3 Ser.). (ENG.). 48p. (J). (gr. 1-4). 2011. pap. 3.99 *(978-0-316-02453-2(8))* 2010. (Illus.). 14.99 *(978-0-316-02452-5(X))* Little, Brown Bks. for Young Readers.
Liu, Carol & Caldarone, Marybeth Sidoti. Arlene on the Scene. 2010. 206p. (J). (gr. 3-5). pap. 7.95 *(978-1-934572-54-2(3))* Emerald Bk. Co.
Loftin, Nikki. Wish Girl. 2015. (ENG.). 256p. (J). (gr. 3-7). 16.99 *(978-1-59514-686-1(5)*, Razorbill) Penguin Young Readers Group.
Long, Ethan. Chamelia. 2011. (ENG., Illus.). 40p. (J). (gr. -1-3). 16.99 *(978-0-316-08612-7(6))* Little, Brown Bks. for Young Readers.
—Chamelia & the New Kid in Class. 2013. (ENG., Illus.). 40p. (J). (gr. -1-3). 16.99 *(978-0-316-21042-3(0))* Little Brown & Co.
Louise, Kate. The Upside-Down Fish. Matine, Laura, illus. 2015. (ENG.). 32p. (J). (gr. -1-k). 16.95 *(978-1-62914-628-7(5)*, Sky Pony Pr.) Skyhorse Publishing Co., Inc.
Lucado, Max. Punchinello & the Most Marvelous Gift: And, Your Special Gift. Martinez, Sergio, illus. 2007. (J). *(978-1-58134-877-4(0))* Crossway.
Lucado, Max, et al. Your Special Gift. Wenzel, David T. & Wenzel, David, illus. 2006. (Max Lucado's Wemmicks Ser.: 6). 32p. (J). (gr. -1-3). 16.99 *(978-1-58134-698-5(0))* Crossway.
Madison, Alan. Velma Gratch & the Way Cool Butterfly. Hawkes, Kevin, illus. 2007. (ENG.). 40p. (J). (gr. -1-3). 17.99 *(978-0-375-83597-1(0)*, Schwartz & Wade Bks.) Random Hse. Children's Bks.
—Velma Gratch & the Way Cool Butterfly. Hawkes, Kevin, illus. 2012. (ENG.). 40p. (J). (gr. -1-3). pap. 7.99 *(978-0-307-97804-2(4)*, Dragonfly Bks.) Random Hse. Children's Bks.
Make Believe Ideas. Paulette the Pinkest Puppy. 2014. (ENG.). 32p. (J). 15.99 *(978-1-78235-975-3(3))* Make Believe Ideas GBR. Dist: Nelson, Thomas Inc.
—Paulette the Pinkest Puppy in the World. 2014. (ENG.). 32p. (J). pap. 6.99 *(978-1-78235-974-6(5))* Make Believe Ideas GBR. Dist: Nelson, Thomas Inc.
Maresca, Beth Anne, illus. Megan Owlet. 2015. (ENG.). 32p. (J). (gr. -1-k). 16.99 *(978-1-63220-404-2(5)*, Sky Pony Pr.) Skyhorse Publishing Co., Inc.
Marien, Donna. Waiting at the Bay: A Young Woman's Reflections on Journeys in the Sea of Life. 2003. 108p. (YA). pap. 10.95 *(978-0-595-26304-2(6)*, Writers Club Pr.) iUniverse, Inc.
Martin, Ann M. Ten Rules for Living with My Sister. 2011. (ENG.). 240p. (J). (gr. 4-7). 16.99 *(978-0-312-36766-4(X)*, 9780312367664) Feiwel & Friends.
—Ten Rules for Living with My Sister. 2012. (ENG.). 256p. (J). (gr. 4-7). pap. 7.99 *(978-1-250-01021-6(7)*, 9781250010216) Square Fish.
Martin, Bill, Jr., et al. The Little Squeegy Bug, 0 vols. Corrigan, Patrick, illus. 2005. (ENG.). 32p. (J). (gr. -1-2). reprint ed. pap. 9.99 *(978-0-7614-5243-0(5)*, 9780761452430, Amazon Children's Publishing) Amazon Publishing.
Mayfield, Sue. I Can, You Can, Toucan! 2006. (Green Bananas Ser.). (ENG., Illus.). 48p. (J). (gr. -1-3). lib. bdg. *(978-0-7787-1032-5(7))* Crabtree Publishing Co.
McCabe, Lauren A. How Many Spots Have I Got? Foulke, Nancy, illus. 2005. (J). 16.00 *(978-1-893516-02-1(4))* Our Child Pr.
McCafferty, Megan. The (Totally Not) Guaranteed Guide to Popularity, Prettiness & Perfection. 2014. (Jessica Darling's It List Ser.: 1). (ENG.). 240p. (J). (gr. 3-7). pap. 8.99 *(978-0-316-24498-5(8)*, Poppy) Little, Brown Bks. for Young Readers.

H
I

McCartney, Tania. Peas in a Pod. Snerling, Tina, illus. 2015. (ENG.). 32p. (J). (gr. -1-2). 17.95 *(978-1-921966-71-2(8))* Exisle Publishing Pty Ltd. AUS. Dist: Hachette Bk. Group.

McCue, Lisa. Quiet Bunny. (ENG., Illus.). (J). (gr. -1-1). 2015. 40p. pap. 6.95 *(978-1-4549-1577-5(3))* 2009. 32p. 14.95 *(978-1-4027-5719-8(0))* Sterling Publishing Co., Inc.

—Quiet Bunny's Many Colors. 2011. (ENG., Illus.). 32p. (J). (gr. -1-1). 14.95 *(978-1-4027-7209-2(2))* Sterling Publishing Co., Inc.

McKee, David. Elmer & Rose. McKee, David, illus. 2010. (ENG., Illus.). 32p. (J). (gr. -1-3). 16.95 *(978-0-7613-5493-2(X))* Lerner Publishing Group.

McKenna, Mark, et al, illus. Banana Tail. 2003. 32p. (J). 12.95 *(978-0-9727681-3-9(0))* Active Media Publishing, LLC.

McKenzie, Heath. My Rules for Being a Pretty Princess. 2015. (ENG., Illus.). 32p. (J). (-3). 16.99 *(978-1-4926-1520-0(X))* Sourcebooks, Inc.

McNamara, Margaret. Class Picture Day. Gordon, Mike, illus. 2011. (Robin Hill School Ser.). (ENG.). 32p. (J). (gr. -1-1). 15.99 *(978-1-4424-3611-4(5))*; pap. 3.99 *(978-1-4169-9173-1(5))* Simon Spotlight. (Simon Spotlight).

McPhail, David. Brothers. 2014. (ENG., Illus.). 32p. (J). (gr. -1-3). 12.99 *(978-0-544-30200-6(1)*, HMH Books For Young Readers) Houghton Mifflin Harcourt Publishing Co.

—Hermanos Brothers. Calvo, Carlos, tr. 2017. (ENG & SPA., Illus.). 28p. (J). (— 1). bds. 4.99 *(978-0-544-91586-2(0)*, HMH Books For Young Readers) Houghton Mifflin Harcourt Publishing Co.

Meister, Cari. What Can I Be? Phillips, Matt, illus. 2003. (Rookie Readers Ser.). 24p. (J). 19.50 *(978-0-516-22876-1(5)*, Children's Pr.) Scholastic Library Publishing.

Mellom, Robin. Hannah Sparkles. Brantley-Newton, Vanessa, illus. 2017. 32p. (J). (gr. -1-3). 17.99 *(978-0-06-232233-3(8))* HarperCollins Pubs.

Meyer, Megan. The Great Adventures of Larriot the Liger. Meyer, Megan, ed. 2010. (ENG., Illus.). 30p. 16.95 *(978-0-9830359-0-9(3))* Brosen Bks.

Milgrim, David. Some Monsters Are Different. Milgrim, David, illus. 2013. (ENG., Illus.). 36p. (J). (gr. -1-k). 16.99 *(978-0-8050-9519-7(5)*, 9780805095197, Holt, Henry & Co. Bks. For Young Readers) Holt, Henry & Co.

Mochizuki, Ken. Beacon Hill Boys. 2004. 200p. 16.00 *(978-0-7569-4281-6(0))* Perfection Learning Corp.

Morrison, Toni & Morrison, Slade. Little Cloud & Lady Wind. Qualls, Sean, illus. 2010. (ENG.). 32p. (J). pap. 7.99 *(978-1-4169-8524-2(7)*, Simon & Schuster Bks. For Young Readers) Simon & Schuster Bks. For Young Readers.

—Little Cloud & Lady Wind. Qualls, Sean, illus. 2010. (ENG.). 32p. (J). (gr. -1-3). 16.99 *(978-1-4169-8523-5(9)*, Simon & Schuster/Paula Wiseman Bks.) Simon & Schuster/Paula Wiseman Bks.

Moss, Peggy & Weber, Penny. One of Us, 1 vol. 2010. (ENG., Illus.). 32p. (gr. 1-7). 16.95 *(978-0-88448-322-9(3)*, 884322) Tilbury Hse. Pubs.

Munsch, Robert. Stephanie's Ponytail. Martchenko, Michael, illus. 16th ed. 2007. (Annikin Ser.). (ENG.). 24p. (J). (gr. -1-2). 1.99 *(978-1-55451-114-3(3)*, 9781554511143) Annick Pr., Ltd. CAN. Dist: Publishers Group West (PGW).

—Stephanie's Ponytail. 2006. (J). 15.10 *(978-0-7569-7162-5(4))* Perfection Learning Corp.

Murray, Andrew. The Very Sleepy Sloth. Tickle, Jack, tr. Tickle, Jack, illus. 2003. 32p. (J). tchr. ed. 15.95 *(978-1-58925-033-8(8))* Tiger Tales.

Murray, Martine. Henrietta: There's No One Better. 2010. (Henrietta Ser.). (ENG., Illus.). 96p. (J). (gr. k-2). pap. 10.99 *(978-1-74114-718-6(2))* Allen & Unwin AUS. Dist: Independent Pubs. Group.

—Henrietta: There's No One Better. 2006. (Illus.). 88p. (J). 9.99 *(978-0-439-80749-4(2)*, Levine, Arthur A. Bks.) Scholastic, Inc.

Myers, Walter Dean. Looking Like Me. Myers, Christopher, illus. 2009. (ENG.). 32p. (J). (gr. k-4). 18.99 *(978-1-60684-001-6(0)*, Carolrhoda Bks.) Lerner Publishing Group.

Myracle, Lauren. Peace, Love, & Baby Ducks. (ENG.). (YA). (gr. 7-18). 2010. 304p. 8.99 *(978-0-14-241527-6(8)*, Speak) 2009. 272p. 16.99 *(978-0-525-47743-3(8)*, Dutton Books for Young Readers) Penguin Young Readers Group.

—Ten. (Winnie Years Ser.). (ENG.). (J). (gr. 3-7). 2012. 240p. pap. 7.99 *(978-0-14-242134-5(0)*, Puffin Books) 2011. 272p. 16.99 *(978-0-525-42356-0(7)*, Dutton Books for Young Readers) Penguin Young Readers Group.

Namioka, Lensey. Ties That Bind, Ties That Break: A Novel. 2006. (Reader's Workshop Ser.). (ENG.). 176p. (C). pap. 19.95 *(978-0-7362-3149-7(8))* CENGAGE Learning.

Namm, Diane. My Best Friend. Gordon, Mike, illus. 2004. (My First Reader Ser.). (ENG.). 32p. (J). (gr. k-1). pap. 3.95 *(978-0-516-25504-0(5)*, Children's Pr.) Scholastic Library Publishing.

—My Best Friend. Gordon, Mike, tr. Gordon, Mike, illus. 2004. (My First Reader Ser.). (ENG.). 31p. (J). 18.50 *(978-0-516-24416-7(7)*, Children's Pr.) Scholastic Library Publishing.

Nash, Margaret. Dog's New Coat. 2011. (Tadpoles Ser.). (ENG., Illus.). 24p. (J). (gr. k-2). lib. bdg. *(978-0-7787-0576-5(5))*; pap. *(978-0-7787-0587-1(0))* Crabtree Publishing Co.

Naylor, Phyllis Reynolds. Anyone Can Eat Squid!, 0 vols. Ramsey, Marcy, illus. 2009. (Simply Sarah Ser.: 0). (ENG.). 80p. (J). (gr. 2-5). pap. 9.99 *(978-0-7614-5540-0(X)*, 9780761455400, Amazon Children's Publishing) Amazon Publishing.

—Eating Enchiladas, 0 vols. Ramsey, Marcy, illus. 2011. (Simply Sarah Ser.: 0). (ENG.). 80p. (J). (gr. 1-4). pap. 9.99 *(978-0-7614-5885-2(9)*, 9780761458852, Amazon Children's Publishing) Amazon Publishing.

Not Every Princess. 2014. (Illus.). (J). *(978-1-4338-1647-5(4)*, Magination Pr.) American Psychological Assn.

Numeroff, Laura Joffe. Would I Trade My Parents? Bernardin, James, illus. 2009. (ENG.). 32p. (J). (gr. k-2). 16.95 *(978-0-8109-0637-2(6)*, Abrams Bks. for Young Readers) Abrams, Inc.

Ocean, Davy. Deep-Sea Disaster. Blecha, Aaron, illus. 2014. (Shark School Ser.: 1). (ENG.). 128p. (J). (gr. 1-4). 17.99 *(978-1-4814-0679-6(5)*, Aladdin) Simon & Schuster Children's Publishing.

O'Connor, Jane. Apples Galore! 2013. (Fancy Nancy - I Can Read! Ser.). (J). lib. bdg. 13.55 *(978-0-606-32150-1(0)*, Turtleback) Turtleback Bks.

—Fancy Nancy. Glasser, Robin Preiss, illus. 2005. (Fancy Nancy Ser.). 32p. (J). (gr. -1-3). 17.89 *(978-0-06-054210-8(1))*; (ENG.). 17.99 *(978-0-06-054209-2(8))* HarperCollins Pubs.

—Fancy Nancy: Too Many Tutus. Glasser, Robin Preiss, illus. 2012. (I Can Read Level 1 Ser.). (ENG.). 32p. (J). (gr. -1-3). 16.99 *(978-0-06-208308-1(2))* HarperCollins Pubs.

—Fancy Nancy & the Posh Puppy. Glasser, Robin Preiss, illus. (Fancy Nancy Ser.). 32p. (J). (gr. -1-2). 2012. (ENG.). 9.99 *(978-0-06-221052-4(1))* 2007. (ENG.). 17.99 *(978-0-06-054213-9(6))* 2007. lib. bdg. 18.89 *(978-0-06-054215-3(2))* HarperCollins Pubs.

—Fancy Nancy Loves! Loves!! Loves!!! Glasser, Robin Preiss & Bracken, Carolyn, illus. 2007. (Fancy Nancy Ser.). (ENG.). 12p. (J). (gr. -1-2). pap. 6.99 *(978-0-06-123599-3(7)*, HarperFestival) HarperCollins Pubs.

—Nancy la Elegante, 1 vol. Valenzuela, Liliana, tr. from ENG. Glasser, Robin Preiss, illus. 2008. (Fancy Nancy Ser.). (SPA.). 32p. (J). (gr. -1-2). 17.99 *(978-0-06-143528-7(7))* HarperCollins Pubs.

—Too Many Tutus. Glasser, Robin Preiss, illus. 2012. (I Can Read Level 1 Ser.). (ENG.). 32p. (J). (gr. -1-3). pap. 3.99 *(978-0-06-208307-4(4))* HarperCollins Pubs.

OHora, Zachariah. My Cousin Momo. 2015. (ENG., Illus.). 32p. (J). (gr. -1-k). 17.99 *(978-0-8037-4011-2(5)*, Dial Bks) Penguin Young Readers Group.

Oliver, Amanda Eaddy. Cheyenne the Cat. 2010. 28p. 13.99 *(978-1-4520-6218-1(8))* AuthorHouse.

Oliver, Lin. Almost Identical. 2012. (Almost Identical Ser.: 1). (ENG.). 224p. (J). (gr. 3-7). pap. 7.99 *(978-0-448-45191-6(3)*, Grosset & Dunlap) Penguin Young Readers Group.

Parker, Amy. The Plans I Have for You, 1 vol. Newton, Vanessa & Brantley-Newton, Vanessa, illus. 2015. (ENG.). 32p. (J). 16.99 *(978-0-310-72410-0(4))* Zonderkidz.

Parker, Emma. Delia Dynamite. 2010. (Illus.). 24p. pap. *(978-1-877561-35-1(5))* First Edition Ltd.

Parkinson, Ethelyn. Good Old Archibald. Stevens, Mary, illus. 2014. 145p. (J). pap. 14.95 *(978-1-932350-42-5(X))* Bethlehem Bks.

Parr, Todd. The Family Book. 2010. (ENG., Illus.). 32p. (J). (gr. -1-1). pap. 8.00 *(978-0-316-07040-9(8))* Little, Brown Bks. for Young Readers.

—It's Okay to Be Different. 2009. (ENG., Illus.). 32p. (J). (gr. -1-1). pap. 8.00 *(978-0-316-04347-2(8))* Little Brown & Co.

Patrick, Cat. The Originals. (ENG.). (YA). (gr. 7-17). 2014. 320p. pap. 10.00 *(978-0-316-21945-7(2))* 2013. 304p. 18.00 *(978-0-316-21943-3(6))* Little, Brown Bks. for Young Readers.

Pavón, Mar. Zaira y los Delfines. 2012. (SPA & ENG., Illus.). 32p. (J). (gr. k-2). *(978-84-15241-02-7(X))* D P & G Military Pubs.

Pearce, Emily Smith. Slowpoke. Ritchie, Scot, illus. 2010. (ENG.). 40p. (J). (gr. 2-4). 16.95 *(978-1-59078-705-2(6))* Boyds Mills Pr.

Pérez, Celia C. The First Rule of Punk. 2017. (ENG., Illus.). 336p. (J). (gr. 4-7). 16.99 ***(978-0-425-29040-8(9)**, Viking Books for Young Readers)* Penguin Young Readers Group.

Perkins, Mitali. Secret Keeper. 2010. (ENG.). 240p. (YA). (gr. 7). pap. 8.99 *(978-0-440-23955-0(9)*, Ember) Random Hse. Children's Bks.

Philbin, Joanna. The Daughters Take the Stage. 2011. (Daughters Ser.: 3). (ENG.). 304p. (J). (gr. 7-17). pap. 8.99 *(978-0-316-04908-5(5)*, Poppy) Little, Brown Bks. for Young Readers.

Phinn, Gervase. Who Am I? Phinn, Gervase, illus. 2012. (Andersen Press Picture Bks). (ENG., Illus.). 32p. (J). (gr. -1-3). 16.95 *(978-0-7613-8996-5(2))* Lerner Publishing Group.

Piven, Hanoch. My Best Friend Is as Sharp as a Pencil: And Other Funny Classroom Portraits. 2010. (ENG., Illus.). 40p. (J). (gr. -1-3). 17.99 *(978-0-375-85338-8(3)*, Schwartz & Wade Bks.) Random Hse. Children's Bks.

—My Dog Is As Smelly As Dirty Socks. 2012. lib. bdg. 18.40 *(978-0-606-26384-9(5)*, Turtleback) Turtleback Bks.

—My Dog Is As Smelly As Dirty Socks: And Other Funny Family Portraits. Piven, Hanoch, illus. 2012. (ENG., Illus.). 40p. (J). (gr. -1-3). pap. 7.99 *(978-0-307-93089-7(0)*, Dragonfly Bks.) Random Hse. Children's Bks.

Plourde, Lynn. You're Wearing That to School?! Cornelison, Sue, illus. 2013. (ENG.). 32p. (J). (gr. -1-3). 16.99 *(978-1-4231-5510-2(6))* Disney Pr.

Polacco, Patricia. The Art of Miss Chew. Polacco, Patricia, illus. 2012. (ENG., Illus.). 40p. (J). (gr. k-3). 17.99 *(978-0-399-25703-2(9)*, G.P. Putnam's Sons Books for Young Readers) Penguin Young Readers Group.

Portis, Antoinette. Froodle. Portis, Antoinette, illus. 2014. (ENG., Illus.). 32p. (J). (gr. -1-3). 16.99 *(978-1-59643-922-1(X)*, 9781596439221) Roaring Brook Pr.

Prasadam-Halls, Smriti. T. Veg: The Story of a Carrot-Crunching Dinosaur. Manolessou, Katherina, illus. 2017. (ENG.). 32p. (J). (gr. -1-3). 16.95 *(978-1-4197-2494-7(0)*, Abrams Bks. for Young Readers) Abrams, Inc.

Proimos, James. Mac & Cheese. Proimos, James, illus. 2016. (ENG., Illus.). 40p. (J). 16.99 *(978-0-8050-9156-4(4)*, 9780805091564, Holt, Henry & Co. Bks. For Young Readers) Holt, Henry & Co.

Pugin-Rodas, M. C. The Eight Ball Club: Ocean of Fire. 2007. (ENG., Illus.). 144p. pap. 15.95 *(978-0-9793761-2-2(2))* ESOL Publishing.

Pulley, Kelly. Ten Unusual Features of Lulu McDunn. Pulley, Kelly, illus. 2010. (Illus.). 32p. (J). (gr. -1). 16.95 *(978-0-9820812-7-3(8)*, Frog Legs Ink) Gauthier Pubns. Inc.

Purkapile, Susan & Peck, Amy. Mumbles the Bumble Bee: The Bee Who Couldn't Buzz. Ducommun, Barbara, illus. 2008. (J). *(978-1-930596-87-0(1))* Amherst Pr.

Raschka, Chris. New York Is English, Chattanooga Is Creek. Raschka, Chris, illus. 2005. (ENG., Illus.). 40p. (J). (gr. -1-2). 17.99 *(978-0-689-84600-7(2)*, Atheneum/Richard Jackson Bks.) Simon & Schuster Children's Publishing.

Rech, Lindsay Faith. It Started with a Dare. 2010. (ENG.). 312p. (YA). (gr. 7-18). pap. 17.99 *(978-0-547-23558-5(5))* Houghton Mifflin Harcourt Publishing Co.

Reger, Rob & Gruner, Jessica. Stranger & Stranger. Reger, Rob & Parker, Buzz, illus. 2010. (Emily the Strange Ser.: 2). (ENG.). 272p. (YA). (gr. 8). pap. 9.99 *(978-0-06-145234-5(3))* HarperCollins Pubs.

Reiser, Lynn. My Way(A Mi Manera) A Margaret & Margarita Story(Un Cuento de Margarita y Margaret) Reiser, Lynn, illus. 2007. (ENG & SPA., Illus.). 32p. (J). (gr. -1-k). 16.99 *(978-0-06-084101-0(X)*, Greenwillow Bks.) HarperCollins Pubs.

Rennert, Laura Joy. Emma, the Extra Ordinary Princess. Florian, Melanie, illus. 2009. (J). *(978-0-525-42152-8(1)*, Dutton Juvenile) Penguin Publishing Group.

Révah, Noémie. Mister Horizontal & Miss Vertical. Zagnoli, Olimpia, illus. 2014. (ENG.). 48p. (J). (gr. -1-3). 17.95 *(978-1-59270-161-2(2))* Enchanted Lion Bks., LLC.

Reynolds, Cynthia Furlong. Grammie's Secret Cupboard. Dodson, Bert, illus. 2007. 32p. (J). (gr. -1-3). 17.95 *(978-1-58726-310-1(6)*, Mitten Pr.) Ann Arbor Editions LLC.

Reynolds, Peter H. Happy Dreamer. 2017. (ENG., Illus.). 32p. (J). (gr. -1-3). 17.99 *(978-0-545-86501-2(8))* Scholastic, Inc.

Richmond, Marianne. Beautiful Blue Eyes. 2011. (ENG.). 32p. (J). (gr. -1-3). 15.99 *(978-1-4022-5639-4(6)*, Sourcebooks Jabberwocky) Sourcebooks, Inc.

—Hooray for You! A Celebration Of "You-Ness" 2015. (Marianne Richmond Ser.: 0). (ENG.). 24p. (J). (-2). bds. 7.99 *(978-1-4926-1555-2(2))* Sourcebooks, Inc.

Rim, Sujean. Birdie's Big-Girl Hair. 2014. (Birdie Ser.). (ENG., Illus.). 40p. (J). (gr. -1-3). 17.00 *(978-0-316-22791-9(9))* Little Brown & Co.

—Chee-Kee: A Panda in Bearland. 2017. (ENG., Illus.). 40p. (J). (gr. -1-3). 17.99 *(978-0-316-40744-1(5))* Little Brown & Co.

Robbins, Jacqui. Two of a Kind. Phelan, Matt, illus. 2009. (ENG.). 32p. (J). (gr. -1-2). 17.99 *(978-1-4169-2437-1(X)*, Atheneum Bks. for Young Readers) Simon & Schuster Children's Publishing.

Robinson, Fiona. Whale Shines: An Artistic Tale. 2013. (ENG., Illus.). 32p. (J). (gr. k-2). 18.95 *(978-1-4197-0848-0(1)*, Abrams Bks. for Young Readers) Abrams, Inc.

Robinson, Gary. Little Brother of War. 2013. (PathFinders Ser.). (ENG.). 113p. (YA). pap. 9.95 *(978-1-939053-02-2(1)*, 7th Generation) Book Publishing Co.

Rosenthal, Amy Krouse, narrated by. Spoon. 2011. (J). (gr. -1-1). 29.95 *(978-0-545-23753-6(X))* Weston Woods Studios, Inc.

Roskifte, Kristin. Animal Beauty. 2015. (ENG., Illus.). 50p. (J). 17.00 *(978-0-8028-5454-4(0)*, Eerdmans Bks For Young Readers) Eerdmans, William B. Publishing Co.

Ross, Fiona. Chilly Milly Moo. 2011. (ENG., Illus.). 32p. (J). (gr. -1-2). 15.99 *(978-0-7636-5693-5(3))* Candlewick Pr.

Rovetch, L. Bob. Frog Went A-Dancing. Berry, Holly, illus. 2006. (J). *(978-1-58987-008-6(5))* Kindermusik International.

Rue, Nancy. You Can't Sit with Us - Mean Girl Makeover, 1 vol. 2014. (Mean Girl Makeover Ser.). (ENG.). 224p. (J). pap. 9.99 *(978-1-4003-2371-5(1))* Nelson, Thomas Inc.

Russell, Natalie. Lost for Words, 1 vol. Russell, Natalie, illus. 2014. (ENG., Illus.). 32p. (J). (gr. -1-3). 16.95 *(978-1-56145-739-7(6))* Peachtree Pubs.

Ryan, Candace. Ewe & Aye. Ruble, Stephanie, illus. 2014. (ENG.). 40p. (J). (gr. -1-k). 17.99 *(978-1-4231-7591-9(3))* Hyperion Bks. for Children.

Salter, Sydney. My Big Nose & Other Natural Disasters. 2009. (ENG., Illus.). 352p. (J). (gr. 7-18). pap. 19.95 *(978-0-15-206643-7(8))* Houghton Mifflin Harcourt Publishing Co.

Saltzberg, Barney. Star of the Week. Saltzberg, Barney, illus. 2010. (ENG., Illus.). 32p. (J). (gr. k-3). pap. 6.99 *(978-0-7636-3076-8(4))* Candlewick Pr.

Sauer, Tammi. Cowboy Camp. Reed, Mike, illus. (ENG.). (J). (gr. -1-k). 2015. 24p. bds. 6.95 *(978-1-4549-1389-4(4))* 2014. 32p. pap. 6.95 *(978-1-4549-1360-3(6))* Sterling Publishing Co., Inc.

—Mostly Monsterly. Magoon, Scott, illus. 2010. (ENG.). 40p. (J). (gr. -1-3). 17.99 *(978-1-4169-6110-9(0)*, Simon & Schuster/Paula Wiseman Bks.) Simon & Schuster/Paula Wiseman Bks.

—Princess in Training. Berger, Joe, illus. (ENG.). 40p. (J). (gr. -1-3). 2015. 6.99 *(978-0-544-45609-9(2)*, HMH Books For Young Readers) 2012. 16.99 *(978-0-15-206599-7(7))* Houghton Mifflin Harcourt Publishing Co.

Scarry, Richard. School Bus Box Set. 2014. (Illus.). (J). *(978-0-7641-6690-7(5))* Barron's Educational Series, Inc.

Schaefer, Lola M. Frankie Stein, 0 vols. Atteberry, Kevan, illus. 2009. (ENG.). 34p. (J). (gr. k-3). pap. 6.99 *(978-0-7614-5608-7(2)*, 9780761456087, Amazon Children's Publishing) Amazon Publishing.

Schanen, Adriana Brad. Quinny & Hopper. Swearingen, Greg, illus. 2014. (ENG.). 240p. (J). (gr. 3-7). 15.99 *(978-1-4231-7829-3(7))* Hyperion Bks. for Children.

Scher, Paula. The Brownstone. 2016. (ENG., Illus.). 32p. (J). (gr. -1-3). 17.95 *(978-1-61689-428-3(8))* Princeton Architectural Pr.

Schnee, Silke. The Prince Who Was Just Himself. Sistig, Heike, illus. 2015. (Prince Noah Book Ser.). (ENG.). 32p. (J). (gr. -1-4). 16.00 *(978-0-87486-682-7(0))* Plough Publishing Hse.

Schoonmaker, Elizabeth. Square Cat. Schoonmaker, Elizabeth, illus. 2011. (ENG., Illus.). 32p. (J). (gr. -1-3). 16.99 *(978-1-4424-0619-3(4)*, Aladdin) Simon & Schuster Children's Publishing.

Schotter, Roni. All about Grandmas. Nadeau, Janice, illus. 2012. (ENG.). 32p. (J). (gr. -1-k). 16.99 *(978-0-8037-3714-3(9)*, Dial Bks) Penguin Young Readers Group.

Scott, Lisa Ann. School of Charm. 2014. (ENG.). 304p. (J). (gr. 3-7). 16.99 *(978-0-06-220758-6(X)*, Tegen, Katherine Bks) HarperCollins Pubs.

Scotto, Michael. Just Flash. Gabriel, Evette et al, illus. 2009. (J). *(978-1-935193-50-0(3))* National Network of Digital Schls.

Sesame Street, Sesame & Kimmelmen, Leslie. Sesame Street - Celebrate You! Celebrate Me! A Peek & Touch Book. 2017. (ENG., Illus.). 10p. (J). (gr. -1-k). 10.99 *(978-0-7944-3871-5(7)*, Reader's Digest Children's Bks.) Studio Fun International.

Seuling, Barbara. Robert & the Lemming Problem. Brewer, Paul, illus. 2003. (Robert Bks.). (ENG.). 120p. (J). 15.95 *(978-0-8126-2686-5(9))* Cricket Bks.

Shaffer, Jody Jensen. Prudence the Part-Time Cow. Laberis, Stephanie, illus. 2017. (ENG.). 32p. (J). 16.99 *(978-1-62779-615-6(0)*, 9781627796156, Holt, Henry & Co. Bks. For Young Readers) Holt, Henry & Co.

Shang, Wendy Wan-Long. The Great Wall of Lucy Wu. 2013. (ENG.). 320p. (J). (gr. 3-7). pap. 7.99 *(978-0-545-16216-6(5)*, Scholastic Paperbacks) Scholastic, Inc.

Shannon, David. A Bad Case of Stripes. 2015. 32p. pap. 7.00 *(978-1-61003-539-2(9))* Center for the Collaborative Classroom.

—A Bad Case of Stripes. 2004. (Scholastic Bookshelf Ser.). (Illus.). (gr. -1-3). 17.00 *(978-0-7569-3183-4(5))* Perfection Learning Corp.

—A Bad Case of Stripes. Shannon, David, illus. 2007. (ENG., Illus.). (J). (gr. -1-3). 9.99 *(978-0-439-92494-8(4))* Scholastic, Inc.

—A Bad Case of Stripes. 2007. (ENG.). (J). (gr. -1-3). 18.95 *(978-0-439-02328-3(9))* Scholastic, Inc.

Shaskan, Stephen. A Dog Is a Dog. 2011. (ENG., Illus.). 40p. (J). (gr. -1-1). 14.99 *(978-0-8118-7896-8(1))* Chronicle Bks. LLC.

Sheldon, Dyan. My Worst Best Friend. 2010. (ENG., Illus.). 304p. (YA). (gr. 7-18). 15.99 *(978-0-7636-4555-7(9))* Candlewick Pr.

Shireen, Nadia. Good Little Wolf. 2011. (ENG.). 32p. (J). (gr. -1-2). 16.99 *(978-0-375-86904-4(2)*, Knopf Bks. for Young Readers) Random Hse. Children's Bks.

Silvermetz, Marcia A. Gertrude the Albino Frog & Her Friend Rupert the Turtle. Doyel, Ginger, illus. 2003. 48p. (J). (gr. 2-3). 19.95 *(978-0-9718724-0-0(6))* Hiccup Cottage Pubns.

Smallman, Steve. Bumbletum. Warnes, Tim, illus. 2006. 24p. (J). (gr. -1-3). 15.95 *(978-1-58925-060-4(5))* Tiger Tales.

—Troll Two — Three — Four. Temairik, Jaime, illus. 2014. (J). *(978-1-4723-2925-7(2))* Parragon Bk. Service Ltd.

Smith, Bryan. Is There an App for That? Wish, Katia, illus. 2015. (ENG.). 32p. (J). pap. 10.95 *(978-1-934490-74-7(1))* Boys Town Pr.

Sommer, Carl. The Eagle & the Chickens. Noé, illus. 2016. (J). *(978-1-57537-945-6(7))* Advance Publishing, Inc.

Spagnol, Estelle Billon. Little Benguin. Spagnol, Estelle Billon, illus. 2014. (ENG., Illus.). 32p. (J). (gr. -1-1). 16.95 *(978-0-8234-2934-9(2))* Holiday Hse., Inc.

Spinelli, Eileen. I Like Noisy, Mom Likes Quiet. Halverson, Lydia, illus. 2006. (ENG.). 32p. (J). (gr. -1-3). 8.95 *(978-0-8249-5517-5(X)*, 1256103, Ideal Pubns.) Worthy Publishing.

Spinelli, Jerry. Jake & Lily. 2012. 352p. (J). (gr. 3-7). (ENG.). 16.99 *(978-0-06-028135-9(9))*; lib. bdg. 16.89 *(978-0-06-028136-6(7))* HarperCollins Pubs.

—Stargirl. 2003. (EMC Masterpiece Series Access Editions). xiv, 199p. (YA). 12.99 *(978-0-8219-2504-1(0)*, 35378) EMC/Paradigm Publishing.

—Stargirl. unabr. ed. 2004. 192p. (J). (gr. 7-18). pap. 40.00 incl. audio *(978-0-8072-0855-7(8)*, LYA 323 SP, Listening Library) Random Hse. Audio Publishing Group.

—Stargirl. 2004. (ENG.). 208p. (YA). (gr. 7). mass mkt. 7.99 *(978-0-440-41677-7(9)*, Laurel Leaf) Random Hse. Children's Bks.

Spruill, Edward L. & Spruill, Sonya. Jordan's Hair. Peringer, Stephen Mercer, illus. 2005. 16p. (J). (gr. -1-3). 8.00 *(978-0-8170-1484-1(5))* Judson Pr.

Stanton, Elizabeth Rose. Henny. Stanton, Elizabeth Rose, illus. 2014. (ENG., Illus.). 40p. (J). (gr. -1-3). 17.99 *(978-1-4424-8436-8(5)*, Simon & Schuster/Paula Wiseman Bks.) Simon & Schuster/Paula Wiseman Bks.

Stern, Beth. Yoda Gets a Buddy. Crane, Devin, illus. 2015. (ENG.). 32p. (J). (gr. -1-3). 17.99 *(978-1-4814-6969-2(X)*, Aladdin) Simon & Schuster Children's Publishing.

Stockland, Patricia M. Peanut Picking, 1 vol. Haugen, Ryan, illus. 2008. (Safari Friends Ser.). (ENG.). 32p. (gr. -1-3). 28.50 *(978-1-60270-085-7(0)*, Looking Glass Library) ABDO Publishing Co.

Street, Emily June. The Velocipede Races. 2016. (Bikes in Space Ser.). (ENG., Illus.). 256p. (J). (gr. 7). pap. 9.95 *(978-1-62106-058-1(6)*, Elly Blue Publishing) Microcosm Publishing.

Sundgaard, Arnold. The Lamb & the Butterfly. Carle, Eric, illus. 2013. (ENG.). 32p. (J). (gr. -1-k). 17.99 *(978-0-545-44326-5(1)*, Orchard Bks.) Scholastic, Inc.

Swenson, Jamie. Woof & Quack in Winter (reader) Sias, Ryan, illus. 2017. (Green Light Readers Level 1 Ser.). (ENG.). 32p. (J). (gr. -1-3). 12.99 ***(978-0-544-95949-1(3)**, HMH Books For Young Readers)* Houghton Mifflin Harcourt Publishing Co.

Tarpley, Todd. My Grandma's a Ninja. Chatzikonstantinou, Danny, illus. 2015. (ENG.). 40p. (J). 17.95 *(978-0-7358-4199-4(3))* North-South Bks., Inc.

Taylor-Butler, Christine. I Am Smart. Borlasca, Hector, illus. (My First Reader Ser.). (ENG.). 32p. (J). (gr. k-1). 2006. per. 3.95 *(978-0-516-24971-1(1))* 2005. lib. bdg. 18.50 *(978-0-516-25176-9(7))* Scholastic Library Publishing. (Children's Pr.).

Ter Haar, Carol. Chris T. Saves the Wetlands. 2008. (J). 20.00 *(978-0-9768310-2-0(3))* BIC Alliance.

Tiano, Danielle. Tillie Is Terrific. 2006. (Illus.). (J). 16.99 *(978-0-9788769-0-0(6))* Beyond Your Words.

Tillman, Nancy. The Crown on Your Head. Tillman, Nancy, illus. (ENG., Illus.). (J). (gr. -1-3). 2014. 34p. 7.99 *(978-1-250-04045-9(0)*, 9781250040459) 2011. 32p. 17.99 *(978-0-312-64521-2(X)*, 9780312645212) Feiwel & Friends.

—You're Here for a Reason. 2015. (ENG., Illus.). 32p. (J). (gr. -1-3). 17.99 *(978-1-250-05626-9(8)*, 9781250056269) Feiwel & Friends.

Todd, Ilima. Remake. 2014. (Remake Ser.: 1). (ENG.). 304p. (YA). (gr. 7). 17.99 *(978-1-60907-924-6(8)*, Shadow Mountain) Shadow Mountain Publishing.

Tomkins, Jasper, illus. Nimby: An Extraordinary Cloud Who Meets a Remarkable Friend. 2011. (ENG.). 60p. 15.95 *(978-1-59583-428-7(1)*, 9781595834287, Green Tiger Pr.) Laughing Elephant.

Trasacco, Christina. Indigo. 2012. (ENG.). 35p. (J). 26.95 *(978-1-4327-7722-7(X))* Outskirts Pr., Inc.

Tuminelly, Nancy. Los Zapatos de la Potranca, 1 vol. Nobens, C. A., illus. 2007. (Cuentos de Animales Ser.). (SPA &

ENG.). 24p. (J). (gr. k-3). lib. bdg. 24.21 *(978-1-59928-677-8(7),* SandCastle) ABDO Publishing Co.

Turner, Sadie & Freedman, Colette. Anomalies. 2016. (ENG.). 336p. (J). (gr. 9-12). 17.95 *(978-1-59079-361-9(7))* Select Bks., Inc.

Ungerer, Tomi. Rufus. 2015. (ENG.). 32p. (gr. -1-2). 16.95 *(978-0-7148-7049-6(8))* Phaidon Pr., Inc.

—Rufus: The Bat Who Loved Colours. 2015. (ENG., Illus.). 32p. 16.95 *(978-0-7148-6972-8(4))* Phaidon Pr., Inc.

Urban, Linda. Mouse Was Mad. Cole, Henry, illus. (ENG.). 40p. (J). (gr. -1-3). 2012. pap. 7.99 *(978-0-547-72750-9(X))* 2009. 16.99 *(978-0-15-205337-6(9))* Houghton Mifflin Harcourt Publishing Co.

Vail, Rachel. Piggy Bunny. Tankard, Jeremy, illus. 2012. (ENG.). 32p. (J). (gr. -1-1). 14.99 *(978-0-312-64988-3(6),* 9780312649883) Feiwel & Friends.

Valdivia, Paloma. Up above & down Below. 2012. (ENG., Illus.). 32p. (J). (gr. -1-2). 15.95 *(978-1-926973-39-5(9),* Owlkids) Owlkids Bks. Inc. CAN. Dist: Publishers Group West (PGW).

van Arsdale, Peternelle. The Beast Is an Animal. 2017. (ENG., Illus.). 352p. (YA). (gr. 9). 17.99 *(978-1-4814-8841-9(4),* McElderry, Margaret K. Bks.) McElderry, Margaret K. Bks.

Velthuijs, Max. Frog & the Stranger. 2014. (ENG., Illus.). 32p. (J). (-k). pap. 12.95 *(978-1-78344-143-3(7))* Andersen Pr. GBR. Dist: Independent Pubs. Group.

Vincent, Rachel. Brave New Girl. 2017. (ENG.). 272p. (YA). (gr. 7). 17.99 ***(978-0-399-55245-8(6)***, Delacorte Pr.) Random Hse. Children's Bks.

Walsh, Vivian. June & August. McCauley, Adam, illus. 2009. (ENG.). 32p. (J). (gr. k-2). 16.95 *(978-0-8109-8410-3(5),* Abrams Bks. for Young Readers) Abrams, Inc.

Ward, Helen. Spots in a Box. Ward, Helen, illus. 2015. (ENG., Illus.). 40p. (J). (gr. -1-2). 16.99 *(978-0-7636-7597-4(0),* Templar) Candlewick Pr.

Warnes, Tim. Chalk & Cheese. Warnes, Tim, illus. 2008. (ENG., Illus.). 32p. (J). (gr. -1-3). 18.99 *(978-1-4169-1378-8(5),* Simon & Schuster Bks. For Young Readers) Simon & Schuster Bks. For Young Readers.

Watson, Jean. Onyx the Butterfly. 2007. 160p. pap. 58.25 *(978-1-4303-2408-9(2))* Lulu Pr., Inc.

Weeks, Sarah. Mac & Cheese. Manning, Jane K., illus. 2010. (I Can Read Level 1 Ser.). (ENG.). 32p. (J). (gr. -1-3). 16.99 *(978-0-06-117079-9(8))* HarperCollins Pubs.

Weidner, Teri. Always Twins. Weidner, Teri, illus. 2015. (ENG., Illus.). 32p. (J). (gr. -1-k). 16.95 *(978-0-8234-3159-5(2))* Holiday Hse., Inc.

Weissman, Elissa Brent. Nerd Camp. (ENG., 272p. (J). (gr. 3-7). 2012. Illus.). pap. 6.99 *(978-1-4424-1704-5(8))* 2011. 17.99 *(978-1-4424-1703-8(X))* Simon & Schuster Children's Publishing. (Atheneum Bks. for Young Readers).

—Nerd Camp 2.0. Willis, Drew, illus. (ENG.). (J). (gr. 3-7). 2015. 304p. pap. 7.99 *(978-1-4424-5295-4(1))* 2014. 288p. 17.99 *(978-1-4424-5294-7(3),* Atheneum Bks. for Young Readers) Simon & Schuster Children's Publishing.

—Standing for Socks. Sonkin, Jessica, illus. (ENG.). 224p. (J). (gr. 3-7). 2010. pap. 6.99 *(978-1-4169-9777-1(6))* 2009. 15.99 *(978-1-4169-4801-8(5))* Simon & Schuster Children's Publishing. (Atheneum Bks. for Young Readers).

West, Tracey. A Ninja's Path. 2012. (Ninjago Readers Ser.: 5). lib. bdg. 13.55 *(978-0-606-26771-7(9),* Turtleback) Turtleback Bks.

Weyn, Suzanne. The Bar Code Tattoo. 2012. (ENG.). 256p. (J). (gr. 7). pap. 9.99 *(978-0-545-47054-4(4),* Scholastic Paperbacks) Scholastic, Inc.

Whamond, Dave. Oddrey. 2017. (Oddrey Ser.: 1). (ENG., Illus.). 32p. (J). (gr. k-3). pap. 7.95 ***(978-1-77147-303-3(7))*** Owlkids Bks. Inc. CAN. Dist: Publishers Group West (PGW).

Whamond, Dave & Owlkids Books Inc. Staff. Oddrey. 2012. (Oddrey Ser.: 1). (ENG., Illus.). 32p. (J). (gr. k-3). 16.95 *(978-1-926973-45-6(3),* Owlkids) Owlkids Bks. Inc. CAN. Dist: Publishers Group West (PGW).

White, Ruth. You'll Like It Here (Everybody Does) 2012. (ENG.). 272p. (J). (gr. 4-7). 7.99 *(978-0-375-86596-1(9),* Yearling) Random Hse. Children's Bks.

White, Tara. I Like Who I Am, 1 vol. 2010. (ENG., Illus.). 44p. pap. 12.95 *(978-1-894778-63-3(4))* Theytus Bks., Ltd. CAN. Dist: Univ. of Toronto Pr.

Whitney, Kim Ablon. See You down the Road. 14.85 *(978-0-7569-5710-0(9))* Perfection Learning Corp.

Willems, Mo. Naked Mole Rat Gets Dressed. Willems, Mo, illus. 2009. (ENG., Illus.). 40p. (J). (gr. -1 — 1). 16.99 *(978-1-4231-1437-6(X))* Hyperion Pr.

Willems, Mo, narrated by. Leonardo, the Terrible Monster. 2011. (Illus.). (J). (gr. -1-3). 29.95 *(978-0-439-02766-3(7),* WHCD801) Weston Woods Studios, Inc.

Willems, Mo, et al, narrated by. Naked Mole Rat Gets Dressed. 2011. (J). (gr. -1-2). 29.95 *(978-0-545-29678-6(1))* Weston Woods Studios, Inc.

Willner-Pardo, Gina. The Hard Kind of Promise. 2011. (ENG.). 204p. (J). (gr. 5-7). pap. 12.99 *(978-0-547-55017-6(0))* Houghton Mifflin Harcourt Publishing Co.

Wilson, Karma. Duddle Puck: The Puddle Duck. Hall, Marcellus, illus. 2015. (ENG.). 40p. (J). (gr. -1-3). 17.99 *(978-1-4424-4927-5(6),* McElderry, Margaret K. Bks.) McElderry, Margaret K. Bks.

Winfrey, Michelle Whitaker. It's My Birthday. . . Finally! A Leap Year Story. Turley, Joyce M., illus. 2003. 88p. (J). (gr. 3-7). per. 11.95 *(978-0-9727179-0-8(0))* Hobby Hse. Publishing Group.

Winkler, Henry & Oliver, Lin. A Brand-New Me! Watson, Jesse Joshua & Heitz, Tim, illus. 2010. (Hank Zipzer Ser.: 17). (ENG.). 160p. (J). (gr. 3-7). pap. 5.99 *(978-0-448-45210-4(3),* Grosset & Dunlap) Penguin Young Readers Group.

Winter, Ariel S. One of a Kind. Hitch, David, illus. 2012. (ENG.). 32p. (J). (gr. -1-2). 15.99 *(978-1-4424-2016-8(2),* Aladdin) Simon & Schuster Children's Publishing.

Wolf, Elisabeth. Lulu in la la Land. 2013. (Lulu in la la Land Ser.: 1). (ENG.). 272p. (J). (gr. 3-6). pap. 6.99 *(978-1-4022-8504-2(3),* 9781402285042, Sourcebooks Jabberwocky) Sourcebooks, Inc.

Wolitzer, Meg. The Fingertips of Duncan Dorfman. 2012. (ENG.). 304p. (J). (gr. 3-7). pap. 7.99 *(978-0-14-242204-5(5),* Puffin Books) Penguin Young Readers Group.

Woloson, Eliza. My Friend Isabelle. Gough, Bryan, tr. Gough, Bryan, illus. 2003. (ENG.). 28p. (J). 14.95 *(978-1-890627-50-8(X))* Woodbine Hse.

Wong, Janet S. & Wong, Janet G. Minn & Jake. Cote, Genevieve, illus. 2008. (ENG.). 160p. (J). (gr. 2-5). pap. 9.99 *(978-0-374-40021-7(0),* 9780374400217, Farrar, Straus & Giroux (BYR)) Farrar, Straus & Giroux.

Yee, Lisa. Bobby the Brave (Sometimes) Santat, Dan, illus. 2012. (ENG.). 160p. (J). (gr. 2-5). pap. 5.99 *(978-0-545-05595-6(4),* Levine, Arthur A. Bks.) Scholastic, Inc.

Yolen, Jane & Stemple, Heidi E. Y. Not All Princesses Dress in Pink. Lanquetin, Anne-Sophie, illus. 2010. (ENG.). 32p. (J). (gr. -1-3). 17.99 *(978-1-4169-8018-6(0),* Simon & Schuster Bks. For Young Readers) Simon & Schuster Bks. For Young Readers.

Yoon, Salina. Be a Friend. 2016. (ENG.). 40p. (J). 17.99 *(978-1-61963-951-5(3),* 9781619639515, Bloomsbury USA Childrens) Bloomsbury Publishing USA.

Yum, Hyewon. The Twins' Blanket. Yum, Hyewon, illus. 2011. (ENG., Illus.). 40p. (J). (gr. -1-1). 17.99 *(978-0-374-37972-8(6),* 9780374379728, Farrar, Straus & Giroux (BYR)) Farrar, Straus & Giroux.

Zachmeyer, Mary L. The Star That Sparkled. Ruzicka, Delores F., illus. Date not set. 26p. (J). pap. 5.00 *(978-0-9646864-1-0(4))* Zachmeyer, Mary L.

Zimmer, Elizabeth & Zimmer, Eric. The Turtle & the Deep Blue Sky. 2007. (ENG., Illus.). 32p. (J). (gr. -1-3). 12.95 *(978-1-55591-597-1(3))* Fulcrum Publishing.

Zimmerman, Brandon. Societal Equilibrium: The First Iteration. 2013. 52p. (J). pap. 15.99 *(978-1-4797-6448-8(5))* Xlibris Corp.

INDOCHINA

see Southeast Asia

INDONESIA

Benoit, Peter. The Krakatau Eruption. 2011. (J). pap. *(978-0-531-29027-9(1))* Children's Pr., Ltd.

—The Krakatau Eruption. 2011. (True Bks.). 48p. (J). (gr. 3-5). 29.00 *(978-0-531-20628-7(9));* (ENG., Illus.). pap. 6.95 *(978-0-531-28997-6(4))* Scholastic Library Publishing. (Children's Pr.).

Brimson, Samuel. Brazil-East Timor, 8 vols. 2003. (Nations of the World Ser.: Vol. 2). (Illus.). 64p. (gr. 5-12). lib. bdg. 31.00 *(978-0-8368-5486-2(1),* Gareth Stevens Secondary Library) Stevens, Gareth Publishing LLLP.

Canavan, Roger. Indonesia. 2007. (Countries in Crisis Ser.). (Illus.). 48p. (J). (gr. 4-8). lib. bdg. 31.36 *(978-1-60044-615-3(9))* Rourke Educational Media.

Cassanos, Lynda Cohen. Indonesia. 2010. (Major Muslim Nations Ser.). 128p. (YA). (gr. 5-18). lib. bdg. 25.95 *(978-1-4222-1405-3(2))* Mason Crest.

Cornell, Kari & Anwar, Merry. Cooking the Indonesian Way: Includes Low-Fat & Vegetarian Recipes. 2nd rev. ed. 2004. (Easy Menu Ethnic Cookbooks 2nd Edition Ser.). (ENG., Illus.). 72p. (J). (gr. 5-12). 25.26 *(978-0-8225-4127-1(0),* Carolrhoda Bks.) Lerner Publishing Group.

Furgang, Kathy. Krakatoa: History's Loudest Volcano. 2009. (Volcanoes of the World Ser.). 24p. (gr. 3-3). 42.50 *(978-1-60854-730-2(2),* PowerKids Pr.) Rosen Publishing Group, Inc., The.

—Tambora: A Killer Volcano from Indonesia. 2009. (Volcanoes of the World Ser.). 24p. (gr. 3-3). 42.50 *(978-1-60854-734-0(5),* PowerKids Pr.) Rosen Publishing Group, Inc., The.

Greenhaven Press Editors & Busby, Barbara Sheen. Foods of Indonesia. 2012. (Taste of Culture Ser.). (ENG., Illus.). 64p. (gr. 3-6). lib. bdg. 35.20 *(978-0-7377-5950-1(X),* Kidhaven) Cengage Gale.

Hibbs, Linda. All about Indonesia: Stories, Songs & Crafts for Kids. 2014. (ENG., Illus.). 64p. (J). (gr. 2-6). 16.95 *(978-0-8048-4085-9(7))* Tuttle Publishing.

Kalman, Bobbie. Spotlight on Indonesia. 2010. (ENG.). 32p. (J). pap. *(978-0-7787-3484-0(6))* Crabtree Publishing Co.

Lim, Robin. Indonesia. 2010. (Country Explorers Ser.). (ENG.). 48p. (gr. 2-4). (J). lib. bdg. 29.27 *(978-1-58013-602-0(8));* pap. 9.95 *(978-0-7613-5535-9(9))* Lerner Publishing Group.

Mirpuri, Gouri, et al. Indonesia. 3rd rev. ed. 2011. (Cultures of the World: 3rd Edition 1 Ser.). (Illus.). 144p. (J). (gr. 6). 47.07 *(978-1-60870-783-6(0))* Marshall Cavendish Corp.

Morgan, Sally. Focus on Indonesia. 2007. (World in Focus Ser.). 64p. (gr. 5-12). pap. 14.05 *(978-0-8368-6757-2(2));* (Illus.). lib. bdg. 34.00 *(978-0-8368-6750-3(5))* Stevens, Gareth Publishing LLLP. (Gareth Stevens Secondary Library).

Nagara, Innosanto. My Night in the Planetarium. 2016. (ENG., Illus.). 24p. (J). (gr. 1-4). 17.95 *(978-1-60980-700-9(6),* Triangle Square) Seven Stories Pr.

Orr, Tamra. Indonesia. 2010. (Explorer Library: Social Studies Explorer Ser.). (ENG.). 48p. (gr. 4-8). lib. bdg. 31.36 *(978-1-60279-826-7(5),* 200518) Cherry Lake Publishing.

Orr, Tamra & Greenblatt, Miriam. Indonesia. 2005. (Enchantment of the World Ser.). (ENG., Illus.). 144p. (YA). (gr. 5-9). 39.00 *(978-0-516-23684-1(9))* Scholastic Library Publishing.

Owings, Lisa. Indonesia. 2012. (Exploring Countries Ser.). (ENG., Illus.). 32p. (J). (gr. 3-7). lib. bdg. 26.95 *(978-1-60014-763-0(1),* Blastoff! Readers) Bellwether Media.

Phillips, Douglas A. Indonesia. 2004. (Modern World Nations Ser.). (Illus.). 120p. (gr. 6-12). 35.00 *(978-0-7910-8022-1(6),* Chelsea Hse.) Facts On File, Inc.

Reynolds, Jan. Cycle of Rice, Cycle of Life: A Story of Sustainable Farming. Reynolds, Jan, photos by. 2009. (ENG., Illus.). 48p. (J). (gr. 2-7). 19.95 *(978-1-60060-254-2(1))* Lee & Low Bks., Inc.

Simpson, Judith. Indonesia. 2004. (Ask about Asia Ser.). (Illus.). 48p. (J). (gr. 4-18). lib. bdg. 19.95 *(978-1-59084-202-7(2))* Mason Crest.

Spilsbury, Louise. Indonesia. 2015. (Emerging Nations Ser.). (ENG., Illus.). 48p. (J). (gr. 4-9). 37.10 *(978-1-59920-990-6(X))* Black Rabbit Bks.

Wiseman, Blaine. Indonesia. 2016. (Illus.). 32p. (J). *(978-1-4896-4611-8(6))* Weigl Pubs., Inc.

Woolf, Alex. My Life in Indonesia. 2015. (J). lib. bdg. *(978-1-62713-337-1(2))* Cavendish Square Publishing.

Yomtov, Nelson. Indonesia. 2015. (ENG., Illus.). 144p. (J). lib. bdg. 40.00 *(978-0-531-21253-0(X),* Orchard Bks.) Scholastic Library Publishing.

INDONESIA—FICTION

Ballantyne, R. M. Blown to Bits; or, the Lonely Man of Rak. 2006. pap. *(978-1-4065-0515-3(3))* Dodo Pr.

Bunanta, Murti. The Tiny Boy & Other Tales from Indonesia, 1 vol. Hardiyono, illus. 2013. (ENG.). 80p. (J). (gr. 3). 24.95 *(978-1-55498-193-9(X))* Groundwood Bks. CAN. Dist: Publishers Group West (PGW).

Burchett, Jan & Vogler, Sara. Poacher Panic, 1 vol. Le Feyer, Diane, illus. 2012. (Wild Rescue Ser.). (ENG.). 152p. (gr. 3-6). 9.95 *(978-1-4342-4593-9(4));* lib. bdg. 25.32 *(978-1-4342-3286-1(7))* Stone Arch Bks.

Irwin, Bindi & Black, Jess. Roar! 2011. (Bindi's Wildlife Adventures Ser.: 6). (ENG.). 112p. (J). (gr. 3-6). pap. 4.99 *(978-1-4022-5931-9(X),* Sourcebooks Jabberwocky) Sourcebooks, Inc.

Jenkins, Jerry B. Crash at Cannibal Valley, 1 vol. 2006. (AirQuest Adventures Ser.). (ENG.). 160p. (J). (gr. 3-7). pap. 6.99 *(978-0-310-71347-0(1))* Zonderkidz.

Joiner, Sara K. After the Ashes. 2015. (ENG., Illus.). 352p. (J). (gr. 5-10). 17.95 *(978-0-8234-3441-1(9))* Holiday Hse., Inc.

Lewis, Richard. The Killing Sea. 2008. (ENG., Illus.). 256p. (YA). (gr. 7-12). mass mkt. 7.99 *(978-1-4169-5372-2(8),* Simon Pulse) Simon Pulse.

Meyer, L. A. The Mark of the Golden Dragon: Being an Account of the Further Adventures of Jacky Faber, Jewel of the East, Vexation of the West & Pearl of the South China Sea. (Bloody Jack Adventures Ser.: 9). (ENG.). (YA). (gr. 9). 2013. 400p. pap. 9.99 *(978-0-544-00328-6(4))* 2011. 384p. 16.99 *(978-0-547-51764-3(5))* Houghton Mifflin Harcourt Publishing Co.

Schrefer, Eliot. Rescued. 2016. (ENG.). 272p. (J). (gr. 7). 18.99 *(978-0-545-65503-3(X),* Scholastic Pr.) Scholastic, Inc.

Taylor, Diane & Tay-Audouard, L. K. Singapore Children's Favorite Stories. 2003. (ENG., Illus.). 96p. (J). (gr. k-8). 18.95 *(978-0-7946-0097-6(2))* Periplus Editions (HK), Ltd. HKG. Dist: Simon & Schuster, Inc.

INDUCTION (LOGIC)

see Logic

INDUCTION MOTORS

see Electric Motors

INDUS RIVER

Aronovsky, Ilona & Gopinath, Sujata. The Indus Valley. 2016. (Excavating the Past Ser.). (ENG.). 48p. (gr. 4-6). pap. 8.99 *(978-1-4846-3644-2(9),* NA-h) Heinemann-Raintree.

INDUSTRIAL CHEMISTRY

see Chemistry, Technical

INDUSTRIAL COUNCILS

see Management—Employee Participation

INDUSTRIAL DRAWING

see Mechanical Drawing

INDUSTRIAL EDUCATION

see Technical Education

INDUSTRIAL ENGINEERING

see Industrial Management

INDUSTRIAL MANAGEMENT

Here are entered works on the application of the principles of management to industrial enterprises, including production, office management, marketing, finance, etc. Works on the technical control of manufacturing processes are entered under Factory Management.

see also Business; Machinery; Marketing

Adamson, Thomas K. The Kids' Guide to Sports Design & Engineering, 1 vol. 2014. (SI Kids Guide Bks.). (ENG.). 48p. (gr. 4-9). lib. bdg. 31.99 *(978-1-4765-4155-6(8))* Capstone Press of Coughlan Cos.

Cohn, Jessica. Great Careers with a High School Diploma: Manufacturing & Transportation. 2008. (Great Careers with a High School Diploma Ser.). 127p. (C). (gr. 9). 32.95 *(978-0-8160-7050-3(4),* Ferguson Publishing Co.) Facts On File, Inc.

Ferguson Publishing Staff, creator. Manufacturing. 3rd rev. ed. 2008. (Careers in Focus Ser.). (Illus.). 188p. (gr. 6-12). 32.95 *(978-0-8160-7273-6(6),* Ferguson Publishing Co.) Facts On File, Inc.

Gregory, Helen. Places to Work, 1 vol. 2013. (Wonder Readers Next Steps: Social Studies). (ENG.). 20p. (gr. -1-1). lib. bdg. 22.65 *(978-1-4765-0043-0(6),* Wonder Readers) Capstone Press of Coughlan Cos.

Haugen, David M. Outsourcing. 2009. (Opposing Viewpoints Ser.). (ENG., Illus.). 240p. (YA). (gr. 10-12). pap. 42.95 *(978-0-7377-4376-0(X),* LML02109-245381); pap. 29.45 *(978-0-7377-4375-3(1),* LML02109-245367) Cengage Gale. (Greenhaven Pr., Inc.).

Leave a Mark, Not a Stain. 2005. (YA). 14.95 *(978-1-59872-138-6(0))* Instant Pub.

Porterfield, Jason. Becoming a Quality Assurance Engineer. 2017. (Tech Track: Building Your Career in IT Ser.). 80p. (J). (gr. 12-12). 35.75 ***(978-1-5081-7562-9(4)***, Rosen Young Adult) Rosen Publishing Group, Inc., The.

Prentzas, Scott. Radar Guns. 2009. (21st Century Skills Library: Global Products Ser.). (ENG., Illus.). 32p. (gr. 4-8). lib. bdg. 28.50 *(978-1-60279-507-5(X),* 200322) Cherry Lake Publishing.

INDUSTRIAL MATERIALS

see Materials

INDUSTRIAL ORGANIZATION

see Industrial Management

INDUSTRIAL PSYCHOLOGY

see Psychology, Applied

INDUSTRIAL REVOLUTION

see Great Britain—History—19th Century; Industries—History

INDUSTRIAL SCHOOLS

see Technical Education

INDUSTRIAL WASTES

see Waste Products

INDUSTRIAL WORKERS OF THE WORLD

Housel, Debra J. Industrial Giants, 1 vol. 2007. (Primary Source Readers Ser.). (ENG.). 32p. (J). (gr. 4-4). pap. 8.99 *(978-0-7439-0661-6(6))* Shell Educational Publishing.

INDUSTRIES

see also Industrial Management; Machinery in the Workplace; Manufactures

Allen, John. Careers in Environmental & Energy Technology. 2017. (ENG.). 80p. (J). (gr. 5-12). *(978-1-68282-110-7(2))* ReferencePoint Pr., Inc.

Brezina, Corona. The Industrial Revolution in America: A Primary Source History of America's Transformation into an Industrial Society. 2005. (Primary Sources in American History Ser.). (Illus.). 64p. (YA). (gr. 5-8). lib. bdg. 31.95 *(978-1-4042-0179-8(3))* Rosen Publishing Group, Inc., The.

Brown, Marty. Webmaster. 2009. (Coolcareers. com Ser.). 48p. (gr. 5-8). 53.00 *(978-1-61511-985-1(X),* Rosen Reference) Rosen Publishing Group, Inc., The.

Buell, Tonya. Careers with Successful Dot-Com Companies. 2009. (Library of E-Commerce & Internet Careers Ser.). 64p. (gr. 5-5). 58.50 *(978-1-60853-584-2(3))* Rosen Publishing Group, Inc., The.

Burgan, Michael. Energy, Vol. 10. 2016. (Stem in Current Events Ser.). (Illus.). 64p. (J). (gr. 7). 23.95 *(978-1-4222-3589-8(0))* Mason Crest.

—Farming Vegetables & Grains, 1 vol. 2011. (Ethics of Food Ser.). (ENG.). 56p. (gr. 6-6). pap. 9.99 *(978-1-4329-6190-9(X))* Heinemann-Raintree.

Doeden, Matt. SpaceX & Tesla Motors Engineer Elon Musk. 2015. (STEM Trailblazer Bios Ser.). (ENG., Illus.). 32p. (J). (gr. 2-5). lib. bdg. 26.60 *(978-1-4677-5791-1(8),* Lerner Pubns.) Lerner Publishing Group.

Edge, Laura Bufano. Andrew Carnegie. 2004. (Lerner Biographies Ser.). (Illus.). 128p. (J). (gr. 6-12). lib. bdg. 27.93 *(978-0-8225-4965-9(4))* Lerner Publishing Group.

Ferguson. Careers in Focus: Energy. 3rd rev. ed. 2011. (Careers in Focus Ser.). (Illus.). 228p. (gr. 6-12). 32.95 *(978-0-8160-8039-7(9),* Ferguson Publishing Co.) Facts On File, Inc.

Frydenborg, Kay. Chocolate: Sweet Science & Dark Secrets of the World's Favorite Treat. 2015. (ENG., Illus.). 256p. (YA). (gr. 7). 18.99 *(978-0-544-17566-2(2),* HMH Books For Young Readers) Houghton Mifflin Harcourt Publishing Co.

Gedacht, Daniel C. Economy & Industry in Ancient Rome. (Primary Sources of Ancient Civilizations Ser.). 24p. 2009. (gr. 3-3). 42.50 *(978-1-60851-557-8(5))* 2004. (ENG., Illus.). (gr. 4-8). pap. 8.25 *(978-0-8239-8946-1(1))* 2004. (Illus.). (J). lib. bdg. 22.60 *(978-0-8239-6780-3(8))* Rosen Publishing Group, Inc., The. (PowerKids Pr.).

Goldish, Meish. Poisoned Air: Bhopal, India. 2017. (Eco-Disasters Ser.). (ENG.). 32p. (J). (gr. 2-7). 19.95 ***(978-1-68402-221-2(5))*** Bearport Publishing Co., Inc.

Gordon, Sherri Mabry & Library. Green & Clean Energy: What You Can Do. 2010. (Green Issues in Focus Ser.). (Illus.). 128p. (J). (gr. 7-12). lib. bdg. 33.27 *(978-0-7660-3348-1(1))* Enslow Pubs., Inc.

Green, Sara. Coca-Cola. 2015. (Brands We Know Ser.). (ENG., Illus.). 24p. (J). (gr. 3-8). lib. bdg. 25.95 *(978-1-62617-287-6(0),* Pilot Bks.) Bellwether Media.

—Crayola. 2015. (Brands We Know Ser.). (ENG., Illus.). 24p. (J). (gr. 3-8). lib. bdg. 25.95 *(978-1-62617-288-3(9),* Pilot Bks.) Bellwether Media.

—Google. 2016. (Brands We Know Ser.). (ENG., Illus.). 24p. (J). (gr. 3-8). lib. bdg. 25.95 *(978-1-62617-347-7(8),* Pilot Bks.) Bellwether Media.

—Sony. 2016. (Brands We Know Ser.). (ENG., Illus.). 24p. (J). (gr. 3-8). 25.95 *(978-1-62617-412-2(1),* Pilot Bks.) Bellwether Media.

Harris, Ashley Rae. Arms Trade, 1 vol. 2011. (Essential Issues Set 2 Ser.). (ENG., Illus.). 112p. (J). (gr. 6-12). lib. bdg. 35.64 *(978-1-61714-770-8(2),* Essential Library) ABDO Publishing Co.

Hayward, Linda. I Am a Pencil. Nicklaus, Carol, illus. 2003. (Silly Millies Ser.). 32p. lib. bdg. 17.90 *(978-0-7613-2904-6(8),* Millbrook Pr.) Lerner Publishing Group.

Houghton, Gillian. Goods & Services. 2009. (Invest Kids Ser.). (Illus.). 24p. (J). (ENG.). (gr. 2-5). pap. 8.25 *(978-1-4358-3210-7(8),* 1291654); lib. bdg. 22.60 *(978-1-4358-2775-2(9),* 1291654) Rosen Publishing Group, Inc., The. (PowerKids Pr.).

Johanson, Paula. Tech Industry. 2017. (Illus.). 32p. (J). ***(978-0-7787-3604-2(0))*** Crabtree Publishing Co.

Kallen, Stuart A. Internet Entrepreneurs. 2016. (ENG.). 80p. (J). (gr. 5-12). lib. bdg. *(978-1-68282-028-5(9))* ReferencePoint Pr., Inc.

Kops, Deborah. The Great Molasses Flood. 2015. (ENG.). 112p. (J). (gr. 4-7). pap. 11.95 *(978-1-58089-349-7(X))* Charlesbridge Publishing, Inc.

—The Great Molasses Flood: Boston 1919. 2015. lib. bdg. 23.25 *(978-0-606-36650-2(4))* Turtleback Bks.

Lukidis, Lydia. Manufacturing. 2017. (J). ***(978-1-5105-1937-4(8))*** SmartBook Media, Inc.

Mara, Wil. Hazmat Removal Worker. 2015. (21st Century Skills Library: Cool STEAM Careers Ser.). (ENG.). 32p. (J). (gr. 4-7). 29.93 *(978-1-63362-004-9(2),* 205928) Cherry Lake Publishing.

Marcovitz, Hal. Energy Security, 1 vol. 2011. (Essential Issues Set 2 Ser.). (ENG., Illus.). 112p. (J). (gr. 6-12). lib. bdg. 35.64 *(978-1-61714-771-5(0),* Essential Library) ABDO Publishing Co.

Mattern, Joanne. Florida's Economy: From the Mouse to the Moon. 2016. (Primary Source Readers Ser.). (Illus.). 32p. (J). (gr. 4-4). pap. 8.99 *(978-1-4938-3548-5(3))* Teacher Created Materials, Inc.

McGinty, Alice B. Software Designer. 2009. (Coolcareers. com Ser.). 48p. (gr. 5-8). 53.00 *(978-1-61511-984-4(1),* Rosen Reference) Rosen Publishing Group, Inc., The.

Meyer, Jared. Working in a War Zone: Military Contractors. 2009. (Extreme Careers Ser.). 64p. (gr. 5-5). 58.50 *(978-1-61512-422-0(5),* Rosen Reference) Rosen Publishing Group, Inc., The.

Nelson, Robin. What Do We Buy? A Look at Goods & Services. 2010. (Lightning Bolt Books — Exploring Economics Ser.). (ENG., Illus.). 32p. (gr. k-2). pap. 7.95 *(978-0-7613-5667-7(3));* lib. bdg. 26.60 *(978-0-7613-3913-7(2))* Lerner Publishing Group.

Olhoff, Jim. Hazmat. 2012. (Emergency Workers Ser.). 32p. (J). (gr. 5-9). lib. bdg. 27.07 *(978-1-61783-514-8(5),* Abdo & Daughters) ABDO Publishing Co.

Rauf, Don. Careers in Janitorial & Cleaning Services, 1 vol. 2015. (ENG.). 80p. (J). 34.25 *(978-1-4777-7880-7(2)*, Rosen Young Adult) Rosen Publishing Group, Inc., The.

Rockwood, Leigh. The Ancient Egyptian Economy. 2013. (Spotlight on Ancient Civilizations: Egypt Ser.). (ENG., Illus.). 24p. (J). (gr. 3-4). pap. 10.00 *(978-1-4777-0863-7(4))*; lib. bdg. 23.60 *(978-1-4777-0765-4(4))* Rosen Publishing Group, Inc., The. (PowerKids Pr.).

Schauer, Pete. General Contractor. 2016. (Careers in Construction Ser.). (ENG., Illus.). 112p. (J). (gr. 7-7). lib. bdg. 42.79 *(978-1-5026-0978-6(9))* Cavendish Square Publishing.

Scherer, Lauri S., ed. Oil. 2013. (Introducing Issues with Opposing Viewpoints Ser.). (ENG., Illus.). 144p. (gr. 7-10). lib. bdg. 36.95 *(978-0-7377-6279-2(9)*, Greenhaven Pr., Inc.) Cengage Gale.

Senker, Cath. Samsung: The Business Behind the Technology. 2016. (Big Brands Ser.). (ENG., Illus.). 32p. (J). (gr. 4-6). 26.65 *(978-1-5124-0591-0(4))*; 39.99 *(978-1-5124-0595-8(7)*, Lerner Pubns.) Lerner Publishing Group.

Sherman, Jill. Fossil Fuels. 2017. (J). pap. ***(978-0-7660-9151-1(1))*** Enslow Pubs., Inc.

Solway, Andrew. The Scientists Behind Energy, 1 vol. 2011. (Sci-Hi: Scientists Ser.). (ENG.). 48p. (gr. 4-4). pap. 9.95 *(978-1-4109-4052-0(7))*; lib. bdg. 33.32 *(978-1-4109-4045-2(4))* Heinemann-Raintree. (Sci-Hi).

Spaulding, Jeffrey. Career Building Through Digital Sampling & Remixing. 2009. (Digital Career Building Ser.). 64p. (gr. 6-6). 58.50 *(978-1-61512-165-6(X))* Rosen Publishing Group, Inc., The.

Spilsbury, Richard. Pharmaceutical Industry. 2010. (Closer Look: Global Industries Ser.). (ENG.). 48p. (YA). lib. bdg. 29.25 *(978-1-4358-9633-8(5)*, Rosen Reference) Rosen Publishing Group, Inc., The.

Staley, Erin. Careers in Hospitality, 1 vol. 2015. (ENG., Illus.). 80p. (J). 34.25 *(978-1-4777-7882-1(9)*, Rosen Young Adult) Rosen Publishing Group, Inc., The.

Technology Pioneers, 8 vols., Set. Incl. Craigslist: The Company & Its Founder. Freese, Susan M. lib. bdg. 35.64 *(978-1-61714-806-4(7))*; EBay: The Company & Its Founder. Gitlin, Martin. lib. bdg. 35.64 *(978-1-61714-807-1(5))*; Google: The Company & Its Founders. Hamen, Susan E. lib. bdg. 35.64 *(978-1-61714-808-8(3))*; Nintendo: The Company & Its Founders. Firestone, Mary. lib. bdg. 35.64 *(978-1-61714-809-5(1))*; Pixar: The Company & Its Founders. Buckley, A. M. lib. bdg. 35.64 *(978-1-61714-810-1(5))*; Social Networking: Myspace, Facebook, & Twitter. Lusted, Marcia Amidon. lib. bdg. 35.64 *(978-1-61714-811-8(3))*; Wikipedia: The Company & Its Founders. Anderson, Jennifer Joline. lib. bdg. 35.64 *(978-1-61714-812-5(1))*; YouTube: The Company & Its Founders. Rowell, Rebecca. lib. bdg. 35.64 *(978-1-61714-813-2(X))*; (J). (gr. 6-12). (Technology Pioneers Set 1 Ser.: 8). (ENG., Illus.). 112p. 2011. Set lib. bdg. 285.12 *(978-1-61714-805-7(9)*, Essential Library) ABDO Publishing Co.

Thaddeus, Eva. Powering the Future: New Energy Technologies. 2010. (World's of Wonder Ser.). (ENG., Illus.). 131p. (J). (gr. 4-18). 34.95 *(978-0-8263-4901-9(3))* Univ. of New Mexico Pr.

The True Cost of Toys. 2014. (ENG., Illus.). 48p. (J). *(978-0-7787-0486-7(6))* Crabtree Publishing Co.

Turner, Donald R. & Tillema, Juliana O. Production of Goods & Services. 2011. (J). 244.80 *(978-1-4488-4860-7(1))*; (J). pap. 12.95 *(978-1-4488-4721-1(4))*; (YA). (gr. 5-9). lib. bdg. 31.95 *(978-1-4488-4711-2(7))* Rosen Publishing Group, Inc., The.

Wooster, Patricia. Music Producer. 2011. (21st Century Skills Library: Cool Arts Careers Ser.). (ENG.). 32p. (gr. 4-8). lib. bdg. 28.50 *(978-1-61080-133-1(4)*, 201144) Cherry Lake Publishing.

INDUSTRIES—GREAT BRITAIN

Anita Roddick. 2010. (Women of Achievement Ser.). (Illus.). 120p. (gr. 6-12). 35.00 *(978-1-60413-688-3(X)*, Chelsea Hse.) Facts On File, Inc.

INDUSTRIES—HISTORY

Brennan, Patricia. Who Is Bill Gates? 2013. (Who Is... ? Ser.). lib. bdg. 16.00 *(978-0-606-30038-4(4)*, Turtleback) Turtleback Bks.

Brezina, Corona. The Industrial Revolution in America: A Primary Source History of America's Transformation into an Industrial Society. (Primary Sources in American History Ser.). 64p. (gr. 5-8). 2009. 58.50 *(978-1-60851-497-7(8))* 2005. (Illus.). (YA). lib. bdg. 31.95 *(978-1-4042-0179-8(3))* Rosen Publishing Group, Inc., The.

Brown, Jonatha A. Bill Gates. 2004. (People We Should Know Ser.). (Illus.). 24p. (gr. 1-4). pap. 8.15 *(978-0-8368-4317-0(7))*; lib. bdg. 22.00 *(978-0-8368-4310-1(X))* Stevens, Gareth Publishing LLLP. (Weekly Reader Leveled Readers).

Buckley, Susan Washburn & National Geographic Learning Staff. The Industrial Revolution. 2006. (Nonfiction Reading & Writing Workshops Ser.). (ENG., Illus.). 40p. (J). pap. 19.95 *(978-0-7922-8685-1(5))* CENGAGE Learning.

Burgan, Michael. The European Industrial Revolution. 2013. (ENG.). 64p. (J). 30.00 *(978-0-531-28202-1(3))*; pap. 8.95 *(978-0-531-27667-9(8))* Scholastic Library Publishing.

Christopher, Nick. The Industrial Revolution, Migration, & Immigration, 01 vols., 1. 2016. (Spotlight on Immigration & Migration Ser.). (ENG., Illus.). 24p. (J). pap. 10.00 *(978-1-5081-4086-3(3)*, PowerKids Pr.) Rosen Publishing Group, Inc., The.

Cunningham, Kevin. Video Games: From Concept to Consumer. 2013. (Calling All Innovators). (ENG.). 64p. (J). pap. 8.95 *(978-0-531-22011-5(7)*, Children's Pr.); lib. bdg. 30.00 *(978-0-531-26523-9(4))* Scholastic Library Publishing.

George, Enzo. The Industrial Revolution. 2016. (Primary Sources in World History Ser.). (ENG.). 48p. (YA). (gr. 6-6). 31.36 *(978-1-5026-1817-7(6))* Cavendish Square Publishing.

Gray, Leon. Horrible Jobs of the Industrial Revolution, Vol. 1. 2014. (History's Most Horrible Jobs Ser.). (ENG.). 48p. (J). (gr. 5-6). 31.95 *(978-1-4824-0343-5(9))* Stevens, Gareth Publishing LLLP.

Grayson, Robert. The U. S. Industrial Revolution, 1 vol. 2010. (Essential Events Set 5 Ser.). (ENG.). 112p. (J). (gr. 6-12). lib. bdg. 35.64 *(978-1-61613-687-1(1))* ABDO Publishing Co.

Housel, Debra J. Industrial Revolution, 1 vol. 2007. (Primary Source Readers Ser.). (ENG.). 32p. (J). (gr. 5-5). pap. 8.99 *(978-0-7439-0660-9(8))* Shell Educational Publishing.

Howell, Brian. U. S. Growth & Change in the 19th Century, 1801 to 1861. 2011. (Explorer Library: Language Arts Explorer Ser.). (ENG.). 32p. (gr. 4-8). lib. bdg. 28.50 *(978-1-61080-202-4(0)*, 201180) Cherry Lake Publishing.

—U.S. Growth & Change in the 19th Century. 2011. (Explorer Library: Language Arts Explorer Ser.). (ENG.). 32p. (gr. 4-8). pap. 14.21 *(978-1-61080-290-1(X)*, 201213) Cherry Lake Publishing.

The Industrial Revolution: PowerPoint Presentations in World History. 2005. cd-rom 49.95 net. *(978-1-56004-210-5(9))* Social Studies Schl. Service.

Industrialism. 2010. (Key Concepts in American History Ser.). (Illus.). 128p. (gr. 6-12). 45.00 *(978-1-60413-222-9(1)*, Chelsea Hse.) Facts On File, Inc.

James, Trisha. Cattle & Oil: The Growth of Texas Industries. 2010. (Spotlight on Texas Ser.). (ENG., Illus.). 32p. (J). (gr. 3-4). pap. 11.75 *(978-1-61532-475-0(5))*; lib. bdg. 26.25 *(978-1-61532-477-4(1))* Rosen Publishing Group, Inc., The.

Jarnow, Jesse. Oil, Steel, & Railroads: America's Big Businesses in the Late 1800s. (America's Industrial Society in the 19th Century Ser.). 32p. 2009. (gr. 4-4). 47.90 *(978-1-61511-337-8(1))* 2004. (ENG., Illus.). (gr. 5-8). pap. 10.00 *(978-0-8239-4276-3(7))* Rosen Publishing Group, Inc., The.

Liberman, Sherri. A Historical Atlas of the Industrial Age & the Growth of America's Cities. 2009. (United States: Historical Atlases of the Growth of a New Nation Ser.). 64p. (gr. 5-5). 61.20 *(978-1-60854-254-3(8))* Rosen Publishing Group, Inc., The.

Marsh, Carole. Industrial Revolution from Muscles to Machines! 2004. (American Milestones Ser.). (Illus.). 28p. (J). (gr. 4-12). pap. 5.95 *(978-0-635-02694-1(5))* Gallopade International.

—Industrial Revolution Reproducible Activity Book (HC) 2004. 28p. (gr. 4-12). 29.95 *(978-0-635-02695-8(3))* Gallopade International.

Meinking, Mary. The Development of U. S. Industry. 2011. (Explorer Library: Language Arts Explorer Ser.). (ENG.). 32p. (gr. 4-8). pap. 14.21 *(978-1-61080-286-4(1)*, 201209) Cherry Lake Publishing.

—The Development of U.S. Industry. 2011. (Explorer Library: Language Arts Explorer Ser.). (ENG.). 32p. (gr. 4-8). lib. bdg. 28.50 *(978-1-61080-198-0(9)*, 201172) Cherry Lake Publishing.

Mooney, Carla. The Industrial Revolution: Investigate How Science & Technology Changed the World with 25 Projects. Vaughn, Jenn, illus. 2011. (Build It Yourself Ser.). (ENG.). 128p. (J). (gr. 3-7). 21.95 *(978-1-936313-81-5(2))*; pap. 15.95 *(978-1-936313-80-8(4))* Open City Bks.

Mooney, Carla. Perspectives on the Industrial Revolution. 2018. (ENG.). 32p. (gr. 3-6). ***(978-1-63235-402-0(0)***, 12-Story Library) Pr. Room Editions LLC.

Mullenbach, Cheryl. The Industrial Revolution for Kids: The People & Technology That Changed the World, with 21 Activities. 2014. (For Kids Ser.). (ENG., Illus.). 144p. (J). (gr. 4). pap. 16.95 *(978-1-61374-690-5(3))* Chicago Review Pr., Inc.

Nardo, Don. The Industrial Revolution in Britain. 2009. (Lucent Library of Historical Eras). (ENG., Illus.). 128p. (YA). (gr. 7-10). lib. bdg. 34.80 *(978-1-4205-0152-0(6)*, LML02109-246064, Lucent Bks.) Cengage Gale.

—The Rise of Industrial America. 2016. (Illus.). 48p. (J). *(978-1-5105-1290-0(X))* SmartBook Media, Inc.

Perritano, John. The Revolution in Industry: How Machines Changed America. 2008. (Graphic America Ser.). (ENG., Illus.). 32p. (J). (gr. 3-6). pap. *(978-0-7787-4216-6(4))*; lib. bdg. *(978-0-7787-4189-3(3))* Crabtree Publishing Co.

Peters, Craig. Bill Gates: Software Genius of Microsoft. 2003. (Internet Biographies Ser.). (Illus.). 48p. (J). (gr. 4-10). lib. bdg. 23.93 *(978-0-7660-1969-0(1))* Enslow Pubs., Inc.

—Larry Ellison: Database Genius of Oracle. 2003. (Internet Biographies Ser.). (Illus.). 48p. (J). (gr. 4-10). lib. bdg. 23.93 *(978-0-7660-1974-4(8))* Enslow Pubs., Inc.

Pierce, Alan. Industrial Revolution, 1 vol. 2005. (American Moments Ser.). (ENG., Illus.). 48p. (gr. 4-8). 27.07 *(978-1-59197-933-3(1)*, Abdo & Daughters) ABDO Publishing Co.

Richardson, Adele D. The Story of Microsoft. 2003. (Built for Success Ser.). (Illus.). 48p. (J). 28.50 *(978-1-58340-294-8(2))* Black Rabbit Bks.

Sakolsky, Josh. Critical Perspectives on the Industrial Revolution. 2005. (Critical Anthologies of Nonfiction Writing Ser.). (Illus.). 176p. (YA). (gr. 7-12). lib. bdg. 37.95 *(978-1-4042-0062-3(2))* Rosen Publishing Group, Inc., The.

Samuels, Charlie. The Rise of Industry (1700-1800) 2010. (Science Highlights: A Gareth Stevens Timeline Ser.). (ENG.). 48p. (J). (gr. 6-8). pap. 14.05 *(978-1-4339-4146-7(5))*; lib. bdg. 31.95 *(978-1-4339-4145-0(7))* Stevens, Gareth Publishing LLLP. (Gareth Stevens Secondary Library).

—A Timeline of the Industrial Revolution. 2010. (History Highlights: A Gareth Stevens Timeline Ser.). (Illus.). 48p. (gr. 6-8). (J). pap. 14.05 *(978-1-4339-3493-3(0))*; (YA). lib. bdg. 31.95 *(978-1-4339-3492-6(2))* Stevens, Gareth Publishing LLLP. (Gareth Stevens Secondary Library).

Schimel, Kate & Collins, Kathleen. The Economic Growth of New York. 2012. (Illus.). 24p. (J). 60.00 *(978-1-4488-5766-1(X))*; pap. 10.00 *(978-1-4488-5765-4(1))*; lib. bdg. 22.60 *(978-1-4488-5746-3(5))* Rosen Publishing Group, Inc., The. (PowerKids Pr.).

Sheppard, Paul. Access to Geography: Economic Activity & Change. 2004. (Access to Geography Ser.). (Illus.). 128p. pap. 32.50 *(978-0-340-81500-7(0)*, Hodder Education) Hodder Education Group GBR. Dist: Trans-Atlantic Pubns., Inc.

Sioux, Tracee. Immigrants, Migration, & the Industrial Revolution. (Primary Sources of Immigration & Migration in America Ser.). 24p. 2009. (gr. 3-4). 42.50 *(978-1-60851-779-4(9))* 2004. (Illus.). (J). lib. bdg. 22.60 *(978-0-8239-6826-8(X))* Rosen Publishing Group, Inc., The. (PowerKids Pr.).

—Immigration, Migration, & the Industrial Revolution. 2004. (Primary Sources of Immigration & Migration in America Ser.). (ENG., Illus.). 24p. (gr. 4-8). pap. 9.40 *(978-0-8239-8998-0(4)*, PowerKids Pr.) Rosen Publishing Group, Inc., The.

Spilsbury, Louise. Industrialization & Empire, 1783 to 1914. 2010. (CC: Atlas of World History Ser.). 112p. (gr. 6-12). 42.80 *(978-1-933834-69-6(2))* Brown Bear Bks.

Stein, R. Conrad. The Industrial Revolution: Manufacturing a Better America. 2006. (American Saga Ser.). (Illus.). 128p. (J). (gr. 5-12). lib. bdg. 31.93 *(978-0-7660-2571-4(3))* Enslow Pubs., Inc.

Sutcliffe, Jane. Milton Hershey. Parlin, Tim, illus. 2003. (History Maker Biographies Ser.). (ENG.). 48p. (gr. 3-6). 27.93 *(978-0-8225-0247-0(X)*, Lerner Pubns.) Lerner Publishing Group.

Vallencourt, Margaret. Technology of the Industrial Revolution, 01 vols., 1. 2016. (History of Technology Ser.). (ENG., Illus.). 112p. (J). lib. bdg. 32.90 *(978-1-68048-275-1(0)*, Britannica Educational Publishing) Rosen Publishing Group, Inc., The.

Vickers, Rebecca. Industrial Age Medicine, 1 vol. 2012. (Medicine Through the Ages Ser.). (ENG.). 48p. (gr. 6-7). pap. 9.49 *(978-1-4109-4651-5(7))*; lib. bdg. 34.65 *(978-1-4109-4645-4(2))* Heinemann-Raintree. (Raintree Freestyle).

Wirkner, Linda. Learning about America's Industrial Growth with Graphic Organizers. 2005. (Graphic Organizers in Social Studies). (Illus.). 24p. (J). (gr. 3-5). lib. bdg. 22.60 *(978-1-4042-2812-2(8)*, PowerKids Pr.) Rosen Publishing Group, Inc., The.

Wolfe, James. The Industrial Revolution: Steam & Steel. 2015. (Age of Revolution Ser.). (ENG., Illus.). 128p. (J). (gr. 9-10). 35.25 *(978-1-68048-026-9(X)*, Britannica Educational Publishing) Rosen Publishing Group, Inc., The.

Wolfe, James, ed. The Industrial Revolution. 2015. (Age of Revolution Ser.). (ENG.). 128p. (YA). (gr. 9-10). 70.50 *(978-1-68048-027-6(8)*, Britannica Educational Publishing) Rosen Publishing Group, Inc., The.

INDUSTRIES—ORGANIZATION

see Industrial Management

INDUSTRIES—UNITED STATES

Benge, Janet & Benge, Geoff. Milton Hershey: More Than Chocolate. 2012. (ENG.). (YA). pap. 9.99 *(978-1-932096-82-8(5))* Emerald Bks.

Bodden, Valerie. The Story of Coca-Cola. (Built for Success Ser.). 2011. (ENG.). 48p. (J). (gr. 4-7). pap. 12.00 *(978-0-89812-753-9(X)*, Creative Paperbacks) 2008. (Illus.). 46p. (YA). (gr. 5-9). 22.95 *(978-1-58341-602-0(1))* Creative Co., The.

Buckley, James, Jr. Who Was Milton Hershey? Hammond, Ted, illus. 2013. (Who Was? Ser.). (ENG.). 112p. (J). (gr. 3-7). 5.99 *(978-0-448-47936-1(2)*, Grosset & Dunlap) Penguin Young Readers Group.

Carroll, Jamuna. The Pharmaceutical Industry. 2008. (Opposing Viewpoints Ser.). (ENG., Illus.). 212p. (YA). (gr. 10-12). 27.50 *(978-0-7377-4239-8(9)*, LML02109-243153); pap. 39.70 *(978-0-7377-4238-1(0)*, LML02109-243118) Cengage Gale. (Greenhaven Pr., Inc.).

Conklin, Wendy. Georgia's Location & Resources. 2016. (Primary Source Readers Ser.). (Illus.). 32p. (gr. 2-2). 8.99 *(978-1-4938-2549-3(6))* Teacher Created Materials, Inc.

Demuth, Patricia Brennan. Who Is Bill Gates? Hammond, Ted & Harrison, Nancy, illus. 2013. (Who Was? Ser.). (ENG.). 112p. (J). (gr. 3-7). pap. 5.99 *(978-0-448-46332-2(6)*, Grosset & Dunlap) Penguin Young Readers Group.

Doeden, Matt. GoPro Inventor Nick Woodman. 2015. (STEM Trailblazer Bios Ser.). (ENG., Illus.). 32p. (J). (gr. 2-5). pap. 7.95 *(978-1-4677-6117-8(6))*; lib. bdg. 26.60 *(978-1-4677-5792-8(6)*, Lerner Pubns.) Lerner Publishing Group.

Fandel, Jennifer & Milgrom, Al. George Eastman & the Kodak Camera, 1 vol. Purcell, Gordon & Milgrom, Al, illus. 2007. (Inventions & Discovery Ser.). (ENG.). 32p. (gr. 3-4). 30.65 *(978-0-7368-6848-8(8)*, Graphic Library) Capstone Press of Coughlan Cos.

Fershee, Joshua P. Energy Law: A Context & Practice Casebook. 2014. (Illus.). 646p. 88.00 *(978-1-59460-799-8(0))* Carolina Academic Pr.

Frisch, Aaron. The Story of Nike. 2008. (Built for Success Ser.). (YA). (gr. 5-9). 22.95 *(978-1-58341-608-2(0))* Creative Co., The.

Ganchinello, Sheena. Tim Westergren & Pandora. 2013. (Internet Biographies Ser.). (ENG., Illus.). 128p. (YA). (gr. 7-12). lib. bdg. 34.60 *(978-1-4488-9526-7(X)*, Rosen Classroom) Rosen Publishing Group, Inc., The.

Garstecki, Julia. Life During the Industrial Revolution, 1 vol. 2014. (Daily Life in US History Ser.). (ENG.). 48p. (gr. 3-6). lib. bdg. 32.79 *(978-1-62403-627-9(9))* ABDO Publishing Co.

Gilbert, Sara. Built for Success: The\Story of Starbucks. 2008. (Built for Success Ser.). (Illus.). 46p. (YA). (gr. 5-9). 22.95 *(978-1-58341-609-9(9))* Creative Co., The.

—The Story of Google. 2008. (Built for Success Ser.). (Illus.). 46p. (J). (gr. 5-9). 22.95 *(978-1-58341-605-1(6))* Creative Co., The.

Grayson, Robert. Estée Lauder: Businesswoman & Cosmetics Pioneer, 1 vol. 2013. (Essential Lives Set 8 Ser.). (ENG.). 112p. (J). (gr. 6-12). lib. bdg. 35.64 *(978-1-61783-892-7(6)*, Essential Library) ABDO Publishing Co.

Green, Sara. Crayola. 2017. (Crayola Ser.). 24p. (J). (gr. 3-8). pap. 7.99 ***(978-1-61891-252-7(6)***, Pilot Bks.) Bellwether Media.

—Hershey's. (Hershey's Ser.). 24p. (J). (gr. 3-8). 2017. pap. 7.99 ***(978-1-61891-248-0(8))*** 2015. (ENG., Illus.). lib. bdg. 25.95 *(978-1-62617-206-7(4))* Bellwether Media. (Pilot Bks.).

—Kraft. 2016. (Brands We Know Ser.). (ENG., Illus.). 24p. (J). (gr. 3-8). 25.95 *(978-1-62617-409-2(1)*, Pilot Bks.) Bellwether Media.

—Lego. 2015. (Brands We Know Ser.). (ENG., Illus.). 24p. (J). (gr. 3-8). lib. bdg. 25.95 *(978-1-62617-208-1(0)*, Pilot Bks.) Bellwether Media.

—Nike. 2015. (Brands We Know Ser.). (ENG., Illus.). 24p. (J). (gr. 3-8). 25.95 *(978-1-62617-210-4(2)*, Pilot Bks.) Bellwether Media.

—Sergey Brin. 2014. (Tech Icons Ser.). (ENG., Illus.). 24p. (J). (gr. 3-8). lib. bdg. 25.95 *(978-1-60014-993-1(6)*, Pilot Bks.) Bellwether Media.

Greene, Jacqueline Dembar. The Triangle Shirtwaist Factory Fire. 2007. (Code Red Ser.). (Illus.). 32p. (YA). (gr. 2-5). lib. bdg. 25.27 *(978-1-59716-359-0(7))* Bearport Publishing Co., Inc.

Harris, Ashley Rae. Microsoft: The Company & Its Founders, 1 vol. 2012. (Technology Pioneers Set 2 Ser.). (ENG.). 112p. (J). (gr. 6-12). lib. bdg. 35.64 *(978-1-61783-333-5(9)*, Essential Library) ABDO Publishing Co.

Haugen, David M. Should the Federal Government Bail Out Private Industry? 2010. (At Issue Ser.). (Illus.). 128p. (J). pap. 24.45 *(978-0-7377-4657-0(2)*, Greenhaven Pr., Inc.) Cengage Gale.

Hillstrom, Kevin & Hillstrom, Laurie Collier, eds. Automobiles, Mining & Petroleum, Textiles, 3 vols., Set. 2006. (Industrial Revolution in America Ser.). (Illus.). 884p. (C). 121.00 *(978-1-85109-749-4(X)*, IRAUTO1C) ABC-CLIO, LLC.

—The Industrial Revolution in America - Overview/Comparison, 3 vols., Set. 2007. (Industrial Revolution in America Ser.). (Illus.). 901p. (C). 121.00 *(978-1-85109-719-7(8)*, IRCOMM1C) ABC-CLIO, LLC.

Jarnow, Jesse. Oil, Steel, & Railroads: America's Big Businesses in the Late 1800s. 2009. (America's Industrial Society in the 19th Century Ser.). 32p. (gr. 4-4). 47.90 *(978-1-61511-337-8(1))* Rosen Publishing Group, Inc., The.

Kovatch, Sarah, text. Giving up Grapes. 2005. (Illus.). 16p. (J). pap. *(978-0-7367-2924-6(0))* Zaner-Bloser, Inc.

Kowalski, Emma. The Story of Konvict Muzik. 2012. (J). pap. *(978-1-4222-2129-7(6))*; 64p. (gr. 4). 22.95 *(978-1-4222-2116-7(4))* Mason Crest.

Lange, Brenda. The Triangle Shirtwaist Factory Fire. 2008. (Great Historic Disasters Ser.). (Illus.). 112p. (gr. 5-8). lib. bdg. 35.00 *(978-0-7910-9641-3(6)*, Chelsea Hse.) Facts On File, Inc.

Llanas, Sheila Griffin. Caleb Davis Bradham: Pepsi-Cola Inventor, 1 vol. 2014. (Food Dudes Set 2 Ser.). (ENG.). 32p. (J). (gr. 8-12). lib. bdg. 27.07 *(978-1-62403-315-5(6)*, Checkerboard Library) ABDO Publishing Co.

Marshall Cavendish. The Miller. 2011. (Colonial People 2 Ser.). 48p. (gr. 3). 29.93 *(978-1-60870-416-3(5))* Marshall Cavendish Corp.

Mattern, Joanne. Ben & Jerry: Ice Cream Manufacturers, 1 vol. 2011. (Food Dudes Ser.). (ENG., Illus.). 32p. (YA). (gr. 3-6). 27.07 *(978-1-61613-554-6(9))* ABDO Publishing Co.

—The Mars Family: M&M Mars Candy Makers, 1 vol. 2011. (Food Dudes Ser.). (ENG., Illus.). 32p. (YA). (gr. 3-6). 27.07 *(978-1-61613-560-7(3))* ABDO Publishing Co.

—Milton Hershey: Hershey's Chocolate Creator, 1 vol. 2011. (Food Dudes Ser.). (ENG., Illus.). 32p. (J). (gr. 3-6). 27.07 *(978-1-61613-557-7(3))* ABDO Publishing Co.

—Robert Cade: Gatorade Inventor, 1 vol. 2011. (Food Dudes Ser.). (ENG., Illus.). 32p. (J). (gr. 3-6). 27.07 *(978-1-61613-556-0(5))* ABDO Publishing Co.

—William Wrigley Jr. Wrigley's Chewing Gum Founder, 1 vol. 2011. (Food Dudes Ser.). (ENG., Illus.). 32p. (J). (gr. 3-6). 27.07 *(978-1-61613-561-4(1))* ABDO Publishing Co.

McAneney, Caitie. Madam C. J. Walker & Her Beauty Empire. 2016. (Great Entrepreneurs in U. S. History Ser.). (Illus.). 32p. (J). (gr. 5-5). pap. 11.75 *(978-1-4994-2131-6(1)*, PowerKids Pr.) Rosen Publishing Group, Inc., The.

McCormick, Anita Louise. The Industrial Revolution in United States History. 2014. (In United States History Ser.). (Illus.). 96p. (J). (gr. 5-12). 27.94 *(978-0-7660-6102-6(7))*; pap. 10.95 *(978-0-7660-6103-3(5))* Enslow Pubs., Inc.

Meinking, Mary. The Development of U. S. Industry. 2011. (Explorer Library: Language Arts Explorer Ser.). (ENG.). 32p. (gr. 4-8). pap. 14.21 *(978-1-61080-286-4(1)*, 201209) Cherry Lake Publishing.

—The Development of U.S. Industry. 2011. (Explorer Library: Language Arts Explorer Ser.). (ENG.). 32p. (gr. 4-8). lib. bdg. 28.50 *(978-1-61080-198-0(9)*, 201172) Cherry Lake Publishing.

Meyer, Jared. Working in a War Zone: Military Contractors. 2006. (Extreme Careers Ser.). (Illus.). 64p. (J). (gr. 5-8). lib. bdg. 31.95 *(978-1-4042-0959-6(X))* Rosen Publishing Group, Inc., The.

Moore, Andrew. New York City's Industries: Jobs for People. 2011. (My Community Ser.). (ENG., Illus.). 12p. (gr. 2-2). pap. 6.95 *(978-1-4488-5721-0(X)*, Rosen Classroom) Rosen Publishing Group, Inc., The.

Musolf, Nell. Built for Success: The\Story of Microsoft. 2008. (Built for Success Ser.). (YA). (gr. 5-9). 22.95 *(978-1-58341-607-5(2))* Creative Co., The.

—The Story of Ford. 2008. (Built for Success Ser.). (Illus.). 46p. (YA). (gr. 5-9). 22.95 *(978-1-58341-604-4(8))* Creative Co., The.

—The Story of Microsoft - Built for Success. 2011. (Built for Success Ser.). (ENG.). 48p. (J). (gr. 4-7). pap. 12.00 *(978-0-89812-757-7(2)*, Creative Paperbacks) Creative Co., The.

Niver, Heather Moore. Eli Whitney & the Industrial Revolution. 2016. (Great Entrepreneurs in U. S. History Ser.). 32p. (J). (gr. 5-5). pap. 11.75 *(978-1-4994-2123-1(0)*, PowerKids Pr.) Rosen Publishing Group, Inc., The.

Petersen, Christine. The Tanner. 2011. (Colonial People 2 Ser.). (Illus.). 48p. (J). (gr. 3). 29.93 *(978-1-60870-418-7(1))* Marshall Cavendish Corp.

Primary Sources of America's Industrial Society in the 19th Century. 2004. (Primary Source Big Bookstm Ser.). (ENG.). 24p. (gr. 4-8). 43.95 *(978-0-8239-4598-6(7))* Rosen Publishing Group, Inc., The.

Ribke, Simone T. Milton Hershey. 2015. (Rookie Biographies(tm) Ser.). (ENG., Illus.). 32p. (J). lib. bdg. 25.00 *(978-0-531-20594-5(0))* Scholastic Library Publishing.

Roza, Greg. Bill & Melinda Gates. 2014. (Making a Difference: Leaders Who Are Changing the World Ser.). 48p. (J). (gr. 5-8). pap. 14.05 *(978-1-62275-452-6(2))* Rosen Publishing Group, Inc., The.

Sakolsky, Josh. Critical Perspectives on the Industrial Revolution. 2005. (Critical Anthologies of Nonfiction Writing Ser.). (Illus.). 176p. (YA). (gr. 7-12). lib. bdg. 37.95 *(978-1-4042-0062-3(2))* Rosen Publishing Group, Inc., The.

Slade, Suzanne. What Can We Do about the Energy Crisis? 2009. (Protecting Our Planet Ser.). (Illus.). 24p. (ENG.). (J). pap. 8.25 *(978-1-4358-2481-2(4)*, PowerKids Pr.); (YA). (gr. 2-5). lib. bdg. 22.60 *(978-1-4042-8081-6(2))* Rosen Publishing Group, Inc., The.

Waxman, Laura Hamilton. W. K. Kellogg. 2006. (History Maker Biographies Ser.). (Illus.). 48p. (J). (gr. 3-7). lib. bdg. 26.60 *(978-0-8225-6578-9(1)*, Lerner Pubns.) Lerner Publishing Group.

Zabludoff, Marc. Ebox. 2010. (Green Cars Ser.). 48p. (J). (gr. 3-6). 28.50 (978-1-60870-009-7(7)) Marshall Cavendish Corp.

INDUSTRY

see Industries

INDUSTRY AND ART

see Art Industries and Trade

INEBRIATES

see Alcoholism

INEQUALITY

see Equality

INFANTILE PARALYSIS

see Poliomyelitis

INFANTS

Here are entered works on children from birth through two years of age.

Aigner-Clark, Julie. Bebes. 2004. (Baby Einstein Ser.). (SPA., Illus.). 20p. (J). bds. (978-970-718-155-7(9), Silver Dolphin en Español) Advanced Marketing, S. de R. L. de C. V.

Allen, Joy. Baby Signs. 2008. (ENG., Illus.). 16p. (J). (gr. -1 — 1). bds. 6.99 (978-0-8037-3193-6(0), Dial Bks) Penguin Young Readers Group.

—Baby Sounds. 2012. (ENG.). 16p. (J). (gr. -1 — 1). bds. 6.99 (978-0-8037-3831-7(5), Dial Bks) Penguin Young Readers Group.

Allen, Kathryn Madeline. I Am a Baby. Gizicki, Rebecca, photos by. 2016. (ENG., Illus.). 24p. (J). (gr. -1-3). 15.99 (978-0-8075-3622-3(9)) Whitman, Albert & Co.

Auld, Mary. Welcoming a New Baby. 2011. (My Family & Me Ser.). (Illus.). 24p. (J). lib. bdg. 24.25 (978-1-59771-232-3(9)) Sea-To-Sea Pubns.

Baby Shakespeare. (Baby Einstein Ser.). (Illus.). 28p. (J). (gr. -1). pap. 19.98 incl. audio, VHS (978-1-892309-15-0(7)) Baby Einstein Co., LLC, The.

Barber, Nicola. A New Baby Arrives. 2009. (Big Day! Ser.). 24p. (J). (gr. k-2). (ENG., Illus.). pap. 8.25 (978-1-4358-2898-8(4), 1291898); lib. bdg. 22.60 (978-1-4358-2842-1(9)) Rosen Publishing Group, Inc., The. (PowerKids Pr.).

BeachHouse Publishing. Noodles for Baby. Jamie, Meckel, illus. 2011. (ENG.). 16p. (J). (gr. -1-1). bds. 7.95 (978-1-933067-40-7(3)) Beachhouse Publishing, LLC.

Bell-Rehwoldt, Sheri, et al. Kids' Guides. 2016. (Kids' Guides). (ENG.). 32p. lib. bdg. 307.89 (978-1-5157-4030-8(7), Edge Bks.) Capstone Press of Coughlan Cos.

bint Robert, Na'ima. Welcome to the World, Baby. 2004. (J). (ENG & RUS.). 16.95 (978-1-84444-638-4(7)); (CHI & ENG.). 16.95 (978-1-84444-624-7(7)); (BEN & ENG.). 16.95 (978-1-84444-623-0(9)); (ENG & VIE.). 16.95 (978-1-84444-644-5(1)) Mantra Lingua GBR. Dist: Chinasprout, Inc.

Burton, Margie, et al. A Pair of Babies. 2011. (Early Connections Ser.). (J). (978-1-61672-280-7(0)) Benchmark Education Co.

Christopher, Matt. All Keyed Up. Vasconcellos, Daniel, illus. 7th ed. 2003. (ENG.). 64p. (J). (gr. 1-4). pap. 13.99 (978-0-316-73821-7(2)) Little, Brown Bks. for Young Readers.

Church, Caroline Jayne. I Will Love You Forever. 2016. (ENG.). 22p. (J). (gr. -1-k). bds. 8.99 (978-0-545-94200-3(4), Cartwheel Bks.) Scholastic, Inc.

Civardi, Anne. The New Baby. Bates, Michelle, ed. Cartwright, Stephen, illus. rev. ed. 2005. 16p. (J). (gr. -1-17). pap. 4.99 (978-0-7945-1003-9(5), Usborne) EDC Publishing.

Dale, Jay. Growing Up, 1 vol. 2012. (Engage Literacy Green Ser.). (ENG.). 32p. (gr. k-2). pap. 5.99 (978-1-4296-9027-0(5), Engage Literacy) Capstone Press of Coughlan Cos.

Danzig, Dianne. Babies Don't Eat Pizza: A Big Kids' Book about Baby Brothers & Baby Sisters. Tilley, Debbie, illus. 2009. (ENG.). 32p. (J). (gr. -1-k). 16.99 (978-0-525-47441-8(2), Dutton Books for Young Readers) Penguin Young Readers Group.

Davis, Caroline. Babies. Davis, Caroline, illus. 2010. (ENG., Illus.). 20p. (J). bds. (978-1-4083-0786-1(3), Orchard Bks.) Hachette Children's Group GBR. Dist: Hachette Bk. Group.

DiCicco, Sue. Peek-a-Boo Baby. 2010. 12p. (J). (gr. -1). 9.95 (978-1-60747-709-9(2), Pickwick Pr.) Phoenix Bks., Inc.

Dorling Kindersley Publishing Staff. Baby - Hide & Seek! 2012. (ENG.). 16p. (J). (gr. -1 — 1). bds. 6.99 (978-0-7566-8999-5(6), DK Children) Dorling Kindersley Publishing, Inc.

—Baby Woof Woof! 2009. (ENG.). 16p. (J). (gr. -1 — 1). bds. 6.99 (978-0-7566-5508-2(0), DK Children) Dorling Kindersley Publishing, Inc.

Dorling Kindersley Publishing Staff, creator. Baby Says Peekaboo! 2006. (ENG., Illus.). 12p. (J). (gr. -1-k). bds. 6.99 (978-0-7566-1621-2(2), DK Children) Dorling Kindersley Publishing, Inc.

Douglas, Ann. Baby Science: How Babies Really Work! Desputeaux, Helene, illus. 2004. 32p. (J). (gr. k-4). reprint ed. pap. 7.00 (978-0-7567-8455-3(7)) DIANE Publishing Co.

Ford, Mindi. Mommy Says: A preemie Story. 2009. 20p. pap. 18.49 (978-1-4343-8138-5(2)) AuthorHouse.

Frazee, Marla. Walk On! A Guide for Babies of All Ages. Frazee, Marla, illus. 2006. (ENG., Illus.). 40p. (J). (gr. -1-k). 16.99 (978-0-15-205573-8(8)) Houghton Mifflin Harcourt Publishing Co.

Global Fund for Children Staff. American Babies. 2010. (ENG., Illus.). 16p. (J). (gr. -1 — 1). bds. 6.95 (978-1-58089-280-3(9)) Charlesbridge Publishing, Inc.

—Global Babies. Su, Keren et al, photos by. 2007. (Global Fund for Children Ser.). (ENG., Illus.). 16p. (J). (gr. -1 — 1). bds. 6.95 (978-1-58089-174-5(8)) Charlesbridge Publishing, Inc.

—Global Babies (Bebes del Mundo) Su, Keren et al, photos by. 2009. (ENG & SPA., Illus.). 16p. (J). (gr. -1 — 1). bds. 6.95 (978-1-58089-250-6(7)) Charlesbridge Publishing, Inc.

Grossman, Rena. Carry Me, 1 vol. 2009. (Babies Everywhere Ser.). (ENG.). 32p. (J). (gr. -1). bds. 6.95 (978-1-59572-180-8(0)) Star Bright Bks., Inc.

—Carry Me (Spanish/English), 1 vol. Fiol, Maria A., tr. 2010. (Babies Everywhere Ser.). (ENG & SPA., Illus.). 16p. (J). (gr. -1). bds. 6.95 (978-1-59572-199-0(1)) Star Bright Bks., Inc.

Guillain, Charlotte. A New Brother or Sister, 1 vol. 2011. (Growing Up Ser.). (ENG.). 24p. (gr. k-2). 23.32 (978-1-4329-4803-0(2), Heinemann Read & Learn) Heinemann-Raintree.

Harrison, Anne-Marie. Babies Are Noisy: A Book for Big Brothers & Sisters Including Those on the Autism Spectrum. Byrne, Beth, illus. 2013. (ENG.). 40p. (J). 15.95 (978-1-84905-459-1(2), 4085) Kingsley, Jessica Pubs. GBR. Dist: Macmillan Distribution Ltd.

Harwood, Beth. Amazing Baby Go Baby Go. 2005. (Illus.). 16p. (J). bds. 5.95 (978-1-59223-526-1(3)) Readerlink Distribution Services, LLC.

Hewitt, Sally. Our New Baby. 2009. (J). 28.50 (978-1-59920-232-7(8)) Black Rabbit Bks.

Higgins, Melissa & Rissman, Rebecca. Babysitter's Backpack, 1 vol. 2014. (Babysitter's Backpack Ser.). (ENG.). 32p. (gr. 3-4). 111.96 (978-1-4914-0771-4(9), Snap Bks.) Capstone Press of Coughlan Cos.

Hughes, Susan. Up! How Families Around the World Carry Their Little Ones. Barron, Ashley, illus. 2017. (ENG.). 24p. (J). (gr. -1-2). 15.95 (978-1-77147-176-3(X)) Owlkids Bks. Inc. CAN. Dist: Publishers Group West (PGW).

I Love Babies. 2004. per. 9.95 (978-0-9754779-1-5(9)) Chosen Word Publishing.

Knight, Margy Burns. Welcoming Babies, 1 vol. O'Brien, Anne Sibley, illus. 2003. (ENG.). 40p. (gr. -1-4). 7.95 (978-0-88448-124-9(7), 884124) Tilbury Hse. Pubs.

Lemay, Violet. Southern Baby. Lemay, Violet, illus. 2015. (ENG., Illus.). 22p. (gr. k — 1). bds. 8.95 (978-1-938093-45-6(3), Duo Pr. Llc (US)) Duo Pr. LLC.

Lindsay, Jeanne Warren & Brunelli, Jean. Nurturing Your Newborn: Young Parents' Guide to Baby's First Month. 2nd ed. 2006. (Illus.). 96p. (J). pap. (978-1-932538-38-0(0)) Morning Glory Pr., Inc.

Litchfield, Jo, illus. Baby Sister Look & Say. 2008. (Look & Say Board Bks). 12p. (J). bds. 7.99 (978-0-7945-2102-8(9), Usborne) EDC Publishing.

MacKinnon, Catherine-Anne, illus. Babies Baby Flashcards. 2007. (Baby Flashcards Ser.). 16p. (J). (gr. -1-k). 9.99 (978-0-7945-1571-3(1), Usborne) EDC Publishing.

Magabala Books Staff. Australian Babies. 2005. (Illus.). 10p. (J). bds. (978-1-875641-92-5(0)) Magabala Bks.

McDougall, Carol & LaRamee-Jones, Shanda. Baby Look, 1 vol. 2013. (Baby Steps Ser.). (ENG., Illus.). 16p. (J). (gr. -1-k). bds. 8.95 (978-1-55109-937-8(3)) Nimbus Publishing, Ltd. CAN. Dist: Orca Bk. Pubs. USA.

Merritt, Kate, illus. Indestructibles: Baby Faces. 2012. (Indestructibles Ser.). (ENG.). 12p. (J). (gr. k — 1). pap. 5.95 (978-0-7611-6881-2(8), 16881) Workman Publishing Co., Inc.

Molinet, Michael & Molinet, Kelly. Just Like You. Molinet, Michael, illus. 2004. (Illus.). 22p. (J). 15.99 (978-1-932587-34-0(9)) Practical Christianity Foundation.

Morris, Alison. I Love to Learn. 2004. (Look at Me... I Love Ser.). (Illus.). 10p. (J). bds. 4.99 (978-1-85854-343-7(6)) Brimax Books Ltd. GBR. Dist: Byeway Bks.

Munoz, Ruby. Tomorrow I Am a Big Sister, but Today I Am Me. Maes, Ame, illus. 2008. 24p. pap. 24.95 (978-1-60672-862-8(8)) America Star Bks.

Murkoff, Heidi. What to Expect When Mommy's Having a Baby. Rader, Laura, illus. 2004. (What to Expect Kids Ser.). (ENG.). 24p. (J). (gr. -1-3). pap. 3.99 (978-0-06-053802-6(3), HarperFestival) HarperCollins Pubs.

Organic Baby Sleep. 2008. (Illus.). (J). (gr. -1-3). bds. (978-0-312-50270-6(2)) Priddy Bks.

Our Baby: Individual Title Six-Packs. (Literatura 2000 Ser.). (gr. -1-1). 28.00 (978-0-7635-0011-5(9)) Rigby Education.

Pandell, Karen. I Love You, Baby, from Head to Toe! Cowen-Fletcher, Jane, illus. 2010. (ENG.). 16p. (J). (— 1). bds. 8.99 (978-0-7636-5089-6(7)) Candlewick Pr.

Pankow, Valerie. No Bigger Than My Teddy Bear. Connelly, Gwen, illus. 2nd ed. 2004. 32p. (J). 6.95 (978-0-9728460-0-4(X)) Family Bks.

Parramore, Helen. Where Do Babies Come From? 2009. 28p. pap. 12.49 (978-1-4490-3589-1(2)) AuthorHouse.

Peekaboo Baby. 2004. (J). bds. 6.99 (978-0-9753127-1-1(5)) Family Bks. at Home.

Piper, Sophie. Blessings for a Baby Boy. Williams, Caroline, illus. 2010. (ENG.). 44p. (J). (gr. k-k). 8.99 (978-0-7459-6184-2(3)) Lion Hudson PLC GBR. Dist: Independent Pubs. Group.

—Blessings for a Baby Girl. Williams, Caroline, illus. 11th ed. 2010. (ENG.). 48p. (J). (gr. k-k). 8.99 (978-0-7459-6185-9(1)) Lion Hudson PLC GBR. Dist: Independent Pubs. Group.

—First Prayers for Baby. Spenceley, Annabel, illus. 2014. (ENG.). 48p. (J). (— 1). 8.99 (978-0-7459-6407-2(9)) Lion Hudson PLC GBR. Dist: Independent Pubs. Group.

Priddy, Roger. Hello Baby - A High Contrast Book. 2012. (Hello Baby Ser.). (ENG., Illus.). 6p. (J). (gr. -1 — 1). bds. 5.99 (978-0-312-51505-8(7), 9780312515058, Priddy Bks.) St. Martin's Pr.

Publishing, Sterling. Hello, Baby! 2008. (Illus.). 10p. (J). bds. (978-1-934618-26-4(8)) Begin Smart LLC.

Rippey, Josie B. It's Ok to Be a Pre-Mie. 2005. 54p. pap. (978-1-931456-75-3(5)) Athena Pr.

Ritchie, Jon. Babies Are Boring. Ritchie, Alex, illus. 2008. 40p. (J). (978-0-9809970-0-2(3)) Purple Possum Publishing Inc.

Rizzi, Kathleen. What's up, Baby?, 1 vol. 2010. (ENG.). 32p. (J). bds. 5.95 (978-1-59572-268-3(8)) Star Bright Bks., Inc.

Robert, Na'ima Bint. Welcome to the World Baby. Brazell, Derek, illus. 2005. 32p. (J). (YOR & ENG.). pap. (978-1-84444-297-3(7)); (ENG & VIE.). pap. (978-1-84444-296-6(9)); (ENG & URD.). pap. (978-1-84444-295-9(0)); (TUR & ENG.). pap. (978-1-84444-293-5(4)); (ENG & SWA.). pap. (978-1-84444-290-4(X)); (SPA & ENG.). pap. (978-1-84444-289-8(6)); (ENG & SOM.). pap. (978-1-84444-288-1(8)); (ENG & RUS.). pap. (978-1-84444-287-4(X)); (ENG & RUM.). pap. (978-1-84444-286-7(1)); (ENG & POR.). pap. (978-1-84444-285-0(3)); (POL & ENG.). pap. (978-1-84444-284-3(5)); (ENG & PAN.). pap. (978-1-84444-283-6(7)); (ENG & KOR.). pap. (978-1-84444-282-9(9)); (JPN & ENG.). pap. (978-1-84444-281-2(0)); (ENG & SNA.). pap. (978-1-84444-450-2(3)); (WEL, ENG, KOR & KUR.). pap. (978-1-84444-633-9(6)); (ENG & ALB.). pap. (978-1-84444-268-3(3)); (ENG & ARA.). pap. (978-1-84444-269-0(1)); (ENG & BEN.). pap. (978-1-84444-270-6(5)); (ENG & CHI.). pap. (978-1-84444-271-3(3)); (ENG & ITA.). pap. (978-1-84444-280-5(2)); (ENG & HIN.). pap. (978-1-84444-279-9(9)); (ENG & GUJ.). pap. (978-1-84444-278-2(0)); (ENG & GER.). pap. (978-1-84444-276-8(4)); (FRE & ENG.). pap. (978-1-84444-275-1(6)); (ENG & PER.). pap. (978-1-84444-274-4(8)); (ENG, HRV & SER.). pap. (978-1-84444-273-7(X)); (ENG & CHI.). pap. (978-1-84444-272-0(1)) Mantra Lingua.

Robert, Na'ima Bint & Petrova-Browning, Nina. Welcome to the World Baby. Brazell, Derek, illus. 2005. (ENG & BUL.). 32p. (J). pap. (978-1-84444-721-3(9)) Mantra Lingua.

Rock, Lois. Now We Have a Baby. Massey, Jane, illus. 2014. (ENG.). 24p. (J). (gr. -1-k). bds. 7.99 (978-0-7459-6345-7(5)) Lion Hudson PLC GBR. Dist: Independent Pubs. Group.

Rookie Toddler(r) (Fall 2014 Set Of 4) 2014. (Rookie Toddler(r) Ser.). (J). bds. 27.80 (978-0-531-24361-9(3)) Scholastic Library Publishing.

Safran, Sheri. All Kinds of Babies. Damon, Emma, illus. 2007. (All Kinds Of... Ser.). (ENG.). 16p. (J). (gr. -1-k). 12.99 (978-1-85707-679-0(6)) Tango Bks. GBR. Dist: Independent Pubs. Group.

Schindel, John & Woodward, Molly. The Babies & Doggies Book. 2015. (ENG., Illus.). 26p. (J). (— 1). bds. 7.99 (978-0-544-44477-5(9), HMH Books For Young Readers) Houghton Mifflin Harcourt Publishing Co.

Sheldon, Annette. Big Brother Now: A Story about Me & Our New Baby. Maizel, Karen, illus. 2008. 32p. (J). (gr. -1-1). 14.95 (978-1-4338-0381-9(X)); pap. 9.95 (978-1-4338-0382-6(8)) American Psychological Assn. (Magination Pr.).

—Big Sister Now: A Story about Me & Our New Baby. Maizel, Karen, illus. 2005. 32p. (J). (gr. -1-1). per. 9.95 (978-1-59147-244-5(X)); 14.95 (978-1-59147-243-8(1)) American Psychological Assn. (Magination Pr.).

Slier, Debby. Babies on the Go!, 1 vol. 2013. (ENG., Illus.). 32p. (J). bds. 5.99 (978-1-59572-173-0(8)) Star Bright Bks., Inc.

Smith, Nikki Siegen. Welcome to the World: A Celebration of Birth & Babies from Many Cultures. 2005. (ENG., Illus.). 48p. (J). 18.99 (978-1-84148-890-5(9)) Barefoot Bks., Inc.

Stanton, Brandon. Little Humans. Stanton, Brandon, photos by. 2014. (ENG., Illus.). 40p. (J). (gr. -1-1). 17.99 (978-0-374-37456-3(2), 9780374374563, Farrar, Straus & Giroux (BYR)) Farrar, Straus & Giroux.

Star Bright Books. Carry Me (Portuguese/English), 1 vol. Icibaci, Neusa, tr. 2009. (Babies Everywhere Ser.). (ENG & POR., Illus.). 20p. (J). (gr. -1). 6.95 (978-1-59572-200-3(9)) Star Bright Bks., Inc.

—Families (Portuguese/English), 1 vol. Icibaci, Neusa, tr. 2009. (Babies Everywhere Ser.). (ENG & POR., Illus.). 20p. (J). (gr. -1). 6.95 (978-1-59572-202-7(5)) Star Bright Bks., Inc.

—Families (Spanish/English), 1 vol. Fiol, Maria A., tr. 2009. (Babies Everywhere Ser.). (ENG & SPA., Illus.). 32p. (J). (gr. -1). bds. 6.95 (978-1-59572-201-0(7)) Star Bright Bks., Inc.

Star Bright Books, creator. Carry Me (Somali/English), 1 vol. 2010. (Babies Everywhere Ser.). (SOM & ENG., Illus.). 20p. (J). 6.95 (978-1-59572-220-1(3)) Star Bright Bks., Inc.

—Carry Me (Vietnamese/English), 1 vol. 2010. (Babies Everywhere Ser.). (VIE & ENG., Illus.). 20p. (J). 6.95 (978-1-59572-217-1(3)) Star Bright Bks., Inc.

Takahashi, Hideko, illus. Hello, New Baby. 2005. 12p. (J). (gr. -1-18). 9.95 (978-1-58117-345-1(8), Intervisual/Piggy Toes) Bendon, Inc.

Thoms, Susan Collins. My First Communion. le Joly Sénoville, Tinou, illus. 2017. (ENG.). 48p. (J). (gr. k). 12.95 (978-1-4549-1453-2(X)) Sterling Publishing Co., Inc.

Tiger, Tales, ed. Baby Firsts. Ward, Sarah, illus. 2016. (To Baby with Love Ser.). (ENG.). (J). (gr. -1-k). 14.99 (978-1-58925-235-6(7)) Tiger Tales.

Toulmin, Sarah. Baby's Little Bible & Prayers, 2 vols. Stephenson, Kristina, illus. 2011. (ENG.). 224p. (J). (gr. k — 1). pap. 19.99 (978-0-7459-6039-5(1)) Lion Hudson PLC GBR. Dist: Independent Pubs. Group.

Tupera, Tupera. What Does Baby Want? Gartner, Maya, ed. 2017. (ENG., Illus.). 22p. (gr. -1 — 1). bds. 12.95 **(978-0-7148-7407-4(8))** Phaidon Pr., Inc.

Uzon, Jorge. Go, Baby, Go!, 1 vol. 2010. (Hello Baby Board Bks.). (ENG., Illus.). 24p. (J). (gr. k — 1). bds. 6.95 (978-0-88899-985-6(2)) Groundwood Bks. CAN. Dist: Publishers Group West (PGW).

—Look Around, Baby!, 1 vol. 2010. (Hello Baby Board Bks.). (ENG., Illus.). 24p. (J). (gr. k — 1). bds. 6.95 (978-0-88899-967-2(4)) Groundwood Bks. CAN. Dist: Publishers Group West (PGW).

—Not a Baby Anymore!, 1 vol. 2010. (Hello Baby Board Bks.). (ENG., Illus.). 24p. (J). (gr. k — 1). bds. 6.95 (978-0-88899-986-3(0)) Groundwood Bks. CAN. Dist: Publishers Group West (PGW).

Verdick, Elizabeth. Pacifiers Are Not Forever. Heinlen, Marieka, illus. 2007. (Best Behavior Ser.). (ENG.). 24p. (J). (gr. -1-k). pap. 7.95 (978-1-57542-257-2(3)) Free Spirit Publishing, Inc.

Verdick, Elizabeth. Teeth Are Not for Biting/Los Dientes No Son para Morder. Heinlen, Marieka, illus. 2017. (Best Behavior Ser.). (ENG, SPA & MUL.). 24p. (J). bds. 7.95 **(978-1-63198-157-9(9))** Free Spirit Publishing, Inc.

Verdick, Elizabeth & Lisovskis, Marjorie. Move. 2013. (Happy Healthy Baby Ser.). (ENG., Illus.). 22p. (J). bds. 6.99 (978-1-57542-422-4(3)) Free Spirit Publishing, Inc.

Watt, Fiona. Christmas Baby Jigsaw Book. Wells, Rachel, illus. 2004. (Jigsaw Books Ser.). 14p. (J). 10.95 (978-0-7945-0809-8(X), Usborne) EDC Publishing.

Welcome to the World, Baby. 2004. (J). (CRO & ENG.). (978-1-84444-626-1(3)); (CHI & ENG.). (978-1-84444-625-4(5)); (ARA & ENG.). (978-1-84444-622-3(0)); (ALB & ENG.). (978-1-84444-621-6(2)); (ENG & ITA.). (978-1-84444-631-5(X)); (ENG & PER.). (978-1-84444-627-8(1)); (ENG & FRE.). (978-1-84444-645-2(X)); (ENG & GRE.). (978-1-84444-628-5(X)); (ENG & GUJ.). (978-1-84444-629-2(8)); (ENG & HIN.). (978-1-84444-630-8(1)); (ENG & URD.). (978-1-84444-643-8(3)); (ENG & TUR.). (978-1-84444-642-1(5)); (ENG & TAM.). (978-1-84444-641-4(7)); (ENG & SPA.). (978-1-84444-640-7(9)); (ENG & SOM.). (978-1-84444-639-1(5)); (ENG & POR.). (978-1-84444-637-7(9)); (ENG & POL.). (978-1-84444-636-0(0)); (ENG & JPN.). (978-1-84444-632-2(8)); (ENG & KUR.). (978-1-84444-634-6(4)); (ENG & PAN.). (978-1-84444-635-3(2)) Mantra Lingua.

Where Do We Come From ? 2006. (J). per. 9.99 (978-0-9777650-0-3(8)) El Assali, Amira.

Williams, Rhonda, photos by. Mommy, Daddy, Where Do Babies Come From? Activity Book. Date not set. (Wonderful World of True Love Ser.). (Illus.). 16p. (J). (gr. k-4). pap. 3.95 (978-0-9675068-0-7(8)) Media For Life.

wintranslation.com, tr. Carry Me (French/English), 1 vol. 2010. (ENG & FRE., Illus.). 20p. (J). 6.95 (978-1-59572-216-4(5)) Star Bright Bks., Inc.

Wyatt, Valerie. Welcome to the World. Newell, Lennette, illus. 2011. (ENG.). 24p. (J). (gr. -1 — 1). 14.95 (978-1-55453-593-4(X)) Kids Can Pr., Ltd. CAN. Dist: Hachette Bk. Group.

Wyrwas, Kim. The Lonely Cat. 2012. 30p. 24.95 (978-1-4626-6459-7(8)) America Star Bks.

Zuravicky, Orli. Baby Faces. 2005. (Babies Everywhere Ser.). (Illus.). (J). (gr. -1-k). bds. 8.95 (978-1-4042-2773-6(3), PowerKids Pr.) Rosen Publishing Group, Inc., The.

INFANTS—DISEASES

see Children—Diseases

INFANTS—FICTION

Aboitiz, Victoria De & Afraz. Mystery of the Breast. 2012. (ENG., Illus.). 32p. (J). (gr. -1-12). pap. 9.99 (978-1-905177-31-8(3)) Pinter & Martin Ltd. GBR. Dist: National Bk. Network.

Adams, Diane. Two Hands to Love You. Davis, Jon & Keiser, Paige, illus. 2014. (ENG.). 40p. (J). (gr. -1 — 1). 15.99 (978-0-8118-7797-8(3)) Chronicle Bks. LLC.

Adams, Jennifer. Edgar & the Tattle-Tale Heart, 1 vol. Stucki, Ron, illus. 2014. (ENG.). 32p. (J). 16.99 (978-1-4236-3766-0(6)) Gibbs Smith, Publisher.

Adler, David A. Andy & Tamika. Hillenbrand, Will, illus. 2005. (Andy Russell Ser.: Bk. 2). 129p. 16.00 (978-0-7569-4898-6(3)) Perfection Learning Corp.

Ahlberg, Janet & Ahlberg, Allan. Adiós Pequeño! Ahlberg, Janet, illus. 2003. (Picture Books Collection).Tr. of Bye Bye Baby. (SPA., Illus.). 32p. (J). (gr. k-3). 12.95 (978-84-372-2315-5(6)) Altea, Ediciones, S.A. - Grupo Santillana ESP. Dist: Santillana USA Publishing Co., Inc.

Ajmera, Maya. Global Baby Bedtimes. 2015. (ENG., Illus.). 16p. (J). (— 1). bds. 6.95 (978-1-58089-708-2(8)) Charlesbridge Publishing, Inc.

Alborozo. And Then... Alborozo, illus. 2016. (Child's Play Library). (ENG., Illus.). 32p. (J). (978-1-84643-696-3(6)) Child's Play International Ltd.

Allen, Page. Madison's Descent: A Child's Journey. (Illus.). (J). 2006. pap. 25.00 (978-0-9752516-2-1(7)) 2004. lib. bdg. 60.00 (978-0-9752516-1-4(9)) Otis & Randolph Pr.

—The Way to Davis: On the River of Stars. collector's ed. 2007. (Illus.). (J). 75.00 (978-0-9752516-3-8(5)) Otis & Randolph Pr.

Andreae, Giles. I Love You, Baby. Dodd, Emma, illus. 2015. (ENG.). 32p. (J). (gr. -1-k). 15.99 (978-1-4847-2230-5(2)) Disney Publishing Worldwide.

Appelt, Kathi. Brand-New Baby Blues. Murphy, Kelly, illus. 2009. (ENG.). 32p. (J). (gr. -1-1). 16.99 (978-0-06-053233-8(5)) HarperCollins Pubs.

Arena, Jen. Besos for Baby: A Little Book of Kisses. 2014. (ENG & SPA., Illus.). 22p. (J). (gr. -1 — 1). bds. 6.99 (978-0-316-23037-7(5)) Little, Brown Bks. for Young Readers.

Ashbe, Jeanne. Adios! 2003. (SPA.). 48p. (J). 15.95 (978-84-95150-68-4(9)) Corimbo, Editorial S.L. ESP. Dist: Lectorum Pubns., Inc., Distribooks, Inc.

—Eso No Se Hace! 2003. (SPA.). 32p. (978-84-95150-35-6(2)) Corimbo, Editorial S.L.

Ashman, Linda. Henry Wants More! Hughes, Brooke Boynton, illus. 2016. (ENG.). 32p. (J). (gr. -1-2). 20.99 (978-0-375-97348-2(6), Random Hse. Bks. for Young Readers) Random Hse. Children's Bks.

—Rock-a-Bye Romp. Mulazzani, Simona, illus. 2016. (ENG.). 36p. (J). (— 1). 16.99 (978-0-399-17150-5(9), Nancy Paulsen Books) Penguin Young Readers Group.

—When I Was King. McPhail, David, illus. 2008. 32p. (J). (gr. -1-3). 17.89 (978-0-06-029052-8(8)) HarperCollins Pubs.

Ashman, Linda & Airgood, Ellen. Little Baby Buttercup. Byun, You, illus. 2015. (ENG.). 32p. (J). (— 1). 16.99 (978-0-399-16763-8(3), Nancy Paulsen Books) Penguin Young Readers Group.

Ault, Kelly. Let's Sign, Baby! A Fun & Easy Way to Talk with Baby. Landry, Leo, illus. abr. ed. 2010. (ENG.). 40p. (J). (gr. k — 1). bds. 7.99 (978-0-547-31596-6(1)) Houghton Mifflin Harcourt Publishing Co.

AZ Books. Babies. 2013. (Guess What? Ser.). (ENG.). 10p. (J). (gr. -1 — 1). 5.95 (978-1-61889-316-1(5)) AZ Bks. LLC.

Bamford, Desmond Nicholas. Beekemose. 2012. (Illus.). 54p. (gr. 2-4). pap. 13.66 (978-1-4685-7773-0(5)) AuthorHouse.

Banks, Lynne Reid. Angela & Diabola. 163p. (J). (gr. 4-6). pap. 4.50 (978-0-8072-1515-9(5), Listening Library) Random Hse. Audio Publishing Group.

Bardaus, Anna W. Bounce, Bounce, Baby! Grove, Christine, illus. 2013. (J). (978-0-545-61897-7(5)) Scholastic, Inc.

—Dance, Dance, Baby! Grove, Christine, illus. 2013. (J). (978-0-545-61899-1(1)) Scholastic, Inc.

—Reach, Reach, Baby! Grove, Christine, illus. 2013. (J). (978-0-545-61900-4(9)) Scholastic, Inc.

—Read, Read, Baby! Grove, Christine, illus. 2013. (J). (978-0-545-61898-4(3)) Scholastic, Inc.

Barnhill, Carla. Rufus & the Very Special Baby: A Frolic Christmas Story. Barnhill, Carla, illus. 2016. (Frolic First Faith Ser.). (ENG., Illus.). 32p. (J). (gr. -1-3). 12.99 (978-1-5064-1762-2(0), Sparkhouse Family) Augsburg Fortress, Pubs.

Baskerville. New Baby. (ENG., Illus.). 32p. (J). pap. (978-0-7136-4111-0(8), 93347, A&C Black) Bloomsbury Publishing Plc.

Bauer, Marion Dane. The Christmas Baby. Cowdrey, Richard, illus. 2009. (ENG.). 32p. (J). (gr. -1-k). 15.99

(978-1-4169-7885-5(2), Simon & Schuster Bks. For Young Readers) Simon & Schuster Bks. For Young Readers.

—Grandmother's Song. Rossi, Pamela, illus. 2007. (ENG.). 32p. (J). (gr. -1-3). 10.99 (978-1-4169-6849-8(0), Simon & Schuster/Paula Wiseman Bks.) Simon & Schuster/Paula Wiseman Bks.

Beaton, Kate. King Baby. 2016. (Dog Tags Ser.). (ENG., Illus.). 40p. (J). (gr. -1-3). 17.99 (978-0-545-63754-1(6)) Scholastic, Inc.

Beaumont, Karen. Crybaby. Yelchin, Eugene, illus. 2015. (ENG.). 40p. (J). (gr. -1-1). 17.99 (978-0-8050-8974-5(8), 9780805089745, Holt, Henry & Co. Bks. For Young Readers) Holt, Henry & Co.

Bently, Peter. A Recipe for Bedtime. Massini, Sarah, illus. 2016. (ENG.). 32p. (J). (— 1). 16.99 (978-0-399-17625-8(X), G.P. Putnam's Sons Books for Young Readers) Penguin Young Readers Group.

Bergstein, Rita M. Your Own Big Bed. Hartung, Susan Kathleen, illus. 2008. (ENG.). 36p. (J). (gr. -1-k). 15.99 (978-0-670-06079-5(8), Viking Books for Young Readers) Penguin Young Readers Group.

Bigler, Ashley Hansen. Once upon a Time: An Adoption Story. Hintz, Amy, illus. 2010. (J). pap. 12.99 (978-1-59955-310-8(4)) Cedar Fort, Inc./CFI Distribution.

Bilik-Franklin, MidiAna & Griffith, Indigo, photos by. The Carseat Tourist. 2006. (Illus.). (J). bds. 7.95 (978-0-9772825-0-0(3)) Critter Camp Inc.

Blackall, Sophie. The Baby Tree. Blackall, Sophie, illus. 2014. (ENG., Illus.). 32p. (J). (gr. k-3). 17.99 (978-0-399-25718-6(7), Nancy Paulsen Books) Penguin Young Readers Group.

Blackstone, Stella & Scribens, Sunny. Mis Primeras Palabras. 2017. (SPA.). 30p. (J). (gr. -1-k). bds. 14.99 **(978-1-78285-325-1(1))** Barefoot Bks., Inc.

Blake, Stephanie. New Baby! 2016. (ENG., Illus.). 40p. (J). 15.95 (978-0-7358-4255-7(8)) North-South Bks., Inc.

Blume, Judy. Superfudge. 2007. (Fudge Bks.: 3).Tr. of Superfudge. lib. bdg. 18.40 (978-1-4177-8843-9(7), Turtleback) Turtleback Bks.

Boie, Kristen. The Little Bitty Story of Austin Q. Peapot, 1 vol. Gentile, Christopher, illus. 2009. 20p. pap. 24.95 (978-1-60749-548-2(1)) America Star Bks.

Borden, Louise. Big Brothers Don't Take Naps. Dodd, Emma, illus. 2011. (ENG.). 32p. (J). (gr. -1-3). 17.99 (978-1-4169-5503-0(8), McElderry, Margaret K. Bks.) McElderry, Margaret K. Bks.

Bowen, Anne. Christmas Is Coming. Bogacki, Tomek, illus. 2007. (Carolrhoda Picture Bks.). 28p. (J). (gr. -1-3). 16.95 (978-1-57505-934-1(7), Carolrhoda Bks.) Lerner Publishing Group.

—When You Visit Grandma & Grandpa. Bogacki, Tomasz, tr. Bogacki, Tomasz, illus. 2004. (Carolrhoda Picture Books Ser.). 32p. (J). (gr. -1-3). 15.95 (978-1-57505-610-4(0)) Lerner Publishing Group.

Bowen, Anne M. I Loved You Before You Were Born. Shed, Greg, illus. 2004. (ENG.). 32p. (J). (gr. -1-3). reprint ed. pap. 6.99 (978-0-06-443631-1(4)) HarperCollins Pubs.

Bozarth, Jan. The Fairy Godmother Academy #6: Trinity's Book. 2013. (Fairy Godmother Academy Ser.). (ENG., Illus.). 240p. (J). (gr. 3-7). 6.99 (978-0-375-86576-3(4), Yearling) Random Hse. Children's Bks.

Brandon, Tanisha Danyette. Bayje's Story: An IVF Tale for Little People, 1 vol. 2010. 20p. pap. 24.95 (978-1-4489-7002-5(4)) PublishAmerica, Inc.

Brantz, Loryn. Feminist Baby. Brantz, Loryn, illus. 2017. (ENG., Illus.). 22p. (J). (gr. -1 — 1). 12.99 (978-1-4847-7858-6(8)) Disney Pr.

Braun, Sebastian. Peekaboo Baby. Braun, Sebastian, illus. 2012. (ENG., Illus.). 16p. (J). (gr. -1 — 1). bds. 6.99 (978-0-7636-5933-2(9)) Candlewick Pr.

Brock-Jaurequi, Dawn. Dream Big, 1 vol. 2009. 27p. pap. 24.95 (978-1-61582-584-4(3)) America Star Bks.

Brown, Marc. Arthur & the Baby. Brown, Marc, illus. 2011. (Classic Arthur Adventure Ser.). (ENG., Illus.). 32p. (J). (gr. -1-3). pap. 7.99 (978-0-316-12905-3(4)) Little Brown & Co.

—Arthur's Reading Trick. 2009. (Step into Reading Ser.). (ENG., Illus.). 24p. (J). (gr. k-3). pap. 3.99 (978-0-375-82977-2(6), Random Hse. Bks. for Young Readers) Random Hse. Children's Bks.

—Monkey: Not Ready for the Baby. 2016. (ENG., Illus.). 32p. (J). (gr. -1-2). 16.99 (978-1-101-93327-5(5), Knopf Bks. for Young Readers) Random Hse. Children's Bks.

Brown, Marc. Monkey: Not Ready for the Baby. 2017. (ENG.). 32p. (J). (gr. -1-2). 5.99 **(978-0-399-55781-1(4)**, Dragonfly Bks.) Random Hse. Children's Bks.

Brown, Margery W. Baby Jesus Like My Brother. 2008. (Illus.). 32p. 6.95 (978-1-60349-000-9(0), Marimba Bks.) Hudson Publishing Group, The.

Bruel, Nick. Bad Kitty Meets the Baby. Bruel, Nick, illus. 2011. (Bad Kitty Ser.). (ENG., Illus.). 144p. (J). (gr. 2-5). 14.99 (978-1-59643-597-1(6), 9781596435971) Roaring Brook Pr.

—Bad Kitty Meets the Baby. Bruel, Nick, illus. 2012. (Bad Kitty Ser.). (ENG., Illus.). 160p. (J). (gr. 2-5). pap. 6.99 (978-0-312-64121-4(4), 9780312641214) Square Fish.

—Bad Kitty Meets the Baby. 2012. (Bad Kitty Chapter Bks.). (J). lib. bdg. 17.20 (978-0-606-23754-3(2), Turtleback) Turtleback Bks.

Bruha, Ginger. Lilly's Breakfast Time. 2004. 20p. pap. 24.95 (978-1-4137-3133-0(3)) PublishAmerica, Inc.

Bunting, Eve. Will It Be a Baby Brother? Spiegel, Beth, illus. 2010. (ENG.). 32p. (J). (gr. -1-1). 16.95 (978-1-59078-439-6(1)) Boyds Mills Pr.

Burgess, Lisa Maria. Juma & Little Sungura. Gugu, Abdul M., illus. 2013. 32p. 19.95 (978-1-939604-06-4(0)); pap. 9.99 (978-1-939604-02-6(8)) Barranca Pr.

Burningham, John. There's Going to Be a Baby. Oxenbury, Helen, illus. 2010. 48p. (J). (978-0-7445-4996-6(5)); (ENG.). (gr. -1-k). 16.99 (978-0-7636-4907-4(4)) Candlewick Pr.

Calaf, Monica. You, Me & the Breast. Fuentes, Mikel, illus. 2012. (ENG.). 40p. (J). (gr. -1-12). pap. 9.99 (978-1-905177-52-3(6)) Pinter & Martin Ltd. GBR. Dist: National Bk. Network.

Cannon, A. E. Charlotte's Rose. 2011. (ENG., Illus.). 256p. (J). (gr. 4). pap. 9.95 (978-1-60781-141-1(3)) Univ. of Utah Pr.

Cantrell, Caley. You're Bringing Me a Baby?! 2013. (Illus.). 40p. (J). 15.95 (978-0-9859358-7-0(1), Belle Isle Bks.) Brandylane Pubs., Inc.

Capucilli, Alyssa Satin. Biscuit & the Baby. Schories, Pat, illus. 2005. (My First I Can Read Ser.). (ENG.). 32p. (J). (gr. -1 — 1). 16.99 (978-0-06-009459-1(1)) HarperCollins Pubs.

—Hannah Is a Big Sister. Stott, Dorothy, illus. 2014. (Hannah & Henry Ser.). (ENG.). 32p. (J). (gr. -1-k). 5.99 (978-0-7641-6750-8(2)) Barron's Educational Series, Inc.

—Henry Is a Big Brother. Stott, Dorothy, illus. 2014. (Hannah & Henry Ser.). (ENG.). 32p. (J). (gr. -1-k). 5.99 (978-0-7641-6749-2(9)) Barron's Educational Series, Inc.

Carlson, Nancy. Poor Carl. Carlson, Nancy, illus. 2012. (Nancy Carlson Picture Bks). (Illus.). 32p. (J). (gr. k-2). 56.72 (978-0-7613-9305-4(6)); (ENG., 9.95 (978-0-7613-8950-7(4)) Lerner Publishing Group. (Carolrhoda Bks.).

Carlstrom, Nancy White & Saport, Linda. Before You Were Born. Saport, Linda, illus. 2004. (Illus.). 32p. (J). (gr. -1-k). 17.00 (978-0-8028-5185-7(1)) Eerdmans, William B. Publishing Co.

Carter, Dorothy. Wilhe'mina Miles: After the Stork Night. Stevenson, Harvey, illus. 2005. 30p. (J). (gr. k-4). reprint ed. 16.00 (978-0-7567-9421-7(8)) DIANE Publishing Co.

Celcer, Irene. The Gift. Gatto, Horacio, illus. 2009. (J). pap. (978-0-9755810-6-3(6)) Graphite Pr.

—The Gift of Egg Donation. Gatto, Horacio, illus. 2007. (Hope & Will Have a Baby Ser.). 32p. (J). (gr. k-3). pap. 19.95 (978-0-9755810-1-8(5), 9780975581018) Graphite Pr.

—The Gift of Embryo Donation. Gatto, Horacio, illus. 2007. (Hope & Will Have a Baby Ser.). 32p. (J). (gr. k-3). pap. 19.95 (978-0-9755810-2-5(3), 9780975581025) Graphite Pr.

—The Gift of Sperm Donation. Gatto, Horacio, illus. 2007. (Hope & Will Have a Baby Ser.). 32p. (J). (gr. k-3). pap. 19.95 (978-0-9755810-3-2(1), 9780975581032) Graphite Pr.

—The Gift of Surrogacy. Gatto, Horacio, illus. 2007. (Hope & Will Have a Baby Ser.). 32p. (J). (gr. k-3). pap. 19.95 (978-0-9755810-4-9(X), 9780975581049) Graphite Pr.

Chapman, Lynne. Baby Goes Baaaaa! Chapman, Lynne, illus. 2013. (ENG., Illus.). 24p. (J). (— 1). 7.99 (978-1-4052-5830-2(6)) Egmont Bks., Ltd. GBR. Dist: Independent Pubs. Group.

Cheng, Andrea. The Year of the Baby. Barton, Patrice, illus. 2014. (Anna Wang Novel Ser.: 2). (ENG.). 176p. (J). (gr. 1-4). pap. 5.99 (978-0-544-22525-1(2), HMH Books For Young Readers) Houghton Mifflin Harcourt Publishing Co.

Cherobin. Zoomy Boomy, the Moon, & the Earth: All in its Season, & Seasons Change. 2010. 24p. pap. 14.99 (978-1-4490-2658-5(3)) AuthorHouse.

Chichester Clark, Emma. My Baby Sister. Chichester Clark, Emma, illus. 2009. (Humber & Plum Ser.: 2). (ENG., Illus.). 32p. (J). (gr. -1-k). 9.99 (978-0-00-727324-9(X), HarperCollins Children's Bks.) HarperCollins Pubs. Ltd. GBR. Dist: HarperCollins Pubs.

Chouette Publishing Staff. Baby Caillou: Good Night! Brignaud, Pierre, illus. 2013. (Baby Caillou Ser.). (ENG.). 10p. (J). (gr. -1 — 1). (978-2-89718-099-7(4)) Filmer Ltd.

Christian, Cheryl. What Happens Next? (Haitian Creole/English), 1 vol. Dwight, Laura, photos by. 2005. (ENG & HAT., Illus.). 12p. (J). (gr. -1). 5.95 (978-1-59572-025-2(1)) Star Bright Bks., Inc.

—Where Does It Go? (Haitian Creole/English), 1 vol. Dwight, Laura, photos by. 2005. (CRP & ENG., Illus.). 12p. (J). 5.95 (978-1-59572-026-9(X)) Star Bright Bks., Inc.

—Where's the Baby? (Haitian Creole/English), 1 vol. Dwight, Laura, photos by. 2005. (Photoflaps Ser.). (HAT & ENG., Illus.). 12p. (J). (gr. -1). 5.95 (978-1-59572-027-6(8)) Star Bright Bks., Inc.

—Where's the Baby? (Korean) Choi, Jin, tr. Dwight, Laura, photos by. 2004. (KOR., Illus.). 12p. (J). bds. 5.95 (978-1-932065-80-0(6)) Star Bright Bks., Inc.

—Where's the Baby? (Russian/English), 1 vol. Dwight, Laura, photos by. 2005. (Photoflaps Ser.). (RUS & ENG., Illus.). 24p. (J). (gr. -1). bds. 5.95 (978-1-932065-86-2(5)) Star Bright Bks., Inc.

—Where's the Baby? (Simplified Mandarin) Dwight, Laura, photos by. 2004. (CHI., Illus.). 12p. (J). bds. 5.95 (978-1-932065-68-8(7)) Star Bright Bks., Inc.

—Where's the Baby? (Vietnamese) Dwight, Laura, photos by. 2004. (VIE., Illus.). 12p. (J). bds. 5.50 (978-1-932065-74-9(1)) Star Bright Bks., Inc.

Chronicle Books Staff. New York, Baby! Jenkins, Ward, illus. 2012. (ENG.). 24p. (J). (gr. -1 — 1). 12.99 (978-1-4521-0619-9(3)) Chronicle Bks. LLC.

—San Francisco, Baby! Jenkins, Ward, illus. 2012. (ENG.). 24p. (J). (gr. -1 — 1). 12.99 (978-1-4521-0620-5(7)) Chronicle Bks. LLC.

Chung, Arree. Out. Chung, Arree, illus. 2017. (ENG., Illus.). 40p. (J). 17.99 (978-1-62779-553-1(7), 9781627795531, Holt, Henry & Co. Bks. For Young Readers) Holt, Henry & Co.

Church, Caroline Jayne. I Am a Big Brother! 2015. (SPA & ENG.). 24p. (J). (gr. -1 — 1). 6.99 (978-0-545-84717-9(6), Scholastic en Espanol) Scholastic, Inc.

—I Am a Big Brother! Church, Caroline Jayne, illus. 2015. (ENG., Illus.). 24p. (J). (gr. -1 — 1). 6.99 (978-0-545-68886-4(8), Cartwheel Bks.) Scholastic, Inc.

—I Am a Big Sister! 2015. (SPA & ENG.). 24p. (J). (gr. -1 — 1). 6.99 (978-0-545-84718-6(4), Scholastic en Espanol) Scholastic, Inc.

—I Am a Big Sister! Church, Caroline Jayne, illus. 2015. (ENG., Illus.). 24p. (J). (gr. -1 — 1). 6.99 (978-0-545-68898-7(1), Cartwheel Bks.) Scholastic, Inc.

—Sweet Child of Mine: A Caroline Jayne Church Treasury. Church, Caroline Jayne, illus. 2014. (ENG., Illus.). 26p. (J). (— 1). bds. 8.99 (978-0-545-64771-7(1), Cartwheel Bks.) Scholastic, Inc.

Claire, Onge. Caillou Que manque t Il. pap. 9.95 (978-2-89450-267-9(2)) Éditions Chouette CAN. Dist: Distribooks, Inc.

Cocca-Leffler, Maryann. Theo's Mood: A Book of Feelings. Cocca-Leffler, Maryann, illus. 2013. (ENG., Illus.). 24p. (J). (gr. -1-3). 15.99 (978-0-8075-7778-3(2)) Whitman, Albert & Co.

Coh, Smiljana. I Have a Brother. 2012. (ENG.). 24p. (J). (978-1-58925-124-3(5)) Tiger Tales.

—I Have a Sister. 2012. (ENG.). 24p. (J). (978-1-58925-125-0(3)) Tiger Tales.

Cohen, Miriam. Backpack Baby (Spanish/English), 1 vol. Fiol, Maria A., tr. 2005. (SPA & ENG., Illus.). 32p. (J). (gr. -1 — 1). bds. 5.95 (978-1-59572-018-4(9)) Star Bright Bks., Inc.

Cohn, Arlen. Firsts. Vasconcellos, Daniel, illus. gif. ed. 2004. (ENG.). 28p. (J). bds. 9.99 (978-1-57939-168-3(0)) Andrews McMeel Publishing.

Cole, Joanna. I'm a Big Brother. Kightley, Rosalinda, illus. 2010. (ENG.). 32p. (J). (gr. -1-3). 6.99 (978-0-06-190065-5(6), HarperFestival) HarperCollins Pubs.

—I'm a Big Sister. Kightley, Rosalinda, illus. 2010. (ENG.). 32p. (J). (gr. -1-3). 6.99 (978-0-06-190062-4(1), HarperFestival) HarperCollins Pubs.

—Soy un Hermano Mayor, 1 vol. Kightley, Rosalinda, illus. 2010. (SPA & ENG.). 32p. (J). (gr. -1-k). 6.99 (978-0-06-190066-2(4)) HarperCollins Pubs.

—Soy una Hermana Mayor, 1 vol. Kightley, Rosalinda, illus. 2010.Tr. of I am a Big Sister. (SPA.). 32p. (J). (gr. -1-k). 6.99 (978-0-06-190063-1(X)) HarperCollins Pubs.

Colman, Michelle Sinclair. Beach Babies Wear Shades. Dion, Nathalie, illus. 2007. (Urban Babies Wear Black Book Ser.). (ENG.). 18p. (J). (gr. k — 1). bds. 6.99 (978-1-58246-204-2(6), Tricycle Pr.) Random Hse. Children's Bks.

—Foodie Babies Wear Bibs. Dion, Nathalie, illus. 2008. (Urban Babies Wear Black Book Ser.). (ENG.). 20p. (J). (— 1). bds. 6.99 (978-1-58246-254-7(2), Tricycle Pr.) Random Hse. Children's Bks.

—Rocker Babies Wear Jeans. Dion, Nathalie, illus. 2009. (Urban Babies Wear Black Book Ser.). (ENG.). 9p. (J). (gr. -1 — 1). bds. 6.99 (978-1-58246-291-2(7), Tricycle Pr.) Random Hse. Children's Bks.

—Urban Babies Wear Black. Dion, Nathalie, illus. 2005. (Urban Babies Wear Black Book Ser.). (ENG.). 20p. (J). (gr. k — 1). bds. 6.99 (978-1-58246-158-8(9), Tricycle Pr.) Random Hse. Children's Bks.

Cooke, Trish. So Much! Oxenbury, Helen, illus. 2008. (J). (gr. -1-1). lib. bdg. 17.20 (978-0-613-08774-2(7), Turtleback) Turtleback Bks.

Cooper, Ilene. Lucy's Holiday Surprise. Fitzgerald, Royce, illus. 2015. (Lucy Ser.: 7). (ENG.). 112p. (J). (gr. 1-4). 12.99 (978-0-385-39131-3(5), Random Hse. Bks. for Young Readers) Random Hse. Children's Bks.

Cordell, Matthew. Dream. Cordell, Matthew, illus. 2017. (Wish Ser.). (ENG., Illus.). 48p. (J). (gr. -1-k). 16.99 (978-1-4847-7340-6(3)) Hyperion Bks. for Children.

Corso, Erika. The Day You Came. Corso, Erika & Corso, Bertina, illus. 2006. (ENG.). 20p. (J). per. 12.95 (978-1-59800-242-3(2)) Outskirts Pr., Inc.

Costales, Amy. Hello Night/Hola Noche. McDonald, Mercedes, illus. 2007. (ENG, SPA & MUL.). 24p. (J). (gr. -1 — 1). 14.95 (978-0-87358-927-7(0)) Cooper Square Publishing Llc.

Crespo, Ana. JP & the Stinky Monster: Feeling Jealous. Sirotich, Erica, illus. 2016. (My Emotions & Me Ser.). (ENG.). 32p. (J). (gr. -1-3). 16.99 (978-0-8075-3979-8(1)) Whitman, Albert & Co.

Cronin, Doreen. Bounce. Menchin, Scott, illus. 2007. (ENG.). 40p. (J). (gr. -1-3). 17.99 (978-1-4169-1627-7(X), Atheneum Bks. for Young Readers) Simon & Schuster Children's Publishing.

Crystal, Billy. Grandpa's Little One. Porfirio, Guy, illus. 2006. 40p. (J). (gr. -1-k). lib. bdg. 17.89 (978-0-06-078174-3(2)) HarperCollins Pubs.

—I Already Know I Love You. Sayles, Elizabeth, illus. 2008. (ENG.). 32p. (J). (gr. -1-3). bds. 7.99 (978-0-06-145057-0(X), HarperFestival) HarperCollins Pubs.

Curtis, Jamie Lee. When I Was Little: A Four-Year-Old's Memoir of Her Youth. braille ed. 2004. (Illus.). (J). (gr. k-3). spiral bd. (978-0-616-01625-1(5)); spiral bd. (978-0-616-01626-8(3)) Canadian National Institute for the Blind/Institut National Canadien pour les Aveugles.

Cushman, Jean, et al. Little Golden Book Mommy Stories. Wilkin, Eloise & Meisel, Paul, illus. 2015. (Little Golden Book Favorites Ser.). (ENG.). 80p. (J). (-k). 6.99 (978-0-385-39273-0(7), Golden Bks.) Random Hse. Children's Bks.

Czarnota, Jennifer. Blessing Baby & the Heart As Big As the Sky. 2013. 28p. pap. 16.99 (978-1-4808-0238-4(7)) Archway Publishing.

Dahl, Michael. Christmas. Ho, Jannie, illus. 2015. (Baby Face Ser.). (ENG.). 10p. (gr. -1 — 1). bds. 7.99 (978-1-62370-292-2(5)) Capstone Young Readers of Coughlan Cos.

—Halloween. Ho, Jannie, illus. 2015. (Baby Face Ser.). (ENG.). 10p. (gr. -1 — 1). bds. 7.99 (978-1-62370-293-9(3)) Capstone Young Readers of Coughlan Cos.

—Me & My Dog. Persico, Zoe, illus. 2016. (Me & My Pet Ser.). (ENG.). 24p. (gr. 1-2). 6.95 (978-1-62370-793-4(5)) Capstone Young Readers of Coughlan Cos.

—Pirate. Ho, Jannie, illus. 2015. (Baby Face Ser.). (ENG.). 10p. (gr. -1 — 1). bds. 9.99 (978-1-62370-294-6(1)) Capstone Young Readers of Coughlan Cos.

—Princess. Ho, Jannie, illus. 2015. (Baby Face Ser.). (ENG.). 10p. (gr. -1 — 1). bds. 7.99 (978-1-62370-295-3(X)) Capstone Young Readers of Coughlan Cos.

Dale, Jay. Our Baby, 1 vol. Everitt-Stewart, Andrew, illus. 2012. (Engage Literacy Green Ser.). (ENG.). 32p. (gr. k-2). pap. 5.99 (978-1-4296-9023-2(2), Engage Literacy) Capstone Press of Coughlan Cos.

Daubert Standards Committee, et al. Discussions of the Committee on Daubert Standards: Summary of Meetings. Hanna, Kathi E. & Mazza, Anne-Marie, eds. 2006. (ENG., Illus.). 46p. pap. 21.00 (978-0-309-10248-3(0)) National Academies Pr.

Daugherty, Deborah Kay. Hair in the Way. 2013. 40p. pap. 15.99 (978-1-4908-0130-8(8), WestBow Pr.) Author Solutions, Inc.

Davis, David. Ten Redneck Babies: A Southern Counting Book, 1 vol. Ward, Sue Marshall, illus. 2004. (ENG.). 32p. (J). (gr. k-k). 16.99 (978-1-58980-232-2(2)) Pelican Publishing Co., Inc.

—Ten Texas Babies, 1 vol. Jackson, Shelley & Crosby, Jeff, illus. 2014. (ENG.). 32p. (J). (gr. k-3). 16.99 (978-1-4556-1874-3(8)) Pelican Publishing Co., Inc.

Day, Alexandra. Carl's Christmas. 2014. (Carl Ser.). (J). lib. bdg. 18.40 (978-0-606-36127-9(8)) Turtleback Bks.

Demps, Rhonda R. The Angel I Left Behind. 2011. 16p. (gr. -1). 8.32 (978-1-4567-5562-1(5)) AuthorHouse.

Dempsey, Kristy. Ten Little Fingers, Two Small Hands. Massey, Jane, illus. 2016. (ENG.). 32p. (J). (gr. -1-2). 16.99 (978-1-4998-0229-0(3)) Little Bee Books Inc.

—Ten Little Toes, Two Small Feet. Massey, Jane, illus. 2016. (ENG.). 32p. (J). (gr. -1-2). 16.99 (978-1-4998-0236-8(6)) Little Bee Books Inc.

Dempsey, Sheena. Bye-Bye Baby Brother! 2013. (ENG., Illus.). 32p. (J). (gr. -1-2). 15.99 (978-0-7636-6241-7(0)) Candlewick Pr.

DeRosa Bodie, Leona. One Is Fun. Davis, Catherine Baptista, illus. 2007. 30p. (J). (gr. -1). bds. 12.95 (978-1-4243-2961-8(2)) Independent Publisher Services.

Dessen, Sarah. Along for the Ride. (ENG.). (YA). (gr. 7-18). 2011. 432p. pap. 10.99 (978-0-14-241556-6(1), Speak) 2009. 416p. 19.99 (978-0-670-01194-0(0), Viking Books for Young Readers) Penguin Young Readers Group.

—Along for the Ride. 2011. lib. bdg. 20.85 (978-0-606-15360-7(8), Turtleback) Turtleback Bks.

DiCamillo, Kate. Where Are You Going, Baby Lincoln? Tales from Deckawoo Drive, Volume Three. Van Dusen, Chris, illus. 2017. (Tales from Deckawoo Drive Ser.: 3). (ENG.). 112p. (J). (gr. 1-4). pap. 5.99 **(978-0-7636-9758-7(3))** Candlewick Pr.

Dipucchio, Kelly. Littles: And How They Grow. Ford, A. G., illus. 2017. (ENG.). 32p. (J). (gr. -1 — 1). 17.99 **(978-0-399-55526-8(9))**; lib. bdg. 20.99 **(978-0-399-55527-5(7))** Random Hse. Children's Bks. (Doubleday Bks. for Young Readers).

Dipucchio, Kelly. Zombie in Love 2 + 1. Campbell, Scott, illus. 2014. (ENG.). 32p. (J). (gr. -1-3). 14.99 (978-1-4424-5937-3(9), Atheneum Bks. for Young Readers) Simon & Schuster Children's Publishing.

Disney Book Group. Disney Baby I Love You This Much! Disney Storybook Art Team, illus. 2016. (ENG.). 24p. (J). (gr. -1 — 1). bds. 6.99 (978-1-4847-7823-4(5)) Disney Pr.

—Disney Baby My First Year: Record & Share Baby's Firsts. Disney Storybook Art Team, illus. 2016. (ENG.). 20p. (J). (gr. -1 — 1). 12.99 (978-1-4847-4367-6(9)) Disney Pr.

DiTerlizzi, Angela. Baby Love. Hughes, Brooke Boynton, illus. 2015. (ENG.). 32p. (J). (gr. -1-3). 17.99 (978-1-4424-3392-2(2), Beach Lane Bks.) Beach Lane Bks.

Dodd, Emma & Nosy Crow Staff. Baby & Me. Dodd, Emma, illus. 2013. (ENG., Illus.). 16p. (J). (gr. -1-2). 14.99 (978-0-7636-6544-9(4), Nosy Crow) Candlewick Pr.

Doerrfeld, Cori. Penny Loves Pink. 2011. (ENG., Illus.). 40p. (J). (gr. -1-3). 15.99 (978-0-316-05458-4(5)) Little, Brown Bks. for Young Readers.

Doman, Regina. Mi Angelito en Las Aguas. Hatke, Ben, illus. 2006. (SPA.). 40p. (J). (gr. -1-3). pap. 6.95 (978-1-933184-22-7(1)) Sophia Institute Pr.

Dorling Kindersley Publishing Staff. Baby Faces! 2011. (ENG.). 16p. (J). (gr. -1 — 1). bds. 6.99 (978-0-7566-7175-4(2), DK Children) Dorling Kindersley Publishing, Inc.

—Baby Talk: 6 Giant Flasp for Baby to Flip. 2005. (Fun Flaps Ser.). (ENG., Illus.). 14p. (J). (gr. -1-k). bds. 4.99 (978-0-7566-0986-3(0), DK Children) Dorling Kindersley Publishing, Inc.

—Noisy Baby Peekaboo! 2015. (ENG.). 12p. (J). (— 1). bds. 12.99 (978-1-4654-3821-8(1), DK Children) Dorling Kindersley Publishing, Inc.

Dorling Kindersley Publishing Staff, creator. Bedtime Peekaboo! 2006. (ENG., Illus.). 12p. (J). (gr. -1-k). bds. 6.99 (978-0-7566-1622-9(0), DK Children) Dorling Kindersley Publishing, Inc.

Drakeford, Lisa. The Baby. 2016. (ENG.). 256p. (J). (gr. 9). 17.99 (978-0-545-94027-6(3)) Scholastic, Inc.

Duke, Shirley Smith. No Bows!, 1 vol. Mattheson, Jenny, illus. 2006. (ENG.). 32p. (J). (gr. k-1). 15.95 (978-1-56145-356-6(0)) Peachtree Pubs.

Dunbar, Joyce. Pat-A-Cake Baby. Dunbar, Polly, illus. 2015. (ENG.). 40p. (J). (-k). 15.99 (978-0-7636-7577-6(6)) Candlewick Pr.

Duncan, Alice Faye. Honey Baby Sugar Child. Keeter, Susan, illus. 2005. (ENG.). 32p. (J). (gr. -1-1). 17.99 (978-0-689-84678-6(9), Simon & Schuster Bks. For Young Readers) Simon & Schuster Bks. For Young Readers.

Dunrea, Olivier. It's Snowing! Dunrea, Olivier, illus. 2009. (ENG., Illus.). 32p. (J). (gr. -1-1). pap. 6.99 (978-0-312-60216-1(2), 9780312602161) Square Fish.

Elliston, Beth. A Baby Book as told by ME! the Big Sister. 2009. 32p. pap. 14.95 (978-0-557-07646-8(3)) Lulu Pr., Inc.

Elya, Susan Middleton. Bebé Goes Shopping. Salerno, Steven, illus. 2008. (ENG.). 36p. (J). (gr. -1-3). pap. 7.99 (978-0-15-206142-5(8)) Houghton Mifflin Harcourt Publishing Co.

Enderle, Judith Ross & Gordon, Stephanie Jacob. Smile, Principessa! Curmi, Serena, illus. 2012. (ENG.). 40p. (J). (gr. -1-1). 16.99 (978-1-4424-3096-9(6), McElderry, Margaret K. Bks.) McElderry, Margaret K. Bks.

Enersen, Adele. When My Baby Dreams. Enersen, Adele, illus. 2012. (ENG., Illus.). 48p. (J). (gr. -1-3). 14.99 (978-0-06-207175-0(0)) HarperCollins Pubs.

—When My Baby Dreams of Fairy Tales. Enersen, Adele, illus. 2013. (ENG., Illus.). 48p. (J). (gr. -1-k). 15.99 (978-0-06-207177-4(7)) HarperCollins Pubs.

Eyre, David. White Rainbow Black Curse. 2007. 31p. 14.95 (978-0-87336-117-0(2)) Kamehameha Publishing.

Falwell, Cathryn. The Nesting Quilt, 1 vol. 2015. (ENG., Illus.). 32p. (gr. -1-3). 16.95 (978-0-88448-418-9(1), 884418) Tilbury Hse. Pubs.

Fearnley, Jan. A Special Something. 2004. (Illus.). 32p. 7.95 (978-0-7497-4639-1(4)) Egmont Bks., Ltd. GBR. Dist: Trafalgar Square Publishing.

Feiffer, Kate. But I Wanted a Baby Brother! Goode, Diane, illus. 2010. (ENG.). 32p. (J). (gr. -1-3). 16.99 (978-1-4169-3941-2(5), Simon & Schuster/Paula Wiseman Bks.) Simon & Schuster/Paula Wiseman Bks.

—No Go Sleep! Feiffer, Jules, illus. 2012. (ENG.). 32p. (J). (gr. -1-2). 16.99 (978-1-4424-1683-3(1), Simon & Schuster/Paula Wiseman Bks.) Simon & Schuster/Paula Wiseman Bks.

—The Wild, Wild Inside: A View from Mommy's Tummy! Huliska-Beith, Laura, illus. 2010. (ENG.). 32p. (J). (gr. -1-3). 15.99 (978-1-4169-4099-9(5), Simon & Schuster/Paula Wiseman Bks.) Simon & Schuster/Paula Wiseman Bks.

Fennell, Kristen & Petruccelli, Jessica, illus. A World of Hope: Written by Hope's Parents Laurie & Mike. l.t. ed. 2005. 18p.

(J). per. 9.99 *(978-1-59879-069-6(2))* Lifevest Publishing, Inc.

Fergus, Maureen. Buddy & Earl & the Great Big Baby, 1 vol. Sookocheff, Carey, illus. 2016. (Buddy & Earl Ser.). (ENG.). 32p. (J). (gr. -1-2). 16.95 *(978-1-55498-716-0(4))* Groundwood Bks. CAN. Dist: Publishers Group West (PGW).

Fisher, Valorie. My Big Sister. Fisher, Valorie, photos by. 2003. (ENG., Illus.). 40p. (J). (gr. -1-3). 17.99 *(978-0-689-85479-8(X),* Atheneum Bks. for Young Readers) Simon & Schuster Children's Publishing.

Fitch, Sheree. Kisses Kisses Baby-O!, 1 vol. Rose, Hilda, illus. 2008. (ENG.). 10p. (J). (gr. -1-2). bds. 6.50 *(978-1-55109-646-9(3))* Nimbus Publishing, Ltd. CAN. Dist: Orca Bk. Pubs. USA.

Flyte, Min. Box. Beardshaw, Rosalind, illus. 2016. (ENG.). 26p. (J). (gr. -1-2). 15.99 *(978-0-7636-8939-1(4),* Nosy Crow) Candlewick Pr.

Fogliano, Julie. Old Dog Baby Baby. Raschka, Chris, illus. 2016. (ENG.). 32p. (J). 17.99 *(978-1-59643-853-8(3),* 9781596438538) Roaring Brook Pr.

Fox, Mem. Baby Bedtime. 2014. (ENG., Illus.). 32p. (J). (gr. -1-3). 17.99 *(978-1-4814-2097-6(6),* Beach Lane Bks.) Beach Lane Bks.

—Diez Deditos de Las Manos y Diez Deditos de Los Pies / Ten Little Fingers & Ten Little Toes Bilingual Board Book. Oxenbury, Helen, illus. 2012. (ENG & SPA.). 38p. (J). (gr. k — 1). bds. 6.99 *(978-0-547-87006-9(X))* Houghton Mifflin Harcourt Publishing Co.

—Hello Baby! Jenkins, Steve, illus. 2009. (ENG.). 32p. (J). (gr. -1-k). 17.99 *(978-1-4169-8513-6(1),* Beach Lane Bks.) Beach Lane Bks.

—Ten Little Fingers & Ten Little Toes. Oxenbury, Helen, illus. (ENG.). (J). 2010. 38p. (gr. k — 1). bds. 8.99 *(978-0-547-36620-3(5))* 2008. 40p. (gr. -1 — 1). 17.99 *(978-0-15-206057-2(X))* Houghton Mifflin Harcourt Publishing Co.

—Ten Little Fingers & Ten Little Toes Lap Board Book. Oxenbury, Helen, illus. 2011. (ENG.). 38p. (J). (gr. k — 1). bds. 11.99 *(978-0-547-58103-3(3))* Houghton Mifflin Harcourt Publishing Co.

Frasier, Debra. On the Day You Were Born. 2006. (ENG., Illus.). 24p. (J). (gr. -1). bds. 7.95 *(978-0-15-205944-6(X))* Houghton Mifflin Harcourt Publishing Co.

Frazee, Marla. The Boss Baby. Frazee, Marla, illus. 2010. (ENG., Illus.). 40p. (J). (gr. -1-3). 17.99 *(978-1-4424-0167-9(2),* Beach Lane Bks.) Beach Lane Bks.

—The Boss Baby. Frazee, Marla, illus. 2013. (Classic Board Bks.). (ENG., Illus.). 36p. (J). (gr. -1 — 1). bds. 7.99 *(978-1-4424-8779-6(8),* Little Simon) Little Simon.

—The Boss Baby. 2016. lib. bdg. 18.40 *(978-0-606-39228-0(9))* Turtleback Bks.

—The Bossier Baby. Frazee, Marla, illus. 2016. (ENG., Illus.). 40p. (J). (gr. -1-3). 17.99 *(978-1-4814-7162-6(7),* Beach Lane Bks.) Beach Lane Bks.

—Hush, Little Baby: A Folk Song with Pictures. 2007. (ENG., Illus.). 42p. (J). (gr. k — 1). bds. 6.95 *(978-0-15-205887-6(7))* Houghton Mifflin Harcourt Publishing Co.

Freedman, Claire. I Love You, Baby! Abbot, Judi, illus. 2017. (ENG.). 32p. (J). (gr. -1-3). 17.99 ***(978-1-4814-9904-0(1),*** Simon & Schuster/Paula Wiseman Bks.) Simon & Schuster/Paula Wiseman Bks.

Freedman, Claire. Oops-a-Daisy! Hansen, Gaby, illus. 32p. (J). 2004. tchr. ed. 15.95 *(978-1-58925-037-6(0))* 2006. reprint ed. 6.95 *(978-1-58925-398-8(1))* Tiger Tales.

Friedman, Laurie. Mallory Mcdonald, Baby Expert. Kalis, Jennifer, illus. 2015. (Mallory Ser.: Vol. 22). (ENG.). 152p. (J). (gr. 2-5). pap. 5.95 *(978-1-4677-0938-5(7),* Darby Creek) Lerner Publishing Group.

Friedman, Laurie B. Mallory McDonald, Baby Expert. Kalis, Jennifer, illus. 2014. (Mallory Ser.: 22). (ENG.). 152p. (J). (gr. 2-5). 15.95 *(978-1-4677-0922-4(0))* Lerner Publishing Group.

Fruchter, Jason, illus. The Baby Is Here! 2015. (Daniel Tiger's Neighborhood Ser.). (ENG.). 24p. (J). (gr. -1-2). pap. 3.99 *(978-1-4814-3013-5(0),* Simon Spotlight) Simon Spotlight.

Fuller, Rachel, illus. Look at Me! 2009. (New Baby Ser.). (ENG.). 12p. (J). (gr. -1). bds. *(978-1-84643-278-1(2))* Child's Play International Ltd.

—My New Baby. 2009. (New Baby Ser.). (ENG.). 12p. (J). (gr. -1). bds. *(978-1-84643-276-7(6))* Child's Play International Ltd.

Furniss, Clare. The Year of the Rat. 2015. (ENG.). 304p. (YA). (gr. 7). pap. 10.99 *(978-1-4814-2100-3(X),* McElderry, Margaret K. Bks.) McElderry, Margaret K. Bks.

Gallagher, Mary. Mulhern Twins. 2007. (ENG., Illus.). 126p. (J). pap. 11.95 *(978-1-905172-17-7(6))* Collins Pr., The IRL. Dist: Dufour Editions, Inc.

Gamble, Adam, et al. Good Night New Baby. 2014. (Good Night Our World Ser.). (ENG., Illus.). 20p. (J). (— 1). bds. 9.95 *(978-1-60219-188-4(3))* Good Night Bks.

Garcia Sanchez, J. L. El Nino Gigante (The Giant Child) (Derechos del Nino Ser.). (SPA., Illus.). 32p. (J). (gr. 3-5). pap. 8.95 *(978-1-56014-580-6(3))* Santillana USA Publishing Co., Inc.

Gartlan, Daniel. Poor Hannah. 2012. 24p. pap. 24.95 *(978-1-4626-6030-8(4))* America Star Bks.

Gates, Susan & Ceredigion, Cymdeithas Lyfrau. Babi Bag Siwgwr. Williams, Dylan, tr. from ENG. Braun, Sebastien, illus. 2005. (WEL.). 80p. pap. *(978-1-902416-96-0(1))* Cymdeithas Lyfrau Ceredigion.

Gaydos, Nora. I'M a New Big Brother: Little Steps for Big Kids. 2010. (ENG., Illus.). 30p. (J). (gr. -1-17). 8.99 *(978-1-60169-010-4(X))* Innovative Kids.

Geddes, Anne. This Little Baby. 2014. (ENG., Illus.). 24p. (J). bds. 8.99 *(978-1-4022-9828-8(5))* Sourcebooks, Inc.

Geis, Patricia. Good-bye Pacifier! Folch, Sergio, illus. 2009. (Good Habits with Coco & Tula Ser.). 16p. (J). (gr. -1-k). bds. 11.40 *(978-1-60754-405-0(9))* Windmill Bks.

Gentieu, Penny. Baby! Talk! Gentieu, Penny, illus. 2015. (ENG., Illus.). 22p. (J). (— 1). bds. 6.99 *(978-0-517-80079-9(9),* Knopf Bks. for Young Readers) Random Hse. Children's Bks.

George R. Cathcart Jr. Ernie's Clever Plan. 2012. 24p. 24.95 *(978-1-4626-6795-6(3))* America Star Bks.

Geran, Chad. Oh, Baby! 2014. (ENG., Illus.). 16p. (J). (— 1). bds. 8.95 *(978-1-57687-704-3(3),* powerHouse Bks.) powerHouse Cultural Entertainment, Inc.

Gerber, Carole. Tuck-In Time. Pearson, Tracey Campbell, illus. 2014. (ENG.). 40p. (J). (gr. -1 — 1). 16.99 *(978-0-374-37860-8(6),* 9780374378608, Farrar, Straus & Giroux (BYR)) Farrar, Straus & Giroux.

Gershator, David. Where Did the Baby Go? Gershator, Phillis, illus. 2016. (J). pap. *(978-1-934370-57-5(6))* Editorial Campana.

Giggle & grow with Plush. 2007. bds. 15.95 *(978-1-58117-644-5(9),* Intervisual/Piggy Toes) Bendon, Inc.

Gillen, Kristin M. Raspberries on Tummies. 2011. 32p. pap. 21.99 *(978-1-4568-9436-8(6))* Xlibris Corp.

Gillingham, Sara. My Little Sweetheart. 2011. (ENG.). 12p. (J). (gr. -1 — 1). 9.99 *(978-1-4521-0226-9(0))* Chronicle Bks. LLC.

Gillingham, Sara, illus. Snuggle the Baby. 2014. (ENG.). 12p. (J). (gr. -1 — 1). bds. 12.99 *(978-1-4197-1124-4(5),* Abrams Appleseed) Abrams, Inc.

Gobo, creator. Santa Baby. 2006. (Illus.). 10p. (gr. -1-k). 9.95 *(978-1-932915-30-3(3))* Sandvik Innovations, LLC.

Godin, Thelma Lynne. How to Dress a Dragon. Barclay, Eric, illus. 2016. (ENG.). 40p. (J). (gr. -1-k). 16.99 *(978-0-545-67846-9(3),* Scholastic Pr.) Scholastic, Inc.

Good, Jason. Must. Push. Buttons! Krosoczka, Jarrett J., illus. 2015. (ENG.). 32p. (J). (gr. -1-1). 16.99 *(978-1-61963-095-6(8),* 9781619630956, Bloomsbury USA Childrens) Bloomsbury Publishing USA.

Gosline, Andrea Alban. Ten Little Wishes: A Baby Animal Counting Book. Bossi, Lisa Burnett, illus. 2007. 40p. (J). (gr. -1-k). 16.89 *(978-0-06-053411-0(7))* HarperCollins Pubs.

Guest, Elissa Haden. Iris & Walter: Lost & Found. Davenier, Christine, illus. 2014. (Green Light Readers Level 3 Ser.). (ENG.). 44p. (J). (gr. 1-4). pap. 3.99 *(978-0-544-22789-7(1),* HMH Books For Young Readers) Houghton Mifflin Harcourt Publishing Co.

—Iris & Walter & Baby Rose. Davenier, Christine, illus. 2012. (Iris & Walter — Green Light Reader Ser.). lib. bdg. 13.55 *(978-0-606-26612-3(7),* Turtleback) Turtleback Bks.

Hakala, Joann. A Baby Brother! Oh No! Shaw-Peterson, Kimberly, illus. 2006. 32p. (J). (gr. -1). per. 10.95 *(978-1-59298-152-6(6))* Beaver's Pond Pr., Inc.

Hale, Bruce. Big Bad Baby. Breen, Steve, illus. 2014. (ENG.). 32p. (J). (gr. -1-k). 17.99 *(978-0-8037-3585-9(5),* Dial Bks) Penguin Young Readers Group.

Hale, Rachael. Baby's Best Friend. 2011. (ENG.). 20p. (J). (gr. -1 — 1). bds. 6.99 *(978-0-316-12962-6(3))* Little, Brown Bks. for Young Readers.

Hall, Hannah. God Bless Our Baby, 1 vol. Whitlow, Steve, illus. 2017. (God Bless Book Ser.). (ENG.). 20p. (J). bds. 9.99 *(978-0-7180-8666-4(X))* Nelson, Thomas Inc.

Hamburg, Jennifer. Daniel Goes to the Playground. 2015. (Daniel Tiger's Neighborhood 8X8 Ser.). lib. bdg. 13.55 *(978-0-606-38256-4(9))* Turtleback Bks.

Hamilton, Clarice. Special Delivery. 2010. 16p. 12.50 *(978-1-4520-4199-5(7))* AuthorHouse.

Hannigan, Katherine. Gwendolyn Grace. Hannigan, Katherine, illus. 2015. (ENG., Illus.). 32p. (J). (gr. -1-3). 17.99 *(978-0-06-234519-6(2),* Greenwillow Bks.) HarperCollins Pubs.

Harper, Anita. It's Not Fair. McQuillan, Mary, illus. 2007. (ENG.). 32p. (J). (gr. -1-3). 16.95 *(978-0-8234-2094-0(9))* Holiday Hse., Inc.

Harris, Dorothy Joan. Cameron & Me. 2004. (Illus.). (J). (gr. k-3). spiral bd. *(978-0-616-01667-1(0));* spiral bd. *(978-0-616-01668-8(9))* Canadian National Institute for the Blind/Institut National Canadien pour les Aveugles.

Harris, Robie H. Mail Harry to the Moon! Emberley, Michael, illus. 2008. (ENG.). 40p. (J). (gr. -1-3). 16.99 *(978-0-316-15376-8(1))* Little, Brown Bks. for Young Readers.

Harvey, Sarah N. The Lit Report, 1 vol. 2008. (ENG.). 208p. (YA). (gr. 7-12). pap. 12.95 *(978-1-55143-905-1(0))* Orca Bk. Pubs. USA.

Hawkes, Kevin. The Wicked Big Toddlah. 2010. (ENG.). 40p. (J). (gr. -1-2). pap. 7.99 *(978-0-440-41788-0(0),* Dragonfly Bks.) Random Hse. Children's Bks.

—The Wicked Big Toddlah Goes to New York. 2011. (ENG., Illus.). 40p. (J). (gr. -1-2). 16.99 *(978-0-375-86188-8(2),* Knopf Bks. for Young Readers) Random Hse. Children's Bks.

Hawkins-Walsh, Elizabeth & Pierson-Solis, Lennard. Katie's Premature Brother = el Hermano Prematuro de Katie. Blake, Anne Catharine, illus. 2006. (J). *(978-1-56123-197-3(5))* Centering Corp.

HB Staff. Where Babies Play. 97th ed. 2003. (First-Place Reading Ser.). (gr. 1-18). pap. 16.50 *(978-0-15-308136-1(8))* Harcourt Schl. Pubs.

Hegg, Tom & Hanson, Warren. Peef & the Baby Sister. Hegg, Tom & Hanson, Warren, illus. 2006. (ENG., Illus.). 36p. (J). (gr. -1-3). 16.95 *(978-0-931674-67-9(0),* Waldman House Pr.) TRISTAN Publishing, Inc.

Henkes, Kevin. Julius, el Rey de la Casa. 2017.Tr. of Julius, the Baby of the World. (SPA.). (J). pap. ***(978-1-63245-668-7(0))*** Lectorum Pubns., Inc.

Henkes, Kevin. Julius, the Baby of the World. braille ed. 2004. (J). (gr. -1-2). spiral bd. *(978-0-616-07239-4(2))* Canadian National Institute for the Blind/Institut National Canadien pour les Aveugles.

Henson, Heather. Angel Coming. Gaber, Susan, illus. 2011. (ENG.). 40p. (J). (gr. -1-1). pap. 16.99 *(978-1-4424-3077-8(X),* Atheneum Bks. for Young Readers) Simon & Schuster Children's Publishing.

Heos, Bridget. Mustache Baby. Ang, Joy, illus. 2016. (ENG.). 36p. (J). (— 1). bds. 7.99 *(978-0-544-78984-5(9),* HMH Books For Young Readers) Houghton Mifflin Harcourt Publishing Co.

—Mustache Baby. Ang, Joy, illus. (Mustache Baby Ser.). (ENG.). 40p. (J). (gr. -1-3). 2015. 16.99 *(978-0-544-36375-5(2))* 2013. 17.99 *(978-0-547-77357-5(9))* Houghton Mifflin Harcourt Trade & Reference Pubs. (Clarion Bks.).

—Queen Dog. O'Keeffe, Alejandro, illus. 2017. (ENG.). 40p. (J). (gr. -1-k). 16.99 *(978-1-4847-2852-9(1))* Disney Pr.

Hesse, Karen. Lavender. Kimmel, Eric A. & Glass, Andrew, illus. 2010. (ENG.). 48p. (J). (gr. 2-5). pap. 9.99 *(978-0-312-37609-3(X),* 9780312376093) Square Fish.

Higginson, Sheila Sweeny. You're Getting a Baby Brother! Williams, Sam, illus. 2012. (ENG.). 24p. (J). (gr. -1-k). bds. 7.99 *(978-1-4424-2021-2(9),* Little Simon) Little Simon.

—You're Getting a Baby Sister! Williams, Sam, illus. 2012. (ENG.). 24p. (J). (gr. -1-k). bds. 7.99 *(978-1-4424-2050-2(2),* Little Simon) Little Simon.

Hill, Susanna Leonard. Not yet, Rose. Rutten, Nicole, illus. 2009. (ENG.). 34p. (J). (gr. -1-3). 16.50 *(978-0-8028-5326-4(9),* Eerdmans Bks For Young Readers) Eerdmans, William B. Publishing Co.

Hillert, Margaret. I Need You, Dear Dragon. Pullan, Jack, illus. 2016. (BeginningtoRead Ser.). (ENG.). 32p. (J). (-2). lib. bdg. 22.60 *(978-1-59953-771-9(0))* Norwood Hse. Pr.

Hissom, Jennie. Wheels on the Move: Driving with Andy. Catusanu, Mircea, illus. 2006. (J). *(978-1-58987-141-0(3))* Kindermusik International.

Hoban, Russell. Soonchild. Deacon, Alexis, illus. 2012. (ENG.). 144p. (YA). (gr. 9). 15.99 *(978-0-7636-5920-2(7))* Candlewick Pr.

Hodgman, Ann. Do Touch! Don't Touch! Barnard, Lucy, illus. 2012. (ENG.). 18p. (J). bds. *(978-1-58925-867-9(3))* Tiger Tales.

—Uh-Oh! Oh No! Barnard, Lucy, illus. 2012. (Into-Everything Baby Stages Ser.). (ENG.). 18p. (gr. -1). bds. 7.95 *(978-1-58925-866-2(5))* Tiger Tales.

Hood, Susan. Mission: New Baby. Lundquist, Mary, illus. 2015. (ENG.). 32p. (J). (gr. -1-2). 16.99 *(978-0-385-37672-3(3),* Random Hse. Bks. for Young Readers) Random Hse. Children's Bks.

Hooks, William H. Mr. Big Brother. Duke, Kate, illus. 2015. (ENG.). 34p. (J). pap. 11.95 *(978-1-899694-58-7(7),* ipicturebooks) ibooks, Inc.

Hopkins, Ellen. Glass. (ENG., (YA). (gr. 9). 2013. Illus.). 720p. pap. 12.99 *(978-1-4424-7182-5(4))* 2007. 688p. 21.99 *(978-1-4169-4090-6(1))* McElderry, Margaret K. Bks. (McElderry, Margaret K. Bks.).

Hornby, Nick. Slam. (ENG.). 320p. (gr. 12). 2009. 16.00 *(978-1-59448-471-1(6))* 2008. 15.00 *(978-1-59448-345-5(0))* Penguin Publishing Group. (Riverhead Bks. (Hardcover)).

Horse, Harry. Little Rabbit's New Baby, 1 vol. Horse, Harry, illus. (Little Rabbit Ser.). (Illus.). 32p. (J). 2016. (ENG.). (gr. -1-k). pap. 7.95 *(978-1-56145-915-5(1))* 2008. (gr. k-1). 16.95 *(978-1-56145-431-0(1))* Peachtree Pubs.

—Little Rabbit's New Baby / Book & Doll Package. 2008. (Illus.). 32p. (J). (gr. k-1). pap., pap. 22.90 *(978-1-56145-453-2(2))* Peachtree Pubs.

Howatt, Sandra J. Sleepyheads. Wan, Joyce, illus. 2014. (ENG.). 32p. (J). (gr. -1-3). 17.99 *(978-1-4424-2266-7(1),* Beach Lane Bks.) Beach Lane Bks.

Hughes, Mair Wynn & Davies, Tracy. Brawd Newydd. 2005. (WEL., Illus.). 15p. pap. *(978-0-86243-453-3(X))* Y Lolfa.

Hurwitz, Johanna. Amazing Monty. McGrory, Anik, illus. 2013. (Monty Ser.). (ENG.). 112p. (J). (gr. k-4). pap. 5.99 *(978-0-7636-6561-6(4))* Candlewick Pr.

ImageBooks Staff. Snow Baby Finger Puppet Book. 2011. (Little Finger Puppet Board Bks.). (ENG.). 12p. (J). (gr. -1 — 1). bds. 6.99 *(978-1-4521-0220-7(1))* Chronicle Bks. LLC.

Inches, Alison. Súper Bebés! Miller, Victoria, illus. 2006. (Dora la Exploradora Ser.). (SPA.). 24p. (J). (gr. -1-3). pap. 3.99 *(978-1-4169-2461-6(2),* Libros Para Ninos) Libros Para Ninos.

Intrater, Roberta Grobel. Peek-a-Boo, You! Intrater, Roberta Grobel, photos by. 2nd rev. l.t. ed. 2005. (Illus.). 14p. (J). 14.99 *(978-0-9764985-0-6(2))* 1212 Pr.

Isadora, Rachel. Bea in the Nutcracker. Isadora, Rachel, illus. 2015. (ENG., Illus.). 32p. (J). (gr. -1-k). 16.99 *(978-0-399-25231-0(2),* Nancy Paulsen Books) Penguin Young Readers Group.

—Peekaboo Morning. Isadora, Rachel, illus. 2008. (ENG., Illus.). 24p. (J). (gr. -1 — 1). bds. 7.99 *(978-0-399-25153-5(7),* G.P. Putnam's Sons Books for Young Readers) Penguin Young Readers Group.

Isol. The Menino: A Story Based on Real Events, 1 vol. Amado, Elisa, tr. from SPA. 2015. (ENG., Illus.). 60p. (J). (-k). 19.95 *(978-1-55498-778-8(4))* Groundwood Bks. CAN. Dist: Publishers Group West (PGW).

Ivers, Steven. The Family Menaces: The Beginning. 2011. 32p. pap. 24.95 *(978-1-4626-2012-8(4))* America Star Bks.

Jack, Keats Ezra. Peter's Chair. 2014. (ENG.). 40p. (J). (gr. k-k). 11.24 *(978-1-63245-276-4(6))* Lectorum Pubns., Inc.

Jam, Teddy. Night Cars, 1 vol. Beddows, Eric, illus. 2006. (ENG.). 32p. (J). (gr. k — 1). bds. 11.95 *(978-0-88899-748-7(5))* Groundwood Bks. CAN. Dist: Publishers Group West (PGW).

James, Helen Foster. Grandma Loves You! Brown, Petra, illus. 2013. (ENG.). 32p. (J). (gr. -1 — 1). 14.99 *(978-1-58536-836-5(9),* 202884) Sleeping Bear Pr.

—Grandpa Loves You! Brown, Petra, illus. 2016. (ENG.). 32p. (J). (gr. -1-1). 15.99 *(978-1-58536-940-9(3),* 204032) Sleeping Bear Pr.

Jenkins, Emily. That New Animal. Jenkins, Emily, illus. 2006. (Illus.). (J). (gr. -1-4). 29.95 *(978-0-439-84925-8(X),* WHCD687) Weston Woods Studios, Inc.

Jethani, Rita. Baby has a Burp. 2006. (Illus.). 24p. (J). 12.00 *(978-0-9774147-0-3(1))* Laasya Design.

Johnson, Angela. The First Part Last. (ENG.). 144p. (YA). (gr. 7). 2010. pap. 9.99 *(978-1-4424-0343-7(8))* 2003. (Illus.). 16.99 *(978-0-689-84922-0(2))* Simon & Schuster Bks. For Young Readers. (Simon & Schuster Bks. For Young Readers).

—The First Part Last. 2005. (ENG.). 144p. (YA). (gr. 7). reprint ed. pap. 7.99 *(978-0-689-84923-7(0),* Simon Pulse) Simon Pulse.

—The First Part Last. l.t. ed. 2005. 241p. pap. 10.95 *(978-0-7862-7379-9(8),* Large Print Pr.) Thorndike Pr.

Johnston, Tony. Laugh-Out-Loud Baby. Gammell, Stephen, illus. 2012. (ENG.). 32p. (J). (gr. -1-3). 16.99 *(978-1-4424-1380-1(8),* Simon & Schuster Bks. For Young Readers) Simon & Schuster/Paula Wiseman Bks.

Joly, Fanny. Atencion, Bebe Ataca! Capdevila, Roser, illus. 2003. (Coleccion Bebe). (SPA.). (J). (gr. 1-3). *(978-84-246-3652-4(X),* GL30758) La Galera, S.A. Editorial ESP. Dist: Lectorum Pubns., Inc.

—Un Bebe? Que Mala Idea! Capdevila, Roser, illus. 2003. (Coleccion Bebe). (SPA.). (J). (gr. 1-3). *(978-84-246-3651-7(1),* GL30757) La Galera, S.A. Editorial ESP. Dist: Lectorum Pubns., Inc.

Jones Crabbe, Ann, T J & His Friend: It's Just a Baby Thing. 2009. 24p. pap. 13.99 *(978-1-4490-1185-7(3))* AuthorHouse.

Jones, Patrick. Raising Heaven. 2015. (J). 9.99 *(978-1-4677-7697-4(1));* (ENG.). 96p. (gr. 6-12). lib. bdg. 27.99 *(978-1-4677-5802-4(7))* Lerner Publishing Group.

Jordan, Apple & Posner-Sanchez, Andrea. Berry's Sweet Surprise. Random House Disney Staff et al, illus. 2016. (Little Golden Book Ser.). (ENG.). 24p. (J). (gr. -1-k). 4.99 *(978-0-7364-3444-7(5),* Golden/Disney) Random Hse. Children's Bks.

Judy Delton Family Trust Staff & Delton, Judy. Angel's Mother's Baby. Weber, Jill, illus. 2003. (ENG.). 144p. (J). (gr. 2-5). pap. 10.95 *(978-0-618-36919-5(8))* Houghton Mifflin Harcourt Publishing Co.

Kantorovitz, Sylvie. The Very Tiny Baby. Kantorovitz, Sylvie, illus. 2014. (ENG., Illus.). 32p. (J). (gr. -1-2). lib. bdg. 14.95 *(978-1-58089-445-6(3))* Charlesbridge Publishing, Inc.

—The Very Tiny Baby. 2014. (J). pap. *(978-1-58089-446-3(1))* Charlesbridge Publishing, Inc.

Karre, Elizabeth. The Campaign. 2015. (Opportunity Ser.). (ENG.). 104p. (YA). (gr. 6-12). 34.65 *(978-1-4677-6013-3(7),* Lerner Digital) Lerner Publishing Group.

Katz, Karen. Baby's Box of Family Fun!, Set. Katz, Karen, illus. gif. ed. 2006. (ENG., Illus.). 56p. (J). (gr. -1 — 1). bds. 27.99 *(978-1-4169-2795-2(6),* Little Simon) Little Simon.

—Baby's Day. Katz, Karen, illus. 2007. (ENG., Illus.). 10p. (J). (gr. -1 — 1). 17.99 *(978-1-4169-3580-3(0),* Little Simon) Little Simon.

—Buzz, Buzz, Baby! Katz, Karen, illus. 2014. (ENG., Illus.). 14p. (J). (gr. -1 — 1). bds. 6.99 *(978-1-4424-9313-1(5),* Little Simon) Little Simon.

—Counting Kisses: Lap Edition. Katz, Karen, illus. 2010. (ENG., Illus.). 26p. (J). (gr. -1 — 1). bds. 12.99 *(978-1-4424-0792-3(1),* Little Simon) Little Simon.

—Daddy Hugs. Katz, Karen, illus. 2007. (Classic Board Bks.). (ENG., Illus.). 32p. (J). (gr. -1 — 1). bds. 7.99 *(978-1-4169-4120-0(7),* Little Simon) Little Simon.

—How Does Baby Feel? A Karen Katz Lift-The-Flap Book. Katz, Karen, illus. 2013. (ENG., Illus.). 14p. (J). (gr. -1 — 1). bds. 6.99 *(978-1-4424-5204-6(8),* Little Simon) Little Simon.

—Kiss Baby's Boo-Boo. Katz, Karen, illus. 2016. (ENG., Illus.). 14p. (J). (gr. -1 — 1). bds. 6.99 *(978-1-4814-4208-4(2),* Little Simon) Little Simon.

—Mommy Hugs: Lap Edition. Katz, Karen, illus. 2010. (ENG., Illus.). 26p. (J). (gr. -1 — 1). bds. 12.99 *(978-1-4424-0791-6(3),* Little Simon) Little Simon.

—Now I'm Big! Katz, Karen, illus. 2013. (ENG., Illus.). 32p. (J). (gr. -1-k). 15.99 *(978-1-4169-3547-6(9),* McElderry, Margaret K. Bks.) McElderry, Margaret K. Bks.

—Peek-a-Baby. Katz, Karen, illus. 2007. (ENG., Illus.). 14p. (J). (gr. -1 — 1). bds. 6.99 *(978-1-4169-3622-0(X),* Little Simon) Little Simon.

—Princess Baby on the Go. Katz, Karen, illus. 2010. (Princess Baby Ser.). (ENG., Illus.). 14p. (J). (— 1). 7.99 *(978-0-375-85664-8(1),* Schwartz & Wade Bks.) Random Hse. Children's Bks.

—Roar, Roar, Baby! Katz, Karen, illus. 2015. (ENG., Illus.). 14p. (J). (gr. -1 — 1). bds. 6.99 *(978-1-4814-1788-4(6),* Little Simon) Little Simon.

—Shake It up, Baby! Katz, Karen, illus. 2009. (ENG., Illus.). 14p. (J). (gr. -1 — 1). bds. 7.99 *(978-1-4169-6737-8(0),* Little Simon) Little Simon.

—Splish, Splash, Baby! Katz, Karen, illus. 2015. (ENG., Illus.). 14p. (J). (gr. -1 — 1). bds. 6.99 *(978-1-4814-1789-1(4),* Little Simon) Little Simon.

—Ten Tiny Babies. Katz, Karen, illus. 2011. (Classic Board Bks.). (ENG., Illus.). 32p. (J). (gr. -1-k). bds. 7.99 *(978-1-4424-1394-8(8),* Little Simon) Little Simon.

—Ten Tiny Babies. Katz, Karen, illus. 2008. (ENG., Illus.). 32p. (J). (gr. -1-k). 17.99 *(978-1-4169-3546-9(0),* McElderry, Margaret K. Bks.) McElderry, Margaret K. Bks.

—Ten Tiny Tickles. Katz, Karen, illus. 2008. (Classic Board Bks.). (ACE & ENG., Illus.). 32p. (J). (gr. -1-k). bds. 7.99 *(978-1-4169-5101-8(6),* Little Simon) Little Simon.

—Ten Tiny Tickles. Katz, Karen, illus. 2005. (ENG., Illus.). 32p. (J). (gr. -1-k). 15.99 *(978-0-689-85976-2(7),* McElderry, Margaret K. Bks.) McElderry, Margaret K. Bks.

—Where Is Baby's Belly Button? Katz, Karen, illus. anniv. ed. 2009. (ENG., Illus.). 14p. (J). (gr. -1 — 1). bds. 12.99 *(978-1-4169-8733-8(9),* Little Simon) Little Simon.

—Where Is Baby's Belly Button? 2005. (CHI.). 12p. (J). 6.95 *(978-986-7517-72-2(5))* Shan Jen Publishing Co., Ltd. TWN. Dist: Chinasprout, Inc.

—Where Is Baby's Puppy? Katz, Karen, illus. 2011. (ENG., Illus.). 14p. (J). (gr. -1 — 1). bds. 6.99 *(978-1-4169-8684-3(7),* Little Simon) Little Simon.

—Where Is Baby's Valentine? Katz, Karen, illus. 2006. (ENG., Illus.). 14p. (J). (gr. -1 — 1). bds. 7.99 *(978-1-4169-0971-2(0),* Little Simon) Little Simon.

—Where Is Baby's Yummy Tummy? Katz, Karen, illus. 2011. (ENG., Illus.). 14p. (J). (gr. -1 — 1). bds. 6.99 *(978-1-4424-2165-3(7),* Little Simon) Little Simon.

Keane, Claire. Little Big Girl. 2016. (ENG., Illus.). 32p. (J). (-k). 17.99 *(978-0-8037-3912-3(5),* Dial Bks) Penguin Young Readers Group.

Keats, Ezra Jack. Peter's Chair. 2015. 40p. pap. 7.00 *(978-1-61003-534-7(8))* Center for the Collaborative Classroom.

—Peter's Chair. (J). (gr. -1-3). pap. 12.95 incl. audio Weston Woods Studios, Inc.

Kelly, J. M. Speed of Life. 2016. (ENG.). 352p. (YA). (gr. 9). 17.99 *(978-0-544-74782-1(8),* HMH Books For Young Readers) Houghton Mifflin Harcourt Publishing Co.

Kelly, L. J. R. Sometimes It's Storks. Hilts, Brothers, illus. 2017. (ENG.). 32p. (J). (-k). 16.99 *(978-0-399-25682-0(2),* G.P. Putnam's Sons Books for Young Readers) Penguin Young Readers Group.

Kelly, Mij. The Bump. Allan, Nicholas, illus. 2012. (ENG.). 32p. (J). *(978-1-58925-107-6(5))* Tiger Tales.

Kennedy, Marlane. The Dog Days of Charlotte Hayes. 2009. (ENG., Illus.). 240p. (J). (gr. 3-7). 15.99 *(978-0-06-145241-3(6),* Greenwillow Bks.) HarperCollins Pubs.

H I

Kent, Renee Holmes. Girl Talk, Vol. 7. 2004. (Adventures in Misty Falls Ser.: Vol. 7). (Illus.). 100p. (J). (gr. 4-7). pap. 4.99 *(978-1-56309-455-2(X)*, N017103) New Hope Pubs.

Kirwan, Wednesday. Baby Loves to Boogie! Kirwan, Wednesday, illus. 2014. (ENG., Illus.). 30p. (J). (gr. -1 — 1). bds. 5.99 *(978-1-4814-0383-2(4)*, Little Simon) Little Simon.

Kleven, Elisa. A Monster in the House. 2013. 34p. 16.99 *(978-1-62352-036-6(3))*; pap. 9.99 *(978-1-62352-041-0(X))* IntoPrint Publishing LLC.

Konrad, Marla Stewart. Just Like You: Beautiful Babies Around the World, 1 vol. Wang, Lin, illus. 2010. (ENG.). 32p. (J). (gr. -1-2). 15.99 *(978-0-310-71478-1(8))* Zonderkidz.

Korngold, Jamie S. Mazel Tov! It's a Boy: Mazel Tov! It's a Girl. Finkelstein, Jeff, illus. Finkelstein, Jeff, photos by. 2015. (J). (ENG.). 32p. (gr. -1-1). lib. bdg. 17.95 *(978-1-4677-1957-5(9))*; 6.99 *(978-1-4677-6206-9(7))* Lerner Publishing Group. (Kar-Ben Publishing).

Krensky, Stephen. We Just Had a Baby. Graux, Amélie, illus. 2016. (ENG.). 32p. (gr. -1-2). 14.95 *(978-1-62370-603-6(3))* Capstone Young Readers of Coughlan Cos.

Krishnaswami, Uma. Bringing Asha Home, 1 vol. Jeyaveeran, Ruth & Akib, Jamel, illus. 2006. (ENG.). 32p. (J). (gr. -1-3). 16.95 *(978-1-58430-259-9(3))* Lee & Low Bks., Inc.

Kroll, Virginia. On the Way to Kindergarten. Schlossberg, Elizabeth, illus. 2008. (ENG.). 32p. (J). (gr. -1-k). pap. 6.99 *(978-0-14-241144-5(2)*, Puffin Books) Penguin Young Readers Group.

—She Is Born. 2010. (ENG.). 32p. (J). (gr. -1-3). 11.99 *(978-1-4424-1656-7(4))* Aladdin/Beyond Words.

Krulik, Nancy. Oh, Baby!, 3 vols., No. 3. John and Wendy Staff, illus. 2005. (Katie Kazoo, Switcheroo Ser.: 3). (ENG.). 80p. (J). (gr. 2-4). pap. 4.99 *(978-0-448-42704-1(4)*, Grosset & Dunlap) Penguin Young Readers Group.

Kulman, Andrea M. Adventures of Charlie & Doo-Doo: Not a Baby Anymore, 1 vol. 2009. 53p. pap. 16.95 *(978-1-60703-861-0(7))* America Star Bks.

Laden, Nina. Grow Up! 2003. (ENG., Illus.). 26p. (J). (gr. -1-7). bds. 6.99 *(978-0-8118-3761-3(0))* Chronicle Bks. LLC.

Lane, Queen, illus. & creator. It's Christmas Time (Babytown Storybook) Lane, Queen, creator. 2005. (BABYTOWN Ser.: Bk. 4). 36p. (J). spiral bd. 15.00 *(978-0-9772738-1-2(4))* Quebla.

Lane, Queen & Boykin, Brian, illus. No No Baby (Babytown Storybook) 2005. (BABYTOWN Ser.: Bk. 1). 30p. (J). spiral bd. 15.00 *(978-0-9772738-0-5(6))* Quebla.

Lane, Sandra & Miles, Brenda. The Moment You Were Born: A NICU Story for You & Your Preemie. Hehenberger, Shelly, illus. 2015. (J). *(978-1-4338-1964-3(3)*, Magination Pr.) American Psychological Assn.

Langrish, Katherine. Troll Mill. 2008. (ENG., Illus.). 336p. (YA). (gr. 7). pap. 7.99 *(978-0-06-058309-5(6)*, Eos) HarperCollins Pubs.

Lauzon, Christi. Where's Owen Goin'? 2009. 40p. pap. 14.75 *(978-1-60860-543-9(4)*, Eloquent Bks.) Strategic Book Publishing & Rights Agency (SBPRA).

Layne, Steven L. Love the Baby, 1 vol. Hoyt, Ard, illus. 2007. (ENG.). 32p. (J). (gr. k-k). 16.99 *(978-1-58980-392-3(2))* Pelican Publishing Co., Inc.

—Over Land & Sea: The Story of International Adoption, 1 vol. Bower, Jan, illus. 2005. (ENG.). 32p. (J). (gr. k-3). 16.99 *(978-1-58980-182-0(2))* Pelican Publishing Co., Inc.

Lee, Katie Bertoch. Ma Ma's Hair Is Everywhere. 2008. 28p. pap. 24.95 *(978-1-60563-435-7(2))* America Star Bks.

Lee, Spike & Lee, Tonya Lewis. Please, Baby, Please. Nelson, Kadir, illus. 2007. (Classic Board Bks.). (ENG.). 32p. (J). (gr. -1-k). bds. 7.99 *(978-1-4169-4911-4(9)*, Little Simon) Little Simon.

Leicht, Martin & Neal, Isla. A Stranger Thing. 2013. (Ever-Expanding Universe Ser.: 2). (ENG., Illus.). 288p. (YA). (gr. 9). 17.99 *(978-1-4424-2963-5(1)*, Simon & Schuster Bks. For Young Readers) Simon & Schuster Bks. For Young Readers.

Leigh, Heather. Hey Little Baby! Côté, Geneviève, illus. 2012. (ENG.). 32p. (J). (gr. -1-1). 14.99 *(978-1-4169-8979-0(X)*, Beach Lane Bks.) Beach Lane Bks.

L'Engle, Madeleine. The Other Dog. Davenier, Christine, illus. 2003. 37p. (J). (gr. 2-5). reprint ed. 16.00 *(978-0-7567-6970-3(1))* DIANE Publishing Co.

Leonard, Barry, contrib. by. Rock a Bye Baby. 2006. (Illus.). 61p. (J). reprint ed. 25.00 *(978-1-4223-5246-5(3))* DIANE Publishing Co.

Lewis, J. Patrick & Lewis, Leigh. It's Not the Baby. Frost, Maddie, illus. 2017. (ENG.). 14p. (J). (gr. -1 — 1). bds. 9.99 ***(978-1-68152-194-7(6))*** Amicus.

L'Heureux, Christine. Baby Caillou, I'm Growing! Brignaud, Pierre, illus. 2013. (Baby Caillou Ser.). (ENG.). 10p. (J). (gr. -1-k). bds. *(978-2-89718-041-6(2))* Filmer Ltd.

Linenthal, Peter, illus. Look at Baby's House! 2008. (ENG.). 18p. (J). (gr. k — 1). bds. 6.99 *(978-0-525-42061-3(4)*, Dutton Books for Young Readers) Penguin Young Readers Group.

Llewellyn, Claire. Go Away, Baby!, 1 vol. Lovsin, Polona, illus. 2013. (Start Reading Ser.). (ENG.). 24p. (gr. k-1). pap. 7.95 *(978-1-4765-3183-0(8))*; pap. 41.94 *(978-1-4765-3214-1(1))* Capstone Press of Coughlan Cos.

—Good Night, Baby!, 1 vol. Lovsin, Polona, illus. 2013. (Start Reading Ser.). (ENG.). 24p. (gr. k-1). pap. 7.95 *(978-1-4765-3184-7(6))*; pap. 41.94 *(978-1-4765-3216-5(8))* Capstone Press of Coughlan Cos.

Lloyd-Jones, Sally. His Royal Highness, King Baby: A Terrible True Story. Roberts, David, illus. 2017. (ENG.). 48p. (J). (gr. -1-3). 16.99 ***(978-0-7636-9793-8(1))*** Candlewick Pr.

—How to Be a Baby: By Me, the Big Sister. Heap, Sue, illus. 2007. (How to Ser.). (ENG.). 40p. (J). (gr. -1-3). 16.99 *(978-0-375-83843-9(0)*, Schwartz & Wade Bks.) Random Hse. Children's Bks.

—How to Be a Baby... by Me, the Big Sister. Heap, Sue, illus. 2011. (How to Ser.). (ENG.). 40p. (J). (gr. -1-3). pap. 7.99 *(978-0-375-87388-1(0)*, Dragonfly Bks.) Random Hse. Children's Bks.

Loeffelholz, Sarah, illus. Can You Just Imagine. 2007. 40p. (J). 14.95 *(978-0-9786850-1-0(6))* Overdue Bks.

London, Jonathan. Froggy's Baby Sister. Remkiewicz, Frank, illus. 2005. (Froggy Ser.). (ENG.). 32p. (J). (gr. -1-k). pap. 6.99 *(978-0-14-240342-6(3)*, Puffin Books) Penguin Young Readers Group.

Long, Melinda. Pirates Don't Change Diapers. Shannon, David, illus. 2007. (ENG.). 44p. (J). (gr. -1-3). 17.99 *(978-0-15-205353-6(0))* Houghton Mifflin Harcourt Publishing Co.

Lovins, Jennifer O. Opihi Baby. 2008. 32p. pap. 14.95 *(978-1-57306-285-5(5))* Bess Pr., Inc.

Luiz, Fernando, illus. Babies Love the Little Things. 2009. (ENG.). 10p. (J). (gr. -1). 7.95 *(978-1-58117-846-3(8)*, Intervisual/Piggy Toes) Bendon, Inc.

Mackall, Dandi Daley. There's a Baby in There!, 0 vols. Whitt, Carlynn, illus. 2012. (ENG.). 32p. (J). (gr. -1-3). 16.99 *(978-0-7614-6191-3(4)*, 9780761461913, Amazon Children's Publishing) Amazon Publishing.

Macken, JoAnn Early. Baby Says Moo! Walker, David, illus. 2015. (ENG.). 30p. (J). (gr. -1 — 1). bds. 8.99 *(978-1-4847-2098-1(9))* Hyperion Bks. for Children.

MacKenzie, Catherine. Going to the Doctor. rev. ed. 2006. (My First Experiences Ser.). (ENG.). 16p. (J). (gr. -1-3). pap. 3.99 *(978-1-85792-608-8(0)*, 1620dddb-8a38-40bb-af49-bb35654fdf5a) Christian Focus Pubns. GBR. Dist: Bookmasters Distribution.

MacLachlan, Patricia. More Perfect Than the Moon. 2005. 16.00 *(978-0-7569-5437-6(1))* Perfection Learning Corp.

Madison's Descent: A Child's Journey. collector's ed. 2004. (J). 75.00 *(978-0-9752516-0-7(0))* Otis & Randolph Pr.

Magabala Books Staff. Aussie Toddlers Can. Delios, Kim, photos by. l.t. ed. 2006. (Illus.). 10p. (J). bds. *(978-1-875641-88-8(2))* Magabala Bks.

Magsamen, Sandra. Welcome Little One. 2015. (ENG., Illus.). 32p. (J). (gr. 3-8). 16.99 *(978-1-4926-1930-7(2)*, Sourcebooks Jabberwocky) Sourcebooks, Inc.

Manushkin, Fran. Big Brothers Are the Best, 1 vol. Richards, Kirsten, illus. 2012. (Fiction Picture Bks.). (ENG.). 24p. (gr. -1 — 1). 6.95 *(978-1-4048-7224-0(8))*; lib. bdg. 22.65 *(978-1-4048-7137-3(3))* Picture Window Bks. (Fiction Picture Bks.).

—Big Sisters Are the Best, 1 vol. Richards, Kirsten, illus. 2012. (Fiction Picture Bks.). (ENG.). 24p. (gr. -1 — 1). 6.95 *(978-1-4048-7225-7(6))*; lib. bdg. 22.65 *(978-1-4048-7138-0(1))* Picture Window Bks. (Fiction Picture Bks.).

Manzano, Sonia. A Box Full of Kittens. Phelan, Matt, illus. 2007. (ENG.). 40p. (J). (gr. -1-3). 17.99 *(978-0-689-83089-1(0)*, Atheneum Bks. for Young Readers) Simon & Schuster Children's Publishing.

Marr, Melissa & Airgood, Ellen. Bunny Roo, I Love You. White, Teagan, illus. 2015. (ENG.). 32p. (J). (gr. -1 — 1). 16.99 *(978-0-399-16742-3(0)*, Nancy Paulsen Books) Penguin Young Readers Group.

Martins, Isabel Minhós. When I Was Born. Matoso, Madalena, illus. 2011. (ENG.). 32p. (gr. -1-3). 12.95 *(978-1-85437-958-0(5))* Tate Publishing, Ltd. GBR. Dist: Abrams, Inc.

McAllister, Margaret. 15 Things Not to Do with a Baby. Sterling, Holly, illus. 2015. (15 Things Not to Do Ser.). (ENG.). 32p. (J). (gr. -1-1). 17.99 *(978-1-84780-752-6(6)*, Frances Lincoln Children's Bks.) Quarto Publishing Group UK GBR. Dist: Hachette Bk. Group.

McC, Meg. Goodnap, Brewer, 1 vol. 2010. 32p. 24.95 *(978-1-4512-1447-5(2))* PublishAmerica, Inc.

Mccain-Buzzelli, Vic. The Adventures of Milly & Mikey: Womb Mates Book #1. 2010. 20p. pap. 10.49 *(978-1-4520-4654-9(9))* AuthorHouse.

McElroy, Jean. Let's Go, Baby! Vase, Catherine, illus. 2010. (ENG.). 12p. (J). (gr. -1 — 1). 4.99 *(978-1-4424-0901-9(0)*, Little Simon) Little Simon.

McElroy, Jean & Childrens Books Staff. Let's Count 1 2 3! 2011. (ENG.). 12p. (J). (gr. -1 — 1). 4.99 *(978-1-4424-1198-2(8)*, Little Simon) Little Simon.

Mchugh, Gelolo. Baby's House. 2010. (Little Golden Book Ser.). (ENG., Illus.). 24p. (J). (gr. -1-2). 4.99 *(978-0-375-85460-6(6)*, Golden Bks.) Random Hse. Children's Bks.

McHugh, Gelolo. Little Golden Book Babies. 2016. (Little Golden Book Favorites Ser.). (ENG., Illus.). 80p. (J). (gr. -1-k). 7.99 *(978-0-553-53668-3(0)*, Golden Bks.) Random Hse. Children's Bks.

McKay, Hilary. Caddy's World. 2013. (ENG.). 288p. (J). (gr. 5-9). pap. 6.99 *(978-1-4424-4106-4(2)*, McElderry, Margaret K. Bks.) McElderry, Margaret K. Bks.

McKay, Sindy. We Both Read-Jack & the Toddler. Zivoin, Jennifer, illus. 2011. (ENG.). 44p. (J). 9.95 *(978-1-60115-249-7(3))*; pap. 4.99 *(978-1-60115-250-3(7))* Treasure Bay, Inc.

McMahon, Kathleen A. Mister Pudge Meets Baby Beth. 2011. 44p. 22.00 *(978-1-4269-5800-7(5))* Trafford Publishing.

McNamara, Joan. Borya & the Burps: An Eastern European Adoption Story. Majewski, Dawn, illus. 2005. 30p. (J). (gr. -1 — 1). 18.00 *(978-0-944934-31-9(5))* Perspectives Pr., Inc.

McPike, Elizabeth. Little Bitty Friends. Barton, Patrice, illus. 2016. (ENG.). 32p. (J). (— 1). 16.99 *(978-0-399-17255-7(6)*, G.P. Putnam's Sons Books for Young Readers) Penguin Young Readers Group.

—Little Sleepyhead. Barton, Patrice, illus. 2015. (ENG.). 26p. (J). (— 1). 16.99 *(978-0-399-16240-4(2)*, G.P. Putnam's Sons Books for Young Readers) Penguin Young Readers Group.

McQuinn, Anna. Lola le Lee Al Pequeño Leo. Beardshaw, Rosalind, illus. 2013. (SPA & ENG.). 28p. (J). (-k). pap. 7.95 *(978-1-58089-599-6(9))* Charlesbridge Publishing, Inc.

—Lola Reads to Leo. Beardshaw, Rosalind, illus. 2012. (ENG.). 28p. (J). (-k). 15.95 *(978-1-58089-403-6(8))*; pap. 6.95 *(978-1-58089-404-3(6))* Charlesbridge Publishing, Inc.

—Lola Reads to Leo. 2012. pap. 19.95 incl. audio compact disk *(978-0-8045-4236-4(8))* Spoken Arts, Inc.

McQuinn, Anna, et al. A Leo le Gusta Bebelandia. Hearson, Ruth, illus. 2015. (SPA & ENG.). 24p. (J). (— 1). lib. bdg. 9.95 *(978-1-58089-704-4(5))* Charlesbridge Publishing, Inc.

McQuinn, Anna, et al. Lola Reads to Leo: Lola le Lee Al Pequeño Leo. Beardshaw, Rosalind, illus. 2017. (SPA & ENG.). (J). pap. ***(978-1-63289-028-3(3))*** Charlesbridge Publishing, Inc.

Melmed, Laura Krauss. The Rainbabies. LaMarche, Jim, illus. 2004. (ENG.). 32p. (J). (gr. -1-3). pap. 6.99 *(978-0-688-15113-3(2))* HarperCollins Pubs.

Menard, Michele R. The Cherub in the Lily Field. 2013. 50p. pap. 13.50 *(978-0-9887969-3-5(7))* Four Menards, The.

Merritt, Kate. Indestructibles: Jingle Baby. 2016. (Indestructibles Ser.). (ENG., Illus.). 12p. (J). pap. 5.95 *(978-0-7611-8726-4(X))* Workman Publishing Co., Inc.

Merritt, Kate, illus. Indestructibles: Baby Night-Night. 2014. (Indestructibles Ser.). (ENG.). 12p. (J). pap. 5.95 *(978-0-7611-8182-8(2)*, 18182) Workman Publishing Co., Inc.

—Indestructibles: Baby Peekaboo. 2014. (Indestructibles Ser.). (ENG.). 12p. (J). pap. 5.95 *(978-0-7611-8181-1(4)*, 18181) Workman Publishing Co., Inc.

—Indestructibles: Beach Baby. 2016. (Indestructibles Ser.). (ENG.). 12p. (J). pap. 5.95 *(978-0-7611-8732-5(4))* Workman Publishing Co., Inc.

Meyers, Susan. Everywhere Babies. Frazee, Marla, illus. (ENG.). 30p. (J). 2016. (— 1). bds. 8.99 *(978-0-544-79120-6(7)*, HMH Books For Young Readers) 2011. (gr. -1 — 1). bds. 11.99 *(978-0-547-51074-3(8))* Houghton Mifflin Harcourt Publishing Co.

—Everywhere Babies. Frazee, Marla, illus. 2004. (ENG.). 30p. (J). (gr. k — 1). bds. 6.95 *(978-0-15-205315-4(8))* Houghton Mifflin Harcourt Publishing Co.

Michels, Dia. Look What I See! Where Can I Be? With My Animal Friends. Bowles, Michael J. N. & Bowles, Michael J. N., photos by. 2007. (ENG., Illus.). 32p. (J). 9.95 *(978-1-930775-08-4(3))* Platypus Media, L.L.C.

Michels, Dia L. Look What I See! Where Can I Be? At Home. Bowles, Michael J. N., photos by. 2005. (ENG., Illus.). 32p. (J). (gr. -1-12). 9.95 *(978-1-930775-06-0(7))* Platypus Media, L.L.C.

—Look What I See! Where Can I Be? In the Neighborhood. Bowles, Michael J. N., illus. 2005. (Look What I See! Where Can I Be? Ser.: Vol. 1). (ENG.). 32p. (J). (gr. -1-12). 9.95 *(978-1-930775-00-8(8))* Platypus Media, L.L.C.

Michels-Gualtieri, Akaela S. I Was Born to Be a Sister. Ramsey, Marcy Dunn, illus. 2005. (ENG.). 32p. (J). (gr. 4-7). 9.95 incl. lp *(978-1-930775-11-4(3))* Platypus Media, L.L.C.

Millard, Glenda. A Small Free Kiss in the Dark. 2010. (ENG.). 192p. (YA). (gr. 7-18). pap. 16.95 *(978-0-8234-2264-7(X))* Holiday Hse., Inc.

Miller, Margaret. Baby Food. Miller, Margaret, photos by. 2009. (Look Baby! Bks.). (ENG., Illus.). 14p. (J). (gr. -1 — 1). bds. 4.99 *(978-1-4169-8996-7(X)*, Little Simon) Little Simon.

—What's on My Head? Miller, Margaret, photos by. 2009. (Look Baby! Bks.). (ENG., Illus.). 14p. (J). (gr. -1 — 1). bds. 4.99 *(978-1-4169-8995-0(1)*, Little Simon) Little Simon.

Mills, Claudia. The Nora Notebooks, Book 2: the Trouble with Babies. Kath, Katie, illus. 2016. (Nora Notebooks Ser.). (ENG.). 192p. (J). (gr. 2-5). 12.99 *(978-0-385-39165-8(X)*, Knopf Bks. for Young Readers) Random Hse. Children's Bks.

Molitoris, Cathy. I've Got Music! McConnell, Sarah, illus. 2006. (J). *(978-0-439-88620-8(1))* Scholastic, Inc.

Moore, Jodi. When a Dragon Moves in Again. McWilliam, Howard, illus. 2015. (When a Dragon Moves In Ser.). (ENG.). 32p. (J). (gr. k-2). 17.95 *(978-1-936261-35-2(9))* Flashlight Pr.

Morgan, Cythia. The Day I Met You & You Met Me! Cable, Annette, illus. 2008. 32p. pap. 5.95 *(978-0-9802497-0-5(8))* King'S Land Pr. Inc.

Morgan, Gwyn & Owen, Dai. Babi Ben. 2005. (WEL., Illus.). 64p. pap. *(978-1-85596-611-6(5))* Dref Wen.

Morris, Kerry Nicole. The Baby Who Just... WON't Sleep! Parker's Story. 2004. 35p. pap. 24.95 *(978-1-4137-3724-0(2))* PublishAmerica, Inc.

Munsch, Robert. Alligator Baby. 2004. (Illus.). (J). (gr. k-3). spiral bd. *(978-0-616-01731-9(6))*; spiral bd. *(978-0-616-01730-2(8))* Canadian National Institute for the Blind/Institut National Canadien pour les Aveugles.

Murphy, Mary Elizabeth. I Kissed the Baby! Murphy, Mary Elizabeth, illus. 2004. (ENG., Illus.). 24p. (J). (— 1). bds. 6.99 *(978-0-7636-2443-9(8))* Candlewick Pr.

Nevin, Judy Carey. What Daddies Like. Six, Stephanie, illus. 2017. (ENG.). 32p. (J). (gr. -1-3). 16.99 *(978-1-4998-0197-2(1))* Little Bee Books Inc.

Nichols, Lori. Maple. Nichols, Lori, illus. 2014. (ENG., Illus.). 32p. (J). (gr. -1-k). 16.99 *(978-0-399-16085-1(X)*, Nancy Paulsen Books) Penguin Young Readers Group.

Noonimals: Presents the New Baby. rev. ed. 2007. (Illus.). 40p. (J). per. 14.99 *(978-0-9796832-0-6(3))* Nooni Publishing.

North, Sherry. Because You Are My Baby. Hall, Marcellus, illus. 2008. (ENG.). 32p. (J). (gr. -1-1). 16.95 *(978-0-8109-9482-9(8)*, Abrams Bks. for Young Readers) Abrams, Inc.

Novak, Matt. A Wish for You. Novak, Matt, illus. 2010. (Illus.). 32p. (J). 16.99 *(978-0-06-155202-1(X)*, Greenwillow Bks.) HarperCollins Pubs.

Nye, Naomi Shihab. Baby Radar. Carpenter, Nancy, illus. 2003. 32p. (J). lib. bdg. 16.89 *(978-0-688-15949-8(4))* HarperCollins Pubs.

O'Brien, Caragh M. Birthmarked. 2010. (Birthmarked Trilogy Ser.: 1). (ENG., Illus.). 368p. (YA). (gr. 7-18). 18.99 *(978-1-59643-569-8(0)*, 9781596435698) Roaring Brook Pr.

O'Brien, Melanie. No More Pacifiers! With Disappearing Pacifiers! Enright, Amanda, illus. 2008. (ENG.). 18p. (J). (gr. -1-k). 10.95 *(978-1-58117-684-1(8)*, Intervisual/Piggy Toes) Bendon, Inc.

O'Connell, Rebecca. The Baby Goes Beep. Wilson-Max, Ken, illus. 2010. (ENG.). 16p. (J). (gr. -1 — 1). bds. 7.99 *(978-0-8075-0508-3(0))* Whitman, Albert & Co.

—Baby Parade. Poole, Susie, illus. 2017. (ENG.). 24p. (J). (gr. -1 — 1). bds. 7.99 ***(978-0-8075-0515-1(3))*** Whitman, Albert & Co.

O'Connell, Rebecca. Baby Party. Poole, Susie, illus. (ENG.). 24p. (J). (gr. -1 — 1). 2017. bds. 7.99 ***(978-0-8075-0514-4(5))*** 2015. 15.99 *(978-0-8075-0512-0(9))* Whitman, Albert & Co.

O'Leary, Sara. Where You Came From. Morstad, Julie, illus. 2008. (ENG.). 32p. (J). (gr. -1-3). 16.95 *(978-1-894965-46-0(9))* Simply Read Bks. CAN. Dist: Ingram Publisher Services.

Oppel, Kenneth. The Nest. Klassen, Jon, illus. (ENG.). (J). (gr. 5). 2016. 272p. pap. 7.99 *(978-1-4814-3233-7(8))* 2015. 256p. 16.99 *(978-1-4814-3232-0(X))* Simon & Schuster Bks. For Young Readers. (Simon & Schuster Bks. For Young Readers).

Oppel, Kenneth & Klassen, Jon. The Nest. Klassen, Jon, illus. 2016. (ENG., Illus.). 272p. (J). (gr. 5). 18.40 *(978-0-606-39233-4(5))* Turtleback Bks.

Oppenheim, Joanne. Wake up, Baby! Lynn, Sweat, illus. 2015. (ENG.). 34p. (J). pap. 11.95 *(978-1-899694-56-3(0)*, ipicturebooks) ibooks, Inc.

Orgill, Roxane & Orgill. Go-Go Baby!, 1 vol. Salerno, Steven, tr. Salerno, Steven, illus. 2004. (ENG.). 32p. (J). 14.95 *(978-0-7614-5157-0(9))* Marshall Cavendish Corp.

Orloff, Karen Kaufman. I Wanna New Room. Catrow, David, III, illus. 2010. (ENG.). 32p. (J). (gr. k-3). 16.99 *(978-0-399-25405-5(6)*, G.P. Putnam's Sons Books for Young Readers) Penguin Young Readers Group.

Ormerod, Jan. The Baby Swap. Joyner, Andrew, illus. 2015. (ENG.). 32p. (J). (gr. -1-1). 16.99 *(978-1-4814-1914-7(5)*, Little Simon) Little Simon.

Ostrovski, Emil. The Paradox of Vertical Flight. 2014. (ENG.). 272p. (YA). (gr. 9). pap. 9.99 *(978-0-06-223853-5(1)*, Greenwillow Bks.) HarperCollins Pubs.

Oud, Pauline. Big Sister Sarah. Oud, Pauline, illus. 2013. (ENG., Illus.). 32p. (J). (gr. -1-k). 15.95 *(978-1-60537-151-1(3))* Cobblestone Publishing Co.

Packard, Mary. The New Baby. Haley, Amanda, illus. 2004. (My First Reader Ser.). (ENG.). 32p. (J). (gr. k-1). pap. 3.95 *(978-0-516-25506-4(1)*, Children's Pr.) Scholastic Library Publishing.

Park, Barbara. Junie B. Jones & a Little Monkey Business, Vol. 2. unabr. ed. 2004. (Junie B. Jones Ser.: Vol. 2). 68p. (J). (gr. k-3). pap. 17.00 incl. audio *(978-0-8072-0779-6(9)*, LFTR 238 SP, Listening Library) Random Hse. Audio Publishing Group.

—Ma! There's Nothing to Do Here! A Word from Your Baby-in-Waiting. Garofoli, Viviana, illus. 2008. (Picture Book Ser.). (ENG.). 40p. (J). (gr. -1-2). 15.99 *(978-0-375-83852-1(X)*, Random Hse. Bks. for Young Readers) Random Hse. Children's Bks.

Parker, Amy. A Night Night Prayer, 1 vol. Pedler, Caroline, illus. 2014. (Night Night Ser.). (ENG.). 20p. (J). bds. 9.99 *(978-1-4003-2431-6(9))* Nelson, Thomas Inc.

Parragon Publishing Staff. I'm a Big Sister. (Big Brother/Sister Ser.). 32p. *(978-1-4054-5024-9(X))* Parragon, Inc.

Partis, Joanne. Look at Me! Partis, Joanne, illus. 2007. (Baby Bks.). (ENG., Illus.). 10p. (J). (gr. k — 1). 4.99 *(978-1-84458-365-2(1))* Pavilion Bks. GBR. Dist: Independent Pubs. Group.

Paschkis, Julie. Mooshka, a Quilt Story, 1 vol. Paschkis, Julie, illus. 2012. (ENG., Illus.). 32p. (J). 16.95 *(978-1-56145-620-8(9))* Peachtree Pubs.

Patricelli, Leslie. Potty/Bacinica. Patricelli, Leslie, illus. 2016. (Leslie Patricelli Board Bks.). (ENG & SPA., Illus.). (J). (— 1). bds. 6.99 *(978-0-7636-8777-9(4))* Candlewick Pr.

—Tickle. Patricelli, Leslie, illus. 2014. (Leslie Patricelli Board Bks.). (ENG., Illus.). 26p. (J). (— 1). bds. 6.99 *(978-0-7636-6322-3(0))* Candlewick Pr.

—Toot. Patricelli, Leslie, illus. 2014. (Leslie Patricelli Board Bks.). (ENG., Illus.). 24p. (J). (— 1). bds. 6.99 *(978-0-7636-6321-6(2))* Candlewick Pr.

—Tubby. Patricelli, Leslie, illus. 2010. (Leslie Patricelli Board Bks.). (ENG., Illus.). 28p. (J). (— 1). bds. 6.99 *(978-0-7636-4567-0(2))* Candlewick Pr.

—Yummy Yucky/¡Ñam! ¡Puaj! Patricelli, Leslie, illus. 2016. (Leslie Patricelli Board Bks.). (ENG & SPA., Illus.). (J). (— 1). bds. 6.99 *(978-0-7636-8776-2(6))* Candlewick Pr.

Paulits, John. Philip & the Case of the Mistaken Identity & Philip & the Baby. 2007. (ENG.). 150p. (YA). pap. 10.95 *(978-1-59705-897-1(1))* Wings ePress, Inc.

Penfold, Alexandra. Eat, Sleep, Poop. Massey, Jane, illus. 2016. (ENG.). 40p. (J). (-k). 16.99 *(978-0-385-75503-0(1)*, Knopf Bks. for Young Readers) Random Hse. Children's Bks.

—We Are Brothers, We Are Friends. Kaban, Eda, illus. 2017. (ENG.). 32p. (J). 16.99 *(978-0-374-30201-6(4)*, 9780374302016, Farrar, Straus & Giroux (BYR)) Farrar, Straus & Giroux.

Pennypacker, Sara. Completely Clementine. Frazee, Marla, illus. 2016. (Clementine Book Ser.). (ENG.). 208p. (J). (gr. 1-3). pap. 5.99 *(978-1-4231-2438-2(3))* Hyperion Bks. for Children.

Peyo. Welcome, Baby Smurf! Peyo, illus. 2014. (Smurfs Classic Ser.). (ENG., Illus.). 24p. (J). (gr. -1-2). pap. 3.99 *(978-1-4424-9542-5(1)*, Simon Spotlight) Simon Spotlight.

—Why Do You Cry, Baby Smurf? Peyo, illus. 2013. (Smurfs Classic Ser.). (ENG., Illus.). 32p. (J). (gr. k-2). 15.99 *(978-1-4424-6193-2(4))*; pap. 3.99 *(978-1-4424-6191-8(8))* Simon Spotlight. (Simon Spotlight).

Phillips, Samantha. Crow: Part 1, Vol. 1. 2006. (ENG., Illus.). 24p. (YA). 3.50 *(978-0-9785891-0-3(6)*, 0001) MANGACANDY, LLC.

Piggy Toes Press, creator. Color Party! 2007. (ENG., Illus.). 12p. (gr. -1-k). bds. 7.99 *(978-1-58117-585-1(X)*, Intervisual/Piggy Toes) Bendon, Inc.

—Giggle & Grow Baby's Body! 2007. (ENG., Illus.). 14p. (gr. -1-k). bds. 7.99 *(978-1-58117-586-8(8)*, Intervisual/Piggy Toes) Bendon, Inc.

Pilkey, Dav. The Adventures of Super Diaper Baby. 2014. (Super Diaper Baby Ser.: 1). lib. bdg. 20.85 *(978-0-606-36273-3(8))* Turtleback Bks.

Posner-Sanchez, Andrea. Two Princesses & a Baby (Disney Junior: Sofia the First) RH Disney Staff & Studio IBOIX Staff, illus. 2015. (Little Golden Book Ser.). (ENG.). 24p. (J). (-k). 4.99 *(978-0-7364-3358-7(9)*, Golden/Disney) Random Hse. Children's Bks.

Pryor, Bonnie. Jenny's New Baby Sister. 2013. (ENG.). 24p. (J). (gr. -1-3). 11.99 *(978-1-4424-8875-5(1)*, Atheneum Bks. for Young Readers) Simon & Schuster Children's Publishing.

Publications International Ltd. Staff, ed. Sesame St Let's Go to School First Look & Find. 2013. 18p. (J). bds. 7.98 *(978-1-4508-2933-5(3)*, 1450829333) Phoenix International Publications, Inc.

Puck. Babies Around the World. Lemay, Violet, illus. 2017. (ENG.). 20p. (J). (gr. -1 — 1). bds. 7.95 *(978-1-938093-87-6(9)*, Duo Pr. Llc (US)) Duo Pr. LLC.

Puttock, Simon. The Day the Baby Blew Away. Gale, Cathy, illus. 2004. (ENG.). 32p. (J). (gr. k-4). 15.95 *(978-1-84507-046-5(1)*, Frances Lincoln) Quarto Publishing Group UK GBR. Dist: Hachette Bk. Group.

Rabe, Tish. Oh, Baby, the Places You'll Go! Seuss, Dr., illus. 2015. (ENG.). 32p. (J). (gr. k-12). 9.99 *(978-0-553-52057-6(1)*, Random Hse. Bks. for Young Readers) Random Hse. Children's Bks.

Raiku, Makoto. Animal Land 7. 2013. (Animal Land Ser.). (ENG., Illus.). 200p. (gr. 8-12). pap. 10.99 *(978-1-61262-249-1(6))* Kodansha America, Inc.

Reid, Camilla. Lulu & the Noisy Baby. Busby, Ailie, illus. 2016. (Lulu Ser.). (ENG.). 20p. (J). (gr. -1-k). 12.99 *(978-1-4088-2818-2(9)*, 9781408828182, Bloomsbury USA Childrens) Bloomsbury Publishing USA.

Renard Roach, Marietta. Come, Bless the Baby. 2006. 28p. pap. 21.95 incl. audio compact disk *(978-0-9768626-0-4(3))* Aaduna.

Repkin, Mark. Mommy Breastfeeds My Baby Brother/ Mama Amamanta A Mi Hermanito. Moneysmith, David, illus. 2011.Tr. of Mama Amamanta A Mi Hermanito. 24p. (J). pap. 9.99 *(978-0-9816538-1-5(2))* Istoria Hse.

Reynolds, Shelly. Baby Steps. 2009. 28p. pap. 15.99 *(978-1-4415-1243-7(8))* Xlibris Corp.

Rhoton, Lesa. Angus & the Triplets. Switzer, Bobby, illus. 2006. 28p. (J). (gr. -1-3). per. 13.95 *(978-1-58939-852-8(1))* Virtualbookworm.com Publishing, Inc.

Richmond, Marianne. You're a Big Brother. 2017. (ENG., Illus.). 32p. (J). (-3). 8.99 *(978-1-4926-5049-2(8)*, 9781492650492, Sourcebooks Jabberwocky) Sourcebooks, Inc.

—You're a Big Sister. 2017. (ENG., Illus.). 32p. (J). (-3). 8.99 *(978-1-4926-5051-5(X)*, 9781492650515, Sourcebooks Jabberwocky) Sourcebooks, Inc.

Rippin, Sally. The Big Sister: Billie B. Brown. Fukuoka, Aki, illus. 2014. (ENG.). 48p. (J). pap. 4.99 *(978-1-61067-184-2(8))* Kane Miller.

Roberts, Willo Davis. The One Left Behind. 2007. (ENG., Illus.). 144p. (J). (gr. 3-7). pap. 7.99 *(978-0-689-85083-7(2)*, Aladdin) Simon & Schuster Children's Publishing.

Rodgers, Phillip W. When Was God Born?, 1 vol. 2008. (Discovering God Ser.). 32p. (J). 12.99 *(978-0-8254-3608-6(7))* Kregel Pubns.

Rokhsar, Lillian. Babytionary. Bell, Liesl, illus. 2012. (ENG.). 40p. 17.99 *(978-0-9884922-0-2(2))* Begoo Bks., LLC.

Root, Phyllis. Flip, Flap, Fly! A Book for Babies Everywhere. Walker, David, illus. 2011. (ENG.). 32p. (J). (gr. -1 — 1). bds. 6.99 *(978-0-7636-5325-5(X))* Candlewick Pr.

Rose, Phyllis & de Brunhoff, Laurent. Babar & the New Baby. 2013. (ENG., Illus.). 22p. (J). (gr. -1 — 1). bds. 7.95 *(978-1-4197-0620-2(9)*, Abrams Appleseed) Abrams, Inc.

Rosemary Wells. McDuff & the Baby. Rusan Jeffers, illus. 2014. 28p. pap. 9.99 *(978-1-61003-384-8(1))* Center for the Collaborative Classroom.

Rosenthal, Amy Krouse. Little Miss, Big Sis. Reynolds, Peter H., illus. 2015. (ENG.). 40p. (J). (gr. -1-3). 17.99 *(978-0-06-230203-8(5))* HarperCollins Pubs.

Rosoff, Meg. Moose Baby. Ercolini, David, illus. 2017. (J). ***(978-0-399-16664-8(5)***, Putnam Juvenile) Penguin Publishing Group.

Ross, Tony & Ross, Tony. I Want a Sister! 2013. (Illus.). 32p. (J). (gr. -1-3). 16.95 *(978-1-4677-2047-2(X))* Andersen Pr. GBR. Dist: Lerner Publishing Group.

Rossetti-Shustak, Bernadette. I Love You Through & Through: Board Book & Plush. Church, Caroline Jayne, illus. 2014. (ENG.). 24p. (J). (— 1). 14.99 *(978-0-545-64792-2(4)*, Cartwheel Bks.) Scholastic, Inc.

Royal, Stephen. The Journey Inside the Womb. 2012. (Illus.). 16p. pap. 18.30 *(978-1-4772-2604-9(4))* AuthorHouse.

Russo, Marisabina. Peter Is Just a Baby. 2011. (ENG., Illus.). 32p. (J). 16.00 *(978-0-8028-5384-4(6))*, Eerdmans Bks For Young Readers) Eerdmans, William B. Publishing Co.

Ryan, Darlene & Manchester, Peter. Kisses, Kisses, Kisses. 2004. (Illus.). 24p. (J). *(978-1-55131-092-3(9))* Univ. of New Brunswick, Dept. of Graphic Services.

Sacks, Nathan & Paty, Miss. May's Wild Walk. MissPaty, illus. 2017. (Whiskers Sisters Ser.: 1). (ENG.). 40p. (J). (gr. k-3). 26.65 ***(978-1-5124-2527-7(3)***, Graphic Universe™) Lerner Publishing Group.

Salerno, Steven. Wild Child. 2015. (ENG., Illus.). 32p. (J). (gr. -1-3). 16.95 *(978-1-4197-1662-1(X)*, Abrams Bks. for Young Readers) Abrams, Inc.

Santomero, Angela C. Big Brother Daniel. Fruchter, Jason, illus. 2015. (Daniel Tiger's Neighborhood Ser.). (ENG.). 14p. (J). (gr. -1-k). bds. 5.99 *(978-1-4814-3172-9(2)*, Simon Spotlight) Simon Spotlight.

Saunders, Katie. Olive the Alien. 2016. (ENG., Illus.). 32p. (J). (gr. -1-1). 16.99 *(978-1-4998-0195-8(5))* Little Bee Books Inc.

Schaefer, Lola. One Special Day. Meserve, Jessica, illus. 2012. (Story for Big Brothers & Sisters Ser.). (ENG.). 40p. (J). (gr. -1-k). 16.99 *(978-1-4231-3760-3(4))* Hyperion Pr.

Schieldt, Corine. Somebody's Gotta Get Rid of That Vacuum. Schieldt, Jodi, illus. 2008. 24p. per. 24.95 *(978-1-4241-9121-5(1))* America Star Bks.

Schoenberg, Jane. The Baby Hustle: An Interactive Book with Wiggles & Giggles! Conrad, Liz, illus. 2010. (ENG.). 12p. (J). (gr. -1 — 1). bds. 7.99 *(978-1-4169-8050-6(4)*, Little Simon) Little Simon.

Scott, Kieran. This Is So Not Happening. 2013. (He's So/She's So Trilogy Ser.). (ENG., Illus.). 320p. (YA). (gr. 7). pap. 9.99 *(978-1-4169-9956-0(6)*, Simon & Schuster Bks. For Young Readers) Simon & Schuster Bks. For Young Readers.

Scott, Lucy. Busy Busy! Scott, Lucy, illus. 2016. (ENG., Illus.). 32p. (J). (gr. -1-k). 15.99 *(978-1-939547-25-5(3))* Creston Bks.

Seuss, Dr. Oh, Baby! Go, Baby! Gerardi, Jan, illus. 2010. (Dr. Seuss Nursery Collection). (ENG.). 14p. (J). (gr. k — 1). 11.99 *(978-0-375-85738-6(9)*, Random Hse. Bks. for Young Readers) Random Hse. Children's Bks.

Shapiro, Jody Fickes. Family Lullaby. Felstead, Cathie, illus. 2007. 40p. (J). (gr. -1). lib. bdg. 17.89 *(978-0-06-051483-9(3))* HarperCollins Pubs.

Shields, Carol Diggory. Baby's Got the Blues. Tobia, Lauren, illus. 2014. (ENG.). 32p. (J). (gr. -1-2). 16.99 *(978-0-7636-3260-1(0))* Candlewick Pr.

Shields, Gillian. When the World Was Waiting for You. Currey, Anna, illus. (ENG.). (J). (gr. -1 — 1). 2012. 26p. bds. 7.99 *(978-1-59990-849-6(2)*, 9781599908496) 2011. 32p. 14.99 *(978-1-59990-531-0(0)*, 9781599905310) Bloomsbury Publishing USA. (Bloomsbury USA Childrens).

—When the World Was Waiting for You Baby Book. Currey, Anna, illus. 2013. (ENG.). 32p. (J). (gr. -1-1). 22.99 *(978-1-4088-4213-3(0)*, 9781408842133, Bloomsbury USA Childrens) Bloomsbury Publishing USA.

Shields, Gillian & Reed, Nathan. Angel Baby. 2006. (ENG., Illus.). 24p. (J). (gr. -1-k). pap. 9.99 *(978-0-00-718006-6(3)*, HarperCollins Children's Bks.) HarperCollins Pubs. Ltd. GBR. Dist: Independent Pubs. Group.

Shipton, Jonathan. Baby Baby Blah Blah Blah! Chessa, Francesca, illus. 2009. (ENG.). 32p. (J). (gr. -1-1). 16.95 *(978-0-8234-2213-5(5))* Holiday Hse., Inc.

Shreve, Susan. The Search for Baby Ruby. 2015. 213p. (J). pap. *(978-0-545-41784-6(8))* Scholastic, Inc.

Shyba, Jessica. Naptime with Theo & Beau. 2015. (ENG., Illus.). 40p. (J). (gr. -1-k). 16.99 *(978-1-250-05906-2(2)*, 9781250059062) Feiwel & Friends.

Simcox, Lorraine. A Single Red Thread. 2008. (J). 21.99 *(978-1-60131-024-8(2))* Big Tent Bks.

Simon, Toby L., et al. Don't Wake the Baby! (Illus.). 25p. (J). *(978-0-340-70935-1(9))*; pap. *(978-0-340-69842-6(X))* Hodder & Stoughton.

Singer, Marilyn. City Lullaby. Cneut, Carll, illus. 2007. (ENG.). 32p. (J). (gr. -1-3). 16.99 *(978-0-618-60703-7(X))* Houghton Mifflin Harcourt Publishing Co.

Slattery, Karen. Piper's Diapers. 2003. (J). pap. 9.00 *(978-0-8059-5765-5(0))* Dorrance Publishing Co., Inc.

Slegers, Liesbet. Guess Where I Am. 2008. (Guess Ser.). (ENG.). 26p. (J). (gr. k — 1). 7.95 *(978-1-60537-001-9(0))* Clavis Publishing.

—Guess Who I Am. 2008. (Guess Ser.). (ENG.). 26p. (J). (gr. k — 1). 7.95 *(978-1-60537-000-2(2))* Clavis Publishing.

Slier, Debby. Babies, Babies, 1 vol. 2012. (ENG., Illus.). 32p. (J). bds. 5.95 *(978-1-59572-368-0(4))* Star Bright Bks., Inc.

—Cradle Me, 1 vol. 2012. (ENG., Illus.). 32p. (J). bds. 6.95 *(978-1-59572-274-4(2))* Star Bright Bks., Inc.

Smith, Laura Rountree. The Fairy Babies. Dulin, Dorothy, illus. 2011. 126p. 40.95 *(978-1-258-09063-0(5))* Literary Licensing, LLC.

Smith, Maggie. My Blue Bunny, Bubbit. 2014. (ENG., Illus.). 40p. (J). (gr. -1-3). 16.99 *(978-0-547-55861-5(9))* Houghton Mifflin Harcourt Publishing Co.

Snyder, Carol. One up, One Down. Chambliss, Maxie, illus. 2013. (ENG.). 32p. (J). (gr. -1-3). 16.99 *(978-1-4814-2144-7(1)*, Atheneum Bks. for Young Readers) Simon & Schuster Children's Publishing.

Sockabasin, Allen & Raye, Rebekah. Thanks to the Animals, 1 vol. 2nd ed. 2014. (ENG., Illus.). 36p. (gr. 1-6). 17.95 *(978-0-88448-414-1(9)*, 884414) Tilbury Hse. Pubs.

Spalding, Andrea. Dance Baby Dance, 1 vol. 2009. (ENG.). 24p. (J). (gr. -1 — 1). bds. 9.95 *(978-1-55469-079-4(X))* Orca Bk. Pubs. USA.

Spanyol, Jessica. Clive & His Babies. Spanyol, Jessica, illus. 2016. (All about Clive Ser.). (ENG., Illus.). 14p. (J). bds. *(978-1-84643-882-0(9))* Child's Play International Ltd.

Spicer, Lin. Faerie Baby. 2006. 148p. pap. 13.50 *(978-1-84426-384-4(3))* Upfront Publishing Ltd. GBR. Dist: Printondemand-worldwide.com.

Springstubb, Tricia. Phoebe & Digger. Newman, Jeff, illus. 2013. (ENG.). 32p. (J). (gr. -1-2). 16.99 *(978-0-7636-5281-4(4))* Candlewick Pr.

St. John, Patricia. A Home for Virginia. Smith, Helen, illus. 2005. (ENG.). 24p. (J). (gr. 4-7). 9.99 *(978-1-85792-961-4(6)*, 61d6526b-9c8a-4a92-bdf8-4e663de02131) Christian Focus Pubns. GBR. Dist: Bookmasters Distribution.

Stamm, Linda J. Phoebe's Family: A Story about Egg Donation. Clipp, Joan, illus. 2015. (J). pap. *(978-0-9755810-7-0(4))* Graphite Pr.

Stamm, Linda J. Scarlett's Story: A Tale about Embryo Donation. Clipp, Joan, illus. 2017. (J). pap. ***(978-1-938313-17-2(8))*** Graphite Pr.

Stortz, Diane M. Baby, Baby! Busby, Ailie, illus. 2016. (J). *(978-0-8249-1988-7(2)*, Ideal Pubns.) Worthy Publishing.

Sturges, Philemon. How Do You Make a Baby Smile? Strevens-Marzo, Bridget, illus. 2007. 24p. (J). (gr. -1-k). lib. bdg. 17.89 *(978-0-06-076073-1(7))* HarperCollins Pubs.

Symes, Sally. Funny Face, Sunny Face. Beardshaw, Rosalind, illus. 2015. (ENG.). 32p. (J). (-k). 14.99 *(978-0-7636-7606-3(3)*, Nosy Crow) Candlewick Pr.

Tafolla, Carmen. Fiesta Babies. Córdova, Amy, illus. 2010. (ENG & SPA.). 24p. (J). (gr. k — 1). 12.99 *(978-1-58246-319-3(0)*, Tricycle Pr.) Random Hse. Children's Bks.

Thiel Annie. The Playdate Kids Chloe's New Baby Brother 2ED 2007. 2007. 32p. 12.95 *(978-1-933721-28-6(6))*; pap. 6.95 *(978-1-933721-24-8(3))* Playdate Kids Publishing.

Thompson, Carol. Climb! Thompson, Carol, illus. 2013. (Little Movers Ser.). (ENG., Illus.). 12p. (J). bds. *(978-1-84643-617-8(6))* Child's Play International Ltd.

—Crawl! Thompson, Carol, illus. 2013. (Little Movers Ser.). (ENG., Illus.). 12p. (J). bds. *(978-1-84643-614-7(1))* Child's Play International Ltd.

—Jump! Thompson, Carol, illus. 2013. (Little Movers Ser.). (ENG., Illus.). 12p. (J). bds. *(978-1-84643-615-4(X))* Child's Play International Ltd.

Thompson, Laurie. Be Gentle with Baby, 1 vol. 2010. 24p. 24.95 *(978-1-4489-3910-7(0))* PublishAmerica, Inc.

Timbaland & Myers, Christopher. Nighttime Symphony. Myers, Christopher, illus. 2014. (ENG., Illus.). 32p. (J). 16.99 *(978-1-4424-1208-8(9)*, Atheneum Bks. for Young Readers) Simon & Schuster Children's Publishing.

Topper, Wendy. Where's the Pacifier? 2008. 8p. pap. 24.95 *(978-1-60563-823-2(4))* America Star Bks.

Valente, Shannon. Why Baby Toes Aren't Big! 2009. 16p. pap. 10.79 *(978-1-4389-4580-4(9))* AuthorHouse.

Van Camp, Richard. Little You, 1 vol. Flett, Julie, illus. 2013. (ENG.). 24p. (J). (gr. -1-k). bds. 9.95 *(978-1-4598-0248-3(9))* Orca Bk. Pubs. USA.

Van Draanen, Wendelin. Sammy Keyes & the Search for Snake Eyes. 2008. (Sammy Keyes Ser.: Bk. 7). (J). 64.99 *(978-1-60640-645-8(0))* Findaway World, LLC.

—Sammy Keyes & the Search for Snake Eyes. 2003. (Sammy Keyes Ser.: Bk. 7). (Illus.). 277p. (gr. 5-9). 17.00 *(978-0-7569-1445-5(0))* Perfection Learning Corp.

—Sammy Keyes & the Search for Snake Eyes. 2003. (Sammy Keyes Ser.: 7). (ENG.). 320p. (J). (gr. 5-7). 7.99 *(978-0-440-41900-6(X)*, Yearling) Random Hse. Children's Bks.

van Genechten, Guido. The Big Baby Book. 2011. (ENG.). 22p. (J). (gr. k — 1). bds. 12.95 *(978-1-60537-079-8(7))* Cobblestone Publishing Co.

Van Laan, Nancy. Scrubba Dub. Pons, Bernadette, illus. 2008. (ENG.). 32p. (J). (gr. -1-1). 8.99 *(978-1-4169-7859-6(3)*, Simon & Schuster/Paula Wiseman Bks.) Simon & Schuster/Paula Wiseman Bks.

van Lieshout, Maria. Bye-Bye Binky: I'm a Big Kid Now. 2016. (Big Kid Power Ser.). (ENG., Illus.). 24p. (J). (gr. -1 — 1). 9.99 *(978-1-4521-3536-6(3))* Chronicle Bks. LLC.

Vaughan, Kathryn Mademann. Little One... Good Night: A Lullaby from Vermont. Edson, Anharad, illus. 2004. (J). per. 19.95 incl. audio compact disk *(978-0-9747447-0-4(0))* Chaser Media LLC.

Verdi, Jessica. What You Left Behind. 2015. (ENG.). 368p. (YA). (gr. 8-12). pap. 9.99 *(978-1-4926-0874-5(2))* Sourcebooks, Inc.

Verdick, Elizabeth & Lisovskis, Marjorie. Cuddle. 2013. (Happy Healthy Baby Ser.). (ENG., Illus.). 22p. (J). bds. 6.99 *(978-1-57542-423-1(1))* Free Spirit Publishing, Inc.

Vernick, Audrey. Edgar's Second Word. Burris, Priscilla, illus. 2014. (ENG.). 32p. (J). (gr. -1-3). 16.99 *(978-0-547-68462-8(2)*, Clarion Bks.) Houghton Mifflin Harcourt Trade & Reference Pubs.

Vogel, Elizabeth. Al Agua Patos. 2004. (Limpieza y Salud Todo el Dia Ser.). (SPA & ENG., Illus.). 24p. (J). (gr. -1-2). lib. bdg. 18.75 *(978-0-8239-6616-5(X))* Rosen Publishing Group, Inc., The.

—Taking My Bath: Al Agua Patos. 2004. (Limpieza y Salud Todo el Dia Ser.). (SPA & ENG., Illus.). 24p. (J). lib. bdg. 18.75 *(978-0-8239-6617-2(8)*, Editorial Buenas Letras) Rosen Publishing Group, Inc., The.

Walker, G. L. Good Morning Baby. 2008. 24p. pap. 10.95 *(978-1-4327-0536-7(9))* Outskirts Pr., Inc.

Ward, Lindsay. Henry Finds His Word. 2015. (ENG., Illus.). 32p. (J). (gr. -1-k). 16.99 *(978-0-8037-3990-1(7)*, Dial Bks) Penguin Young Readers Group.

—Rosco vs. the Baby. Ward, Lindsay, illus. 2016. (ENG., Illus.). 32p. (J). (gr. -1-3). 17.99 *(978-1-4814-3657-1(0)*, Simon & Schuster Bks. For Young Readers) Simon & Schuster Bks. For Young Readers.

Watson, Stephanie. Behold! a Baby. Ang, Joy, illus. 2015. (ENG.). 32p. (J). (gr. -1-1). 16.99 *(978-1-61963-452-7(X)*, 9781619634527, Bloomsbury USA Childrens) Bloomsbury Publishing USA.

Watt, F. Al Agua Patos! 2004. (Mundo del Pequenin Ser.). (SPA., Illus.). 16p. (J). (gr. -1-18). 4.95 *(978-0-7460-3867-3(4))* EDC Publishing.

—Felices Suenos! 2004. (Mundo del Pequenin Ser.).Tr. of Baby's Bedtime. (SPA., Illus.). 16p. (YA). (gr. -1-18). pap. 4.95 *(978-0-7460-3869-7(0))* EDC Publishing.

Watt, Fiona. Baby's Very First Book of Little Babies. 2011. (Baby's Very First Board Bks). 10p. (J). ring bd. 6.99 *(978-0-7945-3109-6(1)*, Usborne) EDC Publishing.

—Sleepy Baby. MacKinnon, Catherine-Anne, illus. 2006. (Snuggletime Board Bks.). 10p. (J). (gr. -1). bds., bds. 8.99 *(978-0-7945-1071-8(X)*, Usborne) EDC Publishing.

—That's Not My Baby (Boy) 2010. (Touchy Feely Board Book Ser.). 43p. (J). bds. 8.99 *(978-0-7945-2604-7(7)*, Usborne) EDC Publishing.

—That's Not My Baby (Girl) 2010. (Touchy Feely Board Book Ser.). 43p. (J). bds. 8.99 *(978-0-7945-2603-0(9)*, Usborne) EDC Publishing.

—That's Not My Monster. Wells, Rachel, illus. 2010. (Usborne Touchy-Feely Bks.). 10p. (J). bds. 8.99 *(978-0-7945-2878-2(3)*, Usborne) EDC Publishing.

—Water Baby. 2011. (Snuggletime Board Books Ser.). 10p. (J). ring bd. 8.99 *(978-0-7945-2038-0(3)*, Usborne) EDC Publishing.

Watt, Fiona & Watt, F. Baby's Mealtime. 2004. (Baby's World Bathbooks Ser.). (ENG., Illus.). 1p. (YA). (gr. -1-k). 7.95 *(978-0-7460-4176-5(4))* EDC Publishing.

Watt, Fiona & Wells, Rachel. Baby's Bedtime. 2004. (Baby's World Ser.). (ENG., Illus.). 1p. (J). (gr. -1-18). pap. 4.95 *(978-0-7460-3374-6(5))* EDC Publishing.

Weeks, Sarah. Sophie Peterman Tells the Truth! Neubecker, Robert, illus. 2009. (ENG.). 32p. (J). (gr. -1-3). 17.99 *(978-1-4169-8686-7(3)*, Beach Lane Bks.) Beach Lane Bks.

Wells, Rosemary. Max & Ruby's Bedtime Book. 2010. (Max & Ruby Ser.). (ENG.). 48p. (J). (gr. -1-k). 17.99 *(978-0-670-01141-4(X)*, Viking Books for Young Readers) Penguin Young Readers Group.

—Use Your Words, Sophie! 2015. (ENG., Illus.). 24p. (J). (gr. -1 — 1). 16.99 *(978-0-670-01663-1(2)*, Viking Books for Young Readers) Penguin Young Readers Group.

Weninger, Brigitte. Davy Loves the Baby. Tharlet, Eve, illus. 2015. (ENG.). 32p. (J). 15.95 *(978-0-7358-4210-6(8))* North-South Bks., Inc.

West, Tracey, adapted by. The Boss Baby Junior Novelization. 2017. (Boss Baby Movie Ser.). (ENG., Illus.). 112p. (J). (gr. 2-5). 17.99 *(978-1-4814-9170-9(9))*; pap. 6.99 *(978-1-4814-7006-3(X))* Simon Spotlight. (Simon Spotlight).

Weston Woods Staff, creator. Elizabeti's Doll. 2011. 18.95 *(978-0-439-73629-9(3))*; 38.75 *(978-0-439-84574-8(2))* Weston Woods Studios, Inc.

—Peter's Chair. 2011. 29.95 *(978-0-439-76006-5(2))* Weston Woods Studios, Inc.

What Does Baby Love? 2014. (ENG., Illus.). 14p. (J). (gr. -1 — 1). bds. 6.99 *(978-1-4814-0521-8(7)*, Little Simon) Little Simon.

Wheeler, Lisa. Jazz Baby. Christie, R. Gregory, illus. 2007. (ENG.). 40p. (J). (gr. -1-3). 17.99 *(978-0-15-202522-9(7))* Houghton Mifflin Harcourt Publishing Co.

Whelan, Olwyn. The Star Child. Maidment, Stella, illus. 2004. 40p. (J). 14.95 *(978-1-84458-039-2(3))* Avalon Publishing Group.

Willems, Mo. Welcome: A Mo Willems Guide for New Arrivals. Willems, Mo, illus. 2017. (ENG., Illus.). 32p. (J). (gr. -1 — 1). 15.99 *(978-1-4847-6746-7(2))* Disney Pr.

Williams, Garth. Baby's First Book. Williams, Garth, illus. 2011. (Golden Baby Ser.). (ENG., Illus.). 24p. (J). (— 1). bds. 6.99 *(978-0-375-85905-2(5)*, Golden Bks.) Random Hse. Children's Bks.

Wilson, Karma. Baby, I Love You. Williams, Sam, illus. 2009. (ENG.). 30p. (J). (gr. -1 — 1). bds., bds. 7.99 *(978-1-4169-1910-0(4)*, Little Simon) Little Simon.

Witek, Jo. Brave as Can Be: A Book of Courage. Roussey, Christine, illus. 2015. (Growing Hearts Ser.). (ENG.). 32p. (J). (gr. -1 — 1). 16.95 *(978-1-4197-1923-3(8)*, Abrams Appleseed) Abrams, Inc.

—Hello in There! A Big Sister's Book of Waiting. Roussey, Christine, illus. 2013. (Growing Hearts Ser.). (ENG.). 28p. (J). (gr. -1 — 1). 16.95 *(978-1-4197-0371-3(4)*, Abrams Appleseed) Abrams, Inc.

Wood, Jacqueline & Wood, Jakki. Baby Parade. 2003. (Illus.). 32p. (J). 14.95 *(978-0-7112-2065-2(4))* Fleming, Randall.

Woodson, Jacqueline. Pecan Pie Baby. Blackall, Sophie, illus. (ENG.). 32p. (J). (gr. k-3). 2013. 7.99 *(978-0-14-751128-7(3)*, Puffin Books) 2010. 16.99 *(978-0-399-23987-8(1)*, G.P. Putnam's Sons Books for Young Readers) Penguin Young Readers Group.

Yolen, Jane. Pumpkin Baby. Mitchell, Susan, illus. 2009. (ENG.). 32p. (J). (gr. -1). *(978-1-55470-141-4(4))* Me to We.

Young, Amy. Don't Eat the Baby! 2013. (ENG.). 32p. (J). (gr. -1-k). 16.99 *(978-0-670-78513-1(X)*, Viking Books for Young Readers) Penguin Young Readers Group.

Yum, Hyewon. The Twins' Little Sister. Yum, Hyewon, illus. 2014. (ENG., Illus.). 40p. (J). (gr. -1-1). 17.99 *(978-0-374-37973-5(4)*, 9780374379735, Farrar, Straus & Giroux (BYR)) Farrar, Straus & Giroux.

Zobel-Nolan, Allia. Hugs for Baby! Mitchell, Susan, illus. 2008. (Lift-the-Flap Hear-the-Sound Ser.). 10p. (J). (gr. -1). 12.95 *(978-1-932915-64-8(8))* Sandvik Innovations, LLC.

INFECTION AND INFECTIOUS DISEASES

see Communicable Diseases

INFIRMARIES

see Hospitals

INFORMATION SERVICES

Balice, Mary Lee, ed. Information Science, 1 vol., 1. 2016. (Study of Science Ser.). (ENG.). 96p. (J). (gr. 8-8). 36.25 *(978-1-68048-232-4(7)*, Britannica Educational Publishing) Rosen Publishing Group, Inc., The.

Digital & Information Literacy: Sets 1-8. 2014. (Digital & Information Literacy Ser.). 48p. (YA). (gr. 5-8). pap. 2256.00 *(978-1-4777-8119-7(6)*, Rosen Reference) Rosen Publishing Group, Inc., The.

INFORMATION STORAGE AND RETRIEVAL SYSTEMS

Allen, Mitchell. Our Field Trip: Gathering Data. 2017. (Computer Science for the Real World Ser.). 8p. (gr. 5-6). pap. 6.20 ***(978-1-5383-5004-1(1)***, Rosen Classroom) Rosen Publishing Group, Inc., The.

Anniss, Matt. What Is a Database & How Do I Use It? 2013. (Practical Technology Ser.). 48p. (J). (gr. 5-8). 25.85 *(978-1-62275-078-8(0))*; pap. 14.05 *(978-1-62275-079-5(9))* Rosen Publishing Group, Inc., The.

Arnone, Marilyn P. & Coatney, Sharon. Mac, Information Detective, in ... the Curious Kids & Why Dolphins Visit Curiosity Creek: A Storybook Approach to Introducing Research Skills Picture Book & Educator's Guide Set, 2 vols. 2008. (Illus.). 128p. (C). pap. 40.00 *(978-1-59158-498-8(1)*, LU4981, Libraries Unlimited) ABC-CLIO, LLC.

—Mac, Information Detective, in the Case Of— Curious Kids & the Squiggly Question, 2 vols. 2005. 32p. (C). 35.00 *(978-1-59158-189-5(3)*, LU1893, Libraries Unlimited) ABC-CLIO, LLC.

Athans, Sandra K. & Parente, Robin W. Tips & Tricks for Evaluating Multimedia Content. 2014. (Common Core Readiness Guide to Reading Ser.). 80p. (YA). (gr. 5-8). 32.95 *(978-1-4777-7563-9(3)*, Rosen Reference) Rosen Publishing Group, Inc., The.

Braxton, Simone. Nina's Nature Walk: Gathering Data. 2017. (Computer Science for the Real World Ser.). 12p. (gr. 6-7). pap. 7.05 ***(978-1-5383-5116-1(1)***, Rosen Classroom) Rosen Publishing Group, Inc., The.

Clasky, Leonard. What Do You See in Nature? Gathering Data. 2017. (Computer Science for the Real World Ser.). 12p. (gr. 6-7). pap. 7.05 ***(978-1-5383-5119-2(6)***, Rosen Classroom) Rosen Publishing Group, Inc., The.

Cowen, Carla Romaine. E-Commerce: Careers in Multimedia. 2009. (Library of E-Commerce & Internet Careers Ser.). 64p. (gr. 5-5). 58.50 *(978-1-60853-586-6(X))* Rosen Publishing Group, Inc., The.

Facts on File, Inc. Staff. Career Skills Library: Research & Information Management, Third Edition. 3rd rev. ed. 2009. (Career Skills Library). (Illus.). 168p. (gr. 6-12). 25.95 *(978-0-8160-7777-9(0)*, Ferguson Publishing Co.) Facts On File, Inc.

Gottfried Hollander, Barbara. Participating in Plays, Skits, & Debates with Cool New Digital Tools. 2013. (Way Beyond PowerPoint: Making 21st Century Presentations Ser.). 48p. (J). (gr. 5-8). 29.95 *(978-1-4777-1838-4(9))*; pap. 11.75 *(978-1-4777-1849-0(4))* Rosen Publishing Group, Inc., The. (Rosen Reference).

Harper, Reggie. The Princess & Her Gems: Putting Data in Order. 2017. (Computer Science for the Real World Ser.). 8p. (gr. 5-6). pap. 6.20 ***(978-1-5383-5016-4(5)***, Rosen Classroom) Rosen Publishing Group, Inc., The.

Johnson, Mary J. Super Smart Information Strategies: Your Fascinating Family History. 2011. (Explorer Library: Information Explorer Ser.). (ENG.). 32p. (gr. 4-8). pap. 14.21 *(978-1-61080-268-0(3)*, 201229) Cherry Lake Publishing.

Kamberg, Mary-Lane. Becoming a Database Administrator. 2017. (Tech Track: Building Your Career in IT Ser.). 80p. (gr. 12-12). 35.75 ***(978-1-5081-7552-0(7)***, Rosen Young Adult) Rosen Publishing Group, Inc., The.

La Bella, Laura. How Do I Use a Database? 2014. (Research Tools You Can Use Ser.). 32p. (J). (gr. 3-6). 23.45 *(978-1-62275-374-1(7))* Rosen Publishing Group, Inc., The.

Meyer, Susan. Performing & Creating Speeches, Demonstrations, & Collaborative Learning Experiences with Cool New Digital Tools. 2013. (Way Beyond PowerPoint: Making 21st Century Presentations Ser.). 48p. (J). (gr. 5-8). 29.95 *(978-1-4777-1837-7(0))*; pap. 11.75 *(978-1-4777-1851-3(6))* Rosen Publishing Group, Inc., The. (Rosen Reference).

O'Dell, Kathryn. Life Online: the Digital Age Low Intermediate Book with Online Access. 2014. (ENG.). 28p. (J). pap. 9.50 *(978-1-107-65069-5(0))* Cambridge Univ. Pr.

H I

Pace, Marisa. Our Class Traits: Gathering Data. 2017. (Computer Science for the Real World Ser.). 16p. (gr. 7-8). pap. 7.95 **(978-1-5383-5188-8(9)**, Rosen Classroom) Rosen Publishing Group, Inc., The.

Participating in Plays, Skits, & Debates with Cool New Digital Tools. 2013. (Way Beyond PowerPoint: Making 21st Century Presentations Ser.). 48p. (J). (gr. 5-8). pap. 70.50 (978-1-4777-1850-6(8), Rosen Reference) Rosen Publishing Group, Inc., The.

Performing & Creating Speeches, Demonstrations, & Collaborative Learning Experiences with Cool New Digital Tools. 2013. (Way Beyond PowerPoint: Making 21st Century Presentations Ser.). 48p. (J). (gr. 5-8). pap. 70.50 (978-1-4777-1852-0(4), Rosen Reference) Rosen Publishing Group, Inc., The.

QEB Let's Start! Computing National Book Stores Edition: Sorting Information. 2006. (J). per. (978-1-59566-296-5(0)) QEB Publishing Inc.

Rabbat, Suzy. Citing Sources: Learning to Use the Copyright Page. 2013. (Explorer Junior Library: Information Explorer Junior Ser.). (ENG.). 24p. (gr. 1-4). 28.50 (978-1-62431-023-2(0), 202543); pap. 12.79 (978-1-62431-047-8(8), 202545) Cherry Lake Publishing.

—Super Smart Information Strategies: Find Your Way Online. 2010. (Explorer Library: Information Explorer Ser.). (ENG.). 32p. (gr. 4-8). lib. bdg. 28.50 (978-1-60279-639-3(4), 200342) Cherry Lake Publishing.

Towne, Isobel & Porterfield, Jason. Strategic Searches Using Digital Tools, 01 vols., 1. 2016. (Digital & Information Literacy Ser.). (ENG.). 48p. (J). pap. 11.75 (978-1-4994-3789-8(7), Rosen Central) Rosen Publishing Group, Inc., The.

Truesdell, Ann. Present It! Creating & Sharing a Slide Show. 2014. (Explorer Junior Library: Information Explorer Junior Ser.). (ENG., Illus.). 24p. (J). (gr. 1-4). 28.50 (978-1-63137-787-7(6), 205391) Cherry Lake Publishing.

Wells, Naomi. I Find Signs: Looking at Data. 2017. (Computer Science for the Real World Ser.). 8p. (gr. 5-6). pap. 6.20 **(978-1-5383-5012-6(2)**, Rosen Classroom) Rosen Publishing Group, Inc., The.

INFORMATION TECHNOLOGY

Abramovitz, Melissa. How Are Digital Devices Impacting Society? 2015. (ENG., Illus.). 96p. (J). lib. bdg. (978-1-60152-772-1(1)) ReferencePoint Pr., Inc.

Apel, Melanie Ann. Careers in Information Technology. rev. ed. 2005. (Career Resource Library). (Illus.). 192p. (YA). (gr. 7-12). lib. bdg. 34.60 (978-0-8239-4085-1(3)) Rosen Publishing Group, Inc., The.

Bidder, Jane. Inventions We Use for Information & Entertainment. 2006. (Everyday Inventions Ser.). (Illus.). 32p. (gr. 1-4). lib. bdg. 26.00 (978-0-8368-6899-9(4), Gareth Stevens Learning Library) Stevens, Gareth Publishing LLLP.

Boritzke, Lauren. Working in Technology. 2018. (ENG.). 32p. (gr. 3-6). **(978-1-63235-450-1(0)**, 12-Story Library) Pr. Room Editions LLC.

Csiszar, John. Information Technology, Vol. 10. 2016. (Stem in Current Events Ser.). (Illus.). 64p. (J). (gr. 7). 23.95 (978-1-4222-3593-5(9)) Mason Crest.

De Arazoza, Ralph. Technology: At Your Service. 2014. (ENG., Illus.). 224p. (C). (gr. 13-13). pap. 108.67 (978-0-07-351687-5(2), 0073516872) McGraw-Hill Cos., The.

Einspruch, Andrew. Wired World. 2012. (Discovery Education: Technology Ser.). (ENG., Illus.). 32p. (J). (gr. 3-6). pap. 10.00 (978-1-4488-7970-0(1)); lib. bdg. 25.25 (978-1-4488-7888-8(8)) Rosen Publishing Group, Inc., The. (PowerKids Pr.).

Ferguson. Discovering Careers for Your Future: Library & Information Science. 2008. (Discovering Careers for Your Future Ser.). 91p. (gr. 4-9). 21.95 (978-0-8160-7282-8(5), Ferguson Publishing Co.) Facts On File, Inc.

Fromm, Megan. Privacy & Digital Security, 1 vol. 2015. (ENG.). 48p. (YA). 30.25 (978-1-4777-8068-8(8), Rosen Reference) Rosen Publishing Group, Inc., The.

Goodwin, Ann. How to Dazzle at Information Technology. 2004. (Illus.). 48p. pap. 30.00 (978-1-897675-67-0(4)) Brilliant Pubns. GBR. Dist: Parkwest Pubns., Inc.

Gordon, Sherri Mabry. Using Technology. 2011. (Life—a How-To Guide Ser.). (Illus.). 128p. (J). lib. bdg. 33.27 (978-0-7660-3441-9(0)); (gr. 6-18). pap. 10.95 (978-1-59845-311-9(4)) Enslow Pubs., Inc.

Gregory, Josh. Information Systems Technician. 2012. (21st Century Skills Library: Cool Military Careers Ser.). (ENG.). 32p. (gr. 4-8). 28.50 (978-1-61080-447-9(3), 202057); pap. 14.21 (978-1-61080-621-3(2), 202231) Cherry Lake Publishing.

Harmon, Daniel E. Powering up a Career in Software Development & Programming. 2015. (Preparing for Tomorrow's Careers Ser.). (ENG., Illus.). 80p. (J). (gr. 7-8). 34.25 (978-1-4994-6095-7(3), Rosen Young Adult) Rosen Publishing Group, Inc., The.

Henderson, Harry. The Digital Age. 2013. (Illus.). 96p. (J). lib. bdg. (978-1-60152-482-9(X)) ReferencePoint Pr., Inc.

Hudak, Heather. Waves & Information Transfer. 2017. (Catch a Wave Ser.). (ENG.). 32p. (J). **(978-0-7787-2962-4(1))**; (Illus.). pap. **(978-0-7787-2970-9(2))** Crabtree Publishing Co.

Indovino, Shaina. Women in Information Technology. Lee-Karlon, Ann, ed. 2013. (Major Women in Science Ser.: 10). 64p. (J). (gr. 7-18). 22.95 (978-1-4222-2928-6(9)) Mason Crest.

JG Ferguson Publishing Company, creator. Computers. 2007. (What Can I Do Now? Ser.). 208p. (YA). (gr. 7-12). 32.95 (978-0-8160-6027-6(4)) Facts On File, Inc.

Kallen, Stuart A. The Information Revolution. 2010. (World History Ser.). (ENG., Illus.). 128p. (gr. 7-10). 39.90 (978-1-4205-0163-6(1), Lucent Bks.) Cengage Gale.

Kamberg, Mary-Lane. Becoming a Database Administrator. 2017. (Tech Track: Building Your Career in IT Ser.). 80p. (gr. 12-12). 35.75 **(978-1-5081-7552-0(7)**, Rosen Young Adult) Rosen Publishing Group, Inc., The.

Kamberg, Mary-Lane. Getting a Job in the IT Industry. 2016. (Job Basics: Getting the Job You Need Ser.). 80p. (J). (gr. 8-8). 35.75 (978-1-4777-8556-0(6)) Rosen Publishing Group, Inc., The.

Kassnoff, David. What Degree Do I Need to Pursue a Career in Information Technology & Information Systems?, 1 vol. 2015. (ENG., Illus.). 80p. (J). 34.60 (978-1-4777-7865-4(9), Rosen Young Adult) Rosen Publishing Group, Inc., The.

La Bella, Laura. Becoming a Data Engineer. 2017. (Tech Track: Building Your Career in IT Ser.). 80p. (gr. 12-12). 35.75 **(978-1-5081-7550-6(0)**, Rosen Young Adult) Rosen Publishing Group, Inc., The.

—Becoming a Systems Analyst. 2017. (Tech Track: Building Your Career in IT Ser.). 80p. (J). (gr. 12-12). 35.75 **(978-1-5081-7558-2(6)**, Rosen Young Adult) Rosen Publishing Group, Inc., The.

Lester, Brian. R U In? Using Technology Responsibly, 1 vol. 2010. (Essential Health: a Guy's Guide Ser.). (ENG.). 112p. (J). (gr. 6-12). lib. bdg. 35.64 (978-1-61613-543-0(3)) ABDO Publishing Co.

Lyons, Heather. Coding in the Real World. Westgate, Alex, illus. 2017. (Kids Get Coding Ser.). (ENG.). 24p. (J). (gr. 1-4). 26.65 **(978-1-5124-3943-4(6))**; pap. 7.99 **(978-1-5124-5586-1(5))** Lerner Publishing Group.

McBride, P. K. Skills Award Information Technology - Standard Level. 2003. (Cambridge International Examinations Ser.). (ENG., Illus.). 146p. (gr. 9-14). per. 17.85 (978-0-521-52528-2(4)) Cambridge Univ. Pr.

Mozer, Mindy. Big Data & You. 2014. (Digital & Information Literacy Ser.). 48p. (YA). (gr. 5-8). 30.25 (978-1-4777-7643-8(5)) Rosen Publishing Group, Inc., The.

Reeves, Diane Lindsey. Career Ideas for Teens in Information Technology. 2006. (Career Ideas for Teens Ser.). (Illus.). 192p. (gr. 8-12). per. 16.95 (978-0-8160-6921-7(2), Checkmark Bks.) Facts On File, Inc.

—Information Technology. 2017. (Bright Futures Press: World of Work Ser.). (ENG., Illus.). 32p. (J). (gr. 4-7). lib. bdg. 29.93 (978-1-63472-625-2(1), 209534) Cherry Lake Publishing.

Reeves, Diane Lindsey & Karlitz, Gail. Information Technology. 2nd rev. ed. 2012. (Career Ideas for Teens Ser.). (Illus.). 192p. (gr. 6-12). 45.00 (978-0-8160-8267-4(7)) Facts On File, Inc.

Reeves, Diane Lindsey, et al. Career Ideas for Teens in Information Technology. 2005. (Career Ideas for Teens Ser.). (Illus.). 192p. (gr. 6-12). 40.00 (978-0-8160-5293-6(X), Ferguson Publishing Co.) Facts On File, Inc.

Solway, Andrew. Communication: The Impact of Science & Technology. 2009. (Pros & Cons Ser.). (ENG.). 64p. (YA). (gr. 5-9). lib. bdg. 35.00 (978-1-4339-1986-2(9)) Stevens, Gareth Publishing LLLP.

Sutherland, Adam. The Story of Google. 2012. (Business of High Tech Ser.). (ENG.). 48p. (YA). (gr. 5-8). pap. 10.00 (978-1-4488-7092-9(5), Rosen Reference); lib. bdg. 29.25 (978-1-4488-7041-7(0)) Rosen Publishing Group, Inc., The.

Teague Meyer, Terry. The Vo-Tech Track to Success in Information Technology. 2014. (Learning a Trade, Preparing for a Career Ser.). (Illus.). 80p. (J). (gr. 7-12). 34.25 (978-1-4777-7724-4(5)) Rosen Publishing Group, Inc., The.

Ward-Johnson, Chris & Gould, William. The Magic Mouse Dictionary of Computers & Information Technology. Laughing Gravy Design Staff, illus. 2003. (Magic Mouse Guides). 64p. (J). lib. bdg. 29.27 (978-0-7660-2264-5(1)) Enslow Pubs., Inc.

Way Beyond Powerpoint: Making 21st Century Presentations. 2013. (Way Beyond PowerPoint: Making 21st Century Presentations Ser.). 48p. (J). (gr. 5-8). 149.75 (978-1-4777-1844-5(3)); pap. 58.75 (978-1-4777-7805-0(5)); pap. 352.50 (978-1-4777-7804-3(7)) Rosen Publishing Group, Inc., The. (Rosen Reference).

Wilcox, Christine. Careers in Information Technology. 2014. (Exploring Careers). (ENG., Illus.). 80p. (J). lib. bdg. (978-1-60152-706-6(3)) ReferencePoint Pr., Inc.

Wilson, Barbara. City & Guilds: Information Technology. 2nd rev. ed. (Illus.). 144p. pap. (978-1-86152-699-1(7)) Cengage Learning.

Wolny, Philip. Creating Electronic Graphic Organizers. 2010. (Digital & Information Literacy Ser.). (ENG.). 48p. (YA). pap. 11.75 (978-1-4488-0596-9(1)); lib. bdg. 29.25 (978-1-4358-9428-0(6)) Rosen Publishing Group, Inc., The. (Rosen Reference).

INJURIES

see First Aid

INJURIOUS INSECTS

see Insect Pests

INK DRAWING

see Pen Drawing

INNS

see Hotels, Motels, etc.

INOCULATION

see Vaccination

INORGANIC CHEMISTRY

see Chemistry, Inorganic

INQUISITION

Bartolotta, Kenneth L. The Inquisition: The Quest for Absolute Religious Power. 2017. (World History Ser.). 104p. (YA). (gr. 7-7). lib. bdg. 39.90 **(978-1-5345-6049-9(1)**, Lucent Pr.) Greenhaven Publishing LLC.

Don Nardo. The Trial of Galileo. 2003. (Famous Trials Ser.). (ENG., Illus.). 112p. (J). 29.95 (978-1-59018-423-3(8)) Cengage Gale.

INQUISITION—FICTION

Dyer, K. C. Shades of Red: An Eagle Glen Trilogy Book. 2005. (Eagle Glen Trilogy Ser.: 3). (ENG.). 272p. (YA). (gr. 7). pap. 12.99 (978-1-55002-545-3(7)) Dundurn CAN. Dist: Ingram Publisher Services.

Hoffman, Alice. Incantation. rev. ed. 2007. (ENG., Illus.). 192p. (YA). (gr. 7-17). per. 10.00 (978-0-316-15428-4(8)) Little, Brown Bks. for Young Readers.

Matas, Carol. The Burning Time, 1 vol. 2007. (ENG.). 112p. (YA). (gr. 7-12). per. 14.95 (978-1-55143-624-1(8)) Orca Bk. Pubs. USA.

Ricci, Dorothy. Through Goya's Eyes: The World of the Spanish Painter & His Friend & Mentor, Gaspar Jovellanos. 2008. (YA). pap. (978-0-88092-763-5(1)); lib. bdg. (978-0-88092-762-8(3)) Royal Fireworks Publishing Co.

Tulien, Sean & Poe, Edgar Allen. The Pit & the Pendulum, 1 vol. Fabul, J. C. & Calero, Dennis, illus. 2013. (Edgar Allan Poe Graphic Novels Ser.). (ENG.). 72p. (gr. 2-3). pap. 6.10 (978-1-4342-4020-0(9)); lib. bdg. 27.99 (978-1-4342-4024-8(X)) Stone Arch Bks.

Walshe, Elizabeth Hely. Under the Inquisition: A Story of the Reformation in Italy. 2009. (Illus.). 315p. (978-1-894666-30-5(5)) Inheritance Pubns.

INQUISITION—SPAIN

Boehme, Gerry. Heresy: The Spanish Inquisition. 2016. (Public Persecutions Ser.). 128p. (J). 45.64 (978-1-5026-2329-4(3)) Cavendish Square Publishing.

Miklowitz, Gloria D. Secrets in the House of Delgado. 2004. 192p. (J). (gr. 4-18). pap. 8.00 (978-0-8028-5210-6(6)) Eerdmans, William B. Publishing Co.

Woog, Adam. Life During the Spanish Inquisition. 2014. (Living History Ser). (ENG., Illus.). 96p. (J). lib. bdg. (978-1-60152-722-6(5)) ReferencePoint Pr., Inc.

INSANE

see Mentally Ill

INSECT PESTS

also individual insects and groups of insects.

see also Insects As Carriers of Disease

Axelrod-Contrada, Joan. Pesky Critters! Squirrels, Raccoons, & Other Furry Invaders, 1 vol. 2013. (Nature's Invaders Ser.). (ENG.). 32p. (gr. 3-4). lib. bdg. 27.99 (978-1-4765-0141-3(6)) Capstone Press of Coughlan Cos.

Bensinger, Lou. Tiny Invaders in Your Backyard. 2010. (Tiny Invaders Ser.). (Illus.). 24p. (J). pap. 8.25 (978-1-4358-9848-6(6)); (gr. 1-5). lib. bdg. 22.60 (978-1-4358-9378-8(6)) Rosen Publishing Group, Inc., The.

—Tiny Invaders in Your Home. 2010. (Tiny Invaders Ser.). (Illus.). 24p. (J). pap. 8.25 (978-1-4358-9846-2(X), PowerKids Pr.) Rosen Publishing Group, Inc., The.

Birch, Ann. Head Lice up Close 6 Pack. 2004. pap. 40.50 (978-1-4109-1154-4(3)) Harcourt Schl. Pubs.

Jackson, Cari. Bugs That Destroy. 2008. (Bug Alert! Ser.). 32p. (gr. 3-18). lib. bdg. 28.50 (978-0-7614-3188-6(8), Benchmark Bks.) Marshall Cavendish Corp.

Lay, Richard & Zamnaal, Laura Nienhaus. A Green Kid's Guide to Garden Pest Removal, 1 vol. 2013. (Green Kid's Guide to Gardening! Ser.). (ENG.). 24p. (J). (gr. -1-4). 27.07 (978-1-61641-944-8(X)) Magic Wagon.

Metz, Lorijo. What Can We Do about Invasive Species? 2009. (Protecting Our Planet Ser.). (Illus.). 24p. (J). pap. 8.25 (978-1-4358-2487-4(3), PowerKids Pr.) Rosen Publishing Group, Inc., The.

Miller, Connie Colwell. Disgusting Bugs. 2016. (That's Disgusting! Ser.). (ENG.). 32p. pap. 7.95 (978-1-5157-6286-7(6), Blazers) Capstone Press of Coughlan Cos.

Reith, Sharon L. Infestation! Roaches, Bedbugs, Ants, & Other Insect Invaders, 1 vol. 2013. (Nature's Invaders Ser.). (ENG.). 32p. (gr. 3-4). 27.99 (978-1-4765-0139-0(4), Edge Bks.) Capstone Press of Coughlan Cos.

Schafer, Susan. Invasive Reptiles & Amphibians. 2016. (Invasive Species Ser.). 48p. (J). (gr. 4-4). 31.36 (978-1-5026-1830-6(3)) Cavendish Square Publishing.

Spilsbury, Richard. Zoom in on House of Horrors. 2013. (Zoom in on... Ser.). 32p. (J). 23.94 (978-0-7660-4312-1(6)) Enslow Pubs., Inc.

INSECTS

see also Bees; Beetles; Beneficial Insects; Cockroaches; Fleas; Flies; Insect Pests; Wasps

ABDO Publishing Company Staff & Hansen, Grace. Insects. 2014. (Insects Ser.: 6). (ENG.). 24p. (J). (gr. 4-8). lib. bdg. 171.00 (978-1-62970-035-9(5)) ABDO Publishing Co.

Accord Publishing Staff & Andrews McMeel Publishing, LLC Staff. Bugs. 2014. (ENG., Illus.). 12p. (J). bds. 5.99 (978-1-4494-6055-6(0)) Andrews McMeel Publishing.

Acorn, John Harrison. Bugs of Ontario, 1 vol. Sheldon, Ian, illus. rev. ed. 2003. (ENG.). 160p. (gr. 4). pap. 16.95 (978-1-55105-287-8(3), 1551052873) Lone Pine Publishing USA.

Act-Two Staff. Bug Safari. 2004. (Illus.). (J). (gr. 1-4). pap. 8.99 incl. cd-rom (978-0-7868-3415-0(3)) Hyperion Bks. for Children.

Aitken, Stephen. Plants & Insects. 2013. 64p. (J). (gr. 5-8). 31.36 (978-1-60870-462-0(9)); pap. 15.28 (978-1-62712-042-5(4)) Cavendish Square Publishing.

Albee, Sarah. Bugged: How Insects Changed History. Leighton, Robert, illus. 2014. (ENG.). 176p. (J). (gr. 3-6). pap. 17.99 (978-0-8027-3422-8(7), 9780802734228, Bloomsbury USA Childrens) Bloomsbury Publishing USA.

Albright, Rosie. Bedbug-Sniffing Beagles & Other Scent Hounds. 2012. (Animal Detectives Ser.). (ENG., Illus.). 24p. (J). (gr. k-3). pap. 8.25 (978-1-4488-6264-1(7)); lib. bdg. 22.60 (978-1-4488-6152-1(7)) Rosen Publishing Group, Inc., The. (PowerKids Pr.).

—Bedbug-Sniffing Beagles & Other Scent Hounds: Beagles Cazadores de Chinches y Otros Sabuesos. Alamán, Eduardo, tr. from ENG. 2012. (Animal Detectives / Detectives Del Reino Animal Ser.). (SPA & ENG., Illus.). 24p. (J). (gr. k-3). lib. bdg. 22.60 (978-1-4488-6726-4(6), PowerKids Pr.) Rosen Publishing Group, Inc., The.

Allen, Francesca, illus. Creepy-Crawlies. 2005. 10p. (J). 4.99 (978-0-7945-0856-2(1), Usborne) EDC Publishing.

Allen, Judy. Are You a Dragonfly? Humphries, Tudor, illus. 2004. (Backyard Bks.). (ENG.). 32p. (J). (gr. k-3). pap. 6.99 (978-0-7534-5805-1(5), 9780753458051, Kingfisher) Roaring Brook Pr.

Aloian, Molly. Life Cycles of Insects. 2013. (ENG., Illus.). 24p. (J). (978-0-7787-1278-7(8)); pap. (978-0-7787-1282-4(6)) Crabtree Publishing Co.

—What Is an Insect? 2013. (ENG., Illus.). 24p. (J). (978-0-7787-1279-4(6)); pap. (978-0-7787-1283-1(4)) Crabtree Publishing Co.

Aloian, Molly & Kalman, Bobbie. Helpful & Harmful Insects. 2005. (World of Insects Ser.). (ENG., Illus.). 32p. (J). lib. bdg. (978-0-7787-2341-7(0)); pap. (978-0-7787-2375-2(5)) Crabtree Publishing Co.

—Insect Bodies. 2005. (World of Insects Ser.). (ENG., Illus.). 32p. (J). lib. bdg. (978-0-7787-2340-0(2)); pap. (978-0-7787-2374-5(7)) Crabtree Publishing Co.

—Insect Life Cycles. 2005. (World of Insects Ser.). (ENG., Illus.). 32p. (J). lib. bdg. (978-0-7787-2343-1(7)); pap. (978-0-7787-2377-6(1)) Crabtree Publishing Co.

—Les Insectes: Utiles Ou Nuisibles? 2010. (FRE., Illus.). 32p. (J). pap. 9.95 (978-2-89579-287-1(9)) Bayard Canada Livres CAN. Dist: Crabtree Publishing Co.

—Insects That Work Together. 2005. (World of Insects Ser.). (ENG., Illus.). 32p. (J). lib. bdg. (978-0-7787-2342-4(9)); pap. (978-0-7787-2376-9(3)) Crabtree Publishing Co.

American Museum of Natural History Staff. ABC Insects. 2014. (AMNH ABC Board Bks.). (ENG., Illus.). 18p. (J). (gr. -1-k). bds. 7.95 (978-1-4549-1194-4(8)) Sterling Publishing Co., Inc.

Ames, Lee J. & Burns, Ray. Draw 50 Creepy Crawlies: The Step-by-Step Way to Draw Bugs, Slugs, Spiders, Scorpions, Butterflies, & Many More... 2013. (ENG., Illus.). 64p. pap. 9.99 (978-0-8230-8614-6(3), Watson-Guptill) Potter/TenSpeed/Harmony.

Amstutz, Lisa. Cicadas, 1 vol. 2013. (Creepy Crawlers Ser.). (ENG.). 24p. (gr. k-1). lib. bdg. 26.65 (978-1-4765-2062-9(3), Pebble Plus) Capstone Press of Coughlan Cos.

Amstutz, Lisa J. Creepy Crawlers. 2013. (Creepy Crawlers Ser.). (ENG.). 24p. (gr. k-1). lib. bdg. 159.90 (978-1-4765-3694-1(5), Pebble Plus) Capstone Press of Coughlan Cos.

—Little Critters. 2016. (Little Critters Ser.). (ENG.). 24p. (gr. k-1). 87.96 (978-1-5157-1955-7(3), Pebble Bks.) Capstone Press of Coughlan Cos.

Amstutz, Lisa J. Praying Mantises. 2017. (Little Critters Ser.). (ENG.). 24p. (gr. k-1). lib. bdg. 21.99 **(978-1-5157-7825-7(8))** Capstone Press of Coughlan Cos.

Anderson, Margaret J. Bugged-Out Insects. 2011. (Bizarre Science Ser.). (Illus.). 48p. (J). (gr. 5-18). pap. 8.95 (978-1-59845-220-4(7)) Enslow Pubs., Inc.

Anderson, Margaret Jean. Bugged-Out Insects. 2011. (Bizarre Science Ser.). (Illus.). 48p. (J). (gr. 5-18). lib. bdg. 25.27 (978-0-7660-3674-1(X)) Enslow Pubs., Inc.

Ard, Catherine. Origami Bugs. 2015. (Amazing Origami Ser.). (ENG.). 32p. (J). (gr. 2-3). 26.60 (978-1-4824-2199-6(2)) Stevens, Gareth Publishing LLLP.

Arlon, Penelope. Bugs. 2012. (Scholastic Discover More Ser.). (ENG.). 80p. (J). (gr. -1-3). 12.99 (978-0-545-36574-1(0), Scholastic Reference) Scholastic, Inc.

—Insectos: Y Otras Criaturas. 2013. (Scholastic Explora Tu Mundo Ser.). (SPA.). 80p. (J). (gr. -1-3). 12.99 (978-0-545-49082-5(0), Scholastic en Espanol) Scholastic, Inc.

Arlon, Penelope & Gordon-Harris, Tory. Bugs. 2012. (J). lib. bdg. (978-0-531-22954-5(8)) Scholastic, Inc.

Arnold, Tedd. Fly Guy Presents: Insects. 2015. (Illus.). (J). (978-0-545-87391-8(6)) Scholastic, Inc.

—Insects. Arnold, Tedd, illus. 2015. (Fly Guy Presents Ser.). (ENG., Illus.). 32p. (J). (gr. 1-3). pap. 3.99 (978-0-545-75714-0(2), Scholastic Reference) Scholastic, Inc.

—Insects. 2015. (Fly Guy Presents Ser.). (Illus.). (J). lib. bdg. 13.55 (978-0-606-36334-1(3)) Turtleback Bks.

Arnosky, Jim. Creep & Flutter: The Secret World of Insects & Spiders. (ENG., Illus.). (J). (gr. 1-5). 2016. 32p. pap. 6.95 (978-1-4549-1910-0(8)) 2012. 40p. 14.95 (978-1-4027-7766-0(3)) Sterling Publishing Co., Inc.

Aronin, Miriam. The Ant's Nest: A Huge, Underground City. 2009. (Spectacular Animal Towns Ser.). (Illus.). 32p. (J). (gr. 2-7). lib. bdg. 25.27 (978-1-59716-868-7(8)) Bearport Publishing Co., Inc.

Artell, Mike. Backyard Bloodsuckers: Questions, Facts & Tongue Twisters about Creepy Crawlers. 2004. (Illus.). 80p. pap. 14.95 (978-0-673-59248-4(0)) Good Year Bks.

—Backyard Bloodsuckers: Questions, Facts & Tongue Twisters about Creepy, Crawly Creatures. 2008. (Illus.). 80p. (J). (gr. 4). pap. 14.95 (978-1-59647-271-6(5)) Good Year Bks.

AZ Books Staff. Buzzing Meadow. Tulup, Natalia, ed. 2012. (How We Speak Ser.). (ENG.). 12p. (J). (gr. -1-k). bds. 10.95 (978-1-61889-095-5(6)) AZ Bks. LLC.

Backyard Bugs. (J). 21.95 (978-0-8136-4252-9(3)) Modern Curriculum Pr.

Baker, Charles F. & Baker, Charles F., III, eds. Bugs. 2005. (ENG., Illus.). 32p. (J). (gr. 1-5). 17.95 (978-0-8126-7926-7(1)) Cobblestone Publishing Co.

Baker, Nancy & Hoffman, Richard L. Exploring Virginia Insects. Date not set. 32p. (J). (gr. 4-6). pap., act. bk. ed. 4.95 (978-0-9625801-8-5(X)) Virginia Museum of Natural History.

Baker, Wendy. Experimenta con Insectos (Experiment with Insects) (SPA.). 56p. (J). (978-84-348-3996-0(2)) SM Ediciones.

Baker, Wendy & Haslam, Andrew. Insects. (Make It Work! Ser.). (Illus.). (J). 48p. pap. 15.95 (978-0-590-24204-2(0)); (FRE., pap. 9.99 (978-0-590-24330-8(6)) Scholastic, Inc.

Ball, Jacqueline A. Animales Migratorios: Por Aire. 2007. (En marcha: Migraciones animales (Spanish- on the Move: Animal Migration) Ser.). (SPA.). 24p. (gr. 1-4). pap. 8.15 (978-0-8368-8432-6(9)); (Illus.). lib. bdg. 22.00 (978-0-8368-8427-2(2)) Stevens, Gareth Publishing LLLP. (Weekly Reader Leveled Readers).

—Migrating Animals of the Air. 2007. (On the Move: Animal Migration Ser.). 24p. (gr. 1-4). pap. 8.15 (978-0-8368-8422-7(1)); (Illus.). lib. bdg. 22.00 (978-0-8368-8417-3(5)) Stevens, Gareth Publishing LLLP. (Weekly Reader Leveled Readers).

Barbaresi, Nina. Glow-in-the-Dark Bugs Stickers. 2006. (Dover Little Activity Books Stickers Ser.). (ENG., Illus.). 2p. (J). (gr. 1-4). 1.99 (978-0-486-44912-8(2)) Dover Pubns., Inc.

Barner, Bob. Bug Safari. Barner, Bob, illus. (ENG., Illus.). 36p. (J). 2004. tchr. ed. 17.95 (978-0-8234-1707-0(7)) 2006. (gr. -1-3). reprint ed. pap. 6.95 (978-0-8234-2038-4(8)) Holiday Hse., Inc.

—Bugs! Bugs! Bugs! 2017. (ENG., Illus.). 32p. (J). pap. 7.99 (978-1-4521-6137-2(2)) Chronicle Bks. LLC.

Bater, Lucy. Incredible Insects. 2006. (Illus.). 48p. (J). lib. bdg. 29.95 (978-1-60044-260-5(9)) Rourke Educational Media.

Bauer, Jeff. What Is an Insect? 2008. (Illus.). 24p. (J). (978-0-545-00736-8(4)) Scholastic, Inc.

Bayley, Kimberly & Lawton, Caroline. Bugs A to Z. 2011. (ENG., Illus.). 32p. (J). (gr. -1-3). pap. 4.99 (978-0-545-27330-5(7), Scholastic Paperbacks) Scholastic, Inc.

Becker, Helaine. The Insecto-Files: Amazing Insect Science & Bug Facts You'll Never Believe. Dávila, Claudia & Owlkids Books Inc. Staff, illus. 2009. (ENG.). 64p. (J). (gr. 3-6). pap. 10.95 (978-1-897349-47-2(5), Maple Tree Pr.) Owlkids Bks. Inc. CAN. Dist: Publishers Group West (PGW).

Bedry, Christa. Insects. 2004. (Prehistoric Life Ser.). (Illus.). 32p. (J). (gr. -1-3). per. 9.95 (978-1-59036-173-3(3)); lib. bdg. 26.00 (978-1-59036-113-9(X)) Weigl Pubs., Inc.

Bell, Samantha S. 12 Insects Back from the Brink. 2014. (ENG., Illus.). 32p. (J). (978-1-63235-002-2(5)) Pr. Room Editions LLC.

Benchmark Education Company, compiled by. Insects Measure up! & ¡Vamos a Medir Insectos! 2005. (J). 62.00 net. (978-1-4108-4496-5(X)) Benchmark Education Co.

Bensinger, Lou. Tiny Invaders, 4 vols., Set. Incl. Tiny Invaders in the Water. lib. bdg. 22.60 (978-1-4358-9380-1(8), PowerKids Pr.); Tiny Invaders in Your Backyard. lib. bdg. 22.60 (978-1-4358-9378-8(6)); Tiny Invaders in Your Body. lib. bdg. 22.60 (978-1-4358-9379-5(4), PowerKids Pr.); (J). (gr. 1-5). (Illus.). 24p. 2010. Set lib. bdg. 85.00 (978-1-4358-9410-5(3), PowerKids Pr.) Rosen Publishing Group, Inc., The.

Bestor, Sheri M. Good Trick Walking Stick. Lambert, Jonny, illus. 2016. (ENG.). 32p. (J). (gr. 1-3). 16.99 (978-1-58536-943-0(8), 204033) Sleeping Bear Pr.

Bibbo, Molly. The Hidden World of Edible Insects: Comparing Fractions (Grade 4) 2017. (Mathematics Readers Ser.). (Illus.). 32p. (gr. 4-4). pap. 9.99 **(978-1-4258-5553-6(9))** Teacher Created Materials, Inc.

Biel, Timothy Levi. Aranas. Rountree, Monica, tr. 2003. (Zoobooks Ser.). Orig. Title: Spiders. (SPA., Illus.). 24p. (J). (gr. 1-7). lib. bdg. 15.95 (978-1-888153-82-8(2)) Wildlife Education, Ltd.

Blobaum, Cindy. Insectigations: 40 Hands-On Activities to Explore the Insect World. 2005. (Young Naturalists Ser.). (ENG., Illus.). 144p. (J). (gr. 1-4). pap. 14.95 (978-1-55652-568-1(0)) Chicago Review Pr., Inc.

Bodden, Valerie. Creepy Creatures: Mites. 2014. (Creepy Creatures Ser.). (ENG.). 24p. (J). (gr. 1-3). pap. 7.99 (978-0-89812-936-6(2), Creative Paperbacks) Creative Co., The.

—Creepy Creatures: Stick Insects. 2014. (Creepy Creatures Ser.). (ENG.). 24p. (J). (gr. 1-3). pap. 9.99 (978-0-89812-938-0(9), Creative Paperbacks) Creative Co., The.

—Creepy Creatures: Ticks. 2013. (Creepy Creatures Ser.). (ENG.). 24p. (J). (gr. 1-3). pap. 7.99 (978-0-89812-797-3(1), Creative Paperbacks) Creative Co., The.

—Mantises. 2011. (Creepy Creatures Ser.). 24p. (J). (gr. 1-3). (ENG.). pap. 8.99 (978-0-89812-567-2(7), Creative Paperbacks); 24.25 (978-1-58341-994-6(2), Creative Education) Creative Co., The.

—Mantises. 2010. (ENG., Illus.). 24p. (J). 8.95 (978-1-926853-74-1(1)) Saunders Bk. Co. CAN. Dist: Creative Co., The.

—Mites. 2014. (Illus.). 24p. (J). (978-1-60818-357-9(2), Creative Education) Creative Co., The.

—Stick Insects. 2014. (J). (978-1-60818-359-3(9), Creative Education) Creative Co., The.

—Ticks. 2013. (Illus.). 24p. (J). 25.65 (978-1-60818-234-3(7), Creative Education) Creative Co., The.

Bone, Emily. Big Book of Big Bugs. 2012. (Big Bks). 16p. (J). bds. 14.99 (978-0-7945-3300-7(0), Usborne) EDC Publishing.

Boor, Daniele, et al. Bajo la Tierra. (Coleccion Mundo Maravilloso). (SPA., Illus.). 40p. (J). (gr. 2-4). (978-84-348-3469-9(3), SM5474) SM Ediciones.

Boothroyd, Jennifer. Insect Pollinators. 2015. (First Step Nonfiction - Pollination Ser.). (ENG., Illus.). 24p. (gr. k-2). 39.99 (978-1-4677-8906-6(2), Lerner Digital); lib. bdg. 23.99 (978-1-4677-5738-6(1), Lerner Pubns.) Lerner Publishing Group.

Bowman, Lucy. Bugs: Level 1. Rivers, Ruth, illus. 2007. (Beginners Nature Ser.). 32p. (J). 4.99 (978-0-7945-1705-2(6), Usborne) EDC Publishing.

Bradley, Timothy. Bug Builders, 1 vol. 2nd rev. ed. 2013. (Nonfiction Readers Ser.). (ENG., Illus.). 48p. (J). (gr. 4-4). pap. 29.96 (978-1-4807-1097-9(0)) Shell Educational Publishing.

—Insectos Constructores. 2017. (TIME for Kids en Español - Level 4 Ser.). (SPA., Illus.). 48p. (gr. 4-4). lib. bdg. 31.99 (978-1-5157-5126-7(0)) Time for Kids Inc AUS. Dist: Capstone Pub.

Bradley, Timothy J. Bug Builders, 1 vol. 2nd rev. ed. 2012. (Nonfiction Readers Ser.). (ENG., Illus.). 48p. (J). (gr. 4-4). pap. 9.99 (978-1-4333-4821-1(7)) Teacher Created Materials, Inc.

—Strange but True Tiny Creatures, 1 vol. 2nd rev. ed. 2012. (Nonfiction Readers Ser.). (ENG.). 48p. (J). (gr. 4-4). pap. 9.99 (978-1-4333-4862-4(4)) Teacher Created Materials, Inc.

Brecke, Nicole & Stockland, Patricia M. Insects You Can Draw. Brecke, Nicole, illus. 2010. (Ready, Set, Draw! Ser.). (ENG., Illus.). 32p. (J). (gr. 2-4). lib. bdg. 25.26 (978-0-7613-4170-3(6), Millbrook Pr.) Lerner Publishing Group.

Bredeson, Carmen. Bomb-Factory Beetles & Other Weird Insects. 2009. (I Like Weird Animals! Ser.). (Illus.). 24p. (J). (gr. 1-3). lib. bdg. 22.60 (978-0-7660-3123-4(3), Enslow Elementary) Enslow Pubs., Inc.

Bredeson, Carmen & Cousins, Lindsey. Can You Find These Bugs? 2012. (All about Nature Ser.). 24p. (J). (gr. -1-1). (Illus.). pap. 7.95 (978-1-4644-0071-1(7)); 22.60 (978-0-7660-3982-7(X)) Enslow Pubs., Inc. (Enslow Elementary).

Bridges, Melanie. The Complete Guide to Bugs & Insects. 2016. (Illus.). 144p. (J). **(978-1-4351-6350-8(8))** Barnes & Noble, Inc.

Brin, Antoine & Valladares, Lionel. My Encyclopedia of Insects & Bugs. 2016. (My Encyclopedia Ser.). (ENG., Illus.). 128p. (J). lib. bdg. 34.00 (978-0-531-22470-0(8), Children's Pr.) Scholastic Library Publishing.

Brookes, Olivia. A Bug. 2009. (Ask Ser.). (Illus.). 32p. (J). lib. bdg. 26.50 (978-1-4358-2514-7(4), PowerKids Pr.) Rosen Publishing Group, Inc., The.

Buellis, Linda. Cicadas. 2016. (Dig Deep! Bugs That Live Underground Ser.). 24p. (J). (gr. 3-3). pap. 8.25 (978-1-4994-2050-0(1), PowerKids Pr.) Rosen Publishing Group, Inc., The.

Bug Adventures. 2015. (Bug Adventures Ser.). (ENG.). 24p. (J). (gr. 1-2). pap., pap., pap. 297.00 (978-1-4777-5675-1(2), Windmill Bks.) Rosen Publishing Group, Inc., The.

Bug Alert!, 6 bks., Set. Incl. Bugs That Build. Jackson, Cari. lib. bdg. 28.50 (978-0-7614-3191-6(8)); Bugs That Destroy. Jackson, Cari. lib. bdg. 28.50 (978-0-7614-3188-6(8)); Bugs That Help. Weir, Kirsten. lib. bdg. 28.50 (978-0-7614-3192-3(6)); Bugs That Kill. Raham, Gary. lib. bdg. 28.50 (978-0-7614-3185-5(3)); Bugs That Live on Animals. Weir, Kirsten. lib. bdg. 28.50 (978-0-7614-3189-3(6)); Bugs That Live on Us. Perritano, John. lib. bdg. 28.50 (978-0-7614-3187-9(X)); 32p. (gr. 3-2). (Bug Alert Ser.). 2008. Set lib. bdg. 171.00 (978-0-7614-3184-8(5), Benchmark Bks.) Marshall Cavendish Corp.

Bug Mania. (Flip Flap Fun Book Ser.). 10p. (J). bds. (978-2-7643-0183-8(9)) Phidal Publishing, Inc./Editions Phidal, Inc.

Bugs! (Early Intervention Levels Ser.). 31.86 (978-0-7362-0626-6(4)) CENGAGE Learning.

Bugs. 2005. (J). per. 4.99 (978-1-933581-22-4(0)) Byeway Bks.

Bugs. 2014. (Animal Q & A Ser.). (Illus.). 24p. (J). (gr. k-3). lib. bdg. 23.60 (978-1-4777-9186-8(8)) Windmill Bks.

Bugs! Bugs! Bugs! [Scholastic]. 2010. (Bugs, Bugs, Bugs! Ser.). pap. 2.60 (978-1-4296-5056-4(7), Pebble Plus) Capstone Press of Coughlan Cos.

Bugs IR. 2017. (Young Beginners Ser.). (ENG.). (J). 4.99 **(978-0-7945-3789-0(8)**, Usborne) EDC Publishing.

Bulion, Leslie. Hey There, Stink Bug! Evans, Leslie, illus. (ENG.). 48p. (J). (gr. 2-5). 2008. per. 5.95 (978-1-58089-340-4(6)) 2006. lib. bdg. 12.95 (978-1-58089-304-6(X)) Charlesbridge Publishing, Inc.

Burnie, David. Bug Hunter. 2015. (ENG., Illus.). 72p. (J). (gr. 3-7). pap. 9.99 (978-1-4654-3016-8(4), DK Children) Dorling Kindersley Publishing, Inc.

Burton, Margie, et al. Insects All Around. 2011. (Early Connections Ser.). (J). (978-1-61672-494-8(3)) Benchmark Education Co.

Bussell, Linda. Measuring at the Pond. 2008. (Math in Our World - Level 3 Ser.). 24p. (gr. 2-5). (J). lib. bdg. 22.00 (978-0-8368-9291-8(7)); pap. 8.15 (978-0-8368-9390-8(5)) Stevens, Gareth Publishing LLLP. (Weekly Reader Leveled Readers).

—Vamos a Medir en el Estanque. 2008. (Matemáticas en Nuestro Mundo - Nivel 3 (Math in Our World - Level 3) Ser.). (SPA.). 24p. (gr. 2-5). (J). lib. bdg. 22.00 (978-0-8368-9299-4(2)); pap. 8.15 (978-0-8368-9398-4(0)) Stevens, Gareth Publishing LLLP. (Weekly Reader Leveled Readers).

Busy Bugs. Date not set. (Sticker Shapes Ser.). (Illus.). 16p. (J). 2.98 (978-0-7525-8138-5(4)) Parragon, Inc.

Butterfield, Moira. Superstats - Bugs. 2016. (Superstats Ser.). (ENG., Illus.). 64p. (J). (gr. 2-4). 11.99 (978-1-4998-0240-5(4)) Little Bee Books Inc.

Cain, Marie Mowery. Insects up Close. 2013. (Big Books, Blue Ser.). (ENG & SPA., Illus.). 16p. pap. 33.00 (978-1-59246-006-9(2)) Big Books, by George!

—Weird Bugs. 2013. (Big Books, Blue Ser.). (ENG & SPA., Illus.). 16p. pap. 33.00 (978-1-59246-021-2(6)) Big Books, by George!

Calabrese, Paul. The Bad Bug Book: (and other Annoying Pests) 2010. 24p. pap. 15.99 (978-1-4500-4067-9(5)) Xlibris Corp.

Candlewick Press Staff. Creepy-Crawlies: a 3D Pocket Guide. KJA Artists Staff, illus. 2013. (Panorama Pops Ser.). (ENG.). 30p. (J). (gr. -1-2). 8.99 (978-0-7636-6662-0(9)) Candlewick Pr.

Caputo, Christine A. Insects & Spiders. 2012. (Illus.). 32p. (J). (978-0-545-46703-2(9)) Scholastic, Inc.

Cardenas, Ernesto A. A Bee Is an Insect. 2009. 23.95 (978-1-60698-032-3(7)); pap. 4.95 (978-1-60698-030-9(0)) Milo Educational Bks. & Resources.

—Insects. 2009. pap. 4.95 (978-1-60698-066-8(1)) Milo Educational Bks. & Resources.

Carr, Aaron. Stick Insects. 2014. (J). (978-1-4896-1046-1(4)) Weigl Pubs., Inc.

Carson, Mary Kay. How Strong Is an Ant? And Other Questions about Bugs & Insects. Schwartz, Carol, illus. 2014. (Good Question! Ser.). (ENG.). 40p. (J). (gr. 1). 12.95 (978-1-4549-0684-1(7)) Sterling Publishing Co., Inc.

Carter, David A. Birthday Bugs. Carter, David A., illus. 2004. (David Carter's Bugs Ser.). (ENG., Illus.). 16p. (J). (gr. -1-3). 12.99 (978-0-689-81858-5(0), Little Simon) Little Simon.

Chambers, Jo. Extreme Earth. 2007. (Trackers-Math Ser.). (gr. 2-5). pap. 5.00 (978-1-59055-913-0(4)) Pacific Learning, Inc.

Charner, Kathy, ed. Learn Every Day about Bugs & Spiders: 100 Best Ideas from Teachers. 2010. (Learn Every Day Ser.). (ENG.). 128p. pap. 12.95 (978-0-87659-128-4(4), Gryphon House Inc) Gryphon Hse., Inc.

Christopher, Nick. Lice. 2015. (Freaky Freeloaders: Bugs That Feed on People Ser.). (ENG.). 24p. (J). (gr. 2-3). 23.60 (978-1-4994-0757-0(2), PowerKids Pr.) Rosen Publishing Group, Inc., The.

Clapper, Nikki Bruno. Creepy Crawlers. 2015. (Creepy Crawlers Ser.). (ENG.). 24p. (gr. k-1). 106.60 (978-1-4914-6931-6(5), Pebble Plus) Capstone Press of Coughlan Cos.

Clarence, S. M. Beat Bugs Activity Book with Stickers. 2017. (Beat Bugs Ser.). 160p. (J). (gr. -1-3). pap. 12.99 (978-0-06-264075-8(5), HarperFestival) HarperCollins Pubs.

Clarke, Ginjer L. Bug Out! The World's Creepiest, Crawliest Critters. Mueller, Pete, illus. 2007. (Penguin Young Readers, Level 3 Ser.). (ENG.). 48p. (J). (gr. 1-3). pap. 3.99 (978-0-448-44543-4(3), Penguin Young Readers) Penguin Young Readers Group.

—Bug Out! The World's Creepiest, Crawliest Critters. Mueller, Pete, illus. 2007. (All Aboard Science Reader Ser.). (gr. -1-3). 14.00 (978-0-7569-8168-6(9)) Perfection Learning Corp.

Claybourne, Anna. A Colony of Ants: And Other Insect Groups, 1 vol. 2012. (Animals in Groups Ser.). (ENG.). 48p. (gr. 4-6). pap. 9.95 (978-1-4329-6487-0(9)); lib. bdg. 33.32 (978-1-4329-6480-1(1)) Heinemann-Raintree. (Heinemann InfoSearch).

—Insects - Weird Wildlife, 6 bks. 2003. (Illus.). (J). pap. 48.30 (978-1-4109-0296-2(X)) Harcourt Schl. Pubs.

Cleary, Brian P. Butterfly, Flea, Beetle, & Bee: What Is an Insect? Goneau, Martin, illus. 2012. (Animal Groups Are CATegorical (tm) Ser.). (ENG.). 32p. (gr. k-3). (J). lib. bdg. 26.60 (978-0-7613-6208-1(8)); pap. 7.95 (978-1-4677-0336-9(2)) Lerner Publishing Group. (Millbrook Pr.).

Cleary, Brian P. & Goneau, Martin. Apples, Cherries, Red Raspberries: What Is in the Fruits Group? 2011. (Food Is CATegorical Ser.). pap. 45.32 (978-0-7613-8348-2(4), Millbrook Pr.) Lerner Publishing Group.

Cleave, Rohan. Phasmid: Saving the Lord Howe Island Stick Insect. Tulloch, Coral, illus. 2015. (ENG.). 32p. (J). (gr. 2-2). 19.95 (978-1-4863-0112-6(6)) CSIRO Publishing AUS. Dist: Stylus Publishing, LLC.

Cole, Joanna. Insects. 2014. (Magic School Bus Presents Ser.). lib. bdg. 17.20 (978-0-606-36330-3(0)) Turtleback Bks.

Cole, Joanna & Jackson, Tom. Magic School Bus Presents: Insects: A Nonfiction Companion to the Original Magic School Bus Series. Degen, Bruce & Bracken, Carolyn, illus. 2014. (Magic School Bus Presents Ser.). (ENG.). 32p. (J). (gr. 1-3). pap. 6.99 (978-0-545-68587-0(7), Scholastic Paperbacks) Scholastic, Inc.

Cole, Tayler. Bloodsucking Leeches. 2016. (Real-Life Vampires Ser.). (ENG., Illus.). 24p. (J). (gr. 2-3). pap. 8.15 (978-1-4824-3951-9(4)) Stevens, Gareth Publishing LLLP.

Collard, Sneed B., III. Insects: The Most Fun Bug Book Ever. 2017. (ENG., Illus.). 48p. (J). (gr. 4-7). lib. bdg. 17.99 (978-1-58089-642-9(1)) Charlesbridge Publishing, Inc.

Collinson, Clare. British Insects & Other Minibeasts. 2017. (Nature in Your Neighbourhood Ser.). (ENG., Illus.). 32p. (J). (gr. 2-4). 17.99 (978-1-4451-3632-5(5), Franklin Watts) Hachette Children's Group GBR. Dist: Hachette Bk. Group.

Connors, Kathleen. Insect Fossils. 2012. (Fossilized! Ser.). (Illus.). 24p. (J). (gr. 2-5). pap. 8.15 (978-1-4339-6418-3(X)); lib. bdg. 22.60 (978-1-4339-6416-9(3)) Stevens, Gareth Publishing LLLP.

Cooper, Jason. Praying Mantises. 2005. (Rourke Discovery Library). (Illus.). 24p. (J). (gr. k-2). per. 5.45 (978-1-59515-743-0(3)) Rourke Educational Media.

Coulter, Catherine. Discovering Bugs. Csotonyi, Julius, illus. 2017. (ENG.). 96p. (J). 19.95 **(978-1-60433-689-4(7)**, Applesauce Pr.) Cider Mill Pr. Bk. Pubs., LLC.

Courtauld, Sarah. Bugs. Scarpa, Daniel, illus. 2008. (Usborne First Reading: Level 3 Ser.). 47p. (J). 8.99 (978-0-7945-1938-4(5), Usborne) EDC Publishing.

Creepy Crawly Creatures. 2007. (ENG., Illus.). 14p. (J). (gr. -1-3). 16.95 (978-1-58117-623-0(6), Intervisual/Piggy Toes) Bendon, Inc.

Creese, Sarah. Extreme Animals: I-Explore Reader. 2013. (ENG.). 32p. (J). pap. 4.99 (978-1-78235-158-0(2)) Make Believe Ideas GBR. Dist: Nelson, Thomas Inc.

—Mad about Insects Spiders & Creepy Crawlies. 2009. (Mad About Ser.). (ENG., Illus.). 24p. (J). (gr. -1-3). pap. 3.99 (978-1-84879-004-9(X)) Make Believe Ideas GBR. Dist: Nelson, Thomas Inc.

Critters & Bugs of the Tropical Rainforest. 2003. (J). spiral bd. 12.95 (978-1-931334-33-4(1)) Pieces of Learning.

Crowl, Janice. Pulelehua & Mamaki. Orme, Harinani, illus. 2009. 36p. (J). 14.95 (978-1-58178-090-1(7), Kamahoi Pr.) Bishop Museum Pr.

Cunningham, Kevin. Stick Insects & Ants. 2016. (21st Century Junior Library: Better Together Ser.). (ENG., Illus.). 24p. (J). (gr. 2-5). 27.07 (978-1-63471-087-9(8), 208427) Cherry Lake Publishing.

Davis, Caroline. Bugs. Davis, Caroline, illus. 2010. (ENG., Illus.). 20p. (J). bds. (978-1-4083-0784-7(7), Orchard Bks.) Hachette Children's Group GBR. Dist: Hachette Bk. Group.

De la Bédoyère, Camilla. Beasties in My Backyard. 2015. (Illus.). 64p. (978-0-545-91749-0(2)) Scholastic, Inc.

Denchfield, Nick & Sharp, Anne, illus. Pop-up Minibeast Adventure. 2004. 16p. (J). (gr. k-4). reprint ed. 25.00 (978-0-7567-8204-7(X)) DIANE Publishing Co.

Dickins, R. Bugs. 2004. (Discovery Program Ser.). (Illus.). 48p. (J). pap. 8.95 (978-0-7945-0267-6(9), Usborne); lib. bdg. 16.95 (978-1-58086-469-5(4)) EDC Publishing.

Dickins, Rosie. Bugs. 2009. (Discovery Nature Ser.). 48p. (YA). (gr. 3-18). 8.99 (978-0-7945-2375-6(7), Usborne) EDC Publishing.

Dig Deep! Bugs That Live Underground. 2016. (Dig Deep! Bugs That Live Underground Ser.). 24p. (gr. 3-3). 141.60 (978-1-4994-1915-3(5)); pap. 49.50 (978-1-4994-2444-7(2)) Rosen Publishing Group, Inc., The. (PowerKids Pr.).

Dixon, Norma. Focus on Flies, 1 vol. 2008. (Focus On Ser.). (ENG., Illus.). 32p. (J). (gr. 3-7). (978-1-55005-128-5(8)) Fitzhenry & Whiteside, Ltd.

Dobkin, Bonnie. The Great Bug Hunt. Dunnington, Tom, illus. 2011. (Rookie Ready to Learn — Animals Ser.). 40p. (J). (gr. -1-k). lib. bdg. 25.00 (978-0-531-26415-7(7)); pap. 5.95 (978-0-531-26696-0(6)) Scholastic Library Publishing. (Children's Pr.).

Dorling Kindersley Publishing Staff. Bugs, Bees, & Other Buzzy Creatures. 2016. (ENG., Illus.). 32p. (J). (-k). 8.99 (978-1-4654-4477-6(7), DK Children) Dorling Kindersley Publishing, Inc.

—DK Eyewitness Books: Insect. 2017. (DK Eyewitness Bks.). (ENG.). 72p. (J). (gr. 3-7). pap. 9.99 **(978-1-4654-6248-0(1)**, DK Children) Dorling Kindersley Publishing, Inc.

—Everything You Need to Know about Bugs. 2015. (Everything You Need to Know Ser.). (ENG., Illus.). 80p. (J). (gr. 2-5). 15.99 (978-1-4654-2894-3(1), DK Children) Dorling Kindersley Publishing, Inc.

—Follow the Trail: Bugs. 2017. (Follow the Trail Ser.). (ENG., Illus.). 14p. (J). (— 1). bds. 9.99 (978-1-4654-5670-0(8), DK Children) Dorling Kindersley Publishing, Inc.

—Insect. 2017. (DK Eyewitness Bks.). (ENG.). 72p. (J). (gr. 3-7). lib. bdg. 19.99 **(978-1-4654-6253-4(8)**, DK Children) Dorling Kindersley Publishing, Inc.

—Pocket Genius: Bugs. 2016. (Pocket Genius Ser.). (ENG., Illus.). 160p. (J). (gr. 3-7). pap. 4.99 (978-1-4654-4560-5(9), DK Children) Dorling Kindersley Publishing, Inc.

—Spot the Bug. 2013. (ENG.). 128p. (J). (gr. k-4). pap. 9.99 (978-1-4654-0247-9(0), DK Children) Dorling Kindersley Publishing, Inc.

—Super Bug Encyclopedia. 2016. (ENG., Illus.). 208p. (J). (gr. 3-7). 24.99 (978-1-4654-4600-8(1), DK Children) Dorling Kindersley Publishing, Inc.

—Ultimate Factivity Collection - Bugs. 2015. (ENG.). 96p. (J). (gr. 2-4). pap. 12.99 (978-1-4654-2929-2(8), DK Children) Dorling Kindersley Publishing, Inc.

—Ultimate Sticker Book: Bugs. 2016. (Ultimate Sticker Bks.). (ENG.). 32p. (J). (gr. k-3). pap. 6.99 (978-1-4654-5120-0(X), DK Children) Dorling Kindersley Publishing, Inc.

Dorling Kindersley Publishing Staff & Mills, Andrea. DK Findout! Bugs. 2017. (DK Find Out! Ser.). (ENG., Illus.). 64p. (J). (gr. 1-4). pap. 10.99 **(978-1-4654-6208-4(2)**, DK Children) Dorling Kindersley Publishing, Inc.

Dover. Bugs Activities Dover Chunky Book. 2009. (Dover Little Activity Bks.). (ENG., Illus.). 320p. (J). (gr. -1-5). 6.99 (978-0-486-47425-0(9)) Dover Pubns., Inc.

—Dover Digital Design Source #6: Spiders, Insects & Crustaceans. 2010. (Dover Electronic Clip Art Ser.). (ENG., Illus.). 128p. pap. 19.95 (978-0-486-99070-5(2)) Dover Pubns., Inc.

Dowling, Lucy. Why Why Why... Do Bees Make Honey? 2010. (Why Why Why Ser.). 32p. (J). (gr. 1-3). lib. bdg. 18.95 (978-1-4222-1579-1(2)) Mason Crest.

Duling, Kaitlyn. Invasive Insects & Diseases. 2016. (Invasive Species Ser.). 48p. (gr. 4-4). 31.36 (978-1-5026-1840-5(0)) Cavendish Square Publishing.

Duopress Labs Staff. Hello, Garden Bugs. Mora, Julissa, illus. 2017. (ENG.). 20p. (J). (gr. -1 — 1). bds. 7.95 (978-1-938093-84-5(4), Duo Pr. Llc (US)) Duo Pr. LLC.

Dussling, Jennifer. Bugs! Bugs! Bugs! 2011. (DK Readers Ser.). (ENG.). 32p. (J). (gr. 1-3). 3.99 (978-0-7566-7205-8(8), DK Children) Dorling Kindersley Publishing, Inc.

Eagen, Rachel. Buzz off, Flies! 2010. (Creepy Crawlies Ser.). (ENG.). 32p. (J). (gr. 3-6). (978-0-7787-2499-5(9)); pap. (978-0-7787-2506-0(5)) Crabtree Publishing Co.

Eco-Craft Bugs on Wheels. 2009. (Vacation Bible School Ser.). (J). 23.79 (978-1-4347-6460-7(5)) Cook, David C.

Editors of Kingfisher. Beastly Bugs. 2016. (It's All About... Ser.). (ENG., Illus.). 32p. (J). pap. 5.99 (978-0-7534-7260-6(0), 9780753472606, Kingfisher) Roaring Brook Pr.

Encyclopaedia Britannica, Inc. Staff, compiled by. My First Britannica: Birds, Insects, Reptiles, & Aquatic Life. 2008. (gr. 7-12). (978-1-59339-411-0(X)) Encyclopaedia Britannica, Inc.

Encyclopedia of Tiny Creatures, 6 Pks. (Discovery World Ser.). 16p. (gr. 1-2). 28.00 (978-0-7635-8468-9(1)) Rigby Education.

Evans, Arthur V., et al. Grzimek's Student Animal Life Resource, 2 vols. 2005. (Illus.). I, 442p. (J). (978-0-7876-9245-2(X)); (978-0-7876-9244-5(1)) Cengage Gale. (UXL).

Fact Atlas: Bugs. 2009. (FACT ATLAS Ser.). 72p. (J). 14.95 (978-0-8437-1915-4(X)) Hammond World Atlas Corp.

Falchetta, Drew. Forest Bugs. 2015. (1G Bugs Ser.). (ENG., Illus.). 20p. (J). pap. 5.99 (978-1-63437-099-8(6)) American Reading Co.

—Rainforest Bugs. 2015. (1G Bugs Ser.). (ENG., Illus.). 20p. (J). pap. 5.99 (978-1-63437-100-1(3)) American Reading Co.

Feldman, Thea & Ganeri, Anita. Creepy Crawlies. 2013. (Kingfisher Readers Ser.). (ENG., Illus.). 32p. (J). (gr. k-3). 12.99 (978-0-7534-7090-9(X), 9780753470909); pap. 3.99 (978-0-7534-7091-6(8), 9780753470916) Roaring Brook Pr. (Kingfisher).

Fiedler, Heidi. Bugs: A Close-Up Photographic Look Inside Your World. 2017. (Up Close Ser.). (ENG., Illus.). (J). (gr. k-6). lib. bdg. 27.99 **(978-1-942875-36-9(3)**, Walter Foster Jr) Quarto Publishing Group USA.

Fisher, Diana. Insects: Step-by-Step Instructions for 26 Creepy Crawlies. 2007. (Learn to Draw Ser.). (ENG., Illus.). 40p. (J). (gr. 1-17). per. 4.95 (978-1-60058-507-4(8), 1600585078) Quarto Publishing Group USA.

Fliess, Sue & dePaola, Tomie. The Bug Book. 2016. (ENG., Illus.). 32p. (J). (-k). pap. 3.99 (978-0-448-48935-3(X), Grosset & Dunlap) Penguin Young Readers Group.

Follow the Bee. 2004. 10p. (J). bds. 5.99 (978-1-85997-874-0(6)) Byeway Bks.

Forrest, Tim & Hamel, Jen. Bug Camp: Where Every Day's an Adventure. 2016. (ENG.). 96p. (J). (gr. 3-7). 14.95 (978-1-63322-116-1(4), Moondance) Quarto Publishing Group USA.

Freaky Freeloaders: Bugs That Feed on People. 2015. (Freaky Freeloaders: Bugs That Feed on People Ser.). (ENG.). 24p. (J). (gr. 2-3). pap., pap., pap. 297.00 (978-1-4994-1292-5(4), PowerKids Pr.) Rosen Publishing Group, Inc., The.

Fredericks, Anthony D. On One Flower: Butterflies, Ticks & a Few More Icks. DiRubbio, Jennifer, illus. 2006. (Sharing Nature with Children Book Ser.). 32p. (J). (gr. -1-5). 7.95 (978-1-58469-087-0(9)); (ENG.). 16.95 (978-1-58469-086-3(0)) Dawn Pubns.

French, Jess. Fluttering Minibeast Adventures. Woodward, Jonathan, illus. 2016. (ENG.). 32p. (J). (gr. -1-k). 10.99 (978-1-4052-7755-6(6)) Egmont Bks., Ltd. GBR. Dist: Independent Pubs. Group.

—Tickly Minibeast Adventures. Woodward, Jonathan, illus. 2016. (ENG.). 32p. (J). (gr. -1-k). 10.99 (978-1-4052-7756-3(4)) Egmont Bks., Ltd. GBR. Dist: Independent Pubs. Group.

Gates Galvin, Laura. First Look at Insects. Oh, Charlotte, illus. 2011. (ENG.). 16p. (J). (978-1-60727-223-6(7)) Soundprints.

Gates, Valerie. The Alphabet of Bugs: An ABC Book. Cutting, Ann, photos by. 2015. (ENG., Illus.). 56p. (J). (gr. -1-k). 14.99 (978-1-63220-407-3(X), Sky Pony Pr.) Skyhorse Publishing Co., Inc.

George, Abigail. Freaky Bug Facts! Understand Place Value, 1 vol. 2015. (InfoMax Common Core Math Readers Ser.). (ENG.). 24p. (J). pap. 8.25 (978-1-4777-4837-4(7), Rosen Classroom) Rosen Publishing Group, Inc., The.

Giebink, Bruce. Minnesota Bug Hunt. Johnson, Bill, photos by. 2013. (ENG., Illus.). 32p. (J). (gr. -1-2). 16.95 (978-0-87351-865-9(9)) Minnesota Historical Society Pr.

Gifford, Clive. Bugs: The World's Longest, Loudest & Most Lethal! 2017. (Record Busters Ser.). (ENG., Illus.). 32p. (J). (gr. 4-6). pap. 11.99 (978-0-7502-8908-5(2), Wayland) Hachette Children's Group GBR. Dist: Hachette Bk. Group.

Giulieri, Anne. Bugs, 1 vol. Vanzet, Gaston, illus. 2012. (Engage Literacy Red Ser.). (ENG.). 32p. (gr. k-2). pap. 5.99 (978-1-4296-8934-2(X), Engage Literacy) Capstone Press of Coughlan Cos.

Gleason, Carrie. Feasting Bedbugs, Mites, & Ticks. 2010. (Creepy Crawlies Ser.). (ENG.). 32p. (J). (gr. 3-6). (978-0-7787-2500-8(6)); pap. (978-0-7787-2507-7(3)) Crabtree Publishing Co.

Gleeson, Michelle. Miniature Lives: Identifying Insects in Your Home & Garden. 2016. (ENG., Illus.). 344p. pap. 28.95 (978-1-4863-0137-9(1)) CSIRO Publishing AUS. Dist: Stylus Publishing, LLC.

H I

Gleisner, Jenna Lee. Bug Exterminator. 2015. (Gross Jobs Ser.). (ENG.). 24p. (J). (gr. 2-5). 27.07 (978-1-63143-684-0(8), 208519) Child's World, Inc., The.

Goddard, Jerome. You Gonna Touch That? Student Edition. 2008. (Illus.). 24p. (J). 9.95 (978-0-9795394-3-5(9)) Father's Pr., LLC.

Goldish, Meish. Hidden Walkingsticks. 2008. (No Backbone! Ser.). (Illus.). 24p. (J). (gr. k-3). lib. bdg. 21.28 (978-1-59716-646-1(4)) Bearport Publishing Co., Inc.

—Red Imported Fire Ants: Attacking Everything. 2015. (They Don't Belong: Tracking Invasive Species Ser.). (ENG., Illus.). 32p. (J). (gr. 2-7). lib. bdg. 26.60 (978-1-62724-831-0(5)) Bearport Publishing Co., Inc.

—Smelly Stink Bugs. 2008. (No Backbone! Ser.). (Illus.). 24p. (J). (gr. k-3). lib. bdg. 21.28 (978-1-59716-580-8(8)) Bearport Publishing Co., Inc.

Goodman, Sarah & Sorkin, Louis N. Bugs - Fandex Family Field Guides. 2009. (ENG., Illus.). 50p. (J). (gr. 4-12). 12.95 (978-0-7611-5414-3(0), 15414) Workman Publishing Co., Inc.

Gordon, David George. Creepy Critters of the Southwest. 2004. (Illus.). 16p. pap. 4.95 (978-1-58369-053-6(0)) Western National Parks Assn.

—La Tarantula. 2004. (Al Descubierto Ser.).Tr. of Uncover a Tarantula. (SPA., Illus.). 16p. (J). bds. 20.85 (978-970-718-212-7(1), Silver Dolphin Bks.) Readerlink Distribution Services, LLC.

Gould, Robert. Bugs, Vol. 7. Epstein, Eugene, illus. 2009. (Big Stuff Ser.: 7 vols.). (ENG.). 16p. (J). bds. 7.95 (978-1-929945-66-5(3)) Big Guy Bks., Inc.

Gravel, Elise. Head Lice. (Disgusting Critters Ser.). (ENG., Illus.). 32p. (J). (gr. 1-4). 2016. pap. 5.99 (978-1-101-91853-1(5)) 2015. 10.99 (978-1-77049-661-3(0)) Tundra Bks. CAN. (Tundra Bks.). Dist: Penguin Random Hse. LLC.

Gray, Leon. Walking Sticks: The World's Longest Insects. 2013. (Even More SuperSized! Ser.). 24p. (J). (gr. k-3). lib. bdg. 23.93 (978-1-61772-733-7(4)) Bearport Publishing Co., Inc.

Gray, Rita. Flowers Are Calling. Pak, Kenard, illus. 2015. (ENG.). 32p. (J). (gr. -1-3). 16.99 (978-0-544-34012-1(4), HMH Books For Young Readers) Houghton Mifflin Harcourt Publishing Co.

Gray, Susan H. Emerald Ash Borer. 2008. (21st Century Skills Library: Animal Invaders Ser.). (ENG.). 32p. (gr. 4-8). lib. bdg. 28.50 (978-1-60279-112-1(0), 200096) Cherry Lake Publishing.

—The Life Cycle of Insects, 1 vol. 2011. (Life Cycles Ser.). (ENG.). 48p. (gr. 3-5). pap. 9.95 (978-1-4329-4990-7(X)); 33.32 (978-1-4329-4983-9(7)) Heinemann-Raintree. (Heinemann InfoSearch).

—Super Cool Science Experiments: Bugs. 2009. (Explorer Library: Science Explorer Ser.). (ENG.). 32p. (gr. 4-8). lib. bdg. 28.50 (978-1-60279-521-1(5), 200281) Cherry Lake Publishing.

Green, Emily K. Walkingsticks. 2006. (World of Insects Ser.). (ENG., Illus.). 24p. (J). (gr. k-3). lib. bdg. 25.95 (978-1-60014-015-0(7)) Bellwether Media.

Green, Jen. Beetles & Bugs. 2014. (ENG., Illus.). 64p. (J). (gr. 3-7). 12.99 (978-1-86147-366-0(4), Armadillo) Anness Publishing GBR. Dist: National Bk. Network.

—Exploring Nature: Incredible Insects. 2014. (ENG., Illus.). 64p. (J). (gr. 3-7). 12.99 (978-1-84322-911-7(0), Armadillo) Anness Publishing GBR. Dist: National Bk. Network.

—Find Out about Insects. 2013. (ENG., Illus.). 64p. 9.99 (978-1-84322-980-3(3), Armadillo) Anness Publishing GBR. Dist: National Bk. Network.

Gregoire, Maryellen. Insects. 2011. (Wonder Readers Emergent Level Ser.). (ENG.). (gr. -1-1). 8p. pap. 35.94 (978-1-4296-8231-2(0)); 32p. pap. 5.99 (978-1-4296-7844-5(5)) Capstone Press of Coughlan Cos. (Wonder Readers).

Greve, Tom. Buzzing Bugs. Rourke Publishing Staff, ed. 2009. 24p. (J). pap. 3.99 (978-0-8249-5144-3(1), Ideal Pubns.) Worthy Publishing.

—Creeping Crawlers. Rourke Publishing Staff, ed. 2009. 24p. (J). pap. 3.99 (978-0-8249-5145-0(X), Ideal Pubns.) Worthy Publishing.

Grolier Educational Staff, contrib. by. Insects & Other Invertebrates, 50 vols. 2004. (World of Animals Ser.: Vol. 3). (Illus.). (J). 499.00 (978-0-7172-5894-9(7)) Scholastic Library Publishing.

Gross Bugs. (Illus.). (J). (gr. k-6). 112.50 (978-1-4042-3292-1(3)) Rosen Publishing Group, Inc., The.

Group/McGraw-Hill, Wright. La Vida de Los Insectos, 6 vols., Vol. 2. (First Explorers, Primeros Exploradores Nonfiction Sets Ser.). (SPA.). (gr. 1-2). 34.95 (978-0-7699-1479-4(9)) Shortland Pubns. (U. S. A.) Inc.

Guillain, Charlotte. Bug Parts, 1 vol. 2010. (Comparing Bugs Ser.). (ENG.). 24p. (gr. -1-1). 22.65 (978-1-4329-3565-8(8)); pap. 6.29 (978-1-4329-3574-0(7)) Heinemann-Raintree. (Acorn).

—Bug Senses, 1 vol. 2010. (Comparing Bugs Ser.). (ENG.). 24p. (gr. -1-1). pap. 6.29 (978-1-4329-3575-7(5)); lib. bdg. 22.65 (978-1-4329-3566-5(6)) Heinemann-Raintree. (Acorn).

—Comparing Bugs, 5 vols., Set. Incl. Bug Babies. pap. 6.29 (978-1-4329-3579-5(8)); Bug Food. pap. 6.29 (978-1-4329-3578-8(X)); Bug Homes. pap. 6.29 (978-1-4329-3577-1(1)); Bug Parts. pap. 6.29 (978-1-4329-3574-0(7)); Bug Senses. pap. 6.29 (978-1-4329-3575-7(5)); Bugs on the Move. pap. 6.29 (978-1-4329-3576-4(3)); (gr. -1-1). (Comparing Bugs Ser.). (ENG.). 24p. 2010. Set pap. 37.74 (978-1-4329-3580-1(1)); 135.90 (978-1-4329-3571-9(2)) Heinemann-Raintree. (Acorn).

—Las Crias de los Insectos. 2010. (Comparar Insectos Ser.).Tr. of Bug Babies. (SPA.). 24p. (gr. -1-1). 22.65 (978-1-4329-4327-1(8)); pap. 6.29 (978-1-4329-4334-9(0)) Heinemann-Raintree. (Bellota).

—Las Partes de los Insectos. 2010. (Comparar Insectos Ser.). (SPA.). 24p. (gr. -1-1). pap. 6.29 (978-1-4329-4329-5(4), Bellota) Heinemann-Raintree.

—Los Sentidos de los Insectos. 2010. (Comparar Insectos Ser.). (SPA., Illus.). 24p. (gr. -1-1). 22.65 (978-1-4329-4323-3(5)); pap. 6.29 (978-1-4329-4330-1(8)) Heinemann-Raintree. (Bellota).

—A World of Bugs, 1 vol. 2011. (ENG.). 24p. (gr. -1-1). pap. 9.95 (978-1-4329-5506-9(3)); 25.99 (978-1-4329-5505-2(5)) Heinemann-Raintree. (Acorn Read-Aloud).

Haffmann, Janet & Richardson, Adele D. Bugbooks, Set. (Illus.). 32p. (J). lib. bdg. 170.40 (978-1-887068-49-9(X)) Black Rabbit Bks.

Hall, Kirsten. Up Close & Gross. Jankowski, Dan, illus. 2009. 64p. (J). (978-0-545-13583-2(4)) Scholastic, Inc.

Hamilton, S. L. Bugs. 2013. (Xtreme Pets Ser.). (Illus.). 32p. (J). (gr. 3-9). lib. bdg. 27.07 (978-1-61783-970-2(1), Abdo & Daughters) ABDO Publishing Co.

—Mantis. 2014. (Xtreme Insects Ser.). (ENG., Illus.). 32p. (J). (gr. 3-9). lib. bdg. 27.07 (978-1-62403-690-3(2), Abdo & Daughters) ABDO Publishing Co.

—Roaches. 2014. (Xtreme Insects Ser.). (ENG.). 32p. (gr. 3-9). lib. bdg. 27.07 (978-1-62403-691-0(0), Abdo & Daughters) ABDO Publishing Co.

—Xtreme Insects. 2014. (Xtreme Insects Ser.: 6). (ENG.). 32p. (gr. 3-9). lib. bdg. 162.42 (978-1-62403-685-9(6), Abdo & Daughters) ABDO Publishing Co.

Hamilton, Sue L. Forensic Entomology: Bugs & Bodies, 1 vol. 2008. (Crime Scene Investigation Ser.). (ENG.). 32p. (gr. 4-8). 27.07 (978-1-59928-991-5(1), Abdo & Daughters) ABDO Publishing Co.

Hansen, Amy S. Bugs & Bugsicles: Insects in the Winter. Kray, Robert C., illus. 2010. (ENG.). 32p. (J). (gr. 2-4). pap. 11.95 (978-1-59078-763-2(3)) Boyds Mills Pr.

Hanson, Anders & Mann, Elissa. Biggest, Baddest Book of Bugs, 1 vol. 2012. (Biggest, Baddest Books for Boys Ser.). (ENG.). 24p. (J). (gr. k-4). 25.65 (978-1-61783-405-9(X)) ABDO Publishing Co.

Hardyman, Robyn. Bugs. 2008. (World of Animals Ser.). 32p. (gr. 2-5). 31.35 (978-1-933834-36-8(0)) Brown Bear Bks.

Harrington, Jane. Extreme Pets. 2007. (ENG., Illus.). 164p. (J). (gr. 2-5). pap., instr.'s hndbk. ed. 12.99 (978-0-439-82948-9(8)) Scholastic, Inc.

Harris, Monica. Walking Stick. 2003. (Bug Bks.). (Illus.). 32p. (J). lib. bdg. 22.79 (978-1-4034-0766-5(5)) Heinemann-Raintree.

Harrison, Paul & Arcturus Publishing Staff. Bugs & the World's Creepiest Microbugs. 2011. (3-D Thrillers Ser.). (ENG.). 32p. (J). (gr. 2-5). pap. 4.99 (978-0-545-28178-2(4), Scholastic Reference) Scholastic, Inc.

Haslam, Andrew. Insects. 2004. (Make It Work! Science Ser.). (Illus.). 48p. (J). (gr. 3-6). 12.95 (978-1-58728-365-9(4), Two-Can Publishing) T&N Children's Publishing.

Haworth, Katie. Little Honey Bee. Ormes, Jane, illus. 2016. (ENG.). 14p. (J). (gr. -1-2). bds. 14.99 (978-0-7636-8531-7(3), Big Picture Press) Candlewick Pr.

Hayes, Amy. A Larva Becomes a Fly. 2016. (Transformations in Nature Ser.). (ENG.). 24p. (J). (gr. 1-1). pap. 8.22 (978-1-5026-0830-7(8)) Cavendish Square Publishing.

Healan, Tammy. A Ladybug's Defense: Part One of the Fascinating Bug's Series. Hill, Malissa, illus. 2011. 24p. pap. 24.95 (978-1-4626-4459-9(7)) America Star Bks.

Helbrough, Emma. 1001 Bugs to Spot. 2009. (1001 Things to Spot Ser.). 32p. (J). 9.99 (978-0-7945-2493-7(1), Usborne) EDC Publishing.

Heos, Bridget. What to Expect When You're Expecting Larvae: A Guide for Insect Parents (And Curious Kids) Jorisch, Stéphane, illus. 2011. (Expecting Animal Babies Ser.). (ENG.). 32p. (gr. 2-5). 25.26 (978-0-7613-5858-9(7)) Lerner Publishing Group.

Herrington, Lisa M. Incredible Insects. 2016. (Rookie Read-About Science(tm): Strange Animals Ser.). (ENG., Illus.). 32p. (J). lib. bdg. 25.00 (978-0-531-22602-5(6), Children's Pr.) Scholastic Library Publishing.

Hewitt, Sally. Minibeasts. (Illus.). 32p. (YA). (gr. 2-18). lib. bdg. 27.10 (978-1-932333-29-9(0)) Chrysalis Education.

Hide to Survive, 6 Packs. (gr. k-1). 23.00 (978-0-7635-8857-1(1)) Rigby Education.

Hilton, Samantha. World of Insects. Holmes, Steve, illus. 2004. (Interfact Ladders Ser.). (ENG.). 48p. (J). (gr. -1-2). 14.95 incl. cd-rom (978-1-58728-419-9(7)) Cooper Square Publishing Llc.

Himmelman, John. Basic Illustrated Guide to Frogs, Snakes, Bugs, & Slugs. 2013. (Basic Illustrated Ser.). (ENG., Illus.). 104p. pap. 10.95 (978-0-7627-8259-8(5), Falcon Guides) Globe Pequot Pr., The.

—There's a Bug on My Book!, 1 vol. Himmelman, John, illus. 2017. (ENG., Illus.). 32p. (J). (gr. -1-3). 16.95 (978-1-58469-587-5(0)) Dawn Pubns.

Hipp, Andrew. Assassin Bugs. (Really Wild Life of Animals Ser.). 24p. 2009. (gr. 3-4). 42.50 (978-1-60854-181-2(9)) 2003. (Illus.). (J). lib. bdg. 22.60 (978-0-8239-6240-2(7)) Rosen Publishing Group, Inc., The. (PowerKids Pr.).

—Leafhoppers. (Really Wild Life of Animals Ser.). 24p. 2009. (gr. 3-4). 42.50 (978-1-60854-196-6(7)) 2003. (Illus.). (J). lib. bdg. 22.60 (978-0-8239-6241-9(5)) Rosen Publishing Group, Inc., The. (PowerKids Pr.).

—Orchid Mantises. (Really Wild Life of Animals Ser.). 24p. 2009. (gr. 3-4). 42.50 (978-1-60854-201-7(7)) 2003. (Illus.). (J). lib. bdg. 22.60 (978-0-8239-6239-6(3)) Rosen Publishing Group, Inc., The. (PowerKids Pr.).

—Peanut-Head Bugs. (Really Wild Life of Animals Ser.). 24p. 2009. (gr. 3-4). 42.50 (978-1-60854-203-1(3), PowerKids Pr.) 2003. (Illus.). (J). lib. bdg. 22.60 (978-0-8239-6242-6(3)) Rosen Publishing Group, Inc., The.

—Really Wild Life of Insects, 4 vols., set. 80.70 (978-0-8239-7275-3(5)) Rosen Publishing Group, Inc., The.

Hirsch, Rebecca E. Monarch Butterflies: A Generational Journey. 2016. (Illus.). 32p. (J). (978-1-4896-4521-0(7)) Weigl Pubs., Inc.

Hisao, Sato, illus. Make & Move - Bugs: 12 Paper Puppets to Press Out & Play. 2017. (ENG.). 56p. (J). (gr. 1-4). 12.99 (978-1-78067-957-0(2)) King, Laurence Publishing GBR. Dist: Hachette Bk. Group.

Holcomb, Carrie E., ed. Buggin' with Ruud. 2007. (Illus.). 48p. (J). per. 6.99 (978-0-696-23690-7(7)) Meredith Bks.

Holden, Pam. Bugs & Beetles. 2015. (ENG., Illus.). 16p. (-2). pap. (978-1-77654-137-9(5), Red Rocket Readers) Flying Start Bks.

Holland, Gay W., illus. An Introduction to Bug-Watching. 2003. (Look Closer Ser.: 4). 32p. lib. bdg. 22.90 (978-0-7613-2664-9(2), Millbrook Pr.) Lerner Publishing Group.

Hopkins, Therese. Insect Homes. 2009. (Home Sweet Home Ser.). 24p. (J). (gr. k-2). (Illus.). pap. 8.25 (978-1-4358-3069-1(5), PowerKids Pr.); lib. bdg. 22.60 (978-1-4358-2695-3(7)) Rosen Publishing Group, Inc., The.

Hudak, Heather C. Insects. 2005. (Animal Facts Ser.). (Illus.). 24p. (J). (gr. 2-3). per. 8.95 (978-1-59036-244-0(6)); lib. bdg. 24.45 (978-1-59036-199-3(7)) Weigl Pubs., Inc.

Hufnal, Amy. Let's Explore Bugs: A Look at God's Smallest Creatures. 2009. 24p. pap. 15.00 (978-1-4490-3676-8(7)) AuthorHouse.

Huggins-Cooper, Lynn. Beastly Bugs. 2006. (Killer Nature! Ser.). (Illus.). 32p. (J). (gr. 3-5). lib. bdg. 28.50 (978-1-58340-936-7(X)) Black Rabbit Bks.

—Minibeasts. 2003. (Starters Ser.). 24p. (J). lib. bdg. 21.35 (978-1-58340-263-4(2)) Black Rabbit Bks.

Hughes, Catherine D. Little Kids First Big Book Collector's Set: Birds & Bugs. 2017. (ENG., Illus.). 288p. (J). (gr. -1-3). 25.00 (**978-1-4263-2948-7(2)**, National Geographic Children's Bks.) National Geographic Society.

Hughes, Catherine D. & National Geographic Kids Staff. Little Kids First Big Book of Bugs. 2014. (National Geographic Little Kids First Big Bks.). (ENG., Illus.). 128p. (J). (gr. -1-3). 14.99 (978-1-4263-1723-1(9), National Geographic Children's Bks.) National Geographic Society.

Hughes, Huw John, et al. Bwystfilod Bychain. 2005. (WEL., Illus.). 40p. pap. (978-1-85596-665-9(4)) Dref Wen.

Hutnick, Theresa & Phillips, Karen. Insectos Insolitos. Fox, Peter, photos by. 2005. (SPA., Illus.). 38p. (J). spiral bd. 17.95 (978-987-1078-43-1(9)) Klutz Latino MEX. Dist: Independent Pubs. Group.

I'm a Bug! 2017. (I'm a Bug! Ser.). 24p. (gr. 4-6). 94.40 (**978-1-5081-5791-5(X)**); pap. 33.00 (**978-1-5081-5803-5(7)**) Rosen Publishing Group, Inc., The. (PowerKids Pr.).

Insects, Set. 2005. (Bugs, Bugs, Bugs Ser.). (YA). (gr. k-3). 297.00 (978-0-7368-4203-7(9), Pebble Bks.) Capstone Press of Coughlan Cos.

Insects. 2007. (Nonfiction Collection). (J). 8.00 (978-1-60343-002-9(4)) Pioneer Valley Bks.

Insects, Set. (gr. k-2). 288.95 (978-0-7368-9040-3(8)) Red Brick Learning.

Insects! (Creatures Corner Ser.). 16p. (J). (978-2-7643-0123-4(5)) Phidal Publishing, Inc./Editions Phidal, Inc.

Insects, Set, Vol. 2. 2005. (Bugs, Bugs, Bugs Ser.). (YA). (gr. k-3). 297.00 (978-0-7368-4204-4(7), Pebble Bks.) Capstone Press of Coughlan Cos.

Insects & Spiders. (Action Bks.). 64p. (J). (gr. 3-7). pap. (978-1-882210-67-1(0)) Action Publishing, Inc.

Interesting Insects; Individual Title Six-Pack. (Story Steps Ser.). (gr. k-2). 23.00 (978-0-7635-9847-1(X)) Rigby Education.

Ipcizade, Catherine. BIG Bugs. 2016. (Big Ser.). (ENG.). 24p. pap. 6.95 (978-1-5157-6235-5(1), Pebble Plus) Capstone Press of Coughlan Cos.

Ipcizade, Catherine & Rustad, Martha E. Bugs Are Beautiful! 2017. (Bugs Are Beautiful! Ser.). (ENG.). 32p. (gr. 1-2). 109.28 (978-1-5157-4517-4(1), Aplus Bks.) Capstone Press of Coughlan Cos.

Jackson, Cari. Bugs That Build. 2008. (Bug Alert! Ser.). 32p. (gr. 3-18). lib. bdg. 28.50 (978-0-7614-3191-6(8), Benchmark Bks.) Marshall Cavendish Corp.

Jackson, Demi. Name That Bug! 2016. (Guess That Animal! Ser.). 24p. (J). (gr. 2-1). 22.60 (978-1-4824-4744-6(4)) Stevens, Gareth Publishing LLLP.

Jackson, Donna M. The Bug Scientists. 2004. (Illus.). 48p. (J). lib. bdg. 13.60 (978-0-7569-5192-4(5)) Perfection Learning Corp.

Jackson, Tom. Beastly Bugs. 2010. (Dangerous Animals Ser.). (ENG.). 32p. (J). (gr. 2-6). pap. 10.50 (978-1-4339-4035-4(3), Gareth Stevens Learning Library); (YA). (gr. 3-6). lib. bdg. 26.60 (978-1-4339-4034-7(5)) Stevens, Gareth Publishing LLLP.

Jacobs, Pat. Why Do Insects Have Six Legs? And Other Questions about Evolution & Classification. 2016. (Wildlife Wonders Ser.). 00032p. (J). (gr. 3-3). pap. 10.00 (978-1-4994-3207-7(0), PowerKids Pr.) Rosen Publishing Group, Inc., The.

James, Lincoln. Bugs up Close. 2009. (Real Life Readers Ser.). 8p. (gr. k-1). pap. 5.15 (978-1-4042-7957-5(1), Rosen Classroom) Rosen Publishing Group, Inc., The.

Jeffries, Joyce. Bedbugs. 2015. (Freaky Freeloaders: Bugs That Feed on People Ser.). (ENG.). 24p. (J). (gr. 2-3). pap. 8.25 (978-1-4994-0742-6(4), PowerKids Pr.) Rosen Publishing Group, Inc., The.

—Freaky Freeloaders: Bugs That Feed on People Set. 2015. (Freaky Freeloaders: Bugs That Feed on People Ser.). (ENG.). 24p. (J). (gr. 2-3). 141.60 (978-1-4994-0781-5(5), PowerKids Pr.) Rosen Publishing Group, Inc., The.

Jeunesse, Gallimard & Peyrols, Sylvaine. Ladybugs & Other Insects. Peyrols, Sylvaine, illus. 2007. (First Discovery Book Ser.). (ENG., Illus.). 24p. (J). (gr. -1-k). pap. 5.99 (978-0-439-91086-6(2)) Scholastic, Inc.

Jobes, Cecily. Bugs & Plants Need Each Other. 2013. (Rosen Readers Ser.). (ENG.). 24p. (J). (gr. 2-3). pap. 8.25 (978-1-4777-2302-9(1)); pap. 49.50 (978-1-4777-2766-9(3)) Rosen Publishing Group, Inc., The. (Rosen Classroom).

Johnson-Farris, Nancy. Critters & Bugs of Africa. 2003. (J). spiral bd. 12.95 (978-1-931334-35-8(8)) Pieces of Learning.

—Critters & Bugs of the Great Sonoran Desert. 2003. (J). spiral bd. 12.95 (978-1-931334-32-7(3)) Pieces of Learning.

Jones, J. Just Bugs: Learning the Short U Sound. 2009. (PowerPhonics Ser.). 24p. (gr. 1-1). 39.90 (978-1-60851-454-0(4), PowerKids Pr.) Rosen Publishing Group, Inc., The.

Junor, Amy. My Giant Fold-Out Bright Bugs. 2014. (My Giant Fold-Outs Ser.). (ENG.). 10p. (J). (gr. -1 — 1). 6.99 (978-0-7641-6668-6(9)) Barron's Educational Series, Inc.

Kahn, Sarah. Creepy Crawlies. Scott, Peter David, illus. 2006. (J). (978-0-439-78702-4(5)) Scholastic, Inc.

Kalman, Bobbie. The ABCs of Insects. 2009. (ABCs of the Natural World Ser.). (ENG., Illus.). 32p. (J). (gr. 1-5). pap. (978-0-7787-3436-9(6)); (gr. 2-4). lib. bdg. (978-0-7787-3416-1(1)) Crabtree Publishing Co.

—El Ciclo de Vida de la Mariposa. Reiach, Margaret Amy, illus. 2005. (Serie Ciclos de Vida Ser.). (SPA.). 32p. (J). (gr. 1-4). pap. (978-0-7787-8708-2(7)) Crabtree Publishing Co.

—Insect Eaters. 2008. (Big Science Ideas Ser.). (ENG., Illus.). 32p. (J). (gr. 1-4). pap. (978-0-7787-3298-3(3)); lib. bdg. (978-0-7787-3278-5(9)) Crabtree Publishing Co.

Kalman, Bobbie & Aloian, Molly. El Ciclo de Vida de los Insectos. 2006. (Mundo de los Insectos Ser.). (SPA & ENG., Illus.). 32p. (J). (gr. 3-7). pap. (978-0-7787-8515-6(7)) Crabtree Publishing Co.

—El Ciclo de Vida de Los Insectos. 2006. (Mundo de los Insectos Ser.). (SPA & ENG., Illus.). 32p. (J). (gr. 3-7). lib. bdg. (978-0-7787-8499-9(1)) Crabtree Publishing Co.

—El Cuerpo de los Insectos. 2006. (Mundo de los Insectos Ser.). (SPA., Illus.). 32p. (J). (gr. 3-7). pap. (978-0-7787-8512-5(2)) Crabtree Publishing Co.

—El Cuerpo de Los Insectos. 2006. (Mundo de los Insectos Ser.). (SPA., Illus.). 32p. (J). (gr. 3-7). lib. bdg. (978-0-7787-8496-8(7)) Crabtree Publishing Co.

—Insectos Que Trabajan en Equipo. 2006. (Mundo de los Insectos Ser.). (SPA., Illus.). 32p. (J). (gr. 3-7). pap. (978-0-7787-8514-9(9)); lib. bdg. (978-0-7787-8498-2(3)) Crabtree Publishing Co.

—Insectos Utiles y Daninos. 2006. (Mundo de los Insectos Ser.). (SPA., Illus.). 32p. (J). (gr. 3-7). lib. bdg. (978-0-7787-8497-5(5)) Crabtree Publishing Co.

—Insectos Utiles y Dañinos. 2006. (Mundo de los Insectos Ser.). (SPA., Illus.). 32p. (J). (gr. 3-7). pap. (978-0-7787-8513-2(0)) Crabtree Publishing Co.

Kalman, Bobbie & Crossingham, John. Los Hogares de los Insectos. 2006. (Mundo de los Insectos Ser.). (SPA., Illus.). 32p. (J). (gr. 3-7). pap. (978-0-7787-8516-3(5)); lib. bdg. (978-0-7787-8500-2(9)) Crabtree Publishing Co.

—Insect Homes. 2006. (World of Insects Ser.). (ENG., Illus.). 32p. (J). (gr. 4-7). pap. (978-0-7787-2379-0(8)); lib. bdg. (978-0-7787-2345-5(3)) Crabtree Publishing Co.

Kalman, Bobbie & Sjonger, Rebecca. Everyday Insects. 2006. (World of Insects Ser.). (ENG., Illus.). 32p. (J). (gr. 3-7). pap. (978-0-7787-2370-7(4)); lib. bdg. (978-0-7787-2336-3(4)) Crabtree Publishing Co.

—Insect Defenses. 2006. (World of Insects Ser.). (ENG., Illus.). 32p. (J). (gr. 3-7). pap. (978-0-7787-2368-4(2)); lib. bdg. (978-0-7787-2334-9(8)) Crabtree Publishing Co.

—Insectos Comunes. 2006. (Mundo de los Insectos Ser.). (SPA., Illus.). 32p. (J). (gr. 3-7). pap. (978-0-7787-8517-0(3)); lib. bdg. (978-0-7787-8501-9(7)) Crabtree Publishing Co.

Kaspar, Anna. What's an Insect? 2012. (All about Animals Ser.). (ENG., Illus.). 24p. (J). (gr. k-3). pap. 8.25 (978-1-4488-6236-8(1)); lib. bdg. 22.60 (978-1-4488-6139-2(X)) Rosen Publishing Group, Inc., The. (PowerKids Pr.).

—What's an Insect? Qué Es un Insecto? 2012. (All about Animals / Todo sobre los animales Ser.). (SPA & ENG., Illus.). 24p. (J). (gr. k-3). lib. bdg. 22.60 (978-1-4488-6704-2(5), PowerKids Pr.) Rosen Publishing Group, Inc., The.

Khan, Sarah. Creepy Crawlies Lift-the-Flap. Scott, Peter, illus. 2005. (Luxury Lift-the-Flap Learners Ser.). 16p. (J). (gr. 1-18). 11.95 (978-0-7945-0763-3(8), Usborne) EDC Publishing.

Kilpatrick, Cathy. Creepy Crawlies. 2007. (Usborne First Nature Ser.). (Illus.). 24p. (J). (gr. k-3). 12.99 (978-1-58086-982-9(3), Usborne) EDC Publishing.

—Creepy Crawlies. Jacquemier, Sue, ed. Shields, Chris et al, illus. rev. ed. 2006. (First Nature Ser.). 24p. (J). pap. 4.99 (978-0-7945-1494-5(4), Usborne) EDC Publishing.

—Creepy Crawlies Kid Kit. rev. ed. 2007. (Kid Kits Ser.). (Illus.). 23p. (J). pap. 10.99 (978-1-60130-021-8(2), Usborne) EDC Publishing.

Knapp, Ron. Bloodsucking Creatures. 2011. (Bizarre Science Ser.). (Illus.). 48p. (J). (gr. 5-18). pap. 8.95 (978-1-59845-219-8(3)) Enslow Pubs., Inc.

Krauczyk, Sabine & Allaire, Caroline. Let's Look at the Vegetable Garden. 2012. (ENG., Illus.). 38p. (J). (gr. 1-4). pap. 11.99 (978-1-85103-361-4(0)) Moonlight Publishing, Ltd. GBR. Dist: Independent Pubs. Group.

Kravetz, Jonathan. Mosquitoes. 2006. (Gross Bugs Ser.). (Illus.). 24p. (J). lib. bdg. 22.60 (978-1-4042-3044-6(0), PowerKids Pr.) Rosen Publishing Group, Inc., The.

—Stink Bugs. (Gross Bugs Ser.). 24p. 2009. (gr. 3-4). 42.50 (978-1-61513-230-0(9), PowerKids Pr.) 2006. (Illus.). (J). lib. bdg. 22.60 (978-1-4042-3045-3(9)) Rosen Publishing Group, Inc., The.

Krawczyk, Sabine & Allaire, Caroline. Let's Look under the Stone. Krawczyk, Sabine, illus. 2013. (ENG., Illus.). 36p. (J). (gr. 1-4). pap. 11.99 (978-1-85103-353-9(X)) Moonlight Publishing, Ltd. GBR. Dist: Independent Pubs. Group.

Krawczyk, Sabine & Delafosse, Claude. Let's Look at Insects. Krawczyk, Sabine, illus. 2012. (ENG., Illus.). 38p. (J). (gr. k-3). pap. 11.99 (978-1-85103-279-2(7)) Moonlight Publishing, Ltd. GBR. Dist: Independent Pubs. Group.

Krawczyk, Sabine & Sautai, Raoul. Insects. Krawczyk, Sabine, illus. 2012. (My First Discoveries Ser.). (ENG., Illus.). 36p. (J). (gr. -1-k). spiral bd. 14.99 (978-1-85103-411-6(0)) Moonlight Publishing, Ltd. GBR. Dist: Independent Pubs. Group.

Kroll, Jennifer. Pequeños Poderosos: Cosas Diminutas - Grandes Resultados. 2016. (TIME for Kids en Español - Level 5 Ser.). (SPA.). 64p. (gr. 5-5). lib. bdg. 31.99 (978-1-5157-2926-6(5)) Time for Kids Inc AUS. Dist: Capstone Pub.

Kulavis, Allyson. Insect-O-Mania! 2013. (Science with Stuff Ser.: 4). (ENG.). 48p. (J). (gr. 1). 11.99 (978-1-935703-58-7(7)) Downtown Bookworks.

Lara, Enrique & Garcia, Luis. Leaves. 2004. (Illus.). (J). (978-81-89020-07-1(2)) Katha.

Leaf, Christina. Cicadas. 2017. (Insects up Close Ser.). (ENG., Illus.). 24p. (J). (gr. k-3). lib. bdg. 25.95 (**978-1-62617-660-7(4)**, Blastoff! Readers) Bellwether Media.

—Damselflies. 2017. (Insects up Close Ser.). (ENG., Illus.). 24p. (J). (gr. k-3). lib. bdg. 25.95 (**978-1-62617-661-4(2)**, Blastoff! Readers) Bellwether Media.

Lee, Celeste & Herndon, Ryan, compiled by. Guinness World Records: Bizarre Bug Records. 2006. (Illus.). 29p. (J). (978-0-439-87416-8(5)) Scholastic, Inc.

Lee, Mi-Ae. Twinkle, Twinkle! Cowley, Joy, ed. Kim, Dong Soo, illus. 2015. (Science Storybooks Ser.). (ENG.). 32p. (J). (gr. k-3). 26.65 (978-1-925233-62-9(6)) Lerner Publishing Group.

Legg, Gerald & Weston, Steve. The World of Insect Life. 2012. (ENG., Illus.). 48p. (J). 15.00 (978-1-899762-73-6(6)) Award Pubns. Ltd. GBR. Dist: Parkwest Pubns., Inc.

Levy, Janey. Tiny Bugs up Close. 2013. (Under the Microscope Ser.). 32p. (J). (gr. 4-6). pap. 11.70 *(978-1-4339-8351-1(6))*; lib. bdg. 26.60 *(978-1-4339-8350-4(8))* Stevens, Gareth Publishing LLLP.

Lewis, Clare. Bug Body Parts. 2015. (J). *(978-1-4846-2555-2(2))* Heinemann-Raintree.

Li, Maggie. Bug Detective. 2015. (ENG., Illus.). 28p. (J). (gr. 1). 14.95 *(978-1-4549-1516-4(1))* Sterling Publishing Co., Inc.

Linde, Barbara M. Insect Fossils. 2016. (Fossil Files Ser.). 00032p. (J). (gr. 5-5). 26.25 *(978-1-4994-2860-5(X))*; pap. 10.00 *(978-1-4994-2744-8(1))* Rosen Publishing Group, Inc., The. (PowerKids Pr.).

Linde, Barbara M. Venus Flytraps Eat Bugs! 2016. (World's Weirdest Plants Ser.). 00024p. (J). pap. 8.15 ***(978-1-4824-5640-0(0))*** Stevens, Gareth Publishing LLLP.

Little & Large Sticker Activity Bugs. 2008. 24p. pap. *(978-1-84810-057-2(4))* Miles Kelly Publishing, Ltd.

Llewellyn, Claire. The Best Book of Bugs. 2005. (Best Book Of Ser.). (ENG., Illus.). 32p. (J). (gr. k-3). per. 6.99 *(978-0-7534-5901-0(9)*, 9780753459010, Kingfisher) Roaring Brook Pr.

—Big Bugs Green Band. 2016. (Cambridge Reading Adventures Ser.). (ENG.). 16p. pap. 6.56 *(978-1-107-55064-3(5))* Cambridge Univ. Pr.

Lluch, Alex A. I Like to Learn Opposites: Amazing Bugs. 2011. (ENG.). 32p. (J). (gr. -1-k). bds. 4.95 *(978-1-934386-03-3(0))* WS Publishing.

Looking at Insects: Individual Title Six-Packs. (Discovery World Ser.). 24p. (gr. 1-2). 33.00 *(978-0-7635-8474-0(6))* Rigby Education.

Looking for Insects. 2003. (J). 28.95 *(978-0-673-78112-3(7))* Celebration Pr.

Lunis, Natalie. Bugs All Around. Date not set. (Thinking Like a Scientist Ser.). (Illus.). 20p. (J). pap. 16.95 *(978-1-58273-091-2(1))* Sundance/Newbridge Educational Publishing.

—Katydids: Leaf Look-Alikes. 2010. (Disappearing Acts Ser.). (Illus.). 24p. (J). (gr. k-3). lib. bdg. 22.61 *(978-1-936087-40-2(5))* Bearport Publishing Co., Inc.

—Making a Bug Habitat. 2011. (Early Connections Ser.). (J). *(978-1-61672-561-7(3))* Benchmark Education Co.

Lynch, Annabelle. Bugs, 01 vols., 1. 2016. (Nature Explorers Ser.). (ENG., Illus.). 24p. (J). pap. 8.25 *(978-1-5081-9057-8(7)*, 1397735, Windmill Bks.) Rosen Publishing Group, Inc., The.

Lyons, Eric. God Made Insects. 2007. (ENG., Illus.). (J). 3.00 *(978-0-932859-86-0(0))* Apologetics Pr., Inc.

Macken, JoAnn Early. The Life Cycle of a Cicada. 2006. (Things with Wings Ser.). (Illus.). 24p. (gr. k-3). lib. bdg. 22.00 *(978-0-8368-6380-2(1)*, Weekly Reader Leveled Readers) Stevens, Gareth Publishing LLLP.

Madsen, Chris. Bugs. 2005. (Glow in the Dark Ser.). (Illus.). 23p. (J). (gr. -1-7). bds. *(978-1-902626-75-8(3))* Red Bird Publishing.

Maley, Adrienne Houk. 20 Fun Facts about Praying Mantises. 2013. (Fun Fact File: Bugs! Ser.). (Illus.). 32p. (gr. 2-5). 25.25 *(978-1-4339-8240-8(4))*; pap. 10.50 *(978-1-4339-8241-5(2))* Stevens, Gareth Publishing LLLP. (Gareth Stevens Learning Library).

Markle, Sandra. Arachnid World: Spring 2012 New Releases. 2012. (Arachnid World Ser.). 48p. (gr. 4-8). lib. bdg. 175.62 *(978-0-7613-8905-7(9)*, Lerner Pubns.) Lerner Publishing Group.

—Harvestmen: Secret Operatives. 2011. (Arachnid World Ser.). (ENG., Illus.). 48p. (gr. 4-8). 29.27 *(978-0-7613-5042-2(X))* Lerner Publishing Group.

—Insect World: Classroom Library. 2008. pap. 70.95 *(978-1-58013-288-6(X))* Lerner Publishing Group.

—Insect World: Complete Library. 2008. pap. 422.95 *(978-1-58013-289-3(8))* Lerner Publishing Group.

—Insects: Biggest! Littlest! Pollard, Simon, photos by. 2011. (Biggest! Littlest! Ser.). (ENG., Illus.). 32p. (J). pap. 10.95 *(978-1-59078-872-1(9))* Boyds Mills Pr.

—Stick Insects. 2008. pap. 52.95 *(978-1-58013-286-2(3))* Lerner Publishing Group.

—Stick Insects: Masters of Defense. 2008. (Insect World Ser.). (ENG., Illus.). 48p. (gr. 4-8). lib. bdg. 27.93 *(978-0-8225-7296-1(6)*, Lerner Pubns.) Lerner Publishing Group.

—Tarantulas: Super-Sized Predators. 2012. (Arachnid World Ser.). (ENG., Illus.). 48p. (gr. 4-8). lib. bdg. 29.27 *(978-0-7613-5043-9(8))* Lerner Publishing Group.

—Ticks: Dangerous Hitchhikers. 2011. (Arachnid World Ser.). (ENG., Illus.). 48p. (gr. 4-8). 29.27 *(978-0-7613-5041-5(1))* Lerner Publishing Group.

Marshall Cavendish Corporation Staff, contrib. by. Insects & Spiders of the World, 11 vols., Set. 2003. (Illus.). 704p. lib. bdg. 471.36 *(978-0-7614-7334-3(3)*, Marshall Cavendish Reference Bks.) Marshall Cavendish Corp.

Marshall, Stephen A. Insects A to Z. 2009. (ENG., Illus.). 32p. (J). (gr. 1-5). 19.95 *(978-1-55407-555-3(6)*, 9781554075553); pap. 7.95 *(978-1-55407-503-4(3)*, 9781554075034) Firefly Bks., Ltd.

Marshall, Stephen A. & Worek, Michael. Weird Insects. 2013. (ENG., Illus.). 64p. (J). (gr. 5-7). pap. 9.95 *(978-1-77085-234-1(4)*, 9781770852341) Firefly Bks., Ltd.

Marsico, Katie. Insects. 2016. (J). *(978-1-4896-5277-5(9))* Weigl Pubs., Inc.

—Lice. 2015. (ENG., Illus.). 48p. (J). lib. bdg. *(978-0-531-21395-7(1))* Grolier Publishing.

—Step-by-Step Experiments with Insects. Ostrom, Bob, illus. 2012. (Step-By-Step Experiments Ser.). (ENG.). 32p. (J). (gr. 1-4). lib. bdg. 29.93 *(978-1-60973-339-1(8)*, 201231) Child's World, Inc., The.

Martin, Isabel. Insects: A Question & Answer Book, 1 vol. 2014. (Animal Kingdom Questions & Answers Ser.). (ENG.). 24p. (gr. k-1). 26.65 *(978-1-4914-0564-2(3))*; (Illus.). pap. 6.95 *(978-1-4914-0632-8(1))* Capstone Press of Coughlan Cos. (Pebble Plus).

Masiello, Ralph. Bug Drawing Book: Simple Steps Make Anyone an Artist. Masiello, Ralph, illus. 2004. (ENG., Illus.). 32p. (J). (gr. k-3). 16.95 *(978-1-57091-525-3(3))* Charlesbridge Publishing, Inc.

—Bug Drawing Book: Simple Steps to Make Anyone an Artist. Masiello, Ralph, illus. 2004. (ENG., Illus.). 32p. (J). (gr. k-3). pap. 7.95 *(978-1-57091-526-0(1))* Charlesbridge Publishing, Inc.

Mason, Paul. Caring for Critters. 2011. (ENG.). 24p. (J). pap. *(978-0-7787-7870-7(3))*; (gr. 3-6). *(978-0-7787-7848-6(7))* Crabtree Publishing Co.

Matt, Bugler. My First Encylopedia of Bugs: A Great Big Book of Amazing Creatures to Discover. 2016. (ENG.). 24p. pap. 7.99 *(978-1-86147-823-8(2)*, Armadillo) Anness Publishing GBR. Dist: National Bk. Network.

McDonald, Jill. Hello, World! Backyard Bugs. 2017. (ENG., Illus.). 26p. (J). (— 1). bds. 7.99 *(978-0-553-52105-4(5)*, Doubleday Bks. for Young Readers) Random Hse. Children's Bks.

McEvey, Shane F. & Australian Museum Archives Staff. Insects & Spiders Series, 6 bks. Incl. Moths & Butterflies. (Illus.). (J). (gr. 4-18). 2001. 16.95 *(978-0-7910-6598-3(7)*, 010555, Chelsea Hse.); (Illus.). 101.70 *(978-0-7910-6594-5(4)*, 010550S, Chelsea Hse.) Facts On File, Inc.

McFadzean, Lesley. Insects. 2014. (Discovery Education: Animals Ser.). 32p. (J). (gr. 3-6). 26.25 *(978-1-4777-6952-2(8))*; pap. 10.00 *(978-1-4777-6953-9(6))* Rosen Publishing Group, Inc., The. (PowerKids Pr.).

McGavin, George. Bugs: A Stunning Pop-Up Look at Insects, Spiders, & Other Creepy-Crawlies. Kay, Jim, illus. 2013. (ENG.). 12p. (J). (gr. 2-5). 19.99 *(978-0-7636-6762-7(5))* Candlewick Pr.

McGavin, George C. Amazing Insects & Spiders. 2008. (Amazing Life Cycles Ser.). (Illus.). 32p. (gr. 2-6). lib. bdg. 26.00 *(978-0-8368-8899-7(5)*, Gareth Stevens Learning Library) Stevens, Gareth Publishing LLLP.

McNab, Chris & Sutherland, Jonathan. Dangerous Insects & Spiders. 2006. (Nature's Monsters Ser.). (Illus.). 32p. (gr. 2-6). lib. bdg. 26.00 *(978-0-8368-6848-7(X)*, Gareth Stevens Learning Library) Stevens, Gareth Publishing LLLP.

—Giant Spiders & Insects. 2006. (Nature's Monsters Ser.). (Illus.). 32p. (gr. 2-6). lib. bdg. 26.00 *(978-0-8368-6850-0(1)*, Gareth Stevens Learning Library) Stevens, Gareth Publishing LLLP.

Merlino, Kim. Insects & Spiders: Grades 2 & 3. (Illus.). (J). pap., wbk. ed. 4.99 *(978-0-88743-960-5(8))* School Zone Publishing Co.

Michele, Tracey. Bugs & Beetles. 2011. (Learn-Abouts Ser.). (Illus.). 16p. (J). pap. 7.95 *(978-1-59920-611-0(0))* Black Rabbit Bks.

Miller, Connie Colwell. Disgusting Bugs. 2016. (That's Disgusting! Ser.). (ENG.). 32p. pap. 7.95 *(978-1-5157-6286-7(6)*, Blazers) Capstone Press of Coughlan Cos.

Miller, Dave. Birds, Bugs, & Bees. 2006. (ENG., Illus.). (J). 3.00 *(978-0-932859-90-7(9))* Apologetics Pr., Inc.

Miller, Heather. Daddy Longlegs (Bugs) 2005. (Bugs Ser.). (ENG., Illus.). 32p. (J). (gr. 3-6). 26.20 *(978-0-7377-1769-3(6)*, Greenhaven Pr., Inc.) Cengage Gale.

Misztal, Yvonne. How Bugs & Plants Live Together. 2013. (InfoMax Readers Ser.). (ENG.). 24p. (J). (gr. 2-3). pap. 49.50 *(978-1-4777-2447-7(8))*; (Illus.). pap. 8.25 *(978-1-4777-2446-0(X))* Rosen Publishing Group, Inc., The. (Rosen Classroom).

Mitchell, Susan K. Biggest vs. Smallest Incredible Insects. 2010. (Biggest vs. Smallest Animals Ser.). (Illus.). 24p. (J). 22.60 *(978-0-7660-3583-6(2)*, Enslow Elementary) Enslow Pubs., Inc.

Morey, Allan. Insects. 2015. (Animal Kingdom Ser.). (Illus.). 32p. (J). 28.50 *(978-1-60753-474-7(6))* Amicus Publishing.

Morgan, Emily R. La Próxima Vez Que Vean a una Cochinilla. 2016. (Next Time You See Ser.). (SPA., Illus.). 32p. (J). (gr. 2-4). pap. 12.95 *(978-1-68140-289-5(0))* National Science Teachers Assn.

Morris, Neil. Minibeasts. 2004. (Knowledge Masters Ser.). (Illus.). 32p. (YA). pap. incl. cd-rom *(978-1-903954-51-5(7)*, Pavilion Children's Books) Pavilion Bks.

Mound, Laurence & Dorling Kindersley Publishing Staff. Insect. 2007. (DK Eyewitness Bks.). (ENG., Illus.). 72p. (J). (gr. 3-7). 16.99 *(978-0-7566-3004-1(5)*, DK Children) Dorling Kindersley Publishing, Inc.

Munson, Victoria. British Insects. 2016. (Nature Detective Ser.). (ENG., Illus.). 64p. (J). (gr. 2-4). pap. 9.99 *(978-0-7502-9321-1(7)*, Wayland) Hachette Children's Group GBR. Dist: Hachette Bk. Group.

Murawski, Darlyne & Honovich, Nancy. Ultimate Bugopedia: The Most Complete Bug Reference Ever. 2013. (ENG.). 272p. (J). (gr. 2-5). lib. bdg. 34.90 *(978-1-4263-1377-6(2))*; (Illus.). 24.95 *(978-1-4263-1376-9(4))* National Geographic Society. (National Geographic Children's Bks.).

Murphy, Daniel. Bug Dance. 2003. (J). pap., tchr. ed. *(978-0-7398-6545-3(5))* Steck-Vaughn.

Murphy, Patricia J. Investigating Insects with a Scientist. 2004. (I Like Science! Ser.). (Illus.). 24p. (J). (gr. 1-3). lib. bdg. 22.60 *(978-0-7660-2270-6(6))* Enslow Pubs., Inc.

Nagelhout, Ryan. Really Strange Insects. 2016. (Really Strange Adaptations Ser.). 00032p. (J). (gr. 5-5). pap. 10.00 *(978-1-4994-2790-5(5)*, PowerKids Pr.) Rosen Publishing Group, Inc., The.

National Geographic Kids. My Bugs Adventure. 2015. (NG Kids Funny Fill In Ser.). (ENG.). 48p. (J). (gr. 3-7). pap. 4.99 *(978-1-4263-2199-3(6)*, National Geographic Children's Bks.) National Geographic Society.

National Geographic Kids Staff. Bugs. 2015. (Look & Learn Ser.). (ENG., Illus.). 24p. (J). (-k). bds. 6.99 *(978-1-4263-1876-4(6)*, National Geographic Children's Bks.) National Geographic Society.

National Geographic Kids Staff & Gleason, Carrie. National Geographic Kids Everything Insects: All the Facts, Photos, & Fun to Make You Buzz. 2015. (National Geographic Kids Everything Ser.). (ENG., Illus.). 64p. (J). (gr. 3-7). pap. 12.99 *(978-1-4263-1891-7(X)*, National Geographic Children's Bks.) National Geographic Society.

Newman-D'Amico, Fran. Bugs Activity & Coloring Book. 2007. (Dover Children's Activity Bks.). (ENG., Illus.). 32p. (J). (gr. 1-3). pap. 3.99 *(978-0-486-46199-1(8))* Dover Pubns., Inc.

Nirgiotis, Nicholas. Killer Ants. Stevenson, Emma, illus. 2009. (ENG.). 32p. (J). (gr. 1-5). 17.95 *(978-0-8234-2034-6(5))* Holiday Hse., Inc.

Nishida, Masaki. Drawing Manga Insects. (How to Draw Manga Ser.). 24p. (gr. 3-3). 2009. 47.90 *(978-1-61513-439-7(5)*, PowerKids Pr.) 2007. (Illus.). (J). lib. bdg. 25.25 *(978-1-4042-3847-3(6))* Rosen Publishing Group, Inc., The.

Niver, Heather Moore. 20 Fun Facts about Stick Bugs. 2013. (Fun Fact File: Bugs! Ser.). (Illus.). 32p. (gr. 2-5). 25.25 *(978-1-4339-8251-4(X))*; pap. 10.50 *(978-1-4339-8252-1(8))* Stevens, Gareth Publishing LLLP. (Gareth Stevens Learning Library).

Noble, Marty. Creative Haven Incredible Insect Designs Coloring Book. 2014. (Adult Coloring Ser.). (ENG., Illus.). 64p. (gr. 3). pap. 5.99 *(978-0-486-49499-9(3))* Dover Pubns., Inc.

Novick, Mary. Bugs. Hale, Jenny, illus. 2003. 16p. (Orig.). pap. *(978-1-877003-32-5(8))* Little Hare Bks. AUS. Dist: HarperCollins Pubs. Australia.

Oberbillig, Deborah Richie. Bug Feats of Montana. Rath, Robert, illus. 2009. 48p. (J). 7.95 *(978-1-56037-444-2(6))* Farcountry Pr.

O'Brien, Lindsy, et al. Bug Battles. 2016. (Bug Wars Ser.). (ENG.). 32p. (gr. 3-4). 111.96 *(978-1-4914-8080-9(7)*, Edge Bks.) Capstone Press of Coughlan Cos.

O'Donnell, Kerri. Ugly Bugs. 2009. (Ugly Animals Ser.). 24p. (gr. 2-3). 42.50 *(978-1-60854-603-9(9)*, PowerKids Pr.) Rosen Publishing Group, Inc., The.

Oelrich, Deborah, photos by. Amazing Creatures. 2009. (Illus.). 48p. pap. 19.00 *(978-1-4343-6713-6(4))* AuthorHouse.

Ogden, Charlie. Insects. 2017. (Animal Classification Ser.). (J). (gr. 3-4). 32p. pap. 10.50 ***(978-1-5345-2013-4(9))***; pap. 63.00 ***(978-1-5345-2014-1(7))***; 32p. lib. bdg. 27.25 ***(978-1-5345-2015-8(5))*** Greenhaven Publishing LLC. (KidHaven Publishing).

Olsen, Alana. What Do You Know about Bugs? Understand Place Value. 2014. (Math Masters: Number & Operations in Base Ten Ser.). (Illus.). 24p. (J). (gr. 2-3). 23.60 *(978-1-4777-6431-2(3))*; (ENG., pap. 8.25 *(978-1-4777-4663-9(3))* Rosen Publishing Group, Inc., The. (Rosen Classroom).

Olson, Carl. 50 Common Insects of the Southwest. 2004. (Illus.). 64p. pap. 11.95 *(978-1-58369-042-0(5))* Western National Parks Assn.

O'Neill, Amanda. I Wonder Why Spiders Spin Webs: And Other Questions about Creepy Crawlies. 2011. (I Wonder Why Ser.). (ENG., Illus.). 32p. (J). (gr. k-3). pap. 6.99 *(978-0-7534-6524-0(8)*, 9780753465240, Kingfisher) Roaring Brook Pr.

Orme, David. Bugs & Spiders. 2010. (Fact to Fiction Grafx Ser.). (Illus.). 36p. (J). lib. bdg. 16.95 *(978-1-60686-465-4(3))* Perfection Learning Corp.

Orr, Tamra. Backyard Insects: Walking Sticks. 2015. (21st Century Junior Library: Creepy Crawly Critters Ser.). (ENG.). 24p. (J). (gr. k-3). 27.07 *(978-1-63362-595-2(8)*, 206564) Cherry Lake Publishing.

Owen, Ruth. Science & Craft Projects with Insects, Spiders, & Other Minibeasts. 2013. (Get Crafty Outdoors Ser.). (ENG., Illus.). 32p. (J). (gr. k-3). 26.50 *(978-1-4777-0245-1(8))*; pap. 11.75 *(978-1-4777-0253-6(9))* Rosen Publishing Group, Inc., The. (PowerKids Pr.).

Packard, Mary. The Real Thing! Stinkbugs: And Other Bugs. 2006. (Illus.). 47p. (J). *(978-0-439-88064-0(5)*, Scholastic) Scholastic, Inc.

Paige, Joy. The Stick Insect: World's Longest Insect. 2009. (Record-Breaking Animals Ser.). 24p. (gr. 1-1). 42.50 *(978-1-60852-444-0(2)*, PowerKids Pr.) Rosen Publishing Group, Inc., The.

—The Stick Insect / el insecto Palo: The World's Longest Insect / el insecto más largo del Mundo. 2009. (Record-Breaking Animals / Campeones del mundo animal Ser.). (ENG & SPA.). 24p. (gr. 1-1). 42.50 *(978-1-60852-450-1(7)*, Editorial Buenas Letras) Rosen Publishing Group, Inc., The.

—The Stick Insect: The World's Longest Insect: El Insecto Palo:El Insecto Mas Largo Del Mundo. 2004. (Campeones Del Mundo Animal Ser.). (SPA & ENG., Illus.). 24p. (J). (gr. 3-6). lib. bdg. 17.25 *(978-0-8239-6897-8(9)*, Editorial Buenas Letras) Rosen Publishing Group, Inc., The.

Pallister, John C. In the Steps of the Great American Entomologist. Elgin, Kathleen, illus. 2014. (ENG.). 128p. (J). (gr. 2-6). pap. 11.95 *(978-1-59077-364-2(0))* Evans, M. & Co., Inc.

Pallotta, Jerry. The Icky Bug Counting Book. Masiello, Ralph, illus. 2004. (ENG.). 30p. (J). (-k). bds. 7.95 *(978-1-57091-624-3(1))* Charlesbridge Publishing, Inc.

Parker, Janice. Insects. 2007. (Life Science (Weigl Hardcover) Ser.). (Illus.). 32p. (J). (gr. 4-7). lib. bdg. 26.00 *(978-1-59036-707-0(3))*; per. 9.95 *(978-1-59036-708-7(1))* Weigl Pubs., Inc.

Parker, Nancy Winslow. Organs! How They Work, Fall Apart, & Can Be Replaced (Gasp!) 2009. (ENG.). 48p. (J). (gr. 1-4). 17.99 *(978-0-688-15105-8(1)*, Greenwillow Bks.) HarperCollins Pubs.

Parker, Steve. Bugs. 2010. (Remarkable Man & Beast Ser.). (Illus.). 48p. (J). (gr. 3-18). lib. bdg. 19.95 *(978-1-4222-1967-6(4))* Mason Crest.

—Bugs. Draper, Richard, illus. 2010. (I Love Animals Ser.). (ENG.). 24p. (J). (gr. 1-5). pap. 8.15 *(978-1-61533-252-6(9))*; lib. bdg. 22.60 *(978-1-61533-246-5(4))* Windmill Bks.

—Insects & Spiders. 2015. (100 Facts You Should Know Ser.). (ENG., Illus.). 48p. (J). (gr. 4-5). pap. 14.05 *(978-1-4824-3203-9(X))* Stevens, Gareth Publishing LLLP.

—Strange Bugs. 2016. (Animals Are Wild! Ser.). 40p. (gr. 4-3). pap. 14.05 *(978-1-4824-5002-6(X))* Stevens, Gareth Publishing LLLP.

—Why Do Bugs Bite & Sting? And Other Questions & Answers about Creepy Crawlies. Rosewarne, Graham, illus. 2016. (ENG.). 32p. 7.99 *(978-1-86147-480-3(6)*, Armadillo) Anness Publishing GBR. Dist: National Bk. Network.

Pascoe, Elaine. Bugs. Kuhn, Dwight, illus. Kuhn, Dwight, photos by. 2003. 48p. (J). 23.70 *(978-1-56711-458-4(X)*, Blackbirch Pr., Inc.) Cengage Gale.

Pebble Books: Bugs, Bugs, Bugs. 2005. (YA). (gr. k-3). 831.60 *(978-0-7368-4220-4(9)*, Pebble Bks.) Capstone Press of Coughlan Cos.

Perios, Sylvaine, et al. Mariquita. (Coleccion Mundo Maravilloso). (SPA., Illus.). 40p. (J). (gr. 2-4). *(978-84-348-3467-5(7)*, SM5480) SM Ediciones ESP. Dist: Lectorum Pubns., Inc.

Perish, Patric. Aphids. 2017. (Insects up Close Ser.). (ENG., Illus.). 24p. (J). (gr. k-3). lib. bdg. 25.95 ***(978-1-62617-658-4(2)***, Black Sheep) Bellwether Media.

—Earwigs. 2017. (Insects up Close Ser.). (ENG., Illus.). 24p. (J). (gr. k-3). lib. bdg. 25.95 ***(978-1-62617-663-8(9)***, Blastoff! Readers) Bellwether Media.

Perish, Patrick. Disgusting Bugs. 2014. (Totally Disgusting Ser.). (ENG.). 24p. (J). (gr. 3-7). 25.95 *(978-1-62617-128-2(9)*, Epic Bks.) Bellwether Media.

Perritano, John. Bugs on Your Body: Nature's Creepiest Creatures Live on You! 2009. (Current Science Ser.). 48p. (YA). (gr. 4-7). lib. bdg. 31.00 *(978-1-4339-2058-5(1))* Stevens, Gareth Publishing LLLP.

Petrie, Kristin. Box Elder Bugs, 1 vol. 2009. (Bugs! Ser.). (ENG.). 32p. (gr. 3-6). 27.07 *(978-1-60453-064-3(2)*, Checkerboard Library) ABDO Publishing Co.

—Lice, 1 vol. 2009. (Bugs! Ser.). (ENG.). 32p. (gr. 3-6). 27.07 *(978-1-60453-070-4(7)*, Checkerboard Library) ABDO Publishing Co.

—Walking Sticks, 1 vol. 2009. (Bugs! Ser.). (ENG.). 32p. (gr. 3-6). 27.07 *(978-1-60453-073-5(1)*, Checkerboard Library) ABDO Publishing Co.

Pftyler. The Principle of Love. 2015. (ENG., Illus.). 66p. (J). pap. 9.99 *(978-1-4984-5220-5(5))* Salem Author Services.

Pike, Katy. Insects. (Make it Work Ser.). 42p. (J). (gr. 4-8). pap. *(978-1-882210-39-8(5))* Action Publishing, Inc.

—Teaching Insects. 2004. (Illus.). lib. bdg., tchr. ed. 7.95 *(978-0-8225-4526-2(8))* Lerner Publishing Group.

Pledger, Maurice, illus. Dinosaurs & Bugs. 2014. (ENG.). 120p. (J). (gr. -1). act. bk. ed. 12.95 *(978-1-62686-106-0(4)*, Silver Dolphin Bks.) Readerlink Distribution Services, LLC.

Preston-Mafham, Rod & Preston-Mafham, Ken. Insects & Other Invertebrates. 2007. (Facts at Your Fingertips Ser.). (Illus.). 64p. (YA). (gr. 7-12). lib. bdg. 31.35 *(978-1-933834-02-3(1))* Brown Bear Books.

Priddy, Roger. Bug Bites. 2015. (Fact Bites Ser.). (ENG.). 62p. (J). (gr. k-3). pap. 12.99 *(978-0-312-51850-9(1)*, 9780312518509, Priddy Bks.) St. Martin's Pr.

—Busy Bugs Cloth Book. 2014. (My First Priddy Ser.). (ENG.). 6p. (J). (gr. -1 — 1). 10.99 *(978-0-312-51746-5(7)*, 9780312517465, Priddy Bks.) St. Martin's Pr.

Pringle, Laurence. Cicadas! Strange & Wonderful. Henderson, Meryle, illus. unabr. ed. 2010. (Strange & Wonderful Ser.). (ENG.). 32p. (J). (gr. 2-4). 16.95 *(978-1-59078-673-4(4))* Boyds Mills Pr.

Prokopowicz, Jen. Look Out for Bugs. 2015. (ENG., Illus.). 32p. (J). (gr. k-2). 17.99 *(978-1-940052-14-4(9))* Craigmore Creations.

Proudfoot, Peter R., et al, illus. Creepy Critters: A Pop-Up Book of Creatures That Jump, Crawl, & Fly. 2012. (ENG.). 14p. (J). (gr. k-3). 15.95 *(978-0-8109-8942-9(5)*, Abrams Bks. for Young Readers) Abrams, Inc.

Pugliano-Martin, Carol. Being a Bug Scout: Set Of 6. 2011. (Navigators Ser.). (J). 48.00 net. *(978-1-4108-0424-2(0))* Benchmark Education Co.

—Being a Bug Scout & Como ser un explorador de Animalitos: 6 English, 6 Spanish Adaptations. 2011. (ENG & SPA.). (J). 97.00 net. *(978-1-4108-5695-1(X))* Benchmark Education Co.

Raham, Gary. Bugs That Kill. 2008. (Bug Alert! Ser.). 32p. (gr. 3-18). lib. bdg. 28.50 *(978-0-7614-3185-5(3)*, Benchmark Bks.) Marshall Cavendish Corp.

Rajczak, Michael. Attack of the Stink Bugs. 2016. (Animal Invaders: Destroying Native Habitats Ser.). 00024p. (J). pap. 8.15 ***(978-1-4824-5674-5(5))*** Stevens, Gareth Publishing LLLP.

Rake, Jody Sullivan. Why Bed Bugs Bite & Other Gross Facts about Bugs. 2012. (Gross Me Out Ser.). (ENG.). 24p. (gr. 1-2). pap. 41.70 *(978-1-4296-8376-0(7))*; lib. bdg. 25.32 *(978-1-4296-7612-0(4))* Capstone Press of Coughlan Cos. (First Facts).

Regan, Lisa. How to Draw Bugs. Roberts, Steve, illus. 2008. (How to Draw Ser.). 47p. (J). (gr. -1-3). *(978-1-84810-065-7(5))* Miles Kelly Publishing, Ltd.

Reher, Matt. The Book of Flies. 2016. (1G Bugs Ser.). (ENG., Illus.). 28p. (J). pap. 5.99 ***(978-1-63437-574-0(2))*** American Reading Co.

—Desert Bugs. 2015. (1G Bugs Ser.). (ENG., Illus.). 20p. (J). pap. 5.99 *(978-1-63437-112-4(7))* American Reading Co.

—She Wants to Be Queen. 2015. (2G Bugs Ser.). (ENG., Illus.). 24p. (J). pap. 5.99 *(978-1-63437-115-5(1))* American Reading Co.

—Swamp Bugs. 2015. (1G Bugs Ser.). (ENG., Illus.). 20p. (J). pap. 5.99 *(978-1-63437-103-2(8))* American Reading Co.

—What Bug Is That? 2015. (1G Bugs Ser.). (ENG., Illus.). 32p. (J). pap. 5.99 *(978-1-63437-094-3(5))* American Reading Co.

Reith, Sharon L. Infestation! Roaches, Bedbugs, Ants, & Other Insect Invaders, 1 vol. 2013. (Nature's Invaders Ser.). (ENG.). 32p. (gr. 3-4). 27.99 *(978-1-4765-0139-0(4)*, Edge Bks.) Capstone Press of Coughlan Cos.

Reyes, Blanca Matilde. Insects. 2006. (Illus.). 16p. (J). act. bk. ed. 0.75 *(978-1-933984-04-9(X))* Two Lands.

Reynolds, Toby & Calver, Paul. Insects & Spiders. 2016. (Visual Explorers Ser.). (ENG., Illus.). 32p. (J). (gr. 3-7). pap. 6.99 *(978-1-4380-0827-1(9))* Barron's Educational Series, Inc.

Rice, Dona Herweck. Going Buggy!, 1 vol. 2nd rev. ed. 2013. (Nonfiction Readers Ser.). (ENG., Illus.). 20p. (J). (gr. 1-1). pap. 19.96 *(978-1-4807-1024-5(5))* Shell Educational Publishing.

—Going Buggy!, 1 vol. 2nd rev. ed. 2011. (Nonfiction Readers Ser.). (ENG.). 20p. (J). (gr. 1-1). pap. 4.99 *(978-1-4333-3591-4(3))* Teacher Created Materials, Inc.

Richardson, Joy. Insects. 2005. (Variety of Life Ser.). (Illus.). 32p. (gr. 1-4). lib. bdg. 26.00 *(978-0-8368-4505-1(6)*, Gareth Stevens Learning Library) Stevens, Gareth Publishing LLLP.

Richmond, Ben. Don't Bug the Insects. 2017. (ENG., Illus.). 32p. (J). (gr. 1-5). 12.95 ***(978-1-4549-2137-0(4))*** Sterling Publishing Co., Inc.

Riehecky, Janet. Insects. 2017. (My First Animal Kingdom Encyclopedias Ser.). (ENG., Illus.). 32p. (gr. 1-2). lib. bdg. 27.32 *(978-1-5157-3925-8(2)*, Aplus Bks.) Capstone Press of Coughlan Cos.

Rigby Education Staff. Bugs on the Menu. (Sails Literacy Ser.). (Illus.). 16p. (gr. 2-3). 27.00 *(978-0-7635-9954-6(9)*, 699549C99) Rigby Education.

—Discovery World Red Insect Body. (Discovery World Ser.). (Illus.). 12p. (gr. 1-2). 31.00 *(978-0-7635-2704-4(1))* Rigby Education.
—Pebble Soup Ever Changing Big Book: Ants & Grasshoppers. (Pebble Soup Explorations Ser.). 16p. (gr. -1-18). tchr. ed. 21.00 *(978-0-7635-6474-2(5))* Rigby Education.
Riggs, Kate. That's Creepy! Dogi, Fiammetta, illus. 2013. (ENG.). 14p. (J). (gr. -1-k). bds. 7.99 *(978-1-56846-236-3(0),* Creative Editions) Creative Co., The.
Rin, Bo. Insects & Spiders. Cowley, Joy, ed. Garrido & Do, Gam, illus. 2015. (Science Storybooks Ser.). (ENG.). 32p. (J). (gr. k-3). 26.65 *(978-1-925233-61-2(8))* Lerner Publishing Group.
Ripley's Believe It Or Not! Staff & Ripley's Believe It Or Not! Editors. Ripley Twists: Spiders & Scary Creepy Crawlies. 2014. (Twist Ser.: 12). (ENG.). 48p. (J). 12.95 *(978-1-60991-115-7(6))* Ripley Entertainment, Inc.
Rissman, Rebecca. Insects. 2013. (Real Size Science Ser.). (ENG.). 24p. (gr. -1-1). 22.65 *(978-1-4329-7881-5(0))*; pap. 6.95 *(978-1-4329-7888-4(8))* Heinemann-Raintree. (Acorn).
Rockwell, Anne. Bugs Are Insects. Jenkins, Steve, illus. 2015. (Let's-Read-And-Find-Out Science 1 Ser.). (ENG.). 40p. (J). (gr. -1-3). pap. 6.99 *(978-0-06-238182-8(2))* HarperCollins Pubs.
—Bugs Are Insects. 2015. (Let's Read & Find Out Science Stage 1 Ser.). (J). lib. bdg. 17.20 *(978-0-606-37896-3(0))* Turtleback Bks.
Rodger, Ellen. Bloodsucking Lice & Fleas. 2010. (Creepy Crawlies Ser.). (ENG.). 32p. (J). (gr. 3-6). *(978-0-7787-2498-8(0))*; pap. *(978-0-7787-2505-3(7))* Crabtree Publishing Co.
Rodhe, Paul, et al. Kids Meet the Bugs. 2013. (Kids Meet Ser.: 1). (ENG.). 96p. (J). 12.95 *(978-1-60433-324-4(3),* Applesauce Pr.) Cider Mill Pr. Bk. Pubs., LLC.
Rodriguez, Ana Maria. The Secret of the Scuba Diving Spider... & More! 2017. (Animal Secrets Revealed! Ser.). 48p. (J). (gr. 4-4). lib. bdg. 27.93 ***(978-0-7660-8629-6(1))*** Enslow Pubs., Inc.
Romero, Libby. Ultimate Explorer Field Guide: Insects: Find Adventure! Go Outside! Have Fun! Be a Backyard Insect Inspector! 2017. (ENG., Illus.). 160p. (J). (gr. 3-7). pap. 12.99 *(978-1-4263-2740-7(4),* National Geographic Children's Bks.) National Geographic Society.
Rooney, Anne. You Wouldn't Want to Live Without Insects! Antram, David, illus. 2015. (You Wouldn't Want to Live Without... Ser.). (ENG.). 40p. (J). pap. 9.95 *(978-0-531-21405-3(2),* Watts, Franklin) Scholastic Library Publishing.
Ross, Kathy. Crafts for Kids Who Are Learning about Dinosaurs. Barger, Jan, illus. 2008. (Crafts for Kids Who Are Learning about Ser.). (ENG.). 48p. (gr. k-3). lib. bdg. 26.60 *(978-0-8225-6809-4(8))* Lerner Publishing Group.
—Crafts for Kids Who Are Learning about Insects. Barger, Jan, illus. 2008. (Crafts for Kids Who Are Learning about Ser.). (ENG.). 48p. (gr. k-3). 26.60 *(978-0-8225-7591-7(4))* Lerner Publishing Group.
Ross, Michael Elsohn. Millipedology. Erickson, Darren, illus. Grogan, Brian, photos by. 2003. (Backyard Buddies Ser.). 48p. (YA). (gr. 3-5). 6.95 *(978-1-57505-436-0(1),* Carolrhoda Bks.) Lerner Publishing Group.
—Rolypolyology. 2003. (Backyard Buddies Ser.). 48p. (YA). (gr. 3-5). 6.95 *(978-0-87614-901-0(8),* Carolrhoda Bks.) Lerner Publishing Group.
Rothstein, Barry & Rothstein, Betsy. Eye-Popping 3-D Bugs: Phantogram Creepy-Crawlies You Can Practically Touch! 2011. (ENG.). 64p. (J). (gr. 3-7). 19.99 *(978-0-8118-7772-5(8))* Chronicle Bks. LLC.
Royston, Angela. Insects. (Illus.). 32p. (YA). (gr. 2-18). lib. bdg. 27.10 *(978-1-932333-36-7(3))* Chrysalis Education.
Roza, Greg. The Bizarre Life Cycle of a Cicada. 2012. (Strange Life Cycles Ser.). 24p. (gr. 2-5). pap. 8.15 *(978-1-4339-7040-5(6))*; lib. bdg. 22.60 *(978-1-4339-7039-9(2))* Stevens, Gareth Publishing LLLP.
—The Bizarre Life Cycle of a Mayfly. 2012. (Strange Life Cycles Ser.). (Illus.). 24p. (J). (gr. 2-5). pap. 8.15 *(978-1-4339-7052-8(X))*; lib. bdg. 22.60 *(978-1-4339-7051-1(1))* Stevens, Gareth Publishing LLLP.
—Mysterious Mantises. 2011. (World of Bugs Ser.). (Illus.). 24p. (gr. k-2). 69.20 *(978-1-4339-6143-4(1))* Stevens, Gareth Publishing LLLP.
—Weird Walking Sticks. 2011. (World of Bugs Ser.). (Illus.). 24p. (gr. k-2). 69.20 *(978-1-4339-6146-5(6))*; (J). (gr. -1-2). lib. bdg. 22.60 *(978-1-4339-4615-8(7))*; (J). (gr. k-2). pap. 8.15 *(978-1-4339-4616-5(5))* Stevens, Gareth Publishing LLLP.
Rupert, Matthews. Visual Factfinder Bugs. 2008. 512p. pap. *(978-1-84810-079-4(5))* Miles Kelly Publishing, Ltd.
Rustad, Martha E. H. Ants & Aphids Work Together. 2011. (Animals Working Together Ser.). (ENG.). 24p. (gr. k-1). pap. 41.70 *(978-1-4296-6366-3(9),* Pebble Plus) Capstone Press of Coughlan Cos.
—Insects, 1 vol. 2014. (Little Scientist Ser.). (ENG.). 32p. (gr. 1-2). lib. bdg. 27.99 *(978-1-4914-0792-9(1))* Capstone Press of Coughlan Cos.
—One More Bug: An Insect Addition Book. 2016. (1, 2, 3 Count with Me Ser.). (ENG., Illus.). 24p. (J). (gr. k-3). 20.95 *(978-1-60753-923-0(3))* Amicus Publishing.
Ruth, Angie. My Adventure Bug Collecting. 2006. 44p. (J). 8.99 *(978-1-59092-448-8(7))* Blue Forge Pr.
Salas, Laura Purdie. Colors of Insects. 2011. (Colors All Around Ser.). (ENG.). 32p. (gr. 1-2). pap. 47.70 *(978-1-4296-6154-6(2),* Aplus Bks.) Capstone Press of Coughlan Cos.
Salzmann, Mary Elizabeth. Pesky Houseflies, 1 vol. 2012. (Bug Bks.). (ENG.). 24p. (J). (gr. k-3). 24.21 *(978-1-61783-194-2(8),* SandCastle) ABDO Publishing Co.
—What Has Wings?, 1 vol. 2007. (Creature Features Ser.). (ENG., Illus.). 24p. (J). (gr. -1-3). lib. bdg. 25.65 *(978-1-59928-876-5(1),* Super SandCastle) ABDO Publishing Co.
Savage, Stephen. Focus on Insects. 2011. (Animal Watch Ser.). 32p. (YA). (gr. 3-6). lib. bdg. 26.60 *(978-1-4339-5987-5(9))* Stevens, Gareth Publishing LLLP.
Sayre, April Pulley. Ant, Ant, Ant! An Insect Chant. Park, Trip, illus. 2005. (American City Ser.). (ENG.). 32p. (J). (gr. k-3). 15.95 *(978-1-55971-922-3(2))* Cooper Square Publishing Llc.
Scholastic & Arlon, Penelope. Bug off! (LEGO Nonfiction) 2017. (LEGO Nonfiction Ser.). (ENG.). 32p. (J). (gr. -1-3). pap. 4.99 *(978-1-338-13015-7(3))* Scholastic, Inc.
School Zone Publishing Company Staff. Insects & Spiders. (Illus.). (J). 19.99 incl. audio compact disk *(978-0-88743-977-3(2))*; 19.99 incl. audio compact disk *(978-0-88743-944-5(6))* School Zone Publishing Co.
Schuetz, Kari. Insects. 2012. (Animal Classes Ser.). (ENG., Illus.). 24p. (J). (gr. k-3). lib. bdg. 25.95 *(978-1-60014-774-6(7),* Blastoff! Readers) Bellwether Media.
Schuh, Mari. Cicadas. 2015. (J). lib. bdg. 25.65 *(978-1-62031-160-8(7),* Bullfrog Bks.) Jump! Inc.
—Praying Mantises. 2015. (J). lib. bdg. 25.65 *(978-1-62031-163-9(1),* Bullfrog Bks.) Jump! Inc.
—Show Me Insects: My First Picture Encyclopedia, 1 vol. 2013. (My First Picture Encyclopedias Ser.). (ENG., Illus.). 32p. (gr. 1-2). 7.95 *(978-1-62065-929-8(8),* Aplus Bks.) Capstone Press of Coughlan Cos.
—Stink Bugs. 2015. (J). lib. bdg. 25.65 *(978-1-62031-164-6(X),* Bullfrog Bks.) Jump! Inc.
—Walkingsticks. 2015. (J). lib. bdg. 25.65 *(978-1-62031-165-3(8),* Bullfrog Bks.) Jump! Inc.
—The World's Biggest Insects. 2015. (Illus.). 24p. (J). lib. bdg. 25.65 *(978-1-62031-208-7(5))* Jump! Inc.
Schwaeber, Barbie Heit. Alphabet of Insects. Buchs, Thomas, illus. 2009. (ENG.). 40p. 9.95 *(978-1-59249-992-2(9))* Soundprints.
—Alphabet of Insects. Bratun, Katy et al, illus. 2007. (ENG.). 40p. (J). (gr. -1-3). 15.95 *(978-1-59249-725-6(X))* Soundprints.
Science Stories Foss Spanish Insects EA CR05. 2005. (J). *(978-1-59242-584-6(4))* Delta Education, LLC.
Sengupta, Monalisa. Discover Bugs. 2008. (Discover Animals Ser.). (Illus.). 48p. (J). (gr. 5-9). lib. bdg. 25.27 *(978-0-7660-3472-3(0))* Enslow Pubs., Inc.
Senior, Kathryn. Bugs. 2016. (Wise Up Ser.). 32p. (gr. 2-6). 31.35 *(978-1-62588-337-7(4),* Smart Apple Media) Black Rabbit Bks.
Senker, Cath. Creepy-Crawlies, 01 vols., 1. 2016. (Adventures in Nature Ser.). (ENG.). 32p. (J). pap. 10.00 *(978-1-5081-4579-0(2),* PowerKids Pr.) Rosen Publishing Group, Inc., The.
Sexton, Colleen. Aphids. 2008. (World of Insects Ser.). (ENG., Illus.). 24p. (J). (gr. k-3). lib. bdg. 25.95 *(978-1-60014-189-8(7))* Bellwether Media.
—Cicadas. 2007. (World of Insects Ser.). (ENG., Illus.). 24p. (J). (gr. k-3). lib. bdg. 25.95 *(978-1-60014-051-8(3))* Bellwether Media.
—Damselflies. 2008. (World of Insects Ser.). (ENG., Illus.). 24p. (J). (gr. k-3). lib. bdg. 25.95 *(978-1-60014-190-4(0))* Bellwether Media.
—Earwigs. 2008. (World of Insects Ser.). (ENG., Illus.). 24p. (J). (gr. k-3). lib. bdg. 25.95 *(978-1-60014-191-1(9))* Bellwether Media.
—Stink Bugs. 2008. (World of Insects Ser.). (ENG., Illus.). 24p. (J). (gr. k-3). lib. bdg. 25.95 *(978-1-60014-192-8(7))* Bellwether Media.
Shannon, Jason. A Calling of Quarrels: Ebook. Hartter, Sean, illus. 2008. (J). per. 12.95 *(978-0-9790889-5-7(X))* CatsCurious Pr.
Shaw, Gina & Bader, Bonnie. The Buzz on Insects. 2016. (Smithsonian Ser.). (ENG., Illus.). 32p. (J). (gr. 1-3). 3.99 *(978-0-448-49022-9(6),* Penguin Young Readers) Penguin Young Readers Group.
Shea, Nicole. Creepy Bugs. 2012. (Nature's Creepiest Creatures Ser.). (ENG.). 24p. (J). (gr. 2-5). pap. 8.15 *(978-1-4339-6491-6(0))*; lib. bdg. 22.60 *(978-1-4339-6489-3(9))* Stevens, Gareth Publishing LLLP. (Gareth Stevens Learning Library).
Shepherd, Matthew, et al. Pollinator Conservation Handbook: A Guide to Understanding, Protecting, & Providing Habitat for Native Pollinator Insects 2003. (Illus.). 145p. pap. 19.95 *(978-0-9744475-0-6(1))* Xerces Society, The.
Sherab, Chodzin & Langham, Tony. Creepy Crawly Calypso. 2012. (ENG., Illus.). 32p. (J). (gr. -1-2). 9.99 *(978-1-84686-828-3(9))* Barefoot Bks., Inc.
Sherman, Janice. Draco the Dragonfly. 2007. (ENG., Illus.). 15p. (J). pap. 4.99 *(978-0-9797139-6-5(X))* Jan's Bks.
—Kyle the Caterpillar. 2007. (ENG., Illus.). 10p. (J). pap. 4.99 *(978-0-9797139-5-8(1))* Jan's Bks.
Shores, Erika L. The Deadliest Bugs on Earth. 2010. (World's Deadliest Ser.). (ENG.). 32p. (gr. 1-2). lib. bdg. 26.65 *(978-1-4296-3930-9(X),* Blazers) Capstone Press of Coughlan Cos.
Shoulders, Michael. Cicada. 2015. (21st Century Junior Library: Creepy Crawly Critters Ser.). (ENG.). 24p. (J). (gr. k-3). 27.07 *(978-1-63362-589-1(3),* 206540) Cherry Lake Publishing.
Sill, Cathryn. About Arachnids: A Guide for Children, 1 vol. Sill, John, illus. 2006. (About... Ser.). (ENG.). 40p. (J). (gr. k-3). pap. 7.95 *(978-1-56145-364-1(1))* Peachtree Pubs.
—About Insects. 2014. 17.95 *(978-1-63419-643-7(0))* Perfection Learning Corp.
—About Insects: A Guide for Children, 1 vol. Sill, John, illus. rev. ed. 2015. (About... Ser.). (ENG.). 48p. (J). (gr. -1-2). 16.95 *(978-1-56145-881-3(3))* Peachtree Pubs.
Silver Dolphin en Español Staff, creator. Bichos y Mas. 2007. (Libro y Modelos 3-D Ser.). (Illus.). 24p. (J). (gr. -1). *(978-970-718-506-7(6),* Silver Dolphin en Español) Advanced Marketing, S. de R. L. de C. V.
Silverman, Buffy. Do You Know about Insects? 2009. (Lightning Bolt Books — Meet the Animal Groups Ser.). (ENG., Illus.). 32p. (gr. k-2). pap. 7.95 *(978-1-58013-859-8(4))*; lib. bdg. 26.60 *(978-0-8225-7544-3(2),* Lerner Pubns.) Lerner Publishing Group.
—¿Sabes Algo Sobre Insectos? (Do You Know about Insects?) 2012. (Libros Rayo — Conoce Los Grupos de Animales (Lightning Bolt Books — Meet the Animal Groups) Ser.). (Illus.). 32p. (gr. k-2). (ENG & SPA.). pap. 7.95 *(978-0-7613-9372-6(2))*; (SPA., lib. bdg. 26.60 *(978-0-7613-9335-1(8))* Lerner Publishing Group. (Ediciones Lerner).
Silverstein, Alvin, et al. Creepy Crawlies. 2003. (What a Pet! Ser.). (ENG., Illus.). 48p. (gr. 3-6). lib. bdg. 23.93 *(978-0-7613-2511-6(5),* Millbrook Pr.) Lerner Publishing Group.
Simon, Seymour. Insects. 2016. (Illus.). 40p. (J). (gr. 1-5). pap. 6.99 *(978-0-06-228914-8(4))* HarperCollins Pubs.
Siy, Alexandra. Bug Shots: The Good, the Bad, & the Bugly. Siy, Alexandra & Kunkel, Dennis, photos by. 2011. (ENG., Illus.). 32p. (J). 16.95 *(978-0-8234-2286-9(0))* Holiday Hse., Inc.
Slade, Suzanne. Do All Bugs Have Wings? And Other Questions Kids Have about Bugs, 1 vol. Pillo, Cary, illus. 2010. (Kids' Questions Ser.). (ENG.). 24p. (gr. 1-2). lib. bdg. 26.65 *(978-1-4048-5761-2(3))* Picture Window Bks.
—Multiply on the Fly, 1 vol. Hunter, Erin E., illus. 2011. (ENG.). 32p. (J). (gr. -1-4). 16.95 *(978-1-60718-128-6(2))*; pap. 8.95 *(978-1-60718-138-5(X))* Arbordale Publishing.
—What If There Were No Bees? A Book about the Grassland Ecosystem, 1 vol. Schwartz, Carol, illus. 2010. (Food Chain Reactions Ser.). (ENG.). 24p. (gr. 2-4). pap. 9.95 *(978-1-4048-6394-1(X))* Picture Window Bks.
Smith, Carrie. Counting Insects: Lap Book. 2009. (My First Reader's Theater Set B Ser.). (J). 28.00 *(978-1-4108-8539-5(9))* Benchmark Education Co.
Smith, Sian. Woodlice, 1 vol. 2012. (Creepy Critters Ser.). (ENG.). 24p. (gr. -1-k). pap. 8.95 *(978-1-4109-4824-3(2))*; lib. bdg. 25.32 *(978-1-4109-4811-3(0))* Heinemann-Raintree.
Smithsonian Institution, ed. Insects A to Z. 2009. (ENG.). 36p. 13.99 *(978-1-59069-824-2(X))* Studio Mouse LLC.
Smithyman, Kathryn & Kalman, Bobbie. Insects in Danger. 2006. (World of Insects Ser.). (ENG., Illus.). 32p. (J). (gr. 3-7). lib. bdg. *(978-0-7787-2344-8(5))*; (gr. 4-7). pap. *(978-0-7787-2378-3(X))* Crabtree Publishing Co.
Snedden, Robert. Insects. (Living Things Ser.). (Illus.). 32p. 2009. (J). (gr. -1-3). pap. 7.95 *(978-1-59920-197-9(6))* 2007. (YA). (gr. 3-6). lib. bdg. 28.50 *(978-1-59920-080-4(5))* Black Rabbit Bks.
Sohn, Emily & Klobuchar, Lisa. Fabric: It's Got You Covered. 2011. (iScience Readers Ser.). (ENG.). 24p. (J). (gr. k-2). pap. 11.94 *(978-1-60357-280-4(5))* Norwood Hse. Pr.
Sohn, Emily & Rothbardt, Karen. Insects: Which One Doesn't Belong? 2011. (iScience Readers Ser.). 24p. (J). (gr. k-2). pap. 11.94 *(978-1-60357-304-7(6))* Norwood Hse. Pr.
Sohn, Emily & Rothbardt, Karen J. Insects: Which One Doesn't Belong? 2011. (iScience Readers Ser.). 24p. (J). (gr. k-2). lib. bdg. 21.27 *(978-1-59953-407-7(X))* Norwood Hse. Pr.
Somervill, Barbara A. Leeches: Waiting in the Water. 2007. (Bloodsuckers Ser.). (Illus.). 24p. (J). (gr. 2-5). lib. bdg. 22.60 *(978-1-4042-3801-5(8))* Rosen Publishing Group, Inc., The.
—Lice: Head Hunters. 2009. (Bloodsuckers Ser.). 24p. (gr. 2-3). 42.50 *(978-1-61511-634-8(6),* PowerKids Pr.) Rosen Publishing Group, Inc., The.
Soundprints Staff, ed. Backyard Collection: Daddy Longlegs, Owl, Armadillo & Ladybug Books, 4 microbks., No. III. (Smithsonian's Backyard Ser.). (Illus.). 128p. (J). (gr. -1-2). 18.95 *(978-1-56899-634-9(9))* Soundprints.
Spilsbury, Louise. Backyard Bugs. 2011. (ENG.). 24p. (J). pap. *(978-0-7787-7863-9(0))*; (gr. 3-6). *(978-0-7787-7841-7(X))* Crabtree Publishing Co.
Spilsbury, Richard. Burrow. Hanna, Gary, illus. 2013. (Look Inside Ser.). (ENG.). 32p. (gr. 1-3). 27.32 *(978-1-4329-7193-9(X))*; pap. 8.29 *(978-1-4329-7200-4(6))* Heinemann-Raintree. (Heinemann First Library).
—Zoom in on Bizarre Bugs. 2013. (Zoom in on... Ser.). 32p. (J). 23.94 *(978-0-7660-4309-1(6))*; (gr. 4-12). pap. 7.95 *(978-1-4644-0563-1(8))* Enslow Pubs., Inc.
Sterry, Paul. Insects - Pb: A Portrait of the Animal World. 2013. (Portrait of the Animal World Ser.). (Illus.). 72p. pap. 9.95 *(978-1-59764-324-5(6))* New Line Bks.
Stevens, Danielle. Minibeasts. 2013. (World of Wonder Ser.). (ENG., Illus.). 32p. (J). (gr. 4-7). lib. bdg. *(978-1-904642-03-9(9))* Book Hse.
—Minibeasts. 2013. (World of Wonder Ser.). (Illus.). 32p. (gr. 1-3). 31.35 ***(978-1-905087-09-9(8))*** Book Hse. GBR. Dist: Black Rabbit Bks.
Stevens, Kathryn. Bugs Rule! 2007. (Reading Rocks! Ser.). (ENG., Illus.). 32p. (J). (gr. 2-5). 28.50 *(978-1-59296-856-5(2),* 200741) Child's World, Inc., The.
Stewart, Melissa. Creepy, Crawly Jokes about Spiders & Other Bugs: Laugh & Learn about Science. Kelley, Gerald, illus. 2012. (Super Silly Science Jokes Ser.). 48p. (J). (gr. 3-4). 25.27 *(978-0-7660-3966-7(8),* Enslow Elementary) Enslow Pubs., Inc.
—Insect or Spider? How Do You Know? 2011. (Which Animal Is Which? Ser.). (Illus.). 24p. (J). (gr. k-18). pap. 7.95 *(978-1-59845-237-2(1),* Enslow Elementary); lib. bdg. 22.60 *(978-0-7660-3681-9(2))* Enslow Pubs., Inc.
—Maggots, Grubs, & More: The Secret Lives of Young Insects. 2003. 64p. lib. bdg. 24.90 *(978-0-7613-2658-8(8),* Millbrook Pr.) Lerner Publishing Group.
Stewart, Pat. Invisible Bugs Magic Picture Book. 2003. (Dover Little Activity Bks.). (ENG., Illus.). 16p. (J). (gr. -1-2). pap. 1.50 *(978-0-486-42635-8(1))* Dover Pubns., Inc.
Stout, Frankie. Bugs: In Flight. 2009. (Things with Wings Ser.). 24p. (gr. 2-3). 42.50 *(978-1-60854-351-9(X),* PowerKids Pr.) Rosen Publishing Group, Inc., The.
—Bugs in Flight. 2009. (Things with Wings Ser.). (Illus.). 24p. (J). (gr. 2-4). lib. bdg. 22.60 *(978-1-4042-4493-1(X),* PowerKids Pr.) Rosen Publishing Group, Inc., The.
Sullivan, Laura. Insects & Arachnids Explained. 2016. (Distinctions in Nature Ser.). 32p. (J). pap. 10.58 *(978-1-5026-2189-4(4))* Cavendish Square Publishing.
Sullivan, Mary C. Bugs! a Counting Book. Sullivan, Mary C., illus. 2013. (Illus.). 32p. 18.95 *(978-0-9859986-6-0(0))* Nectar Pubns.
Superstar Insects. 2014. (Nature's Got Talent Ser.). (Illus.). 32p. (J). (gr. k-5). lib. bdg. 26.25 *(978-1-4777-7064-1(X),* PowerKids Pr.) Rosen Publishing Group, Inc., The.
Sutherland, Jonathan & McNab, Chris. Flying Insects. 2006. (Nature's Monsters Ser.). (Illus.). 32p. (gr. 2-6). lib. bdg. 26.00 *(978-0-8368-6849-4(8),* Gareth Stevens Learning Library) Stevens, Gareth Publishing LLLP.
—Social Insects. 2006. (Nature's Monsters Ser.). (Illus.). 32p. (gr. 2-6). lib. bdg. 26.00 *(978-0-8368-6851-7(X),* Gareth Stevens Learning Library) Stevens, Gareth Publishing LLLP.
Swanson, Diane. Bugs up Close. Davidson, Paul, illus. 2007. (ENG.). 40p. (J). (gr. 2-5). 8.95 *(978-1-55453-139-4(X))*; 17.95 *(978-1-55453-138-7(1))* Kids Can Pr., Ltd. CAN. Dist: Hachette Bk. Group.
Swanson, Jennifer & Leet, Karen M. Tiny Creepy Creatures. 2011. (Tiny Creepy Creatures Ser.). (ENG.). 32p. (gr. 3-4). pap. 190.80 *(978-1-4296-7280-1(3))*; lib. bdg. 111.96 *(978-1-4296-6534-6(3))* Capstone Press of Coughlan Cos. (Edge Bks.).
Tabletop Zoo: Add-on Package. 2003. (J). 26.95 *(978-0-673-76189-7(4))* Celebration Pr.
Tabletop Zoo: Individual 6-pack: Cicadas. 2003. 43.95 *(978-0-673-57975-1(1))* Celebration Pr.
Tabletop Zoo: Stick Insects. 2003. (J). 43.95 *(978-0-673-57976-8(X))* Celebration Pr.
Tabletop Zoo: Tabletop Zoo Complete Package. 2003. (J). 167.95 *(978-0-673-76172-9(X))* Celebration Pr.
Tait, Noel. Insects & Spiders. 2008. (Insiders Ser.). (ENG.). 64p. (J). (gr. 3-7). 17.99 *(978-1-4169-3868-2(0),* Simon & Schuster Bks. For Young Readers) Simon & Schuster Bks. For Young Readers.
Tait, Noel, ed. Bugs. 2007. (Little Guides). (Illus.). 320p. pap. 7.98 *(978-1-74089-346-6(8))* Fog City Pr.
Tan, Richard. Bugs, Bugs, Bugs. 2015. (Rosen REAL Readers: STEM & STEAM Collection). (ENG.). 8p. pap. 5.46 *(978-1-4994-9703-8(2),* Rosen Classroom) Rosen Publishing Group, Inc., The.
Tatchell, Judy. Bugs & Slugs. 2004. (Lift-the-Flap Ser.). (ENG., Illus.). 1p. (J). (gr. 1-18). pap. 8.95 *(978-0-7460-2773-8(7))* EDC Publishing.
—Bugs & Slugs Lift-the-Flap. 2004. (Luxury Lift-the-Flap Ser.). 16p. (J). (gr. 1-18). 11.95 *(978-0-7945-0762-6(X),* Usborne) EDC Publishing.
Taylor, Barbara. Bug Athletes. (Illus.). 32p. (YA). (gr. 1-18). lib. bdg. 27.10 *(978-1-932333-10-7(X))* Chrysalis Education.
—Bug Hunters. (Illus.). 32p. (YA). (gr. 1-18). lib. bdg. 27.10 *(978-1-932333-12-1(6))* Chrysalis Education.
—In Focus: Bugs. 2017. (In Focus Ser.). (ENG.). 64p. (J). 17.99 *(978-0-7534-7345-0(3),* 9780753473450, Kingfisher) Roaring Brook Pr.
—Poisonous Bugs. (Illus.). 32p. (YA). (gr. 1-18). lib. bdg. 27.10 *(978-1-932333-14-5(2))* Chrysalis Education.
—Water Bugs. (Illus.). 32p. (YA). (gr. 1-18). lib. bdg. 27.10 *(978-1-932333-11-4(8))* Chrysalis Education.
Taylor, Barbara & Green, Jen. Explore the Deadly World of Bugs, Snakes, Spiders, Crocodiles: The Dramatic Lives & Conflicts of the World's Strangest Creatures Shown in 1500 Amazing Close-Up Photographs. 2013. (ENG., Illus.). 512p. (J). (gr. -1-12). pap. 17.99 *(978-1-84322-840-0(8),* Armadillo) Anness Publishing GBR. Dist: National Bk. Network.
Taylor, Barbara, et al. Bugs & Minibeasts. 2015. (ENG., Illus.). 256p. 13.99 *(978-1-86147-422-3(9),* Armadillo) Anness Publishing GBR. Dist: National Bk. Network.
—The Deadly World of Bugs, Snakes, Spiders, Crocodiles: And Hundreds of Other Amazing Reptiles & Insects. 2008. (ENG., Illus.). 512p. (J). (gr. 4-7). 29.99 *(978-0-7548-1781-9(4))* Anness Publishing GBR. Dist: National Bk. Network.
Taylor-Butler, Christine. Insects & Spiders. 2013. (ENG.). 48p. (J). 29.00 *(978-0-531-21753-5(1))*; pap. 6.95 *(978-0-531-22338-3(8))* Scholastic Library Publishing.
Taylor, Trace & Sánchez, Lucía M. Avispas. 2011. (2G - Bichos Ser.). (SPA.). 12p. (J). (gr. k-2). pap. 6.99 *(978-1-61541-420-8(7))* American Reading Co.
Taylor, Trace & Sanchez, Lucia M. Avispas (Wasps) 2011. (poder de 100 - Bichos Ser.). 12p. pap. 33.92 *(978-1-61541-421-5(5))* American Reading Co.
—Mantis religiosa (Praying Mantis) 2011. (poder de 100 - Bichos Ser.). (SPA.). 12p. pap. 33.92 *(978-1-61541-293-8(X))* American Reading Co.
Teora, creator. Insects. 2007. (My First Sticker Encyclopedia Ser.). (Illus.). 18p. (J). (gr. -1-3). pap. 5.95 *(978-1-59496-146-5(8))* Teora USA LLC.
Thomas, Isabel. Crazy Creepy Crawlies, 1 vol. 2012. (Extreme Animals Ser.). (ENG.). 32p. (gr. 1-3). pap. 8.29 *(978-1-4109-4685-0(1))*; lib. bdg. 29.99 *(978-1-4109-4679-9(7))* Heinemann-Raintree. (Read Me!).
Tiny Bugs up Close. 2013. (Under the Microscope Ser.). 32p. (J). (gr. 4-6). pap. 70.20 *(978-1-4339-8352-8(4))* Stevens, Gareth Publishing LLLP.
Top That Publishing Staff, ed. Creepy Crawlies. 2005. (Illus.). 24p. *(978-1-84510-539-6(7))* Top That! Publishing PLC.
—Incredible Insects. 2005. 48p. pap. *(978-1-84510-190-9(1))* Top That! Publishing PLC.
Tornio, Stacy & Keffer, Ken. The Secret Lives of Animals: 1,001 Tidbits, Oddities, & Amazing Facts about North America's Coolest Animals. 2015. (ENG., Illus.). 264p. (J). (gr. -1-5). pap. 19.95 *(978-1-4930-1191-9(X),* Falcon Guides) Globe Pequot Pr., The.
Turner, Matt. Extraordinary Insects. Calle, Santiago, illus. 2017. (Crazy Creepy Crawlers Ser.). (ENG.). 32p. (J). (gr. 3-6). 26.65 *(978-1-5124-1556-8(1))*; 7.99 ***(978-1-5124-3600-6(3))***; 39.99 ***(978-1-5124-3599-3(6))***; 39.99 ***(978-1-5124-2716-5(0))*** Lerner Publishing Group.
Turner, Matt. Flying Creepy Crawlers. Calle, Santiago, illus. 2017. (Crazy Creepy Crawlers Ser.). (ENG.). 32p. (J). (gr. 3-6). 26.65 *(978-1-5124-1554-4(5))*; 7.99 ***(978-1-5124-3603-7(8))***; 39.99 ***(978-1-5124-2714-1(4))***; 39.99 ***(978-1-5124-3602-0(X))*** Lerner Publishing Group.
Turpin, Tom. What's Buggin' You Now? Bee's Knees, Bug Lites & Beetles. 2008. (ENG., Illus.). 120p. pap. 12.95 *(978-1-55753-509-2(4),* 96d0e9b0-6e56-4faf-9179-83e986a16f5f) Purdue Univ. Pr.
Ugly Bugs. 2006. (Ugly Animals Ser.). (Illus.). 24p. (J). (gr. 3-7). lib. bdg. 22.60 *(978-1-4042-3527-4(2))* Rosen Publishing Group, Inc., The.
Underwood, Shelley. Insects. 2010. (Weird, Wild, & Wonderful Ser.). 24p. (J). (gr. 2-5). lib. bdg. 22.00 *(978-1-4339-3575-6(9),* Gareth Stevens Learning Library) Stevens, Gareth Publishing LLLP.
—Minibeasts. 2010. (Weird, Wild, & Wonderful Ser.). (Illus.). 24p. (J). (gr. 2-5). lib. bdg. 22.00 *(978-1-4339-3576-3(7),* Gareth Stevens Learning Library) Stevens, Gareth Publishing LLLP.
Uttridge, Sarah. Spiders & Bugs Around the World. 2014. (Animals Around the World Ser.). (Illus.). 32p. (gr. 2-5). 31.35 *(978-1-62588-198-4(3))* Black Rabbit Bks.
Vaughan, Jenny. Minibeasts. 2010. (Science Everywhere! Ser.). 24p. 24.25 *(978-1-84898-290-1(9))* Black Rabbit Bks.
Veitch, Catherine. Learning about Insects, 1 vol. 2013. (Natural World Ser.). (ENG., Illus.). 24p. (gr. -1-1). 22.65

(978-1-4109-5403-9(X)); pap. 6.95 *(978-1-4109-5408-4(0))* Heinemann-Raintree. (NA-r).

Voake, Steve. Insect Detective. Voake, Charlotte, illus. (Read & Wonder Ser.). (J). 2012. (ENG.). 32p. (gr. -1-3). pap. 6.99 *(978-0-7636-5816-8(2))* 2010. 28p. *(978-1-4063-1051-1(4))* Candlewick Pr.

—Insect Detective. Voake, Charlotte, illus. 2015. 32p. pap. 7.00 *(978-1-61003-407-4(4))* Center for the Collaborative Classroom.

—Insect Detective. 2012. (Read & Wonder Ser.). lib. bdg. 17.20 *(978-0-606-23802-1(6)*, Turtleback) Turtleback Bks.

Walker, Maryalice. Entomology & Palynology. Noziglia, Carla Miller & Siegel, Jay A., eds. 2013. (Solving Crimes with Science: Forensics Ser.: 12). (Illus.). 112p. (J). (gr. 7-18). 22.95 *(978-1-4222-2866-1(5))* Mason Crest.

Wallace, Karen. Creepy-Crawlies. Humphries, Tudor, illus. 2012. (Flip the Flaps Ser.). (ENG.). 32p. (J). (gr. -1-1). pap. 6.99 *(978-0-7534-6739-8(9)*, 9780753467398, Kingfisher) Roaring Brook Pr.

Walls, Suzanne L. Insects & Spiders. Maiden, D. W. & Govoni, Dennis, photos by. 2012. (Illus.). 64p. (J). pap. 14.95 *(978-0-9841960-9-8(9))* Chantilly Books.

Washington, Joi. Mantises. (Predator Bugs Ser.). 16p. 2011. pap. 39.62 *(978-1-61541-237-2(9))* 2010. (ENG.). (J). pap. 5.99 *(978-1-61541-220-4(4))* American Reading Co.

—The Wasp. 2011. (Power 50 - Predator Bugs Ser.). 32p. (J). (gr. k-2). pap. 7.95 *(978-1-61541-387-4(1))* American Reading Co.

—Wasps. 2011. (Predator Bugs Ser.). 16p. pap. 39.62 *(978-1-61541-352-2(9))* American Reading Co.

Washington, Joi & Sanchez, Lucia M. Avispas: Wasps. 2011. (Bichos depredadores (Predator Bugs) Ser.). 16p. (J). pap. 6.95 *(978-1-61541-353-9(7))* American Reading Co.

Washington, Joi & Sánchez, Lucía M. Las Mantis: Mantises. 2011. (Bugs, Bugs, & More Bugs Ser.). (SPA., Illus.). 16p. (J). (gr. k-2). pap. 6.99 *(978-1-61541-445-1(2))* American Reading Co.

Washington, Joi & Sanchez, Lucia M. Las Mantis (Mantises) 2011. (Bichos depredadores Ser.). (SPA.). 16p. pap. 39.62 *(978-1-61541-446-8(0))* American Reading Co.

Waxman, Laura Hamilton. Walking Sticks & Other Amazing Camouflage. 2017. (Searchlight Books (tm) — Animal Superpowers Ser.). (ENG.). 40p. (J). (gr. 3-5). 16.99 ***(978-1-5124-3672-3(0)***, Lerner Pubns.); 46.65 ***(978-1-5124-3671-6(2)***, Lerner Pubns.); 46.65 ***(978-1-5124-2824-7(8)***, Lerner Pubns.); (Illus.). 30.65 *(978-1-5124-2549-9(4))* Lerner Publishing Group.

Weakland, Mark. Yogi Bear's Guide to Bugs. Beach, Bryan, illus. 2015. (Yogi Bear's Guide to the Great Outdoors Ser.). (ENG.). 32p. (gr. 1-2). lib. bdg. 27.99 *(978-1-4914-6546-2(8))* Capstone Press of Coughlan Cos.

Weber, Valerie J. Giant Tubeworms. 2005. (Weird Wonders of the Deep Ser.). (Illus.). 24p. (J). (gr. 1-4). lib. bdg. 23.00 *(978-0-8368-4562-4(5)*, Gareth Stevens Learning Library) Stevens, Gareth Publishing LLLP.

Webster, Jean. Daddy-Long-Legs. 2006. 80p. pap. *(978-1-84637-590-3(8))* Echo Library.

Wechsler, Doug. Bizarre Bugs. 2003. (ENG., Illus.). 48p. (J). (gr. 3-6). 17.95 *(978-1-59078-095-4(7))* Boyds Mills Pr.

Werner, Sharon & Forss, Sarah. Bugs by the Numbers Counting Cards. 2011. (ENG., Illus.). 27p. (J). (gr. k-12). 24.99 *(978-1-60905-101-3(7))* Blue Apple Bks.

West, David. Mini Beasts. (Nora the Naturalist's Animals Ser.). 24p. (gr. k-3). 2014. pap. 8.95 *(978-1-62588-051-2(0))* 2013. 28.50 *(978-1-62588-002-4(2))* Black Rabbit Bks.

Wheeler-Toppen, Jodi. Orchid Mantises & Other Extreme Insect Adaptations, 1 vol. 2014. (Extreme Adaptations Ser.). (ENG.). 32p. (gr. 3-4). pap. 7.95 *(978-1-4914-0171-2(0)*, Fact Finders); lib. bdg. 27.32 *(978-1-4914-0166-8(4))* Capstone Press of Coughlan Cos.

William H. Sadlier Staff. Funny Bugs. 2005. (Early Library). (gr. k-2). 24.00 net. *(978-0-8215-8943-4(1))* Sadlier, William H. Inc.

Williamson, Margaret. The First Book of Bugs. 2010. 48p. pap. 15.75 *(978-1-171-85596-5(6))* Creative Media Partners, LLC.

Windsor, Jo. Animal Lights: Early Level Satellite Individual Title Six-Packs. (Sails Literacy Ser.). 16p. (gr. 1-2). 27.00 *(978-0-7578-2938-3(4))* Rigby Education.

Winterbottom, Julie. Frightlopedia: An Encyclopedia of Everything Scary, Creepy, & Spine-Chilling, from Arachnids to Zombies. 2016. (ENG., Illus.). 224p. (J). (gr. 3-7). pap. 9.95 *(978-0-7611-8379-2(5))* Workman Publishing Co., Inc.

Woodward, John. Garden Minibeasts up Close, 8 vols., Set. 2010. (Garden Minibeasts up Close Ser.). (gr. 2-4). 240.00 *(978-1-60413-966-2(8)*, Chelsea Clubhouse) Facts On File, Inc.

Woodward, John & Gray, Leon. Insects. 2007. (Close-up Ser.). (Illus.). 32p. (J). (gr. -1-3). lib. bdg. *(978-1-933834-14-6(5))* Brown Bear Books.

Worek, Michael & Marshall, Stephen A. Weird Insects. 2013. (ENG., Illus.). 64p. (J). (gr. 5-7). 19.95 *(978-1-77085-235-8(2)*, 9781770852358) Firefly Bks., Ltd.

World Book, Inc Staff, contrib. by. Animal Lives, 7 vols. 2009. (Illus.). 336p. (J). (gr. 3-5). 139.00 *(978-0-7166-0401-3(9))* World Bk., Inc.

—Insects & Spiders. (J). 2011. *(978-0-7166-1789-1(7))* 2009. *(978-0-7166-0405-1(1))* World Bk., Inc.

World Book, Inc. Staff, contrib. by. Insects of the United States & Canada. 2004. (World Book's Science & Nature Guides Ser.). (Illus.). 80p. (J). *(978-0-7166-4214-5(X))* World Bk., Inc.

World Book, Inc Staff, contrib. by. Insects, Spiders, & Creepy Crawlers: A Supplement to Childcraft, the How & Why Library. 2007. (J). *(978-0-7166-0618-5(6))* World Bk., Inc.

—World of Insects. 2007. (J). *(978-0-7166-7735-2(0))* World Bk., Inc.

Wyse, Liz & Barnes, Jon. Insects. (Make It Work! Ser.). (Illus.). 48p. (J). pap. 7.95 *(978-0-590-24402-2(7))* Scholastic, Inc.

Yancey, Diane. The Forensic Entomologist. 2008. (Crime Scene Investigations Ser.). (ENG., Illus.). 128p. (gr. 7-10). lib. bdg. 40.40 *(978-1-4205-0070-7(8)*, LML02109-242074, Lucent Bks.) Cengage Gale.

Yoon, Salina. Bug Hunt. 2017. (Lift-The-Flap Adventures Ser.). (ENG., Illus.). 14p. (J). (gr. -1-2). bds. 8.95 *(978-1-4549-2108-0(0))* Sterling Publishing Co., Inc.

Young, Caroline. Big Bug Search. 2010. (Great Searches Ser.). 32p. (J). 9.99 *(978-0-7945-2724-2(8)*, Usborne) EDC Publishing.

Young, Karen Romano. Bug Science: 20 Projects & Experiments about Anthropods - Insects, Arachnids, Algae, Worms, & Other Small Creatures. Goldin, David, illus. 2009. (Science Fair Winners Ser.). (ENG.). 80p. (J). (gr. 5-9). 24.90 *(978-1-4263-0520-7(6)*, National Geographic Children's Bks.) National Geographic Society.

—Bug Science: 20 Projects & Experiments about Anthropods - Insects, Arachnids, Algae, Worms, & Other Small Creatures. Goldin, David, illus. 2009. (Science Fair Winners Ser.). (ENG.). 80p. (J). (gr. 5-9). pap. 12.95 *(978-1-4263-0519-1(2)*, National Geographic Children's Bks.) National Geographic Society.

Zabludoff, Marc. The Insect Class. 2005. (Family Trees Ser.). (Illus.). 96p. (gr. 6-7). lib. bdg. 34.21 *(978-0-7614-1819-1(9)*, Benchmark Bks.) Marshall Cavendish Corp.

Zinke, William. Bugs: Big & Small, God Made Them All. 2014. (Illus.). 80p. (J). *(978-0-89051-835-9(1))* Master Bks.

Zommer, Yuval, et al. The Big Book of Bugs. 2016. (ENG., Illus.). 64p. (J). (gr. -1-2). 19.95 *(978-0-500-65067-7(5)*, 565067) Thames & Hudson.

Zondervan Bibles Staff. Big Bugs, Little Bugs, 1 vol. 2011. (I Can Read! / Made by God Ser.). (ENG., Illus.). 32p. (J). (gr. -1-2). pap. 3.99 *(978-0-310-72186-4(5))* Zonderkidz.

Zondervan Staff & Schriemer, Peter. Ocean Adventures, Volume 3: Winged Creatures, Waterfalls, & Wild Reptiles, 1 vol. 2013. (Nature of God Ser.). (ENG.). (J). 7.99 *(978-0-310-88833-8(6))* Zonderkidz.

INSECTS—COLLECTION AND PRESERVATION

Blanchard, Patricia & Suhr, Joanne. My Bug Box. Sloat, Teri, illus. 2003. (Books for Young Learners). 12p. (J). pap. 15.00 *(978-1-57274-701-2(3)*, BB2473, Bks. for Young Learners) Owen, Richard C. Pubs., Inc.

INSECTS—FICTION

Aardema, Verna. Why Mosquitoes Buzz in People's Ears. 2004. 29.95 *(978-1-55592-491-1(3))*; (J). 38.75 *(978-1-55592-492-8(1))*; (J). 18.95 *(978-1-55592-490-4(5))* Weston Woods Studios, Inc.

Abbott Orloff, Chrissy. Lady Humming Fly's Lesson on Staying Safe. 2009. 80p. pap. 28.99 *(978-1-4389-9938-8(0))* AuthorHouse.

Adams, Alison. Why Mosquitoes Buzz in People's Ears: Classic Tales Edition. Greenhead, Bill, illus. 2011. (Classic Tales Ser.). (J). *(978-1-936258-69-7(2))* Benchmark Education Co.

Adams, Pam, illus. There Was an Old Lady Who Swallowed a Fly. (Classic Books with Holes Ser.). (ENG.). (J). 2005. 20p. (gr. -1-1). bds. *(978-0-85953-314-0(X))* 2003. 16p. pap. *(978-0-85953-134-4(1))* Child's Play International Ltd.

Aldrich, Jodi. Bee Mumble & Wug. 2011. 36p. (J). pap. 20.95 *(978-1-4327-6808-9(5))* Outskirts Pr., Inc.

Alemagna, Beatrice. The Bug Next Door. David, Annette, tr. from FRE. 2012. (ENG., Illus.). 40p. (gr. -1-4). 12.95 *(978-0-7148-6356-6(4))* Phaidon Pr., Inc.

—Bugs in a Blanket. 2009. (ENG.). 42p. (gr. -1-4). 12.95 *(978-0-7148-4970-6(7))* Phaidon Pr., Inc.

—Bugs in the Garden. 2011. (ENG.). 40p. (gr. -1-2). 12.95 *(978-0-7148-6238-5(X))* Phaidon Pr., Inc.

Alemagne, Beatrice. Bugs at Christmas. Gordon, Sam, tr. from FRE. 2013. (ENG., Illus.). 38p. 12.95 *(978-0-7148-6573-7(7))* Phaidon Pr., Inc.

Amundson, Sandi. Zach & Dougie Dragonfly's Adventure. 2011. 55p. pap. 23.95 *(978-1-4327-3536-4(5))* Outskirts Pr., Inc.

Andrade, Maria J. Why Dear Mrs Sullivan Is Distressed! 2012. 30p. 19.95 *(978-0-9706347-8-8(1))* Clara Publishing.

Angelo, Tony. Just Inn Time. Freeman, Angela, illus. 2011. 24p. pap. 24.95 *(978-1-4560-6828-8(8))* America Star Bks.

Angus, Jennifer. In Search of Goliathus Hercules. 2013. (ENG.). 352p. (J). (gr. 3-7). 17.99 *(978-0-8075-2990-4(7))* Whitman, Albert & Co.

Applefield, Annie. The Beetle & the Berry. Applefield, Annie, illus. 2007. (Illus.). 28p. (J). per. 15.95 *(978-0-9748933-9-6(0))* E & E Publishing.

Archambault, Jeanne. The Leaping Grasshopper. Smith, Dwight, illus. 2006. 32p. (J). bds. 15.95 *(978-0-9763031-2-1(4))* Jitterbug Bks.

Arnold, Tedd. Buzz Boy & Fly Guy. Arnold, Tedd, illus. 2010. (Fly Guy Ser.: 9). (ENG., Illus.). 32p. (J). (gr. -1-3). 6.99 *(978-0-545-22274-7(5)*, Cartwheel Bks.) Scholastic, Inc.

—Buzz Boy & Fly Guy. 2010. (Fly Guy Ser.: 9). lib. bdg. 17.20 *(978-0-606-14841-2(8)*, Turtleback) Turtleback Bks.

—Fly Guy & the Frankenfly. 2013. (Fly Guy Ser.: 13). (ENG., Illus.). 32p. (J). (gr. -1-3). 6.99 *(978-0-545-49328-4(5)*, Cartwheel Bks.) Scholastic, Inc.

—Fly Guy Meets Fly Girl! Arnold, Tedd, illus. 2010. (Fly Guy Ser.: 8). (ENG., Illus.). 32p. (J). (gr. -1-3). 6.99 *(978-0-545-11029-7(7)*, Cartwheel Bks.) Scholastic, Inc.

—Fly Guy Meets Fly Girl. 2010. (Fly Guy Ser.: 8). lib. bdg. 17.20 *(978-0-606-07099-7(0)*, Turtleback) Turtleback Bks.

—Fly Guy vs. the Fly Swatter. 2011. (Illus.). 30p. (J). *(978-0-545-38130-7(4)*, Cartwheel Bks.) Scholastic, Inc.

—Fly Guy vs. the Flyswatter! Arnold, Tedd, illus. 2011. (Fly Guy Ser.: 10). (ENG., Illus.). 32p. (J). (gr. -1-3). 6.99 *(978-0-545-31286-8(8)*, Cartwheel Bks.) Scholastic, Inc.

—Fly Guy's Amazing Tricks. 2014. (Illus.). 30p. (J). *(978-0-545-76926-6(4))* Scholastic, Inc.

—Fly Guy's Amazing Tricks. 2014. (Fly Guy Ser.: 14). lib. bdg. 17.20 *(978-0-606-36267-2(3))* Turtleback Bks.

—Fly Guy's Ninja Christmas. Arnold, Tedd, illus. 2016. (Fly Guy Ser.: 16). (ENG., Illus.). 32p. (J). (gr. -1-3). 6.99 *(978-0-545-66277-2(X))* Scholastic, Inc.

—Fly High, Fly Guy! Arnold, Tedd, illus. 2008. (Fly Guy Ser.: 5). (ENG., Illus.). 32p. (J). (gr. -1-3). 6.99 *(978-0-545-00722-1(4))* Scholastic, Inc.

—Hi! Fly Guy. Arnold, Tedd, illus. 2005. (Fly Guy Ser.: 1). (ENG., Illus.). 32p. (J). (gr. -1-3). 6.99 *(978-0-439-63903-3(4)*, Cartwheel Bks.) Scholastic, Inc.

—Hooray for Fly Guy! 2008. (Fly Guy Ser.: 6). (ENG.). 32p. (J). (gr. -1-3). 6.99 *(978-0-545-00724-5(0))* Scholastic, Inc.

—I Spy Fly Guy! Arnold, Tedd, illus. 2009. (Fly Guy Ser.: 7). (ENG., Illus.). 32p. (J). (gr. -1-3). 6.99 *(978-0-545-11028-0(9))* Scholastic, Inc.

—I Spy Fly Guy! Arnold, Tedd, illus. 2009. (Fly Guy Ser.: 7). (Illus.). lib. bdg. 17.20 *(978-0-606-07098-0(2)*, Turtleback) Turtleback Bks.

—A Pet for Fly Guy. Arnold, Tedd, illus. 2014. (Fly Guy Ser.). (ENG., Illus.). 32p. (J). (gr. -1-3). 16.99 *(978-0-545-31615-6(4)*, Orchard Bks.) Scholastic, Inc.

—Ride, Fly Guy, Ride! 2012. (Fly Guy Ser.: 11). (ENG., Illus.). 32p. (J). (gr. -1-3). 6.99 *(978-0-545-22276-1(1)*, Cartwheel Bks.) Scholastic, Inc.

—Shoo, Fly Guy! Arnold, Tedd, illus. 2006. (Fly Guy Ser.: 3). (ENG., Illus.). 32p. (J). (gr. -1-3). 6.99 *(978-0-439-63905-7(0)*, Cartwheel Bks.) Scholastic, Inc.

—There's a Fly Guy in My Soup. 2012. (Fly Guy Ser.: 12). (ENG.). 32p. (J). (gr. -1-3). 6.99 *(978-0-545-31284-4(1)*, Cartwheel Bks.) Scholastic, Inc.

—There's a Fly Guy in My Soup. 2012. (Fly Guy Ser.: 12). lib. bdg. 17.20 *(978-0-606-26533-1(3)*, Turtleback) Turtleback Bks.

Austrian, J. J. Worm Loves Worm. Curato, Mike, illus. 2016. 32p. (J). (gr. -1-3). 17.99 *(978-0-06-238633-5(6))* HarperCollins Pubs.

Avi. A Beginning, a Muddle, & an End: The Right Way to Write Writing. Tusa, Tricia, illus. 2008. (ENG.). 176p. (J). (gr. 2-5). 14.95 *(978-0-15-205555-4(X))* Houghton Mifflin Harcourt Publishing Co.

—The End of the Beginning: Being the Adventures of a Small Snail (and an Even Smaller Ant) Tusa, Tricia, illus. 2008. (ENG.). 144p. (J). (gr. 2-5). pap. 6.95 *(978-0-15-205532-5(0))* Houghton Mifflin Harcourt Publishing Co.

Awad, Shelley. The Greenhouse Kids: Dan Delion's Secret. Zonta, Rose, illus. 2009. 127p. (J). pap. *(978-0-88887-379-8(4))* Borealis Pr.

Axmacher, Denise. Mrs. FireFly. 2008. 32p. 16.50 *(978-1-4357-0864-8(4))* Lulu Pr., Inc.

AZ Books Staff. Busy Insects Moving & Talking. Dubovik, Ludmila, ed. 2012. (Funny Trails Ser.). (ENG.). 10p. (J). (gr. -1-k). bds. 9.95 *(978-1-61889-175-4(8))* AZ Bks. LLC.

Baez, Debra. Fly, Fly, Little Fly. 2008. 15p. pap. 24.95 *(978-1-60474-600-6(9))* America Star Bks.

Bailey, Arthur Scott. The Tale of Freddie Firefly. 2004. reprint ed. pap. 1.99 *(978-1-4192-8478-6(9))*; pap. 15.95 *(978-1-4191-8478-9(4))* Kessinger Publishing, LLC.

—Tuck-Me-in Tales: The Tale of Freddie Fi. 2006. pap. *(978-1-4065-0449-1(1))* Dodo Pr.

Bailey, Linda. The Tiny Hero of Ferny Creek Library. Jamieson, Victoria, illus. 2017. 336p. (J). (gr. 3-7). 16.99 *(978-0-06-244093-8(4)*, Greenwillow Bks.) HarperCollins Pubs.

Baisden, Crystal. Carlie's New Friend. 2012. 24p. pap. 24.95 *(978-1-4626-8405-2(X))* America Star Bks.

Balash, Sue Beth. Mimi the Inchworm. 2009. (ENG.). 32p. pap. 10.95 *(978-1-933916-44-6(3)*, Ferne Pr.) Nelson Publishing & Marketing.

Bama. Lucy Ladybug's Backyard Adventure. 2012. (ENG., Illus.). 48p. 14.95 *(978-1-4697-3868-0(6)*, 2f8a90e6-2c3f-4026-aaad-d311543fc12a) iUniverse, Inc.

Barnes, Brenda J. Silas Watts: The Highly Electric Lightning Bug. Williams, Nancy E., ed. Forrest, Grace Metzger, illus. 2013. 28p. (J). pap. 17.98 *(978-1-938526-36-7(8))* Roxby Media Ltd. GBR. Dist: Laurus Co., The.

Bass, Keisha Y., creator. Ladybug Ladybug. 2005. (Illus.). 60p. (J). per. 7.95 *(978-0-9768129-0-6(8))* KB Publishing.

Beck, Bev. Benny at the Bop. 2011. 28p. pap. 24.95 *(978-1-4560-6151-7(8))* America Star Bks.

The Bee & the Bug, 6 vols. 8p. (gr. k-1). 21.50 *(978-0-322-02076-4(X))* Wright Group/McGraw-Hill.

Bell, Rebecca. Message from Miami: The Adventures of Sharp-Eye, Book 2. Bell, Rebecca, illus. 2005. (Adventures of Sharp-Eye). (Illus.). 30p. (J). 9.95 *(978-1-934138-09-0(6))* Bouncing Ball Bks., Inc.

—A Regular Bug: The Adventures of Sharp-Eye, Book 1. Bell, Rebecca, illus. 2005. (Adventures of Sharp-Eye: Bk. 1). (Illus.). 25p. (J). 9.95 *(978-1-934138-08-3(8))* Bouncing Ball Bks., Inc.

Belt, Christopher R. The Adventures of Nate the Gnat. 2009. 32p. pap. 15.00 *(978-1-4389-6427-0(7))* AuthorHouse.

Bernstein, Nina. Magic by the Book, 4 vols. unabr. ed. 2005. (J). 65.75 *(978-1-4193-3607-2(X)*, 42048) Recorded Bks., Inc.

Bethel, Ellie. Michael Recycle Meets Litterbug Doug. Colombo, Alexandra, illus. 2009. (Michael Recycle Ser.). (ENG.). 24p. (J). (gr. 2-5). 15.99 *(978-1-60010-392-6(8)*, 9781600103926) Idea & Design Works, LLC.

Biedrzycki, David. Ace Lacewing: Bad Bugs Are My Business. Biedrzycki, David, illus. 2011. (ENG., Illus.). 44p. (J). (gr. k-4). pap. 8.95 *(978-1-57091-693-9(4))* Charlesbridge Publishing, Inc.

—Ace Lacewing: Bug Detective. Biedrzycki, David, illus. 2008. (ENG., Illus.). 40p. (J). (gr. k-4). pap. 8.95 *(978-1-57091-684-7(5))* Charlesbridge Publishing, Inc.

—Ace Lacewing, Bug Detective: Bad Bugs Are My Business. Biedrzycki, David, illus. 2009. (ENG., Illus.). 44p. (J). (gr. k-4). 16.95 *(978-1-57091-692-2(6))* Charlesbridge Publishing, Inc.

—Ace Lacewing, Bug Detective: The Big Swat. Biedrzycki, David, illus. 2010. (ENG., Illus.). 44p. (J). (gr. k-4). 16.95 *(978-1-57091-747-9(7))* Charlesbridge Publishing, Inc.

The Black Bug SAT. Date not set. 5.95 *(978-0-89868-319-6(X))* ARO Publishing Co.

Black, Cassandra. Twinkle: A Chapter Book. 2003. 113p. (J). 7.99 *(978-0-9742739-0-7(2))* Lavender Bks.

Blackford, Andy. George & the Dragonfly. Mason, Sue, illus. 2014. (ReadZone Picture Bks.). (ENG.). 32p. (J). (gr. k-3). pap. 8.99 *(978-1-78322-423-4(1))* ReadZone Bks. GBR. Dist: Independent Pubs. Group.

—George & the Dragonfly. Mason, Sue, illus. 2011. (ENG.). 32p. (J). (gr. -1-k). pap. *(978-1-84089-624-4(8))* Zero to Ten, Ltd.

Blackshaw, Win. David's Dinosaur. 2009. 104p. pap. 17.55 *(978-1-4092-3704-4(4))* Lulu Pr., Inc.

Blake-Brekke, Carri. Billy Bully Bug: Learns a Lesson in Hawaii. Melton, Jodi, illus. 2003. (Mrs. B's Story Time... With a Twist! Ser.). 20p. (J). pap. 11.95 incl. audio compact disk *(978-0-9720549-2-8(8))* Mom's Pride Enterprises.

—Juanita Maria Sophia Bug Diva: Lived down South in the West. Melton, Jo Lynn, illus. 2004. (Mrs. B'S Story Time-. . with A Twist! Ser.). 20p. (J). pap. 11.95 incl. audio compact disk *(978-0-9720549-3-5(6))* Mom's Pride Enterprises.

Blechman, R. O. Franklin the Fly. 2008. (ENG., Illus.). 40p. (J). (gr. 1-3). 17.95 *(978-1-56846-148-9(8)*, Creative Editions) Creative Co., The.

Bogart, Jo Ellen. The Big Tree Gang, 1 vol. Griffiths, Dean, illus. 2005. (Orca Echoes Ser.). (ENG.). 64p. (J). (gr. 2-3). per. 6.95 *(978-1-55143-345-5(1))* Orca Bk. Pubs. USA.

Book Company Staff. Be Bop Bugs. 2003. (Novelty Bks.). (J). 15.95 *(978-1-74047-329-3(9))* Book Co. Publishing Pty, Ltd., The AUS. Dist: Penton Overseas, Inc.

—Busy Bugs. 2003. (Puzzles Ser.). (Illus.). (J). bds. 10.95 *(978-1-74047-335-4(3))* Book Co. Publishing Pty, Ltd., The AUS. Dist: Penton Overseas, Inc.

—Counting. 2003. (Bug Chunkie Board Bks.). (Illus.). (J). bds. 2.95 *(978-1-74047-346-0(9))* Book Co. Publishing Pty, Ltd., The AUS. Dist: Penton Overseas, Inc.

Booth-Alberstadt, Sheila. Maggie Mcnair Has Sugar Bugs in There. Hall, Norris, illus. 2013. (ENG.). 36p. (J). (gr. -1-1). 14.95 *(978-0-9711404-6-2(4))* SBA Bks., LLC.

Bouldin, Anthony Roth & Bouldin, Morshica. Tag along with Momo & Jojo: You're IT! Series #1 Jojo's 1st day of School. 2011. 16p. 14.95 *(978-1-4567-2077-3(5))* AuthorHouse.

Box, Marty & McKenna, Allen. The Little Red Beetle Goes Shopping. Box, Marty, illus. 2005. (ENG., Illus.). 40p. pap. *(978-1-84401-521-4(1))* Athena Pr.

Bradley, Timothy J. Paleo Bugs: Survival of the Creepiest. Bradley, Timothy J., illus. 2008. (Paleo Ser.: PALE). (ENG., Illus.). 48p. (J). (gr. 3-7). 15.99 *(978-0-8118-6022-2(1))* Chronicle Bks. LLC.

Bradshaw-White, Karl. The Adventures of Flossy. 2015. (ENG.). 44p. (J). (gr. 1-2). mass mkt. 13.95 *(978-1-78455-971-7(7)*, 51c20d50-dd7c-4585-945d-24d3c8fd00ab) Austin, Stan AUS. Dist: Bookmasters Distribution.

Brandt-Taylor, Diane. The Bunny, the Bear, the Bug & the Bee. Brandt, Michael, illus. 2005. (J). cd-rom 9.88 *(978-0-9773236-0-9(9))* TaySysCo Publishing.

Breckenridge, Trula & Lynch, Todd. Ricca the Ladybug. Breckenridge, Trula & Lynch, Todd, illus. 2004. (Illus.). (J). per. *(978-0-9749480-8-9(X)*, MSPpress) Mama Specific Productions.

Breen, Steve. Stick. 2009. (ENG.). 48p. (J). (gr. -1-k). pap. 6.99 *(978-0-14-241303-6(8)*, Puffin Books) Penguin Young Readers Group.

Brimhall Snow, Virginia. Summer Walk, 1 vol. 2016. (ENG., Illus.). 32p. (J). 16.99 *(978-1-4236-4215-2(5))* Gibbs Smith, Publisher.

Broach, Elise. James to the Rescue. Murphy, Kelly, illus. 2015. (Masterpiece Adventures Ser.: 2). (ENG.). 112p. (J). (gr. 1-4). 15.99 *(978-1-62779-316-2(X)*, 9781627793162, Holt, Henry & Co. Bks. For Young Readers) Holt, Henry & Co.

—Masterpiece. 2010. 18.00 *(978-1-60686-888-1(8))* Perfection Learning Corp.

—Masterpiece. Murphy, Kelly, illus. 2010. (ENG.). 320p. (J). (gr. 4-7). pap. 7.99 *(978-0-312-60870-5(5)*, 9780312608705) Square Fish.

—Masterpiece. 2010. (J). lib. bdg. 18.40 *(978-0-606-14604-3(0)*, Turtleback) Turtleback Bks.

Bryant, G. E. Nirvana's Sunshine Babies. 2009. 28p. pap. 12.95 *(978-1-59858-903-0(2))* Dog Ear Publishing, LLC.

The Bug Guy. Date not set. 9.95 *(978-0-89868-285-4(1))*; pap. 3.95 *(978-0-89868-284-7(3))* ARO Publishing Co.

Bugs & Other Stories: Individual Title Six-Pack. (Story Steps Ser.). (gr. k-2). 48.00 *(978-0-7635-9616-3(7))* Rigby Education.

Bugtime Adventures - Blessing in Disguise. 2005. (J). 3.95 *(978-1-933262-26-0(5))* Lightning Bug Flix.

Buller, Laura. Bugs Hide & Seek. 2014. (DK Readers Ser.). (ENG., Illus.). 32p. (J). (gr. k-4). 14.99 *(978-1-4654-1994-1(2)*, DK Children) Dorling Kindersley Publishing, Inc.

Burch, Sharon, et al. Freddie the Frog & the Secret of Crater Island: 4th Adventure: Crater Island. 2010. (ENG.). 48p. 24.99 incl. audio compact disk *(978-0-9747454-6-6(4)*, 0974745464) Mystic Publishing.

Burns, Helen Marie. Ryleigh's Little Bug Book, 1 vol. Vareberg, Gladys, illus. 2009. 24p. pap. 24.95 *(978-1-60813-701-5(5))* America Star Bks.

Burroway, Janet & Lord, John Vernon. The Giant Jam Sandwich, 1 vol. 2007. (Read along Book & CD Ser.). (ENG., Illus.). 32p. (J). (gr. -1-3). audio compact disk 10.99 *(978-0-618-83952-0(6))* Houghton Mifflin Harcourt Publishing Co.

Burton, Margie, et al. Counting Insects. 2011. (Early Connections Ser.). (J). *(978-1-61672-486-3(2))* Benchmark Education Co.

Busy Bugs. (Dough Craft Ser.). 9p. bds. *(978-1-4054-9443-4(3))* Parragon, Inc.

Butterworth, MyLinda & Day, Linda S. Frogazoom! Day, Linda S., illus. l.t. ed. 2003. (Illus.). 32p. (J). (gr. k-3). pap. 16.95 *(978-1-890905-03-3(8)*, Writers Collective, The) Day to Day Enterprises.

Cain, Janan. Roonie B. Moonie: Lost & Alone. 2007. (Illus.). 32p. (J). (gr. -1-3). 15.95 *(978-0-9740190-8-6(9))* Illumination Arts Publishing Co., Inc.

The Cake: Individual Title Six-Packs. (Story Steps Ser.). (gr. k-2). 29.00 *(978-0-7635-9601-9(9))* Rigby Education.

Calabrese, Paul. The Good Bug Book ... (and Other Cool Creatures) 2012. 24p. pap. 15.99 *(978-1-4797-4131-1(0))* Xlibris Corp.

Campbell, Rod. Colour Bugs. 2003. (ENG., Illus.). 10p. (J). bds. 4.95 *(978-0-333-73338-7(X))* Macmillan Pubs., Ltd. GBR. Dist: Trafalgar Square Publishing.

Cannon, Janell. Crickwing. 2005. (Illus.). (gr. 1-4). 17.00 *(978-0-7569-5051-4(1))* Perfection Learning Corp.

Carbonell, Paula. BUTTERFLY TRIP. 2007. (ENG., Illus.). 48p. (J). 18.95 *(978-84-96788-85-5(7))* OQO, Editora ESP. Dist: Baker & Taylor Bks.

Carle, Eric. Coccinelle Mal Lune. pap. 18.95 *(978-2-87142-287-7(7))* Mijade Editions BEL. Dist: Distribooks, Inc.

—Piccolo Ragno Tesse e Tace. pap. 18.95 *(978-88-04-33198-8(4))* Mondadori ITA. Dist: Distribooks, Inc.

Carretero, Mónica. ROLY-POLIES. 2011. (Mini-Animalist Ser.). (ENG., Illus.). 32p. (J). (gr. k-2). *(978-84-938240-1-3(1))* D P & G Military Pubs.

Carter, David A. Alpha Bugs: A Pop-Up Alphabet. Carter, David A., illus. 2006. (David Carter's Bugs Ser.). (ENG., Illus.). 28p. (J). (gr. -1-2). 12.99 *(978-1-4169-0973-6(7)*, Little Simon) Little Simon.

—Beach Bugs. Carter, David A., illus. 2008. (David Carter's Bugs Ser.). (ENG., Illus.). 16p. (J). (gr. -1-2). 12.99 *(978-1-4169-5055-4(9)*, Little Simon) Little Simon.

—Bedtime Bugs. Carter, David A., illus. 2010. (David Carter's Bugs Ser.). (ENG., Illus.). 18p. (J). (gr. -1-2). 12.99 *(978-1-4169-9960-7(4)*, Little Simon) Little Simon.

—The Big Bug Book. Carter, David A., illus. 2008. (David Carter's Bugs Ser.). (ENG., Illus.). 16p. (J). (gr. -1-2). 24.99 *(978-1-4169-4095-1(2)*, Little Simon) Little Simon.

—Bugs at the Beach. Carter, David A., illus. 2016. (David Carter's Bugs Ser.). (ENG., Illus.). 24p. (J). (gr. -1-1). pap. 3.99 *(978-1-4814-4050-9(0)*, Simon Spotlight) Simon Spotlight.

—Bugs That Go! A Bustling Pop-Up Book. Carter, David A., illus. 2011. (David Carter's Bugs Ser.). (ENG., Illus.). 18p. (J). (gr. -1-1). 12.99 *(978-1-4169-4097-5(9)*, Little Simon) Little Simon.

—Busy Bug Builds a Fort. Carter, David A., illus. 2016. (David Carter's Bugs Ser.). (ENG., Illus.). 24p. (J). (gr. -1-1). pap. 3.99 *(978-1-4814-4047-9(0)*, Simon Spotlight) Simon Spotlight.

—Colors: A Bugs Pop-Up Concept Book. Carter, David A., illus. 2010. (David Carter's Bugs Ser.). (ENG., Illus.). 16p. (J). (gr. -1-1). 8.99 *(978-1-4424-0830-2(8)*, Little Simon) Little Simon.

—Counting: A Bugs Pop-Up Concept Book. Carter, David A., illus. 2010. (David Carter's Bugs Ser.). (ENG., Illus.). 16p. (J). (gr. -1-1). 7.99 *(978-1-4424-0828-9(6)*, Little Simon) Little Simon.

—Feely Bugs. Carter, David A., illus. 2005. (David Carter's Bugs Ser.). (ENG., Illus.). 14p. (J). (gr. -1-2). 12.99 *(978-1-4169-0326-0(7)*, Little Simon) Little Simon.

—Jingle Bugs: A Merry Pop-Up Book with Lights & Music! Carter, David A., illus. 2004. (David Carter's Bugs Ser.). (ENG., Illus.). 22p. (J). (gr. -1-2). 11.99 *(978-0-689-87416-1(2)*, Little Simon) Little Simon.

—Love Bugs. Carter, David A., illus. 2003. (ENG., Illus.). 12p. (J). (gr. 2-5). 6.99 *(978-0-689-85815-4(9)*, Little Simon) Little Simon.

—Princess Bugs: A Touch-And-Feel Fairy Tale. Carter, David A., illus. 2013. (David Carter's Bugs Ser.). (ENG., Illus.). 16p. (J). (gr. -1-2). 12.99 *(978-1-4424-5055-4(X)*, Little Simon) Little Simon.

—A Snowy Day in Bugland! Carter, David A., illus. 2012. (David Carter's Bugs Ser.). (ENG., Illus.). 24p. (J). (gr. -1-1). 15.99 *(978-1-4424-3895-8(9))*; pap. 3.99 *(978-1-4424-3894-1(0))* Simon Spotlight. (Simon Spotlight).

—Springtime in Bugland! Carter, David A., illus. 2012. (David Carter's Bugs Ser.). (ENG., Illus.). 24p. (J). (gr. -1-1). 15.99 *(978-1-4424-3892-7(4))*; pap. 3.99 *(978-1-4424-3890-3(8))* Simon Spotlight. (Simon Spotlight).

—Welcome to Bugland! A Fun Foldout World from David A. Carter. Carter, David A., illus. 2011. (David Carter's Bugs Ser.). (ENG., Illus.). 24p. (J). (gr. -1-3). 12.99 *(978-1-4424-1962-9(8)*, Little Simon) Little Simon.

—The 12 Bugs of Christmas: A Pop-Up Christmas Counting Book. Carter, David A., illus. 2011. (David Carter's Bugs Ser.). (ENG., Illus.). 24p. (J). (gr. -1-1). 12.99 *(978-1-4424-2649-8(7)*, Little Simon) Little Simon.

Cassity, Brittney. Fiddlebug. 2008. 52p. pap. 22.49 *(978-1-4389-2537-0(9))* AuthorHouse.

Catrow, David. The Fly Flew In. Catrow, David, illus. 2012. (I Like to Read(r) Ser.). (ENG., Illus.). 24p. (J). (gr. -1-3). 14.95 *(978-0-8234-2418-4(9))* Holiday Hse., Inc.

Chadwick, Jennie. The Peach Tree Kids: Circus Fleas. 2012. 96p. pap. 9.99 *(978-1-61897-455-6(6)*, Strategic Bk. Publishing) Strategic Book Publishing & Rights Agency (SBPRA).

Childrens Press Staff, contrib. by. The Bug Box: Firefly Friend -The Great Bug Hunt - How Many Ants? 2005. (Rookie Reader Ser.). (ENG.). 96p. (J). (gr. 1-2). pap. 9.95 *(978-0-516-25385-5(9)*, Children's Pr.) Scholastic Library Publishing.

Church, Anna. Hug-A-Bug Travels to Greece. Taylor, Nicole, illus. 2012. 44p. pap. 12.00 *(978-0-9831449-5-3(8))* Mighty Lion Ventures.

Clark, Kent & Snider, Brandon T. Peter Powers & the Itchy Insect Invasion! Bardin, Dave, illus. 2017. (Peter Powers Ser.: 3). (ENG.). 128p. (J). (gr. 1-5). 15.99 *(978-0-316-35947-4(5))* Little, Brown Bks. for Young Readers.

Clarke, Ella. I Am So Beautiful, 1 vol. rev. ed. 2013. (Fiction Readers Ser.). (ENG., Illus.). 20p. (J). (gr. 1-1). 4.99 *(978-1-4333-5485-4(3))*; pap. 15.96 *(978-1-4807-1141-9(1))* Shell Educational Publishing.

Coleman, Candace. Zubie the Lightning Bug - I Want to Remember Your Thoughts. 2006. (J). 15.99 *(978-0-9774998-0-9(4))* Parent Brigade Company, The.

Connell, Karen. The Adventures of Katie & Sam: A Day to Fly, 1 vol. 2009. 16p. pap. 24.95 *(978-1-60813-702-2(3))* America Star Bks.

—Slow Down: The Adventures of Katie & Sam, 1 vol. 2009. 15p. pap. 24.95 *(978-1-61582-420-5(0))* America Star Bks.

Connelly, Wendy. Fiona the Firefly! 2003. (Illus.). (J). 12.95 *(978-1-929039-16-6(6))* Ambassador Bks., Inc.

Cooper, Lynne. Alien Invaders. Leick, Bonnie, illus. 2010. (ENG.). 32p. (J). (gr. 4-7). *(978-1-934960-83-7(7))* Continental Sales.

Cordone Warner, Debra. Buddy & A Walk in the Woods. 2010. 38p. pap. 18.99 *(978-0-557-60690-0(X))* Lulu Pr., Inc.

Corrick, Dave. Louie the Bee: The Insects Prevail. 2010. 358p. 29.99 *(978-1-4500-1603-2(0))*; pap. 19.99 *(978-1-4500-1602-5(2))* Xlibris Corp.

Cosgrove, Stephen. Bee Double Bopp: Respecting Others. Arroyo, Fian, illus. 2004. (J). *(978-1-58804-350-4(9))* P C I Education.

—Big Bubba Bigg, Jr. Dealing with Bullies. Arroyo, Fian, illus. 2004. (J). *(978-1-58804-352-8(5))* P C I Education.

—The Bigg Family: Getting along with Others. Arroyo, Fian, illus. 2004. (J). *(978-1-58804-354-2(1))* P C I Education.

—The Bugglar Brothers: Consequences of Stealing. Arroyo, Fian, illus. 2007. (J). *(978-1-58804-381-8(9))* P C I Education.

—Cricket Clickett: Finding Your Talents. Arroyo, Fian, illus. 2004. (J). *(978-1-58804-382-5(7))* P C I Education.

—Flynn "Flea" Flicker: Sticking to the Truth. Arroyo, Fian, illus. 2004. (J). *(978-1-58804-353-5(3))* P C I Education.

—Hickory B. Hopp: Paying Attention. Arroyo, Fian, illus. 2004. (J). *(978-1-58804-379-5(7))* P C I Education.

—Katy Didd Bigg: Standing up for Yourself. Arroyo, Fian, illus. 2004. (J). *(978-1-58804-378-8(9))* P C I Education.

—Melody Moth: Practice Makes Perfect. Arroyo, Fian, illus. 2004. (J). *(978-1-58804-351-1(7))* P C I Education.

—Mizz Buggly: Doing Your Best. Arroyo, Fian, illus. 2004. (J). *(978-1-58804-380-1(0))* P C I Education.

—Snugg N. Flitter: Facing Your Fears. Arroyo, Fian, illus. 2004. (J). *(978-1-58804-377-1(0))* P C I Education.

Costa, Maria S. How to Find a Friend. 2017. (ENG., Illus.). 32p. (J). (gr. -1-3). 16.99 *(978-0-544-92678-3(1))* Houghton Mifflin Harcourt Publishing Co.

Cottrell, Kim. Jimmy Has the Bugaloo Zoo Flu. 2009. 32p. pap. 12.99 *(978-1-4389-5209-3(0))* AuthorHouse.

Cramer, Gayle Shaw. The Secret of the Dragonfly: A Story of Hope & Promise. Jones, Jan, illus. 2006. (YA). pap. 19.95 *(978-0-9729346-7-1(7))* Ambrosia Press LLC.

Croall, Marie P. & Jolley, Dan. Agent Mongoose & the Attack of the Giant Insects. Wendt, Matt, illus. 2010. (Twisted Journeys (r) Ser.: 15). (ENG.). 112p. (J). (gr. 4-7). lib. bdg. 27.93 *(978-0-8225-9251-8(7))* Lerner Publishing Group.

Cronin, Doreen. Diary of a Fly. Bliss, Harry, illus. (ENG.). 40p. (J). (gr. -1-3). 2013. 9.99 *(978-0-06-223298-4(3))* 2007. 16.99 *(978-0-06-000156-8(9))* HarperCollins Pubs.

—Diary of a Fly. Bliss, Harry, illus. 2008. (J). (gr. -1-3). 25.95 incl. audio *(978-1-4301-0404-9(X))*; 28.95 incl. audio compact disk *(978-1-4301-0407-0(4))* Live Oak Media.

—Diary of a Fly. 2011. (J). (gr. -1-3). 29.95 *(978-0-545-09454-2(2))* Weston Woods Studios, Inc.

—Diary of a Spider. Bliss, Harry, illus. (ENG.). 40p. (J). (gr. -1-3). 2013. 9.99 *(978-0-06-223300-4(9))* 2005. 16.99 *(978-0-06-000153-7(4))* HarperCollins Pubs.

—Diary of a Spider. Bliss, Harry, illus. unabr. ed. 2006. (Picture Book Readalong Ser.). (J). (gr. -1-2). 28.95 incl. audio compact disk *(978-1-59519-486-2(X))* Live Oak Media.

—Diary of a Spider. Bliss, Harry, illus. unabr. ed. 2006. (J). (gr. -1-3). 29.95 *(978-0-439-90579-4(6))* Weston Woods Studios, Inc.

Crowley, Ned. Ugh! a Bug! 2005. (Silly Millies Ser.). (Illus.). 32p. (J). (gr. 4-4). per. 4.99 *(978-0-7613-2475-1(5))*; (gr. -1-3). lib. bdg. 18.60 *(978-0-7613-3450-7(5)*, Millbrook Pr.) Lerner Publishing Group.

Cullagh, Yolanda. Sabina the Beach Fly. 2007. (ENG.). 28p. pap. 10.99 *(978-1-4196-7950-6(3))* CreateSpace Independent Publishing Platform.

D'Agata, Tabatha Jean. Ick the Stick: Yes, I Can Read! Nature Series, Book 1. Lineberger, Judy, illus. 2006. (Yes, I Can Read! Ser.: 1). 24p. (J). pap. 6.95 *(978-1-934138-01-4(0))* Bouncing Ball Bks., Inc.

The Daisy Bug Kids Say Hello New York. 2004. (J). *(978-0-9712349-2-5(2))* Univ. At Buffalo, Child Care Ctr.

Dale, Jay. Up & Down, 1 vol. Bailey, Martin, illus. 2012. (Engage Literacy Magenta Ser.). (ENG.). 32p. (gr. k-2). pap. 5.99 *(978-1-4296-8878-9(5)*, Engage Literacy) Capstone Press of Coughlan Cos.

Daley-Prado, M. J. Buzz. 2008. 36p. pap. 17.95 *(978-1-4357-1352-9(4))* Lulu Pr., Inc.

Davies, Kathern. Bugs, Bugs, Bugs! Sorensen, Heather, illus. 2010. 24p. pap. 12.99 *(978-1-4520-1624-5(0))* AuthorHouse.

Dawson, J. M. Bug, Bug, Where's the Bug? Hoofnagle, Therese, illus. 2008. 26p. pap. 24.95 *(978-1-60474-365-4(4))* America Star Bks.

Day, Robert O. & Day, Linda S. There's a Frog on a Log in the Bog. Day, Linda S., illus. 2003. (Illus.). (J). (gr. 3-6). 212p. pap. 8.95 *(978-1-890905-50-7(X)*, Writers Collective, The); (Just So Wild Ser.: Vol. 1). 14.95 *(978-1-890905-51-4(8)*, Eco Fiction Bks.) Day to Day Enterprises.

De Vicq de Cumptich, Roberto. Counting Insects. Date not set. (J). 15.95 *(978-0-8050-6560-2(1)*, Holt, Henry & Co. Bks. For Young Readers) Holt, Henry & Co.

Deflitch, Jennifer L. Delia the Dragonfly's Grand Adventures: Delia Goes to Washington D. C. 2012. 28p. (-18). pap. 24.95 *(978-1-62709-290-6(0))* America Star Bks.

DeMatteis, J. M. Stardust Kid. Ploog, Mike, illus. 2008. (ENG.). 128p. pap. 14.99 *(978-1-934506-04-2(4))* Boom! Studios.

Depisco, Dorothea. Beetle Bugs Party: A Counting Book. Parry, Jo, illus. 2005. 10p. (J). (gr. -1-3). 10.95 *(978-1-58117-415-1(2)*, Intervisual/Piggy Toes) Bendon, Inc.

Derico, Laura. All God's Bugs. Smith, Matt, illus. 2013. (Happy Day Ser.). (ENG.). 16p. (J). pap. 2.49 *(978-1-4143-9295-0(8))* Tyndale Hse. Pubs.

Derico, Laura Ring. All God's Bugs. Smith, Matt, illus. 2015. (Faith That Sticks Bks.). (ENG.). 30p. (J). pap. 3.99 *(978-1-4964-0317-9(7))* Tyndale Hse. Pubs.

Derrick, Patricia. Sly the Dragonfly. Martinez, J-P Loppo, illus. 2007. 32p. (J). (gr. -1-3). 18.95 incl. audio compact disk *(978-1-933818-16-0(6))* Animalations.

DeSica, Melissa. Gecko & Mosquito. 2007. (Illus.). 32p. (J). 14.95 *(978-0-9790647-6-0(7))* Watermark Publishing, LLC.

DeSpain, Pleasant. Tales of Insects. 2016. (ENG., Illus.). 80p. (J). (gr. 3-4). pap. 9.95 *(978-1-941460-40-5(2))* August Hse. Pubs., Inc.

Dettman, Eric. Any Day Friends. 2012. 28p. pap. 19.99 *(978-1-4685-4297-4(4))* AuthorHouse.

Dewane, Patrick Ryan. What If the Rain Were Bugs? Konecny, John, illus. 2013. 24p. 14.99 *(978-1-937165-39-0(6))* Orange Hat Publishing.

Disney Book Group. Bug Zoo: Walt Disney Animation Studios Artist Showcase Book. Harkness, Andy, illus. 2016. (Walt Disney Animation Studios Artist Showcase Ser.). (ENG.). 40p. (J). (gr. -1-k). 17.99 *(978-1-4847-2054-7(7))* Hyperion Bks. for Children.

Disney Publishing Staff. The Big Bug Hunt, 15 vols. 2003. (It's Fun to Learn Ser.). (Illus.). 32p. (J). (gr. -1-3). 3.99 *(978-1-57973-139-7(2))* Advance Pubs. LLC.

DiTerlizzi, Angela. Some Bugs. Wenzel, Brendan, illus. 2014. (ENG.). 32p. (J). (gr. -1-3). 17.99 *(978-1-4424-5880-2(1)*, Beach Lane Bks.) Beach Lane Bks.

Dodd, Emma. I Love Bugs. Dodd, Emma, illus. 2011. (ENG., Illus.). 32p. (J). pap. 6.95 *(978-0-8234-2345-3(X))* Holiday Hse., Inc.

Dodd, Lynley. Zachary Quack Minimonster. Dodd, Lynley, illus. 2006. (Gold Star First Readers Ser.). (Illus.). 32p. (gr. -1-3). lib. bdg. 23.00 *(978-0-8368-6187-7(6)*, Gareth Stevens Learning Library) Stevens, Gareth Publishing LLLP.

Donaldson, Julia. Superworm. Scheffler, Axel, illus. 2014. (ENG.). 32p. (J). (gr. -1-3). 16.99 *(978-0-545-59176-8(7)*, Levine, Arthur A. Bks.) Scholastic, Inc.

Doodler, Todd H. Super Fly: The World's Smallest Superhero! 2015. (Super Fly Ser.). (ENG., Illus.). 128p. (J). (gr. k-2). 15.99 *(978-1-61963-379-7(5)*, 9781619633797, Bloomsbury USA Childrens) Bloomsbury Publishing USA.

—Super Fly 4: Rise of the Evil Army. 2017. (Super Fly Ser.). (ENG., Illus.). 128p. (J). pap. 6.99 *(978-1-61963-387-2(6)*, 9781619633872, Bloomsbury USA Childrens) Bloomsbury Publishing USA.

—Super Fly vs. Furious Flea! 2016. (Super Fly Ser.). (ENG., Illus.). 128p. (J). 15.99 *(978-1-61963-385-8(X)*, 9781619633858); pap. 6.99 *(978-1-61963-384-1(1)*, 9781619633841) Bloomsbury Publishing USA. (Bloomsbury USA Childrens).

—Super Fly vs. Furious Flea! 2016. (Super Fly Ser.: 3). (J). lib. bdg. 17.20 *(978-0-606-39556-4(3))* Turtleback Bks.

Doman, Rae. Sunbuddy Fables. 2013. 108p. pap. 9.99 *(978-0-9896218-3-0(9))* Sunraehealing.

Douglas, Babette. Rosebud. 2004. (J). 9.99 *(978-1-890343-12-5(9))* Kiss A Me Productions, Inc.

Dower, Laura. Return of Mega Mantis. Schlafman, Dave, illus. 2009. (Monster Squad Ser.: 2). (ENG.). 144p. (J). (gr. 2-4). pap. 5.99 *(978-0-448-44913-5(7)*, Grosset & Dunlap) Penguin Young Readers Group.

Dragonfly Dreams & Other Stories: Individual Title Six-Pack. (Story Steps Ser.). (gr. k-2). 48.00 *(978-0-7635-9843-3(7))* Rigby Education.

Durango, Julia. Pest Fest. Cyrus, Kurt, illus. 2012. (ENG.). 40p. (J). (gr. -1-2). 19.99 *(978-1-4424-3095-2(8)*, Simon & Schuster Bks. For Young Readers) Simon & Schuster Bks. For Young Readers.

Dyan, Penelope. Mikey & Me & the Fly — -the Continuing Story of a Girl & Her Dog. Dyan, Penelope, illus. 2010. (Illus.). 50p. pap. 14.95 *(978-1-935118-94-7(3))* Bellissima Publishing, LLC.

E.A. Budd. Stella Saves the Game. Lucas, Diane, illus. 2012. 24p. pap. 12.95 *(978-1-61244-059-0(2))* Halo Publishing International.

Earnhardt, Heather L. The Wandering Goose: A Modern Fable of How Love Goes. Clements, Frida, illus. 2013. (ENG.). 64p. 15.95 *(978-1-57061-881-9(X))* Sasquatch Bks.

Edgecombe, Jane. Fly Away Home. Martin, Stuart, illus. 2003. (J). 15.95 *(978-1-74047-152-7(0))* Book Co. Publishing Pty, Ltd., The AUS. Dist: Penton Overseas, Inc.

—Whoops! 2003. (J). pap. 12.95 *(978-1-74047-258-6(6))* Book Co. Publishing Pty, Ltd., The AUS. Dist: Penton Overseas, Inc.

Edwards, Karl Newsom. Fly! 2015. (ENG., Illus.). 32p. (J). (-k). 15.99 *(978-0-385-39283-9(4)*, Knopf Bks. for Young Readers) Random Hse. Children's Bks.

Ellis, Carson. Du Iz Tak? Ellis, Carson, illus. 2016. (ENG., Illus.). 48p. (J). (gr. -1-3). 16.99 *(978-0-7636-6530-2(4))* Candlewick Pr.

Emberley, Rebecca & Emberley, Ed. The Ant & the Grasshopper. 2013. 29.95 incl. audio compact disk *(978-0-545-57140-1(5))* Weston Woods Studios, Inc.

Eniwaye, Olu O. Adventures of Jabi-Jabi II: The Return of the King Fly 2nd in the series of adventures of the King Fly Jabi-Jabi. 2011. 48p. pap. 17.30 *(978-1-4634-1974-5(0))* AuthorHouse.

Eterovich-Boynar, Janine. Those Mean Bugs Are Going to Get Me, Mommy! 2011. 28p. pap. 15.99 *(978-1-4583-2429-0(X))* Lulu Pr., Inc.

farahay, m. l. The BUTTERFLY, the BEE & the SPIDER. 2009. 32p. pap. 6.94 *(978-0-557-14043-5(9))* Lulu Pr., Inc.

—The BUTTERFLY, the BEE & the SPIDER, Sc3. 2009. 32p. pap. 14.94 *(978-0-557-15287-2(9))* Lulu Pr., Inc.

Five Shiny Bugs. 2008. (Baby Gold Stars Fabric Ser.). 6p. bds. *(978-1-4075-2521-1(2))* Parragon, Inc.

Fleming, Maria. The Bug Book. Swift, Gary, illus. 2004. (Grammar Tales Ser.). (ENG.). 16p. (J). (gr. 3-7). pap. 3.25 *(978-0-439-45818-4(8))* Scholastic, Inc.

Fox, Kate & Read, Abigail. Dear Mom: A Journal All about You Written by Me. 2014. (ENG.). 96p. 12.99 *(978-1-84601-469-7(7)*, Spruce) Octopus Publishing Group GBR. Dist: Hachette Bk. Group.

Frampton, Colleen Mesler. Margret's Morning. 2011. 24p. pap. 15.99 *(978-1-4568-2101-2(6))* Xlibris Corp.

Frashier, Giva. Bogey the Golf Bug. 2013. 36p. pap. 15.99 *(978-1-4808-0126-4(7))* Archway Publishing.

Frederick, Cynthia. The Gray Beetle. 2005. 20p. 15.00 *(978-1-4116-5732-8(2))* Lulu Pr., Inc.

Freeman, Don. Manuelo the Playing Mantis. 2006. (ENG., Illus.). 32p. (J). (gr. -1-2). reprint ed. pap. 6.99 *(978-0-14-240560-4(4)*, Puffin Books) Penguin Young Readers Group.

Freeman, Tor. Ambrose Goes for Gold. 2008. (ENG., Illus.). 32p. (J). (gr. 3-6). 24.50 *(978-0-230-53146-8(6)*, Macmillan) Pan Macmillan GBR. Dist: Trans-Atlantic Pubns., Inc.

Frenkel, Yetti. The Big, Blue Lump. Frenkel, Yetti, illus. 2004. (Illus.). 32p. (J). 16.95 *(978-0-9749006-0-5(5))* Snow Tree Bks.

Fricke, Paul. Night of the Bedbugs. 2010. (ENG., Illus.). 32p. (J). 12.99 *(978-1-60706-145-8(7)*, 9781607061458) Image Comics.

Frontiera, Deborah. Eric & the Enchanted Leaf: A Night with Echo. Scott, Korey, illus. 2007.Tr. of Eric y la hojita encantada: una noche con Eco. (SPA.). 32p. (J). *(978-0-9795474-2-3(3))* KAM Publishing.

Frontiera, Deborah K. The Re-Creation of Roacheria. 2nd ed. 2004. (Chronicles of Henry Roach-Dairier: Bk. 3). 247p. (YA). (gr. 5-18). per. 15.95 *(978-0-9753410-3-2(0))* Jade Enterprises.

—To Build a Tunnel. 2nd ed. 2004. (Chronicles of Henry Roach-Dairier: Bk. 1). 218p. (YA). (gr. 5-18). per. 15.95 *(978-0-9753410-1-8(4))* Jade Enterprises.

Fultion, T. C. Jan the Cleaning Lady. 2009. 20p. pap. 10.95 *(978-1-60860-447-0(0)*, Strategic Bk. Publishing) Strategic Book Publishing & Rights Agency (SBPRA).

Ganges, Montse. Fly Hunter. Urberuaga, Emilio, illus. 2009. (Cooper Ser.). 24p. (J). (gr. -1-3). pap. 8.15 *(978-1-60754-237-7(4))*; lib. bdg. 22.60 *(978-1-60754-236-0(6))* Windmill Bks.

A Garden Circus. 2003. (J). 9.99 *(978-0-9740847-5-6(1))* GiGi Bks.

Garner, Albert. The Adventures of Dimi. 2013. (ENG.). 48p. (J). 24.95 *(978-1-4787-1677-8(0))* Outskirts Pr., Inc.

Gerth, Melanie. Diez Pequeñas Mariquitas. Huliska-Beith, Laura, illus. 2005. Orig. Title: Ten Little Ladybugs. (SPA & ENG.). 22p. (J). (gr. -1). 10.95 *(978-1-58117-006-1(8)*, Intervisual/Piggy Toes) Bendon, Inc.

—Five Little Ladybugs. Huliska-Beith, Laura, illus. 2006. 12p. (J). bds. 14.95 *(978-1-58117-218-8(4)*, Intervisual/Piggy Toes) Bendon, Inc.

Gibson, Barbara Leonard, illus. The Dragonfly Door. rev. ed. 2007. (ENG.). 40p. (J). (gr. k-5). 17.95 *(978-1-934066-12-6(5))* Feather Rock Bks., Inc.

Gillanders, Ann. Fairy Fleur & Doug the Dragonfly's Adventures in London: Ann Gillanders. 2012. (Illus.). 36p. pap. 22.88 *(978-1-4772-4358-9(5))* AuthorHouse.

Glennon, Michelle. My Big Green Teacher: Please Turn off the Lights. Glennon, Michelle, illus. 2008. (ENG., Illus.). 32p. (J). 19.95 *(978-0-9796625-3-9(2))* GDG Publishing.

—My Big Green Teacher: Recycling: It's Easy Being Green. Glennon, Michelle, illus. 2007. (Illus.). 32p. (J). 19.95 *(978-0-9796625-6-0(7))* GDG Publishing.

Gollub, Matthew. Jazz Fly 2: The Jungle Pachanga. Hanke, Karen, illus. 2010. (J). 32p. (gr. -1-3). 17.95 incl. audio compact disk *(978-1-889910-44-4(9))*; *(978-1-889910-45-1(7))* Tortuga Pr.

Goodnight, Little Bug & Wheres the Chick? 2005. (J). bds. 19.99 *(978-0-9767325-8-7(0))* Toy Quest.

Goodnight, Macy. The Toad & the Dragonfly. 2008. 24p. pap. 24.95 *(978-1-60474-785-0(4))* America Star Bks.

Gopinath, Karin Ursula. Friends in the Garden. Sutanto, Tommy, illus. 2008. 34p. (J). per. 19.95 *(978-0-9800637-0-7(1))* Lotus Art Works Inc.

Grandfeather Press. Roly Poly Napoleon Discovers Colors. 2011. (ENG., Illus.). 36p. (J). pap. 6.99 *(978-0-9832355-0-7(3))* Grandfeather Pr.

Greban, Quentin. Mommy, I Love You. 2007. (ENG., Illus.). 32p. (J). (gr. -1-3). 9.95 *(978-1-59687-184-7(9))* IBks., Inc.

Green, Kevin M. Livy Bug & Ally Gator in Best Friends. 2008. 16p. per. 24.95 *(978-1-4241-9385-1(0))* America Star Bks.

Greenburg, J. C. With the Frogs. Gerardi, Jan, illus. 2008. (Andrew Lost Ser.: 18). (ENG.). 96p. (J). (gr. 1-4). 3.99 *(978-0-375-84668-7(9)*, Random Hse. Bks. for Young Readers) Random Hse. Children's Bks.

Griffith, Christina. Jubilee & Ashanti Find Insects. 2011. 28p. (gr. 2-4). pap. 13.54 *(978-1-4269-7068-9(4))* Trafford Publishing.

Grindley, Sally. Puff Flies. Fuller, Jeremy, illus. 2011. (My Phonics Readers: Level 3 Ser.). 24p. (J). (gr. -1-1). 24.25 *(978-1-84898-514-8(2))* Sea-To-Sea Pubns.

Group/McGraw-Hill, Wright. Bugs don't Bug Me: Level K, 6 vols., Vol. 2. (First Explorers Ser.). 24p. (gr. 1-2). 34.95 *(978-0-7699-1455-8(1))* Shortland Pubns. (U. S. A.) Inc.

Hall, H. Tom. The Golden Tombo. 2011. 42p. 35.95 *(978-1-258-10444-3(X))* Literary Licensing, LLC.

Hall, John. Jeffrey Takes on the World. 2005. 48p. pap. 16.95 *(978-1-4137-9832-6(2))* PublishAmerica, Inc.

Hall, Shirley. Buggy Buggy. Ledger, Faye, illus. 2010. 20p. 12.00 *(978-1-4520-6787-2(2))* AuthorHouse.

Hanson, Warren. Bugtown Boogie. Johnson, Steve & Fancher, Lou, illus. 2008. 32p. (J). (gr. -1-3). 17.89 *(978-0-06-059938-6(3)*, Geringer, Laura Book) HarperCollins Pubs.

Harden, Mark E. The Bug in the Big White Forest. 2009. 32p. pap. 12.99 *(978-1-4389-6477-5(3))* AuthorHouse.

Harrison, Paul. Yummy in My Tummy! Worsley, Belinda, illus. 2009. (Get Ready (Windmill Books) Ser.). 32p. (J). (gr. k-2). lib. bdg. 22.60 *(978-1-60754-263-6(3))* Windmill Bks.

Harter, Gage. Sly the Fly: The Doctor's Office. Teich, Melle, illus. 2003. 16p. (J). 7.95 *(978-1-59466-009-2(3)*, Little Ones) Port Town Publishing.

Harvey, Paul, Jr. E: A Tale For Everybody. Butler, Bryan C., illus. 2013. (ENG.). 44p. (J). 25.00 *(978-0-9887774-0-8(1))* Aurandt, Paul H II.

Hawley, Greg. Don't Let the Bedbugs Bite. Regan, Dana, illus. 2004. (J). *(978-0-9657612-7-7(4))* Paddle Wheel Publishing.

Hays, Barrett K. Mars, Jimmy & Me. 2011. 24p. (gr. 4-6). pap. 11.32 *(978-1-4567-4164-8(0))* AuthorHouse.

Hazen, Lynn E. The Amazing Trail of Seymour Snail. Cushman, Doug, illus. 2009. (ENG.). 64p. (J). (gr. 1-4). 16.99 *(978-0-8050-8698-0(6)*, 9780805086980, Holt, Henry & Co. Bks. For Young Readers) Holt, Henry & Co.

Hector, Julian. The Gentleman Bug. Hector, Julian, illus. 2010. (ENG., Illus.). 40p. (J). (gr. -1-k). 16.99 *(978-1-4169-9467-1(X)*, Atheneum Bks. for Young Readers) Simon & Schuster Children's Publishing.

Henderson, Maryel. Squirt Saves the Day: A Stinkbug's Story. Henderson, Maryel, illus. 2017. (ENG., Illus.). 42p. (J). pap. 8.95 *(978-1-68350-043-8(1))* Morgan James Publishing.

Hensley, Terri Anne. The Silliest Bug & Insect Book Ever. Hall, Norris, illus. 2007. 28p. per. 6.99 *(978-0-9789057-7-4(6))* Huntington Ludlow Media Group.

Hewett, Katherine. Smile Doodle Bug! 2009. 26p. 21.80 *(978-0-578-03065-4(9))* Hewett, Katherine J.E.

Hicks, Betty. The Worm Whisperer. Hatke, Ben, illus. 2013. (ENG.). 192p. (J). (gr. 3-7). 17.99 *(978-1-59643-490-5(2)*, 9781596434905) Roaring Brook Pr.

Hildreth, Ruth Erixon. Fun Lovin' Delanie Jo. Aughe, Roger, illus. 2012. 36p. pap. 24.95 *(978-1-4626-7851-8(3))* America Star Bks.

Hill, Kevin. Lady Bug's Can't Be Tall. 2012. (Illus.). 32p. (J). 19.99 *(978-0-9852146-4-7(3))* AM Ink Publishing.

Hines-Stephens, Sarah & Harper, Benjamin. Bug Girl. Syed, Anoosha, illus. 2017. (Bug Girl Ser.). (ENG.). 304p. (J). 14.99 *(978-1-250-10661-2(3)*, 9781250106612) Imprint IND. Dist: Macmillan.

Hino, Hideshi. The Bug Boy No. 2: Hino Horror: A Graphic Novel. Hino, Hideshi, illus. 2005. (Illus.). 204p. (YA). (gr. 4-9).

reprint ed. pap. 10.00 *(978-0-7567-9709-6(8))* DIANE Publishing Co.
Hoffman, Terri. Sly Fly & the Gray Mare. BURNS, Theresa, illus. 2013. 26p. 15.95 *(978-1-940224-15-2(2))* Taylor and Seale Publishing, LLC.
Holloway, Jamie. Wanda & the Wasp's Nest. 2015. (Rosen REAL Readers: STEM & STEAM Collection). (ENG.). 8p. pap. 5.46 *(978-1-4994-9605-5(2)*, Rosen Classroom) Rosen Publishing Group, Inc., The.
Holub, Joan. Picnic! A Day in the Park. Terry, Will, illus. 2008. (Ant Hill Ser.). (ENG.). 24p. (J). (gr. -1-k). pap. 3.99 *(978-1-4169-5133-9(4)*, Simon Spotlight) Simon Spotlight.
Hood, Susan. Caterpillar Spring, Butterfly Summer. Gévry, Claudine, illus. 2003. (ENG.). 10p. (J). (gr. k-3). bds. 12.99 *(978-0-7944-0149-8(X))* Reader's Digest Assn., Inc., The.
Hooser, Betty J. Kids with Large Insects & Flowers & Unusual Things. 2012. 32p. 24.95 *(978-1-4626-4784-2(7))* America Star Bks.
Hopper, Ada. Invasion of the Insects. Ricks, Sam, illus. 2017. (DATA Set Ser.: 6). (ENG.). 128p. (J). (gr. -1-4). 16.99 *(978-1-4814-7117-6(1)*, Little Simon) Little Simon.
Horácek, Petr. The Fly. Horácek, Petr, illus. 2015. (ENG., Illus.). 32p. (J). (gr. -1-2). 14.99 *(978-0-7636-7480-9(X))* Candlewick Pr.
La Hormiga y el Saltamontes: Lap Book. (Pebble Soup Exploraciones Ser.). (SPA.). 16p. (gr. -1-18). 21.00 *(978-0-7578-1682-6(7))* Rigby Education.
La hormiga y el Saltamontes: Small Book. (Pebble Soup Exploraciones Ser.). (SPA.). 16p. (gr. -1-18). 5.00 *(978-0-7578-1722-9(X))* Rigby Education.
Houston, Anna. Daisy's Bug. 2009. 32p. pap. 14.49 *(978-1-4389-6696-0(2))* AuthorHouse.
Hunter, Mandy. Bug Crazy. 2011. 20p. pap. 10.50 *(978-1-4634-3053-5(1))* AuthorHouse.
Irwin, Gerald. Harry the Spider & His Friend Charlie. 2012. 28p. pap. 19.99 *(978-1-4772-6620-5(8))* AuthorHouse.
Jackson, Tyrone. Save Our Home. 2006. (ENG.). 88p. per. 16.95 *(978-1-4241-0875-6(6))* PublishAmerica, Inc.
James, Ian. Why Mosquitos Buzz in People's Ears: A Folktale from West Africa. 2006. (J). pap. *(978-1-4108-7161-9(4))* Benchmark Education Co.
Jefferson, Barbara. The Luck of the Dragonfly. Jefferson, Daniel E., illus. 2008. 31p. pap. 24.95 *(978-1-60672-283-1(2))* America Star Bks.
Jeffs, Dixie. A Happy Lightning Bug. 2013. 24p. pap. 24.95 *(978-1-62709-633-1(7))* America Star Bks.
Jenkins, Amanda. Mutant Bugs. 2005. (J). pap. *(978-1-4108-4219-0(3))* Benchmark Education Co.
Jenkins, Steven. The Spider House: Battle for the Wall. 2007. 264p. per. 16.95 *(978-0-595-44488-5(1))* iUniverse, Inc.
Johnson, Darlington. Layla the Ladybug - "Honesty" 2011. 24p. pap. 15.99 *(978-1-4568-5214-6(0))* Xlibris Corp.
Joiner, Mica. Petunia Pollie & Her Prolific Purse. 2011. 28p. (gr. -1). pap. 13.59 *(978-1-4567-3400-8(8))* AuthorHouse.
Jolley, Dan & Croall, Marie P. Agent Mongoose & the Attack of the Giant Insects. Wendt, Matt, illus. 2010. (Twisted Journeys (r) Ser.: 15). (ENG.). 112p. (J). (gr. 4-7). pap. 7.95 *(978-0-8225-9257-0(6)*, Graphic Universe™) Lerner Publishing Group.
Joyce, William. The Leaf Men: And the Brave Good Bugs. Joyce, William, illus. 2017. (World of William Joyce Ser.). (ENG., Illus.). 40p. (J). (gr. -1-3). 17.99 ***(978-1-4814-8955-3(0)**, Atheneum/Caitlyn Dlouhy Books)* Simon & Schuster Children's Publishing.
Kamau, G. Why Beetles Roll Cowdung. 2004. 22p. pap. *(978-9966-25-167-1(7))* Heinemann Kenya, Limited (East African Educational Publishers Ltd E.A.E.P.) KEN. Dist: Michigan State Univ. Pr.
Kamke, Bridget. The Story of the Infinipede. Ospital, Geneveive, illus. 2003. (J). 19.95 *(978-0-9744306-0-7(9))* You Can Do It! Productions.
Katz, Karen. Buzz, Buzz, Baby! Katz, Karen, illus. 2014. (ENG., Illus.). 14p. (J). (gr. -1 — 1). bds. 6.99 *(978-1-4424-9313-1(5)*, Little Simon) Little Simon.
Katz, Karin Jill. There's a Fly in My Soup. 2012. 16p. pap. 15.99 *(978-1-4772-6331-0(4))* AuthorHouse.
Keene, Carolyn. Buggy Breakout. Pamintuan, Macky, illus. 2010. (Nancy Drew & the Clue Crew Ser.: 25). (ENG.). 96p. (J). (gr. 1-4). pap. 5.99 *(978-1-4169-7814-5(3)*, Aladdin) Simon & Schuster Children's Publishing.
Kelly, Theresa. Tony the Pony: Bugs Are Not Bad. Sampson, Jody, illus. 2005. (J). per. 7.95 *(978-1-59466-030-6(1))* Port Town Publishing.
Kennedy, Kirk. Mr. Blue Butterfly. Nazario, Rafael, illus. 2013. (ENG.). (J). (gr. -1-3). 14.95 *(978-1-62086-256-8(5))* Mascot Bks., Inc.
Kenner, Crystal R. The King of All Tickle Bugs & Other Stories. 2011. (Illus.). 124p. (gr. -1). pap. 10.95 *(978-1-4502-9466-9(9))* iUniverse, Inc.
Kidd, Jessica A. Zachary Zoom. 2009. 28p. pap. 12.25 *(978-1-60860-502-6(7)*, Eloquent Bks.) Strategic Book Publishing & Rights Agency (SBPRA).
Kimmel, Eric A. Bernal & Florinda: A Spanish Tale. Rayevsky, Robert, illus. 2004. 29p. (J). (gr. k-4). reprint ed. 16.00 *(978-0-7567-7906-1(5))* DIANE Publishing Co.
King-Cason, Jermaine & McCollum, Nicole. From a Caterpillar to a Butterfly. 2012. 40p. pap. 24.95 *(978-1-4626-7777-1(0))* America Star Bks.
Kirk, Bill. There's a Beetle in My Bed. Brown, Suzy, illus. 2009. 16p. pap. 9.95 *(978-1-61633-005-7(8))* Guardian Angel Publishing, Inc.
Kirk, David. Bedtime Story. 2006. (Illus.). 32p. (J). *(978-0-448-44514-4(X))* Penguin Publishing Group.
—Captain Sunny Patch. 2006. (Illus.). 32p. (J). *(978-0-448-44515-1(8))* Callaway Editions, Inc.
—Happy Heartwood Day. 2005. (Illus.). (J). *(978-1-4156-3888-0(8)*, Grosset & Dunlap) Penguin Publishing Group.
Kirk, David & Scholastic / LeapFrog. Miss Spider's Tea Party. 2008. (J). 13.99 *(978-1-59319-934-0(1))* LeapFrog Enterprises, Inc.
Kitten chased a Fly 6 Packs. Individual Title. (gr. 1-2). 22.00 *(978-0-7635-9163-2(7))* Rigby Education.
Knudsen, Michelle. Bugged! Sims, Blanche, illus. 2008. (Science Solves It! Ser.). 32p. (J). (gr. -1-3). pap. 5.95 *(978-1-57565-259-7(5))* Kane Press, Inc.
Knudson, Michelle. Bugged! 2008. pap. 34.95 *(978-1-58013-761-4(X))* Kane Press, Inc.
Kompelien, Tracy. Fly Paper, 1 vol. Haberstroh, Anne, illus. 2007. (Critter Chronicles Ser.). (ENG.). 24p. (J). (gr. k-3). lib. bdg. 24.21 *(978-1-59928-438-5(3)*, SandCastle) ABDO Publishing Co.
Krings, Antoon. Duendecillo Membrillo. 2005. (Bichitos Curiosos Ser.). (SPA & ENG., Illus.). 32p. (J). (gr. -1-k). 5.95 *(978-84-932442-6-2(0))* Blume ESP. Dist: Independent Pubs. Group.
—Gilberto Mariposa. 2005. (Bichitos Curiosos Ser.). (SPA & ENG., Illus.). 32p. (J). (gr. -1-k). 5.95 *(978-84-932442-9-3(5))* Blume ESP. Dist: Independent Pubs. Group.
Kroll, Virginia. Mosquito, 1 vol. LePlatt, Betsy, illus. 2011. (ENG.). 32p. (J). (gr. k-3). 16.99 *(978-1-58980-883-6(5))* Pelican Publishing Co., Inc.
Krulik, Nancy. Lice Check, No. 12. Blecha, Aaron, illus. 2014. (George Brown, Class Clown Ser.: 12). (ENG.). 128p. (J). (gr. 2-4). 4.99 *(978-0-448-46112-0(9)*, Grosset & Dunlap) Penguin Young Readers Group.
Lamb, Anne. Beat Bugs. 2017. (Beat Bugs Ser.). 32p. (J). (gr. -1-3). 9.99 *(978-0-06-264076-5(3)*, HarperFestival) HarperCollins Pubs.
—Beat Bugs: Magical Mystery Tour. 2017. (Beat Bugs Ser.). 24p. (J). (gr. -1-3). pap. 3.99 *(978-0-06-264062-8(3)*, HarperFestival) HarperCollins Pubs.
—Beat Bugs: Meet the Beat Bugs. 2017. (I Can Read Level 1 Ser.). 32p. (J). (gr. -1-3). pap. 3.99 *(978-0-06-264066-6(6))* HarperCollins Pubs.
—Beat Bugs: Rain. 2017. (Beat Bugs Ser.). 16p. (J). (gr. -1 — 1). bds. 6.99 *(978-0-06-264073-4(9)*, HarperFestival) HarperCollins Pubs.
Lambert, Nancy & Lamb, Anne. Help! 2017. (Beat Bugs Ser.). 24p. (J). (gr. -1-3). pap. 3.99 *(978-0-06-264060-4(7)*, HarperFestival) HarperCollins Pubs.
Langham, Tony. Creepy Crawly Calypso. Harter, Debbie, illus. 2004. (ENG.). 32p. (J). 16.99 *(978-1-84148-699-4(X))* Barefoot Bks., Inc.
Langham, Tony & Harter, Debbie. Creepy Crawly Calypso. 2005. (ENG.). 32p. (J). pap. 9.99 *(978-1-902283-46-3(5))* Barefoot Bks., Inc.
Lasseter, John. Disney/Pixar a Bug's Life Read-along. 2007. (ENG., Illus.). (J). (gr. -1-3). *(978-0-7634-2180-9(4))* Walt Disney Records.
LeapFrog Staff. Ozzie & Mack. 2008. (J). pap. 39.99 *(978-1-59319-976-0(7))*; pap. 49.99 *(978-1-59319-924-1(4))* LeapFrog Enterprises, Inc.
Lee, WonKyeong. The Chirping Band. Jang, EunJoo, illus. 2014. (MySELF Bookshelf Ser.). (ENG.). 32p. (J). (gr. k-2). pap. 11.94 *(978-1-60357-698-7(3))*; lib. bdg. 25.27 *(978-1-59953-663-7(3))* Norwood Hse. Pr.
Lehman-Wilzig, Tami. Zvuvi's Israel. Topaz, Ksenia, illus. 2009. (Israel Ser.). (ENG.). 32p. (J). (gr. -1-2). 16.95 *(978-0-8225-8759-0(9)*, Kar-Ben Publishing) Lerner Publishing Group.
Lemberger, Evelyn. Furmin & Clyde Think Positive. 2012. 28p. pap. 16.09 *(978-1-4669-2195-5(1))* Trafford Publishing.
Leonard, M. G. Beetle Boy. (ENG.). (J). (gr. 3-7). 2017. 304p. pap. 6.99 ***(978-0-545-85347-7(8))*** 2016. 288p. 16.99 *(978-0-545-85346-0(X))* Scholastic, Inc. (Chicken Hse., The).
Lewis-Brown, Alscess. Mosquito Get in Trouble Too. Hatfield, Cynthia, illus. 2009. (J). *(978-1-934370-09-4(6))* Editorial Campana.
Lluch, Alex. Big Bugs, Small Bugs: If You Could Be a Bug, Which Bug Would You Be? Defenbaugh, David, illus. 2005. (ENG.). 28p. (J). (gr. -1-k). bds. 7.95 *(978-1-887169-62-2(8))* WS Publishing.
Lobel, Arnold. Saltamontes Va De Viage. Date not set. (SPA.). 68p. 9.95 *(978-84-204-3053-9(6))* Santillana USA Publishing Co., Inc.
Lockhart, E. Fly on the Wall: How One Girl Saw Everything. 2007. (ENG., Illus.). 192p. (YA). (gr. 7-12). pap. 8.99 *(978-0-385-73282-6(1)*, Delacorte Pr) Random House Publishing Group.
Lonborg, Rosemary. Helpin' Bugs. Houghton, Diane R., illus. 2006. 32p. (J). (gr. -1-3). reprint ed. pap. 7.00 *(978-1-4223-5405-6(9))* DIANE Publishing Co.
Long, Olivia. Billy Bumble Is Missing! Long, Olivia, illus. Date not set. (Kaleidoscope Ser.). (Illus.). 32p. (J). (gr. -1-4). *(978-1-880042-02-1(9))* Shelf-Life Bks.
Loper, Kathleen. Angelina Katrina: Bugs in My Backyard. Waltz, Dan, illus. l.t. ed. 2004. 24p. (J). 17.95 *(978-0-9741774-4-1(X))* D. W. Publishing.
Lorraine, Nancy. The Butterfly Adventure. Herron, Dorothy, illus. 2nd ed. 2013. 50p. 22.50 *(978-0-9886194-9-4(0))* ProsePress.
Low-Dumond, Sabrina. Weakling Willie, 1 vol. 2010. 26p. 24.95 *(978-1-4512-1509-0(6))* PublishAmerica, Inc.
Lubar, David. The Bully Bug: A Monsterrific Tale. 2014. (Monsterrific Tales Ser.). (ENG., Illus.). 144p. (J). (gr. 3-7). 24.99 *(978-0-7653-3082-6(2)*, 9780765330826, Starscape) Doherty, Tom Assocs., LLC.
Lucado, Max & Schmidt, Troy. Webster, the Scaredy Spider. 2005. 32p. (J). pap. 3.99 *(978-1-4003-0665-7(5))* Nelson, Thomas Inc.
Luebke, Gayle M. There's A Bug in My Bed. 2005. 17p. 9.58 *(978-1-4116-2635-5(4))* Lulu Pr., Inc.
Lund, Laurel. When Glory Got Her Glow Back: A Glowworm's Tail. 2012. 32p. (-18). pap. 16.99 *(978-1-4525-6011-3(0))* Balboa Pr.
Mack, Jeff. Frog & Fly. 2012. (ENG.). 40p. (J). (gr. -1-k). 12.99 *(978-0-399-25617-2(2)*, Philomel Bks.) Penguin Young Readers Group.
Macmillan, Sue. Hoppy Frog's Fly Spy. Ward, Sarah, illus. 2014. (Cheery Chasers Ser.). (ENG.). 8p. (J). (gr. -1 — 1). bds. 4.99 *(978-0-7641-6700-3(6))* Barron's Educational Series, Inc.
Majors, J. Natty's Adventures. 2011. 28p. pap. 15.99 *(978-1-4568-5949-7(8))* Xlibris Corp.
Man-Kong, Mary. Barbie & the Three Musketeers. Random House Staff, illus. 2009. (Step into Reading Ser.). (ENG.). 32p. (J). (gr. -1-1). pap. 3.99 *(978-0-375-86007-2(X)*, Random Hse. Bks. for Young Readers) Random Hse. Children's Bks.
Manushkin, Fran. Pedro Goes Buggy. Lyon, Tammie, illus. 2016. (Pedro Ser.). (ENG.). 32p. (gr. k-2). lib. bdg. 21.32 *(978-1-5158-0085-9(7))* Pedro Pubns. GBR. Dist: Capstone Pub.
Manzur, Vivian Mansour & Mansour, Vivian. La Vida Util de Pillo Polilla. Flores, Lupita, illus. rev. ed. 2005. (Castillo de la Lectura Naranja Ser.). (SPA & ENG.). 112p. (J). (gr. -1-7). pap. 7.95 *(978-970-20-0129-4(3))* Castillo, Ediciones, S. A. de C. V. MEX. Dist: Macmillan.
Mark, Jessica & Mark, Rebecca. Sky the Fly Explores Philadelphia. 2013. 28p. pap. 11.00 *(978-1-4349-3272-3(9)*, RoseDog Bks.) Dorrance Publishing Co., Inc.
Marquess, Dana. Night of the Lighted Freedom - A Firefly Fantasy. 2006. (ENG., Illus.). 32p. (J). 19.95 *(978-1-932278-06-4(0))* Mayhaven Publishing, Inc.
Marshall, Natalie, illus. Tiny Creatures: Touch & Feel Book. 2015. (J). *(978-1-4351-5935-8(7))* Barnes & Noble, Inc.
Martin, Bill, Jr., et al. The Little Squeegy Bug, 0 vols. Corrigan, Patrick, illus. 2005. (ENG.). 32p. (J). (gr. -1-2). reprint ed. pap. 9.99 *(978-0-7614-5243-0(5)*, 9780761452430, Amazon Children's Publishing) Amazon Publishing.
Mason, Jane B. Battle Bugs of Outer Space, 1 vol. Baltazar, Art, illus. 2011. (DC Super-Pets Ser.). (ENG.). 56p. (gr. 2-2). pap. 4.95 *(978-1-4048-6848-9(8))*; lib. bdg. 23.99 *(978-1-4048-6482-5(2))* Picture Window Bks. (DC Super-Pets).
Matheson, Jason. Buzzbomb: Adventures in the Forbidden Zone. Hope, Bill, illus. 2013. 80p. (J). pap. *(978-1-925011-26-5(7))* Australian Self Publishing Group/ Inspiring Pubs.
Matute, Ana María. El Saltamontes Verde. (SPA.). (YA). (gr. 5-8). pap. 7.96 *(978-84-264-3410-4(X))*; 2003. 96p. *(978-84-264-3001-4(5)*, LM0622); 2003. (Illus.). 133p. *(978-84-264-5051-7(2)*, LM30549) Editorial Lumen ESP. Dist: Lectorum Pubns., Inc.
McBride, Lish. Firebug. 2014. (ENG.). 336p. (YA). (gr. 9-12). 17.99 *(978-0-8050-9862-4(3)*, 9780805098624, Holt, Henry & Co. Bks. For Young Readers) Holt, Henry & Co.
McBride, Peter & McBride, Judith. Bug & Budgie. 2013. 32p. *(978-1-4602-2343-7(8))* FriesenPress.
—Bug & Budgie Fly Away. 2013. 48p. *(978-1-4602-3312-2(3))* FriesenPress.
McDonald, Megan. Beetle Mcgrady Eats Bugs! Manning, Jane K., illus. 2005. (ENG.). 32p. (J). (gr. k-5). 17.99 *(978-0-06-001354-7(0)*, Greenwillow Bks.) HarperCollins Pubs.
McElligott, Matthew. Bean Thirteen. McElligott, Matthew, illus. 2007. (ENG., Illus.). 32p. (J). (gr. k-3). 15.99 *(978-0-399-24535-0(9)*, G.P. Putnam's Sons Books for Young Readers) Penguin Young Readers Group.
McGann, Oisín. The Poison Factory. 2006. (Forbidden Files Ser.). (ENG., Illus.). 96p. (J). pap. 10.95 *(978-0-86278-941-1(9))* O'Brien Pr., Ltd., The IRL. Dist: Dufour Editions, Inc.
McInvale, Rebecca. Emmy the Bug-Gulping Dog. 2009. 16p. pap. 8.99 *(978-1-4389-9954-8(2))* AuthorHouse.
McLean, Wendy. Whizz! 2003. (J). pap. 12.95 *(978-1-74047-276-0(4))* Book Co. Publishing Pty, Ltd., The AUS. Dist: Penton Overseas, Inc.
McOmber, Rachel B., ed. McOmber Phonics Storybooks: A Hum-Bug. rev. ed. (Illus.). (J). *(978-0-944991-20-6(3))* Swift Learning Resources.
—McOmber Phonics Storybooks: Bug. rev. ed. (Illus.). (J). *(978-0-944991-19-0(X))* Swift Learning Resources.
—McOmber Phonics Storybooks: The Hum-Bug Hop. rev. ed. (Illus.). (J). *(978-0-944991-31-2(9))* Swift Learning Resources.
MCP Staff. Good Night Little Bug, Level 4, Bk. 42. (J). (gr. -1-3). 24.50 *(978-0-8136-1971-2(8))* Modern Curriculum Pr.
—That Fly, Level 3, Bk. 12. (J). (gr. -1-3). 24.50 *(978-0-8136-1943-9(2))* Modern Curriculum Pr.
Meadows, Michelle. Super Bugs. Mayer, Bill, illus. 2016. (ENG.). 40p. (J). (gr. -1-k). 16.99 *(978-0-545-68756-0(X))* Scholastic, Inc.
Meister, Cari. Beat Bugs. 2017. (I Can Read Level 1 Ser.). 32p. (J). (gr. -1-3). pap. 3.99 *(978-0-06-264069-7(0))* HarperCollins Pubs.
—Beat Bugs: Penny Lane. 2017. (I Can Read Level 1 Ser.). 32p. (J). (gr. -1-3). pap. 3.99 *(978-0-06-264071-0(2))* HarperCollins Pubs.
Mengis, Heidi A. The Lily Pad & the Dragonfly: A Story of Spiritual Enlightenment as told by Arden L. Johnson. 2009. 24p. pap. 12.00 *(978-1-4490-2535-9(8))* AuthorHouse.
Mercer, Rita C. Earl the Squatchem. 2007. 9.00 *(978-0-8059-8823-9(8))* Dorrance Publishing Co., Inc.
Merry, Lindsay R. Dackshew Dragonfly. 2012. 24p. pap. 17.99 *(978-1-4685-9865-8(6))* AuthorHouse.
Miller, Liza. BusyBugz Adventures: Izzi Goes Missing. Bolton, Bill, illus. 2013. (BusyBugz Adventures Ser.). (ENG.). 16p. (J). (gr. -1). 12.95 *(978-1-60710-714-9(7)*, Silver Dolphin Bks.) Readerlink Distribution Services, LLC.
Mincks, Margaret. Bedbugs. 2017. (Awful, Disgusting Parasites Ser.). (ENG., Illus.). 32p. (J). (gr. 3-7). 31.35 ***(978-1-68072-006-8(6))*** Black Rabbit Bks.
Mitchell, Marianne. Firebug. 2004. (ENG., Illus.). 176p. (J). (gr. 7-6). 16.95 *(978-1-59078-170-8(8))* Boyds Mills Pr.
Monroe, Chris. Bug on a Bike. Monroe, Chris, illus. 2014. (ENG., Illus.). 32p. (J). (gr. -1-2). 16.95 *(978-1-4677-2154-7(9)*, Carolrhoda Bks.) Lerner Publishing Group.
Morris, Lynn. Belinda the Butterfly's Beautiful Colors. 2011. 48p. (gr. -1). pap. 19.26 *(978-1-4567-3521-0(7))* AuthorHouse.
Morrow, Barbara Olenyik. Mr. Mosquito Put on His Tuxedo. Goembel, Ponder, illus. 2009. (ENG.). 32p. (J). (gr. -1-3). 16.95 *(978-0-8234-2072-8(8))* Holiday Hse., Inc.
Mortensen, Denise Dowling. Bug Patrol. Bell, Cece, illus. 2013. (ENG.). 32p. (J). (gr. -1-3). 16.99 *(978-0-618-79024-1(1))* Houghton Mifflin Harcourt Publishing Co.
Moser, Lisa. Stories from Bug Garden. Millward, Gwen, illus. 2016. (ENG.). 32p. (J). (gr. -1-3). 16.99 *(978-0-7636-6534-0(7))* Candlewick Pr.
Moss, Patricia Crocker. Dillie & the Dragonfly. 2012. 32p. pap. 21.99 *(978-1-4691-7821-9(4))* Xlibris Corp.
Munton, Gill. Who Ate All the Lettuce? Top That Publishing Staff, ed. Elliott, Rebecca, illus. 2007. 12p. (gr. -1-k). bds. *(978-1-84666-177-8(3)*, Tide Mill Pr.) Top That! Publishing PLC.
Murdock, Kita Helmetag & Helmetag, Patricia. Cecily Cicada 2004th l.t. ed. 2004. (Illus.). 28p. (J). pap. 9.95 *(978-0-615-12548-0(4))* Possum Products.
Murguia, Bethanie Deeney. Buglette, the Messy Sleeper. Murguia, Bethanie Deeney, illus. 2011. (ENG., Illus.). 32p. (J). (gr. -1-2). 15.99 *(978-1-58246-375-9(1)*, Tricycle Pr.) Random Hse. Children's Bks.
Murphy, Patricia. Mama, Look! Diaz, David, illus. 2017. (ENG.). 40p. (J). (gr. -1-k). 17.99 *(978-1-4998-0080-7(0))* Little Bee Books Inc.
Murray, Alison. The House That Zack Built. Murray, Alison, illus. 2016. (ENG., Illus.). 32p. (J). (-k). 16.99 *(978-0-7636-7844-9(9))* Candlewick Pr.
Myers, Nancy. Super Ben. 2012. 32p. pap. 24.95 *(978-1-4626-9529-4(9))* America Star Bks.
Myers, Stacy Erin. Lil Bug. 2012. 56p. pap. 11.99 *(978-1-929845-56-9(1))* DeFranco Entertainment.
Navarro, Cece P. My Cherry Tree House. 2008. 16p. pap. 24.95 *(978-1-60474-415-6(4))* America Star Bks.
Nelson-Anderson, Joanna. Dragonfly Ceremony. 2008. 24p. pap. 24.95 *(978-1-60813-030-6(4))* America Star Bks.
Nelson-Anderson, Joanna "J. O. ". I Spy a Dragonfly. 2008. 20p. per. 24.95 *(978-1-60441-581-0(9))* America Star Bks.
Nettrour, Nelani. Dragonfly Flight. Lesnick, Tina, illus. l.t. ed. 2003. 62p. (J). pap. 11.94 *(978-1-932657-02-9(9))* Third Millennium Pubns.
—Jodi's Bugs. Nettrour, Heather, illus. l.t. ed. 2003. 66p. (J). pap. 11.95 *(978-1-932657-04-3(5))* Third Millennium Pubns.
Nickel, Scott. Backyard Bug Battle: A Buzz Beaker Brainstorm, 1 vol. Smith, Andy J., illus. 2006. (Buzz Beaker Brainstorm Ser.). (ENG.). 40p. (gr. 1-3). lib. bdg. 23.99 *(978-1-59889-054-9(9))*; per. 5.95 *(978-1-59889-224-6(X))* Stone Arch Bks. (Graphic Sparks).
Niddrie, June. Fly Ladybird, Fly. 2010. 32p. pap. 16.10 *(978-0-557-31862-9(9))* Lulu Pr., Inc.
Norris, Gayle A. Bed Bug, 1 vol. 2009. 23p. pap. 24.95 *(978-1-60836-088-8(1))* America Star Bks.
Noyes, Diana. The Tickle Bug. Noyes, Diana, illus. l.t. ed. 2005. (Illus.). 20p. (J). per. 9.99 *(978-1-59879-080-1(3))* Lifevest Publishing, Inc.
O'Boyle, Laurel. Froggy & Bug, 1 vol. 2010. 28p. pap. 24.95 *(978-1-4489-7068-1(7))* PublishAmerica, Inc.
O'Connor, Jane. Explorer Extraordinaire! Glasser, Robin Preiss, illus. 2009. (Fancy Nancy Ser.). (ENG.). 32p. (J). (gr. -1-2). 12.99 *(978-0-06-168486-9(4))* HarperCollins Pubs.
Ogle, Bonnie. Arthur the Arthropod. 2012. 28p. pap. 15.99 *(978-1-4771-1424-7(6))* Xlibris Corp.
Olowoyeye, Ola. Critters! II: Mary Moth. 2011. 40p. pap. 16.59 *(978-1-4634-3295-9(X))* AuthorHouse.
Opitz, Todd. The Football & the Fly. 2012. 24p. pap. 24.95 *(978-1-4626-9847-9(6))* America Star Bks.
Oppel, Kenneth. The Nest. Klassen, Jon, illus. (ENG.). (J). (gr. 5). 2016. 272p. pap. 7.99 *(978-1-4814-3233-7(8))* 2015. 256p. 16.99 *(978-1-4814-3232-0(X))* Simon & Schuster Bks. For Young Readers. (Simon & Schuster Bks. For Young Readers).
Oram, Hiawyn. Beetle & Bug & the Grissel Hunt. Kitamura, Satoshi, illus. 2015. (ENG.). 36p. (J). (gr. -1-k). pap. 9.99 *(978-1-78344-042-9(2))* Andersen Pr. GBR. Dist: Independent Pubs. Group.
Orlando, Mardi. The Wishall. 2009. 156p. pap. 15.34 *(978-1-4269-1704-2(X))* Trafford Publishing.
Orme, David. Bugs & Spiders. Mongiovi, Jorge, illus. 2010. (Fact to Fiction Ser.). 36p. pap. 7.45 *(978-0-7891-7990-6(3))* Perfection Learning Corp.
Oroma Alikor-Adele. Bugerfly Finds Friends. 2010. 28p. pap. 15.99 *(978-1-4535-6167-6(6))* Xlibris Corp.
—The Lonely Bugerfly. 2010. 28p. pap. 21.99 *(978-1-4535-6225-3(7))* Xlibris Corp.
Osborn, D. W. Why Can't I Ribbit?, 1 vol. 2009. 48p. pap. 16.95 *(978-1-61582-641-4(6))* America Star Bks.
Osburn, Jacquelyn. Willy, the Worried Worm. 2008. 24p. pap. 12.99 *(978-1-4343-8183-5(8))* AuthorHouse.
Owen, Dan. Ellen. 2006. 32p. (J). pap. 11.99 *(978-1-4116-9069-1(9))* Lulu Pr., Inc.
Pagel, Stace. Fletcher the Fly. 2008. (Illus.). 32p. pap. 14.95 *(978-1-4389-2196-9(9))* AuthorHouse.
Palatini, Margie. The Perfect Pet. Whatley, Bruce, illus. 2003. 32p. (J). (gr. -1-2). 16.99 *(978-0-06-000108-7(9))* HarperCollins Pubs.
Pandanas, Ms L A. Zar-Zar the Russian Ladybeetle: Bull Ants, Bindies & Bees. 2013. 26p. pap. *(978-0-9870702-1-0(5))* Reed, Laura.
—Zar-Zar the Russian Ladybeetle: Easter Beetle. 2013. 26p. pap. *(978-0-9870702-4-1(X))* Reed, Laura.
—Zar-Zar the Russian Ladybeetle: The Land of Black & White. 2013. 26p. pap. *(978-0-9870702-7-2(4))* Reed, Laura.
Paranuzzi, Fred. Babak. Prigent, Andrée, illus. 2016. (ENG.). 32p. (J). 17.95 *(978-0-7358-4251-9(5))* North-South Bks., Inc.
Parker, Andy. Ciberbichos: Cyber Bugs, Spanish-Language Edition. 2005. (Mekanimals Ser.). (SPA., Illus.). 8p. (J). bds. *(978-970-718-323-0(3)*, Silver Dolphin en Español) Advanced Marketing, S. de R. L. de C. V.
Parker, Andy, illus. Mekanimals Cyber Bugs. 2004. 8p. (J). bds. 12.95 *(978-1-59223-146-1(2)*, Silver Dolphin Bks.) Readerlink Distribution Services, LLC.
Parnell, Declan. The Big Bug Hunt, 01 vols., 1. 2016. (Rosen REAL Readers: STEM & STEAM Collection). (ENG.). 8p. (J). pap. 5.46 *(978-1-5081-1498-7(6)*, Rosen Classroom) Rosen Publishing Group, Inc., The.
Patton, Jack. The Butterfly Rebellion. 2016. (Battle Bugs Ser.: 9). (ENG.). 128p. (J). (gr. 2-5). pap. 4.99 *(978-0-545-94515-8(1)*, Scholastic Paperbacks) Scholastic, Inc.
—The Chameleon Attack (Battle Bugs #4) 2015. (Battle Bugs Ser.: 4). (ENG., Illus.). 128p. (J). (gr. 2-5). pap. 4.99 *(978-0-545-70784-8(6)*, Scholastic Paperbacks) Scholastic, Inc.
—The Cobra Clash (Battle Bugs #5) 2015. (Battle Bugs Ser.: 5). (ENG.). 128p. (J). (gr. 2-5). pap. 4.99 *(978-0-545-79124-3(3)*, Scholastic Pr.) Scholastic, Inc.
—The Dragonfly Defense. 2016. (Battle Bugs Ser.: 7). (ENG.). 128p. (J). (gr. 2-5). pap. 4.99 *(978-0-545-94509-7(7)*, Scholastic Paperbacks) Scholastic, Inc.

H
I

—The Komodo Conflict. 2016. (Battle Bugs Ser.: 6). (ENG.). 128p. (J). (gr. 2-5). pap. 4.99 *(978-0-545-79148-9(0),* Scholastic Paperbacks) Scholastic, Inc.
—The Poison Frog Assault (Battle Bugs #3) 2015. (Battle Bugs Ser.: 3). (ENG.). 128p. (J). (gr. 2-5). pap. 4.99 *(978-0-545-70744-2(7),* Scholastic Paperbacks) Scholastic, Inc.
—The Snake Fight. 2016. (Battle Bugs Ser.: 8). (ENG.). 128p. (J). (gr. 2-5). pap. 4.99 *(978-0-545-94512-7(7),* Scholastic Paperbacks) Scholastic, Inc.
Peacock-Williams, Carol A. & Williams, Christy Jo. Benny the Beetle. 1 vol. Peacock, Bessie Merle, illus. 2010. 28p. 24.95 *(978-1-4489-8373-5(8))* PublishAmerica, Inc.
Pearl, Beverly. Poison Ivy. 2008. 98p. pap. 9.99 *(978-1-4357-1386-4(9))* Lulu Pr., Inc.
—Poison Ivy, the Pocket Book. 2008. 105p. pap. 14.95 *(978-1-4357-2328-3(7))* Lulu Pr., Inc.
Perez, Jessica. Goodnight, Little Bug. Shelly, Jeff, illus. 2005. (J). bds. 14.99 *(978-0-9767325-2-5(1))* Toy Quest.
Perry, Taily. Saving Sunny Stream, a Wormie Wormald Adventure. 2009. 60p. pap. 22.00 *(978-1-60860-296-4(6),* Eloquent Bks.) Strategic Book Publishing & Rights Agency (SBPRA).
Petracca, C. A. B. The Chronicles of Petr The. 2005. 208p. per. 14.95 *(978-1-59858-012-9(4))* Dog Ear Publishing, LLC.
Petrik, Andrea, illus. Shoo, Fly! 2008. (J). *(978-0-545-03046-5(3))* Scholastic, Inc.
Pettersson, Aline. Ontario, la Mariposa Viajera. Valderrama, Rosario, illus. 2003. (SPA.). 72p. (gr. 3-5). pap. 8.95 *(978-968-19-0276-6(9))* Santillana USA Publishing Co., Inc.
Pfeffer, Wendy. Firefly at Stonybrook Farm. Mikec, Larry, illus. 2004. (Smithsonian's Backyard Ser.). (ENG.). 32p. (J). (gr. -1-2). 8.95 *(978-1-59249-306-7(8),* SC5026); 9.95 *(978-1-59249-308-1(4),* PB5076); 19.95 *(978-1-59249-307-4(6),* BC5026) Soundprints.
Phillips, Gina & Martin, Stuart. Bees & Butterflies. 2003. (Busy Bugs Ser.). 12p. (J). bds. 14.95 *(978-1-74047-239-5(X))* Book Co. Publishing Pty, Ltd., The AUS. Dist: Penton Overseas, Inc.
Pichon, Liz. The Very Ugly Bug. 2005. (Illus.). 32p. (J). 15.95 *(978-1-58925-048-2(6))* Tiger Tales.
Pier, Daniel Wayne. Ferrous the Venus Fly Trap Meets the Cactus. 2008. 36p. pap. 24.95 *(978-1-60441-645-9(9))* PublishAmerica, Inc.
Pig & Small. 1 vol. 2014. (ENG., Illus.). 32p. (J). (gr. -1-3). 15.95 *(978-1-56145-797-7(3))* Peachtree Pubs.
Pixton, Amy, creator. Things with Wings. 2006. (J). *(978-0-9779631-2-6(8))* TyBook.
Plesscher, Marietta. When One Little Bug Gave the World a Big Hug. 2011. 28p. pap. 21.99 *(978-1-4628-5605-3(5))* Xlibris Corp.
Powell, Glenda. Cassie & Mr. Ant. Mitchell, Hazel, illus. 2008. 30p. (J). (gr. -1-3). per. 7.95 *(978-0-9779445-6-9(5))* Zoe Life Publishing.
Prasadam, Smriti. Hello, Bugs! Bolam, Emily, illus. 2010. (Black & White Sparklers Ser.). (ENG.). 10p. (J). (gr. -1). bds. 6.99 *(978-1-58925-862-4(2))* Tiger Tales.
Prayor, Erika. Heavenly Angel Bugs: Do Not Fear God Is Here. 2011. 32p. pap. 16.49 *(978-1-4520-5333-2(2))* AuthorHouse.
Price, David. Sly the Fox & Advice from la Princessa Roja. 2008. (Illus.). 34p. (J). 14.95 *(978-0-9779701-2-4(4))* Wishingstone Publishing.
Priddy Book. In the Yard: Fuzzy Bee & Friends. (Illus.). (J). 17.90 *(978-0-312-49377-6(0),* Priddy Bks.) St. Martin's Pr.
Pritchard, Alicia Michele. Critter Pics. 2008. 53p. pap. 22.50 *(978-1-4357-1134-1(3))* Lulu Pr., Inc.
Random House & Pohlmeyer, Krista. Bug Parade! (Bubble Guppies) Moore, Harry, illus. 2014. (Pictureback(R) Ser.). (ENG.). 24p. (J). (gr. -1-2). 5.99 *(978-0-385-38517-6(X),* Random Hse. Bks. for Young Readers) Random Hse. Children's Bks.
Raphael, Akili & Lewis, Harriet. Malik & the Malaria-Carrying Mosquito. 2012. 32p. pap. 19.99 *(978-1-4772-8813-9(9))* AuthorHouse.
Raschka, Chris. Buggy Bug. 2014. (Thingy Things Ser.). (ENG., Illus.). 24p. (J). (gr. -1-k). 6.95 *(978-1-4197-1200-5(4),* Abrams Appleseed) Abrams, Inc.
Raye, Donna. Edison the Firefly & Ford the Fly. 2013. 28p. pap. 9.99 *(978-0-9894748-2-5(8))* Mindstir Media.
Reasoner, Charles. Bug Babies. Devaney, Adam, illus. 2009. (Baby Animal Board Bks.). 12p. (J). (gr. -1-k). bds. 7.99 *(978-1-934650-51-6(X))* Just For Kids Pr., LLC.
—Insects. Doherty, Paula, illus. 2009. (Little Big Flap Bks.). 10p. (J). (gr. -1-k). bds. 9.99 *(978-1-934650-21-9(8))* Just For Kids Pr., LLC.
Recob, Amy. The BugaBees: Friends with Food Allergies. 2009. (Illus.). 32p. (J). *(978-1-59298-279-0(4))* Beaver's Pond Pr., Inc.
Reitmeyer, Shannon. The Proud Inchworm. Reitmeyer, Shannon, illus. 2013. (Illus.). 24p. pap. 12.00 *(978-1-61286-161-6(X))* Avid Readers Publishing Group.
Reynolds, Aaron. The Dung Beetle Bandits. 1 vol. Lervold, Erik, illus. 2007. (Tiger Moth Ser.). (ENG.). 40p. (gr. 1-3). lib. bdg. 23.99 *(978-1-59889-317-5(3),* Graphic Sparks) Stone Arch Bks.
—The Dung Beetle Bandits: Tiger Moth. Lervold, Erik, illus. 2007. (Graphic Sparks Ser.). (ENG.). 40p. (gr. 1-3). pap. 5.95 *(978-1-59889-412-7(9),* Graphic Sparks) Stone Arch Bks.
—The Fortune Cookies of Weevil: Tiger Moth. Lervold, Erik, illus. 2007. (Graphic Sparks Ser.). (ENG.). 40p. (gr. 1-3). pap. 5.95 *(978-1-59889-413-4(7),* Graphic Sparks) Stone Arch Bks.
—Insect Ninja: Tiger Moth. Lervold, Erik, illus. 2006. (Graphic Sparks Ser.). (ENG.). 40p. (gr. 1-3). per. 5.95 *(978-1-59889-228-4(2),* Graphic Sparks) Stone Arch Bks.
—Kung Pow Chicken: Tiger Moth. Lervold, Erik, illus. 2008. (Graphic Sparks Ser.). (ENG.). 40p. (gr. 1-3). pap. 5.95 *(978-1-4342-0505-6(3),* Graphic Sparks) Stone Arch Bks.
—Tiger Moth: Adventures of an Insect Ninja. 1 vol. Lervold, Erik, illus. 2011. (Tiger Moth Ser.). (ENG.). 128p. (gr. 2-5). pap. 7.95 *(978-1-4342-3032-4(5),* Graphic Sparks) Stone Arch Bks.
Ricci, Christine & Golden Books Staff. Bug Hunt. Savitsky, Steve et al, illus. 2008. (Color Plus Chunky Crayons Ser.). (ENG.). 48p. (J). (gr. -1-2). pap. 3.99 *(978-0-375-84298-6(5),* Golden Bks.) Random Hse. Children's Bks.
Richards, Lucy, illus. Busy Bugs (W/Header Card) 2004. (Cuddly Cuffs Ser.: 6). 12p. (J). tchr. ed. 5.95 *(978-1-58925-730-6(8))* Tiger Tales.
Rights, Lenz-Mulligan, et al. Little Ladybug. 2005. (Little Finger Puppet Board Bks.: FING). (ENG., Illus.). 12p. (J). (gr. -1 — 1). bds. 6.99 *(978-0-8118-4848-0(5))* Chronicle Bks. LLC.
Rinehart, Susie Caldwell. Eliza & Dragonfly. 2014. 18.95 *(978-1-63419-697-0(X))* Perfection Learning Corp.
—Eliza & the Dragonfly. Hovemann, Anisa Claire, illus. 2004. (Sharing Nature with Children Book Ser.). 32p. (J). 16.95 *(978-1-58469-060-3(7));* 8.95 *(978-1-58469-059-7(3))* Dawn Pubns.
Ring, Susan. Honeybees: An Amazing Insect Discovery BK. 2009. (ENG.). 12p. 5.95 *(978-1-58117-910-1(3),* Intervisual/Piggy Toes) Bendon, Inc.
Roark, Algernon Michael. Graylinger Grotto. Triplett, Ginger, illus. 2011. (ENG.). 94p. (J). pap. 22.95 *(978-1-59299-631-5(0))* Inkwater Pr.
Rogers, Bryar Elizabeth. A Special Bug Indeed. 1 vol. Twigg, Craig, illus. 2009. 41p. pap. 19.95 *(978-1-60749-750-9(6))* PublishAmerica, Inc.
Rose, Jeremy. The Frog & the Fly. 2013. 28p. pap. 16.99 *(978-1-4624-0517-6(7),* Inspiring Voices) Author Solutions, Inc.
Rosen, Michael. Tiny Little Fly. Waldron, Kevin, illus. 2010. (ENG.). 32p. (J). (gr. 5-k). 16.99 *(978-0-7636-4681-3(4))* Candlewick Pr.
Ross, Melanie H. & Willis, Jeanne. Mayfly Day. Ross, Tony, illus. 2012. (ENG.). 32p. (J). (gr. -1-k). pap. 10.99 *(978-1-84270-606-0(3))* Andersen Pr. GBR. Dist: Independent Pubs. Group.
Roth, Kapra Lynn. The Healing Bugs. 2008. 24p. pap. 24.95 *(978-1-60703-169-7(8))* America Star Bks.
Rothenberger, Charlene. Kara's Kapers with Katy Pillar. Rothenberger, Boyd & Bays, Gail, illus. 2006. 64p. per. 9.99 *(978-0-9776260-6-9(7))* Bearhead Publishing, LLC.
Rowe, Papa. Itchy Lee & Itchy Dee Mcgee. Wilkins, Kevan & Mason, Shannon, eds. Shortell, Stephen, illus. 2006. (J). 15.99 *(978-0-9778858-0-0(1))* WowZee Works Inc.
Russ, Tim & Roskilly, Jedda. Bugsters! 2008. (Illus.). 32p. (J). 16.95 *(978-0-9795131-7-6(0))* Woods N' Water Pr., Inc.
Ryder, Joanne. My Father's Hands. Graham, Mark, illus. 2014. 32p. pap. 8.00 *(978-1-61003-330-5(2))* Center for the Collaborative Classroom.
Salzano, Tammi. One Little Blueberry. Whelan, Kat, illus. 2011. (ENG.). 22p. (J). (gr. -1-k). 12.95 *(978-1-58925-859-4(2))* Tiger Tales.
Samuels, Linda Nissen. Cuando Elly Fue a la Reserva Ecologica. Samuels, Linda Nissen, illus. 2013. (Illus.). 40p. pap. *(978-0-9511751-8-7(1))* Samuels, Linda Y.
—Elly e il Parco Degli Animali. Samuels, Linda Nissen, illus. 2013. (Illus.). 40p. pap. *(978-0-9511751-7-0(3))* Samuels, Linda Y.
—When Elly Went to the Animal Park... Samuels, Linda Nissen, illus. 2013. (Illus.). 40p. pap. *(978-0-9511751-5-6(7))* Samuels, Linda Y.
Sanders, Terri L. Night Flies. 2003. (J). E-Book 4.95 incl. cd-rom *(978-1-59201-010-3(5))* Bks. Unbound E-Publishing Co.
Santillo, LuAnn. The Seeds. Santillo, LuAnn, ed. 2003. (Half-Pint Kids Readers Ser.). (Illus.). 7p. (J). (gr. -1-1). pap. 1.00 *(978-1-59256-109-4(8))* Half-Pint Kids, Inc.
Sargent, Dave & Sargent, Pat. Lizzy Lightning Bug/Lizzy la Luciérnaga. 10 vols., Vol. 17. Robinson, Laura, illus. 2004. (Learn to Read Ser.: 10).Tr. of Lizzy la Luciernaga. (ENG & SPA.). 18p. (J). (gr. k-2). lib. bdg. 20.95 *(978-1-56763-993-3(3))* Ozark Publishing.
Sayle, Stephen. Cam & Zara the Travel Bugs. 2012. 20p. pap. 11.70 *(978-1-105-42214-0(3))* Lulu Pr., Inc.
Scherzer, Cecilia. The Close Encounter of a Bug. 2011. 28p. (gr. -1). pap. 16.09 *(978-1-4269-6375-9(0))* Trafford Publishing.
Schwartz, Betty Ann. One to Ten... & Back Again. Shakir, Susie, illus. 2009. 24p. bds. 12.99 *(978-0-8249-1436-3(8),* Ideal Pubns.) Worthy Publishing.
Scott, Marilyn. A Lightening Bug's Message of Love. 2009. pap. *(978-1-61658-333-0(9))* Independent Pub.
Seal, Vickie Di-Ann. Edgar Tells the Truth. 2012. 26p. 24.95 *(978-1-4626-0976-5(7))* America Star Bks.
Seitz, J. B. Freddy the Flea. 2009. 23p. pap. 24.95 *(978-1-60836-759-7(2))* America Star Bks.
Shannon, David. Bugs in My Hair! Shannon, David, illus. 2013. (ENG., Illus.). 32p. (J). (gr. -1-3). 17.99 *(978-0-545-14313-4(6),* Blue Sky Pr., The) Scholastic, Inc.
Shaw, Irene. Cosy Cottage. 2006. (Illus.). 48p. pap. *(978-1-84401-792-8(3))* Athena Pr.
Sheets, Katherine. Captured by Henrey. 1 vol. 2010. 48p. pap. 16.95 *(978-1-4489-4538-2(0))* America Star Bks.
Shepherd, Donna J. The Lonely Lightning Bug. 2005. (Illus.). 16p. (J). E-Book 9.95 incl. cd-rom *(978-1-933090-30-6(8))* Guardian Angel Publishing, Inc.
Shields, Carol Diggory. The Bugliest Bug. Nash, Scott, illus. 2005. (ENG.). 32p. (J). (gr. -1-3). pap. 7.99 *(978-0-7636-2293-0(1))* Candlewick Pr.
Shreeve, Elizabeth. Hector Finds a Fortune. Levy, Pamela R., illus. 2004. 68p. (J). lib. bdg. 15.00 *(978-1-4242-0903-3(X))* Fitzgerald Bks.
—Hector Finds a Fortune. Levy, Pamela R., illus. 2004. (Adventures of Hector Fuller Ser.). 68p. (J). (gr. 1-4). 11.65 *(978-0-7569-5527-4(0))* Perfection Learning Corp.
—Hector Springs Loose. Levy, Pamela R., illus. 2004. (Adventures of Hector Fuller Ser.). 67p. (J). (gr. 1-4). 11.65 *(978-0-7569-5528-1(9))* Perfection Learning Corp.
—Hector Springs Loose. Levy, Pamela R., illus. 2004. (Ready-For-Chapters Ser.). (ENG.). 80p. (J). (gr. 1-4). pap. 3.99 *(978-0-689-86414-8(0),* Simon & Schuster/Paula Wiseman Bks.) Simon & Schuster/Paula Wiseman Bks.
Shubert's Choice. 2004. (YA). 9.00 *(978-1-889609-26-3(9))* Loving Guidance, Inc.
Simpson, Caroll. The First Mosquito. 1 vol. 2010. (ENG., Illus.). 32p. (J). *(978-1-926613-67-3(8))* Heritage Hse.
—The First Mosquito. 1 vol. Simpson, Caroll, illus. 2015. (Coastal Spirit Tales Ser.). (ENG., Illus.). 32p. (J). (gr. k-3). pap. 12.95 ***(978-1-77203-063-1(5))*** Heritage Hse. CAN. Dist: Orca Bk. Pubs. USA.
Siomades, Lorianne. Katy Did It! 2009. (ENG., Illus.). 32p. (J). (gr. -1-k). 16.95 *(978-1-59078-602-4(5))* Boyds Mills Pr.
Smith, Andrew. Grasshopper Jungle. 2015. (ENG.). 416p. (YA). (gr. 9). pap. 10.99 *(978-0-14-242500-8(1),* Speak) Penguin Young Readers Group.
Smith, D. K. Sock 'n Boots - Share. 2010. 32p. pap. 13.60 *(978-0-557-52614-7(0))* Lulu Pr., Inc.
Soman, David & Davis, Jacky. Little Box of Ladybug Girl. 4 vols. Soman, David, illus. 2013. (Ladybug Girl Ser.). (ENG., Illus.). 14p. (J). (gr. -1-k). bds. 23.96 *(978-0-8037-4102-7(2),* Dial Bks) Penguin Young Readers Group.
Sommer, Carl. No Longer a Dilly Dally. James, Kennon, illus. 2014. (J). pap. *(978-1-57537-961-6(9))* Advance Publishing, Inc.
—No Longer a Dilly Dally(Nunca Mas a Troche y Moche) James, Kennon, illus. 2009. (Another Sommer-Time Story Bilingual Ser.). (SPA & ENG.). 48p. (J). lib. bdg. 16.95 *(978-1-57537-162-7(6))* Advance Publishing, Inc.
—The Ugly Caterpillar. Budwine, Greg, illus. 2014. (J). pap. *(978-1-57537-971-5(6))* Advance Publishing, Inc.
—The Ugly Caterpillar(La Oruga Fea) Budwine, Greg, illus. 2009. (Another Sommer-Time Story Bilingual Ser.). (SPA & ENG.). 48p. (J). (gr. k-3). lib. bdg. 16.95 *(978-1-57537-171-9(5))* Advance Publishing, Inc.
Sonneborn, Scott. Attack of the Zom-Bees! Esparza, Andres et al, illus. 2013. (Tiger Moth Ser.). (ENG.). 48p. (gr. 1-3). pap. 6.19 *(978-1-4342-3871-9(7))* Stone Arch Bks.
—Tiger Moth: Attack of the Zom-Bees!. 1 vol. Esparza, Andres, illus. 2013. (Tiger Moth Ser.). (ENG.). 48p. (gr. 1-3). lib. bdg. 23.99 *(978-1-4342-3283-0(2))* Stone Arch Bks.
Soundprints Staff. Smithsonian's Backyard Collection Micro 4 Book Set. 2007. (ENG.). 32p. 14.95 *(978-1-59249-750-8(0));* 14.95 *(978-1-59249-751-5(9))* Soundprints.
Spanyol, Jessica. Keith & His Super-Stunt Rally Racer. Spanyol, Jessica, illus. 2008. (MiniBug Bks.). (ENG., Illus.). 24p. (J). (gr. k-k). 5.99 *(978-0-7636-3742-2(4))* Candlewick Pr.
Sparkes, Ali. Beetle Blast. Collins, Ross, illus. 2013. (S. W. I. T. C. H. Ser.: 6). (ENG.). 104p. (J). (gr. 2-5). pap. 7.95 *(978-1-4677-0715-2(5),* Darby Creek); lib. bdg. 27.93 *(978-0-7613-9204-0(1))* Lerner Publishing Group.
—Crane Fly Crash. Collins, Ross, illus. 2013. (S. W. I. T. C. H. Ser.: 5). (ENG.). 104p. (J). (gr. 2-5). pap. 7.95 *(978-1-4677-0714-5(7),* Darby Creek) Lerner Publishing Group.
The Sparkling Beauty. 2006. Orig. Title: Televisual Book. (J). 18.99 *(978-0-9779672-0-9(4))* Karsonkina, Tatiana.
Speck, Katie. Maybelle Goes to School. Tagyos, Paul Rátz de, illus. 2015. (Maybelle Ser.). (ENG.). 64p. (J). (gr. 2-5). 16.99 *(978-0-8050-9158-8(0);* 9780805091588, Holt, Henry & Co. Bks. For Young Readers) Holt, Henry & Co.
Spiegelman, Nadja. Zig & Wikki in the Cow. Loeffler, Trade, illus. 2012. (ENG.). 40p. (J). (gr. -1-3). 12.95 *(978-1-935179-15-3(2))* TOON Books / RAW Junior, LLC.
Spruill, Patricia Thomas. Josie Is Afraid. 2008. 32p. pap. 14.49 *(978-1-4343-7898-9(5))* AuthorHouse.
Stanek, Robert, pseud. Bugville Critters & Catching a Cup of Sunshine. 2011. (Illus.). 36p. pap. 5.99 *(978-1-57545-264-7(2),* Reagent Pr. Bks. for Young Readers) RP Media.
—Bugville Critters & Every Day Is Different. 2011. (Illus.). 32p. pap. 4.99 *(978-1-57545-263-0(4),* Reagent Pr. Bks. for Young Readers) RP Media.
—Bugville Critters Go to Camp. 2011. 34p. pap. 5.99 *(978-1-57545-261-6(8),* Reagent Pr. Bks. for Young Readers) RP Media.
—Bugville Critters Remember Their Manners. 2011. (Illus.). 46p. pap. 6.99 *(978-1-57545-260-9(X),* Reagent Pr. Bks. for Young Readers) RP Media.
—Bugville Critters Save Their Allowance. 2011. (Illus.). 32p. pap. 4.99 *(978-1-57545-258-6(8),* Reagent Pr. Bks. for Young Readers) RP Media.
—Bugville Critters Start Summer Vacation. 2011. (Illus.). 32p. pap. 4.99 *(978-1-57545-257-9(X),* Reagent Pr. Bks. for Young Readers) RP Media.
—Bugville Critters Visit the Library. 2011. (Illus.). 28p. pap. 4.99 *(978-1-57545-259-3(6),* Reagent Pr. Bks. for Young Readers) RP Media.
Stein, Peter. Bugs Galore. Staake, Bob, illus. 2013. (ENG.). 32p. (J). (— 1). bds. 6.99 *(978-0-7636-6220-2(8))* Candlewick Pr.
Steve, Smallman. Very Greedy Bee. Jack, Tickle, illus. 2010. (ENG.). 32p. (J). pap. 7.95 *(978-1-58925-422-0(8))* Tiger Tales.
Stewart, Yale. Creatures from Planet X!. 1 vol. Stewart, Yale, illus. 2014. (Amazing Adventures of Superman! Ser.). (ENG., Illus.). 32p. (gr. k-2). lib. bdg. 25.32 *(978-1-4795-5734-9(X),* DC Super Heroes) Stone Arch Bks.
Stier, Catherine. Bugs in My Hair?! Lyon, Tammie, illus. 2012. (J). 34.28 *(978-1-61913-111-8(0))* Weigl Pubs., Inc.
—Bugs in My Hair?!. 1 vol. Lyon, Tammie, illus. 2010. (ENG.). 32p. (J). (gr. 1-3). pap. 6.99 *(978-0-8075-0909-8(4))* Whitman, Albert & Co.
—What's Bugging Nurse Penny? A Story about Lice. Beaky, Suzanne, illus. 2013. (ENG.). 32p. (J). (gr. -1-3). 16.99 *(978-0-8075-8803-1(2))* Whitman, Albert & Co.
Stone, Jodi. I Want to Catch a Dragonfly. 2008. 28p. per. 24.95 *(978-1-4241-8770-6(2))* America Star Bks.
—Lady Bug. Herring, Kip, illus. 2005. 36p. (J). per. 15.00 *(978-0-9754298-7-7(6),* Ithaca Pr.) Authors & Artists Publishers of New York, Inc.
Straker, Bethany, illus. The Funny Bunny Fly. 2014. (ENG.). 32p. (J). (gr. -1-k). 14.95 *(978-1-62914-610-2(2),* Sky Pony Pr.) Skyhorse Publishing Co., Inc.
Sturges, Philemon. I Love Bugs! Halpern, Shari, illus. 2005. (ENG.). 32p. (J). (gr. -1-3). 17.99 *(978-0-06-056168-0(8))* HarperCollins Pubs.
Suarez de la Prida, Isabel. Los Diminutos. Bouchain, Nava, illus. 2003. (SPA.). 32p. (J). (gr. k-3). pap. 6.95 *(978-968-19-0631-3(4))* Santillana USA Publishing Co., Inc.
Sunday, Bonnie. Sparkles, Dragons, & Dragonfly Land. 2012. 32p. pap. 19.99 *(978-1-4772-2914-9(0))* AuthorHouse.
Surman-Hobbs, Debbi. The Little Brown Moth. 1 vol. 2010. 34p. pap. 24.95 *(978-1-4489-8620-0(6))* PublishAmerica, Inc.
Syddall, Susan. It's a Bad Day to Be a Fly! 2012. 40p. pap. 32.70 *(978-1-4771-1170-3(0))* Xlibris Corp.
Tate, Bernice & Andy. Funspell. 2009. 20p. pap. 14.95 *(978-1-4343-7103-4(4))* AuthorHouse.
Tatro, John L. Bugs Bugs Bugs. 2008. 28p. pap. 12.49 *(978-1-4343-9579-5(0))* AuthorHouse.
Ten Little Lady Bugs. (Mini Whizz Ser.). (Illus.). (J). *(978-1-58209-076-4(9))* Bks. Are Fun, Ltd.
Terpening, Lori. Hey! You Bug Me. 2012. 28p. pap. 21.99 *(978-1-4691-9529-2(1))* Xlibris Corp.
Thompson, Colleen. Claudine & Claudette: A Bug Story. 2010. 12p. 8.49 *(978-1-4520-7902-8(1))* AuthorHouse.
—Claudine & Claudette a Bug Story. 2011. 12p. pap. 8.32 *(978-1-4634-2286-8(5))* AuthorHouse.
Tiger Tales Staff, creator. Busy Bugs. 2004. (Cuddly Cuffs Ser.: 6). (Illus.). 10p. (J). (gr. -1-13). tchr. ed. 5.95 *(978-1-58925-726-9(X))* Tiger Tales.
Tim, Fireball. Big Book of Wacky Rides! 2013. (ENG.). 32p. (J). (gr. -1). 17.95 *(978-1-933492-81-0(3))* Design Studio Pr.
Tisdale, Towanda. Wallace Mack Has a Bug Attack! 2012. 28p. 24.95 *(978-1-4626-6071-1(1))* America Star Bks.
Treviño, Hilda L. Ladybugs on a Mission. 2013. 70p. (gr. 4-6). pap. 8.95 *(978-1-4759-7762-2(X))* iUniverse, Inc.
Troupe, Thomas Kingsley. Lost: a Wild Tale of Survival. Fagan, Kirbi, illus. 2016. (Survive! Ser.). (ENG.). 56p. (gr. 4-6). lib. bdg. 25.32 *(978-1-4965-2557-4(4))* Stone Arch Bks.
Trout, Holly Christian. The Firefly Who Lost Her Way. 2013. 24p. pap. 24.95 *(978-1-62709-594-5(2))* America Star Bks.
Tyson, Leigh Ann. An Interview with Harry the Tarantula. Drescher, Henrik, illus. 2003. (ENG.). 32p. (J). (gr. -1-3). 15.95 *(978-0-7922-5122-4(9),* National Geographic Children's Bks.) National Geographic Society.
Uncle Bobby. Herman & Hariett. 2004. 43p. pap. 24.95 *(978-1-4137-2931-3(2))* PublishAmerica, Inc.
Varner, Carla. The Worrisome Worm. 2003. (J). 11.95 *(978-0-9745787-3-6(8))* I Can Do All Things Productions.
Vaughn, Trudy D. Bugs Beware My Mom Doesn't Care! 2012. 24p. pap. 10.95 *(978-1-4497-3635-4(1),* WestBow Pr.) Author Solutions, Inc.
Vidal, Séverine. Mega Pig. Barroux, Stephane, illus. 2015. (Mega Hero Bks.). (ENG.). 28p. (J). (gr. k-2). 12.95 *(978-1-77085-636-3(6),* 9781770856363) Firefly Bks., Ltd.
—Mega Wolf. Barroux, Stephane, illus. 2015. (Mega Hero Bks.). (ENG.). 28p. (J). (gr. k-2). 12.95 *(978-1-77085-637-0(4),* 9781770856370) Firefly Bks., Ltd.
von Bassewitz, Gerdt. Peter & Anneli's Journey to the Moon. Baluschek, Hans, illus. 2007. 110p. (J). (gr. 3-7). *(978-0-88010-584-2(4),* Bell Pond Bks.) SteinerBooks, Inc.
Wadsworth, Kay. Daisy Moon & the Worm Armies. 2011. (Illus.). 100p. pap. 12.52 *(978-1-4567-7043-3(8))* AuthorHouse.
Wainwright, W. O. O' Mista' Whadda' Wata' Bug!. 1 vol. 2009. pap. 24.95 *(978-1-60749-385-3(3))* PublishAmerica, Inc.
Walsh, Ellen Stoll. Dot & Jabber & the Big Bug Mystery. 2017. (Green Light Readers — Level 2 Ser.: Vol. 3). (ENG.). (J). (gr. -1-3). lib. bdg. 13.55 ***(978-0-606-39827-5(9))*** Turtleback Bks.
Warmus, Paul J. Sue's Zoo & the Magic Garden. 2012. pap. 11.95 *(978-0-7414-7200-7(7))* Infinity Publishing.
Watson-Dubisch, Carolyn. Bug-a-boo. 1. l.t. ed. 2006. (Illus.). 32p. (J). per. 9.95 *(978-0-9779295-1-1(5))* Medusa Road Pr.
Watson, Mary. The Paper Dragonfly. Watson, Mary, illus. 2007. (ENG., Illus.). 32p. (J). (gr. k-3). 15.95 *(978-0-9726614-3-0(3))* Shenanigan Bks.
Watt, Mélanie. Bug in a Vacuum. 2015. (ENG., Illus.). 96p. (J). (gr. k-4). 21.99 *(978-1-77049-645-3(9),* Tundra Bks.) Tundra Bks. CAN. Dist: Penguin Random Hse. LLC.
Webb, Heather. The Frog & the Fly. Sanderson, Constance, illus. 2008. 29p. pap. 24.95 *(978-1-60441-380-9(8))* America Star Bks.
Webb, Ramona. Tee & Tye Learn to Fly. Webb, Terris, illus. 2008. 20p. pap. 24.95 *(978-1-60703-729-3(7))* America Star Bks.
Weston Woods Staff, creator. The Napping House. 2011. 29.95 *(978-0-439-72863-8(0))* Weston Woods Studios, Inc.
Wheeler, Darcy. Lydia the Lazy Ladybug. 2012. 34p. pap. 19.99 *(978-1-4772-3741-0(0))* AuthorHouse.
White, Janet. Tales of Leafy Lane. White, Lee et al, illus. 2007. 88p. per. *(978-1-84748-196-2(5))* Athena Pr.
Whiting, Sue & Martin, Stuart. That's Funny! 2003. (Illus.). 14p. 12.95 *(978-1-74047-272-2(1))* Book Co. Publishing Pty, Ltd., The AUS. Dist: Penton Overseas, Inc.
Wilder, Beth. Bugs in Shoes. 1 vol. 2012. (ENG., Illus.). 64p. (J). 14.99 *(978-0-7643-3967-7(2),* 9780764339677) Schiffer Publishing, Ltd.
Wiley, Melissa. Inch & Roly & the Sunny Day Scare. Jatkowska, Ag, illus. 2014. (Inch & Roly Ser.). (ENG.). 24p. (J). (gr. -1-1). 16.99 *(978-1-4424-9072-7(1),* Simon Spotlight) Simon Spotlight.
—Inch & Roly & the Very Small Hiding Place. Jatkowska, Ag, illus. 2013. (Inch & Roly Ser.). (ENG.). 24p. (J). (gr. -1-1). 16.99 *(978-1-4424-5281-7(1));* pap. 3.99 *(978-1-4424-5279-4(X))* Simon Spotlight. (Simon Spotlight).
—Inch & Roly Make a Wish. Jatkowska, Ag, illus. 2012. (Inch & Roly Ser.). (ENG.). 24p. (J). (gr. -1-1). 15.99 *(978-1-4424-5277-0(3));* pap. 3.99 *(978-1-4424-5276-3(5))* Simon Spotlight. (Simon Spotlight).
Willard, Gerald. Amy Firefly. 2009. 40p. pap. 18.50 *(978-1-60693-448-7(1),* Eloquent Bks.) Strategic Book Publishing & Rights Agency (SBPRA).
Williams, Billie. Angela's Bedtime Adventures. 1 vol. 2009. 31p. pap. 24.95 *(978-1-60749-112-5(5))* America Star Bks.
Williams, Dawn. Very Little Venus & the Very Friendly Fly. Chou, Joey, illus. 2007. 48p. (J). 15.00 *(978-0-9770783-2-5(9))* SunriseHouse Pubs.
Williams, Greg. Townsworth the Turkey. 2011. 28p. pap. 19.00 *(978-1-60746-631-4(7))* FastPrncil, Inc.
—Yarborrow. 2011. 30p. pap. 19.00 *(978-1-60746-506-5(X))* FastPrncil, Inc.
Williams Jr., Floyd. Lenney the Lightning Bug. Roberts, Joel, illus. 2013. 20p. pap. 9.50 *(978-1-4276-1898-6(4))* Witty Publishing.
Willis, Lisa M. The Bug's Picnic. 2008. 28p. pap. 24.95 *(978-1-60563-389-3(5))* America Star Bks.
Wilson, Karma. A Frog in the Bog. Rankin, Joan, illus. (ENG.). 32p. (J). (gr. -1-3). 2007. 7.99 *(978-1-4169-2727-3(1))* 2003. 17.99 *(978-0-689-84081-4(0))* McElderry, Margaret K. Bks. (McElderry, Margaret K. Bks.).
Wolff, Susan. Quackers Wants to Fly. Currie, Justin, illus. 2013. 32p. pap. 8.95 *(978-1-60653-074-0(7))* High Hill Pr.

Wood, Audrey. Napping House / La Casa Adormecida. Wood, Don, illus. 2012. (ENG & SPA.). 32p. (J). (gr. -1 — 1). bds. 6.99 (978-0-547-71920-7(5)) Houghton Mifflin Harcourt Publishing Co.
Woods, Candy Godwin. Shimmer Finds Her Gift. 2009. 32p. pap. 13.00 (978-1-60860-840-9(9), Eloquent Bks.) Strategic Book Publishing & Rights Agency (SBPRA).
Woodson, Vera. Lady Bug, Beetle Boy, & Friends: Bullies Be Gone! 2013. (ENG., Illus.). (J). 14.95 (978-1-62086-049-6(X)) Mascot Bks., Inc.
Wright, Bill, Sr. Gleedus the Happy Grasshopper. Fraser, Jess, illus. 2006. (J). cd-rom 9.99 (978-0-9795190-6-2(3)) Color & Learn.
Yangas, Angela Marie. The Bugguzz: Let There Be Light. 2007. 19.99 (978-0-9801796-0-6(2)) Binx Bks.
Ylitalo, Becky Jean. Gretchen & the Grumpybugs. 2012. 32p. pap. 21.99 (978-1-4691-3074-3(2)) Xlibris Corp.
Yoon, Salina. Wings: A Book to Touch & Feel. Yoon, Salina, illus. 2010. (ENG., Illus.). 14p. (J). (gr. -1 — 1). bds. 8.99 (978-1-4169-8958-5(7), Little Simon) Little Simon.

INSECTS—HABITS AND BEHAVIOR

Act-Two Staff. Bug Safari. 2004. (Illus.). (J). (gr. 1-4). pap. 8.99 incl. cd-rom (978-0-7868-3415-0(3)) Hyperion Bks. for Children.
Aloian, Molly. Where Do Insects Live? 2013. (ENG., Illus.). 24p. (J). (978-0-7787-1280-0(X)); pap. (978-0-7787-1284-8(2)) Crabtree Publishing Co.
Carlin, Lydia. Insect Homes. 2008. (Illus.). 24p. (J). (978-0-545-00739-9(9)) Scholastic, Inc.
de la Bedoyere, Camilla. Bugs in the Backyard. 2016. (ENG., Illus.). 80p. (J). (gr. 3-6). pap. 9.95 (978-1-77085-697-4(8), 9781770856974) Firefly Bks., Ltd.
Farndon, John. Incredible Bugs. Portolano, Cristina, illus. 2016. (Animal Bests Ser.). (ENG.). 32p. (J). (gr. 3-6). lib. bdg. 26.65 (978-1-5124-0640-5(6)) Lerner Publishing Group.
Forsyth, Adrian. Exploring the World of Insects: The Equinox Guide to Insect Behaviour. 2004. (Illus.). 64p. (J). (gr. 4-8). reprint ed. pap. 10.00 (978-0-7567-8497-3(2)) DIANE Publishing Co.
Glaser, Linda. Not a Buzz to Be Found: Insects in Winter. Zollars, Jaime, illus. 2011. (Exceptional Science Titles for Primary Grades Ser.). (ENG.). 32p. (J). (gr. 2-4). lib. bdg. 25.26 (978-0-7613-5644-8(4)) Lerner Publishing Group.
Guillain, Charlotte. Los Alimentos de los Insectos. 2010. (Comparar Insectos Ser.). (SPA.). 24p. (gr. -1-1). 22.65 (978-1-4329-4326-4(X)); pap. 6.29 (978-1-4329-4333-2(2)) Heinemann-Raintree. (Bellota).
—Bug Babies, 1 vol. 2010. (Comparing Bugs Ser.). (ENG.). 24p. (gr. -1-1). 22.65 (978-1-4329-3570-2(4)); pap. 6.29 (978-1-4329-3579-5(8)) Heinemann-Raintree. (Acorn).
—Bug Food, 1 vol. 2010. (Comparing Bugs Ser.). (ENG.). 24p. (gr. -1-1). pap. 6.29 (978-1-4329-3578-8(X)); lib. bdg. 22.65 (978-1-4329-3569-6(0)) Heinemann-Raintree. (Acorn).
—Bug Homes, 1 vol. 2010. (Comparing Bugs Ser.). (ENG.). 24p. (gr. -1-1). pap. 6.29 (978-1-4329-3577-1(1)); lib. bdg. 22.65 (978-1-4329-3568-9(2)) Heinemann-Raintree. (Acorn).
—Bugs on the Move, 1 vol. 2010. (Comparing Bugs Ser.). (ENG.). 24p. (gr. -1-1). 22.65 (978-1-4329-3567-2(4)); pap. 6.29 (978-1-4329-3576-4(3)) Heinemann-Raintree. (Acorn).
—Las Casas de los Insectos. 2010. (Comparar Insectos Ser.).Tr. of Bug Homes. (SPA.). 24p. (gr. -1-1). pap. 6.29 (978-1-4329-4332-5(4), Bellota) Heinemann-Raintree.
—Los Insectos en Movimiento. 2010. (Comparar Insectos Ser.).Tr. of Bugs on the Move. (SPA.). 24p. (gr. -1-1). 22.65 (978-1-4329-4324-0(3)); pap. 6.29 (978-1-4329-4331-8(6)) Heinemann-Raintree. (Bellota).
—Las Casas de Los Insectos, 1 vol. 2010. (Comparar Insectos Ser.).Tr. of Bug Homes. (SPA.). 24p. (gr. -1-1). 22.65 (978-1-4329-4325-7(1), Bellota) Heinemann-Raintree.
Hansen, Amy S. Bugs & Bugsicles: Insects in the Winter. Kray, Robert C., illus. 2010. (ENG.). 32p. (J). (gr. 2-4). 17.95 (978-1-59078-269-9(0)) Boyds Mills Pr.
Hopkins, Therese. Insect Homes. 2009. (Home Sweet Home Ser.). 24p. (gr. 1-1). 42.50 (978-1-61513-402-1(6), PowerKids Pr.) Rosen Publishing Group, Inc., The.
Kopp, Megan. How Do Insects Move? 2015. (ENG., Illus.). 24p. (J). (978-0-7787-1970-0(7)) Crabtree Publishing Co.
—How Do Insects Protect Themselves? 2015. (ENG., Illus.). 24p. (J). (978-0-7787-1971-7(5)) Crabtree Publishing Co.
—How Do Insects Work Together? 2015. (ENG., Illus.). 24p. (J). (978-0-7787-1972-4(3)) Crabtree Publishing Co.
—What Do Insects Eat? 2015. (ENG., Illus.). 24p. (J). (978-0-7787-1973-1(1)) Crabtree Publishing Co.
Lunis, Natalie. Inside the Tarantula's Burrow. 2013. (Science Slam: Snug As a Bug-Where Bugs Live Ser.). 24p. (J). (gr. -1-3). lib. bdg. 23.93 (978-1-61772-907-2(8)) Bearport Publishing Co., Inc.
McCleese, Don. Insects. 2011. (ENG., Illus.). 24p. (gr. 2-5). pap. 8.95 (978-1-61741-980-5(X)) Rourke Educational Media.
Munro, Roxie. Busy Builders, 0 vols. 2012. (ENG.). 40p. (J). (gr. k-6). 17.99 (978-0-7614-6105-0(1), 9780761461050, Amazon Children's Publishing) Amazon Publishing.
Roza, Greg. Inside an Ant Colony. 2009. (Real Life Readers Ser.). 16p. (gr. 2-3). pap. 7.05 (978-1-4358-0224-7(1), Rosen Classroom) Rosen Publishing Group, Inc., The.
Sill, Cathryn. About Insects / Sobre Los Insectos: A Guide for Children / una Guía para Niños, 1 vol. Sill, John, illus. rev. ed. 2015. (About... Ser.). (ENG & SPA.). 48p. (J). (gr. -1-2). pap. 8.95 (978-1-56145-883-7(X)) Peachtree Pubs.
Silverstein, Alvin, et al. Dung Beetles, Slugs, Leeches, & More: The Yucky Animal Book. Kelley, Gerald, illus. 2010. (Yucky Science Ser.). 48p. (J). (gr. 5-9). 25.27 (978-0-7660-3317-7(1)) Enslow Pubs., Inc.
Tagliaferro, Linda. Bees & Their Hives [Scholastic]. 2010. (Animal Homes Ser.). 24p. pap. 0.49 (978-1-4296-5797-6(9), Pebble Plus) Capstone Press of Coughlan Cos.

INSECTS—POETRY

Cricket Books Staff. Ladybug, Ladybug: And Other Favorite Poems. 2007. (ENG., Illus.). 40p. (J). (gr. k-k). 17.95 (978-0-8126-7936-6(9)) Cricket Bks.
Elizabeth Tarquinio Sciulli. Butterfly Milk. 2009. 16p. pap. 14.95 (978-1-4389-5889-7(7)) AuthorHouse.
Frost, Helen. Step Gently Out. Lieder, Rick, photos by. 2012. (ENG., Illus.). 32p. (J). (gr. k-k). 15.99 (978-0-7636-5601-0(1)) Candlewick Pr.
Harley, Avis. The Monarch's Progress: Poems with Wings. Harley, Avis, illus. 2008. (ENG., Illus.). 32p. (J). (gr. 2-3). 16.95 (978-1-59078-558-4(4)) Boyds Mills Pr.
Murray, Carol. Cricket in the Thicket: Poems about Bugs. Sweet, Melissa, illus. 2017. (ENG.). 40p. (J). 17.99 (978-0-8050-9818-1(6), 9780805098181, Holt, Henry & Co. Bks. For Young Readers) Holt, Henry & Co.
Reffett, Frances. Insectaside. Losh, Eric, illus. l.t. ed. 2006. 28p. (J). 8.00 net. (978-0-9785886-0-1(6)) Chicory Pr.
Shane, Molly G. Butterfly Wishes & Popsicle Dreams Deseos de Mariposas y Sue±Os de Paletas: A Collection of Children's Silly Poems una Colecci=n de poemas raros Par. 2009. 92p. pap. 9.95 (978-1-4401-3526-2(6)) iUniverse, Inc.
Yolen, Jane. Bug Off! Creepy, Crawly Poems. Stemple, Jason, photos by. 2012. (ENG., Illus.). 32p. (J). (gr. k). 16.95 (978-1-59078-862-2(1), Wordsong) Boyds Mills Pr.

INSECTS AS CARRIERS OF DISEASE

see also Flies; Mosquitoes
Body Bugs. 2013. (Earth's Grossest Animals Ser.). 32p. (J). (gr. k-5). pap. 60.00 (978-1-61533-782-8(2), PowerKids Pr.) Rosen Publishing Group, Inc., The.
Cefrey, Holly. Yellow Fever. 2009. (Epidemics Ser.). 64p. (gr. 5-5). 58.50 (978-1-61512-309-4(1)) Rosen Publishing Group, Inc., The.
DiConsiglio, John. Bitten! Mosquitoes Infect New York. 2011. (J). (978-0-545-32807-4(1)) Scholastic, Inc.
Orr, Tamra B. Understanding Insects. 2014. (Explorer Library: Follow the Clues Ser.). (ENG., Illus.). 32p. (J). (gr. 4-8). 28.50 (978-1-62431-783-5(9), 203328) Cherry Lake Publishing.
Reith, Sharon L. Infestation! Roaches, Bedbugs, Ants, & Other Insect Invaders, 1 vol. 2013. (Nature's Invaders Ser.). (ENG.). 32p. (gr. 3-4). 27.99 (978-1-4765-0139-0(4), Edge Bks.) Capstone Press of Coughlan Cos.
Wood, Alix. Body Bugs. 2013. (Earth's Grossest Animals Ser.). 32p. (J). (gr. k-5). pap. 10.00 (978-1-61533-781-1(4), PowerKids Pr.) Rosen Publishing Group, Inc., The.

IN-SERVICE TRAINING

see Employees—Training of

INSOLVENCY

see Bankruptcy

INSPECTION OF SCHOOLS

see School Management And Organization

INSPIRATION

see Creation (Literary, Artistic, etc.)

INSTRUCTION

see Education; Teaching

INSTRUMENTS, ASTRONOMICAL

see Astronomical Instruments

INSTRUMENTS, MEASURING

see Measuring Instruments

INSTRUMENTS, METEOROLOGICAL

see Meteorological Instruments

INSTRUMENTS, MUSICAL

see Musical Instruments

INSTRUMENTS, SCIENTIFIC

see Scientific Apparatus and Instruments

INSULIN

Downey, Glen. Miracle Men. Brennan, Anthony, illus. 2007. (Timeline Ser.). 48p. pap. 8.99 (978-1-4190-4410-6(9)) Steck-Vaughn.
Peterson, Amanda. What You Need to Know about Diabetes. 2015. (Focus on Health Ser.). (ENG., Illus.). 32p. (gr. 3-4). pap. 7.95 (978-1-4914-4901-1(2)) Capstone Press of Coughlan Cos.

INSURANCE

Andrews, Carolyn & Bedesky, Baron. What Is Insurance? 2009. (ENG., Illus.). 32p. (J). (gr. 2-5). lib. bdg. (978-0-7787-4444-3(2)); (gr. 3-7). pap. (978-0-7787-4455-9(8)) Crabtree Publishing Co.
Connolly, Sean. Insurance. 2010. (World Economy Explained Ser.). (Illus.). 48p. (YA). (gr. 7-12). 35.65 (978-1-60753-078-7(3)) Amicus Publishing.
—Insurance. 2012. (Illus.). 48p. (gr. 6-10). pap. 9.95 (978-1-926722-76-4(0)) Saunders Bk. Co. CAN. Dist: RiverStream Publishing.
Connolly, Sean & Claybourne, Anna. Insurance. 2011. (On the Edge Ser.). 32p. (YA). (gr. 3-6). 28.50 (978-1-59920-519-9(X)) Black Rabbit Bks.
Gagne, Tammy. Teen Guide to Protecting & Insuring Assests. 2014. (Illus.). 48p. (gr. 4-8). lib. bdg. 29.95 (978-1-61228-473-6(6)) Mitchell Lane Pubs., Inc.
Graham, Amy. Be Smart about Your Future: Risk Management & Insurance. 2014. (Be Smart about Money & Financial Literacy Ser.). 48p. (J). lib. bdg. 22.60 (978-0-7660-4285-8(5)) Enslow Pubs., Inc.
Kowalski, Kathiann M. National Health Care. 2008. (Open for Debate Ser.). 128p. (gr. 7-18). lib. bdg. 42.79 (978-0-7614-2943-2(3), Benchmark Bks.) Marshall Cavendish Corp.
Lynette, Rachel. What to Do When Your Family Can't Afford Health Care. 2010. (Let's Work It Out Ser.). 24p. (ENG.). (J). pap. 8.25 (978-1-4358-9772-4(2), PowerKids Pr.); (Illus.). (YA). (gr. 2-5). lib. bdg. 22.60 (978-1-4358-9342-9(5)) Rosen Publishing Group, Inc., The.
McGuire, Kara. Cover Your Assets: The Teens' Guide to Protecting Their Money, Their Stuff, & Themselves, 1 vol. 2014. (Financial Literacy for Teens Ser.). (ENG.). 64p. (gr. 6-7). lib. bdg. 33.99 (978-0-7565-4921-3(3)) Compass Point Bks.
Stokes, Kathy. Insurance Operations. 2012. (ENG.). 168p. (gr. 9-12). pap., wbk. ed. 24.00 (978-1-60525-776-1(1)) Goodheart-Willcox Pub.
Stokes, Kathy E. Insurance Operations. 2012. (ENG.). 320p. (gr. 9-12). 88.00 (978-1-60525-774-7(5)) Goodheart-Willcox Pub.

INSURANCE, SOCIAL

see Social Security

INTEGRATED CIRCUITS

Lepora, Nathan. Inside Atoms & Molecules. 2010. (Invisible Worlds Ser.). 48p. (gr. 4). 28.50 (978-0-7614-4192-2(1)) Marshall Cavendish GBR. Dist: Marshall Cavendish Corp.

INTEGRATION, RACIAL

see Race Relations

INTEGRATION IN EDUCATION

see Segregation in Education

INTELLECT

see also Creation (Literary, Artistic, etc.); Imagination; Knowledge, Theory of; Logic; Perception; Reasoning; Senses and Sensation; Thought and Thinking
Einspruch, Andrew. Brain Works, 1 vol., 1. 2014. (Discovery Education: How It Works). (ENG.). 32p. (gr. 3-6). 26.25 (978-1-4777-6305-6(8), PowerKids Pr.) Rosen Publishing Group, Inc., The.
MauleDavid. GENIUS BEGINNING BOOK WITH ONLINE ACCESS. 2014. (ENG.). 24p. (J). pap. 9.50 (978-1-107-67865-1(X)) Cambridge Univ. Pr.
Romanek, Trudee. Aha! The Most Interesting Book You'll Ever Read about Intelligence. Cowles, Rose, tr. Cowles, Rose, illus. 2004. (Mysterious You Ser.). (ENG.). 40p. (J). (gr. 4-9). 7.95 (978-1-55337-569-2(6)) Kids Can Pr., Ltd. CAN. Dist: Hachette Bk. Group.
Steckel, Richard, et al. Wise at Heart: Children & Adults Share Words of Wisdom. Steckel, Richard et al, illus. 2011. (ENG.). 72p. (J). (gr. 2-6). 18.95 (978-1-55453-630-6(8)) Kids Can Pr., Ltd. CAN. Dist: Hachette Bk. Group.
Waldron, Melanie. Your Brain: Understand It with Numbers, 1 vol. 2014. (Your Body by Numbers Ser.). (ENG., Illus.). 48p. (gr. 3-5). pap. 9.95 (978-1-4109-5985-0(6)); lib. bdg. 32.65 (978-1-4109-5980-5(5)) Heinemann-Raintree.

INTELLECTUAL LIFE

see Culture; Learning and Scholarship

INTELLIGENCE

see Intellect

INTELLIGENCE OF ANIMALS

see Animal Intelligence

INTELLIGENCE SERVICE

Berlatsky, Noah. The U. S. Intelligence Community. 2011. (Opposing Viewpoints Ser.). (ENG.). 224p. (gr. 12-12). pap. 33.80 (978-0-7377-5246-5(7)); lib. bdg. 48.80 (978-0-7377-5245-8(9)) Cengage Gale. (Greenhaven Pr., Inc.).
Caraccilo, Dominic J. Military Intelligence Technology of the Future. 2009. (Library of Future Weaponry Ser.). 64p. (gr. 6-6). 58.50 (978-1-60853-639-9(4)) Rosen Publishing Group, Inc., The.
Coddington, Andrew. Mass Government Surveillance: Spying on Citizens. 2017. (J). **(978-1-5026-2672-1(1))** Cavendish Square Publishing.
Curley, Robert. Spy Agencies, Intelligence Operations, & the People Behind Them. Curley, Robert, ed. 2013. 120p. (YA). (gr. 9-12). 32.90 (978-1-62275-035-1(7)) Rosen Publishing Group, Inc., The.
Doak, Robin S. National Intelligence. 2012. (Cornerstones of Freedom, Third Ser.). (ENG., Illus.). 64p. (J). pap. 8.95 (978-0-531-28161-1(2)); lib. bdg. 30.00 (978-0-531-23061-9(9)) Scholastic Library Publishing.
Dorling Kindersley Publishing Staff & Platt, Richard. Spy. 2009. (DK Eyewitness Bks.). (ENG.). 72p. (J). (gr. 3-7). 16.99 (978-0-7566-5034-6(8), DK Children) Dorling Kindersley Publishing, Inc.
Engdahl, Sylvia. Espionage & Intelligence. Greenhaven Press Editors, ed. 2012. (Current Controversies Ser.). (ENG.). 224p. (gr. 10-12). 46.40 (978-0-7377-5616-6(0)); pap. 32.00 (978-0-7377-5617-3(9), Greenhaven Pr., Inc.) Cengage Gale.
Goodman, Michael E. The CIA & Other American Spies. 2012. (Spies Around the World Ser.). (Illus.). 48p. (J). (gr. 5-12). 23.95 (978-1-60818-226-8(6)) Creative Co., The.
—The KGB & Other Russian Spies. 2012. (Spies Around the World Ser.). (Illus.). 48p. (J). (gr. 5-12). 23.95 (978-1-60818-227-5(4), Creative Education) Creative Co., The.
—Modern Spies. 2015. (Illus.). 48p. (J). (978-1-60818-600-6(8), Creative Education) Creative Co., The.
—Modern Spies: Wartime Spies. 2016. (Wartime Spies Ser.). (ENG., Illus.). 48p. (J). (gr. 5-9). pap. 12.00 (978-1-62832-205-7(5), Creative Paperbacks) Creative Co., The.
—The SIS & Other British Spies. 2012. (Spies Around the World Ser.). (Illus.). 48p. (J). (gr. 5-12). 23.95 (978-1-60818-229-9(0), Creative Education) Creative Co., The.
—Spies Around the World: The Mossad & Other Israeli Spies. 2012. (Spies Around the World Ser.). (Illus.). 48p. (J). (gr. 5-12). 23.95 (978-1-60818-228-2(2), Creative Education) Creative Co., The.
—Spies Around the World: the CIA & Other American Spies. 2014. (Spies Around the World Ser.). (ENG., Illus.). 48p. (J). (gr. 4-7). pap. 12.00 (978-0-89812-969-4(9), Creative Paperbacks) Creative Co., The.
—Spies Around the World: the KGB & Other Russian Spies. 2014. (Spies Around the World Ser.). (ENG., Illus.). 48p. (J). (gr. 4-7). pap. 12.00 (978-0-89812-970-0(2), Creative Paperbacks) Creative Co., The.
—Spies Around the World: the Mossad & Other Israeli Spies. 2014. (Spies Around the World Ser.). (ENG., Illus.). 48p. (J). (gr. 4-7). pap. 12.00 (978-0-89812-971-7(0), Creative Paperbacks) Creative Co., The.
—Spies Around the World: the SIS & Other British Spies. 2014. (Spies Around the World Ser.). (ENG., Illus.). 48p. (J). (gr. 4-7). pap. 12.00 (978-0-89812-972-4(9), Creative Paperbacks) Creative Co., The.
Harmon, Daniel E. Special Ops: Military Intelligence, 1 vol. 2015. (ENG.). 64p. (J). 32.95 (978-1-4777-7587-5(0), Rosen Reference) Rosen Publishing Group, Inc., The.
Hines, Janet. Inside America's CIA: The Central Intelligence Agency. (Inside the World's Most Famous Intelligence Agencies Ser.). 64p. 2009. (gr. 5-5). 58.50 (978-1-61513-567-7(7)) 2005. (Illus.). (YA). (gr. 7-12). lib. bdg. 31.95 (978-0-8239-3811-7(5)) Rosen Publishing Group, Inc., The.
Inside the World's Most Famous Intelligence Agencies. 2005. (Illus.). (gr. 7-12). lib. bdg. 159.00 (978-0-8239-4061-5(6)) Rosen Publishing Group, Inc., The.
Intelligence & Counterintelligence. 2013. (Intelligence & Counterintelligence Ser.). (YA). (gr. 9-12). 131.60 (978-1-62275-062-7(4)); 65.80 (978-1-62275-040-5(3)) Rosen Publishing Group, Inc., The.
Jeffrey, Gary. Secret Agents. 2009. (Graphic Careers Ser.). (ENG.). 48p. (YA). (gr. 5-5). 58.50 (978-1-61512-891-4(3), Rosen Reference) Rosen Publishing Group, Inc., The.
—Secret Agents. Riley, Terry, illus. 2008. (Graphic Careers Ser.). (ENG.). 48p. (gr. 5-8). per. 14.05 (978-1-4042-1465-1(8)); (YA). lib. bdg. 31.95 (978-1-4042-1464-4(X)) Rosen Publishing Group, Inc., The.
Lockwood, Brad. Domestic Spying & Wiretapping. (In the News Ser.). 64p. 2009. (gr. 6-6). 58.50 (978-1-61513-465-6(4)) 2006. (Illus.). (YA). (gr. 7-12). lib. bdg. 31.95 (978-1-4042-0973-2(5)) Rosen Publishing Group, Inc., The.
McCormack, Shaun. Inside Britain's MI6: Military Intelligence 6. (Inside the World's Most Famous Intelligence Agencies Ser.). 64p. 2009. (gr. 5-5). 58.50 (978-1-61513-568-4(5)) 2005. (Illus.). (YA). (gr. 7-12). lib. bdg. 31.95 (978-0-8239-3812-4(3)) Rosen Publishing Group, Inc., The.
Mitchell, Susan K. The Secret World of Spy Agencies. 2011. (Secret World of Spies Ser.). (Illus.). 48p. (J). (gr. 2-5). lib. bdg. 25.27 (978-0-7660-3714-4(2)); (gr. 4-18). pap. 8.95 (978-1-59845-352-2(1)) Enslow Pubs., Inc.
Murray, Laura K. Spies in the CIA. 2016. 24p. (J). (978-1-60818-616-7(4), Creative Education) Creative Co., The.
—Spies in the Mossad. 2016. (Illus.). 24p. (J). (978-1-60818-618-1(0), Creative Education) Creative Co., The.
—Spies in the SIS. 2016. (Illus.). 24p. (J). (978-1-60818-619-8(9), Creative Education) Creative Co., The.
Pender, Lionel. Spy vs. Spy: Intelligence Organizations. 2016. (Law Enforcement & Intelligence Gathering Ser.). 00104p. (YA). (gr. 8-8). lib. bdg. 36.25 (978-1-5081-0370-7(4), Britannica Educational Publishing) Rosen Publishing Group, Inc., The.
Platt, Richard. Spy. 2009. (DK Eyewitness Bks.). (ENG.). 72p. (J). (gr. 3-7). 19.99 (978-0-7566-5035-3(6), DK Children) Dorling Kindersley Publishing, Inc.
Polisar, Patti. Inside France's DGSE: General Directorate for External Security. 2005. (Inside the World's Most Famous Intelligence Agencies Ser.). (Illus.). 64p. (YA). (gr. 7-12). lib. bdg. 31.95 (978-0-8239-3814-8(X)) Rosen Publishing Group, Inc., The.
—Inside France's DGSE: The General Directorate for External Security. 2009. (Inside the World's Most Famous Intelligence Agencies Ser.). 64p. (gr. 5-5). 58.50 (978-1-61513-569-1(3)) Rosen Publishing Group, Inc., The.
Price, Sean. Modern Spies. 2014. pap. (978-1-4765-3593-7(0)) Capstone Press of Coughlan Cos.
Price, Sean Stewart. Modern Spies, 1 vol. 2013. (Classified Ser.). (ENG.). 48p. (gr. 3-4). 31.99 (978-1-4765-0123-9(8)) Capstone Press of Coughlan Cos.
Rabiger, Joanna. Government Intelligence Agencies, Vol. 20. Gomez, Manny, ed. 2016. (Crime & Detection Ser.). (Illus.). 96p. (J). (gr. 7). 24.95 (978-1-4222-3478-5(9)) Mason Crest.
Rooney, Anne. Secret Services. 2010. (Spies & Spying Ser.). (J). (gr. 4-7). 28.50 (978-1-59920-360-7(X)) Black Rabbit Bks.
Schiel, Katy. Inside Germany's BND: The Federal Intelligence Service. 2005. (Illus.). 63p. (YA). (gr. 4-8). reprint ed. 20.00 (978-0-7567-8669-4(X)) DIANE Publishing Co.
—Inside Germany's BND: The Federal Intelligence Service. (Inside the World's Most Famous Intelligence Agencies Ser.). 64p. 2009. (gr. 5-5). 58.50 (978-1-61513-570-7(7)) 2005. (Illus.). (YA). (gr. 7-12). lib. bdg. 31.95 (978-0-8239-3813-1(1)) Rosen Publishing Group, Inc., The.
Streissguth, Tom. America's Security Agencies: The Department of Homeland Security, FBI, NSA, & CIA. 2008. (Federal Government Ser.). (Illus.). 128p. (J). (gr. 3-7). lib. bdg. 34.60 (978-1-59845-058-3(1), MyReportLinks.com Bks.) Enslow Pubs., Inc.
—The Security Agencies of the United States: How the CIA, FBI, NSA, & Homeland Security Keep Us Safe. 2012. (Constitution & the United States Government Ser.). (Illus.). 104p. (J). (gr. 5-18). 33.27 (978-0-7660-4064-9(X)) Enslow Pubs., Inc.
Suib, Stella. Inside Russia's SVR: The Federal Security Service. 2005. (Inside the World's Most Famous Intelligence Agencies Ser.). (Illus.). 64p. (YA). (gr. 7-12). lib. bdg. 31.95 (978-0-8239-3816-2(6)) Rosen Publishing Group, Inc., The.
—Inside Russia's SVR: The Foreign Intelligence Service. 2005. (Illus.). 63p. (YA). reprint ed. 26.00 (978-0-7567-8668-7(1)) DIANE Publishing Co.
—Inside Russia's SVR: The Foreign Intelligence Service. 2009. (Inside the World's Most Famous Intelligence Agencies Ser.). 64p. (gr. 5-5). 58.50 (978-1-61513-572-1(3)) Rosen Publishing Group, Inc., The.
Sutherland, Adam. Undercover Operations. 2012. (On the Radar: Defend & Protect Ser.). (ENG.). 32p. (gr. 4-8). lib. bdg. 26.60 (978-0-7613-7773-3(5), Lerner Pubns.) Lerner Publishing Group.
Webster, Matt. Inside Israel's Mossad: The Institute for Intelligence & Special Tasks. (Inside the World's Most Famous Intelligence Agencies Ser.). 64p. 2009. (gr. 5-5). 58.50 (978-1-61513-571-4(5)) 2005. (Illus.). (YA). (gr. 7-12). lib. bdg. 31.95 (978-0-8239-3815-5(8)) Rosen Publishing Group, Inc., The.

INTEMPERANCE

see Alcoholism

INTERCOLLEGIATE ATHLETICS

see Athletics

INTERCULTURAL EDUCATION

see Multicultural Education

INTEREST GROUPS

see Lobbying

INTERIOR DECORATION

see also Furniture; Tapestry
Blake, Susannah. Crafts for Revamping Your Room. 2013. (Eco Chic Ser.). 32p. (J). lib. bdg. 23.94 (978-0-7660-4315-2(0)); (gr. 4-12). pap. 7.95 (978-1-4644-0575-4(1)) Enslow Pubs., Inc.
Dreyer, Kira. My New Bedroom: Estimate Lengths in Standard Units. 2014. (Math Masters: Measurement & Data Ser.). 24p. (J). (gr. 2-3). 23.60 (978-1-4777-6438-1(0)); (ENG.). pap. 8.25 (978-1-4777-4801-5(6)) Rosen Publishing Group, Inc., The. (Rosen Classroom).

George, Chris. Things in My Room. 2017. (Early Concepts Ser.). 24p. (gr. 4-6). pap. 8.25 **(978-1-5081-6225-4(5)**, PowerKids Pr.) Rosen Publishing Group, Inc., The.
Gunzi, Christiane. My Home. 2003. (My Very First Look At Ser.). (SPA & ENG., Illus.). 24p. (J). (gr. -1-k). pap. 5.95 *(978-1-58728-685-8(8))*; 9.95 *(978-1-58728-671-1(8))* Cooper Square Publishing Llc.
Harte, May. ABCs in My House. 2004. (Look-And-Learn Books). (Illus.). (J). lib. bdg. 8.95 *(978-1-4042-2824-5(1)*, PowerKids Pr.) Rosen Publishing Group, Inc., The.
—ABC's in My House. 2009. (Board Bks.). 16p. (gr. k-1). 23.90 *(978-1-61511-638-6(9)*, PowerKids Pr.) Rosen Publishing Group, Inc., The.
—1, 2, 3 in My House. 2004. (Look-And-Learn Books). (Illus.). (J). lib. bdg. 8.95 *(978-1-4042-2823-8(3)*, PowerKids Pr.) Rosen Publishing Group, Inc., The.
Kennedy, Marge. See Inside the White House. 2009. (Scholastic News Nonfiction Readers Ser.). (Illus.). 24p. (J). (gr. 1-2). 22.00 *(978-0-531-21097-0(9))* Scholastic Library Publishing.
Klutz Editors. Design Your Dream Room: Interior Design Portfolio. 2016. (ENG.). 80p. (J). (gr. 3-7). 19.99 *(978-1-338-03752-4(8))* Klutz.
Kopp, Megan. Maker Projects for Kids Who Love Designing Spaces. 2016. (Be a Maker! Ser.). (ENG.). 32p. (J). (gr. 5-8). *(978-0-7787-2574-9(X))* Crabtree Publishing Co.
Lim, Annalees. Recycling Crafts, Vol. 1. 2014. (Craft Attack! Ser.). (ENG.). 32p. (J). (gr. 3-3). 26.60 *(978-1-4824-0218-6(1))* Stevens, Gareth Publishing LLLP.
Mason, Helen. Interior Designer. 2014. (Creative Careers Ser.). 48p. (J). (gr. 4-8). pap. 84.30 *(978-1-4824-1291-8(8))* Stevens, Gareth Publishing LLLP.
Maurer, Tracy Nelson. Rock Your Room with Crafts. 2009. (Illus.). 32p. (J). pap. 8.95 *(978-1-60694-507-0(6))* Rourke Educational Media.
Nations, Susan. Things at Home. 2006. (Things in My World Ser.). (Illus.). 16p. (gr. -1-2). lib. bdg. 19.00 *(978-0-8368-6807-4(2)*, Weekly Reader Leveled Readers) Stevens, Gareth Publishing LLLP.
Onyefulu, Ifeoma. Home. 2013. (ENG., Illus.). 32p. (J). (gr. -1-k). 17.99 *(978-1-84780-266-8(4)*, Frances Lincoln) Quarto Publishing Group UK GBR. Dist: Hachette Bk. Group.
Peterson, Megan Cooley & Rustad, Martha E. H. Kid Style: Rockin' Bedrooms for You!, 1 vol. 2014. (Make It Mine Ser.). (ENG.). 24p. (gr. k-1). lib. bdg. 26.65 *(978-1-4765-3970-6(7)*, Pebble Plus) Capstone Press of Coughlan Cos.
Rissman, Rebecca. Counting at Home, 1 vol. 2012. (I Can Count! Ser.). (ENG.). 24p. (gr. -1-k). pap. 9.95 *(978-1-4329-6699-7(5))*; lib. bdg. 25.32 *(978-1-4329-6694-2(4))* Heinemann-Raintree.
Ryan, Nellie. Dream House Doodles. 2013. (ENG., Illus.). 160p. (J). (gr. -1-17). pap. 12.95 *(978-0-7624-5292-7(7)*, Running Pr. Kids) Running Pr. Bk. Pubs.
Smith, Tana. DIY Bedroom Decor: 50 Awesome Ideas for Your Room. 2015. (ENG., Illus.). 192p. pap. 16.99 *(978-1-4405-8802-0(3))* Adams Media Corp.
Torres, Laura. Rock Your Room. 2012. (Illus.). 32p. (gr. 3-5). pap. 8.95 *(978-1-926853-87-1(3))* Saunders Bk. Co. CAN. Dist: RiverStream Publishing.
Warwick, Ellen. Stuff for Your Space. Lum, Bernice, tr. Lum, Bernice, illus. 2004. (Kids Can Do It Ser.). (ENG.). 40p. (J). (gr. 3-7). 6.95 *(978-1-55337-399-5(5))* Kids Can Pr., Ltd. CAN. Dist: Hachette Bk. Group.
Watt, Fiona. Sticker Dolly Dressing Fashion Designer Home Designer. 2015. (Sticker Dolly Dressing Fashion Designer Ser.). (ENG.). 24+10p. (J). (gr. k-5). pap. 9.99 *(978-0-7945-3548-3(8)*, Usborne) EDC Publishing.
Weaver, Janice & Wishinsky, Frieda. It's Your Room: A Decorating Guide for Real Kids. Dávila, Claudia, illus. 2006. (ENG.). 64p. (J). (gr. 4-7). per. 14.95 *(978-0-88776-711-1(7)*, Tundra Bks.) Tundra Bks. CAN. Dist: Penguin Random Hse. LLC.
Weekly Reader Editorial Staff. Things at Home (Las Cosas de Mi Casa) 2006. (Things in My World/ Las cosas de mi mundo Ser.). (SPA., Illus.). 16p. (gr. -1-2). lib. bdg. 19.00 *(978-0-8368-7219-4(3)*, Weekly Reader Leveled Readers) Stevens, Gareth Publishing LLLP.
Weekly Reader Editorial Staff, contrib. by. Things at Home (Las Cosas De Mi Casa) 2006. (Things in My World/ Las cosas de mi mundo Ser.). (ENG & SPA., Illus.). 16p. (gr. -1-2). pap. 5.30 *(978-0-8368-7226-2(6)*, Weekly Reader Leveled Readers) Stevens, Gareth Publishing LLLP.
Wild Garden. 2017. (ENG.). (J). 19.99 **(978-0-7945-3957-3(2)**, Usborne) EDC Publishing.
Wrigley, Annabel. We Love to Sew — Bedrooms: 23 Projects, Cool Stuff for Your Space. 2014. (ENG., Illus.). 176p. (J). (gr. 2-8). pap. 21.95 *(978-1-60705-824-3(3)*, FunStitch Studio) C & T Publishing.
Zondervan Staff. Redo Your Room: 50 Bedroom DIYs You Can Do in a Weekend, 1 vol. Faithgirlz! and Girls' Life Magazine Editors, ed. 2015. (Faithgirlz Ser.). (ENG.). 128p. (J). pap. 14.99 *(978-0-310-74632-4(9))* Zonderkidz.

INTERIOR DECORATION—FICTION

Kompelien, Tracy. Octopus's Garden, 1 vol. 2007. (Critter Chronicles Ser.). (ENG., Illus.). 24p. (J). (gr. k-3). lib. bdg. 24.21 *(978-1-59928-456-9(1)*, SandCastle) ABDO Publishing Co.
Lodge, Jo. La Casa del Senor Coc/ The House of Mr Coc. 2007. 8p. bds. 36.95 *(978-84-263-6454-8(3))* Vives, Luis Editorial (Edelvives) ESP. Dist: Baker & Taylor Bks.
Mellom, Robin. The Classroom Trick Out My School! Gilpin, Stephen, illus. 2014. (Classroom Novel Ser.). (ENG.). 288p. (J). (gr. 3-7). 12.99 *(978-1-4231-5065-7(1))* Hyperion Bks. for Children.
Rylant, Cynthia. Annie & Snowball & the Prettiest House. Stevenson, Sucie, illus. (Annie & Snowball Ser.: 2). (ENG.). 40p. (J). (gr. k-2). 2008. pap. 3.99 *(978-1-4169-1460-0(9))* 2007. 16.99 *(978-1-4169-0939-2(7))* Simon Spotlight. (Simon Spotlight).
Santucci, Barbara. Abby's Chairs. Santini, Debrah L., illus. 2004. 32p. 16.00 *(978-0-8028-5205-2(X))* Eerdmans, William B. Publishing Co.
Slonim, David. He Came with the Couch. Slonim, David, illus. 2005. (ENG., Illus.). 36p. (J). (gr. -1-3). 15.99 *(978-0-8118-4430-7(7))* Chronicle Bks. LLC.

INTERMARRIAGE

see also Interracial Marriage

Haerens, Margaret. Mixed Marriage. Gale, ed. 2014. (Global Viewpoints Ser.). (ENG., Illus.). 224p. (gr. 7-12). lib. bdg. 46.20 *(978-0-7377-6266-2(7)*, Greenhaven Pr., Inc.) Cengage Gale.

INTERMARRIAGE—FICTION

Otey Little, Mimi. Yoshiko & the Foreigner. Otey Little, Mimi, illus. 2004. (Illus.). 31p. (J). (gr. 4-8). reprint ed. 16.00 *(978-0-7567-7510-0(8))* DIANE Publishing Co.

INTERMARRIAGE, RACIAL

see Interracial Marriage

INTERMITTENT FEVER

see Malaria

INTERNAL COMBUSTION ENGINES

see also Automobiles—Engines

Boite, Mari. Amazing Story of the Combustion Engine. Pop Art Properties Staff, illus. 2013. (STEM Adventures Ser.). (ENG.). 32p. (gr. 3-4). 30.65 *(978-1-4765-3103-8(X)*, Graphic Library) Capstone Press of Coughlan Cos.
—Sleepover Girls Crafts: Amazing Recipes You Can Make & Share, 1 vol. Franco, Paula, illus. 2014. (Sleepover Girls Crafts Ser.). (ENG.). 64p. (gr. 3-4). pap. 9.95 *(978-1-62370-197-0(X))* Capstone Press of Coughlan Cos.

INTERNATIONAL COOKING

Alexander, Heather. Easy Desserts from Around the World. 2011. (Easy Cookbooks for Kids Ser.). (Illus.). 48p. (J). lib. bdg. 25.27 *(978-0-7660-3765-6(7))*; (gr. 3-18). pap. 8.95 *(978-1-59845-270-9(3))* Enslow Pubs., Inc. (Enslow Elementary).
—Easy Main Dishes from Around the World. 2011. (Easy Cookbooks for Kids Ser.). (Illus.). 48p. (J). (gr. 3-18). pap. 8.95 *(978-1-59845-273-0(8)*, Enslow Elementary) Enslow Pubs., Inc.
—Easy Snacks from Around the World. 2011. (Easy Cookbooks for Kids Ser.). (Illus.). 48p. (J). lib. bdg. 25.27 *(978-0-7660-3767-0(3))*; (gr. 3-18). pap. 8.95 *(978-1-59845-274-7(6))* Enslow Pubs., Inc. (Enslow Elementary).
Bullard, Lisa. My Food, Your Food. Schneider, Christine, illus. 2015. (Cloverleaf Books (tm) — Alike & Different Ser.). (ENG.). 24p. (gr. k-2). (J). lib. bdg. 23.99 *(978-1-4677-4903-9(6))*; pap. 6.99 *(978-1-4677-6031-7(5))* Lerner Publishing Group. (Millbrook Pr.).
Burton, Margie, et al. Food Around the World. 2011. (Early Connections Ser.). (J). *(978-1-61672-488-7(9))* Benchmark Education Co.
Cook, Deanna F. The Kids' Multicultural Cookbook: Food & Fun Around the World. Kline, Michael P., illus. 2008. (ENG.). 160p. (J). (gr. k). 16.99 *(978-0-8249-6817-5(4)*, Ideal Pubns.) Worthy Publishing.
Cornell, Kari A., ed. Holiday Cooking Around the World. Wolfe, Robert L. & Wolfe, Diane, illus. Wolfe, Robert L. & Wolfe, Diane, photos by. 2nd rev. exp. ed. 2003. (Easy Menu Ethnic Cookbooks). 72p. (J). (gr. 5-12). pap. 7.95 *(978-0-8225-4159-2(9))* Lerner Publishing Group.
Davies, Monika. Art & Culture: Desserts Around the World: Comparing Fractions (Grade 3) 2017. (Mathematics Readers Ser.). (Illus.). 32p. (gr. 3-3). 8.99 **(978-1-4807-5804-9(3))** Teacher Created Materials, Inc.
Drummond, Karen Eich & D'Amico, Joan. The Coming to America Cookbook: Delicious Recipes & Fascinating Stories from America's Many Cultures. 2005. (ENG., Illus.). 192p. (J). (gr. 3-7). pap. 16.95 *(978-0-471-48335-9(4)*, Wiley) Wiley, John & Sons, Inc.
Engfer, Lee. Desserts Around the World. 2nd rev. ed. 2003. (Easy Menu Ethnic Cookbooks 2nd Edition Ser.). (ENG., Illus.). 72p. (J). (gr. 5-12). 25.26 *(978-0-8225-4126-4(2))* Lerner Publishing Group.
Falk, Laine. This Is the Way We Eat Our Food. 2010. (Rise & Shine Ser.). (ENG.). 24p. (C). (gr. 1-2). pap. 11.95 *(978-0-531-21439-8(7))* National Geographic School Publishing, Inc.
—This Is the Way We Eat Our Food. 2009. (Scholastic News Nonfiction Readers Ser.). (ENG.). 24p. (J). (gr. 1-2). lib. bdg. 22.00 *(978-0-531-21339-1(0))* Scholastic Library Publishing.
Gale. Junior Worldmark Encyclopedia of Foods & Recipes of the World, 4 vols. 2nd ed. 2012. (Junior Worldmark Encyclopedia of Foods & Recipes of the World Ser.). (ENG., Illus.). 800p. lib. bdg. 372.00 *(978-1-4144-9071-7(2)*, UXL) Cengage Gale.
Gall, Susan B. & Edgar, Kathleen J. Junior Worldmark Encyclopedia of Foods & Recipes of the World, 4 vols. 2nd ed. 2012. (Illus.). *(978-1-4144-9075-5(5))*; *(978-1-4144-9074-8(7))*; *(978-1-4144-9073-1(9))*; *(978-1-4144-9072-4(0))* Cengage Gale. (UXL).
Gioffre, Rosalba, et al. The Kids' Cookbook: Recipes from Around the World. Wilson, Alison & Farrell, Helen, eds. Lanza, Marco, photos by. 2008. (ENG., Illus.). 120p. (J). (gr. 2-18). 19.95 *(978-88-88166-96-4(3))* McRae Bks. Srl ITA. Dist: Independent Pubs. Group.
Goldish, Meish. Baby Bug Dishes. 2009. (Extreme Cuisine Ser.). (Illus.). 24p. (YA). (gr. 1-4). lib. bdg. 22.61 *(978-1-59716-758-1(4))* Bearport Publishing Co., Inc.
—Bug-a-Licious. 2009. (Extreme Cuisine Ser.). (Illus.). 24p. (J). (gr. 1-4). lib. bdg. 22.61 *(978-1-59716-757-4(6))* Bearport Publishing Co., Inc.
—Mammal Menu. 2009. (Extreme Cuisine Ser.). (Illus.). 24p. (J). (gr. 1-4). lib. bdg. 22.61 *(978-1-59716-760-4(6))* Bearport Publishing Co., Inc.
—Spider-Tizers & Other Creepy Treats. 2009. (Extreme Cuisine Ser.). (Illus.). 24p. (J). (gr. 1-4). lib. bdg. 22.61 *(978-1-59716-759-8(2))* Bearport Publishing Co., Inc.
Gregoire, Maryellen. Morning Meals Around the World, 1 vol. Yesh, Jeff, illus. 2004. (Meals Around the World Ser.). (ENG.). 24p. (gr. k-4). per. 8.95 *(978-1-4048-1130-0(3))* Picture Window Bks.
Kalman, Bobbie. Multicultural Meals: Step-by-Step Healthy Recipes for Kids. 2003. (Kid Power Ser.). (ENG., Illus.). 32p. (J). (gr. 3). lib. bdg. *(978-0-7787-1255-8(9))* Crabtree Publishing Co.
Llanas, Sheila Griffin. Easy Breakfasts from Around the World. 2011. (Easy Cookbooks for Kids Ser.). (Illus.). 48p. (J). lib. bdg. 25.27 *(978-0-7660-3707-6(X))*; (gr. 3-18). pap. 8.95 *(978-1-59845-269-3(X))* Enslow Pubs., Inc. (Enslow Elementary).
—Easy Lunches from Around the World. 2011. (Easy Cookbooks for Kids Ser.). (Illus.). 48p. (J). lib. bdg. 25.27 *(978-0-7660-3708-3(8))*; (gr. 3-18). pap. 8.95 *(978-1-59845-272-3(X))* Enslow Pubs., Inc. (Enslow Elementary).
—Easy Vegetarian Foods from Around the World. 2011. (Easy Cookbooks for Kids Ser.). (Illus.). 48p. (J). lib. bdg. 25.27 *(978-0-7660-3764-9(9))*; (gr. 3-18). pap. 8.95 *(978-1-59845-271-6(1))* Enslow Pubs., Inc. (Enslow Elementary).
Locricchio, Matthew. The 2nd International Cookbook for Kids, 0 vols. 2008. (ENG., Illus.). 176p. (J). (gr. 3-8). 18.99 *(978-0-7614-5513-4(2)*, 9780761455134, Amazon Children's Publishing) Amazon Publishing.
Malerba, Giulia. Food Atlas: Discover All the Delicious Foods of the World. Sillani, Febe, illus. 2017. (ENG.). 72p. (J). (gr. 3-12). 19.95 **(978-1-77085-952-4(7)**, 9781770859524) Firefly Bks., Ltd.
Roten, Lindsay Grace & Webb, Lois Sinaiko. The Multicultural Cookbook for Students. 2nd rev. ed. 2009. (Illus.). 354p. (C). (gr. 6-18). 94.00 *(978-0-313-37558-3(5)*, GR7558, Greenwood) ABC-CLIO, LLC.
Wagner, Lisa. Cool World Cooking: Fun & Tasty Recipes for Kids! 2013. (ENG., Illus.). 160p. (gr. 2-7). pap. 15.95 *(978-1-938063-12-1(0)*, Mighty Media Junior Readers) Mighty Media Pr.
Watt, Fiona. Children's World Cookbook. 2004. (Children's Cooking Ser.). (Illus.). 96p. (J). lib. bdg. 21.95 *(978-1-58086-365-0(5))* EDC Publishing.
Watt, Fiona & Wilkes, Angela. Children's World Cookbook. 2004. (Children's Cooking Ser.). (ENG., Illus.). 1p. (J). pap. 13.95 *(978-0-7945-0098-6(6)*, Usborne) EDC Publishing.
Williams, Dinah. Shocking Seafood. 2009. (Extreme Cuisine Ser.). (Illus.). 24p. (J). (gr. 1-4). lib. bdg. 22.61 *(978-1-59716-761-1(4))* Bearport Publishing Co., Inc.
—Slithery, Slimy, Scaly Treats. 2009. (Extreme Cuisine Ser.). (Illus.). 24p. (J). (gr. 1-4). lib. bdg. 22.61 *(978-1-59716-762-8(2))* Bearport Publishing Co., Inc.

INTERNATIONAL COOPERATION

Here are entered works on international cooperative activities with or without the participation of governments.

see also International Organization; United Nations

Alagna, Magdalena. The Monroe Doctrine: An End to European Colonies in America. (Life in the New American Nation Ser.). 32p. 2009. (gr. 4-4). 47.90 *(978-1-61514-285-9(1))* 2004. (Illus.). (gr. 5-8). pap. 10.00 *(978-0-8239-4258-9(9))* Rosen Publishing Group, Inc., The.
Internationalism. 2010. (Key Concepts in American History Ser.). (Illus.). 128p. (gr. 6-12). 45.00 *(978-1-60413-225-0(6)*, Chelsea Hse.) Facts On File, Inc.
Marriott, Emma. Did Anything Good Come Out of World War II?, 01 vols., 1. 2016. (Innovation Through Adversity Ser.). (ENG.). 48p. (J). 30.25 *(978-1-5081-7070-9(3)*, Rosen Young Adult) Rosen Publishing Group, Inc., The.
Shoveller, Herb. Ryan & Jimmy: And the Well in Africa That Brought Them Together. 2008. (CitizenKid Ser.). (ENG., Illus.). 56p. (J). (gr. 3-7). pap. 9.95 *(978-1-55453-271-1(X))* Kids Can Pr., Ltd. CAN. Dist: Hachette Bk. Group.

INTERNATIONAL ECONOMIC RELATIONS

Brezina, Corona. How the Group of 20 Works: Cooperation among the World's Major Economic Powers. 2012. (Real World Economics Ser.). (ENG., Illus.). 80p. (J). (gr. 7-12). 33.25 *(978-1-4488-6788-2(6))* Rosen Publishing Group, Inc., The.
Harris, Nathaniel. The Debate about Globalization. 2007. (Ethical Debates Ser.). (Illus.). 48p. (YA). (gr. 5-9). lib. bdg. 29.25 *(978-1-4042-3753-7(4))* Rosen Publishing Group, Inc., The.
Heing, Bridey. Critical Perspectives on Free Trade & Globalization. 2017. (J). **(978-0-7660-9168-9(6))** Enslow Pubs., Inc.
McPherson, Stephanie Sammartino. Arctic Thaw: Climate Change & the Global Race for Energy Resources. 2014. (Illus.). 64p. (J). (gr. 6-12). lib. bdg. 34.60 *(978-1-4677-2043-4(7)*, Twenty-First Century Bks.) Lerner Publishing Group.
Spilsbury, Richard. Global Economy, 1 vol. 2012. (Hot Topics Ser.). (ENG.). 64p. (gr. 7-8). 34.65 *(978-1-4329-6038-4(5)*, NA-h) Heinemann-Raintree.
Teichmann, Iris. Globalization. 2003. (In the News Ser.). (J). lib. bdg. 24.25 *(978-1-58340-397-6(3))* Black Rabbit Bks.
Wagner, Heather Lehr, et al. The Organization of the Petroleum Exporting Countries. 2008. (Global Organizations Ser.). (Illus.). 112p. (YA). (gr. 7-12). 35.00 *(978-1-60413-102-4(0))* Facts On File, Inc.

INTERNATIONAL EXHIBITIONS

see Exhibitions

INTERNATIONAL FEDERATION

see International Organization

INTERNATIONAL LAW

see also International Cooperation; International Organization; International Relations; Pirates; Salvage; Slave Trade; War

Cefrey, Holly. The Sherman Antitrust Act: Getting Big Business under Control. 2009. (America's Industrial Society in the 19th Century Ser.). 32p. (gr. 4-4). 47.90 *(978-1-61511-347-7(9))* Rosen Publishing Group, Inc., The.
Nelson, Sheila. International Law & Playing by the Rules, Vol. 10. Russett, Bruce, ed. 2015. (United Nations: Leadership & Challenges in a Global World Ser.). (Illus.). 88p. (J). (gr. 7). lib. bdg. 24.95 *(978-1-4222-3433-4(9))* Mason Crest.
Stearman, Kaye. The Debate about Military Intervention. 2007. (Ethical Debates Ser.). (Illus.). 48p. (YA). (gr. 5-9). lib. bdg. 29.25 *(978-1-4042-3756-8(9))* Rosen Publishing Group, Inc., The.

INTERNATIONAL ORGANIZATION

Here are entered works on theories and efforts leading toward world-wide or regional political organization of nations.

see also International Cooperation; International Law; World Politics

also names of specific organizations, e.g. United Nations, etc.

Exploring World Governments, 8 vols., Set. Incl. Anarchism. Buckley, A. M. lib. bdg. 37.07 *(978-1-61714-788-3(5))*; Communism. Vander Hook, Sue. lib. bdg. 37.07 *(978-1-61714-789-0(3))*; Democracy. Vander Hook, Sue. lib. bdg. 37.07 *(978-1-61714-790-6(7))*; Dictatorships. Marcovitz, Hal. lib. bdg. 37.07 *(978-1-61714-791-3(5))*; Monarchies. Gimpel, Diane. lib. bdg. 37.07 *(978-1-61714-792-0(3))*; Parliaments. Pratt, Mary K. lib. bdg. 37.07 *(978-1-61714-793-7(1))*; Theocracies. Lucerne, Sam. lib. bdg. 37.07 *(978-1-61714-794-4(X))*; Totalitarianism. Cemak, Linda. lib. bdg. 37.07 *(978-1-61714-795-1(8))*; (J). (gr. 9-12). (Exploring World Governments Ser.: 8). (ENG., Illus.). 160p. 2011. Set lib. bdg. 296.56 *(978-1-61714-787-6(7)*, Essential Library) ABDO Publishing Co.
Global Organizations Set, 13-Volumes. 2009. (Global Organizations Ser.). (C). (gr. 9-18). 455.00 *(978-0-7910-9924-7(5)*, Chelsea Hse.) Facts On File, Inc.
Haerens, Margaret. The World Trade Organization. 2010. (Opposing Viewpoints Ser.). (Illus.). 240p. 42.95 *(978-0-7377-4785-0(4))*; pap. 29.45 *(978-0-7377-4786-7(2))* Cengage Gale. (Greenhaven Pr., Inc.).
January, Brendan. Globalize It! The Stories of the IMF, the World Bank, the WTO - And Those Who Protest. 2003. (Single Titles Ser.). (Illus.). 144p. (gr. 7-18). 26.90 *(978-0-7613-2417-1(8)*, Twenty-First Century Bks.) Lerner Publishing Group.
Spalding, Maddie. Guarding the Centers for Disease Control & Prevention. 2016. (Highly Guarded Places Ser.). (ENG.). 24p. (J). (gr. 2-5). 28.50 *(978-1-5038-0810-2(6)*, 210649) Child's World, Inc., The.

INTERNATIONAL RELATIONS

see also Diplomacy; Diplomats; Disarmament; International Cooperation; International Economic Relations; International Law; International Organization; Military Weapons; Monroe Doctrine; Peace; Security, International

also names of countries with the subdivision Foreign Relations, e.g. U. S.—Foreign Relations, etc.

Alagna, Magdalena. The Monroe Doctrine: An End to European Colonies in America. (Life in the New American Nation Ser.). 32p. 2009. (gr. 4-4). 47.90 *(978-1-61514-285-9(1))* 2004. (Illus.). (gr. 5-8). pap. 10.00 *(978-0-8239-4258-9(9))* Rosen Publishing Group, Inc., The.
Challen, Paul C. Migration in the 21st Century: How Will Globalization & Climate Change Affect Migration & Settlement? 2010. (Investigating Human Migration & Settlement Ser.). (ENG., Illus.). 48p. (J). (gr. 5-8). *(978-0-7787-5181-6(3))*; pap. *(978-0-7787-5196-0(1))* Crabtree Publishing Co.
Crayton, Lisa A. & La Bella, Laura. Globalization: What It Is & How It Works. 2016. (Economics in the 21st Century Ser.). (ENG.). 96p. (J). (gr. 8-8). lib. bdg. 34.60 *(978-0-7660-7244-2(4))* Enslow Pubs., Inc.
East, Mike, et al. Global Issues No. 3: Project Organizer. Lelievre, Barclay, ed. 2010. (IB MYP Ser.). (ENG., Illus.). 80p. 19.00 *(978-0-19-918081-3(4))* Oxford Univ. Pr., Inc.
Foreign Policy Research Institute Staff, ed. Modern Middle East Nations & Their Strategic Places in the World, 25 vols., Set. 2003. (Illus.). 112,128p. (YA). (gr. 7-18). lib. bdg. *(978-1-59084-504-2(8))* Mason Crest.
Gale Editors, ed. Worldmark Conflict & Diplomacy: 2 Volume Set, 2 vols. 2014. (Worldmark Conflict & Diplomacy Ser.). (ENG.). 1000p. 329.00 *(978-1-57302-726-7(X))* Cengage Gale.
Haugen, David M. Globalization. 2010. (Opposing Viewpoints Ser.). (Illus.). 240p. (J). pap. 29.45 *(978-0-7377-4772-0(2)*, Greenhaven Pr., Inc.) Cengage Gale.
Hoffman, Aaron M. Building Trust: Overcoming Suspicion in International Conflict. Rosenau, James N. & Stone, Russell, eds. 2005. (SUNY Series in Global Politics Ser.). (Illus.). 232p. 55.00 *(978-0-7914-6635-3(3)*, Suny Pr.) State Univ. of New York Pr.
Immell, Myra. Homeland Security. 2009. (At Issue Ser.). (ENG., Illus.). 128p. (gr. 10-12). pap. 27.80 *(978-0-7377-4421-7(9))* Cengage Gale.
Immell, Myra, ed. Homeland Security. 2009. (At Issue Ser.). (ENG., Illus.). 128p. (gr. 10-12). 39.40 *(978-0-7377-4420-0(0))* Cengage Gale.
Johnson, Cynthia. Worldmark Conflict & Diplomacy. 2014. (J). *(978-1-57302-727-4(8))* Cengage Gale.
Leppman, Elizabeth & Andrews, David. Business Without Borders: Globalization, 1 vol. 2010. (Global Marketplace Ser.). (ENG.). 56p. (gr. 6-9). 34.65 *(978-1-4329-3933-5(5)*, NA-h) Heinemann-Raintree.
McGregor, Harriet. Globalization. 2011. (Global Issues Ser.). (Illus.). 48p. (YA). (gr. 5-8). lib. bdg. 29.25 *(978-1-4488-1878-5(8)*, Rosen Reference) Rosen Publishing Group, Inc., The.
McPherson, Stephanie Sammartino. Arctic Thaw: Climate Change & the Global Race for Energy Resources. 2014. (Illus.). 64p. (J). (gr. 6-12). lib. bdg. 34.60 *(978-1-4677-2043-4(7)*, Twenty-First Century Bks.) Lerner Publishing Group.
Merino, Noël. Globalization. 2009. (Introducing Issues with Opposing Viewpoints Ser.). (ENG., Illus.). 144p. (gr. 10-12). 42.00 *(978-0-7377-4476-7(6))* Cengage Gale.
Nelson, Robin. Working with Others. 2006. (Pull Ahead Bks.). (Illus.). 32p. (J). (gr. 3-7). lib. bdg. 22.60 *(978-0-8225-3486-0(X)*, Lerner Pubns.) Lerner Publishing Group.
Nelson, Sheila. Cultural Globalization & Celebrating Diversity, Vol. 10. Russett, Bruce, ed. 2015. (United Nations: Leadership & Challenges in a Global World Ser.). 88p. (J). (gr. 7). lib. bdg. 24.95 *(978-1-4222-3429-7(0))* Mason Crest.
Pavlovic, Zoran. The Changing Global Economy. 2009. (Global Connections Ser.). (Illus.). 112p. (gr. 5-8). 35.00 *(978-1-60413-283-0(3)*, Chelsea Hse.) Facts On File, Inc.
Prentzas, Scott. Radar Guns. 2009. (21st Century Skills Library: Global Products Ser.). (ENG., Illus.). 32p. (gr. 4-8). lib. bdg. 28.50 *(978-1-60279-507-5(X)*, 200322) Cherry Lake Publishing.
Spilsbury, Louise. World Wars & Globalization, 1914 to 2010. 2010. (Curriculum Connections: Atlas of World History Ser.). 39.95 *(978-1-933834-70-2(6))* Brown Bear Bks.

INTERNATIONAL SECURITY

see Security, International

INTERNATIONAL TRADE

see Commerce

INTERNET

see also World Wide Web

Abramavitz. Online Privacy & Healthcare. 2014. (Privacy in the Online World). (ENG., Illus.). 80p. (YA). lib. bdg. (978-1-60152-652-6(0)) ReferencePoint Pr., Inc.

Abramovitz, Melissa. How Do Computers Talk to One Another? 2015. (ENG., Illus.). 32p. (J). (gr. k-2). 26.65 (978-1-4677-8075-9(8)) Lerner Publishing Group.

—Online Predators. 2016. (ENG.). 80p. (J). (gr. 5-12). lib. bdg. (978-1-68282-092-6(0)) ReferencePoint Pr., Inc.

Adams, Sabrina. Everything You Need to Know about Trolls & Cybermobs. 2017. (Need to Know Library). 64p. (J). (gr. 12-11). 34.45 **(978-1-5081-7420-2(2))**; pap. 12.95 **(978-1-5081-7418-9(0))** Rosen Publishing Group, Inc., The. (Rosen Young Adult).

Albee, Michael J. Elements of Research: The Student's Guide to Avoiding Plagiarism in the Information Age. 2003. (Illus.). 140p. per. (978-0-9745405-0-4(1)) Albee, Michael.

Allman, Toney. Internet Predators. 2007. (Ripped from the Headlines Ser.). 64p. (J). (gr. 7-12). 23.95 (978-1-60217-000-1(2)) Erickson Pr.

Axelrod-Contrada, Joan. Reno V. ACLU Internet Censorship. 2006. (Supreme Court Milestones Ser.). (Illus.). 128p. (gr. 7-7). lib. bdg. 42.79 (978-0-7614-2144-3(0), Benchmark Bks.) Marshall Cavendish Corp.

Bailey, Diane. Cyber Ethics. (Cyber Citizenship & Cyber Safety Ser.). 48p. (gr. 5-5). 2009. 53.00 (978-1-61512-102-1(1), Rosen Reference) 2008. (Illus.). (YA). lib. bdg. 29.25 (978-1-4042-1349-4(X), 1276926) Rosen Publishing Group, Inc., The.

Barbour, William. Censorship. 2010. (Opposing Viewpoints Ser.). (Illus.). 240p. (J). pap. 29.45 (978-0-7377-4762-1(5), Greenhaven Pr., Inc.) Cengage Gale.

Barrington, Richard. Getting Paid to Blog & Vlog. 2016. (Turning Your Tech Hobbies into a Career Ser.). 00080p. (J). (gr. 7-7). 35.75 (978-1-5081-7290-1(0)) Rosen Publishing Group, Inc., The.

Berlatsky, Noah. Netiquette & Online Ethics. 2013. (Opposing Viewpoints Ser.). (ENG., Illus.). 224p. (gr. 10-12). pap. 33.80 (978-0-7377-6429-1(5)); lib. bdg. 48.80 (978-0-7377-6428-4(7)) Cengage Gale. (Greenhaven Pr., Inc.).

—Social Networking. 2013. (Global Viewpoints Ser.). (ENG., Illus.). 224p. (J). (gr. 10-12). pap. 31.70 (978-0-7377-6446-8(5), Greenhaven Pr., Inc.) Cengage Gale.

Berlatsky, Noah, ed. Social Networking. 2013. (Global Viewpoints Ser.). (ENG., Illus.). 224p. (J). (gr. 10-12). lib. bdg. 40.45 (978-0-7377-6270-9(5), Greenhaven Pr., Inc.) Cengage Gale.

Bingham, Jane, et al. The Usborne Internet-Linked Encyclopedia of World History: Prehistoric, Ancient, Medieval, Last 500 Years. 2004. (World History Ser.). (ENG., Illus.). 1p. (J). (gr. 3-18). 39.95 (978-0-7460-4168-0(3)) EDC Publishing.

Birley, Shane. How to Be a Blogger & Vlogger in 10 Easy Lessons: Learn How to Create Your Own Blog, Vlog, or Podcast & Get It Out in the Blogosphere! 2016. (Super Skills Ser.). (ENG.). 64p. (J). (gr. 7-12). spiral bd. 12.95 (978-1-63322-105-5(9), Walter Foster Jr) Quarto Publishing Group USA.

Bodden, Valerie. Internet. 2008. pap. 9.95 (978-0-89812-530-6(8)); (Illus.). 24p. (J). lib. bdg. 24.25 (978-1-58341-557-3(2)) Creative Co., The. (Creative Education).

—Using the Internet. 2012. (Research for Writing Ser.). 48p. (gr. 5-12). 23.95 (978-1-60818-207-7(X), Creative Education) Creative Co., The.

Brezina, Corona. Sergey Brin, Larry Page, Eric Schmidt, & Google. 2012. (Internet Biographies Ser.). (ENG., Illus.). 128p. (J). (gr. 7-12). lib. bdg. 34.60 (978-1-4488-6911-4(0)) Rosen Publishing Group, Inc., The.

Brown, Tracy. Facebook Safety & Privacy. 2013. (21st Century Safety & Privacy Ser.). 64p. (J). (gr. 5-8). 31.95 (978-1-4488-9569-4(3)); pap. 77.70 (978-1-4488-9581-6(2)); pap. 12.95 (978-1-4488-9580-9(4)) Rosen Publishing Group, Inc., The.

Buell, Tonya. Careers with Successful Dot-Com Companies. 2005. (Library of e-Commerce & Internet Careers Ser.). (Illus.). 64p. (YA). (gr. 7-12). lib. bdg. 31.95 (978-0-8239-3424-9(1)) Rosen Publishing Group, Inc., The.

Burgan, Michael. The Making of the Social Network: An Interactive Modern History Adventure, 1 vol. 2014. (You Choose: Modern History Ser.). (ENG.). 112p. (gr. 3-4). pap. 6.95 (978-1-4765-5219-4(3)); 31.99 (978-1-4765-4188-4(4)) Capstone Press of Coughlan Cos. (You Choose Bks.).

Burns, Jan. Build Your Online Community: Blogging, Message Boards, Newsgroups, & More. 2011. (Issues in Focus Today Ser.). (Illus.). 104p. (J). lib. bdg. 33.27 (978-1-59845-130-6(8)) Enslow Pubs., Inc.

Chmielewski, Gary. How Did That Get to My House? Internet. 2009. (Community Connections: How Did That Get to My House? Ser.). (ENG.). 24p. (gr. 2-5). lib. bdg. 25.64 (978-1-60279-477-1(4), 200250) Cherry Lake Publishing.

Coleman, Miriam. Share It: Using Digital Tools & Media. 2012. (Core Skills Ser.). (ENG., Illus.). 32p. (J). (gr. 3-6). pap. 10.00 (978-1-4488-7526-9(9), PowerKids Pr.) Rosen Publishing Group, Inc., The.

Colt, James P. & Rogers, Marcus K. Cyberpredators. 2011. (Cybersafety Ser.). (Illus.). 136p. (gr. 6-12). 39.95 (978-1-60413-698-2(7)) Facts On File, Inc.

Combatting Shaming & Toxic Communities. 2016. (Combatting Shaming & Toxic Communities Ser.). 64p. (gr. 7-7). 172.25 (978-1-4777-8545-4(0), Rosen Young Adult) Rosen Publishing Group, Inc., The.

Cornell, Kari. Facebook Founder & Internet Entrepreneur Mark Zuckerberg. 2016. (STEM Trailblazer Bios Ser.). (ENG.). 32p. (J). (gr. 2-5). 26.65 (978-1-4677-9527-2(5), Lerner Pubns.) Lerner Publishing Group.

Cornwall, Phyllis. Mind Your Manners Online. 2012. (Explorer Junior Library: Information Explorer Junior Ser.). (ENG., Illus.). 24p. (J). (gr. 1-4). pap. 12.79 (978-1-61080-388-5(4), 201325); lib. bdg. 28.50 (978-1-61080-363-2(9), 201260) Cherry Lake Publishing.

—Play It Safe Online. 2012. (Explorer Junior Library: Information Explorer Junior Ser.). (ENG., Illus.). 24p. (J). (gr. 1-4). pap. 12.79 (978-1-61080-389-2(2), 201326); lib. bdg. 28.50 (978-1-61080-364-9(7), 201262) Cherry Lake Publishing.

—Super Smart Information Strategies: Online Etiquette & Safety. 2010. (Explorer Library: Information Explorer Ser.). (ENG.). 32p. (gr. 4-8). lib. bdg. 28.50 (978-1-60279-956-1(3), 200637) Cherry Lake Publishing.

Craig, Tom. Internet: Technology, People, Process. 2003. (Media Wise Ser.). 64p. (J). lib. bdg. 28.50 (978-1-58340-257-3(8)) Black Rabbit Bks.

Culp, Jennifer. Online Gaming Safety & Privacy. 2013. (21st Century Safety & Privacy Ser.). 64p. (J). (gr. 5-8). pap. 77.70 (978-1-4488-9585-4(5)); pap. 12.95 (978-1-4488-9584-7(7)); (Illus.). 31.95 (978-1-4488-9570-0(7)) Rosen Publishing Group, Inc., The.

Curatola Knowles, Carmela N. Piano & Laylee & the Cyberbully. Lewellen, Emily, illus. 2011. (J). pap. (978-1-56484-279-4(7)) International Society for Technology in Education.

—Piano & Laylee Go Online. 2011. (J). (978-1-56484-292-3(4)) International Society for Technology in Education.

—Piano & Laylee Go Online. Lewellen, Emily, illus. 2011. (J). pap. (978-1-56484-277-0(0)) International Society for Technology in Education.

Des Chenes, Elizabeth, ed. The Internet. 2007. (Introducing Issues with Opposing Viewpoints Ser.). (ENG., Illus.). 136p. (YA). (gr. 7-12). lib. bdg. 36.95 (978-0-7377-3567-3(8)) Cengage Gale.

Doherty, Gillian. Birds. 2004. (Discovery Program Ser.). (SPA & ENG., Illus.). (J). (gr. 2-18). 1p. pap. 8.95 (978-0-7460-3738-6(4)); 64p. lib. bdg. 16.95 (978-1-58086-334-6(5)) EDC Publishing.

Dugan, Christine. Tech World: The Language of Social Media (Level 5) 2017. (Exploring Reading Ser.). (Illus.). 48p. (J). (gr. 5-5). pap. 10.99 **(978-1-4258-4989-4(X))** Teacher Created Materials, Inc.

Eck, Michael. The Internet: Inside & Out. (Technology: Blueprints of the Future Ser.). 48p. (gr. 4-4). 2009. 53.00 (978-1-60853-286-5(0)) 2005. (Illus.). (YA). lib. bdg. 29.25 (978-0-8239-6108-5(7)) Rosen Publishing Group, Inc., The.

Ekman, Joseph Anthony. Kids Ultimate Online Homework Resource Guide 2004. 2003. spiral bd. 14.95 (978-0-9745406-0-3(9)) Duke Publishing & Software Corp.

Endsley, Kezia. How to Do Great Online Research. 2015. (J). lib. bdg. (978-1-62713-539-9(1)) Cavendish Square Publishing.

Engdahl, Sylvia. Internet Activism. Greenhaven Press Editors, ed. 2013. (Current Controversies Ser.). (ENG., Illus.). 224p. (gr. 10-12). pap. 32.00 (978-0-7377-6877-0(0)); lib. bdg. 46.40 (978-0-7377-6876-3(2)) Cengage Gale. (Greenhaven Pr., Inc.).

Espejo, Roman. Sexting. 2015. (At Issue Ser.). (ENG.). 128p. (J). (gr. 10-12). pap. 27.80 (978-0-7377-7186-2(0), Greenhaven Pr., Inc.) Cengage Gale.

—What Is the Impact of Twitter? Greenhaven Press Editors, ed. 2013. (At Issue Ser.). (ENG.). 128p. (gr. 10-12). pap. 27.80 (978-0-7377-6216-7(0)); lib. bdg. 39.40 (978-0-7377-6215-0(2)) Cengage Gale. (Greenhaven Pr., Inc.).

Etingoff, Kim. Navigating Cyberspace. Stephens, Ronald, ed. 2014. (Safety First Ser.: 11). 48p. (J). (gr. 5-18). 20.95 (978-1-4222-3049-7(X)) Mason Crest.

Evan Williams, Biz Stone, & Jack Dorsey & Twitter. 2011. (Graphic Nonfiction Biographies Ser.). (ENG.). 48p. (YA). (gr. 5-8). (978-1-4488-5551-3(9)); pap. (978-1-4488-5647-3(7)) Rosen Publishing Group, Inc., The. (Rosen Reference).

Fonticharo, Kristin. Getting Around Online. 2012. (Explorer Junior Library: Information Explorer Junior Ser.). (ENG., Illus.). 24p. (gr. 1-4). pap. 12.79 (978-1-61080-391-5(4), 201328); lib. bdg. 28.50 (978-1-61080-366-3(3), 201266) Cherry Lake Publishing.

Freedman, Jeri. Online Safety. 2011. (J). 167.70 (978-1-4488-4858-4(X), Rosen Reference); (Illus.). 48p. (YA). (gr. 5-9). lib. bdg. 29.25 (978-1-4488-4577-4(7)) Rosen Publishing Group, Inc., The.

Friedman, Lauri S. Web 2. 0. 2011. (Writing the Critical Essay: an Opposing Viewpoints Guide Ser.). 128p. lib. bdg. 33.75 (978-0-7377-5026-3(X), Greenhaven Pr., Inc.) Cengage Gale.

Furgang, Adam. Searching Online for Image, Audio, & Video Files. 2009. (Digital & Information Literacy Ser.). (Illus.). 48p. (YA). (gr. 5-8). lib. bdg. 29.25 (978-1-4358-5318-8(0)) Rosen Publishing Group, Inc., The.

—20 Great Career-Building Activities Using YouTube. 2016. (Social Media Career Building Ser.). 00064p. (J). (gr. 7-7). 34.45 (978-1-5081-7264-2(1)) Rosen Publishing Group, Inc., The.

Furgang, Kathy. Internet Surveillance & How to Protect Your Privacy. 2016. (Digital & Information Literacy Ser.). 00048p. (J). (gr. 6-6). pap. 11.75 (978-1-4994-6519-8(X)) Rosen Publishing Group, Inc., The.

—20 Great Career-Building Activities Using Twitter. 2016. (Social Media Career Building Ser.). 00064p. (J). (gr. 7-7). 34.45 (978-1-5081-7268-0(4)) Rosen Publishing Group, Inc., The.

Gaines, Ann Graham. Ace Your Internet Research. 2009. (Ace It! Information Literacy Ser.). (Illus.). 48p. (J). (gr. 2-5). lib. bdg. 25.27 (978-0-7660-3392-4(9)) Enslow Pubs., Inc.

Gerber, Larry. Cited! Identifying Credible Information Online. 2010. (Digital & Information Literacy Ser.). (ENG.). 48p. (YA). pap. 11.75 (978-1-4488-0599-0(6)); lib. bdg. 29.25 (978-1-4358-9430-3(8)) Rosen Publishing Group, Inc., The. (Rosen Reference).

Gifford, Clive. Super Social Media & Awesome Online Safety. 2017. 32p. (J). **(978-0-7787-3630-1(X))** Crabtree Publishing Co.

—Web Page Design. 2017. 32p. (J). **(978-0-7787-3631-8(8))** Crabtree Publishing Co.

Gilbert, Sara. Built for Success: the Story of Twitter. 2015. (Built for Success Ser.). (ENG.). 48p. (J). (gr. 5-8). pap. 12.00 (978-0-89812-985-4(0), Creative Paperbacks) Creative Co., The.

—The Story of Amazon. Com. 2013. (Built for Success Ser.). (ENG.). 48p. (J). (gr. 4-7). pap. 12.00 (978-0-89812-759-1(9), Creative Paperbacks) Creative Co., The.

—The Story of Amazon.com. 2012. (Built for Success Ser.). (Illus.). 48p. (J). (gr. 5-12). 23.95 (978-1-60818-174-2(X), Creative Education) Creative Co., The.

—The Story of Google. (Illus.). (J). (gr. 5-17). 2011. (ENG.). 48p. pap. 12.00 (978-1-897563-03-8(5), Creative Paperbacks) 2008. 46p. 22.95 (978-1-58341-605-1(6)) Creative Co., The.

Glaser, Jason. Careers in Online Retailing. 2013. 80p. (YA). (gr. 9-12). 33.25 (978-1-4488-9595-3(2)) Rosen Publishing Group, Inc., The.

Goranson, Christopher. Careers as a Webmaster: Maintaining the Site. 2009. (Library of E-Commerce & Internet Careers Ser.). 64p. (gr. 5-5). 58.50 (978-1-60853-579-8(7)) Rosen Publishing Group, Inc., The.

Goranson, Christopher D. Careers as a Webmaster: Maintaining the Site. 2005. (Library of e-Commerce & Internet Careers Ser.). (Illus.). 64p. (YA). (gr. 7-12). lib. bdg. 31.95 (978-0-8239-3419-5(5)) Rosen Publishing Group, Inc., The.

Gordon, Sherri Mabry. Downloading Copyrighted Stuff from the Internet: Stealing or Fair Use? 2005. (Issues in Focus Today Ser.). (Illus.). 104p. (J). (gr. 6-12). lib. bdg. 33.27 (978-0-7660-2164-8(5)) Enslow Pubs., Inc.

Gray, Leon. What Is a Search Engine & How Do I Use It? 2013. (Practical Technology Ser.). 48p. (J). (gr. 5-8). 25.85 (978-1-62275-081-8(0)); pap. 14.05 (978-1-62275-082-5(9)) Rosen Publishing Group, Inc., The.

Grayson, Robert. Managing Your Digital Footprint. 2011. (Digital & Information Literacy Ser.). (Illus.). 48p. (YA). pap. 11.75 (978-1-4488-2290-4(4)); lib. bdg. 29.25 (978-1-4488-1319-3(0)) Rosen Publishing Group, Inc., The. (Rosen Reference).

Green, Lyric & Graham Gaines, Ann. Future Ready Internet Research Skills. 2017. (Future Ready Project Skills Ser.). 48p. (J). (gr. 3-4). pap. 11.70 **(978-0-7660-8769-9(7))**; lib. bdg. 27.93 **(978-0-7660-8655-5(0))** Enslow Pubs., Inc.

Green, Sara. Larry Page. 2014. (Tech Icons Ser.). (ENG., Illus.). 24p. (J). (gr. 3-8). lib. bdg. 25.95 (978-1-60014-990-0(1), Pilot Bks.) Bellwether Media.

Green, Sara. Netflix. 2017. (Brands We Know Ser.). (ENG., Illus.). 24p. (J). (gr. 3-8). 25.95 **(978-1-62617-653-9(1)**, Pilot Bks.) Bellwether Media.

Gregson, Susan R. Cyber Literacy: Evaluating the Reliability of Data. 2008. (Cyber Citizenship & Cyber Safety Ser.). (Illus.). 48p. (YA). (gr. 5-9). lib. bdg. 29.25 (978-1-4042-1353-1(8)) Rosen Publishing Group, Inc., The.

Greve, Meg. The Internet. 2014. (ENG.). 24p. (gr. k-3). 28.50 (978-1-62717-643-9(8)) Rourke Educational Media.

Haegele, Katie. E-Advertising & E-Marketing: Online Opportunities. 2005. (Library of e-Commerce & Internet Careers Ser.). (Illus.). 64p. (YA). (gr. 7-12). lib. bdg. 31.95 (978-0-8239-3426-3(8)) Rosen Publishing Group, Inc., The.

—E-Advertising & E-Marketing Online Opportunities. 2009. (Library of E-Commerce & Internet Careers Ser.). 64p. (gr. 5-5). 58.50 (978-1-60853-585-9(1)) Rosen Publishing Group, Inc., The.

Hall, Kevin. Creating & Building Your Own Youtube Channel. 2016. (Digital & Information Literacy Ser.). 00048p. (J). (gr. 6-6). pap. 11.75 (978-1-5081-7326-7(5), Rosen Reference) Rosen Publishing Group, Inc., The.

Hamilton, John. Internet, 1 vol. 2005. (Straight to the Source Ser.). (ENG., Illus.). 32p. (gr. k-6). 27.07 (978-1-59197-544-1(1), Checkerboard Library) ABDO Publishing Co.

Hamilton, Tracy Brown. Combatting Internet Shaming. 2016. (Combatting Shaming & Toxic Communities Ser.). 64p. (J). (gr. 7-7). 34.45 (978-1-5081-7116-4(5)) Rosen Publishing Group, Inc., The.

Hankison, McP. Surfing the Internet Safely: A Guide for Teens & Adults. 2009. 84p. pap. 11.95 (978-0-595-52405-1(2)) iUniverse, Inc.

Hankison, Whitney. Surfing the Internet Safely: A Workbook for Children. 2007. 68p. per. 9.95 (978-0-595-44630-8(2)) iUniverse, Inc.

Harmon, Daniel E. Careers in Internet Security. 2011. (Careers in Computer Technology Ser.). (ENG.). 80p. (YA). lib. bdg. 33.25 (978-1-4488-1315-5(8)) Rosen Publishing Group, Inc., The.

Harris, Ashley Rae. Facebook: The Company & Its Founders, 1 vol. 2012. (Technology Pioneers Set 2 Ser.). (ENG.). 112p. (J). (gr. 6-12). lib. bdg. 35.64 (978-1-61783-332-8(0), Essential Library) ABDO Publishing Co.

Haugen, Hayley Mitchell. Internet Safety. 2008. (Issues That Concern You Ser.). (ENG., Illus.). 144p. (gr. 10-12). lib. bdg. 42.00 (978-0-7377-3986-2(X), LML02109-239947, Greenhaven Pr., Inc.) Cengage Gale.

Head, Honor. How to Handle Cyberbullying. 2014. (Under Pressure Ser.). (Illus.). 48p. (gr. 4-7). 37.10 (978-1-59920-826-8(1)) Black Rabbit Bks.

Henderson, Harry. Online Privacy & Government. 2014. (Privacy in the Online World). (ENG., Illus.). 80p. (J). lib. bdg. (978-1-60152-726-4(8)) ReferencePoint Pr., Inc.

Henneberg, Susan. 20 Great Career-Building Activities Using Tumblr. 2016. (Social Media Career Building Ser.). 00064p. (J). (gr. 7-7). 34.45 (978-1-5081-7266-6(8)) Rosen Publishing Group, Inc., The.

Heos, Bridget. Be Safe on the Internet. Baroncelli, Silvia, illus. 2015. (Be Safe! Ser.). 24p. (J). 25.65 (978-1-60753-445-7(2)) Amicus Publishing.

Heppermann, Christine. Twitter: The Company & Its Founders, 1 vol. 2012. (Technology Pioneers Set 2 Ser.). (ENG.). 112p. (J). (gr. 6-12). lib. bdg. 35.64 (978-1-61783-337-3(1), Essential Library) ABDO Publishing Co.

Herrington, Lisa M. Internet Safety. 2012. (Rookie Read-About(tm) Safety Ser.). (ENG., Illus.). 32p. (J). lib. bdg. 25.00 (978-0-531-28971-6(0)); (gr. -1-1). pap. 5.95 (978-0-531-29273-0(8)) Scholastic Library Publishing.

Herumin, Wendy. Censorship on the Internet: From Filters to Freedom of Speech. 2004. (Issues in Focus Ser.). (Illus.). 128p. (J). lib. bdg. 27.94 (978-0-7660-1946-1(2)) Enslow Pubs., Inc.

Higa, Ryan. Ryan Higa's How to Write Good. 2017. (ENG.). 208p. (YA). (gr. 7-17). 19.99 **(978-0-316-46407-9(4)**, Poppy) Little, Brown Bks. for Young Readers.

Hile, Lori. Social Networks & Blogs. 2011. (Illus.). 56p. (J). (978-1-4062-1762-9(X)) Heinemann-Raintree.

Hillstrom, Kevin. The Internet Revolution. 2005. (Defining Moments Ser.). (Illus.). 224p. lib. bdg. 55.00 (978-0-7808-0767-9(7)) Omnigraphics, Inc.

Hollander, Barbara Gottfried. I Am a Digital Addict, Now What? 2016. (Teen Life 411 Ser.). 00112p. (J). (gr. 7-7). 37.10 (978-1-5081-7200-0(5)) Rosen Publishing Group, Inc., The.

Hovanec, Erin. Careers as a Content Provider for the Web. 2009. (Library of E-Commerce & Internet Careers Ser.). 64p. (gr. 5-5). 58.50 (978-1-60853-578-1(9)) Rosen Publishing Group, Inc., The.

Hovanec, Erin M. Careers as Content Provider for the Web. 2005. (Library of e-Commerce & Internet Careers Ser.). (Illus.). 64p. (YA). (gr. 7-12). lib. bdg. 31.95 (978-0-8239-3418-8(7)) Rosen Publishing Group, Inc., The.

Hubbard, Ben. Our Digital Planet. 2017. (Our Digital Planet Ser.). (ENG.). 24p. (gr. k-2). 93.28 (978-1-4846-3617-6(1), Heinemann Read & Learn) Heinemann-Raintree.

—Staying Safe Online. 2017. (Our Digital Planet Ser.). (ENG., Illus.). 24p. (gr. k-2). lib. bdg. 23.32 (978-1-4846-3600-8(7), Heinemann Read & Learn) Heinemann-Raintree.

—Using Digital Technology. 2017. (Our Digital Planet Ser.). (ENG., Illus.). 24p. (gr. k-2). lib. bdg. 23.32 (978-1-4846-3597-1(3)) Heinemann-Raintree.

Hunter, Nick. Internet Safety, 1 vol. 2011. (Hot Topics Ser.). (ENG.). 56p. (gr. 7-8). 34.65 (978-1-4329-4871-9(7), NA-h) Heinemann-Raintree.

Hurt, Avery Elizabeth. Everything You Need to Know about Sextortion. 2017. (Need to Know Library). 64p. (J). (gr. 12-11). 34.45 **(978-1-5081-7408-0(3))**; pap. 12.95 **(978-1-5081-7406-6(7))** Rosen Publishing Group, Inc., The. (Rosen Young Adult).

Internet. 3rd rev. ed. 2006. (Careers in Focus Ser.). (Illus.). 192p. (gr. 6-12). 32.95 (978-0-8160-6564-6(0), Ferguson Publishing Co.) Facts On File, Inc.

Internet Career Biographies, 6 vols., Set. Incl. Jerry Yang & David Filo: The Founders of Yahoo! Weston, Michael R. lib. bdg. 34.60 (978-1-4042-0718-9(X)); Marc Andreessen & Jim Clark: The Founders of Netscape. Payment, Simone. lib. bdg. 34.60 (978-1-4042-0719-6(8)); Pierre Omidyar: The Founder of Ebay. Viegas, Jennifer. lib. bdg. 34.60 (978-1-4042-0715-8(5)); Shawn Fanning: The Founder of Napster. Ambrosek, Renee. lib. bdg. 34.60 (978-1-4042-0720-2(1)); (Illus.). 112p. (YA). (gr. 7-12). 2006. 2007. Set lib. bdg. 191.70 (978-1-4042-1021-9(0)) Rosen Publishing Group, Inc., The.

Internet Dos & Don'ts. 2013. (Internet DOs & DON'ts Ser.). 24p. (J). (gr. k-2). 135.60 (978-1-4777-1574-1(6)); pap. 49.50 (978-1-4777-1679-3(3)); pap. 297.00 (978-1-4777-1680-9(7)) Rosen Publishing Group, Inc., The. (PowerKids Pr.).

Internet Guide. 2004. (Internet Guide Ser.). (gr. k-6). 30.00 (978-0-328-02542-8(9)) Addison-Wesley Educational Pubs., Inc.

Jakubiak, David J. Kids Online, 6 vols., Set. Incl. Smart Kid's Guide to Avoiding Online Predators. lib. bdg. 22.60 (978-1-4042-8117-2(7)); Smart Kid's Guide to Doing Internet Research. lib. bdg. 22.60 (978-1-4042-8116-5(9)); Smart Kid's Guide to Internet Privacy. lib. bdg. 22.60 (978-1-4042-8118-9(5)); Smart Kid's Guide to Playing Online Games. lib. bdg. 22.60 (978-1-4042-8115-8(0)); (Illus.). 24p. (J). (gr. 2-6). 2009. 2009. Set lib. bdg. 127.50 (978-1-4358-8460-1(4), PowerKids Pr.) Rosen Publishing Group, Inc., The.

—A Smart Kid's Guide to Avoiding Online Predators. (Illus.). 24p. (J). 2010. pap. 8.25 (978-1-4358-3354-8(6)) 2009. (gr. 2-6). lib. bdg. 22.60 (978-1-4042-8117-2(7)) Rosen Publishing Group, Inc., The. (PowerKids Pr.).

—A Smart Kid's Guide to Doing Internet Research. (Illus.). 24p. (J). 2010. pap. 8.25 (978-1-4358-3352-4(X)) 2009. (gr. 2-6). lib. bdg. 22.60 (978-1-4042-8116-5(9)) Rosen Publishing Group, Inc., The. (PowerKids Pr.).

—A Smart Kid's Guide to Internet Privacy. (J). 2010. pap. 8.25 (978-1-4358-3356-2(2)) 2009. (Illus.). 24p. (gr. 2-6). lib. bdg. 22.60 (978-1-4042-8118-9(5)) Rosen Publishing Group, Inc., The. (PowerKids Pr.).

—A Smart Kid's Guide to Social Networking Online. 2010. (Illus.). 24p. (J). pap. 8.25 (978-1-4358-3358-6(9), 1300427, PowerKids Pr.) Rosen Publishing Group, Inc., The.

Jennings, Rosemary. Safe Online. 2016. (Safety Smarts Ser.). 00024p. (J). (gr. k-1). 23.60 (978-1-4994-2998-5(3)); pap. 8.25 (978-1-4994-2783-7(2)) Rosen Publishing Group, Inc., The. (PowerKids Pr.).

Jones, Leanne. It's Cool to Be Clever: The story of Edson C. Hendricks, the genius who invented the design for the Internet. Mah, Anna, illus. 2011. 40p. (978-1-897435-63-2(0)) Agio Publishing Hse.

Kallen, Stuart A. Mark Zuckerberg & Facebook. 2015. (ENG., Illus.). 80p. (J). lib. bdg. (978-1-60152-876-6(0)) ReferencePoint Pr., Inc.

Kamberg, Mary-Lane. Evan Williams, Biz Stone, Jack Dorsey, & Twitter. 2012. (Internet Biographies Ser.). (ENG., Illus.). 128p. (J). (gr. 7-12). lib. bdg. 34.60 (978-1-4488-6913-8(7)) Rosen Publishing Group, Inc., The.

Kaplan, Arie. Blogs: Finding Your Voice, Finding Your Audience. 2011. (Digital & Information Literacy Ser.). (ENG.). 48p. (YA). (gr. 5-8). pap. 11.75 (978-1-4488-5618-3(3)); lib. bdg. 29.25 (978-1-4488-5556-8(X)) Rosen Publishing Group, Inc., The. (Rosen Reference).

Kenney, Karen Latchana. David Karp: The Mastermind Behind Tumblr. 2015. (Gateway Biographies Ser.). (ENG., Illus.). 48p. (gr. 4-8). 34.65 (978-1-4677-5975-5(9), Lerner Digital) Lerner Publishing Group.

Klein, Rebecca T. Career Building Through Using Digital Publishing Tools. 2013. (Digital Career Building Ser.). (Illus.). 64p. (J). (gr. 7-12). pap. 77.70 (978-1-4777-1742-4(0)); pap. 12.95 (978-1-4777-1741-7(2)); lib. bdg. 31.95 (978-1-4777-1724-0(2)) Rosen Publishing Group, Inc., The.

—Frequently Asked Questions about Texting, Sexting, & Flaming. 2012. (FAQ: Teen Life Ser.). (ENG., Illus.). 64p. (J). (gr. 7-12). lib. bdg. 31.95 (978-1-4488-8331-8(8)) Rosen Publishing Group, Inc., The.

Knittel, John. Everything You Need to Know about the Dangers of Computer Hacking. 2009. (Need to Know Library). 64p. (gr. 5-5). 58.50 (978-1-60854-092-1(8)) Rosen Publishing Group, Inc., The.

Larson, Paul J. Safe & Sound: Social Media. 2017. (Time for Kids Nonfiction Readers Ser.). lib. bdg. 20.85 **(978-0-606-40276-7(4))** Turtleback Bks.

Learning Resources for Kids on the Net. 2003. per. 14.95 (978-0-9722803-0-3(8)) Resources on the Net Publishing.

H
I

Leavitt, Amie Jane. Combatting Toxic Online Communities. 2016. (Combatting Shaming & Toxic Communities Ser.). 64p. (J). (gr. 7-7). 34.45 *(978-1-5081-7117-1(3))* Rosen Publishing Group, Inc., The.

Lee, Sally. Staying Safe Online, 1 vol. 2012. (Staying Safe Ser.). (ENG.). 24p. (gr. 1-2). lib. bdg. 25.32 *(978-1-4296-7617-5(5),* First Facts) Capstone Press of Coughlan Cos.

Lester, Brian. R U In? Using Technology Responsibly, 1 vol. 2010. (Essential Health: a Guy's Guide Ser.). (ENG.). 112p. (J). (gr. 6-12). lib. bdg. 35.64 *(978-1-61613-543-0(3))* ABDO Publishing Co.

Levete, Sarah. Taking Action Against Internet Crime. 2010. (Taking Action Ser.). (Illus.). 48p. (J). pap. 11.75 *(978-1-4358-9669-7(6),* Rosen Reference); (YA). (gr. 5-9). lib. bdg. 29.25 *(978-1-4358-9667-3(X))* Rosen Publishing Group, Inc., The.

Lew, Kristi. 20 Great Career-Building Activities Using Pinterest. 2016. (Social Media Career Building Ser.). 00064p. (J). (gr. 7-7). 34.45 *(978-1-5081-7270-3(6))* Rosen Publishing Group, Inc., The.

Lindeen, Mary. Smart Internet Surfing: Evaluating Websites & Advertising. 2016. (Searchlight Books (tm) — What Is Digital Citizenship? Ser.). (ENG., Illus.). 40p. (J). (gr. 3-5). lib. bdg. 30.65 *(978-1-4677-9492-3(9))* Lerner Publishing Group.

—Smart Online Communication: Protecting Your Digital Footprint. 2016. (Searchlight Books (tm) — What Is Digital Citizenship? Ser.). (ENG.). 40p. (J). (gr. 3-5). 30.65 *(978-1-4677-9487-9(2),* Lerner Pubns.) Lerner Publishing Group.

—Smart Online Searching: Doing Digital Research. 2016. (Searchlight Books (tm) — What Is Digital Citizenship? Ser.). (ENG., Illus.). 40p. (J). (gr. 3-5). lib. bdg. 30.65 *(978-1-4677-9491-6(0))* Lerner Publishing Group.

Little Bee Books Staff. The Vloggers Yearbook. 2015. (ENG., Illus.). 64p. (J). (gr. 4-9). pap. 9.99 *(978-1-4998-0230-6(7))* Little Bee Books Inc.

Loh-Hagan, Virginia. YouTube Channel. 2017. (D. I. Y. Make It Happen Ser.). (ENG., Illus.). 32p. (J). (gr. 4-8). 29.93 *(978-1-63472-145-5(4),* 209152, 45th Parallel Press) Cherry Lake Publishing.

Lombardo, Jennifer & Mooney, Carla. Social Networking: Staying Safe in the Online World. 2017. (Hot Topics Ser.). 120p. (YA). (gr. 7-7). lib. bdg. 39.40 ***(978-1-5345-6021-5(1),*** Lucent Pr.) Greenhaven Publishing LLC.

Lurie, Ian. The Unfun Parent: Keeping your kids safe Online. 2010. 63p. pap. 10.00 *(978-0-557-45677-2(0))* Lulu Pr., Inc.

Lyons, Heather & Tweedale, Elizabeth. Online Safety for Coders. Westgate, Alex, illus. 2016. (Kids Get Coding Ser.). (ENG.). 24p. (J). (gr. 1-4). 26.65 *(978-1-5124-1361-8(5))* Lerner Publishing Group.

Machajewski, Sarah. Mark Pincus & Zynga. 2013. (Internet Biographies Ser.). (ENG., Illus.). 128p. (YA). (gr. 7-12). lib. bdg. 34.60 *(978-1-4488-9530-4(8),* Rosen Classroom) Rosen Publishing Group, Inc., The.

Macken, JoAnn Early. Take a Closer Look at the Internet. 2016. (Core Content Science — Take a Closer Look Ser.). (ENG., Illus.). 40p. (J). (gr. 2-4). lib. bdg. 26.65 *(978-1-63440-053-4(4),* 1401565) Red Chair Pr.

marcovitz, hal. Online information & Research. 2011. (Issues in the Digital Age Ser.). (Illus.). 96p. (YA). (gr. 7-12). lib. bdg. 27.95 *(978-1-60152-192-7(8))* ReferencePoint Pr., Inc.

Mark Zuckerberg & Facebook. 2011. (Graphic Nonfiction Biographies Ser.). (ENG.). 48p. (YA). (gr. 5-8). pap. *(978-1-4488-5652-7(3),* Rosen Reference) Rosen Publishing Group, Inc., The.

Marzilli, Alan. The Internet & Crime. 2009. (Point/Counterpoint Ser.). (Illus.). 120p. (C). (gr. 9-18). 35.00 *(978-1-60413-506-0(9),* Chelsea Hse.) Facts On File, Inc.

Mason, Helen. What Is Digital Entrepreneurship? 2016. (Your Start-Up Starts Now! a Guide to Entrepreneurship Ser.). (ENG.). 48p. (J). (gr. 5-8). *(978-0-7787-2740-8(8));* pap. *(978-0-7787-2763-7(7))* Crabtree Publishing Co.

Mason, Paul. Understanding Computer Search & Research. 2015. (Understanding Computing Ser.). (ENG.). 48p. (gr. 3-6). 33.32 *(978-1-4846-0903-3(4),* Heinemann InfoSearch) Heinemann-Raintree.

McAllister, Jenn. Really Professional Internet Person. 2015. (ENG., Illus.). 240p. (J). (gr. 7). pap. 14.99 *(978-0-545-86112-0(8))* Scholastic, Inc.

Mcaneney, Caitie. La Seguridad en Internet (Online Safety). 1 vol. 2015. (Hablemos Acerca de... (Let's Talk about It) Ser.). (SPA.). 24p. (J). 23.60 *(978-1-4994-0192-9(2),* PowerKids Pr.) Rosen Publishing Group, Inc., The.

McAneney, Caitlin. I Have Been Cyberbullied. Now What? 2015. (Teen Life 411 Ser.). (ENG., Illus.). 112p. (J). (gr. 6-7). 35.60 *(978-1-4994-6138-1(0),* Rosen Young Adult) Rosen Publishing Group, Inc., The.

McClintock Miller, Shannon. Staying Safe Online. Durst, Kathryn, illus. 2017. (Library Skills Ser.). (ENG.). 24p. (gr. 1-3). 33.99 ***(978-1-68410-049-1(6))*** Cantata Learning.

McDonough, Judy. Online Privacy & Hacking. 2014. (Privacy in the Online World). (ENG., Illus.). 80p. (J). lib. bdg. *(978-1-60152-728-8(4))* ReferencePoint Pr., Inc.

McHugh, Jeff. Maintaining a Positive Digital Footprint. 2014. (Explorer Junior Library: Information Explorer Junior Ser.). (ENG.). 24p. (J). (gr. 1-4). 28.50 *(978-1-63137-789-1(2),* 205399); pap. 12.79 *(978-1-63137-809-6(0),* 205400) Cherry Lake Publishing.

McKenzie, Precious. Library Skills & Internet Research. 2014. (ENG.). 24p. (gr. 3-5). 28.50 *(978-1-62717-687-3(X))* Rourke Educational Media.

Meyer, Jared. Making Friends: The Art of Social Networking in Life & Online. 2011. (Communicating with Confidence Ser.). (ENG.). 80p. (YA). (gr. 7-12). pap. 14.15 *(978-1-4488-5633-6(7));* lib. bdg. 33.25 *(978-1-4488-5522-3(5))* Rosen Publishing Group, Inc., The.

Michalski, Pete & Lily, Henrietta M. Research Project Success Using Digital Tools, 01 vols., 1. 2016. (Digital & Information Literacy Ser.). (ENG.). 48p. (J). 30.25 *(978-1-4994-3787-4(0));* pap. 11.75 *(978-1-4994-3785-0(4))* Rosen Publishing Group, Inc., The. (Rosen Central).

Miller, Deborah J. Careers with an Internet Service Provider. 2005. (Library of e-Commerce & Internet Careers Ser.). (Illus.). 64p. (J). (gr. 7-12). lib. bdg. 31.95 *(978-0-8239-3425-6(X))* Rosen Publishing Group, Inc., The.

Miller, Jonathan. Sharks. 2004. (Discovery Program Ser.). (SPA., Illus.). 64p. (J). (gr. 2-18). lib. bdg. 16.95 *(978-1-58086-335-3(3))* EDC Publishing.

Miller, Shannon. Be Nice Online. 2013. (Internet DOs & DON'ts Ser.). (Illus.). 24p. (J). (gr. k-2). 22.60 *(978-1-4777-0756-2(5));* (ENG., pap. 8.25 *(978-1-4777-1566-6(5));* pap. 49.50 *(978-1-4777-1567-3(3))* Rosen Publishing Group, Inc., The. (PowerKids Pr.).

—Don't Share Your Address Online. 2013. (Internet DOs & DON'ts Ser.). (Illus.). 24p. (J). (gr. k-2). 22.60 *(978-1-4777-1536-9(3));* (ENG., pap. 8.25 *(978-1-4777-1558-1(4));* pap. 49.50 *(978-1-4777-1559-8(2))* Rosen Publishing Group, Inc., The. (PowerKids Pr.).

—Don't Share Your Phone Number Online. 2013. (Internet DOs & DON'ts Ser.). (Illus.). 24p. (J). (gr. k-2). 22.60 *(978-1-4777-0753-1(0));* (ENG., pap. 8.25 *(978-1-4777-1556-7(8));* pap. 49.50 *(978-1-4777-1557-4(6))* Rosen Publishing Group, Inc., The. (PowerKids Pr.).

—Don't Share Your Plans Online. 2013. (Internet DOs & DON'ts Ser.). (Illus.). 24p. (J). (gr. k-2). 22.60 *(978-1-4777-0754-8(9));* pap. 49.50 *(978-1-4777-1561-1(4));* (ENG., pap. 8.25 *(978-1-4777-1560-4(6))* Rosen Publishing Group, Inc., The. (PowerKids Pr.).

—Don't Talk to Strangers Online. 2013. (Internet DOs & DON'ts Ser.). (Illus.). 24p. (J). (gr. k-2). 22.60 *(978-1-4777-0755-5(7));* (ENG., pap. 8.25 *(978-1-4777-1564-2(9));* pap. 49.50 *(978-1-4777-1565-9(7))* Rosen Publishing Group, Inc., The. (PowerKids Pr.).

—Keep Your Passwords Secret. 2013. (Internet DOs & DON'ts Ser.). (Illus.). 24p. (J). (gr. k-2). 22.60 *(978-1-4777-1537-6(1));* pap. 49.50 *(978-1-4777-1563-5(0));* (ENG., pap. 8.25 *(978-1-4777-1562-8(2))* Rosen Publishing Group, Inc., The. (PowerKids Pr.).

Mills, J. Elizabeth. Creating Content: Maximizing Wikis, Widgets, Blogs, & More. 2011. (Digital & Information Literacy Ser.). (Illus.). 48p. (YA). 29.25 *(978-1-4488-1322-3(0));* pap. 11.75 *(978-1-4488-2293-5(9))* Rosen Publishing Group, Inc., The. (Rosen Reference).

Minden, Cecilia & Roth, Kate. How to Write an E-Mail. 2011. (Explorer Junior Library: Language Arts Explorer Junior Ser.). (ENG.). 24p. (gr. 1-4). lib. bdg. 25.64 *(978-1-60279-993-6(8),* 200986) Cherry Lake Publishing.

Minton, Eric. Passwords & Security, 1 vol., 1. 2014. (Stay Safe Online Ser.). (ENG.). 32p. (J). (gr. 4-6). 26.25 *(978-1-4777-2942-7(9),* PowerKids Pr.) Rosen Publishing Group, Inc., The.

—Smartphone Safety, 1 vol., 1. 2014. (Stay Safe Online Ser.). (ENG.). 32p. (J). (gr. 4-6). 26.25 *(978-1-4777-2935-9(6),* PowerKids Pr.) Rosen Publishing Group, Inc., The.

—Spam & Scams: Using Email Safely, 1 vol., 1. 2014. (Stay Safe Online Ser.). (ENG.). 32p. (J). (gr. 4-6). 26.25 *(978-1-4777-2934-2(8),* PowerKids Pr.) Rosen Publishing Group, Inc., The.

Mooney, Carla. Getting Paid to Moderate Websites. 2016. (Turning Your Tech Hobbies into a Career Ser.). 00080p. (J). (gr. 7-7). 35.75 *(978-1-5081-7300-7(1))* Rosen Publishing Group, Inc., The.

—How the Internet Is Changing Society. 2015. (ENG., Illus.). 80p. (YA). lib. bdg. *(978-1-60152-900-8(7))* ReferencePoint Pr., Inc.

—Online Privacy & Social Media. 2014. (Privacy in the Online World). (ENG., Illus.). 80p. (J). lib. bdg. *(978-1-60152-730-1(6))* ReferencePoint Pr., Inc.

—Online Social Networking. 2009. (Hot Topics Ser.). (ENG., Illus.). 128p. (YA). (gr. 7-10). lib. bdg. 33.95 *(978-1-4205-0120-9(8),* LML02109-245431, Lucent Bks.) Cengage Gale.

Moore, Kevin M. What You Need to Know about the Law & Cyberspace, 1 vol. 2015. (ENG., Illus.). 64p. (J). 33.25 *(978-1-4777-8008-4(4),* Rosen Reference) Rosen Publishing Group, Inc., The.

Morales, Leslie. Esther Dyson: Internet Visionary. 2003. (Internet Biographies Ser.). (Illus.). 48p. (J). (gr. 4-10). lib. bdg. 23.93 *(978-0-7660-1973-7(X))* Enslow Pubs., Inc.

Morretta, Alison. How to Maintain Your Privacy Online. 2015. (J). lib. bdg. *(978-1-62713-545-0(6));* (ENG.). 48p. (gr. 5-5). lib. bdg. 31.36 *(978-1-5026-0187-2(7))* Cavendish Square Publishing.

Murray, Guillermo. Internet para Nino.Tr. of Internet for Children. (SPA.). 8.98 *(978-970-643-110-3(1))* Selector, S.A. de C.V. MEX. Dist: AIMS International Bks., Inc.

Nagelhout, Ryan. Smart Machines & the Internet of Things, 01 vols., 1. 2016. (Digital & Information Literacy Ser.). (ENG.). 48p. (J). pap. 11.75 *(978-1-4994-3777-5(3),* Rosen Central) Rosen Publishing Group, Inc., The.

Nakaya, Andrea C. Is Social Media Good for Society? 2016. (ENG.). 80p. (J). (gr. 5-12). lib. bdg. *(978-1-68282-068-1(8))* ReferencePoint Pr., Inc.

netzley, patricia D. How Serious a Threat Are Online Predators? 2012. (Illus.). 80p. (J). lib. bdg. *(978-1-60152-450-8(1))* ReferencePoint Pr., Inc.

Netzley, Patricia D. Online Addiction. 2016. (ENG.). 80p. (J). (gr. 5-12). lib. bdg. *(978-1-60152-984-8(8))* ReferencePoint Pr., Inc.

—Online Entertainment. 2016. (ENG.). 80p. (J). (gr. 5-12). lib. bdg. *(978-1-60152-986-2(4))* ReferencePoint Pr., Inc.

—Teens & Sexting. 2015. (Illus.). 80p. (J). 28.95 *(978-1-60152-916-9(3))* ReferencePoint Pr., Inc.

Online Smarts. 2015. (Online Smarts Ser.). (ENG.). 32p. (J). (gr. 3-4). pap., pap., pap. 378.72 *(978-0-7660-6685-4(1));* pap., pap., pap. 63.12 *(978-0-7660-7057-8(3))* Enslow Pubs., Inc.

Orr, Tamra. I Have Been Shamed on the Internet, Now What? 2016. (Teen Life 411 Ser.). 00112p. (J). (gr. 7-7). 37.10 *(978-1-5081-7202-4(1))* Rosen Publishing Group, Inc., The.

Owen, John. #Presidents: Follow the Leaders. 2015. (Illus.). 115p. (J). pap. *(978-0-545-85127-5(0))* Scholastic, Inc.

Owings, Lisa. Stay Safe Online. 2013. (Library Smarts Ser.). (ENG., Illus.). 24p. (gr. -1-2). lib. bdg. 23.93 *(978-1-4677-1505-8(0),* Lerner Pubns.) Lerner Publishing Group.

Oxlade, Chris. Experiments with Electricity & Magnets, 1 vol. 2015. (ENG., Illus.). 32p. (J). 27.50 *(978-1-4777-5804-5(6),* PowerKids Pr.) Rosen Publishing Group, Inc., The.

Parks, Peggy J. The Internet. 2003. (Kidhaven Science Library). (Illus.). 48p. (J). 23.70 *(978-0-7377-1015-1(2),* Greenhaven Pr., Inc.) Cengage Gale.

—Online Privacy. 2016. (ENG.). 80p. (J). (gr. 5-12). lib. bdg. *(978-1-60152-988-6(0))* ReferencePoint Pr., Inc.

—Social Media. 2016. (ENG.). 80p. (J). (gr. 5-12). lib. bdg. *(978-1-60152-992-3(9))* ReferencePoint Pr., Inc.

Pascaretti, Vicki & Wilkie, Sara. Super Smart Information Strategies: Team up Online. 2010. (Explorer Library: Information Explorer Ser.). (ENG.). 32p. (gr. 4-8). lib. bdg. 28.50 *(978-1-60279-644-7(0),* 200347) Cherry Lake Publishing.

—Super Smart Information Strategies: Team Up Online. 2010. (Explorer Library: Information Explorer Ser.). (ENG.). 32p. (gr. 4-8). pap. 14.21 *(978-1-61080-264-2(0),* 200909) Cherry Lake Publishing.

Pelusey, Michael & Pelusey, Jane. Internet. 2005. (Media Ser.). (Illus.). 32p. (gr. 5-8). lib. bdg. 21.95 *(978-0-7910-8803-6(0),* Chelsea Hse.) Facts On File, Inc.

Penna, Christine. Careers in Network Engineering. 2009. (Library of E-Commerce & Internet Careers Ser.). 64p. (gr. 5-5). 58.50 *(978-1-60853-581-1(9))* Rosen Publishing Group, Inc., The.

Perdew, Laura. Internet Addiction, 1 vol. 2014. (Essential Issues Set 4 Ser.). (ENG., Illus.). 112p. (YA). (gr. 6-12). lib. bdg. 35.64 *(978-1-62403-421-3(7),* Essential Library) ABDO Publishing Co.

Peters, Craig. Steve Case: Internet Genius of America Online. 2003. (Internet Biographies Ser.). (Illus.). 48p. (J). (gr. 4-10). lib. bdg. 25.27 *(978-0-7660-1971-3(3))* Enslow Pubs., Inc.

Popek, Emily. Copyright & Digital Ethics. 2011. (Digital & Information Literacy Ser.). (Illus.). 48p. (YA). 29.25 *(978-1-4488-1323-0(9));* pap. 11.75 *(978-1-4488-2294-2(7))* Rosen Publishing Group, Inc., The. (Rosen Reference).

Porterfield, Jason. Conducting Basic & Advanced Searches. 2009. (Digital & Information Literacy Ser.). (Illus.). 48p. (YA). (gr. 5-8). lib. bdg. 29.25 *(978-1-4358-5316-4(4),* Rosen Reference) Rosen Publishing Group, Inc., The.

Rabbat, Suzy. Super Smart Information Strategies: Find Your Way Online. 2010. (Explorer Library: Information Explorer Ser.). (ENG.). 32p. (gr. 4-8). pap. 14.21 *(978-1-61080-256-7(X),* 200904) Cherry Lake Publishing.

Randolph, Ryan P. New Research Techniques: Getting the Most Out of Search Engine Tools. 2011. (Digital & Information Literacy Ser.). (ENG., Illus.). 48p. (J). pap. 11.75 *(978-1-4488-2292-8(0));* lib. bdg. 29.25 *(978-1-4488-1321-6(2))* Rosen Publishing Group, Inc., The. (Rosen Reference).

Rauf, Don. Getting Paid to Manage Social Media. 2016. (Turning Your Tech Hobbies into a Career Ser.). 00080p. (J). (gr. 7-7). 35.75 *(978-1-5081-7294-9(3))* Rosen Publishing Group, Inc., The.

—Powering up a Career in Internet Security. 2015. (Preparing for Tomorrow's Careers Ser.). (ENG., Illus.). 80p. (J). (gr. 7-8). 34.25 *(978-1-4994-6093-3(7),* Rosen Young Adult) Rosen Publishing Group, Inc., The.

Reed, Jennifer. What Are Computer Networks & the Internet? 2017. (J). ***(978-1-5383-0033-6(8))*** Rosen Publishing Group, Inc., The.

Regan Gregson, Susan. Cyber Literacy: Evaluating the Reliability of Data. 2009. (Cyber Citizenship & Cyber Safety Ser.). 48p. (gr. 5-5). 53.00 *(978-1-61512-103-8(X),* Rosen Reference) Rosen Publishing Group, Inc., The.

Richards, Patti. All about Social Networking. 2017. (Cutting-Edge Technology (hardcover) Ser.). (ENG., Illus.). 32p. (J). (gr. 4-7). lib. bdg. 28.50 ***(978-1-63517-016-0(8),*** Focus Readers) North Star Editions.

Rondina, Catherine. The 10 Worst Things about Internet. 2008. 14.99 *(978-1-55448-556-7(8))* Scholastic Library Publishing.

Rooney, Anne. Internet Safety. 2013. (Let's Read & Talk about Ser.). 32p. (gr. 2-5). 28.50 *(978-1-59771-398-6(8))* Sea-To-Sea Pubns.

—You Wouldn't Want to Live Without the Internet! Bergin, Mark, illus. 2015. (You Wouldn't Want to Live Without... Ser.). (ENG.). 32p. (J). lib. bdg. 29.00 *(978-0-531-21931-7(3),* Watts, Franklin) Scholastic Library Publishing.

—You Wouldn't Want to Live Without the Internet! 2015. (You Wouldn't Want to Live Without Ser.). lib. bdg. 20.80 *(978-0-606-37470-5(1))* Turtleback Bks.

Rose, Arden. Almost Adulting: All You Need to Know to Get It Together (Sort Of) 2017. (Illus.). 208p. (YA). (gr. 8). 18.99 *(978-0-06-257410-7(8))* HarperCollins Pubs.

Rosen Publishing Staff. Internet Biographies: Set 3, 1 vol. 2015. (Internet Biographies Ser.). (ENG.). 128p. (YA). 213.60 *(978-1-4777-7929-3(9),* Rosen Young Adult) Rosen Publishing Group, Inc., The.

Roslund, Samantha. Join Forces: Teaming up Online. 2012. (Explorer Junior Library: Information Explorer Junior Ser.). (ENG., Illus.). 24p. (J). (gr. 1-4). 28.50 *(978-1-61080-486-8(4),* 202096); pap. 12.79 *(978-1-61080-660-2(3),* 202270) Cherry Lake Publishing.

Rosner, Marc Alan. Science Fair Success Using the Internet. rev. ed. 2006. (Science Fair Success Ser.). (Illus.). 112p. (J). (gr. 7-12). lib. bdg. 27.94 *(978-0-7660-2425-0(3))* Enslow Pubs., Inc.

Rothman, Kevin F. Coping with Dangers on the Internet. 2005. (Coping Ser.). (Illus.). 192p. (YA). (gr. 7-12). lib. bdg. 34.60 *(978-0-8239-3201-6(X))* Rosen Publishing Group, Inc., The.

Schrier, Allyson Valentine. Gaming Safely, 6 vols. 2013. (Tech Safety Smarts Ser.). (ENG.). 32p. (gr. 3-4). 47.70 *(978-1-62065-801-7(1),* Fact Finders); (Illus.). pap. 8.10 *(978-1-62065-800-0(3));* (Illus.). lib. bdg. 27.32 *(978-1-4296-9946-4(9))* Capstone Press of Coughlan Cos.

Schwartz, Heather E. Safe Social Networking, 1 vol. 2013. (Tech Safety Smarts Ser.). (ENG.). 32p. (gr. 3-4). lib. bdg. 27.32 *(978-1-4296-9943-3(4));* (Illus.). pap. 8.10 *(978-1-62065-802-4(X))* Capstone Press of Coughlan Cos.

Scientific American Staff. The Future of the Web. 2009. (Scientific American Cutting-Edge Science Ser.). 118p. (gr. 9-9). 63.90 *(978-1-60853-081-6(7))* Rosen Publishing Group, Inc., The.

Scott, Celicia. Facebook(Tm) How Mark Zuckerberg Connected More Than a Billion Friends. 2014. (Wizards of Technology Ser.: 10). 64p. (J). (gr. 7-18). 23.95 *(978-1-4222-3181-4(X))* Mason Crest.

Sergey Brin, Larry Page, & Eric Schmidt & Google. 2011. (Graphic Nonfiction Biographies Ser.). (ENG.). 48p. (YA). (gr. 5-8). *(978-1-4488-5548-3(9));* pap. *(978-1-4488-5653-4(1))* Rosen Publishing Group, Inc., The. (Rosen Reference).

Sheikh-Miller, Jonathan. Snakes. 2004. (Discovery Program Ser.). (SPA., Illus.). 64p. (J). (gr. 2-18). pap. 8.95 *(978-0-7945-0004-7(8),* Usborne); lib. bdg. 16.95 *(978-1-58086-344-5(2))* EDC Publishing.

Sherman, Josepha. It's a www. World. 2004. (YA). lib. bdg. 25.90 *(978-0-7613-2353-2(8),* Millbrook Pr.) Lerner Publishing Group.

Smith, Chris & McGrath, Marci. Twitter: Jack Dorsey, Evan Williams & Biz Stone. 2012. (Business Leaders Ser.). (Illus.). 112p. (YA). (gr. 7-12). 28.95 *(978-1-59935-179-7(X))* Reynolds, Morgan Inc.

Social Media Career Building. 2016. (Social Media Career Building Ser.). 00064p. (J). (gr. 7-7). 206.70 *(978-1-5081-7359-5(1),* Rosen Young Adult) Rosen Publishing Group, Inc., The.

Souter, Gerry, et al. Researching on the Internet Using Search Engines, Bulletin Boards, & Listservs. 2003. (Internet Library). (Illus.). 64p. (J). (gr. 4-12). lib. bdg. 23.94 *(978-0-7660-2081-8(9))* Enslow Pubs., Inc.

Spivet, Bonnie. Avoiding Predators Online. 2011. (CyberSmarts: Staying Safe Online Ser.). (ENG.). 24p. (J). (gr. 4-6). pap. 10.00 *(978-1-4488-6416-4(X));* lib. bdg. 21.25 *(978-1-4488-6411-9(9))* Rosen Publishing Group, Inc., The. (PowerKids Pr.).

—Playing Games Online. 2011. (CyberSmarts: Staying Safe Online Ser.). (ENG.). 24p. (J). (gr. 4-6). lib. bdg. 21.25 *(978-1-4488-6414-0(3),* PowerKids Pr.) Rosen Publishing Group, Inc., The.

—Stopping Cyberbullying. 2011. (CyberSmarts: Staying Safe Online Ser.). (ENG.). 24p. (J). (gr. 4-6). pap. 10.00 *(978-1-4488-6420-1(8));* lib. bdg. 21.25 *(978-1-4488-6413-3(5))* Rosen Publishing Group, Inc., The. (PowerKids Pr.).

—Using Social Networks. 2011. (CyberSmarts: Staying Safe Online Ser.). (ENG.). 24p. (J). (gr. 4-6). pap. 10.00 *(978-1-4488-6425-6(9));* lib. bdg. 21.25 *(978-1-4488-6415-7(1))* Rosen Publishing Group, Inc., The. (PowerKids Pr.).

Staley, Erin. Vloggers & Vlogging. 2016. (Digital & Information Literacy Ser.). 00048p. (J). (gr. 6-6). pap. 11.75 *(978-1-5081-7333-5(8))* Rosen Publishing Group, Inc., The.

Steffens, Bradley. Careers in Internet Technology. 2017. (ENG.). 80p. (J). (gr. 5-12). *(978-1-68282-114-5(5))* ReferencePoint Pr., Inc.

—Cutting Edge Internet Technology. 2016. (ENG.). 80p. (J). (gr. 5-12). lib. bdg. *(978-1-68282-090-2(4))* ReferencePoint Pr., Inc.

Stephens, Catherine & National Geographic Learning Staff. Inside the Internet. 2007. (Reading Expeditions Ser.). (ENG., Illus.). 32p. (J). pap. 17.95 *(978-0-7922-8875-6(0))* CENGAGE Learning.

Stuckey, Rachel. Digital Dangers. 2015. (ENG., Illus.). 48p. (J). *(978-0-7787-2202-1(3))* Crabtree Publishing Co.

Suen, Anastasia. Downloading & Online Shopping Safety & Privacy. 2013. (21st Century Safety & Privacy Ser.). (Illus.). 64p. (J). (gr. 5-8). 31.95 *(978-1-4488-9571-7(5));* pap. 12.95 *(978-1-4488-9582-3(0));* pap. 77.70 *(978-1-4488-9583-0(9))* Rosen Publishing Group, Inc., The.

Sutherland, Adam. Being a YouTuber. 2017. (Quick Expert's Guide Ser.). (ENG., Illus.). 64p. (J). (gr. 7-11). pap. 9.99 ***(978-0-7502-9776-9(X),*** Wayland) Hachette Children's Group GBR. Dist: Hachette Bk. Group.

—The Story of Google. 2012. (Business of High Tech Ser.). (ENG.). 48p. (YA). (gr. 5-8). pap. 10.00 *(978-1-4488-7092-9(5),* Rosen Reference); lib. bdg. 29.25 *(978-1-4488-7041-7(0))* Rosen Publishing Group, Inc., The.

—Youtube. 2016. (Big Business Ser.). (ENG., Illus.). 32p. (J). (gr. 4-6). pap. 11.99 *(978-0-7502-8921-4(X),* Wayland) Hachette Children's Group GBR. Dist: Hachette Bk. Group.

Tatchell, Judy. Science Encyclopedia. 2004. (Library of Science Ser.). (Illus.). (J). (gr. 4-18). (ENG.). 1p. 39.95 *(978-0-7460-3833-8(X));* 448p. lib. bdg. 47.95 *(978-1-58086-337-7(X))* EDC Publishing.

Truesdell, Ann. Being Respectful Online. Petelinsek, Kathleen, illus. 2013. (Explorer Junior Library: Information Explorer Junior Ser.). (ENG.). 24p. (J). (gr. 1-4). 28.50 *(978-1-62431-131-4(8),* 202844); pap. 12.79 *(978-1-62431-263-2(2),* 202846) Cherry Lake Publishing.

—Get to the Right Site. 2012. (Explorer Junior Library: Information Explorer Junior Ser.). (ENG., Illus.). 24p. (J). (gr. 1-4). pap. 12.79 *(978-1-61080-390-8(6),* 201327); lib. bdg. 28.50 *(978-1-61080-365-6(5),* 201264) Cherry Lake Publishing.

—How to Handle Cyberbullies. Petelinsek, Kathleen, illus. 2013. (Explorer Library: Information Explorer Ser.). (ENG.). 32p. (J). (gr. 4-8). 28.50 *(978-1-62431-127-7(X),* 202828); pap. 14.21 *(978-1-62431-259-5(4),* 202830) Cherry Lake Publishing.

—Super Smart Information Strategies: Find the Right Site. 2010. (Explorer Library: Information Explorer Ser.). (ENG.). 32p. (gr. 4-8). pap. 14.21 *(978-1-61080-255-0(1),* 200903) Cherry Lake Publishing.

Trunko, Emily. The Last Message Received. Ingram, Zoe, illus. 2017. (ENG.). 176p. (YA). (gr. 9). 14.99 *(978-0-399-55776-7(8),* Crown Books For Young Readers) Random Hse. Children's Bks.

Van Lent, Colleen. More Web Design with HTML5. 2015. (21st Century Skills Innovation Library: Makers As Innovators Ser.). (ENG., Illus.). 32p. (J). (gr. 4-8). lib. bdg. 29.93 *(978-1-63188-868-7(4),* 206052) Cherry Lake Publishing.

Viegas, Jennifer. Pierre Omidyar: The Founder of EBay. 2009. (Internet Career Biographies Ser.). 112p. (gr. 8-8). 63.90 *(978-1-61513-596-7(0))* Rosen Publishing Group, Inc., The.

Wainewright, Max. I'm an HTML Web Page Builder. 2017. 32p. (J). ***(978-0-7787-3516-8(8))*** Crabtree Publishing Co.

Ward-Johnson, Chris. Internet: A Magic Mouse Guide. Laughing Gravy Design Staff, illus. 2003. (Magic Mouse Guides). 32p. (J). lib. bdg. 22.60 *(978-0-7660-2260-7(9))* Enslow Pubs., Inc.

Weber, Sandra. The Internet. 2003. (Transforming Power of Technology Ser.). (Illus.). 112p. (C). (gr. 9-13). 30.00 *(978-0-7910-7449-7(8),* Chelsea Hse.) Facts On File, Inc.

Weston, Michael R. Jerry Yang & David Filo: The Founders of Yahoo! 2009. (Internet Career Biographies Ser.). 112p. (gr. 8-8). 63.90 *(978-1-61513-590-5(1))* Rosen Publishing Group, Inc., The.

White, Casey. Sergey Brin & Larry Page: The Founders of Google. 2009. (Internet Career Biographies Ser.). 112p. (gr. 8-8). 63.90 (978-1-61513-597-4(9)) Rosen Publishing Group, Inc., The.

Wiener, Gary. The Internet. 2010. (Global Viewpoints Ser.). (ENG.). 272p. 40.45 (978-0-7377-4935-9(0)); 224p. (gr. 10-12). pap. 31.70 (978-0-7377-4936-6(9)) Cengage Gale. (Greenhaven Pr., Inc.).

Wilcox, Christine. How Is Online Pornography Affecting Society? 2015. (ENG., Illus.). 96p. (J). lib. bdg. (978-1-60152-882-7(5)) ReferencePoint Pr., Inc.

Wilkinson, Colin. Everything You Need to Know about Digital Privacy. 2017. (Need to Know Library). 64p. (J). (gr. 12-11). 34.45 **(978-1-5081-7400-4(8))**; pap. 12.95 **(978-1-5081-7398-4(2))** Rosen Publishing Group, Inc., The. (Rosen Young Adult).

Wilkinson, Colin. Gaming: Playing Safe & Playing Smart. 2011. (Digital & Information Literacy Ser.). (ENG.). 48p. (YA). (gr. 5-8). pap. 11.75 (978-1-4488-5611-4(6)); lib. bdg. 29.25 (978-1-4488-5552-0(7)) Rosen Publishing Group, Inc., The. (Rosen Reference).

Willoughby, Nick. Making YouTube Videos: Star in Your Won Video! 2015. (Dummies Junior Ser.). (ENG., Illus.). 128p. (J). (gr. 2-8). pap. 9.99 (978-1-119-17724-1(3), For Dummies) Wiley, John & Sons, Inc.

Wittekind, Erika. Amazon. com: The Company & Its Founder, 1 vol. 2012. (Technology Pioneers Set 2 Ser.). (ENG.). 112p. (J). (gr. 6-12). lib. bdg. 35.64 (978-1-61783-330-4(4), Essential Library) ABDO Publishing Co.

Wolinsky, Art. Internet Power Research Using the Big6 Approach. rev. ed. 2005. (Internet Library). (Illus.). 64p. (J). lib. bdg. 23.94 (978-0-7660-1563-0(7)) Enslow Pubs., Inc.

—Safe Surfing on the Internet. 2003. (Internet Library). (Illus.). 64p. (YA). (gr. 4-12). lib. bdg. 22.60 (978-0-7660-2030-6(4)) Enslow Pubs., Inc.

Wolny, Philip. Foursquare & Other Location-Based Services: Checking in, Staying Safe, & Being Savvy. 2011. (Digital & Information Literacy Ser.). (ENG.). 48p. (YA). (gr. 5-8). pap. 11.75 (978-1-4488-5615-2(9)); lib. bdg. 29.25 (978-1-4488-5554-4(3)) Rosen Publishing Group, Inc., The. (Rosen Reference).

Woog, Adam. YouTube. 2008. (Great Idea Ser.). (Illus.). 48p. (J). (gr. 4-6). lib. bdg. 26.60 (978-1-59953-198-4(4)) Norwood Hse. Pr.

Woolf, Alex. Let's Think about the Internet & Social Media, 1 vol. 2014. (Let's Think About Ser.). (ENG., Illus.). 48p. (gr. 3-6). 33.32 (978-1-4846-0293-5(5)); pap. 8.99 (978-1-4846-0298-0(6)) Heinemann-Raintree. (Heinemann InfoSearch).

Yearling, Tricia. E-Mail: What It Is & How to Use It. 2016. (Zoom in on Technology Ser.). (ENG., Illus.). 24p. (J). (gr. 2-2). pap. 9.35 (978-0-7660-7365-4(3)) Enslow Pubs., Inc.

—How Do I Find Information Online? 2015. (Online Smarts Ser.). (ENG., Illus.). 32p. (J). (gr. 3-4). 25.27 (978-0-7660-6839-1(0)); pap. 10.52 (978-0-7660-6837-7(4)) Enslow Pubs., Inc.

—How Do I Keep My Privacy Online? 2015. (Online Smarts Ser.). (ENG.). 32p. (J). (gr. 3-4). 25.27 (978-0-7660-6843-8(9)); pap. 10.52 (978-0-7660-6841-4(2)) Enslow Pubs., Inc.

—How Do I Play Games Online? 2015. (Online Smarts Ser.). (ENG.). 32p. (J). (gr. 3-4). pap. 10.52 (978-0-7660-6845-2(5)); (Illus.). 25.27 (978-0-7660-6847-6(1)) Enslow Pubs., Inc.

—How Do I Stay Safe from Online Predators? 2015. (Online Smarts Ser.). (ENG.). 32p. (J). (gr. 3-4). pap. 10.52 (978-0-7660-6853-7(6)); (Illus.). 25.27 (978-0-7660-6854-4(4)) Enslow Pubs., Inc.

—How Do I Use Social Networking? 2015. (Online Smarts Ser.). (ENG.). 32p. (J). (gr. 3-4). pap. 10.52 (978-0-7660-6856-8(0)); (Illus.). 25.27 (978-0-7660-6858-2(7)) Enslow Pubs., Inc.

—The Internet: What It Is & How to Use It. 2016. (Zoom in on Technology Ser.). (ENG.). 24p. (J). (gr. 2-2). pap. 9.35 (978-0-7660-7380-7(7)); (Illus.). lib. bdg. 22.60 (978-0-7660-7382-1(3)) Enslow Pubs., Inc.

—The World Wide Web: What It Is & How to Use It. 2016. (Zoom in on Technology Ser.). (ENG., Illus.). 24p. (J). (gr. 2-2). pap. 9.35 (978-0-7660-7386-9(6)) Enslow Pubs., Inc.

Yomtov, Nelson. Internet Inventors. 2013. (Cornerstones of Freedom™, Third Ser.). (ENG., Illus.). 64p. (J). pap. 8.95 (978-0-531-21967-6(4)); lib. bdg. 30.00 (978-0-531-23609-3(9)) Scholastic Library Publishing.

—Internet Security: From Concept to Consumer. 2015. (ENG.). 64p. (J). lib. bdg. (978-0-531-21896-9(1), Orchard Bks.) Scholastic, Inc.

Zuchora-Walske, Christine. How Can I Be a Good Digital Citizen? 2015. (ENG., Illus.). 32p. (J). (gr. k-2). 26.65 (978-1-4677-8078-0(2)) Lerner Publishing Group.

INTERNET—FICTION

Amato, Mary. The Naked Mole-Rat Letters. 2007. (ENG., Illus.). 208p. (J). (gr. 4-7). pap. 7.99 (978-0-8234-2098-8(1)) Holiday Hse., Inc.

Anastasiu, Heather & Brown, Anne Greenwood. Girl Last Seen. 2016. (ENG.). 272p. (YA). (gr. 8-12). pap. 9.99 (978-0-8075-8141-4(0)) Whitman, Albert & Co.

Anzalone, Karen. Time in a Bottle. 2003. 100p. (YA). pap. 9.00 (978-0-7599-3840-3(7)) Hard Shell Word Factory.

Asher, Jay & Mackler, Carolyn. The Future of Us. 2012. (ENG., Illus.). 384p. (YA). (gr. 7). pap. 10.99 (978-1-59514-516-1(8), Razorbill) Penguin Young Readers Group.

—The Future of Us. 2012. lib. bdg. 20.85 (978-0-606-26498-3(1), Turtleback) Turtleback Bks.

Baskin, Nora Raleigh. Runt. 2013. (ENG., Illus.). 208p. (J). (gr. 3-7). 15.99 (978-1-4424-5807-9(0), Simon & Schuster Bks. For Young Readers) Simon & Schuster Bks. For Young Readers.

Bernard, Norah S. CLIVE & BRIE. 2006. (YA). per. 8.95 (978-0-615-15932-4(X)) HELORO Publishing Group.

Brege, K. B. Ghost Board Posse London Screaming! 2008. (Ghost Board Posse Ser.: No. 1). (Illus.). 207p. (YA). pap. 6.99 (978-0-9774119-6-2(6)) Team B Creative LLC.

Breslaw, Anna. Scarlett Epstein Hates It Here. 2016. (ENG.). 288p. (YA). (gr. 7). 17.99 (978-1-59514-835-3(3), Razorbill) Penguin Young Readers Group.

Brown, Anne Greenwood & Anastasiu, Heather. Girl Last Seen. 2016. (ENG.). 272p. (YA). (gr. 8-12). 16.99 (978-0-8075-8140-7(2)) Whitman, Albert & Co.

Butcher, Kristin. Chat Room, 1 vol. 2006. (Orca Currents Ser.). (ENG.). 128p. (J). (gr. 5-9). per. 9.95 (978-1-55143-485-8(7)) Orca Bk. Pubs. USA.

—Chat Room. 2006. (Orca Currents Ser.). 102p. (gr. 4-7). 19.95 (978-0-7569-6873-1(9)) Perfection Learning Corp.

Buzzeo, Toni. But I Read It on the Internet! Yoshikawa, Sachiko, illus. 2013. 32p. (J). 17.95 (978-1-60213-062-3(0), Upstart Bks.) Highsmith Inc.

Casanova, Mary. Chrissa Stands Strong, Bks. 2. England, Tamara, ed. Jones, Richard, illus. 2009. (ENG.). 130p. (YA). (gr. 3-18). pap. 6.95 (978-1-59369-567-5(5), American Girl) American Girl Publishing, Inc.

Cook, Julia. Technology Tail: A Digital Footprint Story. DuFalla, Anita, illus. 2017. (ENG.). 32p. (J). (gr. 1-6). pap. 10.95 **(978-1-944882-13-6(8))** Boys Town Pr.

Cowan, Jennifer. Earthgirl, 1 vol. 2009. (ENG.). 192p. (J). (gr. 8-18). 17.95 (978-0-88899-889-7(9)) Groundwood Bks. CAN. Dist: Publishers Group West (PGW).

Cray, Jordan. Firestorm. 2009. (Danger. com Ser.: 2). (ENG.). 208p. (YA). (gr. 7). pap. 9.99 (978-1-4169-9846-4(2), Simon Pulse) Simon Pulse.

—Gemini7. 2009. (Danger. com Ser.: 1). (ENG.). 192p. (YA). (gr. 7). pap. 9.99 (978-1-4169-9847-1(0), Simon Pulse) Simon Pulse.

—Stalker. 2009. (Danger. com Ser.: 5). (ENG.). 224p. (YA). (gr. 7). pap. 10.99 (978-1-4169-9850-1(0), Simon Pulse) Simon Pulse.

Dawson, Dorothy M. Email on a Special Journey. 2008. 32p. per. 24.95 (978-1-4241-9338-7(9)) America Star Bks.

Day, Susie. My Invisible Boyfriend. 2010. (ENG.). 288p. (J). (gr. 7-18). 16.99 (978-0-545-07354-7(5), Scholastic Pr.) Scholastic, Inc.

Doctorow, Cory. In Real Life. Wang, Jen, illus. 2014. (ENG.). 192p. (YA). (gr. 7). pap. 17.99 (978-1-59643-658-9(1), 9781596436589, First Second Bks.) Roaring Brook Pr.

—Pirate Cinema. (ENG.). 384p. (YA). 2013. (gr. 7). pap. 9.99 (978-0-7653-2909-7(3), 9780765329097) 2012. (gr. 8-13). 19.99 (978-0-7653-2908-0(5), 9780765329080) Doherty, Tom Assocs., LLC. (Tor Teen).

Duracell and the National Center for Missing & Exploited Children (NCMEC), creator. The Great Tomato Adventure: A Story about Smart Safety Choices. 2007. 0.00 (978-0-9795307-0-8(9)) Duracell & the National Ctr. for Missing & Exploited Children (NCMEC).

Ferrari, Vincent. Blogosfear. 2005. 143p. (YA). pap. 15.00 (978-1-4116-6814-0(6)) Lulu Pr., Inc.

Ferraro, Lynn. Joey's Day of Discovery. Leslie, Melissa, illus. 2005. (ENG.). 21p. per. 12.99 (978-1-4134-9622-2(9)) Xlibris Corp.

Fink, Jeri & Paltrowitz, Donna. Mathew's Tangled Trails. (YA). pap. 11.95 (978-0-7925-5279-6(2)) Educational Activities, Inc.

Ford, John C. & Wells, Rosemary. The Cipher. 2015. (ENG.). 320p. (YA). (gr. 7). bds. 17.99 (978-0-670-01542-9(3), Viking Books for Young Readers) Penguin Young Readers Group.

Frazier, Sundee T. Cleo Edison Oliver in Persuasion Power. 2017. (ENG.). 256p. (J). (gr. 3-7). 16.99 (978-0-545-82239-8(4), Levine, Arthur A. Bks.) Scholastic, Inc.

Fuzy, Jim. An Internet Adventure with Safari Sam. Melvin, Anita Flannery, illus. 2004. 24p. (J). per. 14.95 (978-0-9760129-7-9(9)) The Publishing Place LLC.

Goedde, Kathy. Blogged Down. 2009. 28p. pap. 13.99 (978-1-4389-5055-6(1)) AuthorHouse.

Gray, Jennifer, et al. Guinea Pigs Online: Viking Victory. 2014. (Guinea PIgs Online Ser.: 3). (ENG., Illus.). 160p. (J). (gr. 1-4). 12.99 (978-1-62365-347-7(9), Quercus) Quercus NA.

Haydu, Corey Ann. Life by Committee. 2014. (ENG.). 304p. (YA). (gr. 9). 17.99 (978-0-06-229405-0(9), Tegen, Katherine Bks) HarperCollins Pubs.

Hildebrand, Jens & Ridge, Sally. Cyberstalker. 2013. 242p. pap. (978-3-929892-45-1(6)) Hildebrand, Jutta Warped Tomato Publishing.

Homzie, Hillary. Queen of Likes. 2016. (Mix Ser.). (ENG., Illus.). 272p. (J). (gr. 4-8). pap. 7.99 (978-1-4814-4521-4(9), Aladdin) Simon & Schuster Children's Publishing.

Ice, Rod. The Cat & the Strat. 2007. 32p. per. 24.95 (978-1-4241-8646-4(3)) America Star Bks.

Jenkins, Jerry B. & Fabry, Chris. Instant Menace. 2006. (Red Rock Mysteries Ser.: 9). (ENG.). 256p. (YA). (gr. 3-7). per. 6.99 (978-1-4143-0148-8(0), Tyndale Kids) Tyndale Hse. Pubs.

Leblanc, Louise. Maddie Surfs for Cyber-Pals. Gay, Marie-Louise, illus. 2004. 64p. (J). lib. bdg. 12.00 (978-1-4242-1226-2(X)) Fitzgerald Bks.

—Maddie Surfs for Cyber-Pals. Cummins, Sarah, tr. from FRE. Gay, Marie-Louise, illus. 2004. (Formac First Novels Ser.: 52). (ENG.). 64p. (gr. 2-5). 14.95 (978-0-88780-639-1(2), 9780887806391) Formac Publishing Co., Ltd. CAN. Dist: Casemate Pubs. & Bk. Distributors, LLC.

—Maddie Surfs for Cyber Pals, 1 vol. Cummins, Sarah, tr. from FRE. Gay, Marie-Louise, illus. 2004. (Formac First Novels Ser.: 52). (ENG.). 64p. (J). (gr. 2-5). 4.95 (978-0-88780-638-4(4), 9780887806384) Formac Publishing Co., Ltd. CAN. Dist: Casemate Pubs. & Bk. Distributors, LLC.

Littman, Sarah Darer. Want to Go Private? 2011. (ENG.). 336p. (J). (gr. 9-9). 17.99 (978-0-545-15146-7(5), Scholastic Pr.) Scholastic, Inc.

Lu, Marie. Warcross, 9 vols. 2017. (ENG.). (YA). 170.91 **(978-0-525-48674-9(7))**; 368p. (gr. 7). 18.99 **(978-0-399-54796-6(7))** Penguin Young Readers Group. (G.P. Putnam's Sons Books for Young Readers).

Marciniak, Christine. Reality Ali. 2012. (J). (978-1-61271-076-1(X)); (978-1-61271-075-4(1)); pap. 13.99 (978-1-61271-074-7(3)) Zumaya Pubns. LLC.

Matthew's Web Unplugged. 2003. (J). per. (978-0-9716567-7-2(0)) Book Web Publishing, Limited.

Messinger, Robert. I've Got Mail! Salerno, John, illus. 2003. 40p. (J). 12.95 (978-1-893237-01-8(X)) Little Mai Pr.

Morgan, Melissa J. Freaky Tuesday, 17 vols. 2007. (Camp Confidential Ser.: 17). (ENG.). 160p. (J). (gr. 3-7). pap. 4.99 (978-0-448-44651-6(0), Grosset & Dunlap) Penguin Young Readers Group.

Plawner, Michael A. Then & Now. 2009. 60p. pap. 10.99 (978-0-557-08595-8(0)) Lulu Pr., Inc.

Purtill, C. Leigh. In Your Face. 2010. 240p. pap. 5.95 (978-1-60747-780-8(7), Pickwick Pr.) Phoenix Bks., Inc.

Reed, Amy. Crazy. 2012. (ENG.). 384p. (YA). (gr. 9). 16.99 (978-1-4424-1347-4(6), Simon Pulse) Simon Pulse.

Rodkey, Geoff. The Tapper Twins Go to War (with Each Other) 2015. (Tapper Twins Ser.: 1). (ENG., Illus.). 240p. (J). (gr. 3-7). 13.99 (978-0-316-29779-0(8)) Little Brown & Co.

Ryan, Jeanne. Nerve. (ENG.). (YA). (gr. 9). 2012. 304p. 17.99 (978-0-8037-3832-4(3), Dial Bks) 2016. 320p. pap. 10.99 (978-0-14-242283-0(5), Speak) Penguin Young Readers Group.

Sak., M. J. The Stone Summons. 2007. 141p. pap. 15.95 (978-1-84799-791-3(0)) Lulu Pr., Inc.

Sanschagrin, Joceline. Le Visage Masqué. Brignaud, Pierre, illus. 2004. (Mon Roman Ser.). (FRE.). 160p. (J). (gr. 2). pap. (978-2-89021-651-8(9)) Diffusion du livre Mirabel (DLM).

Schechter, Lynn R. My Big Fat Secret: How Jenna Takes Control of Her Emotions & Eating. Chin, Jason, illus. 2009. 48p. (J). (gr. 3-7). 14.95 (978-1-4338-0540-0(5)); pap. 9.95 (978-1-4338-0541-7(3)) American Psychological Assn. (Magination Pr.).

Shava, Ryder. Amit's Very Own Website, 01 vols., 1. 2016. (Rosen REAL Readers: STEM & STEAM Collection). (ENG.). 12p. (J). pap. 6.33 (978-1-5081-1617-2(2), Rosen Classroom) Rosen Publishing Group, Inc., The.

Skurzynski, Gloria & Ferguson, Alane. Over the Edge. 2008. (Mysteries in Our National Park Ser.). (ENG., Illus.). 160p. (J). (gr. 3-7). per. 4.99 (978-1-4263-0177-3(4), National Geographic Children's Bks.) National Geographic Society.

StJohn, Amanda. How to Find Information Online. Ostrom, Bob, illus. 2012. (Library Skills Ser.). (ENG.). 24p. (J). (gr. -1-2). 28.50 (978-1-61473-251-8(5), 204953) Child's World, Inc., The.

Strasser, Todd. Wish You Were Dead. 2009. (ENG.). 240p. (gr. 9-18). 16.99 (978-1-60684-007-8(X), Carolrhoda Lab™) Lerner Publishing Group.

Tashjian, Janet. The Gospel According to Larry. 2003. (Illus.). 227p. 17.00 (978-0-7569-1451-6(5)) Perfection Learning Corp.

Toz, Karen Pokras. Millicent Marie Is Not My Name. 2012. (ENG.). 162p. (J). pap. 7.99 (978-0-9848608-5-2(1)) Grand Daisy Pr.

Ure, Jean. Secret Meeting. 2004. (Diary Ser.). (ENG., Illus.). 192p. (J). (gr. 4-7). pap. 8.99 (978-0-00-715620-7(0), Collins) HarperCollins Pubs. Ltd. GBR. Dist: Independent Pubs. Group.

Walters, Eric. Stuffed, 1 vol. 2006. (Orca Soundings Ser.). (ENG.). 136p. (YA). (gr. 8-12). per. 9.95 (978-1-55143-500-8(4)) Orca Bk. Pubs. USA.

Wells, Tina. Mixed Messages. 2010. (Madison Avery Ser.: 4). (ENG.). 208p. (J). (gr. 3-7). 12.99 (978-0-06-158317-9(0)) HarperCollins Pubs.

Wilhelm, Doug. The Revealers. 2011. (ENG.). 240p. (YA). (gr. 5-9). pap. 7.99 (978-0-312-56374-5(4), 9780312563745) Square Fish.

Willis, Jeanne. Chicken Clicking. Ross, Tony, illus. 2015. (ENG.). 32p. (J). (gr. -1-k). pap. 9.99 (978-1-78344-161-7(5)) Andersen Pr. GBR. Dist: Independent Pubs. Group.

Zenescope Entertainment Staff & Brusha, Joe. Sci-Fi & Fantasy: The Perfect Mate. 2012. (Illus.). 168p. (YA). pap. 15.99 (978-1-937068-91-2(9)) Zenescope Entertainment.

INTERNMENT CAMPS

see Concentration Camps

INTERPERSONAL RELATIONS

Here are entered works that deal with the integration of people so that they can live and work together with psychological, social and economic satisfaction.

Alexander, Kwame, et al. Love & Profanity: A Collection of True, Tortured, Wild, Hilarious, Concise, & Intense Tales of Teenage Life. 2015. (ENG.). 232p. (gr. 8-12). 16.95 (978-1-63079-012-7(5)) Switch Pr.

Algranati, Melissa J. Talk about It: Family Fun for Girls 8-11. 2005. (Illus.). 49p. (J). (978-0-88441-696-8(8)) Girl Scouts of the USA.

Allenbaugh, Kay. Chocolate for a Teen's Dreams: Heartwarming Stories about Making Your Wishes Come True. 2003. (ENG., Illus.). 224p. pap. 16.95 (978-0-7432-3703-1(X), Touchstone) Touchstone.

Asugha, Ruby. Little Sisters, Listen Up! A Message of Hope for Girls Growing up in Poverty Racism, & Despair. 2004. 138p. 9.95 (978-1-889322-61-2(X), 25-017) Boys Town Pr.

Baish, Vanessa. Dating. 2007. (FAQ: Teen Life Ser.). (Illus.). 64p. (YA). (gr. 7-12). lib. bdg. 31.95 (978-1-4042-1969-4(2)) Rosen Publishing Group, Inc., The.

—Frequently Asked Questions about Dating. 2009. (FAQ: Teen Life Ser.). 64p. (gr. 5-6). 58.50 (978-1-61512-573-9(6)) Rosen Publishing Group, Inc., The.

Baker, Jed. The Social Skills Picture Book: For High School & Beyond. 2006. (ENG., Illus.). 177p. (J). (gr. 9-12). pap. 39.95 (978-1-932565-35-5(3)) Future Horizons, Inc.

Bartel, Blaine. Little Black Book on How to Get Along with Your Parents. 2004. (Illus.). 80p. (J). pap. 4.99 (978-1-57794-626-7(X)) Harrison House Pubs.

Basen, Ryan. Got Your Back: Dealing with Friends & Enemies, 1 vol. 2010. (Essential Health: a Guy's Guide Ser.). (ENG.). 112p. (J). (gr. 6-12). lib. bdg. 35.64 (978-1-61613-540-9(9)) ABDO Publishing Co.

Bauer, Marion Dane. How Do I Love You? Church, Caroline Jayne, illus. 2009. (ENG.). 26p. (J). (gr. -1-k). bds. 8.99 (978-0-545-07270-0(0), Cartwheel Bks.) Scholastic, Inc.

Bawden, Jennifer. Un Hombre no es la Solucion: Construye una Vida Propia y Luego, una Relacion con Alguien. (SPA.). (J). 12.00 (978-958-04-7015-1(4)) Norma S.A. COL. Dist: Distribuidora Norma, Inc.

Behrens, Janice. We Are Alike, We Are Different. 2009. (Scholastic News Nonfiction Readers Ser.). (ENG.). 24p. (J). (gr. 1-2). pap. 6.95 (978-0-531-21447-3(8), Children's Pr.); lib. bdg. 22.00 (978-0-531-21347-6(1)) Scholastic Library Publishing.

Beisswenger, Iffer & Eldred, Margaret. The Way We See Things: Middle Schoolers Look at Themselves & Issues They Face Everyday. Krusi, Carolynne, ed. 2004. 96p. pap. 14.95 (978-0-9759264-0-6(3)) Anemone Publishing.

Bender, Alexandra Sabina. Alana's Advice... When There's a Clique, You've Got to Think Quick. 2007. (Illus.). 152p. (J). (gr. 4-10). per. 14.95 (978-1-84590-075-5(8)) Crown Hse. Publishing.

Bender, Janet M. Getting Yourself Together When Your Family Comes Apart: Coping with Family Changes. 2004. (Illus.). 50p. per. 19.95 (978-1-931636-28-5(1)) National Ctr. For Youth Issues.

Berry, Joy. Help Me Be Good about Being Bossy. 2009. (Help Me Be Good Ser.). 32p. pap. 7.95 (978-1-60577-126-7(0)) Berry, Joy Enterprises.

—Help Me Be Good about Being Mean. 2009. (Help Me Be Good Ser.). 32p. pap. 7.95 (978-1-60577-129-8(5)) Berry, Joy Enterprises.

—Help Me Be Good about Showing Off. 2009. (Help Me Be Good Ser.). 32p. pap. 7.95 (978-1-60577-107-6(4)) Berry, Joy Enterprises.

—Help Me Be Good about Whining. 2009. (ENG.). 40p. (J). (gr. k-2). pap. 7.95 (978-1-60577-115-1(5)) Berry, Joy Enterprises.

—Help Me Be Good Being Mean. Bartholomew, illus. 2010. (Help Me Be Good Ser.). (ENG.). 32p. (J). (gr. -1-2). pap. 4.99 (978-1-60577-142-7(2)) Berry, Joy Enterprises.

—Help Me Be Good Showing Off. Bartholomew, illus. 2010. (Help Me Be Good Ser.). (ENG.). 32p. (J). (gr. -1-2). pap. 4.99 (978-1-60577-143-4(0)) Berry, Joy Enterprises.

—Help Me Be Good Whining. Bartholomew, illus. 2010. (Help Me Be Good Ser.). (ENG.). 32p. (J). (gr. -1-2). pap. 4.99 (978-1-60577-134-2(1)) Berry, Joy Enterprises.

Berry, Joy Wilt. A Book about Being Mean. 2005. (Illus.). (J). (978-0-7172-8591-4(X)) Scholastic, Inc.

—A Book about Complaining. 2005. (Illus.). (J). (978-0-7172-8595-2(2)) Scholastic, Inc.

—A Book about Interrupting. 2005. (Illus.). (J). (978-0-7172-8599-0(5)) Scholastic, Inc.

—A Book about Showing Off. 2005. (Illus.). (J). (978-0-7172-8597-6(9)) Scholastic, Inc.

Bosworth, Lo. The Lo-Down. 2011. (ENG.). 256p. (YA). (gr. 9-18). pap. 9.99 (978-1-4424-1200-2(3), Simon & Schuster Bks. For Young Readers) Simon & Schuster Bks. For Young Readers.

Buron, Kari D. & Buron, Kari Dunn. When My Worries Get Too Big! A Relaxation Book for Children Who Live with Anxiety. 2006. (Illus.). 124p. pap. 16.95 (978-1-931282-92-5(7)) Autism Asperger Publishing Co.

Cain, Susan, et al. Quiet Power: The Secret Strengths of Introverts. Snider, Grant, illus. (ENG.). 288p. (J). (gr. 5). 2017. 9.99 (978-0-14-750992-5(0), Puffin Books) 2016. 17.99 (978-0-8037-4060-0(3), Dial Bks) 2016. lib. bdg. 20.99 (978-0-399-18672-1(7), Dial Bks) Penguin Young Readers Group.

Cali, Davide. I Love Kissing You. Bloch, Serge, illus. 2011.Tr. of J'aime T'embrasser. (ENG.). 96p. 16.95 (978-0-9804165-0-3(7)) Wilkins Farago Pty, Ltd. AUS. Dist: Independent Pubs. Group.

Carlinsky, Dan. Do You Know Your Boyfriend? 2013. (Do You Know? Ser.). (ENG.). 48p. (YA). (gr. 9-12). pap. 5.99 (978-1-4022-8539-4(6)) Sourcebooks, Inc.

Carlson, Dale Bick. Talk: Teen Art of Communication. Khairnar, Kishore, ed. Nicklaus, Carol, illus. 2006. (ENG.). 154p. (gr. 7-18). pap. 14.95 (978-1-884158-32-2(3)) Team Kreskin Productions, LLC.

Cassella, Lynn. When Parents Divorce. 2003. (YA). pap. 1.95 net. (978-0-7648-1061-9(8)) Liguori Pubns.

Chapman, Gary D. A Teen's Guide to the 5 Love Languages: How to Understand Yourself & Improve Relationships with Those You Care About. 2016. (ENG.). 144p. pap. 13.99 (978-0-8024-1435-9(4)) Northfield Publishing.

Clark, Chap. Next Time I Fall in Love: How to Handle Sex, Intimacy, & Feelings in Dating Relationships. 2004. 144p. pap. 20.00 (978-1-59244-684-1(1), Wipf and Stock) Wipf & Stock Pubs.

Coan, Sharon. Good for Me: Love. 2015. (TIME for KIDS(r) Nonfiction Readers Ser.). (ENG., Illus.). 12p. (gr. k-k). 4.99 (978-1-4938-2153-2(9)) Teacher Created Materials, Inc.

Cobb, Carlene. Coping with an Abusive Relationship. (Coping Ser.). 192p. (gr. 7-12). 2009. 63.90 (978-1-61511-990-5(6)) 2005. (Illus.). (YA). lib. bdg. 34.60 (978-0-8239-2822-4(5)) Rosen Publishing Group, Inc., The.

Colwell, Todd. Get Real about Relationships: Leader's Guide. 2005. (YA). 7.95 (978-0-9748825-6-7(9)) Ampelon Publishing, LLC.

Constantine, Robin. The Season of You & Me. 2016. 352p. (YA). (gr. 9). 17.99 (978-0-06-243883-6(2)) HarperCollins Pubs.

Cook, Julia. Personal Space Camp. 2006. (J). 15.95 (978-1-934073-06-3(7)) National Ctr. For Youth Issues.

Cooper, Scott. Speak up & Get Along! Learn the Mighty Might, Thought Chop, & More Tools to Make Friends, Stop Teasing, & Feel Good about Yourself. 2005. (ENG., Illus.). 128p. (J). (gr. 4-7). pap. 12.99 (978-1-57542-182-7(8)) Free Spirit Publishing, Inc.

Cotta, Susan. I Can Show You I Care: Compassionate Touch for Children. Crawford, Gregory, illus. 2003. (ENG.). 32p. (J). (gr. k-4). 18.95 (978-1-55643-433-4(2)) North Atlantic Bks.

Courtney, Vicki. Can You Relate? How to Handle Parents, Friends, Boys, & More. 2016. (ENG.). 208p. (J). (gr. 3-6). pap. 14.99 (978-1-4336-8785-3(2), B&H Kids) B&H Publishing Group.

Crissy, Pat. Real-World Social Skills Curriculum. 2004. (J). ring bd. 69.95 (978-1-58804-368-9(1)) P C I Education.

Crist, James J. The Survival Guide for Making & Being Friends. 2014. (ENG., Illus.). 128p. (J). (gr. 4-7). pap. 13.99 (978-1-57542-472-9(X)) Free Spirit Publishing, Inc.

Criswell, Patti Kelley. Friendship Troubles. 2013. (Smart Girl's Guide Ser.). lib. bdg. 24.50 (978-0-606-34732-7(1), Turtleback) Turtleback Bks.

—A Smart Girl's Guide to Knowing What to Say: Finding the Words to Fit Any Situation. 2011. (ENG.). 120p. (J). pap. 9.95 (978-1-59369-772-3(4)) American Girl Publishing, Inc.

Davidson, Tish. School Conflict. 2004. (Life Balance Ser.). (ENG., Illus.). 80p. (YA). (gr. 5-8). pap. 6.95 (978-0-531-15571-4(4), Watts, Franklin) Scholastic Library Publishing.

Dennis, Rainey. Passport 2 Purity. 2004. 29.99 (978-1-57229-656-5(9)) FamilyLife.

Diamond, Susan. Social Rules for Kids-the Top 100 Social Rules Kids Need to Succeed. 2011. (ENG.). 132p. (J). pap.

19.95 *(978-1-934575-84-0(4))* Autism Asperger Publishing Co.

DiPiazza, Francesca. Friend Me! Six Hundred Years of Social Networking in America. 2012. (Single Titles Ser.). (ENG.). 112p. (gr. 5-12). lib. bdg. 33.26 *(978-0-7613-5869-5(2),* Twenty-First Century Bks.) Lerner Publishing Group.

Doeden, Matt. Conflict Resolution Smarts: How to Communicate, Negotiate, Compromise, & More. 2012. (USA TODAY Teen Wise Guides: Time, Money, & Relationships Ser.). (ENG., Illus.). 64p. (J). (gr. 8-12). lib. bdg. 31.93 *(978-0-7613-7020-8(X))* Lerner Publishing Group.

Drew, Naomi. The Kids' Guide to Working Out Conflicts: How to Keep Cool, Stay Safe, & Get Along. 2004. (ENG., Illus.). 160p. (YA). (gr. 5-9). pap. 14.99 *(978-1-57542-150-6(X))* Free Spirit Publishing, Inc.

Eastham, Chad. The Truth about Breaking Up, Making Up, & Moving On, 1 vol. 2013. (ENG.). 240p. (YA). pap. 14.99 *(978-1-4003-2115-5(8))* Nelson, Thomas Inc.

Educators for Social Responsibility Staff & Desetta, Al, eds. The Courage to Be Yourself: True Stories by Teens about Cliques, Conflicts, & Overcoming Peer Pressure. 2005. (ENG.). 160p. (YA). (gr. 8-18). pap. 13.99 *(978-1-57542-185-8(2))* Free Spirit Publishing, Inc.

Espeland, Pamela. Knowing Me, Knowing You: The I-Sight Way to Understand Yourself & Others. 2004. (Illus.). 128p. (YA). (gr. 8-12). pap. 13.95 *(978-1-57542-090-5(2))* Free Spirit Publishing, Inc.

Espeland, Pamela & Verdick, Elizabeth. Making Choices & Making Friends: The Social Competencies Assets. 2006. (Adding Assets Series for Kids Ser.). (ENG., Illus.). 80p. (J). (gr. 3-7). pap. 7.99 *(978-1-57542-201-5(8))* Free Spirit Publishing, Inc.

Everly, Nita. Early Social Behavior Books Can You Be a Friend? 2005. (J). spiral bd. 10.95 *(978-0-7606-0633-9(1))* LinguiSystems, Inc.

—Early Social Behavior Books Can you Be Polite? 2005. (J). spiral bd. 10.95 *(978-0-7606-0637-7(4))* LinguiSystems, Inc.

—Early Social Behavior Books Can You Listen with Your Eyes? 2005. (J). spiral bd. 10.95 *(978-0-7606-0630-8(7))* LinguiSystems, Inc.

—Early Social Behavior Books Can You Share? 2005. (J). spiral bd. 10.95 *(978-0-7606-0635-3(8))* LinguiSystems, Inc.

—Early Social Behavior Books Can You Take Turns? 2005. (J). spiral bd. 10.95 *(978-0-7606-0634-6(X))* LinguiSystems, Inc.

—Early Social Behavior Books Can You Tell How Someone Feels? 2005. (J). spiral bd. 14.95 *(978-0-7606-0636-0(6))* LinguiSystems, Inc.

—Early Social Behavior Books Can You Use a Good Voice? 2005. (J). spiral bd. 10.95 *(978-0-7606-0632-2(3))* LinguiSystems, Inc.

—Early Social Behavior Books Can You Use Your Words? 2005. (J). spiral bd. 10.95 *(978-0-7606-0631-5(5))* LinguiSystems, Inc.

—Early Social Behavior Books Set (12) 2007. (J). spiral bd. 143.40 *(978-0-7606-9983-6(6))* LinguiSystems, Inc.

Fallon, Michael. Who Are These People? Coping with Family Dynamics, 1 vol. 2010. (Essential Health: a Guy's Guide Ser.). (ENG., Illus.). 112p. (J). (gr. 6-12). lib. bdg. 35.64 *(978-1-61613-545-4(X))* ABDO Publishing Co.

Fiedler, Julie. How to Deal with Insults. (Let's Work It Out Ser.). 24p. (gr. 2-3). 2009. 42.50 *(978-1-61514-263-7(0),* PowerKids Pr.) 2007. (Illus.). (J). lib. bdg. 22.60 *(978-1-4042-3673-8(2))* Rosen Publishing Group, Inc., The.

Finding a Partner in Later Life. 2005. (YA). per. *(978-1-59872-108-9(9))* Instant Pub.

Fine, Debra. Beyond Texting: The Fine Art of Face-to-Face Communication for Teenagers. 2014. (ENG.). 136p. (YA). pap. 12.95 *(978-0-9889696-0-5(2))* Canon Pubs.

Finnis, Anne & Bond, Denis. It's a Boy/Girl Thing! The Truth... in Their Own Words. 2003. (ENG., Illus.). 144p. (J). pap. 10.95 *(978-0-09-943212-8(9),* Red Fox) Random House Children's Books GBR. Dist: Random Hse. of Canada.

Fischer, James. Earning Money: Jobs. 2010. (Junior Library of Money). 64p. (YA). (gr. 7-18). pap. 9.95 *(978-1-4222-1882-2(1));* lib. bdg. 22.95 *(978-1-4222-1763-4(9))* Mason Crest.

Fixman, Jennifer. Make a Difference with Miss Jenny. 2009. 64p. 19.99 *(978-1-930979-14-7(2))* Edutunes.

Gainer, Cindy. I'm Like You, You're Like Me: A Book about Understanding & Appreciating Each Other. Sakamoto, Miki, illus. (ENG.). 48p. (J). (gr. -1-3). 2013. pap. 9.99 *(978-1-57542-436-1(3))* 2011. 14.99 *(978-1-57542-383-8(9))* Free Spirit Publishing, Inc.

Gizicki-Lipson, Coryn & Gizicki, Carlie. An Angel in the Sky. Gizicki-Lipson, Coryn, illus. 2003. (ENG., Illus.). 32p. (J). 14.95 *(978-0-9740438-0-7(X))* In the Sky Publishing.

Goetchius, Alex. Career Building Through Social Networking. 2009. (Digital Career Building Ser.). 64p. (gr. 6-6). 58.50 *(978-1-61512-172-4(2))* Rosen Publishing Group, Inc., The.

Golden, Pam. Lulu Learns about Reporting: Ending the Tattle Battle. Outohak, Diana, illus. 2007. 28p. (J). pap. 18.95 *(978-0-9659650-8-8(2))* Roedway Pr.

Goodwin, Evelyn. Meet the Children from the Fifty States in Poetry. 2007. 106p. pap. 37.50 *(978-0-615-16145-7(6))* Goodwin, Evelyn.

Graham, Stedman. Move Without the Ball: Put Your Skills & Your Magic to Work for You. 2004. (ENG., Illus.). 208p. pap. 14.99 *(978-0-7432-3440-5(5),* Touchstone) Touchstone.

Graves, Sue. I Don't Want to Be Nice! A Book about Showing Kindness. Carletti, Emanuela & Guicciardini, Desideria, illus. 2017. (Our Emotions & Behavior Ser.). (ENG.). 28p. (J). (gr. -1-3). 12.99 ***(978-1-63198-132-6(3))*** Free Spirit Publishing, Inc.

Gregoire, Maryellen. Help, 1 vol. 2012. (Wonder Readers Emergent Level Ser.). (ENG.). 32p. (gr. -1-1). pap. 5.99 *(978-1-4296-9190-1(5),* Wonder Readers) Capstone Press of Coughlan Cos.

Greven, Alec. How to Talk to Girls. Acedera, Kei, illus. 2008. (ENG.). 48p. (J). (gr. 1-5). 9.99 *(978-0-06-170999-9(9),* Collins) HarperCollins Pubs.

—How to Talk to Moms. Acedera, Kei, illus. 2009. (ENG.). 48p. (J). (gr. 1-5). 9.99 *(978-0-06-171001-8(6),* Collins) HarperCollins Pubs.

Hacker, Caryn Sabes. A Bully Grows Up: Erik Meets the Wizard: Adult Guide Edition, 1. Boureau, Silvere, illus. 2006. 34p. (J). tchr. ed. 15.95 *(978-0-9791046-0-2(2))* Caryn Solutions, LLC.

Hamilton, Lily & Myers, Barbara. Lily & Nana. Sellaro, Brendan, illus. 2010. (J). *(978-0-929915-38-8(0))* Headline Bks., Inc.

Hanson, Anders. Keeping the Peace: The Kids' Book of Peacemaking, 1 vol. 2014. (What We Stand For Ser.). (ENG.). 24p. (gr. 5-10). lib. bdg. 25.65 *(978-1-62403-294-3(X),* Super SandCastle) ABDO Publishing Co.

Hardyman, Robyn. Relationships. 2010. (Being Healthy, Feeling Great Ser.). (ENG.). 32p. (J). pap. 10.60 *(978-1-61532-380-7(5),* PowerKids Pr.); (gr. 3-6). lib. bdg. 26.50 *(978-1-61532-371-5(6))* Rosen Publishing Group, Inc., The.

Harpster, Steve, illus. Growing up Happy: Arnold Gets Angry, Betty Stops the Bully & Catherine Finds Her Courage: the Emotional Literacy Series, 3, 3 vols., Set. 2004. (Emotional Literacy Ser.). 135p. (J). lib. bdg. 52.00 *(978-0-9747789-9-0(0))* CTC Publishing.

Hemmen, Lucie. The Teen Girl's Survival Guide: 10 Tips for Making Friends, Avoiding Drama & Coping with Social Stress. 2015. (Instant Help Solutions Ser.). (ENG.). 208p. (YA). (gr. 5-12). pap. 17.95 *(978-1-62625-306-3(4))* New Harbinger Pubns.

Hentges, Katie. Your First Boyfriend. 2012. (Relationships 101 Ser.). (ENG., Illus.). 48p. (J). (gr. 5-8). pap. 11.75 *(978-1-4488-6833-9(5),* Rosen Reference) Rosen Publishing Group, Inc., The.

Heos, Bridget. Your First Girlfriend. 2012. (Relationships 101 Ser.). (ENG., Illus.). 48p. (J). (gr. 5-8). pap. 11.75 *(978-1-4488-6836-0(X));* lib. bdg. 27.95 *(978-1-4488-6830-8(0))* Rosen Publishing Group, Inc., The.

Hernandez, Roger E. Teens & Relationships. Developed in Association with the Gallup Organization Staff, ed. 2013. (Gallup Youth Survey: Major Issues & Trends Ser.: 14). 112p. (J). (gr. 7-18). 24.95 *(978-1-4222-2956-9(4))* Mason Crest.

—Teens & Relationships. 2008. (Gallup Youth Survey, Major Issues & Trends Ser.). (Illus.). 112p. (J). (gr. -1-7). lib. bdg. 22.95 *(978-1-59084-875-3(6))* Mason Crest.

Holtzman, Claudia Ann. Why Are They Called... Grandparents! 2012. 36p. pap. 24.95 *(978-1-4626-8404-5(1))* America Star Bks.

Howver, Jen, et al. Wisdom on ... Getting along with Parents, 1 vol. 2008. (Wisdom Ser.). (ENG.). 144p. (YA). pap. 9.99 *(978-0-310-27929-7(1))* Zondervan.

Hyde, Natalie. Above & Beyond with Collaboration. 2016. (Fueling Your Future! Going above & Beyond in the 21st Cent Ser.). (ENG., Illus.). 48p. (J). (gr. 5-8). *(978-0-7787-2829-0(3))* Crabtree Publishing Co.

Jablonski, Carrie. Spot the Duck: A Real Story. 2012. 24p. 24.95 *(978-1-4626-7464-0(X));* pap. 24.95 *(978-1-4626-8328-4(2))* America Star Bks.

Jakubiak, David J. A Smart Kid's Guide to Social Networking Online. 2010. (Illus.). 24p. (J). pap. 8.25 *(978-1-4358-3358-6(9),* 1300427, PowerKids Pr.) Rosen Publishing Group, Inc., The.

Jenkins, Susan Padgett. Daddy Comes Back. 2011. 20p. pap. 24.95 *(978-1-4626-2092-0(2))* America Star Bks.

Jessum, Jeffrey E. Diary of a Social Detective: Real-life tales of mystery, intrigue & interpersonal Adventure. 2011. (ENG., Illus.). 293p. (YA). pap. 19.95 *(978-1-934575-71-0(2))* Autism Asperger Publishing Co.

Johnston, Marianne. Dealing with Fighting / Qué hacer con las Peleas. 2009. (Conflict Resolution Library / Biblioteca solución de conflictos Ser.). (ENG & SPA.). 24p. (gr. 2-3). 42.50 *(978-1-60853-414-2(6),* Editorial Buenas Letras) Rosen Publishing Group, Inc., The.

—Dealing with Fighting/Qué Hacer con Las Peleas. Velazquez De Leon, Mauricio, tr. from ENG. 2008. (Conflict Resolution Library / Biblioteca Solución de Conflictos Ser.). (SPA., Illus.). 24p. (J). (gr. k-3). lib. bdg. 22.60 *(978-1-4042-7660-4(2))* Rosen Publishing Group, Inc., The.

—Dealing with Insults / Qué hacer con los Insultos. 2009. (Conflict Resolution Library / Biblioteca solución de conflictos Ser.). (ENG & SPA.). 24p. (gr. 2-3). 42.50 *(978-1-60853-415-9(4),* Editorial Buenas Letras) Rosen Publishing Group, Inc., The.

—Dealing with Insults/Que Hacer con Los Insultos. Velazquez De Leon, Mauricio, tr. from ENG. 2008. (Conflict Resolution Library / Biblioteca Solución de Conflictos Ser.). (SPA., Illus.). 24p. (J). (gr. k-3). lib. bdg. 22.60 *(978-1-4042-7661-1(0))* Rosen Publishing Group, Inc., The.

Kaplan, Arie. Dating & Relationships: Navigating the Social Scene. 2011. (Young Man's Guide to Contemporary Issues Ser.). (ENG.). 104p. (YA). (gr. 9-12). lib. bdg. 34.60 *(978-1-4488-5523-0(3))* Rosen Publishing Group, Inc., The.

Kavanaugh, Dorothy. Feeling Unloved? Girls Dealing with Feelings. 2014. (ENG.). 64p. (J). (gr. 5-12). 15.95 *(978-1-62293-050-0(9))* Enslow Pubs., Inc.

Kerstein, Lauren H. A Week of Switching, Shifting, & Stretching: How to Make My Thinking More Flexible. 2013. (ENG., Illus.). 57p. (J). (gr. -1-5). pap. 18.00 *(978-1-937473-89-1(9))* Autism Asperger Publishing Co.

Khalifé, Fatima & Mouazen, Deema. If Your Mom Was.... What Will You Do? 2012. 28p. pap. 19.99 *(978-1-4772-6951-0(7))* AuthorHouse.

Kihm, Steve. The Lost Candy Bar. 2004. (J). mass mkt. 6.95 *(978-0-9786794-0-8(7))* Lost Candy Bar Pr., LLC.

Lennon, Liz. My Behaviour - I Don't Hit. 2017. (Little Stars,Sea-To-Sea Ser.). (ENG., Illus.). 24p. (J). (gr. -1-k). pap. 6.99 *(978-1-4451-4763-5(7),* Franklin Watts) Hachette Children's Group GBR. Dist: Hachette Bk. Group.

Levy, Barrie. In Love & in Danger: A Teen's Guide to Breaking Free of Abusive Relationships. 3rd rev. ed. 2006. (ENG., Illus.). 144p. (Orig.). per. 13.00 *(978-1-58005-187-3(1))* Seal Pr.

Lightner, Laura. FirstFires. Messina, Linda, illus. 2008. 27p. (J). 31.99 *(978-1-4363-4542-2(1))* Xlibris Corp.

Liles, Rebecca. My Daddy's a Soldier, 2 bks. 2003. (Illus.). 16p. (J). 4.99 *(978-0-9744346-0-5(4))* Rebecca's Bks.

—My Mommy's a Soldier, 2 bks. 2003. (Illus.). 16p. (J). 4.99 *(978-0-9744346-1-2(2))* Rebecca's Bks.

Logan, John. An Unloved Guy's Guide: How to Deal. 2014. (ENG.). 64p. (J). (gr. 5-12). 15.95 *(978-1-62293-020-3(7))* Enslow Pubs., Inc.

Logan, John & Kavanaugh, Dorothy. A Guys' Guide to Love. 2008. (Flip-It-Over Guides to Teen Emotions Ser.). (Illus.). 128p. (J). (gr. k-5). lib. bdg. 33.27 *(978-0-7660-2855-5(0))* Enslow Pubs., Inc.

Lowery, Zoe & Bezdecheck, Bethany. Women in Relationships. 2017. (Women in the World Ser.). 112p. (gr. 12-11). 37.10 ***(978-1-5081-7443-1(1),*** Rosen Young Adult) Rosen Publishing Group, Inc., The.

Lynch, Amy. A Smart Girl's Guide to Understanding Her Family: Feelings, Fighting & Figuring It Out. Scheuer, Lauren, illus. 2009. (ENG.). 64p. (J). (gr. 3-18). pap. 9.95 *(978-1-59369-617-7(5))* American Girl Publishing, Inc.

Macavinta, Courtney & Pluym, Andrea Vander. Respect: A Girl's Guide to Getting Respect & Dealing When Your Line Is Crossed. Lepage, Catherine, illus. 2005. (ENG.). 240p. (YA). (gr. 8-12). pap. 16.99 *(978-1-57542-177-3(1))* Free Spirit Publishing, Inc.

Major, Gail Baccelli. What Do You See in Me I am Who I am. Major, Rebekah, illus. 2013. (ENG.). 32p. (J). pap. 9.95 *(978-1-939289-22-3(X),* Little Creek Bks.) Jan-Carol Publishing, INC.

Makerspace Projects. 2015. (Makerspace Projects Ser.). (ENG.). 32p. (J). (gr. 3-3). pap., pap., pap. 423.00 *(978-1-4777-5680-5(9),* Windmill Bks.) Rosen Publishing Group, Inc., The.

Marcovitz, Hal. Teens & Family Issues. 2008. (Gallup Youth Survey, Major Issues & Trends Ser.). (Illus.). 112,128p. (YA). (gr. 7-9). lib. bdg. 22.95 *(978-1-59084-725-1(3))* Mason Crest.

Margot. The Best Good Night Present Ever. 2010. 32p. pap. 12.99 *(978-1-4389-9168-9(1))* AuthorHouse.

Marx, Trish. Reaching for the Sun: Kids in Cuba. 2003. (Single Titles Ser.: 6). (ENG., Illus.). 48p. (gr. 2-4). lib. bdg. 26.60 *(978-0-7613-2261-0(2),* Millbrook Pr.) Lerner Publishing Group.

Masters, Barbara. King Jack the Fourth. 2011. 24p. 13.00 *(978-1-4567-1344-7(2))* AuthorHouse.

Mathews, Janice. Jack, Jake, Jacque, & Jodie: The Get-Along Doggies. 2015. (J). *(978-0-8163-5734-5(X))* Pacific Pr. Publishing Assn.

McCloud, Carol. Have You Filled a Bucket Today? A Guide to Daily Happiness for Kids. Messing, David, illus. 2006. (ENG.). 32p. (J). (gr. -1-3). pap. 9.95 *(978-0-9785075-1-0(7),* Ferne Pr.) Nelson Publishing & Marketing.

Mccloud, Carol. Have You Filled a Bucket Today: A Guide to Daily Happiness for Kids. 2015. lib. bdg. 20.80 *(978-0-606-38236-6(4))* Turtleback Bks.

McCloud, Carol & Martin, Katherine. Fill a Bucket: A Guide to Daily Happiness for Young Children. David, Messing, illus. 2009. (ENG.). 26p. (J). (-2). 9.95 *(978-1-933916-43-9(5))* Bucket Fillers, Inc.

McGee, Kathleen M. & Buddenberg, Laura J. Unmasking Sexual Con Games: Helping Teens Avoid Emotional Grooming & Dating Violence. 3rd ed. 2004. (Leader's Guide with Session Plans Ser.). (ENG., Illus.). 199p. pap. 29.95 *(978-1-889322-54-4(7),* 25-015) Boys Town Pr.

—Unmasking Sexual Con Games Teen's Guide: A Teen's Guide to Avoiding Emotional Grooming & Dating Violence. 3rd ed. 2004. (Leader's Guide with Session Plans Ser.). (ENG.). 79p. pap. 5.95 *(978-1-889322-55-1(5),* 25-016) Boys Town Pr.

Medina, Sarah. Know the Facts about Relationships. 2009. (J). 70.50 *(978-1-4358-5469-7(1),* Rosen Reference); (ENG.). 48p. (YA). pap. 11.75 *(978-1-4358-5468-0(3),* Rosen Reference); (ENG., Illus.). 48p. (YA). (gr. 5-9). lib. bdg. 29.25 *(978-1-4358-5342-3(3))* Rosen Publishing Group, Inc., The.

Meiners, Cheri J. Accept & Value Each Person. Johnson, Meredith, illus. 2006. (Learning to Get Along(r) Ser.). (ENG.). 40p. (J). (gr. 3-7). pap. 10.95 *(978-1-57542-203-9(4))* Free Spirit Publishing, Inc.

—Be Polite & Kind. 2003. (Learning to Get Along(r) Ser.). (ENG., Illus.). 40p. (J). (gr. -1-3). pap. 10.95 *(978-1-57542-151-3(8))* Free Spirit Publishing, Inc.

—Join in & Play. 2003. (Learning to Get Along(r) Ser.). (ENG., Illus.). 40p. (J). (gr. -1-3). pap. 10.95 *(978-1-57542-152-0(6))* Free Spirit Publishing, Inc.

—Talk & Work It Out. Johnson, Meredith, illus. 2005. (Learning to Get Along(r) Ser.). (ENG.). 40p. (J). (gr. -1-3). pap. 10.95 *(978-1-57542-176-6(3))* Free Spirit Publishing, Inc.

—Talk & Work It Out / Hablar y Resolver. Johnson, Meredith, illus. 2015. (Learning to Get Along(r) Ser.). (ENG, SPA & MUL.). 48p. (J). (gr. -1-3). pap. 12.45 *(978-1-57542-497-2(5))* Free Spirit Publishing, Inc.

Metzger, Julie & Lehman, Robert. Will Puberty Last My Whole Life? Real Answers to Real Questions from Preteens about Body Changes, Sex, & Other Growing-Up Stuff. 2012. (ENG., Illus.). 192p. (YA). (gr. 4-7). pap. 16.95 *(978-1-57061-739-3(2),* Little Bigfoot) Sasquatch Bks.

Mihaly, Mary E. Getting Your Own Way: A Guide to Growing up Assertively. 2014. (ENG.). 176p. pap. 12.95 *(978-1-59077-306-2(3))* Evans, M. & Co., Inc.

Miles, Lisa & Chown, Xanna Eve. How to Survive Dating. 2013. (Girl Talk Ser.). 48p. (J). (gr. 5-8). pap. 70.50 *(978-1-4777-0719-7(0),* Rosen Reference); (ENG., Illus.). pap. 11.75 *(978-1-4777-0718-0(2),* Rosen Classroom); (ENG., Illus.). lib. bdg. 29.25 *(978-1-4777-0705-0(0),* Rosen Reference) Rosen Publishing Group, Inc., The.

—How to Survive Having a Crush. 2013. (Girl Talk Ser.). 48p. (J). (gr. 5-8). pap. 70.50 *(978-1-4777-0727-2(1),* Rosen Reference); (ENG., Illus.). pap. 11.75 *(978-1-4777-0720-3(4),* Rosen Reference); (ENG., Illus.). lib. bdg. 29.25 *(978-1-4777-0706-7(9),* Rosen Classroom) Rosen Publishing Group, Inc., The.

Miller, Connie Colwell. You Can Handle Conflict: Hands or Words? Victoria Assanelli, illus. 2017. (Making Good Choices Ser.). (ENG.). 24p. (J). (gr. 1-4). 20.95 ***(978-1-68151-162-7(2),*** Amicus Illustrated) Amicus Publishing.

Moe, Barbara. Coping with Rejection. (Coping Ser.). 192p. (gr. 7-12). 2009. 63.90 *(978-1-61512-010-9(6))* 2005. (Illus.). (YA). lib. bdg. 34.60 *(978-0-8239-3362-4(8))* Rosen Publishing Group, Inc., The.

Moehn, Heather. Everything You Need to Know about Cliques. (Need to Know Library). 64p. 2009. (gr. 5-5). 58.50 *(978-1-60854-058-7(8))* 2005. (Illus.). (J). (gr. 7-12). 31.95 *(978-0-8239-3326-6(1))* Rosen Publishing Group, Inc., The.

Monckeberg, Paulina. Artilugia Agenda: Diario de Amores y Locuras. 2006. (Pascualina Family of Products Ser.). (SPA., Illus.). 274p. (J). (gr. 3-5). 14.99 *(978-956-8222-46-8(4))* Pascualina Producciones S.A.

Mototsune, Kat. Cliques: Using What You Have Inside, 1 vol. Shannon, Ben, illus. (Lorimer Deal with It Ser.). (ENG.). 32p. (J). (gr. 4-12). 2011. pap. 12.95 *(978-1-55277-544-8(5),* 9781552775448) 2010. lib. bdg. 24.95 *(978-1-55277-545-5(3),* 9781552775455) Lorimer, James & Co., Ltd., Pubs. CAN. Dist: Orca Bk. Pubs. USA, Casemate Pubs. & Bk. Distributors, LLC.

Mutch Miller, Tiwana. Be Encouraging. 2008. (J). per. 10.00 *(978-0-9788937-9-8(4))* Amani Publishing, LLC.

Neal, Angie & Kjesbo, Rynette. Simply Social 7 at School. Bristol, Mark, illus. 2011. 216p. (J). spiral bd. 34.95 net. *(978-1-60723-005-2(4))* Super Duper Pubns.

Nunn, Daniel. I Can Be a Friend. 2014. (Me & My Friends Ser.). (ENG.). 24p. (gr. -1-1). pap. 5.99 *(978-1-4846-0245-4(5),* Acorn) Heinemann-Raintree.

—I Can Listen, 1 vol. 2014. (Me & My Friends Ser.). (ENG.). 24p. (gr. -1-1). pap. 5.99 *(978-1-4846-0246-1(3),* Acorn) Heinemann-Raintree.

Olien, Rebecca. Kids Care! 75 Ways to Make a Difference for People, Animals & the Environment. Kline, Michael, illus. (ENG.). 128p. (J). (gr. 3-7). 2008. pap. 12.99 *(978-0-8249-6792-5(5))* 2007. 16.99 *(978-0-8249-6793-2(3))* Worthy Publishing. (Ideal Pubns.).

Orr, Tamra B. Coping with Breakups & Jealousy. 2017. (Coping Ser.). 112p. (J). (gr. 12-12). 37.10 ***(978-1-5081-7388-5(5),*** Rosen Young Adult) Rosen Publishing Group, Inc., The.

Palmer, Pat. Liking Myself. Shondeck, Betty, illus. 2010. 102p. (J). pap. 12.99 *(978-0-9622834-2-0(8))* Uplift Pr.

Parker, Vic. Buenas Relaciones, 1 vol. 2010. (Explorar el Civismo Ser.). (SPA & ENG.). 32p. (gr. 1-3). 27.32 *(978-1-4329-4463-6(0));* pap. 8.29 *(978-1-4329-4471-1(1))* Heinemann-Raintree.

Payment, Simone. Friendship, Dating, & Relationships. 2010. (Teens: Being Gay, Lesbian, Bisexual, or Transgender Ser.). (Illus.). 80p. (YA). (gr. 7-12). lib. bdg. 33.25 *(978-1-4358-3578-8(6))* Rosen Publishing Group, Inc., The.

Payne, Lauren Murphy. We Can Get Along: A Child's Book of Choices. Iwai, Melissa, illus. 2nd rev. ed. 2015. (ENG.). 40p. (Orig.). (J). (gr. -1-2). pap. 9.99 *(978-1-63198-027-5(0))* Free Spirit Publishing, Inc.

Peavler, Amy & Peavler, Jan. The King the Queen & the Princess. Peavler, Amy & Peavler, Jan, illus. 2006. (Illus.). 40p. (J). per. *(978-0-9787672-2-8(5))* Lotus Petal Publishing.

Polsky, Milton & Gilead, Jack. The Improv Workshop Handbook: Creative Movement & Verbal Interaction for Students K-8: The Object Is Teamwork. Cordero, Chris, ed. Rockwell, Richard, illus. l.t. ed. 2003. 112p. (J). (gr. k-8). pap. 15.00 *(978-0-88734-691-0(X))* Players Pr., Inc.

Poulin, Andree. The Magic Clothesline. Arbona, Marion, illus. 2012. 32p. (J). 14.95 *(978-1-4338-1194-4(4));* pap. 9.95 *(978-1-4338-1195-1(2))* American Psychological Assn. (Magination Pr.).

Priest, Saira, photos by & des. If We Were... Priest, Saira, des. l.t. ed. 2003. (Illus.). 20p. 12.95 *(978-0-9726628-7-1(1))* Niche Publishing & Marketing.

Puppet Rescue, creator. Rosie & Yellowtail Share. 2007. (Illus.). 10p. (J). 4.95 *(978-0-9799958-0-4(9))* Puppet Rescue.

Raatma, Lucia. Social Networks. 2010. (21st Century Skills Innovation Library: Innovation in Entertainment Ser.). (ENG.). 32p. (gr. 4-8). lib. bdg. 28.50 *(978-1-60279-636-2(X),* 200340) Cherry Lake Publishing.

Reed, Cristie. Problem Solving. 2012. (ENG., Illus.). 24p. (gr. k-2). pap. 8.95 *(978-1-61810-266-9(4))* Rourke Educational Media.

Richards, Patti. All about Social Networking. 2017. (Cutting-Edge Technology (hardcover) Ser.). (ENG., Illus.). 32p. (J). (gr. 4-7). lib. bdg. 28.50 ***(978-1-63517-016-0(8),*** Focus Readers) North Star Editions.

Richmond, Marianne. The Do-It-Yourself Guide to - Understanding a Wome. 2005. (Marianne Richmond Ser.: 0). (ENG., Illus.). 40p. 5.95 *(978-0-9763101-6-7(3),* Marianne Richmond Studios, Inc.) Sourcebooks, Inc.

—Thank You Mom. 2004. (Illus.). 40p. (YA). 7.95 *(978-0-9741465-6-0(0),* Marianne Richmond Studios, Inc.) Sourcebooks, Inc.

Riso, Walter. Amar o Depender? Como Superar el Apego Afectivo y Hacer del Amor una Experiencia Plena y Saludable. (SPA.). (J). 10.00 *(978-958-04-5425-0(6))* Norma S.A. COL. Dist: Distribuidora Norma, Inc.

Robinson, Matthew. Making Smart Choices about Relationships. (Making Smart Choices Ser.). 48p. (gr. 5-5). 2009. 53.00 *(978-1-61514-340-5(8),* Rosen Reference) 2008. (Illus.). (YA). lib. bdg. 29.25 *(978-1-4042-1390-6(2))* Rosen Publishing Group, Inc., The.

Roslund, Samantha & Rodgers, Emily Puckett. Makerspaces. 2013. (21st Century Skills Innovation Library: Makers As Innovators Ser.). (ENG.). 32p. (J). (gr. 4-8). pap. 14.21 *(978-1-62431-273-1(X),* 202886); (Illus.). 28.50 *(978-1-62431-141-3(5),* 202884) Cherry Lake Publishing.

Ross, Allison J. Everything You Need to Know about Social Anxiety. 2005. (Need to Know Library). (Illus.). 64p. (YA). (gr. 7-12). 31.95 *(978-0-8239-3324-2(5))* Rosen Publishing Group, Inc., The.

Rue, Nancy N. Everything You Need to Know about Peer Mediation. 2009. (Need to Know Library). 64p. (gr. 5-5). 58.50 *(978-1-60854-080-8(4))* Rosen Publishing Group, Inc., The.

Russell Johnson, Charlotte. A Journey to Hell & Back: The Flip Side. 2004. (Illus.). 255p. per. 15.95 *(978-0-9741893-2-1(4))* Reaching Beyond, Inc.

Ryan, Peter K. Social Networking. 2011. (Digital & Information Literacy Ser.). (ENG.). 48p. (YA). pap. 11.75 *(978-1-4488-2295-9(5));* lib. bdg. 29.25 *(978-1-4488-1922-5(9))* Rosen Publishing Group, Inc., The. (Rosen Reference).

Sasse, Connie R. & McGraw-Hill Education Staff. Families Today, 2 vols. 4th ed. 2003. (Families Today Ser.). (ENG., Illus.). 704p. (gr. 10-12). stu. ed. 85.60 *(978-0-07-829840-0(7),* 0078298407) McGraw-Hill Education.

Scherer, Lauri S. Dating. Gale, ed. 2014. (Issues That Concern You Ser.). (ENG., Illus.). 144p. (gr. 7-10). lib. bdg. 42.00 (978-0-7377-6288-4(8), Greenhaven Pr., Inc.) Cengage Gale.

Scheunemann, Pam. Learning about Differences, 1 vol. 2004. (Keeping the Peace Ser.). (ENG., Illus.). 24p. (J). (gr. k-3). lib. bdg. 24.21 (978-1-59197-561-8(1), SandCastle) ABDO Publishing Co.

Scholastic, Inc. Staff. A Drama-Free Life. Bokram, Karen, ed. Thomas, Bill, illus. 2010. (ENG.). 128p. (J). (gr. 5-9). pap. 8.99 (978-0-545-21493-3(9), Scholastic Paperbacks) Scholastic, Inc.

Seduction by Shakespeare: Advice, Observations & Quotes on Love, Lust, Beauty & Desire. 2004. 128p. (YA). (gr. 11-18). per. 11.95 (978-0-9674898-6-5(5)) TCB-Cafe Publishing.

Senker, Cath. Relationships, 1 vol. 2012. (Teen Issues Ser.). (ENG.). 56p. (gr. 6-10). pap. 9.99 (978-1-4329-6541-9(7)); lib. bdg. 34.65 (978-1-4329-6536-5(0)) Heinemann-Raintree.

Sessoms, Bob. Buscar Arriba para Alcanzar Alrededor: Guia para Lideres. 2005. (SPA., Illus.). 312p. 39.99 (978-1-4158-2115-2(1)) LifeWay Christian Resources.

Shapiro, Lawrence E. & Holmes, Julia. Let's Be Friends: A Workbook to Help Kids Learn Social Skills & Make Great Friends. 2008. (Instant Help Ser.). (ENG., Illus.). 144p. (J). (gr. k-5). pap. 16.95 (978-1-57224-610-2(3), Instant Help Books) New Harbinger Pubns.

Shaul, Joel. Our Brains Are Like Computers! Exploring Social Skills & Social Cause & Effect with Children on the Autism Spectrum. 2016. (ENG., Illus.). 80p. (J). 24.95 (978-1-84905-716-5(8), 8164) Kingsley, Jessica Pubs. GBR. Dist: Macmillan Distribution Ltd.

Sherman, Dean. Relationships: The Key to Love, Sex, & Everything Else. 2003. (ENG.). 208p. pap. 12.99 (978-1-57658-275-6(2)) YWAM Publishing.

Sheva, Marie, mem. The Year of the Dogs: A Chronicle of Redemption, a Story of Love. 2003. (Illus.). 247p. (YA). per. 15.95 (978-0-9741736-0-3(6), 9900) Sheva, Marie.

Simons, Rae. Grandparents Raising Kids. 2010. (Changing Face of Modern Families Ser.). (Illus.). 64p. (YA). (gr. 6-18). lib. bdg. 22.95 (978-1-4222-1496-1(6)) Mason Crest.

Sisler, Stephanie. Gravy on My Mashed Potatoes: A Creative Exploration of Special Relationships. Grzelak, Kyle, illus. 2012. 20p. pap. 11.95 (978-1-61493-123-2(2)) Peppertree Pr., The.

Skeen, Michelle, et al. Communication Skills for Teens: How to Listen, Express, & Connect for Success. 2016. (Instant Help Solutions Ser.). (ENG.). 208p. (YA). (gr. 5-12). pap. 16.95 (978-1-62625-263-9(7)) New Harbinger Pubns.

Smiler, Andrew M. Dating & Sex: A Guide for the 21st Century Teen Boy. 2015. 288p. (J). pap. (978-1-4338-2045-8(5), Magination Pr.) American Psychological Assn.

Snipes, Carol. Mary's Rockin' ABC's. 2005. (Illus.). (J). 17.95 (978-0-9702324-5-8(4)) Pinpoint Printing.

Sommers, Michael A. Great Interpersonal Skills. (Work Readiness Ser.). 64p. 2009. (gr. 6-6). 58.50 (978-1-60854-824-8(4)) 2008. (J). (gr. 3-7). lib. bdg. 31.95 (978-1-4042-1423-1(2)) Rosen Publishing Group, Inc., The.

Spencer, Lauren. Everything You Need to Know about Falling in Love. 2009. (Need to Know Library). 64p. (gr. 5-5). 58.50 (978-1-60854-067-9(7)) Rosen Publishing Group, Inc., The.

Stephens, Ronald, ed. Peer Pressure & Relationships. 2014. (Safety First Ser.: 11). 48p. (J). (gr. 5-18). 20.95 (978-1-4222-3050-3(3)) Mason Crest.

Stewart, Ed & McDowell, Josh. Conflicts with Others. 2008. (Project 17:17 Ser.). (ENG.). 64p. (J). pap. 4.99 (978-1-84550-354-3(6), fb41ae66-973d-4060-8e31-2a08e1f62976) Christian Focus Pubns. GBR. Dist: Bookmasters Distribution.

Tavolacci, Joyce. Teen Wise Guide to Relationships. 2012. (USA TODAY Teen Wise Guides: Time, Money, & Relationships Ser.). (ENG., Illus.). 64p. (gr. 8-12). lib. bdg. 31.93 (978-0-7613-7018-5(8)) Lerner Publishing Group.

Telgemeier, Raina. Sisters. 2014. (ENG., Illus.). 208p. (J). (gr. 3-7). 24.99 (978-0-545-54059-9(3)); pap. 10.99 (978-0-545-54060-5(7)) Scholastic, Inc. (Graphix).

—Sisters. 2014. lib. bdg. 22.10 (978-0-606-36038-8(7)) Turtleback Bks.

Thomas, Natasha. Mommy & Daddy Is There Really Greatness in Me? 2013. (ENG.). 24p. (J). pap. 34.95 (978-1-4327-8767-7(5)) Outskirts Pr., Inc.

Uhl, Xina M. Strengthening Collaborative Project Skills. 2017. (Skills for Success Ser.). 64p. (gr. 12-12). 34.45 **(978-1-5081-7566-7(7)**, Rosen Young Adult) Rosen Publishing Group, Inc., The.

Verdick, Elizabeth. Words Are Not for Hurting. Heinlen, Marieka, illus. 2004. (Best Behavior Ser.). (ENG.). 24p. (J). 7.95 (978-1-57542-155-1(0)) Free Spirit Publishing, Inc.

Vitterito, Joseph A., 2nd. My Sister Is a Preemie: A Children's Guide to the NICU Experience. Chuzzlewit, Abraham R., illus. 2012. 30p. (J). (-18). pap. 15.99 (978-0-9882940-9-7(5)) Bryson Taylor Publishing.

Ward, Shirley. Preventing the Heartaches. 2013. 96p. (gr. 10-12). 21.52 (978-1-4907-0630-6(5)); pap. 11.52 (978-1-4907-0628-3(3)) Trafford Publishing.

Weinick, Suzanne. Professional Connections: Learning How to Network. 2011. (Communicating with Confidence Ser.). (ENG.). 80p. (YA). (gr. 7-12). pap. 14.15 (978-1-4488-5635-0(3)); lib. bdg. 33.25 (978-1-4488-5520-9(9)) Rosen Publishing Group, Inc., The.

White, Kelly & Stacy, Lori. Ask Lucky! The Girls'life Guide to Dealing with Dilemmas. 2003. (Illus.). 120p. (J). (978-0-439-44982-3(0)) Scholastic, Inc.

Whitfield, Kate. The Empowered Gal's 9 Life Lessons: Keys, Tips, Strategies, Advice & Everything You Need to Know to be a Confident, Successful, in Control Gal. 2008. 236p. pap. 18.95 (978-0-595-47829-3(8)) iUniverse, Inc.

Wilcox, Christine. Understanding Family & Personal Relationships. 2017. (Understanding Psychology Ser.). (ENG.). 80p. (YA). (gr. 5-12). **(978-1-68282-273-9(7))** ReferencePoint Pr., Inc.

Wilson, Mike. Domestic Violence. 2008. (Opposing Viewpoints Ser.). (ENG., Illus.). 217p. (YA). (gr. 10-12). 27.50 (978-0-7377-4207-7(0), LML02109-243135); pap. 39.70 (978-0-7377-4206-0(2), LML02109-243102) Cengage Gale. (Greenhaven Pr., Inc.).

Wilson, Rebekah. The Hope Chest: A Legacy of Love 2nd ed. 2003. (Illus.). 380p. (YA). per. 15.00 (978-1-59565-001-6(6)) Hope Chest Legacy, Inc.

Woods, Sara. Identifying As Transgender. 2016. (Transgender Life Ser.). 00064p. (J). (gr. 6-6). pap. 12.95 (978-1-4994-6456-6(8)) Rosen Publishing Group, Inc., The.

Worthy of Honor. 2003. (Humble Heart Ser.). (J). spiral bd., wbk. ed. (978-0-9746148-2-3(3)) Common Courtesy.

INTERPERSONAL RELATIONS—FICTION

Abbott, Hailey. Boy Crazy. 2009. (ENG.). 240p. (YA). (gr. 9). pap. 8.99 (978-0-06-125385-0(5), HarperTeen) HarperCollins Pubs.

Abdul-Jabbar, Kareem. Streetball Crew Book One Sasquatch in the Paint. 2015. (Streetball Crew Ser.). (ENG.). 288p. (J). (gr. 3-7). pap. 7.99 (978-1-4231-9254-1(0)) Hyperion Bks. for Children.

Abdul-Jabbar, Kareem & Obstfeld, Raymond. Sasquatch in the Paint. 2013. (Streetball Crew Ser.). (ENG.). 272p. (J). (gr. 3-7). 16.99 (978-1-4231-7870-5(X)) Hyperion Pr.

Adachi, Mitsuru. Cross Game, Vol. 4. Adachi, Mitsuru, illus. 2011. (ENG., Illus.). 376p. pap. 14.99 (978-1-4215-3768-9(0)) Viz Media.

Adee, Donna & Adee, Ed. Jonathan Finds True Treasure. Rectenbaugh, Marci, illus. 2004. (Jonathan Ser.: Bk. 2). 344p. (J). per. 10.95 (978-0-9654272-5-8(0)) Harvest Pubns.

Adornetto, Alexandra. Ghost Hour. 2017. 272p. 9.99 (978-0-7322-9934-7(9)) HarperCollins Pubs. Australia AUS. Dist: HarperCollins Pubs.

—Halo. 2010. (Halo Trilogy Ser.: 1). (ENG.). 496p. (YA). (gr. 7-12). 16.99 (978-0-312-65626-3(2)) Feiwel & Friends.

—Halo. 2011. (Halo Trilogy Ser.: 1). (ENG.). 512p. (YA). (gr. 7-12). pap. 10.99 (978-0-312-67436-6(8), 9780312674366) Square Fish.

—HALO. 2010. (SPA.). 416p. (YA). pap. 22.95 (978-84-9918-173-8(2)) Roca Editorial ESP. Dist: Spanish Pubs., LLC.

Adrian, Emily. Like It Never Happened. 2015. (ENG.). 368p. (J). (gr. 9). 17.99 (978-0-525-42823-7(2), Dial Bks) Penguin Young Readers Group.

Albin, Gennifer. Altered. 2014. (Crewel World Ser.: 2). (ENG.). 416p. (YA). (gr. 7). pap. 10.99 (978-1-250-05073-1(1), 9781250050731) Square Fish.

Albright, Emily. The Heir & the Spare. 2016. (ENG.). 287p. (YA). 17.99 (978-1-4405-9010-8(9), Simon Pulse) F&W Media, Inc.

Alderson, Sarah. The Sound. 2014. (ENG., Illus.). 320p. (YA). (gr. 9). 17.99 (978-1-4424-9933-1(8), Simon Pulse) Simon Pulse.

Alender, Katie. Marie Antoinette, Serial Killer. (ENG.). 304p. (J). (gr. 7). 2014. pap. 9.99 (978-0-545-46810-7(8), Scholastic Paperbacks) 2013. 18.99 (978-0-545-46809-1(4)) Scholastic, Inc.

Allen, M. E. Gotta Get Some Bish Bash Bosh. 2005. (Illus.). 208p. (J). 15.99 (978-0-06-073198-4(2), HarperTeen) HarperCollins Pubs.

Allen, Skye. Pretty Peg. 2016. (ENG., Illus.). (J). 27.99 **(978-1-63533-064-9(5)**, Harmony Ink Pr.) Dreamspinner Pr.

Almond, David. Raven Summer. 2011. (ENG.). 208p. (YA). (gr. 7). pap. 7.99 (978-0-385-73807-1(2), Ember) Random Hse. Children's Bks.

The (Almost) Perfect Guide to Imperfect Boys. 2014. (Mix Ser.). (ENG., Illus.). 304p. (J). (gr. 4-8). pap. 7.99 (978-1-4814-0563-8(2), Aladdin) Simon & Schuster Children's Publishing.

Alsenas, Linas. Beyond Clueless. 2015. (ENG.). 256p. (YA). (gr. 7-11). 16.95 (978-1-4197-1496-2(1), Amulet Bks.) Abrams, Inc.

Altebrando, Tara. The Best Night of Your (Pathetic) Life. 2013. (ENG.). 256p. (YA). (gr. 9). pap. 8.99 (978-0-14-242640-1(7), Speak) Penguin Young Readers Group.

Amato, Mary. Guitar Notes. (ENG., Illus.). 304p. (J). (gr. 7). 2014. pap. 8.99 (978-1-60684-503-5(9)) 2012. 16.99 (978-1-60684-124-2(6)) Lerner Publishing Group. (Carolrhoda Lab™).

Andersen, Hans Christian. La Reina de las Nieves.Tr. of Snow Queen. (SPA., Illus.). 48p. (J). (gr. 3-5). (978-84-241-5526-1(2), EV1028) Everest Editora ESP. Dist: Lectorum Pubns., Inc.

—La Reina de las Nieves. Bravo-Villasante, Carmen, tr. Catagan, Tino, illus.Tr. of Snow Queen. (SPA.). (J). (gr. 2-4). 6.50 (978-84-355-0695-3(9)) Minon, S.A. ESP. Dist: Lectorum Pubns., Inc.

Anderson, Jessica Lee. Calli. 2011. (ENG.). 198p. (J). (gr. 6). 16.95 (978-1-57131-702-5(3)); pap. 8.00 (978-1-57131-699-8(X)) Milkweed Editions.

Anderson, Jodi Lynn. Love & Peaches. 256p. (YA). 2009. (Peaches Ser.: 3). (ENG.). (gr. 8). pap. 8.99 (978-0-06-073313-1(6)) 2008. (gr. 7-18). lib. bdg. 17.89 (978-0-06-073312-4(8)) HarperCollins Pubs. (HarperTeen).

—Peaches. (ENG.). (YA). 2005. 320p. (gr. 7-12). 15.99 (978-0-06-073305-6(5)) 2012. (Peaches Ser.: 1). 368p. (gr. 9-12). reprint ed. pap. 8.99 (978-0-06-073307-0(1), HarperTeen) HarperCollins Pubs.

—The Secrets of Peaches. 2012. (Peaches Ser.: 2). (ENG.). 368p. (YA). (gr. 9-12). pap. 8.99 (978-0-06-073310-0(1), HarperTeen) HarperCollins Pubs.

Anderson, Laurie Halse. Twisted. 2014. (ENG.). 288p. (YA). (gr. 7-12). 14.24 (978-1-63245-343-3(6)) Lectorum Pubns., Inc.

—Twisted. 2011. 11.04 (978-0-7848-3388-9(5), Everbind) Marco Bk. Co.

—Twisted. 2008. (ENG.). 288p. (YA). (gr. 7-18). 9.99 (978-0-14-241184-1(1), Speak) Penguin Young Readers Group.

—Twisted. l.t. ed. 2007. (Literacy Bridge Young Adult Ser.). 299p. (YA). (gr. 7-12). 23.95 (978-0-7862-9885-3(5)) Thorndike Pr.

Anderson, M. T. No Such Thing as the Real World. 2009. 8.99 (978-0-06-147060-8(0)) HarperCollins Pubs.

Anderson, R. J. Spell Hunter. 2009. (Faery Rebels Ser.). (ENG.). 336p. (J). (gr. 8-18). 16.99 (978-0-06-155474-2(X)) HarperCollins Pubs.

—Wayfarer. 2010. (ENG.). 304p. (J). (gr. 8-18). 16.99 (978-0-06-155477-3(4), HarperTeen) HarperCollins Pubs.

Anderson, Robert L. Dreamland. 2016. 336p. (YA). (gr. 9). pap. 9.99 (978-0-06-233868-6(4), HarperTeen) HarperCollins Pubs.

Angleberger, Tom. Darth Paper Strikes Back. 2011. (Origami Yoda Ser.). (ENG., Illus.). 176p. (J). (gr. 3-7). 13.95 (978-1-4197-0027-9(8), Amulet Bks.); pap. (978-1-4197-0254-9(8)) Abrams, Inc.

—Darth Paper Strikes Back, 3 vols. 2011. (Origami Yoda Ser.: 2). (J). (978-1-4618-4266-8(2)); 1.25 (978-1-4640-2485-6(5)) Recorded Bks., Inc.

—Darth Paper Strikes Back. (Origami Yoda Files Ser.: 2). (J). 2015. lib. bdg. 18.40 (978-0-606-39395-9(1)) 2011. lib. bdg. 25.70 (978-0-606-33075-6(5), Turtleback) Turtleback Bks.

—Emperor Pickletine Rides the Bus. (Origami Yoda Ser.). (ENG., Illus.). (J). (gr. 3-7). 2016. 240p. pap. 7.95 (978-1-4197-2201-1(8)) 2014. 224p. 13.95 (978-1-4197-0933-3(X)) Abrams, Inc. (Amulet Bks.).

—Emperor Pickletine Rides the Bus. 2014. (Origami Yoda Files Ser.: 6). (J). lib. bdg. 25.70 (978-0-606-36168-2(5)) Turtleback Bks.

—Princess Labelmaker to the Rescue! (Origami Yoda Ser.). (ENG., Illus.). (gr. 3-7). 2016. 224p. (J). pap. 7.95 (978-1-4197-2200-4(X)) 2014. 208p. (YA). 13.95 (978-1-4197-1052-0(4)) Abrams, Inc. (Amulet Bks.).

—Princess Labelmaker to the Rescue! 2014. (Origami Yoda Files Ser.: 5). (J). lib. bdg. 25.70 (978-0-606-35237-6(6)) Turtleback Bks.

—The Secret of the Fortune Wookiee. 2015. (Origami Yoda Ser.). (ENG., Illus.). 208p. (J). (gr. 3-7). pap. 7.95 (978-1-4197-1971-4(8), Amulet Bks.) Abrams, Inc.

—The Secret of the Fortune Wookiee. Bell, Cece, illus. 2012. (Origami Yoda Ser.: No. 3). (ENG.). 208p. (J). (gr. 3-7). 13.95 (978-1-4197-0392-8(7), Amulet Bks.) Abrams, Inc.

—The Strange Case of Origami Yoda. 2011. (Illus.). 160p. pap. (978-0-8109-9877-3(7), Amulet Bks.) 2010. (ENG., Illus.). 160p. (J). (gr. 3-7). 13.95 (978-0-8109-8425-7(3), Amulet Bks.) 2010. pap. (978-0-8109-9650-2(2)) Abrams, Inc.

—The Strange Case of Origami Yoda, 2 vols. 2010. (Origami Yoda Ser.: 1). (J). 48.75 (978-1-4498-4583-4(5)) Recorded Bks., Inc.

—The Surprise Attack of Jabba the Puppett. 2016. (Origami Yoda Ser.). (ENG.). 240p. (YA). (gr. 3-7). pap. 7.95 (978-1-4197-2030-7(9), Amulet Bks.) Abrams, Inc.

—The Surprise Attack of Jabba the Puppett: An Origami Yoda Book. 2013. (Origami Yoda Ser.: No. 4). (ENG., Illus.). 224p. (YA). (gr. 3-7). 13.95 (978-1-4197-0858-9(9), Amulet Bks.) Abrams, Inc.

—The Surprise Attack of Jabba the Puppett: An Origami Yoda Book. 2013. (Origami Yoda Ser.: 4). (J). 50.75 (978-1-4703-9686-2(6)); 48.75 (978-1-4703-9677-0(7)); 168.75 (978-1-4703-9641-1(6)); 48.75 (978-1-4703-9650-3(5)); 1.25 (978-1-4703-9695-4(5)) Recorded Bks., Inc.

—The Surprise Attack of Jabba the Puppett: An Origami Yoda Book. (Origami Yoda Files Ser.: 4). (J). 2016. lib. bdg. 18.40 (978-0-606-38208-3(9)) 2013. lib. bdg. 25.70 (978-0-606-33308-5(8), Turtleback) Turtleback Bks.

Apostolina, M. Hazing Meri Sugarman. 2005. (ENG.). 272p. (YA). pap. 8.99 (978-1-4169-0610-0(X), Simon Pulse) Simon Pulse.

Applegate, Katherine. Beach Blondes. 2008. (Summer Ser.: 1). (ENG.). 736p. (YA). (gr. 9). pap. 9.99 (978-1-4169-6133-8(X), Simon Pulse) Simon Pulse.

Archer, Natalie J. Willy, 1 vol. 2009. 50p. pap. 16.95 (978-1-4489-2935-1(0)) America Star Bks.

Arena, Felice & Kettle, Phil. Basketball Buddies. Gordon, Gus, illus. 2004. (J). pap. (978-1-59336-369-7(9)) Mondo Publishing.

Armentrout, Jennifer L. Don't Look Back. 2014. (Novel Ser.: 1). (ENG.). 384p. (YA). (gr. 9-17). 16.99 (978-1-4231-7512-4(3)) Hyperion Bks. for Children.

Arnold, Elizabeth. The Parsley Parcel. 2006. 212p. per. (978-1-904529-22-4(4), Back to Front) Solidus.

Aronson, Marc & Smith, Charles R., Jr., eds. Pick-Up Game: A Full Day of Full Court. Smith, Charles R., Jr., illus. (ENG., Illus.). 176p. (YA). (gr. 9). 2012. pap. 7.99 (978-0-7636-6068-0(X)) 2011. 15.99 (978-0-7636-4562-5(1)) Candlewick Pr.

Asher, Jay. Thirteen Reasons Why. 2014. (ENG.). 336p. (YA). 15.24 (978-1-63245-099-9(2)) Lectorum Pubns., Inc.

—Thirteen Reasons Why. 2009. 11.72 (978-0-7848-3782-5(1), Everbind) Marco Bk. Co.

—Thirteen Reasons Why. (ENG.). (YA). (gr. 7). 2017. 336p. pap. 10.99 **(978-0-451-47829-0(0))** 2011. 336p. pap. 10.99 (978-1-59514-188-0(X)) 2007. 320p. 18.99 (978-1-59514-171-2(5)) 10th anniv. ed. 2016. 352p. 18.99 (978-1-59514-788-2(8)) Penguin Young Readers Group. (Razorbill).

—Thirteen Reasons Why. 2011. (ENG.). (YA). (gr. 7-12). lib. bdg. 21.60 **(978-1-60686-991-8(4))** Perfection Learning Corp.

—Thirteen Reasons Why. 2011. lib. bdg. 22.10 (978-0-606-15085-9(4), Turtleback) Turtleback Bks.

Ashman, Linda. Peace, Baby! Lew-Vriethoff, Joanne, illus. 2013. (ENG.). 32p. (J). (gr. -1-k). 15.99 (978-1-4521-0613-7(4)) Chronicle Bks. LLC.

Atkins, Catherine. Alt Ed. 2004. (ENG.). 208p. (YA). (gr. 7-12). reprint ed. 6.99 (978-0-14-240235-1(4), Speak) Penguin Young Readers Group.

Atwood, Megan. Molly Meets Trouble (Whose Real Name Is Jenna) Fleming, Lucy, illus. 2016. (Dear Molly, Dear Olive Ser.). (ENG.). 96p. (gr. 1-3). lib. bdg. 21.99 (978-1-4795-8696-7(X)) Picture Window Bks.

Auerbach, Annie, adapted by. Despicable Me 2: The Junior Novel. movie tie-in ed. 2013. (ENG.). 144p. (J). (gr. 3-7). pap. 6.99 (978-0-316-23432-0(X)) Little, Brown Bks. for Young Readers.

Auseon, Andrew. Freak Magnet. 2010. (ENG.). 304p. (YA). (gr. 9-18). 16.99 (978-0-06-113926-0(2), HarperTeen) HarperCollins Pubs.

Austen, Jane. Pride & Prejudice. Miralles, Joseph, illus. 2005. (Great Illustrated Classics Ser.). 236p. (gr. 3-8). 21.35 (978-1-59679-249-4(3)) Spotlight.

Austen, Jane & Fisher, Eric Scott. Pride & Prejudice, 1 vol. 2012. (Calico Illustrated Classics Ser.: No. 4). (ENG., Illus.). 112p. (J). (gr. 3-6). 27.07 (978-1-61641-619-5(X)) Magic Wagon.

Auth, Jeannine. Emmy's Question. 2010. 155p. pap. 11.99 (978-0-9790395-3-9(3)) 2007. 151p. (J). (gr. 4-7). 16.99 (978-0-9790395-2-2(5)) Morningtide Pr.

Ayarbe, Heidi. Compulsion. 2011. (ENG.). 304p. (YA). (gr. 9-18). 17.99 (978-0-06-199386-2(7)) HarperCollins Pubs.

Bailey, Christine. Girl in the Middle. 2013. 236p. pap. 8.99 (978-0-9890632-0-3(8)) Vinspire Publishing LLC.

Bailey, Em. Shift. 2016. (ENG.). 288p. (YA). (gr. 9). pap. 17.99 **(978-1-76012-698-8(5))** Hardie Grant Egmont Pty, Ltd. AUS. Dist: Independent Pubs. Group.

Baker, Chandler. Alive. 2017. (YA). lib. bdg. 20.85 **(978-0-606-39171-9(1))** Turtleback Bks.

Ballard, Alexandra. What I Lost. 2017. (ENG., Illus.). 400p. (YA). 17.99 (978-0-374-30463-8(7), 9780374304638, Farrar, Straus & Giroux (BYR)) Farrar, Straus & Giroux.

Banash, Jennifer. The Elite. 2008. (ENG.). 256p. (YA). (gr. 9-18). 9.99 (978-0-425-22157-0(1), Berkley) Penguin Publishing Group.

—In Too Deep. 2009. (ENG.). 256p. (YA). (gr. 9-18). 9.99 (978-0-425-22353-6(1), Berkley) Penguin Publishing Group.

—Silent Alarm. 2015. (ENG.). 336p. (YA). (gr. 7). bds. 17.99 (978-0-399-25789-6(6), G.P. Putnam's Sons Books for Young Readers) Penguin Young Readers Group.

—Simply Irresistible. 2009. (ENG.). 256p. (YA). (gr. 9-18). 9.99 (978-0-425-22783-1(9), Berkley) Penguin Publishing Group.

Banim, Lisa & Minsky, Terri. The Case of the Kate Haters. 2005. (Illus.). 124p. (J). (978-1-4156-3927-6(2)) Disney Pr.

Banks, Jane Whelen. Liam Knows What to Do When Kids Act Snitty: Coping When Friends Are Tactless. 2008. (ENG., Illus.). 32p. 12.95 (978-1-84310-902-0(6), 7167) Kingsley, Jessica Pubs. GBR. Dist: Macmillan Distribution Ltd.

Barnes, Jennifer Lynn. The Fixer. (ENG.). (YA). 2016. 400p. pap. 9.99 (978-1-61963-598-2(4), 9781619635982) 2015. 384p. (gr. 7). 17.99 (978-1-61963-594-4(1), 9781619635944) Bloomsbury Publishing USA. (Bloomsbury USA Childrens).

Barnhill, Kelly. The Mostly True Story of Jack. 2012. (ENG.). 352p. (J). (gr. 3-7). pap. 8.99 (978-0-316-05672-4(3)) Little, Brown Bks. for Young Readers.

Barnholdt, Lauren. Rules for Secret Keeping. 2011. (Mix Ser.). (ENG.). 304p. (J). (gr. 4-8). pap. 7.99 (978-1-4169-8021-6(0), Aladdin) Simon & Schuster Children's Publishing.

—Sometimes It Happens. (ENG.). (YA). (gr. 9). 2012. 336p. pap. 9.99 (978-1-4424-1315-3(8)) 2011. 320p. 16.99 (978-1-4424-1314-6(X)) Simon Pulse. (Simon Pulse).

—Two-Way Street. 2007. (ENG.). 304p. (YA). (gr. 9-18). pap. 10.99 (978-1-4169-1318-4(1), Simon Pulse) Simon Pulse.

—Watch Me. 2010. (ENG.). 304p. (YA). (gr. 7). pap. 9.99 (978-1-4424-0255-3(5), Simon Pulse) Simon Pulse.

Barshaw, Ruth McNally. Ellie McDoodle: Have Pen, Will Travel. Barshaw, Ruth McNally, illus. 2nd ed. 2011. (Ellie Mcdoodle Ser.). (ENG., Illus.). 192p. (YA). (gr. 3-6). pap. 7.99 (978-1-59990-715-4(1), 9781599907154, Bloomsbury USA Childrens) Bloomsbury Publishing USA.

—Have Pen, Will Travel. Barshaw, Ruth McNally, illus. 2013. (Ellie Mcdoodle Diaries). (ENG., Illus.). 192p. (YA). (gr. 3-6). 12.99 (978-1-61963-173-1(3), 9781619631731, Bloomsbury USA Childrens) Bloomsbury Publishing USA.

Barulich-Liederbach, Terri & Liederbach, Tom. The Memory Chair. 2010. 48p. pap. 19.49 (978-1-4520-5672-2(2)) AuthorHouse.

Baskin, Nora Raleigh. All We Know of Love. 2008. (ENG., Illus.). 208p. (YA). (gr. 9). 16.99 (978-0-7636-3623-4(1)) Candlewick Pr.

—Basketball (or Something Like It) 176p. (J). 2007. (ENG.). (gr. 4-7). pap. 6.99 (978-0-06-059612-5(0)) 2005. (ENG.). 15.99 (978-0-06-059610-1(4)) 2005. lib. bdg. 16.89 (978-0-06-059611-8(2)) HarperCollins Pubs.

—The Summer Before Boys. (ENG.). 208p. (J). (gr. 4-7). 2012. pap. 6.99 (978-1-4169-8674-4(X)) 2011. 16.99 (978-1-4169-8673-7(1)) Simon & Schuster Bks. For Young Readers. (Simon & Schuster Bks. For Young Readers).

Bateman, Anya. I Just Got a Letter from Allyson Pringle. 2008. 256p. (YA). pap. 15.95 (978-1-60641-028-8(8)) Deseret Bk. Co.

Bateson, Catherine. The Boyfriend Rules of Good Behavior. 2006. (ENG.). 192p. (YA). (gr. 8-12). 16.95 (978-0-8234-2026-1(4)) Holiday Hse., Inc.

—Stranded in Boringsville. (ENG.). 144p. (J). (gr. 5-9). 2007. pap. 6.95 (978-0-8234-2113-8(9)) 2005. 16.95 (978-0-8234-1969-2(X)) Holiday Hse., Inc.

Bauer, Joan. Squashed. 2005. (ENG.). 208p. (YA). (gr. 7-7). pap. 7.99 (978-0-14-240426-3(8), Speak) Penguin Young Readers Group.

—Squashed. 2005. 194p. (gr. 7-12). 18.00 (978-0-7569-5781-0(8)) Perfection Learning Corp.

Bauer, Marion Dane. The Double-Digit Club. 2004. (ENG.). 126p. (J). (gr. 4-6). tchr. ed. 16.95 (978-0-8234-1805-3(7)) Holiday Hse., Inc.

—Killing Miss Kitty & Other Sins. 2008. (ENG.). 176p. (YA). (gr. 7). pap. 12.95 (978-0-547-07614-0(2)) Houghton Mifflin Harcourt Publishing Co.

Beale, Fleur. The Boy in the Olive Grove. 2013. 368p. pap. (978-1-4596-5723-6(3)) ReadHowYouWant.com, Ltd.

Beck, Nina. This Book Isn't Fat, It's Fabulous. 2009. (ENG.). 256p. (J). (gr. 9). pap. 8.99 (978-0-545-01704-6(1)) Scholastic, Inc.

Bellingham, Brenda. Lilly in the Middle, 1 vol. Owen, Elizabeth, illus. 2003. (Formac First Novels Ser.: 25). (ENG.). 64p. (J). (gr. 1-5). 4.95 (978-0-88780-589-9(2), 9780887805899); 14.95 (978-0-88780-590-5(6), 9780887805905) Formac Publishing Co., Ltd. CAN. Dist: Casemate Pubs. & Bk. Distributors, LLC.

Bennett-Boltinghouse, Jo Ann. Yolandababy: A Pooch Finds Her Purpose! an Adventure in Self-Esteem. Julich, Jenniffer, illus. 2007. (YolandaBaby Ser.). 28p. (J). (gr. -1-3). 16.00 (978-0-9785151-0-2(2)) Ginger Pr., The.

Bennett, Cindy C. Geek Girl. 2011. 280p. (J). pap. 15.99 (978-1-59955-925-4(0)) Bonneville B.V. NLD. Dist: Cedar Fort, Inc./CFI Distribution.

Benoit, Charles. Snow Job. 2016. (ENG.). 288p. (YA). (gr. 7). 17.99 (978-0-544-31886-1(2)) Houghton Mifflin Harcourt Publishing Co.

Benton, Jim. Nobody's Perfect. I'm As Close As It Gets. Benton, Jim, illus. 2013. (Dear Dumb Diary Year Two Ser.: 3). (ENG., Illus.). 144p. (J). (gr. 3-7). pap. 5.99 (978-0-545-37764-5(1), Scholastic Paperbacks) Scholastic, Inc.

—Nobody's Perfect. I'm As Close As It Gets. 2013. (Dear Dumb Diary: Year Two Ser.: 3). lib. bdg. 16.00 *(978-0-606-31535-7(7),* Turtleback) Turtleback Bks.

—School. Hasn't This Gone on Long Enough? Benton, Jim, illus. 2012. (Dear Dumb Diary Year Two Ser.: 1). (ENG., Illus.). 160p. (J). (gr. 3-7). pap. 5.99 *(978-0-545-37761-4(7),* Scholastic Paperbacks) Scholastic, Inc.

—School. Hasn't This Gone on Long Enough? 2012. (Dear Dumb Diary: Year Two Ser.: 1). lib. bdg. 16.00 *(978-0-606-23731-4(3),* Turtleback) Turtleback Bks.

—The Super-Nice Are Super-Annoying. 2012. (Dear Dumb Diary: Year Two Ser.: 2). lib. bdg. 16.00 *(978-0-606-26188-3(5),* Turtleback) Turtleback Bks.

—What I Don't Know Might Hurt Me. Benton, Jim, illus. 2013. (Dear Dumb Diary Year Two Ser.: 4). (ENG., Illus.). 144p. (J). (gr. 3-7). pap. 5.99 *(978-0-545-37765-2(X),* Scholastic Paperbacks) Scholastic, Inc.

Bergen, Lara. Stand up & Cheer. 2013. 134p. (J). pap. *(978-0-545-56280-5(5))* Scholastic, Inc.

Berk, Sheryl. On Pointe. 2014. (Dance Divas Ser.). (ENG.). 144p. (YA). (gr. 3-6). 15.99 *(978-1-61963-585-2(2),* 9781619635852, Bloomsbury USA Childrens) Bloomsbury Publishing USA.

—Two to Tango. 2014. (Dance Divas Ser.). (ENG.). 160p. (YA). (gr. 3-6). 15.99 *(978-1-61963-187-8(3),* 9781619631878, Bloomsbury USA Childrens) Bloomsbury Publishing USA.

Bingham, J. & Brontë, Emily. Wuthering Heights. 2004. (Paperback Classics Ser.). 144p. (J). pap. 4.95 *(978-0-7945-0573-8(2))* EDC Publishing.

Bingham, Kelly. Formerly Shark Girl. (ENG.). 352p. (YA). (gr. 7). 2015. pap. 8.99 *(978-0-7636-7673-5(X))* 2013. 16.99 *(978-0-7636-5362-0(4))* Candlewick Pr.

—Shark Girl. (ENG., Illus.). 288p. (YA). (gr. 7). 2010. pap. 8.99 *(978-0-7636-4627-1(X))* 2007. 16.99 *(978-0-7636-3207-6(4))* Candlewick Pr.

Binns, B. A. & McKenzie, C. Lee. The Princess of Las Pulgas. 2010. 334p. (YA). (gr. 8-18). 16.95 *(978-1-934813-44-7(3))* Westside Bks.

Birdseye, Tom. Attack of the Mutant Underwear. 2006. (ENG., Illus.). 208p. (J). (gr. 3-7). 7.99 *(978-0-14-240734-9(8),* Puffin Books) Penguin Young Readers Group.

Biren, Sara. The Last Thing You Said. 2017. (ENG.). 320p. (YA). 17.95 *(978-1-4197-2304-9(9),* Amulet Bks.) Abrams, Inc.

Birney, Betty G. Surprises According to Humphrey. (Humphrey Ser.: 4). (ENG.). (J). (gr. 3-7). 2009. 160p. 5.99 *(978-0-14-241296-1(1),* Puffin Books) 2008. 144p. 15.99 *(978-0-399-24730-9(0),* G.P. Putnam's Sons Books for Young Readers) Penguin Young Readers Group.

—Surprises According to Humphrey. 2009. (According to Humphrey Ser.: 4). lib. bdg. 16.00 *(978-0-606-00906-5(X),* Turtleback) Turtleback Bks.

—Trouble According to Humphrey. (Humphrey Ser.: 3). (ENG.). (J). (gr. 3-7). 2008. 192p. 5.99 *(978-0-14-241089-9(6),* Puffin Books) 2007. 176p. 15.99 *(978-0-399-24505-3(7),* G.P. Putnam's Sons Books for Young Readers) Penguin Young Readers Group.

Bishop, Jenn. 14 Hollow Road. 2017. (ENG.). 288p. (J). (gr. 3-7). 16.99 ***(978-1-101-93875-1(7))***; lib. bdg. 19.99 ***(978-1-101-93876-8(5))*** Random Hse. Children's Bks. (Knopf Bks. for Young Readers).

Bjorkman, Lauren. Miss Fortune Cookie. 2012. (ENG.). 288p. (YA). (gr. 9-13). 16.99 *(978-0-8050-8951-6(9),* Holt, Henry & Co. Bks. For Young Readers) Holt, Henry & Co.

Black, Allyson. Crushed, Bk. 5. Spaziante, Patrick & Riley, Kellee, illus. 2011. (Scarlett & Crimson Ser.). (ENG.). 112p. (J). pap. 6.99 *(978-1-4169-9648-4(6),* Simon Spotlight) Simon Spotlight.

Blackman, Malorie. Black & White. 2007. (ENG.). 512p. (YA). (gr. 9-12). pap. 12.99 *(978-1-4169-0017-7(9),* Simon & Schuster Bks. For Young Readers) Simon & Schuster Bks. For Young Readers.

Blubaugh, Penny. Blood & Flowers. 2011. (ENG.). 352p. (YA). (gr. 8-18). 16.99 *(978-0-06-172862-4(4),* HarperTeen) HarperCollins Pubs.

Blume, Judy. Double Fudge. 2004. (ENG.). 192p. (J). (gr. 3-7). 5.99 *(978-0-425-19647-2(X),* Berkley) Penguin Publishing Group.

Boggess, Eileen. Mia the Meek. 2006. (ENG.). 155p. (gr. 6-9). per. 14.95 *(978-1-890862-47-3(9))* Bancroft Pr.

—MIA the Meek. 2006. (Mia Fullerton Ser.: Bk. 1). 155p. (J). (gr. 6-11). 16.95 *(978-1-890862-46-6(0))* Bancroft Pr.

—Mia the Melodramatic. 2008. (MIA Fullerton Ser.). 168p. (J). (gr. 6-13). 19.95 *(978-1-890862-56-5(8))* Bancroft Pr.

Boie, Kirsten. The Princess Trap. (ENG.). 416p. (J). (gr. 5-9). 2012. pap. 7.99 *(978-0-545-22262-4(1))* 2010. 17.99 *(978-0-545-22261-7(3))* Scholastic, Inc. (Chicken Hse., The).

Bonin, Liane. Pretty on the Outside: Fame Unlimited. 2007. 288p. (YA). pap. 9.99 *(978-0-451-22122-3(2),* N A L Trade) Penguin Publishing Group.

Booth, Coe. Kinda Like Brothers. 2015. (ENG.). 256p. (J). (gr. 3-7). pap. 6.99 *(978-0-545-22497-0(7),* Scholastic Paperbacks) Scholastic, Inc.

Bosak, Susan V. A Little Something. McGaw, Laurie, illus. 2008. 32p. (J). *(978-1-896232-06-5(X),* TCP Pr.) Communication Project, The.

Bostic, Megan. Never Eighteen. 2012. (ENG.). 208p. (YA). (gr. 7). pap. 8.99 *(978-0-547-55076-3(6))* Houghton Mifflin Harcourt Publishing Co.

Bowe, Julie. My Extra Best Friend. 2013. (Friends for Keeps Ser.: 5). (ENG.). 240p. (J). (gr. 3-7). pap. 6.99 *(978-0-14-242603-6(2),* Puffin Books) Penguin Young Readers Group.

—My Forever Friends. 2012. (Friends for Keeps Ser.). (ENG.). 240p. (J). (gr. 3-7). pap. 6.99 *(978-0-14-242104-8(9),* Puffin Books) Penguin Young Readers Group.

Bower, Gary. The Person I Marry. Bower, Jan, illus. 2008. 32p. (J). pap. 11.99 *(978-0-9704621-7-6(4))* Storybook Meadow Publishing.

Bracken, Alexandra. The Darkest Minds. (Darkest Minds Novel Ser.). (ENG.). 2013. 528p. (YA). (gr. 9-17). pap. 9.99 *(978-1-4231-5932-2(2))* 2012. 496p. (J). (gr. 5-9). 17.99 *(978-1-4231-5737-3(0))* Hyperion Pr.

—The Darkest Minds. 2013. (Darkest Minds Ser.: 1). (YA). lib. bdg. 20.85 *(978-0-606-36533-8(8))* Turtleback Bks.

—In the Afterlight. (Darkest Minds Novel Ser.). (ENG.). (YA). 2015. 592p. (gr. 9-17). pap. 9.99 *(978-1-4231-5934-6(9))* 2014. 544p. (gr. 7-12). 18.99 *(978-1-4231-5752-6(4))* Hyperion Bks. for Children.

—In the Afterlight. 2015. (Darkest Minds Ser.: 3). (YA). lib. bdg. 20.85 *(978-0-606-37505-4(8))* Turtleback Bks.

—Never Fade. 2014. (Darkest Minds Novel Ser.). (ENG.). 544p. (YA). (gr. 7-12). pap. 9.99 *(978-1-4231-5933-9(0))* Hyperion Bks. for Children.

—Never Fade. 2013. (Darkest Minds Novel Ser.: Bk. 2). (ENG.). 512p. (J). (gr. 5-9). 17.99 *(978-1-4231-5751-9(6))* Hyperion Pr.

—Never Fade. 2014. (Darkest Minds Ser.: 2). (YA). lib. bdg. 20.85 *(978-0-606-36534-5(6))* Turtleback Bks.

—Through the Dark: A Darkest Minds Collection. 2015. (Darkest Minds Novel Ser.). (ENG.). 416p. (YA). (gr. 9-17). 18.99 *(978-1-4847-5687-4(8))* Hyperion Bks. for Children.

Bradbury, Bianca. Flight into Spring. 2005. (Sally (Bethlehem Books) Ser.). 184p. (YA). (gr. 7). per. 11.95 *(978-1-932350-01-2(2))* Bethlehem Bks.

Bradbury, Jennifer. A Moment Comes. 2013. (ENG., Illus.). 288p. (YA). (gr. 7). 17.99 *(978-1-4169-7876-3(3))* Simon & Schuster Children's Publishing.

Brashares, Ann. The Here & Now. 2014. 242p. (YA). *(978-0-385-39008-8(4),* Delacorte Pr) Random House Publishing Group.

—The Here & Now. (ENG.). 256p. (YA). (gr. 7). 2015. pap. 10.99 *(978-0-385-73683-1(5),* Ember) 2014. 18.99 *(978-0-385-73680-0(0),* Delacorte Pr.) Random Hse. Children's Bks.

Breese, K. Ryer. Future Imperfect. 2011. (ENG.). 320p. (YA). (gr. 8-18). pap. 22.99 *(978-0-312-64151-1(6),* 9780312641511, St. Martin's Griffin) St. Martin's Pr.

Breslaw, Anna. Scarlett Epstein Hates It Here. 2016. (ENG.). 288p. (YA). (gr. 7). 17.99 *(978-1-59514-835-3(3),* Razorbill) Penguin Young Readers Group.

Brezenoff, Steve. The Absolute Value of -1. 2010. (Carolrhoda YA Ser.). (ENG.). 296p. (YA). (gr. 9-12). lib. bdg. 16.95 *(978-0-7613-5417-8(4),* Carolrhoda Bks.) Lerner Publishing Group.

—The Absolute Value Of -1. 2011. (Carolrhoda YA Ser.). (ENG.). 296p. (YA). (gr. 9-12). pap. 9.95 *(978-0-7613-8130-3(9),* Carolrhoda Lab™) Lerner Publishing Group.

—Brooklyn, Burning. 2011. (Carolrhoda YA Ser.). (ENG.). 208p. (YA). (gr. 9-12). 17.95 *(978-0-7613-7526-5(0),* Carolrhoda Lab™) Lerner Publishing Group.

Brian, Kate, pseud. Fake Boyfriend. 2009. (ENG.). 288p. (YA). (gr. 9). pap. 8.99 *(978-1-4169-1368-9(8),* Simon & Schuster Bks. For Young Readers) Simon & Schuster Bks. For Young Readers.

—Last Christmas: The Private Prequel. 2008. (Private Ser.). (ENG.). 272p. (YA). (gr. 9-18). 16.99 *(978-1-4169-1369-6(6),* Simon & Schuster Bks. For Young Readers) Simon & Schuster Bks. For Young Readers.

—Megan Meade's Guide to the McGowan Boys. 2006. (ENG.). 288p. (YA). (gr. 7-12). pap. 9.99 *(978-1-4169-0031-3(4),* Simon & Schuster Bks. For Young Readers) Simon & Schuster Bks. For Young Readers.

—The Virginity Club. 2008. (ENG.). 304p. (YA). (gr. 9). pap. 8.99 *(978-1-4169-5370-8(1),* Simon & Schuster Bks. For Young Readers) Simon & Schuster Bks. For Young Readers.

Briggs, Elizabeth. Future Shock. 2016. (YA). (Future Shock Ser.: 1). (ENG.). 288p. (gr. 8-12). pap. 9.99 *(978-0-8075-2680-4(0)); (978-0-8075-2683-5(5));* (Future Shock Ser.: 1). (ENG.). 272p. (gr. 8-12). 16.99 *(978-0-8075-2682-8(7))* Whitman, Albert & Co.

Bristow, Catherine. My Strange & Terrible Malady. 2008. (YA). pap. 15.95 *(978-1-934575-19-2(4))* Autism Asperger Publishing Co.

Britt, Paige. Why Am I Me? Qualls, Sean & Alko, Selina, illus. 2017. (ENG.). 40p. (J). (gr. -1-3). 17.99 ***(978-1-338-05314-2(0),*** Scholastic Pr.) Scholastic, Inc.

Brody, Jessica. The Karma Club. 2011. (ENG.). 288p. (YA). (gr. 7-12). pap. 10.99 *(978-0-312-67473-1(2),* 9780312674731) Square Fish.

Brontë, Emily. Wuthering Heights. 2004. (Graphic Novels Ser.). (ENG., Illus.). 72p. (J). pap. 7.99 *(978-0-237-52581-1(X))* Evans Brothers, Ltd. GBR. Dist: Independent Pubs. Group.

—Wuthering Heights. (Classics Illustrated Ser.). (Illus.). 52p. (YA). pap. 4.95 *(978-1-57209-011-8(1))* Classics International Entertainment, Inc.

—Wuthering Heights. Warner, Darrell, illus. 2004. (Paperback Classics Ser.). 158p. (J). (gr. 5). lib. bdg. 12.95 *(978-1-58086-604-0(2))* EDC Publishing.

Brooks, Kevin. The Bunker Diary. 2015. (ENG.). 264p. (YA). (gr. 8-12). 17.99 *(978-1-4677-5420-0(X))* Lerner Publishing Group.

—Naked '76. 2016. (ENG.). 424p. (gr. 9-12). 18.99 *(978-1-5124-0418-0(7),* Carolrhoda Bks.); (YA). 38.65 *(978-1-5124-0445-6(4),* Carolrhoda Lab™) Lerner Publishing Group.

Brooks, Martha. Being with Henry. 1 vol. (ENG.). 174p. pap. 8.95 *(978-0-88899-502-5(4))* Groundwood Bks. CAN. Dist: Publishers Group West (PGW).

—True Confessions of a Heartless Girl. braille ed. 2003. (J). (gr. 2). spiral bd. *(978-0-616-15264-5(7))* Canadian National Institute for the Blind/Institut National Canadien pour les Aveugles.

—True Confessions of a Heartless Girl. 1 vol. (ENG.). 224p. pap. 8.95 *(978-0-88899-569-8(5))* Groundwood Bks. CAN. Dist: Publishers Group West (PGW).

Brooks, Walter R. Freddy Rides Again. Wiese, Kurt, illus. 2013. (ENG.). 240p. (gr. 4-13). pap. 10.99 *(978-1-4683-0724-5(X),* 460724) Overlook Pr., The.

Brosgol, Vera. Anya's Ghost. Brosgol, Vera, illus. 2011. (ENG., Illus.). 224p. (YA). (gr. 7-12). 22.99 *(978-1-59643-713-5(8),* 9781596437135, First Second Bks.) Roaring Brook Pr.

—Anya's Ghost. Brosgol, Vera, illus. 2014. (ENG., Illus.). 240p. (YA). (gr. 7). pap. 10.99 *(978-1-250-04001-5(9),* 9781250040015) Square Fish.

Bross, Lee. Tangled Webs. 2015. (Tangled Webs Ser.). (ENG., Illus.). 304p. (YA). (gr. 9-17). 17.99 *(978-1-4231-8423-2(8))* Hyperion Bks. for Children.

Brouillet, Chrystine. Le Cameleon. 2003. (Roman Jeunesse Ser.). (FRE., Illus.). 96p. (YA). (gr. 4-7). pap. *(978-2-89021-072-1(3))* Diffusion du livre Mirabel (DLM).

Brown, Jennifer. Thousand Words. 2014. (YA). lib. bdg. 20.85 *(978-0-606-35311-3(9))* Turtleback Bks.

Bryant, Jen. The Fortune of Carmen Navarro. 2011. (ENG.). 240p. (YA). (gr. 7). pap. 8.99 *(978-0-375-85097-4(X),* Ember) Random Hse. Children's Bks.

Bulion, Leslie. The Trouble with Rules. 1 vol. (ENG.). 160p. (J). 2011. pap. 6.95 *(978-1-56145-576-8(8))* 2008. (gr. 2-6). 14.95 *(978-1-56145-440-2(0))* Peachtree Pubs.

Burgess, Melvin. Lady: My Life as a Bitch. 2003. (Illus.). 272p. (J). pap. 6.99 *(978-0-06-054033-3(8))* HarperCollins Pubs.

Burkhart, Jessica. Comeback. 2012. (Canterwood Crest Ser.: 15). lib. bdg. 18.40 *(978-0-606-26312-2(8),* Turtleback) Turtleback Bks.

—Home Sweet Drama. 2010. (Canterwood Crest Ser.: 8). (ENG.). 240p. (J). (gr. 4-8). pap. 7.99 *(978-1-4169-9040-6(2),* Aladdin) Simon & Schuster Children's Publishing.

—Popular. 2012. (Canterwood Crest Ser.: 14). lib. bdg. 18.40 *(978-0-606-26311-5(X),* Turtleback) Turtleback Bks.

—Rival Revenge. 2010. (Canterwood Crest Ser.: 7). (ENG.). 240p. (J). (gr. 4-8). pap. 7.99 *(978-1-4169-9039-0(9),* Aladdin) Simon & Schuster Children's Publishing.

Burkhart, Jessica & Haley, Patricia. Chosen: Super Special. 2011. (Canterwood Crest Ser.). (ENG.). 304p. (J). (gr. 5-8). pap. 7.99 *(978-1-4424-1946-9(6),* Aladdin) Simon & Schuster Children's Publishing.

Burkhart, Kiersi, et al. The Long Trail Home. 2017. (Quartz Creek Ranch Ser.). (ENG.). 240p. (gr. 4-8). 6.99 *(978-1-5124-3090-5(0),* Darby Creek) Lerner Publishing Group.

Burnham, Niki. Goddess Games. 2008. (ENG.). 256p. (YA). (gr. 9-12). pap. 8.99 *(978-1-4169-2772-3(7),* Simon Pulse) Simon Pulse.

—Royally Crushed: Royally Jacked; Spin Control; Do-Over. 2011. (ENG.). 624p. (YA). (gr. 7). pap. 11.99 *(978-1-4424-0648-3(8),* Simon Pulse) Simon Pulse.

Burns, Laura J. & Metz, Melinda. Sacrifice. 2011. (ENG.). 272p. (YA). (gr. 9). 17.99 *(978-1-4424-3900-9(9));* pap. 9.99 *(978-1-4424-0818-0(9))* Simon & Schuster Bks. For Young Readers. (Simon & Schuster Bks. For Young Readers).

Bursting at the Seams. 2014. (Sew Zoey Ser.: 10). (ENG., Illus.). 176p. (J). (gr. 3-7). pap. 6.99 *(978-1-4814-1964-2(1),* Simon Spotlight) Simon Spotlight.

Bush, Penelope. Alice in Time. 2011. (ENG., Illus.). 208p. (YA). (gr. 7-18). 17.95 *(978-0-8234-2329-3(8))* Holiday Hse., Inc.

Bushnell, Candace. The Carrie Diaries. (Carrie Diaries: 1). (ENG.). (YA). (gr. 9). 2011. 416p. pap. 9.99 *(978-0-06-172892-1(6))* 2010. 400p. 18.99 *(978-0-06-172891-4(8))* 2012. 416p. pap. 10.99 *(978-0-06-223684-5(9))* HarperCollins Pubs.

Butcher, Kristin. El Plan de Zee. 1 vol. 2008. (Spanish Soundings Ser.).Tr. of Zee's Way. (SPA.). 112p. (YA). (gr. 8-12). pap. 9.95 *(978-1-55469-057-2(9))* Orca Bk. Pubs. USA.

—Zee's Way. 2004. (Orca Soundings Ser.). 104p. (gr. 7-12). 19.95 *(978-0-7569-4360-8(4))* Perfection Learning Corp.

Buyea, Rob. Because of Mr. Terupt. (ENG.). (J). (gr. 3-7). 2011. 304p. 7.99 *(978-0-375-85824-6(5),* Yearling) 2010. 288p. 16.99 *(978-0-385-73882-8(X),* Delacorte Bks. for Young Readers) Random Hse. Children's Bks.

Byars, Betsy. The Animal, the Vegetable, & John D. Jones. 150p. (J). (gr. 4-6). pap. 3.50 *(978-0-8072-1414-5(0),* Listening Library) Random Hse. Audio Publishing Group.

Byler, Linda. Big Decisions: A Novel Based on True Experiences from an Amish Writer!. 1 vol. 2011. (ENG.). 345p. pap. 13.99 *(978-1-56148-700-4(7),* Good Bks.) Skyhorse Publishing Co., Inc.

Cabot, Meg. All-American Girl. 2008. (All-American Girl Ser.: 1). (ENG.). 416p. (YA). (gr. 8). pap. 8.99 *(978-0-06-147989-2(6),* HarperTeen) HarperCollins Pubs.

—All-American Girl. 2008. (All-American Girl Ser.: Vol. 1). 398p. (YA). (gr. 7-12). 19.65 *(978-1-4178-2386-4(0),* Turtleback) Turtleback Bks.

—Princess in Training. (ENG., 2005. (Princess Diaries: Vol. 6). Illus.). 288p. (J). (gr. 7-18). 16.99 *(978-0-06-009613-7(6))* Vol. VI. 2008. (Princess Diaries: 6). 304p. (YA). (gr. 8). pap. 9.99 *(978-0-06-154365-4(9),* HarperTeen) HarperCollins Pubs.

—Ready or Not. 2nd ed. 2005. (All-American Girl Ser.: Vol. 2). 256p. (J). (gr. 7-18). lib. bdg. 16.89 *(978-0-06-072451-1(X))* HarperCollins Pubs.

—Teen Idol. 2005. (ENG., Illus.). 320p. (YA). (gr. 8-18). reprint ed. pap. 9.99 *(978-0-06-009618-2(7),* HarperTeen) HarperCollins Pubs.

—Teen Idol. 2005. 291p. (YA). 16.65 *(978-0-7569-5735-3(4))* Perfection Learning Corp.

Cain, Mary Wimmer. Liver. 1 vol. 2009. 59p. pap. 12.95 *(978-1-4489-9129-7(3))* PublishAmerica, Inc.

Caletti, Deb. Honey, Baby, Sweetheart. 2008. (ENG.). 336p. (YA). (gr. 7-12). pap. 9.99 *(978-1-4169-5783-6(9),* Simon Pulse) Simon Pulse.

—The Queen of Everything. Greenberg, Anne, ed. 2008. (ENG.). 352p. (YA). (gr. 7-12). pap. 8.99 *(978-1-4169-5781-2(2),* Simon Pulse) Simon Pulse.

—The Secret Life of Prince Charming. (ENG.). (YA). (gr. 7). 2010. 352p. pap. 11.99 *(978-1-4169-5941-0(6))* 2009. 336p. 16.99 *(978-1-4169-5940-3(8))* Simon Pulse. (Simon Pulse).

—The Six Rules of Maybe. (ENG.). (YA). (gr. 7). 2011. 352p. pap. 9.99 *(978-1-4169-7971-5(9))* 2010. 336p. 16.99 *(978-1-4169-7969-2(7))* Simon Pulse. (Simon Pulse).

Calin, Marisa. Between You & Me. 2012. (ENG.). 256p. (YA). (gr. 7-12). 16.99 *(978-1-59990-758-1(5),* 9781599907581, Bloomsbury USA Childrens) Bloomsbury Publishing USA.

Callaghan, Cindy. Lost in Paris. 2015. (Mix Ser.). (ENG., Illus.). 192p. (J). (gr. 4-8). pap. 7.99 *(978-1-4814-2601-5(X),* Aladdin) Simon & Schuster Children's Publishing.

—Lost in Rome. 2015. (ENG., Illus.). 208p. (J). (gr. 4-8). 17.99 *(978-1-4814-4282-4(1),* Aladdin) Simon & Schuster Children's Publishing.

Calonita, Jen. Family Affairs. 2009. (Secrets of My Hollywood Life Ser.: 3). (ENG.). 352p. (YA). (gr. 7-17). pap. 7.99 *(978-0-316-11800-2(1),* Poppy) Little, Brown Bks. for Young Readers.

—On Location. 2008. (Secrets of My Hollywood Life Ser.: 2). (ENG.). 256p. (YA). (gr. 7-17). per. 7.99 *(978-0-316-15440-6(7),* Poppy) Little, Brown Bks. for Young Readers.

—Sleepaway Girls. 2010. (ENG.). 320p. (J). (gr. 7-17). pap. 18.99 *(978-0-316-01718-3(3),* Poppy) Little, Brown Bks. for Young Readers.

—Summer State of Mind. 2014. (ENG.). 256p. (YA). (gr. 7-17). pap. 10.00 *(978-0-316-09115-2(4),* Poppy) Little, Brown Bks. for Young Readers.

Calucag, Angela. Little Freddy S Journey. 2012. 32p. pap. 17.99 *(978-1-62419-840-3(6))* Salem Author Services.

Cameron, Peter. Someday This Pain Will Be Useful to You. 2009. (ENG.). 240p. (YA). (gr. 9-13). pap. 16.00 *(978-0-312-42816-7(2),* 9780312428167) Picador.

Cann, Kate. Text Game. 2013. (ENG.). 72p. (YA). (gr. 6-12). pap. 6.95 *(978-1-78112-170-2(2));* lib. bdg. 22.60 *(978-1-78112-169-6(9))* Lerner Publishing Group.

Cannon, A. E. The Loser's Guide to Life & Love. 2008. 272p. (J). (gr. 7-18). lib. bdg. 17.89 *(978-0-06-112847-9(3));* (ENG.). (YA). (gr. 8-18). 16.99 *(978-0-06-112846-2(5))* HarperCollins Pubs. (HarperTeen).

Cantor, Jillian. The Life of Glass. 2010. (ENG.). 352p. (YA). (gr. 8-18). 16.99 *(978-0-06-168651-1(4),* HarperTeen) HarperCollins Pubs.

Carlson, Melody. Homecoming Queen. 1 vol. 2014. (Carter House Girls Ser.). (ENG.). 224p. (YA). pap. 9.99 *(978-0-310-74725-3(2))* Zondervan.

—I Do! 2005. (Diary of a Teenage Girl Ser.: Bk. 9). (ENG.). 272p. (J). (gr. 7). pap. 14.99 *(978-1-59052-320-9(2),* Multnomah) Doubleday Religious Publishing Group, The.

—It's a Green Thing. 2009. (Diary of a Teenage Girl Ser.: Bk. 15). (ENG.). 256p. pap. 14.99 *(978-1-60142-118-0(4),* Multnomah) Doubleday Religious Publishing Group, The.

—Just Ask. 2005. (Diary of a Teenage Girl Ser.: Bk. 10). (ENG.). 256p. (J). (gr. 7-12). per. 14.99 *(978-1-59052-321-6(0),* Multnomah Bks.) Crown Publishing Group.

—Last Dance. 1 vol. 2014. (Carter House Girls Ser.). (ENG.). 208p. (YA). pap. 9.99 *(978-0-310-74900-4(X))* Zondervan.

—Lost in Las Vegas. 1 vol. 2014. (Carter House Girls Ser.). (ENG.). 208p. (YA). pap. 9.99 *(978-0-310-74716-1(3))* Zondervan.

—Mixed Bags. 1 vol. 2014. (Carter House Girls Ser.). (ENG.). 224p. (YA). pap. 9.99 *(978-0-310-74756-7(2))* Zondervan.

—My Name Is Chloe. 2005. (Diary of a Teenage Girl: Bk. 5). 288p. (YA). mass mkt. 7.99 *(978-1-59052-736-8(4),* Multnomah) Doubleday Religious Publishing Group, The.

—New York Debut. 1 vol. 2014. (Carter House Girls Ser.). (ENG.). 224p. (YA). pap. 9.99 *(978-0-310-74779-6(1))* Zondervan.

—Notes from a Spinning Planet - Mexico. 2007. (Notes from a Spinning Planet Ser.). (ENG.). 256p. (YA). (gr. 7). pap. 12.99 *(978-1-4000-7146-3(1),* WaterBrook Pr.) Crown Publishing Group.

—Spring Breakdown. 1 vol. 2014. (Carter House Girls Ser.). (ENG.). 208p. (YA). pap. 9.99 *(978-0-310-74809-0(7))* Zondervan.

—Stealing Bradford. 1 vol. 2014. (Carter House Girls Ser.). (ENG.). 224p. (YA). pap. 9.99 *(978-0-310-74654-6(X))* Zondervan.

—Viva Vermont!. 1 vol. 2014. (Carter House Girls Ser.). (ENG.). 224p. (YA). pap. 9.99 *(978-0-310-74714-7(7))* Zondervan.

—What Matters Most. 2009. (Diary of a Teenage Girl Ser.: Bk. 3). (ENG.). 256p. pap. 13.99 *(978-1-60142-119-7(2),* Multnomah) Doubleday Religious Publishing Group, The.

Carman, Patrick. Dark Eden. Arrasmith, Patrick, illus. 2012. (Dark Eden Ser.: 1). (ENG.). 336p. (YA). (gr. 8). pap. 8.99 *(978-0-06-200971-5(0),* Tegen, Katherine Bks) HarperCollins Pubs.

—Eve of Destruction. Arrasmith, Patrick, illus. 2012. (Dark Eden Ser.: 2). (ENG.). 288p. (YA). (gr. 8). 17.99 *(978-0-06-210182-2(X),* Tegen, Katherine Bks) HarperCollins Pubs.

—Quake: A Pulse Novel. 2016. (Pulse Ser.: 3). 288p. (YA). (gr. 8). pap. 9.99 *(978-0-06-208597-9(2),* Tegen, Katherine Bks) HarperCollins Pubs.

Carmichael, Clay. Brother, Brother. 2013. (ENG.). 320p. (YA). (gr. 7). 17.99 *(978-1-59643-743-2(X))* Roaring Brook Pr.

Carolina, Philip. My Sister Hates Me ... Only Sometimes. 2013. 40p. pap. 19.57 *(978-1-4669-6578-2(9))* Trafford Publishing.

Carter, Aimée. The Goddess Inheritance. 2013. (Goddess Test Ser.: 3). lib. bdg. 20.85 *(978-0-606-26948-3(7),* Turtleback) Turtleback Bks.

Carter, Ally. I'd Tell You I Love You, but Then I'd Have to Kill You (10th Anniversary Edition) 2016. (Gallagher Girls Ser.). (ENG.). 304p. (J). (gr. 5-9). pap. 9.99 *(978-1-4847-8505-8(3))* Hyperion Bks. for Children.

—Only the Good Spy Young. 2016. (Gallagher Girls Ser.: 4). (J). lib. bdg. 20.85 *(978-0-606-38298-4(4))* Turtleback Bks.

—Only the Good Spy Young (10th Anniversary Edition) 2016. (Gallagher Girls Ser.). (ENG.). 288p. (J). (gr. 5-9). pap. 9.99 *(978-1-4847-8506-5(1))* Hyperion Bks. for Children.

Carter, Nikki & Elliott, Kevin. The Break-Up Diaries, Vol. 2. 2011. (ENG.). 288p. (YA). (gr. 9). pap. 9.95 *(978-0-7582-6888-4(2),* K-Teen/Dafina) Kensington Publishing Corp.

Carter, Scott William. Wooden Bones. (ENG., Illus.). 160p. (J). (gr. 3-7). 2013. pap. 6.99 *(978-1-4424-2752-5(3))* 2012. 15.99 *(978-1-4424-2751-8(5))* Simon & Schuster Bks. For Young Readers. (Simon & Schuster Bks. For Young Readers).

Casciano, Christie & Moziak, Rose Mary Casciano, illus. Haunted Hockey in Lake Placid. 2012. 72p. (J). pap. *(978-1-59531-040-8(1))* North Country Bks., Inc.

—The Puck Hog. 2011. 44p. (J). pap. 9.95 *(978-1-59531-037-8(1))* North Country Bks., Inc.

Casella, Jody. Thin Space. 2013. (ENG.). 256p. (YA). (gr. 7). 16.99 *(978-1-58270-435-7(X));* pap. 10.99 *(978-1-58270-392-3(2))* Simon Pulse. (Simon Pulse).

Castan, Mike. The Price of Loyalty. 2011. (ENG., Illus.). 256p. (YA). (gr. 7-18). 17.95 *(978-0-8234-2268-5(2))* Holiday Hse., Inc.

Castellucci, Cecil. Boy Proof. (ENG.). 208p. (YA). (gr. 9-18). 2005. 15.99 *(978-0-7636-2333-3(4))* 2006. reprint ed. per. 8.99 *(978-0-7636-2796-6(8))* Candlewick Pr.

—Boy Proof, 4 vols. 2005. (YA). 62.75 *(978-1-4193-5131-0(1))* Recorded Bks., Inc.

Catchpole, Barbara. Dead Ed in My Head. 2013. 118p. pap. *(978-0-7552-1604-8(0)*, Bright Pen) Authors OnLine, Ltd.

Chambers, Aidan. Dying to Know You. 2013. (ENG.). 288p. (YA). (gr. 9-17). pap. 9.95 *(978-1-4197-0794-0(9)*, Amulet Bks.) Abrams, Inc.

—Postcards from No Man's Land. 2004. (ENG.). 320p. (YA). (gr. 9-18). reprint ed. 8.99 *(978-0-14-240145-3(5)*, Speak) Penguin Young Readers Group.

Chan, Gillian. An Ocean Apart: The Gold Mountain Diary of Chin Mei-Ling. 2004. (Dear Canada Ser.). (ENG., Illus.). 224p. (J). *(978-0-7791-1353-8(5))* Scholastic Canada, Ltd.

A Change of Lace. 2014. (Sew Zoey Ser.: 9). (ENG., Illus.). 176p. (J). (gr. 3-7). pap. 6.99 *(978-1-4814-1961-1(7)*, Simon Spotlight) Simon Spotlight.

Chessen, Sherri. Gorp's Dream: A Tale of Diversity, Tolerance, & Love in Pumpernickel Park. Masel, Christy, illus. 2003. (ENG.). 36p. (J). pap. 7.95 *(978-0-9724249-1-2(1))* Gorp Group Pr., The.

Chibbaro, Julie. Deadly. Sovak, Jean-Marc Superville, illus. (ENG.). 304p. (YA). (gr. 7). 2012. pap. 10.99 *(978-0-689-85739-3(X))* 2011. 17.99 *(978-0-689-85738-6(1))* Simon & Schuster Children's Publishing. (Atheneum Bks. for Young Readers).

Childs, Tera Lynn. Fins Are Forever. 2012. (Forgive My Fins Ser.: 2). (ENG.). 288p. (YA). (gr. 8). pap. 8.99 *(978-0-06-191470-6(3)*, Tegen, Katherine Bks) HarperCollins Pubs.

—Forgive My Fins. (Forgive My Fins Ser.: 1). (ENG.). (YA). (gr. 8). 2011. 336p. pap. 8.99 *(978-0-06-191467-6(3))* 2010. 304p. 16.99 *(978-0-06-191465-2(7))* HarperCollins Pubs. (Tegen, Katherine Bks).

—Ten Things Sloane Hates about Tru. 2015. (ENG., Illus.). 240p. (J). pap. 14.99 *(978-1-943892-44-0(X))* Entangled Publishing, LLC.

Christopher, Lucy. Stolen. (ENG.). (J). 2012. 320p. (gr. 9). pap. 9.99 *(978-0-545-17094-9(X))* 2010. 304p. (gr. 7-18). 17.99 *(978-0-545-17093-2(1))* Scholastic, Inc. (Chicken Hse., The).

—Stolen. 2012. lib. bdg. 20.85 *(978-0-606-23955-4(3)*, Turtleback) Turtleback Bks.

Christopher, Matt. Slam Dunk. 2004. (ENG., Illus.). 128p. (J). (gr. 3-7). pap. 5.99 *(978-0-316-60762-9(2))* Little, Brown Bks. for Young Readers.

Clark, Abbie. Way down Yonder in the Paw Paw Patch. Taylor, Jennifer, illus. 2006. 32p. (J). (gr. -1-3). per. 16.95 *(978-1-59858-129-4(5))* Dog Ear Publishing, LLC.

Clark, Billy C. The Champion of Sourwood Mountain. 2003. (Illus.). 251p. (J). *(978-1-931672-19-1(9))* Stuart, Jesse Foundation, The.

Clark, Bridie. Maybe Tonight? 2013. (Snap Decision Ser.: 1). (ENG.). 224p. (YA). (gr. 7). pap. 9.99 *(978-1-59643-816-3(9))* Roaring Brook Pr.

—You Only Live Once. 2014. (Snap Decision Ser.: 2). (ENG.). 224p. (YA). (gr. 7). pap. 9.99 *(978-1-59643-817-0(7)*, 9781596438170) Roaring Brook Pr.

Clark, Catherine. Banana Splitsville. 2008. (ENG.). 288p. (YA). (gr. 8). pap. 5.99 *(978-0-06-136715-1(X)*, HarperTeen) HarperCollins Pubs.

Clements, Andrew. Bully Buster. 2014. (Jake Drake Ser. Bk. 1 Ser.). (ENG.). 80p. (J). (gr. 2-5). 9.24 *(978-1-63245-290-0(1))* Lectorum Pubns., Inc.

—Bully Buster. Frazee, Marla & Pedersen, Janet, illus. 2008. (Jake Drake Ser.: Bk. 1). 67p. (gr. 2-5). 15.00 *(978-0-7569-9001-5(7))* Perfection Learning Corp.

—Bully Buster. Pedersen, Janet & Frazee, Marla, illus. 2007. (Jake Drake Ser.: Bk. 1). (ENG.). 80p. (J). (gr. 2-5). pap. 5.99 *(978-1-4169-3933-7(4)*, Atheneum Bks. for Young Readers) Simon & Schuster Children's Publishing.

—Lunch Money. Selznick, Brian, illus. 2007. (ENG.). 240p. (J). (gr. 3-7). pap. 7.99 *(978-0-689-86685-2(2)*, Atheneum Bks. for Young Readers) Simon & Schuster Children's Publishing.

—Lunch Money. 2007. 17.20 *(978-1-4177-8116-4(5)*, Turtleback) Turtleback Bks.

Cobot, Meg. All-American Girl. 2004. 416p. (J). (gr. 7-18). pap. 44.00 incl. audio *(978-0-8072-2281-2(X)*, Listening Library) Random Hse. Audio Publishing Group.

Coburn, Jake. Prep. 2005. (ENG.). 192p. (YA). (gr. 7-7). 6.99 *(978-0-14-240307-5(5)*, Speak) Penguin Young Readers Group.

Cocks, Heather & Morgan, Jessica. Messy. 2013. (ENG.). 368p. (YA). (gr. 7-17). pap. 9.00 *(978-0-316-09828-1(0)*, Poppy) Little, Brown Bks. for Young Readers.

Codell, Esmé Raji. Sahara Special. 2003. (ENG., Illus.). 208p. (J). (gr. 3-7). pap. 16.49 *(978-0-7868-2627-8(4))* Hyperion Bks. for Children.

—Sahara Special. 2004. (ENG.). 192p. (J). (gr. 3-7). pap. 6.99 *(978-0-7868-1611-8(2))* Hyperion Pr.

Cohen, Miriam. Layla's Head Scarf, 1 vol. Himler, Ronald, illus. 2009. (ENG.). 32p. (J). (gr. -1-3). 15.95 *(978-1-59572-177-8(0))*; pap. 5.95 *(978-1-59572-178-5(9))* Star Bright Bks., Inc.

Cohen, Paula Marantz. Beatrice Bunson's Guide to Romeo & Juliet. 2016. (ENG.). 200p. (J). (gr. 4-9). pap. 11.95 *(978-1-58988-105-1(2))* Dry, Paul Bks., Inc.

Cohn, Rachel. Shrimp, 7 vols. 2005. (YA). 171.75 *(978-1-4193-5253-9(9))* Recorded Bks., Inc.

—Shrimp. 2006. (ENG.). 352p. (YA). (gr. 7-12). reprint ed. pap. 6.99 *(978-0-689-86613-5(5)*, Simon & Schuster Bks. For Young Readers) Simon & Schuster Bks. For Young Readers.

—You Know Where to Find Me. (ENG.). (YA). (gr. 7). 2009. 224p. pap. 8.99 *(978-0-689-87860-2(5))* 2008. 208p. 16.99 *(978-0-689-87859-6(1))* Simon & Schuster Bks. For Young Readers. (Simon & Schuster Bks. For Young Readers).

Cohn, Rachel & Levithan, David. Naomi & Ely's No Kiss List. 2008. (ENG.). 256p. (YA). (gr. 9). pap. 9.99 *(978-0-375-84441-6(4)*, Ember) Random Hse. Children's Bks.

Cohn, Rachel & Wattenberg, Jane. Gingerbread. 2003. (ENG., Illus.). 224p. (YA). (gr. 9). pap. 8.99 *(978-0-689-86020-1(X)*, Simon & Schuster Bks. For Young Readers) Simon & Schuster Bks. For Young Readers.

Colasanti, Susane. So Much Closer. 2012. (ENG.). 272p. (YA). (gr. 7-18). pap. 8.99 *(978-0-14-242114-7(6)*, Speak) Penguin Young Readers Group.

—Something Like Fate. 2011. (ENG., Illus.). 304p. (YA). (gr. 7-18). 9.99 *(978-0-14-241882-6(X)*, Speak) Penguin Young Readers Group.

—Take Me There. 2009. (ENG.). 320p. (YA). (gr. 7-18). 9.99 *(978-0-14-241435-4(2)*, Speak) Penguin Young Readers Group.

—Waiting for You. 2010. (ENG.). 336p. (YA). (gr. 7-18). 9.99 *(978-0-14-241575-7(8)*, Speak) Penguin Young Readers Group.

—When It Happens. 2008. (ENG.). 336p. (YA). (gr. 7-18). 9.99 *(978-0-14-241155-1(8)*, Speak) Penguin Young Readers Group.

Cole, Cathy. The Trouble with Love. 2015. 200p. (J). **(978-0-545-87877-7(2))** Scholastic, Inc.

Cole, Stephen. Thieves Like Us. 2007. (ENG., Illus.). 368p. (YA). (gr. 7). per. 8.99 *(978-1-59990-041-4(6)*, 9781599900414, Bloomsbury USA Childrens) Bloomsbury Publishing USA.

Collins, Pat Lowery. Hidden Voices: The Orphan Musicians of Venice. 2009. (ENG., Illus.). 352p. (YA). (gr. 7). 17.99 *(978-0-7636-3917-4(6))* Candlewick Pr.

Collins, Suzanne. Catching Fire. 2009. (Hunger Games Trilogy: Bk. 2). (YA). 74.99 *(978-1-61574-572-2(6))* Findaway World, LLC.

—Catching Fire. 2009. 12.04 *(978-0-7848-3842-6(9)*, Everbind) Marco Bk. Co.

—Catching Fire. 2011. 480p. pap. *(978-1-4071-3209-9(1))* Scholastic.

—Catching Fire. (Hunger Games Ser.: 2). (ENG.). (gr. 7). 2014. 448p. (YA). pap. 12.99 *(978-0-545-79188-5(X)*, Tangerine Pr.) 2013. 400p. (YA). pap. 12.99 *(978-0-545-58617-7(8)*, Scholastic Pr.) 2013. 400p. (Illus.). 400p. (J). lib. bdg. 22.99 *(978-0-545-31059-8(8)*, Scholastic Pr.) 2009. 400p. (J). 18.99 *(978-0-439-02349-8(1)*, Scholastic Pr.) 2013. 400p. (J). pap. 12.99 *(978-0-545-60368-3(4)*, Scholastic Paperbacks) Scholastic, Inc.

—Catching Fire. l.t. ed. (Hunger Games Trilogy: 2). (ENG.). (YA). 2012. 498p. (gr. 7-12). pap. 14.99 *(978-1-59413-585-9(1)*, Large Print Pr.) 2009. 500p. 23.95 *(978-1-4104-2044-2(2))* Thorndike Pr.

—Catching Fire. 2013. (Hunger Games Trilogy Ser.: 2). lib. bdg. 24.50 *(978-0-606-32025-2(3)*, Turtleback) Turtleback Bks.

—Catching Fire. 2011. (Hunger Games Trilogy: Bk. 2). (CHI.). 344p. (YA). (gr. 7-12). pap. *(978-7-5063-5566-7(3))* Writers' Publishing Hse.

—EN LLAMAS. 2012. (Hunger Games Trilogy: Bk. 2). (SPA.). 416p. (J). pap. 19.99 *(978-84-272-0213-9(X))* Molino, Editorial ESP. Dist: Lectorum Pubns., Inc.

—En Llamas, Bk. 2. 2010. (Hunger Games Trilogy: Bk. 2).Tr. of Catching Fire. (SPA.). 416p. (J). (gr. 8-12). pap. 19.99 *(978-84-272-0000-5(5))* Lectorum Pubns., Inc.

—The Hunger Games. 2009. (Hunger Games Trilogy: Bk. 1). 10.85 *(978-0-7848-3801-3(1)*, Everbind) Marco Bk. Co.

—The Hunger Games. 2010. (Hunger Games Trilogy: Bk. 1). (ENG.). 374p. (gr. 7-12). 21.00 *(978-1-60686-581-1(1))* Perfection Learning Corp.

—The Hunger Games. Fournier, Guillaume, tr. 2011. (Hunger Games Trilogy: Bk. 1). (FRE.). 398p. (YA). (gr. 7-12). pap. *(978-2-266-18269-0(2))* Presses Pocket.

—The Hunger Games. 2011. (Hunger Games Trilogy: 1). (YA). 69.75 *(978-1-4561-3196-8(6))* Recorded Bks., Inc.

—The Hunger Games. 2010. (Hunger Games Ser.: 1). (ENG.). 384p. (J). (gr. 7-18). pap. 10.99 *(978-0-439-02352-8(1)*, Scholastic Pr.) Scholastic, Inc.

—The Hunger Games. O'Brien, Tim, illus. 2009. 448p. pap. *(978-1-4071-0908-4(1)*, Scholastic) Scholastic, Inc.

—The Hunger Games. (Hunger Games Ser.: 1). (ENG.). (gr. 7). 2008. 384p. (J). 18.99 *(978-0-439-02348-1(3)*, Scholastic Pr.) 2012. 384p. (J). pap. 12.99 *(978-0-545-42511-7(5))*Set. 2014. (YA). pap. 38.97 *(978-0-545-79191-5(X)*, Scholastic Pr.) Scholastic, Inc.

—The Hunger Games. l.t. ed. (Hunger Games Trilogy: Bk. 1). (ENG.). (YA). 2012. 484p. (gr. 7-12). pap. 14.99 *(978-1-59413-587-3(8)*, Large Print Pr.) 2009. 486p. 23.95 *(978-1-4104-1986-6(X))* Thorndike Pr.

—The Hunger Games. 2010. (Hunger Games Trilogy Ser.: 1). lib. bdg. 22.10 *(978-1-4178-3173-9(1)*, Turtleback) Turtleback Bks.

—The Hunger Games. 2010. (Hunger Games Trilogy: Bk. 1). (CHI.). 324p. (YA). (gr. 7-12). pap. *(978-7-5063-5153-9(6))* Writers' Publishing Hse.

—The Hunger Games: Foil Edition. 2014. (Hunger Games Ser.: 1). (ENG.). 448p. (YA). (gr. 7). pap. 12.99 *(978-0-545-79187-8(1)*, Scholastic Pr.) Scholastic, Inc.

—The Hunger Games Trilogy Set: The Hunger Games; Catching Fire; Mockingjay. 2010. (Hunger Games Ser.: 1). (ENG.). (J). (gr. 7-18). 53.97 *(978-0-545-26535-5(5)*, Scholastic Pr.) Scholastic, Inc.

—The Hunger Games Trilogy Collection. 2014. (Hunger Games Ser.). (ENG.). (J). (gr. 9). pap. 36.97 *(978-0-545-67031-9(4)*, Scholastic Pr.) Scholastic, Inc.

—Los Juegos del Hambre. 2009. (Hunger Games Trilogy: Bk. 1).Tr. of Hunger Games. (SPA.). pap. 19.99 *(978-84-9867-539-9(1))* RBA Libros, S.A. ESP. Dist: Lectorum Pubns., Inc.

—Los Juegos del Hambre. 2012. (Hunger Games Trilogy Spanish Ser.: 1).Tr. of Hunger Games. (SPA.). lib. bdg. 33.05 *(978-0-606-26447-1(7)*, Turtleback) Turtleback Bks.

—LOS JUEGOS DEL HAMBRE. 2012. (Hunger Games Trilogy: Bk. 1). (SPA.). 400p. (J). pap. 19.99 *(978-84-272-0212-2(1))* Molino, Editorial ESP. Dist: Lectorum Pubns., Inc.

—Mockingjay. 2011. (Hunger Games Trilogy: Bk. 3). (CHI.). 435p. (YA). (gr. 7-12). pap. *(978-986-213-216-6(7))* Locus Publishing Co.

—Mockingjay. (Hunger Games Trilogy: 3). (YA). 2011. 77.75 *(978-1-4561-3203-3(2))* 2010. 75.75 *(978-1-4561-3205-7(9))* 2010. 1.25 *(978-1-4640-2636-2(X))* Recorded Bks., Inc.

—Mockingjay. 2011. (Hunger Games Ser.: Vol. 3). (ENG.). 448p. (YA). (gr. 8-12). pap. *(978-1-4071-3210-5(5))* Scholastic Canada, Ltd.

—Mockingjay. 2014. (Hunger Games Ser.: 3). (ENG.). 400p. (YA). (gr. 7). pap. 12.99 *(978-0-545-78829-8(3)*, Scholastic Paperbacks) 2014. (Hunger Games Ser.: 3). (ENG.). 448p. (YA). (gr. 7). pap. 12.99 *(978-0-545-79190-8(1)*, Scholastic Pr.) 2014. (Hunger Games Ser.: 3). (ENG.). 400p. (J). (gr. 7). pap. 12.99 *(978-0-545-66326-7(1)*, Scholastic Pr.) 2010. (Hunger Games Ser.: 3). (ENG.). 400p. (J). (gr. 7-7). lib. bdg. 22.99 *(978-0-545-31060-4(1)*, Scholastic Pr.) 2010. (Hunger Games Ser.: 3). (ENG.). 400p. (J). (gr. 7-18). 18.99 *(978-0-439-02351-1(3)*, Scholastic Pr.) 2010. pap. *(978-0-439-02354-2(8)*, Scholastic Pr.) Scholastic, Inc.

—Mockingjay. l.t. ed. (Hunger Games Trilogy: Bk. 3). (ENG.). (YA). 2012. 502p. (gr. 7-12). pap. 14.99 *(978-1-59413-586-6(X)*, Large Print Pr.) 2010. 503p. 23.99 *(978-1-4104-2841-7(9))* Thorndike Pr.

—Mockingjay. 2014. (Hunger Games Trilogy Ser.: 3). lib. bdg. 24.50 *(978-0-606-36328-0(9))*; lib. bdg. 24.50 *(978-0-606-35133-1(7))* Turtleback Bks.

—Sinsajo. 2010. (Hunger Games Trilogy: Bk. 3).Tr. of Mockingjay. (SPA.). 424p. (J). (gr. 8-12). pap. 19.99 *(978-84-272-0038-8(2))* Molino, Editorial ESP. Dist: Lectorum Pubns., Inc.

—SINSAJO. 2012. (Hunger Games Trilogy: Bk. 3). (SPA.). 424p. (J). pap. 19.99 *(978-84-272-0214-6(8))* Molino, Editorial ESP. Dist: Lectorum Pubns., Inc.

—Sinsajo. 2012. (Hunger Games Trilogy Spanish Ser.: 3).Tr. of Mockingjay. (SPA.). lib. bdg. 33.05 *(978-0-606-26449-5(3)*, Turtleback) Turtleback Bks.

Condie, Ally. Crossed. 2013. (Matched Ser.: 2). (ENG.). 400p. (YA). (gr. 7). pap. 9.99 *(978-0-14-242171-0(5)*, Speak) Penguin Publishing Group.

—Crossed, 2 vols. 2011. (Matched Ser.: 2). (ENG.). 384p. (YA). (gr. 7-18). 17.99 *(978-0-525-42365-2(6)*, Dutton Books for Young Readers) Penguin Young Readers Group.

—Crossed. l.t. ed. 2011. (Matched Trilogy: Bk. 2). (ENG.). 448p. (J). 23.99 *(978-1-4104-4325-0(6))* Thorndike Pr.

—Crossed. 2013. (Matched Trilogy Ser.: 2). lib. bdg. 20.85 *(978-0-606-26634-5(8)*, Turtleback) Turtleback Bks.

—Juntos. 2011. (Vintage Espanol Ser.).Tr. of Matched. (SPA.). 352p. (YA). (gr. 7). pap. 10.95 *(978-0-307-94778-9(5)*, Vintage Espanol) Knopf Doubleday Publishing Group.

—Juntos. 2011.Tr. of Matched. (SPA.). lib. bdg. 22.05 *(978-0-606-26417-4(5)*, Turtleback) Turtleback Bks.

—Matched. 2009. (Matched Trilogy: Bk. 1). 11.04 *(978-0-7848-3716-0(3)*, Everbind) Marco Bk. Co.

—Matched. (Matched Ser.: 1). (ENG.). (YA). (gr. 7-18). 2011. 416p. 9.99 *(978-0-14-241977-9(X)*, Speak) 2010. 384p. 17.99 *(978-0-525-42364-5(8)*, Dutton Books for Young Readers) Penguin Young Readers Group.

—Matched. 2011. pap. *(978-0-545-39990-6(4))* Scholastic, Inc.

—Matched. l.t. ed. 2011. (Matched Trilogy: Bk. 1). (ENG.). 450p. 23.99 *(978-1-4104-3954-3(2))* Thorndike Pr.

—Matched. 2011. (Matched Trilogy Ser.: 1). lib. bdg. 20.85 *(978-0-606-23140-4(4)*, Turtleback) Turtleback Bks.

—Reached. 2012. (Matched Ser.: 3). (ENG.). 528p. (YA). (gr. 7-18). 17.99 *(978-0-525-42366-9(4)*, Dutton Books for Young Readers) Penguin Young Readers Group.

—Reached. l.t. ed. 2012. (Matched Trilogy: Bk. 3). (ENG.). 614p. 23.99 *(978-1-4104-5366-2(9))* Thorndike Pr.

Connelly, Neil. Into the Hurricane. 2017. (ENG.). 240p. (J). (gr. 9). 17.99 **(978-0-545-85381-1(8)**, Levine, Arthur A. Bks.) Scholastic, Inc.

Conrad, Lauren. L. A. Candy. (L. A. Candy Ser.: 1). (ENG.). (YA). (gr. 9-18). 2010. 352p. pap. 9.99 *(978-0-06-176759-3(X))* 2009. 336p. 17.99 *(978-0-06-176758-6(1))* HarperCollins Pubs.

—Sugar & Spice. (YA). 2011. (L. A. Candy Ser.: 3). (ENG.). 288p. (gr. 9). pap. 9.99 *(978-0-06-176763-0(8))* 2010. (L. A. Candy Ser.: 3). (ENG.). 288p. (gr. 9-18). 17.99 *(978-0-06-176762-3(X))* 2010. 279p. 9.99 *(978-0-06-201148-0(0))* HarperCollins Pubs.

—Sweet Little Lies. 2010. (L. A. Candy Ser.: 2). (YA). (ENG.). 336p. (gr. 9). pap. 9.99 *(978-0-06-176761-6(1))*; 309p. 9.99 *(978-0-06-198572-0(4))* HarperCollins Pubs.

Conway, K. R. Stormfront, vol. 2. 2014. (The Undertow Ser.). 428p. (YA). (gr. 7-17). pap. 15.95 *(978-0-9897763-4-9(4))* Conway, Kathleen R.

Cook, Eileen. Getting Revenge on Lauren Wood. 2010. (ENG.). (YA). (gr. 9). 288p. pap. 9.99 *(978-1-4424-0976-7(2))*; 272p. 15.99 *(978-1-4169-7433-8(4))* Simon Pulse. (Simon Pulse).

Cook, Julia. Cliques Just Don't Make Cents. DuFalla, Anita, illus. 2012. (ENG.). 32p. (J). pap. 10.95 *(978-1-934490-39-6(3))* Boys Town Pr.

—Decibella & Her 6-Inch Voice. DuFalla, Anita, illus. 2014. (ENG.). 32p. (J). pap. 10.95 *(978-1-934490-58-7(X))* Boys Town Pr.

—I Want to Be the Only Dog! DuFalla, Anita, illus. 2015. (ENG.). 32p. (J). pap. 10.95 *(978-1-934490-86-0(5))* Boys Town Pr.

—My Mouth Is a Volcano! Hartman, Carrie, illus. 2008. 32p. (J). (gr. -1-3). pap. 9.95 *(978-1-931636-85-8(0))* National Ctr. For Youth Issues.

—Personal Space Camp. Hartman, Carrie, illus. 32p. (J). 2009. 15.95 *(978-1-931636-89-6(3))* 2008. (gr. -1-3). pap. 9.95 *(978-1-931636-87-2(7))* National Ctr. For Youth Issues.

—Teamwork Isn't My Thing, & I Don't Like to Share! De Weerd, Kelsey, illus. 2012. (ENG.). 32p. (J). pap. 10.95 *(978-1-934490-35-8(0))* Boys Town Pr.

Cook, Julia. Technology Tail: A Digital Footprint Story. DuFalla, Anita, illus. 2017. (ENG.). 32p. (J). (gr. 1-6). pap. 10.95 **(978-1-944882-13-6(8))** Boys Town Pr.

Cook, Kristi. Magnolia. 2014. (ENG., Illus.). 336p. (YA). (gr. 9). 17.99 *(978-1-4424-8535-8(3))*; pap. 10.99 *(978-1-4424-8534-1(5))* Simon Pulse. (Simon Pulse).

Cooner, Donna. Worthy. 2017. (ENG.). 288p. (J). (gr. 7). 17.99 *(978-0-545-90393-6(9))* Scholastic, Inc.

Cooney, Caroline B. The Lost Songs. 2013. (ENG.). 256p. (YA). (gr. 7). pap. 8.99 *(978-0-385-73967-2(2)*, Ember) Random Hse. Children's Bks.

Cooper, Wendy. My First Ride with Isaiah. Elizabeth Mobley, illus. 2006. 18p. (J). 11.95 *(978-0-9772964-8-4(2))* Kingdom Publishing Group, Inc.

Copeland, Cynthia L. Elin's Island. 2003. (Single Titles Ser.: up). (ENG.). 144p. (YA). (gr. 6-12). lib. bdg. 22.60 *(978-0-7613-2522-2(0)*, Millbrook Pr.) Lerner Publishing Group.

—The 15 Best Things about Being the New Kid. Vargo, Sharon, illus. 2006. (Silly Millies Ser.). 32p. (J). (gr. -1-3). lib. bdg. 21.27 *(978-0-7613-2869-6(0)*, Millbrook Pr.); (gr. 2). per. 5.95 *(978-0-8225-6473-7(4)*, First Avenue Editions) Lerner Publishing Group.

Corbett, Sue. 12 Again. 2007. (ENG.). 240p. (J). (gr. 5-18). 6.99 *(978-0-14-240729-5(1)*, Puffin Books) Penguin Young Readers Group.

Coriell, Shelley. Welcome, Caller, This Is Chloe. 2013. (ENG.). 320p. (YA). (gr. 7-17). pap. 7.95 *(978-1-4197-0545-8(8)*, Amulet Bks.) Abrams, Inc.

Costain, Meredith. Dreams Come True. McDonald, Danielle, illus. 2017. (Ella Diaries Ser.: 4). 144p. (J). pap. 5.99 *(978-1-61067-523-9(1))* Kane Miller.

Cote, Denis. Les Yeux d'Emeraude. 2003. (Roman Jeunesse Ser.). (FRE.). 96p. (YA). (gr. 4-7). pap. *(978-2-89021-165-0(7))* Diffusion du livre Mirabel (DLM).

Cotugno, Katie. Top Ten. 2017. 368p. (YA). (gr. 8). 17.99 **(978-0-06-241830-2(0))** HarperCollins Pubs.

Couloumbis, Audrey. Not Exactly a Love Story. 2014. (ENG.). 288p. (YA). (gr. 7). pap. 9.99 *(978-0-375-86606-7(X)*, Ember) Random Hse. Children's Bks.

Coven, Wanda. Heidi Heckelbeck & the Secret Admirer. Burris, Priscilla, illus. 2012. (Heidi Heckelbeck Ser.: 6). (ENG.). 128p. (J). (gr. k-4). 16.99 *(978-1-4424-4175-0(5))*; pap. 5.99 *(978-1-4424-4174-3(7))* Little Simon. (Little Simon).

—Heidi Heckelbeck & the Secret Admirer. 2012. (Heidi Heckelbeck Ser.: 6). lib. bdg. 16.00 *(978-0-606-26905-6(3)*, Turtleback) Turtleback Bks.

Cowing, Sue. Call Me Drog. 2014. (ENG.). 320p. (J). 13.99 *(978-0-00-757804-7(0))* HarperCollins Pubs. Ltd. GBR. Dist: Independent Pubs. Group.

—You Will Call Me Drog. 2011. (Exceptional Reading & Language Arts Titles for Intermediate Grades Ser.). (ENG.). 288p. (J). (gr. 4-7). 16.95 *(978-0-7613-6076-6(X)*, Carolrhoda Bks.) Lerner Publishing Group.

Coy, John. Love of the Game. 2011. (4 For 4 Ser.: 3). (ENG.). 192p. (J). (gr. 3-7). 16.99 *(978-0-312-37331-3(7)*, 9780312373313) Feiwel & Friends.

—Love of the Game. 2011. (4 For 4 Ser.: 3). (ENG.). 192p. (J). (gr. 3-7). pap. 8.99 *(978-1-250-00637-0(6)*, 9781250006370) Square Fish.

Cozzo, Karole. How to Keep Rolling after a Fall. 2016. (ENG.). 272p. (YA). pap. 9.99 *(978-1-250-07928-2(4)*, 9781250079282) Feiwel & Friends.

Cray, Jordan. Gemini7. 2009. (Danger. com Ser.: 1). (ENG.). 192p. (YA). (gr. 7). pap. 9.99 *(978-1-4169-9847-1(0)*, Simon Pulse) Simon Pulse.

Cremer, Andrea. Nightshade. (Nightshade Ser.: 1). (ENG.). (YA). (gr. 9-18). 2011. 496p. pap. 9.99 *(978-0-14-241980-9(X)*, Speak) 2010. 464p. 17.99 *(978-0-399-25482-6(X)*, Philomel Bks.) Penguin Young Readers Group.

Crilley, Mark. Spring. Crilley, Mark, illus. 2007. (Miki Falls Ser.: 1). (ENG., Illus.). 176p. (YA). (gr. 8-12). pap. 8.99 *(978-0-06-084616-9(X))* HarperCollins Pubs.

—Summer. Crilley, Mark, illus. 2007. (Miki Falls Ser.: 2). (ENG., Illus.). 176p. (YA). (gr. 8-12). pap. 8.99 *(978-0-06-084617-6(8))* HarperCollins Pubs.

Crompton, Laurie Boyle. Blaze (Or, Love in the Time of Supervillains) 2013. (ENG.). 320p. (YA). (gr. 7-12). pap. 8.99 *(978-1-4022-7343-8(6))* Sourcebooks, Inc.

Cross, Mimi. Shining Sea, 0 vols. 2016. (ENG.). 432p. (YA). (gr. 9-12). pap. 9.99 *(978-1-5039-3553-2(1)*, 9781503935532, Skyscape) Amazon Publishing.

Cross, P. C. Summer Job: A Virgil & Cy Mystery. 2008. 260p. pap. 16.95 *(978-0-595-50921-8(5))* iUniverse, Inc.

Cross, Shauna. Whip It. 2009. (ENG.). 272p. (YA). (gr. 9-12). pap. 9.99 *(978-0-312-53599-5(6)*, 9780312535995) Square Fish.

Croteau, Marie-Danielle. Un Vent de Liberte. 2003. (Roman Plus Ser.). (FRE.). 160p. (YA). (gr. 8-18). pap. *(978-2-89021-204-6(1))* Diffusion du livre Mirabel (DLM).

Crowley, Cath. Graffiti Moon. 2012. (ENG.). 272p. (YA). (gr. 9). pap. 8.99 *(978-0-375-87195-5(0)*, Ember); 16.99 *(978-0-375-86953-2(0)*, Knopf Bks. for Young Readers) Random Hse. Children's Bks.

Crutcher, Chris. Ironman. 2004. (ENG.). 288p. (YA). (gr. 8). pap. 9.99 *(978-0-06-059840-2(9)*, Greenwillow Bks.) HarperCollins Pubs.

—Staying Fat for Sarah Byrnes. 2003. (ENG.). 304p. (YA). (gr. 8). pap. 9.99 *(978-0-06-009489-8(3)*, Greenwillow Bks.) HarperCollins Pubs.

Culbertson, Kim. Instructions for a Broken Heart. 2011. (ENG.). 304p. (YA). (gr. 7-12). pap. 9.99 *(978-1-4022-4302-8(2))* Sourcebooks, Inc.

Culbertson, Kim. The Wonder of Us. 2017. (ENG.). 336p. (J). (gr. 7). 17.99 **(978-0-545-73151-5(8))** Scholastic, Inc.

Culverwell, C. Ellen. The Horse Lady. 2009. (J). pap. *(978-0-88092-723-9(2))*; lib. bdg. *(978-0-88092-722-2(4))* Royal Fireworks Publishing Co.

Cusick, John M. Cherry Money Baby. 2013. (ENG.). 400p. (YA). (gr. 9). 16.99 *(978-0-7636-5557-0(0))* Candlewick Pr.

—Girl Parts. (ENG., Illus.). 240p. (YA). (gr. 9). 2012. pap. 7.99 *(978-0-7636-5644-7(5))* 2010. 16.99 *(978-0-7636-4930-2(9))* Candlewick Pr.

Cutler, Dave. When I Wished I Was Alone. Cutler, Dave, illus. 2003. (Illus.). 36p. (J). 16.95 *(978-0-9671851-0-1(6))* GreyCore Pr.

Dale, Mitzi. The Great & Awful Summer, 1 vol. 2007. (ENG.). 192p. (YA). (gr. 8-12). pap. 9.95 *(978-1-55109-614-8(5))* Nimbus Publishing, Ltd. CAN. Dist: Orca Bk. Pubs. USA.

Damico, Gina. Hellhole. (ENG.). (YA). (gr. 9). 2016. 384p. pap. 9.99 *(978-0-544-54117-7(0))* 2015. 368p. 17.99 *(978-0-544-30710-0(0))* Houghton Mifflin Harcourt Publishing Co. (HMH Books For Young Readers).

Danczyk, Kenneth. Grandpas Farm. 2008. 35p. pap. 16.00 *(978-1-4357-4021-1(1))* Lulu Pr., Inc.

Daneshvari, Gitty. Class Is Not Dismissed! 2011. (School of Fear Ser.: 2). (ENG.). 336p. (J). (gr. 3-7). pap. 8.99 *(978-0-316-03329-9(4))* Little, Brown Bks. for Young Readers.

—The Final Exam. (School of Fear Ser.: 3). (ENG.). (J). (gr. 3-7). 2012. 352p. pap. 8.99 *(978-0-316-18285-0(0))* 2011. 336p. 16.99 *(978-0-316-18287-4(7))* Little, Brown Bks. for Young Readers.

—School of Fear. 2010. (School of Fear Ser.: 1). (ENG., Illus.). 368p. (J). (gr. 3-7). pap. 8.99 *(978-0-316-03327-5(8))* Little, Brown Bks. for Young Readers.

Danziger, Paula, et al. Amber Brown Horses Around. Lewis, Anthony, illus. (Amber Brown Ser.: 12). (ENG.). (J). 2015. 224p. (gr. 3-7). 5.99 *(978-0-14-751552-0(1)*, Puffin Books)

H

I

2014. 208p. (gr. 2-5). 14.99 (978-0-399-16170-4(8), G.P. Putnam's Sons Books for Young Readers) Penguin Young Readers Group.

Daviess, Maria Thompson. The Golden Bird. 2007. 92p. per. (978-1-4068-1853-6(4)) Echo Library.

Davis, Heather. The Clearing. 2010. (ENG., Illus.). 224p. (YA). (gr. 9). pap. 8.99 (978-0-547-26367-0(8)) Houghton Mifflin Harcourt Publishing Co.

—Never Cry Werewolf. 2010. (ENG.). 224p. (YA). (gr. 8). pap. 9.99 (978-0-06-134925-6(9), HarperTeen) HarperCollins Pubs.

Day, Susie. My Invisible Boyfriend. 2010. (ENG.). 288p. (J). (gr. 7-18). 16.99 (978-0-545-07354-7(5), Scholastic Pr.) Scholastic, Inc.

de Campi, Alex. Kat & Mouse. 2017. (ENG., Illus.). 96p. pap. 5.99 (978-1-59816-549-4(6), 9781598165494) TOKYOPOP, Inc.

de Lint, Charles. Waifs & Strays. 2004. (ENG.). 416p. (YA). (gr. 7-18). 8.99 (978-0-14-240158-3(7), Firebird) Penguin Young Readers Group.

de Vigan, Delphine. No & Me. Miller, George, tr. from FRE. 2010. (ENG.). 256p. (YA). (gr. 7-12). 16.99 (978-1-59990-479-5(9), 9781599904795, Bloomsbury USA Childrens) Bloomsbury Publishing USA.

Dean, Carolee. Forget Me Not. (ENG.). (YA). (gr. 9). 2013. 400p. pap. 11.99 (978-1-4424-3255-0(1)) 2012. 384p. 16.99 (978-1-4424-3254-3(3)) Simon Pulse. (Simon Pulse).

Dean, Zoey. Blonde Ambition. 2004. (A-List Ser.: 3). (ENG.). 240p. (YA). (gr. 10-17). pap. 9.99 (978-0-316-73474-5(8), Poppy) Little, Brown Bks. for Young Readers.

DeAngelo, Jeremy. The Out Crowd. 2006. (J). pap. (978-0-88092-613-3(9)); lib. bdg. (978-0-88092-612-6(0)) Royal Fireworks Publishing Co.

Dee, Barbara. Solving Zoe. 2010. (Mix Ser.). (ENG.). 256p. (J). (gr. 4-8). pap. 7.99 (978-1-4169-9159-5(X), Aladdin) Simon & Schuster Children's Publishing.

—This Is Me from Now On. 2010. (Mix Ser.). (ENG.). 272p. (J). (gr. 4-8). pap. 7.99 (978-1-4169-9414-5(9), Aladdin) Simon & Schuster Children's Publishing.

DeLaCroix, Alice. How to Survive a Totally Boring Summer. Fisher, Cynthia, illus. 2007. (ENG.). 96p. (J). (gr. 1-4). 16.95 (978-0-8234-2024-7(8)) Holiday Hse., Inc.

Delany, Shannon & Redgrave, Saoirse. Secrets & Shadows: A 13 to Life Novel. 2011. (13 to Life Ser.: 2). (ENG.). 320p. (YA). (gr. 7-18). pap. 9.99 (978-0-312-60915-3(9), 9780312609153, St. Martin's Griffin) St. Martin's Pr.

Delisle, Annette Gonzalez. Nettey Loves Shoeboxes. Leyva, Juan Camilo, illus. 2011. 28p. pap. 9.99 (978-1-61170-015-2(9)) Robertson Publishing.

Dellasega, Cheryl. Nugrl90, 0 vols. LaPierre, Karina, illus. 2007. (Bloggrls Ser.: 1). (ENG.). 192p. (YA). (gr. 7-11). pap. 9.99 (978-0-7614-5396-3(2), 9780761453963, Amazon Children's Publishing) Amazon Publishing.

Delsol, Wendy. Flock. 2013. (ENG.). 400p. (YA). (gr. 7). pap. 8.99 (978-0-7636-6467-1(7)) Candlewick Pr.

—Frost. (ENG., Illus.). (YA). (gr. 7). 2012. 384p. pap. 8.99 (978-0-7636-6249-3(6)) 2011. 376p. 15.99 (978-0-7636-5386-6(1)) Candlewick Pr.

Demetrios, Heather. Exquisite Captive. 2014. (Dark Caravan Cycle Ser.: 1). (ENG., Illus.). 480p. (YA). (gr. 8). 17.99 (978-0-06-231856-5(X)) HarperCollins Pubs.

Derby, Sally. Kyle's Island. 2010. (ENG.). 192p. (J). (gr. 5-8). 16.95 (978-1-58089-316-9(3)) Charlesbridge Publishing, Inc.

Deriso, Christine Hurley. Thirty Sunsets. 2014. (ENG.). 240p. (YA). pap. 9.99 (978-0-7387-3991-5(X), Flux) North Star Editions.

Despain, Bree. The Dark Divine. 2010. (ENG.). 384p. (gr. 7). pap. 9.99 (978-1-60684-154-9(8), Carolrhoda Lab™) Lerner Publishing Group.

—The Lost Saint. 2011. (ENG.). 416p. (J). (gr. 7). pap. 9.99 (978-1-60684-235-5(8), Carolrhoda Lab™) Lerner Publishing Group.

—The Savage Grace. 2013. (ENG.). 496p. (J). (gr. 7). pap. 9.99 (978-1-60684-416-8(4), Carolrhoda Lab™) Lerner Publishing Group.

Dessen, Sarah. Along for the Ride. (ENG.). (YA). (gr. 7-18). 2011. 432p. pap. 10.99 (978-0-14-241556-6(1), Speak) 2009. 416p. 19.99 (978-0-670-01194-0(0), Viking Books for Young Readers) Penguin Young Readers Group.

—Along for the Ride. 2011. lib. bdg. 20.85 (978-0-606-15360-7(8), Turtleback) Turtleback Bks.

—Just Listen. 2008. (ENG.). 400p. (YA). (gr. 7-18). 10.99 (978-0-14-241097-4(7), Speak) Penguin Young Readers Group.

—Just Listen. 2007. 20.00 (978-0-7569-8270-6(7)) Perfection Learning Corp.

—Just Listen. 2008. 22.10 (978-1-4178-2016-0(0), Turtleback) Turtleback Bks.

—Keeping the Moon. 2004. (ENG.). 256p. (YA). (gr. 7-7). pap. 10.99 (978-0-14-240176-7(5), Speak) Penguin Young Readers Group.

—Lock & Key. 2009. (ENG.). 448p. (YA). (gr. 7-18). 10.99 (978-0-14-241472-9(7), Speak) Penguin Young Readers Group.

—Lock & Key. 2009. lib. bdg. 22.10 (978-0-606-14396-7(3), Turtleback) Turtleback Bks.

—That Summer. (ENG.). (YA). (gr. 7-18). 2006. 208p. 17.99 (978-0-670-06110-5(7), Viking Books for Young Readers) 2004. 224p. 10.99 (978-0-14-240172-9(2), Speak) Penguin Young Readers Group.

—This Lullaby. 2004. (ENG.). 368p. (YA). (gr. 7-18). reprint ed. pap. 10.99 (978-0-14-250155-9(7), Speak) Penguin Young Readers Group.

—The Truth about Forever. 2006. (ENG.). 400p. (YA). (gr. 7-18). reprint ed. 10.99 (978-0-14-240625-0(2), Speak) Penguin Young Readers Group.

—The Truth about Forever. 2007. 374p. (gr. 7-12). 20.00 (978-0-7569-8275-1(8)) Perfection Learning Corp.

—The Truth about Forever. (YA). 2006. 1.25 (978-1-4193-2647-9(3)) 2005. 127.75 (978-1-4193-3880-9(3)) 2005. 107.75 (978-1-4193-2650-9(3)) Recorded Bks., Inc.

Deuker, Carl. Night Hoops. 2009. (ENG.). 224p. (YA). (gr. 7). pap. 8.99 (978-0-547-24891-2(1)) Houghton Mifflin Harcourt Publishing Co.

—Night Hoops. 2009. 250p. (gr. 7-12). lib. bdg. 19.65 (978-0-613-61919-6(6), Turtleback) Turtleback Bks.

Devlin, Ivy. Low Red Moon. 2010. (ENG., Illus.). 256p. (YA). (gr. 7-18). 16.99 (978-1-59990-510-5(8), 9781599905105, Bloomsbury USA Childrens) Bloomsbury Publishing USA.

Devoles, Margaret. My Aunt Calls Me Saree. 2007. 88p. per. 19.95 (978-1-4241-7579-6(8)) America Star Bks.

DeWoskin, Rachel. Blind. 2014. (ENG.). 416p. (YA). (gr. 7). 17.99 (978-0-670-78522-3(9), Viking Books for Young Readers) Penguin Young Readers Group.

Dewoskin, Rachel. Blind. 2016. (ENG.). 416p. (YA). (gr. 7). pap. 10.99 (978-0-14-242455-1(2), Speak) Penguin Young Readers Group.

Diallo, Elishia Shelene. Boogalou: A Boogie down Bronx Tale. 2015. (ENG.). 272p. (YA). pap. 14.99 (978-1-4951-7655-5(X)) Independent Pub.

Dickerson, Tim. Napping with Daddy. 2010. 24p. pap. 11.49 (978-1-4490-4718-4(1)) AuthorHouse.

Dionne, Erin. Notes from an Accidental Band Geek. 2012. (ENG.). 304p. (J). (gr. 5). pap. 6.99 (978-0-14-242247-2(9), Puffin Books) Penguin Young Readers Group.

—The Total Tragedy of a Girl Named Hamlet. 2011. (ENG.). 304p. (J). (gr. 3-7). 8.99 (978-0-14-241748-5(3), Puffin Books) Penguin Young Readers Group.

Dirkes, Craig. Sucktown, Alaska. 2017. (ENG.). 352p. (gr. 9-12). 17.95 (978-1-63079-055-4(9)) Switch Pr.

Divine, L. Cold as Ice. 2010. (ENG., Illus.). 256p. (YA). (gr. 9-18). 15.00 (978-0-7582-3113-0(X), K-Teen/Dafina) Kensington Publishing Corp.

—Frenemies. 2008. (Drama High Ser.: Vol. 4). 218p. (gr. 8-12). 19.95 (978-0-7569-8832-6(2)) Perfection Learning Corp.

—Lady J. 2008. (Drama High Ser.: Vol. 5). 214p. (gr. 8-12). 19.95 (978-0-7569-8833-3(0)) Perfection Learning Corp.

Dolby, Tom. Secret Society. 2011. (ENG.). 368p. (YA). (gr. 8). pap. 8.99 (978-0-06-172163-2(8), Tegen, Katherine Bks) HarperCollins Pubs.

—The Trust. 2011. (ENG.). 368p. (YA). (gr. 8-18). 16.99 (978-0-06-172164-9(6), Tegen, Katherine Bks) HarperCollins Pubs.

Donovan, John. I'll Get There. It Better Be Worth the Trip: 40th Anniversary Edition. 40th ed. 2010. (ENG.). 240p. (YA). (gr. 8-18). pap. 11.99 (978-0-7387-2134-7(4), Flux) North Star Editions.

Donovan, Stacey. Who I Am Keeps Happening. 2004. (YA). (978-0-7636-1988-6(4)) Candlewick Pr.

Dowell, Frances O'Roark. Ten Miles Past Normal. (ENG., 224p. (YA). (gr. 7). 2012. Illus.). pap. 9.99 (978-1-4169-9586-9(2)) 2011. 16.99 (978-1-4169-9585-2(4)) Simon & Schuster Children's Publishing. (Atheneum Bks. for Young Readers).

Downham, Jenny. You Against Me. 2012. (ENG.). 416p. (YA). (gr. 9). pap. 9.99 (978-0-385-75266-4(0), Ember) Random Hse. Children's Bks.

Downing, Erin. Best Friends (until Someone Better Comes Along) 2014. (Mix Ser.). (ENG., Illus.). 240p. (J). (gr. 4-8). pap. 6.99 (978-1-4424-8519-8(1), Aladdin) Simon & Schuster Children's Publishing.

—Dancing Queen. 2006. (Romantic Comedies Ser.). (ENG.). 272p. (YA). (gr. 9-12). mass mkt. 6.99 (978-1-4169-2510-1(4), Simon Pulse) Simon Pulse.

—Drive Me Crazy. 2009. (Romantic Comedies Ser.). (ENG.). 240p. (YA). (gr. 7-18). mass mkt. 6.99 (978-1-4169-7484-0(9), Simon Pulse) Simon Pulse.

—A Funny Thing about Love: Dancing Queen; Prom Crashers; Drive Me Crazy. 2011. (ENG.). 656p. (YA). (gr. 7). pap. 9.99 (978-1-4424-0645-2(3), Simon Pulse) Simon Pulse.

—Kiss It. 2010. (ENG.). 288p. (YA). (gr. 9-18). pap. 9.99 (978-1-4169-9700-9(8), Simon Pulse) Simon Pulse.

Drakeford, Lisa. The Baby. 2016. (ENG.). 256p. (J). (gr. 9). 17.99 (978-0-545-94027-6(3)) Scholastic, Inc.

Draper, Sharon M. Just Another Hero. 2017. (Jericho Trilogy Ser.: 3). (ENG., Illus.). 304p. (YA). (gr. 7). pap. 9.99 (978-1-4814-9030-6(3), Atheneum/Caitlyn Dlouhy Books) Simon & Schuster Children's Publishing.

—November Blues. 2009. (Jericho Trilogy Ser.). (ENG.). 400p. (YA). (gr. 7). mass mkt. 8.99 (978-1-4169-0699-5(1), Simon Pulse) Simon Pulse.

—Out of My Mind. 2009. 9.00 (978-0-7848-3780-1(5), Everbind) Marco Bk. Co.

—Out of My Mind. (ENG., Illus.). (J). (gr. 5). 2012. 320p. pap. 9.99 (978-1-4169-7171-9(8)) 2010. 304p. 18.99 (978-1-4169-7170-2(X)) Simon & Schuster Children's Publishing. (Atheneum Bks. for Young Readers).

—Out of My Mind. 2012. lib. bdg. 20.85 (978-0-606-25672-8(5), Turtleback) Turtleback Bks.

Drown, Merle. Lighting the World. 2015. (ENG.). 278p. pap. 18.00 (978-0-9898971-4-3(1)) Whitepoint Pr.

Dunlap, Susanne. The Academie. 2012. (ENG.). 368p. (YA). 16.99 (978-1-59990-586-0(8), 9781599905860, Bloomsbury USA Childrens) Bloomsbury Publishing USA.

—Anastasia's Secret. 2011. (ENG.). 368p. (YA). (gr. 7). pap. 8.99 (978-1-59990-588-4(4), 9781599905884, Bloomsbury USA Childrens) Bloomsbury Publishing USA.

Dunmore, Helen. The Tide Knot. 2008. 330p. (J). 5.99 (978-0-06-081857-9(3)); (Ingo Ser.: 2). (ENG.). 336p. (YA). (gr. 5-8). 16.99 (978-0-06-081855-5(7)) HarperCollins Pubs.

DuPrau, Jeanne. Car Trouble. 2005. 288p. (J). 15.99 (978-0-06-073672-9(0)); lib. bdg. 16.89 (978-0-06-073674-3(7)) HarperCollins Pubs.

Eager, Edward. The Well-Wishers. Bodecker, N. M., illus. 2016. (Tales of Magic Ser.: 6). (ENG.). 240p. (J). (gr. 2-5). pap. 7.99 (978-0-544-67167-6(8), HMH Books For Young Readers) Houghton Mifflin Harcourt Publishing Co.

Earls, Nick. After Summer. 2005. (ENG.). 240p. (YA). (gr. 7). pap. 13.99 (978-0-618-45781-6(X)) Houghton Mifflin Harcourt Publishing Co.

—48 Shades of Brown. 2004. (ENG.). 288p. (YA). (gr. 7-18). pap. 16.99 (978-0-618-45295-8(8)) Houghton Mifflin Harcourt Publishing Co.

Echols, Jennifer. Biggest Flirts. 2014. (Superlatives Ser.). (ENG., Illus.). 336p. (YA). (gr. 9). pap. 9.99 (978-1-4424-7445-1(9), Simon Pulse) Simon Pulse.

—Endless Summer: The Boys Next Door; Endless Summer. 2010. (ENG.). 624p. (YA). (gr. 7). mass mkt. 11.99 (978-1-4424-0659-9(3), Simon Pulse) Simon Pulse.

—The Ex Games. 2011. (Romantic Comedies Ser.). (ENG.). 240p. (YA). (gr. 7). pap. 11.99 (978-1-4424-3083-9(4), Simon Pulse) Simon Pulse.

Edgeworth, Maria. Tomorrow. 2004. reprint ed. pap. 1.99 (978-1-4192-9032-9(0)); pap. 15.95 (978-1-4191-9032-2(6)) Kessinger Publishing, LLC.

Edwards, Asasimone. What's a Mimi-Saurus? 2009. (Illus.). 36p. pap. 16.99 (978-1-4389-7919-9(3)) AuthorHouse.

Edwardson, Debby Dahl. My Name Is Not Easy, 0 vols. 2013. (ENG.). 256p. (YA). (gr. 7-9). pap. 9.99 (978-1-4778-1629-5(1), 9781477816295, Amazon Children's Publishing) Amazon Publishing.

Efaw, Amy. Battle Dress. 2010. (ENG.). 304p. (YA). (gr. 7-18). 8.99 (978-0-14-241397-5(6), Speak) Penguin Young Readers Group.

Egan, Kate. The Hunger Games - Catching Fire. 2013. (ENG., Illus.). 160p. (J). (gr. 7-12). pap. 18.99 (978-0-545-59933-7(4)) Scholastic, Inc.

Elkeles, Simone. How to Ruin a Summer Vacation. 2006. (How to Ruin a Summer Vacation Novel Ser.: 1). (ENG.). 240p. (YA). (gr. 8-12). per. 9.95 (978-0-7387-0961-1(1), Flux) North Star Editions.

—How to Ruin My Teenage Life. 2007. (How to Ruin a Summer Vacation Novel Ser.: 2). (ENG.). 288p. (YA). (gr. 7-12). per. 11.99 (978-0-7387-1019-8(9), Flux) North Star Editions.

—Return to Paradise. 2010. (Leaving Paradise Novel Ser.: 2). (ENG.). 312p. (YA). (gr. 8-18). pap. 9.95 (978-0-7387-1868-2(8), Flux) North Star Editions.

—Return to Paradise. 2010. lib. bdg. 20.80 (978-0-606-14994-5(5), Turtleback) Turtleback Bks.

Ellis, Ann Dee. This Is What I Did. 2011. 9.68 (978-0-7848-3387-2(7), Everbind) Marco Bk. Co.

Ellis, Kat. Breaker. 2016. (ENG.). 336p. (YA). (gr. 2-17). pap. 9.95 (978-0-7624-5908-7(5), Running Pr. Kids) Running Pr. Bk. Pubs.

Ellis, Kim. Bernard & His Dad. 2005. 49p. pap. 16.95 (978-1-4137-7058-2(4)) America Star Bks.

Ellis, Leanne Statland. Tree Huggers. 2010. (J). pap. (978-0-88092-521-1(3)) Royal Fireworks Publishing Co.

Emerson, Kevin. Breakout. 2015. (ENG.). 304p. (YA). (gr. 7). 17.99 (978-0-385-39112-2(9), Crown Books For Young Readers) Random Hse. Children's Bks.

—Encore to an Empty Room. 2016. (Exile Ser.: 2). 336p. (YA). (gr. 9). pap. 9.99 (978-0-06-213399-1(3), Tegen, Katherine Bks) HarperCollins Pubs.

Emery, Anne. Senior Year. Krush, Beth, illus. 2006. (YA). per. 11.95 (978-1-59511-005-3(4)) Image Cascade Publishing.

—Sorority Girl. 2006. (YA). per. 11.95 (978-1-59511-007-7(0)) Image Cascade Publishing.

Emmanuel, Linda. The Angel Children: I Love Who I Am. 2005. (Illus.). (J). E-Book 12.95 incl. cd-rom (978-0-9767418-0-0(6)) Wintermantel Group, LLC, The.

Emond, Stephen. Happyface. 2011. (ENG., Illus.). 336p. (YA). (gr. 7-17). pap. 10.99 (978-0-316-04099-0(1)) Little, Brown Bks. for Young Readers.

Eulberg, Elizabeth. Better off Friends. 2014. (ENG.). 288p. (J). (gr. 7). 17.99 (978-0-545-55145-8(5)) Scholastic, Inc.

—Just Another Girl. 2017. (ENG.). 256p. (J). (gr. 7). 17.99 (978-0-545-95628-4(5)) Scholastic, Inc.

—The Lonely Hearts Club. (ENG.). 304p. (J). 2011. (gr. 3-7). pap. 8.99 (978-0-545-14032-4(3)) 2010. (gr. 9-12). 17.99 (978-0-545-14031-7(5)) Scholastic, Inc.

—Revenge of the Girl with the Great Personality. 2014. (ENG.). 272p. (J). (gr. 7). pap. 10.99 (978-0-545-47700-0(X), Scholastic Paperbacks) Scholastic, Inc.

—Take a Bow. 2013. (ENG.). 288p. (J). (gr. 7). pap. 9.99 (978-0-545-33476-1(4), Scholastic Paperbacks) 2012. (ENG.). 288p. (J). (gr. 7). 17.99 (978-0-545-33474-7(8)) 2012. 280p. (YA). pap. (978-0-545-43982-4(5)) Scholastic, Inc.

—We Can Work It Out. 2015. (ENG.). 320p. (J). (gr. 7). 17.99 (978-0-545-65461-6(0)) Scholastic, Inc.

Evangelista, Kate. No Second Chances. 2017. (Dodge Cove Trilogy Ser.). (ENG.). 224p. (YA). pap. 10.99 (978-1-250-10067-2(4), 9781250100672) Feiwel & Friends.

Ewell, Katherine. Dear Killer. 2014. (ENG.). 368p. (YA). (gr. 8). 17.99 (978-0-06-225780-2(3)) HarperCollins Pubs.

Farrar, Josh. A Song for Bijou. 2013. (ENG.). 304p. (YA). (gr. 5-8). 16.99 (978-0-8027-3394-8(8), 9780802733948, Bloomsbury USA Childrens) Bloomsbury Publishing USA.

Fehlbaum, Beth. Hope in Patience. 2010. 312p. (YA). (gr. 8-18). 16.95 (978-1-934813-41-6(9)) Westside Bks.

Fehler, Gene. Beanball. 2011. (ENG.). 144p. (YA). (gr. 7). pap. 7.99 (978-0-547-55001-5(4)) Houghton Mifflin Harcourt Publishing Co.

Ferguson, Alane. The Angel of Death. 2008. (Forensic Mystery Ser.). 258p. 17.00 (978-0-7569-8929-3(9)) Perfection Learning Corp.

Ferris, Aimee. Girl Overboard. 2007. (S. A. S. S. Ser.). (ENG., Illus.). 224p. (YA). (gr. 7-18). 7.99 (978-0-14-240799-8(2), Speak) Penguin Young Readers Group.

Findlay, Chris. Ae Sma Voice. 2008. 152p. pap. (978-1-84923-144-2(3)) YouWriteOn.

Finn, Katie. Revenge, Ice Cream, & Other Things Best Served Cold. 2015. (Broken Hearts & Revenge Novel Ser.: 2). (ENG.). 400p. (YA). (gr. 8). 17.99 (978-1-250-04525-6(8), 9781250045256) Feiwel & Friends.

Finn, Mary. Belladonna. 2011. (ENG., Illus.). 384p. (YA). (gr. 7-18). 16.99 (978-0-7636-5106-0(0)) Candlewick Pr.

Flack, Sophie. Bunheads. 2012. (ENG.). 320p. (YA). (gr. 7-17). pap. 10.99 (978-0-316-12654-0(3), Poppy) Little, Brown Bks. for Young Readers.

Fliess, Sue. The Hug Book. Kennedy, Anne, illus. 2014. (Little Golden Book Ser.). (ENG.). 24p. (J). (-k). 4.99 (978-0-385-37907-6(2), Golden Bks.) Random Hse. Children's Bks.

Flinn, Alex. Diva. 2007. (ENG.). 288p. (J). (gr. 9-12). pap. 8.99 (978-0-06-056846-7(1)) 2006. 263p. (YA). (gr. 7-12). 16.99 (978-0-06-056843-6(7)) 2006. 263p. (YA). (gr. 7-12). lib. bdg. 18.89 (978-0-06-056845-0(3)) HarperCollins Pubs. (HarperTeen).

Flores-Scott, Patrick. Jumped In. 2013. (ENG.). 304p. (YA). (gr. 7). 16.99 (978-0-8050-9514-2(4), 9780805095142, Holt, Henry & Co. Bks. For Young Readers) Holt, Henry & Co.

Fogelin, Adrian. The Big Nothing. (ENG.). 224p. (J). (gr. 3-7). 2006. pap. 7.95 (978-1-56145-388-7(9)) 2004. 15.95 (978-1-56145-326-9(9)) Peachtree Pubs.

—My Brother's Hero, 1 vol. 2005. (ENG.). 224p. (J). (gr. 3-7). reprint ed. pap. 7.95 (978-1-56145-352-8(8)) Peachtree Pubs.

—The Real Question, 1 vol. (ENG.). 256p. (YA). 2009. pap. 7.95 (978-1-56145-501-0(6)) 2006. (gr. 7-18). 15.95 (978-1-56145-383-2(8)) Peachtree Pubs.

Ford, Juwanda G. Shop Talk. Hoston, Jim, illus. 2004. 32p. (J). lib. bdg. 15.00 (978-1-4242-0236-2(1)) Fitzgerald Bks.

Forman, Gayle. Where She Went. l.t. ed. 2015. (If I Stay Ser.: BK.2). (ENG.). 288p. (YA). 23.99 (978-1-4104-7562-6(X)) Cengage Gale.

—Where She Went. (If I Stay Ser.: BK.2). (ENG.). (YA). (gr. 9-18). 2012. 304p. 10.99 (978-0-14-242089-8(1), Speak) 2011. 272p. 17.99 (978-0-525-42294-5(3), Dutton Books for Young Readers) Penguin Young Readers Group.

—Where She Went. 2012. (If I Stay Ser.: BK.2). (YA). 21.00 (978-1-61383-394-0(6)) Perfection Learning Corp.

—Where She Went. l.t. ed. 2015. (If I Stay Ser.: BK.2). (ENG.). 286p. (YA). pap. 12.99 (978-1-59413-855-3(9), Large Print Pr.) Thorndike Pr.

—Where She Went. 2012. (If I Stay Ser.: BK.2). (YA). lib. bdg. 22.10 (978-0-606-23644-7(9), Turtleback) Turtleback Bks.

Frank, E. R. Friction. 2004. (ENG.). 208p. (YA). (gr. 7). reprint ed. pap. 10.99 (978-0-689-85385-2(8), Simon Pulse) Simon Pulse.

—Life Is Funny. 2016. (ENG., Illus.). 288p. (YA). (gr. 9). 17.99 (978-1-4814-3164-4(1), Atheneum Bks. for Young Readers) Simon & Schuster Children's Publishing.

Frank, Hillary. I Can't Tell You. 2004. (ENG.). 208p. (YA). (gr. 7). pap. 7.99 (978-0-618-49491-0(X)) Houghton Mifflin Harcourt Publishing Co.

—I Can't Tell You. 2004. 208p. (YA). (gr. 7). 16.00 (978-0-618-41202-0(6)) Houghton Mifflin Harcourt Trade & Reference Pubs.

Frazier, Sundee T. Brendan Buckley's Sixth-Grade Experiment. 2013. (ENG.). 288p. (J). (gr. 4-7). 6.99 (978-0-385-74051-7(4), Yearling) Random Hse. Children's Bks.

Frederick, Heather Vogel. Home for the Holidays. 2012. (Mother-Daughter Book Club Ser.). (ENG.). 384p. (J). (gr. 4-9). pap. 8.99 (978-1-4424-0686-5(0), Simon & Schuster Bks. For Young Readers) Simon & Schuster Bks. For Young Readers.

—Mother-Daughter Book Camp. 2016. (Mother-Daughter Book Club Ser.). (ENG., Illus.). 336p. (J). (gr. 5-9). 16.99 (978-1-4424-7183-2(2), Simon & Schuster Bks. For Young Readers) Simon & Schuster Bks. For Young Readers.

—The Mother-Daughter Book Club. (Mother-Daughter Book Club Ser.). (ENG.). (J). 2008. 288p. (gr. 4-7). pap. 7.99 (978-1-4169-7079-8(7)) 2007. (Illus.). 256p. (gr. 5-7). 17.99 (978-0-689-86412-4(4)) Simon & Schuster Bks. For Young Readers. (Simon & Schuster Bks. For Young Readers).

—Much Ado about Anne. 2009. (Mother-Daughter Book Club Ser.). (ENG., Illus.). 352p. (J). (gr. 4-7). pap. 7.99 (978-1-4169-8269-2(8), Simon & Schuster Bks. For Young Readers) Simon & Schuster Bks. For Young Readers.

—Pies & Prejudice. (Mother-Daughter Book Club Ser.). (ENG.). (J). (gr. 4-7). 2011. 400p. pap. 8.99 (978-1-4424-2019-9(7)) 2010. 384p. 15.99 (978-1-4169-7431-4(8)) Simon & Schuster Bks. For Young Readers. (Simon & Schuster Bks. For Young Readers).

—Wish You Were Eyre. 2013. (Mother-Daughter Book Club Ser.). (ENG.). 480p. (J). (gr. 4-9). pap. 7.99 (978-1-4424-3065-5(6), Simon & Schuster Bks. For Young Readers) Simon & Schuster Bks. For Young Readers.

Fredericks, Mariah. Crunch Time. 2007. (ENG.). 336p. (YA). (gr. 7-12). pap. 15.99 (978-1-4169-3973-3(3), Atheneum Bks. for Young Readers) Simon & Schuster Children's Publishing.

Freeman, Martha. 1,000 Reasons Never to Kiss a Boy. 2007. (ENG.). 240p. (YA). (gr. 7-18). 16.95 (978-0-8234-2044-5(2)) Holiday Hse., Inc.

Freitas, Donna. Gold Medal Summer. (ENG.). 240p. (J). 2014. (gr. 5-9). pap. 6.99 (978-0-545-32789-3(X)) 2012. (gr. 4-7). 16.99 (978-0-545-32788-6(1)) Scholastic, Inc. (Levine, Arthur A. Bks.).

Freymann-Weyr, Garret. Stay with Me. 2007. (ENG.). 320p. (YA). (gr. 9-12). pap. 8.99 (978-0-618-88404-9(1)) Houghton Mifflin Harcourt Publishing Co.

Friedman, Laurie. Mallory Goes Green! Kalis, Jennifer, illus. (Mallory Ser.). 160p. (J). 2011. pap. 33.92 (978-0-7613-7606-4(2), Darby Creek) 2011. (ENG.). (gr. 2-5). pap. 5.95 (978-0-7613-3949-6(3)) 2010. (ENG.). (gr. 2-5). 15.95 (978-0-8225-8885-6(4), Carolrhoda Bks.) Lerner Publishing Group.

—Mallory's Guide to Boys, Brothers, Dads, & Dogs. Kalis, Jennifer, illus. (Mallory Ser.). 160p. (J). (gr. 2-5). 2012. pap. 33.92 (978-0-7613-9206-4(8), Darby Creek) 2012. (ENG.). pap. 5.95 (978-0-7613-5250-1(3), Darby Creek) 2011. (ENG.). 15.95 (978-0-8225-8886-3(2), Carolrhoda Bks.) Lerner Publishing Group.

—Too Good to Be True. 2014. (Mostly Miserable Life of April Sinclair Ser.: 2). (ENG., Illus.). 168p. (J). (gr. 5-9). 17.95 (978-1-4677-0926-2(3), Darby Creek) Lerner Publishing Group.

—Too Much Drama. Shaloshvili, Natasha, illus. 2016. (Mostly Miserable Life of April Sinclair Ser.: 6). (ENG.). 184p. (J). (gr. 5-9). 17.95 (978-1-4677-8589-1(X), Darby Creek) Lerner Publishing Group.

—Truth & Kisses. 2015. (ENG.). 168p. (J). (gr. 5-9). pap. 5.95 (978-1-4677-0943-9(3), Darby Creek) Lerner Publishing Group.

Friedman, Laurie B. Truth & Kisses. 2014. (Mostly Miserable Life of April Sinclair Ser.: 3). (ENG.). 168p. (J). (gr. 5-9). 17.95 (978-1-4677-0927-9(1)) Lerner Publishing Group.

Friend, Natasha. Where You'll Find Me. 2016. (ENG.). 272p. (YA). 16.99 (978-0-374-30230-6(8), 9780374302306, Farrar, Straus & Giroux (BYR)) Farrar, Straus & Giroux.

—Where You'll Find Me. 2017. (YA). lib. bdg. 20.85 (978-0-606-39591-5(1)) Turtleback Bks.

Friesen, Jonathan. Rush. 2010. (ENG.). 320p. (YA). (gr. 7-18). 9.99 (978-0-14-241258-9(9), Speak) Penguin Young Readers Group.

Frost, Helen. Keesha's House. 2011. 9.46 (978-0-7848-3534-0(9), Everbind) Marco Bk. Co.

—Keesha's House. 2013. (ENG.). 144p. (YA). (gr. 7-12). pap. 9.99 (978-0-312-64127-6(3), 9780312641276) Square Fish.

—Room 214: a Year in Poems. 2014. (ENG., Illus.). 128p. (J). (gr. 5-9). pap. 8.99 *(978-1-250-04009-1(4)*, 9781250040091) Square Fish.

Fry, Michael. The Odd Squad King Karl. Fry, Michael, illus. 2014. (Odd Squad Book Ser.). (ENG., Illus.). 208p. (J). (gr. 3-7). 12.99 *(978-1-4231-9958-8(8))* Hyperion Bks. for Children.

Gallagher, Diana G. Advice about Family: Claudia Cristina Cortez Uncomplicates Your Life. Garvey, Brann, illus. 2010. (Claudia Cristina Cortez Ser.). (ENG.). 80p. (gr. 2-3). pap. 6.10 *(978-1-4342-2250-3(0)*, Claudia Cristina Cortez) Stone Arch Bks.

—Advice about Friends: Claudia Cristina Cortez Uncomplicates Your Life. Garvey, Brann, illus. 2010. (Claudia Cristina Cortez Ser.). (ENG.). 80p. (gr. 2-3). pap. 6.10 *(978-1-4342-2251-0(9)*, Claudia Cristina Cortez) Stone Arch Bks.

—Beach Blues: The Complicated Life of Claudia Cristina Cortez, 1 vol. Garvey, Brann, illus. 2008. (Claudia Cristina Cortez Ser.). (ENG.). 88p. (gr. 2-3). pap. 6.10 *(978-1-4342-0869-9(9)*, Claudia Cristina Cortez) Stone Arch Bks.

—Camp Can't: The Complicated Life of Claudia Cristina Cortez, 1 vol. Garvey, Brann, illus. 2007. (Claudia Cristina Cortez Ser.). (ENG.). 88p. (gr. 2-3). per. 6.10 *(978-1-59889-878-1(7)*, Claudia Cristina Cortez) Stone Arch Bks.

—Dance Trap: The Complicated Life of Claudia Cristina Cortez, 1 vol. Garvey, Brann, illus. 2007. (Claudia Cristina Cortez Ser.). (ENG.). 88p. (gr. 2-3). per. 6.10 *(978-1-59889-879-8(5)*, Claudia Cristina Cortez) Stone Arch Bks.

—Monica & the Sweetest Song, 1 vol. 2011. (Monica Ser.). (ENG.). 88p. (gr. 2-3). lib. bdg. 26.65 *(978-1-4342-2556-6(9))* Stone Arch Bks.

—Monica & the Unbeatable Bet, 1 vol. 2011. (Monica Ser.). (ENG.). 88p. (gr. 2-3). lib. bdg. 26.65 *(978-1-4342-2555-9(0))* Stone Arch Bks.

—Party! The Complicated Life of Claudia Cristina Cortez, 1 vol. Garvey, Brann, illus. 2008. (Claudia Cristina Cortez Ser.). (ENG.). 88p. (gr. 2-3). pap. 6.10 *(978-1-4342-0867-5(2))*; lib. bdg. 26.65 *(978-1-4342-0771-5(4))* Stone Arch Bks. (Claudia Cristina Cortez).

Gallagher, Toni. Twist My Charm - The Popularity Spell. 2015. (Twist My Charm Ser.). (ENG.). 272p. (J). (gr. 3-7). 16.99 *(978-0-553-51115-4(7)*, Random Hse. Bks. for Young Readers) Random Hse. Children's Bks.

—Twist My Charm: Love Potion #11. 2016. (Twist My Charm Ser.). (ENG.). 272p. (J). (gr. 3-7). 16.99 *(978-0-553-51119-2(X)*, Random Hse. Bks. for Young Readers) Random Hse. Children's Bks.

Galliez, Roxane Marie. Farewell Sadness. Lhomme, Sandrine, illus. 2010. 24p. (J). 9.99 *(978-0-8416-7139-3(7))* Hammond World Atlas Corp.

Ganger, Candace. The Inevitable Collision of Birdie & Bash. 2017. (ENG.). 320p. (YA). 17.99 *(978-1-250-11622-2(8)*, 9781250116222, St. Martin's Griffin) St. Martin's Pr.

Gant, Gene. The Thunder in His Head [Library Edition]. 2012. 200p. (-18). pap. 14.99 *(978-1-62380-903-4(7)*, Harmony Ink Pr.) Dreamspinner Pr.

Garcia, Kami & Stohl, Margaret. Beautiful Redemption. 2013. (Beautiful Creatures Ser.: 4). (YA). lib. bdg. 24.50 *(978-0-606-32282-9(5)*, Turtleback) Turtleback Bks.

Garvey, Amy. Cold Kiss. 2012. (Cold Kiss Ser.: 1). (ENG.). 336p. (YA). (gr. 8). pap. 8.99 *(978-0-06-199623-8(8)*, HarperTeen) HarperCollins Pubs.

Gauthier, Bertrand. La Revanche d'Ani Croche. 2003. (Roman Jeunesse Ser.). (FRE.). 96p. (YA). (gr. 4-7). pap. *(978-2-89021-078-3(2))* Diffusion du livre Mirabel (DLM).

Gaydos, Nora. Now I'm Growing! Hands Are Not for Hurting. Gutierrez, Akemi, illus. 2012. (ENG.). 30p. (J). (gr. -1-17). 8.99 *(978-1-60169-222-1(6))* Innovative Kids.

Geiger, J. C. Wildman. 2017. (ENG.). 1p. (YA). (gr. 9-17). 17.99 ***(978-1-4847-4957-9(X))*** Hyperion Bks. for Children.

Geithner, Carole. If Only. 2012. (ENG.). 336p. (J). (gr. 5-9). 16.99 *(978-0-545-23499-3(9)*, Scholastic Pr.) Scholastic, Inc.

Gemeinhart, Dan. Scar Island. 2017. (ENG.). 256p. (J). (gr. 3-7). 16.99 *(978-1-338-05384-5(1)*, Scholastic Pr.) Scholastic, Inc.

George, Elisabeth. The Edge of the Water. 2014. (Edge of Nowhere Ser.). (ENG.). 448p. (YA). (gr. 7). 18.99 *(978-0-670-01297-8(1)*, Viking Books for Young Readers) Penguin Young Readers Group.

George, Elizabeth. The Edge of the Water. 2015. (Edge of Nowhere Ser.). (ENG.). 464p. (YA). (gr. 7). pap. 9.99 *(978-0-14-242674-6(1)*, Speak) Penguin Young Readers Group.

Gibson, Marley. Radiate. 2012. (ENG.). 416p. (YA). (gr. 7). pap. 21.99 *(978-0-547-61728-2(3))* Houghton Mifflin Harcourt Publishing Co.

Giles, Gail. Right Behind You. 2008. (ENG.). 320p. (J). (gr. 10-17). pap. 10.99 *(978-0-316-16637-9(5))* Little, Brown Bks. for Young Readers.

Gillen, Lynea. Good People Everywhere. Swarner, Kristina, illus. 2012. (ENG.). 32p. (J). (gr. -1-2). 15.95 *(978-0-9799289-8-7(2))* Three Pebble Pr., LLC.

Glass, Lisa. Air. 2016. (Blue Ser.: 2). (ENG.). 320p. 16.99 *(978-1-68144-512-0(3))* Quercus NA.

—Blue. 2015. (Blue Ser.: 1). (ENG.). 352p. (J). (gr. 7-17). 16.99 *(978-1-62365-414-6(9)*, Quercus) Quercus NA.

Glines, Abbi. Just for Now. 2013. (Sea Breeze Ser.). (ENG., Illus.). 336p. (YA). (gr. 11). 17.99 *(978-1-4424-8861-8(1))*; pap. 9.99 *(978-1-4424-8860-1(3))* Simon Pulse. (Simon Pulse).

Godbersen, Anna. Rumors. 2008. (Luxe Ser.: No. 2). (YA). (gr. 9-12). (ENG.). 304p. 17.99 *(978-0-06-134569-2(5))*; 423p. lib. bdg. 18.89 *(978-0-06-134570-8(9))* HarperCollins Pubs. (HarperTeen).

Going, K. L. Fat Kid Rules the World. 2004. (ENG.). 224p. (YA). (gr. 7-18). reprint ed. pap. 9.99 *(978-0-14-240208-5(7)*, Speak) Penguin Young Readers Group.

Goldberg, Whoopi. Terrible Terrel. Roos, Maryn, illus. 2010. (ENG.). 160p. (J). (gr. 1-17). pap. 4.99 *(978-0-7868-5263-5(1)*, Jump at the Sun) Hyperion Bks. for Children.

Goldblatt, Mark. Twerp. 2013. (ENG.). 288p. (J). (gr. 4-7). 16.99 *(978-0-375-97142-6(4)*, Random Hse. Bks. for Young Readers) Random Hse. Children's Bks.

Golding, Julia. The Glass Swallow, 0 vols. 2011. (ENG.). 320p. (gr. 7-12). 17.99 *(978-0-7614-5979-8(0)*, 9780761459798, Amazon Children's Publishing) Amazon Publishing.

Goniwicha, William. Spike a Relli: A Week at the Lake. 2009. 28p. pap. 13.99 *(978-1-4389-2902-6(1))* AuthorHouse.

Gonzales Bertrand, Diane. There's a Name for This Feeling / Hay un Nombre para lo Que Siento. Baeza Ventura, Gabriela, tr. 2014. (ENG & SPA.). 72p. (J). pap. 10.95 *(978-1-55885-784-1(2)*, Piñata Books) Arte Publico Pr.

Gonzalez, Gabriela & Triana, Gaby. Backstage Pass. 2004. (Illus.). 224p. (J). (gr. 7-18). 15.99 *(978-0-06-056017-1(7))*; lib. bdg. 16.89 *(978-0-06-056018-8(5))* HarperCollins Pubs.

Gotsch, Connie. Belle's Trial. Cogan, John, illus. 2010. (ENG & ABK.). 150p. (J). pap. 8.99 *(978-1-932926-12-5(7)*, Kinkajou Pr.) Artemesia Publishing, LLC.

Gottesfeld, Jeff. Choices. 2014. (Campus Confessions Ser.: 3). (YA). lib. bdg. 20.80 *(978-0-606-34000-7(9)*, Turtleback) Turtleback Bks.

—Crush. 2014. (Campus Confessions Ser.: 4). (YA). lib. bdg. 20.80 *(978-0-606-34001-4(7)*, Turtleback) Turtleback Bks.

Gough, Erin. Get It Together, Delilah! 2017. (ENG., Illus.). 336p. (YA). 16.99 *(978-1-4521-5187-8(3))* Chronicle Bks. LLC.

Gow, Kailin. Loving Summer. 2012. 250p. (-18). pap. 9.99 *(978-1-59748-044-4(4)*, The Edge) Sparklesoup LLC.

Gownley, Jimmy. Amelia's Life During Wartime, 1 vol. 2013. (Amelia Rules! Set 2 Ser.). (ENG.). 36p. (J). (gr. 3-6). 24.21 *(978-1-61479-073-0(6))* Spotlight.

—The Meaning of Life ... & Other Stuff. Gownley, Jimmy, illus. 2011. (Amelia Rules! Ser.). (ENG., Illus.). 160p. (J). (gr. 2-7). 19.99 *(978-1-4169-8613-3(8))*; pap. 11.99 *(978-1-4169-8612-6(X))* Simon & Schuster Children's Publishing. (Atheneum Bks. for Young Readers).

Grace, Amanda. But I Love Him. 2011. (ENG.). 264p. (YA). (gr. 7-18). pap. 9.95 *(978-0-7387-2594-9(3)*, Flux) North Star Editions.

Graff, Lisa. The Great Treehouse War. 2017. (ENG.). 288p. (J). (gr. 3-7). 16.99 *(978-0-399-17500-8(8)*, Philomel Bks.) Penguin Young Readers Group.

Graham, Rosemary. Thou Shalt Not Dump the Skater Dude: And Other Commandments I Have Broken. 2008. (ENG.). 288p. (YA). (gr. 7-18). 8.99 *(978-0-14-240851-3(4)*, Speak) Penguin Young Readers Group.

Grahame, Abby. Wentworth Hall. (ENG.). 288p. (YA). (gr. 7). 2013. pap. 9.99 *(978-1-4424-5197-1(1))* 2012. 16.99 *(978-1-4424-5196-4(3))* Simon & Schuster Bks. For Young Readers. (Simon & Schuster Bks. For Young Readers).

Gray, Keith. The Chain. 2013. (ENG.). 80p. (YA). (gr. 6-12). pap. 6.95 *(978-1-78112-173-3(7))*; lib. bdg. 22.60 *(978-1-78112-172-6(9))* Lerner Publishing Group.

Green, John. An Abundance of Katherines. 2008. (J). 69.99 *(978-1-60514-809-0(1))* Findaway World, LLC.

—An Abundance of Katherines. 2009. 9.68 *(978-0-7848-1947-0(5)*, Everbind) Marco Bk. Co.

—An Abundance of Katherines. (ENG., Illus.). (YA). 2008. 272p. (gr. 7-18). 10.99 *(978-0-14-241070-7(5)*, Speak) 2006. 240p. (gr. 9-18). 18.99 *(978-0-525-47688-7(1)*, Dutton Books for Young Readers) Penguin Young Readers Group.

—An Abundance of Katherines. 2008. 20.00 *(978-1-60686-090-8(9))* Perfection Learning Corp.

—Looking for Alaska. 2014. (ENG.). 256p. (YA). (gr. 12-12). 14.24 *(978-1-63245-185-9(9))* Lectorum Pubns., Inc.

—Looking for Alaska. 2009. 11.04 *(978-0-7848-1838-1(X)*, Everbind) Marco Bk. Co.

—Looking for Alaska. 2014. *(978-0-525-42728-5(7)*, Dutton Adult) 2006. 20.00 *(978-0-7569-6726-0(0))* Penguin Publishing Group.

—Looking for Alaska. (ENG.). (YA). 2006. 256p. (gr. 9-18). pap. 10.99 *(978-0-14-240251-1(6)*, Speak) 2005. 160p. (gr. 8-12). 18.99 *(978-0-525-47506-4(0)*, Dutton Books for Young Readers) 10th anniv. ed. 2015. 368p. (gr. 9). 19.99 *(978-0-525-42802-2(X)*, Dutton Books for Young Readers) Penguin Young Readers Group.

—Looking for Alaska. l.t. ed. 2016. (ENG.). pap. 13.99 *(978-1-59413-982-6(2)*, Large Print Pr.) Thorndike Pr.

—Looking for Alaska. 2006. 221p. (gr. 7-12). lib. bdg. 20.85 *(978-1-4177-2915-9(5)*, Turtleback) Turtleback Bks.

—El Teorema Katherine. 2015.Tr. of An Abundance of Katherines. (SPA.). 320p. (YA). (gr. 7). pap. 12.95 *(978-1-101-91056-6(9)*, Vintage Espanol) Knopf Doubleday Publishing Group.

—Will Grayson, Will Grayson. 2011. lib. bdg. 22.10 *(978-0-606-15358-4(6)*, Turtleback) Turtleback Bks.

Green, John & Levithan, David. Will Grayson, Will Grayson. 2015. (SPA.). 336p. (YA). (gr. 7). pap. 12.95 *(978-1-101-91070-2(4)*, Vintage Espanol) Knopf Doubleday Publishing Group.

—Will Grayson, Will Grayson. (ENG., (YA). (gr. 9-18). 2011. Illus.). 352p. 10.99 *(978-0-14-241847-5(1)*, Speak) 2010. 320p. 17.99 *(978-0-525-42158-0(0)*, Dutton Books for Young Readers) Penguin Young Readers Group.

Green, John, et al. Let It Snow: Three Holiday Romances. (ENG.). 368p. (YA). (gr. 7). 2014. mass mkt. 7.99 *(978-0-14-751501-8(7))* 2008. pap. 10.99 *(978-0-14-241214-5(7))* Penguin Young Readers Group. (Speak).

Green, Julia. Hunter's Heart. 2007. 264p. (YA). (gr. 7-12). 16.95 *(978-0-7613-9493-8(1)*, Carolrhoda Bks.) Lerner Publishing Group.

Green, S. E. Killer Instinct. 2014. (ENG., Illus.). 272p. (YA). (gr. 9). 17.99 *(978-1-4814-0285-9(4)*, Simon Pulse) Simon Pulse.

Green, Tim. First Team. 2015. (ENG.). 352p. (J). (gr. 3-7). pap. 6.99 *(978-0-06-220876-7(4))* HarperCollins Pubs.

—First Team. 2014. (ENG.). 336p. (J). (gr. 3-7). 16.99 *(978-0-06-220875-0(6))* HarperCollins Pubs.

—New Kid. (ENG.). (J). (gr. 3-7). 2015. 336p. pap. 6.99 *(978-0-06-220873-6(X))* 2014. 320p. 16.99 *(978-0-06-220872-9(1))* HarperCollins Pubs.

Greenwald, Tommy. Charlie Joe Jackson's Guide to Extra Credit. Coovert, J. P., illus. 2012. (Charlie Joe Jackson Ser.: 2). (ENG.). 272p. (J). (gr. 4-7). 15.99 *(978-1-59643-692-3(1)*, 9781596436923) Roaring Brook Pr.

—Charlie Joe Jackson's Guide to Extra Credit. Coovert, J. P., illus. 2013. (Charlie Joe Jackson Ser.: 2). (ENG.). 288p. (J). (gr. 4-7). pap. 7.99 *(978-1-250-01670-6(3)*, 9781250016706) Square Fish.

—Charlie Joe Jackson's Guide to Extra Credit. 2013. (Charlie Joe Jackson's Guide Ser.: 2). (J). lib. bdg. 18.40 *(978-0-606-28461-5(3)*, Turtleback) Turtleback Bks.

—Charlie Joe Jackson's Guide to Not Reading. Coovert, J. P., illus. 2011. (Charlie Joe Jackson Ser.: 1). (ENG.). 224p. (J). (gr. 4-7). 15.99 *(978-1-59643-691-6(3)*, 9781596436916) Roaring Brook Pr.

—Charlie Joe Jackson's Guide to Not Reading. 2012. (Charlie Joe Jackson's Guide Ser.: 1). (J). lib. bdg. 17.20 *(978-0-606-26127-2(3)*, Turtleback) Turtleback Bks.

—Charlie Joe Jackson's Guide to Planet Girl. Coovert, J. P., illus. 2015. (Charlie Joe Jackson Ser.: 5). (ENG.). 208p. (J). (gr. 4-7). 13.99 *(978-1-59643-841-5(X)*, 9781596438415) Roaring Brook Pr.

—Charlie Joe Jackson's Guide to Summer Vacation. Coovert, J. P., illus. (Charlie Joe Jackson Ser.: 3). (ENG.). 240p. (J). (gr. 5-7). 2014. 13.99 *(978-1-62672-031-2(2)*, 9781626720312) 2013. 14.99 *(978-1-59643-757-9(X)*, 9781596437579) Roaring Brook Pr.

Gresh, Dannah & Anderson, Chizuruoke. Yuzi's False Alarm. 2008. (Secret Keeper Girl Fiction Ser.). (ENG.). 96p. pap. 7.99 *(978-0-8024-8704-9(1))* Moody Pubs.

Griffin, Adele. The Julian Game. 2011. (ENG.). 208p. (YA). (gr. 7-18). 7.99 *(978-0-14-241973-1(7)*, Speak) Penguin Young Readers Group.

Griffin, Paul. The Orange Houses. 2011. (ENG.). 176p. (YA). (gr. 9-18). 8.99 *(978-0-14-241982-3(6)*, Speak) Penguin Young Readers Group.

Grossmann-Hensel, Katharina. How Mommy Met Daddy. Ward, Rachel, tr. from GER. 2008. (ENG., Illus.). 32p. (J). (gr. -1-3). 16.95 *(978-0-7358-2176-7(3))* North-South Bks., Inc.

Grosso, Alissa. Ferocity Summer. 2012. (ENG., Illus.). 288p. (YA). pap. 9.95 *(978-0-7387-3070-7(X)*, Flux) North Star Editions.

Grosso, Mike. I Am Drums. 2016. (ENG.). 256p. (J). (gr. 5-7). 16.99 *(978-0-544-70710-8(9))* Houghton Mifflin Harcourt Publishing Co.

Guerra, Stephanie. Betting Blind, 0 vols. 2014. (ENG.). 256p. (gr. 9-12). pap. 9.99 *(978-1-4778-4785-5(5)*, 9781477847855, Skyscape) Amazon Publishing.

Guibert, Emmanuel. Where's Petula? 2015. (Ariol Ser.: 7). (J). lib. bdg. 20.85 *(978-0-606-37284-8(9))* Turtleback Bks.

Gunn, Robin Jones. Open Your Heart Vol. 3, Vol. 3. 2006. (Sierra Jensen Collection: Bks. 7-9). (ENG.). 480p. (J). (gr. 7-12). 15.99 *(978-1-59052-590-6(6)*, Multnomah) Doubleday Religious Publishing Group, The.

—Sierra Jensen Collection, Vol. 4. 2006. (Sierra Jensen Collection: Bks. 10-12). (ENG.). 464p. (J). (gr. 7-12). 15.99 *(978-1-59052-591-3(4)*, Multnomah) Doubleday Religious Publishing Group, The.

—Sierra Jensen Collection, Vol 1, Vol. 1. 2006. (Sierra Jensen Collection: Bks. 1-3). (ENG.). 432p. (J). (gr. 7-12). 15.99 *(978-1-59052-588-3(4)*, Multnomah) Doubleday Religious Publishing Group, The.

—Whispers. 2004. (Glenbrooke Ser.: Bk. 2). (ENG.). 288p. pap. 14.99 *(978-1-59052-192-2(7)*, Multnomah) Doubleday Religious Publishing Group, The.

Gurtler, Janet. If I Tell. 2011. (ENG.). 256p. (YA). (gr. 7-12). pap. 12.99 *(978-1-4022-6103-9(9))* Sourcebooks, Inc.

—Who I Kissed. 2012. (ENG.). 320p. (YA). (gr. 8-12). pap. 9.99 *(978-1-4022-7054-3(2)*, 1350501) Sourcebooks, Inc.

Gutman, Dan. Back to School, Weird Kids Rule! 2014. (My Weird School Ser.). (J). lib. bdg. 16.00 *(978-0-606-35502-5(2))* Turtleback Bks.

—The Homework Machine. 2014. (ENG.). 176p. (J). (gr. 3-7). 11.24 *(978-1-63245-274-0(X))* Lectorum Pubns., Inc.

—The Homework Machine. 2006. (ENG., Illus.). 160p. (J). (gr. 3-7). 17.99 *(978-0-689-87678-3(5)*, Simon & Schuster Bks. For Young Readers) Simon & Schuster Bks. For Young Readers.

Gwaltney, Doris. Homefront. 2009. (ENG.). 320p. (J). (gr. 5-9). pap. 6.99 *(978-1-4169-9572-2(2)*, Simon & Schuster Bks. For Young Readers) Simon & Schuster Bks. For Young Readers.

Haines, Kathryn Miller. The Girl Is Trouble. 2012. (ENG.). 336p. (YA). (gr. 7-12). 17.99 *(978-1-59643-610-7(7))* Roaring Brook Pr.

Hall, Annalisa. Momma, i hold You. 2009. 32p. pap. 7.99 *(978-0-557-05470-1(2))* Lulu Pr., Inc.

Hall, Barbara. Dixie Storms. 2006. (ENG., Illus.). 224p. (YA). (gr. 7-12). pap. 12.95 *(978-0-15-205756-5(0))* Houghton Mifflin Harcourt Publishing Co.

Han, Jenny. The Complete Summer I Turned Pretty Trilogy: The Summer I Turned Pretty; It's Not Summer Without You; We'll Always Have Summer. 2013. (Summer I Turned Pretty Ser.). (ENG., Illus.). 928p. (YA). (gr. 7). pap. 32.99 *(978-1-4424-9832-7(3)*, Simon & Schuster Bks. For Young Readers) Simon & Schuster Bks. For Young Readers.

—It's Not Summer Without You, 6 vols. 2010. (Summer I Turned Pretty Ser.: 2). (YA). 90.75 *(978-1-4498-2018-3(2))*; 88.75 *(978-1-4498-2020-6(4))*; 230.75 *(978-1-4498-2015-2(8))*; 1.25 *(978-1-4498-2022-0(0))*; 73.75 *(978-1-4498-2016-9(6))* Recorded Bks., Inc.

—It's Not Summer Without You. (Summer I Turned Pretty Ser.). (ENG.). (YA). (gr. 7). 2011. 320p. pap. 10.99 *(978-1-4169-9556-2(0))* 2010. 288p. 18.99 *(978-1-4169-9555-5(2))* Simon & Schuster Bks. For Young Readers. (Simon & Schuster Bks. For Young Readers).

—The Summer I Turned Pretty. (Summer I Turned Pretty Ser.). (ENG.). (YA). (gr. 7). 2010. 304p. pap. 10.99 *(978-1-4169-6829-0(6))* 2009. 288p. 19.99 *(978-1-4169-6823-8(7))* Simon & Schuster Bks. For Young Readers. (Simon & Schuster Bks. For Young Readers).

—The Summer I Turned Pretty. 2010. lib. bdg. 22.10 *(978-0-606-14529-9(X)*, Turtleback) Turtleback Bks.

—We'll Always Have Summer. 2011. (YA). 1.25 *(978-1-4640-1977-7(0))* Recorded Bks., Inc.

—We'll Always Have Summer. (Summer I Turned Pretty Ser.). (ENG.). (YA). (gr. 7). 2012. 320p. pap. 10.99 *(978-1-4169-9559-3(5))* 2011. 304p. 17.99 *(978-1-4169-9558-6(7))* Simon & Schuster Bks. For Young Readers. (Simon & Schuster Bks. For Young Readers).

Handler, Daniel. Why We Broke Up. Kalman, Maira, illus. 2013. (ENG.). 368p. (YA). (gr. 10-17). pap. 15.99 *(978-0-316-12726-4(4))* Little, Brown Bks. for Young Readers.

Hannan, Peter. My Big Mouth: 10 Songs I Wrote That Almost Got Me Killed. Hannan, Peter, illus. 2011. (ENG., Illus.). 240p. (J). (gr. 3-7). 16.99 *(978-0-545-16210-4(6)*, Scholastic Pr.) Scholastic, Inc.

Hapka, Catherine, pseud & Echols, Jennifer. Winter's Kiss: The Ex Games - The Twelve Dates of Christmas. 2012. (ENG.). 496p. (YA). (gr. 7). pap. 9.99 *(978-1-4424-5040-0(1)*, Simon Pulse) Simon Pulse.

Harazin, S. A. Painless. 2015. (ENG.). 304p. (YA). (gr. 8-12). 16.99 *(978-0-8075-6288-8(2))* Whitman, Albert & Co.

Harmon, Michael. Stick. 2015. (ENG.). 240p. (YA). (gr. 9). 17.99 *(978-0-385-75436-1(1))*; lib. bdg. 20.99 *(978-0-385-75437-8(X))* Random Hse. Children's Bks. (Knopf Bks. for Young Readers).

Harold, Gwyneth. Bad Girls in School. 2007. (ENG.). 148p. (YA). (gr. 8-12). per. 17.44 *(978-0-435-21517-0(5)*, 21517) Heinemann.

Harper, Charise Mericle. Just Grace & the Snack Attack. 2010. (Just Grace Ser.: 5). (ENG., Illus.). 176p. (J). (gr. 1-4). pap. 5.99 *(978-0-547-40629-9(0))* Houghton Mifflin Harcourt Publishing Co.

—Just Grace, Star on Stage. 2014. (Just Grace Ser.: 9). (ENG., Illus.). 208p. (J). (gr. 1-4). pap. 5.99 *(978-0-544-22533-6(3)*, HMH Books For Young Readers) Houghton Mifflin Harcourt Publishing Co.

Harper, Suzanne. The Juliet Club. (YA). 2010. (ENG.). 416p. (gr. 8). pap. 9.99 *(978-0-06-136693-2(5)*, Greenwillow Bks.) 2008. 402p. (gr. 7-18). lib. bdg. 18.89 *(978-0-06-136692-5(7)*, HarperTeen) HarperCollins Pubs.

Harrington, Kim. Clarity. (ENG.). 256p. (J). (gr. 9-9). 2012. pap. 8.99 *(978-0-545-23051-3(9))* 2011. 16.99 *(978-0-545-23050-6(0))* Scholastic, Inc.

—Perception. 2012. (ENG.). 288p. (J). (gr. 9). 16.99 *(978-0-545-23053-7(5))* Scholastic, Inc.

Harris, Linda. What Is a Me-Ma? 2011. 30p. 24.50 *(978-1-61204-038-7(1)*, Eloquent Bks.) Strategic Book Publishing & Rights Agency (SBPRA).

Harris, Robie H. Who We Are! All about Being the Same & Being Different. Westcott, Nadine Bernard, illus. 2016. (Let's Talk about You & Me Ser.). (ENG.). 40p. (J). (-k). 15.99 *(978-0-7636-6903-4(2))* Candlewick Pr.

Harrison, Lisi. Alphas. 2009. (Alphas Ser.: 1). (ENG.). 272p. (YA). (gr. 7-17). pap. 9.99 *(978-0-316-03579-8(3)*, Poppy) Little, Brown Bks. for Young Readers.

—Best Friends for Never. 2004. (Clique Ser.: 2). (ENG.). 208p. (YA). (gr. 7-17). pap. 9.99 *(978-0-316-70131-0(9)*, Poppy) Little, Brown Bks. for Young Readers.

—Bratfest at Tiffany's, No. 9. 2008. (Clique Ser.: 9). (ENG., Illus.). 256p. (YA). (gr. 7-17). per. 9.99 *(978-0-316-00680-4(7)*, Poppy) Little, Brown Bks. for Young Readers.

—Dial L for Loser. 2008. (Clique Novels Ser.). 268p. 20.00 *(978-1-60686-291-9(X))* Perfection Learning Corp.

—It's Not Easy Being Mean. 2008. (Clique Ser.). 193p. 20.00 *(978-1-60686-330-5(4))* Perfection Learning Corp.

—Movers & Fakers. 2010. (Alphas Ser.: 2). (ENG.). 240p. (YA). (gr. 7-17). pap. 9.99 *(978-0-316-03580-4(7)*, Poppy) Little, Brown Bks. for Young Readers.

—Revenge of the Wannabes. 2005. (Clique Ser.: 3). (ENG.). 304p. (YA). (gr. 7-17). pap. 9.99 *(978-0-316-70133-4(5)*, Poppy) Little, Brown Bks. for Young Readers.

—Top of the Feud Chain. 2011. (Alphas Ser.: 4). (ENG.). 240p. (YA). (gr. 7-17). pap. 9.99 *(978-0-316-03582-8(3)*, Poppy) Little, Brown Bks. for Young Readers.

Hart, Amber. After Us. 2014. (Before & after Ser.). (ENG.). 368p. (YA). (gr. 13). pap. 9.95 *(978-1-61773-118-1(8)*, K-Teen) Kensington Publishing Corp.

Hartnett, Sonya. Butterfly. (ENG.). 240p. (YA). (gr. 9). 2013. pap. 7.99 *(978-0-7636-6334-6(4))* 2010. (Illus.). 16.99 *(978-0-7636-4760-5(8))* Candlewick Pr.

Hassan, Michael. Crash & Burn. (ENG.). 544p. (YA). (gr. 9). 2014. pap. 9.99 *(978-0-06-211291-0(0))* 2013. 18.99 *(978-0-06-211290-3(2))* HarperCollins Pubs.

Haston, Meg. How to Rock Best Friends & Frenemies. 2013. (How to Rock Ser.: 2). (ENG.). 352p. (J). (gr. 3-7). pap. 8.00 *(978-0-316-06827-7(6)*, Poppy) Little, Brown Bks. for Young Readers.

—How to Rock Braces & Glasses. 2011. (How to Rock Ser.: 1). (ENG.). 336p. (J). (gr. 3-7). 16.99 *(978-0-316-06825-3(X)*, Poppy) Little, Brown Bks. for Young Readers.

—How to Rock Braces & Glasses. 2012. (How to Rock Ser.: 1). (ENG.). 352p. (J). (gr. 3-7). pap. 8.00 *(978-0-316-06824-6(1)*, Poppy) Little, Brown Bks. for Young Readers.

Haus, Jean. With the Band, 0 vols. 2014. (Luminescent Juliet Ser.: 3). (ENG.). 286p. (YA). (gr. 7-12). pap. 7.99 *(978-1-4778-4709-1(X)*, 9781477847091, Amazon Children's Publishing) Amazon Publishing.

Hautman, Pete. Sweetblood. 2010. (ENG.). 208p. (YA). (gr. 7). pap. 8.99 *(978-1-4424-0755-8(7)*, Simon & Schuster Bks. For Young Readers) Simon & Schuster Bks. For Young Readers.

—What Boys Really Want. 2012. (ENG.). 304p. (J). (gr. 7). 17.99 *(978-0-545-11315-1(6)*, Scholastic Pr.) Scholastic, Inc.

Haworth-Attard, Barbara. My Life from Air-Bras to Zits. 2009. (ENG.). 288p. (YA). (gr. 7-10). pap. 9.95 *(978-0-7387-1483-7(6)*, Flux) North Star Editions.

Hawthorne, Nathaniel. Scarlet Letter. 2014. (Differentiated Timeless Classics Ser.). (ENG.). 80p. (YA). (gr. 9-12). 12.95 *(978-1-62250-716-0(9))* Saddleback Educational Publishing, Inc.

Hawthorne, Rachel. The Boyfriend Project. 2015. (ENG.). 352p. (YA). (gr. 9). pap. 9.99 *(978-0-06-233073-4(X)*, HarperTeen) HarperCollins Pubs.

—Labor of Love. 2008. (ENG.). 320p. (YA). (gr. 9-18). pap. 5.99 *(978-0-06-136384-9(7)*, HarperTeen) HarperCollins Pubs.

Haydu, Corey Ann. OCD Love Story. (ENG., Illus.). 352p. (YA). (gr. 9). 2014. pap. 11.99 *(978-1-4424-5733-1(3))* 2013. 17.99 *(978-1-4424-5732-4(5))* Simon Pulse. (Simon Pulse).

Hayes, Nicole. The Whole of My World. l.t. ed. 2013. 618p. pap. *(978-1-4596-6746-4(8))* ReadHowYouWant.com, Ltd.

H
I

Hayes, Sonia. Urban Goddess. 2007. 224p. (YA). per. 9.95 *(978-0-9777573-1-2(5))* NUA Multimedia.

Hayward, Linda. Monster Bug. Palmisciano, Diane, illus. 2004. (Science Solves It Ser.). 32p. (gr. -1-3). 15.00 *(978-0-7569-4313-4(2))* Perfection Learning Corp.

Heasley, Gwendolyn. A Long Way from You. 2012. (Where I Belong Ser.: 2). (ENG.). 336p. (YA). (gr. 8). pap. 8.99 *(978-0-06-197885-2(X)*, HarperTeen) HarperCollins Pubs.

Heffernan, John. Hotaka: Through My Eyes - Natural Disaster Zones. White, Lyn, ed. 2017. (Through My Eyes Ser.). (ENG.). 224p. (J). (gr. 6-9). pap. 12.99 ***(978-1-76011-376-6(X))*** Allen & Unwin AUS. Dist: Independent Pubs. Group.

Heidicker, Christian McKay. Cure for the Common Universe. 2016. (ENG., Illus.). 320p. (YA). (gr. 9). 19.99 *(978-1-4814-5027-0(1)*, Simon & Schuster Bks. For Young Readers) Simon & Schuster Bks. For Young Readers.

Heldring, Thatcher. Toby Wheeler: Eighth Grade Benchwarmer. 2008. (ENG.). 224p. (J). (gr. 3-7). 6.99 *(978-0-440-42183-2(7)*, Yearling) Random Hse. Children's Bks.

Henderson, Lauren. Kiss of Death. 2012. (ENG.). 318p. (YA). (gr. 9). pap. 9.99 *(978-0-385-73780-7(7)*, Ember) Random Hse. Children's Bks.

Hendry, Diana. Oodles of Noodles. Massini, Sarah, illus. 2008. (Tiger Tales Ser.). 32p. (J). (gr. -1-2). 15.95 *(978-1-58925-075-8(3))* Tiger Tales.

Henkes, Kevin. Bird Lake Moon. 2010. (ENG.). 192p. (J). (gr. 3-7). pap. 5.99 *(978-0-06-147079-0(1)*, Greenwillow Bks.) HarperCollins Pubs.

Hennessy, Claire. Afterwards. 2005. 188p. (YA). pap. *(978-1-84223-207-1(X))* Poolbeg Pr.

Henty, George Alfred. With Wolfe in Canad: The Winning of a Continent. 2011. 378p. pap. 19.95 *(978-1-61179-149-5(9))* Fireship Pr.

—With Wolfe in Canada: The Winning of a Continent. 2006. per. 8.95 *(978-1-57646-980-4(8))* Quiet Vision Publishing.

Hickman, Rachel. One Silver Summer. 2016. (ENG.). 272p. (J). (gr. 9). 17.99 *(978-0-545-80892-7(8)*, Scholastic Pr.) Scholastic, Inc.

Hicks, Faith Erin. Friends with Boys. Hicks, Faith Erin, illus. 2012. (ENG., Illus.). 224p. (YA). (gr. 7-11). pap. 16.99 *(978-1-59643-556-8(9)*, 9781596435568, First Second Bks.) Roaring Brook Pr.

Hidaka, Banri. V. B. Rose Volume 10. 2010. (Illus.). 208p. pap. 10.99 *(978-1-4278-1160-8(1))* TOKYOPOP, Inc.

—V. B. Rose Volume 9. 2010. (Illus.). 192p. pap. 10.99 *(978-1-4278-0927-8(5))* TOKYOPOP, Inc.

Hill, C. J. Slayers. 2013. (Slayers Ser.: 1). (ENG.). 400p. (YA). (gr. 7). pap. 9.99 *(978-0-312-67514-1(3))* Square Fish.

—Slayers: Friends & Traitors. 2014. (Slayers Ser.: 2). (ENG.). 416p. (YA). (gr. 7). pap. 10.99 *(978-1-250-05079-3(0)*, 9781250050793) Square Fish.

Hill, Kirkpatrick. Do Not Pass Go. 2011. (ENG.). 240p. (J). (gr. 4-9). pap. 6.99 *(978-1-4424-2122-6(3)*, McElderry, Margaret K. Bks.) McElderry, Margaret K. Bks.

Hills, Tad. Duck & Goose. Hills, Tad, illus. 2006. (Duck & Goose Ser.). (ENG., Illus.). 40p. (J). (gr. -1-2). 17.99 *(978-0-375-83611-4(X)*, Schwartz & Wade Bks.) Random Hse. Children's Bks.

—Duck & Goose, 1, 2, 3. Hills, Tad, illus. 2008. (Duck & Goose Ser.). (ENG., Illus.). 22p. (J). (gr. k — 1). bds. 7.99 *(978-0-375-85621-1(8)*, Schwartz & Wade Bks.) Random Hse. Children's Bks.

Hinwood, Christine. The Returning. 2013. (ENG.). 320p. (YA). (gr. 9). pap. 8.99 *(978-0-14-242477-3(3)*, Speak) Penguin Young Readers Group.

Hirahara, Naomi. 1001 Cranes. 2009. (ENG.). 240p. (J). (gr. 3-7). 7.99 *(978-0-440-42234-1(5)*, Yearling) Random Hse. Children's Bks.

Hobbs, Will. Leaving Protection. 2005. (ENG.). 192p. (J). (gr. 5-18). pap. 8.99 *(978-0-380-73312-5(9))* HarperCollins Pubs.

—Leaving Protection. 2005. 178p. (gr. 5-9). 19.00 *(978-0-7569-5121-4(6))* Perfection Learning Corp.

Hoblin, Paul. False Start. 2017. (Gridiron Ser.). (ENG.). 128p. (YA). (gr. 6-12). 26.65 ***(978-1-5124-3979-3(7))***; pap. 7.99 ***(978-1-5124-5351-5(X))*** Lerner Publishing Group. (Darby Creek).

Hoeffner, Karol Ann. Surf Ed. 2010. (ENG.). 288p. (YA). (gr. 9). pap. 13.99 *(978-1-4424-1418-1(9)*, Simon Pulse) Simon Pulse.

Hoffman, Alice. Nightbird. (ENG., Illus.). 208p. (J). (gr. 5). 2016. pap. 7.99 *(978-0-385-38961-7(2)*, Yearling) 2015. 16.99 *(978-0-385-38958-7(2)*, Lamb, Wendy Bks.) Random Hse. Children's Bks.

—Nightbird. 2016. lib. bdg. 18.40 *(978-0-606-38451-3(0))* Turtleback Bks.

Hogan, Mary. The Serious Kiss. 2005. (ENG.). 256p. (YA). (gr. 8). pap. 7.99 *(978-0-06-072208-1(8)*, HarperTeen); (gr. 7-18). 16.99 *(978-0-06-072206-7(1))* HarperCollins Pubs.

Hohl, Richard. The Prairie: A Novelette. 2006. (Illus.). 67p. pap. 12.50 *(978-1-4120-9073-5(3))* Trafford Publishing.

Holder, Nancy. Pretty Little Devils. 2009. (ENG.). 272p. (YA). (gr. 7-18). 8.99 *(978-1-59514-269-6(X)*, Razorbill) Penguin Young Readers Group.

Holmes, Kathryn. The Distance Between Lost & Found. 2015. (ENG.). 304p. (YA). (gr. 8). 17.99 *(978-0-06-231726-1(1))* HarperCollins Pubs.

Hopkins, Cathy. The Princess of Pop. 2012. (Truth or Dare Ser.). (ENG.). 224p. (YA). (gr. 7). pap. 10.99 *(978-1-4424-6057-7(1)*, Simon Pulse) Simon Pulse.

Hopkins, Ellen. Impulse. (ENG.). (YA). (gr. 9-12). 2008. 688p. pap. 12.99 *(978-1-4169-0357-4(7))* 2007. 672p. 22.99 *(978-1-4169-0356-7(9))* McElderry, Margaret K. Bks. (McElderry, Margaret K. Bks.).

—Perfect. (ENG., (YA). (gr. 9). 2013. Illus.). 656p. pap. 12.99 *(978-1-4169-8325-5(2))* 2011. 640p. 18.99 *(978-1-4169-8324-8(4))* McElderry, Margaret K. Bks. (McElderry, Margaret K. Bks.).

Hopkinson, Nalo. The Chaos. (ENG., 256p. (YA). (gr. 9). 2013. Illus.). pap. 9.99 *(978-1-4424-5926-7(3))* 2012. 16.99 *(978-1-4169-5488-0(0))* McElderry, Margaret K. Bks. (McElderry, Margaret K. Bks.).

Horvath, Polly. Everything on a Waffle. 2008. (Illus.). 154p. (gr. 5-9). 18.00 *(978-0-7569-8776-3(8))* Perfection Learning Corp.

—Everything on a Waffle. 2008. (ENG., Illus.). 176p. (J). (gr. 5-9). pap. 7.99 *(978-0-312-38004-5(6)*, 9780312380045) Square Fish.

—One Year in Coal Harbor. 2014. (ENG.). 224p. (J). (gr. 4-7). 7.99 *(978-0-385-38653-1(2)*, Yearling) Random Hse. Children's Bks.

Howe, James. Addie on the Inside. (Misfits Ser.). (ENG., Illus.). (J). (gr. 5-9). 2012. 240p. pap. 8.99 *(978-1-4169-1385-6(8))* 2011. 224p. 16.99 *(978-1-4169-1384-9(X))* Simon & Schuster Children's Publishing. (Atheneum Bks. for Young Readers).

Howland, Leila. The Forget-Me-Not Summer. Kim, Ji-Hyuk, illus. 2015. (Silver Sisters Ser.: 1). (ENG.). 352p. (J). (gr. 3-7). 16.99 *(978-0-06-231869-5(1))* HarperCollins Pubs.

—Hello, Sunshine. 2017. (ENG.). 368p. (YA). (gr. 9-17). 17.99 ***(978-1-4847-2545-0(X))*** Hyperion Bks. for Children.

Howland, Leila. Nantucket Blue. 2014. (Nantucket Blue Ser.). (ENG.). 320p. (YA). (gr. 9-17). pap. 8.99 *(978-1-4231-6139-4(4))* Hyperion Bks. for Children.

Huang, Charlotte. Going Geek. 2016. (ENG.). 304p. (YA). (gr. 7). 17.99 *(978-0-553-53943-1(4)*, Delacorte Pr.) Random Hse. Children's Bks.

Hubbard, Jennifer. Try Not to Breathe. 2013. (ENG.). 256p. (YA). (gr. 9). pap. 8.99 *(978-0-14-242387-5(4)*, Speak) Penguin Young Readers Group.

Hubbard, Jenny. And We Stay. 2014. (ENG.). 240p. (YA). (gr. 9). lib. bdg. 19.99 *(978-0-375-98955-1(2)*, Delacorte Pr.) Random Hse. Children's Bks.

Hueller, Andy. Dizzy Fantastic & Her Flying Bicycle. 2010. (Illus.). 155p. (J). pap. 8.99 *(978-1-59955-395-5(3))* Cedar Fort, Inc./CFI Distribution.

Hughes, Mark Peter. Lemonade Mouth. movie tie-in ed. 2011. (ENG.). 352p. (YA). (gr. 7-7). pap. 8.99 *(978-0-385-74208-5(8)*, Ember) Random Hse. Children's Bks.

Humphrey, Anna. Ruby Goldberg's Bright Idea. Newton, Vanessa Brantley, illus. 2013. (ENG.). 144p. (J). (gr. 3-7). 15.99 *(978-1-4424-8027-8(0)*, Simon & Schuster Bks. For Young Readers) Simon & Schuster Bks. For Young Readers.

Hunt, Tiffani "Paradise". Glamorous 5: In the City of Garden Valley. 2012. 24p. pap. 17.99 *(978-1-4772-7922-9(9))* AuthorHouse.

Hunter, C. C. Awake at Dawn. 2013. (Shadow Falls Novel Ser.: 2). (ENG.). 400p. (YA). (gr. 7-12). mass mkt. 9.99 *(978-1-250-04679-6(3)*, 9781250046796, St. Martin's Paperbacks) St. Martin's Pr.

—Born at Midnight. 2013. (Shadow Falls Novel Ser.: 1). (ENG.). 416p. (YA). (gr. 7-12). mass mkt. 9.99 *(978-1-250-04680-2(7)*, 9781250046802, St. Martin's Paperbacks) St. Martin's Pr.

Huntley, Amy. The Everafter. 2010. (ENG.). 272p. (YA). (gr. 8). pap. 9.99 *(978-0-06-177681-6(5))* HarperCollins Pubs.

Huser, Glen. Skinnybones & the Wrinkle Queen. 2013. 232p. pap. *(978-1-4596-6507-1(4))* ReadHowYouWant.com, Ltd.

Hutchinson, Shaun David. FML. 2013. (ENG.). 304p. (YA). (gr. 9). pap. 9.99 *(978-1-4424-3287-1(X))*; (Illus.). 17.99 *(978-1-4424-8318-7(0))* Simon Pulse. (Simon Pulse).

—We Are the Ants. 2016. (ENG., Illus.). 464p. (YA). (gr. 9). 17.99 *(978-1-4814-4963-2(X)*, Simon Pulse) Simon Pulse.

I Am Just Like U. 2003. per. *(978-0-9740182-2-5(8))* HuntForMo Creations.

I Like You & I Love You. 2003. (J). per. 5.95 *(978-0-9742714-1-5(1))* I C Creative, Inc.

Ibbotson, Eva. Journey to the River Sea. 5th unabr. ed. 2008. (ENG.). 304p. (J). (gr. 10-14). 14.95 *(978-0-330-39715-5(X)*, Macmillan) Pan Macmillan GBR. Dist: Trans-Atlantic Pubns., Inc.

—Journey to the River Sea. Hawkes, Kevin, illus. 2003. 298p. (gr. 3-7). 18.00 *(978-0-7569-1552-0(X))* Perfection Learning Corp.

Ingalls, Melodi J. Everyone Is Differphant. 2008. 20p. pap. 11.99 *(978-1-4389-1206-6(4))* AuthorHouse.

Jacobson, Jennifer Richard. The Complete History of Why I Hate Her. 2010. (ENG.). 192p. (YA). (gr. 7-18). 16.99 *(978-0-689-87800-8(1)*, Atheneum/Richard Jackson Bks.) Simon & Schuster Children's Publishing.

—Stained. (ENG.). 208p. (YA). (gr. 8). 2012. pap. 10.99 *(978-1-4424-8565-5(5)*, Atheneum Bks. for Young Readers) 2005. (Illus.). 16.95 *(978-0-689-86745-3(X)*, Atheneum/Richard Jackson Bks.) Simon & Schuster Children's Publishing.

Jahn-Clough, Lisa. Country Girl, City Girl. 2009. (ENG.). 192p. (YA). (gr. 7). pap. 12.95 *(978-0-547-22322-3(6))* Houghton Mifflin Harcourt Publishing Co.

—Me, Penelope. 2009. (ENG.). 208p. (YA). (gr. 9). pap. 12.99 *(978-0-547-07632-4(0))* Houghton Mifflin Harcourt Publishing Co.

Jeffrey, Leonard J. Journeys of the Mind-Book. 2011. 116p. (J). pap. *(978-1-4269-9333-6(1))* Trafford Publishing (UK) Ltd.

Jenkins, A. M. Out of Order. 2003. 256p. (J). lib. bdg. 16.89 *(978-0-06-623969-9(9))* HarperCollins Pubs.

Jenkins, Emily. Tiger & Badger. Gay, Marie-Louise, illus. 2016. (ENG.). 32p. (J). (-k). 15.99 *(978-0-7636-6604-0(1))* Candlewick Pr.

Jennings, Patrick. Barb & Dingbat's Crybaby Hotline. 2007. (ENG.). 208p. (YA). (gr. 8-12). 16.95 *(978-0-8234-2055-1(8))* Holiday Hse., Inc.

Jocelyn, Marthe. What We Hide. (ENG.). 288p. (YA). (gr. 9). 2015. pap. 9.99 *(978-0-375-85544-3(0)*, Ember) 2014. 16.99 *(978-0-385-73847-7(1)*, Lamb, Wendy Bks.) Random Hse. Children's Bks.

Johnson, Angela. Bird. 2006. 133p. (gr. 3-7). 16.00 *(978-0-7569-6660-7(4))* Perfection Learning Corp.

—Sweet, Hereafter. 2011. (ENG.). 128p. (YA). (gr. 7). pap. 8.99 *(978-0-689-87386-7(7)*, Simon & Schuster Bks. For Young Readers) Simon & Schuster Bks. For Young Readers.

—Sweet, Hereafter. Bk. 3. 2010. 128p. (YA). (gr. 9-18). pap. 16.99 *(978-1-4169-9995-9(7))* Simon & Schuster Children's Publishing.

Johnson, Antonia. Bianca's Light. 2009. 28p. pap. 14.99 *(978-1-4389-8951-8(2))* AuthorHouse.

Johnson-Choong, Shelly. The Jewelry Box. 2nd ed. 2004. (YA). reprint ed. pap. 10.95 *(978-1-932280-40-1(5)*, 80405) Granite Publishing & Distribution.

Johnson, J. J. This Girl Is Different, 1 vol. 2011. (ENG.). 288p. (YA). (gr. 7-11). 16.95 *(978-1-56145-578-2(4))* Peachtree Pubs.

Johnson, Maureen. Girl at Sea. 2008. (ENG., Illus.). 336p. (YA). (gr. 8-12). pap. 8.99 *(978-0-06-054146-0(6)*, HarperTeen) HarperCollins Pubs.

Johnson, Peter. The Amazing Adventures of John Smith, Jr. Aka Houdini. 2012. (ENG.). 176p. (J). (gr. 3-7). 16.99 *(978-0-06-198890-5(1))* HarperCollins Pubs.

—The Amazing Adventures of John Smith, Jr. AKA Houdini. 2014. (ENG.). 192p. (J). (gr. 3-7). pap. 6.99 *(978-0-06-198891-2(X))* HarperCollins Pubs.

—What Happened. 2007. (ENG.). 136p. (J). (gr. 8-18). 16.95 *(978-1-932425-67-3(5)*, Front Street) Boyds Mills Pr.

Johnston, Julie. Adam & Eve & Pinch-Me. 2003. (ENG.). 232p. (J). (gr. 5). pap. 9.95 *(978-0-88776-648-0(X)*, Tundra Bks.) Tundra Bks. CAN. Dist: Penguin Random Hse. LLC.

—A Very Fine Line. 2008. (ENG.). 208p. (YA). (gr. 5). pap. 10.95 *(978-0-88776-829-3(6)*, Tundra Bks.) Tundra Bks. CAN. Dist: Penguin Random Hse. LLC.

Jonas. JONAS #5: about Face. 5th ed. 2010. 128p. pap. 4.99 *(978-1-4231-1773-5(5))* Disney Pr.

Jones, Jen. The Competition for Gaby, No. 4. 2011. (Team Cheer Ser.). (ENG.). 112p. (gr. 4-4). lib. bdg. 25.32 *(978-1-4342-2997-7(1)*, Team Cheer) Stone Arch Bks.

—The Competition for Gaby: # 4, 1 vol. 2012. (Team Cheer Ser.). (ENG.). 112p. (gr. 4-4). pap. 7.19 *(978-1-4342-4252-5(8)*, Team Cheer) Stone Arch Bks.

—Faith & the Camp Snob, No. 1. 2011. (Team Cheer Ser.). (ENG.). 112p. (gr. 4-4). lib. bdg. 25.32 *(978-1-4342-2994-6(7)*, Team Cheer) Stone Arch Bks.

—Faith & the Camp Snob: # 1, 1 vol. 2012. (Team Cheer Ser.). (ENG.). 112p. (gr. 4-4). pap. 7.19 *(978-1-4342-4249-5(8)*, Team Cheer) Stone Arch Bks.

Jones, Patrick. Barrier. 2014. (Alternative Ser.). (ENG.). 104p. (YA). (gr. 6-12). pap. 7.95 *(978-1-4677-4481-2(6)*, Darby Creek); lib. bdg. 27.93 *(978-1-4677-3899-6(9))* Lerner Publishing Group.

—Guarding Secrets. 2015. (J). 9.99 *(978-1-4677-7694-3(7))*; (ENG.). 96p. (gr. 6-12). lib. bdg. 27.99 *(978-1-4677-5801-7(9))* Lerner Publishing Group.

Juby, Susan. Miss Smithers. 2004. (Illus.). 336p. (J). 15.99 *(978-0-06-051546-1(5)*, HarperTeen) HarperCollins Pubs.

Jules, Jacqueline. Never Say a Mean Word Again: A Tale from Medieval Spain. Bernhard, Durga Yael, illus. 2014. (ENG.). 32p. (J). (gr. -1-3). 16.95 *(978-1-937786-20-5(X)*, Wisdom Tales) World Wisdom, Inc.

Jungle Crossing. 2011. (ENG.). 228p. (J). (gr. 5-7). pap. 13.99 *(978-0-547-55009-1(X))* Houghton Mifflin Harcourt Publishing Co.

Kade, Stacey. The Ghost & the Goth. 2011. (ENG.). 304p. (J). (gr. 7-17). pap. 8.99 *(978-1-4231-2487-0(1))* Hyperion Pr.

Kadence, Sam. Unicorns & Rainbow Poop. (J). 2016. (ENG., Illus.). 27.99 ***(978-1-63477-988-3(6)***, Harmony Ink Pr.) 2014. 246p. pap. *(978-1-63216-417-9(5))* Dreamspinner Pr.

Kantor, Melissa. Better Than Perfect. 2015. (ENG.). 336p. (YA). (gr. 8). 17.99 *(978-0-06-227923-1(8)*, HarperTeen) HarperCollins Pubs.

Karasyov, Carrie & Kargman, Jill. Summer Intern. 2007. 184p. (YA). (gr. 7-18). lib. bdg. 17.89 *(978-0-06-115376-1(1)*, HarperTeen) HarperCollins Pubs.

Kass, Pnina Moed. Real Time. 2006. (ENG.). 192p. (YA). (gr. 7-12). reprint ed. pap. 7.99 *(978-0-618-69174-6(X))* Houghton Mifflin Harcourt Publishing Co.

Kath, Natalie. The Summer I Lost It, 1 vol. (Stone Arch Novels Ser.). (ENG.). 128p. (gr. 4-8). 2012. pap. 6.95 *(978-1-4342-4067-5(3))* 2011. lib. bdg. 26.65 *(978-1-4342-3316-5(2))* Stone Arch Bks. (Stone Arch Novels).

Kaufman, Sashi. Wired Man & Other Freaks of Nature. 2016. (ENG.). 264p. (YA). (gr. 9-12). 17.99 *(978-1-4677-8563-1(6)*, Carolrhoda Bks.); 35.99 *(978-1-4677-9564-7(X)*, Carolrhoda Lab™) Lerner Publishing Group.

Keene, Carolyn. Secret Sabotage, Bk. 1. 2010. (Nancy Drew (All New) Girl Detective Ser.: 42). (ENG.). 144p. (J). (gr. 3-7). pap. 5.99 *(978-1-4169-9069-7(0)*, Aladdin) Simon & Schuster Children's Publishing.

Keil, Melissa. Life in Outer Space, 1 vol. (ENG.). 320p. (YA). (gr. 7-11). 2016. pap. 9.95 ***(978-1-56145-975-9(5))*** 2013. 16.95 *(978-1-56145-742-7(6))* Peachtree Pubs.

Kellerman, Faye & Kellerman, Aliza. Prism. (YA). 2010. (ENG.). 288p. (gr. 8). pap. 8.99 *(978-0-06-168724-2(3))* 2009. 272p. (gr. 7-18). lib. bdg. 17.89 *(978-0-06-168722-8(7)*, HarperTeen) HarperCollins Pubs.

Kelly, Allison Palmer. The Power of Words. 2013. 202p. 24.95 *(978-1-4759-6745-6(4))*; pap. 14.95 *(978-1-4759-6743-2(8))* iUniverse, Inc.

Kelly, Katy. Working Myself to Pieces & Bits. Ferguson, Peter, illus. 2008. (Lucy Rose Ser.). (ENG.). 208p. (J). (gr. 3-7). 6.99 *(978-0-440-42186-3(1)*, Yearling) Random Hse. Children's Bks.

Kelly, Nikki. Gabriel. 2015. (Styclar Saga Ser.: 2). (ENG.). 384p. (YA). (gr. 7). 17.99 *(978-1-250-05153-0(3)*, 9781250051530) Feiwel & Friends.

Kendall, Grace, ed. I See Reality: Twelve Short Stories about Real Life. 2016. (ENG.). 304p. (YA). 17.99 *(978-0-374-30258-0(8)*, 9780374302580, Farrar, Straus & Giroux (BYR)) Farrar, Straus & Giroux.

Kenneally, Miranda. Catching Jordan. 2011. (Hundred Oaks Ser.: Bk. 1). (ENG.). 288p. (YA). (gr. 7-12). pap. 9.99 *(978-1-4022-6227-2(2))* Sourcebooks, Inc.

—Coming up for Air. 2017. (Hundred Oaks Ser.: Bk. 8). (ENG.). 304p. (YA). (gr. 8-12). pap. 10.99 *(978-1-4926-3011-1(X))* Sourcebooks, Inc.

Kennedy, Katie. Learning to Swear in America. 2017. (ENG.). 368p. (YA). pap. 9.99 *(978-1-61963-911-9(4)*, 9781619639119, Bloomsbury USA Childrens) Bloomsbury Publishing USA.

Kenney, Rebecca. The Silent. 2009. (YA). 8.99 *(978-1-60682-054-4(0)*, JourneyForth) BJU Pr.

Kephart, Beth. Small Damages. 2013. (ENG., Illus.). 304p. (YA). (gr. 9). pap. 8.99 *(978-0-14-242641-8(5)*, Speak) Penguin Young Readers Group.

Keplinger, Kody. Lying Out Loud: A Companion to the DUFF. 2015. (ENG.). 288p. (J). (gr. 9). 17.99 *(978-0-545-83109-3(1))* Scholastic, Inc.

—Lying Out Loud: a Companion to the DUFF. 2016. (ENG.). 304p. (J). (gr. 9). pap. 9.99 *(978-0-545-83110-9(5)*, Scholastic Paperbacks) Scholastic, Inc.

Kerr, B. Modern Persona: Valhalla High School. 2007. 296p. (YA). per. 18.95 *(978-0-595-44412-0(1))* iUniverse, Inc.

Kessler, Liz. Emily Windsnap & the Siren's Secret. (Emily Windsnap Ser.: 4). (ENG., Illus.). 304p. (J). (gr. 3-7). 2012. pap. 5.99 *(978-0-7636-6019-2(1))* 2010. 15.99 *(978-0-7636-4374-4(2))* Candlewick Pr.

—Emily Windsnap & the Siren's Secret. 2012. (Emily Windsnap Ser.: 4). lib. bdg. 16.00 *(978-0-606-25601-8(6)*, Turtleback) Turtleback Bks.

Keyser, Amber J. & Burkhart, Kiersi. The Long Trail Home. 2017. (Quartz Creek Ranch Ser.). (ENG.). 240p. (gr. 4-8). lib. bdg. 27.99 *(978-1-4677-9256-1(X))*; 35.99 ***(978-1-5124-2698-4(9))*** Lerner Publishing Group. (Darby Creek).

Killian, Beth. Boy Trouble. 2007. (ENG.). 256p. (gr. 8-12). pap. 16.99 *(978-1-4165-3497-6(0)*, MTV Bks.) MTV Books.

Kim, Susan & Klavan, Laurence. Guardians. (Wasteland Ser.: 3). 432p. (YA). (gr. 9). 2016. pap. 9.99 *(978-0-06-211858-5(7))* 2015. (ENG.). 17.99 *(978-0-06-211857-8(9))* HarperCollins Pubs. (HarperTeen).

—Wanderers: A Wasteland Novel. 2015. (Wasteland Ser.: 2). (ENG.). 384p. (YA). (gr. 9). pap. 9.99 *(978-0-06-211855-4(2)*, HarperTeen) HarperCollins Pubs.

—Wasteland. 2013. (Wasteland Ser.: 1). (ENG.). 336p. (YA). (gr. 9). 17.99 *(978-0-06-211851-6(X)*, HarperTeen) HarperCollins Pubs.

Kimmel, Elizabeth Cody. Lily B. on the Brink of Love. 2005. (ENG.). 192p. (J). 15.99 *(978-0-06-075541-6(5))* HarperCollins Pubs.

King, M. C. Truth or Dare. 2nd ed. 2008. (Hannah Montana Ser.). (Illus.). 126p. (gr. 3-7). 15.00 *(978-0-7569-8336-9(3))* Perfection Learning Corp.

Kingsley, Kate. Kiss & Break Up. 2011. (Young, Loaded, & Fabulous Ser.: 3). (ENG.). 320p. (YA). (gr. 9-18). pap. 9.99 *(978-1-4169-9401-5(7)*, Simon Pulse) Simon Pulse.

—Pretty on the Outside. 2010. (Young, Loaded, & Fabulous Ser.: 1). (ENG.). 320p. (YA). (gr. 9-18). pap. 9.99 *(978-1-4169-9399-5(1)*, Simon Pulse) Simon Pulse.

Kipling, Rudyard. Captains Courageous. 2006. (Classics Ser.). (Illus.). 48p. (YA). per. 17.95 *(978-1-56254-869-8(7))*; 80p. (J). (gr. 4-7). per. *(978-1-56254-868-1(9))* Saddleback Educational Publishing, Inc.

Klass, David. Timelock. 2009. (Caretaker Trilogy Ser.: 3). (ENG.). 256p. (YA). (gr. 9-12). 17.99 *(978-0-374-32309-7(7)*, 9780374323097, Farrar, Straus & Giroux (BYR)) Farrar, Straus & Giroux.

—Timelock. 2010. (Caretaker Trilogy Ser.: 3). (ENG.). 272p. (YA). (gr. 9-12). pap. 8.99 *(978-0-312-60863-7(2)*, 9780312608637) Square Fish.

—Whirlwind. 2009. (Caretaker Trilogy Ser.: 2). (ENG.). 320p. (YA). (gr. 9-12). pap. 18.99 *(978-0-312-38429-6(7)*, 9780312384296) Square Fish.

—You Don't Know Me. 2010. (ENG.). 288p. (YA). (gr. 9-12). pap. 9.99 *(978-0-312-65302-6(9))* Square Fish.

Klassen, Kirsten L. Katelyn's Affection. 2004. (ENG.). 280p. pap. 11.99 *(978-0-8361-9281-0(8))* Herald Pr.

Klausner, Julie. Art Girls Are Easy. 2013. (ENG.). 240p. (YA). (gr. 10-17). pap. 18.99 *(978-0-316-24362-9(0)*, Poppy) Little, Brown Bks. for Young Readers.

Klauss, Lucas. Everything You Need to Survive the Apocalypse. 2012. (ENG.). 416p. (gr. 9). (J). pap. 9.99 *(978-1-4424-2389-3(7))*; (YA). 16.99 *(978-1-4424-2388-6(9))* Simon Pulse. (Simon Pulse).

Klein, Abby. Thanksgiving Turkey Trouble. McKinley, John, illus. 2008. (Ready, Freddy! Ser.: Bk. 15). 95p. (gr. -1-3). 16.00 *(978-0-7569-8838-8(1))* Perfection Learning Corp.

Kluger, Steve. My Most Excellent Year: A Novel of Love, Mary Poppins, & Fenway Park. 2009. (ENG.). 416p. (YA). (gr. 7-18). 9.99 *(978-0-14-241343-2(7)*, Speak) Penguin Young Readers Group.

Knight, Richard, et al. Finn at Clee Point. Hurst, Oliver, illus. 2012. (ENG.). 128p. (J). pap. 12.99 *(978-1-84686-401-8(1))* Barefoot Bks., Inc.

Knowles, Jo. Jumping off Swings. 2011. (ENG., Illus.). 240p. (YA). (gr. 9). pap. 7.99 *(978-0-7636-5296-8(2))* Candlewick Pr.

—Lessons from a Dead Girl. 2009. (ENG., Illus.). 224p. (YA). (gr. 9). pap. 7.99 *(978-0-7636-4485-7(4))* Candlewick Pr.

—Living with Jackie Chan. 2013. (ENG.). 384p. (YA). (gr. 9). 16.99 *(978-0-7636-6280-6(1))* Candlewick Pr.

Koertge, Ron. Shakespeare Makes the Playoffs. 2012. (ENG., Illus.). 176p. (YA). (gr. 7). pap. 6.99 *(978-0-7636-5852-6(9))* Candlewick Pr.

Koertge, Ronald. Shakespeare Makes the Playoffs. 2010. (ENG., Illus.). 176p. (YA). (gr. 7-18). 15.99 *(978-0-7636-4435-2(8))* Candlewick Pr.

Konen, Leah. The Last Time We Were Us. 2016. 368p. (YA). (gr. 8). 17.99 *(978-0-06-240247-9(1)*, Tegen, Katherine Bks) HarperCollins Pubs.

Korman, Gordon. Restart. 2017. (ENG.). 256p. (J). (gr. 3-7). 16.99 ***(978-1-338-05377-7(9)***, Scholastic Pr.) Scholastic, Inc.

Koss, Amy Goldman. Gossip Times Three. 2005. (ENG.). 176p. (J). (gr. 3-7). reprint ed. pap. 6.99 *(978-0-14-240295-5(8)*, Puffin Books) Penguin Young Readers Group.

—Gossip Times Three. 2005. 170p. (gr. 5-9). 16.00 *(978-0-7569-5648-6(X))* Perfection Learning Corp.

Kowalski, William. The Way It Works, 1 vol. 2010. (Rapid Reads Ser.). (ENG.). 128p. pap. 9.95 *(978-1-55469-367-2(5)*, Raven Bks.) Literations.

Kramer, Stacy & Thomas, Valerie. Karma Bites. 2010. (ENG.). 348p. (J). (gr. 5-7). pap. 18.99 *(978-0-547-36301-1(X))* Houghton Mifflin Harcourt Publishing Co.

Kroll, Jennifer. Their Eyes Were Watching God. rev. ed. 2015. (Great Works). (ENG., Illus.). 72p. (gr. 9-12). pap. 9.99 *(978-1-4258-8997-5(2))* Shell Educational Publishing.

Kroll, Steven. The Biggest Valentine Ever. Bassett, Jeni, illus. 2006. (ENG.). 32p. (J). (gr. -1-1). pap. 3.99 *(978-0-439-76419-3(X))* Scholastic, Inc.

Kropp, Paul. Running the Bases: Definitely Not a Book about Baseball. 2008. (ENG.). 208p. (J). (gr. 7). mass mkt. 7.99 *(978-0-7704-2975-1(0)*, Seal Bks.) Penguin Random House Canada Young Readers CAN. Dist: Penguin Random Hse. LLC.

Krossing, Karen. Punch Like a Girl, 1 vol. 2015. (ENG.). 240p. (YA). (gr. 8-12). pap. 12.95 *(978-1-4598-0828-7(2))* Orca Bk. Pubs. USA.

Krovatin, Christopher. Mountain of Bones. (Gravediggers Ser.: 1). (ENG.). (J). (gr. 3-7). 2013. 352p. pap. 6.99 *(978-0-06-207741-7(4))* 2012. 336p. 16.99 *(978-0-06-207740-0(6))* HarperCollins Pubs. (Tegen, Katherine Bks).

—Venomous. Yates, Kelly, illus. 2011. (ENG.). 336p. (YA). (gr. 8). pap. 8.99 *(978-1-4424-1298-9(4),* Atheneum Bks. for Young Readers) Simon & Schuster Children's Publishing.

Krulik, Nancy. Girls Don't Have Cooties. John and Wendy Staff, illus. 2005. (Katie Kazoo, Switcheroo Ser.: 4). (ENG.). 80p. (J). (gr. 2-4). mass mkt. 4.99 *(978-0-448-42705-8(2),* Grosset & Dunlap) Penguin Young Readers Group.

Krumwiede, Lana. Archon. 2015. (Psi Chronicles Ser.). (ENG.). 320p. (J). (gr. 5). pap. 7.99 *(978-0-7636-7659-9(4))* Candlewick Pr.

—Freakling. 2014. (Psi Chronicles Ser.). (ENG.). 320p. (J). (gr. 5). pap. 7.99 *(978-0-7636-6938-6(5))* Candlewick Pr.

Kunze, Lauren & Onur, Rina. The Ivy. (Ivy Ser.: 1). (ENG.). (YA). (gr. 9). 2011. 336p. pap. 8.99 *(978-0-06-196046-8(2))* 2010. 320p. 16.99 *(978-0-06-196045-1(4))* HarperCollins Pubs. (Greenwillow Bks.).

—Rivals. 2012. (Ivy Ser.: 3). (ENG.). 384p. (YA). (gr. 9). 16.99 *(978-0-06-196049-9(7),* Greenwillow Bks.) HarperCollins Pubs.

—Scandal. 2013. (Ivy Ser.: 4). (ENG.). 336p. (YA). (gr. 9). 17.99 *(978-0-06-196051-2(9),* Greenwillow Bks.) HarperCollins Pubs.

—Secrets. 2011. (Ivy Ser.: 2). (ENG.). 320p. (YA). (gr. 9-18). 16.99 *(978-0-06-196047-5(0),* Greenwillow Bks.) HarperCollins Pubs.

Kyi, Tanya Lloyd. Anywhere but Here. 2013. (ENG., Illus.). 320p. (YA). (gr. 9). 17.99 *(978-1-4424-8070-4(X));* pap. 9.99 *(978-1-4424-8069-8(6))* Simon Pulse. (Simon Pulse).

Laban, Elizabeth. The Tragedy Paper. (ENG.). 320p. (YA). (gr. 7). 2014. pap. 9.99 *(978-0-307-93048-4(3),* Ember) 2013. (Illus.). 17.99 *(978-0-375-87040-8(7),* Knopf Bks. for Young Readers) Random Hse. Children's Bks.

Lanagan, Margo. Red Spikes. 2009. (ENG.). 192p. (YA). (gr. 9). pap. 7.99 *(978-0-375-84304-4(3),* Knopf Bks. for Young Readers) Random Hse. Children's Bks.

—White Time. 2006. 224p. (YA). (gr. 7-18). lib. bdg. 16.89 *(978-0-06-074394-9(8))* HarperCollins Pubs.

Lane, Sharmen. Why Am I Special? l.t. ed. 2006. (Illus.). 23p. (J). per. 14.95 *(978-0-9764103-8-6(9))* Daylight Pubs.

Lang, Diane & Buchanan, Michael. The Fat Boy Chronicles. 2010. (Fat Boy Chronicles Ser.). (ENG.). 224p. (J). (gr. 7-11). pap. 9.95 *(978-1-58536-543-2(2),* 202220) Sleeping Bear Pr.

Langan, Paul & Schraff, Anne. Summer of Secrets. 2008. (Bluford High Ser.: 10). (ENG.). 160p. (J). (gr. 7-18). 5.99 *(978-0-439-90491-9(9),* Scholastic Paperbacks) Scholastic, Inc.

Lange, Erin Jade. Rebel, Bully, Geek, Pariah. 2016. (ENG.). 320p. (YA). 17.99 *(978-1-61963-498-5(8),* 9781619634985, Bloomsbury USA Childrens) Bloomsbury Publishing USA.

Laure, Estelle. These Mighty Forces. 2017. (ENG.). 320p. (YA). (gr. 9). 17.99 *(978-0-544-53126-0(4),* HMH Books For Young Readers) Houghton Mifflin Harcourt Publishing Co.

Lavigne, Guy. Pas de Quartier pour les Poires. 2003. (Roman Plus Ser.). (FRE., Illus.). 160p. (YA). (gr. 8-18). pap. *(978-2-89021-250-3(5))* Diffusion du livre Mirabel (DLM).

Lay, Kathryn. Book 4: Time under the Sea. 2016. (Time Twisters Ser.). (ENG.). (J). (gr. 2-6). lib. bdg. 27.07 ***(978-1-62402-180-0(8))*** ABDO Publishing Co.

Lazebnik, Claire. Epic Fail. 2011. (ENG.). 304p. (YA). (gr. 8-18). pap. 9.99 *(978-0-06-192126-1(2),* HarperTeen) HarperCollins Pubs.

—The Last Best Kiss. 2014. (ENG.). 384p. (YA). (gr. 8). pap. 9.99 *(978-0-06-225228-9(3),* HarperTeen) HarperCollins Pubs.

—The Trouble with Flirting. 2013. (ENG.). 336p. (YA). (gr. 8). pap. 9.99 *(978-0-06-192127-8(0),* HarperTeen) HarperCollins Pubs.

Leader, Jessica. Nice & Mean. 2010. (Mix Ser.). (ENG.). 272p. (J). (gr. 4-8). pap. 6.99 *(978-1-4169-9160-1(3),* Aladdin) Simon & Schuster Children's Publishing.

Leaney, Cindy. It's Your Turn Now: Politeness. Wilks, Peter, tr. Wilks, Peter, illus. 2003. 31p. (J). 28.50 *(978-1-58952-735-5(6))* Rourke Educational Media.

Leavitt, Martine. Keturah & Lord Death. (ENG.). (YA). 2012. 224p. (gr. 9-12). pap. 9.95 *(978-1-59078-949-0(0))* 2006. 216p. (gr. 7-7). 16.95 *(978-1-932425-29-1(2),* Front Street) Boyds Mills Pr.

Leavy, Patricia. Blue. 2015. (ENG., Illus.). 168p. pap. *(978-94-6300-353-7(3))* Sense Pubs.

Lee, Kathy. No Means No. 2007. 143p. pap. *(978-1-84427-253-2(2))* Scripture Union.

Lee, Mackenzi. The Gentleman's Guide to Vice & Virtue. 2017. 528p. (YA). (gr. 8). 18.99 *(978-0-06-238280-1(2),* Tegen, Katherine Bks) HarperCollins Pubs.

Lee Wardlaw. Seventh-Grade Weirdo. 2010. 160p. pap. 11.95 *(978-1-4401-8263-1(9))* iUniverse, Inc.

Lefeuvre, Amy. Probable Sons. 2004. reprint ed. pap. 1.99 *(978-1-4192-4306-6(3));* pap. 15.95 *(978-1-4191-4306-9(9))* Kessinger Publishing, LLC.

LeFlore, Lyah B. Can't Hold Me Down. Warfield, D. L., illus. 2010. (Come Up Ser.). (ENG.). 272p. (J). (gr. 9-18). pap. 8.99 *(978-1-4169-7964-7(6),* Simon Pulse) Simon Pulse.

—The World Is Mine. Warfield, D. L., illus. 2009. (Come Up Ser.). (ENG.). 304p. (YA). (gr. 9-18). pap. 8.99 *(978-1-4169-7963-0(8),* Simon Pulse) Simon Pulse.

Leveen, Tom. Party. 2011. (ENG.). 240p. (YA). (gr. 9). pap. 8.99 *(978-0-375-86392-9(3),* Ember) Random Hse. Children's Bks.

Levithan, David. Every You, Every Me. Levithan, David & Farmer, Jonathan, photos by. 2012. (ENG., Illus.). 256p. (YA). (gr. 7). pap. 9.99 *(978-0-375-85451-4(7),* Ember) Random Hse. Children's Bks.

—Every You, Every Me. Farmer, Jonathan, photos by. 2012. (Illus.). lib. bdg. 20.85 *(978-0-606-26816-5(2),* Turtleback) Turtleback Bks.

—Love Is the Higher Law. 2010. (ENG.). 176p. (YA). (gr. 7). pap. 9.99 *(978-0-375-83469-1(9),* Knopf Bks. for Young Readers) Random Hse. Children's Bks.

—The Realm of Possibility. 2006. (ENG.). 224p. (YA). (gr. 7-12). reprint ed. pap. 9.99 *(978-0-375-83657-2(8),* Ember) Random Hse. Children's Bks.

Levithan, David & Ehrenhaft, Daniel. 21 Proms. l.t. ed. 2007. (YA). 22.95 *(978-0-7862-9866-2(9))* Thorndike Pr.

Levy, Janice. Totally Uncool. Monroe, Chris, illus. 2003. (Picture Bks.). 32p. (J). (gr. -1-3). reprint ed. 6.95 *(978-1-57505-555-8(4),* Carolrhoda Bks.) Lerner Publishing Group.

Lewis, Beverly. Holly's Heart. 2008. (ENG., (gr. 7-11). Vol. 2, Bks. 6-10. Illus.). 560p. pap. 13.99 *(978-0-7642-0459-3(9))* Vol. 3, Bks. 11-14. 448p. pap. 16.00 *(978-0-7642-0460-9(2))* Bethany Hse. Pubs.

Lewis, Linda. Loving Two Is Hard to Do. 2008. (ENG.). 160p. (YA). (gr. 7). pap. 8.95 *(978-1-4169-7534-2(9),* Simon Pulse) Simon Pulse.

—My Heart Belongs to That Boy. 2008. (ENG.). 176p. (Orig.). (YA). (gr. 7). pap. 9.95 *(978-1-4169-7536-6(5),* Simon Pulse) Simon Pulse.

Lewis, Richard. The Demon Queen. 2012. (ENG.). 240p. (YA). (gr. 7). pap. 11.99 *(978-1-4169-3590-2(8),* Simon & Schuster Bks. For Young Readers) Simon & Schuster Bks. For Young Readers.

Li, August. Fox-Hat & Neko. 2016. (ENG., Illus.). (YA). 29.99 ***(978-1-63533-018-2(1),*** Harmony Ink Pr.) Dreamspinner Pr.

Lieberman, Leanne. The Book of Trees, 1 vol. 2010. (ENG.). 256p. (YA). (gr. 8-12). pap. 12.95 *(978-1-55469-265-1(2))* Orca Bk. Pubs. USA.

Life Changing Books, creator. Teenage Bluez 2, 2. 2006. 169p. (J). (gr. -1). per. 10.99 *(978-0-9741394-8-7(3))* Power Play Media.

Linch, Tanya. The Owl, the Aat & the Roar. 2005. (ENG., Illus.). 32p. (J). (gr. -1-3). pap. 12.99 *(978-0-7475-6324-2(1))* Bloomsbury Publishing Plc GBR. Dist: Independent Pubs. Group.

Lindsey, Mary. Shattered Souls. 2012. (ENG.). 356p. (YA). (gr. 9). pap. 8.99 *(978-0-14-242190-1(1),* Speak) Penguin Young Readers Group.

Littman, Sarah Darer. Want to Go Private? (ENG.). 336p. (J). 2013. (gr. 7). pap. 10.99 *(978-0-545-15147-4(3))* 2011. (gr. 9-9). 17.99 *(978-0-545-15146-7(5),* Scholastic Pr.) Scholastic, Inc.

Lockhart, E. The Boy Book: A Study of Habits & Behaviors, Plus Techniques for Taming Them. 2008. (Ruby Oliver Quartet Ser.). (ENG.). 224p. (YA). (gr. 7). pap. 8.99 *(978-0-385-73209-3(0),* Delacorte Pr.) Random Hse. Children's Bks.

—The Boyfriend List: 15 Guys, 11 Shrink Appointments, 4 Ceramic Frogs & Me, Ruby Oliver. 2006. (Ruby Oliver Quartet Ser.). (ENG.). 256p. (YA). (gr. 7-12). reprint ed. pap. 9.99 *(978-0-385-73207-9(4),* Ember) Random Hse. Children's Bks.

—The Disreputable History of Frankie Landau-Banks. 2009. (ENG.). 352p. (J). (gr. 5-9). pap. 9.99 *(978-0-7868-3819-6(1))* Hyperion Pr.

—The Disreputable History of Frankie Landau-Banks. l.t. ed. 2009. (ENG.). 502p. (YA). 23.95 *(978-1-4104-1439-7(6))* Thorndike Pr.

—Fly on the Wall: How One Girl Saw Everything. 2007. (ENG., Illus.). 192p. (YA). (gr. 7-12). pap. 8.99 *(978-0-385-73282-6(1),* Delacorte Pr) Random House Publishing Group.

—Real Live Boyfriends: Yes. Boyfriends, Plural. If My Life Weren't Complicated, I Wouldn't Be Ruby Oliver. 2011. (Ruby Oliver Quartet Ser.). (ENG.). 240p. (J). (gr. 7). pap. 8.99 *(978-0-385-73429-5(8),* Ember) Random Hse. Children's Bks.

—The Treasure Map of Boys: Noel, Jackson, Finn, Hutch, Gideon - And Me, Ruby Oliver. 2010. (Ruby Oliver Quartet Ser.). (ENG.). 256p. (J). (gr. 7). pap. 8.99 *(978-0-385-73427-1(1),* Delacorte Pr.) Random Hse. Children's Bks.

Lockwood, Cara. The Scarlet Letterman. 2007. (Bard Academy Ser.: 2). (ENG.). 272p. (gr. 7-12). pap. 17.99 *(978-1-4165-2490-8(8))* Pocket Books.

Logsted, Greg. Alibi Junior High. (ENG.). 256p. (J). (gr. 5-9). 2011. pap. 6.99 *(978-1-4169-4814-8(7))* 2009. (Illus.). 16.99 *(978-1-4169-7959-3(X))* Simon & Schuster/Paula Wiseman Bks. (Simon & Schuster/Paula Wiseman Bks.).

London, Jonathan. Desolation Canyon. London, Sean, illus. 2015. (Aaron's Wilderness Ser.: 1). (ENG.). 168p. (YA). pap. 12.99 *(978-1-941821-29-9(4),* West Winds Pr.) Graphic Arts Ctr. Publishing Co.

Look, Lenore. Alvin Ho: Allergic to Babies, Burglars, & Other Bumps in the Night. Pham, LeUyen, illus. 2013. (Alvin Ho Ser.). (ENG.). 192p. (J). (gr. 1-4). 15.99 *(978-0-375-87033-0(4),* Schwartz & Wade Bks.) Random Hse. Children's Bks.

—Alvin Ho: Allergic to Birthday Parties, Science Projects, & Other Man-Made Catastrophes. Pham, LeUyen, illus. 2011. (Alvin Ho Ser.). (ENG.). 192p. (J). (gr. 1-4). 6.99 *(978-0-375-87369-0(4),* Yearling) Random Hse. Children's Bks.

—Alvin Ho: Allergic to Babies, Burglars, & Other Bumps in the Night. Pham, LeUyen, illus. 2014. (Alvin Ho Ser.). (ENG.). 192p. (J). (gr. 1-4). 6.99 *(978-0-385-38600-5(1),* Yearling) Random Hse. Children's Bks.

Lord, Emery. The Start of Me & You. 2016. (ENG.). 416p. (YA). pap. 9.99 *(978-1-61963-938-6(6),* 9781619639386, Bloomsbury USA Childrens) Bloomsbury Publishing USA.

Lorentz, Dayna. No Safety in Numbers. 2013. (No Safety in Numbers Ser.: 1). (ENG.). 288p. (YA). (gr. 7). pap. 8.99 *(978-0-14-242597-8(4),* Speak) Penguin Young Readers Group.

Love, D. Anne. Picture Perfect. 2010. (ENG.). 304p. (YA). (gr. 7). pap. 8.99 *(978-0-689-87391-1(3),* McElderry, Margaret K. Bks.) McElderry, Margaret K. Bks.

Lowry, Brigid. Follow the Blue. 2004. (ENG.). 205p. (J). (gr. 7-18). tchr. ed. 16.95 *(978-0-8234-1827-5(8))* Holiday Hse., Inc.

—Follow the Blue. 2006. (ENG.). 208p. (YA). (gr. 8-12). pap. 18.99 *(978-0-312-34297-5(7),* 9780312342975, St. Martin's Griffin) St. Martin's Pr.

Lubar, David. Character, Driven: A Novel. 2017. (ENG.). 304p. (YA). pap. 9.99 *(978-0-7653-7694-7(6),* 9780765376947, Tor Teen) Doherty, Tom Assocs., LLC.

—Dunk. 2004. (ENG.). 272p. (YA). (gr. 7-18). reprint ed. pap. 7.99 *(978-0-618-43909-6(9))* Houghton Mifflin Harcourt Publishing Co.

—Sleeping Freshmen Never Lie. 2007. (ENG.). 288p. (YA). (gr. 7-18). 10.99 *(978-0-14-240780-6(1),* Speak) Penguin Young Readers Group.

Ludwig, Elisa. Pretty Wanted. 2015. (Pretty Crooked Trilogy Ser.: 3). (ENG.). 336p. (YA). (gr. 8). 17.99 *(978-0-06-206612-1(9),* Tegen, Katherine Bks) HarperCollins Pubs.

Ludwig, Trudy. Better Than You. Gustavson, Adam, illus. 2011. (ENG.). 32p. (J). (gr. 1-4). 15.99 *(978-1-58246-380-3(8),* Knopf Bks. for Young Readers) Random Hse. Children's Bks.

—Just Kidding. Gustavson, Adam, illus. 2006. (ENG.). 32p. (J). (gr. 1-4). 15.99 *(978-1-58246-163-2(5),* Tricycle Pr.) Random Hse. Children's Bks.

—Trouble Talk. Prevost, Mikela, illus. 2008. (ENG.). 32p. (J). (gr. 1-4). 15.99 *(978-1-58246-240-0(2),* Tricycle Pr.) Random Hse. Children's Bks.

Luper, Eric. Seth Baumgartner's Love Manifesto. 2010. (ENG.). 304p. (YA). (gr. 8-18). 16.99 *(978-0-06-182753-2(3))* HarperCollins Pubs.

Lupica, Mike. Miracle on 49th Street. 2007. (ENG.). 272p. (J). (gr. 5-18). 7.99 *(978-0-14-240942-8(1),* Puffin Books) Penguin Young Readers Group.

—Miracle on 49th Street. 2007. 246p. (gr. 5-9). 18.00 *(978-0-7569-8157-0(3))* Perfection Learning Corp.

Lyga, Barry. The Astonishing Adventures of Fanboy & Goth Girl. 2007. (ENG.). 320p. (YA). (gr. 7-12). pap. 9.99 *(978-0-618-91652-8(0))* Houghton Mifflin Harcourt Publishing Co.

Lyles, Whitney. Party Games. 2012. (Romantic Comedies Ser.). (ENG.). 304p. (YA). (gr. 7). pap. 14.99 *(978-1-4424-6060-7(1),* Simon Pulse) Simon Pulse.

Lynch, Chris. Pieces. 2013. (ENG., (YA). (gr. 7). Illus.). 192p. pap. 9.99 *(978-1-4424-5441-5(5));* 176p. 16.99 *(978-1-4169-2703-7(4))* Simon & Schuster Bks. For Young Readers. (Simon & Schuster Bks. For Young Readers).

Maciejewski, Mark. I Am Fartacus. 2017. (Max Ser.). (ENG., Illus.). 336p. (J). (gr. 4-8). pap. 7.99 *(978-1-4814-6419-2(1),* Simon & Schuster/Paula Wiseman Bks.) Simon & Schuster/Paula Wiseman Bks.

Mackey, Weezie Kerr. Throwing Like a Girl, 0 vols. 2010. (ENG.). 272p. (YA). (gr. 7-9). pap. 9.99 *(978-0-7614-5606-3(6),* 9780761456063, Amazon Children's Publishing) Amazon Publishing.

Mackler, Carolyn. Guyaholic. 2009. (ENG., Illus.). 192p. (YA). (gr. 9). pap. 7.99 *(978-0-7636-2801-7(8))* Candlewick Pr.

—Tangled. (ENG.). (YA). (gr. 9). 2011. 336p. pap. 9.99 *(978-0-06-173106-8(4))* 2009. 320p. 16.99 *(978-0-06-173104-4(8))* HarperCollins Pubs. (HarperTeen).

MacLeod, J.E.. Waiting to Score. 2011. 8.42 *(978-1-934813-17-1(6))* Westside Bks.

Magnason, Andri Snaer. The Story of the Blue Planet. D'Arcy, Julian Meldon, tr. Jonsdottir, Aslaug, illus. 2013. (ENG.). 136p. (J). (gr. 2-5). pap. 9.95 *(978-1-60980-506-7(2),* Triangle Square) Seven Stories Pr.

Magoon, Kekla. 37 Things I Love (in No Particular Order) 2012. (ENG.). 224p. (YA). (gr. 9-13). 16.99 *(978-0-8050-9465-7(2),* Holt, Henry & Co. Bks. For Young Readers) Holt, Henry & Co.

—37 Things I Love (in No Particular Order) 2013. (ENG.). 240p. (YA). (gr. 9-13). pap. 14.99 *(978-1-250-03430-4(2),* 9781250034304) Square Fish.

Mahoney, Karen. The Iron Witch. 2011. (Iron Witch Ser.: 1). (ENG.). 312p. (YA). (gr. 7-18). pap. 9.95 *(978-0-7387-2582-6(X),* Flux) North Star Editions.

Maldonado, Torrey. Secret Saturdays. 2012. (ENG.). 208p. (YA). (gr. 7-18). 7.99 *(978-0-14-241747-8(5),* Puffin Books) Penguin Young Readers Group.

—Secret Saturdays. 2012. lib. bdg. 18.40 *(978-0-606-23645-4(7),* Turtleback) Turtleback Bks.

Malloy, Brian. Twelve Long Months. 2010. (ENG.). 320p. (J). (gr. 7). 9.99 *(978-0-439-87763-3(6),* Scholastic Paperbacks) Scholastic, Inc.

Mammay, Judith. Knowing Joseph. (ENG., Illus.). 256p. (J). (gr. 2-7). 2009. pap. 8.95 *(978-1-933831-06-0(5))* 2008. 13.95 *(978-1-933831-05-3(7))* Blooming Tree Pr.

Mangum, Lisa. The Hourglass Door. (Hourglass Door Trilogy: Bk. 1). (YA). 2010. 408p. mass mkt. 7.99 *(978-1-60641-679-2(0))* 2009. 432p. (gr. 9-18). 18.95 *(978-1-60641-093-6(8))* Shadow Mountain Publishing. (Shadow Mountain).

Manners I. Care. 2005. (J). pap. 5.99 *(978-0-9771143-4-4(1))* Child Life Bks., LLC.

Manning, Sarra. Guitar Girl. 2005. 217p. (gr. 9-12). 17.00 *(978-0-7569-5702-5(8))* Perfection Learning Corp.

Mantchev, Lisa. Perchance to Dream. 2011. (Theatre Illuminata Ser.: 2). (ENG.). 368p. (YA). (gr. 7-12). pap. 9.99 *(978-0-312-67510-3(0),* 9780312675103) Square Fish.

Maple, Daphne. Top Dog. Metayer, Annabelle, illus. 2016. (Roxbury Park Dog Club Ser.: 3). 224p. (J). (gr. 3-7). pap. 6.99 *(978-0-06-232771-0(2))* HarperCollins Pubs.

Margolis, Leslie. Boys Are Dogs. 2008. (Annabelle Unleashed Ser.). (ENG., Illus.). 208p. (YA). (gr. 3-6). 15.99 *(978-1-59990-221-0(4),* 9781599902210, Bloomsbury USA Childrens) Bloomsbury Publishing USA.

—Everybody Bugs Out. (Annabelle Unleashed Ser.). (ENG.). (YA). (gr. 3-12). 2012. 224p. pap. 6.99 *(978-1-59990-828-1(X),* 9781599908281) 2011. 208p. 15.99 *(978-1-59990-526-6(4),* 9781599905266) Bloomsbury Publishing USA. (Bloomsbury USA Childrens).

—Girls Acting Catty. (Annabelle Unleashed Ser.). (ENG.). (YA). (gr. 3-6). 2010. 208p. pap. 6.99 *(978-1-59990-520-4(5),* 9781599905204) 2009. 192p. 15.99 *(978-1-59990-237-1(0),* 9781599902371) Bloomsbury Publishing USA. (Bloomsbury USA Childrens).

—One Tough Chick. 2013. (Annabelle Unleashed Ser.). (ENG.). 176p. (YA). (gr. 3-6). 15.99 *(978-1-59990-961-5(8),* 9781599909615, Bloomsbury USA Childrens) Bloomsbury Publishing USA.

Marien, Donna. Waiting at the Bay: A Young Woman's Reflections on Journeys in the Sea of Life. 2003. 108p. (YA). pap. 10.95 *(978-0-595-26304-2(6),* Writers Club Pr.) iUniverse, Inc.

Marino, Nan. Neil Armstrong Is My Uncle & Other Lies Muscle Man McGinty Told Me. 2012. (ENG.). 176p. (J). (gr. 3-7). pap. 6.99 *(978-0-312-66548-7(2),* 9780312665487) Square Fish.

Martin, C. K. Kelly. The Lighter Side of Life & Death. 2010. (YA). pap. *(978-0-375-84590-1(9))* Random Hse. Children's Bks.

Martinusen-Coloma, Cindy. Ruby Unscripted, 1 vol. 2009. (ENG.). 272p. (YA). (gr. 7-18). pap. 12.99 *(978-1-59554-356-1(2))* Nelson, Thomas Inc.

Mary-Todd, Jonathan. Lock-In. 2011. (Night Fall Ser.). (ENG.). 112p. (YA). (gr. 6-12). pap. 7.95 *(978-0-7613-7815-0(4));* lib. bdg. 27.93 *(978-0-7613-7743-6(3))* Lerner Publishing Group.

—Pig City. 2012. (After the Dust Settled Ser.). (ENG.). 112p. (YA). (gr. 6-12). pap. 7.95 *(978-0-8225-8746-0(7),* Darby Creek); lib. bdg. 27.93 *(978-0-7613-8328-4(X))* Lerner Publishing Group.

—Snakebite. 2012. (After the Dust Settled Ser.). (ENG.). 120p. (YA). (gr. 6-12). pap. 7.95 *(978-0-8225-8745-3(9),* Darby Creek); lib. bdg. 27.93 *(978-0-7613-8327-7(1))* Lerner Publishing Group.

Masel, Christy, illus. Gorp's Dream: A Tale of Diversity, Tolerance, & Love in Pumpernickel Park. 2003. 36p. (J). 14.95 *(978-0-9724249-0-5(3))* Gorp Group Pr., The.

Mason, Jane B. Without Annette. 2016. (ENG.). 336p. (YA). (gr. 7). 18.99 *(978-0-545-81995-4(4),* Scholastic Pr.) Scholastic, Inc.

Mass, Wendy. Leap Day. 2006. (ENG.). 208p. (YA). (gr. 7-17). per. 10.99 *(978-0-316-05828-5(9))* Little, Brown Bks. for Young Readers.

—11 Birthdays. (ENG.). 272p. (J). (gr. 3-7). 2010. pap. 6.99 *(978-0-545-05240-5(8),* Scholastic Paperbacks) 2009. 17.99 *(978-0-545-05239-9(4),* Scholastic Pr.) Scholastic, Inc.

—11 Birthdays. 2010. (Willow Falls Ser.: 1). lib. bdg. 17.20 *(978-0-606-13990-8(7),* Turtleback) Turtleback Bks.

Matson, Morgan. Amy & Roger's Epic Detour. (ENG.). (YA). (gr. 7). 2011. 384p. pap. 10.99 *(978-1-4169-9066-6(6))* 2010. 352p. 19.99 *(978-1-4169-9065-9(8))* Simon & Schuster Bks. For Young Readers. (Simon & Schuster Bks. For Young Readers).

—Second Chance Summer. (ENG.). (YA). (gr. 7). 2013. 496p. pap. 10.99 *(978-1-4169-9068-0(2))* 2012. 480p. 19.99 *(978-1-4169-9067-3(4))* Simon & Schuster Bks. For Young Readers. (Simon & Schuster Bks. For Young Readers).

Mayer, Kirsten. Attack of the Evil Minions! Miller, Ed, illus. 2013. (ENG.). 32p. (J). (gr. -1-3). 12.99 *(978-0-316-23444-3(3))* Little, Brown Bks. for Young Readers.

Mazer, Norma Fox. Babyface. 2007. (ENG., Illus.). 176p. (YA). (gr. 7). pap. 11.95 *(978-0-15-206277-4(7))* Houghton Mifflin Harcourt Publishing Co.

McBride, Kristina. The Tension of Opposites. 2011. (ENG.). 288p. (J). (gr. 9). pap. 8.99 *(978-1-60684-213-3(7),* Carolrhoda Lab™) Lerner Publishing Group.

McBride, Susan. The Debs: Gloves Off. 2010. (YA). *(978-0-385-73796-8(3)); (978-0-385-90703-3(6))* Random House Publishing Group. (Delacorte Pr).

McCaffrey, Kate. Crashing Down. 2015. 304p. (YA). (gr. 7). 14.95 *(978-1-922089-85-4(0))* Fremantle Pr. AUS. Dist: Independent Pubs. Group.

McCahan, Erin. I Now Pronounce You Someone Else. 2010. (ENG.). 272p. (J). (gr. 7-18). 16.99 *(978-0-545-08818-3(6),* Levine, Arthur A. Bks.) Scholastic, Inc.

McCall, Guadalupe Garcia. Shame the Stars, 1 vol. 2016. (ENG.). 320p. (YA). 19.95 *(978-1-62014-278-3(3))* Lee & Low Bks., Inc.

McClintock, Norah. About That Night, 1 vol. 2014. (ENG.). 248p. (YA). (gr. 8-12). pap. 12.95 *(978-1-4598-0594-1(1))* Orca Bk. Pubs. USA.

—Back, 1 vol. 2009. (Orca Soundings Ser.). (ENG.). 112p. (YA). (gr. 8-12). 16.95 *(978-1-55143-991-4(3));* pap. 9.95 *(978-1-55143-989-1(1))* Orca Bk. Pubs. USA.

McClure, Brian D. The Up down Day. Plumlee, Buddy, illus. 2009. (Brian D. Mcclure Childrens Book Collection). 47p. (J). (gr. -1-3). 14.95 *(978-1-933426-07-5(1))* Universal Flag Publishing.

—Who Am I? 2006. (Illus.). 52p. (J). 12.95 *(978-1-933426-03-7(9))* Universal Flag Publishing.

McCombie, Karen. My Big (Strange) Happy Family. Monks, Lydia, illus. 2009. (J). pap. *(978-0-385-73597-1(9),* Yearling) Random Hse. Children's Bks.

McCranie, Stephen. Mal & Chad - The Biggest, Bestest Time Ever! McCranie, Stephen, illus. 2011. (Mal & Chad Ser.: 1). (ENG., Illus.). 224p. (J). (gr. 3-7). 9.99 *(978-0-399-25221-1(5),* Philomel Bks.) Penguin Young Readers Group.

McDaniel, Lurlene. Hit & Run. 2013. (ENG.). 192p. (YA). (gr. 7). pap. 8.99 *(978-0-385-74381-5(5),* Ember) Random Hse. Children's Bks.

—Keep Me in Your Heart: Three Novels. 2010. (ENG.). 624p. (YA). (gr. 7). pap. 10.99 *(978-0-385-73982-5(6),* Ember) Random Hse. Children's Bks.

—Letting Go of Lisa. 2007. (ENG.). 192p. (YA). (gr. 7-12). mass mkt. 6.99 *(978-0-440-23868-3(4),* Laurel Leaf) Random Hse. Children's Bks.

—Losing Gabriel: a Love Story. 2017. (ENG.). 336p. (YA). (gr. 7). pap. 9.99 ***(978-0-385-74422-5(6),*** Ember) Random Hse. Children's Bks.

—Prey. 2010. (ENG.). 208p. (YA). (gr. 7). mass mkt. 7.99 *(978-0-440-24015-0(8),* Laurel Leaf) Random Hse. Children's Bks.

—Red Heart Tattoo. 2013. (ENG.). 224p. (YA). (gr. 7). pap. 8.99 *(978-0-440-24019-8(0),* Ember) Random Hse. Children's Bks.

—The Year of Chasing Dreams. 2014. (ENG.). 336p. (YA). (gr. 7). 16.99 *(978-0-385-74173-6(1),* Delacorte Pr.) Random Hse. Children's Bks.

McDonald, Abby. The Anti-Prom. (ENG., Illus.). 288p. (YA). (gr. 9). 2012. pap. 7.99 *(978-0-7636-5847-2(2))* 2011. 16.99 *(978-0-7636-4956-2(2))* Candlewick Pr.

—Jane Austen Goes to Hollywood. (ENG.). 336p. (YA). (gr. 9). 2015. pap. 8.99 *(978-0-7636-7669-8(1))* 2013. 17.99 *(978-0-7636-5508-2(2))* Candlewick Pr.

McGovern, Cammie. Say What You Will. 2014. (ENG.). 352p. (YA). (gr. 9). 17.99 *(978-0-06-227110-5(5),* HarperTeen) HarperCollins Pubs.

McGowan, Maureen. Glory, 0 vols. 2014. (Dust Chronicles Ser.: 3). (ENG.). 326p. (YA). (gr. 9-12). pap. 9.99

(978-1-4778-4797-8(9), 9781477847978, Amazon Children's Publishing) Amazon Publishing.

McIntosh, Kenneth. The Trickster's Image: Forensic Art. 2009. (J). pap. 24.95 (978-1-4222-1452-7(4)) 2007. (Illus.). 144p. (YA). (gr. 8-12). pap. 9.95 (978-1-4222-0873-1(7)) Mason Crest.

—The Trickster's Image: Forensic Art, 3 vols. Miller, Justin, illus. 2007. (Crime Scene Club Ser.). 144p. (YA). (gr. 9-12). lib. bdg. 24.95 (978-1-4222-0249-4(6)) Mason Crest.

McKay, Hilary. Wishing for Tomorrow: The Sequel to a Little Princess. Maland, Nick, illus. (ENG.). 288p. (J). (gr. 3-7). 2011. pap. 6.99 (978-1-4424-0170-9(2)) 2010. 16.99 (978-1-4424-0169-3(9)) McElderry, Margaret K. Bks. (McElderry, Margaret K. Bks.).

McKenzie, C. Lee. The Princess of Las Pulgas. 2010. (ENG.). (YA). (978-1-934813-46-1(X)) Westside Bks.

McKinley, Mary. Rusty Summer. 2015. (Rusty Winters Ser.: 2). (ENG.). 352p. (YA). (gr. 9). pap. 9.95 (978-1-61773-257-7(5)) Kensington Publishing Corp.

McKnight, Gillian. To Catch a Prince: To Catch a Prince; the Frog Prince. 2011. (ENG., Illus.). 432p. (YA). (gr. 7). pap. 9.99 (978-1-4424-3139-3(3), Simon & Schuster Bks. For Young Readers) Simon & Schuster Bks. For Young Readers.

McLoon, Linda Snow. Crown Prince. 2013. (ENG.). 272p. (gr. 6-9). pap. (978-1-57076-546-9(4)) Verlhac Editions.

—Crown Prince Challenged. 2012. (Brookmeade Young Riders Ser.: 2). (ENG.). 384p. (YA). (gr. 6-9). pap. (978-1-57076-545-2(6)) Verlhac Editions.

McMahon, Kate. That Touch of Magic. 2009. (ENG.). 112p. (J). pap. 12.95 (978-1-901737-60-8(8)) Anvil Bks., Ltd. IRL. Dist: Dufour Editions, Inc.

McMann, Lisa. Cryer's Cross. 2011. (ENG.). (YA). (gr. 9). 256p. pap. 9.99 (978-1-4169-9482-4(3)); (Illus.). 240p. 16.99 (978-1-4169-9481-7(5)) Simon Pulse. (Simon Pulse).

—Fade. (Wake Ser.: Bk. 2). (ENG., (YA). (gr. 9-18). 2010. Illus.). 272p. pap. 10.99 (978-1-4169-7448-2(2)) 2009. 256p. 17.99 (978-1-4169-5358-6(2)) Simon Pulse. (Simon Pulse).

—Wake. 2008. (Wake Ser.: Bk. 1). (ENG.). 224p. (YA). (gr. 9). pap. 11.99 (978-1-4169-7447-5(4)); 17.99 (978-1-4169-5357-9(4)) Simon Pulse. (Simon Pulse).

McNeal, Laura & McNeal, Tom. Crooked. 2007. (ENG.). 368p. (YA). (gr. 7-11). pap. 9.99 (978-0-375-84191-0(1), Ember) Random Hse. Children's Bks.

McStay, Moriah. Everything That Makes You. 2015. (ENG.). 352p. (YA). (gr. 8). 17.99 (978-0-06-229548-4(9), Tegen, Katherine Bks) HarperCollins Pubs.

McVoy, Terra Elan. After the Kiss. (ENG.). (YA). (gr. 9). 2011. 416p. pap. 10.99 (978-1-4424-0216-4(4)) 2010. 400p. 16.99 (978-1-4424-0211-9(3)) Simon Pulse. (Simon Pulse).

—Being Friends with Boys. (ENG., (YA). (gr. 9). 2013. Illus.). 384p. pap. 10.99 (978-1-4424-2160-8(6)) 2012. 368p. 16.99 (978-1-4424-2159-2(2)) Simon Pulse. (Simon Pulse).

—The Summer of Firsts & Lasts. (ENG.). (YA). (gr. 9). 2012. 448p. pap. 9.99 (978-1-4424-0214-0(8)) 2011. 432p. 16.99 (978-1-4424-0213-3(X)) Simon Pulse. (Simon Pulse).

Meacham, Margaret. A Mid-Semester Night's Dream. 2004. (ENG.). 144p. (J). (gr. 4-6). tchr. ed. 16.95 (978-0-8234-1815-2(4)) Holiday Hse., Inc.

Mead, Richelle. Frostbite. 2008. (Vampire Academy Ser.: Bk. 2). (ENG.). 335p. (YA). (gr. 7-18). pap. 10.99 (978-1-59514-175-0(8), Razorbill) Penguin Publishing Group.

—The Glittering Court. 2016. 416p. (YA). pap. (978-0-448-49385-5(3), Razorbill) Penguin Publishing Group.

—The Glittering Court. (Glittering Court Ser.: 1). (ENG.). (YA). (gr. 7). 2017. 432p. pap. 10.99 (978-1-59514-842-1(6)) 2016. 416p. 19.99 (978-1-59514-841-4(8)) Penguin Young Readers Group. (Razorbill).

—The Ruby Circle. 2015. (Bloodlines Ser.: 6). (ENG.). 368p. (YA). (gr. 7). 18.99 (978-1-59514-322-8(X), Razorbill) Penguin Young Readers Group.

—Spirit Bound. 2011. (Vampire Academy Ser.: 5). (ENG.). 512p. (YA). (gr. 7-18). 9.99 (978-1-59514-366-2(1), Razorbill) Penguin Young Readers Group.

Mechling, Lauren & Moser, Laura. All Q, No A: More Tales of a 10th-Grade Social Climber. 2006. (ENG.). 288p. (YA). (gr. 7-12). pap. 15.95 (978-0-618-66378-1(9)) Houghton Mifflin Harcourt Publishing Co.

—Foreign Exposure: The Social Climber Abroad. 2007. (ENG.). 320p. (YA). (gr. 7-18). pap. 18.95 (978-0-618-66379-8(7)) Houghton Mifflin Harcourt Publishing Co.

Melissa, De La Cruz, et al. 21 Proms. Levithan, David & Ehrenhaft, Daniel, eds. 2015. (ENG.). 304p. (J). (gr. 7). pap. 9.99 (978-0-545-79867-9(1), PUSH) Scholastic, Inc.

Mellom, Robin. Ditched: A Love Story. 2013. (ENG.). 288p. (YA). (gr. 7-17). pap. 8.99 (978-1-4231-4351-2(5)) Disney Pr.

Mentyka, Sharon. Chasing at the Surface. 2016. (ENG., Illus.). 228p. (J). pap. 12.99 (978-1-943328-60-4(9), West Winds Pr.) Graphic Arts Ctr. Publishing Co.

Mercado, Nancy E. & Mercado, Nancy, eds. Every Man for Himself: Ten Short Stories about Being a Guy. 2007. (ENG., Illus.). 176p. (YA). (gr. 7-18). 6.99 (978-0-14-240813-1(1), Speak) Penguin Young Readers Group.

Mervyn, Catherine Antolino. Call Me Nona. 2013. 32p. pap. (978-1-4602-1570-8(2)) FriesenPress.

Mesrobian, Carrie. Cut Both Ways. 2015. (ENG.). 352p. (YA). (gr. 9). 17.99 (978-0-06-234988-0(0)) HarperCollins Pubs.

—Perfectly Good White Boy. 2014. (ENG.). 304p. (gr. 8-12). 17.95 (978-1-4677-3480-6(2), Carolrhoda Lab™) Lerner Publishing Group.

—Sex & Violence. 2013. (ENG.). 304p. (YA). (gr. 9-12). 17.95 (978-1-4677-0597-4(7), Carolrhoda Lab™) Lerner Publishing Group.

Meyer, Brad. A Matchless Age. 2006. 302p. pap. 29.95 (978-1-4241-0523-6(4)) PublishAmerica, Inc.

Meyer, Carolyn. Beauty's Daughter: The Story of Hermione & Helen of Troy. (ENG.). 352p. (YA). (gr. 7). 2015. pap. 8.99 (978-0-544-43915-3(5), HMH Books For Young Readers) 2013. (Illus.). 16.99 (978-0-544-10862-2(0)) Houghton Mifflin Harcourt Publishing Co.

Michaelis, Antonia. The Storyteller. 2012. (ENG.). 416p. (YA). (gr. 9-17). 19.95 (978-1-4197-0047-7(2), Amulet Bks.) Abrams, Inc.

Miles, Linda, et al. Amanda Salamander & the Secret of Happily Ever After. 2005. (J). cd-rom 7.99 (978-0-9778623-4-4(8)) Miles & Assocs.

Miller, Jennifer. Jennifer Miller's Run, Rasputin Run! Rasputin's Redemption (Book 3) 2007. (Illus.). 136p. per. 14.50 (978-1-4251-1029-1(0)) Trafford Publishing.

Miller, Lauren. Parallel. 2013. (ENG.). 432p. (YA). (gr. 8). 17.99 (978-0-06-219977-5(3), HarperTeen) HarperCollins Pubs.

Mills, Tricia. Heartbreak River. 2009. (YA). (978-1-59514-220-7(7), Razorbill) Penguin Publishing Group.

Mills, Wendy. All We Have Left. (ENG.). 368p. (YA). 2017. pap. 9.99 (978-1-68119-432-5(5), 9781681194325) 2016. 17.99 (978-1-61963-343-8(4), 9781619633438) Bloomsbury Publishing USA. (Bloomsbury USA Childrens).

Mlynowski, Sarah. Ten Things We Did (and Probably Shouldn't Have) (YA). (gr. 9). 2017. 384p. pap. 9.99 **(978-0-06-268303-8(9))** 2012. (ENG.). 368p. pap. 9.99 (978-0-06-170126-9(2), HarperTeen) 2011. (ENG.). 368p. 16.99 (978-0-06-170124-5(6), HarperTeen) HarperCollins Pubs.

Monaghan, Annabel. Double Digit. (ENG.). 192p. (YA). (gr. 7). 2015. pap. 7.99 (978-0-544-33620-9(8), HMH Books For Young Readers) 2014. 16.99 (978-0-544-10577-5(X)) Houghton Mifflin Harcourt Publishing Co.

—A Girl Named Digit: Under Cover, under Pressure, under Estimated. 2013. (ENG.). 192p. (YA). (gr. 7). pap. 8.99 (978-0-544-02248-5(3)) Houghton Mifflin Harcourt Publishing Co.

—A Girl Named Digit: Undercover, under Pressure, & Underestimated. 2012. (ENG., Illus.). 192p. (YA). (gr. 7). 16.99 (978-0-547-66852-9(X)) Houghton Mifflin Harcourt Publishing Co.

Montgomery, L. M. Anne of the Island. 2006. (ENG.). pap. (978-1-4068-2171-0(3)); pap. (978-1-4068-3175-7(1)) Echo Library.

—Anne of the Island. 2004. reprint ed. pap. 1.99 (978-1-4192-0718-1(0)); pap. 30.95 (978-1-4179-0885-1(8)) Kessinger Publishing, LLC.

—Anne of the Island. l.t. ed. 2004. 396p. 26.00 (978-1-58287-640-5(1)) North Bks.

—Anne of the Island. 2010. (Puffin Classics Ser.). (ENG.). 368p. (J). (gr. 5-7). pap. 5.99 (978-0-14-132736-5(7), Puffin Books) Penguin Young Readers Group.

Moore, Stephanie Perry. Back That Thing. 2015. (Illus.). 103p. (YA). 9.99 (978-1-4677-7892-3(3)) Lerner Publishing Group.

—Experiencing the Joy, 1 vol. 2009. (Yasmin Peace Ser.: 3). (ENG.). 160p. (gr. 7-10). pap. 7.99 (978-0-8024-8604-2(5), Lift Every Voice) Moody Pubs.

—Get What You Give. 2010. (ENG., Illus.). 233p. (YA). (gr. 9-18). 16.00 (978-0-7582-3446-9(5), K-Teen/Dafina) Kensington Publishing Corp.

—Give It Up. 2015. (YA). 9.99 (978-1-4677-7886-2(9)); (Swoop List Ser.: 1). (ENG., Illus.). 128p. (gr. 6-12). lib. bdg. 27.99 (978-1-4677-5804-8(3)) Lerner Publishing Group.

—On Your Knees. 2015. (Swoop List Ser.: 2). (ENG., Illus.). 128p. (YA). (gr. 6-12). lib. bdg. 27.99 (978-1-4677-5805-5(1)) Lerner Publishing Group.

—Sit on Top. 2015. (Swoop List Ser.: 4). (ENG., Illus.). 112p. (YA). (gr. 6-12). pap. 9.99 (978-1-4677-6052-2(8)) Lerner Publishing Group.

Moore, Stephanie Perry & Moody Publishing Staff. Finding Your Faith 2009. (Yasmin Peace Ser.: 1). (ENG.). 176p. (gr. 7-10). pap. 7.99 (978-0-8024-8602-8(9), Lift Every Voice) Moody Pubs.

Morgan, Melissa J. In It to Win It. 2010. (Camp Confidential Ser.: 25). (ENG.). 160p. (J). (gr. 4-7). pap. 4.99 (978-0-448-45402-3(5), Grosset & Dunlap) Penguin Young Readers Group.

—Topsy-Turvy. 2010. (Camp Confidential Ser.: 24). (ENG.). 160p. (J). (gr. 3-7). pap. 4.99 (978-0-448-45372-9(X), Grosset & Dunlap) Penguin Young Readers Group.

—Twilight. 2009. (Summer Confidential Ser.: 3). (ENG.). 240p. (J). (gr. 5-18). pap. 7.99 (978-0-448-44990-6(0), Grosset & Dunlap) Penguin Young Readers Group.

Moriarty, Jaclyn. A Corner of White. 2013. (Colors of Madeleine Ser.: 1). (ENG.). 384p. (J). (gr. 7). 18.99 (978-0-545-39736-0(7), Levine, Arthur A. Bks.) Scholastic, Inc.

—The Cracks in the Kingdom. 2014. (Colors of Madeleine Ser.: 2). (ENG.). 480p. (J). (gr. 7). 18.99 (978-0-545-39738-4(3), Levine, Arthur A. Bks.) Scholastic, Inc.

—The Ghosts of Ashbury High. (ENG.). 496p. (J). (gr. 7). 2012. pap. 10.99 (978-0-545-06973-1(4)) 2010. 18.99 (978-0-545-06972-4(6)) Scholastic, Inc. (Levine, Arthur A. Bks.).

—The Murder of Bindy MacKenzie. 2008. (ENG.). 496p. (J). (gr. 7-12). pap. 9.99 (978-0-439-74052-4(5), Levine, Arthur A. Bks.) Scholastic, Inc.

—The Spell Book of Listen Taylor. 2007. (YA). (978-0-439-84679-0(X), Levine, Arthur A. Bks.) Scholastic, Inc.

—A Tangle of Gold. 2016. (Colors of Madeleine Ser.: 3). (ENG.). 480p. (YA). (gr. 7). 18.99 (978-0-545-39740-7(5), Levine, Arthur A. Bks.) Scholastic, Inc.

Morrill, Lauren. Being Sloane Jacobs. 2015. (ENG.). 352p. (YA). (gr. 7). pap. 9.99 (978-0-385-74180-4(4), Ember) Random Hse. Children's Bks.

—Meant to Be. (ENG.). 304p. (YA). (gr. 7). 2014. pap. 9.99 (978-0-385-74178-1(2), Ember) 2012. 17.99 (978-0-385-74177-4(4), Delacorte Pr.) 2012. E-Book (978-0-375-98711-3(8), Delacorte Pr.) Random Hse. Children's Bks.

Morris, Paula. Dark Souls. 2011. (ENG.). 304p. (J). (gr. 7-7). 17.99 (978-0-545-25132-7(X)) Scholastic, Inc.

Morrison, Megan. Disenchanted: The Trials of Cinderella. 2016. (Tyme Ser.: 2). (ENG., Illus.). 416p. (J). (gr. 3-7). 17.99 (978-0-545-64271-2(X), Levine, Arthur A. Bks.) Scholastic, Inc.

Morty, Ducktor. Can Do & Friends to the Rescue! A Story about Getting along & Working Together. l.t. ed. 2005. Orig. Title: Can Do & the Mall. (Illus.). 34p. (J). pap. (978-0-9768384-2-5(7)) Can Do Duck Publishing.

Moskowitz, Hannah. Not Otherwise Specified: A Novel. 2015. (ENG., Illus.). 304p. (YA). (gr. 9). pap. 11.99 (978-1-4814-0595-9(0), Simon Pulse) Simon Pulse.

Moss, Alexandra. Lara's Leap of Faith. 2005. (Royal Ballet School Diaries). 138p. (J). 12.65 (978-0-7569-5894-7(6)) Perfection Learning Corp.

Moss, Marissa. Amelia's Boy Survival Guide. Moss, Marissa, illus. 2012. (Amelia Ser.). (ENG., Illus.). 80p. (J). (gr. 4-8). 9.99 (978-1-4424-4084-5(8), Simon & Schuster/Paula Wiseman Bks.) Simon & Schuster/Paula Wiseman Bks.

Murdock, Catherine Gilbert. Front & Center. 2011. (ENG.). 288p. (YA). (gr. 7). pap. 8.99 (978-0-547-40305-2(4)) Houghton Mifflin Harcourt Publishing Co.

—Heaven Is Paved with Oreos. (ENG.). 208p. (J). (gr. 5-7). 2015. pap. 6.99 (978-0-544-43932-0(5), HMH Books For Young Readers) 2013. 16.99 (978-0-547-62538-6(3)) Houghton Mifflin Harcourt Publishing Co.

—The off Season. 2011. (ENG.). 304p. (YA). (gr. 7). pap. 8.99 (978-0-618-93493-5(6)) Houghton Mifflin Harcourt Publishing Co.

Murphy, Julie. Ramona Blue. (YA). (gr. 8). 2018. (ENG.). 448p. pap. 9.99 **(978-0-06-241836-4(X))** 2017. 432p. 17.99 (978-0-06-241835-7(1)) HarperCollins Pubs.

Murphy, Julie. Side Effects May Vary. (ENG.). (YA). (gr. 9). 2015. 352p. pap. 9.99 (978-0-06-224537-3(6)) 2014. 336p. 17.99 (978-0-06-224535-9(X)) HarperCollins Pubs.

Murphy, Stuart J. Percy's Neighborhood. 2013. (I See I Learn Ser.). (ENG.). 32p. (J). (-k). lib. bdg. 14.95 (978-1-58089-480-7(1)); (Illus.). pap. 6.95 (978-1-58089-481-4(X)) Charlesbridge Publishing, Inc.

Myers, Anna. Tulsa Burning. 2004. (Illus.). 184p. (J). (gr. 3-7). 16.95 (978-0-8027-8829-0(7)) Walker & Co.

Myers, Edward. Duck & Cover. 2004. 200p. (J). per. 11.95 (978-0-9674477-8-0(X)) Montemayor Pr.

Myers, Walter Dean. The Beast. 2005. 17.00 (978-0-7569-5107-8(0)) Perfection Learning Corp.

—On a Clear Day. 2014. (ENG.). 256p. (YA). (gr. 7). 17.99 (978-0-385-38753-8(9), Crown Books For Young Readers) Random Hse. Children's Bks.

—Somewhere in the Darkness. 2008. 18.00 (978-0-7569-9060-2(2)) Perfection Learning Corp.

—Somewhere in the Darkness. 2008. (ENG., Illus.). 192p. (J). (gr. 7). pap. 8.99 (978-0-545-05577-2(6), Scholastic Paperbacks) Scholastic, Inc.

Myracle, Lauren. Bliss. 2008. (ENG.). 464p. (YA). (gr. 9-17). 16.95 (978-0-8109-7071-7(6), Amulet Bks.) Abrams, Inc.

—Peace, Love, & Baby Ducks. (ENG.). (YA). (gr. 7-18). 2010. 304p. 8.99 (978-0-14-241527-6(8), Speak) 2009. 272p. 16.99 (978-0-525-47743-3(8), Dutton Books for Young Readers) Penguin Young Readers Group.

—Rhymes with Witches. (ENG.). (YA). (gr. 8-17). 2006. 272p. pap. 7.95 (978-0-8109-9215-3(9)) 2005. 224p. 16.95 (978-0-8109-5859-3(7), Amulet Bks.) Abrams, Inc.

—Thirteen. 2009. (Winnie Years Ser.). (ENG.). 272p. (J). (gr. 3-7). 7.99 (978-0-14-241370-8(4), Puffin Books) Penguin Young Readers Group.

—Thirteen Plus One. 2011. (Winnie Years Ser.). (ENG.). 304p. (J). (gr. 5-18). 7.99 (978-0-14-241901-4(X), Puffin Books) Penguin Young Readers Group.

—Twelve. 2008. (Winnie Years Ser.). (ENG.). 224p. (J). (gr. 5-18). 7.99 (978-0-14-241091-2(8), Puffin Books) Penguin Young Readers Group.

—Yolo. 2014. (Internet Girls Ser.). (ENG., Illus.). 208p. (YA). (gr. 8-17). 16.95 (978-1-4197-0871-8(6), Amulet Bks.) Abrams, Inc.

Myracle, Lauren, et al. How to Be Bad. 2015. (ENG.). 352p. (YA). (gr. 9). pap. 9.99 (978-0-06-240568-5(3), HarperTeen) HarperCollins Pubs.

Nall, Gail. Breaking the Ice. 2015. (ENG., Illus.). 320p. (J). (gr. 3-7). 16.99 (978-1-4814-1911-6(0), Aladdin) Simon & Schuster Children's Publishing.

Nancy Mann Israel. The Juggler & His Wife. 2009. 24p. pap. 12.95 (978-1-4389-5334-2(8)) AuthorHouse.

Naylor, Phyllis Reynolds. Alice on the Outside. 2012. (Alice Ser.: 11). (ENG., Illus.). 208p. (J). (gr. 5-9). pap. 6.99 (978-1-4424-3495-0(3), Atheneum Bks. for Young Readers) Simon & Schuster Children's Publishing.

—All but Alice. 2011. (Alice Ser.: 4). (ENG.). 192p. (J). (gr. 5-9). pap. 6.99 (978-1-4424-2756-3(6), Atheneum Bks. for Young Readers) Simon & Schuster Children's Publishing.

—I Like Him, He Likes Her: Alice Alone; Simply Alice; Patiently Alice. 2010. (Alice Ser.). (ENG.). 640p. (YA). (gr. 7). pap. 12.99 (978-1-4424-0978-1(9), Atheneum Bks. for Young Readers) Simon & Schuster Children's Publishing.

—Including Alice. 2005. (Alice McKinley Ser.: No. 16). 277p. (J). (gr. 4-7). 13.65 (978-0-7569-5460-4(6)) Perfection Learning Corp.

—Simply Alice. 2003. (Alice Ser.: 14). (ENG., Illus.). 240p. (YA). (gr. 7). mass mkt. 5.99 (978-0-689-85965-6(1), Simon Pulse) Simon Pulse.

Nelson, Blake. The New Rules of High School. 2004. (ENG.). 240p. (YA). (gr. 7-18). reprint ed. 7.99 (978-0-14-240242-9(7), Speak) Penguin Young Readers Group.

Nelson, Suzanne. Hot Cocoa Hearts: a Wish Novel. 2016. (ENG.). 256p. (J). (gr. 4-7). pap. 6.99 (978-0-545-92889-2(3), Scholastic Paperbacks) Scholastic, Inc.

—Serendipity's Footsteps. 2015. (ENG.). 368p. (YA). (gr. 7). 17.99 (978-0-385-39212-9(5), Knopf Bks. for Young Readers) Random Hse. Children's Bks.

Nelson, Theresa. Ruby Electric. 2004. 264p. (J). (gr. 5-7). 13.65 (978-0-7569-3530-6(X)) Perfection Learning Corp.

—Ruby Electric. 2004. (ENG.). 272p. (J). (gr. 5-7). reprint ed. pap. 12.99 (978-0-689-87146-7(5), Atheneum Bks. for Young Readers) Simon & Schuster Children's Publishing.

Nichols, Lee. Deception. 2010. (Haunting Emma Ser.). (ENG.). 336p. (YA). (gr. 9-12). 16.99 (978-1-59990-308-8(3), 9781599903088); pap. 9.99 (978-1-59990-421-4(7), 9781599904214) Bloomsbury Publishing USA. (Bloomsbury USA Childrens).

Night, P. J. Truth or Dare ..., 1 vol. 2013. (You're Invited to a Creepover Ser.). (ENG.). 160p. (J). (gr. 3-6). lib. bdg. 24.21 (978-1-61479-065-5(5), Essential Library) ABDO Publishing Co.

—Truth or Dare... 2011. (You're Invited to a Creepover Ser.: 1). (ENG., Illus.). 160p. (J). (gr. 3-7). pap. 6.99 (978-1-4424-2096-0(0), Simon Spotlight) Simon Spotlight.

Nighthawk, Tori. Don't Judge a Bird by Its Feathers. Nighthawk, Tori, illus. 2013. (ENG., Illus.). 60p. (J). (gr. -1-3). 17.99 (978-0-9858811-9-1(4)) Stone, Anne Publishing.

Nijkamp, Marieke. This Is Where It Ends. 2016. (ENG.). 288p. (YA). (gr. 8-12). 17.99 (978-1-4926-2246-8(X), 9781492622468) Sourcebooks, Inc.

—This Is Where It Ends. 2016. lib. bdg. 22.10 (978-0-606-39479-6(6)) 2017. lib. bdg. 22.10 **(978-0-606-39992-0(5))** Turtleback Bks.

Nitz, Kristin Wolden. Defending Irene, 1 vol. 2004. (ENG.). 224p. (J). (gr. 3-7). 14.95 (978-1-56145-309-2(9)) Peachtree Pubs.

Noël, Alyson. Art Geeks & Prom Queens. 2011. (ENG.). 240p. (YA). (gr. 7-12). pap. 9.99 (978-0-312-61922-0(7), 9780312619220, St. Martin's Griffin) St. Martin's Pr.

—Forever Summer. 2011. (ENG.). 464p. (YA). (gr. 8-12). pap. 9.99 (978-0-312-60439-4(4), 9780312604394, St. Martin's Griffin) St. Martin's Pr.

Norris, Elizabeth. Unbreakable. 2013. (Unraveling Ser.: 2). (ENG.). 496p. (YA). (gr. 9). 17.99 (978-0-06-210376-5(8)) HarperCollins Pubs.

—Unraveling. (Unraveling Ser.: 1). (ENG.). (YA). (gr. 8). 2013. 480p. pap. 9.99 (978-0-06-210374-1(1)) 2012. 464p. 17.99 (978-0-06-210373-4(3)) HarperCollins Pubs.

Norris, Shana. Something to Blog About. 2008. (ENG.). 256p. (J). (gr. 2-7). 16.95 (978-0-8109-9474-4(7), Amulet Bks.) Abrams, Inc.

Northrop, Michael. Trapped. (ENG.). 240p. (J). 2012. (gr. 7). pap. 9.99 (978-0-545-21013-3(5)) 2011. (gr. 9-10). 17.99 (978-0-545-21012-6(7)) Scholastic, Inc. (Scholastic Pr.).

Norton, Tamra. Molly Married? 2003. 158p. pap. 12.95 (978-1-55517-694-5(1), 76941) Cedar Fort, Inc./CFI Distribution.

Oakes, Colleen. Blood of Wonderland. 2017. (Queen of Hearts Ser.: 2). (YA). (gr. 8). 352p. pap. 9.99 **(978-0-06-240977-5(8))**; 336p. 17.99 (978-0-06-240976-8(X)) HarperCollins Pubs. (HarperTeen).

O'Connell, Jenny. Local Girls: An Island Summer Novel. 2008. (ENG.). 320p. pap. 19.99 (978-1-4165-6335-8(0)) Pocket Books.

O'connell, Tyne. A Royal Match. 2011. (Calypso Chronicles Ser.). (ENG.). 512p. (YA). pap. 9.99 (978-1-59990-751-2(8), 9781599907512, Bloomsbury USA Childrens) Bloomsbury Publishing USA.

O'Connor, Barbara. Fame & Glory in Freedom, Georgia. 2008. (ENG.). 112p. (J). (gr. 3-7). pap. 8.99 (978-0-374-40018-7(0), 9780374400187) Square Fish.

—Greetings from Nowhere. 2008. (ENG.). 208p. (J). (gr. 5-8). 17.99 (978-0-374-39937-5(9), 9780374399375, Farrar, Straus & Giroux (BYR)) Farrar, Straus & Giroux.

—How to Steal a Dog. 2009. (ENG.). 192p. (J). (gr. 3-7). pap. 6.99 (978-0-312-56112-3(1), 9780312561123) Square Fish.

O'Dell, Kathleen. Agnes Parker... Keeping Cool in Middle School. 2008. (ENG.). 160p. (J). (gr. 3-7). 6.99 (978-0-14-241181-0(7), Puffin Books) Penguin Young Readers Group.

O'Donnell, Kerri. Sue Helps Out. 2006. (Neighborhood Readers Ser.). (ENG.). 8p. (gr. -1-3). pap. 5.15 (978-1-4042-5684-2(9), Rosen Classroom) Rosen Publishing Group, Inc., The.

O'Keefe, Susan Heyboer. My Life & Death by Alexandra Canarsie, 1 vol. 2006. (ENG.). 217p. (YA). (gr. 7-18). pap. 7.95 (978-1-56145-387-0(0)) Peachtree Pubs.

Okimoto, Jean Davies. Dear Ichiro. Keith, Doug, illus. 2006. 29p. (J). (gr. 4-8). reprint ed. 17.00 (978-1-4223-5803-0(8)) DIANE Publishing Co.

Oliver, Lauren. Before I Fall. (ENG.). (YA). (gr. 9). 2016. 544p. pap. 10.99 (978-0-06-172681-1(8)) 2010. 480p. 17.99 (978-0-06-172680-4(X)) HarperCollins Pubs.

—Before I Fall. 2010. 368p. pap. (978-0-340-98090-3(7), Hodder Paperbacks) Hodder & Stoughton.

—Before I Fall. 2016. (YA). lib. bdg. 22.10 (978-0-606-23576-1(0), Turtleback) Turtleback Bks.

Oppel, Kenneth. Starclimber. 400p. (YA). (gr. 8). 2010. pap. 9.99 (978-0-06-085059-3(0)) 2009. (Illus.). 17.99 (978-0-06-085057-9(4)) HarperCollins Pubs.

Orczy, Emmuska. Unto Caesar. 2008. 260p. 29.95 (978-1-60664-863-6(2)); pap. 15.95 (978-1-60664-110-1(7)) Aegypan.

Ostow, Micol. Gettin' Lucky. 2012. (Romantic Comedies Ser.). (ENG.). 256p. (YA). (gr. 9). pap. 12.99 (978-1-4424-8568-6(X), Simon Pulse) Simon Pulse.

Owens, Robert. Butterfly Love. 2008. 34p. pap. 16.70 (978-0-557-01168-1(X)) Lulu Pr., Inc.

Padian, Maria. Brett McCarthy: Work in Progress. 2009. (ENG.). 288p. (YA). (gr. 7). pap. 8.99 (978-0-440-24055-6(7), Knopf Bks. for Young Readers) Random Hse. Children's Bks.

Pagel, Beth. What's Wrong with Grandma? 2008. 32p. pap. 11.96 (978-0-557-00302-0(4)) Lulu Pr., Inc.

Palmer, Robin. Geek Charming. 2009. (ENG.). 368p. (YA). (gr. 7-18). 7.99 (978-0-14-241122-3(1), Speak) Penguin Young Readers Group.

—Sealed with a Kiss, 2 vols., No. 2. 2010. (Yours Truly, Lucy B. Parker Ser.: 2). (ENG.). 224p. (J). (gr. 5-18). 6.99 (978-0-14-241501-6(4), Puffin Books) Penguin Young Readers Group.

Paratore, Coleen Murtagh. Dreamsleeves. 2012. (ENG.). 288p. (J). (gr. 5-9). 16.99 (978-0-545-31020-8(2), Scholastic Pr.) Scholastic, Inc.

—Willa by Heart. 2008. (Wedding Planner's Daughter Ser.). (ENG.). 240p. (J). (gr. 3-7). 15.99 (978-1-4169-4076-0(6), Simon & Schuster Bks. For Young Readers) Simon & Schuster Bks. For Young Readers.

—Willa by Heart. 2009. (Wedding Planner's Daughter Ser.). (ENG.). 240p. (J). (gr. 4-8). pap. 6.99 (978-1-4169-7470-3(9), Aladdin) Simon & Schuster Children's Publishing.

Parker, Francis W. Uncle Robert's Geography, Uncle Robert's, Vol. 3. 2004. reprint ed. pap. 20.95 (978-1-4191-9175-6(6)) Kessinger Publishing, LLC.

—Uncle Robert's Geography, Uncle Robert's Visit, Vol. 3. 2004. reprint ed. pap. 1.99 (978-1-4192-9175-3(0)) Kessinger Publishing, LLC.

Pascal, Francine. Fearless 2: Twisted; Kiss; Payback. 2013. (Fearless Ser.). (ENG.). 656p. (YA). (gr. 9). pap. 12.99 (978-1-4424-6860-3(2), Simon Pulse) Simon Pulse.

Patron, Susan. The Higher Power of Lucky. 2008. (JPN., Illus.). 215p. (J). *(978-4-7515-2209-7(4))* Asunaro Shobo.
—The Higher Power of Lucky. 2009. 9.00 *(978-0-7848-2460-3(6),* Everbind) Marco Bk. Co.
—The Higher Power of Lucky. 2008. 17.00 *(978-1-60686-088-5(7))* Perfection Learning Corp.
—The Higher Power of Lucky. Phelan, Matt, illus. (ENG.). (J). (gr. 4-6). 2008. 160p. pap. 7.99 *(978-1-4169-7557-1(8),* Atheneum Bks. for Young Readers) 2006. 144p. 17.99 *(978-1-4169-0194-5(9),* Atheneum/Richard Jackson Bks.) Simon & Schuster Children's Publishing.
—The Higher Power of Lucky. 2008. lib. bdg. 18.40 *(978-0-606-08934-0(9),* Turtleback) Turtleback Bks.
—Lucky Breaks. Phelan, Matt, illus. 2010. (ENG.). 208p. (J). (gr. 3-7). pap. 7.99 *(978-1-4169-9772-6(5),* Atheneum Bks. for Young Readers) Simon & Schuster Children's Publishing.
—Lucky for Good. McGuire, Erin, illus. 2012. (ENG.). 224p. (J). (gr. 3-7). pap. 6.99 *(978-1-4169-9059-8(3),* Atheneum Bks. for Young Readers) Simon & Schuster Children's Publishing.
—Lucky for Good. McGuire, Erin K., illus. 2011. (ENG.). 224p. (J). (gr. 3-7). 16.99 *(978-1-4169-9058-1(5),* Atheneum Bks. for Young Readers) Simon & Schuster Children's Publishing.
Patterson, James & Papademetriou, Lisa. Homeroom Diaries. Keino, illus. 2014. (ENG.). 272p. (YA). (gr. 7-17). 18.00 *(978-0-316-20762-1(4),* Jimmy Patterson) Little Brown & Co.
Patti, Caroline. The World Spins Madly On. 2008. 144p. 21.95 *(978-0-595-71087-4(5));* pap. 11.95 *(978-0-595-47439-4(X))* iUniverse, Inc.
Paulsen, Gary. Crush: The Theory, Practice & Destructive Properties of Love. (ENG.). 144p. (J). (gr. 4-7). 2013. pap. 6.99 *(978-0-385-74231-3(2),* Yearling) 2012. 12.99 *(978-0-385-74230-6(4),* Lamb, Wendy Bks.) Random Hse. Children's Bks.
—Family Ties. 2014. (ENG.). 144p. (J). (gr. 4-7). 12.99 *(978-0-385-37380-7(5),* Lamb, Wendy Bks.) Random Hse. Children's Bks.
—Liar, Liar. 2012. (ENG.). 128p. (J). (gr. 3-7). 6.99 *(978-0-375-86611-1(6),* Yearling) Random Hse. Children's Bks.
—Vote. 2013. (ENG.). 144p. (J). (gr. 4-7). 12.99 *(978-0-385-74228-3(2),* Lamb, Wendy Bks.) Random Hse. Children's Bks.
—Vote: The Theory, Practice, & Destructive Properties of Politics. 2014. (ENG.). 144p. (J). (gr. 4-7). pap. 6.99 *(978-0-385-74229-0(0),* Yearling) Random Hse. Children's Bks.
Pearsall, Shelley. All of the Above. Steptoe, Javaka, illus. 2008. (ENG.). 256p. (J). (gr. 3-7). per. 8.00 *(978-0-316-11526-1(6))* Little, Brown Bks. for Young Readers.
Pearson, Joanna. The Rites & Wrongs of Janice Wills. 2011. (YA). pap. *(978-0-545-19774-8(0));* (ENG.). 224p. (J). (gr. 9-7). 16.99 *(978-0-545-19773-1(2))* Scholastic, Inc. (Levine, Arthur A. Bks.).
Pearson, Mary E. A Room on Lorelei Street. 2008. (ENG.). 288p. (YA). (gr. 9-13). pap. 19.99 *(978-0-312-38019-9(4),* 9780312380199) Square Fish.
Penn, Tony. The Misadventures of Michael Mcmichaels: The Creepy Campers, vol. 3. Martin, Brian, illus. 2017. (Michael Mcmichaels Ser.: 3). (ENG.). 84p. (J). pap. 7.95 ***(978-1-944882-10-5(3))*** Boys Town Pr.
Perez, Marlene. Dead Is a Battlefield. 2012. (Dead Is Ser.: 6). (ENG.). 240p. (YA). (gr. 7). pap. 7.99 *(978-0-547-60734-4(2))* Houghton Mifflin Harcourt Publishing Co.
—Dead Is a Battlefield. 2012. (Dead Is Ser.: 6). lib. bdg. 18.40 *(978-0-606-24759-7(9),* Turtleback) Turtleback Bks.
—Dead Is a Killer Tune. 2012. (Dead Is Ser.: 7). lib. bdg. 18.40 *(978-0-606-26623-9(2),* Turtleback) Turtleback Bks.
—Dead Is Just a Dream. 2014. (Dead Is Ser.: 8). (ENG.). 176p. (YA). (gr. 7). pap. 7.99 *(978-0-544-33634-6(8),* HMH Books For Young Readers) Houghton Mifflin Harcourt Publishing Co.
—Dead Is Just a Dream. 2014. (Dead Is Ser.: 8). lib. bdg. 18.40 *(978-0-606-35990-0(7))* Turtleback Bks.
—Dead Is Not an Option. 2011. (Dead Is Ser.: 5). (ENG.). 256p. (YA). (gr. 7-18). pap. 7.99 *(978-0-547-34593-2(3))* Houghton Mifflin Harcourt Publishing Co.
—Dead Is the New Black. 2008. (Dead Is Ser.: 1). (ENG., Illus.). 208p. (YA). (gr. 7-18). pap. 8.99 *(978-0-15-206408-2(7))* Houghton Mifflin Harcourt Publishing Co.
Perkins, Stephanie. Anna & the French Kiss. 2010. (ENG.). 384p. (YA). (gr. 7-18). 16.99 *(978-0-525-42327-0(3),* Dutton Books for Young Readers) Penguin Young Readers Group.
Perkins, Stephanie, ed. Summer Days & Summer Nights: Twelve Summer Romances. 2016. (ENG., Illus.). 400p. (YA). 19.99 *(978-1-250-07912-1(8),* 9781250079121, St. Martin's Griffin) St. Martin's Pr.
Perry, Jolene. All the Forever Things. 2017. (ENG.). 272p. (YA). (gr. 8-12). 16.99 *(978-0-8075-2532-6(4));* pap. 9.99 ***(978-0-8075-2534-0(0))*** Whitman, Albert & Co.
—Has to Be Love. 2015. (ENG.). 272p. (YA). (gr. 8-12). 16.99 *(978-0-8075-6557-5(1))* Whitman, Albert & Co.
Peters, Julie Anne. Keeping You a Secret. 2005. (ENG., Illus.). 272p. (YA). (gr. 10-17). pap. 10.00 *(978-0-316-00985-0(7),* Tingley, Megan Bks.) Little, Brown Bks. for Young Readers.
Peterson, Donna. Pip Goes to Camp. 2012. 9.99 *(978-1-4621-1077-3(0))* Cedar Fort, Inc./CFI Distribution.
Peterson, Matt. The Epic Tales of a Misfit Hero. 2012. pap. 8.99 *(978-1-59955-999-5(4),* Bonneville Bks.) Cedar Fort, Inc./CFI Distribution.
Peterson, Willa. It's a Mommy Day! 2011. 28p. pap. 13.99 *(978-1-4634-3592-9(4))* AuthorHouse.
Pfeffer, Susan Beth. The Shade of the Moon. (Life As We Knew It Ser.: 4). (ENG.). 304p. (YA). (gr. 7). 2014. pap. 8.99 *(978-0-544-33615-5(1),* HMH Books For Young Readers) 2013. 17.99 *(978-0-547-81337-0(6))* Houghton Mifflin Harcourt Publishing Co.
Philips, A. If You Believe in Mermaids Don't Tell. 2007. 160p. per. 12.95 *(978-1-59858-359-5(X))* Dog Ear Publishing, LLC.
Phillips, Dee. Dumped, 1 vol. unabr. ed. 2011. (Right Now! Ser.). (ENG.). 45p. (YA). (gr. 9-12). pap. 8.95 *(978-1-61651-247-7(4))* Saddleback Educational Publishing, Inc.
Pierre, Eileen. Why Is Life So Confusing? 2009. 40p. pap. 12.00 *(978-1-60693-025-0(7),* Eloquent Bks.) Strategic Book Publishing & Rights Agency (SBPRA).
Pike, Aprilynne. Destined. (Wings Ser.: 4). (ENG.). (YA). (gr. 8). 2013. 336p. pap. 9.99 *(978-0-06-166814-2(1))* 2012. 320p. 17.99 *(978-0-06-166812-8(5))* HarperCollins Pubs. (HarperTeen).
—Hechizos. 2012.Tr. of Spells. (UND & SPA.). 352p. (YA). pap. 18.95 *(978-84-96886-27-8(1))* Ediciones Urano S. A. ESP. Dist: Spanish Pubs., LLC.
—Illusions. 2012. (Wings Ser.: 3). (ENG.). 400p. (YA). (gr. 8). pap. 8.99 *(978-0-06-166811-1(7),* HarperTeen) HarperCollins Pubs.
—Spells. (Wings Ser.: 2). (ENG.). (YA). (gr. 8). 2011. 384p. pap. 9.99 *(978-0-06-166808-1(7))* 2010. 368p. 16.99 *(978-0-06-166806-7(0))* HarperCollins Pubs. (HarperTeen).
—Spells, 7 vols. 2010. (YA). 78.75 *(978-1-4407-8375-3(6))* Recorded Bks., Inc.
—Wings. 2011. (Wings Ser.: 1). (ENG.). 320p. (YA). (gr. 8). pap. 8.99 *(978-0-06-166805-0(2),* HarperTeen) HarperCollins Pubs.
Pinkney, Andrea Davis. Raven in a Dove House. 2014. (ENG.). 224p. (J). (gr. 5-7). pap. 8.99 *(978-0-544-23016-3(7),* HMH Books For Young Readers) Houghton Mifflin Harcourt Publishing Co.
Pitchford, Dean. Captain Nobody. 2010. (ENG.). 208p. (J). (gr. 3-7). 6.99 *(978-0-14-241667-9(3),* Puffin Books) Penguin Young Readers Group.
Pitcock, Tiffany. Just Friends. 2017. (ENG.). 320p. (YA). pap. 10.99 *(978-1-250-08405-7(9),* 9781250084057) Feiwel & Friends.
Plum-Ucci, Carol. Fire Will Fall. 2011. (ENG.). 492p. (YA). (gr. 9). pap. 25.99 *(978-0-547-55007-7(3))* Houghton Mifflin Harcourt Publishing Co.
Polacco, Patricia. The Junkyard Wonders. Polacco, Patricia, illus. 2010. (ENG., Illus.). 48p. (J). (gr. 1-4). 17.99 *(978-0-399-25078-1(6),* Philomel Bks.) Penguin Young Readers Group.
Pons, Lele & De la Cruz, Melissa. Surviving High School: Do It for the Vine: A Novel. 2017. (ENG.). 272p. (gr. 8). pap. 11.99 *(978-1-5011-2054-1(9),* Gallery Bks.) Gallery Bks.
Porter, Eleanor H. Miss Billy's Decision. 2006. pap. *(978-1-4068-3240-2(5))* Echo Library.
—Pollyanna. 2007. (ENG.). 184p. pap. 19.99 *(978-1-4346-0972-4(3))* Creative Media Partners, LLC.
—Pollyanna. 2016. (J). pap. *(978-1-5124-2614-4(8))* Lerner Publishing Group.
—Pollyanna. McKowen, Scott, illus. 2013. (Sterling Unabridged Classics Ser.). (ENG.). 208p. (J). (gr. 5). 9.95 *(978-1-4027-9718-7(4))* Sterling Publishing Co., Inc.
—Pollyanna. Akib, Jamel, illus. 2007. (Classic Starts(tm) Ser.). (ENG.). 160p. (J). (gr. 2-4). 6.95 *(978-1-4027-3692-6(4))* Sterling Publishing Co., Inc.
—Pollyanna. abr. ed. 2006. 210p. (J). (gr. 3-7). per. 8.99 *(978-1-59166-669-1(4))* BJU Pr.
—Pollyanna. l.t. ed. 2007. (ENG.). 206p. pap. 22.99 *(978-1-4346-1071-3(3))* Creative Media Partners, LLC.
Porter, Sarah. Lost Voices. 2011. (Lost Voices Trilogy Ser.: 1). (ENG.). 304p. (YA). (gr. 7-18). 16.99 *(978-0-547-48250-7(7))* Houghton Mifflin Harcourt Publishing Co.
—The Twice Lost. (Lost Voices Trilogy Ser.: 3). (ENG.). 480p. (YA). (gr. 7). 2014. pap. 8.99 *(978-0-547-48255-2(8),* HMH Books For Young Readers) 2013. 16.99 *(978-0-547-48252-1(3))* Houghton Mifflin Harcourt Publishing Co.
Porter, Tracey. Lark. 2011. (ENG.). 192p. (YA). (gr. 8-18). 15.99 *(978-0-06-112287-3(4),* HarperTeen) HarperCollins Pubs.
Posner, Richard. Goodnight Cinderella. 2014. (ENG.). 248p. (J). (gr. 8-11). pap. 15.95 *(978-1-59077-314-7(4))* Evans, M. & Co., Inc.
Poupart, Jean-Marie. Des Crayons Qui Trichent. 2003. (Roman Jeunesse Ser.). (FRE.). 96p. (YA). (gr. 4-7). pap. *(978-2-89021-197-1(5))* Diffusion du livre Mirabel (DLM).
—Des Photos Qui Parlent. 2003. (Roman Jeunesse Ser.). (FRE.). 96p. (YA). (gr. 4-7). pap. *(978-2-89021-162-9(2))* Diffusion du livre Mirabel (DLM).
Pratchett, Terry. Nation. 2009. 384p. (YA). (gr. 8-18). pap. 9.99 *(978-0-06-143303-0(9))* 2008. 504p. (J). pap. 16.99 *(978-0-06-170913-5(1))* 2008. 384p. (YA). (gr. 8-18). 17.99 *(978-0-06-143301-6(2))* HarperCollins Pubs.
Precious, Precious & Williams, Kashamba. Best Kept Secret. 2008. 124p. (YA). pap. 6.99 *(978-0-9729325-5-4(0))* Precioustymes Entertainment, LLC.
Prendergast, Gabrielle. Audacious, 1 vol. 2015. (ENG.). 336p. (YA). (gr. 8-12). pap. 12.95 *(978-1-4598-0264-3(0))* Orca Bk. Pubs. USA.
—Capricious, 1 vol. 2014. (ENG.). 352p. (YA). (gr. 8-12). 19.95 *(978-1-4598-0267-4(5))* Orca Bk. Pubs. USA.
Prinz, Yvonne. The Vinyl Princess. 2011. 336p. (J). pap. 8.99 *(978-0-06-171585-3(9),* HarperTeen) 2009. (ENG.). 320p. (YA). (gr. 8-18). 16.99 *(978-0-06-171583-9(2))* HarperCollins Pubs.
Prom Crashers. 2014. (Romantic Comedies Ser.). (ENG., Illus.). 256p. (YA). (gr. 9). pap. 12.99 *(978-1-4814-2747-0(4),* Simon Pulse) Simon Pulse.
Psanis, Maria. I Love My Sister but Sometimes I Don't. 2013. 70p. pap. 14.99 *(978-1-4817-0846-3(5))* AuthorHouse.
Puppy Love. 2014. (Flirt Ser.). (ENG., Illus.). 240p. (YA). (gr. 7). pap. 10.99 *(978-1-4424-8412-2(8),* Simon Pulse) Simon Pulse.
Purtill, C. Leigh. In Your Face. 2010. 240p. pap. 5.95 *(978-1-60747-780-8(7),* Pickwick Pr.) Phoenix Bks., Inc.
Rahlens, Holly-Jane. Prince William, Maximilian Minsky, & Me. 2007. (ENG.). 320p. (YA). (gr. 7-11). per. 7.99 *(978-0-7636-3299-1(6))* Candlewick Pr.
Ramsaroop, Bibi. As I Remember. 2007. 20p. per. 11.95 *(978-1-4327-0838-2(4))* Outskirts Pr., Inc.
Randle, Kristen D. Slumming. 2003. (Illus.). 240p. (J). lib. bdg. 16.89 *(978-0-06-001023-2(1),* HarperTeen) HarperCollins Pubs.
Rayban, Chloe. Drama Queen. 2004. (ENG.). 288p. (J). pap. 12.99 *(978-0-7475-6325-9(X))* Bloomsbury Publishing Plc GBR. Dist: Independent Pubs. Group.
Reed, Amy. Clean. (ENG.). (YA). (gr. 9). 2012. 304p. pap. 10.99 *(978-1-4424-1345-0(X))* 2011. 288p. 16.99 *(978-1-4424-1344-3(1))* Simon Pulse. (Simon Pulse).
—Crazy. (ENG., (YA). (gr. 9). 2013. Illus.). 416p. pap. 9.99 *(978-1-4424-1348-1(4))* 2012. 384p. 16.99 *(978-1-4424-1347-4(6))* Simon Pulse. (Simon Pulse).
Reed, Jaime. Keep Me in Mind. 2016. (ENG.). 336p. (J). (gr. 7). 17.99 *(978-0-545-88381-8(4))* Scholastic, Inc.
Refrolo, C. T. Grandchild of Mine: You & I. 2006. (J). 12.00 *(978-0-8059-6845-3(8))* Dorrance Publishing Co., Inc.
Reid, Roger. Space. 2008. (ENG.). 160p. (J). 19.95 *(978-1-58838-230-6(3),* NewSouth Bks.) NewSouth, Inc.
Reinhardt, Dana. Harmless. 2008. (ENG.). 240p. (YA). (gr. 9). pap. 8.99 *(978-0-553-49497-6(X),* Ember) Random Hse. Children's Bks.
—How to Build a House. 2009. (ENG.). 240p. (YA). (gr. 9-11). pap. 8.99 *(978-0-375-84454-6(6),* Ember) Random Hse. Children's Bks.
—The Summer I Learned to Fly. 2012. (ENG.). 224p. (YA). (gr. 7). pap. 8.99 *(978-0-385-73955-9(9),* Ember) Random Hse. Children's Bks.
—Tell Us Something True. 2016. (ENG.). 208p. (YA). (gr. 9). lib. bdg. 20.99 *(978-0-375-99066-3(6),* Lamb, Wendy Bks.) Random Hse. Children's Bks.
Reisner, Molly & Ostrow, Kim. Camp Spongebob. Martinez, Heather, illus. 2005. (Spongebob Squarepants Ser.). 32p. (gr. k-2). 14.00 *(978-0-7569-5424-6(X))* Perfection Learning Corp.
Rennison, Louise. Are These My Basoomas I See Before Me? Final Confessions of Georgia Nicolson. 2010. (Confessions of Georgia Nicolson Ser.: 10). (ENG.). 336p. (YA). (gr. 8-9). pap. 8.99 *(978-0-06-145937-5(2),* HarperTeen) HarperCollins Pubs.
—Dancing in My Nuddy-Pants. 2006. (Confessions of Georgia Nicolson Ser.: 4). (ENG.). 240p. (YA). (gr. 8). reprint ed. pap. 8.99 *(978-0-06-009748-6(5),* HarperTeen) HarperCollins Pubs.
—Knocked Out by My Nunga-Nungas. 2006. (Confessions of Georgia Nicolson Ser.: No. 3). 183p. (gr. 7-12). 19.00 *(978-0-7569-6729-1(5))* Perfection Learning Corp.
—Love Is a Many Trousered Thing. 2008. (Confessions of Georgia Nicolson Ser.: 8). (ENG.). 304p. (YA). (gr. 8). pap. 9.99 *(978-0-06-085389-1(1),* HarperTeen) HarperCollins Pubs.
—Startled by His Furry Shorts. (Confessions of Georgia Nicolson Ser.: 7). (YA). 2007. (ENG.). 304p. (gr. 8-12). pap. 9.99 *(978-0-06-085386-0(7))* 2006. 288p. (gr. 7-12). 16.99 *(978-0-06-085384-6(0))* 2006. 278p. (gr. 7-12). lib. bdg. 17.89 *(978-0-06-085385-3(9))* HarperCollins Pubs. (HarperTeen).
—Stop in the Name of Pants! (Confessions of Georgia Nicolson Ser.: 9). (YA). 2009. (ENG.). 336p. (gr. 8). pap. 9.99 *(978-0-06-145934-4(8))* 2008. 256p. (gr. 7-18). 16.99 *(978-0-06-145932-0(1))* 2008. 320p. (gr. 7-18). lib. bdg. 17.89 *(978-0-06-145933-7(X))* HarperCollins Pubs. (HarperTeen).
—Stop in the Name of Pants!, 6 vols. 2010. (Confessions of Georgia Nicolson Ser.: 9). (YA). 85.75 *(978-1-4407-7775-2(6));* 82.75 *(978-1-4407-7777-6(2));* 172.75 *(978-1-4407-7772-1(1));* 1.25 *(978-1-4407-7779-0(9));* 70.75 *(978-1-4407-7771-4(3));* 67.75 *(978-1-4407-7773-8(X))* Recorded Bks., Inc.
—The Taming of the Tights. 2013. (Misadventures of Tallulah Casey Ser.: 3). (ENG.). 320p. (YA). (gr. 8). 17.99 *(978-0-06-222620-4(7),* HarperTeen) HarperCollins Pubs.
—Then He Ate My Boy Entrancers: More Mad, Marvy Confessions of Georgia Nicolson. (Confessions of Georgia Nicolson Ser.: 6). 2006. (ENG.). 336p. (YA). (gr. 8-12). pap. 9.99 *(978-0-06-058939-4(6))* 2005. 320p. (J). lib. bdg. 16.89 *(978-0-06-058938-7(8))* HarperCollins Pubs. (HarperTeen).
—Withering Tights. (Misadventures of Tallulah Casey Ser.: 1). (ENG.). (YA). (gr. 8). 2012. 304p. pap. 8.99 *(978-0-06-179933-4(5))* 2011. 288p. 16.99 *(978-0-06-179931-0(9))* HarperCollins Pubs. (HarperTeen).
Resau, Laura. The Ruby Notebook. 2012. (ENG.). 384p. (YA). (gr. 7). pap. 9.99 *(978-0-375-84525-3(9),* Ember) Random Hse. Children's Bks.
Rettig, Liz. My Desperate Love Diary. 2007. (ENG.). 314p. (YA). (gr. 9-12). 16.95 *(978-0-8234-2033-9(7))* Holiday Hse., Inc.
Reul, Robin. My Kind of Crazy. 2016. (ENG.). 336p. (YA). (gr. 8-12). pap. 10.99 *(978-1-4926-3176-7(0),* 9781492631767) Sourcebooks, Inc.
Ricci, Christine. Helping Hands. Hall, Susan, illus. 2007. (J). pap. *(978-1-4127-8921-9(4))* Publications International, Ltd.
Rice, Luanne. The Beautiful Lost. 2017. (ENG.). 304p. (J). (gr. 7). 18.99 ***(978-1-338-11107-1(8))*** Scholastic, Inc.
Rice, Morgan. Before Dawn (Vampire, Fallen-Book 1) 2016. (ENG., Illus.). 118p. (J). pap. 6.99 *(978-1-63291-611-2(8))* Morgan Rice Bks.
Richards, Natalie D. My Secret to Tell. 2015. (ENG.). 320p. (YA). (gr. 7-12). pap. 9.99 *(978-1-4926-1571-2(4),* 9781492615712) Sourcebooks, Inc.
Ripken, Cal. Cal Ripken, Jr. 's All-Stars Out at Home. 2016. (Cal Ripken, Jr. 's All Stars Ser.). (ENG.). 224p. (J). (gr. 3-7). pap. 6.99 *(978-1-4847-2789-8(4))* Hyperion Bks. for Children.
Ripken Jr., Cal. Cal Ripken, Jr. 's All-Stars Out at Home. 2015. (Cal Ripken, Jr. 's All Stars Ser.). (ENG.). 208p. (J). (gr. 3-7). 16.99 *(978-1-4231-7867-5(X))* Hyperion Bks. for Children.
Risco, Elle D. Dora Had a Little Lamb. Savitsky, Steve, illus. 2007. (Dora the Explorer Ser.). (J). (gr. -1-2). 11.65 *(978-0-7569-8294-2(4))* Perfection Learning Corp.
Ritter, John H. Under the Baseball Moon. 2008. (ENG., Illus.). 320p. (J). (gr. 5-18). 9.99 *(978-0-14-241090-5(X),* Puffin Books) Penguin Young Readers Group.
—Under the Baseball Moon. 2008. (Illus.). 283p. (gr. 8-12). 17.00 *(978-0-7569-8934-7(5))* Perfection Learning Corp.
Rivers, Karen. The Encyclopedia of Me. 2012. (ENG., Illus.). 256p. (J). (gr. 4-7). 16.99 *(978-0-545-31028-4(8),* Levine, Arthur A. Bks.) Scholastic, Inc.
Rivers, Phoebe. Kindred Spirits. 2013. (Saranormal Ser.: 8). (ENG.). 160p. (J). (gr. 3-7). 15.99 *(978-1-4424-6853-5(X));* (Illus.). pap. 5.99 *(978-1-4424-6852-8(1))* Simon Spotlight. (Simon Spotlight).
Robico. My Little Monster 3. 2014. (My Little Monster Ser.). (ENG., Illus.). 176p. (YA). (gr. 9). pap. 10.99 *(978-1-61262-599-7(1))* Kodansha America, Inc.
—My Little Monster 4. 2014. (My Little Monster Ser.). (ENG., Illus.). 176p. (YA). pap. 10.99 *(978-1-61262-600-0(9))* Kodansha America, Inc.
Robins, Eleanor. Time to Move On, 1 vol. unabr. ed. 2011. (Carter High Senior Year Ser.). (ENG.). 50p. (YA). (gr. 9-12). pap. 7.95 *(978-1-61651-329-0(2))* Saddleback Educational Publishing, Inc.
—A Very Good Year, 1 vol. unabr. ed. 2011. (Carter High Senior Year Ser.). (ENG.). 49p. (YA). (gr. 9-12). pap. 7.95 *(978-1-61651-332-0(2))* Saddleback Educational Publishing, Inc.
—The Worst Year Ever, 1 vol. unabr. ed. 2011. (Carter High Senior Year Ser.). (ENG.). 50p. (YA). (gr. 9-12). pap. 7.95 *(978-1-61651-330-6(6))* Saddleback Educational Publishing, Inc.
Robison, Dan. Death Chant: Kimo's Battle with the Shamanic Forces. 2006. 194p. (J). pap. *(978-0-922993-52-9(1))* Marquette Bks., LLC.
Rock, J. K. Camp Forget-Me-Not. 2014. (Camp Boyfriend Ser.: 3). (ENG.). 272p. (YA). (gr. 4-6). pap. 9.95 *(978-1-939392-30-5(6),* Spencer Hill Contemporary) Spencer Hill Pr.
Ross, Elizabeth. Belle Epoque. 2014. (ENG.). 352p. (YA). (gr. 7). pap. 9.99 *(978-0-385-74147-7(2),* Ember) Random Hse. Children's Bks.
Røssland, Ingelin. Minus Me. Dawkin, Deborah, tr. from NOR. 2015. (ENG.). 288p. (gr. 4-9). pap. 10.99 *(978-1-78074-694-4(6))* Oneworld Pubns. GBR. Dist: Publishers Group West (PGW).
Roter, Jordan. Camp Rules. 2007. 260p. (J). *(978-1-4287-4603-9(X),* Dutton Adult) Penguin Publishing Group.
Rowlands, Samuel. The Bride. 2004. reprint ed. pap. 15.95 *(978-1-4191-5524-6(5));* pap. 1.99 *(978-1-4192-5524-3(X))* Kessinger Publishing, LLC.
Roy, Jennifer. Mindblind, 0 vols. unabr. ed. 2013. (ENG.). 254p. (J). (gr. 7-9). pap. 9.99 *(978-1-4778-1712-4(3),* 9781477817124, Amazon Children's Publishing) Amazon Publishing.
Ruby, Laura. Bone Gap. 368p. (YA). (gr. 9). 2016. pap. 9.99 *(978-0-06-231762-9(8))* 2015. (ENG.). 17.99 *(978-0-06-231760-5(1))* HarperCollins Pubs.
—Bone Gap. 2016. (YA). lib. bdg. 20.85 *(978-0-606-38739-2(0))* Turtleback Bks.
—Good Girls. 2008. (ENG.). 304p. (YA). (gr. 9-12). pap. 8.99 *(978-0-06-088225-9(5))* 2006. 288p. (J). lib. bdg. 17.89 *(978-0-06-088224-2(7))* 2006. (ENG.). 288p. (YA). (gr. 9-12). 16.99 *(978-0-06-088223-5(9))* HarperCollins Pubs. (HarperTeen).
—Lily's Ghosts. 2005. (Illus.). 258p. (J). (gr. 5-9). 13.65 *(978-0-7569-5115-3(1))* Perfection Learning Corp.
—Play Me. 2009. (ENG.). 336p. (YA). (gr. 9). pap. 9.99 *(978-0-06-124329-5(9),* HarperTeen) HarperCollins Pubs.
Rundell, Katherine. Cartwheeling in Thunderstorms. Castrillón, Melissa, illus. 2014. (ENG.). 256p. (J). (gr. 3-7). 17.99 *(978-1-4424-9061-1(6),* Simon & Schuster Bks. For Young Readers) Simon & Schuster Bks. For Young Readers.
—Cartwheeling in Thunderstorms. 2016. lib. bdg. 18.40 *(978-0-606-38273-1(9))* Turtleback Bks.
Rupp, Rebecca. After Eli. (ENG.). 256p. (J). (gr. 4-7). 2015. pap. 8.99 *(978-0-7636-7674-2(8))* 2012. (Illus.). 15.99 *(978-0-7636-5810-6(3))* Candlewick Pr.
—Sarah Simpson's Rules for Living. 2008. (ENG., Illus.). 96p. (J). (gr. 3-7). 14.99 *(978-0-7636-3220-5(1))* Candlewick Pr.
Russell, Paul. Immaculate Blue: A Novel. 2015. (ENG., Illus.). 340p. pap. 16.95 *(978-1-62778-095-7(5))* Cleis Pr.
Russon, Penni. Breathe. 2007. (ENG., Illus.). 368p. (YA). (gr. 9-18). 16.99 *(978-0-06-079393-7(7))* HarperCollins Pubs.
Ryan, Amy Kathleen. Vibes. 2010. (ENG.). 264p. (YA). (gr. 9). pap. 14.95 *(978-0-547-24889-9(X))* Houghton Mifflin Harcourt Publishing Co.
—Zen & Xander Undone. 2011. (ENG.). 228p. (YA). (gr. 9). pap. 13.99 *(978-0-547-55030-5(8))* Houghton Mifflin Harcourt Publishing Co.
Rylant, Cynthia. A Fine White Dust. 2006. (ENG.). 112p. (J). (gr. 5-9). pap. 6.99 *(978-1-4169-2769-3(7),* Atheneum Bks. for Young Readers) Simon & Schuster Children's Publishing.
Sachar, Louis. The Cardturner. 2011. (ENG.). 352p. (YA). (gr. 7). pap. 9.99 *(978-0-385-73663-3(0),* Ember) Random Hse. Children's Bks.
—The Cardturner. 2011. lib. bdg. 20.85 *(978-0-606-23428-3(4),* Turtleback) Turtleback Bks.
—Small Steps. 2008. (Readers Circle Ser.). 257p. (gr. 5-9). 20.00 *(978-0-7569-9130-2(7))* Perfection Learning Corp.
—Small Steps. 2008. (ENG.). 288p. (YA). (gr. 7-9). pap. 9.99 *(978-0-385-73315-1(1),* Ember) Random Hse. Children's Bks.
—Small Steps. rev. l.t. ed. 2006. 339p. 23.95 *(978-0-7862-8297-5(5))* Thorndike Pr.
Sáenz, Benjamin Alire. He Forgot to Say Goodbye. 2008. (ENG.). 336p. (YA). (gr. 7-12). 18.99 *(978-1-4169-4963-3(1),* Simon & Schuster Bks. For Young Readers) Simon & Schuster Bks. For Young Readers.
Sales, Leila. Past Perfect. 2012. (ENG.). 336p. (YA). (gr. 9). pap. 10.99 *(978-1-4424-0683-4(6),* Simon Pulse) Simon Pulse.
—This Song Will Save Your Life. 2013. (ENG.). 288p. (YA). (gr. 7). 18.99 *(978-0-374-35138-0(4),* 9780374351380, Farrar, Straus & Giroux (BYR)) Farrar, Straus & Giroux.
—Tonight the Streets Are Ours. 2015. (ENG.). 352p. (YA). (gr. 7). 17.99 *(978-0-374-37665-9(4),* 9780374376659, Farrar, Straus & Giroux (BYR)) Farrar, Straus & Giroux.
Salisbury, Graham. Extra Famous. Rogers, Jacqueline, illus. 2014. (Calvin Coconut Ser.). (ENG.). 176p. (J). (gr. 2-5). pap. 6.99 *(978-0-307-93075-0(0),* Yearling) Random Hse. Children's Bks.
—Kung Fooey. Rogers, Jacqueline, illus. 2012. (Calvin Coconut Ser.). (ENG.). 144p. (J). (gr. 2-5). 6.99 *(978-0-375-86506-0(3),* Yearling) Random Hse. Children's Bks.
—Night of the Howling Dogs. 2009. (ENG.). 208p. (YA). (gr. 7-7). mass mkt. 6.99 *(978-0-440-23839-3(0),* Laurel Leaf) Random Hse. Children's Bks.
Salisbury, Linda G. No Sisters Sisters Club: A Bailey Fish Adventure. Grotke, Christopher A., illus. 2005. 188p. (J). per. 8.95 *(978-1-881539-40-7(7))* Tabby Hse. Bks.
Sanchez, Alex. Boyfriends with Girlfriends. (ENG.). 224p. (YA). (gr. 7). 2012. pap. 10.99 *(978-1-4169-3775-3(7))* 2011. 16.99 *(978-1-4169-3773-9(0))* Simon & Schuster Bks. For Young Readers. (Simon & Schuster Bks. For Young Readers).
—Rainbow Boys. 2003. (ENG., Illus.). 262p. (YA). (gr. 7). pap. 9.99 *(978-0-689-85770-6(5),* Simon & Schuster Bks. For

H
I

Young Readers) Simon & Schuster Bks. For Young Readers.

—Rainbow Road. 2007. (ENG., Illus.). 266p. (YA). (gr. 7-12). pap. 11.99 *(978-1-4169-1191-3(X)*, Simon & Schuster Bks. For Young Readers) Simon & Schuster Bks. For Young Readers.

—So Hard to Say. Weiss, Jennifer, ed. 2006. (ENG., Illus.). 232p. (YA). (gr. 7-12). reprint ed. pap. 11.99 *(978-1-4169-1189-0(8)*, Simon & Schuster Bks. For Young Readers) Simon & Schuster Bks. For Young Readers.

Sanchez, Alex & Louth, Jack. Rainbow Road. 2005. (ENG., Illus.). 256p. (J). (gr. 7). 16.95 *(978-0-689-86565-7(1)*, Simon & Schuster Bks. For Young Readers) Simon & Schuster Bks. For Young Readers.

Sanchez, Jenny Torres. Death, Dickinson, & the Demented Life of Frenchie Garcia. 2013. (ENG.). 272p. (YA). (gr. 2-17). pap. 10.95 *(978-0-7624-4680-3(3)*, Running Pr. Kids) Running Pr. Bk. Pubs.

Sandell, Lisa Ann. A Map of the Known World. (ENG.). 288p. (J). (gr. 7-7). 2011. pap. 8.99 *(978-0-545-06971-7(8))* 2009. 16.99 *(978-0-545-06970-0(X))* Scholastic, Inc. (Scholastic Pr.).

Santopolo, Jill. Bad News Nails. 2015. (Sparkle Spa Ser.: 5). (ENG., Illus.). 128p. (J). (gr. 2-5). pap. 5.99 *(978-1-4814-2384-7(3)*, Aladdin) Simon & Schuster Children's Publishing.

—Wedding Bell Blues. 2016. (Sparkle Spa Ser.: 8). (ENG., Illus.). 112p. (J). (gr. 2-5). pap. 5.99 *(978-1-4814-2393-9(2)*, Aladdin) Simon & Schuster Children's Publishing.

Sarfati, Sonia. Comme une Peau De Chagrin. 2003. (Roman Plus Ser.). (FRE.). 160p. (YA). (gr. 8-18). pap. *(978-2-89021-242-8(4))* Diffusion du livre Mirabel (DLM).

Sasse, Connie R. & McGraw-Hill Education Staff. Families Today, 2 vols. 4th ed. 2003. (Families Today Ser.). (ENG., Illus.). 704p. (gr. 10-12). stu. ed. 85.60 *(978-0-07-829840-0(7)*, 0078298407) McGraw-Hill Education.

Say, Allen. The Favorite Daughter. 2013. (J). pap. *(978-0-545-17663-7(8)*, Levine, Arthur A. Bks.) Scholastic, Inc.

—The Favorite Daughter. Say, Allen, illus. 2013. (ENG., Illus.). 32p. (J). (gr. -1-3). 17.99 *(978-0-545-17662-0(X)*, Levine, Arthur A. Bks.) Scholastic, Inc.

Schmatz, Pat. Mousetraps. Hauser, Bill, illus. 2008. (ENG.). 192p. (YA). (gr. 7-12). 17.95 *(978-0-8225-8657-9(6)*, Carolrhoda Bks.) Lerner Publishing Group.

Schneider, Robyn. The Beginning of Everything. (ENG.). 352p. (YA). (gr. 8). 2014. pap. 9.99 *(978-0-06-221714-1(3)*, Tegen, Katherine Bks) 2013. 17.99 *(978-0-06-221713-4(5))* HarperCollins Pubs.

Scholastic, Inc. Staff & Ford, Juwanda G. Shop Talk. Hoston, Jim, illus. 2004. (Just for You Ser.). (ENG.). 32p. (gr. k-3). pap. 3.99 *(978-0-439-56873-9(0)*, Teaching Resources) Scholastic, Inc.

Schraff, Anne. The Burning of the Valley. 2008. (Passages to History Ser.). 115p. (J). (gr. 4-6). lib. bdg. 13.95 *(978-0-7569-8400-7(9))* Perfection Learning Corp.

—Just Another Name for Lonely. 2008. (Passages Ser.). 107p. (J). (gr. 4-7). pap. 8.50 *(978-0-7891-7560-1(6))* Perfection Learning Corp.

—The Lost, 1 vol. unabr. ed. 2011. (Urban Underground Ser.). (ENG.). 198p. (YA). (gr. 9-12). pap. 9.95 *(978-1-61651-585-0(6))* Saddleback Educational Publishing, Inc.

—Lost & Found. Langan, Paul, ed. 2007. (Bluford High Ser.). 133p. (gr. 8-12). 16.00 *(978-0-7569-8076-4(3))* Perfection Learning Corp.

—Lost & Found. 2007. (Bluford High — Scholastic Ser.: 1). lib. bdg. 16.00 *(978-1-4177-7141-7(0)*, Turtleback) Turtleback Bks.

Schraff, Anne E. Misjudged. 2014. (Urban Underground — Cesar Chavez High School Ser.). (YA). lib. bdg. 20.80 *(978-0-606-35589-6(8))* Turtleback Bks.

Schreiber, Ellen. The Beginning. 2009. (Vampire Kisses Ser.: Nos. 1-3). (ENG.). 576p. (YA). (gr. 8). pap. 9.99 *(978-0-06-177894-0(X)*, Tegen, Katherine Bks) HarperCollins Pubs.

—Vampire Kisses. 2003. (Vampire Kisses Ser.: 1). (ENG.). 208p. (YA). (gr. 8-18). 17.99 *(978-0-06-009334-1(X)*, Tegen, Katherine Bks) HarperCollins Pubs.

—Vampire Kisses: Finstere Sehnsucht / Dunkle Ahnung / Düsteres Versprechen. 2005. (Vampire Kisses Ser.: No. 1). 272p. (YA). (gr. 7-18). reprint ed. pap. 5.99 *(978-0-06-009336-5(6)*, Harper Trophy) HarperCollins Pubs.

—Vampire Kisses: Finstere Sehnsucht / Dunkle Ahnung / Düsteres Versprechen. l.t. ed. 2008. (Vampire Kisses Ser.: No. 1). 294p. (YA). 22.95 *(978-1-4104-0727-6(6))* Thorndike Pr.

—Vampire Kisses Boxed Set: Vampire Kisses; Kissing Coffins; Vampireville. 2008. (Vampire Kisses Ser.: Nos. 1-3). (J). pap. 15.99 *(978-0-06-169160-7(7)*, HarperTeen) HarperCollins Pubs.

Schreiber, Joe. Lenny Cyrus, School Virus. Smith, Matt, illus. 2014. (ENG.). 288p. (J). (gr. 5-7). pap. 6.99 *(978-0-544-33628-5(3)*, HMH Books For Young Readers) Houghton Mifflin Harcourt Publishing Co.

Schroeder, Lisa. Chasing Brooklyn. (ENG.). 432p. (YA). (gr. 9). 2011. pap. 11.99 *(978-1-4169-9174-8(3))* 2010. 15.99 *(978-1-4169-9168-7(9))* Simon Pulse. (Simon Pulse).

—The Day Before. (ENG.). (YA). (gr. 9). 2012. 336p. pap. 9.99 *(978-1-4424-1744-1(7))* 2011. 320p. 16.99 *(978-1-4424-1743-4(9))* Simon Pulse. (Simon Pulse).

Schroeder, Lisa. Keys to the City. 2017. (ENG.). 240p. (J). (gr. 3-7). 16.99 ***(978-0-545-90738-5(1)***, Scholastic Pr.) Scholastic, Inc.

Schumacher, Julie. The Unbearable Book Club for Unsinkable Girls. 2013. (ENG.). 240p. (YA). (gr. 7). pap. 8.99 *(978-0-375-85127-8(5)*, Ember) Random Hse. Children's Bks.

Schutz, Samantha. You Are Not Here. 2010. (ENG.). 304p. (J). (gr. 9-18). 17.99 *(978-0-545-16911-0(9)*, PUSH) Scholastic, Inc.

Schwemm, Diane. The Year I Turned Sixteen: Rose, Daisy, Laurel, Lily. 2010. (ENG.). 720p. (YA). (gr. 7). pap. 12.99 *(978-1-4169-8597-6(2)*, Simon Pulse) Simon Pulse.

Scott, Elizabeth. The Unwritten Rule. (ENG.). (YA). (gr. 9). 2011. 240p. pap. 9.99 *(978-1-4169-7892-3(5))* 2010. 224p. 16.99 *(978-1-4169-7891-6(7))* Simon Pulse. (Simon Pulse).

Scott, Kieran. He's So Not Worth It. (He's So/She's So Trilogy Ser.). (ENG.). (YA). (gr. 7). 2012. 384p. pap. 9.99 *(978-1-4169-9954-6(X))* 2011. 368p. 17.99 *(978-1-4169-9953-9(1))* Simon & Schuster Bks. For Young Readers. (Simon & Schuster Bks. For Young Readers).

—She's So Dead to Us. (He's So/She's So Trilogy Ser.). (ENG.). (YA). (gr. 7). 2011. 304p. pap. 9.99 *(978-1-4169-9952-2(3))* 2010. 288p. 16.99 *(978-1-4169-9951-5(5))* Simon & Schuster Bks. For Young Readers. (Simon & Schuster Bks. For Young Readers).

Scott, Kieran & Scott, Kiernan. Brunettes Strike Back. 2007. (ENG.). 272p. (YA). (gr. 7-18). 8.99 *(978-0-14-240778-3(X)*, Speak) Penguin Young Readers Group.

Scott, Mary Ann. New Girl, 1 vol. 2003. (ENG.). 208p. (YA). *(978-1-55041-725-8(8))* Fitzhenry & Whiteside, Ltd.

Scott, Mindi. Freefall. 2010. (ENG.). 336p. (YA). (gr. 9-18). pap. 8.99 *(978-1-4424-0278-2(4)*, Simon Pulse) Simon Pulse.

Second Look. 64p. (YA). (gr. 6-12). pap. *(978-0-8224-2385-0(5))* Globe Fearon Educational Publishing.

Seles, Monica. Love Match. 2014. (Academy Ser.). (ENG.). 224p. (YA). (gr. 7). pap. 9.99 *(978-1-59990-902-8(2)*, 9781599909028, Bloomsbury USA Childrens) Bloomsbury Publishing USA.

Seles, Monica & LaRosa, James. Game On. 2013. (Academy Ser.). (ENG.). 256p. (YA). (gr. 7). 17.99 *(978-1-59990-976-9(6)*, 9781599909769); pap. 9.99 *(978-1-59990-901-1(4)*, 9781599909011) Bloomsbury Publishing USA. (Bloomsbury USA Childrens).

Serle, Rebecca. The Edge of Falling. 2014. (ENG., Illus.). 304p. (YA). (gr. 9). 17.99 *(978-1-4424-3316-8(7)*, Simon Pulse) Simon Pulse.

Serrano, Pet. Best Friends No Matter What. 2007. (Illus.). 32p. (J). pap. *(978-0-9770497-9-0(5)*, Itty Bitty Kitty) Singing Moon Pr.

Shade, Jeff. An Unusual Education. 2010. (J). pap. *(978-0-88092-317-0(2))* Royal Fireworks Publishing Co.

Shapiro, Lawrence E. Freddy Fights Fat: An Emotional Literacy Book. Harpster, Steve, illus. 2004. (Emotional Literacy Ser.). 54p. (J). (gr. 2-18). 14.95 *(978-0-9747789-5-2(8)*, 67873) CTC Publishing.

Sharafeddine, Fatima. The Servant, 1 vol. 2017. (ENG.). 160p. (J). (gr. 6). pap. 9.95 *(978-1-55498-308-7(8))* Groundwood Bks. CAN. Dist: Publishers Group West (PGW).

Shaw-Burns, Carol. Grandma's House: Jacob's Adventure. 2012. 24p. pap. 17.99 *(978-1-4685-5318-5(6))* AuthorHouse.

Shaw, Tucker. The Girls. 2010. (ENG.). 224p. (YA). (gr. 7-11). pap. 7.95 *(978-0-8109-8991-7(3)*, Amulet Bks.) Abrams, Inc.

Shaw, Tucker & Luce, Clare Boothe. The Girls. 2009. (ENG.). 208p. (YA). (gr. 7-11). 17.95 *(978-0-8109-8348-9(6)*, Amulet Bks.) Abrams, Inc.

Sheldon, Dyan. Confessions of a Teenage Drama Queen. movie tie-in ed. 2004. (J). 107.82 *(978-0-7636-2538-2(8))* Candlewick Pr.

—Confessions of a Teenage Hollywood Star. 2007. (ENG., Illus.). 208p. (YA). (gr. 7-12). per. 7.99 *(978-0-7636-3408-7(5))* Candlewick Pr.

—The Crazy Things Girls Do for Love. (ENG.). 352p. (YA). (gr. 7). 2013. pap. 8.99 *(978-0-7636-6468-8(5))* 2011. (Illus.). 16.99 *(978-0-7636-5018-6(8))* Candlewick Pr.

—My Worst Best Friend. 2010. (ENG., Illus.). 304p. (YA). (gr. 7-18). 15.99 *(978-0-7636-4555-7(9))* Candlewick Pr.

—One or Two Things I Learned about Love. 2013. (ENG.). 304p. (YA). (gr. 7). 15.99 *(978-0-7636-6665-1(3))* Candlewick Pr.

—Planet Janet. (ENG., 240p. (YA). (gr. 9-18). 2004. Illus.). pap. 6.99 *(978-0-7636-2556-6(6))* 2003. 14.99 *(978-0-7636-2048-6(3))* Candlewick Pr.

—Sophie Pitt-Turnbull Discovers America. 2007. (ENG.). 192p. (YA). (gr. 7-12). per. 7.99 *(978-0-7636-3295-3(3))* Candlewick Pr.

Sherman, Susan & Poryes, Michael. That's So Raven, 2 vols., Vol. 1. 2004. (Illus.). 192p. pap. 14.99 *(978-1-59182-806-8(6)*, Tokyopop Kids) TOKYOPOP, Inc.

Sheth, Kashmira. Koyal Dark, Mango Sweet. (ENG.). 224p. (gr. 7-17). 2006. 15.99 *(978-0-7868-3857-8(4))* 2007. pap. 7.99 *(978-0-7868-3858-5(2))* Hyperion Pr.

Shoup, Barbara. Wish You Were Here. 2008. (ENG.). 336p. (YA). (gr. 7). pap. 9.95 *(978-0-7387-1355-7(4)*, Flux) North Star Editions.

Shull, Megan. The Swap. 2014. (ENG.). 400p. (J). (gr. 5-9). 16.99 *(978-0-06-231169-6(7)*, Tegen, Katherine Bks) HarperCollins Pubs.

Shulman, Polly. Enthusiasm. 2007. (ENG.). 224p. (YA). (gr. 7-18). pap. 8.99 *(978-0-14-240935-0(9)*, Speak) Penguin Young Readers Group.

Shusterman, Neal. Antsy Does Time. 2010. (ENG.). 256p. (J). (gr. 5-18). pap. 6.99 *(978-0-14-241487-3(5)*, Puffin Books) Penguin Young Readers Group.

—Bruiser. 2010. (ENG.). 336p. (YA). (gr. 9-18). 17.99 *(978-0-06-113408-1(2)*, HarperTeen) HarperCollins Pubs.

Siddoway, Richard M. The Cottage Park Puzzle. 2015. 200p. (YA). pap. 14.99 *(978-1-4621-1562-4(4))* Cedar Fort, Inc./CFI Distribution.

Silver, Eve. Crash. 2015. (Game Ser.: 3). (ENG.). 368p. (YA). (gr. 9). 17.99 *(978-0-06-219219-6(1)*, Tegen, Katherine Bks) HarperCollins Pubs.

—Rush. (Game Ser.: 1). (ENG.). (YA). (gr. 9). 2014. 384p. pap. 9.99 *(978-0-06-219214-1(0)*, Tegen, Katherine Bks) 2013. 368p. 17.99 *(978-0-06-219213-4(2))* HarperCollins Pubs.

Silver, Gail. Peace, Bugs, & Understanding: An Adventure in Sibling Harmony. Ly, Youme Nguyen, illus. 2014. (ENG.). 48p. (J). (gr. -1-3). 16.95 *(978-1-937006-63-1(8)*, Plum Blossom Bks.) Parallax Pr.

Silvey, Craig. Jasper Jones. 2012. 20.00 *(978-1-61383-806-8(9))* Perfection Learning Corp.

—Jasper Jones. 2012. (ENG.). 320p. (YA). (gr. 7). pap. 9.99 *(978-0-375-86627-2(2)*, Ember) Random Hse. Children's Bks.

Simmons, Vikk. Divided Loyalties. 2004. 150p. (YA). per. 12.95 *(978-1-58749-484-0(1)*, Byte/Me Teen Bk.) Awe-Struck Publishing.

Simner, Janni Lee. Secret of the Three Treasures. 2006. (ENG.). 160p. (YA). (gr. 8-12). 16.95 *(978-0-8234-1914-2(2))* Holiday Hse., Inc.

Simon, Coco. Alexis & the Perfect Recipe. 2013. (Cupcake Diaries: 4). (ENG., Illus.). 160p. (J). (gr. 3-7). 15.99 *(978-1-4424-7493-2(9)*, Simon Spotlight) Simon Spotlight.

—Alexis Cupcake Crush. 2016. (Cupcake Diaries: 28). (ENG., Illus.). 160p. (J). (gr. 3-7). pap. 6.99 *(978-1-4814-6060-6(9)*, Simon Spotlight) Simon Spotlight.

—Alexis Cupcake Crush. 2016. (Cupcake Diaries: 28). lib. bdg. 17.20 *(978-0-606-38968-6(7))* Turtleback Bks.

Simone, Ni-Ni & London, Kelli. The Break-Up Diaries. 2011. (ENG.). 272p. (YA). (gr. 9-18). 9.95 *(978-0-7582-6316-2(3)*, K-Teen/Dafina) Kensington Publishing Corp.

Singer, Marilyn, ed. Face Relations: 11 Stories about Seeing Beyond Color. 2013. (ENG., Illus.). 240p. (YA). (gr. 7). pap. 11.99 *(978-1-4424-9616-3(9)*, Simon & Schuster Bks. For Young Readers) Simon & Schuster Bks. For Young Readers.

Skovron, Jon. Struts & Frets. (ENG.). 304p. (YA). 2011. (gr. 9-17). pap. 7.95 *(978-1-4197-0028-6(6))* 2009. (gr. 7-11). 16.95 *(978-0-8109-4174-8(0))* Abrams, Inc. (Amulet Bks.).

Skye, Evelyn. The Crown's Game. (Crown's Game Ser.: 1). (ENG.). (YA). (gr. 8). 2017. 432p. pap. 9.99 *(978-0-06-242259-0(6))* 2016. 416p. 17.99 *(978-0-06-242258-3(8))* HarperCollins Pubs.

—The Crown's Game. 2017. (Crown's Game Ser.: bk.1). (ENG.). (J). lib. bdg. 20.85 ***(978-0-606-39645-5(4))*** Turtleback Bks.

Slater, David Michael. The Sharpest Tool in the Shed, 1 vol. Reibeling, Brandon, illus. 2007. (Missy Swiss & More Ser.). (ENG.). 32p. (gr. -1-4). 28.50 *(978-1-60270-013-0(3)*, Looking Glass Library) ABDO Publishing Co.

Sloan, Brian. A Really Nice Prom Mess. 2008. (ENG., Illus.). 320p. (YA). (gr. 9-12). pap. 8.99 *(978-1-4169-5389-0(2)*, Simon & Schuster Bks. For Young Readers) Simon & Schuster Bks. For Young Readers.

Smale, Holly. Geek Girl. 2015. (Geek Girl Ser.: 1). 384p. (YA). (gr. 8). 17.99 *(978-0-06-233357-5(7)*, HarperTeen) HarperCollins Pubs.

Smiletown's Upside Down. 2007. (J). per. 14.95 *(978-0-9785132-3-8(1))* Smile-a-Lot, LLP.

Smith, Andrew. Stand-off. Bosma, Sam, illus. 2016. (ENG.). 432p. (YA). (gr. 7). pap. 10.99 *(978-1-4814-1830-0(0)*, Simon & Schuster Bks. For Young Readers) Simon & Schuster Bks. For Young Readers.

—Winger. Bosma, Sam, illus. (ENG.). (YA). (gr. 7). 2014. 464p. pap. 11.99 *(978-1-4424-4493-5(2))* 2013. 448p. 16.99 *(978-1-4424-4492-8(4))* Simon & Schuster Bks. For Young Readers. (Simon & Schuster Bks. For Young Readers).

Smith, Bryan. Of Course It's a Big Deal. Griffin, Lisa, illus. 2017. (Executive Function Ser.: 3). (ENG.). 32p. (J). (gr. k-5). pap. 10.95 ***(978-1-944882-11-2(1))*** Boys Town Pr.

Smith, D. James. Probably the World's Best Story about a Dog & the Girl Who Loved Me. 2011. (ENG.). 256p. (J). pap. 5.99 *(978-1-4169-9652-1(4)*, Atheneum Bks. for Young Readers) Simon & Schuster Children's Publishing.

—Probably the World's Best Story about a Dog & The Girl Who Loved Me. 2010. (ENG.). 240p. (J). (gr. 4-7). pap. 11.99 *(978-1-4424-2194-3(0)*, Atheneum Bks. for Young Readers) Simon & Schuster Children's Publishing.

Smith, Jennifer E. The Comeback Season. 2008. (ENG.). 256p. (YA). (gr. 8). 15.99 *(978-1-4169-3847-7(8)*, Simon & Schuster Bks. For Young Readers) Simon & Schuster Bks. For Young Readers.

Smith, L. J. The Awakening & the Struggle, 2 vols. 2007. (Vampire Diaries: 1). 492p. (YA). (gr. 7). lib. bdg. 20.85 *(978-1-4178-2599-8(5)*, Turtleback) Turtleback Bks.

—Dark Visions: The Strange Power - The Possessed - The Passion. 2009. (Dark Visions Ser.: Bks 1-3). (ENG.). 752p. (YA). (gr. 7). pap. 9.99 *(978-1-4169-8956-1(0)*, Simon Pulse) Simon Pulse.

—Destiny Rising. 2012. (Vampire Diaries: the Hunters Ser.: 3). (ENG.). 400p. (YA). (gr. 9). 17.99 *(978-0-06-201773-4(X)*, HarperTeen) HarperCollins Pubs.

—Midnight. (Vampire Diaries: the Return Ser.: 3). (ENG.). (YA). (gr. 8). 2012. 592p. pap. 9.99 *(978-0-06-172086-4(0))* 2011. 576p. 17.99 *(978-0-06-172085-7(2))* HarperCollins Pubs. (HarperTeen).

—Moonsong Vol. 9. 2013. (Vampire Diaries: the Hunters Ser.: 2). (ENG.). 416p. (YA). (gr. 9). pap. 10.99 *(978-0-06-201771-0(3)*, HarperTeen) HarperCollins Pubs.

—Nightfall. (Vampire Diaries: the Return Ser.: 1). (ENG.). (YA). (gr. 8). 2010. 608p. pap. 9.99 *(978-0-06-172080-2(1))* 2009. 592p. 17.99 *(978-0-06-172077-2(1))* HarperCollins Pubs. (HarperTeen).

—Phantom. (Vampire Diaries: the Hunters Ser.: 1). (ENG.). (YA). (gr. 9). 2012. 432p. pap. 9.99 *(978-0-06-201769-7(1))* 2011. 416p. 17.99 *(978-0-06-201768-0(3))* HarperCollins Pubs. (HarperTeen).

—Shadow Souls. (Vampire Diaries: the Return Ser.: 2). (ENG.). (YA). (gr. 8). 2011. 624p. pap. 9.99 *(978-0-06-172083-3(6))* 2010. (Illus.). 608p. 17.99 *(978-0-06-172081-9(X))* HarperCollins Pubs. (HarperTeen).

Smith, L. J. & Williamson, Kevin. The Asylum. 2012. (Vampire Diaries: Stefan's Diaries: 5). (ENG.). 256p. (YA). (gr. 9). pap. 9.99 *(978-0-06-211395-5(X)*, HarperTeen) HarperCollins Pubs.

Smith, Michelle. Play On. 2015. (Lewis Creek Ser.: 1). (ENG.). 296p. (YA). (gr. 10-12). pap. 9.95 *(978-1-939392-59-6(4)*, Spencer Hill Contemporary) Spencer Hill Pr.

Smith, Yeardley. I, Lorelei. 2009. 352p. (J). (gr. 3-7). lib. bdg. 17.89 *(978-0-06-149345-4(7)*, Geringer, Laura Book) HarperCollins Pubs.

Snow, Carol. Bubble World. 2014. (ENG.). 352p. (YA). (gr. 7). pap. 9.99 *(978-1-250-04441-9(3)*, 9781250044419) Square Fish.

—Switch. 2009. (ENG.). 240p. (YA). (gr. 8). pap. 8.99 *(978-0-06-145210-9(6)*, HarperTeen) HarperCollins Pubs.

Sommer, Bill & Tilghman, Natalie. A 52-Hertz Whale. 2015. (ENG.). 200p. (YA). (gr. 8-12). 18.99 *(978-1-4677-7917-3(2))* Lerner Publishing Group.

Sommer, Bill & Tilghman, Natalie Haney. A 52-Hertz Whale. 2015. (ENG.). 200p. (YA). (gr. 8-12). 18.99 *(978-1-4677-8811-3(2)*, Carolrhoda Lab™) Lerner Publishing Group.

Sones, Sonya. One of Those Hideous Books Where the Mother Dies. (ENG., (YA). (gr. 7). 2013. Illus.). 288p. pap. 9.99 *(978-1-4424-9383-4(6))* 2005. 272p. reprint ed. pap. 7.99 *(978-1-4169-0788-6(2))* Simon & Schuster Bks. For Young Readers. (Simon & Schuster Bks. For Young Readers).

Spangler, Brie. Beast. 2016. (ENG.). 336p. (YA). (gr. 7). 17.99 *(978-1-101-93716-7(5)*, Knopf Bks. for Young Readers) Random Hse. Children's Bks.

Spera, Carole. Oh My Goodness! 2009. 28p. pap. 12.99 *(978-1-4389-4874-4(3))* AuthorHouse.

Spooner, M. Entrapment. 2010. (ENG.). 320p. (YA). (gr. 8). pap. 8.99 *(978-1-4424-0366-6(7)*, McElderry, Margaret K. Bks.) McElderry, Margaret K. Bks.

—Entr@pment: A High School Comedy in Chat. 2009. (ENG.). 320p. (YA). (gr. 8-18). 16.99 *(978-1-4169-5889-5(4)*, McElderry, Margaret K. Bks.) McElderry, Margaret K. Bks.

Spyri, Johanna. Rico & Stineli. 2006. 148p. (gr. 4-7). per. 11.95 *(978-1-59818-873-8(9))* Aegypan.

St. Anthony, Jane. Grace above All. 2015. (Fesler-Lampert Minnesota Heritage Ser.). (ENG.). 176p. pap. 9.95 *(978-0-8166-9814-1(7))* Univ. of Minnesota Pr.

—The Summer Sherman Loved Me. 2015. (Fesler-Lampert Minnesota Heritage Ser.). (ENG.). 144p. pap. 9.95 *(978-0-8166-9815-8(5))* Univ. of Minnesota Pr.

Standiford, Natalie. Ex-Rating. 4th rev. ed. 2006. (ENG.). 224p. (YA). (gr. 7-17). per. 17.99 *(978-0-316-15876-3(3))* Little, Brown Bks. for Young Readers.

Stangl, Katrin, illus. Strong As a Bear. 2016. (ENG.). 40p. (J). (gr. -1-3). 16.95 *(978-1-59270-198-8(1))* Enchanted Lion Bks., LLC.

Steinkellner, Teddy. Trash Can Days: A Middle School Saga. 2013. (Trash Can Days Ser.). (ENG.). 352p. (J). (gr. 5-9). 16.99 *(978-1-4231-6632-0(9))* Disney Pr.

Stevens, Travis. I Ain't Mad at YA. 2006. (Illus.). 208p. per. 15.00 *(978-0-9745075-5-2(5))* Amiaya Entertainment.

Stevenson, Robin. Ben's Robot, 1 vol. Parkins, David, illus. 2010. (Orca Echoes Ser.). (ENG.). 64p. (J). (gr. 2-3). pap. 6.95 *(978-1-55469-153-1(2))* Orca Bk. Pubs. USA.

Stine, R. L. The Lost Girl: A Fear Street Novel. 2015. (Fear Street Ser.). (ENG.). 272p. (YA). 17.99 *(978-1-250-05163-9(0)*, 9781250051639, St. Martin's Griffin) St. Martin's Pr.

Stoehr, Shelley. Tomorrow Wendy: A Love Story. 2003. 176p. (YA). pap. 14.95 *(978-0-595-26954-9(0)*, Backinprint.com) iUniverse, Inc.

Stokes, Jordan & Belinkie, Matt. Gilded Delirium. 2007. (YA). pap. *(978-1-4114-9670-5(1)*, Spark Publishing Group) Sterling Publishing Co., Inc.

Stokes, Paula. The Art of Lainey. 2014. (Art of Lainey Ser.). (ENG.). 384p. (YA). (gr. 9). pap. 9.99 *(978-0-06-223842-9(6)*, HarperTeen) HarperCollins Pubs.

Stone, Heather Duffy. This Is What I Want to Tell You. 2009. (ENG.). 240p. (YA). (gr. 7-18). pap. 9.95 *(978-0-7387-1450-9(X)*, Flux) North Star Editions.

Stone, Tamara Ireland. Time & Time Again. 2017. (ENG.). 736p. (YA). (gr. 7-12). pap. 11.99 ***(978-1-4847-8133-3(3))*** Hyperion Bks. for Children.

Stork, Francisco X. Marcelo in the Real World. 2011. 9.64 *(978-0-7848-3609-5(4)*, Everbind) Marco Bk. Co.

—Marcelo in the Real World. (ENG.). 320p. (J). (gr. 7-7). 2011. pap. 9.99 *(978-0-545-05690-8(X)*, Scholastic Paperbacks) 2009. (Illus.). 17.99 *(978-0-545-05474-4(5)*, Levine, Arthur A. Bks.) Scholastic, Inc.

—Marcelo in the Real World. l.t. ed. 2010. (ENG.). 420p. 23.99 *(978-1-4104-2751-9(X))* Thorndike Pr.

Strasnick, Lauren. Her & Me & You. (ENG.). 208p. (YA). (gr. 9). 2011. pap. 9.99 *(978-1-4169-8267-8(1))* 2010. 16.99 *(978-1-4169-8266-1(3))* Simon Pulse. (Simon Pulse).

Strasnick, Lauren. 16 Ways to Break a Heart. 2017. 208p. (YA). (gr. 9). 17.99 ***(978-0-06-241872-2(6)***, Tegen, Katherine Bks) HarperCollins Pubs.

Strasser, Todd. Boot Camp. 2012. (ENG.). 272p. (YA). (gr. 7). pap. 11.99 *(978-1-4424-3358-8(2)*, Simon & Schuster Bks. For Young Readers) Simon & Schuster Bks. For Young Readers.

—Boot Camp. 2007. (ENG.). 256p. (YA). (gr. 7-12). 16.99 *(978-1-4169-0848-7(X))* Simon & Schuster Children's Publishing.

—Boot Camp. 2008. (ENG., Illus.). 256p. (YA). (gr. 7). mass mkt. 7.99 *(978-1-4169-5942-7(4)*, Simon Pulse) Simon Pulse.

Stratton-Porter, Gene. At the Foot of the Rainbow. 2007. 180p. 18.95 *(978-1-934169-52-0(8))*; pap. 7.95 *(978-1-934169-53-7(6))* Norilana Bks.

Streblow, Mary. The Family of Man. 2005. 28p. 14.01 *(978-1-4116-5564-5(8))* Lulu Pr., Inc.

Strohm, Stephanie Kate. Confederates Don't Wear Couture: A Tale of Heartache, Haunting, & Hoop Skirts. 2013. (ENG.). 240p. (YA). (gr. 7). pap. 13.99 *(978-0-547-97258-9(X))* Houghton Mifflin Harcourt Publishing Co.

—It's Not Me, It's You. (ENG.). 288p. (gr. 7). 2017. (J). pap. 9.99 ***(978-1-338-16066-6(4))*** 2016. (YA). 17.99 *(978-0-545-95258-3(1))* Scholastic, Inc.

Strohm, Stephanie Kate. Pilgrims Don't Wear Pink. 2012. (ENG.). 208p. (YA). (gr. 7). pap. 8.99 *(978-0-547-56459-3(7))* Houghton Mifflin Harcourt Publishing Co.

Stuart, Tara. Tara's Tales: Lake. 2013. 34p. pap. 17.99 *(978-1-4575-2187-4(3))* Dog Ear Publishing, LLC.

Suen, Anastasia. New Girl: An Up2U Character Education Adventure, 1 vol. Dippold, Jane, illus. 2013. (Up2U Adventures Ser.). (ENG.). 80p. (J). (gr. 2-5). lib. bdg. 27.07 *(978-1-61641-968-4(7)*, Calico Chapter Bks) Magic Wagon.

Sugg, Zoe. Girl Online: On Tour. 2016. (ENG.). (Girl Online Book Ser.: 2). 368p. (gr. 7). pap. 11.99 *(978-1-5011-0034-5(3)*, Atria Bks.); (J). pap. 13.00 ***(978-1-5011-5958-9(5))*** Simon & Schuster.

—Girl Online - On Tour. 2015. (Girl Online Book Ser.: 2). (ENG., Illus.). 352p. (gr. 7-12). 17.99 *(978-1-5011-0033-8(5)*, Atria Bks.) Simon & Schuster.

Summers, Courtney. All the Rage. (ENG.). 336p. (YA). 2016. pap. 10.99 *(978-1-250-06915-3(7)*, 9781250069153) 2015. (gr. 9-13). 18.99 *(978-1-250-02191-5(X)*, 9781250021915) St. Martin's Pr. (St. Martin's Griffin).

—Cracked up to Be. 2008. (ENG.). 224p. (YA). (gr. 9-18). pap. 12.99 *(978-0-312-38369-5(X)*, 9780312383695, St. Martin's Griffin) St. Martin's Pr.

—Fall for Anything. 2010. (ENG.). 240p. (YA). (gr. 7-18). pap. 15.99 *(978-0-312-65673-7(4)*, 9780312656737, St. Martin's Griffin) St. Martin's Pr.

Supplee, Suzanne. Artichoke's Heart. 2009. (ENG.). 288p. (YA). (gr. 7-18). 8.99 *(978-0-14-241427-9(1)*, Speak) Penguin Young Readers Group.

Sutcliffe, Kathy. When Romeo Kissed Mercutio. 2012. (ENG.). 240p. pap. *(978-1-922120-28-1(6)*, IP Digital) Interactive Pubns. Pty, Ltd.

Sutherland, Tui T. This Must Be Love. 256p. (J). 2005. pap. 7.99 *(978-0-06-056477-3(6)*, Harper Trophy) 2004. (gr. 7-18). lib. bdg. 16.89 *(978-0-06-056476-6(8))* HarperCollins Pubs.

Sutton, Kelsey. The Lonely Ones. 2016. (ENG.). 240p. (J). (gr. 5). 16.99 *(978-0-399-17289-2(0)*, Philomel Bks.) Penguin Young Readers Group.

Swaab, Neil. Class Election. 2016. (Secrets to Ruling School Ser.: 2). (ENG., Illus.). 240p. (YA). (gr. 5-9). 13.95 *(978-1-4197-2126-7(7)*, Amulet Bks.) Abrams, Inc.

—Without Even Trying, Bk. 1. 2015. (Secrets to Ruling School Ser.). (ENG., Illus.). 240p. (J). (gr. 5-9). 13.95 *(978-1-4197-1221-0(7)*, Amulet Bks.) Abrams, Inc.

Swallow, Pamela. It Only Looks Easy. 2009. (ENG.). 192p. (J). (gr. 3-7). pap. 9.99 *(978-0-312-56114-7(8)*, 9780312561147) Square Fish.

Tabak, Lawrence. In Real Life. 2014. (ENG.). 288p. (J). (gr. 7-12). 16.99 *(978-0-8048-4478-9(X))* Tuttle Publishing.

Taekema, Sylvia. Ripple Effect, 1 vol. 2015. (ENG.). 144p. (J). (gr. 4-7). pap. 9.95 *(978-1-4598-0872-0(X))* Orca Bk. Pubs. USA.

Tahir "Z", Zarghuna. The Lazy Froggies. 2012. 28p. (-18). pap. 19.99 *(978-1-4772-8907-5(0))* AuthorHouse.

Tamaki, Mariko. This One Summer. Tamaki, Jillian, illus. 2014. (ENG.). 320p. (YA). (gr. 7). 21.99 *(978-1-62672-094-7(0)*, 9781626720947); pap. 18.99 *(978-1-59643-774-6(X)*, 9781596437746) Roaring Brook Pr. (First Second Bks.).

Tanen, Sloane. Appetite for Detention. Hagen, Stefan, illus. Hagen, Stefan, photos by. 2008. (ENG.). 80p. (YA). (gr. 7-18). 14.99 *(978-1-59990-075-9(0)*, 9781599900759, Bloomsbury USA Childrens) Bloomsbury Publishing USA.

Tanner, Lian. Battlesong. Szabla, Liz, ed. 2017. (Icebreaker Trilogy Ser.: 3). (ENG.). 304p. (J). 16.99 *(978-1-250-05218-6(1)*, 9781250052186) Feiwel & Friends.

Tarshis, Lauren. Emma-Jean Lazarus Fell in Love. 2010. (ENG.). 176p. (J). (gr. 5-18). 6.99 *(978-0-14-241568-9(5)*, Puffin Books) Penguin Young Readers Group.

—Emma-Jean Lazarus Fell Out of a Tree. 2008. (ENG., Illus.). 224p. (J). (gr. 5-18). 7.99 *(978-0-14-241150-6(7)*, Puffin Books) Penguin Young Readers Group.

Taylor, Chloé. Clothes Minded. Zhang, Nancy, illus. 2015. (Sew Zoey Ser.: 11). (ENG.). 160p. (J). (gr. 3-7). pap. 6.99 *(978-1-4814-2927-6(2)*, Simon Spotlight) Simon Spotlight.

—Cute As a Button. Zhang, Nancy, illus. 2014. (Sew Zoey Ser.: 5). (ENG.). 176p. (J). (gr. 3-7). pap. 5.99 *(978-1-4814-0248-4(X)*, Simon Spotlight) Simon Spotlight.

—Dressed to Frill. Zhang, Nancy, illus. 2015. (Sew Zoey Ser.: 12). (ENG.). 160p. (J). (gr. 3-7). pap. 6.99 *(978-1-4814-2930-6(2)*, Simon Spotlight) Simon Spotlight.

Taylor, Chloe. On Pins & Needles. Christy, Jana & Zhang, Nancy, illus. 2013. (Sew Zoey Ser.: 2). (ENG.). 160p. (J). (gr. 3-7). 15.99 *(978-1-4424-7937-1(X))*; pap. 6.99 *(978-1-4424-7936-4(1))* Simon Spotlight. (Simon Spotlight).

—Swatch Out! Zhang, Nancy, illus. 2014. (Sew Zoey Ser.: 8). (ENG.). 176p. (J). (gr. 3-7). pap. 5.99 *(978-1-4814-1535-4(2)*, Simon Spotlight) Simon Spotlight.

Taylor, Michelle M. What's Happily Ever after, Anyway? 2004. (Illus.). 178p. (YA). (gr. 9-12). per. 10.95 *(978-0-9746481-3-2(2))* Brown Barn Bks.

Telgemeier, Raina. Drama. 2012. lib. bdg. 22.10 *(978-0-606-26738-0(7)*, Turtleback) Turtleback Bks.

Teller, Janne. Nothing. Aitken, Martin, tr. (ENG., 240p. (YA). (gr. 7). 2012. Illus.). pap. 10.99 *(978-1-4424-4116-3(X))* 2010. 16.99 *(978-1-4169-8579-2(4))* Simon & Schuster Children's Publishing. (Atheneum Bks. for Young Readers).

Theo & the Sisters of Sage: From the Creator of We Are All the Same Inside. 2003. (We Are All the Same Inside Ser.: Vol. 3). (Illus.). 32p. (J). pap. 9.95 *(978-0-9718232-1-1(9))* T.I.M.M.-E. Co., Inc.

Thomas, Jacquelin. Split Ends. 2010. (ENG.). 272p. pap. 17.99 *(978-1-4165-9879-4(0))* Pocket Books.

Thomas, Lex. The Loners. (Quarantine Ser.: No. 1). (ENG.). 416p. (gr. 9). 2013. (J). pap. 9.99 *(978-1-60684-438-0(5))* 2012. 17.99 *(978-1-60684-329-1(X))* Lerner Publishing Group. (Carolrhoda Lab™).

—Quarantine: The Saints Book 2. 2014. (Quarantine Ser.: No. 2). (ENG.). 400p. (J). (gr. 9). pap. 9.99 *(978-1-60684-540-0(3))* Lerner Publishing Group.

Thompson, Alicia. Psych Major Syndrome. 2010. (ENG.). 336p. pap. 8.99 *(978-1-4231-1549-6(X))* Disney Pr.

Thorpe, Kiki, adapted by. Broken Hearts. 2003. (Lizzie Mcguire Ser.). (Illus.). 138p. (J). 12.65 *(978-0-7569-2718-9(8))* Perfection Learning Corp.

Tibensky, Arlaina. And Then Things Fall Apart. 2011. (ENG.). 272p. (YA). (gr. 9). pap. 9.99 *(978-1-4424-1323-8(9)*, Simon Pulse) Simon Pulse.

Tiller, Steve. Connectada al Corazon. Cremeans, Robert, illus. Date not set. (SPA.). (J). 15.95 *(978-1-932317-01-5(5))* Right Stuff Kids Bks.

Tobias, Jerry E. There's No Better Place Than the U. S. of A. 2004. (Illus.). 30p. (J). 4.95 *(978-0-9700582-2-5(5))* Factors Pr.

Todd, Pamela. The Blind Faith Hotel. (ENG.). 320p. (YA). (gr. 7). 2010. pap. 8.99 *(978-1-4169-9509-8(9))* 2008. 16.99 *(978-1-4169-5494-1(5))* McElderry, Margaret K. Bks. (McElderry, Margaret K. Bks.).

Top Ten Clues You're Clueless. 2014. (ENG.). 304p. (YA). (gr. 8). pap. 9.99 *(978-0-06-227242-3(X))* HarperCollins Pubs.

Townsend, Wendy. Lizard Love. 2013. 198p. 18.95 *(978-1-60898-151-9(7))* namelos llc.

Tregay, Sarah. Love & Leftovers. 2011. (ENG.). 448p. (YA). (gr. 8). 17.99 *(978-0-06-202358-2(6)*, Tegen, Katherine Bks) HarperCollins Pubs.

Triana, Gaby. Cubanita. 2005. 195p. (YA). (gr. 7-17). 15.99 *(978-0-06-056020-1(7)*, Rayo) HarperCollins Pubs.

Trigiani, Adriana. Viola in Reel Life. (Viola Ser.: 1). (ENG.). (YA). (gr. 8). 2011. 304p. pap. 8.99 *(978-0-06-145104-1(5))* 2009. 288p. 17.99 *(978-0-06-145102-7(9))* HarperCollins Pubs. (HarperTeen).

—Viola in the Spotlight. 2012. (Viola Ser.: 2). (ENG.). 288p. (YA). (gr. 8). pap. 8.99 *(978-0-06-145107-2(X)*, HarperTeen) HarperCollins Pubs.

Tsang, Evonne. I Love Him to Pieces. Görrissen, Janina, illus. 2011. (My Boyfriend Is a Monster Ser.: 1). (ENG.). 128p. (YA). (gr. 7-12). 29.27 *(978-0-7613-6004-9(2))* Lerner Publishing Group.

Ungermann Marshall, Yana. Gilda Gets Wise. Ungermann Marshall, Yana, illus. 2008. (Illus.). 34p. (J). pap. *(978-0-9670982-6-5(2))* Yana's Kitchen.

Urban, Linda. The Center of Everything. (ENG.). 208p. (J). (gr. 5-7). 2015. pap. 7.99 *(978-0-544-34069-5(8)*, HMH Books For Young Readers) 2013. 15.99 *(978-0-547-76348-4(4))* Houghton Mifflin Harcourt Publishing Co.

—A Crooked Kind of Perfect. (ENG., Illus.). 224p. (J). (gr. 5-7). 2009. pap. 7.99 *(978-0-15-206608-6(X))* 2007. 16.00 *(978-0-15-206007-7(3))* Houghton Mifflin Harcourt Publishing Co.

Vail, Rachel. Gorgeous. (Avery Sisters Trilogy Ser.: 2). (ENG.). (YA). (gr. 8). 2010. 304p. pap. 9.99 *(978-0-06-089048-3(7))* 2009. 288p. 16.99 *(978-0-06-089046-9(0))* HarperCollins Pubs.

—If We Kiss. 2005. (If We Kiss Ser.: Bk. 1). (ENG.). 272p. (J). 15.99 *(978-0-06-056914-3(X))* HarperCollins Pubs.

—If You Only Knew. 2014. (Friendship Ring Ser.: 1). (ENG.). 176p. (J). (gr. 5). pap. 7.99 *(978-0-14-751118-6(6)*, Puffin Books) Penguin Young Readers Group.

—Kiss Me Again. 2012. (If We Kiss Ser.: 2). (ENG.). 256p. (YA). (gr. 8). 17.99 *(978-0-06-194717-9(2)*, HarperTeen) HarperCollins Pubs.

—You, Maybe: The Profound Asymmetry of Love in High School. (YA). 2007. (ENG.). 224p. (gr. 8-12). pap. 7.99 *(978-0-06-056919-8(0))* 2006. (ENG.). 208p. (gr. 7-12). 15.99 *(978-0-06-056917-4(4))* 2006. 199p. (gr. 7-12). lib. bdg. 16.89 *(978-0-06-056918-1(2))* HarperCollins Pubs.

Van Draanen, Wendelin. Confessions of a Serial Kisser. 2009. (ENG.). 304p. (YA). (gr. 7-18). pap. 9.99 *(978-0-375-84249-8(7)*, Ember) Random Hse. Children's Bks.

—Flipped. 2003. (ENG.). 256p. (YA). (gr. 7-9). pap. 9.99 *(978-0-375-82544-6(4)*, Ember) Random Hse. Children's Bks.

Vance, Alexander. The Heartbreak Messenger. 2014. (ENG.). 304p. (J). (gr. 5-8). pap. 7.99 *(978-1-250-04416-7(2)*, 9781250044167) Square Fish.

Vanished. 64p. (YA). (gr. 6-12). pap. *(978-0-8224-2367-6(7))* Globe Fearon Educational Publishing.

Vaughan, Kathryn Mademann. What's under the Sea? 2005. (Illus.). (J). per. 19.95 incl. audio compact disk *(978-0-9747447-2-8(7))* Chaser Media LLC.

Vaughn, Carrie. Voices of Dragons. (ENG.). (YA). (gr. 8). 2011. 336p. pap. 8.99 *(978-0-06-154790-4(5))* 2010. 320p. 16.99 *(978-0-06-179894-8(0))* HarperCollins Pubs. (HarperTeen).

Vaughn, Lauren Roedy. OCD, the Dude, & Me. 2013. (ENG.). 240p. (YA). (gr. 9). 16.99 *(978-0-8037-3843-0(9)*, Dial Bks) Penguin Young Readers Group.

Vaught, Susan. Going Underground. (ENG.). (YA). (gr. 9-12). 2012. 352p. pap. 9.99 *(978-1-59990-919-6(7)*, 9781599909196) 2011. 336p. 16.99 *(978-1-59990-640-9(6)*, 9781599906409) Bloomsbury Publishing USA. (Bloomsbury USA Childrens).

Vawter, Vince. Paperboy. 2013. (ENG.). 240p. (J). (gr. 5). 16.99 *(978-0-385-74244-3(4))*; lib. bdg. 19.99 *(978-0-375-99058-8(5))* Random Hse. Children's Bks. (Delacorte Bks. for Young Readers).

Vega, Denise. Click Here: (To Find Out How I Survived Seventh Grade) 2006. (ENG., Illus.). 224p. (J). (gr. 5-17). reprint ed. per. 7.99 *(978-0-316-98559-8(7))* Little, Brown Bks. for Young Readers.

Viguié, Debbie. The Spring of Candy Apples, 1 vol. 2009. (Sweet Seasons Novel Ser.). (ENG.). 208p. (YA). (gr. 8-11). pap. 9.99 *(978-0-310-71753-9(1))* Zondervan.

Vipont, Elfrida. The Lark on the Wing. Freeman, T. R., illus. 2008. 233p. (J). pap. 12.95 *(978-1-932350-11-1(X))* Bethlehem Bks.

Vivian, Siobhan. A Little Friendly Advice. 2015. (ENG.). 256p. (J). (gr. 7). pap. 9.99 *(978-0-545-75801-7(7)*, PUSH) Scholastic, Inc.

Vizzini, Med. Be More Chill. 2011. 9.68 *(978-0-7848-3414-5(8)*, Everbind) Marco Bk. Co.

Vizzini, Ned. Be More Chill. 2005. (ENG.). 304p. (J). (gr. 5-9). per. 8.99 *(978-0-7868-0996-7(5))* Disney Publishing Worldwide.

Voigt, Cynthia & Marcus, Barry David. Bad Girls in Love. 2004. (ENG., Illus.). 240p. (J). (gr. 4-8). pap. 11.99 *(978-0-689-86620-3(8)*, Atheneum Bks. for Young Readers) Simon & Schuster Children's Publishing.

Voyer, Dorothy May. Henry Hedgehog's Holiday. 2012. (ENG.). (J). pap. *(978-1-4675-2084-3(5))* Independent Pub.

Walker, Kristin. A Match Made in High School. 2010. (ENG.). 288p. (YA). (gr. 7-18). 9.99 *(978-1-59514-257-3(6)*, Razorbill) Penguin Young Readers Group.

Walker, Rysa. Time's Edge, 0 vols. 2014. (Chronos Files Ser.: 2). (ENG.). 450p. (J). (gr. 7-12). pap. 9.99 *(978-1-4778-2582-2(7)*, 9781477825822, Skyscape) Amazon Publishing.

Wallace, Kim. Erik & Isabelle Senior Year at Foresthill High. 2008. (Foresthill High Ser.). 220p. (YA). (gr. 8-12). per. 12.00 *(978-0-9755848-3-5(9))* Foglight Pr.

Ward, Rachel. The Chaos. 2011. (Numbers Ser.: 2). (ENG.). 352p. (J). (gr. 9-9). 17.99 *(978-0-545-24269-1(X)*, Chicken Hse., The) Scholastic, Inc.

—Infinity: 2012. (Numbers Ser.: 3). (ENG.). 256p. (J). (gr. 9-9). 17.99 *(978-0-545-35092-1(1)*, Chicken Hse., The) Scholastic, Inc.

—Numbers. 2010. (Numbers Ser.: 1). (ENG.). 336p. (J). (gr. 7-12). 17.99 *(978-0-545-14299-1(7)*, Chicken Hse., The) Scholastic, Inc.

Wardlaw, Lee. 101 Ways to Bug Your Friends & Enemies. 2011. (ENG.). 288p. (J). (gr. 5-18). 6.99 *(978-0-14-241949-6(4)*, Puffin Books) Penguin Young Readers Group.

Warner, Sally. Only Emma. Harper, Jamie, illus. 2006. (Emma Ser.). (ENG.). 144p. (J). (gr. 3-7). 6.99 *(978-0-14-240711-0(9)*, Puffin Books) Penguin Young Readers Group.

Warner, Sally & Harper, Jamie. Only Emma. 2005. (Emma Ser.). (ENG., Illus.). 128p. (J). (gr. 3-7). 14.99 *(978-0-670-05979-9(X)*, Viking Books for Young Readers) Penguin Young Readers Group.

Wasserman, Robin. Lust. 2005. (Seven Deadly Sins Ser.: 1). (ENG.). 256p. (YA). (gr. 9-12). pap. 9.99 *(978-0-689-87782-7(X)*, Simon Pulse) Simon Pulse.

—Lust; Envy. 2013. (Seven Deadly Sins Ser.: 1). (ENG., Illus.). 592p. (YA). (gr. 9). pap. 9.99 *(978-1-4424-7504-5(8)*, Simon Pulse) Simon Pulse.

—Pride. 2006. (Seven Deadly Sins Ser.: 3). (ENG.). 256p. (YA). (gr. 9-12). pap. 8.99 *(978-0-689-87784-1(6)*, Simon Pulse) Simon Pulse.

—Pride - Wrath Vol. 2. 2013. (Seven Deadly Sins Ser.: 2). (ENG., Illus.). 592p. (YA). (gr. 9). pap. 9.99 *(978-1-4424-7506-9(4)*, Simon Pulse) Simon Pulse.

—Seven Deadly Sins Vol. 3: Sloth; Gluttony; Greed. 2013. (ENG., Illus.). 880p. (YA). (gr. 9). pap. 10.99 *(978-1-4424-7508-3(0)*, Simon Pulse) Simon Pulse.

—Sloth. 2006. (Seven Deadly Sins Ser.: 5). (ENG.). 256p. (YA). (gr. 9). pap. 9.99 *(978-1-4169-0718-3(1)*, Simon Pulse) Simon Pulse.

—Wrath. 2006. (Seven Deadly Sins Ser.: 4). (ENG., Illus.). 256p. (YA). (gr. 9-12). pap. 9.99 *(978-0-689-87785-8(4)*, Simon Pulse) Simon Pulse.

Weatherly, L. A. Them. 2013. (ENG.). 80p. (YA). (gr. 6-12). pap. 6.95 *(978-1-78112-185-6(0))*; lib. bdg. 22.60 *(978-1-78112-184-9(2))* Lerner Publishing Group.

Weaver, Will. Saturday Night Dirt. 2009. (Motor Novels Ser.: 1). (ENG.). 192p. (YA). (gr. 7-12). pap. 14.99 *(978-0-312-56131-4(8)*, 9780312561314) Square Fish.

Webb, Sarah. Ask Amy Green: Wedding Belles. 2014. (Ask Amy Green Ser.: 6). (ENG.). 240p. (YA). (gr. 7). 16.99 *(978-0-7636-5584-6(8))* Candlewick Pr.

Weisberg, E. Gathering Roses. 2007. pap. *(978-1-84747-118-5(8))* Chipmunkapublishing.

Weissman, Elissa Brent. Nerd Camp. (ENG., 272p. (J). (gr. 3-7). 2012. Illus.). pap. 6.99 *(978-1-4424-1704-5(8))* 2011. 17.99 *(978-1-4424-1703-8(X))* Simon & Schuster Children's Publishing. (Atheneum Bks. for Young Readers).

—Nerd Camp 2.0. Willis, Drew, illus. (ENG.). (J). (gr. 3-7). 2015. 304p. pap. 7.99 *(978-1-4424-5295-4(1))* 2014. 288p. 17.99 *(978-1-4424-5294-7(3)*, Atheneum Bks. for Young Readers) Simon & Schuster Children's Publishing.

Wells, Donna. You & Me Brother. 2008. 16p. pap. 8.49 *(978-1-4389-0556-3(4))* AuthorHouse.

Wells, Helen. Cherry Ames, Boarding School Nurse. 10th ed. 2007. (Cherry Ames Nurse Stories Ser.). 224p. (YA). (gr. 7-12). 14.95 *(978-0-8261-0413-7(4))* Springer Publishing Co., Inc.

—Cherry Ames, Cruise Nurse. 2007. (Cherry Ames Nurse Stories Ser.). 232p. (YA). (gr. 7-12). 14.95 *(978-0-8261-0411-3(8))* Springer Publishing Co., Inc.

Wells, Pamela. The Crushes. 2009. (ENG.). 352p. (J). (gr. 7). pap. 8.99 *(978-0-439-92560-0(6))* Scholastic, Inc.

Wells, Robison. Variant. (Variant Ser.: 1). (ENG.). (YA). (gr. 8). 2012. 400p. pap. 9.99 *(978-0-06-202609-5(7))* 2011. 384p. 17.99 *(978-0-06-202608-8(9))* HarperCollins Pubs. (HarperTeen).

Wells, Rosemary. Hands Off, Harry! Wells, Rosemary, illus. 2011. (ENG., Illus.). 40p. (J). (gr. -1-1). 14.99 *(978-0-06-192112-4(2)*, Tegen, Katherine Bks) HarperCollins Pubs.

Wells, Tina. Friends Forever? 2013. (Mackenzie Blue Ser.: 3). (ENG.). 208p. (J). (gr. 3-7). pap. 6.99 *(978-0-06-158316-2(2))* HarperCollins Pubs.

—Mackenzie Blue. 2013. (Mackenzie Blue Ser.: 1). (ENG.). 224p. (J). (gr. 3-7). pap. 6.99 *(978-0-06-158310-0(3))* HarperCollins Pubs.

—Mackenzie Blue. Segawa, Michael, illus. 2009. (Mackenzie Blue Ser.: 1). (ENG.). 224p. (J). (gr. 3-7). 12.99 *(978-0-06-158308-7(1))* HarperCollins Pubs.

—Mixed Messages. (Mackenzie Blue Ser.: 4). (ENG.). (J). (gr. 3-7). 2013. 224p. pap. 6.99 *(978-0-06-158319-3(7))* 2010. 208p. 12.99 *(978-0-06-158317-9(0))* HarperCollins Pubs.

—The Secret Crush. 2013. (Mackenzie Blue Ser.: 2). (ENG.). 240p. (J). (gr. 3-7). pap. 6.99 *(978-0-06-158313-1(8))* HarperCollins Pubs.

—The Secret Crush. Segawa, Michael, illus. 2009. (Mackenzie Blue Ser.: 2). (ENG.). 240p. (J). (gr. 3-7). 10.99 *(978-0-06-158311-7(1))* HarperCollins Pubs.

Welshman, Kate. Anais Butt & the Hairy-Handed Gent. 2013. 164p. pap. 16.50 *(978-1-61213-187-0(5))* Writer's Coffee Shop, The.

Wenberg, Michael. Stringz. 2010. 216p. (YA). (gr. 6-10). 16.95 *(978-1-934813-33-1(8))* Westside Bks.

West, Kathryn E. Garden of Roses. 2007. 328p. 29.95 *(978-0-595-70333-3(X))* iUniverse, Inc.

Westerfeld, Scott & Lanagan, Margo. Swarm. 2018. (Zeroes Ser.: 2). lib. bdg. 24.50 ***(978-0-606-40832-5(0))*** Turtleback Bks.

Westerfeld, Scott, et al. Swarm. 2016. (Zeroes Ser.: 2). (ENG., Illus.). 464p. (YA). (gr. 9). 19.99 *(978-1-4814-4339-5(9)*, Simon Pulse) Simon Pulse.

—Zeroes. (Zeroes Ser.: 1). (ENG.). (YA). (gr. 9). 2016. 576p. pap. 12.99 *(978-1-4814-4337-1(2))* 2015. (Illus.). 560p. 19.99 *(978-1-4814-4336-4(4))* Simon Pulse. (Simon Pulse).

Weyland, Jack. Brianna, My Brother, & the Blog. 2009. (YA). *(978-1-60641-140-7(3))* Deseret Bk. Co.

Weyn, Suzanne. Bionic. 2016. (ENG.). 240p. (YA). (gr. 7). 17.99 *(978-0-545-90677-7(6)*, Scholastic Pr.) Scholastic, Inc.

Whaley, John Corey. Noggin. (ENG., Illus.). (YA). (gr. 9). 2015. 368p. pap. 12.99 *(978-1-4424-5873-4(9))* 2014. 352p. 18.99 *(978-1-4424-5872-7(0))* Simon & Schuster Children's Publishing. (Atheneum Bks. for Young Readers).

—Where Things Come Back. (ENG., Illus.). (YA). (gr. 9). 2012. 256p. pap. 11.99 *(978-1-4424-1334-4(4))* 2011. 240p. 16.99 *(978-1-4424-1333-7(6))* Simon & Schuster Children's Publishing. (Atheneum Bks. for Young Readers).

Whamond, Dave. Oddrey. 2017. (Oddrey Ser.: 1). (ENG., Illus.). 32p. (J). (gr. k-3). pap. 7.95 ***(978-1-77147-303-3(7))*** Owlkids Bks. Inc. CAN. Dist: Publishers Group West (PGW).

Whamond, Dave & Owlkids Books Inc. Staff. Oddrey. 2012. (Oddrey Ser.: 1). (ENG., Illus.). 32p. (J). (gr. k-3). 16.95 *(978-1-926973-45-6(3)*, Owlkids) Owlkids Bks. Inc. CAN. Dist: Publishers Group West (PGW).

Whelen-Banks, Jane. Liam Says "Hi" Learning to Greet a Friend. 2008. (ENG., Illus.). 32p. 12.95 *(978-1-84310-901-3(8)*, 5372) Kingsley, Jessica Pubs. GBR. Dist: Macmillan Distribution Ltd.

Whipple, Natalie. Transparent. 2013. (ENG.). 368p. (YA). (gr. 8). pap. 9.99 *(978-0-06-212016-8(6)*, HarperTeen) HarperCollins Pubs.

White, Kiersten. The Chaos of Stars. (ENG.). (YA). 2014. 304p. (gr. 8). pap. 9.99 *(978-0-06-213587-2(2))* 2013. 288p. (gr. 8). 17.99 *(978-0-06-213592-6(9))* 2013. 288p. pap. *(978-0-06-229412-8(1))* HarperCollins Pubs. (HarperTeen).

White, Sarah. Our Broken Pieces. 2017. 288p. (YA). (gr. 9). pap. 9.99 ***(978-0-06-247313-4(1)***, HarperTeen) HarperCollins Pubs.

Who Needs a Hug. 2003. (J). per. *(978-1-57657-877-3(1))* Paradise Pr., Inc.

Whytock, Cherry. My Cup Runneth Over: The Life of Angelica Cookson Potts. Whytock, Cherry, illus. 2012. (ENG., Illus.). 192p. (YA). (gr. 7). pap. 9.99 *(978-1-4424-6055-3(5)*, Simon Pulse) Simon Pulse.

—My Scrumptious Scottish Dumplings: The Life of Angelica Cookson Potts. Whytock, Cherry, illus. 2006. (ENG., Illus.). 192p. (YA). mass mkt. 5.99 *(978-0-689-86552-7(X)*, Simon Pulse) Simon Pulse.

Wiggin, Kate Douglas & Fisher, Eric Scott. Rebecca of Sunnybrook Farms, 1 vol. 2012. (Calico Illustrated Classics Ser.: No. 4). (ENG., Illus.). 112p. (J). (gr. 3-6). 27.07 *(978-1-61641-620-1(3))* Magic Wagon.

Wild, Margaret. Jinx. Gould, Jason, photos by. 2004. (ENG., Illus.). 224p. (YA). (gr. 9). reprint ed. pap. 11.95 *(978-0-689-86541-1(4)*, Simon Pulse) Simon Pulse.

Wilkinson, Lili. Pink. (ENG.). 320p. (YA). (gr. 8). 2012. pap. 9.99 *(978-0-06-192654-9(X))* 2011. 16.99 *(978-0-06-192653-2(1))* HarperCollins Pubs. (HarperTeen).

Willard, Elizabeth Kimmel. Mary Ingalls on Her Own. 2007. (Little House Sequel Ser.). (ENG.). 192p. (J). (gr. 3-7). 16.99 *(978-0-06-000905-2(5))* HarperCollins Pubs.

Williams, Joyce. A Daddy's Love Through a Girl's Eye. Petroff, Kathryn, illus. 2012. 58p. pap. 9.99 *(978-0-9852729-3-7(7))* Faith Bks. & MORE.

Williams, Kathryn. Pizza, Love, & Other Stuff That Made Me Famous. 2013. (ENG.). 256p. (YA). (gr. 7-12). pap. 11.99 *(978-1-250-02745-0(4)*, 9781250027450) Square Fish.

Williams, Nicole. Trusting You & Other Lies. 2017. (ENG.). 304p. (YA). (gr. 9). 17.99 ***(978-0-553-49877-6(0)***, Crown Books For Young Readers) Random Hse. Children's Bks.

Willis, Meredith Sue. Meli's Way. 2015. 178p. (YA). *(978-1-932727-15-9(9))* Montemayor Pr.

Wilson, F. Paul. Jack: Secret Histories. 2009. (Repairman Jack Ser.). (ENG.). 320p. (YA). (gr. 7). pap. 6.99 *(978-0-7653-5811-0(5)*, 9780765358110, Tor Teen) Doherty, Tom Assocs., LLC.

Winerip, Michael. Adam Canfield: The Last Reporter. 2009. (Adam Canfield of the Slash Ser.: 3). (ENG., Illus.). 384p. (J). (gr. 3-7). 16.99 *(978-0-7636-2342-5(3))* Candlewick Pr.

—Adam Canfield the Last Reporter. 2010. (Adam Canfield of the Slash Ser.: 3). (ENG., Illus.). 384p. (J). (gr. 3-7). 7.99 *(978-0-7636-4838-1(8))* Candlewick Pr.

Wittlinger, Ellen. Heart on My Sleeve. 2006. (ENG., Illus.). 240p. (YA). (gr. 7). reprint ed. pap. 10.99 *(978-0-689-84999-2(0)*, Simon & Schuster Bks. For Young Readers) Simon & Schuster Bks. For Young Readers.

—Love & Lies: Marisol's Story. (ENG.). (YA). 2009. 272p. (gr. 7). pap. 8.99 *(978-1-4169-7914-2(X))* 2008. 256p. (gr. 9-18). 16.99 *(978-1-4169-1623-9(7))* Simon & Schuster Bks. For Young Readers. (Simon & Schuster Bks. For Young Readers).

—Zigzag. (ENG., Illus.). (YA). (gr. 7). 2003. 272p. 16.95 *(978-0-689-84996-1(6))* 2005. 288p. reprint ed. pap. 9.99 *(978-0-689-84998-5(2))* Simon & Schuster Bks. For Young Readers. (Simon & Schuster Bks. For Young Readers).

Wolff, Virginia Euwer. This Full House. (ENG.). 496p. (YA). (gr. 9). 2011. pap. 9.99 *(978-0-06-158306-3(5))* 2009. (Make Lemonade Trilogy: No. 3). 17.99 *(978-0-06-158304-9(9))* HarperCollins Pubs. (HarperTeen).

Wolitzer, Meg. The Fingertips of Duncan Dorfman. 2012. (ENG.). 304p. (J). (gr. 3-7). pap. 7.99 *(978-0-14-242204-5(5)*, Puffin Books) Penguin Young Readers Group.

Wood, Fiona. Six Impossible Things. 2015. (ENG.). 304p. (YA). (gr. 7-17). 18.00 *(978-0-316-24216-5(0))* Little Brown & Co.

—Six Impossible Things. 2016. (ENG.). 304p. (YA). (gr. 7-17). pap. 9.99 *(978-0-316-29941-1(3)*, Poppy) Little, Brown Bks. for Young Readers.

Woods, Brenda. Emako Blue. 2005. (ENG.). 128p. (YA). (gr. 7-18). 6.99 *(978-0-14-240418-8(7)*, Speak) Penguin Young Readers Group.

—Emako Blue. 2005. 124p. (gr. 7). 16.00 *(978-0-7569-5495-6(9))* Perfection Learning Corp.

Woodson, Jacqueline. Behind You. 2010. (ENG.). 176p. (YA). (gr. 7-18). 7.99 *(978-0-14-241554-2(5)*, Puffin Books) Penguin Young Readers Group.

—Behind You. 2010. lib. bdg. 18.40 *(978-0-606-14598-5(2)*, Turtleback) Turtleback Bks.

—If You Come Softly & Behind You. 2010. (ENG.). 352p. (YA). (gr. 7-18). 8.99 *(978-0-14-241918-2(4)*, Puffin Books) Penguin Young Readers Group.

Wyatt, Melissa. Funny How Things Change. 2009. (ENG.). 208p. (YA). (gr. 9-13). 26.99 *(978-0-374-30233-7(2)*, Farrar, Straus & Giroux (BYR)) Farrar, Straus & Giroux.

Wynne-Jones, Tim. Rex Zero & the End of the World. 2013. (ENG.). 208p. (J). (gr. 3-7). pap. 8.99 *(978-0-312-64460-4(4)*, 9780312644604) Square Fish.

—Rex Zero, King of Nothing. 2013. (ENG.). 240p. (J). (gr. 3-7). pap. 6.99 *(978-0-312-67478-6(3)*, 9780312674786) Square Fish.

Young, Suzanne. So Many Boys. 2010. (Naughty List Ser.: No. 2). (ENG.). 256p. (YA). (gr. 7-18). 9.99 *(978-1-59514-267-2(3)*, Razorbill) Penguin Young Readers Group.

Yovanoff, Brenna. The Space Between. 2012. (ENG., Illus.). 384p. (YA). (gr. 9). pap. 8.99 *(978-1-59514-483-6(8)*, Razorbill) Penguin Young Readers Group.

Zadoff, Allen. Boy Nobody. 2013. (Unknown Assassin Ser.: 1). (ENG.). 352p. (YA). (gr. 10-17). 18.00 *(978-0-316-19968-1(0))* Little Brown & Co.

Zarins, Kim. Sometimes We Tell the Truth. 2016. ***(978-1-4814-7554-9(1))*** Simon & Schuster, Inc.

—Sometimes We Tell the Truth. 2016. (ENG., Illus.). 448p. (YA). (gr. 9). 17.99 *(978-1-4814-6499-4(X),* Simon Pulse) Simon Pulse.

Zarr, Sara. How to Save a Life. 2012. (ENG.). 368p. (YA). (gr. 7-17). pap. 10.99 *(978-0-316-03605-4(6))* Little, Brown Bks. for Young Readers.

—Story of a Girl. 2008. (ENG.). 224p. (YA). (gr. 7-17). per. 10.99 *(978-0-316-01454-0(0))* Little, Brown Bks. for Young Readers.

Zephaniah, Benjamin. Gangsta Rap. 2004. (ENG.). 336p. (YA). (gr. 9-13). pap. 8.99 *(978-1-58234-886-5(3),* 9781582348865, Bloomsbury USA Childrens) Bloomsbury Publishing USA.

Ziegesar, Cecily von. Adored. 2009. (It Girl Ser.: 8). (ENG.). 240p. (YA). (gr. 10-17). pap. 9.99 *(978-0-316-02509-6(7),* Tingley, Megan Bks.) Little, Brown Bks. for Young Readers.

—It Had to Be You. 2009. (Gossip Girl Ser.). (ENG.). 432p. (YA). (gr. 10-17). pap. 10.99 *(978-0-316-01769-5(8),* Poppy) Little, Brown Bks. for Young Readers.

Ziegesar, Cecily von, creator. Notorious. 2006. (It Girl Ser.: 2). (ENG.). 288p. (YA). (gr. 10-17). per. 9.99 *(978-0-316-01186-0(X),* Poppy) Little, Brown Bks. for Young Readers.

Ziegler, Jennifer. Sass & Serendipity. 2012. (ENG.). 384p. (YA). (gr. 7). pap. 9.99 *(978-0-375-85964-9(0),* Ember) Random Hse. Children's Bks.

Zink, Michelle. Lies I Told. 2015. (Lies I Told Ser.: 1). (ENG.). 352p. (YA). (gr. 8). pap. 9.99 *(978-0-06-232713-0(5),* HarperTeen); 17.99 *(978-0-06-232712-3(7))* HarperCollins Pubs.

—Promises I Made. 2015. (Lies I Told Ser.: 2). (ENG.). 304p. (YA). (gr. 8). 17.99 *(978-0-06-232715-4(1))* HarperCollins Pubs.

INTERPLANETARY COMMUNICATION

see Interstellar Communication

INTERPLANETARY VOYAGES

see also Outer Space—Exploration; Rockets (Aeronautics); Space Flight

Aldrin, Buzz. Look to the Stars. Minor, Wendell, illus. 2009. (ENG.). 40p. (J). (gr. 1-3). 17.99 *(978-0-399-24721-7(1),* G.P. Putnam's Sons Books for Young Readers) Penguin Young Readers Group.

Carson, Mary Kay. The Mission to Pluto: The First Visit to an Ice Dwarf & the Kuiper Belt. Uhlman, Tom, photos by. 2017. (Scientists in the Field Ser.). (ENG., Illus.). 80p. (J). (gr. 5-7). 18.99 *(978-0-544-41671-0(6),* HMH Books For Young Readers) Houghton Mifflin Harcourt Publishing Co.

DeYoe, Aaron. Space Travel, 1 vol. 2015. (ENG., Illus.). 24p. (J). *(978-1-62403-745-0(3),* 1391272) ABDO Publishing Co.

Goodman, Susan E. How Do You Burp in Space? And Other Tips Every Space Tourist Needs to Know. Slack, Michael H., illus. 2013. (ENG.). 80p. (J). (gr. 3-6). 16.99 *(978-1-59990-068-1(8),* 9781599900681, Bloomsbury USA Childrens) Bloomsbury Publishing USA.

—How Do You Burp in Space? And Other Tips Every Space Tourist Needs to Know. Slack, Michael, illus. 2013. (ENG.). 80p. (J). (gr. 3-6). 17.89 *(978-1-59990-934-9(0),* 9781599909349, Bloomsbury USA Childrens) Bloomsbury Publishing USA.

Hamilton, John. Spaceships, 1 vol. 2006. (World of Science Fiction Ser.). (ENG., Illus.). 32p. (gr. 4-7). 27.07 *(978-1-59679-995-0(1),* Abdo & Daughters) ABDO Publishing Co.

Jackson, Ellen. Worlds Around Us: A Space Voyage. Miller, Ron, illus. 2006. (Exceptional Science Title for Intermediate Grades). 37p. (J). (gr. 3-7). lib. bdg. 23.93 *(978-0-7613-3405-7(X),* Millbrook Pr.) Lerner Publishing Group.

Laser-Sailing Starships: Meet NASA Inventor Philip Lubin & His Team's. 2017. (J). ***(978-0-7166-6159-7(4))*** World Bk., Inc.

Mazurkiewicz, Jessica, et al. Skyscapes. 2012. (Adult Coloring Ser.). (ENG.). 32p. (J). (gr. 3). pap. 5.99 *(978-0-486-48834-9(9))* Dover Pubns., Inc.

Space Travel. (Jump Ser.). 36p. (J). (gr. 2-7). pap. *(978-1-882210-22-0(0))* Action Publishing, Inc.

INTERRACIAL MARRIAGE

Alko, Selina. The Case for Loving: The Fight for Interracial Marriage. Alko, Selina & Qualls, Sean, illus. 2015. (ENG.). 40p. (J). (gr. -1-3). 18.99 *(978-0-545-47853-3(7))* Scholastic, Inc.

Fields, Julianna. Multiracial Families. 2010. (Changing Face of Modern Families Ser.). (Illus.). 64p. (YA). (gr. 5-18). lib. bdg. 22.95 *(978-1-4222-1494-7(X))* Mason Crest.

Gold, Susan Dudley. Loving V. Virginia: Lifting the Ban Against Interracial Marriage. 2007. (Supreme Court Milestones Ser.). (Illus.). 128p. (gr. 7-18). lib. bdg. 42.79 *(978-0-7614-2586-1(1),* Benchmark Bks.) Marshall Cavendish Corp.

Haugen, David M. Interracial Relationships. 2006. (At Issue Ser.). (ENG.). 128p. (gr. 10-12). 39.40 *(978-0-7377-2390-8(4));* 98p. (YA). (gr. 8-12). 24.45 *(978-0-7377-2391-5(2),* Greenhaven Pr., Inc.) Cengage Gale.

Poole, H. W. Multiracial Families, Vol. 12. 2016. (Families Today Ser.). (Illus.). 48p. (J). (gr. 5). 20.95 *(978-1-4222-3622-2(6))* Mason Crest.

Poole, Hilary W. Military Families. 2017. (Illus.). 48p. (J). *(978-1-4222-3612-3(9))* Mason Crest.

INTERRACIAL MARRIAGE—FICTION

Blackstone, Stella & Scribens, Sunny. Mis Primeras Palabras. 2017. (SPA.). 30p. (J). (gr. -1-k). bds. 14.99 ***(978-1-78285-325-1(1))*** Barefoot Bks., Inc.

Sanders, Dori. Clover. 2013. (ENG.). 208p. pap. 13.95 *(978-1-61620-340-5(4),* 73340) Algonquin Bks. of Chapel Hill.

Woodson, Jacqueline. The House You Pass on the Way. 2010. (ENG.). 160p. (YA). (gr. 7-18). 8.99 *(978-0-14-241706-5(8),* Puffin Books) Penguin Young Readers Group.

INTERSTELLAR COMMUNICATION

Firestone, Mary. Seti Science. 2005. (Weird Careers in Science Ser.). (Illus.). 88p. (gr. 5-8). lib. bdg. 25.00 *(978-0-7910-8701-5(8),* Chelsea Hse.) Facts On File, Inc.

Kortemeier, Todd. Searching for Alien Life. 2017. (Science Frontiers Ser.). (ENG., Illus.). 32p. (J). (gr. 3-6). 21.95 *(978-1-63235-380-1(6))* Pr. Room Editions LLC.

INTERSTELLAR VOYAGES

see Interplanetary Voyages

INTERVIEWING IN JOURNALISM

see Journalism

INTOLERANCE

see Toleration

INTOXICATION

see Alcoholism; Drug Addiction

INUIT

Here are entered works limited to the indigenous Arctic peoples of Greenland, Canada, and northern Alaska. Works discussing collectively the Inuit peoples and the related Eskimo peoples of southern and western Alaska and adjacent regions of Siberia, or works for which the individual group cannot be identified, are entered under Eskimos.

Alexander, Cherry & Alexander, Bryan. Inuit. 2009. (Flashback History Ser.). (Illus.). 48p. (J). pap. 11.75 *(978-1-4358-5508-3(6),* PowerKids Pr.); (YA). (gr. 3-6). 29.25 *(978-1-4358-5507-6(8))* Rosen Publishing Group, Inc., The.

Arnaquq-Baril, Alethea. The Blind Boy & the Loon, 1 vol. Arnaquq-Baril, Alethea, illus. 2014. (ENG., Illus.). 48p. (J). (gr. k-2). 16.95 *(978-1-927095-57-7(3))* Inhabit Media Inc. CAN. Dist: Independent Pubs. Group.

Arnéz, Lynda. Native Peoples of the Arctic. 2016. (Native Peoples of North America Ser.). (Illus.). 32p. (J). (gr. 3-2). 25.25 *(978-1-4824-4807-8(6))* Stevens, Gareth Publishing LLLP.

Bennett, Doraine. The Inuit. 2013. (Illus.). 32p. (J). pap. *(978-1-935884-95-8(6));* lib. bdg. *(978-1-935884-89-7(1))* State Standards Publishing, LLC.

Bial, Raymond. The People & Culture of the Inuit. 2016. (First Peoples of North America Ser.). (ENG., Illus.). 128p. (J). (gr. 6-6). 45.70 *(978-1-5026-1006-5(X))* Cavendish Square Publishing.

Burgan, Michael. Inuit. 2004. (Native American Peoples Ser.). (Illus.). 32p. (gr. 3-7). lib. bdg. 26.00 *(978-0-8368-4219-7(7),* Gareth Stevens Learning Library) Stevens, Gareth Publishing LLLP.

—Inuit History & Culture. 2011. (Native American Library). 48p. (J). (gr. 3-6). pap. 14.05 *(978-1-4339-5972-1(0));* lib. bdg. 31.95 *(978-1-4339-5970-7(4))* Stevens, Gareth Publishing LLLP. (Gareth Stevens Learning Library).

Caravantes, Peggy. Marooned in the Arctic: The True Story of Ada Blackjack, the Female Robinson Crusoe. 2016. (Women of Action Ser.). (ENG., Illus.). 208p. (YA). (gr. 7). 19.95 *(978-1-61373-098-0(5))* Chicago Review Pr., Inc.

Chesterfield, Jayson. Inuit. 2015. (Spotlight on Native Americans Ser.). (ENG., Illus.). 32p. (J). (gr. 4-6). 26.25 *(978-1-4994-1673-2(3),* PowerKids Pr.) Rosen Publishing Group, Inc., The.

Christopher, Neil. Arctic Giants, 1 vol. Widermann, Eva, illus. 2010. (ENG.). 128p. (J). (gr. 3). 24.95 *(978-1-926569-09-3(1))* Inhabit Media Inc. CAN. Dist: Independent Pubs. Group.

—Those That Cause Fear, 1 vol. Arnaktauyok, Germaine, illus. 2016. (ENG.). 40p. (J). (gr. 2-4). 16.95 *(978-1-77227-085-3(7))* Inhabit Media Inc. CAN. Dist: Independent Pubs. Group.

Comveau, Danielle. The Inuit of Canada. 2005. (First Peoples Ser.). (Illus.). 48p. (gr. 4-8). lib. bdg. 23.95 *(978-0-8225-4850-8(X))* Lerner Publishing Group.

Cunningham, Kevin & Benoit, Peter. The Inuit. 2011. (True Bk Ser.). 48p. (J). (ENG.). pap. 6.95 *(978-0-531-29302-7(5));* (gr. 3-5). 29.00 *(978-0-531-20760-4(9))* Scholastic Library Publishing. (Children's Pr.).

Diemer, Lauren. Igloos. 2010. (Illus.). 24p. *(978-1-77071-578-3(9));* pap. *(978-1-77071-585-1(1))* Weigl Educational Pubs. Ltd.

—Les Iglous or les Igloos [Check Which Translator Used]: Les Emblèmes Canadiens. McMann, Julie, tr. from ENG. 2011. (FRE.). 24p. (YA). (gr. 2-4). *(978-1-77071-408-3(1))* Weigl Educational Pubs. Ltd.

Doak, Robin S. Arctic Peoples, 1 vol. 2011. (First Nations of North America Ser.). (ENG.). 48p. (gr. 3-3). pap. 9.95 *(978-1-4329-4956-3(X),* Heinemann InfoSearch) Heinemann-Raintree.

Falconer, Shelley & White, Shawna. Stones, Bones & Stitches: Storytelling Through Inuit Art. 2007. (Lord Museum Book Ser.). (ENG., Illus.). 48p. (J). (gr. k-12). 22.95 *(978-0-88776-854-5(7),* Tundra Bks.) Tundra Bks. CAN. Dist: Penguin Random Hse. LLC.

Flaherty, Louise & Christopher, Neil. The Country of Wolves, 1 vol. Perez, Ramon, illus. 2013. (ENG.). 108p. (J). (gr. 7). 24.95 *(978-1-927095-04-1(2))* Inhabit Media Inc. CAN. Dist: Independent Pubs. Group.

Hainnu, Rebecca & Ziegler, Anna. A Walk on the Tundra, 1 vol. Leng, Qin, illus. 2011. (ENG.). 40p. (J). (gr. 1-3). 13.95 *(978-1-926569-43-7(1))* Inhabit Media Inc. CAN. Dist: Independent Pubs. Group.

Ipellie, Alootook. The Inuit Thought of It: Amazing Arctic Innovations. 2007. (We Thought of It Ser.). (ENG., Illus.). 32p. (J). (gr. 5-7). 2nd ed. 19.95 *(978-1-55451-088-7(0),* 9781554510887) 7th ed. pap. 9.95 *(978-1-55451-087-0(2),* 9781554510870) Annick Pr., Ltd. CAN. Dist: Publishers Group West (PGW).

Issaluk, Johnny. Games of Survival: Traditional Inuit Games for Elementary Students, 1 vol. Maruyama, Ed, photos by. 2013. (ENG., Illus.). 62p. (J). (gr. 3-6). 12.95 *(978-1-927095-21-8(2))* Inhabit Media Inc. CAN. Dist: Independent Pubs. Group.

Jordan-Fenton, Christy & Pokiak-Fenton, Margaret. Fatty Legs: A True Story. Amini-Holmes, Liz, illus. 9th ed. 2010. (ENG.). 112p. (J). (gr. 4-7). pap. 12.95 *(978-1-55451-246-1(8),* 9781554512461) Annick Pr., Ltd. CAN. Dist: Publishers Group West (PGW).

—Not My Girl. Grimard, Gabrielle, illus. 2014. (ENG.). 36p. (J). (gr. 1-4). 21.95 *(978-1-55451-625-4(0),* 9781554516254); pap. 9.95 *(978-1-55451-624-7(2),* 9781554516247) Annick Pr., Ltd. CAN. Dist: Publishers Group West (PGW).

—A Stranger at Home: A True Story. Amini-Holmes, Liz, illus. 2011. (ENG.). 112p. (J). (gr. 3-7). 21.95 *(978-1-55451-362-8(6),* 9781554513628); 3rd ed. pap. 12.95 *(978-1-55451-361-1(8),* 9781554513611) Annick Pr., Ltd. CAN. Dist: Publishers Group West (PGW).

—When I Was Eight. Grimard, Gabrielle, illus. 2nd ed. 2013. (ENG.). 32p. (J). (gr. 1-4). 21.95 *(978-1-55451-491-5(6),* 9781554514915); pap. 9.95 *(978-1-55451-490-8(8),* 9781554514908) Annick Pr., Ltd. CAN. Dist: Publishers Group West (PGW).

Jordan-Fenton, Christy, et al. Fatty Legs: A True Story. Amini-Holmes, Liz, illus. 8th ed. 2010. (ENG.). 112p. (J). (gr. 4-7). 21.95 *(978-1-55451-247-8(6),* 9781554512478) Annick Pr., Ltd. CAN. Dist: Publishers Group West (PGW).

Kallen, Stuart A. Native Peoples of the Arctic. 2016. (North American Indian Nations Ser.). (ENG., Illus.). 48p. (J). (gr. 3-5). 33.32 *(978-1-4677-7937-1(7))* Lerner Publishing Group.

—Native Peoples of the Subarctic. 2016. (North American Indian Nations Ser.). (ENG., Illus.). 48p. (J). (gr. 3-5). 33.32 *(978-1-4677-7938-8(5))* Lerner Publishing Group.

Kent, Deborah. The Inuit: A Proud People. 2005. (American Indians Ser.). (Illus.). 48p. (J). lib. bdg. 25.27 *(978-0-7660-2451-9(2),* Enslow Elementary) Enslow Pubs., Inc.

King, David C. The Inuit. 2007. (First Americans Ser.). 48p. (J). (gr. 1-4). lib. bdg. 31.36 *(978-0-7614-2679-0(5),* Benchmark Bks.) Marshall Cavendish Corp.

Koestler-Grack, Rachel A. The Inuit: Ivory Carvers of the Far North. 2016. (America's First Peoples Ser.). (ENG.). 32p. (gr. 3-4). pap. 8.99 *(978-1-5157-4215-9(6),* Blue Earth Bks.) Capstone Press of Coughlan Cos.

Lajiness, Katie. Inuit, 1 vol. 2016. (ENG., Illus.). 32p. (J). *(978-1-68078-199-1(5))* ABDO Publishing Co.

Lomberg, Michelle. Grand Canyon: Wonders of the World. 2012. (J). *(978-1-61913-524-6(8));* pap. *(978-1-61913-437-9(3))* Weigl Pubs., Inc.

Manning, Jack. Igloos, 1 vol. 2014. (American Indian Homes Ser.). (ENG.). 24p. (gr. 1-2). lib. bdg. 25.32 *(978-1-4914-0314-3(4))* Capstone Press of Coughlan Cos.

Meredith, Susan Markowitz. The Inupiaq Live Here. 2011. (Early Connections Ser.). (J). *(978-1-61672-602-7(4))* Benchmark Education Co.

—The Inupiaq Live Here: Set Of 6. 2011. (Early Connections Ser.). (J). pap. 37.00 net. *(978-1-4108-1087-8(9))* Benchmark Education Co.

Mikkigak, Qaunaq & Schwartz, Joanne. The Legend of the Fog, 1 vol. Christopher, Danny, illus. 2017. (ENG.). 40p. (J). (gr. k-2). pap. 10.95 ***(978-1-77227-136-2(5))*** Inhabit Media Inc. CAN. Dist: Independent Pubs. Group.

Miller, Connie R. The Inuit. 2003. (Uncovering Native American History Ser.). (J). pap. *(978-1-58417-114-0(6));* lib. bdg. *(978-1-58417-051-8(4))* Lake Street Pubs.

Qitsualik-Tinsley, Rachel & Qitsualik-Tinsley, Sean. Tuniit: Mysterious Folk of the Arctic, 1 vol. Bigham, Sean, illus. 2014. (ENG.). 60p. (J). (gr. 2-4). 16.95 *(978-1-927095-76-8(X))* Inhabit Media Inc. CAN. Dist: Independent Pubs. Group.

Reynolds, Jan. Frozen Land, 1 vol. 2007. (Vanishing Cultures Ser.). (ENG., Illus.). 32p. (J). (gr. 4-7). 16.95 *(978-1-60060-143-9(X));* 10.95 *(978-1-60060-128-6(6))* Lee & Low Bks., Inc.

Rhodes, Sam. Native American Rhymes: The People of the Far North, 9 vols. Howard, Kimberley, ed. Haas, Deborah, illus. 2003. 92p. (J). (gr. 3-5). mass mkt. 7.50 *(978-0-9743214-0-0(0))* Rhodes Educational Pubns.

Spilsbury, Louise. Igloos & Inuit Life. 2011. (Big Picture: Homes Ser.). (ENG.). 24p. (gr. 1-2). pap. 41.70 *(978-1-4296-6730-2(3),* First Facts) Capstone Press of Coughlan Cos.

Strudwick, Leslie. Inuit. (J). 2012. 28.55 *(978-1-61913-092-0(0))* 2003. (Illus.). 32p. lib. bdg. 26.00 *(978-1-59036-122-1(9))* Weigl Pubs., Inc.

—Inuit with Code. 2012. (World Cultures Ser.). (ENG., Illus.). 32p. (J). (gr. 3-7). pap. 13.95 *(978-1-61913-530-7(2),* AV2 by Weigl) Weigl Pubs., Inc.

Wallace, Mary. An Inuksuk Means Welcome. 2015. (ENG., Illus.). 32p. (J). (gr. -1-2). 17.95 *(978-1-77147-137-4(9),* Owlkids) Owlkids Bks. Inc. CAN. Dist: Publishers Group West (PGW).

Wallace, Mary & Owlkids Books Inc. Staff. Make Your Own Inuksuk. 2004. (Wow Canada! Ser.). (ENG., Illus.). 32p. (J). (gr. 3-6). pap. 11.95 *(978-1-897066-14-0(7),* Maple Tree Pr.) Owlkids Bks. Inc. CAN. Dist: Publishers Group West (PGW).

Williams, Suzanne Morgan. The Inuit. 2003. (Watts Library). (Illus.). 64p. (J). 25.50 *(978-0-531-12172-6(0),* Watts, Franklin) Scholastic Library Publishing.

Wolfson, Evelyn. Mythology of the Inuit. 2014. (Mythology, Myths, & Legends Ser.). (Illus.). 96p. (J). (gr. 6-12). 27.94 *(978-0-7660-6177-4(9))* Enslow Pubs., Inc.

World Book, Inc Staff, contrib. by. Peoples of the Arctic & Subarctic. 2009. (J). *(978-0-7166-2132-4(0))* World Bk., Inc.

Young, Dan. Life among the Inuit. 2013. (InfoMax Readers Ser.). (ENG.). 24p. (J). (gr. 3-4). pap. 8.25 *(978-1-4777-2770-6(1));* pap. 49.50 *(978-1-4777-2605-1(5))* Rosen Publishing Group, Inc., The. (Rosen Classroom).

INUIT—FICTION

Brereton, Libby. A Visit with Moon & Sun: A Tale from the Inuit. Peluso, Martina, illus. 2016. 24p. (J). pap. *(978-1-927244-60-9(9))* Flying Start Bks.

—A Visit with Moon & Sun (Big Book Edition) A Tale from the Inuit. Peluso, Martina, illus. 2016. 24p. (J). pap. *(978-1-927244-70-8(6))* Flying Start Bks.

Brouwer, Sigmund. Oil King Courage, 1 vol. 2009. (Orca Sports Ser.). (ENG.). 240p. (YA). (gr. 6-10). pap. 9.95 *(978-1-55469-197-5(4))* Orca Bk. Pubs. USA.

Christopher, Danny. Putuguq & Kublu, 1 vol. Arijanto, Astrid, illus. 2017. (ENG.). 40p. (J). (gr. k-2). pap. 5.95 ***(978-1-77227-143-0(8))*** Inhabit Media Inc. CAN. Dist: Independent Pubs. Group.

Christopher, Neil. The Hidden: A Compendium of Arctic Giants, Dwarves, Gnomes, Trolls, Faeries & Other Strange Beings from Inuit Oral History, 1 vol. Austin, Mike, illus. 2014. (ENG.). 256p. (YA). (gr. 7). 29.95 *(978-1-927095-59-1(X))* Inhabit Media Inc. CAN. Dist: Independent Pubs. Group.

Dumont, Claire. Noel: An Unforgettable Night! 2017. (ENG., Illus.). 32p. (J). 14.95 ***(978-0-8091-6780-7(8))*** Paulist Pr.

Edwardson, Debby Dahl. Whale Snow. Patterson, Annie, illus. 2004. (ENG.). 32p. (J). (gr. -1-3). pap. 7.95 *(978-1-57091-394-5(3))* Charlesbridge Publishing, Inc.

Feagan, Robert. Napachee. 2006. (ENG.). 128p. (J). (gr. 7). pap. 9.99 *(978-1-55002-636-8(4),* Sandcastle Bks.) Dundurn CAN. Dist: Ingram Publisher Services.

Foresman, Timothy. The Last Little Polar Bear: A Global Change Adventure Story. Laura Lee, Cundiff, illus. 2007. 60p. (J). per. 19.95 *(978-0-9776906-2-6(8))* Blueline Publishing.

Hamel, Mike. Rylan the Renegade, 6. 2007. (Matterhorn the Brave Ser.: 6). (ENG.). 192p. (J). (gr. 8-7). per. 9.99 *(978-0-89957-838-5(1))* AMG Pubs.

Heinz, Brian J. Kayuktuk: An Arctic Quest. Van Zyle, Jon, illus. 2004. (J). pap. 6.95 *(978-0-936335-09-4(2));* 14.95 *(978-0-936335-08-7(4))* Ballyhoo BookWorks, Inc.

—Nanuk, Lord of the Ice. Manchess, Gregory, illus. 2005. (J). *(978-0-936335-13-1(0));* pap. *(978-0-936335-14-8(9))* Ballyhoo BookWorks, Inc.

Hobbs, Will. Never Say Die. 224p. (J). (gr. 3-7). 2014. (ENG.). pap. 6.99 *(978-0-06-170880-0(1))* 2013. (ENG.). 16.99 *(978-0-06-170878-7(X))* 2013. lib. bdg. 17.89 *(978-0-06-170879-4(8))* HarperCollins Pubs.

Immi's Gift, 1 vol. 2014. (ENG., Illus.). 32p. (J). (gr. -1-3). 7.95 *(978-1-56145-813-4(9))* Peachtree Pubs.

Kilabuk, Elisha. The Qalupalik, 1 vol. Ang, Joy, illus. 2011. (ENG.). 32p. (J). (gr. 1-3). 12.95 *(978-1-926569-31-4(8))* Inhabit Media Inc. CAN. Dist: Independent Pubs. Group.

Kirkpatrick, Katherine. Between Two Worlds. (ENG.). 304p. (YA). (gr. 9). 2015. pap. 9.99 *(978-0-375-87221-1(3),* Ember) 2014. 16.99 *(978-0-385-74047-0(6),* Lamb, Wendy Bks.) Random Hse. Children's Bks.

Lewis, Marion. Kaugjagjuk, 1 vol. Smith, Kim, illus. 2011. (ENG.). 40p. (J). (gr. 1-3). 13.95 *(978-1-926569-39-0(3))* Inhabit Media Inc. CAN. Dist: Independent Pubs. Group.

Littlewood, Karin. Immi's Gift, 1 vol. Littlewood, Karin, illus. 2010. (ENG., Illus.). 32p. (J). (gr. -1-3). 15.95 *(978-1-56145-545-4(8))* Peachtree Pubs.

McGrath, Robin. Livyers World. 2007. (ENG.). 150p. (J). (gr. 4-7). per. *(978-1-897174-15-9(2))* Creative Bk. Publishing.

Meredith, Susan Markowitz. A Happy Summer Day: Set Of 6. 2010. (Early Connections Ser.). (J). 37.00 net. *(978-1-4108-1371-8(1))* Benchmark Education Co.

Noah, Jennifer. Nala's Magical Mitsiaq: A Story of Inuit Adoption, 1 vol. Leng, Qin, illus. 2013. (ENG.). 32p. (J). (gr. 1-3). 10.95 *(978-1-927095-26-3(3))* Inhabit Media Inc. CAN. Dist: Independent Pubs. Group.

Noah, Jennifer & Giroux, Chris. Our First Caribou Hunt, 1 vol. Lim, Hwei, illus. 2015. (ENG.). 32p. (J). (gr. k-2). 10.95 *(978-1-77227-022-8(9))* Inhabit Media Inc. CAN. Dist: Independent Pubs. Group.

Oelschlager, Vanita. Magic Words: From the Ancient Oral Tradition of the Inuit. Blanc, Mike, illus. 2013. (ENG.). 24p. (J). (gr. -1-3). 15.95 *(978-0-9832904-6-9(6));* pap. 8.95 *(978-0-9832904-7-6(4))* VanitaBooks.

Polak, Monique. The Middle of Everywhere, 1 vol. 2009. (ENG., Illus.). 208p. (YA). (gr. 7-12). pap. 12.95 *(978-1-55469-090-9(0))* Orca Bk. Pubs. USA.

Qaunaq, Sakiasi. The Orphan & the Polar Bear, 1 vol. Widermann, Eva, illus. 2011. (ENG.). 40p. (J). (gr. 1-3). 13.95 *(978-1-926569-44-4(X))* Inhabit Media Inc. CAN. Dist: Independent Pubs. Group.

Qitsualik, Rachel A. The Shadows That Rush Past: A Collection of Frightening Inuit Folktales, 1 vol. MacDougall, Larry & Fiegenschuh, Emily, illus. 2011. (ENG.). 42p. (J). (gr. 3-6). 13.95 *(978-1-926569-46-8(6))* Inhabit Media Inc. CAN. Dist: Independent Pubs. Group.

Qitsualik-Tinsley, Rachel & Qitsualik-Tinsley, Sean. How Things Came to Be: Inuit Stories of Creation, 1 vol. Lewis-MacDougall, Patricia Ann & Fiegenschuh, Emily, illus. 2015. (ENG.). 60p. (J). (gr. -1-k). 16.95 *(978-1-927095-78-2(6))* Inhabit Media Inc. CAN. Dist: Independent Pubs. Group.

—Skraelings: Clashes in the Old Arctic, 1 vol. Trabbold, Andrew, illus. 2014. (Arctic Moon Magick Ser.). (ENG.). 120p. (YA). (gr. 7). pap. 10.95 *(978-1-927095-54-6(9))* Inhabit Media Inc. CAN. Dist: Independent Pubs. Group.

Qitsualik-Tinsley, Rachel, et al. Stories of Survival & Revenge: From Inuit Folklore, 1 vol. 2015. (ENG., Illus.). 80p. (YA). (gr. 7). pap. 12.95 *(978-1-77227-001-3(6))* Inhabit Media Inc. CAN. Dist: Independent Pubs. Group.

Renaud, Anne. Missuk's Snow Geese. Côté, Geneviève, illus. 2008. (ENG.). 36p. (J). (gr. -1-3). 16.95 *(978-1-894965-82-8(5))* Simply Read Bks. CAN. Dist: Ingram Publisher Services.

Riel, Jörn & Chodzin, Sherab. The Raiders Vol. 2: The Inuk Quartet. Cann, Helen, illus. 2013. (ENG.). 128p. (J). (gr. 4-6). pap. 9.99 *(978-1-84686-744-6(4))* Barefoot Bks., Inc.

Riel, Jørn, et al. The Snowstorm. Cann, Helen, illus. 2012. (ENG.). 128p. (J). (gr. 4-6). pap. 9.99 *(978-1-84686-797-2(5))* Barefoot Bks., Inc.

Rivera, Raquel. Arctic Adventures: Tales from the Lives of Inuit Artists, 1 vol. Marton, Jirina, illus. 2007. (ENG.). 36p. (J). (gr. 2-18). 18.95 *(978-0-88899-714-2(0))* Groundwood Bks. CAN. Dist: Publishers Group West (PGW).

—Tuk & the Whale, 1 vol. Gerber, Mary Jane, illus. (ENG.). (J). (gr. 2-5). 2009. 88p. pap. 7.95 *(978-0-88899-891-0(0))* 2008. 96p. 15.95 *(978-0-88899-689-3(6))* Groundwood Bks. CAN. Dist: Publishers Group West (PGW).

Stafford, Liliana. Snow Bear. Davis, Lambert, illus. 32p. (J). pap. *(978-0-88899-441-7(9))* Groundwood Bks.

Taylor, Theodore & Taylor, Theodore. Ice Drift. 2006. (ENG., Illus.). 240p. (J). (gr. 2-5). pap. 7.99 *(978-0-15-205550-9(9))* Houghton Mifflin Harcourt Publishing Co.

Teevee, Ningeokuluk. Alego, 1 vol. Manning-Toonoo, Nina, tr. 2009. (ENG., Illus.). 24p. (J). (gr. -1-2). 17.95 *(978-0-88899-943-6(7))* Groundwood Bks. CAN. Dist: Publishers Group West (PGW).

Ulmer, Mike. The Gift of the Inuksuk. Rose, Melanie, illus. rev. ed. 2004. (ENG.). 32p. (J). (gr. k-6). 17.95 *(978-1-58536-214-1(X))* Sleeping Bear Pr.

van Keuren, Luise. Raven, Stay by Me. 2012. (ENG.). 162p. pap. *(978-1-894377-30-0(3))* Breakwater Bks., Ltd.

INVALIDS

see People with Disabilities; Sick

INVASION OF PRIVACY
see Privacy, Right of
INVENTIONS
see also Creation (Literary, Artistic, etc.); Inventors
AZ Books Staff. Discoveries & Inventions. Kazimirova, Karina, ed. 2012. (Encyclopedia with Flaps Ser.). (ENG.). 22p. (J). (gr. 1-3). bds. 13.95 *(978-1-61889-152-5(9))* AZ Bks. LLC.
Banting, Erinn. Inventing the Automobile. 2006. (Breakthrough Inventions Ser.). (ENG., Illus.). 32p. (J). (gr. 3-7). pap. *(978-0-7787-2834-4(X))* Crabtree Publishing Co.
—Inventing the Telephone. 2006. (Breakthrough Inventions Ser.). (ENG., Illus.). 32p. (J). (gr. 4-7). pap. *(978-0-7787-2837-5(4))*; lib. bdg. *(978-0-7787-2815-3(3))* Crabtree Publishing Co.
Bark, Jasper. The Inventions of Leonardo Da Vinci. 2015. (ENG., Illus.). 14p. (J). (gr. 4). 21.95 *(978-1-62686-446-7(2)*, Silver Dolphin Bks.) Readerlink Distribution Services, LLC.
Barretta, Gene. Now & Ben: The Modern Inventions of Benjamin Franklin. 2007. (J). (gr. 2-5). 29.95 incl. audio compact disk *(978-0-8045-4175-6(2))*; 27.95 incl. audio *(978-0-8045-6952-1(5))* Spoken Arts, Inc.
—Now & Ben: The Modern Inventions of Benjamin Franklin. Barretta, Gene, illus. 2008. (ENG., Illus.). 40p. (J). (gr. k-4). pap. 8.99 *(978-0-312-53569-8(4)*, 9780312535698) Square Fish.
—Timeless Thomas: How Thomas Edison Changed Our Lives. Barretta, Gene, illus. 2012. (ENG., Illus.). 40p. (J). (gr. 1-5). 18.99 *(978-0-8050-9108-3(4)*, 9780805091083, Holt, Henry & Co. Bks. For Young Readers) Holt, Henry & Co.
Bearce, Stephanie. Insane Inventors. 2017. (Twisted True Tales from Science Ser.: 0). (ENG., Illus.). 125p. (J). (gr. 4-7). pap. 8.95 *(978-1-61821-570-3(1))* Prufrock Pr.
Beattie, Rob. Invent It! 2017. (ENG., Illus.). 64p. (J). (gr. 3). 12.95 *(978-1-4549-2349-7(0))* Sterling Publishing Co., Inc.
Beaty, Andrea. Rosie Revere's Big Project Book for Bold Engineers. Roberts, David, illus. 2017. (ENG.). 96p. (J). (gr. k-2). pap. 14.95 *(978-1-4197-1910-3(6)*, Abrams Bks. for Young Readers) Abrams, Inc.
Benchmark Education Company, LLC Staff, compiled by. Invention & Technology: Theme Set. 2006. (J). 158.00 *(978-1-4108-7100-8(2))* Benchmark Education Co.
Bender, Lionel. DK Eyewitness Books: Invention: Invention. 2013. (DK Eyewitness Bks.). (ENG.). 72p. (J). (gr. 3-7). 19.99 *(978-1-4654-0902-7(5)*, DK Children) Dorling Kindersley Publishing, Inc.
Bender, Lionel & Dorling Kindersley Publishing Staff. Invention. 2013. (DK Eyewitness Bks.). (ENG.). 72p. (J). (gr. 3-7). 16.99 *(978-1-4654-0901-0(7)*, DK Children) Dorling Kindersley Publishing, Inc.
Berger, Melvin. Think Factory: Amazing Inventions. 2006. (Illus.). 47p. *(978-0-439-51913-7(6))* Scholastic, Inc.
Bergin, Mark. Inventions. 2016. (Wise Up Ser.). 32p. (gr. 2-6). 31.35 *(978-1-62588-341-4(2)*, Smart Apple Media) Black Rabbit Bks.
Bidder, Jane. Inventions We Use at Home. 2006. (Everyday Inventions Ser.). (Illus.). 32p. (gr. 1-4). lib. bdg. 26.00 *(978-0-8368-6898-2(6)*, Gareth Stevens Learning Library) Stevens, Gareth Publishing LLLP.
—Inventions We Use for Information & Entertainment. 2006. (Everyday Inventions Ser.). (Illus.). 32p. (gr. 1-4). lib. bdg. 26.00 *(978-0-8368-6899-9(4)*, Gareth Stevens Learning Library) Stevens, Gareth Publishing LLLP.
Biskup, Agnieszka. The Science Behind Batman's Tools. Vecchio, Luciano, illus. 2016. (Science Behind Batman Ser.). (ENG.). 24p. (J). (gr. 1-2). lib. bdg. 25.32 *(978-1-5157-2038-6(1)*, DC Super Heroes) Stone Arch Bks.
Bloopers of Invention. 2015. (Bloopers of Invention Ser.). (ENG.). 24p. (J). (gr. 2-3). 135.60 *(978-1-4824-2546-8(7))*; pap., pap., pap. 293.40 *(978-1-4824-3442-2(3))*; pap., pap., pap. 48.90 *(978-1-4824-3443-9(1))* Stevens, Gareth Publishing LLLP.
Bonavista, Rufito & Beascoa, Santiago. Then & Now: A Journey Through the History of Things. Altarriba, Eduard, illus. 2016. (ENG.). 44p. (J). (gr. 1-5). 14.95 *(978-1-4549-1962-9(0))* Sterling Publishing Co., Inc.
Booth, Jack. The 10 Greatest Accidental Inventions. 2007. (J). 14.99 *(978-1-55448-510-9(X))* Scholastic Library Publishing.
Brasch, Nicolas. The Industrial Revolution: Age of Invention. 2013. (Discovery Education: Discoveries & Inventions Ser.). 32p. (J). (gr. 3-6). pap. 60.00 *(978-1-4777-1507-9(X))*; pap. 10.00 *(978-1-4777-1506-2(1))*; lib. bdg. 25.25 *(978-1-4777-1332-7(8))* Rosen Publishing Group, Inc., The. (PowerKids Pr.).
Braun, Sandra. Women Inventors Who Changed the World. 2011. (Great Women of Achievement Ser.). (ENG., Illus.). 112p. (YA). (gr. 5-8). lib. bdg. 34.60 *(978-1-4488-5996-2(4)*, Rosen Reference) Rosen Publishing Group, Inc., The.
Brewer, Duncan. Inventions. 2010. (Mosaic of Magical Information Ser.). (Illus.). 48p. (YA). (gr. 3-18). 19.95 *(978-1-4222-1990-4(9))* Mason Crest.
—100 Facts Inventions. 2013. (Illus.). 48p. (J). *(978-1-4351-5092-8(9))* Barnes & Noble, Inc.
Britannica, Learning Library. Technology & Inventions. 2003. (Illus.). 64p. 14.95 *(978-1-59339-034-1(3))* Encyclopaedia Britannica, Inc.
Brown, Don. A Wizard from the Start: The Incredible Boyhood & Amazing Inventions of Thomas Edison. Brown, Don, illus. 2010. (ENG., Illus.). 32p. (J). (gr. -1-3). 17.99 *(978-0-547-19487-5(0))* Houghton Mifflin Harcourt Publishing Co.
Brown Reference Group. History of Invention Set. 2004. (History of Invention Ser.). 96p. (gr. 6-12). 175.00 *(978-0-8160-5435-0(5))* Facts On File, Inc.
Burns Chong, Susan. Step-By-Step Guide to Innovating at School & Work. 2014. (Winning at Work Readiness Ser.). 64p. (J). (gr. 9-12). 32.95 *(978-1-4777-7786-2(5))* Rosen Publishing Group, Inc., The.
Canfield, Michael. Freaky Stories about Inventions. 2016. (Freaky True Science Ser.). (Illus.). 32p. (J). (gr. 5-4). pap. 10.50 *(978-1-4824-4819-1(X))* Stevens, Gareth Publishing LLLP.
Capstone Press Staff, et al. Famous Firsts, 1 vol. 2014. (Famous Firsts Ser.). (ENG.). 24p. (J). (gr. k-1). 106.60 *(978-1-4914-0672-4(0)*, Pebble Plus) Capstone Press of Coughlan Cos.
Carlson, Laurie M. Queen of Inventions: How the Sewing Machine Changed the World. 2003. (Illus.). 32p. lib. bdg. 22.90 *(978-0-7613-2706-6(1)*, Millbrook Pr.) Lerner Publishing Group.
Carmichael, Lindsey. Innovations in Entertainment. 2016. (Problem Solved! Your Turn to Think Big Ser.). (ENG.). 32p. (J). (gr. 3-6). *(978-0-7787-2671-5(1))* Crabtree Publishing Co.
Casey, Susan. Kids Inventing! A Handbook for Young Inventors. 2005. (ENG., Illus.). 148p. (J). (gr. 1-12). pap. 15.95 *(978-0-471-66086-6(8)*, Jossey-Bass) Wiley, John & Sons, Inc.
Castaldo, Nancy F. Greatest Inventions. Random House, illus. 2016. (Stepping Stone Book(TM) Ser.). (ENG.). 80p. (J). (gr. 2-5). pap. 7.99 *(978-1-101-93340-4(2))*; lib. bdg. 12.99 *(978-1-101-93341-1(0))* Random Hse. Children's Bks. (Random Hse. Bks. for Young Readers).
Catala, Ellen. What Has Changed? 2005. (Yellow Umbrella Fluent Level Ser.). (ENG., Illus.). 16p. (gr. k-1). pap. 35.70 *(978-0-7368-5307-1(3)*, Yellow Umbrella Bks.) Capstone Press of Coughlan Cos.
Claybourne, A. & Larkum, A. Inventor's Portfolio Kit (Bag). 2008. (Kid Kits Ser.). 96p. (J). pap. 24.99 *(978-1-60130-105-5(7)*, Usborne) EDC Publishing.
—Inventor's Portfolio Kit (Box) 2008. (Kid Kits Ser.). 96p. (J). pap. 24.99 *(978-1-60130-107-9(3)*, Usborne) EDC Publishing.
Claybourne, Anna. The Story of Inventions. Chisholm, Jane, ed. 2007. (Story of Inventions Ser.). (Illus.). 96p. (J). (gr. 4-7). per. 10.99 *(978-0-7945-1710-6(2)*, Usborne) EDC Publishing.
Cobb, William, Jr. Willie Cobb's Invention: Inventing with a Motive. 2008. 212p. pap. 17.95 *(978-0-595-52103-6(7))* iUniverse, Inc.
Colson, Mary. Get Inventing!, 1 vol. 2014. (Dream It, Do It! Ser.). (ENG., Illus.). 32p. (gr. 1-3). pap. 8.95 *(978-1-4109-6269-0(5)*, Read Me!) Heinemann-Raintree.
Culp, Jennifer. Ancient Chinese Technology. 2016. (Spotlight on the Rise & Fall of Ancient Civilizations Ser.). 48p. (J). (gr. 6-6). pap. 11.75 *(978-1-4777-8897-4(2))* Rosen Publishing Group, Inc., The.
Currie, Stephen. African-American Inventors. 2010. (Lucent Library of Black History Ser.). (Illus.). 128p. (gr. 7-10). 34.80 *(978-1-4205-0121-6(6)*, Lucent Bks.) Cengage Gale.
Cutting, Robert. The 10 Most Revolutionary Inventions. 2007. (J). 14.99 *(978-1-55448-460-7(X))* Scholastic Library Publishing.
Davis, Lynn. Amazing Inventors & Innovators. 2015. (Amazing Inventors & Innovators Ser.: Vol. 6). (ENG.). 24p. (J). (gr. 4-7). lib. bdg. 153.90 *(978-1-62403-720-7(8))* ABDO Publishing Co.
Daynes, Katie. Toilets, Telephones & Other Useful Inventions. (Young Reading Ser. 1 Gift Bks). 48p. (J). 2010. pap. 5.99 *(978-0-7945-2818-8(X))* 2005. (gr. 2-18). pap. 5.95 *(978-0-7945-0888-3(X))* EDC Publishing. (Usborne).
Demuth, Patricia Brennan. Thomas Edison & His Bright Idea. Tuya, Jez, illus. 2016. (Penguin Young Readers, Level 3 Ser.). (ENG.). 32p. (J). (gr. 1-3). pap. 3.99 *(978-0-448-48830-1(2)*, Penguin Young Readers) Penguin Young Readers Group.
Discovery Education: Discoveries & Inventions. 2013. (Discovery Education: Discoveries & Inventions Ser.). 32p. (J). (gr. 3-6). 151.50 *(978-1-4777-1551-2(7))*; pap. 60.00 *(978-1-4777-2699-0(3))*; pap. 360.00 *(978-1-4777-2700-3(0))* Rosen Publishing Group, Inc., The. (PowerKids Pr.).
Dorling Kindersley Publishing Staff. Ideas That Changed the World. 2013. (ENG.). 256p. (J). (gr. 5-12). pap. 16.99 *(978-1-4654-1423-6(1)*, DK Children) Dorling Kindersley Publishing, Inc.
—Pocket Genius: Inventions. 2016. (Pocket Genius Ser.). (ENG., Illus.). 160p. (J). (gr. 3-7). pap. 4.99 *(978-1-4654-4606-0(0)*, DK Children) Dorling Kindersley Publishing, Inc.
—1,000 Inventions & Discoveries. 2014. (ENG., Illus.). 256p. (J). (gr. 4-7). pap. 16.99 *(978-1-4654-2038-1(X)*, DK Children) Dorling Kindersley Publishing, Inc.
Dowling, Lucy. Why Why Why... Do Clocks Have Hands? 2010. (Why Why Why Ser.). 32p. (J). (gr. 1-3). lib. bdg. 18.95 *(978-1-4222-1580-7(6))* Mason Crest.
Downey, Glen R. The 10 Most Revolutionary Military Inventions. 2008. 14.99 *(978-1-55448-500-0(2))* Scholastic Library Publishing.
Draze, Dianne. Inventions, Inventors & You. 2005. (ENG.). 64p. (Orig.). (gr. 3-7). pap. 14.95 *(978-1-59363-082-9(4))* Prufrock Pr.
Dunham, Bandhu Scott. We Like to Invent! Stark, Ryan, illus. 2010. (J). pap. *(978-1-935387-13-8(8))* Hohm Pr.
Dunn, Karen Lewit. What's the Problem? 2008. (Discovering & Exploring Science Ser.). (Illus.). 16p. (J). (gr. -1-3). lib. bdg. 12.95 *(978-0-7569-8421-2(1))* Perfection Learning Corp.
Eggleton, Jill. An Idea Seed. 2007. (Connectors Ser.). (gr. 2-5). pap. *(978-1-877453-09-0(9))* Global Education Systems Ltd.
Enz, Tammy & Biskup, Agnieszka. Batman Science, 1 vol. 2014. (Batman Science Ser.). (ENG.). 32p. (gr. 3-4). lib. bdg. 109.28 *(978-1-4765-6188-2(5)*, DC Super Heroes) Stone Arch Bks.
Erlbach, Arlene & National Geographic Learning Staff. The Kids' Invention Book. 2010. (ENG., Illus.). 64p. (C). (gr. 3-6). pap. 15.95 *(978-0-8225-9844-2(2))* National Geographic School Publishing, Inc.
Fielder, Scott. The 10 Greatest 21st Century Innovations. 2008. 14.99 *(978-1-55448-550-5(9))* Scholastic Library Publishing.
Fontichiaro, Kristin. Organizing a MakerFest. 2017. (21st Century Skills Innovation Library: Makers As Innovators Junior Ser.). (ENG., Illus.). 24p. (J). (gr. 2-5). lib. bdg. 28.50 *(978-1-63472-190-5(X)*, 209332) Cherry Lake Publishing.
Freedman, Jeri. Strategic Inventions of the Napoleonic Wars. 2016. (Tech in the Trenches Ser.). 112p. (J). 42.79 *(978-1-5026-2351-5(X))* Cavendish Square Publishing.
Frith, Alex & King, Colin. See Inside Inventions IR. 2012. (See Inside Board Bks). 16p. (J). ring bd. 13.99 *(978-0-7945-3239-0(X)*, Usborne) EDC Publishing.
Getting the Most Out of Makerspaces to Go from Idea to Market. 2014. (Makerspaces Ser.). 64p. (J). (gr. 6-12). 32.95 *(978-1-4777-7795-4(4)*, Rosen Reference) Rosen Publishing Group, Inc., The.
Gilby, Nancy Benovich. FIRST Robotics. 2015. (21st Century Skills Innovation Library: Makers As Innovators Ser.). (ENG., Illus.). 32p. (J). (gr. 4-8). 29.93 *(978-1-63362-378-1(5)*, 206932) Cherry Lake Publishing.
Goldish, Meish. Accidental Inventions: (Or Made by Mistake) 2005. (Illus.). 64p. (J). pap. *(978-0-669-51406-3(3))* Great Source Education Group, Inc.
Gomez, Rebecca. Thomas Edison, 1 vol. 2003. (First Biographies Ser.). (ENG., Illus.). 32p. (gr. k-4). 27.07 *(978-1-57765-945-7(7)*, Buddy Bks.) ABDO Publishing Co.
Graham, Ian. Machines & Inventions. Antram, David et al, illus. 2008. (World of Wonder Ser.). (ENG.). 32p. (J). (gr. 1-4). 29.00 *(978-0-531-24027-4(4))*; pap. 9.95 *(978-0-531-23823-3(7))* Scholastic Library Publishing. (Children's Pr.).
Great Inventions, 5 bks., Group 2. Incl. Airplane. Faber, Harold. 128p. (J). (gr. 3-7). lib. bdg. *(978-0-7614-1876-4(8))*; Automobile. Collier, James Lincoln. 112p. (J). (gr. 3-7). lib. bdg. *(978-0-7614-1877-1(6))*; Electricity & the Lightbulb. Collier, James Lincoln. 112p. (YA). (gr. 8-12). lib. bdg. *(978-0-7614-1878-8(4))*; Steam Engine. Collier, James Lincoln. 112p. (YA). (gr. 8-12). lib. bdg. *(978-0-7614-1880-1(6))*; Telephone. Stefoff, Rebecca. 127p. (YA). (gr. 8-12). lib. bdg. *(978-0-7614-1879-5(2))*; (Illus.). 2005. *(978-0-7614-1875-7(X)*, Benchmark Bks.) Marshall Cavendish Corp.
Great Inventions Classroom Library. (gr. 2-5). lib. bdg. 34.95 *(978-0-7368-4545-8(3))* Red Brick Learning.
Great Inventions Group 3, 5 bks., Set. Incl. Medical Imaging. Sherrow, Victoria. (gr. 8-10). lib. bdg. 29.95 *(978-0-7614-2231-0(5))*; Microscopes & Telescopes. Stefoff, Rebecca. (J). (gr. 3-7). lib. bdg. 39.93 *(978-0-7614-2230-3(7))*; Rockets. Otfinoski, Steven. (gr. 8-7). lib. bdg. 29.95 *(978-0-7614-2232-7(3))*; Submarines. Stefoff, Rebecca. (gr. 8-7). lib. bdg. 29.95 *(978-0-7614-2229-7(3))*; Television. Otfinoski, Steven. (gr. 8-7). lib. bdg. 29.95 *(978-0-7614-2228-0(5))*; (Illus.). 128p. 2006. 2007. Set lib. bdg. 199.64 *(978-0-7614-2227-3(7)*, Benchmark Bks.) Marshall Cavendish Corp.
Great Inventions [NASCO]. 2010. (Great Inventions Ser.). 32p. pap. 71.55 *(978-1-4296-4632-1(2)*, Fact Finders) Capstone Press of Coughlan Cos.
Great Mistakes. 2014. (ENG.). 144p. (J). (gr. 3-7). pap. 12.95 *(978-1-59077-346-8(2))* Evans, M. & Co., Inc.
Green, Jen. Medicine. 2004. (Routes of Science Ser.). (Illus.). 40p. (J). (gr. 4-7). 23.70 *(978-1-4103-0168-0(0)*, Blackbirch Pr., Inc.) Cengage Gale.
Gregory, Josh. From Butterfly Wings to Display Technology. 2014. (21st Century Skills Innovation Library: Innovations from Nature Ser.). (ENG., Illus.). 32p. (J). (gr. 4-8). pap. 14.21 *(978-1-62431-760-6(X)*, 203285); lib. bdg. 28.50 *(978-1-62431-754-5(5)*, 203284) Cherry Lake Publishing.
Grossman, Max & Benchmark Education Co., LLC. The Idea Machine: My Inventor's Journal. 2014. (Text Connections Ser.). (J). (gr. 3). *(978-1-4509-9655-6(8))* Benchmark Education Co.
Hall, Derek, ed. Philosophy, Invention, & Engineering. 2009. (FAYFT: Great Scientists Ser.). 64p. (gr. 4-10). 39.95 *(978-1-933834-48-1(X))* Brown Bear Bks.
Hamilton Waxman, Laura & Waxman, Laura. Fabulous Fashion Inventions. 2013. (Awesome Inventions You Use Every Day Ser.). (ENG., Illus.). 32p. (gr. 3-6). lib. bdg. 26.60 *(978-1-4677-1093-0(8)*, Lerner Pubns.) Lerner Publishing Group.
Happy Accidents!, 6 Pack. (Action Packs Ser.). 104p. (gr. 3-5). 44.00 *(978-0-7635-3303-8(3))* Rigby Education.
HarrisNic. THE GREATEST INVENTION OF ALL TIME LOW INTERMEDIATE BOOK WITH ONLINE ACCESS. 2014. (ENG., Illus.). 24p. (J). pap. 9.50 *(978-1-107-62161-9(5))* Cambridge Univ. Pr.
Hello From 2030: The Science of the Future & You. 2014. (ENG., Illus.). 224p. (J). (gr. 3-7). 15.99 *(978-1-58270-474-6(0))* Aladdin/Beyond Words.
Higgins, Nadia. Fun Food Inventions. 2013. (Awesome Inventions You Use Every Day Ser.). (ENG., Illus.). 32p. (gr. 3-6). lib. bdg. 26.60 *(978-1-4677-1091-6(1)*, Lerner Pubns.) Lerner Publishing Group.
—The World's Oddest Inventions. 2015. (Library of Weird Ser.). (ENG.). 32p. (gr. 3-4). lib. bdg. 27.99 *(978-1-4914-2016-4(2))* Capstone Press of Coughlan Cos.
Hollar, Sherman. Pioneers of the Industrial Age: Breakthroughs in Technology. 2012. (Inventors & Innovators Ser.). (ENG., Illus.). 112p. (YA). (gr. 7-12). 65.80 *(978-1-61530-789-0(3))*; 32.90 *(978-1-61530-696-1(X))* Rosen Publishing Group, Inc., The.
Holper, Paul & Torok, Simon. Imagining the Future: Invisibility, Immortality & 40 Other Incredible Ideas. 2017. (ENG., Illus.). 146p. (gr. 4-10). pap. 17.95 *(978-1-4863-0272-7(6))* CSIRO Publishing AUS. Dist: Stylus Publishing, LLC.
Holzweiss, Kristina & Barth, Amy. I Can Make Marvelous Movers. 2017. (Rookie Star — MakerSpace Projects Ser.). (ENG.). 32p. (J). lib. bdg. 25.00 ***(978-0-531-23413-6(4)***, Children's Pr.) Scholastic Library Publishing.
Hopkins, Lee Bennett. Incredible Inventions. Sarcone-Roach, Julia, illus. 2009. 32p. (J). (gr. k-5). (ENG.). 17.99 *(978-0-06-087245-8(4))*; lib. bdg. 18.89 *(978-0-06-087246-5(2))* HarperCollins Pubs. (Greenwillow Bks.).
Hubbard, Ben. Hi Tech World: Cool Stuff. 2010. (ENG., Illus.). 32p. (J). lib. bdg. *(978-0-7787-7529-4(1))* Crabtree Publishing Co.
Hughes, Susan & Wandelmaier, Michael. Case Closed? Nine Mysteries Unlocked by Modern Science. Wandelmaier, Michael, illus. 2013. (ENG., Illus.). 88p. (J). (gr. 3-7). pap. 12.95 *(978-1-55453-363-3(5))* Kids Can Pr., Ltd. CAN. Dist: Hachette Bk. Group.
Indovino, Shaina. Women Inventors. Lee-Karlon, Ann, ed. 2013. (Major Women in Science Ser.: 10). 64p. (J). (gr. 7-18). 22.95 *(978-1-4222-2932-3(7))* Mason Crest.
Inventions & Discoveries. (Action Bks.). 64p. (J). (gr. 3-7). pap. *(978-1-882210-68-8(9))* Action Publishing, Inc.
Inventions & Discoveries, 12 vols., Set. 2009. (J). (gr. 4-6). lib. bdg. 239.00 *(978-0-7166-0380-1(2))* World Bk., Inc.
Inventions & Discovery. 2016. (Inventions & Discovery Ser.). (ENG.). 32p. (gr. 3-4). lib. bdg. 429.10 *(978-1-5157-4020-9(X)*, Graphic Library) Capstone Press of Coughlan Cos.
Inventors & Inventions - Group 2, 6 bks., Set. Incl. Biotechnology. Wells, Donna K. lib. bdg. 25.64 *(978-0-7614-0046-2(X))*; Nuclear Power. Holland, Gini. lib. bdg. 25.64 *(978-0-7614-0047-9(8))*; Radiology. Winkler, Kathy. lib. bdg. 25.64 *(978-0-7614-0075-2(3))*; Satellites. Fox, Mary Virginia. lib. bdg. 25.64 *(978-0-7614-0049-3(4))*; Television. Riehecky, Janet. lib. bdg. 25.64 *(978-0-7614-0045-5(1))*; Video. Biel, Jackie. lib. bdg. 25.64 *(978-0-7614-0048-6(6))*; 64p. (YA). (gr. 5-9). 1996. (Illus.). Set lib. bdg. 153.86 *(978-0-7614-0044-8(3)*, Benchmark Bks.) Marshall Cavendish Corp.
Jacobson, Ryan. Exciting Entertainment Inventions. 2013. (Awesome Inventions You Use Every Day Ser.). (ENG., Illus.). 32p. (gr. 3-6). lib. bdg. 26.60 *(978-1-4677-1094-7(6)*, Lerner Pubns.) Lerner Publishing Group.
Jango-Cohen, Judith. Ben Franklin's Big Shock. Lepp, Kevin, illus. 2006. (On My Own Science Ser.). 48p. (J). (gr. k-3). lib. bdg. 25.26 *(978-1-57505-873-3(1)*, Millbrook Pr.) Lerner Publishing Group.
Jedicke, Peter. Great Inventions of the 20th Century. 2007. (Scientific American Ser.). (Illus.). 72p. (YA). (gr. 5-9). lib. bdg. 30.00 *(978-0-7910-9048-0(5))* Facts On File, Inc.
Jones, Charlotte. Mistakes That Worked. O'Brien, John, illus. 2016. (ENG.). 96p. (J). (gr. 3-7). 12.99 *(978-0-399-55202-1(2)*, Delacorte Bks. for Young Readers) Random Hse. Children's Bks.
Keener, Joan N. God Thought of It First. Petrova, Valeria, illus. 2006. 28p. (J). 14.99 *(978-0-7847-1432-4(0)*, 04016) Standard Publishing.
Kennelly, Sean. American Inventors & Innovators. Paiva, Johannah Gilman, ed. 2014. (ENG., Illus.). 48p. (J). (gr. 4). 8.99 *(978-1-4867-0258-9(9))* Flowerpot Children's Pr. Inc. CAN. Dist: Cardinal Pubs. Group.
Kerrigan, Juliet. Ancient Greeks & Why They Matter to Us, Bd. 16. 2017. (ENG., Illus.). 56p. (J). pap. 8.99 ***(978-0-00-820892-9(1))*** HarperCollins Pubs. Ltd. GBR. Dist: Independent Pubs. Group.
Kespert, Deborah. Genius! The Most Astonishing Inventions of All Time. 2015. (ENG., Illus.). 96p. (J). (gr. 4-6). 19.95 *(978-0-500-65043-1(8)*, 565043) Thames & Hudson.
Klutz Editors & Boyle, Brendan. The Klutz Book of Inventions. Cassidy, John, ed. 2010. (ENG.). 200p. (J). (gr. 3-18). 19.99 *(978-1-59174-879-3(8))* Klutz.
Kobasa, Paul A. Personal & Household Items. 2009. (J). *(978-0-7166-0390-0(X))* World Bk., Inc.
Kops, Deborah. Were Early Computers Really the Size of a School Bus? And Other Questions about Inventions. 2011. (Is That a Fact? Ser.). (ENG.). 40p. (gr. 4-6). 26.60 *(978-0-7613-6098-8(0))* Lerner Publishing Group.
Kramer, Alan. The Ogs Discover Fire & Other Stuff. 2011. (Navigators Ser.). (J). pap. *(978-1-61672-970-7(8))* Benchmark Education Co.
Kroll, Jennifer. The Cutting Edge: Breakthroughs in Technology, 1 vol. 2nd rev. ed. 2013. (TIME for KIDS(r) Nonfiction Readers Ser.). (ENG.). 64p. (J). (gr. 5-5). pap. 10.99 *(978-1-4333-4947-8(7))*; (Illus.). pap. 31.96 *(978-1-4333-7446-3(3))* Teacher Created Materials, Inc.
Kuskowski, Alex. Amazing Super Simple Inventions. 2015. (Amazing Super Simple Inventions Ser.: Vol. 6). (ENG.). 32p. (J). (gr. 4-7). lib. bdg. 162.42 *(978-1-62403-727-6(5))* ABDO Publishing Co.
—Super Simple Telegraph Projects: Inspiring & Educational Science Activities, 1 vol. 2016. (ENG., Illus.). 32p. (J). *(978-1-62403-732-0(1))* ABDO Publishing Co.
—Super Simple Telephone Projects: Inspiring & Educational Science Activities, 1 vol. 2016. (ENG., Illus.). 32p. (J). *(978-1-62403-733-7(X))* ABDO Publishing Co.
Kuskowski, Alex & Craig, Diane. Super Simple Automobile Projects: Inspiring & Educational Science Activities, 1 vol. 2016. (ENG., Illus.). 32p. (J). 18.95 *(978-1-62403-729-0(1))* ABDO Publishing Co.
Landon, Rocky. A Native American Thought of It: Amazing Inventions & Innovations. 3rd ed. 2013. (We Thought of It Ser.). (ENG., Illus.). 48p. (J). (gr. 5-7). pap. 9.95 *(978-1-55451-154-9(2)*, 9781554511549) Annick Pr., Ltd. CAN. Dist: Publishers Group West (PGW).
Layton, Neal. The Story of Things: From the Stone Age to the Modern Age in 10 Pop-Up Spreads. 2010. (ENG., Illus.). 24p. (J). (gr. k-2). 15.99 *(978-0-340-94532-2(X)*, Hodder Children's Books) Hachette Children's Group GBR. Dist: Hachette Bk. Group.
Leavitt, Amie Jane. Physical Computing & Makerspaces. 2014. (Digital & Information Literacy Ser.). (Illus.). 48p. (J). (gr. 5-8). 30.25 *(978-1-4777-7659-9(1)*, Rosen Reference) Rosen Publishing Group, Inc., The.
Lindeen, Mary. Then & Now, 1 vol. 2012. (Wonder Readers: Social Studies). (ENG.). 20p. (gr. -1-2). lib. bdg. 22.65 *(978-1-4296-9616-6(8)*, Wonder Readers) Capstone Press of Coughlan Cos.
Litmanovich, Ellina. How to Create Digital Portfolios for Problem Solving & Innovation. 2017. (Project Learning Using Digital Portfolios Ser.). 64p. (J). (gr. 12-12). 34.45 ***(978-1-5081-7526-1(8)***, Rosen Young Adult) Rosen Publishing Group, Inc., The.
Littleton, Baron J. Your Little Black Book on African American Inventions & Inventors. 2006. vi, 153p. (J). per. 9.95 *(978-0-9791883-0-5(X))* Disciple One Publishing.
Lomask, Milton. Invention & Technology. 2012. (ENG.). 288p. (J). (gr. 4-6). pap. 13.99 *(978-1-4424-8324-8(5)*, Atheneum Bks. for Young Readers) Simon & Schuster Children's Publishing.
Lovett, Amber. LittleBits. 2016. (21st Century Skills Innovation Library: Makers As Innovators Ser.). (ENG., Illus.). 32p. (J). (gr. 4-8). lib. bdg. 29.93 *(978-1-63471-415-0(6)*, 208439) Cherry Lake Publishing.
Lowell, Barbara. George Ferris, What a Wheel! Hoare, Jerry, illus. 2014. (Penguin Core Concepts Ser.). (ENG.). 32p. (J). (gr. -1-k). 3.99 *(978-0-448-47925-5(7)*, Grosset & Dunlap) Penguin Young Readers Group.
Lunis, Natalie. Household Inventions: From Toilets to Toasters. 2006. (Which Came First? Ser.). (Illus.). 32p. (YA). (gr. 3-6). lib. bdg. 25.27 *(978-1-59716-131-2(4))* Bearport Publishing Co., Inc.
Macaulay, David. The Way Things Work Now. 2016. (ENG., Illus.). 400p. (YA). (gr. 7). 35.00 *(978-0-544-82438-6(5)*, HMH Books For Young Readers) Houghton Mifflin Harcourt Publishing Co.

H
I

MacLeod, Elizabeth, et al. A History of Just about Everything: 180 Events, People & Inventions That Changed the World. Leng, Qin, illus. 2013. (ENG.). 124p. (J). (gr. 3-7). 21.95 (978-1-55453-775-4(4)) Kids Can Pr., Ltd. CAN. Dist: Hachette Bk. Group.

MacLeod, Jilly. Great Inventions. (Eyes on Adventure Ser.). 32p. (J). (gr. 1). pap. (978-1-882210-80-0(8)) Action Publishing, Inc.

Major Inventions Through History, 7 bks., Set. 2006. (J). (gr. 5-7). 61.95 (978-0-8225-5822-4(X)) Lerner Publishing Group.

Major Inventions Through History, 7 bks., Set. Incl. History of Communication. Woods, Michael & Woods, Mary B. (J). (gr. 4-7). lib. bdg. 26.60 (978-0-8225-3807-3(5)); History of Energy. Landau, Elaine. (gr. 5-8). lib. bdg. 26.60 (978-0-8225-3806-6(7)); History of Food. Jango-Cohen, Judith. (gr. 5-8). lib. bdg. 26.60 (978-0-8225-2484-7(8)); History of Medicine. Woods, Michael & Woods, Mary B. (gr. 5-8). lib. bdg. 26.60 (978-0-8225-2636-0(0)); History of Transportation. Herbst, Judith. (gr. 5-8). lib. bdg. 26.60 (978-0-8225-2496-0(1)); History of Weapons. Herbst, Judith. (gr. 5-8). lib. bdg. 26.60 (978-0-8225-3805-9(9)); (Illus.). 56p. 2005. 2006. 186.20 (978-0-8225-2475-5(9), Twenty-First Century Bks.) Lerner Publishing Group.

Mara, Wil. The Clock. 2006. (Inventions That Shaped the World Ser.). (ENG., Illus.). 80p. (J). (gr. 5-8). per. 9.95 (978-0-531-16743-4(7), Watts, Franklin) Scholastic Library Publishing.

—From Gecko Feet to Adhesive Tape. 2014. (21st Century Skills Innovation Library: Innovations from Nature Ser.). (ENG., Illus.). 32p. (J). (gr. 4-8). 28.50 (978-1-62431-752-1(9), 203276) Cherry Lake Publishing.

Marsico, Katie. Stinky Sanitation Inventions. 2013. (Awesome Inventions You Use Every Day Ser.). (ENG., Illus.). 32p. (gr. 3-6). lib. bdg. 26.60 (978-1-4677-1090-9(3), Lerner Pubns.) Lerner Publishing Group.

—Tremendous Technology Inventions. 2013. (Awesome Inventions You Use Every Day Ser.). (ENG., Illus.). 32p. (gr. 3-6). lib. bdg. 26.60 (978-1-4677-1092-3(X), Lerner Pubns.) Lerner Publishing Group.

Mason, Helen. Agricultural Inventions: At the Top of the Field. 2013. (ENG., Illus.). 48p. (J). (978-0-7787-0213-9(8)); (gr. 4-7). pap. (978-0-7787-0233-7(2)) Crabtree Publishing Co.

McArdle, Matthew. 19th Century Innovations: Paving the Way. 2017. (Primary Source Readers Ser.). (Illus.). 32p. (J). (gr. 4-5). pap. 8.99 (978-1-4938-3796-0(6)) Teacher Created Materials, Inc.

McHugh, Michael J. & Bachman, Frank P. The Story of Inventions. 2007. (Illus.). 350p. (J). (gr. 5-7). pap. 8.95 (978-1-930092-40-2(7), CLP29660) Christian Liberty Pr.

Media, Cont. Inventions. 2008. (ENG.). 96p. (YA). 17.99 (978-1-931703-07-9(8)) Creative Publishing Consultants.

Meister, Cari. Totally Amazing Facts about Outrageous Inventions. 2017. (Mind Benders Ser.). (ENG.). 112p. (gr. 1-3). lib. bdg. 23.32 (978-1-5157-4752-9(2)) Capstone Press of Coughlan Cos.

Mooney, Carla. The Industrial Revolution: Investigate How Science & Technology Changed the World with 25 Projects. Vaughn, Jenn, illus. 2011. (Build It Yourself Ser.). (ENG.). 128p. (J). (gr. 3-7). 21.95 (978-1-936313-81-5(2)); pap. 15.95 (978-1-936313-80-8(4)) Open City Bks.

Morris, Neil. Gadgets & Inventions, 1 vol. 2010. (From Fail to Win! Learning from Bad Ideas Ser.). (ENG., Illus.). 56p. (gr. 5-8). 34.65 (978-1-4109-3909-8(X), Raintree Freestyle) Heinemann-Raintree.

Morrison, Heather S. Inventors of Everyday Technology. 2015. (Designing Engineering Solutions Ser.). (ENG.). 144p. (J). (gr. 8-8). 42.79 (978-1-5026-0660-0(7)) Cavendish Square Publishing.

—Inventors of Industrial Technology. 2015. (Designing Engineering Solutions Ser.). (ENG.). 144p. (J). (gr. 8-8). lib. bdg. 42.79 (978-1-5026-0666-2(6)) Cavendish Square Publishing.

Morrison, Ian. Skiing in the Desert: Asian Innovation. 2007. (Shockwave: Science in Practice Ser.). (ENG., Illus.). 36p. (J). (gr. 3-5). 25.00 (978-0-531-17583-5(9), Children's Pr.) Scholastic Library Publishing.

Murphy, Glenn. Inventions. 2009. (Insiders Ser.). (ENG.). 64p. (J). (gr. 3-7). 17.99 (978-1-4169-3865-1(6), Simon & Schuster Bks. For Young Readers) Simon & Schuster Bks. For Young Readers.

National Geographic. 125 Cool Inventions. 2015. lib. bdg. 24.50 (978-0-606-36422-5(6)) Turtleback Bks.

National Geographic Kids Staff. 125 Cool Inventions: Super Smart Machines & Wacky Gadgets You Never Knew You Wanted. 2015. (ENG., Illus.). 112p. (J). (gr. 3-7). pap. 12.99 (978-1-4263-1885-6(5), National Geographic Children's Bks.) National Geographic Society.

Ng, Sandy. Makey Makey. 2016. (21st Century Skills Innovation Library: Makers As Innovators Ser.). (ENG.). 32p. (J). (gr. 4-8). lib. bdg. 29.93 (978-1-63471-414-3(8), 208435) Cherry Lake Publishing.

Norlander, Britt. I've Discovered Electricity! 2008. (Eureka! Ser.). 32p. (gr. 4-18). lib. bdg. 28.50 (978-0-7614-3195-4(0), Benchmark Bks.) Marshall Cavendish Corp.

Norman, Penny. Science One Two Three Inventions. Einstein, Ann, ed. 2005. 32p. 15.95 (978-1-886978-67-6(0)) Norman & Globus, Inc.

Oachs, Emily Rose. The 12 Most Influential Inventions of All Time. 2018. (ENG.). 32p. (gr. 3-6). 31.35 **(978-1-63235-409-9(8)**, 12-Story Library) Pr. Room Editions LLC.

O'Brien, Cynthia. Innovations in Safety. 2016. (Problem Solved! Your Turn to Think Big Ser.). (ENG., Illus.). 32p. (J). (gr. 3-6). (978-0-7787-2679-1(7)) Crabtree Publishing Co.

Opini, Bathseba & Lee, Richard B. Africans Thought of It: Amazing Innovations. 2nd ed. 2011. (We Thought of It Ser.). (ENG., Illus.). 48p. (J). (gr. 5-7). 21.95 (978-1-55451-277-5(8), 9781554512775); pap. 11.95 (978-1-55451-276-8(X), 9781554512768) Annick Pr., Ltd. CAN. Dist: Publishers Group West (PGW).

Osborne, J. E. Inventions. Date not set. (Early Science Big Bks.). (Illus.). 16p. (J). (gr. -1-2). pap. 16.95 (978-1-58273-117-9(9)) Sundance/Newbridge Educational Publishing.

Oxlade, Chris. Inventions. 2003. (Knowledge Masters Ser.). (Illus.). 32p. (YA). pap. incl. cd-rom (978-1-903954-59-1(2), Pavilion Children's Books) Pavilion Bks.

—Inventors' Secret Scrapbook. 2010. (ENG.). 32p. (J). lib. bdg. (978-0-7787-9909-2(3)); (Crabtree Connections Ser.: No. 2). (gr. 3-6). pap. (978-0-7787-9930-6(1)) Crabtree Publishing Co.

—The Top Ten Inventions That Changed the World. 2009. 32p. (YA). (ENG.). pap. 10.00 (978-1-4358-9174-6(0), PowerKids Pr.); (Illus.). (gr. 3-6). 26.50 (978-1-4358-9173-9(2)) Rosen Publishing Group, Inc., The.

Paris, Stephanie. Technology Feats & Failures, 1 vol. 2nd rev. ed. 2013. (Nonfiction Readers Ser.). (ENG., Illus.). 48p. (J). (gr. 4-4). pap. 29.96 (978-1-4807-1121-1(7)) Shell Educational Publishing.

—Technology Feats & Failures, 1 vol. 2nd rev. ed. 2012. (Nonfiction Readers Ser.). (ENG.). 48p. (J). (gr. 4-4). pap. 9.99 (978-1-4333-4869-3(1)) Teacher Created Materials, Inc.

Parker, Steve. Satellites. West, David, illus. 2015. (Story of Space Ser.). (ENG.). 32p. (J). (gr. 3-6). 31.35 (978-1-62588-079-6(0)) Black Rabbit Bks.

Payne, Jan, et al. Penicillin Was Discovered by Accident: The Truth about Inventions & Discoveries. 2016. (True or False? Ser.). (Illus.). 48p. (J). (gr. 3-3). pap. 11.70 (978-0-7660-7739-3(X)) Enslow Pubs., Inc.

Perry, Andrea J. & Perry, Andrea. Here's What You Do When You Can't Find Your Shoe: Ingenious Inventions for Pesky Problems. Snow, Alan, illus. 2003. (ENG.). 40p. (J). (gr. -1-3). 18.99 (978-0-689-83067-9(X), Atheneum Bks. for Young Readers) Simon & Schuster Children's Publishing.

Podesto, Martine. Inventions. 2008. (My Science Notebook Ser.). (Illus.). 104p. (J). (gr. 5-9). lib. bdg. 31.00 (978-0-8368-9214-7(3)) Stevens, Gareth Publishing LLLP.

Powell, Jillian. Greatest Inventions of All Time. 2016. (ENG., Illus.). 32p. (J). (gr. 4-6). pap. 11.99 (978-0-7502-9780-6(8), Wayland) Hachette Children's Group GBR. Dist: Hachette Bk. Group.

Pringle, Laurence. Ice! The Amazing History of the Ice Business. 2012. (ENG.). 80p. (J). (gr. 4-6). 17.95 (978-1-59078-801-1(X), Calkins Creek) Boyds Mills Pr.

Publishers, Chelsea House, creator. Milestones in Discovery & Invention Set, 8-Volumes. 2007. (Milestones in Discovery & Invention Ser.). (gr. 6-12). 280.00 (978-0-8160-7219-4(1), Chelsea Hse.) Facts On File, Inc.

Question & Answer Inventions. (Children's Reference Ser.). 224p. (978-1-4054-9462-5(X)) Parragon, Inc.

Red Brick Learning Staff. Famous Firsts, 1 vol. 2014. (Famous Firsts Ser.). (ENG.). 24p. (gr. k-1). pap. 27.80 (978-1-4914-0673-1(9), Pebble Plus) Capstone Press of Coughlan Cos.

Regan, Michael. Bad Days in Science & Invention. 2017. (Whoops! a History of Bad Days Ser.). (ENG., Illus.). 48p. (gr. 5-8). lib. bdg. 33.32 (978-1-4109-8563-7(6)) Heinemann-Raintree.

Rhatigan, Joe & Owsley, Anthony. Inventions That Could Have Changed the World... But Didn't! 2015. (ENG., Illus.). 80p. (J). (gr. 3-7). 14.95 (978-1-62354-024-1(0)) Charlesbridge Publishing, Inc.

Richter, Joanne. Inventing the Camera. 2006. (Breakthrough Inventions Ser.). (ENG., Illus.). 32p. (J). (gr. 4-7). pap. (978-0-7787-2836-8(6)) Crabtree Publishing Co.

Rieger, Linda. Flying Animals. Bianchi, John, illus. 2006. 20p. (J). (978-0-9779427-1-8(6)) Pathways into Science.

Roslund, Samantha & Fontichiaro, Kristin. Maker Faire. 2013. (21st Century Skills Innovation Library: Makers As Innovators Ser.). (ENG., Illus.). 32p. (J). (gr. 4-8). 28.50 (978-1-62431-136-9(9), 202864); pap. 14.21 (978-1-62431-268-7(3), 202866) Cherry Lake Publishing.

Rossi, Ann. The Age of Inventions. 2007. (Rise & Shine Ser.). (ENG., Illus.). 40p. (J). pap. 19.95 (978-0-7922-8696-7(0)) CENGAGE Learning.

Rowell, Rebecca. The 12 Most Amazing American Inventions. 2014. (ENG.). 32p. (J). (978-1-63235-008-4(4)) Pr. Room Editions LLC.

Royston, Angela. Inventors Who Changed the World. 2010. (ENG., Illus.). 32p. (J). (978-0-7787-9902-3(6)); pap. (978-0-7787-9923-8(9)) Crabtree Publishing Co.

Ryles, Briony & Hall, Derek. The Ages of Steam & Electricity. 2010. (Curriculum Connections: Technology Through the Ages Ser.). 112p. 39.95 (978-1-933834-86-3(2)) Brown Bear Bks.

Saddleback, creator. Machines & Inventions. 2008. (Factoscope Ser.). (Illus.). 64p. (YA). (gr. 8-12). per. 10.95 (978-1-59905-235-9(0)) Saddleback Educational Publishing, Inc.

Salinas, Eva. Lo Inventaron los Latinoamericanos: Innovaciones Asombrosas. 2012. (SPA & ENG., Illus.). 48p. (J). (gr. 3-7). 21.95 (978-1-55451-379-6(0), 9781554513796) Annick Pr., Ltd. CAN. Dist: Publishers Group West (PGW).

—Lo Inventarons los Latinamericanos: Innovaciones Asombrosas. 2016. (We Thought of It Ser.). (ENG & SPA., Illus.). 48p. (J). (gr. 3-7). pap. 9.95 (978-1-55451-378-9(2)) Annick Pr., Ltd. CAN. Dist: Publishers Group West (PGW).

—Latin Americans Thought of It: Amazing Innovations. 2012. (We Thought of It Ser.). (ENG., Illus.). 48p. (J). (gr. 5-7). 21.95 (978-1-55451-377-2(4), 9781554513772); pap. 11.95 (978-1-55451-376-5(6), 9781554513765) Annick Pr., Ltd. CAN. Dist: Publishers Group West (PGW).

Salzmann, Mary Elizabeth. Aircraft, 1 vol. 2016. (ENG., Illus.). 24p. (J). (978-1-62403-707-8(0)) ABDO Publishing Co.

—Automobile, 1 vol. 2016. (ENG., Illus.). 24p. (J). (978-1-62403-708-5(9)) ABDO Publishing Co.

—Camera, 1 vol. 2016. (ENG., Illus.). 24p. (J). (978-1-62403-709-2(7)) ABDO Publishing Co.

—Phonograph, 1 vol. 2016. (ENG., Illus.). 24p. (J). (978-1-62403-710-8(0)) ABDO Publishing Co.

—Telegraph, 1 vol. 2016. (ENG., Illus.). 24p. (J). (978-1-62403-711-5(9)) ABDO Publishing Co.

—Telephone, 1 vol. 2016. (ENG., Illus.). 24p. (J). (978-1-62403-712-2(7)) ABDO Publishing Co.

Samuels, Charlie. The Age of the Atom (1900-1946) 2010. (Science Highlights: A Gareth Stevens Timeline Ser.). (ENG.). 48p. (J). (gr. 6-8). pap. 14.05 (978-1-4339-4152-8(X)); lib. bdg. 31.95 (978-1-4339-4151-1(1)) Stevens, Gareth Publishing LLLP. (Gareth Stevens Secondary Library).

—The Digital Age (1947-Present Day) 2010. (Science Highlights: A Gareth Stevens Timeline Ser.). (ENG.). 48p. (J). (gr. 6-8). pap. 14.05 (978-1-4339-4155-9(4), Gareth Stevens Secondary Library) Stevens, Gareth Publishing LLLP.

—The Rise of Industry (1700-1800) 2010. (Science Highlights: A Gareth Stevens Timeline Ser.). (ENG.). 48p. (J). (gr. 6-8). pap. 14.05 (978-1-4339-4146-7(5)); lib. bdg. 31.95 (978-1-4339-4145-0(7)) Stevens, Gareth Publishing LLLP. (Gareth Stevens Secondary Library).

Schonberg, Marcia. I Is for Idea: An Inventions Alphabet. Radzinski, Kandy, illus. (Science Ser.). (ENG.). (J). 2006. 40p. (gr. -1-3). pap. 7.95 (978-1-58536-327-8(8)) 2005. 48p. (gr. k-5). 16.95 (978-1-58536-257-8(3)) Sleeping Bear Pr.

Science Stories Foss Spanish Ideas & Inventions EA CR05. 2005. (J). (978-1-59242-588-4(7)) Delta Education, LLC.

Sechrist, Darren. Inventions & Inventors. 2008. (ENG.). 32p. (J). pap. (978-0-7787-4213-5(X)) Crabtree Publishing Co.

Senker, Cath. Ideas That Changed the World. 2017. (10 Ser.). (ENG., Illus.). 32p. (J). (gr. 4-6). pap. 12.99 **(978-0-7502-9141-5(9)**, Wayland) Hachette Children's Group GBR. Dist: Hachette Bk. Group.

Snedden, Robert. Aztec, Inca & Maya. 2009. (Technology in Times Past Ser.). (J). 32.80 (978-1-59920-299-0(9)) Black Rabbit Bks.

—Aztec, Inca, & Maya. 2009. (Technology in Times Past Ser.). (Illus.). 46p. (J). (gr. 4-7). pap. (978-1-897563-64-9(7)) Saunders Bk. Co.

—The Medieval World. 2009. (Technology in Times Past Ser.). (Illus.). 46p. (J). (gr. 4-7). pap. (978-1-897563-65-6(5)) Saunders Bk. Co.

Spengler, Kremena T. An Illustrated Timeline of Inventions & Inventors, 1 vol. Morgan, Rick, illus. 2011. (Visual Timelines in History Ser.). (ENG.). 32p. (gr. 3-4). pap. 7.49 (978-1-4048-7017-8(2)); pap. 41.70 (978-1-4048-7021-5(0), Nonfiction Picture Bks.) Picture Window Bks.

—An Illustrated Timeline of Inventions & Inventors, 1 vol. Morgan, Rick, illus. 2011. (Visual Timelines in History Ser.). (ENG.). 32p. (gr. 3-4). lib. bdg. 28.65 (978-1-4048-6662-1(0)) Picture Window Bks.

St. George, Judith. So You Want to Be an Inventor? Small, David, illus. 2005. (ENG.). 56p. (J). (gr. 2-5). pap. 7.99 (978-0-14-240460-7(8), Puffin Books) Penguin Young Readers Group.

Sturm, Jeanne. Inventors & Discoveries. 2011. (ENG., Illus.). 48p. (gr. 4-6). pap. 10.95 (978-1-61741-987-4(7)) Rourke Educational Media.

Sundance/Newbridge LLC Staff. How Life Changed. 2004. (Reading PowerWorks Ser.). (gr. 1-3). 37.50 (978-0-7608-7815-6(3)); pap. 6.10 (978-0-7608-7816-3(1)) Sundance/Newbridge Educational Publishing.

—Inventions. 2007. (Early Science Ser.). (gr. k-3). 18.95 (978-1-4007-6630-7(3)); pap. 6.10 (978-1-4007-6626-0(5)) Sundance/Newbridge Educational Publishing.

Taylor, Barbara. I Wonder Why Zippers Have Teeth. 2012. (I Wonder Why Ser.). (ENG., Illus.). 32p. (J). (gr. k-3). 6.99 (978-0-7534-6801-2(8), 9780753468012, Kingfisher) Roaring Brook Pr.

Thomson, Ruth. The Science & Inventions Creativity Book: Games, Models to Make, High-Tech Craft Paper, Stickers, & Stencils. 2013. (Creativity Bks.). (ENG., Illus.). 80p. (J). (gr. 1-6). pap. 12.99 (978-1-4380-0251-4(3)) Barron's Educational Series, Inc.

TickTock Books Ltd. Amazing Inventions. 2010. (Top Tens Ser.). (ENG.). 32p. (J). (gr. 1-3). pap. 6.95 (978-1-84898-199-7(6), TickTock Books) Octopus Publishing Group GBR. Dist: Independent Pubs. Group.

Top That Publishing Staff, ed. Inventions. 2004. (Know How Know Why Ser.). (Illus.). 48p. (J). pap. (978-1-84510-030-8(1)) Top That! Publishing PLC.

Turner, Matt. Genius Communication Inventions: From Morse Code to the Internet. Conner, Sarah, illus. 2017. (Incredible Inventions Ser.). (ENG.). 32p. (J). (gr. 3-6). 26.65 **(978-1-5124-3210-7(5))** Lerner Publishing Group.

—Genius Engineering Inventions: From the Plow to 3D Printing. Conner, Sarah, illus. 2017. (Incredible Inventions Ser.). (ENG.). 32p. (J). (gr. 3-6). 26.65 **(978-1-5124-3211-4(3)**, Hungry Tomato (r)) Lerner Publishing Group.

Unlocking the Secrets of Science, 40 Bks, Set. (Illus.). (gr. 4-10). lib. bdg. (978-1-58415-255-2(9)) Mitchell Lane Pubs., Inc.

Vallencourt, Margaret. Technology of the Industrial Revolution, 01 vols., 1. 2016. (History of Technology Ser.). (ENG., Illus.). 112p. (J). lib. bdg. 32.90 (978-1-68048-275-1(0), Britannica Educational Publishing) Rosen Publishing Group, Inc., The.

Verstraete, Larry. Innovations in Everyday Technologies. 2016. (Problem Solved! Your Turn to Think Big Ser.). (ENG., Illus.). 32p. (J). (gr. 3-6). (978-0-7787-2678-4(9)) Crabtree Publishing Co.

—Innovations in Transportation. 2016. (Problem Solved! Your Turn to Think Big Ser.). (ENG., Illus.). 32p. (J). (gr. 3-6). (978-0-7787-2680-7(0)) Crabtree Publishing Co.

Walker, Robert. Transportation Inventions: Moving Our World Forward. 2013. (ENG., Illus.). 48p. (J). (978-0-7787-0223-8(5)) Crabtree Publishing Co.

Walter Foster Jr. Creative Team & Rhatigan, Joe. 50 Wacky Inventions Throughout History: Unbelievable Inventions That Seem Too Crazy to Be Real! Aires, Celeste, illus. 2017. (Wacky Ser.). (ENG.). 112p. (J). (gr. 2-7). 14.95 (978-1-63322-294-6(2), Walter Foster Jr) Quarto Publishing Group USA.

Warren, Mike. The Gadget Inventor Handbook. 2017. (ENG., Illus.). 64p. (J). (gr. 3). 12.95 (978-1-4549-2347-3(4)) Sterling Publishing Co., Inc.

Washburne, Sophie. African American Inventors: Overcoming Challenges to Change America. 2017. (J). **(978-1-5345-6071-0(8))** Greenhaven Publishing LLC.

Weldon, Andrew. Clever Trevor's Stupendous Inventions. 2016. (ENG.). 96p. (J). (gr. 2-4). 8.99 **(978-0-14-330915-4(3))** Random Hse. Australia AUS. Dist: Independent Pubs. Group.

Winterberg, Jenna. Tech World: 20th Century Inventions (Level 3) 2017. (Exploring Reading Ser.). (Illus.). 32p. (J). (gr. 3-3). pap. 8.99 **(978-1-4258-4971-9(7))** Teacher Created Materials, Inc.

World Book, Inc Staff, contrib. by. Economics. 2009. (J). (978-0-7166-0392-4(6)) World Bk., Inc.

—Industry & Manufacturing. 2009. (J). (978-0-7166-0389-4(6)) World Bk., Inc.

—Inventions & Discoveries. 2011. (J). (978-0-7166-1790-7(0)) World Bk., Inc.

Worth, Bonnie. Oh, the Things They Invented! All about Great Inventors. 2015. (Cat in the Hat's Learning Library). (ENG., Illus.). 48p. (J). (gr. k-3). lib. bdg. 13.99 (978-0-375-97170-9(X), Random Hse. Bks. for Young Readers) Random Hse. Children's Bks.

—Oh, the Things They Invented! All about Great Inventors. Ruiz, Aristides & Mathieu, Joe, illus. 2015. (Cat in the Hat's Learning Library). (ENG.). 48p. (J). (gr. k-3). 9.99 (978-0-449-81497-0(1), Random Hse. Bks. for Young Readers) Random Hse. Children's Bks.

Wulffson, Don. Toys! Keller, Laurie, illus. 2014. (ENG.). 208p. (J). (gr. 3-7). pap. 9.99 (978-1-250-03409-0(4), 9781250034090) Square Fish.

Wyatt, Valerie. Inventions. Fernandes, Matthew, illus. 2003. (Faq Ser.). (ENG.). 40p. (J). (gr. 3-7). 6.95 (978-1-55337-404-6(5)) Kids Can Pr., Ltd. CAN. Dist: Hachette Bk. Group.

Ye, Ting-Xing. The Chinese Thought of It: Amazing Inventions & Innovations. 2009. (Jobs in History Ser.). (ENG., Illus.). 48p. (J). (gr. 5-7). 19.95 (978-1-55451-196-9(8), 9781554511969); pap. 9.95 (978-1-55451-195-2(X), 9781554511952) Annick Pr., Ltd. CAN. Dist: Publishers Group West (PGW).

Young Discovery Library, 6 bks. (Illus.). (J). (gr. k-6). lib. bdg. 17.94 (978-1-56674-941-1(7)) Forest Hse. Publishing Co., Inc.

Zdrok, Jodie L. 1880-1900 (Events That Changed the World) 2004. (gr. 10-12). 22.45 (978-0-7377-2038-9(7), Greenhaven Pr., Inc.) Cengage Gale.

Zuchora-Walske, Christine. Key Discoveries in Engineering & Design. 2015. (Science Discovery Timelines Ser.). (ENG.). 48p. (J). (gr. 6-8). pap. 8.99 (978-1-4677-6158-1(3)); lib. bdg. 30.65 (978-1-4677-5788-1(8)) Lerner Publishing Group. (Lerner Pubns.).

100 Inventions That Made History. 2014. (ENG.). 128p. (J). (gr. 2-5). 16.99 (978-1-4654-1670-4(6), DK Children) Dorling Kindersley Publishing, Inc.

INVENTIONS—FICTION

Alger Jr. Horatio Staff. Herbert Carter's Legacy. rev. ed. 2006. 264p. 28.95 (978-1-4218-1756-9(X)); pap. 13.95 (978-1-4218-1856-6(6)) 1st World Publishing, Inc. (1st World Library - Literary Society).

Anderson, Jessica. Milkshakes with Maria Mitchell. 2016. (Time Hop Sweets Shop Ser.). (ENG.). 32p. (gr. k-3). 25.65 (978-1-68191-374-2(7)) Rourke Educational Media.

Anholt, Laurence. Leonardo & the Flying Boy. 2007. (Anholt's Artists Books for Children Ser.). (ENG., Illus.). 36p. (J). (gr. -1-3). 8.99 (978-0-7641-3851-5(0)) Barron's Educational Series, Inc.

Appleton, Victor. Tom Swift & his Great Searchlight. 2005. 27.95 (978-1-4218-1090-4(5), 1st World Library - Literary Society) 1st World Publishing, Inc.

—Tom Swift & His Great Searchlight or O. 2006. pap. (978-1-4065-0903-8(5)) Dodo Pr.

Arps, Melissa & Lagonegro, Melissa. Gwen's Great Gizmos (Disney Junior: Sofia the First) Random House Disney Staff, illus. 2016. (Little Golden Book Ser.). (ENG.). 24p. (J). (gr. -1-k). 4.99 (978-0-7364-3448-5(8), Golden/Disney) Random Hse. Children's Bks.

Asch, Frank. Gravity Buster: Journal #2 of a Cardboard Genius. Asch, Frank, illus. 2007. (Journals of a Cardboard Genius Ser.). (ENG., Illus.). 144p. (J). (gr. 2-5). 5.95 (978-1-55453-069-4(5)) Kids Can Pr., Ltd. CAN. Dist: Hachette Bk. Group.

—Gravity Buster: Journal 2 of a Cardboard Genius. Asch, Frank, illus. 2007. (Journals of a Cardboard Genius Ser.). (ENG., Illus.). 144p. (J). (gr. 2-5). 15.95 (978-1-55453-068-7(7)) Kids Can Pr., Ltd. CAN. Dist: Hachette Bk. Group.

AZ Books, creator. Little Magician. 2012. (Millions of Inventions Ser.). (ENG., Illus.). 16p. (J). (gr. 1-3). pap. 5.95 (978-1-61889-302-4(5)) AZ Bks. LLC.

Azose, Elana & Amancio, Brandon. Never Insult a Killer Zucchini. Clark, David, illus. 2016. (ENG.). 32p. (J). (gr. 2-5). lib. bdg. 16.95 (978-1-58089-618-4(9)) Charlesbridge Publishing, Inc.

Bailey, Kristin. Rise of the Arcane Fire. 2014. (Secret Order Ser.: 2). (ENG., Illus.). 464p. (YA). (gr. 9). 17.99 (978-1-4424-6802-3(5), Simon Pulse) Simon Pulse.

Baker, Keith. Cookies: A Mr. & Mrs. Green Adventure. 2012. (Green Light Readers Level 2 Ser.). (ENG., Illus.). 24p. (J). (gr. -1-3). pap. 3.99 (978-0-547-74561-9(3)) Houghton Mifflin Harcourt Publishing Co.

—On the Go with Mr. & Mrs. Green, 1 vol. Baker, Keith, illus. 2007. (Mr. & Mrs. Green Ser.). (ENG., Illus.). 72p. (gr. 2-4). 27.07 (978-1-59961-303-1(4)) Spotlight.

Bancks, Tristan. Mac Slater vs. the City. (Mac Slater Hunts the Cool Ser.). (ENG.). 192p. (J). (gr. 3-7). 2012. pap. 6.99 (978-1-4169-8577-8(8)) 2011. 15.99 (978-1-4169-8576-1(X)) Simon & Schuster Bks. For Young Readers. (Simon & Schuster Bks. For Young Readers).

Bean, Raymond. Benji Franklin: Kid Zillionaire. Vimislik, Matthew, illus. 2014. (Benji Franklin: Kid Zillionaire Ser.). (ENG.). 160p. (gr. 2-3). 9.95 (978-1-4342-6419-0(X)) Stone Arch Bks.

—Benji Franklin: Kid Zillionaire, 2 vols. Vimislik, Matthew, illus. 2015. (Benji Franklin: Kid Zillionaire Ser.). (ENG.). 88p. (gr. 2-3). 45.30 (978-1-4965-1992-4(2)) Stone Arch Bks.

—Benji Franklin: Kid Zillionare, 1 vol. Vimislik, Matthew, illus. 2014. (Benji Franklin: Kid Zillionaire Ser.). (ENG.). 88p. (gr. 2-3). 45.30 (978-1-4342-8927-8(3)) Stone Arch Bks.

—Blown Away, 0 vols. unabr. ed. 2012. (Sweet Farts Ser.: 3). (ENG.). 172p. (J). (gr. 4-6). pap. 9.95 (978-1-61218-251-3(8), 9781612182513, Amazon Children's Publishing) Amazon Publishing.

—Building Wealth (and Superpowered Rockets!), 1 vol. Vimislik, Matthew, illus. 2014. (Benji Franklin: Kid Zillionaire Ser.). (ENG.). 88p. (gr. 2-3). 22.65 (978-1-4342-6418-3(1)) Stone Arch Bks.

—Saving Money (and the World from Killer Dinos!), 1 vol. Vimislik, Matthew, illus. 2014. (Benji Franklin: Kid Zillionaire

Ser.). (ENG.). 88p. (gr. 2-3). 22.65 *(978-1-4342-6417-6(3))* Stone Arch Bks.

Bellisario, Gina. An Extra-Ordinary Girl. Von Innerebner, Jessika, illus. 2016. (Ellie Ultra Ser.). (ENG.). 128p. (gr. 2-3). lib. bdg. 25.99 *(978-1-4965-3139-1(6))* Stone Arch Bks.

—Super Fluffy to the Rescue. Von Innerebner, Jessika, illus. 2016. (Ellie Ultra Ser.). (ENG.). 128p. (gr. 2-3). lib. bdg. 25.99 *(978-1-4965-3142-1(6))* Stone Arch Bks.

Bernasconi, Pablo. El Zoo de Joaquin. 2006. (Illus.). 32p. (YA). (gr. 7-9). 15.99 *(978-84-96388-36-9(0))* Lectorum Pubns., Inc.

Blanchard, Anne & Cerisier, Emmanuel. Arab Science & Invention in the Golden Age. Brent, R. M., tr. from FRE. 2009. (ENG., Illus.). 80p. (J). (gr. 3). 19.95 *(978-1-59270-080-6(2))* Enchanted Lion Bks., LLC.

Bowditch, Eden Unger. The Atomic Weight of Secrets or the Arrival of the Mysterious Men in Black. 2011. (Young Inventors Guild Ser.: 1). (ENG.). 320p. (YA). 19.95 *(978-1-61088-002-2(1),* 33471904-45bf-4a52-9f65-44ef10fff3b6) Bancroft Pr.

Brannon, Tom, illus. What's the Big Idea, Charlie Brown? 2014. (Peanuts Great American Adventure Ser.). (ENG.). 40p. (J). (gr. -1). 16.99 *(978-1-62157-257-2(9),* Little Patriot Pr.) Regnery Publishing, Inc., An Eagle Publishing Co.

Cameron, Sharon. The Dark Unwinding. (ENG.). 336p. (J). (gr. 7). 2013. pap. 9.99 *(978-0-545-32787-9(3),* Scholastic Paperbacks) 2012. 17.99 *(978-0-545-32786-2(5),* Scholastic Pr.) Scholastic, Inc.

—A Spark Unseen. 2013. (ENG.). 352p. (J). (gr. 7). 17.99 *(978-0-545-32813-5(6),* Scholastic Pr.) Scholastic, Inc.

Carman, Patrick. Floozombies! Sheesley, Brian, illus. 2016. (Fizzopolis Ser.: 2). 176p. (J). (gr. 3-7). 12.99 *(978-0-06-239392-0(8),* Tegen, Katherine Bks) HarperCollins Pubs.

—The Trouble with Fuzzwonker Fizz. Sheesley, Brian, illus. 2016. (Fizzopolis Ser.: 1). 160p. (J). (gr. 3-7). 12.99 *(978-0-06-239390-6(1))* HarperCollins Pubs.

Chand, Emlyn. Izzy the Inventor: A Bird Brain Book. Giffin, Noelle, illus. l.t. ed. 2013. 7. (ENG.). 56p. (gr. k-3). 21.95 *(978-1-62253-123-3(X));* pap. 10.95 *(978-1-62253-122-6(1))* Evolved Publishing.

Chapman, Allen. Radio Boys First Wireless. 2006. 136p. per. *(978-1-897312-19-3(9))* Adlibbed Ltd.

Cohen, Rich. Alex & the Amazing Time Machine. Murphy, Kelly, illus. 2013. (ENG.). 176p. (J). (gr. 3-7). pap. 6.99 *(978-1-250-02729-0(2),* 9781250027290) Square Fish.

Cole, Dylan. The Other Worldly Adventures of Tyler Washburn: the New Kid. 2012. (ENG., Illus.). 48p. (J). (gr. -1). 19.95 *(978-1-933492-77-3(5))* Design Studio Pr.

Cornwell, Betsy. Mechanica. (ENG.). 320p. (gr. 7). 2016. (YA). pap. 8.99 *(978-0-544-66868-3(5),* HMH Books For Young Readers) 2015. (J). 17.99 *(978-0-547-92771-8(1),* Clarion Bks.) Houghton Mifflin Harcourt Publishing Co.

Cross, Gillian. Sam Sorts It Out. Mier, Colin, illus. 2005. (ENG.). 24p. (J). lib. bdg. 23.65 *(978-1-59646-702-6(9))* Dingles & Co.

David, Erica. The Great Ice Engine. RH Disney Staff et al, illus. 2015. (Stepping Stone Book(TM) Ser.: 4). (ENG.). 128p. (J). (gr. 1-4). 9.99 *(978-0-7364-3431-7(3),* RH/Disney) Random Hse. Children's Bks.

DeStefano, Lauren. The Girl with the Ghost Machine. 2017. (ENG.). 224p. (J). 16.99 *(978-1-68119-444-8(9),* 9781681194448, Bloomsbury USA Childrens) Bloomsbury Publishing USA.

Deutsch, Stacia, adapted by. Cloudy with a Chance of Meatballs 2 Movie Novelization. 2013. (Cloudy with a Chance of Meatballs Movie Ser.). (ENG., Illus.). 128p. (J). (gr. 3-7). pap. 5.99 *(978-1-4424-9551-7(0),* Simon Spotlight) Simon Spotlight.

Dube, Pierrette. How to Become a Perfect Knight in Five Days. Hamel, Caroline, illus. 2009. (Rainy Day Readers Ser.). 32p. (J). (gr. -1-3). 22.60 *(978-1-60754-373-2(7));* pap. 10.55 *(978-1-60754-374-9(5))* Windmill Bks.

Durand, Hallie. No Room for Dessert. Davenier, Christine, illus. (ENG.). 192p. (J). (gr. 2-5). 2012. pap. 6.99 *(978-1-4424-0361-1(6))* 2011. 15.99 *(978-1-4424-0360-4(8))* Simon & Schuster Children's Publishing. (Atheneum Bks. for Young Readers).

Eddleman, Peggy. Escape One Danger - Jump into Another.... 2013. (Sky Jumpers Ser.: 1). (ENG.). 288p. (J). (gr. 3-7). lib. bdg. 19.99 *(978-0-307-98128-8(2),* Random Hse. Bks. for Young Readers) Random Hse. Children's Bks.

—Sky Jumpers. 2013. (Sky Jumpers Ser.). (ENG.). 288p. (J). (gr. 3-7). 16.99 *(978-0-307-98127-1(4),* Random Hse. Bks. for Young Readers) Random Hse. Children's Bks.

—Sky Jumpers: Book 1. 2014. (Sky Jumpers Ser.). (ENG.). 304p. (J). (gr. 3-7). 7.99 *(978-0-307-98130-1(4),* Yearling) Random Hse. Children's Bks.

Eliopoulis, Chris, text. Franklin Richards: Son of a Genius Ultimate Collection - Book 1. 2010. (ENG., Illus.). 208p. (J). (gr. -1-17). pap., pap. 19.99 *(978-0-7851-4924-8(4))* Marvel Worldwide, Inc.

Everett-Camplin, Helen. Grandad's Magic Gadgets. 2009. (ENG.). 64p. pap. 12.00 *(978-84-8323-522-5(6))* Cambridge Univ. Pr.

Fields, Bryan W. Lunchbox & the Aliens. Atteberry, Kevan, illus. 2009. (Froonga Ser.). (ENG.). 208p. (J). (gr. 4-7). pap. 11.99 *(978-0-312-56115-4(6),* 9780312561154) Square Fish.

Fields, Jan. Big City Blues: Back to Wonderland, 1 vol. Altmann, Scott, illus. 2013. (Adventures in Extreme Reading Ser.). (ENG.). 112p. (J). (gr. 3-6). 27.07 *(978-1-61641-923-3(7))* Magic Wagon.

—The Calm Before the Storm: A Night in Sleepy Hollow, 1 vol. Altmann, Scott, illus. 2013. (Adventures in Extreme Reading Ser.). (ENG.). 112p. (J). (gr. 3-6). 27.07 *(978-1-61641-920-2(2))* Magic Wagon.

—Hack Attack: A Trip to Wonderland, 1 vol. Altmann, Scott, illus. 2013. (Adventures in Extreme Reading Ser.). (ENG.). 112p. (J). (gr. 3-6). 27.07 *(978-1-61641-919-6(9))* Magic Wagon.

—Lightning Strikes Twice: Escaping Great Expectations, 1 vol. Altmann, Scott, illus. 2013. (Adventures in Extreme Reading Ser.). (ENG.). 112p. (J). (gr. 3-6). 27.07 *(978-1-61641-922-6(9))* Magic Wagon.

—Trapped in Stormy Seas: Sailing to Treasure Island, 1 vol. Altmann, Scott, illus. 2013. (Adventures in Extreme Reading Ser.). (ENG.). 112p. (J). (gr. 3-6). 27.07 *(978-1-61641-921-9(0))* Magic Wagon.

Ford, Martyn. The Imagination Box. 2016. (ENG.). 240p. (J). (gr. 4-7). 16.99 *(978-1-101-93627-6(4),* Delacorte Pr.) Random Hse. Children's Bks.

Freedman, Claire. Monstersaurus! Cort, Ben, illus. 2011. (ENG.). 32p. *(978-1-84738-904-6(X))* Simon & Schuster, Ltd.

Gale, Emily. My Explosive Diary. Dreidemy, Joëlle, illus. 2014. (Eliza Boom Ser.: 1). (ENG.). 128p. (J). (gr. 1-4). 15.99 *(978-1-4814-0650-5(7),* Simon & Schuster/Paula Wiseman Bks.) Simon & Schuster/Paula Wiseman Bks.

Grabenstein, Chris. The Island of Dr. Libris. 2016. (ENG.). 272p. (J). (gr. 3-7). 7.99 *(978-0-385-38845-0(4),* Yearling) Random Hse. Children's Bks.

GrandPré, Mary. Cleonardo, the Little Inventor. 2016. (ENG., Illus.). 48p. (J). (gr. -1-3). 18.99 *(978-0-439-35764-7(0))* Scholastic, Inc.

Gray, Claudia. Ten Thousand Skies above You. 2016. (Firebird Ser.: 2). 448p. (YA). (gr. 9). pap. 9.99 *(978-0-06-227900-2(9),* HarperTeen) HarperCollins Pubs.

Greenburg, J. C. In Time. Gerardi, Jan, illus. 2004. (Andrew Lost Ser.: 9). (ENG.). 96p. (J). (gr. 1-4). 3.99 *(978-0-375-82949-9(0),* Random Hse. Bks. for Young Readers) Random Hse. Children's Bks.

—On Earth. Gerardi, Jan, illus. 10th ed. 2005. (Andrew Lost Ser.: 10). (ENG.). 96p. (J). (gr. 1-4). 3.99 *(978-0-375-82950-5(4),* Random Hse. Bks. for Young Readers) Random Hse. Children's Bks.

—On the Reef. Reed, Mike, tr. Reed, Mike & Gerardi, Jan, illus. 2004. (Andrew Lost Ser.: 7). (ENG.). 96p. (J). (gr. 1-4). 3.99 *(978-0-375-82525-5(8),* Random Hse. Bks. for Young Readers) Random Hse. Children's Bks.

—Under Water. Reed, Mike, illus. 2003. (Andrew Lost Ser.: 5). (ENG.). 96p. (J). (gr. 1-4). mass mkt. 3.99 *(978-0-375-82523-1(1),* Random Hse. Bks. for Young Readers) Random Hse. Children's Bks.

Groth-fleming. Professor Fergus Fahrenheit & His Wonderful Weat. 2009. (ENG.). 36p. (J). (gr. -1-3). pap. 10.99 *(978-1-4424-0220-1(2),* Simon & Schuster Bks. For Young Readers) Simon & Schuster Bks. For Young Readers.

Gutman, Dan. Mrs. Master Is a Disaster! 2017. (My Weirdest School Ser.: 8). lib. bdg. 14.75 ***(978-0-606-40078-7(8))*** Turtleback Bks.

—Mrs. Yonkers Is Bonkers! Paillot, Jim, illus. 2007. (My Weird School Ser.: 18). (J). 14.75 *(978-1-4177-8222-2(6),* Turtleback) Turtleback Bks.

—My Weirdest School #8: Mrs. Master Is a Disaster! Paillot, Jim, illus. 2017. (My Weirdest School Ser.: 8). 112p. (J). (gr. 1-5). pap. 4.99 *(978-0-06-242933-9(7))* HarperCollins Pubs.

Hale, Bruce. From Russia with Lunch: A Chet Gecko Mystery. 2010. (Chet Gecko Ser.: 14). (ENG., Illus.). 128p. (J). (gr. 2-5). pap. 6.99 *(978-0-547-32882-9(6))* Houghton Mifflin Harcourt Publishing Co.

Hall / Waltz. Mortimer Jones: The Bubble Gum Nerd, 1. l.t. ed. 2003. (Illus.). 32p. 19.95 *(978-0-9741774-2-7(3))* D. W. Publishing.

Hamilton, Kersten. The Ire of Iron Claw. Hamilton, James, illus. (Gadgets & Gears Ser.: 2). (ENG.). (J). (gr. 2-5). 2016. 192p. pap. 6.99 *(978-0-544-66854-6(5),* HMH Books For Young Readers) 2015. 176p. 16.99 *(978-0-544-22502-2(3))* Houghton Mifflin Harcourt Publishing Co.

Hansen, Dustin. Microsaurs: Adventure Awaits. Hansen, Dustin, illus. 2017. (Microsaurs Ser.: 1). (ENG., Illus.). 224p. (J). 13.99 *(978-1-250-09021-8(0),* 9781250090218) Feiwel & Friends.

—Microsaurs: Tiny-Raptor Pack Attack. Hansen, Dustin, illus. 2017. (Microsaurs Ser.: 2). (ENG., Illus.). 240p. (J). 13.99 *(978-1-250-09025-6(3),* 9781250090256) Feiwel & Friends.

Harvey, Sharon M. One Egg-stra-Ordinary Invention. 2012. (ENG.). 94p. pap. 35.95 *(978-1-4327-7210-9(4))* Outskirts Pr., Inc.

Hawking, Stephen W. & Hawking, Lucy. George's Secret Key to the Universe. Parsons, Garry, illus. l.t. ed. 2008. (Literacy Bridge Middle Reader Ser.). 359p. (J). (gr. 3-7). 24.95 *(978-1-4104-0638-5(5))* Thorndike Pr.

Hicks, Clifford B. Alvin Fernald, Foreign Trader. Schluenderfritz, Theodore, illus. 2007. (Alvin Fernald Mysteries Ser.). 181p. (J). (gr. 4). per. 11.95 *(978-1-883937-74-4(4))* Bethlehem Bks.

—The Marvelous Inventions of Alvin Fernald. Geer, Charles, illus. 2006. 119p. (J). (gr. 3-7). 16.95 *(978-1-930900-21-9(X))* Purple Hse. Pr.

Hirsch, Jeff. Magisterium. 2012. (ENG.). 320p. (J). (gr. 7). 17.99 *(978-0-545-29018-0(X),* Scholastic Pr.) Scholastic, Inc.

Hoban, Russell. A Near Thing for Captain Najork. Blake, Quentin, illus. 2006. (ENG.). 32p. (J). (gr. -1-3). pap. 7.95 *(978-1-56792-323-0(2))* Godine, David R. Pub.

Hopper, Ada. Invasion of the Insects. Ricks, Sam, illus. 2017. (DATA Set Ser.: 6). (ENG.). 128p. (J). (gr. -1-4). 16.99 *(978-1-4814-7117-6(1),* Little Simon) Little Simon.

—March of the Mini Beasts. Ricks, Sam, illus. 2016. (DATA Set Ser.: bk.1). (ENG.). 128p. (J). (gr. k-4). pap. 5.99 *(978-1-4814-5728-6(4),* Little Simon) Little Simon.

—Robots Rule the School. Ricks, Sam, illus. 2016. (DATA Set Ser.: bk.4). (ENG.). 128p. (J). (gr. k-4). pap. 5.99 *(978-1-4814-6312-6(8),* Little Simon) Little Simon.

—The Sky Is Falling. Ricks, Sam, illus. 2016. (DATA Set Ser.: bk.3). (ENG.). 128p. (J). (gr. k-4). pap. 5.99 *(978-1-4814-6309-6(8),* Little Simon) Little Simon.

Houtman, Jacqueline. The Reinvention of Edison Thomas. (ENG.). 192p. (J). (gr. 3-7). 2012. pap. 8.95 *(978-1-59078-951-3(2))* 2010. 17.95 *(978-1-59078-708-3(0),* Front Street) Boyds Mills Pr.

Humphrey, Anna. Ruby Goldberg's Bright Idea. Newton, Vanessa Brantley, illus. 2013. (ENG.). 144p. (J). (gr. 3-7). 15.99 *(978-1-4424-8027-8(0),* Simon & Schuster Bks. For Young Readers) Simon & Schuster Bks. For Young Readers.

Hutchins, Hazel. TJ & the Rockets, 1 vol. 2004. (Orca Young Readers Ser.). (ENG., Illus.). 112p. (J). (gr. 3-6). pap., tchr. ed. 4.99 *(978-1-55143-300-4(1),* 1234543) Orca Bk. Pubs. USA.

Ishida, S. E. M. Nick Newton Is Not a Genius. 2016. (Illus.). 151p. (J). *(978-1-62856-235-4(8))* BJU Pr.

The Island of Dr. Libris. 2015. (ENG.). 256p. (J). (gr. 3-7). 16.99 *(978-0-385-38844-3(6));* lib. bdg. 19.99 *(978-0-385-38846-7(2))* Random Hse. Children's Bks. (Random Hse. Bks. for Young Readers).

Joyce, William. A Day with Wilbur Robinson. Joyce, William, illus. 2017. (World of William Joyce Ser.). (ENG., Illus.). 40p. (J). (gr. -1-3). 17.99 *(978-1-4814-8951-5(8),* Atheneum/Caitlyn Dlouhy Books) Simon & Schuster Children's Publishing.

Jules, Jacqueline. Freddie Ramos Springs into Action. Benitez, Miguel, illus. 2011. (Zapato Power Ser.: Book 2). (ENG.). 96p. (J). (gr. 1-5). pap. 4.99 *(978-0-8075-9483-4(0))* Whitman, Albert & Co.

—Freddie Ramos Stomps the Snow. Benitez, Miguel, illus. 2014. (Zapato Power Ser.: Book 5). (ENG.). 96p. (J). (gr. 1-5). 14.99 *(978-0-8075-9487-2(3))* Whitman, Albert & Co.

Jury, Walter & Fine, Sarah. Burn. 2015. (ENG.). 352p. (YA). (gr. 7). bds. 17.99 *(978-0-399-16068-4(X),* G.P. Putnam's Sons Books for Young Readers) Penguin Young Readers Group.

Kehoe, Tim. The Unusual Mind of Vincent Shadow. Francis, Guy & Wohnoutka, Mike, illus. 2009. (Vincent Shadow Ser.: 1). (ENG.). 192p. (J). (gr. 3-7). 9.99 *(978-0-316-05665-6(0))* Little, Brown Bks. for Young Readers.

Kidd, Ronald. Undercover Kid: The Comic Book King. Sklar, Andy, illus. 2007. (All Aboard Mystery Reader Ser.). (ENG.). 48p. (J). pap. 3.99 *(978-0-448-44438-3(0),* Grosset & Dunlap) Penguin Publishing Group.

Korman, Gordon. Jackpot. 2014. (Swindle Ser.: 6). (ENG.). 208p. (J). (gr. 3-7). pap. 6.99 *(978-0-545-56147-1(7));* 16.99 *(978-0-545-56146-4(9))* Scholastic, Inc. (Scholastic Pr.).

—Jackpot. 2014. (Swindle Ser.: 6). lib. bdg. 17.20 *(978-0-606-36032-6(8))* Turtleback Bks.

—Unleashed. 2015. (Swindle Ser.: 7). (ENG.). 208p. (J). (gr. 3-7). 16.99 *(978-0-545-70935-4(0),* Scholastic Pr.) Scholastic, Inc.

Kunce, Craig. Spring Is for Gardening. 2011. (Edrick the Inventor Ser.: 2). (ENG., Illus.). 24p. (J). (gr. k-2). 16.00 *(978-0-9844828-1-8(4))* Windhill Bks. LLC.

Lachenmeyer, Nathaniel. Eureka! Jack, Colin, illus. 2013. (J). *(978-0-8037-3514-9(6),* Dial) Penguin Publishing Group.

Lawson, Janet. The Alberts & Me. 2009. (J). *(978-0-15-205327-7(1))* Harcourt Trade Pubs.

Liberto, Lorenzo, et al. Matt the Rat's Incredible Creations / Las Creaciones Increíbles de Ratón Mateo. Torres, Irving, illus. 2004. (ENG & SPA.). 32p. (J). lib. bdg. 20.00 *(978-0-9743668-3-8(8))* Harvest Sun Pr., LLC.

Livingston, A. A. B. Bear & Lolly: Catch That Cookie! Chou, Joey, illus. 2015. (ENG.). 32p. (J). (gr. -1-3). 15.99 *(978-0-06-219791-7(6))* HarperCollins Pubs.

Matt & Dave. Yuck's Robotic Butt Blast. Baines, Nigel, illus. 2013. (Yuck Ser.). (ENG.). 112p. (J). (gr. 2-5). pap. 4.99 *(978-1-4424-8309-5(1),* Simon & Schuster/Paula Wiseman Bks.) Simon & Schuster/Paula Wiseman Bks.

Matthews, Morgan & Sinden, David. Yuck's Robotic Butt Blast. Baines, Nigel, illus. 2013. (Yuck Ser.). (ENG.). 112p. (J). (gr. 2-5). 15.99 *(978-1-4424-8308-8(3),* Simon & Schuster/Paula Wiseman Bks.) Simon & Schuster/Paula Wiseman Bks.

McBee, Travis. A Little Holiday Thrill. 2008. 66p. pap. 10.99 *(978-0-557-03276-1(8))* Lulu Pr., Inc.

Meister, Cari. Buzz Beaker & the Cave Creatures. McGuire, Bill, illus. 2010. (Buzz Beaker Bks.). (ENG.). 32p. (gr. 2-3). pap. 6.25 *(978-1-4342-2797-3(9));* 22.65 *(978-1-4342-2060-8(5))* Stone Arch Bks.

—Buzz Beaker & the Cool Caps, 1 vol. McGuire, Bill, illus. 2011. (Buzz Beaker Bks.). (ENG.). 32p. (gr. 2-3). pap. 6.25 *(978-1-4342-3055-3(4))* Stone Arch Bks.

—Buzz Beaker & the Putt-Putt Contest. McGuire, Bill, illus. 2010. (Buzz Beaker Bks.). (ENG.). 32p. (gr. 2-3). pap. 6.25 *(978-1-4342-2799-7(5));* 22.65 *(978-1-4342-2062-2(1))* Stone Arch Bks.

—Buzz Beaker & the Race to School, 1 vol. McGuire, Bill, illus. 2011. (Buzz Beaker Bks.). (ENG.). 32p. (gr. 2-3). pap. 6.25 *(978-1-4342-3057-7(0));* lib. bdg. 22.65 *(978-1-4342-2528-3(3))* Stone Arch Bks.

—Buzz Beaker & the Speed Secret. McGuire, Bill, illus. 2010. (Buzz Beaker Bks.). (ENG.). 32p. (gr. 2-3). pap. 6.25 *(978-1-4342-2798-0(7));* 22.65 *(978-1-4342-2061-5(3))* Stone Arch Bks.

Mermelstein, Yael. Izzy the Whiz & Passover McClean. Hartman, Carrie, illus. 2012. (Passover Ser.). (ENG.). 32p. (J). (gr. -1-2). lib. bdg. 17.95 *(978-0-7613-5653-0(3),* Kar-Ben Publishing) Lerner Publishing Group.

—Izzy the Whiz & Passover Mcclean. Hartman, Carrie, illus. 2012. (Passover Ser.). (ENG.). 32p. (J). (gr. -1-2). pap. 7.95 *(978-0-7613-5654-7(1),* Kar-Ben Publishing) Lerner Publishing Group.

Myers, Bill. Choices: A Truth Seekers Novel. 2014. (Truth Seekers Ser.). (ENG.). 224p. (J). (gr. 4-8). 10.99 *(978-1-4336-9081-5(0),* B&H Kids) B&H Publishing Group.

—My Life as a Supersized Superhero... with Slobber, 1 vol. 2007. (Incredible Worlds of Wally Mcdoogle Ser.: 28). (ENG.). 128p. (gr. 3-7). per. 6.99 *(978-1-4003-0637-4(X))* Nelson, Thomas Inc.

Nickel, Scott. Wind Power Whiz Kid: A Buzz Beaker Brainstorm. Smith, Andy J., illus. 2008. (Graphic Sparks Ser.). (ENG.). 40p. (gr. 1-3). pap. 5.95 *(978-1-4342-0854-5(0),* Graphic Sparks) Stone Arch Bks.

Oneka, Angelo O. Mary & Jackie Discovered Jupiter. 2012. 30p. 19.95 *(978-1-4626-2495-9(2))* America Star Bks.

Oppel, Kenneth. Skybreaker. (Illus.). 2007. 560p. (YA). (gr. 8). per. 9.99 *(978-0-06-053229-1(7))* 2005. (ENG., 384p. (J). (gr. 6-10). 16.99 *(978-0-06-053227-7(0))* HarperCollins Pubs.

—Skybreaker. 2007. (Illus.). 544p. (YA). (gr. 8-12). lib. bdg. 20.85 *(978-1-4177-8130-0(0),* Turtleback) Turtleback Bks.

The Perfect Person, 6 Packs. (Bookweb Ser.). 32p. (gr. 4-18). 34.00 *(978-0-7635-3734-0(9))* Rigby Education.

The Perfect Pet, 6 Packs. (Bookweb Ser.). 32p. (gr. 5-18). 34.00 *(978-0-7635-3781-4(0))* Rigby Education.

Perritano, John. Battle of the Bots, 1 vol. 2014. (Kid Squad Saves the World Ser.). (ENG.). 112p. (J). (gr. 8-12). lib. bdg. 27.07 *(978-1-62402-037-7(2),* Calico Chapter Bks.) Magic Wagon.

—The Comet of Doom, 1 vol. Laughead, Mike, illus. 2014. (Kid Squad Saves the World Ser.). (ENG.). 112p. (J). (gr. 8-12). 27.07 *(978-1-62402-038-4(0))* Magic Wagon.

—Madness of Captain Cyclops, 1 vol. 2014. (Kid Squad Saves the World Ser.). (ENG.). 112p. (J). (gr. 8-12). lib. bdg. 27.07 *(978-1-62402-040-7(2),* Calico Chapter Bks) Magic Wagon.

—The Snickerblooms & the Age Bug, 1 vol. Laughead, Mike, illus. 2014. (Kid Squad Saves the World Ser.). (ENG.). 112p. (J). (gr. 8-12). 27.07 *(978-1-62402-041-4(0))* Magic Wagon.

Pilkey, Dav. Captain Underpants & the Sensational Saga of Sir Stinks-a-Lot. Pilkey, Dav, illus. 2015. (Captain Underpants Ser.: 12). (ENG., Illus.). 208p. (J). (gr. 2). 9.99 *(978-0-545-50492-8(9))* Scholastic, Inc.

—Captain Underpants & the Sensational Saga of Sir Stinks-a-Lot. Pilkey, Dav, illus. 2015. (Captain Underpants Ser.: 12). (ENG., Illus.). 208p. (J). (gr. 2). lib. bdg. 20.85 *(978-0-606-37924-3(X))* Turtleback Bks.

Polacco, Patricia. The Junkyard Wonders. Polacco, Patricia, illus. 2010. (ENG., Illus.). 48p. (J). (gr. 1-4). 17.99 *(978-0-399-25078-1(6),* Philomel Bks.) Penguin Young Readers Group.

Posner-Sanchez, Andrea. Oaken's Invention. Random House Disney, illus. 2016. (Frozen 8X8 Ser.). (ENG.). 24p. (J). (gr. -1-2). 14.75 *(978-0-606-39347-8(1))* Turtleback Bks.

Potter, Ellen. Slob. 2009. (ENG.). 208p. (J). (gr. 3-7). 16.99 *(978-0-399-24705-7(X),* Philomel Bks.) Penguin Young Readers Group.

Pugin-Rodas, M. C. The Eight Ball Club: Ocean of Fire. 2007. (ENG., Illus.). 144p. pap. 15.95 *(978-0-9793761-2-2(2))* ESOL Publishing.

Rabley, Stephen. The Twins & the Time Machine/Les Jumeaux et la Machine du Temps. Bougard, Marie-Therese, tr. Eudes-Pascal, Elisabeth, illus. 2008. (Let's Read! Bks.). (ENG & FRE.). 32p. (J). (gr. 3-7). pap. 5.99 *(978-0-7641-4048-8(5))* Barron's Educational Series, Inc.

Rash, Andy. Archie the Daredevil Penguin. Rash, Andy, illus. 2015. (ENG., Illus.). 34p. (J). (gr. -1-3). 16.99 *(978-0-451-47123-9(7),* Viking Books for Young Readers) Penguin Young Readers Group.

Reedy, Trent. Stealing Air. 2012. (ENG.). 288p. (J). (gr. 3-7). 16.99 *(978-0-545-38307-3(2),* Levine, Arthur A. Bks.) Scholastic, Inc.

Salisbury, Linda G. Trouble in Contrary Woods: A Bailey Fish Adventure. Tomatore, Carol, illus. 2009. (J). 8.85 *(978-1-881539-46-9(6))* Tabby Hse. Bks.

Scholastic, Inc. Staff. Dolphin Rescue. 2014. (LEGO Friends Ser.). (ENG., Illus.). 64p. (J). (gr. 2-5). pap. 4.99 *(978-0-545-51655-6(2))* Math Solutions.

Sharpe, Luke. And the Stink Spectacular. Ross, Graham, illus. 2015. (Billy Sure Kid Entrepreneur Ser.: 2). (ENG.). 160p. (J). (gr. 3-7). 17.99 *(978-1-4814-3951-0(0),* Simon Spotlight) Simon Spotlight.

—Billy Sure Kid Entrepreneur & the Haywire Hovercraft. Ross, Graham, illus. 2016. (Billy Sure Kid Entrepreneur Ser.: 7). (ENG.). 160p. (J). (gr. 3-7). pap. 6.99 *(978-1-4814-6193-1(1),* Simon Spotlight) Simon Spotlight.

—Billy Sure Kid Entrepreneur & the Invisible Inventor. Ross, Graham, illus. 2016. (Billy Sure Kid Entrepreneur Ser.: 8). (ENG.). 160p. (J). (gr. 3-7). pap. 6.99 *(978-1-4814-6196-2(6),* Simon Spotlight) Simon Spotlight.

—Billy Sure Kid Entrepreneur Is NOT a Singer! Ross, Graham, illus. 2016. (Billy Sure Kid Entrepreneur Ser.: 9). (ENG.). 160p. (J). (gr. 3-7). pap. 6.99 *(978-1-4814-6895-4(2),* Simon Spotlight) Simon Spotlight.

—The No-Trouble Bubble. Ross, Graham, illus. 2016. (Billy Sure Kid Entrepreneur Ser.: 5). (ENG.). 160p. (J). (gr. 3-7). 17.99 *(978-1-4814-5275-5(4),* Simon Spotlight) Simon Spotlight.

—The No-Trouble Bubble. Ross, Graham, illus. 2016. (Billy Sure Kid Entrepreneur Ser.: 5). (ENG.). 160p. (J). (gr. 3-7). pap. 6.99 *(978-1-4814-5274-8(6),* Simon Spotlight) Simon Spotlight.

—The Stink Drink. Ross, Graham, illus. 2015. (Billy Sure Kid Entrepreneur Ser.: 2). (ENG.). 160p. (J). (gr. 3-7). pap. 6.99 *(978-1-4814-3950-3(2),* Simon Spotlight) Simon Spotlight.

Shusterman, Neal. The Accelerati Trilogy Book Three Hawking's Hallway. 2017. (Accelerati Trilogy Ser.). (ENG.). 368p. (J). (gr. 5-9). pap. 8.99 *(978-1-4231-5521-8(1))* Hyperion Bks. for Children.

—Edison's Alley. 2016. (Accelerati Trilogy Ser.: Bk. 2). (ENG.). 256p. (J). (gr. 5-9). pap. 7.99 *(978-1-4231-5517-1(3))* Hyperion Bks. for Children.

Shusterman, Neal & Elfman, Eric. Edison's Alley. 2015. (Accelerati Trilogy Ser.: Bk. 2). (ENG.). 256p. (J). (gr. 5-9). 16.99 *(978-1-4231-4806-7(1))* Hyperion Bks. for Children.

—Hawking's Hallway. 2016. (Accelerati Trilogy Ser.: Bk. 3). (ENG.). 368p. (J). (gr. 5-9). 16.99 *(978-1-4231-4805-0(3))* Hyperion Bks. for Children.

—Tesla's Attic. 2014. (Accelerati Trilogy Ser.: Bk. 1). (ENG.). 256p. (J). (gr. 3-7). 16.99 *(978-1-4231-4803-6(7))* Hyperion Bks. for Children.

Soup, Cuthbert. Another Whole Nother Story. Timmins, Jeffrey Stewart, illus. (Whole Nother Story Ser.). (ENG.). (YA). (gr. 3-6). 2012. 320p. pap. 7.99 *(978-1-59990-737-6(2),* 9781599907376) 2010. 304p. 16.99 *(978-1-59990-436-8(5),* 9781599904368) Bloomsbury Publishing USA. (Bloomsbury USA Childrens).

—No Other Story. (Whole Nother Story Ser.). (ENG., Illus.). 256p. (YA). (gr. 3-6). 2013. pap. 7.99 *(978-1-61963-120-5(2),* 9781619631205) 2012. 16.99 *(978-1-59990-824-3(7),* 9781599908243) Bloomsbury Publishing USA. (Bloomsbury USA Childrens).

—A Whole Nother Story. Timmins, Jeffrey Stewart, illus. 2010. (Whole Nother Story Ser.). (ENG.). 288p. (YA). (gr. 3-6). pap. 7.99 *(978-1-59990-518-1(3),* 9781599905181, Bloomsbury USA Childrens) Bloomsbury Publishing USA.

Steinkraus, Kyla. Toffee with Thomas Edison. 2016. (Time Hop Sweets Shop Ser.). (ENG.). 32p. (gr. k-3). 25.65 *(978-1-68191-372-8(0))* Rourke Educational Media.

Stevenson, Robin. Ben the Inventor, 1 vol. Parkins, David, illus. 2011. (Orca Echoes Ser.). (ENG.). 64p. (J). (gr. 2-3). pap. 6.95 *(978-1-55469-802-8(2))* Orca Bk. Pubs. USA.

Stewart, Paul & Riddell, Chris. Far-Flung Adventures: Fergus Crane. 2011. (Far-Flung Adventures Ser.). (ENG.). 240p. (J). (gr. 3-7). 7.99 *(978-0-385-75112-4(5),* Yearling) Random Hse. Children's Bks.

Stine, R. L. Punk'd & Skunked, 1 vol. Park, Trip, illus. 2011. (Rotten School Ser.: No. 11). (ENG.). 128p. (gr. 2-5). 24.21 *(978-1-59961-835-7(4))* Spotlight.

Strand, Kai. Save the Lemmings. 2012. 108p. pap. 8.99 *(978-1-60820-710-7(2))* MLR Pr., LLC.

Stupniker, Yehudit. The Remarkable Invention That Saves Zion: A Tale of Triz. 2007. 292p. 18.95

(978-1-932687-74-3(2), Devora Publishing) Simcha Media Group.

Tatulli, Mark, et al. Lio: Making Friends. 2013. (Lio Ser.: 8). (ENG., Illus.). 224p. (J). pap. 9.99 *(978-1-4494-2558-6(5))* Andrews McMeel Publishing.

Taylor, Dereen. Robo-Pup to the Rescue! Hutchinson, Tim, illus. 2013. (ENG.). 12p. (J). (gr. 1-8). 16.99 *(978-1-84322-821-9(1)*, Armadillo) Anness Publishing GBR. Dist: National Bk. Network.

Terry, Alana. What, No Sushi? Steffen, Jeremy, illus. 2013. 116p. pap. 7.99 *(978-1-937848-04-0(3))* Do Life Right, Inc.

Theurer, Heather, illus. Thaddeus Macdonald III: Aka the Boss. 2011. (ENG.). 64p. (gr. -1). 16.95 *(978-0-9826137-8-8(4)*, Channel Kids) Channel Photographics.

Thomas, Isabel. Cindy-Ella & the Incredible Techno-Slippers. Moor, Becka, illus. 2015. (Fairy Tales Today Ser.). (ENG.). 24p. (gr. 1-2). 23.99 *(978-1-4795-8616-5(1))* Picture Window Bks.

Trussell-Cullen, Alan. Sam the Incredible Inventor, 1 vol. rev. ed. 2013. (Fiction Readers Ser.). (ENG., Illus.). 32p. (J). (gr. 3-3). pap. 8.99 *(978-1-4333-5610-0(4))* Shell Educational Publishing.

—Sam the Incredible Inventor. rev. ed. 2013. (Fiction Readers Ser.). (ENG., Illus.). 32p. (gr. 3-3). pap. 19.96 *(978-1-4807-1732-9(0))* Teacher Created Materials, Inc.

van Reek, Wouter. Coppernickel: The Invention. 2008. (ENG., Illus.). 32p. (J). (gr. -1-3). 14.95 *(978-1-59270-100-1(0))* Enchanted Lion Bks., LLC.

Voake, Steve. Hooey Higgins & the Tremendous Trousers. Dodson, Emma, illus. 2014. (ENG.). 144p. (J). (gr. 2-5). 14.99 *(978-0-7636-6923-2(7))* Candlewick Pr.

Wardlaw, Lee. 101 Ways to Bug Your Friends & Enemies. 2011. (ENG.). 288p. (J). (gr. 5-18). 6.99 *(978-0-14-241949-6(4)*, Puffin Books) Penguin Young Readers Group.

Weston, Greg. The Inventors. 2009. 202p. pap. 13.95 *(978-1-4092-6096-7(8))* Lulu Pr., Inc.

Weston, Robert Paul. The Creature Department. Framestore, illus. 2014. (Creature Department Ser.: 1). (ENG.). 352p. (J). (gr. 3-7). pap. 8.99 *(978-1-59514-684-7(9)*, Razorbill) Penguin Young Readers Group.

Weston, Robert Paul & Loftin, Nikki. Gobbled by Ghorks. Framestore, illus. 2015. (Creature Department Ser.: 2). (ENG.). 240p. (J). (gr. 3-7). 8.99 *(978-1-59514-751-6(9)*, Razorbill) Penguin Young Readers Group.

Wildavsky, Rachel. The Secret of Rover. Caparo, Antonio, illus. 2011. (ENG.). 368p. (J). (gr. 3-7). 17.95 *(978-0-8109-9710-3(X)*, Amulet Bks.) Abrams, Inc.

Yasuda, Anita. The Mystery Coins, 1 vol. Harpster, Steve, illus. 2013. (Dino Detectives Ser.). (ENG.). 32p. (gr. 1-2). lib. bdg. 22.65 *(978-1-4342-5972-1(2))* Stone Arch Bks.

—Mystery Coins. Harpster, Steve, illus. 2013. (Dino Detectives Ser.). (ENG.). 32p. (gr. 1-2). pap. 5.95 *(978-1-4342-6201-1(4))* Stone Arch Bks.

Yasuda, Anita & Harpster, Steve. The Mystery Coins. 2013. (Dino Detectives Ser.). (ENG.). 32p. (gr. 1-2). pap. 29.70 *(978-1-4342-6228-8(6))* Stone Arch Bks.

Young, Jessica. Fin-Tastic Fashion. Secheret, Jessica, illus. 2017. (Finley Flowers Ser.). (ENG.). 128p. (gr. 2-3). lib. bdg. 25.32 ***(978-1-4795-9804-5(6)***, Finley Flowers) Picture Window Bks.

—Finley Flowers Collection. Secheret, Jessica, illus. 2016. (Finley Flowers Ser.). (ENG.). 256p. (gr. 2-3). 9.99 *(978-1-4795-9850-2(X)*, Finley Flowers) Picture Window Bks.

—New & Improved. Secheret, Jessica, illus. 2015. (Finley Flowers Ser.). (ENG.). 128p. (gr. 2-3). 8.95 *(978-1-4795-5959-6(8)*, Finley Flowers) Picture Window Bks.

INVENTORS

see also Inventions

Abbey, Cherie D., ed. Biography Today: Profiles of People of Interest to Young Readers. 2003. (Biography Today Subject Ser.: 8). 200p. lib. bdg. 44.00 *(978-0-7808-0656-6(5))* Omnigraphics, Inc.

Abbey, Cherie D. & Hillstrom, Kevin, eds. Biography Today: Scientists & Inventors Volume 9. 2004. (Biography Today Subject Ser.: Vol. 9). (Illus.). 200p. (gr. 4-7). 44.00 *(978-0-7808-0711-2(1))* Omnigraphics, Inc.

Abdul-Jabbar, Kareem & Obstfeld, Raymond. What Color Is My World? The Lost History of African-American Inventors. Boos, Ben & Ford, A. G., illus. (ENG.). (J). (gr. 3-7). 2013. 96p. pap. 6.99 *(978-0-7636-6442-8(1))* 2012. 44p. 17.99 *(978-0-7636-4564-9(8))* Candlewick Pr.

Adams, Colleen. Benjamin Franklin: American Inventor. 2009. (Reading Room Collection 2 Ser.). 24p. (gr. 3-4). 42.50 *(978-1-60851-959-0(7)*, PowerKids Pr.) Rosen Publishing Group, Inc., The.

Adler, David A. A Picture Book of Benjamin Franklin. Wallner, John & Wallner, Alexandra, illus. 2008. (Picture Book Biography Ser.). (J). (gr. k-3). 28.95 incl. audio compact disk *(978-1-4301-0340-0(X))*;Set. pap. 37.95 incl. audio *(978-1-4301-0338-7(8))* Live Oak Media.

—A Picture Book of George Washington Carver. Brown, Dan, illus. 2008. (Picture Book Biography Ser.). (J). (gr. -1-2). 28.95 incl. audio compact disk *(978-1-4301-0348-6(5))* Live Oak Media.

Aldrich, Lisa J. Nikola Tesla & the Taming of Electricity. 2005. (Profiles in Science Ser.). (Illus.). 160p. (J). (gr. 3-7). lib. bdg. 26.95 *(978-1-931798-46-4(X))* Reynolds, Morgan Inc.

Aller, Susan Bivin. George Eastman. 2003. (History Maker Biographies Ser.). (ENG., Illus.). 48p. (gr. 3-6). lib. bdg. 27.93 *(978-0-8225-0200-5(3))* Lerner Publishing Group.

Anderson, Kirsten & dePaola, Tomie. Who Was Milton Bradley? Foley, Tim & Harrison, Nancy, illus. 2016. (Who Was? Ser.). (ENG.). 112p. (J). (gr. 3-7). lib. bdg. 15.99 *(978-0-399-54236-7(1)*, Grosset & Dunlap) Penguin Young Readers Group.

Anorak Press Staff. Anorak Vol. 3: The Happy Mag for Kids. Wright, Jay, illus. 2013. (ENG.). 68p. (J). pap. 9.99 *(978-1-4236-3389-1(X)*, Anorak Pr.) Gibbs Smith, Publisher.

Auch, Allison. Electrifying Personalities & Personalidades Electrizantes: 6 English, 6 Spanish Adaptations. 2011. (ENG & SPA.). (J). 97.00 net. *(978-1-4108-5713-2(1))* Benchmark Education Co.

Bader, Bonnie. Who Was Alexander Graham Bell? Groff, David, illus. 2013. (Who Was? Ser.). (ENG.). 112p. (J). (gr. 3-7). 5.99 *(978-0-448-46460-2(8)*, Grosset & Dunlap) Penguin Young Readers Group.

—Who Was Alexander Graham Bell? 2013. (Who Was... ? Ser.). lib. bdg. 16.00 *(978-0-606-32132-7(2)*, Turtleback) Turtleback Bks.

Bankston, John. Alexander Graham Bell & the Story of the Telephone. 2004. (Uncharted, Unexplored, & Unexplained Ser.). (Illus.). 48p. (J). (gr. 4-8). lib. bdg. 29.95 *(978-1-58415-243-9(5))* Mitchell Lane Pubs., Inc.

—Karl Benz & the Single Cylinder Engine. 2004. (Uncharted, Unexplored, & Unexplained Ser.). (Illus.). 48p. (J). (gr. 4-8). lib. bdg. 29.95 *(978-1-58415-244-6(3))* Mitchell Lane Pubs., Inc.

Barnham, Kay. Thomas Edison, 1 vol. 2014. (Science Biographies Ser.). (ENG.). 32p. (gr. 2-4). lib. bdg. 30.65 *(978-1-4109-6239-3(3)*, Raintree Perspectives) Heinemann-Raintree.

Barretta, Gene. Neo Leo: The Ageless Ideas of Leonardo da Vinci. Barretta, Gene, illus. 2009. (ENG., Illus.). 40p. (J). (gr. -1-4). 17.99 *(978-0-8050-8703-1(6)*, 9780805087031, Holt, Henry & Co. Bks. For Young Readers) Holt, Henry & Co.

—Now & Ben: The Modern Inventions of Benjamin Franklin. 2007. (J). (gr. 2-5). 29.95 incl. audio compact disk *(978-0-8045-4175-6(2))*; 27.95 incl. audio *(978-0-8045-6952-1(5))* Spoken Arts, Inc.

—Now & Ben: The Modern Inventions of Benjamin Franklin. Barretta, Gene, illus. 2008. (ENG., Illus.). 40p. (J). (gr. k-4). pap. 8.99 *(978-0-312-53569-8(4)*, 9780312535698) Square Fish.

Barton, Chris. Whoosh! Lonnie Johnson's Super-Soaking Stream of Inventions. Tate, Don, illus. 2016. (ENG.). 32p. (J). (gr. 2-5). lib. bdg. 16.95 *(978-1-58089-297-1(3))* Charlesbridge Publishing, Inc.

Bearce, Stephanie. Insane Inventors. 2017. (Twisted True Tales from Science Ser.: 0). (ENG., Illus.). 125p. (J). (gr. 4-7). pap. 8.95 *(978-1-61821-570-3(1))* Prufrock Pr.

Benge, Janet & Benge, Geoff. Heroes of History - Benjamin Franklin: Live Wire. 2005. (Heroes of History Ser.). (ENG., Illus.). 208p. (YA). (gr. 5). pap. 9.99 *(978-1-932096-14-9(0))* Emerald Bks.

—Heroes of History - Thomas Edison: Inspiration & Hard Work. 2007. (Heroes of History Ser.). (ENG.). 208p. (YA). (gr. 3-7). pap. 9.99 *(978-1-932096-37-8(X))* Emerald Bks.

Bennett, Doraine & Scott, Clark C. Benjamin Franklin. 2012. (Illus.). 24p. (J). *(978-1-935884-38-5(7))*; pap. *(978-1-935884-47-7(6))* State Standards Publishing, LLC.

Bergin, Mark. Inventions. 2016. (Wise Up Ser.). 32p. (gr. 2-6). 31.35 *(978-1-62588-341-4(2)*, Smart Apple Media) Black Rabbit Bks.

Bethea, Nikole Brooks. The Invention of the Cotton Gin. 2017. (Engineering That Made America Ser.). (ENG.). 32p. (J). (gr. 3-6). lib. bdg. 28.50 *(978-1-5038-1642-8(7)*, 211158) Child's World, Inc., The.

Boekhoff, P. M. & Kallen, Stuart A. Benjamin Franklin. 2006. (Illus.). 48p. (J). (gr. 4-8). 17.00 *(978-1-4223-5322-6(2))* DIANE Publishing Co.

Boothroyd, Jennifer. Robert Fulton: A Life of Innovation. 2007. (Pull Ahead Bks.). (Illus.). 32p. (J). (gr. 3-7). lib. bdg. 22.60 *(978-0-8225-6458-4(0)*, Lerner Pubns.) Lerner Publishing Group.

Borden, Louise. Sea Clocks: The Story of Longitude. Blegvad, Erik, illus. 2004. (ENG.). 48p. (J). (gr. 2-5). 19.99 *(978-0-689-84216-0(3)*, McElderry, Margaret K. Bks.) McElderry, Margaret K. Bks.

Braun, Sandra. Incredible Women Inventors, 1 vol. 2007. (Women's Hall of Fame Ser.). (ENG., Illus.). 120p. (J). (gr. 3-8). pap. 10.95 *(978-1-897187-15-9(7))* Second Story Pr. CAN. Dist: Orca Bk. Pubs. USA.

—Women Inventors Who Changed the World. 2011. (Great Women of Achievement Ser.). (ENG., Illus.). 112p. (YA). (gr. 5-8). lib. bdg. 34.60 *(978-1-4488-5996-2(4)*, Rosen Reference) Rosen Publishing Group, Inc., The.

Brown, Natalie. Who Was Alexander Graham Bell? 2012. (InfoMax Readers Ser.). (ENG., Illus.). 24p. (J). (gr. 1-2). pap. 8.25 *(978-1-4488-9085-9(3)*, Rosen Classroom) Rosen Publishing Group, Inc., The.

Bryant, Tamera. Thomas Alva Edison. 2003. (World Was Never the Same Ser.). (J). *(978-1-58417-260-4(6))*; pap. *(978-1-58417-261-1(4))* Lake Street Pubs.

Buckley, James, Jr. Who Were the Wright Brothers? Foley, Tim & Harrison, Nancy, illus. 2014. (Who Was? Ser.). (ENG.). 112p. (J). (gr. 3-7). 5.99 *(978-0-448-47951-4(6)*, Grosset & Dunlap) Penguin Young Readers Group.

Buckley, James. Who Were the Wright Brothers? Foley, Tim, illus. 2014. 106p. (J). *(978-1-101-99527-3(0))* Penguin Publishing Group.

Burke, Michelle Prater. The Story of the Wright Brothers. Johnson, Meredith, illus. 2008. (ENG.). 26p. (J). (gr. -1-3). bds. 6.99 *(978-0-8249-6729-1(1)*, Ideal Pubns.) Worthy Publishing.

Byrd, Robert. Electric Ben: The Amazing Life & Times of Benjamin Franklin. 2012. (ENG.). 40p. (J). (gr. k-3). 17.99 *(978-0-8037-3749-5(1)*, Dial Bks) Penguin Young Readers Group.

Camp, Carole Ann. American Women Inventors. 2004. (Collective Biographies Ser.). (Illus.). 104p. (J). lib. bdg. 27.94 *(978-0-7660-1913-3(6))* Enslow Pubs., Inc.

Carson, Mary Kay. Who Invented Home Video Games? Ralph Baer. 2012. (I Like Inventors! Ser.). (Illus.). 24p. (J). (gr. k-3). pap. 7.95 *(978-1-4644-0135-0(7)*, Enslow Elementary) Enslow Pubs., Inc.

—Who Invented Television? — Philo Farnsworth. 2012. (I Like Inventors! Ser.). 24p. (J). (gr. k-3). 22.60 *(978-0-7660-3974-2(9)*, Enslow Elementary) Enslow Pubs., Inc.

Cefrey, Holly. The Inventions of Alexander Graham Bell: The Telephone. (19th Century American Inventors Ser.). 24p. 2009. (gr. 2-3). 42.50 *(978-1-60854-949-8(6))* 2003. (Illus.). (J). lib. bdg. 22.60 *(978-0-8239-6441-3(8))* Rosen Publishing Group, Inc., The. (PowerKids Pr.).

—The Inventions of Amanda Jones: The Vacuum Method of Canning & Food Preservation. 2009. (19th Century American Inventors Ser.). 24p. (gr. 2-3). 42.50 *(978-1-60854-950-4(X)*, PowerKids Pr.) Rosen Publishing Group, Inc., The.

—The Inventions of Eli Whitney: The Cotton Gin. 2009. (19th Century American Inventors Ser.). 24p. (gr. 2-3). 42.50 *(978-1-60854-951-1(8)*, PowerKids Pr.) Rosen Publishing Group, Inc., The.

—The Inventions of Granville Woods: The Railroad Telegraph System & the "Third Rail" 2003. (19th Century American Inventors Ser.). (Illus.). 24p. (J). lib. bdg. 22.60 *(978-0-8239-6442-0(6)*, PowerKids Pr.) Rosen Publishing Group, Inc., The.

—The Inventions of Granville Woods: The Railroad Telegraph System & the Third Rail. 2009. (19th Century American Inventors Ser.). 24p. (gr. 2-3). 42.50 *(978-1-60854-952-8(6)*, PowerKids Pr.) Rosen Publishing Group, Inc., The.

—The Inventions of Martha Coston: Signal Flares That Save Sailors' Lives. 2009. (19th Century American Inventors Ser.). 24p. (gr. 2-3). 42.50 *(978-1-60854-953-5(4)*, PowerKids Pr.) Rosen Publishing Group, Inc., The.

—The Inventions of Martha Coston: Signal Flares That Saved Sailors' Lives. 2003. (19th Century American Inventors Ser.). (Illus.). 24p. (J). lib. bdg. 22.60 *(978-0-8239-6444-4(2)*, PowerKids Pr.) Rosen Publishing Group, Inc., The.

—The Inventions of Thomas Alva Edison: Father of the Light Bulb & the Motion Picture Camera. 2009. (19th Century American Inventors Ser.). 24p. (gr. 2-3). 42.50 *(978-1-60854-954-2(2)*, PowerKids Pr.) Rosen Publishing Group, Inc., The.

—The Inventions of Thomas Alva Edison: Father of the Lightbulb & the Motion Picture Camera. 2003. (19th Century American Inventors Ser.). (Illus.). 24p. (J). lib. bdg. 22.60 *(978-0-8239-6440-6(X)*, PowerKids Pr.) Rosen Publishing Group, Inc., The.

Challoner, Jack. Exploring the Mysteries of Genius & Invention. 2016. (STEM Guide to the Universe Ser.). (ENG.). 96p. (J). (gr. 9-9). lib. bdg. 46.10 *(978-1-4994-6410-8(X))* Rosen Publishing Group, Inc., The.

Chambers, Catherine. Alexander Graham Bell, 1 vol. 2014. (Science Biographies Ser.). (ENG.). 32p. (gr. 2-4). lib. bdg. 30.65 *(978-1-4109-6238-6(5)*, Raintree Perspectives) Heinemann-Raintree.

Claybourne, Anna. The Story of Inventions. Chisholm, Jane, ed. 2007. (Story of Inventions Ser.). (Illus.). 96p. (J). (gr. 4-7). per. 10.99 *(978-0-7945-1710-6(2)*, Usborne) EDC Publishing.

Colbert, David. Benjamin Franklin. 2008. (10 Days Ser.). (ENG.). 160p. (J). (gr. 3-8). pap. 8.99 *(978-1-4169-6446-9(0)*, Simon & Schuster/Paula Wiseman Bks.) Simon & Schuster/Paula Wiseman Bks.

Collard, Sneed B., III. Benjamin Franklin: The Man Who Could Do Just about Anything. 2006. (American Heroes Ser.). (Illus.). 48p. (gr. 3-7). lib. bdg. 29.93 *(978-0-7614-2161-0(0)*, Benchmark Bks.) Marshall Cavendish Corp.

Cooper, Sharon Katz, et al. The Story Behind the Name. 2015. (Story Behind the Name Ser.). (ENG.). 32p. (gr. 2-3). pap. 31.80 *(978-1-4795-8252-5(2))* Picture Window Bks.

Crawford, Laura. Benjamin Franklin from A to Z, 1 vol. Hierstein, Judith, illus. 2013. (ENG.). 32p. (J). (gr. k-3). 16.99 *(978-1-4556-1713-5(X))* Pelican Publishing Co., Inc.

Crompton, Samuel Willard. Alexander Graham Bell & the Telephone: The Invention That Changed Communication. 2008. (Milestones in American History Ser.). (Illus.). 120p. (J). (gr. 7-12). 35.00 *(978-1-60413-004-1(0))* Facts On File, Inc.

—The Wright Brothers: First in Flight. 2007. (Milestones in American History Ser.). (Illus.). 128p. (YA). (gr. 7-12). lib. bdg. 35.00 *(978-0-7910-9356-6(5))* Facts On File, Inc.

Dakers, Diane. Orville & Wilbur Wright: Pioneers of the Age of Flight. 2016. (Crabtree Groundbreaker Biographies Ser.). (ENG.). 112p. (J). (gr. 5-8). *(978-0-7787-2609-8(6))* Crabtree Publishing Co.

Davidson, Tish. African American Scientists & Inventors. 2012. (J). pap. *(978-1-4222-2388-8(4))* Mason Crest.

—African American Scientists & Inventors. Hill, Marc Lamont, ed. 2012. (Major Black Contributions from Emancipation to Civil Rights Ser.). 64p. (J). (gr. 5). 22.95 *(978-1-4222-2375-8(2))* Mason Crest.

Davis, Kathryn Gibbs. Mr. Ferris & His Wheel. Ford, Gilbert, illus. 2014. (ENG.). 40p. (J). (gr. -1-3). 17.99 *(978-0-547-95922-1(2)*, HMH Books For Young Readers) Houghton Mifflin Harcourt Publishing Co.

Davis, Lynn. Alexander Graham Bell, 1 vol. 2016. (ENG.). 24p. (J). *(978-1-62403-721-4(6))* ABDO Publishing Co.

—George Eastman, 1 vol. 2016. (ENG., Illus.). 24p. (J). *(978-1-62403-722-1(4))* ABDO Publishing Co.

—Samuel Morse, 1 vol. 2016. (ENG., Illus.). 24p. (J). *(978-1-62403-725-2(9))* ABDO Publishing Co.

—Thomas Edison, 1 vol. 2016. (ENG., Illus.). 24p. (J). 25.65 *(978-1-62403-723-8(2))* ABDO Publishing Co.

—The Wright Brothers, 1 vol. 2016. (ENG., Illus.). 24p. (J). *(978-1-62403-726-9(7))* ABDO Publishing Co.

Davis, Marc & Santella, Andrew. The Wright Brothers: Inventors & Aviators. 2003. (Our People Ser.). (ENG., Illus.). 32p. (J). (gr. 3-6). 29.93 *(978-1-56766-369-3(9)*, 200657) Child's World, Inc., The.

Delano, Marfe Ferguson. Inventing the Future: A Photobiography of Thomas Alva Edison. 2006. (Photobiographies Ser.). (ENG., Illus.). 64p. (J). (gr. 5-7). per. 7.95 *(978-0-7922-5934-3(3)*, National Geographic Children's Bks.) National Geographic Society.

Delano, Marfe Ferguson & National Geographic Kids Staff. Inventing the Future: A Photobiography of Thomas Alva Edison. 2015. (Photobiographies Ser.). (ENG., Illus.). 64p. (J). (gr. 5). pap. 7.99 *(978-1-4263-2220-4(8)*, National Geographic Children's Bks.) National Geographic Society.

Demuth, Patricia Brennan. Thomas Edison & His Bright Idea. Tuya, Jez, illus. 2016. (Penguin Young Readers, Level 3 Ser.). (ENG.). 32p. (J). (gr. 1-3). pap. 3.99 *(978-0-448-48830-1(2)*, Penguin Young Readers) Penguin Young Readers Group.

Diggory, Nikki. Inventor Nikola Tesla. 2013. (Rosen Readers Ser.). (ENG.). 24p. (J). (gr. 3-4). pap. 49.50 *(978-1-4777-2507-8(5))*; pap. 8.25 *(978-1-4777-2506-1(7))* Rosen Publishing Group, Inc., The. (Rosen Classroom).

Doeden, Matt. Steve Jobs: Technology Innovator & Apple Genius. 2012. (Gateway Biographies Ser.). (ENG.). 48p. (gr. 4-8). lib. bdg. 26.60 *(978-1-4677-0215-7(3)*, Lerner Pubns.) Lerner Publishing Group.

Dolan, Ellen M. Thomas Alva Edison: American Inventor & Businessman. 2015. (Legendary American Biographies Ser.). 96p. (J). (gr. 6-12). 27.94 *(978-0-7660-6510-9(3))*; pap. 10.95 *(978-0-7660-6511-6(1))* Enslow Pubs., Inc.

Dooling, Michael. Young Thomas Edison. Dooling, Michael, illus. 2005. (ENG., Illus.). 40p. (J). (gr. -1-3). 17.95 *(978-0-8234-1868-8(5))* Holiday Hse., Inc.

Draze, Dianne. Inventions, Inventors & You. 2005. (ENG.). 64p. (Orig.). (gr. 3-7). pap. 14.95 *(978-1-59363-082-9(4))* Prufrock Pr.

Dunn, Joe. The Wright Brothers, 1 vol. Dunn, Ben, illus. 2007. (Bio-Graphics Ser.). (ENG.). 32p. (gr. 3-6). 28.50 *(978-1-60270-071-0(0)*, Graphic Planet- Nonfiction) ABDO Publishing Co.

Dykstra, Danell. The Man Who Invented the Ferris Wheel: The Genius of George Ferris. 2013. (Genius Inventors & Their Great Ideas Ser.). (Illus.). 48p. (J). (gr. 3-18). 25.27 *(978-0-7660-4136-3(0))* Enslow Pubs., Inc.

Eamer, Claire. Before the World Was Ready: Stories of Daring Genius in Science. Boothroyd, Sa, illus. 2013. (ENG.). 128p. (J). (gr. 4-7). pap. 14.95 *(978-1-55451-535-6(1)*, 9781554515356) Annick Pr., Ltd. CAN. Dist: Publishers Group West (PGW).

Edwards, Roberta. Who Was Leonardo da Vinci? Kelley, True, illus. 2005. (Who Was... ? Ser.). 106p. (J). (gr. 2-6). 12.65 *(978-0-7569-6971-4(9))* Perfection Learning Corp.

Eldridge, Alison & Eldridge, Stephen. The Coolest Inventor: Willis Haviland Carrier & His Air Conditioner. 2014. (Inventors at Work! Ser.). 48p. (J). lib. bdg. 25.27 *(978-0-7660-4216-2(2)*, Enslow Elementary) Enslow Pubs., Inc.

Endsley, Kezia, et al. Inventors of Computer Technology. 2015. 144p. (J). lib. bdg. *(978-1-5026-0654-9(2))* Musa Publishing.

Espinosa, Rod. Benjamin Franklin, 1 vol. Espinosa, Rod, illus. 2007. (Bio-Graphics Ser.). (ENG., Illus.). 32p. (gr. 3-6). 28.50 *(978-1-60270-066-6(4)*, Graphic Planet- Nonfiction) ABDO Publishing Co.

Fandel, Jennifer. The Light Bulb. 2004. (What in the World? Ser.). (Illus.). 48p. 19.95 *(978-1-58341-271-8(9)*, Creative Education) Creative Co., The.

Feinstein, Stephen. Alexander Graham Bell: The Genius Behind the Phone. 2008. (Inventors Who Changed the World Ser.). (Illus.). 128p. (J). (gr. 6-18). lib. bdg. 34.60 *(978-1-59845-055-2(7)*, MyReportLinks.com Bks.) Enslow Pubs., Inc.

Fleming, Candace. Ben Franklin's Almanac: Being a True Account of the Good Gentleman's Life. 2003. (ENG., Illus.). 128p. (J). (gr. 5-9). 21.99 *(978-0-689-83549-0(3)*, Atheneum Bks. for Young Readers) Simon & Schuster Children's Publishing.

Fleming, Thomas. Ben Franklin: Inventing America. (Great Leaders & Events Ser.). (ENG.). 208p. (J). (gr. 4-8). 2017. lib. bdg. 35.99 ***(978-1-942875-23-9(1))*** 2016. (Illus.). pap. 12.99 *(978-0-7603-5228-1(3))* Quarto Publishing Group USA. (Voyageur Pr.).

Ford, Carin T. George Eastman: The Kodak Camera Man. 2004. (Famous Inventors Ser.). (Illus.). 32p. (J). lib. bdg. 22.60 *(978-0-7660-2247-8(1))* Enslow Pubs., Inc.

—The Wright Brothers: Heroes of Flight. 2003. (Famous Inventors Ser.). (Illus.). 32p. (J). (gr. 1-4). lib. bdg. 23.94 *(978-0-7660-2002-3(9))* Enslow Pubs., Inc.

Foster, Leila Merrell. Benjamin Franklin: Statesman & Inventor. 2015. (Legendary American Biographies Ser.). 96p. (J). (gr. 6-12). 27.94 *(978-0-7660-6445-4(X))*; pap. 10.95 *(978-0-7660-6446-1(8))* Enslow Pubs., Inc.

Fradin, Dennis Brindell. Who Was Ben Franklin? O'brien, John, illus. 2003. (Who Was... ? Ser.). 105p. (gr. 4-7). 15.00 *(978-0-7569-1589-6(9))* Perfection Learning Corp.

Franklin, Benjamin. Benjamin Franklin's Wise Words. Harper, Fred, illus. 2017. (ENG.). 128p. (J). (gr. 3-7). 16.99 *(978-1-4263-2699-8(8))*; lib. bdg. 26.90 *(978-1-4263-2700-1(5))* National Geographic Society. (National Geographic Children's Bks.).

Fraser, Mary Ann. Alexander Graham Bell Answers the Call. Fraser, Mary Ann, illus. 2017. (ENG., Illus.). 32p. (J). (gr. 1-4). lib. bdg. 16.99 *(978-1-58089-721-1(5))* Charlesbridge Publishing, Inc.

Freedman, Russell. Becoming Ben Franklin: How a Candle-Maker's Son Helped Light the Flame of Liberty. 2013. (ENG.). 96p. (J). (gr. 5). 24.95 *(978-0-8234-2374-3(3))* Holiday Hse., Inc.

Frith, Margaret. Who Was Thomas Alva Edison? O'brien, John, illus. 2005. (Who Was... ? Ser.). 106p. (gr. 3-7). 15.00 *(978-0-7569-5830-5(X))* Perfection Learning Corp.

Garcia, Tracy J. Eli Whitney. 2013. (Jr. Graphic American Inventors Ser.). (ENG., Illus.). 24p. (J). (gr. 3-6). pap. 10.60 *(978-1-4777-0135-5(4))*; lib. bdg. 25.25 *(978-1-4777-0075-4(7))* Rosen Publishing Group, Inc., The. (PowerKids Pr.).

—Thomas Edison. 2013. (Jr. Graphic American Inventors Ser.). (ENG., Illus.). 24p. (J). (gr. 3-6). pap. 10.60 *(978-1-4777-0137-9(0))*; lib. bdg. 25.25 *(978-1-4777-0076-1(5))* Rosen Publishing Group, Inc., The. (PowerKids Pr.).

Gaustad, Edwin S. Benjamin Franklin: Inventing America. 2006. 143p. (J). (gr. 4-8). reprint ed. 22.00 *(978-1-4223-5227-4(7))* DIANE Publishing Co.

Giblin, James Cross. The Amazing Life of Benjamin Franklin. Dooling, Michael, illus. 2006. 48p. (gr. -1-3). 18.00 *(978-0-7569-6551-8(9))* Perfection Learning Corp.

Gibson, Karen Bush. Eli Whitney. 2006. (Profiles in American History Ser.). (Illus.). 48p. (J). (gr. 3-7). lib. bdg. 29.95 *(978-1-58415-434-1(9))* Mitchell Lane Pubs., Inc.

Gilman, Sarah. Ben Franklin. 2016. (Explore Colonial America Ser.). (Illus.). 48p. (J). (gr. 5-4). 27.93 *(978-0-7660-7873-4(6))* Enslow Pubs., Inc.

Glass, Andrew. Flying Cars: The True Story. 2015. (ENG., Illus.). 128p. (J). (gr. 5-7). 17.99 *(978-0-618-98482-4(8))* Houghton Mifflin Harcourt Publishing Co.

Glass, Maya. Benjamin Franklin: Early American Genius. 2009. (Primary Sources of Famous People in American History Ser.). 32p. (gr. 2-3). 47.90 *(978-1-60851-654-4(7))* Rosen Publishing Group, Inc., The.

—Benjamin Franklin: Early American Genius / Político e inventor Estadounidense. 2009. (Famous People in American History/Grandes personajes en la historia de los Estados Unidos Ser.). (ENG & SPA.). 32p. (gr. 2-3). 47.90 *(978-1-61512-538-8(8)*, Editorial Buenas Letras) Rosen Publishing Group, Inc., The.

—Benjamin Franklin: Político e inventor estadounidense (Benjamin Franklin: Early American Genius) 2009. (Grandes personajes en la historia de los Estados Unidos (Famous People in American History) Ser.). (SPA.). 32p. (gr. 2-3). 47.90 *(978-1-61512-790-0(9)*, Editorial Buenas Letras) Rosen Publishing Group, Inc., The.
Glatzer, Jenna. George Ferris' Grand Idea: The Ferris Wheel. Dominguez, Stephanie, illus. 2015. (Story Behind the Name Ser.). (ENG.). 32p. (gr. 2-3). pap. 7.95 *(978-1-4795-7165-9(2))*; lib. bdg. 28.65 *(978-1-4795-7135-2(0))* Picture Window Bks.
—The Story Behind the Name. 2015. (Story Behind the Name Ser.). (ENG.). 32p. (gr. 2-3). 114.60 *(978-1-4795-8008-8(2))* Picture Window Bks.
Goldish, Meish. Accidental Inventions: (Or Made by Mistake) 2005. (Illus.). 64p. (J). pap. *(978-0-669-51406-3(3))* Great Source Education Group, Inc.
Goldsmith, Howard. Thomas Edison to the Rescue! DiVito, Anna, illus. 2003. (Ready-To-read COFA Ser.). (ENG.). 32p. (J). (gr. k-2). pap. 3.99 *(978-0-689-85331-9(9))*, Simon Spotlight) Simon Spotlight.
Gosman, Gillian. Benjamin Franklin. 2011. (Life Stories Ser.). (Illus.). 24p. (J). pap. 8.25 *(978-1-4488-2759-6(0))*; (gr. 1-4). lib. bdg. 22.60 *(978-1-4488-2585-1(7))* Rosen Publishing Group, Inc., The. (PowerKids Pr.).
—Benjamín Franklin. 2011. (Life Stories / Biografías Ser.). (ENG & SPA., Illus.). 24p. (J). (gr. 1-4). lib. bdg. 22.60 *(978-1-4488-3219-4(5))* Rosen Publishing Group, Inc., The.
Gould, Jane H. Benjamin Franklin. 2012. (Jr. Graphic Founding Fathers Ser.). (ENG., Illus.). 24p. (J). (gr. 3-6). pap. 10.60 *(978-1-4488-7990-8(6))*; lib. bdg. 25.25 *(978-1-4488-7896-3(9))* Rosen Publishing Group, Inc., The. (PowerKids Pr.).
Graham, Amy. Thomas Edison: Wizard of Light & Sound. 2007. (Inventors Who Changed the World Ser.). (Illus.). 128p. (J). (gr. 5-9). lib. bdg. 34.60 *(978-1-59845-052-1(2)*, MyReportLinks.com Bks.) Enslow Pubs., Inc.
Grandes Inventos, 6 vols. (Explorers. Exploradores Nonfiction Sets Ser.). (SPA.). 32p. (gr. 3-6). 44.95 *(978-0-7699-0634-8(6))* Shortland Pubns. (U. S. A.) Inc.
Great Inventions Group 3, 5 bks., Set. Incl. Medical Imaging. Sherrow, Victoria. (gr. 8-10). lib. bdg. 29.95 *(978-0-7614-2231-0(5))*; Microscopes & Telescopes. Stefoff, Rebecca. (J). (gr. 3-7). lib. bdg. 39.93 *(978-0-7614-2230-3(7))*; Rockets. Otfinoski, Steven. (gr. 8-7). lib. bdg. 29.95 *(978-0-7614-2232-7(3))*; Submarines. Stefoff, Rebecca. (gr. 8-7). lib. bdg. 29.95 *(978-0-7614-2229-7(3))*; Television. Otfinoski, Steven. (gr. 8-7). lib. bdg. 29.95 *(978-0-7614-2228-0(5))*; (Illus.). 128p. 2006. 2007. Set lib. bdg. 199.64 *(978-0-7614-2227-3(7)*, Benchmark Bks.) Marshall Cavendish Corp.
Gregory, Josh. Henry Ford: Father of the Auto Industry. 2013. (True Book(tm), a — Great American Business Ser.). (ENG.). 48p. (J). 31.00 *(978-0-531-24777-8(5))*; pap. 6.95 *(978-0-531-28463-6(8))* Scholastic Library Publishing.
Grossman, Max & Benchmark Education Co., LLC. The Idea Machine: My Inventor's Journal. 2014. (Text Connections Ser.). (J). (gr. 3). *(978-1-4509-9655-6(8))* Benchmark Education Co.
Groundbreakers Series, 24 bks., Set. (Illus.). (J). (gr. 4-6). lib. bdg. 612.96 *(978-1-58810-133-4(9))* Heinemann-Raintree.
Gunderson, Jessica Sarah, et al. Eli Whitney & the Cotton Gin, 1 vol. Acerno, Gerry, illus. 2007. (Inventions & Discovery Ser.). (ENG.). 32p. (gr. 3-4). per. 8.10 *(978-0-7368-7895-1(5)*, Graphic Library) Capstone Press of Coughlan Cos.
—Eli Whitney & the Cotton Gin, 1 vol. Acerno, Gerry et al, illus. 2007. (Inventions & Discovery Ser.). (ENG.). 32p. (gr. 3-4). 30.65 *(978-0-7368-6843-3(7)*, Graphic Library) Capstone Press of Coughlan Cos.
Haldy, Emma E. Benjamin Franklin. Bane, Jeff, illus. 2016. (My Early Library: My Itty-Bitty Bio Ser.). (ENG.). 24p. (J). (gr. k-1). 28.50 *(978-1-63470-478-6(9)*, 207643) Cherry Lake Publishing.
Hall, Derek, ed. Philosophy, Invention, & Engineering. 2009. (FAYFT: Great Scientists Ser.). 64p. (gr. 4-10). 39.95 *(978-1-933834-48-1(X))* Brown Bear Bks.
Hall, M. C. Leonardo Da Vinci, 1 vol. 2007. (Essential Lives Set 1 Ser.). (ENG., Illus.). 112p. (J). (gr. 6-12). lib. bdg. 35.64 *(978-1-59928-844-4(3))* ABDO Publishing Co.
Hantula, Richard. Thomas Edison. 2004. (Trailblazers of the Modern World Ser.). (Illus.). 48p. (J). (gr. 5-12). pap. 14.05 *(978-0-8368-5265-3(6))*; lib. bdg. 31.00 *(978-0-8368-5496-1(9))* Stevens, Gareth Publishing LLLP. (Gareth Stevens Secondary Library).
Hardyman, Robyn. Nikola Tesla & Thomas Edison. 2014. (Dynamic Duos of Science Ser.). 48p. (YA). (gr. 5-8). pap. 84.30 *(978-1-4824-1285-7(3))* Stevens, Gareth Publishing LLLP.
Harness, Cheryl. The Remarkable Benjamin Franklin. 2008. (ENG., Illus.). 48p. (J). (gr. 2-5). 7.95 *(978-1-4263-0297-8(5)*, National Geographic Children's Bks.) National Geographic Society.
—The Remarkable Benjamin Franklin. Harness, Cheryl, illus. 2005. (National Geographic Ser.). (ENG., Illus.). 48p. (J). (gr. 2-5). 17.95 *(978-0-7922-7882-5(8)*, National Geographic Children's Bks.) National Geographic Society.
—The Remarkable Benjamin Franklin. 2005. (ENG., Illus.). 48p. (J). (gr. 2-5). 27.90 *(978-0-7922-7884-9(4)*, National Geographic Children's Bks.) National Geographic Society.
Harris, Laurie Lanzen. Biography for Beginners: Inventors. 2006. (J). lib. bdg. 55.00 *(978-1-931360-27-2(8))* Favorable Impressions.
Haven, Kendall F. Alexander Graham Bell: Inventor & Visionary. 2003. (Great Life Stories: Inventors & Scientists Ser.). (Illus.). 128p. (J). 30.50 *(978-0-531-12314-0(6)*, Watts, Franklin) Scholastic Library Publishing.
Head, David L. Granville T. Woods: African American Communication & Transportation Pioneer. 2013. 140p. pap. 30.00 *(978-1-4349-7841-7(9)*, RoseDog Bks.) Dorrance Publishing Co., Inc.
Herweck, Don. Making It Go: The Life & Work of Robert Fulton, 1 vol. 2007. (Science Readers Ser.). (ENG.). 32p. (J). (gr. 3-3). pap. 8.99 *(978-0-7439-0578-7(4))* Shell Educational Publishing.
Hesleden, Michael. Benjamin Franklin: American Diplomat. 2015. (Spotlight on American History Ser.). (ENG., Illus.). 24p. (J). (gr. 4-6). pap. 10.00 *(978-1-4994-1782-1(9)*, PowerKids Pr.) Rosen Publishing Group, Inc., The.
Hirschmann, Kris. Jonathan Ive: Designer of the iPod. 2007. (Innovators Ser.). (ENG., Illus.). 48p. (J). (gr. 3-7). lib. bdg. 28.75 *(978-0-7377-3533-8(3)*, Kidhaven) Cengage Gale.
Hollar, Sherman. Pioneers of the Industrial Age: Breakthroughs in Technology. 2012. (Inventors & Innovators Ser.). (ENG., Illus.). 112p. (YA). (gr. 7-12). 65.80 *(978-1-61530-789-0(3))*; 32.90 *(978-1-61530-696-1(X))* Rosen Publishing Group, Inc., The.
Huff, Regan A. Eli Whitney: The Cotton Gin & American Manufacturing. 2009. (Library of American Lives & Times Ser.). 112p. (gr. 5-5). 69.20 *(978-1-60853-478-4(2))* Rosen Publishing Group, Inc., The.
Indovino, Shaina. Women Inventors. Lee-Karlon, Ann, ed. 2013. (Major Women in Science Ser.: 10). 64p. (J). (gr. 7-18). 22.95 *(978-1-4222-2932-3(7))* Mason Crest.
Inventors & Inventions - Group 2, 6 bks., Set. Incl. Biotechnology. Wells, Donna K. lib. bdg. 25.64 *(978-0-7614-0046-2(X))*; Nuclear Power. Holland, Gini. lib. bdg. 25.64 *(978-0-7614-0047-9(8))*; Radiology. Winkler, Kathy. lib. bdg. 25.64 *(978-0-7614-0075-2(3))*; Satellites. Fox, Mary Virginia. lib. bdg. 25.64 *(978-0-7614-0049-3(4))*; Television. Riehecky, Janet. lib. bdg. 25.64 *(978-0-7614-0045-5(1))*; Video. Biel, Jackie. lib. bdg. 25.64 *(978-0-7614-0048-6(6))*; 64p. (YA). (gr. 5-9). 1996. (Illus.). Set lib. bdg. 153.86 *(978-0-7614-0044-8(3)*, Benchmark Bks.) Marshall Cavendish Corp.
Jacobson, Bob. Ole Evinrude & His Outboard Motor. 2009. (Badger Biographies Ser.). (ENG., Illus.). 78p. (J). (gr. 3-7). pap. 12.95 *(978-0-87020-420-3(3))* Wisconsin Historical Society.
James, Emily. Alexander Graham Bell. 2017. (Great Scientists & Inventors Ser.). (ENG.). 24p. (gr. k-1). lib. bdg. 26.65 *(978-1-5157-3883-1(3)*, Pebble Plus) Capstone Press of Coughlan Cos.
—Great Scientists & Inventors. 2017. (Great Scientists & Inventors Ser.). (ENG.). 24p. (gr. k-1). 159.90 *(978-1-5157-3910-4(4)*, Pebble Plus) Capstone Press of Coughlan Cos.
—The Wright Brothers. 2017. (Great Scientists & Inventors Ser.). (ENG.). 24p. (gr. k-1). lib. bdg. 26.65 *(978-1-5157-3885-5(X))* Capstone Press of Coughlan Cos.
Jankowski, Connie. Pioneers of Light & Sound, 1 vol. 2007. (Science Readers Ser.). (ENG.). 32p. (J). (gr. 3-3). pap. 8.99 *(978-0-7439-0580-0(6))* Shell Educational Publishing.
Jeffrey, Laura S. Amazing American Inventors of the 20th Century. 2013. (Inspiring Collective Biographies Ser.). 112p. (J). (gr. 5-12). pap. 10.95 *(978-1-4644-0245-6(0))*; lib. bdg. 33.27 *(978-0-7660-4162-2(X))* Enslow Pubs., Inc.
Jenner, Caryn. First Flight Vol. 4: The Story of the Wright Brothers. 2004. (DK Readers Ser.). (Illus.). 48p. (gr. -1-3). 14.00 *(978-0-7569-3361-6(7))* Perfection Learning Corp.
Jenner, Caryn & Garrett, Leslie. First Flight, Level 4: The Story of the Wright Brothers. 2003. (DK Readers Ser.). (ENG., Illus.). 48p. (J). (gr. 3-7). pap. 3.99 *(978-0-7894-9291-3(1)*, DK Children) Dorling Kindersley Publishing, Inc.
Kamkwamba, William. The Boy Who Harnessed the Wind: Creating Currents of Electricity & Hope. 2009. 14.44 *(978-0-7848-3872-3(0)*, Everbind) Marco Bk. Co.
—The Boy Who Harnessed the Wind: Creating Currents of Electricity & Hope. Hymas, Anna, illus. 2015. (ENG.). 304p. (J). (gr. 5). 18.99 *(978-0-8037-4080-8(8)*, Dial Bks) Penguin Young Readers Group.
Kamkwamba, William & Mealer, Bryan. The Boy Who Harnessed the Wind: Young Readers Edition. Zunon, Elizabeth, illus. (ENG.). (J). 2016. 304p. (gr. 5). 8.99 *(978-0-14-751042-6(2)*, Puffin Books) 2012. 32p. (gr. 1-3). 17.99 *(978-0-8037-3511-8(1)*, Dial Bks) Penguin Young Readers Group.
Kelly, David A. Miracle Mud: Lena Blackburne & the Secret Mud That Changed Baseball. Dominguez, Oliver, illus. 2013. (ENG.). 32p. (J). (gr. 2-5). lib. bdg. 16.95 *(978-0-7613-8092-4(2)*, Millbrook Pr.) Lerner Publishing Group.
Kelly, Jack. Benjamin Franklin. Tafalla, Ortiz, illus. 2005. (Heroes of America Ser.). 239p. (gr. 3-8). 27.07 *(978-1-59679-257-9(4)*, Abdo & Daughters) ABDO Publishing Co.
Kenison, Misti. Cheer up, Ben Franklin! 2017. (ENG.). 28p. (J). bds. 9.99 ***(978-1-4926-5247-2(4)***, Sourcebooks Jabberwocky) Sourcebooks, Inc.
Kennelly, Sean. American Inventors & Innovators. Flowerpot Press, ed. 2012. (Illus.). 48p. (J). *(978-1-926988-95-5(7))* Flowerpot Children's Pr. Inc.
—American Inventors & Innovators. Paiva, Johannah Gilman, ed. 2014. (ENG., Illus.). 48p. (J). (gr. 4). 8.99 *(978-1-4867-0258-9(9))* Flowerpot Children's Pr. Inc. CAN. Dist: Cardinal Pubs. Group.
Klingel, Cynthia Fitterer & Klingel, Cynthia. Alexander Graham Bell: Inventor. 2003. (Our People Ser.). (ENG., Illus.). 32p. (J). (gr. 3-6). 29.93 *(978-1-56766-367-9(2)*, 200625) Child's World, Inc., The.
Kobayashi, Tatsuyoshi, illus. Thomas Edison: Genius of the Electric Age. 2011. (Biographical Comic Ser.). (ENG.). 152p. (J). (gr. 2-6). 18.99 *(978-1-4215-4236-2(6))* Shogakukan JPN. Dist: Simon & Schuster, Inc.
Koestler-Grack, Rachel A. Leonardo Da Vinci: Artist, Inventor, & Renaissance Man. 2005. (Makers of the Middle Ages & Renaissance Ser.). (Illus.). 152p. (gr. 5-8). lib. bdg. 32.95 *(978-0-7910-8626-1(7)*, Chelsea Hse.) Facts On File, Inc.
Kortemeier, Todd. 12 Unsung Heroes of Technology. 2017. (Unsung Heroes Ser.). (ENG., Illus.). 32p. (J). (gr. 3-6). 21.95 *(978-1-63235-311-5(3))* Pr. Room Editions LLC.
Kraft, Betsy Harvey. The Fantastic Ferris Wheel: The Story of Inventor George Ferris. Salerno, Steven, illus. 2015. (ENG.). 42p. (J). (gr. k-4). 17.99 *(978-1-62779-072-7(1)*, 9781627790727, Holt, Henry & Co. Bks. For Young Readers) Holt, Henry & Co.
Kramer, Barbara. Alexander Graham Bell. 2015. (Readers Bios Ser.). (ENG.). 32p. (J). (gr. k-3). pap. 3.99 *(978-1-4263-1935-8(5)*, National Geographic Children's Bks.) National Geographic Society.
Krensky, Stephen & Dorling Kindersley Publishing Staff. Benjamin Franklin. 2007. (DK Biography Ser.). (ENG., Illus.). 128p. (J). (gr. 5-12). pap. 6.99 *(978-0-7566-3528-2(4)*, DK Children) Dorling Kindersley Publishing, Inc.
Krieg, Katherine. Thomas Edison: World-Changing Inventor, 1 vol. 2014. (Great Minds of Science Ser.). (ENG.). 48p. (gr. 8-12). lib. bdg. 32.79 *(978-1-62403-378-0(4))* ABDO Publishing Co.
Krull, Kathleen. Benjamin Franklin. Kulikov, Boris, illus. 2014. (Giants of Science Ser.). (ENG.). 128p. (J). (gr. 3-7). pap. 7.99 *(978-0-14-751178-2(X)*, Puffin Books) Penguin Young Readers Group.
—The Boy Who Invented TV: The Story of Philo Farnsworth. Couch, Greg, illus. (ENG.). 40p. (J). (gr. 1-4). 2014. 7.99 *(978-0-385-75557-3(0)*, Dragonfly Bks.) 2009. 16.99 *(978-0-375-84561-1(5)*, Knopf Bks. for Young Readers) Random Hse. Children's Bks.
Kulling, Monica. Clean Sweep! Frank Zamboni's Ice Machine. Benoit, Renné, illus. 2017. (ENG.). 32p. (J). (gr. k-3). pap. 6.99 *(978-1-77049-796-2(X)*, Tundra Bks.) Tundra Bks. CAN. Dist: Penguin Random Hse. LLC.
—Clean Sweep! Frank Zamboni's Ice Machine. Benoit, Renne, illus. 2016. (ENG.). 32p. (J). (gr. k-3). 17.99 *(978-1-77049-795-5(1)*, Tundra Bks.) Tundra Bks. CAN. Dist: Penguin Random Hse. LLC.
—Going Up! Elisha Otis's Trip to the Top. Parkins, David, illus. 2014. (Great Idea Ser.). (ENG.). 32p. (J). (gr. k-3). pap. 7.99 *(978-1-77049-516-6(9)*, Tundra Bks.) Tundra Bks. CAN. Dist: Penguin Random Hse. LLC.
—In the Bag! Margaret Knight Wraps It Up. Parkins, David, illus. (Great Idea Ser.). (ENG.). 32p. (J). (gr. k-3). 2013. pap. 7.95 *(978-1-77049-515-9(0))* 2011. 17.95 *(978-1-77049-239-4(9))* Tundra Bks. CAN. (Tundra Bks.). Dist: Penguin Random Hse. LLC.
—It's a Snap! George Eastman's First Photograph. Slavin, Bill, illus. (Great Idea Ser.). (ENG.). 32p. (J). (gr. k-3). 2013. pap. 7.95 *(978-1-77049-513-5(4))* 2009. 17.95 *(978-0-88776-881-1(4))* Tundra Bks. CAN. (Tundra Bks.). Dist: Penguin Random Hse. LLC.
—Listen Up! Alexander Graham Bell's Talking Machine. Walz, Richard, illus. 2007. (Step into Reading Ser.). (ENG.). 48p. (J). (gr. k-3). per. 3.99 *(978-0-375-83115-7(0)*, Random Hse. Bks. for Young Readers) Random Hse. Children's Bks.
—Making Contact! Marconi Goes Wireless. 2016. (Great Idea Ser.). (ENG., Illus.). 32p. (J). (gr. k-3). pap. 6.99 *(978-1-101-91842-5(X)*, Tundra Bks.) Tundra Bks. CAN. Dist: Penguin Random Hse. LLC.
—Making Contact! Marconi Goes Wireless. Rudnicki, Richard, illus. 2013. (Great Idea Ser.). (ENG.). 32p. (J). (gr. k-3). 17.95 *(978-1-77049-378-0(6)*, Tundra Bks.) Tundra Bks. CAN. Dist: Penguin Random Hse. LLC.
—Sky High: George Ferris's Big Wheel. Barretta, Gene, illus. 2016. (Step into Reading Ser.). (ENG.). 48p. (J). (gr. k-3). pap. 3.99 *(978-1-101-93452-4(2)*, Random Hse. Bks. for Young Readers) Random Hse. Children's Bks.
—To the Rescue! Garrett Morgan Underground. Parkins, David, illus. (Great Idea Ser.). (ENG.). 32p. (J). (gr. k-3). 2017. pap. 6.99 *(978-1-101-91882-1(9))* 2016. 17.99 *(978-1-77049-520-3(7))* Tundra Bks. CAN. (Tundra Bks.). Dist: Penguin Random Hse. LLC.
Kulling, Monica & Parkins, David. Going Up! Elisha Otis's Trip to the Top. 2012. (Great Idea Ser.). (ENG., Illus.). 32p. (J). (gr. k-3). 17.95 *(978-1-77049-240-0(2)*, Tundra Bks.) Tundra Bks. CAN. Dist: Penguin Random Hse. LLC.
Kulling, Monica & Slavin, Bill. Zap! Nikola Tesla Takes Charge. 2016. (Great Idea Ser.). (ENG., Illus.). 32p. (J). (gr. k-3). 17.99 *(978-1-77049-522-7(3)*, Tundra Bks.) Tundra Bks. CAN. Dist: Penguin Random Hse. LLC.
Kurlansky, Mark. Frozen in Time: Clarence Birdseye's Outrageous Idea about Frozen Food. 2014. (ENG.). 176p. (J). (gr. 5). lib. bdg. 18.99 *(978-0-375-99135-6(2)*, Delacorte Bks. for Young Readers) Random Hse. Children's Bks.
La Bella, Laura. Steve Jobs & Steve Wozniak, 01 vols., 1. 2016. (Tech Pioneers Ser.). (ENG.). 112p. (J). 35.60 *(978-1-4994-6286-9(7)*, Rosen Young Adult) Rosen Publishing Group, Inc., The.
Labrecque, Ellen. Maria Beasley & Life Rafts. 2017. (21st Century Junior Library: Women Innovators Ser.). (ENG., Illus.). 24p. (J). (gr. 2-5). lib. bdg. 27.07 *(978-1-63472-179-0(9)*, 209288) Cherry Lake Publishing.
—Mary Anderson & Windshield Wipers. 2017. (21st Century Junior Library: Women Innovators Ser.). (ENG., Illus.). 24p. (J). (gr. 2-5). lib. bdg. 27.07 *(978-1-63472-178-3(0)*, 209284) Cherry Lake Publishing.
—Patricia Bath & Laser Surgery. 2017. (21st Century Junior Library: Women Innovators Ser.). (ENG., Illus.). 24p. (J). (gr. 2-5). lib. bdg. 27.07 *(978-1-63472-180-6(2)*, 209292) Cherry Lake Publishing.
—Sarah Mather & Underwater Telescopes. 2017. (21st Century Junior Library: Women Innovators Ser.). (ENG., Illus.). 24p. (J). (gr. 2-5). lib. bdg. 27.07 *(978-1-63472-181-3(0)*, 209296) Cherry Lake Publishing.
—Stephanie Kwolek & Bulletproof Material. 2017. (21st Century Junior Library: Women Innovators Ser.). (ENG., Illus.). 24p. (J). (gr. 2-5). lib. bdg. 27.07 *(978-1-63472-183-7(7)*, 209304) Cherry Lake Publishing.
—Yvonne Brill & Satellite Propulsion. 2017. (21st Century Junior Library: Women Innovators Ser.). (ENG., Illus.). 24p. (J). (gr. 2-5). lib. bdg. 27.07 *(978-1-63472-184-4(5)*, 209308) Cherry Lake Publishing.
Lace, William W. Benjamin Franklin. 2010. (Leaders of the Colonial Era Ser.). (Illus.). 120p. (gr. 5-8). 35.00 *(978-1-60413-737-8(1)*, Chelsea Hse.) Facts On File, Inc.
Landau, Elaine. Meet Ben Franklin with Elaine Landau. 2006. (Explore Colonial America with Elaine Landau Ser.). (Illus.). 48p. (J). (gr. 3-4). lib. bdg. 25.27 *(978-0-7660-2555-4(1)*, Enslow Elementary) Enslow Pubs., Inc.
Landon, Rocky. A Native American Thought of It: Amazing Inventions & Innovations. 2nd ed. 2008. (We Thought of It Ser.). (ENG., Illus.). 48p. (J). (gr. 5-7). 19.95 *(978-1-55451-155-6(0)*, 9781554511556) Annick Pr., Ltd. CAN. Dist: Publishers Group West (PGW).
Latta, Sara L. Microwave Man: Percy Spencer & His Sizzling Invention. 2014. (Inventors at Work! Ser.). 48p. (J). 25.27 *(978-0-7660-4201-8(4))*; pap. 8.95 *(978-1-4644-0345-3(7))* Enslow Pubs., Inc. (Enslow Elementary).
—Who Fixed Babies' Hearts? Vivien Thomas. 2012. (I Like Inventors! Ser.). (Illus.). 24p. (J). (gr. k-3). pap. 7.95 *(978-1-4644-0130-5(6)*, Enslow Elementary) Enslow Pubs., Inc.
—Who Invented Basketball? James Naismith. 2012. (I Like Inventors! Ser.). (Illus.). 24p. (J). (gr. k-3). pap. 7.95 *(978-1-4644-0131-2(4)*, Enslow Elementary) Enslow Pubs., Inc.
—Who Invented the Ferris Wheel? George Ferris. 2012. (I Like Inventors! Ser.). (Illus.). 24p. (J). (gr. k-3). pap. 7.95 *(978-1-4644-0132-9(2)*, Enslow Elementary) Enslow Pubs., Inc.
—The Woman Who Invented Windshield Wipers: Mary Anderson & Her Wonderful Invention. 2014. (Inventors at Work! Ser.). 48p. (J). pap. 8.95 *(978-1-4644-0349-1(X)*, Enslow Elementary) Enslow Pubs., Inc.
Latta, Sara L. & Anderson, Mary. The Woman Who Invented Windshield Wipers: Mary Anderson & Her Wonderful Invention. 2014. (Inventors at Work! Ser.). 48p. (J). 25.27 *(978-0-7660-4203-2(0))* Enslow Pubs., Inc.
Lee, T. S. The Thomas Edison Story: The First Thomas Edison Comic Biography. 2010. 179p. (J). pap. 14.95 *(978-0-9819542-5-7(1))* DASANBOOKS.
Lin, Yoming S. Alexander Graham Bell & the Telephone. 2012. (Eureka! Ser.). (Illus.). 24p. (J). (gr. 3-6). lib. bdg. 22.60 *(978-1-4488-5034-1(7))* Rosen Publishing Group, Inc., The.
Littleton, Baron J. Your Little Black Book on African American Inventions & Inventors. 2006. vi, 153p. (J). per. 9.95 *(978-0-9791883-0-5(X))* Disciple One Publishing.
Lomask, Milton. Invention & Technology. 2012. (ENG.). 288p. (J). (gr. 4-6). pap. 13.99 *(978-1-4424-8324-8(5)*, Atheneum Bks. for Young Readers) Simon & Schuster Children's Publishing.
Lowell, Barbara. George Ferris, What a Wheel! Hoare, Jerry, illus. 2014. (Penguin Core Concepts Ser.). (ENG.). 32p. (J). (gr. -1-k). 3.99 *(978-0-448-47925-5(7)*, Grosset & Dunlap) Penguin Young Readers Group.
Machajewski, Sarah. Elon Musk: Engineer & Inventor for the Future. 2017. (Breakout Biographies Ser.). 32p. (gr. 9-10). 26.25 ***(978-1-5081-6056-4(2)***, PowerKids Pr.) Rosen Publishing Group, Inc., The.
MacLeod, Elizabeth. Alexander Graham Bell. Krystoforski, Andrej, illus. 2007. (ENG.). 32p. (J). (gr. 1-3). 3.95 *(978-1-55453-002-1(4))*; 14.95 *(978-1-55453-001-4(6))* Kids Can Pr., Ltd. CAN. Dist: Hachette Bk. Group.
—Thomas Edison. Krystoforski, Andrej, illus. 2008. (ENG.). 32p. (J). (gr. 1-3). 14.95 *(978-1-55453-057-1(1))*; pap. 3.95 *(978-1-55453-058-8(X))* Kids Can Pr., Ltd. CAN. Dist: Hachette Bk. Group.
Malam, John. Leonardo Da Vinci: El Genio Que Definio el Renacimiento. P. López, Wendy, tr. from ENG. 2007. (Altea Biografías Ser.).Tr. of Leonardo da Vinci. (SPA., Illus.). 64p. (J). (gr. -1-3). 17.99 *(978-84-372-2467-1(5))* Altea, Ediciones, S.A. - Grupo Santillana ESP. Dist: Santillana USA Publishing Co., Inc.
Mara, Wil. Benjamin Franklin. (Rookie Biographies(r) Ser.). (Illus.). (J). 2014. (ENG.). 32p. pap. 5.95 *(978-0-531-21201-1(7))* 2014. (ENG., 32p. lib. bdg. 25.00 *(978-0-531-20558-7(4))* 2007. 31p. (gr. 1-2). pap. 4.95 *(978-0-531-12591-5(2)*, Children's Pr.) Scholastic Library Publishing.
Marcovitz, Hal. Benjamin Franklin: Scientist, Inventor, Printer, & Statesman. 2006. (Leaders of the American Revolution Ser.). (Illus.). 100p. (gr. 5-8). lib. bdg. 30.00 *(978-0-7910-9219-4(4)*, Chelsea Hse.) Facts On File, Inc.
Marsh, Carole. Alexander Graham Bell. 2003. 12p. (gr. k-4). 2.95 *(978-0-635-02354-4(7))* Gallopade International.
—Charles Kettering: Patent Giant. 2004. (1000 Readers Ser.). (Illus.). 14p. (J). (gr. k-4). pap. 2.95 *(978-0-635-02525-8(6))* Gallopade International.
—Garrett Morgan, Innovative Inventor. 2004. 12p. (gr. k-4). 2.95 *(978-0-635-02526-5(4))* Gallopade International.
—Granville Woods: Excellent Inventor. 2004. (1000 Readers Ser.). (Illus.). 14p. (J). (gr. k-4). pap. 2.95 *(978-0-635-02527-2(2))* Gallopade International.
Marsico, Katie. Inventor, Engineer, & Physicist Nikola Tesla. 2017. (STEM Trailblazer Bios Ser.). (ENG.). 32p. (J). (gr. 2-5). 26.65 ***(978-1-5124-3448-4(5))*** Lerner Publishing Group.
Martin, Justin. Easy Reader Biographies: Alexander Graham Bell: A Famous Inventor. 2007. (ENG.). 16p. pap. 2.99 *(978-0-439-77415-4(2)*, Teaching Resources) Scholastic, Inc.
Mason, Paul. Bonkers Boffins, Inventors & Other Eccentric Eggheads. 2017. (Barmy Biogs Ser.). (ENG., Illus.). 96p. (J). (gr. 4-6). pap. 7.99 ***(978-0-7502-8391-5(2)***, Wayland) Hachette Children's Group GBR. Dist: Hachette Bk. Group.
Mattern, Joanne. Clarence Birdseye: Frozen Food Innovator, 1 vol. 2014. (Food Dudes Set 1 Ser.). (ENG.). 32p. (gr. 3-6). lib. bdg. 27.07 *(978-1-62403-492-3(6)*, Checkerboard Library) ABDO Publishing Co.
—Robert Cade: Gatorade Inventor, 1 vol. (Food Dudes Set 1 Ser.). (ENG.). 32p. (gr. 3-6). 2014. lib. bdg. 27.07 *(978-1-62403-493-0(4)*, Checkerboard Library) 2011. (Illus.). (J). 27.07 *(978-1-61613-556-0(5))* ABDO Publishing Co.
Matthews, Tom L. Always Inventing: A Photobiography of Alexander Graham Bell. 2006. (Photobiographies Ser.). (ENG., Illus.). 64p. (J). (gr. 5-7). per. 7.95 *(978-0-7922-5932-9(7)*, National Geographic Children's Bks.) National Geographic Society.
Matthews, Tom L. & National Geographic Kids Staff. Always Inventing: A Photobiography of Alexander Graham Bell. 2015. (Photobiographies Ser.). (ENG.). 64p. (J). (gr. 5). pap. 7.99 *(978-1-4263-2217-4(8)*, National Geographic Children's Bks.) National Geographic Society.
McCarthy, Meghan. Earmuffs for Everyone! How Chester Greenwood Became Known As the Inventor of Earmuffs. McCarthy, Meghan, illus. 2015. (ENG., Illus.). 48p. (J). (gr. -1-3). 17.99 *(978-1-4814-0637-6(X)*, Simon & Schuster/Paula Wiseman Bks.) Simon & Schuster/Paula Wiseman Bks.
McCully, Emily Arnold. Marvelous Mattie: How Margaret E. Knight Became an Inventor. 2006. (ENG., Illus.). 32p. (J). (gr. 2-6). 17.99 *(978-0-374-34810-6(3)*, 9780374348106, Farrar, Straus & Giroux (BYR)) Farrar, Straus & Giroux.
McCurdy, Michael. So Said Ben. 2007. (ENG., Illus.). 32p. (J). (gr. 1-3). 17.95 *(978-1-56846-147-2(X)*, Creative Editions) Creative Co., The.
McDowell, Pamela. Benjamin Franklin. 2013. *(978-1-62127-307-3(5))*; pap. *(978-1-62127-313-4(X))* Weigl Pubs., Inc.

H I

McLeese, Don. Robert Fulton. 2005. (Rourke Discovery Library). (Illus.). 24p. (J). (gr. 2-5). lib. bdg. *(978-1-59515-434-7(5),* 1244323) Rourke Educational Media.

McPherson, Stephanie Sammartino. Alexander Graham Bell. 2008. pap. 52.95 *(978-0-8225-9385-0(8))* Lerner Publishing Group.

—Alexander Graham Bell. Butler, Tad, illus. 2007. (History Maker Biographies Ser.). (ENG.). 48p. (gr. 3-6). lib. bdg. 27.93 *(978-0-8225-7606-8(6),* Lerner Pubns.) Lerner Publishing Group.

Miller, Brandon Marie. Benjamin Franklin, American Genius: His Life & Ideas with 21 Activities. 2009. (For Kids Ser.). (ENG., Illus.). 144p. (J). (gr. 4-7). pap. 16.95 *(978-1-55652-757-9(8))* Chicago Review Pr., Inc.

Mills, Lois. Three Together: Story of the Wright Brothers & Their Sister. Moyers, William, illus. 2011. 160p. 41.95 *(978-1-258-05968-2(1))* Literary Licensing, LLC.

Mills, Nathan & Weir, William. The Wright Brothers: The First to Fly. 2012. (Rosen Readers Ser.). (ENG., Illus.). 24p. (J). (gr. 1-2). pap. 8.25 *(978-1-4488-8863-4(8),* Rosen Classroom) Rosen Publishing Group, Inc., The.

Morlock, Theresa. 20 Fun Facts about Benjamin Franklin. 2017. (Fun Fact File: Founding Fathers Ser.). 32p. (gr. 2-3). pap. 63.00 ***(978-1-5382-0271-5(9))*** Stevens, Gareth Publishing LLLP.

Morrison, Heather S. Inventors of Communications Technology. 2015. (Designing Engineering Solutions Ser.). (ENG.). 144p. (J). (gr. 8-8). 42.79 *(978-1-5026-0656-3(9))* Cavendish Square Publishing.

—Inventors of Everyday Technology. 2015. (Designing Engineering Solutions Ser.). (ENG.). 144p. (J). (gr. 8-8). 42.79 *(978-1-5026-0660-0(7))* Cavendish Square Publishing.

—Inventors of Food & Agriculture Technology. 2015. (Designing Engineering Solutions Ser.). (ENG., Illus.). 144p. (J). (gr. 8-8). lib. bdg. 42.79 *(978-1-5026-0664-8(X))* Cavendish Square Publishing.

—Inventors of Health & Medical Technology. 2015. (Designing Engineering Solutions Ser.). (ENG., Illus.). 144p. (J). (gr. 8-8). 42.79 *(978-1-5026-0658-7(5))* Cavendish Square Publishing.

—Inventors of Industrial Technology. 2015. (Designing Engineering Solutions Ser.). (ENG.). 144p. (J). (gr. 8-8). lib. bdg. 42.79 *(978-1-5026-0666-2(6))* Cavendish Square Publishing.

—Inventors of Transportation Technology. 2015. (Designing Engineering Solutions Ser.). (ENG.). 144p. (J). (gr. 8-8). lib. bdg. 42.79 *(978-1-5026-0662-4(3))* Cavendish Square Publishing.

Mortensen, Lori & Picture Window Books Staff. Thomas Edison: Inventor, Scientist, & Genius, 1 vol. Thompson, Jeffrey, illus. 2007. (Biographies Ser.). (ENG.). 24p. (gr. k-3). 26.65 *(978-1-4048-3105-6(3))* Picture Window Bks.

Murphy, Patricia J. Garrett Morgan: Inventor of the Traffic Light & Gas Mask. 2004. (Famous Inventors Ser.). (Illus.). 32p. (J). lib. bdg. 23.94 *(978-0-7660-2274-4(9))* Enslow Pubs., Inc.

—Grace Hopper: Computer Pioneer. 2004. (Famous Inventors Ser.). (Illus.). 32p. (J). lib. bdg. 22.60 *(978-0-7660-2273-7(0))* Enslow Pubs., Inc.

Nagelhout, Ryan. Elon Musk: Space Entrepreneur. 2017. (People in the News Ser.). 104p. (YA). (gr. 7-7). lib. bdg. 39.40 ***(978-1-5345-6035-2(1),*** Lucent Pr.) Greenhaven Publishing LLC.

National Geographic Learning Staff. Thomas Edison, Level 3 - World Windows. 2011. (World Windows Ser.). (ENG., Illus.). 16p. (J). stu. ed. 9.95 *(978-1-133-49279-5(7))* Cengage Heinle.

Nelson, Maria. The Life of Ben Franklin. 2012. (Famous Lives Ser.). (ENG.). 24p. (J). (gr. k-3). lib. bdg. 22.60 *(978-1-4339-6345-2(0));* (gr. 1-4). pap. 8.15 *(978-1-4339-6347-6(7))* Stevens, Gareth Publishing LLLP.

—The Life of Ben Franklin / la Vida de BenjamiN Franklin. 2012. (Famous Lives / Vidas extraordinarias Ser.). (ENG & SPA., Illus.). 24p. (J). (gr. k-3). 22.60 *(978-1-4339-6653-8(0))* Stevens, Gareth Publishing LLLP.

Niver, Heather Moore. Eli Whitney & the Industrial Revolution. 2016. (Great Entrepreneurs in U. S. History Ser.). 32p. (J). (gr. 5-5). pap. 11.75 *(978-1-4994-2123-1(0),* PowerKids Pr.) Rosen Publishing Group, Inc., The.

Northrup, Mary. Pioneering American Computer Geniuses. 2013. (Inspiring Collective Biographies Ser.). 112p. (J). (gr. 5-12). pap. 10.95 *(978-1-4644-0273-9(6));* lib. bdg. 33.27 *(978-0-7660-4167-7(0))* Enslow Pubs., Inc.

Old, Wendie C. The Wright Brothers: Aviation Pioneers & Inventors. 2015. (Legendary American Biographies Ser.). 96p. (J). (gr. 6-12). 27.94 *(978-0-7660-6505-5(7));* pap. 10.95 *(978-0-7660-6506-2(5))* Enslow Pubs., Inc.

Older, Jules. Snowmobile: Bombardier's Dream Machine. Lauritano, Michael, illus. 2012. (ENG.). 64p. (J). (gr. 3-7). pap. 6.95 *(978-1-58089-335-0(X))* Charlesbridge Publishing, Inc.

Orr, Tamra B. The Dawn of Aviation: The Story of the Wright Brothers. 2005. (Monumental Milestones Ser.). (Illus.). 48p. (YA). (gr. 4-7). lib. bdg. 29.95 *(978-1-58415-396-2(2),* 1244922) Mitchell Lane Pubs., Inc.

O'Shei, Tim. Marconi & Tesla: Pioneers of Radio Communication. 2008. (Inventors Who Changed the World Ser.). (Illus.). 128p. (J). (gr. 3-7). lib. bdg. 34.60 *(978-1-59845-076-7(X),* MyReportLinks.com Bks.) Enslow Pubs., Inc.

—Philo T. Farnsworth: Visionary Inventor of Television. 2008. (Inventors Who Changed the World Ser.). (Illus.). 128p. (J). (gr. 6-18). lib. bdg. 34.60 *(978-1-59845-075-0(1),* MyReportLinks.com Bks.) Enslow Pubs., Inc.

Owen, Ruth. Inventors: Designing & Creating Tomorrow's World. 2016. (Get to Work with Science & Technology Ser.). (ENG.). 32p. (J). (gr. 2-7). 19.95 *(978-1-910549-91-9(6))* Bearport Publishing Co., Inc.

Owens, L. L. Benjamin Franklin, 1 vol. 2007. (Essential Lives Set 1 Ser.). (ENG., Illus.). 112p. (J). (gr. 6-12). lib. bdg. 35.64 *(978-1-59928-840-6(0))* ABDO Publishing Co.

Oxlade, Chris. The Top Ten Inventions That Changed the World. 2009. 32p. (YA). (ENG.). pap. 10.00 *(978-1-4358-9174-6(0),* PowerKids Pr.); (Illus.). (gr. 3-6). 26.50 *(978-1-4358-9173-9(2))* Rosen Publishing Group, Inc., The.

Parker, Lewis K. The Inventions of Amanda Jones: The Vacuum Method of Canning & Food Preservation. 2003. (19th Century American Inventors Ser.). (Illus.). 24p. (J). lib. bdg. 22.60 *(978-0-8239-6445-1(0),* PowerKids Pr.) Rosen Publishing Group, Inc., The.

Parks, Peggy J. Robert Fulton: Innovator with Steam Power. 2003. (Giants of Science Ser.). (ENG., Illus.). 64p. (J). 28.35 *(978-1-56711-492-8(X),* Blackbirch Pr., Inc.) Cengage Gale.

Pederson, Charles E. Thomas Edison, 1 vol. 2007. (Essential Lives Set 1 Ser.). (ENG., Illus.). 112p. (J). (gr. 6-12). lib. bdg. 35.64 *(978-1-59928-845-1(1))* ABDO Publishing Co.

Photo-Illustrated Biographies. 2010. (Photo-Illustrated Biographies Ser.). (ENG.). 24p. (gr. 2-3). pap. 662.40 *(978-1-4296-5209-4(8),* Bridgestone Bks.) Capstone Press of Coughlan Cos.

Pierce, Morris A. Robert Fulton & the Development of the Steamboat. (Library of American Lives & Times Ser.). 112p. 2009. (gr. 5-5). 69.20 *(978-1-60853-502-6(9))* 2005. (Illus.). (YA). (gr. 4-8). lib. bdg. 34.60 *(978-0-8239-5737-8(3))* Rosen Publishing Group, Inc., The.

Polette, Nancy. Blunder or Brainstorm: Fact & Fiction of Famous Inventors & Inventions. Dillon, Paul, illus. 2006. (YA). pap. 11.95 *(978-1-931334-91-4(9))* Pieces of Learning.

Pollack, Pam, et al. Who Was Steve Jobs? Harrison, Nancy et al, illus. 2012. (Who Was? Ser.). (ENG.). 112p. (J). (gr. 3-7). pap. 5.99 *(978-0-448-46211-0(7),* Grosset & Dunlap) Penguin Young Readers Group.

Pollack, Pamela & Belviso, Meg. Who Was Steve Jobs? 2012. (Who Was... ? Ser.). lib. bdg. 16.00 *(978-0-606-26649-9(6),* Turtleback) Turtleback Bks.

Proudfit, Benjamin. Benjamin Franklin. 2015. (What You Didn't Know about History Ser.). (ENG., Illus.). 24p. (J). (gr. 2-3). pap. 8.15 *(978-1-4824-1926-9(2))* Stevens, Gareth Publishing LLLP.

Randolph, Joanne. African American Inventors & Scientists. 2017. (J). ***(978-0-7660-9248-8(8))*** Enslow Pubs., Inc.

Randolph, Ryan P. Benjamin Franklin: Inventor, Writer & Patriot. 2005. (Library of American Lives & Times). (Illus.). 112p. (YA). (gr. 4-8). lib. bdg. 34.60 *(978-0-8239-5751-4(9))* Rosen Publishing Group, Inc., The.

—Benjamin Franklin: Inventor, Writer, & Patriot. 2009. (Library of American Lives & Times Ser.). 112p. (gr. 5-5). 69.20 *(978-1-60853-472-2(3))* Rosen Publishing Group, Inc., The.

Rausch, Monica. Benjamin Franklin. 2007. (Grandes personajes (Spanish- Great Americans) Ser.). 24p. (gr. 1-4). (ENG & SPA.). pap. 8.15 *(978-0-8368-7988-9(0));* (Illus.). pap. 8.15 *(978-0-8368-7689-5(X));* (Illus.). lib. bdg. 22.00 *(978-0-8368-7682-6(2))* Stevens, Gareth Publishing LLLP. (Weekly Reader Leveled Readers).

Rausch, Monica L. Benjamin Franklin. 2007. (Grandes personajes (Great Americans) Ser.). (ENG & SPA., Illus.). 24p. (gr. 1-4). lib. bdg. 22.00 *(978-0-8368-7981-0(3),* Weekly Reader Leveled Readers) Stevens, Gareth Publishing LLLP.

—George Eastman & the Camera. 2007. (Inventors & Their Discoveries Ser.). (Illus.). 24p. (gr. 1-4). pap. 8.15 *(978-0-8368-7730-4(6));* lib. bdg. 22.00 *(978-0-8368-7499-0(4))* Stevens, Gareth Publishing LLLP. (Weekly Reader Leveled Readers).

—George Eastman y la Cámara. 2007. (Inventores y sus descubrimientos (Inventors & Their Discoveries) Ser.). (ENG & SPA., Illus.). 24p. (gr. 1-4). pap. 8.15 *(978-0-8368-7999-5(6));* lib. bdg. 22.00 *(978-0-8368-7994-0(5))* Stevens, Gareth Publishing LLLP. (Weekly Reader Leveled Readers).

—Henry Ford & the Model T Car. 2007. (Inventors & Their Discoveries Ser.). (Illus.). 24p. (gr. 1-4). lib. bdg. 22.00 *(978-0-8368-7500-3(1),* Weekly Reader Leveled Readers) Stevens, Gareth Publishing LLLP.

—Henry Ford y el Automovil Modelo T. 2007. (Inventores y sus descubrimientos (Inventors & Their Discoveries) Ser.). (ENG & SPA., Illus.). 24p. (gr. 1-4). pap. 8.15 *(978-0-8368-8000-7(5));* lib. bdg. 22.00 *(978-0-8368-7995-7(3))* Stevens, Gareth Publishing LLLP. (Weekly Reader Leveled Readers).

—Los Hermanos Wright y el Avion. 2007. (Inventores y sus descubrimientos (Inventors & Their Discoveries) Ser.). (SPA., Illus.). 24p. (gr. 1-4). pap. 8.15 *(978-0-8368-8001-4(3),* Weekly Reader Leveled Readers) Stevens, Gareth Publishing LLLP.

—Thomas Edison & the Light Bulb. 2007. (Inventors & Their Discoveries Ser.). (Illus.). 24p. (gr. 1-4). pap. 8.15 *(978-0-8368-7732-8(2),* Weekly Reader Leveled Readers) Stevens, Gareth Publishing LLLP.

—Thomas Edison & the Lightbulb. 2007. (Inventors & Their Discoveries Ser.). (Illus.). 24p. (gr. 1-4). lib. bdg. 22.00 *(978-0-8368-7501-0(X),* Weekly Reader Leveled Readers) Stevens, Gareth Publishing LLLP.

—Thomas Edison y la bombilla Eléctrica. 2007. (Inventores y sus descubrimientos (Inventors & Their Discoveries) Ser.). (SPA., Illus.). 24p. (gr. 1-4). lib. bdg. 22.00 *(978-0-8368-7997-1(X),* Weekly Reader Leveled Readers) Stevens, Gareth Publishing LLLP.

—Thomas Edison y la Bombilla Eléctrica. 2007. (Inventores y sus descubrimientos (Inventors & Their Discoveries) Ser.). (SPA., Illus.). 24p. (gr. 1-4). pap. 8.15 *(978-0-8368-8002-1(1),* Weekly Reader Leveled Readers) Stevens, Gareth Publishing LLLP.

—The Wright Brothers & the Airplane. 2007. (Inventors & Their Discoveries Ser.). (Illus.). 24p. (gr. 1-4). pap. 8.15 *(978-0-8368-7733-5(0));* lib. bdg. 22.00 *(978-0-8368-7502-7(8))* Stevens, Gareth Publishing LLLP. (Weekly Reader Leveled Readers).

Rich, Mari. Inventors, Vol. 10. Gilmore, Malinda & Pouson, Mel, eds. 2016. (Black Achievement in Science Ser.). 64p. (J). (gr. 7). 23.95 *(978-1-4222-3560-7(2))* Mason Crest.

Riley, Gail Blasser. Benjamin Franklin & Electricity. 2004. (Cornerstones of Freedom Ser.). (ENG., Illus.). 48p. (YA). (gr. 4-7). 26.00 *(978-0-516-24240-8(7))* Scholastic Library Publishing.

Riley, John B. Benjamin Franklin: A Photo Biography. l.t. ed. 2004. (First Biographies Ser.). (Illus.). 24p. (YA). (gr. 5-18). 16.95 *(978-1-883846-64-0(1),* First Biographies) Reynolds, Morgan Inc.

Rivera, Sheila. Alexander Graham Bell: A Life of Helpfulness. 2007. (Pull Ahead Bks.). (Illus.). 32p. (J). (gr. 3-7). lib. bdg. 22.60 *(978-0-8225-6463-8(7),* Lerner Pubns.) Lerner Publishing Group.

Roberts, Steven. Robert Fulton. 2013. (Jr. Graphic American Inventors Ser.). (ENG., Illus.). 24p. (J). (gr. 3-6). pap. 10.60 *(978-1-4777-0139-3(7));* lib. bdg. 25.25 *(978-1-4777-0077-8(3))* Rosen Publishing Group, Inc., The. (PowerKids Pr.).

Rogers, Kate. Robert Fulton Invents the Steamboat. 2013. (Rosen Readers Ser.). (ENG.). 24p. (J). (gr. 3-4). pap. 49.50 *(978-1-4777-2604-4(7));* pap. 8.25 *(978-1-4777-2603-7(9))* Rosen Publishing Group, Inc., The. (Rosen Classroom).

Rosenstock, Barb. Ben Franklin's Big Splash: The Mostly True Story of His First Invention. Schindler, S. D., illus. 2014. (ENG.). 32p. (J). (gr. 3). 16.95 *(978-1-62091-446-5(8),* Calkins Creek) Boyds Mills Pr.

Rossi, Ann. The Age of Inventions. 2007. (Rise & Shine Ser.). (ENG., Illus.). 40p. (J). pap. 19.95 *(978-0-7922-8696-7(0))* CENGAGE Learning.

Rowell, Rebecca. The 12 Most Amazing American Inventions. 2014. (ENG.). 32p. (J). *(978-1-63235-008-4(4))* Pr. Room Editions LLC.

Royston, Angela. Inventors Who Changed the World. 2010. (ENG., Illus.). 32p. (J). *(978-0-7787-9902-3(6));* pap. *(978-0-7787-9923-8(9))* Crabtree Publishing Co.

—Robert Fulton & the Steamboat, 01 vols., 1. 2016. (Inventions That Changed the World Ser.). (ENG.). 32p. (J). pap. 10.00 *(978-1-5081-4635-3(7),* PowerKids Pr.) Rosen Publishing Group, Inc., The.

Roza, Greg. Henry Ford: Pioneer of Modern Industry. 2009. (Real Life Readers Ser.). 24p. (gr. 3-4). pap. 8.25 *(978-1-4358-0137-0(7),* Rosen Classroom) Rosen Publishing Group, Inc., The.

—Thomas Alva Edison, 1 vol. 2015. (ENG., Illus.). 32p. (J). 23.45 *(978-1-62275-693-3(2),* Britannica Educational Publishing) Rosen Publishing Group, Inc., The.

Rusch, Elizabeth. Electrical Wizard. 2015. (Candlewick Biographies Ser.). lib. bdg. 14.75 *(978-0-606-36873-5(6))* Turtleback Bks.

—Electrical Wizard: How Nikola Tesla Lit up the World. Dominguez, Oliver, illus. 2015. (Candlewick Biographies Ser.). (ENG.). 56p. (J). (gr. 3-7). 14.99 *(978-0-7636-7978-1(X))* Candlewick Pr.

Sabin, Louis & Macken, JoAnn Early. Thomas Edison: Incredible Inventor. 2006. (Illus.). 52p. (J). *(978-0-439-88006-0(8))* Scholastic, Inc.

Saddleback Educational Publishing Staff, ed. Alexander Graham Bell, 1 vol. unabr. ed. 2008. (Graphic Biographies Ser.). (ENG., Illus.). 25p. (YA). (gr. 9-12). pap. 7.95 *(978-1-59905-213-7(X))* Saddleback Educational Publishing, Inc.

—Benjamin Franklin, 1 vol. unabr. ed. 2008. (Graphic Biographies Ser.). (ENG., Illus.). 25p. (YA). (gr. 9-12). pap. 7.95 *(978-1-59905-217-5(2))* Saddleback Educational Publishing, Inc.

—Thomas Edison, 1 vol. unabr. ed. 2008. (Graphic Biographies Ser.). (ENG., Illus.). 25p. (YA). (gr. 9-12). pap. 7.95 *(978-1-59905-228-1(8))* Saddleback Educational Publishing, Inc.

Salzmann, Mary Elizabeth. Benjamin Franklin, 1 vol. 2016. (ENG., Illus.). 24p. (J). *(978-1-68078-157-1(X))* ABDO Publishing Co.

Sandler, Martin W. Inventors. 2014. (Library of Congress Classics). (ENG., Illus.). 96p. (J). (gr. 3-18). pap. 12.99 *(978-0-06-446746-9(5))* HarperCollins Pubs.

Satterfield, Kathryn Hoffman. Benjamin Franklin A Man of Many Talents. 2005. 44p. (J). lib. bdg. 15.00 *(978-1-4242-0846-3(7))* Fitzgerald Bks.

Schraff, Anne E. Ellen Ochoa: Astronaut & Inventor. 2009. (Latino Biography Library). (Illus.). 128p. (J). (gr. 6-18). lib. bdg. 33.27 *(978-0-7660-3163-0(2))* Enslow Pubs., Inc.

Schroeder, Alan. Ben Franklin: His Wit & Wisdom from A to Z. O'brien, John, illus. 2011. (ENG.). 32p. (J). (gr. 1-5). 16.95 *(978-0-8234-1950-0(9))* Holiday Hse., Inc.

—Ben Franklin: His Wit & Wisdom from A-Z. O'brien, John, illus. 2012. (ENG.). 32p. (J). pap. 7.95 *(978-0-8234-2435-1(9))* Holiday Hse., Inc.

Schuette, Sarah L. Garrett Morgan, 1 vol. 2014. (Great African-Americans Ser.). (ENG.). 24p. (gr. k-1). lib. bdg. 21.99 *(978-1-4914-0504-8(X),* Pebble Bks.) Capstone Press of Coughlan Cos.

Schuman, Michael. Alexander Graham Bell: Scientist & Inventor. 2015. (Legendary American Biographies Ser.). 96p. (J). (gr. 6-12). 27.94 *(978-0-7660-6430-0(1))* Enslow Pubs., Inc.

Schuman, Michael A. Alexander Graham Bell: Scientist & Inventor. 2015. (Legendary American Biographies Ser.). 96p. (J). (gr. 6-12). pap. 10.95 *(978-0-7660-6431-7(X))* Enslow Pubs., Inc.

Schwartz, Heather E. Super Soaker Inventor Lonnie Johnson. 2017. (STEM Trailblazer Bios Ser.). (ENG.). 32p. (J). (gr. 2-5). 26.65 ***(978-1-5124-3447-7(7))*** Lerner Publishing Group.

Sechrist, Darren. Inventions & Inventors. 2008. (ENG.). 32p. (J). pap. *(978-0-7787-4213-5(X))* Crabtree Publishing Co.

Segel, Robert G. Machine Gun Inventors: A Military History Coloring Book. Pajot, Lauren, illus. 2016. 16p. 4.95 *(978-0-9823918-2-2(X))* Chipotle Publishing, LLC.

Seidman, David & Williams, Keith. Samuel Morse & the Telegraph, 1 vol. Whigham, Rod & Barnett, Charles, III, illus. 2007. (Inventions & Discovery Ser.). (ENG.). 32p. (gr. 3-4). pap. 8.10 *(978-0-7368-7898-2(X),* Graphic Library) Capstone Press of Coughlan Cos.

Seidman, David, et al. Samuel Morse & the Telegraph, 1 vol. Whigham, Rod, illus. 2007. (Inventions & Discovery Ser.). (ENG.). 32p. (gr. 3-4). 30.65 *(978-0-7368-6846-4(1),* Graphic Library) Capstone Press of Coughlan Cos.

Silver, Tony. What's the Big Idea? The Story of Thomas Edison. (Illus.). 16p. *(978-0-7367-2880-5(5))* Zaner-Bloser, Inc.

Slade, Suzanne. The Inventor's Secret: What Thomas Edison Told Henry Ford. Reinhardt, Jennifer Black, illus. 2015. (ENG.). 48p. (J). (gr. 1-4). lib. bdg. 16.95 *(978-1-58089-667-2(7))* Charlesbridge Publishing, Inc.

Slater, Lee. Board Game Builder: Milton Bradley, 1 vol. 2016. (Toy Trailblazers Ser.). (ENG., Illus.). 32p. (J). (gr. 3-6). lib. bdg. 27.07 *(978-1-62403-975-1(8),* Checkerboard Library) ABDO Publishing Co.

—Play-Doh Pioneer: Joseph Mcvicker, 1 vol. 2016. (Toy Trailblazers Ser.). (ENG., Illus.). 32p. (J). (gr. 3-6). lib. bdg. 27.07 *(978-1-62403-978-2(2),* Checkerboard Library) ABDO Publishing Co.

—Toy Trailblazers. 2016. (Toy Trailblazers Ser.: 6). (ENG.). 32p. (J). (gr. 3-6). lib. bdg. 162.42 *(978-1-62403-973-7(1),* Checkerboard Library) ABDO Publishing Co.

Sneed, Dani. The Man Who Invented the Ferris Wheel: The Genius of George Ferris. 2013. (Genius Inventors & Their Great Ideas Ser.). 48p. (J). (gr. 3-4). pap. 8.95 *(978-1-4644-0206-7(X),* Enslow Elementary) Enslow Pubs., Inc.

Spengler, Kremena T. An Illustrated Timeline of Inventions & Inventors, 1 vol. Morgan, Rick, illus. 2011. (Visual Timelines in History Ser.). (ENG.). 32p. (gr. 3-4). pap. 7.49 *(978-1-4048-7017-8(2))* Picture Window Bks.

—An Illustrated Timeline of Inventions & Inventors, 1 vol. Morgan, Rick, illus. 2011. (Visual Timelines in History Ser.). (ENG.). 32p. (gr. 3-4). lib. bdg. 28.65 *(978-1-4048-6662-1(0))* Picture Window Bks.

Spilsbury, Louise. Alexander Graham Bell & the Telephone, 01 vols., 1. 2016. (Inventions That Changed the World Ser.). (ENG.). 32p. (J). pap. 10.00 *(978-1-5081-4623-0(3),* PowerKids Pr.) Rosen Publishing Group, Inc., The.

—Robert Goddard & the Rocket, 01 vols., 1. 2016. (Inventions That Changed the World Ser.). (ENG.). 32p. (J). pap. 10.00 *(978-1-5081-4639-1(X),* PowerKids Pr.) Rosen Publishing Group, Inc., The.

Sprunger, Reed. Thomas Edison: Incredible Inventor, 1 vol. 2013. (Beginner Biographies Set 2 Ser.). (ENG.). 32p. (J). (gr. -1-4). lib. bdg. 28.50 *(978-1-61641-936-3(9),* Looking Glass Library) Magic Wagon.

St. George, Judith. So You Want to Be an Inventor? Small, David, illus. 2005. (ENG.). 56p. (J). (gr. 2-5). pap. 7.99 *(978-0-14-240460-7(8),* Puffin Books) Penguin Young Readers Group.

Stevenson, Robert Louis. Memoir of Fleeming Jenkin. 2005. 192p. 26.95 *(978-1-4218-0858-1(7),* 1st World Library - Literary Society) 1st World Publishing, Inc.

Stewart, Gail B. Stephanie Kwolek: Creator of Kevlar. 2008. (Innovators Ser.). (ENG., Illus.). 48p. (J). (gr. 4-8). lib. bdg. 29.95 *(978-0-7377-4040-0(X),* LML02109-239897, Kidhaven) Cengage Gale.

Streissguth, Tom. Benjamin Franklin. 2005. (Bios for Challenged Readers Ser.). (Illus.). 112p. (J). (gr. 6-12). lib. bdg. 27.93 *(978-0-8225-2210-2(1))* Lerner Publishing Group.

Sullivan, Erin. Mathematical Thinkers & Los Matemáticos: 6 English, 6 Spanish Adaptations, 122 vols., Vol. 2. 2011. (Navigators Ser.). (ENG & SPA.). (J). instr.'s gde. ed. 97.00 net. *(978-1-4108-1773-0(3),* 17733) Benchmark Education Co.

Sullivan, Otha Richard. African American Inventors. Haskins, Jim, ed. 2011. (Black Stars Ser.). (ENG., Illus.). 176p. (J). (gr. 5-9). pap. 27.00 *(978-1-118-11599-2(6),* Wiley) Wiley, John & Sons, Inc.

Swaby, Rachel. Trailblazers: 33 Women in Science Who Changed the World. (ENG.). 208p. (J). (gr. 5). 2017. 6.99 ***(978-0-399-55418-6(1),*** Yearling) 2016. 15.99 *(978-0-399-55396-7(7),* Delacorte Bks. for Young Readers) Random Hse. Children's Bks.

Tagliaferro, Linda. Thomas Edison: Inventor of the Age of Electricity. 2003. (Lerner Biographies Ser.). (ENG., Illus.). 128p. (gr. 6-12). 27.93 *(978-0-8225-4689-4(2),* Lerner Pubns.) Lerner Publishing Group.

Thatcher Murcia, Rebecca. Thomas Edison: Great Inventor. 2004. (Uncharted, Unexplored, & Unexplained Ser.). (Illus.). 48p. (J). (gr. 4-8). lib. bdg. 29.95 *(978-1-58415-306-1(7))* Mitchell Lane Pubs., Inc.

Thayer, William Makepeace. From Boyhood to Manhood: Life of Benjamin Franklin. 2006. pap. *(978-1-4068-0906-0(3))* Echo Library.

Thompson, Craig. ABC's of Black Inventors: A Children's Guide. 2009. (ENG.). 32p. (J). 14.95 *(978-0-9823876-2-7(8))* Beckham Pubns. Group, Inc.

Time for Kids Editors. Alexander Graham Bell: Inventor of the Telephone. 2006. (Time for Kids Ser.). (ENG., Illus.). 48p. (J). (gr. 2-4). pap. 3.99 *(978-0-06-057618-9(9))* HarperCollins Pubs.

—Benjamin Franklin - A Man of Many Talents. 2005. (Time for Kids Ser.). (ENG., Illus.). 48p. (J). (gr. 2-4). pap. 3.99 *(978-0-06-057609-7(X))* HarperCollins Pubs.

—Time for Kids - Thomas Edison: A Brilliant Inventor. 2005. (Time for Kids Ser.). (ENG., Illus.). 48p. (J). (gr. 2-4). pap. 3.99 *(978-0-06-057611-0(1))* HarperCollins Pubs.

Tracy, Kathleen. Henry Bessemer: Making Steel from Iron. 2005. (Uncharted, Unexplored, & Unexplained Ser.). (Illus.). 48p. (J). (gr. 4-8). lib. bdg. 29.95 *(978-1-58415-366-5(0))* Mitchell Lane Pubs., Inc.

Troupe, Thomas Kingsley. The Wright Brothers' First Flight: a Fly on the Wall History. Tejido, Jomike, illus. 2017. (Fly on the Wall History Ser.). (ENG.). 32p. (gr. 1-3). pap. 7.95 *(978-1-4795-9791-8(0));* lib. bdg. 27.32 *(978-1-4795-9787-1(2))* Picture Window Bks.

Unlocking the Secrets of Science: Set of 15 Inventors. (Illus.). 26p. (gr. 4-10). lib. bdg. *(978-1-58415-232-3(X))* Mitchell Lane Pubs., Inc.

Van Steenwyk, Elizabeth. One Fine Day: A Radio Play. Farnsworth, Bill, illus. 2004. 32p. (J). (gr. 3-5). 16.00 *(978-0-8028-5234-2(3))* Eerdmans, William B. Publishing Co.

Van Vleet, Carmella. Amazing Ben Franklin Inventions. 2007. (Build It Yourself Ser.). (ENG., Illus.). 128p. (J). (gr. 3-7). 19.95 *(978-0-9792268-8-5(0))* Octavio Publishing.

—Amazing Ben Franklin Inventions: You Can Build Yourself. 2007. (Build It Yourself Ser.). (ENG., Illus.). 128p. (J). (gr. 3-7). per. 15.95 *(978-0-9771294-7-8(0))* Octavio Publishing.

Vance, Ashlee. Elon Musk & the Quest for a Fantastic Future Young Readers' Edition. 2017. 288p. (J). (gr. 3). pap. 6.99 *(978-0-06-246327-2(6));* (Illus.). 16.99 *(978-0-06-246328-9(4))* HarperCollins Pubs.

Venezia, Mike. Alexander Graham Bell: Setting the Tone for Communication. Venezia, Mike, illus. 2009. (Getting to Know the World's Greatest Inventors & Scientists Ser.). (ENG., Illus.). 32p. (J). (gr. 3-4). pap. 6.95 *(978-0-531-22207-2(1),* Children's Pr.) Scholastic Library Publishing.

—Benjamin Franklin: Electrified the World with New Ideas. Venezia, Mike, illus. 2009. (Getting to Know the World's Greatest Inventors & Scientists Ser.). (ENG., Illus.). 32p. (J).

(gr. 2-5). 28.00 (978-0-531-23701-4(X)) Scholastic Library Publishing.
—Getting to Know the World's Greatest Inventors & Scientists, 4 vols., Set. Venezia, Mike, illus. Incl. Charles Drew: Doctor Who Got the World Pumped up to Donate Blood. 28.00 (978-0-531-23725-0(7)); Henry Ford: Big Wheel in the Auto Industry. 28.00 (978-0-531-23726-7(5)); Mary Leakey - Archaeologist Who Really Dug Her Work. 28.00 (978-0-531-23727-4(3)); Stephen Hawking: Cosmologist Who Gets a Big Bang Out of the Universe. 28.00 (978-0-531-23728-1(1)); 32p. (J). (gr. 2-5). 2009. (Illus.). 2009. Set lib. bdg. 112.00 (978-0-531-26130-9(1), Watts, Franklin) Scholastic Library Publishing.
—Thomas Edison: Inventor with a Lot of Bright Ideas. Venezia, Mike, illus. (Getting to Know the World's Greatest Inventors & Scientists Ser.). (ENG., Illus.). 32p. (J). 2009. (gr. 3-4). pap. 6.95 (978-0-531-22209-6(8), Children's Pr.) 2008. (gr. 2-5). 28.00 (978-0-531-14978-2(1)) Scholastic Library Publishing.
Ventura, Marne. Google Glass & Robotics Innovator Sebastian Thrun. 2014. (STEM Trailblazer Bios Ser.). (ENG., Illus.). 32p. (gr. 2-5). lib. bdg. 26.60 (978-1-4677-2459-3(9), Lerner Pubns.) Lerner Publishing Group.
Ventura, Marne & Feynman, Drew. The Creators of the iPhone. Glass, Simon, illus. 2017. (Awesome Minds Ser.). (ENG.). 56p. (J). (gr. 1-5). 14.99 (978-1-938093-77-7(1), Duo Pr. Llc (US)) Duo Pr. LLC.
Wadsworth, Ginger. The Wright Brothers. 2004. (History Maker Bios Ser.). (Illus.). 47p. (J). 26.60 (978-0-8225-0199-2(6), Lerner Pubns.) Lerner Publishing Group.
Washburne, Sophie. African American Inventors: Overcoming Challenges to Change America. 2017. (J). **(978-1-5345-6071-0(8))** Greenhaven Publishing LLC.
Washburne, Sophie & Sheen, Barbara. Steve Jobs: Computer Visionary. 2017. (People in the News Ser.). 104p. (J). (gr. 7-7). lib. bdg. 39.40 **(978-1-5345-6031-4(9)**, Lucent Pr.) Greenhaven Publishing LLC.
Weakland, Mark. When Thomas Edison Fed Someone Worms. Radcliffe, Thomas, illus. 2017. (J). (978-1-5158-0139-9(X)) 2016. (ENG.). 32p. (gr. 2-3). lib. bdg. 27.99 (978-1-4795-9683-6(3)) Picture Window Bks.
Weir, William. The Wright Brothers: The First to Fly. 2012. (Beginning Biographies Ser.). (ENG., Illus.). 24p. (J). (gr. 1-3). 22.60 (978-1-4488-8597-8(3), PowerKids Pr.) Rosen Publishing Group, Inc., The.
Welch, Catherine A. Farmland Innovator: A Story about Cyrus Mccormick. Jones, Jan Naimo, illus. 2007. (Creative Minds Biographies Ser.). (ENG.). 64p. (gr. 4-8). lib. bdg. 22.60 (978-0-8225-5988-7(9)) Lerner Publishing Group.
Welvaert, Scott R. Thomas Edison & the Lightbulb, 1 vol. Miller, Phil et al, illus. 2006. (Inventions & Discovery Ser.). (ENG.). 32p. (gr. 3-4). 30.65 (978-0-7368-6489-3(X), Graphic Library) Capstone Press of Coughlan Cos.
Whiting, Jim. Benjamin Franklin. 2006. (Profiles in American History Ser.). (Illus.). 48p. (J). (gr. 3-7). lib. bdg. 29.95 (978-1-58415-435-8(7)) Mitchell Lane Pubs., Inc.
—James Watt & the Steam Engine. 2005. (Uncharted, Unexplored, & Unexplained Ser.). (Illus.). 48p. (J). (gr. 4-8). lib. bdg. 29.95 (978-1-58415-371-9(7)) Mitchell Lane Pubs., Inc.
Williams, Marcia. Hooray for Inventors! Williams, Marcia, illus. 2013. (ENG., Illus.). 40p. (J). (gr. 3-7). pap. 7.99 (978-0-7636-6749-8(8)) Candlewick Pr.
Woodside, Martin. Thomas Edison: The Man Who Lit up the World. 2007. (Sterling Biographies(r) Ser.). (ENG., Illus.). 128p. (J). (gr. 5-9). pap. 5.95 (978-1-4027-3229-4(5)) Sterling Publishing Co., Inc.
Wooldridge, Connie N. & Wooldridge, Connie Nordhielm. Thank You Very Much, Captain Ericsson! Glass, Andrew, photos by. 2004. (ENG., Illus.). 32p. (J). (gr. k-3). tchr. ed. 16.95 (978-0-8234-1626-4(7)) Holiday Hse., Inc.
Worth, Bonnie. Oh, the Things They Invented! All about Great Inventors. 2015. (Cat in the Hat's Learning Library). (ENG., Illus.). 48p. (J). (gr. k-3). lib. bdg. 13.99 (978-0-375-97170-9(X), Random Hse. Bks. for Young Readers) Random Hse. Children's Bks.
Wyckoff, Edwin Brit. Electric Guitar Man: The Genius of les Paul. 2008. (Genius at Work! Great Inventor Biographies Ser.). (Illus.). 32p. (J). (gr. 3-7). lib. bdg. 23.94 (978-0-7660-2847-0(X), Enslow Elementary) Enslow Pubs., Inc.
—The Guy Who Invented Home Video Games: Ralph Baer & His Awesome Invention. 2010. (Genius at Work! Great Inventor Biographies Ser.). (Illus.). 32p. (J). (gr. 2-5). 23.94 (978-0-7660-3450-1(X)) Enslow Pubs., Inc.
—The Man Who Invented the Electric Guitar: The Genius of les Paul. 2013. (Genius Inventors & Their Great Ideas Ser.). (Illus.). 48p. (J). (gr. 3-18). 25.27 (978-0-7660-4137-0(9)); pap. 8.95 (978-1-4644-0207-4(8), Enslow Elementary) Enslow Pubs., Inc.
—Stopping Bullets with a Thread: Stephanie Kwolek & Her Incredible Invention. 2008. (Genius at Work! Great Inventor Biographies Ser.). (Illus.). 32p. (J). (gr. 3-7). lib. bdg. 23.94 (978-0-7660-2850-0(X), Enslow Elementary) Enslow Pubs., Inc.
—The Teen Who Invented Television: Philo T. Farnsworth & His Awesome Invention. 2007. (Genius at Work! Great Inventor Biographies Ser.). (Illus.). 32p. (J). (gr. 4-7). lib. bdg. 23.94 (978-0-7660-2845-6(3), Enslow Elementary) Enslow Pubs., Inc.
—The Woman Who Invented the Thread That Stops Bullets: The Genius of Stephanie Kwolek. 2013. (Genius Inventors & Their Great Ideas Ser.). 48p. (J). (gr. 3-4). pap. 8.95 (978-1-4644-0211-1(6), Enslow Elementary); (Illus.). 25.27 (978-0-7660-4141-7(7)) Enslow Pubs., Inc.
Yomtov, Nelson. Internet Inventors. 2013. (Cornerstones of Freedom™, Third Ser.). (ENG., Illus.). 64p. (J). pap. 8.95 (978-0-531-21967-6(4)); lib. bdg. 30.00 (978-0-531-23609-3(9)) Scholastic Library Publishing.
Young, Jeff C. Inspiring African-American Inventors: Nine Extraordinary Lives. 2009. (Great Scientists & Famous Inventors Ser.). (Illus.). 128p. (J). (gr. 5-9). lib. bdg. 34.60 (978-1-59845-080-4(8)) Enslow Pubs., Inc.
Yount, Lisa. Nikola Tesla. 2011. (Trailblazers in Science & Technology Ser.). 146p. (gr. 6-12). 35.00 (978-1-60413-670-8(7), Chelsea Hse.) Facts On File, Inc.
Zannos, Susan. Guglielmo Marconi & Radio Waves. 2004. (Uncharted, Unexplored, & Unexplained Ser.). (Illus.). 48p. (J). (gr. 4-8). lib. bdg. 29.95 (978-1-58415-265-1(6)) Mitchell Lane Pubs., Inc.
—Samuel Morse & the Telegraph. 2004. (Uncharted, Unexplored, & Unexplained Ser.). (Illus.). 48p. (J). (gr. 4-8). lib. bdg. 29.95 (978-1-58415-269-9(9)) Mitchell Lane Pubs., Inc.
Zemlicka, Shannon. Thomas Edison. 2003. (History Maker Biographies Ser.). (ENG., Illus.). 48p. (gr. 3-6). lib. bdg. 27.93 (978-0-8225-0239-5(9), Lerner Pubns.) Lerner Publishing Group.

INVENTORS—FICTION

ABDO Publishing Company Staff. Tom Swift, Young Inventor - 4 Titles. 2007. (Tom Swift, Young Inventor Ser.). (ENG.). 165p. 108.28 (978-1-59961-349-9(2)) Spotlight.
Appleton, Victor. Into the Abyss. 2007. (Tom Swift, Young Inventor Ser.). (ENG.). 160p. (gr. 3-7). 27.07 (978-1-59961-350-5(6)) Spotlight.
—The Robot Olympics. 2006. (Tom Swift, Young Inventor Ser.: 2). (ENG.). 176p. (J). (gr. 3-7). pap. 4.99 (978-1-4169-1361-0(0), Aladdin) Simon & Schuster Children's Publishing.
—The Robot Olympics. 2007. (Tom Swift, Young Inventor Ser.). (ENG.). 160p. (gr. 4-7). 27.07 (978-1-59961-351-2(4)) Spotlight.
—Rocket Racers. 2007. (Tom Swift, Young Inventor Ser.: 4). (ENG.). 160p. (J). (gr. 3-7). pap. 8.99 (978-1-4169-3488-2(X), Aladdin) Simon & Schuster Children's Publishing.
—The Space Hotel. 2007. (Tom Swift, Young Inventor Ser.). (ENG.). 160p. (gr. 4-7). 27.07 (978-1-59961-353-6(0)) Spotlight.
—Tom Swift Circling the Globe. 2007. 224p. 29.95 (978-1-4344-9464-1(0)); per. 19.95 (978-1-4344-9463-4(2)) Wildside Pr., LLC.
Appleton, Victor & Appleton, Victor, II. Into the Abyss. 2006. (Tom Swift, Young Inventor Ser.: 1). (ENG.). 176p. (J). (gr. 3-7). pap. 4.99 (978-1-4169-1518-8(4), Aladdin) Simon & Schuster Children's Publishing.
—Under the Radar. 2007. (Tom Swift, Young Inventor Ser.: 6). (ENG.). 160p. (J). (gr. 3-7). pap. 8.99 (978-1-4169-3644-2(0), Simon & Schuster/Paula Wiseman Bks.) Simon & Schuster/Paula Wiseman Bks.
Bailey, Gerry & Foster, Karen. The Wright Brothers' Glider. Radford, Karen & Noyes, Leighton, illus. 2008. (Stories of Great People Ser.). (ENG.). 40p. (J). (gr. 3-8). pap. (978-0-7787-3715-5(2)); lib. bdg. (978-0-7787-3693-6(8)) Crabtree Publishing Co.
Bancks, Tristan. Mac Slater vs. the City. (Mac Slater Hunts the Cool Ser.). (ENG.). 192p. (J). (gr. 3-7). 2012. pap. 6.99 (978-1-4169-8577-8(8)) 2011. 15.99 (978-1-4169-8576-1(X)) Simon & Schuster Bks. For Young Readers. (Simon & Schuster Bks. For Young Readers).
Bean, Raymond. Benji Franklin: Kid Zillionaire. Vimislik, Matthew, illus. 2014. (Benji Franklin: Kid Zillionaire Ser.). (ENG.). 160p. (gr. 2-3). 9.95 (978-1-4342-6419-0(X)) Stone Arch Bks.
—Benji Franklin: Kid Zillionaire, 2 vols. Vimislik, Matthew, illus. 2015. (Benji Franklin: Kid Zillionaire Ser.). (ENG.). 88p. (gr. 2-3). 45.30 (978-1-4965-1992-4(2)) Stone Arch Bks.
—Benji Franklin: Kid Zillionaire: Money Troubles. Vimislik, Matthew, illus. 2016. (Benji Franklin: Kid Zillionaire Ser.). (ENG.). 160p. (gr. 2-3). pap. 6.95 (978-1-4965-4137-6(5)) Stone Arch Bks.
—Benji Franklin: Kid Zillionare, 1 vol. Vimislik, Matthew, illus. 2014. (Benji Franklin: Kid Zillionaire Ser.). (ENG.). 88p. (gr. 2-3). 45.30 (978-1-4342-8927-8(3)) Stone Arch Bks.
—Building Wealth (and Superpowered Rockets!), 1 vol. Vimislik, Matthew, illus. 2014. (Benji Franklin: Kid Zillionaire Ser.). (ENG.). 88p. (gr. 2-3). 22.65 (978-1-4342-6418-3(1)) Stone Arch Bks.
—Buying Stocks (and Solid Gold Submarines!) Vimislik, Matthew, illus. 2015. (Benji Franklin: Kid Zillionaire Ser.). (ENG.). 88p. (gr. 2-3). lib. bdg. 22.65 (978-1-4965-0367-1(8)) Stone Arch Bks.
—Investing Well (in Supersonic Spaceships!) Vimislik, Matthew, illus. 2015. (Benji Franklin: Kid Zillionaire Ser.). (ENG.). 88p. (gr. 2-3). lib. bdg. 22.65 (978-1-4965-0368-8(6)) Stone Arch Bks.
—Money Troubles. Vimislik, Matthew, illus. 2015. (Benji Franklin: Kid Zillionaire Ser.). (ENG.). 160p. (gr. 2-3). 9.95 (978-1-4965-0369-5(4)) Stone Arch Bks.
—Saving Money (and the World from Killer Dinos!), 1 vol. Vimislik, Matthew, illus. 2014. (Benji Franklin: Kid Zillionaire Ser.). (ENG.). 88p. (gr. 2-3). 22.65 (978-1-4342-6417-6(3)) Stone Arch Bks.
—Sweet Farts, 0 vols. unabr. ed. 2012. (Sweet Farts Ser.: 1). (ENG.). 138p. (J). (gr. 4-6). pap. 9.95 (978-1-61218-250-6(X), 9781612182506, Amazon Children's Publishing) Amazon Publishing.
Beaty, Andrea. Rosie Revere, Engineer. Roberts, David, illus. 2013. (ENG.). 32p. (J). (gr. k-17). 17.95 (978-1-4197-0845-9(7), Abrams Bks. for Young Readers) Abrams, Inc.
Becker, Lindsey. The Star Thief. 2017. (ENG., Illus.). 416p. (J). (gr. 3-7). 16.99 (978-0-316-34856-0(2)) Little, Brown Bks. for Young Readers.
Bowditch, Eden Unger. The Ravens of Solemano or the Order of the Mysterious Men in Black. 2015. (Young Inventors Guild Ser.: 2). (ENG.). 464p. (YA). 22.95 (978-1-61088-121-0(4), 631f4bac-0739-447d-b5b4-f9b46c4c02b3) Bancroft Pr.
Breen, Steve. Violet the Pilot. 2016. (ENG.). 40p. (J). (gr. -1-3). 19.65 (978-0-606-39324-9(2)) Turtleback Bks.
Butler, Dave. The Kidnap Plot. 2016. (Extraordinary Journeys of Clockwork Charlie Ser.). (ENG.). 336p. (J). (gr. 3-7). 16.99 (978-0-553-51295-3(1), Knopf Bks. for Young Readers) Random Hse. Children's Bks.
Carlson, Drew. Attack of the Turtle. Johnson, David A., illus. 2008. (ENG.). 157p. (YA). (gr. 4-9). per. 8.00 (978-0-8028-5338-7(2)) Eerdmans, William B. Publishing Co.
Carroll, Claudia. Old Dumpling & the Rainy Day. 2008. 55p. pap. 9.95 (978-0-557-01565-8(0)) Lulu Pr., Inc.
Cole, Dylan. The Other Worldly Adventures of Tyler Washburn: the New Kid. 2012. (ENG., Illus.). 48p. (J). (gr. -1). 19.95 (978-1-933492-77-3(5)) Design Studio Pr.
Colfer, Eoin. Airman. 2009. (ENG.). 416p. (J). (gr. 5-9). pap. 8.99 (978-1-4231-0751-4(9)) Hyperion Pr.
—Airman. 2009. (J). lib. bdg. 19.65 (978-0-606-12534-5(5), Turtleback) Turtleback Bks.
Cornwell, Betsy. Venturess. 2017. (ENG.). 320p. (J). (gr. 7). 17.99 (978-0-544-31927-1(3), Clarion Bks.) Houghton Mifflin Harcourt Trade & Reference Pubs.
Damiron, Anya. Inventor Boy. Pino, Pablo, illus. 2010. (SPA.). 26p. (J). (978-9945-00-157-0(4)) Lucia Stories.
—Nino Inventor. Pino, Pablo, illus. 2010. 26p. (J). (978-9945-00-153-2(1)) Lucia Stories.
Davis, Eleanor. Secret Science Alliance. 2010. (J). (978-1-59990-143-5(9)) Bloomsbury Publishing USA.
—The Secret Science Alliance. Davis, Eleanor, illus. 2009. (ENG., Illus.). 160p. (YA). (gr. 3-6). pap. 16.99 (978-1-59990-396-5(2), 9781599903965, Bloomsbury USA Childrens) Bloomsbury Publishing USA.
—The Secret Science Alliance & the Copycat Crook. Davis, Eleanor, illus. 2009. (ENG., Illus.). 160p. (J). (gr. 3-6). 18.99 (978-1-59990-142-8(0), 9781599901428, Bloomsbury USA Childrens) Bloomsbury Publishing USA.
Deutsch, Stacia & Cohon, Rhody. Bell's Breakthrough. Wenzel, David, illus. 2013. (Blast to the Past Ser.: 3). (ENG.). 128p. (J). (gr. 2-5). pap. 5.99 (978-1-4424-9536-4(7), Simon & Schuster/Paula Wiseman Bks.) Simon & Schuster/Paula Wiseman Bks.
d'Lacey, Chris. Frankin's Bear. Taylor, Thomas, illus. 2005. (Red Go Bananas Ser.). (ENG.). 48p. (J). (gr. 2-3). lib. bdg. (978-0-7787-2674-6(6)) Crabtree Publishing Co.
Domanska, Mary Ann. Emic Rizzle, Tinkerer. 2016. (J). pap. **(978-1-59021-777-1(2))** Lethe Pr.
Doubleday, Russell. Stories of Inventors. 2004. reprint ed. pap. 1.99 (978-1-4192-4959-4(2)); pap. 15.95 (978-1-4191-4959-7(8)) Kessinger Publishing, LLC.
Fields, Jan. Hack Attack: A Trip to Wonderland, 1 vol. Altmann, Scott, illus. 2013. (Adventures in Extreme Reading Ser.). (ENG.). 112p. (J). (gr. 3-6). 27.07 (978-1-61641-919-6(9)) Magic Wagon.
Fleming, Candace. Papa's Mechanical Fish. Kulikov, Boris, illus. 2013. (ENG.). 40p. (J). (gr. k-3). 17.99 (978-0-374-39908-5(5), 9780374399085, Farrar, Straus & Giroux (BYR)) Farrar, Straus & Giroux.
Friedlander, Mark P., Jr. Innovators in Action! Leonardo Da Vinci Gets a Do-Over. Sakprayoonpong, Worachet Boon, illus. 2014. (Innovators in Action Ser.: 1). (ENG.). 208p. (J). (gr. 5-9). pap. 12.95 (978-0-9678020-6-0(7)) Science, Naturally!
Gale Research Staff. Industrial Revolution: Biographies. 2003. (Industrial Revolution Reference Library). (ENG., Illus.). 240p. (J). (gr. 6-10). 106.00 (978-0-7876-6514-2(2), GML00502-182382, UXL) Cengage Gale.
Gall, Chris. Awesome Dawson. 2013. (ENG., Illus.). 40p. (J). (gr. -1-3). 17.99 (978-0-316-21330-1(6)) Little, Brown Bks. for Young Readers.
Giff, Patricia Reilly. Flying Feet. Bright, Alasdair, illus. 2011. (Zigzag Kids Ser.). (ENG.). 80p. (J). (gr. 1-4). 4.99 (978-0-375-85911-3(X), Yearling) Random Hse. Children's Bks.
—Sky High. 2012. (Zigzag Kids Ser.). (ENG., Illus.). 80p. (J). (gr. 1-4). 4.99 (978-0-307-97701-4(3), Yearling); 12.99 (978-0-385-74274-0(6), Lamb, Wendy Bks.); lib. bdg. 15.99 (978-0-375-99074-8(7), Lamb, Wendy Bks.) Random Hse. Children's Bks.
Glass, Andrew. The Wondrous Whirligig: The Wright Brothers¿ First Flying Machine. Glass, Andrew, illus. 2007. (Illus.). 30p. (J). reprint ed. 17.00 (978-1-4223-6765-0(7)) DIANE Publishing Co.
Golden Books. Rusty's Robot Rescue (Rusty Rivets) Dynamo Limited, illus. 2017. (Color Plus Crayons & Sticker Ser.). (ENG.). 48p. (J). (gr. -1-2). pap. 4.99 **(978-1-5247-1675-2(8)**, Golden Bks.) Random Hse. Children's Bks.
Guillain, Charlotte & Guillain, Adam. Cinderella & the Amazing Techno-Slippers. Moor, Becka, illus. 2016. (Fairy Tales Today Ser.). (ENG.). 24p. (gr. 1-2). 9.95 (978-1-4795-8750-6(8)) Picture Window Bks.
Harper, Charise Mericle. Wedgieman & the Big Bunny Trouble. Shea, Bob, illus. 2014. (Step into Reading Ser.). (ENG.). 48p. (J). (gr. k-3). 3.99 (978-0-307-93073-6(4), Random Hse. Bks. for Young Readers) Random Hse. Children's Bks.
Hatke, Ben. Zita the Spacegirl. Hatke, Ben, illus. 2011. (Zita the Spacegirl Ser.: 1). (ENG., Illus.). 192p. (J). (gr. 3-7). 19.99 (978-1-59643-695-4(6), 9781596436954); pap. 12.99 (978-1-59643-446-2(5), 9781596434462) Roaring Brook Pr. (First Second Bks.).
—Zita the Spacegirl. 2011. (Zita the Spacegirl Ser.: 1). (J). lib. bdg. 24.50 (978-0-606-21623-4(5), Turtleback) Turtleback Bks.
Helfand, Lewis. They Changed the World: Bell, Edison & Tesla. Kumar, Naresh, illus. 2014. (Campfire Graphic Novels Ser.). (ENG.). 102p. (YA). (gr. 8-12). pap. 12.99 (978-93-80741-87-1(1), Campfire) Steerforth Pr.
Hood, Susan. The Fix-It Man. Chung, Arree, illus. 2016. 40p. (J). (gr. -1-3). 17.99 (978-0-06-237085-3(5)) HarperCollins Pubs.
Houtman, Jacqueline. The Reinvention of Edison Thomas. (ENG.). 192p. (J). (gr. 3-7). 2012. pap. 8.95 (978-1-59078-951-3(2)) 2010. 17.95 (978-1-59078-708-3(0), Front Street) Boyds Mills Pr.
Hunter, Norman. The Incredible Adventures of Professor Branestawm. 2013. (ENG., Illus.). 288p. (J). (gr. 4-7). pap. 10.99 (978-0-09-958249-6(X)) Random Hse. GBR. Dist: Independent Pubs. Group.
—The Peculiar Triumph of Professor Branestawm. 2003. (Red Fox Classics Ser.). (ENG., Illus.). 128p. (J). (gr. 4-7). pap. 9.99 (978-0-09-941756-9(1)) Random Hse. GBR. Dist: Independent Pubs. Group.
Ingalls, Ann. Fairy Floss. Blanco, Migy, illus. 2017. (ENG.). 40p. (J). (gr. -1-3). 17.99 (978-1-4998-0238-2(2)) Little Bee Books Inc.
Kehoe, Tim. Vincent Shadow: Toy Inventor. Francis, Guy & Wohnoutka, Mike, illus. 2011. (Vincent Shadow Ser.: 1). (ENG.). 224p. (J). (gr. 3-7). pap. 6.99 (978-0-316-05666-3(9)) Little, Brown Bks. for Young Readers.
Kelly, Katy. Melonhead. Johnson, Gillian, illus. 2010. (Melonhead Ser.). (ENG.). 240p. (J). (gr. 3-7). 6.99 (978-0-440-42187-0(X), Yearling) Random Hse. Children's Bks.
Lachenmeyer, Nathaniel. Eureka! Jack, Colin, illus. 2013. (J). (978-0-8037-3514-9(6), Dial) Penguin Publishing Group.
Lackey, Mercedes & Edghill, Rosemary. Dead Reckoning. 2012. (ENG.). 336p. (YA). (gr. 7-12). 16.99 (978-1-59990-684-3(8), 9781599906843, Bloomsbury USA Childrens) Bloomsbury Publishing USA.
Lombardi, Kristine A. Mr. Biddles. Lombardi, Kristine A., illus. 2017. (Illus.). 40p. (J). (gr. -1-3). 17.99 **(978-0-06-244114-0(0))** HarperCollins Pubs.
Long, Ilana. Ziggy's Big Idea. Joni, Rasa, illus. 2014. (Kar-Ben Favorites Ser.). (ENG.). 32p. (J). (gr. -1-4). 17.95 (978-0-7613-9053-4(7)); 7.95 (978-0-7613-9054-1(5)) Lerner Publishing Group. (Kar-Ben Publishing).
Mathis, Mandy. The Littlest Inventor. 2016. (ENG., Illus.). 32p. (J). pap. 11.95 (978-1-935567-62-2(4)) Sensory Resources.
McCann, Jesse Leon. The Science Project. Fruchter, Jason, illus. 2003. 61p. (J). (978-0-439-56271-3(6)) Scholastic, Inc.
McGowan, Keith. The Witch's Guide to Cooking with Children. Tanaka, Yoko, illus. 2011. (ENG.). 192p. (J). (gr. 4-7). pap. 8.99 (978-0-312-67486-1(4), 9780312674861) Square Fish.
Meister, Cari. Buzz Beaker & the Cave Creatures. McGuire, Bill, illus. 2010. (Buzz Beaker Bks.). (ENG.). 32p. (gr. 2-3). pap. 6.25 (978-1-4342-2797-3(9)); 22.65 (978-1-4342-2060-8(5)) Stone Arch Bks.
—Buzz Beaker & the Cool Caps, 1 vol. McGuire, Bill, illus. 2011. (Buzz Beaker Bks.). (ENG.). 32p. (gr. 2-3). pap. 6.25 (978-1-4342-3055-3(4)) Stone Arch Bks.
—Buzz Beaker & the Growing Goo, 1 vol. McGuire, Bill, illus. 2011. (Buzz Beaker Bks.). (ENG.). 32p. (gr. 2-3). pap. 6.25 (978-1-4342-3056-0(2)); lib. bdg. 22.65 (978-1-4342-2527-6(5)) Stone Arch Bks.
—Buzz Beaker & the Outer Space Trip. McGuire, Bill, illus. 2010. (Buzz Beaker Bks.). (ENG.). 32p. (gr. 2-3). pap. 6.25 (978-1-4342-2800-0(2)) Stone Arch Bks.
—Buzz Beaker & the Putt-Putt Contest. McGuire, Bill, illus. 2010. (Buzz Beaker Bks.). (ENG.). 32p. (gr. 2-3). pap. 6.25 (978-1-4342-2799-7(5)); 22.65 (978-1-4342-2062-2(1)) Stone Arch Bks.
—Buzz Beaker & the Race to School, 1 vol. McGuire, Bill, illus. 2011. (Buzz Beaker Bks.). (ENG.). 32p. (gr. 2-3). pap. 6.25 (978-1-4342-3057-7(0)); lib. bdg. 22.65 (978-1-4342-2528-3(3)) Stone Arch Bks.
—Buzz Beaker & the Speed Secret. McGuire, Bill, illus. 2010. (Buzz Beaker Bks.). (ENG.). 32p. (gr. 2-3). pap. 6.25 (978-1-4342-2798-0(7)); 22.65 (978-1-4342-2061-5(3)) Stone Arch Bks.
—Buzz Beaker & the Super Fast Car, 1 vol. McGuire, Bill, illus. 2011. (Buzz Beaker Bks.). (ENG.). 32p. (gr. 2-3). pap. 6.25 (978-1-4342-3058-4(9)) Stone Arch Bks.
Montgomery, R. A. The Brilliant Dr. Wogan. 2005. (Choose Your Own Adventure Ser.). (Illus.). 112p. (gr. 4-8). pap. 5.50 (978-0-7608-9705-8(0)) Sundance/Newbridge Educational Publishing.
Moriarty, Chris. The Inquisitor's Apprentice. Geyer, Mark Edward, illus. 2011. (ENG.). 352p. (J). (gr. 5-7). 16.99 (978-0-547-58135-4(1)) Houghton Mifflin Harcourt Publishing Co.
My Super-Spy Diary. 2014. (Eliza Boom Ser.: 2). (ENG., Illus.). 128p. (J). (gr. 1-4). pap. 5.99 (978-1-4814-0652-9(3), Aladdin) Simon & Schuster Children's Publishing.
Nelson, Peter. Herbert's Wormhole. Rao, Rohitash, illus. 2010. (Herbert's Wormhole Ser.: 1). (ENG.). 304p. (J). (gr. 3-7). pap. 6.99 (978-0-06-168870-6(3)) HarperCollins Pubs.
Nesbø, Jo. Bubble in the Bathtub. Chace, Tara F., tr. Lowery, Mike, illus. 2011. (Doctor Proctor's Fart Powder Ser.). (ENG.). 448p. (J). (gr. 3-7). pap. 7.99 (978-1-4169-7975-3(1), Aladdin) Simon & Schuster Children's Publishing.
—Bubble in the Bathtub. Chace, Tara, tr. from NOR. Lowery, Mike, illus. 2011. (Doctor Proctor's Fart Powder Ser.). (ENG.). 432p. (J). (gr. 3-7). 17.99 (978-1-4169-7974-6(3), Aladdin) Simon & Schuster Children's Publishing.
—Doctor Proctor's Fart Powder. Chace, Tara F., tr. Lowery, Mike, illus. 2010. (Doctor Proctor's Fart Powder Ser.). (ENG.). 288p. (J). (gr. 3-7). pap. 7.99 (978-1-4169-7973-9(5), Aladdin) Simon & Schuster Children's Publishing.
—Doctor Proctor's Fart Powder. Chace, Tara, tr. from GER. Lowery, Mike, illus. 2009. (Doctor Proctor's Fart Powder Ser.). (ENG.). 272p. (J). (gr. 3-7). 17.99 (978-1-4169-7972-2(7), Aladdin) Simon & Schuster Children's Publishing.
—Doctor Proctor's Fart Powder. 2010. (Dr. Proctor's Fart Powder Ser.: 1). lib. bdg. 18.40 (978-0-606-15419-2(1), Turtleback) Turtleback Bks.
—The Magical Fruit. 2014. (Doctor Proctor's Fart Powder Ser.). (ENG., Illus.). 320p. (J). (gr. 3-7). pap. 7.99 (978-1-4424-9343-8(7), Aladdin) Simon & Schuster Children's Publishing.
—The Magical Fruit. Chace, Tara F., tr. from NOR. Lowery, Mike, illus. 2013. (Doctor Proctor's Fart Powder Ser.). (ENG.). 320p. (J). (gr. 3-7). 17.99 (978-1-4424-9342-1(9), Aladdin) Simon & Schuster Children's Publishing.
—Silent (but Deadly) Night. Lowery, Mike, illus. 2017. (J). pap. **(978-1-5344-1000-8(7)**, Simon & Schuster/Paula Wiseman Bks.) Simon & Schuster/Paula Wiseman Bks.
Nesbø, Jo. Who Cut the Cheese? Chace, Tara F., tr. Lowery, Mike, illus. 2012. (Doctor Proctor's Fart Powder Ser.). (ENG.). 464p. (J). (gr. 3-7). pap. 7.99 (978-1-4424-3308-3(6), Aladdin) Simon & Schuster Children's Publishing.
—Who Cut the Cheese? Chace, Tara, tr. from NOR. Lowery, Mike, illus. 2012. (Doctor Proctor's Fart Powder Ser.). (ENG.). 464p. (J). (gr. 3-7). 17.99 (978-1-4424-3307-6(8), Aladdin) Simon & Schuster Children's Publishing.
Nickel, Scott. Wind Power Whiz Kid: A Buzz Beaker Brainstorm. Smith, Andy J., illus. 2008. (Graphic Sparks Ser.). (ENG.). 40p. (gr. 1-3). pap. 5.95 (978-1-4342-0854-5(0), Graphic Sparks) Stone Arch Bks.
Nix, Garth. One Beastly Beast: Two Aliens, Three Inventors, Four Fantastic Tales. Biggs, Brian, illus. 2007. 176p. (J). (gr. 2-6). lib. bdg. 16.89 (978-0-06-084320-5(9), Eos) HarperCollins Pubs.

Odgers, Sally. Felix & His Flying Machine, 1 vol. rev. ed. 2013. (Fiction Readers Ser.). (ENG., Illus.). 28p. (J). (gr. 3-3). pap. 8.99 *(978-1-4333-5604-9(X))* Shell Educational Publishing.

—Felix & His Flying Machine. rev. ed. 2013. (Fiction Readers Ser.). (ENG., Illus.). 28p. (gr. 3-3). pap. 19.96 *(978-1-4807-1726-8(6))* Teacher Created Materials, Inc.

Orton, J. R. Trial Trip of the Flying Cloud. 2004. reprint ed. pap. 1.99 *(978-1-4192-9109-8(2))* Kessinger Publishing, LLC.

Patterson, James. House of Robots: Robot Revolution. Neufeld, Juliana, illus. 2017. (House of Robots Ser.: 3). (ENG.). 336p. (J). (gr. 3-7). 13.99 *(978-0-316-34958-1(5),* Jimmy Patterson) Little Brown & Co.

Patterson, James & Grabenstein, Chris. House of Robots. Neufeld, Juliana, illus. (House of Robots Ser.: 1). (ENG.). (J). (gr. 3-7). 2015. 336p. pap. 7.99 *(978-0-316-34679-5(9))* 2014. 352p. 13.99 *(978-0-316-40591-1(4))* Little Brown & Co. (Jimmy Patterson).

—House of Robots. 2015. (J). lib. bdg. 18.40 *(978-0-606-37527-6(9))* Turtleback Bks.

—Robots Go Wild. Neufeld, Juliana, illus. 2015. (House of Robots Ser.: 2). (ENG.). 336p. (J). (gr. 3-7). 13.99 *(978-0-316-28479-0(3),* Jimmy Patterson) Little Brown & Co.

Pettenati, Jeanne. Galileo's Journal, 1609-1610. Rui, Paolo, illus. 2006. (ENG.). 32p. (J). (gr. 1-4). pap. 7.95 *(978-1-57091-880-3(5))* Charlesbridge Publishing, Inc.

Roy, Philip. Eco Warrior. 2015. (ENG., Illus.). 232p. pap. 11.95 *(978-1-55380-347-8(7))* Ronsdale Pr. CAN. Dist: SPD-Small Pr. Distribution.

Rubin, Sarah. The Impossible Clue. 2017. (J). pap. ***(978-0-545-94272-0(1),*** Chicken Hse., The) Scholastic, Inc.

Sabuda, Robert. Uh-Oh, Leonardo! The Adventures of Providence Traveler. Sabuda, Robert, illus. 2007. (ENG., Illus.). 48p. (J). (gr. k-3). 12.99 *(978-1-4169-6164-2(X),* Aladdin) Simon & Schuster Children's Publishing.

Sargent, Dave & Sargent, Pat. Ginger: (Lilac Roan) Be Likeable, 30 vols., Vol. 27. Lenoir, Jane, illus. 2003. (Saddle up Ser.: Vol. 27). 42p. (J). pap. 10.95 *(978-1-56763-812-7(0));* lib. bdg. 23.60 *(978-1-56763-811-0(2))* Ozark Publishing.

Scieszka, Jon. The Brain Turbo. Biggs, Brian, illus. 2015. (Frank Einstein Ser.). (ENG.). 192p. (J). (gr. 3-7). 13.95 *(978-1-4197-1643-0(3),* Amulet Bks.) Abrams, Inc.

—Frank Einstein & the Antimatter Motor. Biggs, Brian, illus. 2014. (Frank Einstein Ser.: 1). (ENG.). 192p. (J). (gr. 2-6). 13.95 *(978-1-4197-1218-0(7),* Amulet Bks.) Abrams, Inc.

—Frank Einstein & the Antimatter Motor. 2017. (Frank Einstein Ser.: 1). (J). lib. bdg. 18.40 ***(978-0-606-39683-7(7))*** Turtleback Bks.

—Frank Einstein & the Antimatter Motor (Frank Einstein Series #1) Book One. Biggs, Brian, illus. 2017. (Frank Einstein Ser.). (ENG.). 208p. (J). (gr. 3-7). pap. 7.95 *(978-1-4197-2492-3(4),* Amulet Bks.) Abrams, Inc.

—Frank Einstein & the BrainTurbo. Biggs, Brian, illus. 2015. (ENG.). 192p. (J). (gr. 3-7). pap. 8.95 *(978-1-4197-1924-0(6))* Abrams, Inc.

—Frank Einstein & the Electro-Finger. Biggs, Brian, illus. 2015. (Frank Einstein Ser.: 2). (ENG.). 176p. (J). (gr. 3-7). 13.95 *(978-1-4197-1483-2(X),* Amulet Bks.) Abrams, Inc.

—Frank Einstein & the Electro-Finger (Frank Einstein Series #2) Book Two. Biggs, Brian, illus. 2017. (Frank Einstein Ser.). (ENG.). 192p. (J). (gr. 3-7). pap. 7.95 *(978-1-4197-2493-0(2),* Amulet Bks.) Abrams, Inc.

—Frank Einstein & the Evoblaster Belt, Bk. 4. Biggs, Brian, illus. 2016. (Frank Einstein Ser.). (ENG.). 208p. (J). (gr. 3-7). pap. 7.95 *(978-1-4197-2379-7(0))* Abrams, Inc.

—Frank Einstein & the EvoBlaster Belt (Frank Einstein Series #4) Book Four. Biggs, Brian, illus. 2016. (Frank Einstein Ser.). (ENG.). 208p. (J). (gr. 3-7). 13.95 *(978-1-4197-1887-8(8),* Amulet Bks.) Abrams, Inc.

Scieszka, Jon. Frank Einstein & the EvoBlaster Belt (Frank Einstein Series #4) Book Four. Biggs, Brian, illus. 2017. (Frank Einstein Ser.). (ENG.). 224p. (J). (gr. 3-7). pap. 7.99 ***(978-1-4197-2736-8(2),*** Amulet Bks.) Abrams, Inc.

Scieszka, Jon & Brian Biggs. Frank Einstein & the Electro-Finger. 2017. (Frank Einstein Ser.: 2). (J). lib. bdg. 18.40 ***(978-0-606-39684-4(5))*** Turtleback Bks.

Sharpe, Luke. And the Stink Spectacular. Ross, Graham, illus. 2015. (Billy Sure Kid Entrepreneur Ser.: 2). (ENG.). 160p. (J). (gr. 3-7). 17.99 *(978-1-4814-3951-0(0),* Simon Spotlight) Simon Spotlight.

—Billy Sure, Kid Entrepreneur. Ross, Graham, illus. 2015. (Billy Sure Kid Entrepreneur Ser.: 1). (ENG.). 160p. (J). (gr. 3-7). pap. 6.99 *(978-1-4814-3947-3(2),* Simon Spotlight) Simon Spotlight.

—Billy Sure Kid Entrepreneur & the Haywire Hovercraft. Ross, Graham, illus. 2016. (Billy Sure Kid Entrepreneur Ser.: 7). (ENG.). 160p. (J). (gr. 3-7). pap. 6.99 *(978-1-4814-6193-1(1),* Simon Spotlight) Simon Spotlight.

—Billy Sure Kid Entrepreneur Is NOT a Singer! Ross, Graham, illus. 2016. (Billy Sure Kid Entrepreneur Ser.: 9). (ENG.). 160p. (J). (gr. 3-7). pap. 6.99 *(978-1-4814-6895-4(2),* Simon Spotlight) Simon Spotlight.

—The No-Trouble Bubble. Ross, Graham, illus. 2016. (Billy Sure Kid Entrepreneur Ser.: 5). (ENG.). 160p. (J). (gr. 3-7). 17.99 *(978-1-4814-5275-5(4),* Simon Spotlight) Simon Spotlight.

—The No-Trouble Bubble. Ross, Graham, illus. 2016. (Billy Sure Kid Entrepreneur Ser.: 5). (ENG.). 160p. (J). (gr. 3-7). pap. 6.99 *(978-1-4814-5274-8(6),* Simon Spotlight) Simon Spotlight.

Stevenson, Robin. Ben the Inventor, 1 vol. Parkins, David, illus. 2011. (Orca Echoes Ser.). (ENG.). 64p. (J). (gr. 2-3). pap. 6.95 *(978-1-55469-802-8(2))* Orca Bk. Pubs. USA.

Stilton, Geronimo & Mckeon, Kathryn. Mouse in Space! 2013. (Geronimo Stilton Ser.: 52). lib. bdg. 18.40 *(978-0-606-31525-8(X),* Turtleback) Turtleback Bks.

Stilton, Geronimo, et al. Robot Attack. Usai, Luca & Verzini, Daniele, illus. 2015. 117p. (J). *(978-0-545-86796-2(7))* Scholastic, Inc.

Strambini, Karla. The Extraordinary Mr. Qwerty. Strambini, Karla, illus. 2014. (ENG., Illus.). 32p. (J). (gr. k-3). 16.99 *(978-0-7636-7324-6(2))* Candlewick Pr.

Sutton, Felix. We Were There at the First Airplane Flight. Matulay, Laszlo, illus. 2013. (ENG.). 192p. (J). (gr. 3-8). pap. 6.99 *(978-0-486-49258-2(3))* Dover Pubns., Inc.

Tacang, Brian. Bully-Be-Gone: The Misadventures of Millicent Madding #1. 2006. (Illus.). 216p. (J). (gr. 3-7). 17.89 *(978-0-06-073912-6(6))* HarperCollins Pubs.

Timmers, Leo. Gus's Garage. Timmers, Leo, illus. 2017. (ENG., Illus.). 32p. (gr. -1-k). 16.99 ***(978-1-77657-092-8(8));*** 9.99 ***(978-1-77657-094-2(4))*** Gecko Pr. NZL. Dist: Lerner Publishing Group.

Trod, Mariano, et al, illus. The Brilliant Dr. Wogan. 2007. (Choose Your Own Adventure Ser.: No. 17). 112p. (J). (gr. 4-7). per. 6.99 *(978-1-933390-17-8(4),* CHC:17) Chooseco LLC.

Trussell-Cullen, Alan. Sam the Incredible Inventor, 1 vol. rev. ed. 2013. (Fiction Readers Ser.). (ENG., Illus.). 32p. (J). (gr. 3-3). pap. 8.99 *(978-1-4333-5610-0(4))* Shell Educational Publishing.

—Sam the Incredible Inventor. rev. ed. 2013. (Fiction Readers Ser.). (ENG., Illus.). 32p. (gr. 3-3). pap. 19.96 *(978-1-4807-1732-9(0))* Teacher Created Materials, Inc.

Wasson, Dave. The Big Ideas of Buster Bickles. Wasson, Dave, illus. 2015. (ENG., Illus.). 40p. (J). (gr. -1-3). 17.99 *(978-0-06-229178-3(5))* HarperCollins Pubs.

Weiner, Ellis. The Templeton Twins Have an Idea. Holmes, Jeremy, illus. 2012. (ENG.). 232p. (J). (gr. 4-7). 16.99 *(978-0-8118-6679-8(3))* Chronicle Bks. LLC.

—The Templeton Twins Have an Idea: Book 1. Holmes, Jeremy, illus. 2013. (Templeton Twins Ser.). (ENG.). 240p. (J). (gr. 3-7). pap. 6.99 *(978-1-4521-2704-0(2))* Chronicle Bks. LLC.

—The Templeton Twins Make a Scene: Book 2. Holmes, Jeremy, illus. 2014. (ENG.). 272p. (J). (gr. 3-7). pap. 6.99 *(978-1-4521-2872-6(3))* Chronicle Bks. LLC.

Weston, Greg. The Inventors. 2009. 202p. pap. 13.95 *(978-1-4092-6096-7(8))* Lulu Pr., Inc.

Wurge, B. B. The Last Notebook of Leonardo. 2010. (LeapKids Ser.). (ENG., Illus.). 154p. (J). (gr. 1-7). pap. 9.95 *(978-1-935248-14-9(6))* Leapfrog Pr.

Zafón, Carlos Ruiz. The Watcher in the Shadows. (ENG.). (YA). (gr. 7-17). 2014. 288p. pap. 10.99 *(978-0-316-04475-2(X))* 2013. 272p. 18.00 *(978-0-316-04476-9(8))* Little, Brown Bks. for Young Readers.

INVERTEBRATES

see also Corals; Insects; Mollusks; Protozoa; Worms

Adamson, Heather. Sea Urchins. 2017. (Ocean Life up Close Ser.). (ENG., Illus.). 24p. (J). (gr. k-3). lib. bdg. 25.95 ***(978-1-62617-646-1(9),*** Blastoff! Readers) Bellwether Media.

Boothroyd, Jennifer. Endangered & Extinct Invertebrates. 2014. (Lightning Bolt Books Animals in Danger Ser.). (ENG., Illus.). 32p. (gr. k-2). pap. 7.95 *(978-1-4677-2371-8(1));* lib. bdg. 26.60 *(978-1-4677-1333-7(3),* Lerner Pubns.) Lerner Publishing Group.

—Under the Ground. 2006. (First Step Nonfiction - Animal Homes Ser.). (ENG., Illus.). 8p. (gr. -1-1). pap. 4.95 *(978-0-8225-5661-9(8),* Lerner Pubns.) Lerner Publishing Group.

Coldiron, Deborah. Sea Sponges, 1 vol. 2007. (Underwater World Ser.). (ENG.). 32p. (gr. 3-7). 27.07 *(978-1-59928-812-3(5),* Buddy Bks.) ABDO Publishing Co.

Collinson, Clare. British Insects & Other Minibeasts. 2017. (Nature in Your Neighbourhood Ser.). (ENG., Illus.). 32p. (J). (gr. 2-4). 17.99 *(978-1-4451-3632-5(5),* Franklin Watts) Hachette Children's Group GBR. Dist: Hachette Bk. Group.

Didier, Dominique A. Sea Anemone. 2014. (21st Century Skills Library: Exploring Our Oceans Ser.). (ENG., Illus.). 32p. (J). (gr. 3-6). 28.50 *(978-1-63188-022-3(5),* 205495) Cherry Lake Publishing.

Downer, Ann. Smart & Spineless: Brainy Without a Backbone. 2015. (ENG., Illus.). 88p. (J). (gr. 5-12). lib. bdg. 33.32 *(978-1-4677-3739-5(9),* Twenty-First Century Bks.) Lerner Publishing Group.

—Smart & Spineless: Exploring Invertebrate Intelligence. 2015. (ENG., Illus.). 88p. (gr. 5-12). 33.32 *(978-1-4677-8805-2(8),* Twenty-First Century Bks.) Lerner Publishing Group.

Duke, Shirley Smith. Vertebrates & Invertebrates Explained. 2016. (Distinctions in Nature Ser.). (Illus.). 32p. (J). (gr. 3-3). pap. 10.58 *(978-1-5026-1779-8(X))* Cavendish Square Publishing.

Encyclopaedia Britannica, Inc. Staff. Britannica Illustrated Science Library Series (18 Title Series), 18 vols. 2010. 599.00 *(978-1-61535-423-8(9))* Encyclopaedia Britannica, Inc.

Encyclopaedia Britannica, Inc. Staff, compiled by. Britannica Illustrated Science Library: Invertebrates. 2008. (J). *(978-1-59339-587-2(6))* Encyclopaedia Britannica, Inc.

Encyclopaedia Britannica Staff, creator. Invertebrates. 2011. (Britannica Illustrated Science Library Ser.). 104p. (J). 37.44 *(978-1-61535-462-7(X))* Encyclopaedia Britannica, Inc.

Flad, Antje, illus. Creeping, Crawling, Who Goes There? 2016. (Mini Movers Ser.). (ENG.). 12p. (J). (gr. -1 — 1). bds. 4.99 *(978-0-7641-6865-9(7))* Barron's Educational Series, Inc.

Galko, Francine. Classifying Invertebrates. 2016. (Classifying Living Things Ser.). (ENG.). 32p. (gr. 3-5). pap. 7.99 *(978-1-4846-4017-3(9),* NA-h) Heinemann-Raintree.

Grolier Educational Staff, contrib. by. Insects & Other Invertebrates, 50 vols. 2004. (World of Animals Ser.: Vol. 3). (Illus.). (J). 499.00 *(978-0-7172-5894-9(7))* Scholastic Library Publishing.

Harrison, Lorraine. Mites. 2015. (Freaky Freeloaders: Bugs That Feed on People Ser.). (ENG.). 24p. (J). (gr. 2-3). 23.60 *(978-1-4994-0761-7(0),* PowerKids Pr.) Rosen Publishing Group, Inc., The.

Holt, Rinehart and Winston Staff. Holt Science & Technology Chapter 15: Life Science: Invertebrates. 5th ed. 2004. (Illus.). pap. 12.86 *(978-0-03-030219-0(6))* Holt McDougal.

Housel, Debra J. Incredible Invertebrates, 1 vol. 2nd rev. ed. 2013. (Nonfiction Readers Ser.). (ENG., Illus.). 28p. (J). (gr. 3-3). pap. 25.96 *(978-1-4807-1075-7(X))* Shell Educational Publishing.

—Incredible Invertebrates, 1 vol. 2nd rev. ed. 2011. (Nonfiction Readers Ser.). (ENG.). 28p. (J). (gr. 3-3). pap. 8.99 *(978-1-4333-3660-7(X))* Teacher Created Materials, Inc.

Housel, Debra J. Los Invertebrados Increíbles. 2017. (TIME for Kids en Español - Level 3 Ser.). (SPA.). 32p. (gr. 3-3). lib. bdg. 31.99 ***(978-1-5157-5173-1(2))*** Time for Kids Inc AUS. Dist: Capstone Pub.

Invertebrates. 2005. (Invertebrates Ser.). (Illus.). 32p. (gr. 4-6). 168.00 *(978-0-7910-7058-1(1),* Chelsea Hse.) Facts On File, Inc.

Jenkins, Jean & Loewer, Peter. The Inside-Out Stomach: An Introduction to Animals Without Backbones. 2013. (ENG.). 72p. (J). (gr. -1-3). pap. 13.99 *(978-1-4814-2158-4(1),* Atheneum Bks. for Young Readers) Simon & Schuster Children's Publishing.

Kalman, Bobbie. Animals Without Backbones. 2008. (Big Science Ideas Ser.). (ENG., Illus.). 32p. (J). (gr. 1-4). pap. *(978-0-7787-3299-0(1));* lib. bdg. *(978-0-7787-3279-2(7))* Crabtree Publishing Co.

Kilpatrick, Cathy. Creepy Crawlies. 2007. (Usborne First Nature Ser.). (Illus.). 24p. (J). (gr. k-3). 12.99 *(978-1-58086-982-9(3),* Usborne) EDC Publishing.

—Creepy Crawlies. Jacquemier, Sue, ed. Shields, Chris et al, illus. rev. ed. 2006. (First Nature Ser.). 24p. (J). pap. 4.99 *(978-0-7945-1494-5(4),* Usborne) EDC Publishing.

—Creepy Crawlies Kid Kit. rev. ed. 2007. (Kid Kits Ser.). (Illus.). 23p. (J). pap. 10.99 *(978-1-60130-021-8(2),* Usborne) EDC Publishing.

Ladybird. Minibeasts. 2016. (Read It Yourself with Ladybird Ser.). (ENG., Illus.). 48p. (J). 5.99 *(978-0-241-23737-3(8))* Penguin Bks., Ltd. GBR. Dist: Independent Pubs. Group.

Legg, Gerald. Minibeasts. 2008. (Hot Topics Ser.). (Illus.). 32p. (J). (gr. 3-7). *(978-1-84239-936-1(5))* Alligator Bks. Ltd.

Lewis, Clare. Bug Body Parts. 2015. (J). *(978-1-4846-2555-2(2))* Heinemann-Raintree.

Li, Maggie. Bug Detective. 2015. (ENG., Illus.). 28p. (J). (gr. 1). 14.95 *(978-1-4549-1516-4(1))* Sterling Publishing Co., Inc.

Lunis, Natalie. Squishy Sponges. 2016. (No Backbone! Marine Invertebrates Ser.). (ENG.). 24p. (J). (gr. k-3). pap. 7.95 *(978-1-944998-80-6(2))* Bearport Publishing Co., Inc.

Magby, Meryl. Sea Anemones. 2012. (Under the Sea Ser.). (ENG., Illus.). 24p. (J). (gr. k-5). 22.60 *(978-1-4488-7401-9(7));* pap. 8.25 *(978-1-4488-7480-4(7))* Rosen Publishing Group, Inc., The. (PowerKids Pr.).

—Sponges. 2012. (Under the Sea Ser.). (ENG., Illus.). 24p. (J). (gr. k-5). pap. 8.25 *(978-1-4488-7478-1(5));* lib. bdg. 22.60 *(978-1-4488-7399-9(1))* Rosen Publishing Group, Inc., The. (PowerKids Pr.).

McNeil, Niki, et al. HOCPP 1131 Invertebrates. 2006. spiral bd. 22.00 *(978-1-60308-131-3(3))* In the Hands of a Child.

Miller, Sara Swan. Secret Lives of Soil Creatures. 2010. (Secret Lives Ser.). 48p. (gr. 4). 29.93 *(978-0-7614-4229-5(4))* Marshall Cavendish Corp.

Miller, Tori. Sea Urchins. 2009. (Freaky Fish Ser.). (ENG., Illus.). 24p. (J). (gr. 2-5). pap. 8.25 *(978-1-4358-3173-5(X),* PowerKids Pr.); 24p. (gr. 2-3). 42.50 *(978-1-61512-649-1(X),* PowerKids Pr.); (YA). (gr. 1-4). lib. bdg. 22.60 *(978-1-4358-2756-1(2))* Rosen Publishing Group, Inc., The.

Moore, Heidi. Giant Isopod: And Other Crafty Crustaceans. 2011. (Creatures of the Deep Ser.). (ENG.). 32p. (gr. 3-5). 30.65 *(978-1-4109-4198-5(1),* NA-r) Heinemann-Raintree.

—Giant Isopods & Other Crafty Crustaceans, 1 vol. 2011. (Creatures of the Deep Ser.). (ENG.). 32p. (gr. 3-5). pap. 8.95 *(978-1-4109-4205-0(8),* NA-r) Heinemann-Raintree.

Morgan, Sally. Under a Stone & Other Rocky Places. 2006. (Hidden Habitats Ser.). (J). *(978-1-59389-285-2(3))* Chrysalis Education.

O'Hare, Ted. Invertebrates. 2005. (What Is an Animal Ser.). (Illus.). 24p. (J). (gr. 3-7). lib. bdg. 14.95 *(978-1-59515-419-4(1))* Rourke Educational Media.

Pascoe, Elaine. Animals Without Backbones. (Kid's Guide to the Classification of Living Things Ser.). 32p. 2009. (gr. 3-4). 47.90 *(978-1-61511-201-2(4))* 2003. (J). lib. bdg. 25.25 *(978-0-8239-6311-9(X))* Rosen Publishing Group, Inc., The. (PowerKids Pr.).

Pearson, Scott. Zebra Mussels. 2017. (Invasive Species Takeover Ser.). (ENG., Illus.). 32p. (J). (gr. 3-7). 31.35 ***(978-1-68072-019-8(8),*** Bolt) Black Rabbit Bks.

Pietras, Jamie & Breheny, Jamie. Creepy & Crawly: Incredible Invertebrates. 2007. (Illus.). 32p. (J). pap. *(978-0-439-02573-7(7))* Scholastic, Inc.

Pugliano-Martin, Carol. Being a Bug Scout & Como ser un explorador de Animalitos: 6 English, 6 Spanish Adaptations. 2011. (ENG & SPA.). (J). 97.00 net. *(978-1-4108-5695-1(X))* Benchmark Education Co.

Rose, Simon. Sea Urchins. 2011. (Ocean Life Ser.). (Illus.). 24p. (J). (gr. 3-6). 27.13 *(978-1-61690-691-7(X))* Weigl Pubs., Inc.

Rose, Simon & McDowell, Pamela. Sea Urchins. 2011. (J). (gr. 2-4). pap. 12.95 *(978-1-61690-695-5(2),* AV2 by Weigl) Weigl Pubs., Inc.

Royston, Angela. Invertebrates. 2015. (Animal Classifications Ser.). (ENG.). 32p. (gr. 1-3). 27.32 *(978-1-4846-0752-7(X),* Heinemann First Library) Heinemann-Raintree.

Rustad, Martha E. H. Clown Fish & Sea Anemones Work Together, 1 vol. 2011. (Animals Working Together Ser.). (ENG., Illus.). 24p. (gr. k-1). pap. 7.29 *(978-1-4296-6198-0(4),* Pebble Plus) Capstone Press of Coughlan Cos.

—What's in the Dirt? 2015. (What's in There? Ser.). (ENG., Illus.). 24p. (gr. k-1). lib. bdg. 21.99 *(978-1-4914-6012-2(1),* Pebble Bks.) Capstone Press of Coughlan Cos.

Silverstein, Alvin, et al. Creepy Crawlies. 2003. (What a Pet! Ser.). (ENG., Illus.). 48p. (gr. 3-6). lib. bdg. 23.93 *(978-0-7613-2511-6(5),* Millbrook Pr.) Lerner Publishing Group.

—Dung Beetles, Slugs, Leeches, & More: The Yucky Animal Book. Kelley, Gerald, illus. 2010. (Yucky Science Ser.). 48p. (J). (gr. 5-9). 25.27 *(978-0-7660-3317-7(1))* Enslow Pubs., Inc.

Smalley, Carol. A Project Guide to Sponges, Worms, & Mollusks. 2010. (Life Science Projects for Kids Ser.). (Illus.). 48p. (J). (gr. 4-8). lib. bdg. 29.95 *(978-1-58415-876-9(X))* Mitchell Lane Pubs., Inc.

Turner, Matt. Tiny Creepy Crawlers. Calle, Santiago, illus. 2017. (Crazy Creepy Crawlers Ser.). (ENG.). 32p. (J). (gr. 3-6). 26.65 *(978-1-5124-1555-1(3));* 7.99 ***(978-1-5124-3606-8(2));*** 39.99 ***(978-1-5124-3605-1(4));*** 39.99 ***(978-1-5124-2715-8(2))*** Lerner Publishing Group.

Underwood, Shelley. Minibeasts. 2010. (Weird, Wild, & Wonderful Ser.). (Illus.). 24p. (J). (gr. 2-5). lib. bdg. 22.00 *(978-1-4339-3576-3(7),* Gareth Stevens Learning Library) Stevens, Gareth Publishing LLLP.

INVESTIGATIONS

Green, Sara. Fire Dogs. 2013. (Dogs to the Rescue! Ser.). (ENG., Illus.). 24p. (J). (gr. 3-8). lib. bdg. 25.95 *(978-1-60014-953-5(7),* Pilot Bks.) Bellwether Media.

Hodge, Susie & Mason, Paul. Investigating UFOs & Aliens. 2010. (Extreme! Ser.). (ENG.). 32p. (gr. 3-4). pap. 47.70 *(978-1-4296-5115-8(6),* Fact Finders) Capstone Press of Coughlan Cos.

Mendez, Antonio J. & Mendez, Jonna. Going Undercover: Disguise & Secret Identities. 2007. (Illus.). 32p. (J). pap. *(978-0-545-01558-5(8))* Scholastic, Inc.

Spilsbury, Richard, et al. Anatomy of an Investigation. 2013. (Anatomy of an Investigation Ser.). (ENG.). 56p. (gr. 7-8). pap. 47.45 *(978-1-4329-7611-8(7));* lib. bdg. 103.95 *(978-1-4329-7605-7(2))* Heinemann-Raintree.

INVESTMENTS

see also Bonds; Stock Exchanges; Stocks

Bamber, Lori. Sleep-Easy Investing: The Canadian Guide to Lower-Risk & Income Investing. 2004. (ENG.). 288p. pap. 17.38 *(978-0-470-83431-2(5))* Wiley, John & Sons, Inc.

Bateman, Katherine R. The Young Investor: Projects & Activities for Making Your Money Grow. 2nd ed. 2010. (ENG., Illus.). 144p. (J). (gr. 4). pap. 14.95 *(978-1-56976-546-3(4))* Chicago Review Pr., Inc.

Benjamin, Tina. My Piggy Bank. 2015. (Inside My World Ser.). (ENG.). 24p. (J). (gr. k-k). lib. bdg. 22.60 *(978-1-4824-1808-8(8))* Stevens, Gareth Publishing LLLP.

Best, B. J. Investing Your Money. 2015. (J). lib. bdg. *(978-1-62713-391-3(7));* (ENG.). 48p. (gr. 4-4). 31.36 *(978-1-5026-0103-2(6))* Cavendish Square Publishing.

Bonnice, Sherry. Financial Advisor. Riggs, Ernestine G. & Gholar, Cheryl, eds. 2013. (Careers with Character Ser.: 18). 96p. (J). (gr. 7-18). 22.95 *(978-1-4222-2755-8(3))* Mason Crest.

Crayton, Lisa A. & Furang, Kathy. The Stock Market: What It Is & How It Works. 2016. (Economics in the 21st Century Ser.). (ENG.). 96p. (J). (gr. 8-8). 34.60 *(978-0-7660-7384-5(X))* Enslow Pubs., Inc.

Dakers, Diane. It Doesn't Grow on Trees: Sources of Income. 2017. (Financial Literacy for Life Ser.). (ENG.). 48p. (J). ***(978-0-7787-3096-5(4));*** pap. ***(978-0-7787-3105-4(7))*** Crabtree Publishing Co.

—Money for Your Life: Invest in Your Financial Future. 2017. (Financial Literacy for Life Ser.). (ENG.). 48p. (J). ***(978-0-7787-3098-9(0));*** pap. ***(978-0-7787-3107-8(3))*** Crabtree Publishing Co.

Dugan, Christine. From Rags to Riches, 1 vol. 2nd rev. ed. 2013. (Nonfiction Readers Ser.). (ENG., Illus.). 64p. (J). (gr. 5-5). pap. 31.96 *(978-1-4333-7433-3(1))* Teacher Created Materials, Inc.

—Where Does Your Money Go?, 1 vol. 2nd rev. ed. 2013. (Nonfiction Readers Ser.). (ENG., Illus.). 64p. (J). (gr. 5-5). pap. 31.96 *(978-1-4333-7432-6(3))* Teacher Created Materials, Inc.

Einspruch, Andrew. Managing Money. 2012. (Money Sense Ser.). (Illus.). 32p. (gr. 4-6). lib. bdg. 28.50 *(978-1-59920-432-1(0))* Black Rabbit Bks.

Fabris, Judith. Money...Cool! Brolin, Carol, illus. l.t. ed. 2003. 155p. (YA). pap. 9.95 *(978-1-893335-12-7(7))* Archipelago Pr.

Fitzgerald, Lee. Goods & Services. 2013. (InfoMax Readers Ser.). (ENG.). 24p. (J). (gr. 2-3). pap. 8.25 *(978-1-4777-2415-6(X));* pap. 49.50 *(978-1-4777-2416-3(8))* Rosen Publishing Group, Inc., The. (Rosen Classroom).

Fradin, Dennis B. & Fradin, Judith Bloom. Saving. 2010. (Money Smart Ser.). 64p. (gr. 4). 32.79 *(978-1-60870-125-4(5))* Marshall Cavendish GBR. Dist: Marshall Cavendish Corp.

Fradin, Dennis Brindell & Fradin, Judith Bloom. Investing. 2010. (Money Smart Ser.). 64p. (gr. 4). 32.79 *(978-1-60870-124-7(7))* Marshall Cavendish Corp.

Gagne, Tammy. A Dividend Stock Strategy for Teens. 2013. (Illus.). 48p. (gr. 4-8). lib. bdg. 29.95 *(978-1-61228-426-2(4))* Mitchell Lane Pubs., Inc.

—Investment Options for Teens. 2013. (ENG., Illus.). 48p. (gr. 4-8). lib. bdg. 29.95 *(978-1-61228-540-5(6))* Mitchell Lane Pubs., Inc.

—A Teen Guide to Buying Bonds. 2013. (ENG., Illus.). 48p. (gr. 4-8). lib. bdg. 29.95 *(978-1-61228-424-8(8))* Mitchell Lane Pubs., Inc.

—A Teen Guide to Safe-Haven Savings. 2013. (Illus.). 48p. (gr. 4-8). lib. bdg. 29.95 *(978-1-61228-428-6(0))* Mitchell Lane Pubs., Inc.

—Teen Guide to Saving & Investing. 2014. (Illus.). 48p. (gr. 4-8). lib. bdg. 29.95 *(978-1-61228-471-2(X))* Mitchell Lane Pubs., Inc.

Healy, Aaron. Making the Trade: Stocks, Bonds, & Other Investments. 2011. (Global Marketplace Ser.). (ENG.). 56p. (gr. 6-9). pap. 9.95 *(978-1-4329-5478-9(4),* NA-h) Heinemann-Raintree.

Hollander, Barbara. Top 10 Secrets for Investing Successfully. 2013. (Student's Guide to Financial Empowerment Ser.). (Illus.). 64p. (YA). (gr. 7-12). pap. 12.95 *(978-1-4488-9371-3(2))* Rosen Publishing Group, Inc., The.

Hollander, Barbara & Gottfried Hollander, Barbara. Top 10 Secrets for Investing Successfully. 2013. (Illus.). 64p. (YA). (gr. 7-12). 31.95 *(978-1-4488-9357-7(7))* Rosen Publishing Group, Inc., The.

Karlitz, Gail & Honig, Debbie. Growing Money: A Complete Investing Guide for Kids. Lewis, Stephen, illus. 2010. (ENG.). 144p. (J). (gr. 3-7). 8.99 *(978-0-8431-9905-5(9),* Price Stern Sloan) Penguin Young Readers Group.

Kiyosaki, Robert T. Rich Dad Poor Dad for Teens. 2011. 14.44 *(978-0-7848-3384-1(2),* Everbind) Marco Bk. Co.

—Rich Dad's Escape from the Rat Race: How to Become a Rich Kid by Following Rich Dad's Advice. 2013. (ENG.). 64p. (J). pap. 12.95 *(978-1-61268-055-2(0))* Plata Publishing.

Kiyosaki, Robert T. & Lechter, Sharon L. Rich Dad's Escape from the Rat Race: How to Become a Rich Kid by Following Rich Dad's Advice. Hoseley, Rantz, illus. 2005. (ENG.). 64p. (J). (gr. 3-7). pap. 9.99 *(978-0-316-00047-5(7))* Little, Brown Bks. for Young Readers.

—The Secrets about Money: That You Don't Learn in School! 2004. (ENG.). 160p. (J). (gr. 7-17). pap. 14.99 *(978-0-446-69321-9(9))* Little, Brown Bks. for Young Readers.

Kjelle, Marylou Morano. A Teen Guide to Buying Mutual Funds. 2013. (Illus.). 48p. (gr. 4-8). lib. bdg. 29.95 *(978-1-61228-427-9(2))* Mitchell Lane Pubs., Inc.
Kowalski, Kathiann M. Be Smart about Investing: Planning, Saving, & the Stock Market. 2014. (Be Smart about Money & Financial Literacy Ser.). 48p. (J). lib. bdg. 22.60 *(978-0-7660-4281-0(2))* Enslow Pubs., Inc.
Kulp, Donald. Money Puppies: America's #1 Money Management Book for Kids. 2010. 36p. pap. 14.99 *(978-1-4490-8977-1(1))* AuthorHouse.
Marsico, Katie. Investing: Making Your Money Work for You. 2015. (21st Century Skills Library: Real World Math Ser.). (ENG., Illus.). 32p. (J). (gr. 4-7). 29.93 *(978-1-63362-571-6(0)*, 206468) Cherry Lake Publishing.
Matheson, Murdoch H. Building Wealth for Teens: Answers to Questions Teens Care About. 2007. 116p. 24.65 *(978-1-4251-2358-1(9))* Trafford Publishing.
McGuire, Kara. Making Money Work: A Teen's Guide to Saving, Investing, & Building Wealth, 1 vol. 2014. (Financial Literacy for Teens Ser.). (ENG.). 64p. (gr. 6-7). lib. bdg. 33.99 *(978-0-7565-4922-0(1)*, CPB Grades 4-8) Compass Point Bks.
Meachen Rau, Dana. Saving Money. 2010. (Money & Banks Ser.). (Illus.). 24p. (gr. 2-5). pap. 8.15 *(978-1-4339-3387-5(X))* Stevens, Gareth Publishing LLLP.
Minden, Cecilia. Investing: Making Your Money Work for You. 2007. (21st Century Skills Library: Real World Math Ser.). (ENG., Illus.). 32p. (gr. 4-8). lib. bdg. 28.50 *(978-1-60279-003-2(5)*, 200069) Cherry Lake Publishing.
Monroe Peterson, Judy. Smart Strategies for Investing Wisely & Successfully. 2014. (Financial Security & Life Success for Teens Ser.). 80p. (J). (gr. 7-12). pap. 84.90 *(978-1-4777-7621-6(4))* Rosen Publishing Group, Inc., The.
Morrison, Jessica. Investing. 2017. (J). ***(978-1-5105-1945-9(9))*** SmartBook Media, Inc.
—Investing. 2009. (Everyday Economics Ser.). (Illus.). 32p. (J). (gr. 4-6). pap. 9.95 *(978-1-60596-650-2(9))*; lib. bdg. 26.00 *(978-1-60596-649-6(5))* Weigl Pubs., Inc.
—Saving. 2009. (Everyday Economics Ser.). (Illus.). 32p. (J). (gr. 4-6). pap. 9.95 *(978-1-60596-648-9(7))*; lib. bdg. 26.00 *(978-1-60596-647-2(9))* Weigl Pubs., Inc.
Murray, Laura K. Berkshire-Hathaway: Built for Success. 2016. (Built for Success Ser.). (ENG., Illus.). 48p. (J). (gr. 5-9). pap. 12.00 *(978-1-62832-158-6(X)*, Creative Paperbacks) Creative Co., The.
—The Story of Berkshire Hathaway. 2015. (Illus.). 48p. (J). *(978-1-60818-557-3(5)*, Creative Education) Creative Co., The.
O'Neal, Claire. A Teen Guide to Buying Stocks. 2013. (ENG., Illus.). 48p. (gr. 4-8). lib. bdg. 29.95 *(978-1-61228-425-5(6))* Mitchell Lane Pubs., Inc.
Orr, Tamra. A Kid's Guide to Stock Market Investing. 2008. (Money Matters Ser.). (Illus.). 48p. (YA). (gr. 3-6). lib. bdg. 29.95 *(978-1-58415-642-0(2))* Mitchell Lane Pubs., Inc.
Randolph, Ryan P. How to Save & Invest. 2013. (Smart Kid's Guide to Personal Finance Ser.). (Illus.). 24p. (J). (gr. 3-6). pap. 49.50 *(978-1-4777-0826-2(X))*; pap. 8.25 *(978-1-4777-0825-5(1))*; lib. bdg. 22.60 *(978-1-4777-0742-5(5))* Rosen Publishing Group, Inc., The. (PowerKids Pr.).
Rau, Dana Meachen. Saving Money. 2010. (Money & Banks Ser.). (Illus.). 24p. (J). (gr. 2-5). lib. bdg. 22.00 *(978-1-4339-3386-8(1))* Stevens, Gareth Publishing LLLP.
Reynolds, Mattie. Saving for the Future: An Introduction to Financial Literacy. 2013. (Start Smart: Money Ser.). (Illus.). 24p. (gr. k-2). (J). lib. bdg. 17.95 net. *(978-1-937529-42-0(8))*; (ENG., pap. 5.95 *(978-1-937529-38-3(X))* Red Chair Pr.
Rumsch, BreAnn. Saving & Investing, 1 vol. 2012. (Economy in Action! Ser.). (ENG.). 32p. (J). (gr. 3-6). lib. bdg. 27.07 *(978-1-61783-490-5(4)*, Checkerboard Library) ABDO Publishing Co.
Swanson, Jennifer A. Top 10 Secrets for Saving Successfully. 2013. (Student's Guide to Financial Empowerment Ser.). 64p. (YA). (gr. 7-12). 31.95 *(978-1-4488-9356-0(9))*; pap. 77.70 *(978-1-4488-9379-9(8))*; (ENG., Illus.). pap. 12.95 *(978-1-4488-9378-2(X)*, Rosen Classroom) Rosen Publishing Group, Inc., The.
Thompson, Helen. Understanding the Stock Market. 2010. (Junior Library of Money). 64p. (YA). (gr. 7-18). lib. bdg. 22.95 *(978-1-4222-1773-3(6))* Mason Crest.

IOWA

Brown, Vanessa. Iowa. (Bilingual Library of the United States of America Ser.). (ENG & SPA.). 32p. 2009. (gr. 2-2). 47.90 *(978-1-60853-360-2(3)*, Editorial Buenas Letras) 2005. (Illus.). (J). (gr. 3-6). lib. bdg. 25.25 *(978-1-4042-3080-4(7))* Rosen Publishing Group, Inc., The.
Daily Nonpareil Staff, prod. Heroes Remembered. 2003. (Illus.). 192p. per. 27.95 *(978-0-9745410-2-0(8))* Omaha Bks.
Deinard, Jenny. How to Draw Iowa's Sights & Symbols. 2009. (Kid's Guide to Drawing America Ser.). 32p. (gr. k-k). 50.50 *(978-1-61511-064-3(X)*, PowerKids Pr.) Rosen Publishing Group, Inc., The.
Dykstra, Mary. Iowa. 2006. (Portraits of the States Ser.). (Illus.). 32p. (gr. 2-6). (J). lib. bdg. 26.00 *(978-0-8368-4664-5(8))*; pap. 10.50 *(978-0-8368-4683-6(4))* Stevens, Gareth Publishing LLLP. (Gareth Stevens Learning Library).
Freedman, Jeri. Iowa: Past & Present. 2010. (United States: Past & Present Ser.). (ENG., Illus.). 48p. (J). pap. 11.75 *(978-1-4358-8485-4(X))*; lib. bdg. 29.25 *(978-1-4358-3517-7(4))* Rosen Publishing Group, Inc., The. (Rosen Reference).
Haack, Kelly J. Iowa: A MyReportLinks. Com Book. 2003. (States Ser.). (Illus.). 48p. (J). lib. bdg. 25.26 *(978-0-7660-5146-1(3)*, MyReportLinks.com Bks.) Enslow Pubs., Inc.
King, David C. Iowa. 2006. (It's My State! Ser.). (Illus.). 80p. (J). (gr. 4-7). lib. bdg. 29.93 *(978-0-7614-1928-0(4)*, Benchmark Bks.) Marshall Cavendish Corp.
LaDoux, Rita. Iowa. 2012. (J). lib. bdg. 25.26 *(978-0-7613-4532-9(9)*, Lerner Pubns.) Lerner Publishing Group.
Lusted, Marcia Amidon. Iowa: The Hawkeye State. 2010. (Our Amazing States Ser.). (ENG.). 24p. (J). pap. 8.25 *(978-1-4358-9790-8(0))*; lib. bdg. 22.60 *(978-1-4358-9348-1(4))* Rosen Publishing Group, Inc., The. (PowerKids Pr.).
Marsh, Carole. Iowa Current Events Projects: 30 Cool, Activities, Crafts, Experiments & More for Kids to Do to Learn about Your State! 2003. (Iowa Experience Ser.). 32p. (gr. k-5). pap. 5.95 *(978-0-635-02034-5(3)*, Marsh, Carole Bks.) Gallopade International.
—Iowa Geography Projects: 30 Cool, Activities, Crafts, Experiments & More for Kids to Do to Learn about Your State! 2003. (Iowa Experience Ser.). 32p. (gr. k-5). pap. 5.95 *(978-0-635-01834-2(9)*, Marsh, Carole Bks.) Gallopade International.
—Iowa Government Projects: 30 Cool, Activities, Crafts, Experiments & More for Kids to Do to Learn about Your State! 2003. (Iowa Experience Ser.). 32p. (gr. k-5). pap. 5.95 *(978-0-635-01934-9(5)*, Marsh, Carole Bks.) Gallopade International.
—Iowa People Projects: 30 Cool, Activities, Crafts, Experiments & More for Kids to Do to Learn about Your State! 2003. (Iowa Experience Ser.). 32p. (gr. k-5). pap. 5.95 *(978-0-635-01984-4(1)*, Marsh, Carole Bks.) Gallopade International.
—Iowa Symbols & Facts Projects: 30 Cool, Activities, Crafts, Experiments & More for Kids to Do to Learn about Your State! 2003. (Iowa Experience Ser.). 32p. (gr. k-5). pap. 5.95 *(978-0-635-01884-7(5)*, Marsh, Carole Bks.) Gallopade International.
Morrice, Polly Alison & Hart, Joyce. Iowa. 2nd rev. ed. 2006. (Celebrate the States Ser.). (Illus.). 144p. (gr. 6-7). lib. bdg. 42.79 *(978-0-7614-2350-8(8)*, Benchmark Bks.) Marshall Cavendish Corp.
Murray, Julie. Iowa, 1 vol. 2006. (United States Ser.). (ENG., Illus.). 32p. (gr. 2-4). 27.07 *(978-1-59197-674-5(X)*, Buddy Bks.) ABDO Publishing Co.
Myron, Vicki & Witter, Bret. Dewey: There's a Cat in the Library! James, Steve, illus. 2009. (ENG.). 40p. (J). (gr. -1-3). 16.99 *(978-0-316-06874-1(8))* Little, Brown Bks. for Young Readers.
—Dewey the Library Cat. 2011. (ENG., Illus.). 224p. (J). (gr. 3-7). pap., pap. 8.99 *(978-0-316-06870-3(5))* Little, Brown Bks. for Young Readers.
Patricia Pierce. Numbers in a Row: An Iowa Number Book. Rohner, Dorothia, illus. 2006. (Count Your Way Across the U. S. A. Ser.). (ENG.). 40p. (J). (gr. -1-3). 17.95 *(978-1-58536-164-9(X))* Sleeping Bear Pr.
Peterson, Sheryl. Iowa. 2008. (This Land Called America Ser.). (Illus.). 32p. (YA). (gr. 3-6). 22.95 *(978-1-58341-640-2(4))* Creative Co., The.
Pierce, Patricia A. H Is for Hawkeye: An Iowa Alphabet. Langton, Bruce, tr. Langton, Bruce, illus. 2003. (Discover America State by State Ser.). (ENG.). 40p. (J). 17.95 *(978-1-58536-114-4(3))* Sleeping Bear Pr.
Ryan, Pat. Iowa. 2013. (Exploring the States Ser.). (ENG., Illus.). 32p. (gr. 3-7). lib. bdg. 26.95 *(978-1-62617-014-8(2)*, Blastoff! Readers) Bellwether Media.
Sapre, Reshma & Vargus, Nanci Reginelli. Iowa. 2004. (Rookie Read-About Geography Ser.). (J). 20.50 *(978-0-516-22753-5(X)*, Children's Pr.) Scholastic Library Publishing.
Swanson, Angie. Iowa. 2016. (States Ser.). (ENG., Illus.). 32p. (gr. 3-4). lib. bdg. 27.32 *(978-1-5157-0402-7(5))* Next Page Pr., The.
Wheeler, Jill C. Iowa, 1 vol. 2009. (United States Ser.). (ENG., Illus.). 48p. (YA). (gr. 2-5). 27.07 *(978-1-60453-650-8(0))* ABDO Publishing Co.
Winans, Jay D. Iowa. 2011. (Guide to American States Ser.). (Illus.). 48p. (YA). (gr. 3-6). 29.99 *(978-1-61690-787-7(8))* Weigl Pubs., Inc.
Woods, Jessica I. Iowa. 2003. (Seeds of a Nation Ser.). (Illus.). 48p. (J). 23.70 *(978-0-7377-1396-1(8)*, Greenhaven Pr., Inc.) Cengage Gale.

IOWA—FICTION

Atwood, Megan. Dear Molly, Dear Olive. Fleming, Lucy, illus. 2016. (Dear Molly, Dear Olive Ser.). (ENG.). 96p. (gr. 1-3). 87.96 *(978-1-4795-8701-8(X))* Picture Window Bks.
—Molly Discovers Magic (Then Wants to Un-Discover It) Fleming, Lucy, illus. 2017. (Dear Molly, Dear Olive Ser.). (ENG.). 96p. (gr. 1-3). pap. 5.95 *(978-1-62370-616-6(5))* Picture Window Bks.
—Molly Meets Trouble (Whose Real Name Is Jenna) Fleming, Lucy, illus. 2016. (Dear Molly, Dear Olive Ser.). (ENG.). 96p. (gr. 1-3). lib. bdg. 21.99 *(978-1-4795-8696-7(X))* Picture Window Bks.
—Olive Finds Treasure (of the Most Precious Kind) Fleming, Lucy, illus. (Dear Molly, Dear Olive Ser.). (ENG.). 96p. (gr. 1-3). 2017. pap. 5.95 *(978-1-62370-615-9(7))* 2016. lib. bdg. 21.99 *(978-1-4795-8693-6(5))* Picture Window Bks.
—Olive Spins a Tale (and It's a Doozy!) Fleming, Lucy, illus. 2016. (Dear Molly, Dear Olive Ser.). (ENG.). 96p. (gr. 1-3). lib. bdg. 21.99 *(978-1-4795-8695-0(1))* Picture Window Bks.
Backes, M. Molly. The Princesses of Iowa. (ENG.). 464p. (YA). (gr. 9). 2014. pap. 9.99 *(978-0-7636-7161-7(4))* 2012. (Illus.). 16.99 *(978-0-7636-5312-5(8))* Candlewick Pr.
Barnhill, Kelly. The Mostly True Story of Jack. 2012. (ENG.). 352p. (J). (gr. 3-7). pap. 8.99 *(978-0-316-05672-4(3))* Little, Brown Bks. for Young Readers.
Bauer, Joan. Squashed. 2005. (ENG.). 208p. (YA). (gr. 7-7). pap. 7.99 *(978-0-14-240426-3(8)*, Speak) Penguin Young Readers Group.
—Squashed. 2005. 194p. (gr. 7-12). 18.00 *(978-0-7569-5781-0(8))* Perfection Learning Corp.
Burd, Nick. The Vast Fields of Ordinary. 2009. (ENG.). 320p. (YA). (gr. 9-18). 16.99 *(978-0-8037-3340-4(2)*, Dial Bks) Penguin Young Readers Group.
Butler, Dori Hillestad. Sliding into Home, 1 vol. 2005. (ENG.). 192p. (J). (gr. 3-7). pap. 7.95 *(978-1-56145-341-2(2))* Peachtree Pubs.
Carr, Elias & Karre, Andrew. Fight the Wind. 2012. (After the Dust Settled Ser.). (ENG.). 104p. (YA). (gr. 6-12). pap. 7.95 *(978-0-8225-9034-7(4)*, Darby Creek); lib. bdg. 27.93 *(978-0-7613-8331-4(X))* Lerner Publishing Group.
Chan, Crystal. Bird. (ENG.). (J). (gr. 3-7). 2015. 320p. pap. 8.99 *(978-1-4424-5091-2(6))* 2014. (Illus.). 304p. 16.99 *(978-1-4424-5089-9(4)*, Atheneum Bks. for Young Readers) Simon & Schuster Children's Publishing.
Cornelison, Sue F., illus. The Twelve Days of Christmas in Iowa. 2010. (Twelve Days of Christmas in America Ser.). (ENG.). 40p. (J). (gr. k). 12.95 *(978-1-4027-6710-4(2))* Sterling Publishing Co., Inc.
Cottrell-Bentley, Lisa M. Wright on Time: Iowa. Bauerle, Tanja, illus. 2013. 164p. pap. 12.99 *(978-1-937848-06-4(X))* Do Life Right, Inc.
Delashmutt, Amy. Hello, Cy! Torgeson, Sarah, illus. 2007. 24p. (J). lib. bdg. 14.95 *(978-1-932888-53-9(5))* Mascot Bks., Inc.
Duey, Kathleen & Grosset and Dunlap Staff. Katie & the Mustang, Bk. 1. 2004. (Hoofbeats Ser.: 1). (ENG.). 144p. (J). (gr. 3-7). pap. 5.99 *(978-0-14-240090-6(4)*, Puffin Books) Penguin Young Readers Group.
Gorman, Carol & Findley, Ron J. The Stumptown Kid, 1 vol. 2005. (ENG.). 224p. (J). (gr. 3-7). 15.95 *(978-1-56145-337-5(4))* Peachtree Pubs.
Hautman, Pete. The Flinkwater Factor: A Novel in Five Thrilling Episodes. 2015. (Flinkwater Chronicles Ser.: 1). (ENG.). 256p. (J). (gr. 4-8). 16.99 *(978-1-4814-3251-1(6)*, Simon & Schuster Bks. For Young Readers) Simon & Schuster Bks. For Young Readers.
Jacobs, Lily. The Littlest Bunny in Iowa: An Easter Adventure. 2015. (ENG.). 32p. (J). (-3). 9.99 *(978-1-4926-1087-8(9)*, Sourcebooks Jabberwocky) Sourcebooks, Inc.
James, Eric. A Halloween Scare in Iowa. Le Ray, Marina, illus. 2014. (ENG.). 32p. (J). (-5). 9.99 *(978-1-4926-0594-2(8)*, 9781492605942, Sourcebooks Jabberwocky) Sourcebooks, Inc.
—Santa's Sleigh Is on Its Way to Iowa. Dunn, Robert, illus. 2015. (ENG.). 32p. (J). (-2). 12.99 *(978-1-4926-2749-4(6)*, Sourcebooks Jabberwocky) Sourcebooks, Inc.
Judybee. Danny Strikes Out in Americ: A R. E. A. d Book. Kecskés, Anna, illus. 2013. 32p. pap. *(978-1-78092-335-2(X))* MX Publishing, Ltd.
Keast, Ellen Frances. A Rainy Week. 2011. 16p. pap. 10.00 *(978-1-60976-777-8(2)*, Eloquent Bks.) Strategic Book Publishing & Rights Agency (SBPRA).
Kraus, Daniel. Scowler. 2014. (ENG.). 304p. (YA). (gr. 9). pap. 9.99 *(978-0-385-74310-5(6)*, Ember) Random Hse. Children's Bks.
Mahmoodian, Maryam. Muslim Teens In: Pitfalls & Pranks. 2008. (YA). per. 10.95 *(978-0-9793577-3-2(X))* Muslim Writers Publishing.
Mary-Todd, Jonathan. Pig City. 2012. (After the Dust Settled Ser.). (ENG.). 112p. (YA). (gr. 6-12). pap. 7.95 *(978-0-8225-8746-0(7)*, Darby Creek); lib. bdg. 27.93 *(978-0-7613-8328-4(X))* Lerner Publishing Group.
Night, P. J. The Ride of Your Life. 2014. (You're Invited to a Creepover Ser.: 18). (ENG., Illus.). 160p. (J). (gr. 3-7). pap. 6.99 *(978-1-4424-9729-0(7)*, Simon Spotlight) Simon Spotlight.
—The Ride of Your Life. 2014. (Creepover Ser.: 18). lib. bdg. 17.20 *(978-0-606-35431-8(X))* Turtleback Bks.
Ray, Delia. Here Lies Linc. (ENG.). 320p. (J). (gr. 3-7). 2012. 7.99 *(978-0-375-86538-1(1)*, Yearling) 2011. 16.99 *(978-0-375-86757-6(0)*, Knopf Bks. for Young Readers) Random Hse. Children's Bks.
Rylant, Cynthia. Old Town in the Green Groves. 2007. (Little House Ser.). (ENG.). 192p. (J). (gr. 3-7). pap. 6.99 *(978-0-06-088546-5(7))* HarperCollins Pubs.
Silvano, Wendi. Love Is All Around Iowa. Czernichowska, Joanna, illus. 2016. (ENG.). 32p. (J). (-6). 12.99 *(978-1-4926-2924-5(3)*, Sourcebooks Jabberwocky) Sourcebooks, Inc.
Smallman, Steve. Santa Is Coming to Iowa. Dunn, Robert, illus. 2013. (ENG.). 32p. (J). (-3). 9.99 *(978-1-4022-8818-0(2)*, Sourcebooks Jabberwocky) Sourcebooks, Inc.
Smith, Andrew. Grasshopper Jungle. 2015. (ENG.). 416p. (YA). (gr. 9). pap. 10.99 *(978-0-14-242500-8(1)*, Speak) Penguin Young Readers Group.
Stromberg, Ronica. A Shadow in the Dark. 2009. (J). pap. *(978-0-88092-751-2(8))*; lib. bdg. *(978-0-88092-750-5(X))* Royal Fireworks Publishing Co.
Tyler, Maggie Ann. Fantasy on 4th Street. 2011. 36p. pap. 20.99 *(978-1-4670-3591-0(2))* AuthorHouse.
Walter-Sereg, D. Bonnie, the Trapeze Artist. 2012. 32p. pap. 24.95 *(978-1-4626-5858-9(X))* America Star Bks.
—Bonnie Tracks a Jungle Animal. 2012. 24p. 24.95 *(978-1-4626-5857-2(1))* America Star Bks.
Warner, Gertrude Chandler. The Clue in the Corn Maze. 2004. (Boxcar Children Ser.: No. 101). (Illus.). 128p. (J). (gr. 2-7). 14.99 *(978-0-8075-5556-9(8))* Whitman, Albert & Co.
Warner, Gertrude Chandler, creator. The Clue in the Corn Maze. 2004. (Boxcar Children Mysteries Ser.: 101). (ENG., Illus.). 136p. (J). (gr. 1-5). 6.99 *(978-0-8075-5557-6(6))* Whitman, Albert & Co.
Weber, John. Orphan. 2010. 266p. (YA). (gr. 7-18). 16.95 *(978-1-934813-38-6(9))* Westside Bks.
Wells, Helen. Cherry Ames, Rural Nurse. 2007. (Cherry Ames Nurse Stories Ser.). 224p. (J). (gr. 3-7). 14.95 *(978-0-8261-0425-0(8))* Springer Publishing Co., Inc.
Wetterer, Margaret K. The Midnight Adventure of Kate Shelley, Train Rescuer. 2010. pap. 51.02 *(978-0-7613-6919-6(8))* Lerner Publishing Group.
—The Midnight Adventure of Kate Shelley, Train Rescuer. Trover, Zachary, illus. 2010. (History's Kid Heroes Ser.). (ENG.). 32p. (gr. 3-5). 26.60 *(978-0-7613-6173-2(1))*; pap. 8.95 *(978-0-7613-6192-3(8)*, Graphic Universe™) Lerner Publishing Group.
Wood, Nathaniel. Play Me Backwards. 2014. (ENG., Illus.). 288p. (YA). (gr. 9). 18.99 *(978-1-4814-0102-9(5)*, Simon & Schuster Bks. For Young Readers) Simon & Schuster Bks. For Young Readers.
Woodson, Jacqueline. Beneath a Meth Moon: An Elegy. (ENG.). (YA). (gr. 7). 2013. 240p. pap. 8.99 *(978-0-14-242392-9(0)*, Speak) 2012. 144p. 16.99 *(978-0-399-25250-1(9)*, Nancy Paulsen Books) Penguin Young Readers Group.
—Beneath a Meth Moon: An Elegy. 2013. lib. bdg. 19.65 *(978-0-606-30566-2(1)*, Turtleback) Turtleback Bks.
Yansky, Brian. Utopia, Iowa. 2015. (ENG.). 336p. (YA). (gr. 9). 17.99 *(978-0-7636-6533-3(9))* Candlewick Pr.
Ylvisaker, Anne. Button Down. (ENG.). 192p. (J). (gr. 3-7). 2013. pap. 6.99 *(978-0-7636-6463-3(4))* 2012. (Illus.). 15.99 *(978-0-7636-5396-5(9))* Candlewick Pr.
—The Curse of the Buttons. 2014. (ENG.). 240p. (J). (gr. 3-7). 15.99 *(978-0-7636-6138-0(4))* Candlewick Pr.
—The Luck of the Buttons. 2012. (ENG., Illus.). 240p. (J). (gr. 3-7). pap. 6.99 *(978-0-7636-6061-1(2))* Candlewick Pr.

IOWA—HISTORY

Blashfield, Jean F. Iowa (Revised Edition) 2014. (America the Beautiful, Third Ser. (Revised Edition) Ser.). (ENG.). 144p. (J). lib. bdg. 40.00 *(978-0-531-28279-3(1))* Scholastic Library Publishing.
Gamble, Adam & Jasper, Mark. Good Night Iowa. 2013. (Good Night Our World Ser.). (ENG., Illus.). 20p. (J). (— 1). bds. 9.95 *(978-1-60219-085-6(2))* Good Night Bks.
Gillespie, Sarah. Diary of Sarah Gillespie: A Pioneer Farm Girl, 1 vol. 2014. (First-Person Histories Ser.). (ENG.). 32p. (gr. 3-4). lib. bdg. 27.32 *(978-1-4765-4194-5(9)*, Fact Finders) Capstone Press of Coughlan Cos.
Jerome, Kate B. Lucky to Live in Iowa. 2017. (Arcadia Kids Ser.). (ENG., Illus.). 32p. (J). 16.99 ***(978-0-7385-2801-4(3))*** Arcadia Publishing.
Kavanaugh, Dorothy. Central Mississippi River Basin: Arkansas, Iowa, Missouri, Vol. 19. 2015. (Let's Explore the States Ser.). (Illus.). 64p. (J). (gr. 5). lib. bdg. 23.95 *(978-1-4222-3321-4(9))* Mason Crest.
King, David C. Iowa. 2014. (J). lib. bdg. *(978-1-62712-222-1(2))* Musa Publishing.
King, David C. & Stanmyre, Jackie F. Iowa. 2016. (It's My State! (r) Ser.). 80p. (J). (gr. 4-4). 34.21 *(978-1-62713-238-1(4))* Cavendish Square Publishing.
Marciniak, Kristin. What's Great about Iowa? 2015. (Our Great States Ser.). (ENG.). 32p. (gr. 2-5). pap. 7.95 *(978-1-4677-6092-8(7))*; lib. bdg. 26.60 *(978-1-4677-3868-2(9))* Lerner Publishing Group. (Lerner Pubns.).
Marsh, Carole. Exploring Iowa Through Project-Based Learning. 2016. (Iowa Experience Ser.). (ENG.). (J). pap. 9.99 *(978-0-635-12339-8(8))* Gallopade International.
—Iowa History Projects: 30 Cool, Activities, Crafts, Experiments & More for Kids to Do to Learn about Your State! 2003. (Iowa Experience Ser.). 32p. (gr. k-5). pap. 5.95 *(978-0-635-01784-0(9)*, Marsh, Carole Bks.) Gallopade International.
Murray, Julie. Iowa, 1 vol. 2012. (Explore the United States Ser.). (ENG.). 32p. (J). (gr. 2-5). 28.50 *(978-1-61783-353-3(3))* ABDO Publishing Co.
Poole, Marcia. Building a Dream: The Story of the Sioux City Lewis & Clark Interpretive Center. 2004. (Illus.). 60p. per. 10.95 *(978-0-9753860-0-2(X))* Sioux City Lewis & Clark Interpretive Ctr., The.
Schwieder, Dorothy, et al. Iowa Past to Present: The People & the Prairie. 3rd rev. ed. 2011. (Iowa & the Midwest Experience Ser.). (ENG., Illus.). 352p. pap. 39.95 *(978-1-60938-036-6(3))* Univ. of Iowa Pr.
Wagner, Jay. H Is for Hawkeye. Potts Dawson, Eileen, illus. 2003. (J). 16.95 *(978-1-931599-11-5(4))*, Trails Bks.) Bower Hse.
Winans, Jay D. Iowa: The Hawkeye State. 2016. (J). *(978-1-4896-4860-0(7))* Weigl Pubs., Inc.
Yasuda, Anita. Iowa: The Hawkeye State. 2012. (J). 27.13 *(978-1-61913-349-5(0))* Weigl Pubs., Inc.

IRAN

Bauder, Julia. Is Iran a Threat to Global Security? (At Issue Ser.). (ENG., Illus.). 114p. (J). (gr. 10-12). 2006. pap. 31.80 *(978-0-7377-3526-0(0))* 2004. 22.50 *(978-0-7377-3527-7(9))* Cengage Gale. (Greenhaven Pr., Inc.).
DiPrimio, Pete. We Visit Iran. 2011. (Your Land & My Land Ser.). (Illus.). 64p. (J). (gr. 4-7). lib. bdg. 33.95 *(978-1-58415-954-4(5))* Mitchell Lane Pubs., Inc.
Gray, Leon & U. S. National Geographic Society Staff. National Geographic Countries of the World - Iran. 2008. (National Geographic Countries of the World Ser.). (ENG., Illus.). 64p. (J). (gr. 5). lib. bdg. 27.90 *(978-1-4263-0200-8(2)*, National Geographic Children's Bks.) National Geographic Society.
Haugen, David M. Iran. 2010. (Opposing Viewpoints Ser.). (ENG.). 224p. (gr. 10-12). 48.80 *(978-0-7377-4972-4(5))*; pap. 33.80 *(978-0-7377-4973-1(3))* Cengage Gale. (Greenhaven Pr., Inc.).
Kaplan, Leslie C. A Primary Source Guide to Iran. (Countries of the World). 24p. 2009. (gr. 2-3). 42.50 *(978-1-61512-034-5(3))* 2005. (Illus.). (J). (gr. k-5). lib. bdg. 22.60 *(978-1-4042-2754-5(7))* Rosen Publishing Group, Inc., The. (PowerKids Pr.).
Kenney, Karen Latchana. Iran, 1 vol. 2011. (Countries of the World Set 1 Ser.). (ENG., Illus.). 144p. (J). (gr. 6-12). lib. bdg. 37.07 *(978-1-61783-112-6(3))* ABDO Publishing Co.
Mara, Wil. Iran. 2006. (Discovering Cultures Ser.). (Illus.). 48p. lib. bdg. 28.50 *(978-0-7614-1986-0(1)*, Benchmark Bks.) Marshall Cavendish Corp.
Mattern, Joanne. Iran. 2017. ***(978-1-5026-2494-9(X))*** Cavendish Square Publishing.
Miller, William. Tales of Persia: Missionary Stories from Islamic Iran. Van Patten, Bruce, illus. 2005. 163p. per. 9.99 *(978-0-87552-615-7(2))* P & R Publishing.
Orr, Tamra. Iran & Nuclear Weapons. 2009. (Understanding Iran Ser.). (Illus.). 80p. (YA). (gr. 7-12). lib. bdg. 33.25 *(978-1-4358-5281-5(8))* Rosen Publishing Group, Inc., The.
Prentzas. It's Cool to Learn about Countries: Iran. 2012. (Explorer Library: Social Studies Explorer Ser.). (ENG.). 48p. (gr. 4-8). 31.36 *(978-1-61080-440-0(6)*, 202050); pap. 15.64 *(978-1-61080-614-5(X)*, 202224) Cherry Lake Publishing.
Rajendra, Vijeya & Kaplan, Gisela T. Iran. 2nd rev. ed. 2003. (Cultures of the World Ser.). (Illus.). 144p. (gr. 6-18). lib. bdg. 42.79 *(978-0-7614-1665-4(X)*, Marshall Cavendish Reference Bks.) Marshall Cavendish Corp.
Reece, Katherine E. The Persians: Warriors of the Ancient World. 2004. (Ancient Civilizations Ser.). (Illus.). 48p. (gr. 4-8). lib. bdg. *(978-1-59515-238-1(5))* Rourke Educational Media.
Richardson, Adele. Iran. 2006. (My First Look at Countries Ser.). (Illus.). 24p. (J). (gr. -1-3). lib. bdg. 15.95 *(978-1-58341-446-0(0)*, Creative Education) Creative Co., The.
Simmons, Walter. Iran. 2011. (Exploring Countries Ser.). (ENG., Illus.). 32p. (J). (gr. 3-7). lib. bdg. 26.95 *(978-1-60014-591-9(4)*, Blastoff! Readers) Bellwether Media.
Spencer, Lauren. Iran: A Primary Source Cultural Guide. 2009. (Primary Sources of World Cultures Ser.). 128p. (gr. 4-5). 79.90 *(978-1-60851-924-8(4))* Rosen Publishing Group, Inc., The.

H
I

Zimmerman, W. Frederick. Cool Maps of Iran: Persian History, Oil Wealth, Politics, Population, Religion, Satellite, WMD & More. 2007. 32p. per. 17.36 *(978-1-934840-13-9(0))* Nimble Bks. LLC.

IRAN—FICTION

Ahour, Paravish. All Children of the World Smile in the Same Language: Iran, the Cradle of Civilization. 2006. (Illus.). 103p. (J). (gr. 4-7). per. 16.95 *(978-1-60002-015-5(1),* 3593) Mountain Valley Publishing, LLC.

Akbarpour, Ahmad. Good Night, Commander, 1 vol. Eskandani, Shadi & Mixter, Helen, trs. from PER. Zahedi, Morteza, illus. 2010. (ENG.). 24p. (J). (gr. 1). 17.95 *(978-0-88899-989-4(5))* Groundwood Bks. CAN. Dist: Publishers Group West (PGW).

Disney Press Staff. Valley of Vipers. 2010. 144p. pap. 4.99 *(978-1-4231-1007-1(2))* Disney Pr.

Dumas, Firoozeh. It Ain't So Awful, Falafel. 2017. (ENG.). 384p. (J). (gr. 5-7). pap. 7.99 ***(978-1-328-74096-0(X),*** HMH Books For Young Readers) Houghton Mifflin Harcourt Publishing Co.

Ellis, Deborah. Moon at Nine, 1 vol. 2014. (ENG.). 224p. (YA). (gr. 8-12). 15.95 *(978-1-927485-57-6(6))* Pajama Pr. CAN. Dist: Ingram Publisher Services.

Farizan, Sara. If You Could Be Mine. (ENG.). (YA). (gr. 9-12). 2014. 272p. pap. 9.95 *(978-1-61620-455-6(9),* 73455) 2013. 256p. 16.95 *(978-1-61620-251-4(3),* 73251) Algonquin Bks. of Chapel Hill.

Fletcher, Susan. Alphabet of Dreams. 2008. (ENG., Illus.). 432p. (YA). (gr. 7-12). mass mkt. 7.99 *(978-0-689-85152-0(9),* Simon Pulse) Simon Pulse.

Kiah Odom, Danayla Odom-West. Emily's Way. 2012. (ENG.). (J). pap. 18.00 *(978-1-4675-2036-2(5))* Independent Pub.

Launier, Veronique. Deliverance. 2014. (Hearts of Stone Ser.: 2). (ENG.). 288p. (YA). pap. 9.99 *(978-0-7387-3075-2(0),* Flux) Llewellyn Pubns.

Lee, Howard. Jamshid & the Lost Mountain of Light. 2008. (ENG.). 248p. pap. 14.99 *(978-1-4196-8958-1(4))* CreateSpace Independent Publishing Platform.

Nahali Nikoo Fells. Drowning in the Mainstream: Confessions of a Sister. 2010. 284p. 27.95 *(978-1-4502-0552-8(6))* iUniverse, Inc.

Napoli, Donna Jo. Beast. 2004. (ENG., Illus.). 272p. (YA). (gr. 7). mass mkt. 8.99 *(978-0-689-87005-7(1),* Simon Pulse) Simon Pulse.

Sadeghian, Alireza, illus. The Knight, the Princess, & the Magic Rock: A Classic Persian Tale. 2012. (ENG.). 32p. (J). (gr. -1-3). 15.95 *(978-1-937786-01-4(3))* World Wisdom, Inc.

Shahegh, Mahvash. The Green Musician. Ewart, Claire, illus. 2015. (ENG.). 36p. (J). (gr. k-3). 16.95 *(978-1-937786-42-7(0),* Wisdom Tales) World Wisdom, Inc.

Tak, Bibi Dumon & Dumon Tak, Bibi. Soldier Bear. Hopman, Philip, illus. 2011. (ENG.). 158p. (J). 13.00 *(978-0-8028-5375-2(7),* Eerdmans Bks For Young Readers) Eerdmans, William B. Publishing Co.

Townsend, S. P. The Star of Persia. 2007. 120p. 33.50 *(978-1-84799-236-9(6))* Lulu Pr., Inc.

IRAN—HISTORY

Abbott, Jacob. History of Xerxes the Great. 2003. 302p. 99.00 *(978-0-7950-4614-8(6))* New Library Press LLC.

Adl, Shirin & Quarto Generic Staff. I Is for Iran. Adl, Kamyar, photos by. 2012. (ENG., Illus.). 32p. (J). (gr. -1-2). 17.99 *(978-1-84780-211-8(7),* Frances Lincoln) Quarto Publishing Group UK GBR. Dist: Hachette Bk. Group.

Barter, James. The Ancient Persians. 2005. (Lost Civilizations Ser.). (Illus.). 112p. (J). (gr. 4-7). lib. bdg. 29.95 *(978-1-59018-621-3(4),* Lucent Bks.) Cengage Gale.

Bramwell, Neil D. Ancient Persia: A MyReportLinks. com Book. 2004. (Civilizations of the Ancient World Ser.). (Illus.). 48p. (J). lib. bdg. 26.60 *(978-0-7660-5251-2(6),* MyReportLinks.com Bks.) Enslow Pubs., Inc.

—Discover Ancient Persia. 2014. (Discover Ancient Civilizations Ser.). 104p. (J). pap. 10.95 *(978-1-4644-0339-2(2));* (Illus.). (gr. 5-18). 33.27 *(978-0-7660-4198-1(0))* Enslow Pubs., Inc.

Bridges, Shirin Yim & Yim Bridges, Shirin. Qutlugh Terkan Khatun of Kirman. Nguyen, Albert, illus. 2010. (Thinking Girl's Treasury of Real Princesses Ser.). (ENG.). 24p. (J). (gr. 3-8). 18.95 *(978-0-9845098-3-6(6))* Goosebottom Bks. LLC.

Burgan, Michael. Empire of Ancient Persia. 2009. (Great Empires of the Past Ser.). (Illus.). 160p. (gr. 6-12). 35.00 *(978-1-60413-156-7(X),* Chelsea Hse.) Facts On File, Inc.

Capek, Michael. Understanding Iran Today. 2014. (Illus.). 64p. (gr. 3-6). 33.95 *(978-1-61228-647-1(X))* Mitchell Lane Pubs., Inc.

Caravantes, Peggy. Exploring the Persian Empire. 2018. (ENG.). 32p. (gr. 3-6). ***(978-1-63235-468-6(3),*** 12-Story Library) Pr. Room Editions LLC.

Donaldson, Madeline. Iran. 2010. (Country Explorers Ser.). (ENG.). 48p. (gr. 2-4). pap. 9.95 *(978-0-7613-5541-0(3));* (Illus.). (J). lib. bdg. 29.27 *(978-1-58013-606-8(0))* Lerner Publishing Group.

Downing, David & Marshall Cavendish Corporation Staff. Iran. 2008. (Global Hotspots Ser.). 32p. (gr. 5-18). lib. bdg. 18.56 *(978-0-7614-3179-4(9),* Benchmark Bks.) Marshall Cavendish Corp.

Ejaz, Khadija. The Persian Empire. 2009. (How'd They Do That? Ser.). (Illus.). 64p. (J). (gr. 4-8). lib. bdg. 33.95 *(978-1-58415-825-7(5))* Mitchell Lane Pubs., Inc.

Fast, April. Iran: The People. 3rd rev. ed. 2010. (ENG., Illus.). 32p. (J). *(978-0-7787-9277-2(3));* pap. *(978-0-7787-9647-3(7))* Crabtree Publishing Co.

Fast, April & Richter, Joanne. Iran - The Land. 3rd rev. ed. 2010. (ENG., Illus.). 32p. (J). *(978-0-7787-9276-5(5));* pap. *(978-0-7787-9646-6(9))* Crabtree Publishing Co.

Glynne, Andy. Navid's Story: A Real-Life Account of His Journey from Iran. 2017. (Seeking Refuge Ser.). (ENG.). 32p. (gr. 3-4). 27.32 ***(978-1-5158-1415-3(7))*** Picture Window Bks.

Graham, Amy. Iran in the News: Past, Present, & Future. 2006. (Middle East Nations in the News Ser.). (Illus.). 128p. (J). (gr. 4-10). lib. bdg. 34.60 *(978-1-59845-022-4(0),* MyReportLinks.com Bks.) Enslow Pubs., Inc.

Habeeb, William Mark. Iran. 2008. (YA). pap. 14.95 *(978-1-4222-1431-2(1))* 2010. 128p. (YA). (gr. 4-8). lib. bdg. 25.95 *(978-1-4222-1401-5(X))* Vol. 13. 2015. (Illus.). 128p. (J). (gr. 7). lib. bdg. 25.95 *(978-1-4222-3441-9(X))* Mason Crest.

Haskins, James & Benson, Kathleen. Count Your Way Through Iran. Zaman, Farida, illus. 2006. (Count Your Way Ser.). 40p. (J). (gr. -1-3). lib. bdg. 19.93 *(978-1-57505-881-8(2),* Millbrook Pr.) Lerner Publishing Group.

The Iranian Revolution. 2010. (Milestones in World History Ser.). (Illus.). 112p. (C). (gr. 9-18). 35.00 *(978-1-60413-490-2(9),* Chelsea Hse.) Facts On File, Inc.

January, Brendan. The Iranian Revolution. 2008. (Pivotal Moments in History Ser.). (ENG., Illus.). 160p. (gr. 9-12). lib. bdg. 38.60 *(978-0-8225-7521-4(3))* Lerner Publishing Group.

Jestice, Phyllis G. Ancient Persian Warfare. 2009. (Ancient Warfare Ser.). (Illus.). 32p. (J). (gr. 5-8). lib. bdg. 26.00 *(978-1-4339-1973-2(7),* Gareth Stevens Learning Library) Stevens, Gareth Publishing LLLP.

Khanlari, Parviz-Natel. A Young Persons History of Iran. Yazdanfar, Farzin, tr. 2006. (YA). pap. *(978-1-58814-042-5(3))* Ibex Pubs., Inc.

Kheirabadi, Masoud & Gritzner, Charles F. Iran. 2nd rev. ed. 2011. (Modern World Nations Ser.). (Illus.). 160p. (J). (gr. 6-12). 35.00 *(978-1-60413-939-6(0),* Chelsea Hse.) Facts On File, Inc.

Markovics, Joyce L. Iran. 2017. (Countries We Come From Ser.). (ENG., Illus.). 32p. (J). (gr. -1-3). 19.95 ***(978-1-68402-057-7(3))*** Bearport Publishing Co., Inc.

McKinley, Herald. Persia, the Rise of Islam, & the Holy Roman Empire. 2015. (Exploring the Ancient & Medieval Worlds Ser.). (ENG., Illus.). 160p. (J). (gr. 8-8). 45.64 *(978-1-5026-0677-8(1))* Cavendish Square Publishing.

Miller, Debra A. Iran. Gale Editors, ed. 2010. (Current Controversies Ser.). (ENG.). 240p. 40.95 *(978-0-7377-5181-9(9));* pap. 28.45 *(978-0-7377-5182-6(7))* Cengage Gale. (Greenhaven Pr., Inc.).

Murray, Julie. Iran, 1 vol. 2016. (Explore the Countries Set 3 Ser.). (ENG.). 40p. (J). (gr. 2-5). 29.93 *(978-1-68078-067-3(0))* ABDO Publishing Co.

Peppas, Lynn. Cultural Traditions in Iran. 2015. (ENG., Illus.). 32p. (J). *(978-0-7787-8061-8(9))* Crabtree Publishing Co.

Piddock, Charles. Iran. 2006. (Nations in the News Ser.). (Illus.). 48p. (gr. 5-12). pap. 14.05 *(978-0-8368-6714-5(9));* lib. bdg. 31.00 *(978-0-8368-6707-7(6))* Stevens, Gareth Publishing LLLP. (Gareth Stevens Secondary Library).

Pohl, Kathleen. Descubramos Iran. 2008. (Descubramos países del mundo (Looking at Countries) Ser.). (SPA., Illus.). 32p. (gr. 1-5). lib. bdg. 26.00 *(978-0-8368-8782-2(4),* Gareth Stevens Learning Library) Stevens, Gareth Publishing LLLP.

—Descubramos Irán. 2008. (Descubramos Países Del Mundo Ser.). (SPA.). 32p. (gr. 1-5). pap. 10.50 *(978-0-8368-8789-1(1),* Gareth Stevens Learning Library) Stevens, Gareth Publishing LLLP.

—Looking at Iran. 2008. (Looking at Countries Ser.). (Illus.). 32p. (gr. 1-5). pap. 10.50 *(978-0-8368-8775-4(1));* lib. bdg. 26.00 *(978-0-8368-8768-6(9))* Stevens, Gareth Publishing LLLP. (Gareth Stevens Learning Library).

Poolos, J. Darius the Great. 2008. (Ancient World Leaders Ser.). (Illus.). 128p. (gr. 6-12). lib. bdg. 30.00 *(978-0-7910-9633-8(5),* Chelsea Hse.) Facts On File, Inc.

Price, Massoume. Ancient Iran. 2008. (Culture of Iran Ser.). (Illus.). 72p. (J). (gr. 4-8). *(978-0-9809714-0-8(3))* Anahita Productions Ltd.

Rajendra, Vijeya, et al. Iran. 2014. (Cultures of the World (r) Ser.). 144p. (YA). (gr. 5-10). lib. bdg. 47.07 *(978-0-7614-4993-5(0))* Cavendish Square Publishing.

Ramen, Fred. A Historical Atlas of Iran. 2009. (Historical Atlases of South Asia, Central Asia, & the Middle East Ser.). 64p. (gr. 6-6). 61.20 *(978-1-61513-319-2(4))* Rosen Publishing Group, Inc., The.

Richardson, Adele. Iran. 2011. (My First Look At Ser.). (ENG.). 24p. (J). (gr. 1-17). pap. 7.99 *(978-1-926722-36-8(1),* Creative Paperbacks) Creative Co., The.

Richter, Joanne. Iran: The Culture. 3rd rev. ed. 2010. (ENG., Illus.). 32p. (J). pap. *(978-0-7787-9648-0(5))* Crabtree Publishing Co.

—Iran - The Culture. 3rd rev. ed. 2010. (ENG., Illus.). 32p. (J). *(978-0-7787-9278-9(1))* Crabtree Publishing Co.

Robbins, Gerald. The Ottoman & Qajar Empires in the Age of Reform. 2009. (Making of the Middle East Ser.). (Illus.). 80p. (YA). (gr. 7-18). lib. bdg. 22.95 *(978-1-4222-0167-1(8))* Mason Crest.

Schomp, Virginia & Firdawsi. The Ancient Persians. 2009. (Myths of the World Ser.). 96p. (gr. 6-7). 34.21 *(978-0-7614-4218-9(9))* Marshall Cavendish Corp.

Sheen, Barbara. Foods of Iran. 2006. (Taste of Culture Ser.). (ENG., Illus.). 64p. (J). (gr. 3-7). lib. bdg. 28.75 *(978-0-7377-3453-9(1),* Greenhaven Pr., Inc.) Cengage Gale.

Somervill, Barbara A. Iran. 2012. (Enchantment of the World, Second Ser.). (ENG., Illus.). 144p. (J). (gr. 5-9). lib. bdg. 40.00 *(978-0-531-25311-3(2),* Children's Pr.) Scholastic Library Publishing.

Spilsbury, Richard & Spilsbury, Louise. Iran, 1 vol. 2011. (Countries Around the World Ser.). (ENG.). 48p. (gr. 3-6). pap. 9.95 *(978-1-4329-5233-4(1),* NA-h) Heinemann-Raintree.

Steele, Philip. Iran & the West. 2012. (Our World Divided Ser.). (ENG., Illus.). 48p. (J). (gr. 5-8). 27.95 *(978-1-4488-6031-9(8),* Rosen Reference) Rosen Publishing Group, Inc., The.

Understanding Iran, 4 vols., Set. Incl. Iran & Iraq: Religion, War, & Geopolitics. Wolny, Philip. lib. bdg. 33.25 *(978-1-4358-5280-8(X));* Iran & Nuclear Weapons. Orr, Tamra. lib. bdg. 33.25 *(978-1-4358-5281-5(8));* Iran & the Shia. Levy, Janey. lib. bdg. 33.25 *(978-1-4358-5282-2(6));* Iran's Religious Leaders. Shapera, Paul M. lib. bdg. 33.25 *(978-1-4358-5283-9(4));* (Illus.). 80p. (YA). (gr. 7-12). 2009. 2009. Set lib. bdg. 122.40 *(978-1-4358-5645-5(7))* Rosen Publishing Group, Inc., The.

Wagner, Heather Lehr. Iran. 2nd rev. ed. 2008. (Creation of the Modern Middle East Ser.). (Illus.). 116p. (gr. 6-12). 35.00 *(978-1-60413-022-5(9),* Chelsea Hse.) Facts On File, Inc.

Willett, Edward. Ayatollah Khomeini. (Middle East Leaders Ser.). 112p. (gr. 5-8). 2009. 66.50 *(978-1-61514-645-1(8),* Rosen Reference) 2004. (Illus.). (YA). lib. bdg. 34.60 *(978-0-8239-4465-1(4))* Rosen Publishing Group, Inc., The.

Wilson, Rosie. Discover Iran. 2012. (Discover Countries Ser.). (ENG., Illus.). 32p. (J). (gr. 3-5). pap. 10.60 *(978-1-4488-7050-9(X));* lib. bdg. 26.50 *(978-1-4488-6624-3(3))* Rosen Publishing Group, Inc., The. (PowerKids Pr.).

Wiseman, Blaine. Iran. 2016. ***(978-1-4896-5411-3(9))*** Weigl Pubs., Inc.

Wiseman, Blaine. Persians. 2016. (Illus.). 32p. (J). *(978-1-5105-1102-6(4))* SmartBook Media, Inc.

IRAQ

Arbuthnot, Felicity & Van Der Gaag, Nikki. Baghdad. 2005. (Great Cities of the World Ser.). (Illus.). 48p. (gr. 5-12). lib. bdg. 31.00 *(978-0-8368-5049-9(1),* Gareth Stevens Secondary Library) Stevens, Gareth Publishing LLLP.

Coleman, Wim & Perrin, Pat. Iraq in the News: Past, Present, & Future. 2006. (Middle East Nations in the News Ser.). (Illus.). 128p. (J). (gr. 5-9). lib. bdg. 34.60 *(978-1-59845-027-9(1),* MyReportLinks.com Bks.) Enslow Pubs., Inc.

Dennis, Brian, et al. Nubs: The True Story of a Mutt, a Marine & a Miracle. 2009. (ENG., Illus.). 48p. (J). (gr. -1-3). 18.99 *(978-0-316-05318-1(X))* Little, Brown Bks. for Young Readers.

Friedman, Mel. Iraq. 2009. (True Book(tm), A — Countries Ser.). (ENG., 48p. (J). Illus.). (gr. 2-5). 31.00 *(978-0-531-16891-2(3));* (gr. 3-5). pap. 6.95 *(978-0-531-21358-2(7),* Children's Pr.) Scholastic Library Publishing.

Hassig, Susan M. & Muhmood, Laith. Iraq. 2nd rev. ed. 2003. (Cultures of the World Ser.). (Illus.). 144p. (gr. 6-18). lib. bdg. 42.79 *(978-0-7614-1668-5(4),* Marshall Cavendish Reference Bks.) Marshall Cavendish Corp.

Hollar, Sherman. Mesopotamia. 2011. (Illus.). 88p. (J). lib. bdg. 31.70 *(978-1-61530-526-1(2))* Rosen Publishing Group, Inc., The.

Kotapish, Dawn. Daily Life in Ancient & Modern Baghdad. Webb, Ray, illus. 2005. (Cities Through Time Ser.). 64p. (gr. 5-12). 25.26 *(978-0-8225-3219-4(0))* Lerner Publishing Group.

Lightfoot, Dale. Iraq. 2nd rev. ed. 2006. (Modern World Nations Ser.). (Illus.). 117p. (YA). (gr. 7-12). lib. bdg. 35.00 *(978-0-7910-9247-7(X))* Facts On File, Inc.

Malaspina, Ann. The Iroquois: A Proud People. 2005. (American Indians Ser.). (Illus.). 48p. (J). lib. bdg. 23.93 *(978-0-7660-2450-2(4),* Enslow Elementary) Enslow Pubs., Inc.

Malhotra, Sonali. Welcome to Iraq. 2004. (Welcome to My Country Ser.). (Illus.). 48p. (gr. 2-5). lib. bdg. 27.00 *(978-0-8368-2559-6(4))* Stevens, Gareth Publishing LLLP.

Mason, Paul. Iraq, 1 vol. 2011. (Countries Around the World Ser.). (ENG.). 48p. (gr. 3-6). pap. 9.95 *(978-1-4329-5234-1(X),* NA-h) Heinemann-Raintree.

O'Neal, Claire. We Visit Iraq. 2011. (Your Land & My Land Ser.). (Illus.). 64p. (J). (gr. 4-7). lib. bdg. 33.95 *(978-1-58415-955-1(3))* Mitchell Lane Pubs., Inc.

Owings, Lisa. Iraq. 2011. (Exploring Countries Ser.). (ENG., Illus.). 32p. (J). (gr. 3-7). lib. bdg. 26.95 *(978-1-60014-592-6(2),* Blastoff! Readers) Bellwether Media.

Phillips, Larissa. A Historical Atlas of Iraq. 2003. (Historical Atlases of South Asia, Central Asia, & the Middle East Ser.). (Illus.). 64p. (YA). lib. bdg. 31.95 *(978-0-8239-3865-0(4))* Rosen Publishing Group, Inc., The.

Roberts, Russell. The Evolution of Government & Politics in Egypt. 2014. 48p. (gr. 4-8). 29.95 *(978-1-61228-585-6(6))* Mitchell Lane Pubs., Inc.

Romero, Libby. Ibn Al-Haytham: The Man Who Discovered How We See. 2016. (Readers Bios Ser.). (ENG., Illus.). 48p. (J). (gr. 1-4). pap. 3.99 *(978-1-4263-2500-7(2),* National Geographic Children's Bks.) National Geographic Society.

Roraback, Amanda. Iraq in a Nutshell. Gerber, Kathryn, illus. 2003. (Nutshell Notes). 36p. 5.95 *(978-0-9702908-5-4(3))* Enisen Publishing.

—Iraq in a Nutshell. 2nd rev. exp. ed. 2004. (Nutshell Notes). (Illus.). 60p. (YA). pap. 7.95 *(978-0-9702908-6-1(1))* Enisen Publishing.

Steele, Philip, et al. Mesopotamia. 2007. (DK Eyewitness Bks.). (ENG., Illus.). 72p. (J). (gr. 3-7). 16.99 *(978-0-7566-2972-4(1),* DK Children) Dorling Kindersley Publishing, Inc.

Taus-Bolstad, Stacy. Iraq in Pictures. 2nd ed. 2003. (Visual Geography Series, Second Ser.). (ENG., Illus.). 80p. (gr. 5-12). 31.93 *(978-0-8225-0934-9(2))* Lerner Publishing Group.

Walsh, Kieran. Iraq. 2003. (Countries in the News Ser.). (Illus.). 24p. (J). 25.64 *(978-1-58952-678-5(3))* Rourke Educational Media.

Zimmerman, W. Frederick. Cool Maps of Iraq: History, Oil Wealth, Politics, Population, Religion, Satellite, & More. 2007. 32p. per. 17.36 *(978-1-934840-07-8(6))* Nimble Bks. LLC.

IRAQ—HISTORY

Bill & Thompson, Dorcas. Iraq, Vol. 13. 2015. (Major Nations of the Modern Middle East Ser.). (Illus.). 128p. (J). (gr. 7). lib. bdg. 25.95 *(978-1-4222-3442-6(8))* Mason Crest.

Bjorklund, Ruth. Iraq. 2016. (Exploring World Cultures Ser.). 32p. (J). pap. 10.58 *(978-1-5026-2157-3(6))* Cavendish Square Publishing.

Blesch, Will. Understanding Iraq Today. 2014. (Illus.). 64p. (J). (gr. 3-6). 33.95 *(978-1-61228-648-8(8))* Mitchell Lane Pubs., Inc.

Bryant, Tamera. The Life & Times of Hammurabi. 2005. (Biography from Ancient Civilizations Ser.). (Illus.). 48p. (J). (gr. -1-7). lib. bdg. 29.95 *(978-1-58415-338-2(5),* 1244807) Mitchell Lane Pubs., Inc.

Cooper, Candy J. Reporting from Iraq: On the Ground in Fallujah. 2012. pap. *(978-0-545-32799-2(7))* Scholastic, Inc.

Crean, Susan. Iraq in Our World. 2010. (Countries in Our World Ser.). 32p. (YA). (gr. 3-6). lib. bdg. 28.50 *(978-1-59920-443-7(6))* Black Rabbit Bks.

Doeden, Matt. Tools & Treasures of Ancient Mesopotamia. 2014. (Searchlight Books: What Can We Learn from Early Civilizations? Ser.). (ENG., Illus.). 40p. (gr. 3-5). 27.93 *(978-1-4677-1432-7(1),* Lerner Pubns.) Lerner Publishing Group.

Faiella, Graham. The Technology of Mesopotamia. 2009. (Technology of the Ancient World Ser.). 48p. (gr. 6-6). 61.20 *(978-1-60854-243-7(2),* Rosen Reference) Rosen Publishing Group, Inc., The.

Fast, April. Iraq: The Culture. 3rd rev. ed. 2010. (ENG., Illus.). 32p. (J). pap. *(978-0-7787-9651-0(5))* Crabtree Publishing Co.

—Iraq: The Land. 3rd rev. ed. 2010. (ENG., Illus.). 32p. (J). pap. *(978-0-7787-9649-7(3))* Crabtree Publishing Co.

—Iraq - The Culture. 3rd rev. ed. 2010. (ENG., Illus.). 32p. (J). *(978-0-7787-9281-9(1))* Crabtree Publishing Co.

—Iraq - The Land. 3rd rev. ed. 2010. (ENG., Illus.). 32p. (J). *(978-0-7787-9279-6(X))* Crabtree Publishing Co.

—Iraq - The People. 3rd rev. ed. 2010. (ENG., Illus.). 32p. (J). *(978-0-7787-9280-2(3));* pap. *(978-0-7787-9650-3(7))* Crabtree Publishing Co.

Fattah, Hala & Caso, Frank. Iraq. 2008. (Brief History Ser.). 352p. (C). (gr. 9-18). pap. 19.95 *(978-0-8160-7737-3(1),* Checkmark Bks.) Facts On File, Inc.

Fattah, Hala Mundhir, et al. A Brief History of Iraq. 2008. (Brief History Ser.). (Illus.). 336p. (C). (gr. 9). 49.50 *(978-0-8160-5767-2(2))* Facts On File, Inc.

Feinstein, Stephen. Discover Ancient Mesopotamia. 2014. (Discover Ancient Civilizations Ser.). 104p. (J). pap. 10.95 *(978-1-4644-0337-8(6));* (Illus.). (gr. 5-18). 33.27 *(978-0-7660-4197-4(2))* Enslow Pubs., Inc.

Goldish, Meish. Baghdad Pups. 2011. (Dog Heroes Ser.). (Illus.). 32p. (J). (gr. 2-5). lib. bdg. 25.27 *(978-1-61772-150-2(6),* 1321528) Bearport Publishing Co., Inc.

Gruber, Beth. Ancient Iraq: Archaeology Unlocks the Secrets of Iraq's Past. 2007. (National Geographic Investigates Ser.). (ENG., Illus.). 64p. (gr. 5). 17.95 *(978-0-7922-5382-2(5));* 27.90 *(978-0-7922-5383-9(3))* National Geographic Society. (National Geographic Children's Bks.).

Hardwick, Susan. Iraq: World-Wise Kids Guides. 2004. 96p. *(978-1-59258-093-4(9))* Hylas Publishing.

Hassig, Susan M. & Al Adely, Laith Muhmood. Iraq. 2014. (Cultures of the World (r) Ser.). (Illus.). 144p. (J). (gr. 5-10). lib. bdg. 47.07 *(978-0-7614-4994-2(9))* Cavendish Square Publishing.

Holl, Kristi. Ancient Mesopotamian Technology. 2016. (Spotlight on the Rise & Fall of Ancient Civilizations Ser.). 48p. (YA). (gr. 6-6). pap. 11.75 *(978-1-4777-8953-7(7))* Rosen Publishing Group, Inc., The.

Hynson, Colin. Mesopotamia. 2006. (Ancient Civilizations Ser.). (Illus.). 48p. (gr. 5-12). lib. bdg. 31.00 *(978-0-8368-6192-1(2),* Gareth Stevens Secondary Library) Stevens, Gareth Publishing LLLP.

Krasner, Barbara. Ancient Mesopotamian Daily Life. 2016. (Spotlight on the Rise & Fall of Ancient Civilizations Ser.). 48p. (J). (gr. 6-6). pap. 11.75 *(978-1-4777-8905-6(7))* Rosen Publishing Group, Inc., The.

Malhotra, Sonali. Iraq. 2010. (Welcome to My Country Ser.). 48p. (gr. 3). 28.50 *(978-1-60870-155-1(7))* Marshall Cavendish Corp.

Mason, Paul. Iraq, 1 vol. 2011. (Countries Around the World Ser.). (ENG.). 48p. (gr. 3-6). 33.32 *(978-1-4329-5209-9(9),* NA-h) Heinemann-Raintree.

Mason, Paul & Marshall Cavendish Corporation Staff. Iraq. 2008. (Global Hotspots Ser.). 32p. (gr. 5-18). lib. bdg. 18.56 *(978-0-7614-3180-0(2),* Benchmark Bks.) Marshall Cavendish Corp.

Matthews, Rupert. Assyrian Soldier! An Ancient Army You'd Rather Not Join. Antram, David, illus. 2007. (You Wouldn't Want to... Ser.). (ENG.). 32p. (J). (gr. 2-5). 29.00 *(978-0-531-18727-2(6))* Scholastic Library Publishing.

Miller, Mara. The Iraq War: A Controversial War in Perspective. 2010. (Issues in Focus Today Ser.). 128p. (J). (gr. 7-12). 33.27 *(978-0-7660-3488-4(7))* Enslow Pubs., Inc.

Murray, Julie. Iraq, 1 vol. 2016. (Explore the Countries Set 3 Ser.). (ENG., Illus.). 40p. (J). (gr. 2-5). 29.93 *(978-1-68078-068-0(9))* ABDO Publishing Co.

Nardo, Don. Arts & Literature in Ancient Mesopotamia. 2008. (Lucent Library of Historical Eras Ser.). (ENG., Illus.). 104p. (YA). (gr. 7-12). lib. bdg. 37.45 *(978-1-4205-0099-8(6),* LML02109-244222) Cengage Gale.

—Life & Worship in Ancient Mesopotamia. 2008. (Lucent Library of Historical Eras). (ENG., Illus.). 104p. (YA). (gr. 7-12). lib. bdg. 34.80 *(978-1-4205-0100-1(3),* LML02109-244223) Cengage Gale.

—Science, Technology, & Warfare of Ancient Mesopotamia. 2008. (Lucent Library of Historical Eras). (ENG., Illus.). 104p. (YA). (gr. 7-12). lib. bdg. 34.80 *(978-1-4205-0102-5(X),* LML02109-244225) Cengage Gale.

Oachs, Emily Rose. Iraq. 2017. (Country Profiles Ser.). (ENG., Illus.). 32p. (J). (gr. 3-8). lib. bdg. 26.95 ***(978-1-62617-682-9(5),*** Blastoff! Discovery) Bellwether Media.

Orr, Tamra. Long Ago & Far Away Mesopotamia: Mesopotamia. 2015. (ENG., Illus.). 32p. (J). 26.50 *(978-1-62469-130-0(7))* Purple Toad Publishing, Inc.

Platt, Richard. The Golden Age of Baghdad. 2017. (ENG.). 56p. (J). pap. 8.99 ***(978-0-00-820895-0(6))*** HarperCollins Pubs. Ltd. GBR. Dist: Independent Pubs. Group.

Randolph, Joanne, ed. Living & Working in Ancient Mesopotamia. 2017. (Back in Time Ser.). 48p. (gr. 5-6). 27.93 ***(978-0-7660-8958-7(4))*** Enslow Pubs., Inc.

Rodger, Ellen. Ancient Mesopotamia Inside Out. 2017. (Ancient Worlds Inside Out Ser.). (ENG.). 32p. (J). ***(978-0-7787-2880-1(3));*** (Illus.). pap. ***(978-0-7787-2894-8(3))*** Crabtree Publishing Co.

—A Refugee's Journey from Iraq. 2017. (Leaving My Homeland Ser.). (ENG., Illus.). 32p. (J). pap. ***(978-0-7787-3157-3(X))*** Crabtree Publishing Co.

Rowell, Rebecca. Iraq, 1 vol. 2011. (Countries of the World Set 1 Ser.). (ENG., Illus.). 144p. (J). (gr. 6-12). lib. bdg. 37.07 *(978-1-61783-113-3(1))* ABDO Publishing Co.

Roxburgh, Ellis. The Mesopotamian Empires. 2015. (Great Empires Ser.). (ENG., Illus.). 48p. (J). (gr. 7-7). 31.36 *(978-1-5026-0630-3(5))* Cavendish Square Publishing.

Samuels, Charlie. National Geographic Countries of the World - Iraq. 2007. (National Geographic Countries of the World Ser.). (ENG., Illus.). 64p. (J). (gr. 5-9). lib. bdg. 27.90 *(978-1-4263-0061-5(1),* National Geographic Children's Bks.) National Geographic Society.

Sonnebom, Liz. Iraq. 2012. (Enchantment of the World, Second Ser.). (ENG., Illus.). 144p. (J). (gr. 5-9). lib. bdg. 40.00 *(978-0-531-25312-0(0),* Children's Pr.) Scholastic Library Publishing.

Stamaty, Mark Alan. Alia's Mission: Saving the Books of Iraq. 2010. (ENG.). 32p. (J). (gr. k-3). pap. 7.99 (978-0-375-85763-8(X), Dragonfly Bks.) Random Hse. Children's Bks.

Thompson, William & Thompson, Dorcas. Iraq. (YA). 2009. pap. 14.95 (978-1-4222-1414-5(1)) 2010. 136p. (gr. 4-8). lib. bdg. 25.95 (978-1-4222-1384-1(6)) Mason Crest.

Tracy, Kathleen. The Evolution of Government & Politics in Iraq. 2014. (gr. 4-8). 29.95 (978-1-61228-580-1(5)) Mitchell Lane Pubs., Inc.

IRAQ—HISTORY—TO 634

Ancient Mesopotamia/India. 2003. (Mr. Donn & Maxie's Always Something You Can Use Ser.). spiral bd. 19.95 (978-1-56004-166-5(8)) Social Studies Schl. Service.

Apte, Sunita. Mesopotamia. (True Book Ser.). (ENG., 48p. (J). 2010. Illus.). pap. 6.95 (978-0-531-24111-0(4)) 2009. (gr. 2-5). 29.00 (978-0-531-25230-7(2)) Scholastic Library Publishing.

—Mesopotamia: Set Of 6. 2011. (Navigators Ser.). (J). pap. 50.00 net. (978-1-4108-5111-6(7)) Benchmark Education Co.

—Mesopotamia: Text Pairs. 2008. (Bridges/Navigators Ser.). (J). (gr. 6). 89.00 (978-1-4108-8446-6(5)) Benchmark Education Co.

Benchmark Education Company. The Empires of Mesopotamia (Teacher Guide) 2005. (978-1-4108-4661-7(X)) Benchmark Education Co.

Brannon, Barbara. Discover the Empires of Mesopotamia. 2005. (J). pap. (978-1-4108-5161-1(3)) Benchmark Education Co.

Conklin, Wendy. Ancient Civilizations - China - India - Africa - Mesopotamia: All-in-One Resource with Background Information, Map Activities, Simulations & Games, & a Read-Aloud Play to Support Comprehension & Critical Thinking in Social Studies, Grades 5 & Up. 2006. (Ancient Civilizations Ser.). (ENG., Illus.). 96p. (gr. 5). per. 14.99 (978-0-439-53993-7(5), Teaching Resources) Scholastic, Inc.

Empire of Ancient Mesopotamia. 2009. (Great Empires of the Past Ser.). (Illus.). 152p. (gr. 6-12). 35.00 (978-1-60413-157-4(8), Chelsea Hse.) Facts On File, Inc.

Faiella, Graham. The Technology of Mesopotamia. 2005. (Technology of the Ancient World Ser.). (Illus.). 48p. (J). (gr. 5-8). lib. bdg. 30.60 (978-1-4042-0560-4(8)) Rosen Publishing Group, Inc., The.

Feinstein, Stephen. Ancient Mesopotamia: A Myreportlinks.com Book. 2005. (Civilizations of the Ancient World Ser.). (Illus.). 48p. (J). (gr. 4-10). lib. bdg. 26.60 (978-0-7660-5254-3(0), MyReportLinks.com Bks.) Enslow Pubs., Inc.

Greeley, August. Writing in Ancient Mesopotamia. 2009. (Writing in the Ancient World Ser.). 24p. (gr. 3-3). 42.50 (978-1-60854-907-8(0), PowerKids Pr.) Rosen Publishing Group, Inc., The.

Head, Tom. Ancient Mesopotamia, 1 vol. 2014. (Ancient Civilizations Ser.). (ENG.). 112p. (J). (gr. 6-12). lib. bdg. 35.64 (978-1-62403-541-8(8), Essential Library) ABDO Publishing Co.

Hunt, Norman Bancroft. Living in Ancient Mesopotamia. 2008. (Living in the Ancient World Ser.). (Illus.). 96p. (YA). (gr. 7-12). 35.00 (978-0-8160-6337-6(0)) Facts On File, Inc.

Hunter, Erica C. D. Ancient Mesopotamia. 3rd rev. ed. 2007. (Cultural Atlas for Young People Ser.). (Illus.). 96p. (YA). (gr. 5-9). 35.00 (978-0-8160-6824-1(0)) Facts On File, Inc.

Hunter, Nick. Daily Life in Ancient Sumer. 2015. (Daily Life in Ancient Civilizations Ser.). (ENG., Illus.). 48p. (gr. 3-6). pap. 8.99 (978-1-4846-2583-5(8)) Heinemann-Raintree.

Kerrigan, Michael. Mesopotamians. 2010. (Ancients in Their Own Words Ser.). 64p. (gr. 5). 32.79 (978-1-60870-066-0(6)) Marshall Cavendish GBR. Dist: Marshall Cavendish Corp.

Lassieur, Allison. Ancient Mesopotamia. 2012. (Ancient World Ser.). (ENG., Illus.). 112p. (J). pap. 9.95 (978-0-531-25982-5(X)); (gr. 6-9). lib. bdg. 34.00 (978-0-531-25182-9(9)) Scholastic Library Publishing.

Mayfield, Christine & Quinn, Kristine M. Mesopotamia, 1 vol. 2007. (Primary Source Readers Ser.). (ENG.). 32p. (J). (gr. 5-5). pap. 8.99 (978-0-7439-0440-7(0)) Shell Educational Publishing.

Mehta-Jones, Shilpa. Life in Ancient Mesopotamia. 2004. (Peoples of the Ancient World Ser.). (ENG., Illus.). 32p. (J). pap. (978-0-7787-2066-9(7)) Crabtree Publishing Co.

Morley, Jacqueline. Be a Sumerian Slave! A Life of Hard Labor You'd Rather Avoid. Antram, David, illus. 2007. (You Wouldn't Want to... Ser.). (ENG.). 32p. (J). (gr. 4-7). 29.00 (978-0-531-18728-9(4), Watts, Franklin); pap. 9.95 (978-0-531-18921-4(X)) Scholastic Library Publishing.

Nardo, Don. Mesopotamia. 2012. (Exploring the Ancient World Ser.). (ENG., Illus.). 48p. (gr. 5-6). 29.32 (978-0-7565-4567-3(6)) Compass Point Bks.

—Peoples & Empires of Ancient Mesopotamia. 2008. (Lucent Library of Historical Eras Ser.). (ENG., Illus.). 104p. (YA). (gr. 7-12). lib. bdg. 37.45 (978-1-4205-0101-8(1), LML02109-244224) Cengage Gale.

Oakes, Lorna. Hands-On History! Mesopotamia. 2013. (ENG., Illus.). 64p. (J). (gr. -1-12). 12.99 (978-1-84322-970-4(6)) Anness Publishing GBR. Dist: National Bk. Network.

—Mesopotamia. 2009. (Passport to the Past Ser.). (Illus.). 64p. (J). (gr. 4-7). lib. bdg. 31.95 (978-1-4358-5172-6(2)) Rosen Publishing Group, Inc., The.

Ryall, Michael. The Empires of Mesopotamia. 2005. (J). pap. (978-1-4108-4613-6(X)) Benchmark Education Co.

Samuels, Charlie. Technology in Ancient Mesopotamia. 2013. (Technology in the Ancient World Ser.). 48p. (J). (gr. 4-6). pap. 84.30 (978-1-4339-9642-9(1)); pap. 14.05 (978-1-4339-9641-2(3)) Stevens, Gareth Publishing LLLP.

—Technology in Mesopotamia. 2013. (Technology in the Ancient World Ser.). (ENG., Illus.). 48p. (J). (gr. 4-6). lib. bdg. 31.95 (978-1-4339-9640-5(5)) Stevens, Gareth Publishing LLLP.

Scholl, Elizabeth. Ancient Mesopotamia. 2009. (How'd They Do That? Ser.). (Illus.). 64p. (J). (gr. 4-8). lib. bdg. 33.95 (978-1-58415-818-9(2)) Mitchell Lane Pubs., Inc.

Shuter, Jane. Mesopotamia. 2016. (Excavating the Past Ser.). (ENG.). 48p. (gr. 4-6). pap. 8.99 (978-1-4846-3643-5(0), NA-h) Heinemann-Raintree.

Spotlight on the Rise & Fall of Ancient Civilizations: Mesopotamia. 2016. (Spotlight on the Rise & Fall of Ancient Civilizations Ser.). 48p. (gr. 6-6). 190.50 (978-1-4777-8958-2(8)); pap. 70.50 (978-1-4994-6421-4(5)) Rosen Publishing Group, Inc., The. (Rosen Young Adult).

Tarchon The Etruscan. Nubian Gold: A Conspiracy of Jewish Proportions. 2008. 436p. pap. 15.95 (978-1-4327-2064-3(3)) Outskirts Pr., Inc.

Wildwood, Gretchen. Ancient Mesopotamian Civilization. Cantucci, Alessandro & Morandi, Andrea, illus. 2009. (Ancient Civilizations & Their Myths & Legends Ser.). (YA). (gr. 5-9). lib. bdg. 29.25 (978-1-4042-8037-3(5)) Rosen Publishing Group, Inc., The.

Wood, Alix. Uncovering the Culture of Ancient Mesopotamia, 01 vols., 1. 2016. (Archaeology & Ancient Cultures Ser.). (ENG.). 32p. (J). pap. 10.00 (978-1-5081-4663-6(2), PowerKids Pr.) Rosen Publishing Group, Inc., The.

IRAQ-KUWAIT CRISIS, 1990-1991

Skip Press Staff. The Kuwaiti Oil Fires. Miller, Zachary N., ed. Taylor, Marjorie, illus. rev. ed. 2003. (Take Ten Ser.). 46p. (J). (gr. 4-18). pap. 4.95 (978-1-58659-024-6(3)) Artesian Pr.

IRAQ-KUWAIT CRISIS, 1990-1991—FICTION

Simmons, Ted. Sandstorm. 2006. (Illus.). 140p. (YA). pap. 13.95 (978-0-9776958-4-3(0)) CyPress Pubns.

IRAQ WAR, 2003-2011

Aronin, Miriam & Pushies, Fred J. Today's Air Force Heroes. 2012. (Acts of Courage: Inside America's Military Ser.). (Illus.). 32p. (J). (gr. 2-7). lib. bdg. 25.27 (978-1-61772-447-3(5)) Bearport Publishing Co., Inc.

Campbell, Geoffrey A. Weapons of War. 2004. (American War Library). (Illus.). 112p. (J). (gr. 7-10). 30.85 (978-1-59018-544-5(7), Lucent Bks.) Cengage Gale.

Carlisle, Rodney P. Iraq War. 3rd rev. ed. 2010. (America at War Ser.). (Illus.). 224p. (gr. 6-12). 45.00 (978-0-8160-8191-2(3), Chelsea Hse.) Facts On File, Inc.

Cooper, Candy J. P.O.W. 2011. (J). (978-0-531-22553-0(4)) Scholastic, Inc.

Dennis, Brian, et al. Nubs: The True Story of a Mutt, a Marine & a Miracle. 2009. (ENG., Illus.). 48p. (J). (gr. -1-3). 18.99 (978-0-316-05318-1(X)) Little, Brown Bks. for Young Readers.

Doak, Robin. Conflicts in Iraq & Afghanistan. 2006. (Wars That Changed American History Ser.). (Illus.). 48p. (gr. 5-12). pap. 14.05 (978-0-8368-7305-4(X), Gareth Stevens Secondary Library) Stevens, Gareth Publishing LLLP.

Doak, Robin Santos. Conflicts in Iraq & Afghanistan. 2006. (Wars That Changed American History Ser.). (Illus.). 48p. (gr. 5-12). lib. bdg. 31.00 (978-0-8368-7296-5(7), Gareth Stevens Secondary Library) Stevens, Gareth Publishing LLLP.

Ellis, Deborah. Children of War: Voices of Iraqi Refugees, 1 vol. 2010. (ENG., Illus.). 128p. (J). (gr. 6-9). pap. 9.95 (978-0-88899-908-5(9)) Groundwood Bks. CAN. Dist: Publishers Group West (PGW).

Fiscus, James W. Iraqi Insurgents: Iraqi Resistance to America after the Defeat of Saddam Hussein. 2004. (Frontline Coverage of Current Events Ser.). (Illus.). 48p. (YA). lib. bdg. 29.25 (978-1-4042-0277-1(3)) Rosen Publishing Group, Inc., The.

Fishkin, Rebecca Love. Vehicles of the Iraq War, 1 vol. 2013. (War Vehicles Ser.). (ENG.). 32p. (gr. 3-4). 27.99 (978-1-4296-9914-3(0), Edge Bks.) Capstone Press of Coughlan Cos.

Gabe: The Dog Who Sniffs Out Danger. 2014. (Hero Dog Ser.). (ENG., Illus.). 32p. (J). (gr. k-2). pap. 3.99 (978-1-4814-2237-6(5), Simon Spotlight) Simon Spotlight.

Goldish, Meish. Baghdad Pups. 2011. (Dog Heroes Ser.). (Illus.). 32p. (J). (gr. 2-5). lib. bdg. 25.27 (978-1-61772-150-2(6), 1321528) Bearport Publishing Co., Inc.

Gunderson, Cory Gideon. Battle in Baghdad. 2004. (War in Iraq Ser.). 48p. (gr. 4-8). 27.07 (978-1-59197-494-9(1), Abdo & Daughters) ABDO Publishing Co.

—When Diplomacy Fails. 2004. (War in Iraq Ser.). (Illus.). 48p. (gr. 4-8). 27.07 (978-1-59197-502-1(6), Abdo & Daughters) ABDO Publishing Co.

Gunderson, Jessica. Pivotal Moments. 2011. (War on Terror Ser.). (J). (gr. 5-9). 34.25 (978-1-60818-102-5(2)) Creative Co., The.

Halls, Kelly Milner & Sumner, William. Saving the Baghdad Zoo: A True Story of Hope & Heroes. Sumner, William, illus. 2010. (ENG., Illus.). 64p. (J). (gr. 3-18). 17.99 (978-0-06-177202-3(X), Greenwillow Bks.) HarperCollins Pubs.

Hamilton, John. Allied Forces. 2004. (War in Iraq Ser.). (Illus.). 48p. (gr. 4-8). 27.07 (978-1-59197-491-8(7), Abdo & Daughters) ABDO Publishing Co.

—America's Military. 2004. (War in Iraq Ser.). (Illus.). 48p. (gr. 4-8). 27.07 (978-1-59197-492-5(5), Abdo & Daughters) ABDO Publishing Co.

—Real-Time Reporting. 2004. (War in Iraq Ser.). (Illus.). 48p. (gr. 4-8). 27.07 (978-1-59197-497-0(6), Abdo & Daughters) ABDO Publishing Co.

—Weapons of the Twenty-First Century. 2004. (War in Iraq Ser.). (Illus.). 48p. (gr. 4-8). 27.07 (978-1-59197-501-4(8), Abdo & Daughters) ABDO Publishing Co.

Hatton, Thomas & George, Enzo. The Afghanistan & Iraq Wars: War Against Extremism. 2014. (Voices of War Ser.). 48p. (J). (gr. 4-6). lib. bdg. 31.36 (978-1-62712-879-7(4)) Cavendish Square Publishing.

Haugen, David M., et al. Iraq. 2009. (Opposing Viewpoints Ser.). (ENG., Illus.). 240p. (YA). (gr. 10-12). 29.45 (978-0-7377-4525-2(8), LML02109-246006);No. 9. pap. 42.95 (978-0-7377-4524-5(X), LML02109-245978) Cengage Gale. (Greenhaven Pr., Inc.).

Hunnicutt, Susan C. Casualties of War. 2011. (At Issue Ser.). (ENG.). 128p. (gr. 12-12). lib. bdg. 39.40 (978-0-7377-4880-2(X), Greenhaven Pr., Inc.) Cengage Gale.

Kiland, Taylor Baldwin & Teitelbaum, Michael. Military Humvees: Armored Mobility. 2015. (Military Engineering in Action Ser.). (ENG.). 48p. (J). (gr. 6-6). pap. 11.70 (978-0-7660-7065-3(4)); (Illus.). 27.93 (978-0-7660-6914-5(1)) Enslow Pubs., Inc.

Langley, Andrew. Bush, Blair, & Iraq: Days of Decision, 1 vol. Della-Rovere, Cynthia, illus. 2013. (Days of Decision Ser.). (ENG.). 64p. (gr. 7-8). pap. 10.95 (978-1-4329-7640-8(0)) Heinemann-Raintree.

Lankford, Ronald D. The Iraq War. 2010. (Social Issues Firsthand Ser.). (ENG.). 192p. (gr. 10-12). 38.30 (978-0-7377-5010-2(3), Greenhaven Pr., Inc.) Cengage Gale.

Lansford, Tom. The War in Iraq. 2009. (Global Viewpoints Ser.). (ENG., Illus.). 224p. (gr. 10-12). pap. 31.70 (978-0-7377-4163-6(5), LML02109-243060, Greenhaven Pr., Inc.); (YA). (gr. 9-12). lib. bdg. 40.45 (978-0-7377-4162-9(7), LML02109-243054) Cengage Gale.

Lowery, Zoe. Key Figures of the Wars in Iraq & Afghanistan. 2015. (Biographies of War Ser.). (ENG., Illus.). 112p. (J). (gr. 7-8). 32.90 (978-1-68048-066-5(9), Britannica Educational Publishing) Rosen Publishing Group, Inc., The.

Lowery, Zoe, ed. Key Figures of the Wars in Iraq & Afghanistan. 2015. (Biographies of War Ser.). (ENG.). 112p. (YA). (gr. 7-8). 65.80 (978-1-68048-067-2(7), Britannica Educational Publishing) Rosen Publishing Group, Inc., The.

Miller, Debra A. The Middle East. 2007. (Current Controversies Ser.). (ENG., Illus.). 224p. (gr. 10-12). 46.40 (978-0-7377-3960-2(6)); pap. 32.00 (978-0-7377-3961-9(4), Greenhaven Pr., Inc.) Cengage Gale.

—The War Against Iraq. 2003. (Lucent Terrorism Library). (ENG., Illus.). 112p. (J). 30.85 (978-1-59018-522-3(6), Lucent Bks.) Cengage Gale.

Miller, Mara. The Iraq War: A Controversial War in Perspective. 2010. (Issues in Focus Today Ser.). 128p. (J). (gr. 7-12). 33.27 (978-0-7660-3488-4(7)) Enslow Pubs., Inc.

Moe, Barbara. The Search for Weapons of Mass Destruction in Iraq. 2009. (Library of Weapons of Mass Destruction Ser.). 64p. (gr. 5-5). 58.50 (978-1-60853-958-1(X)) Rosen Publishing Group, Inc., The.

Moe, Barbara A. The Search for Weapons of Mass Destruction in Iraq. 2004. (Library of Weapons of Mass Destruction Ser.). (Illus.). 64p. (J). lib. bdg. 31.95 (978-1-4042-0295-5(1)) Rosen Publishing Group, Inc., The.

Monteverde, Matthew. American Presence in Iraq: Winning the Peace. 2004. (Frontline Coverage of Current Events Ser.). (Illus.). 48p. (J). lib. bdg. 29.25 (978-1-4042-0276-4(5)) Rosen Publishing Group, Inc., The.

—America's Presence in Iraq: Winning the Peace. 2009. (Frontline Coverage of Current Events Ser.). 48p. (gr. 5-5). 53.00 (978-1-61512-652-1(X)) Rosen Publishing Group, Inc., The.

Payment, Simone. Finding & Capturing Saddam Hussein: A Successful Military Manhunt. (Frontline Coverage of Current Events Ser.). 48p. 2009. (gr. 5-5). 53.00 (978-1-61512-654-5(6)) 2004. (Illus.). (J). lib. bdg. 29.25 (978-1-4042-0280-1(3)) Rosen Publishing Group, Inc., The.

Pipe, Jim. Hoping for Peace in Iraq. 2012. (Peace Pen Pals Ser.). (Illus.). 48p. (J). (gr. 6-8). 31.95 (978-1-4339-7731-2(1)); pap. 14.05 (978-1-4339-7732-9(X)) Stevens, Gareth Publishing LLLP. (Gareth Stevens Secondary Library).

Poffenberger, Nancy. Iraq, 2003. Gottesman, Val, illus. 2003. 32p. (YA). per. 9.95 (978-0-938293-11-8(7)) Fun Publishing Co.

Ritland, Mike, et al. Navy SEAL Dogs: My Tale of Training Canines for Combat. 2013. (ENG., Illus.). 208p. (YA). (gr. 7). 17.99 (978-1-250-04182-1(1), 9781250041821, St. Martin's Griffin) St. Martin's Pr.

Rivera, Sheila. Operation Iraqi Freedom. 2004. (War in Iraq Ser.). (Illus.). 48p. (gr. 4-8). 27.07 (978-1-59197-496-3(8), Abdo & Daughters) ABDO Publishing Co.

—Rebuilding Iraq. 2004. (War in Iraq Ser.). (Illus.). 48p. (gr. 4-8). 27.07 (978-1-59197-498-7(4), Abdo & Daughters) ABDO Publishing Co.

Rudolph, Jessica & Pushies, Fred J. Today's Navy Heroes. 2012. (Acts of Courage: Inside America's Military Ser.). 32p. (J). (gr. 2-7). lib. bdg. 25.27 (978-1-61772-446-6(7)) Bearport Publishing Co., Inc.

Sandler, Michael & Pushies, Fred J. Today's Marine Heroes. 2012. (Acts of Courage: Inside America's Military Ser.). 32p. (J). (gr. 2-7). lib. bdg. 25.27 (978-1-61772-444-2(0)) Bearport Publishing Co., Inc.

Schafer, Christopher. Attack in Iraq. 2004. (War in Iraq Ser.). (Illus.). 48p. (gr. 4-8). 27.07 (978-1-59197-493-2(3), Abdo & Daughters) ABDO Publishing Co.

—War Protesters. 2004. (War in Iraq Ser.). (Illus.). 48p. (gr. 4-8). 27.07 (978-1-59197-500-7(X), Abdo & Daughters) ABDO Publishing Co.

Scheppler, Bill. Iraqi Insurgents: Resisting America's Nation-Building in Iraq. 2009. (Frontline Coverage of Current Events Ser.). 48p. (gr. 5-5). 53.00 (978-1-61512-656-9(2)) Rosen Publishing Group, Inc., The.

Scholastic Library Publishing. The War in Iraq: From the Front Lines to the Home Front. 2009. (24/7: Behind the Headlines Ser.). (ENG., Illus.). 64p. (J). (gr. 6-12). 29.00 (978-0-531-21807-5(4)) Scholastic Library Publishing.

Shostak, Arthur B., ed. Defeating Terrorism/Developing Dreams: Beyond 9/11 & the Iraq War. 2005. (Defeating Terrorism/Developing Dreams: Beyond 9/11 & the Iraq War Ser.). (Illus.). 185p. (gr. 6-12). 159.75 (978-0-7910-8421-2(3), Chelsea Hse.) Facts On File, Inc.

Smithson, Ryan. Ghosts of War: The True Story of a 19-Year-Old GI. 2010. (ENG.). 352p. (YA). (gr. 9). pap. 9.99 (978-0-06-166471-7(5), Collins) HarperCollins Pubs.

A Soldier Comes Home. 2011. (ENG., Illus.). 32p. (J). pap. 9.99 (978-0-578-06838-1(9)) Yari Publishing.

Souter, Gerry & Souter, Janet. War in Afghanistan & Iraq: The Daily Life of the Men & Women Serving in Afghanistan & Iraq. Carlton Books Staff, ed. 2011. (ENG., Illus.). 48p. (J). (gr. 3). 16.95 (978-1-84732-895-3(4)) Carlton Bks., Ltd. GBR. Dist: Sterling Publishing Co., Inc.

Stamaty, Mark Alan. Alia's Mission: Saving the Books of Iraq. 2010. (ENG.). 32p. (J). (gr. k-3). pap. 7.99 (978-0-375-85763-8(X), Dragonfly Bks.) Random Hse. Children's Bks.

—Alia's Mission: Saving the Books of Iraq: Inspired by a True Story. 2005. (Reader's Workshop Ser.). (ENG., Illus.). 32p. (C). pap. 21.95 (978-0-7362-2802-2(0)) CENGAGE Learning.

—Muhimat Al Sayyda Alia: Inkaz Kuttub Al Irag. 2005.Tr. of Alia's Mission - Saving the Books of Iraq. 32p. pap. 12.00 (978-977-6171-01-5(X), 706-001) Al-Balsam Pubng. Hse. EGY. Dist: Bookmasters Distribution.

Summers, Elizabeth. Weapons & Vehicles of the Iraq War. 2015. (Tools of War Ser.). (ENG., Illus.). 32p. (gr. 1-2). lib. bdg. 26.65 (978-1-4914-4081-0(3)) Capstone Press of Coughlan Cos.

Tougas, Shelley. Weapons, Gear, & Uniforms of the Iraq War, 1 vol. 2012. (Equipped for Battle Ser.). (ENG.). 32p. (gr. 3-4). lib. bdg. 27.99 (978-1-4296-7652-6(3), Edge Bks.) Capstone Press of Coughlan Cos.

Westmark, Jon. The Iraq War: 12 Things to Know. 2017. (America at War Ser.). (ENG., Illus.). 32p. (J). (gr. 3-6). 21.95 (978-1-63235-266-8(4)) Pr. Room Editions LLC.

Wheeler, Jill C. Coalition Leaders. 2004. (War in Iraq Ser.). (Illus.). 48p. (gr. 4-8). 27.07 (978-1-59197-495-6(X), Abdo & Daughters) ABDO Publishing Co.

—Saddam Hussein. 2004. (War in Iraq Ser.). 48p. (gr. 4-8). 27.07 (978-1-59197-499-4(2), Abdo & Daughters) ABDO Publishing Co.

Willett, Edward. The Iran-Iraq War. 2004. (War & Conflict in the Middle East Ser.). (Illus.). 64p. (gr. 7-12). lib. bdg. 31.95 (978-0-8239-4547-4(2)) Rosen Publishing Group, Inc., The.

Wimmer, Teresa. Controversies. 2011. (War on Terror Ser.). (Illus.). 48p. (J). (gr. 5-9). 34.25 (978-1-60818-098-1(0)) Creative Co., The.

Wingate, Brian. Saddam Hussein. 2009. (Middle East Leaders Ser.). 112p. (gr. 5-8). 66.50 (978-1-61514-648-2(2), Rosen Reference) Rosen Publishing Group, Inc., The.

Winter, Jeanette. The Librarian of Basra: A True Story from Iraq. Winter, Jeanette, illus. 2005. (ENG., Illus.). 32p. (J). (gr. -1-3). 17.99 (978-0-15-205445-8(6)) Houghton Mifflin Harcourt Publishing Co.

Yomtov, Nel. Combat. 2016. (Military Missions Ser.). (ENG., Illus.). 24p. (J). (gr. 3-7). 25.95 (978-1-62617-433-7(4), Epic Bks.) Bellwether Media.

Young, Jeff C. Operation Iraqi Freedom: A MyReportLinks.Com Book. 2003. (U.S. Wars Ser.). (Illus.). 48p. (J). lib. bdg. 26.60 (978-0-7660-5088-4(2)) Enslow Pubs., Inc.

Zullo, Allan. War Heroes: Voices from Iraq. (10 True Tales Ser.). (J). 2014. (ENG.). 160p. (gr. 3-7). pap. 5.99 (978-0-545-81840-7(0), Scholastic Nonfiction) 2009. 48p. pap. (978-0-545-09026-1(1)) Scholastic, Inc.

Zwier, Lawrence J. & Weltig, Matthew S. The Persian Gulf & Iraqi Wars. 2005. (Chronicle of America's Wars Ser.). (Illus.). 96p. (J). (gr. 3-7). lib. bdg. 27.93 (978-0-8225-0848-9(6)) Lerner Publishing Group.

IRELAND

Adams, Colleen. A Primary Source Guide to Italy. 2009. (Countries of the World). 24p. (gr. 2-3). 42.50 (978-1-61512-036-9(X), PowerKids Pr.) Rosen Publishing Group, Inc., The.

Atkinson, Tim. Discover the United Kingdom. 2012. (Discover Countries Ser.). (Illus.). 32p. (YA). (gr. 4-7). lib. bdg. 26.50 (978-1-4488-5265-9(X)) Rosen Publishing Group, Inc., The.

Blomquist, Christopher. A Prmiary Source Guide to the United Kingdom. 2005. (Countries of the World). (Illus.). 24p. (J). (gr. k-5). lib. bdg. 22.60 (978-1-4042-2760-6(1), PowerKids Pr.) Rosen Publishing Group, Inc., The.

Bunting, Eve. S Is for Shamrock: An Ireland Alphabet. Faulkner, Matt & Bunting, Matt, illus. rev. ed. 2007. (Discover the World Ser.). (ENG.). 40p. (J). (gr. -1-3). 17.95 (978-1-58536-290-5(5)) Sleeping Bear Pr.

—S Is for Shamrock: An Ireland Alphabet. 2016. (Av2 Fiction Readalong 2017 Ser.). (ENG.). (J). (gr. k-6). 34.28 **(978-1-4896-5224-9(8)**, AV2 by Weigl) Weigl Pubs., Inc.

Burke, John, et al. Irelandopedia. 2016. (ENG., Illus.). 96p. 39.00 (978-0-7171-6938-2(3)) M.H. Gill & Co. U. C. IRL. Dist: Dufour Editions, Inc.

Campbell, Kumari. United Kingdom in Pictures. 2nd rev. expurg. ed. 2004. (Visual Geography Series, Second Ser.). (ENG., Illus.). 80p. (gr. 5-12). 31.93 (978-0-8225-1995-9(X)) Lerner Publishing Group.

Fazzi, Cindy. How to Draw Ireland's Sights & Symbols. 2009. (Kid's Guide to Drawing the Countries of the World Ser.). 48p. (gr. 4-4). 53.00 (978-1-61511-114-5(X), PowerKids Pr.) Rosen Publishing Group, Inc., The.

Fouberg, Erin Hogan & Hogan, Edward Patrick. Ireland. 2003. (Modern World Nations Ser.). (Illus.). 150p. (gr. 6-12). 35.00 (978-0-7910-7377-3(7), Chelsea Hse.) Facts On File, Inc.

Friedman, Lita. Mary Robinson: Fighter for Human Rights. 2004. (Avisson Young Adult Ser.). (Illus.). 142p. (YA). pap. 19.95 (978-1-888105-65-0(8)) Avisson Pr., Inc.

Givens, David, ed. For the Kids! A Family-Friendly Guide to Outings & Activities. 2003. (ENG., Illus.). 220p. pap. 24.95 (978-1-904148-27-2(1)) Liffey Pr., The IRL. Dist: Dufour Editions, Inc.

Hardwick, Susan, ed. Ireland. 2005. (World-Wise Kids Project Guides). (Illus.). 96p. (978-1-59258-068-2(8)) Hylas Publishing.

Koponen, Libby. Ireland. 2009. (True Book(tm), A — Countries Ser.). (ENG., Illus.). 48p. (J). (gr. 2-5). 31.00 (978-0-531-16892-9(1)) Scholastic Library Publishing.

MacCurtain, Fionnuala. The Story of Tomás Mac Curtáin. 2011. (Irish Heros for Children Ser.). (ENG.). 128p. (J). 16.95 (978-1-85635-716-6(3)) Mercier Pr., Ltd., The IRL. Dist: Dufour Editions, Inc.

Pittman, Rickey E. Irish Alphabet, 1 vol. 2011. (ENG., Illus.). 32p. (J). (gr. k-3). 16.99 (978-1-58980-745-7(6)) Pelican Publishing Co., Inc.

Rose, Elizabeth. A Primary Source Guide to Ireland. (Countries of the World). 24p. 2009. (gr. 2-3). 42.50 (978-1-61512-035-2(1)) 2004. (Illus.). (J). (gr. k). lib. bdg. 22.60 (978-0-8239-6731-5(X)) Rosen Publishing Group, Inc., The. (PowerKids Pr.).

Rudolph, Janice Clark. Ireland. 2017. (Countries We Come From Ser.). (ENG.). 32p. (J). (gr. k-3). 19.95 **(978-1-68402-254-0(1))** Bearport Publishing Co., Inc.

Sasek, M. This Is Ireland. 2005. (ENG., Illus.). 64p. (J). (gr. 2-12). 17.95 (978-0-7893-1224-2(7)) Universe Publishing.

Sheen, Barbara. Foods of Ireland. 2010. (Taste of Culture Ser.). (ENG.). 64p. (gr. 3-6). 35.20 (978-0-7377-5114-7(2), Kidhaven) Cengage Gale.

Walker, Ida. Ireland. 2007. (European Union Ser.). (Illus.). 88p. (YA). (gr. 4-7). lib. bdg. 21.95 (978-1-4222-0051-3(5)) Mason Crest.

Webb, Mary & Ni Laoghaire, Ide. My Ireland Counting Book. Ryan, Eoin, illus. (ENG.). 32p. (J). 2012. pap. 12.95 (978-1-84717-278-5(4)) 2nd rev. ed. 2017. pap. 12.00 **(978-1-84717-931-9(2))** O'Brien Pr., Ltd., The IRL. Dist: Dufour Editions, Inc.

IRELAND—FICTION

Andrisano, Micheal. Harold the High Knight & Princess Megan: Harold & Megan. 2013. (ENG.). 221p. (YA). pap. 16.95 (978-1-4327-9451-4(5)) Outskirts Pr., Inc.

Arrigan, Mary & Quarto Generic Staff. Esty's Gold. 2010. (ENG.). 224p. (J). (gr. 6-9). pap. 8.95 (978-1-84507-965-9(5), Frances Lincoln) Quarto Publishing Group UK GBR. Dist: Hachette Bk. Group.

Aryal, Aimee. Let's Go Irish! Shrestha, Anuj, illus. 2004. 24p. (J). 19.95 (978-0-9743442-5-6(7)) Mascot Bks., Inc.

Awdry, Wilbert V. Valentine's Day in Vicarstown. 2008. (Thomas in Town Ser.). (ENG., Illus.). 32p. (J). (gr. -1-2). 5.99 (978-0-375-84755-4(3), Random Hse. Bks. for Young Readers) Random Hse. Children's Bks.

Banville, Vincent. Hennessy. 180p. pap. (978-0-7022-2505-5(3)) Univ. of Queensland Pr.

Barrett, Phillip. Where's Larry This Time? 2016. (ENG., Illus.). 32p. (J). pap. 15.00 (978-1-84717-745-2(X)) O'Brien Pr., Ltd., The IRL. Dist: Dufour Editions, Inc.

Barrett, Phillip, illus. Where's Larry? 2016. (ENG.). 32p. (J). pap. 15.00 (978-1-84717-276-1(8)) O'Brien Pr., Ltd., The IRL. Dist: Dufour Editions, Inc.

Bateman, Teresa. Fiona's Luck. Murphy, Kelly, illus. 2009. (ENG.). 32p. (J). (gr. -1-3). pap. 7.95 (978-1-57091-643-4(8)) Charlesbridge Publishing, Inc.

Batt, Tanya Robyn. The Faerie's Gift. Ceccoli, Nicoletta, illus. 2008. (ENG.). 32p. (J). (gr. -1-3). 17.99 (978-1-84686-230-4(2)) Barefoot Bks., Inc.

Bennett, Holly. The Warrior's Daughter, 1 vol. 2007. (ENG., Illus.). 240p. (YA). (gr. 8-12). per. 9.95 (978-1-55143-607-4(8)) Orca Bk. Pubs. USA.

Bo, Ben. Skullcrack. 2003. (ENG.). 168p. (YA). (gr. 5-12). pap. 6.95 (978-0-8225-3311-5(1)) Lerner Publishing Group.

Bowie, Sarah. Let's See Ireland! Bowie, Sarah, illus. 2016. (ENG., Illus.). 32p. (J). 18.00 (978-1-84717-731-5(X)) O'Brien Pr., Ltd., The IRL. Dist: Dufour Editions, Inc.

Bowling, Athena. Malice: The Magicka Barney Chronicles, 1 vol. 2010. 388p. pap. 29.95 (978-1-4489-4066-0(4)) PublishAmerica, Inc.

Brennan, Ann. The Hawthorn Bush. 2005. (Illus.). 163p. pap. (978-0-88887-316-3(6)) Borealis Pr.

Bunting, Eve. Ballywhinney Girl. McCully, Emily Arnold, illus. 2012. (ENG.). 32p. (J). (gr. -1-3). 16.99 (978-0-547-55843-1(0)) Houghton Mifflin Harcourt Publishing Co.

—The Banshee. McCully, Emily Arnold, illus. 2009. (ENG.). 32p. (J). (gr. -1-3). 16.00 (978-0-618-82162-4(7)) Houghton Mifflin Harcourt Publishing Co.

—That's What Leprechauns Do. McCully, Emily Arnold, illus. 2006. (ENG.). 32p. (J). (gr. -1-3). 17.99 (978-0-618-35410-8(7)) Houghton Mifflin Harcourt Publishing Co.

Burgard, Anna Marlis. Flying Feet: A Story of Irish Dance. Dees, Leighanne, illus. 2006. 31p. (J). (gr. 4-8). 16.00 (978-1-4223-5255-7(2)) DIANE Publishing Co.

Byrne, Jean Livingstone. Legends of Newgrange. 2014. 54p. pap. 12.99 (978-1-84386-818-7(0)) Vanguard Pr.

Callaghan, Cindy. Lost in Ireland. 2016. (Mix Ser.). (ENG., Illus.). 224p. (J). (gr. 4-8). pap. 7.99 (978-1-4814-6206-8(7), Aladdin) Simon & Schuster Children's Publishing.

—Lucky Me. 2014. (Mix Ser.). (ENG., Illus.). 224p. (J). (gr. 4-8). pap. 6.99 (978-1-4424-8950-9(2), Aladdin) Simon & Schuster Children's Publishing.

Carroll, Yvonne. Great Irish Legends for Children, 1 vol. Lawrie, Robin, illus. 2005. (ENG.). 64p. (J). (gr. k-3). 18.99 (978-1-58980-345-9(0)) Pelican Publishing Co., Inc.

Carville, Declan. A Day to Remember at the Giant's Causeway. Ellis, Brendan, illus. 29p. (J). (gr. 2-5). pap. 7.95 (978-0-9538222-0-1(6)) Discovery Pubns. GBR. Dist: Irish Bks. & Media, Inc.

Cavanagh, Peter J. Fungie: The Dingle Dolphin. 2008. 48p. per. 24.95 (978-1-4241-8356-2(1)) America Star Bks.

Colfer, Eoin. Airman. 2009. (ENG.). 416p. (J). (gr. 5-9). pap. 8.99 (978-1-4231-0751-4(9)) Hyperion Pr.

—Airman. 2009. (J). lib. bdg. 19.65 (978-0-606-12534-5(5), Turtleback) Turtleback Bks.

Collard, Claire. Footpaths on the Sea. 2015. (ENG., Illus.). 292p. (J). pap. (978-1-78222-420-4(3)) Paragon Publishing, Rothersthorpe.

Colum, Padraic. The King of Ireland's Son. Pogány, Willy, illus. 2009. 308p. pap. 12.95 (978-1-59915-083-3(2)) Yesterday's Classics.

Conlon-McKenna, Marita. The Fields of Home. 2009. (ENG.). 176p. (J). (gr. 4-6). pap. 7.99 (978-1-4022-1908-5(3), Sourcebooks Jabberwocky) Sourcebooks, Inc.

—Under the Hawthorn Tree. Teskey, Donald, illus. 2003. 160p. pap. 5.95 (978-0-86278-206-1(6)) O'Brien Pr., Ltd., The IRL. Dist: Independent Pubs. Group.

—Under the Hawthorn Tree. 2009. (ENG.). 144p. (J). (gr. 4-6). pap. 7.99 (978-1-4022-1906-1(7), Sourcebooks Jabberwocky) Sourcebooks, Inc.

Costanza, Stephen, illus. Smudge & the Book of Mistakes: A Christmas Story. 2012. (ENG.). 48p. (J). (gr. 1-5). 17.95 (978-1-58536-483-1(5)) Sleeping Bear Pr.

Creech, Sharon. The Great Unexpected. 2013. (ENG.). 256p. (J). (gr. 3-7). pap. 6.99 (978-0-06-189234-9(3)) HarperCollins Pubs.

Creech, Sharon. Walk Two Moons: a Harper Classic. 2017. (Harper Classic Ser.). 288p. (J). (gr. 3-7). 16.99 **(978-0-06-265877-7(8))** HarperCollins Pubs.

Cregan, Mairin. Old John. Sewell, Helen, illus. 2012. 198p. 44.95 (978-1-258-23306-8(1)); pap. 29.95 (978-1-258-24727-0(5)) Literary Licensing, LLC.

Curtin, Judi. Alice Again. Fox, Woody, illus. 2006. (ENG.). 240p. (J). pap. 12.95 (978-0-86278-956-5(7)) O'Brien Pr., Ltd., The IRL. Dist: Dufour Editions, Inc.

dePaola, Tomie. Jamie O'Rourke & the Big Potato. 2009. (ENG.). 14p. (J). (gr. -1-k). bds. 5.99 (978-0-448-45090-2(9), Grosset & Dunlap) Penguin Young Readers Group.

Dillon, Eilis. The Island of Horses. 2004. (New York Review Children's Collection). (ENG.). 224p. (J). (gr. 4-7). 17.95 (978-1-59017-102-8(0), NYR Children's Collection) New York Review of Bks., Inc., The.

—The Lost Island. Kennedy, Richard, illus. 2006. (New York Review Children's Collection). (ENG.). 208p. (J). (gr. 4-7). 17.95 (978-1-59017-205-6(1), NYR Children's Collection) New York Review of Bks., Inc., The.

Dinsdale, Christopher. The Emerald Key. 2013. 356p. pap. (978-1-4596-6395-4(0)) ReadHowYouWant.com, Ltd.

—Stolen Away. 2006. (ENG., Illus.). 240p. (J). per. 10.95 (978-1-894917-20-9(0), Napoleon & Co.) Dundurn CAN. Dist: Ingram Publisher Services.

Doherty, Ellen. William's Journal. 2011. (Early Connections Ser.). (J). (978-1-61672-680-5(6)) Benchmark Education Co.

Dougherty, John. Bansi O'Hara & the Edges of Halloween. 2011. (Bansi O'Hara Ser.: 2). (ENG.). 416p. (J). (gr. 4-7). pap. 8.99 (978-0-440-86792-0(4)) Transworld Publishers Ltd. GBR. Dist: Independent Pubs. Group.

Dowd, Siobhan. Bog Child. 2010. (ENG.). 336p. (YA). (gr. 7). pap. 9.99 (978-0-375-84135-4(0)) Fickling, David Bks. GBR. Dist: Penguin Random Hse. LLC.

—A Swift Pure Cry. 2008. (ENG.). 320p. (YA). (gr. 7). pap. 8.99 (978-0-440-42218-1(3)) Fickling, David Bks. GBR. Dist: Penguin Random Hse. LLC.

—A Swift Pure Cry. 2011. 10.54 (978-0-7848-3500-5(4), Everbind) Marco Bk. Co.

Doyle, Malachy. Tales from Old Ireland. Sharkey, Niamh, illus. 2008. (ENG.). 96p. (J). 21.99 (978-1-84686-241-0(8)) Barefoot Bks., Inc.

Doyle, Marissa. Betraying Season. 2010. (ENG.). 336p. (YA). (gr. 9-13). pap. 19.99 (978-0-312-62916-8(8), 9780312629168) Square Fish.

Emery, Joanna. Brothers of the Falls. Erickson, David, illus. 2004. (Adventures in America Ser.). (gr. 4). 14.95 (978-1-893110-37-3(0)) Silver Moon Pr.

Epstein, Alex. The Circle Cast, 1 vol. 2011. (ENG., Illus.). 304p. (YA). (gr. 2-4). pap. 12.95 (978-1-896580-63-0(7)) Tradewind Bks. CAN. Dist: Orca Bk. Pubs. USA.

Fallon, Leigh. Carrier of the Mark. 2011. (Carrier of the Mark Ser.: 1). (ENG.). 352p. (YA). (gr. 8). pap. 8.99 (978-0-06-202787-0(5), HarperTeen) HarperCollins Pubs.

—Shadow of the Mark. 2013. (Carrier of the Mark Ser.: 2). (ENG.). 320p. (YA). (gr. 8). pap. 9.99 (978-0-06-212800-3(0), HarperTeen) HarperCollins Pubs.

Farley, Steven. The Black Stallion & the Shape-Shifter. 2010. (Black Stallion Ser.). (ENG.). 272p. (J). (gr. 3-7). 8.99 (978-0-375-84532-1(1), Yearling) Random Hse. Children's Bks.

Farrell, Liam. Goldilocks the Babysitter from Hell. 2007. (ENG.). 64p. (J). pap. 11.95 (978-1-901737-57-8(8)) Anvil Bks., Ltd. IRL. Dist: Dufour Editions, Inc.

Flannigan, Liz. Cara & the Wizard, 2 vols. Docampo, Valeria, illus. 2013. (Magic Stories Ser.). (ENG.). 48p. (J). (gr. 1-4). pap. 8.99 (978-1-84686-780-4(0)) Barefoot Bks., Inc.

Flor Ada, Alma. Celebra el Dia De3 San Patricio con Samantha y Lola. Lavandeira, Sandra, illus. 2006. (Cuentos para Celebrar / Stories to Celebrate Ser.). (SPA.). 30p. (gr. k-6). per. 11.95 (978-1-59820-117-8(4), Alfaguara) Santillana USA Publishing Co., Inc.

Fowley-Doyle, Moïra. The Accident Season. 2016. (ENG.). 320p. (YA). (gr. 9). 22.10 (978-0-606-39325-6(0)) Turtleback Bks.

Friesner, Esther M. Deception's Pawn. 2015. (ENG.). 336p. (YA). (gr. 7). 17.99 (978-0-449-81867-1(5), Random Hse. Bks. for Young Readers) Random Hse. Children's Bks.

Gallagher, Brian. Friend or Foe. 2015. (ENG.). 240p. (J). pap. 12.00 (978-1-84717-631-8(3)) O'Brien Pr., Ltd., The IRL. Dist: Dufour Editions, Inc.

Gannon, Gretchen. Rince: The Fairytale of Irish Dance. 2012. (ENG.). 32p. (J). pap. 20.95 (978-1-4327-8237-5(1)); pap. 12.95 (978-1-4327-8235-1(5)) Outskirts Pr., Inc.

Garland, Michael. King Puck. Garland, Michael, illus. 2009. (ENG., Illus.). 32p. (J). (gr. -1-3). pap. 6.99 (978-0-06-084811-8(1)) HarperCollins Pubs.

Giff, Patricia Reilly. Maggie's Door. 2005. 158p. (gr. 3-7). 17.00 (978-0-7569-5102-3(X)) Perfection Learning Corp.

—Maggie's Door. 2005. (ENG.). 176p. (J). (gr. 3-7). 6.99 (978-0-440-41581-7(0), Yearling) Random Hse. Children's Bks.

—Nory Ryan's Song. 2004. 160p. (J). (gr. 4-7). pap. 36.00 incl. audio (978-0-8072-2093-1(0), Listening Library) Random Hse. Audio Publishing Group.

Graves, Alfred Perceval. The Irish Fairy Book. 2007. 376p. per. 33.95 (978-0-548-65710-2(6)) Kessinger Publishing, LLC.

Hale, Linda. Activity Story Book: Sunshine & Her Big Blarney Smile. Liao, Yivian, illus. 2013. 26p. pap. (978-1-927915-03-5(1)) Chase Enterprises.

—Sunshine & Her Big Blarney Smile. Liao, Yivian, illus. 2013. 26p. pap. (978-1-927915-02-8(3)) Chase Enterprises.

Harrington, James. The Last Laugh. 2009. (Illus.). 24p. pap. 11.50 (978-1-60860-187-5(0), Strategic Bk. Publishing) Strategic Book Publishing & Rights Agency (SBPRA).

Harrison, Cora. Secret Spy from Drumshee. Wolfhound Publishing Editors, ed. 2003. (Drumshee Timeline Ser.: No. 13). (ENG.). 240p. (J). pap. 6.95 (978-0-86327-902-7(3)) Wolfhound Pr. IRL. Dist: Interlink Publishing Group, Inc.

—Titanic Voyage from Drumshee. 2nd ed. 2003. (Drumshee Timeline Ser.). 134p. (J). (gr. 4-7). per. (978-0-86327-905-8(8)) Wolfhound Pr.

Heneghan, James. Safe House, 1 vol. 2006. (ENG.). 160p. (J). (gr. 5-9). per. 8.95 (978-1-55143-640-1(X)) Orca Bk. Pubs. USA.

Heneghan, James B. Torn Away, 1 vol. 2003. (ENG.). 256p. (YA). (gr. 8-12). pap. 9.95 (978-1-55143-263-2(3)) Orca Bk. Pubs. USA.

Hennessy, Claire. Afterwards. 2005. 188p. (YA). pap. (978-1-84223-207-1(X)) Poolbeg Pr.

Holmes, Victoria. The Horse from the Sea. 2005. (ENG.). 320p. (J). (gr. 5-18). 15.99 (978-0-06-052028-1(0)) HarperCollins Pubs.

—The Horse from the Sea: An Epic Horse Story. 2005. 320p. (J). (gr. k-9). lib. bdg. 16.89 (978-0-06-052029-8(9)) HarperCollins Pubs.

Hope, Kathleen. Jack Eagle the Pirate & Other Mysterious Tales. 2012. (Illus.). 48p. pap. 24.40 (978-1-4678-9611-5(X)) AuthorHouse.

Hush: An Irish Princess' Tale. 2014. (ENG., Illus.). 336p. (YA). (gr. 7). pap. 11.99 (978-1-4424-9496-1(4), Simon & Schuster/Paula Wiseman Bks.) Simon & Schuster/Paula Wiseman Bks.

Hyland, Betty. Tressa & the Lost Circus of Ireland. 2004. 85p. (YA). pap. 10.95 (978-0-7414-2268-2(9)) Infinity Publishing.

Johnson, Lois Walfrid. The Raider's Promise. 2006. (Viking Quest Ser.: 5). (ENG., Illus.). 304p. (J). (gr. 3-7). per. 8.99 (978-0-8024-3116-5(X)) Moody Pubs.

Jones, Heulwen. O'Grady's Well. 2005. (Illus.). 96p. pap. (978-1-84401-578-8(5)) Athena Pr.

Judge, Chris. Brian & the Vikings. 2015. (ENG., Illus.). 32p. (J). pap. 13.00 (978-1-84717-687-5(9)) O'Brien Pr., Ltd., The IRL. Dist: Dufour Editions, Inc.

Judge, Chris & Wickham, Mark. Brian & the Giant. 2016. (ENG., Illus.). 32p. (J). pap. 11.00 (978-1-84717-773-5(5)) O'Brien Pr., Ltd., The IRL. Dist: Dufour Editions, Inc.

Kasony_O'Malley, Michael R. An Irish Tale: Tom Moore & the Seal Woman. Rowland, Michael J., illus. 2007. (J). lib. bdg. 19.95 incl. audio compact disk (978-0-9776170-3-6(3)) Green Igric Pr.

Kavanagh, Herminie Templeton. Darby O'Gill & the Crocks of Gold: And Other Irish Tales. Schluenderfritz, Ted, illus. 2003. ix, 155p. (J). pap. 14.95 (978-1-928832-85-0(7)) Sophia Institute Pr.

Keily, Kevin. A Horse Called el Dorado. 2005. (ENG.). 144p. (J). pap. 10.95 (978-0-86278-907-7(9)) O'Brien Pr., Ltd., The IRL. Dist: Dufour Editions, Inc.

Krensky, Stephen. Too Many Leprechauns: Or How That Pot O' Gold Got to the End of the Rainbow. Andreasen, Dan, illus. 2007. (ENG.). 32p. (J). (gr. -1-1). 12.99 (978-0-689-85112-4(X), Simon & Schuster Bks. For Young Readers) Simon & Schuster Bks. For Young Readers.

Krichilsky, Lauren. The Great Hunger. Madden, Colleen, illus. 2017. (Text Connections Guided Close Reading Ser.). (J). (gr. 2). (978-1-4900-1862-1(X)) Benchmark Education Co.

Lane, Andrew. Knife Edge. 2015. (Sherlock Holmes: the Legend Begins Ser.: 6). (ENG.). 320p. (YA). (gr. 7). 18.99 (978-0-374-38011-3(2), 9780374380113, Farrar, Straus & Giroux (BYR)) Farrar, Straus & Giroux.

Lenihan, Eddie. Eddie Lenihan's Irish Tales of Mystery. Clarke, Alan, illus. 2006. (ENG.). 224p. (J). 33.95 (978-1-85635-519-3(5)) Mercier Pr., Ltd., The IRL. Dist: Dufour Editions, Inc.

Lennon, Tom. When Love Comes to Town. 2013. (ENG.). 304p. (J). (gr. 10-12). 15.99 (978-0-8075-8916-8(0)) Whitman, Albert & Co.

Limke, Jeff. Tristan & Isolde: The Warrior & the Princess [A British Legend]. Randall, Ron, illus. 2009. (Graphic Myths & Legends Ser.). (ENG.). 48p. (gr. 4-8). pap. 8.95 (978-1-58013-889-5(6)) Lerner Publishing Group.

Llywelyn, Morgan. Cave of Secrets. 2013. (ENG.). 272p. (J). pap. 12.95 (978-1-84717-207-5(5)) O'Brien Pr., Ltd., The IRL. Dist: Dufour Editions, Inc.

Maloney, Andrew. The Master Song. 2014. (Illus.). 352p. (YA). (978-1-62911-176-6(7)) Whitaker Hse.

—Verse of Valor. 2015. 285p. (YA). (978-1-62911-357-9(3)) Whitaker Hse.

Massey, Eithne. Best-Loved Irish Legends: Mini Edition. Jackson, Lisa, illus. 2012. (ENG.). 64p. (J). 8.95 (978-1-84717-237-2(7)) O'Brien Pr., Ltd., The IRL. Dist: Dufour Editions, Inc.

—The Silver Stag of Bunratty. 2012. (ENG., Illus.). 240p. (J). pap. 12.95 (978-1-84717-206-8(7)) O'Brien Pr., Ltd., The IRL. Dist: Dufour Editions, Inc.

Matthews, Caitlín, et al. Tales from Celtic Lands. Whelan, Olwyn, illus. 2008. (ENG.). 80p. (J). (gr. -1-3). 21.99 (978-1-84686-213-7(2)) Barefoot Bks., Inc.

McCann, David. Garda Gaby: The Danger of Playing Truant. Brundige, Britt, ed. Bauknecht, Julie, illus. l.t. ed. 2003. 14p. (J). (gr. k-5). spiral bd. 5.99 (978-1-929063-92-5(X), 324) Moons & Stars Publishing For Children.

McCaughren, Tom. Children of the Forge. (Illus.). 128p. 3.95 (978-0-900068-98-0(1)) Penguin Publishing Group.

—Legend of the Corrib King. 2nd rev. ed. 2012. (McCaughren's Legends Trilogy Ser.). (ENG., Illus.). 128p. (J). pap. 14.95 (978-1-85635-801-9(1)) Mercier Pr., Ltd., The IRL. Dist: Dufour Editions, Inc.

—Legend of the Corrib King. (Illus.). 96p. 2.25 (978-0-900068-86-7(8)) Penguin Publishing Group.

—Legend of the Golden Key. 2nd rev. ed. 2012. (McCaughren's Legends Trilogy Ser.). (ENG., Illus.). 190p. (J). pap. 14.95 (978-1-85635-803-3(8)) Mercier Pr., Ltd., The IRL. Dist: Dufour Editions, Inc.

—Legend of the Phantom Highwayman. 2nd rev. ed. 2012. (McCaughren's Legends Trilogy Ser.). (ENG., Illus.). 128p. (J). pap. 14.95 (978-1-85635-802-6(X)) Mercier Pr., Ltd., The IRL. Dist: Dufour Editions, Inc.

McDaniels, Preston, illus. The Prince of Ireland & the Three Magic Stallions. 2003. (ENG.). 32p. (J). (gr. k-3). tchr. ed. 16.95 (978-0-8234-1573-1(2)) Holiday Hse., Inc.

McKinty, Adrian. The Lighthouse Keepers. 2008. (ENG.). 400p. (YA). (gr. 7-11). 17.95 (978-0-8109-7070-0(8), Amulet Bks.) Abrams, Inc.

—The Lighthouse War. 2007. (ENG.). 414p. (J). (gr. 7-17). 16.95 (978-0-8109-9354-9(6)) Abrams, Inc.

McMahon, Susan. Sean O'Grady. 2009. 12p. pap. 9.50 (978-1-4389-5149-2(3)) AuthorHouse.

Melling, O. R. The Chronicles of Faerie: The Book of Dreams. 2010. (Chronicles of Faerie Ser.). (ENG.). 720p. (YA). (gr. 2-8). pap. 12.95 (978-0-8109-8418-9(0), Amulet Bks.) Abrams, Inc.

—The Light-Bearer's Daughter. 2008. (ENG.). 368p. (YA). (gr. 2-8). pap. 9.95 (978-0-8109-7123-3(2), Amulet Bks.) Abrams, Inc.

—The Summer King. 2006. (ENG., Illus.). 380p. (YA). (gr. 5-10). 16.95 (978-0-8109-5969-9(0)) Abrams, Inc.

Millen, C. M. The Ink Garden of Brother Theophane. Wisnewski, Andrea, illus. 2010. (ENG.). 32p. (J). (gr. k-3). 17.95 (978-1-58089-179-0(9)) Charlesbridge Publishing, Inc.

Molly's Magic: Evaluation Guide. 2006. (J). (978-1-55942-417-2(6)) Witcher Productions.

Morpurgo, Michael. Twist of Gold. (ENG.). 304p. (J). 2004. pap. 8.99 (978-0-7497-4687-2(4)) 2nd ed. 2009. (gr. 4-7). pap. 10.99 (978-1-4052-2928-9(4)) Egmont Bks., Ltd. GBR. Dist: Trafalgar Square Publishing, Independent Pubs. Group.

Murray, Kirsty. Bridie's Fire. 2005. (ENG.). 264p. (J). (gr. 4-8). pap. 13.99 (978-1-86508-727-6(0)) Allen & Unwin AUS. Dist: Independent Pubs. Group.

Neale, Cynthia G. The Irish Dresser: A Story of Hope During the Great Hunger (an Gorta Mor, 1845-1850) 2003. 148p. (J). pap. 7.95 (978-1-57249-344-5(5), White Mane Kids) White Mane Publishing Co., Inc.

Newhall, Mary & Campbell, Joanna. Samantha's Irish Luck. 2005. (Thoroughbred Ser.). (Illus.). 156p. (gr. 3-7). 15.00 (978-0-7569-5350-8(2)) Perfection Learning Corp.

No Way Home: Individual Title Six-Packs. (Bookweb Ser.). 32p. (gr. 6-18). 34.00 (978-0-7578-0896-8(4)) Rigby Education.

Norris, Christine. The Sword of Danu. 2012. (J). 268p. (gr. 3-7). pap. 14.99 (978-1-61271-095-2(6)); (978-1-61271-097-6(2)); (978-1-61271-096-9(4)) Zumaya Pubns. LLC.

O'Guilin, Peadar. The Call. 2016. (ENG.). 320p. (YA). (gr. 9). 18.99 (978-1-338-04561-1(X)) Scholastic, Inc.

O'Neill, Louise. Asking for It. 2016. (ENG.). 336p. (gr. 7-12). 16.99 (978-1-68144-537-3(9)) Quercus NA.

Osborne, Mary Pope. Leprechaun in Late Winter. Murdocca, Sal, illus. (Magic Tree House Merlin Mission Ser.: No. 15). (ENG.). 128p. (J). (gr. 2-5). 2012. 5.99 (978-0-375-85651-8(X)) 2010. 12.99 (978-0-375-85650-1(1)) Random Hse. Children's Bks. (Random Hse. Bks. for Young Readers).

—Leprechaun in Late Winter. 2012. (Magic Tree House Merlin Missions Ser.: 15). lib. bdg. 16.00 (978-0-606-23860-1(3), Turtleback) Turtleback Bks.

—Viking Ships at Sunrise. unabr. ed. 2004. (Magic Tree House Ser.: No. 15). 71p. (J). (gr. k-3). pap. 17.00 incl. audio (978-0-8072-0784-0(5), LFTR 243 SP, Listening Library) Random Hse. Audio Publishing Group.

Parkinson, Siobhan. Spellbound: Tales of Enchantment from Ancient Ireland. Whelan, Olwyn, illus. 2013. (ENG.). 64p. (J). (gr. 1-4). 19.99 (978-1-84780-140-1(4), Frances Lincoln) Quarto Publishing Group UK GBR. Dist: Hachette Bk. Group.

Perkins, Lucy Fitch. The Irish Twins. 2008. 164p. pap. 9.95 (978-1-59915-122-9(7)) Yesterday's Classics.

Perkyns, Dorothy. Bridget's Black '47. 2009. (ENG.). 160p. (J). (gr. 5-18). pap. 12.99 (978-1-55488-400-1(4)) Dundurn CAN. Dist: Ingram Publisher Services.

Porter, Duane. Molly O'Malley & the Leprechaun. 2007. (Illus.). 224p. (J). per. 12.95 (978-0-9800993-0-0(7)) Buried Treasure Publishing.

Raphael, Marie. A Boy from Ireland. 2007. (Karen & Michael Braziller Bks.). (ENG.). 224p. (YA). (gr. 8-12). 19.95 (978-0-89255-331-0(6)) Persea Bks., Inc.

Regan, Peter. Riverside: Spring Fever. 2007. (ENG.). 112p. (J). pap. 10.95 (978-1-901737-56-1(X)) Anvil Bks., Ltd. IRL. Dist: Dufour Editions, Inc.

—Riverside: The Spy. 2007. (ENG.). 112p. (J). pap. 10.95 (978-1-901737-53-0(5)) Anvil Bks., Ltd. IRL. Dist: Dufour Editions, Inc.

Roberts, Scott A. The Rollicking Adventures of Tam O'Hare. Roberts, Scott A., illus. 2007. (ENG., Illus.). 228p. (J). (gr. 4-7). per. 16.95 (978-1-60037-289-6(9)) Morgan James Publishing.

Russel, Mary. Flickertail & Paint, Barnyard Sleuths, 1 vol. 2010. 96p. pap. 19.95 (978-1-4489-7248-7(5)) America Star Bks.

Ryan, Frank P. The Snowmelt River. 2013. (Three Powers Ser.: 1). (ENG.). 720p. (J). (gr. 7-17). 15.95 (978-1-62365-048-3(8), Jo Fletcher Books) Quercus NA.

Sanderson, Whitney. Darcy. Sanderson, Ruth, illus. 2013. (Horse Diaries). (ENG.). 160p. (J). (gr. 3-7). pap. 7.99 (978-0-307-97635-2(1), Random Hse. Bks. for Young Readers) Random Hse. Children's Bks.

—Darcy. 2013. (Horse Diaries: 10). lib. bdg. 18.40 (978-0-606-27001-4(9), Turtleback) Turtleback Bks.

Schlesinger, Gretchen. Send Me the Soap #1: The Emerald Isle Adventure. Pietila, David, illus. 2006. (J). 11.95 (978-0-9778536-0-1(8)) Eco-thumb Publishing Co.

—Send Me the Soap #1: The Emerald Isle Adventure (lib. Bdg.) Pietila, David, illus. 2006. (J). lib. bdg. (978-0-9778536-1-8(6)) Eco-thumb Publishing Co.

Schmidt, Gary D. Anson's Way. 2009. (ENG.). 224p. (J). (gr. 2-5). pap. 15.95 (978-0-547-23761-9(8)) Houghton Mifflin Harcourt Publishing Co.

Schneider, Mical. Annie Quinn in America. 2003. (Adventures in Time Ser.). (Illus.). 252p. (J). (gr. 4-7). 15.95 (978-1-57505-510-7(4), Carolrhoda Bks.) Lerner Publishing Group.

Sexton, Jessa R. Mobert's Irish Experience. Sexton, Jessa R., photos by. 2012. (Illus.). 34p. pap. 10.00 (978-0-9860150-3-8(2)) O'More Publishing.

Sharkey-Wilmot. The Mysterious Golden Horse. 2007. 168p. 22.95 (978-0-595-69325-2(3)); per. 12.95 (978-0-595-45162-3(4)) iUniverse, Inc.

Siggins, Gerard. Rugby Rebel. 2015. (ENG.). 176p. (J). 12.00 (978-1-84717-677-6(1)) O'Brien Pr., Ltd., The IRL. Dist: Dufour Editions, Inc.

—Rugby Warrior: Back in School. Back in Sport. Back in Time. 2014. (ENG., Illus.). 176p. (J). pap. 14.00 (978-1-84717-591-5(0)) O'Brien Pr., Ltd., The IRL. Dist: Dufour Editions, Inc.

Smith, Cathy Jo. Seamus Mcseamus, an Irish Rover. 2005. (Illus.). 104p. per. 11.95 (978-0-9766666-0-8(X)) Arcadian Hse.

Smyth, Jimmy. Causeway Coast. 2013. 34p. pap. (978-0-9569314-6-7(4)) Smith, Jimmy.

Stengel, Joyce A. St. Patrick & the Three Brave Mice, 1 vol. Leonhard, Herb, illus. 2009. (ENG.). 32p. (J). (gr. k-3). 16.99 (978-1-58980-663-4(8)) Pelican Publishing Co., Inc.

Su, Lucy, illus. Irish Legends for Children, 1 vol. 2004. (ENG.). 64p. (J). (gr. k-3). 18.99 (978-1-58980-278-0(0)) Pelican Publishing Co., Inc.

Tegen, Katherine Brown. The Story of the Jack O'Lantern. Dorman, Brandon, illus. 2010. (ENG.). 32p. (J). (gr. -1-3). 12.99 (978-0-06-143088-6(9)) HarperCollins Pubs.

Thomas, Shelley Moore. Secrets of Selkie Bay. 2015. (ENG.). 208p. (J). (gr. 3-7). 15.99 (978-0-374-36749-7(3), 9780374367497, Farrar, Straus & Giroux (BYR)) Farrar, Straus & Giroux.

Thompson, Kate. The Last of the High Kings. (YA). 2010. (New Policeman Trilogy Ser.: 2). (ENG.). 336p. (gr. 8). pap. 8.99 (978-0-06-117597-8(8), Greenwillow Bks.) 2008. 323p. (gr. 7-18). lib. bdg. 17.89 (978-0-06-117596-1(X), HarperTeen) HarperCollins Pubs.

—The New Policeman. (Illus.). 2008. (New Policeman Trilogy Ser.: 1). (ENG.). 464p. (YA). (gr. 8-12). pap. 9.99 (978-0-06-117429-2(7)) 2007. 448p. (J). (gr. 7-12). 16.99

(978-0-06-117427-8(0)) HarperCollins Pubs. (Greenwillow Bks.).

—The New Policeman. pap. 1.00 *(978-1-4074-4550-2(2))* Recorded Bks., Inc.

—Switchers. 220p. (J). (gr. 4-7). pap. 5.99 *(978-0-8072-1553-1(8))*; 2004. (Switchers Ser.: Vol. 1). (gr. 5-9). pap. 38.00 incl. audio *(978-0-8072-8138-3(7)*, YA115SP) Random Hse. Audio Publishing Group. (Listening Library).

—The White Horse Trick. 2010. (New Policeman Trilogy Ser.: 3). (ENG.). 416p. (YA). (gr. 8-18). 17.99 *(978-0-06-200416-1(6)*, Greenwillow Bks.) HarperCollins Pubs.

Walsh, Stephen & O'Donovan, Marita. Brendan & the Blarney Stone. Le Feyer, Diane, illus. 2017. (ENG.). 32p. (J). pap. 13.00 ***(978-1-84717-723-0(9))*** O'Brien Pr., Ltd., The IRL. Dist: Dufour Editions, Inc.

Warner, Gertrude Chandler, creator. The Legend of the Irish Castle. 2016. (Boxcar Children Mysteries Ser.: 142). (ENG., Illus.). 128p. (J). (gr. 1-5). 15.99 *(978-0-8075-0705-6(9))* Whitman, Albert & Co.

Warren, Wendy Ann. Potato Chip, an Irish Tale. 2008. 28p. pap. 15.99 *(978-1-4363-0551-8(9))* Xlibris Corp.

Webb, Sarah. Ask Amy Green: Boy Trouble. 2010. (Ask Amy Green Ser.: 1). (ENG., Illus.). 288p. (YA). (gr. 7-18). 16.99 *(978-0-7636-5006-3(4))* Candlewick Pr.

—Ask Amy Green: Love & Other Drama-Ramas! 2012. (Ask Amy Green Ser.: 4). (ENG., Illus.). 224p. (YA). (gr. 7). 15.99 *(978-0-7636-5582-2(1))* Candlewick Pr.

—Boy Trouble. 2011. (Ask Amy Green Ser.: 1). (ENG., Illus.). 288p. (YA). (gr. 7). 6.99 *(978-0-7636-5063-6(3))* Candlewick Pr.

—Summer Secrets. (Ask Amy Green Ser.: 2). (ENG., Illus.). 288p. (YA). (gr. 7). 2012. pap. 6.99 *(978-0-7636-5705-5(0))* 2011. 16.99 *(978-0-7636-5071-1(4))* Candlewick Pr.

Whelan, Gloria. Megan's Year: An Irish Traveler's Story. Peck, Beth, illus. 2011. (Tales of the World Ser.). (ENG.). 32p. (gr. k-5). lib. bdg. 16.95 *(978-1-58536-449-7(5))* Sleeping Bear Pr.

Wiggin, Kate Douglas. Penelope's Irish Experiences. 2004. reprint ed. pap. 1.99 *(978-1-4192-4072-0(2))*; pap. 22.95 *(978-1-4191-4072-3(8))* Kessinger Publishing, LLC.

—Penelope's Irish Experiences. 2011. 186p. (gr. 4-7). 26.95 *(978-1-4638-9985-1(8))* Rodgers, Alan Bks.

Winks, P. M. Romany Gnomanies in the Emerald Isle. 2011. 124p. pap. 13.32 *(978-1-4567-7556-8(1))* AuthorHouse.

IRELAND—HISTORY

Allan, Tony. The Irish Famine: The Birth of Irish America. 2003. (Point of Impact Ser.). (Illus.). 32p. (J). (gr. 5-7). per. 7.50 *(978-1-4034-4113-3(8))* Heinemann-Raintree.

Allen, Tony. The Irish Famine: The Birth of Irish America, 1 vol. 2nd ed. 2006. (Point of Impact Ser.). (ENG., Illus.). 32p. (gr. 3-7). pap. 8.49 *(978-1-4034-9153-4(4)*, NA-h) Heinemann-Raintree.

Barnham, Kay. Ireland. 2010. (Illus.). 32p. (J). *(978-1-84234-550-4(8))* Cherrytree Bks.

Bartoletti, Susan Campbell. Black Potatoes: The Story of the Great Irish Famine, 1845-1850. 2005. (ENG., Illus.). 192p. (J). (gr. 5-7). pap. 9.95 *(978-0-618-54883-5(1))* Houghton Mifflin Harcourt Publishing Co.

Blashfield, Jean F. Ireland. 2013. (ENG., Illus.). 144p. (J). 40.00 *(978-0-531-23676-5(5))* Scholastic Library Publishing.

Bowden, Rob & Foley, Ronan. Focus on Ireland. 2007. (World in Focus Ser.). 64p. (gr. 5-12). pap. 14.05 *(978-0-8368-6758-9(0))*; (Illus.). lib. bdg. 34.00 *(978-0-8368-6751-0(3))* Stevens, Gareth Publishing LLLP. (Gareth Stevens Secondary Library).

Burke, Fatti & Burke, John. Historopedia. 2017. (ENG., Illus.). 96p. (J). 39.00 ***(978-0-7171-7113-2(2))*** M.H. Gill & Co. U. C. IRL. Dist: Dufour Editions, Inc.

Burke, Shauna. The Historopedia Quiz Book: An 'Ask Me Questions' Book. 2017. (ENG.). 60p. (J). pap. 14.00 ***(978-0-7171-7574-1(X))*** M.H. Gill & Co. U. C. IRL. Dist: Dufour Editions, Inc.

Cosford, Nina, illus. Dublin. 2012. (Panorama Pops Ser.). (ENG.). 30p. (J). (gr. k-4). 8.99 *(978-0-7636-6153-3(8))* Candlewick Pr.

Darraj, Susan Muaddi. Mairead Corrigan & Betty Williams: Partners in Peace in Northern Ireland. 2006. (Modern Peacemakers Ser.). (Illus.). 106p. (J). (gr. 9-12). lib. bdg. 30.00 *(978-0-7910-9001-5(9))* Facts On File, Inc.

Derkins, Susie. The Irish Republican Army. (Inside the World's Most Infamous Terrorist Organizations Ser.). 64p. 2009. (gr. 5-5). 58.50 *(978-1-61513-579-0(0))* 2005. (Illus.). (YA). (gr. 7-12). lib. bdg. 31.95 *(978-0-8239-3822-3(0))* Rosen Publishing Group, Inc., The.

Donaldson, Madeline. Ireland. 2011. (Country Explorers Ser.). 48p. pap. 51.02 *(978-0-7613-7625-5(9))*; (ENG.). (gr. 2-4). pap. 9.95 *(978-0-7613-7062-6(X))*; (ENG.). (gr. 2-4). lib. bdg. 29.27 *(978-0-7613-6415-3(3))* Lerner Publishing Group.

Edgar, Sherra G. Ireland. 2015. (One World, Many Countries Ser.). (ENG.). 32p. (J). (gr. 1-4). 28.50 *(978-1-63407-048-5(8)*, 208884) Child's World, Inc., The.

Fradin, Dennis Brindell & Fradin, Judith Bloom. The Irish Potato Famine. 2011. (Great Escapes Ser.). (Illus.). 80p. (J). (gr. 6). 34.21 *(978-1-60870-473-6(4))* Marshall Cavendish Corp.

Gallagher, Tara. 100 Greatest Moments in Irish History. Bailey, Hannah, illus. 2011. (ENG.). 64p. (J). 23.95 *(978-0-7171-4970-4(6))* M.H. Gill & Co. U. C. IRL. Dist: Dufour Editions, Inc.

Ganeri, Anita. Republic of Ireland. Isik, Semur, illus. 2015. (Country Guides, with Benjamin Blog & His Inquisitive Dog Ser.). (ENG.). 32p. (gr. 1-3). 29.99 *(978-1-4109-6849-4(9)*, Read Me!) Heinemann-Raintree.

Hill, George. The Fall of Irish Chiefs & Clans & the Plantation of Ulster: Including the Names of Irish Catholics, & Protestant Settlers. 2004. Orig. Title: An Historical Account of the Plantation in Ulster at the Commencement of the 17th Century. (Illus.). 276p. lib. bdg. 39.00 *(978-0-940134-42-3(X))* Irish Genealogical Foundation.

Israel, Susan E. Be Just Me. 2012. 26p. pap. *(978-0-9827449-6-3(X))* Roxby Media Ltd.

Levy, Patricia & Nevins, Debbie. Ireland. 2015. (Cultures of the World Ser.). (ENG., Illus.). 144p. (J). (gr. 6-6). 47.07 *(978-1-5026-0075-2(7))* Cavendish Square Publishing.

Lisson, Deborah. Red Hugh: The Kidnap of Hugh O'Donnell. 2003. (Illus.). 224p. (YA). (gr. 5-18). pap. 7.95 *(978-0-86278-604-5(5))* O'Brien Pr., Ltd., The IRL. Dist: Independent Pubs. Group.

Lynette, Rachel. Let's Throw a St. Patrick's Day Party! 2011. (J). 49.50 *(978-1-4488-2738-1(8))*; pap. 8.25 *(978-1-4488-2737-4(X))*; lib. bdg. 22.60 *(978-1-4488-2574-5(1))* Rosen Publishing Group, Inc., The. (PowerKids Pr.).

Lyons, Mary E., ed. Feed the Children First: Irish Memories of the Great Hunger. 2012. (ENG.). 48p. (J). (gr. 3-6). pap. 22.99 *(978-1-4424-8292-0(3)*, Atheneum Bks. for Young Readers) Simon & Schuster Children's Publishing.

Mac a'Bháird, Natasha & Nolan, Alan. My Ireland. 2016. (ENG., Illus.). 24p. (J). pap., act. bk. ed. 12.00 *(978-1-84717-834-3(0))* O'Brien Pr., Ltd., The IRL. Dist: Dufour Editions, Inc.

Macken, Ultan. The Story of Daniel O'Connell. 2009. (Irish Heroes for Children Ser.). (ENG., Illus.). 128p. (J). 17.95 *(978-1-85635-596-4(9))* Mercier Pr., Ltd., The IRL. Dist: Dufour Editions, Inc.

McDonnell, Vincent. Ireland Our Island Story. 2011. (ENG., Illus.). 178p. (J). pap. 16.95 *(978-1-84889-118-0(0))* Collins Pr., The IRL. Dist: Dufour Editions, Inc.

—Michael Collins: Most Wanted Man. 2009. (ENG.). 136p. (J). pap. 15.95 *(978-1-905172-62-7(1))* Collins Pr., The IRL. Dist: Dufour Editions, Inc.

McHale, Conor. Ancient Ireland Colouring Book: From Newgrange to the Vikings. McHale, Conor, illus. 2014. (ENG., Illus.). 32p. (J). pap. 12.00 *(978-1-84717-629-5(1))* O'Brien Pr., Ltd., The IRL. Dist: Dufour Editions, Inc.

McQuinn, Anna & National Geographic Kids Staff. Ireland. 2008. (Countries of the World Ser.). (ENG., Illus.). 64p. (J). (gr. 5). lib. bdg. 27.90 *(978-1-4263-0299-2(1)*, National Geographic Children's Bks.) National Geographic Society.

Murray, Julie. Ireland, 1 vol. 2014. (Explore the Countries Set 2 Ser.). (ENG.). 40p. (gr. 7-11). lib. bdg. 29.93 *(978-1-62403-343-8(1)*, Big Buddy Bks.) ABDO Publishing Co.

Ní Dheirg, Iosold. The Story of Michael Collins. 2009. (Irish Heroes for Children Ser.). (ENG.). 123p. (J). 17.95 *(978-1-85635-595-7(0))* Mercier Pr., Ltd., The IRL. Dist: Dufour Editions, Inc.

Ní Dheirg, Iosold. The Story of Michael Collins. 2017. (ENG.). 140p. (J). pap. 10.00 ***(978-1-78117-491-3(1))*** Mercier Pr., Ltd., The IRL. Dist: Dufour Editions, Inc.

O'Donoghue, Sean. The Disaster of the Irish Potato Famine: Irish Immigrants Arrive in America (1845-1850), 01 vols., 1. 2016. (Spotlight on Immigration & Migration Ser.). (ENG., Illus.). 24p. (J). pap. 10.00 *(978-1-5081-4066-5(9)*, PowerKids Pr.) Rosen Publishing Group, Inc., The.

O'Neill, Joseph R. The Irish Potato Famine, 1 vol. 2009. (Essential Events Set 3 Ser.). (ENG., Illus.). 112p. (J). (gr. 6-12). lib. bdg. 35.64 *(978-1-60453-514-3(8))* ABDO Publishing Co.

O'Neill, Mary. Pick Your Brains about Ireland. Williams, Caspar, illus. 2005. (Pick Your Brains - Cadogan Ser.). (ENG.). 128p. pap. 9.95 *(978-1-86011-221-8(8))* Cadogan Guides GBR. Dist: Globe Pequot Pr., The.

Parker, Lewis K. Why Irish Immigrants Came to America. 2009. (Coming to America Ser.). 24p. (gr. 2-3). 42.50 *(978-1-61511-884-7(5)*, PowerKids Pr.) Rosen Publishing Group, Inc., The.

Pipe, Jim. Sail on an Irish Famine Ship! A Trip Across Teh Atlantic You'd Rather Not Make. Antram, David, illus. 2008. (You Wouldn't Want to Ser.). (ENG.). 32p. (J). (gr. 4-7). 29.00 *(978-0-531-13913-4(1))* Scholastic Library Publishing.

—You Wouldn't Want to Sail on an Irish Famine Ship! A Trip Across the Atlanic You'd Rather Not Make. Antram, David, illus. 2008. (You Wouldn't Want to...: History of the World Ser.). (ENG.). 32p. (J). (gr. 4-7). pap. 9.95 *(978-0-531-14854-9(8)*, Watts, Franklin) Scholastic Library Publishing.

Pohl, Kathleen. Descubramos Irlanda. 2008. (Descubramos Países Del Mundo Ser.). (SPA.). 32p. (gr. 1-5). pap. 10.50 *(978-0-8368-8790-7(5))*; (Illus.). lib. bdg. 26.00 *(978-0-8368-8783-9(2))* Stevens, Gareth Publishing LLLP. (Gareth Stevens Learning Library).

—Looking at Ireland. 2008. (Looking at Countries Ser.). (Illus.). 32p. (gr. 1-5). pap. 10.50 *(978-0-8368-8776-1(X))*; lib. bdg. 26.00 *(978-0-8368-8769-3(7))* Stevens, Gareth Publishing LLLP. (Gareth Stevens Learning Library).

Pollard, Michael. Rivers of Britain & Ireland: The Avon, Yorkshire Ouse, Tyne, Wye, Forth, Liffey, Lagan. (Illus.). 46p. (J). *(978-0-237-51805-9(8))* Evans Brothers, Ltd.

Sexton, Colleen. Ireland. 2010. (Exploring Countries Ser.). (ENG., Illus.). 32p. (J). (gr. 3-7). lib. bdg. 26.95 *(978-1-60014-483-7(7)*, Blastoff! Readers) Bellwether Media.

Sherman, Jill. The Irish Potato Famine: A Cause-And-Effect Investigation. 2016. (Cause-And-Effect Disasters Ser.). (ENG., Illus.). 40p. (J). (gr. 4-6). lib. bdg. 30.65 *(978-1-5124-1119-5(1))*; 46.65 *(978-1-5124-1131-7(0)*, Lerner Pubns.) Lerner Publishing Group.

Sonneborn, Liz. The Great Irish Famine. 2011. (Milestones in Modern World History Ser.). (Illus.). 124p. (C). (gr. 9). 35.00 *(978-1-60413-918-1(8)*, Chelsea Hse.) Facts On File, Inc.

Waldron, Melanie. Ireland, 1 vol. 2012. (Countries Around the World Ser.). (ENG.). 48p. (gr. 3-6). pap. 9.95 *(978-1-4329-6126-8(8))*; lib. bdg. 33.32 *(978-1-4329-6100-8(4))* Heinemann-Raintree. (NA-h).

Walker, Ida & Indovino, Shaina Carmel. Ireland. 2012. (J). pap. *(978-1-4222-2278-2(0))* Mason Crest.

—Ireland. Bruton, John, ed. 2012. (Major European Union Nations Ser.). 64p. (J). (gr. 7). 22.95 *(978-1-4222-2247-8(0))* Mason Crest.

Wallenfeldt, Jeff, ed. Ireland. 2013. (Britannica Guide to Countries of the European Union Ser.). (ENG., Illus.). 136p. (YA). (gr. 9-12). lib. bdg. 53.00 *(978-1-62275-058-0(6))* Rosen Publishing Group, Inc., The.

IRISH AMERICANS

Allan, Tony. The Irish Famine: The Birth of Irish America. 2003. (Point of Impact Ser.). (Illus.). 32p. (J). (gr. 5-7). per. 7.50 *(978-1-4034-4113-3(8))* Heinemann-Raintree.

Allen, Tony. The Irish Famine: The Birth of Irish America, 1 vol. 2nd ed. 2006. (Point of Impact Ser.). (ENG., Illus.). 32p. (gr. 3-7). pap. 8.49 *(978-1-4034-9153-4(4)*, NA-h) Heinemann-Raintree.

Goldstein, Margaret J. Irish in America. 2004. (In America Ser.). (ENG., Illus.). 80p. (gr. 5-8). lib. bdg. 27.93 *(978-0-8225-3950-6(0))* Lerner Publishing Group.

Graves, Kerry A. Irish Americans. 2003. (Immigrants in America Ser.). (Illus.). 112p. (gr. 6-12). 30.00 *(978-0-7910-7128-1(6)*, Chelsea Hse.) Facts On File, Inc.

Hall, Margaret C. Irish Americans. 2003. (We Are America Ser.). (Illus.). 32p. (J). (gr. 2-4). lib. bdg. 24.22 *(978-1-4034-0734-4(7))* Heinemann-Raintree.

Hossell, Karen Price. The Irish Americans. 2003. (Immigrants in America Ser.). (ENG., Illus.). 112p. (J). 30.85 *(978-1-56006-752-8(7)*, Lucent Bks.) Cengage Gale.

Moreno, Barry. The Irish Americans. 2007. (Major American Immigration Ser.). (YA). pap. 9.95 *(978-1-4222-0675-1(0))* Mason Crest.

Moreno, Barry & Haugen, Brenda. The Irish Americans. 2010. (Major American Immigration Ser.). (Illus.). 64p. (YA). (gr. 9-12). 22.95 *(978-1-4222-0608-9(4))* Mason Crest.

Nichol, Bryan. Irish Americans, 1 vol. 2004. (One Nation Set 2 Ser.). (ENG.). 32p. (gr. k-6). 27.07 *(978-1-59197-528-1(X)*, Checkerboard Library) ABDO Publishing Co.

Nickles, Greg. The Irish: We Came to North America. 2006. (Illus.). 32p. (J). (gr. 4-8). reprint ed. 19.00 *(978-0-7567-9909-0(0))* DIANE Publishing Co.

O'Donoghue, Sean. The Disaster of the Irish Potato Famine: Irish Immigrants Arrive in America (1845-1850), 01 vols., 1. 2016. (Spotlight on Immigration & Migration Ser.). (ENG., Illus.). 24p. (J). pap. 10.00 *(978-1-5081-4066-5(9)*, PowerKids Pr.) Rosen Publishing Group, Inc., The.

Parker, Lewis K. Why Irish Immigrants Came to America. (Coming to America Ser.). 24p. 2009. (gr. 2-3). 42.50 *(978-1-61511-884-7(5))* 2003. (Illus.). (J). lib. bdg. 22.60 *(978-0-8239-6462-8(0))* Rosen Publishing Group, Inc., The. (PowerKids Pr.).

Paulson, Timothy J. Irish Immigrants. Asher, Robert, ed. 2004. (Immigration to the United States Ser.). (Illus.). 96p. (gr. 4-9). 35.00 *(978-0-8160-5682-8(X))* Facts On File, Inc.

Thornton, Jeremy. The Irish Potato Famine: Irish Immigrants Come to America, 1845-1850. 2004. (Primary Sources of Immigration & Migration in America Ser.). (ENG., Illus.). 24p. (gr. 4-8). pap. 9.40 *(978-0-8239-8957-7(7)*, PowerKids Pr.) Rosen Publishing Group, Inc., The.

Trumbauer, Lisa. Hopes Fulfilled: The Irish Immigrants in Boston. 2005. (Illus.). 32p. (J). pap. *(978-0-7367-2881-2(3))* Zaner-Bloser, Inc.

Uschan, Michael V. Irish Americans. 2006. (World Almanac Library of American Immigration). (Illus.). 48p. (gr. 5-12). pap. 14.05 *(978-0-8368-7324-5(6))*; lib. bdg. 31.00 *(978-0-8368-7311-5(4))* Stevens, Gareth Publishing LLLP. (Gareth Stevens Secondary Library).

IRISH AMERICANS—FICTION

Acheson, A. S. Fighting Words. 2014. (Bareknuckle Ser.). 96p. (YA). (gr. 6-12). lib. bdg. 27.93 *(978-1-4677-1461-7(5)*, Darby Creek) Lerner Publishing Group.

Alger, Horatio. Only an Irish Boy: Or, Andy Burke's Fortunes & Misfortunes. 2006. pap. *(978-1-4065-0716-4(4))* Dodo Pr.

Alger Jr. Horatio Staff. Only an Irish Boy. rev. ed. 2006. 284p. 28.95 *(978-1-4218-1759-0(4))*; pap. 13.95 *(978-1-4218-1859-7(0))* 1st World Publishing, Inc. (1st World Library - Literary Society).

Auch, Mary Jane. Ashes of Roses. 2004. 250p. (YA). (gr. 8-12). 14.15 *(978-0-7569-4069-0(9))* Perfection Learning Corp.

Barker, M. P. A Difficult Boy. 2009. (ENG.). 272p. (YA). (gr. 5-18). pap. 7.95 *(978-0-8234-2244-9(5))* Holiday Hse., Inc.

—Mending Horses. 2014. (ENG.). 320p. (J). (gr. 5). 17.95 *(978-0-8234-2948-6(2))* Holiday Hse., Inc.

Bouthyette, Valerie, illus. The Leprechaun Trap. 2008. 40p. (J). pap. 10.95 *(978-0-9800835-0-7(8))* Clinch Media.

Chance, Megan. The Veil, 0 vols. 2015. (Fianna Trilogy Ser.: 3). (ENG.). 366p. (YA). (gr. 7-12). 16.99 *(978-1-5039-4571-5(5)*, 9781503945715, Skyscape) Amazon Publishing.

Collins, David Paul. Shanghaied. 2011. 320p. 29.95 *(978-1-4620-3184-9(6))*; pap. 19.95 *(978-1-4620-3183-2(8))* iUniverse, Inc.

Durbin, William. Until the Last Spike: The Journal of Sean Sullivan, a Transcontinental Railroad Worker, Nebraska & Points West 1867. 2013. (My Name Is America Ser.). lib. bdg. 17.20 *(978-0-606-32342-0(2)*, Turtleback) Turtleback Bks.

Emery, Joanna. Brothers of the Falls. Erickson, David, illus. 2004. (Adventures in America Ser.). (gr. 4). 14.95 *(978-1-893110-37-3(0))* Silver Moon Pr.

Fitzgerald, Laura Marx. The Gallery. 2016. (ENG.). 336p. (J). (gr. 5-7). 16.99 *(978-0-525-42865-7(8)*, Dial Bks) Penguin Young Readers Group.

Giff, Patricia Reilly. Water Street. 2008. (ENG.). 176p. (J). (gr. 3-7). 6.99 *(978-0-440-41921-1(2)*, Yearling) Random Hse. Children's Bks.

Haas, Jessie. Chase. 2007. 256p. (J). (gr. 5-9). lib. bdg. 17.89 *(978-0-06-112851-6(1))* HarperCollins Pubs.

Hamilton, Kersten. Tyger Tyger. 2011. (ENG.). 336p. (YA). (gr. 7). pap. 18.99 *(978-0-547-57732-6(X))* Houghton Mifflin Harcourt Publishing Co.

—When the Stars Threw down Their Spears. 2014. (ENG.). 400p. (YA). (gr. 7). pap. 8.99 *(978-0-544-22771-2(9)*, HMH Books For Young Readers) Houghton Mifflin Harcourt Publishing Co.

Hungry No More (Irish) 76p. (YA). (gr. 6-12). pap. 9.95 *(978-0-8224-3680-5(9))* Globe Fearon Educational Publishing.

Ingle, Sheila. Courageous Kate: A Daughter of the American Revolution. 2006. (ENG.). 130p. pap. 11.95 *(978-1-891885-52-5(9))* Hub City Pr.

LaFaye, A. Water Steps. 2009. (ENG., Illus.). 208p. (J). (gr. 2-7). 16.95 *(978-1-57131-687-5(6))*; pap. 6.95 *(978-1-57131-686-8(8))* Milkweed Editions.

Loughrey, Eithne. Annie Moore: First in Line for America. l.t. ed. 2006. (Dales Ser.). 224p. (J). (gr. 4-7). 23.99 *(978-1-84262-446-3(6))* Magna Large Print Bks. GBR. Dist: Ulverscroft Large Print Bks., Ltd.

—Annie Moore: New York City Girl. l.t. ed. 2006. (Dales Ser.). 208p. 23.99 *(978-1-84262-448-7(2))* Dales Large Print Bks. GBR. Dist: Ulverscroft Large Print Bks., Ltd.

—Annie Moore: The Golden Dollar Girl. l.t. ed. 2006. (Dales Ser.). 208p. (J). 23.99 *(978-1-84262-447-0(4))* Magna Large Print Bks. GBR. Dist: Ulverscroft Large Print Bks., Ltd.

Massachusetts Sabbath School Society Staff. Winnie Malone Written for the Mass S S Society, & Approved by the Committee of Publication. 2006. 144p. per. 18.99 *(978-1-4255-1163-0(5))* Michigan Publishing.

McDavid-Jones, Elizabeth. Secrets on 26th Street. 2009. (Mysteries Through Time Ser.). 144 - 176p. (YA). (gr. 4-8). 31.95 *(978-1-60754-200-1(5))*; pap. 15.25 *(978-1-60754-201-8(3))* Windmill Bks.

McNamara, Margaret & Gordon, Mike. The Luck of the Irish. 2007. (Robin Hill School Ser.). (SPA & ENG., Illus.). 32p. (J). (gr. -1-1). pap. 3.99 *(978-1-4169-1539-3(7)*, Simon Spotlight) Simon Spotlight.

Morpurgo, Michael. Twist of Gold. 2nd ed. 2009. (ENG.). 304p. (J). (gr. 4-7). pap. 10.99 *(978-1-4052-2928-9(4))* Egmont Bks., Ltd. GBR. Dist: Independent Pubs. Group.

Neale, Cynthia. Hope in New York City: The Continuing Story of the Irish Dresser. 2008. (ENG.). 176p. (J). pap. 7.95 *(978-1-57249-387-2(9)*, White Mane Kids) White Mane Publishing Co., Inc.

Polacco, Patricia. Fiona's Lace. Polacco, Patricia, illus. 2014. (ENG., Illus.). 48p. (J). (gr. -1-3). 17.99 *(978-1-4424-8724-6(0)*, Simon & Schuster/Paula Wiseman Bks.) Simon & Schuster/Paula Wiseman Bks.

Quick, Matthew. Boy21. 2013. (ENG.). 272p. (YA). (gr. 7-17). pap. 10.99 *(978-0-316-12796-7(5))* Little, Brown Bks. for Young Readers.

Rue, Nancy N. Sophie Steps Up, 1 vol. 2009. (Faithgirlz! Ser.: No. 4). (ENG.). 128p. (J). pap. 6.99 *(978-0-310-71841-3(4))* Zonderkidz.

Schneider, Mical. Annie Quinn in America. 2003. (Adventures in Time Ser.). (Illus.). 252p. (J). (gr. 4-7). 15.95 *(978-1-57505-510-7(4)*, Carolrhoda Bks.) Lerner Publishing Group.

Shepherd, David & Plummer, William K. We Were There at the Driving of the Golden Spike. 2013. (ENG., Illus.). 192p. (J). (gr. 3-8). pap. 6.99 *(978-0-486-49259-9(1))* Dover Pubns., Inc.

Sullivan, Paul. Breaker at Dawn. 2010. (J). pap. *(978-0-88092-705-5(4))* Royal Fireworks Publishing Co.

Whitney, Kim Ablon. See You down the Road. 14.85 *(978-0-7569-5710-0(9))* Perfection Learning Corp.

Wilson, Diane Lee. Tracks. (ENG., (J). (gr. 5-9). 2013. Illus.). 304p. pap. 6.99 *(978-1-4424-2014-4(6))* 2012. 288p. 16.99 *(978-1-4424-2013-7(8))* McElderry, Margaret K. Bks. (McElderry, Margaret K. Bks.).

IRISH—UNITED STATES—FICTION

Bennese, Ray & Bennese, Kristian. Till the Train Runs Out of Track. 2007. 76p. per. 19.95 *(978-1-4241-7567-3(4))* America Star Bks.

Lawson, Robert. The Great Wheel. Lawson, Robert, illus. 2004. (ENG., Illus.). 192p. (YA). (gr. 5). pap. 9.99 *(978-0-8027-7705-8(8)*, 9780802777058, Bloomsbury USA Childrens) Bloomsbury Publishing USA.

Meyer, L. A. Boston Jacky: Being an Account of the Further Adventures of Jacky Faber, Taking Care of Business. 2015. (Bloody Jack Adventures Ser.: 11). (ENG.). 384p. (YA). (gr. 9). pap. 9.99 *(978-0-544-43914-6(7)*, HMH Books For Young Readers) Houghton Mifflin Harcourt Publishing Co.

O'Neill, Joan. Rainbow's End. 2007. (ENG.). 288p. (J). (gr. 7-17). pap. 10.95 *(978-0-340-91149-5(2))* Hachette Children's Group GBR. Dist: Hachette Bk. Group.

IRISH LITERATURE

Bloom, Harold, ed. James Joyce, New Edition. 2nd rev. ed. 2009. (Bloom's Modern Critical Views Ser.). 270p. (C). (gr. 9-18). 45.00 *(978-1-60413-396-7(1)*, Chelsea Hse.) Facts On File, Inc.

Jarvie, Gordon, ed. Irish Folk & Fairy Tales. 2nd rev. ed. 2009. (ENG.). 224p. pap. 16.95 *(978-0-85640-836-6(0))* Blackstaff Pr., Ltd. GBR. Dist: Dufour Editions, Inc.

Priddy, Roger. Mo Chéad Focóir. Ó Murchadha, Niall, tr. 2013. (GLE & IRI.). 10p. (J). 19.00 *(978-0-7171-5807-2(1))* M.H. Gill & Co. U. C. IRL. Dist: Dufour Editions, Inc.

Saddleback Educational Publishing Staff, ed. Gulliver's Travels. 2011. (Timeless Classics Ser.). (ENG.). 48p. (YA). (gr. 9-12). pupil's gde. ed. 19.95 incl. cd-rom *(978-1-61651-136-4(2))* Saddleback Educational Publishing, Inc.

IRON

Capaccio, George. Iron: Set Of 6. 2011. (Navigators Ser.). (J). pap. 48.00 net. *(978-1-4108-6237-2(2))* Benchmark Education Co.

—Iron: Text Pairs. 2008. (Bridges/Navigators Ser.). (J). (gr. 5). 89.00 *(978-1-4108-8419-0(8))* Benchmark Education Co.

Hasan, Heather. Iron. (Understanding the Elements of the Periodic Table Ser.). 48p. 2009. (gr. 6-6). 53.00 *(978-1-60854-658-9(6)*, Rosen Reference) 2005. (Illus.). (J). (gr. 5-8). lib. bdg. 29.25 *(978-1-4042-0157-6(2))* Rosen Publishing Group, Inc., The.

Kassinger, Ruth. Iron & Steel: From Thor's Hammer to the Space Shuttle. 2003. (Material World Ser.). (ENG., Illus.). 80p. (gr. 5-9). lib. bdg. 26.60 *(978-0-7613-2111-8(X)*, Twenty-First Century Bks.) Lerner Publishing Group.

Kennon, Caroline. How Iron Ore Forms. 2016. (From the Earth: How Resources Are Made Ser.). (Illus.). 32p. (J). (gr. 4-3). pap. 10.50 *(978-1-4824-4713-2(4))* Stevens, Gareth Publishing LLLP.

Perritano, John. Iron, Vol. 12. 2015. (North American Natural Resources Ser.). (Illus.). 64p. (J). (gr. 7). 23.95 *(978-1-4222-3383-2(9))* Mason Crest.

Zemlicka, Shannon. From Iron to Car. 2003. (Start to Finish Ser.). (ENG., Illus.). 24p. (gr. k-3). 19.93 *(978-0-8225-0943-1(1)*, Lerner Pubns.) Lerner Publishing Group.

IRON AGE

Butterfield, Moira. Everyday Life. 2016. (ENG., Illus.). 32p. (J). (gr. 2-4). 17.99 *(978-1-4451-4815-1(3)*, Franklin Watts) Hachette Children's Group GBR. Dist: Hachette Bk. Group.

—Iron Age. 2017. (Britain in the Past Ser.). (ENG., Illus.). 32p. (J). (gr. 2-5). pap. 12.99 ***(978-1-4451-4065-0(9)***, Franklin Watts) Hachette Children's Group GBR. Dist: Hachette Bk. Group.

Butterfield, Moira. Warriors & Weapons. 2016. (ENG., Illus.). 32p. (J). (gr. 2-4). 17.99 *(978-1-4451-4816-8(1)*, Franklin

H
I

Watts) Hachette Children's Group GBR. Dist: Hachette Bk. Group.

Coulter, Laurie. Kings & Carpenters: One Hundred Bible Land Jobs You Might Have Praised or Panned. Newbigging, Martha, illus. 2010. (Jobs in History Ser.). (ENG.). 96p. (J). (gr. 3-6). 25.95 *(978-1-55451-227-0(1)*, 9781554512270); pap. 16.95 *(978-1-55451-226-3(3)*, 9781554512263) Annick Pr., Ltd. CAN. Dist: Publishers Group West (PGW).

Green, Jen. The Celts & the Iron Age. 2016. (Discover Through Craft Ser.). (ENG., Illus.). 32p. (J). (gr. 2-4). pap. 12.99 *(978-1-4451-3749-0(6)*, Franklin Watts) Hachette Children's Group GBR. Dist: Hachette Bk. Group.

Hibbert, Clare. Stone Age to Iron Age. 2017. (History Detective Investigates Ser.). (ENG., Illus.). 32p. (J). (gr. 4-6). pap. 12.99 ***(978-0-7502-8197-3(9)***, Wayland) Hachette Children's Group GBR. Dist: Hachette Bk. Group.

Howell, Izzi. Stone Age to Iron Age. 2017. (Fact Cat: History: Early Britons Ser.). (ENG., Illus.). 24p. (J). (gr. k-2). pap. 9.99 *(978-0-7502-9938-1(X)*, Wayland) Hachette Children's Group GBR. Dist: Hachette Bk. Group.

Kerrigan, Juliet. Life & Death in a Hill Fort. 2015. (Collins Big Cat Ser.). (ENG., Illus.). 32p. (J). (gr. 3-3). pap. 8.95 *(978-0-00-812773-2(5))* HarperCollins Pubs. Ltd. GBR. Dist: Independent Pubs. Group.

IRON INDUSTRY AND TRADE

see also Steel Industry and Trade

Hiller, Sandra J. The Life of a Colonial Blacksmith. 2013. (Jr. Graphic Colonial America Ser.). (ENG., Illus.). 24p. (J). (gr. 3-6). pap. 10.60 *(978-1-4777-1433-1(2))*; lib. bdg. 25.25 *(978-1-4777-1308-2(5))* Rosen Publishing Group, Inc., The. (PowerKids Pr.).

Kresse, Alfred L. Alleghany Iron. 2012. (Illus.). 63p. *(978-0-939487-54-7(3))* Chesapeake & Ohio Historical Society, Inc.

The Life of a Colonial Blacksmith. 2013. (Jr. Graphic Colonial America Ser.). 24p. (J). (gr. 3-6). pap. 63.60 *(978-1-4777-1434-8(0)*, PowerKids Pr.) Rosen Publishing Group, Inc., The.

Orr, Tamra. Careers in Sheet Metal & Ironwork, 01 vols., 1. 2016. (Essential Careers Ser.). (ENG.). 80p. (J). 34.25 *(978-1-4994-6221-0(2)*, Rosen Young Adult) Rosen Publishing Group, Inc., The.

IRRIGATION

see also Dams; Windmills

Burns, Kylie. William Kamkwamba: Powering His Village. 2016. (Remarkable Lives Revealed Ser.). (ENG., Illus.). 32p. (J). (gr. 2-5). *(978-0-7787-2690-6(8))* Crabtree Publishing Co.

Hofer, Charles. How Do Irrigation Systems Work? 2016. (STEM Waterworks Ser.). (Illus.). 32p. (J). (gr. 5-5). pap. 11.75 *(978-1-4994-2007-4(2)*, PowerKids Pr.) Rosen Publishing Group, Inc., The.

Kamkwamba, William. The Boy Who Harnessed the Wind: Creating Currents of Electricity & Hope. 2009. 14.44 *(978-0-7848-3872-3(0)*, Everbind) Marco Bk. Co.

—The Boy Who Harnessed the Wind: Creating Currents of Electricity & Hope. Hymas, Anna, illus. 2015. (ENG.). 304p. (J). (gr. 5). 18.99 *(978-0-8037-4080-8(8)*, Dial Bks) Penguin Young Readers Group.

Kamkwamba, William & Mealer, Bryan. The Boy Who Harnessed the Wind: Young Readers Edition. Zunon, Elizabeth, illus. (ENG.). (J). 2016. 304p. (gr. 5). 8.99 *(978-0-14-751042-6(2)*, Puffin Books) 2012. 32p. (gr. 1-3). 17.99 *(978-0-8037-3511-8(1)*, Dial Bks) Penguin Young Readers Group.

Phillips, Cynthia & Priwer, Shana. Dams & Waterways. 2009. (ENG., Illus.). 112p. (C). (gr. 6-18). lib. bdg. 158.00 *(978-0-7656-8122-5(6)*, Y181910) Routledge.

IRVING, WASHINGTON, 1783-1859

Collins, David R. Washington Irving: Storyteller for a New Nation. 2004. (World Writers Ser.). (Illus.). 112p. (YA). (gr. 6-12). 23.95 *(978-1-883846-50-3(1)*, First Biographies) Reynolds, Morgan Inc.

Harasymiw, Mark J. The Legend of Rip Van Winkle. 2015. (Famous Legends Ser.). (ENG., Illus.). 32p. (J). (gr. 2-3). pap. 10.50 *(978-1-4824-2744-8(3))* Stevens, Gareth Publishing LLLP.

Harness, Cheryl. The Literary Adventures of Washington Irving: American Storyteller. 2008. (ENG., Illus.). 48p. (J). (gr. 2-5). 17.95 *(978-1-4263-0438-5(2))*; lib. bdg. 27.90 *(978-1-4263-0439-2(0))* National Geographic Society. (National Geographic Children's Bks.).

ISABELLA I, QUEEN OF SPAIN, 1451-1504

Bridges, Shirin Yim. Isabella of Castile. Nguyen, Albert, illus. 2010. (Thinking Girl's Treasury of Real Princesses Ser.). (ENG.). 24p. (J). (gr. 3-8). 18.95 *(978-0-9845098-4-3(4))* Goosebottom Bks. LLC.

Whitelaw, Nancy. Queen Isabella & the Unification of Spain. 2004. (World Leaders Ser.). (Illus.). 160p. (YA). (gr. 6-12). lib. bdg. 26.95 *(978-1-931798-25-9(7))* Reynolds, Morgan Inc.

ISLAM

Here are entered works on the religion of which Muhammad is the prophet. Works on the community of believers in Islam are entered under Muslims.

see also Muslims

Abdullah, Noorah Kathryn. What Do We Say... A Guide to Islamic Manners. 2nd ed. 2010. (ENG., Illus.). 24p. (J). (gr. -1-k). 8.95 *(978-0-86037-350-6(9))* Kube Publishing Ltd. GBR. Dist: Consortium Bk. Sales & Distribution.

Ahamed, Syed Vickar, tr. from ARA. The Quran: English Translation of the Meaning Of. 2005. (ENG.). 396p. per. 14.95 *(978-0-9773009-0-7(0))* Bk. of Signs Foundation.

Ahmad, Tazeen. Abc's of Islam. 2012. 38p. pap. 20.99 *(978-1-4772-7328-9(X))* AuthorHouse.

—Ali's Special Cure. 2010. 36p. 15.99 *(978-1-4520-5199-4(2))* AuthorHouse.

Ahmedi, Waqar, et al. World Religions: Judaism, Christianity & Islam. 2017. (ENG.). 120p. (J). (gr. 6-9). pap. 29.99 ***(978-0-00-822768-5(3))*** HarperCollins Pubs. Ltd. GBR. Dist: Independent Pubs. Group.

Ali-Karamali, Sumbul. Growing up Muslim: Understanding the Beliefs & Practices of Islam. 2013. (ENG.). 224p. (J). (gr. 5). pap. 7.99 *(978-0-385-74096-8(4)*, Ember) Random Hse. Children's Bks.

Alkouatli, Claire. Islam. 2006. (World Religions Ser.). (Illus.). 144p. (J). (gr. 3-7). lib. bdg. 39.93 *(978-0-7614-2120-7(3))* Marshall Cavendish Corp.

Allah in Person, Royall. The Center Page, Volume 1. 2003. (Illus.). 241p. 51.00 *(978-0-9768502-0-5(6))* United Nation of Islam, The.

Aloian, Molly. Ramadan. 2008. (Celebrations in My World Ser.). (ENG., Illus.). 32p. (J). (gr. k-3). pap. *(978-0-7787-4303-3(9))*; lib. bdg. *(978-0-7787-4285-2(7))* Crabtree Publishing Co.

Aman, Israa. The Monotheistic Faiths: Judaism, Christianity, & Islam, Vol. 8. Pecastaing, Camille, ed. 2016. (Understanding Islam Ser.: Vol. 8). (ENG., Illus.). 112p. (J). (gr. 7-12). 25.95 *(978-1-4222-3674-1(9))* Mason Crest.

Amer, Fatmah. Islam. 2007. (QEB World of Faiths Ser.). (Illus.). 32p. (J). (gr. 4-7). lib. bdg. 27.10 *(978-1-59566-208-8(1))* QEB Publishing Inc.

Anderson, Sheila. Ramadan, 1 vol. Conger, Holli, illus. 2009. (Cultural Holidays Ser.). (ENG.). 32p. (gr. -1-4). 28.50 *(978-1-60270-605-7(0)*, Looking Glass Library- Nonfiction) Magic Wagon.

Azm, Mohsen Abou El, illus. Muhammad: The Life of the Prophet - Based on Original Sources. adapted ed. 2014. (ENG.). 64p. pap. 6.95 *(978-1-906230-62-3(5))* Real Reads Ltd. GBR. Dist: Casemate Pubs. & Bk. Distributors, LLC.

Baig, Khalid. First Things First: For Inquiring Minds & Yearning Hearts. 2004. 432p. pap. 20.00 *(978-0-9755157-0-9(5))* Open Mind Pr.

Blake, Philip. We Are Muslims. 2016. (ENG., Illus.). 32p. (J). (gr. 4-6). pap. 11.99 *(978-1-4451-3888-6(3)*, Franklin Watts) Hachette Children's Group GBR. Dist: Hachette Bk. Group.

Bodden, Valerie. Mosques. 2008. (Built to Last Ser.). (Illus.). 24p. (J). (gr. 3-7). lib. bdg. 24.25 *(978-1-58341-562-7(9)*, Creative Education) Creative Co., The.

Brewer, Paul. September 11 & Radical Islamic Terrorism. 2006. (Terrorism in Today's World Ser.). (Illus.). 48p. (gr. 5-12). pap. 14.05 *(978-0-8368-6567-7(7))*; lib. bdg. 31.00 *(978-0-8368-6560-8(X))* Stevens, Gareth Publishing LLLP. (Gareth Stevens Secondary Library).

The Britannica Guide to Islam. 2017. (Britannica Guide to Islam Ser.). 128p. (gr. 14-15). 181.25 ***(978-1-5081-0548-0(0)***, Britannica Educational Publishing) Rosen Publishing Group, Inc., The.

Bryfonski, Dedria. Islamophobia. 2012. (Current Controversies Ser.). (ENG.). 224p. (gr. 10-12). lib. bdg. 46.40 *(978-0-7377-6235-8(7)*, Greenhaven Pr., Inc.) Cengage Gale.

Bryfonski, Dedria, ed. Islamophobia. 2012. (Current Controversies Ser.). (ENG.). 240p. (gr. 10-12). pap. 28.45 *(978-0-7377-6236-5(5)*, Greenhaven Pr., Inc.) Cengage Gale.

Cara, Anwar. 5 Pillars of Islam. Zulkifli, Azhari, illus. 2015. (ENG.). 16p. (J). bds. 9.95 *(978-0-86037-574-6(9))* Kube Publishing Ltd. GBR. Dist: Consortium Bk. Sales & Distribution.

Carr, Melissa S. Who Are the Muslims? 2005. (Introducing Islam Ser.). (Illus.). 112p. (YA). lib. bdg. 24.95 *(978-1-59084-701-5(6))* Mason Crest.

Chaudhry, Saida. Call to Prophethood. (Illus.). (J). (gr. 2-5). pap. 4.00 *(978-0-89259-046-9(7))* American Trust Pubns.

Clark, Charles. Islam. 2004. (Religions of the World Ser.). (ENG., Illus.). 104p. (YA). 30.85 *(978-1-56006-986-7(4)*, LML00902-178231, Lucent Bks.) Cengage Gale.

Conover, Sarah & Crane, Freda, adapted by. Ayay Jamilah: Beautiful Signs: A Treasury of Islamic Wisdom for Children & Parents. 2010. (ENG., Illus.). 212p. (YA). pap. 19.95 *(978-1-55896-569-0(6)*, Skinner Hse. Bks.) Unitarian Universalist Assn.

Cooper, Alison. Facts about Islam. 2010. (World Religions Ser.). (Illus.). 48p. (J). (gr. 3-6). lib. bdg. 29.25 *(978-1-61532-322-7(8)*, Rosen Reference) Rosen Publishing Group, Inc., The.

Delgado, Linda D. Saying Goodbye. 2006. (YA). per. *(978-0-9767861-8-4(4))* Muslim Writers Publishing.

—Stories. 2006. (YA). per. *(978-0-9767861-7-7(6))* Muslim Writers Publishing.

Denffer, Ahmad Von. Islam for Children. 2009. (ENG., Illus.). 176p. (J). (gr. 2-6). pap. 9.95 *(978-0-86037-085-7(2))* Kube Publishing Ltd. GBR. Dist: Consortium Bk. Sales & Distribution.

Dicker, K. I Belong to the Muslim Faith. Azizi, Z., photos by. 2009. (Illus.). 24p. (YA). pap. 8.25 *(978-1-4358-8624-7(0))* Rosen Publishing Group, Inc., The.

Dicker, Katie & Azizi, Zoha. I Belong to the Muslim Faith. 2009. (I Belong Ser.). (Illus.). 24p. (J). (gr. 1-4). lib. bdg. 22.60 *(978-1-4358-3035-6(0))* Rosen Publishing Group, Inc., The.

Douglass, Susan L. Ramadan. Reeves, Jeni, illus. (On My Own Holidays Ser.). (gr. 2-4). 2004. (J). lib. bdg. 25.26 *(978-0-87614-932-4(8))* 2003. (ENG.). pap. 6.95 *(978-1-57505-584-8(6))* Lerner Publishing Group.

D'Oyen, Fatima. Islamic Manners. Zulkifli, Azhar, illus. 2012. (ENG.). 64p. (J). (gr. -1-2). pap., act. bk. ed. 5.95 *(978-0-86037-463-3(7))* Kube Publishing Ltd. GBR. Dist: Consortium Bk. Sales & Distribution.

D'Oyen, Fatima M. & Chachi, Abdelkader. In the Prophet's Garden: A Selection of Ahadith for the Young. 2010. (ENG., Illus.). 132p. (J). (gr. 3). pap. 22.50 *(978-0-86037-372-8(X))* Kube Publishing Ltd. GBR. Dist: Consortium Bk. Sales & Distribution.

Emerick, Yahiya. It's All about Islam. 2014. (ARA & ENG., Illus.). 407p. (J). *(978-1-933269-14-6(6))* Noorart, Inc.

Ergün, Erol. The All-Merciful Master: The Beautiful Names of God. Egitim, Hasan, illus. 2009. 127p. (J). pap. *(978-1-59784-223-5(0))* Tughra Bks.

Fadl, Khaled Abou El. Introducing Islam, 8 vols., Set. 2003. (Illus.). 112p. (YA). lib. bdg. *(978-1-59084-696-4(6))* Mason Crest.

Foreign Policy Research Institute Staff, ed. The Growth & Influence of Islam in the Nations of Asia & Central Asia, 17 vols., Set. 2006. (Illus.). 112,128p. (YA). lib. bdg. 441.15 *(978-1-59084-832-6(2))* Mason Crest.

Ganeri, Anita. Hajj Story. 2003. (Festival Stories Ser.). (ENG., Illus.). 24p. (J). pap. 10.99 *(978-0-237-52732-7(4))* Evans Brothers, Ltd. GBR. Dist: Independent Pubs. Group.

—Islamic Stories. Phillips, Rachael, illus. 2014. (Storyteller Ser.). (ENG.). 32p. (J). (gr. 2-4). pap. 10.99 *(978-1-78388-009-6(0))* Tulip Books GBR. Dist: Independent Pubs. Group.

—Muslim Festivals Through the Year. 2003. (Year of Festivals Ser.). 30p. (J). lib. bdg. 24.25 *(978-1-58340-371-6(X))* Black Rabbit Bks.

—The Qur'an & Islam. Fennell, Tracy, illus. 2003. 30p. (J). lib. bdg. 24.25 *(978-1-58340-241-2(1))* Black Rabbit Bks.

Garcha, Rajinder & Russell, Patricia Yates. The World of Islam in Literature for Youth: A Selective Annotated Bibliography for K-12, Vol. 2006. (Literature for Youth Ser.: 7). (ENG.). 242p. (gr. 3-7). per. 70.00 *(978-0-8108-5488-8(0))* Scarecrow Pr., Inc.

Gemer, Katy. Islam. 2008. (Religions Around the World Ser.). 32p. (gr. 3-18). lib. bdg. 18.56 *(978-0-7614-3167-1(5)*, Benchmark Bks.) Marshall Cavendish Corp.

Ghani, Aisha. I Can Pray Anywhere! Zulkifli, Azhari, illus. 2010. (ENG.). 15p. (J). (gr. -1-k). bds. 9.95 *(978-0-86037-339-1(8))* Kube Publishing Ltd. GBR. Dist: Consortium Bk. Sales & Distribution.

Gnojewski, Carol. Ramadan: A Muslim Time of Fasting, Prayer, & Celebration. 2004. (Finding Out about Holidays Ser.). (Illus.). 48p. (J). (gr. 2-5). lib. bdg. 25.27 *(978-0-7660-2275-1(7))* Enslow Pubs., Inc.

Gordon, Matthew. Islam. 2009. (Understanding Religions Ser.). (YA). (gr. 7-12). lib. bdg. 34.60 *(978-1-4358-5618-9(X))* Rosen Publishing Group, Inc., The.

Green, Alice. Celebrating Id-Ul-Adha: A Muslim Festival. 2009. (We Love Holidays Ser.). 24p. (J). (gr. k-5). (ENG., Illus.). pap. 8.25 *(978-1-4358-2905-3(0)*, 1291609); lib. bdg. 22.60 *(978-1-4358-2845-2(3))* Rosen Publishing Group, Inc., The. (PowerKids Pr.).

Guillain, Charlotte. Islamic Culture, 1 vol. 2012. (Global Cultures Ser.). (ENG.). 48p. (gr. 4-6). pap. 9.95 *(978-1-4329-6788-8(6))*; 32.65 *(978-1-4329-6779-6(7))* Heinemann-Raintree. (NA-h).

Gunes, Aysenur. All about Wudu (Ablution) Polat, Ercan, illus. 2017. (Discover Islam Sticker Activity Bks.). (ENG.). 32p. (J). (gr. -1-2). pap., act. bk. ed. 5.95 *(978-0-86037-681-1(8))* Kube Publishing Ltd. GBR. Dist: Consortium Bk. Sales & Distribution.

—Makkah & Madinah Activity Book. Polat, Ercan, illus. 2015. (Discover Islam Sticker Activity Bks.). (ENG.). 32p. (J). 5.95 *(978-0-86037-544-9(7))* Kube Publishing Ltd. GBR. Dist: Consortium Bk. Sales & Distribution.

—Prayer & Wudu. Polat, Ercan, illus. 2015. (Discover Islam Sticker Activity Bks.). (ENG.). 32p. (J). act. bk. ed. 5.95 *(978-0-86037-610-1(9))* Kube Publishing Ltd. GBR. Dist: Consortium Bk. Sales & Distribution.

Habeeb, William Mark. Islamic Fundamentalism. 2005. (Introducing Islam Ser.). (Illus.). 112p. (YA). lib. bdg. 24.95 *(978-1-59084-703-9(2))* Mason Crest.

Hackney Blackwell, Amy & Matters, Print. Ramadan. 2009. (Holidays & Celebration Ser.). (Illus.). 112p. (gr. 5-8). 40.00 *(978-1-60413-098-0(9)*, Chelsea Hse.) Facts On File, Inc.

Haqq, Shahada Sharelle Abdul. Noble Women of Faith: Asiya, Mary, Khadija, Fatima. 2012. (ENG., Illus.). 31p. (J). (gr. 2-4). 12.95 *(978-1-59784-268-6(0))* Tughra Bks.

Haugen, David M. Islam. 2009. (Opposing Viewpoints Ser.). (ENG., Illus.). (J). (gr. 10-12). 224p. 48.80 *(978-0-7377-4526-9(6))*;No. 9. 240p. pap. 29.45 *(978-0-7377-4527-6(4))* Cengage Gale. (Greenhaven Pr., Inc.).

Hawke, Rosanne. The Truth about Peacock Blue: A Powerful Story about One Girl's Fight for Justice in Pakistan. 2016. (ENG.). 272p. (YA). (gr. 8-11). pap. 11.99 *(978-1-74331-994-9(0))* Allen & Unwin AUS. Dist: Independent Pubs. Group.

Hiber, Amanda. Islamic Militancy. 2009. (Opposing Viewpoints Ser.). (ENG., Illus.). 224p. (gr. 10-12). pap. 33.80 *(978-0-7377-4217-6(8)*, LML02109-243140); lib. bdg. 48.80 *(978-0-7377-4216-9(X)*, LML02109-243107) Cengage Gale. (Greenhaven Pr., Inc.).

Hilliam, David. Richard the Lionheart & the Third Crusade: The English King Confronts Saladin in AD 1191. 2009. (Library of the Middle Ages Ser.). 64p. (gr. 5-8). 58.50 *(978-1-60853-902-4(4)*, Rosen Reference) Rosen Publishing Group, Inc., The.

Hipps, Amelia. Islam, Christianity, Judaism. 2005. (Introducing Islam Ser.). (Illus.). 112p. (J). lib. bdg. 24.95 *(978-1-59084-698-8(2))* Mason Crest.

Hodges, Rick. What Muslims Think, & How They Live. 2005. (Introducing Islam Ser.). (Illus.). 112p. (YA). lib. bdg. 24.95 *(978-1-59084-702-2(4))* Mason Crest.

Hunt, Demi & Barks, Coleman. Painting Heaven: Polishing the Mirror of the Heart. 2015. (ENG., Illus.). 44p. (J). (gr. k-2). 19.95 *(978-1-941610-13-8(7))* Fons Vitae of Kentucky, Inc.

Ibrahim, Yasmin. I Can Make Du'a Anywhere! Zulkifli, Azhari, illus. 2010. (ENG.). 15p. (J). (gr. -1-k). bds. 9.95 *(978-0-86037-324-7(X))* Kube Publishing Ltd. GBR. Dist: Consortium Bk. Sales & Distribution.

—I Can Say Bismillah Anywhere! Zulkifli, Azhari, illus. 2010. (ENG.). 15p. (J). (gr. -1-k). bds. 9.95 *(978-0-86037-314-8(2))* Kube Publishing Ltd. GBR. Dist: Consortium Bk. Sales & Distribution.

Interaction Publishers, Inc. Staff. Into Islam. 2004. (Illus.). (YA). (gr. 6-12). 48.00 *(978-1-57336-401-0(0)*, I3011) Interaction Pubs., Inc.

Jeffrey, Laura S. Celebrate Ramadan. 2007. (Celebrate Holidays Ser.). (Illus.). 112p. (J). (gr. 5-9). lib. bdg. 33.27 *(978-0-7660-2774-9(0))* Enslow Pubs., Inc.

Jones, Rob Lloyd. The Story of Islam. Chisholm, Jane, ed. 2007. (Young Reading Series 3 Gift Bks). (Illus.). 61p. (J). 8.99 *(978-0-7945-1865-3(6)*, Usborne) EDC Publishing.

Juettner, Bonnie. Genies. 2010. (Monsters Ser.). (ENG., Illus.). 48p. (gr. 4-8). 35.20 *(978-0-7377-5051-5(0)*, Kidhaven) Cengage Gale.

Kabbani, Shaykh Muhamma & Kabbani, Muhammad Hisham. Links of Light: The Golden Chain: A Child's Version of the Naqshbandi Sufi Way. Sperling, Karima & Sperling, Alia, illus. 2009. xi, 217p. (J). *(978-1-930409-68-2(0))* Islamic Supreme Council of America.

Kemmetmueller, Donna Jean. My Muslim Friend: A Young Catholic Learns about Islam. Jacobsen, Laura, illus. 2006. 47p. (J). 15.95 *(978-0-8198-4844-4(1))* Pauline Bks. & Media.

Khan, Aisha Karen. What You Will See Inside a Mosque. Pepis, Aaron, photos by. (What You Will See Inside ... Ser.). (Illus.). 32p. (J). 2008. (ENG.). pap. 8.99 *(978-1-59473-257-7(4)*, 9781594732577) 2003. (gr. 1-5). 16.95 *(978-1-893361-60-7(8))* LongHill Partners, Inc. (Skylight Paths Publishing).

—What You Will See Inside a Mosque. Pepis, Aaron, photos by. 2003. (Illus.). 32p. *(978-2-89507-398-7(8))* Novalis Publishing.

Khan, Hena. Golden Domes & Silver Lanterns: A Muslim Book of Colors. Amini, Mehrdokht, illus. 2015. (ENG.). 32p. (J). (gr. -1-k). 7.99 *(978-1-4521-4121-3(5))* Chronicle Bks. LLC.

Kidwai, Abdur Raheem. The Qur'an: Essential Teachings. 2015. (ENG.). 192p. pap. 14.95 *(978-0-86037-410-7(6))* Kube Publishing Ltd. GBR. Dist: Consortium Bk. Sales & Distribution.

Knight, Khadijah. My Muslim Faith. (Illus.). 32p. *(978-0-237-51898-1(8))* Evans Brothers, Ltd.

Leadbeater, Tim. Islamic Empires, 600-1650. 2004. (Illus.). 48p. pap. 32.50 *(978-0-340-81200-6(1))* Hodder Education Group GBR. Dist: Trans-Atlantic Pubns., Inc.

Leadbeater, Tim & Clare, John. Islamic Empires, 600-1650. 2004. (Illus.). 48p. (YA). pap. 32.50 *(978-0-340-81199-3(4))* Hodder Education Group GBR. Dist: Trans-Atlantic Pubns., Inc.

Lemu, B.Aisha. Animals in Islam. 2005. (Illus.). 52p. pap. *(978-978-2462-33-6(0))* Spectrum Bks., Ltd. NGA. Dist: Michigan State Univ. Pr.

Luxenberg, Alan H. Radical Islam. 2010. (World of Islam Ser.). (Illus.). 64p. (YA). (gr. 4-7). lib. bdg. 22.95 *(978-1-4222-0536-5(3))* Mason Crest.

Mahdi, Nasreen. Islam: Core Beliefs & Practices, Vol. 8. Pecastaing, Camille, ed. 2016. (Understanding Islam Ser.: Vol. 8). (ENG., Illus.). 112p. (J). (gr. 7-12). 25.95 *(978-1-4222-3672-7(2))* Mason Crest.

Mansoor, Musheer. Muslim Heroes & Holy Places, Vol. 8. Pecastaing, Camille, ed. 2016. (Understanding Islam Ser.: Vol. 8). (ENG., Illus.). 112p. (J). (gr. 7-12). 25.95 *(978-1-4222-3675-8(7))* Mason Crest.

Marcovitz, Hal. Islam in Africa. Ojakorotu, Victor & Rotberg, Robert I., eds. 2013. (Africa: Progress & Problems Ser.: 13). (Illus.). 112p. (J). (gr. 7-18). 24.95 *(978-1-4222-2943-9(2))* Mason Crest.

Marsico, Katie. Islam. 2017. (21st Century Skills Library: Global Citizens: World Religions Ser.). (ENG., Illus.). 32p. (J). (gr. 4-7). lib. bdg. 29.93 *(978-1-63472-156-1(X)*, 209196) Cherry Lake Publishing.

McKissack, Fredrick L. & McKissack, Lisa Beringer. Ramadan-Count & Celebrate! 2009. (Holidays—Count & Celebrate! Ser.). (Illus.). 32p. (J). (gr. k-3). lib. bdg. 23.94 *(978-0-7660-3100-5(4))* Enslow Pubs., Inc.

Melman, Anna. Islam, Law & Human Rights. 2010. (World of Islam Ser.). (Illus.). 64p. (YA). (gr. 6-10). lib. bdg. 22.95 *(978-1-4222-1362-9(5))* Mason Crest.

—Muslims in America. 2010. (World of Islam Ser.). (Illus.). 64p. (YA). (gr. 4-7). lib. bdg. 22.95 *(978-1-4222-0535-8(5))* Mason Crest.

Mobin-Uddin, Asma. A Party in Ramadan. Jacobsen, Laura, illus. 2009. (ENG.). 34p. (J). (gr. 2-4). 16.95 *(978-1-59078-604-8(1))* Boyds Mills Pr.

Morretta, Alison. Islamophobia: Religious Intolerance Against Muslims Today. 2016. (Public Persecutions Ser.). 128p. (YA). lib. bdg. 45.64 *(978-1-5026-2331-7(5))* Cavendish Square Publishing.

Mowjood, Siraj. The Boy & the Owl: A Story about the Attributes of God Based on the Poem the Creed of Salvation. Changezi, Aisha, illus. 2015. (ENG.). 24p. (J). (gr. k-3). 17.95 *(978-1-941610-14-5(5))* Fons Vitae of Kentucky, Inc.

Mrowiec, Katia, et al. God, Yahweh, Allah. 2014. (Illus.). 192p. 19.95 *(978-0-8091-6771-5(9))* Paulist Pr.

Nason, Ruth. Visiting a Mosque. 2014. (Start up Religion Ser.). (ENG., Illus.). 32p. (J). (gr. -1-k). pap. 10.99 *(978-0-237-54409-6(1))* Evans Brothers, Ltd. GBR. Dist: Independent Pubs. Group.

Omar, Tayyib. The Struggle for Identity: Islam & the West, Vol. 8. Pecastaing, Camille, ed. 2016. (Understanding Islam Ser.: Vol. 8). (ENG., Illus.). 112p. (J). (gr. 7-12). 25.95 *(978-1-4222-3678-9(1))* Mason Crest.

Oral, Osman. I Believe in Allah. 2013. (J). *(978-1-59784-302-7(4))* Tughra Bks.

—I Believe in the Angels. 2013. (J). *(978-1-59784-303-4(2))* Tughra Bks.

—I Believe in the Books. 2013. (J). *(978-1-59784-304-1(0))* Tughra Bks.

—I Believe in the Divine Destiny & Decree. 2013. (J). *(978-1-59784-307-2(5))* Tughra Bks.

—I Believe in the Hereafter. 2013. (J). *(978-1-59784-306-5(7))* Tughra Bks.

—I Believe in the Prophets. 2013. (J). *(978-1-59784-305-8(9))* Tughra Bks.

Orr, Tamra. Egyptian Islamic Jihad. 2009. (Inside the World's Most Infamous Terrorist Organizations Ser.). 64p. (gr. 5-5). 58.50 *(978-1-61513-574-5(X))* Rosen Publishing Group, Inc., The.

Overbeeke-Rippen, Francina van. Abraham & Ibrahim: The Bible & the Qur'an Told to Children. 2006. (J). pap. *(978-1-57153-072-1(X)*, Witherspoon Pr.) Curriculum Publishing, Presbyterian Church (U. S. A.).

Öze, Özkan. I Wonder about Allah, Bk. 1. Ayduz, Selma, tr. from TUR. 2014. (I Wonder about Islam Ser.). (ENG., Illus.). 128p. (J). (gr. 3). pap. 11.95 *(978-0-86037-592-0(7))* Kube Publishing Ltd. GBR. Dist: Consortium Bk. Sales & Distribution.

Physicians, Scientists, & Mathematicians of the Islamic World. 2016. (Physicians, Scientists, & Mathematicians of the Islamic World Ser.). 112p. (gr. 6-6). 259.70 *(978-1-4777-8547-8(7)*, Rosen Young Adult) Rosen Publishing Group, Inc., The.

Pirotta, Saviour. Id-Ul-Fitr. 2007. (We Love Holidays Ser.). (Illus.). 24p. (J). (gr. 3-7). lib. bdg. 22.60 *(978-1-4042-3708-7(9)*, PowerKids Pr.) Rosen Publishing Group, Inc., The.

Quran Made Easy with Tajweed. 2004. 89p. (J). pap. 6.50 net. *(978-0-9760681-0-5(9))* Quranic Educational Society.

Rice Jr., Earle. Muslim Brotherhood. 2017. lib. bdg. 29.95 ***(978-1-68020-057-7(7))*** Mitchell Lane Pubs., Inc.

Saeed, Mahmud S. The Model of the Muslim Youth in the Story of Prophet Yusuf. (ARA.). 32p. (YA). pap. *(978-1-882837-28-1(2))* WAMY International, Inc.

Sanna, Ellyn. Gallup Guides for Youth Facing Persistent Prejudice Muslims. 2012. (Gallup Guides for Youth Facing Persistent Prejudice Ser.). 64p. (J). (gr. 7-8). 22.95 *(978-1-4222-2468-7(6))* Mason Crest.

—People with Mental & Physical Challenges. 2012. (Gallup Guides for Youth Facing Persistent Prejudice Ser.). 64p. (J). (gr. 7-8). 22.95 *(978-1-4222-2470-0(8))* Mason Crest.

Saqr, Abdul B. How to Call People to Islam. Ahmad, Shakil, tr. 154p. (Orig.). (YA). pap. *(978-1-882837-16-8(9))* WAMY International, Inc.

Sears, Evelyn. Muslims & the West. 2005. (Introducing Islam Ser.). (Illus.). 112p. (YA). lib. bdg. 24.95 *(978-1-59084-700-8(8))* Mason Crest.

Self, David. Islam. 2005. (Religions of the World Ser.). (Illus.). 48p. (J). (gr. 5-12). pap. 14.05 *(978-0-8368-5874-7(3))*; lib. bdg. 31.00 *(978-0-8368-5868-6(9))* Stevens, Gareth Publishing LLLP. (Gareth Stevens Secondary Library).

Senker, Cath. Islam: Signs, Symbols, Stories. 2009. (Religious Signs, Symbols, & Stories Ser.). (Illus.). 32p. (J). (ENG.). pap. 10.00 *(978-1-4358-3048-6(2))*; lib. bdg. 25.25 *(978-1-4358-3040-0(7))* Rosen Publishing Group, Inc., The. (PowerKids Pr.).

—My Muslim Year. 2007. (Year of Religious Festivals Ser.). (Illus.). 32p. (J). (gr. 4-7). lib. bdg. 23.95 *(978-1-4042-3728-5(3)*, PowerKids Pr.) Rosen Publishing Group, Inc., The.

Steer, Malcolm. A Christian's Evangelistic Pocket Guide to Islam. 2015. (ENG.). 80p. pap. 6.99 *(978-1-85792-915-7(2)*, cfcf1379-a4b8-4893-9f7d-cc0543024c54, Christian Focus) Christian Focus Pubns. GBR. Dist: Bookmasters Distribution.

Studies and Research Unit of Wamy Staff. Principles of Dialogue. (ARA.). 79p. (YA). pap. *(978-1-882837-00-7(2))* WAMY International, Inc.

Syed, Ibrahim. Quranic Inspirations. 2007. 688p. (YA). per. 37.95 *(978-0-595-45003-9(2))* iUniverse, Inc.

Tamer, Abdul Hakeem. Ideas & Daily Life in the Muslim World Today, Vol. 8. Pecastaing, Camille, ed. 2016. (Understanding Islam Ser.: Vol. 8). (ENG., Illus.). 112p. (J). (gr. 7-12). 25.95 *(978-1-4222-3671-0(4))* Mason Crest.

Taykutgul, Selcuk & Akin, Ferruh. Uthman: Bearer of Two Pure Lights. 2012. (ENG.). 98p. (J). (gr. 8-12). pap. 7.50 *(978-1-59784-267-9(2))* Tughra Bks.

Thompson, Jan. Islam. (Illus.). 64p. (YA). (gr. 4-18). lib. bdg. 29.95 *(978-1-59389-133-6(4))* Chrysalis Education.

Tomljanovic, Tatiana. Ramadan. 2006. (American Holidays Ser.). (Illus.). 24p. (J). (gr. 3-7). per. 8.95 *(978-1-59036-464-2(3))*; lib. bdg. 24.45 *(978-1-59036-461-1(9))* Weigl Pubs., Inc.

Townsend, Chris. Life under the Caliphate. 2017. (J). ***(978-0-7660-9218-1(6))*** Enslow Pubs., Inc.

Wachal, Barbara S. The American Encounter with Islam. 2005. (Introducing Islam Ser.). (Illus.). 112p. (YA). lib. bdg. 24.95 *(978-1-59084-699-5(0))* Mason Crest.

Wali, Anbara. An Overview: Who Are the Muslims?, Vol. 8. Pecastaing, Camille, ed. 2016. (Understanding Islam Ser.: Vol. 8). (ENG., Illus.). 112p. (J). (gr. 7-12). 25.95 *(978-1-4222-3677-2(3))* Mason Crest.

Walker, Robert. Eid Al-Adha. 2010. (ENG., Illus.). 32p. (J). (gr. 2-4). *(978-0-7787-4761-1(1))*; pap. *(978-0-7787-4779-6(4))* Crabtree Publishing Co.

White, Bender Richardson, et al. Islam. 4th rev. ed. 2009. (World Religions Ser.). (Illus.). 144p. (gr. 6-12). 40.00 *(978-1-60413-109-3(8)*, Chelsea Hse.) Facts On File, Inc.

Willett, Edward. Ayatollah Khomeini. 2009. (Middle East Leaders Ser.). 112p. (gr. 5-8). 66.50 *(978-1-61514-645-1(8)*, Rosen Reference) Rosen Publishing Group, Inc., The.

Williams, Julie. Islam: Understanding the History, Beliefs, & Culture. 2008. (Issues in Focus Today Ser.). (Illus.). 112p. (J). (gr. 3-7). lib. bdg. 33.27 *(978-0-7660-2686-5(8))* Enslow Pubs., Inc.

Wolny, Philip. Muslims Around the World Today. 2009. (Understanding Islam Ser.). 64p. (gr. 6-6). 58.50 *(978-1-60854-626-8(8))* Rosen Publishing Group, Inc., The.

ISLAM—FICTION

Abdel-Fattah, Randa. Does My Head Look Big in This? 2007. 360p. (YA). 25.66 *(978-1-4287-4610-7(2)*, Follettbound) Follett School Solutions.

—Does My Head Look Big in This? 2008. (ENG.). 368p. (J). (gr. 7). pap. 9.99 *(978-0-439-92233-3(X)*, Scholastic Paperbacks) Scholastic, Inc.

Abdelsalam, Lisa. A Song for Me: A Muslim Holiday Story. Nielsen, Janet Marie, illus. 2006. 34p. (J). *(978-0-9755975-1-4(5))* Abdelsalam Corp.

Addasi, Maha. Time to Pray. Albitar, Nuha, tr. Gannon, Ned, illus. 2010. (ENG & ARA.). 32p. (J). (gr. 2-4). 17.95 *(978-1-59078-611-6(4))* Boyds Mills Pr.

Aktar, Nasreen. Samira's Eid. Attard, Enebor, illus. 2004. 24p. (J). *(978-1-85269-538-5(2))*; *(978-1-85269-539-2(0))*; *(978-1-85269-540-8(4))*; (ENG & PAN.). pap. *(978-1-85269-183-7(2))*; (ENG & ALB.). pap. *(978-1-85269-572-9(2))*; (ENG & PER.). pap. *(978-1-85269-503-3(X))*; (ENG & FRE.). pap. *(978-1-85269-502-6(1))*; (ENG & ARA.). pap. *(978-1-85269-122-6(0))*; (ENG & BEN.). pap. *(978-1-85269-131-8(X))*; (ENG & GUJ.). pap. *(978-1-85269-132-5(8))*; (ENG & SOM.). pap. *(978-1-85269-133-2(6))*; (ENG & TUR.). pap. *(978-1-85269-134-9(4))*; (ENG & URD.). pap. *(978-1-85269-135-6(2))* Mantra Lingua.

Al-Kinani, Maarja. Islamic. 2010. 74p. pap. 69.50 *(978-1-4461-6416-7(0))* Lulu Pr., Inc.

Albert, Edoardo. Call to Prayer: The Story of Bilal. 2009. (ENG., Illus.). 26p. (J). (gr. 2-6). 6.95 *(978-0-86037-456-5(4))* Kube Publishing Ltd. GBR. Dist: Consortium Bk. Sales & Distribution.

Delgado, Linda D. The Visitors. 2006. 169p. (J). per. *(978-0-9767861-1-5(7))* Muslim Writers Publishing.

Ergun, Erol. The All-Merciful Master. 2009. (Beautiful Names of God Ser.). (ENG.). 128p. (J). (gr. 4-7). 14.95 *(978-1-59784-202-0(8))* Tughra Bks.

Ertekin, Betul. I Love My Prophet: This World I Love. 2011. (ENG.). 48p. pap. 4.95 *(978-1-59784-236-5(2))* Tughra Bks.

Faruqi, Reem & Lyon, Lea. Lailah's Lunchbox, 1 vol. 2015. (ENG., Illus.). 32p. (gr. 1-7). 16.95 *(978-0-88448-431-8(9)*, 884431) Tilbury Hse. Pubs.

Gilani, Fawzia & Adams, Shireen. Snow White: An Islamic Tale. Adams, Shireen, illus. 2013. (Islamic Fairy Tales Ser.). (ENG., Illus.). 40p. (J). (gr. k-3). 14.00 *(978-0-86037-526-5(9))* Kube Publishing Ltd. GBR. Dist: Consortium Bk. Sales & Distribution.

Gutta, Razeena. Faatimah & Ahmed - We're Little Muslims. 2015. (ENG., Illus.). 34p. (J). pap. *(978-1-925209-24-2(5))* Vivid Publishing.

Hamed, Maissa. The Last Night of Ramadan. El Wakil, Mohamed, illus. 2007. (J). (gr. -1-3). *(978-0-88010-586-6(0)*, Bell Pond Bks.) SteinerBooks, Inc.

Imam, Seema & Imam, Ibrahim. I am Listening. 2007. (I Am Good Ser.). (Illus.). 32p. (J). mass mkt. *(978-0-9787849-8-0(7))* Lucent Interpretations, LLC.

Jalali, Reza. Moon Watchers: Shirin's Ramadan Miracle, 1 vol. Sibley O'Brien, Anne, illus. 2017. (ENG.). 32p. (gr. 1-7). pap. 8.95 *(978-0-88448-587-2(0)*, 884587) Tilbury Hse. Pubs.

Jolin, Paula. In the Name of God. 2008. (ENG.). 224p. (YA). (gr. 9-12). pap. 18.99 *(978-0-312-38455-5(6)*, 9780312384555) Square Fish.

Khan, Hena. Golden Domes & Silver Lanterns: A Muslim Book of Colors. Amini, Mehrdokht, illus. 2012. (ENG.). 32p. (J). (gr. -1-2). 17.99 *(978-0-8118-7905-7(4))* Chronicle Bks. LLC.

—The Night of the Moon: A Muslim Holiday Story. Paschkis, Julie, illus. 2008. (ENG.). 32p. (J). (gr. -1-3). 16.99 *(978-0-8118-6062-8(0))* Chronicle Bks. LLC.

Mair, J. Samia. Amira's Totally Chocolate World. 2010. (ENG., Illus.). 29p. (J). (gr. k-3). 8.95 *(978-0-86037-408-4(4))* Kube Publishing Ltd. GBR. Dist: Consortium Bk. Sales & Distribution.

Marsh, Sarah Glenn. Fear the Drowning Deep. 2016. (ENG.). 312p. (YA). (gr. 6). 16.99 *(978-1-5107-0348-3(9)*, Sky Pony Pr.) Skyhorse Publishing Co., Inc.

Nazeer, Tasnim & Publishing, Greenbirdbooks Childrens. Allah's Gifts. Frongia, Daniela, illus. 2012. 26p. pap. *(978-0-9562141-7-1(7))* Greenbird Bks.

Noor, Razana & Burgess, Omar. My Special Angels: Two Noble Scribes. Burgess, Omar, illus. 2017. (ENG., Illus.). 24p. (J). (gr. -1-2). 8.95 *(978-0-86037-645-3(1))* Kube Publishing Ltd. GBR. Dist: Consortium Bk. Sales & Distribution.

Ondaatje, Griffin. The Camel in the Sun, 1 vol. Wolfsgruber, Linda, illus. 2013. (ENG.). 32p. (J). (gr. k). 17.95 *(978-1-55498-381-0(9))* Groundwood Bks. CAN. Dist: Publishers Group West (PGW).

Sezgin, Orhan. The Adventures of Little Selim. 2011. (ENG., Illus.). 48p. pap. 4.95 *(978-1-59784-237-2(0))* Tughra Bks.

Suphandagi, Lale. The Dream Bird. 2013. (ENG., Illus.). 54p. (J). (gr. k-1). pap. 9.95 *(978-1-59784-282-2(6))* Tughra Bks.

Turan, Kemal. The Essence of Wisdom: Parables from Prophet Muhammad. 2011. (ENG.). 192p. (J). (gr. 7-10). pap. 9.95 *(978-1-59784-263-1(X))* Tughra Bks.

Ulker, Munise. Little Batul's Eid Celebration: The Most Pleasant Festival of Sacrifice. 2013. (ENG., Illus.). 32p. (J). (gr. -1-3). pap. 6.95 *(978-1-59784-294-5(X))* Tughra Bks.

Zia, Farhana. The Garden of My Imaan, 1 vol. (ENG.). (J). (gr. 3-6). 2016. 232p. pap. 7.95 *(978-1-56145-921-6(6))* 2013. 192p. 15.95 *(978-1-56145-698-7(5))* Peachtree Pubs.

ISLAM—HISTORY

Barnard, Bryn. The Genius of Islam: How Muslims Made the Modern World. 2011. (ENG., Illus.). 40p. (J). (gr. 3-7). 17.99 *(978-0-375-84072-2(9)*, Knopf Bks. for Young Readers) Random Hse. Children's Bks.

Cohn, Jessica. The Medieval Islamic World, 1 vol. 2012. (Primary Source Readers Ser.). (ENG.). 32p. (J). (gr. 5-5). pap. 8.99 *(978-1-4333-5003-0(3))* Teacher Created Materials, Inc.

Cooke, Tim. Your Guide to the Islamic Golden Age. 2017. (Destination: Middle Ages Ser.). (ENG., Illus.). 32p. (J). ***(978-0-7787-2993-8(1))***; pap. ***(978-0-7787-2999-0(0))*** Crabtree Publishing Co.

Durkee, Noura. The Fall of the Giant. Durkee, Noura, illus. 2007. (ENG., Illus.). 26p. (J). (gr. k-5). 16.00 *(978-1-879402-63-8(7))* Tahrike Tarsile Quran, Inc.

Hawker, Frances & Alicavusoglu, Leyla. Islam in Turkey. Campbell, Bruce, photos by. 2009. (ENG., Illus.). 32p. (J). (gr. 3-6). *(978-0-7787-5009-3(4))*; pap. *(978-0-7787-5026-0(4))* Crabtree Publishing Co.

Haylamaz, Resit. Abu Bakr: The Pinnacle of Truthfulness. 2011. (ENG.). 175p. (gr. 8-11). pap. 8.95 *(978-1-59784-250-1(8))* Tughra Bks.

—Ali: Hero of Chivalry. 2011. (ENG.). 142p. pap. 9.95 *(978-1-59784-253-2(2))* Tughra Bks.

—Zayd: The Rose That Bloomed in Captivity. 2011. (ENG.). 88p. (gr. 8-11). pap. 6.95 *(978-1-59784-247-1(8))* Tughra Bks.

Howell, Izzi. Early Islamic Civilisation. 2017. (Explore! Ser.). (ENG., Illus.). 32p. (J). (gr. 4-6). 16.99 ***(978-1-5263-0082-9(6)**, Wayland)* Hachette Children's Group GBR. Dist: Hachette Bk. Group.

Jessa, Azra. Ramadhan & Eid-Ul-Fitr. Jessa, Azra, illus. 2008. (ENG., Illus.). 16p. (J). (gr. -1). 12.95 *(978-1-879402-23-2(8))* Tahrike Tarsile Quran, Inc.

Kavanaugh, Dorothy. The Muslim World: An Overview. 2010. (World of Islam Ser.). (Illus.). 64p. (YA). (gr. 4-7). lib. bdg. 22.95 *(978-1-4222-0532-7(0))* Mason Crest.

McAdam, Jessica & Aitchison, Kathleen. Symbols of Freedom. 2004. (Illus.). (J). (gr. 2-6). cd-rom 38.00 *(978-1-57336-400-3(2)*, I8025D) Interaction Pubs., Inc.

Nardo, Don. The Birth of Islam. 2011. (World Religions & Beliefs Ser.). 110p. (gr. 7-12). 28.95 *(978-1-59935-146-9(3))* Reynolds, Morgan Inc.

—Daily Life in the Islamic Golden Age. 2015. (Daily Life in Ancient Civilizations Ser.). (ENG., Illus.). 48p. (gr. 3-6). pap. 8.99 *(978-1-4846-0836-4(4)*, Heinemann InfoSearch) Heinemann-Raintree.

—The Islamic Empire. 2011. (World History Ser.). (ENG., Illus.). 128p. (gr. 7-10). lib. bdg. 39.90 *(978-1-4205-0634-1(X))* Cengage Gale.

O'Connor, Frances. History of Islam. 2009. (Understanding Islam Ser.). 64p. (gr. 6-6). 58.50 *(978-1-60854-617-6(9))*; (Illus.). (J). lib. bdg. 31.95 *(978-1-4358-5064-4(5))* Rosen Publishing Group, Inc., The.

—Understanding Islam: History of Islam. 2009. (Understanding Islam Ser.). (ENG., Illus.). 64p. (J). (gr. 9-12). pap. 12.95 *(978-1-4358-5382-9(2))* Rosen Publishing Group, Inc., The.

Romanek, Trudee. Government & Law in the Early Islamic World. 2013. (Life in the Early Islamic World Ser.). (ENG., Illus.). 48p. (J). pap. *(978-0-7787-2175-8(2))* Crabtree Publishing Co.

Roraback, Amanda. Islam in a Nutshell. 2nd exp. rev. ed. 2004. (Nutshell Notes). (Illus.). 60p. (YA). pap. 7.95 *(978-0-9702908-8-5(8))* Enisen Publishing.

Rostom, Mustafa. Four Arabian Tales: Educating Children about Islam. 2011. (Illus.). 52p. pap. 33.83 *(978-1-4567-8266-5(5))* AuthorHouse.

Rubin, Barry M. & Garton, Leora. The History of Islam. 2010. (World of Islam Ser.). (Illus.). 64p. (J). (gr. 4-7). lib. bdg. 22.95 *(978-1-4222-0531-0(2))* Mason Crest.

Samuels, Charlie. Timeline of the Muslim World. 2010. (History Highlights: A Gareth Stevens Timeline Ser.). (Illus.). 48p. (gr. 6-8). (J). pap. 14.05 *(978-1-4339-3490-2(6))*; (YA). lib. bdg. 31.95 *(978-1-4339-3489-6(2))* Stevens, Gareth Publishing LLLP. (Gareth Stevens Secondary Library).

Stokes, Jamie. The Muslim World. 2010. (Global Issues Ser.). 400p. (C). (gr. 9). 45.00 *(978-0-8160-8086-1(0))* Facts On File, Inc.

Townsend, Chris. The Violent Rise of ISIS. 2017. (J). ***(978-0-7660-9210-5(0))*** Enslow Pubs., Inc.

World of Islam, 10 vols., Set. Incl. Divisions in Islam. Calvert, John. (Illus.). (YA). (gr. 4-7). lib. bdg. 22.95 *(978-1-4222-0533-4(9))*; History of Islam. Rubin, Barry M. & Garton, Leora. (Illus.). (J). (gr. 4-7). lib. bdg. 22.95 *(978-1-4222-0531-0(2))*; Islam in Europe. Radu, Michael. (Illus.). (YA). (gr. 6-10). lib. bdg. 22.95 *(978-1-4222-1363-6(3))*; Islam, Law & Human Rights. Melman, Anna. (Illus.). (YA). (gr. 6-10). lib. bdg. 22.95 *(978-1-4222-1362-9(5))*; Islamic Festivals & Celebrations. Kavanaugh, Dorothy. (Illus.). (YA). (gr. 4-7). lib. bdg. 22.95 *(978-1-4222-0534-1(7))*; Islamic-Jewish Relations Before 1947. Sklar, Tanya. (Illus.). (YA). (gr. 6-10). lib. bdg. 22.95 *(978-1-4222-1361-2(7))*; Monotheistic Religions: Islam, Christianity & Judaism. Cohen, Abe M. (YA). (gr. 7-12). lib. bdg. 22.95 *(978-1-4222-0537-2(1))*; Muslim World: An Overview. Kavanaugh, Dorothy. (Illus.). (YA). (gr. 4-7). lib. bdg. 22.95 *(978-1-4222-0532-7(0))*; Muslims in America. Melman, Anna. (Illus.). (YA). (gr. 4-7). lib. bdg. 22.95 *(978-1-4222-0535-8(5))*; Radical Islam. Luxenberg, Alan H. (Illus.). (YA). (gr. 4-7). lib. bdg. 22.95 *(978-1-4222-0536-5(3))*; 2010. (Illus.). 64p. 2010. Set lib. bdg. 229.50 *(978-1-4222-0530-3(4))* Mason Crest.

ISLAMIC ART

Barkow, Henriette. Tom & Sofia Start School. Lamont, Priscilla, illus. 2004. (J). (BEN, ENG & MAL.). *(978-1-84444-573-8(9))*; (MAL & ENG.). 32p. pap. *(978-1-84444-587-5(9))*; (SPA & ENG.). 32p. pap. *(978-1-84444-586-8(0))*; (ENG & VIE.). 32p. pap. *(978-1-84444-584-4(4))*; (SOM & ENG.). 32p. pap. *(978-1-84444-585-1(2))*; (URD & ENG.). 32p. pap. *(978-1-84444-583-7(6))*; (ENG & TUR.). 32p. pap. *(978-1-84444-582-0(8))*; (TAM & ENG.). 32p. pap. *(978-1-84444-581-3(X))*; (ENG & TGL.). 32p. pap. *(978-1-84444-580-6(1))*; (ENG & RUS.). 32p. pap. *(978-1-84444-579-0(8))*; (ENG & POR.). 32p. pap. *(978-1-84444-577-6(1))*; (ENG & POL.). 32p. pap. *(978-1-84444-576-9(3))*; (ENG & PAN.). 32p. pap. *(978-1-84444-575-2(5))*; (ENG & KUR.). 32p. pap. *(978-1-84444-574-5(7))*; (ENG & JPN.). 32p. pap. *(978-1-84444-572-1(0))*; (ENG & ITA.). 32p. pap. *(978-1-84444-571-4(2))* Mantra Lingua.

Beardwood, Mary. Discovering Islamic Art: A Childrens' Guide with Activity Sheets. 2015. (ENG., Illus.). 68p. pap. 9.99 *(978-1-909339-04-0(0))* Medina Publishing, Ltd. GBR. Dist: Casemate Pubs. & Bk. Distributors, LLC.

Flatt, Lizann. Arts & Culture in the Early Islamic World. 2012. (Life in the Early Islamic World Ser.). (ENG., Illus.). 48p. (J). pap. *(978-0-7787-2174-1(4))*; lib. bdg. *(978-0-7787-2167-3(1))* Crabtree Publishing Co.

Journey Through Islamic Art. 2004. (ENG & TUR.). (J). *(978-1-84444-591-2(7))*; *(978-1-84444-590-5(9))*; *(978-1-84444-593-6(3))*; *(978-1-84444-592-9(5))*; *(978-1-84444-589-9(5))*; *(978-1-84444-588-2(7))*; *(978-1-84444-578-3(X))*; *(978-1-84444-669-8(7))* Mantra Lingua.

Levy, Janey. Islamic Art: Recognizing Geometric Ideas in Art. (Math for the Real World Ser.). 32p. 2009. (ENG., Illus.). (gr. 6-7). pap. 10.00 *(978-1-4042-6081-8(1))* 2009. (gr. 5-5). 47.90 *(978-1-60851-360-4(2)*, PowerKids Pr.) 2006. (Illus.). (YA). (gr. 5-9). lib. bdg. 25.25 *(978-1-4042-3364-5(4))* Rosen Publishing Group, Inc., The.

Smith, A. G. Arabic Patterns Stained Glass Coloring Book. 2006. (Dover Design Stained Glass Coloring Book Ser.). (ENG., Illus.). 32p. (J). (gr. 3-8). pap. 6.99 *(978-0-486-44839-8(8))* Dover Pubns., Inc.

ISLAND ECOLOGY

Anderson, Sheila. Islands. 2008. (First Step Nonfiction - Landforms Ser.). (Illus.). 24p. (J). (gr. -1-3). lib. bdg. 18.60 *(978-0-8225-8594-7(4)*, Lerner Pubns.); pap. 34.95 *(978-0-8225-9936-4(8))* Lerner Publishing Group.

Kalman, Bobbie. Baby Animals on Islands. 2013. (ENG., Illus.). 24p. (J). *(978-0-7787-1016-5(5))*; pap. *(978-0-7787-1027-1(0))* Crabtree Publishing Co.

Kopp, Megan. Islands Inside Out. 2015. (ENG.). 32p. (J). *(978-0-7787-1497-2(7))* Crabtree Publishing Co.

Silva Lee, Alfonso. My Island & I: The Nature of the Caribbean. Hayskar, Bonnie J., ed. Lago, Alexis, illus. 2010. 32p. (J). pap. 9.95 *(978-1-929165-14-8(5))* PANGAEA.

World Book, Inc Staff, contrib. by. Oceans, Islands, & Polar Regions. 2008. (J). *(978-0-7166-1402-9(2))* World Bk., Inc.

ISLANDS

see also Coral Reefs and Islands

also names of islands and groups of islands, e.g. Cuba

Anderson, Sheila. Islands. (First Step Nonfiction - Landforms Ser.). 2015. (ENG., Illus.). 24p. (gr. k-2). 23.99 *(978-1-5124-1042-6(X)*, Lerner Pubns.) 2008. (Illus.). 24p. (J). (gr. -1-3). lib. bdg. 18.60 *(978-0-8225-8594-7(4)*, Lerner Pubns.) 2008. pap. 34.95 *(978-0-8225-9936-4(8))* Lerner Publishing Group.

Bailey, Gerry. Stranded on an Island. 2014. (ENG., Illus.). 32p. (J). *(978-0-7787-0430-0(0))* Crabtree Publishing Co.

Barber, Nicola. Island Homes. 2007. (Homes Around the World Ser.). (ENG., Illus.). 32p. (J). (gr. 4-7). pap. *(978-0-7787-3555-7(9))* Crabtree Publishing Co.

Best, B. J. How Are Islands Formed? 2017. (J). pap. 16.95 ***(978-1-5026-2537-3(7))*** Cavendish Square Publishing.

Cheong-Lum, Roseline Ng & NgCheong-Lum, Roseline. Maldives. 2nd rev. ed. 2010. (Cultures of the World 21 Ser.). 144p. (gr. 6). lib. bdg. 42.79 *(978-1-60870-217-6(0))* Marshall Cavendish GBR. Dist: Marshall Cavendish Corp.

Dyan, Penelope. By the Sea — -A Kid's Guide to Valletta, Malt. Weigand, John D., photos by. 2011. (Illus.). 36p. pap. 11.95 *(978-1-935630-55-5(5))* Bellissima Publishing, LLC.

Famighetti, Robert, et al. How Do Islands Form? 2009. (Science in the Real World Ser.). (Illus.). 32p. (gr. 4-6). 28.00 *(978-1-60413-474-2(7)*, Chelsea Clubhouse) Facts On File, Inc.

French, Cathy. Make an Island & Haz una Isla: 6 English, 6 Spanish Adaptations. 2011. (ENG & SPA.). (J). 75.00 net. *(978-1-4108-5632-6(1))* Benchmark Education Co.

Gibbons, Gail. Surrounded by Sea: Life on a New England Fishing Island. Gibbons, Gail, illus. 2006. (ENG., Illus.). 32p. (J). (gr. -1-3). 17.95 *(978-0-8234-1941-8(X))*; 6.95 *(978-0-8234-2021-6(3))* Holiday Hse., Inc.

Green, Jen. Islands Around the World. 2009. (Geography Now! Ser.). (ENG., Illus.). 32p. (J). (gr. 4-6). pap. 10.00 *(978-1-4358-2958-9(1)*, PowerKids Pr.); (YA). (gr. 3-6). lib. bdg. 26.50 *(978-1-4358-2872-8(0))* Rosen Publishing Group, Inc., The.

Heinrichs, Ann. Islands. 2009. (21st Century Skills Library: Real World Math Ser.). (ENG.). 32p. (gr. 4-8). lib. bdg. 28.50 *(978-1-60279-494-8(4)*, 200315) Cherry Lake Publishing.

Hutmacher, Kimberly M. Islands, 1 vol. 2011. (Natural Wonders Ser.). (ENG., 24p. (gr. k-1). Illus.). pap. 7.29 *(978-1-4296-6219-2(0))*; pap. 41.70 *(978-1-4296-6390-8(1))* Capstone Press of Coughlan Cos. (Pebble Plus).

Kennard, Philippa. Bunny Island. Fukuda, Yukihiro, photos by. 2015. (ENG., Illus.). 32p. (J). (gr. -1-1). pap. 4.99 *(978-1-77085-657-8(9)*, 9781770856578) Firefly Bks., Ltd.

Labrecque, Ellen. Islands, 1 vol. 2014. (Learning about Landforms Ser.). (ENG., Illus.). 32p. (gr. 1-3). lib. bdg. 27.32 *(978-1-4329-9534-8(0)*, Heinemann First Library) Heinemann-Raintree.

Mis, Melody S. Exploring Islands. 2009. (Geography Zone: Landforms Ser.). 24p. (Illus.). (J). (gr. 2-4). pap. 8.25 *(978-1-4358-3110-0(1))*; (gr. 2-3). 42.50 *(978-1-61512-703-0(8))*; (J). lib. bdg. 22.60 *(978-1-4358-2712-7(0))* Rosen Publishing Group, Inc., The. (PowerKids Pr.).

Moore, David. Expl on Your Own the Island /Formed in 1 Day. 2009. (Explore on Your Own Ser.). (ENG., Illus.). 12p. (J). pap. 7.95 *(978-0-7362-5522-6(2))* National Geographic School Publishing, Inc.

Nadeau, Isaac. Islands. (Library of Landforms Ser.). 24p. (gr. 3-4). 2009. 42.50 *(978-1-60853-726-6(9)*, PowerKids Pr.) 2006. (Illus.). (J). lib. bdg. 22.60 *(978-1-4042-3126-9(9))* Rosen Publishing Group, Inc., The.

Rigby Education Staff. Our Home on the Island. (Illus.). (J). bds. 3.95 *(978-0-7635-6455-1(9)*, 764559C99) Rigby Education.

Salaka, Michael. Islands & Archipelagos. 2016. (Spotlight on Earth Science Ser.). 00024p. (J). (gr. 4-6). pap. 10.00 *(978-1-4994-2517-8(1)*, PowerKids Pr.) Rosen Publishing Group, Inc., The.

Sheehan, Thomas F. Islands. 2007. (Landforms Ser.). (Illus.). 32p. (J). (gr. 4-7). lib. bdg. 28.50 *(978-1-60044-545-3(4))* Rourke Educational Media.

Tagliaferro, Linda. How Does a Volcano Become an Island? 2016. (How Does It Happen Ser.). (ENG.). 32p. (gr. 3-5). pap. 8.29 *(978-1-4109-8530-9(X)*, Raintree Perspectives) Heinemann-Raintree.

Vale, Janice. Where Do You Live? Band 15. 2007. (Collins Big Cat Ser.). (ENG., Illus.). 48p. (J). (gr. 3-4). pap. 8.99 *(978-0-00-723098-3(2))* HarperCollins Pubs. Ltd. GBR. Dist: Independent Pubs. Group.

Williams, Dinah. Creepy Islands. 2015. (Illus.). 32p. (J). lib. bdg. *(978-1-62724-294-3(5))* Bearport Publishing Co., Inc.

ISLANDS—FICTION

Acton, Vanessa. Radioactive. 2016. (Atlas of Cursed Places Ser.). (ENG.). 104p. (YA). (gr. 6-12). lib. bdg. 26.65 *(978-1-5124-1327-4(5)*, Darby Creek) Lerner Publishing Group.

Adams, Jackie. Without a Blink. 2008. 40p. (J). 10.99 *(978-0-9800327-0-3(9))* Speranza's Pr.

Aguiar, Nadia. The Great Wave of Tamarind. 2017. (Book of Tamarind Ser.: 3). (ENG.). 384p. (J). 16.99 *(978-0-312-38031-1(3)*, 9780312380311) Feiwel & Friends.

Anderson, Al. Adventures with Bingo Borden. Agora Publications Staff, tr. Kurzyca, Krystyna Emilia, illus. 2010. 77p. (J). pap. 9.50 *(978-1-887250-46-7(8))* Agora Pubns., Inc.

Appleton, Victor. Tom Swift & His Wireless Message. 2007. 220p. 24.95 *(978-1-4344-9231-9(1))*; per. 14.95 *(978-1-4344-9137-4(4))* Wildside Pr., LLC.

Ashes to Ashes. 2014. (ENG., Illus.). 400p. (YA). (gr. 9). 18.99 *(978-1-4424-4081-4(3)*, Simon & Schuster Bks. For Young Readers) Simon & Schuster Bks. For Young Readers.

Atkinson, Elizabeth. The Island of Beyond. 2016. (ENG.). 288p. (gr. 4-7). 17.99 *(978-1-4677-8116-9(9))*; 35.99 *(978-1-4677-9557-9(7))* Lerner Publishing Group. (Carolrhoda Bks.).

Awdry, Wilbert V. Full Steam Ahead! Golden Books, illus. 2012. (Color Plus Tattoos Ser.). (ENG.). 48p. (J). (gr. -1-2). pap. 3.99 *(978-0-307-93120-7(X)*, Golden Bks.) Random Hse. Children's Bks.

—The Lost Crown of Sodor. Random House Staff, illus. 2013. (Pictureback Ser.). (ENG.). 24p. (J). (gr. -1-2). 3.99 *(978-0-449-81533-5(1)*, Random Hse. Bks. for Young Readers) Random Hse. Children's Bks.

Baldwin, Robert F. The Fish House Door. Sheckels, Astrid, illus. 2010. (ENG.). 36p. (J). 16.95 *(978-1-934031-30-8(5)*, 10b511a5-c2dc-4bc7-8d33-85991c0a158b) Islandport Pr., Inc.

Ballantyne, R. The Coral Island. 2006. pap. 14.95 *(978-1-55742-666-6(X))* Wildside Pr., LLC.

H I

Ballantyne, R. M. Blown to Bits; or, the Lonely Man of Rak. 2006. pap. (978-1-4065-0515-3(3)) Dodo Pr.

Bannerman, Helen. The Story of Little Black Mingo (Illustr. 2006. pap. (978-1-4065-0770-6(9)) Dodo Pr.

Bardwell, Harrison. The Airplane Girls & the Mystery of Seal Islands. 2003. (ENG.). 223p. (J). pap. 13.95 (978-1-55753-337-1(7), cb32f1de-2660-4a6d-a577-d92ff5815b0e) Purdue Univ. Pr.

Barnum, Vance. Frank & Andy Afloat: The Cave on the Island. 2007. (ENG.). 160p. pap. 19.99 (978-1-4346-3226-5(1)); 180p. pap. 21.99 (978-1-4346-3227-2(X)) Creative Media Partners, LLC.

Barry, Dave & Pearson, Ridley. Peter & the Starcatchers. Call, Greg, illus. rev. ed. 2006. (Peter & the Starcatchers Ser.). (ENG.). 480p. (J). (gr. 5-9). reprint ed. pap. 9.99 (978-0-7868-4907-9(X), Disney Editions) Disney Pr.

Base, Graeme & Children of Gununa Staff. Our Island. 2016. (ENG.). 34p. (J). (gr. -1-k). 14.99 **(978-0-14-350593-8(9))** Random Hse. Australia AUS. Dist: Independent Pubs. Group.

Baum, L. Frank. Enchanted Island of Yew. 2006. 268p. pap. 11.45 (978-1-59462-396-7(1), Book Jungle) Standard Pubns., Inc.

—Sky Island. 2007. 144p. (gr. 4-7). per. 11.95 (978-1-60312-253-5(2)) Aegypan.

Beadling, Marilyn. The Apple Pie Pickle. 2008. 52p. pap. 9.95 (978-1-4327-2302-6(2)) Outskirts Pr., Inc.

Beaufrand, M. J. Useless Bay. 2016. (ENG.). 240p. (YA). (gr. 8-17). 17.95 (978-1-4197-2138-0(0), Amulet Bks.) Abrams, Inc.

Bial, Raymond. Shadow Island: A Tale of Lake Superior. 2006. 172p. (J). (gr. 3-7). 18.95 (978-1-883953-37-9(5)); per. 12.95 (978-1-883953-36-2(7)) Great Lakes Literary, LLC. (Blue Horse Books).

Bigonette, John, Jr. The Island. 2005. 334p. (YA). 29.95 (978-0-595-78170-6(5)) iUniverse, Inc.

Binch, Caroline. Gregory Cool. 2012. (ENG., Illus.). 32p. (J). (gr. k-3). pap. 8.99 (978-1-84780-258-3(3), Frances Lincoln) Quarto Publishing Group UK GBR. Dist: Hachette Bk. Group.

Blackstone, Stella. Una Isla Bajo el Sol. Ceccoli, Nicoletta, illus. 2003. (SPA.). 24p. (J). pap. 6.99 (978-1-84148-144-9(0)) Barefoot Bks., Inc.

—Secret Seahorse. Beaton, Clare, illus. 2005. (J). (gr. -1-2). 24p. bds. 7.99 (978-1-905236-15-2(8)); 24p. 15.99 (978-1-84148-704-5(X)); 32p. pap. 7.99 (978-1-84148-937-7(9)) Barefoot Bks., Inc.

Blackstone, Stella & Barefoot Books Staff. An Island in the Sun. Ceccoli, Nicoletta, illus. 2005. (ENG.). 24p. (J). pap. 6.99 (978-1-84148-079-4(7)) Barefoot Bks., Inc.

Blanks, Morgan Georgia. The Desert Island. 2008. 52p. pap. 20.49 (978-1-4343-9006-6(3)) AuthorHouse.

Boggs, Patdee. Island of Angels. 2006. 55p. pap. 16.95 (978-1-4241-3758-9(6)) PublishAmerica, Inc.

Bond, A. Russell. Scientific American Boy: Or the Camp at Willow Clump Island. 2006. (ENG., Illus.). 320p. (J). (gr. 4-7). per. 19.95 (978-1-55709-185-7(4)) Applewood Bks.

Boone, Martina. Illusion. 2016. (Heirs of Watson Island Ser.). (ENG., Illus.). 480p. (YA). (gr. 9). 17.99 (978-1-4814-1128-8(4), Simon Pulse) Simon Pulse.

—Persuasion. 2015. (Heirs of Watson Island Ser.). (ENG., Illus.). 464p. (YA). (gr. 9). 17.99 (978-1-4814-1125-7(X), Simon Pulse) Simon Pulse.

Bowler, Ann Martin & Bowler, Anna. Gecko's Complaint: A Balinese Folktale. Sukanada, I. Gusti Made, illus. 2009. (ENG & IND.). 32p. (J). (gr. k-3). 14.95 (978-0-7946-0484-4(6)) Tuttle Publishing.

Brian, Kate. Endless (a Shadowlands Novel) 2014. (Shadowlands Ser.). (ENG.). 336p. (YA). (gr. 7-12). 17.99 (978-1-4231-6485-2(7)) Hyperion Bks. for Children.

—Hereafter (a Shadowlands Novel) 2014. (Shadowlands Ser.). (ENG.). 336p. (YA). (gr. 9-17). pap. 9.99 (978-1-4231-6526-2(8)) Hyperion Bks. for Children.

—Shadowlands. 2013. (Shadowlands Ser.). (ENG.). 352p. (YA). (gr. 9-17). pap. 9.99 (978-1-4231-6525-5(X)) Hyperion Pr.

Brown, Margaret Wise. The Little Island. Weisgard, Leonard, illus. 2003. (ENG.). 48p. (J). (gr. -1-2). 15.99 (978-0-385-74640-3(7), Doubleday Bks. for Young Readers) Random Hse. Children's Bks.

Brown, Peter. The Wild Robot. 2016. (ENG., Illus.). 288p. (J). (gr. 3-7). 16.99 (978-0-316-38199-4(3)) Little, Brown Bks. for Young Readers.

Buchholz, Quint. El Coleccionista de Momentos. 2nd ed. 2003. (Rosa y Manzana Ser.). (SPA., Illus.). 48p. (J). (978-84-89804-16-6(8)) Lóguez Ediciones ESP. Dist: Lectorum Pubns., Inc.

Caletti, Deb. The Queen of Everything. Greenberg, Anne, ed. 2008. (ENG.). 352p. (YA). (gr. 7-12). pap. 8.99 (978-1-4169-5781-2(2), Simon Pulse) Simon Pulse.

—Stay. (ENG.). (YA). (gr. 7). 2012. 336p. pap. 9.99 (978-1-4424-0374-1(8)) 2011. 320p. 16.99 (978-1-4424-0373-4(X)) Simon Pulse. (Simon Pulse).

Calmenson, Stephanie. There Are No Moose on This Island, 1 vol. Thermes, Jennifer, illus. 2013. (ENG.). 32p. (J). 17.95 (978-1-934031-34-6(8), a2b39bfc-ad16-4e21-bc2e-5db5168164a8) Islandport Pr., Inc.

Calu, John & Hart, Dave. The Treasure of Tucker's Island. 2003. 80p. (YA). pap. 8.95 (978-0-595-27953-1(8)) iUniverse, Inc.

Cann, Kate. Mediterranean Holiday: Or, How I Moved to a Tiny Island & Found the Love of My Life. 2007. (ENG.). 416p. (YA). (gr. 9-12). pap. 5.99 (978-0-06-115216-0(1), HarperTeen) HarperCollins Pubs.

Carey, Janet Lee. Dragon's Keep. 2007. 302p. (J). (978-1-4287-3929-1(7)) Harcourt Trade Pubs.

—Dragon's Keep. 2008. (ENG., Illus.). 320p. (YA). (gr. 7-18). pap. 7.95 (978-0-15-206401-3(X)) Houghton Mifflin Harcourt Publishing Co.

Casanova, Mary. Wake up, Island. Wroblewski, Nick, illus. 2016. (J). (ENG.). 40p. 14.95 (978-0-8166-8935-4(0)); pap. (978-0-8166-8936-1(9)) Univ. of Minnesota Pr.

Cashore, Kristin. Jane, Unlimited. 2017. (ENG.). 464p. (YA). (gr. 9). 18.99 **(978-0-8037-4149-2(9)**, Kathy Dawson Books) Penguin Young Readers Group.

Castlemon, Harry. No Moss; or, the Career of a Rolling Stone, by Harry Castlemon [Pseud.]. 2006. 328p. per. 23.99 (978-1-4255-3290-1(X)) Michigan Publishing.

Cattell, Bob & Agard, John. Butter-Finger. Smy, Pam, illus. 2006. (ENG.). 128p. (J). (gr. 2-17). per. 7.95 (978-1-84507-376-3(2), Frances Lincoln) Quarto Publishing Group UK GBR. Dist: Hachette Bk. Group.

Causton, Linda. Lester's Rainy Lake Pony. Lt. ed. 2004. (Illus.). 32p. (J). 12.00 (978-1-930374-09-6(7)) DeForest Pr.

Chand, Emlyn. Larry the Lonely: A Bird Brain Book. Giffin, Noelle, illus. Lt. ed. 2013. 9. (ENG.). 62p. (gr. k-3). pap. 10.95 (978-1-62253-128-8(0)) Evolved Publishing.

Charles, Antoinette. My Favorite Island Games. 2012. 20p. pap. 17.99 (978-1-4685-5678-0(9)) AuthorHouse.

Chen, Sam. A Real Meal Table Fable. Peschel, Georgia, illus. 2007. 60p. (J). (978-0-9800764-0-0(4)) Uncle Jim's Publishing.

Chin, Oliver. Welcome to Monster Isle. Miracola, Jeff, illus. 2008. (ENG.). 36p. (J). (gr. -1-3). 15.95 (978-1-59702-016-9(8)) Immedium.

Citak, Michael J. The Adventures of Leo- & the Treasure Cave. 2009. 51p. pap. 22.95 (978-0-557-02994-5(5)) Lulu Pr., Inc.

Climo, Liz. Rory the Dinosaur: Me & My Dad. 2015. (ENG., Illus.). 40p. (J). (gr. -1-3). 17.00 (978-0-316-27728-0(2)) Little Brown & Co.

Cohn, Edith. Spirit's Key. 2014. (ENG.). 320p. (J). (gr. 4-7). 16.99 (978-0-374-30011-1(9), 9780374300111, Farrar, Straus & Giroux (BYR)) Farrar, Straus & Giroux.

Cohn, Rachel. Beta. 2013. (Beta Novel Ser.). (ENG., Illus.). 336p. (YA). (gr. 9-17). pap. 9.99 (978-1-4231-5734-2(6)) Hyperion Pr.

—Emergent. 2014. (Beta Novel Ser.). (ENG.). 288p. (YA). (gr. 9-17). 17.99 (978-1-4231-5720-5(6)) Hyperion Bks. for Children.

Cole, Bob. Power Reading: Comic Book/Treasure Island. Lee, loe, illus. 2005. 70p. (J). (gr. 4-6). vinyl bd. (978-1-883186-78-4(1), PPCLC3) National Reading Styles Institute, Inc.

Colfer, Eoin. Airman. 2009. (ENG.). 416p. (J). (gr. 5-9). pap. 8.99 (978-1-4231-0751-4(9)) Hyperion Pr.

—Airman. 2009. (J). lib. bdg. 19.65 (978-0-606-12534-5(5), Turtleback) Turtleback Bks.

Collins, Pat Lowery. The Fattening Hut. 2005. (ENG.). 192p. (YA). (gr. 7). pap. 12.95 (978-0-618-55209-2(X)) Houghton Mifflin Harcourt Publishing Co.

Connell, Richard. The Most Dangerous Game. 2006. pap. 9.99 (978-1-59986-969-8(1)) Filiquarian Publishing, LLC.

—The Most Dangerous Game. 2004. reprint ed. pap. 1.99 (978-1-4192-7460-2(0)) Kessinger Publishing, LLC.

Connell, Richard Edward. The Most Dangerous Game. 2010. (Creative Short Stories Ser.). (Illus.). 48p. (J). (gr. 5-18). 19.95 (978-1-58341-920-5(9), Creative Education) Creative Co., The.

Cook, Eileen. Unraveling Isobel. 2012. (ENG.). (YA). (gr. 9). 320p. pap. 9.99 (978-1-4424-1328-3(X)); 304p. 16.99 (978-1-4424-1327-6(1)) Simon Pulse. (Simon Pulse).

Cooper, Michelle. A Brief History of Montmaray. 2011. (Montmaray Journals). (ENG.). 324p. (YA). (gr. 7). pap. 8.99 (978-0-375-85154-4(2), Knopf Bks. for Young Readers) Random Hse. Children's Bks.

Copeland, Cynthia L. Elin's Island. 2003. (Single Titles Ser.: up). (ENG.). 144p. (YA). (gr. 6-12). lib. bdg. 22.60 (978-0-7613-2522-2(0), Millbrook Pr.) Lerner Publishing Group.

Covey, S. K. The Road to Rincon, 1 vol. 2010. 40p. 24.95 (978-1-4489-4929-8(7)) PublishAmerica, Inc.

Crossman, D. A. The Legend of Burial Island: A Bean & Ab Mystery. 2009. (J). pap. (978-0-89272-812-1(4)) Down East Bks.

Crowley-Ranelli, D. Holiday Island: Santa in a Bathing Suit? 2009. 56p. pap. 9.95 (978-1-60860-268-1(0), Eloquent Bks.) Strategic Book Publishing & Rights Agency (SBPRA).

Cue, Ian J. The Renewal: First Encounter. 2003. 192p. (YA). per. 9.95 (978-0-9741989-0-3(0)) Mill Creek Metro Publishing.

Cummings, Diana M. Hardy. Trimp II Mystic Island. 2012. (ENG.). 60p. pap. 18.95 (978-1-4327-8925-1(2)) Outskirts Pr., Inc.

Dalton, Michelle. Pulled Under. 2014. (Sixteenth Summer Ser.). (ENG., Illus.). 288p. (YA). (gr. 7). pap. 9.99 (978-1-4814-0700-7(7), Simon Pulse) Simon Pulse.

Davidson, Michele R. Stowaways to Smith Island: Hayden & Chloe's Enchanted Journey with the Nurses to Maryland's Mysterious Smith Island. Watjen, Laureen, illus. 2004. 128p. (J). pap. 8.95 (978-0-9754170-1-0(0)) Smith Island Foundation.

Davies, Anna. Wrecked. (ENG., Illus.). 336p. (YA). (gr. 9). 2013. pap. 9.99 (978-1-4424-3279-6(9)) 2012. 16.99 (978-1-4424-3278-9(0)) Simon & Schuster Bks. For Young Readers. (Simon & Schuster Bks. For Young Readers).

de Brunhoff, Laurent. Babar on Paradise Island. 2014. (ENG., Illus.). 48p. (J). (gr. k-2). 18.95 (978-1-4197-1038-4(9), Abrams Bks. for Young Readers) Abrams, Inc.

Defoe, Daniel. Robinson Crusoe. McKowen, Scott, illus. 2011. (Sterling Unabridged Classics Ser.). (ENG.). 288p. (J). 9.95 (978-1-4027-8406-4(6)) Sterling Publishing Co., Inc.

—Robinson Crusoe. Akib, Jamel, illus. 2006. (Classic Starts(tm) Ser.). (ENG.). 160p. (J). (gr. 2-4). 6.95 (978-1-4027-2664-4(3)) Sterling Publishing Co., Inc.

Defoe, Daniel, et al. Robinson Crusoe: The Complete Story of Robinson Crusoe. (Classics Illustrated Ser.). (Illus.). 52p. (YA). pap. 4.95 (978-1-57209-021-7(9)) Classics International Entertainment, Inc.

Dell, Scott O. L Isola Dei Delfini Blu. pap. 16.95 (978-88-09-02504-2(0)) Giunti Gruppo Editoriale ITA. Dist: Distribooks, Inc.

Depken, Kristen L. Island of the Lost Horses (Dora & Friends) Aikins, David, illus. 2015. (Step into Reading Ser.). (ENG.). 24p. (J). (gr. -1-1). 4.99 (978-0-553-52093-4(8), Random Hse. Bks. for Young Readers) Random Hse. Children's Bks.

Derby, Sally. Kyle's Island. (ENG.). 192p. (J). (gr. 5). 2014. pap. 7.95 (978-1-58089-317-6(1)) 2010. 16.95 (978-1-58089-316-9(3)) Charlesbridge Publishing, Inc.

Dingwell, Carson. Rory of Cain's Mountain. 2005. pap. 16.95 (978-1-4137-8756-6(8)) America Star Bks.

Dixon, Franklin W. & Walker, Jeff. Typhoon Island, Vol. 180. 2003. (Hardy Boys Ser.: 180). (ENG., Illus.). 160p. (J). (gr. 3-7). pap. 5.99 (978-0-689-85884-0(1), Aladdin) Simon & Schuster Children's Publishing.

Doan, Lisa. Jack the Castaway. Stevanovic, Ivica, illus. 2014. (Berenson Schemes Ser.: 1). (ENG.). 152p. (J). (gr. 4-6). 17.95 (978-1-4677-1076-3(8), Darby Creek) Lerner Publishing Group.

Doherty, Berlie. The Company of Ghosts. 2015. (ENG., Illus.). 272p. (YA). (gr. 7). 9.99 (978-1-84939-729-2(5)) Andersen Pr. GBR. Dist: Independent Pubs. Group.

Dorros, Arthur. La Isla. 2004. (SPA., Illus.). (J). (gr. k-3). spiral bd. (978-0-616-07275-2(9)) Canadian National Institute for the Blind/Institut National Canadien pour les Aveugles.

Douglas, H. I. Voyage to the Stars: David's First Adventure. 2006. 156p. pap. 24.95 (978-1-4241-1176-3(5)) America Star Bks.

Duddle, Jonny. The Jolley-Rogers & the Monster's Gold. Duddle, Jonny, illus. 2017. (ENG., Illus.). 160p. (J). (gr. 1-4). pap. 6.99 (978-0-7636-9292-6(1), Templar) Candlewick Pr.

Dunrea, Olivier. Me & Annie McPhee. Hillenbrand, Will, illus. 2016. (ENG.). 32p. (J). (gr. -1-2). 16.99 (978-0-399-16808-6(7), Philomel Bks.) Penguin Young Readers Group.

Dyer-Groves, Beverly E. Spooky Nights on the Island. 2011. 64p. (gr. -1). pap. 11.99 (978-1-4567-2040-7(6)) AuthorHouse.

Eagland, Jane. Wild Song. 2013. (ENG.). 80p. (YA). (gr. 6-12). pap. 6.95 (978-1-78112-182-5(6)); lib. bdg. 22.60 (978-1-78112-181-8(8)) Lerner Publishing Group.

Eames, Brian. The Dagger X. 2013. (Dagger Chronicles Ser.). (ENG.). 368p. (J). (gr. 3-7). 15.99 (978-1-4424-6855-9(6), Simon & Schuster Bks. For Young Readers) Simon & Schuster Bks. For Young Readers.

—The Dagger X. 2013. (Dagger Chronicles Ser.). (ENG., Illus.). 368p. (J). (gr. 3-7). pap. 6.99 (978-1-4424-6856-6(4), Simon & Schuster/Paula Wiseman Bks.) Simon & Schuster/Paula Wiseman Bks.

East, Bob. Tommy Cat & the Giant Chickens. East, Matt, illus. 2008. 24p. per. 24.95 (978-1-4241-9242-7(0)) America Star Bks.

—Tommy Cat & the Haunted Well, 1 vol. 2009. 42p. pap. 24.95 (978-1-60703-754-5(8)) America Star Bks.

Eastman, Peter. Fred & Ted Like to Fly. 2011. (Bright & Early Board Books Ser.). (ENG., Illus.). 24p. (J). (— 1). bds. 4.99 (978-0-375-86802-3(X), Random Hse. Bks. for Young Readers) Random Hse. Children's Bks.

Eaton, Maxwell, III. Birds vs. Bunnies. 2013. (Flying Beaver Brothers Ser.). (ENG., Illus.). 96p. (J). (gr. 1-4). pap. 7.99 (978-0-449-81022-4(4), Knopf Bks. for Young Readers) Random Hse. Children's Bks.

—Birds vs. Bunnies. 2013. (Flying Beaver Brothers Ser.: 4). lib. bdg. 18.40 (978-0-606-32234-8(5), Turtleback) Turtleback Bks.

—The Flying Beaver Brothers & the Crazy Critter Race. 2015. (Flying Beaver Brothers Ser.). (ENG., Illus.). 96p. (J). (gr. 1-4). pap. 7.99 (978-0-385-75469-9(8), Knopf Bks. for Young Readers) Random Hse. Children's Bks.

—The Flying Beaver Brothers & the Evil Penguin Plan. 2012. (Flying Beaver Brothers Ser.). (ENG.). 96p. (J). (gr. 1-4). pap. 7.99 (978-0-375-86447-6(4), Knopf Bks. for Young Readers) Random Hse. Children's Bks.

—The Flying Beaver Brothers & the Evil Penguin Plan. 2012. (Flying Beaver Brothers Ser.: 1). lib. bdg. 17.20 (978-0-606-23869-4(7), Turtleback) Turtleback Bks.

—The Flying Beaver Brothers & the Fishy Business. 2012. (Flying Beaver Brothers Ser.). (ENG.). 96p. (J). (gr. 1-4). pap. 7.99 (978-0-375-86448-3(2), Knopf Bks. for Young Readers) Random Hse. Children's Bks.

—The Flying Beaver Brothers & the Fishy Business. 2012. (Flying Beaver Brothers Ser.: 2). lib. bdg. 18.40 (978-0-606-23870-0(0), Turtleback) Turtleback Bks.

—The Flying Beaver Brothers & the Hot Air Baboons. 2014. (Flying Beaver Brothers Ser.). (ENG., Illus.). 96p. (J). (gr. 1-4). pap. 6.99 (978-0-385-75466-8(3), Knopf Bks. for Young Readers) Random Hse. Children's Bks.

—The Flying Beaver Brothers & the Mud-Slinging Moles. 2013. (Flying Beaver Brothers Ser.). (ENG., Illus.). 96p. (J). (gr. 1-4). pap. 7.99 (978-0-449-81019-4(4), Knopf Bks. for Young Readers) Random Hse. Children's Bks.

—The Flying Beaver Brothers & the Mud-Slinging Moles. 2013. (Flying Beaver Brothers Ser.: 3). lib. bdg. 17.20 (978-0-606-32233-1(7), Turtleback) Turtleback Bks.

Epner, Paul. Herbert Hilligan's Tropical Adventure. Kuon, Vuthy & Nguyen, Duke, illus. 2003. 32p. (J). 15.95 (978-0-9743335-2-6(2)) Imaginative Publishing, Ltd.

Finlay, Roger Thompson. The Wonder Island Boys: Conquest of the Savages. 2007. (ENG.). 188p. pap. 19.99 (978-1-4346-5001-6(4)); 204p. pap. 22.99 (978-1-4346-5002-3(2)) Creative Media Partners, LLC.

—The Wonder Island Boys: Treasures of the Island. 2007. (ENG.). 180p. pap. 19.99 (978-1-4346-4905-8(9)); 198p. pap. 21.99 (978-1-4346-4906-5(7)) Creative Media Partners, LLC.

Fiona Fox Staff, ed. The Swiss Family Robinson. 2012. (ENG., Illus.). 224p. (J). 15.00 (978-1-84135-839-0(8)) Award Pubns. Ltd. GBR. Dist: Parkwest Pubns., Inc.

Fitzpatrick, Huntley. What I Thought Was True. 2014. (ENG.). 416p. (YA). (gr. 9). 17.99 (978-0-8037-3909-3(5), Dial Bks) Penguin Young Readers Group.

Francis, Mamie, et al. Green Isles of the Ocean. Evans, Fran et al, illus. 2005. (ENG.). 32p. pap. 12.95 (978-1-84323-421-0(1)) Beekman Bks., Inc.

Fred. Cast Away on the Letter A. Fred, illus. 2013. (Philemon Adventures Ser.). (ENG., Illus.). 48p. (J). (gr. 2-7). 16.95 (978-1-935179-63-4(2)) TOON Books / RAW Junior, LLC.

Friedman, Aimee. Sea Change. (ENG.). (J). (gr. 7). 2010. 320p. 8.99 (978-0-439-92230-2(5)) 2009. 304p. 16.99 (978-0-439-92228-9(3)) Scholastic, Inc.

Fujisaki, Ryu. The Sennin World War. Fujisaki, Ryu, illus. 2009. (Hoshin Engi Ser.: 13). (ENG., Illus.). 200p. pap. 7.99 (978-1-4215-2402-3(3)) Viz Media.

Fuller, Harvey. Tommy & the Island. Fuller, Harvey, illus. 2007. (Illus.). (J). pap. 18.95 (978-0-9773725-7-7(X)) Flat Hammock Pr.

Fultz, Steven D. The Adventures of the Barnyard Detectives: Where's Mr. Peacock, 1 vol. 2009. 79p. pap. 19.95 (978-1-60749-965-7(7)) America Star Bks.

Garis, Howard R. The Curlytops on Star Island; or, Camping Out with Grandpa. 2007. 164p. per. (978-1-4065-2764-3(5)) Dodo Pr.

Garlick, Nicholas. Storm Horse. 2017. (J). pap. **(978-0-545-90415-5(3))** Scholastic, Inc.

Gay, Marie-Louise. Sur Mon Ile. 2004. (FRE.). (J). (gr. k-3). spiral bd. (978-0-616-07261-5(9)) Canadian National Institute for the Blind/Institut National Canadien pour les Aveugles.

Giff, Patricia Reilly. Jubilee. (ENG.). 160p. (J). (gr. 3-7). 2017. 6.99 **(978-0-385-74489-8(7)**, Yearling) 2016. 16.99 (978-0-385-74486-7(2), Lamb, Wendy Bks.) Random Hse. Children's Bks.

Gilleland, Rebecca. The Swiss Family Robinson Study Guide. 2003. stu. ed., ring bd. 14.99 (978-1-58609-194-1(8)) Progeny Pr.

Gilligan, Shannon. Ghost Island. Newton, Keith, illus. 2008. (Dragonlarks Ser.). 80p. (J). (gr. k-3). pap. 7.99 (978-1-933390-57-4(3)) Chooseco LLC.

Godolphin, Mary. The Swiss Family Robinson Told in Words. 2004. reprint ed. pap. 15.95 (978-1-4191-8466-6(0)) Kessinger Publishing, LLC.

—The Swiss Family Robinson Told in Words of One Syllable. 2004. reprint ed. pap. 1.99 (978-1-4192-8466-3(5)) Kessinger Publishing, LLC.

Goodman, Allegra. The Other Side of the Island. 2009. (ENG.). 288p. (YA). (gr. 7-18). pap. 8.99 (978-1-59514-196-5(0), Razorbill) Penguin Young Readers Group.

Greene, John McBride. Encounter at Ogre Island. Julich, Jenniffer, illus. 2006. 96p. pap. 9.50 (978-0-9772809-0-2(X)) Comprecom.

Gregory, Kristiana. Bronte's Book Club. 2008. (ENG., Illus.). 160p. (J). (gr. 3-7). pap. 7.95 (978-0-8234-2209-8(7)) Holiday Hse., Inc.

Guerra, R. R. Gabirochi y la Isla de la Vid. 2010. 168p. pap. 31.90 (978-1-59754-554-9(6)) Editorial Libros en Red.

Gurney, James. Dinotopia: The World Beneath. 20th anniv. ed. 2012. (Calla Editions Ser.). (ENG., Illus.). 192p. (gr. 3). 30.00 (978-1-60660-033-7(8)) Dover Pubns., Inc.

—Dinotopia - First Flight. 20th anniv. ed. 2014. (ENG., Illus.). 112p. (gr. 5). 25.00 (978-1-60660-057-3(5)) Dover Pubns., Inc.

Gutzschhahn, Uwe-Michael. The Lighthouse under the Clouds. Docherty, Thomas, illus. 2008. (ENG.). 32p. (J). (gr. -1-k). 19.00 (978-1-906367-03-9(5)) National Maritime Museum GBR. Dist: Independent Pubs. Group.

Haen, Teri R. Treasure to Love. 2012. 74p. pap. 27.95 (978-1-4497-4207-2(6), WestBow Pr.) Author Solutions, Inc.

Halam, Ann. Dr. Franklin's Island. 2003. (ENG.). 272p. (YA). (gr. 7). mass mkt. 6.99 (978-0-440-23781-5(5), Laurel Leaf) Random Hse. Children's Bks.

Hammond, Jo. Home Before Dark, 1 vol. 2005. (ENG.). 144p. (YA). (gr. 7-12). per. 7.95 (978-1-55143-340-0(0)) Orca Bk. Pubs. USA.

Han, Jenny & Vivian, Siobhan. Burn for Burn. (ENG., (YA). (gr. 9). 2013. Illus.). 400p. pap. 10.99 (978-1-4424-4076-0(7)) 2012. 368p. 17.99 (978-1-4424-4075-3(9)) Simon & Schuster Bks. For Young Readers. (Simon & Schuster Bks. For Young Readers).

—Fire with Fire. 2013. (ENG., Illus.). 528p. (YA). (gr. 9). 17.99 (978-1-4424-4078-4(3), Simon & Schuster Bks. For Young Readers) Simon & Schuster Bks. For Young Readers.

Hardy, Cindy & Masterman, Lorrine A. Egg Island Reader, 1 vol. 2003. (ENG., Illus.). 76p. pap. 14.95 (978-1-55059-246-7(7)) Brush Education CAN. Dist: Univ. of Toronto Pr.

Hargrave, Kiran Millwood. The Cartographer's Daughter. 2016. (ENG.). 224p. (J). (gr. 5). 16.99 (978-0-553-53528-0(5), Knopf Bks. for Young Readers) Random Hse. Children's Bks.

Harvey, Pam & Panckridge, Michael. Ghost of a Chance. 2007. 208p. (978-0-207-20063-2(7)) HarperCollins Pubs. Australia.

Haugaard, Erik. Prince Boghole. 2013. (ENG., Illus.). 32p. (J). (gr. -1-3). 16.99 (978-1-4814-2167-6(0), Simon & Schuster Bks. For Young Readers) Simon & Schuster Bks. For Young Readers.

Hawley, Mabel C. Four Little Blossoms on Apple Tree Island. 2004. reprint ed. pap. 1.99 (978-1-4192-2050-0(0)) Kessinger Publishing, LLC.

Hawthorne, Rachel. Island Girls & Boys. 2005. (ENG.). 336p. (YA). (gr. 9). pap. 8.99 (978-0-06-075546-1(6), HarperTeen) HarperCollins Pubs.

Hedderwick, Mairi. Katie Morag of Course! 2003. (Katie Morag Ser.: 1). (ENG., Illus.). 64p. (J). (gr. 2-7). pap. 11.99 (978-0-09-943205-0(6)) Random Hse. GBR. Dist: Independent Pubs. Group.

Henry, William. Tir na NOg: A New Adventure. Arnault, Delphine, illus. 2009. (ENG.). 128p. (J). pap. 25.95 (978-1-85635-597-1(7)) Mercier Pr., Ltd., The IRL. Dist: Dufour Editions, Inc.

Henty, George Alfred. The Stone Chest or the Secret of Cedar Island. 2004. reprint ed. pap. 1.99 (978-1-4192-8354-3(5)); pap. 15.95 (978-1-4191-8354-6(0)) Kessinger Publishing, LLC.

Herron, Edward A. The Return of the Alaskan: Mailboat in the Outpost. Langley, Gene, illus. 2011. 190p. 42.95 (978-1-258-09093-7(7)) Literary Licensing, LLC.

Hofmeyr, Dianne & Daly, Jude. The Faraway Island. Daly, Jude, illus. 2008. (ENG., Illus.). 32p. (J). (gr. 1-4). 16.95 (978-1-84507-644-3(3), Frances Lincoln Children's Bks.) Quarto Publishing Group UK GBR. Dist: Hachette Bk. Group.

Hogan, Jamie. Seven Days of Daisy, 1 vol. Hogan, Jamie, illus. 2011. (ENG., Illus.). 32p. (J). (gr. -1-3). 14.95 (978-0-89272-919-7(8)) Down East Bks.

Holden, Pam. Surprise from the Sky, 6 pack. Whimp, Pauline, illus. 2009. (Red Rocket Readers Ser.). (ENG.). 16p. (gr. 2-1). pap. (978-1-877363-68-9(5)) Flying Start Bks.

Hope, B. T. The Curse of the Bone Pirates: Nui Island Eco-Logical Adventures. 2008. 198p. (J). pap. 9.95 (978-0-9817388-0-2(X)) Nui Media & Entertainment, LLC.

Hope, Laura Lee. The Outdoor Girls on Pine Island: Or A Cave & What It Contained. 2007. (ENG.). 144p. pap. 18.99 (978-1-4264-9638-7(9)) Creative Media Partners, LLC.

Hortten, Jacqueline Faye. Pu Beach. l.t. ed. 2004. (Illus.). 27p. (J). pap. 14.95 *(978-0-9728393-0-3(5))* Children's Bookshoppe Stop, The.

Hsiao, Christie. Journey to Rainbow Island. 2013. (ENG., Illus.). 40p. (J). (gr. 2-7). 17.95 *(978-1-939529-24-4(7))* BenBella Bks.

Hueller, Andy. Skipping Stones at the Center of the Earth: A Middle Grade Novel. 2011. (J). pap. 8.99 *(978-1-59955-488-4(7),* Bonneville Bks.) Cedar Fort, Inc./CFI Distribution.

Hunter, Erin. Spirits in the Stars. 2012. (Seekers Ser.: 6). (ENG.). 304p. (J). (gr. 3-7). pap. 6.99 *(978-0-06-087142-0(3))* HarperCollins Pubs.

Hutchinson, Kerrian. The Fish People. 2011. 18p. pap. 16.95 *(978-1-4626-2692-2(0))* PublishAmerica, Inc.

Ikeda, Daisaku. Over the Deep Blue Sea. McCraughrean, Geraldine, tr. from JPN. Wildsmith, Brian, illus. 2013. 6.95 *(978-1-935523-59-8(7))* World Tribune Pr.

Inkpen, Mick. Beachmoles & Bellvine. 2005. (ENG., Illus.). 32p. (J). (gr. -1-k). pap. 9.99 *(978-0-340-87866-8(5))* Hodder & Stoughton GBR. Dist: Hachette Bk. Group.

—Ploo & the Terrible Gnobbler. 2006. (Blue Nose Island Ser.: Bk. 1). (ENG., Illus.). (J). (gr. -1). 11.95 *(978-1-84032-988-9(2))* Hodder & Stoughton GBR. Dist: Trafalgar Square Publishing.

Ito, Jerilyn. Double Rainbow Island: The Mauka Adventure. Wong, Melissa Olaivar, illus. 2013. 36p. pap. 10.95 *(978-1-937260-99-6(2))* Sleepytown Pr.

Jacques, Florence Page. There Once Was a Puffin. Halpern, Shari, illus. 2016. (ENG.). 32p. (J). 15.95 *(978-0-7358-4245-8(0))* North-South Bks., Inc.

Jamieson, Mark. Ico Island. 2007. (J). pap. 11.95 *(978-0-9792518-0-1(X))* Gequalsa.

Jansson, Tove. Moominpappa at Sea. Hart, Kingsley, tr. Jansson, Tove, illus. 2010. (Moomins Ser.: 7). (ENG., Illus.). 240p. (J). (gr. 4-7). pap. 7.99 *(978-0-312-60892-7(6),* 9780312608927) Square Fish.

—Moomin's Desert Island. 2014. (Moomin Ser.). (ENG., Illus.). 48p. (J). (gr. 4-7). pap. 9.95 *(978-1-77046-134-5(5),* 9781770461345) Drawn & Quarterly Pubs. CAN. Dist: Macmillan.

Johann David Wyss Staff. The Swiss Family Robinson. 2005. pap. *(978-1-905432-50-9(X))* Dodo Pr.

Johnson, Sandi. Lost Island. Johnson, Britt & Durant, Sybrina, eds. Sturgeon, Bobbi, illus. l.t. ed. 2014. 28p. (J). (gr. k-5). pap. 12.99 *(978-1-929063-69-7(5),* 168) Moons & Stars Publishing For Children.

Jones, Gareth P. Ninja Meerkats (#7) the Ultimate Dragon Warrior. Finlayson, Luke, illus. 2014. (Ninja Meerkats Ser.: 7). (ENG.). 128p. (J). (gr. 2-4). pap. 5.99 *(978-1-250-04665-9(3),* 9781250046659) Square Fish.

Jones, Kimberly K. Sand Dollar Summer. 2008. (ENG., Illus.). 224p. (J). (gr. 4-8). pap. 5.99 *(978-1-4169-5834-5(7),* McElderry, Margaret K. Bks.) McElderry, Margaret K. Bks.

Kamata, Suzanne. A Girls' Guide to the Islands. 2017. (Gemma Open Door Ser.). (ENG.). mass mkt. 10.00 ***(978-1-936846-57-3(8))*** GemmaMedia.

Kellogg, Elijah. The Ark of Elm Island. 2005. reprint ed. pap. 28.95 *(978-1-4191-1833-3(1))* Kessinger Publishing, LLC.

—Charlie Bell, the Waif of Elm Island by Rev Elijah Kellogg. 2006. 352p. per. 23.99 *(978-1-4255-3559-9(3))* Michigan Publishing.

Kephart, Beth. This Is the Story of You. 2016. (ENG., Illus.). 264p. (YA). (gr. 7-12). 17.99 *(978-1-4521-4284-5(X))* Chronicle Bks. LLC.

Kerr, Gordon. Story of Robinson Crusoe. 2006. 100p. per. *(978-1-4067-2131-7(X),* Hesperides Pr.) Read Bks.

Kibuishi, Kazu. The Lost Islands. 2013. (Explorer Ser.: 1). (J). lib. bdg. 22.05 *(978-0-606-33456-3(4),* Turtleback) Turtleback Bks.

Kimpton, Diana. Pony-Crazed Princess Super Special: Princess Ellie's Summer Vacation. Finlay, Lizzie, illus. 2007. (ENG.). 144p. (gr. 1-4). pap. 4.99 *(978-1-4231-0616-6(4))* Hyperion Pr.

Kipling, Rudyard. The White Seal. Jones, Chuck, illus. 2006. (ENG.). 32p. (J). (gr. -1-3). 8.95 *(978-0-8249-6598-3(1),* Ideal Pubns.) Worthy Publishing.

Kodiath, Alex. Elephant Escapes to an Island. 2012. 104p. pap. 31.99 *(978-1-4685-8138-6(4))* AuthorHouse.

Korman, Gordon. Escape. 2008. (Island (Playaway Audio) Ser.). (J). 34.99 *(978-1-60514-854-0(7))* Findaway World, LLC.

Kositsky, Lynne. Minerva's Voyage. 2009. (ENG., Illus.). 240p. (YA). (gr. 6-18). pap. 10.99 *(978-1-55488-439-1(X),* Dundurn Pr.) Dundurn CAN. Dist: Ingram Publisher Services.

Krebs, Laurie. We're Sailing to Galapagos: A Week in the Pacific. Restelli, Grazia, illus. 2007. (ENG.). 32p. (J). (gr. k-1). pap. 8.99 *(978-1-84686-102-4(0))* Barefoot Bks., Inc.

Krpata, Mitch. The Secret Society. Merritt, Kory, illus. 2017. (Poptropica Ser.). (ENG.). 112p. (J). (gr. 1-4). 9.95 *(978-1-4197-2311-7(1),* Amulet Bks.) Abrams, Inc.

Kutner, Richard, tr. from FRE. The Suspended Castle: a Philemon Adventure: A TOON Graphic. Fred, illus. 2015. (Philemon Adventures Ser.). (ENG.). 56p. (J). (gr. 2). 16.95 *(978-1-935179-86-3(1))* TOON Books / RAW Junior, LLC.

—The Wild Piano. Fred, illus. 2015. (Philemon Adventures Ser.). (ENG.). 48p. (J). (gr. 2-7). 16.95 *(978-1-935179-83-2(7))* TOON Books / RAW Junior, LLC.

Lacey, Josh. The Dragonsitter. Parsons, Garry, illus. 2016. (Dragonsitter Ser.: 4). (ENG.). 96p. (J). (gr. 1-5). pap. 5.99 *(978-0-316-29908-4(1))* Little, Brown Bks. for Young Readers.

—Island of Thieves. 2013. (ENG.). 240p. (J). (gr. 5-7). pap. 7.99 *(978-0-544-10485-3(4))* Houghton Mifflin Harcourt Publishing Co.

Lacey, Josh & Pakenham, Sarah. Island of Thieves. 2012. (ENG.). 240p. (J). (gr. 5-7). 15.99 *(978-0-547-76327-9(1))* Houghton Mifflin Harcourt Publishing Co.

LaFer, Jenni. Ben Dhere! Don Dhat! Tall Tales from the Island of Gullah. Weitzel, Erica, illus. 2007. 96p. (J). per. 18.95 *(978-0-9800816-0-2(2))* Bread & Butter Bks.

Lanagan, Margo. The Brides of Rollrock Island. (ENG.). (YA). (gr. 9). 2013. 318p. pap. 9.99 *(978-0-375-87336-2(8),* Ember) 2012. 320p. 17.99 *(978-0-375-86919-8(0),* Knopf Bks. for Young Readers) Random Hse. Children's Bks.

Landrón, Rafael & Landrón, José Rafael. Beba y la Isla Nena: Beba & the Little Island. Ordóñez, María Antonia, illus. 2010. (SPA & ENG.). 32p. (J). *(978-1-934370-05-6(3),* Campanita Bks.) Editorial Campana.

Larry, H. I. Poison Island. Oswald, Ash, illus. 2008. (Zac Power Ser.: 1). (ENG.). 96p. (J). (gr. 3-6). pap. 5.99 *(978-0-312-34659-1(X),* 9780312346591) Square Fish.

Lasky, Kathryn. May. (Daughters of the Sea Ser.). (ENG.). 336p. (J). (gr. 7-7). 2012. pap. 9.99 *(978-0-545-24331-5(9))* 2011. 17.99 *(978-0-439-78311-8(9))* Scholastic, Inc. (Scholastic Pr.).

Latsch, Oliver, tr. from GER. The Pirate Pig. 2015. (ENG., Illus.). 80p. (J). (gr. 2-5). 9.99 *(978-0-385-37544-3(1),* Random Hse. Bks. for Young Readers) Random Hse. Children's Bks.

Law, Felicia & Way, Steve. Castaway Code: Sequencing in Action. Law, Felicia et al, illus. 2010. (Mandrill Mountain Math Mysteries Ser.). 32p. (J). (gr. 2-6). 22.60 *(978-1-60754-817-1(8));* pap. 10.55 *(978-1-60754-822-5(4))* Windmill Bks.

—Crocodile Teeth: Geometric Shapes in Action. Spoor, Mike & Mostyn, David, illus. 2010. (Mandrill Mountain Math Mysteries Ser.). 32p. (J). (gr. 2-6). 22.60 *(978-1-60754-816-4(X));* pap. 10.55 *(978-1-60754-821-8(6))* Windmill Bks.

—Mirage in the Mist: Measurement in Action. Spoor, Mike & Mostyn, David, illus. 2010. (Mandrill Mountain Math Mysteries Ser.). 32p. (J). (gr. 2-6). pap. 10.55 *(978-1-60754-823-2(2))* Windmill Bks.

—Mirage in the Mist: Measurements in Action. Spoor, Mike & Mostyn, David, illus. 2010. (Mandrill Mountain Math Mysteries Ser.). 32p. (J). (gr. 2-6). 22.60 *(978-1-60754-818-8(6))* Windmill Bks.

—The Mystery of Nine: Number Place & Value in Action. Spoor, Mike & Mostyn, David, illus. 2010. (Mandrill Mountain Math Mysteries Ser.). 32p. (J). (gr. 2-6). 22.60 *(978-1-60754-819-5(4));* pap. 10.55 *(978-1-60754-824-9(0))* Windmill Bks.

LeapFrog Staff. Pirates: The Treasure of Turtle Island. 2008. (J). 13.99 *(978-1-59319-927-2(9))* LeapFrog Enterprises, Inc.

Lee, Joshua. The Mysterious Quest of Johnathan Davis. 2012. 24p. pap. 16.95 *(978-1-4626-9672-7(4))* America Star Bks.

Legend of the Island Horse. 2006. (J). *(978-1-933343-22-8(2))* Stabenfeldt Inc.

Levin, Betty. Thorn. 2005. (ENG.). 176p. (J). (gr. 9-12). 16.95 *(978-1-932425-46-8(2),* Lemniscaat) Boyds Mills Pr.

Lewis, Lisa. Tsunaxen's Journey. 2013. (ENG.). 23p. (J). pap. 14.95 *(978-1-4787-1979-3(5))* Outskirts Pr., Inc.

Libhart, Virginia B. Carrie's Dream. 2005. *(978-0-9652963-7-3(7))* Harborseal Publishing Co.

Likins, Kim. Charlie's Perfect Day. Magalinska, Ingrid, illus. l.t. ed. 2003. 32p. (J). bds. *(978-0-9729987-0-3(5))* Island Friends LLC.

Lindeman, Craig. The Big Black Dog & the Big Blue Se. Shoop, Johanna, illus. 2009. 40p. pap. 15.95 *(978-1-60844-047-4(8))* Dog Ear Publishing, LLC.

Lindgren, Astrid. Seacrow Island. Ramsden, Evelyn, tr. from SWE. 2015. (ENG.). 400p. (J). (gr. 3-7). 17.95 *(978-1-59017-868-3(8),* NYR Children's Collection) New York Review of Bks., Inc., The.

Lloyd, Sam R. Yummy Yummy! Food for My Tummy. Tickle, Jack, illus. 2004. 32p. (J). tchr. ed. 15.95 *(978-1-58925-035-2(4))* Tiger Tales.

Lord, Cynthia. Touch Blue. 2012. (ENG.). 192p. (J). (gr. 3-7). pap. 6.99 *(978-0-545-03532-3(5),* Scholastic Pr.) Scholastic, Inc.

Lumley, Jemima. The Journey Home from Grandpa's. Fatus, Sophie, illus. 2010. (ENG.). 16p. (J). (gr. -1-3). pap. 5.99 *(978-1-84686-277-9(9))* Barefoot Bks., Inc.

MacLachlan, Patricia & MacLachlan, Emily. Painting the Wind. Schneider, Katy, illus. 2006. (Joanna Cotler Bks.). (ENG.). 40p. (J). (gr. -1-3). reprint ed. pap. 7.99 *(978-0-06-443825-4(2))* HarperCollins Pubs.

MacNeil, Stephen. Woolies & Worms. Sandford, John, illus. 2007. (ENG.). 192p. (J). (gr. 1-5). 16.95 *(978-0-8126-2751-0(2))* Cricket Bks.

MacPherson, D. R. The Sport of Kings. 2011. 92p. pap. 25.00 *(978-1-60911-294-3(6),* Strategic Bk. Publishing) Strategic Book Publishing & Rights Agency (SBPRA).

Majumdar, Anuradha. Island of Infinity: Marina's Dream. 2005. 300p. (J). *(978-0-14-333513-9(8),* Puffin) Penguin Publishing Group.

Mara, Sarah Robinson. A Snug Little Island Hammond, Nancy Robinson, illus. 2005. 60p. (J). 18.50 *(978-0-9766737-0-5(3))* Pink Granite Pr.

Marsh, Carole. The Secret of Eyesocket Island. 2007. (Pretty Darn Scary Mysteries Ser.). (Illus.). 113p. (J). (gr. 3-5). per. 5.99 *(978-0-635-06236-9(4));* (YA). (gr. 7-14). 14.95 *(978-0-635-06240-6(2))* Gallopade International.

Martineck, Michael J. The Wrong Channel. 2005. 160p. (J). (gr. 4-8). 8.00 *(978-0-9720978-1-9(3))* Our Little Secret Pr.

Mason, Jo-Anne. Paddy, the Goat That Saved Rainbow Island. 2003. 48p. (gr. -1-3). 13.95 *(978-0-333-97062-1(4))* Macmillan Caribbean GBR. Dist: Interlink Publishing Group, Inc.

Mathieson, Karen. Thirteen Times Three: Book One of the Rosemary Ridge Trilogy. 2013. 164p. (J). pap. 7.99 *(978-1-940350-02-8(6))* Portable COO, The.

Matic, Mia. Ocean Blue: Delphi Island. 2012. 80p. (gr. 4-6). pap. 8.99 *(978-1-4525-0640-1(X))* Balboa Pr.

Matson, Lynne. Nil. 2014. (Nil Ser.: 1). (ENG.). 384p. (YA). (gr. 9-13). 18.99 *(978-0-8050-9771-9(6),* 9780805097719, Holt, Henry & Co. Bks. For Young Readers) Holt, Henry & Co.

—Nil Unlocked. 2015. (Nil Ser.: 2). (ENG.). 432p. (YA). (gr. 9). 17.99 *(978-1-62779-293-6(7),* 9781627792936, Holt, Henry & Co. Bks. For Young Readers) Holt, Henry & Co.

Matter, Sandy. The Great Sea Chase. 2011. 20p. pap. 24.95 *(978-1-4626-2488-1(X))* America Star Bks.

Matthew-Barnes, David. Wonderland. 2013. (ENG.). 264p. (gr. 7). pap. 11.95 *(978-1-60282-788-2(5))* Bold Strokes Bks.

McDonald, John. The Tempest: The Graphic Novel. Gale Editor, ed. 2011. (Classic Graphic Novel Collection). (ENG.). 160p. (gr. 7-10). lib. bdg. 39.40 *(978-1-4205-0632-7(3))* Cengage Gale.

Mcghee, Alison. Pablo & Birdy. Juan, Ana, illus. 2017. (ENG.). 304p. (J). (gr. 3-7). 17.99 ***(978-1-4814-7026-1(4),*** Atheneum/Caitlyn Dlouhy Books) Simon & Schuster Children's Publishing.

McGinnis, Mindy. Given to the Sea. 2017. (Given Duet Ser.). (ENG.). 352p. (YA). (gr. 9). 17.99 *(978-0-399-54461-3(5),* G.P. Putnam's Sons Books for Young Readers) Penguin Young Readers Group.

McMann, Lisa. Dragon Captives. 2017. (Unwanteds Quests Ser.: 1). (ENG., Illus.). 432p. (J). (gr. 3-7). 17.99 *(978-1-4814-5681-4(4),* Simon & Schuster/Paula Wiseman Bks.) Simon & Schuster/Paula Wiseman Bks.

—Dragon Captives. 2018. (Unwanteds Quests Ser.: 1). lib. bdg. 18.40 ***(978-0-606-40846-2(0))*** Turtleback Bks.

McMullan, Kate. Revenge of the Dragon Lady, 1 vol. Basso, Bill, illus. 2007. (Dragon Slayers' Academy Ser.: No. 2). (ENG.). 109p. (gr. -1-3). 24.21 *(978-1-59961-378-9(6))* Spotlight.

—Sir Lancelot, Where Are You?, 1 vol. Basso, Bill, illus. 2007. (Dragon Slayers' Academy Ser.: No. 6). (ENG.). 109p. (gr. 2-5). 24.21 *(978-1-59961-379-6(4))* Spotlight.

Meadows, Daisy. Isabella the Air Fairy. 2014. (Rainbow Magic — the Earth Fairies Ser.). lib. bdg. 14.75 *(978-0-606-35831-6(5))* Turtleback Bks.

—Joy the Summer Vacation Fairy. Ripper, Georgie, illus. 2007. (Rainbow Magic — Special Edition Ser.). 177p. (gr. -1-3). lib. bdg. 17.20 *(978-1-4177-7081-6(3),* Turtleback) Turtleback Bks.

—Louise the Lily Fairy. 2009. (Petal Fairies Ser.: 3). (ENG., Illus.). 80p. (J). (gr. 2-5). pap. 4.99 *(978-0-545-07092-8(9),* Scholastic Paperbacks) Scholastic, Inc.

—Nicole the Beach Fairy. 2014. (Rainbow Magic — the Earth Fairies Ser.). lib. bdg. 14.75 *(978-0-606-35830-9(7))* Turtleback Bks.

Meeks, John R. Dugan's Magical Island. 2011. 28p. pap. 12.40 *(978-1-4567-3947-8(6))* AuthorHouse.

Meunier, Sylvain. Raffi's Island Adventure, 1 vol. Cummins, Sarah, tr. from FRE. Eudes-Pascal, Elisabeth, illus. 2008. (Formac First Novels Ser.). (ENG.). 64p. (J). (gr. 2-5). 5.95 *(978-0-88780-755-8(0),* 9780887807558) Formac Publishing Co., Ltd. CAN. Dist: Casemate Pubs. & Bk. Distributors, LLC.

Miller, Ed, illus. Minions Paradise: Phil Saves the Day! 2016. (ENG.). 24p. (J). (gr. -1-3). pap. 5.99 *(978-0-316-39296-9(0))* Little, Brown Bks. for Young Readers.

Miller, Kyle Linda. Dillo - A Baby Armadillo's Adventure on Sanibel Island. Eddy, Randon T., illus. l.t. ed. 2005. (ENG.). 64p. (J). 16.95 *(978-0-9769332-0-5(9))* Jungle Hse. Pubns.

Mongoose, Mongoose, Stop! Don't Run. 2004. (J). 11.95 *(978-0-931548-65-9(9))* Island Heritage Publishing.

Montgomery, L. M. Anne of Avonlea. 2005. (Aladdin Classics Ser.). (ENG., Illus.). 416p. (J). (gr. 4-7). pap. 5.99 *(978-1-4169-0328-4(3),* Aladdin) Simon & Schuster Children's Publishing.

—Anne of Avonlea. Andreasen, Dan, illus. 2009. (Classic Starts(tm) Ser.). (ENG.). 160p. (J). (gr. 2-4). 6.95 *(978-1-4027-5424-1(8))* Sterling Publishing Co., Inc.

—Anne of Avonlea. McKowen, Scott, illus. 2008. (Sterling Unabridged Classics Ser.). (ENG.). 256p. (J). 9.95 *(978-1-4027-5428-9(0))* Sterling Publishing Co., Inc.

—Anne of Green Gables. 2005. 400p. 33.95 *(978-1-4218-0660-0(6),* 1st World Library - Literary Society) 1st World Publishing, Inc.

—Anne of Green Gables. 2009. 292p. 27.99 *(978-1-60512-375-2(7));* pap. 14.99 *(978-1-60512-475-9(3))* Akasha Publishing, LLC. (Akasha Classics).

—Anne of Green Gables. 2008. 316p. 29.99 *(978-0-554-23545-5(5))* 2008. 316p. 28.99 *(978-0-554-32848-5(8))* 2007. (ENG.). 312p. pap. 24.99 *(978-1-4264-4662-7(4))* Creative Media Partners, LLC.

—Anne of Green Gables. 2008. (Anne of Green Gables Ser.). (ENG.). 366p. (J). (gr. 4-7). pap. 9.95 *(978-0-9782552-6-8(7))* Davenport Pr. CAN. Dist: Independent Pubs. Group.

—Anne of Green Gables. 2007. 284p. per. *(978-1-4065-6399-3(4))* Dodo Pr.

—Anne of Green Gables. 2007. 572p. *(978-1-84702-773-3(3))* 2006. pap. *(978-1-4068-2170-3(5))* Echo Library.

—Anne of Green Gables. 2008. 316p. pap. 16.95 *(978-1-60096-565-4(2));* pap. 16.95 *(978-1-60096-101-4(0))* Editorium, The.

—Anne of Green Gables. 2009. 242p. pap. 8.58 *(978-0-217-43952-7(7))* General Bks. LLC.

—Anne of Green Gables. 2005. 21.99 *(978-1-4142-5125-7(4))* IndyPublish.com.

—Anne of Green Gables. 2008. (ENG.). 376p. (gr. k-12). pap. 14.95 *(978-0-7710-9368-5(3),* New Can Library) McClelland & Stewart CAN. Dist: Penguin Random Hse. LLC.

—Anne of Green Gables. Rubio, Mary Henley & Waterston, Elizabeth, eds. 2007. (Norton Critical Editions Ser.: 0). (ENG., Illus.). 464p. (C). (gr. 9-12). per. 15.02 *(978-0-393-92695-8(8),* 92695) Norton, W. W. & Co., Inc.

—Anne of Green Gables. 2003. 320p. (J). (gr. 4-7). 12.60 *(978-0-7569-1848-4(0))* Perfection Learning Corp.

—Anne of Green Gables. 2013. (Word Cloud Classics Ser.). (ENG.). 264p. pap. 14.99 *(978-1-60710-728-6(7),* Thunder Bay Pr.) Readerlink Distribution Services, LLC.

—Anne of Green Gables. 2009. 224p. pap. 15.45 *(978-1-4385-1847-3(1),* Book Jungle) Standard Pubns., Inc.

—Anne of Green Gables. 2008. (Modern Library Classics Ser.). (ENG.). 320p. pap. 9.00 *(978-0-8129-7903-9(6),* Modern Library) Random House Publishing Group.

—Anne of Green Gables. rev. ed. 2007. 280p. pap. 21.99 *(978-1-4264-4611-5(X))* Creative Media Partners, LLC.

—Anne of Green Gables. l.t. ed. 2006. pap. *(978-1-4068-3174-0(3))* Echo Library.

—Anne of Green Gables. 2004. reprint ed. pap. 27.95 *(978-1-4191-0717-7(8));* pap. 1.99 *(978-1-4192-0717-4(2))* Kessinger Publishing, LLC.

—Anne of Green Gables. l.t. ed. 2009. (World Classics Ser.). 288p. pap. 21.95 *(978-1-59688-123-5(2))* Large Print Bk. Co., The.

Montgomery, R. A. Island of Time. Louie, Wes & Cannella, Marco, illus. 2008. 144p. (J). (gr. 2-7). pap. 6.99 *(978-1-933390-28-4(X))* Chooseco LLC.

Mooney, Tara. Tot Island. 2011. 24p. pap. 16.95 *(978-1-4461-5907-1(8))* Lulu Pr., Inc.

Morgan, Clay. The Boy Who Returned from the Sea. 2009. (ENG.). 256p. (J). (gr. 3-7). pap. 7.99 *(978-0-14-241395-1(X),* Puffin Books) Penguin Young Readers Group.

—The Boy Who Spoke Dog. 2005. (ENG.). 176p. (J). (gr. 3-7). 5.99 *(978-0-14-240343-3(1),* Puffin Books) Penguin Young Readers Group.

Morley, P. Kevin. The Stinky Pirate & the Princess. 2009. 36p. pap. 17.99 *(978-1-4490-4062-8(4))* AuthorHouse.

Morton-Shaw, Christine. The Riddles of Epsilon. 384p. 2006. (ENG.). (YA). (gr. 8). per. 7.99 *(978-0-06-072821-2(3),* Tegen, Katherine Bks) Vol. 1. 2005. (gr. 7-18). 16.99 *(978-0-06-072819-9(1))* HarperCollins Pubs.

Moskowitz, Hannah. Teeth. 2013. (ENG.). 288p. (YA). (gr. 9). 17.99 *(978-1-4424-6532-9(8));* pap. 9.99 *(978-1-4424-4946-6(2))* Simon Pulse. (Simon Pulse).

Murphy, Anne. Animal Island. 2009. 44p. pap. 16.99 *(978-1-4389-4263-6(X))* AuthorHouse.

Murphy, Thomas. Island Boy. 2007. 124p. per. 19.95 *(978-1-4241-7940-4(8))* America Star Bks.

Murray, Eva & Hogan, Jamie. Island Birthday, 1 vol. 2015. (ENG., Illus.). 32p. (gr. 1-7). 16.95 *(978-0-88448-425-7(4),* 884425) Tilbury Hse. Pubs.

My Time on Nantucket Coloring Book. 2005. (J). 3.95 *(978-0-9755078-1-0(8))* Sweet Punkin Pr.

Myers, Suzanne. Stone Cove Island. (ENG., Illus.). (YA). (gr. 9). 2015. 256p. pap. 10.99 *(978-1-61695-575-5(9))* 2014. 236p. 17.99 *(978-1-61695-437-6(X))* Soho Pr., Inc. (Soho Teen).

Myklusch, Matt. The Lost Prince. 2015. (Seaborne Ser.: No. 1). (ENG.). 400p. (J). (gr. 3-7). 16.99 *(978-1-60684-525-7(X),* Carolrhoda Bks.) Lerner Publishing Group.

Norris, Zack. The Secret of Skull Island. 2012. (Double Detectives Ser.). (ENG.). 144p. (J). (gr. 3-7). pap. 4.95 *(978-1-4027-7912-1(7))* Sterling Publishing Co., Inc.

O'Dell, Scott. La Isla de los Delfines Azules. (SPA., Illus.). (YA). (gr. 5-8). 7.96 net. *(978-1-56137-541-7(1),* NU5722) Novel Units, Inc.

—Island of the Blue Dolphins. Lewin, Ted, illus. gif. ed. 2010. (ENG.). 192p. (J). (gr. 2-5). 22.00 *(978-0-547-42483-5(3))* Houghton Mifflin Harcourt Publishing Co.

—Island of the Blue Dolphins. 184p. (J). (gr. 3-5). pap. 5.99 *(978-0-8072-8327-1(4));* 2004. (gr. 5-9). pap. 36.00 incl. audio *(978-0-8072-8326-4(6),* YA163SP) Random Hse. Audio Publishing Group. (Listening Library).

—Island of the Blue Dolphins. l.t. ed. 2005. (ENG.). 223p. pap. 10.95 *(978-0-7862-7254-9(6),* Large Print Pr.) Thorndike Pr.

—Island of the Blue Dolphins. 2010. lib. bdg. 18.40 *(978-0-606-10724-2(X),* Turtleback) Turtleback Bks.

—Island of the Blue Dolphins. Schwebel, Sara L., ed. 2016. (ENG., Illus.). 256p. 29.95 *(978-0-520-28937-6(4))* Univ. of California Pr.

—Island of the Blue Dolphins: And Related Readings. 2006. (McDougal Littell Literature Connections Ser.). (ENG., Illus.). 208p. (gr. 6-8). 18.50 *(978-0-395-87473-8(4),* 2-70833) Great Source Education Group, Inc.

Ormondroyd, Edward. Castaways on Long Ago. 2003. (Illus.). 188p. (gr. 5-18). 12.95 *(978-0-9714612-8-4(7))* Green Mansion Pr. LLC.

Orr, Wendy. Nim's Island. Millard, Kerry, illus. 2008. (ENG.). 128p. (J). (gr. 3-7). 6.99 *(978-0-385-73606-0(1),* Yearling) Random Hse. Children's Bks.

Owen, Chris. Hairy Mole & the Precious Islands. 2008. (ENG., Illus.). 132p. pap. *(978-1-84167-564-0(4))* Ransom Publishing Ltd.

Papish, Ram. The Little Fox: An Alaska Adventure. Papish, Ram & Papish, Ram, illus. 2008. (ENG., Illus.). 38p. (gr. 3-7). 15.95 *(978-1-889963-87-7(9))* Univ. of Alaska Pr.

Parker, S. M. The Rattled Bones. 2017. (ENG., Illus.). 384p. (YA). (gr. 9). 17.99 ***(978-1-4814-8204-2(1),*** Simon Pulse) Simon Pulse.

Pascal, Francine. My First Love & Other Disasters. 2011. (ENG.). 256p. (YA). (gr. 4-9). pap. 11.99 *(978-1-4424-5234-3(X),* Simon Pulse) Simon Pulse.

Patchett, Mary Elwyn. The Great Barrier Reef. Monroe, Joan Kiddell, illus. 2011. 210p. 44.95 *(978-1-258-08492-9(9))* Literary Licensing, LLC.

Patchett, Terry. Nation. 2011. 10.36 *(978-0-7848-3498-5(9),* Everbind) Marco Bk. Co.

Patton, Jack. The Komodo Conflict. 2016. (Battle Bugs Ser.: 6). (ENG.). 128p. (J). (gr. 2-5). pap. 4.99 *(978-0-545-79148-9(0),* Scholastic Paperbacks) Scholastic, Inc.

Paulsen, Gary. The Island. 2006. (Point Ser.). 202p. (gr. 7-12). 16.00 *(978-0-7569-6382-8(6))* Perfection Learning Corp.

Payne, M. D. Fartsunami. Dockery, Amanda, illus. 2013. (Monster Juice Ser.: 2). (ENG.). 192p. (J). (gr. 3-7). pap. 5.99 *(978-0-448-46227-1(3),* Grosset & Dunlap) Penguin Young Readers Group.

Pearson, Ridley & Barry, Dave. Peter & the Secret of Rundoon. Call, Greg, illus. rev. ed. 2009. (Peter & the Starcatchers Ser.: Bk. 3). (ENG.). 496p. (J). (gr. 5-9). pap. 9.99 *(978-1-4231-2326-2(3))* Hyperion Pr.

Peretti, Frank E. The Cooper Kids Adventure Series. 2004. (Cooper Kids Adventure Ser.). (gr. 5-7). 23.96 *(978-0-89107-901-9(7))* Crossway.

—Escape from the Island of Aquarius, Vol. 2. 2004. (Cooper Kids Adventure Ser.: 2). 160p. (J). pap. 6.99 *(978-1-58134-619-0(0))* Crossway.

Pfister, Marcus. Milo & the Mysterious Island. 2014. (Milo Ser.). (ENG., Illus.). 32p. (J). (gr. k-3). 17.95 *(978-0-7358-4173-4(X))* North-South Bks., Inc.

Piper, Danny W. Skinny Boy's Close Call. 2008. 28p. per. 24.95 *(978-1-60441-534-6(7))* America Star Bks.

Poblocki, Dan. The House on Stone's Throw Island. 2015. (ENG.). 272p. (J). (gr. 5-9). 16.99 *(978-0-545-64556-0(5),* Scholastic Pr.) Scholastic, Inc.

Ponti, Claude. DeZert Isle. Holliday, Mary Martin, tr. from FRE. Ponti, Claude, illus. 2003. (ENG., Illus.). 64p. (J). 16.95 *(978-1-56792-237-0(6))* Godine, David R. Pub.

Potter, Ellen. Going Places. Leng, Qin, illus. 2017. 108p. (J). *(978-1-101-93961-1(3))* Knopf, Alfred A. Inc.

—The Humming Room. 2012. (ENG.). 192p. (J). (gr. 4-7). 16.99 *(978-0-312-64438-3(8),* 9780312644383) Feiwel & Friends.

—The Humming Room. 2013. (ENG.). 208p. (J). (gr. 4-7). pap. 6.99 *(978-1-250-01666-9(5),* 9781250016669) Square Fish.

—Piper Green & the Fairy Tree. Leng, Qin, illus. 2015. (Piper Green & the Fairy Tree Ser.). (ENG.). 112p. (J). (gr. 2-4). pap. 5.99 *(978-0-553-49926-1(2),* Yearling) Random Hse. Children's Bks.

H
I

—Piper Green & the Fairy Tree: Going Places. Leng, Qin, illus. 2017. (Piper Green & the Fairy Tree Ser.). (ENG.). (J). (gr. 2-4). 20.95 **(978-1-4301-2680-5(9))** Live Oak Media.
—Piper Green & the Fairy Tree: Going Places. Leng, Qin, illus. 2017. (Piper Green & the Fairy Tree Ser.). (ENG.). 128p. (J). (gr. 2-4). lib. bdg. 17.99 *(978-1-101-93962-8(1)*, Knopf Bks. for Young Readers) Random Hse. Children's Bks.
—Piper Green & the Fairy Tree: Pie Girl. Leng, Qin, illus. 2017. (Piper Green & the Fairy Tree Ser.: 5). (ENG.). 144p. (J). (gr. 2-4). pap. 5.99 **(978-1-101-93968-0(0))**; lib. bdg. 17.99 **(978-1-101-93966-6(4))** Random Hse. Children's Bks. (Yearling).
—Piper Green & the Fairy Tree: the Sea Pony. Leng, Qin, illus. 2016. (Piper Green & the Fairy Tree Ser.). (ENG.). 128p. (J). (gr. 2-4). 14.99 *(978-0-553-49931-5(9)*, Knopf Bks. for Young Readers) Random Hse. Children's Bks.
—Piper Green & the Fairy Tree: Too Much Good Luck. Leng, Qin, illus. 2015. (Piper Green & the Fairy Tree Ser.). (ENG.). 128p. (J). (gr. 2-4). 14.99 *(978-0-553-49927-8(0)*, Knopf Bks. for Young Readers) Random Hse. Children's Bks.
Pratchett, Terry. Jingo. 2014. (Discworld Ser.: 21). (gr. 5-8). 20.85 *(978-0-613-57231-6(9)*, Turtleback) Turtleback Bks.
Quixley, Barbara. Island Adventures of Jacki-Jacki. 2012. 116p. pap. 61.99 *(978-1-4771-4616-3(4))* Xlibris Corp.
R. M. Ballantyne. The Coral Island. 2007. 316p. per. 14.95 *(978-1-4218-4004-8(9)*, 1st World Library - Literary Society) 1st World Publishing, Inc.
Randall, Alice. The Diary of B. B. Bright, Possible Princess. 2012. (J). *(978-1-61858-016-0(7))* Turner Publishing Co.
Randall, Alice & Williams, Caroline Randall. The Diary of B. B. Bright, Possible Princess. Strickland, Shadra, illus. 2012. (ENG.). 192p. (J). (gr. 2-6). 19.95 *(978-1-61858-015-3(9))* Turner Publishing Co.
Random House Disney. Moana Junior Novelization. Random House Disney, illus. 2016. (Junior Novel Ser.). (ENG., Illus.). 144p. (J). (gr. 2-5). 17.20 *(978-0-606-39357-7(9))* Turtleback Bks.
Raven, Margot Theis. Circle Unbroken. Lewis, E. B., illus. 2007. (ENG.). 48p. (J). (gr. -1-3). per. 8.99 *(978-0-312-37603-1(0)*, 9780312376031) Square Fish.
Reeve, Philip. Oliver & the Sea Monkeys. Mcintyre, Sarah, illus. 2016. (Not-So-Impossible Tale Ser.). (ENG.). 224p. (J). (gr. 2-5). pap. 6.99 *(978-0-385-38789-7(X)*, Yearling) Random Hse. Children's Bks.
—Oliver & the Seawigs. Mcintyre, Sarah, illus. 2014. (Not-So-Impossible Tale Ser.). (ENG.). 208p. (J). (gr. 2-5). 12.99 *(978-0-385-38788-0(1)*, Random Hse. Bks. for Young Readers) Random Hse. Children's Bks.
Regis, Tessa. The Hibiscus Conspiracies: Loss of Innocence. 2009. 116p. 20.95 *(978-0-595-69133-3(1))*; pap. 10.95 *(978-0-595-44978-1(6))* iUniverse, Inc.
Reichs, Kathy. Code. 2013. (Virals Ser.: 3). (ENG.). 432p. (J). (gr. 5). pap. 8.99 *(978-1-59514-572-7(9)*, Puffin Books) Penguin Young Readers Group.
—Virals. 2014. lthr. 79.00 *(978-1-62715-582-3(1))* Leatherbound Bestsellers.
—Virals. (Virals Ser.: 1). (ENG.). (J). (gr. 5-18). 2011. 480p. 10.99 *(978-1-59514-426-3(9)*, Puffin Books) 2010. 464p. 17.99 *(978-1-59514-342-6(4)*, Razorbill) Penguin Young Readers Group.
—Virals. 2011. 20.00 *(978-1-61383-226-4(5))* Perfection Learning Corp.
Reichs, Kathy & Reichs, Brendan. Code. 2013. (Virals Ser.: 3). lib. bdg. 19.65 *(978-0-606-32140-2(3)*, Turtleback) Turtleback Bks.
—Virals. 2011. (Virals Ser.: 1). lib. bdg. 20.85 *(978-0-606-23069-8(6)*, Turtleback) Turtleback Bks.
Reiter, Naomi. Sandy the Stingray. 2007. 24p. per. 24.95 *(978-1-4241-8619-8(6))* America Star Bks.
Remole, Arnulf. The Island of Alphebia. 2007. 34p. 24.55 *(978-1-4303-2720-2(0))* Lulu Pr., Inc.
Rigby Education Staff. The Island of Wingo. (Sails Literacy Ser.). (Illus.). 16p. (gr. 2-3). 27.00 *(978-0-7635-9946-1(8)*, 699468C99) Rigby Education.
Robison, Dan. Death Chant: Kimo's Battle with the Shamanic Forces. 2006. 194p. (J). pap. *(978-0-922993-52-9(1))* Marquette Bks., LLC.
Roddy, Lee. Mystery of the Island Jungle. 2006. (Ladd Family Adventure Ser.: Vol. 3). (Illus.). 128p. (Orig.). (J). (gr. 3-7). per. 7.99 *(978-0-88062-252-3(0))* Mott Media.
Rodkey, Geoff. Deadweather & Sunrise. 2013. (Chronicles of Egg Ser.: 1). (ENG.). 320p. (J). (gr. 5). pap. 7.99 *(978-0-14-242662-3(8)*, Puffin Books) Penguin Young Readers Group.
Rogers, Jean. Goodbye, My Island. Munoz, Rie, illus. 2015. (ENG.). 96p. (J). (gr. 7-9). 21.99 *(978-1-943328-15-4(3)*, Alaska Northwest Bks.) Graphic Arts Ctr. Publishing Co.
Rooney-Freedman, Isabelle. Angus MacDream & the Roktopus Rogue. 2011. 206p. pap. 11.95 *(978-0-9843064-3-5(9))* Word with You Pr., A.
Sage, Angie. Skeleton Island. 2016. (Araminta Spookie Adventure Ser.: 2). (ENG.). 176p. (J). 16.99 *(978-1-61963-945-4(9)*, 9781619639454, Bloomsbury USA Childrens) Bloomsbury Publishing USA.
—Syren. Zug, Mark, illus. 2009. (Septimus Heap Ser.: 5). 640p. (J). (gr. 4). lib. bdg. 18.89 *(978-0-06-088211-2(5))*; (ENG.). 17.99 *(978-0-06-088210-5(7))* HarperCollins Pubs. (Tegen, Katherine Bks).
Salter, Charlotte. The Bone Snatcher. 2017. (ENG.). 352p. (J). (gr. 5-9). 16.99 *(978-0-399-18634-9(4)*, Dial Bks) Penguin Young Readers Group.
Sansone, V. K. WANTED: Children for Toys. 2009. 32p. pap. 14.98 *(978-0-557-16717-3(5))* Lulu Pr., Inc.
Santa Takes A Vacation. 2005. (J). 5.95 *(978-0-9769321-4-7(8))* Steingart, Nathan Publishing.
Schaefer, Lola M. An Island Grows. Felstead, Cathie, illus. 2006. (ENG.). 40p. (J). (gr. -1-3). 17.99 *(978-0-06-623930-9(3)*, Greenwillow Bks.) HarperCollins Pubs.
Scholastic Editors & Howard, Kate. Return of the Djinn. 2016. (Ninjago Readers Ser.: 15). lib. bdg. 13.55 *(978-0-606-38830-6(3))* Turtleback Bks.
Scott, Michael Rhys. Island's unto Himself. 2012. 28p. pap. 16.09 *(978-1-4669-0880-2(7))* Trafford Publishing.
Sedgwick, Marcus. Midwinterblood. 2013. (ENG.). 272p. (YA). (gr. 7). 17.99 *(978-1-59643-800-2(2)*, 9781596438002) Roaring Brook Pr.
—Midwinterblood. 2014. (ENG., Illus.). 288p. (YA). (gr. 7). pap. 9.99 *(978-1-250-04007-7(8)*, 9781250040077) Square Fish.
—Midwinterblood. 2014. (YA). lib. bdg. 20.85 *(978-0-606-35221-5(X))* Turtleback Bks.
Sheckels, Astrid, illus. Nic & Nellie, 1 vol. 2013. (ENG.). 32p. (J). (gr. 1-4). 17.95 *(978-1-934031-52-0(6)*, 9781934031520) Islandport Pr., Inc.
Sherrow, Victoria. Galapagos Fur Seal: At Home in the Tropics. Wertheim, Anne, illus. 2011. (ENG.). 32p. (J). pap. 8.95 *(978-1-60727-613-5(5))* Soundprints.
Sherry, Kevin. Turtle Island. 2014. (ENG.). 40p. (J). (gr. -1-k). 16.99 *(978-0-8037-3391-6(7)*, Dial Bks) Penguin Young Readers Group.
Shue, Jenna. Animal Island. Herzog, Inge, illus. 2005. 27p. (J). (gr. -1-3). per. 14.95 *(978-1-4259-0039-7(9))* AuthorHouse.
Sims, Lesley. Island Adventures. 2004. (Puzzle Adventures Ser.). (Illus.). 48p. (J). pap. 4.95 *(978-0-7945-0091-7(9)*, Usborne) EDC Publishing.
Skye, obert. The Ruins of Alder. Sowards, Ben, illus. 2010. (Leven Thumps Ser.: 5). (ENG.). 416p. (J). (gr. 4-9). pap. 9.99 *(978-1-4169-9093-2(3)*, Aladdin) Simon & Schuster Children's Publishing.
Smithey, Donna. Nichisan & the Ancient Ones. 2012. 36p. pap. 24.99 *(978-1-62419-240-1(8))* Salem Author Services.
Snedeker, Caroline. Downright Dencey. Barney, Maginel Wright, illus. 2003. (Young Adult Library). 268p. (YA). pap. 12.95 *(978-1-883937-79-9(5))* Bethlehem Bks.
Solod, Margo. Coyote Summer: A Summerhood Island Book. 2014. 1. (Illus.). 118p. (J). pap. 15.00 *(978-1-939930-18-7(9))* Brandylane Pubs., Inc.
Spalding, Andrea. An Island of My Own. 2008. (ENG., Illus.). 112p. (YA). (gr. 8-12). pap. 11.99 *(978-1-55002-635-1(6)*, Sandcastle Bks.) Dundurn CAN. Dist: Ingram Publisher Services.
Spalding, Esta. Knock about with the Fitzgerald-Trouts. Smith, Sydney, illus. 2017. (ENG.). 320p. (J). (gr. 3-7). 16.99 *(978-0-316-29860-5(3))* Little, Brown Bks. for Young Readers.
—Look Out for the Fitzgerald-Trouts. Smith, Sydney, illus. 2016. (ENG.). 256p. (J). (gr. 3-7). 16.99 *(978-0-316-29858-2(1))* Little, Brown Bks. for Young Readers.
Spoor, Mike, illus. Desperate Measures: Units of Measurement in Action. 2010. (Mandrill Mountain Math Mysteries Ser.). (ENG.). 32p. (J). (gr. 2-6). pap. 10.55 *(978-1-60754-925-3(5))* Windmill Bks.
—Desperate Measures: Units of Measurement in Action. 2010. (Mandrill Mountain Math Mysteries Ser.). (ENG.). 32p. (J). (gr. 2-6). lib. bdg. 22.60 *(978-1-60754-920-8(4))* Windmill Bks.
—The Emperor's Guards: Concepts of Time. 2010. (Mandrill Mountain Math Mysteries Ser.). (ENG.). 32p. (J). (gr. 2-6). pap. 10.55 *(978-1-60754-927-7(1))*; lib. bdg. 22.60 *(978-1-60754-922-2(0))* Windmill Bks.
—The Emperor's Last Command: Problem-solving in Action. 2010. (Mandrill Mountain Math Mysteries Ser.). (ENG.). 32p. (J). (gr. 2-6). pap. 10.55 *(978-1-60754-928-4(X))* Windmill Bks.
—The Emperor's Last Command: Problem-Solving in Action. 2010. (Mandrill Mountain Math Mysteries Ser.). (ENG.). 32p. (J). (gr. 2-6). lib. bdg. 22.60 *(978-1-60754-923-9(9))* Windmill Bks.
—The Hidden Valley: Reasoning in Action. 2010. (Mandrill Mountain Math Mysteries Ser.). (ENG.). 32p. (J). (gr. 2-6). pap. 10.55 *(978-1-60754-924-6(7))*; lib. bdg. 22.60 *(978-1-60754-919-2(0))* Windmill Bks.
—Lightning Flash: Probability in Action. 2010. (Mandrill Mountain Math Mysteries Ser.). (ENG.). 32p. (J). (gr. 2-6). pap. 10.55 *(978-1-60754-926-0(3))*; lib. bdg. 22.60 *(978-1-60754-921-5(2))* Windmill Bks.
Springer, Susan Woodward. Seldovia Sam & the Very Large Clam. Meissner, Amy, illus. 2003. (Misadventures of Seldovia Sam Ser.: 1). (ENG.). 64p. (J). (gr. -1-4). pap. 6.95 *(978-0-88240-570-4(5))* Graphic Arts Ctr. Publishing Co.
Springstubb, Tricia. Moonpenny Island. Ford, Gilbert, illus. 2015. (ENG.). 304p. (J). (gr. 3-7). 16.99 *(978-0-06-211293-4(7))* HarperCollins Pubs.
—Moonpenny Island. 2016. (J). lib. bdg. 17.20 *(978-0-606-38742-2(0))* Turtleback Bks.
St George, Colleen. Don't Pollute Our Island. 2011. 40p. pap. 24.95 *(978-1-4626-3484-2(2))* America Star Bks.
Staake, Bob. Beachy & Me. 2016. (ENG., Illus.). 40p. (J). (gr. -1-2). 16.99 *(978-0-385-37314-2(7))*; lib. bdg. 19.99 *(978-0-375-97198-3(X))* Random Hse. Children's Bks. (Random Hse. Bks. for Young Readers).
Steig, William. Abel's Island. 2007. (Newbery Award & Honor Bks.). (Illus.). 117p. (gr. 3-7). 17.00 *(978-0-7569-8290-4(1))* Perfection Learning Corp.
Stephens, Sarah. Seeing Red. 2016. (J). lib. bdg. 13.55 *(978-0-606-38189-5(9))* Turtleback Bks.
Sterns, Michael. Kokopelli & the Island of Change. Hageman, Erik, illus. 2nd ed. 2005. 64p. (J). 17.95 net. *(978-0-615-12724-8(X))* Grasshopper Dream Productions.
Stevenson, Robert Louis. Treasure Island. Date not set. (Nelson Readers Ser.). (J). pap. *(978-0-17-556699-0(2))* Addison-Wesley Longman, Inc.
Stiles, Gannett Ruth. My Father's Dragon. 2014. (My Father's Dragon Ser.). (ENG.). 96p. (J). (gr. 4-7). 11.24 *(978-1-63245-265-8(0))* Lectorum Pubns., Inc.
Stilton, Geronimo. Lost Treasure of the Emerald Eye. Wolf, Matt, illus. 2004. (Geronimo Stilton Ser.: No. 1). 116p. (J). lib. bdg. 10.00 *(978-1-4242-0695-7(2))* Fitzgerald Bks.
—Lost Treasure of the Emerald Eye. Wolf, Matt & Keys, Larry, illus. 2004. (Geronimo Stilton Ser.: 1). (ENG.). 128p. (J). (gr. 2-5). pap. 7.99 *(978-0-439-55963-8(4)*, Scholastic Paperbacks) Scholastic, Inc.
—Shipwreck on the Pirate Islands. 2005. (Geronimo Stilton Ser.: 18). (ENG., Illus.). 128p. (J). (gr. 2-5). 7.99 *(978-0-439-69141-3(9)*, Scholastic Paperbacks) Scholastic, Inc.
Stilton, Geronimo & Stilton, Thea. Thea Stilton & the Ghost of the Shipwreck. 2010. (Thea Stilton Ser.: 3). (ENG., Illus.). 176p. (J). (gr. 2-5). mass mkt. 8.99 *(978-0-545-15059-0(0)*, Scholastic Paperbacks) Scholastic, Inc.
Stilton, Thea. Revenge of the Lizard Club. Cooper-McGuinness, Nanette, tr. from ITA. 2013. (Thea Stilton Graphic Novels Ser.). (ENG., Illus.). 56p. (J). (gr. 1-5). 9.99 *(978-1-59707-430-8(6)*, 9781597074308) Papercutz.
Stine, R. L. Fear Street Super Thriller: Party Games & Don't Stay up Late. 2015. (Fear Street Ser.). (ENG.). 592p. (YA). (gr. 7-12). pap. 11.99 *(978-1-250-07693-9(5)*, 9781250076939, St. Martin's Griffin) St. Martin's Pr.
Streib, Sally. Octopus Encounter. 2007. (Illus.). 126p. (J). 6.97 *(978-0-8163-2210-7(4))* Pacific Pr. Publishing Assn.
Strong, Louise. The Island Adventures of Frodo Mcadoo. 2005. (Illus.). 196p. (J). per. 12.95 *(978-0-9770950-0-1(2))* Strong, Louise dev.
Suhay, Lisa. Our Fantasy Island: An Interactive Book. Hundley, Sam, illus. 2006. 30p. (J). pap. 8.00 *(978-0-9766628-0-8(9))* Fantasy Island Pr.
Summers, Kim. Senor Mundo & Me: A Happy Birthday Story. Mariscal, Javier, illus. 2004. 31p. (J). (gr. k-4). 20.00 *(978-0-7567-7759-3(3))* DIANE Publishing Co.
Swift, Jonathan. Los Viajes de Gulliver. (SPA., Illus.). 144p. (YA). 14.95 *(978-84-7281-080-8(1)*, AF1080) Auriga, Ediciones S.A. ESP. Dist: Continental Bk. Co., Inc.
—Los Viajes de Gulliver. (Coleccion Clasicos de la Juventud). (SPA., Illus.). 204p. (J). 12.95 *(978-84-7189-062-7(3)*, ORT322) Ortells, Alfredo Editorial S.L. ESP. Dist: Continental Bk. Co., Inc.
Tait, Chris & Wyss, Johann David. The Swiss Family Robinson. Akib, Jamel, illus. 2007. 151p. (J). *(978-1-4287-4213-0(1))* Sterling Publishing Co., Inc.
Tanen, Sloane. Are You Going to Kiss Me Now? 2011. (ENG.). 368p. (YA). (gr. 8-12). pap. 8.99 *(978-1-4022-5461-1(X))* Sourcebooks, Inc.
Taylor, Jessica. A Map for Wrecked Girls. 2017. (ENG.). 368p. (YA). (gr. 9). 17.99 **(978-0-7352-2811-5(6)**, Dial Bks) Penguin Young Readers Group.
Taylor, Tom. The Deep: The Vanishing Island, Vol. 2. Edwards, Gary, ed. 2013. (ENG., Illus.). 80p. (J). pap. 11.95 *(978-1-922023-05-6(1))* Gestalt Publishing Pty, Ltd. AUS. Dist: Diamond Comic Distributors, Inc.
TenNapel, Doug. Bad Island. 2011. (ENG.). 224p. (J). (gr. 4-7). pap. 10.99 *(978-0-545-31480-0(1)*, Graphix) Scholastic, Inc.
Terry, Michael. Captain Wag & the Big Blue Whale. Terry, Michael, illus. 2008. (Captain Wag Ser.). (ENG., Illus.). 32p. (J). (gr. k-k). pap. 13.95 *(978-0-7475-9254-9(3))* Bloomsbury Publishing Plc GBR. Dist: Independent Pubs. Group.
Thor, Annika. A Faraway Island. Schenck, Linda, tr. 2011. (ENG.). 256p. (J). (gr. 3-7). 6.99 *(978-0-375-84495-9(3)*, Yearling) Random Hse. Children's Bks.
Tiffany, Grace. Ariel. 2005. 240p. (J). 16.99 *(978-0-06-075327-6(7))* HarperCollins Pubs.
Tolman, Marije & Tolman, Ronald. The Island. 2012. (ENG., Illus.). 32p. (J). (gr. -1). 17.95 *(978-1-935954-19-4(9)*, 9781935954194) Lemniscaat USA.
Tomkins, Jasper, illus. Nimby: An Extraordinary Cloud Who Meets a Remarkable Friend. 2011. (ENG.). 60p. 15.95 *(978-1-59583-428-7(1)*, 9781595834287, Green Tiger Pr.) Laughing Elephant.
Treasures of the Barrier Reef. 2005. (J). audio, cd-rom 24.95 *(978-0-9771381-7-3(8))* Williams, Geoffrey T.
Trudeau, Scott & Holzbauer, David. A Treasure to Share: Adventures in Social Skills. Trudeau, Scott, illus. 2003. (Illus.). 68p. (J). *(978-0-9743805-0-6(4))* Intellipop, LLC.
Tyler, Tanith. Aegis Rising. 2007. (Illus.). 179p. *(978-0-9800860-0-3(0))* TNT Publishing Co.
Unexpected Treasure, 6 vols. (Ragged Island Mysteriestm Ser.). 161p. (gr. 5-7). 42.50 *(978-0-322-01650-7(9))* Wright Group/McGraw-Hill.
Ungerer, Tomi. Fog Island IBook. 2013. (ENG.). 48p. 5.99 *(978-0-7148-6777-9(2))* Phaidon Pr., Inc.
Ungureanu, Dan. Nara & the Island. Ungureanu, Dan, illus. 2016. (ENG., Illus.). 32p. (J). (gr. -1-3). 17.99 *(978-1-5124-1793-7(9))* Andersen Pr. GBR. Dist: Lerner Publishing Group.
—Nara & the Island. Ungureanu, Dan, illus. 2016. (ENG., Illus.). 32p. (gr. -1-3). 35.99 *(978-1-5124-1794-4(7))* Lerner Publishing Group.
Vachon, Mary Beth. Mac s Mackinac Island Adventure. Rusky, Ann G., illus. 2005. 216p. (J). pap. 17.95 *(978-0-9766104-1-0(8))* Arbutus Pr.
Varveris, Ariana Eleni. The Adventures of Magic Island: Book I- Welcome to Magic Island. 2012. 122p. (gr. 2-2). pap. 9.95 *(978-1-4620-5751-1(9))* iUniverse, Inc.
Veneziano, Chuckie. My Time on Nantucket. 2005. (Illus.). 56p. (J). lib. bdg. 17.95 *(978-0-9755078-0-3(X))* Sweet Punkin Pr.
Verne, Jules. La Isla Misteriosa. (SPA., Illus.). 192p. (YA). 11.95 *(978-84-7281-105-8(0)*, AF1105) Auriga, Ediciones S.A. ESP. Dist: Continental Bk. Co., Inc.
Wacker, Eileen. Black Tortoise & the Dynasty Dragon. Low, Alan M., illus. 2012. (Fujimini Adventure Ser.: Vol. 5). (ENG.). 40p. (J). (gr. -1-3). 10.99 *(978-1-4675-1741-6(0))* Oncekids.
—The Fujimini Adventure Series Box Set. 2013. (Fujimini Adventure Ser.). (ENG.). 128p. (J). (gr. 1-3). 29.99 *(978-1-4675-1747-8(X))* Oncekids.
—Rainbow Panda & the Firecracker Fiasco. 2013. (Fujimini Adventure Ser.). (ENG.). 40p. (J). 10.99 *(978-1-4675-1749-2(6))* Oncekids.
Wade, Judith. The Mermaid's Gift. 2004. 140p. (J). per. 5.99 *(978-0-9728958-1-1(7)*, 750) Riley Pr.
—The Secret of Mermaid Island. 2003. 136p. (J). mass mkt. 5.99 *(978-0-9728958-0-4(9))* Riley Pr.
Walford, N. E. The Island Hunters Bk. 1. 2011. (ENG.). 130p. pap. 14.99 *(978-1-4196-6072-6(1))* CreateSpace Independent Publishing Platform.
Walton, O. F. Saved at Sea: A Young Boy in a Dramatic Rescue. 2007. (Classic Stories Ser.). (ENG., Illus.). 144p. (J). mass mkt. 7.99 *(978-1-85792-795-5(8)*, 9781857927955) Christian Focus Pubns. GBR. Dist: Bookmasters Distribution.
Warner, Larry. Chocolate Island, 1 vol. 2010. 42p. pap. 24.95 *(978-1-4489-7372-9(4))* PublishAmerica, Inc.
Wells, Helen. Cherry Ames, Island Nurse. 2007. (Cherry Ames Nurse Stories Ser.). 224p. (J). (gr. 3-7). 14.95 *(978-0-8261-0423-6(1))* Springer Publishing Co., Inc.
Weston Woods Staff, creator. The Island of the Skog. 2011. 38.75 *(978-0-545-23367-5(4))*; 29.95 *(978-0-545-23365-1(8))*; 18.95 *(978-0-545-23366-8(6))* Weston Woods Studios, Inc.
—Time of Wonder. 2011. 29.95 *(978-0-439-73525-4(4))*; 18.95 *(978-0-439-72905-5(X))*; 38.75 *(978-0-439-72906-2(8))* Weston Woods Studios, Inc.
Wheeler, Lisa. Castaway Cats. Goembel, Ponder, illus. 2006. (ENG.). 32p. (J). (gr. -1-2). 17.99 *(978-0-689-86232-8(6)*, Atheneum/Richard Jackson Bks.) Simon & Schuster Children's Publishing.
Wiebe, Joanna. The Wicked Awakening of Anne Merchant. 2015. (V Trilogy Ser.: Bk. 2). (ENG.). 320p. (gr. 7). pap. 12.95 *(978-1-940363-29-5(2))* BenBella Bks.
Wigington, Patti. Summer's Ashes. 2007. (ENG.). 208p. (gr. 8-12). per. 15.00 *(978-0-9766805-9-8(9))* Keene Publishing.
Wiley. The Extraordinary Adventures of Ordinary Basil: Island of the Volcano Monkeys. 2007. (Ordinary Basil Ser.). (J). pap. *(978-0-439-86133-5(0))* Blue Sky Pr.
Wilkinson, Carole. Buried at Sea. 2007. 96p. (YA). pap. *(978-1-4207-0738-0(8))* Sundance/Newbridge Educational Publishing.
Williams, Geoffrey T. Manatees & Mermaids. 2010. (ENG., Illus.). 64p. (J). (gr. 3-7). 8.95 *(978-0-9800444-3-0(X))* Save Our Seas, Ltd.
Windham, Ryder. Island of Lost Masks. Scholastic, Inc. Staff, illus. 2015. (LEGO Bionicle Ser.: 1). (ENG.). 128p. (J). (gr. 2-5). pap. 5.99 *(978-0-545-87325-3(8))* Scholastic, Inc.
Winfield, Arthur M. The Rover Boys on Snowshoe Island or the Old Lumberman's. 2006. (ENG.). 332p. per. 30.95 *(978-1-4286-4114-3(9))* Kessinger Publishing, LLC.
Wirt, Mildred A. Swamp Island. 2011. 176p. pap. 12.99 *(978-1-935774-85-3(9)*, Resurrected Pr.) Intrepid Ink, LLC.
Wolk, Lauren. Beyond the Bright Sea. 2017. (ENG.). 304p. (J). (gr. 5). 16.99 **(978-1-101-99485-6(1)**, Dutton Books for Young Readers) Penguin Young Readers Group.
Wolverton, Barry. Neversink. Nielson, Sam, illus. (ENG.). (J). (gr. 3-7). 2013. 320p. pap. 6.99 *(978-0-06-202793-1(X))* 2012. 304p. 16.99 *(978-0-06-202791-7(3))* HarperCollins Pubs. (Waldon Pond Pr.).
—Neversink. Nielson, Sam, illus. 2012. xiii, 287p. (J). *(978-0-06-202792-4(1))* Longman Publishing.
Wyss, Johann. The Swiss Family Robinson. 2006. (Illus.). 61p. (J). lib. bdg. 30.77 *(978-1-4242-1334-4(7))* Fitzgerald Bks.
—The Swiss Family Robinson. 2005. pap. 16.95 *(978-1-59818-422-8(9))* Rodgers, Alan Bks.
Wyss, Johann David. Swiss Family Robinson. 2008. (Bring the Classics to Life Ser.). (ENG., Illus.). 72p. (gr. 1-12). pap., act. bk. ed. 10.95 *(978-1-55576-049-6(X)*, EDCTR-104B) EDCON Publishing Group.
—The Swiss Family Robinson. Akib, Jamel, illus. 2007. (Classic Starts(tm) Ser.). (ENG.). 160p. (J). (gr. 2-4). 6.95 *(978-1-4027-3694-0(0))* Sterling Publishing Co., Inc.
—The Swiss Family Robinson. McKowen, Scott, illus. 2006. (Sterling Unabridged Classics Ser.). (ENG.). 352p. (J). (gr. 5-7). 14.95 *(978-1-4027-2602-6(3))* Sterling Publishing Co., Inc.
—Swiss Family Robinson. Hunt, Robert, illus. 2006. (Stepping Stone Book(TM) Ser.). (ENG.). 112p. (J). (gr. 1-4). per. 3.99 *(978-0-375-87525-0(5)*, Random Hse. Bks. for Young Readers) Random Hse. Children's Bks.
—Swiss Family Robinson: A Classic Story about Initiative. 2003. (Illus.). 32p. per. 3.95 *(978-0-9747133-3-5(3)*, Values to Live By Classic Stories) Thomas, Frederic Inc.
—Swiss Family Robinson: With a Discussion of Teamwork. Butterfield, Ned, illus. 2003. (Values in Action Illustrated Classics Ser.). 191p. (J). *(978-1-59203-036-1(X))* Learning Challenge, Inc.
Wyss, Johann David, illus. The Swiss Family Robinson. 2004. reprint ed. pap. 30.95 *(978-1-4191-5012-8(X))*; pap. 1.99 *(978-1-4192-5012-5(4))* Kessinger Publishing, LLC.
Wyss, Johann David & Kingston, William Henry Giles. The Swiss Family Robinson: A Translation from the Original German. 2016. (J). pap. *(978-1-5124-2612-0(1))* Lerner Publishing Group.

ISLANDS OF THE PACIFIC

Beales, R. A. James Cook: The Pacific Coast & Beyond. 2005. (In the Footsteps of Explorers Ser.). (ENG., Illus.). 32p. (J). (gr. 4-5). pap. *(978-0-7787-2451-3(4))*; lib. bdg. *(978-0-7787-2415-5(8))* Crabtree Publishing Co.
Blackwell, Amy Hackney. East Asia & the Pacific, Vol. 10. 2016. (Social Progress & Sustainability Ser.). (Illus.). 80p. (J). (gr. 7). 24.95 *(978-1-4222-3494-5(0))* Mason Crest.
Comire, S. Joshua & Porter, Malcolm. Atlas of Australia & the Pacific. 2009. (Atlases of the World Ser.). (Illus.). 48p. (YA). (gr. 5-8). 29.25 *(978-1-4358-8456-4(6)*, Rosen Reference) Rosen Publishing Group, Inc., The.
Currie, Stephen. Australia & the Pacific Islands. 2004. (Exploration & Discovery Ser.). (ENG.). (J). (gr. 7-10). 30.85 *(978-1-59018-496-7(3)*, Lucent Bks.) Cengage Gale.
Darian-Smith, Kate. Australia, Antarctica, & the Pacific. 2005. (Continents of the World Ser.). 64p. (gr. 5-12). pap. 14.05 *(978-0-8368-5919-5(7))*; (Illus.). lib. bdg. 34.00 *(978-0-8368-5912-6(X))* Stevens, Gareth Publishing LLLP. (Gareth Stevens Secondary Library).
Exploring the Pacific, Revised Edition. 2nd rev. ed. 2009. (Discovery & Exploration Ser.). (Illus.). 120p. (YA). (gr. 7-12). 35.00 *(978-1-60413-197-0(7))* Facts On File, Inc.
Feinstein, Stephen. Captain Cook: Great Explorer of the Pacific. 2010. (Great Explorers of the World Ser.). (Illus.). 112p. (J). (gr. 7-12). 33.27 *(978-1-59845-102-3(2))* Enslow Pubs., Inc.
Friedman, Mel. Australia & Oceania. (True Book(tm), A — Continents Ser.). (ENG., 48p. (J). 2008. Illus.). (gr. 2-5). 31.00 *(978-0-531-16866-0(2))* 2009. pap. 6.95 *(978-0-531-21828-0(7)*, Children's Pr.) Scholastic Library Publishing.
Kalman, Bobbie & Sjonger, Rebecca. Explora Australia y Oceania. 2007. (Explora Los Continentes Ser.). (SPA & ENG., Illus.). 32p. (J). (gr. 6-10). pap. *(978-0-7787-8298-8(0))* Crabtree Publishing Co.
—Explore Australia & Oceania. rev. ed. 2007. (Explore the Continents Ser.). (ENG., Illus.). 32p. (J). (gr. 1-5). pap. *(978-0-7787-3087-3(5))* Crabtree Publishing Co.
Lace, William W. Captain James Cook. 2009. (Great Explorers Ser.). (Illus.). 112p. (gr. 6-12). 30.00 *(978-1-60413-416-2(X)*, Chelsea Hse.) Facts On File, Inc.
Leppman, Elizabeth J. Australia & the Pacific. 2005. (Modern World Cultures Ser.). (Illus.). 128p. (gr. 6-12). lib. bdg. 30.00 *(978-0-7910-8150-1(8)*, Chelsea Hse.) Facts On File, Inc.

Petrie, Kristin. James Cook, 1 vol. 2004. (Explorers Set 1 Ser.). (ENG., Illus.). 32p. (gr. k-6). 27.07 *(978-1-59197-596-0(4),* Checkerboard Library) ABDO Publishing Co.

Proujan, Carl & National Geographic Learning Staff. Oceania & Antarctica. 2007. (Reading Expeditions Ser.). (ENG., Illus.). 64p. (J). pap. 25.95 *(978-0-7922-4366-3(8))* CENGAGE Learning.

—Oceania & Antarctica - People & Places. 2007. (Reading Expeditions Ser.). (ENG., Illus.). 64p. (J). pap. 25.95 *(978-0-7922-4367-0(6))* CENGAGE Learning.

Willett, Edward. The Bounty Mutiny: From the Court Case to the Movie. 2009. (Famous Court Cases That Became Movies Ser.). (Illus.). 128p. (J). (gr. 6-18). lib. bdg. 33.27 *(978-0-7660-3128-9(4))* Enslow Pubs., Inc.

ISLANDS OF THE PACIFIC—FICTION

Ballantyne, R. M. The Coral Island. 2014. (ENG.). 368p. (J). (gr. 4-7). pap. 14.99 *(978-1-84391-481-5(6))* Hesperus Pr. GBR. Dist: Independent Pubs. Group.

Cantor, Jillian. Searching for Sky. 2014. (ENG.). 288p. (YA). (gr. 7-12). 17.99 *(978-1-61963-351-3(5),* 9781619633513, Bloomsbury USA Childrens) Bloomsbury Publishing USA.

Collingwood, Harry. The Strange Adventures of Eric Blackburn. 2008. 164p. 25.95 *(978-1-60664-711-0(3))* Rodgers, Alan Bks.

David, Christopher. Denholme & the Skeleton Mystery. 2006. 274p. pap. 22.52 *(978-1-4120-8014-9(2))* Trafford Publishing.

Hager, Mandy. Into the Wilderness. 2014. (Blood of the Lamb Ser.). (ENG.). 335p. (YA). (gr. 9). 17.99 *(978-1-61614-863-8(2))* Prometheus Bks., Pubs.

—Resurrection. 2014. (Blood of the Lamb Ser.). (ENG.). 361p. (YA). (gr. 9). 17.99 *(978-1-61614-909-3(4))* Prometheus Bks., Pubs.

Island of the Blue Dolphins. 2011. 9.00 *(978-0-7848-3655-2(8),* Everbind) Marco Bk. Co.

Jonell, Bob. Katie the Cricket. Prince, Brian, illus. 2009. 12p. pap. 24.95 *(978-1-61546-280-3(5))* America Star Bks.

Knox, Elizabeth. Mortal Fire. 2013. (ENG.). 448p. (YA). (gr. 7). 17.99 *(978-0-374-38829-4(6),* 9780374388294, Farrar, Straus & Giroux (BYR)) Farrar, Straus & Giroux.

Pratchett, Terry. Nation. 2008. 504p. (J). pap. 16.99 *(978-0-06-170913-5(1));* 384p. (YA). (gr. 8-18). 17.99 *(978-0-06-143301-6(2))* HarperCollins Pubs.

Probst, Jeff & Tebbetts, Chris. Stranded. 2013. (Stranded Ser.: 1). (ENG.). 208p. (J). (gr. 3-7). pap. 6.99 *(978-0-14-242424-7(2),* Puffin Books) Penguin Young Readers Group.

—Stranded. 2013. (Stranded Ser.: 1). lib. bdg. 17.20 *(978-0-606-36788-2(8))* Turtleback Bks.

—Trial by Fire. 2013. (Stranded Ser.: 2). (ENG.). 192p. (J). (gr. 3). pap. 6.99 *(978-0-14-242425-4(0),* Puffin Books) Penguin Publishing Group.

Probst, Jeff & Tebbetts, Christopher. The Sabotage. 2015. (Stranded Ser.: 5). (ENG.). 224p. (J). (gr. 3-7). 6.99 *(978-0-14-751389-2(8),* Puffin Books) Penguin Young Readers Group.

—Survivors. 2013. (Stranded Ser.: 3). (ENG.). 224p. (J). (gr. 3). pap. 6.99 *(978-0-14-242426-1(9),* Puffin Books) Penguin Publishing Group.

—Trial by Fire. 2013. 174p. (J). *(978-0-14-751195-9(X))* Penguin Publishing Group.

RH Disney. Moana Junior Novelization. RH Disney, illus. 2016. (Junior Novel Ser.). (ENG., Illus.). 144p. (J). (gr. 2-5). 6.99 *(978-0-7364-3600-7(6),* RH/Disney) Random Hse. Children's Bks.

Scollon, Bill. Moana Guide Book (Disney Moana) Random House Disney Staff, illus. 2016. (Essential Guide Ser.). (ENG.). 64p. (J). (gr. 4-7). pap. 7.99 *(978-0-7364-3673-1(1),* RH/Disney) Random Hse. Children's Bks.

Slade, Arthur. Island of Doom: Hunchback Assignments 4. 2013. (Hunchback Assignments Ser.). (ENG.). 320p. (YA). (gr. 7). pap. 9.99 *(978-0-375-85406-4(1),* Ember) Random Hse. Children's Bks.

Sundaram, Renuka. Sammy, the Galapagos Sea Lion. 2011. 32p. pap. 15.00 *(978-1-61286-015-2(X))* Avid Readers Publishing Group.

Verne, Jules. The Secret of the Island. Kingston, W. H. G., tr. 2008. 160p. 24.95 *(978-1-60664-753-0(9))* Rodgers, Alan Bks.

Wells, Helen. Cherry Ames, Chief Nurse. 2005. (Cherry Ames Nurse Stories Ser.: Bk. 4). 224p. (YA). (gr. 8-12). 14.95 *(978-0-9771597-3-4(6))* Springer Publishing Co., Inc.

ISLANDS OF THE PACIFIC—HISTORY

Gray, Leon. Giant Pacific Octopus: The World's Largest Octopus. 2013. (Even More SuperSized! Ser.). 24p. (J). (gr. k-3). lib. bdg. 23.93 *(978-1-61772-730-6(X))* Bearport Publishing Co., Inc.

Greig, Charlotte. Oceania. 2004. (Cultures & Costumes Ser.). (Illus.). 64p. (YA). (gr. 7-18). lib. bdg. 19.95 *(978-1-59084-432-8(7))* Mason Crest.

Harmon, Daniel E. Explorers of the South Pacific. 2004. (Exploration & Discovery Ser.). (Illus.). 64p. (YA). (gr. 5-18). lib. bdg. 19.95 *(978-1-59084-057-3(7))* Mason Crest.

Rockett, Paul. Mapping Australia & Oceania, & Antarctica. 2016. (Illus.). 32p. (J). *(978-0-7787-2614-2(2))* Crabtree Publishing Co.

Stenson, Marcia. Illustrated History of the South Pacific. 2006. (Illus.). 112p. (J). pap. *(978-1-86941-718-5(6))* Random Hse. New Zealand.

ISRAEL

Adler, David A. Golda Meir: A Strong Determined Leader. 2015. (Women of Our Time Ser.). (ENG., Illus.). 80p. (J). (gr. 3-7). 7.99 *(978-0-14-751660-2(9),* Puffin Books) Penguin Young Readers Group.

Aretha, David. Israel in the News: Past, Present, & Future. 2006. (Middle East Nations in the News Ser.). (Illus.). 128p. (J). (gr. 3-7). lib. bdg. 34.60 *(978-1-59845-028-6(X),* MyReportLinks.com Bks.) Enslow Pubs., Inc.

Bascomb, Neal. The Nazi Hunters: How a Team of Spies & Survivors Captured the World's Most Notorious Nazi. 2013. (ENG., Illus.). 256p. (J). (gr. 7). 17.99 *(978-0-545-43099-9(2),* Levine, Arthur A. Bks.) Scholastic, Inc.

Blumenthal, Scott. The Great Israel Scavenger Hunt. 2003. (Illus.). 96p. (J). 8.95 *(978-0-87441-711-1(2))* Behrman Hse., Inc.

Dietrick, Ellen. It's Israel's Birthday! Cohen, Tod, photos by. 2008. (ENG., Illus.). 24p. (J). (gr. -1-1). pap. 12.95 *(978-0-8225-7668-6(6),* Kar-Ben Publishing) Lerner Publishing Group.

DuBois, Jill & Rosh, Mair. Israel. 2nd rev. ed. 2003. (Cultures of the World Ser.). (Illus.). 144p. (gr. 6-18). lib. bdg. 42.79 *(978-0-7614-1669-2(2),* Benchmark Bks.) Marshall Cavendish Corp.

Fontes, Justine & Fontes, Ron. Israel. 2004. (A to Z Ser.). (ENG.). 40p. (J). (gr. 2-4). pap. 6.95 *(978-0-516-26811-8(2),* Children's Pr.) Scholastic Library Publishing.

Garfinkle, Adam M. Israel. 144p. 2015. (Illus.). (J). *(978-1-4222-3438-9(X))* 2010. (YA). (gr. 5-18). lib. bdg. 25.95 *(978-1-4222-1402-2(8))* Mason Crest.

Goldstein, Margaret J. Israel in Pictures. 80p. (gr. 5-12). (YA). 20.95 *(978-1-58013-088-2(7),* Kar-Ben Publishing); 2nd ed. 2003. (ENG., Illus.). (J). lib. bdg. 31.93 *(978-0-8225-0935-6(0))* Lerner Publishing Group.

Gresko, Marcia. Israel. 2009. pap. 52.95 *(978-0-7613-4729-3(1))* Lerner Publishing Group.

Gresko, Marcia S. Israel. 48p. 16.95 *(978-0-929371-63-4(1),* Kar-Ben Publishing); 2005. (Illus.). (gr. 2-4). 22.60 *(978-1-57505-143-7(5))* Lerner Publishing Group.

—A Ticket to Israel. 2003. (Illus.). 48p. (J). (gr. 1-2). 16.95 *(978-1-58013-077-6(1),* Kar-Ben Publishing) Lerner Publishing Group.

Grossman, Laurie. Children of Israel. Grossman, Laurie, photos by. 2003. (Illus.). 48p. (J). 17.95 *(978-1-58013-072-1(0),* Kar-Ben Publishing) Lerner Publishing Group.

—Colors of Israel. Byers, Helen, illus. (Colors of the World Ser.). 24p. 2005. (gr. 3-6). lib. bdg. 19.93 *(978-1-57505-382-0(9))* 2003. (J). (gr. 1-4). pap. 5.95 *(978-1-57505-523-7(6))* Lerner Publishing Group.

Hintz, Martin. Israel. rev. ed. 2006. (Enchantment of the World Ser.). (ENG., Illus.). 144p. (YA). (gr. 5-9). 39.00 *(978-0-516-24854-7(5))* Scholastic Library Publishing.

Immell, Myra. Israel. 2010. (Opposing Viewpoints Ser.). (ENG.). 224p. (gr. 12-12). 48.80 *(978-0-7377-4974-8(1));* pap. 33.80 *(978-0-7377-4975-5(X))* Cengage Gale. (Greenhaven Pr., Inc.).

Kimmelman, Leslie A. Everybody Says Shalom. 2015. (ENG., Illus.). 40p. (J). (gr. -1-2). lib. bdg. 20.99 *(978-0-375-97343-7(5),* Random Hse. Bks. for Young Readers) Random Hse. Children's Bks.

Klepeis, Alicia. Israel. 2016. (Exploring World Cultures Ser.). 32p. (J). pap. 10.58 *(978-1-5026-2154-2(1))* Cavendish Square Publishing.

Lenhart, Crystal. One Nation under God: A Family Study of Biblical Israel. 2003. (Illus.). 76p. (J). (gr. 5-18). pap. 12.00 *(978-1-886987-16-6(5))* Key of David Publishing.

Matray, James I., ed. Arbitrary Borders: Political Boundaries in World History. (Illus.). (gr. 9-13). lib. bdg. 242.55 *(978-0-7910-8422-9(1),* Chelsea Hse.) Facts On File, Inc.

Murray, Laura K. Spies in the Mossad. 2016. (Illus.). 24p. (J). *(978-1-60818-618-1(0),* Creative Education) Creative Co., The.

Owings, Lisa. Israel, 1 vol. 2013. (Countries of the World Set 2 Ser.). (ENG.). 144p. (J). (gr. 6-12). lib. bdg. 37.07 *(978-1-61783-630-5(3),* Essential Library) ABDO Publishing Co.

Pohl, Kathleen. Descubramos Israel. 2008. (Descubramos países del mundo (Looking at Countries) Ser.). (SPA., Illus.). 32p. (gr. 1-5). lib. bdg. 26.00 *(978-0-8368-8784-6(0),* Gareth Stevens Learning Library) Stevens, Gareth Publishing LLLP.

Richardson, Adele. Israel. 2006. (My First Look at: Countries Ser.). (Illus.). 24p. (J). (gr. -1-3). lib. bdg. 15.95 *(978-1-58341-447-7(9),* Creative Education) Creative Co., The.

Saul, Laya. Meet Our New Student from Israel. 2008. (Meet Our New Student Ser.). (Illus.). 48p. (J). (gr. 3-7). lib. bdg. 29.95 *(978-1-58415-651-2(1))* Mitchell Lane Pubs., Inc.

—We Visit Israel. 2011. (Your Land & My Land Ser.). (Illus.). 64p. (J). (gr. 4-7). lib. bdg. 33.95 *(978-1-58415-957-5(X))* Mitchell Lane Pubs., Inc.

Sheen, Barbara, ed. Foods of Israel. 2011. (Taste of Culture Ser.). (Illus.). 65p. (YA). (gr. 9-12). 30.45 *(978-0-7377-5882-5(1))* Cengage Gale.

Slavicek, Louise Chipley. Israel. 2nd rev. ed. 2008. (Creation of the Modern Middle East Ser.). (Illus.). 128p. (gr. 6-12). 35.00 *(978-0-7910-9775-5(7),* Chelsea Hse.) Facts On File, Inc.

Smith, Debbie. Israel: The Land. 3rd rev. ed. 2007. (Lands, Peoples & Cultures Ser.). (ENG., Illus.). 32p. (J). (gr. 3-7). pap. *(978-0-7787-9679-4(5));* lib. bdg. *(978-0-7787-9311-3(7))* Crabtree Publishing Co.

—Israel - The People. 3rd rev. ed. 2007. (Lands, Peoples & Cultures Ser.). (ENG., Illus.). 32p. (J). (gr. 3-7). pap. *(978-0-7787-9680-0(9));* lib. bdg. *(978-0-7787-9312-0(5))* Crabtree Publishing Co.

Sofer, Barbara. Keeping Israel Safe: Serving the Israel Defense Forces. 2008. (Israel Ser.). (ENG., Illus.). 56p. (J). (gr. 3-7). lib. bdg. 16.95 *(978-0-8225-7221-3(4),* Kar-Ben Publishing) Lerner Publishing Group.

Thomas, Kenneth W. & Thomas, Joyce Carol. In the Land of Milk & Honey. Cooper, Floyd, illus. 2012. (ENG.). 32p. (J). (gr. -1-3). 16.99 *(978-0-06-025383-7(5),* Amistad) HarperCollins Pubs.

Webster, Matt. Inside Israel's Mossad: The Institute for Intelligence & Special Tasks. (Inside the World's Most Famous Intelligence Agencies Ser.). 64p. 2009. (gr. 5-5). 58.50 *(978-1-61513-571-4(5))* 2005. (Illus.). (YA). (gr. 7-12). lib. bdg. 31.95 *(978-0-8239-3815-5(8))* Rosen Publishing Group, Inc., The.

Werner, Aviva. Experience Modern Israel: Explore, Discover, Connect. 2011. (J). *(978-0-87441-800-2(3))* Behrman Hse., Inc.

Woolf, Alex. Focus on Israel. 2007. (World in Focus Ser.). (Illus.). 64p. (gr. 5-12). pap. 14.05 *(978-0-8368-6742-8(4));* lib. bdg. 34.00 *(978-0-8368-6735-0(1))* Stevens, Gareth Publishing LLLP. (Gareth Stevens Secondary Library).

ISRAEL—FICTION

Abraham, Michelle Shapiro. My Cousin Tamar Lives in Israel. Koffsky, Ann D., illus. 2006. 14p. (J). (gr. -1). pap. 6.95 *(978-0-8074-0989-3(8))* URJ Pr.

Balsley, Tilda & Fischer, Ellen. Grover & Big Bird's Passover Celebration. Leigh, Tom, illus. 2013. (Passover Ser.). (ENG.). 24p. (J). (gr. -1-1). 6.95 *(978-0-7613-8492-2(8),* Kar-Ben Publishing) Lerner Publishing Group.

—I'm Sorry, Grover! A Rosh Hashanah Tale. Leigh, Tom, illus. 2013. (High Holidays Ser.). (ENG.). 24p. (J). (gr. -1-k). lib. bdg. 16.95 *(978-0-7613-7560-9(0),* Kar-Ben Publishing) Lerner Publishing Group.

—I'm Sorry, Grover: A Rosh Hashanah Tale. Leigh, Tom, illus. 2013. (High Holidays Ser.). (ENG.). 24p. (J). (gr. -1-k). 6.95 *(978-0-7613-7561-6(9),* Kar-Ben Publishing) Lerner Publishing Group.

—It's a Mitzvah, Grover! Leigh, Tom, illus. 2013. (ENG.). 24p. (J). (gr. -1-1). 6.95 *(978-0-7613-7563-0(5));* lib. bdg. 16.95 *(978-0-7613-7562-3(7))* Lerner Publishing Group. (Kar-Ben Publishing).

—Shalom Everybodeee! Leigh, Tom, illus. 2016. (ENG.). 24p. (gr. -1-2). 16.99 *(978-0-7613-7558-6(9),* Kar-Ben Publishing) Lerner Publishing Group.

Carlson, Claudia. Avi the Ambulance to the Rescue! 2016. (J). *(978-1-68115-512-8(5))* Behrman Hse., Inc.

Carlson, Claudia, illus. Avi the Ambulance Goes to School. 2015. (J). *(978-0-87441-941-2(7)); (978-1-68115-503-6(6))* Behrman Hse., Inc.

Carlson, Claudia & Koffsky, Ann D. Avi the Ambulance & the Snowy Day. Decker, C. B., illus. 2017. (J). *(978-1-68115-528-9(1))* Behrman Hse., Inc.

Cohen, Deborah Bodin. Engineer Arielle & the Israel Independence Day Surprise: High, Low, & on the Go. Orrelle, Yael Kimhi, illus. 2017. (ENG.). 32p. (gr. k-3). 17.99 ***(978-1-5124-2094-4(8))***; pap. 7.99 ***(978-1-5124-2095-1(6))*** Lerner Publishing Group. (Kar-Ben Publishing).

Dillon, Sally Pierson. Exile of the Chosen: God's Heroes from Solomon to Malachi. 2003. (Pathfinder Junior Book Club Ser.). 223p. (J). pap. 10.99 *(978-0-8280-1703-9(4),* 58-710) Review & Herald Publishing Assn.

Edwards, Michelle. Chicken Man. 2008. (J). *(978-1-58838-237-5(0));* 3rd ed. (Illus.). 32p. 16.95 *(978-1-58838-223-8(0))* NewSouth, Inc. (Junebug Bks.).

Eisner, Fern. Saba's Room. 2009. 28p. pap. 15.99 *(978-1-4415-1843-9(6))* Xlibris Corp.

Elkeles, Simone. How to Ruin a Summer Vacation Novel Ser.: 3). (ENG.). 264p. (YA). (gr. 7-18). pap. 9.95 *(978-0-7387-1879-8(3),* Flux) North Star Editions.

Ellis, Deborah. The Cat at the Wall, 1 vol. (ENG., Illus.). (J). 2015. 152p. pap. 9.95 *(978-1-55498-707-8(5))* 2014. 144p. (gr. 3-7). 16.95 *(978-1-55498-491-6(2))* Groundwood Bks. CAN. Dist: Publishers Group West (PGW).

Ellis, Gwen. The First Christmas, 1 vol. Pichon, Liz, illus. 2007. 10p. (J). bds. 15.99 *(978-0-8254-5538-4(3))* Kregel Pubns.

Friedman, Maya. Three Falafels in My Pita. Mack, Steve, illus. 2015. (ENG.). 12p. (J). (gr. -1 — 1). bds. 5.95 *(978-1-4677-3472-1(1),* Kar-Ben Publishing) Lerner Publishing Group.

Gibson, Beatrice. The Legend of the Sandals. 2008. 28p. pap. 15.99 *(978-1-4363-9169-6(5))* Xlibris Corp.

Gilani-Williams, Fawzia. Yaffa & Fatima: Shalom, Salaam. Fedele, Chiara, illus. 2017. (ENG.). 24p. (gr. -1-3). 17.99 *(978-1-4677-8938-7(0),* Kar-Ben Publishing) Lerner Publishing Group.

Goldman, Karen. Jordan & the Dreadful Golem. Moseley, Rachel, illus. 2013. (ENG.). 224p. (J). (gr. 4-7). 15.95 *(978-0-9838685-2-1(2))* Penlight Pubns.

Haley, Jeannette. The Adventures of Zack & Mira. 2013. 116p. pap. 12.95 *(978-0-9891683-0-4(1))* Hidden Manna Pubns.

Henry, Juliann. The Little Shepherd Girl: A Christmas Story. Madsen, Jim, illus. 2007. 32p. (J). (gr. -1-3). 14.99 *(978-0-7814-4513-9(2))* Cook, David C.

Jacobs, Z. D. Ari & the Dybbuk. 2012. 144p. (gr. 4-6). pap. 14.95 *(978-1-4685-3671-3(0))* AuthorHouse.

Kalechofsky, Roberta. A Boy, a Chicken & the Lion of Judah: How Ari Became a Vegetarian. 2012. (ENG., Illus.). 50p. (J). pap. 12.00 *(978-0-916288-58-7(7))* Micah Pubns.

Kass, Pnina Moed. Real Time. 2006. (ENG.). 192p. (YA). (gr. 7-12). reprint ed. pap. 7.99 *(978-0-618-69174-6(X))* Houghton Mifflin Harcourt Publishing Co.

Kir-on, Callanitte. The 3-D Files: Prisoner on the Loose. 2003. (Illus.). (J). 10.95 *(978-1-931681-47-6(3))* Israel Bookshop Pubns.

Lapidot, Gila. Shakel Shakelovitz Finds a Treasure. 2013. 40p. pap. *(978-965-550-200-8(7))* Contento De Semrik.

Lehman-Wilzig, Tami. Stork's Landing. Shuttlewood, Anna, illus. 2014. (ENG.). 32p. (J). (gr. -1-2). 17.95 *(978-1-4677-1395-5(3),* Kar-Ben Publishing) Lerner Publishing Group.

—Zvuvi's Israel. Topaz, Ksenia, illus. 2009. (Israel Ser.). (ENG.). 32p. (J). (gr. -1-2). 16.95 *(978-0-8225-8759-0(9));* pap. 7.95 *(978-0-8225-8760-6(2))* Lerner Publishing Group. (Kar-Ben Publishing).

Levine, Anna. Jodie's Hanukkah Dig. Topaz, Ksenia, illus. 2008. (Hanukkah Ser.). (ENG.). 32p. (J). (gr. k-3). 17.95 *(978-0-8225-7391-3(1));* pap. 7.95 *(978-0-8225-7402-6(0))* Lerner Publishing Group. (Kar-Ben Publishing).

Levy, Marilyn. Checkpoints. 2009. (ENG.). 256p. (gr. 7). pap. 14.95 *(978-0-8276-0870-2(5))* Jewish Pubn. Society.

McOmber, Rachel B., ed. McOmber Phonics Storybooks: Razz Visits Raz in Israel. rev. ed. (Illus.). (J). *(978-0-944991-75-6(0))* Swift Learning Resources.

Newman, Vivian. Ella's Trip to Israel. Nathan, Cheryl & Gutierrez, Akemia, illus. 2011. (Israel Ser.). (ENG.). 24p. (J). (gr. -1 — 1). pap. 8.95 *(978-0-7613-6029-2(8),* Kar-Ben Publishing) Lerner Publishing Group.

Ofanansky, Allison. Cheesecake for Shavuot. Alpern, Eliyahu, illus. 2013. (Lag B'Omer & Shavuot Ser.). (ENG.). 32p. (J). (gr. -1-2). lib. bdg. 15.95 *(978-0-7613-8126-6(0),* Kar-Ben Publishing) Lerner Publishing Group.

—Cheesecake for Shavuot. Alpern, Eliyahu, photos by. 2013. (Lag B'Omer & Shavuot Ser.). (ENG., Illus.). 32p. (J). (gr. -1-2). 8.95 *(978-1-4677-1411-2(9),* Kar-Ben Publishing) Lerner Publishing Group.

—Harvest of Light. Alpern, Eliyahu, photos by. 2008. (Hanukkah Ser.). (ENG., Illus.). 32p. (J). (gr. -1-5). 15.95 *(978-0-8225-7389-0(X),* Kar-Ben Publishing) Lerner Publishing Group.

—Sukkot Treasure Hunt. Alpern, Eliyahu, illus. Alpern, Eliyahu, photos by. 2009. (Sukkot & Simchat Torah Ser.). (ENG.). 32p. (J). (gr. -1-5). 15.95 *(978-0-8225-8763-7(7),* Kar-Ben Publishing) Lerner Publishing Group.

—Tisha B'Av: A Jerusalem Journey. Alpern, Eliyahu, photos by. 2017. (ENG., Illus.). 32p. (gr. -1-3). 16.99 *(978-1-4677-8930-1(5),* Kar-Ben Publishing) Lerner Publishing Group.

—What's the Buzz? Honey for a Sweet New Year. Alpern, Eliyahu, photos by. 2014. (ENG., Illus.). 32p. (J). (gr. -1-5). 8.95 *(978-1-4677-5706-5(3),* Kar-Ben Publishing) Lerner Publishing Group.

—What's the Buzz? Honey for a Sweet New Year. Alpern, Eliyahu, illus. Alpern, Eliyahu, photos by. 2011. (High Holidays Ser.). (J). (gr. -1-k). lib. bdg. 15.95 *(978-0-7613-5640-0(1))* Lerner Publishing Group.

Ofanansky, Allison Maile. Tisha B'Av: A Jerusalem Journey. Alpern, Eliyahu, photos by. 2017. (Kar-Ben Favorites Ser.). (ENG., Illus.). 32p. (gr. -1-3). 23.99 ***(978-1-5124-2719-6(5),*** Kar-Ben Publishing) Lerner Publishing Group.

Ramsay, Elizabeth. The Burning Light. Katz, Avi, illus. 2005. 144p. (J). (gr. 4-9). 14.95 *(978-1-930143-43-2(5));* pap. 9.95 *(978-1-930143-44-9(3))* Simcha Media Group. (Devora Publishing).

Rauchwerger, Diane Levin. Dinosaur Goes to Israel. Wolff, Jason, illus. 2012. (Israel Ser.). (ENG.). 24p. (J). (gr. -1-1). pap. 7.95 *(978-0-7613-5134-4(5));* lib. bdg. 16.95 *(978-0-7613-5133-7(7))* Lerner Publishing Group. (Kar-Ben Publishing).

Rouss, Sylvia A. & Kahn, Katherine Janus. Sammy Spider's Israel Fun Book. 2004. (ENG., Illus.). 24p. (J). (gr. -1-2). pap. 4.95 *(978-1-58013-119-3(0),* Kar-Ben Publishing) Lerner Publishing Group.

Shem-Tov, Tami & Sandbank, Rachella. A Concert in the Sand. Ofer, Avi, illus. 2017. (ENG.). 32p. (gr. -1-3). 17.99 *(978-1-5124-0099-1(8),* Kar-Ben Publishing) Lerner Publishing Group.

Simpson, Lesley. Yuvi's Candy Tree. Porter, Janice Lee, illus. 2011. (ENG.). 32p. (J). (gr. k-3). pap. 7.95 *(978-0-7613-5652-3(5));* lib. bdg. 17.95 *(978-0-7613-5651-6(7))* Lerner Publishing Group. (Kar-Ben Publishing).

Snir, Mirik. When I First Held You: A Lullaby from Isarel. Shubow, Mary Jane, tr. from HEB. Snir, Eleyor, illus. 2009. (Kar-Ben Favorites Ser.). (ENG.). 32p. (J). (gr. k-3). pap. 9.95 *(978-0-7613-5098-9(5),* Kar-Ben Publishing) Lerner Publishing Group.

Stampler, Ann Redisch. The Cats on Ben Yehuda Street. Carabelli, Francesca, illus. 2013. (Israel Ser.). (ENG.). 32p. (J). (gr. -1-2). 7.95 *(978-0-7613-8124-2(4));* lib. bdg. 16.95 *(978-0-7613-8123-5(6))* Lerner Publishing Group. (Kar-Ben Publishing).

Stein, Tammar. The Six-Day Hero. 2017. (ENG.). 256p. (gr. 4-7). 16.99 ***(978-1-5124-5871-8(6),*** Kar-Ben Publishing) Lerner Publishing Group.

Stupniker, Yehudit. The Remarkable Invention That Saves Zion: A Tale of Triz. 2007. 292p. 18.95 *(978-1-932687-74-3(2),* Devora Publishing) Simcha Media Group.

Wilson, Heather Gemmen. Lydia Barnes & the Mystery of the Broken Cross. 2007. (Global Warning Ser.). 157p. (J). (gr. 3-7). per. 7.99 *(978-0-89827-351-9(X))* Wesleyan Publishing Hse.

Zenatti, Valerie. A Bottle in the Gaza Sea. Hunter, Adriana, tr. from FRE. 2008. (ENG.). 160p. (YA). (gr. 7-13). 17.99 *(978-1-59990-200-5(1),* 9781599902005, Bloomsbury USA Childrens) Bloomsbury Publishing USA.

ISRAEL—HISTORY

Aloian, Molly. Cultural Traditions in Israel. 2014. (ENG., Illus.). 32p. (J). *(978-0-7787-0303-7(7))* Crabtree Publishing Co.

Bar-Hillel, Gili. I Is for Israel. 2016. (World Alphabets Ser.). (ENG., Illus.). 32p. (J). 18.99 *(978-1-84780-708-3(9),* Frances Lincoln Children's Bks.) Quarto Publishing Group UK GBR. Dist: Littlehampton Bk Services, Ltd.

Barber, Nicola. The Arab-Israeli Conflict. 2012. (Both Sides of the Story Ser.). (ENG., Illus.). 48p. (YA). (gr. 5-8). lib. bdg. 29.25 *(978-1-4488-7183-4(2),* Rosen Reference) Rosen Publishing Group, Inc., The.

Bard, Mitchell Geoffrey. Israel Matters: Understand the Past, Look to the Future. 2012. (Illus.). 216p. (J). *(978-0-87441-858-3(5))* Behrman Hse., Inc.

Blashfield, Jean F. Golda Meir. 2010. (Leading Women Ser.). 96p. (YA). (gr. 7-12). 39.93 *(978-0-7614-4960-7(4))* Marshall Cavendish GBR. Dist: Marshall Cavendish Corp.

Byrne, Judy. A New Queen. 2013. 28p. pap. 13.95 *(978-1-4908-0887-1(6),* WestBow Pr.) Author Solutions, Inc.

Coulter, Laurie. Kings & Carpenters: One Hundred Bible Land Jobs You Might Have Praised or Panned. Newbigging, Martha, illus. 2010. (Jobs in History Ser.). (ENG.). 96p. (J). (gr. 3-6). 25.95 *(978-1-55451-227-0(1),* 9781554512270); pap. 16.95 *(978-1-55451-226-3(3),* 9781554512263) Annick Pr., Ltd. CAN. Dist: Publishers Group West (PGW).

Derovan, David. Israeli Culture in Perspective. 2014. 64p. (gr. 4-8). 33.95 *(978-1-61228-566-5(X))* Mitchell Lane Pubs., Inc.

DuBois, Jill, et al. Israel. 2014. (Cultures of the World (r) Ser.). 144p. (YA). (gr. 5-10). lib. bdg. 47.07 *(978-0-7614-4995-9(7))* Cavendish Square Publishing.

Durkee, Noura. The Fall of the Giant. Durkee, Noura, illus. 2007. (ENG., Illus.). 26p. (J). (gr. k-5). 16.00 *(978-1-879402-63-8(7))* Tahrike Tarsile Quran, Inc.

Edgar, Sherra G. Israel. 2015. (One World, Many Countries Ser.). (ENG.). 32p. (J). (gr. 1-4). 28.50 *(978-1-63407-049-2(6),* 208885) Child's World, Inc., The.

Foy, Don. Israel. 2010. (Festivals of the World Ser.). 32p. (gr. 3). 28.50 *(978-0-60870-102-5(6))* Marshall Cavendish Corp.

Garfinkle, Adam M. Israel, Vol. 13. 2015. (Major Nations of the Modern Middle East Ser.). (Illus.). 144p. (J). (gr. 7). lib. bdg. 25.95 *(978-1-4222-3443-3(6))* Mason Crest.

Goodman, Michael E. Spies Around the World: the Mossad & Other Israeli Spies. 2014. (Spies Around the World Ser.). (ENG., Illus.). 48p. (J). (gr. 4-7). pap. 12.00 *(978-0-89812-971-7(0),* Creative Paperbacks) Creative Co., The.

Greenfeld, Howard. A Promise Fulfilled: Theodor Herzl, Chaim Weizmann, David Ben-Gurion, & the Creation of the State of Israel. 2005. (Illus.). 144p. (J). (gr. 7-18). 19.89 *(978-0-06-051505-8(8))* HarperCollins Pubs.

Gregory, Joy. Israel. 2014. (J). *(978-1-4896-1014-0(6))* Weigl Pubs., Inc.

H
I

Gresko, Marcia S. Israel. 2008. (Country Explorers Ser.). (ENG.). 48p. (gr. 2-4). 29.27 *(978-0-8225-9414-7(5))* Lerner Publishing Group.
Hawker, Frances & Taub, Daniel. Judaism in Israel. Campbell, Bruce, photos by. 2009. (ENG., Illus.). 32p. (J). (gr. 3-6). *(978-0-7787-5010-9(8))*; pap. *(978-0-7787-5027-7(2))* Crabtree Publishing Co.
Hayhurst, Chris. Israel's War of Independence. 2009. (War & Conflict in the Middle East Ser.). 64p. (gr. 5-5). 58.50 *(978-1-60854-736-4(1))* Rosen Publishing Group, Inc., The.
—Israel's War of Independence: Al-Nakba. 2004. (War & Conflict in the Middle East Ser.). (Illus.). 64p. (gr. 7-12). lib. bdg. 31.95 *(978-0-8239-4548-1(0))* Rosen Publishing Group, Inc., The.
Hurt, Avery. Arab Nationalism & Zionism. 2017. (J). ***(978-1-5026-2720-9(5))*** Cavendish Square Publishing.
Immell, Myra. The Creation of the State of Israel. 2009. (Perspectives on Modern World History Ser.). (Illus.). 224p. (YA). (gr. 10-18). 42.45 *(978-0-7377-4556-6(8)*, Greenhaven Pr., Inc.) Cengage Gale.
Israel in Pictures. 2003. (Illus.). 64p. (J). 15.95 *(978-1-58013-076-9(3)*, Kar-Ben Publishing) Lerner Publishing Group.
Karsh, Efraim. The Arab-Israeli Conflict: The 1948 War. 2008. (Essential Histories: War & Conflict in Modern Times Ser.). (Illus.). 96p. (YA). (gr. 9-12). lib. bdg. 33.25 *(978-1-4042-1842-0(4))* Rosen Publishing Group, Inc., The.
Langley, Andrew. Israel in Our World. 2011. (Countries in Our World Ser.). 32p. (gr. 4-7). lib. bdg. 31.35 *(978-1-59920-388-1(X))* Black Rabbit Bks.
Lehman, Emil. Israel: Idea & Reality. (Illus.). (J). (gr. 8-18). 3.95 *(978-0-8381-0205-3(0)*, 10-205) United Synagogue of America Bk. Service.
Mason, Paul & Marshall Cavendish Staff. Israel & Palestine. 2008. (Global Hotspots Ser.). 32p. (gr. 5-18). lib. bdg. 18.56 *(978-0-7614-3181-7(0)*, Benchmark Bks.) Marshall Cavendish Corp.
Murray, Julie. Israel, 1 vol. 2013. (Explore the Countries Ser.). (ENG.). 40p. (J). (gr. 2-5). lib. bdg. 29.93 *(978-1-61783-813-2(6)*, Big Buddy Bks.) ABDO Publishing Co.
Ofanansky, Allison. Harvest of Light. Alpern, Eliyahu, photos by. 2011. (Hanukkah Ser.). (ENG., Illus.). 32p. (J). (gr. -1-5). pap. 8.95 *(978-0-7613-8305-5(0)*, Kar-Ben Publishing) Lerner Publishing Group.
Pohl, Kathleen. Descubramos Israel. 2008. (Descubramos países del mundo (Looking at Countries) Ser.). (SPA.). 32p. (gr. 1-5). pap. 10.50 *(978-0-8368-8791-4(3)*, Gareth Stevens Learning Library) Stevens, Gareth Publishing LLLP.
—Looking at Israel. 2008. (Looking at Countries Ser.). 32p. (gr. 1-5). pap. 10.50 *(978-0-8368-8777-8(8))*; (Illus.). lib. bdg. 26.00 *(978-0-8368-8770-9(0))* Stevens, Gareth Publishing LLLP. (Gareth Stevens Learning Library).
Raz, Rachel. The Colors of Israel. Raz, Rachel, photos by. 2015. (ENG., Illus.). 24p. (J). (gr. -1-2). lib. bdg. 17.99 *(978-1-4677-5539-9(7)*, Kar-Ben Publishing) Lerner Publishing Group.
Richardson, Adele. Israel. 2011. (My First Look At Ser.). (ENG.). 24p. (J). (gr. 1-17). pap. 7.99 *(978-1-926722-37-5(X)*, Creative Paperbacks) Creative Co., The.
Romano, Amy. A Historical Atlas of Israel. 2009. (Historical Atlases of South Asia, Central Asia, & the Middle East Ser.). 64p. (gr. 6-6). 61.20 *(978-1-61513-321-5(6))* Rosen Publishing Group, Inc., The.
Rosenberg, Aaron. The Yom Kippur War. 2009. (War & Conflict in the Middle East Ser.). 64p. (gr. 5-5). 58.50 *(978-1-60854-742-5(6))* Rosen Publishing Group, Inc., The.
Royston, Angela. Hoping for Peace in the Middle East. 2012. (Peace Pen Pals Ser.). (Illus.). 48p. (J). (gr. 6-8). 31.95 *(978-1-4339-7743-5(5))*; pap. 14.05 *(978-1-4339-7744-2(3))* Stevens, Gareth Publishing LLLP.
Sasek, Miroslav. This Is Israel. 2008. (ENG., Illus.). 62p. (J). (gr. 2-12). 17.95 *(978-0-7893-1595-3(5))* Universe Publishing.
Sexton, Colleen & Simmons, Walter. Israel. 2010. (Exploring Countries Ser.). (ENG., Illus.). 32p. (J). (gr. 3-7). lib. bdg. 26.95 *(978-1-60014-484-4(5)*, Blastoff! Readers) Bellwether Media.
Shepherd, Good. Our Almighty God: A Bible Study. 2008. 48p. pap. 13.49 *(978-1-4389-1850-1(X))* AuthorHouse.
Sherman, Josepha. Your Travel Guide to Ancient Israel. 80p. (J). (gr. 4-8). 19.95 *(978-1-58013-093-6(3)*, Kar-Ben Publishing); 2005. (Illus.). 96p. (YA). (gr. 5-9). 26.60 *(978-0-8225-3072-5(4))* Lerner Publishing Group.
Silverman, Elisa. Understanding Israel Today. 2014. (Illus.). 64p. (J). (gr. 3-6). 33.95 *(978-1-61228-650-1(X))* Mitchell Lane Pubs., Inc.
Singer, David. Yisrael Sheli/My Israel: People & Places. 2011. (ENG., Illus.). 95p. (J). (gr. 4-7). pap. 11.95 *(978-1-934527-25-2(4))* Torah Aura Productions.
Slavicek, Louise Chipley. The Establishment of the State of Israel. 2011. (Milestones in Modern World History Ser.). (Illus.). 128p. (C). (gr. 9). 35.00 *(978-1-60413-917-4(X)*, Chelsea Hse.) Facts On File, Inc.
Smith, Debbie. Israel: The Culture. 3rd rev. ed. 2007. (Lands, Peoples & Cultures Ser.). (ENG., Illus.). 32p. (J). (gr. 3-7). lib. bdg. *(978-0-7787-9313-7(3))* Crabtree Publishing Co.
—Israel - The Culture. 3rd rev. ed. 2007. (Lands, Peoples & Cultures Ser.). (ENG., Illus.). 32p. (J). (gr. 3-7). pap. *(978-0-7787-9681-7(7))* Crabtree Publishing Co.
Throp, Claire. Israel, 1 vol. 2012. (Countries Around the World Ser.). (ENG.). 48p. (gr. 3-6). lib. bdg. 33.32 *(978-1-4329-6101-5(2)*, NA-h) Heinemann-Raintree.
Vinberger, Naftali Yehiel ben Shelomoh Avraham, et al. The Story of Rebbetzin Kanievsky: A Biography for Young Readers. 2012. (Illus.). 204p. (J). *(978-1-4226-1333-7(X))* Mesorah Pubns., Ltd.
Woolf, Alex. The Arab-Israeli War Since 1948, 1 vol. 2012. (Living Through... Ser.). (ENG.). 80p. (gr. 7-8). lib. bdg. 37.32 *(978-1-4329-5995-1(6))* Heinemann-Raintree.
Worth, Richard. The Arab-Israeli Conflict. 2006. (Open for Debate Ser.). (Illus.). 128p. (gr. 7-7). lib. bdg. 42.79 *(978-0-7614-2295-2(1)*, Benchmark Bks.) Marshall Cavendish Corp.
Yomtov, Nelson. Israel. 2012. (Enchantment of the World, Second Ser.). (ENG., Illus.). 144p. (J). (gr. 5-9). lib. bdg. 40.00 *(978-0-531-25313-7(9)*, Children's Pr.) Scholastic Library Publishing.
Young, Emma. National Geographic Countries of the World - Israel. 2008. (Countries of the World Ser.). (ENG., Illus.). 64p. (J). (gr. 5). lib. bdg. 27.90 *(978-1-4263-0258-9(4)*, National Geographic Children's Bks.) National Geographic Society.
Zeigler, Donald J. Israel. 2nd rev. ed. 2006. (Modern World Nations Ser.). (Illus.). 120p. (YA). (gr. 7-12). lib. bdg. 35.00 *(978-0-7910-9210-1(0))* Facts On File, Inc.

ISRAEL—HISTORY—FICTION

Clark, Marian. Benji's Sicarii Sword. 2007. 156p. per. 13.99 *(978-1-60266-022-9(0))* Salem Author Services.
Gregerson, Lajuan. A Child's Tour of the Holy Land. 2008. 73p. pap. 19.95 *(978-1-60610-367-8(9))* America Star Bks.
Hennessey, David G. A Cricket's Christmas: the Bethlehem Story. 2009. 151p. pap. 15.30 *(978-0-557-04685-0(8))* Lulu Pr., Inc.
Jasper, Mark. Good Night Israel. Rosen, Anne, illus. 2010. (Good Night Our World Ser.). (ENG.). 24p. (J). (gr. k — 1). bds. 9.95 *(978-1-60219-043-6(7))* Good Night Bks.
Kaplan, Kathy Walden. The Dog of Knots. 2005. 139p. (J). pap. 7.50 *(978-0-8028-5274-8(2))* Eerdmans, William B. Publishing Co.
Schram, Scott. The Last Noel: A Christmas Musical for Children. 2007. (ENG.). pap. 64.95 *(978-0-7390-4487-2(7))* Alfred Publishing Co., Inc.
Shapiro, David L. Sara's Journey. 2005. (ENG.). 224p. (gr. 7-12). per. 16.95 *(978-0-8276-0776-7(8))* Jewish Pubn. Society.
Stein, Tammar. The Six-Day Hero. 2017. (J). *(978-1-5124-2855-1(8)*, Kar-Ben Publishing) Lerner Publishing Group.

ISRAEL—HISTORY, MILITARY

Finkelstein, Norman H. Ariel Sharon. 128p. (J). (gr. 6-18). 20.95 *(978-1-58013-205-3(7)*, Kar-Ben Publishing); 2005. (Illus.). 112p. (YA). (gr. 7-12). lib. bdg. 29.27 *(978-0-8225-2370-3(1)*, Lerner Pubns.) Lerner Publishing Group.
Sofer, Barbara. Keeping Israel Safe: Serving in the Israel Defense Forces. 2008. (Israel Ser.). (ENG., Illus.). 56p. (J). (gr. 3-7). per. 7.95 *(978-0-8225-7222-0(2)*, Kar-Ben Publishing) Lerner Publishing Group.

ISRAEL—POLITICS AND GOVERNMENT

Crompton, Samuel Willard. Ariel Sharon. 2nd rev. ed. 2007. (Modern World Leaders Ser.). (Illus.). 111p. (J). (gr. 7-12). lib. bdg. 30.00 *(978-0-7910-9263-7(1))* Facts On File, Inc.
Ellis, Deborah. Three Wishes: Palestinian & Israeli Children Speak, 1 vol. 2006. (ENG., Illus.). 144p. (J). (gr. 5-7). pap. 9.95 *(978-0-88899-645-9(4))* Groundwood Bks. CAN. Dist: Publishers Group West (PGW).
Ellis, Deborah, ed. Three Wishes: Palestinian & Israeli Children Speak. 2004. (YA). 16.95 *(978-0-88899-608-4(X)*, Libros Tigrillo) Groundwood Bks. CAN. Dist: Publishers Group West (PGW).
Fiscus, James. The Suez Crisis. 2009. (War & Conflict in the Middle East Ser.). 64p. (gr. 5-5). 58.50 *(978-1-60854-741-8(8))* Rosen Publishing Group, Inc., The.
Mason, Paul & Marshall Cavendish Staff. Israel & Palestine. 2008. (Global Hotspots Ser.). 32p. (gr. 5-18). lib. bdg. 18.56 *(978-0-7614-3181-7(0)*, Benchmark Bks.) Marshall Cavendish Corp.
Shahak, Bat-Chen. The Bat-Chen Diaries. Rubanenko, Diana, tr. from HEB. 2008. (Israel Ser.). (ENG., Illus.). 112p. (J). (gr. 5-7). per. 7.95 *(978-0-8225-7223-7(0)*, Kar-Ben Publishing) Lerner Publishing Group.
Sommers, Michael. Ehud Olmert: Prime Minister of Israel. 2009. (Newsmakers Ser.). 112p. (gr. 9-10). 63.90 *(978-1-60851-131-0(6))* Rosen Publishing Group, Inc., The.
Sommers, Michael A. Ehud Olmert: Prime Minister of Israel. 2007. (Newsmakers Ser.). (Illus.). 112p. (YA). (gr. 7-12). lib. bdg. 34.60 *(978-1-4042-1904-5(8))* Rosen Publishing Group, Inc., The.

ISRAEL-ARAB BORDER CONFLICTS

see Jewish-Arab Relations

ISRAEL-ARAB WAR, 1967

Baughan, Brian. Arab-Israeli Relations, 1950-1979. 2009. (Making of the Middle East Ser.). (Illus.). 80p. (YA). (gr. 3-7). lib. bdg. 22.95 *(978-1-4222-0171-8(6))* Mason Crest.
Broyles, Matthew. The Six-Day War. 2004. (War & Conflict in the Middle East Ser.). (Illus.). 64p. (gr. 7-12). lib. bdg. 31.95 *(978-0-8239-4549-8(9))* Rosen Publishing Group, Inc., The.
Hay, Jeff. The Arab-Israeli Six-Day War. 2012. (Perspectives on Modern World History Ser.). (ENG., Illus.). 224p. (gr. 10-12). lib. bdg. 47.80 *(978-0-7377-6361-4(2)*, Greenhaven Pr., Inc.) Cengage Gale.
Matray, James I., ed. Arbitrary Borders: Political Boundaries in World History. (Illus.). (gr. 9-13). lib. bdg. 242.55 *(978-0-7910-8422-9(1)*, Chelsea Hse.) Facts On File, Inc.

ISRAEL-ARAB WAR, 1967—FICTION

Breen, Mirka M. G. The Voice of Thunder. 2012. (ENG.). 118p. (J). pap. 12.95 *(978-1-937178-17-8(X))* WiDo Publishing.
Stein, Tammar. The Six-Day Hero. 2017. (ENG.). 256p. (gr. 4-7). 16.99 ***(978-1-5124-5871-8(6))***; (J). *(978-1-5124-2855-1(8))* Lerner Publishing Group. (Kar-Ben Publishing).

ISRAELITES

see Jews

ISTANBUL (TURKEY)

Bowden, Rob. Istanbul. Parker, Edward, photos by. 2007. (Global Cities Ser.). (Illus.). 61p. (gr. 5-8). lib. bdg. 30.00 *(978-0-7910-8850-0(2)*, Chelsea Hse.) Facts On File, Inc.

ISTANBUL (TURKEY)—FICTION

Johnson, Elizabeth. And Then Nicholas Sang: The Story of the Trisagion Hymn. Lobastov, Masha, illus. 2010. 32p. (J). 18.95 *(978-1-936270-05-7(6))* Ancient Faith Publishing.
Marillier, Juliet. Cybele's Secret. 2011. (ENG.). 444p. (YA). (gr. 7). pap. 9.99 *(978-0-553-49486-0(4)*, Knopf Bks. for Young Readers) Random Hse. Children's Bks.
Murray, Maturin. The Circassian Slave. 2009. 116p. 23.95 *(978-1-60664-664-9(8))*; pap. 9.95 *(978-1-60664-292-4(8))* Rodgers, Alan Bks.
Stilton, Geronimo & Stilton, Thea. Thea Stilton & the Mystery on the Orient Express. 2012. (Thea Stilton Ser.: 13). (ENG.). 176p. (J). (gr. 2-5). pap. 8.99 *(978-0-545-34105-9(1)*, Scholastic Paperbacks) Scholastic, Inc.
Westerfeld, Scott. Behemoth. Thompson, Keith, illus. (Leviathan Trilogy Ser.). (ENG.). (YA). (gr. 7). 2011. 512p. pap. 12.99 *(978-1-4169-7176-4(9))* 2010. 496p. 18.99 *(978-1-4169-7175-7(0))* Simon Pulse. (Simon Pulse).
—Behemoth. Thompson, Keith, illus. l.t. ed. 2010. (Leviathan Trilogy: Bk. 2). (ENG.). 540p. 23.99 *(978-1-4104-3066-3(9))* Thorndike Pr.
—Behemoth. 2011. (Leviathan Ser.: 2). lib. bdg. 24.50 *(978-0-606-22407-9(6)*, Turtleback) Turtleback Bks.
White, Kiersten. Now I Rise. 2017. (And I Darken Ser.: 2). (ENG.). 480p. (YA). (gr. 7). 18.99 ***(978-0-553-52235-8(3))***; lib. bdg. 21.99 ***(978-0-553-52236-5(1))*** Random Hse. Children's Bks. (Delacorte Pr.).

ISTANBUL (TURKEY)—HISTORY

Donovan, Sue. Istanbul, Once Constantinople. 2008. (Illus.). 36p. pap. *(978-0-531-15490-8(4))* Children's Pr., Ltd.
—Istanbul, Once Constantinople. 2007. (Shockwave: History & Politics Ser.). (ENG., Illus.). 36p. (J). (gr. 4-8). 25.00 *(978-0-531-17755-6(6)*, Children's Pr.) Scholastic Library Publishing.
Fall of Rome/Byzantium DBA. 2003. spiral bd. 16.95 *(978-1-56004-155-9(2))* Social Studies Schl. Service.
Feldman, Ruth Tenzer. The Fall of Constantinople. 2008. (Pivotal Moments in History Ser.). (ENG., Illus.). 160p. (gr. 9-12). lib. bdg. 38.60 *(978-0-8225-5918-4(8))* Lerner Publishing Group.
Lace, William W. The Unholy Crusade: The Ransacking of Medieval Constantinople. 2006. (Lucent Library of Historical Eras). (ENG., Illus.). 104p. (J). (gr. 3-7). lib. bdg. 33.45 *(978-1-59018-846-0(2)*, Lucent Bks.) Cengage Gale.

ITALIAN AMERICANS

Aldridge, Rebecca. Italian Americans. 2003. (Immigrants in America Ser.). (Illus.). 112p. (gr. 6-12). 30.00 *(978-0-7910-7129-8(4)*, Chelsea Hse.) Facts On File, Inc.
Anderson, Dale. Italian Americans. 2006. (World Almanac Library of American Immigration). 48p. (gr. 5-12). pap. 14.05 *(978-0-8368-7325-2(4))*; (Illus.). lib. bdg. 31.00 *(978-0-8368-7312-2(2))* Stevens, Gareth Publishing LLLP. (Gareth Stevens Secondary Library).
Behnke, Alison. Italians in America. 2005. (In America Ser.). (Illus.). 80p. (J). (gr. 5-8). lib. bdg. 27.93 *(978-0-8225-4696-2(5))* Lerner Publishing Group.
Bryan, Nichol. Italian Americans, 1 vol. 2004. (One Nation Set 1 Ser.). (ENG.). 32p. (gr. k-6). 27.07 *(978-1-57765-985-3(6)*, Checkerboard Library) ABDO Publishing Co.
Burgan, Michael. Italian Immigrants. 2004. (Immigration to the United States Ser.). (Illus.). 96p. (gr. 4-9). 35.00 *(978-0-8160-5681-1(1))* Facts On File, Inc.
Ciongoli, A. Kenneth & Parini, Jay. Passage to Liberty: The Story of Italian Immigration & the Rebirth of America. 2003. (Illus.). 32p. (YA). (gr. 9-12). 30.00 *(978-0-7567-6841-6(1))* DIANE Publishing Co.
Deiters, Erika & Deiters, Jim. The Italian Community in America. 2003. (J). pap. *(978-1-58417-091-4(3))*; lib. bdg. *(978-1-58417-028-0(X))* Lake Street Pubs.
Moreno, Barry. The Italian Americans. 2007. (Major American Immigration Ser.). (YA). pap. 9.95 *(978-1-4222-0676-8(9))* Mason Crest.
Moreno, Barry & Bowen, Richard A. The Italian Americans. 2010. (Major American Immigration Ser.). (Illus.). 64p. (YA). (gr. 9-12). 22.95 *(978-1-4222-0609-6(2))* Mason Crest.
Nickles, Greg. The Italians: We Came to North America. 2006. (Illus.). 32p. (J). (gr. 4-8). reprint ed. 19.00 *(978-0-7567-9906-9(6))* DIANE Publishing Co.
Parker, Lewis K. Why Italian Immigrants Came to America. (Coming to America Ser.). 24p. 2009. (gr. 2-3). 42.50 *(978-1-61511-885-4(3))* 2003. (Illus.). (J). lib. bdg. 22.60 *(978-0-8239-6460-4(4))* Rosen Publishing Group, Inc., The. (PowerKids Pr.).
Spinelli, Jerry. Knots in My Yo-Yo String. Gentieu, Penny, photos by. 2014. (Illus.). 158p. pap. 11.00 *(978-1-61003-375-6(2))* Center for the Collaborative Classroom.
Yoder, Carolyn. Italian Americans. 2003. (We Are America Ser.). (Illus.). 32p. (J). (gr. 2-4). lib. bdg. *(978-1-4034-0166-3(7))* Heinemann-Raintree.

ITALIAN AMERICANS—FICTION

Askew, Kim & Helmes, Amy. Anyone but You. 2014. (Twisted Lit Ser.). (ENG.). 224p. (YA). 17.99 *(978-1-4405-7001-8(9)*, Simon Pulse) Simon Pulse.
Ayres, Katherine. Under Copp's Hill. 2009. (Mysteries Through Time Ser.). 176p. (YA). (gr. 4-8). 31.95 *(978-1-60754-185-1(8))*; pap. 15.25 *(978-1-60754-186-8(6))* Windmill Bks.
Bartone, Elisa. Peppe the Lamplighter. Lewin, Ted, illus. 2015. 32p. pap. 7.00 *(978-1-61003-612-2(3))* Center for the Collaborative Classroom.
Blundell, Judy. Strings Attached. (ENG.). 320p. (J). (gr. 7). 2012. pap. 9.99 *(978-0-545-22127-6(7)*, Scholastic Paperbacks) 2011. 17.99 *(978-0-545-22126-9(9)*, Scholastic Pr.) Scholastic, Inc.
Creech, Sharon. Granny Torrelli Makes Soup. Raschka, Chris, illus. 2012. (ENG.). 160p. (J). (gr. 3-7). reprint ed. pap. 6.99 *(978-0-06-440960-5(0))* HarperCollins Pubs.
—Granny Torrelli Makes Soup. Raschka, Chris, illus. 2004. (Joanna Cotler Bks.). 141p. (gr. 3-7). 17.00 *(978-0-7569-4604-3(2))* Perfection Learning Corp.
Gambini, Josephine. Poetino Piccolino Saves the Day. Stafford, Jordan, illus. 2011. (ENG.). (J). pap. 19.95 *(978-0-9829496-3-4(4))* Giusti-Gambini, J.M. Publishing, LLC.
Holm, Jennifer L. Penny from Heaven. 2007. 265p. (gr. 3-7). 17.00 *(978-0-7569-8206-5(5))* Perfection Learning Corp.
—Penny from Heaven. 2007. (ENG., Illus.). 304p. (J). (gr. 3-7). 7.99 *(978-0-375-83689-3(6)*, Yearling) Random Hse. Children's Bks.
—Penny from Heaven. l.t. ed. 2007. (Literacy Bridge Middle Reader Ser.). (Illus.). 285p. (J). (gr. 5-7). 23.95 *(978-0-7862-9698-9(4))* Thorndike Pr.
Hopkinson, Deborah. A Bandit's Tale: The Muddled Misadventures of a Pickpocket. 2016. (ENG.). 304p. (J). (gr. 3-7). lib. bdg. 19.99 *(978-0-385-75500-9(7)*, Knopf Bks. for Young Readers) Random Hse. Children's Bks.
Kroll, Steven. Sweet America: An Immigrant's Story. 2004. 172p. (J). lib. bdg. 16.92 *(978-1-4242-0773-2(8))* Fitzgerald Bks.
—When I Dream of Heaven: Angelina's Story. 2004. 156p. (J). lib. bdg. 16.92 *(978-1-4242-0770-1(3))* Fitzgerald Bks.
Little Italy (Italians) 76p. (YA). (gr. 6-12). pap. 9.95 *(978-0-8224-3677-5(9))* Globe Fearon Educational Publishing.
Napoli, Donna Jo. Alligator Bayou. 2010. (ENG.). 288p. (YA). (gr. 7). pap. 8.99 *(978-0-553-49417-4(1)*, Lamb, Wendy Bks.) Random Hse. Children's Bks.
Nobisso, Josephine. En Ingles, por Supuesto. Ziborova, Dasha, illus. 2003. Orig. Title: In English, of Course. (SPA & ENG.). 32p. (J). (gr. k-2). 16.95 *(978-0-940112-14-8(0))* Gingerbread Hse.
—En ingles, por Supuesto. Ziborova, Dasha, illus. 2003. Orig. Title: In English, of Course. (SPA & ENG.). 32p. (J). (gr. k-2). pap. 8.95 *(978-0-940112-16-2(7))* Gingerbread Hse.
Palatini, Margie. Isabella for Real. Pham, LeUyen, illus. 2016. (ENG.). 208p. (J). (gr. 5-7). 16.99 *(978-0-544-14846-8(0)*, HMH Books For Young Readers) Houghton Mifflin Harcourt Publishing Co.
Smith, D. James. The Boys of San Joaquin. 2006. (ENG.). 240p. (J). (gr. 3-7). pap. 11.99 *(978-1-4169-1619-2(9)*, Atheneum Bks. for Young Readers) Simon & Schuster Children's Publishing.
Testa, Maria. Becoming Joe Dimaggio. Hunt, Scott, illus. 2005. (ENG.). 64p. (J). (gr. 5-9). reprint ed. pap. 6.99 *(978-0-7636-2444-6(6))* Candlewick Pr.

ITALIAN LANGUAGE

Amery, Heather. First Thousand Words: With Internet-Linked Pronunciation Guide. MacKinnon, Mairi, ed. Cartwright, Stephen, illus. 2007. (Usborne Internet-Linked First Thousand Words Ser.). 63p. (J). (gr. -1). 20.99 *(978-1-58086-987-4(4)*, Usborne) EDC Publishing.
—First Thousand Words in Italian. Cartwright, Stephen, illus. rev. ed. 2004. (First Thousand Words Ser.). (ITA & ENG.). 64p. (J). (gr. -1-6). 12.99 *(978-0-7945-0286-7(5)*, Usborne) EDC Publishing.
Berlitz Publishing Staff. Italian - Berlitz Picture Dictionary. 2nd ed. 2004. (Kids Picture Dictionary Ser.). (ITA & ENG., Illus.). 128p. (J). (gr. -1-4). pap. 12.95 *(978-981-246-390-6(9)*, 463909) APA Publications Services SGP. Dist: Ingram Publisher Services.
Campaniello, Don. 1000 First Words in Italian. Lacome, Susie, illus. 2013. (ENG & ITA.). 96p. (J). (gr. k-4). 12.99 *(978-1-84322-956-8(0))* Anness Publishing GBR. Dist: National Bk. Network.
Dai Zovi, Lonnie. Canti,Ritmi e Rime: Chants, Rhythms & Rhymes for the Italian Classroom. 2004. 30.50 *(978-0-935301-87-8(9))* Vibrante Pr.
Davies, Helen. Italian Dictionary for Beginners. Irving, Nicole, ed. Shackell, John, illus. 2006. (Beginner's Dictionaries Ser.). (ITA.). 128p. (J). (gr. 4). lib. bdg. 20.95 *(978-1-58086-555-5(0))* EDC Publishing.
Davies, Helen & Iannaco, G. Italian Dictionary for Beginners. 2004. (Beginner's Dictionaries Ser.). (ITA & ENG.). 127p. (J). pap. 12.95 *(978-0-7945-0290-4(3)*, Usborne) EDC Publishing.
Fedoruk, Dennis, prod. Bilingual Baby - Flashcard Set - Italian. 2013. (ITA.). (J). 7.99 *(978-1-892703-77-4(7))* Small Fry Beginnings.
Fulcher, Roz. Color & Learn Easy Italian Phrases for Kids. 2015. (Dover Little Activity Bks.). (ENG.). 64p. (J). (gr. k-3). pap. 1.99 *(978-0-486-80359-3(7))* Dover Pubns., Inc.
Goodman, Marlene. Let's Learn Italian Picture Dictionary. 2003. (ENG & ITA., Illus.). 80p. 13.00 *(978-0-07-140826-4(6)*, 0071408266) McGraw-Hill Education.
Graziano, Carlo. Dialoghi Simpatici. (ITA.). (J). (gr. 7-10). audio 15.00 *(978-0-8442-8034-9(8)*, National Textbook Co.) McGraw-Hill/Contemporary.
Hochstatter, Daniel J., illus. Italian. 2003. (Just Look 'n Learn Picture Dictionary Ser.). (ITA & ENG.). 96p. (J). (gr. 4-7). pap. 11.95 *(978-0-8442-8057-8(7)*, 80577) McGraw-Hill Trade.
Kudela, Katy R. My First Book of Italian Words, 1 vol. Translations.com Staff, tr. 2011. (Bilingual Picture Dictionaries Ser.). 32p. (gr. 1-2). (ENG, ITA & MUL., Illus.). pap. 8.10 *(978-1-4296-6159-1(3))*; (MUL.). pap. 47.70 *(978-1-4296-6160-7(7))* Capstone Press of Coughlan Cos. (Aplus Bks.).
Milet Publishing Staff. Animals. 2011. (My First Bilingual Book Ser.). (ENG & ITA., Illus.). 24p. (J). (gr. k — 1). bds. 7.99 *(978-1-84059-614-4(7))* Milet Publishing.
—Bilingual Visual Dictionary. (Milet Bilingual Visual Dictionary Ser.). (ENG & ITA., Illus.). (J). (gr. k-2). 2012. 148p. 34.95 *(978-1-84059-690-8(2))* 2011. 1p. cd-rom 19.95 *(978-1-84059-586-4(8))* Milet Publishing.
—Fruit - My First Bilingual Book. 2011. (My First Bilingual Book Ser.). (ENG & ITA., Illus.). 24p. (J). (gr. k — 1). bds. 8.99 *(978-1-84059-630-4(9))* Milet Publishing.
—Home. 2011. (My First Bilingual Book Ser.). (ENG & ITA., Illus.). 24p. (J). (gr. k — 1). bds. 7.99 *(978-1-84059-646-5(5))* Milet Publishing.
—My Bilingual Book-Hearing (English-Italian) 2014. (My Bilingual Book Ser.). (ENG & ITA., Illus.). 28p. (J). (gr. -1-k). 9.95 *(978-1-84059-778-3(X))* Milet Publishing.
—My Bilingual Book-Sight (English-Italian) 2014. (My Bilingual Book Ser.). (ENG & ITA., Illus.). 28p. (J). (gr. -1-k). 9.95 *(978-1-84059-794-3(1))* Milet Publishing.
—My Bilingual Book-Smell (English-Italian) 2014. (My Bilingual Book Ser.). (ENG & ITA., Illus.). 28p. (J). (gr. -1-k). 9.95 *(978-1-84059-810-0(7))* Milet Publishing.
—My Bilingual Book-Taste (English-Italian) 2014. (My Bilingual Book Ser.). (ENG & ITA., Illus.). 28p. (J). (gr. -1-k). 9.95 *(978-1-84059-826-1(3))* Milet Publishing.
—My Bilingual Book-Touch (English-Italian) 2014. (My Bilingual Book Ser.). (ENG & ITA., Illus.). 28p. (J). (gr. -1-k). 9.95 *(978-1-84059-842-1(5))* Milet Publishing.
—Vegetables (Le Verdure) 2011. (My First Bilingual Book Ser.). (ENG & ITA., Illus.). 24p. (J). (gr. k — 1). bds. 7.99 *(978-1-84059-662-5(7))* Milet Publishing.
Mio Primo Dizionario Illustrato de Italia. (ITA., Illus.). pap. 9.95 *(978-88-8148-840-7(X))* European Language Institute ITA. Dist: Distribooks, Inc.
Mio Primo Dizionario Illustrato de Italiano. (ITA., Illus.). pap. 9.95 *(978-88-8148-830-8(2))*; pap. 9.95

(978-88-8148-845-2(0)); pap. 9.95 (978-88-8148-835-3(3)) European Language Institute ITA. Dist: Distribooks, Inc.

Nunn, Daniel. Colors in Italian: I Colori, 1 vol. 2012. (World Languages - Colors Ser.). (ENG, ITA & MUL.). 24p. (gr. 1-3). pap. 6.29 (978-1-4329-6662-1(6)); lib. bdg. 22.65 (978-1-4329-6655-3(3)) Heinemann-Raintree. (Acom).

—Families in Italian: le Famiglie, 1 vol. 2013. (World Languages - Families Ser.). (ENG, MUL & ITA.). 24p. (gr. 1-3). pap. 6.29 (978-1-4329-7183-0(2)); lib. bdg. 22.65 (978-1-4329-7176-2(X)) Heinemann-Raintree. (Acom).

—Numbers in Italian. 2012. (World Languages - Numbers Ser.). (ENG, ITA & MUL.). 24p. (gr. 1-3). lib. bdg. 22.65 (978-1-4329-6676-8(6), Acom) Heinemann-Raintree.

—Numbers in Italian: I Numeri - 1 2 3. 2012. (World Languages - Numbers Ser.). (ENG, ITA & MUL.). 24p. (gr. 1-3). pap. 6.29 (978-1-4329-6683-6(9), Acom) Heinemann-Raintree.

The Rosetta Stone Language Library: Italian Level 2. 2005. (J). (gr. 1-18). cd-rom 239.00 (978-1-883972-73-8(6)) Rosetta Stone Ltd.

Rossi, Sophia. Buon Natale: Learning Songs & Traditions in Italian. Kelleher, Kathie, illus. 2007. (Teach Me Ser.). (ITA & SPA.). 32p. (J). (gr. -1-3). 19.95 (978-1-59972-067-8(1)) Teach Me Tapes, Inc.

ITALIAN LANGUAGE—CONVERSATION AND PHRASE BOOKS

Gorjanc, Adele A. Italian Conversation: A Practical Guide for Students & Travelers. (Illus.). 202p. (J). pap. 11.95 (978-0-8283-1670-5(8)) Branden Bks.

Mahoney, Judy. Teach Me Everyday Italian: Celebrating the Seasons, 22 vols., Vol. 2. Girouard, Patrick, illus. adapted ed. 2010. (ITA & ENG.). 32p. (J). 19.95 (978-1-59972-207-8(0), 1286051) Teach Me Tapes, Inc.

Sansone, Emma. Getting to Know Italy & Italian. Woolley, Kim, illus. 2005. 33p. (J). reprint ed. pap. 13.00 (978-0-7567-9579-5(6)) DIANE Publishing Co.

Wightwick, Jane. Way Cool Italian Phrasebook. 2005. (ENG., Illus.). 96p. 12.95 (978-0-07-144841-3(1), 0071448411) McGraw-Hill Cos., The.

ITALIAN LANGUAGE—GRAMMAR

Melling, David, illus. First Italian Words. 2009. (First Words Ser.). (ITA & ENG.). 48p. (J). (gr. 3-18). pap. 12.95 (978-0-19-911100-8(6)) Oxford Univ. Pr., Inc.

Milet Publishing Staff. Music - My First Bilingual Book. 2012. (My First Bilingual Book Ser.). (ENG & ITA., Illus.). 24p. (J). (gr. k — 1). bds. 7.99 (978-1-84059-722-6(4)) Milet Publishing.

—Opposites - My First Bilingual Book. 2012. (My First Bilingual Book Ser.). (ENG & ITA., Illus.). 24p. (J). (gr. k — 1). bds. 8.99 (978-1-84059-738-7(0)) Milet Publishing.

—Sports (English-Italian) 2012. (My First Bilingual Book Ser.). (ENG & ITA., Illus.). 24p. (J). (gr. k — 1). bds. 7.99 (978-1-84059-754-7(2)) Milet Publishing.

ITALIAN LANGUAGE—READERS

Bella Addormentata Nel. pap. 14.95 (978-88-04-46595-9(6)) Mondadori ITA. Dist: Distribooks, Inc.

Burke, David. Beauty & the Beast (English to Italian - Level 3) Learn ITALIAN Through Fairy Tales. 2007. (Learn Italian Through Fairy Tales Ser.). (ENG & ITA., Illus.). (J). per. 14.95 incl. audio compact disk (978-1-891888-89-2(7)) Slangman Publishing.

—Cinderella: Level 1: Learn Italian Through Fairy Tales. Bobrick, Julie, ed. Filippi, Alessio, tr. Sandoval, Migs, illus. 2006. (Learn Italian Through Fairy Tales Ser.). (ENG & ITA.). 29p. pap. 14.95 incl. audio compact disk (978-1-891888-77-9(3)) Slangman Publishing.

—Goldilocks (English to Italian - Level 2) Learn ITALIAN Through Fairy Tales. 2007. (Learn Italian Through Fairy Tales Ser.). (ENG & ITA., Illus.). (J). per. 14.95 incl. audio compact disk (978-1-891888-82-3(X)) Slangman Publishing.

Eva & Vincent. (GER & ENG., Illus.). 80p. (J). pap., wbk. ed. 13.95 (978-88-8148-178-1(2)) European Language Institute ITA. Dist: Distribooks, Inc.

Howell, Heather. Emanuele Goes to the Zoo. 2010. 20p. 10.49 (978-1-4490-4816-7(1)) AuthorHouse.

Milet Publishing Staff. Colours - My First Bilingual Book. 2010. (My First Bilingual Book Ser.). (ENG & ITA., Illus.). 24p. (J). (gr. k — 1). bds. 8.99 (978-1-84059-537-6(X)) Milet Publishing.

—Numbers - My First Bilingual Book. 2010. (My First Bilingual Book Ser.). (ENG & ITA., Illus.). 24p. (J). (gr. k — 1). bds. 7.99 (978-1-84059-543-7(4)) Milet Publishing.

Mistero en las Olimpiadas Acuaticas. (SPA., Illus.). 70p. (YA). (gr. 6-8). pap. (978-88-8148-456-0(0)) EMC/Paradigm Publishing.

ITALIAN LANGUAGE—STUDY AND TEACHING

Hanson, Tracie, des. New World Baby - Italian. 2007. (ENG, ITA, FRE, GER & SPA., Illus.). 28p. (J). 14.00 (978-0-9799185-3-7(7)) Hanson, Tracie.

Mahoney, Judy. Teach Me Everyday Italian: Celebrating the Seasons, 22 vols., Vol. 2. Girouard, Patrick, illus. adapted ed. 2010. (ITA & ENG.). 32p. (J). 19.95 (978-1-59972-207-8(0), 1286051) Teach Me Tapes, Inc.

ITALY

Adams, Colleen. A Primary Source Guide to Italy. 2003. (Countries of the World). (Illus.). 24p. (ENG.). (gr. 3-6). pap. 8.25 (978-0-8239-8077-2(4)); (J). lib. bdg. 22.60 (978-0-8239-6593-9(7)) Rosen Publishing Group, Inc., The.

Anderson, Robert. Italy. 2006. (Countries of the World Ser.). (ENG., Illus.). 64p. (gr. 5-9). lib. bdg. 27.90 (978-0-7922-7666-1(3), National Geographic Children's Bks.) National Geographic Society.

—Italy - National Geographic. 2009. (Countries of the World Ser.). (ENG., Illus.). 64p. (J). (gr. 5). pap. 12.95 (978-1-4263-0567-2(2), National Geographic Children's Bks.) National Geographic Society.

Bailey, Gerry & Foster, Karen. Galileo's Telescope. Noyes, Leighton & Radford, Karen, illus. 2008. (Stories of Great People Ser.). (ENG.). 40p. (J). (gr. 3-6). lib. bdg. (978-0-7787-3694-3(6)); pap. (978-0-7787-3716-2(0)) Crabtree Publishing Co.

Bauer, Helen. Verdi for Kids: His Life & Music with 21 Activities. 2013. (For Kids Ser.). (ENG., Illus.). 144p. (J). (gr. 4). pap. 16.95 (978-1-61374-500-7(1)) Chicago Review Pr., Inc.

Bell, Rachael. Italy. 2016. (Visit To Ser.). (ENG.). 32p. pap. 8.29 (978-1-4846-3874-3(3), Heinemann First Library) Heinemann-Raintree.

Brooks, Susie. Let's Visit Italy. 2009. (Around the World Ser.). (Illus.). 32p. (J). (gr. 2-5). (ENG.). pap. 10.00 (978-1-4358-8612-4(7)); lib. bdg. 25.25 (978-1-4358-3029-5(6)) Rosen Publishing Group, Inc., The. (PowerKids Pr.).

Cook, Diane. Michelangelo: Renaissance Artist. 2013. (People of Importance Ser.: 21). (Illus.). 32p. (J). (gr. 4-18). 19.95 (978-1-4222-2851-7(7)) Mason Crest.

Dalrymple, Lisa & O'Brien, Cynthia. Explore with John Cabot. 2015. (Travel with the Great Explorers Ser.). (ENG., Illus.). 32p. (J). (gr. 3-6). (978-0-7787-1702-7(X)) Crabtree Publishing Co.

Demi. Saint Francis of Assisi. 2012. (ENG., Illus.). 56p. (J). (gr. -1-3). 19.95 (978-1-937786-04-5(8)) World Wisdom, Inc.

Demuth, Patricia Brennan. Who Was Galileo? 2015. (Who Was... ? Ser.). lib. bdg. 16.00 (978-0-606-36594-9(X)) Turtleback Bks.

Denham, Joyce. Saint Francis of Assisi. Temporin, Elena, illus. 2008. (ENG.). 32p. (J). (gr. k-6). pap. 9.95 (978-1-55725-571-6(7)) Paraclete Pr., Inc.

Donaldson, Madeline. Italy. 2010. pap. 51.02 (978-0-7613-6976-9(7)) Lerner Publishing Group.

Dyan, Penelope. On the Way to Rome — - a Kid's Guide to Civitavecchia , Italy. Weigand, John D., photos by. 2011. (Illus.). 34p. pap. 11.95 (978-1-935630-59-3(8)) Bellissima Publishing, LLC.

Favor, Lesli J. Italy: A Primary Source Cultural Guide. 2009. (Primary Sources of World Cultures Ser.). 128p. (gr. 4-5). 79.90 (978-1-60851-925-5(2)) Rosen Publishing Group, Inc., The.

Feinstein, Stephen. Columbus: Opening up the New World. 2009. (Great Explorers of the World Ser.). (Illus.). 112p. (J). (gr. 7-12). lib. bdg. 33.27 (978-1-59845-101-6(4)) Enslow Pubs., Inc.

Furgang, Kathy. Mount Vesuvius: Europe's Mighty Volcano of Smoke & Ash. 2009. (Volcanoes of the World Ser.). 24p. (gr. 3-3). 42.50 (978-1-60854-733-3(7), PowerKids Pr.) Rosen Publishing Group, Inc., The.

Green, Jen. Focus on Italy. 2007. (World in Focus Ser.). (Illus.). 64p. (gr. 5-12). pap. 14.05 (978-0-8368-6743-5(2)); lib. bdg. 34.00 (978-0-8368-6736-7(X)) Stevens, Gareth Publishing LLLP. (Gareth Stevens Secondary Library).

Grodin, Elissa D., et al. C Is for Ciao: An Italy Alphabet. Ventura, Marco, illus. 2008. (Discover the World Ser.). (ENG.). 40p. (J). (gr. 1-5). 17.95 (978-1-58536-361-2(8)) Sleeping Bear Pr.

Hardyman, Robyn. Celebrate: Italy. 2009. (Celebrate Country Ser.). 32p. (gr. 4-6). 28.00 (978-1-60413-269-4(8), Chelsea Clubhouse) Facts On File, Inc.

January, Brendan. Leonardo Da Vinci: Renaissance Painter. 2013. (People of Importance Ser.: 21). (Illus.). 32p. (J). (gr. 4-18). 19.95 (978-1-4222-2848-7(7)) Mason Crest.

Klepeis, Alicia. Italy. 2016. (Exploring World Cultures Ser.). 32p. (J). pap. 10.58 (978-1-5026-2138-2(X)) Cavendish Square Publishing.

Kohen, E. Italy. 3rd ed. 2013. 144p. (J). (gr. 6-9). 47.07 (978-1-60870-870-3(5)) Cavendish Square Publishing.

Levinson, Debra. Italy's Best with Kids: Extraordinary Places to Sleep, Eat & Play. 2003. (J). pap. 19.95 (978-0-9633577-4-8(3)) Max Publication, Inc.

Marsh, Carole. Italy: The Country of Amazing Fountains & Awesome Arts! 2009. (It's Your World Ser.). 48p. (J). (gr. 2-9). pap. 7.99 (978-0-635-06817-0(6)) Gallopade International.

Obregón, José María. Italy: Italia. 2009. (Great National Soccer Teams / Grandes selecciones del fútbol mundial Ser.). (SPA & ENG.). 24p. pap. 8.25 (978-1-4358-2491-1(1), PowerKids Pr.) Rosen Publishing Group, Inc., The.

Pavlovic, Zoran. Italy. 2003. (Modern World Nations Ser.). (Illus.). 150p. (gr. 6-12). 35.00 (978-0-7910-7608-8(3), Chelsea Hse.) Facts On File, Inc.

Popper, Garry. Mario in Italy. Johnson, Andi, illus. 2004. 36p. (gr. -1-7). 4.00 (978-1-84161-059-7(3)) Ravette Publishing, Ltd. GBR. Dist: Parkwest Pubns., Inc.

Powell, Jillian. Descubramos Italia. 2007. (Descubramos paises del mundo (Looking at Countries) Ser.). (ENG & SPA., Illus.). 32p. (gr. 1-5). pap. 10.50 (978-0-8368-7962-9(7)); lib. bdg. 26.00 (978-0-8368-7955-1(4)) Stevens, Gareth Publishing LLLP. (Gareth Stevens Learning Library).

—Looking at Italy. 2007. (Looking at Countries Ser.). (Illus.). 32p. (gr. 1-5). pap. 10.50 (978-0-8368-7677-2(6)); lib. bdg. 26.00 (978-0-8368-7670-3(9)) Stevens, Gareth Publishing LLLP. (Gareth Stevens Learning Library).

Rechner, Amy. Italy. 2017. (Country Profiles Ser.). (ENG., Illus.). 32p. (J). (gr. 3-8). lib. bdg. 26.95 **(978-1-62617-683-6(3)**, Blastoff! Discovery) Bellwether Media.

Riddle, John. Marco Polo: 13th Century Italian Trader. 2013. (People of Importance Ser.: 21). (Illus.). 32p. (J). (gr. 4-18). 19.95 (978-1-4222-2850-0(9)) Mason Crest.

Sansone, Emma. Getting to Know Italy & Italian. Woolley, Kim, illus. 2005. 33p. (J). reprint ed. pap. 13.00 (978-0-7567-9579-5(6)) DIANE Publishing Co.

Savery, Annabel. Italy. 2011. (ENG., Illus.). 32p. (J). pap. 10.95 (978-1-77092-025-5(0)) Saunders Bk. Co. CAN. Dist: RiverStream Publishing.

Tecco, Betsy Dru. How to Draw Italy's Sights & Symbols. 2009. (Kid's Guide to Drawing the Countries of the World Ser.). 48p. (gr. 4-4). 53.00 (978-1-61511-115-2(8), PowerKids Pr.) Rosen Publishing Group, Inc., The.

Wagner, Heather Lehr. Pompeii. 2012. (Lost Worlds & Mysterious Civilizations Ser.). (Illus.). 104p. (gr. 6-12). 35.00 (978-1-60413-971-6(4), Chelsea Hse.) Facts On File, Inc.

Walsh, Alison. Hugh O'Flaherty: His Wartime Adventures. 2011. (ENG., Illus.). 114p. (J). pap. 4.99 (978-1-84889-058-9(3)) Collins Pr., The IRL. Dist: Vearsa.

Winter, Jane Kohen. Italy. 2013. (Cultures of the World 4 Ser.). 144p. (J). (gr. 6-9). pap. 23.51 (978-1-62712-161-3(7)) Cavendish Square Publishing.

ITALY—CIVILIZATION

Boekhoff, P. M. & Kallen, Stuart A. The Italian Renaissance. 2003. (History of the World Ser.). (Illus.). 48p. (J). (gr. 3-5). 23.70 (978-0-7377-1036-6(5), Kidhaven) Cengage Gale.

Dubois, Muriel L. Ancient Rome: A Mighty Empire. 2011. (Great Civilizations Ser.). (ENG.). 32p. (gr. 3-4). pap. 47.70 (978-1-4296-7240-5(4), Fact Finders) Capstone Press of Coughlan Cos.

ITALY—FICTION

Abbott, Jacob. Rollo in Naples. 2008. 108p. 23.95 (978-1-60664-821-6(7)); pap. 9.95 (978-1-60664-066-1(6)) Aegypan.

Las Aventuras de Pinocho. (SPA., Illus.). 160p. (YA). 14.95 (978-84-7281-190-4(5), AF1905) Auriga, Ediciones S.A. ESP. Dist: Continental Bk. Co., Inc.

Avi. Magia de Medianoche. 2004. (SPA.). 194p. (YA). 10.99 (978-84-348-9112-8(3)) SM Ediciones ESP. Dist: Lectorum Pubns., Inc.

—Murder at Midnight. (ENG.). (J). (gr. 3-7). 2011. 256p. pap. 6.99 (978-0-545-08091-0(6), Scholastic Paperbacks) 2009. 272p. 17.99 (978-0-545-08090-3(8), Scholastic Pr.) Scholastic, Inc.

Balit, Christina. Escape from Pompeii. 2013. (ENG., Illus.). 32p. (J). (gr. 1-4). pap. 8.99 (978-1-84507-059-5(3), Frances Lincoln) Quarto Publishing Group UK GBR. Dist: Hachette Bk. Group.

Barry, Todd J. Pierogies with the Pope: A Tribute to Pope John Paul II, & New Beginnings with Pope Benedict XVI for Young Readers, 1 vol. Evenwel, Patricia L., illus. 2009. 58p. pap. 16.95 (978-1-60836-325-4(2)) America Star Bks.

Bastianich, Lidia Matticchio. Lidia's Family Kitchen: Nonna's Birthday Surprise. Graef, Renee, illus. 2013. (ENG.). 60p. (J). (gr. -1-17). 16.95 (978-0-7624-4655-1(2), Running Pr. Kids) Running Pr. Bk. Pubs.

—Nonna Tell Me a Story: Lidia's Christmas Kitchen. Logan, Laura, illus. 2010. (ENG.). 56p. (J). (gr. -1-3). 15.95 (978-0-7624-3692-7(1)) Running Pr. Bk. Pubs.

Bergren, Lisa T. Season of Fire, 1 vol. 2015. (Remnants Novel Ser.: Bk. 2). (ENG.). 384p. (YA). 16.99 (978-0-310-73565-6(3)) Blink.

Bertanzetti, Eileen Dunn. Poor Pio. 2008. (Illus.). 48p. (J). pap. 4.95 (978-0-7599-0241-1(0)) Hard Shell Word Factory.

Burg, Ann. Rebekkah's Journey: A World War II Refugee Story. Iskowitz, Joel, illus. 2006. (Tales of Young Americans Ser.). (ENG.). 32p. (J). (gr. 3-7). 17.95 (978-1-58536-275-2(1)) Sleeping Bear Pr.

Campillo, Carlo Collodi. Ilustrado por Susana. Las Aventuras de Pinocho. (Coleccion Cuentos Universales). (SPA.). (YA). (gr. 4-18). (978-84-261-3145-4(X), JV30301) Juventud, Editorial ESP. Dist: Lectorum Pubns., Inc.

Chandler, Ann. Siena Summer, 1 vol. 2009. (ENG., Illus.). 142p. (YA). (gr. 6-9). pap. 12.95 (978-1-896580-17-3(3)) Tradewind Bks. CAN. Dist: Orca Bk. Pubs. USA.

Collodi, Carlo. The Adventures of Pinocchio. Staino, Franco & Innocenti, Roberto, illus. rev. ed. 2004. (ENG.). 192p. (J). (gr. 1-3). 35.00 (978-1-56846-190-8(9)) Creative Co., The.

Creech, Sharon. The Castle Corona. Diaz, David, illus. (J). 2013. (ENG.). 352p. (gr. 3-7). pap. 7.99 (978-0-06-206395-3(2)) 2007. 336p. (gr. 4-7). lib. bdg. 19.89 (978-0-06-084622-0(4), Cotler, Joanna Books) HarperCollins Pubs.

Culbertson, Kim. Instructions for a Broken Heart. 2011. (ENG.). 304p. (YA). (gr. 7-12). pap. 9.99 (978-1-4022-4302-8(2)) Sourcebooks, Inc.

Dane Rehagen. How Katie Got Her Meow. 2010. 42p. pap. 15.00 (978-1-4251-8664-7(5)) Trafford Publishing.

Davidson L. Haworth. The Dragon of Prali. 2010. 168p. 22.95 (978-1-4502-0147-6(4)); pap. 12.95 (978-1-4502-0145-2(8)) iUniverse, Inc.

De La Ramee, Louise & Ouida. Bimbi. 2007. 152p. per. 13.95 (978-1-60312-344-0(X)); 24.95 (978-1-60312-682-3(1)) Aegypan.

dePaola, Tomie. Days of the Blackbird: A Tale of Northern Italy. dePaola, Tomie, illus. 2005. (Illus.). (J). 13.65 (978-0-7569-5888-6(1)) Perfection Learning Corp.

—Strega Nona. dePaola, Tomie, illus. 2011. (Strega Nona Book Ser.). (ENG., Illus.). 40p. (J). (gr. -1-3). pap. 9.99 (978-1-4424-3355-7(8), Little Simon) Little Simon.

DeSio, Delores. Annie's Journey Through the Golden Door, 1 vol. 2009. 114p. pap. 19.95 (978-1-4489-8470-1(X)) America Star Bks.

Elliott, L. M. Da Vinci's Tiger. (YA). (gr. 8). 2017. 320p. pap. 9.99 **(978-0-06-074426-7(X))** 2015. (ENG.). 304p. 17.99 (978-0-06-074424-3(3)) HarperCollins Pubs. (Tegen, Katherine Bks).

Falconer, Ian. Olivia Goes to Venice. Falconer, Ian, illus. 2010. (ENG., Illus.). 48p. (J). (gr. -1-2). 17.99 (978-1-4169-9674-3(5), Atheneum Bks. for Young Readers) Simon & Schuster Children's Publishing.

Fillion, Susan. Pizza in Pienza. Fillion, Susan, illus. 2013. (ENG & ITA., Illus.). 32p. (J). 17.95 (978-1-56792-459-6(X)) Godine, David R. Pub.

Francia, Giada, ed. Ballooning over Italy: An Extraordinary Voyage Packed with Games & Fantastic Adventures; Special Agents. Ezrin, Amy, tr. Colombo, Angelo, illus. 2007. (Alex & Penny Ser.). (ENG.). 80p. (J). (gr. 2-5). 14.95 (978-88-544-0160-0(9), White Star) Rizzoli International Pubns., Inc.

Funke, Cornelia. Inkheart. Bell, Anthea, tr. 2005. (Inkheart Trilogy Ser.: Bk. 1).Tr. of Tintenherz. (ENG., Illus.). 576p. (J). (gr. 3-7). pap. 10.99 (978-0-439-70910-1(5)) Scholastic, Inc.

—Inkheart Trilogy Boxed Set: Inkheart, Inkspell, Inkdeath. 2003. (Inkheart Trilogy: Bks. 1-3). 544p. (J). 60.00 (978-0-439-61671-3(9), Chicken Hse., The) Scholastic, Inc.

—Inkspell. 2007. (Inkheart Trilogy Ser.: 2). lib. bdg. 22.10 (978-1-4177-7471-5(1), Turtleback) Turtleback Bks.

—Thief Lord. Birmingham, Christian, illus. 2010. (ENG.). 376p. (J). (gr. 3-7). 7.99 (978-0-545-22770-4(4), Chicken Hse., The) Scholastic, Inc.

Gale, Audra. The Adventures of Buddy & Me. 2007. 32p. (YA). pap. 8.00 (978-0-8059-7277-1(3)) Dorrance Publishing Co., Inc.

Gale Editor, ed. Romeo & Juliet: The Graphic Novel. 2011. (Classic Graphic Novel Collection Ser.). (Illus.). 160p. (J). (gr. 7-12). lib. bdg. 34.80 (978-1-4205-0631-0(5)) Cengage Gale.

Garant, Andre J. The Elite Eight. 2011. 120p. (gr. 4-6). pap. 10.99 (978-1-4567-4302-4(3)) AuthorHouse.

Giles, Susan. Lola & Luigi. 2011. 32p. pap. 14.39 (978-1-4567-0063-8(4)) AuthorHouse.

Gonzalez, Christina Diaz. Moving Target. 2015. (ENG.). 256p. (J). (gr. 3-7). 17.99 (978-0-545-77318-8(0), Scholastic Pr.) Scholastic, Inc.

Gonzalez, Jorge & Shakespeare, William. Romeo & Juliet, 1 vol. Cabrera, Eva, illus. 2011. (Shakespeare Graphics Ser.). (ENG.). 88p. (gr. 2-3). pap. 7.15 (978-1-4342-3448-3(7)); lib. bdg. 27.99 (978-1-4342-2563-4(1)) Stone Arch Bks. (Shakespeare Graphics).

Grant, Crystal. Warrior Boy. 2007. (ENG.). 92p. per. 16.95 (978-1-4241-3978-1(3)) PublishAmerica, Inc.

Graziani, E. War in My Town, 1 vol. 2015. (ENG., Illus.). 152p. (YA). (gr. 8-10). pap. 11.95 (978-1-927583-71-5(3)) Second Story Pr. CAN. Dist: Orca Bk. Pubs. USA.

Hamilton, Martha & Weiss, Mitch. Priceless Gifts: A Tale from Italy. Kanzler, John, illus. 2006. (ENG.). 32p. (J). (gr. k-3). 16.95 (978-0-87483-788-9(X)) August Hse. Pubs., Inc.

Harper, Suzanne. The Juliet Club. (YA). 2010. (ENG.). 416p. (gr. 8). pap. 9.99 (978-0-06-136693-2(5), Greenwillow Bks.) 2008. 402p. (gr. 7-18). lib. bdg. 18.89 (978-0-06-136692-5(7), HarperTeen) HarperCollins Pubs.

Henry, Marguerite. Gaudenzia, Pride of the Palio. Ward, Lynd, illus. 2014. (ENG.). 304p. (J). (gr. 3-7). pap. 5.99 (978-1-4814-0397-9(4), Aladdin) Simon & Schuster Children's Publishing.

Hinds, Gareth. Romeo & Juliet. Hinds, Gareth, illus. 2013. (ENG., Illus.). 144p. (YA). (gr. 7). 21.99 (978-0-7636-5948-6(7)); pap. 12.99 (978-0-7636-6807-5(9)) Candlewick Pr.

—Romeo & Juliet (Graphic Adaptation) 2013. lib. bdg. 24.50 (978-0-606-32098-6(9), Turtleback) Turtleback Bks.

Hoffman, Mary. City of Secrets. (Stravaganza Ser.). (ENG.). (YA). 2010. 416p. (gr. 7). pap. 8.99 (978-1-59990-451-1(9), 9781599904511) 2008. 400p. (gr. 5-18). 17.99 (978-1-59990-202-9(8), 9781599902029) Bloomsbury Publishing USA. (Bloomsbury USA Childrens).

—City of Ships. 2010. (Stravaganza Ser.). (ENG.). 368p. (YA). (gr. 7-18). 17.99 (978-1-59990-491-7(8), 9781599904917, Bloomsbury USA Childrens) Bloomsbury Publishing USA.

—The Falconer's Knot: A Story of Friars, Flirtation & Foul Play. 2008. (ENG., Illus.). 304p. (YA). (gr. 7). pap. 7.99 (978-1-59990-229-6(X), 9781599902296, Bloomsbury USA Childrens) Bloomsbury Publishing USA.

—Stravaganza: City of Ships. 2012. (Stravaganza Ser.). (ENG.). 384p. (YA). (gr. 7). pap. 9.99 (978-1-59990-832-8(8), 9781599908328, Bloomsbury USA Childrens) Bloomsbury Publishing USA.

—Stravaganza: City of Swords. 2012. (Stravaganza Ser.). (ENG.). 368p. (YA). (gr. 7-12). 18.99 (978-1-59990-842-7(5), 9781599908427, Bloomsbury USA Childrens) Bloomsbury Publishing USA.

Hogan, Mary. Pretty Face. (ENG.). 224p. (J). 2009. pap. 8.99 (978-0-06-084113-3(3)) 2008. (gr. 9-18). 16.99 (978-0-06-084111-9(7)) HarperCollins Pubs. (HarperTeen).

Hood, Ann. Leonardo Da Vinci No. 9: Renaissance Master. Zilber, Denis, illus. 2014. (Treasure Chest Ser.: 9). (ENG.). 224p. (J). (gr. 3-7). 15.99 (978-0-448-46768-9(2), Grosset & Dunlap) Penguin Young Readers Group.

Horowitz, Anthony. Scorpia. (Alex Rider Ser.). (ENG.). (J). (gr. 5-18). 2006. 416p. pap. 8.99 (978-0-14-240578-9(7), Puffin Books) 2005. 336p. 17.99 (978-0-399-24151-2(5), Philomel Bks.) Penguin Young Readers Group.

Jo, Eun-jeong. Grandfather Whisker's Table. Landmann, Bimba, illus. 2017. (J). **(978-0-8028-5474-2(5)**, Eerdmans Bks For Young Readers) Eerdmans, William B. Publishing Co.

Johnson, Maureen. Girl at Sea. 2008. (ENG., Illus.). 336p. (YA). (gr. 8-12). pap. 8.99 (978-0-06-054146-0(6), HarperTeen) HarperCollins Pubs.

Kieffer, Jean-Francois. The Adventures of Loupio, Volume 3: The Tournament. Chevrier, Janet, tr. 2013. (ENG., Illus.). 40p. (J). (gr. 4-7). pap. 6.99 (978-1-58617-853-6(9)) Ignatius Pr.

Langton, Jane P. Saint Francis & the Wolf. Plume, Ilse, illus. 2007. (ENG.). 32p. (J). (gr. -1-3). 16.95 (978-1-56792-320-9(8)) Godine, David R. Pub.

Lapucci, Carlo. Fiabe toscane di maghi, fate, animali, diavoli e Giganti: Edizione economica. Volume I. 2nd ed. 2011. (ITA., Illus.). 228p. (J). pap. 20.00 (978-88-563-0058-1(3)) Polistampa ITA. Dist: Casemate Academic.

Lawrence, Caroline. The Secrets of Vesuvius. 2004. (Roman Mysteries Ser.). (Illus.). 173p. (J). (gr. 3-7). 13.65 (978-0-7569-5947-0(0)) Perfection Learning Corp.

Levithan, David. Are We There Yet? 2007. (ENG.). 224p. (YA). (gr. 7-12). per. 8.99 (978-0-375-83956-6(9), Knopf Bks. for Young Readers) Random Hse. Children's Bks.

Lim, Rebecca. The Sweet Life. 2012. (ENG.). 196p. (YA). (gr. 7). pap. 11.99 (978-1-74237-770-4(X)) Allen & Unwin AUS. Dist: Independent Pubs. Group.

Lollino, Jessica. Lily & the Big Italian Wedding. Lollino, Jessica, ed. 2008. (Little Lily Mays Ser.: vol. 2). (ENG., Illus.). 32p. (J). pap. 12.95 (978-0-9712383-2-9(4)) Culturatti Ink.

Mann, T. L. The Adventures of Magellan. 2009. 23p. (J). pap. 13.95 (978-1-4327-3490-9(3)) Outskirts Pr., Inc.

Mcallister, Bruce. The Village Sang to the Sea. 2013. 172p. pap. (978-0-9534784-9-1(1)) Aeon Pr.

McCaughrean, Geraldine. Monacello: The Little Monk. Diemberger, Jana, illus. 2013. (Monacello Trilogy Ser.: 1). (ENG.). 64p. (J). (gr. 4-7). pap. 12.99 (978-1-907912-03-0(7)) Phoenix Yard Bks. GBR. Dist: Independent Pubs. Group.

—The Wish-Bringer. Diemberger, Jana, illus. 2014. (Monacello Trilogy Ser.). (ENG.). 56p. (J). (gr. 4-7). pap. 12.99 (978-1-907912-06-1(1)) Phoenix Yard Bks. GBR. Dist: Independent Pubs. Group.

Meyer, Kai. Arcadia Burns. 2013. (Arcadia Ser.: 2). (ENG.). 432p. (YA). (gr. 9). 17.99 (978-0-06-200608-0(8)) HarperCollins Pubs.

Napoli, Donna Jo. Three Days. 2003. (ENG., Illus.). 160p. (J). (gr. 5-18). pap. 5.99 (978-0-14-250025-5(9), Puffin Books) Penguin Young Readers Group.

—Three Days. 2003. 151p. (J). (gr. 5-9). 13.65 (978-0-7569-6313-2(3)) Perfection Learning Corp.

Nitz, Kristin Wolden. Saving the Griffin, 1 vol. Jaeggi, Yoshiko, illus. 2007. (ENG.). 192p. (J). (gr. 3-7). 14.95 (978-1-56145-380-1(3)) Peachtree Pubs.

Nobisso, Josephine. In English, of Course. Ziborova, Dasha, illus. 2003.Tr. of En Ingles, Por Supuesto. 32p. (J). (gr. -1).

H
I

(SPA & ENG.). 16.95 *(978-0-940112-07-0(8))*; (ENG.). pap. 8.95 *(978-0-940112-08-7(6))* Gingerbread Hse.

Oda, Matthew K. The Time MacHine: Mario's Box A Journey into Creativity. 2011. 36p. pap. 24.95 *(978-1-4626-3892-5(9))* America Star Bks.

Optic, Oliver, pseud. Sunny Shores; or, Young America in Italy & Austria a Story of Travel & Adventure by William T Adams. 2006. 428p. per. 26.99 *(978-1-4255-4627-4(7))* Michigan Publishing.

Osborne, Mary Pope. Vacation under the Volcano. unabr. ed. 2004. (Magic Tree House Ser.: No. 13). 74p. (J). (gr. k-3). pap. 17.00 incl. audio *(978-0-8072-0782-6(9))*, LFTR 241 SP, Listening Library) Random Hse. Audio Publishing Group.

Parkinson, Curtis. Domenic's War: A Story of the Battle of Monte Cassino. 2006. (ENG.). 200p. (J). (gr. 5-9). per. 9.95 *(978-0-88776-751-7(6))*, Tundra Bks.) Tundra Bks. CAN. Dist: Penguin Random Hse. LLC.

Parrish, Amanda. Greyhound Travels: Puma Travels to Italy. 2010. 28p. pap. 12.49 *(978-1-4490-9453-9(8))* AuthorHouse.

Peacock, L. A. Panic in Pompeii. Hale, Nathan, illus. 2011. 92p. (J). pap. *(978-0-545-34062-5(4))* Scholastic, Inc.

Peterfreund, Diana. Rampant. 2010. (ENG.). 432p. (YA). (gr. 9). pap. 8.99 *(978-0-06-149004-0(0))*, HarperTeen) HarperCollins Pubs.

Rae, Kristin. Wish You Were Italian: An If Only Novel. 2014. (If Only... Ser.). (ENG.). 352p. (YA). (gr. 7). pap. 9.99 *(978-1-61963-286-8(1))*, 9781619632868, Bloomsbury USA Childrens) Bloomsbury Publishing USA.

Raynham, Alex. Factfiles Leonardo da Vinci. 3rd ed. 2013. (ENG., Illus.). 64p. pap. 10.00 *(978-0-19-423670-6(6))* Oxford Univ. Pr., Inc.

Roberts, Kelly Hughes. The Road to Chianti. 2012. 214p. (gr. 4-6). 33.99 *(978-1-4525-5963-6(5))*; pap. 15.99 *(978-1-4525-5961-2(9))* Balboa Pr.

Ruiz, Margarita, illus. Pinocho. (SPA & ENG.). (J). (gr. -1-5). pap. 5.95 incl. audio compact disk *(978-88-8148-253-5(3))* EMC/Paradigm Publishing.

Russo, Richard. Bridge of Sighs. 2007. *(978-0-7393-2751-7(8))* Random Hse. Large Print.

Salten, Felix. The Hound of Florence. Paterson, Huntley, tr. from GER. 2014. (Bambi's Classic Animal Tales Ser.). (ENG., Illus.). 288p. (J). (gr. 3-7). pap. 6.99 *(978-1-4424-8748-2(8))*, Aladdin) Simon & Schuster Children's Publishing.

Scieszka, Jon. Da Wild, Da Crazy, Da Vinci, No. 14. McCauley, Adam & Adam, Mccauley, illus. 2006. (Time Warp Trio Ser.: 14). (ENG.). 96p. (J). (gr. 2-4). 5.99 *(978-0-14-240465-2(9))*, Puffin Books) Penguin Young Readers Group.

Seven, John. The Dragon of Rome, 1 vol. Phillips, Craig, illus. 2013. (Time-Tripping Faradays Ser.). (ENG.). 160p. (gr. 4-5). 9.95 *(978-1-62370-012-6(4))*; lib. bdg. 26.65 *(978-1-4342-6029-1(1))* Stone Arch Bks.

Seven, John & Phillips, Craig. The Dragon of Rome, 1 vol. 2013. (ENG.). 160p. (YA). pap. *(978-1-4342-6439-8(4))* Stone Arch Bks.

Shakespeare, William. Romeo & Juliet. Peluso, Martina, illus. 2013. (Big Picture Book Ser.). (ENG.). 40p. (J). (gr. 1). 14.95 *(978-2-7338-2119-0(9))* Auzou, Philippe Editions FRA. Dist: Consortium Bk. Sales & Distribution.

Slocombe, Megan. A Trip to Italy. 2013. 34p. pap. *(978-3-7103-0389-0(3))* united p.c. Verlag.

Smallman, Steve. Santa Is Coming to Naples. Dunn, Robert, illus. 2013. (ENG.). 32p. (J). (-3). 9.99 *(978-1-4022-9048-0(9))*, Sourcebooks Jabberwocky) Sourcebooks, Inc.

Smith, Annie Laura. Saving da Vinci. 2005. (YA). mass mkt. 6.99 *(978-0-9753367-6-2(2))* Onstage Publishing, LLC.

Snyder, Zilpha Keatley. The Famous Stanley Kidnapping Case. 2012. (Stanley Family Ser.). (ENG.). 216p. (J). (gr. 3-7). pap. 10.99 *(978-1-4424-8446-7(2))*, Atheneum Bks. for Young Readers) Simon & Schuster Children's Publishing.

Stevenson, Steve. The Crown of Venice. 2014. (Agatha Girl of Mystery Ser.: 7). lib. bdg. 16.00 *(978-0-606-36164-4(2))* Turtleback Bks.

Stilton, Geronimo. Play It Again, Mozart! Cooper-McGuinness, Nanette, tr. 2011. (Geronimo Stilton Graphic Novels Ser.). (ENG., Illus.). 56p. (J). (gr. 2-6). 9.99 *(978-1-59707-276-2(1))*, 9781597072762) Papercutz.

Tarshis, Lauren. I Survived the Destruction of Pompeii, 79 A. D. 2014. (I Survived . Ser.: No. 10). (Illus.). 95p. (J). lib. bdg. 14.75 *(978-0-606-36067-8(0))* Turtleback Bks.

Walshe, Elizabeth Hely. Under the Inquisition: A Story of the Reformation in Italy. 2009. (Illus.). 315p. *(978-1-894666-30-5(5))* Inheritance Pubns.

Weisleder, Stanley. Wings of the Panther. 2010. (ENG.). 224p. pap. 15.00 *(978-0-936783-38-3(9))* Merril Pr.

Welborn, Amy. Adventures in Assisi: on the Path with St. Francis: On the Path with St. Francis. Engelhart, Ann Kissane, illus. 2014. (ENG.). 32p. (J). (gr. k-3). 15.99 *(978-1-61636-650-6(8))* Franciscan Media.

—Bambinelli Sunday: A Christmas Blessing. Engelhart, Ann, illus. 2013. (ENG.). 32p. (J). (gr. k-2). 15.99 *(978-1-61636-649-0(4))* Franciscan Media.

Weston Woods Staff, creator. Clown of God. 2011. 38.75 *(978-0-545-14915-0(0))* Weston Woods Studios, Inc.

—The Clown of God. 2011. 29.95 *(978-0-545-08638-7(8))*; 18.95 *(978-0-545-08632-5(9))* Weston Woods Studios, Inc.

Zaugg, Sandy. Murdock Mystery #2: The Cats of Rome. 2010. 88p. pap. 10.95 *(978-1-4327-5062-6(3))* Outskirts Pr., Inc.

ITALY—HISTORY

Anderson, Dale. Italian Americans. 2006. (World Almanac Library of American Immigration). 48p. (gr. 5-12). pap. 14.05 *(978-0-8368-7325-2(4))*; (Illus.). lib. bdg. 31.00 *(978-0-8368-7312-2(2))* Stevens, Gareth Publishing LLLP. (Gareth Stevens Secondary Library).

Bach, Nancy. Cristoforo Colombo e la Pasta Al Pomodoro - Christopher Columbus & the Pasta with Tomato Sauce: A Bilingual Picture Book (Italian-English Text) Lätti, Leo, illus. 2013. 30p. pap. *(978-1-938712-06-7(4))* Roxby Media Ltd.

—Giuseppe Verdi, Compositore d'Opera Italiano - Giuseppe Verdi, Italian Opera Composer: A Bilingual Picture Book (Italian-English Text) Lätti, Leo, illus. 2013. 28p. pap. *(978-1-938712-12-8(9))* Roxby Media Ltd.

Ball, Karen. Pompeii. Cerisier, Emmanuel, illus. 2006. (Usborne Young Reading Ser.). 64p. (J). (gr. 3-7). 8.99 *(978-0-7945-1270-5(4))*, Usborne) EDC Publishing.

Blashfield, Jean F. Italy. 2013. (ENG.). 144p. (J). 40.00 *(978-0-531-23677-2(3))* Scholastic Library Publishing.

Brandeis, Madeline. Little Tony of Italy. 2011. 160p. 41.95 *(978-1-258-09804-9(0))* Literary Licensing, LLC.

Briggs, Raymond. Nuvolari & the Alfa Romeo. 2006. (Illus.). (J). *(978-0-9766683-1-2(9))* Racemaker Pr.

Buckley, A. M. Italy, 1 vol. 2011. (Countries of the World Set 1 Ser.). (ENG., Illus.). 144p. (J). (gr. 6-12). lib. bdg. 37.07 *(978-1-61783-114-0(X))* ABDO Publishing Co.

Cain, Marie Mowery. George Takes a Road Trip, Italy. 2013. (Big Books, Red Ser.). (ENG & SPA., Illus.). 16p. pap. 33.00 *(978-1-59246-205-6(7))* Big Books, by George!

Conklin, Wendy. You Are There! Pompeii 79. 2017. (Time for Kids Nonfiction Readers Ser.). lib. bdg. 19.65 ***(978-0-606-40293-4(4))*** Turtleback Bks.

De Almeida, Guilherme, et al. Galileo Galilei. 2010. (Me Llamo... Ser.). (SPA., Illus.). 63p. (J). pap. *(978-84-342-3617-2(6))* Parramon Ediciones S.A.

Demuth, Patricia Brennan & dePaola, Tomie. Who Was Galileo? O'Brien, John & Harrison, Nancy, illus. 2015. (Who Was? Ser.). (ENG.). 112p. (J). (gr. 3-7). 5.99 *(978-0-448-47985-9(0))*, Grosset & Dunlap) Penguin Young Readers Group.

Donaldson, Madeline. Italy. 2010. (Country Explorers Ser.). (ENG.). 48p. (gr. 2-4). pap. 9.95 *(978-0-7613-6036-0(0))*; lib. bdg. 29.27 *(978-0-7613-5316-4(X))* Lerner Publishing Group.

Ford, Nick. Niccolo Machiavelli: Florentine Statesman, Playwright, & Poet. 2004. (Rulers, Scholars, & Artists of the Renaissance Ser.). (J). lib. bdg. 34.60 *(978-1-4042-0316-7(8))* Rosen Publishing Group, Inc., The.

Francia, Giada. Alex & Penny's Italy Jigsaw Book. Colombo, Angelo, illus. 2007. (ENG.). 14p. (gr. 1-3). pap. 14.95 *(978-88-544-0242-3(7))*, White Star) Rizzoli International Pubns., Inc.

Gregory, Joy. Italy. 2016. (J). ***(978-1-4896-5414-4(3))*** Weigl Pubs., Inc.

Hancock, Lee. Lorenzo de' Medici: Florence's Great Leader & Patron of the Arts. 2004. (Rulers, Scholars, & Artists of the Renaissance Ser.). (Illus.). 112p. (J). lib. bdg. 34.60 *(978-1-4042-0315-0(X))* Rosen Publishing Group, Inc., The.

Herold, Vickey. Discover the Renaissance in Italy. 2006. (J). pap. *(978-1-4108-6465-9(0))* Benchmark Education Co.

—The Renaissance in Italy. 2006. (J). pap. *(978-1-4108-6462-8(6))* Benchmark Education Co.

Hightower, Paul W. Galileo: Genius Astronomer. 2015. (Genius Scientists & Their Genius Ideas Ser.). 96p. (J). (gr. 5-12). 27.94 *(978-0-7660-6560-4(X))*; pap. 10.95 *(978-0-7660-6561-1(8))* Enslow Pubs., Inc.

Kalman, Bobbie. Spotlight on Italy. 2011. (Spotlight on My Country Ser.: No. 17). (ENG.). 32p. (J). (gr. k-3). pap. *(978-0-7787-3488-8(9))* Crabtree Publishing Co.

Kaplan, Sarah Pitt. Pompeii: City of Ashes. 2005. (High Interest Bks.). (ENG., Illus.). 48p. (J). (gr. 3-7). per. 6.95 *(978-0-516-25091-5(4))*, Children's Pr.) Scholastic Library Publishing.

Kenison, Misti, illus. The Tiny Traveler: Italy: A Book of Numbers. 2016. (ENG.). 24p. (J). (— 1). bds. 5.99 *(978-1-5107-0466-4(3))*, Sky Pony Pr.) Skyhorse Publishing Co., Inc.

Knight, Patricia. Mussolini & Fascism. 2003. (Questions & Analysis in History Ser.). (ENG., Illus.). 144p. (C). 115.00 *(978-0-415-27921-5(6))*, 0415279216); per. 30.95 *(978-0-415-27922-2(4))* Routledge.

Kulling, Monica. Making Contact! Marconi Goes Wireless. 2016. (Great Idea Ser.). (ENG., Illus.). 32p. (J). (gr. k-3). pap. 6.99 *(978-1-101-91842-5(X))*, Tundra Bks.) Tundra Bks. CAN. Dist: Penguin Random Hse. LLC.

—Making Contact! Marconi Goes Wireless. Rudnicki, Richard, illus. 2013. (Great Idea Ser.). (ENG.). 32p. (J). (gr. k-3). 17.95 *(978-1-77049-378-0(6))*, Tundra Bks.) Tundra Bks. CAN. Dist: Penguin Random Hse. LLC.

Lin, Yoming S. Galileo & the Telescope. 2012. (Eureka! Ser.). (Illus.). 24p. (J). (gr. 3-6). lib. bdg. 22.60 *(978-1-4488-5030-3(4))* Rosen Publishing Group, Inc., The.

Lindeen, Mary. Ashes to Ashes: Uncovering Pompeii. 2007. (Shockwave: People & Communities Ser.). (ENG., Illus.). 36p. (J). (gr. 3-5). 25.00 *(978-0-531-17745-7(9))*, Children's Pr.) Scholastic Library Publishing.

Markovics, Joyce L. Italy. 2017. (Countries We Come From Ser.). (ENG., Illus.). 32p. (J). (gr. -1-3). 19.95 *(978-1-68402-058-4(1))* Bearport Publishing Co., Inc.

Mincieli, Rose Laura & Ross, Rose Laura. Tales Merry & Wise. Werth, Kurt, illus. 2011. 130p. 40.95 *(978-1-258-09714-1(1))* Literary Licensing, LLC.

Murray, Lorraine, ed. Italy. 2013. (Britannica Guide to Countries of the European Union Ser.). (ENG., Illus.). 320p. (YA). (gr. 9-12). lib. bdg. 53.00 *(978-1-61530-966-5(7))* Rosen Publishing Group, Inc., The.

Obregón, José María. Italy: Italia. Benson, Megan, tr. 2009. (Great National Soccer Teams / Grandes Selecciones Del Fútbol Mundial Ser.). (SPA & ENG., Illus.). 24p. (J). (gr. 2-5). lib. bdg. 22.60 *(978-1-4042-8086-1(3))*, PowerKids Pr.) Rosen Publishing Group, Inc., The.

Parker, Lewis K. Why Italian Immigrants Came to America. 2009. (Coming to America Ser.). 24p. (gr. 2-3). 42.50 *(978-1-61511-885-4(3))*, PowerKids Pr.) Rosen Publishing Group, Inc., The.

Perkins, Chloe. Living in ... Italy. Silva, Reg & Woolley, Tom, illus. 2016. (Living In... Ser.). (ENG.). 32p. (J). (gr. k-2). pap. 3.99 *(978-1-4814-5200-7(2))* Simon & Schuster Children's Publishing.

Potter, Giselle. The Year I Didn't Go to School. Potter, Giselle, illus. 2015. (ENG., Illus.). 40p. (J). (gr. -1-3). 13.99 *(978-1-4814-7995-0(4))*, Atheneum Bks. for Young Readers) Simon & Schuster Children's Publishing.

Rinaldo, Denise. Julius Caesar. rev. ed. 2015. (Wicked History Ser.). (ENG., Illus.). 144p. (J). lib. bdg. 33.00 *(978-0-531-22123-5(7))*, Children's Pr.) Scholastic Library Publishing.

Roberts, Russell. Mt. Vesuvius & the Destruction of Pompei, A. D. 79. 2005. (Natural Disasters Ser.). (Illus.). 32p. (J). (gr. 1-4). lib. bdg. 25.70 *(978-1-58415-419-8(5))* Mitchell Lane Pubs., Inc.

Roberts, Steven. John Cabot. 2013. (Jr. Graphic Famous Explorers Ser.). (ENG., Illus.). 24p. (J). (gr. 3-6). pap. 10.60 *(978-1-4777-0129-4(X))*; lib. bdg. 25.25 *(978-1-4777-0072-3(2))* Rosen Publishing Group, Inc., The. (PowerKids Pr.).

Robinson, Joanna J. Italy. 2015. (One World, Many Countries Ser.). (ENG.). 32p. (J). (gr. 1-4). 28.50 *(978-1-63407-050-8(X))*, 208891) Child's World, Inc., The.

Sadek, Ademola O. & Indovino, Shaina C. Italy. Bruton, John, ed. 2012. (Major European Union Nations Ser.). 64p. (J). (gr. 7). 22.95 *(978-1-4222-2248-5(9))* Mason Crest.

Sadik, Ademola O. & Indovino, Shaina Carmel. Italy. 2012. (J). pap. *(978-1-4222-2279-9(9))* Mason Crest.

Schoell, William. Giuseppe Verdi & Italian Opera. 2007. (Classical Composers Ser.). (Illus.). 128p. (J). (gr. 3-7). lib. bdg. 27.95 *(978-1-59935-041-7(6))* Reynolds, Morgan Inc.

Sharpe, Paula A. Maria Montessori. Ward, Patricia R. & Pigford, Grady A., illus. 2010. 51p. (J). *(978-1-892142-47-4(3))* Cedar Tree Bks.

Tanaka, Shelley. The Buried City of Pompeii: What It Was Like When Vesuvius Exploded. Ruhl, Greg, illus. Christopher, Peter, photos by. 2003. 48p. (J). (gr. 4-9). reprint ed. 17.00 *(978-0-7567-6722-8(9))* DIANE Publishing Co.

Throp, Claire. Italy, 1 vol. 2011. (Countries Around the World Ser.). (ENG.). 48p. (J). (gr. 3-6). pap. 9.95 *(978-1-4329-5235-8(8))*, NA-h) Heinemann-Raintree.

Tieck, Sarah. Italy, 1 vol. 2013. (Explore the Countries Ser.). (ENG.). 40p. (J). (gr. 2-5). lib. bdg. 29.93 *(978-1-61783-814-9(4))*, Big Buddy Bks.) ABDO Publishing Co.

Venezia, Mike. Sandro Boticelli. Venezia, Mike, illus. rev. ed. 2016. (Getting to Know the World's Greatest Artists Ser.). (ENG., Illus.). 40p. (J). pap. 7.95 *(978-0-531-22086-3(9))*, Children's Pr.) Scholastic Library Publishing.

Wallace, Susan Helen. Saint Gianna Beretta Molla: The Gift of Life. 2012. (ENG., Illus.). 101p. (J). pap. 7.95 *(978-0-8198-7182-4(6))* Pauline Bks. & Media.

Waxman, Laura Hamilton. Mysteries of Pompeii. 2017. (Ancient Mysteries Ser.). (ENG.). 32p. (J). (gr. 3-6). 27.99 ***(978-1-5124-4017-1(5))*** Lerner Publishing Group.

Weil, Ann. Italy in Our World. 2011. (Countries in Our World Ser.). 32p. (YA). (gr. 4-7). lib. bdg. 28.50 *(978-1-59920-389-8(8))* Black Rabbit Bks.

ITALY—HISTORY—FICTION

Avery, Ben & Zondervan Staff. Time Trap, 1 vol. Wong, Scott, illus. 2009. (Z Graphic Novels / TimeFlyz Ser.). (ENG.). 160p. (J). pap. 6.99 *(978-0-310-71366-1(8))* Zondervan.

Bolognese, Don. The Warhorse. Bolognese, Don, illus. 2010. (ENG., Illus.). 176p. (J). (gr. 5-9). pap. 9.99 *(978-1-4424-2942-0(9))*, Simon & Schuster Bks. For Young Readers) Simon & Schuster Bks. For Young Readers.

Castaldo, Nancy F. Pizza for the Queen. Potter, Melisande, illus. 2005. (ENG.). 32p. (J). (gr. -1-3). 16.95 *(978-0-8234-1865-7(0))* Holiday Hse., Inc.

Christopher, Nicholas. The True Adventures of Nicolo Zen: A Novel. 2015. (ENG.). 288p. (YA). (gr. 7). pap. 9.99 *(978-0-375-86492-6(X))*, Ember) Random Hse. Children's Bks.

Collins, Pat Lowery. Hidden Voices: The Orphan Musicians of Venice. 2009. (ENG., Illus.). 352p. (YA). (gr. 7). 17.99 *(978-0-7636-3917-4(6))* Candlewick Pr.

Duble, Kathleen Benner. Phantoms in the Snow. 2011. (ENG.). 240p. (J). (gr. 7-7). 17.99 *(978-0-545-19770-0(8))*, Scholastic Pr.) Scholastic, Inc.

Eco, Umberto. The Story of the Betrothed. Lorenzetti, Marco, illus. 2017. (Save the Story Ser.). (ENG.). 104p. (J). (gr. 3-7). 19.95 *(978-1-78269-022-1(0))*, Pushkin Press) Steerforth Pr.

Fern, Tracey E. Pippo the Fool. Estrada, Pau, illus. 2011. (ENG.). 48p. (J). (gr. k-3). pap. 7.95 *(978-1-57091-793-6(0))* Charlesbridge Publishing, Inc.

Flavin, Teresa. The Blackhope Enigma. 2011. (ENG., Illus.). 304p. (J). (gr. 4-7). 15.99 *(978-0-7636-5694-2(1))*, Templar) Candlewick Pr.

Fletcher, Susan. Falcon in the Glass. (ENG., Illus.). (J). (gr. 5-9). 2014. 336p. pap. 9.99 *(978-1-4424-2991-8(7))* 2013. 320p. 16.99 *(978-1-4424-2990-1(9))* McElderry, Margaret K. Bks. (McElderry, Margaret K. Bks.).

Gregory, Philippa. Stormbringers. van Deelen, Fred, illus. 2013. (Order of Darkness Ser.: 2). (ENG.). 336p. (YA). (gr. 9). pap. 9.99 *(978-1-4424-7688-2(5))*; 17.99 *(978-1-4424-7687-5(7))* Simon Pulse. (Simon Pulse).

Hawes, Louise & Sharratt, Mary. The Vanishing Point. 2007. (ENG.). 240p. (J). (gr. 5-7). pap. 15.95 *(978-0-618-74788-7(5))* Houghton Mifflin Harcourt Publishing Co.

Hemphill, Stephanie. Sisters of Glass. 2013. (ENG.). 160p. (YA). (gr. 7). pap. 7.99 *(978-0-307-98141-7(X))*, Ember) Random Hse. Children's Bks.

Hoffman, Mary. The Falconer's Knot: A Story of Friars, Flirtation & Foul Play. 2007. (ENG., Illus.). 304p. (YA). (gr. 7-18). 16.95 *(978-1-59990-056-8(4))*, 9781599900568, Bloomsbury USA Childrens) Bloomsbury Publishing USA.

Konigsburg, E. L. The Second Mrs. Giaconda. 3rd ed. (J). pap. 4.95 *(978-0-13-800061-5(1))* Prentice Hall (Schl. Div.).

Lawrence, Caroline. The Pirates of Pompeii. 2004. (Roman Mysteries Ser.). (Illus.). 159p. (J). (gr. 3-7). 13.65 *(978-0-7569-5938-8(1))* Perfection Learning Corp.

Lovric, Michelle. The Undrowned Child. 2012. (ENG.). 464p. (J). (gr. 5). 7.99 *(978-0-375-86597-8(7))*, Yearling) Random Hse. Children's Bks.

Marsden, Carolyn. Take Me with You. 2010. (ENG., Illus.). 176p. (J). (gr. 5-18). 14.99 *(978-0-7636-3739-2(4))* Candlewick Pr.

Meyer, Carolyn. Duchessina: A Novel of Catherine de' Medici. 2009. (Young Royals Ser.). (ENG., Illus.). 272p. (J). (gr. 9). pap. 8.99 *(978-0-15-206620-8(9))* Houghton Mifflin Harcourt Publishing Co.

Napoli, Donna Jo. Daughter of Venice. 2003. (ENG.). 288p. (YA). (gr. 7). mass mkt. 7.99 *(978-0-440-22928-5(6))*, Laurel Leaf) Random Hse. Children's Bks.

—Fire in the Hills. 2008. (ENG.). 240p. (YA). (gr. 7-18). 7.99 *(978-0-14-241200-8(7))*, Speak) Penguin Young Readers Group.

—The Wager. 2010. (ENG.). 272p. (YA). (gr. 7-12). 16.99 *(978-0-8050-8781-9(8))*, 9780805087819, Holt, Henry & Co. Bks. For Young Readers) Holt, Henry & Co.

Nobisso, Josephine. Francis Woke up Early. Hyde, Maureen, illus. 2011. (ENG.). 32p. (J). (gr. k-2). 17.95 *(978-0-940112-20-9(5))*; pap. 9.95 *(978-0-940112-22-3(1))* Gingerbread Hse.

O'Dell, Scott. The Road to Damietta. 2004. (ENG.). 320p. (YA). (gr. 7). pap. 17.99 *(978-0-618-49493-4(6))* Houghton Mifflin Harcourt Publishing Co.

Osborne, Mary Pope. Monday with a Mad Genius. 2009. (Magic Tree House Merlin Missions Ser.: 10). lib. bdg. 16.00 *(978-0-606-01777-0(1))*, Turtleback) Turtleback Bks.

Osborne, Mary Pope, et al. Carnaval a Media Luz. Murdocca, Sal, illus. 2016. (SPA.). (J). (gr. 2-4). pap. 5.99 ***(978-1-63245-643-4(5))*** Lectorum Pubns., Inc.

Shecter, Vicky Alvear. Curses & Smoke: A Novel of Pompeii. 2014. (ENG.). 336p. (J). (gr. 7). 17.99 *(978-0-545-50993-0(9))*, Levine, Arthur A. Bks.) Scholastic, Inc.

Shefelman, Janice Jordan. Anna Maria's Gift. Papp, Robert, illus. 2011. (Stepping Stone Book Ser.). (ENG.). 112p. (J). (gr. 2-5). pap. 4.99 *(978-0-375-85882-6(2))*, Random Hse. Bks. for Young Readers) Random Hse. Children's Bks.

Tak, Bibi Dumon & Dumon Tak, Bibi. Soldier Bear. Hopman, Philip, illus. 2011. (ENG.). 158p. (J). 13.00 *(978-0-8028-5375-2(7))*, Eerdmans Bks For Young Readers) Eerdmans, William B. Publishing Co.

ITALY—POLITICS AND GOVERNMENT

Darraj, Susan Muaddi. Silvio Berlusconi: Prime Minister of Italy. Schlesinger, Arthur M., Jr., ed. 2005. (Major World Leaders Ser.). (Illus.). 112p. (J). (gr. 6-12). 30.00 *(978-0-7910-8260-7(1))*, Chelsea Hse.) Facts On File, Inc.

Gagne, Tammy. The Evolution of Government & Politics in Italy. 2014. (gr. 4-8). 29.95 *(978-1-61228-586-3(4))* Mitchell Lane Pubs., Inc.

ITALY—SOCIAL LIFE AND CUSTOMS

Bisignano, Alphonse. Cooking the Italian Way. 2nd rev. exp. ed. 2003. (Easy Menu Ethnic Cookbooks). (Illus.). 72p. (J). (gr. 5-12). pap. 7.95 *(978-0-8225-4161-5(0))* Lerner Publishing Group.

Centore, Michael. Italy, Vol. 12. 2015. (Major Nations in a Global World: Tradition, Culture, & Daily Life Ser.). (Illus.). 64p. (J). (gr. 7). 23.95 *(978-1-4222-3346-7(4))* Mason Crest.

Challen, Paul. The Culture & Crafts of Italy. 2015. (Cultural Crafts Ser.). (ENG., Illus.). 32p. (J). (gr. 4-6). pap. 11.75 *(978-1-4994-1123-2(5))*, 1391365, PowerKids Pr.) Rosen Publishing Group, Inc., The.

Elgin, Kathy. Italy. 2008. (Costume Around the World Ser.). (Illus.). 32p. (gr. 4-6). 28.00 *(978-0-7910-9769-4(2))*, Chelsea Clubhouse) Facts On File, Inc.

Hammond, Paula. Italy & Switzerland. 2004. (Cultures & Costumes Ser.). (Illus.). 64p. (YA). (gr. 7-18). lib. bdg. 19.95 *(978-1-59084-438-0(6))* Mason Crest.

Hardyman, Robyn. Celebrate: Italy. 2009. (Celebrate Country Ser.). 32p. (gr. 4-6). 28.00 *(978-1-60413-269-4(8))*, Chelsea Clubhouse) Facts On File, Inc.

Manning, Jack. Christmas in Italy, 1 vol. 2013. (Christmas Around the World Ser.). (ENG.). 24p. (gr. 1-2). 25.32 *(978-1-4765-3100-7(5))*, First Facts) Capstone Press of Coughlan Cos.

Matthew, John. Foods of Italy. 2011. (Culture in the Kitchen Ser.). 24p. (J). (gr. 2-5). pap. 8.15 *(978-1-4339-5712-3(4))*; lib. bdg. 22.60 *(978-1-4339-5710-9(8))* Stevens, Gareth Publishing LLLP. (Gareth Stevens Learning Library).

Mehta-Jones, Shilpa. Life in Ancient Rome. 2004. (Peoples of the Ancient World Ser.). (ENG., Illus.). 32p. (J). pap. *(978-0-7787-2064-5(0))*; lib. bdg. *(978-0-7787-2034-8(9))* Crabtree Publishing Co.

Morganelli, Adrianna. Cultural Traditions in Italy. 2016. (ENG., Illus.). 32p. (J). *(978-0-7787-8087-8(2))* Crabtree Publishing Co.

Parks, Peggy J. Growing up in Italy. 2017. (ENG.). 80p. (YA). (gr. 5-12). ***(978-1-68282-217-3(6))*** ReferencePoint Pr., Inc.

Roholt, Christine VeLure. Foods of Italy. 2014. (Cook with Me Ser.). (ENG.). 24p. (J). (gr. 3-7). lib. bdg. 25.95 *(978-1-62617-119-0(X))*, Express Bks.) Bellwether Media.

Roscoe, Kelly. The Italian & Northern Renaissance. 2017. (Power & Religion in Medieval & Renaissance Times Ser.). 112p. (gr. 14-15). 36.25 ***(978-1-68048-627-8(6))***, Britannica Educational Publishing) Rosen Publishing Group, Inc., The.

Rossi, Sophia. Buon Natale: Learning Songs & Traditions in Italian. Kelleher, Kathie, illus. 2007. (Teach Me Ser.). (ITA & SPA.). 32p. (J). (gr. -1-3). 19.95 *(978-1-59972-067-8(1))* Teach Me Tapes, Inc.

Sexton, Colleen & Simmons, Walter. Italy. 2010. (Exploring Countries Ser.). (ENG., Illus.). 32p. (J). (gr. 3-7). lib. bdg. 26.95 *(978-1-60014-485-1(3))*, Blastoff! Readers) Bellwether Media.

IVAN IV, CZAR OF RUSSIA, 1530-1584

Nagelhout, Ryan. Ivan the Terrible. 2016. (History's Most Murderous Villains Ser.). (Illus.). 32p. (J). (gr. 5-4). pap. 10.50 *(978-1-4824-4794-1(0))* Stevens, Gareth Publishing LLLP.

Price, Sean. Ivan the Terrible: Tsar of Death. 2008. (Wicked History Ser.). (ENG.). 128p. (J). (gr. 6-18). pap. 5.95 *(978-0-531-20500-6(2))*, Watts, Franklin); (Illus.). (gr. 3-7). 31.00 *(978-0-531-12597-7(1))*, Children's Pr.) Scholastic Library Publishing.

IVORY COAST

see Cote d'Ivoire

IWO JIMA, BATTLE OF, JAPAN, 1945

Bradley, James & Powers, Ron. Flags of Our Fathers: A Young People's Edition. 2005. (ENG., Illus.). 224p. (YA). (gr. 4-7). mass mkt. 7.99 *(978-0-440-22920-9(0))*, Laurel Leaf) Random Hse. Children's Bks.

—Flags of Our Fathers: Heroes of Iwo Jima. 2003. (ENG., Illus.). 232p. (YA). (gr. 4-7). reprint ed. pap. 8.99 *(978-0-385-73064-8(0))*, Delacorte Bks. for Young Readers) Random Hse. Children's Bks.

Burgan, Michael. Raising the Flag: How a Photograph Gave a Nation Hope in Wartime, 1 vol. 2011. (Captured History Ser.). (ENG.). 64p. (gr. 5-7). pap. 9.10 *(978-0-7565-4449-2(1))*; lib. bdg. 34.65 *(978-0-7565-4395-2(9))* Compass Point Bks. (CPB Grades 4-8).

Hama, Larry. The Battle of Iwo Jima: Guerilla Warfare in the Pacific. 2008. (Graphic Battles of World War II Ser.). (ENG., Illus.). 48p. (gr. 5-8). pap. 14.05 *(978-1-4042-6030-6(7))* Rosen Publishing Group, Inc., The.

—The Battle of Iwo Jima: Guerilla Warfare in the Pacific. Williams, Anthony, illus. 2007. (Graphic Battles of World War II Ser.). (ENG.). 48p. (YA). (gr. 4-7). lib. bdg. 31.95 *(978-1-4042-0781-3(3))* Rosen Publishing Group, Inc., The.

—The Battle of Iwo Jima: Guerrilla Warfare in the Pacific. 2009. (Graphic Battles of World War II Ser.). (ENG., Illus.). 48p. (YA). (gr. 5-5). 58.50 *(978-1-61512-821-1(2)*, Rosen Reference) Rosen Publishing Group, Inc., The.
Nelson, S. D. Quiet Hero: The Ira Hayes Story. 2006. (ENG., Illus.). 32p. (J). 16.95 *(978-1-58430-263-6(1))* Lee & Low Bks., Inc.

J

JACKSON, ANDREW, 1767-1845
Behrman, Carol H. Andrew Jackson. 2004. (History Maker Biographies Ser.). (ENG., Illus.). 48p. (gr. 3-6). 27.93 *(978-0-8225-1543-2(1))* Lerner Publishing Group.
Byers, Ann. The Trail of Tears: A Primary Source History of the Forced Relocation of the Cherokee Nation. (Primary Sources in American History Ser.). 64p. (gr. 5-8). 2009. 58.50 *(978-1-60851-504-2(4))* 2004. (Illus.). (J). lib. bdg. 31.95 *(978-0-8239-4007-3(1)*, Rosen Reference) Rosen Publishing Group, Inc., The.
Frost, J. Old Hickory. reprint ed. 150.00 *(978-0-7222-8720-0(8))* Library Reprints, Inc.
Gregory, Josh. Andrew Jackson: The 7th President. 2015. (First Look at America's Presidents Ser.). (ENG.). 24p. (J). (gr. -1-3). lib. bdg. 23.93 *(978-1-62724-556-2(1))* Bearport Publishing Co., Inc.
Gunderson, Megan M. Andrew Jackson, 1 vol. (ENG., Illus.). 40p. 2016. (J). *(978-1-68078-101-4(4))* 2009. (YA). (gr. 3-6). 27.07 *(978-1-60453-459-7(1))* ABDO Publishing Co.
Harmon, Daniel E. Andrew Jackson. 2004. (Childhoods of the Presidents Ser.). (Illus.). 48p. (J). (gr. 4-18). lib. bdg. 17.95 *(978-1-59084-274-4(X))* Mason Crest.
Hollar, Sherman, contrib. by. Andrew Jackson. 2012. (Pivotal Presidents: Profiles in Leadership Ser.). (ENG., Illus.). 80p. (gr. 7-12). (J). lib. bdg. 32.90 *(978-1-61530-941-2(1))*; (YA). 65.80 *(978-1-61530-954-2(3))* Rosen Publishing Group, Inc., The.
Hunsicker, Jennifer. Young Andrew Jackson in the Carolinas: A Revolutionary Boy. 2014. Orig. Title: Young Andrew Jackson in the Carolinas: a Revolutionary Boy. (ENG., Illus.). 160p. (J). (gr. 4-7). pap. 12.99 *(978-1-62619-359-8(2)*, History Pr., The) Arcadia Publishing.
Marsh, Carole. Andrew Jackson. 2003. 12p. (gr. k-4). 2.95 *(978-0-635-02360-5(1))* Gallopade International.
Marsico, Katie. Andrew Jackson. 2010. (Presidents & Their Times 4 Ser.). 96p. (gr. 6). 34.21 *(978-0-7614-4813-6(6))* Marshall Cavendish GBR. Dist: Marshall Cavendish Corp.
Mis, Melody S. How to Draw the Life & Times of Andrew Jackson. (Kid's Guide to Drawing the Presidents of the United States of America Ser.). 2009. 32p. (gr. 4-4). 50.50 *(978-1-61511-131-2(X)*, PowerKids Pr.) 2006. (YA). (gr. 2-5). 26.50 *(978-1-4042-2984-6(1))* Rosen Publishing Group, Inc., The.
Rausch, Monica. Andrew Jackson. 2007. (Grandes personajes (Spanish- Great Americans) Ser.). 24p. (gr. 1-4). (ENG & SPA.). pap. 8.15 *(978-0-8368-7989-6(9))*; (Illus.). pap. 8.15 *(978-0-8368-7690-1(3))*; (Illus.). lib. bdg. 22.00 *(978-0-8368-7683-3(0))* Stevens, Gareth Publishing LLLP. (Weekly Reader Leveled Readers).
Rausch, Monica L. Andrew Jackson. 2007. (Grandes personajes (Great Americans) Ser.). (ENG & SPA., Illus.). 24p. (gr. 1-4). lib. bdg. 22.00 *(978-0-8368-7982-7(1)*, Weekly Reader Leveled Readers) Stevens, Gareth Publishing LLLP.
Rissman, Rebecca. Andrew Jackson. 2017. (Premier Presidents Ser.). (ENG.). 24p. (J). (gr. 1-4). lib. bdg. 27.07 *(978-1-5038-1643-5(5)*, 211486) Child's World, Inc., The.
Stanley, George Edward. Andrew Jackson: Young Patriot. Henderson, Meryl, illus. 2003. (Childhood of Famous Americans Ser.). (ENG.). 192p. (J). (gr. 3-7). pap. 6.99 *(978-0-689-85744-7(6)*, Simon & Schuster/Paula Wiseman Bks.) Simon & Schuster/Paula Wiseman Bks.
Venezia, Mike. Andrew Jackson. Venezia, Mike, illus. 2005. (Getting to Know the U. S. Presidents Ser.). (ENG., Illus.). 32p. (J). (gr. 3-4). 28.00 *(978-0-516-22612-5(6)*, Children's Pr.) Scholastic Library Publishing.
—Andrew Jackson: Seventh President, 1829-1837. Venezia, Mike, illus. 2005. (Getting to Know the U. S. Presidents Ser.). (ENG., Illus.). 32p. (J). (gr. 3-4). per. 7.95 *(978-0-516-27481-2(3)*, Children's Pr.) Scholastic Library Publishing.
Whitelaw, Nancy. Andrew Jackson: Frontier President. 2004. (Notable Americans Ser.). (Illus.). 128p. (J). (gr. 6-12). 23.95 *(978-1-883846-67-1(6)*, First Biographies) Reynolds, Morgan Inc.
Wilson, Steve. Andrew Jackson's Presidency: Democracy in Action. 2016. (Spotlight on American History Ser.). (Illus.). 24p. (J). (gr. 6-4). 26.25 *(978-1-5081-4938-5(0)*, PowerKids Pr.) Rosen Publishing Group, Inc., The.
Yacka, Douglas. Who Was Andrew Jackson? Murray, Jake, illus. 2017. (Who Was? Ser.). (ENG.). 112p. (J). (gr. 3-7). 5.99 ***(978-0-399-53990-9(5))***; lib. bdg. 15.99 ***(978-0-399-53992-3(1))*** Penguin Young Readers Group. (Penguin Workshop).
Yomtov, Nel. Andrew Jackson: Heroic Leader or Cold-Hearted Ruler?, 1 vol. 2013. (Perspectives on History Ser.). (ENG.). 32p. (gr. 3-4). 27.32 *(978-1-4765-0245-8(5))*; pap. 7.95 *(978-1-4765-3409-1(8))* Capstone Press of Coughlan Cos. (Fact Finders).
Zuchora-Walske, Christine. Andrew Jackson's Presidency. 2016. (Presidential Powerhouses Ser.). (ENG., Illus.). 104p. (J). (gr. 6-12). 35.99 *(978-1-4677-7926-5(1))*; 53.32 *(978-1-4677-8548-8(2))* Lerner Publishing Group. (Lerner Pubns.).

JACKSON, JESSE, 1941-
Linde, Barbara M. Jesse Jackson. 2011. (Civil Rights Crusaders Ser.). 24p. (gr. 2-5). (J). pap. 8.15 *(978-1-4339-5684-3(5)*, Gareth Stevens Learning Library); (YA). lib. bdg. 22.60 *(978-1-4339-5682-9(9))* Stevens, Gareth Publishing LLLP.
Mis, Melody S. Meet Jesse Jackson. (Civil Rights Leaders Ser.). 24p. (gr. 2-3). 2009. 42.50 *(978-1-61511-852-6(7)*, PowerKids Pr.) 2008. (Illus.). (YA). lib. bdg. 22.60 *(978-1-4042-4212-8(0))* Rosen Publishing Group, Inc., The.
Woog, Dan. Jesse Jackson. 2003. (People in the News Ser.). (ENG., Illus.). 118p. (YA). (gr. 6-9). 33.45 *(978-1-56006-631-6(8)*, Lucent Bks.) Cengage Gale.

JACKSON, MAHALIA, 1911-1972
Dunham, Montrew. Mahalia Jackson: Gospel Singer & Civil Rights Champion, 7 vols. Underdown, Harold D., ed. Morrison, Cathy, illus. 3rd rev. ed. 2003. (Young Patriots Ser.: 7). (ENG.). 120p. (J). (gr. 4-7). pap. 9.95 *(978-1-882859-39-9(1))*; 15.95 *(978-1-882859-38-2(3))* Patria Pr., Inc.
Kramer, Barbara. Mahalia Jackson: The Voice of Gospel & Civil Rights. 2003. (African-American Biographies Ser.). (Illus.). 128p. (J). lib. bdg. 26.60 *(978-0-7660-2115-0(7))* Enslow Pubs., Inc.
Nolan, Nina. Mahalia Jackson: Walking with Kings & Queens. Holyfield, John, illus. 2015. (ENG.). 32p. (J). (gr. -1-3). 17.99 *(978-0-06-087944-0(0))* HarperCollins Pubs.
Pinkney, Andrea Davis. Martin & Mahalia: His Words, Her Song. 2013. (ENG., Illus.). 40p. (J). (gr. 1-17). 18.99 *(978-0-316-07013-3(0))* Little Brown & Co.

JACKSON, STONEWALL, 1824-1863
Brager, Bruce L. There He Stands: The Story of Stonewall Jackson. 2005. (Civil War Leaders Ser.). (Illus.). 176p. (J). (gr. 6-12). 26.95 *(978-1-931798-44-0(3))* Reynolds, Morgan Inc.
Hale, Sarah Elder, ed. Stonewall Jackson: Spirit of the South. 2005. (ENG., Illus.). 48p. (J). (gr. 3-9). 17.95 *(978-0-8126-7907-6(5))* Cobblestone Publishing Co.
Koestler-Grack, Rachel A. Stonewall Jackson. 2009. (Leaders of the Civil War Era Ser.). (Illus.). 136p. (gr. 6-12). 35.00 *(978-1-60413-299-1(X)*, Chelsea Hse.) Facts On File, Inc.
McLeese, Don. Stonewall Jackson. 2005. (Civil War Military Leaders Ser.). (Illus.). 32p. (J). (gr. 3-6). lib. bdg. 19.95 *(978-1-59515-477-4(9))* Rourke Educational Media.
Pflueger, Lynda. Stonewall Jackson: General of the Confederate Army. 2015. (J). *(978-0-7660-6495-9(6))* Enslow Pubs., Inc.
Power, J. Tracey. Stonewall Jackson: Hero of the Confederacy. 2009. (Library of American Lives & Times Ser.). 112p. (gr. 5-5). 69.20 *(978-1-60853-507-1(X))* Rosen Publishing Group, Inc., The.

JACKSON, STONEWALL, 1824-1863—FICTION
Altsheler, Joseph A. The Scouts of Stonewall: The Story of the Great Valley Campaign. 2006. (Civil War Ser.: Vol. 3). 312p. (J). reprint ed. 29.95 *(978-1-4218-1779-8(9))*; pap. 14.95 *(978-1-4218-1879-5(5))* 1st World Publishing, Inc. (1st World Library - Literary Society).
—The Scouts of Stonewall: The Story of the Great Valley Campaign. l.t. ed. (Civil War Ser.: Vol. 3). (J). reprint ed. 2007. (ENG.). 240p. pap. 22.99 *(978-1-4264-1531-9(1))* 2011. 370p. (gr. 4-7). pap. 32.75 *(978-1-245-65787-7(9))* 2008. 244p. 27.99 *(978-0-554-22030-7(X))* 2008. 244p. 24.99 *(978-0-554-31333-7(2))* 2006. 250p. pap. 20.99 *(978-1-4264-1498-5(6))* Creative Media Partners, LLC.
—The Scouts of Stonewall: The Story of the Great Valley Campaign. 2006. (Civil War Ser.: Vol. 3). (J). reprint ed. pap. *(978-1-4065-0820-8(9))* Dodo Pr.
—The Scouts of Stonewall: The Story of the Great Valley Campaign. 2007. (Civil War Ser.: Vol. 3). 184p. (J). reprint ed. per. *(978-1-4068-1684-6(1))* Echo Library.
—The Scouts of Stonewall: The Story of the Great Valley Campaign. 2010. (Civil War Ser.: Vol. 3). (Illus.). 166p. (J). (gr. 4-7). reprint ed. pap. 19.99 *(978-1-153-72009-0(4))* General Bks. LLC.
—The Scouts of Stonewall: The Story of the Great Valley Campaign. reprint ed. 2010. (Civil War Ser.: Vol. 3). 252p. (J). (gr. 4-7). 33.56 *(978-1-169-30265-5(3))* 2010. (Civil War Ser.: Vol. 3). 252p. (J). (gr. 4-7). pap. 21.56 *(978-1-162-70768-6(2))* 2010. (Civil War Ser.: Vol. 3). 252p. (J). 41.95 *(978-1-161-47632-3(6))* 2004. pap. 26.95 *(978-1-4191-8162-7(9))* 2004. (Civil War Ser.: Vol. 3). (J). pap. 1.99 *(978-1-4192-8162-4(3))* Kessinger Publishing, LLC.
—The Scouts of Stonewall: The Story of the Great Valley Campaign. 2011. (Civil War Ser.: Vol. 3). 278p. (J). (gr. 4-7). reprint ed. pap. *(978-3-8424-6100-0(3))* Tredition GmbH.

JACKSON, THOMAS JONATHAN, 1824-1863
see Jackson, Stonewall, 1824-1863

JACOB (BIBLICAL PATRIARCH)
Hoak, Benjamin T. Jacob. (Money at its Best: Millionaires of the Old Testament Ser.). 112p. (YA). (gr. 7-12). 2009. 24.95 *(978-1-4222-0470-2(7))* 2007. pap. 14.95 *(978-1-4222-0845-8(1))* Mason Crest.
Larsen, Carolyn. Abraham, Isaac, & Jacob. 2012. (Standard Bible Storybook Ser.). (ENG., Illus.). 32p. (J). 7.99 *(978-0-7847-3563-3(8))* Standard Publishing.
Nakhat, Shamim. The Story of Yaqub & Yusuf: Based on Qur'anic Facts. 2005. (Me & My Holy Qur'an Ser.). (Illus.). 24p. (J). *(978-81-7231-618-1(6))* Islamic Bk. Service.
Racklin-Siegel, Alison, illus. Jacob's Travels. 2005. (ENG & HEB.). 32p. (J). per. 10.95 *(978-0-939144-53-2(0))* EKS Publishing Co.

JAGUAR
Archer, Claire. Jaguars, 1 vol. 2014. (Big Cats Ser.). (ENG.). 24p. (J). (gr. 4-8). lib. bdg. 28.50 *(978-1-62970-002-1(9))* ABDO Publishing Co.
Archer, Claire, et al. Jaguares. 2015. (Grandes Felinos Ser.). (SPA., Illus.). 24p. (gr. k-1). pap. 7.95 *(978-1-4966-0459-0(8))* Capstone Classroom.
Arnold, Quinn M. Jaguars. (Seedlings Ser.). 24p. (J). (gr. k-2). 2017. (ENG.). pap. 7.99 *(978-1-62832-334-4(5)*, Creative Paperbacks) 2016. (Illus.). *(978-1-60818-738-6(1)*, Creative Education) Creative Co., The.
Bodden, Valerie. Amazing Animals: Jaguars. 2013. (Amazing Animals Ser.). (ENG.). 24p. (J). (gr. 1-3). pap. 8.99 *(978-0-89812-788-1(2)*, Creative Paperbacks) Creative Co., The.
—Jaguars. 2013. (Illus.). 24p. (J). 25.65 *(978-1-60818-086-8(7)*, Creative Education) Creative Co., The.
Diemer, Lauren. Jaguars. 2014. (J). pap. *(978-1-4896-0919-9(9))* Weigl Pubs., Inc.
Feinstein, Stephen. The Jaguar: Help Save This Endangered Species! 2008. (Saving Endangered Species Ser.). (Illus.). 128p. (J). (gr. 3-7). lib. bdg. 34.60 *(978-1-59845-065-1(4)*, MyReportLinks.com Bks.) Enslow Pubs., Inc.
Franchino, Vicky. Jaguars. 2013. (ENG.). 48p. (J). 28.00 *(978-0-531-23360-3(X))*; pap. 6.95 *(978-0-531-25158-4(6))* Scholastic Library Publishing.
Gagne, Tammy. Jaguars, 1 vol. 2012. (Big Cats Ser.). (ENG.). 32p. (gr. 3-4). lib. bdg. 27.99 *(978-1-4296-7642-7(6)*, Edge Bks.) Capstone Press of Coughlan Cos.
Ganeri, Anita. Jaguar, 1 vol. 2010. (Day in the Life: Rain Forest Animals Ser.). (ENG., Illus.). 24p. (gr. k-2). 23.32 *(978-1-4329-4106-2(2))*; pap. 6.79 *(978-1-4329-4117-8(8))* Heinemann-Raintree. (Heinemann Read & Learn).
Gates, Margo. Jaguars. 2013. (Animal Safari Ser.). (ENG., Illus.). 24p. (J). (gr. k-3). lib. bdg. 25.95 *(978-1-60014-911-5(1)*, Blastoff! Readers) Bellwether Media.
Gish, Melissa. Jaguars. (Living Wild Ser.). (J). 2012. (ENG.). 48p. (gr. 4-7). pap. 12.00 *(978-0-89812-671-6(1)*, Creative Paperbacks) 2011. (Illus.). 46p. 35.65 *(978-1-60818-079-0(4)*, Creative Education) Creative Co., The.
Guidone, Julie. Jaguars. 2009. (Animals That Live in the Rain Forest Ser.). 24p. (J). (gr. -1-3). pap. 8.15 *(978-1-4339-0105-8(6))*; lib. bdg. 22.60 *(978-1-4339-0023-5(8))* Stevens, Gareth Publishing LLLP. (Weekly Reader Leveled Readers).
—Jaguars (Jaguares) 2009. (Animals That Live in the Rain Forest/Animales de la selva Ser.). (SPA & ENG.). 24p. (gr. -1-3). pap. 8.15 *(978-1-4339-0112-6(9))*; lib. bdg. 22.60 *(978-1-4339-0062-4(9))* Stevens, Gareth Publishing LLLP. (Weekly Reader Leveled Readers).
Guillain, Charlotte. Jaguars, 1 vol. 2014. (Living in the Wild: Big Cats Ser.). (ENG., Illus.). 48p. (gr. 3-6). lib. bdg. 33.32 *(978-1-4329-8106-8(4)*, Heinemann InfoSearch) Heinemann-Raintree.
Guillain, Charlotte, et al. Living in the Wild: Big Cats, 1 vol. 2014. (Living in the Wild: Big Cats Ser.). (ENG.). 48p. (gr. 3-6). lib. bdg. 199.92 *(978-1-4329-8111-2(0)*, Heinemann InfoSearch) Heinemann-Raintree.
Huntrods, David. Jaguars. 2006. (Amazing Animals Ser.). (Illus.). 24p. (J). (gr. 3-7). pap. 8.95 *(978-1-59036-398-0(1))*; lib. bdg. 24.45 *(978-1-59036-392-8(2))* Weigl Pubs., Inc.
Kenan, Tessa. Es un Jaguar! 2017. (Bumba Books (tm) en Español — Animales de la Selva Tropical (Rain Forest Animals) Ser.). (SPA., Illus.). 24p. (J). (gr. -1-1). pap. 6.99 ***(978-1-5124-5410-9(9))*** Lerner Publishing Group.
—It's a Jaguar! 2017. (Bumba Books (tm) — Rain Forest Animals Ser.). (ENG.). 24p. (J). (gr. -1-1). 12.99 ***(978-1-5124-3756-0(5)***, Lerner Pubns.); 38.65 ***(978-1-5124-2760-8(8)***, Lerner Pubns.); 38.65 ***(978-1-5124-3755-3(7)***, Lerner Pubns.); (Illus.). 25.32 *(978-1-5124-2571-0(0))* Lerner Publishing Group.
Lawrence, Ellen. Jaguar. 2017. (Apex Predators of the Amazon Rain Forest Ser.). (ENG., Illus.). 24p. (J). (gr. -1-3). 17.95 ***(978-1-68402-030-0(1))*** Bearport Publishing Co., Inc.
Luna, Tom. The Spots on the Jaguar: A Counting Book. Luna, Tom & Alvarez, Laura, illus. 2005. (SPA & ENG.). 20p. (J). *(978-0-9716580-4-2(8))* Lectura Bks.
Lynette, Rachel. Jaguars. 2013. (Jungle Babies of the Amazon Rain Forest Ser.). 24p. (J). (gr. -1-3). lib. bdg. 21.32 *(978-1-61772-755-9(5))* Bearport Publishing Co., Inc.
Macleod, Steve. Jaguar. 2011. (J). *(978-1-61690-758-7(4))*; pap. *(978-1-61690-851-5(3))* Weigl Pubs., Inc.
—Soy el Jaguar. 2012. (SPA.). (J). *(978-1-61913-177-4(3))* Weigl Pubs., Inc.
Marks, Jennifer L. Jaguars, 1 vol. 2010. (Wildcats Ser.). (ENG.). 24p. (gr. k-1). lib. bdg. 26.65 *(978-1-4296-4481-5(8)*, Pebble Plus) Capstone Press of Coughlan Cos.
Marsico, Katie. Jaguars. 2012. (21st Century Basic Skills Library: Baby Zoo Animals Ser.). (ENG.). 24p. (gr. k-3). 22.79 *(978-1-61080-454-7(6)*, 202064); pap. 12.79 *(978-1-61080-628-2(X)*, 202238) Cherry Lake Publishing.
Mezzanotte, Jim. The Story of Jaguar. 2005. (Classic Cars Ser.). (Illus.). 24p. (gr. 1-4). lib. bdg. 23.00 *(978-0-8368-4535-8(8)*, Gareth Stevens Learning Library) Stevens, Gareth Publishing LLLP.
Miller, Reagan & Johnson, Robin. Jaguar. 2010. (ENG., Illus.). 64p. (J). lib. bdg. *(978-0-7787-2143-7(4))* Crabtree Publishing Co.
Morgan, Elizabeth. Jaguar, 01 vols., 1. 2016. (North America's Biggest Beasts Ser.). (ENG., Illus.). 24p. (J). pap. 8.25 *(978-1-5081-4303-1(X)*, PowerKids Pr.) Rosen Publishing Group, Inc., The.
Murray, Julie. Jaguars, 1 vol. 2005. (Animal Kingdom Set Ii Ser.). (ENG., Illus.). 24p. (gr. k-4). 25.65 *(978-1-59197-322-5(8)*, Buddy Bks.) ABDO Publishing Co.
Otfinoski, Steven. Jaguars. 2010. (Animals Animals Ser.). 48p. (gr. 3-6). 23.95 *(978-0-7614-4839-6(X))* Marshall Cavendish Corp.
Ringstad, Arnold. Jaguars. 2014. (Illus.). 24p. (J). 27.10 *(978-1-60753-601-7(3))* Amicus Publishing.
Ryndak, Rob. Leopard or Jaguar? 2015. (Animal Look-Alikes Ser.). (ENG., Illus.). 24p. (J). (gr. 1-2). pap. 8.15 *(978-1-4824-2720-2(6))* Stevens, Gareth Publishing LLLP.
Schuh, Mari. Jaguars. 2014. (Illus.). 24p. (J). lib. bdg. 25.65 *(978-1-62031-111-0(9)*, Bullfrog Bks.) Jump! Inc.
Stacy, Lee. Jaguar. 2004. (Hot Cars Ser.). (Illus.). 32p. (gr. 4-8). lib. bdg. *(978-1-59515-211-4(3))* Rourke Educational Media.
Vail, Grace. Jaguars. 2012. (Killer Cats Ser.). (Illus.). 24p. (J). (gr. 2-5). pap. 8.15 *(978-1-4339-7004-7(X))*; lib. bdg. 22.60 *(978-1-4339-7003-0(1))* Stevens, Gareth Publishing LLLP.
Vogel, Elizabeth. Jaguars. 2009. (Big Cats (Powerkids Readers) Ser.). 24p. (gr. 1-1). 37.50 *(978-1-61511-568-6(4)*, PowerKids Pr.) Rosen Publishing Group, Inc., The.
Von Zumbusch, Amelie. Jaguars: World's Strongest Cats. 2007. (Dangerous Cats Ser.). (Illus.). 24p. (J). (gr. 3-7). lib. bdg. 22.60 *(978-1-4042-3628-8(7)*, PowerKids Pr.) Rosen Publishing Group, Inc., The.
von Zumbusch, Amelie. Jaguars: World's Strongest Cats. 2009. (Dangerous Cats Ser.). 24p. (gr. 2-3). 42.50 *(978-1-61512-127-4(7)*, PowerKids Pr.) Rosen Publishing Group, Inc., The.
Walker, Sally M. Jaguars. 2008. (Nature Watch Ser.). (ENG.). 48p. (gr. 4-8). 27.93 *(978-0-8225-7510-8(8)*, Lerner Pubns.) Lerner Publishing Group.
Williams, Zella. Jaguars & Other Latin American Wild Cats: Jaguares y Otros Felinos de Latino América. 2009. (Animals of Latin America / Animales de Latinoamérica Ser.). (SPA & ENG., Illus.). 24p. pap. 8.25 *(978-1-4358-3378-4(3))*; (J). (gr. 1-3). lib. bdg. 22.60 *(978-1-4042-8125-7(8))* Rosen Publishing Group, Inc., The. (PowerKids Pr.).
Woods, Theresa. Jaguars. 2015. (Animals of the Rain Forest Ser.). (ENG.). 24p. (J). (gr. 2-5). 27.07 *(978-1-63143-748-9(8)*, 208577) Child's World, Inc., The.

JAGUAR—FICTION
Albert, Burton. Journey of the Nightly Jaguar. Roth, Robert, illus. 2007. (ENG.). 32p. (J). (gr. k-3). 10.99 *(978-1-4169-7092-7(4)*, Simon & Schuster/Paula Wiseman Bks.) Simon & Schuster/Paula Wiseman Bks.
Ballantyne, Robert Michael. The Rover of the Andes: A Tale of Adventure in South America. 2007. (ENG.). 266p. pap. 21.99 *(978-1-4346-3753-6(0))*; 296p. pap. 23.99 *(978-1-4346-3767-3(0))* Creative Media Partners, LLC.
Cowcher, Helen. Jaguar. (CHI, ENG, URD, TUR & VIE., Illus.). 40p. 16.95 *(978-1-84059-009-8(2))* Milet Publishing.
—Jaguar. (J). (gr. 1-2). *(978-0-590-36037-1(X))*; (SPA., Illus.). pap. 3.96 net. *(978-0-590-87599-8(X)*, SO30738, Scholastic Pr.) Scholastic, Inc.
Driscoll, Laura. Where Is Baby Jaguar? Mangano, Tom & Miller, Victoria, illus. 2011. (Dora & Diego Ser.). (ENG.). 24p. (J). pap. 3.99 *(978-1-4424-1398-6(0)*, Simon Spotlight/Nickelodeon) Simon Spotlight/Nickelodeon.
Flor Ada, Alma. Eyes of the Jaguar. Davalos, Felipe, illus. 2004. (Puertas Al Sol / Gateways to the Sun Ser.). 48p. (gr. k-6). pap. 17.95 *(978-1-58105-970-0(1))* Santillana USA Publishing Co., Inc.
Gosse, Jim. Jimmy Jaguar: Collection of Stories. 2006. 17.00 *(978-0-8059-9373-8(8))* Dorrance Publishing Co., Inc.
Nickelodeon Staff & Nickelodeon / LeapFrog. Go Diego Go! Underwater Mystery. 2008. (J). 13.99 *(978-1-59319-925-8(2))* LeapFrog Enterprises, Inc.
Sargent, Pat L. The Jaguar, 8 vols. Lenoir, Jane, illus. 2007. (Barney the Bear Killer Ser.: 8). 164p. (YA). lib. bdg. 26.25 *(978-1-59381-424-3(0))* Ozark Publishing.

JAILS
see Prisons

JAM
Owings, Lisa. From Strawberry to Jam. 2015. (Start to Finish, Second Ser.). (ENG.). 24p. (J). (gr. k-3). pap. 6.95 *(978-1-4677-6110-9(9))*; lib. bdg. 23.93 *(978-1-4677-6022-5(6))* Lerner Publishing Group. (Lerner Pubns.).
Zemlicka, Shannon. From Fruit to Jelly. 2004. (Start to Finish Ser.). (J). pap. 5.95 *(978-0-8225-0748-2(X))*; (Illus.). 24p. 18.60 *(978-0-8225-0942-4(3)*, Lerner Pubns.) Lerner Publishing Group.

JAMAICA
Barraclough, John. Jamaica. (World Focus Ser.). (Illus.). 31p. (J). (gr. 3-7). pap. 3.99 *(978-0-431-07266-1(3))* Oxfam Publishing GBR. Dist: Stylus Publishing, LLC.
Bastrya, Judy. Living in Jamaica. 2006. (Living In- Ser.). (Illus.). 32p. (J). (gr. 4-7). lib. bdg. 27.10 *(978-1-59771-047-3(4))* Sea-To-Sea Pubns.
Bjorklund, Ruth. Jamaica. 2015. (ENG., Illus.). 144p. (J). lib. bdg. 40.00 *(978-0-531-21252-3(1)*, Orchard Bks.) Scholastic Library Publishing.
Capek, Michael. Jamaica. 2010. (Country Explorers Ser.). (ENG.). 48p. (gr. 2-4). (J). lib. bdg. 29.27 *(978-1-58013-604-4(4))*; pap. 9.95 *(978-0-7613-5545-8(6))* Lerner Publishing Group.
Carman, Lucy. Social Studies. 2014. (ENG.). 76p. tchr. ed., spiral bd. 33.00 *(978-0-7487-9976-3(1))* Oxford Univ. Pr., Inc.
Colleen Madonna Flood Williams. Jamaica, Vol. 11. Henderson, James D., ed. 2015. (Discovering the Caribbean: History, Politics, & Culture Ser.). (Illus.). 64p. (J). (gr. 7). lib. bdg. 22.95 *(978-1-4222-3313-9(8))* Mason Crest.
Crespi, Jess. Exploring Jamaica with the Five Themes of Geography. (Library of the Western Hemisphere Ser.). 24p. 2009. (gr. 4-4). 42.50 *(978-1-60853-927-7(X)*, PowerKids Pr.) 2005. (Illus.). (J). lib. bdg. 22.60 *(978-1-4042-2674-6(5)*, PowerKids Pr.) 2005. (ENG., Illus.). (gr. 3-8). pap. 8.25 *(978-0-8239-4634-1(7))* Rosen Publishing Group, Inc., The.
Gritzner, Janet H. Jamaica. 2004. (Modern World Nations Ser.). (Illus.). 144p. (gr. 6-12). 35.00 *(978-0-7910-7913-3(9)*, Chelsea Hse.) Facts On File, Inc.
Hamilton, Janice. Jamaica in Pictures. 2005. (Visual Geography Series, Second Ser.). (ENG., Illus.). 80p. (gr. 5-12). 31.93 *(978-0-8225-2394-9(9))* Lerner Publishing Group.
Harris, Devon & Cortés, Ricardo. Yes, I Can! The Story of the Jamaican Bobsled Team. 2008. (Illus.). *(978-0-9764082-5-3(2))* Waterhouse Publishing.
Heinrichs, Ann. Jamaica. 2003. (True Bks.). (ENG., Illus.). 48p. (J). (gr. 3-5). pap. 6.95 *(978-0-516-27751-6(0)*, Children's Pr.) Scholastic Library Publishing.
Horst, Heather A. & Garner, Andrew. Jamaican Americans. 2007. (New Immigrants Ser.). (Illus.). 144p. (gr. 6-12). lib. bdg. 30.00 *(978-0-7910-8790-9(5)*, Chelsea Hse.) Facts On File, Inc.
Irving, Barrington & Peppe, Holly. Touch the Sky. 2012. (J). *(978-0-531-22525-7(9))* Scholastic, Inc.
Kwek, Karen. Welcome to Jamaica. 2004. (Welcome to My Country Ser.). 48p. (gr. 2-5). lib. bdg. 27.00 *(978-0-8368-2564-0(0))* Stevens, Gareth Publishing LLLP.
Miller, Calvin Craig. Reggae Poet: The Story of Bob Marley. 2007. (Modern Music Masters Ser.). (Illus.). 128p. (YA). (gr. 9-18). lib. bdg. 27.95 *(978-1-59935-071-4(8))* Reynolds, Morgan Inc.
Morris, Kerry-Ann. Jamaica. 2003. (Countries of the World Ser.). (Illus.). 96p. (gr. 5-12). lib. bdg. 31.00 *(978-0-8368-2364-6(8))* Stevens, Gareth Publishing LLLP.
Owings, Lisa. Jamaica. 2014. (Exploring Countries Ser.). (ENG., Illus.). 32p. (J). (gr. 3-7). lib. bdg. 26.95 *(978-1-62617-067-4(3)*, Blastoff! Readers) Bellwether Media.
Peppas, Lynn. Cultural Traditions in Jamaica. 2015. (ENG., Illus.). 32p. (J). *(978-0-7787-8062-5(7))* Crabtree Publishing Co.
Rudolph, Jessica. Jamaica. 2016. (Countries We Come From Ser.). (ENG.). 32p. (J). (gr. -1-3). lib. bdg. 19.95 *(978-1-944102-72-2(8))* Bearport Publishing Co., Inc.
Savage, Jeff. Usain Bolt. 2012. (Amazing Athletes Ser.). (ENG., Illus.). 32p. (gr. 2-5). lib. bdg. 25.26 *(978-1-4677-1088-6(1)*, Lerner Pubns.) Lerner Publishing Group.

J K L

Sheehan, Sean. Jamaica. 2nd rev. ed. 2004. (Cultures of the World Ser.). (Illus.). 144p. (gr. 6). 42.79 *(978-0-7614-1785-9(0))* Marshall Cavendish Corp.
Sheehan, Sean, et al. Jamaica. 2015. (Cultures of the World Ser.). (ENG., Illus.). 144p. (J). (gr. 6-6). lib. bdg. 47.07 *(978-1-5026-0077-6(3))* Cavendish Square Publishing.
Stone, Vicky. Jamaica. 2008. (Countries of the World Ser.). (ENG., Illus.). 64p. (J). (gr. 5). lib. bdg. 27.90 *(978-1-4263-0300-5(9),* National Geographic Children's Bks.) National Geographic Society.
Sullivan, Laura L. Sir Henry Morgan. 2015. (J). lib. bdg. *(978-1-62713-308-1(9))* Cavendish Square Publishing.
Williams, Colleen Madonna Flood. Jamaica. (Caribbean Today Ser.). 64p. (YA). 2010. (Illus.). (gr. 9-12). 21.95 *(978-1-4222-0626-3(2))* 2006. (gr. 7-18). pap. 9.95 *(978-1-4222-0693-5(9))* Mason Crest.

JAMAICA—FICTION

Angelou, Maya. Cedric of Jamaica. Rockwell, Lizzy, illus. 2005. (Random House Pictureback Book Ser.). (J). *(978-0-375-83269-7(6))* Random Hse., Inc.
Bell, Ted. The Time Pirate. 2011. (Nick Mciver Adventures Through Time Ser.: 2). (ENG., Illus.). 480p. (J). (gr. 5-9). pap. 10.99 *(978-0-312-66549-4(0),* 9780312665494) Square Fish.
Bryant, Annie. Katani's Jamaican Holiday. 2008. (Beacon Street Girls Ser.: No. 4). (ENG., Illus.). 192p. (J). (gr. 4-8). pap. 6.99 *(978-1-4169-6443-8(6),* Aladdin) Simon & Schuster Children's Publishing.
Burford, Lorrimer. A Jamaican Storyteller's Tale. 2005. (ENG., Illus.). 197p. pap. 7.99 *(978-976-8184-84-9(1))* Penguin Publishing Group.
Curtatone, Raffaello. The Adventures of Mr Greenwood from Jamaic. 2011. 50p. (J). pap. 9.99 *(978-0-557-91852-2(9))* Lulu Pr., Inc.
D'Costa, Jean. Sprat Morrison. Date not set. (ENG., Illus.). 192p. pap. 26.00 *(978-0-582-05207-9(6))* Addison-Wesley Longman, Ltd. GBR. Dist: Trans-Atlantic Pubns., Inc.
Grant Sr, Hector J. Sybil: The Trials & Triumphs of a Jamaican Girl. 2008. 208p. per. 15.95 *(978-1-4327-1889-3(4))* Outskirts Pr., Inc.
Hall, Rose. After the Storm. Jazvic, Beryl, illus. 2005. (J). bds. 19.95 *(978-0-9770503-0-7(0))* Institute For Behavior Change Incorporated The.
Harris, Angela Brent -. Sweet Jamaican Summertime at Grandma's. 2011. 28p. pap. 21.99 *(978-1-4628-7271-8(9))* Xlibris Corp.
Isbell, Tessa J. Animal Adventures: Goosey & Beauty Take a Mystery Magic Carpet Ride to Jamaica. 2013. 48p. pap. 21.99 *(978-1-4669-7217-9(3))* Trafford Publishing.
Magnus, Kellie. Little Lion Goes to School. Robinson, Michael, illus. l.t. ed. 2003. 16p. (J). 9.99 *(978-0-9744211-0-0(3))* Media Magic New York.
McKnight, Penny. Nix. 2006. (Illus.). 84p. (J). (gr. 3-7). per. 8.99 *(978-1-59166-610-3(4))* BJU Pr.
Montague, Chester. Timmy's Vacation. 2008. 40p. pap. 24.95 *(978-1-60441-225-3(9))* America Star Bks.
Peacock, Shane. Double You, 1 vol. 2014. (Seven Sequels Ser.). (ENG., Illus.). 272p. (J). (gr. 5-10). pap. 10.95 *(978-1-4598-0534-7(8))* Orca Bk. Pubs. USA.
Rees, Celia. Pirates! 2003. (ENG.). 384p. (YA). (gr. 7). 16.95 *(978-1-58234-816-2(2),* 9781582348162, Bloomsbury USA Childrens) Bloomsbury Publishing USA.
Richmond, Beulah. Anancy & Friends: A Grandmother's Anancy Stories for Her Grandchildren. Brown, Clovis, illus. 2004. (ENG.). 52p. pap. 5.99 *(978-976-8184-48-1(5))* Penguin Publishing Group.
Salkey, Andrew. Drought. 2011. (Caribbean Modern Classics Ser.). (ENG., Illus.). 128p. (J). (gr. 7). pap. 13.95 *(978-1-84523-183-5(X))* Peepal Tree Pr., Ltd. GBR. Dist: Independent Pubs. Group.
—Earthquake. 2011. (Caribbean Modern Classics Ser.). (ENG., Illus.). 108p. (J). (gr. 7). pap. 13.95 *(978-1-84523-182-8(1))* Peepal Tree Pr., Ltd. GBR. Dist: Independent Pubs. Group.
—Hurricane. 2011. (Caribbean Modern Classics Ser.). (ENG., Illus.). 104p. (J). (gr. 7-7). pap. 13.95 *(978-1-84523-180-4(5))* Peepal Tree Pr., Ltd. GBR. Dist: Independent Pubs. Group.
—Riot. 2011. (Caribbean Modern Classics Ser.). (ENG., Illus.). 176p. (J). (gr. 7). pap. 14.95 *(978-1-84523-181-1(3))* Peepal Tree Pr., Ltd. GBR. Dist: Independent Pubs. Group.
Smith, Vicki. Jamaican Adventure with Tori & Paul. 2012. (ENG., Illus.). 24p. (J). pap. 13.95 *(978-1-4327-8578-9(8))* Outskirts Pr., Inc.
Walker, Charmaine. Jon & Alex Goes to School. 2012. 34p. pap. *(978-1-105-62383-7(1))* Lulu.com.
Weathers, Marlon. Henry Baldpate & His Treetop Friends. 2008. 24p. pap. 24.95 *(978-1-60672-923-6(3))* America Star Bks.
Wilson, Heather Gemmen. Lydia Barnes & the Escape from Shark Bay. 2008. 160p. (J). 9.99 *(978-0-89827-352-6(8))* Wesleyan Publishing Hse.
Wohlt, Julia. Naughty Eddie Larue. Brown, Clovis, illus. 27p. *(978-976-610-173-2(6))* Creative Links.

JAMAICA—HISTORY—FICTION

Rees, Celia. Pirates! The True & Remarkable Adventures of Minerva Sharpe & Nancy Kington, Female Pirates. 2005. (Illus.). 379p. (YA). (gr. 9-12). 16.60 *(978-0-7569-6304-0(4))* Perfection Learning Corp.

JAMAICAN AMERICANS

Caravantes, Peggy. Marcus Garvey: Black Nationalist. 2004. (Twentieth Century Leaders Ser.). (Illus.). 128p. (YA). (gr. 6-12). 23.95 *(978-1-931798-14-3(1))* Reynolds, Morgan Inc.
Horst, Heather A. & Garner, Andrew. Jamaican Americans. 2007. (New Immigrants Ser.). (Illus.). 144p. (gr. 6-12). lib. bdg. 30.00 *(978-0-7910-8790-9(5),* Chelsea Hse.) Facts On File, Inc.
Kallen, Stuart A. Marcus Garvey & the Back to Africa Movement. 2006. (Lucent Library of Black History). (ENG., Illus.). 112p. (YA). (gr. 7-10). lib. bdg. 34.80 *(978-1-59018-838-5(1),* Lucent Bks.) Cengage Gale.
Mohamed, Paloma. A Man Called Garvey: The Life & Times of the Great Leader Marcus Garvey. Braithwaithe, Barrington, illus. l.t. ed. 2004. (Majority Press Inc., Wisdom for Children Ser.: No. 1). (ENG.). 36p. (J). 12.95 *(978-0-912469-40-9(4))* Majority Pr., The.

JAMAICAN AMERICANS—FICTION

Dower, Laura. Kiki Takes the Cake. Lazuli, Lilly, illus. 2016. (Dessert Diaries). (ENG.). 160p. (gr. 4-5). lib. bdg. 26.65 *(978-1-4965-3120-9(5))* Stone Arch Bks.
Gunning, Monica. A Shelter in Our Car. Pedlar, Elaine, illus. 2013. (ENG.). 32p. (J). pap. 9.95 *(978-0-89239-308-4(4),* Children's Book Press) Lee & Low Bks., Inc.
Never So Good (Jamaicans) 76p. (YA). (gr. 6-12). pap. 9.95 *(978-0-8224-3806-9(2))* Globe Fearon Educational Publishing.
Vigilante, Danette. The Trouble with Half a Moon. 2015. (ENG.). 208p. (J). (gr. 5). 7.99 *(978-0-14-751550-6(5),* Puffin Books) Penguin Young Readers Group.

JAMES, JESSE, 1847-1882

Burlingame, Jeff. Jesse James: I Will Never Surrender. 2010. (Americans—the Spirit of a Nation Ser.). (Illus.). 128p. (J). lib. bdg. 33.27 *(978-0-7660-3353-5(8))* Enslow Pubs., Inc.
Collins, Kathleen. Jesse James: Bank Robber of the American West. 2009. (Primary Sources of Famous People in American History Ser.). 32p. (gr. 2-3). 47.90 *(978-1-60851-690-2(3))* Rosen Publishing Group, Inc., The.
—Jesse James: Bank Robber of the American West / Legendario bandido del oeste Americano. 2009. (Famous People in American History/Grandes personajes en la historia de los Estados Unidos Ser.). (ENG & SPA.). 32p. (gr. 2-3). 47.90 *(978-1-61512-547-0(7),* Editorial Buenas Letras) Rosen Publishing Group, Inc., The.
—Jesse James: Legendario Bandido del Oeste Americano. 2004. (Grandes personajes en la historia de los Estados Unidos Ser.). (SPA.). 32p. (gr. 3-6). pap. 10.00 *(978-0-8239-4230-5(9),* Rosen Classroom) Rosen Publishing Group, Inc., The.
—Jesse James: Legendario bandido del oeste americano (Jesse James: Bank Robber of the American West) 2009. (Grandes personajes en la historia de los Estados Unidos (Famous People in American History) Ser.). (SPA.). 32p. (gr. 2-3). 47.90 *(978-1-61512-801-3(8),* Editorial Buenas Letras) Rosen Publishing Group, Inc., The.
—Jesse James: Western Bank Robber. 2004. (Famous People in American History Ser.). (ENG., Illus.). 32p. (gr. 4-8). pap. 10.00 *(978-0-8239-4184-1(1))* Rosen Publishing Group, Inc., The.
Cooke, Tim. Jesse James: A Notorious Bank Robber of the Wild West. 2016. (Wanted! Famous Outlaws Ser.). (ENG., Illus.). 48p. (J). (gr. 6-8). pap. 14.05 *(978-1-4824-4259-5(0))* Stevens, Gareth Publishing LLLP.
Cunningham, Meghan Engsberg. Jesse James. Lapegüe, Matías, illus. 2016. (American Legends & Folktales Ser.). 32p. (J). 28.50 *(978-1-5026-2197-9(5))* Cavendish Square Publishing.
Frisch, Aaron. Jesse James. 2005. (Legends of the West (Creative Education) Ser.). (Illus.). 48p. (J). (gr. 5-9). lib. bdg. 21.95 *(978-1-58341-338-8(3),* Creative Education) Creative Co., The.
Green, Carl R. & Sanford, William R. Jesse James. rev. ed. 2008. (Outlaws & Lawmen of the Wild West, Revised Edition Ser.). (Illus.). 48p. (J). (gr. 5-18). lib. bdg. 25.27 *(978-0-7660-3172-2(1))* Enslow Pubs., Inc.
Jesse James. 2010. (Legends of the Wild West Ser.). (Illus.). 128p. (gr. 6-12). 35.00 *(978-1-60413-598-5(0),* Chelsea Hse.) Facts On File, Inc.
Landau, Elaine. Jesse James: Wild West Train Robber. 2004. (Best of the West Biographies Ser.). (Illus.). 48p. (J). lib. bdg. 25.27 *(978-0-7660-2208-9(0))* Enslow Pubs., Inc.
Randolph, Ryan. A Bank Robber's End: The Death of Jesse James. 2009. (Great Moments in American History Ser.). 32p. (gr. 3-3). 47.90 *(978-1-61513-138-9(8))* Rosen Publishing Group, Inc., The.
Woog, Adam & Triplett, Frank. Jesse James: The Wild West for Kids. 2014. (ENG., Illus.). 128p. (J). (gr. 2-7). pap. 12.95 *(978-1-62636-160-7(6),* 263160, Sky Pony Pr.) Skyhorse Publishing Co., Inc.

JAMES, WILL, 1892-1942

James, Will. The Will James Cowboy Book, Vol. 1. rev. ed. (Illus.). 128p. (J). (gr. 4). *(978-0-87842-469-6(5),* 816) Mountain Pr. Publishing Co., Inc.

JAMESTOWN (VA.)—FICTION

Archambault, Jeanne. Larry the Lawnmower. Corey, Victoria, illus. 2004. 32p. (J). 14.95 *(978-0-9763031-0-7(8));* per. 10.00 *(978-0-9763031-1-4(6))* Jitterbug Bks.
Campbell, L. A. Cartboy Goes to Camp. 2014. (Cartboy Ser.: 2). (ENG., Illus.). 224p. (J). (gr. 3-7). 12.99 *(978-0-7653-3327-8(9),* 9780765333278, Starscape) Doherty, Tom Assocs., LLC.
Carbone, Elisa. Blood on the River: James Town 1607. 2007. (ENG.). 256p. (J). (gr. 5-18). 7.99 *(978-0-14-240932-9(4),* Puffin Books) Penguin Young Readers Group.
—Blood on the River: James Town 1607. 2009. (Illus.). 237p. 17.00 *(978-1-60686-385-5(1))* Perfection Learning Corp.
Hall, Lucy. From England to Jamestowne: A Journey to Find My Father. 2007. (J). *(978-0-9763706-5-9(4))* Tendril Pr., LLC.
Lapallo, Connie. Dark Enough to See the Stars in a Jamestown Sky. 2006. (YA). (gr. 7-18). pap. 19.95 *(978-1-59526-421-3(3))* Aeon Publishing Inc.
Smith, Andrea P. Pocahontas & John Smith. 2012. (Jr. Graphic Colonial America Ser.). (Illus.). 24p. (J). lib. bdg. 25.25 *(978-1-4488-5190-4(4),* PowerKids Pr.) Rosen Publishing Group, Inc., The.
Stone, Marie. On Their Own: A Journey to Jamestown. 2006. (Illus.). 166p. (J). (gr. 3-7). per. 8.95 *(978-1-57249-385-8(2),* White Mane Kids) White Mane Publishing Co., Inc.

JAMESTOWN (VA.)—HISTORY

Becker, Sandra. Pocahontas. 2003. (Folk Heroes Ser.). (Illus.). 24p. (J). lib. bdg. 24.45 *(978-1-59036-074-3(5))* Weigl Pubs., Inc.
Benge, Janet & Benge, Geoff. Heroes of History - John Smith: A Foothold in the New World. 2006. (Heroes of History Ser.). (ENG., Illus.). 224p. (YA). (gr. 3-7). pap. 9.99 *(978-1-932096-36-1(1))* Emerald Bks.
Benoit, Peter. Cornerstones of Freedom, Third Series: the Jamestown Colony. 2012. (ENG.). 64p. (J). lib. bdg. 30.00 *(978-0-531-23058-9(9),* Children's Pr.) Scholastic Library Publishing.
—The Jamestown Colony. 2012. (Cornerstones of Freedom, Third Ser.). (ENG.). 64p. (J). pap. 8.95 *(978-0-531-28158-1(2))* Scholastic Library Publishing.
Brannon, Barbara. Discover Jamestown. 2005. (J). pap. *(978-1-4108-5142-0(7))* Benchmark Education Co.
Braun, Eric. The Story of Jamestown, 1 vol. Erwin, Steve et al, illus. 2005. (Graphic History Ser.). (ENG.). 32p. (gr. 3-4). 30.65 *(978-0-7368-4967-8(X),* Graphic Library) Capstone Press of Coughlan Cos.
Bridy, Dan & Solomon, Sharon K. Christopher Newport: Jamestown Explorer, 1 vol. 2013. (ENG., Illus.). 32p. (J). (gr. k-3). 16.99 *(978-1-4556-1752-4(0))* Pelican Publishing Co., Inc.
Broyles, Janell. A Timeline of the Jamestown Colony. 2009. (Timelines of American History Ser.). 32p. (gr. 4-4). 47.90 *(978-1-60854-385-4(4),* Rosen Reference) Rosen Publishing Group, Inc., The.
Bruchac, Joseph. Pocahontas. 2005. (ENG., Illus.). 192p. (YA). (gr. 7-12). pap. 6.99 *(978-0-15-205465-6(0))* Houghton Mifflin Harcourt Publishing Co.
—Pocahontas. 2005. (Illus.). 173p. (gr. 7). 15.95 *(978-0-7569-5604-2(8))* Perfection Learning Corp.
Cipriano, Jeri. Three Historical Communities of North America: Text Pairs. 2008. (Bridges/Navigators Ser.). (J). (gr. 3). 89.00 *(978-1-4108-8375-9(2))* Benchmark Education Co.
Cooper, Michael L. Jamestown 1607. 2007. (ENG., Illus.). 112p. (J). (gr. 3-7). 18.95 *(978-0-8234-1948-7(7))* Holiday Hse., Inc.
Early Jamestown (NCHS) (YA). (gr. 5-8). spiral bd., tchr.'s planning gde. ed. 11.50 *(978-0-382-40928-8(0))* Cobblestone Publishing Co.
Fradin, Dennis Brindell. Jamestown, Virginia. 2007. (Turning Points in U. S. History Ser.). (Illus.). 48p. (gr. 3-7). lib. bdg. 31.36 *(978-0-7614-2122-1(X),* Benchmark Bks.) Marshall Cavendish Corp.
Harkins, William H. & Harkins, Susan Sales. Jamestown: The First Colony. 2006. (Building America Ser.). (Illus.). 48p. (J). (gr. 3-7). lib. bdg. 29.95 *(978-1-58415-458-7(6))* Mitchell Lane Pubs., Inc.
Higgins, Melissa. Jamestown Colony, 1 vol. 2013. (Foundations of Our Nation Ser.). (ENG.). 48p. (J). (gr. 3-6). lib. bdg. 32.79 *(978-1-61783-710-4(5));* (Illus.). pap. 15.64 *(978-1-61783-760-9(1),* Core Library) ABDO Publishing Co.
Jenner, Caryn. Pocahontas, Level 2. 2009. (DK Readers Ser.). (ENG.). 32p. (J). (gr. 1-3). 3.99 *(978-0-7566-5611-9(7),* DK Children) Dorling Kindersley Publishing, Inc.
Jones, Victoria Garrett. Pocahontas: A Life in Two Worlds. 2010. (Sterling Biographies(r) Ser.). (ENG., Illus.). 128p. (J). (gr. 5-18). pap. 5.95 *(978-1-4027-5158-5(3))* Sterling Publishing Co., Inc.
Kells, Deanne. The Jamestown Community. 2005. (J). pap. *(978-1-4108-4624-2(5))* Benchmark Education Co.
Kirkman, Marissa. The Life & Times of Pocahontas & the First Colonies. 2016. (Life & Times Ser.). (ENG., Illus.). 24p. (gr. 1-2). lib. bdg. 25.32 *(978-1-5157-2477-3(8),* First Facts) Capstone Press of Coughlan Cos.
Landau, Elaine. Explore Colonial Jamestown with Elaine Landau. 2006. (Explore Colonial America with Elaine Landau Ser.). (Illus.). 48p. (J). (gr. 3-7). lib. bdg. 25.27 *(978-0-7660-2554-7(3),* Enslow Elementary) Enslow Pubs., Inc.
Lange, Karen. 1607: A New Look at Jamestown. Block, Ira, photos by. 2007. (ENG., Illus.). 48p. (J). (gr. 4-7). 17.95 *(978-1-4263-0012-7(3));* 27.90 *(978-1-4263-0013-4(1))* National Geographic Society. (National Geographic Children's Bks.).
Levy, Janey. Life in Jamestown Colony, Vol. 1. 2014. (What You Didn't Know about History Ser.). (ENG.). 24p. (J). (gr. 2-3). 22.60 *(978-1-4824-0586-6(5))* Stevens, Gareth Publishing LLLP.
Loker, Aleck. Fearless Captain: The Adventures of John Smith. 2006. (Founders of the Republic Ser.). (Illus.). 176p. (J). (gr. 6-12). lib. bdg. 26.95 *(978-1-931798-83-9(4))* Reynolds, Morgan Inc.
Lusted, Marcia Amidon. The Jamestown Colony Disaster: A Cause-And-Effect Investigation. 2016. (Cause-And-Effect Disasters Ser.). (ENG., Illus.). 40p. (J). (gr. 4-6). 46.65 *(978-1-5124-1127-0(2),* Lerner Pubns.) Lerner Publishing Group.
Marsh, Carole. I'm Reading About Jamestown. 2016. (I'm Reading About Ser.). (ENG., Illus.). (J). lib. bdg. 24.99 ***(978-0-635-12187-5(5));*** pap. 7.99 ***(978-0-635-12188-2(3))*** Gallopade International.
Marsh, Carole. Jamestown: America's First Permanent English Settlement. 2006. (American Milestones Ser.). (Illus.). 32p. (J). (gr. -1-3). pap. 7.99 *(978-0-635-06323-6(9))* Gallopade International.
McAneney, Caitie. Hidden History: Uncovering the Jamestown Colony. 2016. (Hidden History Ser.). 00032p. (J). pap. 10.50 *(978-1-4824-5806-0(3))* Stevens, Gareth Publishing LLLP.
McNeese, Tim. Jamestown. 2007. (Colonial Settlements in America Ser.). (Illus.). 112p. (YA). (gr. 5-9). lib. bdg. 30.00 *(978-0-7910-9335-1(2))* Facts On File, Inc.
—John Smith. 2010. (Leaders of the Colonial Era Ser.). 128p. (gr. 5-8). 35.00 *(978-1-60413-742-2(8),* Chelsea Hse.) Facts On File, Inc.
Morley, Jacqueline. You Wouldn't Want to Be an American Colonist! A Settlement You'd Rather Not Start. 2013. (You Wouldn't Want To Ser.). lib. bdg. 20.80 *(978-0-606-31628-6(0),* Turtleback) Turtleback Bks.
Oney, Yannick. First American Colonies. 2004. (World Discovery History Readers Ser.). (Illus.). 32p. (J). pap. *(978-0-439-66555-1(8))* Scholastic, Inc.
Pederson, Charles E. The Jamestown Colony, 1 vol. 2009. (Essential Events Set 3 Ser.). (ENG., Illus.). 112p. (J). (gr. 6-12). lib. bdg. 35.64 *(978-1-60453-515-0(6))* ABDO Publishing Co.
Petrie, Kristin. John Smith, 1 vol. 2007. (Explorers Set 2 Ser.). (ENG., Illus.). 32p. (gr. 4-7). 27.07 *(978-1-59679-751-2(7),* Checkerboard Library) ABDO Publishing Co.
Pierce, Alan. Jamestown Colony, 1 vol. 2005. (American Moments Ser.). (ENG., Illus.). 48p. (gr. 4-8). 27.07 *(978-1-59197-733-9(9),* Abdo & Daughters) ABDO Publishing Co.
Quasha, Jennifer. Jamestown: Hands-on Projects about One of America's First Communities. 2009. (Great Social Studies Projects Ser.). 24p. (gr. 3-3). 42.50 *(978-1-61513-210-2(4),* PowerKids Pr.) Rosen Publishing Group, Inc., The.
Ransom, Candice. Why Did English Settlers Come to Virginia? And Other Questions about the Jamestown Settlement. 2011. (Six Questions of American History Ser.). (ENG.). 48p. (gr. 4-6). 30.60 *(978-0-7613-5228-0(7));* pap. 9.95 *(978-0-7613-7133-5(8));* pap. 56.72 *(978-0-7613-7301-8(2))* Lerner Publishing Group.
Rosen, Daniel & National Geographic Learning Staff. Jamestown & the Virginia Colony. 2007. (Reading Expeditions Ser.). (ENG., Illus.). 40p. (J). pap. 19.95 *(978-0-7922-4547-6(4))* CENGAGE Learning.
Rossi, Anne. Bright Ideas: The Age of Invention in America 1870-1910. 2005. (Crossroads America Ser.). (ENG., Illus.). 40p. (J). (gr. 5-9). 12.95 *(978-0-7922-8276-1(0),* National Geographic Children's Bks.) National Geographic Society.
Rudolph, Ellen K. Willi Gets a History Lesson: In Virginia's Historic Triangle. Rudolph, Ellen K., photos by. 2007. (ENG., Illus.). 80p. pap. 24.00 *(978-0-9791348-0-7(3))* EKR Pubns.
Ruffin, Frances E. Jamestown. 2006. (Places in American History Ser.). (Illus.). 24p. (gr. 1-4). lib. bdg. 22.00 *(978-0-8368-6410-6(7),* Weekly Reader Leveled Readers) Stevens, Gareth Publishing LLLP.
Schanzer, Rosalyn. John Smith Escapes Again! 2006. (ENG., Illus.). 64p. (J). (gr. 4-7). 16.95 *(978-0-7922-5930-5(0));* lib. bdg. 25.90 *(978-0-7922-5931-2(9))* National Geographic Society. (National Geographic Children's Bks.).
Sita, Lisa. Pocahontas: The Powhatan Culture & the Jamestown Colony. 2009. (Library of American Lives & Times Ser.). 112p. (gr. 5-5). 69.20 *(978-1-60853-500-2(2))* Rosen Publishing Group, Inc., The.
Tieck, Sarah. Jamestown, 1 vol. 2008. (All Aboard America Ser.). (ENG.). 24p. (J). (gr. 1-4). 25.65 *(978-1-59928-936-6(9))* ABDO Publishing Co.

JAMESTOWN (VA.)—HISTORY—FICTION

Johnston, Tony & Mazellan, Ron. The Harmonica. Mazellan, Ron, illus. 2008. (ENG., Illus.). 32p. (J). (gr. 2-5). pap. 7.95 *(978-1-57091-489-8(3))* Charlesbridge Publishing, Inc.
Kudlinski, Kathleen V. My Lady Pocahontas, 0 vols. unabr. ed. 2013. (ENG.). 288p. (gr. 5-9). pap. 9.99 *(978-1-4778-1711-7(5),* 9781477817117, Amazon Children's Publishing) Amazon Publishing.
LeSourd, Nancy. Adventures in Jamestown, 1 vol. 2008. (Liberty Letters Ser.). (ENG.). 240p. (J). pap. 7.99 *(978-0-310-71392-0(7))* Zonderkidz.
Lincoln Collier, James. The Corn Raid. 2004. 142p. (J). lib. bdg. 16.92 *(978-1-4242-0768-8(1))* Fitzgerald Bks.
Marsh, Carole. The Mystery at Jamestown: First Permanent English Colony in America! 2009. (Real Kids, Real Places Ser.). (Illus.). 137p. (J). lib. bdg. 18.99 *(978-0-635-07023-4(5),* Marsh, Carole Mysteries) Gallopade International.
Ransom, Candice. Sam Collier & the Founding of Jamestown. Archambault, Matthew, illus. (On My Own History Ser.). 48p. 2007. (ENG.). (gr. 2-4). pap. 6.95 *(978-0-8225-6451-5(3),* First Avenue Editions) 2006. (J). (gr. 1-2). 25.26 *(978-1-57505-874-0(X),* Millbrook Pr.) Lerner Publishing Group.
Smith, Andrea P. Pocahontas & John Smith. 2012. (Illus.). 24p. (J). 63.60 *(978-1-4488-5219-2(6));* pap. 10.60 *(978-1-4488-5218-5(8))* Rosen Publishing Group, Inc., The. (PowerKids Pr.).

JAMESTOWN (VA.)—SOCIAL LIFE AND CUSTOMS

Quasha, Jennifer. Jamestown: Hands-on Projects about One of America's First Communities. 2009. (Great Social Studies Projects Ser.). 24p. (gr. 3-3). 42.50 *(978-1-61513-210-2(4),* PowerKids Pr.) Rosen Publishing Group, Inc., The.

JANIE (FICTITIOUS CHARACTER: COONEY)—FICTION

Cooney, Caroline B. The Face on the Milk Carton. 2009. 9.14 *(978-0-7848-0397-4(8),* Everbind) Marco Bk. Co.

JANSEN, CAM (FICTITIOUS CHARACTER)—FICTION

Adler, David A. Cam Jansen: The Mystery of the Babe Ruth Baseball. (Cam Jansen Ser.: No. 6). 57p. (J). (gr. 2-4). pap. 3.99 *(978-0-8072-1347-6(0),* Listening Library) Random Hse. Audio Publishing Group.
—Cam Jansen - The Mystery Writer Mystery. Allen, Joy, illus. 27th ed. 2008. (Cam Jansen Ser.: 27). (ENG.). 64p. (J). (gr. 2-5). 4.99 *(978-0-14-241194-0(9),* Puffin Books) Penguin Young Readers Group.
—Cam Jansen & the Sports Day Mysteries: A Super Special. 2009. (Cam Jansen Ser.). lib. bdg. 16.00 *(978-0-606-00110-6(7),* Turtleback) Turtleback Bks.
—Mystery at the Haunted House, 13 vols. Natti, Susanna, illus. 2004. (Cam Jansen Ser.: 13). (ENG.). 64p. (J). (gr. 2-5). 4.99 *(978-0-14-240210-8(9),* Puffin Books) Penguin Young Readers Group.
—The Mystery of the Carnival Prize, 9 vols. Natti, Susanna, illus. 2004. (Cam Jansen Ser.: 9). (ENG.). 64p. (J). (gr. 2-5). 4.99 *(978-0-14-240018-0(1),* Puffin Books) Penguin Young Readers Group.
—The Mystery of the Circus Clown, 7 vols. Natti, Susanna, illus. 2004. (Cam Jansen Ser.: 7). (ENG.). 64p. (J). (gr. 2-5). 4.99 *(978-0-14-240016-6(5),* Puffin Books) Penguin Young Readers Group.
—The Mystery of the Gold Coins, 5 vols. Natti, Susanna, illus. 2004. (Cam Jansen Ser.: 5). (ENG.). 64p. (J). (gr. 2-5). 4.99 *(978-0-14-240014-2(9),* Puffin Books) Penguin Young Readers Group.
—The Mystery of the Monkey House. Natti, Susanna, illus. 2004. (Cam Jansen Ser.: 10). (ENG.). 64p. (J). (gr. 2-5). 4.99 *(978-0-14-240019-7(X),* Puffin Books) Penguin Young Readers Group.
—The Mystery of the Monster Movie, 8 vols. Natti, Susanna, illus. 2004. (Cam Jansen Ser.: 8). (ENG.). 64p. (J). (gr. 2-5). 4.99 *(978-0-14-240017-3(3),* Puffin Books) Penguin Young Readers Group.
—The Mystery of the Stolen Diamonds. Natti, Susanna, illus. 2004. (Cam Jansen Ser.: 1). (ENG.). 64p. (J). (gr. 2-5). pap. 4.99 *(978-0-14-240010-4(6),* Puffin Books) Penguin Young Readers Group.
—The Mystery of the Television Dog, 4 vols. Natti, Susanna, illus. 2004. (Cam Jansen Ser.: 4). (ENG.). 64p. (J). (gr. 2-5). 4.99 *(978-0-14-240013-5(0),* Puffin Books) Penguin Young Readers Group.
—The Mystery of the U. F. O., 2 vols. Natti, Susanna, illus. 2004. (Cam Jansen Ser.: 2). (ENG.). 64p. (J). (gr. 2-5). 4.99

(978-0-14-240011-1(4), Puffin Books) Penguin Young Readers Group.
—The Summer Camp Mysteries. Allen, Joy, illus. 2007. (Cam Jansen Ser.). (ENG.). 128p. (J). (gr. 2-5). 5.99 (978-0-14-240742-4(9), Puffin Books) Penguin Young Readers Group.
—The Valentine Baby Mystery. Natti, Susanna, illus. 25th ed. 2006. (Cam Jansen Ser.: 25). (ENG.). 80p. (J). (gr. 2-5). 4.99 (978-0-14-240694-6(5), Puffin Books) Penguin Young Readers Group.
—Young Cam Jansen & the 100th Day of School, 15 vols. Natti, Susanna, illus. 2010. (Young Cam Jansen Ser.: 15). (ENG.). 32p. (J). (gr. 1-3). mass mkt. 3.99 (978-0-14-241685-3(1), Penguin Young Readers) Penguin Young Readers Group.
—Young Cam Jansen & the 100th Day of School Mystery, 15 vols. Natti, Susanna, illus. 2009. (Young Cam Jansen Ser.: 15). (ENG.). 32p. (J). (gr. 1-3). 13.99 (978-0-670-06172-3(7), Viking Books for Young Readers) Penguin Young Readers Group.
—Young Cam Jansen & the Circus Mystery. Natti, Susanna, illus. 2013. (Young Cam Jansen Ser.: 17). (ENG.). 32p. (J). (gr. 1-3). pap. 3.99 (978-0-448-46614-9(7), Penguin Young Readers) Penguin Young Readers Group.
—Young Cam Jansen & the Double Beach Mystery. Natti, Susanna, illus. 2003. (Young Cam Jansen Ser.: 8). (ENG.). 32p. (J). (gr. 1-3). mass mkt. 3.99 (978-0-14-250079-8(8), Penguin Young Readers) Penguin Young Readers Group.
—Young Cam Jansen & the Double Beach Mystery. Natti, Susanna, illus. 2003. (Young Cam Jansen — Penguin Young Readers Level 3 Ser.: 8). 30p. (gr. -1-3). lib. bdg. 13.55 (978-0-613-67477-5(4), Turtleback) Turtleback Bks.
—Young Cam Jansen & the Knock, Knock Mystery. Natti, Susanna, illus. 2015. (Young Cam Jansen Ser.: 20). (ENG.). 32p. (J). (gr. 1-3). pap. 3.99 (978-0-14-242225-0(8), Penguin Young Readers) Penguin Young Readers Group.
—Young Cam Jansen & the New Girl Mystery. Natti, Susanna, illus. 2005. (Young Cam Jansen Ser.: 10). (ENG.). 32p. (J). (gr. 1-3). mass mkt. 3.99 (978-0-14-240353-2(9), Penguin Young Readers) Penguin Young Readers Group.

JAPAN

Antram, David. Manga Action Figures. 2012. (How to Draw Ser.). (ENG.). 32p. (J). (gr. 4-6). pap. 11.75 (978-1-4488-6469-0(0)); lib. bdg. 26.50 (978-1-4488-6460-7(7)) Rosen Publishing Group, Inc., The. (PowerKids Pr.).
Bjorklund, Ruth. Japan. 2017. (Enchantment of the World Ser.). (ENG.). 144p. (J). lib. bdg. 40.00 **(978-0-531-23569-0(6)**, Children's Pr.) Scholastic Library Publishing.
Blevins, Wiley. Japan. 2017. (Follow Me Around Ser.). (ENG.). 32p. (J). lib. bdg. 27.00 **(978-0-531-23705-2(2)**, Children's Pr.) Scholastic Library Publishing.
Buckley, A. M. Japan, 1 vol. 2011. (Countries of the World Set 1 Ser.). (ENG., Illus.). 144p. (J). (gr. 6-12). lib. bdg. 37.07 (978-1-61783-115-7(8)) ABDO Publishing Co.
Crean, Susan. Discover Japan. 2012. (Discover Countries Ser.). (Illus.). 32p. (YA). (gr. 4-7). lib. bdg. 26.50 (978-1-4488-5269-7(2)) Rosen Publishing Group, Inc., The.
Eppard, Jon. Manga. 2012. (ENG., Illus.). 24p. (J). pap. (978-1-60014-857-6(3)); (gr. 3-8). lib. bdg. 25.95 (978-1-60014-812-5(3), Express Bks.) Bellwether Media.
Freed, Kira. Surviving the 2011 Japanese Earthquake & Tsunami. 2015. (Surviving Disaster Ser.). (ENG., Illus.). 48p. (J). (gr. 5-6). 30.25 (978-1-4994-3645-7(9), Rosen Central) Rosen Publishing Group, Inc., The.
Gitlin, Marty. Japan. 2017. (Country Profiles Ser.). (ENG., Illus.). 32p. (J). (gr. 3-8). lib. bdg. 26.95 **(978-1-62617-684-3(1)**, Blastoff! Discovery) Bellwether Media.
Green, Yuko. Let's Learn about JAPAN: Activity & Coloring Book. 2013. (Dover Children's Activity Bks.). (ENG.). 48p. (J). (gr. 1-5). pap. 4.99 (978-0-486-48993-3(0)) Dover Pubns., Inc.
Greene, Meg. Japan: A Primary Source Cultural Guide. (Primary Sources of World Cultures Ser.). 128p. (gr. 4-5). 2009. 79.90 (978-1-60851-926-2(0)) 2005. (Illus.). (J). lib. bdg. 37.25 (978-1-4042-2912-9(4)) Rosen Publishing Group, Inc., The.
Gritzner, Charles F. & Phillips, Douglas. Japan. 2003. (Modern World Nations Ser.). (Illus.). 150p. (gr. 6-12). 35.00 (978-0-7910-7239-4(8), Chelsea Hse.) Facts On File, Inc.
Hardyman, Robyn. Celebrate: Japan. 2009. (Celebrate Country Ser.). 32p. (gr. 4-6). 28.00 (978-1-60413-268-7(X), Chelsea Clubhouse) Facts On File, Inc.
Hepperman, Christina. Samurai, 1 vol. 2013. (Great Warriors Ser.). (ENG.). 48p. (J). (gr. 3-6). lib. bdg. 32.79 (978-1-61783-727-2(X)) ABDO Publishing Co.
Juarez, Christine. Japan, 1 vol. 2013. (Countries Ser.). (ENG.). 24p. (gr. k-1). 26.65 (978-1-4765-3080-2(7), Pebble Plus); pap. 6.95 (978-1-4765-3520-3(5), Pebble Bks.) Capstone Press of Coughlan Cos.
Kalman, Bobbie. Japan: The Land. 3rd rev. ed. 2008. (Lands, Peoples, & Cultures Ser.). (ENG., Illus.). 32p. (J). (gr. 3-9). pap. (978-0-7787-9664-0(7)) Crabtree Publishing Co.
—Japan the Land. 3rd rev. ed. 2008. (Lands, Peoples, & Cultures Ser.). (ENG., Illus.). 32p. (J). (gr. 3-9). lib. bdg. (978-0-7787-9296-3(X)) Crabtree Publishing Co.
—Spotlight on Japan. 2010. (Spotlight on My Country Ser.). (ENG.). 32p. (J). (gr. 2-5). lib. bdg. (978-0-7787-3459-8(5)) Crabtree Publishing Co.
March, Michael. Japan. 2003. (Country Files Ser.). 32p. (J). lib. bdg. 24.25 (978-1-58340-237-5(3)) Black Rabbit Bks.
Marsh, Carole. Japan: An Island Country of Endless Intrigue! 2009. (It's Your World Ser.). 48p. (J). (gr. 2-9). pap. 7.99 (978-0-635-06819-4(2)) Gallopade International.
Moon, Walt K. Let's Explore Japan. 2017. (Bumba Books (tm) — Let's Explore Countries Ser.). (ENG.). 24p. (J). (gr. -1-1). 12.99 **(978-1-5124-3738-6(7)**, Lerner Pubns.); 38.65 **(978-1-5124-3737-9(9)**, Lerner Pubns.); 38.65 **(978-1-5124-3020-2(X)**, Lerner Pubns.); (Illus.). 25.32 (978-1-5124-3008-0(0)) Lerner Publishing Group.
Phillips, Charles. Japan. (Countries of the World Ser.). (ENG., Illus.). 64p. (J). (gr. 5). 2009. pap. 12.95 (978-1-4263-0571-9(0)) 2007. lib. bdg. 27.90 (978-1-4263-0029-5(8)) National Geographic Society. (National Geographic Children's Bks.).
Pipe, Jim. Japan in Our World. 2011. (Countries in Our World Ser.). 32p. (YA). (gr. 4-7). lib. bdg. 28.50 (978-1-59920-390-4(1)) Black Rabbit Bks.
Popper, Garry. Keito in Japan. Johnson, Andi, illus. 2004. 36p. (gr. -1-7). 4.00 (978-1-84161-058-0(5)) Ravette Publishing, Ltd. GBR. Dist: Parkwest Pubns., Inc.
Powell, Jillian. Descubramos Japón (Looking at Japan) 2007. (Descubramos paises del mundo (Spanish- Looking at Countries) Ser.). (SPA.). 32p. (gr. 1-5). pap. 10.50 (978-0-8368-8192-9(3), Gareth Stevens Learning Library) Stevens, Gareth Publishing LLLP.
—Looking at Japan. 2007. (Looking at Countries Ser.). 32p. (gr. 1-5). pap. 10.50 (978-0-8368-8178-3(8)); (Illus.). lib. bdg. 26.00 (978-0-8368-8171-4(0)) Stevens, Gareth Publishing LLLP. (Gareth Stevens Learning Library).
Roberts, Jeremy. Japanese Mythology A to Z, Second Edition. 2nd rev. ed. 2009. (Mythology A to Z Ser.). (Illus.). 168p. (gr. 5-8). 45.00 (978-1-60413-435-3(6), Chelsea Hse.) Facts On File, Inc.
Roop, Peter & Roop, Connie. Japan. 2016. (Visit To Ser.). (ENG.). 32p. pap. 8.29 (978-1-4846-3873-6(5), Heinemann First Library) Heinemann-Raintree.
Singh, Asavari. How to Draw the Most Exciting, Awesome Manga, 1 vol. James, Martin et al, illus. 2011. (Drawing Ser.). (ENG.). 48p. (gr. 3-4). lib. bdg. 31.99 (978-1-4296-6593-3(9)) Capstone Press of Coughlan Cos.
Somervill, Barbara. Japan. 2010. (Explorer Library: Social Studies Explorer Ser.). (ENG.). 48p. (gr. 4-8). lib. bdg. 31.36 (978-1-60279-832-8(X), 200530) Cherry Lake Publishing.
Somervill, Barbara A. Japan. 2011. (Enchantment of the World Ser.). (ENG., Illus.). 144p. (J). (gr. 5-9). lib. bdg. 40.00 (978-0-531-25354-0(6)) Scholastic Library Publishing.
Southgate, Anna & Sparrow, Keith. Drawing Manga Boys. 2011. (J). 84.30 (978-1-4488-4807-2(5)); pap. 14.05 (978-1-4488-4803-4(2)); lib. bdg. 33.25 (978-1-4488-4799-0(0)) Rosen Publishing Group, Inc., The. (Rosen Reference).
—Drawing Manga Expressions & Poses. 2011. (J). pap. 14.05 (978-1-4488-4804-1(0)); lib. bdg. 33.25 (978-1-4488-4800-3(8)) Rosen Publishing Group, Inc., The. (Rosen Reference).
—Drawing Manga Weapons, Vehicles, & Accessories. 2011. (Illus.). 80p. (J). 84.30 (978-1-4488-4809-6(1)); pap. 14.05 (978-1-4488-4805-8(9)); lib. bdg. 33.25 (978-1-4488-4801-0(6)) Rosen Publishing Group, Inc., The. (Rosen Reference).
Stewart, Tobi Stanton. A Primary Source Guide to Japan. (Countries of the World). 24p. 2009. (gr. 2-3). 42.50 (978-1-61512-037-6(8)) 2003. (ENG., Illus.). (gr. 3-6). pap. 8.25 (978-0-8239-8078-9(2)) 2003. (Illus.). (J). lib. bdg. 22.60 (978-0-8239-6594-6(5)) Rosen Publishing Group, Inc., The. (PowerKids Pr.).
Streissguth, Thomas. Japan. 2008. (Country Explorers Ser.). (ENG., Illus.). 48p. (gr. 2-4). lib. bdg. 29.27 (978-0-8225-8659-3(2)) Lerner Publishing Group.
Streissguth, Tom. Japan. 2008. pap. 40.95 (978-0-8225-9303-4(3)) Lerner Publishing Group.
Taylor, Des. Cartoons & Manga. 2012. (Master This! Ser.). (Illus.). 32p. (J). lib. bdg. 25.25 (978-1-4488-5283-3(8), PowerKids Pr.) Rosen Publishing Group, Inc., The.
Tecco, Betsy Dru. How to Draw Japan's Sights & Symbols. 2009. (Kid's Guide to Drawing the Countries of the World Ser.). 48p. (gr. 4-4). 53.00 (978-1-61511-116-9(6), PowerKids Pr.) Rosen Publishing Group, Inc., The.
Thomas, Mark. The Akashi-Kaikyo Bridge: World's Longest Bridge. 2009. (Record-Breaking Structures Ser.). 24p. (gr. 1-2). 42.50 (978-1-60852-453-2(1), PowerKids Pr.) Rosen Publishing Group, Inc., The.
—El puente Akashi Kaikyo: El puente más largo del mundo (the Akashi-Kaikyo Bridge: World's Longest Bridge) 2009. (Estructuras extraordinarias (Record-Breaking Structures) Ser.). (SPA.). 24p. (gr. 1-2). 42.50 (978-1-61512-311-7(3), Editorial Buenas Letras) Rosen Publishing Group, Inc., The.
Tidmarsh, Celia. Focus on Japan. 2006. (World in Focus Ser.). (Illus.). 64p. (gr. 5-12). pap. 14.05 (978-0-8368-6729-9(7)); lib. bdg. 34.00 (978-0-8368-6722-0(X)) Stevens, Gareth Publishing LLLP. (Gareth Stevens Secondary Library).
Whelan, Gloria & Nolan, Jenny. K Is for Kabuki: A Japan Alphabet. Han, Oki S., illus. 2009. (Discover the World Ser.). (ENG.). 40p. (J). (gr. 1-3). 17.95 (978-1-58536-444-2(4), 202169) Sleeping Bear Pr.
White, Bender Richardson. Shinto. 3rd rev. ed. 2009. (World Religions Ser.). (Illus.). 144p. (gr. 6-12). 40.00 (978-1-60413-113-0(6), Chelsea Hse.) Facts On File, Inc.
Zocchi, Judy. In Japan. Brodie, Neale, illus. 2005. (Global Adventures II Ser.). 32p. (J). per. 10.95 (978-1-59646-140-6(3)) Dingles & Co.
—In Japan/en Japón. Brodie, Neale, illus. 2005. (Global Adventures II Ser.).Tr. of En Japón. (ENG & SPA.). 32p. (J). per. 10.95 (978-1-59646-142-0(X)) Dingles & Co.

JAPAN—BIOGRAPHY

Benge, Janet & Benge, Geoff. Jacob Deshazer: Forgive Your Enemies. 2009. (ENG.). 224p. (YA). pap. 9.99 (978-1-57658-475-0(5)) YWAM Publishing.
Bloom, Harold, intro. The Tale of Genji. 2003. (Bloom's Modern Critical Interpretations Ser.). (Illus.). 176p. (C). (gr. 9-13). 45.00 (978-0-7910-7584-5(2), Chelsea Hse.) Facts On File, Inc.
Christopher, Matt. At the Plate with... Ichiro. 2003. (ENG., Illus.). 112p. (J). (gr. 5-8). pap. 15.99 (978-0-316-13679-2(4)) Little, Brown Bks. for Young Readers.
Grayson, Robert. Sony: The Company & Its Founders, 1 vol. 2012. (Technology Pioneers Set 2 Ser.). (ENG.). 112p. (J). (gr. 6-12). lib. bdg. 35.64 (978-1-61783-335-9(5), Essential Library) ABDO Publishing Co.
Hillenbrand, Laura. Unbroken: An Olympian's Journey from Airman to Castaway to Captive (Young Readers Edition) 2017. lib. bdg. 22.10 **(978-0-606-39867-1(8))** Turtleback Bks.
Lenburg, Jeff. Hayao Miyazaki. 2012. (Legends of Animation Ser.). (Illus.). 120p. (gr. 6-12). 34.95 (978-1-60413-841-2(6), Chelsea Hse.) Facts On File, Inc.
Levin, Judith. Ichiro Suzuki. (Baseball Superstars Ser.). (Illus.). 2008. 144p. (gr. 6-12). pap. 11.95 (978-0-7910-9849-3(4), Checkmark Bks.) 2007. 135p. (YA). (gr. 7-12). lib. bdg. 30.00 (978-0-7910-9440-2(5)) Facts On File, Inc.
Mochizuki, Ken. Passage to Freedom: The Sugihara Story. 2004. (Illus.). (J). (gr. k-3). spiral bd. (978-0-616-03098-1(3)) Canadian National Institute for the Blind/Institut National Canadien pour les Aveugles.
—Passage to Freedom: The Sugihara Story. 2005. 19.45 (978-0-7569-4773-6(1)) Perfection Learning Corp.
Mortensen, Lori. Satoshi Tajiri: Pokemon Creator. 2009. (Innovators Ser.). (ENG., Illus.). 64p. (J). (gr. 4-8). lib. bdg. 29.95 (978-0-7377-4269-5(0), LML02109-243872, Kidhaven) Cengage Gale.
Savage, Jeff. Ichiro Suzuki. (Amazing Athletes Ser.). 2007. (J). pap. 6.95 (978-0-8225-7266-4(4), Lerner Pubns.) 2005. (Illus.). 32p. (gr. 3-4). lib. bdg. 22.60 (978-0-8225-1344-5(7)) Lerner Publishing Group.
Turner, Pamela S. Samurai Rising: The Epic Life of Minamoto Yoshitsune. Hinds, Gareth, illus. 2016. (ENG.). 256p. (YA). (gr. 7-12). 16.95 (978-1-58089-584-2(0)) Charlesbridge Publishing, Inc.
Viola, Herman J. & Layson, Annelex Hofstra. Lost Childhood: My Life in a Japanese Prison Camp During World War II. 2008. (ENG., Illus.). (J). (gr. 5). 112p. 15.95 (978-1-4263-0321-0(1)); 128p. lib. bdg. 23.90 (978-1-4263-0322-7(X)) National Geographic Society. (National Geographic Children's Bks.).

JAPAN—CIVILIZATION

Centore, Michael. Japan, Vol. 12. 2015. (Major Nations in a Global World: Tradition, Culture, & Daily Life Ser.). (Illus.). 64p. (J). (gr. 7). 23.95 (978-1-4222-3347-4(2)) Mason Crest.
Greene, Meg. The Technology of Ancient Japan. (Technology of the Ancient World Ser.). 48p. 2009. (gr. 6-6). 61.20 (978-1-60854-241-3(6), Rosen Reference) 2005. (Illus.). (J). (gr. 5-8). lib. bdg. 29.25 (978-1-4042-0559-8(4)) Rosen Publishing Group, Inc., The.
Heapy, Teresa. Japanese Culture, 1 vol. 2012. (Global Cultures Ser.). (ENG., Illus.). 48p. (gr. 4-6). pap. 9.95 (978-1-4329-6789-5(4)); 32.65 (978-1-4329-6780-2(0)) Heinemann-Raintree. (NA-h).
Kalman, Bobbie. Japan: The Culture. 3rd rev. ed. 2008. (ENG., Illus.). 32p. (J). (gr. 3-9). pap. (978-0-7787-9666-4(3)) Crabtree Publishing Co.
Kuskowski, Alex. Super Simple Japanese Art: Fun & Easy Art from Around the World, 1 vol. 2014. (Super Simple Cultural Art Set 2 Ser.). (ENG.). 32p. (gr. 5-10). lib. bdg. 27.07 (978-1-62403-281-3(8), Super SandCastle) ABDO Publishing Co.
Sepahban, Lois. Samurai Warriors. 2015. (Ancient Warriors Ser.). (ENG.). 32p. (J). (gr. 2-5). 28.50 (978-1-63143-759-5(3), 208591) Child's World, Inc., The.

JAPAN—FICTION

Ando, Natsumi. Arisa 1. 2012. (Arisa Ser.). (ENG., Illus.). 208p. pap. 10.99 (978-1-61262-335-1(2)) Kodansha America, Inc.
Ann, Dee. Burden of Silence. 2013. 136p. pap. (978-1-4602-2099-3(4)) FriesenPress.
Asai, Carrie. The Book of the Shadow. Alarcao, Renato, illus. 2013. (Samurai Girl Ser.: 2). (ENG.). 224p. (YA). (gr. 11). pap. 13.99 (978-1-4814-1540-8(9), Simon Pulse) Simon Pulse.
Avila, Kat. Hanako Loves Monsters. 2008. 32p. 14.98 (978-1-4357-0188-5(7)) Lulu Pr., Inc.
Benwell, Sarah. The Last Leaves Falling. 2015. (ENG., Illus.). 368p. (YA). (gr. 9). 17.99 (978-1-4814-3065-4(3)) Simon & Schuster Children's Publishing.
Bidoli, Katie. Karate Adventures of Kisho, Hana, & Nobu: Karate Is for Everyone! 2006. (Illus.). 16p. (J). 10.00 (978-1-60243-029-7(2)) Keen's Martial Arts Academy.
Bradford, Chris. The Ring of Earth. 4th ed. 2010. (Young Samurai Ser.: 4). (ENG., Illus.). 336p. (YA). (gr. 7). pap. 8.99 (978-0-14-133253-6(0), Penguin Global) Penguin Publishing Group.
—The Ring of Fire. 6th ed. 2011. (Young Samurai Ser.: 6). (ENG., Illus.). 352p. (YA). (gr. 7). pap. 10.95 (978-0-14-133255-0(7)) Penguin Bks., Ltd. GBR. Dist: Independent Pubs. Group.
—The Ring of Sky. 8th ed. 2012. (Young Samurai Ser.: 8). (ENG., Illus.). 384p. (YA). (gr. 7). pap. 10.95 (978-0-14-133972-6(1)) Penguin Bks., Ltd. GBR. Dist: Independent Pubs. Group.
—The Ring of Water. 5th ed. 2011. (Young Samurai Ser.: 5). (ENG., Illus.). 320p. (YA). (gr. 7). pap. 8.99 (978-0-14-133254-3(9)) Penguin Bks., Ltd. GBR. Dist: Independent Pubs. Group.
—The Ring of Wind. 7th ed. 2012. (Young Samurai Ser.: 7). (ENG., Illus.). 368p. (YA). (gr. 7). 8.99 (978-0-14-133971-9(3), Penguin Global) Penguin Publishing Group.
—The Way of the Warrior, Bk. 1. 2008. (Young Samurai Ser.: 1). (ENG., Illus.). 352p. (J). (gr. 6-10). pap. 12.99 **(978-0-14-132430-2(9))** Penguin Bks., Ltd. GBR. Dist: Independent Pubs. Group.
—Young Samurai the Way of the Dragon. l.t. ed. 2012. (Young Samurai Ser.). (ENG.). 644p. (J). (gr. 9-12). 23.99 (978-1-4104-4466-0(X)) Thorndike Pr.
—Young Samurai: the Way of the Sword. 2011. 448p. pap. 7.99 (978-1-4231-2937-0(7)) Hyperion Pr.
—Young Samurai the Way of the Sword. l.t. ed. 2012. (Young Samurai Ser.). (ENG.). 547p. (J). (gr. 6-9). 23.99 (978-1-4104-4404-2(X)) Thorndike Pr.
Burkinshaw, Kathleen. The Last Cherry Blossom. 2016. (ENG.). 240p. (J). (gr. 5-8). 16.99 (978-1-63450-693-9(6), Sky Pony Pr.) Skyhorse Publishing Co., Inc.
Canning, Charlie. The 89th Temple. 2012. (ENG.). 211p. pap. 14.95 (978-1-4787-1763-8(7)) Outskirts Pr., Inc.
The Case of the Secret Box. 2007. 56p. pap. 7.75 (978-0-8341-2288-8(X), 083-412-288X) Beacon Hill Pr. of Kansas City.
Chrystyn, Julie. Hachiko: The Story of a Loyal Akita & the Royal Dogs of Japan. 2009. 48p. pap. 7.95 (978-1-59777-629-5(7)) Phoenix Bks., Inc.
Clum, James. Koji's Ninja Secrets. 2011. 36p. pap. 15.96 (978-0-557-60314-5(5)) Lulu Pr., Inc.
Coatsworth, Elizabeth. The Cat Who Went to Heaven. 2011. 7.64 (978-0-7848-3455-8(5), Everbind) Marco Bk. Co.
—The Cat Who Went to Heaven. Vitale, Raoul, illus. 2008. (ENG.). 96p. (J). (gr. 3-7). pap. 6.99 (978-1-4169-4973-2(9), Simon & Schuster/Paula Wiseman Bks.) Simon & Schuster/Paula Wiseman Bks.
—Gata Que Se Fue para el Cielo. 2011. (SPA.). 104p. (gr. 5-8). pap. 12.99 (978-958-04-1530-5(7), NR4853) Norma S.A. COL. Dist: Lectorum Pubns., Inc.
Coerr, Eleanor. Circus Day in Japan: Bilingual English & Japanese Text. Matsunari, Yumi, tr. 2010. (ENG & JPN., Illus.). 48p. (J). (gr. -1-3). 15.95 (978-4-8053-1059-5(6)) Tuttle Publishing.
Coerr, Eleanor & Matsunari, Yumi. Circus Day in Japan: Bilingual English & Japanese Text. 2016. (ENG & JPN., Illus.). 48p. (J). (gr. -1-3). 9.95 (978-0-8048-4743-8(6)) Tuttle Publishing.
Dahl, Michael. Monster Hunter, 1 vol. Aime, Luigi, illus. 2012. (Dragonborn Ser.). (ENG.). 72p. (gr. 1-3). pap. 7.10 (978-1-4342-4256-3(0)); lib. bdg. 23.99 (978-1-4342-4040-8(1)) Stone Arch Bks.
Dalton, Annie. Budding Star: Mission - Rescue a Pop Princess. 2008. (Mel Beeby Agent Angel Ser.). (ENG.). 208p. (J). (gr. 4-7). pap. 6.95 (978-0-00-720478-6(7)) HarperCollins Pubs. Ltd. GBR. Dist: Independent Pubs. Group.
—The Divine Collection: Three Amazing Missions in One Book! 2008. (Mel Beeby Agent Angel Ser.). (ENG., Illus.). 608p. (J). (gr. 4-7). pap. 19.95 (978-0-00-719074-4(3)) HarperCollins Pubs. Ltd. GBR. Dist: Independent Pubs. Group.
Dilloway, Margaret. Momotaro Xander & the Dream Thief. Yoon, Choong, illus. 2017. (Momotaro Ser.). (ENG.). 336p. (J). (gr. 3-7). 16.99 (978-1-4847-2488-0(7)) Hyperion Bks. for Children.
Duey, Kathleen. Samurai. Epstein, Eugene, illus. Gould, Robert, photos by. 2007. (Time Soldiers Ser.). (ENG.). 96p. (gr. k-2). 24.21 (978-1-59961-229-4(1)) Spotlight.
Egan, Tim. Dodsworth in Tokyo. Egan, Tim, illus. 2014. (Green Light Readers Level 3 Ser.). (ENG., Illus.). 48p. (J). (gr. 1-4). pap. 3.99 (978-0-544-33915-6(0), HMH Books For Young Readers) Houghton Mifflin Harcourt Publishing Co.
Falk, Nick. The Battle for the Golden Egg. Flowers, Tony, illus. 2015. (Samurai vs Ninja Ser.: 1). (ENG.). 96p. (J). (gr. 1-3). pap. 7.99 (978-0-85798-605-4(8)) Random Hse. Australia AUS. Dist: Independent Pubs. Group.
—The Curse of the Oni. Flowers, Tony, illus. 2016. (Samurai vs Ninja Ser.: 4). (ENG.). 96p. (J). (gr. 1-3). pap. 7.99 (978-0-85798-640-5(6)) Random Hse. Australia AUS. Dist: Independent Pubs. Group.
—The Race for the Shogun's Treasure. Flowers, Tony, illus. 2015. (Samurai vs Ninja Ser.: 2). (ENG.). 96p. (J). (gr. 1-3). pap. 7.99 (978-0-85798-636-8(8)) Random Hse. Australia AUS. Dist: Independent Pubs. Group.
Fanning, Kieran. The Black Lotus: The Samurai Wars. 2016. (ENG.). 304p. (J). (gr. 3-7). 16.99 (978-0-545-94028-3(1), Chicken Hse., The) Scholastic, Inc.
Friesner, Esther. Spirit's Chosen. 2013. (Princesses of Myth Ser.). (ENG., Illus.). 496p. (YA). (gr. 7). 17.99 (978-0-375-86908-2(5), Random Hse. Bks. for Young Readers) Random Hse. Children's Bks.
Friesner, Esther M. Spirit's Bride. 2014. (Princesses of Myth Ser.). (ENG., Illus.). 512p. (YA). (gr. 7). pap. 10.99 (978-0-375-87316-4(3), Ember) Random Hse. Children's Bks.
—Spirit's Princess. (Princesses of Myth Ser.). (ENG.). (YA). (gr. 7). 2013. 480p. pap. 10.99 (978-0-375-87314-0(7), Bluefire) 2012. 464p. 17.99 (978-0-375-86907-5(7), Random Hse. Bks. for Young Readers) Random Hse. Children's Bks.
—Spirit's Princess. 2012. 449p. (YA). (978-0-375-87315-7(5)) Random Hse., Inc.
Fussell, Sandy. Owl Ninja. James, Rhian Nest, illus. 2011. (Samurai Kids Ser.: 2). (ENG.). 272p. (J). (gr. 4-7). 15.99 (978-0-7636-5003-2(X)) Candlewick Pr.
—Shaolin Tiger. James, Rhian Nest, illus. 2011. (Samurai Kids Ser.: 3). (ENG.). 272p. (J). (gr. 4-7). pap. 6.99 (978-0-7636-5702-4(6)) Candlewick Pr.
—White Crane. James, Rhian Nest, illus. 2010. (Samurai Kids Ser.: 1). (ENG.). 256p. (J). (gr. 4-7). 15.99 (978-0-7636-4503-8(6)) Candlewick Pr.
Gerber, Linda. Now & Zen. 2006. (S. A. S. S. Ser.). (ENG., Illus.). 224p. (YA). (gr. 7-18). 7.99 (978-0-14-240657-1(0), Speak) Penguin Young Readers Group.
Gerstein, Mordicai, illus. Three Samurai Cats: A Story from Japan. 2004. (ENG.). 32p. (J). (gr. k-3). 6.95 (978-0-8234-1877-0(4)) Holiday Hse., Inc.
—Three Samurai Cats: A Story from Japan. 2004. (J). (978-0-439-69256-4(3)) Scholastic, Inc.
Gilligan, Shannon. The Mystery of Ura Senke. 2005. (Illus.). 120p. (Orig.). (J). (978-0-7608-9701-0(8)) Sundance/Newbridge Educational Publishing.
Gollub, Matthew. Ten Oni Drummers. Stone, Kazuko G., illus. 2013. (JPN & ENG.). 32p. (J). (gr. -1-3). 16.95 (978-1-58430-011-3(6)) Lee & Low Bks., Inc.
—Ten Oni Drummers. Stone, Kazuko G., illus. 2017. (J). (978-1-889910-51-2(1)) Tortuga Pr.
Goto, Scott. Perfect Sword. Goto, Scott, illus. 2010. (ENG., Illus.). 48p. (J). (gr. 1-4). pap. 8.95 (978-1-57091-698-4(5)) Charlesbridge Publishing, Inc.
Gratz, Alan. Samurai Shortstop. 2008. (ENG.). 288p. (YA). (gr. 7-18). 7.99 (978-0-14-241099-8(3), Speak) Penguin Young Readers Group.
Haibara, Yak & Haibara, Yak. Sengoku Basara: Samurai Legends Volume 2: Samurai Legends Volume 2, 2 vols. 2013. (ENG., Illus.). 424p. (YA). pap. 19.99 (978-1-926778-59-4(6), 9781926778594) URON Entertainment Corp. CAN. Dist: Diamond Comic Distributors, Inc.
Haidar, Hanna. Earl's Big Adventure in Japan. Newton, Kimberly, illus. 2012. 26p. (J). (978-0-9800975-1-1(7)) Old Silver Pr.
Hall, H. Tom. The Golden Tombo. 2011. 42p. 35.95 (978-1-258-10444-3(X)) Literary Licensing, LLC.
Hamazaki, Tatsuya. . hack //Legend of the Twilight, Volume 1: Kaplan SAT/ACT Vocabulary-Building Manga. Izumi, Rei, illus. 2007. (Kaplan SAT/ACT Score-Raising Manga Ser.). 192p. pap. 9.99 (978-1-4277-5497-4(7)) Kaplan Publishing.
Hana's Year: Evaluation Guide. 2006. (J). (978-1-55942-408-0(7)) Witcher Productions.
Harrington, Claudia. My Mom & Dad, 1 vol. Persico, Zoe, illus. 2016. (ENG.). 32p. (J). (978-1-62402-107-7(7)) Magic Wagon.
Haugaard, Erik Christian & Haugaard, Erik C. The Revenge of the Forty-Seven Samurai. 2005. (ENG.). 240p. (J). (gr. 5-7). pap. 14.95 (978-0-618-54896-5(3)) Houghton Mifflin Harcourt Publishing Co.

—The Samurai's Tale. 2005. (ENG.). 256p. (J). (gr. 5-7). pap. 7.99 *(978-0-618-61512-4(1))* Houghton Mifflin Harcourt Publishing Co.

Hearn, Lian. Leyendas de los Otori I. 2004. (SPA.). 312p. (YA). (gr. 8-12). pap. 13.95 *(978-956-239-300-3(3))* Santillana USA Publishing Co., Inc.

Heffernan, John. Hotaka: Through My Eyes - Natural Disaster Zones. White, Lyn, ed. 2017. (Through My Eyes Ser.). (ENG.). 224p. (J). (gr. 6-9). pap. 12.99 ***(978-1-76011-376-6(X))*** Allen & Unwin AUS. Dist: Independent Pubs. Group.

Henrichs, Wendy. I Am Tama, Lucky Cat: A Japanese Legend, 1 vol. Jaeggi, Yoshiko, illus. 2011. (ENG.). 32p. (J). (gr. k-4). 16.95 *(978-1-56145-589-8(X),* Peachtree Junior) Peachtree Pubs.

Higgins, Nadia. Issun Boshi (One-Inch Boy) A Japanese Folktale. Morrow, J. T., illus. 2011. (Folktales from Around the World Ser.). (ENG.). 24p. (J). (gr. k-3). 28.50 *(978-1-60973-139-7(5),* 201143) Child's World, Inc., The.

Higgins, Simon. Moonshadow #2: the Nightmare Ninja. 2012. (Moonshadow Ser.: 2). (ENG.). 384p. (J). (gr. 3-7). pap. 6.99 *(978-0-316-05534-5(4))* Little, Brown Bks. for Young Readers.

—Moonshadow: Rise of the Ninja. 2011. (Moonshadow Ser.: 1). (ENG.). 352p. (J). (gr. 3-7). pap. 6.99 *(978-0-316-05532-1(8))* Little, Brown Bks. for Young Readers.

Hiwatari, Saki. Please Save My Earth, Vol. 18. Hiwatari, Saki, illus. 2006. (Please Save My Earth Ser.: 18). (ENG., Illus.). 208p. pap. 9.99 *(978-1-4215-0551-0(7))* Viz Media.

—Please Save My Earth, Vol. 17. Hiwatari, Saki, illus. 2006. (ENG., Illus.). 208p. pap. 9.99 *(978-1-4215-0550-3(9))* Viz Media.

Hoobler, Dorothy & Hoobler, Thomas. The Demon in the Teahouse. 2005. 181p. (J). (gr. 4-7). 13.65 *(978-0-7569-6725-3(2))* Perfection Learning Corp.

—The Ghost in the Tokaido Inn. 2005. (ENG.). 240p. (J). (gr. 3-7). 6.99 *(978-0-14-240541-3(8),* Puffin Books) Penguin Young Readers Group.

—The Ghost in the Tokaido Inn. 2005. 214p. (J). (gr. 4-7). 14.65 *(978-0-7569-6403-0(2))* Perfection Learning Corp.

—In Darkness, Death. 2005. (Puffin Sleuth Novels Ser.). 195p. (J). (gr. 5-9). 14.65 *(978-0-7569-5457-4(6))* Perfection Learning Corp.

—Seven Paths to Death. 2009. (ENG.). 208p. (YA). (gr. 7-7). 7.99 *(978-0-14-241466-8(2),* Puffin Books) Penguin Young Readers Group.

—The Sword That Cut the Burning Grass. 2006. 211p. (gr. 5-9). 17.00 *(978-0-7569-6907-3(7))* Perfection Learning Corp.

Hulme-Cross, Benjamin. The Samurai's Assassin. Rinaldi, Angelo, illus. 2015. (ENG.). 160p. (J). *(978-0-7787-1766-9(6))* Crabtree Publishing Co.

Hunt, Elizabeth Singer & Weinstein Books Staff. The Theft of the Samurai Sword: Japan. Williamson, Brian, illus. 2009. (Secret Agent Jack Stalwart Ser.: 11). (ENG.). 128p. (J). (gr. 1-4). pap. 5.99 *(978-1-60286-098-8(X),* Weinstein Bks.) Perseus Bks. Group.

Ihara, Shigekatsu. Pokémon Vol. 8: Diamond & Pearl Adventure! Ihara, Shigekatsu, illus. 2010. (ENG., Illus.). 192p. (J). pap. 9.99 *(978-1-4215-3671-2(4))* Viz Media.

Iinuma, Yuuki. Itsuwaribito, Vol. 14. 2015. (ENG.). 192p. pap. 9.99 *(978-1-4215-6525-5(0))* Viz Media.

Ikeda, Daisaku. The Cherry Tree. McCaughrean, Geraldine, tr. from JPN. Wildsmith, Brian, illus. 2013. 6.95 *(978-1-935523-57-4(0))* World Tribune Pr.

Inui, Tomiko. The Secret of the Blue Glass. Takemori, Ginny Tapley, tr. from JPN. 2016. (ENG., Illus.). 192p. (YA). (gr. 5-12). pap. 12.95 *(978-1-78269-034-4(4),* Pushkin Press) Steerforth Pr.

Inzana, Ryan. Ichiro. (ENG., Illus.). 288p. (YA). (gr. 7). 2014. pap. 12.99 *(978-0-547-61789-3(5),* HMH Books For Young Readers) 2012. 24.99 *(978-0-547-25269-8(2))* Houghton Mifflin Harcourt Publishing Co.

Inzer, Christine Mari. Diary of a Tokyo Teen. 2016. (ENG., Illus.). 128p. (J). (gr. 6-12). pap. 14.99 *(978-4-8053-1396-1(X))* Tuttle Publishing.

Izumi, Kaneyoshi. Seiho Boys' High School!, Vol. 3. Izumi, Kaneyoshi, illus. 2010. (ENG., Illus.). 200p. pap. 9.99 *(978-1-4215-3733-7(8))* Viz Media.

Kajikawa, Kimiko. Tsunami! Young, Ed, illus. 2010. (Rise & Shine Ser.). (ENG.). 32p. (C). (gr. -1-k). 27.95 *(978-0-399-25006-4(9))* National Geographic School Publishing, Inc.

Kajikawa, Kimiko, et al. Yoshi's Feast. Heo, Yumi, illus. 2003. (Avenues Ser.). (ENG.). 32p. (C). (gr. -1-3). pap. 21.95 *(978-0-7894-2607-9(2))* National Geographic School Publishing, Inc.

Kamachi, Kazuma. A Certain Magical Index, Vol. 1. Haimura, Kiyotaka, illus. 2014. (Certain Magical Index Ser.: 1). (ENG.). 224p. (YA). (gr. 8-17). 14.00 *(978-0-316-33912-4(1),* Yen Pr.) Orbit.

Kann, Victoria. Cherry Blossom. Kann, Victoria, illus. 2015. (I Can Read Level 1 Ser.). (ENG., Illus.). 32p. (J). (gr. -1-3). 16.99 *(978-0-06-224593-9(7));* pap. 3.99 *(978-0-06-224594-6(5))* HarperCollins Pubs.

Kishimoto, Masashi. Naruto: Chapter Book, Vol. 11. Kishimoto, Masashi, illus. 2010. (ENG., Illus.). 80p. (J). pap. 4.99 *(978-1-4215-3041-3(4))* Viz Media.

—Naruto: Chapter Book, Vol. 13. Kishimoto, Masashi, illus. 2010. (ENG., Illus.). 80p. (J). pap. 4.99 *(978-1-4215-3043-7(0))* Viz Media.

—Naruto: Chapter Book, Vol. 16. Kishimoto, Masashi, illus. 2010. (ENG., Illus.). 80p. (J). pap. 4.99 *(978-1-4215-3046-8(5))* Viz Media.

—Naruto: Chapter Book, Vol. 2. Kishimoto, Masashi, illus. 2008. (ENG., Illus.). 80p. (J). (gr. 1-5). pap. 4.99 *(978-1-4215-2213-5(6))* Viz Media.

—Naruto: Chapter Book, Vol. 5. Kishimoto, Masashi, illus. 2009. (ENG., Illus.). 80p. (J). (gr. 1). pap. 4.99 *(978-1-4215-2315-6(9))* Viz Media.

Kline, Spencer. The Adventures of Fujimori-San. Brown, E. Jackie, illus. 2010. 20p. 12.99 *(978-1-4520-6275-4(7))* AuthorHouse.

Krensky, Stephen. Bokuden & the Bully: [A Japanese Folktale]. Noll, Cheryl, illus. 2009. (On My Own Folklore Ser.). (ENG.). 48p. (gr. 2-4). pap. 6.95 *(978-1-58013-847-5(0),* First Avenue Editions) Lerner Publishing Group.

Krulik, Nancy. Don't Mess with the Ninja Puppy!, No. 6. Braun, Sebastien, illus. 2014. (Magic Bone Ser.: 6). (ENG.). 128p. (J). (gr. 1-3). 5.99 *(978-0-448-48095-4(6),* Grosset & Dunlap) Penguin Young Readers Group.

—Don't Mess with the Ninja Puppy! 2014. (Magic Bone Ser.: 6). lib. bdg. 14.75 *(978-0-606-36162-0(6))* Turtleback Bks.

Kusaka, Hidenori. Pokémon Black & White, Vol. 12. Yamamoto, Satoshi, illus. 2013. (ENG.). 96p. (J). pap. 4.99 *(978-1-4215-5896-7(3))* Viz Media.

—Pokémon Black & White, Vol. 13. Yamamoto, Satoshi, illus. 2013. (ENG.). 96p. (J). pap. 4.99 *(978-1-4215-5897-4(1))* Viz Media.

Lake, Nick. The Betrayal of the Living. (ENG., Illus.). 368p. (YA). (gr. 9). 2013. (Blood Ninja Ser.: Bk. 3). pap. 9.99 *(978-1-4424-2680-1(2))* 2012. 17.99 *(978-1-4424-2679-5(9))* Simon & Schuster Bks. For Young Readers. (Simon & Schuster Bks. For Young Readers).

—Blood Ninja. 2010. (Blood Ninja Ser.: Bk. 1). (ENG., Illus.). 400p. (YA). (gr. 7). pap. 9.99 *(978-1-4169-8628-7(6),* Simon & Schuster Bks. For Young Readers) Simon & Schuster Bks. For Young Readers.

—The Revenge of Lord Oda. (ENG., Illus.). (YA). (gr. 7). 2011. (Blood Ninja Ser.: Bk. 2). 416p. pap. 9.99 *(978-1-4169-8630-0(8))* 2010. 400p. 16.99 *(978-1-4169-8629-4(4))* Simon & Schuster Bks. For Young Readers. (Simon & Schuster Bks. For Young Readers).

Lane, Dakota. Gothic Lolita: A Mystical Thriller. Lane, Dakota, illus. 2008. (ENG., Illus.). 208p. (YA). (gr. 7-18). 17.99 *(978-1-4169-1396-2(3),* Atheneum Bks. for Young Readers) Simon & Schuster Children's Publishing.

Leibold, Jay. Secret of the Ninja. Nugent, Suzanne & Marron, Jose, illus. 2007. (Choose Your Own Adventure Ser.: Vol. 16). 124p. (J). (gr. 4-7). per. 6.99 *(978-1-933390-16-1(6))* Chooseco LLC.

Lemke, Donald B. The Awakening, 1 vol. 2011. (Good vs Evil Ser.). (ENG.). 48p. (J). (gr. 1-2). lib. bdg. 23.99 *(978-1-4342-2089-9(3),* Good vs Evil) Stone Arch Bks.

Lendroth, Susan. Maneki Neko: The Tale of the Beckoning Cat. Otoshi, Kathryn, illus. 2010. (J). *(978-1-885008-39-8(2),* Shen's Bks.) Lee & Low Bks., Inc.

Li, August. Fox-Hat & Neko. 2016. (ENG., Illus.). (YA). 29.99 ***(978-1-63533-018-2(1),*** Harmony Ink Pr.) Dreamspinner Pr.

Libster, Bernard. The Bonsai Bear. Cheung, Aries, illus. 2006. 31p. (J). (gr. k-4). reprint ed. 16.00 *(978-1-4223-5857-3(7))* DIANE Publishing Co.

Lifton, Betty Jean. Taka-Chan & I: A Dog's Journey to Japan by Runcible. Hosoe, Eikoh, photos by. 2012. (ENG., Illus.). 64p. (J). (gr. k-4). 16.95 *(978-1-59017-502-6(6),* NYR Children's Collection) New York Review of Bks., Inc., The.

London, C. Alexander. Blood in the Water. 2014. (Tides of War Ser.: 1). (ENG.). 224p. (J). (gr. 5-9). pap. 5.99 *(978-0-545-66298-7(2),* Scholastic Paperbacks) Scholastic, Inc.

Low, Chen-Chen-Chen. Lizzie May & Oshin. 2009. 46p. pap. 29.99 *(978-1-4092-5740-0(1))* Lulu Pr., Inc.

Lowitz, Leza. Up from the Sea. 2016. (ENG.). 272p. (YA). (gr. 7). 17.99 *(978-0-553-53474-0(2),* Crown Books For Young Readers) Random Hse. Children's Bks.

Lowitz, Leza & Oketani, Shogo. Jet Black & the Ninja Wind. 2013. (ENG., Illus.). 320p. (J). (gr. 7-12). 17.99 *(978-4-8053-1284-1(X))* Tuttle Publishing.

Lydia Jane. Fifth Moon: The First Installment in the Gates Trilogy. 2007. 480p. 35.95 *(978-0-595-91408-1(X));* per. 25.95 *(978-0-595-43671-2(4))* iUniverse, Inc.

Manley, Ruth. The Plum-Rain Scroll. 2005. (UQP Children's Classics Ser.). 378p. (J). pap. *(978-0-7022-3505-4(9))* Univ. of Queensland Pr.

Marriott, Zoë. The Name of the Blade. 2014. (ENG.). 368p. (YA). (gr. 7). 16.99 *(978-0-7636-6957-7(1))* Candlewick Pr.

Marsh, Carole. The Mystery at Mt. Fuji: Tokyo, Japan. 2009. (Around the World in 80 Mysteries Ser.). 131p. (J). 18.99 *(978-0-635-07016-6(2),* Marsh, Carole Mysteries) Gallopade International.

Martin, Benjamin. Revenge of the Akuma Clan. 2013. (ENG.). 320p. (J). (gr. 7-12). 17.99 *(978-4-8053-1274-2(2))* Tuttle Publishing.

—Revenge of the Akuma Clan: (Samurai Awakening Book 2) 2016. (ENG.). 320p. (J). (gr. 7-12). 8.99 *(978-0-8048-4738-4(X))* Tuttle Publishing.

—Samurai Awakening. 2012. (ENG.). 320p. (J). (gr. 7-12). 17.99 *(978-4-8053-1228-5(9))* Tuttle Publishing.

—Samurai Awakening: (Samurai Awakening Book 1) 2016. (ENG.). 320p. (J). (gr. 7-12). 8.99 *(978-0-8048-4737-7(1))* Tuttle Publishing.

Matsumoto, Reiko Odate. The Princess with the Magic Bowl: As retold from the Japanese folk tale By. 2008. 48p. pap. 22.49 *(978-1-4389-1225-7(0))* AuthorHouse.

Mayer, Mercer. Shibumi & the Kitemaker, 1 vol. 2003. (ENG., Illus.). 32p. (J). (gr. -1-3). pap. 5.95 *(978-0-7614-5145-7(5))* Marshall Cavendish Corp.

McCune, D. J. Fault Lines. 2016. (Death & Co Ser.: 3). (ENG.). 352p. (YA). (gr. 8). pap. 11.99 *(978-1-4714-0271-5(1))* Bonnier Publishing GBR. Dist: Independent Pubs. Group.

Meshon, Aaron. Take Me Out to the Yakyu. Meshon, Aaron, illus. 2013. (ENG., Illus.). 40p. (J). (gr. -1-3). 16.99 *(978-1-4424-4177-4(1),* Atheneum Bks. for Young Readers) Simon & Schuster Children's Publishing.

Moore, Sandra. The Peace Tree from Hiroshima: A Little Japanese Bonsai with a Big Story. Wilds, Kazumi, illus. 2015. (ENG.). 32p. (J). (gr. 2-6). 14.95 *(978-4-8053-1347-3(1))* Tuttle Publishing.

Myers, Tim J. The Outfoxed Fox: Based on a Japanese Kyogen, 0 vols. 2013. (ENG.). 32p. (J). (gr. k-3). pap. 9.99 *(978-1-4778-1681-3(X),* 9781477816813, Amazon Children's Publishing) Amazon Publishing.

Namioka, Lensey. Valley of the Broken Cherry Trees. 2005. (ENG.). 1p. pap. 7.95 *(978-0-8048-3610-4(8))* Tuttle Publishing.

Narita, Ryohgo & Yasuda, Suzuhito. Drrr!! 2016. (Durarara!! (novel) Ser.: 5). (ENG., Illus.). 192p. (YA). (gr. 8-17). pap. 14.00 *(978-0-316-30479-5(4),* Yen Pr.) Orbit.

Nelson, Carmen R. Jacob & Katie in Japan: The Adventures of Tcks in a New Home. 2013. 26p. pap. 13.95 *(978-1-935986-38-6(4))* Liberty University Press.

Newman, Lesléa. Hachiko Waits. Kodaira, Machiyo, illus. 2008. (ENG.). 96p. (J). (gr. 3-5). pap. 7.99 *(978-0-312-55806-2(6),* 9780312558062) Square Fish.

Nomura, Mizuki. Book Girl & the Captive Fool. 2011. (Book Girl Ser.: 3). (ENG., Illus.). 240p. (YA). (gr. 8-17). pap. 13.00 *(978-0-316-07693-7(7),* Yen Pr.) Orbit.

—Book Girl & the Corrupted Angel. 2012. (Book Girl Ser.: 4). (ENG., Illus.). 240p. (YA). (gr. 8-17). pap. 13.00 *(978-0-316-07694-4(5),* Yen Pr.) Orbit.

—Book Girl & the Suicidal Mime. 2010. (Book Girl Ser.: 1). (ENG., Illus.). 192p. (YA). (gr. 8-17). pap. 13.00 *(978-0-316-07690-6(2),* Yen Pr.) Orbit.

—Book Girl & the Undine Who Bore a Moonflower. 2013. (Book Girl Ser.: 6). (ENG., Illus.). 240p. (YA). (gr. 8-17). pap. 11.99 *(978-0-316-07696-8(1),* Yen Pr.) Orbit.

Nosaka, Akiyuki. The Whale That Fell in Love with a Submarine. Takemori, Ginny Tapley, tr. from JPN. 2015. (ENG., Illus.). 192p. (YA). (gr. 3-7). pap. 14.95 *(978-1-78269-027-6(1),* Pushkin Press) Steerforth Pr.

Ohi, Ruth. Kenta & the Big Wave. 2nd ed. 2013. (ENG., Illus.). 32p. (J). (gr. -1-2). pap. 9.95 *(978-1-55451-576-9(9),* 9781554515769) Annick Pr., Ltd. CAN. Dist: Publishers Group West (PGW).

Ohnogi, Hiroshi. Rahxephon, Vol. 4. 2006. (RahXephon (Dr Masterbook) Ser.). (ENG., Illus.). 200p. (YA). pap. 7.95 *(978-1-59796-003-8(9))* DrMaster Pubns. Inc.

—Rahxephon, Vol. 5. 2006. (RahXephon (Dr Masterbook) Ser.). (ENG., Illus.). 200p. (YA). pap. 7.95 *(978-1-59796-004-5(7))* DrMaster Pubns. Inc.

Ohtaka, Shinobu. The Strongest Bride on Earth, 12 vols. 2012. (Sumomomo, Momomo Ser.: 12). (ENG., Illus.). 240p. (gr. 11-17). pap. 13.00 *(978-0-316-20470-5(6),* Yen Pr.) Orbit.

Okei-san: The Girl from Wakamatsu. 2006. (J). pap. 11.95 *(978-0-9642112-8-5(9))* Barsotti Bks.

Orlean, Susan & Bradford, Chris. Young Samurai the Way of the Warrior. l.t. ed. 2011. (Young Samurai Ser.). (ENG.). 628p. (J). 23.99 *(978-1-4104-4329-8(9))* Thorndike Pr.

Orsak, Lane Rockford. Keiko the Fairy, the Kujiki. 2010. 192p. pap. 14.95 *(978-0-557-47206-2(7))* Lulu Pr., Inc.

Osborne, Mary Pope. Dragon of the Red Dawn. Murdocca, Sal, illus. 2008. (Magic Tree House Merlin Mission Ser.: 9). (ENG.). 144p. (J). (gr. 2-5). 5.99 *(978-0-375-83728-9(0),* Random Hse. Bks. for Young Readers) Random Hse. Children's Bks.

—La Noche de los Ninjas. 2004. (Casa del Arbol Ser.: 5).Tr. of Night of the Ninjas. (SPA., Illus.). (J). pap. 5.99 *(978-1-930332-66-9(1))* Lectorum Pubns., Inc.

Otey Little, Mimi. Yoshiko & the Foreigner. Otey Little, Mimi, illus. 2004. (Illus.). 31p. (J). (gr. 4-8). reprint ed. 16.00 *(978-0-7567-7510-0(8))* DIANE Publishing Co.

Ozaki, Yei. Warriors of Old Japan. 2007. 168p. per. 14.95 *(978-1-59654-553-3(4))* Disruptive Publishing.

Parenteau, Shirley. Dolls of Hope. 2015. (ENG.). 336p. (J). (gr. 3-7). 16.99 *(978-0-7636-7752-7(3))* Candlewick Pr.

Parot, Annelore. Kimonos. 2011. (ENG.). 36p. (J). (gr. k-17). 17.99 *(978-1-4521-0493-5(X))* Chronicle Bks. LLC.

Paterson, Katherine. The Master Puppeteer. 3rd ed. (J). pap. 3.95 *(978-0-13-800095-0(6))* Prentice Hall (Schl. Div.).

—El Signo del Crisantemo. 2003.Tr. of Sign of the Chrysanthemum. (SPA., Illus.). 142p. (YA). (gr. 5-8). *(978-84-348-6699-7(4),* SM30544) SM Ediciones ESP. Dist: Lectorum Pubns., Inc.

Pearce, Jacqueline. L' Effet Manga, 1 vol. 2010.Tr. of Manga Touch. (FRE.). 136p. (J). (gr. 5-9). pap. 9.95 *(978-1-55469-379-5(9))* Orca Bk. Pubs. USA.

—Manga Touch, 1 vol. 2007. (Orca Currents Ser.). (ENG.). (J). (gr. 5-9). 136p. pap. 9.95 *(978-1-55143-746-0(5));* 112p. lib. bdg. 14.95 *(978-1-55143-748-4(1))* Orca Bk. Pubs. USA.

Perkins, Lucy Fitch. The Japanese Twins. 2005. 26.95 *(978-1-4218-0369-2(0),* 1st World Library - Literary Society) 1st World Publishing, Inc.

—The Japanese Twins. 2004. reprint ed. pap. 15.95 *(978-1-4191-6781-2(2));* pap. 1.99 *(978-1-4192-6781-9(7))* Kessinger Publishing, LLC.

—The Japanese Twins (Yesterday's Classics) 2006. (J). per. 9.95 *(978-1-59915-058-1(1))* Yesterday's Classics.

Pham, Thien. Sumo. Pham, Thien, illus. 2012. (ENG., Illus.). 112p. (YA). (gr. 9-12). pap. 14.99 *(978-1-59643-581-0(X),* First Second Bks.) Roaring Brook Pr.

Phillipps, J. C. Wink: The Ninja Who Wanted to Be Noticed. 2009. (ENG.). 40p. (J). (gr. -1-k). 15.99 *(978-0-670-01092-9(8),* Viking Books for Young Readers) Penguin Young Readers Group.

Place, Francois. The Old Man Mad about Drawing: A Tale of Hokusai. Rodarmor, William, tr. from FRE. 2004. (ENG., Illus.). 112p. (J). 19.95 *(978-1-56792-260-8(0))* Godine, David R. Pub.

Preus, Margi. The Bamboo Sword. (ENG., Illus.). (YA). (gr. 5-9). 2016. 368p. pap. 8.95 *(978-1-4197-0824-4(4))* 2015. 352p. 16.95 *(978-1-4197-0807-7(4))* Abrams, Inc. (Amulet Bks.).

—Heart of a Samurai. (ENG.). (YA). (gr. 3-7). 2012. 336p. pap. 8.95 *(978-1-4197-0200-6(9))* 2010. 320p. 18.95 *(978-0-8109-8981-8(6))* Abrams, Inc. (Amulet Bks.).

—Heart of a Samurai, 5 vols. (YA). 77.75 *(978-1-4618-0507-6(4));* 77.75 *(978-1-4618-0343-0(8));* 2011. 1.25 *(978-1-4618-4275-0(1));* 2011. 79.75 *(978-1-4618-0358-4(6))* Recorded Bks., Inc.

—Heart of a Samurai. 2012. (J). lib. bdg. 19.60 *(978-0-606-38363-9(8))* Turtleback Bks.

Puccini, Giacomo. Madame Butterfly. Fučíková, Renata, illus. 2005. (ENG.). 40p. (Orig.). (J). 15.95 *(978-1-933327-04-4(9))* Purple Bear Bks., Inc.

Randall, Thomas. The Waking: Dreams of the Dead. 2nd ed. 2010. (ENG., Illus.). 304p. (YA). (gr. 7-18). pap. 8.99 *(978-1-59990-585-3(X),* 9781599905853, Bloomsbury USA Childrens) Bloomsbury Publishing USA.

Randall, Thomas & Golden, Christopher. Spirits of the Noh. 2011. (ENG.). 272p. (YA). (gr. 7-18). pap. 9.99 *(978-1-59990-251-7(6),* 9781599902517, Bloomsbury USA Childrens) Bloomsbury Publishing USA.

Reibstein, Mark. Wabi Sabi. Young, Ed, illus. 2008. (ENG.). 40p. (J). (gr. -1-3). 18.99 *(978-0-316-11825-5(7))* Little Brown & Co.

—Wabi Sabi, 2 vols. 2009. (J). 39.75 *(978-1-4407-1922-6(5));* 39.75 *(978-1-4407-1918-9(7));* 37.75 *(978-1-4407-1924-0(1));* 192.75 *(978-1-4407-1919-6(5));* 37.75 *(978-1-4407-1920-2(9));* 1.25 *(978-1-4407-1925-7(X))* Recorded Bks., Inc.

Renn, Diana. Tokyo Heist. 2013. (ENG.). 384p. (YA). (gr. 7). pap. 8.99 *(978-0-14-242654-8(7),* Speak) Penguin Young Readers Group.

Reynolds, Betty. Japanese Celebrations: Cherry Blossoms, Lanterns & Stars! 2006. (ENG., Illus.). 48p. (J). (gr. 2-6). 16.95 *(978-0-8048-3658-6(2))* Tuttle Publishing.

Ripley's Believe It or Not Editors & Ripley's Believe It Or Not! Staff. The Dragon's Triangle. 2010. (Rbi Ser.: 2). (ENG.). 128p. (J). pap. 4.99 *(978-1-893951-53-2(7))* Ripley Entertainment, Inc.

Roberts, Deborah. Mr Otagiri's Promise. Ju-Young Im, Joy & Da-Young Im, Linda, illus. 2012. 40p. pap. *(978-1-77067-719-7(4))* FriesenPress.

Rohan, Jason. The Sword of Kuromori. 2017. (J). pap. 6.99 *(978-1-61067-355-6(7))* Kane Miller.

Roman, Javier. Adventures of Tinturu & Kumachan the M. 2007. (Illus.). 48p. pap. 16.95 *(978-1-4241-1626-3(0))* PublishAmerica, Inc.

Rooks, Elizabeth. Where Does Santa Go on Vacation after Christmas? 2012. 24p. pap. 17.99 *(978-1-4772-6535-2(X))* AuthorHouse.

Saijyo, Shinji. Iron Wok Jan!, 27 vols. 2005. (ENG., Illus.). (YA). 2nd ed. 190p. pap. 9.95 *(978-1-58899-256-7(X))* Vol. 5. 200p. pap. 9.95 *(978-1-58899-260-4(8))* ComicsOne Corp./Dr. Masters.

Sakade, Florence & Hayashi, Yoshio. Kintaro's Adventures & Other Japanese Children's Favorite Stories. rev. ed. 2008. (ENG., Illus.). 48p. (J). (gr. -1-3). 12.95 *(978-4-8053-0994-0(6))* Tuttle Publishing.

—Urashima Taro & Other Japanese Children's Favorite Stories. Kurosaki, Yoshisuke, illus. 2008. (ENG.). 48p. (J). (gr. -1-3). 12.95 *(978-4-8053-0997-1(0))* Tuttle Publishing.

Say, Allen. The Boy in the Garden. 2010. (ENG., Illus.). 32p. (J). (gr. -1-3). 17.99 *(978-0-547-21410-8(3))* Houghton Mifflin Harcourt Publishing Co.

—Grandfather's Journey. Say, Allen, illus. 2008. (ENG., Illus.). 32p. (J). (gr. -1-3). 7.99 *(978-0-547-07680-5(0))* Houghton Mifflin Harcourt Publishing Co.

—Grandfather's Journey. 20th anniv. ed. 2013. (ENG., Illus.). 32p. (J). (gr. -1-3). 17.99 *(978-0-544-05050-1(9))* Houghton Mifflin Harcourt Publishing Co.

—Grandfather's Journey. 2008. (ENG.). 32p. (J). (gr. -1-3). pap. 7.99 *(978-0-547-14178-7(5),* Sandpiper) Houghton Mifflin Harcourt Trade & Reference Pubs.

—Grandfather's Journey. 2011. (J). (gr. k-5). 29.95 *(978-0-545-10696-2(6));* 18.95 *(978-0-545-12708-0(4))* Weston Woods Studios, Inc.

—The Ink-Keeper's Apprentice. 2006. 149p. (YA). 14.60 *(978-0-7569-6811-3(9))* Perfection Learning Corp.

—Kamishibai Man. 2005. (ENG., Illus.). 32p. (J). (gr. -1-3). 17.99 *(978-0-618-47954-2(6))* Houghton Mifflin Harcourt Publishing Co.

—Tree of Cranes. Say, Allen, illus. 2009. (ENG., Illus.). 32p. (J). (gr. -1-3). pap. 7.99 *(978-0-547-24830-1(X))* Houghton Mifflin Harcourt Publishing Co.

Schulz, Charles & Scott, Vicki. It's Tokyo, Charlie Brown! Braddock, Paige, illus. 2012. (Peanuts Ser.). (ENG.). 96p. (J). (gr. 2). pap. 9.99 *(978-1-60886-270-2(4))* Boom! Studios.

Scieszka, Jon. Sam Samurai. McCauley, Adam, illus. 2004. (Time Warp Trio Ser.: 10). (ENG.). 96p. (J). (gr. 2-4). pap. 5.99 *(978-0-14-240088-3(2),* Puffin Books) Penguin Young Readers Group.

—Sam Samurai. McCauley, Adam, illus. 2006. (Time Warp Trio Ser.: No. 10). 85p. (gr. 4-7). 15.00 *(978-0-7569-6779-6(1))* Perfection Learning Corp.

See, Jonny. On the Walk Trail - Japan. 2011. 32p. pap. 18.65 *(978-1-4568-9463-4(3))* Xlibris Corp.

Seki, Sunny. The Last Kappa of Old Japan: A Magical Journey of Two Friends. rev. ed. 2016. (ENG & JPN., Illus.). 32p. (J). (gr. k-8). 12.95 *(978-4-8053-1399-2(4))* Tuttle Publishing.

—The Tale of the Lucky Cat. Seki, Sunny, illus. 2008. (ENG & SPA., Illus.). 32p. (J). 18.95 *(978-0-9669437-9-5(1))* East West Discovery Pr.

—Yuko-Chan & the Daruma Doll: The Adventures of a Blind Japanese Girl Who Saves Her Village. 2012. (ENG., Illus.). 32p. (J). (gr. -1-3). 15.95 *(978-4-8053-1187-5(8))* Tuttle Publishing.

Seki, Sunny, illus. & retold by. The Tale of the Lucky Cat. Seki, Sunny, retold by. 2008. 32p. (J). *(978-0-9669437-6-4(7))* East West Discovery Pr.

Seven, John. The Terror of the Tengu, 1 vol. Hans, Stephanie, illus. 2014. (Time-Tripping Faradays Ser.). (ENG.). 192p. (gr. 4-5). 26.65 *(978-1-4342-9173-8(1))* Stone Arch Bks.

Shakespeare, William & Appignanesi, Richard. Romeo & Juliet. Leong, Sonia, illus. 2007. (ENG.). 208p. (J). (gr. 2-8). pap. 14.95 *(978-0-8109-9325-9(2),* Abrams Bks. for Young Readers) Abrams, Inc.

Shaw, Carol Anne. Hannah & the Wild Woods. 2015. (ENG.). 240p. pap. 11.95 *(978-1-55380-440-6(6))* Ronsdale Pr. CAN. Dist: SPD-Small Pr. Distribution.

Smale, Holly. Geek Girl: Model Misfit. 2016. (Geek Girl Ser.: 2). 416p. (YA). (gr. 8). pap. 9.99 *(978-0-06-233361-2(5),* HarperTeen) HarperCollins Pubs.

Smith, Lindsay. A Darkly Beating Heart. 2016. (ENG.). 272p. (YA). 17.99 *(978-1-62672-044-2(4),* 9781626720442) Roaring Brook Pr.

Snow, Maya. Chasing the Secret. 2010. (Sisters of the Sword Ser.: 2). (ENG.). 272p. (J). (gr. 5). pap. 6.99 *(978-0-06-124392-9(2))* HarperCollins Pubs.

So-Un, Kim. The Tigers of the Kumgang Mountains: A Korean Folktale. Kyoung-Sim, Jeong, illus. 2005. (ENG.). 1p. (J). (gr. 4-11). 16.95 *(978-0-8048-3653-1(1))* Tuttle Publishing.

Sorachi, Hideaki. Gin Tama, Vol. 4. (JPN., Illus.). 186p. (YA). pap. *(978-4-08-873672-3(9))* Shuei-Sha.

Souhami, Jessica & Quarto Generic Staff. The Strongest Boy in the World. 2016. (ENG., Illus.). 32p. (J). (gr. k-3). pap. 12.99 *(978-1-84780-603-1(1),* Frances Lincoln) Quarto Publishing Group UK GBR. Dist: Littlehampton Bk Services, Ltd.

Spradlin, Michael P. Prisoner of War. 2017. (ENG.). 272p. (J). (gr. 7). 17.99 ***(978-0-545-85783-3(X),*** Scholastic Pr.) Scholastic, Inc.

Stilton, Geronimo. The First Samurai. Cooper-McGuinness, Nanette, tr. from ITA. 2013. (Geronimo Stilton Graphic

Novels Ser.). (ENG., Illus.). 56p. (J). (gr. 2-6). 9.99 *(978-1-59707-385-1(7)*, 9781597073851) Papercutz.

—The Way of the Samurai. 2012. (Geronimo Stilton Ser.: No. 49). (ENG.). 128p. (J). (gr. 2-5). pap. 7.99 *(978-0-545-34101-1(9)*, Scholastic Paperbacks) Scholastic, Inc.

—The Way of the Samurai. 2012. (Geronimo Stilton Ser.: 49). lib. bdg. 18.40 *(978-0-606-26094-7(3)*, Turtleback) Turtleback Bks.

Stokes, Katherine. Motor Maids in Fair Japan. 2006. pap. *(978-1-4068-3090-3(9))* Echo Library.

Stutzman, D. J. The Promise Ring. 2007. (J). pap. 9.00 *(978-0-8059-7365-5(6))* Dorrance Publishing Co., Inc.

Sylvester, Kevin. Neil Flambé & the Tokyo Treasure. Sylvester, Kevin, illus. 2014. (Neil Flambe Capers Ser.: 4). (ENG., Illus.). 368p. (J). (gr. 3-7). pap. 7.99 *(978-1-4424-4289-4(1)*, Simon & Schuster Bks. For Young Readers) Simon & Schuster Bks. For Young Readers.

Takahashi, Rumiko. Inuyasha Ani-Manga. (Inuyasha Ser.: 15). (ENG., Illus.). Vol. 15. 2006. 208p. pap. 11.99 *(978-1-4215-0482-7(0))* Vol. 20. 2007. 216p. pap. 11.99 *(978-1-4215-0904-4(0))* Viz Media.

Tamura, Mitsuhisa. BakéGyamon, Vol. 4. Tamura, Mitsuhisa, illus. 2009. (Bakégyamon Ser.: 4). (ENG., Illus.). 216p. (J). pap. 7.99 *(978-1-4215-1882-4(1))* Viz Media.

Tanaka, Shelley. Nobody Knows, 1 vol. 2012. (ENG.). 144p. (J). (gr. 4). 16.95 *(978-1-55498-140-3(9))* Groundwood Bks. CAN. Dist: Publishers Group West (PGW).

Tanigawa, Nagaru. The Boredom of Haruhi Suzumiya. 2010. (Haruhi Suzumiya Ser.: 3). (ENG., Illus.). 224p. (YA). (gr. 10-17). 24.00 *(978-0-316-03886-7(5))*; pap. 18.00 *(978-0-316-03887-4(3))* Little, Brown Bks. for Young Readers.

—The Disappearance of Haruhi Suzumiya. 2010. (Haruhi Suzumiya Ser.: 4). (ENG., Illus.). 192p. (YA). (gr. 10-17). pap. 18.00 *(978-0-316-03889-8(X))* Little, Brown Bks. for Young Readers.

—The Dissociation of Haruhi Suzumiya. 2013. (Haruhi Suzumiya Ser.: 9). (ENG., Illus.). 192p. (YA). (gr. 10-17). pap. 8.99 *(978-0-316-03894-2(6))* Little, Brown Bks. for Young Readers.

—The Intrigues of Haruhi Suzumiya. 2012. (Haruhi Suzumiya Ser.: 7). (ENG.). 288p. (YA). (gr. 10-17). 15.99 *(978-0-316-03895-9(4))*; pap. 18.00 *(978-0-316-03896-6(2))* Little, Brown Bks. for Young Readers.

—The Rampage of Haruhi Suzumiya. 2011. (Haruhi Suzumiya Ser.: 4). (ENG.). 240p. (YA). (gr. 10-17). pap. 18.00 *(978-0-316-03884-3(9))* Little, Brown Bks. for Young Readers.

—The Sigh of Haruhi Suzumiya. 2009. (Haruhi Suzumiya Ser.: Bk. 1). (Illus.). 208p. (YA). (gr. 10-18). 14.99 *(978-0-316-03881-2(4))* Hachette Bk. Group.

—The Surprise of Haruhi Suzumiya. 2013. (Haruhi Suzumiya Ser.: 10). (ENG., Illus.). 368p. (YA). (gr. 10-17). 24.00 *(978-0-316-03898-0(9))*; pap. 10.99 *(978-0-316-03897-3(0))* Little, Brown Bks. for Young Readers.

—The Wavering of Haruhi Suzumiya. 2011. (Haruhi Suzumiya Ser.: 6). (ENG & JPN.). 208p. (YA). (gr. 10-17). pap. 18.00 *(978-0-316-03892-8(X))* Little, Brown Bks. for Young Readers.

Tarshis, Lauren. I Survived the Japanese Tsunami 2011. 2013. (I Survived Ser.: No. 8). (ENG., Illus.). 112p. (J). (gr. 2-5). pap. 4.99 *(978-0-545-45937-2(0))* Scholastic, Inc.

—I Survived the Japanese Tsunami 2011. Dawson, Scott, illus. 2013. (I Survived Ser.: No. 8). 83p. (J). *(978-0-545-62981-2(0))* Scholastic, Inc.

—I Survived the Japanese Tsunami 2011. 2013. (I Survived Ser.: No. 8). lib. bdg. 14.75 *(978-0-606-32390-1(2)*, Turtleback) Turtleback Bks.

Terheyden, Jerry, reader. Crow Boy. 2004. (Illus.). (J). (gr. -1-2). 28.95 incl. audio compact disk *(978-1-59112-802-1(1))* Live Oak Media.

Thompson, Holly. Falling into the Dragon's Mouth. Huynh, Matt, illus. 2016. (ENG.). 352p. (J). 17.99 *(978-1-62779-134-2(5)*, 9781627791342, Holt, Henry & Co. Bks. For Young Readers) Holt, Henry & Co.

—Orchards. 2012. (ENG.). 336p. (YA). (gr. 7). pap. 9.99 *(978-0-385-73978-8(8)*, Ember) Random Hse. Children's Bks.

Umezu, Kazuo. The Drifting Classroom. Roman, Annette, ed. Umezu, Kazuo, illus. 2007. (Drifting Classroom Ser.: 8). (ENG., Illus.). 192p. pap. 9.99 *(978-1-4215-0960-0(1))* Viz Media.

Vernon, Ursula. Attack of the Ninja Frogs. 2nd ed. (Dragonbreath Ser.: 2). (ENG.). 208p. (J). (gr. 3-7). 2012. pap. 6.99 *(978-0-14-242066-9(2)*, Puffin Books) 2010. 12.99 *(978-0-8037-3365-7(8)*, Dial Bks) Penguin Young Readers Group.

—Attack of the Ninja Frogs. 2012. (Dragonbreath Ser.: 2). lib. bdg. 17.20 *(978-0-606-26666-6(6)*, Turtleback) Turtleback Bks.

Vinesse, Cecilia. Seven Days of You. 2017. (ENG.). 336p. (YA). (gr. 10-17). 17.99 *(978-0-316-39111-5(5))* Little Brown & Co.

Watkins, Yoko Kawashima & Watkins, Yoko K. So Far from the Bamboo Grove. 2008. (ENG., Illus.). 192p. (J). (gr. 3-7). reprint ed. pap. 5.99 *(978-0-688-13115-9(8))* HarperCollins Pubs.

Watson, Mary. The Paper Dragonfly. Watson, Mary, illus. 2007. (ENG., Illus.). 32p. (J). (gr. k-3). 15.95 *(978-0-9726614-3-0(3))* Shenanigan Bks.

Welles, Lee. Way of Water. Coogan, Carol, illus. 2007. (Gaia Girls Ser.: 2). (ENG.). 336p. (YA). (gr. 4-7). pap. 19.95 *(978-1-933609-03-4(6))* Chelsea Green Publishing.

Wells, Rosemary. Yoko Finds Her Way. 2014. (Yoko Book Ser.). (ENG.). 32p. (J). (gr. -1-k). 16.99 *(978-1-4231-6512-5(8))* Hyperion Pr.

Weston Woods Staff, creator. Grandfather's Journey. 2011. 38.75 *(978-0-545-12710-3(6))* Weston Woods Studios, Inc.

Whelan, Gloria. Yuki & the One Thousand Carriers. Nascimbene, Yan, illus. 2008. (Tales of the World Ser.). (ENG.). 32p. (J). (gr. -1-3). 17.95 *(978-1-58536-352-0(9))* Sleeping Bear Pr.

Whitney, Daisy. When You Were Here. (ENG.). 272p. (YA). (gr. 7-17). 2014. pap. 9.00 *(978-0-316-20975-5(9))* 2013. 18.00 *(978-0-316-20974-8(0))* Little, Brown Bks. for Young Readers.

Williams, Jan. An Amazing Storytelling Cat. Peecock, Simon & McKissock, Charmaine, illus. 2013. 120p. pap. *(978-0-9568148-6-9(7))* Swift Publishing.

Wynne-Jones, Tim. The Emperor of Any Place. 2015. (ENG.). 336p. (YA). (gr. 9). 17.99 *(978-0-7636-6973-7(3))* Candlewick Pr.

Yashima, Taro. Crow Boy. Yashima, Taro, illus. 2004. (Illus.). 34p. (J). (gr. k-3). reprint ed. pap. 14.00 *(978-0-7567-7102-7(1))* DIANE Publishing Co.

—Crow Boy. Yashima, Taro, illus. (Illus.). pap. 35.95 incl. audio compact disk *(978-1-59112-803-8(X))* Live Oak Media.

Yasuda, Yuri & Yasuda, Yuri Old tales of Japan. A Treasury of Japanese Folktales. Matsunari, Yumi & Yamaguchi, Yumi, trs. Sakakura, Yoshinobu & Mitsui, Eiichi, illus. 2010. (ENG & JPN.). 112p. (J). (gr. k-8). 19.95 *(978-4-8053-1079-3(0))* Tuttle Publishing.

Yoshikawa, Sachiko, illus. The Boy from the Dragon Palace: A Folktale from Japan. 2012. (J). *(978-1-61913-110-1(2))* Weigl Pubs., Inc.

JAPAN—FOREIGN RELATIONS—UNITED STATES

Blumberg, Rhoda. Commodore Perry in the Land of the Shogun. 2003. (ENG., Illus.). 144p. (J). (gr. 3-18). pap. 9.99 *(978-0-06-008625-1(4))* HarperCollins Pubs.

—Commodore Perry in the Land of the Shogun. 2003. (Illus.). 144p. (gr. 3-7). 20.00 *(978-0-7569-1440-0(X))* Perfection Learning Corp.

Dougherty, Steve. Attack on Pearl Harbor: World War II Strikes Home in the USA. 2011. (J). pap. *(978-0-545-32930-9(2))* Scholastic, Inc.

Johnson, Robin. Pearl Harbor. 2014. (ENG., Illus.). 48p. (J). *(978-0-7787-1367-8(9))* Crabtree Publishing Co.

Marshall Cavendish. The Attack on Pearl Harbor. 2011. (Perspectives on 3 Ser.). (Illus.). 112p. (J). (gr. 7). 39.93 *(978-1-60870-448-4(3))* Marshall Cavendish Corp.

McNeese, Tim. The Perry Expedition & the Opening of Japan. 2012. (J). 35.00 *(978-1-60413-924-2(2)*, Chelsea Hse.) Facts On File, Inc.

Ross, Stewart & Woodward, Joe. Pearl Harbor. 2011. (Place in History Ser.). (Illus.). 48p. (YA). (gr. 5-9). lib. bdg. 34.25 *(978-1-84837-676-2(6))* Arcturus Publishing GBR. Dist: Black Rabbit Bks.

Samuels, Charlie. The Attack on Pearl Harbor, Vol. 1. 2014. (Turning Points in US Military History Ser.). (ENG.). 48p. (J). (gr. 5-6). 31.95 *(978-1-4824-0409-8(5))* Stevens, Gareth Publishing LLLP.

Yomtov, Nel. The Attack on Pearl Harbor: December 7 1941, 1 vol. 2014. (24-Hour History Ser.). (ENG.). 48p. (gr. 3-5). pap. 8.95 *(978-1-4329-9299-6(6))*; (Illus.). lib. bdg. 33.32 *(978-1-4329-9293-4(7))* Heinemann-Raintree. (NA-h).

Zimmerman, Andrea. Eliza's Cherry Trees: Japan's Gift to America, 1 vol. Chen, Ju-Hong, illus. 2011. (ENG.). 32p. (J). (gr. k-3). 16.99 *(978-1-58980-954-3(8))* Pelican Publishing Co., Inc.

JAPAN—HISTORY

Allen, John. Anime & Manga. 2014. (Discovering Art). (ENG., Illus.). 80p. (J). lib. bdg. *(978-1-60152-696-0(2))* ReferencePoint Pr., Inc.

Anderson, Dale. Japanese Americans. 2006. (World Almanac Library of American Immigration). (Illus.). 48p. (gr. 5-12). pap. 14.05 *(978-0-8368-7326-9(2))*; lib. bdg. 31.00 *(978-0-8368-7313-9(0))* Stevens, Gareth Publishing LLLP. (Gareth Stevens Secondary Library).

Arato, Rona. Fukushima Nuclear Disaster. 2013. (ENG., Illus.). 32p. (J). *(978-0-7787-1192-6(7))*; pap. *(978-0-7787-1194-0(3))* Crabtree Publishing Co.

Ball, Jacqueline A. Himeji Castle: Japan's Samurai Past. 2005. (Castles, Palaces, & Tombs Ser.). 32p. (J). lib. bdg. 25.27 *(978-1-59716-001-8(6))* Bearport Publishing Co., Inc.

Baxter, Roberta. The Dropping of the Atomic Bombs: A History Perspectives Book. 2014. (Perspectives Library). (ENG., Illus.). 32p. (J). (gr. 4-8). 28.50 *(978-1-62431-665-4(4)*, 203224) Cherry Lake Publishing.

Blumberg, Rhoda. Commodore Perry in the Land of the Shogun. 2003. (ENG., Illus.). 144p. (J). (gr. 3-18). pap. 9.99 *(978-0-06-008625-1(4))* HarperCollins Pubs.

—Commodore Perry in the Land of the Shogun. 2003. (Illus.). 144p. (gr. 3-7). 20.00 *(978-0-7569-1440-0(X))* Perfection Learning Corp.

—Shipwrecked! The True Adventures of a Japanese Boy. 2003. (ENG., Illus.). 80p. (J). (gr. 3-18). pap. 8.99 *(978-0-688-17485-9(X))* HarperCollins Pubs.

Bolte, Mari. Harajuku Style: Fun Fashions You Can Sketch, 1 vol. Hagel, Brooke, illus. 2013. (Drawing Fun Fashions Ser.). (ENG.). 32p. (gr. 3-4). lib. bdg. 27.99 *(978-1-62065-034-9(7)*, Snap Bks.) Capstone Press of Coughlan Cos.

Candlewick Press, Candlewick. Japan: Panorama Pops. Smith, Anne, illus. 2015. (Panorama Pops Ser.). (ENG.). 30p. (J). (gr. k-4). 8.99 *(978-0-7636-7504-2(0))* Candlewick Pr.

Catel, Patrick. Japan, 1 vol. 2012. (Countries Around the World Ser.). (ENG.). 48p. (gr. 3-6). pap. 9.95 *(978-1-4329-6128-2(4))*; lib. bdg. 33.32 *(978-1-4329-6102-2(0))* Heinemann-Raintree. (NA-h).

Chambers, Catherine. A Shogun's Guide. Pentney, Ryan, illus. 2017. (How-To Guides for Fiendish Rulers Ser.). (ENG.). 32p. (J). (gr. 3-6). 26.65 *(978-1-5124-1552-0(9))*; 7.99 ***(978-1-5124-3630-3(5))***; 39.99 ***(978-1-5124-3629-7(1))***; 39.99 ***(978-1-5124-2708-0(X))*** Lerner Publishing Group.

Chant, Christopher. The End of World War II: The Japanese Surrender. 2017. (World War II Ser.: Vol. 5). (ENG.). (YA). (gr. 7-12). 24.95 ***(978-1-4222-3898-1(9))*** Mason Crest.

Cunningham, Mark E. & Zwier, Lawrence J. The End of the Shoguns & the Birth of Modern Japan. 2009. (Pivotal Moments in History Ser.). (ENG.). 160p. (gr. 9-12). 38.60 *(978-0-8225-8747-7(5))* Lerner Publishing Group.

Florence, Debbi Michiko. Japan. Caputo, James, illus. 2009. (Kaleidoscope Kids Ser.). (ENG.). 96p. (J). (gr. 3-8). 19.99 *(978-0-8249-6828-1(X))*; pap. 12.99 *(978-0-8249-6829-8(8))* Worthy Publishing. (Ideal Pubns.).

Ganeri, Anita. Japan: A Benjamin Blog & His Inquisitive Dog Guide, 1 vol. Isik, Semur, illus. 2014. (Country Guides, with Benjamin Blog & His Inquisitive Dog Ser.). (ENG.). 32p. (gr. 1-3). 29.99 *(978-1-4109-6666-7(6)*, Read Me!) Heinemann-Raintree.

Giannotta, Andres Bernardo & Drawing Staff. How to Draw Manga. 2010. (Dover How to Draw Ser.). (ENG., Illus.). 64p. (J). (gr. 3-5). pap. 5.99 *(978-0-486-47662-9(6))* Dover Pubns., Inc.

Grant, R. G. Why Did Hiroshima Happen? 2010. (Moments in History Ser.). (Illus.). 48p. (YA). (gr. 5-9). lib. bdg. 31.95 *(978-1-4339-4163-4(5))*; (gr. 6-8). pap. 14.05 *(978-1-4339-4164-1(3)*, Gareth Stevens Secondary Library) Stevens, Gareth Publishing LLLP.

Green, Sara. Sony. 2016. (Brands We Know Ser.). (ENG., Illus.). 24p. (J). (gr. 3-8). 25.95 *(978-1-62617-412-2(1)*, Pilot Bks.) Bellwether Media.

Heppermann, Christine. Samurai. 2013. (Great Warriors EBook Ser.). (ENG., Illus.). 48p. (J). pap. 15.64 *(978-1-61783-777-7(6)*, Core Library) ABDO Publishing Co.

Idee, Ari. Delicious Japan by Month. 2013. 40p. pap. 9.49 *(978-0-9798991-1-9(7))* Technology & Imagination Pr.

Jones, Richard & Santillan, Jorge. Manga Animals. 2012. (Learn to Draw Manga Ser.). (ENG., Illus.). 32p. (J). (gr. 4-6). pap. 11.75 *(978-1-4488-7943-4(4))*; lib. bdg. 26.50 *(978-1-4488-7872-7(1))* Rosen Publishing Group, Inc., The. (PowerKids Pr.).

—Manga Dragons. 2012. (Learn to Draw Manga Ser.). (ENG., Illus.). 32p. (J). (gr. 4-6). pap. 11.75 *(978-1-4488-7945-8(0))*; lib. bdg. 26.50 *(978-1-4488-7874-1(8))* Rosen Publishing Group, Inc., The. (PowerKids Pr.).

—Manga Martial Arts Figures. 2012. (Learn to Draw Manga Ser.). (ENG., Illus.). 32p. (J). (gr. 4-6). pap. 11.75 *(978-1-4488-7946-5(9))*; lib. bdg. 26.50 *(978-1-4488-7875-8(6))* Rosen Publishing Group, Inc., The. (PowerKids Pr.).

—Manga Superheroes. 2012. (Learn to Draw Manga Ser.). (ENG., Illus.). 32p. (J). (gr. 4-6). pap. 11.75 *(978-1-4488-7948-9(5))*; lib. bdg. 26.50 *(978-1-4488-7877-2(2))* Rosen Publishing Group, Inc., The. (PowerKids Pr.).

Kalman, Bobbie. Spotlight on Japan. 2010. (Spotlight on My Country Ser.). (ENG.). 32p. (J). (gr. 2-5). pap. *(978-0-7787-3485-7(4))* Crabtree Publishing Co.

Lee, Adrienne. Samurai, 1 vol. Martin, Cynthia, illus. 2013. (Legendary Warriors Ser.). (ENG.). 32p. (gr. 1-2). 26.65 *(978-1-4765-3113-7(7)*, Blazers) Capstone Press of Coughlan Cos.

Lusted, Marcia Amidon. 2011 Japan Disasters, 1 vol. 2011. (Essential Events Set 7 Ser.). (ENG.). 112p. (J). (gr. 6-12). lib. bdg. 35.64 *(978-1-61783-179-9(4))* ABDO Publishing Co.

Macdonald, Fiona. Ancient Japan: Step Back to the Time of Shoguns & Samurai, with 15 Step-by-Step Projects & over 330 Exciting Pictures. 2014. (ENG., Illus.). 64p. (J). (gr. k-8). pap. 12.99 *(978-1-84322-824-0(6)*, Armadillo) Anness Publishing GBR. Dist: National Bk. Network.

McDowell, Pamela. Japan. 2016. (J). ***(978-1-5105-1903-9(3))*** SmartBook Media, Inc.

—Japan. 2014. (J). *(978-1-4896-1018-8(9))* Weigl Pubs., Inc.

McLeese, Don. Samurai. 2009. 32p. pap. 7.99 *(978-0-8249-1444-8(9)*, Ideal Pubns.) Worthy Publishing.

McManus, Lori. Meet Our New Student from Japan. 2009. (Meet Our New Student Ser.). 48p. (J). (gr. 2-5). 29.95 *(978-1-58415-780-9(1))* Mitchell Lane Pubs., Inc.

Miller, Karen. Japan. 2009. (Opposing Viewpoints Ser.). (ENG., Illus.). 240p. (YA). (gr. 10-12). pap. 29.45 *(978-0-7377-4371-5(9)*, LML02109-245359, Greenhaven Pr., Inc.) Cengage Gale.

—Japan. 2009. (Opposing Viewpoints Ser.). (ENG., Illus.). 224p. (gr. 10-12). 48.80 *(978-0-7377-4372-2(7)*, LML02109-245377, Greenhaven Pr., Inc.) Cengage Gale.

Miocevich, Grant. Investigating Japan: Prehistory to Postwar. Cheng & Tsui, ed. 2005. (Illus.). 84p. (YA). (gr. 10-12). per. 24.99 *(978-0-7339-0163-8(8))* Pearson Education Australia AUS. Dist: Cheng & Tsui Co.

Miyake, Okiko, ed. Miyake: Japan in English Books for Boys & Girls, 1819-1935. 2008. (ENG.). 2700p. (C). 1355.00 *(978-4-86166-061-0(0)*, RU0610) Synapse, Edition JPN. Dist: Taylor & Francis Group.

Moon, Walt K. Exploremos Japón. 2017. (Bumba Books (tm) en Español — Exploremos Países (Let's Explore Countries) Ser.). (SPA.). 24p. (J). (gr. -1-1). lib. bdg. 25.32 ***(978-1-5124-4124-6(4))*** Lerner Publishing Group.

Murray, Julie. Japan, 1 vol. 2013. (Explore the Countries Ser.). (ENG.). 40p. (J). (gr. 2-5). lib. bdg. 29.93 *(978-1-61783-815-6(2)*, Big Buddy Bks.) ABDO Publishing Co.

Murrell, Deborah Jane & Dennis, Peter. Samurai. 2012. (Illus.). 32p. (gr. 3-5). pap. 8.95 *(978-1-926853-55-0(5))* Saunders Bk. Co. CAN. Dist: RiverStream Publishing.

Osborne, Mary Pope & Boyce, Natalie Pope. Ninjas & Samurai: A Nonfiction Companion to Magic Tree House #5: Night of the Ninjas. Murdocca, Sal, illus. 2014. (Magic Tree House - Fact Tracker Ser.: 30). (ENG.). 128p. (J). (gr. 2-5). 6.99 *(978-0-385-38632-6(X)*, Random Hse. Bks. for Young Readers) Random Hse. Children's Bks.

Park, Louise & Love, Timothy. The Japanese Samurai. 2009. (Ancient & Medieval People Ser.). 32p. (gr. 5). 28.50 *(978-0-7614-4448-0(3))* Marshall Cavendish Corp.

Parker, Lewis K. Why Japanese Immigrants Came to America. 2009. (Coming to America Ser.). 24p. (gr. 2-3). 42.50 *(978-1-61511-886-1(1)*, PowerKids Pr.) Rosen Publishing Group, Inc., The.

Persano, Thomas. Japan. 2017. (Countries We Come From Ser.). (ENG.). 32p. (J). (gr. k-3). 19.95 ***(978-1-68402-253-3(3))*** Bearport Publishing Co., Inc.

Redmond, Shirley Raye. Hiroshima. 2009. (J). *(978-1-58415-784-7(4))* Mitchell Lane Pubs., Inc.

Richardson, Hazel. Life in Ancient Japan. 2005. (Peoples of the Ancient World Ser.). (ENG., Illus.). 32p. (J). (gr. -1-9). pap. *(978-0-7787-2071-3(3))* Crabtree Publishing Co.

Riggs, Kate. Samurai. 2011. (Great Warriors Ser.). 24p. (J). (gr. k-2). 16.95 *(978-1-60818-003-5(4)*, Creative Education) Creative Co., The.

Rissman, Rebecca. Swept Away: The Story of the 2011 Japanese Tsunami. 2017. (Tangled History Ser.). (ENG., Illus.). 112p. (gr. 3-4). lib. bdg. 31.99 *(978-1-5157-3605-9(9))* Capstone Press of Coughlan Cos.

Ross, Stewart. Hiroshima. 2011. (Place in History Ser.). 48p. (YA). (gr. 5-9). lib. bdg. 34.25 *(978-1-84837-674-8(X))* Arcturus Publishing GBR. Dist: Black Rabbit Bks.

Shelley, Rex. Japan. 3rd rev. ed. 2011. (Cultures of the World: 3rd Edition 1 Ser.). (Illus.). 144p. (J). (gr. 6). 47.07 *(978-1-60870-784-3(9))* Marshall Cavendish Corp.

Spivak, Dawnine. Grass Sandals: The Travels of Basho. Demi, illus. 2009. (ENG.). 40p. (J). (gr. 4-6). 13.99 *(978-1-4424-0936-1(3)*, Atheneum Bks. for Young Readers) Simon & Schuster Children's Publishing.

Stelson, Caren. Sachiko: A Nagasaki Bomb Survivor's Story. 2016. (ENG., Illus.). (gr. 5-12). 120p. 19.99 *(978-1-4677-8903-5(8))*; 144p. 38.65 *(978-1-5124-1885-9(4))*; 144p. 38.65 *(978-1-5124-0893-5(X))*; (YA). 9.99 *(978-1-5124-1884-2(6))* Lerner Publishing Group. (Carolrhoda Bks.).

Turnbull, Stephen R. The Most Daring Raid of the Samurai. 2011. (Most Daring Raids in History Ser.). (Illus.). 64p. (YA). (gr. 7-12). lib. bdg. 31.95 *(978-1-4488-1872-3(9))* Rosen Publishing Group, Inc., The.

Whyte, Harlinah & Frank, Nicole. Japan. 2010. (Welcome to My Country Ser.). 48p. (gr. 3). 28.50 *(978-1-60870-156-8(5))* Marshall Cavendish Corp.

Winter, Max. Japan. 2015. (One World, Many Countries Ser.). (ENG.). 32p. (J). (gr. 1-4). 28.50 *(978-1-63407-051-5(8)*, 208876) Child's World, Inc., The.

Zocchi, Judy. In Japan. Brodie, Neale, illus. 2005. (Global Adventures I Ser.). 32p. (J). pap. 10.95 *(978-1-59646-139-0(X))*; lib. bdg. 21.65 *(978-1-59646-004-1(0))* Dingles & Co.

—In Japan/en Japón. Brodie, Neale, illus. 2005. (Global Adventures I Ser.).Tr. of En Japón. (ENG & SPA.). 32p. (J). pap. 10.95 *(978-1-59646-141-3(1))*; lib. bdg. 21.65 *(978-1-59646-005-8(9))* Dingles & Co.

JAPAN—HISTORY—1868-1945

Bodden, Valerie. The Bombing of Hiroshima & Nagasaki. 2007. (Days of Change Ser.). (Illus.). 48p. (J). (gr. 4-7). lib. bdg. 31.35 *(978-1-58341-545-0(9)*, Creative Education) Creative Co., The.

JAPAN—SOCIAL LIFE AND CUSTOMS

Bingham, Jane. Japan. 2008. (Costume Around the World Ser.). (Illus.). 32p. (gr. 4-6). 28.00 *(978-0-7910-9770-0(6)*, Chelsea Clubhouse) Facts On File, Inc.

Brooks, Susie. Japan. 2016. (Land & the People Ser.). 48p. (gr. 5-5). pap. 14.05 *(978-1-4824-5103-0(4))* Stevens, Gareth Publishing LLLP.

Byers, Helen & National Geographic Learning Staff. Japan. 2007. (Reading Expeditions Ser.). (ENG., Illus.). 24p. (J). pap. 14.95 *(978-0-7922-4540-7(7))* CENGAGE Learning.

Centore, Michael. Japan, Vol. 12. 2015. (Major Nations in a Global World: Tradition, Culture, & Daily Life Ser.). (Illus.). 64p. (J). (gr. 7). 23.95 *(978-1-4222-3347-4(2))* Mason Crest.

Chambers, Catherine. A Shogun's Guide. Pentney, Ryan, illus. 2017. (How-To Guides for Fiendish Rulers Ser.). (ENG.). 32p. (J). (gr. 3-6). 26.65 *(978-1-5124-1552-0(9))*; 7.99 ***(978-1-5124-3630-3(5))***; 39.99 ***(978-1-5124-2708-0(X))***; 39.99 ***(978-1-5124-3629-7(1))*** Lerner Publishing Group.

Coleman, Miriam. The Culture & Crafts of Japan. 2015. (Cultural Crafts Ser.). (ENG., Illus.). 32p. (J). (gr. 4-6). pap. 11.75 *(978-1-4994-1125-6(1)*, PowerKids Pr.) Rosen Publishing Group, Inc., The.

Heapy, Teresa. Japanese Culture, 1 vol. 2012. (Global Cultures Ser.). (ENG., Illus.). 48p. (gr. 4-6). pap. 9.95 *(978-1-4329-6789-5(4))*; 32.65 *(978-1-4329-6780-2(0))* Heinemann-Raintree. (NA-h).

Idee, Ari. Delicious Japan by Month. 2013. 40p. pap. 9.49 *(978-0-9798991-1-9(7))* Technology & Imagination Pr.

Kalman, Bobbie. Japan: The Culture. 3rd rev. ed. 2008. (ENG., Illus.). 32p. (J). (gr. 3-9). pap. *(978-0-7787-9666-4(3))* Crabtree Publishing Co.

—Japan: The People. 3rd rev. ed. 2008. (Lands, Peoples, & Cultures Ser.). (ENG., Illus.). 32p. (J). (gr. 3-9). lib. bdg. *(978-0-7787-9297-0(8))* Crabtree Publishing Co.

—Japan - The People. 3rd rev. ed. 2008. (Lands, Peoples, & Cultures Ser.). (ENG., Illus.). 32p. (J). (gr. 3-9). pap. *(978-0-7787-9665-7(5))* Crabtree Publishing Co.

McKay, Susan. Japan. 2010. (Festivals of the World Ser.). 32p. (gr. 3). 28.50 *(978-1-60870-103-2(4))* Marshall Cavendish Corp.

Moore, Willamarie & Wilds, Kazumi. All about Japan: Stories, Songs, Crafts & Games for Kids. 2017. (ENG., Illus.). 64p. (J). (gr. 3-6). 14.95 *(978-4-8053-1440-1(0))* Tuttle Publishing.

Nakaya, Andrea C. Growin up in Japan. 2017. (ENG.). 80p. (YA). (gr. 5-12). ***(978-1-68282-219-7(2))*** ReferencePoint Pr., Inc.

Otowa, Rebecca. My Awesome Japan Adventure: A Diary about the Best 4 Months Ever! 2013. (ENG., Illus.). 48p. (J). (gr. 2-6). 14.95 *(978-4-8053-1216-2(5))* Tuttle Publishing.

Peppas, Lynn. Cultural Traditions in Japan. 2012. (ENG.). 32p. (J). pap. *(978-0-7787-7593-5(3))*; lib. bdg. *(978-0-7787-7586-7(0))* Crabtree Publishing Co.

Reynolds, Betty. Tokyo Friends. 2nd rev. ed. 2012. (ENG., Illus.). 64p. (J). (gr. 1-3). 14.95 *(978-4-8053-1075-5(8))* Tuttle Publishing.

Rich, Mari. My Teenage Life in Japan. 2017. (Custom & Cultures of the World Ser.). (ENG.). (YA). (gr. 7-12). 23.95 ***(978-1-4222-3906-3(3))*** Mason Crest.

Rolbin, Cyrus. Art & Life in Rural Japan: Toho Village Throught the Eyes of Its Youth. 2011. 176p. (J). (gr. 3-6). pap. 24.95 *(978-0-9815595-3-7(0))* Next Generation Pr.

Sexton, Colleen. Japan. 2010. (Exploring Countries Ser.). (ENG., Illus.). 32p. (J). (gr. 3-7). lib. bdg. 26.95 *(978-1-60014-486-8(1)*, Blastoff! Readers) Bellwether Media.

Sexton, Colleen A. Japan. 2011. (ENG., Illus.). 32p. (J). *(978-0-531-26467-6(X)*, Blastoff! Readers) Bellwether Media.

Takabayashi, Mari. I Live in Tokyo. 2004. (ENG., Illus.). 32p. (J). (gr. -1-3). reprint ed. pap. 6.95 *(978-0-618-49484-2(7))* Houghton Mifflin Harcourt Publishing Co.

Teacher Created Resources Staff. Japan: Come on a Journey of Discovery. 2008. (Qeb Travel Through Ser.). (ENG., Illus.). 32p. (gr. 4-7). pap. 7.99 *(978-1-4206-8284-7(9))* Teacher Created Resources, Inc.

Temko, Florence. Traditional Crafts from Japan. Gooch, Randall, illus. 2005. (Culture Crafts Ser.). 64p. (gr. 3-8). 23.93 *(978-0-8225-2938-5(6))* Lerner Publishing Group.

West, Patricia. East Meets West: Japan & America. 2005. (ENG., Illus.). 12p. (J). (gr. 3-3). pap. 5.97 net. *(978-0-328-13382-6(5)*, Scott Foresman) Pearson Schl.

Zocchi, Judy. In Japan. Brodie, Neale, illus. 2005. (Global Adventures I Ser.). 32p. (J). pap. 10.95 *(978-1-59646-139-0(X))*; lib. bdg. 21.65 *(978-1-59646-004-1(0))* Dingles & Co.

J
K
L

—In Japan/en Japón. Brodie, Neale, illus. 2005. (Global Adventures I Ser.).Tr. of En Japón. (ENG & SPA.). 32p. (J). lib. bdg. 21.65 (978-1-59646-005-8(9)) Dingles & Co.

JAPANESE—UNITED STATES

Aihara, Chris. Nikkei Donburi: A Japanese American Cultural Survival Guide. Iwasaki, Glen, illus. 2004. 124p. (J). (gr. 1-4). pap. 18.95 (978-1-879965-18-8(6)) Polychrome Publishing Corp.

Heinrichs, Ann. The Japanese-American Internment: Innocence, Guilt, & Wartime Justice. 2010. (Perspectives on 2 Ser.). 112p. (gr. 7-10). 39.93 (978-0-7614-4983-6(3)) Marshall Cavendish Corp.

Kaelberer, Angie Peterson & Burgan, Michael. Japanese American Internment. 2017. (Eyewitness to World War II Ser.). (ENG.). 112p. (gr. 5-7). pap. 8.95 **(978-0-7565-5585-6(X))**; lib. bdg. 35.99 **(978-0-7565-5581-8(7))** Compass Point Bks. (CPB Grades 4-8).

Uchida, Yoshiko. Journey to Topaz. 2005. 160p. pap. 9.95 (978-1-890771-91-1(0)) Heyday.

JAPANESE—UNITED STATES—FICTION

Berry, Eileen M. Haiku on Your Shoes. Regan, Dana, illus. 2005. 56p. (J). (gr. -1-3). per. 7.49 (978-1-59166-374-4(1)) BJU Pr.

Hathaway, Lucinda Churchman. 'Round the World: Takashi Sails Home. 2008. (Illus.). 135p. (J). 12.95 (978-1-59322-034-1(0)) Down The Shore Publishing Corp.

Okei-san: The Girl from Wakamatsu. 2006. (J). pap. 11.95 (978-0-9642112-8-5(9)) Barsotti Bks.

Preus, Margi. Heart of a Samurai. (ENG.). (YA). (gr. 3-7). 2012. 336p. pap. 8.95 (978-1-4197-0200-6(9)) 2010. 320p. 18.95 (978-0-8109-8981-8(6)) Abrams, Inc. (Amulet Bks.).

—Heart of a Samurai, 5 vols. (YA). 77.75 (978-1-4618-0343-0(8)); 77.75 (978-1-4618-0507-6(4)); 2011. 1.25 (978-1-4618-4275-0(1)); 2011. 79.75 (978-1-4618-0358-4(6)) Recorded Bks., Inc.

—Heart of a Samurai. 2012. (J). lib. bdg. 19.60 (978-0-606-38363-9(8)) Turtleback Bks.

Simmons, Andrew & Averdonz, N. R. I Was an Eighth-Grade Ninja, 1 vol. Padilla, Ariel, illus. 2007. (Z Graphic Novels / Tomo Ser.). (ENG.). 160p. (J). (gr. 3-7). pap. 6.99 (978-0-310-71300-5(5)) Zondervan.

Van Dolzer, Krista. The Sound of Life & Everything. 2015. (ENG.). 272p. (J). (gr. 5). 16.99 (978-0-399-16775-1(7), G.P. Putnam's Sons Books for Young Readers) Penguin Young Readers Group.

Yashima, Taro. Umbrella. unabr. ed. (J). (gr. k-3). 24.95 incl. audio (978-0-670-73864-9(6)) Live Oak Media.

JAPANESE AMERICANS

Anderson, Dale. Japanese Americans. 2006. (World Almanac Library of American Immigration). (Illus.). 48p. (gr. 5-12). pap. 14.05 (978-0-8368-7326-9(2)); lib. bdg. 31.00 (978-0-8368-7313-9(0)) Stevens, Gareth Publishing LLLP. (Gareth Stevens Secondary Library).

Atkins, Laura & Yogi, Stan. Fred Korematsu Speaks Up. 2017. (Illus.). 103p. (J). (978-1-59714-368-4(5)) Heyday.

Bailey, Rachel A. The Japanese Internment Camps: A History Perspectives Book. 2014. (Perspectives Library). (ENG., Illus.). 32p. (J). (gr. 4-8). 28.50 (978-1-62431-666-1(2), 203228) Cherry Lake Publishing.

Becker, Peggy Daniels. Japanese-American Internment During World War II. 2013. (Defining Moments Ser.). 240p. lib. bdg. 55.00 (978-0-7808-1333-5(2)) Omnigraphics, Inc.

Bjorklund, Ruth. Internment: Japanese Americans in World War II. 2016. (Public Persecutions Ser.). 128p. (J). 45.64 (978-1-5026-2323-2(4)) Cavendish Square Publishing.

Blegen, Daniel. Bob Sakata: American Farmer. 2009. (Now You Know Bio Ser.: 13). (Illus.). 102p. (J). pap. 8.95 (978-0-86541-093-0(3)) Filter Pr., LLC.

Bryan, Nichol. Japanese Americans, 1 vol. 2004. (One Nation Set 2 Ser.). (ENG.). 32p. (gr. k-6). 27.07 (978-1-59197-529-8(8), Checkerboard Library) ABDO Publishing Co.

Christopher, Matt. At the Plate with... Ichiro. 2003. (Matt Christopher Sports Bio Bookshelf Ser.). (Illus.). 101p. (J). (gr. 4-7). 12.65 (978-0-7569-1606-0(2)) Perfection Learning Corp.

Duncan, E. E. Ralph Carr: Defender of Japanese Americans. 2011. (ENG & SPA., Illus.). 66p. (J). pap. 8.95 (978-0-86541-116-6(6)) Filter Pr., LLC.

Fremon, David K. The Internment of Japanese Americans in United States History. 2014. (In United States History Ser.). (Illus.). 96p. (J). (gr. 5-12). 27.94 (978-0-7660-6068-5(3)) Enslow Pubs., Inc.

Goldstein, Margaret J. Japanese in America. 2006. (In America Ser.). (ENG., Illus.). 80p. (gr. 5-8). 27.93 (978-0-8225-3952-0(7), Lerner Pubns.) Lerner Publishing Group.

Hale, Christy. The East-West House: Noguchi's Childhood in Japan. Hale, Christy, illus. 2012. (ENG., Illus.). 32p. (J). (gr. 2-7). 17.95 (978-1-60060-363-1(7)) Lee & Low Bks., Inc.

Hasday, Judy L. Japanese Americans. (Successful Americans Ser.). 64p. (YA). 2009. (gr. 9-12). 22.95 (978-1-4222-0519-8(3)) 2007. (gr. 7-18). pap. 9.95 (978-1-4222-0863-2(X)) Mason Crest.

Hay, Jeff. Japanese American Internment. Wukovits, John, ed. 2012. (World History Ser.). (ENG., Illus.). 128p. (gr. 7-10). lib. bdg. 39.90 (978-1-4205-0824-6(5), Lucent Bks.) Cengage Gale.

Heinrichs, Ann. The Japanese-American Internment: Innocence, Guilt, & Wartime Justice. 2010. (Perspectives on 2 Ser.). 112p. (gr. 7-10). 39.93 (978-0-7614-4983-6(3)) Marshall Cavendish Corp.

Hyde, Natalie. Internment Camps. 2016. (Uncovering the Past: Analyzing Primary Sources Ser.). (ENG., Illus.). 48p. (J). (gr. 5-8). (978-0-7787-2860-3(9)) Crabtree Publishing Co.

Ingram, Scott. Japanese Immigrants. 2004. (Immigration to the United States Ser.). (Illus.). 96p. (gr. 4-9). 35.00 (978-0-8160-5688-0(9)) Facts On File, Inc.

The Internment of Japanese Americans During World War II: Detention of American Citizens. 2010. (Milestones in American History Ser.). (Illus.). 128p. (gr. 6-12). 35.00 (978-1-60413-681-4(2), Chelsea Hse.) Facts On File, Inc.

Kaelberer, Angie Peterson & Burgan, Michael. Japanese American Internment. 2017. (Eyewitness to World War II Ser.). (ENG.). 112p. (gr. 5-7). pap. 8.95 **(978-0-7565-5585-6(X))**; lib. bdg. 35.99 **(978-0-7565-5581-8(7))** Compass Point Bks. (CPB Grades 4-8).

Kenney, Karen Latchana & Friedman, Richard D. Korematsu v. the United States: World War II Japanese-American Internment Camps, 1 vol. 2012. (Landmark Supreme Court Cases Ser.). (ENG., Illus.). 160p. (J). (gr. 6-12). 37.07 (978-1-61783-473-8(4)) ABDO Publishing Co.

Kops, Deborah. Racial Profiling. 2006. (Open for Debate Ser.). (Illus.). 128p. (gr. 7-7). lib. bdg. 42.79 (978-0-7614-2298-3(6), Benchmark Bks.) Marshall Cavendish Corp.

Marrin, Albert. Uprooted: The Japanese American Experience During World War II. 2016. (ENG., Illus.). 256p. (YA). (gr. 7). 17.99 (978-0-553-50936-6(5), Knopf Bks. for Young Readers) Random Hse. Children's Bks.

Mattern, Joanne. Japanese Americans. 2003. (Immigrants in America Ser.). (Illus.). 112p. (gr. 6-12). 30.00 (978-0-7910-7130-4(8), Chelsea Hse.) Facts On File, Inc.

Moreno, Barry. The Japanese Americans. (Major American Immigration Ser.). (YA). 2010. (Illus.). 64p. (gr. 9-12). 22.95 (978-1-4222-0610-2(6)) 2007. pap. 9.95 (978-1-4222-0677-5(7)) Mason Crest.

Moss, Marissa. Barbed Wire Baseball. Shimizu, Yuko, illus. 2013. (ENG.). 48p. (J). (gr. 1-4). 19.95 (978-1-4197-0521-2(0), Abrams Bks. for Young Readers) Abrams, Inc.

Nickles, Greg. The Japanese: We Came to North America. 2006. (Illus.). 32p. (J). (gr. 4-8). reprint ed. 19.00 (978-0-7567-9908-3(2)) DIANE Publishing Co.

Oppenheim, Joanne F. Dear Miss Breed: True Stories of the Japanese American Incarceration During World War II & a Librarian Who Made a Difference. 2006. (ENG., Illus.). 288p. (J). (gr. 7-12). 22.99 (978-0-439-56992-7(3)) Scholastic, Inc.

Parker, Lewis K. Why Japanese Immigrants Came to America. (Coming to America Ser.). 24p. 2009. (gr. 2-3). 42.50 (978-1-61511-886-1(1)) 2003. (Illus.). (J). lib. bdg. 22.60 (978-0-8239-6463-5(9)) Rosen Publishing Group, Inc., The. (PowerKids Pr.).

Sandler, Martin W. Imprisoned: The Betrayal of Japanese Americans During World War II. 2013. (ENG., Illus.). 176p. (J). (gr. 5-8). 24.99 (978-0-8027-2277-5(6), 9780802722775, Bloomsbury USA Childrens) Walker & Co.

Say, Allen. Drawing from Memory. 2011. (978-0-545-17687-3(5), Scholastic Pr.) Scholastic, Inc.

—Drawing from Memory. Say, Allen, illus. 2011. (ENG., Illus.). 64p. (J). (gr. 5-18). 18.99 (978-0-545-17686-6(7), Scholastic Pr.) Scholastic, Inc.

Slavicek, Louise Chipley. Daniel Inouye. 2nd ed. 2007. (Asian Americans of Achievement Ser.). (Illus.). 128p. (YA). (gr. 7-12). lib. bdg. 35.00 (978-0-7910-9271-2(2)) Facts On File, Inc.

Taylor, Charlotte & Kent, Deborah. The Internment of Japanese Americans. 2015. (Our Shared History Ser.). (ENG.). 128p. (J). (gr. 7-7). lib. bdg. 37.27 (978-0-7660-7008-0(5)) Enslow Pubs., Inc.

Tiger, Caroline. Isamu Noguchi. 2007. (Asian Americans of Achievement Ser.). (Illus.). 112p. (YA). (gr. 7-12). lib. bdg. 35.00 (978-0-7910-9276-7(3)) Facts On File, Inc.

Welch, Catherine A. Children of the Relocation Camps. 2005. (Picture the American Past Ser.). (Illus.). 48p. (gr. 2-5). lib. bdg. 22.60 (978-1-57505-350-9(0)) Lerner Publishing Group.

Welky, Ali. A Captive Audience: Voices of Japanese American Youth in World War II Arkansas. 2015. (ENG., Illus.). 124p. pap. 21.95 (978-1-935106-86-9(4)) Butler Ctr. for Arkansas Studies.

West, Patricia. East Meets West: Japan & America. 2005. (ENG., Illus.). 12p. (J). (gr. 3-3). pap. 5.97 net. (978-0-328-13382-6(5), Scott Foresman) Pearson Schl.

JAPANESE AMERICANS—FICTION

Banks, Jacqueline Turner. A Day for Vincent Chin & Me. 2005. (ENG.). 128p. (J). (gr. 5-7). pap. 11.95 (978-0-618-54879-8(3)) Houghton Mifflin Harcourt Publishing Co.

Bunting, Eve. So Far from the Sea. Soentpiet, Chris K., illus. 2009. (ENG.). 32p. (J). (gr. 5-7). pap. 7.99 (978-0-547-23752-7(9)) Houghton Mifflin Harcourt Publishing Co.

Cheaney, J. B. My Friend the Enemy. 2007. 266p. (gr. 4-7). 16.50 (978-0-7569-7946-1(3)) Perfection Learning Corp.

Ching, Tokie. Boy's Day in Hawaii. Arai, Setsuo, illus. 2008. 32p. (J). 12.95 (978-1-56647-852-6(9)) Mutual Publishing LLC.

—Girl's Day in Hawaii with Yuki Chan. 2006. 40p. (J). 14.95 (978-1-56647-820-5(0)) Mutual Publishing LLC.

Conkling, Winifred. Sylvia & Aki. (ENG.). 160p. (J). 2013. (gr. 4-7). 6.99 (978-1-58246-345-2(X), Yearling) 2011. (Illus.). (gr. 3-7). 16.99 (978-1-58246-337-7(9), Tricycle Pr.) Random Hse. Children's Bks.

Crilley, Mark. Akiko Flights of Fancy. exp. ed. 2007. (Illus.). 264p. pap. 24.95 (978-1-57989-088-9(1)) Sirius Entertainment, Inc.

—The Battle for Boach's Keep Vol. 7. 2004. (Illus.). 144p. pap. 14.95 (978-1-57989-064-3(4)) Sirius Entertainment, Inc.

Dallas, Sandra. Red Berries, White Clouds, Blue Sky. (ENG.). 216p. (J). (gr. 3-6). 2015. pap. 9.99 (978-1-58536-907-2(1), 203820) 2014. 15.95 (978-1-58536-906-5(3), 203673) Sleeping Bear Pr.

DeNomme, Donna & Proctor, Tina. Ophelia's Oracle: Discovering the Healthy, Happy, Self-aware, & Competant Girl in the Mirror. 2009. (YA). pap. 16.95 (978-1-61539-958-1(5)) Independent Pub.

Falwell, Cathryn. Butterflies for Kiri. Falwell, Cathryn, illus. 2003. (ENG., Illus.). 32p. (J). (978-1-58430-100-4(7)) Lee & Low Bks., Inc.

—Butterflies for Kiri, 1 vol. 2003. (ENG., Illus.). 32p. (J). pap. 9.95 (978-1-60060-342-6(4)) Lee & Low Bks., Inc.

Faulkner, Matt. Gaijin: American Prisoner of War. 2014. (ENG., Illus.). 144p. (J). (gr. 3-7). 19.99 (978-1-4231-3735-1(3)) Hyperion Bks. for Children.

Fein, Eric. Mystery at Manzanar: A WWII Internment Camp Story, 1 vol. Hartman, Kurt, illus. 2008. (Historical Fiction Ser.). (ENG.). 56p. (gr. 2-3). pap. 6.25 (978-1-4342-0847-7(8), Graphic Flash) Stone Arch Bks.

Fitzmaurice, Kathryn. A Diamond in the Desert. (ENG.). 272p. (J). (gr. 5). 2013. pap. 6.99 (978-0-14-242437-7(4), Puffin Books) 2012. 16.99 (978-0-670-01292-3(0), Viking Books for Young Readers) Penguin Young Readers Group.

Florence, Debbi Michiko. Jasmine Toguchi, Mochi Queen. 2017. (J). pap. **(978-0-374-30411-9(4))** Farrar, Straus & Giroux.

—Jasmine Toguchi, Mochi Queen. Vukovic, Elizabet, illus. 2017. (Jasmine Toguchi Ser.: 1). (ENG.). 128p. (J). pap. 5.99 **(978-0-374-30834-6(9)**, 9780374308346, Farrar, Straus & Giroux (BYR)) Farrar, Straus & Giroux.

—Jasmine Toguchi, Super Sleuth. Vukovic, Elizabet, illus. 2017. (J). pap. **(978-0-374-30414-0(9))**; (Jasmine Toguchi Ser.: 2). (ENG.). 128p. pap. 5.99 **(978-0-374-30835-3(7)**, 9780374308353, Farrar, Straus & Giroux (BYR)) Farrar, Straus & Giroux.

Harrington, Claudia. My Mom & Dad, 1 vol. Persico, Zoe, illus. 2016. (ENG.). 32p. (J). (978-1-62402-107-7(7)) Magic Wagon.

Hirahara, Naomi. 1001 Cranes. 2009. (ENG.). 240p. (J). (gr. 3-7). 7.99 (978-0-440-42234-1(5), Yearling) Random Hse. Children's Bks.

Hughes, Dean. Four-Four-Two. 2016. (ENG., Illus.). 272p. (YA). (gr. 7). 17.99 (978-1-4814-6252-5(0), Atheneum Bks. for Young Readers) Simon & Schuster Children's Publishing.

—Missing in Action. 2010. (ENG.). 240p. (J). (gr. 5-9). 16.99 (978-1-4169-1502-7(8), Atheneum Bks. for Young Readers) Simon & Schuster Children's Publishing.

Inzana, Ryan. Ichiro. (ENG., Illus.). 288p. (YA). (gr. 7). 2014. pap. 12.99 (978-0-547-61789-3(5), HMH Books For Young Readers) 2012. 24.99 (978-0-547-25269-8(2)) Houghton Mifflin Harcourt Publishing Co.

Kadohata, Cynthia. Kira-Kira. (ENG., Illus.). (J). (gr. 5-9). 2004. 256p. 17.99 (978-0-689-85639-6(3)) 2006. 272p. reprint ed. pap. 7.99 (978-0-689-85640-2(7)) Simon & Schuster Children's Publishing. (Atheneum Bks. for Young Readers).

—The Thing about Luck. Kuo, Julia, illus. (ENG.). (J). (gr. 5-9). 2014. 304p. pap. 8.99 (978-1-4424-7465-9(3), Atheneum Bks. for Young Readers) 2013. 288p. 16.99 (978-1-4169-1882-0(5)) Simon & Schuster Children's Publishing.

—The Thing about Luck. 2014. lib. bdg. 18.40 (978-0-606-35798-2(X)) Turtleback Bks.

—Weedflower. (ENG.). 272p. (J). (gr. 5-9). 2009. pap. 7.99 (978-1-4169-7566-3(7)) 2006. (Illus.). 19.99 (978-0-689-86574-9(0)) Simon & Schuster Children's Publishing. (Atheneum Bks. for Young Readers).

Karalius, Kimberly. Love Charms & Other Catastrophes. 2016. (Grimbaud Ser.). (ENG.). 384p. (YA). pap. 10.99 (978-1-250-08404-0(0), 9781250084040) Feiwel & Friends.

Larson, Kirby. Dash. (Dogs of World War II Ser.). (ENG.). 256p. (J). (gr. 3-7). 2016. pap. 7.99 (978-0-545-41636-8(1), Scholastic Paperbacks) 2014. 17.99 (978-0-545-41635-1(3), Scholastic Pr.) Scholastic, Inc.

—The Fences Between Us: The Diary of Piper Davis. 2010. (Dear America Ser.). (J). (ENG.). 320p. (gr. 3-7). 12.99 (978-0-545-22418-5(7)); (Illus.). 313p. pap. (978-0-545-27094-6(4)) Scholastic, Inc.

Lee-Tai, Amy. A Place Where Sunflowers Grow. Hoshino, Felicia, illus. 32p. (J). 2015. (ENG & JPN.). pap. 9.95 (978-0-89239-274-2(6), Children's Book Press) 2006. (JPN & ENG.). 17.95 (978-0-89239-215-5(0)) Lee & Low Bks., Inc.

Lieurance, Suzanne. The Lucky Baseball: My Story in a Japanese-American Internment Camp. 2009. (Historical Fiction Adventures (HFA) Ser.). (Illus.). 160p. (J). (gr. 3-6). lib. bdg. 29.27 (978-0-7660-3311-5(2)) Enslow Pubs., Inc.

Lorenzi, Natalie Dias. Flying the Dragon. (ENG.). 240p. (J). (gr. 4-7). 2014. pap. 8.95 (978-1-58089-435-7(6)) 2012. 16.95 (978-1-58089-434-0(8)) Charlesbridge Publishing, Inc.

Maetani, Valynne E. Ink & Ashes. 2015. (ENG.). 368p. (YA). 19.95 (978-1-62014-211-0(2), Tu Bks.) Lee & Low Bks., Inc.

Maruno, Jennifer. When the Cherry Blossoms Fell. 2009. (Cherry Blossom Book Ser.: 1). (ENG.). 144p. (J). (gr. 4-7). pap. 9.95 (978-1-894917-83-4(9), Napoleon & Co.) Dundurn CAN. Dist: Ingram Publisher Services.

May, Kyla. Mika: My New Life. 2013. (Lotus Lane Ser.: 4). lib. bdg. 14.75 (978-0-606-32365-9(1), Turtleback) Turtleback Bks.

Mazer, Harry. A Boy No More. 2007. 136p. (gr. 5-9). 16.00 (978-0-7569-8112-9(3)) Perfection Learning Corp.

Michiko Florence, Debbi. Jasmine Toguchi, Mochi Queen. Vukovic, Elizabet, illus. 2017. (Jasmine Toguchi Ser.). (ENG.). 128p. (J). 15.99 (978-0-374-30410-2(6), 9780374304102, Farrar, Straus & Giroux (BYR)) Farrar, Straus & Giroux.

—Jasmine Toguchi, Super Sleuth. Vukovic, Elizabet, illus. 2017. (Jasmine Toguchi Ser.). (ENG.). 128p. (J). 15.99 (978-0-374-30413-3(0), 9780374304133, Farrar, Straus & Giroux (BYR)) Farrar, Straus & Giroux.

Mitsui Brown, Janet, illus. Oshogatsu with Obaachan. 2005. (J). (978-1-879965-24-9(0)) Polychrome Publishing Corp.

Mochizuki, Ken. Baseball Saved Us. 97th rev. ed. 2014. (ENG.). 30p. (J). (gr. k-12). 15.65 (978-1-63245-249-8(9)) Lectorum Pubns., Inc.

—Baseball Saved Us. Lee, Dom, illus. (Picture Book Readalong Ser.). pap. 39.95 incl. audio compact disk (978-1-59112-917-2(6)); 2004. (J). (gr. -1-2). 25.95 incl. audio (978-1-59112-456-6(5)) Live Oak Media.

—Beacon Hill Boys. 2004. 200p. 16.00 (978-0-7569-4281-6(0)) Perfection Learning Corp.

Noguchi, Rick & Jenks, Deneen. Flowers from Mariko. Kumata, Michelle Reiko, illus. 2013. (ENG.). 32p. (J). (gr. 1-18). 16.95 (978-1-58430-032-8(9)) Lee & Low Bks., Inc.

—Flowers from Mariko, 1 vol. Kumata, Michelle Reiko, illus. 2016. (ENG.). 32p. (J). pap. 9.95 (978-1-62014-315-5(1)) Lee & Low Bks., Inc.

Parkhurst, Liz S. Under One Flag: A Year at Rohwer. Clifton, Tom, illus. 2006. (ENG.). 32p. (J). (gr. 3-7). 16.95 (978-0-87483-759-9(6), 1241971) August Hse. Pubs., Inc.

Parry, Rosanne. The Turn of the Tide. 2016. (ENG., Illus.). 304p. (J). (gr. 3-7). 16.99 (978-0-375-86972-3(7), Random Hse. Bks. for Young Readers) Random Hse. Children's Bks.

Patneaude, David. Thin Wood Walls. 2008. (ENG., Illus.). 240p. (J). (gr. 5-7). pap. 7.99 (978-0-618-80915-8(5)) Houghton Mifflin Harcourt Publishing Co.

Pyle, Kevin C. Take What You Can Carry. Pyle, Kevin C., illus. 2012. (ENG., Illus.). 176p. (YA). (gr. 7-12). pap. 14.99 (978-0-8050-8286-9(7), 9780805082869) Square Fish.

Reece, Colleen L. Last Page in the Diary. 2011. 94p. pap. 8.95 (978-1-61633-179-5(8)) Guardian Angel Publishing, Inc.

Robbins, Trina. The Bark in Space. Page, Tyler, illus. 2013. (Chicagoland Detective Agency Ser.: 5). (ENG.). 64p. (gr. 4-8). (J). lib. bdg. 29.27 (978-0-7613-8166-2(X)); pap. 6.95 (978-1-4677-0725-1(2)) Lerner Publishing Group. (Graphic Universe™).

—The Big Flush. Page, Tyler, illus. 2012. (Chicagoland Detective Agency Ser.: 4). (ENG.). 64p. (gr. 4-8). pap. 6.95 (978-0-8225-9161-0(8)); lib. bdg. 29.27 (978-0-7613-8165-5(1)) Lerner Publishing Group. (Graphic Universe™).

—The Drained Brains Caper. Page, Tyler, illus. 2010. (Chicagoland Detective Agency Ser.: 1). (ENG.). 64p. (gr. 4-8). pap. 6.95 (978-0-7613-5635-6(5), Graphic Universe™); lib. bdg. 29.27 (978-0-7613-4601-2(5)) Lerner Publishing Group.

—Night of the Living Dogs. Page, Tyler, illus. 2012. (Chicagoland Detective Agency Ser.). 64p. (J). (gr. 4-8). pap. 39.62 (978-0-7613-9313-9(7), Graphic Universe™); (ENG.). lib. bdg. 29.27 (978-0-7613-4616-6(3)) Lerner Publishing Group.

Salisbury, Graham. House of the Red Fish. (ENG.). (YA). (gr. 7). 2014. 318p. pap. 9.99 (978-0-385-38657-9(5), Ember) 2008. 320p. mass mkt. 6.50 (978-0-440-23838-6(2), Laurel Leaf) Random Hse. Children's Bks.

—Hunt for the Bamboo Rat. 2014. (ENG., Illus.). 336p. (YA). (gr. 7). 16.99 (978-0-375-84266-5(7), Lamb, Wendy Bks.) Random Hse. Children's Bks.

—Under the Blood Red Sun. 246p. (YA). 22.00 (978-0-8446-7322-6(6)) Smith, Peter Pub., Inc.

—Under the Blood-Red Sun. 2014. (ENG.). 272p. (YA). (gr. 7-7). pap. 9.99 (978-0-385-38655-5(9), Ember) Random Hse. Children's Bks.

Say, Allen. The Favorite Daughter. 2013. (J). pap. (978-0-545-17663-7(8), Levine, Arthur A. Bks.) Scholastic, Inc.

—The Favorite Daughter. Say, Allen, illus. 2013. (ENG., Illus.). 32p. (J). (gr. -1-3). 17.99 (978-0-545-17662-0(X), Levine, Arthur A. Bks.) Scholastic, Inc.

—Grandfather's Journey. Say, Allen, illus. 2008. (ENG., Illus.). 32p. (J). (gr. -1-3). 7.99 (978-0-547-07680-5(0)) Houghton Mifflin Harcourt Publishing Co.

—Grandfather's Journey. 20th anniv. ed. 2013. (ENG., Illus.). 32p. (J). (gr. -1-3). 17.99 (978-0-544-05050-1(9)) Houghton Mifflin Harcourt Publishing Co.

—Grandfather's Journey. 2008. (ENG.). 32p. (J). (gr. -1-3). pap. 7.99 (978-0-547-14178-7(5), Sandpiper) Houghton Mifflin Harcourt Trade & Reference Pubs.

—Grandfather's Journey. 2011. (J). (gr. k-5). 29.95 (978-0-545-10696-2(6)); 18.95 (978-0-545-12708-0(4)) Weston Woods Studios, Inc.

Sepahban, Lois. Paper Wishes. 2016. (ENG.). 192p. (J). 16.99 (978-0-374-30216-0(2), 9780374302160, Farrar, Straus & Giroux (BYR)) Farrar, Straus & Giroux.

—Paper Wishes. 2017. (J). lib. bdg. 18.40 **(978-0-606-39942-5(9))** Turtleback Bks.

Sugiura, Misa. It's Not Like It's a Secret. 2017. 400p. (YA). (gr. 8). 17.99 (978-0-06-247341-7(7), HarperTeen) HarperCollins Pubs.

Terasaki, Stanley Todd. Ghosts for Breakfast. Shinjo, Shelly, illus. 2013. (ENG.). 32p. (J). (gr. k-4). 16.95 (978-1-58430-046-5(9)) Lee & Low Bks., Inc.

Terry, Alana. What, No Sushi? Steffen, Jeremy, illus. 2013. 116p. pap. 7.99 (978-1-937848-04-0(3)) Do Life Right, Inc.

Thompson, Holly. Orchards. 2012. (ENG.). 336p. (YA). (gr. 7). pap. 9.99 (978-0-385-73978-8(8), Ember) Random Hse. Children's Bks.

Uchida, Yoshiko. Samurai of Gold Hill. Forberg, Ati, illus. 2005. 119p. (J). (gr. 2). per. 8.95 (978-1-59714-015-7(5)) Heyday.

Villani, Donna. The Capture of Art. 2008. 244p. pap. 14.95 (978-1-60693-104-2(0), Eloquent Bks.) Strategic Book Publishing & Rights Agency (SBPRA).

Wahl, Jan. Candy Shop. Wong, Nicole E., illus. 2004. (ENG.). 32p. (J). (gr. -1-3). 15.95 (978-1-57091-508-6(3)) Charlesbridge Publishing, Inc.

Wells, Rosemary. Yoko. Wells, Rosemary, illus. 2009. (ENG., Illus.). 32p. (J). (gr. -1-1). pap. 6.99 (978-1-4231-1983-8(5)) Hyperion Pr.

Weston Woods Staff, creator. Grandfather's Journey. 2011. 38.75 (978-0-545-12710-3(6)) Weston Woods Studios, Inc.

Yamasaki, Katie. Fish for Jimmy. Yamasaki, Katie, illus. 2013. (ENG., Illus.). 32p. (J). (gr. 1-5). 16.95 (978-0-8234-2375-0(1)) Holiday Hse., Inc.

Yamasaki, Katie, illus. When the Cousins Came. 2016. (J). (978-0-8234-3457-2(5)) Holiday Hse., Inc.

JAPANESE LANGUAGE

Ace Academics, ed. Japanese: A Whole Course in a Box! 2007. (Exambusters Ser.). 384p. (gr. 7-18). 12.95 (978-1-881374-96-1(3), Exambusters) Ace Academics, Inc.

Brown, Michelle Haney. My First Book of Japanese Words: An ABC Rhyming Book. Padron, Aya, illus. 2013. (ENG & JPN.). 32p. (J). (gr. -1-3). 12.95 (978-4-8053-1201-8(7)) Tuttle Publishing.

Evans, Meg, et al. Mirai Stage 1: Course Book, 6 vols., Stage 2. 2004. (JPN & ENG., Illus.). (gr. 7-10). 168p. stu. ed., per. 49.95 (978-0-7339-0929-0(9)); 158p. tchr. ed., per. 100.00 (978-0-7339-1367-9(9)) Pearson Education Australia AUS. Dist: Cheng & Tsui Co.

Fedoruk, Dennis, prod. Bilingual Baby - Flashcard Set - Japanese. 2013. (JPN.). (J). 7.99 (978-1-892703-78-1(5)) Small Fry Beginnings.

Galan, Christian. I'm Learning Japanese! A Language Adventure for Young People. Lerot-Calvo, Florence, illus. 2010. (ENG & JPN.). 128p. (J). (gr. 3-8). spiral bd. 19.95 (978-4-8053-1074-8(X)) Tuttle Publishing.

Green, Yuko. Japanese Word Book. 2004. (JPN., Illus.). 112p. pap. 14.95 (978-1-57306-196-4(4)) Bess Pr., Inc.

Kalz, Jill. My First Japanese Phrases, 1 vol. TransPerfect Translations Staff, tr. Fabbri, Daniele, illus. 2012. (Speak Another Language! Ser.). (JPN & ENG.). 32p. (gr. 1-3). lib. bdg. 26.65 (978-1-4048-7514-2(X)) Picture Window Bks.

Kardy, Glenn. Kanji de Manga Special Edition: Yoji-Jukugo: Yoji-Jukugo. 2008. (JPN & ENG., Illus.). 112p. pap. 9.99 (978-4-921205-22-5(1), 9784921205225) Japanime Co., Ltd. JPN. Dist: Diamond Comic Distributors, Inc.

Konda, Cynthia. Okasan & Me: Japanese American Educational Program. 2003. (JPN., Illus.). 26p. (J). (gr.

-1-18). spiral bd. 19.99 *(978-0-9743613-0-7(5))* Okasan & Me.

Lee, Margaret. Tsumiki, 2 vols. 2004. (JPN & ENG., Illus.). (gr. 7-9). 177p. pap., stu. ed. 45.95 *(978-0-17-010267-4(X))*; 194p. pap., tchr. ed. 135.00 *(978-0-17-010268-1(8))* Cengage Learning Australia AUS. Dist: Cheng & Tsui Co.

Mahoney, Judy. Teach Me Everyday Japanese V 1, Vol 1. Girouard, Patrick, illus. 2008. (JPN & ENG.). 32p. (J). (gr. -1). 19.95 *(978-1-59972-104-0(X))* Teach Me Tapes, Inc.

McBride, Helen, et al. Kimono, Level 3. (JPN.). 160p. (J). pap., wbk. ed. 29.95 *(978-0-8219-1038-2(8)*, 58653) EMC/Paradigm Publishing.

—Kimono, Level 3. Incl. Level 3. pap., wbk. ed. 29.95 *(978-0-8219-1038-2(8)*, 58653); Level 3. tchr. ed. 189.95 *(978-0-8219-1049-8(3)*, 58653); (J). (gr. k-5). (JPN.). 160p. Set stu. ed. 47.95 *(978-0-8219-1037-5(X)*, 58253) EMC/Paradigm Publishing.

Passport Books Staff, ed. Japanese Picture Dictionary: Elementary Through Junior High. Goodman, Marlene, illus. 2003. (Let's Learn... Picture Dictionary Ser.). (JPN.). 80p. (J). (gr. 4-7). pap. 11.95 *(978-0-8442-8494-1(7)*, 84947) McGraw-Hill Trade.

Peterson, Hiromi & Omizo, Naomi. Adventures in Japanese, Vol. 2. Muronaka, Michael & Kaylor, Emiko, illus. 2004. (JPN & ENG.). 210p. (gr. 7-10). pap., wbk. ed. 19.95 *(978-0-88727-321-6(1))* Cheng & Tsui Co.

—Adventures in Japanese: Field Test Edition. 2004. (JPN & ENG., Illus.). (gr. 9-12). 462p. pap. 45.00 *(978-0-88727-416-9(1))*; 116p. pap., wbk. ed. 21.95 *(978-0-88727-417-6(X))* Cheng & Tsui Co.

York, M. J. Learn Japanese Words. Petelinsek, Kathleen, illus. 2014. (Foreign Language Basics Ser.). (ENG.). 24p. (J). (gr. 2-5). 27.07 *(978-1-62687-376-6(3)*, 207123) Child's World, Inc., The.

JAPANESE LANGUAGE—GRAMMAR

Brenda, Stapleton. Grammar Keys: A Guide for Japanese Students. 3rd ed. 2005. pap. *(978-0-9770443-0-6(0))* Top Shelf Publishing.

Evans, Meg, et al. Mirai Stage 1: Course Book, 6 vols. 2004. (JPN & ENG., Stage 1. Illus.). 191p. (gr. 6-9). stu. ed., per. 49.95 *(978-0-7339-0425-7(4))*Stage 1. (Illus.). 141p. (gr. 6-9). tchr. ed., per. 100.00 *(978-0-7339-0504-9(8))*Stage 2. (gr. 7-10). per. 100.00 *(978-0-7339-1214-6(1))* Pearson Education Australia AUS. Dist: Cheng & Tsui Co.

Goodman, Marlene. Let's Learn Japanese Picture Dictionary. 2003. (JPN & ENG., Illus.). 80p. 13.00 *(978-0-07-140827-1(4)*, 0071408274) McGraw-Hill Cos., The.

Green, Yuko. Japanese Word Book. 2004. (JPN., Illus.). 112p. pap. 14.95 *(978-1-57306-196-4(4))* Bess Pr., Inc.

Kardy, Glenn. Kana de Manga: the Fun, Easy Way to Learn the ABCs of Japanese: The Fun, Easy Way to Learn the ABCs of Japanese. 2005. (ENG., Illus.). 144p. (YA). pap. 9.99 *(978-4-921205-01-0(9)*, 9784921205010) Japanime Co., Ltd. JPN. Dist: Diamond Comic Distributors, Inc.

Kudela, Katy R. My First Book of Japanese Words, 1 vol. Translations.com Staff, tr. 2011. (Bilingual Picture Dictionaries Ser.). 32p. (gr. 1-2). (ENG & MUL.). pap. 8.10 *(978-1-4296-6337-3(5))*; (MUL.). pap. 47.70 *(978-1-4296-6464-6(9))* Capstone Press of Coughlan Cos. (Aplus Bks.).

Milet Publishing Staff. My First Bilingual Book - Colors. 2011. (My First Bilingual Book Ser.). (ENG.). 24p. (J). (gr. k — 1). bds. 7.99 *(978-1-84059-600-7(7))* Milet Publishing.

Milles, Harriet. Japanese, 1 vol. 2012. (Languages of the World Ser.). (ENG & JPN.). 32p. (gr. 1-3). lib. bdg. 27.32 *(978-1-4329-5836-7(4)*, Heinemann First Library) Heinemann-Raintree.

Stout, Timothy G. Japanese for Kids, Kit. 2008. (Tuttle Flash Cards Ser.). (ENG., Illus.). 1p. (J). (gr. -1-8). 19.95 *(978-4-8053-0904-9(0))* Tuttle Publishing.

Takahashi, Peter X. Jimi's Book of Japanese: A Motivating Method to Learn Japanese (Kanji) Moto, Mikki, ed. Toka, Yumie, illus. 2006. (J). pap. 24.95 *(978-0-9723247-5-5(5)*, PB&J OmniMedia) Takahashi & Black.

—Jimi's Book of Japanese: A Motivating Method to Learn Japanese (Katakana) Moto, Mikki, ed. Toka, Yumie, illus. 2005. (JPN & ENG.). 76p. (J). pap. 18.95 *(978-0-9723247-2-4(0)*, PB&J OmniMedia) Takahashi & Black.

—Jimi's Sumo Stack: A Motivating Method to Memorize Japanese. Toka, Yumie, illus. 2006. pap. 19.95 *(978-0-9723247-8-6(X)*, PB&J OmniMedia) Takahashi & Black.

Uchiyama, Akira & Kodaira, Hiromi. Yubisashi Yubinazori Aiueo. 2011. (JPN., Illus.). 96p. (J). (gr. -1-3). *(978-4-564-00493-3(X))* Hikari no Kuni.

JAY, JOHN, 1745-1829

Miller, Chuck. John Jay. 2003. (America's Founders Ser.). (J). pap. *(978-1-58417-083-9(2))*; lib. bdg. *(978-1-58417-020-4(4))* Lake Street Pubs.

White, Casey. John Jay: Diplomat of the American Experiment. (Library of American Thinkers Ser.). 112p. 2009. (gr. 6-6). 66.50 *(978-1-60853-515-6(0)*, Rosen Reference) 2005. (Illus.). (YA). (gr. 5-9). lib. bdg. 34.60 *(978-1-4042-0507-9(1))* Rosen Publishing Group, Inc., The.

JAZZ

Allen, Richard, contrib. by. Mysterious Thelonious. abr. ed. 2003. (Illus.). (J). (gr. -1-2). audio compact disk 28.95 *(978-1-59112-422-1(0))* Live Oak Media.

Barron, Rachel Stiffler. John Coltrane: Jazz Revolutionary. 2004. (Masters of Music Ser.). (Illus.). 112p. (YA). (gr. 6-12). 23.95 *(978-1-883846-57-2(9)*, First Biographies) Reynolds, Morgan Inc.

Battaglia, Stephen. Mr. Mcsymphony's It's All about Jazz. 2008. (ENG.). 28p. pap. 9.99 *(978-1-4196-8086-1(2))* CreateSpace Independent Publishing Platform.

Batten, Jack. Oscar Peterson: The Man & His Jazz. 2012. (ENG., Illus.). 192p. (YA). (gr. 5). 19.95 *(978-1-77049-269-1(0)*, Tundra Bks.) Tundra Bks. CAN. Dist: Penguin Random Hse. LLC.

Ben-Hur, Roni Amos, text. Talk Jazz: A Comprehensive Collection of Be Bop Studies for All Instrumentalists & Vocalists. Ben-Hur, Roni Amos, . 2003. 54p. (YA). pap. 19.00 net. *(978-0-9744943-0-2(5)*, (201 862-1692) Bohobza Music.

Burch, Sharon. Scat Singing for Kids: A Step-By-Step Journey in Jazz. 2012. (ENG.). 32p. pap. 12.99 *(978-1-4768-1204-5(7)*, 1476812047) Leonard, Hal Corp.

Collins, Terry. Louis Armstrong: Jazz Legend. Pope, Richie, illus. 2012. (American Graphic Ser.). (ENG.). 32p. (gr. 3-4). pap. 47.70 *(978-1-4296-9337-0(1)*, Graphic Library) Capstone Press of Coughlan Cos.

Hal Leonard Corp. Staff, creator. Jazzy Opera Classix: For Clarinet. 2005. (ENG.). 36p. pap. 19.95 incl. audio compact disk *(978-1-902455-29-7(0)*, 1902455290) Schott Music Corp.

—Jazzy Opera Classix: For Violin. 2005. (ENG.). 36p. pap. 19.95 incl. audio compact disk *(978-1-902455-32-7(0)*, 1902455320) Schott Music Corp.

Josephson, Judith Pinkerton. Louis Armstrong. 2008. pap. 52.95 *(978-0-8225-9392-8(0))* Lerner Publishing Group.

Lynette, Rachel. Miles Davis. 2010. (Innovators Ser.). (Illus.). 64p. (J). 29.95 *(978-0-7377-5034-8(0)*, Kidhaven) Cengage Gale.

McDonough, Yona Zeldis. Who Was Louis Armstrong? O'Brien, John A. & Harrison, Nancy, illus. 2004. (Who Was? Ser.). (ENG.). 112p. (J). (gr. 3-7). pap. 5.99 *(978-0-448-43368-4(0)*, Grosset & Dunlap) Penguin Young Readers Group.

Orgill, Roxane. Skit-Scat Raggedy Cat: Ella Fitzgerald. Qualls, Sean, illus. 2012. (Candlewick Biographies Ser.). (ENG.). 48p. (J). (gr. 3-7). 14.99 *(978-0-7636-6459-6(6))*; pap. 4.99 *(978-0-7636-6458-9(8))* Candlewick Pr.

Pinkney, Andrea Davis. Ella Fitzgerald: The Tale of a Vocal Virtuosa. Pinkney, Brian, illus. 2007. (ENG.). 32p. (J). (gr. k-4). pap. 6.99 *(978-0-7868-1416-9(0)*, Jump at the Sun) Hyperion Bks. for Children.

Raschka, Chris. Mysterious Thelonious. Raschka, Chris, illus. (Illus.). pap. 18.95 incl. audio compact disk *(978-1-59112-421-4(2))* Live Oak Media.

Russell-Brown, Katheryn. Little Melba & Her Big Trombone. Morrison, Frank, illus. 2014. (ENG.). 40p. (J). 18.95 *(978-1-60060-898-8(1))* Lee & Low Bks., Inc.

Watson, Cindy. Out of Darkness: The Jeff Healey Story. 2010. (ENG., Illus.). 144p. (YA). (gr. k-6). pap. 19.99 *(978-1-55488-706-4(2)*, 9781554887064) Dundurn CAN. Dist: Ingram Publisher Services.

Weinstein, Muriel Harris. Play, Louis, Play! The True Story of a Boy & His Horn. Morrison, Frank, illus. 2010. (ENG.). 112p. (J). (gr. 2-4). 15.99 *(978-1-59990-375-0(X)*, 9781599903750, Bloomsbury USA Childrens) Bloomsbury Publishing USA.

Weston Woods Staff, creator. Ella Fitzgerald. 2011. 38.75 *(978-0-545-02763-2(2))*; 18.95 *(978-0-545-02761-8(6))* Weston Woods Studios, Inc.

What Jazz & Blues Can I Play - Alto Sax. 20p. 6.95 *(978-1-85909-426-6(0)*, Warner Bros. Pubns.) Alfred Publishing Co., Inc.

What Jazz & Blues Can I Play - Flute. 20p. 6.95 *(978-1-85909-422-8(8)*, Warner Bros. Pubns.) Alfred Publishing Co., Inc.

What Jazz & Blues Can I Play - Trumpet. 20p. 6.95 *(978-1-85909-425-9(2)*, Warner Bros. Pubns.) Alfred Publishing Co., Inc.

What Jazz & Blues Can I Play - Violin. 24p. 6.95 *(978-1-85909-424-2(4)*, Warner Bros. Pubns.) Alfred Publishing Co., Inc.

What Jazz Blues Can I Play. 20p. 6.95 *(978-1-85909-423-5(6)*, Warner Bros. Pubns.) Alfred Publishing Co., Inc.

Winter, Jonah. Dizzy. Qualls, Sean, illus. 2006. (J). 16.99 *(978-0-439-50736-3(7)*, Levine, Arthur A. Bks.) Scholastic, Inc.

—How Jelly Roll Morton Invented Jazz. Mallett, Keith, illus. 2015. (ENG.). 32p. (J). (gr. k-3). 17.99 *(978-1-59643-963-4(7)*, 9781596439634) Roaring Brook Pr.

JAZZ—FICTION

Alexander, Kwame. Acoustic Rooster & His Barnyard Band. Bowers, Tim, illus. 2011. (ENG.). 32p. (gr. k-5). lib. bdg. 15.95 *(978-1-58536-688-0(9))* Sleeping Bear Pr.

Bell, Krista & Smith, Craig. If the Shoe Fits. 2008. (Illus.). (Orig.). (J). 60p. (gr. -1-3). 14.95 *(978-1-58089-338-1(4))*; (ENG., 64p. (gr. 4-7). pap. 5.95 *(978-1-58089-339-8(2))* Charlesbridge Publishing, Inc.

Calmenson, Stephanie. Jazzmatazz! Degen, Bruce, illus. 2008. 32p. (J). (gr. -1). lib. bdg. 17.89 *(978-0-06-077290-1(5))* HarperCollins Pubs.

Carlon, Mick. Riding on Duke's Train. 2011. (LeapKids Ser.). (ENG.). 160p. (J). (gr. k-7). pap. 9.95 *(978-1-935248-06-4(5))* Leapfrog Pr.

—Travels with Louis. 2012. (LeapKids Ser.). (ENG.). 240p. (J). (gr. 2-10). pap. 9.95 *(978-1-935248-35-4(9))* Leapfrog Pr.

Cobb, Amy. Notes from a Pro, 1 vol. Cattish, Anna, illus. 2015. (ENG.). 112p. (J). *(978-1-62402-075-9(5))* Magic Wagon.

Ehrhardt, Karen. This Jazz Man. Roth, R G, illus. 2006. (ENG.). 32p. (J). (gr. -1-3). 17.99 *(978-0-15-205307-9(7))* Houghton Mifflin Harcourt Publishing Co.

—This Jazz Man. Roth, R. G., illus. 2010. (J). (gr. 1-5). 28.95 incl. audio compact disk *(978-1-4301-0740-8(5))* Live Oak Media.

Farley, Robin. Mia Jazzes It Up! 2013. (Mia I Can Read Bks.). (J). lib. bdg. 13.55 *(978-0-606-32164-8(0)*, Turtleback) Turtleback Bks.

Friedman, Carol. Nicky the Jazz Cat. 2004. (Illus.). 32p. (J). (gr. -1-3). 16.95 *(978-0-9726092-0-3(2))* Dominick Pictures.

Golio, Gary. Spirit Seeker: John Coltrane's Musical Journey. Gutierrez, Rudy, illus. 2012. (ENG.). 48p. (J). (gr. 5-7). 17.99 *(978-0-547-23994-1(7))* Houghton Mifflin Harcourt Publishing Co.

Gollub, Matthew. Jazz Fly 2: The Jungle Pachanga. Hanke, Karen, illus. 2010. (J). 32p. (gr. -1-3). 17.95 incl. audio compact disk *(978-1-889910-44-4(9))*; *(978-1-889910-45-1(7))* Tortuga Pr.

Gordon, Gus. Herman & Rosie. Gordon, Gus, illus. 2013. (ENG., Illus.). 32p. (J). (gr. 2-5). 17.99 *(978-1-59643-856-9(8)*, 9781596438569) Roaring Brook Pr.

Howarth, Kylie. Fish Jam. 2015. (ENG., Illus.). 40p. (J). (gr. -1-2). 16.99 *(978-1-4998-0098-2(3))* Little Bee Books Inc.

Jennings, Patrick. Bat & Rat. Cordell, Matthew, illus. 2012. (ENG.). 40p. (J). (gr. k-2). 16.95 *(978-1-4197-0160-3(6)*, Abrams Bks. for Young Readers) Abrams, Inc.

Kehoe, Stasia Ward. The Sound of Letting Go. 2014. (ENG.). 400p. (YA). (gr. 7). 17.99 *(978-0-670-01553-5(9)*, Viking Books for Young Readers) Penguin Young Readers Group.

Miller, William. Rent Party Jazz. Riley-Webb, Charlotte, illus. 2011. (ENG.). 32p. (J). pap. 9.95 *(978-1-60060-344-0(0))* Lee & Low Bks., Inc.

Mullarkey, Lisa & Mullarkey, John. Get Ella to the Apollo, 1 vol. Bernard, Courtney, illus. 2015. (ENG.). 128p. (J). *(978-1-62402-087-2(9))* Magic Wagon.

Myers, Walter Dean & Myers, Christopher. Jazz. Myers, Christopher, illus. 2006. (ENG., Illus.). 48p. (J). (gr. -1-3). 18.95 *(978-0-8234-1545-8(7))* Holiday Hse., Inc.

Neftzger, Amy. All That the Dog Ever Wanted. 2005. (Illus.). 32p. (J). lib. bdg. 21.99 *(978-0-9746296-1-2(8)*, FOG104) Fields of Gold Publishing, Inc.

Osborne, Mary Pope. A Good Night for Ghosts. 2010. (Magic Tree House Merlin Missions Ser.: No. 14). (Illus.). 157p. (J). pap. *(978-4-8401-3411-8(1))* Fukuinkan Shoten.

—A Good Night for Ghosts. Murdocca, Sal, illus. 2011. (Magic Tree House Merlin Mission Ser.: 14). (ENG.). 144p. (J). (gr. 2-5). 5.99 *(978-0-375-85649-5(8)*, Random Hse. Bks. for Young Readers) Random Hse. Children's Bks.

Pinfold, Levi. The Django. Pinfold, Levi, illus. 2010. (ENG., Illus.). 40p. (J). (gr. k-4). 16.99 *(978-0-7636-4788-9(8)*, Templar) Candlewick Pr.

Raschka, Chris. John Coltrane's Giant Steps. Raschka, Chris, illus. (Illus.). pap. 18.95 incl. audio compact disk *(978-1-59112-416-0(6))*; pap. incl. audio *(978-0-87499-974-7(X))*; pap. incl. audio compact disk *(978-1-59112-603-4(7))*; pap. 16.95 incl. audio *(978-0-87499-972-3(3))* Live Oak Media.

—John Coltrane's Giant Steps. 2003. (Live Oak Readalong Ser.). (Illus.). (J). (gr. -1-2). audio compact disk 28.95 *(978-1-59112-417-7(4))* Live Oak Media.

Shahan, Sherry. The Jazzy Alphabet. Thelen, Mary, illus. 2006. 30p. (J). (gr. k-4). reprint ed. 16.00 *(978-1-4223-5730-9(9))* DIANE Publishing Co.

Taylor, Debbie & Morrison, Frank. Sweet Music in Harlem, 1 vol. 2004. (ENG., Illus.). 32p. (J). 17.95 *(978-1-58430-165-3(1))* Lee & Low Bks., Inc.

Taylor, Debbie A. Sweet Music in Harlem. Morrison, Frank, illus. 2014. 32p. pap. 9.00 *(978-1-61003-220-9(9))* Center for the Collaborative Classroom.

Townley, Roderick. Sky. 2010. (ENG.). 272p. (YA). (gr. 7). pap. 12.99 *(978-1-4423-3973-6(X)*, Atheneum Bks. for Young Readers) Simon & Schuster Children's Publishing.

Volponi, Paul. Hurricane Song. 2009. (ENG.). 160p. (YA). (gr. 7-18). 6.99 *(978-0-14-241418-7(2)*, Speak) Penguin Young Readers Group.

Weatherford, Carole Boston. Becoming Billie Holiday. Cooper, Floyd, illus. 2008. (ENG.). 120p. (YA). (gr. 9-18). 19.95 *(978-1-59078-507-2(X)*, Wordsong) Boyds Mills Pr.

JAZZ—HISTORY AND CRITICISM

Asirvatham, Sandy. The History of Jazz. 2006. (Illus.). 108p. (J). (gr. 4-8). reprint ed. 25.00 *(978-1-4223-5545-9(4))* DIANE Publishing Co.

Greenhaven Press Editors. The History of Jazz. 2012. (Music Library). (ENG., Illus.). 128p. (J). (gr. 7-10). lib. bdg. 34.45 *(978-1-4205-0820-8(2))* Cengage Gale.

Handyside, Chris. A History of Jazz. 2006. (J). *(978-1-4109-1812-3(2))* Steck-Vaughn.

Riggs, Kate. Jazz Music. 2008. (World of Music Ser.). (Illus.). 24p. (J). (gr. -1). lib. bdg. 24.25 *(978-1-58341-567-2(X)*, Creative Education) Creative Co., The.

Weatherford, Carole Boston. The Sound That Jazz Makes, 0 vols. Velasquez, Eric, illus. 2010. (ENG.). 34p. (J). (gr. k-4). pap. 9.99 *(978-0-7614-5732-9(1)*, 9780761457329, Amazon Children's Publishing) Amazon Publishing.

JEALOUSY

Berry, Joy. Let's Talk about Feeling Jealous. Smith, Maggie, illus. 2010. (Let's Talk About Ser.). (ENG.). 32p. (J). (gr. -1-k). pap. 4.99 *(978-1-60577-223-3(2))* Berry, Joy Enterprises.

Croft, Priscilla. Dealing with Jealousy/Que Hacer con Los Celos. Velazquez De Leon, Mauricio, tr. from ENG. 2008. (Conflict Resolution Library / Biblioteca Solución de Conflictos Ser.). (SPA., Illus.). 24p. (J). (gr. k-3). lib. bdg. 22.60 *(978-1-4042-7662-8(9))* Rosen Publishing Group, Inc., The.

Dougherty, Karla. Jealousy: Triumphing over Rivalry & Envy. 2003. (Teen Issues Ser.). (Illus.). 64p. (J). lib. bdg. 23.94 *(978-0-7660-1909-6(8))* Enslow Pubs., Inc.

Hewitt, Sally, et al. Teimlo'n Genfigennus. 2005. (WEL., Illus.). 32p. *(978-0-86174-097-0(1))* Drake Educational Assocs. Ltd.

Hill, Z. B. Envy & Jealousy. Croft, Cindy, ed. 2014. (Causes & Effects of Emotions Ser.: 13). 64p. (J). (gr. 7-18). 23.95 *(978-1-4222-3072-5(4))* Mason Crest.

Jealousy Is Not for Me: A Guide for Freeing Yourself from Envy. 2008. (Elf-Help Books for Kids Ser.). (Illus.). 28p. (J). (gr. -1-3). per. 7.95 *(978-0-87029-408-2(3))* Abbey Pr.

Johnston, Marianne. Dealing with Jealousy / Qué hacer con los Celos. 2009. (Conflict Resolution Library / Biblioteca solución de conflictos Ser.). (ENG & SPA.). 24p. (gr. 2-3). 42.50 *(978-1-60853-416-6(2)*, Editorial Buenas Letras) Rosen Publishing Group, Inc., The.

Kravetz, Jonathan. How to Deal with Jealousy. (Let's Work It Out Ser.). 24p. (gr. 2-3). 2009. 42.50 *(978-1-61514-264-4(9)*, PowerKids Pr.) 2007. (Illus.). (YA). lib. bdg. 22.60 *(978-1-4042-3674-5(0))* Rosen Publishing Group, Inc., The.

Marcovitz, Hal. A Jealous Guy's Guide: How to Deal. 2014. (ENG.). 64p. (J). (gr. 5-12). 15.95 *(978-1-62293-015-9(0))* Enslow Pubs., Inc.

Marcovitz, Hal & Snyder, Gail. A Guys' Guide to Jealousy. 2008. (Flip-It-Over Guides to Teen Emotions Ser.). (Illus.). 128p. (J). (gr. k-5). lib. bdg. 33.27 *(978-0-7660-2854-8(2))* Enslow Pubs., Inc.

Orr, Tamra B. Coping with Breakups & Jealousy. 2017. (Coping Ser.). 112p. (J). (gr. 12-12). 37.10 ***(978-1-5081-7388-5(5)***, Rosen Young Adult) Rosen Publishing Group, Inc., The.

Smith, Brendan Powell. Joseph & the Colorful Coat: The Brick Bible for Kids. 2015. (Brick Bible for Kids Ser.). (ENG., Illus.). 32p. (J). (gr. -1-k). 12.99 *(978-1-63220-409-7(6)*, Sky Pony Pr.) Skyhorse Publishing Co., Inc.

Snyder, Gail. Jealous Girl? Girls Dealing with Feelings. 2014. (ENG.). 64p. (J). (gr. 5-12). 15.95 *(978-1-62293-045-6(2))* Enslow Pubs., Inc.

Thomas, Isabel. Dealing with Feeling... Jealous. 2013. (Dealing with Feeling... Ser.). (ENG.). 24p. (J). (gr. 1-2). pap. 6.79 *(978-1-4329-7115-1(8))*; lib. bdg. 23.32 *(978-1-4329-7106-9(9))* Heinemann-Raintree. (Heinemann Read & Learn).

Toner, Jacqueline B. & Freeland, Claire A.B. What to Do When It's Not Fair: A Kid's Guide to Handling Envy & Jealousy. 2013. (Illus.). 96p. pap. 15.95 *(978-1-4338-1341-2(6))* American Psychological Assn.

JEALOUSY—FICTION

Allen, Elise & Stanford, Halle. Winter's Flurry Adventure. Pooler, Paige, illus. 2014. (Enchanted Sisters Ser.). (ENG.). 128p. (YA). (gr. 2-4). pap. 5.99 *(978-1-61963-267-7(5)*, 9781619632677, Bloomsbury USA Childrens) Bloomsbury Publishing USA.

—Winter's Flurry Adventure. Pooler, Paige, illus. 2014. (Enchanted Sisters Ser.: 2). (YA). lib. bdg. 16.00 *(978-0-606-36217-7(7))* Turtleback Bks.

Barden, Stephanie. Cinderella Smith. Goode, Diane, illus. (Cinderella Smith Ser.: 1). (ENG.). (J). 2011. 160p. (gr. 3-7). 16.99 *(978-0-06-196423-7(9))* Vol. 3. 2013. 144p. (gr. 1-5). 16.99 *(978-0-06-200443-7(3))* HarperCollins Pubs.

—The More the Merrier. Goode, Diane, illus. (Cinderella Smith Ser.: 2). (ENG.). (J). (gr. 3-7). 2013. 160p. pap. 5.99 *(978-0-06-200442-0(5))* 2012. 144p. 15.99 *(978-0-06-200440-6(9))* HarperCollins Pubs.

Benton, Jim. Let's Pretend This Never Happened. Benton, Jim, illus. 2004. (Dear Dumb Diary Ser.: 1). (ENG., Illus.). 128p. (J). (gr. 4-7). pap. 6.99 *(978-0-439-62904-1(7)*, Scholastic Paperbacks) Scholastic, Inc.

—School. Hasn't This Gone on Long Enough? Benton, Jim, illus. 2012. (Dear Dumb Diary Year Two Ser.: 1). (ENG., Illus.). 160p. (J). (gr. 3-7). pap. 5.99 *(978-0-545-37761-4(7)*, Scholastic Paperbacks) Scholastic, Inc.

—School. Hasn't This Gone on Long Enough? 2012. (Dear Dumb Diary: Year Two Ser.: 1). lib. bdg. 16.00 *(978-0-606-23731-4(3)*, Turtleback) Turtleback Bks.

Bowe, Julie. So Much Drama. 2016. (Victoria Torres, Unfortunately Average Ser.). (ENG., Illus.). 160p. (gr. 4-4). pap. 5.95 *(978-1-4965-3807-9(2))*; lib. bdg. 26.65 *(978-1-4965-3799-7(8))* Stone Arch Bks.

Bowman, Crystal. Little David & His Best Friend. Hartung, Susan Kathleen & Endersly, Frank, illus. 2010. (I Can Read! / Little David Ser.). (ENG.). 32p. (J). pap. 3.99 *(978-0-310-71710-2(8))* Zonderkidz.

Bracken, Beth & Fraser, Kay. A Wish in the Woods, 1 vol. Sawyer, Odessa, illus. 2012. (Faeriegeround Ser.). (ENG.). 96p. (gr. 1-3). lib. bdg. 23.99 *(978-1-4342-3303-5(0)*, Faeriegeround) Stone Arch Bks.

Brouwer, Sigmund. Sewer Rats, 1 vol. 2006. (Orca Currents Ser.). (ENG.). 128p. (J). (gr. 5-9). per. 9.95 *(978-1-55143-488-9(1))* Orca Bk. Pubs. USA.

—Sewer Rats. 2006. (Orca Currents Ser.). 106p. (gr. 4-7). 19.95 *(978-0-7569-6872-4(0))* Perfection Learning Corp.

Bucay, Jorge. The King & the Magician. Gusti, illus. 2014. (ENG.). 52p. (J). (gr. -1). 14.95 *(978-0-7892-1204-7(8)*, Abbeville Kids) Abbeville Pr., Inc.

Cameron, Jill. Miffy, the Crooked-Eyed Cat. 2009. 28p. pap. 12.99 *(978-1-60860-353-4(9)*, Eloquent Bks.) Strategic Book Publishing & Rights Agency (SBPRA).

Carlson, Melody. Deep Green: Color Me Jealous. 2004. (Truecolors Ser.: 2). (ENG.). 208p. (YA). pap. 14.99 *(978-1-57683-530-2(8)*, Th1nk Bks.) NavPress Publishing Group.

Choi, SeoYun. Let's Be Friends. Furukawa, Masumi, illus. rev. ed. 2014. (MySELF Bookshelf Ser.). (ENG.). 32p. (J). (gr. k-2). pap. 11.94 *(978-1-60357-658-1(4))*; lib. bdg. 25.27 *(978-1-59953-649-1(8))* Norwood Hse. Pr.

Clarke, Kathryn. The Breakable Vow. 2004. 480p. (YA). (gr. 7-18). 16.89 *(978-0-06-051822-6(7))* HarperCollins Pubs.

Clarke, Kathryn Ann. The Breakable Vow. 2004. (ENG.). 480p. (YA). (gr. 8-18). pap. 7.99 *(978-0-06-051821-9(9)*, HarperTeen) HarperCollins Pubs.

Cosby, Bill. Friends of a Feather: One of Life's Little Fables. Cosby, Erika, illus. 2003. (ENG.). 64p. (gr. k-3). 16.95 *(978-0-06-009147-7(9))* HarperCollins Pubs.

Covey, Sean. Sammy & the Pecan Pie. Curtis, Stacy, illus. 2013. (7 Habits of Happy Kids Ser.: 4). (ENG.). 32p. (J). (gr. -1-1). 7.99 *(978-1-4424-7647-9(8)*, Simon & Schuster Bks. For Young Readers) Simon & Schuster Bks. For Young Readers.

Dadey, Debby & Dadey, Debbie. Secret Sea Horse, 1 vol., Bk. 6. 2015. (Mermaid Tales Ser.). (ENG.). 96p. (J). (gr. 2-4). 24.21 *(978-1-61479-327-4(1)*, Spotlight) ABDO Publishing Co.

De la Cruz, Melissa. The Ashley Project. 2014. (Ashley Project Ser.: 1). (ENG., Illus.). 288p. (J). (gr. 4-8). pap. 6.99 *(978-1-4424-9033-8(0)*, Aladdin) Simon & Schuster Children's Publishing.

—Jealous? 2008. (Ashleys Ser.: Bk. 2). (ENG.). 256p. (J). (gr. 4-8). pap. 9.99 *(978-1-4169-3407-3(3)*, Simon & Schuster Bks. For Young Readers) Simon & Schuster Bks. For Young Readers.

—Social Order. 2014. (Ashley Project Ser.: 2). (ENG., Illus.). 288p. (J). (gr. 4-8). 16.99 *(978-1-4814-0667-3(1)*, Simon & Schuster/Paula Wiseman Bks.) Simon & Schuster/Paula Wiseman Bks.

DeFelice, Cynthia. The Ghost & Mrs. Hobbs. 2010. (Ghost Mysteries Ser.: 2). (ENG.). 208p. (J). (gr. 3-7). pap. 8.99 *(978-0-312-62909-0(5)*, 9780312629090) Square Fish.

Elliott, Rebecca. Eva & the New Owl. 2016. (Owl Diaries: 4). (ENG., Illus.). 80p. (J). (gr. k-2). pap. 4.99 *(978-0-545-82559-7(6))* Scholastic, Inc.

Feiffer, Jules. The House Across the Street. Feiffer, Jules, illus. 2003. (Illus.). 28p. (J). (gr. 1-4). reprint ed. 16.00 *(978-0-7567-6845-4(4))* DIANE Publishing Co.

Friedman, Laurie. Three's Company, Mallory! Kalis, Jennifer, illus. 2014. (Mallory Ser.: 21). (ENG.). 160p. (J). (gr. 2-5). 15.95 *(978-1-4677-0921-7(2)*, Darby Creek) Lerner Publishing Group.

Gassman, Julie A. Lucille Gets Jealous, 1 vol. Cooke, Charlotte, illus. 2012. (Little Boost Ser.). (ENG.). 32p. (gr. k-3). lib. bdg. 23.99 *(978-1-4048-6797-0(X)*, Little Boost) Picture Window Bks.

Genhart, Michael. Peanut Butter & Jellyous: ...sometimes Friendships Get Sticky. Mack, Steve, illus. 2017. (J). ***(978-1-4338-2337-4(3)***, Magination Pr.) American Psychological Assn.

Greene, Stephanie. Princess Posey & the New First Grader. Sisson, Stéphanie Roth, illus. 2013. (Princess Posey, First

Grader Ser.: 6). (ENG.). 96p. (J). pap. 4.99 *(978-0-14-242763-7(2),* Puffin Books) Penguin Young Readers Group.

Guest, Elissa Haden. Iris & Walter & the Substitute Teacher. Davenier, Christine, illus. 2006. (Iris & Walter Ser.). 44p. (gr. 1-4). 15.95 *(978-0-7569-7122-9(5))* Perfection Learning Corp.

Hahn, Mary Downing. The Ghost of Crutchfield Hall. (ENG.). 160p. (J). (gr. 5-7). 2011. pap. 6.99 *(978-0-547-57715-9(X))* 2010. 17.00 *(978-0-547-38560-0(9))* Houghton Mifflin Harcourt Publishing Co.

Hale, Bruce. Key Lardo: A Chet Gecko Mystery. Hale, Bruce, illus. 2007. (Chet Gecko Ser.: 12). (ENG., Illus.). 128p. (J). (gr. 2-5). pap. 5.99 *(978-0-15-205235-5(6))* Houghton Mifflin Harcourt Publishing Co.

Hannan, Peter. Freddy! King of Flurb. Hannan, Peter, illus. 2011. (Freddy! Ser.: 1). (ENG., Illus.). 160p. (J). (gr. 2-6). pap. 5.99 *(978-0-06-128466-3(1))* HarperCollins Pubs.

Harper, Charise Mericle. Just Grace, Star on Stage. 2014. (Just Grace Ser.: 9). (ENG., Illus.). 208p. (J). (gr. 1-4). pap. 5.99 *(978-0-544-22533-6(3),* HMH Books For Young Readers) Houghton Mifflin Harcourt Publishing Co.

Harper, Meg. My Mum & the Green-Eyed Monster. 2006. (My Mum Ser.). (ENG.). 160p. (J). (gr. 4-7). per. 8.99 *(978-0-7459-4993-2(2))* Lion Hudson PLC GBR. Dist: Independent Pubs. Group.

Hautman, Pete. What Boys Really Want. 2012. (ENG.). 304p. (J). (gr. 7). 17.99 *(978-0-545-11315-1(6),* Scholastic Pr.) Scholastic, Inc.

Hermes, Patricia. Emma Dilemma & the Camping Nanny, 0 vols. Carter, Abby, illus. 2009. (Emma Dilemma Ser.: 4). (ENG.). 144p. (J). (gr. 3-6). 15.99 *(978-0-7614-5534-9(5),* 9780761455349, Amazon Children's Publishing) Amazon Publishing.

Hooks, Gwendolyn. Three's a Crowd. Walker, Sylvia, illus. 2004. 32p. (J). lib. bdg. 15.00 *(978-1-4242-0240-9(X))* Fitzgerald Bks.

Johnston, Gail. The Shaggy Pony & the Spotted Pup. 2010. 24p. 11.32 *(978-1-4520-9653-7(8))* AuthorHouse.

Jones, Jen. The New Ashley. Franco, Paula, illus. 2014. (Sleepover Girls Ser.). (ENG.). 128p. (gr. 3-5). lib. bdg. 22.65 *(978-1-4342-9758-7(6))* Stone Arch Bks.

Jones, Patrick. Friend or Foe. 2016. (Unbarred Ser.). (ENG.). 120p. (YA). (gr. 6-12). lib. bdg. 27.99 *(978-1-5124-0005-2(X),* Darby Creek) Lerner Publishing Group.

—Friend or Foe. 2016. (Unbarred Ser.). (ENG.). 120p. (YA). (gr. 6-12). pap. 7.99 *(978-1-5124-0095-3(5),* Darby Creek) Lerner Publishing Group.

—Friend or Foe. 2016. (Unbarred Ser.). (ENG.). 120p. (YA). (gr. 6-12). 42.65 *(978-1-5124-0096-0(3),* Darby Creek) Lerner Publishing Group.

Kantorovitz, Sylvie. The Very Tiny Baby. Kantorovitz, Sylvie, illus. 2014. (ENG., Illus.). 32p. (J). (gr. -1-2). lib. bdg. 14.95 *(978-1-58089-445-6(3))* Charlesbridge Publishing, Inc.

—The Very Tiny Baby. 2014. (J). pap. *(978-1-58089-446-3(1))* Charlesbridge Publishing, Inc.

Keene, Carolyn. Princess Mix-Up Mystery, No. 24. Pamintuan, Macky, illus. 2009. (Nancy Drew & the Clue Crew Ser.: 24). (ENG.). 96p. (J). (gr. 1-4). pap. 5.99 *(978-1-4169-7811-4(9),* Aladdin) Simon & Schuster Children's Publishing.

Kingsley, Kate. Pretty on the Outside. 2010. (Young, Loaded, & Fabulous Ser.: 1). (ENG.). 320p. (YA). (gr. 9-18). pap. 9.99 *(978-1-4169-9399-5(1),* Simon Pulse) Simon Pulse.

Kowitt, Holly, illus. Revenge of the Loser. 2012. 233p. (J). *(978-0-545-42611-4(1),* Scholastic Pr.) Scholastic, Inc.

Krulik, Nancy. Eww! What's on My Shoe? 2013. (George Brown, Class Clown Ser.: 11). lib. bdg. 14.75 *(978-0-606-32126-6(8),* Turtleback) Turtleback Bks.

Lamb, Charles & Lamb, Mary. Tales from Shakespeare: "Othello" Strang, Kay, ed. Andrews, Gary, illus. rev. ed. 2005. 36p. pap. 4.95 *(978-0-9542905-4-2(2))* Capercaillie Bks., Ltd GBR. Dist: Wilson & Assocs.

Lester, Julius & Shakespeare, William. Othello: A Novel. 2006. (Reader's Workshop Ser.). (ENG.). 200p. (J). pap. 19.95 *(978-0-7362-3196-1(X))* CENGAGE Learning.

Long, Ethan. Chamelia & the New Kid in Class. 2013. (ENG., Illus.). 40p. (J). (gr. -1-3). 16.99 *(978-0-316-21042-3(0))* Little Brown & Co.

Mackall, Dandi Daley. Natalie Really Very Much Wants to Be a Star, 1 vol. Blakeslee, Lys, illus. 2009. (That's Nat! Ser.). (ENG.). 96p. (J). (gr. 1-4). pap. 4.99 *(978-0-310-71567-2(9))* Zonderkidz.

—A Perfect Pony, 1 vol. Wolf, Claudia, illus. 2011. (I Can Read! / a Horse Named Bob Ser.). (ENG.). 32p. (J). pap. 3.99 *(978-0-310-71783-6(3))* Zonderkidz.

Manushkin, Fran. Keep Dancing, Katie, 1 vol. 2014. (Katie Woo Ser.). (ENG.). 32p. (gr. k-2). 21.32 *(978-1-4795-5187-3(2))* Picture Window Bks.

Mazer, Norma Fox. Ten Ways to Make My Sister Disappear. 2007. (ENG.). 128p. (J). (gr. 4-7). 16.99 *(978-0-439-83983-9(1),* Levine, Arthur A. Bks.) Scholastic, Inc.

McKee, David. Denver. McKee, David, illus. 2012. (ENG., Illus.). 32p. (J). (gr. -1-k). pap. 9.99 *(978-1-84939-389-8(3))* Andersen Pr. GBR. Dist: Independent Pubs. Group.

Metz, Melinda. The Mars Mission Mayhem. McKenzie, Heath, illus. 2016. (S. M. A. R. T. S. Ser.). (ENG.). 128p. (gr. 3-6). pap. 9.95 *(978-1-4965-3018-9(7))* Stone Arch Bks.

—S. M. A. R. T. S. & the 3-D Danger. McKenzie, Heath, illus. 2015. (S. M. A. R. T. S. Ser.). (ENG.). 128p. (gr. 3-6). 22.65 *(978-1-4965-0465-4(8))* S.M.A.R.T.S. Learning System.

—S. M. A. R. T. S. & the Mars Mission Mayhem. McKenzie, Heath, illus. 2016. (S. M. A. R. T. S. Ser.). (ENG.). 128p. (gr. 3-6). lib. bdg. 22.65 *(978-1-4965-3016-5(0))* S.M.A.R.T.S. Learning System.

Misra, Michelle. Secrets & Sapphires. Chaffey, Samantha, illus. 2016. (Angel Wings Ser.: 3). (ENG.). 128p. (J). (gr. 1-4). pap. 5.99 *(978-1-4814-5803-0(5),* Aladdin) Simon & Schuster Children's Publishing.

Myracle, Lauren. Friends of a Feather. Henry, Jed, illus. 2015. (Life of Ty Ser.: 3). (ENG.). 144p. (J). (gr. 1-4). 5.99 *(978-0-14-242320-2(3),* Puffin Books); 12.99 *(978-0-525-42288-4(9),* Dutton Books for Young Readers) Penguin Young Readers Group.

Ormerod, Jan. The Baby Swap. Joyner, Andrew, illus. 2015. (ENG.). 32p. (J). (gr. -1-1). 16.99 *(978-1-4814-1914-7(5),* Little Simon) Little Simon.

Osiyemi, Linda Omonike. The Pot & the Necklace. 2012. (Illus.). 72p. (gr. -1). pap. 13.66 *(978-1-4772-3104-3(8))* AuthorHouse.

Pakkala, Christine. Last-But-Not-Least Lola & the Wild Chicken. Hoppe, Paul, illus. 2015. (Last-But-Not-Least Lola Ser.). (ENG.). 216p. (J). (gr. 1-5). pap. 7.95 *(978-1-62979-404-4(X))* Boyds Mills Pr.

Petrovic, Svetlana. Brown Bear, White Bear. Hardy, Vincent, illus. 2009. 28p. (J). (gr. -1-3). 17.00 *(978-0-8028-5353-0(6),* Eerdmans Bks For Young Readers) Eerdmans, William B. Publishing Co.

Rippin, Sally. The Best Party Ever. Spartels, Stephanie, illus. 2014. (ENG.). 48p. (J). pap. 4.99 *(978-1-61067-261-0(5))* Kane Miller.

—The Playground Problem. Spartels, Stephanie, illus. 2015. (ENG.). 48p. (J). pap. 4.99 *(978-1-61067-260-3(7))* Kane Miller.

Roberts, Daniel. Harrison & His Dinosaur Robot & the Super-Fast Race Car. 2009. (Illus.). 32p. pap. 14.95 *(978-1-4389-2847-0(5))* AuthorHouse.

Robins, Eleanor. Pay Back, 1 vol. unabr. ed. 2011. (Choices Ser.). (ENG.). 52p. (YA). (gr. 9-12). 7.95 *(978-1-61651-594-2(5))* Saddleback Educational Publishing, Inc.

Russo, Marisabina. The Trouble with Baby. Russo, Marisabina, illus. 2003. (Illus.). 32p. (J). (gr. -1-18). 16.89 *(978-0-06-008925-2(3))* HarperCollins Pubs.

Sareva, Ibrahim. West of Kilimanjaro 1: Book 1. 2010. 44p. pap. 16.99 *(978-1-4520-3006-7(5))* AuthorHouse.

Scholastic, Inc. Staff & Hooks, Gwendolyn. Three's a Crowd. Walker, Sylvia, illus. 2004. (Just for You Ser.). (ENG.). 32p. (gr. k-3). pap. 3.99 *(978-0-439-56865-4(X),* Teaching Resources) Scholastic, Inc.

Schraff, Anne E. Bad Blood. 2014. (Urban Underground — Cesar Chavez High School Ser.). (YA). lib. bdg. 20.80 *(978-0-606-35591-9(X))* Turtleback Bks.

Selvadurai, Shyam. Swimming in the Monsoon Sea. 2007. (ENG.). 280p. (YA). (gr. 9-12). per. 12.95 *(978-0-88776-834-7(2),* Tundra Bks.) Tundra Bks. CAN. Dist: Penguin Random Hse. LLC.

Shaw, Tucker. The Girls. 2010. (ENG.). 224p. (YA). (gr. 7-11). pap. 7.95 *(978-0-8109-8991-7(3),* Amulet Bks.) Abrams, Inc.

Shaw, Tucker & Luce, Clare Boothe. The Girls. 2009. (ENG.). 208p. (YA). (gr. 7-11). 17.95 *(978-0-8109-8348-9(6),* Amulet Bks.) Abrams, Inc.

Sheldon, Dyan. One or Two Things I Learned about Love. 2013. (ENG.). 304p. (YA). (gr. 7). 15.99 *(978-0-7636-6665-1(3))* Candlewick Pr.

Sommer, Isabell & Reinhardt, Swen. CHIP CHIPS JAM - 4: Der Schatz in der Elbe. 2010. 86p. pap. *(978-3-8391-0219-0(7))* Books on Demand GmbH.

Spelman, Cornelia Maude. When I Feel Jealous. Parkinson, Kathy, illus. 2003. (Way I Feel Bks.). (ENG.). 24p. (J). (gr. -1-3). 6.99 *(978-0-8075-8902-1(0))* Whitman, Albert & Co.

Spires, Sharlene. The Grandsisters. 2010. 56p. pap. 15.99 *(978-1-4535-3004-7(5))* Xlibris Corp.

Swan, Bill. Corner Kick, 1 vol. 2004. (Lorimer Sports Stories Ser.: 66). (ENG.). 144p. (J). (gr. 4-8). 16.95 *(978-1-55028-817-9(2),* 9781550288179) Lorimer, James & Co., Ltd., Pubs. CAN. Dist: Casemate Pubs. & Bk. Distributors, LLC.

Townsend, Michael. Cute & Cuter. 2013. (ENG., Illus.). 40p. (J). (gr. k-3). lib. bdg. 18.99 *(978-0-375-95718-5(9),* Knopf Bks. for Young Readers) Random Hse. Children's Bks.

Trueit, Trudi. The Sister Solution. Valencia, Adrian, illus. 2015. (Mix Ser.). (ENG.). 240p. (J). (gr. 4-8). pap. 7.99 *(978-1-4814-3239-9(7),* Aladdin) Simon & Schuster Children's Publishing.

Wesley, Valerie Wilson. How to Fish for Trouble. Roos, Maryn, illus. 2004. 89p. (J). lib. bdg. 15.00 *(978-1-4242-0643-8(X))* Fitzgerald Bks.

Wiggins, Thalia. Greg & the Mural, 1 vol. Tate, Don, illus. 2012. (Making Choices: the Mcnair Cousins Ser.). (ENG.). 64p. 27.07 *(978-1-61641-631-7(9),* Calico Chapter Bks) Magic Wagon.

—James the Rock's Boys, 1 vol. Tate, Don, illus. 2012. (Making Choices: the Mcnair Cousins Ser.). (ENG.). 64p. 27.07 *(978-1-61641-635-5(1),* Calico Chapter Bks) Magic Wagon.

Wisler, Joelle. Ariana Gold. 2016. (What's Your Dream? Ser.). (ENG., Illus.). 96p. (gr. 3-4). lib. bdg. 25.32 *(978-1-4965-3442-2(5))* Capstone Press of Coughlan Cos.

Young, Amy. A New Friend for Sparkle. 2017. (ENG., Illus.). 40p. (J). 16.99 *(978-0-374-30553-6(6),* 9780374305536, Farrar, Straus & Giroux (BYR)) Farrar, Straus & Giroux.

Ziegesar, Cecily von. Dark Horses. 2016. (ENG.). 336p. (YA). (gr. 9). 18.99 *(978-1-61695-517-5(1),* Soho Teen) Soho Pr., Inc.

JEEPS

see Automobiles; Trucks

JEFFERSON, THOMAS, 1743-1826

Albee, Sarah & Benchmark Education Co., LLC. Thomas Jefferson: American Architect. 2014. (Text Connections Ser.). (J). (gr. 3). *(978-1-4509-9658-7(2))* Benchmark Education Co.

Anderson, Michael, contrib. by. Thomas Jefferson. 2012. (Pivotal Presidents: Profiles in Leadership Ser.). (ENG.). 80p. (YA). (gr. 7-12). lib. bdg. 32.90 *(978-1-61530-940-5(3));* (Illus.). 65.80 *(978-1-61530-959-7(4))* Rosen Publishing Group, Inc., The.

Behrman, Carol H. Thomas Jefferson. 2004. (Presidential Leaders Ser.). (Illus.). 112p. (J). 29.27 *(978-0-8225-0822-9(2),* Lerner Pubns.) Lerner Publishing Group.

Bennett, Doraine. Thomas Jefferson. 2012. (Illus.). 24p. (J). *(978-1-935884-39-2(5));* pap. *(978-1-935884-48-4(4))* State Standards Publishing, LLC.

Bober, Natalie S. Thomas Jefferson: Draftsman of a Nation. 2008. (ENG., Illus.). 376p. per. 16.95 *(978-0-8139-2732-9(3))* University of Virginia Pr.

Carr, Aaron. Jefferson Memorial. 2014. (J). *(978-1-4896-2898-5(3))* Weigl Pubs., Inc.

Chew, Elizabeth V. A Day at Monticello. Elliott, Mark, illus. 2014. (ENG.). 56p. (J). (gr. 3-7). 18.95 *(978-1-4197-0541-0(5),* Abrams Bks. for Young Readers) Abrams, Inc.

Ching, Jacqueline & Dorling Kindersley Publishing Staff. Thomas Jefferson. 2009. (DK Biography Ser.). (ENG.). 128p. (J). (gr. 5-12). 6.99 *(978-0-7566-4506-9(9),* DK Children) Dorling Kindersley Publishing, Inc.

Clickard, Carrie. Thomas Jefferson & the Mammoth Hunt. Carpenter, Nancy, illus. 2017. (J). *(978-1-4814-4268-8(6),* Beach Lane Bks.) Beach Lane Bks.

Coddington, Andrew. Thomas Jefferson: Architect of the Declaration of Independence. 2016. (Great American Thinkers Ser.). (Illus.). 128p. (J). (gr. 9-9). 45.64 *(978-1-5026-1924-2(5))* Cavendish Square Publishing.

Collard, Sneed B., III. Thomas Jefferson: Let Freedom Ring! 2008. (American Heroes Ser.). 48p. (gr. 3-18). lib. bdg. 29.93 *(978-0-7614-3067-4(9),* Benchmark Bks.) Marshall Cavendish Corp.

Doeden, Matt. Thomas Jefferson: Great American, 1 vol. Purcell, Gordon & Beatty, Terry, illus. 2006. (Graphic Biographies Ser.). (ENG.). 32p. (gr. 3-4). 30.65 *(978-0-7368-5488-7(6),* Graphic Library) Capstone Press of Coughlan Cos.

Dunn, Joeming. Thomas Jefferson, 1 vol. Espinosa, Rod, illus. 2008. (Bio-Graphics Ser.). (ENG.). 32p. 28.50 *(978-1-60270-174-8(1),* Graphic Planet- Nonfiction) ABDO Publishing Co.

Elston, Heidi M. D. Thomas Jefferson, 1 vol. 2009. (United States Presidents Ser.). (ENG., Illus.). 40p. (YA). (gr. 3-6). 27.07 *(978-1-60453-460-3(5))* ABDO Publishing Co.

Ferry, Joseph. Thomas Jefferson. 2004. (Childhood of the Presidents Ser.). (Illus.). 48p. (J). (gr. 4-18). lib. bdg. 17.95 *(978-1-59084-271-3(5))* Mason Crest.

Ford, Carin T. Thomas Jefferson: The Third President. 2003. (Heroes of American History Ser.). (Illus.). 32p. (J). (gr. 1-4). lib. bdg. 22.60 *(978-0-7660-1861-7(X))* Enslow Pubs., Inc.

Fradin, Dennis Brindell. Who Was Thomas Jefferson? Harrison, Nancy & O'brien, John, illus. 2003. (Who Was? Ser.). (ENG.). 112p. (J). (gr. 3-7). pap. 5.99 *(978-0-448-43145-1(9),* Grosset & Dunlap) Penguin Young Readers Group.

Fradin, Dennis Brindell & Fradin, Dennis. Who Was Thomas Jefferson? 2003. (Who Was... ? Ser.). (Illus.). 103p. (J). (gr. 3-7). 16.00 *(978-0-613-63486-1(1),* Turtleback) Turtleback Bks.

Furgang, Kathy. The Declaration of Independence & Thomas Jefferson of Virginia. 2009. (Framers of the Declaration of Independence Ser.). 24p. (gr. 3-3). 42.50 *(978-1-61512-633-0(3),* PowerKids Pr.) Rosen Publishing Group, Inc., The.

Gaines, Ann Graham. Thomas Jefferson. 2004. (Triangle History of the American Revolution Ser.). (Illus.). 104p. (J). 27.45 *(978-1-56711-781-3(3),* Blackbirch Pr., Inc.) Cengage Gale.

Gomez, Rebecca. Thomas Jefferson, 1 vol. 2003. (First Biographies Ser.). (ENG., Illus.). 32p. (gr. k-4). 27.07 *(978-1-57765-947-1(3),* Buddy Bks.) ABDO Publishing Co.

Gosman, Gillian. Thomas Jefferson. 2011. (Life Stories Ser.). (Illus.). 24p. (J). pap. 8.25 *(978-1-4488-3180-7(6),* PowerKids Pr.); (gr. 1-4). lib. bdg. 22.60 *(978-1-4488-3178-4(4),* PowerKids Pr.); (SPA & ENG., (gr. 1-4). lib. bdg. 22.60 *(978-1-4488-3221-7(7))* Rosen Publishing Group, Inc., The.

Gregory, Josh. Thomas Jefferson: The 3rd President. 2015. (First Look at America's Presidents Ser.). (ENG.). 24p. (J). (gr. -1-3). lib. bdg. 23.93 *(978-1-62724-553-1(7))* Bearport Publishing Co., Inc.

Harness, Cheryl. Thomas Jefferson. (ENG., Illus.). 48p. (J). (gr. 2-5). 2007. per. 7.95 *(978-1-4263-0043-1(3))* 2004. 17.95 *(978-0-7922-6496-5(7))* National Geographic Society. (National Geographic Children's Bks.).

Jeffrey, Gary. Thomas Jefferson & the Declaration of Independence. 2011. (Graphic Heroes of the American Revolution Ser.). (Illus.). 24p. (J). (gr. 3-6). 23.95 *(978-1-4339-6025-3(7));* pap. 8.15 *(978-1-4339-6026-0(5),* Gareth Stevens Learning Library) Stevens, Gareth Publishing LLLP.

Jurmain, Suzanne Tripp. Worst of Friends: Thomas Jefferson, John Adams, & the True Story of an American Feud. Day, Larry, illus. 2011. (ENG.). 32p. (J). (gr. 1-3). 16.99 *(978-0-525-47903-1(1),* Dutton Books for Young Readers) Penguin Young Readers Group.

Kalman, Maira. Thomas Jefferson: Life, Liberty & the Pursuit of Everything. Kalman, Maira, illus. 2014. (ENG., Illus.). 40p. (J). (gr. k-3). 17.99 *(978-0-399-24040-9(3),* Nancy Paulsen Books) Penguin Young Readers Group.

Keppeler, Jill. 20 Fun Facts about Thomas Jefferson. 2017. (Fun Fact File: Founding Fathers Ser.). 32p. (J). (gr. 2-3). pap. 63.00 ***(978-1-5382-0274-6(3))*** Stevens, Gareth Publishing LLLP.

Kerley, Barbara. Those Rebels, John & Tom. Fotheringham, Edwin, illus. 2012. (ENG.). 48p. (J). (gr. 2-5). 17.99 *(978-0-545-22268-6(0),* Scholastic Pr.) Scholastic, Inc.

Kishel, Ann-Marie. Thomas Jefferson: A Life of Patriotism. 2006. (Pull Ahead Books-Biographies Ser.). (ENG.). 32p. (gr. k-3). pap. 7.95 *(978-0-8225-5695-4(2));* (Illus.). lib. bdg. 22.60 *(978-0-8225-3480-8(0),* Lerner Pubns.) Lerner Publishing Group.

—Thomas Jefferson: Una Vida de Patriotismo. Translations.com Staff, tr. 2006. (Libros para Avanzar-Biografías (Pull Ahead Books-Biographies) Ser.). (ENG & SPA., Illus.). 32p. (gr. k-3). lib. bdg. 22.60 *(978-0-8225-6238-2(3),* Ediciones Lerner) Lerner Publishing Group.

—Thomas Jefferson: Una vida de patriotismo (A Life of Patriotism) 2006. (Libros para Avanzar-Biografías (Pull Ahead Books-Biographies Ser.). (Illus.). 32p. (J). (gr. 3-7). per. 6.95 *(978-0-8225-6554-3(4),* Ediciones Lerner) Lerner Publishing Group.

Kit, Oscar. A Timeline of the Life of Thomas Jefferson. 2009. (Timelines of American History Ser.). 32p. (gr. 4-4). 47.90 *(978-1-60854-389-2(7),* Rosen Reference) Rosen Publishing Group, Inc., The.

Kukla, Amy. Thomas Jefferson: Life, Liberty, & the Pursuit of Happiness. 2009. (Library of American Lives & Times Ser.). 112p. (gr. 5-5). 69.20 *(978-1-60853-508-8(8))* Rosen Publishing Group, Inc., The.

Landau, Elaine. Jefferson's Louisiana Purchase: Would You Make the Deal of the Century? 2015. (What Would You Do? Ser.). 48p. (J). (gr. 3-4). 25.27 *(978-0-7660-6305-1(4));* pap. 8.95 *(978-0-7660-6306-8(2),* Enslow Elementary) Enslow Pubs., Inc.

—The Louisiana Purchase: Would You Close the Deal? (What Would You Do? Ser.). (Illus.). 48p. (J). 2010. pap. 8.95 *(978-1-59845-196-2(0))* 2008. (gr. 3-7). lib. bdg. 25.27 *(978-0-7660-2902-6(6))* Enslow Pubs., Inc. (Enslow Elementary).

Lusted, Marcia Amidon. Revolution & the New Nation: 1750-Early 1800s. 2007. (Presidents of the United States Ser.). (Illus.). 48p. (J). (gr. 4-7). lib. bdg. 29.05 *(978-1-59036-739-1(1));* per. 10.95 *(978-1-59036-740-7(5))* Weigl Pubs., Inc.

Maloof, Torrey. Thomas Jefferson & the Empire of Liberty. 2017. (Primary Source Readers Ser.). (Illus.). 32p. (J). (gr. 4-5). pap. 8.99 *(978-1-4938-3792-2(3))* Teacher Created Materials, Inc.

Manolis, Kay & Leslie, Tonya. Thomas Jefferson: A Life of Patriotism. 2007. (People of Character Ser.). (ENG., Illus.). 24p. (J). (gr. 2-5). lib. bdg. 25.95 *(978-1-60014-093-8(9))* Bellwether Media.

McLeese, Don. Thomas Jefferson. 2005. (Heroes of the American Revolution Ser.). (Illus.). 32p. (gr. 2-5). 19.95 *(978-1-59515-217-6(2))* Rourke Educational Media.

Meacham, Jon. Thomas Jefferson: President & Philosopher. (ENG., Illus.). 336p. (J). (gr. 5). 2016. pap. 12.99 *(978-0-385-38752-1(0),* Yearling) 2014. 19.99 *(978-0-385-38749-1(0),* Crown Books For Young Readers) 2014. lib. bdg. 22.99 *(978-0-385-38750-7(4),* Crown Books For Young Readers) Random Hse. Children's Bks.

Miller, Brandon Marie. Thomas Jefferson for Kids: His Life & Times with 21 Activities. 2011. (For Kids Ser.). (ENG., Illus.). 144p. (J). (gr. 4). pap. 16.95 *(978-1-56976-348-3(8))* Chicago Review Pr., Inc.

Mis, Melody S. How to Draw the Life & Times of Thomas Jefferson. (Kid's Guide to Drawing the Presidents of the United States of America Ser.). 2009. 32p. (gr. 4-4). 50.50 *(978-1-61511-161-9(1),* PowerKids Pr.) 2006. (YA). (gr. 2-5). 26.50 *(978-1-4042-2980-8(9))* Rosen Publishing Group, Inc., The.

Mortensen, Lori. Thomas Jefferson: A Founding Father of the United States of America, 1 vol. Ebert, Len, illus. 2008. (Biographies Ser.). (ENG.). 24p. (gr. k-3). lib. bdg. 26.65 *(978-1-4048-3729-4(9))* Picture Window Bks.

Mullin, Rita Thievon. Sterling Biographies - Thomas Jefferson: Architect of Freedom. 2007. (Sterling Biographies(r) Ser.). (ENG., Illus.). 128p. (J). (gr. 5). pap. 5.95 *(978-1-4027-3397-0(6))* Sterling Publishing Co., Inc.

Murphy, Frank. Thomas Jefferson's Feast. Walz, Richard, illus. 2004. (Step into Reading Ser.). 48p. 14.00 *(978-0-7569-3235-0(1))* Perfection Learning Corp.

—Thomas Jefferson's Feast. Walz, Richard, illus. 2003. (Step into Reading Ser.). (ENG.). 48p. (J). (gr. 2-4). pap. 3.99 *(978-0-375-82289-6(5),* Random Hse. Bks. for Young Readers) Random Hse. Children's Bks.

Nelson, Sheila. Thomas Jefferson's America: The Louisiana Purchase (1800-1811) 2006. (How America Became America Ser.). (Illus.). 96p. (YA). lib. bdg. 22.95 *(978-1-59084-904-0(3))* Mason Crest.

Oachs, Emily Rose. Thomas Jefferson's Presidency. 2016. (Presidential Powerhouses Ser.). (ENG., Illus.). 104p. (J). (gr. 6-12). 35.99 *(978-1-4677-7923-4(7));* 53.32 *(978-1-4677-8602-7(0))* Lerner Publishing Group. (Lerner Pubns.).

O'Donoghue, Sean. Thomas Jefferson & the Louisiana Purchase. 2016. (Spotlight on American History Ser.). (Illus.). 24p. (J). (gr. 6-4). 26.25 *(978-1-5081-4948-4(8),* PowerKids Pr.) Rosen Publishing Group, Inc., The.

Pelleschi, Andrea. Thomas Jefferson. 2012. (Jr. Graphic Founding Fathers Ser.). (ENG., Illus.). 24p. (J). (gr. 3-6). pap. 10.60 *(978-1-4488-7994-6(9));* lib. bdg. 25.25 *(978-1-4488-7900-7(0))* Rosen Publishing Group, Inc., The. (PowerKids Pr.).

Pflueger, Lynda. Thomas Jefferson: Creating a Nation. 2004. (America's Founding Fathers Ser.). (Illus.). 128p. (J). lib. bdg. 26.60 *(978-0-7660-2212-6(9))* Enslow Pubs., Inc.

Pingry, Patricia A. Discover Thomas Jefferson: Architect, Inventor, President. Johnson, Meredith, illus. 2005. (Discovery Readers Ser.). (ENG.). 32p. (J). (gr. 1-2). pap. 4.35 *(978-0-8249-5510-6(2),* Ideal Pubns.) Worthy Publishing.

—Meet Thomas Jefferson. Johnson, Meredith, ed. Johnson, Meredith, illus. 2003. 32p. (J). 9.95 *(978-0-8249-5459-8(9),* Ideal Pubns.) Worthy Publishing.

—The Story of Thomas Jefferson. Johnson, Meredith, illus. 2003. (ENG.). 26p. (J). (gr. -1-k). bds. 7.69 *(978-0-8249-6502-0(7),* Ideal Pubns.) Worthy Publishing.

Qaiser, Annie. How to Analyze the Works of Thomas Jefferson, 1 vol. 2013. (Essential Critiques Set 4 Ser.). (ENG.). 112p. (J). (gr. 6-12). lib. bdg. 35.64 *(978-1-61783-648-0(6),* Essential Library) ABDO Publishing Co.

Raabe, Emily. Thomas Jefferson & the Louisiana Purchase. (Westward Ho! Ser.). 24p. 2009. (gr. 2-3). 42.50 *(978-1-60854-763-0(9))* 2003. (Illus.). (J). lib. bdg. 22.60 *(978-0-8239-6499-4(X))* Rosen Publishing Group, Inc., The. (PowerKids Pr.).

Rausch, Monica. Thomas Jefferson. 2007. (Grandes personajes (Spanish- Great Americans) Ser.). 24p. (gr. 1-4). (ENG & SPA.). pap. 8.15 *(978-0-8368-7990-2(2));* (Illus.). pap. 8.15 *(978-0-8368-7691-8(1));* (Illus.). lib. bdg. 22.00 *(978-0-8368-7684-0(9))* Stevens, Gareth Publishing LLLP. (Weekly Reader Leveled Readers).

Rausch, Monica L. Thomas Jefferson. 2007. (Grandes personajes (Great Americans) Ser.). (ENG & SPA., Illus.). 24p. (gr. 1-4). lib. bdg. 22.00 *(978-0-8368-7983-4(X),* Weekly Reader Leveled Readers) Stevens, Gareth Publishing LLLP.

Redmond, Shirley Raye. Lewis & Clark: A Prairie Dog for the President. Manders, John, illus. 2003. (Step into Reading Ser.). 48p. 14.00 *(978-0-7569-1697-8(6))* Perfection Learning Corp.

Ribke, Simone T. Thomas Jefferson. (Rookie Biographies(tm) Ser.). 32p. (J). 2014. (ENG.). lib. bdg. 25.00 *(978-0-531-20560-0(6))* 2014. (ENG.). pap. 5.95 *(978-0-531-21203-5(3))* 2004. (ENG., Illus.). (gr. 1-2). pap. 4.95 *(978-0-516-27927-5(0),* Children's Pr.) 2003. (Illus.). 20.50 *(978-0-516-25884-3(2),* Children's Pr.) Scholastic Library Publishing.

Roberts, Russell. Thomas Jefferson: The Life & Times Of. 2007. (Profiles in American History Ser.). (Illus.). 48p. (J). (gr. 3-7). lib. bdg. 29.95 *(978-1-58415-439-6(X))* Mitchell Lane Pubs., Inc.

Rosenstock, Barb. Thomas Jefferson Builds a Library. O'brien, John, illus. 2013. (ENG.). 32p. (J). (gr. 3-6). 16.95 *(978-1-59078-932-2(6)*, Calkins Creek) Boyds Mills Pr.

Roxburgh, Ellis. Thomas Jefferson vs. John Adams: Founding Fathers & Political Rivals. 2016. (History's Greatest Rivals Ser.). (ENG., Illus.). 48p. (J). (gr. 6-8). pap. 14.05 *(978-1-4824-4239-7(6))* Stevens, Gareth Publishing LLLP.

Ruffin, Frances E. Sally Hemings. 2009. (American Legends Ser.). 24p. (gr. 3-3). 42.50 *(978-1-61511-386-6(X)*, PowerKids Pr.) Rosen Publishing Group, Inc., The.

Saddleback Educational Publishing Staff, ed. Thomas Jefferson, 1 vol. unabr. ed. 2008. (Graphic Biographies Ser.). (ENG., Illus.). 25p. (YA). (gr. 9-12). pap. 7.95 *(978-1-59905-229-8(6))* Saddleback Educational Publishing, Inc.

Sharp, Constance. Thomas Jefferson & the Growing United States (1800-1811) 2012. (J). pap. *(978-1-4222-2414-4(7))* Mason Crest.

—Thomas Jefferson & the Growing United States (1800-1811) Rakove, Jack N., ed. 2012. (How America Became America Ser.). 48p. (J). (gr. 3-4). 19.95 *(978-1-4222-2400-7(7))* Mason Crest.

Shea, John M. Thomas Jefferson in His Own Words, Vol. 1. 2014. (Eyewitness to History Ser.). 32p. (J). (gr. 4-5). (ENG.). pap. 10.50 *(978-1-4339-9933-8(1))*; 26.60 *(978-1-4339-9873-7(4))* Stevens, Gareth Publishing LLLP.

Slepian, Curtis. Hamilton vs. Jefferson (Alexander Hamilton) 2017. (Primary Source Readers Focus On Ser.). (Illus.). 32p. (J). (gr. 4-8). pap. 8.99 ***(978-1-4258-6354-8(X))*** Teacher Created Materials, Inc.

Thomas, Peggy. Thomas Jefferson Grows a Nation. Innerst, Stacy, illus. 2015. (ENG.). 48p. (J). (gr. 3-7). 16.95 *(978-1-62091-628-5(2)*, Calkins Creek) Boyds Mills Pr.

Tieck, Sarah. Monticello, 1 vol. 2008. (All Aboard America Ser.). (ENG.). 24p. (J). (gr. 1-4). 25.65 *(978-1-59928-937-3(7))* ABDO Publishing Co.

Trueit, Trudi Strain. Thomas Jefferson. 2009. (Presidents & Their Times 3 Ser.). 96p. (gr. 6). 34.21 *(978-0-7614-3622-5(7))* Marshall Cavendish Corp.

Uhl, Xina M. Thomas Jefferson. 2016. (Premier Presidents Ser.). (ENG.). 24p. (J). (gr. 1-4). 27.07 *(978-1-5038-0877-5(7)*, 210727) Child's World, Inc., The.

Venezia, Mike. Thomas Jefferson: Third President, 1801-1809. Venezia, Mike, illus. (Getting to Know the U. S. Presidents Ser.). (ENG., Illus.). (J). 2005. 32p. (gr. 3-4). pap. 7.95 *(978-0-516-27477-5(5))* 2004. 28.00 *(978-0-516-22608-8(8))* Scholastic Library Publishing. (Children's Pr.).

Whitelaw, Nancy. Thomas Jefferson: Philospher & President. 2004. (Notable Americans Ser.). (Illus.). 144p. (YA). (gr. 6-12). 23.95 *(978-1-883846-81-7(1)*, First Biographies) Reynolds, Morgan Inc.

Winter, Jonah. My Name Is James Madison Hemings. Widener, Terry, illus. 2016. (ENG.). 40p. (J). (gr. k-4). 17.99 *(978-0-385-38342-4(8)*, Schwartz & Wade Bks.) Random Hse. Children's Bks.

JEFFERSON, THOMAS, 1743-1826—FICTION

Bradley, Kimberly Brubaker. Jefferson's Sons: A Founding Father's Secret Children. 2013. (ENG.). 400p. (J). (gr. 3-7). pap. 7.99 *(978-0-14-242184-0(7)*, Puffin Books) Penguin Young Readers Group.

Edwards, Myrtice J. Dirty Sally. 2007. 44p. per. 18.95 *(978-1-4327-0774-3(4))* Outskirts Pr., Inc.

Fleming, Candace. A Big Cheese for the White House: The True Tale of a Tremendous Cheddar. Schindler, S. D., illus. 2004. (ENG.). 32p. (J). (gr. -1-3). reprint ed. pap. 8.99 *(978-0-374-40627-1(8)*, 9780374406271) Square Fish.

Fleming, Candace, et al. The Hatmaker's Sign: A Story Benjamin Franklin. Parker, Robert Andrew, illus. 2003. (Avenues Ser.). (ENG.). 40p. (C). (gr. k-4). pap. 10.95 *(978-0-531-07174-8(X))* National Geographic School Publishing, Inc.

Fox, Mary Virginia. Treasure of the Revolution. Cary, illus. 2011. 192p. 42.95 *(978-1-258-09675-5(7))* Literary Licensing, LLC.

Goldsmith, Howard. Thomas Jefferson & the Ghostriders. Rose, Drew, illus. 2008. (Ready-To-read COFA Ser.). (ENG.). 32p. (J). (gr. k-2). pap. 3.99 *(978-1-4169-2692-4(5))*; lib. bdg. 13.89 *(978-1-4169-2749-5(2))* Simon Spotlight. (Simon Spotlight).

Grigsby, Susan. First Peas to the Table: How Thomas Jefferson Inspired a School Garden. Tadgell, Nicole, illus. 2012. (ENG.). 32p. (J). (gr. 1-3). 16.99 *(978-0-8075-2452-7(2))* Whitman, Albert & Co.

Limbaugh, Rush H., III & Limbaugh, Kathryn Adams. Rush Revere & the Presidency. 2016. (Rush Revere Ser.: 5). (ENG., Illus.). 272p. (gr. 4-7). 19.99 *(978-1-5011-5689-2(6)*, Threshold Editions) Threshold Editions.

Roy, Ron. The Secret at Jefferson's Mansion. Bush, Timothy, illus. 2009. (Capital Mysteries Ser.: 11). (ENG.). 96p. (J). (gr. 1-4). 4.99 *(978-0-375-84533-8(X)*, Random Hse. Bks. for Young Readers) Random Hse. Children's Bks.

Thomson, Sarah L. The Eagle's Quill. 2017. (Secrets of the Seven Ser.). (ENG.). 224p. (J). 16.99 *(978-1-61963-733-7(2)*, 9781619637337, Bloomsbury USA Childrens) Bloomsbury Publishing USA.

Turner, Ann Warren. When Mr. Jefferson Came to Philadelphia: What I Learned of Freedom 1776. Hess, Mark, illus. 2004. 32p. (J). (gr. -1-3). 15.99 *(978-0-06-027579-2(0))* HarperCollins Pubs.

JEKYLL, DOCTOR (FICTITIOUS CHARACTER)—FICTION

Stevenson, Robert Louis. Dr. Jekyll & Mr. Hyde. 2008. (Bring the Classics to Life Ser.). (ENG., Illus.). 72p. (gr. 4-12). pap., act. bk. ed. 10.95 *(978-0-931334-50-4(0)*, EDCTR-402B) EDCON Publishing Group.

—Dr. Jekyll & Mr. Hyde, 1 vol. 2010. (Illustrated Classics Ser.). (ENG., Illus.). 64p. (YA). (gr. 9-12). per. 9.95 *(978-1-56254-894-0(8))* Saddleback Educational Publishing, Inc.

—The Strange Case of Dr. Jekyll & Mr. Hyde. (Classics Illustrated Ser.). (Illus.). 52p. (YA). pap. 4.95 *(978-1-57209-008-8(1))* Classics International Entertainment, Inc.

—The Strange Case of Dr. Jekyll & Mr. Hyde. Andrews, Gary, illus. 2008. (Fast Track Classics Ser.). (ENG.). 48p. pap. 10.00 *(978-1-4190-5082-4(6))* Steck-Vaughn.

—The Strange Case of Dr. Jekyll & Mr. Hyde. McKowen, Scott, illus. 2011. (Sterling Unabridged Classics Ser.). (ENG.). 96p. (J). 9.95 *(978-1-4027-8402-6(3))* Sterling Publishing Co., Inc.

—The Strange Case of Dr. Jekyll & Mr. Hyde. Akib, Jamel, illus. 2006. (Classic Starts(tm) Ser.). (ENG.). 160p. (J). (gr. 2-4). 6.95 *(978-1-4027-2667-5(8)*, 1252057) Sterling Publishing Co., Inc.

—Strange Case of Dr. Jekyll & Mr. Hyde. Kennedy, Cam, illus. 2008. (ENG.). 48p. (YA). (gr. 5). pap. 11.95 *(978-0-88776-882-8(2)*, Tundra Bks.) Tundra Bks. CAN. Dist: Penguin Random Hse. LLC.

—The Strange Case of Dr. Jekyll & Mr. Hyde (Quality Library Classics) 2008. (YA). pap. 14.95 *(978-1-57545-703-1(2))* RP Media.

Stevenson, Robert Louis & Venable, Alan. The Strange Case of Dr. Jekyll & Mr. Hyde. 2005. (Classic Literature Ser.). 108p. pap. 9.95 *(978-1-4105-0119-6(1))*; pap., E-Book 69.00 incl. audio compact disk *(978-1-4105-0117-2(5))* Johnston, Don Inc.

JELLYFISHES

Allen, Catherine Judge. Corals, Jellyfish, Sponges & Other Simple Animals. Harris, Madeline S. et al, eds. 2005. (Grzimek's Student Animal Life Resource Ser.). (ENG., Illus.). 368p. (J). (gr. 3-7). 106.00 *(978-0-7876-9412-8(6)*, UXL) Cengage Gale.

Bodden, Valerie. Amazing Animals: Jellyfish. 2017. (Amazing Animals Ser.). (ENG.). 24p. (J). (gr. 1-3). pap. 8.99 ***(978-1-62832-363-4(9)***, Creative Paperbacks) Creative Co., The.

Bodden, Valerie. Jellyfish. 2017. (J). *(978-1-60818-755-3(1)*, Creative Education) Creative Co., The.

Cheshire, Gerard. Jellyfish - Scary Creatures. 2008. (Scary Creatures Ser.). (ENG., Illus.). 32p. (J). (gr. 2-7). 27.00 *(978-0-531-20446-7(4)*, Children's Pr.) Scholastic Library Publishing.

Coldiron, Deborah. Jellyfish, 1 vol. 2007. (Underwater World Ser.). (ENG., Illus.). 32p. (J). (gr. 3-7). 27.07 *(978-1-59928-810-9(9)*, Buddy Bks.) ABDO Publishing Co.

Douglas, Lloyd G. Jellyfish. 2005. (Ocean Life Ser.). (ENG., Illus.). 24p. (J). (gr. -1-2). per. 4.95 *(978-0-516-23738-1(1)*, Children's Pr.) Scholastic Library Publishing.

Gibbs, Maddie. Jellyfish. 2013. (PowerKids Readers: Fun Fish Ser.). 24p. (J). (gr. k-2). 22.60 *(978-1-4777-0759-3(X))*; pap. 8.25 *(978-1-4777-0851-4(0))* Rosen Publishing Group, Inc., The. (PowerKids Pr.).

Gibbs, Maddie & Alamán, Eduardo. Jellyfish: Las Medusas. 2013. (PowerKids Readers: Fun Fish / Peces Divertidos Ser.). (SPA & ENG.). 24p. (J). (gr. k-2). lib. bdg. 22.60 *(978-1-4777-1217-7(8)*, PowerKids Pr.) Rosen Publishing Group, Inc., The.

Gish, Melissa. Jellyfish. 2015. (Illus.). 46p. (J). *(978-1-60818-568-9(0)*, Creative Education) Creative Co., The.

—Jellyfish: Living Wild. 2016. (Living Wild Ser.). (ENG.). 48p. (J). (gr. 5-9). pap. 12.00 *(978-1-62832-169-2(5)*, Creative Paperbacks) Creative Co., The.

Gray, Susan H. Australian Spotted Jellyfish. 2010. (21st Century Skills Library: Animal Invaders Ser.). (ENG.). 32p. (gr. 4-8). lib. bdg. 28.50 *(978-1-60279-628-7(9)*, 200333) Cherry Lake Publishing.

—Jellyfish. 2014. (21st Century Skills Library: Exploring Our Oceans Ser.). (ENG., Illus.). 32p. (J). (gr. 3-6). 28.50 *(978-1-62431-600-5(X)*, 203184) Cherry Lake Publishing.

Gross, Miriam J. The Jellyfish. (Weird Sea Creatures Ser.). 24p. (gr. 3-3). 2009. 42.50 *(978-1-60854-751-7(5))* 2006. (Illus.). (J). lib. bdg. 22.60 *(978-1-4042-3192-4(7))* Rosen Publishing Group, Inc., The. (PowerKids Pr.).

Hansen, Grace. Jellyfish, 1 vol. 2014. (Ocean Life Ser.). (ENG.). 24p. (J). (gr. 2-4). lib. bdg. 28.50 *(978-1-62970-709-9(0))* ABDO Publishing Co.

Herriges, Ann. Jellyfish. 2006. (Oceans Alive Ser.). (ENG., Illus.). 24p. (J). (gr. k-3). lib. bdg. 25.95 *(978-1-60014-018-1(1))* Bellwether Media.

Jellyfish. 2013. (PowerKids Readers: Fun Fish Ser.). 24p. (J). (gr. k-2). pap. 49.50 *(978-1-4777-0852-1(9)*, PowerKids Pr.) Rosen Publishing Group, Inc., The.

Jellyfish. 2014. (ENG.). 48p. (J). lib. bdg. 28.00 *(978-0-531-20664-5(5))* Scholastic Library Publishing.

Kenan, Tessa. Look, a Jellyfish! 2016. (Bumba Books (tm) — I See Ocean Animals Ser.). (ENG., Illus.). 24p. (J). (gr. -1-1). 25.32 *(978-1-5124-1421-9(2))* Lerner Publishing Group.

—¡Mira, una Medusa! (Look, a Jellyfish!) 2017. (Bumba Books (tm) en Español — Veo Animales Marinos (I See Ocean Animals) Ser.). (SPA., Illus.). 24p. (J). (gr. -1-1). 25.32 *(978-1-5124-2866-7(3))* Lerner Publishing Group.

Laughlin, Kara L. Jellyfish. 2017. (In the Deep Blue Sea Ser.). (ENG.). 24p. (J). (gr. k-3). lib. bdg. 27.07 *(978-1-5038-1686-2(9)*, 211520) Child's World, Inc., The.

Leaf, Christina. Jellyfish. (Jellyfish Ser.). 24p. (J). (gr. k-3). 2017. pap. 6.99 ***(978-1-61891-266-4(6))*** 2016. (ENG., Illus.). 25.95 *(978-1-62617-418-4(0))* Bellwether Media. (Blastoff! Readers).

Lunis, Natalie. Box Jellyfish: Killer Tentacles. 2009. (Afraid of the Water Ser.). (Illus.). 24p. (YA). (gr. 2-5). lib. bdg. 22.61 *(978-1-59716-945-5(5))* Bearport Publishing Co., Inc.

—Gooey Jellyfish. (No Backbone! Marine Invertebrates Ser.). 24p. (J). (gr. k-3). 2016. (ENG.). pap. 7.95 *(978-1-59716-776-5(2))* 2007. (Illus.). lib. bdg. 21.28 *(978-1-59716-510-5(7))* Bearport Publishing Co., Inc.

—Portuguese Man-of-War: Floating Misery. 2009. (Afraid of the Water Ser.). (Illus.). 24p. (YA). (gr. 2-5). lib. bdg. 22.61 *(978-1-59716-946-2(3))* Bearport Publishing Co., Inc.

Magby, Meryl. Jellyfish. 2012. (Under the Sea Ser.). (ENG., Illus.). 24p. (J). (gr. k-5). pap. 8.25 *(978-1-4488-7476-7(9))*; lib. bdg. 22.60 *(978-1-4488-7397-5(5))* Rosen Publishing Group, Inc., The. (PowerKids Pr.).

McFee, Shane. Jellyfish. (Poison! Ser.). 24p. (gr. 2-3). 2009. 42.50 *(978-1-60851-324-6(6)*, PowerKids Pr.) 2007. (Illus.). (J). lib. bdg. 22.60 *(978-1-4042-3799-5(2))* Rosen Publishing Group, Inc., The.

McKenzie, Michelle. Jellyfish Inside Out. 2003. (Illus.). 48p. (J). 14.95 *(978-1-878244-43-7(4))* Monterey Bay Aquarium.

Meister, Cari. Jellyfish. 2014. (Illus.). 24p. (J). lib. bdg. 25.65 *(978-1-62031-098-4(8)*, Bullfrog Bks.) Jump! Inc.

Metz, Lorijo. Discovering Jellyfish. 2012. (Along the Shore Ser.). 24p. (J). (gr. k-3). lib. bdg. 22.60 *(978-1-4488-4997-0(7))* Rosen Publishing Group, Inc., The.

Owen, Ruth. Box Jellyfish, 1 vol., 1. 2014. (Real Life Sea Monsters Ser.). (ENG.). 32p. (J). (gr. k-5). pap. 10.00 *(978-1-4777-6269-1(8)*, PowerKids Pr.) Rosen Publishing Group, Inc., The.

Rajczak, Kristen. Jellyfish, 1 vol. 2015. (ENG., Illus.). 24p. (J). pap. 8.25 *(978-1-4777-5827-4(5)*, PowerKids Pr.) Rosen Publishing Group, Inc., The.

Rake, Jody S. Jellyfish. 2016. (Faceless, Spineless, & Brainless Ocean Animals Ser.). (ENG., Illus.). 24p. (gr. 1-2). lib. bdg. 25.32 *(978-1-5157-2141-3(8)*, First Facts) Capstone Press of Coughlan Cos.

Raum, Elizabeth. Box Jellyfish. 2015. (Poisonous Animals Ser.). (ENG., Illus.). 32p. (J). (gr. 2-4). 19.95 *(978-1-60753-786-1(9))* Amicus Publishing.

Roza, Greg. Jellyfish. 2015. (Things That Sting Ser.). (ENG., Illus.). 24p. (J). (gr. 2-3). lib. bdg. 22.60 *(978-1-4824-1702-9(2))* Stevens, Gareth Publishing LLLP.

Schuh, Mari C. Jellyfish. 2015. (Sea Life Ser.). (ENG., Illus.). 24p. (gr. k-1). lib. bdg. 26.65 *(978-1-4914-6043-6(1))* Capstone Press of Coughlan Cos.

Sexton, Colleen. The Box Jellyfish. 2011. (Nature's Deadliest Ser.). (ENG., Illus.). 24p. (YA). (gr. 3-8). lib. bdg. 25.95 *(978-1-60014-664-0(3)*, Pilot Bks.) Bellwether Media.

Spilsbury, Louise. Jellyfish, 1 vol. 2010. (Day in the Life: Sea Animals Ser.). (ENG.). 24p. (gr. k-2). 23.32 *(978-1-4329-4000-3(7))*; pap. 6.79 *(978-1-4329-4007-2(4))* Heinemann-Raintree. (Heinemann Read & Learn).

Stone, Lynn M. Jellyfish. 2005. (Rourke Discovery Library). (Illus.). 24p. (J). (gr. 1-4). lib. bdg. 14.95 *(978-1-59515-439-2(6))* Rourke Educational Media.

Sullivan, Laura L. The Box Jellyfish. 2017. (J). ***(978-1-5026-2579-3(2))*** Cavendish Square Publishing.

Trueit, Trudi Strain. Jellyfish. 2010. (Benchmark Rebus: Ocean Life Ser.). 24p. (gr. k-1). 15.95 *(978-0-7614-4891-4(8))* Marshall Cavendish Corp.

Wearing, Judy. Jellyfish. 2009. (World of Wonder Ser.). (Illus.). 24p. (J). (gr. k-3). lib. bdg. 24.45 *(978-1-60596-100-2(0))* Weigl Pubs., Inc.

—Jellyfish: World of Wonder: Underwater Life. 2009. (Illus.). 24p. (J). pap. 8.95 *(978-1-60596-101-9(9))* Weigl Pubs., Inc.

JEMISON, MARY, 1743-1833

Aller, Susan Bivin. Living with the Senecas: A Story about Mary Jemison. Harden, Laurie, illus. 2007. (Creative Minds Biographies Ser.). 64p. (J). (gr. 3-7). lib. bdg. 22.60 *(978-0-8225-5989-4(7))* Lerner Educational Publishing Group.

JENGHIS KHAN, 1162-1227

see Genghis Khan, 1162-1227

JENNER, EDWARD, 1749-1823

Rodríguez, Ana María. Edward Jenner: Conqueror of Smallpox. 2006. (Great Minds of Science Ser.). (Illus.). 128p. (J). (gr. 4-10). lib. bdg. 33.27 *(978-0-7660-2504-2(7))* Enslow Pubs., Inc.

JERUSALEM

Ashabranner, Brent. Gavriel & Jemal: Two Boys of Jerusalem. Conklin, Paul, photos by. 2005. (Illus.). 94p. (J). (gr. 4-10). reprint ed. 12.00 *(978-0-7567-9758-4(6))* DIANE Publishing Co.

Bowden, Rob. Jerusalem. 2005. (Great Cities of the World Ser.). (Illus.). 48p. (gr. 5-12). lib. bdg. 31.00 *(978-0-8368-5051-2(3)*, Gareth Stevens Secondary Library) Stevens, Gareth Publishing LLLP.

Ford, Nick. Jerusalem under Muslim Rule in the Eleventh Century: Christian Pilgrims under Islamic Government. (Library of the Middle Ages Ser.). 64p. (gr. 5-8). 2009. 58.50 *(978-1-60853-899-7(0))* 2004. (Illus.). lib. bdg. 31.95 *(978-0-8239-4216-9(3))* Rosen Publishing Group, Inc., The. (Rosen Reference).

Furstinger, Nancy. Jerusalem, 1 vol. 2005. (Cities Set 1 Ser.). (ENG., Illus.). 32p. (gr. k-6). 27.07 *(978-1-59197-860-2(2)*, Checkerboard Library) ABDO Publishing Co.

Jerusalem 30 A. D. When Yeshua (Jesus) Walked. 2004. (YA). 0.00 net. *(978-0-9748424-0-0(0))* Magee, Burke & Glenna.

Levy, Leah. The Waiting Wall. Rosenfeld, D. L. & Leverton, Yossi, eds. 2009. (Illus.). 26p. (J). (gr. -1-1). 12.95 *(978-1-929628-49-0(8))* Hachai Publishing.

Slavik, Diane. Daily Life in Ancient & Modern Jerusalem. Webb, Ray, illus. (Cities Through Time Ser.). 64p. 2005. (gr. 5-12). 25.26 *(978-0-8225-3218-7(2))* 2003. (J). 18.95 *(978-1-58013-075-2(5)*, Kar-Ben Publishing) Lerner Publishing Group.

JERUSALEM—FICTION

Benjamin, Amanda. Journey Through Jerusalem. Blumenfeld, Tamar, illus. 2016. (J). *(978-1-68115-531-9(1))* Behrman Hse., Inc.

Breen, Mirka M. G. The Voice of Thunder. 2012. (ENG.). 118p. (J). pap. 12.95 *(978-1-937178-17-8(X))* WiDo Publishing.

Buxton, Jamie. Temple Boys. 2015. (ENG.). 288p. (YA). (gr. 7). 17.99 *(978-1-62672-036-7(3))* Roaring Brook Pr.

Dateno, Maria Grace. Discovery at Dawn. Cunningham, Paul, illus. 2014. (ENG.). 79p. (J). pap. 5.95 *(978-0-8198-1895-9(X))* Pauline Bks. & Media.

Eddy, Daniel. Walter's Tours in the East: Walter in Je. 2005. pap. 16.95 *(978-1-59605-437-0(9)*, Cosimo Classics) Cosimo, Inc.

Emmer, E. R. The Dolphin Project. 2004. (Going to Ser.). (ENG., Illus.). 202p. (J). (gr. 4-8). pap. 6.95 *(978-1-893577-12-1(0))* Fruitbearer Publishing, LLC.

Fals, Mary. The Chosen Colt. 2009. 40p. pap. 18.49 *(978-1-4389-9417-8(6))* AuthorHouse.

Greene, Janice. The Dark Lady, 1 vol. unabr. ed. 2010. (Q Reads Ser.). (ENG.). 32p. (YA). (gr. 9-12). pap. 6.95 *(978-1-61651-215-6(6))* Saddleback Educational Publishing, Inc.

Haggard, H. Rider. Pearl-Maiden. Kou, Christopher D. & McHugh, Michael J., eds. 2003. 372p. (YA). pap. 9.95 *(978-1-930367-89-0(9))* Christian Liberty Pr.

Holliday, Bobby. Hamor: The Road to Jerusalem. 2013. (ENG., Illus.). 32p. (J). 18.99 *(978-0-9829082-3-5(7))* Lady Hawk Pr.

—A Lump of Clay. Price, Rebecca, illus. 2010. 28p. (J). 18.99 *(978-0-9829082-1-1(0))* Lady Hawk Pr.

Hotz, Donna. Aaron's Surprise! 2010. 32p. pap. 14.49 *(978-1-4520-4522-1(4))* AuthorHouse.

Hyman, Frieda Clark. Victory on the Walls: A Story of Nehemiah. 2005. (Living History Library). 182p. (YA). (gr. 4-7). pap. 12.95 *(978-1-883937-96-6(5))* Bethlehem Bks.

King, Bonnie. Left Behind: Marion's Story. 2005. 57p. pap. 16.95 *(978-1-4137-9286-7(3))* PublishAmerica, Inc.

Levine, Anna. Jodie's Passover Adventure. Topaz, Ksenia, illus. 2012. (Passover Ser.). (ENG.). 32p. (J). (gr. k-3). pap. 7.95 *(978-0-7613-5642-4(8))*; lib. bdg. 17.95 *(978-0-7613-5641-7(X))* Lerner Publishing Group. (Kar-Ben Publishing).

Levy, Marilyn. Checkpoints. 2009. (ENG.). 256p. (gr. 7). pap. 14.95 *(978-0-8276-0870-2(5))* Jewish Pubn. Society.

Lieberman, Leanne. The Book of Trees, 1 vol. 2010. (ENG.). 256p. (YA). (gr. 8-12). pap. 12.95 *(978-1-55469-265-1(2))* Orca Bk. Pubs. USA.

Magni, Aurora. The 10 Marys & the Little Gabriel. Vignaga, Francesca Dafne, illus. 2011. (J). *(978-0-8091-6764-7(6))* Paulist Pr.

Manzione, Lisa. Let's Visit Jerusalem! Adventures of Bella & Harry. Lucco, Kristine, illus. 2013. (Adventures of Bella & Harry Ser.: 10). (ENG.). 35p. (J). (gr. k-3). 16.95 *(978-1-937616-00-7(2))* Bella & Harry, LLC.

Mindel, Nissan. Eight Chanukah Tales. Toron, Eli & Graybar, Shmuel, illus. 2007. 78p. (J). 10.95 *(978-0-8266-0039-4(5))* Kehot Pubn. Society.

Molina, Maria Isabel. De Victoria para Alejandro. (SPA., Illus.). 136p. (YA). (gr. 5-8). 8.95 *(978-84-204-4861-9(3))* Ediciones Alfaguara ESP. Dist: Lectorum Pubns., Inc.

Monson, Marianne. The Enchanted Tunnel Vol. 3: Journey to Jerusalem. Burr, Dan, illus. 2011. (J). (gr. 3-6). pap. 7.99 *(978-1-60908-068-6(8))* Deseret Bk. Co.

Ofanansky, Allison. Tisha B'Av: A Jerusalem Journey. Alpern, Eliyahu, photos by. 2017. (ENG., Illus.). 32p. (gr. -1-3). 16.99 *(978-1-4677-8930-1(5)*, Kar-Ben Publishing) Lerner Publishing Group.

Ofanansky, Allison Maile. Tisha B'Av: A Jerusalem Journey. Alpern, Eliyahu, photos by. 2017. (Kar-Ben Favorites Ser.). (ENG., Illus.). 32p. (gr. -1-3). 23.99 ***(978-1-5124-2719-6(5)***, Kar-Ben Publishing) Lerner Publishing Group.

Ogorek, Keith. Eli the Stable Boy. 2009. 28p. pap. 13.99 *(978-1-4490-4116-8(7))* AuthorHouse.

Petersen, Alicia. Out of Darkness. 2007. (Illus.). 177p. (J). (gr. 3-7). per. 8.99 *(978-1-59166-822-0(0))* BJU Pr.

Pushker, Gloria Teles & Tarman, Mel. Toby Belfer Learns about Heroes & Martyrs, 1 vol. Henriquez, Emile, illus. 2009. (Toby Belfer Ser.). (ENG.). 128p. (J). (gr. 3-7). 14.95 *(978-1-58980-647-4(6))* Pelican Publishing Co., Inc.

Rouss, Sylvia A. Tali's Jerusalem Scrapbook. Oppenheimer, Nancy, illus. 2003. 32p. (J). (gr. 1-4). 14.95 *(978-1-930143-68-5(0))*; pap. 9.95 *(978-1-930143-69-2(9))* Simcha Media Group. (Pitspopany Pr.).

Rucinski, Sandra. The Story of Jesus According to Tobin. 2009. 32p. pap. 14.50 *(978-1-60860-372-5(5)*, Eloquent Bks.) Strategic Book Publishing & Rights Agency (SBPRA).

Smith, Chris. One City, Two Brothers. Fronty, Aurélia, illus. 2007. (ENG.). 32p. (J). (gr. -1-3). 16.99 *(978-1-84686-042-3(3))* Barefoot Bks., Inc.

Smith, Chris & Barefoot Books. One City, Two Brothers: A Story from Jerusalem. Fronty, Aurélia, illus. 2015. 32p. (J). (gr. 1-4). 9.99 *(978-1-78285-252-0(2))* Barefoot Bks., Inc.

Smith, Jimmie. Jonas Little Donkey, Big Job. 2013. 20p. pap. 11.99 *(978-1-62509-331-8(4))* Salem Author Services.

star, celina. Paw Prints on the Road. 2008. 79p. pap. 9.96 *(978-0-557-02420-9(X))* Lulu Pr., Inc.

Stever, Karen Malloy. Jabin, the Talking Donkey: In Jerusalem. 2012. 24p. pap. 24.95 *(978-1-4626-8285-0(5))* America Star Bks.

Tenney, Richard L. Conflict & Calling. 2012. 184p. *(978-1-77097-461-6(X))*; pap. *(978-1-77097-462-3(8))* FriesenPress.

Toska, Mary Lou. The Shepherd Boy. 2013. 32p. pap. 24.95 *(978-1-62709-475-7(X))* America Star Bks.

JESUS CHRIST

see also Christianity

Adams, Michelle Medlock. What Is Easter? Wummer, Amy, illus. (ENG.). 26p. (J). 2007. bds. 12.99 *(978-0-8249-6691-1(0))* 2005. (gr. -1-k). bds. 6.95 *(978-0-8249-6639-3(2))* Worthy Publishing. (Ideal Pubns.).

Adelsperger, Charlotte. Amazing Miracles of Jesus. 2014. (Happy Day Ser.). (ENG.). 16p. (J). pap. 2.49 *(978-1-4143-9528-9(0)*, Happy Day) Tyndale Hse. Pubs.

Ahmed, Shabbir, et al. Jesus: Prophet of Islam. rev. ed. 2003. (ENG.). 320p. pap. 12.00 *(978-1-879402-73-7(4))* Tahrike Tarsile Quran, Inc.

Almquist, Beth, et al. Growing up in Jesus: Weekly Meeting Plans for Voyager Leaders. 2007. (J). 19.95 *(978-0-9743503-5-6(4))* Pioneer Clubs.

Amya Penny Anysia Turpin. Jesus & Me. 2009. 52p. pap. 25.49 *(978-1-4389-6818-6(3))* AuthorHouse.

Arthur, Kay & Arndt, Janna. Jesus, to Eternity & Beyond. 2005. (Discover-4-Yourself for Kids Ser.). 143p. (J). pap. 8.99 *(978-1-888655-90-2(9))* Precept Ministries.

Arthur, Kay & Shearer, Cyndy. Jesus in the Spotlight. (Discover-4-Yourself for Kids Ser.). 128p. (J). 2006. pap. 8.99 *(978-1-888655-24-7(0))* 2004. pap. 8.99 *(978-1-888655-73-5(9))* Precept Ministries.

Arthur, Kay, et al. Jesus, Awesome Power, Awesome Love. 2004. (Discover-4-Yourself for Kids Ser.). 138p. (J). pap. 8.99 *(978-1-888655-75-9(5))* Precept Ministries.

B&H Kids Editorial Staff. Jesus. Conger, Holli, illus. 2015. (Little Words Matter(tm) Ser.). (ENG.). 24p. (J). (— 1). bds. 8.99 *(978-1-4336-8648-1(1)*, B&H Kids) B&H Publishing Group.

Bader, Joanne. He's Risen! He's Alive! Heroldt, Richard, illus. 2003. (Arch Bks.). (ENG.). 16p. (J). 1.99 *(978-0-570-07563-7(1))* Concordia Publishing Hse.

—Jesus Heals the Centurion's Servant. 2010. (Arch Bks.). (Illus.). 16p. (J). (gr. k-4). pap. 2.49 *(978-0-7586-1864-1(6))* Concordia Publishing Hse.

Bagley, Val Chadwick, illus. I Will Trust in Heavenly Father & Jesus. 2006. (J). *(978-1-59811-056-2(X))* Covenant Communications.

Balika, Susan. Jesus Is My Special Friend. Bolling, Vickey, illus. 2003. 24p. (J). 2.49 *(978-0-7847-1270-2(0))* Standard Publishing.

J K L

Balika, Susan S. Jesus Is My Special Friend. Bolling, Vickey, illus. 2013. (Happy Day Ser.). (ENG.). 16p. (J). pap. 2.49 *(978-1-4143-9294-3(X))* Tyndale Hse. Pubs.

Benjamin, M. A. Jesus the Good Shepherd. 2008. 16p. pap. 24.95 *(978-1-60441-029-7(9))* America Star Bks.

The Birth of Jesus Bible Sticker Book. 2003. (Illus.). 16p. (J). 2.98 *(978-1-4054-1559-0(2))* Parragon, Inc.

Bishop, Jennie. Jesus Must Be Really Special. Wummer, Amy, illus. 2006. (Heritage Builders Ser.). 32p. (J). 14.99 *(978-0-7847-1379-2(0)*, 04029) Standard Publishing.

Blundell, Trevor, et al. On the Way for 3 - 9's Vol. 2: The Christmas Story & Miracles of Jesus. 2006. (On the Way (3-9's) Ser.). (ENG.). 96p. (J). pap. 17.99 *(978-1-85792-319-3(7)*, 9781857923193) Christian Focus Pubns. GBR. Dist: Bookmasters Distribution.

Blyton, Enid. Story of Jesus. 2012. (ENG.). 24p. (J). pap. 9.95 *(978-1-84135-744-7(8))* Award Pubns. Ltd. GBR. Dist: Parkwest Pubns., Inc.

Bohnet, Eric C. Arch Books: The Centurion at the Cross. Murphy, Terri, illus. 2007. (Arch Bks.). (J). 1.99 *(978-0-7586-1260-1(5))* Concordia Publishing Hse.

Bostrom, Kathleen Long. Why Is There a Cross? Kucharik, Elena, illus. 2006. (Little Blessings Ser.). (ENG.). 64p. (J). (gr. 4-7). 9.99 *(978-1-4143-0288-1(6))* Tyndale Hse. Pubs.

Bowman, Crystal. Jesus Feeds the Five Thousand, 1 vol. Sokolova, Valerie, illus. 2011. (I Can Read! / Bible Stories Ser.). (ENG.). 32p. (J). (gr. -1-2). pap. 3.99 *(978-0-310-72157-4(1))* Zonderkidz.

—Jesus Raises Lazarus, 1 vol. Sokolova, Valerie, illus. 2011. (I Can Read! / Bible Stories Ser.). (ENG.). 32p. (J). (gr. -1-2). pap. 3.99 *(978-0-310-72158-1(X))* Zonderkidz.

Breems, Beau. The Promise. Breems, Beau, illus. 2006. (Illus.). (YA). 10.00 *(978-0-9768680-9-5(1))*; 20.00 *(978-0-9768680-8-8(3))* Burning Bush Creation.

Breems, Beau A. La Gran Historia: The Illustrated Gospel from Creation to Resurrection. Breems, Beau A., illus. 2005.Tr. of His Story. (SPA., Illus.). (J). 10.99 *(978-0-9768680-5-7(9))* Burning Bush Creation.

Breems, Beau Alan. His Story: The Illustrated Gospel from Creation to Resurrection. Breems, Beau Alan, illus. 2005. (Illus.). (J). per. 14.95 *(978-0-9768680-2-6(4))* Burning Bush Creation.

Brown-Johnson, G. C. O. T. K. A City Called Heaven: Revelations. 2012. 36p. pap. 21.32 *(978-1-4691-2616-6(8))* Xlibris Corp.

Bryant, Patricia White. Jesus, Is Your Daddy Mean? 112p. (J). 7.95 *(978-1-56794-148-7(6)*, C-2485) Star Bible & Tract Corp.

Buck, Deanna. My First Story of the First Easter. 2008. 32p. (J). 13.95 *(978-1-59038-871-6(2))* Deseret Bk. Co.

Budensiek, Joy. Jesus, My Very Best Friend. 2003. (J). *(978-0-9618730-8-0(6))* FEA Ministries.

Buehner, Caralyn. In the Garden. Dorman, Brandon, illus. 2007. (J). 18.95 *(978-1-59038-403-9(2))* Deseret Bk. Co.

Burchett, Author Walter, BA. Christian children's questions & answers resurrection of christ Volume 7. 2009. 32p. pap. 14.28 *(978-0-557-08245-2(5))* Lulu Pr., Inc.

Burkart, Jeffrey, narrated by. The Week That Led to Easter/Jesus Washes Peter's Feet. 2005. (Arch Books on CD Ser.). (Illus.). 16p. (J). (gr. -1-3). pap. 7.99 incl. audio compact disk *(978-5-559-30143-3(4))* Concordia Publishing Hse.

Busch, Melinda Kay. Jesus & the Woman at the Well. Clark, Bill, illus. 2005. (Arch Bks.). (ENG.). 16p. (J). 1.99 *(978-0-7586-0675-4(3))* Concordia Publishing Hse.

Carolyn, Berg. Jesus Walks Away. Paris, Pat, illus. 2003. (Arch Bks.). 16p. (J). 2.49 *(978-0-7586-0504-7(8))* Concordia Publishing Hse.

Carruth, Jane. More Bible Stories for Children. Cloke, Rene, illus. 2012. (ENG.). 32p. (J). 9.95 *(978-0-86163-770-6(4))* Award Pubns. Ltd. GBR. Dist: Parkwest Pubns., Inc.

Choi, Young-Jin. Jesus Feeds Everybody! 2007.Tr. of Jesus' Breadbasket. (Illus.). 26p. bds. 5.95 *(978-0-8198-3987-9(6))* Pauline Bks. & Media.

—Mary's Big Surprise. 2007.Tr. of Mary, Crying & Laughing. (Illus.). 26p. (J). (gr. -1-k). bds. 5.95 *(978-0-8198-4853-6(0))* Pauline Bks. & Media.

Choi, Young-Jin & Kim, Jung-cho. A Walk on the Waves. 2007. (Illus.). 26p. bds. 5.95 *(978-0-8198-8315-5(8))* Pauline Bks. & Media.

Christian Art Gifts, creator. The Miracles of Jesus Puzzle Bible. 2008. (Illus.). 10p. (J). (gr. -1-3). bds. *(978-1-86920-787-8(4))* Christian Art Pubs.

Consuegra, Claudio & Consuegra, Pamela. Making Jesus My Best Friend: Baptism Preparation for Younger Children (Ages 8-10) 2005. (Illus.). 95p. (J). (gr. 4-7). per. 8.99 *(978-0-8280-1836-4(7))* Review & Herald Publishing Assn.

Cooley, Karen. Jesus Blesses the Children. Julien, Terry, illus. 2015. (Faith That Sticks Bks.). (ENG.). 26p. (J). pap. 3.99 *(978-1-4964-0316-2(9))* Tyndale Hse. Pubs.

Copland, Steve. Just Because. 2007. 224p. per. 14.99 *(978-1-60266-916-1(3))* Salem Author Services.

Creek, Lorie. Who Is This Jesus? A Hidden Picture Book. Creek, Chris, illus. 2012. (J). 18.99 *(978-1-60908-909-2(X))* Deseret Bk. Co.

Dateno, Maria Grace. The Stations of the Cross for Children. Pompei, Maria Teresa, tr. Richards, Virginia Helen, illus. 2006. (SPA.). 24p. (J). 1.25 *(978-0-8198-7095-7(1))* Pauline Bks. & Media.

David, Juliet. Candle Day by Day Walk with Jesus: The Story of Jesus Retold in 40 Days, 1 vol. Heyes, Jane, illus. 2016. (ENG.). 48p. (J). 9.99 *(978-1-78128-291-5(9)*, Candle Bks.) Lion Hudson PLC GBR. Dist: Kregel Pubns.

—My Friend Jesus, 1 vol. Prole, Helen, illus. 2016. (Candle Bible for Toddlers Ser.). (ENG.). 32p. (J). pap. 4.99 *(978-1-78128-280-9(3)*, Candle Bks.) Lion Hudson PLC GBR. Dist: Kregel Pubns.

—My Very First Easter, 1 vol. Prole, Helen, illus. 2016. (ENG.). 24p. (J). pap. 4.99 *(978-1-78128-244-1(7)*, Candle Bks.) Lion Hudson PLC GBR. Dist: Kregel Pubns.

—A Stable in Bethlehem. Denham, Gemma & Scott, Richard, illus. 2007. 14p. (J). (gr. -1-3). 16.99 *(978-0-8254-7341-8(1)*, Candle Bks.) Lion Hudson PLC GBR. Dist: Kregel Pubns.

Davis, Mary J. Five-Minute Sunday School Activities for Preschoolers: Jesus Shows Me. Galey, Chuck, illus. 2005. 96p. (J). pap. 11.95 *(978-1-58411-047-7(3))* Rainbow Pubs. & Legacy Pr.

Demars, Sue. Jesus Loves You More. 2009. 20p. pap. 10.95 *(978-1-60860-695-5(3)*, Eloquent Bks.) Strategic Book Publishing & Rights Agency (SBPRA).

Demi. Jesus. Demi, illus. 2005. (ENG., Illus.). 48p. (J). (gr. 2-5). 24.99 *(978-0-689-86905-1(3)*, McElderry, Margaret K. Bks.) McElderry, Margaret K. Bks.

dePaola, Tomie. The Miracles of Jesus. 2008. (ENG., Illus.). 32p. (J). (gr. -1-3). pap. 7.99 *(978-0-14-241068-4(3)*, Puffin Books) Penguin Young Readers Group.

DeWitt, Becky. Destiny's Closet: Circle of Friends. 2010. 68p. pap. 17.99 *(978-1-4520-8364-3(9))* AuthorHouse.

Dobson, Cynthia Lund. I'm Trying to Be Like Jesus. Dewey, Simon, illus. 2010. (J). 19.99 *(978-1-60641-846-8(7))* Deseret Bk. Co.

Doxey, Heidi. Jesus Was Just Like Me. 2017. (ENG.). (J). bds. 10.99 ***(978-1-4621-1925-7(5))*** Cedar Fort, Inc./CFI Distribution.

Doyle, Christopher. The Story of Easter. Haysom, John, illus. 2008. 29p. (J). (gr. k-3). pap. 7.49 *(978-0-7586-1495-7(0))* Concordia Publishing Hse.

Dudley, Cathy D. Toddler Theology: Childlike Faith for Everyone. 2012. 24p. pap. 13.99 *(978-1-4685-5728-2(9))* AuthorHouse.

Ellis, Gwen. The Story of Easter, 1 vol. Smallman, Steve, illus. 2008. (Read & Share (Tommy Nelson) Ser.). (ENG.). 32p. (gr. -1-2). 7.99 *(978-1-4003-0855-2(0))* Nelson, Thomas Inc.

Esquinaldo, Virginia. What Did Baby Jesus Do? Esquinaldo, Virginia, illus. 2006. (Illus.). 12p. (J). bds. 6.95 *(978-0-8198-8310-0(7))* Pauline Bks. & Media.

Fawcett, Cheryl & Newman, Robert C. Kids' Questions about God & Jesus. Mazellan, Ron, illus. 2003. 71p. pap. *(978-1-59402-081-0(7))* Regular Baptist Pr.

Ferguson, Sinclair B. Big Book of Bible Truths, Vol. 1. Apps, Fred, illus. 2012. (ENG.). 64p. (J). pap. 14.99 *(978-1-84550-371-0(6)*, df9d28c0-46d4-40ea-9ab5-380c71e316dc) Christian Focus Pubns. GBR. Dist: Bookmasters Distribution.

Fitzgerald, Josephine. Christ, Our Burden Bearer. Skorackiji, Olga et al, eds. 2003. 168p. (YA). pap. 8.95 *(978-0-910487-55-9(3))* Royalty Publishing Co.

Five Small Loaves & Two Small Fish. 2014. (Happy Day Ser.). (ENG., Illus.). 16p. (J). pap. 2.49 *(978-1-4143-9519-7(1))* Tyndale Hse. Pubs.

Flanagan, Anne. Miracles of Jesus Act/Col Bk. 24p. pap. 1.25 *(978-0-8198-4836-9(0)*, 332-225) Pauline Bks. & Media.

Fogle, Robin. Itty-bitty Bible Activity Book, the Legend of the Candy Cane. 2007. (Illus.). 48p. (J). pap. 1.49 *(978-1-59317-212-1(5))* Warner Pr., Inc.

Frank, Penny. Jesus on Trial. 2nd rev. ed. (ENG., Illus.). 24p. pap. 2.99 *(978-0-7459-4122-6(2)*, Lion Books) Lion Hudson PLC GBR. Dist: Trafalgar Square Publishing.

Frank, Penny & Allsopp, Sophie. The First Easter. 2nd rev. ed. (ENG., Illus.). 24p. pap. 2.99 *(978-0-7459-4123-3(0)*, Lion Books) Lion Hudson PLC GBR. Dist: Trafalgar Square Publishing.

Frey, Daniel J., illus. Jacy's Coloring & Activity Book. 2006. 32p. (J). 3.00 *(978-0-9755314-2-6(5))* Majestic Publishing, LLC.

Fryar, Jane L. Jesus Enters Jerusalem. Dorenkamp, Michelle, illus. 2004. (ENG.). 16p. (J). 1.99 *(978-0-7586-0641-9(9))* Concordia Publishing Hse.

Galloway, Tammy. I Am Healed: Praying God's Word for Children. 2010. 28p. 13.95 *(978-1-4497-0428-5(X)*, WestBow Pr.) Author Solutions, Inc.

Ganeri, Anita. The Easter Story. Phillips, Rachael, illus. 2003. (Festival Stories Ser.). 24p. (J). pap. *(978-0-237-52475-3(9))* Evans Brothers, Ltd.

Garris, Norma, illus. The Story of Christmas. 2013. (Happy Day Ser.). (ENG.). 16p. (J). pap. 2.49 *(978-1-4143-9524-1(8))* Tyndale Hse. Pubs.

Glavich, Mary Kathleen. A Child's Book of Miracles. 2004. *(978-0-8294-1038-9(4))* Loyola Pr.

Godfrey, Jan. The Road to Easter Day. Piwowarski, Marcin, illus. 2009. 32p. (J). (gr. -1-1). 14.95 *(978-0-8198-6486-4(2))* Pauline Bks. & Media.

God's Gift: The Birth of Jesus. (Illus.). 16p. (J). pap. 1.50 *(978-0-87162-855-8(4)*, E4573) Warner Pr., Inc.

Grack, Rachel. Easter. 2017. (Easter Ser.). 24p. (J). (gr. k-3). pap. 6.99 ***(978-1-61891-273-2(9)***, Blastoff! Readers) Bellwether Media.

Greendyk, William, tr. from ENG. El Hijo de la Viuda. l.t. ed. 2004. Orig. Title: The Widow's Son. (SPA., Illus.). 92p. (J). pap. *(978-1-932789-11-9(1))* Editorial Sendas Antiguas, LLC.

Group Publishing Staff, creator. Flip Flops, Pre-K - K: Group's Buzz: the Instant Sunday School Three-Lesson Mini-Kit. 2013. (ENG.). 19.99 incl. audio compact disk *(978-1-4707-0468-1(4))* Group Publishing, Inc.

Gudmundson, C. J. When I Take the Sacrament, I Remember Jesus. Tenney, Shawna J. C., illus. 2012. (J). *(978-1-62108-020-6(X))* Covenant Communications, Inc.

Gunney, Lynn Tuttle. Meet Jesus: The Life & Lessons of a Beloved Teacher. Conteh-Morgan, Jane, illus. 2008. (ENG.). 36p. (J). (gr. 3-7). pap. 12.00 *(978-1-55896-524-9(6)*, Skinner Hse. Bks.) Unitarian Universalist Assn.

Gynux, illus. Jesus Loves Me, 1 vol. 2017. (Sing-Along Book Ser.). (ENG.). 20p. (J). bds. 8.99 *(978-0-310-75894-5(7))* Zonderkidz.

Halpin, D. I Learn about Jesus Col/Act Bk. 32p. pap. 1.25 *(978-0-8198-3686-1(9)*, 332-139) Pauline Bks. & Media.

Handloser, Rick. Sneezy Neezy. Byous, Shawn, illus. 2006. 48p. pap. 19.97 *(978-1-59800-291-1(0))* Outskirts Pr., Inc.

Harman, Debbie G. Jesus Said- 2004. (Illus.). 17.95 *(978-1-59156-091-3(8))* Covenant Communications, Inc.

Hartman, Sara. Mary Magdalene's Easter Story. Koehler, Ed, illus. 2005. (ENG.). 16p. (J). 1.99 *(978-0-7586-0722-5(9))* Concordia Publishing Hse.

Harvest House Publishers. Jesus the Miracle Worker Sticker Book. 2015. (ENG.). 20p. (J). pap. 3.99 *(978-0-7369-6160-8(7))* Harvest Hse. Pubs.

Hascall, Glenn. It All Matters to Jesus Devotional for Boys: Bullies, Bikes, & Baseball... He Cares about It All! 2016. (ENG.). 264p. (J). pap. 5.99 *(978-1-63058-921-9(7)*, Barbour Bks.) Barbour Publishing, Inc.

Hendricks, Brenda K. Much More to Christmas. Hendricks, Brenda K., illus. 2013. (Illus.). 30p. pap. 9.99 *(978-0-9826582-5-3(7))* Two Small Fish Pubns.

Hendrix, John. Miracle Man: The Story of Jesus. 2016. (ENG., Illus.). 40p. (J). (gr. 1-4). 18.95 *(978-1-4197-1899-1(1)*, Abrams Bks. for Young Readers) Abrams, Inc.

Heyer, Carol. The First Easter. Heyer, Carol, illus. 2008. (ENG., Illus.). 28p. (J). (gr. -1-3). 8.99 *(978-0-8249-5576-2(5)*, Ideal Pubns.) Worthy Publishing.

—The First Easter. 2nd ed. 2015. (Illus.). 32p. (J). pap. *(978-0-8249-1955-9(6)*, Ideal Pubns.) Worthy Publishing.

Hinkle, Cynthia. Star of Wonder. van der Sterre, Johanna, illus. 2005. (Arch Bks.). (ENG.). 16p. (J). 1.99 *(978-0-7586-0724-9(5))* Concordia Publishing Hse.

Hinkle, Cynthia A. The Thankful Leper: The Story of the Ten Lepers: Luke 17:11-19 & 2 Kings 5:1-15 for Children. Collier-Morales, Roberta, illus. 2006. (Arch Bks.). (J). 2.49 *(978-0-7586-1284-7(2))* Concordia Publishing Hse.

Hoffa, Darlene. Bible Stories about Jesus. 2004. (Illus.). 96p. (J). (gr. -1-k). pap. 11.95 *(978-0-937282-05-2(7)*, RB36112); (gr. 1-2). pap. 11.95 *(978-0-937282-06-9(5)*, RB36113); (gr. 3-4). pap. 11.95 *(978-0-937282-07-6(3)*, RB36114) Rainbow Pubs. & Legacy Pr.

Holder, Jennifer. My Story of Jesus. Munger, Nancy, illus. 2014. (Happy Day Ser.). (ENG.). 16p. (J). pap. 2.49 *(978-1-4143-9325-4(3))* Tyndale Hse. Pubs.

Hook, Katie. Momma Loves You. Hook, Katie, illus. 2015. (ENG., Illus.). 32p. pap. 9.99 *(978-1-63047-495-9(9))* Morgan James Publishing.

Hudson, Angus. Localiza la Diferencia (Find the Difference) Parabolas Que Jesus Relato. (SPA.). (J). 1.89 *(978-1-56063-965-7(2)*, 497756) Editorial Unilit.

I Can Follow Jesus. 2014. (Happy Day Ser.). (ENG., Illus.). 16p. (J). pap. 2.49 *(978-1-4143-9419-0(5))* Tyndale Hse. Pubs.

Jackson, Antonia. The Easter Story. Ferri, Giuliano, illus. 2015. (ENG.). 32p. (J). (gr. k-4). 14.99 *(978-0-7459-6508-6(3))* Lion Hudson PLC GBR. Dist: Independent Pubs. Group.

Jakubowsky, Frank. God Looked down & Saw a Baby. 2012. 56p. (gr. 4-6). pap. 9.95 *(978-1-4497-7319-9(2)*, WestBow Pr.) Author Solutions, Inc.

James, Ben, illus. Los Tres Reyes Magos, the Three Wise Men. 2006. (J). bds. *(978-0-9786863-2-1(2))* ITRON Publishing.

James, Betsy, illus. The Word & Picture Books Set 1: For Year B/C, 6 vols. Incl. Breakfast at the Lake. Wehreim, Carol. bds. 4.95 *(978-0-8298-1186-5(9))*; Come to Jesus. Wehreim, Carol, ed. bds. 4.95 *(978-0-8298-1183-4(4))*; First Church. Wehreim, Carol, ed. bds. 4.95 *(978-0-8298-1188-9(5))*; Jesus, a Special Baby. Wehreim, Carol, ed. bds. 4.95 *(978-0-8298-1184-1(2))*; Jesus Goes Fishing. Wehreim, Carol, ed. bds. 4.95 *(978-0-8298-1185-8(0))*; Loving Shepherd. Wehreim, Carol, ed. bds. 4.95 *(978-0-8298-1187-2(7))*; 12p. (J). (gr. -1-4). 1997. (Word & Picture Bks.). (Illus.). 29.70 *(978-0-8298-1189-6(3))* Pilgrim Pr., The/United Church Pr.

Jeffs, Stephanie. Where's Jesus. Laver, Sarah, 8th, illus. 2004. 32p. 13.95 *(978-0-8294-1728-9(1))* Loyola Pr.

Jesus & His Disciples: Coloring Book. (Illus.). 16p. (J). pap. 1.50 *(978-0-87162-856-5(2)*, E6040) Warner Pr., Inc.

Jesus Is Born. 2004. *(978-0-8294-9909-4(1))* Loyola Pr.

Jesus Is Everything I Need: Challenging Bible Activities on Jesus & All He Is to Us! (Illus.). 16p. (J). pap. 1.50 *(978-0-87162-818-3(X)*, E4512) Warner Pr., Inc.

Jesus Loves Me Pre-School Activity Book. 2006. (Illus.). 32p. (J). pap. 6.95 *(978-0-8091-6734-0(4)*, 6734-4) Paulist Pr.

Jesus, our Righteousness. 2005. (YA). 14.00 *(978-1-59872-121-8(6))* Instant Pub.

Johnson, Alice. Believe & You're There (4 vol. Set), 4 vols. 2009. pap. 24.99 *(978-1-60641-186-5(1))* Deseret Bk. Co.

Johnson, Alice W. & Warner, Allison H. Believe & You're There at the Miracles of Jesus. Nelson, Holly, illus. 2009. 96p. (J). pap. 8.95 *(978-1-59038-722-1(8))* Deseret Bk. Co.

—Believe & You're There When the Stone Was Rolled Away. Nelson, Holly, illus. 2009. 96p. (J). pap. 8.95 *(978-1-59038-723-8(6))* Deseret Bk. Co.

—Believe & You're There When the White Dove Descended. Nelson, Holly, illus. 2009. 96p. (J). pap. 8.95 *(978-1-59038-721-4(X))* Deseret Bk. Co.

Jones, Ron, ed. Jesus: Passages from the Gospel Records. 2003. *(978-0-9747452-0-6(0))* Titus Institute of California.

Julien, Terry & Carter, Nancy, illus. Jesus Loves Me. 2015. (Faith That Sticks Bks.). (ENG.). 24p. (J). pap. 3.99 *(978-1-4964-0315-5(0))* Tyndale Hse. Pubs.

Keable, Ruth. Jesus A True Story. 2006. (Illus.). 108p. per. *(978-0-901860-41-5(7))* Scripture Truth Pubns.

Keating, Susan K. Jesus Christ. 2004. (Great Names Ser.). (Illus.). 32p. (J). (gr. 3-18). lib. bdg. 19.95 *(978-1-59084-138-9(7))* Mason Crest.

KH Pathways. Kindergarten Stepping Stones: Jesus Is God's Best Gift Lapbook. rev. ed. 2013. (ENG.). 32p. pap. 25.00 *(978-1-4652-0019-8(3))* Kendall Hunt Publishing Co.

Knight, Chris. The Body of Jesus. 2010. 24p. pap. 12.99 *(978-1-4520-7413-9(5))* AuthorHouse.

Kovacs, Victoria. Jesus' Miracles/Martha Flip-Over Book. Krome, Mike & Ryley, David, illus. 2015. (Little Bible Heroes(tm) Ser.). (ENG.). 32p. (J). (gr. k-2). pap. 3.99 *(978-1-4336-8714-3(3)*, B&H Kids) B&H Publishing Group.

Krenzer, Rolf. Jesus Is Risen. Maloney, Linda M., tr. from GER. Droop, Constanza, illus. 2005. 24p. (gr. -1-3). 14.95 *(978-0-8146-2764-8(1))* Liturgical Pr.

Kueker, Donald, illus. The Easter Story According to Matthew. 2007. 32p. (J). per. 7.49 *(978-0-7586-1008-9(4))* Concordia Publishing Hse.

Lafond, Pascale. The Story of Jesus. Flowerpot Press, ed. 2012. (Illus.). 32p. (J). *(978-1-77093-387-3(5))* Flowerpot Children's Pr. Inc.

Land Fairer Than Day. 7.50 *(978-0-8054-5937-1(5))* B&H Publishing Group.

Lane, Leena. Come to the Party with Jesus. Reynolds, Annette, ed. Saunderson, Chris, illus. 2007. (Action Rhymes Ser.). (ENG.). 16p. (J). (gr. -1-2). pap. 4.99 *(978-0-9789056-5-1(2))* New Day Publishing, Inc.

Larsen, Carolyn. Stories about Jesus for Little Ones. Incrocci, Rick, illus. 2008. 35p. (gr. -1-k). bds. *(978-1-86920-173-9(6))* Christian Art Pubs.

Later Life of Jesus: Pict O Graph. (Pict-O-Graph Ser.). (Illus.). (J). 10.99 *(978-0-7847-1028-9(7)*, 02228) Standard Publishing.

Lee, Otha. Mrs. Lee's Stories about Jesus. 2013. 274p. pap. 19.95 *(978-1-58427-388-2(7))* Guardian of Truth Foundation.

Lesson in a Bag-Eucharist Lesson 1. 2012. (ENG.). (J). 24.99 *(978-1-59982-387-4(X))* St. Mary's Pr. of MN.

Lesson in a Bag-Eucharist Lesson 10. 2012. (ENG.). 24.99 *(978-1-59982-396-6(9))* St. Mary's Pr. of MN.

Lesson in a Bag-Eucharist Lesson 2. 2012. (ENG.). 24.99 *(978-1-59982-388-1(8))* St. Mary's Pr. of MN.

Lesson in a Bag-Eucharist Lesson 3. 2012. (ENG.). (gr. 6-8). 24.99 *(978-1-59982-389-8(6))* St. Mary's Pr. of MN.

Lesson in a Bag-Eucharist Lesson 4. 2012. (ENG.). 24.99 *(978-1-59982-390-4(X))* St. Mary's Pr. of MN.

Lesson in a Bag-Eucharist Lesson 5. 2012. (ENG.). 24.99 *(978-1-59982-391-1(8))* St. Mary's Pr. of MN.

Lesson in a Bag-Eucharist Lesson 6. 2012. (ENG.). 24.99 *(978-1-59982-392-8(6))* St. Mary's Pr. of MN.

Lesson in a Bag-Eucharist Lesson 7. 2012. (ENG.). 24.99 *(978-1-59982-393-5(4))* St. Mary's Pr. of MN.

Lesson in a Bag-Eucharist Lesson 8. 2012. (ENG.). 24.99 *(978-1-59982-394-2(2))* St. Mary's Pr. of MN.

Lesson in a Bag-Eucharist Lesson 9. 2012. (ENG.). 24.99 *(978-1-59982-395-9(0))* St. Mary's Pr. of MN.

Lesson in a Bag-Reconciliation Lesson 1. 2012. (ENG.). 24.99 *(978-1-59982-398-0(5))* St. Mary's Pr. of MN.

Lesson in a Bag-Reconciliation Lesson 2. 2012. (ENG.). 24.99 *(978-1-59982-399-7(3))* St. Mary's Pr. of MN.

Lesson in a Bag-Reconciliation Lesson 3. 2012. (ENG.). 24.99 *(978-1-59982-400-0(0))* St. Mary's Pr. of MN.

Lesson in a Bag-Reconciliation Lesson 4. 2012. (ENG.). 24.99 *(978-1-59982-401-7(9))* St. Mary's Pr. of MN.

Lesson in a Bag-Reconciliation Lesson 5. 2012. (ENG.). 24.99 *(978-1-59982-402-4(7))* St. Mary's Pr. of MN.

Lesson in a Bag-Reconciliation Lesson 6. 2012. (ENG.). 24.99 *(978-1-59982-403-1(5))* St. Mary's Pr. of MN.

Lesson in a Bag-Reconciliation Lesson 7. 2012. (ENG.). 24.99 *(978-1-59982-404-8(3))* St. Mary's Pr. of MN.

Lesson in a Bag-Reconciliation Lesson 8. 2012. (ENG.). 24.99 *(978-1-59982-405-5(1))* St. Mary's Pr. of MN.

Lewis, Jan. Baby's First Stories of Jesus. 2015. (ENG., Illus.). 24p. (J). (gr. -1-2). bds. 6.99 *(978-1-86147-415-5(6)*, Armadillo) Anness Publishing GBR. Dist: National Bk. Network.

Librado. Thank You Jesus. l.t. ed. 2006. (Illus.). 29p. (J). (gr. -1-3). per. 11.99 *(978-1-59879-209-6(1))* Lifevest Publishing, Inc.

Lloyd-Jones, Sally. Biblia para Niños - Historias de Jesús: Cada historia susurra Su Nombre, 1 vol. 2008. (SPA.). 352p. (J). 17.99 *(978-0-8297-5606-7(X))* Vida Pubs.

Lord, Jill Roman. If Jesus Came to Visit Me. Graef, Renee, illus. (ENG.). (J). 2008. 28p. bds. 6.95 *(978-0-8249-6568-6(X))* 2006. 26p. (gr. -1-k). 12.95 *(978-0-8249-6651-5(1))* Worthy Publishing. (Ideal Pubns.).

—If Jesus Lived Inside My Heart. Wummer, Amy, illus. (If Jesus Ser.). (J). 2014. 22p. bds. 6.99 *(978-0-8249-1937-5(8))* 2007. (ENG.). 26p. (gr. -1-k). bds. 6.99 *(978-0-8249-6686-7(4))* Worthy Publishing. (Ideal Pubns.).

—If Jesus Walked Beside Me. Graef, Renee, illus. 2006. (ENG.). 26p. (J). (gr. -1-3). bds. 6.95 *(978-0-8249-6638-6(4)*, Ideal Pubns.) Worthy Publishing.

Lounsbury, Pete. Jesus & the Blind Man. 2007. (J). per. 12.95 *(978-1-59879-408-3(6))* Lifevest Publishing, Inc.

Lucado, Max. Next Door Savior, 1 vol. 2008. (ENG.). 212p. pap. 13.99 *(978-1-4041-7544-0(X))* Nelson, Thomas Inc.

MacKenzie, Carine. God, the Ten Commandments & Jesus. 2003. (ENG.). 48p. (J). 12.99 *(978-1-85792-850-1(4)*, 2c94907f-0368-4d78-82a2-be1bc134e3fd) Christian Focus Pubns. GBR. Dist: Bookmasters Distribution.

Mackenzie, Carine. Little Hands Life of Jesus. Cosco, Rafaella, illus. 2008. (ENG.). 144p. (J). 10.99 *(978-1-84550-339-0(2)*, 2fdce463-aebe-497c-a405-33622bcfa7d7) Christian Focus Pubns. GBR. Dist: Bookmasters Distribution.

MacKenzie, Carine. My First Book about Jesus. 2014. (My First Bks.). (ENG., Illus.). 64p. (J). pap. 3.99 *(978-1-84550-463-2(1)*, bec911fb-f239-4a45-9b23-a38b1eaf171a) Christian Focus Pubns. GBR. Dist: Bookmasters Distribution.

MacKenzie, Catherine. Jesus Christ the Best King of All. 2010. (Colour Bks.). (ENG., Illus.). 64p. (J). 6.99 *(978-1-84550-568-4(9)*, 9781845505684) Christian Focus Pubns. GBR. Dist: Bookmasters Distribution.

—Jesus Helps His People. Apps, Fred, illus. 2008. (Sent to Save Ser.). (ENG.). 16p. (J). (gr. -1-3). bds. 3.99 *(978-1-84550-322-2(8)*, 9781845503222) Christian Focus Pubns. GBR. Dist: Bookmasters Distribution.

—Jesus Rescues His People. Apps, Fred, illus. 2008. (Sent to Save Ser.). (ENG.). 16p. (J). (gr. 4-7). 3.99 *(978-1-84550-321-5(X)*, 9781845503215) Christian Focus Pubns. GBR. Dist: Bookmasters Distribution.

—Jesus Rose from the Dead - The Evidence. 2010. (ENG., Illus.). 96p. (J). 7.99 *(978-1-84550-537-0(9)*, c1967fb3-066c-446d-84ee-1bc9c8837321) Christian Focus Pubns. GBR. Dist: Bookmasters Distribution.

—Jesus Saves His People. Apps, Fred, illus. 2008. (Sent to Save Ser.). (ENG.). 16p. (J). (gr. -1-3). 3.99 *(978-1-84550-323-9(6)*, 9781845503239) Christian Focus Pubns. GBR. Dist: Bookmasters Distribution.

—What Is the Truth? 2013. (Little Lights Ser.). (ENG., Illus.). 24p. (J). 7.99 *(978-1-84550-560-8(3)*, 281bfc81-447c-4f63-85f8-daa6919a36b7) Christian Focus Pubns. GBR. Dist: Bookmasters Distribution.

—What Should I Do? 2013. (Little Lights Ser.). (ENG., Illus.). 24p. (J). 7.99 *(978-1-84550-561-5(1)*, 9781845505615) Christian Focus Pubns. GBR. Dist: Bookmasters Distribution.

Maier, Paul L. The Very First Easter. 32p. (J). 9.99 *(978-0-570-07195-2(X))* Concordia Publishing Hse.

—The Very First Easter. Ordaz, Francisco, illus. 2004. 32p. (J). pap. 7.49 *(978-0-7586-0627-3(3))*; 13.49 *(978-0-570-07053-5(8))* Concordia Publishing Hse.

Maltese, Donna K. Know Your Bible for Kids: All about Jesus. 2015. (ENG., Illus.). 128p. (J). pap. 4.99 *(978-1-63058-852-6(0)*, Barbour Bks.) Barbour Publishing, Inc.

Marsh, Dilleen, tr. & illus. What Happens When People Die? Marsh, Dilleen, illus. 2003. (J). 12.95 *(978-1-57008-954-1(X))* Deseret Bk. Co.

Martin, Peter. Jesus Detective: A Puzzle Search Book. Kent, Peter, illus. 2014. (ENG.). 48p. (J). (gr. 2-4). 14.99 *(978-0-7459-6444-7(3))* Lion Hudson PLC GBR. Dist: Independent Pubs. Group.

McClendon, Kimberli A. Have You Heard? Jesus Walks on Water. 2012. 30p. pap. 13.99 *(978-1-4497-4179-2(7),* WestBow Pr.) Author Solutions, Inc.

McGuire, George. God & Me. 2006. 36p. pap. 13.99 *(978-1-4116-9218-3(7))* Lulu Pr., Inc.

Milbourne, Anna & Roberti, Alessandra. The Story of the Nativity. 2010. (Illus.). (J). 10.99 *(978-0-7945-2552-1(0),* Usborne) EDC Publishing.

Miracles of Jesus. (Pict-O-Graph Ser.). (Illus.). (J). 10.99 *(978-0-7847-1026-5(0),* 02226) Standard Publishing.

Miracles of Jesus. (Illus.). 16p. (J). pap. 1.50 *(978-0-87162-858-9(9),* E6039) Warner Pr., Inc.

Moore, Alan & Tavner, Gill. Jesus of Nazareth. Donnelly, Karen, illus. 2014. (New Testament Ser.). (ENG.). 64p. pap. 6.95 *(978-1-906230-24-1(2))* Real Reads Ltd. GBR. Dist: Casemate Pubs. & Bk. Distributors, LLC.

Moore, Angela Hays. Maggie Seeks the Kingdom of God. Kiel, Casey Kizer, illus. 2007. 32p. (J). 19.99 *(978-1-59879-323-9(3))* Lifevest Publishing, Inc.

Mortimer, F. L. More about Jesus. 288p. (J). pap. 7.99 *(978-1-85792-592-0(0))* Christian Focus Pubns. GBR. Dist: Riverside.

My Story of Jesus. 2006. 32p. (J). pap. 2.89 *(978-0-7847-1281-8(6),* 22094) Standard Publishing.

Neeley, Deta Petersen & Neeley, Nathan Glen. Paul of Tarsus, V2: A Child's Story of the New Testament. 2011. 152p. 41.95 *(978-1-258-07519-4(9))* Literary Licensing, LLC.

Neff, LaVonne. The Jesus Book: 40 Bible Stories. Goffe, Toni, illus. 2004. (Life of Christ for Children Ser.). 84p. (gr. -1-k). 9.95 *(978-0-8294-1373-1(1))* Loyola Pr.

Nielson, Mark S. I Believe in Jesus Too. Stapley, Craig, illus. 2011. (J). 17.99 *(978-1-60908-741-8(0))* Deseret Bk. Co.

Nyland, Richard. Jesus. 2005. 18.99 *(978-1-59467-983-4(5));* per. 10.99 *(978-1-59467-982-7(7))* Salem Author Services.

Oakes, Loretta. Peek-a-Boo Jesus! Hall, Mary, illus. 2010. 16p. (J). (gr. -1). pap. 9.95 *(978-0-8091-6755-5(7),* Ambassador Bks.) Paulist Pr.

Olson, Marc. The World Jesus Knew: A Curious Kid's Guide to Life in First-Century Palestine. Maybank, Jem, illus. 2017. (ENG.). 64p. (J). (gr. 4-6). 19.99 ***(978-1-5064-2500-9(3),*** Sparkhouse Family) Augsburg Fortress, Pubs.

O'Neal, Debbie Trafton. J Is for Jesus: An Easter Alphabet & Activity Book. Bryan-Hunt, Jan, illus. 2005. 32p. (J). (gr. 3-7). per., act. bk. ed. 11.99 *(978-0-8066-5123-1(7),* Augsburg Bks.) Augsburg Fortress, Pubs.

O'Neill-McGrath, Michael. Jesus A to Z. O'Neill-McGrath, Michael, illus. 2007. (Illus.). 32p. 16.99 *(978-1-58459-332-4(6))* World Library Pubns.

Palmer, Alison. Simply Singing Time. 2009. 96p. (J). pap. 8.99 *(978-0-88290-970-7(3))* Cedar Fort, Inc./CFI Distribution.

Pascucci, Mary Ann. Adventures on Green Pasture Farm Scruff: An Orphan Lamb. 2013. 48p. pap. 20.45 *(978-1-4908-1184-0(2),* WestBow Pr.) Author Solutions, Inc.

Perez III, Librado. Thank You Jesus. l.t. ed. 2006. (Illus.). 36p. (J). 23.99 *(978-1-59879-317-8(9))* Lifevest Publishing, Inc.

Pingry, Patricia A. Bible Story Cards: The Story of Jesus. 2006. (ENG., Illus.). 10p. 7.95 *(978-0-8249-1704-3(9),* Ideal Pubns.) Worthy Publishing.

—The Easter Story. Utt, Mary Ann, illus. (ENG.). (J). 2006. 32p. (gr. -1-3). per. 3.95 *(978-0-8249-5531-1(5))* 2003. 26p. bds. 6.95 *(978-0-8249-4231-1(0))* Worthy Publishing. (Ideal Pubns.).

—Jesus in the Temple: Based on Luke 2:40/52. Munger, Nancy, illus. 2008. (ENG.). 26p. (J). bds. 6.95 *(978-0-8249-6569-3(8),* Ideal Pubns.) Worthy Publishing.

—The Story of Easter. Wells, Lorraine, illus. 2006. (ENG.). 26p. (gr. -1-k). 12.95 *(978-0-8249-6649-2(X),* Ideal Pubns.) Worthy Publishing.

—The Story of Jesus. Pulley, Kelly, illus. 2011. (Little Bible Bks). 22p. (J). (gr. -1-k). bds. 6.99 *(978-0-8249-1854-5(1),* Ideal Pubns.) Worthy Publishing.

—The Story of Loaves & Fishes. Venturi-Pickett, Stacy, illus. 2003. 26p. (J). bds. 6.95 *(978-0-8249-6518-1(3),* Ideal Pubns.) Worthy Publishing.

Pipkin, Evelyn Ruth. The Pretty Little Red Bird. l.t. ed. 2004. 19p. (J). (gr. 1-3). 7.95 *(978-0-9755789-0-2(1))* Two Seed Planters Inc.

Plante, Patty. Joy for Jesus: Friends with God, 1. 2nd ed. 2003. (Joy for Jesus Ser.: 1). Orig. Title: Joy for Jesus: Friends with God. 91p. (J). ring bd. 24.95 *(978-1-889723-31-0(2))* Family Harvest Church.

—Joy for Jesus: Jesus in Me. 2003. (Joy for Jesus Ser.: 2). 78p. (J). ring bd. 24.95 *(978-1-889723-40-2(1))* Family Harvest Church.

—Viviendo Como Jesus, Libro 1. Garcia de Ortiz, Lic. Rosalinda, tr. from ENG. 2003. (SPA.). 71p. (J). ring bd. 24.95 *(978-1-889723-32-7(0))* Family Harvest Church.

Poelman, Heidi. I Can Love Like Jesus. 2017. (ENG., Illus.). (J). (gr. -1-2). 14.99 ***(978-1-4621-1940-0(9))*** Cedar Fort, Inc./CFI Distribution.

Poole, Susie. The Amazing Journey: Jesus, Creation, Death & Life! 2nd ed. 2007. (ENG., Illus.). 44p. pap. 10.99 *(978-1-904637-43-1(4),* 1904637434) Authentic Media GBR. Dist: EMI CMG Distribution.

Puhalo, Lazar. Twelve Great Feast Days. Date not set. (Illus.). 45p. (J). pap. 5.00 *(978-1-879038-43-1(9),* 9011) Synaxis Pr.

Pulley, Kelly. Jesus & His Friends, 1 vol. 2007. (I Can Read! / the Beginner's Bible Ser.). (ENG., Illus.). 32p. (J). (gr. -1-1). pap. 3.99 *(978-0-310-71461-3(3))* Zonderkidz.

Redding, David Asbury. He Never Spoke Without a Parable: His Kingdom, Your Antagonist, It's up to You, 3 bks, 5 vols. l.t. ed. 2003. pap. 16.00 *(978-0-9671701-3-8(3),* 0-9671701-3-3) Redding, Marion T.

Redford, Marjorie. My Bible Says. Marlin, Kathryn, illus. 2013. (Happy Day Ser.). (ENG.). 16p. (J). pap. 2.49 *(978-1-4143-9301-8(6))* Tyndale Hse. Pubs.

—My Bible Says. Marlin, Kathryn, illus. 2013. (Happy Day Ser.). (ENG.). 18p. (J). bds. 4.99 *(978-1-4143-9291-2(5))* Tyndale Hse. Pubs.

Reeves, Eira. Jesus & Me Every Day Book 1, 1 vol. 2009. (ENG., Illus.). 64p. (J). pap. *(978-1-85345-518-6(0))* Crusade for World Revival.

—Jesus & Me Every Day Book 2, 1 vol. 2009. (ENG., Illus.). 64p. (J). pap. *(978-1-85345-519-3(9))* Crusade for World Revival.

Reeves, Eira & Jefferson, Graham. Would You Like to Know Jesus?, 1 vol. 2015. (ENG., Illus.). 28p. (J). 2.99 *(978-1-78128-103-1(3),* Candle Bks.) Lion Hudson PLC GBR. Dist: Kregel Pubns.

The Revolutionary Revelation on the Book of Revelation & its all about Jesus. 2005. (YA). per. *(978-1-59872-168-3(2))* Instant Pub.

Rhodes, Karen. Do You Know Jesus? 2005. (J). pap. 1.79 *(978-1-59317-111-7(0))* Warner Pr., Inc.

Rhydderch, Gwyn, et al. Iesu'r Ffrind: 16 Sesiwn Yn Cyflwyno Bywyd Iesu Ar Gyfer Plant Cynradd Yn Seiliedig Ar Efengyl Luc. 2005. (WEL., Illus.). 120p. pap. *(978-1-85994-007-5(2))* Cyhoeddiadau'r Gair.

Rikkers, Doris Wynbeek. Little Jesus, Little Me, 1 vol. 2017. (ENG., Illus.). 14p. (J). bds. 6.99 ***(978-0-310-76177-8(8))*** Zonderkidz.

Risen Today. 7.50 *(978-0-8054-5925-8(1))* B&H Publishing Group.

Robinson, Timothy. What Happens When People Die? Reprint. 2009. 32p. 10.95 *(978-1-60641-114-8(4))* Deseret Bk. Co.

Roche, Maite. The Gospel for Little Ones. 2011. (ENG., Illus.). 32p. (J). (gr. -1-k). bds. 12.99 *(978-1-58617-507-8(6))* Ignatius Pr.

—My First Pictures of Jesus. 2012. 14p. 6.99 *(978-1-58617-651-8(X))* Ignatius Pr.

Rock, Lois. A Little Life of Jesus - To Read & Treasure. Langton, Roger W., illus. 2nd ed. 2015. (ENG.). 352p. (J). (gr. -1-k). pap. 8.99 *(978-0-7459-6567-3(9))* Lion Hudson PLC GBR. Dist: Independent Pubs. Group.

—Look Inside the Time of Jesus. Orlandi, Lorenzo, illus. 2014. (ENG.). 8p. (J). (gr. k-2). bds. 14.99 *(978-0-7459-6398-3(6))* Lion Hudson PLC GBR. Dist: Independent Pubs. Group.

—Tiny Tots Easter. Widdowson, Kay, illus. 2016. (Tiny Tots Ser.). (ENG.). 32p. (J). (gr. -1 — 1). 7.99 *(978-0-7459-6456-0(7))* Lion Hudson PLC GBR. Dist: Independent Pubs. Group.

Rose, Drew, illus. God's Son, Jesus. 2005. (Bible Activity Bks.). 94p. (J). (gr. -1-3). 2.99 *(978-0-7814-4314-2(8),* 0781443148) Cook, David C.

Rottmann, Erik. The Easter Victory. Billin-Frye, Paige, illus. 2006. (Arch Bks.). (ENG.). 16p. (J). (gr. -1-3). 2.49 *(978-0-7586-0869-7(1))* Concordia Publishing Hse.

—Jesus, My Good Shepherd. Miyake, Yoski, illus. 2005. (ENG.). 16p. (J). 1.99 *(978-0-7586-0725-6(3))* Concordia Publishing Hse.

Sanders, Nancy I. Jesus Walks on the Water. Swisher, Elizabeth, illus. 2005. (ENG.). 16p. (J). 1.99 *(978-0-7586-0864-2(0))* Concordia Publishing Hse.

Sanderson, Harvelene. Hello, Jesus Loves You. 2012. 16p. pap. 7.99 *(978-1-4624-0120-8(1),* Inspiring Voices) Author Solutions, Inc.

Schkade, Jonathan. Jesus Shows His Glory. 2008. (Arch Bks.). 16p. (J). (gr. k-4). pap. 1.99 *(978-0-7586-1452-0(7))* Concordia Publishing Hse.

—The Love Bridge. 2017. (ENG., Illus.). (J). (gr. -1-3). 10.99 ***(978-0-7586-5777-0(3))*** Concordia Publishing Hse.

Schkade, Jonathan. Nicodemus & Jesus. Miyake, Yoshi, illus. 2014. (Arch Bks.). (ENG.). 16p. (J). (gr. k-4). pap. 2.49 *(978-0-7586-4606-4(2))* Concordia Publishing Hse.

Schlitt, D. Celebrate the Names of Jesus. 2004. 52p. 6.99 *(978-0-8054-0825-6(8))* B&H Publishing Group.

Schmertz Navarro, Christine, ed. Student Activity Workbook for Breakthrough! the Bible for Young Catholics: Getting to Know Jesus. 2007. (Illus.). 32p. pap. 8.50 *(978-0-88489-978-5(0))* St. Mary's Pr. of MN.

Scrimshire, Hazel. Jesus Loves You: A Colouring Book. 2006. (Bible Art Ser.). (ENG.). 16p. (J). pap., act. bk. ed. 1.99 *(978-1-85792-305-6(7),* f07d9e80-1067-468f-8800-0d756c8e469f) Christian Focus Pubns. GBR. Dist: Bookmasters Distribution.

Seifert, Sheila. Happy Birthday Jesus. 2007. (DSJ Ser.). (Illus.). 112p. (J). per. 16.99 *(978-0-7814-4511-5(6))* Cook, David C.

Setzer, Lee Ann. Tiny Talks: My Savior, Jesus Christ, Vol. 10. 2009. 86p. (J). pap. 8.99 *(978-1-59955-375-7(9))* Cedar Fort, Inc./CFI Distribution.

Sharpe, Jean Ann, ed. The Saving Name of God the Son. 2009. (Illus.). 22p. (J). bds. 9.95 *(978-1-932350-30-2(6))* Bethlehem Bks.

Shegog, Jakeenya. My Friend Jesus. 2013. 24p. pap. 9.95 *(978-0-9896581-6-4(3))* Kingdom Publishing Group, Inc.

Simmons, JoAnne. It All Matters to Jesus Devotional for Girls: Mean Girls, Manicures, & Mondays... He Cares about It All. 2016. (ENG.). 264p. (J). pap. 5.99 *(978-1-63058-933-2(0),* Barbour Bks.) Barbour Publishing, Inc.

Slattery, Kathryn. My Friend Jesus, 1 vol. 2013. (ENG., Illus.). 32p. (J). 12.99 *(978-1-4003-2267-1(7))* Nelson, Thomas Inc.

Smart, Dominic. 40 Days with Jesus: A Journey Through Mark's Gospel. 2006. (Daily Readings Ser.). (ENG., Illus.). 144p. (J). per. 10.99 *(978-1-84550-193-8(4),* 4ae05e0c-fa9c-48fd-8b6d-360a73b461fc) Christian Focus Pubns. GBR. Dist: Bookmasters Distribution.

Smart Kidz, creator. Jesus Loves the Little Children. 2013. (Bible Sing along Bks.). (ENG., Illus.). 12p. (gr. -1). bds. 12.99 *(978-1-891100-34-5(3),* Smart Kids) Penton Overseas, Inc.

Smith, Evans. The Christmas Angel. 2009. 40p. pap. 18.49 *(978-1-4490-4056-7(X))* AuthorHouse.

Smith, Judah. Jesus Is Student Edition, 1 vol. 2014. (ENG.). 224p. (J). pap. 12.99 *(978-0-7180-2245-7(9))* Nelson, Thomas Inc.

Smith, Martina. The Story of Easter: A Spark Bible Story. Grosshauser, Peter, illus. 2016. (Spark Bible Stories Ser.). (ENG.). 32p. (J). (gr. -1-2). 12.99 *(978-1-5064-0230-7(5),* Sparkhouse Family) Augsburg Fortress, Pubs.

Southall, M. Renee. My Daddy Loves Me & He Can Do Anything. 2012. 28p. pap. 19.99 *(978-1-4772-8221-2(1))* AuthorHouse.

St. Pierre, Stephanie. Jesus, the Good Shepherd. Bolam, Emily, illus. 2003. 14p. (J). bds. 7.99 *(978-0-7847-1272-6(7),* 04032) Standard Publishing.

Stanton, Sue. Child's Guide to the Stations of the Cross. Blake, Anne Catharine, illus. 2008. 32p. (J). (gr. k-4). 10.95 *(978-0-8091-6739-5(5),* 6739-5) Paulist Pr.

Stayton, Claudia Grace. Day by Day the Jesus Way: What Jesus Has to Say about Life, Love, & the Way to God. 2003. 144p. per. 5.95 *(978-0-9728900-0-7(9),* 888-899-3207) Good News Connections.

Steigemeyer, Julie. My Little Easter Book. Regan, Dana, illus. 2008. 20p. (J). (gr. -1-k). bds. 6.49 *(978-0-7586-1444-5(6))* Concordia Publishing Hse.

Stephens Landoll, Mary. A Vision from Heaven. 2013. 50p. pap. 9.95 *(978-1-4908-0604-4(0),* WestBow Pr.) Author Solutions, Inc.

Stiegemeyer, Julie. Things I See at Christmas. Mitter, Kathryn, illus. 2005. 16p. (J). (gr. -1-17). bds. 5.49 *(978-0-7586-0809-3(8))* Concordia Publishing Hse.

Stohs, Anita Reith. Hush, Little One: A Lullaby for God's Children. Kanzler, John, tr. Kanzler, John, illus. 2004. 32p. (J). 12.99 *(978-0-570-07144-0(5))* Concordia Publishing Hse.

—Hush Little One: A Lullaby for God's Children. Kanzler, John, illus. 2006. 20p. (J). (gr. -1). bds. 5.49 *(978-0-7586-0861-1(6))* Concordia Publishing Hse.

Stoner, Diane. Do You Know My Friend, Jesus? 2012. (ENG.). 20p. (J). pap. 16.95 *(978-1-4327-9049-3(8))* Outskirts Pr., Inc.

Story of Jesus. 2004. 16p. (J). act. bk. ed. 8.99 *(978-0-570-07178-5(X))* Concordia Publishing Hse.

Story of Jesus for Children. 2004. pap. 14.98 *(978-0-7378-0584-0(6))* Brentwood Home Video.

Strobel, Lee & Suggs, Rob. The Case for Christ for Kids, 1 vol. enl. rev. expurg. ed. 2010. (Case for... Series for Kids Ser.). (ENG., Illus.). 144p. (J). pap. 7.99 *(978-0-310-71990-8(9))* Zonderkidz.

Stuckey, Denise. Jesus, I Feel Close to You. Saroff, Phyllis, illus. 2005. 32p. (J). 10.95 *(978-0-8091-6718-0(2),* 6718-2) Paulist Pr.

Student Life Staff & Navigators Staff, The. 31 Verses - Community: Every Teenager Should Know. 2009. 80p. (YA). pap. 4.99 *(978-1-935040-16-3(2))* NavPress Publishing Group.

Summerer, Marilyn. The First Christmas Present. van der Sterre, Johanna, illus. 2009. 32p. (J). (gr. -1). 14.99 *(978-0-7586-1663-0(5))* Concordia Publishing Hse.

Taylor, Mark A. Breakfast with Jesus. 2014. (Happy Day Ser.). (ENG.). 16p. (J). pap. 2.49 *(978-1-4143-9484-8(5))* Tyndale Hse. Pubs.

—One Tiny Baby. Burroughs, Scott, illus. 2014. (Happy Day Ser.). (ENG.). 16p. (J). pap. 2.49 *(978-1-4143-9478-7(0))* Tyndale Hse. Pubs.

Tebo, Mary Elizabeth. My First Book about Jesus. Peterson, Mary Joseph, illus. 2008. 64p. (J). (gr. 1-3). pap. 7.95 *(978-0-8198-4865-9(4))* Pauline Bks. & Media.

Thomas-Logan, Sharon. The Miracles of Jesus Christ. 2009. 24p. pap. 12.99 *(978-1-4389-4615-3(5))* AuthorHouse.

Thornborough, Tim. The Fright of Your Life, 25 vols. 2010. 6p. (J). *(978-1-906334-27-7(7))* Good Bk. Co.

Thorne, Rick. The Hidden Secrets of Jesus & Other Revelations. 2004. (Illus.). 268p. (YA). pap. 19.95 *(978-0-937327-04-3(2))* Soul Pubns.

True God, True Man. 2004. (Effective Dre Ser.). pap. *(978-0-8294-1499-8(1))* Loyola Pr.

Turton, Karalynn Teresa. The Passion for Children: Bilingual (English & Spanish) Guide to the Passion of Christ, 1 bk. Ruiz, Jeanette, tr. Burnett, Anne, illus. 2005. (J). 3.00 *(978-0-9765180-0-6(7))* Catholic World Mission.

Twin Sisters(r), et al. Jesus Loves the Little Children/Jesus Loves Me: Sing-A-Story Book with CD. 2016. (Let's Share a Story Ser.). (ENG., Illus.). 18p. (J). bds. 9.99 *(978-1-63409-767-3(X))* Barbour Publishing, Inc.

Twin Sisters(r) Staff. The Story of Jesus Handlebox-4books. 2009. 12.99 *(978-1-59922-111-3(X))* Twin Sisters IP, LLC.

Twin Sisters(r) Staff, et al. Jesus Loves Me More Than... 2015. (Let's Share a Story Ser.). (ENG., Illus.). 10p. (J). (gr. -1-k). bds. 9.99 *(978-1-63058-896-0(2))* Barbour Publishing, Inc.

Understanding Scripture: The Genesis Creation Story. 2004. (Our Catholic Tradition Handbooks Ser.). *(978-0-8294-1044-0(9))* Loyola Pr.

Van der Veer, Andrew. Bible Lessons for Juniors, Book 3: The Life of Christ. 2007. (ENG.). 88p. (J). 6.00 *(978-1-60178-014-0(1))* Reformation Heritage Bks.

Van Leeuwen, Wendy. Miracle Man Activity Book. 2007. (Illus.). 16p. (J). pap. 1.89 *(978-1-59317-209-1(5))* Warner Pr., Inc.

Walker, Joni. Jesus Is with Me. Walker, Joni, illus. 2004. (Illus.). 20p. (J). bds. 5.49 *(978-0-7586-0628-0(1))* Concordia Publishing Hse.

—Jesus Knows Me. Walker, Joni, illus. 2003. (Illus.). 14p. (J). (gr. -1-k). bds. 5.49 *(978-0-7586-0507-8(2))* Concordia Publishing Hse.

Warner, Anna Bartlett. Yes Jesus Loves Me. 2006. (Illus.). 36p. (J). 14.99 *(978-0-7847-1512-3(2),* 04154) Standard Publishing.

Warner Press Staff. Jesus in My Heart Coloring Books Intermediate. 2005. 2.69 *(978-0-87162-939-5(9))* Warner Pr., Inc.

—Jesus Loves Me Coloring Book Pre-K. 2005. (J). pap. 2.69 *(978-1-59317-017-2(3))* Warner Pr., Inc.

Warnes, Tim. Jesus Loves Me! Warnes, Tim, illus. 2006. (ENG., Illus.). 32p. (J). (gr. -1-3). 15.99 *(978-1-4169-0065-8(9),* Simon & Schuster Bks. For Young Readers) Simon & Schuster Bks. For Young Readers.

Warnes, Tim, illus. Jesus Loves Me! 2008. (ENG.). 26p. (J). (gr. -1-k). bds. 7.99 *(978-1-4169-5367-8(1),* Little Simon) Little Simon.

Wedeven, Carol. The Easter Cave. 2007. (Illus.). 28p. (J). (gr. -1). per. 7.49 *(978-0-7586-1213-7(3))* Concordia Publishing Hse.

Wesley, Misty Lynn. The Dancing Easter Lilies. 2012. 36p. pap. 16.95 *(978-1-4626-6819-9(4))* America Star Bks.

White, Susan K. Jesus Does Good Things. McQuitty, LaVonia Corbin, illus. 2013. 24p. (J). 15.00 *(978-0-9832570-6-6(X))* Scribe's Closet Pubns., The.

Wildsmith, Brian. The Easter Story. Wildsmith, Brian, illus. 2004. (Illus.). 24p. (gr. -1-7). 18.00 *(978-0-8028-5189-5(4))* Eerdmans, William B. Publishing Co.

—Jesus. Wildsmith, Brian, illus. 2004. (Illus.). 24p. (gr. 3-7). 20.00 *(978-0-8028-5212-0(2))* Eerdmans, William B. Publishing Co.

Wildwood Forest Customizable Outdoor Banner. 2009. (Vacation Bible School Ser.). (J). 35.00 *(978-2-608-00908-1(5))* Cook, David C.

Williams, Lynda Anne. This Is Why I Talk to Jesus. 2005. (J). act. bk. ed. 10.00 *(978-0-9771015-0-4(9))* Let's Learn Library of Knowledge Series.

Wood, Minister Dorothy F. Samuel's New Suit. 2012. 20p. pap. 17.99 *(978-1-4343-7605-3(2))* AuthorHouse.

Zobel-Nolan, Allia. Amazing Life of Jesus. Cox, Steve, illus. 2005. 10p. (J). 10.99 *(978-0-8254-5522-3(7))* Kregel Pubns.

Zondervan. Jesus: A 365-Day Devotional, 1 vol. 2016. (ENG.). 384p. (J). 15.99 *(978-0-310-75809-9(2))* Zonderkidz.

Zondervan Staff. The Beginner's Bible All about Jesus Sticker & Activity Book, 1 vol. Pulley, Kelly, illus. 2015. (Beginner's Bible Ser.). (ENG.). 16p. (J). pap. 3.99 *(978-0-310-74693-5(0))* Zonderkidz.

—The Beginner's Bible Stories about Jesus, 1 vol. Pulley, Kelly, illus. 2015. (Beginner's Bible Ser.). (ENG.). 22p. (J). bds. 9.99 *(978-0-310-74740-6(6))* Zonderkidz.

—The First Easter Ever, 1 vol. Jones, Dennis, illus. 2015. (ENG.). 32p. (J). pap. 1.99 *(978-0-310-74084-1(3))* Zonderkidz.

—Jesus & His Friends, 1 vol. Pulley, Kelly, illus. 2009. (I Can Read! / the Beginner's Bible / ¡Yo Sé Leer! Ser.). (SPA & ENG.). 32p. (J). pap. 3.99 *(978-0-310-71889-5(9))* Zonderkidz.

—Jesus Feeds the People, 1 vol. Pulley, Kelly, illus. 2010. (I Can Read! / the Beginner's Bible Ser.). (ENG.). 32p. (J). pap. 3.99 *(978-0-310-71779-9(5))* Zonderkidz.

—Jesus God's Only Son, 1 vol. Jones, Dennis, illus. 2010. (I Can Read! / Dennis Jones Ser.). (ENG.). 32p. (J). (gr. -1-2). pap. 3.99 *(978-0-310-71880-2(5))* Zonderkidz.

—Jesus Loves Me, 1 vol. Borlasca, Hector, illus. 2008. (I Can Read! / Song Ser.). (ENG.). 32p. (J). (gr. -1-3). pap. 3.99 *(978-0-310-71619-8(5))* Zonderkidz.

—Jesus Loves the Little Children, 1 vol. Trasler, Janee, illus. 2008. (I Can Read! / Song Ser.). (ENG.). 32p. (J). (gr. -1-3). pap. 3.99 *(978-0-310-71620-4(9))* Zonderkidz.

—Jesus Saves the World, 1 vol. Pulley, Kelly, illus. 2008. (I Can Read! / the Beginner's Bible Ser.). (ENG.). 32p. (J). (gr. -1-1). pap. 3.99 *(978-0-310-71553-5(9))* Zonderkidz.

—Miracles of Jesus, 1 vol. Miles, David, illus. 2014. (I Can Read! / Adventure Bible Ser.). (ENG.). 32p. (J). pap. 3.99 *(978-0-310-73242-6(5))* Zonderkidz.

—The Very First Easter, 1 vol. Pulley, Kelly, illus. 2009. (Beginner's Bible Ser.). (ENG.). 32p. (J). pap. 47.76 *(978-0-310-71817-8(1));* pap. 1.99 *(978-0-310-71827-7(9))* Zonderkidz.

JESUS CHRIST—ART

see also Bible—Pictorial Works; Christian Art and Symbolism

Daily, Eileen M. Beyond the Written Word: Exploring Faith Through Christian Art. 2005. (Illus.). 32p. (YA). pap. 6.25 *(978-0-88489-849-8(0))* St. Mary's Pr. of MN.

Newton, Richard. The Life of Jesus Christ for the Young. 2007. (ENG.). 204p. pap. 20.99 *(978-1-4346-2211-2(8));* 224p. pap. 22.99 *(978-1-4346-2271-6(1))* Creative Media Partners, LLC.

—The Life of Jesus Christ for the Young. 2004. reprint ed. pap. 1.99 *(978-1-4192-6962-2(3));* pap. 22.95 *(978-1-4191-6962-5(9))* Kessinger Publishing, LLC.

—The Life of Jesus Christ for the Young. 2005. pap. 32.00 *(978-1-932474-89-3(7));* pap. 30.00 *(978-1-932474-88-6(9))* Solid Ground Christian Bks.

Olsen, Greg. Beautiful Savior. 2004. (Illus.). (J). *(978-1-59156-553-6(7))* Covenant Communications.

JESUS CHRIST—BIOGRAPHY

see also Jesus Christ—Nativity

Adams, Michelle Medlock. The Story of Jesus Activity Book. Reed, Lisa, illus. 2014. 18p. (J). 4.99 *(978-0-8249-5659-2(1),* Ideal Pubns.) Worthy Publishing.

Avril, Adeline & Gravier, Anne. Little Life of Jesus. 2013. (ENG., Illus.). 24p. (gr. -1). bds. 9.99 *(978-1-58617-814-7(8))* Ignatius Pr.

Award, Anna. The Story of Jesus. 2012. (ENG., Illus.). 24p. (J). pap. 6.50 *(978-1-84135-604-4(2))* Award Pubns. Ltd. GBR. Dist: Parkwest Pubns., Inc.

Boon, Fiona. The Story of Jesus. Ede, Lara, illus. 2014. (ENG.). 22p. (J). bds. *(978-1-78235-883-1(8))* Make Believe Ideas.

Brennan, Gerald T. The Man Who Never Died: The Life & Adventures of St. Peter, the First Pope. 2005. (Illus.). 87p. (J). (gr. 3-7). per. 11.95 *(978-1-933184-09-8(4))* Sophia Institute Pr.

Brierley, Jane. Life of Jesus Puzzle Book. Lebedev, Aleksandr, illus. 2006. (Play & Learn Puzzle Bks.). (J). 12.95 *(978-0-88271-854-5(1))* Regina Pr., Malhame & Co.

Concordia Publishing House. The Story of Jesus Coloring & Activity Book. 2015. (ENG.). 96p. (J). pap. 3.99 *(978-0-7586-5222-5(4))* Concordia Publishing Hse.

Conn, Robert. Jesus Christ for Youth Leader, 2 vols. rev. ed. 2006. (Illus.). 152p. (gr. 3-7). per. 10.99 *(978-0-687-33276-2(1))* Abingdon Pr.

Conn, Robert A. Jesus Christ for Youth, 2 vols. 2006. (Illus.). 112p. stu. ed., per. 8.99 *(978-0-687-33286-1(9))* Abingdon Pr.

Cram101 Textbook Reviews Staff. Studyguide for Jesus of History Christ of Faith by Zanzig, Isbn 9780884895305. 3rd ed. 2014. (ENG.). 184p. (C). pap. 30.95 *(978-1-61812-856-0(6))* Cram101 Inc.

Cuyler, Margery. Jesus, 0 vols. Spirin, Gennady, illus. 2010. (ENG.). 36p. (J). (gr. 3-7). 21.00 *(978-0-7614-5630-8(9),* 9780761456308, Amazon Children's Publishing) Amazon Publishing.

Daily, Eileen M. Beyond the Written Word: Exploring Faith Through Christian Art. 2005. (Illus.). 32p. (YA). pap. 6.25 *(978-0-88489-849-8(0))* St. Mary's Pr. of MN.

Dearmer, Mabel. A Child's Life of Christ. 2006. pap. 30.95 *(978-1-4286-0075-1(2))* Kessinger Publishing, LLC.

Dickens, Charles. The Life of Our Lord: Illustrated 200th Anniversary Edition. Dewey, Simon, illus. 2012. 17.99 *(978-1-60907-185-1(9),* Shadow Mountain) Shadow Mountain Publishing.

—The Life of Our Lord: The Story of Jesus Told by Charles Dickens. 2009. 144p. 29.99 *(978-1-86118-960-8(5))* Third Millennium Pr., Ltd. GBR. Dist: Send The Light Distribution LLC.

J
K
L

—The Life of Our Lord: Written for His Children During the Years 1846 To 1849. 2004. 60p. pap. 7.95 *(978-1-57646-705-3(8))* Quiet Vision Publishing.

Dumont, C. & Lacoursiere, Suzanne. Jesus: A Story of Love. Merola, Caroline, tr. from FRE. Merola, Caroline, illus. 2003. 32p. (J). mass mkt. 5.95 *(978-0-8198-3977-0(9)*, 332-153) Pauline Bks. & Media.

Ferguson, Sinclair B. Big Book of Questions & Answers about Jesus: A Family Guide to Jesus' Life & Ministry. 2008. (Bible Teaching Ser.). (ENG., Illus.). 100p. (J). (gr. -1-3). pap. 14.99 *(978-1-85792-559-3(9)*, 7c99498f-3479-4298-b67c-3254ddce3da3) Christian Focus Pubns. GBR. Dist: Bookmasters Distribution.

Foster, Charles. Story of the Gospel. 2004. reprint ed. pap. 33.95 *(978-1-4191-1372-7(0))* Kessinger Publishing, LLC.

Glaser, Rebecca. The Holy Moly Easter Story. Ferenc, Bill, illus. 2016. (Holy Moly Bible Storybooks Ser.). (ENG.). 32p. (J). (gr. k-3). 12.99 *(978-1-5064-0256-7(9)*, Sparkhouse Family) Augsburg Fortress, Pubs.

—Jesus Feeds 5,000 & Other Bible Stories. Ferenc, Bill, illus. 2015. (Holy Moly Bible Storybooks Ser.). (ENG.). 32p. (J). (gr. k-3). 12.99 *(978-1-5064-0252-9(6)*, Sparkhouse Family) Augsburg Fortress, Pubs.

Hemenway, Priya. The Little Book of Jesus. 2004. (Illus.). 152p. *(978-0-7607-5447-4(0))* Barnes & Noble, Inc.

Heyer, Carol, illus. The First Easter. 2003. (ENG.). 32p. (J). 14.95 *(978-0-8249-5463-5(7)*, Ideal Pubns.) Worthy Publishing.

Hook, Richard & Hook, Frances, illus. Jesus the Friend of Children. 6th ed. 2006. (David C Cook Read to Me Bible Stories Ser.). 112p. (J). (gr. 3-7). 14.99 *(978-0-7814-4390-6(3))* Cook, David C.

Hudgins, Ellis A. A Good Man Who Came Out of Nazareth: A Biography of Jesus for Young Teen Readers. 2009. 240p. pap. 15.99 *(978-1-61579-140-8(X))* Salem Author Services.

Humble-Jackson, Sally. The Miracle Maker: The Greatest Story Ever Told. (Illus.). 48p. (J). pap. *(978-0-340-74958-6(X))* Hodder & Stoughton.

Hunt, Marigold. A Life of Our Lord for Children. 2003. (Illus.). v, 189p. (J). pap. 14.95 *(978-1-928832-64-5(4))* Sophia Institute Pr.

Jeffs, Stephanie. Bywyd Iesu. Wyn, Delyth, tr. from ENG. Tulip, Jenny, illus. 2005. (WEL.). 94p. *(978-1-85994-496-7(5))* Cyhoeddiadau'r Gair.

—People Jesus Met. Tulip, Jenny, illus. 2004. (My First Find Out about Book Ser.). 24p. (gr. -1-18). pap. 3.95 *(978-0-8294-1731-9(1))* Loyola Pr.

—Things Jesus Did. Tulip, Jenny, illus. 2004. 24p. (gr. -1-18). pap. 3.95 *(978-0-8294-1734-0(6))* Loyola Pr.

Jesus Christ - the Passion: And the Gospels of Matthew, Mark, Luke & John. 2004. mass mkt. 14.95 net. *(978-0-9749755-4-2(0))* Science Pubs.

Keating, Susan. Jesus Christ: Influential Religious Leader. 2013. (People of Importance Ser.: 21). (Illus.). 32p. (J). (gr. 4-18). 19.95 *(978-1-4222-2847-0(9))* Mason Crest.

Kredell, Janine. Jesus, the Brother of James & Jude, & the Savior of the World. 2013. 68p. pap. 13.95 *(978-1-4908-0953-3(8)*, WestBow Pr.) Author Solutions, Inc.

Kucharik, Elena & Goodings, Christina. Who Is Jesus? Royse, Maria, illus. 2016. (ENG.). 64p. (J). (gr. 2-4). 16.99 *(978-0-7459-6596-3(2))* Lion Hudson PLC GBR. Dist: Independent Pubs. Group.

Langford, Norman F. King Nobody Wanted. 2006. 25.95 *(978-1-4218-3214-2(3))*; pap. 10.95 *(978-1-4218-3215-9(1))* 1st World Publishing, Inc.

—The King Nobody Wanted. Lear, John, illus. 2007. (ENG.). 142p. pap. 18.99 *(978-1-4264-9571-7(4))*; 154p. pap. 21.99 *(978-1-4264-9952-4(3))* Creative Media Partners, LLC.

Larsen, Carolyn. Jesus: His Last Days. 2012. (Standard Bible Storybook Ser.). (ENG., Illus.). 32p. (J). 7.99 *(978-0-7847-3566-4(2))* Standard Publishing.

Laubach, Frank. The Story of Jesus: Part 1. Woodworth, Ralph, ed. Aldredge, Terry Beckham, illus. 2005. per. *(978-0-9749168-6-6(2))* FEA Ministries.

—The Story of Jesus: Part 2. Woodworth, Ralph, ed. Aldredge, Terry Beckham, illus. 2005. per. *(978-0-9749168-8-0(9))* FEA Ministries.

Le Guillou, Philippe. Jesús. Pérez, Berta Herreros, tr. Pommier, Maurice, illus. 2008. (Tras Los Pasos de ... Ser.). (SPA.). 128p. (J). (gr. 4-7). pap. 14.95 *(978-84-9801-197-5(3))* Blume ESP. Dist: Independent Pubs. Group.

Malone, Jean M. The Miracle of Easter. Langdo, Bryan, illus. 2010. (Penguin Young Readers, Level 3 Ser.). (ENG.). 48p. (J). (gr. 1-3). pap. 3.99 *(978-0-448-45265-4(0)*, Penguin Young Readers) Penguin Young Readers Group.

Mears, Henrietta C. What Jesus Is All About: Meet the Man Whose Life - & Death - Changed the Course of History. 2004. 140p. pap. 9.99 *(978-0-8307-3332-3(9)*, Gospel Light) Gospel Light Pubns.

Moore, Christopher. Lamb: The Gospel According to Biff, Christ's Childhood Pal. 2004. (gr. 7-12). lib. bdg. 26.95 *(978-0-613-70985-9(3)*, Turtleback) Turtleback Bks.

Morgan, Ellen. Who Was Jesus? 2015. (Who Was... ? Ser.). lib. bdg. 16.00 *(978-0-606-36593-2(1))* Turtleback Bks.

Morgan, Ellen & dePaola, Tomie. Who Was Jesus? Marchesi, Stephen & Harrison, Nancy, illus. 2015. (Who Was? Ser.). (ENG.). 112p. (J). (gr. 3-7). 5.99 *(978-0-448-48320-7(3)*, Grosset & Dunlap) Penguin Young Readers Group.

National Gallery of Art Staff. Jesus of Nazareth: The National Gallery of Art, Washington. (Illus.). 40p. (J). (gr. 1-18). *(978-0-7112-0871-1(9))* ReiseArt Buchhandlung GmbH.

Neff, Merlin L. The Mighty Prince. 2008. (J). *(978-0-8163-2267-1(8))* Pacific Pr. Pubns.

Newton, Richard. The Life of Jesus Christ for the Young. 2007. (ENG.). 204p. pap. 20.99 *(978-1-4346-2211-2(8))*; 224p. pap. 22.99 *(978-1-4346-2271-6(1))* Creative Media Partners, LLC.

—The Life of Jesus Christ for the Young. 2004. reprint ed. pap. 22.95 *(978-1-4191-6962-5(9))*; pap. 1.99 *(978-1-4192-6962-2(3))* Kessinger Publishing, LLC.

—The Life of Jesus Christ for the Young. 2005. pap. 32.00 *(978-1-932474-89-3(7))*; pap. 30.00 *(978-1-932474-88-6(9))* Solid Ground Christian Bks.

O'Reilly, Bill. The Last Days of Jesus: His Life & Times. Low, William & Cobalt Illustrations Studio Staff, illus. 2014. (ENG.). 320p. (J). (gr. 5-12). 19.99 *(978-0-8050-9877-8(1)*, 9780805098778, Holt, Henry & Co. Bks. For Young Readers) Holt, Henry & Co.

—Los Últimos Días de Jesús. Uxó, Carlos, tr. from ENG. Low, William & Cobalt Illustrations Studio Staff, illus. 2015.Tr. of Last Days of Jesus. (SPA & ENG.). 320p. (J). (gr. 5). 25.99 *(978-1-62779-278-3(3)*, 9781627792783, Holt, Henry & Co. Bks. For Young Readers) Holt, Henry & Co.

Paris, Pilar, et al. Jesus Grows Up. 2003. (Illus.). 64p. *(978-2-89088-895-1(9))* Novalis Publishing.

Paterson, Katherine. Life of Jesus for Children. Roca, François, illus. 2008. (J). *(978-0-545-01173-0(6)*, Levine, Arthur A. Bks.) Scholastic, Inc.

Piantedosi, John J. The Gospel for Children. Cioffi, Ben, illus. 2011. (J). pap. *(978-1-56548-370-5(7))* New City Community Pr.

Pingry, Patricia A. The Story of Jesus. Thornburgh, Rebecca, illus. 2008. (ENG.). 32p. (J). (gr. -1-3). pap. 3.95 *(978-0-8249-5545-8(5)*, Ideal Pubns.) Worthy Publishing.

Pulley, Kelly & Zondervan Staff. Jesus Saves the World, 1 vol. Pulley, Kelly, illus. 2009. (I Can Read! / the Beginner's Bible / ¡Yo Sé Leer! Ser.). (SPA & ENG., Illus.). 32p. (J). pap. 3.99 *(978-0-310-71893-2(7))* Zonderkidz.

Roche, Maite. The Beautiful Story of Jesus. Roche, Maite, illus. 2010.Tr. of belle histoire de Jesus. (Illus.). 64p. (J). (gr. k-2). 14.95 *(978-0-8198-1177-6(7))* Pauline Bks. & Media.

Rock, Lois. A Little Life of Jesus. 2004. (Illus.). 352p. (J). pap. 8.99 *(978-0-7459-4878-2(2))* Lion Hudson PLC GBR. Dist: Trafalgar Square Publishing.

—Who Is Jesus? 2007. Orig. Title: Tell Me about Jesus. (Illus.). 21p. (J). 12.95 *(978-0-8198-8313-1(1))* Pauline Bks. & Media.

Sanders, Nancy I. Jesus, 1 vol. 2014. (Get to Know Ser.). (ENG.). 128p. (J). pap. 7.99 *(978-0-310-74516-7(0))* Zonderkidz.

Skevington, Andrea. The Story of Jesus. Ruta, Angelo, illus. 2008. (ENG.). 128p. (J). (gr. 2-4). pap. 16.95 *(978-0-7459-6121-7(5))* Lion Hudson PLC GBR. Dist: Independent Pubs. Group.

Smith, Elwyn Allen. Men Called Him Master. 2007. (ENG.). 188p. pap. 19.99 *(978-1-4264-9607-3(9))*; 208p. pap. 22.99 *(978-1-4264-9988-3(4))* Creative Media Partners, LLC.

Smither, Ethel L. Stories of Jesus. Wiese, Kurt, illus. 2012. 82p. 37.95 *(978-1-258-23282-5(0))*; pap. 22.95 *(978-1-258-24854-3(9))* Literary Licensing, LLC.

Snow, Eliza R. The Story of Jesus. 2011. *(978-1-59955-940-7(4))* Cedar Fort, Inc./CFI Distribution.

St. John, P. Historias Que Jesus Conto (Stories That Jesus Told) (SPA.). 56p. (J). 9.99 *(978-1-56063-589-5(4)*, 498751) Editorial Unilit.

Stiegemeyer, Julie. Bright Easter Day. Spellman, Susan, illus. 2005. 32p. (J). 10.49 *(978-0-7586-0818-5(7))* Concordia Publishing Hse.

Sturtz, Maria Ester H. La Vida de Jesus. 2005. (Illus.). 32p. (J). (gr. -1-4). pap. 6.99 *(978-0-7586-1241-0(9))* Concordia Publishing Hse.

Taylor, Jane & MacKenzie, Carine. Jesus: The Promised Child. 2015. (Bible Wise Ser.). (ENG., Illus.). 32p. (J). (gr. -1-k). pap. 4.50 *(978-1-85792-297-4(2)*, 9781857922974, CF4Kids) Christian Focus Pubns. GBR. Dist: Bookmasters Distribution.

Taylor, Kenneth N. La Vida de Jesús para Ninos Pequenos, 1 vol. 2006.Tr. of Jesus in Pictures for Little Eyes. (SPA.). 128p. (J). (gr. -1-3). 9.99 *(978-0-8254-1704-7(X)*, Editorial Portavoz) Kregel Pubns.

Thomas, Sylvia. Jesus, My Lord. 2012. 36p. pap. 19.99 *(978-1-61904-638-2(5))* Salem Author Services.

Watson, Jane Werner. The Story of Jesus. Smath, Jerry, illus. 2007. (Little Golden Book Ser.). (ENG.). 24p. (J). (gr. -1-k). 4.99 *(978-0-375-83941-2(0)*, Golden Bks.) Random Hse. Children's Bks.

White, Ellen Gould Harmon. Story of Jesus. 2003. (Review Kids Ser.). (Illus.). 142p. (J). 19.99 *(978-0-8280-1765-7(4)*, 196-010) Review & Herald Publishing Assn.

Wilder, John Watson. His Name Is Jesus. 2005. pap. 19.95 *(978-1-4179-9157-0(7))* Kessinger Publishing, LLC.

Williamson, Karen. My Little Life of Jesus, 1 vol. Enright, Amanda, illus. 2014. (ENG.). 68p. (J). 8.99 *(978-1-78128-131-4(9)*, Candle Bks.) Lion Hudson PLC GBR. Dist: Kregel Pubns.

JESUS CHRIST—BIRTH

see Jesus Christ—Nativity

JESUS CHRIST—FICTION

Adams, Michelle Medlock. Little Colt's Palm Sunday. Parmenter, Wayne, illus. 2005. (ENG.). 28p. (J). 14.95 *(978-0-8249-5503-8(X)*, Ideal Pubns.) Worthy Publishing.

—Memories of the Manger. Ettinger, Doris, illus. (J). 2009. (ENG.). 32p. (gr. -1-3). 8.99 *(978-0-8249-5614-1(1))* 2005. (ENG.). 32p. (gr. -1-3). 16.95 *(978-0-8249-5476-5(9))* 2005. *(978-0-8249-5484-0(X))* Worthy Publishing. (Ideal Pubns.).

—The Sparrow's Easter Song. Eldridge, Marion, illus. (ENG.). 32p. (J). 2009. pap. 7.99 *(978-0-8249-5608-0(7))* 2003. 14.95 *(978-0-8249-5470-3(X))* Worthy Publishing. (Ideal Pubns.).

Alborghetti, Marci. The Miracle of the Myrrh. Blondon, Herve, illus. 2003. (J). 16.95 *(978-0-87946-249-9(3)*, 708) ACTA Pubns.

Alexander, Florence & Alexander, Stanley. Jesus Child Is Born: Dare to Be Great. l.t. ed. 2003. (Illus.). 32p. (YA). 7.99 net. *(978-0-915960-85-9(0))* Ebon Research Systems Publishing, LLC.

Alexander, Janice Marie. Princess Panny - Not Princess Nobody. Arkanov, Elvira, illus. 2013. 46p. pap. 21.95 *(978-0-9890410-1-0(8))* Artistic Angels Corp.

Alexander, Marilee. The Wise Man's Last Wish: A Christmas Tale. Nash, Gisele, illus. 2012. (ENG.). 23p. (J). 23.95 *(978-1-4327-8307-5(6))*; pap. 14.95 *(978-1-4327-8040-1(9))* Outskirts Pr., Inc.

Anderson, Ashley. My Day with Jesus. 2010. 26p. pap. 7.99 *(978-0-88144-017-1(5)*, Thorncrown Publishing) Yorkshire Publishing Group.

Anderson, Debby. Jesus Is Alive. 2017. (Cuddle & Sing Ser.). (ENG.). 18p. (J). bds. 5.99 *(978-1-4347-1115-1(3))* Cook, David C.

Aoki, Hisako. Santa's Favorite Story: Santa Tells the Story of the First Christmas. Gantschev, Ivan, illus. 2007. (ENG.). 28p. (J). (gr. -1-3). 9.99 *(978-1-4169-5029-5(X)*, Simon & Schuster Bks. For Young Readers) Simon & Schuster Bks. For Young Readers.

Arroyo, Kritzia. Angel Princess Star. 2008. 18p. 10.28 *(978-1-4303-2776-9(6))* Lulu Pr., Inc.

Arroyo, Madeline. What Matthias Found. Vavak, S. Dean, illus. 2005. 32p. (J). (gr. -1-3). 16.95 *(978-0-9740061-1-6(4))* Stairway Pubns.

Arruda, Suzanne M. A Stocking for Jesus. Ogden, Betina, illus. 2005. (J). pap. 7.95 *(978-0-8198-7076-6(5)*, 332-372) Pauline Bks. & Media.

Austin, Diane Vaughan. The Hideout: A Child's Conversations with Jesus. 2012. 108p. (gr. -1). pap. 12.00 *(978-1-4772-4464-7(6))* AuthorHouse.

Ballou, Bert. Anthony's Amazing Garden. 2011. 20p. pap. 9.99 *(978-1-936750-12-2(0))* Yorkshire Publishing Group.

Banks, Celia. Issy's Gift: A Story about Giving. 2006. (Illus.). 41p. 14.99 *(978-0-9764460-7-1(3))* HonorNet.

Barnhill, Carla. Rufus & the Very Special Baby: A Frolic Christmas Story. Barnhill, Carla, illus. 2016. (Frolic First Faith Ser.). (ENG., Illus.). 32p. (J). (gr. -1-3). 12.99 *(978-1-5064-1762-2(0)*, Sparkhouse Family) Augsburg Fortress, Pubs.

Basal, Patricia. Sammy Discovers Jesus. 2008. 28p. per. 24.95 *(978-1-4241-8400-2(2))* America Star Bks.

Basye, Dottie. The Angel with Big Feet. 2012. 32p. pap. 13.95 *(978-1-4497-3595-1(9)*, WestBow Pr.) Author Solutions, Inc.

Bauer, Marion Dane. The Christmas Baby. Cowdrey, Richard, illus. 2009. (ENG.). 32p. (J). (gr. -1-k). 15.99 *(978-1-4169-7885-5(2)*, Simon & Schuster Bks. For Young Readers) Simon & Schuster Bks. For Young Readers.

Beatty, Connie. Why Owls Say Who. Beatty, Connie & Phillippi, Faith, illus. 2008. 20p. per. 24.95 *(978-1-4137-6715-5(X))* America Star Bks.

Bell, Cheryl. Boy Jesus. 2011. 24p. pap. 10.95 *(978-1-4497-1636-3(9)*, WestBow Pr.) Author Solutions, Inc.

Benoist, Cathy & Gilmore, Cathy. El Conejito de Pascua: El Cuento de un Día Extraordinario. Sundy, Jonathan, illus. 2014. (SPA.). 40p. (J). (gr. 4-7). 16.99 *(978-0-7648-2456-2(2)*, Libros Liguori) Liguori Pubns.

Benton, Ann. Ferdinand: The Engine That Went off the Rails. 2009. (Colour Bks.). (ENG., Illus.). 40p. (J). 7.99 *(978-1-84550-444-1(5)*, 506364f9-0f36-4fc3-909c-1010b7b811f6) Christian Focus Pubns. GBR. Dist: Bookmasters Distribution.

Berenstain, Jan & Berenstain, Mike. The Berenstain Bears, the Very First Christmas, 1 vol. 2015. (Berenstain Bears/Living Lights Ser.). (ENG., Illus.). 24p. (J). pap. 3.99 *(978-0-310-75102-1(0))* Zonderkidz.

Bertola, Ann Marie, et al, contrib. by. Four in the Afternoon. 2003. 118p. pap. 11.99 *(978-0-9743661-0-4(2))* Circle Pr.

Black, Chuck. Kingdom's Reign, 4 bks. Black, Andrea & Black, Brittney, eds. Johnson, Marcella, illus. 2004. 160p. (YA). per. 9.95 *(978-0-9679240-3-8(0))* Perfect Praise Publishing.

Bolme, Edward Sarah. Baby Bible Board Books Collection No. 1: Stories of Jesus, 4 vols. Gillette, Tim, illus. l.t. ed. 2003. 20p. (J). bds. 23.99 *(978-0-9725546-4-0(5))* CREST Pubns.

—Jesus Feeds the People. Gillette, Tim, illus. l.t. ed. 2003. 20p. (J). bds. 6.99 *(978-0-9725546-0-2(2))* CREST Pubns.

—Jesus Heals a Little Girl. Gillette, Tim, illus. l.t. ed. 2003. 20p. (J). bds. 6.99 *(978-0-9725546-1-9(0))* CREST Pubns.

—Jesus Helps a Blind Man. Gillette, Tim, illus. l.t. ed. 2003. 20p. (J). bds. 6.99 *(978-0-9725546-2-6(9))* CREST Pubns.

—Jesus Stops a Storm. Gillette, Tim, illus. l.t. ed. 2003. 20p. (J). bds. 6.99 *(978-0-9725546-3-3(7))* CREST Pubns.

Booth, Anne. Refuge. Usher, Sam, illus. 2016. (ENG.). 32p. (J). (gr. -1-3). 15.99 *(978-0-316-36172-9(0))* Little, Brown Bks. for Young Readers.

Booth, Bradley. Adventures in Galilee. 2011. (J). pap. *(978-0-8163-2506-1(5))* Pacific Pr. Publishing Assn.

Bostrom, Kathleen. The Secret of the Twelve Days of Christmas. Bostrom, Christopher, illus. 2005. 68p. (gr. -1-7). per. 10.95 *(978-1-931195-74-4(9))* KiwE Publishing, Ltd.

Bowman, Crystal. A Star for Jesus, 1 vol. 2014. (ENG.). 14p. (J). bds. 6.99 *(978-0-310-73826-8(1))* Zonderkidz.

—The Story of the Resurrection Eggs, 1 vol. Johnson, Richard G., illus. 2013. (ENG.). 40p. (J). 7.99 *(978-0-310-72595-4(X))* Zonderkidz.

Brent, Isabelle. The Christmas Horse & the Three Wise Men. 2016. (ENG., Illus.). 28p. (J). (gr. k-3). 17.95 *(978-1-937786-61-8(7)*, Wisdom Tales) World Wisdom, Inc.

Brock Bryant, Anita. Abcs of Advent. 2009. 40p. pap. 16.99 *(978-1-4490-3151-0(X))* AuthorHouse.

Broughton, Pamela & Watson, Jane Werner. Miracles of Jesus. Smath, Jerry, illus. 2009. (Little Golden Book Ser.). (ENG.). 24p. (J). (gr. -1-2). 4.99 *(978-0-375-85623-5(4)*, Golden Inspirational) Random Hse. Children's Bks.

Brown, Donna. Crippled Like Me. 2009. 36p. pap. 14.75 *(978-1-60693-986-4(6)*, Eloquent Bks.) Strategic Book Publishing & Rights Agency (SBPRA).

Brown, Margery W. Baby Jesus Like My Brother. 2008. (Illus.). 32p. 6.95 *(978-1-60349-000-9(0)*, Marimba Bks.) Hudson Publishing Group, The.

Burow, Ginger. The Night That Was Christmas, 1 vol. 2009. 21p. pap. 24.95 *(978-1-4489-9842-5(5))* America Star Bks.

Buxton, Jamie. Temple Boys. 2015. (ENG.). 288p. (YA). (gr. 7). 17.99 *(978-1-62672-036-7(3))* Roaring Brook Pr.

Bynum, Jeff. Blinky. 2008. 24p. pap. 10.49 *(978-1-4389-2331-4(7))* AuthorHouse.

Campbell, Jeffrey. St. Francis & the Christmas Miracle of Greccio. Bianco, Francesca, illus. 2014. (ENG.). 28p. (J). 14.95 *(978-0-9796766-3-5(0)*, Tau Publishing) Vesuvius Pr. Inc.

Campos Eichelberger, Misty. Who Is Santa? & Where Did He Come From? 2009. 16p. pap. 9.49 *(978-1-4490-1857-3(2))* AuthorHouse.

Cannon, Sherrill S. Santa's Birthday Gift. 2009. 24p. pap. 11.50 *(978-1-60860-824-9(7)*, Eloquent Bks.) Strategic Book Publishing & Rights Agency (SBPRA).

Carlson, Melody. Benjamin's Box: The Story of the Resurrection Eggs, 1 vol. Stockman, Jack, illus. rev. ed. 2008. (ENG.). 40p. (J). (gr. -1-3). 8.99 *(978-0-310-71505-4(9))* Zonderkidz.

Carroll, Harlisha. Miracle Mouse & Jesus Book #3: Short Stories 2. 2013. 32p. pap. 24.95 *(978-1-4626-6647-8(7))* America Star Bks.

Chavez, Joe. Benny the Bunny & Jesus. 2013. 136p. (J). pap. 9.99 *(978-1-62697-463-0(2))* Salem Author Services.

Christ Legends & Other Stories. 2012. 204p. pap. *(978-1-84902-141-8(4))* Benediction Classics.

Christensen, Catherine. Emily's Perfect Christmas Tree. 2015. (J). 14.99 *(978-1-4621-1750-5(3))* Cedar Fort, Inc./CFI Distribution.

Church, Peggy Pond. Shoes for the Santo Niño. Carrillo, Charles M., illus. 2013. 64p. 25.95 *(978-1-936744-23-7(6)*, Rio Grande Bks.) LPD Pr.

—Shoes for the Santo Niño: Zapitillos para el Santo Niño: A Bilingual Tale. Carrillo, Charles M., illus. 2009. (SPA & ENG.). 61p. (J). pap. *(978-1-890689-64-3(5)*, Rio Grande Bks.) LPD Pr.

Columbro, Judy. The Gift of Rainbows. Scottorosano, Deborah, illus. 2011. 24p. pap. 24.95 *(978-1-4626-0355-8(6))* PublishAmerica, Inc.

Colvin, Adele Bibb. The Donkey's Easter Tale, 1 vol. Carmichael, Peyton, illus. 2008. (Donkey Tales Ser.). (ENG.). 32p. (J). (gr. k-3). 16.99 *(978-1-58980-593-4(3))* Pelican Publishing Co., Inc.

Correa, Alvaro. Mountain Miracle: A Navtivity Story. Lorenzo, Gloria, illus. 2008. 94p. (J). (gr. -1). pap. 14.95 *(978-1-933271-23-1(X))* Circle Pr.

Cowan, Dolly. Yeehaw, the Chosen Donkey. 2012. 26p. pap. 13.95 *(978-1-4497-6675-7(7)*, WestBow Pr.) Author Solutions, Inc.

Dacey, Richard. Spinner McClock & the Christmas Visit. Gillett, Hallie, illus. 2004. 32p. (J). 13.95 *(978-1-929039-24-1(7))* Ambassador Bks., Inc.

Dateno, Maria Grace. Braving the Storm, 6 vols., Vol. 2. Cunningham, Paul, illus. 2013. 70p. (J). pap. 5.95 *(978-0-8198-1204-9(8))* Pauline Bks. & Media.

—Courageous Quest. Cunningham, Paul, illus. 2014. 81p. (J). pap. 5.95 *(978-0-8198-1628-3(0))* Pauline Bks. & Media.

—Danger at Sea. Cunningham, Paul, illus. 2013. 80p. (J). pap. 5.95 *(978-0-8198-1891-1(7))* Pauline Bks. & Media.

—Mystery of the Missing Jars. Cunningham, Paul, illus. 2014. 77p. (J). 5.95 *(978-0-8198-4922-9(7))* Pauline Bks. & Media.

—Shepherds to the Rescue, 6 vols., Vol. 1. Cunningham, Paul, illus. 2013. 71p. (J). pap. 5.95 *(978-0-8198-7251-7(2))* Pauline Bks. & Media.

David, Juliet. The First Christmas, 1 vol. Denham, Gemma, illus. 2008. (Candle Playbook Ser.). 18p. (J). bds. 7.99 *(978-0-8254-7377-7(2)*, Candle Bks.) Lion Hudson PLC GBR. Dist: Kregel Pubns.

—The Midnight Visitors, 1 vol. Parry, Jo, illus. 2015. 32p. (J). 14.99 *(978-1-78128-233-5(1)*, Candle Bks.) Lion Hudson PLC GBR. Dist: Kregel Pubns.

Davidson, Alice Joyce. My Day with Jesus, 1 vol. Clar, David Austin, illus. 2005. (Easter Board Bks.). (ENG.). 16p. (J). bds. 3.99 *(978-0-310-70843-8(5))* Zonderkidz.

Debecker, Benoit & Benoît, Debecker. La Primera Navidad de los Animales. 2005. (Montana Encantada Ser.). (SPA., Illus.). 48p. (J). (gr. k-2). pap. 8.50 *(978-84-241-1675-0(5))* Lectorum Pubns., Inc.

Denger, Monique. Who Colored the Rainbow, Mimi? 2010. 40p. pap. 16.99 *(978-1-4490-6166-1(4))* AuthorHouse.

dePaola, Tomie. The Birds of Bethlehem. dePaola, Tomie, illus. 2012. (ENG., Illus.). 40p. (J). (gr. -1-k). 16.99 *(978-0-399-25780-3(2)*, Nancy Paulsen Books) Penguin Young Readers Group.

Derico, Laura Ring. Easter Surprises. Harris, Phyllis, illus. 2015. (Faith That Sticks Bks.). (ENG.). 26p. (J). pap. 3.99 *(978-1-4964-0311-7(8))* Tyndale Hse. Pubs.

DeStefano, Anthony. Little Star. Elliott, Mark, illus. 2013. (ENG.). 36p. (J). 14.99 *(978-0-7369-5859-2(2))* Harvest Hse. Pubs.

—The Puppy That No One Wanted. Cowdrey, Richard, illus. 2015. (ENG.). 32p. 14.99 *(978-1-61636-928-6(0)*, Servant Bks.) Franciscan Media.

Deweerd, Jamison. Priceless. 2013. 32p. pap. 13.95 *(978-1-4497-9077-6(1)*, WestBow Pr.) Author Solutions, Inc.

Dineen, Kaite. What Santa Wants You to Know: A Story of Santa's Love for Jesus, 1 vol. 2010. 34p. pap. 24.95 *(978-1-4489-7071-1(7))* PublishAmerica, Inc.

Dumont, Claire. Noel: An Unforgettable Night! 2017. (ENG., Illus.). 32p. (J). 14.95 **(978-0-8091-6780-7(8))** Paulist Pr.

Edwards, Carol. Jacy Faces Evil: Jacy's Search for Jesus Book III. Frey, Daniel J., illus. 2008. 32p. (J). 15.95 *(978-0-9755314-3-3(3))* Majestic Publishing, LLC.

—Jacy's Search for Jesus Frey, Daniel J., illus. 2005. 31p. (J). (gr. -1-3). 15.95 *(978-0-9755314-0-2(9))* Majestic Publishing, LLC.

Elkins, Christy. Sir Stinks-A-Lot. 2010. (ENG.). 43p. pap. 12.00 *(978-0-557-34847-3(1))* Lulu Pr., Inc.

Elliott, Rebecca. Not So Silent Night! Elliott, Rebecca, illus. 2016. (ENG., Illus.). 5p. (J). (— 1). bds. 7.99 *(978-0-7459-6560-4(1))* Lion Hudson PLC GBR. Dist: Independent Pubs. Group.

Entinger, Chad. A Deaf Boy Meets Jesus. Schofield-Farmer, Twila, illus. 2011. 42p. (J). 10.00 *(978-1-59799-082-0(5))* Deaf Missions.

Falk, Karen. Tacianna & the Endless Ball of String. 2006. 83p. pap. 19.95 *(978-1-4241-3287-4(8))* PublishAmerica, Inc.

Fals, Mary. The Chosen Colt. 2009. 40p. pap. 18.49 *(978-1-4389-9417-8(6))* AuthorHouse.

Felden, Georgia. When Jesus Hired Santa. 2006. (J). pap. *(978-0-9790444-8-9(0))* Dynasty Publishing, Inc.

Felton, Jerilyn E. The Master's Companion: A Christian Midrash. 2007. (Illus.). 134p. 16.75 *(978-0-88489-936-5(5))* St. Mary's Pr. of MN.

Ferguson, Sinclair B. Big Book of Bible Truths 2. Apps, Fred, illus. 2008. (ENG.). 64p. (J). pap. 14.99 *(978-1-84550-372-7(4)*, 9781845503727) Christian Focus Pubns. GBR. Dist: Bookmasters Distribution.

Fischer, Jean & Thomas Nelson Publishing Staff. A Star for Me, 1 vol. Steele-Morgan, Alexandra, illus. 2014. (ENG.). 20p. (J). bds. 14.99 *(978-0-529-11212-5(4))* Nelson, Thomas Inc.

Fleming, Theresa. Going Home with Jesus, 1 vol. Fleming, Yvonne B., illus. 2009. 22p. pap. 24.95 *(978-1-60813-703-9(1))* America Star Bks.

Fletcher, Susan. Alphabet of Dreams. 2008. (ENG., Illus.). 432p. (YA). (gr. 7-12). mass mkt. 7.99 *(978-0-689-85152-0(9)*, Simon Pulse) Simon Pulse.

Flinn, Lias. Unwrapping the Christmas Creche. 18.00 *(978-0-687-05441-1(9))* Abingdon Pr.

Flinn, Lisa & Younger, Barbara. The Christmas Garland. Corvino, Lucy, tr. Corvino, Lucy, illus. 2003. 32p. (J). 14.95 *(978-0-8249-5460-4(2),* Ideal Pubns.) Worthy Publishing.
Fogle, Robin. The Legend of the Candy Cane. 2006. (J). pap. 1.79 *(978-1-59317-158-2(7))* Warner Pr., Inc.
Foster, Lisa. 5 Little Tomatoes. 2008. 44p. pap. 17.95 *(978-1-4327-2306-4(5))* Outskirts Pr., Inc.
Fox, Ruth M. The Bible, in Story, from the Beginning. 2012. 156p. pap. 53.99 *(978-1-4497-7351-9(6),* WestBow Pr.) Author Solutions, Inc.
Freddie. The Rooster's Story. 2009. 28p. pap. 13.99 *(978-1-4389-8827-6(3))* AuthorHouse.
Freeman, Emily. God Bless Your Way: A Christmas Journey. Burr, Dan, illus. 2007. 32p. (J). (gr. -1-3). 19.95 incl. audio compact disk *(978-1-59038-806-8(2))* Deseret Bk. Co.
Froeb, Lori C. The Most Holy Night. Sakamoto, Miki, illus. 2015. (Pop & Play Ser.). (ENG.). 12p. (J). (gr. -1-k). 12.99 *(978-0-7944-3239-3(5))* Reader's Digest Assn., Inc., The.
Gamble, Adam. Good Night Baby Jesus. 2010. (Good Night Our World Ser.). (ENG.). 20p. (J). (gr. k — 1). bds. 9.95 *(978-1-60219-049-8(6))* Good Night Bks.
Gibson, Beatrice. The Legend of the Sandals. 2008. 28p. pap. 15.99 *(978-1-4363-9169-6(5))* Xlibris Corp.
Gilmore, Cathy & Benoist, Carol. Easter Bunny's AMAZING Day. Sundy, Jonathan, illus. 2011. (ENG.). 40p. (J). 15.99 *(978-0-9847656-1-4(1))* I.H.S. Pubs.
Ginolfi, Art. The Tiny Star. 2005. 32p. (J). pap. 3.99 *(978-1-4003-0683-1(3))* Nelson, Thomas Inc.
Giordano, Paula J. The Honey Bees Going to a New School. 2012. 30p. 29.99 *(978-1-61996-501-0(1));* pap. 19.99 *(978-1-61996-500-3(3))* Salem Author Services.
Gloria, Truitt. Baby Jesus Is Born. 2004. (Illus.). 16p. (J). 1.99 *(978-0-7586-0635-8(4))* Concordia Publishing Hse.
Godwin, Laura & Buck, Nola. A Christmas Goodnight. Wright, Sarah Jane, illus. 2011. (ENG.). 24p. (J). (gr. -1-k). 12.99 *(978-0-06-166491-5(X),* Tegen, Katherine Bks) HarperCollins Pubs.
Gooch-Anderson, Stacy. The Legend of the Star. 2009. (Illus.). (J). 15.99 *(978-1-59955-243-9(4))* Cedar Fort, Inc./CFI Distribution.
Gorla, Stefano. A Donkey's Tale. Marchetti, Angela, illus. 2013. 64p. (J). pap. 9.95 *(978-0-8198-1901-7(8))* Pauline Bks. & Media.
Gould, M. & Gould, R. About Gossip: What Would Jesus Do, 1 vol. Hurst, Debbie, illus. 2009. 28p. pap. 24.95 *(978-1-60749-680-9(1))* America Star Bks.
Grant, Cindy M. Itty-Bitty Jesus Is Born Christmas Storybook. 2005. (J). pap. 1.29 *(978-1-59317-117-9(X))* Warner Pr., Inc.
Guiffre, William. Angelita's Song. Baron, Cheri Ann, illus. 2008. 32p. (J). (gr. -1-3). pap. 9.95 *(978-1-931650-36-6(5))* Bks. for Children Publishing.
—The First Gift of Christmas. Baron, Cheri Ann, illus. 2008. 32p. (J). (gr. -1-3). pap. 9.95 *(978-1-931650-33-5(0))* Bks. for Children Publishing.
Guiffre, William A. Angelita's Song. Baron, Cheri Ann, illus. 2008. 32p. (J). (gr. -1-3). lib. bdg. 17.95 *(978-1-931650-30-4(6))* Bks. for Children Publishing.
Hall, Stephen M. The Shepherd's Son. 2013. 36p. 25.99 *(978-1-4808-0112-7(7));* pap. 16.99 *(978-1-4808-0078-6(3))* Archway Publishing.
Hallinan, P. K. I Know Jesus Loves Me. Hallinan, P. K., illus. 2014. (Illus.). 18p. (J). pap. 6.99 *(978-0-8249-5663-9(X),* Ideal Pubns.) Worthy Publishing.
—I Know Jesus Loves Me. 2007. (ENG., Illus.). 28p. (J). (gr. -1-3). 8.99 *(978-0-8249-5553-3(6),* Ideal Pubns.) Worthy Publishing.
—That's What a Friend Is! 2003. (ENG.). 24p. (J). bds. 6.95 *(978-0-8249-5468-0(8),* Ideal Pubns.) Worthy Publishing.
Harp, Georgeanna. This Is Your Earthday. 2009. 32p. pap. 14.62 *(978-1-4251-7064-6(1))* Trafford Publishing.
Harrast, Tracy. Oh Holy Night. Corke, Estelle, illus. 2006. 10p. (J). (gr. -1-k). bds. 10.49 *(978-0-7586-1129-1(3))* Concordia Publishing Hse.
Hartman, Bob. The Big Pig Stampede: And a Bunch More Amazing Miracles. 2015. (Goat Boy Chronicles Ser.). (ENG., Illus.). 192p. (J). 12.99 *(978-1-4964-0865-5(9))* Tyndale Hse. Pubs.
—Easter Angels. Williams, Sophy, illus. 2010. (ENG.). 32p. (J). (gr. 2-4). 14.99 *(978-0-7459-6922-0(4))* Lion Hudson PLC GBR. Dist: Independent Pubs. Group.
Hartman, Bob & Abel, Simone. Who Frightened the Fishermen? (Illus.). 48p. pap. 6.99 *(978-0-7459-4987-1(8))* Lion Hudson PLC GBR. Dist: Trafalgar Square Publishing.
Harvey, Charlene A. The Adventures of the Tiger Club. 2011. 14p. pap. 10.99 *(978-1-61215-027-7(6))* Salem Author Services.
Hays, Phillip. Porka-Bella-Snu & the Mystery of the Letters. Spencer, Chip, illus. 2013. 54p. pap. 6.95 *(978-1-938679-05-6(9))* Written World Communications.
Helldorfer, M. C. Daniel's Gift. 2013. (ENG., Illus.). 32p. (J). (gr. -1-3). 16.99 *(978-1-4814-2141-6(7),* Atheneum Bks. for Young Readers) Simon & Schuster Children's Publishing.
Hennessey, David G. A Cricket's Christmas: the Bethlehem Story. 2009. 151p. pap. 15.30 *(978-0-557-04685-0(8))* Lulu Pr., Inc.
Henry, Juliann. The Little Shepherd Girl: A Christmas Story. Madsen, Jim, illus. 2007. 32p. (J). (gr. -1-3). 14.99 *(978-0-7814-4513-9(2))* Cook, David C.
Herzog, Kimberly. All That We Could Give. 2013. 24p. pap. 24.95 *(978-1-63000-830-7(3))* America Star Bks.
Heyer, Carol. Humphrey's First Christmas. Heyer, Carol, illus. 2008. (ENG., Illus.). 32p. (J). (gr. -1-3). 14.99 *(978-0-8249-5559-5(5),* Ideal Pubns.) Worthy Publishing.
—Humphrey's First Palm Sunday. Heyer, Carol, illus. 2012. (Illus.). 32p. (J). 14.99 *(978-0-8249-5636-3(2),* Ideal Pubns.) Worthy Publishing.
Hildahl, Melita K. Life Is an Adventure with Ernie. 2008. 156p. per. 15.99 *(978-1-60477-139-8(9))* Salem Author Services.
Hillenbrand, Will. Asleep in the Stable. 2004. (ENG., Illus.). 32p. (J). (gr. k-3). tchr. ed. 16.95 *(978-0-8234-1824-4(3))* Holiday Hse., Inc.
Hopkins, Lee Bennett. Mary's Song. Alcorn, Stephen, illus. 2012. (ENG.). 32p. (J). 17.00 *(978-0-8028-5397-4(8),* Eerdmans Bks For Young Readers) Eerdmans, William B. Publishing Co.
Horner, Susan. The Mission: An Angel's Most Important Assignment. Allen, Joe, illus. 2006. pap. 10.99 *(978-1-59317-148-3(X))* Warner Pr., Inc.
Howie, Vicki. The Easter Swallows. Grudina, Paola Bertolini, illus. 2007. 32p. (J). 10.95 *(978-0-8198-2360-1(0))* Pauline Bks. & Media.
Hulslander, Dyan. I Just Love You So Much. Heaton, Jr., illus. 2009. 28p. pap. 14.49 *(978-1-4490-0454-5(7))* AuthorHouse.
Hunt, Angela Elwell. Los Tres Árboles: Cento Tradicional. Jonke, Tim, illus. 2010. Orig. Title: The Tale of Three Trees - A Traditional Folktale. (SPA & ENG.). 32p. (J). 5.99 *(978-1-4143-3737-1(X))* Tyndale Hse. Pubs.
Ippolito, Eva Marie. The Donkey's Tale. Ippolito, Eva Marie, illus. 2003. (Illus.). lll, 15p. (J). (gr. -1-3). pap. 1.95 *(978-0-9705350-3-0(1))* Ippolito, Eva Marie.
Jackson, Leona Novy. The Littlest Christmas Kitten. Dupre, Kelly, illus. 2005. 32p. (J). 16.00 *(978-0-930643-18-8(6),* 1250560) Images Unlimited Publishing.
Jacob's Gift. 2004. (Max Lucado Ser.). 32p. 19.99 incl. DVD *(978-1-4003-0182-9(3))* Nelson, Thomas Inc.
Jaxland, Sheila. Mylo. 2013. 32p. pap. 12.95 *(978-0-578-12595-4(1))* Roald Publishing.
Jeanmarie, Michele. Curiosity, Curiosity: Lost in an Array. 2008. 74p. pap. 19.95 *(978-1-60610-169-8(2))* America Star Bks.
Jeffs, Stephanie. Llygoden y Nadolig. Wyn, Delyth, tr. from ENG. Thorne, Jenny, illus. 2005. (WEL.). 28p. *(978-1-85994-497-4(3))* Cyhoeddiadau'r Gair.
Jenkins, Barbie. The Legend of the Christmas Kiss. 2010. (ENG.). 32p. pap. 11.99 *(978-1-4391-9623-6(0),* Howard Bks.) Howard Books.
Jensen, Kimberly. Always the Elf. Harmon, Glenn, illus. 2007. 38p. (J). (gr. -1-3). 15.99 *(978-1-59955-086-2(5))* Cedar Fort, Inc./CFI Distribution.
Johnson-Carrigan, Ettarose. Old Rugged: How the Tree Became the Cross. 2008. 24p. pap. 11.99 *(978-1-4389-2781-7(9))* AuthorHouse.
Joslin, Mary. The Fourth Wise Man. Johnson, Richard, illus. 2007. 28p. (J). (gr. -1-2). 14.99 *(978-0-7814-4545-0(0))* Cook, David C.
Kennedy, Pamela. Easter in the Garden. Wenzel, David T., illus. 2008. (ENG.). 32p. (J). (gr. -1-3). 12.99 *(978-0-8249-5577-9(3),* Ideal Pubns.) Worthy Publishing.
King, Emily. Clopper & the Lost Boy, 1 vol. Olson, Ed, illus. 2009. 32p. (J). 12.99 *(978-0-8254-2946-0(3))* Kregel Pubns.
—Clopper & the Night Travelers. Olson, Ed, illus. 2007. 32p. (J). (gr. -1-3). 10.99 *(978-0-8254-3066-4(6))* Kregel Pubns.
Koch, Theresa F. The Gift of Laughter. 2007. 16p. per. 24.95 *(978-1-4241-8343-2(X))* America Star Bks.
Konecny, Linda. Dave's First Christmas. 2011. 26p. pap. 9.99 *(978-1-61379-817-1(2))* Salem Author Services.
Lagerlöf, Selma. Christ Legends. 2004. pap. 14.95 *(978-0-8095-9388-0(2));* 196p. 29.95 *(978-0-8095-9883-0(3))* Wildside Pr., LLC.
—Christ Legends: & Other Stories. 2010. 200p. pap. 44.50 *(978-1-4092-0934-8(2))* Lulu Pr., Inc.
Lamson, Deborah Ann. The Nativity Lighting. 2008. (Illus.). 36p. pap. 15.95 *(978-1-4343-9521-4(9))* AuthorHouse.
Lang, Gordon. Everyday Encounters: Face to Face with Jesus. 2003. 115p. per. 14.95 *(978-1-932338-19-5(5))* Lifevest Publishing, Inc.
Lewis, Norma. Where Jesus Slept. Hudson, Katy, illus. 2016. (J). *(978-0-8249-5679-0(6),* Ideal Pubns.) Worthy Publishing.
Lingenfelter, Libby. The Watermelon Story. 2010. 36p. pap. 21.99 *(978-1-4535-2683-5(8))* Xlibris Corp.
Little Fish Jesus Merchandiser. (J). 128.16 *(978-0-8307-2907-4(0),* Gospel Light) Gospel Light Pubns.
Lloyd-Jones, Sally. The Jesus Storybook Bible: Every Story Whispers His Name, 1 vol. Jago, illus. 2007. (ENG.). 352p. (J). (gr. -1-3). 17.99 *(978-0-310-70825-4(7))* Zonderkidz.
—Song of the Stars, 1 vol. Jay, Alison, illus. 2015. (ENG.). 32p. (J). bds. 7.99 *(978-0-310-73630-1(7))* Zonderkidz.
Lockhart, Linda J. A Little Angel Dressed in Red. 2006. (J). pap. 8.00 *(978-0-8059-6923-8(3))* Dorrance Publishing Co., Inc.
Logan, Laura, illus. Jesus Loves Me. 2008. (ENG.). 20p. (J). (gr. -1). bds. 12.99 *(978-0-8249-6730-7(5),* Ideal Pubns.) Worthy Publishing.
Long, Mary Evelyn Curton. The First Christmas Gift. 2012. 16p. (-18). pap. 15.99 *(978-1-4772-8836-8(8))* AuthorHouse.
Lord, Jill Roman. If Jesus Walked Beside Me. Wummer, Amy, illus. 2014. (If Jesus Ser.). 22p. (J). bds. 6.99 *(978-0-8249-1920-7(3),* Ideal Pubns.) Worthy Publishing.
Lozano, Neal. Will You Bless Me? Hatke, Ben, illus. 2009. 32p. (J). lib. bdg. 16.95 *(978-1-883551-32-2(3),* MCP-323, Maple Corners Press) Attic Studio Publishing Hse.
Lucado, Max. Itsy Bitsy Christmas: You're Never Too Little for His Love, 1 vol. 2013. (ENG., Illus.). 32p. (J). pap. 9.99 *(978-1-4003-2404-0(1))* Nelson, Thomas Inc.
Luther, Martin. Away in a Manger. Julien, Terry, illus. 2015. (Faith That Sticks Bks.). (ENG.). 24p. (J). pap. 3.99 *(978-1-4964-0318-6(5))* Tyndale Hse. Pubs.
MacDonald, Maryann. The Christmas Cat. Bates, Amy June, illus. 2013. (ENG.). 32p. (J). (gr. -1-k). 16.99 *(978-0-8037-3498-2(0),* Dial Bks) Penguin Young Readers Group.
Mackall, Dandi Daley. One Small Donkey, 1 vol. 2016. (ENG., Illus.). 32p. (J). 14.99 *(978-0-7180-8747-0(X))* Nelson, Thomas Inc.
—The Shepherd's Christmas Story. Catalano, Dominic, illus. 2005. 32p. (J). (gr. 1-5). 12.99 *(978-0-7586-0904-5(3))* Concordia Publishing Hse.
—The Story of the Easter Robin, 1 vol. Vojtech, Anna, illus. 2010. (ENG.). 32p. (J). (gr. -1-2). 15.99 *(978-0-310-71331-9(5))* Zonderkidz.
Mackall, Dandi Daley, adapted by. El Pastorcito: Para ninos de 4-7 Anos.Tr. of Little Shepherd. (SPA.). 32p. 3.99 *(978-0-7586-0362-3(2))* Concordia Publishing Hse.
MacKenzie, Carine. How God Changes People: Conversion Stories from the Bible. 2012. (ENG., Illus.). 48p. (J). 9.99 *(978-1-84550-822-7(X),* e5e27b55-010c-4952-912d-4d962f516ac6) Christian Focus Pubns. GBR. Dist: Bookmasters Distribution.
Marsh, Carole. The Legend of the Candy Cane. 2003. 12p. (J). (gr. k-4). pap. 2.95 *(978-0-635-02124-3(2))* Gallopade International.
Marshall, Geraldine Ann. Spider's Gift: A Christmas Story. Sorge, Rebecca, illus. 2016. 40p. (J). pap. 14.95 *(978-0-8198-9058-0(8))* Pauline Bks. & Media.
Martin, Jann. This Babe So Small. 2007. 32p. pap. 11.95 *(978-1-933916-13-2(3))* Nelson Publishing & Marketing.
Martinez, Roland. The Angel with Red Wings. Graphic Manufacture, illus. 2008. 27p. pap. 24.95 *(978-1-60672-713-3(3))* America Star Bks.
Matson, Carole. Jesus Loves Dirt Bikes Too!! 2009. 33p. pap. 15.40 *(978-0-557-15092-2(2))* Lulu Pr., Inc.
McCarthy, Margaret. The Cat Did Not Know. Molloy, Sophie, illus. 2006. (ENG.). 36p. (J). pap. 14.95 *(978-1-85390-923-8(8))* Veritas Pubns. IRL. Dist: Dufour Editions, Inc.
McCaughrean, Geraldine. The Jesse Tree. Willey, Bee, illus. 2005. 93p. (J). (gr. k). 20.00 *(978-0-8028-5288-5(2),* Eerdmans Bks For Young Readers) Eerdmans, William B. Publishing Co.
McCoy, Jacquelyn. The Heavenly Hen. 2010. 28p. 13.54 *(978-1-4269-4606-6(6))* Trafford Publishing.
McCurdy, Steve. Keeper at the Inn. Lohmann, Stephanie, illus. 2007. 36p. 17.95 *(978-0-9761179-2-6(4))* StoryMaster Pr.
McElligott, Walter Lee. A Blessed Bethlehem Birth: As told by Abraham & Anna Mousenstern. Collier, Kevin Scott, illus. 2006. 28p. (J). E-Book 5.00 incl. cd-rom *(978-1-933090-21-4(9))* Guardian Angel Publishing, Inc.
McKissick, Angela Lorraine (Dame). Jonathan & Elizabeth Meet Jesus of Nazareth. 2013. 28p. pap. 24.95 *(978-1-4626-8916-3(7))* America Star Bks.
Metlen, Ryan W. & Metlen, Ryan. Ewe. 2009. (J). *(978-1-58768-054-0(8),* HiddenSpring) Paulist Pr.
Meyers, David. The Illustrated Life of Jesus: Through the Gospels, Arranged Chronologically. 2005. (Illus.). 304p. *(978-1-59258-125-2(0))* Hylas Publishing.
Michaels, M. J. The Snow Angels' Christmas. Nausley, Kathy, illus. 2016. (ENG.). 24p. (J). (gr. -1-1). 14.95 *(978-1-63322-124-6(5),* Seagrass) Quarto Publishing Group USA.
Milbourne, Anna. Very First Christmas. 2006. 24p. (J). 9.99 *(978-0-7945-1474-7(X),* Usborne) EDC Publishing.
Monson, Marianne. The Enchanted Tunnel Vol. 3: Journey to Jerusalem. Burr, Dan, illus. 2011. (J). (gr. 3-6). pap. 7.99 *(978-1-60908-068-6(8))* Deseret Bk. Co.
Montgomery Gibson, Jane. Jesus Is! Montgomery Gibson, Jane, illus. 2005. (Illus.). (J). bds. 8.99 *(978-1-4183-0033-3(0))* Christ Inspired, Inc.
—Jesus Loves Me. Montgomery Gibson, Jane, illus. 2005. (Illus.). (J). bds. 8.99 *(978-1-4183-0048-7(9))* Christ Inspired, Inc.
Morning, Carey. The Shepherd Girl of Bethlehem: A Nativity Story. Marks, Alan, illus. 2016. (ENG.). 32p. (J). (gr. -1-k). pap. 8.99 *(978-0-7459-6232-0(7))* Lion Hudson PLC GBR. Dist: Independent Pubs. Group.
Murphy, Patty. I Wonder Who? 2012. 32p. pap. 24.95 *(978-1-4626-6258-6(7))* America Star Bks.
Murphy, Paul. The 13th Apostle. 2004. 224p. pap. 11.99 *(978-1-58169-142-9(4),* 3000, Evergreen Pr.) Genesis Communications, Inc.
Napoli, Donna Jo. Song of the Magdalene. 2004. (ENG., Illus.). 256p. (YA). (gr. 7). pap. 12.99 *(978-0-689-87396-6(4),* Simon Pulse) Simon Pulse.
Navillus, Nell. God's Christmas Gift. McCallum, Jodie, illus. 2006. (J). *(978-1-58173-595-6(2))* Sweetwater Pr.
—Happy Birthday, Jesus. McCallum, Jodie, illus. 2007. (J). *(978-1-60261-264-8(1))* Cliff Road Bks.
Neuhofer, Sheri L. Courageous Warrior. Amory, Deanna & O'Hara, Cynthia, illus. 2010. 28p. pap. 10.95 *(978-0-9787472-7-5(5))* Ajoyin Publishing, Inc.
Nikola-lisa, W. & Nikola-lisa, W. Hallelujah! A Christmas Celebration. Saint James, Synthia, illus. 2009. (ENG.). 36p. (J). (gr. -1-3). 10.99 *(978-1-4424-0224-9(5),* Atheneum Bks. for Young Readers) Simon & Schuster Children's Publishing.
Nunes, Ernest. Oh! How I Wish I Could Play Soccer with Ernie & the Dreamers. 2013. 70p. pap. 12.99 *(978-1-62509-705-7(0))* Salem Author Services.
Obasi, Lucy. My Short Story of Jesus on Earth. 2012. 26p. pap. 10.95 *(978-1-4497-3920-1(2),* WestBow Pr.) Author Solutions, Inc.
Olsen, Bevan. Bethlehem's Star. 2008. 16p. pap. 2.99 *(978-1-59955-181-4(0))* Cedar Fort, Inc./CFI Distribution.
—The Innkeeper's Christmas. 2010. (Illus.). 12p. (J). pap. 2.99 *(978-1-59955-433-4(X))* Cedar Fort, Inc./CFI Distribution.
—The Magi. 2011. (Illus.). 12p. (J). pap. 2.99 *(978-1-59955-924-7(2),* Bonneville Bks.) Cedar Fort, Inc./CFI Distribution.
Olson, Kris C. The Shepherd & the Wolf. 2006. 51p. pap. 16.95 *(978-1-4241-1655-3(4))* PublishAmerica, Inc.
Page, Nick & Page, Claire. Finger Puppet Books Christmas Story. 2009. (Finger Puppet Bks.). (Illus.). 12p. (gr. -1-k). bds. 12.99 *(978-1-84610-573-9(0))* Make Believe Ideas GBR. Dist: Nelson, Thomas Inc.
Pantelides, Sherry. It's Red Like Me! A Story about the Blood of Jesus. Perez, Debi, illus. 2007. (J). lib. bdg. 12.99 *(978-0-9771076-0-5(4))* Lacey Productions.
Park, Linda Sue. The Third Gift. Ibatoulline, Bagram, illus. 2011. (ENG.). 32p. (J). (gr. 1-4). 16.99 *(978-0-547-20195-5(8))* Houghton Mifflin Harcourt Publishing Co.
Petersen, Alicia. Out of Darkness. 2007. (Illus.). 177p. (J). (gr. 3-7). per. 8.99 *(978-1-59166-822-0(0))* BJU Pr.
—A Sparrow Alone. 2004. 154p. (YA). 8.99 *(978-1-59166-204-4(4))* BJU Pr.
Phillips, Dixie. Angel Eyes. Sponaugle, Kim, illus. 2008. 24p. pap. 10.95 *(978-1-933090-74-0(X))* Guardian Angel Publishing, Inc.
—Baby Jesus Is Missing. Snider, K. C., illus. 2009. 16p. pap. 9.95 *(978-1-61633-000-2(7))* Guardian Angel Publishing, Inc.
Phillips, Dixie & Sharon, et al. Bethlehem's King Size Bed. 2013. 24p. pap. 7.95 *(978-1-61633-423-9(1))* Guardian Angel Publishing, Inc.
Phillips, Shirley. The Best Gift. 2012. 20p. pap. 10.95 *(978-1-4497-4229-4(7),* WestBow Pr.) Author Solutions, Inc.
Pigman, Shari. Little Frog Finds Jesus. 2005. 23p. (J). 12.67 *(978-1-4116-5779-3(9))* Lulu Pr., Inc.
Pingry, Patricia A. The Christmas Story. Edelson, Wendy, illus. 2008. (ENG.). 32p. (J). pap. 3.95 *(978-0-8249-5512-0(9),* Ideal Pubns.) Worthy Publishing.
—One Baby Jesus. Edleson, Wendy, illus. 2008. (Ideals Christmas Classic Ser.). (ENG.). 30p. (J). (gr. -1-k). pap. 3.95 *(978-0-8249-5511-3(0),* Ideal Pubns.) Worthy Publishing.
Piper, Sophie. The Angel & the Dove: A Story for Easter. Stephenson, Kristina, illus. 2010. (ENG.). 28p. (J). (gr. -1-k). 12.99 *(978-0-7459-6123-1(1))* Lion Hudson PLC GBR. Dist: Independent Pubs. Group.
Prime, Derek. Sarah & Paul Have a Visitor: Discover about the Lord Jesus Christ. 2006. (Sarah & Paul Ser.). (ENG., Illus.). 128p. (J). (gr. 2-5). per. 6.99 *(978-1-84550-158-7(6),* 9fc8ce77-737f-45af-9bdb-cf0fca10e370) Christian Focus Pubns. GBR. Dist: Bookmasters Distribution.
Ramos, Peregrina. The Little Clay Jar: La Vasijita de Barro. Graham, Dennis, illus. 2006.Tr. of vasijita de Barro. (SPA & ENG.). (J). per. 15.95 *(978-0-9788381-0-2(6))* Word Gift Pubns.
Ranga, Katherine. Jesus Loves Me: A Bedtime Prayer. Ang, Selvi, illus. 2011. 26p. pap. 11.95 *(978-1-60976-989-5(9),* Eloquent Bks.) Strategic Book Publishing & Rights Agency (SBPRA).
Rangel, Graciela. Anthony's Christmas Journey. 2006. (ENG.). 80p. pap. 9.95 *(978-1-59526-650-7(X),* Llumina Christian Bks.) Aeon Publishing Inc.
Raum, Elizabeth. Christmas Crossroads. 2015. 133p. (J). *(978-1-62856-046-6(0),* Bloomsbury Visual Arts) BJU Pr.
—Crossroads in Galilee. 2016. (Illus.). xii, 139p. (J). *(978-1-62856-239-2(0))* BJU Pr.
Reeve, Penny. The Back Leg of a Goat: A Tania Abbey Adventure. Apps, Fred, illus. 2008. (Tania Abbey Adventure Ser.). (ENG.). 96p. (J). pap. 6.99 *(978-1-84550-340-6(6),* c8e23bb3-9904-4201-971e-e57faa66b8f3) Christian Focus Pubns. GBR. Dist: Bookmasters Distribution.
—Water or Goo? Apps, Fred, illus. 2008. (Tania Abbey Adventure Ser.). (ENG.). 96p. (J). pap. 6.99 *(978-1-84550-341-3(4),* 748295d7-9d18-4862-90d7-b454340bafc1) Christian Focus Pubns. GBR. Dist: Bookmasters Distribution.
Reid, Pamela Carrington. Little One. Tolman, Tom, illus. 2010. (J). *(978-1-59811-574-1(X))* Covenant Communications.
Reyes, Cameron. In Your Heart. DeBroech, Sarah, illus. 2011. 28p. pap. 24.95 *(978-1-4560-1009-6(3))* America Star Bks.
Reynolds, Peter H., illus. Star Bright: A Christmas Story. 2014. (ENG.). 40p. (J). (gr. -1-3). 17.99 *(978-1-4169-5858-1(4),* Atheneum Bks. for Young Readers) Simon & Schuster Children's Publishing.
Rhodes, Tiffany. What I Learned This Christmas. 2013. (Illus.). 42p. pap. 15.99 *(978-0-9899099-1-4(3))* Bee Creative, LLC.
—Where the Seeds Fall. 2013. (Illus.). 32p. pap. 9.99 *(978-0-9899099-0-7(5))* Bee Creative, LLC.
Rikkers, Don. Jesus Loves Me. 2009. 16p. 6.95 *(978-1-60349-025-2(6),* Marimba Bks.) Hudson Publishing Group, The.
Robinson, Ella M. Happy Home Stories. 2005. 137p. per. 6.95 *(978-1-57258-313-9(4))* TEACH Services, Inc.
Roesti, Delores. Mareena Maree Mulligan & the Flying Wheel Chair: Book 1: School Days. 2007. 81p. pap. 9.95 *(978-0-7414-4048-8(2))* Infinity Publishing.
Roesti, Delores Anne. Mareena Maree Mulligan & the Flying Wheelchair Book #3: Temptation's Talking, 1 vol. 2010. 93p. pap. 16.95 *(978-1-4489-6692-9(2))* PublishAmerica, Inc.
Rowe, Kysha D. What Creatures Teach Us, 1. 2005. (Illus.). 112p. (J). per. *(978-0-9769339-0-8(X))* Rowe, Kysha.
Rowland, Wilmer. Wise & Silly: The Reason for Christmas. 2012. (Illus.). (J). *(978-1-56722-948-6(4))* Word Aflame Pr.
Rowley, Deborah Pace. Easter Walk: A Treasure Hunt for the Real Meaning of Easter. Burr, Dan, illus. 2010. (J). *(978-1-60641-055-4(5))* Deseret Bk. Co.
RR. Priscilla. 2008. 32p. pap. 24.95 *(978-1-60813-213-3(7))* America Star Bks.
Rucinski, Sandra. The Story of Jesus According to Tobin. 2009. 32p. pap. 14.50 *(978-1-60860-372-5(5),* Eloquent Bks.) Strategic Book Publishing & Rights Agency (SBPRA).
Sanchez, Elizabeth. Jesus, It's Me Nicholas! Gutierrez, Chris, illus. 2005. 12p. (J). per. 9.99 *(978-1-59879-062-7(5))* Lifevest Publishing, Inc.
Sassi, Laura. Goodnight, Manger, 1 vol. Chapman, Jane, illus. 2015. (ENG.). 32p. (J). 16.99 *(978-0-310-74556-3(X))* Zonderkidz.
Scherm, Deedra. Cinco Panes y un Par de Peces: Una Historia de la Fe y de Dar. Dreyer, Laura, illus. 2008. (SPA.). 20p. (J). (gr. -1-3). bds. 7.99 *(978-1-934789-06-3(2))* Lemon Vision Productions.
Schomberger, Mary. The Adventures of Goldy the Mouse. 2013. 36p. pap. 16.95 *(978-1-4908-0375-3(0),* WestBow Pr.) Author Solutions, Inc.
Schram, Scott. The Last Noel: A Christmas Musical for Children. 2007. (ENG.). pap. 64.95 *(978-0-7390-4487-2(7))* Alfred Publishing Co., Inc.
Scull, Paul E. Los Animales Cuentan Su Histori. 2011. 20p. pap. *(978-1-4269-7319-2(5))* Trafford Publishing (UK) Ltd.
Sellers, Amy C., ed. Finding Jesus: Contemporary Children's Story. Behan, Rachel A., illus. l.t. ed. 2006. 19p. (J). 24.95 *(978-1-934194-00-3(X))* Olmstead Publishing LLC.
Seres, Frank & Seres, Nancy. The Jacob Series: Book #1 Fearfully & Wonderfully Made. 2009. 24p. (J). pap. 16.95 *(978-1-4327-3862-4(3))* Outskirts Pr., Inc.
Shultz, Carrie. V. I. P. Stepkid. 2013. 24p. pap. 10.95 *(978-1-4908-0831-4(0),* WestBow Pr.) Author Solutions, Inc.
Simon, Mary Manz. My March to the Manger (die-Cut) A Celebration of Jesus' Birth. Scudamore, Angelika, illus. 2016. (ENG.). 14p. (J). (gr. -1 — 1). bds. 12.99 *(978-1-4336-4525-9(4),* B&H Kids) B&H Publishing Group.
Sisk, Liza. Clay Birds of Jesus. 2007. 28p. pap. 10.95 *(978-1-59526-897-6(9),* Llumina Christian Bks.) Aeon Publishing Inc.
Skevington, Andrea. The Little Christmas Tree. Hussey, Lorna, illus. 2015. (ENG.). 32p. (J). (gr. -1-k). 16.99 *(978-0-7459-6579-6(2))* Lion Hudson PLC GBR. Dist: Independent Pubs. Group.
Smart Kidz, creator. Jesus Loves Me! 2013. (Bible Sing along Bks.). (ENG., Illus.). 12p. (gr. -1). bds. 12.99 *(978-1-891100-33-8(5),* Smart Kids) Penton Overseas, Inc.
Speed, Evelyn. Digger Rabbit & the First Easter. 2009. (Illus.). 24p. pap. 11.49 *(978-1-4389-6105-7(7))* AuthorHouse.

J
K
L

Spellman, Rhonda J., as told by. When I Was a Little Boy, by Jesus: Written for Children, Illustrated by Children: Experience the Life Jesus Lived When Jesus Was a Little Boy. l.t. ed. 2003. (Illus.). 32p. (J). per. 19.95 *(978-0-9741009-0-6(0))* Creative Cranium Concept, The.

Stockstill, Gloria McQueen. The Blind Man by the Road. Girouard, Patricia L., illus. 2003. (Listen! Look! Ser.). 20p. (J). bds. 5.49 *(978-0-7586-0144-5(1))* Concordia Publishing Hse.

Stohs, Anita Reith. Oh, Come, Little Children. Huang, Benrei, illus. 2006. 22p. (J). (gr. -1-3). 14.99 *(978-0-7586-1215-1(X))* Concordia Publishing Hse.

Strasser, Myrna A. Saint Francis & the Nativity, 1 vol. Bianchi, Fausto, illus. 2010. (ENG.). 40p. (J). (gr. -1-2). 16.99 *(978-0-310-70890-2(7))* Zonderkidz.

Summers, Susan. The Greatest Gift: The Story of the Other Wise Man. Morris, Jackie, illus. 2011. (ENG.). 30p. (J). 16.99 *(978-1-84686-578-7(6))* Barefoot Bks., Inc.

Tangvald, Christine Harder. The Best Thing about Christmas. Nobens, C. A., illus. 2014. (Faith That Sticks Bks.). (ENG.). 27p. (J). pap. 3.99 *(978-1-4964-0087-1(9))* Tyndale Hse. Pubs.

Taylor, Shirley A. The Stable Boy. Hall, Wendell E., illus. 2012. (ENG.). 40p. (J). (gr. 2-17). 17.95 *(978-1-935166-79-5(4))* Parkhurst Brothers, Inc., Pubs.

Terbay, Susan Handle. Jeremiah & the Man, 6 vols., Vol. 1. Mariants, tr. Children-Oln, illus. 2007. 43p. (J). (gr. 1-6). pap. *(978-0-9628309-8-3(4))* Marianist Pr.

Thomas, Joan G. If Jesus Came to My House. McElrath-Eslick, Lori, illus. 2008. (HarperBlessings Ser.). (ENG.). 40p. (J). (gr. -1-3). 16.99 *(978-0-06-083942-0(2))* HarperCollins Pubs.

Thompson, Lauren. One Starry Night. Bean, Jonathan, illus. (ENG.). 32p. (J). 2011. (gr. -1-3). lib. bdg. 17.99 *(978-0-689-82851-5(9))* 2003. 6.99 *(978-0-689-84215-3(5))* McElderry, Margaret K. Bks. (McElderry, Margaret K. Bks.).

Tolan, Stephanie S. Bartholomew's Blessing. Moore, Margie, illus. 2004. 32p. (J). (gr. -1-3). lib. bdg. 16.89 *(978-0-06-001198-7(X))* HarperCollins Pubs.

Traditional. Away in a Manger. Reed, Lisa & Bennett, Randle Paul, illus. 2012. (VeggieTales Bk Ser.). 16p. (J). 12.99 *(978-0-8249-1882-8(7)*, Ideal Pubns.) Worthy Publishing.

—Jesus Loves the Little Children. Gulliver, Amanda, illus. 2014. 16p. (J). 12.99 *(978-0-8249-1922-1(X)*, Ideal Pubns.) Worthy Publishing.

—Silent Night. Pulley, Kelly & Reed, Lisa, illus. 2014. (VeggieTales Book Ser.). 16p. (J). bds. 12.99 *(978-0-8249-1934-4(3)*, Ideal Pubns.) Worthy Publishing.

Tucker, David J. The Fourth Gift. 2010. 96p. 12.99 *(978-1-59955-438-9(0))* Cedar Fort, Inc./CFI Distribution.

Twin Sisters(r), et al. Where Is Baby Jesus? a Lift-The-Flap Book. 2016. (ENG.). 10p. (J). bds. 9.99 *(978-1-63409-806-9(4))* Barbour Publishing, Inc.

Underhill, Marjorie Fay. Jeremiah. Garrett, Caroline S., tr. Garrett, Caroline S., illus. 2003. (J). 12.00 *(978-1-887905-75-6(8))* Parkway Pubs., Inc.

Van Dyke, Henry. The Other Wise Man. 2004. pap. 11.95 incl. audio compact disk *(978-1-932226-34-8(6))* Wizard Academy Pr.

—The Other Wise Man. Barrett, Robert, illus. 2008. (ENG.). 30p. (J). (gr. -1-3). 8.99 *(978-0-8249-5565-6(X)*, Ideal Pubns.) Worthy Publishing.

—The Story of the Other Wise Man. 2007. 52p. per. *(978-1-4065-4728-3(X))* Dodo Pr.

Van Scott, Miriam. Candy Canes in Bethlehem. Van Wagoner, Traci, illus. 2012. (J). 7.95 *(978-0-8198-1606-1(X))* Pauline Bks. & Media.

Vardamaskos, Angela. Everlasting Truth. Bournakis, Maria, illus. 2008. 48p. pap. 24.95 *(978-1-60610-950-2(2))* America Star Bks.

Villarreal, Carlos C. The Light Beneath the Shadow: Sharing God's Love with Your Child as You Read Together: A Bedtime Story Intended to Awaken Your Parental Christian Spirit. 2006. 48p. pap. 16.95 *(978-1-4241-1247-0(8))* PublishAmerica, Inc.

Visconti, Guido. One Night in a Stable. Cimatoribus, Alessandra, illus. 2004. 32p. (J). 16.00 *(978-0-8028-5279-3(3))* Eerdmans, William B. Publishing Co.

Vivas, Julie. The Nativity. 2006. (ENG., Illus.). 36p. (J). (gr. -1-3). pap. 7.99 *(978-0-15-206085-5(5))* Houghton Mifflin Harcourt Publishing Co.

Vonnegut, Kurt. Sun Moon Star. Chermayeff, Ivan, illus. 2016. (ENG.). 64p. (J). (gr. k-4). 22.95 *(978-1-60980-724-5(3)*, Triangle Square) Seven Stories Pr.

Waddell, Martin. Room for a Little One: A Christmas Tale. Cockcroft, Jason, illus. 2008. (ENG.). 26p. (J). (gr. -1-2). bds. 7.99 *(978-1-4169-6177-2(1)*, Little Simon) Little Simon.

—Room for a Little One: A Christmas Tale. Cockcroft, Jason, illus. (ENG.). 32p. (J). (gr. -1-3). 2006. 11.99 *(978-1-4169-2518-7(X))* 2004. 18.99 *(978-0-689-86841-2(3))* McElderry, Margaret K. Bks. (McElderry, Margaret K. Bks.).

Walburg, Lori. The Legend of the Candy Cane: The Inspirational Story of Our Favorite Christmas Candy, 1 vol. Bernardin, James & Cowdrey, Richard, illus. ed. 2012. (ENG.). 32p. (J). 15.99 *(978-0-310-73012-5(0))* Zonderkidz.

Wallace, Lew. Ben-Hur. (SPA., Illus.). (YA). 11.95 *(978-84-7281-099-0(2)*, AF1099) Auriga, Ediciones S.A. ESP. Dist: Continental Bk. Co., Inc.

Wallace, Sally. A Big Secret: A Nativity Story. 2009. 40p. pap. 16.99 *(978-1-4490-1660-9(X))* AuthorHouse.

Warren, G. A. Starr Light & the Christmas Story. Ciesinska, Izabela, illus. 2009. 32p. (J). 14.95 *(978-1-935268-09-3(0))* Halo Publishing International.

Washington, LaVonne & Washington, LaShawn. The Parables of Humpty Dumpty: Volume 1. 2011. 40p. pap. 24.95 *(978-1-4626-0989-5(9))* America Star Bks.

Webber, Jerry. The Game: None. 2007. 52p. per. 9.95 *(978-1-4327-0911-2(9))* Outskirts Pr., Inc.

Weiner-Booth, Patsy. The Day Santa Met Jesus: A Christmas story & Play. 2009. 56p. pap. 10.99 *(978-1-4490-1090-4(3))* AuthorHouse.

Wiersum, Gale. The Animals' Christmas Eve. 2007. (Little Golden Book Ser.). (ENG., Illus.). 24p. (J). (gr. -1-k). 4.99 *(978-0-375-83923-8(2)*, Golden Bks.) Random Hse. Children's Bks.

Wright, Boyd. Donkey Tales. 2006. 74p. pap. 16.95 *(978-1-4241-1900-4(6))* PublishAmerica, Inc.

Wright, Sally Ann. Christmas Baby. 2008. 14p. (J). 12.99 *(978-1-4003-1301-3(5))* Nelson, Thomas Inc.

Young, Norman, illus. The Christmas Story. rev. ed. 2006. (Usborne Bible Tales Ser.). 16p. (J). (gr. -1-3). pap. 4.99 *(978-0-7945-1286-6(0)*, Usborne) EDC Publishing.

—The Story of Jesus for Young Children. 2005. (Usborne Bible Tales Ser.). 98p. (J). (gr. -1-k). 14.99 incl. audio compact disk *(978-0-7945-0831-9(6)*, Usborne) EDC Publishing.

Ytreeide, Arnold. Amon's Adventure: A Family Story for Easter, 1 vol. 2010. 192p. (J). (gr. 2-7). pap. 16.99 *(978-0-8254-4171-4(4))* Kregel Pubns.

Zemanick, Patty. A Walk with Papa. Hammack, Sandra, illus. 2006. pap. 14.95 *(978-0-9788289-0-5(9))* Dragonfly Ministries.

Zondervan Staff. Story Early Elementary Curriculum: 31 Lessons, 1 vol. 2011. (Story Ser.). (ENG.). cd-rom 34.99 *(978-0-310-71921-2(6))* Zonderkidz.

—Story Preschool Curriculum: 31 Lessons, 1 vol. 2011. (Story Ser.). (ENG.). (J). cd-rom 34.99 *(978-0-310-71920-5(8))* Zonderkidz.

Zondervan Staff & Walburg, Lori. The Legend of the Candy Cane, 1 vol. Cowdrey, Richard, illus. 2014. (ENG.). 30p. (J). bds. 9.99 *(978-0-310-74672-0(8))* Zonderkidz.

JESUS CHRIST—ICONOGRAPHY

see Jesus Christ—Art

JESUS CHRIST—NATIVITY

see also Christmas

Adams, Michelle Medlock. What Is Christmas? 2008. (ENG., Illus.). 26p. (J). (gr. -1-k). bds. 6.95 *(978-0-8249-6668-3(6)*, Ideal Pubns.) Worthy Publishing.

Alexander, Florence & Alexander, Stanley. Jesus Christ Is Born. l.t. ed. 2003. (Dare to Be Great Ser.). (Illus.). 36p. (J). 7.99 *(978-0-915960-02-6(8))* Ebon Research Systems Publishing, LLC.

Anderson, Raymond & Anderson, Georgene. The Jesse Tree: Stories & Symbols of Advent. 2004. (Illus.). 64p. (J). 5.99 *(978-0-8066-2524-9(4)*, 10-25244, Augsburg Bks.) Augsburg Fortress, Pubs.

Arensen, Shel. The First Christmas: Nativity Puzzle Book with 6 Play Pieces. 2003. (Illus.). 16p. (J). 10.99 *(978-0-8254-5509-4(X))* Kregel Pubns.

Armadillo Publishing Staff. Baby's Bible Stories: The Birth of Jesus. Lewis, Jan, illus. 2015. (ENG.). 24p. pap. 6.99 *(978-1-86147-484-1(9)*, Armadillo) Anness Publishing GBR. Dist: National Bk. Network.

Aston, Al. The Shepherds' Surprise. Hutchinson, Joy, illus. 2005. 16p. pap., pap. 2.00 *(978-1-84427-178-8(1))* Scripture Union GBR. Dist: Send The Light Distribution LLC.

Baby Jesus. 16p. (J). 1.89 *(978-0-7847-1386-0(3))* Standard Publishing.

Barker, Stephen, illus. My First Christmas. 2016. (ENG.). 12p. (J). (-k). bds. 9.99 *(978-1-62686-813-7(1)*, Silver Dolphin Bks.) Readerlink Distribution Services, LLC.

Beavers, David R. I Am a Manger. 2007. 48p. per. 14.95 *(978-0-9801674-0-5(X))* Global Education Advance.

Benson, Lyn. Who Were the Magi. Joshua, Benson Benson Joshua, illus. 2007. 56p. pap. 23.99 *(978-0-615-13524-3(2))* Benson, Lyn.

Bierhorst, John. El Nino Espiritu: Una Historia de la Navidad. Aramburu, Francisco Gonzalez, tr. Cooney, Barbara, illus. 2003.Tr. of Spirit Child: A Story of the Nativity. (SPA.). 26p. (J). (gr. 3-7). reprint ed. 20.00 *(978-0-7567-6882-9(9))* DIANE Publishing Co.

Boadt, Lawrence. Stations of the Nativity. 2017. (ENG., Illus.). 32p. pap. 10.95 ***(978-0-8091-6778-4(6))*** Paulist Pr.

Bowman, Crystal & McKinley, Teri. M Is for Manger. Keay, Claire, illus. 2015. (ENG.). 64p. (J). 7.99 *(978-1-4964-0195-3(6))* Tyndale Hse. Pubs.

Bowman, David, illus. Beyond Bethlehem: A Book of Mormon Christmas. 2008. 32p. (J). pap. 11.95 *(978-1-59038-991-1(3))* Deseret Bk. Co.

Box, Su. Baby Jesus. 2014. (Bible Dial-A-Picture Bks.). (ENG., Illus.). 8p. (J). (gr. -1-k). bds. 6.99 *(978-0-7641-6694-5(8))* Barron's Educational Series, Inc.

Brooks, Felicity. Nativity Jigsaw Bk. 2006. 14p. (J). bds. 12.99 *(978-0-7945-1188-3(0)*, Usborne) EDC Publishing.

Burchett, Author Walter, BA. Christian children's questions & answers birth of christ Volume 5. 2009. 33p. pap. 14.32 *(978-0-557-08275-9(7))* Lulu Pr., Inc.

Burrin, Angela M. Jesus Speaks to Me on My First Holy Communion. Lo Cascio, Maria Cristina, illus. 2009. 39p. (J). (gr. 1-5). 12.95 *(978-1-59325-149-9(1))* Word Among Us Pr.

Busch, Melinda Kay. Born on Christmas Morn. Hall, Melanie, illus. 2003. (Arch Bks.). (ENG.). 16p. (J). (gr. k-4). 1.99 *(978-0-570-07584-4(X))* Concordia Publishing Hse.

—Savior of the Nations-Mini BK. Hall, Melanie, illus. 2009. 16p. pap. 2.29 *(978-0-7586-1756-9(9))* Concordia Publishing Hse.

Carter, Jason Andrew. Stations of the Nativity. 2012. (ENG.). (J). pap. *(978-1-4675-4331-6(4))* Independent Pub.

Carton, Gerard. We Four Kings. 2009. (Illus.). 52p. pap. *(978-1-84748-474-1(3))* Athena Pr.

Chand, Candy. The Twelve Prayers of Christmas. Bernardin, James, illus. 2009. (HarperBlessings Ser.). (ENG.). 32p. (J). (gr. -1-2). 16.99 *(978-0-06-077636-7(6))* HarperCollins Pubs.

Charette, Beverly. Story of Christmas for Children. 2004. pap. 3.95 *(978-0-8249-5338-6(X)*, Ideal Pubns.) Worthy Publishing.

Che, Akwanwi Mfonyam. The Baby King: Born in a Stable. 2012. (Illus.). 16p. pap. 18.30 *(978-1-4772-4756-3(4))* AuthorHouse.

Christmas Stable, 1 vol. 2014. (Candle Tiny Tots Ser.). (ENG., Illus.). 16p. (J). 11.99 *(978-1-78128-122-2(X)*, Candle Bks.) Lion Hudson PLC GBR. Dist: Kregel Pubns.

Clark, Lisa. The Song of Christmas. Dyrud, Chris Wold, illus. 2014. (Arch Bks.). (ENG.). 16p. (J). (gr. k-4). pap. 2.49 *(978-0-7586-4605-7(4))* Concordia Publishing Hse.

Copenhagen Publishing Company, prod. When Jesus Was Born. 2015. (ENG.). 10p. (J). 4.99 *(978-1-4964-0464-0(5)*, Tyndale Kids) Tyndale Hse. Pubs.

Cotten, Cynthia. This Is the Stable. Bettoli, Delana, illus. 2008. (ENG.). 32p. (J). (gr. -1-3). pap. 7.99 *(978-0-312-38421-0(1)*, 9780312384210) Square Fish.

Crump, Fred, Jr. Three Kings & a Star. Crump, Fred, Jr., illus. 2010. (Illus.). 40p. (J). (gr. -1-3). 12.95 *(978-1-932715-52-1(5))* UMI (Urban Ministries, Inc.).

Dalton, Pamela, illus. The Story of Christmas. 2011. (ENG.). 32p. (J). (gr. -1-17). 17.99 *(978-1-4521-0470-6(0))* Chronicle Bks. LLC.

David, Juliet. The Christmas Story, 1 vol. Ellis, Elina, illus. 2016. (ENG.). 24p. (J). 8.99 *(978-1-78128-282-3(X)*, Candle Bks.) Lion Hudson PLC GBR. Dist: Kregel Pubns.

—Follow the Star, 1 vol. Prole, Helen, illus. 2005. (Poster Sticker Bks.). 8p. (J). (gr. k-2). pap. 6.99 *(978-0-8254-7304-3(7)*, Candle Bks.) Lion Hudson PLC GBR. Dist: Kregel Pubns.

—My Very First Christmas Story, 1 vol. Siewert, Pauline, illus. 2015. 14p. (J). 7.99 *(978-1-78128-231-1(5)*, Candle Bks.) Lion Hudson PLC GBR. Dist: Kregel Pubns.

—The Nativity Story, 1 vol. Prole, Helen, illus. 2015. (ENG.). 12p. (J). 16.99 *(978-1-78128-226-7(9)*, Candle Bks.) Lion Hudson PLC GBR. Dist: Kregel Pubns.

—The Shepherds, 1 vol. Wood, Hannah, illus. 2009. (Christmas Trio Ser.). 18p. (J). bds. 4.99 *(978-0-8254-7406-4(X)*, Candle Bks.) Lion Hudson PLC GBR. Dist: Kregel Pubns.

—The Wise Men, 1 vol. Wood, Hannah, illus. 2009. (Christmas Trio Ser.). 18p. (J). bds. 4.99 *(978-0-8254-7407-1(8)*, Candle Bks.) Lion Hudson PLC GBR. Dist: Kregel Pubns.

Davidson, Alice Joyce. Baby Blessings Christmas. 2009. (Baby Blessings Ser.). (ENG.). 18p. (J). (gr. -1-k). bds. 12.99 *(978-0-7847-2374-6(5)*, B&H Kids) B&H Publishing Group.

Davidson, Susanna. Story of Baby Jesus. 2015. (Picture Bks.). (ENG.). 24p. (J). 9.99 *(978-0-7945-3419-6(8)*, Usborne) EDC Publishing.

—Story of the Nativity. 2011. (Story of the Nativity Ser.). 24p. (J). ring bd. 9.99 *(978-0-7945-3188-1(1)*, Usborne) EDC Publishing.

Denton, Lynette Harris. Christmas Greetings, My Little Friend. 2011. 24p. pap. 12.99 *(978-1-4520-5614-2(5))* AuthorHouse.

Dodd, Sarah J. Christmas Stories for Little Angels. Kolanovic, Dubravka, illus. 2010. (Little Angels Ser.). (ENG.). 32p. (J). (gr. -1-k). 12.99 *(978-0-7459-6917-6(8))* Lion Hudson PLC GBR. Dist: Independent Pubs. Group.

Dodd, Sarah J. & Stone, Julia. The Christmas Story for Little Angels. Kolanovic, Dubravka, illus. 2016. (Little Angels Ser.). (ENG.). 32p. (J). (gr. -1-k). 7.99 *(978-0-7459-7610-5(7))* Lion Hudson PLC GBR. Dist: Independent Pubs. Group.

Donaghy, Thomas J. My Golden Christmas Book. 2009. (Illus.). 42p. (J). bds. 9.95 *(978-0-89942-361-6(2))* Catholic Bk. Publishing Corp.

Dowley, Tim. Would You Like to Know the Story of Christmas?, 1 vol. Reeves, Eira, illus. 2015. (ENG.). 28p. (J). pap. 2.99 *(978-1-78128-197-0(1)*, Candle Bks.) Lion Hudson PLC GBR. Dist: Kregel Pubns.

Edwards, Josh. Christmas, 1 vol. Embleton-Hall, Chris, illus. 2014. (ENG.). 10p. (J). bds. 11.99 ***(978-1-85985-999-5(2)***, Lion Children's) Lion Hudson PLC GBR. Dist: Kregel Pubns.

The First Christmas. 2003. (Illus.). (J). bds. 6.98 *(978-1-4054-0967-4(3))* Parragon, Inc.

The First Christmas. (Illus.). 12p. (J). 4.95 *(978-1-58989-102-9(3))* Thurman Hse., LLC.

Fogle, Robin. A Christmas Story. 2006. (J). pap. 1.79 *(978-1-59317-159-9(5))* Warner Pr., Inc.

Follow That Star. (Hear Me Read Classroom Sets Ser.). 32.00 *(978-0-570-07172-3(0))* Concordia Publishing Hse.

Four Story Creative, illus. Deep Blue Bible Storybook Christmas. 2016. 9.99 *(978-1-5018-3315-1(4))* Abingdon Pr.

—Deep Blue Bible Storybook Christmas, Spanish Edition. 2016. 40p. 9.99 *(978-1-5018-3566-7(1))* Abingdon Pr.

Ganeri, Anita. The Christmas Story. 2003. (Festival Stories Ser.). (Illus.). 24p. (J). pap. *(978-0-237-52468-5(6))* Evans Brothers, Ltd.

Gifts of the Nativity. 2017. (ENG.). (J). (gr. 1-4). 14.99 ***(978-1-4621-2060-4(1))*** Cedar Fort, Inc./CFI Distribution.

Glaser, Rebecca. The Holy Moly Christmas Story. Ferenc, Bill, illus. 2015. (Holy Moly Bible Storybooks Ser.). (ENG.). 32p. (J). (gr. k-3). 12.99 *(978-1-5064-0257-4(7)*, Sparkhouse Family) Augsburg Fortress, Pubs.

Godfrey, Jan. The Road to Christmas Day. Piwowarski, Marcin, illus. 2008. 32p. (J). (gr. -1-1). 14.95 *(978-0-8198-6487-1(0))* Pauline Bks. & Media.

Godwin, Laura. This First Christmas Night. Cobalt Illustrations Studio, Inc & Low, William, illus. 2016. (ENG.). 32p. (J). 16.99 *(978-1-250-08102-5(5)*, 9781250081025) Feiwel & Friends.

Goodings, Christina. My Carry-Along Nativity: Activity Book with Stickers. Hughes, Cathy, illus. 2016. (ENG.). 32p. (J). (gr. -1-2). pap. 9.99 *(978-0-7459-6511-6(3))* Lion Hudson PLC GBR. Dist: Independent Pubs. Group.

Goodwin, John. The Lion Book of Five-Minute Christmas Stories. Johnson, Richard A., illus. 2014. (ENG.). 48p. (J). (gr. k-2). pap. 12.99 *(978-0-7459-6926-8(7))* Lion Hudson PLC GBR. Dist: Independent Pubs. Group.

Grack, Rachel. Christmas. 2017. (Christmas Ser.). 24p. (J). (gr. k-3). pap. 6.99 ***(978-1-61891-271-8(2))***; (ENG., Illus.). lib. bdg. 25.95 *(978-1-62617-592-1(6))* Bellwether Media. (Blastoff! Readers).

Green, Yuko. The Nativity Activity & Coloring Book. 2013. (Dover Holiday Coloring Book Ser.). (ENG.). 48p. (J). (gr. k-4). pap. 4.99 *(978-0-486-49717-4(8))* Dover Pubns., Inc.

Grimes, Nikki. Voices of Christmas, 1 vol. Velasquez, Eric, illus. 2009. (ENG.). 32p. (J). (gr. -1-2). 16.99 *(978-0-310-71192-6(4))* Zonderkidz.

Guess Who? Christmas: A Flip-The-Flap Book. 2015. (ENG., Illus.). 6p. (J). (— 1). bds. 9.99 *(978-0-7459-6408-9(7))* Lion Hudson PLC GBR. Dist: Independent Pubs. Group.

Hands-On Nativity Craft Book. 2015. (ENG., Illus.). 24p. (J). (gr. k-2). pap. 7.99 *(978-0-7459-6431-7(1))* Lion Hudson PLC GBR. Dist: Independent Pubs. Group.

Hansen, Janis. Jesus: The Birthday of the King, 5 vols. Francisco, Wendy, illus. 2003. (Bible Adventure Club Ser.). 36p. wbk. ed. 19.99 incl. audio, cd-rom *(978-1-58134-331-1(0))* Crossway.

Harmon, Ruth. The Christmas Story. Date not set. 4.95 *(978-0-88271-132-4(6)*, 1415) Regina Pr., Malhame & Co.

Harrast, Tracy. My Giant Fold-Out Book: Christmas. Doherty, Paula, illus. 2008. 10p. (J). (gr. -1). bds. 13.49 *(978-0-7586-1425-4(X))* Concordia Publishing Hse.

Hartman, Bob. The Noisy Stable & Other Christmas Stories. Hudson, Brett, illus. 2004. (Storyteller Tales Ser.). (ENG.). 64p. (J). (gr. k-4). pap. 6.99 *(978-0-7459-4824-9(3))* Lion Hudson PLC GBR. Dist: Independent Pubs. Group.

Hartman, Sara. When Jesus Was Born. Mitter, Kathy, illus. 2007. 16p. (J). (gr. k-4). 1.99 *(978-0-7586-1281-6(8))* Concordia Publishing Hse.

Harvest House Publishers. The Very Special Baby. 2014. (ENG.). 24p. (J). 9.99 *(978-0-7369-6154-7(2))* Harvest Hse. Pubs.

—The Very Special Baby Sticker Book. 2014. (ENG.). 20p. (J). pap. 3.99 *(978-0-7369-6158-5(5))* Harvest Hse. Pubs.

Henning, Heather. Christmas. Bull, Nicola, ed. Chapman, Gillian, illus. 2007. (Touch & Feel Ser.). 14p. (J). (gr. -1-3). bds. 10.49 *(978-0-7586-1383-7(0))* Concordia Publishing Hse.

Heyer, Carol. The First Christmas. 2003. (ENG., Illus.). 30p. (J). 14.95 *(978-0-8249-5469-7(6)*, Ideal Pubns.) Worthy Publishing.

Heyer, Carol, illus. The Christmas Story. (J). 6.95 *(978-0-8249-5347-8(9)*, Ideal Pubns.) Worthy Publishing.

Hoffman, Patricia. Bethlehem Town: Where Jesus Was Born. Munger, Nancy, illus. 2003. 32p. (J). 9.49 *(978-0-7586-0412-5(2))* Concordia Publishing Hse.

Howie, Vicky & MacLean, Moira. Cnoc, Cnoc! Pwy Sy 'Na? Llyfr Fflapiau Stori'r Nadolig. Wyn, Delyth, tr. from ENG. 2005. (WEL., Illus.). 16p. *(978-1-85994-498-1(1))* Cyhoeddiadau'r Gair.

Hudak, Michal. The Uproar at Bethlehem. 2005. (Illus.). 24p. (gr. -1-4). 14.95 *(978-0-8146-2774-7(9))* Liturgical Pr.

The Incarnation of Christ: Immanuel l.t. ed. 2004. (CHI., Illus.). 52p. (J). *(978-0-9752775-0-8(2)*, 0-9752775-0-2) Unitrust Design.

Jackson, Antonia & Nagy, Krisztina Kallai. My Advent Calendar Christmas Book. 2014. (ENG., Illus.). 32p. (J). (-2). 9.99 *(978-0-7459-6392-1(7))* Lion Hudson PLC GBR. Dist: Independent Pubs. Group.

Jaroszko, Mike, illus. Away in a Manger Devotional. 2008. pap. 2.29 *(978-0-7586-1449-0(7))* Concordia Publishing Hse.

Jeffs, Stephanie. Baby Jesus. Tulip, Jenny, illus. 2004. (My First Find Out about Book Ser.). 24p. (gr. -1-18). pap. 3.95 *(978-0-8294-1730-2(3))* Loyola Pr.

Jesus' Birth. (Bulletin Board Jumbo Cutouts Ser.). (Illus.). 96p. (J). 9.99 *(978-0-7847-0551-3(8)*, 02588) Standard Publishing.

Johnson, Alice W. & Warner, Allison H. Believe & You're There When the Night Was Bright As Day. Harston, Jerry, illus. 2010. viii, 81p. (J). *(978-1-60641-249-7(3))* Deseret Bk. Co.

—Believe & You're There When the Prince of Peace Was Born. Harston, Jerry, illus. 2009. 74p. (J). *(978-1-60641-200-8(0))* Deseret Bk. Co.

Jones, Sherilyn. Can't Keep up with the Joneses: Created to Be. Jones, Sherilyn, illus. 2015. (ENG., Illus.). (J). pap. 9.99 *(978-0-9864191-0-2(9))* Concept Media Group, LLC, The.

Joslin, Mary. The Story of Christmas. Massari, Alida, illus. 2014. (ENG.). 32p. (J). (gr. k-2). 14.99 *(978-0-7459-6937-4(2))* Lion Hudson PLC GBR. Dist: Independent Pubs. Group.

Kay, Terry. To Whom the Angel Spoke: A Story of the Christmas, 1 vol. Blyth, Eileen, illus. 2nd ed. 2009. (ENG.). 32p. (J). (gr. k-4). 14.95 *(978-1-56145-502-7(4))* Peachtree Pubs.

Kennedy, Anne Vittur & Kennedy, Anne V. One Shining Star, 1 vol. 2006. (ENG., Illus.). 22p. (J). (gr. -1). bds. 6.99 *(978-0-310-71029-5(4))* Zonderkidz.

King James Bible Staff. Christmas Is Here. Castillo, Lauren, illus. 2010. (ENG.). 32p. (J). (gr. -1-2). 12.99 *(978-1-4424-0822-7(7)*, Simon & Schuster Bks. For Young Readers) Simon & Schuster Bks. For Young Readers.

Kinkade, Thomas, illus. Away in a Manger. 2005. 32p. (J). lib. bdg. 17.89 *(978-0-06-078733-2(3))* HarperCollins Pubs.

Kramer, Janice. The Christmas Baby. Rooney, Ronnie, illus. 2008. (Arch Bks.). 16p. (J). (gr. k-4). pap. 1.99 *(978-0-7586-1454-4(3))* Concordia Publishing Hse.

Lafortune, Claude. The Wonderful Story of Christmas. 2003. (Illus.). 48p. act. bk. ed. *(978-2-89507-439-7(9))*; 24p. *(978-2-89507-438-0(0))* Novalis Publishing.

Litchfield, Jo. Usborne Lift-The-Flap Nitivity. Allman, Howard, photos by. 2004. (Illus.). (J). *(978-0-439-68683-9(0))* Scholastic, Inc.

Lucado, Max. The Christmas Story for Children, 1 vol. 2014. (ENG.). 32p. (J). pap. 6.99 *(978-0-310-73598-4(X))* Zonderkidz.

MacKenzie, Catherine. The Greatest Gift: A Puzzle Book about the Birth of Jesus. 2010. (Puzzle Ser.). (ENG., Illus.). 24p. (J). pap. 4.99 *(978-1-84550-593-6(X)*, 0e3f1c04-517a-4e78-a6a4-7b5d47255af3) Christian Focus Pubns. GBR. Dist: Bookmasters Distribution.

—The Shepherds Find Jesus. Apps, Fred, illus. 2006. (Born to Be King (Board Books) Ser.). (ENG.). 16p. (J). (gr. -1-k). 3.99 *(978-1-84550-185-3(3)*, 9781845501853, Christian Focus) Christian Focus Pubns. GBR. Dist: Bookmasters Distribution.

Maier, Paul L. The Very First Christmas. 32p. (J). 9.99 *(978-0-570-07186-0(0))* Concordia Publishing Hse.

—The Very First Christmas. Ordaz, Francisco, illus. (J). 2004. 20p. (gr. -1-k). bds. 7.49 *(978-0-7586-0689-1(3))* 2003. 32p. (gr. 1-5). 7.49 *(978-0-7586-0616-7(8))* Concordia Publishing Hse.

Malone, Jean M. No Room at the Inn: The Nativity Story. Langdo, Bryan, illus. 2009. (Penguin Young Readers, Level 3 Ser.). (ENG.). 48p. (J). (gr. 1-3). mass mkt. 3.99 *(978-0-448-45217-3(0)*, Penguin Young Readers) Penguin Young Readers Group.

Martin, Oscar, Jr., creator. Birth of Jesus l.t. ed. 2003. (Illus.). 25p. (J). E-Book 19.95 incl. cd-rom *(978-0-9748416-4-9(1))* Build Your Story.

McCaughrean, Geraldine & Dubravka, Kolanovic. The Nativity Story. Williams, Sophy, illus. 2009. (ENG.). 48p. (J). (gr. 2-4). 14.95 *(978-0-7459-6092-0(8))* Lion Hudson PLC GBR. Dist: Independent Pubs. Group.

McDermott, Gerald. The Light of the World. McDermott, Gerald, illus. 2006. (Illus.). 32p. (J). 16.99 *(978-0-525-47488-3(9)*, Dutton Juvenile) Penguin Publishing Group.

McKinley, Teri & Bowman, Crystal. M Is for Manger. Keay, Claire, illus. 2016. (ENG.). 32p. (J). bds. 6.99 *(978-1-4964-2004-6(7)*, Tyndale Kids) Tyndale Hse. Pubs.

Michael, Sally. Jesus Is Most Special. Apps, Fred, illus. 2014. (ENG.). 24p. (J). (gr. 4-7). 9.99 *(978-1-62995-029-7(7))* P & R Publishing.

Miller, Claire. The Christmas Message. Dorenkamp, Michelle, illus. 2006. (Arch Bks.). 16p. (J). 1.99 (978-0-7586-0872-7(1)) Concordia Publishing Hse.

Milligan, Bryce. Brigid's Cloak: An Ancient Irish Story. Cann, Helen, illus. 2004. 32p. (J). (gr. k-18). 16.00 (978-0-8028-5224-3(6)) Eerdmans, William B. Publishing Co.

Miralles, Jose & McTeigue, Jane, illus. Christmas Star: A Light-up Shadow-Box Book. 2005. 10p. (J). (gr. k-4). reprint ed. 10.00 (978-0-7567-9559-7(1)) DIANE Publishing Co.

Miras, Christie. The First Christmas Day. 2011. 28p. pap. 15.99 (978-1-4628-7660-0(9)) Xlibris Corp.

My Little Story of Christmas, 1 vol. 2015. (ENG., Illus.). 20p. (J). pap. 3.99 (978-1-78128-151-2(3), Candle Bks.) Lion Hudson PLC GBR. Dist: Kregel Pubns.

Neff, Larry M. Ha Nacido Jesus (Vida de Cristo)Tr. of Jesus Is Born. (SPA.). 12p. (J). 5.99 (978-0-7899-0033-3(5), 497759) Editorial Unilit.

Nellist, Glenys. Christmas Love Letters from God: Bible Stories, 1 vol. Clowes, Rachel, illus. 2016. (Love Letters from God Ser.). (ENG.). 32p. (J). 16.99 (978-0-310-74824-3(0)) Zonderkidz.

Noble, Marty. Nativity Stained Glass Coloring Book. 2004. (Holiday Stained Glass Coloring Book Ser.). (ENG., Illus.). 32p. (J). (gr. -1-5). pap. 7.99 (978-0-486-43527-5(X)) Dover Pubns., Inc.

Nye, Christopher. The Old Shepherd's Tale. 2004. (Illus.). 32p. (J). 16.95 (978-0-913098-85-1(X)) Orion Society, The.

Oakes, Loretta. A Peek-a-Boo Christmas! Hall, Mary, illus. 2010. 16p. (J). (gr. -1). pap. 9.95 (978-0-8091-6754-8(9), Ambassador Bks.) Paulist Pr.

Parry, Alan & Parry, Linda. The Herald Angels. 2003. (Illus.). 16p. 9.99 (978-1-85608-253-2(9)) Hunt, John Publishing Ltd. GBR. Dist: Send The Light Distribution LLC.

Pasquali, Elena. The Animals' Christmas. Ferri, Giuliano, illus. 2016. (ENG.). 32p. (J). (gr. 2-4). 8.99 (978-0-7459-6249-8(1)) Lion Hudson PLC GBR. Dist: Independent Pubs. Group.

Peak, Cindy. The Little Star That Shines for Jesus. 2011. (ENG., Illus.). 36p. (J). 19.99 (978-1-937008-01-7(0)) Heart to Heart Publishing, Inc.

Pienkowski, Jan. The First Christmas. 2014. (ENG.). 24p. (J). (gr. k-12). 15.99 (978-0-385-75518-4(X), Knopf Bks. for Young Readers) Random Hse. Children's Bks.

Pingry, Patricia A. The Christmas Story. Edelson, Wendy, illus. 2004. (ENG.). 26p. (J). bds. 6.95 (978-0-8249-6549-5(3), Ideal Pubns.) Worthy Publishing.

—The Story of Christmas. Thornburgh, Rebecca, illus. 2012. 24p. (J). pap. 4.99 (978-0-8249-5645-5(1), Ideal Pubns.) Worthy Publishing.

—The Story of Christmas. 2010. (Illus.). 22p. (J). 6.99 (978-0-8249-1845-3(2), Ideal Pubns.) Worthy Publishing.

Piper, Sophie. The Christmas Story. Spenceley, Annabel, illus. 2017. (ENG.). 32p. (J). (gr. -1-k). 7.99 **(978-0-7459-6519-2(9))** Lion Hudson PLC GBR. Dist: Independent Pubs. Group.

Piper, Sophie. Jesus Is Born. Gilbert, Anne Yvonne, illus. 2016. (ENG.). 32p. (J). (gr. -1-3). 16.99 (978-1-68099-187-1(6), Good Bks.) Skyhorse Publishing Co., Inc.

Poole, Susie. A Christmas Journey. Poole, Susie, illus. 2014. (ENG., Illus.). 48p. (gr. -1-3). 12.99 (978-1-4336-8343-5(1), B&H Kids) B&H Publishing Group.

Prole, Helen, illus. The Story of Christmas, 1 vol. 2016. (Candle Bible for Toddlers Ser.). (ENG.). 26p. (J). pap. 6.99 (978-1-78128-309-7(5), Candle Bks.) Lion Hudson PLC GBR. Dist: Kregel Pubns.

Roche, Maite. The First Noel. Roche, Maite, illus. 2009.Tr. of plus belle histoire de Noël. (Illus.). 48p. (J). (gr. -1-1). 16.95 (978-0-8198-2687-9(1)) Pauline Bks. & Media.

Rock, Lois. The First Christmas. Allsopp, Sophie, illus. 2008. (ENG.). 32p. (J). (gr. k-2). 12.95 (978-0-7459-4956-7(8)) Lion Hudson PLC GBR. Dist: Independent Pubs. Group.

—My Very First Nativity Story. Ayliffe, Alex, illus. 2015. (My Very First Ser.). (ENG.). 48p. (J). (gr. -1-k). 7.99 (978-0-7459-6911-4(9)) Lion Hudson PLC GBR. Dist: Independent Pubs. Group.

—On That Christmas Night. Jay, Alison, illus. 2016. (ENG.). 32p. (J). (gr. k-4). 16.99 (978-0-7459-6588-8(1)) Lion Hudson PLC GBR. Dist: Independent Pubs. Group.

Sanderson, Ruth. The Nativity. 2010. (ENG.). 32p. 15.00 (978-0-8028-5371-4(4), Eerdmans Bks For Young Readers) Eerdmans, William B. Publishing Co.

Schulze, Marc-Alexander, illus. A Child Is Born: The Nativity Story. 2010. (ENG.). 32p. (gr. -1 — 1). 16.95 (978-0-7358-2321-1(9)) North-South Bks., Inc.

Schuon, Catherine & Fitzgerald, Michael Oren, eds. King James Christmas: Biblical Selections with Illustrations from Around the World. 2012. (ENG., Illus.). 80p. (J). (gr. 3-7). 19.95 (978-1-937786-03-8(X)) World Wisdom, Inc.

Slegers, Liesbet. The Child in the Manger. Slegers, Liesbet, illus. 2010. (ENG., Illus.). 30p. (J). (gr. k — 1). 15.95 (978-1-60537-084-2(3)) Cobblestone Publishing Co.

Smith, Martina. La Historia de la Navidad: Un Relato de la Biblia Chispita. Grosshauser, Peter & Temple, Ed, illus. 2016. (SPA.). (J). (978-1-5064-2102-5(4)) Augsburg Fortress, Pubs.

—The Story of Christmas: A Spark Bible Story. Grosshauser, Peter, illus. 2015. (Spark Bible Stories Ser.). (ENG.). 32p. (J). (gr. -1-2). 12.99 (978-1-5064-0224-6(0), Sparkhouse Family) Augsburg Fortress, Pubs.

Stevenson, Peter, illus. Baby's First Nativity. 2016. (ENG.). 20p. (J). (gr. -1-k). bds. 9.99 (978-0-7944-3850-0(4)) Studio Fun International.

—Baby's First Nativity: A CarryAlong Treasury. 2016. (Carry along Treasury Ser.: 1). (ENG.). 20p. (J). (gr. -1-k). bds. 14.99 (978-0-7944-3836-4(9)) Studio Fun International.

Tebbs, Victoria. Christmas Story. Mitchell, Melanie, illus. 2009. (See & Say! Ser.). (ENG.). 20p. (J). (gr. k — 1). 6.95 (978-0-7459-4900-0(2)) Lion Hudson PLC GBR. Dist: Independent Pubs. Group.

—What Can You See? On Christmas Night. Julian, Russell, illus. 2010. (ENG.). 32p. (J). (gr. -1-k). 9.99 (978-0-7459-6142-2(8)) Lion Hudson PLC GBR. Dist: Independent Pubs. Group.

Tietz, Heather. Rockabye Baby Jesus. Miller, Nancy, illus. 2011. 20p. 12.95 (978-0-8091-6760-9(3)) Paulist Pr.

Tiny Tots Christmas. 2015. (Tiny Tots Ser.). (ENG., Illus.). 32p. (J). (gr. -1 — 1). 8.99 (978-0-7459-6455-3(9)) Lion Hudson PLC GBR. Dist: Independent Pubs. Group.

Twin Sisters(r) Staff, et al. Happy Birthday, Jesus: A Sing-Along Storybook. 2015. (ENG., Illus.). 14p. (J). (-5). 9.99 (978-1-63409-025-4(X)) Barbour Publishing, Inc.

—Play & Learn Bible Stories: Jesus Is Born: Wipe-Clean Storybook. 2015. (I'm Learning the Bible Activity Book Ser.). (ENG.). 16p. (J). (-5). pap. 6.99 (978-1-63409-026-1(8)) Barbour Publishing, Inc.

Tyrrell, Frances, illus. The Huron Carol. 2004. 32p. 16.00 (978-0-8028-5263-2(7)) Eerdmans, William B. Publishing Co.

Walker, Joni. Tell Me the Christmas Story. Walker, Joni, illus. 2003. (Illus.). 14p. (J). (gr. -1-k). bds. 5.49 (978-0-7586-0508-5(0)) Concordia Publishing Hse.

Wallace, Dora J. Twas the Night Before Jesus Was Born. 2012. 36p. pap. 16.99 (978-1-4497-5807-3(X), WestBow Pr.) Author Solutions, Inc.

Wallace, Ian. The Huron Carol, 1 vol. 2013. (ENG., Illus.). 32p. (J). (gr. -1). 14.95 (978-1-55498-394-0(0)) Groundwood Bks. CAN. Dist: Publishers Group West (PGW).

Whitaker-Taylor, Kandice. A Child Is Born. 2012. 20p. pap. 9.99 (978-1-62419-090-2(1)) Salem Author Services.

Wilkeshuis, Cornelius. The Gift for the Child. Verstegen, Jeska, illus. (ENG.). 28p. (J). 16.95 (978-0-86315-349-5(6)) Floris Bks. GBR. Dist: SteinerBooks, Inc.

Williamson, Karen. Baby Jesus, 1 vol. Conner, Sarah, illus. 2015. (Candle Little Lambs Ser.). (ENG.). 24p. (J). pap. 2.99 (978-1-78128-188-8(2), Candle Bks.) Lion Hudson PLC GBR. Dist: Kregel Pubns.

—The Christmas Story, 1 vol. Barnard, Lucy, illus. 2016. (Bible Mini-Pops Ser.). (ENG.). 10p. (J). 9.99 (978-1-78128-284-7(6), Candle Bks.) Lion Hudson PLC GBR. Dist: Kregel Pubns.

—The Wise Men's Story, 1 vol. Barnard, Lucy, illus. 2016. (Bible Mini-Pops Ser.). (ENG.). 10p. (J). 9.99 (978-1-78128-283-0(8), Candle Bks.) Lion Hudson PLC GBR. Dist: Kregel Pubns.

Windham, Sophie, illus. The Story of the Nativity. 2015. (ENG.). 32p. (J). (gr. k). 16.99 (978-0-7459-6352-5(8)) Lion Hudson PLC GBR. Dist: Independent Pubs. Group.

Woodward, Antonia. The Extra Special Baby: The Story of the Christmas Promise. 2017. (ENG., Illus.). 32p. (J). (gr. -1-k). 14.99 **(978-0-7459-7699-0(9))** Lion Hudson PLC GBR. Dist: Independent Pubs. Group.

Yamamoto, Makoto. O Holy Night: The First Christmas. Moritsu, Wakako, illus. 2005. 24p. (J). (gr. -1-3). per. 16.95 (978-0-8198-5440-7(9)) Pauline Bks. & Media.

Zobel-Nolan, Allia. Lift-the-Flap Nativity. Moroney, Trace, illus. 2015. (Lift-The Flap Ser.). (ENG.). 20p. (J). (gr. -1-k). 10.99 (978-0-7944-3527-1(0), Reader's Digest Children's Bks.) Studio Fun International.

Zondervan, A. The First Christmas Ever, 1 vol. Jones, Dennis, illus. 2014. (ENG.). 32p. (J). pap. 1.99 (978-0-310-74083-4(5)) Zonderkidz.

Zondervan Staff. Baby Jesus Is Born, 1 vol. Pulley, Kelly, illus. 2009. (I Can Read! / the Beginner's Bible Ser.). (ENG.). 32p. (J). (gr. -1-2). pap. 3.99 (978-0-310-71780-5(9)) Zonderkidz.

—Jesus God's Great Gift, 1 vol. Jones, Dennis G., illus. 2010. (I Can Read! / Dennis Jones Ser.). (ENG.). 32p. (J). (gr. -1-2). pap. 3.99 (978-0-310-71881-9(3)) Zonderkidz.

JESUS CHRIST—NATIVITY—DRAMA

Edwards, Emyr. O Achos y Mab Bychan: Casgliad o Ddramâu I Blant Ar Gyfer y Nadolig. 2005. (WEL.). 150p. pap. (978-0-86381-601-7(0)) Gwasg Carreg Gwalch.

JESUS CHRIST—PARABLES

Amery, Heather. Little Book of Stories of Jesus. Edwards, Linda, illus. 2007. (ENG.). 72p. (978-0-7460-8492-2(7)) Usborne Publishing, Ltd.

Archbold, Tim & Rock, Lois. The Good Bad Guy & Other Peculiar Parables. 2004. (ENG., Illus.). 64p. (J). (gr. 2-4). pap. 6.99 (978-0-7459-4695-5(X)) Lion Hudson PLC GBR. Dist: Independent Pubs. Group.

Berendes, Mary. The Good Samaritan. Johnson, Pamela & Squier, Robert, illus. 2011. (Parables Ser.). (ENG.). 24p. (J). (gr. k-3). lib. bdg. 28.50 (978-1-60954-391-4(2), 201186) Child's World, Inc., The.

Bowman, Crystal. The Prodigal Son, 1 vol. Sokolova, Valerie, illus. 2011. (I Can Read! / Bible Stories Ser.). (ENG.). 32p. (J). (gr. -1-2). pap. 3.99 (978-0-310-72155-0(5)) Zonderkidz.

Burgdorf, Larry. The Wise & Foolish Builders: A Parable of Jesus, Matthew 7:24-27 & Luke 6:47-49 for Children. Billen-Frye, Paige, illus. 2007. (Arch Bks.). 16p. (J). 2.49 (978-0-7586-1263-2(X)) Concordia Publishing Hse.

Burgdorf, Larry, et al. Best-Loved Parables of Jesus. Billen-Frye, Paige et al, illus. 2014. (ENG.). 101p. (J). 9.99 (978-0-7586-4662-0(3)) Concordia Publishing Hse.

Butterworth, Nick & Inkpen, Mick. Favorite Parables from the Bible: Stories Jesus Told, 1 vol. 2012. (ENG.). 216p. (J). 9.99 (978-0-310-72432-2(5)) Zonderkidz.

Carlson, Melody. The Other Brother. Björkman, Steve, illus. 2004. 40p. (gr. -1-3). 9.99 (978-1-58134-122-5(9)) Crossway.

Clark, Paul. The Good Wagon. Preston, Graham, illus. 2012. (J). lthr. (978-1-921633-88-1(3), Even Before Publishing) Wombat Bks.

David C. Cook Publishing Company Staff. Ring, Robe & Shoes, 10, Pack. 2008. (Pencil Fun Bks). 16p. (J). pap. 9.90 (978-1-4347-6822-3(8)) Cook, David C.

Dreyer, Nicole E. The Lost Coin. Collier-Morales, Roberta, illus. 2006. 16p. (J). 1.99 (978-0-7586-0873-4(X)) Concordia Publishing Hse.

—The Parable of the Talents. Morris, Susan, illus. 2007. 16p. (J). (gr. k-4). 1.99 (978-0-7586-1282-3(6)) Concordia Publishing Hse.

Edwards, Josh & David, Juliet. The Helpful Donkey, 1 vol. Barnard, Lucy, illus. 2015. (Bible Animals Ser.). (ENG.). 14p. (J). bds. 9.99 (978-1-78128-180-2(7), Candle Bks.) Lion Hudson PLC GBR. Dist: Kregel Pubns.

Froeb, Lori. A Child's Book of Parables. Mioroney, Tracy, illus. 2003. 32p. (J). 15.99 (978-0-7847-1278-8(6), 04344) Standard Publishing.

Glaser, Rebecca. The Good Samaritan & Other Bible Stories. Ferenc, Bill, illus. 2015. (Holy Moly Bible Storybooks Ser.). (ENG.). 32p. (J). (gr. k-3). 12.99 (978-1-5064-0251-2(8), Sparkhouse Family) Augsburg Fortress, Pubs.

Glavich, Mary Kathleen. A Child's Book of Parables. 2004. (978-0-8294-1039-6(2)) Loyola Pr.

Haines, Geri Berger. The Little Lost Lamb. Haines, Geri Berger, illus. 2009. (Illus.). 40p. (J). (gr. -1-k). 8.95 (978-0-8198-4528-3(0)) Pauline Bks. & Media.

Hartman, Bob. The Lion Storyteller Book of Parables. Nagy, Krisztina Kallai, illus. 2015. (ENG.). 64p. (J). (gr. k-4). 14.99 (978-0-7459-6446-1(X)) Lion Hudson PLC GBR. Dist: Independent Pubs. Group.

Jeffs, Stephanie. Stories Jesus Told. Tulip, Jenny, illus. 2004. (My First Find Out about Book Ser.). 24p. (gr. -1-18). pap. 3.95 (978-0-8294-1733-3(8)) Loyola Pr.

Kieffer, Jean-Francois & Ponsard, Christine. The Illustrated Parables of Jesus. 2012. 47p. 14.99 (978-1-58617-649-5(8)) Ignatius Pr.

Larsen, Carolyn. Teachings of Jesus. 2012. (Standard Bible Storybook Ser.). (ENG., Illus.). 32p. (J). 7.99 (978-0-7847-3565-7(4)) Standard Publishing.

Lindvall, Ella K. Read-Aloud Bible Stories, Vol. 5. 2015. (ENG.). 160p. (J). 15.99 (978-0-8024-1264-5(5)) Moody Pubs.

Littleton, Mark. Stories Jesus Told. Moroney, Trace, illus. 2004. 20p. (J). bds. 10.99 (978-0-8254-5519-3(7)) Kregel Pubns.

Lumsden, Colin, illus. Parables of Jesus. 2003. (Bible Colour & Learn Ser.). 32p. pap. 2.50 (978-1-903087-47-3(3)) DayOne Pubns. GBR. Dist: Send The Light Distribution LLC.

—People in the Life of Jesus. 2003. (Bible Colour & Learn Ser.). 32p. pap. 2.50 (978-1-903087-49-7(X)) DayOne Pubns. GBR. Dist: Send The Light Distribution LLC.

Make Believe Ideas, Ltd., creator. Read with Me: the Good Samaritan. 2006. (Read with Me (Make Believe Ideas) Ser.). (Illus.). 32p. (J). (gr. -1-3). pap. 8.97 (978-1-59145-529-5(4)) Nelson, Thomas Inc.

—Read with Me: the Loaves & Fish. 2006. (Read with Me (Make Believe Ideas) Ser.). (Illus.). 32p. (J). (gr. -1-3). pap. 8.97 (978-1-59145-528-8(6)) Nelson, Thomas Inc.

Mathews, Janice. Jack's Hats. 2013. (Illus.). 31p. (J). (978-0-8280-2718-2(8)) Review & Herald Publishing Assn.

Miller, Claire. La parabola de la oveja perdida (The Parable of the Lost Sheep) 2011. 16p. pap. 2.49 (978-0-7586-3065-0(4)) Concordia Publishing Hse.

Rabbit. Parables That Jesus Told. (J). pap. 19.95 (978-0-689-80229-4(3), Simon & Schuster Bks. For Young Readers) Simon & Schuster Bks. For Young Readers.

Rock, Lois. The Lion First Book of Parables. Vagnozzi, Barbara, illus. 2014. (ENG.). 64p. (J). (gr. k-2). 14.99 (978-0-7459-6409-6(5)) Lion Hudson PLC GBR. Dist: Independent Pubs. Group.

Rottmann, Erik. Parable of the Prodigal Son. 2009. 16p. (J). (gr. k-4). pap. 2.49 (978-0-7586-1613-5(9)) Concordia Publishing Hse.

Schantin, Diane. Parables from Twilight: A Bible Study. 2009. 80p. pap. 10.49 (978-1-4389-7757-7(3)) AuthorHouse.

Sexton, Clarence. The Parables of Jesus: The Greatest Stories Ever Told. (Complete Junior High Bible Study Resource Bks.: No. 3). (Illus.). (J). (gr. 6-9). pap. 16.99 (978-0-8307-1699-9(8)) Gospel Light Pubns.

Smouse, Phil. Born Again! 2004. 64p. (J). pap. 4.97 (978-1-59310-099-5(X)) Barbour Publishing, Inc.

Stockstill, Gloria McQueen. Jesus Rose on Easter Morn: A Listen! Look! Book. Durrell, Julie, illus. 2004. 20p. (J). bds. 5.49 (978-0-7586-0143-8(3)) Concordia Publishing Hse.

Teresa, Olive. The Story of the Good Samaritan. 2005. (Illus.). 16p. (J). 1.99 (978-0-7586-0863-5(2)) Concordia Publishing Hse.

Tnt. Gospel Parables, the Easter Story & Parables on the Second Coming. 2014. (On the Way (3-9's) Ser.). (ENG.). 100p. (J). pap. 17.99 (978-1-85792-403-9(7), 9781857924039) Christian Focus Pubns. GBR. Dist: Bookmasters Distribution.

Wach, Randy-Lynne. A Child's Collection of Parables. Harston, Jerry, illus. 2007. 13.95 (978-1-59038-724-5(4)) Deseret Bk. Co.

Zondervan Staff. A Father's Love, 1 vol. Miles, David, illus. 2014. (I Can Read! / Adventure Bible Ser.). (ENG.). 32p. (J). pap. 3.99 (978-0-310-73240-2(9)) Zonderkidz.

JESUS CHRIST—POETRY

Butcher, A D. Grandma Can You Tell Me. Dugan, Alan, illus. 2007. 16p. per. 10.95 (978-1-4327-1316-4(7)) Outskirts Pr., Inc.

Hopkins, Lee Bennett. Manger. Cann, Helen, illus. 2014. (ENG.). 34p. (J). 16.00 (978-0-8028-5419-3(2), Eerdmans Bks For Young Readers) Eerdmans, William B. Publishing Co.

Jeffs, Stephanie. Share Out the Food with Jesus. Reynolds, Annette, ed. Saunderson, Chris, illus. 2007. (Action Rhymes Ser.). (ENG.). 16p. (J). (gr. -1-2). pap. 4.99 (978-0-9789056-1-3(X)) New Day Publishing, Inc.

Lane, Leena. Sail in the Boat with Jesus. Reynolds, Annette, ed. Saunderson, Chris, illus. 2007. (Action Rhymes Ser.). (ENG.). 16p. (J). (gr. -1-2). pap. 4.99 (978-0-9789056-0-6(1)) New Day Publishing, Inc.

—Stand up & Walk with Jesus. Reynolds, Annette, ed. Saunderson, Chris, illus. 2007. (Action Rhymes Ser.). (ENG.). 16p. (J). (gr. -1-2). pap. 4.99 (978-0-9789056-4-4(4)) New Day Publishing, Inc.

pierce, km. The Very First Christmas. 2008. 52p. pap. 22.50 (978-0-615-15984-3(2)) Saeligstone.

Stiegemeyer, Julie. Baby in a Manger. Wong, Nicole, illus. 2004. 32p. (J). (gr. k-4). 9.99 (978-0-7586-0726-3(1)) Concordia Publishing Hse.

JESUS CHRIST—SERMON ON THE MOUNT

see Sermon on the Mount

JESUS CHRIST—TEACHINGS

Buck, Bryant. My First Christian Abc Bk. 2009. 32p. 14.95 (978-1-58169-322-5(2), Evergreen Pr.) Genesis Communications, Inc.

Cantrell, Pete. The Happy Angel: A Fractured Fairy Tale. Farris, Kim, illus. 2010. (ENG.). 32p. (J). 9.95 (978-1-61005-010-4(X)) BookLogix.

Carmody, Michael A. Life with Jesus: Bible Study Workbook. 2003. 32p. (YA). pap. 10.00 (978-0-910487-54-2(5)) Royalty Publishing Co.

Conn, Robert. Jesus Christ for Youth Leader, 2 vols. rev. ed. 2006. (Illus.). 152p. (gr. 3-7). per. 10.99 (978-0-687-33276-2(1)) Abingdon Pr.

Conn, Robert A. Jesus Christ for Youth, 2 vols. 2006. (Illus.). 112p. stu. ed., per. 8.99 (978-0-687-33286-1(9)) Abingdon Pr.

Craft, Sandra. Jesus Whispers in My Ear. 2013. 20p. pap. 10.95 (978-1-4497-8083-8(0), WestBow Pr.) Author Solutions, Inc.

Elkins, Stephen. Just Like Jesus Bible Storybook. 2015. (Wonder Kids Ser.). (ENG.). 176p. (J). 14.99 (978-1-4964-0821-1(7)) Tyndale Hse. Pubs.

Fair, Barbara A. Children Following the Teachings of Jesus: An Activity Book for Kids. Date not set. (J). (gr. k-2). pap. (978-0-9621174-3-5(9)) Fair, Barbara A.

Ficocelli, Elizabeth. The Imitation of Christ for Children: A Guide to Following Jesus. Sabatino, Chris, illus. 2006. 49p. (J). (gr. 3-7). per. 9.95 (978-0-8091-6733-3(6), 6733-6) Paulist Pr.

Flamini, Lorella, illus. Growing in Love: Virtues for Little Ones. 2006. 40p. (J). (gr. -1-k). bds. 11.95 (978-0-8198-3105-7(0)) Pauline Bks. & Media.

Fogg, Paul, illus. Jesus Said. 2008. 36p. pap. 10.95 (978-0-9814878-2-3(3)) Little Hands Bk. Co., LLC.

Kline, Tom. God's Love in Action: The Amazing Gift of Jesus. Weber, Penny, illus. 2015. (ENG.). 62p. pap. 8.99 (978-0-9863364-0-9(8)) Kline, Tom.

Larsen, Carolyn. Teachings of Jesus. 2012. (Standard Bible Storybook Ser.). (ENG., Illus.). 32p. (J). 7.99 (978-0-7847-3565-7(4)) Standard Publishing.

Lee, Ella Dolbear, illus. The Wonderful Story of Jesus. 2004. reprint ed. pap. 20.95 (978-1-4179-3177-4(9)) Kessinger Publishing, LLC.

Maes, Adolfo P. Christ & the Children. 2011. 16p. (gr. -1). pap. 9.99 (978-1-4567-6217-9(6)) AuthorHouse.

Moran, Mary Y. & Myers, Theresa F. Jesus Teaches Us. 77p. (J). (gr. 3). pap. 2.25 (978-0-8198-3925-1(6)) Pauline Bks. & Media.

Notto, E. T. Light of God Bible Books: Book 1 (Creation, God's Commandments, Faith) 2008. 52p. pap. 22.49 (978-1-4389-1702-3(3)) AuthorHouse.

Pingry, Patricia A. The Story of the Lord's Prayer. Garvin, Elaine, illus. 2008. (ENG.). 24p. (J). bds. 6.95 (978-0-8249-6519-8(1), Ideal Pubns.) Worthy Publishing.

Scherm, Deedra. Five Loaves & a Couple of Fish: A Story of Faith & Giving. Dreyer, Laura, illus. 2007. (ENG.). 20p. 7.99 (978-1-934789-01-8(1)) Lemon Vision Productions.

Schuon, Catherine & Fitzgerald, Michael Oren, eds. King James Christmas: Biblical Selections with Illustrations from Around the World. 2012. (ENG., Illus.). 80p. (J). (gr. 3-7). 19.95 (978-1-937786-03-8(X)) World Wisdom, Inc.

Schut, Jessie. Telling Your Friends about Jesus. (Friendship Ser.). stu. ed. 3.25 (978-1-56212-744-2(6), 300550); 55p. mentor's hndbk. ed. 6.25 (978-1-56212-251-5(7), 300555) Faith Alive Christian Resources.

Young, Sarah. Jesus Today Devotions for Kids, 1 vol. 2016. (ENG.). 368p. (J). 15.99 (978-0-7180-3805-2(3)) Nelson, Thomas Inc.

JESUS CHRIST IN ART

see Jesus Christ—Art

JET PLANES

Alvarez, Carlos & Finn, Denny Von. Supersonic Jets. 2009. (World's Fastest Ser.). (ENG., Illus.). 24p. (J). (gr. 3-7). lib. bdg. 25.95 (978-1-60014-287-1(7)) Bellwether Media.

Amato, William. Supersonic Jets. 2009. (High-Tech Vehicles Ser.). 24p. (gr. 2-3). 42.50 (978-1-61513-307-9(0), PowerKids Pr.) Rosen Publishing Group, Inc., The.

Byers, Ann. The Crash of the Concorde. 2009. (When Disaster Strikes! Ser.). 48p. (gr. 5-8). 53.00 (978-1-60854-779-1(5), Rosen Reference) Rosen Publishing Group, Inc., The.

—The Crash of the Concorde: When Disaster Strikes! 2005. (When Disaster Strikes! Ser.). (Illus.). 48p. (J). (gr. 5-8). lib. bdg. 29.25 (978-0-8239-3673-1(2)) Rosen Publishing Group, Inc., The.

Cefrey, Holly. Super Jumbo Jets: Inside & Out. 2009. (Technology: Blueprints of the Future Ser.). 48p. (gr. 4-4). 53.00 (978-1-60853-285-8(2)) Rosen Publishing Group, Inc., The.

—Super Jumbo Jets: Por dentro y por fuera (Super Jumbo Jets: Inside & Out) 2009. (Tecnología: Mapas para el Futuro Ser.). (SPA.). 48p. (gr. 4-4). 53.00 (978-1-60853-289-6(5), Editorial Buenas Letras) Rosen Publishing Group, Inc., The.

David, Jack. F-14 Tomcats. 2008. (Torque Ser.). (ENG.). 24p. (J). (gr. 3-7). 20.00 (978-0-531-21643-9(8), Children's Pr.) Scholastic Library Publishing.

—F-15 Eagles. 2008. (Torque Ser.). (ENG.). 24p. (J). (gr. 3-7). 20.00 (978-0-531-21644-6(6), Children's Pr.) Scholastic Library Publishing.

Doeden, Matt. Air Show Jets. 2009. pap. 52.95 (978-0-7613-4791-0(7)); (ENG.). 48p. (gr. 4-7). 26.60 (978-0-8225-9430-7(7)) Lerner Publishing Group.

Eason, Sarah. How Does a Jet Plane Work? 2010. (How Does It Work? Ser.). 32p. (J). (gr. 3-6). lib. bdg. 26.00 (978-1-4339-3471-1(X)); (Illus.). pap. 10.50 (978-1-4339-3472-8(8)) Stevens, Gareth Publishing LLLP. (Gareth Stevens Learning Library).

Fighter Jets. (Mighty MacHines Ser.). 16p. (J). (978-2-7643-0172-2(3)) Phidal Publishing, Inc./Editions Phidal, Inc.

Finn, Denny Von. F-16 Fighting Falcons. 2013. (Military Vehicles Ser.). (ENG., Illus.). 24p. (J). (gr. 3-7). lib. bdg. 25.95 (978-1-60014-884-2(0), Epic Bks.) Bellwether Media.

Hamilton, John. B-2 Spirit Stealth Bomber. 2012. (ENG., Illus.). 32p. (J). 27.07 (978-1-61783-267-3(7), Abdo & Daughters) ABDO Publishing Co.

—F-16 Fighting Falcon. 2012. 32p. 27.07 (978-1-61783-268-0(5), Abdo & Daughters) ABDO Publishing Co.

—F-35 Lightning II. 2012. 32p. 27.07 (978-1-61783-269-7(3), Abdo & Daughters) ABDO Publishing Co.

—F/A-18 Super Hornet. 2012. 32p. 27.07 (978-1-61783-270-3(7), Abdo & Daughters) ABDO Publishing Co.

High Flying: Level P, 6 vols., Vol. 3. (Explorers Ser.). 32p. (gr. 3-6). 44.95 (978-0-7699-0619-5(2)) Shortland Pubns. (U. S. A.) Inc.

Hill, Lee Sullivan. Jets. 2004. (Pull Ahead Bks.). (ENG., Illus.). 32p. (gr. k-2). (J). pap. 6.95 (978-0-8225-2383-3(3)); lib. bdg. 22.60 (978-0-8225-1541-8(5)) Lerner Publishing Group.

Jackson, Robert. Military Jets up Close, 01 vols., 1. Pearson, Colin, illus. 2016. (Military Technology: Top Secret Clearance Ser.). (ENG.). 224p. (YA). 43.60 *(978-1-5081-7080-8(0)*, Rosen Young Adult) Rosen Publishing Group, Inc., The.
Kennedy, Robert. Would You Dare Fly a Fighter Jet? 2016. (Would You Dare? Ser.). 00032p. (J). lib. bdg. 26.60 ***(978-1-4824-5812-1(8))*** Stevens, Gareth Publishing LLLP.
Macaulay, David & Keenan, Sheila. Jet Plane: How It Works. 2015. (ENG., Illus.). 32p. (J). (gr. -1-k). 17.99 *(978-1-62672-210-1(2)*, 9781626722101, Macaulay, David Studio) Roaring Brook Pr.
Mattern, Joanne. Pilotos (Pilots) 2009. (Trabajo en grupo (Working Together) Ser.). (SPA.). 24p. (gr. 1-2). 42.50 *(978-1-60854-577-3(6)*, Editorial Buenas Letras) Rosen Publishing Group, Inc., The.
—Pilots. 2009. (Working Together Ser.). 24p. (gr. 1-2). 42.50 *(978-1-60854-832-3(5)*, PowerKids Pr.) Rosen Publishing Group, Inc., The.
Maynard, Christopher & Christopher, Maynard. Los Aviones Tienen Alas. 2003. (Enciclopedia Me Pregunto Por Que). (SPA., Illus.). 32p. (J). (gr. 3-5). 12.99 *(978-84-241-2169-3(4)*, EV2031) Everest Editora ESP. Dist: Lectorum Pubns., Inc.
Morey, Allan. Fighter Jets. 2014. (Illus.). 24p. (J). lib. bdg. 25.65 *(978-1-62031-107-3(0)*, Bullfrog Bks.) Jump! Inc.
Mullins, Matt. How Does It Fly? Jet Plane. 2011. (Community Connections: How Does It Fly? Ser.). (ENG.). 24p. (gr. 2-5). lib. bdg. 25.64 *(978-1-61080-069-3(9)*, 201064) Cherry Lake Publishing.
Petruccio, Steven James. Shiny Jet Planes Stickers. 2006. (Dover Little Activity Books Stickers Ser.). (ENG., Illus.). 2p. (J). (gr. -1-5). 1.50 *(978-0-486-44925-8(4))* Dover Pubns., Inc.
Phillips, Karen & Klutz Editors. Straw Shooter Jets: Make Your Own Mini Air Force. 2014. (ENG.). 60p. (J). (gr. 3). 16.99 *(978-0-545-64779-3(7))* Klutz.
Riggs, Kate. Jets. (J). 2015. *(978-1-60818-521-4(4))* 2010. 24p. (gr. -1-3). 16.95 *(978-1-58341-913-7(6))* Creative Co., The. (Creative Education).
—Seedlings: Jets. 2015. (Seedlings Ser.). (ENG.). 24p. (J). (gr. -1-1). pap. 7.99 *(978-1-62832-121-0(0)*, Creative Paperbacks) Creative Co., The.
Scheff, Matt. Jets, 1 vol. 2014. (Speed Machines Ser.). (ENG.). 32p. (gr. 3-6). lib. bdg. 27.07 *(978-1-62403-612-5(0)*, SportsZone) ABDO Publishing Co.
Schuh, Mari. Jet Planes, 1 vol. 2013. (Aircraft Ser.). (ENG.). 24p. (gr. k-1). lib. bdg. 26.65 *(978-1-62065-113-1(0)*, Pebble Plus) Capstone Press of Coughlan Cos.
Silverman, Buffy. How Do Jets Work? 2013. (Lightning Bolt Books (tm) — How Flight Works). (ENG., Illus.). 32p. (gr. k-2). pap. 7.95 *(978-1-4677-0786-2(4))*; lib. bdg. 26.60 *(978-0-7613-8967-5(9)*, Lerner Pubns.) Lerner Publishing Group.
Smith, Sian. Machines at the Airport, 1 vol. 2013. (Machines at Work Ser.). (ENG., Illus.). 24p. (gr. 1-2). pap. 6.95 *(978-1-4329-7504-3(8))*; 23.32 *(978-1-4329-7499-2(8))* Heinemann-Raintree. (Heinemann Read & Learn).
Tieck, Sarah. Jets, 1 vol. 2011. (Amazing Vehicles Set 2 Ser.). (ENG., Illus.). 32p. (J). (gr. 2-5). 28.50 *(978-1-61714-699-2(4))* ABDO Publishing Co.
Zobel, Derek. F-22 Raptors. 2008. (Torque Ser.). (ENG.). 24p. (J). (gr. 3-7). 20.00 *(978-0-531-21645-3(4)*, Children's Pr.) Scholastic Library Publishing.

JET PLANES—FICTION

Biedrzycki, David. Santa's New Jet. Biedrzycki, David & Bonnet, Rosalinde, illus. 2011. (ENG.). 32p. (J). (gr. -1-2). 16.95 *(978-1-58089-291-9(4))*; pap. 7.95 *(978-1-58089-292-6(2))* Charlesbridge Publishing, Inc.
—Santa's New Jet. 2007. (Illus.). (J). pap. *(978-0-545-00238-7(9))* Scholastic, Inc.
Cook, Sherry & Johnson, Terri. Jazzy Jet, 26 vols. Kuhn, Jesse, illus. l.t. ed. 2006. (Quirkles — Exploring Phonics through Science Ser.: 10). 32p. (J). 7.99 *(978-1-933815-09-1(4)*, Quirkles, The) Creative 3, LLC.

JET STREAM

Randolph, Joanne, ed. Jet Stream Steering the Winds! 2017. (Weather Report). 32p. (J). (gr. 3-3). pap. 10.52 ***(978-0-7660-9017-0(5))*** Enslow Pubs., Inc.

JETER, DEREK, 1974-

Anniss, Matt. Derek Jeter in the Community, 1 vol., 1. 2014. (Making a Difference: Athletes Who Are Changing the World Ser.). (ENG.). 48p. (J). (gr. 5-8). 25.85 *(978-1-62275-185-3(X)* Rosen Publishing Group, Inc., The.
Bednar, Chuck. Derek Jeter: All-Star Major League Baseball Player. 2012. (Transcending Race Ser.). 64p. (J). (gr. 5). 22.95 *(978-1-4222-2728-2(6))* Mason Crest.
Bradley, Michael. Derek Jeter. 2004. (Benchmark All-Stars Ser.). (Illus.). 48p. (gr. 4-18). lib. bdg. 27.07 *(978-0-7614-1626-5(9)*, Benchmark Bks.) Marshall Cavendish Corp.
Donovan, Sandy. Derek Jeter. 2011. 32p. (gr. 2-5). 25.26 *(978-0-7613-7203-5(2))* 2008. pap. 40.95 *(978-1-58013-718-8(0))* 2004. 32p. (J). (gr. 2-5). pap. 6.95 *(978-0-8225-2038-2(9))* 2004. (Illus.). 32p. (J). (gr. 3-4). lib. bdg. 23.93 *(978-0-8225-3674-1(9))* 2011. (ENG.). 32p. (gr. 2-5). pap. 7.95 *(978-0-7613-7067-3(6))* 2011. (ENG., Illus.). 32p. (gr. 2-5). lib. bdg. 25.26 *(978-0-7613-7065-9(X))* Lerner Publishing Group.
—Derek Jeter (Revised Edition) 2011. (Amazing Athletes Ser.). 32p. (J). pap. 45.32 *(978-0-7613-7652-1(6))* Lerner Publishing Group.
Edwards, Ethan. Meet Derek Jeter: Baseball's Superstar Shortstop. 2009. (All-Star Players Ser.). 32p. (gr. 4-5). 47.90 *(978-1-61511-279-1(0)*, PowerKids Pr.) Rosen Publishing Group, Inc., The.
—Meet Derek Jeter: Captain of the New York Yankees. 2009. (All-Star Players Ser.). (Illus.). 32p. (YA). (gr. 4-7). lib. bdg. 25.25 *(978-1-4042-4488-7(3))* Rosen Publishing Group, Inc., The.
Feldman, Heather. Derek Jeter: Baseball's Best / Estrella del Béisbol. 2009. (Superstars of Sports/Superestrellas del deporte Ser.). (ENG & SPA.). 24p. (gr. 1-2). 42.50 *(978-1-60853-237-7(2)*, Editorial Buenas Letras) Rosen Publishing Group, Inc., The.
—Derek Jeter: Estrella del Béisbol (Baseball's Best) 2009. (Superestrellas del Deporte (Superstars of Sports) Ser.). (SPA.). 24p. (gr. 1-2). 42.50 *(978-1-60853-225-4(9)*, Editorial Buenas Letras) Rosen Publishing Group, Inc., The.
—Derek Jeter, Baseball's Best/Estrella del Beisbol. De Leon, Mauricio Velzaquez, tr. 2008. (Reading Power Ser.). (ENG., Illus.). 24p. (gr. 1-6). pap. 8.85 *(978-0-8239-6213-6(X))* Rosen Publishing Group, Inc., The.
Gatto, Kimberly. Derek Jeter: A Baseball Star Who Cares. 2013. (Sports Stars Who Care Ser.). 48p. (J). lib. bdg. 25.27 *(978-0-7660-4298-8(7))*; (gr. 3-4). pap. 8.95 *(978-1-4644-0541-9(7))* Enslow Pubs., Inc. (Enslow Elementary).
Greenberg, Keith Elliot. Derek Jeter. 2005. (Sports Heroes & Legends Ser.). (Illus.). 106p. (J). (gr. 3-7). lib. bdg. 27.93 *(978-0-8225-3068-8(6)*, Lerner Pubns.) Lerner Publishing Group.
—Derek Jeter: Spectacular Shortstop. 2011. (USA TODAY Lifeline Biographies Ser.). (ENG.). 112p. (gr. 6-12). 34.60 *(978-0-7613-6422-1(6))* Lerner Publishing Group.
Herman, Gail. Who Is Derek Jeter? 2015. (Who Is... ? Ser.). lib. bdg. 16.00 *(978-0-606-37552-8(X))* Turtleback Bks.
Herman, Gail & dePaola, Tomie. Who Is Derek Jeter? Thomson, Andrew, illus. 2015. (Who Was? Ser.). (ENG.). 112p. (J). (gr. 3-7). 5.99 *(978-0-448-48697-0(0)*, Grosset & Dunlap) Penguin Young Readers Group.
Howell, Brian. Derek Jeter: Yankee Great, 1 vol. 2011. (Playmakers Ser.). (ENG., Illus.). 32p. (J). (gr. 3-6). 27.07 *(978-1-61714-747-0(8))* ABDO Publishing Co.
Kennedy, Mike. Derek Jeter. 2009. (Today's Superstars Ser.). 48p. (J). (gr. 5-8). pap. 14.05 *(978-1-4339-2162-9(5))*; lib. bdg. 31.95 *(978-1-4339-1969-5(9))* Stevens, Gareth Publishing LLLP.
Marcovitz, Hal. Derek Jeter. (Modern Role Models Ser.). (Illus.). 64p. (YA). 2010. (gr. 7-12). lib. bdg. 22.95 *(978-1-4222-0482-5(0))* 2007. pap. 9.95 *(978-1-4222-0770-3(6))* Mason Crest.
Mattern, Joanne. Derek Jeter: Baseball Superstar, 1 vol. 2011. (Superstar Athletes Ser.). (ENG.). 24p. (gr. 1-2). pap. 7.29 *(978-1-4296-7303-7(6))*; pap. 41.70 *(978-1-4296-7304-4(4))*; lib. bdg. 25.32 *(978-1-4296-6560-5(2))* Capstone Press of Coughlan Cos.
Mills, Clifford W. Derek Jeter. (Baseball Superstars Ser.). (Illus.). 2008. 128p. (gr. 6-12). pap. 11.95 *(978-0-7910-9846-2(X)*, Checkmark Bks.) 2007. 122p. (YA). (gr. 7-12). lib. bdg. 30.00 *(978-0-7910-9422-8(7))* Facts On File, Inc.
O'Connell, Jack. Derek Jeter: The Yankee Kid. Rains, Rob, ed. 2003. (Super Star Ser.). 96p. (J). pap. 4.95 *(978-1-58261-043-6(6))* Sports Publishing, LLC.
Rappoport, Ken. Derek Jeter: Champion Baseball Star. 2012. (Sports Star Champions Ser.). (Illus.). 48p. (J). (gr. 5-18). 25.27 *(978-0-7660-4025-0(9))* Enslow Pubs., Inc.
Robinson, Tom. Derek Jeter: Captain on & off the Field. 2006. (Sports Stars with Heart Ser.). (Illus.). 128p. (J). (gr. 5-9). lib. bdg. 33.27 *(978-0-7660-2819-7(4))* Enslow Pubs., Inc.
Sandler, Michael. Derek Jeter & the New York Yankees: 2000 World Series. 2008. (World Series Superstars). (Illus.). 24p. (J). (gr. 1-4). lib. bdg. 22.61 *(978-1-59716-641-6(3))* Bearport Publishing Co., Inc.
Sheen, Barbara. Derek Jeter. 2008. (People in the News Ser.). (ENG., Illus.). 104p. (YA). (gr. 7-12). lib. bdg. 33.95 *(978-1-4205-0089-9(9)*, LML02109-242093) Cengage Gale.
Thornley, Stew. Derek Jeter: Daring to Dream. 2004. (Sports Leaders Ser.). (Illus.). 104p. (J). lib. bdg. 27.94 *(978-0-7660-2035-1(5))* Enslow Pubs., Inc.
Tieck, Sarah. Derek Jeter: Baseball Superstar, 1 vol. 2010. (Big Buddy Bks.). (ENG.). 32p. (J). (gr. 2-5). 28.50 *(978-1-61613-975-9(7))* ABDO Publishing Co.
Torres, John Albert. Derek Jeter. 2004. (Blue Banner Biography Ser.). (Illus.). 32p. (J). lib. bdg. 25.70 *(978-1-58415-333-7(4))* Mitchell Lane Pubs., Inc.
Torsiello, David P. Read about Derek Jeter. 2011. (I Like Sports Stars! Ser.). (Illus.). 24p. (J). (gr. k-18). pap. 7.95 *(978-1-59845-301-0(7)*, Enslow Elementary); (gr. 1-4). lib. bdg. 22.60 *(978-0-7660-3829-5(7))* Enslow Pubs., Inc.

JEWELRY

see also Gems

AZ Books Staff. Favorite Jewelry. 2012. (My Collection). (ENG., Illus.). 14p. (J). (gr. 1-3). bds. 12.95 *(978-1-61889-078-8(6))* AZ Bks. LLC.
Chen, D. M. & Sun, Michelle. Tie a Wish with Bracelets: Easy & Fun Chinese Knotting. 2012. (ENG., Illus.). 71p. (J). (gr. 4). pap. 10.95 *(978-1-937489-01-4(9))* StoryRobin Co.
Design your own Jewelry. 2004. (How 2 Kits Ser.). (Illus.). 48p. (J). *(978-1-84229-927-2(1))* Top That! Publishing PLC.
Everett, Felicity. Make Your Own Jewelry. (Fashion Guides Ser.). (Illus.). 32p. (YA). (gr. 6-18). pap. 6.95 *(978-0-7460-0077-9(4))* EDC Publishing.
Felix, Rebecca. Mini Wearables. 2017. (Mini Makers Ser.). (ENG.). 32p. (J). (gr. 2-5). 12.99 ***(978-1-5124-3843-7(X)***, Lerner Pubns.); 39.99 ***(978-1-5124-2813-1(2)***, Lerner Pubns.); 39.99 ***(978-1-5124-3842-0(1)***, Lerner Pubns.); (Illus.). 26.65 *(978-1-5124-2635-9(0))* Lerner Publishing Group.
French, Cathy. Make a Necklace. 2011. (Early Connections Ser.). (J). *(978-1-61672-235-7(5))* Benchmark Education Co.
Gordon, Stephen G. Expressing the Inner Wild: Tattoos, Piercings, Jewelry, & Other Body Art. 2014. (Illus.). 56p. (J). (gr. 6-12). lib. bdg. 33.26 *(978-1-4677-1467-9(4)*, Twenty-First Century Bks.) Lerner Publishing Group.
Holzach, Cornelie. Schatzsuche MIT Schmucki der Perlsau: Im Schmuckmuseum Pforzheim Für Groß und Klein. 2012. (ENG., Illus.). 80p. 35.00 *(978-3-89790-351-7(2))* Arnoldsche Art Pubs. DEU. Dist: Antique Collectors' Club.
Johnson, Anne Akers. Pulseras Rusticas. 2005. (SPA., Illus.). 32p. (J). (gr. 1). 17.95 *(978-968-5528-11-5(X))* Klutz Latino MEX. Dist: Independent Pubs. Group.
Klutz Editors. Grow Your Own Crystal Jewelry. 2016. (ENG.). 48p. (J). (gr. 3-7). 22.99 *(978-1-338-03749-4(8))* Klutz.
Leisure Arts, creator. Rubber Band Loom Fun! 2013. (ENG., Illus.). 48p. (J). (gr. 4-7). pap. 9.99 *(978-1-4647-1578-5(5))* Leisure Arts, Inc.
McDonald, Fiona. Jewelry & Makeup Through History. 2006. (Why Do We Wear? Ser.). (Illus.). 32p. (gr. 2-6). lib. bdg. 26.00 *(978-0-8368-6856-2(0)*, Gareth Stevens Learning Library) Stevens, Gareth Publishing LLLP.
Nichols, Kaitlyn. Toolbox Jewelry. 2013. (ENG.). 60p. (J). (gr. 3). 21.99 *(978-0-545-56134-1(5))* Klutz.
Schiffer, Nancy N. Rhinestones! A Collector's Handbook & Price Guide, 1 vol. 4th rev. ed. 2003. (ENG., Illus.). 160p. (gr. 10-13). pap. 16.95 *(978-0-7643-1751-4(2)*, 9780764317514) Schiffer Publishing, Ltd.
—Silver Jewelry Treasures, 1 vol. 3rd rev. ed. 2003. (ENG., Illus.). 144p. (gr. 10-13). pap. 16.95 *(978-0-7643-1852-8(7)*, 9780764318528) Schiffer Publishing, Ltd.
Stillerman, Robbie. Glitter Jewelry Sticker Activity Book. 2008. (Dover Little Activity Books Stickers Ser.). (ENG., Illus.). 2p. (J). (gr. 1-4). 1.50 *(978-0-486-46576-0(4))* Dover Pubns., Inc.
Torres, Laura. Brazaletes de la Amistad. 2005. (SPA., Illus.). 57p. (J). (gr. 3). 17.95 *(978-968-5528-05-4(5))* Klutz Latino MEX. Dist: Independent Pubs. Group.
Turnbull, Stephanie. Wardrobe Makeovers. 2016. (Sleepover Secrets Ser.). 24p. (gr. 2-6). 28.50 *(978-1-62588-381-0(1)*, Smart Apple Media) Black Rabbit Bks.
Ward, Charlotte, ed. Gem Care. Ward, Fred, photos by. 2nd ed. 2003. (Fred Ward Gem Book Ser.). (Illus.). 32p. pap. 9.95 *(978-1-887651-07-3(1))* Gem Bk. Pubs.

JEWELRY MAKING

Berne, Emma Carlson. Jewelry Tips & Tricks. Heschke, Elena, illus. 2015. (ENG.). 32p. (gr. 4-8). (J). lib. bdg. 26.65 *(978-1-4677-5220-6(7))*; 26.65 *(978-1-4677-8654-6(3))* Lerner Publishing Group. (Lerner Pubns.).
Blake, Susannah. Crafts for Accessorizing That Look. 2013. (Eco Chic Ser.). 32p. (J). lib. bdg. 23.94 *(978-0-7660-4313-8(4))*; (gr. 4-12). pap. 7.95 *(978-1-4644-0571-6(9))* Enslow Pubs., Inc.
Brothers Grimm & Sweeney, Monica. Loom Magic Charms! 25 Cool Designs That Will Rock Your Rainbow. 2014. (ENG., Illus.). 128p. (J). (gr. k). 12.95 *(978-1-63220-259-8(X)*, Sky Pony Pr.) Skyhorse Publishing Co., Inc.
Dorsey, Colleen. Epic Rubber Band Crafts: Totally Cool Gadget Gear, Never Before Seen Bracelets, Awesome Action Figures, & More! 2014. (ENG., Illus.). 48p. pap. 7.99 *(978-1-57421-914-2(6)*, 9781574219142, Design Originals) Fox Chapel Publishing Co., Inc.
—Totally Awesome Rubber Band Jewelry: Make Bracelets, Rings, Belts & More with Rainbow Loom(r), Cra-Z-Loom & FunLoom. 2013. lib. bdg. 18.40 *(978-0-606-35178-2(7))* Turtleback Bks.
Dybvik, Tina. Trendy Jewelry for the Crafty Fashionista, 1 vol. 2011. (Fashion Craft Studio Ser.). (ENG.). 32p. (gr. 3-4). lib. bdg. 27.99 *(978-1-4296-6549-0(1)*, Snap Bks.) Capstone Press of Coughlan Cos.
Etchison, Denise. Kids! Picture Yourself Making Jewelry. 2008. (Picture Yourself Ser.). (ENG.). 104p. pap. 12.99 *(978-1-59863-526-3(3))* Course Technology.
Hollis, Matthew. Jada Makes Jewelry: Use Place Value Understanding & Properties of Operations to Add & Subtract. 2014. (Math Masters: Number & Operations in Base Ten Ser.). 24p. (J). (gr. 2-3). 23.60 *(978-1-4777-6402-2(X))*; (ENG.). pap. 8.25 *(978-1-4777-4742-1(7))* Rosen Publishing Group, Inc., The. (Rosen Classroom).
Jewelry. 2013. (From Trash to Treasure Ser.). 32p. (J). (gr. 3-6). pap. 70.50 *(978-1-4777-1361-7(1)*, PowerKids Pr.) Rosen Publishing Group, Inc., The.
Johnson, Anne Akers. Loop Loom Bracelets: Make Super-Stretchy Beaded Bracelets. 2014. (ENG.). 40p. (J). (gr. 3). 21.99 *(978-0-545-70318-5(2))* Klutz.
Kachidurian, Debbie, et al. Bring on the Bling! Bracelets, Anklets, & Rings for All Occasions. 2016. (Accessorize Yourself! Ser.). (ENG., Illus.). 48p. (gr. 4-5). lib. bdg. 34.65 *(978-1-4914-8231-5(1))* Capstone Press of Coughlan Cos.
Kachidurian, Debbie Prestine, et al. Bring on the Bling! Bracelets, Anklets, & Rings for All Occasions. 2017. (Illus.). 47p. (J). pap. *(978-1-4914-8621-4(X))* Capstone Press of Coughlan Cos.
Kenney, Karen Latchana. Super Simple Jewelry: Fun & Easy-to-Make Crafts for Kids, 1 vol. 2009. (Super Simple Crafts Ser.). (ENG., Illus.). 32p. (gr. k-4). 27.07 *(978-1-60453-625-6(X)*, Super SandCastle) ABDO Publishing Co.
Kollabora, Inc. Super Simple Jewelry: 10 Modern, Versatile Pieces to Make in 30 Minutes or Less. 2015. (ENG., Illus.). 32p. 9.95 *(978-1-63186-363-9(0)*, 9781631863639) Taunton Pr., Inc.
Kollmar, Elizabeth M. Hooked on Rubber Band Jewelry: 12 Off-the-Loom Designs for Bracelets, Necklaces, & Other Accessories. 2014. (ENG., Illus.). 52p. pap. 9.99 *(978-1-57421-915-9(4)*, 9781574219159, Design Originals) Fox Chapel Publishing Co., Inc.
Kuskowski, Alex. Cool Refashioned Hardware: Fun & Easy Fashion Projects, 1 vol. 2016. (ENG.). 32p. (J). *(978-1-62403-700-9(3))* ABDO Publishing Co.
Laughlin, Kara L. Sparkle & Shine! Trendy Earrings, Necklaces, & Hair Accessories for All Occasions. 2016. (Accessorize Yourself! Ser.). (ENG., Illus.). 48p. (gr. 4-5). lib. bdg. 34.65 *(978-1-4914-8228-5(1))* Capstone Press of Coughlan Cos.
Lim, Annalees. Jewelry Crafts, Vol. 1. 2014. (Craft Attack! Ser.). (ENG.). 32p. (J). (gr. 3-3). 26.60 *(978-1-4824-0199-8(1))* Stevens, Gareth Publishing LLLP.
MacFarlane, Katherine. The Jeweler's Art. 2007. (Eye on Art Ser.). (ENG., Illus.). 128p. (J). (gr. 4-7). lib. bdg. 39.40 *(978-1-59018-984-9(1)*, 1270197, Lucent Bks.) Cengage Gale.
Nichols, Kaitlyn. Safety Pin Bracelets: Turn Ordinary Safety Pins into Extraordinary Bracelets. 2011. (ENG.). 48p. (J). (gr. 3-7). 19.99 *(978-1-59174-932-5(8))* Klutz.
Owen, Ruth. Jewelry. 2013. 32p. (J). (gr. 3-6). 26.50 *(978-1-4777-1283-2(6))*; pap. 11.75 *(978-1-4777-1360-0(3))* Rosen Publishing Group, Inc., The. (PowerKids Pr.).
Petelinsek, Kathleen. Making Jewelry with Rubber Bands. Petelinsek, Kathleen, illus. 2014. (How-To Library). (ENG., Illus.). 32p. (J). (gr. 3-6). 28.50 *(978-1-63137-781-5(7)*, 205367) Cherry Lake Publishing.
Phillips, Karen. Shrink Art Jewelry. 2007. (Klutz Ser.). (ENG., Illus.). 66p. (J). (gr. 7-12). 24.95 *(978-1-59174-437-5(7))* Klutz.
Quinn, Amy. Sewing Circuits. 2017. (21st Century Skills Innovation Library: Makers As Innovators Junior Ser.). (ENG., Illus.). 24p. (J). (gr. 2-5). lib. bdg. 28.50 *(978-1-63472-191-2(8)*, 209336) Cherry Lake Publishing.
Rau, Dana Meachen. Making Jewelry. 2012. (How-To Library). (ENG.). 32p. (gr. 3-6). 28.50 *(978-1-61080-475-2(9)*, 202085); pap. 14.21 *(978-1-61080-649-7(2)*, 202259) Cherry Lake Publishing.
Ross, Kathy. Jazzy Jewelry, Pretty Purses, & More! Bosch, Nicole in den, illus. 2009. (Girl Crafts Ser.). (ENG.). 48p. (gr. 2-5). 26.60 *(978-0-8225-9212-9(6))*; pap. 7.95 *(978-1-58013-883-3(7)*, Millbrook Pr.) Lerner Publishing Group.
Sadler, Judy Ann. Beads.Tr. of Perles. (FRE., Illus.). (J). pap. 7.99 *(978-0-590-24194-6(X))* Scholastic, Inc.
Sadler, Judy Ann & Sadler, Judy. Hemp Jewelry. Bradford, June, illus. 2005. (Kids Can Do It Ser.). (ENG.). 40p. (J). (gr. 3-7). 6.95 *(978-1-55337-775-7(3))* Kids Can Pr., Ltd. CAN. Dist: Hachette Bk. Group.
Warwick, Ellen & Di Salle, Rachel. Junk Drawer Jewelry. Kurisu, Jane, illus. 2006. (Kids Can Do It Ser.). (ENG.). 40p. (J). (gr. 3-7). 6.95 *(978-1-55337-966-9(7))* Kids Can Pr., Ltd. CAN. Dist: Hachette Bk. Group.

JEWELS

see Gems; Jewelry; Precious Stones

JEWISH-ARAB RELATIONS

Ellis, Deborah. Three Wishes: Palestinian & Israeli Children Speak, 1 vol. 2006. (ENG., Illus.). 144p. (J). (gr. 5-7). pap. 9.95 *(978-0-88899-645-9(4))* Groundwood Bks. CAN. Dist: Publishers Group West (PGW).
Ellis, Deborah, ed. Three Wishes: Palestinian & Israeli Children Speak. 2004. (YA). 16.95 *(978-0-88899-608-4(X)*, Libros Tigrillo) Groundwood Bks. CAN. Dist: Publishers Group West (PGW).
Hanel, Rachel. The Israeli-Palestine Conflict. 2007. (Days of Change Ser.). (Illus.). 48p. (YA). (gr. 4-7). lib. bdg. 31.35 *(978-1-58341-548-1(3))* Creative Co., The.
Israel & Palestine: The Roots of Conflict; Fight for Peace, 2 cass.; set. 2003. (YA). (gr. 9-12). tchr. ed. 89.95 *(978-1-58738-432-5(9))* Discovery Education.
Katz, Samuel M. Jerusalem or Death: Palestinian Terrorism. 72p. (YA). (gr. 9-18). 19.95 *(978-1-58013-208-4(1)*, Kar-Ben Publishing); 2003. (Illus.). (J). (gr. 6-12). 26.60 *(978-0-8225-4033-5(9))* Lerner Publishing Group.
Luxenberg, Alan. The Palestine Mandate & the Creation of Israel, 1920-1949. 2007. (Making of the Middle East Ser.). (Illus.). 80p. (J). (gr. 3-7). lib. bdg. 22.95 *(978-1-4222-0170-1(8))* Mason Crest.
Marx, Trish. Sharing Our Homeland: Palestinian & Jewish Children at Summer Peace Camp, 1 vol. Karp, Cindy, illus. 2010. (ENG.). 48p. (J). (gr. 1-6). 19.95 *(978-1-58430-260-5(7))* Lee & Low Bks., Inc.
Robson, David. Israeli-Palestinian Conflict. 2010. (World History Ser.). (Illus.). 128p. (J). 34.95 *(978-1-4205-0239-8(5)*, Lucent Bks.) Cengage Gale.
Ruelle, Karen Gray. The Grand Mosque of Paris: A Story of How Muslims Rescued Jews During the Holocaust. DeSaix, Deborah Durland, illus. 2010. (ENG.). 40p. (J). (gr. 3-18). pap. 8.95 *(978-0-8234-2304-0(2))* Holiday Hse., Inc.
Whiting, Jim. The Creation of Isreal. 2007. (Monumental Milestones Ser.). (Illus.). 48p. (YA). (gr. 4-7). lib. bdg. 29.95 *(978-1-58415-538-6(8))* Mitchell Lane Pubs., Inc.

JEWISH-ARAB RELATIONS—FICTION

Clinton, Cathryn. A Stone in My Hand. 2010. (ENG., Illus.). 208p. (J). (gr. 5). pap. 6.99 *(978-0-7636-4772-8(1))* Candlewick Pr.

JEWISH COOKING

Grossman, Chaya. The Cherry on Top: A Kosher Junior Cookbook. 2009. 79p. 16.99 *(978-1-58330-310-8(3))* Feldheim Pubs.
Harkham, Rachel & Thomas, Doni Zasloff. Get Cooking: A Jewish American Family Cookbook & Rockin' Mmama Doni Celebration. 2012. (ENG., Illus.). 128p. (J). (gr. 3-7). 19.95 incl. audio compact disk *(978-0-87441-948-1(4))* Behrman Hse., Inc.
Hepker, Sue. This Is the Challah. Wummer, Amy, illus. 2012. (J). *(978-0-87441-522-3(5))*; *(978-0-87441-922-1(0))* Behrman Hse., Inc.
Newman, Lesléa. Here Is the World: A Year of Jewish Holidays. Gal, Susan, illus. 2014. (ENG.). 48p. (J). (gr. k-2). 18.95 *(978-1-4197-1185-5(7)*, Abrams Bks. for Young Readers) Abrams, Inc.
Rauchwerger, Lisa. Chocolate Chip Challah: And Other Twists on the Jewish Holiday Table. Rauchwerger, Lisa, illus. 2004. (Illus.). 127p. (J). (gr. k-3). pap. 17.95 *(978-0-8074-0700-4(3)*, 510606) URJ Pr.
Schapira, Leah & Dwek, Victoria. Kids Cooking Made Easy. Lailah, Daniel, photos by. 2013. (ENG., Illus.). 144p. (J). pap. 15.99 *(978-1-4226-1435-8(2))* Mesorah Pubns., Ltd.
Sheen, Barbara, ed. Foods of Israel. 2011. (Taste of Culture Ser.). (Illus.). 65p. (YA). (gr. 9-12). 30.45 *(978-0-7377-5882-5(1))* Cengage Gale.
Tabs, Judy & Steinberg, Barbara. Matzah Meals: A Passover Cookbook for Kids. Hauser, Bill, illus. 2004. (Passover Ser.). (ENG.). 64p. (J). (gr. 3-5). pap. 7.95 *(978-1-58013-086-8(0)*, Kar-Ben Publishing) Lerner Publishing Group.
Yolen, Jane & Stemple, Heidi E. Y. Jewish Fairy Tale Feasts: A Literary Cookbook. Shefrin, Sima Elizabeth, illus. 2013. (ENG.). 200p. (J). 25.00 *(978-1-56656-909-5(5)*, Crocodile Bks.) Interlink Publishing Group, Inc.
Zakon, Miriam. Kids' Kosher Cookbook. 2005. (Illus.). 111p. (J). 16.99 *(978-1-56871-376-2(2))* Targum Pr., Inc.

JEWISH HOLIDAYS

see Fasts and Feasts—Judaism

JEWISH LANGUAGE

see Hebrew Language

JEWISH LEGENDS

Borlasca, Hector, illus. It's Too Crowded in Here! And Other Jewish Folktales. 2010. 64p. (J). pap. 7.95 *(978-0-87441-850-7(X))* Behrman Hse., Inc.
Gale Editor & Redmond, Shirley Raye, eds. Golem. 2011. (Monsters Ser.). (Illus.). 48p. (YA). (gr. 7-12). lib. bdg. 30.45 *(978-0-7377-5866-5(X))* Cengage Gale.
Goldin, Barbara Diamond. The Family Book of Midrash: 52 Jewish Stories from the Sages. 2006. Orig. Title: A Child's Book of Midrash. (ENG.). 128p. per. 28.00 *(978-0-7425-5285-2(3))* Rowman & Littlefield Publishers, Inc.
Lumer, Marc, illus. When Miracles Happened- Wondrous Stories of Tzaddikim. 2009. 22p. (J). *(978-1-56871-484-4(X))* Targum Pr., Inc.

Paulette (Pesha Razela) Fein Lieberman. Jewish Stories & Ideas for Children: A book for bonding, educational fun, & fund-raising purposes for children & Adults! 2009. 180p. pap. 16.95 *(978-1-4401-1914-9(7))* iUniverse, Inc.

Schwartz, Howard. A Journey to Paradise: And Other Jewish Tales. Carmi, Giora, illus. 2005. (Jewish Storyteller Ser.). 48p. (J). (gr. -1-3). 16.95 *(978-0-943706-21-4(1))*; pap. 9.95 *(978-0-943706-16-0(5))* Simcha Media Group. (Devora Publishing).

Sherman, Josepha. Rachel the Clever & Other Jewish Folktales. 2005. (American Storytelling Ser.). (ENG., Illus.). 171p. (J). (gr. 4-17). pap. 12.95 *(978-0-87483-307-2(8))* August Hse. Pubs., Inc.

Spero, Yechiel. Touched by a Story: For Children. Schonfeld, Shaya, illus. 2004. (ArtScroll Youth Ser.). 48p. (J). *(978-1-57819-436-0(9))* Mesorah Pubns., Ltd.

Wein, Berel & Mahr, Aryeh. Of Heaven & Earth: Stories of the Chassidic Masters. 2008. 56p. 18.99 *(978-1-58330-953-7(5))* Feldheim Pubs.

JEWISH LITERATURE

see also Bible

Karkowsky, Nancy. The Ten Commandments: Text. (J). (gr. 3-4). pap., act. bk. ed. 6.50 *(978-0-87441-477-6(6))* Behrman Hse., Inc.

JEWISH RELIGION

see Judaism

JEWITT, JOHN RODGERS, 1783-1821—FICTION

Goldfield, Rebecca & Short, Mike. Captive of Friendly Cove: Based on the Secret Journals of John Jewitt. 2015. (ENG., Illus.). 168p. (J). (gr. 7-7). pap. 25.95 *(978-1-936218-11-0(9))* Fulcrum Publishing.

JEWS

see also Discrimination

Blake, Philip. We Are Jews. 2016. (ENG., Illus.). 32p. (J). (gr. 4-6). pap. 11.99 *(978-1-4451-3892-3(1)*, Franklin Watts) Hachette Children's Group GBR. Dist: Hachette Bk. Group.

Bliss, John. Jewish Migration, 1 vol. 2011. (Children's True Stories: Migration Ser.). (ENG., Illus.). 32p. (gr. 3-3). 30.65 *(978-1-4109-4075-9(6)*, Raintree Perspectives) Heinemann-Raintree.

Byrne, Judy. A New Queen. 2013. 28p. pap. 13.95 *(978-1-4908-0887-1(6)*, WestBow Pr.) Author Solutions, Inc.

Chait, Baruch. The Lost Treasure of Tikkun Hamiddos Island. Pollack, Gadi, illus. (Good Middos Ser.: Vol. 2). 62p. 25.99 *(978-1-58330-478-5(9))* Feldheim Pubs.

Cone, Molly. Hello, Hello, Are You There, God? Kaye, Rosalind Charney, illus. rev. ed. 2004. viii, 55p. (gr. k-3). pap. 13.95 *(978-0-8074-0648-9(1)*, 102553) URJ Pr.

Dion, L. M. The Opposites of My Jewish Year. Olson, Julie, illus. 2005. (Very First Board Bks.). (ENG.). 12p. (J). (gr. -1 — 1). 5.95 *(978-1-58013-113-1(1)*, Kar-Ben Publishing) Lerner Publishing Group.

Hollingsworth, Tamara. Anne Frank: Una Luz en la Oscuridad. 2017. (TIME for Kids en Español - Level 4 Ser.). (SPA & ENG., Illus.). 48p. (gr. 4-4). lib. bdg. 31.99 *(978-1-5157-5146-5(5))* Time for Kids Inc AUS. Dist: Capstone Pub.

Horton, Casey. The Jews: We Came to North America. 2006. (Illus.). 32p. (J). (gr. 4-8). reprint ed. 19.00 *(978-0-7567-9905-2(8))* DIANE Publishing Co.

Katz, Yoni, prod. Virtual I'Shana Tovah. 2003. (J). cd-rom 12.00 *(978-1-932349-23-8(5)*, 20,000) Jewish Educational Media.

Kimmel, Eric A. Joseph & the Sabbath Fish. Peluso, Martina, illus. 2011. (Shabbat Ser.). (ENG.). 32p. (J). (gr. k-3). pap. 7.95 *(978-0-7613-5909-8(5)*, Kar-Ben Publishing) Lerner Publishing Group.

Lehman-Wilzig, Tami. Keeping the Promise: A Torah's Journey. Orback, Craig, illus. 2004. 32p. (J). (ENG.). (gr. k-3). pap. 9.95 *(978-1-58013-118-6(2))*; (gr. 1-5). 16.95 *(978-1-58013-117-9(4))* Lerner Publishing Group. (Kar-Ben Publishing).

McKay, Jenny. Children of the Holocaust. 2015. (ENG., Illus.). 80p. (J). (gr. 5-12). lib. bdg. *(978-1-60152-838-4(8))* ReferencePoint Pr., Inc.

Rosenthal, Zelda B. Precious Jewels: The Roadmap to a Child's Heart - a Delightful Resources for Mothers & Teachers. 2006. (ArtScroll Ser.). (Illus.). 268p. *(978-1-4226-0075-7(0))*; pap. *(978-1-4226-0076-4(9))* Mesorah Pubns., Ltd.

Seidman, Lauren. What Makes Someone a Jew? 2007. (ENG., Illus.). 32p. pap. 8.99 *(978-1-58023-321-7(X)*, 9781580233217, Jewish Lights Publishing) LongHill Partners, Inc.

Shahak, Bat-Chen. The Bat-Chen Diaries. Rubanenko, Diana, tr. from HEB. 2008. (Israel Ser.). (ENG., Illus.). 112p. (J). (gr. 5-7). per. 7.95 *(978-0-8225-7223-7(0)*, Kar-Ben Publishing) Lerner Publishing Group.

Skolnik, Fred & Berenbaum, Michael. Encyclopedia Judaica, 22 vols., Set. 2nd rev. ed. 2006. (ENG., Illus.). 1000p. 3297.00 *(978-0-02-865928-2(7)*, Macmillan Reference USA) Cengage Gale.

Thompson, Gare, et al. Our New Life in America: The Marks Family Lives the American Dream. 2007. (Nonfiction Reading & Writing Workshops Ser.). (ENG., Illus.). 40p. (J). pap. 19.95 *(978-0-7922-8701-8(0))* CENGAGE Learning.

Verzov, Ella & Oirechman, Chana. Moshe of Japan. 2013. (Illus.). 50p. (J). *(978-1-61465-171-0(X))* Menucha Pubs. Inc.

—Tamar of Venice. 2013. (Illus.). 54p. (J). *(978-1-61465-170-3(1))* Menucha Pubs. Inc.

Yanofsky, Tsivia. Take Me to Europe: Jewish Life in England, Spain, France, & Italy. 2013. (Illus.). 85p. (J). *(978-1-4226-1349-8(6))* Mesorah Pubns., Ltd.

Zeligs, Dorothy Freda. A Child's History of the Hebrew People: From Nomadic Times to the Destruction of the Second Temple. 2012. 200p. 44.95 *(978-1-258-25277-9(5))*; pap. 29.95 *(978-1-258-25530-5(8))* Literary Licensing, LLC.

JEWS—BIOGRAPHY

see also Rabbis

Abramson, Ann. Who Was Anne Frank? Harrison, Nancy, illus. 2007. (Who Was? Ser.). (ENG.). 112p. (J). (gr. 3-7). pap. 5.99 *(978-0-448-44482-6(8)*, Grosset & Dunlap) Penguin Young Readers Group.

Amler, Jane Frances. Haym Salomon: Patriot Banker of the American Revolution. 2009. (Library of American Lives & Times Ser.). 112p. (gr. 5-5). 69.20 *(978-1-60853-487-6(1))* Rosen Publishing Group, Inc., The.

Ashby, Ruth. Anne Frank: Young Diarist. 2005. 186p. (J). lib. bdg. 18.46 *(978-1-4242-2208-7(7))* Fitzgerald Bks.

Avital, Moshe. Not to Forget, Impossible to Forgive: Poignant Reflections on the Holocaust. 2004. (Illus.). 339p. (YA). 29.95 *(978-965-90462-4-9(3))* Mazo Pubs.

Bayer, Linda N. Elie Wiesel: Spokesman for Remembrance. 2005. (Holocaust Biographies Ser.). (Illus.). 112p. (J). (gr. 7-12). lib. bdg. 34.60 *(978-0-8239-3306-8(7)*, HBWIES) Rosen Publishing Group, Inc., The.

Boas, Jacob. We Are Witnesses: Five Diaries of Teenagers Who Died in the Holocaust. 2009. (ENG.). 208p. (YA). (gr. 6-10). pap. 9.99 *(978-0-312-53567-4(8)*, 9780312535674) Square Fish.

Borden, Louise & Borden, Louise W. The Journey That Saved Curious George: The True Wartime Escape of Margret & H. A. Rey. Drummond, Allan, illus. 2005. (Curious George Ser.). (ENG.). 80p. (J). (gr. 2-5). 17.99 *(978-0-618-33924-2(8))* Houghton Mifflin Harcourt Publishing Co.

Bornstein, Michael & Holinstat, Debbie Bornstein. Survivors Club: The True Story of a Very Young Prisoner of Auschwitz. 2017. (Illus.). (J). (ENG.). 352p. 16.99 *(978-0-374-30571-0(4)*, 9780374305710, Farrar, Straus & Giroux (BYR)); xviii, 348p. pap. *(978-1-250-11875-2(1))* Farrar, Straus & Giroux.

Byers, Ann. Saving Children from the Holocaust: The Kindertransport. 2011. (Holocaust Through Primary Sources Ser.). (Illus.). 128p. (J). (gr. 6-18). pap. 10.95 *(978-1-59845-344-7(0))*; (gr. 9-12). lib. bdg. 33.27 *(978-0-7660-3323-8(6))* Enslow Pubs., Inc.

Callahan, Kerry P. Mordechai Anielewicz: Hero of the Warsaw Ghetto Uprising. 2009. (Holocaust Biographies Ser.). 112p. (gr. 7-12). 63.90 *(978-1-61513-389-5(5))* Rosen Publishing Group, Inc., The.

Deutsch, Stacia & Cohon, Rhody. Hot Pursuit: Murder in Mississippi. Orback, Craig, illus. 2010. (ENG.). 40p. (J). (gr. 3-5). lib. bdg. 17.95 *(978-0-7613-3955-7(8)*, Kar-Ben Publishing) Lerner Publishing Group.

Dunn, Joe. Anne Frank, 1 vol. 2007. (Bio-Graphics Ser.). (ENG., Illus.). 32p. (J). (gr. 3-6). 28.50 *(978-1-60270-065-9(6)*, Graphic Planet- Nonfiction) ABDO Publishing Co.

Eisenberg, Azriel. Fill a Blank Page: A Biography of Solomon Schechter. (Illus.). (J). (gr. 6-11). 3.75 *(978-0-8381-0730-0(3)*, 10-730) United Synagogue of America Bk. Service.

Finkelstein, Norman H. Jewish Comedy Stars: Classic to Cutting Edge. 2010. (ENG., Illus.). 96p. (J). (gr. 5-12). pap. 9.95 *(978-0-8225-9942-5(2)*, Kar-Ben Publishing) Lerner Publishing Group.

Frank, Ana. The Diary of a Anne Frank. adapted ed. pap., tchr. ed. 4.95 *(978-0-8359-0138-3(6))* Globe Fearon Educational Publishing.

Friedman, Laurie. Angel Girl. Amit, Ofra, illus. 2008. 32p. (J). (gr. 3-7). 16.95 *(978-0-8225-8739-2(4)*, Carolrhoda Bks.) Lerner Publishing Group.

Gertner, Sheina Sachar. The Tree Stood Still. 2006. 96p. per. 9.95 *(978-1-58939-886-3(6))* Virtualbookworm.com Publishing, Inc.

Glaser, Linda. Emma's Poem: The Voice of the Statue of Liberty. Nivola, Claire A., illus. 2010. (ENG.). 32p. (J). (gr. -1-3). 17.99 *(978-0-547-17184-5(6))* Houghton Mifflin Harcourt Publishing Co.

Golabek, Mona, et al. The Children of Willesden Lane: A True Story of Hope & Survival During World War II. 2017. (Illus.). 213p. (J). **(978-0-316-55489-3(8))** Little Brown & Co.

Goldman, David J. Jewish Jocks: Athletic Stars Past & Present. 2004. (General Jewish Interest Ser.). (Illus.). 96p. (J). (gr. 6-18). pap. 8.95 *(978-1-58013-085-1(2)*, Kar-Ben Publishing) Lerner Publishing Group.

—Jewish Sports Stars: Athletic Heroes Past & Present. 2006. (Illus.). 96p. (J). (gr. 6-9). per. 9.95 *(978-1-58013-183-4(2)*, Kar-Ben Publishing) Lerner Publishing Group.

Gruenbaum, Michael. Somewhere There Is Still a Sun: A Memoir of the Holocaust. 2015. (ENG., Illus.). 384p. (J). (gr. 5-9). 17.99 *(978-1-4424-8486-3(1)*, Aladdin) Simon & Schuster Children's Publishing.

Gruenbaum, Michael & Hasak-Lowy, Todd. Somewhere There Is Still a Sun: A Memoir of the Holocaust. 2017. (ENG., Illus.). 384p. (J). (gr. 5-9). pap. 8.99 *(978-1-4424-8487-0(X)*, Simon & Schuster/Paula Wiseman Bks.) Simon & Schuster/Paula Wiseman Bks.

Harris, Samuel R. Sammy Child Survivor of the Holocaust. 2005. (Illus.). 128p. pap. 14.95 *(978-0-9759253-0-0(X))* Harris, Samuel.

Hermann, Spring. Anne Frank: Hope in the Shadows of the Holocaust. 2005. (Holocaust Heroes & Nazi Criminals Ser.). (Illus.). 160p. (YA). (gr. 6-12). lib. bdg. 29.27 *(978-0-7660-2531-8(4))* Enslow Pubs., Inc.

Hillman, Laura. I Will Plant You a Lilac Tree: A Memoir of a Schindler's List Survivor. 2008. (ENG., Illus.). 288p. (YA). (gr. 9-12). mass mkt. 7.99 *(978-1-4169-5366-1(3)*, Simon Pulse) Simon Pulse.

Hoffman, Betty N. Liberation: Stories of Survival from the Holocaust. 2011. (Holocaust Through Primary Sources Ser.). (Illus.). 128p. (J). (gr. 6-18). pap. 10.95 *(978-1-59845-348-5(3))*; (gr. 9-12). lib. bdg. 33.27 *(978-0-7660-3319-1(8))* Enslow Pubs., Inc.

Houghton, Sarah. Elie Wiesel: A Holocaust Survivor Cries Out for Peace. 2003. (High Five Reading - Green Ser.). (ENG., Illus.). 48p. (J). (gr. 3-4). per. 9.00 *(978-0-7368-2833-8(8)*, High Five Reading (RBL)) Capstone Press of Coughlan Cos.

—Elie Wiesel Set: A Holocaust Survivor Cries Out for Peace, 6. 2003. (High Five Reading - Green Ser.). (ENG.). 48p. (gr. 3-4). pap. 54.00 *(978-0-7368-2843-7(5)*, High Five Reading (RBL)) Capstone Press of Coughlan Cos.

Kacer, Kathy. Hiding Edith: A True Story, 1 vol. 2006. (Holocaust Remembrance Ser.). (ENG., Illus.). 120p. (J). (gr. 4-8). pap. 14.95 *(978-1-897187-06-7(8))* Second Story Pr. CAN. Dist: Orca Bk. Pubs. USA.

Killcoyne, Hope Lourie. Anne Frank: Heroic Diarist of the Holocaust, 01 vols., 1. 2016. (Britannica Beginner Bios Ser.). (ENG., Illus.). 32p. (J). pap. 12.90 *(978-1-5081-0061-4(6)*, Britannica Educational Publishing) Rosen Publishing Group, Inc., The.

Koestler-Grack, Rachel. Elie Wiesel: Witness for Humanity. 2009. (Life Portraits Ser.). (Illus.). 112p. (gr. 7-12). lib. bdg. 36.00 *(978-1-4339-0054-9(8)*, 1293616) Stevens, Gareth Publishing LLLP.

Kramer, Ann. Anne Frank: The Young Writer Who Told the World Her Story. 2009. (National Geographic World History Biographies Ser.). (ENG., Illus.). 64p. (J). (gr. 3-7). 7.99 *(978-1-4263-0414-9(5)*, National Geographic Children's Bks.) National Geographic Society.

Landau, Abraham, et al. Branded on My Arm & in My Soul: A Holocaust Memoir. 2011. (Illus.). 144p. 50.00 *(978-0-932027-20-7(2))* Spinner Pubns., Inc.

—Branded on My Arm & in My Soul: The Holocaust Memoir of Abraham Landau. 2011. (Illus.). 144p. pap. 25.00 *(978-0-932027-19-1(9))* Spinner Pubns., Inc.

Lee, Carol Ann. Anne Frank & the Children of the Holocaust. 2008. (ENG., Illus.). 256p. (J). (gr. 5-18). 7.99 *(978-0-14-241069-1(1)*, Puffin Books) Penguin Young Readers Group.

Levy, Max. Brief Jewish Biographies in Biblical, Post-Biblical & Talmudical Times. 2011. 190p. 42.95 *(978-1-258-06674-1(2))* Literary Licensing, LLC.

Leyson, Leon. The Boy on the Wooden Box: How the Impossible Became Possible ... on Schindler's List. (ENG., Illus.). (J). (gr. 4-9). 2015. 256p. pap. 9.99 *(978-1-4424-9782-5(3))* 2013. 240p. 17.99 *(978-1-4424-9781-8(5))* Simon & Schuster Children's Publishing. (Atheneum Bks. for Young Readers).

—The Boy on the Wooden Box: How the Impossible Became Possible ... on Schindler's List. 2015. lib. bdg. 19.65 *(978-0-606-36097-5(2))* Turtleback Bks.

Lobel, Anita. No Pretty Pictures: A Child of War. 2008. (ENG.). 288p. (J). (gr. 5). pap. 7.99 *(978-0-06-156589-2(X)*, Greenwillow Bks.) HarperCollins Pubs.

—No Pretty Pictures: A Child of War. 2008. (J). (gr. 5-8). lib. bdg. 18.40 *(978-0-613-28590-2(5)*, Turtleback) Turtleback Bks.

McDowell, Pamela. Anne Frank. 2014. (J). *(978-1-4896-2456-7(2))* Weigl Pubs., Inc.

Michelson, Richard. As Good As Anybody. Colón, Raúl, illus. 2013. (ENG.). 40p. (J). (gr. 1-4). 7.99 *(978-0-385-75387-6(X)*, Dragonfly Bks.) Random Hse. Children's Bks.

—Lipman Pike: America's First Home Run King. Pullen, Zachary, illus. 2011. (ENG.). 32p. (J). (gr. 1-4). 16.95 *(978-1-58536-465-7(7)*, 202186) Sleeping Bear Pr.

Miklowitz, Gloria. Anne Frank. 2009. pap. 13.25 *(978-1-60559-053-0(3))* Hameray Publishing Group, Inc.

Otfinoski, Steve. Drake: Actor & Hip-Hop Artist, 1 vol. 2013. (Contemporary Lives Set 2 Ser.). (ENG.). 112p. (J). (gr. 6-12). lib. bdg. 35.64 *(978-1-61783-618-3(4)*, Essential Library) ABDO Publishing Co.

Parks, Peggy J. Anne Frank. 2016. (ENG.). 80p. (J). (gr. 5-12). 38.60 *(978-1-60152-946-6(5))* ReferencePoint Pr., Inc.

Rogow, Sally M. Faces of Courage: Young Heroes of World War II. 2008. (ENG., Illus.). 162p. pap. *(978-1-894694-67-4(8))* Granville Island Publishing.

Rose, Or N. Abraham Joshua Heschel: Man of Spirit, Man of Action. 2003. (ENG., Illus.). 80p. pap. 9.95 *(978-0-8276-0758-3(X))* Jewish Pubn. Society.

Rubin, Susan Goldman. The Anne Frank Case: Simon Wiesenthal's Search for the Truth. Farnsworth, Bill, illus. 2009. (ENG.). 40p. (J). (gr. 5-18). 18.95 *(978-0-8234-2109-1(0))* Holiday Hse., Inc.

Rubin, Susan Goldman & Weissberger, Ela. The Cat with the Yellow Star: Coming of Age in Terezin. (ENG., Illus.). 40p. 2008. (J). (gr. 3-9). pap. 8.99 *(978-0-8234-2154-1(6))* 2006. (YA). (gr. 8-12). 16.95 *(978-0-8234-1831-2(6))* Holiday Hse., Inc.

Rubinstein, Robert. Zishe the Strongman. Miller, Woody, illus. 2010. (Kar-Ben Favorites Ser.). (ENG.). 32p. (J). (gr. k-3). pap. 7.95 *(978-0-7613-3960-1(4)*, Kar-Ben Publishing) Lerner Publishing Group.

Russo, Marisabina. Always Remember Me: How One Family Survived World War II. Russo, Marisabina, illus. 2005. (ENG., Illus.). 48p. (J). (gr. 1-5). 19.99 *(978-0-689-86920-4(7)*, Atheneum Bks. for Young Readers) Simon & Schuster Children's Publishing.

Sanders, Nancy I. King David, 1 vol. 2014. (Get to Know Ser.). (ENG.). 128p. (J). pap. 7.99 *(978-0-310-74475-7(X))* Zonderkidz.

Schloss, Eva & Powers, Barbara. The Promise: The Moving Story of a Family in the Holocaust. Yaron, Sophie, illus. 2006. (ENG.). 160p. (J). (gr. 13-18). 10.99 *(978-0-14-132081-6(8))* Penguin Bks., Ltd. GBR. Dist: Independent Pubs. Group.

Singer, Flora M. Flora - I Was but A Child. 2007. 180p. (J). pap. 26.50 *(978-0-9760739-8-7(6))* Yad Vashem Pubns. ISR. Dist: Coronet Bks.

Snyder, Elaine. Anna & Solomon. Bliss, Harry, illus. 2014. (ENG.). 32p. (J). (gr. -1-3). 17.99 *(978-0-374-30362-4(2)*, 9780374303624, Farrar, Straus & Giroux (BYR)) Farrar, Straus & Giroux.

Speregen, Debra Newberger. Ilan Ramon: Jewish Star. 2004. (ENG., Illus.). 120p. (J). pap. 13.00 *(978-0-8276-0769-9(5))* Jewish Pubn. Society.

Spielman, Gloria. Janusz Korczak's Children. Archambault, Matthew, illus. 2007. (Kar-Ben for Older Readers Ser.). 40p. (J). (gr. 3-7). lib. bdg. 17.95 *(978-1-58013-255-8(3))*; (ENG.). pap. 7.95 *(978-0-8225-7050-9(5))* Lerner Publishing Group. (Kar-Ben Publishing).

Thomson, Ruth. Terezín: Voices from the Holocaust. 2013. (ENG., Illus.). 64p. (YA). (gr. 5-9). pap. 9.99 *(978-0-7636-6466-4(9))* Candlewick Pr.

Van Maarsen, Jacqueline. A Friend Called Anne: One Girl's Story of War, Peace, & a Unique Friendship with Anne Frank. 2007. (Illus.). 163p. (J). (gr. 5-9). 14.65 *(978-0-7569-8146-4(8))* Perfection Learning Corp.

Van Maarsen, Jacqueline & Lee, Carol Ann. A Friend Called Anne. 2007. (ENG., Illus.). 176p. (J). (gr. 3-7). 6.99 *(978-0-14-240719-6(4)*, Puffin Books) Penguin Young Readers Group.

Waxman, Laura Hamilton. Anne Frank. 2009. (History Maker Biographies Ser.). (ENG.). 48p. (gr. 3-6). 27.93 *(978-0-7613-4221-2(4)*, Lerner Pubns.) Lerner Publishing Group.

Winkelstein, Steven Paul. Brisko: A True Tale of Holocaust Survival. Juliano, Dana, illus. 2014. 104p. (J). *(978-0-9824498-6-8(0))* Mystic Waters Publishing.

Winter, Jonah. Ruth Bader Ginsburg: The Case of R. B. G. vs. Inequality. Innerst, Stacy, illus. 2017. (ENG.). 48p. (J). (gr. 1-4). 18.95 **(978-1-4197-2559-3(9)**, Abrams Bks. for Young Readers) Abrams, Inc.

JEWS—CZECH REPUBLIC—FICTION

Kimmel, Eric A. The Golem's Latkes, 0 vols. Jasinski, Aaron, illus. 2011. (ENG.). 40p. (J). (gr. k-3). 17.99 *(978-0-7614-5904-0(9)*, 9780761459040, Amazon Children's Publishing) Amazon Publishing.

JEWS—FESTIVALS

see Fasts and Feasts—Judaism

JEWS—FICTION

A. L. O. E. The Triumph over Midian. 2006. 344p. per. 23.99 *(978-1-4255-3466-0(X))* Michigan Publishing.

Aaron, Chester. Gideon. 2009. (ENG., Illus.). 190p. (YA). pap. 12.99 *(978-1-934841-62-4(5)*, Zumaya Thresholds) Zumaya Pubns. LLC.

Abraham, Michelle Shapiro. Good Morning, Boker Tov. Alko, Selina, illus. 2004. pap. 6.95 *(978-0-8074-0783-7(6)*, 101974) URJ Pr.

—Good Night, Lilah Tov. Alko, Selina, illus. 2004. pap. 6.95 *(978-0-8074-0784-4(4)*, 101975) URJ Pr.

—My Cousin Tamar Lives in Israel. Koffsky, Ann D., illus. 2006. 14p. (J). (gr. -1). pap. 6.95 *(978-0-8074-0989-3(8))* URJ Pr.

Abramson, Susan & Dvorkin, Aaron. Who Hogged the Hallah? A Shabbat Shabang. 2008. (Illus.). 80p. (J). pap. 9.95 *(978-0-9659546-5-5(X))* Oak Leaf Systems.

Adelson, Leone. The Mystery Bear: A Purim Story. Howland, Naomi, tr. Howland, Naomi, illus. 2004. 32p. (J). (gr. -1-2). 15.00 *(978-0-618-33727-9(X)*, Clarion Bks.) Houghton Mifflin Harcourt Trade & Reference Pubs.

Appelfeld, Aharon. Adam & Thomas. Green, Jeffrey M., tr. from HEB. Dumas, Philippe, illus. 2017. (ENG.). 160p. (J). (gr. 3-7). pap. 14.95 *(978-1-60980-744-3(8)*, Triangle Square) Seven Stories Pr.

Arato, Rona. Mrs. Kaputnik's Pool Hall & Matzo Ball Emporium. 2010. (ENG., Illus.). 192p. (J). (gr. 4-7). pap. 9.95 *(978-0-88776-967-2(5)*, Tundra Bks.) Tundra Bks. CAN. Dist: Penguin Random Hse. LLC.

Aronson, Sarah. Believe. 2013. (ENG.). 296p. (YA). (gr. 7-12). 17.95 *(978-1-4677-0697-1(3)*, Carolrhoda Lab™) Lerner Publishing Group.

Asner, Anne-Marie. Klutzy Boy. Asner, Anne-Marie, illus. l.t. ed. 2007. (Illus.). 32p. (J). (gr. -1-2). per. 6.95 *(978-0-9753629-4-5(1))* Matzah Ball Bks.

Balsley, Tilda & Fischer, Ellen. I'm Sorry, Grover! A Rosh Hashanah Tale. Leigh, Tom, illus. 2013. (High Holidays Ser.). (ENG.). 24p. (J). (gr. -1-k). lib. bdg. 16.95 *(978-0-7613-7560-9(0)*, Kar-Ben Publishing) Lerner Publishing Group.

—I'm Sorry, Grover: A Rosh Hashanah Tale. Leigh, Tom, illus. 2013. (High Holidays Ser.). (ENG.). 24p. (J). (gr. -1-k). 6.95 *(978-0-7613-7561-6(9)*, Kar-Ben Publishing) Lerner Publishing Group.

—It's a Mitzvah, Grover! Leigh, Tom, illus. 2013. (ENG.). 24p. (J). (gr. -1-1). 6.95 *(978-0-7613-7563-0(5))*; lib. bdg. 16.95 *(978-0-7613-7562-3(7))* Lerner Publishing Group. (Kar-Ben Publishing).

Baraitser, Marion. Home Number One. 2006. (Illus.). 63p. (YA). pap. *(978-0-9529426-7-2(4))* Loki Books Ltd.

Belasen, Amy & Osborn, Jacob. Jenny Green's Killer Junior Year. 2008. (ENG.). 304p. (YA). (gr. 9-18). pap. 14.99 *(978-1-4169-6792-7(3)*, Simon Pulse) Simon Pulse.

Benenfeld, Rikki. Let's Go to the Park. 2015. (ENG., Illus.). 36p. (J). 10.95 *(978-1-929628-82-7(X))* Hachai Publishing.

—Let's Meet Community Helpers. Benenfeld, Rikki, illus. 2013. (Illus.). 32p. (J). 10.95 *(978-1-929628-75-9(7))* Hachai Publishing.

Benjamin, Amanda. Journey Through Jerusalem. Blumenfeld, Tamar, illus. 2016. (J). *(978-1-68115-531-9(1))* Behrman Hse., Inc.

Berlin, Bill & Berlin, Susan Isakoff. The Kvetch Who Stole Hanukkah, 1 vol. Welling, Peter J., illus. 2010. (ENG.). 32p. (J). (gr. k-3). 16.99 *(978-1-58980-798-3(7))* Pelican Publishing Co., Inc.

Berman, Seryl. Around the Shabbos Table. Binus, Ari, illus. 2008. 40p. (J). (gr. -1-k). pap. 10.95 *(978-1-929628-44-5(7))* Hachai Publishing.

Biers-Ariel, Matt. The Seven Species. Goodman, Tama, illus. 2003. 48p. 19.95 *(978-0-8074-0852-0(2)*, 161902) URJ Pr.

—Solomon & the Trees. Silverberg-Kiss, Esti, illus. 2004. (J). (gr. k-3). 13.95 *(978-0-8074-0749-3(6)*, 101055) URJ Pr.

Bietz, Barbara. The Sundown Kid. 2017. (ENG., Illus.). 32p. (J). (gr. k-2). pap. 8.95 *(978-1-939160-94-2(4))* August Hse. Pubs., Inc.

Blanc, Esther Silverstein & Eagle, Godeane. Long Johns for a Small Chicken. Dixon, Tennessee, illus. 2003. (J). 16.95 *(978-1-884244-23-0(8))* volcano pr.

Blankman, Anne. Prisoner of Night & Fog. (ENG.). (YA). (gr. 8). 2015. 432p. pap. 9.99 *(978-0-06-227882-1(7))* 2014. 416p. 17.99 *(978-0-06-227881-4(9))* HarperCollins Pubs.

Blitz, Shmuel. The Adventures of Aliza & Dovid: Holidays at the Farm. Katz, Tova, illus. 2005. (ArtScroll Youth Ser.). 48p. (J). *(978-1-4226-0021-4(1))* Mesorah Pubns., Ltd.

—Bedtime Stories to Make You Smile. 2003. (ArtScroll Youth Ser.). 14.99 *(978-1-57819-745-3(7)*, BEDS) Mesorah Pubns., Ltd.

—Every Story Has a Soul. Katz, Tova, illus. 2006. 47p. (J). 15.99 *(978-1-4226-0224-9(9))* Mesorah Pubns., Ltd.

Brahmachari, Sita. Mira in the Present Tense. 2013. (ENG.). 288p. (J). (gr. 3-7). 16.99 *(978-0-8075-5149-3(X))* Whitman, Albert & Co.

Brightwood, Laura, illus. Wise People of Helm. Brightwood, Laura, . 2006. (J). *(978-0-9779290-4-7(3))* 3-C Institute for Social Development.

Brown, Jason Robert. Tickety Tock. GrandPré, Mary, illus. 2008. 32p. (J). (gr. -1-3). lib. bdg. 18.89 *(978-0-06-078753-0(8)*, Geringer, Laura Book) HarperCollins Pubs.

Carlson, Claudia. Avi the Ambulance to the Rescue! 2016. (J). *(978-1-68115-512-8(5))* Behrman Hse., Inc.

Carlson, Claudia, illus. Avi the Ambulance Goes to School. 2015. (J). *(978-0-87441-941-2(7))*; *(978-1-68115-503-6(6))* Behrman Hse., Inc.

Carlson, Claudia & Koffsky, Ann D. Avi the Ambulance & the Snowy Day. Decker, C. B., illus. 2017. (J). *(978-1-68115-528-9(1))* Behrman Hse., Inc.

J
K
L

Cerrito, Angela. The Safest Lie. 2015. (ENG.). 192p. (J). (gr. 3-7). 16.95 *(978-0-8234-3310-0(2))* Holiday Hse., Inc.

Chaikin, Miriam. Hardlucky: The Story of a Boy Who Learns How to Think Before He Acts. Lisowski, Gabriel, illus. 2012. (ENG.). 40p. (J). (gr. -1-3). 16.95 *(978-1-61608-963-4(6)*, 608963, Sky Pony Pr.) Skyhorse Publishing Co., Inc.

Chotjewitz, David. Daniel Half Human. Orgel, Doris, tr. from GER. 2006. (ENG., Illus.). 336p. (YA). (gr. 7). reprint ed. mass mkt. 8.99 *(978-0-689-85748-5(9)*, Simon Pulse) Simon Pulse.

Cleveland, Rob. The Magic Apple: A Middle Eastern Folktale. Hoffmire, Baird, illus. 2006. (Story Cove Ser.). (ENG.). 32p. (J). (gr. -1-3). pap. 4.95 *(978-0-87483-800-8(2))* August Hse. Pubs., Inc.

Cohen, Barbara. The Carp in the Bathtub. 48p. (J). (gr. 2-4). pap. 5.95 *(978-0-8072-1332-2(2)*, Listening Library) Random Hse. Audio Publishing Group.

Cohen, Deborah. The Seventh Day. Hall, Melanie, illus. 2005. (ENG.). 24p. (J). (gr. -1-2). 16.95 *(978-0-929371-24-5(0))*; per. 8.95 *(978-1-58013-125-4(5))* Lerner Publishing Group. (Kar-Ben Publishing).

Cohen, Deborah Bodin. Engineer Ari & the Hanukkah Mishap. Kober, Shahar, illus. 2011. (Hanukkah Ser.). (ENG.). 32p. (J). (gr. k-3). pap. 7.95 *(978-0-7613-5146-7(9))*; lib. bdg. 17.95 *(978-0-7613-5145-0(0))* Lerner Publishing Group. (Kar-Ben Publishing).

—Engineer Ari & the Sukkah Express. Kober, Shahar, illus. 2010. (Sukkot & Simchat Torah Ser.). (ENG.). 32p. (J). (gr. k-3). pap. 7.95 *(978-0-7613-5128-3(0))*; lib. bdg. 17.95 *(978-0-7613-5126-9(4))* Lerner Publishing Group. (Kar-Ben Publishing).

Cohen, Deborah Bodin. Engineer Arielle & the Israel Independence Day Surprise: High, Low, & on the Go. Orrelle, Yael Kimhi, illus. 2017. (ENG.). 32p. (gr. k-3). 17.99 ***(978-1-5124-2094-4(8))***; pap. 7.99 ***(978-1-5124-2095-1(6))*** Lerner Publishing Group. (Kar-Ben Publishing).

Cohen, Leslie, et al. Jewish Love Stories for Kids: An Anthology of Short Stories. 2005. (Jewish Stories for Kids Ser.). 232p. (J). 16.95 *(978-1-930143-45-6(1)*, 3451); pap. 12.95 *(978-1-930143-46-3(X)*, 346X) Simcha Media Group. (Devora Publishing).

Cohen, R. G. The Place That I Love. Levitas, Alexander, illus. 2006. 30p. (J). 10.95 *(978-1-929628-29-2(3))* Hachai Publishing.

Cooper, Alexandra. Spin the Dreidel! Gévry, Claudine, illus. 2004. (ENG.). 14p. (J). (gr. -1-2). bds. 7.99 *(978-0-689-86430-8(2)*, Little Simon) Little Simon.

Dauvillier, Loïc & Salsedo, Greg. Hidden. Lizano, Marc, illus. 2014. (ENG.). 80p. (J). (gr. 1-5). 16.99 *(978-1-59643-873-6(8)*, 9781596438736, First Second Bks.) Roaring Brook Pr.

Davis, Aubrey. Kishka for Koppel, 1 vol. Cohen, Sheldon, illus. 2011. (ENG.). 32p. (J). (gr. -1-3). 19.95 *(978-1-55469-299-6(7))* Orca Bk. Pubs. USA.

Deutsch, Barry. Hereville: How Mirka Got Her Sword. 2012. (Hereville Ser.). (ENG., Illus.). 144p. (J). (gr. 3-7). pap. 9.95 *(978-1-4197-0619-6(5)*, Amulet Bks.) Abrams, Inc.

Deutsch, Barry & Hansen Literary Agency Staff. Hereville: How Mirka Got Her Sword. 2010. (Hereville Ser.). (ENG., Illus.). 144p. (J). (gr. 3-7). 17.99 *(978-0-8109-8422-6(9)*, Amulet Bks.) Abrams, Inc.

Djilmand, Shira Yehudit. The Secret of the Ruined Castle: And Other Stories. 2009. 148p. (J). *(978-1-56871-521-6(8))* Targum Pr., Inc.

Dostis, Isaac & Haddad Ikonomopoulos, Marcia. Ten Gold Medals: Glory or Freedom. 2005. (Illus.). ii, 72p. (J). *(978-0-8197-0770-3(8))* Bloch Publishing Co.

Draus, Naudia Burtwell. My Grandma Wears A Number: How One Girl Survived World War Ii. 2011. 40p. (gr. 4-6). pap. 19.57 *(978-1-4269-3351-6(7))* Trafford Publishing.

Dublin, Anne. The Baby Experiment: A Novel (Large Print 16pt) 2013. 172p. pap. *(978-1-4596-6337-4(3))* ReadHowYouWant.com, Ltd.

Edwards, Michelle. Chicken Man. 2008. (J). *(978-1-58838-237-5(0))*; 3rd ed. (Illus.). 32p. 16.95 *(978-1-58838-223-8(0))* NewSouth, Inc. (Junebug Bks.).

Elissa, Barbara. The Remarkable Journey of Josh's Kippah. Zaman, Farida, illus. 2010. 32p. (J). (gr. -1-3). pap. 7.95 *(978-0-8225-9933-3(3)*, Kar-Ben Publishing) Lerner Publishing Group.

Elkeles, Simone. How to Ruin a Summer Vacation. 2006. (How to Ruin a Summer Vacation Novel Ser.: 1). (ENG.). 240p. (YA). (gr. 8-12). per. 9.95 *(978-0-7387-0961-1(1)*, Flux) North Star Editions.

Elovitz Marshall, Sylvia A. & Marshall, Linda. The Mitzvah Magician. Engel, Christiane, illus. 2012. (Kar-Ben Favorites Ser.). (ENG.). 24p. (J). (gr. -1-2). 7.95 *(978-0-7613-5656-1(8)*, Kar-Ben Publishing) Lerner Publishing Group.

Fabiyi, Jan Goldin. Where Shabbat Lives. Ramá, Sue, illus. 2008. (ENG.). 12p. (J). (gr. -1 — 1). pap. 5.95 *(978-0-8225-8946-4(X)*, Kar-Ben Publishing) Lerner Publishing Group.

Flam, Chanie. Erev Shabbos. (Goldie Gold Board Book Ser.: Vol. 2). (Illus.). (J). (gr. -1-1). bds. 4.95 *(978-1-58330-026-8(0))* Feldheim Pubs.

Fleischman, Sid. The Entertainer & the Dybbuk. 2009. (ENG.). 192p. (J). (gr. 4-9). pap. 6.99 *(978-0-06-177140-8(6)*, Greenwillow Bks.) HarperCollins Pubs.

Flor Ada, Alma. Celebrate Hanukkah with Bubbe's Tales. Hayes, Joe & Franco, Sharon, trs. Epelbaum, Mariano, illus. 2007. (Cuentos para Celebrar / Stories to Celebrate Ser.). 30p. (gr. k-6). per. 11.95 *(978-1-59820-134-5(4))* Santillana USA Publishing Co., Inc.

Fridman, Sashi. The Great Friday Clean-up (French Flap) Salem, Iosi, illus. 2009. 32p. 12.95 *(978-1-934440-77-3(9)*, Pitspopany Pr.) Simcha Media Group.

—The Great Friday Clean-up (Hard Cover) Salem, Iosi, illus. 2009. 32p. 17.95 *(978-1-934440-93-3(0)*, Pitspopany Pr.) Simcha Media Group.

Fruchter, Yaakov. Best of Olomeinu - Series 2: Stories for All Year 'Round. 2003. 136p. 13.99 *(978-1-57819-398-1(2)*, BO1H); pap. 10.99 *(978-1-57819-399-8(0)*, BO1P) Mesorah Pubns., Ltd.

Ganz, Yaffa. The Adventures of Jeremy & Heddy Levi. Katz, Avi, illus. 2005. 204p. (J). 16.95 *(978-1-930143-50-0(8)*, 3508); pap. 12.95 *(978-1-930143-51-7(6)*, 3516) Simcha Media Group. (Devora Publishing).

—The Travels & Tales of Dr. Emanuel J. Mitzva. 2003. (J). 15.99 *(978-1-58330-581-2(5))* Feldheim Pubs.

Geller, Beverly. Ellies Shabbat Surprise. 2008. 32p. 13.95 *(978-965-229-390-9(3))* Gefen Publishing Hse., Ltd ISR. Dist: Gefen Bks.

Gellman, Ellie B. Netta & Her Plant. Ugliano, Natascia, illus. 2014. (Tu B'Shevat Ser.). (ENG.). 32p. (J). (gr. -1-2). 17.95 *(978-1-4677-0422-9(9)*, Kar-Ben Publishing) Lerner Publishing Group.

—Shai's Shabbat Walk. Conger, Holli, illus. 2014. (ENG.). 12p. (gr. -1). 5.95 *(978-1-4677-4949-7(4)*, Kar-Ben Publishing) Lerner Publishing Group.

—Tamar's Sukkah. Kahn, Katherine Janus, illus. rev. ed. 2015. (ENG.). 32p. (J). (gr. -1-2). pap. 7.99 *(978-1-4677-5637-2(7)*, Kar-Ben Publishing) Lerner Publishing Group.

Gibbs, Noni & Kahrs, Christina. Rahab's Promise. Vieira, Andrei, illus. 2007. 32p. (J). (gr. -1-2). pap. 9.99 *(978-0-8127-0432-7(0))* Autumn Hse. Publishing Co.

Gidwitz, Adam. The Inquisitor's Tale: Or, the Three Magical Children & Their Holy Dog. Aly, Hatem, illus. 2016. (ENG.). 384p. (J). (gr. 5). 17.99 *(978-0-525-42616-5(7)*, Dutton Books for Young Readers) Penguin Young Readers Group.

Gilani-Williams, Fawzia. Yaffa & Fatima: Shalom, Salaam. Fedele, Chiara, illus. 2017. (ENG.). 24p. (gr. -1-3). 17.99 *(978-1-4677-8938-7(0)*, Kar-Ben Publishing) Lerner Publishing Group.

Glaser, Linda. Hannah's Way. Gustavson, Adam, illus. 2012. (Shabbat Ser.). (ENG.). 32p. (J). (gr. k-3). pap. 7.95 *(978-0-7613-5138-2(8)*, Kar-Ben Publishing) Lerner Publishing Group.

Glaser, Linda. Way Too Many Latkes: A Chelm Hanukkah Story. Zolotic, Aleksander, illus. 2017. (ENG.). 32p. (gr. -1-2). 17.99 ***(978-1-5124-2092-0(1)***, Kar-Ben Publishing) Lerner Publishing Group.

Glasthal, Jacqueline B. Liberty on 23rd Street. Reingold, Alan, illus. 2006. (Adventures in America Ser.). (gr. 4). 14.95 net. *(978-1-893110-45-8(1))* Silver Moon Pr.

Glatshteyn, Yankev. Emil & Karl. Shandler, Jeffrey, tr. 2008. (ENG.). 208p. (J). (gr. 4-9). per. 9.99 *(978-0-312-37387-0(2)*, 9780312373870) Square Fish.

Gleitzman, Morris. Now. 2012. (Once Ser.: 3). (ENG.). 192p. (YA). (gr. 7). 16.99 *(978-0-8050-9378-0(8)*, 9780805093780, Holt, Henry & Co. Bks. For Young Readers) Holt, Henry & Co.

—Now. 2013. (Once Ser.: 3). (ENG.). 192p. (YA). (gr. 7). pap. 9.99 *(978-1-250-03417-5(5)*, 9781250034175) Square Fish.

—Once. 2005. 160p. (J). pap. *(978-0-14-330195-0(0)*, Puffin) Penguin Publishing Group.

—Then. 2013. (Once Ser.: 2). (ENG.). 224p. (YA). (gr. 7). pap. 9.99 *(978-1-250-00341-6(5)*, 9781250003416) Square Fish.

Goelman, Ari. The Path of Names. 2013. (Illus.). 339p. (J). pap. *(978-0-545-47431-3(0)*, Levine, Arthur A. Bks.) Scholastic, Inc.

Gold-Vukson, Marji E. The Numbers of My Jewish Year. Oeltjenbruns, Joni, illus. 2006. (ENG.). 12p. (J). (gr. -1 — 1). 5.95 *(978-1-58013-148-3(4)*, Kar-Ben Publishing) Lerner Publishing Group.

Goldberg, Barbara. Mindy's Passover Parsley. 2008. 24p. per. 24.95 *(978-1-4241-9779-8(1))* America Star Bks.

Goldberg, Malky. What Else Do I Say? A Lift the Flap Book. Argoff, Patti, illus. 2007. (J). (gr. -1-k). bds. 9.95 *(978-1-929628-34-6(X))* Hachai Publishing.

Goldin, Barbara Diamond. Mountain of Blintzes, 0 vols. McGrory, Anik, illus. 2010. (ENG.). 32p. (J). (gr. -1-2). pap. 6.99 *(978-0-7614-5790-9(9)*, 9780761457909, Amazon Children's Publishing) Amazon Publishing.

Gonzalez, Christina Diaz. A Thunderous Whisper. 2013. (ENG., Illus.). 320p. (J). (gr. 5). pap. 7.99 *(978-0-375-87371-3(6)*, Yearling) Random Hse. Children's Bks.

Gordon, Meryl G. The Flower Girl Wore Celery. Clifton-Brown, Holly, illus. 2016. (ENG.). 32p. (J). (gr. -1-5). 17.99 *(978-1-4677-7844-2(3)*, Kar-Ben Publishing) Lerner Publishing Group.

Gosline, Andrea & Alban, Andrea. Anya's War. 2011. (ENG.). 208p. (YA). (gr. 6-9). 16.99 *(978-0-312-37093-0(8)*, 9780312370930) Feiwel & Friends.

Gottesfeld, Jeff. The Tree in the Courtyard: Looking Through Anne Frank's Window. McCarty, Peter, illus. 2016. (ENG.). 40p. (J). (gr. k-3). 17.99 *(978-0-385-75397-5(7))*; lib. bdg. 20.99 *(978-0-385-75398-2(5))* Random Hse. Children's Bks. (Knopf Bks. for Young Readers).

Gratz, Alan, et al. Prisoner B-3087. 2013. (ENG.). 272p. (J). (gr. 4-7). 16.99 *(978-0-545-45901-3(X)*, Scholastic Pr.) Scholastic, Inc.

Graudin, Ryan. Blood for Blood. (Wolf by Wolf Ser.: 1). (ENG.). (YA). (gr. 10-17). 2017. 592p. pap. 10.99 ***(978-0-316-40516-4(7))*** 2016. 496p. 17.99 *(978-0-316-40515-7(9))* Little, Brown Bks. for Young Readers.

Greenberg, David E. The Ugly Brown Pear. 2010. 40p. pap. 12.96 *(978-0-557-28055-1(9))* Lulu Pr., Inc.

Greenberger, Tehilla. Gifts to Treasure. Toron, Eli, illus. 2007. (Fun to Read Book). 224p. (J). per. 10.95 *(978-1-929628-32-2(3))* Hachai Publishing.

Grubman, Bonnie. Oy Vey! Life in a Shoe. Mottram, Dave, illus. 2016. (J). *(978-1-68115-515-9(X))* Behrman Hse., Inc.

Hannigan, Lynne. Sam's Passover. 2004. (ENG., Illus.). 32p. pap. 5.95 *(978-0-7136-4084-7(7)*, 93342, A&C Black) Bloomsbury Publishing Plc GBR. Dist: Consortium Bk. Sales & Distribution.

Heller, Linda. How Dalia Put a Big Yellow Comforter Inside a Tiny Blue Box: And Other Wonders of Tzedakah. McQueen, Stacey Dressen, illus. 2011. (ENG.). 32p. (J). (gr. -1-2). 16.99 *(978-1-58246-378-0(6)*, Tricycle Pr.) Random Hse. Children's Bks.

Hering, Marianne & Younger, Marshal. Escape to the Hiding Place. 2012. (AIO Imagination Station Bks.: 9). (ENG., Illus.). 128p. (J). pap. 4.99 *(978-1-58997-693-1(2))* Tyndale Hse. Pubs.

Herman, Charlotte. My Chocolate Year: A Novel with 12 Recipes. Pham, LeUyen, illus. 2008. (ENG.). 176p. (J). (gr. 3-7). 15.99 *(978-1-4169-3341-0(7)*, Simon & Schuster Bks. For Young Readers) Simon & Schuster Bks. For Young Readers.

Herman, Debbie. Rosie Saves the World. Lyon, Tammie, illus. 2017. (ENG.). 32p. (gr. -1-2). 17.99 ***(978-1-5124-2085-2(9)***, Kar-Ben Publishing) Lerner Publishing Group.

Herman, Michael. Under the Sabbath Lamp. Massari, Alida, illus. 2017. (ENG.). 32p. (J). (gr. -1-2). 17.99 *(978-1-5124-0841-6(7)*, Kar-Ben Publishing) Lerner Publishing Group.

Hershenhorn, Esther. Chicken Soup by Heart. Litzinger, Rosanne, illus. 2010. (ENG.). 40p. (J). (gr. -1-3). 16.99 *(978-1-4424-2197-4(5)*, Simon & Schuster Bks. For Young Readers) Simon & Schuster Bks. For Young Readers.

Hesse, Karen. The Cats in Krasinski Square. Watson, Wendy, illus. 2004. (ENG.). 32p. (J). (gr. 2-5). 18.99 *(978-0-439-43540-6(4)*, Scholastic Pr.) Scholastic, Inc.

—Letters from Rifka. 2009. 9.00 *(978-0-7848-2599-0(8)*, Everbind) Marco Bk. Co.

—Letters from Rifka. 2008. (ENG.). 148p. 17.00 *(978-1-60686-224-7(3))* Perfection Learning Corp.

—Letters from Rifka. 2009. (ENG.). 176p. (J). (gr. 5-9). pap. 6.99 *(978-0-312-53561-2(9)*, 9780312535612) Square Fish.

Hest, Amy. When Jessie Came Across the Sea. 2003. 17.20 *(978-0-613-69484-1(8)*, Turtleback) Turtleback Bks.

Hyde, Heidi Smith. Feivel's Flying Horses. van der Sterre, Johanna, illus. 2010. (ENG.). 32p. (J). (gr. k-4). lib. bdg. 17.95 *(978-0-7613-3957-1(4))*; pap. 7.95 *(978-0-7613-3959-5(0))* Lerner Publishing Group. (Kar-Ben Publishing).

—Shanghai Sukkah. Tsong, Jing Jing, illus. 2015. (ENG.). 32p. (J). (gr. k-4). 17.99 *(978-1-4677-3474-5(8))*; pap. 7.99 *(978-1-4677-3475-2(6))* Lerner Publishing Group. (Kar-Ben Publishing).

Ioannides, Mara W. Cohen. A Shout in the Sunshine. 2007. (ENG.). 120p. (gr. 5). per. 14.95 *(978-0-8276-0838-2(1))* Jewish Pubn. Society.

Ish-Kishor, Sulamith. A Boy of Old Prague. Shahn, Ben, illus. 2008. (Dover Children's Classics Ser.). (ENG.). 96p. (J). (gr. 4-6). pap. 3.99 *(978-0-486-46766-5(X))* Dover Pubns., Inc.

Jablonski, Carla. Defiance, Bk. 2. Purvis, Leland, illus. 2011. (Resistance Ser.: 2). (ENG.). 128p. (YA). (gr. 7-12). pap. 18.99 *(978-1-59643-292-5(6)*, 9781596432925, First Second Bks.) Roaring Brook Pr.

—Resistance, Bk. 1. Purvis, Leland, illus. 2010. (Resistance Ser.: 1). (ENG.). 128p. (YA). (gr. 7-12). pap. 17.99 *(978-1-59643-291-8(8)*, 9781596432918, First Second Bks.) Roaring Brook Pr.

Jane, Yolen. The Devil's Arithmetic. 2014. (ENG.). 176p. (J). 11.24 *(978-1-63245-218-4(9))* Lectorum Pubns., Inc.

Joffo, Joseph. A Bag of Marbles: The Graphic Novel. 2013. 128p. pap. 29.27 *(978-1-4677-1651-2(0))* Lerner Publishing Group.

—A Bag of Marbles: The Graphic Novel. Gauvin, Edward, tr. Bailly, Vincent, illus. 2013. (ENG.). 128p. (gr. 7-12). pap. 9.95 *(978-1-4677-1516-4(6))*; lib. bdg. 29.27 *(978-1-4677-0700-8(7))* Lerner Publishing Group. (Graphic Universe™).

Jules, Jacqueline. Happy Hanukkah Lights. Shapiro, Michelle, illus. 2010. (Hanukkah Ser.). (ENG.). 12p. (J). (gr. -1 — 1). 5.95 *(978-0-7613-5120-7(5)*, Kar-Ben Publishing) Lerner Publishing Group.

—What a Way to Start a New Year! A Rosh Hashanah Story. Stead, Judy, illus. 2013. (High Holidays Ser.). (ENG.). 24p. (J). (gr. -1-2). 7.95 *(978-0-7613-8117-4(1)*, Kar-Ben Publishing) Lerner Publishing Group.

Jules, Jacqueline & Hechtkopf, Jacqueline. Goodnight Sh'ma. Hall, Melanie W., illus. 2008. (ENG.). 12p. (J). (gr. -1 — 1). pap. 5.95 *(978-0-8225-8945-7(1)*, Kar-Ben Publishing) Lerner Publishing Group.

—Picnic at Camp Shalom. Melmon, Deborah, illus. 2011. (Kar-Ben Favorites Ser.). (ENG.). 32p. (J). (gr. k-3). 17.95 *(978-0-7613-6661-4(X)*, Kar-Ben Publishing) Lerner Publishing Group.

—The Ziz & the Hanukkah Miracle. Kahn, Katherine Janus, illus. 2006. (ENG.). 32p. (J). (gr. -1-2). lib. bdg. 17.95 *(978-1-58013-160-5(3)*, Kar-Ben Publishing) Lerner Publishing Group.

Kacer, Kathy. The Diary of Laura's Twin, 1 vol. 2008. (Holocaust Remembrance Ser.). (ENG., Illus.). 208p. (J). (gr. 4-8). pap. 14.95 *(978-1-897187-39-5(4))* Second Story Pr. CAN. Dist: Orca Bk. Pubs. USA.

—Shanghai Escape, 1 vol. 2013. (Holocaust Remembrance Ser.). (ENG.). 204p. (J). (gr. 6-8). pap. 14.95 *(978-1-927583-10-4(1))* Second Story Pr. CAN. Dist: Orca Bk. Pubs. USA.

Kalechofsky, Roberta. A Boy, a Chicken & the Lion of Judah: How Ari Became a Vegetarian. 2012. (ENG., Illus.). 50p. (J). pap. 12.00 *(978-0-916288-58-7(7))* Micah Pubns.

Kamin, Rachel & The Association of Jewish Libraries Staff. The 2011 Sydney Taylor Book Award: Quest for the Best. 2011. 228p. (YA). pap. 18.00 *(978-0-929262-02-4(6))* Association of Jewish Libraries.

Karlin, Ann Bell. Eight Bedtime Stories for Jewish Children. Mazo, Chaim, ed. 2012. 64p. pap. 11.95 *(978-1-936778-67-6(X))* Mazo Pubs.

Kasnett, Yitzchak. The Studen't Guide to the Cohens of Tzefat. (J). pap. 3.99 *(978-0-89906-849-7(9)*, SGCO) Mesorah Pubns., Ltd.

Katies Choice. 2005. (YA). per. *(978-1-59872-217-8(4))* Instant Pub.

Kaurin, Marianne. Almost Autumn. Hedger, Rosie, tr. from NOR. 2017. (ENG.). 288p. (J). (gr. 7). 17.99 *(978-0-545-88965-0(0)*, Levine, Arthur A. Bks.) Scholastic, Inc.

Kimmel, Eric A. Even Higher! A Rosh Hashanah Story by I. L. Peretz. Weber, Jill, illus. 2010. (ENG.). 32p. (J). (gr. -1-3). pap. 6.95 *(978-0-8234-2298-2(4))* Holiday Hse., Inc.

—Hanukkah Bear. Wohnoutka, Mike, illus. (ENG.). 32p. (J). (gr. -1-3). 2014. 6.99 *(978-0-8234-3169-4(X))* 2013. 17.95 *(978-0-8234-2855-7(9))* Holiday Hse., Inc.

—Joseph & the Sabbath Fish. Peluso, Martina, illus. 2011. (Shabbat Ser.). (ENG.). 32p. (J). (gr. k-3). lib. bdg. 17.95 *(978-0-7613-5908-1(7)*, Kar-Ben Publishing) Lerner Publishing Group.

—Onions & Garlic: An Old Tale. Arnold, Katya, illus. 2005. 29p. (J). (gr. k-4). reprint ed. 16.00 *(978-0-7567-9638-9(5))* DIANE Publishing Co.

—Scarlett & Sam: Escape from Egypt. Stevanovic, Ivica, illus. 2015. (J). 6.99 *(978-1-4677-6207-6(5))*; (ENG.). 168p. (gr. 1-3). lib. bdg. 15.95 *(978-1-4677-3850-7(6))* Lerner Publishing Group. (Kar-Ben Publishing).

Kimmel, Eric A. & Trueman, Matthew. Simon & the Bear: A Hanukkah Tale. 2014. (ENG., Illus.). 40p. (J). (gr. -1-k). 16.99 *(978-1-4231-4355-0(8))* Hyperion Bks. for Children.

Kimmelman, Leslie. The Little Red Hen & the Passover Matzah. Meisel, Paul, illus. (ENG.). 32p. (J). 2011. pap. 6.95 *(978-0-8234-2327-9(1))* 2010. (gr. -1-3). 16.95 *(978-0-8234-1952-4(5))* Holiday Hse., Inc.

—The Shabbat Puppy, 0 vols. Zollars, Jaime, illus. 2012. (Shofar Ser.: 0). (ENG.). 32p. (J). (gr. -1-3). 17.99 *(978-0-7614-6145-6(0)*, 9780761461456, Amazon Children's Publishing) Amazon Publishing.

Kleinberg, Naomi. Elmo's Little Dreidel (Sesame Street) Moroney, Christopher, illus. 2011. (ENG.). 12p. (J). (gr. k — 1). bds. 5.99 *(978-0-375-87396-6(1)*, Random Hse. Bks. for Young Readers) Random Hse. Children's Bks.

Korngold, Jamie S. Mazel Tov! It's a Boy: Mazel Tov! It's a Girl. Finkelstein, Jeff, illus. Finkelstein, Jeff, photos by. 2015. (J). 6.99 *(978-1-4677-6206-9(7)*, Kar-Ben Publishing) Lerner Publishing Group.

—Sadie's Sukkah Breakfast. Fortenberry, Julie, illus. 2011. (Sukkot & Simchat Torah Ser.). (ENG.). 24p. (J). (gr. -1-1). pap. 7.95 *(978-0-7613-5648-6(7))*; lib. bdg. 16.95 *(978-0-7613-5647-9(9))* Lerner Publishing Group. (Kar-Ben Publishing).

Kosofsky, Chaim. Much, Much Better. 2006. (Illus.). 32p. (J). (gr. -1-3). 14.95 *(978-1-929628-22-3(6))* Hachai Publishing.

Krantz, Hazel. In the Garden of the Caliph. 2012. 132p. (gr. 4-6). 23.14 *(978-1-4669-2888-6(3))*; (J). pap. 13.14 *(978-1-4669-2886-2(7))* Trafford Publishing.

Kranzler, Gershon. Seder in Herlin: And Other Stories. Kotler, Arkady & Kotler, Elina, illus. 2003. 108p. (gr. 5-9). reprint ed. 13.95 *(978-0-8266-0343-2(2))* Merkos L'Inyonei Chinuch.

Kubert, Joe. The Adventures of Yaakov & Isaac. 64p. 9.99 *(978-1-58330-741-0(9))* Feldheim Pubs.

Kushner, Lawrence & Schmidt, Gary. In God's Hands. Baek, Matthew J., illus. 2005. (ENG.). 32p. (gr. k-3). 16.99 *(978-1-58023-224-1(8)*, 9781580232241, Jewish Lights Publishing) LongHill Partners, Inc.

Lang, Andrew, ed. & compiled by. The Orange Fairy Book. Lang, Andrew, compiled by. 2011. 234p. 27.95 *(978-1-4638-9520-4(8))* Rodgers, Alan Bks.

Lanton, Sandy. The Littlest Levine. Keay, Claire, illus. 2014. (Passover Ser.). (ENG.). 24p. (J). (gr. -1-2). 7.95 *(978-0-7613-9046-6(4)*, Kar-Ben Publishing) Lerner Publishing Group.

—Lots of Latkes: A Hanukkah Story. Redenbaugh, Vicki Jo, illus. 2003. (ENG.). 32p. (J). (gr. -1-3). 14.95 *(978-1-58013-091-2(7)*, Kar-Ben Publishing) Lerner Publishing Group.

Lasky, Kathryn. Broken Song. 2007. (ENG.). 160p. (J). (gr. 5-18). 6.99 *(978-0-14-240741-7(0)*, Puffin Books) Penguin Young Readers Group.

—The Night Journey. 2005. (ENG., Illus.). 160p. (J). (gr. 3-7). pap. 5.99 *(978-0-14-240322-8(9)*, Puffin Books) Penguin Young Readers Group.

Lawton, Wendy G. Shadow of His Hand: A Story Based on the Life of Holocaust Survivor Anita Dittman. 2004. (Daughters of the Faith Ser.). (ENG.). 160p. (J). (gr. 3). pap. 7.99 *(978-0-8024-4074-7(6))* Moody Pubs.

Lazewnik, Libby. Out of the Woods. Scheinberg, Shepsil, illus. 2011. 320p. (J). *(978-1-4226-1176-0(0))* Mesorah Pubns., Ltd.

Lehman, Theodore H. Defying Odds. 2014. (YA). pap. *(978-1-935604-63-1(5))* Gaon Bks.

Lehman-Wilzig, Tami. Zvuvi's Israel. Topaz, Ksenia, illus. 2009. (Israel Ser.). (ENG.). 32p. (J). (gr. -1-2). 16.95 *(978-0-8225-8759-0(9))*; pap. 7.95 *(978-0-8225-8760-6(2))* Lerner Publishing Group. (Kar-Ben Publishing).

Lenhard, Elizabeth. The Ball of Clay That Rolled Away, 0 vols. Wolff, Jason, illus. 2012. (Shofar Ser.: 0). (ENG.). 24p. (J). (gr. k-3). 16.99 *(978-0-7614-6142-5(6)*, 9780761461425, Amazon Children's Publishing) Amazon Publishing.

Lester, Julius. Pharaoh's Daughter: A Novel of Ancient Egypt. 2009. (ENG., Illus.). 192p. (J). (gr. 7). pap. 6.99 *(978-0-15-206662-8(4))* Houghton Mifflin Harcourt Publishing Co.

Levine, Anna. Jodie's Hanukkah Dig. Topaz, Ksenia, illus. 2008. (Hanukkah Ser.). (ENG.). 32p. (J). (gr. k-3). 17.95 *(978-0-8225-7391-3(1))*; pap. 7.95 *(978-0-8225-7402-6(0))* Lerner Publishing Group. (Kar-Ben Publishing).

—Jodie's Passover Adventure. Topaz, Ksenia, illus. 2012. (Passover Ser.). (ENG.). 32p. (J). (gr. k-3). lib. bdg. 17.95 *(978-0-7613-5641-7(X)*, Kar-Ben Publishing) Lerner Publishing Group.

—Jodie's Shabbat Surprise. Topaz, Ksenia, illus. 2015. (J). (gr. k-3). (ENG.). 32p. lib. bdg. 17.95 *(978-1-4677-3465-3(9))*; 6.99 *(978-1-4677-6204-5(0))* Lerner Publishing Group. (Kar-Ben Publishing).

Levy, Marilyn. Checkpoints. 2009. (ENG.). 256p. (gr. 7). pap. 14.95 *(978-0-8276-0870-2(5))* Jewish Pubn. Society.

Levy, Rochel. Moshe Goes to Yeshiva. David, Racheli, illus. 2012. 24p. 11.95 *(978-1-60091-212-2(5))* Israel Bookshop Pubns.

Liddiment, Carol, illus. The Wooden Sword: A Jewish Folktale from Afghanistan. 2012. (ENG.). 32p. (J). (gr. k-3). 16.99 *(978-0-8075-9201-4(3))* Whitman, Albert & Co.

Lieberman, Leanne. The Book of Trees, 1 vol. 2010. (ENG.). 256p. (YA). (gr. 8-12). pap. 12.95 *(978-1-55469-265-1(2))* Orca Bk. Pubs. USA.

—Lauren Yonofsky Hates the Holocaust, 1 vol. 2013. (ENG.). 240p. (YA). (gr. 8-12). pap. 12.95 *(978-1-4598-0109-7(1))* Orca Bk. Pubs. USA.

Littlefield, Holly. The Rooftop Adventure of Minnie & Tessa, Factory Fire Survivors. Hammond, Ted & Carbajal, Richard, illus. 2011. (History's Kid Heroes Ser.). 32p. pap. 51.02 *(978-0-7613-7639-2(9))*; (ENG.). (gr. 3-5). pap. 8.95 *(978-0-7613-7071-0(4))* Lerner Publishing Group. (Graphic Universe™).

Lois, Lowry. Compte les Etoiles. pap. 16.95 *(978-2-211-03436-4(5))* Archimede Editions FRA. Dist: Distribooks, Inc.

—Number the Stars. 2011. (ENG.). 160p. (J). (gr. 5-7). pap. 7.99 *(978-0-547-57709-8(5))* Houghton Mifflin Harcourt Publishing Co.

—Number the Stars. 2004. 144p. (J). (gr. 5-9). pap. 29.00 incl. audio (978-1-4000-8637-5(X), Listening Library) Random Hse. Audio Publishing Group.

Londner, Renee. The Missing Letters: A Dreidel Story. Bodnaruk, Iryna, illus. 2017. (ENG.). 32p. (gr. -1-3). 17.99 (978-1-4677-8933-2(X), Kar-Ben Publishing) Lerner Publishing Group.

Long, Ilana. Ziggy's Big Idea. Joni, Rasa, illus. 2014. (Kar-Ben Favorites Ser.). (ENG.). 32p. (J). (gr. -1-4). 17.95 (978-0-7613-9053-4(7)); 7.95 (978-0-7613-9054-1(5)) Lerner Publishing Group. (Kar-Ben Publishing).

MacDonald, Maryann. Odette's Secrets. 2013. (ENG., Illus.). 240p. (YA). (gr. 5-8). 16.99 (978-1-59990-750-5(X), 9781599907505, Bloomsbury USA Childrens) Bloomsbury Publishing USA.

Manushkin, Fran. Many Days, One Shabbat, 0 vols. Monescillo, Maria, illus. 2011. (ENG.). 24p. (J). (gr. -1-3). 12.99 (978-0-7614-5965-1(0), 9780761459651, Amazon Children's Publishing) Amazon Publishing.

Maristella. One Step to Freedom. 2010. 82p. pap. (978-1-84748-756-8(4)) Athena Pr.

Mark, Yudel. The Jewish Pope: A Yiddish Tale. Goodman, Ruth Fisher, tr. from YID. Krupin, Connie G., illus. 2015. (ENG.). 100p. per. 14.95 (978-1-56474-459-3(0), Fithian Pr) Daniel & Daniel, Pubs., Inc.

Marshall, Linda Elovitz. Grandma Rose's Magic. Jatkowska, Ag, illus. 2012. (Shabbat Ser.). (ENG.). 32p. (J). (gr. -1-2). pap. 7.95 (978-0-7613-5216-7(3), Kar-Ben Publishing) Lerner Publishing Group.

—The Mitzvah Magician. Engel, Christiane, illus. 2012. (Kar-Ben Favorites Ser.). (ENG.). 24p. (J). (gr. -1-2). lib. bdg. 17.95 (978-0-7613-5655-4(X), Kar-Ben Publishing) Lerner Publishing Group.

—The Passover Lamb. Mai-Wyss, Tatjana, illus. 2013. (ENG.). 32p. (J). (gr. 1-4). 17.99 (978-0-307-93177-1(3), Random Hse. Bks. for Young Readers) Random Hse. Children's Bks.

Martinez, Mario X. Abran & Isabella's Hidden Faith. 2015. 103p. (J). pap. (978-1-935604-73-0(2)) Gaon Bks.

Mayer, Pamela. Don't Sneeze at the Wedding. Avilés, Martha, illus. 2013. (Life Cycle Ser.). (ENG.). 32p. (J). (gr. k-3). 7.95 (978-1-4677-0429-8(6), Kar-Ben Publishing) Lerner Publishing Group.

—Don't Sneeze at the Wedding. Aviles, Martha, illus. 2013. (Life Cycle Ser.). (ENG.). 32p. (J). (gr. k-3). lib. bdg. 17.95 (978-1-4677-0428-1(8), Kar-Ben Publishing) Lerner Publishing Group.

Mazer, Harry. The Last Mission. 192p. (YA). (gr. 7-18). pap. 4.99 (978-0-8072-1366-7(7), Listening Library) Random Hse. Audio Publishing Group.

McDonough, Yona Zeldis. The Bicycle Spy. 2016. (ENG.). 208p. (J). (gr. 3-7). 16.99 (978-0-545-85095-7(9), Scholastic Pr.) Scholastic, Inc.

Medoff, Francine. The Mouse in the Matzah Factory. Bosch, Nicole in den, illus. 2003. (ENG.). 32p. (J). (gr. -1-3). pap. 6.95 (978-1-58013-048-6(8), Kar-Ben Publishing) Lerner Publishing Group.

Meltzer, Amy. A Mezuzah on the Door. Fried, Janice, illus. 2007. (Jewish Identity Ser.). 32p. (J). (gr. -1-3). 17.95 (978-1-58013-249-7(9)); (ENG.). 7.95 (978-1-58013-251-0(0)) Lerner Publishing Group. (Kar-Ben Publishing).

—The Shabbat Princess. Avilés, Martha, illus. 2011. (Shabbat Ser.). (ENG.). 32p. (J). (gr. -1-2). pap. 7.95 (978-0-7613-5106-1(X), Kar-Ben Publishing) Lerner Publishing Group.

Mermelstein, Yael. Izzy the Whiz & Passover McClean. Hartman, Carrie, illus. 2012. (Passover Ser.). (ENG.). 32p. (J). (gr. -1-2). lib. bdg. 17.95 (978-0-7613-5653-0(3), Kar-Ben Publishing) Lerner Publishing Group.

—Izzy the Whiz & Passover Mcclean. Hartman, Carrie, illus. 2012. (Passover Ser.). (ENG.). 32p. (J). (gr. -1-2). pap. 7.95 (978-0-7613-5654-7(1), Kar-Ben Publishing) Lerner Publishing Group.

—The Stupendous Adventures of Shragi & Shia. Katz, Avi, illus. 2008. 93p. (J). pap. (978-1-4226-0865-4(4)) Mesorah Pubns., Ltd.

Meyer, Susan Lynn. Black Radishes. 2011. (ENG.). 240p. (J). (gr. 3-7). 6.99 (978-0-375-85822-2(9), Yearling) Random Hse. Children's Bks.

Miklowitz, Gloria D. The Enemy Has a Face. 2004. 143p. (YA). pap. 8.00 (978-0-8028-5261-8(0)) Eerdmans, William B. Publishing Co.

Miller, Deborah U. & Ostrove, Karen. Fins & Scales: A Kosher Tale. Ostrove, Karen, illus. 2004. (Israel Ser.). (Illus.). 32p. (J). (gr. 1-3). pap. 4.95 (978-0-929371-25-2(9), Kar-Ben Publishing) Lerner Publishing Group.

Morgan, Anna. Daughters of the Ark, 1 vol. 2005. (ENG., Illus.). 200p. (J). (gr. 5-12). pap. 9.95 (978-1-896764-92-4(4)) Second Story Pr. CAN. Dist: Orca Bk. Pubs. USA.

Muñiz-Huberman, Angelina & Menton, Seymour. Dreaming of Safed. 2014. 126p. (YA). pap. (978-1-935604-61-7(9)) Gaon Bks.

Naomi, Aunt. Jewish Fairy Tales & Legends. 2006. pap. 28.95 (978-1-4254-9788-0(8)) Kessinger Publishing, LLC.

Narváez, Concha López. El Tiempo y la Promesa.Tr. of Time & the Promise. (SPA.). (YA). (gr. 5-8). 164p. (978-84-216-2558-3(6), BU7323); 9th ed. (Illus.). 208p. (978-84-216-1538-6(6), BU6188) Bruño, Editorial ESP. Dist: Lectorum Pubns., Inc.

Newman, Tracy. Sukkot Is Coming! Garófoli, Viviana, illus. 2017. (ENG.). 12p. (gr. -1 — 1). bds. 5.99 (978-1-5124-0828-7(X), Kar-Ben Publishing) Lerner Publishing Group.

Newman, Vivian. Ella's Trip to Israel. Nathan, Cheryl & Gutierrez, Akemia, illus. 2011. (Israel Ser.). (ENG.). 24p. (J). (gr. -1 — 1). pap. 8.95 (978-0-7613-6029-2(8), Kar-Ben Publishing) Lerner Publishing Group.

Newman, Vivian. Moti the Mitzvah Mouse. Knopp-Kilpert, Inga, illus. 2017. (ENG.). 24p. (gr. -1-k). 17.99 **(978-1-5124-2647-2(4))**; pap. 7.99 **(978-1-5124-2649-6(0))** Lerner Publishing Group. (Kar-Ben Publishing).

Nislick, June Levitt. Zayda Was a Cowboy. 2005. (ENG.). 88p. pap. 11.95 (978-0-8276-0817-7(9)) Jewish Pubn. Society.

North, Phoebe. Starbreak. 2014. (Starglass Sequence Ser.). (ENG., Illus.). 432p. (YA). (gr. 7). 17.99 (978-1-4424-5956-4(5), Simon & Schuster Bks. For Young Readers) Simon & Schuster Bks. For Young Readers.

—Starglass. (Starglass Sequence Ser.). (ENG., Illus.). (YA). (gr. 7). 2014. 464p. pap. 9.99 (978-1-4424-5954-0(9)) 2013. 448p. 17.99 (978-1-4424-5953-3(0)) Simon & Schuster Bks. For Young Readers. (Simon & Schuster Bks. For Young Readers).

Now I Am Thee. (Yoni Gold Board Book Ser.). (J). bds. 4.95 (978-1-58330-153-1(4)) Feldheim Pubs.

Ofanansky, Allison. Cheesecake for Shavuot. Alpern, Eliyahu, illus. 2013. (Lag B'Omer & Shavuot Ser.). (ENG.). 32p. (J). (gr. -1-2). lib. bdg. 15.95 (978-0-7613-8126-6(0), Kar-Ben Publishing) Lerner Publishing Group.

—Cheesecake for Shavuot. Alpern, Eliyahu, photos by. 2013. (Lag B'Omer & Shavuot Ser.). (ENG., Illus.). 32p. (J). (gr. -1-2). 8.95 (978-1-4677-1411-2(9), Kar-Ben Publishing) Lerner Publishing Group.

—Sukkot Treasure Hunt. Alpern, Eliyahu, illus. Alpern, Eliyahu, photos by. 2009. (Sukkot & Simchat Torah Ser.). (ENG.). 32p. (J). (gr. -1-5). 15.95 (978-0-8225-8763-7(7), Kar-Ben Publishing) Lerner Publishing Group.

Olswanger, Anna. Shlemiel Crooks. Koz, Paula Goodman, illus. 2005. 36p. (J). (gr. 2-4). 15.95 (978-1-58838-165-1(X)) NewSouth, Inc.

Orgel, Doris. Devil in Vienna. 2004. (ENG.). 256p. (J). (gr. 3-7). 7.99 (978-0-14-240236-8(2), Speak) Penguin Young Readers Group.

Osborne, William. Winter's Bullet. 2016. (ENG.). 240p. (J). (gr. 7). 18.99 (978-0-545-85344-6(3), Chicken Hse., The) Scholastic, Inc.

Ostow, Micol. Emily Goldberg Learns to Salsa. 2007. (ENG.). 208p. (YA). (gr. 7-18). 8.99 (978-1-59514-144-6(8), Razorbill) Penguin Young Readers Group.

Packer, Rachel Ornstein. Sky-High Sukkah. Zemke, Deborah, illus. 2016. (J). (978-1-68115-513-5(3)) Behrman Hse., Inc.

Pearl, Sydelle. Elijah's Tears: Stories for the Jewish Holidays, 1 vol. Skortcheva, Rossitza, illus. 2004. (ENG.). 80p. (J). (gr. 3-7). 14.95 (978-1-58980-178-3(4)) Pelican Publishing Co., Inc.

Penn, Audrey. The Miracle Jar: A Hanukkah Story. Lyon, Lea, illus. 2009. (ENG.). 32p. (J). (gr. -1-3). pap. 8.95 (978-1-933718-26-2(9)) Tanglewood Pr.

Peretz, I. L. & Goldin, Barbara Diamond. The Magician's Visit: A Passover Tale. Parker, Robert Andrew, illus. 2006. 28p. (J). (gr. 4-8). reprint ed. 15.00 (978-1-4223-5408-7(3)); pap. 5.00 (978-1-4223-5400-1(8)) DIANE Publishing Co.

Perl, Erica S. When Life Gives You O. J. 2013. (ENG.). 224p. (J). (gr. 3-7). 6.99 (978-0-375-85902-1(0), Yearling) Random Hse. Children's Bks.

Perl, Lila. Isabel's War. 2014. (ENG.). 224p. (J). (gr. 2-7). pap. 12.95 (978-1-939601-27-8(4)) Ig Publishing, Inc.

Perrin, Randy, et al. Time Like a River. 2004. 144p. (gr. 5-18). 14.95 (978-1-57143-061-8(X)) RDR Bks.

Petersen, Alicia. A Sparrow Alone. 2004. 154p. (YA). 8.99 (978-1-59166-204-4(4)) BJU Pr.

Peysin, Shainy. Whatever the Weather. Rosenfeld, Dina & Leverton, Yossi, eds. Owens, Emily, illus. 2011. 32p. (J). 12.95 (978-1-929628-56-8(0)) Hachai Publishing.

Pfeiffer, Chaviva Krohn. Making Hashem Proud: Stories of Kiddush Hashem in Everyday Life. Stern, Chani, illus. 2014. 48p. (J). (978-1-4226-1464-8(6)) Mesorah Pubns., Ltd.

Polacco, Patricia. The Blessing Cup. Polacco, Patricia, illus. 2013. (ENG., Illus.). 48p. (J). (gr. -1-3). 17.99 (978-1-4424-5047-9(9), Simon & Schuster Bks. For Young Readers) Simon & Schuster Bks. For Young Readers.

—The Butterfly. 2009. (ENG.). 48p. (J). (gr. 1-4). pap. 7.99 (978-0-14-241306-7(2), Puffin Books) Penguin Young Readers Group.

—The Keeping Quilt. 2007. 18.00 (978-0-7569-1720-3(4)) Perfection Learning Corp.

—The Keeping Quilt: 25th Anniversary Edition. Polacco, Patricia, illus. 25th ed. 2013. (ENG., Illus.). 64p. (J). (gr. -1-3). 17.99 (978-1-4424-8237-1(0), Simon & Schuster/Paula Wiseman Bks.) Simon & Schuster/Paula Wiseman Bks.

—Someone for Mr. Sussman. Polacco, Patricia, illus. 2008. (ENG., Illus.). 40p. (J). (gr. 1-3). 17.99 (978-0-399-25075-0(1), Philomel Bks.) Penguin Young Readers Group.

Polikoff, Barbara Garland. Her Mother's Secret. 2012. (ENG.). 184p. (YA). pap. 14.99 (978-0-9831938-7-6(8)) Allium Pr. of Chicago.

Pressler, Mirjam. Malka. Murdoch, Brian, tr. 2005. 280p. (YA). (gr. 7-12). 13.65 (978-0-7569-5217-4(4)) Perfection Learning Corp.

Prins, Piet. Hideout in the Swamp. 2006. (Illus.). 136p. (J). pap. (978-1-894666-73-2(9)) Inheritance Pubns.

Propp, Vera W. When the Soldiers Were Gone: A Novel. 2006. 101p. (J). (gr. 4-8). reprint ed. 15.00 (978-1-4223-5310-3(9)) DIANE Publishing Co.

Pruzansky, Binyomin. Stories for a Child's Heart. Katz, Tova, illus. 2009. 48p. (J). (978-1-4226-0915-6(4)) Mesorah Pubns., Ltd.

Pryor, Bonnie. Simon's Escape: A Story of the Holocaust. 2010. (Historical Fiction Adventures (HFA) Ser.). (Illus.). 160p. (J). pap. 10.95 (978-1-59845-216-7(9)); (gr. 3-6). 29.27 (978-0-7660-3388-7(0)) Enslow Pubs., Inc.

Pullman, Philip. The Tiger in the Well. 2008. (Sally Lockhart Ser.: Bk. 3). (ENG.). 432p. (YA). (gr. 7). pap. 9.99 (978-0-375-84517-8(8), Ember) Random Hse. Children's Bks.

Radding, Alan. Miracles: Stories for Jewish Children & Their Families. 2003. 135p. (J). pap. 13.95 (978-1-59113-309-4(2)) Booklocker.com, Inc.

Rahlens, Holly-Jane. Prince William, Maximilian Minsky, & Me. 2007. (ENG.). 320p. (YA). (gr. 7-11). per. 7.99 (978-0-7636-3299-1(6)) Candlewick Pr.

Reinhardt, Dana. The Things a Brother Knows. 2011. (ENG.). 256p. (YA). (gr. 9). pap. 8.99 (978-0-375-84456-0(2), Ember) Random Hse. Children's Bks.

Rocklin, Joanne. Fleabrain Loves Franny. (ENG.). 288p. (J). (gr. 3-7). 2015. pap. 8.95 (978-1-4197-1676-8(X)) 2014. 16.95 (978-1-4197-1068-1(0)) Abrams, Inc. (Amulet Bks.).

Rose, Robert. Godintoxicated Becoming Paranoid. 2007. 260p. pap. 29.95 (978-1-4327-0041-6(3)) Outskirts Pr., Inc.

Rosen, Michael. Happy Harry's Cafe. Holland, Richard, illus. 2012. (ENG.). 32p. (J). (gr. -1-2). 16.99 (978-0-7636-6239-4(9)) Candlewick Pr.

Rosenbaum, Andria Warmflash. A Grandma Like Yours: A Grandpa Like Yours. Björnson, Barbara, illus. 2006. 32p. (J). 16.95 (978-1-58013-167-4(0), Kar-Ben Publishing) Lerner Publishing Group.

Rosenberg, Madelyn. Happy Birthday, Tree! A Tu B'Shevat Story. Christy, Jana, illus. 2012. (ENG.). 24p. (J). (gr. -1-3). 15.99 (978-0-8075-3151-8(0)) Whitman, Albert & Co.

Rosenfeld, Dina. A Chanukah Story for Night Number Three. 2009. (Illus.). 32p. (J). 12.95 (978-1-929628-54-4(4)) Hachai Publishing.

Rossoff, Donald. The Perfect Prayer. Keiser, Tammy L., illus. 2003. (gr. k-3). 13.95 (978-0-8074-0853-7(0), 164005) URJ Pr.

Rostoker-Gruber, Karen. Maddie the Mitzvah Clown. 2016. (J). (978-1-68115-523-4(0)) Behrman Hse., Inc.

Rostoker-Gruber, Karen & Isaacs, Ronald H. Farmer Kobi's Hanukkah Match. Decker, C. B., illus. 2015. (J). (978-1-68115-501-2(X)) Behrman Hse., Inc.

Rouss, Sylvia. Sammy Spider's First Haggadah. Kahn, Katherine, illus. 2007. (Passover Ser.). (ENG.). 32p. (J). (gr. -1-3). per. 6.95 (978-1-58013-230-5(8), Kar-Ben Publishing) Lerner Publishing Group.

Rouss, Sylvia A. Aaron's Bar Mitzvah. Dubois, Liz Goulet, tr. Dubois, Liz Goulet, illus. 2003. (J). 14.95 (978-0-8246-0447-9(4)) David, Jonathan Pubs., Inc.

—Jaekob, the Dreamer. 2015. (Illus.). (J). (978-1-68115-506-7(0)) Behrman Hse., Inc.

—The Littlest Candlesticks. Hannon, Holly, illus. 2005. (Littlest Ser.). 32p. (J). 14.95 (978-1-930143-48-7(6), Devora Publishing) Simcha Media Group.

—A Sammy Spider Hanukkah Colors. Kahn, Katherine, illus. 2017. (ENG.). 12p. (gr. -1 — 1). bds. 5.99 (978-1-4677-5238-1(X), Kar-Ben Publishing) Lerner Publishing Group.

—Sammy Spider's First Day of School. Kahn, Katherine, illus. 2009. (Kar-Ben Favorites Ser.). (ENG.). 32p. (J). (gr. -1-2). 16.95 (978-0-8225-8583-1(9), Kar-Ben Publishing) Lerner Publishing Group.

—Sammy Spider's First Shavuot. Kahn, Katherine Janus, illus. 2008. (Sammy Spider's First Bks.). (ENG.). 32p. (J). (gr. -1-3). lib. bdg. 15.95 (978-0-8225-7224-4(9), Kar-Ben Publishing) Lerner Publishing Group.

Rouss, Sylvia A. & Lanton, Sandy. Lots of Latkes: A Hanukkah Story. Kahn, Katherine Janus & Redenbaugh, Vicki Jo, illus. 2003. (ENG.). 32p. (J). (gr. -1-3). pap. 6.95 (978-1-58013-061-5(5), Kar-Ben Publishing) Lerner Publishing Group.

Roy, Jennifer. Yellow Star, 0 vols. 2014. (ENG.). 256p. (gr. 5-7). pap. 9.99 (978-0-7614-6310-8(0), 9780761463108, Amazon Children's Publishing) Amazon Publishing.

Rubens, Michael. Sons of The 613. 2012. (ENG.). 320p. (YA). (gr. 7). 16.99 (978-0-547-61216-4(8)) Houghton Mifflin Harcourt Publishing Co.

Ruby, Lois. Shanghai Shadows. 2006. (ENG.). 256p. (YA). 16.95 (978-0-8234-1960-9(6)) Holiday Hse., Inc.

Rudetsky, Seth. My Awesome - Awful Popularity Plan. 2013. (ENG.). 224p. (YA). (gr. 7). pap. 8.99 (978-0-375-89997-3(9), Ember) Random Hse. Children's Bks.

Russo, Marisabina. I Will Come Back for You. 2014. (ENG.). 40p. (J). (gr. k-4). 7.99 (978-0-385-39149-8(8), Dragonfly Bks.) Random Hse. Children's Bks.

Safran, Faigy. Uncle Moishy Visits Torah Island. Snowden, Linda, illus. (J). pap. 5.99 (978-0-89906-806-0(5), UM1P) Mesorah Pubns., Ltd.

Salem, Iosi, illus. The Mr. Mentch Coloring Book. 2008. (J). (gr. -1-3). 6.95 (978-1-934440-37-7(X), Pitspopany Pr.) Simcha Media Group.

Sasso, Sandy Eisenberg. Butterflies under Our Hats. Rothenberg, Joani Keller, illus. 2014. (ENG.). 32p. (J). (gr. k-5). pap. 15.99 (978-1-61261-583-7(X)) Paraclete Pr., Inc.

—The Shema in the Mezuzah: Listening to Each Other. Rothenberg, Joani Keller, illus. 2012. (ENG.). 32p. (J). 18.99 (978-1-58023-506-8(9), 9781580235068, Jewish Lights Publishing) LongHill Partners, Inc.

Saturen, Myra. Journey to a New World. 2006. (J). pap. 9.99 (978-0-88092-494-8(2)) Royal Fireworks Publishing Co.

—Journey to a New World: Mystic River of the West. 2006. (J). pap. (978-0-88092-495-5(0)) Royal Fireworks Publishing Co.

—Julietta. (YA). pap. 9.99 (978-0-88092-538-9(8)) Royal Fireworks Publishing Co.

Savedoff, Barbara E. & Elissa, Barbara. The Remarkable Journey of Josh's Kippah. Jamana, Pharida & Zaman, Farida, illus. 2010. (ENG.). 24p. (J). (gr. -1-2). lib. bdg. 7.95 (978-0-8225-9911-1(2), Kar-Ben Publishing) Lerner Publishing Group.

Sax, Aline. The War Within These Walls. 2013. (ENG., Illus.). 176p. (YA). 17.00 (978-0-8028-5428-5(1), Eerdmans Bks For Young Readers) Eerdmans, William B. Publishing Co.

Schmidt, Gary D. Mara's Stories: Glimmers in the Darkness. 2008. (ENG.). 160p. (YA). (gr. 5-9). per. 14.99 (978-0-312-37388-7(0), 9780312373887) Square Fish.

Schotter, Roni. Passover Magic, 0 vols. Hafner, Marylin, illus. 2011. (ENG.). 34p. (J). (gr. -1-3). pap. 7.99 (978-0-7614-5842-5(5), 9780761458425, Amazon Children's Publishing) Amazon Publishing.

Schram, Peninnah. The Magic Pomegranate. Hall, Melanie, illus. (On My Own Folklore Ser.). 48p. 2008. (ENG.). (gr. 2-4). pap. 6.95 (978-0-8225-6746-2(6), First Avenue Editions) 2007. (J). lib. bdg. 17.95 (978-0-8225-8856-6(0), Kar-Ben Publishing) Lerner Publishing Group.

—The Magic Pomegranate: A Jewish Folktale. Hall, Melanie, illus. 2007. (On My Own Folklore Ser.). (ENG.). 48p. (gr. 2-4). lib. bdg. 25.26 (978-0-8225-6742-4(3), Millbrook Pr.) Lerner Publishing Group.

Schuman, Burt E. Chanukah on the Prairie. Kaye, Rosalind Charney, illus. 2004. (gr. k-3). 13.95 (978-0-8074-0814-8(X), 381780) URJ Pr.

Schwartz, Howard. Gathering Sparks. Swarner, Kristina, illus. 2010. (ENG.). 32p. (J). (gr. -1-3). 16.99 (978-1-59643-280-2(2), 9781596432802) Roaring Brook Pr.

Scott, Walter, ed. Ivanhoe. (SPA., Illus.). 176p. (YA). 14.95 (978-84-7281-096-9(8), AF1096) Auriga, Ediciones S.A. ESP. Dist: Continental Bk. Co., Inc.

—Ivanhoe. 2008. (Bring the Classics to Life Ser.). (Illus.). 72p. (gr. 5-12). pap., act. bk. ed. 10.95 (978-1-55576-099-1(6), EDN506B) EDCON Publishing Group.

Segal, Nechamy. The Torah Book of Opposites. Lumer, Marc, illus. 2012. 12p. (J). pap. 7.95 (978-1-929628-67-4(6)) Hachai Publishing.

Seltzer, Sara Leah. A Day Full of Mitzvos. Katz, Avi, illus. 2009. 26p. (J). (978-1-4226-0949-1(9)) Mesorah Pubns., Ltd.

Seyforth, Edward L. A Horribly Frightening Deception, 1 vol. 2009. 75p. pap. 19.95 (978-1-61546-260-5(0)) America Star Bks.

Sharenow, Robert. The Berlin Boxing Club. 2011. (ENG.). 416p. (YA). (gr. 8-18). 17.99 (978-0-06-157968-4(8), HarperTeen) HarperCollins Pubs.

—The Berlin Boxing Club. 2012. (YA). lib. bdg. 20.85 (978-0-606-26871-4(5), Turtleback) Turtleback Bks.

Shazak. Out of Egypt. 2007. 104p. 24.99 (978-1-930925-11-3(5)) Feldheim Pubs.

Sher, Steven. Where the Shouting Began. 2008. (J). (978-1-932727-08-1(6)) Montemayor Pr.

Shollar, Leah Pearl. Shadow Play: A True Story of Tefillah. Gerber, Pesach, illus. 2006. 32p. (J). 11.95 (978-1-929628-21-6(8)) Hachai Publishing.

Shulman, Lisa. The Matzo Ball Boy. Litzinger, Rosanne, illus. 2007. (ENG.). 32p. (J). (gr. -1-2). pap. 6.99 (978-0-14-240769-1(0), Puffin Books) Penguin Young Readers Group.

Sigal, Maxine Handelman. Shabbat Angels. Rothenberg, Joani, illus. 2003. (gr. k-3). 13.95 (978-0-8074-0865-0(4), 164051) URJ Pr.

Silberman, Shoshana. A Family Haggadah II, Vol. 2. Kahn, Katherine Janus, illus. l.t. ed. 2003. 64p. (J). pap. 6.95 (978-1-58013-014-1(3), Kar-Ben Publishing) Lerner Publishing Group.

Simon, Tanya & Simon, Richard. Oskar & the Eight Blessings. Siegel, Mark, illus. 2015. (ENG.). 40p. (J). (gr. -1-3). 17.99 (978-1-59643-949-8(1), 9781596439498) Roaring Brook Pr.

Simpson, Lesley. The Purim Surprise. Church, Peter, illus. 2004. (Purim Ser.). 32p. (J). (gr. -1-3). pap. 6.95 (978-1-58013-090-5(9), Kar-Ben Publishing) Lerner Publishing Group.

—Yuvi's Candy Tree. Porter, Janice Lee, illus. 2011. (ENG.). 32p. (J). (gr. k-3). pap. 7.95 (978-0-7613-5652-3(5)); lib. bdg. 17.95 (978-0-7613-5651-6(7)) Lerner Publishing Group. (Kar-Ben Publishing).

Simpson, Martha Seif. The Dreidel That Wouldn't Spin: A Toyshop Tale of Hanukkah. Bernhard, Durga Yael, illus. 2014. (ENG.). 32p. (J). (gr. -1-2). 16.95 (978-1-937786-28-1(5), Wisdom Tales) World Wisdom, Inc.

Snir, Mirik. When I First Held You: A Lullaby from Isarel. Shubow, Mary Jane, tr. from HEB. Snir, Eleyor, illus. 2009. (Kar-Ben Favorites Ser.). (ENG.). 32p. (J). (gr. k-3). pap. 9.95 (978-0-7613-5098-9(5), Kar-Ben Publishing) Lerner Publishing Group.

Soci Et E de La Faune Et Des Parcs Du Qu Ebec. Sarah de Cordoba. Sanchez, Andres & Tagle, illus. 2003. (la Orilla del Viento Ser.). (SPA.). 136p. (J). per. 8.50 (978-968-16-7020-7(5)) Fondo de Cultura Economica USA.

Spinelli, Jerry. Milkweed. (ENG.). 240p. (YA). (gr. 7). 2010. pap. 9.99 (978-0-375-86147-5(5), Ember) 2005. mass mkt. 7.99 (978-0-440-42005-7(9), Laurel Leaf) Random Hse. Children's Bks.

Spradlin, Michael P. The Enemy Above. 2016. (ENG.). 240p. (J). (gr. 3-7). 16.99 (978-0-545-85782-6(1), Scholastic Pr.) Scholastic, Inc.

Spring, Debbie. The Righteous Smuggler, 1 vol. 2006. (Holocaust Remembrance Ser.). (ENG., Illus.). 160p. (J). (gr. 4-7). pap. 9.95 (978-1-896764-97-9(5)) Second Story Pr. CAN. Dist: Orca Bk. Pubs. USA.

Sschweiger-dmiel, Izhak. Hanna's Sabbath Dress. Eitan (tchernov), Ora, illus. 2012. (ENG.). 32p. (J). (gr. -1-3). 16.99 (978-1-4424-7439-0(4), Simon & Schuster Bks. For Young Readers) Simon & Schuster Bks. For Young Readers.

Starting First Grade. (Tami & Moishy Ser.: Vol. 4). (J). bds. 6.95 (978-1-58330-968-1(3)) Feldheim Pubs.

Stavans, Ilan. Golemito. Villegas, Teresa, illus. 2013. (ENG.). 32p. (J). 16.95 (978-1-58838-292-4(3), NewSouth Bks.) NewSouth, Inc.

Strauss, Linda Leopold. The Elijah Door. Natchev, Alexi, illus. 2012. (ENG.). 32p. (J). 16.95 (978-0-8234-1911-1(8)) Holiday Hse., Inc.

Strom, Yale. The Wedding That Saved a Town. Prosmitsky, Jenya, illus. 2008. (J). (gr. -1). 17.95 (978-0-8225-7376-0(8)); (ENG.). 32p. (gr. 2-4). pap. 7.95 (978-0-8225-7380-7(6)) Lerner Publishing Group. (Kar-Ben Publishing).

Stuchner, Joan Betty. Can Hens Give Milk?, 1 vol. Weissmann, Joe, illus. 2013. (ENG.). 32p. (J). (gr. -1-3). 9.95 (978-1-4598-0427-2(9)) Orca Bk. Pubs. USA.

—The Kugel Valley Klezmer Band. Row, Richard, illus. 2005. 30p. (J). (gr. 2-6). reprint ed. 16.00 (978-0-7567-8605-2(3)) DIANE Publishing Co.

—The Kugel Valley Klezmer Band. Row, Richard, illus. 2009. (PJ Library). (ENG.). 32p. (J). (gr. -1-3). pap. 7.95 (978-1-56656-782-4(3), Crocodile Bks.) Interlink Publishing Group, Inc.

—A Time to Be Brave. Nugent, Cynthia, illus. 2014. (Stepping Stone Book(TM) Ser.). (ENG.). 112p. (J). (gr. 2-5). 4.99 (978-0-385-39205-1(2), Random Hse. Bks. for Young Readers) Random Hse. Children's Bks.

Sugarman, Brynn Olenberg. Rebecca's Journey Home. Shapiro, Michelle, illus. 2006. 32p. (J). (gr. -1-3). lib. bdg. 17.95 (978-1-58013-157-5(3), Kar-Ben Publishing) Lerner Publishing Group.

Sutton, Jane. Esther's Hanukkah Disaster. Rowland, Andrew, illus. 2013. (Hanukkah Ser.). 32p. (J). (gr. -1-3). lib. bdg. 17.95 (978-0-7613-9043-5(X), Kar-Ben Publishing) Lerner Publishing Group.

—Esther's Hanukkah Disaster. Rowland, Andy, illus. 2013. (Hanukkah Ser.). (ENG.). 32p. (J). (gr. -1-3). 7.95 (978-0-7613-9044-2(8), Kar-Ben Publishing) Lerner Publishing Group.

Swartz, Daniel J. Bim & Bom: A Shabbat Tale. Iwai, Melissa, illus. rev. ed. 2011. (Shabbat Ser.). (ENG.). 24p. (J). (gr. -1-1). pap. 8.95 (978-0-7613-6717-8(9), Kar-Ben Publishing) Lerner Publishing Group.

Tal, Eve. Double Crossing. 2007. (ENG.). 262p. (J). (gr. 7-9). pap. 9.95 (978-1-933693-15-6(0)) Cinco Puntos Pr.

—Double Crossing: A Jewish Immigration Story. 2005. (ENG.). 216p. (J). (gr. 7-9). 16.95 (978-0-938317-94-4(6)) Cinco Puntos Pr.

Tarshis, Lauren. I Survived the Nazi Invasion 1944. 2014. (I Survived Ser.: 9). (ENG.). 112p. (J). (gr. 2-5). pap. 4.99 *(978-0-545-45938-9(9))* Scholastic, Inc.

—I Survived the Nazi Invasion 1944. 2014. (I Survived . Ser.: No. 9). lib. bdg. 14.75 *(978-0-606-35397-7(6))* Turtleback Bks.

Taylor, Sydney. All-Of-a-Kind Family Uptown. 2014. (ENG.). 200p. (J). (gr. 3). pap. 12.95 *(978-1-939601-17-9(7))* Ig Publishing, Inc.

Terwilliger, Kelly. Bubbe Isabella & the Sukkot Cake. Hornung, Phyllis, illus. 2005. 24p. (J). (gr. -1-3). 15.95 *(978-1-58013-187-2(5))*; (gr. 3-8). per. 6.95 *(978-1-58013-128-5(X))* Lerner Publishing Group. (Kar-Ben Publishing).

Tetzner, Annika. Lullabies for Annik. 2012. 120p. pap. 12.33 *(978-1-4669-6581-2(9))* Trafford Publishing.

The Mamas. Meet the Yids: Mr. Mentch. 2007. pap. 18.95 *(978-965-91048-0-2(4),* Pitspopany Pr.) Simcha Media Group.

Thor, Annika. A Faraway Island. Schenck, Linda, tr. 2011. (ENG.). 256p. (J). (gr. 3-7). 6.99 *(978-0-375-84495-9(3),* Yearling) Random Hse. Children's Bks.

—The Lily Pond. Schenck, Linda, tr. 2012. (ENG.). 224p. (J). (gr. 4-7). 7.99 *(978-0-385-74040-1(9),* Yearling) Random Hse. Children's Bks.

Thor, Annika & Schenck, Linda. Deep Sea. 2015. (ENG.). 240p. (YA). (gr. 9). 20.99 *(978-0-375-99132-5(8),* Delacorte Pr.) Random Hse. Children's Bks.

Toro, Sandra. Dona Gracia: Beacon of Hope. 2016. 292p. (YA). pap. *(978-1-935604-75-4(9))* Gaon Bks.

Travis, Lucille. Tirzah. Garber, S. David, ed. 2004. (ENG.). 160p. (YA). (gr. 4-7). pap. 9.99 *(978-0-8361-3546-6(6))* Herald Pr.

Ungar, Richard. Rachel's Library. 2004. (ENG.). 32p. (J). (gr. 2-5). 15.95 *(978-0-88776-678-7(1),* Tundra Bks.) Tundra Bks. CAN. Dist: Penguin Random Hse. LLC.

Vander Zee, Ruth. Erika's Story. Innocenti, Roberto, illus. 2013. (ENG.). 24p. (J). (gr. 1-3). pap. 10.99 *(978-0-89812-891-8(9),* Creative Paperbacks) Creative Co., The.

Vogiel, Eva. Facing the Music. 2003. 284p. 19.95 *(978-1-880582-94-7(5))* Judaica Pr., Inc., The.

Vogiel, Eva & Steinberg, Ruth. A Light for Greytowers. 252p. 11.99 *(978-0-87306-598-6(0))* Feldheim Pubs.

Waldman, Debby. A Sack Full of Feathers, 1 vol. Revell, Cindy, illus. 2007. (ENG.). 32p. (J). (gr. -1-3). 9.95 *(978-1-55143-863-4(1))* Orca Bk. Pubs. USA.

Walfish, Miriam. The Jewel & the Journey. 2007. 208p. (J). 16.95 *(978-1-932443-81-3(9))* Judaica Pr., Inc., The.

Wasserman, Mira. Too Much of a Good Thing. Carolan, Christine, illus. 2003. 32p. (J). (gr. -1-3). pap. 6.95 *(978-1-58013-066-0(6))*; (ENG.). 15.95 *(978-1-58013-082-0(8))* Lerner Publishing Group. (Kar-Ben Publishing).

Watts, Irene N. A Telling Time, 1 vol. Shoemaker, Kathryn E., illus. 2004. (ENG.). 32p. (J). (gr. 2-5). pap. 7.95 *(978-1-896580-72-2(6))* Tradewind Bks. CAN. Dist: Orca Bk. Pubs. USA.

Weber, Ilse. Mendel Rosenbusch: Tales for Jewish Children. Fisher, Hans, tr. from GER. Burden, P. John, illus. 2006. Orig. Title: Mendel Rosenbusch: Geschichten Fur Jud Kinder. 128p. (J). pap. 18.00 *(978-1-933480-05-3(X))* Bunim and Bannigan Ltd.

—Mendel Rosenbusch: Tales for Jewish Children, 1 vol. Fisher, Hans & Fisher, Ruth, trs. from GER. Burden, P. John, illus. 2006. Orig. Title: Mendel Rosenbusch: Geschichen Fur Jud Kinder. (ENG.). 58p. (J). lib. bdg. 18.95 *(978-1-933480-04-6(1))* Bunim and Bannigan Ltd.

Werlin, Nancy. Are You Alone on Purpose? 2007. (ENG.). 208p. (YA). (gr. 7-18). 7.99 *(978-0-14-240777-6(1),* Speak) Penguin Young Readers Group.

Whitney, Kim Ablon. The Other Half of Life. 2010. (ENG.). 256p. (YA). (gr. 7). mass mkt. 7.99 *(978-0-375-84422-5(8),* Laurel Leaf) Random Hse. Children's Bks.

Wigden, Susan & Salem, I. A Mitzva for Zelda. 2008. 32p. 12.95 *(978-1-934440-54-4(X),* Pitspopany Pr.) Simcha Media Group.

Williams, Laura E. Behind the Bedroom Wall. Goldstein, A. Nancy, illus. 2006. 169p. (gr. -1-7). 17.45 *(978-0-7569-6389-7(3))* Perfection Learning Corp.

Wing, Natasha. The Night Before Hanukkah. 2014. (Night Before Ser.). lib. bdg. 13.55 *(978-0-606-36160-6(X))* Turtleback Bks.

The Winter Horses. 2014. (ENG., Illus.). 288p. (YA). (gr. 7). 16.99 *(978-0-385-75543-6(0),* Knopf Bks. for Young Readers) Random Hse. Children's Bks.

Wiseman, Eva. The World Outside. 2014. (ENG., Illus.). 236p. (YA). (gr. 7). 19.99 *(978-0-88776-981-8(0),* Tundra Bks.) Tundra Bks. CAN. Dist: Penguin Random Hse. LLC.

Wisniewski, David. Golem. Wisniewski, David, illus. 2007. (ENG., Illus.). 32p. (J). (gr. 5-7). 7.99 *(978-0-618-89424-6(1))* Houghton Mifflin Harcourt Publishing Co.

Wiviott, Meg. Benno & the Night of Broken Glass. Bisaillon, Josée, illus. 2010. (ENG.). 32p. (J). (gr. 2-5). pap. 7.95 *(978-0-8225-9975-3(9))*; lib. bdg. 17.95 *(978-0-8225-9929-6(5))* Lerner Publishing Group. (Kar-Ben Publishing).

Wohl, Lauren L. The Eighth Menorah. Hughes, Laura, illus. 2013. (ENG.). 32p. (J). (gr. -1-3). 16.99 *(978-0-8075-1892-2(1))* Whitman, Albert & Co.

Wulf, Linda Press. The Night of the Burning. 2007. (ENG.). 224p. pap. *(978-0-7475-9051-4(6))* Bloomsbury Publishing Plc.

Yavin, T. S. All-Star Season. 2006. 160p. (J). (gr. 3-7). lib. bdg. 15.95 *(978-1-58013-211-4(1),* Kar-Ben Publishing) Lerner Publishing Group.

Yerushalmi, Miriam. Feivel the Falafel Ball Who Wanted to Do a Mitzvah. Ginsberg, Dvora, illus. 2007. 28p. (J). 16.50 *(978-0-911643-37-4(0))* Aura Printing, Inc.

—Gedalia the Goldfish Who Wanted Be Just Like the King. Weinberg, Devorah, illus. 2007. 26p. (J). (gr. -1-3). 16.50 *(978-0-911643-36-7(2))* Aura Printing, Inc.

—Let's Go Camping & Discover Our Nature. Perez, Esther Ido, illus. 2007. 28p. (J). (gr. 2-4). 16.50 *(978-0-911643-38-1(9))* Aura Printing, Inc.

Yolen, Jane. The Devil's Arithmetic. 2004. (Puffin Modern Classics Ser.). (ENG.). 176p. (J). (gr. 5-3). pap. 7.99 *(978-0-14-240109-5(9),* Puffin Books) Penguin Young Readers Group.

—Stone Angel. Green, Katie May, illus. 2015. (ENG.). 40p. (J). (gr. k-3). 16.99 *(978-0-399-16741-6(2),* Philomel Bks.) Penguin Young Readers Group.

Yoon, Salina. My First Menorah. Yoon, Salina, illus. 2005. (ENG., Illus.). 20p. (J). (gr. -1-2). bds. 7.99 *(978-0-689-87746-9(3),* Little Simon) Little Simon.

Yorinks, Arthur. The Flying Latke. 2004. (Illus.). (J). (gr. k-3). spiral bd. *(978-0-616-03066-0(5))* Canadian National Institute for the Blind/Institut National Canadien pour les Aveugles.

Zirkind, Chaya Sara. Bas Mitzvah X 3. 2008. 156p. (J). *(978-1-56871-448-6(3))* Targum Pr., Inc.

Zolkower, Edie Stoltz. When It's Purim. Bjornson, Barb, illus. 2009. (Very First Board Bks.). (ENG.). 12p. (J). (gr. -1 — 1). 5.95 *(978-0-8225-8947-1(8),* Kar-Ben Publishing) Lerner Publishing Group.

Zucker, Jonny. Four Special Questions: A Passover Story. Cohen, Jan Barger, illus. 2003. (Festival Time Ser.). (ENG.). 24p. (J). (gr. -1-2). pap. 6.95 *(978-0-7641-2267-5(3))* Barron's Educational Series, Inc.

Zusak, Markus. La Ladrona de Libros. 2010. (Vintage Espanol Ser.).Tr. of Book Thief. (SPA.). 544p. (YA). (gr. 7). pap. 12.99 *(978-0-307-47573-2(5),* Vintage Espanol) Knopf Doubleday Publishing Group.

JEWS—FOLKLORE

Here are entered works on post-Biblical Jewish folklore and Jews as a theme in folklore.

Forest, Heather. A Big Quiet House: A Yiddish Folktale. Gaber, Susan & Greenstein, Susan, illus. 2005. (ENG.). 32p. (J). (gr. k-3). pap. 7.95 *(978-0-87483-604-2(2))* August Hse. Pubs., Inc.

—A Big Quiet House: A Yiddish Folktale from Eastern Europe. Greenstein, Susan, illus. 2005. (ENG.). 32p. (J). (gr. k-3). 15.95 *(978-0-87483-462-8(7))* August Hse. Pubs., Inc.

Gelfand, Shoshana Boyd. The Barefoot Book of Jewish Tales. 2017. (ENG., Illus.). 96p. (J). (gr. 1-4). 16.99 ***(978-1-78285-354-1(5))*** Barefoot Bks., Inc.

Gelfand, Shoshana Boyd. Jewish Tales. Hall, Amanda, illus. 2013. (ENG.). 80p. (J). (gr. 4-6). 19.99 *(978-1-84686-884-9(X))* Barefoot Bks., Inc.

Gilman, Phoebe. Something from Nothing. (J). (gr. k-13). pap. *(978-0-590-47281-4(X),* SO8818) Scholastic, Inc.

Goldin, Barbara Diamond. The Family Book of Midrash: 52 Jewish Stories from the Sages. 2006. Orig. Title: A Child's Book of Midrash. (ENG.). 128p. per. 28.00 *(978-0-7425-5285-2(3))* Rowman & Littlefield Publishers, Inc.

Labensohn, Judy, et al. Jewish Sports Stories for Kids. 2005. (Illus.). 224p. (J). (gr. 3-7). 16.95 *(978-1-930143-66-1(4))*; pap. 12.95 *(978-1-930143-67-8(2))* Simcha Media Group. (Devora Publishing).

Matov, G. Tales of Tzaddikim. Weinbach, Shaindel, tr. Bardugo, Miriam, illus. (J). pap. 56.99 *(978-0-89906-842-8(1))* Mesorah Pubns., Ltd.

Peretz, I. L. Even Higher! A Rosh Hashanah Story. Weber, Jill, illus. 2009. (ENG.). 32p. (J). (gr. -1-3). 16.95 *(978-0-8234-2020-9(5))* Holiday Hse., Inc.

Rogasky, Barbara & Fisher, Leonard Everett. The Dybbuk: A Version. 2005. (ENG., Illus.). 64p. (J). (gr. 5-9). 16.95 *(978-0-8234-1616-5(X))* Holiday Hse., Inc.

Schram, Peninnah, comment & intro. Solomon & the Ant: And Other Jewish Folktales. Schram, Peninnah, intro. 2006. (ENG.). 168p. (J). (gr. 2-8). 19.95 *(978-1-59078-307-8(7))* Boyds Mills Pr.

Schwartz, Howard. The Day the Rabbi Disappeared: Jewish Holiday Tales of Magic. Passicot, Monique, illus. 2003. (ENG.). 80p. pap. 13.00 *(978-0-8276-0757-6(1))* Jewish Pubn. Society.

—A Journey to Paradise: And Other Jewish Tales. Carmi, Giora, illus. 2005. (Jewish Storyteller Ser.). 48p. (J). (gr. -1-3). 16.95 *(978-0-943706-21-4(1))*; pap. 9.95 *(978-0-943706-16-0(5))* Simcha Media Group. (Devora Publishing).

Sherman, Josepha. Rachel the Clever & Other Jewish Folktales. 2005. (American Storytelling Ser.). (ENG., Illus.). 171p. (J). (gr. 4-17). pap. 12.95 *(978-0-87483-307-2(8))* August Hse. Pubs., Inc.

Sokoloff, David. Classic Jewish Tales. 2003. (Illus.). 96p. pap. 8.95 *(978-1-56171-948-8(X))* SPI Bks.

Story of Pnei Yehoshua. (J). 6.99 *(978-0-89906-845-9(6),* PNYH) Mesorah Pubns., Ltd.

Weston Woods Staff, creator. Joseph Had a Little Overcoat. 2004. 29.95 *(978-1-55592-109-5(4))* Weston Woods Studios, Inc.

JEWS—GERMANY

Altman, Linda Jacobs. Warsaw, Lodz, Vilna: The Holocaust Ghettos. 2014. (Remembering the Holocaust Ser.). 96p. (J). (gr. 6-12). pap. 10.95 *(978-0-7660-6208-5(2))* Enslow Pubs., Inc.

Byers, Ann. Anti-Semitism & the Final Solution: The Holocaust Overview. 2014. (Remembering the Holocaust Ser.). 96p. (J). (gr. 6-12). pap. 10.95 *(978-0-7660-6193-4(0))* Enslow Pubs., Inc.

—Kristallnacht & Living in Nazi Germany. 2014. (Documentary History of the Holocaust Ser.). 80p. (YA). (gr. 7-12). 34.25 *(978-1-4777-7595-0(1))* Rosen Publishing Group, Inc., The.

—Remembering the Holocaust: Anti-Semitism & the "Final Solution": The Holocaust Overview. 2014. (Remembering the Holocaust Ser.). (Illus.). 96p. (J). (gr. 6-12). 27.94 *(978-0-7660-6192-7(2))* Enslow Pubs., Inc.

Deem, James M. Kristallnacht: The Nazi Terror That Began the Holocaust. 2011. (Holocaust Through Primary Sources Ser.). (Illus.). 128p. (J). (gr. 6-18). pap. 10.95 *(978-1-59845-345-4(9))*; (gr. 9-12). lib. bdg. 33.27 *(978-0-7660-3324-5(4))* Enslow Pubs., Inc.

Hillman, Laura. I Will Plant You a Lilac Tree: A Memoir of a Schindler's List Survivor. 2005. (ENG., Illus.). 256p. (YA). (gr. 7). 16.95 *(978-0-689-86980-8(0),* Atheneum Bks. for Young Readers) Simon & Schuster Children's Publishing.

Langley, Andrew. Hitler & Kristallnacht: Days of Decision, 1 vol. 2013. (Days of Decision Ser.). (ENG.). 64p. (gr. 7-8). 35.99 *(978-1-4329-7636-1(2))*; pap. 10.95 *(978-1-4329-7643-9(5))* Heinemann-Raintree.

Mara, Wil. Kristallnacht: Nazi Persecution of the Jews in Europe. 2009. (Perspectives on Ser.). 112p. (gr. 7). 39.93 *(978-0-7614-4026-0(7))* Marshall Cavendish Corp.

Perl, Lila & Lazan, Marion Blumenthal. Four Perfect Pebbles: A True Story of the Holocaust. 2016. 160p. (J). (gr. 7-7). pap. 6.99 *(978-0-06-248996-8(8),* Greenwillow Bks.) HarperCollins Pubs.

Russo, Marisabina. Always Remember Me: How One Family Survived World War II. Russo, Marisabina, illus. 2005. (ENG., Illus.). 48p. (J). (gr. 1-5). 19.99 *(978-0-689-86920-4(7),* Atheneum Bks. for Young Readers) Simon & Schuster Children's Publishing.

Shoup, Kate. Nazi Propaganda: Jews in Hitler's Germany. 2016. (Public Persecutions Ser.). 128p. (J). 45.64 *(978-1-5026-2321-8(8))* Cavendish Square Publishing.

JEWS—HISTORY

Aretha, David. Israel in the News: Past, Present, & Future. 2006. (Middle East Nations in the News Ser.). (Illus.). 128p. (J). (gr. 3-7). lib. bdg. 34.60 *(978-1-59845-028-6(X),* MyReportLinks.com Bks.) Enslow Pubs., Inc.

Bader, Joanne. Moses & the Long Walk. von der Sterre, Johanna, illus. 2006. 16p. (J). 1.99 *(978-0-7586-0874-1(8))* Concordia Publishing Hse.

Bartoletti, Susan Campbell. Hitler Youth: Growing up in Hitler's Shadow. 2005. (ENG., Illus.). 176p. (J). (gr. 7). 21.99 *(978-0-439-35379-3(3))* Scholastic, Inc.

Behar, Yvonne. Out of Spain Vol. 3: Celebrating Sephardi Culture. Brooks, Andree Aelion, ed. (Illus.). 58p. (J). (gr. 5-7). pap. 4.95 *(978-0-9702700-3-0(8))* Brooks, Andree Aelion.

Botnick, Julie & Linden, Becca. Min Ha'aretz: Making Meaning from Our Food. 2016. *(978-0-87441-938-2(7))* Behrman Hse., Inc.

Bower, Gary. The Hurry-Up Exit from Egypt. Chotiner, Barbara, illus. 2017. (Faith That God Built Book Ser.). (ENG.). 32p. (J). 14.99 *(978-1-4964-1745-9(3))* Tyndale Hse. Pubs.

Broida, Marian. Ancient Israelites & Their Neighbors. 2003. (ENG., Illus.). 160p. (J). (gr. 4). act. bk. ed. 16.95 *(978-1-55652-457-8(9))* Chicago Review Pr., Inc.

Brown, Jonatha A. Anne Frank. Acosta, Tatiana & Gutierrez, Guillermo, trs. 2004. (Gente Que Hay Que Conocer Ser.). (SPA., Illus.). 24p. (gr. 1-4). lib. bdg. 22.00 *(978-0-8368-4351-4(7),* Weekly Reader Leveled Readers) Stevens, Gareth Publishing LLLP.

Charry, Elias & Segal, Abraham. The Eternal People. (Illus.). 448p. (J). (gr. 9-11). 7.50 *(978-0-8381-0206-0(9),* 10-206) United Synagogue of America Bk. Service.

Draper, Allison Stark. Pastor Andre Trocme: Spiritual Leader of the French Village, Le Chambon. 2005. (Holocaust Biographies Ser.). (Illus.). 112p. (YA). (gr. 7-12). lib. bdg. 34.60 *(978-0-8239-3378-5(4))* Rosen Publishing Group, Inc., The.

—Pastor André Trocmé: Spiritual Leader of the French Village le Chambon. 2009. (Holocaust Biographies Ser.). 112p. (gr. 7-12). 63.90 *(978-1-61513-390-1(9))* Rosen Publishing Group, Inc., The.

Eisenberg, Azriel. Fill a Blank Page: A Biography of Solomon Schechter. (Illus.). (J). (gr. 6-11). 3.75 *(978-0-8381-0730-0(3),* 10-730) United Synagogue of America Bk. Service.

Engel, Barbara, et al. From Ur to Eternity: The Historical Adventures of the Jewish People. 2010. (J). *(978-1-60280-034-2(0))*; (Illus.). pap. *(978-1-60280-035-9(9))* Ktav Publishing Hse., Inc.

Goldstein, Jessica & Inker, Inna, eds. Let My People Go! Carol, Racklin-Siegel, illus. 2011. (ENG & HEB.). 32p. (J). pap. 10.95 *(978-0-939144-67-9(0))* EKS Publishing Co.

Immell, Myra. The Creation of the State of Israel. 2009. (Perspectives on Modern World History Ser.). (Illus.). 224p. (YA). (gr. 10-18). 42.45 *(978-0-7377-4556-6(8),* Greenhaven Pr., Inc.) Cengage Gale.

Jones, Graham. How They Lived in Bible Times. Deverell, Richard, illus. 2003. 48p. 6.49 *(978-1-85999-435-1(0))* Scripture Union GBR. Dist: Gabriel Resources.

Kacer, Kathy. To Hope & Back: The Journey of the St. Louis, 1 vol. 2011. (Holocaust Remembrance Ser.). (ENG., Illus.). 200p. (J). (gr. 6-8). pap. 14.95 *(978-1-897187-96-8(3))* Second Story Pr. CAN. Dist: Orca Bk. Pubs. USA.

Kor, Eva Mozes & Buccieri, Lisa Rojany. Surviving the Angel of Death: The True Story of a Mengele Twin in Auschwitz. 2012. lib. bdg. 19.60 *(978-0-606-23838-0(7),* Turtleback) Turtleback Bks.

Krasner, Jonathan B., et al. The History of the Jewish People: A Story of Tradition & Change, 2 vols. 2006. (Illus.). (J). *(978-0-87441-192-8(0))* Behrman Hse., Inc.

Krohn, Genendel. When We Left Yerushalayim: Stories of the Churban Beis HaMikdash. 2009. 48p. (J). (gr. 1-5). 14.99 *(978-1-59826-393-0(5))* Feldheim Pubs.

Laurel Corona. Jewish Americans. 2004. (Immigrants in America Ser.). (ENG., Illus.). 112p. (J). 30.85 *(978-1-59018-431-8(9))* Cengage Gale.

Lefcourt, Jack. Four Thousand Years of Jewish History: Then & Now. 2009. 108p. (YA). (gr. 6-18). 16.95 *(978-1-60280-132-5(0))* Ktav Publishing Hse., Inc.

Leiman, Sondra. The Atlas of Great Jewish Communities: A Voyage Through History. 2004. (gr. 4-6). pap. 13.95 *(978-0-8074-0801-8(8),* 123941) URJ Pr.

Levinger, Elma Ehrli. The Story of the Jew for Young People. 2005. pap. 30.95 *(978-1-4191-5468-3(0))* Kessinger Publishing, LLC.

Maalos, text. Baruch & Berel. 2011. (YID.). 21.00 *(978-0-9832102-4-5(1))* Roth Pubs.

Rappaport, Doreen. Beyond Courage: The Untold Story of Jewish Resistance During the Holocaust. 2012. (ENG., Illus.). 240p. (J). (gr. 5). 22.99 *(978-0-7636-2976-2(6))* Candlewick Pr.

Rosenfield, Geraldine. The Heroes of Masada. Sugarman, S. Allan, illus. 38p. (J). (gr. 6-10). pap. 1.50 *(978-0-8381-0733-1(8),* 10-732) United Synagogue of America Bk. Service.

Schiffman, Lawrence H. Understanding Second Temple & Rabbinic Judaism. 2003. (Illus.). xviii, 409p. (YA). 29.50 *(978-0-88125-813-4(X))* Ktav Publishing Hse., Inc.

Senker, Cath. Judaism. 2007. (Atlas of World Faiths/Arcturus Ser.). (Illus.). 48p. (YA). (gr. 7-12). lib. bdg. 32.80 *(978-1-59920-056-9(2))* Black Rabbit Bks.

Slavicek, Louise Chipley. The Establishment of the State of Israel. 2011. (Milestones in Modern World History Ser.). (Illus.). 128p. (C). (gr. 9). 35.00 *(978-1-60413-917-4(X),* Chelsea Hse.) Facts On File, Inc.

Stadtler, Bea. The Adventures of Gluckel of Hameln. (J). (gr. 6-10). 3.75 *(978-0-8381-0731-7(1),* 10-731) United Synagogue of America Bk. Service.

Suneby, Liz & Heiman, Diane. The Mitzvah Project Book: Making Mitzvah Part of Your Bar/Bat Mitzvah & Your Life. 2011. (ENG., Illus.). 224p. (J). pap. 16.99 *(978-1-58023-458-0(5),* 9781580234580, Jewish Lights Publishing) LongHill Partners, Inc.

Taylor, Peter Lane & Nicola, Christos. The Secret of Priest's Grotto: A Holocaust Survival Story. 2007. (Holocaust Ser.). (ENG., Illus.). 64p. (YA). (gr. 5-12). per. 8.95 *(978-1-58013-261-9(8),* Kar-Ben Publishing) Lerner Publishing Group.

Weilerstein, Sadie Rose. Jewish Heroes, 2 bks. Cassel, Lili, illus. 208p. (J). (gr. 2-3). Bk. 1. 4.25 *(978-0-8381-0180-3(1))*Bk. 2. 4.25 *(978-0-8381-0177-3(1))* United Synagogue of America Bk. Service.

Worth, Richard & Asher, Robert. Jewish Immigrants. 2004. (Immigration to the United States Ser.). (Illus.). 96p. (gr. 4-9). 35.00 *(978-0-8160-5684-2(6))* Facts On File, Inc.

Yeatts, Tabatha. Weisel, Wiesenthal, Klarsfeld: The Holocaust Survivors. 2014. (Remembering the Holocaust Ser.). 96p. (J). (gr. 6-12). 27.94 *(978-0-7660-6202-3(3))* Enslow Pubs., Inc.

—Wiesel, Wiesenthal, Klarsfeld: The Holocaust Survivors. 2014. (Remembering the Holocaust Ser.). 96p. (J). (gr. 6-12). pap. 10.95 *(978-0-7660-6203-0(1))* Enslow Pubs., Inc.

JEWS—HISTORY—FICTION

Anton, Maggie. Secret Scholar. 2008. (ENG.). 160p. (gr. 4-7). pap. 14.00 *(978-0-8276-0869-6(1))* Jewish Pubn. Society.

Benderly, Beryl Lieff. Jason's Miracle: A Hanukkah Story. 2004. 114p. (J). (gr. 4-8). reprint ed. *(978-0-7567-7792-0(5))* DIANE Publishing Co.

Booth, Bradley. Escape from Egypt. 2009. (J). pap. 11.99 *(978-0-8163-2305-0(4))* Pacific Pr. Publishing Assn.

—Esther: A Star Is Born. 2009. (J). pap. 12.99 *(978-0-8163-2359-3(3))* Pacific Pr. Publishing Assn.

—Plagues in the Palace. 2006. 159p. (J). 10.99 *(978-0-8163-2143-8(4))* Pacific Pr. Publishing Assn.

—Prince of Dreams. 2008. (J). pap. 10.99 *(978-0-8163-2253-4(8))* Pacific Pr. Publishing Assn.

Chotjewitz, David & Orgel, Doris. Daniel, Half Human: And the Good Nazi. 2004. 298p. (J). *(978-3-551-58045-0(6))* Carlsen Verlag DEU. Dist: Distribooks, Inc.

Deutsch, Barry. Hereville: How Mirka Met a Meteorite. 2012. (Hereville Ser.). (ENG., Illus.). 128p. (J). (gr. 3-7). 17.95 *(978-1-4197-0398-0(6),* Amulet Bks.) Abrams, Inc.

Elvgren, Jennifer. The Whispering Town. Santomauro, Fabio, illus. 2014. (Holocaust Ser.). (ENG.). 32p. (J). (gr. 2-5). 17.95 *(978-1-4677-1194-4(2))*; 7.95 *(978-1-4677-1195-1(0))* Lerner Publishing Group.

Focus on the Family Staff & Hering, Marianne. Light in the Lions' Den. 2017. (AIO Imagination Station Bks.: 19). (ENG.). 144p. (J). pap. 4.99 *(978-1-58997-878-2(1))* Focus on the Family Publishing.

Greene, Jacqueline Dembar. The Secret Shofar of Barcelona. Chayka, Doug, illus. 2009. (High Holidays Ser.). (ENG.). 32p. (J). (gr. k-3). 17.95 *(978-0-8225-9915-9(5),* Kar-Ben Publishing) Lerner Publishing Group.

—The Secret Shofar of Barcelona. Chayka, Douglas, illus. 2009. (High Holidays Ser.). (ENG.). 32p. (J). (gr. k-3). pap. 7.95 *(978-0-8225-9944-9(9),* Kar-Ben Publishing) Lerner Publishing Group.

Hernandez, David. Land of the Pharaohs, 1 vol. 2003. (Adventures of Toby Digz Ser.: 1). (ENG., Illus.). 96p. pap. 5.99 *(978-1-4003-0195-9(5))* Nelson, Thomas Inc.

Hesse, Monica. Girl in the Blue Coat. (ENG.). 320p. (gr. 7-17). 2017. (YA). pap. 9.99 *(978-0-316-26063-3(0))* 2016. 17.99 *(978-0-316-26060-2(6))* 2016. (YA). E-Book *(978-0-316-26064-0(9))* Little, Brown Bks. for Young Readers.

—Girl in the Blue Coat. 2017. (YA). lib. bdg. 20.85 ***(978-0-606-39918-0(6))*** Turtleback Bks.

Jules, Jacqueline. The Ziz & the Hanukkah Miracle. Kahn, Katherine Janus, illus. 2006. (ENG.). 32p. (J). (gr. -1-2). per. 9.95 *(978-1-58013-164-3(6),* Kar-Ben Publishing) Lerner Publishing Group.

Kaplan, Kathy Walden. The Dog of Knots. 2005. 139p. (J). pap. 7.50 *(978-0-8028-5274-8(2))* Eerdmans, William B. Publishing Co.

Kerr, Judith. When Hitler Stole Pink Rabbit. (SPA.). 172p. (J). 11.95 *(978-84-204-3201-4(6))* Santillana USA Publishing Co., Inc.

—When Hitler Stole Pink Rabbit. 2009. (gr. 3-6). lib. bdg. 17.20 *(978-0-8085-9123-8(1),* Turtleback) Turtleback Bks.

Lawrence, Caroline. The Assassins of Rome. 2005. (Roman Mysteries Ser.). (Illus.). 161p. (J). (gr. 3-7). 14.65 *(978-0-7569-5879-4(2))* Perfection Learning Corp.

Lawton, Wendy. A La Sombra de Su Mano, 1 vol. 2009. Orig. Title: Shadow of His Hand. (SPA.). 160p. pap. 4.99 *(978-0-8254-1379-7(6),* Editorial Portavoz) Kregel Pubns.

Lawton, Wendy G. Shadow of His Hand: A Story Based on the Life of Holocaust Survivor Anita Dittman. 2004. (Daughters of the Faith Ser.). (ENG.). 160p. (J). (gr. 3). pap. 7.99 *(978-0-8024-4074-7(6))* Moody Pubs.

Lehmann, R' Marcus, contrib. by. The Family y Aguilar. 12.95 *(978-0-87306-318-0(X))* Feldheim Pubs.

Lois, Lowry. Number the Stars: And Related Readings. 2006. (Literature Connections Ser.). 172p. (gr. 6-12). *(978-0-395-88457-7(8),* 2-70863) Holt McDougal.

Martin, Gary & Zondervan Bibles Staff. The Sword of Revenge, 1 vol. Rogers, Bud, ed. Cariello, Sergio, illus. 2009. (Z Graphic Novels / Son of Samson Ser.). (ENG.). 160p. (J). pap. 6.99 *(978-0-310-71285-5(8))* Zondervan.

Martin, Gary & Zondervan Staff. The Heroes of God, 1 vol. Cariello, Sergio, illus. 2009. (Z Graphic Novels / Son of Samson Ser.). (ENG.). 160p. (J). pap. 6.99 *(978-0-310-71284-8(X))* Zondervan.

Martin, Gary, et al. The Maiden of Thunder, 1 vol. Cariello, Sergio & Lanphear, Dave, illus. 2008. (Z Graphic Novels / Son of Samson Ser.). (ENG.). 160p. (J). (gr. 4-7). pap. 6.99 *(978-0-310-71281-7(5))* Zondervan.

Matas, Carol. Lisa's War. 2007. (ENG.). 128p. (J). (gr. 3-7). pap. 11.95 *(978-1-4169-6163-5(1),* Aladdin) Simon & Schuster Children's Publishing.

—Rosie in New York City: Gotcha! 2003. (ENG., Illus.). 128p. (J). (gr. 4-7). pap. 9.95 *(978-0-689-85714-0(4),* Simon &

Schuster/Paula Wiseman Bks.) Simon & Schuster/Paula Wiseman Bks.

—Turned Away: The World War II Diary of Devorah Bernstein. 2005. (Dear Canada Ser.). (ENG., Illus.). 208p. (J). *(978-0-439-96946-8(8))* Scholastic Canada, Ltd.

McKay, Sharon E. Esther. 2004. (ENG.). 336p. (J). pap. *(978-0-14-331204-8(9))* Penguin Canada.

Merritt, Ginny. The Window in the Wall. 2013. 78p. (J). *(978-1-60682-781-9(2))* BJU Pr.

Michelson, Richard. Across the Alley. Lewis, E. B., illus. 2006. (ENG.). 32p. (J). (gr. -1-3). 16.99 *(978-0-399-23970-0(7),* G.P. Putnam's Sons Books for Young Readers) Penguin Young Readers Group.

Miklowitz, Gloria D. Masada: The Last Fortress. 2004. 198p. (YA). (gr. 4-7). 16.00 *(978-0-8028-5165-9(7))* Eerdmans, William B. Publishing Co.

—Secrets in the House of Delgado. 2004. 192p. (J). (gr. 4-18). pap. 8.00 *(978-0-8028-5210-6(6))* Eerdmans, William B. Publishing Co.

Morgan-Cole, Trudy J. Esther: Courage to Stand. 2010. 144p. (J). pap. 12.99 *(978-0-8280-2430-3(8))* Review & Herald Publishing Assn.

Napoli, Donna Jo. Daughter of Venice. 2003. (ENG.). 288p. (YA). (gr. 7). mass mkt. 7.99 *(978-0-440-22928-5(6),* Laurel Leaf) Random Hse. Children's Bks.

Nelson, Suzanne. Serendipity's Footsteps. 2015. (ENG.). 368p. (YA). (gr. 7). 17.99 *(978-0-385-39212-9(5),* Knopf Bks. for Young Readers) Random Hse. Children's Bks.

Orgad, Dorit. The Boy from Seville. Silverston, Sondra, tr. from HEB. Katz, Avi, illus. 2007. (Kar-Ben for Older Readers Ser.). (ENG.). 200p. (J). (gr. 5-7). lib. bdg. 16.95 *(978-1-58013-253-4(7),* Kar-Ben Publishing) Lerner Publishing Group.

Petersen, Alicia. Out of Darkness. 2007. (Illus.). 177p. (J). (gr. 3-7). per. 8.99 *(978-1-59166-822-0(0))* BJU Pr.

Shapiro, David L. Sara's Journey. 2005. (ENG.). 224p. (gr. 7-12). per. 16.95 *(978-0-8276-0776-7(8))* Jewish Pubn. Society.

Sharenow, Robert. The Berlin Boxing Club. 2012. (ENG.). 432p. (YA). (gr. 8). pap. 9.99 *(978-0-06-157970-7(X),* HarperTeen) HarperCollins Pubs.

Silverberg, Selma Kritzer. Naomi's Song. 2009. (ENG.). 142p. (gr. 7-18). pap. 14.00 *(978-0-8276-0886-3(1))* Jewish Pubn. Society.

Snyder, Laurel. The Longest Night: A Passover Story. Chien, Catia, illus. 2013. (ENG.). 40p. (J). (gr. -1-3). 17.99 *(978-0-375-86942-6(5),* Schwartz & Wade Bks.) Random Hse. Children's Bks.

Weil, Sylvie. Elvina's Mirror. 2009. (ENG.). 150p. (gr. 5-18). pap. 14.00 *(978-0-8276-0885-6(3))* Jewish Pubn. Society.

—My Guardian Angel. Rosner, Gillian, tr. from FRE. 2014. (ENG., Illus.). 208p. (J). pap. 14.95 *(978-0-8276-1211-2(7))* Jewish Pubn. Society.

Wiseman, Eva. The Last Song. 2012. (ENG., Illus.). 228p. (YA). (gr. 5). 17.95 *(978-0-88776-979-5(9),* Tundra Bks.) Tundra Bks. CAN. Dist: Penguin Random Hse. LLC.

—Puppet. 2012. (ENG., Illus.). 248p. (YA). (gr. 5). pap. 9.95 *(978-1-77049-296-7(8),* Tundra Bks.) Tundra Bks. CAN. Dist: Penguin Random Hse. LLC.

Zusak, Markus. The Book Thief. 2014. (ENG.). 576p. (YA). 17.24 *(978-1-63245-052-4(6))* Lectorum Pubns., Inc.

—The Book Thief. 2009. 12.64 *(978-0-7848-1941-8(6),* Everbind) Marco Bk. Co.

—The Book Thief. 2008. 552p. (gr. 7-12). 23.00 *(978-0-7569-8440-3(8))* Perfection Learning Corp.

—The Book Thief. (ENG., Illus.). (YA). (gr. 7). 2016. 592p. lib. bdg. 22.99 *(978-0-399-55652-4(4))* 2007. 592p. pap. 12.99 *(978-0-375-84220-7(9))* 2013. 576p. pap. 12.99 *(978-0-385-75472-9(8))* 2016. 592p. 19.99 *(978-1-101-93418-0(2))* Random Hse. Children's Bks. (Knopf Bks. for Young Readers).

—The Book Thief. l.t. ed. 2006. (ENG.). 552p. 23.99 *(978-1-4104-6806-2(2));* 757p. (YA). (gr. 7-12). 24.95 *(978-0-7862-9021-5(8))* Thorndike Pr.

—The Book Thief. 2008. (ENG., Illus.). 560p. pap. *(978-0-552-77389-8(1),* Black Swan) Transworld Publishers Ltd.

—The Book Thief. 2007. 552p. lib. bdg. 24.50 *(978-1-4177-9738-7(X))* 2013. lib. bdg. 24.50 *(978-0-606-34656-6(2))* Turtleback Bks. (Turtleback).

JEWS—LANGUAGE

see Hebrew Language

JEWS—LITERATURE

see Jewish Literature

JEWS—NETHERLANDS

Abramson, Ann. Who Was Anne Frank? Harrison, Nancy, illus. 2007. (Who Was? Ser.). (ENG.). 112p. (J). (gr. 3-7). pap. 5.99 *(978-0-448-44482-6(8),* Grosset & Dunlap) Penguin Young Readers Group.

—Who Was Anne Frank? Harrison, Nancy, illus. 2007. (Who Was... ? Ser.). 103p. (gr. 2-6). 15.00 *(978-0-7569-8166-2(2))* Perfection Learning Corp.

—Who Was Anne Frank? Harrison, Nancy, illus. 2007. (Who Was... ? Ser.). 103p. (J). (gr. 4-7). 16.00 *(978-1-4177-6854-7(1),* Turtleback) Turtleback Bks.

Ashby, Ruth. Anne Frank: Young Diarist. 2005. 186p. (J). lib. bdg. 18.46 *(978-1-4242-2208-7(7))* Fitzgerald Bks.

Brown, Jonatha A. Anne Frank. 2004. (People to Know Ser.). (Illus.). 24p. (gr. 1-4). lib. bdg. 22.00 *(978-0-8368-4309-5(6),* Weekly Reader Leveled Readers) Stevens, Gareth Publishing LLLP.

Brown, Jonatha A. & Goff, Elizabeth Hudson. Ana Frank. McHargue, D. et al, illus. 2007. (Biografías Gráficas (Graphic Biographies) Ser.). (SPA.). 32p. (gr. 5-8). lib. bdg. 27.00 *(978-0-8368-7880-6(9))* Stevens, Gareth Publishing LLLP.

—Anne Frank. Floor, Guus & Timmons, Jonathan, illus. 2006. (Graphic Biographies (World Almanac Library (Firm))). 32p. (gr. 5-8). lib. bdg. 27.00 *(978-0-8368-6196-9(5))* Stevens, Gareth Publishing LLLP.

Dunn, Joe. Anne Frank, 1 vol. 2007. (Bio-Graphics Ser.). (ENG., Illus.). 32p. (gr. 3-6). 28.50 *(978-1-60270-065-9(6),* Graphic Planet- Nonfiction) ABDO Publishing Co.

Gil, Carmen & Gali, Merce. Ana Frank. 2010. (Me Llamo... Ser.). (SPA., Illus.). 63p. (J). pap. *(978-84-342-3339-3(8))* Parramon Ediciones S.A.

Goff, Elizabeth Hudson & Brown, Jonatha A. Anne Frank. 2006. (Graphic Biographies (World Almanac Library (Firm))). (Illus.). 32p. (gr. 5-8). pap. 10.50 *(978-0-8368-6248-5(1))* Stevens, Gareth Publishing LLLP.

Heims, Neil. Reading the Diary of Anne Frank. 2005. (Engaged Reader Ser.). (Illus.). 104p. (gr. 5-8). lib. bdg. 25.00 *(978-0-7910-8829-6(4),* Chelsea Hse.) Facts On File, Inc.

Hollingsworth, Tamara. Anne Frank: A Light in the Dark, 1 vol. 2nd rev. ed. 2013. (Nonfiction Readers Ser.). (ENG., Illus.). 48p. (J). (gr. 4-4). pap. 29.96 *(978-1-4807-1117-4(9))* Shell Educational Publishing.

—Anne Frank: A Light in the Dark, 1 vol. 2nd rev. ed. 2012. (TIME for KIDS(r) Nonfiction Readers Ser.). (ENG.). 48p. (J). (gr. 4-4). pap. 9.99 *(978-1-4333-4865-5(9))* Teacher Created Materials, Inc.

Hudson Goff, Elizabeth & Brown, Jonatha A. Ana Frank. 2007. (Biografías Gráficas (Graphic Biographies) Ser.). (SPA.). 32p. (gr. 5-8). pap. 10.50 *(978-0-8368-7887-5(6))* Stevens, Gareth Publishing LLLP.

Kramer, Ann. Anne Frank: The Young Writer Who Told the World Her Story. 2009. (National Geographic World History Biographies Ser.). (ENG., Illus.). 64p. (J). (gr. 3-7). 7.99 *(978-1-4263-0414-9(5),* National Geographic Children's Bks.) National Geographic Society.

Mara, Wil. Anne Frank: A Life in Hiding. 2016. (Rookie Biographies(tm) Ser.). (ENG., Illus.). 32p. (J). lib. bdg. 25.00 *(978-0-531-21683-5(7),* Children's Pr.) Scholastic Library Publishing.

McDowell, Pamela. Anne Frank. 2014. (J). *(978-1-4896-2456-7(2))* Weigl Pubs., Inc.

Miklowitz, Gloria. Anne Frank. 2009. pap. 13.25 *(978-1-60559-053-0(3))* Hameray Publishing Group, Inc.

Parks, Peggy J. Anne Frank. 2016. (ENG.). 80p. (J). (gr. 5-12). 38.60 *(978-1-60152-946-6(5))* ReferencePoint Pr., Inc.

Poole, Josephine. Ana Frank. Barrett, Angela, illus. 2005. (SPA.). 32p. (J). (gr. 3-4). 17.99 *(978-1-930332-87-4(4))* Lectorum Pubns., Inc.

Waxman, Laura Hamilton. Anne Frank. 2009. (History Maker Biographies Ser.). (ENG.). 48p. (gr. 3-6). 27.93 *(978-0-7613-4221-2(4),* Lerner Pubns.) Lerner Publishing Group.

Whiting, Jim. Anne Frank. 2007. (What's So Great About... ? Ser.). (Illus.). 32p. (YA). (gr. 2-4). lib. bdg. 25.70 *(978-1-58415-581-2(7))* Mitchell Lane Pubs., Inc.

JEWS—NEW YORK (STATE)—NEW YORK—FICTION

Crowder, Melanie & Mack, Jeff. Audacity. 2015. (ENG.). 400p. (YA). (gr. 7). bds. 17.99 *(978-0-399-16899-4(0),* Philomel Bks.) Penguin Young Readers Group.

Freedman, Paula J. My Basmati Bat Mitzvah. 2013. (ENG., Illus.). 256p. (YA). (gr. 3-7). 17.95 *(978-1-4197-0806-0(6),* Amulet Bks.) Abrams, Inc.

Greene, Jacqueline. Rebecca Story Collection. Hirsch, Jennifer, ed. Hunt, Robert, illus. 2009. (ENG.). 456p. (YA). (gr. 3-18). 29.95 *(978-1-59369-626-9(4))* American Girl Publishing, Inc.

Hest, Amy. When Jessie Came Across the Sea. Lynch, P. J., illus. 2003. (ENG.). 40p. (J). (gr. 1-4). pap. 6.99 *(978-0-7636-1274-0(X))* Candlewick Pr.

Levine, Gail Carson. Dave at Night. 2006. (ENG.). 304p. (J). (gr. 3-7). reprint ed. pap. 7.99 *(978-0-06-440747-2(0))* HarperCollins Pubs.

—Dave at Night. 2004. 281p. (gr. 3-7). 17.00 *(978-0-7569-4101-7(6))* Perfection Learning Corp.

—Dave at Night. unabr. ed. 2004. 278p. (J). (gr. 4-7). pap. 38.00 incl. audio *(978-0-8072-8379-0(7),* YA174SP, Listening Library) Random Hse. Audio Publishing Group.

Moriarty, Chris. The Inquisitor's Apprentice. Geyer, Mark Edward, illus. 2011. (ENG.). 352p. (J). (gr. 5-7). 16.99 *(978-0-547-58135-4(1))* Houghton Mifflin Harcourt Publishing Co.

—The Watcher in the Shadows. Geyer, Mark Edward, illus. 2014. (ENG.). 336p. (J). (gr. 5-7). pap. 7.99 *(978-0-544-22776-7(X),* HMH Books For Young Readers) Houghton Mifflin Harcourt Publishing Co.

JEWS—PERSECUTIONS

Altman, Linda Jacobs. Warsaw, Lodz, Vilna: The Holocaust Ghettos. 2014. (Remembering the Holocaust Ser.). 96p. (J). (gr. 6-12). pap. 10.95 *(978-0-7660-6208-5(2));* (Illus.). 27.94 *(978-0-7660-6207-8(4))* Enslow Pubs., Inc.

Brezina, Corona. Nazi Architects of the Holocaust. 2014. (Documentary History of the Holocaust Ser.). 80p. (YA). (gr. 7-12). 34.25 *(978-1-4777-7597-4(8))* Rosen Publishing Group, Inc., The.

Byers, Ann. Kristallnacht & Living in Nazi Germany. 2014. (Documentary History of the Holocaust Ser.). 80p. (YA). (gr. 7-12). 34.25 *(978-1-4777-7595-0(1))* Rosen Publishing Group, Inc., The.

—Remembering the Holocaust: Anti-Semitism & the "Final Solution": The Holocaust Overview. 2014. (Remembering the Holocaust Ser.). (Illus.). 96p. (J). (gr. 6-12). 27.94 *(978-0-7660-6192-7(2))* Enslow Pubs., Inc.

—Rescuing the Danish Jews: A Heroic Story from the Holocaust. 2011. (Holocaust Through Primary Sources Ser.). (Illus.). 128p. (J). (gr. 6-18). pap. 10.95 *(978-1-59845-343-0(2));* (gr. 9-12). lib. bdg. 33.27 *(978-0-7660-3321-4(X))* Enslow Pubs., Inc.

Darman, Peter, ed. The Holocaust & Life under Nazi Occupation. 2012. (World War II Ser.). (ENG., Illus.). 64p. (YA). (gr. 7-12). lib. bdg. 31.95 *(978-1-4488-9235-8(X))* Rosen Publishing Group, Inc., The.

Deem, James M. Auschwitz: Voices from the Death Camp. 2011. (Holocaust Through Primary Sources Ser.). (Illus.). 128p. (J). (gr. 6-18). pap. 10.95 *(978-1-59845-346-1(7));* (gr. 9-12). lib. bdg. 33.27 *(978-0-7660-3322-1(8))* Enslow Pubs., Inc.

—Kristallnacht: The Nazi Terror That Began the Holocaust. 2011. (Holocaust Through Primary Sources Ser.). (Illus.). 128p. (J). (gr. 6-18). pap. 10.95 *(978-1-59845-345-4(9));* (gr. 9-12). lib. bdg. 33.27 *(978-0-7660-3324-5(4))* Enslow Pubs., Inc.

Forest, Jim. Silent As a Stone: Mother Maria of Paris & the Trash Can Rescue. Pancheshnaya, Dasha, illus. 2007. (ENG.). 32p. (J). 18.00 *(978-0-88141-314-4(3))* St. Vladimir's Seminary Pr.

Kaelberer, Angie Peterson & Fitzgerald, Stephanie. Kristallnacht. 2017. (Eyewitness to World War II Ser.). (ENG.). 112p. (gr. 5-7). lib. bdg. 35.99 ***(978-0-7565-5583-2(3),*** CPB Grades 4-8) Compass Point Bks.

Kor, Eva Mozes & Buccieri, Lisa Rojany. Surviving the Angel of Death: The True Story of a Mengele Twin in Auschwitz. 2012. (ENG.). 175p. (J). (gr. 6). pap. 8.95 *(978-1-933718-57-6(9))* Tanglewood Pr.

Kor, Eva Mozes, et al. Surviving the Angel of Death: The Story of a Mengele Twin in Auschwitz. 2009. (ENG., Illus.). 141p. (J). (gr. 6-18). 14.95 *(978-1-933718-28-6(5))* Tanglewood Pr.

Lensky, Mordechai. A Physician Inside the Warswa Ghetto. 2009. 257p. (YA). pap. 27.50 *(978-0-9814686-3-1(2))* Yad Vashem Pubns. ISR. Dist: Coronet Bks.

Lombardo, Jennifer & Robson, David. The Horrors of Auschwitz. 2017. (World History Ser.). 104p. (YA). (gr. 7-7). 39.90 ***(978-1-5345-6054-3(8),*** Lucent Pr.) Greenhaven Publishing LLC.

Mara, Wil. Kristallnacht: Nazi Persecution of the Jews in Europe. 2009. (Perspectives on Ser.). 112p. (gr. 7). 39.93 *(978-0-7614-4026-0(7))* Marshall Cavendish Corp.

Norton, James. The Holocaust: Jews, Germany, & the National Socialists. 2009. (Genocide in Modern Times Ser.). 64p. (gr. 6-6). 58.50 *(978-1-61512-677-4(5))* Rosen Publishing Group, Inc., The.

Norton, James R. The Holocaust: Jews, Germany, & the National Socialists. 2008. (Genocide in Modern Times Ser.). (Illus.). 64p. (YA). (gr. 9-12). lib. bdg. 31.95 *(978-1-4042-1821-5(1))* Rosen Publishing Group, Inc., The.

Robson, David. Auschwitz. 2009. (World History Ser.). (ENG., Illus.). 128p. (J). (gr. 7-10). 34.95 *(978-1-4205-0131-5(3),* Lucent Bks.) Cengage Gale.

Russo, Marisabina. Always Remember Me: How One Family Survived World War II. Russo, Marisabina, illus. 2005. (ENG., Illus.). 48p. (J). (gr. 1-5). 19.99 *(978-0-689-86920-4(7),* Atheneum Bks. for Young Readers) Simon & Schuster Children's Publishing.

Sheehan, Sean. Auschwitz. 2011. (Place in History Ser.). 48p. (YA). (gr. 5-9). lib. bdg. 34.25 *(978-1-84837-672-4(3))* Arcturus Publishing GBR. Dist: Black Rabbit Bks.

Thornton, Jeremy. Religious Intolerance: Jewish Immigrants Come to America (1881-1914) 2004. (Primary Sources of Immigration & Migration in America Ser.). (Illus.). 24p. (J). lib. bdg. 22.60 *(978-0-8239-6834-3(0))* Rosen Publishing Group, Inc., The.

—Religious Intolerance: Jewish Immigrants Come to America, 1890-1924. 2004. (Primary Sources of Immigration & Migration in America Ser.). (ENG., Illus.). 24p. (J). (gr. 4-8). pap. 9.40 *(978-0-8239-8960-7(7))* Rosen Publishing Group, Inc., The.

Toll, Nelly S. Behind the Secret Window: A Memoir of a Hidden Childhood During World War II. 2003. (ENG.). 176p. (J). (gr. 3-7). 5.99 *(978-0-14-230241-5(4),* Puffin Books) Penguin Young Readers Group.

Ziemian, Joseph. The Cigarette Sellers of Three Crosses Square. 2005. (Library of Holocaust Testimonies Ser.). (Illus.). 168p. pap. 24.95 *(978-0-85303-686-9(1))* Vallentine Mitchell Pubs. GBR. Dist: ISBS Publisher Services.

JEWS—POLAND

Altman, Linda Jacobs. The Warsaw Ghetto Uprising: Striking a Blow Against the Nazis. 2011. (Holocaust Through Primary Sources Ser.). (Illus.). 128p. (J). (gr. 6-18). pap. 10.95 *(978-1-59845-347-8(5));* (gr. 9-12). lib. bdg. 33.27 *(978-0-7660-3320-7(1))* Enslow Pubs., Inc.

—Warsaw, Lodz, Vilna: The Holocaust Ghettos. 2014. (Remembering the Holocaust Ser.). 96p. (J). (gr. 6-12). pap. 10.95 *(978-0-7660-6208-5(2))* Enslow Pubs., Inc.

Beyer, Mark. Emmanuel Ringelblum: Historian of the Warsaw Ghetto. (Holocaust Biographies Ser.). 112p. (gr. 7-12). 2009. 63.90 *(978-1-61513-384-0(4))* 2005. (Illus.). (YA). lib. bdg. 34.60 *(978-0-8239-3375-4(X))* Rosen Publishing Group, Inc., The.

Brophy Down, Susan. Irena Sendler: Bringing Life to Children of the Holocaust. 2012. (ENG.). 112p. (J). pap. *(978-0-7787-2556-5(1));* (Illus.). *(978-0-7787-2553-4(7))* Crabtree Publishing Co.

Callahan, Kerry P. Mordechai Anielewicz: Hero of the Warsaw Ghetto Uprising. 2009. (Holocaust Biographies Ser.). 112p. (gr. 7-12). 63.90 *(978-1-61513-389-5(5))* Rosen Publishing Group, Inc., The.

Friedman, Laurie. Angel Girl. Amit, Ofra, illus. 2008. 32p. (J). (gr. 3-7). 16.95 *(978-0-8225-8739-2(4),* Carolrhoda Bks.) Lerner Publishing Group.

Lensky, Mordechai. A Physician Inside the Warswa Ghetto. 2009. 257p. (YA). pap. 27.50 *(978-0-9814686-3-1(2))* Yad Vashem Pubns. ISR. Dist: Coronet Bks.

Lobel, Anita. No Pretty Pictures: A Child of War. 2008. (ENG.). 288p. (J). (gr. 5). pap. 7.99 *(978-0-06-156589-2(X),* Greenwillow Bks.) HarperCollins Pubs.

Ludwig, Trudy. Gifts from the Enemy. Orback, Craig, illus. 2014. (HumanKIND Project Ser.). (ENG.). 32p. (gr. 2-7). 16.95 *(978-1-935952-97-8(8))* White Cloud Pr.

Rubin, Susan Goldman. Irena Sendler & the Children of the Warsaw Ghetto. Farnsworth, Bill, illus. (ENG.). 40p. (J). 2016. (gr. 4-7). pap. 8.99 *(978-0-8234-2595-2(9))* 2011. (gr. 1-5). 18.95 *(978-0-8234-2251-7(8))* Holiday Hse., Inc.

Rubinstein, Robert. Zishe the Strongman. Miller, Woody, illus. 2010. (Kar-Ben Favorites Ser.). (ENG.). 32p. (J). (gr. k-3). pap. 7.95 *(978-0-7613-3960-1(4),* Kar-Ben Publishing) Lerner Publishing Group.

Rubinstein, Robert E. Zishe the Strongman. Miller, Woody, illus. 2010. (Kar-Ben Favorites Ser.). (ENG.). 32p. (J). (gr. k-3). lib. bdg. 17.95 *(978-0-7613-3958-8(2),* Kar-Ben Publishing) Lerner Publishing Group.

Vaughan, Marcia. Irena's Jars of Secrets, 1 vol. Mazellan, Ron, illus. 2011. (ENG.). 40p. (J). 18.95 *(978-1-60060-439-3(0))* Lee & Low Bks., Inc.

Ziemian, Joseph. The Cigarette Sellers of Three Crosses Square. 2005. (Library of Holocaust Testimonies Ser.). (Illus.). 168p. pap. 24.95 *(978-0-85303-686-9(1))* Vallentine Mitchell Pubs. GBR. Dist: ISBS Publisher Services.

JEWS—RELIGION

see Judaism

JEWS—RITES AND CEREMONIES

Abraham, Michelle Shapiro & Koffsky, Ann D. Shavua Tov! A Good Week. 2008. (HEB & ENG.). (J). *(978-0-8074-1084-4(5))* URJ Pr.

Chanover, Hyman & Zusman, Evelyn. A Book of Prayer for Junior Congregations: Sabbath & Festivals. (ENG & HEB.). 256p. (J). (gr. 4-7). 4.50 *(978-0-8381-0174-2(7),* 10-174) United Synagogue of America Bk. Service.

Eisenberg, Azriel & Robinson, Jessie B. My Jewish Holidays. 208p. (J). (gr. 5-6). 3.95 *(978-0-8381-0176-6(3),* 10-176) United Synagogue of America Bk. Service.

Kunda, Shmuel. Boruch Learns His Brochos. Kunda, Shmuel, illus. 2005. (Illus.). 40p. (J). 17.95 *(978-1-932443-41-7(X))* Judaica Pr., Inc., The.

Metter, Bert & Metter, Bertram. Bar Mitzvah, Bat Mitzvah: The Ceremony, the Party, & How the Day Came to Be. Reilly, Joan & Katz, Avi, illus. 2007. (ENG.). 80p. (J). (gr. 5-7). pap. 8.95 *(978-0-618-76773-1(8))* Houghton Mifflin Harcourt Publishing Co.

JEWS—SOVIET UNION

Taybert, Efim. I Kedriy Tojze Plachyt. 2003.Tr. of And Cedars Also Cry. (RUS.). 254p. (YA). pap. *(978-0-9728301-2-6(X))* Publishing Hse. Gelany.

JEWS—SOVIET UNION—FICTION

Blumberg, Margie. Avram's Gift. McGaw, Laurie, illus. (ENG.). 48p. 2005. (YA). pap. 11.95 *(978-0-9624166-3-7(0))* 2003. (J). (gr. 3-18). 15.95 *(978-0-9624166-2-0(2))* MB Publishing, LLC.

Howland, Naomi. Latkes, Latkes, Good to Eat: A Chanukah Story. 2004. (ENG., Illus.). 32p. (J). (gr. -1-3). pap. 6.99 *(978-0-618-49295-4(X))* Houghton Mifflin Harcourt Publishing Co.

Lasky, Kathryn. The Night Journey. 2005. 151p. (gr. 3-7). 16.00 *(978-0-7569-5062-0(7))* Perfection Learning Corp.

Rosen, Michael J. Chanukah Lights Everywhere. 2010. (ENG.). 22p. (J). pap. 6.00 *(978-1-4379-7172-9(5))* DIANE Publishing Co.

Watts, Irene N. Good-Bye Marianne: A Story of Growing up in Nazi Germany. Shoemaker, Kathryn E., illus. 2008. (ENG.). 128p. (J). (gr. 4-7). pap. 12.95 *(978-0-88776-830-9(X),* Tundra Bks.) Tundra Bks. CAN. Dist: Penguin Random Hse. LLC.

JEWS—UNITED STATES

Amler, Jane Frances. Haym Salomon: Patriot Banker of the American Revolution. 2009. (Library of American Lives & Times Ser.). 112p. (gr. 5-5). 69.20 *(978-1-60853-487-6(1))* Rosen Publishing Group, Inc., The.

Borden, Louise W. The Journey That Saved Curious George: The True Wartime Escape of Margret & H. A. Rey. Drummond, Allan, illus. 2010. (Curious George Ser.). (ENG.). 80p. (J). (gr. 2-5). pap. 8.99 *(978-0-547-41746-2(2))* Houghton Mifflin Harcourt Publishing Co.

Bryan, Nichol. Jewish Americans, 1 vol. 2004. (One Nation Set 1 Ser.). (ENG.). 32p. (gr. k-6). 27.07 *(978-1-57765-986-0(4),* Checkerboard Library) ABDO Publishing Co.

Deutsch, Stacia & Cohon, Rhody. Hot Pursuit: Murder in Mississippi. Orback, Craig, illus. 2010. (ENG.). 40p. (J). (gr. 3-5). pap. 7.95 *(978-0-7613-3956-4(6));* lib. bdg. 17.95 *(978-0-7613-3955-7(8))* Lerner Publishing Group. (Kar-Ben Publishing).

Glaser, Linda. Emma's Poem: The Voice of the Statue of Liberty. Nivola, Claire A., illus. 2013. (ENG.). 32p. (J). (gr. -1-3). pap. 7.99 *(978-0-544-10508-9(7))* Houghton Mifflin Harcourt Publishing Co.

Laurel Corona. Jewish Americans. 2004. (Immigrants in America Ser.). (ENG., Illus.). 112p. (J). 30.85 *(978-1-59018-431-8(9))* Cengage Gale.

Lewin, Rhoda. Reform Jews of Minneapolis. 2004. (Images of America Ser.). (ENG., Illus.). 128p. pap. 21.99 *(978-0-7385-3217-2(7))* Arcadia Publishing.

Michelson, Richard. As Good As Anybody. Colón, Raúl, illus. 2013. (ENG.). 40p. (J). (gr. 1-4). 7.99 *(978-0-385-75387-6(X),* Dragonfly Bks.) Random Hse. Children's Bks.

Moreno, Barry. The Jewish Americans. (Major American Immigration Ser.). (YA). 2010. (Illus.). 64p. (gr. 9-12). 22.95 *(978-1-4222-0611-9(4))* 2007. pap. 9.95 *(978-1-4222-0678-2(5))* Mason Crest.

Palmer, Bill. Gallup Guides for Youth Facing Persistent Prejudice. 2012. (Gallup Guides for Youth Facing Persistent Prejudice Ser.). 64p. (J). (gr. 7-8). 22.95 *(978-1-4222-2466-3(X))* Mason Crest.

Rubinstein, Robert. Zishe the Strongman. Miller, Woody, illus. 2010. (Kar-Ben Favorites Ser.). (ENG.). 32p. (J). (gr. k-3). pap. 7.95 *(978-0-7613-3960-1(4),* Kar-Ben Publishing) Lerner Publishing Group.

Rubinstein, Robert E. Zishe the Strongman. Miller, Woody, illus. 2010. (Kar-Ben Favorites Ser.). (ENG.). 32p. (J). (gr. k-3). lib. bdg. 17.95 *(978-0-7613-3958-8(2),* Kar-Ben Publishing) Lerner Publishing Group.

Sohn, Ruth H. Crossing Cairo: A Jewish Woman's Encounter with Egypt. 2013. 272p. pap. 18.95 *(978-1-935604-50-1(3))* Gaon Bks.

Stein, Robert. Jewish Americans: Coming to America. 2006. (Illus.). 128p. (J). (gr. 4-8). reprint ed. 15.00 *(978-1-4223-5576-3(4))* DIANE Publishing Co.

Stone, Amy. Jewish Americans. 2006. (World Almanac Library of American Immigration). (Illus.). 48p. (gr. 5-12). pap. 14.05 *(978-0-8368-7327-6(0));* lib. bdg. 31.00 *(978-0-8368-7314-6(9))* Stevens, Gareth Publishing LLLP. (Gareth Stevens Secondary Library).

Taylor, Peter Lane. The Secret of Priest's Grotto: A Holocaust Survival Story. 2007. (Holocaust Ser.). (Illus.). 64p. (J). (gr. 3-7). lib. bdg. 18.95 *(978-1-58013-260-2(X),* Kar-Ben Publishing) Lerner Publishing Group.

Thornton, Jeremy. Religious Intolerance: Jewish Immigrants Come to America (1881-1914) (Primary Sources of Immigration & Migration in America Ser.). 24p. 2009. (gr. 3-4). 42.50 *(978-1-60851-783-1(7),* PowerKids Pr.) 2004. (Illus.). (J). lib. bdg. 22.60 *(978-0-8239-6834-3(0))* Rosen Publishing Group, Inc., The.

—Religious Intolerance: Jewish Immigrants Come to America, 1890-1924. 2004. (Primary Sources of Immigration & Migration in America Ser.). (ENG., Illus.). 24p. (J). (gr. 4-8). pap. 9.40 *(978-0-8239-8960-7(7))* Rosen Publishing Group, Inc., The.

Worth, Richard & Asher, Robert. Jewish Immigrants. 2004. (Immigration to the United States Ser.). (Illus.). 96p. (gr. 4-9). 35.00 *(978-0-8160-5684-2(6))* Facts On File, Inc.

J
K
L

JEWS—UNITED STATES—FICTION

Abdul-Jabbar, Kareem. Streetball Crew Book One Sasquatch in the Paint. 2015. (Streetball Crew Ser.). (ENG.). 288p. (J). (gr. 3-7). pap. 7.99 *(978-1-4231-9254-1(0))* Hyperion Bks. for Children.

Abdul-Jabbar, Kareem & Obstfeld, Raymond. Sasquatch in the Paint. 2013. (Streetball Crew Ser.). (ENG.). 272p. (J). (gr. 3-7). 16.99 *(978-1-4231-7870-5(X))* Hyperion Pr.

Adler, David A. Hanukkah Cookies with Sprinkles. Ebbeler, Jeffrey, illus. 2015. (J). *(978-0-87441-918-4(2))*; *(978-1-68115-500-5(1))* Behrman Hse., Inc.

—House on the Roof. Hirsh, Marilyn, illus. 2009. (ENG.). 32p. (J). (gr. -1-3). pap. 7.95 *(978-0-8234-2232-6(1))* Holiday Hse., Inc.

Adler, David A. Yom Kippur Shortstop. Ceolin, Andre, illus. 2017. (J). ***(978-1-68115-521-0(4))*** Behrman Hse., Inc.

Andrews, Jesse. Me & Earl & the Dying Girl. (ENG.). 304p. (YA). (gr. 9-17). 2012. 17.95 *(978-1-4197-0176-4(2)*, Amulet Bks.) 2015. 17.95 *(978-1-4197-2027-7(9))* 2015. 17.95 *(978-1-4197-2013-0(9)*, Amulet Bks.) 2015. pap. 9.95 *(978-1-4197-1960-8(2)*, Amulet Bks.) Abrams, Inc.

—Me & Earl & the Dying Girl. 2015. (CHI.). 320p. (YA). (gr. 9-17). pap. *(978-986-344-282-0(8))* Rye Field Publishing, Co.

—Me & Earl & the Dying Girl. 2015. lib. bdg. 20.80 *(978-0-606-37113-1(3))* Turtleback Bks.

Aronson, Sarah. Beyond Lucky. 2011. (ENG.). 256p. (J). (gr. 3-7). 16.99 *(978-0-8037-3520-0(0)*, Dial Bks) Penguin Young Readers Group.

Asher, Diana Harmon. Sidetracked. 2017. (ENG.). 240p. (J). (gr. 3-7). 16.99 ***(978-1-4197-2601-9(3)***, Amulet Bks.) Abrams, Inc.

Avrech, Robert J. The Hebrew Kid & the Apache Maiden. 2006. (Illus.). 220p. (J). (gr. 4-7). per. 11.95 *(978-0-9754382-2-0(0))* Seraphic Pr.

Axe-Bronk, Susan. The Vanishing Gourds: A Sukkot Mystery. Monelli, Marta, illus. 2012. (Sukkot & Simchat Torah Ser.). (ENG.). 24p. (J). (gr. -1-3). 7.95 *(978-0-7613-7504-3(X))*; lib. bdg. 17.95 *(978-0-7613-7503-6(1))* Lerner Publishing Group. (Kar-Ben Publishing).

Baer, Julie, illus. & text. I Only Like What I Like. Baer, Julie, text. 2003. 32p. (J). 15.99 *(978-1-932188-00-4(2))* Bollix Bks.

Barash, Chris. One Fine Shabbat. Mai-Wyss, Tatjana, illus. 2016. (ENG.). 12p. (gr. -1 — 1). (J). 5.99 *(978-1-4677-5871-0(X))*; 23.99 *(978-1-4677-9614-9(X))* Lerner Publishing Group. (Kar-Ben Publishing).

Barbara, Cohen. Molly's Pilgrim. 97th rev. ed. 2014. (ENG.). 32p. (J). (gr. 1-5). 8.24 *(978-1-63245-244-3(8))* Lectorum Pubns., Inc.

Barnhart, Aaron. Firebrand. 2015. (ENG., Illus.). 168p. (J). 19.95 *(978-0-9669258-6-9(6))* Quindaro Pr.

Baron, Jeff. Sean Rosen Is Not for Sale. (ENG.). 384p. (J). (gr. 3-7). 2015. pap. 6.99 *(978-0-06-218751-2(1))* 2014. 16.99 *(978-0-06-218750-5(3))* HarperCollins Pubs. (Greenwillow Bks.).

Baskin, Nora Raleigh. The Truth about My Bat Mitzvah. 2009. (Mix Ser.). (ENG.). 144p. (J). (gr. 4-8). pap. 7.99 *(978-1-4169-7469-7(5)*, Aladdin) Simon & Schuster Children's Publishing.

Benjamin, Ruth. The Lost Treasure of Chelton. 2004. viii, 170p. (J). 13.95 *(978-1-932443-02-8(9))* Judaica Pr., Inc., The.

—The Mysterious Lighthouse of Chelton. 2006. (ENG.). 160p. (J). 14.95 *(978-1-932443-57-8(6))* Judaica Pr., Inc., The.

Bick, Ilsa J. Draw the Dark. (Carolrhoda YA Ser.). (ENG.). 344p. (YA). (gr. 9-12). 2011. pap. 9.95 *(978-0-7613-8131-0(7))* 2010. 16.95 *(978-0-7613-5686-8(X))* Lerner Publishing Group. (Carolrhoda Lab™).

Blume, Judy. Starring Sally J. Freedman As Herself. 2014. (ENG., Illus.). (J). (gr. 3-7). 384p. 17.99 *(978-1-4814-1437-1(2))*; 400p. pap. 7.99 *(978-1-4814-1355-8(4))* Simon & Schuster Children's Publishing. (Atheneum Bks. for Young Readers).

Brandeis, Gayle. My Life with the Lincolns. 2010. (ENG.). 256p. (J). (gr. 5-9). 34.99 *(978-0-8050-9013-0(4)*, 9780805090130, Holt, Henry & Co. Bks. For Young Readers) Holt, Henry & Co.

Brown, Monica. Lola Levine & the Ballet Scheme. 2016. (Lola Levine Ser.: 3). (ENG., Illus.). 112p. (J). (gr. 1-5). 14.99 *(978-0-316-25844-9(X))* Little, Brown Bks. for Young Readers.

Burkhart, Kiersi, et al. The Long Trail Home. 2017. (Quartz Creek Ranch Ser.). (ENG.). 240p. (gr. 4-8). 6.99 *(978-1-5124-3090-5(0)*, Darby Creek) Lerner Publishing Group.

Chapman, Fern Schumer. Is It Night or Day? 2010. (ENG.). 224p. (J). (gr. 5-9). 17.99 *(978-0-374-17744-7(9)*, 9780374177447, Farrar, Straus & Giroux (BYR)) Farrar, Straus & Giroux.

Cohen, Barbara. Molly's Pilgrim. Duffy, Daniel Mark & Deraney, Michael J., illus. 97th rev. ed. 2005. (ENG.). 32p. (J). (gr. 2-5). pap. 3.99 *(978-0-688-16280-1(0))* HarperCollins Pubs.

—Molly's Pilgrim. (Literature to Go Ser.). pap., tchr. ed. incl. VHS *(978-0-7919-2685-7(0))* Phoenix Films & Video.

Crowder, Melanie. Audacity. 2016. (ENG.). 400p. (YA). (gr. 7). pap. 10.99 *(978-0-14-751249-9(2)*, Speak) Penguin Young Readers Group.

Crowder, Melanie & Mack, Jeff. Audacity. 2015. (ENG.). 400p. (YA). (gr. 7). bds. 17.99 *(978-0-399-16899-4(0)*, Philomel Bks.) Penguin Young Readers Group.

Da Costa, Deborah. Hanukkah Moon. Mosz, Gosia, illus. 2007. (Hanukkah Ser.). (ENG.). 32p. (J). (gr. 1-4). 10.95 *(978-1-58013-245-9(6)*, Kar-Ben Publishing) Lerner Publishing Group.

Dembar Greene, Jacqueline. Speak up, Tommy! Melmon, Deborah, illus. 2012. (Kar-Ben Favorites Ser.). (ENG.). 32p. (J). (gr. -1-3). 7.95 *(978-0-7613-7498-5(1)*, Kar-Ben Publishing) Lerner Publishing Group.

Edwards, Michelle. A Hat for Mrs. Goldman: A Story about Knitting & Love. Karas, G. Brian, illus. 2016. (ENG.). 40p. (J). (gr. -1-3). 17.99 *(978-0-553-49710-6(3)*, Schwartz & Wade Bks.) Random Hse. Children's Bks.

Elkeles, Simone. How to Ruin My Teenage Life. 2007. (How to Ruin a Summer Vacation Novel Ser.: 2). (ENG.). 288p. (YA). (gr. 7-12). per. 11.99 *(978-0-7387-1019-8(9)*, Flux) North Star Editions.

Faigen, Anne G. New World Waiting. 2006. iii, 188p. (J). pap. *(978-0-9744715-5-6(0))* Local History Co., The.

Fields, Terri. One Good Deed. Melmon, Deborah, illus. 2015. (ENG.). 24p. (J). (gr. -1-3). 6.99 *(978-1-4677-8841-0(4)*, Kar-Ben Publishing) Lerner Publishing Group.

Fireside, Bryna J. Private Joel & the Sewell Mountain Seder. Costello, Shawn, illus. 2008. (Passover Ser.). (J). (gr. 3-6). 47p. lib. bdg. 16.95 *(978-0-8225-7240-4(0))*; (ENG.). 48p. per. 6.95 *(978-0-8225-9050-7(6))* Lerner Publishing Group. (Kar-Ben Publishing).

Fischer, Debbie Reed. This Is Not the Abby Show. 2016. (ENG.). 320p. (J). (gr. 4-7). 16.99 *(978-0-553-53634-8(6)*, Delacorte Bks. for Young Readers) Random Hse. Children's Bks.

Fox, Tamar. No Baths at Camp. Vasquez, Natalia, illus. 2013. (ENG.). 32p. (J). (gr. -1-3). pap. 7.95 *(978-0-7613-8121-1(X))*; lib. bdg. 17.95 *(978-0-7613-8120-4(1))* Lerner Publishing Group. (Kar-Ben Publishing).

Frank, Steven B. Armstrong & Charlie. 2017. (ENG.). 304p. (J). (gr. 5-7). 16.99 *(978-0-544-82608-3(6)*, HMH Books For Young Readers) Houghton Mifflin Harcourt Publishing Co.

Freedman, Paula J. My Basmati Bat Mitzvah. 2015. (ENG., Illus.). 272p. (YA). (gr. 3-7). pap. 7.95 *(978-1-4197-1368-2(X)*, Amulet Bks.) Abrams, Inc.

Fuks, Menuhah & Tager, Gavriella. Smile with Avigayil #1: Avigayil & the Little Student. Haas, Esti, illus. 2006. 64p. (J). 12.95 *(978-1-932443-60-8(6))* Judaica Pr., Inc., The.

—Smile with Avigayil #2: Avigayil & the Black Cat. Haas, Esti, illus. 2006. (ENG.). 64p. (J). 12.95 *(978-1-932443-58-5(4))* Judaica Pr., Inc., The.

Gadot, A. S. The First Gift. Lafrance, Marie, illus. 2006. (ENG.). 24p. (J). (gr. -1-3). lib. bdg. 15.95 *(978-1-58013-146-9(8)*, Kar-Ben Publishing) Lerner Publishing Group.

Gagnon, Mary. Are Those Your Shoes? 2008. 120p. pap. 11.95 *(978-1-4357-2942-1(0))* Lulu Pr., Inc.

Gardner, Sheldon. The Converso Legacy. 2005. 264p. (J). 18.95 *(978-1-932687-18-7(1)*, Devora Publishing) Simcha Media Group.

Geras, Adèle. Voyage. 2006. (Illus.). 116p. (J). (gr. 4-7). per. 6.95 *(978-1-903015-00-1(6))* Barn Owl Bks, London GBR. Dist: Independent Pubs. Group.

Glaser, Linda. Hannah's Way. Gustavson, Adam, illus. 2012. (Shabbat Ser.). 32p. (J). (gr. k-3). lib. bdg. 17.95 *(978-0-7613-5137-5(X)*, Kar-Ben Publishing) Lerner Publishing Group.

Goldblatt, Mark. Finding the Worm. 2015. (ENG.). 352p. (J). (gr. 4-7). 16.99 *(978-0-385-39108-5(0)*, Random Hse. Bks. for Young Readers) Random Hse. Children's Bks.

—Finding the Worm (Twerp Sequel) 2016. (ENG.). 368p. (J). (gr. 4-7). 7.99 *(978-0-385-39111-5(0)*, Yearling) Random Hse. Children's Bks.

Goldin, Barbara Diamond. Night Lights: A Sukkot Story. Carmi, Giora, illus. 2004. (gr. k-3). 13.95 *(978-0-8074-0803-2(4)*, 142687) URJ Pr.

Goodman, Gabriel. Lightning's Run. 2014. (Bareknuckle Ser.). (ENG.). 104p. (YA). (gr. 6-12). pap. 7.95 *(978-1-4677-2162-2(X)*, Darby Creek) Lerner Publishing Group.

Greene, Bette. Summer of My German Soldier. 2006. (Puffin Modern Classics Ser.). (ENG.). 240p. (J). (gr. 5-18). 7.99 *(978-0-14-240651-9(1)*, Puffin Books) Penguin Young Readers Group.

Greene, Jacqueline. Secrets at Camp Nokomis: A Rebecca Mystery. Hirsch, Jennifer, ed. Tibbles, JeanPaul, illus. 2010. (ENG.). 192p. (J). (gr. 4-8). pap. 6.95 *(978-1-59369-657-3(4))* American Girl Publishing, Inc.

Greene, Jacqueline Dembar. Speak up, Tommy! Melmon, Deborah, illus. 2012. (Kar-Ben Favorites Ser.). (ENG.). 32p. (J). (gr. -1-3). lib. bdg. 17.95 *(978-0-7613-7497-8(3)*, Kar-Ben Publishing) Lerner Publishing Group.

Griffis, Molly Levite. Simon Says. 2004. vi, 263p. (J). 22.95 *(978-1-57168-836-1(6))*; pap. *(978-1-57168-847-7(1))* Eakin Pr. (Eakin Pr.).

Heller, Linda. The Castle on Hester Street. Kulikov, Boris, illus. 25th ed. 2007. (ENG.). 40p. (J). (gr. -1-3). 18.99 *(978-0-689-87434-5(0)*, Simon & Schuster Bks. For Young Readers) Simon & Schuster Bks. For Young Readers.

Herman, Michael. The Cholent Brigade. Harmer, Sharon, illus. 2017. (ENG.). 24p. (J). (gr. -1-2). 17.99 ***(978-1-5124-0844-7(1)***, Kar-Ben Publishing) Lerner Publishing Group.

Hesse, Karen. Brooklyn Bridge. Sheban, Chris, illus. 2011. (ENG.). 256p. (J). (gr. 5-9). pap. 9.99 *(978-0-312-67428-1(7)*, 9780312674281) Square Fish.

Hoberman, Mary Ann. Strawberry Hill. 2010. (ENG., Illus.). 240p. (J). (gr. 3-7). pap. 7.99 *(978-0-316-04135-5(1))* Little, Brown Bks. for Young Readers.

Houston, Julian. New Boy. 2008. (ENG.). 288p. (YA). (gr. 7-12). pap. 7.99 *(978-0-618-88405-6(X))* Houghton Mifflin Harcourt Publishing Co.

—New Boy. 2007. 282p. (gr. 7-12). 18.00 *(978-0-7569-8139-6(5))* Perfection Learning Corp.

Hubner, Carol Korb. The Devora Doresh Mysteries. 2006. (Illus.). 288p. (J). 16.95 *(978-1-932443-59-2(2))* Judaica Pr., Inc., The.

—The Devora Doresh Mysteries 2. 2007. (Illus.). 280p. (J). 16.95 *(978-1-932443-68-4(1))* Judaica Pr., Inc., The.

Hyde, Heidi Smith. Elan, Son of Two Peoples. Prevost, Mikela, illus. 2014. (Life Cycle Ser.). (ENG.). 32p. (J). (gr. k-3). 17.95 *(978-0-7613-9051-0(0)*, Kar-Ben Publishing) Lerner Publishing Group.

—Emanuel & the Hanukkah Rescue. Akib, Jamel, illus. 2012. (Hanukkah Ser.). (SPA & ENG.). 32p. (J). (gr. k-3). 7.95 *(978-0-7613-6627-0(X)*, Kar-Ben Publishing) Lerner Publishing Group.

—Emanuel & the Whale Oil Lamp. Akib, Jamel, illus. 2012. (Hanukkah Ser.). (ENG.). 32p. (J). (gr. -1-1). lib. bdg. 17.95 *(978-0-7613-6625-6(3)*, Kar-Ben Publishing) Lerner Publishing Group.

Izzy, Joel Ben. Dreidels on the Brain. 2016. (ENG.). 320p. (J). (gr. 5-9). 17.99 *(978-0-8037-4097-6(2)*, Dial Bks) Penguin Young Readers Group.

Jules, Jacqueline. Picnic at Camp Shalom. Melmon, Deborah, illus. 2011. (ENG.). 32p. (J). (gr. k-3). pap. 7.95 *(978-0-7613-6662-1(8)*, Kar-Ben Publishing) Lerner Publishing Group.

Karwoski, Gail Langer. When Hurricane Katrina Hit Home. Marshall, Julia, illus. 2013. Orig. Title: When Hurricane Katrina Hit Home. (ENG.). 192p. (gr. 4-7). 15.99 *(978-1-62619-083-2(6)*, History Pr., The) Arcadia Publishing.

Keyser, Amber J. & Burkhart, Kiersi. The Long Trail Home. 2017. (Quartz Creek Ranch Ser.). (ENG.). 240p. (gr. 4-8). lib. bdg. 27.99 *(978-1-4677-9256-1(X))*; 35.99 ***(978-1-5124-2698-4(9))*** Lerner Publishing Group. (Darby Creek).

Kimmelman, Leslie. Sam & Charlie (and Sam Too) at Camp! Owl, William, illus. 2015. (ENG.). 48p. (J). (gr. k-3). 13.99 *(978-0-8075-7217-7(9))* Whitman, Albert & Co.

Koffsky, Ann D. Judah Maccabee Goes to the Doctor. Shipman, Talitha, illus. 2017. (J). ***(978-1-68115-522-7(2))*** Behrman Hse., Inc.

Koffsky, Ann D. Noah's Swim-A-Thon. 2010. (J). *(978-0-8074-1168-1(X))* URJ Pr.

Konigsburg, E. L. About the B'nai Bagels. Konigsburg, E. L., illus. 2008. (ENG., Illus.). 208p. (J). (gr. 3-7). pap. 7.99 *(978-1-4169-5798-0(7)*, Atheneum Bks. for Young Readers) Simon & Schuster Children's Publishing.

Korngold, Jamie. Sadie & Ori & the Blue Blanket. Fortenberry, Julie, illus. 2015. (ENG.). 32p. (J). (gr. -1-2). 17.99 *(978-1-4677-1191-3(8)*, Kar-Ben Publishing) Lerner Publishing Group.

—Sadie & the Big Mountain. Fortenberry, Julie, illus. 2012. (Lag B'Omer & Shavuot Ser.). (ENG.). 32p. (J). (gr. -1-1). pap. 7.95 *(978-0-7613-6494-8(3))*; lib. bdg. 17.95 *(978-0-7613-6492-4(7))* Lerner Publishing Group. (Kar-Ben Publishing).

—Sadie, Ori, & Nuggles Go to Camp. Fortenberry, Julie, illus. 2014. (ENG.). 24p. (J). (gr. -1-1). 17.95 *(978-1-4677-0424-3(5)*, Kar-Ben Publishing) Lerner Publishing Group.

—Sadie's Lag Ba'Omer Mystery. Fortenberry, Julie, illus. 2014. (Lag Ba'Omer & Shavuot Ser.). (ENG.). 32p. (J). (gr. -1-3). 7.95 *(978-0-7613-9048-0(0))*; 17.95 *(978-0-7613-9047-3(2))* Lerner Publishing Group. (Kar-Ben Publishing).

Kushner, Elisabeth. The Purim Superhero. Byrne, Mike, illus. 2013. (Purim Ser.). (ENG.). 32p. (J). (gr. -1-3). 7.95 *(978-0-7613-9062-6(6))*; lib. bdg. 17.95 *(978-0-7613-9061-9(8))* Lerner Publishing Group. (Kar-Ben Publishing).

Lakritz, Deborah. Joey & the Giant Box. Byrne, Mike, illus. 2015. (J). (ENG.). 32p. (gr. -1-2). lib. bdg. 17.95 *(978-1-4677-1953-7(6))*; 6.99 *(978-1-4677-6205-2(9))* Lerner Publishing Group. (Kar-Ben Publishing).

Levinson, Robin K. Shoshana & the Native Rose. Kehl, Drusilla, illus. 2006. 103p. (J). (gr. 3-5). per. 12.00 *(978-0-9773673-2-0(0))* Gali Girls, Inc.

Levy, Joanne. Small Medium at Large. 2012. (ENG.). 208p. (YA). (gr. 3-12). 15.99 *(978-1-59990-836-6(0)*, 9781599908366, Bloomsbury USA Childrens) Bloomsbury Publishing USA.

Lieurance, Suzanne. The Locket: Surviving the Triangle Shirtwaist Fire. 2008. (Historical Fiction Adventures (HFA) Ser.). (Illus.). 160p. (J). (gr. 3-7). lib. bdg. 29.27 *(978-0-7660-2928-6(X))* Enslow Pubs., Inc.

Littlefield, Holly. The Rooftop Adventure of Minnie & Tessa, Factory Fire Survivors. Trover, Zachary et al, illus. 2011. (History's Kid Heroes Ser.). (ENG.). 32p. (gr. 3-5). 26.60 *(978-0-7613-6179-4(0))* Lerner Publishing Group.

Littman, Sarah Darer. Confessions of a Closet Catholic. 2006. (ENG.). 208p. (J). (gr. 5-18). reprint ed. 7.99 *(978-0-14-240597-0(3)*, Puffin Books) Penguin Young Readers Group.

—Life, After. 2010. (ENG.). 288p. (J). (gr. 7-18). 17.99 *(978-0-545-15144-3(9)*, Scholastic Pr.) Scholastic, Inc.

Manushkin, Fran. Sophie & the Shofar. Kaye, Rosalind Charney, illus. 2004. (J). (gr. k-3). 13.95 *(978-0-8074-0751-6(8)*, 101078) URJ Pr.

Matas, Carol. Rosie in Los Angeles: Action! 2004. (HEB & ENG., Illus.). 128p. (J). (gr. 4-7). pap. 9.95 *(978-0-689-85716-4(0)*, Simon & Schuster/Paula Wiseman Bks.) Simon & Schuster/Paula Wiseman Bks.

Mayer, Pamela. Chicken Soup, Chicken Soup. Melmon, Deborah, illus. 2016. (ENG.). 32p. (J). (gr. -1-3). 17.99 *(978-1-4677-8934-9(8)*, Kar-Ben Publishing) Lerner Publishing Group.

—Don't Sneeze at the Wedding. Avilés, Martha, illus. 2013. 32p. 17.95 *(978-1-4677-1641-3(3))* Lerner Publishing Group.

Mazer, Norma Fox. Good Night, Maman. 2006. 185p. (J). (gr. k-4). reprint ed. 16.00 *(978-1-4223-5862-7(3))* DIANE Publishing Co.

—Good Night, Maman. 2010. (ENG., Illus.). 192p. (J). (gr. 5-7). pap. 12.95 *(978-0-15-206173-9(8))* Houghton Mifflin Harcourt Publishing Co.

McDonough, Yona Zeldis. The Cats in the Doll Shop. Maione, Heather, illus. 2012. (ENG.). 160p. (J). (gr. 3-7). pap. 5.99 *(978-0-14-242198-7(7)*, Puffin Books) Penguin Young Readers Group.

—The Doll Shop Downstairs. Maione, Heather, illus. 2011. (ENG.). 128p. (J). (gr. 2-5). 5.99 *(978-0-14-241691-4(6)*, Puffin Books) Penguin Young Readers Group.

Mermelstein, Yael. A Car That Goes Far. Rosenfeld, Dina, ed. Romanenko, Vitaliy & Romanenko, Vasilisa, illus. 2009. 30p. (J). (gr. 1-3). 12.95 *(978-1-929628-47-6(1))* Hachai Publishing.

Meyer, Susan Lynn. Skating with the Statue of Liberty. 2016. (ENG.). 320p. (J). (gr. 3-7). 19.99 *(978-0-375-99010-6(0)*, Delacorte Bks. for Young Readers) Random Hse. Children's Bks.

Moriarty, Chris. The Inquisitor's Apprentice. Geyer, Mark Edward, illus. 2013. (ENG.). 352p. (J). (gr. 5-7). pap. 7.99 *(978-0-547-85084-9(0))* Houghton Mifflin Harcourt Publishing Co.

—The Watcher in the Shadows. Geyer, Mark Edward, illus. 2013. (ENG.). 336p. (J). (gr. 5-7). 16.99 *(978-0-547-46632-3(3))* Houghton Mifflin Harcourt Publishing Co.

Napoli, Donna Jo. The King of Mulberry Street. 2007. 245p. (gr. 3-7). 17.00 *(978-0-7569-7945-4(5))* Perfection Learning Corp.

—The King of Mulberry Street. 2007. (ENG.). 256p. (J). (gr. 3-7). 6.99 *(978-0-553-49416-7(3)*, Yearling) Random Hse. Children's Bks.

Newman, Lesléa. My Name Is Aviva. Jatkowska, Ag, illus. 2015. (ENG.). 32p. (J). (gr. -1-2). pap. 7.99 *(978-1-4677-2656-6(7))*; lib. bdg. 17.99 *(978-1-4677-2654-2(0))* Lerner Publishing Group. (Kar-Ben Publishing).

Newman, Tracy. Shabbat Hiccups. Exelby, Ilana, illus. 2016. (ENG.). 32p. (J). (gr. -1-3). 16.99 *(978-0-8075-7312-9(4))* Whitman, Albert & Co.

—Uncle Eli's Wedding. Isik, Semur, illus. 2015. (ENG.). 32p. (J). (gr. -1-3). 16.99 *(978-0-8075-8293-0(X))* Whitman, Albert & Co.

Newman, Vivian. Tikkun Olam Ted. Mack, Steve, illus. 2013. (Life Cycle Ser.). (ENG.). 12p. (J). (gr. -1 — 1). pap. 5.95 *(978-0-7613-9040-4(5)*, Kar-Ben Publishing) Lerner Publishing Group.

O'Connell, Rebecca. Penina Levine Is a Hard-boiled Egg. Lue Sue, Majella, illus. 2009. (ENG.). 192p. (J). (gr. 3-7). pap. 18.99 *(978-0-312-55026-4(X)*, 9780312550264) Square Fish.

Ofanansky, Allison. The Patchwork Torah. Oriol, Elsa, illus. 2014. (Sukkot & Simchat Torah Ser.). (ENG.). 32p. (J). (gr. -1-5). 7.95 *(978-1-4677-0427-4(X))*; 17.95 *(978-1-4677-0426-7(1))* Lerner Publishing Group. (Kar-Ben Publishing).

Old Ways, New Ways (Eastern European Jews) 76p. (YA). (gr. 6-12). pap. 9.95 *(978-0-8224-3682-9(5))* Globe Fearon Educational Publishing.

Olswanger, Anna. Greenhorn. Nerlove, Miriam, illus. 2012. (ENG.). (J). E-Book 9.99 *(978-1-60306-159-9(2))*; 48p. 17.95 *(978-1-58838-235-1(4))* NewSouth, Inc. (NewSouth Bks.).

—Shlemiel Crooks. Goodman Koz, Paula, illus. 2008. 36p. (J). pap. 11.95 *(978-1-58838-236-8(2)*, Junebug Bks.) NewSouth, Inc.

Ostrove, Karen. Rise & Shine: A Challah-Day Tale. Scott, Kimberley, illus. 2013. (Shabbat Ser.). (ENG.). 24p. (J). (gr. -1-3). 7.95 *(978-0-7613-7500-5(7))*; lib. bdg. 17.95 *(978-0-7613-7499-2(X))* Lerner Publishing Group. (Kar-Ben Publishing).

Palmer, Robin. Little Miss Red. 2010. (ENG.). 320p. (YA). (gr. 7-18). 9.99 *(978-0-14-241123-0(X)*, Speak) Penguin Young Readers Group.

Peet, Amanda & Troyer, Andrea. Dear Santa, Love, Rachel Rosenstein. Davenier, Christine, illus. 2015. (ENG.). 40p. (J). (gr. -1-2). 17.99 *(978-0-553-51061-4(4))*; 20.99 *(978-0-553-51062-1(2))* Random Hse. Children's Bks. (Doubleday Bks. for Young Readers).

Pellicioli, Anna. Where You End. 2015. (ENG.). 312p. (YA). pap. 9.99 *(978-0-7387-4403-2(4)*, Flux) North Star Editions.

Perl, Erica S. Aces Wild. (ENG.). 224p. (J). (gr. 3-7). 2015. 7.99 *(978-0-307-93173-3(0)*, Yearling) 2013. 15.99 *(978-0-307-93172-6(2)*, Knopf Bks. for Young Readers) Random Hse. Children's Bks.

—When Life Gives You O. J. 2011. (ENG.). 224p. (J). (gr. 3-7). 15.99 *(978-0-375-85924-3(1)*, Knopf Bks. for Young Readers) Random Hse. Children's Bks.

Perlov, Betty Rosenberg. Rifka Takes a Bow. Kawa, Cosei, illus. 2013. (ENG.). 32p. (J). (gr. k-3). 7.95 *(978-0-7613-8128-0(7))*; 17.95 *(978-0-7613-8127-3(9))* Lerner Publishing Group. (Kar-Ben Publishing).

Pinkham, Mark Amaru. Love Me Later. 2005. 202p. 14.95 *(978-1-932188-02-8(9))* Adventures Unlimited Pr.

Pixley, Marcella. Without Tess. 2014. (ENG.). 304p. (YA). (gr. 7-12). pap. 9.99 *(978-1-250-04435-8(9)*, 9781250044358) Square Fish.

Powell, Maud Macrory. City of Grit & Gold. 2017. (ENG.). 164p. (J). (gr. 4-6). pap. 16.99 ***(978-0-9967558-5-6(3))*** Allium Pr. of Chicago.

Pushker, Gloria Teles. Toby Belfer Visits Ellis Island, 1 vol. Hierstein, Judith, illus. 2003. (Toby Belfer Ser.). (ENG.). 32p. (J). (gr. k-3). 16.99 *(978-1-58980-117-2(2))* Pelican Publishing Co., Inc.

Reinhardt, Dana. A Brief Chapter in My Impossible Life. 2007. (ENG.). 256p. (YA). (gr. 9-12). pap. 8.99 *(978-0-375-84691-5(3)*, Ember) Random Hse. Children's Bks.

Reiss, Kathryn. A Bundle of Trouble: A Rebecca Mystery. Giovine, Sergio, illus. 2011. (ENG.). 192p. (YA). (gr. 4-18). pap. 6.95 *(978-1-59369-754-9(6))* American Girl Publishing, Inc.

Robinson, Sharon. The Hero Two Doors Down: A Story of Friendship Between a Boy & a Baseball Legend. 2017. (ENG.). 208p. (J). (gr. 3-7). pap. 6.99 ***(978-0-545-80452-3(3)***, Scholastic Paperbacks) Scholastic, Inc.

Rosen, Michael J. Chanukah Lights. Sabuda, Robert, illus. 2011. (ENG.). 16p. (J). (gr. k-4). 34.99 *(978-0-7636-5533-4(3))* Candlewick Pr.

—Chanukah Lights Everywhere. Iwai, Melissa, illus. 2006. (ENG.). 32p. (J). (gr. -1-3). pap. 7.99 *(978-0-15-205675-9(0))* Houghton Mifflin Harcourt Publishing Co.

Rosenberg, Madelyn & Shang, Wendy Wan-Long. This Is Just a Test: A Novel. 2017. (ENG.). 256p. (J). (gr. 3-7). 17.99 ***(978-1-338-03772-2(2)***, Scholastic Pr.) Scholastic, Inc.

Rosenthal, Betsy R. It's Not Worth Making a Tzimmes Over! Rivers, Ruth, illus. 2006. 32p. (J). (gr. k-3). lib. bdg. 16.99 *(978-0-8075-3677-3(6))* Whitman, Albert & Co.

—Looking for Me: In This Great Big Family. 2013. (ENG., Illus.). 176p. (J). (gr. 5-7). pap. 6.99 *(978-0-544-02271-3(8))* Houghton Mifflin Harcourt Publishing Co.

Rosenthal, Sally. Matzo Frogs. Sheldon, David, illus. 2014. (ENG.). 32p. (J). 17.95 *(978-1-58838-302-0(4)*, NewSouth Bks.) NewSouth, Inc.

Rothenberg, Joan. Matzah Ball Soup. Rothenberg, Joan, illus. 2005. (Illus.). 29p. (J). (gr. -1-2). reprint ed. 15.00 *(978-0-7567-8930-5(3))* DIANE Publishing Co.

Rouss, Sylvia. Holiday for Ari Ant. 2016. (Illus.). 24p. (J). pap. *(978-965-229-664-1(3))* Gefen Bks.

—Sammy Spider's First Mitzvah. Janus Kahn, Katherine, illus. 2014. (ENG.). 24p. (J). (gr. -1-3). 17.95 *(978-1-4677-1947-6(1)*, Kar-Ben Publishing) Lerner Publishing Group.

Rouss, Sylvia A. A Holiday for Ari Ant. Kahn, Katherine, illus. 2016. (J). *(978-1-68115-507-4(9))* Behrman Hse., Inc.

—Sammy Spider's First Sukkot. Kahn, Katherine Janus, illus. 2004. (ENG.). 32p. (J). (gr. -1-3). 17.95 *(978-1-58013-142-1(5))*; pap. 7.95 *(978-1-58013-083-7(6))* Lerner Publishing Group. (Kar-Ben Publishing).

—Sammy Spider's New Friend. Kahn, Katherine, illus. 2012. (Kar-Ben Favorites Ser.). (ENG.). 32p. (J). (gr. -1-2). lib. bdg.

17.95 *(978-0-7613-6663-8(6),* Kar-Ben Publishing) Lerner Publishing Group.

Rouss, Sylvia A. & Janus Kahn, Katherine. Sammy Spider's New Friend. 2012. (Kar-Ben Favorites Ser.). (ENG., Illus.). 32p. (J). (gr. -1-3). 7.95 *(978-0-7613-6664-5(4),* Kar-Ben Publishing) Lerner Publishing Group.

Schnur, Susan. Tashlich at Turtle Rock. Schnur-Fishman, Anna & Steele-Morgan, Alexandra, illus. 2010. (High Holidays Ser.). 32p. (J). (gr. k-4). lib. bdg. 17.95 *(978-0-7613-4509-1(4),* Kar-Ben Publishing) Lerner Publishing Group.

Schnur, Susan & Schnur-Fishman, Anna. Tashlich at Turtle Rock. Steele-Morgan, Alex, illus. 2010. (High Holidays Ser.). (ENG.). 32p. (J). (gr. k-3). pap. 7.95 *(978-0-7613-4510-7(8),* Kar-Ben Publishing) Lerner Publishing Group.

Sharenow, Robert. The Girl in the Torch. 2015. (ENG.). 304p. (J). (gr. 3-7). 16.99 *(978-0-06-222795-9(5))* HarperCollins Pubs.

Silverman, Erica. The Hanukkah Hop! D'Amico, Steven, illus. 2011. (ENG.). 32p. (J). (gr. -1-3). 12.99 *(978-1-4424-0604-9(6),* Simon & Schuster Bks. For Young Readers) Simon & Schuster Bks. For Young Readers.

Simhaee, Rebeka. Sara Finds A Mitzva. Leverton, Yossi, ed. 2010. (Illus.). 28p. (J). 10.95 *(978-1-929628-46-9(3))* Hachai Publishing.

Singer, Isaac Bashevis. The Parakeet Named Dreidel. Berkson, Suzanne Raphael, illus. 2015. (J). pap. *(978-0-374-30096-8(8));* (ENG.). 32p. 17.99 *(978-0-374-30094-4(1),* 9780374300944, Farrar, Straus & Giroux (BYR)) Farrar, Straus & Giroux.

Snyder, Laurel. Baxter, the Pig Who Wanted to Be Kosher. Goldin, David, illus. 2010. (ENG.). 32p. (J). (gr. -1-2). 15.99 *(978-1-58246-315-5(8),* Tricycle Pr.) Random Hse. Children's Bks.

—Baxter, the Pig Who Wanted to Be Kosher. 2010. (J). pap. 2.46 *(978-1-58246-373-5(5),* Tricycle Pr.) Ten Speed Pr.

Steinberg, Jessica. Not This Turkey! Pike, Amanda, illus. 2016. (ENG.). 32p. (J). (gr. -1-3). 16.99 *(978-0-8075-7908-4(4))* Whitman, Albert & Co.

Steinberg, Laya. The Best Sukkot Pumpkin Ever. Madden, Colleen M., illus. 2017. (ENG.). 32p. (gr. -1-3). 17.99 ***(978-1-5124-0863-8(8),*** Kar-Ben Publishing) Lerner Publishing Group.

Sugarman, Brynn Olenberg. Rebecca's Journey Home. Shapiro, Michelle, illus. 2014. (Life Cycle Ser.). (ENG.). 32p. (J). (gr. k-4). 8.95 *(978-1-4677-4937-4(0),* Kar-Ben Publishing) Lerner Publishing Group.

Thompson, Holly. Orchards. 2012. (ENG.). 336p. (YA). (gr. 7). pap. 9.99 *(978-0-385-73978-8(8),* Ember) Random Hse. Children's Bks.

Vander Zee, Ruth & Sneider, Marian. Eli Remembers. Farnsworth, Bill, illus. 2007. (ENG.). 32p. (J). (gr. -1-3). 18.00 *(978-0-8028-5309-7(9),* Eerdmans Bks For Young Readers) Eerdmans, William B. Publishing Co.

Vernick, Shirley Reva. The Blood Lie. 2011. (ENG.). 144p. (J). (gr. 7). 15.95 *(978-1-933693-84-2(3))* Cinco Puntos Pr.

Weber, Judith Eichler. Seeking Safety. Martin, John F., illus. 2006. (Adventures in America Ser.). (J). *(978-1-893110-46-5(X))* Silver Moon Pr.

Werlin, Nancy. Extraordinary. 2011. (ENG.). 416p. (YA). (gr. 7-18). 9.99 *(978-0-14-241974-8(5),* Speak) Penguin Young Readers Group.

JIUJITSU

see Judo

JOAN, OF ARC, SAINT, 1412-1431

Boutet de Monvel, Maurice. The Story of Joan of Arc. 2010. (Dover Children's Classics Ser.). (ENG., Illus.). 64p. (J). (gr. 4-7). pap. 14.99 *(978-0-486-47026-9(1))* Dover Pubns., Inc.

Demi. Joan of Arc, 0 vols. 2011. (ENG.). 56p. (J). (gr. 3-7). 19.99 *(978-0-7614-5953-8(7),* 9780761459538, Amazon Children's Publishing) Amazon Publishing.

Hilliam, David. Joan of Arc: Heroine of France. 2004. (Leaders of the Middle Ages Ser.). (Illus.). 112p. (J). lib. bdg. 34.60 *(978-1-4042-0164-4(5))* Rosen Publishing Group, Inc., The.

Joan of Arc. 2010. (Women of Achievement Ser.). (Illus.). 128p. (gr. 6-12). 35.00 *(978-1-60413-710-1(X),* Chelsea Hse.) Facts On File, Inc.

Kudlinski, Kathleen. Joan of Arc. 2008. (DK Biography Ser.). (ENG., Illus.). 128p. (J). (gr. 5-12). pap. 6.99 *(978-0-7566-3526-8(8),* DK Children) Dorling Kindersley Publishing, Inc.

Lace, William W. Joan of Arc & the Hundred Years' War in World History. 2003. (In World History Ser.). (Illus.). 128p. (J). (gr. 5-12). lib. bdg. 27.94 *(978-0-7660-1938-6(1))* Enslow Pubs., Inc.

Macdonald, Fiona. You Wouldn't Want to Be Joan of Arc! A Mission You Might Want to Miss. Antram, David, illus. 2010. (You Wouldn't Want to Ser.). (ENG.). 32p. (J). 29.00 *(978-0-531-20473-3(1));* (gr. 3-18). pap. 9.95 *(978-0-531-22828-9(2))* Scholastic Library Publishing.

Pollack, Pam & Belviso, Meg. Who Was Joan of Arc? Thomson, Andrew, illus. 2016. 105p. (J). ***(978-1-4844-7648-2(4),*** Grosset & Dunlap) Penguin Publishing Group.

Pollack, Pamela D. & Belviso, Meg. Who Was Joan of Arc? Thomson, Andrew & Harrison, Nancy, illus. 2016. (Who Was? Ser.). (ENG.). 112p. (J). (gr. 3-7). pap. 5.99 *(978-0-448-48304-7(1),* Grosset & Dunlap) Penguin Young Readers Group.

—Who Was Joan of Arc? 2016. (Who Was...? Ser.). lib. bdg. 16.00 *(978-0-606-38395-0(6))* Turtleback Bks.

Ross, Nancy Wilson. Joan of Arc. 2003. vii, 182p. pap. 29.00 *(978-0-7581-5017-2(2))* Textbook Pubs.

Thiel, Kristin. Joan of Arc. 2017. (J). ***(978-1-5026-2791-9(4))*** Cavendish Square Publishing.

Thompson, Paul B. Joan of Arc: Warrior Saint of France. 2007. (Rulers of the Middle Ages Ser.). (Illus.). 160p. (YA). (gr. 6-12). lib. bdg. 35.94 *(978-0-7660-2716-9(3))* Enslow Pubs., Inc.

Whiting, Jim. The Life & Times of Joan of Arc. 2005. (Biography from Ancient Civilizations Ser.). (Illus.). 48p. (J). (gr. 4-8). lib. bdg. 29.95 *(978-1-58415-345-0(8))* Mitchell Lane Pubs., Inc.

Wilkinson, Philip. Joan of Arc: The Teenager Who Saved Her Nation. (National Geographic World History Biographies Ser.). (ENG., Illus.). 64p. (J). (gr. 3-7). 2009. pap. 7.99 *(978-1-4263-0415-6(3))* 2007. 17.95 *(978-1-4263-0116-2(2))* 2007. lib. bdg. 27.90 *(978-1-4263-0117-9(0))* National Geographic Society. (National Geographic Children's Bks.).

Wolny, Philip. Joan of Arc: French Soldier & Saint. 2017. (Women Who Changed History Ser.). 48p. (gr. 10-12). pap. 14.05 ***(978-1-68048-645-2(4),*** Britannica Educational Publishing) Rosen Publishing Group, Inc., The.

JOAN, OF ARC, SAINT, 1412-1431—FICTION

Chandler, Pauline. Warrior Girl: A Novel of Joan of Arc. 2006. 354p. (J). (gr. 5-9). 17.89 *(978-0-06-084103-4(6))* HarperCollins Pubs.

Everett-Green, Evelyn. A Heroine of France. 2006. (ENG.). 188p. pap. 19.99 *(978-1-4264-7060-8(6))* 2007. 206p. pap. 22.99 *(978-1-4264-7136-0(X))* Creative Media Partners, LLC.

Johnson, Vargie. Joan of Arc the Messenger: What Made Them Famous? 2006. 156p. (J). per. 15.00 *(978-1-931195-95-9(1))* KiwE Publishing, Ltd.

Lee, Tony. Messenger: the Legend of Joan of Arc. Hart, Sam, illus. 2015. (ENG.). 112p. (J). (gr. 5). 21.99 *(978-0-7636-7613-1(6))* Candlewick Pr.

JOB DISCRIMINATION

see Discrimination in Employment

JOB HUNTING

Byers, Ann. Great Resume, Application, & Interview Skills. (Work Readiness Ser.). 64p. 2009. (gr. 6-6). 58.50 *(978-1-60854-827-9(9))* 2008. (Illus.). (J). lib. bdg. 31.95 *(978-1-4042-1425-5(9))* Rosen Publishing Group, Inc., The.

Coon, Nora. Teen Dream Jobs: How to Find the Job You Really Want Now! 2004. (Illus.). 132p. (YA). (gr. 8-12). per. 9.95 *(978-1-58270-093-9(1))* Beyond Words Publishing, Inc.

Donovan, Sandra. Job Smarts: How to Find Work or Start a Business, Manage Earnings, & More. 2012. (USA TODAY Teen Wise Guides: Time, Money, & Relationships Ser.). (ENG., Illus.). 64p. (gr. 8-12). lib. bdg. 31.93 *(978-0-7613-7015-4(3))* Lerner Publishing Group.

Essential Careers: Set 3. 2013. (Essential Careers Ser.). 80p. (YA). (gr. 7-12). 199.50 *(978-1-4488-9485-7(9))* Rosen Publishing Group, Inc., The.

Essential Careers: Set 4. 2013. (Essential Careers Ser.). 80p. (YA). (gr. 7-12). 166.25 *(978-1-4777-1800-1(1))* Rosen Publishing Group, Inc., The.

Essential Careers: Sets 1 - 3. 2013. (Essential Careers Ser.). 80p. (YA). (gr. 7-12). 731.50 *(978-1-4777-0615-2(1))* Rosen Publishing Group, Inc., The.

Farr, Michael. Job Search Basics, Third Edition. 3rd ed. 2006. (ENG., Illus.). 256p. (YA). pap., wbk. ed. 21.95 *(978-1-59357-313-3(8),* J3138, JIST Works) JIST Publishing.

Fischer, James. Earning Money: Jobs. 2010. (Junior Library of Money). 64p. (YA). (gr. 7-18). lib. bdg. 22.95 *(978-1-4222-1763-4(9))* Mason Crest.

Gagne, Tammy. Teen Guide to Earning Income. 2014. (ENG., Illus.). 48p. (gr. 4-6). lib. bdg. 29.95 *(978-1-61228-470-5(1))* Mitchell Lane Pubs., Inc.

Hagler, Gina. Money-Making Opportunities for Teens Who Are Artistic. 2013. (Make Money Now! Ser.). (Illus.). 80p. (YA). (gr. 7-12). lib. bdg. 33.25 *(978-1-4488-9387-4(9))* Rosen Publishing Group, Inc., The.

Henneberg, Susan. Step-By-Step Guide to Effective Job Hunting & Career Preparedness. 2014. (Winning at Work Readiness Ser.). 64p. (YA). (gr. 9-12). 32.95 *(978-1-4777-7774-9(1))* Rosen Publishing Group, Inc., The.

Jacobson, Ryan. Get a Job at a Business. Cannell, Jon, illus. 2014. (You're in Business! Ser.). (ENG.). 40p. (gr. 5-9). lib. bdg. 27.93 *(978-1-4677-3838-5(7),* Lerner Pubns.) Lerner Publishing Group.

—Get a Summer Adventure Job. Cannell, Jon, illus. 2014. (You're in Business! Ser.). (ENG.). 40p. (gr. 5-9). lib. bdg. 27.93 *(978-1-4677-3839-2(5),* Lerner Pubns.) Lerner Publishing Group.

Marsh, Carole. Would You Hire This Person? A Look at Getting Hired (or Not!)... from the Point of View of Your (Possible!) Future Employer. 2012. (Carole Marsh's Careers Curriculum Ser.). (ENG., Illus.). 82p. (J). pap. 19.99 *(978-0-635-10553-0(5))* Gallopade International.

Mccormick, Anita Louise. How to Create Digital Portfolios to Showcase Your Achievements & Interests. 2017. (Project Learning Using Digital Portfolios Ser.). 64p. (J). (gr. 12-12). 34.45 ***(978-1-5081-7534-6(9),*** Rosen Young Adult) Rosen Publishing Group, Inc., The.

Orr, Tamra B. Money-Making Opportunities for Teens Who Like Working Outside. 2013. (Make Money Now! Ser.). (Illus.). 80p. (YA). (gr. 7-12). lib. bdg. 33.25 *(978-1-4488-9383-6(6))* Rosen Publishing Group, Inc., The.

Project Learning Using Digital Portfolios. 2017. (Project Learning Using Digital Portfolios Ser.). 64p. (gr. 12-12). 206.70 ***(978-1-4994-6635-5(8),*** Rosen Young Adult) Rosen Publishing Group, Inc., The.

Timmons-Hanselka, Angela. How to Create Digital Portfolios to Show What You Know. 2017. (Project Learning Using Digital Portfolios Ser.). 64p. (J). (gr. 12-12). 34.45 ***(978-1-5081-7532-2(2),*** Rosen Young Adult) Rosen Publishing Group, Inc., The.

Troutman, Kathryn K. Creating Your High School Resume, Second Edition: A Step-by-Step Guide to Preparing an Effective Resume for Jobs, College & Training Programs. 2nd ed. 2003. (Illus.). 160p. pap. 10.95 *(978-1-56370-902-9(3),* JIST Works) JIST Publishing.

Wilkes, Donald & Hamilton-Wilkes, Viola. Teen Guide Job Search: 10 Easy Steps to Your Future. 2006. (ENG., Illus.). 122p. (YA). (gr. 10-12). per. 12.95 *(978-0-595-39696-2(8))* iUniverse, Inc.

The World of Work. 2005. (Illus.). (gr. 7-12). lib. bdg. 682.20 *(978-0-8239-3909-1(X))* Rosen Publishing Group, Inc., The.

World of Work: Choose the Right Career for You!, 7 bks. Incl. Choosing a Career in Child Care. Weintraub, Aileen. 2005. lib. bdg. 31.95 *(978-0-8239-3241-2(9),* WWCHCA); Choosing a Career in Computers. Weigant, Chris. 2005. lib. bdg. 31.95 *(978-0-8239-3044-9(0),* WWCOMP); Choosing a Career in Hotels, Motels & Resorts. Rue, Nancy N. 1999. lib. bdg. 27.95 *(978-0-8239-2999-3(X),* WWHOMO); Choosing a Career in Law Enforcement. Wirths, Claudine G. 2005. lib. bdg. 31.95 *(978-0-8239-3282-5(6),* WWLAEN); Choosing a Career in the Restaurant Industry. Beal, Eileen J. 1999. lib. bdg. 31.95 *(978-0-8239-3002-9(5),* WWREST); 64p. (YA). (gr. 7-12). (Illus.). Set lib. bdg. 167.65 *(978-0-8239-9306-2(X))* Rosen Publishing Group, Inc., The.

World of Work: Exciting World of Careers, 7 bks. Incl. Choosing a Career in Carpentry. Ross, Allison J. & Harrison, Scott. lib. bdg. 31.95 *(978-0-8239-3294-8(X));* Choosing a Career in the Pulp & Paper Industry. Draper, Allison Stark. lib. bdg. 31.95 *(978-0-8239-3333-4(4));* 64p. (YA). (gr. 7-12). 2005. (Illus.). Set lib. bdg. 167.65 *(978-0-8239-9208-9(X))* Rosen Publishing Group, Inc., The.

The World of Work Set 1. 2005. (Illus.). (gr. 7-12). lib. bdg. 176.75 *(978-0-8239-9727-5(8))* Rosen Publishing Group, Inc., The.

The World of Work Set 2. 2005. (Illus.). (gr. 7-12). lib. bdg. 202.00 *(978-0-8239-9444-1(9))* Rosen Publishing Group, Inc., The.

The World of Work Set 3. 2005. (Illus.). (gr. 7-12). lib. bdg. 202.00 *(978-0-8239-9443-4(0))* Rosen Publishing Group, Inc., The.

The World of Work Set 4. 2005. (Illus.). (gr. 7-12). lib. bdg. 202.00 *(978-0-8239-9442-7(2))* Rosen Publishing Group, Inc., The.

The World of Work Set 5. 2005. (Illus.). (gr. 7-12). lib. bdg. 126.25 *(978-0-8239-9716-9(2))* Rosen Publishing Group, Inc., The.

JOB HUNTING—FICTION

Brundin, Anders & Dranger, Joanna Rubin. Dudley the Daydreamer. Perry, Frank, tr. from SWE. 2008. (ENG., Illus.). 32p. (J). (gr. k-2). pap. 12.95 *(978-1-905341-10-8(5))* WingedChariot Pr. GBR. Dist: Independent Pubs. Group.

Buyer, Robert L. & Coute, Ursula T. Following the North Star. 2013. 52p. pap. 23.95 *(978-1-4624-0611-1(4),* Inspiring Voices) Author Solutions, Inc.

Durham, Kathryn. Mom, Can You Buy Me This? Richard Gets a Job 2004. 115p. (YA). spiral bd. 11.95 *(978-0-9703876-2-2(8))* Pen & Paper Publishing.

Elga Learns to Juggle. 2006. (J). 6.99 *(978-0-9770918-0-5(5))* Forelle Graphics.

A Job for Little Elf. 2006. (Little Elf Set 1 Ser.). (ENG., Illus.). (J). pap. 7.33 *(978-1-932570-72-4(1))* Pioneer Valley Bks.

Kowalski, William. The Way It Works, 1 vol. 2010. (Rapid Reads Ser.). (ENG.). 128p. pap. 9.95 *(978-1-55469-367-2(5),* Raven Bks.) Literations.

Lynn, Michelle. Sasha Discovers There Is a Job for Everyone. 2013. 28p. pap. 24.95 *(978-1-4241-0153-5(0))* America Star Bks.

Regan, Peter. Riverside: Exit Point. 2009. (ENG., Illus.). 128p. (J). pap. 10.95 *(978-1-901737-59-2(4))* Anvil Bks., Ltd. IRL. Dist: Dufour Editions, Inc.

JOBS, STEVE, 1955-2011

Blumenthal, Karen. Steve Jobs: The Man Who Thought Different. 2012. (ENG., Illus.). 320p. (YA). (gr. 7-12). 17.99 *(978-1-250-01557-0(X),* 9781250015570) Feiwel & Friends.

—Steve Jobs: The Man Who Thought Different. 2012. (ENG., Illus.). 320p. (YA). (gr. 7-12). pap. 10.99 *(978-1-250-01445-0(X),* 9781250014450) Square Fish.

Brackett, Virginia. Steve Jobs: Computer Genius of Apple. 2003. (Internet Biographies Ser.). (Illus.). 48p. (J). (gr. 4-10). lib. bdg. 23.93 *(978-0-7660-1970-6(5))* Enslow Pubs., Inc.

Corrigan, Jim. Steve Jobs. 2008. (Business Leaders Ser.). 128p. (YA). (gr. 7-12). lib. bdg. 27.95 *(978-1-59935-076-9(9))* Reynolds, Morgan Inc.

Doeden, Matt. Steve Jobs: Technology Innovator & Apple Genius. 2012. (Gateway Biographies Ser.). (ENG.). 48p. (gr. 4-8). lib. bdg. 26.60 *(978-1-4677-0215-7(3),* Lerner Pubns.) Lerner Publishing Group.

Gillam, Scott. Steve Jobs: Apple & iPod Wizard, 1 vol. 2008. (Essential Lives Set 2 Ser.). (ENG., Illus.). 112p. (J). (gr. 6-12). lib. bdg. 35.64 *(978-1-60453-037-7(5))* ABDO Publishing Co.

—Steve Jobs: Apple ICon, 1 vol. 2012. (Essential Lives Set 2 Ser.). (ENG.). 112p. (J). (gr. 6-12). lib. bdg. 35.64 *(978-1-60453-997-4(6),* Essential Library) ABDO Publishing Co.

Goldsworthy, Steve. Steve Jobs. 2011. (J). (gr. 4-6). pap. 12.95 *(978-1-61690-675-7(8),* AV2 by Weigl); (Illus.). 24p. (YA). (gr. 3-6). 27.13 *(978-1-61690-670-2(7))* Weigl Pubs., Inc.

Gould, Jane H. Steve Jobs. 2013. (Jr. Graphic American Inventors Ser.). (ENG., Illus.). 24p. (J). (gr. 3-6). pap. 10.60 *(978-1-4777-0145-4(1));* lib. bdg. 25.25 *(978-1-4777-0080-8(3))* Rosen Publishing Group, Inc., The. (PowerKids Pr.).

Green, Sara. Steve Jobs. 2014. (Tech Icons Ser.). (ENG., Illus.). 24p. (J). (gr. 3-8). lib. bdg. 25.95 *(978-1-60014-994-8(4),* Pilot Bks.) Bellwether Media.

Gregory, Josh. Steve Jobs. 2013. (True Book(tm), A — Biographies Ser.). (ENG., Illus.). (J). 48p. lib. bdg. 31.00 *(978-0-531-21907-2(0));* 64p. pap. 8.95 *(978-0-531-21964-5(X));* 48p. pap. 6.95 *(978-0-531-23878-3(4));* 64p. lib. bdg. 30.00 *(978-0-531-23606-2(4))* Scholastic Library Publishing.

Hartland, Jessie. Steve Jobs: Insanely Great. 2015. (ENG., Illus.). 240p. (YA). (gr. 7). 22.95 *(978-0-307-98295-7(5),* Schwartz & Wade Bks.) Random Hse. Children's Bks.

Honders, Christine. Steve Jobs: Father of the Digital Revolution. 2015. (Britannica Beginner Bios Ser.). (ENG., Illus.). 32p. (J). (gr. 2-3). 23.45 *(978-1-62275-921-7(4),* Britannica Educational Publishing) Rosen Publishing Group, Inc., The.

—Steve Jobs: Visionary of the Digital Revolution. 2015. (Britannica Beginner Bios Ser.). (ENG.). 32p. (J). (gr. 2-3). 46.90 *(978-1-62275-924-8(9),* Britannica Educational Publishing) Rosen Publishing Group, Inc., The.

Hunter, Nick. Steve Jobs, 1 vol. 2012. (Titans of Business Ser.). (ENG.). 48p. (gr. 4-6). pap. 8.99 *(978-1-4329-6435-1(6));* lib. bdg. 32.00 *(978-1-4329-6428-3(3))* Heinemann-Raintree. (NA-h).

Imbimbo, Anthony. Steve Jobs: The Brilliant Mind Behind Apple. 2009. (Life Portraits Ser.). (Illus.). 112p. (YA). (gr. 7-12). lib. bdg. 36.00 *(978-1-4339-0060-0(2))* Stevens, Gareth Publishing LLLP.

Isabella, Jude. Steve Jobs: Visionary Entrepreneur of the Digital Age. 2013. (ENG.). 112p. (J). E-Book ***(978-1-4271-8936-3(6));*** (Illus.). *(978-0-7787-1189-6(7));* (Illus.). pap. *(978-0-7787-1191-9(9))* Crabtree Publishing Co.

Jackson, Aurelia. Disney's Pixar(r): How Steve Jobs Changed Hollywood. 2014. (Wizards of Technology Ser.: 10). 64p. (J). (gr. 7-18). 23.95 *(978-1-4222-3180-7(1))* Mason Crest.

Kjelle, Marylou Morano. Steve Jobs: Visionary Founder of Apple, 1 vol. 2014. (Newsmakers Ser.). (ENG.). 48p. (gr. 3-6). lib. bdg. 32.79 *(978-1-62403-642-2(2))* ABDO Publishing Co.

Klein, Adria F. Steve Jobs. 2009. pap. 13.25 *(978-1-60559-071-4(1))* Hameray Publishing Group, Inc.

La Bella, Laura. Steve Jobs & Steve Wozniak, 01 vols., 1. 2016. (Tech Pioneers Ser.). (ENG.). 112p. (J). 35.60 *(978-1-4994-6286-9(7),* Rosen Young Adult) Rosen Publishing Group, Inc., The.

Lakin, Patricia. Steve Jobs: Thinking Differently. 2012. (ENG.). 192p. (J). (gr. 3-7). pap. 7.99 *(978-1-4424-5393-7(1),* Aladdin) Simon & Schuster Children's Publishing.

—Steve Jobs: Thinking Differently. 2012. (ENG.). 192p. (J). (gr. 3-7). 17.99 *(978-1-4424-5394-4(X),* Simon & Schuster/Paula Wiseman Bks.) Simon & Schuster/Paula Wiseman Bks.

Lemke, Donald B. Steve Jobs, Steve Wozniak, & the Personal Computer, 1 vol. Smith, Tod G. & Milgrom, Al, illus. 2006. (Inventions & Discovery Ser.). (ENG.). 32p. (gr. 3-4). 30.65 *(978-0-7368-6488-6(1),* Graphic Library) Capstone Press of Coughlan Cos.

—Steve Jobs, Steve Wozniak, & the Personal Computer, 1 vol. Milgrom, Al & Smith, Tod G., illus. 2006. (Inventions & Discovery Ser.). (ENG.). 32p. (gr. 3-4). pap. 8.10 *(978-0-7368-9650-4(3));* pap. 47.70 *(978-0-7368-9762-4(3))* Capstone Press of Coughlan Cos. (Graphic Library).

Lusted, Marcia Amidon. Apple: The Company & Its Visionary Founder, Steve Jobs, 1 vol. 2012. (Technology Pioneers Set 2 Ser.). (ENG., Illus.). 112p. (J). (gr. 6-12). lib. bdg. 35.64 *(978-1-61783-331-1(2),* Essential Library) ABDO Publishing Co.

Lusted, Marcia Amidon & National Geographic Learning Staff. Apple: The Company & Its Visionary Founder, Steve Jobs. 2013. (ENG.). 112p. (C). pap. 14.95 *(978-1-60453-998-1(4))* National Geographic School Publishing, Inc.

Mattern, Joanne. Steve Jobs. 2013. (Rookie Biographies(r) Ser.). (ENG.). 32p. (J). pap. 5.95 *(978-0-531-24705-1(8),* Children's Pr.); lib. bdg. 23.00 *(978-0-531-24739-6(2))* Scholastic Library Publishing.

Nakaya, Andrea C. Steve Jobs & Apple. 2015. (ENG., Illus.). 80p. (J). lib. bdg. *(978-1-60152-880-3(9))* ReferencePoint Pr., Inc.

Pollack, Pam, et al. Who Was Steve Jobs? Harrison, Nancy et al, illus. 2012. (Who Was? Ser.). (ENG.). 112p. (J). (gr. 3-7). pap. 5.99 *(978-0-448-46211-0(7),* Grosset & Dunlap) Penguin Young Readers Group.

Pollack, Pamela & Belviso, Meg. Who Was Steve Jobs? 2012. (Who Was...? Ser.). lib. bdg. 16.00 *(978-0-606-26649-9(6),* Turtleback) Turtleback Bks.

Shea, Therese. Steve Jobs & Apple. 2012. (Internet Biographies Ser.). (ENG., Illus.). 128p. (YA). (gr. 7-12). lib. bdg. 34.60 *(978-1-4488-6910-7(2))* Rosen Publishing Group, Inc., The.

Sheen, Barbara. Steve Jobs. 2009. (People in the News Ser.). (ENG., Illus.). 128p. (YA). (gr. 7-12). 33.95 *(978-1-4205-0160-5(7))* Cengage Gale.

Steve Jobs & Apple. 2011. (Graphic Nonfiction Biographies Ser.). (ENG.). 48p. (YA). (gr. 5-8). *(978-1-4488-5546-9(2));* pap. *(978-1-4488-5645-9(0))* Rosen Publishing Group, Inc., The. (Rosen Reference).

Venezia, Mike. Steve Jobs & Steve Wozniak: Geek Heroes Who Put the Personal in Computers. 2010. (Getting to Know the World's Greatest Inventors & Scientists Ser.). 32p. (J). pap. 6.95 *(978-0-531-22351-2(5),* Children's Pr.) Scholastic Library Publishing.

Ventura, Marne & Feynman, Drew. The Creators of the iPhone. Glass, Simon, illus. 2017. (Awesome Minds Ser.). (ENG.). 56p. (J). (gr. 1-5). 14.99 *(978-1-938093-77-7(1),* Duo Pr. Llc (US)) Duo Pr. LLC.

Washburne, Sophie & Sheen, Barbara. Steve Jobs: Computer Visionary. 2017. (People in the News Ser.). 104p. (J). (gr. 7-7). lib. bdg. 39.40 ***(978-1-5345-6031-4(9),*** Lucent Pr.) Greenhaven Publishing LLC.

Ziller, Amanda. Steve Jobs: American Genius. 2012. (ENG.). 176p. (J). (gr. 3-7). pap. 5.99 *(978-0-06-219765-8(7),* Collins) HarperCollins Pubs.

JOBS

see Occupations; Professions

JOGUES, ISAAC, SAINT, 1607-1646

Pelous, Donald. A Dream Come True: A Story of St. Isaac Jogues. Jagodits, Carolyn Lee, illus. 2011. 94p. 38.95 *(978-1-258-06266-8(6))* Literary Licensing, LLC.

JOHN, THE APOSTLE, SAINT

Woodman, Ros. Bible Detectives: John. 2006. (Activity Ser.). (ENG.). 64p. (J). pap., act. bk. ed. 7.99 *(978-1-85792-759-7(1),* 8f47f354-1752-4c64-a52d-9fb0afebdb32) Christian Focus Pubns. GBR. Dist: Bookmasters Distribution.

JOHN, THE BAPTIST, SAINT

Johnson, Alice W. & Warner, Allison H. Believe & You're There When the White Dove Descended. Nelson, Holly, illus. 2009. 96p. (J). pap. 8.95 *(978-1-59038-721-4(X))* Deseret Bk. Co.

Lumsden, Colin, illus. John the Baptist. 2003. (Bible Colour & Learn Ser.). 32p. pap. 2.50 *(978-1-903087-44-2(9))* DayOne Pubns. GBR. Dist: Send The Light Distribution LLC.

MacKenzie, Carine. John: The Baptist. McLaren, Duncan, illus. 2013. (Bible Time Ser.). (ENG.). 32p. (J). (gr. -1-2). pap. 3.99 *(978-1-84550-164-8(0),* 9781845501648) Christian Focus Pubns. GBR. Dist: Bookmasters Distribution.

JOHN, THE BAPTIST, SAINT—FICTION

Rivera-Ashford, Roni Capin & Johnson, Richard. Hip Hip Hooray, It's Monsoon Day! 2007. (ENG & SPA.). (YA). pap. 15.95 *(978-1-886679-36-8(3))* Arizona Sonora Desert Museum Pr.

JOHN, ELTON, 1947-

Anderson, Kirsten. Who Is Elton John? 2016. (Who Is...? Ser.). lib. bdg. 16.00 *(978-0-606-38396-7(4))* Turtleback Bks.

O'Mahony, John. Elton John. 2003. (World Musicmakers Ser.). (Illus.). 64p. (J). 26.20 *(978-1-56711-972-5(7),* Blackbirch Pr., Inc.) Cengage Gale.

Schlesinger, Ethan. Elton John. (Pop Rock Ser.). (Illus.). 64p. (YA). (gr. 3-7). 2008. lib. bdg. 22.95 *(978-1-4222-0189-3(9))* 2007. pap. 7.95 *(978-1-4222-0316-3(6))* Mason Crest.

White, Katherine. Elton John. (Rock & Roll Hall of Famers Ser.). 112p. (gr. 5-8). 2009. 63.90 *(978-1-60852-473-0(6),* Rosen Reference) 2006. (Illus.). (YA). lib. bdg. 34.60 *(978-0-8239-3641-0(4))* Rosen Publishing Group, Inc., The.

JKL

JOHN HENRY (LEGENDARY CHARACTER)

Gould, Jane H. John Henry. 2014. (Jr. Graphic American Legends Ser.). (Illus.). 24p. (J). (gr. 3-6). lib. bdg. 26.25 *(978-1-4777-7197-6(2),* PowerKids Pr.) Rosen Publishing Group, Inc., The.

Keats, Ezra Jack. John Henry: An American Legend. 50th anniv. ed. 2014. (ENG., Illus.). 32p. (J). (gr. -1-2). 17.99 *(978-0-553-51307-3(9),* Knopf Bks. for Young Readers) Random Hse. Children's Bks.

—John Henry: an American Legend 50th Anniversary Edition. 2014. (ENG.). 32p. (J). (gr. -1-2). lib. bdg. 20.99 *(978-0-553-51308-0(7),* Knopf Bks. for Young Readers) Random Hse. Children's Bks.

Kessler, Brad. John Henry. Jackson, Barry, illus. 2005. (Rabbit Ears-A Classic Tale Ser.). 36p. (J). (gr. k-5). 25.65 *(978-1-59197-764-3(9))* Spotlight.

Krensky, Stephen. John Henry. Oldroyd, Mark, illus. 2006. (On My Own Folklore Ser.). (ENG.). 48p. (gr. 2-4). lib. bdg. 25.26 *(978-1-57505-887-0(1),* Millbrook Pr.) Lerner Publishing Group.

Meister, Cari. John Henry vs. the Mighty Steam Drill, 1 vol. Rivas, Victor, illus. 2014. (American Folk Legends Ser.). (ENG.). 32p. (gr. k-2). 27.32 *(978-1-4795-5430-0(8))* Picture Window Bks.

JOHNSON, ANDREW, 1808-1875

Gunderson, Megan M. Andrew Johnson, 1 vol. (ENG., Illus.). 40p. 2016. (J). *(978-1-68078-103-8(0))* 2009. (YA). (gr. 3-6). 27.07 *(978-1-60453-461-0(3))* ABDO Publishing Co.

Harper, Judith E. Andrew Johnson. 2008. (Presidents of the U. S. A. Ser.). (ENG., Illus.). 48p. (J). (gr. 3-6). 32.79 *(978-1-60253-046-1(7),* 200685) Child's World, Inc., The.

Havelin, Kate. Andrew Johnson. 2005. (Presidential Leaders Ser.). (Illus.). 112p. (J). (gr. 6-12). lib. bdg. 29.27 *(978-0-8225-1000-0(6))* Lerner Publishing Group.

Powell, Walter. How to Draw the Life & Times of Andrew Johnson. 2009. (Kid's Guide to Drawing the Presidents of the United States of America Ser.). 32p. (gr. 4-4). 50.50 *(978-1-61511-132-9(8),* PowerKids Pr.) Rosen Publishing Group, Inc., The.

Randolph, Ryan P. How to Draw the Life & Times of Andrew Johnson. 2006. (Kid's Guide to Drawing the Presidents of the United States of America Ser.). (YA). (gr. 2-5). 26.50 *(978-1-4042-2994-5(9))* Rosen Publishing Group, Inc., The.

Venezia, Mike. Andrew Johnson: Seventeenth President. Venezia, Mike, illus. 2005. (Getting to Know the U. S. Presidents Ser.). (ENG., Illus.). 32p. (J). (gr. 3-7). lib. bdg. 28.00 *(978-0-516-22622-4(3),* Children's Pr.) Scholastic Library Publishing.

JOHNSON, JAMES WELDON, 1871-1938

Shull, Jodie A. Words of Promise: A Story about James Weldon Johnson. Stetz, Ken, illus. 2005. (Creative Minds Biographies Ser.). (ENG.). 64p. (gr. 4-8). lib. bdg. 22.60 *(978-1-57505-755-2(7),* Carolrhoda Bks.) Lerner Publishing Group.

JOHNSON, LADY BIRD, 1912-2007

Appelt, Kathi. Miss Lady Bird's Wildflowers: How a First Lady Changed America. Hein, Joy Fisher, illus. 2005. 40p. (J). lib. bdg. 17.89 *(978-0-06-001108-6(4));* (ENG.). (gr. 2-5). 17.99 *(978-0-06-001107-9(6))* HarperCollins Pubs.

Collard, Sneed B., III. American Heroes, 6 vols., Group 3. Incl. Cesar Chavez: The Farm Workers' Best Friend. 29.93 *(978-0-7614-4055-0(0));* George Washington: Our First President. 29.93 *(978-0-7614-4060-4(7));* Jacob Lawrence: A Painter's Story. 29.93 *(978-0-7614-4058-1(5));* Lady Bird Johnson: Keeping America Green. 29.93 *(978-0-7614-4056-7(9));* Phillis Wheatley: She Loved Words. 29.93 *(978-0-7614-4057-4(7));* Sitting Bull: Tatanka-Iyotake. 29.93 *(978-0-7614-4059-8(3));* 48p. (gr. 3-18). (American Heroes 3 Ser.). 2009. Set lib. bdg. 179.57 o.p. *(978-0-7614-4054-3(2))* Marshall Cavendish Corp.

—Lady Bird Johnson: Keeping America Green. 2009. (American Heroes Ser.). 48p. (gr. 3-18). 29.93 *(978-0-7614-4056-7(9))* Marshall Cavendish Corp.

Mattern, Joanne. Lady Bird Johnson, 1 vol. 2008. (First Ladies Set 1 Ser.). (ENG., Illus.). 32p. (YA). (gr. 1-4). 27.07 *(978-1-59928-795-9(1))* ABDO Publishing Co.

Yasuda, Anita. Lady Bird Johnson. 2010. (My Life Ser.). 24p. (J). (gr. 2-4). lib. bdg. 25.70 *(978-1-61690-062-5(8))* Weigl Pubs., Inc.

—Lady Bird Johnson: My Life. 2010. pap. 9.95 *(978-1-61690-063-2(6))* Weigl Pubs., Inc.

JOHNSON, LYNDON B. (LYNDON BAINES), 1908-1973

Baxter, Kathleen & McConnell, Robert L., contrib. by. Assassination & Its Aftermath: How a Photograph Reassured a Shocked Nation, 1 vol. 2013. (Captured History Ser.). (ENG.). 64p. (gr. 5-7). 34.65 *(978-0-7565-4692-2(3),* CPB Grades 4-8) Compass Point Bks.

Blake, Kevin. Lyndon B. Johnson. 2016. (First Look at America's Presidents Ser.). (ENG., Illus.). 24p. (J). (gr. -1-3). lib. bdg. 17.95 *(978-1-943553-32-7(7))* Bearport Publishing Co., Inc.

Colbert, Nancy A. Great Society: The Story of Lyndon Baines Johnson. 2004. (Notable Americans Ser.). (Illus.). 144p. (YA). (gr. 6-12). 23.95 *(978-1-883846-84-8(6),* First Biographies) Reynolds, Morgan Inc.

Day, Meredith, ed. Lyndon B. Johnson. 2016. (Pivotal Presidents: Profiles in Leadership Ser.). 80p. (gr. 8-8). lib. bdg. 33.90 *(978-1-68048-527-1(X))* Rosen Publishing Group, Inc., The.

Gimpel, Diane Marczely. Lyndon B. Johnson. 2016. (Premier Presidents Ser.). (ENG.). 24p. (J). (gr. 1-4). 27.07 *(978-1-5038-0870-6(X),* 210720) Child's World, Inc., The.

Gold, Susan Dudley. Lyndon B. Johnson. 2008. (Presidents & Their Times Ser.). 96p. (gr. 6-18). lib. bdg. 34.21 *(978-0-7614-2837-4(2),* Benchmark Bks.) Marshall Cavendish Corp.

Gunderson, Megan M. Lyndon B. Johnson, 1 vol. 2009. (United States Presidents Ser.). (ENG., Illus.). 40p. (YA). (gr. 3-6). 27.07 *(978-1-60453-462-7(1))* ABDO Publishing Co.

Hasselius, Michelle M. Lyndon B. Johnson, 1 vol. 2014. (Presidential Biographies Ser.). (ENG.). 24p. (gr. k-1). lib. bdg. 26.65 *(978-1-4765-9611-2(5),* Pebble Plus) Capstone Press of Coughlan Cos.

Isecke, Harriet. Lyndon B. Johnson: A Texan in the White House, 1 vol. 2012. (Primary Source Readers Ser.). (ENG.). 32p. (J). (gr. 3-3). pap. 8.99 *(978-1-4333-5052-8(1))* Teacher Created Materials, Inc.

—Lyndon B. Johnson: Un Texano en la Casa Blanca / Lyndon B. Johnson - A Texan in the White House. 2013. (Primary Source Readers Ser.). (SPA.). lib. bdg. 19.65 *(978-0-606-31873-0(9),* Turtleback) Turtleback Bks.

Levy, Debbie. Lyndon B. Johnson. 2003. (Presidential Leaders Ser.). (Illus.). 112p. (J). 29.27 *(978-0-8225-0097-1(3),* Lerner Pubns.) Lerner Publishing Group.

Lüsted, Marcia Amidon. Lyndon B. Johnson & the Civil Rights ACT. 2017. (J). ***(978-1-5383-8048-2(X))***; pap. ***(978-1-5081-7746-3(5))*** Rosen Publishing Group, Inc., The.

Mattern, Joanne. Lady Bird Johnson, 1 vol. 2008. (First Ladies Set 1 Ser.). (ENG., Illus.). 32p. (YA). (gr. 1-4). 27.07 *(978-1-59928-795-9(1))* ABDO Publishing Co.

McConnell, Robert L., contrib. by. Assassination & Its Aftermath: How a Photograph Reassured a Shocked Nation, 1 vol. 2013. (Captured History Ser.). (ENG.). 64p. (gr. 5-7). pap. 9.10 *(978-0-7565-4698-4(2),* CPB Grades 4-8) Compass Point Bks.

Mis, M. S. How to Draw the Life & Times of Lyndon B. Johnson. 2009. (Kid's Guide to Drawing the Presidents of the United States of America Ser.). 32p. (gr. 4-4). 50.50 *(978-1-61511-154-1(9),* PowerKids Pr.) Rosen Publishing Group, Inc., The.

Mis, Melody S. How to Draw the Life & Times of Lyndon B. Johnson. 2007. (Kid's Guide to Drawing the Presidents of the United States of America Ser.). (Illus.). 32p. (YA). (gr. 2-5). 26.50 *(978-1-4042-3012-5(2))* Rosen Publishing Group, Inc., The.

Porterfield, Jason. How Lyndon B. Johnson Fought the Vietnam War. 2017. (Presidents at War Ser.). 128p. (J). (gr. 8-8). lib. bdg. 37.27 ***(978-0-7660-8531-2(7))*** Enslow Pubs., Inc.

Venezia, Mike. Lyndon B. Johnson: Thirty-Sixth President, 1963-1969. Venezia, Mike, illus. 2007. (Getting to Know the U. S. Presidents Ser.). (Illus.). 32p. (J). (gr. 3-4). 28.00 *(978-0-516-22640-8(1),* Children's Pr.) Scholastic Library Publishing.

Yasuda, Anita. Lady Bird Johnson. 2010. (My Life Ser.). 24p. (J). (gr. 2-4). lib. bdg. 25.70 *(978-1-61690-062-5(8))* Weigl Pubs., Inc.

—Lady Bird Johnson: My Life. 2010. pap. 9.95 *(978-1-61690-063-2(6))* Weigl Pubs., Inc.

JOHNSTOWN (PA.)—FLOOD, 1889

see Floods—Pennsylvania—Johnstown (Cambria County)

JOKES

see Wit and Humor

JOLIET, LOUIS, 1645-1700

Donaldson-Forbes, Jeff. Jacques Marquette & Louis Jolliet. 2009. (Primary Source Library of Famous Explorers Ser.). 24p. (gr. 4-4). 42.50 *(978-1-60854-127-0(4),* PowerKids Pr.) Rosen Publishing Group, Inc., The.

Larkin, Tanya. Jacques Marquette & Louis Jolliet: Explorers of the Mississippi. 2009. (Library of Explorers & Exploration Ser.). 112p. (gr. 5-8). 66.50 *(978-1-60853-608-5(4),* Rosen Reference) Rosen Publishing Group, Inc., The.

Petrie, Kristin. Marquette & Jolliet, 1 vol. 2007. (Explorers Set 2 Ser.). (ENG., Illus.). 32p. (gr. 4-7). 27.07 *(978-1-59679-745-1(2),* Checkerboard Library) ABDO Publishing Co.

Zelenyi, Alexander & Zelenyj, Alexander. Marquette & Jolliet: Quest for the Mississippi. 2006. (In the Footsteps of Explorers Ser.). (ENG., Illus.). 32p. (J). (gr. 4-7). pap. *(978-0-7787-2467-4(0));* lib. bdg. *(978-0-7787-2431-5(X))* Crabtree Publishing Co.

JONAH (BIBLICAL PROPHET)

Amery, H. Jonah & the Whale. 2004. (Bible Tales Readers Ser.). 16p. (J). lib. bdg. 12.95 *(978-1-58086-632-3(8),* Usborne); (Illus.). pap. 4.95 *(978-0-7945-0414-4(0))* EDC Publishing.

Arthur, Kay & Domeij, Scoti. Wrong Way Jonah. 2006. (Discover-4-Yourself for Kids Ser.). 93p. (J). pap. 8.99 *(978-1-888655-21-6(6))* Precept Ministries.

Arthur, Kay, et al. Wrong Way, Jonah! Jonah. 2010. (ENG.). 128p. (J). pap. 10.99 *(978-0-7369-2819-9(7))* Harvest Hse. Pubs.

Balsley, Tilda. Oh No, Jonah! Silver, Jago, illus. 2012. (Bible Ser.). (ENG.). 32p. (J). (gr. k-4). lib. bdg. 17.95 *(978-0-7613-5139-9(6),* Kar-Ben Publishing) Lerner Publishing Group.

Balsley, Tilda & Jago. Oh No, Jonah! 2012. (Bible Ser.). (ENG., Illus.). 32p. (J). (gr. k-4). 7.95 *(978-0-7613-5140-5(X),* Kar-Ben Publishing) Lerner Publishing Group.

Bishop, Jennie. Jonah & the Big Fish Coloring Book. 2007. (Illus.). 16p. (J). pap. 1.89 *(978-1-59317-206-0(0))* Warner Pr., Inc.

Copenhagen Publishing Company, prod. Jonah & the Big Fish. 2015. (Carry Me Puzzle Bks.). (ENG.). 8p. (J). bds. 11.99 *(978-1-4964-1086-3(6))* Tyndale Hse. Pubs.

Denham, Joyce. The Hard to Swallow Tale of Jonah & the Whale. Hall, Amanda, illus. 2015. (ENG.). 32p. (J). (gr. -1-3). pap. 8.99 *(978-0-7459-6584-0(9))* Lion Hudson PLC GBR. Dist: Independent Pubs. Group.

Gay, Susana. Jonah & the Big Fish. 2017. (Illus.). 16p. (J). ***(978-0-8249-1666-4(2))*** Worthy Publishing.

Goodings, Christina. My Look & Point Jonah & the Whale Stick-a-Story Book. Hudson, Annabel, illus. 2014. (ENG.). 16p. (J). (gr. -1-k). 6.99 *(978-0-7459-6454-6(0))* Lion Hudson PLC GBR. Dist: Independent Pubs. Group.

Gressman, Carylee Anne. Draw & Write Through History: Creation Through Jonah. Wolf, Aaron D., ed. Dick, Peggy, illus. 2006. (J). per. 12.95 *(978-0-9778597-0-2(3))* CPR Pubng.

Grosche, Erwin. Jonah & the Whale. Teich, Karsten, illus. 2016. (ENG.). 28p. (J). (gr. k-3). 12.99 *(978-1-5064-0882-8(6),* Sparkhouse Family) Augsburg Fortress, Pubs.

Hansen, Janis. Jonah & His Amazing Voyage, 5 vols. Francisco, Wendy, illus. 2003. (Bible Adventure Club Ser.). 36p. wbk. ed. 19.99 incl. audio, cd-rom *(978-1-58134-326-7(4))* Crossway.

Holder, Jennifer. Go, Jonah, Go! Julien, Terry, illus. 2014. (Happy Day Ser.). (ENG.). 16p. (J). pap. 2.49 *(978-1-4143-9526-5(4))* Tyndale Hse. Pubs.

Jonah Bible Sticker Book. 2003. (Illus.). 16p. (J). 2.98 *(978-1-4054-1555-2(X))* Parragon, Inc.

Mackall, Dandi Daley. Jonah & the Fish. Marlin, Lissy, illus. 2016. (Flipside Stories Ser.). (ENG.). 48p. (J). 14.99 *(978-1-4964-1120-4(X))* Tyndale Hse. Pubs.

Mackenzie, Carine. Jonah: The Runaway Preacher. McLaren, Duncan, illus. 2013. (Bible Time Ser.). (ENG.). 32p. (J). (gr. -1-2). pap. 3.99 *(978-1-84550-165-5(9),* 95a31c43-f5e1-4925-9bde-d4dcdcad6fea) Christian Focus Pubns. GBR. Dist: Bookmasters Distribution.

MacLean, Ruth. The Man Who Ran: A Puzzle Book about Jonah. rev. ed. 2009. (Puzzle Ser.). (ENG., Illus.). 24p. (J). 4.99 *(978-1-84550-496-0(8),* 9781845504960) Christian Focus Pubns. GBR. Dist: Bookmasters Distribution.

Pingry, Patricia A. Jonah & the Fish: Based on Jonah 1-3:3. Venturi-Pickett, Stacy, illus. 2005. (Stories from the Bible Ser.). (ENG.). 26p. (J). (gr. -1-k). bds. 6.95 *(978-0-8249-6626-3(0),* Ideal Pubns.) Worthy Publishing.

Powell Smith, Brendan. Jonah & the Whale: The Brick Bible for Kids. 2014. (Brick Bible for Kids Ser.). (ENG., Illus.). 32p. (J). (gr. -1-k). 12.95 *(978-1-62873-589-5(9),* Sky Pony Pr.) Skyhorse Publishing Co., Inc.

Pulley, Kelly. Jonah & the Big Fish, 1 vol. 2007. (I Can Read! / the Beginner's Bible Ser.). (ENG., Illus.). 32p. (J). (gr. -1-1). pap. 3.99 *(978-0-310-71459-0(1))* Zonderkidz.

Pulley, Kelly & Zondervan Staff. Jonas y el Gran Pez, 1 vol. Pulley, Kelly, illus. 2009. (I Can Read! / the Beginner's Bible / ¡Yo Sé Leer! Ser.). Tr. of Jonah & the Big Fish. (SPA & ENG., Illus.). 32p. (J). pap. 3.99 *(978-0-310-71887-1(2))* Zonderkidz.

Scherm, Deedra. The Whale & Jonah: A Story of Obedience & Forgiveness. Dreyer, Laura, illus. 2007. (ENG.). 20p. 7.99 *(978-1-934789-00-1(3))* Lemon Vision Productions.

Schmidt, Troy. The Whale & Jonah. Jones, Cory, illus. 2015. (Their Side of the Story Ser.). (ENG.). 32p. (J). (gr. -1-3). pap. 3.99 *(978-1-4336-8723-5(2),* B&H Kids) B&H Publishing Group.

Simon, Mary Mans. Jonah & the Big Fish: Read & Learn the Bible. 2005. (ENG., Illus.). 24p. (J). pap. 2.99 *(978-1-4037-1158-8(5),* Spirit Pr.) Bendon, Inc.

Smart Kids Publishing Staff. Jonah & the Whale: A Story about Responsibility. Sharp, Chris, illus. 2006. (I Can Read the Bible Ser.). (ENG.). 12p. (J). (gr. -1-3). 14.95 *(978-0-8249-6661-4(9),* Ideal Pubns.) Worthy Publishing.

Smith, Brendan Powell. Jonah & the Whale: The Brick Bible for Kids. 2014. (Brick Bible for Kids Ser.). (ENG., Illus.). 32p. (J). (gr. -1-k). 3.99 *(978-1-63450-055-5(5),* Sky Pony Pr.) Skyhorse Publishing Co., Inc.

Thoms, Susan Collins. Jonah & the Big Fish. Stoop, Naoko, illus. 2016. (ENG.). 22p. (J). (— 1). bds. 6.95 *(978-1-4549-1493-8(9),* 1402423) Sterling Publishing Co., Inc.

Wickenden, Nadine, illus. The Story of Jonah. 2006. 10p. (J). (gr. k-4). reprint ed. 8.00 *(978-0-7567-9923-6(6))* DIANE Publishing Co.

Zondervan Bibles Staff. Jonah, God's Messenger, 1 vol. Jones, Dennis, illus. 2011. (I Can Read! / Dennis Jones Ser.). (ENG.). 32p. (J). pap. 3.99 *(978-0-310-71835-2(X))* Zonderkidz.

JONATHAN (BIBLICAL FIGURE)

Dietrich, Julie. David & His Friend, Jonathan. Ramsey, Marcy, illus. 2005. (Arch Bks.). (ENG.). 16p. (J). 1.99 *(978-0-7586-0723-2(7))* Concordia Publishing Hse.

MacKenzie, Carine. David the Fugitive: True Friendship. 2009. (Bible Alive Ser.). (ENG., Illus.). 24p. (J). 3.99 *(978-1-84550-487-8(9),* cf0ac043-f2de-40dc-874b-d61d7396ad4f) Christian Focus Pubns. GBR. Dist: Bookmasters Distribution.

Mackenzie, Carine. Jonathan: The Faithful Friend. Apps, Fred, illus. 2007. (Bible Wise Ser.). (ENG.). 32p. (J). (gr. -1-2). 3.99 *(978-1-84550-289-8(2),* b8e20eae-3f28-43e7-b1a4-6f744d81f802) Christian Focus Pubns. GBR. Dist: Bookmasters Distribution.

JONES, HERCULEAH (FICTITIOUS CHARACTER)—FICTION

Byars, Betsy. The Black Tower. 2007. (Herculeah Jones Mystery Ser.). (ENG.). 144p. (J). (gr. 3-7). 6.99 *(978-0-14-240937-4(5),* Puffin Books) Penguin Young Readers Group.

—The Dark Stairs. (Herculeah Jones Mystery Ser.). 160p. (J). (gr. 3-5). pap. 4.99 *(978-0-8072-1478-7(7),* Listening Library) Random Hse. Audio Publishing Group.

—Death's Door. 2006. (Herculeah Jones Mystery Ser.). (ENG.). 144p. (J). (gr. 3-7). 6.99 *(978-0-14-240565-9(5),* Puffin Books) Penguin Young Readers Group.

—Disappearing Acts. 2006. (Herculeah Jones Mystery Ser.). (ENG.). 144p. (J). (gr. 3-7). 6.99 *(978-0-14-240566-6(3),* Puffin Books) Penguin Young Readers Group.

—King of Murder. 2007. (Herculeah Jones Mystery Ser.). (ENG.). 144p. (J). (gr. 3-7). 5.99 *(978-0-14-240759-2(3),* Puffin Books) Penguin Young Readers Group.

—Tarot Says Beware. 2006. (Herculeah Jones Mystery Ser.). 151p. (gr. 3-7). 16.00 *(978-0-7569-6737-6(6))* Perfection Learning Corp.

JONES, INDIANA (FICTITIOUS CHARACTER)—FICTION

Windham, Ryder & Weyn, Suzanne. Indiana Jones Collector's Edition. 2008. (Illus.). 657p. (J). *(978-0-545-09183-1(7))* Scholastic, Inc.

JONES, JOHN PAUL, 1747-1792

Alphin, Elaine Marie & Alphin, Arthur B. I Have Not Yet Begun to Fight: A Story about John Paul Jones. Casale, Paul, tr. Casale, Paul, illus. 2004. (Creative Minds Biography Ser.). 64p. (J). 22.60 *(978-1-57505-601-2(1),* Carolrhoda Bks.); (ENG.). (gr. 4-8). pap. 8.95 *(978-1-57505-635-7(6))* Lerner Publishing Group.

Bradford, James C. John Paul Jones: And the American Navy. 2005. (Library of American Lives & Times). (Illus.). 112p. (J). (gr. 4-8). lib. bdg. 34.60 *(978-0-8239-5726-2(8))* Rosen Publishing Group, Inc., The.

—John Paul Jones & the American Navy. 2009. (Library of American Lives & Times Ser.). 112p. (gr. 5-5). 69.20 *(978-1-60853-490-6(1))* Rosen Publishing Group, Inc., The.

Brager, Bruce L. John Paul Jones: America's Sailor. 2006. (Founders of the Republic Ser.). (Illus.). 160p. (J). (gr. 6-12). lib. bdg. 26.95 *(978-1-931798-84-6(2))* Reynolds, Morgan Inc.

Cooper, Michael L. Hero of the High Seas: John Paul Jones & the American Revolution. 2006. (ENG., Illus.). 128p. (gr. 5-7). 21.95 *(978-0-7922-5547-5(X));* lib. bdg. 32.90 *(978-0-7922-5548-2(8))* National Geographic Society. (National Geographic Children's Bks.).

Crickard, Sarah. John Paul Jones & the Birth of the American Navy. 2015. (Spotlight on American History Ser.). (ENG., Illus.). 24p. (J). (gr. 4-6). pap. 10.00 *(978-1-4994-1759-3(4),* PowerKids Pr.) Rosen Publishing Group, Inc., The.

Egan, Tracie. John Paul Jones. 2004. (Famous People in American History Ser.). (ENG., Illus.). 32p. (gr. 4-8). pap. 10.00 *(978-0-8239-4185-8(X),* Rosen Reference) Rosen Publishing Group, Inc., The.

—John Paul Jones: American Naval Hero. 2009. (Primary Sources of Famous People in American History Ser.). 32p. (gr. 2-3). 47.90 *(978-1-60851-693-3(8))* Rosen Publishing Group, Inc., The.

—John Paul Jones: American Naval Hero / Héroe de la marina Estadounidense. 2009. (Famous People in American History/Grandes personajes en la historia de los Estados Unidos Ser.). (ENG & SPA.). 32p. (gr. 2-3). 47.90 *(978-1-61512-548-7(5),* Editorial Buenas Letras) Rosen Publishing Group, Inc., The.

—John Paul Jones: Heroe de la Marina Estadounidense. 2004. (Grandes personajes en la historia de los Estados Unidos Ser.). (ENG & SPA.). 32p. (gr. 3-6). pap. 10.00 *(978-0-8239-4231-2(7))* Rosen Publishing Group, Inc., The.

—John Paul Jones: Héroe de la marina estadounidense (John Paul Jones: American Naval Hero) 2009. (Grandes personajes en la historia de los Estados Unidos (Famous People in American History) Ser.). (SPA.). 32p. (gr. 2-3). 47.90 *(978-1-61512-802-0(6),* Editorial Buenas Letras) Rosen Publishing Group, Inc., The.

Harkins, Susan Sales & Harkins, William H. The Life & Times of John Paul Jones. 2007. (Profiles in American History Ser.). (Illus.). 48p. (J). (gr. 4-8). lib. bdg. 29.95 *(978-1-58415-529-4(9))* Mitchell Lane Pubs., Inc.

Heinrichs, Ann & Burgan, Michael. John Paul Jones. 2004. (Our People Ser.). (ENG., Illus.). 32p. (J). (gr. 3-6). 29.93 *(978-1-59296-175-7(4),* 200642) Child's World, Inc., The.

Sonneborn, Liz. John Paul Jones: American Naval Hero. 2005. (Leaders of the American Revolution Ser.). (Illus.). 100p. (gr. 5-8). lib. bdg. 30.00 *(978-0-7910-8621-6(6))* Facts On File, Inc.

Sperry, Armstrong. John Paul Jones: The Pirate Patriot. (Great Leaders & Events Ser.). (ENG.). (J). (gr. 4-8). 2017. lib. bdg. 35.99 ***(978-1-942875-42-0(8))*** 2016. (Illus.). 168p. pap. 12.99 *(978-0-7603-5230-4(5),* Voyageur Pr.) Quarto Publishing Group USA.

Waldman, Scott. Victory at Sea: John Paul Jones & the Continental Navy. 2009. (Great Moments in American History Ser.). 32p. (gr. 3-3). 47.90 *(978-1-61513-156-3(6))* Rosen Publishing Group, Inc., The.

JONES, JUNIE B. (FICTITIOUS CHARACTER)—FICTION

Park, Barbara. Aloha-Ha-Ha! Brunkus, Denise, illus. 2006. (Junie B. Jones Ser.: No. 9). (ENG.). 128p. (J). (gr. 1-4). lib. bdg. 13.95 *(978-0-375-93403-2(0),* Random Hse. Bks. for Young Readers) Random Hse. Children's Bks.

—Boo... & I Mean It! Brunkus, Denise, illus. 2004. (Junie B. Jones Ser.: No. 7). (ENG.). 96p. (J). (gr. 1-4). lib. bdg. 13.99 *(978-0-375-92806-2(5),* Random Hse. Bks. for Young Readers) Random Hse. Children's Bks.

—Boss of Lunch. 2003. (Junie B. Jones Ser.: 19). (gr. k-3). lib. bdg. 14.75 *(978-0-613-63168-6(4),* Turtleback) Turtleback Bks.

—Cheater Pants. Brunkus, Denise, tr. Brunkus, Denise, illus. 2004. (Junie B. Jones Ser.: No. 4). (ENG.). 96p. (J). (gr. 1-4). 4.99 *(978-0-375-82302-2(6),* Random Hse. Bks. for Young Readers) Random Hse. Children's Bks.

—Cheater Pants. Brunkus, Denise, illus. 2003. (Junie B. Jones Ser.: No. 4). (ENG.). 96p. (J). (gr. 1-4). lib. bdg. 13.99 *(978-0-375-92301-2(2),* Random Hse. Bks. for Young Readers) Random Hse. Children's Bks.

—Junie B., First Grader - Boo...and I Mean It! Brunkus, Denise, illus. 2005. (Junie B. Jones Ser.: No. 7). (ENG.). 96p. (J). (gr. 1-4). 4.99 *(978-0-375-82807-2(9),* Random Hse. Bks. for Young Readers) Random Hse. Children's Bks.

—Junie B., First Grader - Boss of Lunch. Brunkus, Denise, illus. 2003. (Junie B., First Grader Ser.: No. 2). 96p. (J). (gr. k-3). lib. bdg. 11.99 *(978-0-375-90294-9(5),* Golden Bks.) Random Hse. Children's Bks.

—Junie B. Jones & a Little Monkey Business, Vol. 2. unabr. ed. 2004. (Junie B. Jones Ser.: Vol. 2). 68p. (J). (gr. k-3). pap. 17.00 incl. audio *(978-0-8072-0779-6(9),* LFTR 238 SP, Listening Library) Random Hse. Audio Publishing Group.

—Junie B. Jones & the Mushy Gushy Valentine. unabr. ed. 2004. (Junie B. Jones Ser.: No. 14). 69p. (J). (gr. k-3). pap. 17.00 incl. audio *(978-0-8072-0335-4(1),* Listening Library) Random Hse. Audio Publishing Group.

—Junie B. Jones & the Stupid Smelly Bus. unabr. ed. 2004. (Junie B. Jones Ser.: Vol. 1). 69p. (J). (gr. k-3). pap. 17.00 incl. audio *(978-0-8072-0778-9(0),* LFTR 237 SP, Listening Library) Random Hse. Audio Publishing Group.

—Junie B. Jones Has a Monster under Her Bed. unabr. ed. 2004. (Junie B. Jones Ser.: No. 8). 69p. (J). (gr. k-3). pap. 17.00 incl. audio *(978-0-8072-0644-7(X),* Listening Library) Random Hse. Audio Publishing Group.

—Junie B. Jones's Fifth Boxed Set Ever!, 4 vols. Brunkus, Denise, illus. 2008. (ENG.). (J). (gr. 1-4). 19.96 *(978-0-375-85570-2(X),* Random Hse. Bks. for Young Readers) Random Hse. Children's Bks.

—Junie B. Jones's Fourth Boxed Set Ever!, 4 vols. Brunkus, Denise, illus. 2004. (ENG.). (J). (gr. 1-4). 19.96 *(978-0-375-82829-4(X),* Random Hse. Bks. for Young Readers) Random Hse. Children's Bks.

—Junie B. Jones's Third Boxed Set Ever!, 4 vols., Bks. 9-12. Brunkus, Denise, illus. 2003. (Junie B. Jones Ser.). (ENG.). (J). (gr. 1-4). 19.96 *(978-0-375-82552-1(5),* Random Hse. Bks. for Young Readers) Random Hse. Children's Bks.

—Junie B.'s Essential Survival Guide to School. Brunkus, Denise, illus. 2013. (Junie B. Jones Ser.). (ENG.). 144p. (J). (gr. 1-4). 12.99 *(978-0-449-81783-4(0),* Random Hse. Bks. for Young Readers) Random Hse. Children's Bks.

—One-Man Band. Brunkus, Denise, illus. 2003. (Junie B. Jones Ser.: No. 5). (ENG.). 96p. (J). (gr. 1-4). lib. bdg. 13.99 *(978-0-375-92522-1(8),* Random Hse. Bks. for Young Readers) Random Hse. Children's Bks.

—Shipwrecked, No. 23. Brunkus, Denise, illus. 2005. (Junie B. Jones Ser.: No. 6). (ENG.). 96p. (J). (gr. 1-4). mass mkt. 4.99 *(978-0-375-82805-8(2)*, Random Hse. Bks. for Young Readers) Random Hse. Children's Bks.

—Toothless Wonder. Brunkus, Denise, illus. 2003. (Junie B. Jones Ser.: No. 3). (ENG.). 96p. (J). (gr. 1-4). pap. 4.99 *(978-0-375-82223-0(2)*, Random Hse. Bks. for Young Readers) Random Hse. Children's Bks.

—Toothless Wonder. 2003. (Junie B. Jones Ser.: 20). (gr. k-3). lib. bdg. 14.75 *(978-0-613-71014-5(2)*, Turtleback) Turtleback Bks.

—Turkeys We Have Loved & Eaten (and Other Thankful Stuff) 2014. (Junie B. Jones Ser.: 28). lib. bdg. 14.75 *(978-0-606-36015-9(8))* Turtleback Bks.

JONES, MOTHER, 1830-1930

Cole, Peter. Ben Fletcher: The Life & Times of a Black Wobbly: Including Fellow Worker Fletcher's Writings & Speeches. 10th annot. ed. 2006. (Labor Classics Ser.). (Illus.). 149p. per. 15.00 *(978-0-88286-311-5(8))* Kerr, Charles H. Publishing Co.

Gay, Kathlyn. Mother Jones. 2006. (American Workers Ser.). (Illus.). 144p. (J). (gr. 3-7). lib. bdg. 28.95 *(978-1-59935-016-5(5))* Reynolds, Morgan Inc.

Kraft, Betsy Harvey. Mother Jones: One Woman's Fight for Labor. 2006. (Illus.). 116p. (YA). (gr. 6-10). reprint ed. 17.00 *(978-1-4223-5443-8(1))* DIANE Publishing Co.

Miller, Connie Colwell. Mother Jones: Labor Leader. Erwin, Steve & Barnett, Charles, III, illus. 2006. (Graphic Biographies Ser.). (ENG.). 32p. (gr. 3-4). 30.65 *(978-0-7368-5487-0(8)*, Graphic Library) Capstone Press of Coughlan Cos.

—Mother Jones: Labor Leader, 1 vol. Erwin, Steve & Barnett, Charles, III, illus. 2006. (Graphic Biographies Ser.). (ENG.). 32p. (gr. 3-4). per. 8.10 *(978-0-7368-9662-7(7)*, Graphic Library) Capstone Press of Coughlan Cos.

JORDAN

Carew-Miller, Anna. Jordan. (Major Muslim Nations Ser.). 112p. 2010. (YA). (gr. 5-18). lib. bdg. 25.95 *(978-1-4222-1383-4(8))* Vol. 13. 2015. (Illus.). (J). (gr. 7). lib. bdg. 25.95 *(978-1-4222-3444-0(4))* Mason Crest.

Etheredge, Laura. Syria, Lebanon, & Jordan. 2011. (Middle East: Region in Transition Ser.). (Illus.). 248p. (YA). (gr. 9-12). lib. bdg. 40.00 *(978-1-61530-329-8(4))* Rosen Publishing Group, Inc., The.

Jankowski, Susan. Jordan in the News: Past, Present, & Future. 2006. (Middle East Nations in the News Ser.). (Illus.). 128p. (J). (gr. 5-9). lib. bdg. 34.60 *(978-1-59845-030-9(1)*, MyReportLinks.com Bks.) Enslow Pubs., Inc.

Kummer, Patricia K. Jordan. 2006. (Enchantment of the World Ser.). (ENG., Illus.). 144p. (J). (gr. 5-9). 39.00 *(978-0-516-24870-7(7)*, Children's Pr.) Scholastic Library Publishing.

Perdew, Laura. Understanding Jordan Today. 2014. (Illus.). 64p. (J). (gr. 3-6). 33.95 *(978-1-61228-654-9(2))* Mitchell Lane Pubs., Inc.

Pundyk, Grace. Welcome to Jordan. 2004. (Welcome to My Country Ser.). (Illus.). 48p. (gr. 2-5). lib. bdg. 27.00 *(978-0-8368-2565-7(9))* Stevens, Gareth Publishing LLLP.

Romano, Amy. A Historical Atlas of Jordan. (Historical Atlases of South Asia, Central Asia, & the Middle East Ser.). 64p. 2009. (gr. 6-6). 61.20 *(978-1-61513-322-2(4))* 2004. (Illus.). (gr. 7-12). lib. bdg. 31.95 *(978-0-8239-3980-0(4))* Rosen Publishing Group, Inc., The.

Skinner, Patricia. Jordan. 2003. (Countries of the World Ser.). (Illus.). 96p. (gr. 5-12). lib. bdg. 31.00 *(978-0-8368-2365-3(6))* Stevens, Gareth Publishing LLLP.

South, Coleman. Jordan. 2nd rev. ed. 2007. (Cultures of the World Ser.). 144p. (gr. 6). lib. bdg. 42.79 *(978-0-7614-2080-4(0)*, Benchmark Bks.) Marshall Cavendish Corp.

South, Coleman & Newsome, Joel. Jordan. 2017. ***(978-1-5026-2608-0(X))*** Cavendish Square Publishing.

Wagner, Heather Lehr. King Abdullah II: King of Jordan. Schlesinger, Arthur M., Jr., ed. 2005. (Major World Leaders Ser.). (Illus.). 112p. (gr. 6-12). 30.00 *(978-0-7910-8259-1(8)*, Chelsea Hse.) Facts On File, Inc.

JORDAN, MICHAEL, 1963-

Aaseng, Nathan. Michael Jordan: Hall of Fame Basketball Superstar. (Hall of Fame Sports Greats Ser.). 64p. (J). (gr. 4-9). 2014. pap. 9.95 *(978-1-62285-036-5(X))* 2013. 15.95 *(978-1-62285-035-8(1))* Enslow Pubs., Inc.

Christopher, Matt. Michael Jordan: Legends in Sports. rev. ed. 2008. (ENG., Illus.). 176p. (gr. 3-7). pap. 6.99 *(978-0-316-02380-1(9))* Little, Brown Bks. for Young Readers.

Hasday, Judy L. Michael Jordan. 2012. (Role Model Athletes Ser.). 64p. (J). (gr. 7). 22.95 *(978-1-4222-2711-4(1))* Mason Crest.

Jordan, Michael. Michael Jordan. 2015. (Quotes from the Greatest Athletes Ser.). (ENG., Illus.). 24p. (J). lib. bdg. 12.95 *(978-1-4896-3369-9(3)*, 1393457); lib. bdg. 28.55 *(978-1-4896-3368-2(5)*, 1393457) Weigl Pubs., Inc. (AV2 by Weigl).

Kirkpatrick, Rob. Michael Jordan: Basketball Superstar. 2009. (Great Record Breakers in Sports Ser.). 24p. (gr. 3-3). 42.50 *(978-1-61513-190-7(6)*, PowerKids Pr.) Rosen Publishing Group, Inc., The.

Taylor, Nancy & Pearson Longman Staff. Michael Jordan. 2nd ed. 2008. (ENG., Illus.). 20p. pap. 11.99 *(978-1-4058-8151-7(8))* Pearson Education.

Taylor, Nancy & Taylor, Nancy. Michael Jordan, Pack. 2nd ed. 2015. (ENG., Illus.). 16p. pap. 14.65 incl. audio compact disk ***(978-1-4058-7812-8(6))*** Pearson Education.

JORDAN RIVER

Bowman, Crystal. Joshua Crosses the Jordan, 1 vol. Sokolova, Valerie, illus. 2011. (I Can Read! / Bible Stories Ser.). (ENG.). 32p. (J). (gr. -1-2). pap. 3.99 *(978-0-310-72156-7(3))* Zonderkidz.

JOSEPH, NEZ PERCE CHIEF, 1840-1904

Biskup, Agnieszka. Thunder Rolling down the Mountain: The Story of Chief Joseph & the Nez Perce, 1 vol. Zimmerman, Rusty, illus. (American Graphic Ser.). (ENG.). 32p. (gr. 3-4). 2011. pap. 8.10 *(978-1-4296-6270-3(0))* 2011. pap. 47.70 *(978-1-4296-6437-0(1))* 2010. lib. bdg. 30.65 *(978-1-4296-5472-2(4))* Capstone Press of Coughlan Cos. (Graphic Library).

Gunther, Vanessa. Chief Joseph: A Biography, 1 vol. 2010. (Greenwood Biographies Ser.). (Illus.). 178p. (C). 39.00 *(978-0-313-37920-8(3)*, GR7920, Greenwood) ABC-CLIO, LLC.

Hopping, Lorraine Jean. Chief Joseph: The Voice for Peace. 2010. (Sterling Biographies(r) Ser.). (ENG., Illus.). 128p. (J). (gr. 5-18). pap. 5.95 *(978-1-4027-6004-4(3))* Sterling Publishing Co., Inc.

Miller, Barbara Kiely. Chief Joseph. 2007. (Great Americans Ser.). 24p. (gr. 1-4). pap. 8.15 *(978-0-8368-8321-3(7))*; lib. bdg. 22.00 *(978-0-8368-8314-5(4))* Stevens, Gareth Publishing LLLP. (Weekly Reader Leveled Readers).

—Jefe Joseph. 2007. (Grandes Personajes (Great Americans) Ser.). (SPA.). 24p. (gr. 1-4). lib. bdg. 22.00 *(978-0-8368-8331-2(4)*, Weekly Reader Leveled Readers) Stevens, Gareth Publishing LLLP.

—Jefe Joseph (Chief Joseph) 2007. (Grandes Personajes (Great Americans) Ser.). (SPA.). 24p. (gr. 1-4). pap. 8.15 *(978-0-8368-8338-1(1)*, Weekly Reader Leveled Readers) Stevens, Gareth Publishing LLLP.

Sanford, William R. Nez Percé Chief Joseph. 2013. (Native American Chiefs & Warriors Ser.). 48p. (J). (gr. 5-18). 22.60 *(978-0-7660-4092-2(5))*; pap. 8.95 *(978-1-4644-0251-7(5))* Enslow Pubs., Inc.

Schwartz, Heather E. Seeking Freedom: Causes & Effects of the Flight of the Nez Perce. 2015. (Cause & Effect: American Indian History Ser.). (ENG.). 32p. (gr. 3-4). lib. bdg. 27.32 *(978-1-4914-2034-8(0))* Capstone Press of Coughlan Cos.

Sutcliffe, Jane. Chief Joseph. 2004. (History Maker Bios Ser.). (J). pap. 6.95 *(978-0-8225-2068-9(0))* Lerner Publishing Group.

—Chief Joseph. Parlin, Tim, tr. Parlin, Tim, illus. 2004. (History Maker Bios Ser.). 48p. (J). (gr. 3-5). lib. bdg. 26.60 *(978-0-8225-0696-6(3))* Lerner Publishing Group.

JOSEPH, SAINT

Drake, Tim. From an Angel in a Dream, the Story of Saint Joseph, Marys Husband: De un Angel en un Sueño, la Historia de San José, Esposo de María. Alvarado, Tomas, tr. Webber, John & Cohee, Ron, illus. 2nd ed. 2003. (SPA.). (J). 5.00 *(978-0-9747571-0-0(1))* Catholic World Mission.

Lovasik, Lawrence G. El Buen San Jose. (SPA.). (J). 1.50 *(978-0-89942-464-4(3))* Catholic Bk. Publishing Corp.

JOSEPH (SON OF JACOB)

Amery, H. Joseph & the Amazing Coat. 2004. (Bible Tales Readers Ser.). (SPA., Illus.). 16p. (J). pap. 4.95 *(978-0-7945-0417-5(5))* EDC Publishing.

Boon, Fiona & Wickenden, Nadine. My Story - Joseph, 1 vol. 2013. (ENG.). 24p. (J). pap. 4.99 *(978-1-4003-2279-4(0))* Nelson, Thomas Inc.

David, R., illus. Joseph & His Brothers. 2010. 12p. *(978-965-91286-0-0(6))* Sifrei Bet Shearim Ltd.

Gallaudet, Thomas H. Scripture Biography for the Young: Vol. 2 - Joseph. 2009. 220p. pap. 18.00 *(978-1-59925-234-6(1))* Solid Ground Christian Bks.

Harvest House Publishers. Joseph the Dreamer. 2014. (ENG.). 32p. (J). 9.99 *(978-0-7369-6156-1(9))* Harvest Hse. Pubs.

—Joseph the Dreamer Sticker Book. 2014. (ENG.). 20p. (J). pap. 3.99 *(978-0-7369-6165-3(8))* Harvest Hse. Pubs.

Hoak, Benjamin T. Joseph. 2007. (Money at its Best: Millionaires of the Old Testament Ser.). 112p. (YA). (gr. 7-18). pap. 14.95 *(978-1-4222-0847-2(8))* Mason Crest.

Holder, Jennifer. God Was with Joseph. 2014. (Happy Day Ser.). (ENG.). 16p. (J). pap. 2.49 *(978-1-4143-9482-4(9))* Tyndale Hse. Pubs.

Joseph: A Bible Story to Color. (Illus.). 16p. (J). pap. 1.50 *(978-0-87162-812-1(0)*, E6026) Warner Pr., Inc.

Joseph & the Colorful Coat: A Little Story in Color. (Illus.). 16p. (J). pap. 1.50 *(978-0-87162-733-9(7)*, E4313) Warner Pr., Inc.

Joseph Bible Sticker Book. 2003. (Illus.). 16p. (J). 2.98 *(978-1-4054-1556-9(8))* Parragon, Inc.

Koralek, Jenny. The Coat of Many Colors. Baynes, Pauline, illus. 2004. 32p. (J). 16.00 *(978-0-8028-5277-9(7))* Eerdmans, William B. Publishing Co.

Kovacs, Victoria. Joseph/the Good Samaritan Flip-Over Book. Krome, Mike, illus. 2015. (Little Bible Heroes(tm) Ser.). (ENG.). 32p. (J). (gr. k-2). pap. 3.99 *(978-1-4336-8715-0(1)*, B&H Kids) B&H Publishing Group.

Laff, Becky. Joseph the Dreamer. Laff, Becky, illus. 2016. (ENG., Illus.). 48p. (J). (gr. k-4). 17.99 *(978-1-4677-7845-9(1)*, Blackbirch Pr., Inc.) Lerner Publishing Group.

MacKenzie, Carine. Bible Heroes Joseph. 2005. (Bible Art Ser.). (ENG.). 16p. (J). act. bk. ed. 1.99 *(978-1-84550-091-7(1)*, 75cca856-6fd6-454b-a66f-ffec2e980d5d) Christian Focus Pubns. GBR. Dist: Bookmasters Distribution.

Mendenhall, Cheryl, illus. Joseph & His Coat of Many Colors. 2004. (ENG.). 24p. (J). 2.99 *(978-1-4037-0966-0(1)*, Spirit Pr.) Bendon, Inc.

Miles, David, illus. Joseph the Dreamer, 1 vol. 2015. (I Can Read! / Adventure Bible Ser.). 32p. (J). (ENG.). pap. 3.99 *(978-0-310-75084-0(9))*; *(978-1-5182-0994-9(7))* Zonderkidz.

Murdock, Hy. Joseph. (Bible Stories Ser.: No. S846-4). (Illus.). (J). (gr. -1-2). 3.95 *(978-0-7214-5067-4(9)*, Dutton Juvenile) Penguin Publishing Group.

Nakhat, Shamim. The Story of Yaqub & Yusuf: Based on Qur'anic Facts. 2005. (Me & My Holy Qur'an Ser.). (Illus.). 24p. (J). *(978-81-7231-618-1(6))* Islamic Bk. Service.

Pennington, Jack & Tank, Daniel, illus. Joseph. 2004. 87p. (J). pap. *(978-0-8280-1855-5(3))* Review & Herald Publishing Assn.

Pingry, Patricia A. Joseph & the Dream: Based on Genesis 37/46:7. Spence, Jim, illus. 2005. (Stories from the Bible Ser.). (ENG.). 26p. (J). (gr. -1-k). bds. 6.95 *(978-0-8249-6625-6(2)*, Ideal Pubns.) Worthy Publishing.

Rice, Tim & Webber, Andrew Lloyd. Joseph & the Amazing Technicolor Dreamcoat. Blake, Quentin, illus. 2012. (ENG.). 48p. (J). (gr. 2-4). 16.99 *(978-1-84365-103-1(3)*, Pavilion Children's Books) Pavilion Bks. GBR. Dist: Independent Pubs. Group.

Smith, Brendan Powell. Joseph & the Colorful Coat: The Brick Bible for Kids. 2015. (Brick Bible for Kids Ser.). (ENG., Illus.). 32p. (J). (gr. -1-k). 12.99 *(978-1-63220-409-7(6)*, Sky Pony Pr.) Skyhorse Publishing Co., Inc.

Zondervan Staff. Joseph & His Brothers, 1 vol. Pulley, Kelly, illus. 2009. (I Can Read! / the Beginner's Bible Ser.). (ENG.). 32p. (J). pap. 3.99 *(978-0-310-71731-7(0))* Zonderkidz.

JOURNALISM

ABDO Publishing. Special Reports. 2016. (Special Reports: 8). (ENG.). 112p. (J). (gr. 6-12). lib. bdg. 285.12 *(978-1-62403-897-6(2)*, Essential Library) ABDO Publishing Co.

Adams, Simon. Politics. 2010. (Media Power Ser.). 48p. (YA). (gr. 5-9). 35.65 *(978-1-60753-114-2(3))* Amicus Publishing.

Anderson, Judith. Crime. 2010. (Media Power Ser.). 48p. (YA). (gr. 5-9). 35.65 *(978-1-60753-113-5(5))* Amicus Publishing.

Bausum, Ann. Muckrackers: How Ida Tarbell, Upton Sinclair, & Lincoln Steffens Helped Expose Scandal, Inspire Reform, & Invent Investigative Journalism (Large P. I.t. ed. 2013. 238p. pap. *(978-1-4596-6718-1(2))* ReadHowYouWant.com, Ltd.

Beutel, Roger & Spencer, Lauren. Writing about Issues. 2011. 77.70 *(978-1-4488-4746-4(X))*; pap. 12.95 *(978-1-4488-4688-7(9))*; (YA). (gr. 5-9). lib. bdg. 31.95 *(978-1-4488-4682-5(X))* Rosen Publishing Group, Inc., The.

Bodden, Valerie. Journalistic Articles. (Nonfiction Writing Ser.). 48p. 2011. (ENG.). (J). (gr. 4-7). pap. 12.00 *(978-0-89812-546-7(4))* 2010. (YA). (gr. 5-18). 23.95 *(978-1-58341-934-2(9))* Creative Co., The. (Creative Education).

Bonnice, Sherry. Journalist. Riggs, Ernestine G. & Gholar, Cheryl, eds. 2013. (Careers with Character Ser.: 18). 96p. (J). (gr. 7-18). 22.95 *(978-1-4222-2758-9(8))* Mason Crest.

Burden, Peter. News of the World? Fake Sheikhs & Royal Trappings. Dillon, Julia & Hiscocks, Dan, eds. 2009. (ENG., Illus.). 320p. pap. 13.95 *(978-1-903070-72-7(4))* Eye Bks. GBR. Dist: Independent Pubs. Group.

Colin Macfarlane. Hit the Headlines: Exciting Journalism Activities for Improving Writing & Thinking Skills. 2012. (ENG., Illus.). 192p. (C). pap. 50.95 *(978-0-415-69511-4(2)*, 0415695112) Routledge.

DiConsiglio, John. Reporting Live. 2011. (J). *(978-0-531-22552-3(6))* Scholastic, Inc.

Emmer, Rae. School Newspaper. 2009. (School Activities Ser.). 24p. (gr. 1-1). 42.50 *(978-1-60852-999-5(1)*, PowerKids Pr.) Rosen Publishing Group, Inc., The.

—School Newspaper / Periódico Escolar. 2009. (School Activities / Actividades escolares Ser.). (ENG & SPA.). 24p. (gr. 1-2). 42.50 *(978-1-60853-005-2(1)*, Editorial Buenas Letras) Rosen Publishing Group, Inc., The.

Fandel, Jennifer. Picture Yourself Writing Nonfiction: Using Photos to Inspire Writing. 2011. (See It, Write It Ser.). (ENG.). 32p. (gr. 3-4). pap. 47.70 *(978-1-4296-7208-5(0)*, Fact Finders) Capstone Press of Coughlan Cos.

—You Can Write a Terrific Opinion Piece. 2012. (You Can Write Ser.). (ENG.). 24p. (gr. 1-2). pap. 41.70 *(978-1-4296-9317-2(7)*, First Facts) Capstone Press of Coughlan Cos.

—You Can Write a Terrific Opinion Piece, 1 vol. 2012. (You Can Write Ser.). (ENG., Illus.). 24p. (gr. 1-2). pap. 7.29 *(978-1-4296-9316-5(9))*; lib. bdg. 25.32 *(978-1-4296-8409-5(7))* Picture Window Bks.

Fromm, Megan. Accuracy in Media, 1 vol. 2015. (ENG.). 48p. (YA). 30.25 *(978-1-4777-8070-1(X)*, Rosen Reference) Rosen Publishing Group, Inc., The.

—Digital Content Creation, 1 vol. 2015. (ENG.). 48p. (YA). 30.25 *(978-1-4777-8060-2(2)*, Rosen Reference) Rosen Publishing Group, Inc., The.

—Gathering & Sharing Digital Information, 1 vol. 2015. (ENG.). 48p. (YA). 30.25 *(978-1-4777-8062-6(9)*, Rosen Reference) Rosen Publishing Group, Inc., The.

—Understanding Advertising & Monetization, 1 vol. 2015. (ENG.). 48p. (YA). 30.25 *(978-1-4777-8064-0(5)*, Rosen Reference) Rosen Publishing Group, Inc., The.

Fromowitz, Lori. 12 Great Moments that Changed Newspaper History. 2015. (ENG., Illus.). 32p. (J). pap. 9.95 *(978-1-63235-085-5(8))* RiverStream Publishing.

Gish, Melissa. A Newspaper Publisher. 2003. 24p. (J). lib. bdg. 21.35 *(978-1-58340-324-2(8))* Black Rabbit Bks.

Hall, Homer L. Junior High Journalism. 2009. (Junior High Journalism Ser.). 352p. 73.00 *(978-1-61513-873-9(0))* Rosen Publishing Group, Inc., The.

Hamilton, John. Real-Time Reporting. 2004. (War in Iraq Ser.). (Illus.). 48p. (gr. 4-8). 27.07 *(978-1-59197-497-0(6)*, Abdo & Daughters) ABDO Publishing Co.

Hernandez, Roger E. Teens & the Media. Developed in Association with the Gallup Organization Staff, ed. 2013. (Gallup Youth Survey: Major Issues & Trends Ser.: 14). 112p. (J). (gr. 7-18). 24.95 *(978-1-4222-2954-5(8))* Mason Crest.

Hollingsworth, Tamara. Noticias Que Marcaron la Historia. 2016. (TIME for Kids en Español - Level 5 Ser.). (SPA.). 64p. (gr. 5-5). lib. bdg. 31.99 *(978-1-5157-2943-3(5))* Time for Kids Inc AUS. Dist: Capstone Pub.

Jordano, Kimberly & Adsit, Kim. Jumping into Journals: Guided Journaling for Beginning Readers & Writers. Cernek, Kim, ed. Weller, Linda, illus. 2006. 112p. pap. 15.99 *(978-1-59198-227-2(8)*, 2229) Creative Teaching Pr., Inc.

Journalism. 2nd rev. ed. (Careers in Focus Ser.). 224p. (gr. 6-12). 2011. (Illus.). 32.95 *(978-0-8160-8031-1(3))* 2010. 32.95 *(978-0-8160-8080-9(1))* Facts On File, Inc. (Ferguson Publishing Co.).

Kokino, Olga. Journalism Student Activity Book: Student Activities Book. Matthews, Douglas L., ed. 2003. (Illus.). stu. ed., per., wbk. ed. *(978-1-931680-16-5(7)*, Expert Systems for Teachers) Teaching Point, Inc.

Krasner, Barbara. 12 Great Tips on Writing a Blog. 2017. (Great Tips on Writing Ser.). (ENG., Illus.). 32p. (gr. 3-6). 21.95 *(978-1-63235-273-6(7))* Pr. Room Editions LLC.

Mahoney, Ellen. Nellie Bly & Investigative Journalism for Kids: Mighty Muckrakers from the Golden Age to Today, with 21 Activities. 2015. (For Kids Ser.). (ENG., Illus.). 144p. (J). (gr. 4). pap. 16.95 *(978-1-61374-997-5(X))* Chicago Review Pr., Inc.

Mattern, Joanne. Katherine Graham & 20th Century American Journalism. 2009. (Women Who Shaped History Ser.). 24p. (gr. 2-3). 42.50 *(978-1-60854-820-0(1)*, PowerKids Pr.) Rosen Publishing Group, Inc., The.

Mooney, Carla. Asking Questions about How the News Is Created. 2015. (21st Century Skills Library: Asking Questions about Media Ser.). (ENG., Illus.). 32p. (J). (gr. 4-8). 29.93 *(978-1-63362-489-4(7)*, 206864) Cherry Lake Publishing.

Palser, Barb. Choosing News: What Gets Reported & Why, 1 vol. 2012. (Exploring Media Literacy Ser.). (ENG., Illus.). 80p. (gr. 6-7). pap. 9.10 *(978-0-7565-4537-6(4))*; lib. bdg. 34.65 *(978-0-7565-4517-8(X))* Compass Point Bks. (CPB Grades 4-8).

Pelleschi, Andrea. Olivia & Oscar Build an Opinion Piece. Hu, Caroline, illus. 2014. (Writing Builders Ser.). (ENG.). 32p. (J). (gr. 2-4). pap. 11.94 *(978-1-60357-556-0(1))*; lib. bdg. 25.27 *(978-1-59953-582-1(3))* Norwood Hse. Pr.

Pelusey, Michael & Pelusey, Jane. Newspapers. 2005. (Media Ser.). (Illus.). 32p. (gr. 5-8). lib. bdg. 21.95 *(978-0-7910-8800-5(6)*, Chelsea Hse.) Facts On File, Inc.

Peters, Jennifer. Critical Perspectives on Media Bias. 2017. (J). ***(978-0-7660-9169-6(4))*** Enslow Pubs., Inc.

Pettiford, Rebecca. Reporters. 2015. (Illus.). 24p. (J). lib. bdg. 25.65 *(978-1-62031-159-2(3)*, Bullfrog Bks.) Jump! Inc.

Rustad, Martha E. H. Learning about Fact & Opinion. 2015. (Media Literacy for Kids Ser.). (ENG.). 24p. (gr. k-1). lib. bdg. 26.65 *(978-1-4914-1831-4(1)*, Pebble Plus) Capstone Press of Coughlan Cos.

Saenger, Diana. Everyone Wants My Job! The ABCs of Entertainment Writing. Fife, Bruce, ed. unabr. ed. 2003. (Writing & Publishing Ser.). (Illus.). 159p. (YA). (gr. 8-12). pap. 15.00 *(978-0-941599-53-5(1))* Piccadilly Bks., Ltd.

Sullivan, George. Journalists at Risk: Reporting America's Wars. 2005. (People's History Ser.). (ENG., Illus.). 96p. (J). (gr. 5-12). 33.26 *(978-0-7613-2745-5(2))* Lerner Publishing Group.

Townsend, Beth. Publishing, 1 vol. 2011. (Inside the Industry Ser.). (ENG., Illus.). 112p. (J). (gr. 6-12). lib. bdg. 35.64 *(978-1-61714-803-3(2)*, Essential Library) ABDO Publishing Co.

Wagner, Sy. I Write for the Newspaper. 2003. (Real Readers - Upper Emergent Ser.). (ENG., Illus.). 12p. (gr. 1-2). pap. 5.90 *(978-0-8239-6364-5(0))* Rosen Publishing Group, Inc., The.

JOURNALISM—FICTION

Alger, Horatio. Risen from the Ranks. 2005. 28.95 *(978-1-4218-1458-2(7))*; 292p. pap. 13.95 *(978-1-4218-1558-9(3))* 1st World Publishing, Inc. (1st World Library - Literary Society).

Bauer, Joan. Peeled. 2009. (ENG.). 256p. (YA). (gr. 7-18). 8.99 *(978-0-14-241430-9(1)*, Speak) Penguin Young Readers Group.

Bennardo, Charlotte & Zaman, Natalie. Blonde Ops. 2014. (ENG.). 288p. (YA). (gr. 7). 17.99 *(978-1-250-03039-9(0)*, 9781250030399, St. Martin's Griffin) St. Martin's Pr.

Brennan, Sarah Rees. Untold. Fochesato, Giorgio, illus. 2013. (Lynburn Legacy Ser.: Bk. 2). (ENG.). 384p. (YA). (gr. 7). 18.99 *(978-0-375-87042-3(3)*, Random Hse. Bks. for Young Readers) Random Hse. Children's Bks.

Buchanan, Paul & Buchanan, P. The Last Place I Want to Be, 1 vol. 2009. 176p. (J). pap. 7.99 *(978-0-8254-2408-3(9))* Kregel Pubns.

Butler, Dori Hillestad. The Truth about Truman School, 1 vol. (ENG.). (J). (gr. 3-7). 2009. 192p. pap. 7.99 *(978-0-8075-8096-7(1))* 2008. (Illus.). 176p. lib. bdg. 15.99 *(978-0-8075-8095-0(3))* Whitman, Albert & Co.

Caroll, Robin. Samantha Sanderson at the Movies, 1 vol. 2014. (FaithGirlz / Samantha Sanderson Ser.). (ENG.). 272p. (J). pap. 8.99 *(978-0-310-74245-6(5))* Zonderkidz.

—Samantha Sanderson on the Scene, 1 vol. 2014. (FaithGirlz / Samantha Sanderson Ser.). (ENG.). 256p. (J). pap. 8.99 *(978-0-310-74247-0(1))* Zonderkidz.

Clark, Sherryl. Kim's Fake Cake Bake. McKenzie, Heath, illus. 2015. (J). pap. *(978-1-4966-0256-5(0))* Capstone Classroom.

Clement-Moore, Rosemary. Hell Week. 2009. (Maggie Quinn: Girl vs Evil Ser.). (ENG.). 336p. (YA). (gr. 9). pap. 9.99 *(978-0-385-73415-8(8)*, Delacorte Bks. for Young Readers) Random Hse. Children's Bks.

Crane, Cheri J. Moment of Truth: A Novel. 2005. 238p. (YA). *(978-1-59156-727-1(0))* Covenant Communications.

Dairman, Tara. All Four Stars. 2014. (All Four Stars Ser.: Bk. 1). (ENG.). 288p. (J). (gr. 3-7). 16.99 *(978-0-399-16252-7(6)*, G.P. Putnam's Sons Books for Young Readers) Penguin Young Readers Group.

—The Stars of Summer. 2015. (All Four Stars Ser.: Bk. 2). (ENG.). 336p. (J). (gr. 3-7). 16.99 *(978-0-399-17069-0(3)*, G.P. Putnam's Sons Books for Young Readers) Penguin Young Readers Group.

—Stars So Sweet. 2016. (All Four Stars Ser.: Bk. 3). (ENG.). 288p. (J). (gr. 3-7). 16.99 *(978-1-101-99648-5(X)*, G.P. Putnam's Sons Books for Young Readers) Penguin Young Readers Group.

Devlin, Calla. Right Where You Left Me. 2017. (ENG., Illus.). 256p. (YA). (gr. 9). 17.99 ***(978-1-4814-8699-6(3)***, Atheneum Bks. for Young Readers) Simon & Schuster Children's Publishing.

Doktorski, Jennifer Salvato. Famous Last Words. 2013. (ENG.). 288p. (YA). (gr. 7). 17.99 *(978-0-8050-9367-4(2)*, 9780805093674, Holt, Henry & Co. Bks. For Young Readers) Holt, Henry & Co.

Duff, Hilary. Devoted: An Elixir Novel. 2012. (Elixir Ser.). (ENG.). 368p. (YA). (gr. 9). pap. 9.99 *(978-1-4424-0856-2(1)*, Simon & Schuster Bks. For Young Readers) Simon & Schuster Bks. For Young Readers.

—True: An Elixir Novel. (Elixir Ser.). (ENG., 304p. (YA). (gr. 7). 2014. Illus.). pap. 9.99 *(978-1-4424-0858-6(8))* 2013. 17.99 *(978-1-4424-0857-9(X))* Simon & Schuster Bks. For Young Readers. (Simon & Schuster Bks. For Young Readers).

Feinstein, John. Change-Up. 2010. (Sports Beat Ser.). (ENG.). 336p. (J). (gr. 5). 8.99 *(978-0-375-84759-2(6)*, Yearling) Random Hse. Children's Bks.

—Cover-Up: Mystery at the Super Bowl. 2008. (Sports Beat Ser.). (ENG.). 320p. (J). (gr. 5). 7.99 *(978-0-440-42205-1(1)*, Yearling) Random Hse. Children's Bks.

—Last Shot - Mystery at the Final Four. 2006. (Sports Beat Ser.). (ENG.). 272p. (J). (gr. 7-9). reprint ed. per. 8.99 *(978-0-553-49460-0(0)*, Yearling) Random Hse. Children's Bks.

—Vanishing Act: Mystery at the U. S. Open. 2008. (Sports Beat Ser.). (ENG.). 304p. (J). (gr. 3-7). 7.99 *(978-0-440-42125-2(X)*, Yearling) Random Hse. Children's Bks.

J
K
L

Frampton, David. Beastie ABC. Frampton, David, illus. Date not set. (Illus.). 32p. (J). (gr. -1-1). pap. 5.99 *(978-0-06-443653-3(5))* HarperCollins Pubs.

Goo, Maurene. Since You Asked... 2013. (YA). pap. *(978-0-545-44822-2(0))*; (ENG.). 272p. (J). (gr. 7). 17.99 *(978-0-545-44821-5(2))* Scholastic, Inc. (Scholastic Pr.).

Halliday, Gemma. Social Suicide. 2012. (Deadly Cool Ser.: 2). (ENG.). 288p. (YA). (gr. 8). pap. 8.99 *(978-0-06-200332-4(1)*, HarperTeen) HarperCollins Pubs.

Hutchins, Hazel J. & Hutchins, Hazel. Robyn Makes the News, 1 vol. Cathcart, Yvonne, illus. 2003. (Formac First Novels Ser.: 27). (ENG.). 64p. (J). (gr. 1-5). 4.95 *(978-0-88780-593-6(0)*, 9780887805936) Formac Publishing Co., Ltd. CAN. Dist: Casemate Pubs. & Bk. Distributors, LLC.

Ingold, Jeanette. Paper Daughter. 2013. (ENG.). 224p. (YA). (gr. 7). pap. 7.99 *(978-0-544-10484-6(6))* Houghton Mifflin Harcourt Publishing Co.

Kraft, Erik P. Lenny & Mel after-School Confidential. Kraft, Erik P., illus. 2012. (Lenny & Mel Ser.). (ENG., Illus.). 64p. (J). (gr. 2-5). pap. 6.99 *(978-1-4424-6314-1(7)*, Simon & Schuster/Paula Wiseman Bks.) Simon & Schuster/Paula Wiseman Bks.

Kunze, Lauren & Onur, Rina. Rivals. 2012. (Ivy Ser.: 3). (ENG.). 384p. (YA). (gr. 9). 16.99 *(978-0-06-196049-9(7)*, Greenwillow Bks.) HarperCollins Pubs.

Meddaugh, Susan. Martha Speaks: Martha's Nose for News (chapter Book) 2013. (Martha Speaks Ser.). (ENG., Illus.). 96p. (J). (gr. 1-4). 14.99 *(978-0-544-13567-3(9))* Houghton Mifflin Harcourt Publishing Co.

—Nose for News. 2013. (Martha Speaks Ser.). (ENG., Illus.). 96p. (J). (gr. 1-4). pap. 5.99 *(978-0-544-08572-5(8))* Houghton Mifflin Harcourt Publishing Co.

Mendle, Jane. My Ultimate Sister Disaster: A Novel. 2010. (ENG.). 208p. (YA). (gr. 7-18). pap. 18.99 *(978-0-312-36904-0(2)*, 9780312369040, St. Martin's Griffin) St. Martin's Pr.

Messina, Lynn. Savvy Girl. 2008. (ENG., Illus.). 272p. (YA). (gr. 7-18). pap. 15.99 *(978-0-15-206161-6(4))* Houghton Mifflin Harcourt Publishing Co.

Miller-Lachmann, Lyn. Gringolandia. 2009. (ENG.). 288p. (YA). (gr. 9-18). 18.95 *(978-1-931896-49-8(6))* Curbstone Pr.

Moore, Stephanie Perry. Truth & Nothing But. 2014. (Sharp Sisters Ser.: 4). (ENG.). 160p. (YA). (gr. 6-12). pap. 7.95 *(978-1-4677-4489-8(1)*, Darby Creek); lib. bdg. 27.93 *(978-1-4677-3727-2(5))* Lerner Publishing Group.

Nagda, Ann Whitehead. The Valentine Cat. Roth, Stephanie, illus. 2008. (ENG.). 32p. (J). (gr. 2-5). 16.95 *(978-0-8234-2123-7(6))* Holiday Hse., Inc.

Paige, D. M. Going to Press. (Opportunity Ser.). (ENG.). 104p. (YA). (gr. 6-12). 2015. 34.65 *(978-1-4677-6016-4(1)*, Lerner Digital) 2013. pap. 7.95 *(978-1-4677-1495-2(X)*, Darby Creek) 2013. lib. bdg. 27.93 *(978-1-4677-1373-3(2)*, Darby Creek) Lerner Publishing Group.

Peet, Mal. The Penalty. 2016. (ENG.). 272p. (J). (gr. 7). pap. 8.99 *(978-0-7636-8747-2(2))* Candlewick Pr.

Pratchett, Terry. The Truth. 2014. (Discworld Ser.: 25). (gr. 5-8). 20.85 *(978-0-613-57290-3(4)*, Turtleback) Turtleback Bks.

Sacks, Nathan. The Big Fix. 2014. (Bareknuckle Ser.). 112p. (YA). (gr. 6-12). lib. bdg. 27.93 *(978-1-4677-1459-4(3)*, Darby Creek) Lerner Publishing Group.

Stilton, Geronimo. Cavemice: Get the Scoop, Geronimo! 2015. (Geronimo Stilton Cavemice Ser.: 9). (ENG., Illus.). 128p. (J). (gr. 2-5). pap. 6.99 *(978-0-545-83550-3(X)*, Scholastic Paperbacks) Scholastic, Inc.

—I'm Too Fond of My Fur! Wolf, Matt, illus. 2004. (Geronimo Stilton Ser.: No. 4). 116p. (J). lib. bdg. 10.00 *(978-1-4242-0698-8(7))* Fitzgerald Bks.

—It's Halloween, You 'Fraidy Mouse! Wolf, Matt, illus. 2004. 113p. (J). lib. bdg. 10.00 *(978-1-4242-0280-5(9))* Fitzgerald Bks.

—Lost Treasure of the Emerald Eye. Wolf, Matt, illus. 2004. (Geronimo Stilton Ser.: No. 1). 116p. (J). lib. bdg. 10.00 *(978-1-4242-0695-7(2))* Fitzgerald Bks.

—The Mona Mousa Code. Wolf, Matt, illus. 2005. (Geronimo Stilton Ser.: No. 15). 113p. (J). lib. bdg. 10.00 *(978-1-4242-0284-3(1))* Fitzgerald Bks.

—The Phantom of the Subway. Wolf, Matt, illus. 2004. (Geronimo Stilton Ser.: No. 13). 112p. (J). lib. bdg. 10.00 *(978-1-4242-0282-9(5))* Fitzgerald Bks.

—Valentine's Day Disaster. Keys, Larry et al, illus. 2006. (Geronimo Stilton Ser.: No. 23). 122p. (J). lib. bdg. 18.46 *(978-1-4242-0292-8(2))* Fitzgerald Bks.

Stilton, Geronimo, et al. Get the Scoop, Geronimo! Facciotto, Giuseppe & Costa, Alessandro, illus. 2015. 113p. (J). ***(978-1-5182-0417-3(1))*** Scholastic, Inc.

Vernick, Audrey. Screaming at the Ump. 2014. (ENG.). 272p. (J). (gr. 5-7). 16.99 *(978-0-544-25208-0(X)*, Clarion Bks.) Houghton Mifflin Harcourt Trade & Reference Pubs.

Whybrow, Ian. Dear Little Wolf. Ross, Tony, illus. 2005. (Little Wolf Adventures Ser.). 64p. (gr. 3-6). pap., lib. bdg. 14.95 *(978-0-87614-902-7(6))* Lerner Publishing Group.

Williams, Maiya. Kaboom Academy. 2016. (ENG.). 240p. (J). (gr. 5). 6.99 *(978-0-449-81615-8(X)*, Yearling) Random Hse. Children's Bks.

Winerip, Michael. Adam Canfield: The Last Reporter. 2009. (Adam Canfield of the Slash Ser.: 3). (ENG., Illus.). 384p. (J). (gr. 3-7). 16.99 *(978-0-7636-2342-5(3))* Candlewick Pr.

—Adam Canfield of the Slash. 2005. (Adam Canfield of the Slash Ser.: 1). (ENG., Illus.). 336p. (J). (gr. 3-7). 15.99 *(978-0-7636-2340-1(7))* Candlewick Pr.

—Adam Canfield the Last Reporter. 2010. (Adam Canfield of the Slash Ser.: 3). (ENG., Illus.). 384p. (J). (gr. 3-7). 7.99 *(978-0-7636-4838-1(8))* Candlewick Pr.

—Adam Canfield Watch Your Back! 2009. (Adam Canfield of the Slash Ser.: 2). (ENG., Illus.). 352p. (J). (gr. 3-7). 7.99 *(978-0-7636-4412-3(9))* Candlewick Pr.

Wise, Rachel. Cast Your Ballot! 2013. (Dear Know-It-All Ser.: 9). (ENG., Illus.). 160p. (J). (gr. 3-7). 15.99 *(978-1-4424-8793-2(3))*; pap. 5.99 *(978-1-4424-8792-5(5))* Simon Spotlight. (Simon Spotlight).

—Texting 1, 2, 3. 2013. (Dear Know-It-All Ser.: 8). (ENG., Illus.). 160p. (J). (gr. 3-7). 16.99 *(978-1-4424-7520-5(X))*; pap. 6.99 *(978-1-4424-7519-9(6))* Simon Spotlight. (Simon Spotlight).

JOURNALISM—UNITED STATES

Bausum, Ann. Muckrakers: How Ida Tarbell, Upton Sinclair, & Lincoln Steffens Helped Expose Scandal, Inspire Reform, & Invent Investigative Journalism. 2007. (ENG., Illus.). 112p. (J). (gr. 5-18). 32.90 *(978-1-4263-0138-4(3))*; 21.95 *(978-1-4263-0137-7(5))* National Geographic Society. (National Geographic Children's Bks.).

Christensen, Bonnie. The Daring Nellie Bly: America's Star Reporter. 2009. (ENG., Illus.). 32p. (J). (gr. k-3). pap. 7.99 *(978-0-375-85118-6(6)*, Dragonfly Bks.) Random Hse. Children's Bks.

Engdahl, Sylvia. Blogs. 2008. (Current Controversies Ser.). (ENG., Illus.). 224p. (gr. 10-12). lib. bdg. 46.40 *(978-0-7377-3954-1(1))*; pap. 32.00 *(978-0-7377-3955-8(X))* Cengage Gale. (Greenhaven Pr., Inc.).

Fromowitz, Lori. 12 Great Moments That Changed Newspaper History. 2015. (ENG., Illus.). 32p. (J). *(978-1-63235-025-1(4))* Pr. Room Editions LLC.

Gallagher, Aileen. The Muckrakers: American Journalism During the Age of Reform. 2009. (Progressive Movement 1900-1920: Efforts to Reform America's New Industrial Society Ser.). 32p. (gr. 3-4). 47.90 *(978-1-60854-173-7(8))* Rosen Publishing Group, Inc., The.

Hall, Homer L. High School Journalism. 2009. (High School Journalism Ser.). (ENG.). 464p. (YA). 159.90 *(978-1-61513-265-2(1))*; 352p. 159.90 *(978-1-61513-264-5(3))* Rosen Publishing Group, Inc., The.

—High School Journalism Teacher's Workbook & Guide. 2009. (High School Journalism Ser.). 136p. 53.00 *(978-1-61513-266-9(X))* Rosen Publishing Group, Inc., The.

—Student's Workbook for Junior High Journalism. (Junior High Journalism Ser.). 88p. 2009. 53.00 *(978-1-61513-874-6(9))* 2003. (ENG., Illus.). (YA). pap., wbk. ed. 26.50 *(978-0-8239-4046-2(2))* Rosen Publishing Group, Inc., The.

Hall, Homer L. & Aimone, Logan. Student's Workbook for Junior High Journalism. 2010. (ENG.). 92p. (J). pap. 26.50 *(978-1-4042-8188-2(6))* Rosen Publishing Group, Inc., The.

Robinson, Tom. The Evolution of News Reporting, 1 vol. 2010. (Essential Viewpoints Set 5 Ser.). (ENG.). 112p. (J). (gr. 6-12). lib. bdg. 35.64 *(978-1-61613-521-8(2)*, Essential Library) ABDO Publishing Co.

JOURNALISM—VOCATIONAL GUIDANCE

Alagna, Magdalena. War Correspondents: Life under Fire. 2005. (Extreme Careers Ser.). (Illus.). 64p. (YA). (gr. 5-8). 31.95 *(978-0-8239-3798-1(4))* Rosen Publishing Group, Inc., The.

Ferguson Publishing Staff, creator. Careers in Focus. 2007. (Careers in Focus Ser.). (Illus.). 192p. (gr. 6-12). 32.95 *(978-0-8160-6573-8(X)*, Ferguson Publishing Co.) Facts On File, Inc.

Reeves, Diane Lindsey. TV Journalist. 2008. (Virtual Apprentice Ser.). (Illus.). 64p. (gr. 4-9). per. 9.95 *(978-0-8160-7553-9(0)*, Checkmark Bks.) Facts On File, Inc.

Roberts, Laura. Careers in Digital Media. 2017. (Exploring Careers Ser.). (ENG.). 80p. (YA). (gr. 5-12). ***(978-1-68282-196-1(X))*** ReferencePoint Pr., Inc.

Thomas, William David. Journalist. 2009. (Cool Careers: on the Go Ser.). 32p. (gr. 5-8). pap. 10.50 *(978-1-4339-0168-3(4))*; (YA). lib. bdg. 26.00 *(978-1-4339-0004-4(1))* Stevens, Gareth Publishing LLLP.

JOURNALISTIC PHOTOGRAPHY

see Photojournalism

JOURNALISTS

Anderson, Kirsten. Who Was Robert Ripley? 2015. (Who Was... ? Ser.). lib. bdg. 16.00 *(978-0-606-36596-3(6))* Turtleback Bks.

Anderson, Kirsten & dePaola, Tomie. Who Was Robert Ripley? Foley, Tim & Harrison, Nancy, illus. 2015. (Who Was? Ser.). (ENG.). 112p. (J). (gr. 3-7). 5.99 *(978-0-448-48298-9(3)*, Grosset & Dunlap) Penguin Young Readers Group.

Bankston, John. Nellie Bly. 2011. (Women of Achievement Ser.). (Illus.). 128p. (gr. 6-12). 35.00 *(978-1-60413-908-2(0)*, Chelsea Hse.) Facts On File, Inc.

Barbara Walters. 2010. (Women of Achievement Ser.). (Illus.). 128p. (J). (gr. 6-12). 35.00 *(978-1-60413-686-9(3)*, Chelsea Hse.) Facts On File, Inc.

Caravantes, Peggy. A Great & Sublime Fool: The Story of Mark Twain. 2010. (World Writers Ser.). (Illus.). 176p. (YA). (gr. 8-18). lib. bdg. 28.95 *(978-1-59935-088-2(2))* Reynolds, Morgan Inc.

Castaldo, Nancy F. The Race Around the World (Totally True Adventures) Lowe, Wesley, illus. 2015. (Totally True Adventures Ser.). (ENG.). 112p. (J). (gr. 2-5). 4.99 *(978-0-553-52278-5(7)*, Random Hse. Bks. for Young Readers) Random Hse. Children's Bks.

Christensen, Bonnie. The Daring Nellie Bly: America's Star Reporter. 2009. (ENG., Illus.). 32p. (J). (gr. k-3). pap. 7.99 *(978-0-375-85118-6(6)*, Dragonfly Bks.) Random Hse. Children's Bks.

Dublin, Anne. June Callwood: A Life of Action, 1 vol. 2007. (ENG., Illus.). 156p. (J). (gr. 3-12). pap. 14.95 *(978-1-897187-14-2(9))* Second Story Pr. CAN. Dist: Orca Bk. Pubs. USA.

Gitlin, Martin. Joseph Pulitzer: Historic Newspaper Publisher, 1 vol. 2009. (Publishing Pioneers Ser.). (ENG., Illus.). 112p. (J). (gr. 6-12). lib. bdg. 35.64 *(978-1-60453-765-9(5)*, Essential Library) ABDO Publishing Co.

Higgins, Melissa. Julian Assange: WikiLeaks Founder, 1 vol. 2011. (Essential Lives Set 7 Ser.). (ENG., Illus.). 112p. (J). (gr. 6-12). lib. bdg. 35.64 *(978-1-61783-001-3(1))* ABDO Publishing Co.

Hoge, Robert. Ugly. Robinson, Keith, illus. 2016. (ENG.). 208p. (J). (gr. 3-7). 16.99 *(978-0-425-28775-0(0)*, Viking Books for Young Readers) Penguin Young Readers Group.

Hunter-Gault, Charlayne. To the Mountaintop: My Journey Through the Civil Rights Movement. 2014. (New York Times Ser.). (ENG., Illus.). 224p. (YA). (gr. 7). pap. 12.99 *(978-1-250-04062-6(0)*, 9781250040626) Square Fish.

Marshall Cavendish. The Khmer Rouge. 2011. (Great Escapes Ser.). (Illus.). 80p. (J). (gr. 6). 34.21 *(978-1-60870-474-3(2))* Marshall Cavendish Corp.

McCully, Emily Arnold. Ida M. Tarbell: The Woman Who Challenged Big Business-and Won! 2014. (ENG., Illus.). 288p. (YA). (gr. 7). 18.99 *(978-0-547-29092-8(6)*, Clarion Bks.) Houghton Mifflin Harcourt Trade & Reference Pubs.

McKissack, Patricia C. & McKissack, Fredrick L. Ida B. Wells-Barnett: Fighter for Justice. 2013. (Famous African Americans Ser.). 24p. (J). (gr. k-3). pap. 7.95 *(978-1-4644-0198-5(5)*, Enslow Elementary); (Illus.). 22.60 *(978-0-7660-4108-0(5))* Enslow Pubs., Inc.

Noyes, Deborah. Ten Days a Madwoman: The Daring Life & Turbulent Times of the Original Girl Reporter Nellie Bly. 2016. (ENG., Illus.). 144p. (J). (gr. 5). 18.99 *(978-0-8037-4017-4(4)*, Viking Books for Young Readers) Penguin Young Readers Group.

Pingelton, Timothy J. A Student's Guide to Ernest Hemingway. 2005. (Understanding Literature Ser.). (Illus.). 160p. (YA). (gr. 7-13). lib. bdg. 29.27 *(978-0-7660-2431-1(8))* Enslow Pubs., Inc.

Reef, Catherine. Ernest Hemingway: A Writer's Life. 2009. (ENG., Illus.). 192p. (J). (gr. 5-7). 20.00 *(978-0-618-98705-4(3))* Houghton Mifflin Harcourt Publishing Co.

Robson, David. Soledad O'Brien. 2009. (Transcending Race in America: Biographies of Biracial Achievers Ser.). (Illus.). 64p. (J). (gr. 5-18). pap. 9.95 *(978-1-4222-1631-6(4))* Mason Crest.

Rubini, Julie K. Missing Millie Benson: The Secret Case of the Nancy Drew Ghostwriter & Journalist. 2015. (Biographies for Young Readers Ser.). (ENG., Illus.). 136p. (J). (gr. 1-6). 28.95 *(978-0-8214-2183-3(2))* Ohio Univ. Pr.

Sauerwein, Stan. Ma Murray: The Story of Canada's Crusty Queen of Publishing. 2003. (ENG., Illus.). 144p. per. *(978-1-55153-979-9(9))* Heritage Hse.

Scarbrough, Mary Hertz. African American Writers & Journalists. 2012. pap. *(978-1-4222-2389-5(2))* Mason Crest.

—African American Writers & Journalists. Hill, Marc Lamont, ed. 2012. (Major Black Contributions from Emancipation to Civil Rights Ser.). 64p. (J). (gr. 5). 22.95 *(978-1-4222-2376-5(0))* Mason Crest.

Somervill, Barbara A. Ida Tarbell: Pioneer Investigative Reporter. 2004. (World Writers Ser.). (Illus.). 112p. (YA). (gr. 6-12). 23.95 *(978-1-883846-87-9(0)*, First Biographies) Reynolds, Morgan Inc.

Towsend, Dana. Lonely Orphan Girl: The Story of Nellie Bly. 2005. (Illus.). 32p. (J). *(978-0-7367-2902-4(X))* Zaner-Bloser, Inc.

Whitelaw, Nancy. Joseph Pulitzer & the New York World. rev. exp. ed. 2004. (Makers of the Media Ser.). (Illus.). 128p. (J). lib. bdg. 21.95 *(978-1-931798-36-5(2))* Reynolds, Morgan Inc.

Wint, Eleanor. Marcus Teaches Us. 2012. 36p. pap. 15.50 *(978-1-4669-5620-9(8))* Trafford Publishing.

Zuchora-Walske, Christine. The Dust Bowl: A History Perspectives Book. 2013. (Perspectives Library). (ENG., Illus.). 32p. (J). (gr. 4-8). 28.50 *(978-1-62431-417-9(1)*, 202788); pap. 14.21 *(978-1-62431-493-3(7)*, 202790) Cherry Lake Publishing.

JOURNEYS

see Voyages and Travels; Voyages around the World

JUAREZ, BENITO, 1806-1872

Flor Ada, Alma & Campoy, F. Isabel, contrib. by. Sonrisas. (Literature Collection of Puertas Al Sol Ser.). (SPA.). 32p. (J). (gr. k-6). pap. 13.95 *(978-1-59437-701-3(4))* Santillana USA Publishing Co., Inc.

Kaplan, Leslie. Cinco de Mayo. 2003. (Library of Holidays Ser.). (Illus.). 24p. (J). (gr. 4-7). lib. bdg. 22.60 *(978-0-8239-6662-2(3)*, PowerKids Pr.) Rosen Publishing Group, Inc., The.

Kaplan, Leslie C. Cinco de Mayo. 2009. (Library of Holidays Ser.). 24p. (gr. 2-3). 42.50 *(978-1-60853-708-2(0)*, PowerKids Pr.) Rosen Publishing Group, Inc., The.

MacMillan, Dianne M. Mexican Independence Day & Cinco de Mayo. rev. ed. 2008. (Best Holiday Bks.). (Illus.). 48p. (J). (gr. 4-7). lib. bdg. 25.27 *(978-0-7660-3044-2(X))* Enslow Pubs., Inc.

JUDAISM

see also Jews; Sabbath; Synagogues

Abraham, Michelle Shapiro. The Be a Mensch Campaign. 2004. (gr. 4-6). stu. ed. 5.95 *(978-0-8074-0743-1(7)*, 571206); pap., tchr. ed., tchr.'s training gde. ed. 11.95 *(978-0-8074-0745-5(3)*, 208056) URJ Pr.

Abrams, Judith Z. The Secret World of Kabbalah. 2006. (Illus.). 80p. (J). (gr. 5-9). per. 9.95 *(978-1-58013-224-4(3)*, Kar-Ben Publishing) Lerner Publishing Group.

Adelman, Penina, et al. The JGirl's Guide: The Young Jewish Woman's Handbook for Coming of Age. 2005. (ENG.). 240p. pap. 16.99 *(978-1-58023-215-9(9)*, 9781580232159, Jewish Lights Publishing) LongHill Partners, Inc.

Adler, David A. The Story of Hanukkah. Weber, Jill, illus. 2012. (ENG.). 32p. (J). (gr. -1-2). pap. 6.99 *(978-0-8234-2547-1(9))* Holiday Hse., Inc.

Ahmedi, Waqar, et al. World Religions: Judaism, Christianity & Islam. 2017. (ENG.). 120p. (J). (gr. 6-9). pap. 29.99 ***(978-0-00-822768-5(3))*** HarperCollins Pubs. Ltd. GBR. Dist: Independent Pubs. Group.

Aman, Israa. The Monotheistic Faiths: Judaism, Christianity, & Islam, Vol. 8. Pecastaing, Camille, ed. 2016. (Understanding Islam Ser.: Vol. 8). (ENG., Illus.). 112p. (J). (gr. 7-12). 25.95 *(978-1-4222-3674-1(9))* Mason Crest.

Amar, Elisheva. One Word Too Many: Stories for Kids about the Life Changing Impact of Words. 2008. 119p. 26.99 *(978-1-59826-210-0(6))* Feldheim Pubs.

Auerbach, Annie. Eight Chanukah Lights. Iwai, Melissa, illus. 2005. (ENG.). 18p. (J). 10.95 *(978-1-58117-326-0(1)*, Intervisual/Piggy Toes) Bendon, Inc.

Bardack, Amy & Naditch, Beth, eds. Halleli Nafshi: A Weekday Siddur for Children. 2011. (Illus.). 144p. 25.00 *(978-0-9836623-2-7(0))* Solomon Schechter Day Schl. of Greater Boston.

Bernay, Emma. Judaism. 2008. (Introducing Issues with Opposing Viewpoints Ser.). (ENG., Illus.). 144p. (gr. 10-12). 42.00 *(978-0-7377-3976-3(2)*, Greenhaven Pr., Inc.) Cengage Gale.

Bernstein, Jordan. The Bible According to Grandpa. Doehring, Aurora, illus. 2011. 34p. pap. 6.50 *(978-0-9743414-3-9(6))* Adventure in Discovery.

Blake, Philip. We Are Jews. 2016. (ENG., Illus.). 32p. (J). (gr. 4-6). pap. 11.99 *(978-1-4451-3892-3(1)*, Franklin Watts) Hachette Children's Group GBR. Dist: Hachette Bk. Group.

Blitz, Shmuel. ArtScroll Children's Book of Berachos: [Sefer Ha-Berakhot Sheli]. Katz, Tova, illus. 2011. (ENG & HEB.). 48p. (J). *(978-1-4226-1170-8(1))* Mesorah Pubns., Ltd.

Blitz, Shmuel & Katz, Tova. Artscroll Children's Machzor: [ha-Mahazor Ha-Rishon: Rosh Ha-Shanah Ve-Yom Kipur]. 2009. (HEB., Illus.). 96p. *(978-1-4226-0910-1(3))* Mesorah Pubns., Ltd.

Bob, Steven M. & Howard, Lisa Bob. The Bar & Bat Mitzvah Manual: Six Steps to a Meaningful Family Celebration. 2008. (J). *(978-0-87441-812-5(7))* Behrman Hse., Inc.

Bobbie, Match. Havdallah Three Stars in the Sky. 2012. (ENG.). (J). pap. 14.99 *(978-1-4675-2709-5(2))* Independent Pub.

Borlasca, Hector, illus. It's Too Crowded in Here! And Other Jewish Folktales. 2010. 64p. (J). pap. 7.95 *(978-0-87441-850-7(X))* Behrman Hse., Inc.

Botnick, Julie & Linden, Becca. Min Ha'aretz: Making Meaning from Our Food. 2016. *(978-0-87441-938-2(7))* Behrman Hse., Inc.

Cato, Vivienne. The Torah & Judaism. 2003. 30p. (J). lib. bdg. 16.95 *(978-1-58340-244-3(6))* Black Rabbit Bks.

Ccar, ed. Mishkan T'filah for Youth, 2 vols., Vol. 1. 2013. (J). *(978-0-88123-201-1(7))* Central Conference of American Rabbis/CCAR Pr.

Chaikin, Miriam. Menorahs, Mezuzas, & Other Jewish Symbols. Weihs, Erika, illus. 2003. (ENG.). 112p. (J). (gr. 5-7). pap. 7.95 *(978-0-618-37835-7(9))* Houghton Mifflin Harcourt Publishing Co.

Chait, Baruch. The Terrifying Trap of the Bad Middos Pirates, 2 vols. Pollack, Gadi, illus. (Good Middos Ser.). 96p. 25.99 *(978-1-58330-664-2(1))* Feldheim Pubs.

Cisner, Naftali. Get Ready for Shabbos with Mendel. Cisner, Naftali, illus. 2003. (Illus.). 10p. (J). bds. 5.95 *(978-1-880582-03-9(1))* Judaica Pr., Inc., The.

Clement, Janet. Jewish Alphabet, 1 vol. Rodriguez, Albert G., illus. 2006. (ENG.). 32p. (J). (gr. k-3). 16.99 *(978-1-58980-414-2(7))* Pelican Publishing Co., Inc.

Cone, Molly. Hello, Hello, Are You There, God? Kaye, Rosalind Charney, illus. rev. ed. 2004. viii, 55p. (gr. k-3). pap. 13.95 *(978-0-8074-0648-9(1)*, 102553) URJ Pr.

Cook, Esky. Jewish Artwork by Esky: Children, Borders, Hebrew Alphabets. (Illus.). 128p. (Orig.). (J). (gr. 1-8). pap. 19.95 *(978-1-885143-02-0(8))* Preferred Enterprises.

—Jewish Artwork by Esky: Complete Set of Jewish Graphics. (Illus.). 384p. (Orig.). (J). (gr. 1-8). pap. 59.95 *(978-1-885143-00-6(1))* Preferred Enterprises.

—Jewish Artwork by Esky: Mitzvot, Animals, Food & Brachot. Whitman, Jonathan, ed. (Illus.). 128p. (Orig.). (J). (gr. 1-8). pap. 19.95 *(978-1-885143-03-7(6))* Preferred Enterprises.

Dick, Judy. Our Community. 2012. (J). *(978-0-87441-861-3(5))* Behrman Hse., Inc.

—Sacred Time: The Jewish Calendar & Life Cycle. 2012. (J). *(978-0-87441-863-7(1))* Behrman Hse., Inc.

—The Seder Activity Book. Dick, Judy, illus. 2004. (Illus.). 39p. (gr. k-3). pap., act. bk. ed. 9.95 *(978-0-8074-0728-8(3)*, 101097) URJ Pr.

Dicker, Katie & Sheldon, Sam. I Belong to the Jewish Faith. 2009. (I Belong Ser.). (Illus.). 24p. (J). (ENG.). pap. 8.25 *(978-1-4358-8622-3(4)*, 1300557, PowerKids Pr.); (gr. 1-4). lib. bdg. 22.60 *(978-1-4358-3034-9(2)*, 1300557) Rosen Publishing Group, Inc., The.

Dickmann, Nancy. Hanukkah, 1 vol. 2010. (Holidays & Festivals Ser.). (ENG., Illus.). 24p. (gr. -1-1). pap. 6.29 *(978-1-4329-4071-3(6)*, Acorn) Heinemann-Raintree.

Dorling Kindersley Publishing Staff. DK Eyewitness Books: Judaism. 2016. (DK Eyewitness Bks.). (ENG., Illus.). 64p. (J). (gr. 3-7). pap. 9.99 *(978-1-4654-5176-7(5)*, DK Children) Dorling Kindersley Publishing, Inc.

—Judaism. 2016. (DK Eyewitness Bks.). (ENG., Illus.). 64p. (J). (gr. 3-7). lib. bdg. 19.99 *(978-1-4654-5177-4(3)*, DK Children) Dorling Kindersley Publishing, Inc.

Dowley, Tim. The Kregel Pictorial Guide to the Tabernacle, 1 vol. Parry, Alan, illus. 2003. (Kregel Pictorial Guide Ser.). 32p. pap. 11.99 *(978-0-8254-2468-7(2))* Kregel Pubns.

Ehrlich, Carl S. Judaism. 2009. (Understanding Religions Ser.). (YA). (gr. 7-12). lib. bdg. 34.60 *(978-1-4358-5622-6(8))* Rosen Publishing Group, Inc., The.

Elie Wiesel's Night. 2009. (Bloom's Guides). 136p. (C). (gr. 9-18). 30.00 *(978-1-60413-198-7(5)*, Chelsea Hse.) Facts On File, Inc.

Feinstein, Edward. Tough Questions Jews Ask: A Young Adult's Huide to Building a Jewish Life. 2nd ed. 2012. (ENG.). 160p. (YA). pap. 17.99 *(978-1-58023-454-2(2)*, 9781580234542, Jewish Lights Publishing) LongHill Partners, Inc.

Finkelman, Shimon. The Story of Reb Moshe: A Biography for Young Readers. 2015. (Illus.). 308p. (J). ***(978-1-4226-1665-9(7)***, ArtScroll Series) Mesorah Pubns., Ltd.

Ganeri, Anita. Jewish Stories. 2014. (Storyteller Ser.). (ENG., Illus.). 32p. (J). (gr. 2-4). pap. 10.99 *(978-1-78388-010-2(4))* Tulip Books GBR. Dist: Independent Pubs. Group.

Gerner, Katy. Judaism. 2008. (Religions Around the World Ser.). 32p. (gr. 3-18). 18.56 *(978-0-7614-3170-1(5)*, Benchmark Bks.) Marshall Cavendish Corp.

Gevirtz, Gila. Count Me In: Jewish Wisdom in Action. 2005. (Illus.). 143p. (J). *(978-0-87441-194-2(7))* Behrman Hse., Inc.

Ginsburgh, Judy. The Complete Jewish Songbook for Children , Vol. 2. 2004. (ENG.). 288p. (gr. k-3). pap. 39.95 *(978-0-8074-0822-3(0)*, 0807408220) Transcontinental Music Pubns.

Glazer, Devorah. A Touch of the High Holidays: A Touch & Feel Book. Seva, illus. 2006. 16p. (J). bds. 7.95 *(978-0-8266-0020-2(4))* Merkos L'Inyonei Chinuch.

Gold, Avie. Pirkei Avos, Vol. 2. Horen, Michael & Halasz, Andras, illus. (J). pap. 12.99 *(978-0-89906-199-3(0)*, PIYP) Mesorah Pubns., Ltd.

Goldner, Harriet. Please, Don't Pass over the Seder Plate: A Haggadah for the Young & Young-at-Heart. 2006. *(978-0-9779676-0-5(3))* Goldner, Harriet LLC.

Graham, Ian. Judaism. (Illus.). 64p. (YA). (gr. 4-18). lib. bdg. 29.95 *(978-1-59389-132-9(6))* Chrysalis Education.

Greenberg, Sidney & Silverman, Morris. Siddurenu. (J). (gr. 3-7). 8.95 *(978-0-87677-099-3(5))* Prayer Bk. Pr., Inc.

Greenwald, Zee. Loving Kindness: Stories of Chessed from Our Sages. 2008. 48p. 17.99 *(978-1-59826-267-4(X))* Feldheim Pubs.

Grinvald, Zeev & Zryl, Laya. Watching My Words: An Illustrated Children's Guide to the Laws of Shemiras Halashon. Baifus, Rut, illus. 2013. 63p. (J). *(978-1-56871-539-1(0))* Menucha Pubs. Inc.

Groner, Judyth & Wikler, Madeline. Thank You, God! A Jewish Child's Book of Prayers. Haas, Shelly, illus. 2003. (ENG.). 32p. (J). (gr. -1-2). pap. 7.95 *(978-1-58013-101-8(8),* Kar-Ben Publishing) Lerner Publishing Group.

Halper, Sharon. To Learn Is to Do: A Tikkun Olam Road Map. Koffsky, Ann D., illus. 2004. vi, 56p. (gr. 4-6). pap. 11.95 *(978-0-8074-0729-5(1),* 123935) URJ Pr.

Hawker, Frances & Taub, Daniel. Judaism in Israel. Campbell, Bruce, photos by. 2009. (ENG., Illus.). 32p. (J). (gr. 3-6). *(978-0-7787-5010-9(8));* pap. *(978-0-7787-5027-7(2))* Crabtree Publishing Co.

Head, Honor. Celebrating Yom Kippur: The Jewish New Year. 2009. (We Love Holidays Ser.). (ENG., Illus.). 24p. (J). (gr. k-5). pap. 8.25 *(978-1-4358-2906-0(9))* Rosen Publishing Group, Inc., The.

Heiligman, Deborah. Celebrate Rosh Hashanah & Yom Kippur: With Honey, Prayers, & the Shofar. 2016. (Holidays Around the World Ser.). (ENG.). 32p. (J). (gr. 2-5). pap. 7.99 *(978-1-4263-2628-8(9),* National Geographic Children's Bks.) National Geographic Society.

Hipps, Amelia. Islam, Christianity, Judaism. 2005. (Introducing Islam Ser.). (Illus.). 112p. (J). lib. bdg. 24.95 *(978-1-59084-698-8(2))* Mason Crest.

Hoffman, Lawrence A. & Wolfson, Ron. What You Will See Inside a Synagogue. Aron, Bill, photos by. 2008. (What You Will See Inside ... Ser.). (ENG., Illus.). 32p. (J). pap. 8.99 *(978-1-59473-256-0(6),* 9781594732560, Skylight Paths Publishing) LongHill Partners, Inc.

Horen, Michael, illus. My Blessings for Food. 2003. (ArtScroll Ser.). (ENG, ARC & HEB.). (J). 49.99 *(978-0-89906-702-5(6),* TCH3) Mesorah Pubns., Ltd.

Jules, Jacqueline. Before We Eat: A Thank You Prayer. Iwai, Melissa, illus. 2010. (ENG.). 12p. (J). (gr. -1-1). 5.95 *(978-0-7613-3954-0(X),* Kar-Ben Publishing) Lerner Publishing Group.

Karesh, Sara E. & Hurvitz, Mitchell M. Encyclopedia of Judaism. 2007. (Encyclopedia of World Religions Ser.). (Illus.). 640p. (C). (gr. 9). per. 21.95 *(978-0-8160-7337-5(6),* Checkmark Bks.) Facts On File, Inc.

Katz, Karen A., et al. What Does Being Jewish Mean? Read-Aloud Responses to Questions Jewish Children Ask about History, Culture, & Religion. 2003. (ENG.). 160p. pap. 12.95 *(978-0-7432-5413-7(9),* Touchstone) Touchstone.

Keene, Michael. Judaism. 2005. (Religions of the World Ser.). (Illus.). 48p. (gr. 5-12). pap. 14.05 *(978-0-8368-5875-4(1));* lib. bdg. 31.00 *(978-0-8368-5869-3(7))* Stevens, Gareth Publishing LLLP. (Gareth Stevens Secondary Library).

Kimmel, Eric A. Bar Mitzvah: A Jewish Boy's Coming of Age. Weihs, Erika, illus. 2004. 143p. (J). (gr. 6-9). reprint ed. pap. 15.00 *(978-0-7567-7261-1(3))* DIANE Publishing Co.

—Wonders & Miracles: A Passover Companion. Kimmel, Eric A., illus. 2004. (Wonders & Miracles Ser.). (ENG., Illus.). 144p. (J). 21.99 *(978-0-439-07175-8(5))* Scholastic, Inc.

Kripke, Dorothy Karp. Let's Talk about God. Tripp, Christine, tr. Tripp, Christine, illus. 2003. (J). 9.95 *(978-1-881283-34-8(8))* Alef Design Group.

Kunda, Shmuel. Boruch Learns His Brochos. Kunda, Shmuel, illus. 2005. (Illus.). 40p. (J). 17.95 *(978-1-932443-41-7(X))* Judaica Pr., Inc., The.

Laurel Corona. Jewish Americans. 2004. (Immigrants in America Ser.). (ENG., Illus.). 112p. (J). 30.85 *(978-1-59018-431-8(9))* Cengage Gale.

Lefcourt, Jack. Four Thousand Years of Jewish History: Then & Now. 2009. 108p. (YA). (gr. 6-18). 16.95 *(978-1-60280-132-5(0))* Ktav Publishing Hse., Inc.

Lehman-Wilzig, Tami. Keeping the Promise: A Torah's Journey. Orback, Craig, illus. 2004. 32p. (J). (ENG.). (gr. k-3). pap. 9.95 *(978-1-58013-118-6(2));* (gr. 1-5). 16.95 *(978-1-58013-117-9(4))* Lerner Publishing Group. (Kar-Ben Publishing).

Leon, Carol Boyd. Dayenu! A Passover Haggadah for Families & Children. Connelly, Gwen, illus. 2008. 32p. (J). (gr. 1-3). 16.95 incl. audio compact disk *(978-1-60280-041-0(3));* pap. 8.95 incl. audio compact disk *(978-1-60280-039-7(1));* spiral bd. 16.95 incl. audio compact disk *(978-1-60280-040-3(5));* bds. 24.95 incl. audio compact disk *(978-1-60280-042-7(1))* Ktav Publishing Hse., Inc.

Levy, Leah. The Waiting Wall. Rosenfeld, D. L. & Leverton, Yossi, eds. 2009. (Illus.). 26p. (J). (gr. -1-1). 12.95 *(978-1-929628-49-0(8))* Hachai Publishing.

Lewinsky, Adam. Judaism. 2017. (J). **(978-1-4222-3820-2(2))** Mason Crest.

Lewis, Andy. Judaism. 2017. (ENG.). 40p. (J). (gr. 6-9). pap. 11.99 **(978-0-00-822771-5(3))** HarperCollins Pubs. Ltd. GBR. Dist: Independent Pubs. Group.

Lewis, Jaime & Katz, Michelle V. Mahazor Katan: Machzor Katan: High Holiday Prayer Book for Families with Young Children. 2012. (ENG & HEB., Illus.). 11p. (J). *(978-0-87441-910-8(7))* Behrman Hse., Inc.

Maalos, text. Baruch & Berel. 2011. (YID.). 21.00 *(978-0-9832102-4-5(1))* Roth Pubs.

Manushkin, Fran. Come, Let Us Be Joyful! The Story of Hava Nagila. Kaye, Rosalind Charney, illus. 2004. (gr. k-3). 13.95 *(978-0-8074-0731-8(3),* 101073) URJ Pr.

Marx, Trish. Sharing Our Homeland: Palestinian & Jewish Children at Summer Peace Camp, 1 vol. Karp, Cindy, illus. 2010. (ENG.). 48p. (J). (gr. 1-6). 19.95 *(978-1-58430-260-5(7))* Lee & Low Bks., Inc.

Merkaz le-Inyene hinukh (Brooklyn, New York, N.Y.) Staff, contrib. by. Hagadah Shel Pesach: Haggadah Shel Pesach for Youth: With Explanatory English Translation & Selected Insights from the Rebbe's Haggadah. 2013. (HEB & ENG., Illus.). 135p. (J). *(978-0-8266-0632-7(6))* Merkos L'Inyonei Chinuch.

Michels, Dia L. Look What I See! Where Can I Be? At the Synagogue. Bowles, Michael J. N., photos by. 2005. (ENG., Illus.). 32p. (J). (gr. -1-3). 9.95 *(978-1-930775-16-9(4))* Platypus Media, L.L.C.

Miller, Woody, illus. Tefilat Haderech: The Traveler's Prayer. 2012. (ENG.). 32p. (J). 17.95 *(978-0-939144-69-3(7))* EKS Publishing Co.

—Tefilat Haderech: The Traveler's Pryaer. 2012. (ENG.). 32p. (J). pap. 10.95 *(978-0-939144-68-6(9))* EKS Publishing Co.

Mrowiec, Katia, et al. God, Yahweh, Allah. 2014. (Illus.). 192p. 19.95 *(978-0-8091-6771-5(9))* Paulist Pr.

Musleah, Rahel & Jarrett, Judy. Apples & Pomegranates: A Family Seder for Rosh Hashanah. 2004. (ENG & HEB., Illus.). 64p. (J). (gr. k-5). pap. 7.95 *(978-1-58013-123-0(9),* Kar-Ben Publishing) Lerner Publishing Group.

Nason, Ruth. The Jewish Faith. 2013. (Start up Religion Ser.). (ENG., Illus.). 32p. (J). (gr. -1-k). pap. 10.99 *(978-0-237-54374-7(5))* Evans Brothers, Ltd. GBR. Dist: Independent Pubs. Group.

Ochs, Carol. Reaching Godward: Voices from Jewish Spiritual Guidance. Kofsky, Ann, illus. 2004. 250p. pap. 14.95 *(978-0-8074-0866-7(2),* 142612) URJ Pr.

Ofanansky, Allison. How It's Made: Torah Scroll. Alpern, Andrew, photos by. 2016. (Illus.). (J). *(978-1-68115-516-6(8))* Behrman Hse., Inc.

Oren, Rony. The Animaged Haggadah. 2012. (ENG., Illus.). 48p. *(978-965-524-118-1(1),* Lambda) Urim Pubns.

Pasachoff, Naomi E. Basic Judaism for Young People Vol. 3: God. (Basic Judaism Ser.). (J). (gr. 6-7). pap. 9.95 *(978-0-87441-425-7(3));* pap., wbk. ed. 5.25 *(978-0-87441-473-8(3))* Behrman Hse., Inc.

Plaut, W. Gunther & Meyer, Michael. The Reform Judaism Reader: North American Documents. 2004. xi, 228p. (gr. 10-12). pap. 15.95 *(978-0-8074-0732-5(1),* 386054) URJ Pr.

Rocklin, Joanne. I Say Shehechiyanu. Filipina, Monika, illus. 2015. (J). (ENG.). 24p. (gr. -1-2). lib. bdg. 16.95 *(978-1-4677-3467-7(5));* 6.99 *(978-1-4677-6203-8(2))* Lerner Publishing Group. (Kar-Ben Publishing).

Rose, Or N. Abraham Joshua Heschel: Man of Spirit, Man of Action. 2003. (ENG., Illus.). 80p. pap. 9.95 *(978-0-8276-0758-3(X))* Jewish Pubn. Society.

Roseman, Kenneth D. Until the Messiah Comes. 2004. (Do-It-Yourself Jewish Adventure Ser.). (Illus.). 145p. (gr. 4-6). pap. 11.95 *(978-0-8074-0706-6(2),* 140073) URJ Pr.

Rosenberg, concept. Reach Your Goal. 2011. (YID.). 198p. (YA). 21.00 *(978-0-9832102-1-4(7))* Roth Pubs.

Rosenberg, Amye. Mitzvot. (Illus.). 30p. (J). (gr. 1-5). pap. 4.95 *(978-0-87441-387-8(7))* Behrman Hse., Inc.

Rosenthal, Zelda B. Precious Jewels: The Roadmap to a Child's Heart - a Delightful Resources for Mothers & Teachers. 2006. (ArtScroll Ser.). (Illus.). 268p. *(978-1-4226-0075-7(0));* pap. *(978-1-4226-0076-4(9))* Mesorah Pubns., Ltd.

Rossel, Seymour. The Storybook Haggadah. Zwebner, Janet, illus. 2006. 72p. (J). pap. 9.95 *(978-1-932687-84-2(X),* Pitspopany Pr.) Simcha Media Group.

—Torah Portion-by-Portion. 2007. (Illus.). 368p. (J). pap. 15.95 *(978-1-891662-94-2(5))* Torah Aura Productions.

Salkin, Jeffrey K. For Kids - Putting God on Your Guest List: How to Claim the Spiritual Meaning of Your Bar or Bat Mitzvah. 2nd ed. 2007. (ENG., Illus.). 144p. (J). (gr. 5-8). per. 16.99 *(978-1-58023-308-8(2),* 9781580233088, Jewish Lights Publishing) LongHill Partners, Inc.

Schiffman, Lawrence H. Understanding Second Temple & Rabbinic Judaism. 2003. (Illus.). xviii, 409p. (YA). 29.50 *(978-0-88125-813-4(X))* Ktav Publishing Hse., Inc.

Schwartz, Barry L. & Levine, Mark H. Judaism's Great Debates. Klossner, John & Ricceri, David, illus. 2012. 72p. (J). pap. *(978-0-87441-852-1(6))* Behrman Hse., Inc.

Schwarz, Jacob D., ed. In the Land of Kings & Prophets. 2004. reprint ed. pap. 22.95 *(978-1-4179-4135-3(9))* Kessinger Publishing, LLC.

Seidman, Lauren. What Makes Someone a Jew? 2007. (ENG., Illus.). 32p. pap. 8.99 *(978-1-58023-321-7(X),* 9781580233217, Jewish Lights Publishing) LongHill Partners, Inc.

Senker, Cath. Judaism. 2007. (Atlas of World Faiths/Arcturus Ser.). (Illus.). 48p. (YA). (gr. 7-12). lib. bdg. 32.80 *(978-1-59920-056-9(2))* Black Rabbit Bks.

—Judaism: Signs, Symbols, Stories. 2009. (Religious Signs, Symbols, & Stories Ser.). (Illus.). 32p. (J). (ENG.). pap. 10.00 *(978-1-4358-3047-9(4));* lib. bdg. 25.25 *(978-1-4358-3039-4(3))* Rosen Publishing Group, Inc., The. (PowerKids Pr.).

Sharer, Avigail. Here, There, Everywhere: Kids' True Stories about Finding Hashem in Their Lives. 2012. 159p. (J). *(978-1-4226-1179-1(5))* Mesorah Pubns., Ltd.

Shazak Productions Inc. Staff, Shazak Productions. Miracle Lights: The Complete Story of Chanukah... Like You've Never Seen Before! 2004. (Illus.). 64p. (J). 15.95 *(978-1-930925-06-9(9))* Torah Excel.

Simon, Solomon & Bial, Morrison D. The Rabbi's Bible Vol. 1: Torah, 2 pts. (J). (gr. 5-6). wbk. ed. 8.95 *(978-0-87441-020-4(7))* Behrman Hse., Inc.

Singer, Howard. With Mind & Heart. (J). (gr. 8-18). 3.95 *(978-0-8381-0203-9(4),* 10-203) United Synagogue of America Bk. Service.

Sirois, Celia. My Jewish Friend: A Young Catholic Learns about Judaism. Santillan, Mariano, illus. 2008. 47p. (J). (gr. 5-7). 15.95 *(978-0-8198-4857-4(3))* Pauline Bks. & Media.

Stone, Amy. Jewish Americans. 2006. (World Almanac Library of American Immigration). (Illus.). 48p. (gr. 5-12). pap. 14.05 *(978-0-8368-7327-6(0));* lib. bdg. 31.00 *(978-0-8368-7314-6(9))* Stevens, Gareth Publishing LLLP. (Gareth Stevens Secondary Library).

Stren, Ariella. Bracha Do You Know? Argoff, Patti, illus. 2015. 28p. (J). 9.95 *(978-1-929628-76-6(5))* Hachai Publishing.

Suneby, Liz & Heiman, Diane. It's a ... It's a ... It's a Mitzvah. Molk, Laurel, illus. 2012. (ENG.). 38p. (J). 24.99 *(978-1-58023-509-9(3),* 9781580235099, Jewish Lights Publishing) LongHill Partners, Inc.

Swamer, Kristina, illus. The Bedtime Sh'ma: A Good Night Book. 2007. (ENG & HEB.). 40p. (J). 17.95 *(978-0-939144-55-6(7));* pap. 10.95 *(978-0-939144-54-9(9))* EKS Publishing Co.

—The BEDTIME SH'MA, Book & CD Set. 2007. (ENG & HEB.). 40p. (J). 24.95 incl. audio compact disk *(978-0-939144-58-7(1))* EKS Publishing Co.

—Modeh Ani: A Good Morning Book. 2010. 32p. (J). (HEB.). 17.95 *(978-0-939144-64-8(6));* pap. 10.95 *(978-0-939144-63-1(8))* EKS Publishing Co.

Tarcov, Susan. Maya Prays for Rain. Ochoa, Ana, illus. 2016. (ENG.). 32p. (J). (gr. -1-3). 17.99 *(978-1-4677-8929-5(1))* Lerner Publishing Group.

Touger, Malka. A Door That's Never Locked. 2011. (ENG.). 64p. (J). 14.95 *(978-0-8266-0131-5(6))* Kehot Pubn. Society.

Walker, Robert. Bar & Bat Mitzvahs. 2012. (ENG., Illus.). 32p. (J). *(978-0-7787-4086-5(2),* 1340852); pap. *(978-0-7787-4091-9(9),* 1340852) Crabtree Publishing Co.

Watson, Emma, et al. Religions to InspiRE for KS3: Judaism. 2012. (Illus.). 72p. (gr. 7-9). pap., stu. ed. 29.50 *(978-1-4441-2224-4(X))* Hodder Education Group GBR. Dist: Trans-Atlantic Pubns., Inc.

Weiss, Bernard P. I Am Jewish. (Religions of the World Ser.). 24p. 2009. (gr. 3-3). 42.50 *(978-1-60852-460-0(4))* 2003. (Illus.). (J). (gr. -1-3). lib. bdg. 22.60 *(978-0-8239-6810-7(3))* Rosen Publishing Group, Inc., The. (PowerKids Pr.).

White, Bender Richardson. Judaism. 4th rev. ed. 2009. (World Religions Ser.). (Illus.). 144p. (gr. 6-12). 40.00 *(978-1-60413-110-9(1),* Chelsea Hse.) Facts On File, Inc.

Whitman, Jonathan, ed. Jewish Artwork by Esky: Shabbat & Jewish Holidays. (Illus.). (Orig.). (J). (gr. 1-8). pap. 19.95 *(978-1-885143-01-3(X))* Preferred Enterprises.

Wood, Angela Gluck. Judaism. 2006. (QEB World of Faiths Ser.). (Illus.). 32p. (J). lib. bdg. 19.95 *(978-1-59566-209-5(X))* QEB Publishing Inc.

Zoldan, Yael. We Can Do Mitzvos from Aleph to Tav. Allen, Shira, illus. 2009. 46p. (J). (gr. -1-2). 14.99 *(978-1-59826-395-4(1))* Feldheim Pubs.

JUDGES

see also Courts; Lawyers

Abrams, Dennis. Sandra Day O'Connor: U. S. Supreme Court Justice. 2009. (Women of Achievement Ser.). (Illus.). 136p. (gr. 6-12). 35.00 *(978-1-60413-337-0(6),* Chelsea Hse.) Facts On File, Inc.

Barrington, Richard. Sonia Sotomayor. 2014. (Making a Difference: Leaders Who Are Changing the World Ser.). 48p. (YA). (gr. 5-8). 25.85 *(978-1-62275-435-9(2))* Rosen Publishing Group, Inc., The.

Benson, Michael. William H. Taft. 2004. (Presidential Leaders Ser.). (ENG., Illus.). 112p. (gr. 6-12). 29.27 *(978-0-8225-0849-6(4),* Lerner Pubns.) Lerner Publishing Group.

Boerst, William J. Galileo Galilei & the Science of Motion. 2004. (Profiles in Science Ser.). (Illus.). 144p. (YA). (gr. 6-12). lib. bdg. 26.95 *(978-1-931798-00-6(1))* Reynolds, Morgan Inc.

Branscomb, Leslie Wolf. Earl Warren. 2011. (Supreme Court Justices Ser.). (Illus.). 112p. 28.95 *(978-1-59935-158-2(7))* Reynolds, Morgan Inc.

Chavez, Emilio. Thurgood Marshall: Supreme Court Justice. 2013. (InfoMax Readers Ser.). (ENG.). 24p. (J). (gr. 3-4). pap. 49.50 *(978-1-4777-2600-6(4));* pap. 8.25 *(978-1-4777-2599-3(7))* Rosen Publishing Group, Inc., The. (Rosen Classroom).

Colins, Luke. Thurgood Marshall, 1 vol. 2014. (Great African-Americans Ser.). (ENG.). 24p. (gr. k-1). lib. bdg. 21.99 *(978-1-4765-3956-0(1),* Pebble Bks.) Capstone Press of Coughlan Cos.

Collins, David R. Clarence Thomas: Fighter with Words, 1 vol. Lauve, Celia & Shepherd, Rosalie M., illus. 2003. (ENG.). 32p. (J). (gr. 1-3). 16.99 *(978-1-56554-862-6(0))* Pelican Publishing Co., Inc.

Corrigan, Jim. John Marshall: The Story of John Marshall. 2011. (Supreme Court Justices Ser.). (Illus.). 112p. (J). 28.95 *(978-1-59935-159-9(5))* Reynolds, Morgan Inc.

Cox, Vicki. Clarence Thomas. 2008. (Black Americans of Achievement Ser.). (Illus.). 120p. (YA). (gr. 7-12). 35.00 *(978-1-60413-048-5(2))* Facts On File, Inc.

De Capua, Sarah. Sandra Day O'Connor. 2013. 96p. (YA). (gr. 7-12). 39.93 *(978-0-7614-4961-4(2))* Cavendish Square Publishing.

DeCapua, Sarah. Sandra Day O'Connor. 2013. (Leading Women 2 Ser.). 96p. (YA). (gr. 7-12). pap. 19.99 *(978-1-62712-117-0(X))* Cavendish Square Publishing.

Gagne, Tammy. What Its Like to Be Sonia Sotomayor. de la Vega, Eida, tr. from SPA. 2010. (What It's Like to Be/Que se Siente al Ser Ser.). (ENG & SPA., Illus.). 32p. (J). (gr. -1-2). lib. bdg. 25.70 *(978-1-58415-853-0(0))* Mitchell Lane Pubs., Inc.

Gallagher, Brigid. Sonia Sotomayor, 1 vol. 2014. (Extraordinary Women Ser.). (ENG., Illus.). 48p. (gr. 6-6). pap. 9.95 *(978-1-4109-5954-6(6));* lib. bdg. 32.65 *(978-1-4109-5946-1(5))* Heinemann-Raintree.

Gitlin, Martin. Sonia Sotomayor: Supreme Court Justice, 1 vol. 2010. (Essential Lives Set 5 Ser.). (ENG.). 112p. (J). (gr. 6-12). lib. bdg. 35.64 *(978-1-61613-518-8(2))* ABDO Publishing Co.

Gorman, Jacqueline Laks. Judge. 2009. (Know Your Government Ser.). 24p. (J). (gr. 2-4). pap. 8.15 *(978-1-4339-0120-1(X));* lib. bdg. 22.00 *(978-1-4339-0092-1(0))* Stevens, Gareth Publishing LLLP. (Weekly Reader Leveled Readers).

—Juez (Judge) 2009. (Conoce tu gobierno (Know Your Government) Ser.). (SPA., Illus.). 24p. (J). (gr. 2-4). lib. bdg. 22.00 *(978-1-4339-0099-0(8),* Weekly Reader Leveled Readers) Stevens, Gareth Publishing LLLP.

Harris, Nancy. What's the State Judicial Branch? 2016. (First Guide to Government Ser.). (ENG.). 32p. (gr. 1-3). pap. 8.29 *(978-1-4846-3691-6(0),* Heinemann First Library) Heinemann-Raintree.

Horn, Geoffrey M. Thurgood Marshall. 2004. (Trailblazers of the Modern World Ser.). (Illus.). 48p. (gr. 5-12). pap. 14.05 *(978-0-8368-5258-5(3));* lib. bdg. 31.00 *(978-0-8368-5098-7(X))* Stevens, Gareth Publishing LLLP. (Gareth Stevens Secondary Library).

Howse, Jennifer. Sandra Day O'Connor. 2007. (Remarkable People Ser.). (Illus.). 24p. (J). (gr. 3-7). pap. 8.95 *(978-1-59036-648-6(4));* lib. bdg. 24.45 *(978-1-59036-647-9(6))* Weigl Pubs., Inc.

Isle, Mick. A Timeline of the Supreme Court. 2009. (Timelines of American History Ser.). 32p. (gr. 4-4). 47.90 *(978-1-60854-391-5(9),* Rosen Reference) Rosen Publishing Group, Inc., The.

Jakubiak, David J. What Does a Supreme Court Justice Do? 2010. (How Our Government Works Ser.). 24p. (J). (gr. 3-6). lib. bdg., E-Book 42.50 *(978-1-4488-0031-5(5));* (Illus.). pap. 8.25 *(978-1-4358-9818-9(4),* PowerKids Pr.); (Illus.). (J). (gr. 3-6). lib. bdg. 22.60 *(978-1-4358-9361-0(1),* PowerKids Pr.) Rosen Publishing Group, Inc., The.

Jarrow, Gail. Robert H. Jackson: New Deal Lawyer, Supreme Court Justice, Nuremberg Prosecutor. 2008. (ENG., Illus.). 104p. (J). (gr. 4-6). 18.95 *(978-1-59078-511-9(8),* Calkins Creek) Boyds Mills Pr.

Jones, Brenn. Learning about Equal Rights from the Life of Ruth Bader Ginsburg. 2009. (Character Building Book Ser.). 24p. (gr. 2-3). 42.50 *(978-1-61511-000-1(3),* PowerKids Pr.) Rosen Publishing Group, Inc., The.

Kemp, Kristin. Amazing Americans: Thurgood Marshall, 1 vol. rev. ed. 2014. (Primary Source Readers Content & Literacy Ser.). (ENG., Illus.). 32p. (gr. 3-3). pap. 8.99 *(978-1-4333-7374-9(2))* Teacher Created Materials, Inc.

Kramer, Barbara. National Geographic Kids Readers: Sonia Sotomayor. 2016. (J). pap. *(978-1-4263-2291-4(7))* National Geographic Society.

Krull, Kathleen. Sonia Sotomayor: I'll Be the Judge of That! Dominguez, Angela N., illus. 2015. (Women Who Broke the Rules Ser.). (ENG.). 48p. (J). (gr. 1-4). 16.99 *(978-0-8027-3797-7(8),* 9780802737977, Bloomsbury USA Childrens) Bloomsbury Publishing USA.

Laks Gorman, Jacqueline. Juez (Judge) 2009. (Conoce tu gobierno (Know Your Government) Ser.). (SPA., Illus.). 24p. (gr. 2-4). pap. 8.15 *(978-1-4339-0127-0(7),* Weekly Reader Leveled Readers) Stevens, Gareth Publishing LLLP.

Levy, Debbie. I Dissent: Ruth Bader Ginsburg Makes Her Mark. Baddeley, Elizabeth, illus. 2016. (ENG.). 40p. (J). (gr. -1-3). 17.99 *(978-1-4814-6559-5(7),* Simon & Schuster Bks. For Young Readers) Simon & Schuster Bks. For Young Readers.

Linde, Barbara. Thurgood Marshall. 2011. (Civil Rights Crusaders Ser.). (Illus.). 24p. (gr. 2-5). (J). pap. 8.15 *(978-1-4339-5700-0(0),* Gareth Stevens Learning Library); (YA). 22.60 *(978-1-4339-5698-0(5))* Stevens, Gareth Publishing LLLP.

Linde, Barbara M. Becoming a Supreme Court Justice. 2016. (Who's Your Candidate? Choosing Government Leaders Ser.). (ENG., Illus.). 32p. (J). (gr. 3-4). pap. 10.50 *(978-1-4824-4051-5(2))* Stevens, Gareth Publishing LLLP.

Littlefield, Sophie. Oliver Wendell Holmes Jr: The Supreme Court & American Legal Thought. 2009. (Library of American Lives & Times Ser.). 112p. (gr. 5-5). 69.20 *(978-1-60853-496-8(0))* Rosen Publishing Group, Inc., The.

Littlefield, Sophie W. & Wiecek, William. Oliver Wendell Holmes Jr: The Supreme Court & American Legal Thought. 2005. (Library of American Lives & Times). (Illus.). 112p. (J). (gr. -1-3). lib. bdg. 34.60 *(978-1-4042-2652-4(4),* PowerKids Pr.) Rosen Publishing Group, Inc., The.

Mara, Wil. Thurgood Marshall: Champion for Civil Rights. 2004. (Great Life Stories Ser.). (ENG., Illus.). 125p. (J). 30.50 *(978-0-531-12058-3(9),* Watts, Franklin) Scholastic Library Publishing.

Marshall, Thurgood. Thurgood Marshall. 2004. (Black Americans of Achievement Ser.). (Illus.). 112p. (gr. 6-12). 35.00 *(978-0-7910-8163-1(X),* Chelsea Hse.) Facts On File, Inc.

McElroy, Lisa Tucker. John G. Roberts, Jr: Chief Justice. 2006. (Gateway Biographies Ser.). (ENG., Illus.). 48p. (gr. 4-8). lib. bdg. 26.60 *(978-0-8225-6389-1(4),* Lerner Pubns.) Lerner Publishing Group.

McPherson, Stephanie Sammartino. Sonia Sotomayor: Supreme Court Justice. 2015. (Exceptional Latinos Ser.). (ENG., Illus.). 24p. (J). (gr. 3-4). pap. 9.35 *(978-0-7660-6722-6(X))* Enslow Pubs., Inc.

Mead, Wendy. William H. Taft. 2011. (Presidents & Their Times 5 Ser.). 96p. (gr. 6). 34.21 *(978-1-60870-186-5(7))* Marshall Cavendish Corp.

My Children Publishing, prod. I am the Judge. 2008. (Illus.). 154p. (YA). pap. 19.95 *(978-0-9799376-0-6(4))* My Children Publishing Inc.

National Geographic Kids Staff & Kramer, Barbara. Sonia Sotomayor. 2016. (Readers Bios Ser.). (ENG., Illus.). 48p. (J). (gr. 1-4). pap. 3.99 *(978-1-4263-2289-1(5),* National Geographic Children's Bks.) National Geographic Society.

Rohan, Rebecca Carey. Thurgood Marshall: The First African-American Supreme Court Justice. 2016. (Great American Thinkers Ser.). 128p. (J). (gr. 9-9). 45.64 *(978-1-5026-1932-7(6))* Cavendish Square Publishing.

Roland, James. Ruth Bader Ginsburg: Iconic Supreme Court Justice. 2016. (Gateway Biographies Ser.). (ENG., Illus.). 48p. (J). (gr. 4-8). 26.65 *(978-1-5124-0596-5(5));* 39.99 *(978-1-5124-0597-2(3))* Lerner Publishing Group. (Lerner Pubns.).

Rumsch, BreAnn. William Taft, 1 vol. 2009. (United States Presidents Ser.). (ENG., Illus.). 40p. (YA). (gr. 3-6). 27.07 *(978-1-60453-474-0(5))* ABDO Publishing Co.

Shichtman, Sandra H. Sonia Sotomayor. 2011. (Supreme Court Justices Ser.). (Illus.). 111p. 28.95 *(978-1-59935-156-8(0))* Reynolds, Morgan Inc.

Sikora, Frank & Batcheler, Michelle. Frank M. Johnson, Jr: Courageous Judge. 2009. (Illus.). 104p. *(978-1-59421-045-7(4))* Seacoast Publishing, Inc.

Stine, Megan. Who Is Sonia Sotomayor? Putra, Dede & Harrison, Nancy, illus. 2017. (Who Was? Ser.). (ENG.). 112p. (J). (gr. 3-7). 5.99 *(978-0-399-54192-6(6),* Grosset & Dunlap) Penguin Young Readers Group.

—Who Is Sonia Sotomayor? 2017. (Who Is... ? Ser.). lib. bdg. 16.00 **(978-0-606-39779-7(5))** Turtleback Bks.

Tol, Alex Van. Sonia Sotomayor: U.S. Supreme Court Justice. 2010. (Crabtree Groundbreaker Biographies Ser.). (ENG., Illus.). 112p. (J). pap. *(978-0-7787-2546-6(4))* Crabtree Publishing Co.

Torres, John. Sonia Sotomayor: First Latina Supreme Court Justice. 2015. (Influential Latinos Ser.). (ENG., Illus.). 128p. (J). (gr. 7-7). 37.27 *(978-0-7660-7001-1(8))* Enslow Pubs., Inc.

Van Tol, Alex. Sonia Sotomayor: U. S. Supreme Court Justice. 2010. (Crabtree Groundbreaker Biographies Ser.). (ENG., Illus.). 112p. (J). (gr. 5-8). lib. bdg. *(978-0-7787-2537-4(5))* Crabtree Publishing Co.

Wetterer, Charles M. & Wetterer, Margaret K. Chief Justice. Walters, Kurt K. C., illus. 2005. 32p. (J). *(978-1-59336-306-2(0));* pap. *(978-1-59336-307-9(9))* Mondo Publishing.

Wheeler, Jill C. Thurgood Marshall. 2003. (Breaking Barriers Ser.). 64p. (gr. 3-8). 27.07 *(978-1-57765-907-5(4),* Abdo & Daughters) ABDO Publishing Co.

White, Casey. John Jay: Diplomat of the American Experiment. (Library of American Thinkers Ser.). 112p. 2009. (gr. 6-6). 66.50 *(978-1-60853-515-6(0),* Rosen Reference) 2005.

J K L

(Illus.). (YA). (gr. 5-9). lib. bdg. 34.60 *(978-1-4042-0507-9(1))* Rosen Publishing Group, Inc., The.

Whitelaw, Nancy. Mr. Civil Rights: The Story of Thurgood Marshall. 2nd rev. exp. ed. 2004. (Notable Americans Ser.). (Illus.). 144p. (YA). (gr. 6-12). 23.95 *(978-1-931798-02-0(8))* Reynolds, Morgan Inc.

—Thurgood Marshall. 2011. (Supreme Court Justices Ser.). (Illus.). 128p. 28.95 *(978-1-59935-157-5(9))* Reynolds, Morgan Inc.

Williams, Zella. Sonia Sotomayor: Supreme Court Justice. 2010. (Hispanic Headliners Ser.). (ENG.). 24p. (J). pap. 8.25 *(978-1-4488-1474-9(X))*; lib. bdg. 22.60 *(978-1-4488-1455-8(3))* Rosen Publishing Group, Inc., The. (PowerKids Pr.).

—Sonia Sotomayor: Supreme Court Justice - Sonia Sotomayor: Jueza de la Corte Suprema. 2010. (Hispanic Headliners / Hispanos en Las Noticias Ser.). (ENG & SPA.). 24p. (J). (gr. 2-5). lib. bdg. 22.60 *(978-1-4488-0711-6(5))* Rosen Publishing Group, Inc., The.

Wilson, Natashya. How to Draw the Life & Times of William Howard Taft. 2009. (Kid's Guide to Drawing the Presidents of the United States of America Ser.). 32p. (gr. 4-4). 50.50 *(978-1-61511-165-7(4)*, PowerKids Pr.) Rosen Publishing Group, Inc., The.

Winter, Jonah. Ruth Bader Ginsburg: The Case of R. B. G. vs. Inequality. Innerst, Stacy, illus. 2017. (ENG.). 48p. (J). (gr. 1-4). 18.95 ***(978-1-4197-2559-3(9)***, Abrams Bks. for Young Readers) Abrams, Inc.

—Sonia Sotomayor. Rodriguez, Edel, illus. 2015. 40p. pap. 8.00 *(978-1-61003-616-0(6))* Center for the Collaborative Classroom.

—Sonia Sotomayor: A Judge Grows in the Bronx. Ziegler, Argentina Palacios, tr. from SPA. Rodriguez, Edel, illus. 2009. (ENG & SPA.). 40p. (J). (gr. -1-3). 17.99 *(978-1-4424-0303-1(9)*, Atheneum Bks. for Young Readers) Simon & Schuster Children's Publishing.

JUDO

see also Karate

Brousse, Michel & Matsumoto, David. A Century of Dedication, the History of Judo in America. 2003. (YA). pap. 25.00 *(978-0-9729790-0-9(X))*; pap. 30.00 *(978-0-9729790-1-6(8))* United States Judo Federation, Inc.

Brown, Heather E. & Martin, Ashley. How to Improve at Judo. 2009. (How to Improve at... Ser.). (ENG., Illus.). 48p. (J). (gr. 3-9). pap. *(978-0-7787-3596-0(6))*; (gr. 4-8). lib. bdg. *(978-0-7787-3574-8(5))* Crabtree Publishing Co.

Chesterman, Barnaby. Judo: Winning Ways. James, Adam, ed. 2015. (Mastering Martial Arts Ser.). 96p. (J). (gr. 5). lib. bdg. 24.95 *(978-1-4222-3236-1(0))* Mason Crest.

Chesterman, Barnaby & Willingham, Bob. Judo. 2004. (Martial Arts Ser.). (Illus.). 32p. (gr. 3-6). lib. bdg. 26.00 *(978-0-8368-4192-3(1)*, Gareth Stevens Learning Library) Stevens, Gareth Publishing LLLP.

Crossingham, John & Kalman, Bobbie. Judo in Action. 2005. (Sports in Action Ser.). (ENG., Illus.). 32p. (J). (gr. 2-3). lib. bdg. *(978-0-7787-0342-6(8))* Crabtree Publishing Co.

—Judo in Action. Crabtree, Marc, photos by. 2005. (Sports in Action Ser.). (ENG., Illus.). 32p. (J). (gr. 2-3). pap. *(978-0-7787-0362-4(2))* Crabtree Publishing Co.

Crossingham, John, et al. Le Judo. 2010. (Sans Limites! Ser.). (FRE., Illus.). 32p. (J). pap. 9.95 *(978-2-89579-318-2(2))* Bayard Canada Livres CAN. Dist: Crabtree Publishing Co.

Ellis, Carole & Ellis, Carol. Judo & Jujitsu. 2011. (Martial Arts in Action 2 Ser.). (Illus.). 48p. (J). (gr. 6). lib. bdg. 29.93 *(978-0-7614-4933-1(7))* Marshall Cavendish Corp.

Ghetti, Roberto. A Complete Guide to Judo. 2017. (Mastering Martial Arts Ser.). 128p. (J). (gr. 6-6). lib. bdg. 37.27 ***(978-0-7660-8547-3(3))*** Enslow Pubs., Inc.

Mason, Paul. Judo. 2010. (Combat Sports Ser.). 32p. lib. bdg. 28.50 *(978-1-59771-274-3(4))* Sea-To-Sea Pubns.

Sander, Hedda & Deling, Bjorn. Judo: From White/Yellow Belt to Brown Belt. 2004. (Illus.). 184p. pap. 17.95 *(978-1-84126-076-1(2))* Meyer & Meyer Sport, Ltd. GBR. Dist: Lewis International, Inc.

Tometich, Annabelle. Judo, 1 vol. 2014. (Inside Martial Arts Ser.). (ENG., Illus.). 48p. (J). (gr. 3-6). lib. bdg. 32.79 *(978-1-62403-602-6(3)*, SportsZone) ABDO Publishing Co.

Wells, Garrison. Brazilian Jiujitsu: Ground-Fighting Combat. 2012. (Martial Arts Sports Zone Ser.). (ENG., Illus.). 32p. (gr. 4-8). lib. bdg. 26.60 *(978-0-7613-8456-4(1)*, Lerner Pubns.) Lerner Publishing Group.

Wood, Alix. Judo. 2013. (Kid's Guide to Martial Arts Ser.). (ENG., Illus.). 32p. (J). (gr. 3-6). 26.50 *(978-1-4777-0318-2(7))*; pap. 11.75 *(978-1-4777-0358-8(6))* Rosen Publishing Group, Inc., The. (PowerKids Pr.).

—Jujitsu. 2013. (Kid's Guide to Martial Arts Ser.). (ENG., Illus.). 32p. (J). (gr. 3-6). pap. 11.75 *(978-1-4777-0356-4(X))*; lib. bdg. 26.50 *(978-1-4777-0317-5(9))* Rosen Publishing Group, Inc., The. (PowerKids Pr.).

JUGGLING

Beak, Nick Huckleberry. How to Juggle: 25 Fantastic Juggling Tricks & Techniques to Try! 2013. (ENG., Illus.). 64p. (J). (gr. 3-7). 9.99 *(978-1-84322-865-3(3)*, Armadillo) Anness Publishing GBR. Dist: National Bk. Network.

Juggling. Date not set. 64p. (J). 5.98 *(978-1-4054-0408-2(6))* Parragon, Inc.

Juggling Kid Kit. 2004. (Kid Kits Ser.). (Illus.). 32p. (J). 9.95 *(978-1-58086-417-6(1))* EDC Publishing.

Juggling Skills. 2004. (Formula Fun Ser.). (Illus.). 48p. (J). *(978-1-84229-588-5(8))* Top That! Publishing PLC.

Just Juggling. 2004. (Whizz Kits Ser.). (Illus.). 48p. (J). *(978-1-84229-940-1(9))* Top That! Publishing PLC.

Top That Publishing Staff, ed. Boob Juggling. 2004. (Naughty Shenanigans Ser.). (Illus.). 48p. *(978-1-84510-218-0(5))* Top That! Publishing PLC.

JUNGLE ANIMALS

AZ Books Staff. About Wildlife. Petrovskaya, Olga, ed. 2012. (Million Whys Ser.). (ENG.). 12p. (J). (gr. -1-4). bds. 18.95 *(978-1-61889-059-7(X))* AZ Bks. LLC.

—Forest Animals. Gorojan, Elena, ed. 2012. (My First Library). (ENG.). 12p. (J). (gr. -1-k). bds. 8.95 *(978-1-61889-120-4(0))* AZ Bks. LLC.

—In the Jungle. Efimova, Tatiana, ed. 2012. (Animal Sounds Ser.). (ENG.). 14p. (J). (gr. -1-k). bds. 7.95 *(978-1-61889-125-9(1))* AZ Bks. LLC.

—Jungle Animals. Gorojan, Elena, ed. 2012. (My First Library). (ENG.). 12p. (J). (-k). bds. 8.95 *(978-1-61889-121-1(9))* AZ Bks. LLC.

—Living Book of the Jungle. Gasteva, Julia, ed. 2012. (Our Amazing World Ser.). (ENG.). 12p. (J). (gr. 1-3). bds. 19.95 *(978-1-61889-024-5(7))* AZ Bks. LLC.

—Living Book of the Savanna. Aksimovich, Natalja, ed. 2012. (Our Amazing World Ser.). (ENG.). 12p. (J). (gr. 1-3). bds. 19.95 *(978-1-61889-023-8(9))* AZ Bks. LLC.

—Savanna Animals. Gorojan, Elena, ed. 2012. (My First Library). (ENG.). 12p. (J). (-k). bds. 8.95 *(978-1-61889-118-1(9))* AZ Bks. LLC.

—Scouting the Forest. Vasilkova, Elena, ed. 2012. (Wild Theater Ser.). (ENG.). 8p. (J). (gr. -1-3). bds. 17.95 *(978-1-61889-018-4(2))* AZ Bks. LLC.

—Sounds of the Forest. Sheljagovich, Yana, ed. 2012. (Sounds Around Us Ser.). (ENG.). 16p. (J). (gr. 1-3). bds. 17.95 *(978-1-61889-028-3(X))* AZ Bks. LLC.

—Sounds of the Jungle. Migiz, Anna, ed. 2012. (Sounds Around Us Ser.). (ENG.). 16p. (J). (gr. 1-3). bds. 17.95 *(978-1-61889-030-6(1))* AZ Bks. LLC.

—Sounds of the Savanna & Desert. Migiz, Anna, ed. 2012. (Sounds Around Us Ser.). (ENG.). 16p. (J). (gr. 1-3). bds. 17.95 *(978-1-61889-031-3(X))* AZ Bks. LLC.

—Sounds of Wild Nature. Naumovets, Elena, ed. 2012. (Sounds Around Us Ser.). (ENG.). 16p. (J). (gr. 1-3). bds. 17.95 *(978-1-61889-026-9(3))* AZ Bks. LLC.

Bradley, Timothy. Terror en Los Trópicos. 2016. (TIME for Kids en Español - Level 5 Ser.). (SPA.). 64p. (gr. 5-5). lib. bdg. 31.99 *(978-1-5157-2939-6(7))* Time for Kids Inc AUS. Dist: Capstone Pub.

Bradley, Timothy J. Terror in the Tropics, 1 vol. 2nd rev. ed. 2013. (Nonfiction Readers Ser.). (ENG., Illus.). 64p. (J). (gr. 5-5). pap. 31.96 *(978-1-4333-7421-0(8))* Teacher Created Materials, Inc.

Casado, Dami & Casado, Alicia. Bebes de la Selva. 2003. (Bebes Ser.). (SPA., Illus.). 12p. (J). bds. 7.99 *(978-84-272-6061-0(X))* Molino, Editorial ESP. Dist: Santillana USA Publishing Co., Inc.

Cocoretto, illus. In the Jungle. 2016. (Peekaboo! Ser.: 4). (ENG.). 12p. (J). bds. *(978-1-84643-866-0(7))* Child's Play International Ltd.

Daly, Bob. Popposites: in the Wild. 2017. (Popposites! Ser.). (ENG., Illus.). 12p. (J). (gr. -1). 12.99 *(978-1-62686-765-9(8)*, Silver Dolphin Bks.) Readerlink Distribution Services, LLC.

de Lambilly-Bresson, Elisabeth. Animals in the Jungle. 2007. (Animal Show & Tell Ser.). (Illus.). 16p. (gr. -1-3). lib. bdg. 19.00 *(978-0-8368-8206-3(7)*, Gareth Stevens Learning Library) Stevens, Gareth Publishing LLLP.

Delafosse, Claude & Broutin, Christian. Let's Look at the Jungle. Broutin, Christian, illus. 2012. (ENG., Illus.). 38p. (J). (gr. k-3). pap. 11.99 *(978-1-85103-332-4(7))* Moonlight Publishing, Ltd. GBR. Dist: Independent Pubs. Group.

Dorling Kindersley Publishing Staff. Jungle Animals. 2012. (Touch & Feel Ser.). (ENG.). 12p. (J). (gr. -1-k). bds. 6.99 *(978-0-7566-9289-6(X)*, DK Children) Dorling Kindersley Publishing, Inc.

Dorling Kindersley Publishing Staff & Gersh, Camilla. DK Readers L1: Jungle Animals. 2016. (DK Readers Ser.). (ENG., Illus.). 24p. (J). (gr. -1-1). pap. 3.99 *(978-1-4654-4962-7(0)*, DK Children) Dorling Kindersley Publishing, Inc.

Dorling Kindersley Publishing Staff, et al. Jungle Adventure. 2015. (DK Adventures Ser.). (ENG., Illus.). 128p. (J). (gr. 3-7). pap. 5.99 *(978-1-4654-2931-5(X)*, DK Children) Dorling Kindersley Publishing, Inc.

—Jungle Adventures. 2015. (DK Adventures Ser.). (ENG., Illus.). 128p. (J). (gr. 3-7). 16.99 *(978-1-4654-2930-8(1)*, DK Children) Dorling Kindersley Publishing, Inc.

Fennell, Clare, illus. Noisy Jungle. 2017. (Push & Pull Ser.). (ENG.). 8p. (J). (gr. -1 — 1). bds. 5.99 *(978-0-7641-6889-5(4))* Barron's Educational Series, Inc.

Guettier, Bénédicte. In the Jungle. 2010. (Funny Faces Ser.). (Illus.). 14p. bds. *(978-1-84089-645-9(0))* Zero to Ten, Ltd.

Jungle Fun. 2017. (Jungle Fun Ser.). 24p. (gr. 4-6). pap. 24.75 ***(978-1-5081-6184-4(4)***, PowerKids Pr.) Rosen Publishing Group, Inc., The.

Kainen, Dan & Wollard, Kathy. Jungle: A Photicular Book. 2016. (Photicular Ser.). (ENG., Illus.). 24p. 25.95 *(978-0-7611-8953-4(0))* Workman Publishing Co., Inc.

Kingfisher Editors. Baby Animals in the Jungle. 2011. (Baby Animals Ser.). (ENG., Illus.). 14p. (J). (gr. -1-k). bds. 5.99 *(978-0-7534-6491-5(8))*, 9780753464915, Kingfisher) Roaring Brook Pr.

Kuskowski, Alex. A Streak of Tigers: Animal Groups in the Jungle, 1 vol. 2012. (Animal Groups Ser.). (ENG.). 24p. (J). (gr. k-3). lib. bdg. 24.21 *(978-1-61783-542-1(0)*, SandCastle) ABDO Publishing Co.

little bee books, little bee & Seal, Julia. Jungle. 2016. (ENG., Illus.). 12p. (J). (gr. -1 — 1). bds. 6.99 *(978-1-4998-0259-7(5))* Little Bee Books Inc.

Look Who's Popping Up: In the Jungle. 2003. (J). (gr. -1-k). 4.98 *(978-0-7525-8902-2(4))* Parragon, Inc.

Martin, Ruth. Noisy Nature: in the Jungle. Pledger, Maurice, illus. 2015. (ENG.). 12p. (J). (gr. -1). 16.95 *(978-1-62686-104-6(8)*, Silver Dolphin Bks.) Readerlink Distribution Services, LLC.

Moran, Shelby. Animals of the Jungle. 2017. (Animals in My World Ser.). 24p. (gr. 4-6). 49.50 ***(978-1-5383-2141-6(6)***, PowerKids Pr.) Rosen Publishing Group, Inc., The.

Ottina, Laura. In the Jungle. Ranchetti, Sebastiano, illus. 2009. (Learn with Animals Ser.). (ENG.). 24p. (J). (gr. -1-2). pap. 8.15 *(978-1-4339-2090-5(5))*; lib. bdg. 22.00 *(978-1-4339-1913-8(3))* Stevens, Gareth Publishing LLLP. (Weekly Reader Leveled Readers).

Radley, Gail. Forests & Jungles. Sherlock, Jean, illus. (Vanishing from Ser.). 32p. 2005. (gr. 6-12). lib. bdg. 22.60 *(978-1-57505-405-6(1))* 2003. (J). (gr. 3-5). 6.95 *(978-1-57505-567-1(8))* Lerner Publishing Group.

Reasoner, Charles. Animals in the Jungle. Pitt, Sarah, illus. 2009. (3D Board Bks.). 12p. (J). (gr. -1-k). bds. 9.99 *(978-1-934650-38-7(2))* Just For Kids Pr., LLC.

—Fan-Tab-U-Lus: Jungle Animals. Devaney, Adam, illus. 2011. (Fan-Tab-U-Lus Bks.). (ENG.). 12p. (J). (gr. -1-3). bds. 9.99 *(978-1-935498-55-1(X))* Just For Kids Pr., LLC.

Rice, William. Animales de la Jungla en Peligro. 2016. (TIME for Kids en Español - Level 5 Ser.). (SPA.). 64p. (gr. 5-5). lib. bdg. 31.99 *(978-1-5157-2933-4(8))* Time for Kids Inc AUS. Dist: Capstone Pub.

Rice, William B. Endangered Animals of the Jungle, 1 vol. 2nd rev. ed. 2013. (Nonfiction Readers Ser.). (ENG.). 64p. (J). (gr. 5-5). pap. 10.99 *(978-1-4333-4937-9(X))*; (Illus.). pap. 31.96 *(978-1-4333-7436-4(6))* Teacher Created Materials, Inc.

Ryndak, Rob. Jungle Animals. 2015. (Jungle Animals Ser.). (ENG.). 24p. (J). (gr. k-k). 135.60 *(978-1-4824-1630-5(1))* Stevens, Gareth Publishing LLLP.

Tejido, Jomike. Jungle Animals. 2016. (Jumbo Stickers for Little Hands Ser.). (ENG.). 24p. (J). (gr. -1-k). pap. 7.95 *(978-1-63322-119-2(9)*, Moondance) Quarto Publishing Group USA.

Uttridge, Sarah. Jungle Animals Around the World. 2014. (Animals Around the World Ser.). (Illus.). 32p. (gr. 2-5). 31.35 *(978-1-62588-194-6(0))* Black Rabbit Bks.

Watt, Fiona. Jungle. Elkerton, Andy, illus. 2009. (Luxury Touchy-Feely Board Bks). 10p. (J). (gr. -1). bds. 15.99 *(978-0-7945-2433-3(8)*, Usborne) EDC Publishing.

West, David. Jungle Animals. 2016. (Safari Sam's Wild Animals Ser.). 24p. (gr. k-3). 28.50 *(978-1-62588-072-7(3)*, Smart Apple Media) Black Rabbit Bks.

Wilson, Hannah. Flip the Flaps: Jungle Animals. Palin, Nicki, illus. 2012. (Flip the Flaps Ser.). (ENG.). 32p. (J). (gr. -1-1). pap. 6.99 *(978-0-7534-6859-3(X)*, 9780753468593, Kingfisher) Roaring Brook Pr.

Wren, Jenny, illus. In the Jungle. 2017. (First Explorers Ser.). (ENG.). 10p. (J). (— 1). bds. 8.95 ***(978-1-4549-2656-6(2))*** Sterling Publishing Co., Inc.

Zimmerman, Beverly. Bridal Planner. 2013. (ENG.). 49p. pap. 29.99 *(978-1-932676-80-8(5))* Vision Pubs., LLC.

Zondervan Staff. Jungle Beasts, 1 vol. 2011. (I Can Read! / Made by God Ser.). (ENG.). 32p. (J). pap. 3.99 *(978-0-310-72191-8(1))* Zonderkidz.

JUNGLE ANIMALS—FICTION

Alborough, Jez. Hug. Alborough, Jez, illus. (ENG., Illus.). 32p. (J). 2009. (gr. -1-k). pap. 3.99 *(978-0-7636-4510-6(9))* 2005. (— 1). bds. 11.99 *(978-0-7636-2893-2(X))* Candlewick Pr.

Alegria, Ciro. Sacha en el Reino de los Arboles. (SPA.). 96p. (YA). (gr. 5-8). *(978-84-204-3693-7(3)*, AF1748) Ediciones Alfaguara ESP. Dist: Lectorum Pubns., Inc.

—Sacha en el Reino de los Arboles. (SPA.). (YA). (gr. 5-8). *(978-956-11-0965-0(4)*, UV6346) Universitaria, Editorial S.A.

Allen, Nancy Kelly. On the Banks of the Amazon/en las orillas del Amazonas. de la Vega, Eida, tr. Driessen, Elizabeth, illus. 2003.Tr. of En las orillas del Amazonas. (SPA & ENG.). 32p. (J). (gr. -1-3). 16.95 *(978-0-9720192-7-9(8)*, 626999, Raven Tree Pr.,Csi) Continental Sales, Inc.

Andreae, Giles. Leo, the Lovable Lion. 2004. (Illus.). *(978-0-439-65567-5(6))* Scholastic, Inc.

—Rumble in Jungle. 2011. (ENG.). 24p. (J). bds. 9.95 *(978-1-58925-864-8(9))* Tiger Tales.

AZ Books Staff. Forest Animals Moving & Talking. Dubovik, Ludmila, ed. 2012. (Funny Trails Ser.). (ENG.). 10p. (J). (gr. -1-k). bds. 9.95 *(978-1-61889-176-1(6))* AZ Bks. LLC.

—My Forest. Yaroshevich, Angelica, ed. 2012. (Open the Book-I Am Alive Ser.). (ENG.). 8p. (J). (— 1). bds. 5.95 *(978-1-61889-042-9(5))* AZ Bks. LLC.

—Our Faraway Jungle. Zayceva, Irina, ed. 2012. (Hook-And-Loop-Pictures Ser.). (ENG.). 12p. (J). (-k). bds. 11.95 *(978-1-61889-158-7(8))* AZ Bks. LLC.

—Who Lives in the Jungle? Gridina, Anna, ed. 2012. (Funny Animals Ser.). (ENG.). 10p. (J). (-k). bds. 8.95 *(978-1-61889-048-1(4))* AZ Bks. LLC.

Baena, Gloria. Invitacion a la Fiesta del Gran Gorila. Osorno, Laura, illus. 2003. (SPA.). 32p. (J). 8.95 *(978-958-04-7072-4(3))* Norma S.A. COL. Dist: Distribuidora Norma, Inc.

Baggott, Stella, illus. Baby's Very First Stroller Book Jungle. 2015. (Baby's Very First Stroller Bks.). (ENG.). 8p. (J). 7.99 *(978-0-7945-3533-9(X)*, Usborne) EDC Publishing.

Balouch, Kristen. The Little Little Girl with the Big Big Voice. Balouch, Kristen, illus. 2011. (ENG., Illus.). 32p. (J). (gr. -1-k). 12.99 *(978-1-4424-0808-1(1)*, Little Simon) Little Simon.

Base, Graeme. Jungle Drums. 2004. (ENG., Illus.). 40p. (J). (gr. -1-3). 19.95 *(978-0-8109-5044-3(8))* Abrams, Inc.

—The Last King of Angkor Wat. 2014. (ENG., Illus.). 36p. (J). (gr. k-2). 17.95 *(978-1-4197-1354-5(X)*, Abrams Bks. for Young Readers) Abrams, Inc.

Beaton, Clare & Blackstone, Stella. How Loud Is a Lion? Beaton, Clare, illus. 2007. (ENG., Illus.). 24p. (J). (gr. -1-k). bds. 7.99 *(978-1-84686-000-3(8))* Barefoot Bks., Inc.

Bergin, Jennifer J. Jungle Jim & Jungle Jen in the African Savannahs. 2012. 68p. pap. 8.99 *(978-1-4525-5314-6(9))* Balboa Pr.

The Big Game. 2007. (Little Dinosaur Chapter Ser.). (J). per. 7.67 *(978-1-932570-68-7(3))* Pioneer Valley Bks.

Blackford, Andy. The Hungry Little Monkey. 2011. (Tadpoles Ser.). (ENG., Illus.). 24p. (J). (gr. k-2). lib. bdg. *(978-0-7787-0581-9(1))*; pap. *(978-0-7787-0592-5(7))* Crabtree Publishing Co.

Blackstone, Stella & Beaton, Clare. How Loud Is a Lion? Beaton, Clare, illus. 2011. (ENG., Illus.). 24p. (J). (gr. -1-2). 6.99 *(978-1-84686-534-3(4))* Barefoot Bks., Inc.

Bland, Nick. The Very Cranky Bear. Bland, Nick, illus. 2014. (ENG., Illus.). 32p. (J). (gr. -1-k). 16.99 *(978-0-545-61269-2(1)*, Orchard Bks.) Scholastic, Inc.

Bolam, Emily. In the Jungle. 2013. (ENG., Illus.). 10p. (J). bds. *(978-0-230-76713-3(3))* Barron's Educational Series, Inc.

Broach, Elise. Gumption! Egielski, Richard, illus. 2010. (ENG.). 40p. (J). (gr. k-3). 18.99 *(978-1-4169-1628-4(8)*, Atheneum Bks. for Young Readers) Simon & Schuster Children's Publishing.

Brooks, David. You Can Count in the Jungle. 2005. (You Can Count Ser.). (ENG., Illus.). 24p. (J). (gr. -1 — 1). bds. 6.95 *(978-1-55971-931-5(1))* Cooper Square Publishing Llc.

Brown, J. A. Hurray for Elephant. 2003. (Funny Faces Ser.). (Illus.). (J). 3.95 *(978-1-58925-717-7(0))* Tiger Tales.

Burgess, Thornton W. Billy Mink. Cady, Harrison, illus. 2012. (Dover Children's Thrift Classics Ser.). (ENG.). 128p. (J). (gr. k-3). pap. 4.00 *(978-0-486-48107-4(7))* Dover Pubns., Inc.

Butler, John. Bedtime in the Jungle. Butler, John, illus. 2009. (Illus.). 32p. (J). (gr. -1-1). 16.95 *(978-1-56145-486-0(9))* Peachtree Pubs.

Carle, Eric. "Slowly, Slowly, Slowly," Said the Sloth. Carle, Eric, illus. 2007. (ENG., Illus.). 32p. (J). (gr. -1-2). pap. 7.99 *(978-0-14-240847-6(6)*, Puffin Books) Penguin Young Readers Group.

—"Slowly, Slowly, Slowly," Said the Sloth. Carle, Eric, illus. 2007. (Illus.). (gr. -1-3). 18.00 *(978-0-7569-8002-3(X))* Perfection Learning Corp.

—"Slowly, Slowly, Slowly," Said the Sloth. 2007. 18.40 *(978-1-4177-7475-3(4)*, Turtleback) Turtleback Bks.

Carter, Wade. The Adventures of Ernie & Ike: Lessons in Life Series. 2008. 44p. pap. 16.99 *(978-1-4343-9087-5(X))* AuthorHouse.

Chachas, George & Wojtak, James. The Adventures of Dynamic Doolittle: The Problem with Paulie Python. De Soto, Ben, illus. 2011. 31p. (J). pap. 9.95 *(978-0-9793144-1-4(0))* Double Dap Bks.

—The Story of Doolittle: An Exceptional Young Gorilla. De Soto, Ben, illus. 2011. 32p. (J). pap. 9.95 *(978-0-9793144-0-7(2))* Dragonetti.

Chapman, Jason. Who's That Singing? A Pull-the-Tab Book. Chapman, Jason, illus. 2010. (ENG., Illus.). 12p. (J). (gr. -1-1). bds. 9.99 *(978-1-4169-8736-9(3)*, Little Simon) Little Simon.

Charles, Faustin. The Selfish Crocodile. Terry, Michael, illus. 2010. (Selfish Crocodile Ser.). (ENG.). 32p. (J). (gr. -1-k). pap. 9.99 *(978-0-7475-4193-6(0)*, 9780747541936, Bloomsbury USA Childrens) Bloomsbury Publishing USA.

Charles, Faustin & Terry, Michael. The Selfish Crocodile Book of Nursery Rhymes. Terry, Michael, illus. 2008. (ENG., Illus.). 1p. (J). (gr. -1-k). 25.95 *(978-0-7475-9523-6(2))* Bloomsbury Publishing Plc GBR. Dist: Independent Pubs. Group.

Chichester Clark, Emma, illus. No More Kissing! 2015. (J). ***(978-1-4351-5751-4(6))*** Barnes & Noble, Inc.

Chorao, Kay. Ed & Kip. Chorao, Kay, illus. (I Like to Read(r) Ser.). (ENG., Illus.). 24p. (J). (gr. -1-3). 2015. 6.99 *(978-0-8234-3398-8(6))* 2014. 14.95 *(978-0-8234-2903-5(2))* Holiday Hse., Inc.

Chukovsky, Kornei. Doctor Ouch. Seabaugh, Jan, tr. from RUS. Seabaugh, Jan, illus. 2004. (Children's International Ser.: 1). Orig. Title: Aibolit. 43p. (J). pap. 6.99 *(978-0-9740551-0-7(7))* Smith, Viveca Publishing.

Clarke, Jane. Who Woke the Baby? Fuge, Charles, illus. 2016. (ENG.). (J). (gr. -1-2). 12.99 *(978-0-7636-8662-8(X)*, Nosy Crow) Candlewick Pr.

Cole, Babette. Tarzana. 2nd ed. 2003. (Babette Cole Ser.).Tr. of Tarzanna! (SPA., Illus.). 34p. (J). 12.95 *(978-84-233-2274-9(2))* Ediciones Destino ESP. Dist: Planeta Publishing Corp.

Cole, Bob. Power Reading: Classics/Jungle Book. Connor, Robin, illus. 2004. 94p. (J). (gr. 4-18). vinyl bd. 39.95 *(978-1-883186-61-6(7)*, PPCL2) National Reading Styles Institute, Inc.

Cooke, Brandy. What's Following Us? Reasoner, Charles & Reasoner, John, illus. 2011. (ENG.). 20p. (J). (gr. -1 — 1). bds. 6.99 *(978-1-4169-9673-6(7)*, Little Simon) Little Simon.

Crowson, Andrew. Flip Flap Safari. Crowson, Andrew, illus. 2003. (Illus.). 12p. (J). bds. *(978-1-85602-473-0(3)*, Pavilion Children's Books) Pavilion Bks.

Dahl, Roald. The Enormous Crocodile. 2009. (gr. k-3). lib. bdg. 18.40 *(978-0-613-87826-5(4)*, Turtleback) Turtleback Bks.

Daniels, Katie C. Danny's Adventure in Afric. 2009. 24p. pap. 12.99 *(978-1-4389-3404-4(1))* AuthorHouse.

Davies, Gill. A Special Wish: A Story of Confidence. O'Neill, Rachael, illus. 2009. (Let's Grow Together Ser.). 32p. (J). (gr. -1-2). pap. 10.55 *(978-1-60754-769-3(4))*; lib. bdg. 22.60 *(978-1-60754-760-0(0))* Windmill Bks.

DePrisco, Dorothea. Who's in the Jungle? Gilvan-Cartwright, Chris, illus. 2006. (ENG.). 10p. (J). bds. 4.95 *(978-1-58117-507-3(8)*, Intervisual/Piggy Toes) Bendon, Inc.

Derrick, David G., Jr., illus. I'm the Scariest Thing in the Jungle! 2013. (ENG.). 36p. (J). (gr. -1-3). 15.95 *(978-1-59702-087-9(7))* Immedium.

Desai, Naina. Fun Jungle. 2009. 28p. pap. 13.99 *(978-1-4490-2058-3(5))* AuthorHouse.

Dillingham Pierson, Clara. Among the Forest People. 2008. 92p. pap. 8.15 *(978-1-60459-501-7(9))* Wilder Pubns., Corp.

Dinerstein, Eric. What Elephants Know. 2016. (ENG.). 288p. (J). (gr. 3-7). 16.99 *(978-1-4847-2854-3(8))* Disney Publishing Worldwide.

DiPerna, Kaitlyn. Who's Hiding? in the Wild. Capizzi, Giusi, illus. 2016. (Who's Hiding? Ser.). (ENG.). 16p. (J). (gr. -1). bds. 12.99 *(978-1-62686-747-5(X)*, Silver Dolphin Bks.) Readerlink Distribution Services, LLC.

Disney Storybook Artists Staff, et al, illus. Disney's the Lion King. 2007. (Play-A-Sound Ser.). 16p. (J). (gr. -1-3). 16.98 *(978-1-4127-8776-5(9))* Publications International, Ltd.

Donaldson, Julia. Where's My Mom? Scheffler, Axel, illus. 2008. (ENG.). 32p. (J). (gr. -1-2). 18.99 *(978-0-8037-3228-5(7)*, Dial Bks) Penguin Young Readers Group.

Douglas, Babette. Noreen: The Real King of the Jungle. Johnson, John, illus. 2006. (Kiss a Me Teacher Creature Stories Ser.). 20p. (J). (gr. -1-3). 9.99 *(978-1-890343-25-5(0))* Kiss A Me Productions, Inc.

Durant, Alan. If You Go Walking in Tiger Wood. Boon, Debbie, illus. 2005. (ENG.). 100p. (J). (gr. -1-k). pap. 9.99 *(978-0-00-710390-4(5)*, HarperSport) HarperCollins Pubs. Ltd. GBR. Dist: Independent Pubs. Group.

Dutson, Shelly. Jingle Jangle Jungle Jeepers. Christenson, Maren, illus. 2009. 24p. pap. 12.50 *(978-1-4490-1061-4(X))* AuthorHouse.

Edwards, Pamela Duncan. Roar! A Noisy Counting Book. Cole, Henry, illus. Date not set. 32p. (J). (gr. -1-2). pap. 5.99 *(978-0-06-443572-7(5))* HarperCollins Pubs.

Ellery, Amanda. If I Were a Jungle Animal. Ellery, Tom, illus. 2009. (ENG.). 40p. (J). (gr. -1-3). 17.99 *(978-1-4169-3778-4(1)*, Simon & Schuster Bks. For Young Readers) Simon & Schuster Bks. For Young Readers.

Ely, Kosa. The Peaceable Forest: India's Tale of Kindness to Animals. Johansson, Anna, illus. 2012. (ENG.). 32p. (gr. k). 16.99 *(978-1-60887-115-5(0))* Mandala Publishing.

Emmett, Jonathan. Through the Heart of the Jungle. Gomez, Elena, illus. 2003. 32p. (J). tchr. ed. 15.95 *(978-1-58925-029-1(X))*; pap. 5.95 *(978-1-58925-380-3(9))* Tiger Tales.

Foster, Claudie. Princess Vanilla of the Amazon Jungle. 2011. 48p. pap. 24.95 *(978-1-60749-297-9(0))* America Star Bks.

Frampton, David. The Whole Night Through. Frampton, David, illus. Date not set. (Illus.). 32p. (J). (gr. -1-1). pap. 5.99 (978-0-06-443652-6(7)) HarperCollins Pubs.

—The Whole Night Through: A Lullaby. Frampton, David, illus. 2004. (Illus.). 30p. (J). (gr. k-4). reprint ed. (978-0-7567-7723-4(2)) DIANE Publishing Co.

Freedman, Claire & Cabban, Vanessa. Gooseberry Goose. 2003. (Illus.). 32p. (J). (gr. -1-2). tchr. ed. 15.95 (978-1-58925-030-7(3)) Tiger Tales.

Friden, Chris. Bedtime Safari. 2008. (Illus.). 27p. (J). bds. 14.99 (978-0-9758785-4-5(9)) Haydenburri Lane.

—Bedtime Safari. Otoshi, Kathryn & Ciccarelli, Gary, illus. 2007. (J). (978-0-9758785-3-8(0)) Haydenburri Lane.

—Sleepytime with Rory. 2008. (Illus.). 27p. (J). bds. 14.99 (978-0-9758785-5-2(7)) Haydenburri Lane.

—Sleepytime with Rory. Zapater Oliva, Carlos & Glazier, Garth, illus. 2008. (J). (978-0-9801849-1-4(6)) Haydenburri Lane.

Gale, Eric Kahn. The Zoo at the Edge of the World. Nielson, Sam, illus. 2014. (ENG.). 240p. (J). (gr. 3-7). 16.99 (978-0-06-212516-3(8)) HarperCollins Pubs.

Gerver, Jane E. Who's at Home? Davis, Nancy & Davis, Kathryn Lynn, illus. 2010. (ENG.). 14p. (J). (gr. -1 — 1). bds. 6.99 (978-1-4169-9758-0(X), Little Simon) Little Simon.

Gibbs, Edward. Little Bee. 2012. (ENG.). 24p. (J). (gr. -1-17). bds. 8.99 (978-0-316-12707-3(8)) Little, Brown Bks. for Young Readers.

Guzman, Lila. Kichi in Jungle Jeopardy. Johnson, Regan, illus. (J). 2007. (ENG.). 135p. (gr. 2-7). pap. 8.95 (978-0-9769417-2-9(4)) 2006. 144p. 13.95 (978-0-9769417-1-2(6)) Blooming Tree Pr.

Hanton, Sophie. Numbers in the Jungle. 2009. (Mag-NUT-Tics! Ser.). (Illus.). (J). bds. 9.99 (978-1-934650-76-9(5)) Just For Kids Pr., LLC.

Harris, Patricia. Do You Wonder Why? 2017. (Jungle Fun Ser.). 24p. (gr. 4-6). pap. 8.25 **(978-1-5383-2132-4(7)**, PowerKids Pr.) Rosen Publishing Group, Inc., The.

—Hide & Seek in the Jungle. 2017. (Jungle Fun Ser.). 24p. (gr. 4-6). pap. 8.25 **(978-1-5383-2136-2(X)**, PowerKids Pr.) Rosen Publishing Group, Inc., The.

Harter, Debbie. Animal Boogie. 2008. (ENG., Illus.). 32p. (J). 16.99 (978-1-84686-231-1(0)) Barefoot Bks., Inc.

Hewitt, Sally. Face to Face Safari. Gilvan-Cartwright, Chris, illus. 2011. (ENG.). 12p. (J). (gr. -1-1). 15.95 (978-0-8109-4261-5(5)) Abrams, Inc.

Hicks, Michael Christopher. Tales of Drake: The Tale of the Lost Dog. 2011. 40p. pap. 18.99 (978-1-4634-1823-6(X)) AuthorHouse.

Holden, Pam. Fire in the Jungle, 6 pack. Hatam, Samer, illus. 2009. (Red Rocket Readers Ser.). (ENG.). 16p. (gr. 2-2). pap. (978-1-877363-73-3(1)) Flying Start Bks.

I Can Swim, 6 Packs. (Sails Literacy Ser.). 16p. (gr. k-18). 27.00 (978-0-7635-4399-0(3)) Rigby Education.

Jarkins, Sheila. The Adventures of Marco Flamingo in the Jungle. Jarkins, Sheila, illus. 2012. (Illus.). 32p. (J). 1.99 (978-1-936299-31-7(3), Raven Tree Pr.) Delta Systems Company, Inc.

Jarocki, Martin. The Daily Zoo. 2013. 12p. pap. 12.68 (978-1-4669-9683-0(8)) Trafford Publishing.

Johnson, Amy. Tales of the Forest. 2011. (Illus.). 64p. pap. 13.95 (978-1-4670-1976-7(3)) AuthorHouse.

Johnson, Sandra, adapted by. Shoobie, 1 vol. 2009. 15p. pap. 24.95 (978-1-60813-705-3(8)) America Star Bks.

Jones, Vanessa. I Dreamed It Snowed in Afric. 2007. 40p. per. 14.95 (978-1-4327-1535-9(6)) Outskirts Pr., Inc.

The Jungle: Individual Title Six-Packs. (Sails Literacy Ser.). 16p. (gr. k-18). 27.00 (978-0-7635-4388-4(8)) Rigby Education.

Kim, Hanmin & Lee, Sera. Tiptoe Tapirs. 2015. (ENG., Illus.). 40p. (J). (gr. -1-3). 16.95 (978-0-8234-3395-7(1)) Holiday Hse., Inc.

Kipling, Rudyard. The Jungle Book. Thorne, Jenny, illus. 2014. (ENG.). 48p. (J). (gr. k-5). pap. 7.99 (978-1-84322-882-0(3), Armadillo) Anness Publishing GBR. Dist: National Bk. Network.

—The Jungle Book. Daily, Don, illus. 2014. (ENG.). 68p. (J). (gr. -1). 18.95 (978-1-60433-475-3(4)) Cider Mill Pr. Bk. Pubs., LLC.

—The Jungle Book. 2010. 318p. (gr. 3-7). pap. 30.75 (978-1-142-79715-7(5)) Creative Media Partners, LLC.

—The Jungle Book. Detmold, Edward J. & Detmold, Maurice, illus. 2010. (Calla Editions Ser.). (ENG.). 192p. 30.00 (978-1-60660-009-2(5)) Dover Pubns., Inc.

—The Jungle Book. 2008. (Bring the Classics to Life Ser.). (ENG., Illus.). 72p. (gr. 1-12). pap., act. bk. ed. 10.95 (978-1-55576-355-8(3), EDCTR-109B) EDCON Publishing Group.

—The Jungle Book. 2009. 122p. (gr. 3-7). pap. 19.99 (978-1-4589-2084-3(4)) General Bks. LLC.

—The Jungle Book. 2011. (ENG., Illus.). 96p. (gr. 2). pap. 20.95 (978-1-84943-010-4(1)) Oberon Bks., Ltd. GBR. Dist: Consortium Bk. Sales & Distribution.

—The Jungle Book. Drake, W. H., Jr., illus. 2015. (Macmillan Classics Ser.). (ENG.). 320p. (J). (gr. 2-4). 17.99 (978-1-4472-7307-3(9)) Pan Macmillan GBR. Dist: Independent Pubs. Group.

—The Jungle Book. Basford, Johanna, illus. 2013. (ENG.). 256p. (J). (gr. 4-7). pap. 10.99 (978-0-09-957302-9(4)) Random Hse. GBR. Dist: Independent Pubs. Group.

—The Jungle Book. 2014. (Word Cloud Classics Ser.). (ENG., Illus.). 320p. pap. 14.99 (978-1-62686-258-6(3), Thunder Bay Pr.) Readerlink Distribution Services, LLC.

—The Jungle Book: A Classic Story about Uniqueness. 2003. (Illus.). 32p. per. 3.95 (978-0-9747133-1-1(7), Values to Live By Classic Stories) Thomas, Frederic Inc.

—The Jungle Books. 2013. (ENG.). 384p. (gr. 12). mass mkt. 5.95 (978-0-451-41918-7(9), Signet) Penguin Publishing Group.

—Jungle Books. Nagai, Kaori, ed. 2013. (ENG.). 448p. (gr. 12). 11.00 (978-0-14-119665-7(3), Penguin Classics) Penguin Publishing Group.

Kipling, Rudyard & Kipling, John Lockwood, illus. The Jungle Book. 2014. (J). 13.32 (978-1-4677-5836-9(1), First Avenue Editions) Lerner Publishing Group.

Krebs, Laurie. We're Roaming in the Rainforest. Wilson, Anne, illus. 2010. (ENG.). 40p. (J). (gr. -1-5). 16.99 (978-1-84686-331-8(7)) Barefoot Bks., Inc.

Kroll, Steven. Jungle Bullies, 0 vols. Nguyen, Vincent, illus. 2006. (ENG.). 34p. (J). (gr. -1-2). pap. 7.99 (978-0-7614-5620-9(1), 9780761456209, Amazon Children's Publishing) Amazon Publishing.

Laird, Elizabeth. Beautiful Bananas, 1 vol. Pichon, Liz, illus. 2013. (ENG.). 32p. pap. 7.95 (978-1-56145-691-8(8)) Peachtree Pubs.

—Beautiful Bananas. Pichon, Liz, tr. Pichon, Liz, illus. 2004. (ENG.). 32p. (J). 15.95 (978-1-56145-305-4(6)) Peachtree Pubs.

Levy, Janey. Jenny in the Jungle. 2006. (Neighborhood Readers Ser.). (ENG.). 8p. (gr. -1-3). pap. 5.15 (978-1-4042-5702-3(0), Rosen Classroom) Rosen Publishing Group, Inc., The.

Lewis, J. Patrick. That's What Friends Are For. Denise, Christopher, illus. 2012. (I Am A Reader! Ser.). (ENG.). 40p. (gr. k-3). pap. 3.99 (978-1-58536-687-3(0)) Sleeping Bear Pr.

—Tugg & Teeny: That's What Friends Are For. Denise, Christopher, illus. 2012. (I Am A Reader! Ser.). (ENG.). 40p. (gr. k-3). lib. bdg. 9.95 (978-1-58536-516-6(5)) Sleeping Bear Pr.

—Tugg & Teeny - Jungle Suprises, Bk. 2. Denise, Christopher, illus. 2011. (I am a Reader Ser.). (ENG.). 40p. (J). (gr. k-2). lib. bdg. 9.95 (978-1-58536-515-9(7)) Sleeping Bear Pr.

—Tugg & Tweeny - Jungle Surprises, Bk. 2. Denise, Christopher, illus. 2011. (I am a Reader Ser.). (ENG.). 40p. (J). (gr. k-2). pap. 3.99 (978-1-58536-686-6(2)) Sleeping Bear Pr.

little bee books, little bee & Powell, Richard. If You See a Tiger. Larranaga, Ana Martin, illus. 2015. (ENG.). 12p. (J). (gr. -1-k). 4.99 (978-1-4998-0113-2(0)) Little Bee Books Inc.

Litton, Jonathan. Peek-Through Jungle. Nowowiejska, Kasia, illus. 2015. (Little Snappers Ser.). (ENG.). 12p. (J). (gr. -1-2). bds. 9.99 (978-1-68010-504-9(3)) Tiger Tales.

Lomsen, Boy. El Bosque en Peligro. (SPA.). 141p. (J). (gr. 3-5). (978-84-279-3451-1(3), NG0993) Noguer y Caralt Editores, S. A. ESP. Dist: Lectorum Pubns., Inc.

Madden, Gloria. Grandmothers Bedtime Stories. 2008. 68p. (gr. -1-7). pap. 10.49 (978-1-4343-9201-5(5)) AuthorHouse.

Maelor, Gwawr, et al. Tân Yn y Jyngl. 2005. (WEL., Illus.). 16p. pap. (978-1-85644-842-0(8)) CAA.

Mathy, Vincent, illus. Who's Hiding with Tiger? 2016. (ENG.). 10p. (J). (gr. -1 — 1). bds. 8.99 (978-1-4521-5662-0(X)) Chronicle Bks. LLC.

McDonnell, Flora. Splash! 2004. (Illus.). (J). 25p. (978-1-85269-489-0(0)); 25p. (978-1-85269-488-3(2)); (ENG & URD., 28p. pap. (978-1-85269-492-0(0)); (ENG & BEN., 28p. pap. (978-1-85269-486-9(6)) Mantra Lingua.

McElligott, Matthew. The Lion's Share. McElligott, Matthew, illus. 2012. (ENG., Illus.). 40p. (J). (gr. k-8). pap. 8.99 (978-0-8027-2360-4(8), 9780802723604, Bloomsbury USA Childrens) Bloomsbury Publishing USA.

—The Lion's Share: A Tale of Halving Cake & Eating It, Too. McElligott, Matthew, illus. 2009. (ENG., Illus.). 32p. (J). (gr. k-3). 16.99 (978-0-8027-9768-1(7), 9780802797681, Bloomsbury USA Childrens) Bloomsbury Publishing USA.

McKee, David. Elmer & the Monster. McKee, David, illus. 2014. (Illus.). 32p. (J). (gr. -1-3). 16.95 (978-1-4677-4200-9(7)) Lerner Publishing Group.

Milgrim, David. Ride, Otto, Ride! Milgrim, David, illus. 2016. (Adventures of Otto Ser.). (ENG., Illus.). 32p. (J). (gr. -1-k). pap. 3.99 (978-1-4814-6793-3(X), Simon Spotlight) Simon Spotlight.

Moore, Judith. Jessica the Furry Baroo. Brown, Karen, illus. 2007. 44p. per. 14.95 (978-1-59858-364-9(6)) Dog Ear Publishing, LLC.

Murray, Andrew. The Very Sleepy Sloth. Tickle, Jack, tr. Tickle, Jack, illus. 2003. 32p. (J). tchr. ed. 15.95 (978-1-58925-033-8(8)) Tiger Tales.

Okeke, Paulicap Okechukwu. Biribamba the Lonely Elephant. 2011. (Illus.). 28p. pap. 13.50 (978-1-4634-2992-8(4)) AuthorHouse.

Omari Jr. The Jungle Save. 2009. 20p. pap. 13.99 (978-1-4490-4205-9(8)) AuthorHouse.

Osborne, Mary Pope. Tigers at Twilight. unabr. ed. 2004. (Magic Tree House Ser.: No. 19). 72p. (J). (gr. k-3). pap. 17.00 incl. audio (978-0-8072-0928-8(7), S FTR 251 SP, Listening Library) Random Hse. Audio Publishing Group.

Osborne, Mary Pope, et al. Tigres Al Anochecer. Murdocca, Sal, illus. 2008. (Casa del Arbol Ser.: 19).Tr. of Tigers at Twilight. (SPA.). (J). (gr. 2-4). pap. 5.99 (978-1-933032-49-8(9)) Lectorum Pubns., Inc.

Parragon Staff. Lion King. 2010. (Disney Diecut Classics). 72p. (J). (gr. -1-1). (978-1-4075-8936-7(9)) Parragon, Inc.

Phinn, Gervase. Who Am I? Phinn, Gervase, illus. 2012. (Andersen Press Picture Bks). (ENG., Illus.). 32p. (J). (gr. -1-3). 16.95 (978-0-7613-8996-5(2)) Lerner Publishing Group.

Poitier, Anton. Flippy Floppy Jungle Animals. Touliatou, Sophia, illus. 2013. 16p. (J). 12.99 (978-1-61067-169-9(4)) Kane Miller.

Poulin, Andree. Monkey in the Mud. Eudes-Pascal, Elisabeth, illus. 2009. (Rainy Day Readers Ser.). 32p. (J). (gr. -1-3). pap. 10.55 (978-1-60754-371-8(0)) Windmill Bks.

Poulin, Andrée. Monkey in the Mud. Eudes-Pascal, Elisabeth, illus. 2009. (Rainy Day Readers Ser.). 32p. (J). (gr. -1-3). 22.60 (978-1-60754-370-1(2)) Windmill Bks.

Pritchett, Dylan. The First Music. Banks, Erin, illus. 2006. (ENG.). 32p. (J). (gr. -1-3). 16.95 (978-0-87483-776-6(6)) August Hse. Pubs., Inc.

Publishing, Arcturus. Jungle. 2016. (ENG.). 10p. (J). 9.95 (978-1-78599-102-8(7), 9781785991028) Arcturus Publishing GBR. Dist: Bookmasters Distribution.

Reasoner, Charles. Jungle. Devaney, Adam, illus. 2009. (Learning Tab Board Bks.). 10p. (J). (gr. -1-k). bds. 9.99 (978-1-934650-79-0(X)) Just For Kids Pr., LLC.

—Jungle Animals. Doherty, Paula, illus. 2009. (Little Big Flap Bks.). 10p. (J). (gr. -1-k). 9.99 (978-1-934650-22-6(6)) Just For Kids Pr., LLC.

—Jungle Babies. Devaney, Adam & Doherty, Paula, illus. 2009. (Baby Animal Board Bks.). 12p. (J). (gr. -1-k). bds. 7.99 (978-1-934650-50-9(1)) Just For Kids Pr., LLC.

Redbank, Tennant & Jackson, Kathryn. The Saggy Baggy Elephant. DiCicco, Sue & Hathi, Garva, illus. 2016. (Step into Reading Ser.). (ENG.). 32p. (J). (gr. -1-1). pap. 3.99 (978-0-553-53588-4(9), Random Hse. Bks. for Young Readers) Random Hse. Children's Bks.

Redlich, Ben. Who Flung Dung? 2013. (ENG., Illus.). 28p. (J). (gr. -1-k). 16.95 (978-1-62087-543-8(8), 620543, Sky Pony Pr.) Skyhorse Publishing Co., Inc.

Reece, William James. The Great Hippo Migration. 2007. 92p. per. 19.95 (978-1-4241-9770-5(8)) America Star Bks.

Rhatigan, Joe & Numberg, Charles. The Jungle Book: Mowgli's Adventures. Dacey, Bob & Bandelin, Debra, illus. 2016. (Modern Retelling Ser.). (ENG.). 28p. (J). (gr. -1-1). 17.95 (978-1-63322-113-0(X), Moondance) Quarto Publishing Group USA.

Rigby Education Staff. The Jungle Sun. (Sails Literacy Ser.). (Illus.). 16p. (gr. 2-3). 27.00 (978-0-7635-9941-6(7), 699417C99) Rigby Education.

Robinson, Michelle. What to Do If an Elephant Stands on Your Foot. Reynolds, Peter H., illus. 2012. (ENG.). 32p. (J). (gr. -1-k). 16.99 (978-0-8037-3398-5(4), Dial Bks) Penguin Young Readers Group.

Roddie, Shen. The Gossipy Parrot. Terry, Michael, tr. Terry, Michael, illus. 2004. (ENG.). 32p. (J). (gr. k-2). 20.00 (978-0-7475-6079-1(X)) Bloomsbury Publishing Plc GBR. Dist: Independent Pubs. Group.

Rose, Gerald. Horrible Melena. (SPA.). (J). 8.95 (978-958-04-7343-5(9)) Norma S.A. COL. Dist: Distribuidora Norma, Inc.

Rosen, Michael. Tiny Little Fly. Waldron, Kevin, illus. 2010. (ENG.). 32p. (J). (gr. 5-k). 16.99 (978-0-7636-4681-3(4)) Candlewick Pr.

Salerno, Steven. Wild Child. 2015. (ENG., Illus.). 32p. (J). (gr. -1-3). 16.95 (978-1-4197-1662-1(X), Abrams Bks. for Young Readers) Abrams, Inc.

Sams II, Carl R. & Stoick, Jean, photos by. When Snowflakes Fall. 2009. (ENG., Illus.). 14p. bds. 7.95 (978-0-9770108-9-9(9)) Sams, II, Carl R. Photography, Inc.

Sattler, Jennifer. Frankie the Blankie. 2016. (ENG., Illus.). 32p. (J). 16.99 (978-1-61963-675-0(1), 9781619636750, Bloomsbury USA Childrens) Bloomsbury Publishing USA.

Scott, Nathan Kumar & Chitara, Jagdish. The Great Race. 2012. (ENG., Illus.). 32p. (J). (gr. -1). 17.95 (978-93-80340-15-9(X)) Tara Books Agency IND. Dist: Publishers Group West (PGW).

Shumway, Gail. Stripey Follows His Dream. 2010. 60p. (J). 19.95 (978-0-9824611-7-4(8)) Snow In Sarasota Publishing.

Simon, Kristen Koerner. Jack's Knack: Book Three of the Blue Forest Series: Book Three of the Blue Forest Series. 2010. (Illus.). 32p. (J). 12.99 (978-1-60706-190-8(2)) Image Comics.

Squillace, Elisa, illus. Down in the Jungle. (Classic Books with Holes Big Book Ser.). (ENG.). (J). (gr. -1-3). 2006. 16p. (978-1-84643-009-1(7)) 2005. 14p. bds. (978-1-904550-61-7(4)) Child's Play International Ltd.

Sykes, Julie. I Don't Want to Go to Bed! Warnes, Tim, illus. 2013. (ENG.). 32p. (J). (978-1-58925-148-9(2)) Tiger Tales.

Tashiro, Chisato. Chameleon's Colors. Martens, Marianne, tr. from JPN. 2007. (Michael Neugebauer Books Ser.). (ENG., Illus.). 32p. (J). (gr. -1-3). pap. 7.95 (978-0-7358-2111-8(9)) North-South Bks., Inc.

Tatsuyama, Sayuri. Happy Happy Clover, Vol. 4. Tatsuyama, Sayuri, illus. 2010. (ENG., Illus.). 192p. (J). pap. 7.99 (978-1-4215-2735-2(9)) Viz Media.

Taylor, Thomas. The Loudest Roar. 2003. (Illus.). (J). pap. (978-0-439-50131-6(8), Levine, Arthur A. Bks.) Scholastic, Inc.

Thorne, Jenny, illus. The Jungle Book. 2016. (ENG.). 24p. pap. 7.99 (978-1-86147-814-6(3), Armadillo) Anness Publishing GBR. Dist: National Bk. Network.

Ticktock Media, Ltd. Staff. Jungle. 2009. (Animal Fun Touch & Feel Ser.). (ENG.). 10p. (J). (gr. -1-k). bds. 4.95 (978-1-84696-828-0(3), TickTock Books) Octopus Publishing Group GBR. Dist: Independent Pubs. Group.

Top That Publishing Staff, ed. Jungle Numbers. Parry, Jo, illus. 2007. (Magnetic - Numbers Ser.). 10p. (J). (gr. -1). bds. (978-1-84666-163-1(3), Tide Mill Pr.) Top That! Publishing PLC.

Top That! Jungle Numbers (large Version) Parry, Jo, illus. 2007. 10p. (J). (gr. -1). (978-1-84666-552-3(3), Tide Mill Pr.) Top That! Publishing PLC.

Vetsch, Rita Kaye. The Many Colors of Friendship. 2009. 40p. pap. 16.50 (978-1-60693-756-3(1), Eloquent Bks.) Strategic Book Publishing & Rights Agency (SBPRA).

Walter-Sereg, D. Bonnie Tracks a Jungle Animal. 2012. 24p. 24.95 (978-1-4626-5857-2(1)) America Star Bks.

Ward, Jennifer. The Busy Tree, 0 vols. Falkenstern, Lisa, illus. 2009. (ENG.). 32p. (J). (gr. k-3). 17.99 (978-0-7614-5550-9(7), 9780761455509, Amazon Children's Publishing) Amazon Publishing.

Watt, Fiona. Baby's Very First Noisy Book Jungle. 2017. (Picture Bks.). (ENG.). 10p. (J). 15.99 **(978-0-7945-3986-3(6)**, Usborne) EDC Publishing.

Weston Woods Staff, creator. Fletcher & the Snowflake Christmas. 2011. 29.95 (978-0-545-42619-0(7)) Weston Woods Studios, Inc.

The Wildlife Adventures of Mugwa & Washtucna. 2008. (Illus.). 54p. (J). 19.95 (978-0-9799493-0-2(0)) Carol Kalhagen-Tamanaha.

Willis, Jeanne. Elephants Can't Jump! Reynolds, Adrian, illus. 2015. (J). (ENG.). 32p. (gr. -1-3). 16.99 (978-1-4677-6316-5(0)); 17.32 (978-1-4677-6320-2(9)) Lerner Publishing Group.

—Hippospotamus. Ross, Tony, illus. 2012. (Andersen Press Picture Bks). (ENG.). 32p. (J). (gr. -1-3). 16.95 (978-1-4677-0316-1(8)) Lerner Publishing Group.

—El Nino Que Perdio el Ombligo. Ross, Tony, illus. (SPA.). (J). 8.95 (978-958-04-5632-2(1)) Norma S.A. COL. Dist: Distribuidora Norma, Inc., Lectorum Pubns., Inc.

Wilson, Karma. Bear's New Friend. Chapman, Jane, illus. 2009. (Bear Bks.). (ENG.). 34p. (J). (gr. -1-2). bds. 7.99 (978-1-4169-5438-5(4), Little Simon) Little Simon.

—Hilda Must Be Dancing. Watts, Suzanne, illus. (ENG.). 32p. (J). (gr. -1-3). 2008. 7.99 (978-1-4169-5083-7(4)) 2004. 17.99 (978-0-689-84788-2(2)) McElderry, Margaret K. Bks. (McElderry, Margaret K. Bks.).

Winnick, Karen B. Good Night, Baby Animals: You've Had a Busy Day. Watkins, Laura, illus. 2017. (ENG.). 64p. (J). 17.99 (978-0-8050-9883-9(6), 9780805098839, Holt, Henry & Co. Bks. For Young Readers) Holt, Henry & Co.

Woodman, Melissa. Lessons with Our Jungle Friends. 2011. 32p. pap. 24.95 (978-1-4626-1902-3(9)) America Star Bks.

Wright, Johanna. The Orchestra Pit. Wright, Johanna, illus. 2014. (ENG., Illus.). 32p. (J). (gr. -1-1). 16.99 (978-1-59643-769-2(3), 9781596437692) Roaring Brook Pr.

Wright, Maureen. Earth Day, Birthday!, 0 vols. Kim, Violet, illus. 2012. (ENG.). 32p. (J). (gr. k-3). 17.99 (978-0-7614-6109-8(4), 9780761461098, Amazon Children's Publishing) Amazon Publishing.

Wyss, Tyan. African Dream. Immelman, Sarita, illus. 2006. 48p. (J). pap. 15.95 (978-1-58939-915-0(3)) Virtualbookworm.com Publishing, Inc.

Zadrozny, Alicia & Church, Caroline Jayne. The Wild Little Jungle: A Mix-and-Match Flap Book. 2008. (ENG.). 10p. (J). bds. 12.99 (978-0-7944-1605-8(5)) Reader's Digest Assn., Inc., The.

Ziefert, Harriet. Monkey's Noisy Jungle. Newton, Jill, illus. 2007. bds. 7.95 (978-1-59354-598-7(3)) Blue Apple Bks.

JUNGLES

AZ Books Staff. Living Book of the Jungle. Gasteva, Julia, ed. 2012. (Our Amazing World Ser.). (ENG.). 12p. (J). (gr. 1-3). bds. 19.95 (978-1-61889-024-5(7)) AZ Bks. LLC.

Bowsher, Alice, illus. Lift-The-Flap & Color Jungle. 2017. (Lift-The-flap & Color Ser.). (ENG.). 10p. (J). (gr. -1-k). pap. 8.99 **(978-1-84780-931-5(6)**, Frances Lincoln Children's Bks.) Quarto Publishing Group UK GBR. Dist: Hachette Bk. Group.

Bradley, Timothy J. Terror in the Tropics, 1 vol. 2nd rev. ed. 2013. (TIME for KIDS(r) Nonfiction Readers Ser.). (ENG.). 64p. (J). (gr. 5-5). pap. 10.99 (978-1-4333-4898-3(5)) Teacher Created Materials, Inc.

Doane, Beth. From the Jungle: Stories & Original Art from Children Living in Rainforests. 2012. 40p. pap. 15.95 (978-1-4525-6090-8(0)) Balboa Pr.

Doeden, Matt. Can You Survive the Jungle? An Interactive Survival Adventure. 2011. (You Choose: Survival Ser.). (ENG.). 112p. (gr. 3-4). pap. 41.70 (978-1-4296-7350-1(8), You Choose Bks.) Capstone Press of Coughlan Cos.

Doeden, Matt & Penn, Jim. Can You Survive the Jungle? An Interactive Survival Adventure, 1 vol. 2011. (You Choose: Survival Ser.). (ENG.). 112p. (gr. 3-4). pap. 6.95 (978-1-4296-7349-5(4)); lib. bdg. 31.99 (978-1-4296-6588-9(2)) Capstone Press of Coughlan Cos. (You Choose Bks.).

Dorling Kindersley Publishing Staff. Ultimate Sticker Book: Jungle. 2017. (Ultimate Sticker Bks.). (ENG.). 32p. (J). (gr. k-2). pap. 6.99 (978-1-4654-5694-6(5), DK Children) Dorling Kindersley Publishing, Inc.

Jungle. (Push & Pop Ser.). 5p. bds. (978-1-4054-6874-9(2)) Parragon, Inc.

Jungle Fun. 2003. 32p. 12.98 (978-1-4054-2004-4(9)) Parragon, Inc.

Labrecque, Ellen. Jungle Worlds, 1 vol. 2014. (Earth's Last Frontiers Ser.). (ENG.). 32p. (gr. 1-3). lib. bdg. 29.99 (978-1-4109-6180-8(X), Read Me!) Heinemann-Raintree.

Levete, Sarah. Jungle Crash! 2011. (ENG.). 24p. (J). pap. (978-0-7787-7871-4(1)); (gr. 3-6). (978-0-7787-7849-3(5)) Crabtree Publishing Co.

MacKenzie, Catherine. Helen Roseveare: What's in the Parcel? 2012. (Little Lights Ser.). (ENG.). 24p. (J). 7.99 (978-1-84550-383-3(X), 30e4822e-2a72-488e-8b19-1af61b42efe4) Christian Focus Pubns. GBR. Dist: Bookmasters Distribution.

Markovics, Joyce L. Patterns in the Jungle. 2014. (Math Blast!: Seeing Patterns All Around Ser.). (ENG.). 32p. (J). (gr. -1-3). lib. bdg. 26.60 (978-1-62724-338-4(0)) Bearport Publishing Co., Inc.

Natural History Museum. Sticker Art Jungle. Craig & Karl, illus. 2017. (Sticker Art Ser.). (ENG.). 24p. (J). (gr. -1-k). pap. 7.99 **(978-1-78603-004-7(7)**, Frances Lincoln Children's Bks.) Quarto Publishing Group UK GBR. Dist: Hachette Bk. Group.

Patkau, Karen. Who Needs a Jungle? 2012. (Ecosystem Ser.). (ENG., Illus.). 32p. (J). (gr. 2-5). 17.95 (978-0-88776-992-4(6), Tundra Bks.) Tundra Bks. CAN. Dist: Penguin Random Hse. LLC.

Peek Inside the Jungle. 2017. (Peek Inside BDs Ser.). (ENG.). (J). bds. 11.99 **(978-0-7945-3920-7(3)**, Usborne) EDC Publishing.

Rettore. Jungle. 2016. (Baby Sees Cloth Bks.). (ENG.). 6p. (J). (gr. -1 — 1). 10.99 (978-1-4380-7759-8(9)) Barron's Educational Series, Inc.

Rice, William B. Survival! Jungle, 1 vol. 2nd rev. ed. 2012. (Nonfiction Readers Ser.). (ENG., Illus.). 48p. (J). (gr. 4-4). pap. 9.99 (978-1-4333-4820-4(9)) Teacher Created Materials, Inc.

Robinson, Fay. In the Jungle. Lopez, Paul, illus. 2004. (Treasure Tree Ser.). 32p. (J). (978-0-7166-1604-7(1)) World Bk., Inc.

Uttridge, Sarah. Jungle Animals Around the World. 2014. (Animals Around the World Ser.). (Illus.). 32p. (gr. 2-5). 31.35 (978-1-62588-194-6(0)) Black Rabbit Bks.

West, David. Ten of the Best Adventures in the Jungle. 2015. (Ten of the Best: Stories of Exploration & Adventure Ser.). (ENG., Illus.). 24p. (J). (gr. 3-6). (978-0-7787-1837-6(9)) Crabtree Publishing Co.

JUNGLES—FICTION

Achebe, Chinua & Iroaganachi, John. How the Leopard Got His Claws. GrandPré, Mary, illus. 2011. (ENG.). 32p. (J). (gr. 2-5). 16.99 (978-0-7636-4805-3(1)) Candlewick Pr.

Adams, Pam. Tiger. 2005. (ENG., Illus.). 12p. (J). (gr. -1-k). bds. (978-1-904550-28-0(2)) Child's Play International Ltd.

Alcott, Louisa May. The Louisa Alcott Reader: A Supplementar. 2006. pap. (978-1-4065-0590-0(0)) Dodo Pr.

Aristizabal, Nora. La Selva Maravillosa/the Wonderful Jungle. Reyes, Maria Margarita, illus. 2005. (Bilingual Collection). (SPA.). 31p. (J). (978-958-30-1966-1(6)) Panamericana Editorial.

Ballantyne, R. M. Gorilla Hunters A Tale of the Wilds of A. 2006. pap. 36.95 (978-1-4286-5952-0(8)) Kessinger Publishing, LLC.

Bannerman, Helen. The Boy & the Tigers. Petrone, Valeria, illus. 2004. (Little Golden Book Ser.). (ENG.). 24p. (J). (gr. -1-2). 4.99 (978-0-375-82719-8(6), Golden Bks.) Random Hse. Children's Bks.

Barroux. Where's the Elephant? Barroux, illus. 2016. (ENG., Illus.). 32p. (J). (gr. -1-2). 14.99 (978-0-7636-8110-4(5)) Candlewick Pr.

Bell-Jackson, Sylvia. Bree's Bubble Gum Adventures: The Pajamas from the Bahamas. 2012. 36p. pap. 13.97 *(978-1-61204-299-2(6)*, Strategic Bk. Publishing) Strategic Book Publishing & Rights Agency (SBPRA).

Bell, Michele Ashman. Rescue: A Jungle Adventure. 2006. 246p. (J). pap. *(978-1-59811-093-7(4))* Covenant Communications.

Beresford, Shane. In the Jungle. 2008. 36p. 19.95 *(978-1-4357-0351-3(0))* Lulu Pr., Inc.

Bhandari, D. Growing Wings: Parrot's Day Out. 2010. 28p. 17.99 *(978-1-4520-1102-8(8))* AuthorHouse.

The Big Game. 2007. (Little Dinosaur Chapter Ser.). (J). per. 7.67 *(978-1-932570-68-7(3))* Pioneer Valley Bks.

Bolam, Emily, illus. In the Jungle. 2013. (Peekabooks Ser.). (ENG.). 8p. (J). (gr. -1 — 1). bds. 5.99 *(978-0-7641-6629-7(8))* Barron's Educational Series, Inc.

Bollinger/Papp, illus. King Kong: Meet Kong & Ann. 2005. 32p. (J). lib. bdg. 13.85 *(978-1-4242-0615-5(4))* Fitzgerald Bks.

Bramucci, Stephen. The Danger Gang & the Pirates of Borneo! Chung, Arree, illus. 2017. (ENG.). 384p. (J). 16.99 *(978-1-61963-692-7(1)*, 9781619636927, Bloomsbury USA Childrens) Bloomsbury Publishing USA.

Broutin, Christian. In the Jungle. Broutin, Christian, illus. 2013. (ENG., Illus.). 36p. (J). (gr. -1-k). 12.99 *(978-1-85103-417-8(X))* Moonlight Publishing, Ltd. GBR. Dist: Independent Pubs. Group.

Brown, Bruce. Mwumba. O'Reilly, Sean Patrick, ed. 2011. (Illus.). 48p. (J). pap. 7.95 *(978-1-897548-03-5(6))* Arcana Studio, Inc.

Bush, John & Geraghty, Paul. The Bungle in the Jungle. (Illus.). 32p. (J). 17.95 *(978-0-09-174056-6(8))* Random Hse. GBR. Dist: Trafalgar Square Publishing.

Carter, Jani R. Long Ago in the African Jungle. 2008. 108p. pap. 10.99 *(978-1-4389-1233-2(1))* AuthorHouse.

Chapman, Bunny. Shanu the Watcher. 2013. 138p. pap. 9.99 *(978-0-9855008-4-9(0))* Champlain Avenue Bks., Inc.

Cline, Renee. Kawndra the Tiger. 2009. 28p. pap. 15.49 *(978-1-4389-6484-3(6))* AuthorHouse.

Cole, Bob. Power Reading: Classics/Jungle Book. Connor, Robin, illus. 2004. 94p. (J). (gr. 4-18). vinyl bd. 39.95 *(978-1-883186-61-6(7)*, PPCL2) National Reading Styles Institute, Inc.

—Power Reading: Comic Book/Jungle Book. Connor, Robin, illus. 2005. 62p. (J). (gr. 3-18). vinyl bd. 39.95 *(978-1-883186-74-6(9)*, PPCLC2) National Reading Styles Institute, Inc.

Condon, Bill. How to Survive in the Jungle by the Person Who Knows, 1 vol. rev. ed. 2013. (Fiction Readers Ser.). (ENG., Illus.). 28p. (J). (gr. 3-3). pap. 8.99 *(978-1-4333-5599-8(X))* Shell Educational Publishing.

—How to Survive in the Jungle by the Person Who Knows. rev. ed. 2013. (Fiction Readers Ser.). (ENG., Illus.). 28p. (gr. 3-3). pap. 19.96 *(978-1-4807-1721-3(5))* Teacher Created Materials, Inc.

Costello, Judi. Gertrude & the Creature. Bouthyette, Valerie, illus. 2008. 28p. pap. 24.95 *(978-1-60672-737-9(0))* America Star Bks.

Curtis, Jamie Lee. A Donde Van los Globos? Cornell, Laura, illus. 2004. (SPA.). 28p. (J). 21.99 *(978-84-8488-056-1(7))* Serres, Ediciones, S. L. ESP. Dist: Lectorum Pubns., Inc.

Cyrus, Kurt. Invisible Lizard. Atkins, Andy, illus. 2017. (ENG.). 32p. (J). (gr. k-2). 16.99 ***(978-1-58536-378-0(2)***, 204320) Sleeping Bear Pr.

Demois, Agathe & Godeau, Vincent. The Great Journey. 2016. (ENG., Illus.). 32p. (J). (gr. k-2). 19.95 *(978-1-84976-375-2(5))* Tate Publishing, Ltd. GBR. Dist: Abrams, Inc.

Disney Book Group, et al. Mowgli's Jungle Book: The Tale of a Man-Cub. Howell, Corin, illus. 2016. (ENG.). 336p. (J). (gr. 3-7). 12.99 *(978-1-4847-2579-5(4))* Disney Pr.

Drake, Christina M. Milo the Monkey. 2013. 88p. *(978-1-4602-2323-9(3))* FriesenPress.

Dubuvoy, Silvia, et al. Murmullos de la Selva. Tsuda, Efrain Rodriguez, illus. 2004. (Montana Encantada Ser.). (SPA.). 60p. (J). (gr. 3-5). pap. 9.99 *(978-84-241-8660-9(5))* Everest Editora ESP. Dist: Lectorum Pubns., Inc.

Dumortier, Marjorie. Zoe & Her Zany Animals. 2006. (ENG., Illus.). 32p. (J). (gr. -1-3). 14.99 *(978-0-7145-3306-3(8))* Boyars, Marion Pubs., Ltd. GBR. Dist: Consortium Bk. Sales & Distribution.

Eldridge, VonDa. Wiggles the Worm, 1 vol. 2010. 26p. pap. 24.95 *(978-1-4489-2547-6(9))* PublishAmerica, Inc.

Elliott, David. Evangeline Mudd & the Golden-Haired Apes of the Ikkinasti Jungle. Wesson, Andrea, illus. 2004. 208p. pap. *(978-0-7445-8379-3(9))* Walker Bks., Ltd.

Evans, Michelle D. I Don't Belong in the Jungle. 2011. 20p. pap. 24.95 *(978-1-4626-1382-3(9))* America Star Bks.

Foreman, Michael. Can't Catch Me! 2013. (Silver Tales Ser.). (ENG., Illus.). 28p. (J). (gr. -1-1). pap. *(978-1-74352-442-8(0))* Hinkler Bks. Pty. Ltd.

Fraser, Jess, illus. Jungle Jingles. 2007. (J). cd-rom 9.99 *(978-0-9795190-8-6(X))* Color & Learn.

Freedman, Claire. Aliens Love Dinopants. Cort, Ben, illus. 2016. (Underpants Bks.). (ENG.). 32p. (J). (gr. -1-2). 17.99 *(978-1-4814-6736-0(0)*, Aladdin) Simon & Schuster Children's Publishing.

Freer, Ida. Panama Girl. 2011. 116p. (gr. 4-6). 20.95 *(978-1-4620-3081-1(5))*; pap. 10.95 *(978-1-4620-3079-8(3))* iUniverse, Inc.

Gilchrist, J. Into the Land of Nede. 2010. 108p. (gr. 4-6). 20.95 *(978-1-4502-5433-5(0))*; pap. 10.95 *(978-1-4502-5432-8(2))* iUniverse, Inc.

Gillingham, Sara. In My Jungle. Siminovich, Lorena, illus. 2011. (ENG.). 12p. (J). (gr. -1 — 1). bds. 8.99 *(978-0-8118-7716-9(7))* Chronicle Bks. LLC.

Gollub, Matthew. Jazz Fly 2: The Jungle Pachanga. Hanke, Karen, illus. 2010. (J). 32p. (gr. -1-3). 17.95 incl. audio compact disk *(978-1-889910-44-4(9))*; *(978-1-889910-45-1(7))* Tortuga Pr.

Gondek, Heather. Who's in the Jungle? Lift-the-Flap 'n' Learn. Gilvan-Cartwright, Chris, illus. 2005. (Fun with Animals Ser.). 10p. (J). 9.95 *(978-1-58117-075-7(0)*, Intervisual/Piggy Toes) Bendon, Inc.

Grimm, Jacob & Grimm, Wilhelm K. Hut in the Forest, 1 vol. Lawson, Polly, tr. from GER. Stietencron, Bettina, illus. 2007. (Grimm's Fairy Tales Ser.). (ENG.). 28p. (J). *(978-0-86315-615-1(0))* Floris Bks.

Hapka, Catherine, pseud. One Big Blue Family. 2014. (I Can Read! Level 2 Ser.). (J). lib. bdg. 13.55 *(978-0-606-35063-1(2)*, Turtleback) Turtleback Bks.

—Vacation in the Wild. 2014. (I Can Read! Level 2 Ser.). (J). lib. bdg. 13.55 *(978-0-606-35064-8(0)*, Turtleback) Turtleback Bks.

Hapka, Cathy, pseud. Jungle Adventure. 2014. (LEGO Friends Chapter Bks.: 6). lib. bdg. 14.75 *(978-0-606-36363-1(7))* Turtleback Bks.

Hart, Teresa. The Ant & the Lost Spider, 1 vol. 2009. 76p. pap. 19.95 *(978-1-60749-296-2(2))* America Star Bks.

Harter, Debbie. The Animal Boogie. Harter, Debbie, illus. (Illus.). 32p. pap. 6.99 *(978-1-84148-996-4(4))*; 2005. (ENG., (J). (gr. -1-2). 6.99 *(978-1-905236-60-2(3))* Barefoot Bks., Inc.

—The Animal Boogie. 2005. (ENG., Illus.). 32p. (J). (gr. -1-2). 9.99 *(978-1-905236-22-0(0))* Barefoot Bks., Inc.

—Cha-Cha-Cha en la Selva. Harter, Debbie, illus. 2003. (SPA., Illus.). 32p. (J). (gr. -1-1). 9.99 *(978-1-84148-913-1(1))* Barefoot Bks., Inc.

—De Paseo Por la Selva. Ugalde, Raquel, tr. Harter, Debbie, illus. 2003. (SPA., Illus.). 32p. (J). pap. 6.99 *(978-1-84148-995-7(6))* Barefoot Bks., Inc.

Hayes, Celeste. Cacao & the Jaded Orb: A Sphinx & Trevi Adventure. 2011. (Illus.). 62p. (J). pap. 22.95 *(978-0-9785695-2-5(0))* Adam's Creations Publishing, LLC.

Hoppey, Tim. Jungle Scout: A Vietnam War Story, 1 vol. Espinoza, Ramon, illus. 2008. (Historical Fiction Ser.). (ENG.). 56p. (gr. 2-3). pap. 6.25 *(978-1-4342-0846-0(X)*, Graphic Flash) Stone Arch Bks.

Illek, Nuala. The Chinese Sausage Dog, the Panicky Porcupine & Mrs Shoo an Animal Tale of Friendship in Chin. 2009. 50p. pap. 9.99 *(978-1-60860-781-5(X)*, Eloquent Bks.) Strategic Book Publishing & Rights Agency (SBPRA).

Jenisch, Betty. Rennie. 2007. 9.00 *(978-0-8059-8947-2(1))* Dorrance Publishing Co., Inc.

John A. MacDonald. Pachung. 2010. 256p. 26.95 *(978-1-4502-1823-8(7))* iUniverse, Inc.

Jones, Allan Frewin. Legend of the Anaconda King. 2006. 186p. (J). pap. *(978-0-439-85670-6(1))* Scholastic, Inc.

Kayler, Ralph. The Tea Party in the Tree Tops. 2009. 48p. pap. 19.49 *(978-1-4389-8000-3(0))* AuthorHouse.

Kehret, Peg. Secret Journey. 2008. (ENG.). 144p. (J). (gr. 3-7). pap. 8.99 *(978-1-4169-9112-0(3)*, Simon & Schuster/Paula Wiseman Bks.) Simon & Schuster/Paula Wiseman Bks.

Kendrick, Robert. Treasure Quest: Journey to the Jungle. 2004. (ENG.). 46p. 24.95 *(978-1-4137-1467-8(6))* PublishAmerica, Inc.

Kim, Hanmin & Lee, Sera. Tiptoe Tapirs. 2015. (ENG., Illus.). 40p. (J). (gr. -1-3). 16.95 *(978-0-8234-3395-7(1))* Holiday Hse., Inc.

Kipling, Rudyard. The Jungle Book. 2010. 318p. (gr. 3-7). pap. 30.75 *(978-1-142-79715-7(5))* Creative Media Partners, LLC.

—The Jungle Book. 2008. (Bring the Classics to Life Ser.). (ENG., Illus.). 72p. (gr. 1-12). pap., act. bk. ed. 10.95 *(978-1-55576-355-8(3)*, EDCTR-109B) EDCON Publishing Group.

—The Jungle Book. 2009. 122p. (gr. 3-7). pap. 19.99 *(978-1-4589-2084-3(4))* General Bks. LLC.

—The Jungle Book. Drake, W. H., Jr., illus. 2015. (Macmillan Classics Ser.). (ENG.). 320p. (J). (gr. 2-4). 17.99 *(978-1-4472-7307-3(9))* Pan Macmillan GBR. Dist: Independent Pubs. Group.

—The Jungle Book. Basford, Johanna, illus. 2013. (ENG.). 256p. (J). (gr. 4-7). pap. 10.99 *(978-0-09-957302-9(4))* Random Hse. GBR. Dist: Independent Pubs. Group.

—The Jungle Book. 2014. (Word Cloud Classics Ser.). (ENG., Illus.). 320p. pap. 14.99 *(978-1-62686-258-6(3)*, Thunder Bay Pr.) Readerlink Distribution Services, LLC.

—The Jungle Book. Corvino, Lucy, illus. 2008. (Classic Starts(tm) Ser.). (ENG.). 160p. (J). (gr. 2-4). 6.95 *(978-1-4027-4576-8(1))* Sterling Publishing Co., Inc.

—The Jungle Book. Rowe, John, ed. 2008. (Jungle Book Ser.: 1). (ENG.). 164p. pap. 8.95 *(978-1-84232-943-6(X))* House of Stratus, Inc. GBR. Dist: Gardners Bks. Ltd.

—The Jungle Book: Rikki-Tikki-Tavi Moves In. Madsen, Jim, illus. 2008. (Easy Reader Classics Ser.). (ENG.). 32p. (gr. 4-7). lib. bdg. 24.21 *(978-1-59961-336-9(0))* Spotlight.

—The Jungle Books. 2004. (Barnes & Noble Classics Ser.). (ENG., Illus.). 432p. pap. 7.95 *(978-1-59308-109-6(X))* Barnes & Noble, Inc.

—The Jungle Books. 2013. (ENG.). 384p. (gr. 12). mass mkt. 5.95 *(978-0-451-41918-7(9)*, Signet) Penguin Publishing Group.

—Rikki-Tikki-Tavi & Toomai of the Elephants. 2008. (Unabridged Classics (in Audio) Ser.). (J). pap. 36.00 incl. audio compact disk *(978-1-58472-431-5(5)*, In Audio) Sound Room Pubs., Inc.

Kipling, Rudyard & Landolf, Diane Wright. The Jungle Book. Rowe, John, illus. 2008. (Stepping Stone Book(TM) Ser.). (ENG.). 112p. (J). (gr. 1-4). per. 3.99 *(978-0-375-84276-4(4)*, Random Hse. Bks. for Young Readers) Random Hse. Children's Bks.

Kipling, Rudyard & Wolek, Guy. The Jungle Book, 1 vol. 2012. (Calico Illustrated Classics Ser.: No. 4). (ENG., Illus.). 112p. (J). (gr. 3-6). 27.07 *(978-1-61641-616-4(5))* Magic Wagon.

Kirk, Trish. I Think There's a Bear Out There. 2009. 36p. pap. 16.99 *(978-1-4389-6097-5(2))* AuthorHouse.

Lannen, Jon Jon. The Giraffe That Taught Me How to Laugh. 2010. 28p. pap. 14.99 *(978-1-4490-5930-9(9))* AuthorHouse.

Lawati, A. The Jungle Adventure of Chimpoo. 2011. 40p. pap. 21.99 *(978-1-4634-2921-8(5))* AuthorHouse.

LeapFrog Staff. Disney Lion King - U. K. 2003. (Illus.). spiral bd. 14.99 *(978-1-59319-006-4(9))* LeapFrog Enterprises, Inc.

Lomsen, Boy. El Bosque en Peligro. (SPA.). 141p. (J). (gr. 3-5). *(978-84-279-3451-1(3)*, NG0993) Noguer y Caralt Editores, S. A. ESP. Dist: Lectorum Pubns., Inc.

Ludy, Mark. Jujo: The Youngest Tribesman. Ludy, Mark, illus. 2007. (ENG., Illus.). 32p. (J). (gr. k-2). 16.95 *(978-0-9664276-5-3(3))* Scribble & Sons.

Lynch, Stephen D. The Travels of Kui, the African Spurred Tortoise. Richard, Keisha Luana, illus. 2007. 36p. per. 24.95 *(978-1-4137-1802-7(7))* America Star Bks.

MacCracken, Joan. Trisba & Sula: A Miskitu Folktale from Nicaragua (Una Leyenda de los Miskitos de Nicaragua) Macdonald, Isabel et al, trs. Silva, Augusto Alves da, illus. 2005. (ENG & SPA.). 16.95 *(978-0-9646018-2-6(6))* Tiffin Pr. of Maine.

MacDonald, John A. Pachung. 2010. 256p. pap. 16.95 *(978-1-4502-1821-4(0))* iUniverse, Inc.

Madden, Gloria. Grandmothers Bedtime Stories. 2008. 68p. (gr. -1-7). pap. 10.49 *(978-1-4343-9201-5(5))* AuthorHouse.

Maggs, William Alan. The Jungle Adventures of Henry Littlejohn. 2012. 96p. pap. 11.52 *(978-1-4669-1252-6(9))* Trafford Publishing.

Magic Painting Jungle. 2017. (Magic Painting Bks.). (ENG.). (J). pap. 9.99 ***(978-0-7945-3982-5(3)***, Usborne) EDC Publishing.

Martin, Nicole. The Werewolf. 2006. 146p. pap. 14.99 *(978-1-4120-8802-2(X))* Trafford Publishing.

Mason, Charlene. Landon's Backyard Adventures. 2012. 24p. pap. 24.95 *(978-1-4626-7470-1(4))* America Star Bks.

Mason, Christine. The Mystery of Nan Madol a Pacific Island Adventure. 2011. 166p. pap. 11.95 *(978-1-61170-025-1(6))* Robertson Publishing.

McBrayer, Cassidy. You Can, Toucan! You Can. 2008. 20p. pap. 15.95 *(978-1-4327-1132-0(6))* Outskirts Pr., Inc.

McCall Smith, Alexander. The Mystery of the Missing Lion: A Precious Ramotswe Mystery for Young Readers. 2014. (Precious Ramotswe Mysteries for Young Readers Ser.: 3). (ENG., Illus.). 112p. (J). (gr. 2-5). pap. 6.99 *(978-0-8041-7327-8(3)*, Anchor) Knopf Doubleday Publishing Group.

McLisky, Marie. Kancil the Mouse Deer. 2017. (ENG.). 31p. (J). pap. 13.95 ***(978-1-78554-253-4(2)***, deae15c5-5838-4e02-b48b-54e9f8d82a01) Austin, Stan AUS. Dist: Bookmasters Distribution.

McMullan, Kate. A Wedding for Wiglaf?, 1 vol. Basso, Bill, illus. 2007. (Dragon Slayers' Academy Ser.: No. 4). (ENG.). 109p. (gr. 4-7). 24.21 *(978-1-59961-380-2(8))* Spotlight.

McNaney, Jeanne. Miracle in Sumatra: The Story of Gutsy Gus. Cochard, David, illus. 2009. (ENG.). 32p. (J). (gr. -1-3). 16.95 *(978-0-9814534-6-0(5))* Ovation Bks.

Meloy, Maile. The Apprentices. Schoenherr, Ian, illus. 2014. (Apothecary Ser.: 2). (ENG.). 432p. (J). (gr. 5). pap. 8.99 *(978-0-14-242598-5(2)*, Puffin Books) Penguin Young Readers Group.

Merberg, Julie & Bober, Suzanne. Dreaming with Rousseau. 2007. (Mini Masters Ser.: MINI). (ENG., Illus.). 22p. (J). (gr. -1 — 1). bds. 6.99 *(978-0-8118-5712-3(3))* Chronicle Bks. LLC.

Miedzybrodzka, Wiktoria. Jungle. Fretczak-Rodak, Monika, illus. 2014. (Mommy & Me Bath Bks.). (ENG.). 6p. (J). (gr. -1 — 1). 4.99 *(978-1-4380-7485-6(9))* Barron's Educational Series, Inc.

Mikaelsen, Ben. Jungle of Bones. 2014. (ENG.). 224p. (J). (gr. 3-7). 16.99 *(978-0-545-44287-9(7))* Scholastic, Inc.

Millett, Peter & Morden, Richard. It's a Jungle Out There. 2008. (Rigby Focus Forward: Level N Ser.). (Illus.). 24p. (J). (gr. -1-3). pap. *(978-1-4190-3838-9(9)*, Rigby) Pearson Education Australia.

Mitchell, Melanie, illus. Deep in the Jungle. 2011. (ENG.). 6p. (J). (gr. -1-k). 14.95 *(978-1-61524-471-3(9)*, Intervisual/Piggy Toes) Bendon, Inc.

Moll, Amanda. Liam's Lost It. 2013. 24p. 15.99 *(978-0-9886409-4-8(5))* Mindstir Media.

The Mystery of the Missing Lion: A Precious Ramotswe Mystery for Young Readers. 2014. (Precious Ramotswe Mysteries for Young Readers Ser.: 3). (ENG., Illus.). 112p. (J). (gr. 2-5). 12.99 *(978-1-101-87202-4(0)*, Anchor) Knopf Doubleday Publishing Group.

Napoli, Donna Jo & Johnston, Shelagh. Hotel Jungle. Spengler, Kenneth, tr. Spengler, Kenneth, illus. 2004. 33p. (J). 15.95 *(978-1-59336-002-3(9))*; pap. *(978-1-59336-003-0(7))* Mondo Publishing.

Nino, Jairo Anibal. Zoro. 2003. (SPA., Illus.). 97p. (YA). (gr. -1-7). pap. *(978-958-30-0291-5(7)*, PV4489) Panamericana Editorial COL. Dist: Lectorum Pubns., Inc.

Okorafor-Mbachu, Nnedi. Zahrah the Windseeker. 2008. (ENG., Illus.). 320p. (J). (gr. 5-7). pap. 8.99 *(978-0-547-02028-0(7))* Houghton Mifflin Harcourt Publishing Co.

Peretti, Frank E. The Deadly Curse of Toco-Rey. Life Publishers International Staff, tr. from ENG. 2005. (RUS., Illus.). 156p. (J). *(978-0-7361-0347-3(3))* Life Pubs. International.

Phillips, Helen. Here Where the Sunbeams Are Green. (ENG.). 304p. (J). (gr. 5). 2013. 7.99 *(978-0-307-93145-0(5)*, Yearling) 2012. E-Book *(978-0-307-97487-7(1)*, Delacorte Bks. for Young Readers) Random Hse. Children's Bks.

Pixton, Kaaren. Jungle, Rumble! Hey Baby! Look at These Wild Animals! 2010. (Indestructibles Ser.). (ENG., Illus.). 12p. (J). (gr. k — 1). pap. 5.95 *(978-0-7611-5858-5(8)*, 15858) Workman Publishing Co., Inc.

The Quest for Forgiveness. 2006. (Amazing Travels of Wannabe Ser.). (Illus.). 32p. (J). (gr. -1-3). 8.99 *(978-0-7847-1803-2(2)*, 04129) Standard Publishing.

Rhatigan, Joe & Nurnberg, Charles. The Jungle Book: Mowgli's Adventures. Dacey, Bob & Bandelin, Debra, illus. 2016. (Modern Retelling Ser.). (ENG.). 28p. (J). (gr. -1-1). 17.95 *(978-1-63322-113-0(X)*, Moondance) Quarto Publishing Group USA.

Richards, Lucy, illus. Jumping Jungle (W/Hang Tag) 2004. (Cuddly Cuffs Ser.: No. 7). 12p. (J). tchr. ed. 5.95 *(978-1-58925-727-6(8))* Tiger Tales.

—Jumping Jungle (W/Header Card) 2004. (Cuddly Cuffs Ser.: 7). 6p. (J). tchr. ed. 5.95 *(978-1-58925-731-3(6))* Tiger Tales.

Richardson, Dick. The Oglin: A Hero's Journey Across Africa... Towards the Tomorrows. Feek, Cathy, illus. 2004. 417p. (J). 24.95 *(978-0-9759440-3-5(7))* Savanna Pr.

Robertson, Betsey. Frisky's Forest Friends: Robin Rescue. 2009. 28p. pap. 12.49 *(978-1-4389-1906-5(9))* AuthorHouse.

Rowe, John, ed. The Jungle Book. Alexander, Gregory, illus. 2003. (Chrysalis Childrens Classics Ser.). 159p. (YA). pap. *(978-1-84365-038-6(X)*, Pavilion Children's Books) Pavilion Bks.

—The Jungle Book. 2007. (Illustrated Classics Ser.). (Illus.). 40p. (gr. 3-6). lib. bdg. 26.00 *(978-0-8368-7663-5(6)*, Gareth Stevens Learning Library) Stevens, Gareth Publishing LLLP.

Ruben's Jungle. 2003.Tr. of Selva de Ruben. (SPA., Illus.). 26p. bds. 16.95 *(978-0-9706953-1-4(4))* Globo Libros.

Saddleback Educational Publishing Staff, ed. River, 1 vol. unabr. ed. 2011. (Heights Ser.). (ENG.). 49p. (gr. 5-8). pap. 7.95 *(978-1-61651-281-1(4))* Saddleback Educational Publishing, Inc.

Sams, Carl R., II & Stoick, Jean. Lost in the Woods: A Photographic Fantasy. Herrick, Mark J., illus. 2005. (Connect-It Ser.). 68p. (J). (gr. -1-3). pap. 24.95 *(978-0-9749412-2-6(0))* EDCO Publishing, Inc.

San Souci, Robert D. Double-Dare to Be Scared: Another Thirteen Chilling Tales. Ouimet, David, illus. 2004. (Dare to Be Scared Ser.). (ENG.). 144p. (J). 17.95 *(978-0-8126-2716-9(4))* Cricket Bks.

San Souci, Robert D. & Burroughs, Edgar Rice. Tarzan. McCurdy, Michael, illus. 2004. 31p. (J). (gr. k-4). reprint ed. 16.00 *(978-0-7567-7576-6(0))* DIANE Publishing Co.

Saunders, Harry M. Teenagers on an Adventure: Journey of Two Boys & a Girl. 2013. 168p. pap. 19.95 *(978-1-62709-466-5(0))* America Star Bks.

Schick, Joel, illus. The Jungle Book: A Story about Loyalty. 2006. (J). 6.99 *(978-1-59939-023-9(X))* Cornerstone Pr.

The Show: Individual Title Six-Packs. (Sails Literacy Ser.). 16p. (gr. k-18). 27.00 *(978-0-7635-4413-3(2))* Rigby Education.

Sithole, Thelma. The Little Monkey & the Crocodile. Montague, Christine, illus. 2007. 32p. per. 12.00 *(978-1-59858-204-8(6))* Dog Ear Publishing, LLC.

Slack, Michael H. & Slack, Mike. Monkey Truck. Slack, Michael H. & Slack, Mike, illus. 2011. (ENG., Illus.). 32p. (J). (gr. -1 — 1). 12.99 *(978-0-8050-8878-6(4)*, 9780805088786, Holt, Henry & Co. Bks. For Young Readers) Holt, Henry & Co.

Slade, Nicholas. Joon the Zsun & His Magical Spoon. 2009. (Illus.). 32p. pap. 12.99 *(978-1-4389-3496-9(3))* AuthorHouse.

Smith, Crystal. The Lioness. 2010. 35p. (J). pap. 19.95 *(978-1-4327-3968-3(9))* Outskirts Pr., Inc.

Smith, Roland. Cryptid Hunters. 2006. (ENG.). 352p. (J). (gr. 5-17). pap. 6.99 *(978-0-7868-5162-1(7))* Hyperion Pr.

—Mutation. (ENG.). 352p. (J). (gr. 3-7). 2016. (Cryptid Hunters Ser.: 4). pap. 6.99 *(978-0-545-08181-8(5))* 2014. 16.99 *(978-0-545-08180-1(7))* Scholastic, Inc. (Scholastic Pr.).

Spann, Bill. The Agents of Little Woods. 2005. 116p. pap. 19.95 *(978-1-4137-6574-8(2))* America Star Bks.

Squillace, Elisa, illus. Down in the Jungle. (Classic Books with Holes Big Book Ser.). (ENG.). (J). (gr. -1-3). 2006. 16p. *(978-1-84643-009-1(7))* 2005. 14p. bds. *(978-1-904550-61-7(4))* Child's Play International Ltd.

Steig, William. The Zabajaba Jungle. 2nd ed. 2016. (ENG., Illus.). 32p. (J). (gr. -1-3). pap. 8.99 *(978-1-250-05761-7(2)*, 9781250057617) Square Fish.

Stephenson, Omri. Freddie Finds Out. 2010. 34p. pap. 21.50 *(978-1-4457-5726-1(5))* Lulu Pr., Inc.

Stilton, Geronimo. Four Mice Deep in the Jungle. Wolf, Matt & Keys, Larry, illus. 2004. (Geronimo Stilton Ser.: 5). (ENG.). 128p. (J). (gr. 2-5). pap. 7.99 *(978-0-439-55967-6(7)*, Scholastic Paperbacks) Scholastic, Inc.

—Rumble in the Jungle. 2013. (Geronimo Stilton Ser.: 53). lib. bdg. 18.40 *(978-0-606-31527-2(6)*, Turtleback) Turtleback Bks.

Storey, Mike. Teddycats. 2016. (Teddycats Ser.: 1). (ENG.). 240p. (J). (gr. 3-7). 16.99 *(978-1-101-99883-0(0)*, Razorbill) Penguin Young Readers Group.

Taylor, Christine. Red Riding Hood & the Toad. 2009. (Illus.). 44p. (gr. -1 — 1). 18.49 *(978-1-4389-3483-9(1))* AuthorHouse.

Taylor, Mark. Henry Explores the Jungle. Booth, Graham, illus. 2012. (ENG.). 48p. (J). (gr. -1-3). 18.95 *(978-1-930900-56-1(2))* Purple Hse. Pr.

Thornewell, Danielle. The Mems. 2007. (ENG.). 52p. per. 16.95 *(978-1-4241-6106-5(1))* PublishAmerica, Inc.

Thottam, Meena, adapted by. Brothers of the Jungle. 2006. (J). 3.95 *(978-0-9776917-4-6(8)*, Curcumin Bks.) Davlaw Press.

ToyBox Innovations, creator. Deep in the Jungle. abr. ed. 2006. (Disney's Read along Collection). (ENG.). (J). (gr. -1-3). pap. *(978-0-7634-2182-3(0))* Walt Disney Records.

Tub Tales: The Jungle. 2003. (Illus.). 10p. (J). 6.00 *(978-0-9713507-2-4(8)*, 843) Panline U.S.A., Inc.

Tulip, Jenny, illus. Who's Hiding in the Jungle? A Mystery Touch-and-Feel Flap Book! 2008. 10p. (gr. -1-k). bds. 6.99 *(978-1-57755-784-5(0))* Flying Frog Publishing.

Vetsch, Rita Kaye. The Many Colors of Friendship. 2009. 40p. pap. 16.50 *(978-1-60693-756-3(1)*, Eloquent Bks.) Strategic Book Publishing & Rights Agency (SBPRA).

Wallace, Dianne. Jungle in the Sky. 2012. (ENG.). 27p. (J). pap. 16.95 *(978-1-4327-4527-1(1))* Outskirts Pr., Inc.

Walser, David. Meg in the Jungle. Pienkowski, Jan, illus. 2017. (ENG.). 32p. (J). (gr. 2-5). pap. 9.99 *(978-0-14-136740-8(7))* Penguin Bks., Ltd. GBR. Dist: Independent Pubs. Group.

Wehrmeijer, Annelien. Noah & Dexter. van de Liejgraaf, Deborah, illus. 2014. (My Best Friend & Me Ser.). (ENG.). 10p. (J). (gr. -1 — 1). bds. 6.99 *(978-0-7641-6662-4(X))* Barron's Educational Series, Inc.

West, Robert. Attack of the Spider Bots, 1 vol. 2008. (Star-Fighters of Murphy Street Ser.). (ENG., Illus.). 160p. (J). (gr. 4-7). pap. 6.99 *(978-0-310-71426-2(5))* Zonderkidz.

White, Paul. Jungle Doctor Looks for Trouble. 2009. (Flamingo Fiction 9-13s Ser.). (ENG., Illus.). 160p. (J). pap. 8.99 *(978-1-84550-499-1(2)*, 9302ad19-8b28-4030-be88-ef9afc9f3a6c) Christian Focus Pubns. GBR. Dist: Bookmasters Distribution.

—Jungle Doctor on Safari. 2011. (Flamingo Fiction 9-13s Ser.). (ENG., Illus.). 144p. (J). 8.99 *(978-1-84550-391-8(0)*, 9781845503918) Christian Focus Pubns. GBR. Dist: Bookmasters Distribution.

—Jungle Doctor Operates. 2009. (Flamingo Fiction 9-13s Ser.). (ENG., Illus.). 160p. (J). pap. 8.99 *(978-1-84550-500-4(X)*, 5b5acc8e-b6fe-4477-b9ac-b1a8ea9426ea) Christian Focus Pubns. GBR. Dist: Bookmasters Distribution.

—Jungle Doctor's Africa. 2011. (Flamingo Fiction 9-13s Ser.). (ENG., Illus.). 144p. (J). 8.99 *(978-1-84550-388-8(0)*, 97eef3f6-1cd9-4ca5-866c-66b47f498800) Christian Focus Pubns. GBR. Dist: Bookmasters Distribution.

Whited, Melissa F. The Bear Brothers' Big Adventure, 1 vol. 2009. 23p. pap. 24.95 *(978-1-60749-258-0(X))* America Star Bks.

Wildsmith, Brian. Jungle Party. 1 vol. Wildsmith, Brian, illus. 2006. (ENG., Illus.). 32p. (J). pap. 6.95 *(978-1-59572-053-5(7))* Star Bright Bks., Inc.

—Jungle Party. 1 vol. 2006. (ENG., Illus.). 32p. (J). (gr. -1-3). 17.95 *(978-1-59572-052-8(9))* Star Bright Bks., Inc.

Willis, Tacey Lynn. Ellie, Tellie & Mellie: Best Jungle Friends Forever. 2010. 28p. pap. 12.49 *(978-1-4520-1903-1(7))* AuthorHouse.

Winskill, John. Jungle Friends. Disney Global Artists Staff & Random House Disney Staff, illus. 2003. (Step into Reading Ser.). (ENG.). 32p. (J). (gr. -1-1). pap. 3.99 *(978-0-7364-2089-1(4),* RH/Disney) Random Hse. Children's Bks.

Youngberg, Norma R. Jungle Thorn. 2010. (Illus.). 132p. reprint ed. per. 11.95 *(978-1-57258-157-9(3),* 945-6024) TEACH Services, Inc.

Zadrozny, Alicia & Church, Caroline Jayne. The Wild Little Jungle: A Mix-and-Match Flap Book. 2008. (ENG.). 10p. (J). bds. 12.99 *(978-0-7944-1605-8(5))* Reader's Digest Assn., Inc., The.

JUNK

see Waste Products

JUPITER (PLANET)

Adamson, Thomas K. Jupiter [Scholastic]: Revised Edition. 2010. (Exploring the Galaxy Ser.). (ENG.). 24p. pap. 0.49 *(978-1-4296-5810-2(X),* Pebble Plus) Capstone Press of Coughlan Cos.

—The Secrets of Jupiter. 2015. (Planets Ser.). (ENG., Illus.). 32p. (gr. 2-4). lib. bdg. 31.99 *(978-1-4914-5864-8(X))* Capstone Press of Coughlan Cos.

Alexander, Richard. Exploring Jupiter. 2017. (J). ***(978-1-5345-2251-0(4),*** KidHaven Publishing) Greenhaven Publishing LLC.

Allyn, Daisy. Jupiter: The Largest Planet. 2010. (Our Solar System Ser.). 24p. (J). (gr. k-3). (ENG.). pap. 8.15 *(978-1-4339-3822-1(7));* (Illus.). lib. bdg. 22.60 *(978-1-4339-3821-4(9))* Stevens, Gareth Publishing LLLP.

Asimov, Isaac & Hantula, Richard. Júpiter. Porras, Carlos & D'Andrea, Patricia, trs. from ENG. 2003. (Isaac Asimov's Biblioteca del Universo del Siglo XXI). (SPA., Illus.). 32p. (gr. 2-6). lib. bdg. 26.00 *(978-0-8368-3854-1(8),* Gareth Stevens Learning Library) Stevens, Gareth Publishing LLLP.

Bloom, J. P. Jupiter. 1 vol. 2014. (Planets Ser.). (ENG., Illus.). 24p. (J). (gr. 2-4). lib. bdg. 28.50 *(978-1-62970-716-7(3))* ABDO Publishing Co.

Capaccio, George. Jupiter. 2009. (Space!). 64p. (gr. 5-18). lib. bdg. 32.79 *(978-0-7614-4244-8(8))* Marshall Cavendish Corp.

Carson, Mary Kay. Far-Out Guide to Jupiter. 2010. (Far-Out Guide to the Solar System Ser.). (Illus.). 48p. (J). pap. 8.95 *(978-1-59845-186-3(3),* Enslow Elementary) Enslow Pubs., Inc.

Carson, Mary Kay & Library Association Staff. Far-Out Guide to Jupiter. 2010. (Far-Out Guide to the Solar System Ser.). (Illus.). 48p. (J). (gr. 2-5). 25.27 *(978-0-7660-3184-5(5))* Enslow Pubs., Inc.

Chiger, Arielle & Elkin, Matthew. 20 Fun Facts about Gas Giants. 2014. (Fun Fact File: Space! Ser.). 32p. (J). (gr. 2-5). 25.25 *(978-1-4824-1001-3(X));* pap. 10.50 *(978-1-4824-1002-0(8))* Stevens, Gareth Publishing LLLP.

Cunningham, Greg P. Journey to Jupiter. 1 vol. 2014. (Spotlight on Space Science Ser.). (ENG.). 32p. (J). (gr. 5-5). pap. 11.75 *(978-1-4994-0370-1(4),* PowerKids Pr.) Rosen Publishing Group, Inc., The.

Dorling Kindersley Publishing Staff. DK Readers L2: Space Quest: Jump to Jupiter. 2015. (DK Readers Ser.). (ENG., Illus.). 48p. (J). (gr. 1-3). 14.99 *(978-1-4654-3826-3(2),* DK Children) Dorling Kindersley Publishing, Inc.

Feinstein, Stephen. Jupiter: A Myreportlinks. com Book. 2005. (Solar System Ser.). (Illus.). 48p. (J). (gr. 4-10). lib. bdg. 26.60 *(978-0-7660-5303-8(2),* MyReportLinks.com Bks.) Enslow Pubs., Inc.

Geiger, Beth. The Inside Story of Jupiter. 2006. (J). 7.80 *(978-1-933798-07-3(6))* Sally Ride Science.

Glaser, Chaya. JÚPiter: El Mayor de Los Planetas. 2015. (Fuera de Este Mundo Ser.). (SPA., Illus.). 24p. (J). (gr. -1-3). lib. bdg. 23.93 *(978-1-62724-590-6(1))* Bearport Publishing Co., Inc.

—Jupiter: The Biggest Planet. 2015. (Out of This World Ser.). (ENG.). 24p. (J). (gr. -1-3). lib. bdg. 23.93 *(978-1-62724-565-4(0))* Bearport Publishing Co., Inc.

Goldstein, Margaret J. Jupiter. 2005. (Pull Ahead Bks.). (Illus.). 32p. (gr. 2-4). lib. bdg. 22.60 *(978-0-8225-4652-8(3))* Lerner Publishing Group.

Hansen, Rosanna. Jupiter. 2009. (Early Bird Astronomy Ser.). (ENG.). 48p. (gr. 2-5). lib. bdg. 26.60 *(978-0-7613-4153-6(6));* (Illus.). pap. 8.95 *(978-0-7613-4979-2(0),* Lerner Pubns.) Lerner Publishing Group.

Higgins, Nadia. Your Mission to Jupiter. 1 vol. 2011. (Planets Ser.). (ENG., Illus.). 32p. (J). (gr. k-3). 28.50 *(978-1-61641-678-2(5))* Magic Wagon.

Howard, Fran. Jupiter. 1 vol. 2007. (Planets Ser.). (ENG.). 32p. (gr. 3-7). 27.07 *(978-1-59928-827-7(3),* Buddy Bks.) ABDO Publishing Co.

Jefferis, David. Mighty Megaplanets: Jupiter & Saturn. 2008. (Exploring Our Solar System Ser.). (ENG., Illus.). 32p. (J). (gr. 3-7). pap. *(978-0-7787-3753-7(5))* Crabtree Publishing Co.

Jupiter. 2nd rev. ed. 2008. (New Solar System Ser.). 32p. (YA). (gr. 3-6). 23.00 *(978-1-60413-212-0(4))* Facts On File, Inc.

Jupiter. 2013. (Explore Outer Space Ser.). 32p. (J). (gr. 3-6). pap. 60.00 *(978-1-61533-770-5(9),* PowerKids Pr.) Rosen Publishing Group, Inc., The.

Kazunas, Ariel. Jupiter. 2011. (21st Century Junior Library: Solar System Ser.). (ENG.). 24p. (gr. 2-5). lib. bdg. 25.64 *(978-1-61080-086-0(9),* 201082) Cherry Lake Publishing.

Lawrence, Ellen. Jupiter: The Giant of the Solar System. 2013. (Zoom into Space Ser.). 24p. (J). (gr. -1-3). lib. bdg. 23.93 *(978-1-909673-12-0(9))* Ruby Tuesday Books Limited GBR. Dist: Bearport Publishing Co., Inc.

Orme, Helen & Orme, David. Let's Explore Jupiter. 2007. (Space Launch! Ser.). 24p. (gr. 1-4). pap. 8.15 *(978-0-8368-8125-7(7));* (Illus.). lib. bdg. 23.00 *(978-0-8368-7940-7(6))* Stevens, Gareth Publishing LLLP. (Gareth Stevens Learning Library).

Owen, Ruth. Jupiter. 2013. (Explore Outer Space Ser.). 32p. (J). (gr. 3-6). 25.25 *(978-1-61533-726-2(1));* pap. 10.00 *(978-1-61533-769-9(5))* Rosen Publishing Group, Inc., The. (PowerKids Pr.).

Owens, L. L. Jupiter. McGeehan, Dan, illus. 2011. (Space Neighbors Ser.). (ENG.). 32p. (J). (gr. 1-4). lib. bdg. 27.07 *(978-1-60954-382-2(3),* 200887) Child's World, Inc., The.

Oxlade, Chris. Jupiter, Neptune, & Other Outer Planets. 2007. (Earth & Space Ser.). (Illus.). 48p. (YA). (gr. 5-9). lib. bdg. 29.25 *(978-1-4042-3736-0(4))* Rosen Publishing Group, Inc., The.

Ring, Susan. Jupiter. (J). 2013. *(978-1-62127-264-9(8))* 2013. pap. *(978-1-62127-273-1(7))* 2004. pap. 8.95 *(978-1-59036-230-3(6))* Weigl Pubs., Inc.

Ring, Susan & Roumanis, Alexis. Jupiter. 2016. (Illus.). 24p. (J). *(978-1-5105-0974-0(7))* SmartBook Media, Inc.

Roumanis, Alexis. Jupiter. 2016. ***(978-1-5105-2047-9(3))*** SmartBook Media, Inc.

—Jupiter. 2015. (J). *(978-1-4896-3284-5(0))* Weigl Pubs., Inc.

Slade, Suzanne. A Look at Jupiter. (Astronomy Now! Ser.). 24p. (gr. 2-3). 2009. 42.50 *(978-1-61511-468-9(8),* PowerKids Pr.) 2007. (Illus.). (J). lib. bdg. 22.60 *(978-1-4042-3829-9(8))* Rosen Publishing Group, Inc., The.

Solway, Andrew. Jupiter & the Outer Planets. 1 vol. 2012. (Astronaut Travel Guides). (ENG.). 48p. (gr. 3-6). lib. bdg. 32.65 *(978-1-4109-4569-3(3),* NA-r) Heinemann-Raintree.

Sparrow, Giles. Destination Jupiter. 32p. (J). 2010. (Illus.). pap. 10.00 *(978-1-4358-3487-3(9))* 2009. (ENG.). lib. bdg. 25.25 *(978-1-4358-3444-6(5))* Rosen Publishing Group, Inc., The. (PowerKids Pr.).

Squire, Ann O. Planet Jupiter. 2014. (True Book(tm), A — Space Ser.). (ENG.). 48p. (J). lib. bdg. 31.00 *(978-0-531-21151-9(7))* Scholastic Library Publishing.

Steinkraus, Kyla. Giant Gas Planets: Jupiter, Saturn, Uranus, & Neptune. 2014. (ENG.). 24p. (gr. k-3). 28.50 *(978-1-62717-728-3(0))* Rourke Educational Media.

Taylor-Butler, Christine. Jupiter. 2007. (Scholastic News Nonfiction Readers Ser.). (ENG., Illus.). 24p. (J). (gr. 1-2). 22.00 *(978-0-531-14696-5(0))* Scholastic Library Publishing.

Wimmer, Teresa. Jupiter. 2007. (My First Look at: Planets Ser.). (Illus.). 24p. (J). (gr. -1-3). lib. bdg. 24.25 *(978-1-58341-517-7(3),* Creative Education) Creative Co., The.

World Book, contrib. by. Jupiter, Ceres & the Asteroids. 2nd ed. 2006. (World Book's Solar System & Space Exploration Library). (Illus.). 64p. (J). *(978-0-7166-9515-8(4))* World Bk., Inc.

World Book, Inc Staff, contrib. by. Jupiter. 2006. (World Book's Solar System & Space Exploration Library). (Illus.). 63p. (J). *(978-0-7166-9505-9(7))* World Bk., Inc.

—Jupiter & the Asteroids. 2010. (J). *(978-0-7166-9537-0(5))* World Bk., Inc.

Young, Abby. Jupiter. (Library of Planets Ser.). 2009. 48p. (gr. 5-8). 55.90 *(978-1-60853-816-4(8),* Rosen Reference) 2006. (J). 29.25 *(978-1-4042-1967-0(6))* Rosen Publishing Group, Inc., The.

Zobel, Derek. Jupiter. 2010. (Exploring Space Ser.). (ENG., Illus.). 24p. (J). (gr. k-3). lib. bdg. 25.95 *(978-1-60014-406-6(3),* Blastoff! Readers) Bellwether Media.

JURISPRUDENCE

see Law

JURISTS

see Lawyers

JURY

De Capua, Sarah. Serving on a Jury. 2012. (True Book Ser.). (ENG., Illus.). 48p. (J). pap. 6.95 *(978-0-531-26214-6(6))* Scholastic Library Publishing.

—A True Book - Civics: Serving on a Jury. 2012. (ENG., Illus.). 48p. (J). lib. bdg. 29.00 *(978-0-531-26042-5(9),* Children's Pr.) Scholastic Library Publishing.

Furgang, Kathy. Seventh Amendment: The Right to a Jury Trial. 2011. (Amendments to the United States Constitution: the Bill of Rights Ser.). (ENG.). 64p. (YA). pap. 12.95 *(978-1-4488-2308-6(0),* Rosen Reference) Rosen Publishing Group, Inc., The.

—The Seventh Amendment: The Right to a Jury Trial. 2011. (Amendments to the United States Constitution: the Bill of Rights Ser.). (Illus.). 64p. (YA). (gr. 5-9). lib. bdg. 31.95 *(978-1-4488-1262-2(3))* Rosen Publishing Group, Inc., The.

Manning, Jack. Serving on a Jury. 1 vol. 2014. (Our Government Ser.). (ENG.). 24p. (gr. 1-2). lib. bdg. 25.32 *(978-1-4914-0333-4(0))* Capstone Press of Coughlan Cos.

Murray, Hallie. The Right to a Jury Trial: The Seventh Amendment. 2017. (Bill of Rights Ser.). 48p. (J). (gr. 5-6). lib. bdg. 27.93 ***(978-0-7660-8561-9(9))*** Enslow Pubs., Inc.

Smith, Rich. Seventh Amendment: The Right to a Trial by Jury. 1 vol. 2007. (Bill of Rights Ser.). (ENG.). 32p. (J). (gr. 3-7). lib. bdg. 27.07 *(978-1-59928-919-9(9),* Abdo & Daughter) ABDO Publishing Co.

—Sixth Amendment: The Right to a Fair Trial. 1 vol. 2007. (Bill of Rights Ser.). (ENG.). 32p. (gr. 4-8). 27.07 *(978-1-59928-918-2(0),* Abdo & Daughters) ABDO Publishing Co.

JUSTICE, ADMINISTRATION OF

see also Courts; Crime

Beier, Anne. The Supreme Court & the Judicial Branch. 2009. (Primary Source Library of American Citizenship Ser.). 32p. (gr. 5-5). 47.90 *(978-1-61511-230-2(8),* Rosen Reference) Rosen Publishing Group, Inc., The.

Cohen, Laura. The Gault Case & Young People's Rights: Debating Supreme Court Decisions. 2006. (Debating Supreme Court Decisions Ser.). (Illus.). 128p. (J). (gr. 7-12). lib. bdg. 27.94 *(978-0-7660-2476-2(8))* Enslow Pubs., Inc.

Cuthbert, Megan & Siemens, Jared. Courthouse. 2016. (J). ***(978-1-5105-1883-4(5))*** SmartBook Media, Inc.

Dupont, Ellen. The U. S. Justice System, Vol. 20. Gomez, Manny, ed. 2016. (Crime & Detection Ser.). (Illus.). 96p. (J). (gr. 7). 24.95 *(978-1-4222-3488-4(6))* Mason Crest.

—The United States Justice System. 2004. (Crime & Detection Ser.). (Illus.). 96p. (YA). (gr. 7-18). lib. bdg. 22.95 *(978-1-59084-377-2(0))* Mason Crest.

Emert, Phyllis Raybin. Attorneys General: Enforcing the Law. 2005. (In the Cabinet Ser.). (Illus.). 176p. (J). (gr. 7-18). lib. bdg. 24.95 *(978-1-881508-66-3(8))* Oliver Pr., Inc.

Genocide & International Justice. 2009. (Global Issues Ser.). 400p. (C). (gr. 9-18). 45.00 *(978-0-8160-7310-8(4))* Facts On File, Inc.

Gold, Susan Dudley. In Re Gault: Do Minors Have the Same Rights as Adults? 2007. (Supreme Court Milestones Ser.). (Illus.). 128p. (gr. 7-16). lib. bdg. 42.79 *(978-0-7614-2584-7(5),* Benchmark Bks.) Marshall Cavendish Corp.

Grinapol, Corinne. Racial Profiling & Discrimination: Your Legal Rights. 2015. (Know Your Rights Ser.). (ENG., Illus.). 64p. (J). (gr. 6-6). 33.25 *(978-1-4777-8020-6(3),* Rosen Young Adult) Rosen Publishing Group, Inc., The.

Hand, Carol. Using Computer Science in High Tech Criminal Justice Careers. 2017. (Coding Your Passion Ser.). 80p. (J). (gr. 12-12). 35.75 ***(978-1-5081-7511-7(X),*** Rosen Young Adult) Rosen Publishing Group, Inc., The.

Hanrahan, Clare. Legal System. 2007. (Opposing Viewpoints Ser.). (ENG., Illus.). 237p. (YA). (gr. 10-12). pap. 29.45 *(978-0-7377-3758-5(1),* LML02109-234418, Greenhaven Pr., Inc.) Cengage Gale.

Hanrahan, Clare M. Legal System. Hanrahan, Clare, ed. 2007. (Opposing Viewpoints Ser.). (ENG., Illus.). 224p. (gr. 10-12). 48.80 *(978-0-7377-3757-8(3),* LML02109-234427, Greenhaven Pr., Inc.) Cengage Gale.

Harris, Nancy. What's the State Judicial Branch? 2016. (First Guide to Government Ser.). (ENG.). 32p. (gr. 1-3). pap. 8.29 *(978-1-4846-3691-6(0),* Heinemann First Library) Heinemann-Raintree.

Hunter, David. Unequal Justice. 2017. (J). ***(978-1-4222-3789-2(3))*** Mason Crest.

Jacobs, Thomas A. They Broke the Law - You Be the Judge: True Cases of Teen Crime. 2003. (ENG.). 224p. (YA). (gr. 7-18). pap. 15.99 *(978-1-57542-134-6(8))* Free Spirit Publishing, Inc.

Juvenile Justice. 2nd rev. ed. 2010. (Point/Counterpoint Ser.). (Illus.). 104p. (C). (gr. 9-18). 35.00 *(978-1-60413-508-4(5),* Chelsea Hse.) Facts On File, Inc.

Krueger, Naomi J. How the Judicial Branch Works. 2016. (How America Works). (ENG.). 24p. (J). (gr. 3-6). 28.50 *(978-1-5038-0905-5(6),* 210662) Child's World, Inc., The.

Lange, Donna. On the Edge of Disaster: Youth in the Juvenile Court System. 2003. (Youth with Special Needs Ser.). (Illus.). 127p. (YA). (gr. 7). pap. 14.95 *(978-1-4222-0428-3(6))* Mason Crest.

Lansford, Tom. Justice, Policing, & the Rule of Law, Vol. 8. Lansford, Tom, ed. 2016. (Foundations of Democracy Ser.). (Illus.). 64p. (J). (gr. 7). 23.95 *(978-1-4222-3630-7(7))* Mason Crest.

LeVert, Suzanne. State Courts. 2003. (Kaleidoscope Ser.). (Illus.). 48p. (gr. 3-18). lib. bdg. 20.95 *(978-0-7614-1594-7(7),* Benchmark Bks.) Marshall Cavendish Corp.

Libal, Autumn. The True Costs of Prisons. 2017. (J). ***(978-1-4222-3781-6(8))*** Mason Crest.

Mattern, Joanne. Attorney General. 2003. (America's Leaders Ser.). (Illus.). 32p. (J). 24.94 *(978-1-56711-278-8(1),* Blackbirch Pr., Inc.) Cengage Gale.

Merino, Noel. Criminal Justice. 2012. (Opposing Viewpoints Ser.). (ENG., Illus.). 224p. (gr. 10-12). lib. bdg. 48.80 *(978-0-7377-6306-5(X),* Greenhaven Pr., Inc.) Cengage Gale.

Merino, No'l, ed. Criminal Justice. 2012. (Opposing Viewpoints Ser.). (ENG., Illus.). 240p. (gr. 10-12). pap. 29.45 *(978-0-7377-6307-2(8),* Greenhaven Pr., Inc.) Cengage Gale.

My Children Publishing, prod. I am the Judge. 2008. (Illus.). 154p. (YA). pap. 19.95 *(978-0-9799376-0-6(4))* My Children Publishing Inc.

Ogden, Charlie. Law & Justice. 2017. 32p. (J). ***(978-0-7787-3721-6(7))*** Crabtree Publishing Co.

Park, Peggy J. Is the Death Penalty Just? 2014. (In Controversy Ser.). (ENG., Illus.). 80p. (J). lib. bdg. *(978-1-60152-714-1(4))* ReferencePoint Pr., Inc.

Schauer, Peter J. What You Need to Know about Violent Crimes, Felonies, & the Law. 1 vol. 2015. (ENG., Illus.). 64p. (J). 33.25 *(978-1-4777-8024-4(6),* Rosen Reference) Rosen Publishing Group, Inc., The.

Smith, Roger & McIntosh, Martha. Juveniles Growing up in Prison. 2017. (J). ***(978-1-4222-3783-0(4))*** Mason Crest.

Trials & the Courts. 2010. (Criminal Justice Ser.). (Illus.). 128p. (gr. 6-12). 35.00 *(978-1-60413-616-6(2),* Chelsea Hse.) Facts On File, Inc.

JUSTINIAN I, EMPEROR OF THE EAST, 483?-565

Rodgers, Kelly. Justinian I: Byzantine Emperor. 1 vol. 2012. (Primary Source Readers Ser.). (ENG.). 32p. (J). (gr. 4-4). pap. 8.99 *(978-1-4333-5002-3(5))* Teacher Created Materials, Inc.

JUVENILE DELINQUENCY

see also Child Welfare

Barrington, Richard. The Junevile Court System: Your Legal Rights. 2015. (Know Your Rights Ser.). (ENG., Illus.). 64p. (J). (gr. 6-6). pap. 12.95 *(978-1-4777-8621-5(X),* Rosen Young Adult) Rosen Publishing Group, Inc., The.

Becnel, Barbara, ed. Gangs & the Abuse of Power: Stanley Tookie Williams Street Peace Series. 8 bks., Vol. 1, Bk. 7. 2008. 24p. (J). 6.95 *(978-0-9753584-7-4(2))* Damamli Publishing Co.

—Gangs & Violence: Stanley Tookie Williams Street Peace Series. 8 bks., Vol. 1, Bk. 3. 2008. 24p. (J). 6.95 *(978-0-9753584-4-3(8))* Damamli Publishing Co.

—Gangs & Your Neighborhood: Stanley Tookie Williams Street Peace Series. 8 bks., Vol. 1, Bk. 8. 2008. 24p. (J). 6.95 *(978-0-9753584-8-1(0))* Damamli Publishing Co.

Brennan, Janette. Child Convicts. 2015. (ENG., Illus.). 32p. (J). (gr. 3-7). 16.99 *(978-0-7636-7326-0(9))* Candlewick Pr.

Brezina, Corona. Deadly School & Campus Violence. 2008. (Violence & Society Ser.). (Illus.). 64p. (YA). (gr. 9-12). lib. bdg. 31.95 *(978-1-4042-1792-8(4))* Rosen Publishing Group, Inc., The.

—Frequently Asked Questions about Juvenile Detention. 2011. (FAQ: Teen Life Ser.). (ENG.). 64p. (YA). (gr. 7-12). lib. bdg. 31.95 *(978-1-4488-5560-5(8))* Rosen Publishing Group, Inc., The.

Gottfried Hollander, Barbara. Conduct Disorder. 2013. (Teen Mental Health Ser.). 48p. (YA). (gr. 7-12). 29.95 *(978-1-4777-1752-3(8))* Rosen Publishing Group, Inc., The.

Haerens, Margaret, ed. Juvenile Crime. 2013. (Global Viewpoints Ser.). (ENG., Illus.). 224p. (gr. 10-12). pap. 27.95 *(978-0-7377-6443-7(0));* lib. bdg. 40.45 *(978-0-7377-6267-9(5))* Cengage Gale. (Greenhaven Pr., Inc.).

Hiber, Amanda. Gangs. 2013. (Issues That Concern You Ser.). (ENG., Illus.). 144p. (gr. 7-10). lib. bdg. 42.00 *(978-0-7377-6294-5(2),* Greenhaven Pr., Inc.) Cengage Gale.

Jones, Patrick. Teen Incarceration: From Cell Bars to Ankle Bracelets. 2016. (ENG., Illus.). 120p. (YA). (gr. 7-12). lib. bdg. 37.32 *(978-1-4677-7572-4(X));* 55.99 *(978-1-5124-1138-6(8),* Twenty-First Century Bks.) Lerner Publishing Group.

Juvenile Justice. 2nd rev. ed. 2010. (Point/Counterpoint Ser.). (Illus.). 104p. (C). (gr. 9-18). 35.00 *(978-1-60413-508-4(5),* Chelsea Hse.) Facts On File, Inc.

Krygier, Leora. Juvenile Court: A Judge's Guide for Young Adults & Their Parents, Vol. 2008. (ENG., Illus.). 196p. (gr. 9-18). 45.00 *(978-0-8108-6127-5(5))* Scarecrow Pr., Inc.

Lange, Donna. On the Edge of Disaster: Youth in the Juvenile Court System. 2004. (Youth with Special Needs Ser.). (Illus.). 128p. (YA). lib. bdg. 24.95 *(978-1-59084-741-1(5))* Mason Crest.

—On the Edge of Disaster: Youth in the Juvenile Court System. 2003. (Youth with Special Needs Ser.). (Illus.). 127p. (YA). (gr. 7). pap. 14.95 *(978-1-4222-0428-3(6))* Mason Crest.

Langwith, Jacqueline. Juvenile Crime. Gale, ed. 2014. (Introducing Issues with Opposing Viewpoints Ser.). (ENG., Illus.). 144p. (gr. 10-12). lib. bdg. 42.00 *(978-0-7377-6925-8(4),* Greenhaven Pr., Inc.) Cengage Gale.

Latchana Kenney, Karen. The Hidden Story of Gangs & Crime. 1 vol., 1. 2014. (Undercover Story Ser.). (ENG.). 48p. (J). (gr. 5-8). 30.25 *(978-1-4777-2799-7(X),* Rosen Reference) Rosen Publishing Group, Inc., The.

Leverich, Jean. Juvenile Justice. 2009. (Issues on Trial Ser.). (ENG., Illus.). 240p. (gr. 10-12). 48.30 *(978-0-7377-4178-0(3),* Greenhaven Pr., Inc.) Cengage Gale.

Merino, Noël & Williams, Heidi. Juvenile Crime. 2010. (Issues That Concern You Ser.). (Illus.). 112-144p. (J). 36.95 *(978-0-7377-4955-7(5))* Cengage Gale.

Meyer, Terry Teague. Juvenile Detention Centers: Your Legal Rights. 2015. (Know Your Rights Ser.). (ENG., Illus.). 64p. (J). (gr. 6-6). 33.25 *(978-1-4777-8036-7(X),* Rosen Young Adult) Rosen Publishing Group, Inc., The.

mooney, carla. Teen Violence. 2013. (ENG.). 96p. (YA). lib. bdg. *(978-1-60152-496-6(X))* ReferencePoint Pr., Inc.

Parks, Peggy J. School Violence. 2008. (Compact Research Ser.). 104p. (YA). (gr. 7-12). lib. bdg. 25.95 *(978-1-60152-057-9(3))* ReferencePoint Pr., Inc.

Robinson, Tony. Bad Kids Vol. 1: The Naughtiest Children in History, 1. 2012. (ENG., Illus.). 96p. (J). (gr. 4-7). pap. 12.99 *(978-0-330-51080-6(0))* Pan Macmillan GBR. Dist: Independent Pubs. Group.

—Bad Kids Vol. 1: The Worst Behaved Children in History, 1. Phillips, Mike, illus. unabr. ed. 2009. (ENG.). 144p. 28.50 *(978-0-230-73787-7(0),* Macmillan) Pan Macmillan GBR. Dist: Trans-Atlantic Pubns., Inc.

Smith, Roger & McIntosh, Martha. Juveniles Growing up in Prison. 2017. (J). ***(978-1-4222-3783-0(4))*** Mason Crest.

Spencer, Betty. Life Is Fragile: One Girl's Story of the Bath School Disaster. Gallinger, Jared, illus. 2007. 68p. per. 19.95 *(978-1-60441-772-2(2))* America Star Bks.

Watson, Stephanie. Incarcerated Youth. 2016. (ENG.). 80p. (J). (gr. 5-12). lib. bdg. *(978-1-60152-982-4(1))* ReferencePoint Pr., Inc.

Wolny, Philip. Defeating Gangs in Your Neighborhood & Online. 01 vols., 1. 2016. (Effective Survival Strategies Ser.). (ENG.). 64p. (J). 32.95 *(978-1-4994-6151-0(8),* Rosen Young Adult) Rosen Publishing Group, Inc., The.

JUVENILE DELINQUENCY—FICTION

Berry, Julie & Gardner, Sally Faye. The Rat Brain Fiasco. 2010. (Splurch Academy Ser.: 1). (ENG.). 208p. (J). (gr. 3-7). pap. 6.99 *(978-0-448-45359-0(2),* Grosset & Dunlap) Penguin Young Readers Group.

De la Peña, Matt. We Were Here. 2010. (ENG.). 368p. (YA). (gr. 9). pap. 9.99 *(978-0-385-73670-1(3),* Ember) Random Hse. Children's Bks.

Deen, Natasha. Sleight of Hand. 1 vol. 2015. (Orca Soundings Ser.). (ENG.). 144p. (YA). (gr. 8-12). pap. 9.95 *(978-1-4598-1120-1(8))* Orca Bk. Pubs. USA.

Ducie, Joe. Crystal Force. 2016. (ENG.). 288p. (YA). (gr. 7). pap. 9.99 *(978-1-4714-0455-9(2))* Bonnier Publishing GBR. Dist: Independent Pubs. Group.

Frye, Mark. School Shooter: In His Own Words. 2005. 194p. (J). per. 14.95 *(978-0-595-34751-3(7))* iUniverse, Inc.

Gantos, Jack. The Follower. 2015. (ENG.). 224p. (YA). (gr. 7-10). 17.99 *(978-0-374-37995-7(5),* 9780374379957, Farrar, Straus & Giroux (BYR)) Farrar, Straus & Giroux.

Ghislain, Gary. How I Stole Johnny Depp's Alien Girlfriend. 2011. (ENG., Illus.). 208p. (YA). (gr. 7-17). 16.99 *(978-0-8118-7460-1(5))* Chronicle Bks. LLC.

Griffin, Paul. Ten Mile River. 2011. (ENG.). 208p. (YA). (gr. 7-18). 7.99 *(978-0-14-241983-0(4),* Speak) Penguin Young Readers Group.

Herrndorf, Wolfgang. Why We Took the Car. Mohr, Tim, tr. from GER. 2014. (ENG.). 256p. (J). (gr. 9). 17.99 *(978-0-545-48180-9(5),* Levine, Arthur A. Bks.) Scholastic, Inc.

Ius, Dawn. Overdrive. 2016. (ENG., Illus.). 352p. (YA). (gr. 9). 17.99 *(978-1-4814-3944-2(8),* Simon Pulse) Simon Pulse.

Korman, Gordon. The Juvie Three. 2010. (ENG.). 256p. (YA). (gr. 7-17). pap. 8.99 *(978-1-4231-0162-8(6))* Hyperion Pr.

Lange, Erin Jade. Rebel, Bully, Geek, Pariah. 2016. (ENG.). 320p. (YA). 17.99 *(978-1-61963-498-5(8),* 9781619634985, Bloomsbury USA Childrens) Bloomsbury Publishing USA.

McClintock, Norah. Down. 1 vol. 2007. (Orca Soundings Ser.). (ENG.). 128p. (YA). (gr. 8-12). pap. 9.95 *(978-1-55143-766-8(X))* Orca Bk. Pubs. USA.

—In Too Deep. 2013. (Robyn Hunter Mysteries Ser.: 8). (ENG.). 224p. (YA). (gr. 6-12). pap. 8.95 *(978-1-4677-0702-2(3));* lib. bdg. 27.93 *(978-0-7613-8318-5(2))* Lerner Publishing Group.

—Last Chance. 2012. (Robyn Hunter Mysteries Ser.: 1). (ENG.). 232p. (YA). (gr. 6-12). pap. 8.95

(978-0-7613-8529-5(0), Darby Creek); lib. bdg. 27.93 (978-0-7613-8311-6(5)) Lerner Publishing Group.
McLaughlin, Lauren. The Free. 2017. (ENG.). 288p. (YA). (gr. 9). 18.99 (978-1-61695-731-5(X), Soho Teen) Soho Pr., Inc.
Morgan, Kass. Homecoming. 2015. (100 Ser.: 3). (ENG.). 352p. (J). (gr. 10-17). pap. 12.99 (978-0-316-38196-3(9)) Little, Brown Bks. for Young Readers.
Myers, Walter Dean. Lockdown. (YA). (gr. 8). 2011. (ENG.). 272p. pap. 9.99 (978-0-06-121482-0(5)) 2010. 256p. lib. bdg. 17.89 (978-0-06-121481-3(7)) 2010. (ENG.). 256p. 16.99 (978-0-06-121480-6(9)) HarperCollins Pubs. (Amistad).
Northrop, Michael. Rotten. 2013. (ENG.). 256p. (J). (gr. 7). 17.99 (978-0-545-49587-5(3), Scholastic Pr.) Scholastic, Inc.
Pérez, Ashley Hope. The Knife & the Butterfly. 2012. (Carolrhoda YA Ser.). (ENG.). 216p. (YA). (gr. 9-12). 17.95 (978-0-7613-6156-5(1), Carolrhoda Lab™) Lerner Publishing Group.
Sachar, Louis. Buracos. pap. 29.95 (978-85-336-1280-8(X)) Livraria Martins Editora BRA. Dist: Distribooks, Inc.
—Holes. 2008. (KOR., Illus.). 334p. (J). pap. (978-89-364-5602-3(4)) Chang-jag and Bipyeong Co.
—Holes. 10th ed. 2008. (ENG., Illus.). 272p. (J). (gr. 4-8). 18.99 (978-0-374-33266-2(5), 9780374332662, Farrar, Straus & Giroux (BYR)) Farrar, Straus & Giroux.
—Holes. 2008. (ENG.). (J). 39.99 (978-0-7393-7103-9(7)) Findaway World, LLC.
—Holes. 2014. (CHI & ENG.). 246p. (J). (gr. 4-8). pap. (978-7-5442-7158-5(7)) Fukuinkan Shoten.
—Holes. 2009. 9.14 (978-0-7848-1394-2(9), Everbind) Marco Bk. Co.
—Holes. 240p. (J). (gr. 4-6). pap. 5.99 (978-0-8072-8073-7(9), Listening Library) Random Hse. Audio Publishing Group.
—Holes, 4 vols. (J). 2006. 46.75 (978-1-4193-6136-4(8)) 2004. 1.25 (978-1-4025-6758-2(8)) Recorded Bks., Inc.
—Holes. l.t. ed. 2003. 288p. pap. 10.95 (978-0-7862-6190-1(0)) Thorndike Pr.
—Small Steps. 2008. (Readers Circle Ser.). 257p. (gr. 5-9). 20.00 (978-0-7569-9130-2(7)) Perfection Learning Corp.
—Small Steps. 2008. (ENG.). 288p. (YA). (gr. 7-9). pap. 9.99 (978-0-385-73315-1(1), Ember) Random Hse. Children's Bks.
—Small Steps. rev. l.t. ed. 2006. 339p. 23.95 (978-0-7862-8297-5(5)) Thorndike Pr.
Schuh, Eileen. The Traz. 2012. 148p. pap. (978-1-926997-61-2(1)) Imajin Bks.
Spradlin, Michael P. Live & Let Shop. 2005. (Spy Goddess Ser.: Bk. 1). (ENG., Illus.). 224p. (gr. 7-18). 15.99 (978-0-06-059407-7(1)) HarperCollins Pubs.
Strasser, Todd. Boot Camp. 2012. (ENG.). 272p. (YA). (gr. 7). pap. 11.99 (978-1-4424-3358-8(2), Simon & Schuster Bks. For Young Readers) Simon & Schuster Bks. For Young Readers.
—Boot Camp. 2007. (ENG.). 256p. (YA). (gr. 7-12). 16.99 (978-1-4169-0848-7(X)) Simon & Schuster Children's Publishing.
—Boot Camp. 2008. (ENG., Illus.). 256p. (YA). (gr. 7). mass mkt. 7.99 (978-1-4169-5942-7(4), Simon Pulse) Simon Pulse.
Tagged. 2015. (ENG.). 288p. (YA). (gr. 7). lib. bdg. 16.95 (978-1-58089-583-5(2)) Charlesbridge Publishing, Inc.
Trueman, Terry. Inside Out. 128p. 2003. (J). lib. bdg. 16.89 (978-0-06-623963-7(X)) 2004. (ENG.). (YA). (gr. 9). reprint ed. pap. 8.99 (978-0-06-447376-7(7), HarperTeen) HarperCollins Pubs.
Volponi, Paul. Rikers High. (ENG.). (YA). (gr. 7-18). 2011. 272p. 7.99 (978-0-14-241778-2(5), Speak) 2010. 256p. 16.99 (978-0-670-01107-0(X), Viking Books for Young Readers) Penguin Young Readers Group.
Voorhees, Coert. On the Free. 2017. (ENG.). 280p. (YA). (gr. 9-12). 17.99 **(978-1-5124-2913-8(9))** Lerner Publishing Group.

JUVENILE LITERATURE

see Children's Literature

K

KAFKA, FRANZ, 1883-1924

Férriz, Ramón Gónzalez. Franz Kafka -el miedo a la Vida. 2005. (SPA.). 96p. (YA). (978-958-30-1360-7(9)) Panamericana Editorial.
Kafka, Franz. The Metamorphosis. Bloom, Harold, ed. 2007. (Bloom's Guides). 87p. (YA). (gr. 9-12). lib. bdg. 30.00 (978-0-7910-9298-9(4)) Facts On File, Inc.

KAHLO, FRIDA, 1910-1954

Alvarez, Mateo. Frida Kahlo: Famous Mexican Artist. 2015. (Exceptional Latinos Ser.). (ENG.). 24p. (J). (gr. 3-4). pap. 9.35 (978-0-7660-6714-1(9)) Enslow Pubs., Inc.
Anholt, Laurence. Frida Kahlo & the Bravest Girl in the World. 2016. (Anholt's Artists Ser.). (ENG.). 32p. (J). (gr. -1-3). 16.99 (978-0-7641-6837-6(1)) Barron's Educational Series, Inc.
Berne, Emma Carlson. Frida Kahlo: Groundbreaking Artist, 1 vol. 2009. (Essential Lives Set 4 Ser.). (ENG., Illus.). 112p. (J). (gr. 6-12). lib. bdg. 35.64 (978-1-60453-701-7(9)) ABDO Publishing Co.
Brown, Monica. Frida Kahlo & Her Animalitos. Parra, John, illus. 2017. (ENG.). 40p. (J). (gr. -1-3). 17.95 **(978-0-7358-4269-4(8))** North-South Bks., Inc.
Colbert, David & Chambers, Mark. Frida Kahlo. 2009. (10 Days Ser.). (ENG.). 160p. (J). (gr. 3-8). pap. 6.99 (978-1-4169-6809-2(1), Simon & Schuster/Paula Wiseman Bks.) Simon & Schuster/Paula Wiseman Bks.
Fabiny, Sarah. Who Was Frida Kahlo? Hoare, Jerry, illus. 2013. (Who Was? Ser.). (ENG.). 112p. (J). (gr. 3-7). 5.99 (978-0-448-47938-5(9), Grosset & Dunlap) Penguin Young Readers Group.
—Who Was Frida Kahlo? 2013. (Who Was... ? Ser.). lib. bdg. 16.00 (978-0-606-34164-6(1), Turtleback) Turtleback Bks.
Guzman, Lila & Guzman, Rick. Frida Kahlo: Painting Her Life. 2006. (Famous Latinos Ser.). (Illus.). 32p. (J). (gr. 3-4). lib. bdg. 22.60 (978-0-7660-2643-8(4), Enslow Elementary) Enslow Pubs., Inc.
Guzmán, Lila & Guzmán, Rick. Frida Kahlo: Pinto su Vida. 2007. (Latinos Famosos Ser.). (SPA., Illus.). 32p. (J). (gr. 3-7). lib. bdg. 23.94 (978-0-7660-2678-0(7), Enslow Elementary) Enslow Pubs., Inc.
Hillstrom, Laurie. Frida Kahlo, Painter. 2008. (Twentieth Century Most Influential Hispanics Ser.). (ENG., Illus.). 96-128p. (YA). (gr. 7-12). 34.80 (978-1-4205-0019-6(8)) Cengage Gale.
Holzhey, Magdalena. Frida Kahlo: The Artist in the Blue House. 2003. (Adventures in Art Ser.). (Illus.). 30p. (J). (gr. 5-18). 14.95 (978-3-7913-2863-8(8)) Prestel Publishing.
Kent, Deborah. Frida Kahlo: An Artist Celebrates Life. 2004. (Proud Heritage: the Hispanic Library). (ENG., Illus.). 40p. (J). (gr. 3-6). 29.93 (978-1-59296-167-2(3), 200008) Child's World, Inc., The.
Klein, Adam G. Frida Kahlo, 1 vol. 2007. (Great Artists Set 2 Ser.). (ENG., Illus.). 32p. (J). (gr. -1-3). 27.07 (978-1-59679-731-4(2), Checkerboard Library) ABDO Publishing Co.
Laidlaw, Jill A. Frida Kahlo. 2003. (Artists in Their Time Ser.). (ENG., Illus.). 48p. (J). (gr. 5-7). pap. 6.95 (978-0-531-16642-0(2), Watts, Franklin) Scholastic Library Publishing.
Lenero, Carmen. Frida Kahlo. Mesquita, Camila, illus. 2004. (Niñez de... Ser.). 24p. pap. 6.95 (978-85-7416-216-4(7)) Callis Editora Ltda BRA. Dist: Independent Pubs. Group.
Medina, Mariana & Wooten, Sara McIntosh. Frida Kahlo: Self-Portrait Artist. 2015. (Influential Latinos Ser.). (ENG., Illus.). 128p. (J). (gr. 7-7). 37.27 (978-0-7660-6997-8(4)) Enslow Pubs., Inc.
Morales, Yuyi. Viva Frida. O'Meara, Tim, photos by. 2014. (ENG., Illus.). 40p. (J). (gr. -1-3). 17.99 (978-1-59643-603-9(4), 9781596436039) Roaring Brook Pr.
Morrison, John. Frida Kahlo. 2nd rev. ed. 2010. (Great Hispanic Heritage Ser.). (Illus.). 128p. (J). (gr. 6-12). 35.00 (978-1-60413-846-7(7), Chelsea Hse.) Facts On File, Inc.
Nardo, Don, ed. Frida Kahlo. 2012. (Eye on Art Ser.). (ENG., Illus.). 128p. (J). (gr. 7-10). lib. bdg. 34.80 (978-1-4205-0850-5(4), Lucent Bks.) Cengage Gale.
Reef, Catherine. Frida & Diego: Art, Love, Life. 2014. (ENG., Illus.). 176p. (J). (gr. 7-12). 18.99 (978-0-547-82184-9(0), Clarion Bks.) Houghton Mifflin Harcourt Publishing Co.
Sabbeth, Carol. Frida Kahlo & Diego Rivera: Their Lives & Ideas, 24 Activities. 2005. (For Kids Ser.). (ENG., Illus.). 160p. (J). (gr. 4). pap. 17.95 (978-1-55652-569-8(9), 1241061) Chicago Review Pr., Inc.
Sanchez Vegara, Isabel & Eng, Gee Fan. Frida Kahlo. 2016. (Little People, Big Dreams Ser.). (ENG.). 32p. (J). (gr. k-3). 14.99 (978-1-84780-783-0(6), Frances Lincoln Children's Bks.) Quarto Publishing Group UK GBR. Dist: Hachette Bk. Group.
Sanchez Vegara, Isabel & Fan, Eng Gee. Frida Kahlo. 2016. (Little People, Big Dreams Ser.). (ENG., Illus.). 32p. (J). 14.99 (978-1-84780-770-0(4), Frances Lincoln Children's Bks.) Quarto Publishing Group UK GBR. Dist: Littlehampton Bk Services, Ltd.
Venezia, Mike. Frida Kahlo. Venezia, Mike, illus. 2015. (Getting to Know the World's Greatest Artists Ser.). (ENG., Illus.). 40p. (J). lib. bdg. 29.00 (978-0-531-21259-2(9), Children's Pr.) Scholastic Library Publishing.
Wooten, Sara McIntosh. Frida Kahlo: Her Life in Paintings. 2005. (Latino Biography Library). (Illus.). 128p. (J). (gr. 6-13). lib. bdg. 31.93 (978-0-7660-2487-8(3)) Enslow Pubs., Inc.

KAIULANI, PRINCESS OF HAWAII, 1875-1899

McDonnell, Peter. The Last Princess. 2005. (Illus.). 16p. (978-0-7367-2910-9(0)) Zaner-Bloser, Inc.

KAKURO

Pazzelli, John. Kids' Kakuro. Zourelias, Diana, illus. 2006. (Dover Children's Activity Bks.). (ENG.). 62p. (J). (gr. 3). per. 5.95 (978-0-486-45344-6(8)) Dover Pubns., Inc.

KALAHARI DESERT

Aloian, Molly. The Kalahari Desert. 2012. (ENG.). 32p. (J). lib. bdg. (978-0-7787-0712-7(1)); (Illus.). pap. (978-0-7787-0720-2(2)) Crabtree Publishing Co.
Clarke, Nadine. Get Bushwise: on Safari Desert, River, Bushveld: A Young Explorer's Guide. 2013. 192p. pap. 23.00 (978-1-4317-0206-0(4)) Penguin Random House Grupo Editorial ESP. Dist: Casemate Pubs. & Bk. Distributors, LLC.

KAMEHAMEHA I, THE GREAT, KING OF THE HAWAIIAN ISLANDS, -1819

Crowe, Ellie. Kamehameha: The Boy Who Became a Warrior King. Robinson, Don, illus. rev. ed. 2008. (ENG.). 62p. (J). (gr. k-k). pap. (978-1-59700-591-3(6)) Island Heritage Publishing.

KANGAROO RATS

Phillips, Dee. Kangaroo Rat's Burrow. 2015. (Illus.). 24p. (J). lib. bdg. (978-1-62724-310-0(0)) Bearport Publishing Co., Inc.

KANGAROOS

Arnold, Quinn M. & Riggs, Kate. Kangaroos. 2017. (Seedlings Ser.). (ENG., Illus.). 24p. (J). (gr. k-2). pap. 7.99 (978-1-62832-335-1(3), Creative Paperbacks) Creative Co., The.
Austen, Amy. The Life Cycle of a Kangaroo. 2015. (Watch Them Grow! Ser.). (ENG., Illus.). 24p. (J). (gr. 1-1). pap. 8.25 (978-1-4994-0672-6(X), PowerKids Pr.) Rosen Publishing Group, Inc., The.
Borgert-Spaniol, Megan. Baby Kangaroos. 2016. (Super Cute! Ser.). (ENG., Illus.). 24p. (J). (gr. k-3). 25.95 (978-1-62617-389-7(3), Blastoff! Readers) Bellwether Media.
Bredeson, Carmen. Kangaroos up Close. (Zoom in on Animals! Ser.). (Illus.). 24p. (J). 2012. (gr. k-18). pap. 7.95 (978-1-59845-416-1(1)) 2008. (gr. 1-3). lib. bdg. 22.60 (978-0-7660-3079-4(2)) Enslow Pubs., Inc. (Enslow Elementary).
Burke, Johanna. A Kangaroo Mob. 2013. (Animal Groups Ser.). (Illus.). 24p. (J). (gr. 1-3). pap. 8.15 (978-1-4339-8200-2(5)); lib. bdg. 22.60 (978-1-4339-8199-9(8)) Stevens, Gareth Publishing LLLP.
—A Kangaroo Mob / una Manada de Canguros. 2013. (Animal Groups / Grupos de animales Ser.). (ENG & SPA., Illus.). 24p. (gr. 1-3). 22.60 (978-1-4339-8804-2(6)) Stevens, Gareth Publishing LLLP.
Calhoun, Kelly. High-Speed Hoppers: Kangaroo. 2015. (Guess What Ser.). (ENG.). 24p. (J). (gr. k-2). pap. 12.79 (978-1-63362-712-3(8), 206681) Cherry Lake Publishing.
—Saltarines de Alta Velocidad (High-Speed Hoppers) Canguro (Kangaroo) 2016. (Adivina (Guess What) Ser.). (SPA., Illus.). 24p. (J). (gr. k-2). 28.50 (978-1-63471-449-5(0), 208859) Cherry Lake Publishing.
Clark, Willow. Tree Kangaroos. 2012. (Up a Tree Ser.). (ENG., Illus.). 24p. (J). (gr. k-3). lib. bdg. 22.60 (978-1-4488-6189-7(6)); pap. 8.25 (978-1-4488-6337-2(6), PowerKids Pr.) Rosen Publishing Group, Inc., The.
Costain, Meredith. Kangaroo. Jackson-Carter, Stuart, illus. 2016. (Wild World Ser.). 00032p. (J). (gr. 1-2). pap. 10.00 (978-1-4994-8212-6(4), Windmill Bks.) Rosen Publishing Group, Inc., The.
Davin, Rose. Kangaroos. 2017. (Meet Desert Animals Ser.). (ENG., Illus.). 24p. (gr. k-1). lib. bdg. 26.65 (978-1-5157-4604-1(6), Pebble Plus) Capstone Press of Coughlan Cos.
De la Bédoyère, Camilla. Joey to Kangaroo. 2012. (Illus.). 24p. (gr. 1-3). pap. 7.95 (978-1-926853-38-3(5)) Saunders Bk. Co. CAN. Dist: RiverStream Publishing.
De Luca, Daniela. Buster the Kangaroo. 2008. (It's a Wildlife, Buddy! Ser.). (ENG., Illus.). 30p. (J). (gr. -1-1). 12.95 (978-88-89272-62-6(7)) McRae Bks. Srl ITA. Dist: Independent Pubs. Group.
Doudna, Kelly. It's a Baby Kangaroo!, 1 vol. 2010. (Baby Australian Animals Ser.). (ENG., Illus.). 24p. (J). (gr. k-3). lib. bdg. 24.21 (978-1-60453-576-1(8), SandCastle) ABDO Publishing Co.
Franks, Katie. Kangaroos. 2014. (Zoo's Who's Who Ser.). (Illus.). 24p. (J). (gr. k-2). pap. 49.50 (978-1-4777-6573-9(5), PowerKids Pr.) Rosen Publishing Group, Inc., The.
French, Jackie. How High Can a Kangaroo Hop? Whatley, Bruce, illus. 2008. 256p. pap. (978-0-7322-8544-9(5)) HarperCollins Pubs. Australia.
Ganeri, Anita. Discover the Kangaroo. 2016. (Fabulous Animals Ser.). (ENG., Illus.). 32p. (gr. 1-3). lib. bdg. 27.32 (978-1-4846-2709-9(1), Heinemann First Library) Heinemann-Raintree.
—Red Kangaroo, 1 vol. 2011. (Day in the Life: Desert Animals Ser.). (ENG.). 24p. (gr. k-2). 23.32 (978-1-4329-4774-3(5), Heinemann Read & Learn) Heinemann-Raintree.
Gareth Stevens Publishing Staff, contrib. by. Kangaroos. 2004. (All about Wild Animals Ser.). (Illus.). 32p. (gr. k-4). lib. bdg. 26.00 (978-0-8368-4119-0(0), Gareth Stevens Learning Library) Stevens, Gareth Publishing LLLP.
Gish, Melissa. Kangaroos. 2011. (Living Wild Ser.). (ENG.). 48p. (J). (gr. 4-7). pap. 12.00 (978-0-89812-553-5(7), Creative Paperbacks) Creative Co., The.
Gordon, Sharon. Guess Who Hops: Adivina Quién Salta. 2007. (Bookworms — Bilingual Editions: Guess Who/Adivina Quien 2 Ser.). (SPA & ENG.). 32p. (gr. k-2). 15.95 (978-0-7614-2884-8(4)); 15.95 (978-0-7614-2867-1(4)) Marshall Cavendish Corp.
Hewett, Joan. A Kangaroo Joey Grows Up. Hewett, Richard, photos by. 2005. (Baby Animals Ser.). (Illus.). 32p. (J). (gr. k-3). lib. bdg. 21.27 (978-1-57505-165-9(6)) Lerner Publishing Group.
Jango-Cohen, Judith. Kangaroos. 2005. (Animals Animals Ser.). (Illus.). 48p. (J). (gr. 3-7). lib. bdg. 29.93 (978-0-7614-1869-6(5), Benchmark Bks.) Marshall Cavendish Corp.
Lawrence, Ellen. A Kangaroo's Life. 2012. (Animal Diaries: Life Cycles Ser.). 24p. (J). (gr. -1-3). lib. bdg. 23.93 (978-1-61772-415-2(7)) Bearport Publishing Co., Inc.
Leigh, Anna. Meet a Baby Kangaroo. 2017. (Lightning Bolt Books (tm) — Baby Australian Animals Ser.). (ENG.). (J). (gr. 1-3). 24p. 25.32 **(978-1-5124-3384-5(5))**; pap. 6.99 **(978-1-5124-5588-5(1))** Lerner Publishing Group.
—Meet a Baby Wallaby. 2017. (Lightning Bolt Books (tm) — Baby Australian Animals Ser.). (ENG.). (J). (gr. 1-3). 24p. 25.32 **(978-1-5124-3386-9(1))**; pap. 6.99 **(978-1-5124-5591-5(1))** Lerner Publishing Group.
Levine, Michelle. Jumping Kangaroos. 2005. (Pull Ahead Bks.). (J). 22.60 (978-0-8225-2421-2(X), Lerner Pubns.); (ENG., Illus.). 32p. pap. 7.95 (978-0-8225-2440-3(6)) Lerner Publishing Group.
Linde, Barbara M. The Bizarre Life Cycle of A Kangaroo. 2012. (Strange Life Cycles Ser.). (Illus.). 24p. (J). (gr. 2-5). 22.60 (978-1-4339-7047-4(3)); pap. 8.15 (978-1-4339-7048-1(1)) Stevens, Gareth Publishing LLLP. (Gareth Stevens Learning Library).
Lunde, Darrin P. Hello, Mama Wallaroo. Wynne, Patricia J., illus. 2013. (ENG.). 32p. (J). (gr. -1-2). pap. 6.95 (978-1-57091-797-4(3)); lib. bdg. 15.95 (978-1-57091-796-7(5)) Charlesbridge Publishing, Inc.
Lunis, Natalie. Red Kangaroo: The World's Largest Marsupial. 2010. (More SuperSized! Ser.). (Illus.). 24p. (J). (gr. k-3). lib. bdg. 22.61 (978-1-936087-24-2(3)) Bearport Publishing Co., Inc.
McNeil, Niki, et al. HOCPP 1121 Kangaroos. 2006. spiral bd. 12.50 (978-1-60308-121-4(6)) In the Hands of a Child.
McRae, Anne & Morris, Neil. Buster the Kangaroo. De Luca, Daniela, illus. 2017. (J). **(978-0-7166-3523-9(2))** World Bk., Inc.
Meister, Cari. Do You Really Want to Meet a Kangaroo? Fabbri, Daniele, illus. 2015. (Do You Really Want to Meet ... ? Ser.). (ENG.). 24p. (J). (gr. 1-3). 19.95 (978-1-60753-734-2(6)) Amicus Publishing.
Montgomery, Sy. Quest for the Tree Kangaroo: An Expedition to the Cloud Forest of New Guinea. Bishop, Nic, photos by. 2006. (Scientists in the Field Ser.). (ENG., Illus.). 80p. (J). (gr. 5-7). 18.99 (978-0-618-49641-9(6)) Houghton Mifflin Harcourt Publishing Co.
Murray, Julie. Kangaroos, 1 vol. (Australian Animals Ser.). (ENG., Illus.). 2011. 32p. (J). (gr. 2-5). 28.50 (978-1-61783-011-2(9)) 2005. 24p. (gr. k-4). 25.65 (978-1-59197-338-6(4), Buddy Bks.) ABDO Publishing Co.
Nickel, Bonnie. Those Kooky Kangaroos. 2012. (Those Amazing Animals Ser.). (ENG., Illus.). 56p. (J). 14.95 (978-1-56164-534-3(6)); pap. 9.95 (978-1-56164-535-0(4)) Pineapple Pr., Inc.
Owings, Lisa. From Joey to Kangaroo. 2016. (Start to Finish, Second Ser.). (ENG., Illus.). 24p. (J). (gr. k-3). lib. bdg. 23.99 (978-1-5124-1830-9(7), Lerner Pubns.) Lerner Publishing Group.
Phillips, Dee. Tree Kangaroo. 2013. (Science Slam: Treed-Animal Life in the Trees Ser.). 24p. (J). (gr. -1-3). lib. bdg. 23.93 (978-1-61772-914-0(0)) Bearport Publishing Co., Inc.
Pohl, Kathleen. Kangaroos. 2007. (Let's Read about Animals Ser.). (Illus.). 24p. (gr. k-3). pap. 8.15 (978-0-8368-7824-0(8)); lib. bdg. 22.00 (978-0-8368-7817-2(5)) Stevens, Gareth Publishing LLLP. (Weekly Reader Leveled Readers).
—Kangaroos/Canguros. 2007. (Let's Read about Animals/ Conozcamos a los animales Ser.). (ENG & SPA., Illus.). 24p. (gr. k-3). (J). lib. bdg. 22.00 (978-0-8368-8006-9(4)); pap. 8.15 (978-0-8368-8013-7(7)) Stevens, Gareth Publishing LLLP. (Weekly Reader Leveled Readers).
Rebus, Anna. Kangaroos. 2006. (Amazing Animals Ser.). (Illus.). 24p. (J). (gr. 3-7). pap. 8.95 (978-1-59036-399-7(X)); lib. bdg. 24.45 (978-1-59036-393-5(0)) Weigl Pubs., Inc.
Reilly, Pauline. Kangaroo. Russell, Gayle, illus. (Picture Roo Bks.). 32p. (J). pap. (978-0-86417-538-0(8), Kangaroo Pr.) Simon & Schuster Australia.
Rigby Education Staff. Kangaroo. (Illus.). (J). suppl. ed. 20.00 (978-0-7635-6461-2(3), 764613C99) Rigby Education.
Riggs, Kate. Amazing Animals: Kangaroos. 2012. (Amazing Animals Ser.). (ENG., Illus.). 24p. (J). (gr. 1-3). pap. 8.99 (978-0-89812-693-8(2), Creative Paperbacks) Creative Co., The.
—Kangaroos. (J). 2016. (Illus.). 24p. (978-1-60818-739-3(X)) 2012. 25.65 (978-1-60818-108-7(1)) Creative Co., The. (Creative Education).
Robbins, Lynette. Kangaroos. 2012. (J). 49.50 (978-1-4488-5160-7(2), PowerKids Pr.); pap. 8.25 (978-1-4488-5159-1(9), PowerKids Pr.); lib. bdg. 22.60 (978-1-4488-5013-6(4)) Rosen Publishing Group, Inc., The.
Saxby, Claire. Big Red Kangaroo. Byrne, Graham, illus. 2015. (ENG.). 32p. (J). (gr. k-3). 16.99 (978-0-7636-7075-7(8)) Candlewick Pr.
Schuetz, Kari. Kangaroos. 2013. (Animal Safari Ser.). (ENG., Illus.). 24p. (J). (gr. k-3). lib. bdg. 25.95 (978-1-60014-864-4(6), Blastoff! Readers) Bellwether Media.
Schuh, Mari. Kangaroos. 2015. (J). lib. bdg. 25.65 (978-1-62031-175-2(5), Bullfrog Bks.) Jump! Inc.
Stockburger, Susan. Adventures of Sugar Pie! 2011. 20p. (gr. -1). pap. 11.00 (978-1-4567-5356-6(8)) AuthorHouse.
Turnbull, Stephanie. Kangaroo. 2015. (Big Beasts Ser.). (Illus.). 24p. (gr. k-3). 28.50 (978-1-62588-166-3(5)) Black Rabbit Bks.
—Kangaroo. 2015. (ENG., Illus.). 24p. (J). pap. 8.95 (978-1-77092-214-3(8)) RiverStream Publishing.
Twine, Alice. Kangaroos. (Baby Animals Ser.). 24p. 2009. (gr. 1-1). 42.50 (978-1-61511-491-7(2)) 2008. (Illus.). (J). (gr. 3-7). lib. bdg. 22.60 (978-1-4042-4145-9(0)) Rosen Publishing Group, Inc., The. (PowerKids Pr.).
—Kangaroos/Canguros. 2009. (Baby Animals/Animales bebé Ser.). (ENG & SPA.). 24p. (gr. 1-1). 42.50 (978-1-61511-503-7(X), Editorial Buenas Letras) Rosen Publishing Group, Inc., The.
—Kangaroos/Canguros. Obregon, Jose Maria, tr. from ENG. 2008. (Baby Animals / Animales Bebé Ser.). (SPA., Illus.). 24p. (J). (gr. k-3). lib. bdg. 22.60 (978-1-4042-7684-0(X)) Rosen Publishing Group, Inc., The.
Wilsdon, Christina. Kangaroos. 2010. (Amazing Animals Ser.). (ENG.). 48p. (J). (gr. 2-6). pap. 10.50 (978-1-4339-4017-0(5)); lib. bdg. 28.00 (978-1-4339-4016-3(7)) Stevens, Gareth Publishing LLLP. (Gareth Stevens Learning Library).
—Kangaroos. 2006. (J). (978-1-59939-078-9(7), Reader's Digest Young Families, Inc.) Studio Fun International.

KANGAROOS—FICTION

Aldrick, Shirley H. F. Hazel, the Hoppity Kangaroo. 2010. 28p. pap. 12.50 (978-1-60860-743-3(7), Strategic Bk. Publishing) Strategic Book Publishing & Rights Agency (SBPRA).
Angel, Ido. Vipo in Australia: The Koala & the Kangaroo. 2015. (AV2 Animated Storytime Ser.). (ENG.). (J). lib. bdg. 29.99 (978-1-4896-3905-9(5), AV2 by Weigl) Weigl Pubs., Inc.
Baker, David. The Roos, A home for Baby. 2005. 14p. 12.49 (978-1-4116-2290-6(1)) Lulu Pr., Inc.
—The Roos, Baby's new Friend. 2006. 18p. 12.49 (978-1-4116-9123-0(7)) Lulu Pr., Inc.
Baldree, Travis. Jumpin' Joey. 2nd ed. 2013. 28p. pap. 9.99 (978-0-9855312-9-4(0)) Bolton Publishing LLC.
Barraza, Cindy Lou. Mexiroo Dice, ¡Qué Importa! 2013. 32p. pap. 12.99 (978-1-890900-80-9(X)) Insight Publishing Group.
Benjamin, A. H. Baa! Moo! What Will We Do? Chapman, Jane, tr. Chapman, Jane, illus. 2003. 32p. (J). pap. 6.95 (978-1-58925-381-0(7)) Tiger Tales.
Berg, Dick. Padunkapoo: The Hawaiian Kangaroo. Berg, Gary, ed. l.t. ed. 2005. (Illus.). 28p. (J). per. 6.99 (978-0-9769985-1-8(3)) Grace Publishing.
Blackstone, Stella. Who Are You, Baby Kangaroo? Beaton, Clare, illus. 2005. (ENG.). 24p. (J). (gr. -1-2). bds. 6.99 (978-1-905236-19-0(0)) Barefoot Bks., Inc.
Blyton, Enid. Mister Meddle's Muddles. (ENG., Illus.). 111p. (J). pap. 6.95 (978-0-7475-3860-8(3)) Bloomsbury Publishing Plc GBR. Dist: Trafalgar Square Publishing.
Bornemann, Elsa. Cuentos a Salto de Canguro. 2003. (SPA., Illus.). 97p. (J). (gr. 3-5). pap. 9.95 (978-950-511-245-6(9)) Alfaguara S.A. de Ediciones ARG. Dist: Santillana USA Publishing Co., Inc.
Bourguignon, Laurence. Heart in the Pocket. D'heur, Valérie, illus. 2008. 26p. (J). (gr. -1-3). 16.50 (978-0-8028-5343-1(9)) Eerdmans, William B. Publishing Co.
Bright, J. E. The Fastest Pet on Earth, 1 vol. Baltazar, Art, illus. 2011. (DC Super-Pets Ser.). (ENG.). 56p. (J). (gr. 2-2). pap. 4.95 (978-1-4048-6623-2(X)); lib. bdg. 23.99 (978-1-4048-6264-7(1)) Picture Window Bks. (DC Super-Pets).
Bump! KinderReaders Individual Title, 6 pack. (Kinderstarters Ser.). 8p. (gr. -1-1). 21.00 (978-0-7635-8649-2(8)) Rigby Education.
Butler, Ethel And Steven, creator. Callie the Kangie Traveling America. 2012. 32p. pap. 15.99 (978-1-4685-6197-5(9)) AuthorHouse.
Cadet, John. The Kangaroo's Adventure. 2012. 24p. pap. 24.95 (978-1-4560-2861-9(8)) America Star Bks.
Collins, Diana Sue. Elfin, the Elf. 2011. 44p. pap. 24.95 (978-1-4560-8493-6(3)) America Star Bks.

Cook, Sherry & Johnson, Terri. Kitchen Chemistry Kal, 26 vols. Kuhn, Jesse, illus. I.t. ed. 2006. (Quirkles — Exploring Phonics through Science Ser.: 11). 32p. (J). 7.99 *(978-1-933815-10-7(8),* Quirkles, The) Creative 3, LLC.

Cox, Robert & Robins, Jim. The Kangaroo Who Couldn't Hop. 2005. (Illus.). 32p. (J). (gr. -1 — 1). pap., pap. *(978-0-7344-0717-7(3),* Lothian Children's Bks.) Hachette Australia.

Crouch, Cheryl. Troo Makes a Big Splash, 1 vol. Zimmer, Kevin, illus. 2011. (I Can Read! / Rainforest Friends Ser.). (ENG.). 32p. (J). (gr. -1-2). pap. 3.99 *(978-0-310-71810-9(4))* Zonderkidz.

—Troo's Big Climb, 1 vol. Zimmer, Kevin, illus. 2011. (I Can Read! / Rainforest Friends Ser.). (ENG.). 32p. (J). (gr. -1-2). pap. 3.99 *(978-0-310-71808-6(2))* Zonderkidz.

—Troo's Secret Clubhouse, 1 vol. Zimmer, Kevin, illus. 2011. (I Can Read! / Rainforest Friends Ser.). (ENG.). 32p. (J). (gr. -1-2). pap. 3.99 *(978-0-310-71809-3(0))* Zonderkidz.

Dean, Natalia. The Dream. 2012. 30p. 24.95 *(978-1-4626-6008-7(8))* America Star Bks.

Dellolio, Kristina. Penelope's Tea Party Oh No Where's Kangaroo. 2012. 28p. pap. 24.95 *(978-1-4626-9748-9(8))* America Star Bks.

DeLuise, Dom & Carter, Derek. Pouch Potato. 2007. 33p. pap. 9.95 *(978-0-9717952-0-4(7))* Bacchus Bks.

deRubertis, Barbara. Kylie Kangaroo's Karate Kickers. Alley, R. W., illus. 2011. (Animal Antics A to Z Ser.). 32p. (J). pap. 45.32 *(978-0-7613-7657-6(7));* (ENG.). lib. bdg. 22.60 *(978-1-57565-332-7(X));* (gr. -1-3). pap. 7.95 *(978-1-57565-323-5(0))* Kane Press, Inc.

deRubertis, Barbara & DeRubertis, Barbara. Kylie Kangaroo's Karate Kickers. Alley, R. W., illus. 2012. (Animal Antics A to Z Ser.). 32p. (J). (gr. 2 — 1). cd-rom 7.95 *(978-1-57565-404-1(0))* Kane Press, Inc.

Duckers, John. The Amazing Adventures of the Silly Six. 2013. (Illus.). 188p. pap. *(978-1-78148-626-9(3))* Grosvenor Hse. Publishing Ltd.

Edwards, Pamela Duncan. McGillycuddy Could! Date not set. 32p. (J). (gr. -1-1). pap. 5.99 *(978-0-06-443688-5(8))* HarperCollins Pubs.

—McGillycuddy Could! Porter, Sue, illus. 2005. 32p. (J). (gr. -1-1). 14.99 *(978-0-06-029001-6(3))* HarperCollins Pubs.

Evans, Hilda Clark. Karbee the Kangaroo Says. 2013. (ENG.). 24p. (J). pap. 11.95 *(978-1-4787-2076-8(X))* Outskirts Pr., Inc.

ffoulkes, Joy. Kitty Kangaroo. 2010. (Illus.). 84p. pap. *(978-1-84748-685-1(1))* Athena Pr.

Finke, Margot. Kangaroo Clues. Delioglu, Mustafa, illus. 2013. 16p. pap. 9.95 *(978-1-61633-368-3(5))* Guardian Angel Publishing, Inc.

Flora, James, creator. Kangaroo for Christmas. 2011. (ENG., Illus.). 40p. (J). (gr. -1-3). 16.95 *(978-1-59270-113-1(2))* Enchanted Lion Bks., LLC.

Foust, Cindy. Kristy Kangaroo. 2008. (J). 12.94 *(978-0-9749220-6-5(4))* Alpha-kidZ.

French, Jackie. Josephine Wants to Dance. Whatley, Bruce, illus. 2007. (ENG.). 32p. (J). (gr. -1-1). 17.95 *(978-0-8109-9431-7(3),* Abrams Bks. for Young Readers) Abrams, Inc.

Glover, Matt. But It's True. 2012. (Illus.). 32p. pap. 13.50 *(978-1-78035-330-2(8),* Fastprint Publishing) Upfront Publishing Ltd. GBR. Dist: Printondemand-worldwide.com.

Goodhart, Pippa. Hoppy Birthday, Jo-Jo! Birkett, Georgie, illus. 2005. (Green Bananas Ser.). (ENG.). 48p. (J). lib. bdg. *(978-0-7787-1025-7(4))* Crabtree Publishing Co.

Hamilton, Elizabeth L. Katie Kangaroo's Leap of Courage. I.t. ed. 2005. (Character Critters Ser.: No. 9). (Illus.). 32p. (J). per. 5.95 *(978-0-9754629-6-6(2),* Character-in-Action) Quiet Impact, Inc.

Hanson, Anders. Kangaroo Boxers, 1 vol. Nobens, Cheryl A., illus. 2006. (Animal Tales Ser.). (ENG.). 24p. (J). (gr. k-3). lib. bdg. 24.21 *(978-1-59679-945-5(5),* SandCastle) ABDO Publishing Co.

—Kangaroo Boxers. Nobens, C. A., illus. 2006. (Fact & Fiction Ser.). 24p. (J). pap. 48.42 *(978-1-59679-946-2(3))* ABDO Publishing Co.

—Los Pantaloncillos del Canguro, 1 vol. Nobens, C. A., illus. 2007. (Cuentos de Animales Ser.). (SPA & ENG.). 24p. (J). (gr. k-3). lib. bdg. 24.21 *(978-1-59928-655-6(6),* SandCastle) ABDO Publishing Co.

Heaton, Maria. Kangaroos Say Sorry, Too. 2006. (Neighborhood Readers Ser.). (ENG.). 12p. (gr. 1-3). pap. 5.90 *(978-1-4042-7030-5(2),* Rosen Classroom) Rosen Publishing Group, Inc., The.

Henderson, Milagros. Lulu the Bouncing Kangaroo. 2012. 36p. (-18). pap. 20.99 *(978-1-4772-8899-3(6))* AuthorHouse.

Hiebert, Elfrieda H. & Juel, Connie. Kangaroo in the Kitchen. (Little Book Practice Reader Ser.). (J). 9.90 *(978-0-8136-0742-9(6))* Modern Curriculum Pr.

Jenkins, Jacqueline. The Kangaroo Tale: Matilda. Minoza, Kersly, illus. 2013. 24p. (J). 28.03 *(978-1-4836-9159-6(4))* Xlibris Corp.

Jones, Elwynn. Frank's Frantic Friday. 2010. 40p. pap. 16.95 *(978-1-60911-750-4(6),* Eloquent Bks.) Strategic Book Publishing & Rights Agency (SBPRA).

Joyce, Rita. Wandawillie. 2005. (J). lib. bdg. 17.95 *(978-1-59094-095-2(4))* Jawbone Publishing Corp.

Kangaroo at the Zoo IR. 2017. (Phonics Readers Ser.). (ENG.). (J). pap. 6.99 ***(978-0-7945-3716-6(2),*** Usborne) EDC Publishing.

Kim, HoJeong. Kanga & Anger. Kim, SookKyeong, illus. rev. ed. 2014. (MySELF Bookshelf Ser.). (ENG.). 32p. (J). (gr. k-2). pap. 11.94 *(978-1-60357-652-9(5));* lib. bdg. 25.27 *(978-1-59953-643-9(9))* Norwood Hse. Pr.

Krulik, Nancy E. Never Box with a Kangaroo. 2016. (Magic Bone Ser.: 11). lib. bdg. 14.75 *(978-0-606-38842-9(7))* Turtleback Bks.

Laconi, Kristin. Karma the Kangaroo Takes the Court. 2010. 24p. pap. 12.99 *(978-1-4490-3227-2(3))* AuthorHouse.

Langeland, Deirdre. Be Careful, Kangaroo! Ordaz, Frank, illus. 2005. (Soundprints' Read-and-Discover Ser.). (ENG.). 48p. (J). (gr. -1-1). 12.95 *(978-1-59249-146-9(4),* PS2010) Soundprints.

—Be Careful, Kangaroo!, Level 1. 2005. (ENG., Illus.). 32p. (J). (gr. -1-1). pap. 3.95 *(978-1-59249-145-2(6),* S2010) Soundprints.

—Kangaroo Island: A Story of an Australian Mallee Forest. 2005. (Soundprints' Wild Habitats Ser.). (ENG., Illus.). 32p. (J). (gr. 1-4). 8.95 *(978-1-59249-095-0(6))* Soundprints.

Lee, Brian. Bouncey the Elf & Friends - Bedtime St. 2005. (ENG., Illus.). 53p. pap. *(978-0-7552-1023-7(9))* Authors OnLine, Ltd.

Lee, Karin. Zangadoo Kangaroo & the Mysterious Boomerang. Porterfield, Scott, illus. 2012. 94p. pap. 6.99 *(978-0-9847428-2-0(4))* Zangadoo Entertainment.

Lewis, Edwina. Who Jumps? Parker, Ant, illus. 2003. (Who... Ser.). 16p. (YA). *(978-1-85602-447-1(4),* Pavilion Children's Books) Pavilion Bks.

Liora, Iimma. Flick Goes Bush. 2013. 32p. pap. 16.95 *(978-1-4525-0819-1(4),* Balboa Pr.) Author Solutions, Inc.

Maar, Paul. El Canguro Aprende a Volar (Kangaroo Learns to Fly) (SPA.). 56p. (J). (gr. 2). 7.95 *(978-958-04-1490-2(4),* 10266271) Norma S.A. COL. Dist: Distribuidora Norma, Inc.

MacKey, Garry. Joey: The Christmas Kangaroo. 2012. 24p. pap. 9.95 *(978-1-4575-1592-7(X))* Dog Ear Publishing, LLC.

Martinez Jover, Carmen. The Twin Kangaroo Treasure Hunt, a Gay Parenting Story. Martinez, Rosemary, illus. 2013. 32p. pap. *(978-607-00-6545-3(X))* Martinez Jover, Maria del Carmen Dorotea.

Mary-Todd, Jonathan. The Giant. 2014. (Bareknuckle Ser.). 104p. (YA). (gr. 6-12). lib. bdg. 27.93 *(978-1-4677-1457-0(7),* Darby Creek) Lerner Publishing Group.

Mayer, Mercer. What Do You Do with a Kangaroo? Mayer, Mercer, illus. 2008. (ENG., Illus.). (J). (gr. -1-3). 9.99 *(978-0-545-07457-5(6))* Scholastic, Inc.

McBratney, Sam. I Love It When You Smile. Fuge, Charles, illus. 2012. 32p. (J). (gr. -1-3). 9.99 *(978-0-06-222133-9(7))* HarperCollins Pubs.

McDonald, Dawn M. Kiki Koala Wanders Away. 2008. 28p. per. 24.95 *(978-1-4241-9924-2(7))* America Star Bks.

Moncure, Jane Belk. A Pocketful of Pets: A Search-and-Count Adventure. Billin-Frye, Paige, illus. 2013. (Magic Castle Readers Ser.). (ENG.). 32p. (J). (gr. -1-2). 25.64 *(978-1-62323-584-0(7),* 206317) Child's World, Inc., The.

—What Do You Do with a Grumpy Kangaroo? A Book about Feelings. Gallagher-Cole, Mernie, illus. 2013. (Magic Castle Readers Ser.). (ENG.). 32p. (J). (gr. -1-2). 25.64 *(978-1-62323-589-5(8),* 206324) Child's World, Inc., The.

Morecroft, Judith. Malu Kangaroo. Bancroft, Bronwyn, illus. 2008. (ENG.). 40p. (J). (gr. k-2). pap. 11.95 *(978-1-921272-51-6(1))* Little Hare Bks. AUS. Dist: Independent Pubs. Group.

Most, Bernard & National Geographic Learning Staff. The Very Boastful Kangaroo. 2010. (Rise & Shine Ser.). (ENG., Illus.). 24p. (C). (gr. -1-3). pap. 6.95 *(978-0-15-204840-2(5))* National Geographic School Publishing, Inc.

Mueller, Kirk Jay. Harriet Can Carry It, 1 vol. Vonthron-Laver, Sarah, illus. 2014. (ENG.). 32p. (J). 16.99 *(978-1-59572-675-9(6))* Star Bright Bks., Inc.

Nancee Jean. The Boomerang Babies Club. 2012. 36p. pap. 13.95 *(978-1-4525-5243-9(6))* Balboa Pr.

Neusner, Sam. Bounce Bounce Bounce. 2012. 24p. pap. 12.56 *(978-1-4669-4558-6(3))* Trafford Publishing.

Nixon, Sidney. Chikka the Kangaroo. 2012. (Illus.). 28p. pap. 21.35 *(978-1-4772-4264-1(8))* AuthorHouse.

Numeroff, Laura Joffe & Munsinger, Lynn. Nighty-Night, Cooper. Munsinger, Lynn, illus. 2013. (ENG., Illus.). 32p. (J). (gr. -1-3). 16.99 *(978-0-547-40205-5(8))* Houghton Mifflin Harcourt Publishing Co.

Owens, Carmen. Katy, the Cooking Kangaroo. Otis, Michelle, ed. Middleton, Taquon, illus. 2013. (J). pap. 12.95 *(978-0-9888644-5-0(2))* Knowledge Power Communications.

Parish, Steve, illus. The Kangaroos' Great Escape. 2005. (Animal Storybooks Ser.). 24p. (gr. k-3). lib. bdg. 22.00 *(978-0-8368-5971-3(5),* Gareth Stevens Learning Library) Stevens, Gareth Publishing LLLP.

Pedley, Ethel C. Dot & the Kangaroo. 2004. reprint ed. pap. 15.95 *(978-1-4191-1659-9(2));* pap. 1.99 *(978-1-4192-1659-6(7))* Kessinger Publishing, LLC.

Phillips, Dee & Ticktock Media, Ltd. Staff. What Do Kangaroos Do? 2009. (What Do Animals Do? Ser.). (ENG.). 5p. (J). (gr. k — 1). bds. 4.95 *(978-1-84696-959-1(X),* TickTock Books) Octopus Publishing Group GBR. Dist: Independent Pubs. Group.

Price, W. Morris. A Gnu with a Shoe. 2009. 20p. pap. 10.49 *(978-1-4389-4388-6(1))* AuthorHouse.

Rebuck, Anthony. Skippy's Favourite Honey. Plagerson, Crock, illus. 2016. 42p. (J). 44.35 *(978-1-5144-4613-3(8));* (ENG.). pap. 28.22 *(978-1-5144-4612-6(X))* Xlibris Corp.

Richardson, Kiowa. The Christmas Kangaroo: Written & Illustrated by Kiowa Richardson. 2012. 16p. pap. 7.95 *(978-1-4497-4329-1(3),* WestBow Pr.) Author Solutions, Inc.

Roberson, Margaret. Maggie Poo the Kangaroo Adventures. 2008. 36p. pap. 14.95 *(978-1-4327-0674-6(8))* Outskirts Pr., Inc.

Roderick, Judith. Katie the Kangaroo & Her Five Acts of Kindness. 2011. 24p. pap. 11.50 *(978-1-4634-7457-7(1))* AuthorHouse.

Rose, M. E. Kangaroo Christmas. Keenan, Brona, illus. 2007. (ENG.). 140p. (YA). 10.95 *(978-1-896209-89-0(0))* Bayeux Arts, Inc. CAN. Dist: Chicago Distribution Ctr.

Sakmar-Sullivan, Eva M. Kangaroo's Out of This World Restaurant, 1 vol. Sakmar-Sullivan, Eva M., illus. 2013. (ENG., Illus.). 32p. (J). 14.99 *(978-0-7643-4519-7(2),* 9780764345197) Schiffer Publishing, Ltd.

Saunders, Len. Joey the Kangaroo: An Adventure in Exercise. 2010. 32p. pap. 14.95 *(978-1-4389-3992-6(2))* AuthorHouse.

Shepherd, Sandra. Kangapoo & the Monster at Kakadu. 2012. 40p. pap. 32.70 *(978-1-4691-6123-5(0))* Xlibris Corp.

Simms, Mattie. Q. 2006. (J). pap. 2.99 *(978-0-9772077-1-8(4))* Kanleam, Inc.

Simon, Francesca. Pablo Diablo Y la Cangura Fantasma. 2005. (Pablo Diablo Ser.).Tr. of Horrid Harry & the Kangaroo Ghost. (SPA., Illus.). (J). (gr. 2-3). pap. 8.95 *(978-84-348-9684-0(2))* SM Ediciones ESP. Dist: Iaconi, Mariuccia Bk. Imports.

Slinkard, Doreen. Wicky Wacky Farm Stories: Peppi Goes to China. 2012. 44p. pap. 14.97 *(978-1-60976-309-1(2),* Strategic Bk. Publishing) Strategic Book Publishing & Rights Agency (SBPRA).

Smith, Marvelyn A. The Kangaroo & the Crocodile. 2008. 28p. pap. 12.49 *(978-1-4343-9650-1(9))* AuthorHouse.

Stein, David Ezra. Pouch! Stein, David Ezra, illus. 2010. (Rise & Shine Ser.). (ENG., Illus.). 32p. (C). (gr. -1-k). 25.95 *(978-0-399-25051-4(4))* National Geographic School Publishing, Inc.

—Pouch! Stein, David Ezra, illus. 2012. (ENG., Illus.). 32p. (J). (gr. -1 — 1). bds. 7.99 *(978-0-399-25738-4(1),* Nancy Paulsen Books) Penguin Young Readers Group.

Thomas, Pam. Mamarswpial. 2005. (WEL., Illus.). 128p. pap. *(978-0-86243-360-4(6))* Y Lolfa.

Thomson, Jeanette. Hurry up Joey: It's Time to Go! 2010. 44p. 18.49 *(978-1-4490-6331-3(4))* AuthorHouse.

Tonderum, Angela. Kaycee Kangaroo Lost in Alphabet Forest: Adventures of Kaycee Kangaroo. Carlson, Christine, illus. 2008. 41p. pap. 24.95 *(978-1-60672-601-3(3))* America Star Bks.

Torres, Jos A. & Torres, Jose A. Joey Kanga Roo: Plays the Trumpet. 2009. 36p. pap. 15.99 *(978-1-4389-7434-7(5))* AuthorHouse.

Torres, Jose A. Joey Kanga Roo: First Day of School. 2009. 36p. pap. 15.99 *(978-1-4389-3964-3(7))* AuthorHouse.

Ungerer, Tomi. Adelaide: The Flying Kangaroo. 2011. (ENG., Illus.). 40p. (gr. -1-3). 16.95 *(978-0-7148-6083-1(2))* Phaidon Pr., Inc.

van Genechten, Guido. Kangaroo Christine. van Genechten, Guido, illus. 2005. (Illus.). 24p. (J). (gr. 3-7). pap. 6.95 *(978-1-58925-396-4(5))* Tiger Tales.

Waterhouse, Raymond & Lawrie, Gabrielle. Yoppi A Bear Story. 2007. 158p. pap. 19.50 *(978-1-84753-876-5(2))* Lulu Pr., Inc.

KANSAS

Bjorklund, Ruth & Trueit, Trudi Strain. Kansas. 2nd rev. ed. 2008. (Celebrate the States Ser.). 144p. (gr. 6-18). lib. bdg. 42.79 *(978-0-7614-3400-9(3),* Benchmark Bks.) Marshall Cavendish Corp.

Deinard, Jenny. How to Draw Kansas's Sights & Symbols. 2009. (Kid's Guide to Drawing America Ser.). 32p. (gr. k-k). 50.50 *(978-1-61511-065-0(8),* PowerKids Pr.) Rosen Publishing Group, Inc., The.

Drummond, Allan. Green City. 2016. (ENG., Illus.). 40p. (J). 17.99 *(978-0-374-37999-5(8),* 9780374379995, Farrar, Straus & Giroux (BYR)) Farrar, Straus & Giroux.

Fredeen, Charles. Kansas. 2012. (J). lib. bdg. 25.26 *(978-0-7613-4533-6(7),* Lerner Pubns.) Lerner Publishing Group.

Kansas: The Sunflower State. 2014. (Illus.). 32p. (J). *(978-0-531-29166-5(9))* Bellwether Media.

Labairon, Cassandra Sharri. Kansas. 2008. (This Land Called America Ser.). 32p. (YA). (gr. 3-6). 22.95 *(978-1-58341-641-9(2))* Creative Co., The.

Marsh, Carole. The Cool Kansas Coloring Book. 2004. (Carole Marsh Kansas Bks.). (Illus.). 32p. (J). (gr. k-2). pap. 3.95 *(978-0-7933-9856-0(8))* Gallopade International.

—Kansas Current Events Projects: 30 Cool, Activities, Crafts, Experiments & More for Kids to Do to Learn about Your State! 2003. (Kansas Experience Ser.). 32p. (gr. k-5). pap. 5.95 *(978-0-635-02035-2(1),* Marsh, Carole Bks.) Gallopade International.

—Kansas Geography Projects: 30 Cool, Activities, Crafts, Experiments & More for Kids to Do to Learn about Your State! 2003. (Kansas Experience Ser.). 32p. (gr. k-5). pap. 5.95 *(978-0-635-01835-9(7),* Marsh, Carole Bks.) Gallopade International.

—Kansas Government Projects: 30 Cool, Activities, Crafts, Experiments & More for Kids to Do to Learn about Your State! 2003. (Kansas Experience Ser.). 32p. (gr. k-5). pap. 5.95 *(978-0-635-01935-6(3),* Marsh, Carole Bks.) Gallopade International.

—Kansas Jeopardy! Answers & Questions about Our State! 2004. (Carole Marsh Kansas Bks.). (Illus.). 32p. (J). (gr. 3-8). pap. 7.95 *(978-0-7933-9798-3(7))* Gallopade International.

—Kansas "Jography" A Fun Run Thru Your State! 2004. 32p. (J). (gr. 3-8). pap. 7.95 *(978-0-7933-9827-0(4))* Gallopade International.

—Kansas People Projects: 30 Cool, Activities, Crafts, Experiments & More for Kids to Do to Learn about Your State! 2003. (Kansas Experience Ser.). 32p. (gr. k-5). pap. 5.95 *(978-0-635-01985-1(X),* Marsh, Carole Bks.) Gallopade International.

—Kansas Symbols & Facts Projects: 30 Cool, Activities, Crafts, Experiments & More for Kids to Do to Learn about Your State! 2003. (Kansas Experience Ser.). 32p. (gr. k-5). pap. 5.95 *(978-0-635-01885-4(3),* Marsh, Carole Bks.) Gallopade International.

—My First Book about Kansas. 2004. (Carole Marsh Kansas Bks.). (Illus.). 32p. (J). (gr. k-4). pap. 7.95 *(978-0-7933-9885-0(1))* Gallopade International.

McNeese, Tim. Brown V. Board of Education: Integrating America's Schools. 2006. (Great Supreme Court Decisions Ser.). (Illus.). 144p. (YA). (gr. 5-9). lib. bdg. 32.95 *(978-0-7910-9238-5(0))* Facts On File, Inc.

Meyer, Diana Lambdin. A Kid's Guide to Kansas City. 3rd ed. 2005. 184p. (J). per. 14.95 *(978-0-9763873-0-5(1))* Kansas City Guidebooks.

Murray, Julie. Kansas, 1 vol. 2006. (Buddy Book Ser.). (ENG., Illus.). 32p. (gr. 2-4). 27.07 *(978-1-59197-675-2(8),* Buddy Bks.) ABDO Publishing Co.

Nault, Jennifer. Kansas. 2011. (Guide to American States Ser.). (Illus.). 48p. (YA). (gr. 3-6). 29.99 *(978-1-61690-788-4(6))* Weigl Pubs., Inc.

—Kansas: The Sunflower State. 2016. (J). *(978-1-4896-4863-1(1))* Weigl Pubs., Inc.

Obregon, Jose Maria. Kansas. 2005. (Bilingual Library of the United States of America Ser.: Set 1). (ENG & SPA., Illus.). 32p. (J). (gr. 3-6). lib. bdg. 25.25 *(978-1-4042-3081-1(5))* Rosen Publishing Group, Inc., The.

Obregón, José María. Kansas. 2009. (Bilingual Library of the United States of America Ser.). (ENG & SPA.). 32p. (gr. 2-2). 47.90 *(978-1-60853-361-9(1),* Editorial Buenas Letras) Rosen Publishing Group, Inc., The.

Reed, Jennifer. Kansas: A MyReportLinks. Com Book. 2003. (States Ser.). (Illus.). 48p. (J). lib. bdg. 25.26 *(978-0-7660-5140-9(4),* MyReportLinks.com Bks.) Enslow Pubs., Inc.

Ryan, Pat & Hoena, Blake. Kansas. 2013. (Exploring the States Ser.). (ENG., Illus.). 32p. (gr. 3-7). lib. bdg. 26.95 *(978-1-62617-015-5(0),* Blastoff! Readers) Bellwether Media.

Scillian, Devin & Scillian, Corey. One Kansas Farmer: A Kansas Number Book. Bowles, Doug, illus. 2009. (Discover America State by State Ser.). (ENG.). 40p. (J). (gr. k-6). 16.95 *(978-1-58536-182-3(8))* Sleeping Bear Pr.

—S Is for Sunflower: A Kansas Alphabet. Bowles, Doug, illus. 2004. (State Ser.). (ENG.). 40p. (J). 17.95 *(978-1-58536-061-1(9),* 1235980) Sleeping Bear Pr.

Taylor-Butler, Christine. Kansas. 2006. (Rookie Read-About Geography Ser.). (ENG., Illus.). 32p. (J). (gr. 1-2). lib. bdg. 20.50 *(978-0-516-24966-7(5),* Children's Pr.) Scholastic Library Publishing.

Thomas, William David. Kansas. 2006. (Portraits of the States Ser.). (Illus.). 32p. (gr. 2-6). lib. bdg. 26.00 *(978-0-8368-4665-2(6),* Gareth Stevens Learning Library) Stevens, Gareth Publishing LLLP.

Thomas, William David & Thomas, Bill. Kansas. 2006. (Portraits of the States Ser.). (Illus.). 32p. (gr. 2-6). pap. 10.50 *(978-0-8368-4684-3(2),* Gareth Stevens Learning Library) Stevens, Gareth Publishing LLLP.

Wheeler, Jill C. Kansas, 1 vol. 2009. (United States Ser.). (ENG., Illus.). 48p. (YA). (gr. 2-5). 27.07 *(978-1-60453-651-5(9))* ABDO Publishing Co.

KANSAS—FICTION

Abbott, E. F. Nettie & Nellie Crook: Orphan Train Sisters. 2016. (Based on a True Story Ser.). (ENG., Illus.). 176p. (J). 15.99 *(978-1-250-06835-4(5),* 9781250068354) Feiwel & Friends.

Adee, Donna & Adee, Ed. Jonathan Finds True Treasure. Rectenbaugh, Marci, illus. 2004. (Jonathan Ser.: Bk. 2). 344p. (J). per. 10.95 *(978-0-9654272-5-8(0))* Harvest Pubns.

Barnes, Derrick D. We Could Be Brothers. 2010. (J). *(978-0-545-13574-0(5),* Scholastic Pr.) Scholastic, Inc.

Baum, L. Frank. Mago di Oz. pap. 14.95 *(978-88-451-2500-3(9))* Fabbri Editori - RCS Libri ITA. Dist: Distribooks, Inc.

Bird, Roy & Harp, Kim. Hark! I Hear a Meadowlark! Battis, Gwen, illus. 2013. 34p. 16.99 *(978-1-939054-08-1(7));* 36p. pap. 10.99 *(978-1-939054-07-4(9))* Rowe Publishing and Design.

Boushell, Mike. Gridiron Hero. (J). pap. 9.99 *(978-0-88092-601-0(5))* Royal Fireworks Publishing Co.

Busch, Darcy J. Lily & the Hidden Secrets, 1 vol. 2009. 164p. pap. 24.95 *(978-1-60836-498-5(4))* America Star Bks.

Cheaney, J. B. & Cheaney, Janie. The Middle of Somewhere. 2008. (ENG.). 224p. (J). (gr. 3-7). 7.99 *(978-0-440-42165-8(9),* Yearling) Random Hse. Children's Bks.

Dunn, Pintip. Girl in Between. 2017. (ENG.). 256p. (YA). pap. 9.95 ***(978-1-4967-0360-6(X))*** Kensington Publishing Corp.

Duvall, Deborah L. Rabbit Goes to Kansas. Jacob, Murv, illus. 2007. (ENG.). 32p. (J). (gr. 1-18). 16.95 *(978-0-8263-4181-5(0))* Univ. of New Mexico Pr.

Gallagher, Diana G. Monica & the Crushworthy Cowboy, 1 vol. 2011. (Monica Ser.). (ENG.). 88p. (gr. 2-3). lib. bdg. 26.65 *(978-1-4342-2554-2(2))* Stone Arch Bks.

Garner, Phillip. Biff Cardova from Rooster Poot Kansas. 2010. 56p. pap. 21.99 *(978-1-4490-7664-1(5))* AuthorHouse.

Garretson, Jerri. Kansas Tall Tales: Tenth Anniversary Anthology. Garretson, Jerri & Dollar, Diane A., illus. 2008. 106p. (J). pap. 19.95 *(978-0-9659712-7-0(9))* Ravenstone Pr.

Garris, Rebekah. Whither Thou Goest, i Will Go. 2005. pap. 24.95 *(978-1-4137-8823-5(8))* PublishAmerica, Inc.

Grigsby, Cynthia. Hollow Creek: A Haunted Beginning, 01. 2006. 163p. (J). 14.95 *(978-0-9786840-0-6(1))* Grigsby, Cynthia.

Gutman, Dan. The Talent Show. 2010. (ENG.). 224p. (J). (gr. 3-7). 17.99 *(978-1-4169-9003-1(8),* Simon & Schuster Bks. For Young Readers) Simon & Schuster Bks. For Young Readers.

Harkrader, L. D. Airball: My Life in Briefs. 2008. (ENG.). 208p. (J). (gr. 3-7). per. 9.99 *(978-0-312-37382-5(1),* 9780312373825) Square Fish.

Hill, Janet Muirhead. Kendall & Kyleah. Leonhard, Herb, illus. 2012. (J). pap. 13.00 *(978-1-937849-05-4(8))* Raven Publishing Inc. of Montana.

—Kyleah's Tree. Leonhard, Herb, illus. 2011. (J). pap. 12.00 *(978-0-9827377-9-8(3))* Raven Publishing Inc. of Montana.

Hopkinson, Deborah. Our Kansas Home. Faricy, Patrick, illus. 2005. 64p. (J). lib. bdg. 15.00 *(978-1-59054-910-0(4))* Fitzgerald Bks.

—Our Kansas Home. Faricy, Patrick, illus. 2003. (Prairie Skies Ser.). 69p. (J). 11.65 *(978-0-7569-3448-4(6))* Perfection Learning Corp.

Jacobs, Lily. The Littlest Bunny in Kansas: An Easter Adventure. 2015. (ENG.). 32p. (J). (-3). 9.99 *(978-1-4926-1090-8(9),* Sourcebooks Jabberwocky) Sourcebooks, Inc.

—The Littlest Bunny in Kansas City: An Easter Adventure. Dunn, Robert, illus. 2015. (ENG.). 32p. (J). (-3). 9.99 *(978-1-4926-1093-9(3),* Sourcebooks Jabberwocky) Sourcebooks, Inc.

James, Eric. A Halloween Scare in Kansas. Le Ray, Marina, illus. 2015. (ENG.). 32p. (J). (-5). 9.99 *(978-1-4926-2376-2(8),* 9781492623762, Sourcebooks Jabberwocky) Sourcebooks, Inc.

—A Halloween Scare in Kansas City. Le Ray, Marina, illus. 2015. (ENG.). 32p. (J). (-5). 9.99 *(978-1-4926-2377-9(6),* 9781492623779, Sourcebooks Jabberwocky) Sourcebooks, Inc.

—Santa's Sleigh Is on Its Way to Kansas: A Christmas Adventure. Dunn, Robert, illus. 2016. (ENG.). 32p. (J). (-2). 12.99 *(978-1-4926-4330-2(0),* 9781492643302, Sourcebooks Jabberwocky) Sourcebooks, Inc.

—Santa's Sleigh Is on Its Way to Kansas City: A Christmas Adventure. Dunn, Robert, illus. 2016. (ENG.). 32p. (J). (-2). 12.99 *(978-1-4926-4331-9(9),* 9781492643319, Sourcebooks Jabberwocky) Sourcebooks, Inc.

Kadohata, Cynthia. The Thing about Luck. Kuo, Julia, illus. (ENG.). (J). (gr. 5-9). 2014. 304p. pap. 8.99 *(978-1-4424-7465-9(3),* Atheneum Bks. for Young Readers) 2013. 288p. 16.99 *(978-1-4169-1882-0(5))* Simon & Schuster Children's Publishing.

—The Thing about Luck. 2014. lib. bdg. 18.40 *(978-0-606-35798-2(X))* Turtleback Bks.

J
K
L

Keeley, Jenny Conner. The Hollow: A Kansas Fairytale. 2011. 154p. pap. 15.95 *(978-1-4327-6670-2(8))* Outskirts Pr., Inc.
Kelly, David A. The All-Star Joker. Meyers, Mark, illus. 2012. (Ballpark Mysteries Ser.: Bk. 5). lib. bdg. 14.75 *(978-0-606-26401-3(9))*, Turtleback Bks.
Ketchen, Susan. Made That Way. 2010. (ENG.). 160p. (J). pap. 12.95 *(978-0-88982-270-2(0))* Oolichan Bks. CAN. Dist: Univ. of Toronto Pr.
King, Judy. When Summer Comes Again. King, Judy, illus. 2013. (Illus.). 160p. (J). pap. *(978-1-884377-20-4(3))* Green Pastures Pr.
Kurtz, Jane. Anna Was Here. 2013. (ENG.). 288p. (J). (gr. 3-7). 16.99 *(978-0-06-056493-3(8))*, Greenwillow Bks.) HarperCollins Pubs.
—Lemon Sand. 2011. (J). lib. bdg. 17.89 *(978-0-06-056494-0(6))*, Greenwillow Bks.) HarperCollins Pubs.
Marie, Tina. Raccoon Round-Up at the Diamond R Ranch. 2012. 30p. 24.95 *(978-1-62709-237-1(4))*; 32p. pap. 24.95 *(978-1-4626-7599-9(9))* America Star Bks.
McMullan, Kate. For This Land Bk. 2: Meg's Prairie Diary. 2003. (My America Ser.). (ENG., Illus.). 112p. (J). 10.95 *(978-0-439-37059-2(0)*, Scholastic Pr.) Scholastic, Inc.
McPhail, J. A. Dawn of Day. Battis, Gwen, illus. 2012. 200p. pap. 10.99 *(978-0-9851196-1-4(6))* Rowe Publishing and Design.
Meyer, Linda Ross. The Recipe Box. 2010. 73p. pap. 7.99 *(978-0-557-54210-9(3))* Lulu Pr., Inc.
Moss, Marissa. Rose's Journal: The Story of a Girl in the Great Depression. 2003. (Young American Voices Ser.). (ENG., Illus.). 56p. (J). (gr. 2-5). pap. 7.99 *(978-0-15-204605-7(4))* Houghton Mifflin Harcourt Publishing Co.
Murphy, Thomas. Island Boy. 2007. 124p. per. 19.95 *(978-1-4241-7940-4(8))* America Star Bks.
Nadol, Jen. The Mark. (ENG.). (YA). (gr. 9-12). 2011. 256p. pap. 8.99 *(978-1-59990-660-7(0)*, 9781599906607) 2010. 240p. 16.99 *(978-1-59990-431-3(4)*, 9781599904313) Bloomsbury Publishing USA. (Bloomsbury USA Childrens).
Osborne, Mary Pope. Twister on Tuesday. 2004. (Magic Tree House Ser.: No. 23). 70p. (J). (gr. k-3). pap. 17.00 incl. audio *(978-0-8072-9932-6(4)*, Listening Library) Random Hse. Audio Publishing Group.
Peck, Dale. Sprout. 2009. (ENG.). 288p. (YA). (gr. 9-12). 16.99 *(978-1-59990-160-2(9)*, 9781599901602, Bloomsbury USA Childrens) Bloomsbury Publishing USA.
Penner, Evelyn. The Kid Who Ate Dog Food. Chullabrahm, T. M., illus. 2008. 32p. (J). 15.99 *(978-0-9796500-0-0(3))* Peppernut Publishing.
Peters, Julie Anne. Pretend You Love Me. 2011. (ENG.). 304p. (YA). (gr. 10-17). pap. 10.99 *(978-0-316-12741-7(8))* Little, Brown Bks. for Young Readers.
Phelan, Matt. The Storm in the Barn. 2011. (ENG., Illus.). 208p. (J). (gr. 5). pap. 14.99 *(978-0-7636-5290-6(3))* Candlewick Pr.
Powell, Anthony. Our Cat Hogan - Could He Be Part Dog? Stodden, Lindsay, illus. 2012. 24p. (J). 19.95 *(978-1-61863-358-3(9))* Bookstand Publishing.
Redgate, Riley. Seven Ways We Lie. 2017. (ENG.). 368p. (YA). pap. 9.95 *(978-1-4197-2348-3(0)*, Amulet Bks.) Abrams, Inc.
Reiss, Kathryn. Riddle of the Prairie Bride. 2009. (Mysteries Through Time Ser.). 144 - 176p. (YA). (gr. 4-8). 31.95 *(978-1-60754-421-0(0))*; pap. 15.25 *(978-1-60754-420-3(2))* Windmill Bks.
Richardson, Steve. Billy's Mountain. Leonhard, Herb, illus. 2007. 52p. 14.95 *(978-0-9786422-0-4(1))* Impossible Dreams Publishing Co.
Richardson, Travis. Lost in Clover. 2012. 198p. pap. 9.99 *(978-1-61187-466-2(1))* Untreed Reads Publishing, LLC.
Robinson, Robin, illus. L. Frank Baum's Wizard of Oz. 2013. (Penguin Young Readers, Level 4 Ser.). (ENG.). 48p. (J). (gr. 3-4). mass mkt. 3.99 *(978-0-448-45588-4(9)*, Penguin Young Readers) Penguin Young Readers Group.
Sargent, Daina. Kansas: Conquer Fear. Lenoir, Jane, illus. l.t. ed. 2004. (Double Trouble Ser.). 48p. (J). pap. 10.95 *(978-1-59381-125-9(X))*; lib. bdg. 23.60 *(978-1-59381-124-2(1))* Ozark Publishing.
Sawyer, Kim Vogel. Katy's Debate, 1 vol. 2010. (Katy Lambright Ser.: No. 2). (ENG.). 208p. (YA). (gr. 8-11). pap. 9.99 *(978-0-310-71923-6(2))* Zondervan.
—Katy's New World, 1 vol. 2010. (Katy Lambright Ser.: No. 1). (ENG.). 208p. (YA). (gr. 8-11). pap. 9.99 *(978-0-310-71924-3(0))* Zondervan.
Schantz, Sarah Elizabeth. Fig. 2016. (ENG.). 352p. (YA). (gr. 9). pap. 10.99 *(978-1-4814-2359-5(2)*, McElderry, Margaret K. Bks.) McElderry, Margaret K. Bks.
Scillian, Devin. Johnny Kaw: A Tall Tale. Sneed, Brad, illus. 2013. (ENG.). 32p. (J). (gr. 1-4). 15.95 *(978-1-58536-791-7(5)*, 202353) Sleeping Bear Pr.
Silvano, Wendi. Love Is All Around Kansas. Czernichowska, Joanna, illus. 2016. (ENG.). 32p. (J). (-6). 12.99 *(978-1-4926-2925-2(1)*, Sourcebooks Jabberwocky) Sourcebooks, Inc.
—Love Is All Around Kansas City. Czernichowska, Joanna, illus. 2016. (ENG.). 32p. (J). (-6). 12.99 *(978-1-4926-2926-9(X)*, Sourcebooks Jabberwocky) Sourcebooks, Inc.
Smallman, Steve. Santa Is Coming to Kansas. Dunn, Robert, illus. 2013. (ENG.). 32p. (J). (-3). 9.99 *(978-1-4022-9121-0(3)*, Sourcebooks Jabberwocky) Sourcebooks, Inc.
—Santa Is Coming to Kansas City. Dunn, Robert, illus. 2013. (ENG.). 32p. (J). (-3). 9.99 *(978-1-4022-8855-5(7)*, Sourcebooks Jabberwocky) Sourcebooks, Inc.
—Santa Is Coming to Wichita. Dunn, Robert, illus. 2015. (ENG.). 32p. (J). (-3). 9.99 *(978-1-4926-2638-1(4)*, Sourcebooks Jabberwocky) Sourcebooks, Inc.
Sully, Katherine. Night-Night Kansas. Kolanovic, Dubravka & Poole, Helen, illus. 2016. (ENG.). 20p. (J). (-1). bds. 9.99 *(978-1-4926-3941-1(9)*, 9781492639411, Sourcebooks Jabberwocky) Sourcebooks, Inc.
Sundstrom, Dainel H. The Return of Oz. 2007. pap. 10.00 *(978-0-8059-8944-1(7))* Dorrance Publishing Co., Inc.
Sutton, Laurie S. The Secret of the Flying Saucer. Neely, Scott, illus. 2015. (You Choose Stories: Scooby-Doo Ser.). (ENG.). 112p. (gr. 2-3). lib. bdg. 32.65 *(978-1-4965-0478-4(X))* Stone Arch Bks.
Trivas, Tracy. The Wish Stealers. 2011. (ENG.). 288p. (J). (gr. 3-7). pap. 7.99 *(978-1-4169-8726-0(6)*, Aladdin) Simon & Schuster Children's Publishing.
Uncle Markie. Piglettè & Bobo in Kansas City. 2003. (YA). ring bd. 9.95 *(978-1-933129-08-2(5))* Studio 403.
Vanderpool, Clare. Moon over Manifest. (ENG.). (J). (gr. 3-7). 2011. 384p. 7.99 *(978-0-375-85829-1(6)*, Yearling) 2010. 368p. 16.99 *(978-0-385-73883-5(8)*, Delacorte Bks. for Young Readers) Random Hse. Children's Bks.
—Moon over Manifest. l.t. ed. 2011. (ENG.). 452p. 23.99 *(978-1-4104-3780-8(9))* Thorndike Pr.
—Moon over Manifest. 2011. lib. bdg. 18.40 *(978-0-606-23875-5(1)*, Turtleback) Turtleback Bks.
Volkov, Alexander. Tales of Magic Land 1. 2010. 360p. pap. 22.95 *(978-0-557-44825-8(5))* Lulu Pr., Inc.
Waggoner, Sandra. Maggie's Treasure, 4 vols., Vol. 1. 2005. (Gatlin Fields Ser.: One). (ENG.). 108p. (J). per. 9.95 *(978-0-9766823-0-1(3))* Sable Creek Pr. LLC.
—Son of an Honest Man. 2013. 136p. (J). pap. 10.95 *(978-0-9890667-2-3(X))* Sable Creek Pr. LLC.
Walter, Dan. Hello, Willie! 2007. (J). 14.95 *(978-1-932888-52-2(7))* Mascot Bks., Inc.
Wasserman, Robin. The Waking Dark. 2013. (ENG.). 464p. (YA). (gr. 9). 17.99 *(978-0-375-86877-1(1)*, Knopf Bks. for Young Readers) Random Hse. Children's Bks.
Wentz, Lorraine. Who Has Barney. 2013. 38p. pap. 10.99 *(978-1-62697-124-0(2))* Salem Author Services.
Wilder, Laura Ingalls. Little House on the Prairie. Williams, Garth, illus. (Little House Ser.: 3). (ENG.). 352p. (J). (gr. 3-7). 2008. pap. 7.99 *(978-0-06-440002-2(6))* 2004. pap. 8.99 *(978-0-06-058181-7(6))* HarperCollins Pubs.
Wilson, N. D. The Chestnut King. 2011. (100 Cupboards Ser.: 3). (ENG., Illus.). 512p. (J). (gr. 3-7). 8.99 *(978-0-375-83886-6(4)*, Yearling) Random Hse. Children's Bks.
—Dandelion Fire. 2009. (100 Cupboards Ser.: 2). (ENG.). 480p. (J). (gr. 3-7). 8.99 *(978-0-375-83884-2(8)*, Yearling) Random Hse. Children's Bks.
—100 Cupboards. 2008. (100 Cupboards Ser.: 1). (ENG.). 320p. (J). (gr. 3-7). 7.99 *(978-0-375-83882-8(1)*, Yearling) Random Hse. Children's Bks.

KANSAS—HISTORY

Baginski, Deanna Fisher. Harvest Time at the Fisher Farms. 2011. 24p. pap. 12.79 *(978-1-4670-2643-7(3))* AuthorHouse.
Bailer, Darice. What's Great about Kansas? 2015. (ENG., Illus.). 32p. (J). (gr. 2-5). 26.65 *(978-1-4677-3884-2(0))* Lerner Publishing Group.
Bailey, Diane. Kansas: Past & Present. 2010. (United States: Past & Present Ser.). (ENG.). 48p. (YA). pap. 11.75 *(978-1-4358-9508-9(8))*; lib. bdg. 29.25 *(978-1-4358-9481-5(2))* Rosen Publishing Group, Inc., The. (Rosen Reference).
Cannarella, Deborah. Kansas (Revised Edition) 2014. (America the Beautiful, Third Ser. (Revised Edition) Ser.). (ENG., Illus.). 144p. (J). lib. bdg. 40.00 *(978-0-531-28280-9(5))* Scholastic Library Publishing.
Connery-Boyd, Peg. Kansas City Royals. 2016. (Hawk's Nest Activity Bks.: 0). (ENG.). 64p. (J). (gr. k-3). pap., act. bk. ed. 8.99 *(978-1-4926-3561-1(8))* Sourcebooks, Inc.
Fleming, Alice. The King of Prussia & a Peanut Butter Sandwich. 2009. (ENG.). 48p. (J). (gr. 2-4). pap. 6.99 *(978-1-4424-1215-6(1)*, Atheneum Bks. for Young Readers) Simon & Schuster Children's Publishing.
Glaser, Jason. Kansas: The Sunflower State. 2010. (Our Amazing States Ser.). (Illus.). 24p. (J). pap. 8.25 *(978-1-4358-9782-3(X))*; (gr. 2-3). lib. bdg. 22.60 *(978-1-4358-9395-5(6))* Rosen Publishing Group, Inc., The. (PowerKids Pr.).
Herschbach, Elisabeth. Lower Plains: Kansas, Nebraska, Vol. 19. 2015. (Let's Explore the States Ser.). (Illus.). 64p. (J). (gr. 5). 23.95 *(978-1-4222-3326-9(X))* Mason Crest.
Ingram, W. Scott. Kansas. 2009. (From Sea to Shining Sea, Second Ser.). (ENG.). 80p. (J). pap. 7.95 *(978-0-531-21131-1(2)*, Children's Pr.) Scholastic Library Publishing.
Jerome, Kate B. Lucky to Live in Kansas. 2017. (Arcadia Kids Ser.). (ENG., Illus.). 32p. (J). 16.99 ***(978-0-7385-2798-7(X))*** Arcadia Publishing.
Marsh, Carole. Exploring Kansas Through Project-Based Learning. 2016. (Kansas Experience Ser.). (ENG.). (J). pap. 9.99 *(978-0-635-12340-4(1))* Gallopade International.
—I'm Reading about Kansas. 2014. (Kansas Experience Ser.). (ENG., Illus.). (J). pap., pap. 8.99 *(978-0-635-11291-0(4))* Gallopade International.
—Jeopardy. 2004. (New York Experience! Ser.). 32p. (J). (gr. 3-8). pap. 7.95 *(978-0-635-00161-0(6))* Gallopade International.
—Kansas History Projects: 30 Cool, Activities, Crafts, Experiments & More for Kids to Do to Learn about Your State! 2003. (Kansas Experience Ser.). 32p. (gr. k-5). pap. 5.95 *(978-0-635-01785-7(7)*, Marsh, Carole Bks.) Gallopade International.
McArthur, Debra. The Kansas-Nebraska Act & Bleeding Kansas in American History. 2003. (In American History Ser.). (Illus.). 128p. (J). lib. bdg. 27.94 *(978-0-7660-1988-1(8))* Enslow Pubs., Inc.
Mead, James R., et al. Hunting & Trading in Kansas, 1859-1875. 2015. (J). *(978-1-929731-25-1(6))* Rowfant Pr.
Murray, Julie. Kansas, 1 vol. 2012. (Explore the United States Ser.). (ENG.). 32p. (J). (gr. 2-5). lib. bdg. 28.50 *(978-1-61783-354-0(1)*, Big Buddy Bks.) ABDO Publishing Co.
Reece, Richard. Bleeding Kansas, 1 vol. 2012. (Essential Events Set 8 Ser.). (ENG.). 112p. (J). (gr. 6-12). lib. bdg. 35.64 *(978-1-61783-307-6(X))* ABDO Publishing Co.
Robertson, Theda Robinson. Journey to a Free Land: The Story of Nicodemus, the First All Black Town West of the Mississippi. 2006. (Illus.). (J). *(978-0-9705721-6-5(6))* Written Images, Inc.
Swanson, Angie. Kansas. 2016. (States Ser.). (ENG., Illus.). 32p. (gr. 3-4). lib. bdg. 27.32 *(978-1-5157-0403-4(3))* Next Page Pr., The.
Yasuda, Anita. Kansas: The Sunflower State. 2012. (J). *(978-1-61913-351-8(2))*; pap. *(978-1-61913-352-5(0))* Weigl Pubs., Inc.
Young, Jeff C. Bleeding Kansas & the Violent Clash over Slavery in the Heartland. 2006. (Wild History of the American West Ser.). (Illus.). 128p. (J). (gr. 5-9). lib. bdg. 34.60 *(978-1-59845-013-2(1)*, MyReportLinks.com Bks.) Enslow Pubs., Inc.

KANSAS—HISTORY—FICTION

Anderson, Jodi Lynn. Midnight at the Electric. 2017. 272p. (YA). (gr. 9). 17.99 *(978-0-06-239354-8(5)*, HarperTeen) HarperCollins Pubs.
Barnhart, Aaron. Firebrand. 2015. (ENG., Illus.). 168p. (J). 19.95 *(978-0-9669258-6-9(6))* Quindaro Pr.
Boeve, Eunice. Echoes of Kansas Past. Peterson-Shea, Julie, illus. 2012. 176p. pap. 10.99 *(978-0-9851196-9-0(1))* Rowe Publishing and Design.
Breault, Christie Merriman. Logan West, Printer's Devil. Archembault, Matthew, illus. 2006. 142p. (J). pap. *(978-1-59336-762-6(7))* Mondo Publishing.
Brown, Irene Bennett. Before the Lark. 2011. (ENG.). 208p. (J). (gr. 4-7). pap. 18.95 *(978-0-89672-727-4(0))* Texas Tech Univ. Pr.
Helget, Nicole. Wonder at the Edge of the World. 2015. (ENG., Illus.). 384p. (J). (gr. 3-7). 17.00 *(978-0-316-24510-4(0))* Little, Brown Bks. for Young Readers.
Helwani, Najiyah Diana. Sophia's Journal: Time Warp 1857. 2008. (YA). per. *(978-0-9793577-2-5(1))* Muslim Writers Publishing.
Kimmel, E. Cody. In the Eye of the Storm. Snow, Scott, illus. 2003. (Adventures of Young Buffalo Bill Ser.). (ENG.). 144p. (J). (gr. 3-7). 15.99 *(978-0-06-029115-0(X))* HarperCollins Pubs.
Kimmel, Elizabeth Cody. In the Eye of the Storm. Snow, Scott, illus. 2003. (Adventures of Young Buffalo Bill Ser.). 144p. (J). (gr. 3-7). lib. bdg. 16.89 *(978-0-06-029116-7(8))* HarperCollins Pubs.
McClure, Wendy. Wanderville. 2014. (Wanderville Ser.: 1). (ENG.). (J). (gr. 3-7). 240p. pap. 7.99 *(978-1-59514-701-1(2))*; 224p. 16.99 *(978-1-59514-700-4(4))* Penguin Young Readers Group. (Razorbill).
McMullan, Kate. A Fine Start Bk. 3: Meg's Prairie Diary. 2003. (My America Ser.). (ENG.). 112p. (J). 12.95 *(978-0-439-37061-5(2))* Scholastic, Inc.
McPhail, J. A. Dawn of Day. Battis, Gwen, illus. 2012. 200p. 17.99 *(978-0-9851196-2-1(4))* Rowe Publishing and Design.
Moss, Marissa. Rose's Journal: The Story of a Girl in the Great Depression. 2004. (Young American Voice Bks.). (Illus.). (gr. 3-7). 17.00 *(978-0-7569-4230-4(6))* Perfection Learning Corp.
Rose, Caroline Starr. May B. 2012. (ENG.). 240p. (J). (gr. 3-7). 15.99 *(978-1-58246-393-3(X)*, Schwartz & Wade Bks.) Random Hse. Children's Bks.
Thomas, Carroll. The Town on Rambling Creek: A Matty Trescott Novel. 2004. (Illus.). ix, 185p. (J). *(978-1-57525-376-3(3))* Smith & Kraus Pubs., Inc.
Villani, Donna. The Capture of Art. 2008. 244p. pap. 14.95 *(978-1-60693-104-2(0)*, Eloquent Bks.) Strategic Book Publishing & Rights Agency (SBPRA).

KANSAS CITY CHIEFS (FOOTBALL TEAM)

Burgess, Zack. Meet the Kansas City Chiefs. 2016. (Big Picture Sports Ser.). (ENG., Illus.). 24p. (J). (gr. k-3). lib. bdg. 22.60 *(978-1-59953-730-6(3))* Norwood Hse. Pr.
Caffrey, Scott. The Story of the Kansas City Chiefs. 2009. (NFL Today Ser.). 48p. (YA). (gr. 5-9). 22.95 *(978-1-58341-760-7(5))* Creative Co., The.
Frisch, Aaron. Kansas City Chiefs. 2011. (Super Bowl Champions Ser.). (J). (gr. 1-3). 24.25 *(978-1-60818-020-2(4))* Creative Co., The.
—Kansas City Chiefs. 2014. (Illus.). 24p. (J). *(978-1-60818-378-4(5)*, Creative Education) Creative Co., The.
Frisch, Nate. NFL Today: Kansas City Chiefs. 2013. (NFL Today Ser.). (ENG., Illus.). 176p. (J). (gr. 4-7). pap. 12.00 *(978-0-89812-860-4(9)*, Creative Paperbacks) Creative Co., The.
—The Story of the Kansas City Chiefs. 2013. (Illus.). 48p. (J). 35.65 *(978-1-60818-307-4(6)*, Creative Education) Creative Co., The.
Hawkes, Brian. The History of the Kansas City Chiefs. 2004. (NFL Today Ser.). (Illus.). 32p. (YA). (gr. 5-9). 18.95 *(978-1-58341-301-2(4))* Creative Co., The.
Howell, Brian. Kansas City Chiefs. 2015. (Insider's Guide to Pro Football Ser.). (ENG.). 32p. (J). (gr. k-3). 28.50 *(978-1-63407-000-3(3)*, 208835) Child's World, Inc., The.
Lester, Brian. Kansas City Chiefs, 1 vol. 2010. (Inside the NFL Ser.). (ENG.). 48p. (YA). (gr. 3-6). lib. bdg. 32.79 *(978-1-61714-016-7(3))* ABDO Publishing Co.
Peters, Rob, illus. Kansas City Chiefs ABCs And 1-2-3s. 2015. (ENG.). 26p. (J). bds. 18.95 *(978-0-9961944-0-2(1))* Ascend Bks., LLC.
Stewart, Mark. The Kansas City Chiefs. rev. ed. 2012. (Team Spirit Ser.). (ENG.). 48p. (J). (gr. 3-6). lib. bdg. 29.27 *(978-1-59953-527-2(0))* Norwood Hse. Pr.
Wyner, Zach. Kansas City Chiefs. (Illus.). 32p. (J). 2015. pap. *(978-1-4896-0843-7(5))* 2014. (ENG., (gr. 4-7). lib. bdg. 28.55 *(978-1-4896-0842-0(7)*, AV2 by Weigl) Weigl Pubs., Inc.

KANSAS CITY ROYALS (BASEBALL TEAM)

Bowker, Paul. Kansas City Royals, 1 vol. 2011. (Inside MLB Ser.). (ENG., Illus.). 48p. (YA). (gr. 3-6). lib. bdg. 32.79 *(978-1-61714-046-4(5))* ABDO Publishing Co.
Gilbert, Sara. The Story of the Kansas City Royals. 2007. (Baseball, the Great American Game Ser.). (Illus.). 48p. (YA). (gr. 4-7). lib. bdg. 32.80 *(978-1-58341-490-3(8))* Creative Co., The.
LeBoutillier, Nate. The Story of the Kansas City Royals. 2011. (J). 35.65 *(978-1-60818-043-1(3)*, Creative Education) Creative Co., The.
Stewart, Mark. The Kansas City Royals. 2012. (Team Spirit Ser.). 48p. (J). (gr. 3-6). lib. bdg. 29.27 *(978-1-59953-484-8(3))* Norwood Hse. Pr.

KARATE

see also Tae Kwon Do

Capucilli, Alyssa Satin. My First Karate Class: A Book with Foldout Pages. Jensen, Leyah, photos by. 2012. (My First Ser.). (ENG., Illus.). 14p. (J). (gr. -1-k). 9.99 *(978-1-4424-2748-8(5)*, Little Simon) Little Simon.
Cook, Harry. Karate. 2004. (Martial Arts Ser.). (Illus.). 32p. (gr. 3-6). lib. bdg. 26.00 *(978-0-8368-4193-0(X)*, Gareth Stevens Learning Library) Stevens, Gareth Publishing LLLP.
Craats, Rennay. For the Love of Karate. Nault, Jennifer & Turner, Kara, eds. 2003. (For the Love of Sports Ser.). (Illus.). 24p. (J). pap. 8.95 *(978-1-59036-071-2(0))* Weigl Pubs., Inc.
Di Marino, Stefano & Ghetti, Roberto. A Complete Guide to Karate. 2017. (Mastering Martial Arts Ser.). 128p. (J). (gr. 6-6). lib. bdg. 37.27 ***(978-0-7660-8539-8(2))*** Enslow Pubs., Inc.
Drewett, Jim & Martin, Ashley. How to Improve at Karate. 2007. (How to Improve At- Ser.). (ENG., Illus.). 48p. (J). (gr. 3-9). lib. bdg. *(978-0-7787-3568-7(0))* Crabtree Publishing Co.
Gifford, Clive. Karate. 2010. (Combat Sports Ser.). 32p. (J). (gr. 2-5). lib. bdg. 28.50 *(978-1-59771-275-0(2))* Sea-To-Sea Pubns.
Hicks, Terry Allan. Karate. 2010. (Martial Arts in Action Ser.). 48p. (gr. 6-7). lib. bdg. 29.93 *(978-0-7614-4934-8(5))* Marshall Cavendish GBR. Dist: Marshall Cavendish Corp.
Johnson, Nathan. Karate: Winning Ways. James, Adam, ed. 2015. (Mastering Martial Arts Ser.). (Illus.). 96p. (J). (gr. 5). lib. bdg. 24.95 *(978-1-4222-3238-5(7))* Mason Crest.
Kalman, Bobbie & MacAulay, Kelley. Karate in Action. 2005. (Sports in Action Ser.). (ENG., Illus.). 32p. (J). (gr. 2-3). pap. *(978-0-7787-0361-7(4))* Crabtree Publishing Co.
Karate: A Master's Secrets of Uechi-Ryu. 2003. (Illus.). 576p. (YA). pap. 49.95 *(978-0-9746989-0-8(3))* Iron Arm International.
MacAulay, Kelley & Kalman, Bobbie. Le Karaté. 2009. (Sans Limites Ser.). (FRE., Illus.). 32p. (J). (gr. 1-7). pap. 9.95 *(978-2-89579-251-2(8))* Bayard Canada Livres CAN. Dist: Crabtree Publishing Co.
Mackay, Jenny. Taekwondo. Greenhaven Press Staff, ed. 2014. (Science Behind Sports Ser.). (ENG., Illus.). 128p. (gr. 7-10). lib. bdg. 39.40 *(978-1-4205-0940-3(3)*, Lucent Bks.) Cengage Gale.
Macken, JoAnn Early. Karate. 2005. (After-School Fun Ser.). (Illus.). 24p. (gr. k-3). lib. bdg. 21.00 *(978-0-8368-4514-3(5)*, Weekly Reader Leveled Readers) Stevens, Gareth Publishing LLLP.
Mara, Wil. Karate. 2012. (J). pap. *(978-0-531-20925-7(3))*; lib. bdg. *(978-0-531-20856-4(7))* Children's Pr., Ltd.
Martin, Ashley. How to Improve at Karate. 2007. (How to Improve At- Ser.). (ENG., Illus.). 48p. (J). (gr. 3-7). pap. *(978-0-7787-3590-8(7))* Crabtree Publishing Co.
McNulty, Mark. Karate, 1 vol. 2014. (Inside Martial Arts Ser.). (ENG., Illus.). 48p. (J). (gr. 3-6). lib. bdg. 32.79 *(978-1-62403-603-3(1)*, SportsZone) ABDO Publishing Co.
O'Brien, Andrew & O'Brien, Emma. The Little Bubishi: A History of Karate for Children. 2010. 172p. pap. 40.00 *(978-1-60911-717-7(4)*, Eloquent Bks.) Strategic Book Publishing & Rights Agency (SBPRA).
Ollhoff, Jim. Karate, 1 vol. 2008. (World of Martial Arts Ser.). (ENG.). 32p. (gr. 4-8). 27.07 *(978-1-59928-977-9(6)*, Abdo & Daughters) ABDO Publishing Co.
—Sport Karate, 1 vol. 2008. (World of Martial Arts Ser.). (ENG.). 32p. (gr. 4-8). 27.07 *(978-1-59928-984-7(9)*, Abdo & Daughters) ABDO Publishing Co.
Pawlett, Ray. The Karate Handbook. (Martial Arts Ser.). 256p. 2009. (gr. 8-8). 79.90 *(978-1-61514-367-2(X))* 2008. (Illus.). (YA). (gr. 7-12). lib. bdg. 42.60 *(978-1-4042-1394-4(5))* Rosen Publishing Group, Inc., The.
Schuetz, Kari. Karate. 2011. (My First Sports Ser.). (ENG., Illus.). 24p. (J). (gr. 2-5). lib. bdg. 25.95 *(978-1-60014-570-4(1)*, Blastoff! Readers) Bellwether Media.
—Karate. 2011. pap. *(978-0-531-20636-2(X))* Grolier Publishing.
Wood, Alix. Karate. 2013. (Kid's Guide to Martial Arts Ser.). (ENG., Illus.). 32p. (J). (gr. 3-6). pap. 11.75 *(978-1-4777-0350-2(0))*; lib. bdg. 26.50 *(978-1-4777-0314-4(4))* Rosen Publishing Group, Inc., The. (PowerKids Pr.).

KARATE—FICTION

Barnes, Susan. Kelly Karate: Discovers the Ice Princess. 2004. 138p. (J). (gr. 4-8). pap. 5.95 *(978-0-9705777-3-3(7))* McBook Pubs., LLC.
Barriman, Lydia. The Runaway Puppy: A Mystery with Probability. Grutzik, Becky, illus. 2010. (Manga Math Mysteries Ser.: 8). (ENG.). 48p. (gr. 3-5). 29.27 *(978-0-7613-4910-5(3))* Lerner Publishing Group.
Bidoli, Katie. Karate Adventures of Kisho, Hana, & Nobu: Karate Is for Everyone! 2006. (Illus.). 16p. (J). 10.00 *(978-1-60243-029-7(2))* Keen's Martial Arts Academy.
Bowman, Rachael Ann. Sammy the Karate Squirrel. 2013. 28p. pap. 13.95 *(978-1-4624-0800-9(1)*, Inspiring Voices) Author Solutions, Inc.
Carey, Michael. Little Kathy Likes Karate. Connors, Jackie, ed. 2003. (Illus.). 30p. (J). spiral bd. 10.95 *(978-0-9743679-1-0(5))* Reiki Blessings.
Chin, Oliver Clyde. Julie Black Belt: The Kung Fu Chronicles. Chua, Charlene, illus. 2008. (ENG.). 36p. (J). (gr. k-1). 15.95 *(978-1-59702-009-1(5))* Immedium.
deRubertis, Barbara. Kylie Kangaroo's Karate Kickers. Alley, R. W., illus. 2011. (Animal Antics A to Z Ser.). 32p. (J). pap. 45.32 *(978-0-7613-7657-6(7))*; (ENG.). lib. bdg. 22.60 *(978-1-57565-332-7(X))*; (gr. -1-3). pap. 7.95 *(978-1-57565-323-5(0))* Kane Press, Inc.
deRubertis, Barbara & DeRubertis, Barbara. Kylie Kangaroo's Karate Kickers. Alley, R. W., illus. 2012. (Animal Antics A to Z Ser.). 32p. (J). (gr. 2 — 1). cd-rom 7.95 *(978-1-57565-404-1(0))* Kane Press, Inc.
Gelsey, James & Duendes Del Sur Staff. Scooby-Doo & the Karate Caper, 1 vol. 2011. (Scooby-Doo Mysteries Ser.). (ENG., Illus.). 64p. (J). (gr. 3-6). 24.21 *(978-1-59961-891-3(5))* Spotlight.
Hearst, Allyson. White Pajamas: A Karate Story. 2011. 68p. pap. 19.95 *(978-1-4626-3871-0(6))* America Star Bks.
Katschke, Judy. Karate Kangaroos (Disney Junior: Doc Mcstuffins) Random House Disney Staff & Martinez, Heather, illus. 2016. (Little Golden Book Ser.). (ENG.). 24p. (J). (gr. -1-k). 4.99 *(978-0-7364-3382-2(1)*, Golden/Disney) Random Hse. Children's Bks.
Knowles, Jo. Living with Jackie Chan. (ENG.). 384p. (YA). (gr. 9). 2015. pap. 8.99 *(978-0-7636-7663-6(2))* 2013. 16.99 *(978-0-7636-6280-6(1))* Candlewick Pr.

Krulik, Nancy. Karate Katie, 18 vols. John and Wendy Staff, illus. 2006. (Katie Kazoo, Switcheroo Ser.: 18). (ENG.). 80p. (J). (gr. 2-4). pap. 4.99 *(978-0-448-43767-5(8)*, Grosset & Dunlap) Penguin Young Readers Group.

Maddox, Jake. Karate Countdown, 1 vol. Tiffany, Sean, illus. 2009. (Jake Maddox Sports Stories Ser.). (ENG.). 72p. (gr. 2-3). lib. bdg. 25.32 *(978-1-4342-1200-9(9))* Stone Arch Bks.

Nevius, Carol. Karate Hour, 0 vols. Thomson, Bill, illus. 2011. (ENG.). 34p. (J). (gr. -1-2). pap. 7.99 *(978-0-7614-5840-1(9)*, 9780761458401, Amazon Children's Publishing) Amazon Publishing.

Noppe-Brandon, Gail. Tilly Takes A Try. 2010. 36p. 15.49 *(978-1-4520-7662-1(6))* AuthorHouse.

Potter, Noel Gyro. A Very Sticky Situation, 1 vol. Cannon, Joseph, illus. 2008. (Adventures of Marshall & Art Ser.). (ENG.). 32p. (gr. -1-4). 28.50 *(978-1-60270-201-1(2)*, Looking Glass Library) ABDO Publishing Co.

—A Wheel Life Lesson, 1 vol. Cannon, Joseph, illus. 2008. (Adventures of Marshall & Art Ser.). (ENG.). 32p. (gr. -1-4). 28.50 *(978-1-60270-202-8(0)*, Looking Glass Library) ABDO Publishing Co.

Shammas, Anna. Recorder Karate. Guiza, Victor, illus. 2012. 32p. pap. 8.95 *(978-0-9843869-2-5(0)*, Castlebridge Bks.) Big Tent Bks.

Sookraj, Esther. Good with Words Bueno con las Palabras. 2010. 24p. pap. 15.99 *(978-1-4500-4169-0(8))* Xlibris Corp.

Stevens, Elizabeth. Mister D. Frongia, Daniela, illus. 2012. 24p. (J). 16.95 *(978-1-60131-114-6(1))* Big Tent Bks.

Stilton, Geronimo. The Karate Mouse. 2010. (Geronimo Stilton Ser.: 40). (ENG., Illus.). 128p. (J). (gr. 2-5). 7.99 *(978-0-545-10369-5(X)*, Scholastic Paperbacks) Scholastic, Inc.

—The Karate Mouse. 2010. (Geronimo Stilton Ser.: 40). lib. bdg. 18.40 *(978-0-606-06847-5(3)*, Turtleback) Turtleback Bks.

Thielbar, Melinda. The Ancient Formula No. 5: A Mystery with Fractions. Pantoja, Tintin, illus. 2010. (Manga Math Mysteries Ser.: 5). (ENG.). 48p. (gr. 3-5). 29.27 *(978-0-7613-4907-5(3))* Lerner Publishing Group.

—The Secret Ghost: A Mystery with Distance & Measurement. Ota, Yuko, illus. 2010. (Manga Math Mysteries Ser.: 3). (ENG.). 46p. (gr. 3-5). pap. 6.95 *(978-0-7613-5245-7(7)*, Graphic Universe™) Lerner Publishing Group.

Tosten, Sharon. Troy's Amazing Universe: K for Karate. 2006. 144p. per. 13.95 *(978-0-9743185-2-3(3))* Booklocker.com, Inc.

KARTS AND KARTING

Challen, Paul C. Kart Racing, 1 vol. 2015. (ENG., Illus.). 32p. (J). lib. bdg. 26.25 *(978-1-4994-0163-9(9)*, PowerKids Pr.) Rosen Publishing Group, Inc., The.

David, Jack. Go-Kart Racing. 2008. (Action Sports Ser.). (ENG., Illus.). 24p. (J). (gr. 3-7). lib. bdg. 25.95 *(978-1-60014-123-2(4))* Bellwether Media.

Dugan, Christine. Final Lap! Go-Kart Racing, 1 vol. 2nd rev. ed. 2013. (Nonfiction Readers Ser.). (ENG., Illus.). 48p. (J). (gr. 4-4). pap. 29.96 *(978-1-4807-1108-2(X))* Shell Educational Publishing.

—Final Lap! Go-Kart Racing, 1 vol. 2nd rev. ed. 2012. (TIME for KIDS(r) Nonfiction Readers Ser.). (ENG.). 48p. (J). (gr. 4-4). pap. 9.99 *(978-1-4333-4832-7(2))* Teacher Created Materials, Inc.

—¡Última Vuelta! Carreras de Kartings. 2017. (TIME for Kids en Español - Level 4 Ser.). (SPA.). 48p. (gr. 4-4). lib. bdg. 31.99 *(978-1-5157-5137-3(6))* Time for Kids Inc AUS. Dist: Capstone Pub.

Hamilton, John. Go-Kart Racing. 2014. (Action Sports Ser.). (ENG., Illus.). 32p. (J). (gr. 8-15). lib. bdg. 27.07 *(978-1-62403-440-4(3)*, A&D Xtreme) ABDO Publishing Co.

Icanberry, Mark, creator. Electric Lunch. 2010. (Look, Learn & Do Ser.). (Illus.). 48p. (J). 7.95 *(978-1-893327-03-0(5))* Look, Learn & Do Pubns.

Randolph, Ryan. Karts. 2011. (Fast Lane: Open-Wheel Racing Ser.). (Illus.). 24p. (gr. 2-5). 22.60 *(978-1-4339-5758-1(2))*; pap. 8.15 *(978-1-4339-5760-4(4))* Stevens, Gareth Publishing LLLP. (Gareth Stevens Learning Library).

KARTS AND KARTING—FICTION

Maddox, Jake. Go-Kart Rush. Tiffany, Sean, illus. 2007. (Jake Maddox Sports Stories Ser.). (ENG.). 72p. (gr. 2-3). pap. 5.95 *(978-1-59889-415-8(3))* Stone Arch Bks.

—Kart Crash, 1 vol. Tiffany, Sean, illus. 2008. (Jake Maddox Sports Stories Ser.). (ENG.). 72p. (gr. 2-3). 25.32 *(978-1-4342-0777-7(3))*; pap. 5.95 *(978-1-4342-0873-6(7))* Stone Arch Bks.

Midnight Lightning, 6 vols., Pack. (Bookweb Ser.). 32p. (gr. 5-18). 34.00 *(978-0-7635-3790-6(X))* Rigby Education.

Montanari, Eva. Go-Cart Number 1. 2005. (Picture Books/Quality Time Ser.). (Illus.). 32p. (gr. k-3). lib. bdg. 26.00 *(978-0-8368-4478-8(5)*, Gareth Stevens Learning Library) Stevens, Gareth Publishing LLLP.

KEATS, JOHN, 1795-1821

Kirkpatrick, Patricia. John Keats. Delessert, Etienne, illus. 2005. (Voices in Poetry Ser.). 43p. (J). (gr. 5-9). 21.95 *(978-1-58341-345-6(6)*, Creative Education) Creative Co., The.

KELLER, HELEN, 1880-1968

Adams, Colleen. The Courage of Helen Keller. (Reading Room Collection 2 Ser.). 24p. 2009. (gr. 3-4). 42.50 *(978-1-60851-992-7(9)*, PowerKids Pr.) 2003. (Illus.). (J). lib. bdg. 22.60 *(978-0-8239-3710-3(0))* Rosen Publishing Group, Inc., The.

Adler, David A. Helen Keller. Wallner, John, illus. 2006. (ENG.). 32p. (J). (gr. -1-3). 4.95 *(978-0-8234-2042-1(6))* Holiday Hse., Inc.

—Helen Keller. Wallner, John C. & Wallner, John, illus. 2003. (ENG.). 32p. (J). (gr. k-3). tchr. ed. 14.95 *(978-0-8234-1606-6(2))* Holiday Hse., Inc.

Auster, Michael A. They Led the Way. 2005. (Yellow Umbrella Fluent Level Ser.). (ENG.). 16p. (gr. k-1). pap. 35.70 *(978-0-7368-5315-6(4)*, Yellow Umbrella Bks.) Capstone Press of Coughlan Cos.

Barry, Holly M. Helen Keller's Best Friend Belle. Thermes, Jennifer, illus. 2013. (ENG.). 32p. (J). (gr. -1-3). 16.99 *(978-0-8075-3198-3(7))* Whitman, Albert & Co.

Benge, Janet. Helen Keller: Facing Her Challenges - Challenging the World, 1 bk. James, Kennon, illus. 2003. (Another Great Achiever Ser.). (J). lib. bdg. 23.95 incl. audio *(978-1-57537-793-3(4))* Advance Publishing, Inc.

Berne, Emma Carlson. What's Your Story, Helen Keller? 2015. (ENG., Illus.). 32p. (J). (gr. k-3). 26.65 *(978-1-4677-7968-5(7))* Lerner Publishing Group.

Berne, Emma Carlson & Hodge, Marie. Helen Keller: Courage in Darkness. 2009. (Sterling Biographies(r) Ser.). (ENG., Illus.). 128p. (J). (gr. 5-18). pap. 5.95 *(978-1-4027-5147-9(8))* Sterling Publishing Co., Inc.

Butler, Darren J. Helen Keller: Leader Without Sight or Sound. 2012. (Illus.). 108p. (J). pap. *(978-1-59421-083-9(7))* Seacoast Publishing, Inc.

Chally, Jeanne. Helen Keller: A Triumph of Spirit. 2003. (Shutterbug Books: Social Studies). (Illus.). 16p. (J). (gr. -1-3). pap. 4.10 *(978-0-7398-7648-0(1))* Steck-Vaughn.

Cline-Ransome, Lesa. Helen Keller: The World in Her Heart. Ransome, James E., illus. 2008. 32p. (J). (gr. k-4). lib. bdg. 17.89 *(978-0-06-057075-0(X)*, Collins) HarperCollins Pubs.

Delano, Marfe Ferguson. Helen's Eyes: A Photobiography of Annie Sullivan, Helen Keller's Teacher. 2008. (Photobiographies Ser.). (ENG., Illus.). 64p. (J). (gr. 5). 27.90 *(978-1-4263-0210-7(X))*; 17.95 *(978-1-4263-0209-1(6))* National Geographic Society. (National Geographic Children's Bks.).

Devillier, Christy. Helen Keller, 1 vol. 2004. (First Biographies Set Iv Ser.). (ENG., Illus.). 32p. (gr. k-4). 27.07 *(978-1-59197-514-4(X)*, Buddy Bks.) ABDO Publishing Co.

Dolan, Sean J. Helen Keller. 2006. (Rookie Biographies Ser.). (ENG., Illus.). 32p. (J). (gr. 1-2). per. 4.95 *(978-0-516-25481-4(2)*, Children's Pr.) Scholastic Library Publishing.

Edison, Erin. Helen Keller, 1 vol. 2014. (Great Women in History Ser.). (ENG.). 24p. (gr. k-1). lib. bdg. 21.99 *(978-1-4765-4217-1(1)*, Pebble Bks.) Capstone Press of Coughlan Cos.

Feinstein, Stephen. Read about Helen Keller. 2004. (I Like Biographies! Ser.). (Illus.). 24p. (J). lib. bdg. 22.60 *(978-0-7660-2299-7(4))* Enslow Pubs., Inc.

Fetty, Margaret. Helen Keller: Break down the Walls! 2006. (Defining Moments Ser.). (Illus.). 32p. (J). (gr. 2-5). lib. bdg. 25.27 *(978-1-59716-271-5(X))* Bearport Publishing Co., Inc.

Garrett, Leslie & Dorling Kindersley Publishing Staff. Helen Keller, Level 3. 2013. (DK Readers Ser.). (ENG., Illus.). 48p. (J). (gr. 2-4). pap. 3.99 *(978-1-4654-0946-1(7)*, DK Children) Dorling Kindersley Publishing, Inc.

Garrett, Leslie, et al. Helen Keller. 2004. (DK Biography Ser.). (ENG., Illus.). 128p. (J). (gr. 5-12). pap. 6.99 *(978-0-7566-0339-7(0)*, DK Children) Dorling Kindersley Publishing, Inc.

Ghiglieri, Carol. Easy Reader Biographies: Helen Keller: An Inspiring Life. 2007. (ENG.). 16p. pap. 2.99 *(978-0-439-77417-8(9)*, Teaching Resources) Scholastic, Inc.

Haldy, Emma E. Helen Keller. Bane, Jeff, illus. 2016. (My Early Library: My Itty-Bitty Bio Ser.). (ENG.). 24p. (J). (gr. k-1). 28.50 *(978-1-63471-020-6(7)*, 208160) Cherry Lake Publishing.

Helenthal, Janet. Helen Keller. 2005. (Illus.). 16p. (J). *(978-0-7367-2853-9(8))* Zaner-Bloser, Inc.

Hollingsworth, Tamara. Helen Keller: A New Vision, 1 vol. 2nd rev. ed. 2013. (Nonfiction Readers Ser.). (ENG., Illus.). 48p. (J). (gr. 4-4). pap. 29.96 *(978-1-4807-1115-0(2))* Shell Educational Publishing.

—Helen Keller: A New Vision, 1 vol. 2nd rev. ed. 2012. (Nonfiction Readers Ser.). (ENG.). 48p. (J). (gr. 4-4). pap. 9.99 *(978-1-4333-4863-1(2))* Teacher Created Materials, Inc.

—Helen Keller: Una Nueva Visión. 2017. (TIME for Kids en Español - Level 4 Ser.). (SPA & ENG., Illus.). 48p. (gr. 4-4). lib. bdg. 31.99 *(978-1-5157-5144-1(9))* Time for Kids Inc AUS. Dist: Capstone Pub.

Hopkinson, Deborah. Annie & Helen. Colón, Raúl, illus. 2012. (ENG.). 48p. (J). (gr. -1-3). 17.99 *(978-0-375-85706-5(0)*, Schwartz & Wade Bks.) Random Hse. Children's Bks.

Jazynka, Kitson. Helen Keller. 2017. (Readers Bios Ser.). (ENG., Illus.). 32p. (J). (gr. k-3). pap. 3.99 *(978-1-4263-2669-1(6)*, National Geographic Children's Bks.) National Geographic Society.

Kennon, Caroline. Helen Keller in Her Own Words. 2014. (Eyewitness to History Ser.). 32p. (J). (gr. 4-6). pap. 63.00 *(978-1-4824-0812-6(0))* Stevens, Gareth Publishing LLLP.

Koestler-Grack, Rachel A. Helen Keller. 2nd rev. ed. 2009. (Women of Achievement Ser.). (Illus.). 144p. (gr. 6-12). 35.00 *(978-1-60413-502-2(6)*, Chelsea Hse.) Facts On File, Inc.

Kudlinski, Kathleen V. Helen Keller: A Light for the Blind. Diamond, Donna, illus. 2015. (Women of Our Time Ser.). (ENG.). 80p. (J). (gr. 3-7). 7.99 *(978-0-14-751467-7(3)*, Puffin Books) Penguin Young Readers Group.

Lawson, Barbara Spilman. Helen Keller Against All Odds. 2016. (Spring Forward Ser.). (J). (gr. 2). *(978-1-4900-9472-4(5))* Benchmark Education Co.

Leavitt, Amie Jane. Helen Keller. 2007. (What's So Great About... ? Ser.). (Illus.). 32p. (J). (gr. 2-4). lib. bdg. 25.70 *(978-1-58415-583-6(3))* Mitchell Lane Pubs., Inc.

MacLeod, Elizabeth. Helen Keller. Krystoforski, Andrej, illus. 2007. (Kids Can Read Ser.). (ENG.). 32p. (J). (gr. 1-3). 3.95 *(978-1-55453-000-7(8))*; 14.95 *(978-1-55337-999-7(3))* Kids Can Pr., Ltd. CAN. Dist: Hachette Bk. Group.

—Helen Keller: A Determined Life. 2004. (Snapshots: Images of People & Places in History Ser.). (ENG., Illus.). 32p. (J). (gr. 3-7). 7.95 *(978-1-55337-509-8(2))* Kids Can Pr., Ltd. CAN. Dist: Hachette Bk. Group.

McDonald, Caryl. Who Was Helen Keller? 2012. (InfoMax Readers Ser.). (ENG., Illus.). 24p. (J). (gr. 1-2). pap. 8.25 *(978-1-4488-9040-8(3)*, Rosen Classroom) Rosen Publishing Group, Inc., The.

Meltzer, Brad. I Am Helen Keller. Eliopoulos, Christopher, illus. 2015. (Ordinary People Change the World Ser.). (ENG.). 40p. (J). (gr. k-3). 14.99 *(978-0-525-42851-0(8)*, Dial Bks) Penguin Young Readers Group.

Mills, Nathan & Peck, Audrey. Helen Keller: Miracle Child. 2012. (Rosen Readers Ser.). (ENG., Illus.). 24p. (J). (gr. 1-2). pap. 8.25 *(978-1-4488-8824-5(7)*, Rosen Classroom) Rosen Publishing Group, Inc., The.

Norwich, Grace. I Am Helen Keller. Elliot, Mark, illus. 2012. (I Am Ser.). (ENG.). 128p. (J). (gr. 3-7). pap. 5.99 *(978-0-545-44779-9(8)*, Scholastic Paperbacks) Scholastic, Inc.

O'Brien, John A. Who Was Helen Keller? Harrison, Nancy, illus. 2003. (Who Was... ? Ser.). 107p. (J). (gr. 3-7). 12.65 *(978-0-7569-1596-4(1))* Perfection Learning Corp.

O'Brien, John A. & Thompson, Gare. Who Was Helen Keller? Harrison, Nancy, illus. 2003. (Who Was... ? Ser.). 107p. (J). (gr. 3-7). 16.00 *(978-0-613-63485-4(3)*, Turtleback) Turtleback Bks.

Peck, Audrey. Helen Keller: Miracle Child. 2012. (Beginning Biographies Ser.). (ENG., Illus.). 24p. (J). (gr. 1-3). 22.60 *(978-1-4488-8593-0(0)*, PowerKids Pr.) Rosen Publishing Group, Inc., The.

Rappaport, Doreen. Helen's Big World: The Life of Helen Keller. Tavares, Matt, illus. 2017. (Big Words Ser.). (ENG.). 48p. (J). (gr. 1-3). pap. 8.99 *(978-1-4847-4960-9(X))* Hyperion Bks. for Children.

—Helen's Big World: The Life of Helen Keller. Tavares, Matt, illus. 2012. (Big Words Ser.). (ENG.). 48p. (J). (gr. 1-3). 17.99 *(978-0-7868-0890-8(X))* Hyperion Pr.

Sabin, Francene & Mattern, Joanne. Helen Keller, Girl of Courage. Meyer, Jean, illus. 2006. 56p. (J). *(978-0-439-66043-3(2))* Scholastic, Inc.

Sullivan, George. Helen Keller: Her Life in Pictures. 2007. (Helen Keller Ser.). (ENG., Illus.). 80p. (J). (gr. 2-5). 17.99 *(978-0-439-91815-2(4)*, Scholastic Nonfiction) Scholastic, Inc.

Sutcliffe, Jane. Helen Keller. 2009. (History Maker Biographies Ser.). (gr. k-2). 27.93 *(978-0-7613-4223-6(0)*, Lerner Pubns.) Lerner Publishing Group.

—Helen Keller. Verstraete, Elaine, illus. 2003. (On My Own Biographies Ser.). 48p. (J). (gr. 1-3). 6.95 *(978-0-87614-903-4(4)*, Carolrhoda Bks.) Lerner Publishing Group.

Takase, Naoko, illus. Helen Keller: From Darkness to Light. 2011. (Biographical Comic Ser.). (ENG.). 152p. (J). (gr. 2-6). 18.99 *(978-1-4215-4238-6(2))*; pap. 9.99 *(978-1-4215-4239-3(0))* Shogakukan JPN. Dist: Simon & Schuster, Inc.

Thompson, Gare. Who Was Helen Keller? O'Brien, John A. & Harrison, Nancy, illus. 2003. (Who Was? Ser.). (ENG.). 112p. (J). (gr. 3-7). pap. 5.99 *(978-0-448-43144-4(0)*, Grosset & Dunlap) Penguin Young Readers Group.

Walker, Pam & National Geographic Learning Staff. Helen Keller. 2010. (Rise & Shine Ser.). (ENG., Illus.). 24p. (C). (gr. -1-3). per. 8.95 *(978-0-516-23588-2(5))* National Geographic School Publishing, Inc.

KELLER, HELEN, 1880-1968—FICTION

Miller, Sarah. Miss Spitfire: Reaching Helen Keller. (ENG.). (J). (gr. 5-7). 2010. 256p. pap. 7.99 *(978-1-4424-0851-7(0))* 2007. 240p. 17.99 *(978-1-4169-2542-2(2))* Simon & Schuster Children's Publishing. (Atheneum Bks. for Young Readers).

KENNEDY, EDWARD M. (EDWARD MOORE), 1932-2009

Goldsworthy, Steve. Edward Kennedy. 2010. (Remarkable People Ser.). (Illus.). 24p. (J). (gr. 4-6). pap. 11.95 *(978-1-61690-170-7(5))*; lib. bdg. 25.70 *(978-1-61690-169-1(1))* Weigl Pubs., Inc.

Kennedy, Edward M. My Senator & Me: A Dog's-Eye View of Washington, D. C. Small, David, illus. 2011. (J). (gr. 2-5). 29.95 *(978-0-545-04379-3(4))* Weston Woods Studios, Inc.

Krull, Kathleen. The Brothers Kennedy: John, Robert, Edward. Bates, Amy June, illus. 2010. (ENG.). 40p. (J). (gr. -1-3). 16.99 *(978-1-4169-9158-8(1)*, Simon & Schuster Bks. For Young Readers) Simon & Schuster Bks. For Young Readers.

McElroy, Lisa Tucker. Ted Kennedy: A Remarkable Life in the Senate. 2009. (Gateway Biographies Ser.). (ENG.). 48p. (gr. 4-8). 26.60 *(978-0-7613-4457-5(8))* Lerner Publishing Group.

Ted Kennedy. 2009. (Political Profiles Ser.). 144p. (YA). (gr. 5-9). 28.95 *(978-1-59935-089-9(0))* Reynolds, Morgan Inc.

KENNEDY, JOHN F. (JOHN FITZGERALD), 1917-1963

Anderson, Catherine Corley. John F. Kennedy. 2004. (Presidential Leaders Ser.). (ENG., Illus.). 112p. (gr. 6-12). 29.27 *(978-0-8225-0812-0(5)*, Lerner Pubns.) Lerner Publishing Group.

Bader, Bonnie. Who Was Jackie Kennedy? Qiu, Joseph J. M., illus. 2016. (Who Was? Ser.). (ENG.). 112p. (J). (gr. 3-7). lib. bdg. 15.99 *(978-0-399-54242-8(6)*, Grosset & Dunlap) Penguin Young Readers Group.

Barretta, Gene. Lincoln & Kennedy: A Pair to Compare. Barretta, Gene, illus. 2016. (ENG., Illus.). 40p. (J). 17.99 *(978-0-8050-9945-4(X)*, 9780805099454, Holt, Henry & Co. Bks. For Young Readers) Holt, Henry & Co.

Baxter, Kathleen & McConnell, Robert L., contrib. by. Assassination & Its Aftermath: How a Photograph Reassured a Shocked Nation, 1 vol. 2013. (Captured History Ser.). (ENG.). 64p. (gr. 5-7). 34.65 *(978-0-7565-4692-2(3)*, CPB Grades 4-8) Compass Point Bks.

Bodden, Valerie. The Assassination of John F. Kennedy. (Turning Points Ser.). 48p. (J). 2017. (ENG.). (gr. 7-12). pap. 12.00 *(978-1-62832-342-9(6)*, Creative Paperbacks) 2016. (Illus.). *(978-1-60818-746-1(2)*, Creative Education) Creative Co., The.

Brown, Jonatha A. John F. Kennedy. 2005. (People We Should Know Ser.). 24p. (gr. 1-4). (SPA.). pap. 8.15 *(978-0-8368-4768-0(7))*; (Illus.). lib. bdg. 22.00 *(978-0-8368-4747-5(4))*; (SPA., Illus.). lib. bdg. 22.00 *(978-0-8368-4761-1(X))* Stevens, Gareth Publishing LLLP. (Weekly Reader Leveled Readers).

Burgan, Michael. John F. Kennedy, 1 vol. HL Studios Staff, illus. 2013. (ENG.). 56p. (gr. 4-8). 33.32 *(978-1-4329-8096-2(3))*; pap. 10.95 *(978-1-4329-8097-9(1))* Heinemann-Raintree. (NA-h).

Corey, Shana. A Time to Act: John F. Kennedy's Big Speech. Christie, R. Gregory, illus. 2017. (ENG.). 56p. (J). (gr. 3). 18.95 *(978-0-7358-4275-5(2))* North-South Bks., Inc.

Duffield, Katy S. John F. Kennedy. 2016. (Premier Presidents Ser.). (ENG.). 24p. (J). (gr. 1-4). 27.07 *(978-1-5038-0867-6(X)*, 210717) Child's World, Inc., The.

Edison, Erin. John F. Kennedy, 1 vol. (Presidential Biographies Ser.). (ENG.). 24p. (gr. k-1). 2014. pap. 6.29 *(978-1-4765-9632-7(8)*, Pebble Bks.) 2012. lib. bdg. 26.65 *(978-1-4296-8738-6(X)*, Pebble Plus) Capstone Press of Coughlan Cos.

Edwards, Roberta. Hail to the Chiefs, 5 vols. 2013. (Who Was? Ser.). (ENG.). 560p. (J). (gr. 3-7). pap. 24.95 *(978-0-448-48122-7(7)*, Grosset & Dunlap) Penguin Young Readers Group.

Ford, Carin T. John F. Kennedy: The 35th President. 2006. (Heroes of American History Ser.). (Illus.). 32p. (J). (gr. 4-7). lib. bdg. 23.94 *(978-0-7660-2601-8(9)*, Enslow Elementary) Enslow Pubs., Inc.

Goldsmith, Howard. John F. Kennedy & the Stormy Sea. Benoit, Renné, illus. 2006. 32p. (J). lib. bdg. 15.00 *(978-1-4242-0958-3(7))* Fitzgerald Bks.

—John F. Kennedy & the Stormy Sea. Benoit, Renne, illus. 2006. (Ready-To-read COFA Ser.). (ENG.). 32p. (J). (gr. k-2). pap. 3.99 *(978-0-689-86816-0(2)*, Simon Spotlight) Simon Spotlight.

Gunderson, Megan M. John F. Kennedy, 1 vol. 2009. (United States Presidents Ser.). (ENG., Illus.). 40p. (YA). (gr. 3-6). 27.07 *(978-1-60453-463-4(X))* ABDO Publishing Co.

Hansen, Grace. John F. Kennedy, 1 vol. 2014. (United States President Biographies Ser.). (ENG.). 24p. (J). (gr. 4-8). lib. bdg. 28.50 *(978-1-62970-090-8(8))* ABDO Publishing Co.

—John F. Kennedy. 2015. (Biografías de Los Presidentes de Los Estados Unidos Ser.). (SPA., Illus.). 24p. (gr. k-1). pap. 7.95 *(978-1-4966-0411-8(3))* Capstone Classroom.

Heiligman, Deborah. High Hopes: A Photobiography of John F. Kennedy. Feresten, Nancy, ed. 2003. (Photobiographies Ser.). (ENG., Illus.). 64p. (J). (gr. 5). 17.95 *(978-0-7922-6141-4(0)*, National Geographic Children's Bks.) National Geographic Society.

Hollar, Sherman, contrib. by. John F. Kennedy. 2012. (Pivotal Presidents: Profiles in Leadership Ser.). (ENG.). 80p. (YA). (gr. 7-12). lib. bdg. 32.90 *(978-1-61530-943-6(8))*; (Illus.). 65.80 *(978-1-61530-957-3(8))* Rosen Publishing Group, Inc., The.

Jones, Brenn. Learning about Public Service from the Life of John F. Kennedy Jr. 2009. (Character Building Book Ser.). 24p. (gr. 2-3). 42.50 *(978-1-61511-002-5(X)*, PowerKids Pr.) Rosen Publishing Group, Inc., The.

Jones, Veda Boyd. John F. Kennedy. 2006. (Rookie Biographies Ser.). (ENG., Illus.). 32p. (J). (gr. 1-2). pap. 4.95 *(978-0-516-29797-2(X)*, Children's Pr.) Scholastic Library Publishing.

Kaplan, Howard S. John F. Kennedy: A Photographic Story of a Life. 2004. (DK Biography Ser.). (ENG., Illus.). 128p. (J). (gr. 5-12). pap. 6.99 *(978-0-7566-0340-3(4)*, DK Children) Dorling Kindersley Publishing, Inc.

Keenan, Sheila. John F. Kennedy the Brave. Ko, Chin, illus. 2017. (I Can Read Level 2 Ser.). 32p. (J). (gr. -1-3). pap. 3.99 *(978-0-06-243258-2(3))* HarperCollins Pubs.

Krull, Kathleen. The Brothers Kennedy: John, Robert, Edward. Bates, Amy June, illus. 2010. (ENG.). 40p. (J). (gr. -1-3). 16.99 *(978-1-4169-9158-8(1)*, Simon & Schuster Bks. For Young Readers) Simon & Schuster Bks. For Young Readers.

Manolis, Kay & Todd, Anne. John F. Kennedy: A Life of Citizenship. 2007. (People of Character Ser.). (ENG., Illus.). 24p. (J). (gr. 2-5). lib. bdg. 25.95 *(978-1-60014-087-7(4))* Bellwether Media.

Mara, Wil. John F. Kennedy. 2009. (Presidents & Their Times 3 Ser.). 96p. (gr. 6). 34.21 *(978-0-7614-3628-7(6))* Marshall Cavendish Corp.

Marcovitz, Hal. John F. Kennedy. 2004. (Childhood of the Presidents Ser.). (Illus.). 48p. (J). (gr. 4-18). lib. bdg. 17.95 *(978-1-59084-272-0(3))* Mason Crest.

Margaret, Amy. John F. Kennedy Library & Museum. (Presidential Libraries Ser.). 24p. 2009. (gr. 3-3). 42.50 *(978-1-60851-487-8(0))* 2004. (Illus.). (J). lib. bdg. 22.60 *(978-0-8239-6269-3(5))* Rosen Publishing Group, Inc., The. (PowerKids Pr.).

Marsh, Carole. John F. Kennedy. 2003. 12p. (gr. k-4). 2.95 *(978-0-635-02127-4(7))* Gallopade International.

Mattern, Joanne. Jacqueline Kennedy, 1 vol. 2008. (First Ladies Set 1 Ser.). (ENG., Illus.). 32p. (YA). (gr. 1-4). 27.07 *(978-1-59928-796-6(X))* ABDO Publishing Co.

McConnell, Robert L., contrib. by. Assassination & Its Aftermath: How a Photograph Reassured a Shocked Nation, 1 vol. 2013. (Captured History Ser.). (ENG.). 64p. (gr. 5-7). pap. 9.10 *(978-0-7565-4698-4(2)*, CPB Grades 4-8) Compass Point Bks.

McDonough, Yona Zeldis. Who Was John F. Kennedy? Weber, Jill & Harrison, Nancy, illus. 2004. (Who Was? Ser.). (ENG.). 112p. (J). (gr. 3-7). pap. 5.99 *(978-0-448-43743-9(0)*, Grosset & Dunlap) Penguin Young Readers Group.

Norwich, Grace. I Am #9: John F. Kennedy. 2013. (I Am Ser.: 9). (ENG.). 128p. (J). (gr. 2-5). pap. 5.99 *(978-0-545-56883-8(8)*, Scholastic Paperbacks) Scholastic, Inc.

Olson, Nathan. John F. Kennedy: American Visionary, 1 vol. Bascle, Brian, illus. 2007. (Graphic Biographies Ser.). (ENG.). 32p. (gr. 3-4). per. 8.10 *(978-0-7368-7904-0(8)*, 1264943, Graphic Library) Capstone Press of Coughlan Cos.

Olson, Nathan & Capstone Press Staff. John F. Kennedy: American Visionary, 1 vol. Bascle, Brian, illus. 2007. (Graphic Biographies Ser.). (ENG.). 32p. (gr. 3-4). 30.65 *(978-0-7368-6852-5(6)*, Graphic Library) Capstone Press of Coughlan Cos.

Rappaport, Doreen. Jack's Path of Courage: The Life of John F. Kennedy. Tavares, Matt, illus. 2016. (Big Words Ser.). (ENG.). 48p. (J). (gr. 1-3). pap. 8.99 *(978-1-4847-4961-6(8))* Hyperion Bks. for Children.

—Jack's Path of Courage: The Life of John F. Kennedy. Tavares, Matt & Borgens, Matthew Todd, illus. 2010. (Big Words Ser.). (ENG.). 48p. (J). (gr. 1-3). 17.99 *(978-1-4231-2272-2(0))* Hyperion Pr.

Rowell, Rebecca. John F. Kennedy's Presidency. 2016. (Presidential Powerhouses Ser.). (ENG.). 104p. (J). (gr. 6-12). 53.32 *(978-1-4677-8600-3(4)*, Lerner Pubns.) Lerner Publishing Group.

Roxburgh, Ellis. John F. Kennedy vs. Nikita Khrushchev. 2015. (History's Greatest Rivals Ser.). (ENG., Illus.). 48p. (J). (gr. 6-8). lib. bdg. 31.95 *(978-1-4824-2221-4(2))* Stevens, Gareth Publishing LLLP.

Senker, Cath. Kennedy & the Cuban Missile Crisis: Days of Decision, 1 vol. 2013. (Days of Decision Ser.). (ENG.). 64p. (gr. 7-8). 35.99 *(978-1-4329-7637-8(0))* Heinemann-Raintree.

Sommer, Shelley. John F. Kennedy: His Life & Legacy. 2005. (Illus.). 160p. (J). 16.99 *(978-0-06-054135-4(0))* HarperCollins Pubs.

Sutcliffe, Jane. John F. Kennedy. (History Maker Bios Ser.). (J). 2005. (Illus.). 48p. 26.60 *(978-0-8225-1546-3(6))* 2004. pap. 8.95 *(978-0-8225-2540-0(2))* Lerner Publishing Group. (Lerner Pubns.).

Upadhyay, Ritu. John F Kennedy the Making of a Leader. 2005. 44p. (J). lib. bdg. 15.00 *(978-1-4242-0851-7(3))* Fitzgerald Bks.

Upadhyay, Ritu & Time for Kids Editors. The Making of a Leader. 2005. (Time for Kids Ser.). (ENG., Illus.). 48p. (J). (gr. 2-4). pap. 3.99 *(978-0-06-057602-8(2))* HarperCollins Pubs.

Winter, Jonah. JFK. Ford, A. G., illus. 2013. (ENG.). 32p. (J). (gr. -1-3). 17.99 *(978-0-06-176807-1(3))* HarperCollins Pubs.

Zamora, Dulce. How to Draw the Life & Times of John F. Kennedy. 2005. (Kid's Guide to Drawing the Presidents of the United States of America Ser.). (Illus.). 32p. (YA). (gr. 2-5). lib. bdg. 25.25 *(978-1-4042-3011-8(4))* Rosen Publishing Group, Inc., The.

—How to Draw the Life & Times of John Fitzgerald Kennedy. 2009. (Kid's Guide to Drawing the Presidents of the United States of America Ser.). 32p. (gr. 4-4). 50.50 *(978-1-61511-151-0(4),* PowerKids Pr.) Rosen Publishing Group, Inc., The.

KENNEDY, JOHN F. (JOHN FITZGERALD), 1917-1963—ASSASSINATION

Benoit, Peter. The Assassination of JFK. 2013. (ENG.). 64p. (J). 30.00 *(978-0-531-28200-7(7))*; pap. 8.95 *(978-0-531-27665-5(1))* Scholastic Library Publishing.

Coates, Tim. The Shooting of John F. Kennedy 1963: The Warren Commission. 2003. (Moments of History Ser.). (Illus.). 320p. *(978-1-84381-025-4(5))* Coates, Tim.

Collins, Terry. The Assassination of John F. Kennedy: November 22 1963, 1 vol. 2014. (24-Hour History Ser.). (ENG.). 48p. (gr. 3-5). pap. 8.95 *(978-1-4329-9300-9(3))*; (Illus.). lib. bdg. 33.32 *(978-1-4329-9294-1(5))* Heinemann-Raintree. (NA-h).

Engdahl, Sylvia. The John F. Kennedy Assassination. Gale Editors, ed. 2010. (Perspectives on Modern World History Ser.). (Illus.). 224p. (YA). (gr. 10-12). 42.45 *(978-0-7377-5006-5(5),* Greenhaven Pr., Inc.) Cengage Gale.

Harkins, Susan Sales & Harkins, William H. The Assassination of John F. Kennedy 1963. 2007. (Monumental Milestones Ser.). (Illus.). 48p. (YA). (gr. 4-7). lib. bdg. 29.95 *(978-1-58415-540-9(X))* Mitchell Lane Pubs., Inc.

Hibbert, Clare. A Day That Changed History: The Assassination of John F Kennedy. 2013. (Turning Points in History Ser.). 48p. (gr. 5-12). 37.10 *(978-1-59920-971-5(3))* Black Rabbit Bks.

Kallen, Stuart A. The John F. Kennedy Assassination. 2009. (Crime Scene Investigations Ser.). (ENG., Illus.). 128p. (J). (gr. 7-10). lib. bdg. 35.45 *(978-1-4205-0110-0(0),* LML02109-245421, Lucent Bks.) Cengage Gale.

Kelley, Tracey. Assassination of John F. Kennedy. 2013. (Turning Points in History Ser.). 48p. (gr. 5-9). 24.95 *(978-1-59920-771-1(0))* Black Rabbit Bks.

Mara, Wil. The Assassination of President John F. Kennedy. 2015. (ENG., Illus.). 112p. (J). lib. bdg. 32.50 *(978-0-531-20999-8(7),* Watts, Franklin) Scholastic Library Publishing.

Mishkin, Dan. The Warren Commission Report: A Graphic Investigation into the Kennedy Assassination. Colón, Ernie & Drozd, Jerzy, illus. 2014. (ENG.). 160p. 29.95 *(978-1-4197-1230-2(6))*; pap. 17.95 *(978-1-4197-1231-9(4))* Abrams, Inc. (Abrams ComicArts).

O'Reilly, Bill. Kennedy's Last Days: The Assassination That Defined a Generation. 2013. (ENG., Illus.). 336p. (J). (gr. 5). 19.99 *(978-0-8050-9802-0(X),* 9780805098020, Holt, Henry & Co. Bks. For Young Readers) Holt, Henry & Co.

—Kennedy's Last Days: The Assassination That Defined a Generation. 2015. (ENG., Illus.). 352p. (J). (gr. 5). pap. 12.99 *(978-1-250-06042-6(7),* 9781250060426) Square Fish.

Otfinoski, Steven. Tragedy in Dallas: The Story of the Assassination of John F. Kennedy. 2016. (Tangled History Ser.). (ENG., Illus.). 112p. (gr. 3-4). lib. bdg. 31.99 *(978-1-4914-8451-7(9))* Capstone Press of Coughlan Cos.

Rivera, Sheila. Assassination of John F. Kennedy, 1 vol. 2004. (American Moments Ser.). (ENG.). 48p. (gr. 4-8). 27.07 *(978-1-59197-277-8(9),* Abdo & Daughters) ABDO Publishing Co.

Spencer, Lauren. The Assassination of John F. Kennedy. (Library of Political Assassinations Ser.). 64p. 2009. (gr. 5-5). 58.50 *(978-1-60853-826-3(5))* 2003. (Illus.). (YA). (gr. 7-12). lib. bdg. 31.95 *(978-0-8239-3541-3(8))* Rosen Publishing Group, Inc., The.

Stockland, Patricia M. The Assassination of John F. Kennedy, 1 vol. 2007. (Essential Events Set 1 Ser.). (ENG., Illus.). 112p. (J). (gr. 6-12). lib. bdg. 35.64 *(978-1-59928-848-2(6))* ABDO Publishing Co.

Swanson, James L. The President Has Been Shot! The Assassination of John F. Kennedy. 2013. (ENG., Illus.). 336p. (J). (gr. 7). 18.99 *(978-0-545-49007-8(3),* Scholastic Pr.) Scholastic, Inc.

KENNEDY, ROBERT F., 1925-1968

Krull, Kathleen. The Brothers Kennedy: John, Robert, Edward. Bates, Amy June, illus. 2010. (ENG.). 40p. (J). (gr. -1-3). 16.99 *(978-1-4169-9158-8(1),* Simon & Schuster Bks. For Young Readers) Simon & Schuster Bks. For Young Readers.

KENNEDY, ROBERT F., 1925-1968—ASSASSINATION

Ching, Juliet. The Assassination of Robert F. Kennedy. (Library of Political Assassinations Ser.). 64p. 2009. (gr. 5-5). 58.50 *(978-1-60853-829-4(X))* 2003. (Illus.). (YA). (gr. 7-12). lib. bdg. 31.95 *(978-0-8239-3545-1(0))* Rosen Publishing Group, Inc., The.

Koestler-Grack, Rachel A. Assassination of Robert F. Kennedy, 1 vol. 2005. (American Moments Ser.). (ENG.). 48p. (gr. 4-8). 27.07 *(978-1-59197-931-9(5),* Abdo & Daughters) ABDO Publishing Co.

KENNEDY FAMILY

Krull, Kathleen. The Brothers Kennedy: John, Robert, Edward. Bates, Amy June, illus. 2010. (ENG.). 40p. (J). (gr. -1-3). 16.99 *(978-1-4169-9158-8(1),* Simon & Schuster Bks. For Young Readers) Simon & Schuster Bks. For Young Readers.

KENOBI, OBI-WAN (FICTITIOUS CHARACTER)—FICTION

Blackman, Haden & Caldwell, Ben. Star Wars: Clone Wars Adventures, 1 vol. 2012. (Star Wars Digests Ser.). (ENG., Illus.). 96p. (J). (gr. 4-7). 27.07 *(978-1-59961-904-0(0))* Spotlight.

Blackman, Haden & The Fillbach Brothers. Star Wars: Clone Wars Adventures, 1 vol. 2012. (Star Wars Digests Ser.). (ENG., Illus.). 96p. (J). (gr. 4-7). 27.07 *(978-1-59961-905-7(9))*; 27.07 *(978-1-59961-906-4(7))* Spotlight.

BookSource Staff, compiled by. Obi-Wan Kenobi: Jedi Knight. 2012. (Star Wars DK Readers Level 3 Ser.). lib. bdg. 13.55 *(978-0-606-26678-9(X),* Turtleback) Turtleback Bks.

Fillbach Brothers. Star Wars: Clone Wars Adventures, 1 vol. 2013. (Star Wars Digests Set 2 Ser.). (ENG.). 80p. (J). (gr. 4-8). lib. bdg. 27.07 *(978-1-61479-058-7(2))*; lib. bdg. 27.07 *(978-1-61479-059-4(0))* ABDO Publishing Co. (Essential Library).

Fillbach, Brothers & The Fillbach Brothers. Star Wars: Clone Wars Adventures, 1 vol. 2012. (Star Wars Digests Ser.). (ENG., Illus.). (J). (gr. 4-7). 88p. 27.07 *(978-1-59961-909-5(1))*; 96p. 27.07 *(978-1-59961-907-1(5))* Spotlight.

Gilroy, Henry. The Clone Wars: Hero of the Confederacy Vol. 1: Breaking Bread with the Enemy!, 1 vol. Koschak, Brian, illus. 2011. (Star Wars: the Clone Wars Ser.: No. 2). (ENG.). 24p. (J). (gr. 7-12). 24.21 *(978-1-59961-841-8(9))* Spotlight.

Landers, Ace. Anakin to the Rescue. 2012. (LEGO Star Wars 8X8 Ser.). lib. bdg. 13.55 *(978-0-606-26774-8(3),* Turtleback) Turtleback Bks.

Lucas Film Book Group. Trouble on Tatooine. 2017. (Star Wars: World of Reading Ser.). (J). lib. bdg. 14.75 ***(978-0-606-39963-0(1))*** Turtleback Bks.

Watson, Jude. The Desperate Mission. 2005. (Star Wars Ser.: No. 1). 168p. (J). lib. bdg. 20.00 *(978-1-4242-0774-9(6))* Fitzgerald Bks.

KENTUCKY

Allen, Nancy Kelly. Daniel Boone: Trailblazer, 1 vol. Waites, Joan C., illus. 2005. (ENG.). 32p. (J). (gr. k-3). 16.99 *(978-1-58980-212-4(8))* Pelican Publishing Co., Inc.

Barrett, Tracy. Kentucky. 2nd rev. ed. 2007. (Celebrate the States Ser.). 144p. (gr. 6). lib. bdg. 42.79 *(978-0-7614-2715-5(5),* Benchmark Bks.) Marshall Cavendish Corp.

Brandt, Keith & Macken, JoAnn Early. Daniel Boone: Frontier Explorer. Lawn, John, illus. 2008. 55p. (J). pap. *(978-0-439-02020-6(4))* Scholastic, Inc.

Brown, Dottie. Kentucky. 2012. (J). lib. bdg. 25.26 *(978-0-7613-4534-3(5),* Lerner Pubns.) Lerner Publishing Group.

Brown, Vanessa. Kentucky. 2009. (Bilingual Library of the United States of America Ser.). (ENG & SPA.). 32p. (gr. 2-2). 47.90 *(978-1-60853-362-6(X),* Editorial Buenas Letras) Rosen Publishing Group, Inc., The.

—Kentucky. Brusca, Maria Cristina, tr. 2005. (Bilingual Library of the United States of America Ser.: Set 1). (ENG & SPA., Illus.). 32p. (J). (gr. 3-6). lib. bdg. 25.25 *(978-1-4042-3082-8(3))* Rosen Publishing Group, Inc., The.

Burton, K. Melissa. Now That's Interesting Kentucky's Capitol. Asher, James, photos by. 2007. (Illus.). 40p. (J). per. 14.95 *(978-0-913383-96-4(1))* McClanahan Publishing Hse., Inc.

Davidson, Tish. East South-Central States: Kentucky & Tennessee, Vol. 19. 2015. (Let's Explore the States Ser.). (Illus.). 64p. (J). (gr. 5). 23.95 *(978-1-4222-3322-1(7))* Mason Crest.

Deinard, Jenny. How to Draw Kentucky's Sights & Symbols. 2009. (Kid's Guide to Drawing America Ser.). 32p. (gr. k-k). 50.50 *(978-1-61511-066-7(6),* PowerKids Pr.) Rosen Publishing Group, Inc., The.

Evdokimoff, Natasha. Kentucky. 2011. (Illus.). 48p. (YA). (gr. 3-6). 29.99 *(978-1-61690-789-1(4))*; (J). *(978-1-61690-465-4(8))* Weigl Pubs., Inc.

Gaines, Ann Graham. Kentucky. 2013. (It's My State 2nd Ed 4 Ser.). 80p. (J). (gr. 4-8). pap. 17.64 *(978-1-62712-093-7(9))* Cavendish Square Publishing.

Johnston, Marianne. Daniel Boone. 2009. (American Legends Ser.). 24p. (gr. 3-3). 42.50 *(978-1-61511-380-4(0),* PowerKids Pr.) Rosen Publishing Group, Inc., The.

Kadair, Deborah, illus. Today Is Monday in Kentucky, 1 vol. 2012. (ENG.). 32p. (J). (gr. k-k). 16.99 *(978-1-4556-1533-9(1))* Pelican Publishing Co., Inc.

Kramer, Sydelle. Who Was Daniel Boone? Ulrich, George, illus. 2006. (Who Was? Ser.). (ENG.). 112p. (J). (gr. 3-7). pap. 5.99 *(978-0-448-43902-0(6),* Grosset & Dunlap) Penguin Young Readers Group.

Labairon, Cassandra Sharri. Kentucky. 2008. (This Land Called America Ser.). 32p. (YA). (gr. 3-6). 22.95 *(978-1-58341-642-6(0))* Creative Co., The.

Lantier, Patricia. Kentucky. 2006. (Portraits of the States Ser.). (Illus.). 32p. (gr. 2-6). pap. 10.50 *(978-0-8368-4685-0(0),* Gareth Stevens Learning Library) Stevens, Gareth Publishing LLLP.

Lantier-Sampon, Patricia. Kentucky. 2006. (Portraits of the States Ser.). (Illus.). 32p. (gr. 2-6). lib. bdg. 26.00 *(978-0-8368-4666-9(4),* Gareth Stevens Learning Library) Stevens, Gareth Publishing LLLP.

Marsh, Carole. The Kentucky Coloring Book. 2004. (Kentucky Experience! Ser.). (Illus.). 32p. (J). (gr. k-2). pap. 3.95 *(978-0-7933-9471-5(6))* Gallopade International.

—The Kentucky Experience Pocket Guide. 2004. (Kentucky Experience! Ser.). (Illus.). 96p. (J). (gr. 3-8). pap. 6.95 *(978-0-7933-9451-7(1))* Gallopade International.

—Kentucky Geography Projects: 30 Cool, Activities, Crafts, Experiments & More for Kids to Do to Learn about Your State! 2003. (Kentucky Experience Ser.). 32p. (gr. k-5). pap. 5.95 *(978-0-635-01836-6(5),* Marsh, Carole Bks.) Gallopade International.

—Kentucky Government Projects #4: 30 Cool Activities, Crafts, Experiments & More for Kids to Do! 2003. (Kentucky Experience Ser.). (Illus.). 32p. (J). (gr. k-5). pap. 5.95 *(978-0-635-01936-3(1),* Marsh, Carole Bks.) Gallopade International.

—Kentucky Jeopardy! Answers & Questions about Our State! 2004. (Kentucky Experience! Ser.). (Illus.). 32p. (J). (gr. 3-8). pap. 7.95 *(978-0-7933-9516-3(X))* Gallopade International.

—Kentucky "Jography" A Fun Run Thru Our State! 2004. (Kentucky Experience! Ser.). (Illus.). 32p. (J). (gr. 3-8). pap. 7.95 *(978-0-7933-9517-0(8))* Gallopade International.

—Kentucky People Projects: 30 Cool, Activities, Crafts, Experiments & More for Kids to Do to Learn about Your State! 2003. (Kentucky Experience Ser.). 32p. (gr. k-5). pap. 5.95 *(978-0-635-01986-8(8),* Marsh, Carole Bks.) Gallopade International.

—Kentucky Symbols & Facts Projects: 30 Cool, Activities, Crafts, Experiments & More for Kids to Do to Learn about Your State! 2003. (Kentucky Experience Ser.). 32p. (gr. k-5). pap. 5.95 *(978-0-635-01886-1(1),* Marsh, Carole Bks.) Gallopade International.

—My First Book about Kentucky. 2004. (Kentucky Experience! Ser.). (Illus.). 32p. (J). (gr. k-4). pap. 7.95 *(978-0-7933-9515-6(1))* Gallopade International.

Murray, Julie. Kentucky, 1 vol. 2006. (United States (BB) Ser.). (ENG.). 32p. (gr. k-4). 27.07 *(978-1-59197-676-9(6),* Buddy Bks.) ABDO Publishing Co.

Nemerson, Roy. Daniel Boone. 2005. (Heroes of America Ser.). 239p. (gr. 3-8). 27.07 *(978-1-59679-256-2(6),* Abdo & Daughters) ABDO Publishing Co.

Petrie, Kristin. Daniel Boone, 1 vol. 2004. (Explorers Set 1 Ser.). (ENG.). 32p. (gr. k-6). 27.07 *(978-1-59197-592-2(1),* Checkerboard Library) ABDO Publishing Co.

Sanford, William R. & Green, Carl R. Daniel Boone: Courageous Frontiersman. 2012. (Courageous Heroes of the American West Ser.). (Illus.). 48p. (J). pap. 8.95 *(978-1-4644-0085-8(7))*; (gr. 5-18). 22.60 *(978-0-7660-4002-1(X))* Enslow Pubs., Inc.

Santella, Andrew. Kentucky. 2014. (America the Beautiful Ser.: 3). (ENG.). 144p. (J). lib. bdg. 40.00 *(978-0-531-24885-0(2))* Scholastic Library Publishing.

Schaffer, David. Kentucky: A MyReportLinks. Com Book. 2003. (States Ser.). (Illus.). 48p. (J). (gr. 4-10). lib. bdg. 25.26 *(978-0-7660-5126-3(9),* MyReportLinks.com Bks.) Enslow Pubs., Inc.

Smith, Andrea P. Daniel Boone. 2012. (Illus.). 24p. (J). 63.60 *(978-1-4488-5227-7(7))*; pap. 10.60 *(978-1-4488-5226-0(9))*; lib. bdg. 25.25 *(978-1-4488-5194-2(7))* Rosen Publishing Group, Inc., The. (PowerKids Pr.).

Smith, Rich. Kentucky, 1 vol. 2009. (United States Ser.). (ENG., Illus.). 48p. (YA). (gr. 2-5). 27.07 *(978-1-60453-652-2(7))* ABDO Publishing Co.

Valzania, Kimberly. Kentucky. 2003. (Rookie Read-About Geography Ser.). (ENG., Illus.). 32p. (J). (gr. 1-2). 20.50 *(978-0-516-22697-2(5),* Children's Pr.) Scholastic Library Publishing.

Zronik, John Paul & Zronik, John. Daniel Boone: Woodsman of Kentucky. 2006. (In the Footsteps of Explorers Ser.). (ENG., Illus.). 32p. (J). (gr. 4-7). pap. *(978-0-7787-2464-3(6),* 1253442); lib. bdg. *(978-0-7787-2428-5(X),* 1253442) Crabtree Publishing Co.

KENTUCKY—FICTION

Allen, Nancy. Amazing Grace: A Kentucky Girl with Gumption During World War II. 2014. Orig. Title: Amazing Grace: a Kentucky Girl with Gumption During World War II. (ENG., Illus.). 160p. (gr. 4-7). pap. 14.99 *(978-1-62619-405-2(X),* History Pr., The) Arcadia Publishing.

Altsheler, Joseph A. The Forest Runners: A Story of the Great War Trail in Early Kentucky. (Young Trailers Ser.: Vol. 2). (J). 25.95 *(978-0-8488-1236-2(0))* Amereon Ltd.

—The Forest Runners: A Story of the Great War Trail in Early Kentucky. l.t. ed. (Young Trailers Ser.: Vol. 2). (J). 2007. 178p. pap. 22.99 *(978-1-4264-8301-1(5))* 2010. 386p. reprint ed. pap. 33.75 *(978-1-149-35494-0(1),* BiblioLife) 2008. 248p. reprint ed. 24.99 *(978-0-554-34443-0(2))* 2008. 248p. reprint ed. 27.99 *(978-0-554-25140-0(X))* 2007. (ENG.). 218p. reprint ed. pap. 20.99 *(978-1-4264-8264-9(7))* Creative Media Partners, LLC.

—The Forest Runners: A Story of the Great War Trail in Early Kentucky. 2006. (Young Trailers Ser.: Vol. 2). (J). reprint ed. pap. *(978-1-4065-0810-9(1))* Dodo Pr.

—The Forest Runners: A Story of the Great War Trail in Early Kentucky. 2010. (Young Trailers Ser.: Vol. 2). (Illus.). 142p. (J). (gr. 4-7). reprint ed. pap. 19.99 *(978-1-153-70291-1(6))* General Bks. LLC.

—The Keepers of the Trail: A Story of the Great Woods. 2008. (Young Trailers Ser.: Vol. 3). 256p. (J). reprint ed. pap. *(978-1-4099-1719-9(3))* Dodo Pr.

—The Keepers of the Trail: A Story of the Great Woods. 2009. (Young Trailers Ser.: Vol. 3). 224p. (gr. 4-7). reprint ed. pap. 15.45 *(978-1-4385-1899-2(4),* Book Jungle) Standard Pubns., Inc.

—The Riflemen of the Ohio: A Story of Early Days along the Beautiful River. (Young Trailers Ser.: Vol. 6). (J). reprint ed. 25.95 *(978-0-8488-1239-3(5))* Amereon Ltd.

—The Riflemen of the Ohio: A Story of Early Days along the Beautiful River. 2009. (Young Trailers Ser.: Vol. 6). 312p. (J). reprint ed. pap. *(978-1-4099-2567-5(6))* Dodo Pr.

—The Riflemen of the Ohio: A Story of Early Days along the Beautiful River. 2008. (Young Trailers Ser.: Vol. 6). 192p. (J). reprint ed. pap. *(978-1-4068-2807-8(6))* Echo Library.

—The Riflemen of the Ohio: A Story of Early Days along the Beautiful River. 2010. (Young Trailers Ser.: Vol. 6). (Illus.). 180p. (J). (gr. 4-7). reprint ed. pap. 19.99 *(978-1-153-79466-4(7))* General Bks. LLC.

—The Riflemen of the Ohio: A Story of Early Days along the Beautiful River. 2012. (Young Trailers Ser.: Vol. 6). 340p. (J). (gr. 4-7). pap. *(978-3-8472-2473-0(5))* Tredition GmbH.

—The Young Trailers. 2007. (Young Trailers Ser.: Vol. 1). 248p. reprint ed. per. 12.45 *(978-1-60424-031-3(8),* Book Jungle) Standard Pubns., Inc.

—The Young Trailers: A Story of Early Kentucky. 2006. (Young Trailers Ser.: Vol. 1). (J). 27.95 *(978-1-4218-2970-8(3))*; reprint ed. pap. 12.95 *(978-1-4218-3070-4(1))* 1st World Publishing, Inc.

—The Young Trailers: A Story of Early Kentucky. (Young Trailers Ser.: Vol. 1). (J). reprint ed. 25.95 *(978-0-89190-824-1(2))* Amereon Ltd.

—The Young Trailers: A Story of Early Kentucky. l.t. ed. (Young Trailers Ser.: Vol. 1). (J). reprint ed. 2007. 222p. pap. 22.99 *(978-1-4346-3289-0(X))* 2008. 224p. 24.99 *(978-0-554-36772-9(6))* 2008. 224p. 27.99 *(978-0-554-27469-0(8))* 2007. (ENG.). 202p. pap. 20.99 *(978-1-4346-3288-3(1))* Creative Media Partners, LLC.

—The Young Trailers: A Story of Early Kentucky. 2007. (Young Trailers Ser.: Vol. 1). 228p. (J). reprint ed. per. *(978-1-4065-6553-9(9))* Dodo Pr.

—The Young Trailers: A Story of Early Kentucky. 2007. (Young Trailers Ser.: Vol. 1). 144p. (J). reprint ed. per. *(978-1-4068-1694-5(9))* Echo Library.

—The Young Trailers: A Story of Early Kentucky. (Young Trailers Ser.: Vol. 1). (J). reprint ed. 2010. 180p. (gr. 4-7). 30.36 *(978-1-169-27791-5(8))* 2010. 180p. (gr. 4-7). pap. 18.36 *(978-1-162-71336-6(4))* 2010. 37.95 *(978-1-161-48200-3(8))* 2004. pap. 22.95 *(978-1-4191-8924-1(7))* 2004. pap. 1.99 *(978-1-4192-8924-8(1))* Kessinger Publishing, LLC.

—The Young Trailers: A Story of Early Kentucky. 2012. (Young Trailers Ser.: Vol. 1). 200p. (J). (gr. 4-7). reprint ed. pap. *(978-3-8472-3210-0(X))* Tredition GmbH.

—The Young Trailers - A Story of Early Kentucky. 2008. (Young Trailers Ser.: Vol. 1). 244p. reprint ed. pap. 14.45 *(978-1-60597-191-9(X),* Book Jungle) Standard Pubns., Inc.

Barkley, Roger C. Johnny Grasshopper. 2006. 52p. pap. 16.95 *(978-1-4241-0221-1(9))* PublishAmerica, Inc.

Birdseye, Tom. A Tough Nut to Crack. 2006. (ENG.). 128p. (J). (gr. 3-7). 16.95 *(978-0-8234-1967-8(3))* Holiday Hse., Inc.

Bonnie, Compton-Hanson. Holly Jean & the Secret of Razorback Ridge, 5 vols., Vol. 1. 2011. (ENG.). 164p. (J). pap. 7.99 *(978-1-59317-431-6(4))* Warner Pr., Inc.

Booher, Brock. Healing Stone. 2014. pap. 15.99 *(978-1-4621-1394-1(X),* Horizon Pubs.) Cedar Fort, Inc./CFI Distribution.

Bradbury, Jennifer. River Runs Deep. 2015. (ENG., Illus.). 336p. (J). (gr. 4-8). 17.99 *(978-1-4424-6824-5(6),* Atheneum Bks. for Young Readers) Simon & Schuster Children's Publishing.

Brogle, Jennifer. The Adventures of Jennifer & Sherry: Summertime. 2013. 60p. pap. 25.36 *(978-1-4669-7560-6(1))* Trafford Publishing.

Brouwer, Sigmund. Cobra Strike, 1 vol. 2007. (Orca Sports Ser.). (ENG.). 176p. (YA). (gr. 6-10). per. 9.95 *(978-1-55143-725-5(2))* Orca Bk. Pubs. USA.

Bryan, Jennifer Liu & Kendle, Hazel Cole. Cole Family Christmas. Julich, Jenniffer, illus. 2008. 80p. (J). (gr. 4-7). 17.95 *(978-0-9816265-0-5(5))* Next Chapter Pr.

Buhlig Meister, Victoria. Tell Me a Story, Please, Mi-Mi! 2009. 36p. pap. 16.99 *(978-1-4389-2430-4(5))* AuthorHouse.

Byars, Betsy. Keeper of the Doves. 2004. (ENG., Illus.). 128p. (J). (gr. 3-7). reprint ed. 7.99 *(978-0-14-240063-0(7),* Puffin Books) Penguin Young Readers Group.

Caudill, Rebecca. Up & down the River. Merwin, Decie, illus. 2005. 143p. (J). (gr. -1-17). pap. 11.95 *(978-1-883937-81-2(7))* Bethlehem Bks.

Christensen, Evelyn B. The Twelve Days of Christmas in Kentucky. Culotta, Kent, illus. 2016. (Twelve Days of Christmas in America Ser.). (ENG.). 32p. (J). (gr. k). 12.95 *(978-1-4549-1959-9(0))* Sterling Publishing Co., Inc.

Clarke, Nancy & Muire, Penny. Stormy Hill's Challenge. 2013. 248p. 26.00 *(978-1-62212-803-7(6),* Strategic Bk. Publishing) Strategic Book Publishing & Rights Agency (SBPRA).

Clevenger, Lee. IncrediBoy: Be Careful What You Wish. 2004. 267p. (J). pap. 12.95 *(978-0-9764052-0-7(2))* Thomas Max Publishing.

Combs, Sarah. Breakfast Served Anytime. (ENG.). 272p. (gr. 7). 2016. (YA). pap. 7.99 *(978-0-7636-8752-6(9))* 2014. (J). 16.99 *(978-0-7636-6791-7(9))* Candlewick Pr.

Crum, Shutta. My Mountain Song. 2007. (Illus.). 32p. (J). 16.00 *(978-1-4223-6590-8(5))* DIANE Publishing Co.

Dowell, Frances O'Roark. Trouble the Water. (ENG.). (J). (gr. 4-8). 2017. 304p. pap. 7.99 *(978-1-4814-2464-6(5))* 2016. (Illus.). 288p. 16.99 *(978-1-4814-2463-9(7))* Simon & Schuster Children's Publishing.

—Trouble the Water. 2017. lib. bdg. 18.40 ***(978-0-606-40126-5(1))*** Turtleback Bks.

Duncan-Pauley, Chadney. A Bull's Paradise. 2009. 32p. pap. 15.60 *(978-0-557-17660-1(3))* Lulu Pr., Inc.

Elliott, R. Kenley. Stories from a Kentucky Boy. 2012. 74p. pap. 12.95 *(978-1-4772-5429-5(3))* AuthorHouse.

Ernst, Kathleen. Midnight in Lonesome Hollow: A Kit Mystery. 2007. (American Girl Mysteries Ser.). (ENG., Illus.). 192p. (gr. 4-7). 10.95 *(978-1-59369-161-5(0),* American Girl) American Girl Publishing, Inc.

—Midnight in Lonesome Hollow: A Kit Mystery. Tibbles, Jean-Paul, illus. 2007. (ENG.). 192p. (gr. 4-7). pap. 6.95 *(978-1-59369-160-8(2),* American Girl) American Girl Publishing, Inc.

Florence, Leigh Anne. The Adoption. Asher, James, illus. 2003. (Woody: the Kentucky Wiener Ser.). 32p. (J). (gr. -1-3). per. 12.95 *(978-0-9741417-0-1(4))* HotDiggetyDog Pr.

—Welcomes a Dad, Vol. 2. Asher, James, illus. 2004. (Woody: the Kentucky Wiener Ser.). 32p. (J). (gr. -1-3). per. 12.95 *(978-0-9741417-1-8(2))* HotDiggetyDog Pr.

Fuchs-Rice, Dwayne. Shades of Ember. 2008. 456p. pap. 24.95 *(978-0-595-53315-2(9))* iUniverse, Inc.

Giurco, Diane. The Adventures of Willy & Nilly. 2008. (Illus.). 32p. pap. 14.49 *(978-1-4389-1134-2(3))* AuthorHouse.

Godby, Ron. The King of Imperial Hill. 2006. 76p. pap. 16.95 *(978-1-4241-1061-2(0))* PublishAmerica, Inc.

Hart, Alison. Gabriel's Horses, 1 vol. 2007. (Racing to Freedom Trilogy). (ENG.). 160p. (J). (gr. 3-7). 14.95 *(978-1-56145-398-6(6))* Peachtree Pubs.

—Gabriel's Journey, 1 vol. (Racing to Freedom Ser.). (ENG.). 160p. (J). 2011. pap. 4.99 *(978-1-56145-530-0(X))* 2008. (Illus.). (gr. 3-7). 14.95 *(978-1-56145-442-6(7))* Peachtree Pubs.

Hemphill, Helen. Runaround. (ENG.). 117p. (J). (gr. 6-9). 2009. pap. 10.95 *(978-1-59078-777-9(3))* 2007. (Illus.). 16.95 *(978-1-932425-83-3(7))* Boyds Mills Pr. (Front Street).

Henry, Emily. The Love That Split the World. (ENG.). (YA). (gr. 7). 2017. 416p. pap. 9.99 *(978-1-59514-851-3(5))* 2016. 400p. 17.99 *(978-1-59514-850-6(7))* Penguin Young Readers Group. (Razorbill).

Henson, Heather. Dream of Night. 2010. (ENG.). 224p. (J). (gr. 3-7). 15.99 *(978-1-4169-4899-5(6),* Atheneum Bks. for Young Readers) Simon & Schuster Children's Publishing.

Jacobs, Lily. The Littlest Bunny in Kentucky: An Easter Adventure. Dunn, Robert, illus. 2015. (ENG.). 32p. (J). (-3).

9.99 *(978-1-4926-1096-0(8)*, Sourcebooks Jabberwocky) Sourcebooks, Inc.

James, Eric. A Halloween Scare in Kentucky. Le Ray, Marina, illus. 2014. (ENG.). 32p. (J). (-5). 9.99 *(978-1-4926-0597-3(2)*, 9781492605973, Sourcebooks Jabberwocky) Sourcebooks, Inc.

—Santa's Sleigh Is on Its Way to Kentucky. Dunn, Robert, illus. 2015. (ENG.). 32p. (J). (-2). 12.99 *(978-1-4926-2761-6(5)*, Sourcebooks Jabberwocky) Sourcebooks, Inc.

James L. Fuller. The Lost Coal Mine to Oz. 2009. 184p. pap. 16.60 *(978-1-4269-1829-2(1))* Trafford Publishing.

Johnson, Paul Brett. Fearless Jack. Johnson, Paul Brett, illus. 2007. (ENG., Illus.). 32p. (J). (gr. -1-3). 10.99 *(978-1-4169-6833-7(4)*, Simon & Schuster/Paula Wiseman Bks.) Simon & Schuster/Paula Wiseman Bks.

Johnston, Annie Fell. The Little Colonel. 2006. (Illus.). pap. *(978-1-4065-1132-1(3))* Dodo Pr.

—The Little Colonel. 2005. reprint ed. pap. 21.95 *(978-0-7661-9402-1(7))* Kessinger Publishing, LLC.

Johnston, Annie Fellows. The Giant Scissors. Barry, Etheldred B., illus. 2005. reprint ed. pap. 22.95 *(978-1-4179-0341-2(4))* Kessinger Publishing, LLC.

—In the Desert of Waiting the Legend of Camel Back Mountain. 2005. reprint ed. pap. 15.95 *(978-1-4179-3370-9(4))* Kessinger Publishing, LLC.

—The Little Colonel's House Party. Meynell, Louis, illus. 2007. 176p. per. *(978-1-4065-3514-3(1))* Dodo Pr.

—Mary Ware the Little Colonel's Chum. Barry, Etheldred B., illus. 2004. reprint ed. pap. 30.95 *(978-1-4179-1704-4(0))* Kessinger Publishing, LLC.

Knight, Mary. Saving Wonder. 2016. (ENG.). 288p. (J). (gr. 3-7). 16.99 *(978-0-545-82893-2(7)*, Scholastic Pr.) Scholastic, Inc.

Lafantasie, Shilo. House of Love. 2012. 32p. pap. 24.95 *(978-1-4560-9404-1(1))* America Star Bks.

Leet, Karen M. Sarah's Courage: A Kentucky Frontier Kidnapping. 2014. (ENG., Illus.). 144p. (gr. 4-7). 14.99 *(978-1-62619-477-9(7)*, History Pr., The) Arcadia Publishing.

Marsh, Carole. The Mystery at the Kentucky Derby. 2009. (Real Kids, Real Places Ser.). (Illus.). 146p. (J). lib. bdg. 18.99 *(978-0-635-07002-9(2)*, Marsh, Carole Mysteries) Gallopade International.

Martinez, Jessica. The Vow. (ENG., (YA). (gr. 9). 2014. Illus.). 448p. pap. 11.99 *(978-1-4424-5865-9(8))* 2013. 432p. 17.99 *(978-1-4424-5864-2(X))* Simon Pulse. (Simon Pulse).

Mary-Todd, Jonathan. Shot Down. 2012. (After the Dust Settled Ser.). (ENG.). 104p. (YA). (gr. 6-12). pap. 7.95 *(978-0-7613-9399-3(4)*, Darby Creek); lib. bdg. 27.93 *(978-0-7613-8329-1(8))* Lerner Publishing Group.

Meister, Victoria Buhlig. Our Playtime Friend. 2011. 28p. 13.59 *(978-1-4567-2883-0(0))* AuthorHouse.

Newhall, Mary & Campbell, Joanna. Bridal Dreams. 2005. (Thoroughbred Ser.). (Illus.). 163p. (gr. 3-7). 15.00 *(978-0-7569-5359-1(6))* Perfection Learning Corp.

—Samantha's Irish Luck. 2005. (Thoroughbred Ser.). (Illus.). 156p. (gr. 3-7). 15.00 *(978-0-7569-5350-8(2))* Perfection Learning Corp.

Paine, Ralph D. First down, Kentucky! 2011. 354p. 51.95 *(978-1-258-07497-5(4))* Literary Licensing, LLC.

Payne, C. C. Something to Sing About. 2008. (ENG.). 167p. (J). (gr. 4-7). pap. 8.50 *(978-0-8028-5344-8(7))* Eerdmans, William B. Publishing Co.

Ramage, Rosalyn Rikel. The Graveyard: N/a. 2012. 184p. (gr. 4-6). pap. 11.88 *(978-1-4669-5033-7(1))* Trafford Publishing.

Rand, Johnathan. American Chillers #27 Kentucky Komodo Dragons. 2009. 208p. (J). pap. 5.99 *(978-1-893699-90-8(0))* AudioCraft Publishing, Inc.

Ransom, Candice. The Underground Adventure of Arly Dunbar, Cave Explorer. Hammond, Ted & Carbajal, Richard Pimentel, illus. 2011. (History's Kid Heroes Set III Ser.). pap. 51.02 *(978-0-7613-7640-8(2)*, Graphic Universe™) Lerner Publishing Group.

—The Underground Adventure of Arly Dunbar, Cave Explorer. Hammond, Ted & Carbajal, Richard, illus. 2011. (History's Kid Heroes Ser.). (ENG.). 32p. (gr. 3-5). (J). 26.60 *(978-0-7613-6182-4(0))*; pap. 8.95 *(978-0-7613-7074-1(9)*, Graphic Universe™) Lerner Publishing Group.

Raven, Margot Theis. Night Boat to Freedom. Lewis, E. B., illus. 2008. (ENG.). 40p. (J). (gr. 1-4). pap. 8.99 *(978-0-312-55018-9(9)*, 9780312550189) Square Fish.

Rice, Alice Caldwell Hegan. Mrs. Wiggs of the Cabbage Patch. (Illus.). 153p. reprint ed. lib. bdg. 88.00 *(978-0-7222-4934-5(9))* Library Reprints, Inc.

Rice, Alice Hegan. Mrs. Wiggs of the Cabbage Patch. 2004. (ENG.). 168p. pap. 19.95 *(978-0-8131-9074-7(6))* Univ. Pr. of Kentucky.

Ritchie, Polly. A Pocket Full of Frogs. 2007. 124p. pap. 10.00 *(978-0-9795103-2-8(5))* Ascended Ideas.

Silvano, Wendi. Love Is All Around Kentucky. Czernichowska, Joanna, illus. 2016. (ENG.). 32p. (J). (-6). 12.99 *(978-1-4926-2927-6(8)*, 9781492629276, Sourcebooks Jabberwocky) Sourcebooks, Inc.

Skinner, Constance Lindsay. Becky Landers: Frontier Warrior. 2006. (Living History Library). 198p. (YA). (gr. 10). per. 12.95 *(978-1-932350-06-7(3))* Bethlehem Bks.

Smallman, Steve. Santa Is Coming to Kentucky. Dunn, Robert, illus. 2013. (ENG.). 32p. (J). (-3). 9.99 *(978-1-4022-8824-1(7)*, Sourcebooks Jabberwocky) Sourcebooks, Inc.

—Santa Is Coming to Louisville. Dunn, Robert, illus. 2015. (ENG.). 32p. (J). (-3). 9.99 *(978-1-4926-2639-8(2)*, Sourcebooks Jabberwocky) Sourcebooks, Inc.

Standish, Burt L. Frank Merriwell in Kentucky. Rudman, Jack, ed. 2003. (Frank Merriwell Ser.). 29.95 *(978-0-8373-9363-6(9))*; pap. 9.95 *(978-0-8373-9063-5(X))* Merriwell, Frank Inc.

Steinkraus, Kyla. Dessert with Daniel Boone. 2016. (Time Hop Sweets Shop Ser.). (ENG.). 32p. (gr. k-3). 25.65 *(978-1-68191-373-5(9))* Rourke Educational Media.

Stevens, Courtney. Dress Codes for Small Towns. 2017. 352p. (YA). (gr. 9). 17.99 ***(978-0-06-239851-2(2)***, HarperTeen) HarperCollins Pubs.

Taylor, Pearl Fleming. Snowbird Weenie, 1 vol. 2009. 59p. pap. 16.95 *(978-1-60836-745-0(2))* America Star Bks.

Varble, Rachel McBrayer. Beth & Seth. Reynolds, Doris, illus. 2012. 208p. 44.95 *(978-1-258-25079-9(9))*; pap. 29.95 *(978-1-258-25542-8(1))* Literary Licensing, LLC.

Watts, Julia. Kindred Spirits. 2008. (ENG.). 147p. (gr. 3-18). pap. 8.95 *(978-0-9667359-9-4(4))* Harren Communications, LLC.

—Revived Spirits. 2011. (ENG.). 170p. (J). (gr. 7). pap. 8.95 *(978-0-9831032-2-6(4)*, BeanPole Bks.) Harren Communications, LLC.

Wedekind, Annie. A Horse of Her Own. 2009. (ENG.). 288p. (YA). (gr. 5-9). pap. 8.99 *(978-0-312-58146-6(7)*, 9780312581466) Square Fish.

Whitaker, Alecia. The Queen of Kentucky. 2013. (ENG.). 384p. (YA). (gr. 7-17). pap. 8.99 *(978-0-316-12494-2(X)*, Poppy) Little, Brown Bks. for Young Readers.

White, Herman H. Valley of the Flames. 2004. (ENG.). 96p. 19.95 *(978-1-932278-09-5(5))* Mayhaven Publishing, Inc.

Wiechman, Kathy Canon. Empty Places. 2016. (ENG., Illus.). 240p. (J). (gr. 3-7). 17.95 *(978-1-62979-451-8(1)*, Calkins Creek) Boyds Mills Pr.

Williamson, Linda. Groundhog Breakfast, Soft Petals, & a Roof That Don't Leak Too Much, 1 vol. Mollett, Irene, illus. 2009. 23p. pap. 24.95 *(978-1-60749-618-2(6))* America Star Bks.

Wyatt, Leslie J. Poor Is Just a Starting Place. 2005. (ENG.). 192p. (J). (gr. 6-17). 16.95 *(978-0-8234-1884-8(7))* Holiday Hse., Inc.

KENTUCKY—HISTORY

Adler, David A. & Adler, Michael S. A Picture Book of Daniel Boone. Collins, Matt, illus. 2013. (ENG.). 32p. (J). (gr. -1-3). 17.95 *(978-0-8234-2748-2(X))* Holiday Hse., Inc.

Blair, Eric. Daniel Boone, 1 vol. Chambers-Goldberg, Micah, illus. (My First Classic Story Ser.). (ENG.). 32p. (gr. k-3). 2013. pap. 7.10 *(978-1-4795-1859-3(X))* 2011. lib. bdg. 22.65 *(978-1-4048-6578-5(0))* Picture Window Bks. (My First Classic Story).

Burgan, Michael. Death at Kent State: How a Photograph Brought the Vietnam War Home to America. 2016. (Captured History Ser.). (ENG., Illus.). 64p. (gr. 5-7). lib. bdg. 34.65 *(978-0-7565-5424-8(1)*, CPB Grades 4-8) Compass Point Bks.

Burton, K. Melissa. Kentucky's Boone: The Pioneer Spirit. Asher, James, illus. 2008. 30p. (J). (gr. 4-7). pap. 14.95 *(978-1-934898-03-1(1))* McClanahan Publishing Hse., Inc.

Christensen, Evelyn B. Kentucky Puzzles: Bluegrass Brainteasers for Ages 6 To 106. 2014. Orig. Title: Kentucky Puzzles: Bluegrass Brainteasers for Ages 6 To 106. (ENG., Illus.). 48p. pap. 9.99 *(978-1-62619-328-4(2)*, History Pr., The) Arcadia Publishing.

Cook, Colleen Ryckert. Kentucky: Past & Present. 2010. (United States: Past & Present Ser.). (ENG.). 48p. (YA). pap. 11.75 *(978-1-4358-9509-6(6))*; lib. bdg. 29.25 *(978-1-4358-9482-2(0))* Rosen Publishing Group, Inc., The. (Rosen Reference).

Dean, Arlan. The Wilderness Trail: From the Shenandoah Valley to the Ohio River. 2009. (Famous American Trails Ser.). 24p. (gr. 3-3). 42.50 *(978-1-61512-493-0(4)*, PowerKids Pr.) Rosen Publishing Group, Inc., The.

Doeden, Matt. The Haunted Sanatorium: A Chilling Interactive Adventure. 2017. (You Choose: Haunted Places Ser.). (ENG., Illus.). 112p. (gr. 3-4). lib. bdg. 31.99 *(978-1-5157-3651-6(2)*, You Choose Bks.) Capstone Press of Coughlan Cos.

Edgar, Sherra G. What's Great about Kentucky? 2015. (ENG., Illus.). 32p. (J). (gr. 2-5). 26.65 *(978-1-4677-3878-1(6)*, Lerner Pubns.) Lerner Publishing Group.

Evdokimoff, Natasha. Kentucky: The Bluegrass State. 2016. (J). *(978-1-4896-4866-2(6))* Weigl Pubs., Inc.

Gaines, Ann, et al. Kentucky. 2016. (It's My State! (r) Ser.). 80p. (J). (gr. 4-4). 34.21 *(978-1-62713-198-8(1))* Cavendish Square Publishing.

Gaines, Ann Graham. Kentucky. 2nd ed. 2013. 80p. (J). (gr. 4-8). 31.36 *(978-1-60870-880-2(2))* Cavendish Square Publishing.

Gamble, Adam, et al. Good Night Kentucky. 2014. (Good Night Our World Ser.). (ENG., Illus.). 20p. (J). (— 1). bds. 9.95 *(978-1-60219-089-4(5))* Good Night Bks.

Glaser, Jason. Kentucky: The Bluegrass State. 2010. (Our Amazing States Ser.). (Illus.). 24p. (J). pap. 8.25 *(978-1-4358-9784-7(6))*; lib. bdg. 22.60 *(978-1-4358-9396-2(4))* Rosen Publishing Group, Inc., The. (PowerKids Pr.).

Hamilton, S. L. Kentucky Derby. 2013. (Xtreme Races Ser.). 32p. (J). (gr. 3-9). lib. bdg. 27.07 *(978-1-61783-695-4(8)*, Abdo & Daughters) ABDO Publishing Co.

The Hatfields & the McCoys. 2014. (Jr. Graphic American Legends Ser.). (Illus.). 24p. (J). (gr. 3-6). lib. bdg. 26.25 *(978-1-4777-7193-8(X)*, PowerKids Pr.) Rosen Publishing Group, Inc., The.

Jerome, Kate B. Lucky to Live in Kentucky. 2017. (Arcadia Kids Ser.). (ENG., Illus.). 32p. (J). 16.99 ***(978-0-7385-2797-0(1))*** Arcadia Publishing.

Kennedy, Emily. Daniel Boone. 2014. (Illus.). 31p. (J). lib. bdg. *(978-1-62712-280-1(X))* Cavendish Square Publishing.

The Kentucky Adventure Program Kit: All program components for the Kentucky Adventure, 1 vol. 2009. 129.95 *(978-1-4236-0717-5(1))* Gibbs Smith, Publisher.

Linda Bartlett & Wen Marcec. Keby the Earth-Friendly Bear. 2009. 36p. pap. 21.32 *(978-1-4415-3989-2(1))* Xlibris Corp.

Lyon, George Ella. Which Side Are You On? The Story of a Song. Cardinale, Christopher, illus. 2011. (ENG.). 40p. (J). (gr. 2-4). 17.95 *(978-1-933693-96-5(7))* Cinco Puntos Pr.

Marsh, Carole. Exploring Kentucky Through Project-Based Learning. 2016. (Kentucky Experience Ser.). (ENG.). (J). pap. 9.99 *(978-0-635-12341-1(X))* Gallopade International.

—Kentucky History Projects #1: 30 Cool Activities, Crafts, Experiments & More for Kids to Do! 2003. (Kentucky Experience Ser.). (Illus.). 32p. (J). (gr. k-5). pap. 5.95 *(978-0-635-01786-4(5)*, Marsh, Carole Bks.) Gallopade International.

—Let's Discover Kentucky! 2004. (J). (gr. 2-8). cd-rom 14.95 *(978-0-7933-9490-6(2))* Gallopade International.

Murray, Julie. Kentucky, 1 vol. 2012. (Explore the United States Ser.). (ENG., Illus.). 32p. (J). (gr. 2-5). lib. bdg. 28.50 *(978-1-61783-355-7(X)*, Big Buddy Bks.) ABDO Publishing Co.

Saddleback Educational Publishing Staff, ed. Daniel Boone, 1 vol. unabr. ed. 2008. (Graphic Biographies Ser.). (ENG., Illus.). 25p. (YA). (gr. 9-12). pap. 7.95 *(978-1-59905-219-9(9))* Saddleback Educational Publishing, Inc.

Simon, Barbara Brooks. Escape to Freedom: The Underground Railroad Adventures of Callie & William. 2004. (I Am American Ser.). (ENG., Illus.). 40p. (J). (gr. 3-7). pap. 6.99 *(978-0-7922-6551-1(3)*, National Geographic Children's Bks.) National Geographic Society.

Williams, Suzanne. Kentucky. 2008. (ENG.). 80p. (J). pap. 7.95 *(978-0-531-20805-2(2)*, Children's Pr.) Scholastic Library Publishing.

Yasuda, Anita. Kentucky: The Bluegrass State. 2012. (J). 27.13 *(978-1-61913-353-2(9))* Weigl Pubs., Inc.

KENYA

Alembi, Ezekiel. Jaramogi Oginga Odinga: People's Revolutionary. 2004. (Lion Books). (Illus.). x, 78p. (J). *(978-9966-951-24-3(5))* Sasa Sema Publications Ltd.

Bankston, John. We Visit Kenya. 2012. (J). lib. bdg. 33.95 *(978-1-61228-304-3(7))* Mitchell Lane Pubs., Inc.

Bartell, Jim. Kenya. 2011. (Exploring Countries Ser.). (ENG., Illus.). 32p. (J). (gr. 3-7). lib. bdg. 26.95 *(978-1-60014-576-6(0)*, Blastoff! Readers) Bellwether Media.

Barysh, Ann, et al. The Suitcase Scholar Goes to Kenya, Set. Lerner Publications, Department of Geography Staff, ed. (Suitcase Scholar Ser.). (J). (gr. 4-6). lib. bdg., tchr. ed. 66.95 *(978-0-8225-4001-4(0)*, Lerner Pubns.) Lerner Publishing Group.

Bentley, Joyce. Kenya: Our Lives, Our World. 2005. 32p. 18.95 *(978-1-59389-225-8(X))* Chrysalis Education.

Burgan, Michael. Kenya. 2015. (ENG., Illus.). 144p. (J). lib. bdg. 40.00 *(978-0-531-21254-7(8)*, Orchard Bks.) Scholastic Library Publishing.

Burgess, Maryellen. Life in Kenya. 2012. (InfoMax Readers Ser.). (ENG., Illus.). 24p. (J). (gr. 1-2). pap. 8.25 *(978-1-4488-9022-4(5)*, Rosen Classroom) Rosen Publishing Group, Inc., The.

Burns, Kylie. Cultural Traditions in Kenya. 2015. (ENG., Illus.). 32p. (J). *(978-0-7787-8063-2(1))* Crabtree Publishing Co.

Corrigan, Jim. Kenya. Rotberg, Robert I., ed. 2012. (Evolution of Africa's Major Nations Ser.). (Illus.). 80p. (J). (gr. 7). 22.95 *(978-1-4222-2180-8(6))* Mason Crest.

—Kenya. 2011. (J). pap. *(978-1-4222-2208-9(X))* Mason Crest.

Deedy, Carmen Agra. 14 Cows for America, 1 vol. González, Thomas, illus. 2009. (ENG.). 36p. (J). (gr. 1-5). 17.95 *(978-1-56145-490-7(7))* Peachtree Pubs.

—14 Cows for America. Gonzalez, Thomas, illus. 2016. (ENG.). 36p. (J). (gr. -1-3). lib. bdg. 19.60 *(978-0-606-39065-1(0))* Turtleback Bks.

Deedy, Carmen Agra & Naiyomah, Wilson Kimeli. 14 Cows for America, 1 vol. González, Thomas, illus. 2016. (ENG.). 36p. (J). (gr. 1-5). pap. 8.95 *(978-1-56145-961-2(5))* Peachtree Pubs.

Dorling Kindersley Publishing Staff & Lock, Deborah. African Adventure. 2014. (DK Readers Ser.). (ENG.). 48p. (J). (gr. 2-4). pap. 3.99 *(978-1-4654-1719-0(2)*, DK Children) Dorling Kindersley Publishing, Inc.

Edgar, Sherra G. Kenya. 2015. (One World, Many Countries Ser.). (ENG.). 32p. (J). (gr. 1-4). 28.50 *(978-1-63407-052-2(6)*, 208886) Child's World, Inc., The.

Ferguson, Amanda. The Attack Against the U. S. Embassies in Kenya & Tanzania. (Terrorist Attacks Ser.). 64p. 2009. (gr. 5-5). 58.50 *(978-1-60853-309-1(3))* 2005. (Illus.). (J). (gr. 7-12). lib. bdg. 31.95 *(978-0-8239-3652-6(X))* Rosen Publishing Group, Inc., The.

Fontes, Justine & Fontes, Ron. Kenya - A-Z. 2004. (A to Z Ser.). (ENG.). 40p. (J). (gr. 2-4). pap. 6.95 *(978-0-516-26813-2(9)*, Children's Pr.) Scholastic Library Publishing.

Giles, Bridget. Kenya. (Countries of the World Ser.). (ENG., Illus.). 64p. (J). (gr. 5). 2009. pap. 12.95 *(978-1-4263-0568-9(0))* 2006. lib. bdg. 27.90 *(978-0-7922-7668-5(X))* National Geographic Society. (National Geographic Children's Bks.).

Gogerly, Liz & Hunt, Rob. Kenya. 2016. (Journey Through Ser.). (ENG., Illus.). 32p. (J). (gr. 4-6). 16.99 *(978-1-4451-3687-5(2)*, Franklin Watts) Hachette Children's Group GBR. Dist: Hachette Bk. Group.

Graham, Ian. Kenya. 2003. (Country Files Ser.). 32p. (J). lib. bdg. 24.25 *(978-1-58340-238-2(1))* Black Rabbit Bks.

Gregory, Joy. Kenya. 2016. (J). ***(978-1-4896-5417-5(8))*** Weigl Pubs., Inc.

Haskins, James & Benson, Kathleen. Count Your Way Through Kenya. Leveque, Lyne, illus. 2006. (Count Your Way Ser.). 24p. (J). (gr. -1-3). lib. bdg. 19.93 *(978-1-57505-884-9(7)*, Millbrook Pr.) Lerner Publishing Group.

Hibbert, Clare. Elephant Orphans, 1 vol. 2015. (ENG.). 32p. (J). pap. 10.00 *(978-1-4777-5896-0(8)*, PowerKids Pr.) Rosen Publishing Group, Inc., The.

Juarez, Christine. Kenya, 1 vol. 2014. (Countries Ser.). (ENG.). 24p. (gr. k-1). lib. bdg. 26.65 *(978-1-4765-4229-4(5)*, Pebble Plus) Capstone Press of Coughlan Cos.

Kalman, Bobbie. Spotlight on Kenya. 2013. (ENG.). 32p. (J). *(978-0-7787-0866-7(7))*; (Illus.). pap. *(978-0-7787-0870-4(5))* Crabtree Publishing Co.

Kirk, Daniel. Rhino in the House: The Story of Saving Samia. 2017. (ENG., Illus.). 40p. (J). (gr. -1-3). 17.95 *(978-1-4197-2316-2(2)*, Abrams Bks. for Young Readers) Abrams, Inc.

Klepeis, Alicia. Kenya. 2017. (J). pap. 19.95 ***(978-1-5026-2504-5(0))*** Cavendish Square Publishing.

Kras, Sara Louise. Kenya: A Question & Answer Book. 2016. (Questions & Answers: Countries Ser.). (ENG.). 32p. (gr. 3-4). pap. 7.95 *(978-1-5157-5851-8(6)*, Fact Finders) Capstone Press of Coughlan Cos.

Levy, Janey. A Primary Source Guide to Kenya. (Countries of the World). 24p. 2009. (gr. 2-3). 42.50 *(978-1-61512-038-3(6))* 2003. (ENG., Illus.). (gr. 3-6). pap. 8.25 *(978-0-8239-8074-1(X))* 2003. (Illus.). (J). lib. bdg. 22.60 *(978-0-8239-6590-8(2))* Rosen Publishing Group, Inc., The. (PowerKids Pr.).

Marshall, David & Sayer, Geoff. Kenya. (World Focus Ser.). (Illus.). 32p. (J). (gr. 3-7). pap. 3.99 *(978-0-431-07255-5(8))* Oxfam Publishing GBR. Dist: Stylus Publishing, LLC.

McCollum, Sean. Kenya. 2008. (Country Explorers Ser.). (Illus.). 48p. (J). (gr. 2-5). lib. bdg. 27.93 *(978-0-8225-8661-6(4))*; pap. 40.95 *(978-0-8225-9304-1(1))* Lerner Publishing Group.

Mills, Nathan & Cortland, Riley. I'm from Kenya. 2012. (Rosen Readers Ser.). (ENG., Illus.). 24p. (J). (gr. 1-2). pap. 8.25 *(978-1-4488-8803-0(4)*, Rosen Classroom) Rosen Publishing Group, Inc., The.

Mis, Melody S. How to Draw Kenya's Sights & Symbols. 2009. (Kid's Guide to Drawing the Countries of the World Ser.). 48p. (gr. 4-4). 53.00 *(978-1-61511-117-6(4)*, PowerKids Pr.) Rosen Publishing Group, Inc., The.

Napoli, Donna Jo. Mama Miti: Wangari Maathai & the Trees of Kenya. Nelson, Kadir, illus. 2010. (ENG.). 40p. (J). (gr. -1-3). 18.99 *(978-1-4169-3505-6(3)*, Simon & Schuster/Paula Wiseman Bks.) Simon & Schuster/Paula Wiseman Bks.

Oelschlager, Vanita. Bonyo Bonyo. Blackwood, Kristin & Blanc, Mike, illus. 2010. (ENG.). 42p. (J). (gr. -1-3). pap. 8.95 *(978-0-9819714-4-5(X))*; 15.95 *(978-0-9819714-3-8(1))* VanitaBooks.

Oppong, Joseph R. & Oppong, Esther D. Kenya. 2003. (Modern World Nations Ser.). (Illus.). 150p. (gr. 6-12). 35.00 *(978-0-7910-7474-9(9)*, Chelsea Hse.) Facts On File, Inc.

Parkes, Elle. Let's Explore Kenya. 2017. (Bumba Books (tm) — Let's Explore Countries Ser.). (ENG.). 24p. (J). (gr. -1-1). 25.32 ***(978-1-5124-3364-7(0))*** Lerner Publishing Group.

Pateman, Robert & Elias, Josie. Kenya. 3rd ed. 2014. (Cultures of the World, Third Ser.). (ENG., Illus.). 144p. (YA). (gr. 7). lib. bdg. 47.07 *(978-0-7614-8012-9(9))* Cavendish Square Publishing.

Reynolds, Jan. Only the Mountains Do Not Move: A Maasai Story of Culture & Conservation. Reynolds, Jan, photos by. 2011. (ENG., Illus.). 40p. (J). pap. 9.95 *(978-1-60060-844-5(2))*; (gr. 1-6). pap. 18.95 *(978-1-60060-333-4(5))* Lee & Low Bks., Inc.

Sheen, Barbara. Foods of Kenya. 2010. (Taste of Culture Ser.). (Illus.). 64p. (J). 30.45 *(978-0-7377-4813-0(3)*, Kidhaven) Cengage Gale.

Taylor, Trace. Kenya. 2010. pap. 39.62 *(978-1-61541-133-7(X))* American Reading Co.

Taylor, Trace & Sánchez, Lucia M. Kenya. 2010. (1Y Nuestro Mundo Ser.). (SPA.). 16p. (J). (gr. k-1). pap. 6.99 *(978-1-61541-155-9(0))* American Reading Co.

Taylor, Trace & SáNchez, LucíA M. Kenya. 2010. pap. 39.62 *(978-1-61541-156-6(9))* American Reading Co.

Thomson, Ruth. Living in Kenya. Hampton, David, photos by. 2006. (Living In- Ser.). (Illus.). 32p. (J). (gr. 4-7). lib. bdg. 27.10 *(978-1-59771-044-2(X))* Sea-To-Sea Pubns.

UNESCO. Wangari Maathai. 2016. (ENG., Illus.). 112p. (J). (gr. 3-7). 13.95 *(978-0-00-814935-2(6))* HarperCollins Pubs. Ltd. GBR. Dist: Independent Pubs. Group.

Ward, Chris. Discover Kenya. 2010. (Illus.). 32p. (J). 63.60 *(978-1-61532-298-5(1)*, 1307264); pap. 10.60 *(978-1-61532-297-8(3))* Rosen Publishing Group, Inc., The. (PowerKids Pr.).

KENYA—FICTION

Ahern, Carolyn L. Tino Turtle Travels to Kenya - the Great Safari. Burt Sullivan, Neallia, illus. 2009. (ENG & SWA.). 32p. (J). (gr. -1-4). 19.95 incl. audio compact disk *(978-0-9793158-3-1(2))* Tino Turtle Travels, LLC.

Allende, Isabel. Forest of the Pygmies. 2009. (City of the Beasts Ser.: Bk. 3).Tr. of Bosque de los Pigmeos. (ENG.). 320p. pap. 14.99 *(978-0-06-182510-1(7)*, Harper Perennial) HarperCollins Pubs.

—Forest of the Pygmies. Peden, Margaret Sayers, tr. from SPA. (City of the Beasts Ser.: Bk. 3).Tr. of Bosque de los Pigmeos. 304p. (J). (gr. 5-12). 2006. (ENG.). pap. 10.99 *(978-0-06-076198-1(9))* 2005. 19.99 *(978-0-06-076196-7(2))* HarperCollins Pubs. (Rayo).

—Forest of the Pygmies. l.t. ed. 2005. (City of the Beasts Ser.: Bk. 3).Tr. of Bosque de los Pigmeos. 304p. (J). (gr. 5-18). pap. 19.99 *(978-0-06-076200-1(4)*, Rayo) HarperCollins Pubs.

Anderson, Natalie C. City of Saints & Thieves. 2017. (ENG.). 432p. (YA). (gr. 7). 18.99 *(978-0-399-54758-4(4)*, G.P. Putnam's Sons Books for Young Readers) Penguin Young Readers Group.

Arensen, Shel. The Poison Arrow Tree. 2003. (Rugendo Rhino Ser.). (Illus.). 128p. (J). pap. 5.99 *(978-0-8254-2041-2(5))* Kregel Pubns.

Barasch, Lynne. First Come the Zebra. Barasch, Lynne, illus. (ENG., Illus.). 40p. (J). 2009. (gr. 1-6). 18.95 *(978-1-60060-365-5(3))* 2005. pap. 10.95 *(978-1-62014-029-1(2))* Lee & Low Bks., Inc.

Browne, Eileen. Handa's Hen. 2011. (ENG., Illus.). 32p. (J). (gr. -1-2). pap. 6.99 *(978-0-7636-5361-3(6))* Candlewick Pr.

—Handa's Surprise. Browne, Eileen, illus. 2011. (Reading & Math Together Ser.). (ENG., Illus.). 32p. (J). (gr. -1-2). pap. 24.99 *(978-0-7636-5385-9(3))* Candlewick Pr.

—Handa's Surprise: Read & Share. Browne, Eileen, illus. 2004. (ENG & SPA., Illus.). 32p. (J). pap. *(978-1-85269-515-6(3))*; pap. *(978-1-85269-476-0(9))*; pap. *(978-1-85269-514-9(5))*; pap. *(978-1-85269-513-2(7))*; pap. *(978-1-85269-512-5(9))* Mantra Lingua.

—Handa's Surprise: Read & Share. 2004. (ENG., Illus.). 32p. (J). pap. *(978-1-85269-511-8(0))* Mantra Lingua.

—Handa's Surprise: Read & Share. Browne, Eileen, illus. 2004. (ENG & POR., Illus.). 32p. (J). pap. *(978-1-85269-510-1(2))*; pap. *(978-1-85269-509-5(9))*; pap. *(978-1-85269-508-8(0))*; pap. *(978-1-85269-507-1(2))*; pap. *(978-1-85269-478-4(5))*; pap. *(978-1-85269-477-7(7))*; pap. *(978-1-85269-475-3(0))*; pap. *(978-1-85269-474-6(2))*; pap. *(978-1-85269-472-2(6))*; pap. *(978-1-85269-473-9(4))* Mantra Lingua.

Browne, Eileen & Habashi, Azza. Handa's Surprise: Read & Share. 2004. (ENG & ARA., Illus.). 32p. (J). pap. *(978-1-85269-471-5(8))* Mantra Lingua.

Burchett, Jan & Vogler, Sara. Safari Survival, 1 vol. Le Feyer, Diane, illus. 2013. (Wild Rescue Ser.). (ENG.). 152p. (gr. 3-6). 9.95 *(978-1-4342-4890-9(9))* Stone Arch Bks.

—Safari Survival, 1 vol. Le Feyer, Diane & Kennedy, Sam, illus. 2012. (Wild Rescue Ser.). (ENG.). 152p. (gr. 3-6). lib. bdg. 25.32 *(978-1-4342-3770-5(2))* Stone Arch Bks.

Bustani, Juma. Adventure in Nairobi. 2005. 72p. pap. *(978-9966-46-842-0(0))* Heinemann Kenya, Limited (East African Educational Publishers Ltd E.A.E.P.) KEN. Dist: Michigan State Univ. Pr.

J
K
L

Carlson, Martin D. Rfaud Tastes Wisdom. Oketch, Alphonce Omondi, illus. 2013. 36p. pap. 11.00 *(978-0-9848791-2-0(9))* BeCook Publishing.

Chamberlain, Mary, et al. Las Crepes de Mama Panya: Un Relato de Kenia. Cairns, Julia, illus. 2016. (SPA.). 40p. (J). (gr. k-5). pap. 8.99 *(978-1-78285-072-4(4))* Barefoot Bks., Inc.

Chamberlin, Mary and Rich. Les Pancakes de Maman Panya. Cairns, Julia, illus. 2016. (FRE.). 40p. (J). (gr. k-5). 8.99 *(978-1-78285-299-5(9))* Barefoot Bks., Inc.

Chamberlin, Richard & Chamberlin, Mary. Mama Panya's Pancakes: A Market Day in Kenya. Cairns, Julia, illus. 2005. 40p. (J). *(978-1-84148-160-9(2))* Barefoot Bks., Inc.

Chamberlin, Richard, et al. Mama Panya's Pancakes. Cairns, Julia, illus. 2006. (ENG.). 40p. (J). (gr. k-5). 8.99 *(978-1-905236-64-0(6))* Barefoot Bks., Inc.

Conway, David. Lila & the Secret of Rain. Daly, Jude, illus. 2011. (ENG.). 32p. (J). (gr. k-3). pap. 8.95 *(978-1-84780-035-0(1),* Frances Lincoln) Quarto Publishing Group UK GBR. Dist: Hachette Bk. Group.

—Lila & the Secret of Rain. Daly, Jude, illus. 2008. (ENG.). 32p. (J). (gr. k-4). *(978-1-84507-407-4(6))* Rough Guides, Ltd.

Cunnane, Kelly. For You Are a Kenyan Child. Juan, Ana, illus. 2006. (ENG.). 40p. (J). (gr. -1-3). 17.99 *(978-0-689-86194-9(X),* Atheneum Bks. for Young Readers) Simon & Schuster Children's Publishing.

Grey, Chelsea Gillian. Leperit the Zebra. Denman, Michael & Huiett, William, illus. 2005. (Internet Interactive Ser.). (ENG.). 36p. (J). (gr. -1-3). 8.95 *(978-1-59249-440-8(4),* SD6505); (gr. 2-2). 14.95 *(978-1-59249-438-5(2),* H6505); (gr. 2-2). pap. 6.95 *(978-1-59249-439-2(0),* S6505) Soundprints.

—Leperit the Zebra: African Wildlife Foundation. Denman, Michael & Huiett, William J., illus. 2005. (Meet Africa's Animals Ser.). (ENG.). 36p. (J). (gr. -1-2). 2.95 *(978-1-59249-441-5(2),* S6555) Soundprints.

Horowitz, Anthony. Crocodile Tears. (Alex Rider Ser.: Bk. 8). (ENG.). (J). (gr. 5-18). 2010. 416p. 8.99 *(978-0-14-241719-5(X),* Puffin Books) 2009. 400p. 18.99 *(978-0-399-25056-9(5),* Philomel Bks.) Penguin Young Readers Group.

—Crocodile Tears, 9 vols. 2010. (Alex Rider Adventure Ser.: 8). (J). 81.75 *(978-1-4407-5451-7(9));* 102.75 *(978-1-4407-5456-2(X));* 1.25 *(978-1-4407-5459-3(4));* 100.75 *(978-1-4407-5458-6(6));* 79.75 *(978-1-4407-5453-1(5))* Recorded Bks., Inc.

—Crocodile Tears. 2010. (Alex Rider Ser.: 8). lib. bdg. 19.65 *(978-0-606-23639-3(2),* Turtleback) Turtleback Bks.

Hunt, Elizabeth Singer. The Pursuit of the Ivory Poachers: Kenya. Williams, Brian, illus. 2008. (Secret Agent Jack Stalwart Ser.: 6). (ENG.). 144p. (J). (gr. 1-4). pap. 5.99 *(978-1-60286-021-6(1),* Weinstein Bks.) Perseus Bks. Group.

Kim, YeShil. My Best Buddy. Tanco, Miguel, illus. 2014. (MySELF Bookshelf Ser.). (ENG.). 32p. (J). (gr. k-2). pap. 11.94 *(978-1-60357-693-2(2));* lib. bdg. 25.27 *(978-1-59953-658-3(7))* Norwood Hse. Pr.

Larkin, Jim & Rambo, Lee Elliot. Books for Oliver. Brown, Dan, illus. 2006. (J). *(978-1-59336-336-9(2));* pap. *(978-1-59336-337-6(0))* Mondo Publishing.

Macgoye, Marjorie Oludhe. The Black Hand Gang. 2003. (Illus.). 64p. (gr. 4-7). pap. *(978-9966-46-016-5(0))* Heinemann Kenya, Limited (East African Educational Publishers Ltd E.A.E.P.) KEN. Dist: Michigan State Univ. Pr.

Malaika: Safari Adventure to Kenya. 2006. (J). 4.99 *(978-0-9765982-0-6(5))* Simba Publishing Co.

Mbuthia, Waithira. My Sister's Wedding: A Story of Kenya. Karanja, Geoffrey Gacheru, illus. 2005. (Make Friends Around the World Ser.). (ENG.). 32p. (J). (gr. k-3). 19.95 *(978-1-56899-898-5(8),* BC8006); 15.95 *(978-1-56899-896-1(1),* B8006) Soundprints.

Milway, Katie Smith. Mimi's Village & How Basic Health Care Transformed It. Fernandes, Eugenie, illus. 2012. (CitizenKid Ser.). (ENG.). 32p. (J). (gr. 3-7). 18.95 *(978-1-55453-722-8(3))* Kids Can Pr., Ltd. CAN. Dist: Hachette Bk. Group.

The Mystery of the Lion's Tail. 2014. (Greetings from Somewhere Ser.: 5). (ENG., Illus.). 128p. (J). (gr. -1-4). pap. 5.99 *(978-1-4814-1464-7(X),* Little Simon) Little Simon.

Naidoo, Beverley. Burn My Heart. 2008. (ENG.). 224p. (J). (gr. 5-18). 16.99 *(978-0-06-143297-2(0),* Amistad) HarperCollins Pubs.

Odhiambo, Eucabeth. Auma's Long Run. 2017. (ENG.). 304p. (J). (gr. 3-6). 17.99 ***(978-1-5124-2784-4(5),*** Carolrhoda Bks.) Lerner Publishing Group.

Odhiambo, Tori. Close to Home: The African Savannah. 2012. 32p. pap. 21.99 *(978-1-4691-9510-0(0))* Xlibris Corp.

Osborne, Jill. Riley Mae & the Sole Fire Safari, 1 vol. 2014. (Faithgirlz / the Good News Shoes Ser.). (ENG.). 256p. (J). pap. 7.99 *(978-0-310-74283-8(8))* Zonderkidz.

Peattie, Cindy & Benchmark Education Co. Staff. The Secret Language of Elephants. 2014. (Text Connections Ser.). (J). (gr. 5). *(978-1-4900-1367-1(9))* Benchmark Education Co.

Pedraza, M. Eugenia Rueda. Nico's Voyage. 2013. 32p. pap. *(978-1-4602-2360-4(8))* FriesenPress.

Peterson, Lois. The Paper House, 1 vol. 2012. (Orca Young Readers Ser.). (ENG.). 108p. (J). (gr. 3-6). pap. 7.95 *(978-1-4598-0051-9(6))* Orca Bk. Pubs. USA.

Richardson, Justin & Parnell, Peter. Christian, the Hugging Lion. Bates, Amy June, illus. 2010. (ENG.). 32p. (J). (gr. -1-3). 16.99 *(978-1-4169-8662-1(6),* Simon & Schuster Bks. For Young Readers) Simon & Schuster Bks. For Young Readers.

Richler, Mordecai. Jacob Two-Two & the Dinosaur. Petricic, Dusan, illus. 2009. (Jacob Two-Two Ser.). (ENG.). 104p. (J). (gr. 4-7). 10.95 *(978-0-88776-926-9(8))* Tundra Bks. CAN. Dist: Random Hse., Inc.

Simwenyi, Robbinson Namasaka. The Young Detectives. 2012. 84p. pap. 17.95 *(978-1-4512-2168-8(1))* America Star Bks.

Sorrells, W. A. Nairobi Nightmare. Bancroft, Tom & Corley, Rob, illus. 2007. 144p. (J). *(978-0-9792912-1-0(6))* KidsGive, LLC.

Stegall, Kim. Mumsi Meets a Lion. Batti, Kimberly Rose, illus. 2008. (gr. -1-1). pap. 7.99 *(978-1-59166-871-8(9))* BJU Pr.

Stilton, Thea. Thea Stilton & the Journey to the Lion's Den. 2013. (Thea Stilton Ser.: 17). (ENG.). 176p. (J). (gr. 2-5). pap. 8.99 *(978-0-545-55627-9(9),* Scholastic Paperbacks) Scholastic, Inc.

Tomaselli, Mela. The Magic Pot: Folk Tales & Legends of the Giriama of Kenya. 2004. (Illus.). 80p. *(978-9966-21-950-3(1))* Paulines Pubns., Africa.

Walters, Eric. Hope Springs. Fernandes, Eugenie, illus. 2014. (ENG.). 32p. (J). (gr. 1-4). 17.99 *(978-1-77049-530-2(4),* Tundra Bks.) Tundra Bks. CAN. Dist: Penguin Random Hse. LLC.

—The Matatu, 1 vol. Campbell, Eva, illus. 2012. (ENG.). 32p. (J). (gr. -1-3). 19.95 *(978-1-55469-301-6(2))* Orca Bk. Pubs. USA.

—My Name Is Blessing. Fernandes, Eugenie, illus. 2013. (ENG.). 32p. (J). (gr. 1-4). 17.95 *(978-1-77049-301-8(8),* Tundra Bks.) Tundra Bks. CAN. Dist: Penguin Random Hse. LLC.

—Today Is the Day. Fernandes, Eugenie, illus. 2015. (ENG.). 36p. (J). (gr. 1-4). 16.99 *(978-1-77049-648-4(3),* Tundra Bks.) Tundra Bks. CAN. Dist: Penguin Random Hse. LLC.

—Walking Home. 2014. (ENG.). 304p. (J). (gr. 5). pap. 10.99 *(978-0-385-68157-5(7),* Doubleday Canada) Penguin Random House Canada Young Readers CAN. Dist: Penguin Random Hse. LLC.

Williams, Alexandra & Williams, David, illus. Fairy Nyumbani. 2005. 24p. *(978-9966-956-41-5(7))* Jacaranda Designs Ltd.

KEPLER, JOHANNES, 1571-1630

Bortz, Fred. Johannes Kepler & the Three Laws of Planetary Motion. 2013. (Revolutionary Discoveries of Scientific Pioneers Ser.). 80p. (YA). (gr. 7-12). 33.25 *(978-1-4777-1805-6(2))* Rosen Publishing Group, Inc., The.

Gow, Mary. Johannes Kepler: Discovering the Laws of Planetary Motion. 2003. (Great Minds of Science Ser.). (Illus.). 128p. (J). lib. bdg. 27.94 *(978-0-7660-2098-6(3))* Enslow Pubs., Inc.

Harmon, Daniel E. Johannes Kepler. 2017. (Leaders of the Scientific Revolution Ser.). 112p. (gr. 12-13). 37.10 ***(978-1-5081-7472-1(5),*** Rosen Young Adult) Rosen Publishing Group, Inc., The.

Hasan, Heather. Kepler & the Laws of Planetary Motion. (Primary Sources of Revolutionary Scientific Discoveries & Theories Ser.). 64p. 2009. (gr. 5-5). 58.50 *(978-1-60851-845-6(0))* 2004. (Illus.). (J). lib. bdg. 31.95 *(978-1-4042-0308-2(7))* Rosen Publishing Group, Inc., The.

Ruiz, Jaime Alejandro Rodriguez. Johannes Kepler -Del otro lado está Dios. 2005. (SPA.). 124p. (YA). *(978-958-30-1647-9(0))* Panamericana Editorial.

KEROSENE

see Petroleum

KETTERING, CHARLES FRANKLIN, 1876-1958

Marsh, Carole. Charles Kettering: Patent Giant. 2004. (1000 Readers Ser.). (Illus.). 14p. (J). (gr. k-4). pap. 2.95 *(978-0-635-02525-8(6))* Gallopade International.

KEY, FRANCIS SCOTT, 1779-1843

Brannon, Cecelia H. Zoom in on the National Anthem. 2016. (Zoom in on American Symbols Ser.). (Illus.). 24p. (J). pap. 9.35 *(978-0-7660-8446-9(9))* Enslow Pubs., Inc.

Craven, Tracy Leininger. Our Flag Was Still There: The Story of the Star-Spangled Banner. Farnsworth, Bill, illus. 2004. (J). *(978-0-9724287-3-6(9))* Vision Forum, Inc., The.

Crewe, Sabrina & Ingram, Scott. The Writing of "The Star-Spangled Banner" 2004. (Events That Shaped America Ser.). (Illus.). 32p. (gr. 3-6). lib. bdg. 26.00 *(978-0-8368-3409-3(7),* Gareth Stevens Learning Library) Stevens, Gareth Publishing LLLP.

Damanda, Lori. The Story of the "Star-Spangled Banner" 2009. (Real Life Readers Ser.). 32p. (J). (ENG., Illus.). (gr. 5-6). pap. 10.00 *(978-1-4358-0205-6(5));* (gr. 4-6). lib. bdg. 25.25 *(978-1-4358-3015-8(6))* Rosen Publishing Group, Inc., The. (PowerKids Pr.).

—The Story of the Star-Spangled Banner. 2009. (American History Milestones Ser.). 32p. (gr. 5-5). 47.90 *(978-1-61511-375-0(4),* PowerKids Pr.) Rosen Publishing Group, Inc., The.

Ferry, Joseph. The Star-Spangled Banner: Story of Our National Anthem. Moreno, Barry, ed. 2014. (Patriotic Symbols of America Ser.: 20). 48p. (J). (gr. 4-18). 20.95 *(978-1-4222-3132-6(1))* Mason Crest.

Gaspar, Joe. The National Anthem. 2013. (PowerKids Readers: American Symbols Ser.). 24p. (J). (gr. k-2). 22.60 *(978-1-4777-0740-1(9));* (ENG., Illus.). pap. 8.25 *(978-1-4777-0821-7(9))* Rosen Publishing Group, Inc., The. (PowerKids Pr.).

—The National Anthem / el Himno Nacional. Alamn, Eduardo, ed. 2013. (PowerKids Readers: American Symbols / Smbolos de Amrica Ser.). (ENG & SPA.). 24p. (J). (gr. k-2). 22.60 *(978-1-4777-1208-5(9),* PowerKids Pr.) Rosen Publishing Group, Inc., The.

Hall, M. C. The National Anthem, 1 vol. Ouren, Todd, illus. 2008. (Our Nation's Pride Ser.). (ENG.). 32p. (gr. -1-3). 28.50 *(978-1-60270-113-7(X),* Looking Glass Library- Nonfiction) Magic Wagon.

Healy, Nick. The Star-Spangled Banner. 2003. (J). *(978-1-58417-055-6(7));* pap. *(978-1-58417-116-8(9))* Lake Street Pubs.

Hess, Deborah. The Star-Spangled Banner. 2007. (J). pap. 6.99 *(978-0-7614-3392-7(9))* Marshall Cavendish Corp.

Ingram, Scott. The Writing of The Star-Spangled Banner. 2004. (Landmark Events in American History Ser.). (Illus.). 48p. (gr. 5-12). pap. 14.05 *(978-0-8368-5418-3(7),* Gareth Stevens Secondary Library) Stevens, Gareth Publishing LLLP.

Jacobson, Ryan. The Story of the Star-Spangled Banner, 1 vol. Martin, Cynthia & Beatty, Terry, illus. 2006. (Graphic History Ser.). (ENG.). 32p. (gr. 3-4). 30.65 *(978-0-7368-5493-1(2),* Graphic Library) Capstone Press of Coughlan Cos.

Kjelle, Marylou Morano. Francis Scott Key. 2006. (What's So Great About...? Ser.). (Illus.). 32p. (YA). (gr. 2-4). lib. bdg. 25.70 *(978-1-58415-474-7(8))* Mitchell Lane Pubs., Inc.

Kulling, Monica. Francis Scott Key's Star-Spangled Banner. 2012. (Step into Reading Level 3 Ser.). lib. bdg. 13.55 *(978-0-606-23857-1(3),* Turtleback) Turtleback Bks.

Lambert, Nancy. The Star-Spangled Banner. 2016. (Smithsonian Ser.). (ENG., Illus.). 48p. (J). (gr. 3-4). pap. 3.99 *(978-1-101-99607-2(2),* Penguin Young Readers) Penguin Young Readers Group.

Landau, Elaine. The National Anthem. (True Book(tm), a — American History Ser.). (ENG., Illus.). 48p. (J). (gr. 3-5). 2007. lib. bdg. 31.00 *(978-0-531-12633-2(1))* 2008. pap. 6.95 *(978-0-531-14783-2(5))* Scholastic Library Publishing. (Children's Pr.).

Lowitz, Sadyebeth & Lowitz, Anson. Mr Key's Song: The Star Spangled Banner. 2011. 58p. 36.95 *(978-1-258-10511-2(X))* Literary Licensing, LLC.

Monroe, Tyler. Star-Spangled Banner. 2013. (U. S. Symbols Ser.). (ENG.). 24p. (gr. k-1). 26.65 *(978-1-4765-3087-1(4));* pap. 7.95 *(978-1-4765-3536-4(1))* Capstone Press of Coughlan Cos. (Pebble Plus).

The National Anthem. 2013. (PowerKids Readers: American Symbols Ser.). 24p. (J). (gr. k-2). pap. 49.50 *(978-1-4777-0822-4(7),* PowerKids Pr.) Rosen Publishing Group, Inc., The.

Nelson, Maria. The National Anthem. 2015. (Symbols of America Ser.). (ENG.). 24p. (J). (gr. 1-2). 22.60 *(978-1-4824-1874-3(6))* Stevens, Gareth Publishing LLLP.

Ouren, Todd, illus. The Star-Spangled Banner: America's National Anthem & Its History, 1 vol. 2003. (Patriotic Songs Ser.). (ENG.). 24p. (gr. -1-4). 26.65 *(978-1-4048-0175-2(8))* Picture Window Bks.

Owens, Tom. The Star-Spangled Banner: The Flag & Its Anthem. 2003. (Illus.). 48p. (J). pap. *(978-0-7891-5890-1(6))* Perfection Learning Corp.

Pearl, Norman. Our National Anthem. Skeens, Matthew, illus. 2006. (American Symbols Ser.). (ENG.). 24p. (gr. 1-2). lib. bdg. 26.65 *(978-1-4048-2215-3(1))* Picture Window Bks.

Pingry, Patricia A. O Little Town of Bethlehem. 2008. (ENG., Illus.). 16p. (J). bds. 12.99 *(978-0-8249-6566-2(3),* Ideal Pubns.) Worthy Publishing.

—The Story of the Star-Spangled Banner. Munger, Nancy, illus. 2014. (Story of Ser.). 24p. (J). bds. 6.99 *(978-0-8249-1930-6(0),* Ideal Pubns.) Worthy Publishing.

Reed, Cristie. The Star Spangled Banner. 2014. (ENG.). 32p. (gr. 3-6). 32.79 *(978-1-62717-737-5(X))* Rourke Educational Media.

Rustad, Martha. Can You Sing the Star-Spangled Banner? Poling, Kyle, illus. 2014. (Cloverleaf Books — Our American Symbols Ser.). 24p. (gr. k-2). (J). lib. bdg. 23.93 *(978-1-4677-2136-3(0));* pap. 6.95 *(978-1-4677-4469-0(7))* Lerner Publishing Group. (Millbrook Pr.).

Schwaeber, Barbie. The Star-Spangled Banner. 2006. (American Favorites Ser.). (ENG., Illus.). 32p. (J). (gr. 3-7). 9.85 *(978-1-59249-652-5(0))* Soundprints.

Sonneborn, Liz. The Star-Spangled Banner: The Story Behind Our National Anthem. 2003. (America in Words & Song Ser.). (Illus.). 32p. (gr. 4-6). 23.00 *(978-0-7910-7337-7(8),* Chelsea Hse.) Facts On File, Inc.

Spier, Peter. The Star-Spangled Banner. 2014. (ENG., Illus.). 56p. (J). (gr. k-4). 17.99 *(978-0-385-37618-1(9),* Doubleday Bks. for Young Readers) Random Hse. Children's Bks.

Welch, Catherine A. La Bandera de Estrellas Centelleantes: El Himno Nacional. Translations.com Staff, tr. from ENG. Warwick, Carrie H., illus. 2005. (Yo Solo - Historia (on My Own - History) Ser.). Tr. of Star-Spangled Banner. (SPA.). 48p. (gr. 2-4). lib. bdg. 25.26 *(978-0-8225-3114-2(3))* Lerner Publishing Group.

—La Bandera de Estrellas Centelleantes; the Star-Spangled Banner. 2008. pap. 40.95 *(978-0-7613-3867-3(5))* Lerner Publishing Group.

—The Star-Spangled Banner. Warwick, Carrie, illus. 2004. (On My Own History Ser.). 48p. (J). (gr. 1-3). pap. 6.95 *(978-1-57505-697-5(6));* (ENG.). (gr. 2-4). 25.26 *(978-1-57505-590-9(2))* Lerner Publishing Group.

Wesolowski, Harriet. The Songs We Sing: Honoring Our Country. 2012. (I'm an American Citizen Ser.). (ENG., Illus.). 24p. (J). (gr. 1-3). 22.60 *(978-1-4488-8581-7(7),* PowerKids Pr.) Rosen Publishing Group, Inc., The.

KEY, FRANCIS SCOTT, 1779-1843—FICTION

Winstead, Amy. The Star-Spangled Banner. Dacey, Bob & Bandelin, Debra, illus. 2003. (ENG.). 32p. (J). 18.65 *(978-0-8249-5462-8(9),* Ideal Pubns.) Worthy Publishing.

KEYS

see Locks and Keys

KHRUSHCHEV, NIKITA SERGEEVICH, 1894-1971

Roxburgh, Ellis. John F. Kennedy vs. Nikita Khrushchev. 2015. (History's Greatest Rivals Ser.). (ENG., Illus.). 48p. (J). (gr. 6-8). lib. bdg. 31.95 *(978-1-4824-2221-4(2))* Stevens, Gareth Publishing LLLP.

KIBBUTZIM—FICTION

Edwards, Michelle. Chicken Man. 2008. (J). *(978-1-58838-237-5(0));* 3rd ed. (Illus.). 32p. 16.95 *(978-1-58838-223-8(0))* NewSouth, Inc. (Junebug Bks.).

KIDD, WILLIAM, -1701

Hamilton, Sue L. Captain Kidd, 1 vol. 2007. (Pirates! Ser.). (ENG., Illus.). 32p. (gr. 4-8). 27.07 *(978-1-59928-759-1(5),* Abdo & Daughters) ABDO Publishing Co.

Stefoff, Rebecca. Captain Kidd. 2015. (J). lib. bdg. *(978-1-62713-529-0(4));* (ENG.). 48p. (gr. 3-3). 31.36 *(978-1-5026-0205-3(9))* Cavendish Square Publishing.

Weintraub, Aileen. Captain Kidd: 17th-Century Pirate of the Indian Ocean & African Coast. 2009. (Library of Pirates Ser.). 24p. (gr. 3-3). 42.50 *(978-1-60853-811-9(7),* PowerKids Pr.) Rosen Publishing Group, Inc., The.

KIDD, WILLIAM, -1701—FICTION

Farber, E. S. Fish Finelli (Book 1) Seagulls Don't Eat Pickles. Beene, Jason, illus. 2014. (Fish Finelli Ser.). (ENG.). 168p. (J). (gr. 3-7). pap. 6.99 *(978-1-4521-2853-5(7))* Chronicle Bks. LLC.

Farber, Erica. Fish Finelli: Seagulls Don't Eat Pickles. Beene, Jason, illus. 2013. (Fish Finelli Ser.). (ENG.). 155p. (J). (gr. 2-5). 15.99 *(978-1-4521-0820-9(X))* Chronicle Bks. LLC.

Stewart, Shannon. Captain Jake, 1 vol. Hodson, Ben, illus. 2008. (Orca Echoes Ser.). (ENG.). 64p. (J). (gr. 2-3). pap. 6.95 *(978-1-55143-896-2(8))* Orca Bk. Pubs. USA.

KIDNAPPING

Burns, Jan. Kidnapping. 2007. (Crime Scene Investigations Ser.). (Illus.). 104p. (J). (gr. 7-12). lib. bdg. 35.45 *(978-1-59018-989-4(2))* Cengage Gale.

Carpentiere, Elizabeth. Kidnapped, 1 vol. unabr. ed. 2012. (Astonishing Headlines Ser.). (ENG.). 92p. (YA). (gr. 9-12). 8.95 *(978-1-61651-921-6(5))* Saddleback Educational Publishing, Inc.

Guard, Anara. What If a Stranger Approaches You?, 1 vol. Madden, Colleen M., illus. 2011. (Danger Zone Ser.). (ENG.). 24p. (gr. 1-2). pap. 7.49 *(978-1-4048-7031-4(8));* lib. bdg. 25.99 *(978-1-4048-6683-6(3))* Picture Window Bks.

Mara, Wil. What Should I Do? If a Stranger Comes Near. 2011. (Community Connections: What Should I Do? Ser.). (ENG.). 24p. (gr. 2-5). lib. bdg. 25.64 *(978-1-61080-049-5(4),* 201040) Cherry Lake Publishing.

Mcdonald, P. J. A Cry for Help No One Heard. 2011. 148p. (gr. 10-12). pap. 14.95 *(978-1-4670-7105-5(6))* AuthorHouse.

O'Brien, Susan. Child Abduction & Kidnapping. 2008. (Criminal Investigations Ser.). (Illus.). 160p. (J). (gr. 9-12). 35.00 *(978-0-7910-9403-7(0),* Chelsea Hse.) Facts On File, Inc.

Raatma, Lucia. Staying Safe Around Strangers, 1 vol. 2011. (Staying Safe Ser.). (ENG.). 24p. (gr. 1-2). pap. 7.29 *(978-1-4296-7195-8(5));* pap. 41.70 *(978-1-4296-7196-5(3));* lib. bdg. 25.32 *(978-1-4296-6821-7(0))* Capstone Press of Coughlan Cos. (First Facts).

Ridenour, Melissa Harker. What Would You Do? A Kid's Guide to Staying Safe in a World of Strangers. Fehling, Leslie, illus. 2011. (J). *(978-0-938467-11-3(5))* Headline Bks., Inc.

Roensch, Greg. The Lindbergh Baby Kidnapping Trial: A Primary Source Account. 2004. (Great Trials of the Twentieth Century Ser.). (Illus.). 64p. (gr. 5-8). lib. bdg. 31.95 *(978-0-8239-3971-8(5),* Rosen Reference) Rosen Publishing Group, Inc., The.

Rooney, Anne. Kidnaps. 2010. (Solve It with Science Ser.). (YA). (gr. 5-9). 34.25 *(978-1-59920-331-7(6))* Black Rabbit Bks.

Spikes, James L. Taffey Pop Kids Presents the Adventures of Lemmon Head & Mudd Duck: What to Do if Someone Tries to Grab YOU!!! Spikes, Leon, Jr., illus. 2007. 32p. (J). 14.95 *(978-0-9771438-0-1(5))* Taffey Pop Kids Publishing.

Steele, Philip. Hostage Takers. 2016. (Illus.). 48p. (J). *(978-0-7787-2587-9(1))* Crabtree Publishing Co.

Stephens, Ronald, ed. Stranger Danger. 2014. (Safety First Ser.: 11). 48p. (J). (gr. 5-18). 20.95 *(978-1-4222-3054-1(6))* Mason Crest.

Turner, Queen of England Patrenia. Queen Patrenialla - A Canadian Story Poem. Turner, Keeng of England Troyius, ed. 2015. (Illus.). pap. *(978-0-578-18000-7(6))* Royalty Patrenia Turner Publications.

KIDNAPPING—FICTION

Abbott, Tony. The Serpent's Curse. 2014. (Illus.). 496p. pap. 9.99 *(978-0-06-235159-3(1))* HarperCollins Pubs.

Adams, Carolyn Lee. Ruthless. 2015. (ENG., Illus.). 256p. (YA). (gr. 9). 17.99 *(978-1-4814-2262-8(6),* Simon Pulse) Simon Pulse.

Adler, Irene. The Soprano's Last Song, 1 vol. Iacopo, Bruno & Bruno, Iacopo, illus. 2014. (Sherlock, Lupin, & Me Ser.). (ENG.). 240p. (gr. 4-8). lib. bdg. 26.65 *(978-1-4342-6522-7(6))* Stone Arch Bks.

The adventures of officer Byrd. 2007. (J). 16.99 *(978-0-9787322-0-2(0))* Officer Byrd Publishing Co.

Akins, Karen. Twist. 2015. (ENG.). 336p. (YA). (gr. 7-12). 18.99 *(978-1-250-03100-6(1),* 9781250031006, St. Martin's Griffin) St. Martin's Pr.

Albano, Lydia. Finding You. 2017. (ENG.). 320p. (YA). 17.99 ***(978-1-250-09858-0(0),*** 9781250098580) Feiwel & Friends.

Alger, Horatio. Helping Himself. 2006. 180p. pap. 19.99 *(978-1-4264-0881-6(1));* (ENG.). 168p. pap. 21.99 *(978-1-4264-0862-5(5))* Creative Media Partners, LLC.

—Helping Himself. 2006. pap. *(978-1-4065-0709-6(1))* Dodo Pr.

—Jack's Ward. 2005. 28.95 *(978-1-4218-1454-4(4));* 260p. pap. 13.95 *(978-1-4218-1554-1(0))* 1st World Publishing, Inc. (1st World Library - Literary Society).

—Jack's Ward. 2006. pap. *(978-1-4065-0711-9(3))* Dodo Pr.

—Jack's Ward: Or, The Boy Guardian. 2006. 176p. pap. 19.99 *(978-1-4264-0882-3(X));* (ENG.). 168p. pap. 21.99 *(978-1-4264-0863-2(3))* Creative Media Partners, LLC.

—Timothy Crump's Ward. 2005. 27.95 *(978-1-4218-1451-3(X));* 220p. pap. 12.95 *(978-1-4218-1551-0(6))* 1st World Publishing, Inc. (1st World Library - Literary Society).

Allan, Nicholas. Android in the Attic. 2013. (ENG., Illus.). 192p. (J). (gr. 2-4). pap. 7.99 *(978-0-340-99706-2(0))* Hodder & Stoughton GBR. Dist: Hachette Bk. Group.

Altebrando, Tara. The Leaving. 2016. (ENG.). 432p. (YA). 17.99 *(978-1-61963-803-7(7),* 9781619638037, Bloomsbury USA Childrens) Bloomsbury Publishing USA.

Anstey, Cindy. Duels & Deception. 2017. (ENG.). 368p. (YA). pap. 10.99 *(978-1-250-11909-4(X),* 9781250119094) Feiwel & Friends.

Antieau, Kim. Broken Moon. 2007. (ENG.). 192p. (YA). (gr. 9-12). 16.99 *(978-1-4169-1767-0(5),* McElderry, Margaret K. Bks.) McElderry, Margaret K. Bks.

Argyle, Michelle Davidson. The Breakaway. 2012. 320p. pap. 15.99 *(978-1-936850-61-7(3))* Rhemalda Publishing.

Avery, Ben & Rogers, Bud. Berlin Breakout, 1 vol. Gaudiamo, Adi Darda, illus. 2008. (Z Graphic Novels / TimeFlyz Ser.). (ENG.). 160p. (J). (gr. 4-7). pap. 6.99 *(978-0-310-71363-0(3))* Zondervan.

Awiakta, Marilou. Rising Fawn & the Fire Mystery. Bringle, Beverly, illus. 2007. (ENG.). 96p. (J). (gr. 4-7). pap. 14.95 *(978-1-55591-600-8(7))* Fulcrum Publishing.

Axelsson, Carina. Paris. 2014. (Model Undercover Ser.: 1). (ENG.). 368p. (J). (gr. 4-7). pap. 6.99 *(978-1-4022-8587-5(6),* Sourcebooks Jabberwocky) Sourcebooks, Inc.

Babbitt, Natalie. Tuck Everlasting. 2008. (J). 39.99 *(978-0-7393-7111-4(8))* Findaway World, LLC.

—Tuck Everlasting. 139p. (J). (gr. 4-6). pap. 4.95 *(978-0-8072-1385-8(3),* Listening Library) Random Hse. Audio Publishing Group.

Bailey, Em. The Special Ones. 2017. (ENG.). 304p. (YA). (gr. 7). 17.99 *(978-0-544-91229-8(2),* HMH Books For Young Readers) Houghton Mifflin Harcourt Publishing Co.

Baker, E. D. Fairy Lies. (ENG., (YA). 2013. Illus.). 272p. (gr. 1-8). pap. 7.99 *(978-1-61963-035-2(4),* 9781619630352) 2012. 256p. (gr. 5-8). 16.99 *(978-1-59990-550-1(7),* 9781599905501) Bloomsbury Publishing USA. (Bloomsbury USA Childrens).

—A Prince among Frogs. 2nd ed. (Tales of the Frog Princess Ser.). (ENG.). (YA). 2010. 224p. (gr. 5-8). 16.99 *(978-1-59990-349-1(0),* 9781599903491) 2015. 240p. (gr.

3-6). pap. 8.99 *(978-1-61963-624-8(7)*, 9781619636248) Bloomsbury Publishing USA. (Bloomsbury USA Childrens).
Barrett, Ron. Cats Get Famous. Barrett, Ron, illus. 2015. (ENG., Illus.). 32p. (J). (gr. -1-3). 17.99 *(978-1-4424-9453-4(0)*, Simon & Schuster Bks. For Young Readers) Simon & Schuster Bks. For Young Readers.
Bath, K. P. Flip Side. 2009. (YA). 16.99 *(978-0-316-03836-2(9))* Little Brown & Co.
Bauer, Deidre. Silver Mountain. 2008. 38p. pap. 8.00 *(978-0-8059-7672-4(8))* Dorrance Publishing Co., Inc.
Bayerl, Katie. A Psalm for Lost Girls. 2017. (ENG.). 368p. (YA). (gr. 7). 17.99 *(978-0-399-54525-2(5)*, G.P. Putnam's Sons Books for Young Readers) Penguin Young Readers Group.
Beck, Ricky. A Puzzled Heart. 2008. 85p. pap. 19.95 *(978-1-60441-385-4(9))* America Star Bks.
Beil, Michael D. Lantern Sam & the Blue Streak Bandits. (ENG., Illus.). 288p. (J). (gr. 3-7). 2015. pap. 7.99 *(978-0-385-75320-3(9)*, Yearling) 2014. 15.99 *(978-0-385-75317-3(9)*, Knopf Bks. for Young Readers) Random Hse. Children's Bks.
Bell, Braden. The Kindling. 2012. (YA). *(978-1-4621-1027-8(4))* Cedar Fort, Inc./CFI Distribution.
Bell, Ted. Nick of Time. 2009. (Nick Mciver Adventures Through Time Ser.: 1). (ENG., Illus.). 464p. (J). (gr. 5-9). pap. 8.99 *(978-0-312-58143-5(2)*, 9780312581435) Square Fish.
—The Time Pirate. 2011. (Nick Mciver Adventures Through Time Ser.: 2). (ENG., Illus.). 480p. (J). (gr. 5-9). pap. 10.99 *(978-0-312-66549-4(0)*, 9780312665494) Square Fish.
Bennett, Cindy C. Rapunzel Untangled. 2013. (ENG.). 294p. (gr. 7). 16.99 *(978-1-4621-1156-5(4)*, Sweetwater Bks.) Cedar Fort, Inc./CFI Distribution.
Bennett, Holly. The Bonemender's Choice, 1 vol. 2007. (Bonemender Ser.: 3). (ENG.). 234p. (YA). (gr. 7-12). per. 13.00 *(978-1-55143-718-7(X))* Orca Bk. Pubs. USA.
Berenato, Dave. Medlocks: The Peractio Blackout. 2011. 284p. (gr. 10-12). 27.95 *(978-1-4620-5219-6(3))*; pap. 17.95 *(978-1-4620-5217-2(7))* iUniverse, Inc.
Biedrzycki, David. Ace Lacewing: Bug Detective. Biedrzycki, David, illus. 2008. (ENG., Illus.). 40p. (J). (gr. k-4). pap. 8.95 *(978-1-57091-684-7(5))* Charlesbridge Publishing, Inc.
Biggs, K. E. The Dawn of Hope. 2010. 112p. pap. 10.99 *(978-1-4490-8931-3(3))* AuthorHouse.
Billingsley, ReShonda Tate. Truth or Dare. 2014. (Rumor Central Ser.). (ENG., Illus.). 208p. (YA). (gr. 13). pap. 9.95 *(978-0-7582-8957-5(X)*, K-Teen) Kensington Publishing Corp.
Blackstock, Terri. Southern Storm, 1 vol. 2014. (Cape Refuge Ser.). (ENG.). 400p. pap. 15.99 *(978-0-310-34280-9(5))* Zondervan.
Bladek, John. Lost in Ghostville. 2016. (Middle-Grade Novels Ser.). (ENG.). 208p. (gr. 4-7). lib. bdg. 25.99 *(978-1-4965-3360-9(7))* Stone Arch Bks.
Blair, Jamie. Leap of Faith. 2013. (ENG., Illus.). 240p. (YA). (gr. 9). 16.99 *(978-1-4424-4713-4(3)*, Simon & Schuster Bks. For Young Readers) Simon & Schuster Bks. For Young Readers.
Blair, Jamie M. Leap of Faith. 2014. (ENG.). 240p. (YA). (gr. 9). pap. 11.99 *(978-1-4424-4716-5(8)*, Simon & Schuster Bks. For Young Readers) Simon & Schuster Bks. For Young Readers.
Bloor, Edward. Taken. 2009. (ENG.). 256p. (YA). (gr. 7). pap. 8.99 *(978-0-440-42128-3(4)*, Knopf Bks. for Young Readers) Random Hse. Children's Bks.
Bodeen, S. A. The Detour. 2015. (ENG.). 224p. (YA). (gr. 7). 17.99 *(978-1-250-05554-5(7)*, 9781250055545) Feiwel & Friends.
Boissery, Beverley. Sophie's Exile. 2008. (ENG.). 280p. (J). (gr. 5-8). pap. 12.99 *(978-1-55002-810-2(3)*, Boardwalk Bks.) Dundurn CAN. Dist: Ingram Publisher Services.
Bosch, Pseudonymous. The Name of This Book Is Secret. (Secret Ser.: 1). (ENG.). 400p. (J). (gr. 3-7). 2008. pap. 8.99 *(978-0-316-11369-4(7))* 2015. 12.99 *(978-0-316-26502-7(0))* Little, Brown Bks. for Young Readers.
—The Name of This Book Is Secret. Ford, Gilbert, illus. rev. ed. 2007. (Secret Ser.: 1). (ENG.). 384p. (J). (gr. 3-7). 17.99 *(978-0-316-11366-3(2))* Little, Brown Bks. for Young Readers.
—The Name of This Book Is Secret. 2009. 18.00 *(978-1-60686-518-7(8))* Perfection Learning Corp.
—The Name of This Book Is Secret. 2008. (Secret Ser.: 1). (J). lib. bdg. 19.65 *(978-1-4178-2975-0(3)*, Turtleback) Turtleback Bks.
Boulton, M. T. Megan Button & the Brim-Tree. 2012. 106p. pap. *(978-1-909039-06-3(3))* Legend Pr.
Bowditch, Eden Unger. The Atomic Weight of Secrets or the Arrival of the Mysterious Men in Black. 2011. (Young Inventors Guild Ser.: 1). (ENG.). 320p. (YA). 19.95 *(978-1-61088-002-2(1)*, 33471904-45bf-4a52-9f65-44ef10fff3b6) Bancroft Pr.
—The Ravens of Solemano or the Order of the Mysterious Men in Black. 2015. (Young Inventors Guild Ser.: 2). (ENG.). 464p. (YA). 22.95 *(978-1-61088-121-0(4)*, 631f4bac-0739-447d-b5b4-f9b46c4c02b3) Bancroft Pr.
Bowen, Carl. Black Anchor, 1 vol. Tortosa, Wilson & Fuentes, Benny, illus. 2013. (Shadow Squadron Ser.). (ENG.). 112p. (gr. 4-8). lib. bdg. 26.65 *(978-1-4342-4605-9(1))* Stone Arch Bks.
Bowen, Carl & Fuentes, Benny. Sand Spider, 1 vol. Tortosa, Wilson, illus. 2014. (Shadow Squadron Ser.). (ENG.). 112p. (gr. 4-8). 26.65 *(978-1-4342-9169-1(3))* Stone Arch Bks.
Bowler, Tim. Storm Catchers. 2003. (ENG., Illus.). 208p. (YA). (gr. 7). 18.99 *(978-0-689-84573-4(1)*, McElderry, Margaret K. Bks.) McElderry, Margaret K. Bks.
Bradford, Chris. Hostage, Bk. 2. 2017. (Bodyguard Ser.). (ENG.). 224p. (J). (gr. 5). pap. 8.99 *(978-1-5247-3699-6(6)*, Philomel Bks.) Penguin Young Readers Group.
Bramucci, Stephen. The Danger Gang & the Pirates of Borneo! Chung, Arree, illus. 2017. (ENG.). 384p. (J). 16.99 *(978-1-61963-692-7(1)*, 9781619636927, Bloomsbury USA Childrens) Bloomsbury Publishing USA.
Breitrose, Prudence & Yue, Stephanie. Mousemobile: When Mice Hit the Road. 2014. (Mousenet Book Ser.). (ENG., Illus.). 288p. (J). (gr. 3-7). pap. 7.99 *(978-1-4231-7438-7(0))* Hyperion Bks. for Children.
Brezenoff, Steve. The Yellowstone Kidnapping That Wasn't, 1 vol. Calo, Marcos, illus. 2012. (Field Trip Mysteries Ser.). (ENG.). 88p. (gr. 2-3). pap. 6.10 *(978-1-4342-4200-6(5))*; lib. bdg. 25.32 *(978-1-4342-3789-7(3))* Stone Arch Bks.
Brindley, John. The Rule of Claw. Benfold Haywood, Ian P., illus. 2009. (Exceptional Reading & Language Arts Titles for Intermediate Grades Ser.). (ENG.). 408p. (YA). (gr. 7-12). 18.95 *(978-1-58013-608-2(7))* Lerner Publishing Group.
Brockmann, Suzanne & Brockmann, Melanie. Night Sky. 2014. (Night Sky Ser.: 1). (ENG.). 496p. (YA). (gr. 8-12). 16.99 *(978-1-4926-0144-9(6))* Sourcebooks, Inc.
Brook, Harry, retold by. Kidnapped. 2004. (Paperback Classics Ser.). 144p. (J). lib. bdg. 12.95 *(978-1-58086-640-8(9)*, Usborne) EDC Publishing.
Brooks, Kevin. The Bunker Diary. 2015. (ENG.). 264p. (YA). (gr. 8-12). 17.99 *(978-1-4677-5420-0(X))* Lerner Publishing Group.
Brooks-Scrivanich, Olivia. Fiscal Pear & Shimmer in the Call of River Whale. 2008. (ENG.). 92p. pap. 14.99 *(978-1-4196-9589-6(4))* CreateSpace Independent Publishing Platform.
Brown, Anne. The Dumari Chronicles: Year One: Year One. 2007. 376p. (YA). per. 20.95 *(978-0-595-45725-0(8))* iUniverse, Inc.
Bruchac, Joseph. Skeleton Man. Comport, Sally Wern, illus. 2003. (Skeleton Man Ser.: 1). (ENG.). 128p. (J). (gr. 5-18). pap. 5.99 *(978-0-06-440888-2(4))* HarperCollins Pubs.
—Skeleton Man. Comport, Sally Wern, illus. 2003. 114p. (J). (gr. 5). 12.65 *(978-0-7569-3399-9(4))* Perfection Learning Corp.
Bruzon, Louise A. The Grimstone Galleries. 2010. 192p. pap. *(978-1-907652-17-2(5))* Grosvenor Hse. Publishing Ltd.
Bryers, Paul. Kobal. 2009. 1.00 *(978-1-4074-4320-1(8))* Recorded Bks., Inc.
Buckley, Michael. Attack of the Bullies. 2013. (Nerds Ser.). (ENG.). 336p. (YA). (gr. 3-7). 16.95 *(978-1-4197-0857-2(0)*, Amulet Bks.) Abrams, Inc.
—The Problem Child. 2017. (Sisters Grimm Ser.: 3). (J). lib. bdg. 19.60 ***(978-0-606-39687-5(X))*** Turtleback Bks.
Buckley, Michael. The Sisters Grimm: The Problem Child. Ferguson, Peter, illus. 10th ed. 2017. (Sisters Grimm Ser.). (ENG.). 288p. (J). (gr. 3-7). pap. 8.95 *(978-1-4197-2004-8(X)*, Amulet Bks.) Abrams, Inc.
Bunting, Eve. The Lambkins. Keegan, Jonathan, illus. 2005. (ENG.). 192p. (J). (gr. 5-18). 15.99 *(978-0-06-059906-5(5)*, Cotler, Joanna Books) HarperCollins Pubs.
Butler, Dave. The Kidnap Plot. 2016. (Extraordinary Journeys of Clockwork Charlie Ser.). (ENG.). 336p. (J). (gr. 3-7). 16.99 *(978-0-553-51295-3(1)*, Knopf Bks. for Young Readers) Random Hse. Children's Bks.
Cameron, Ann. Colibrí. 2005. (Readers Circle Ser.). (ENG.). 256p. (YA). (gr. 7). mass mkt. 5.99 *(978-0-440-42052-1(0)*, Laurel Leaf) Random Hse. Children's Bks.
Carey, Janet Lee. In the Time of Dragon Moon. 2015. (ENG.). 480p. (YA). (gr. 7). 17.99 *(978-0-8037-3810-2(2)*, Kathy Dawson Books) Penguin Young Readers Group.
Carlson, Melody. Spring Breakdown, 1 vol. 2014. (Carter House Girls Ser.). (ENG.). 208p. (YA). pap. 9.99 *(978-0-310-74809-0(7))* Zondervan.
Carter, Aimée. Simon Thorn & the Viper's Pit. 2017. (Simon Thorn Ser.). (ENG.). 304p. (J). 16.99 *(978-1-61963-715-3(4)*, 9781619637153, Bloomsbury USA Childrens) Bloomsbury Publishing USA.
—Simon Thorn & the Wolf's Den. 2016. (Simon Thorn Ser.). (ENG.). 320p. (YA). (gr. 3-6). 16.99 *(978-1-61963-704-7(9)*, 9781619637047, Bloomsbury USA Childrens) Bloomsbury Publishing USA.
—Simon Thorn & the Wolf's Den. 2017. (Simon Thorn Ser.). (ENG.). 336p. (J). pap. 7.99 *(978-1-61963-706-1(5)*, 9781619637061, Bloomsbury USA Childrens) Bloomsbury Publishing USA.
Cartwright, Ran. The Adventures of Billy Space Boy, 1 vol. 2010. 208p. pap. 24.95 *(978-1-4489-3901-5(1))* America Star Bks.
Cassidy, Cathy. Dizzy. 2005. (ENG.). 272p. (J). (gr. 3-7). 6.99 *(978-0-14-240474-4(8)*, Puffin Books) Penguin Young Readers Group.
Chantler, Scott. The Captive Prince. Chantler, Scott, illus. 2012. (Three Thieves Ser.: 3). (ENG., Illus.). 116p. (J). (gr. 4-7). 17.95 *(978-1-55453-776-1(2))*; pap. 7.95 *(978-1-55453-777-8(0))* Kids Can Pr., Ltd. CAN. Dist: Hachette Bk. Group.
Chee, Traci. The Reader. (Sea of Ink & Gold Ser.: 1). (ENG.). 464p. (YA). (gr. 7). 2017. pap. 10.99 ***(978-0-14-751805-7(9)***, Speak)Bk. 1. 2016. 19.99 *(978-0-399-17677-7(2)*, G.P. Putnam's Sons Books for Young Readers) Penguin Young Readers Group.
—The Reader. 2017. (Sea of Ink & Gold Ser.: 1). lib. bdg. 22.10 ***(978-0-606-40001-5(X))*** Turtleback Bks.
Chiu, Harry. Enve Lopt Unfolded. 2007. 268p. per. 17.95 *(978-0-595-44707-7(4))* iUniverse, Inc.
Christopher, Lucy. Stolen. (ENG.). (J). 2012. 320p. (gr. 9). pap. 9.99 *(978-0-545-17094-9(X))* 2010. 304p. (gr. 7-18). 17.99 *(978-0-545-17093-2(1))* Scholastic, Inc. (Chicken Hse., The).
—Stolen. 2012. lib. bdg. 20.85 *(978-0-606-23955-4(3)*, Turtleback) Turtleback Bks.
C.J. Eigert. The Elder Brothers & the Padstow Crystals. 2009. 284p. 27.95 *(978-1-4401-7678-4(7))*; pap. 17.95 *(978-1-4401-7676-0(0))* iUniverse, Inc.
Clarke, Cat. The Lost & the Found. 2016. (ENG.). 368p. (YA). (gr. 9). 17.99 *(978-1-101-93204-9(X)*, Crown Books For Young Readers) Random Hse. Children's Bks.
Clayton, Emma. The Roar. 2012. (ENG.). 512p. (J). (gr. 2-7). pap. 10.99 *(978-0-439-92785-7(4)*, Chicken Hse., The) Scholastic, Inc.
Clement-Moore, Rosemary. Spirit & Dust. 2014. (ENG.). 400p. (YA). (gr. 7). pap. 9.99 *(978-0-385-74081-4(6)*, Ember) Random Hse. Children's Bks.
Coatsworth, Elizabeth. The White Horse. Sewell, Helen, illus. 2006. (Sally (Bethlehem Books) Ser.). 169p. (J). (gr. 5-7). per. 11.95 *(978-1-883937-86-7(8))* Bethlehem Bks.
Cochrane, Mick. Fitz. (ENG.). 192p. (YA). (gr. 7). 2013. pap. 8.99 *(978-0-375-84611-3(5)*, Ember) 2012. 16.99 *(978-0-375-85683-9(8)*, Knopf Bks. for Young Readers) Random Hse. Children's Bks.
Colbert, Brandy. Pointe. (ENG.). 352p. (YA). (gr. 9). 2015. pap. 9.99 *(978-0-14-751441-7(X)*, Speak) 2014. 17.99 *(978-0-399-16034-9(5)*, G.P. Putnam's Sons Books for Young Readers) Penguin Young Readers Group.
Coley, Liz. Pretty Girl-13. 2013. (ENG.). 352p. (YA). (gr. 9). 17.99 *(978-0-06-212737-2(3)*, Tegen, Katherine Bks) HarperCollins Pubs.
Colfer, Eoin. The Arctic Incident. 2009. (Artemis Fowl Ser.). (ENG.). 304p. (J). (gr. 5-9). pap. 8.99 *(978-1-4231-2454-2(5))* Hyperion Pr.
—The Arctic Incident. 2003. (Artemis Fowl Ser.: 2). 277p. (J). (gr. 5-7). lib. bdg. 19.65 *(978-0-613-62927-0(2)*, Turtleback) Turtleback Bks.
—Artemis Fowl, 3 vols., Set. 2010. (Artemis Fowl Ser.). (ENG.). 944p. (J). (gr. 5-17). pap. 19.99 *(978-1-4231-3681-1(0))* Disney Pr.
—Artemis Fowl. (Artemis Fowl Ser.: Bk. 1). (FRE.). pap. 34.95 *(978-2-07-054681-7(0))* Gallimard, Editions FRA. Dist: Distribooks, Inc.
—Artemis Fowl. rev. ed. 2009. (Artemis Fowl Ser.). (ENG.). 304p. (J). (gr. 5-9). pap. 8.99 *(978-1-4231-2452-8(9))* Hyperion Pr.
—Artemis Fowl. (Artemis Fowl Ser.: Bk. 1). pap. 34.95 *(978-88-04-49788-2(2))* Mondadori ITA. Dist: Distribooks, Inc.
—Artemis Fowl. (Artemis Fowl Ser.: 1). (YA). 2007. 1.25 *(978-1-4193-6020-6(5))* 2006. 52.75 *(978-1-4193-6023-7(X))* 2006. 54.75 *(978-1-4193-6021-3(3))* 2006. 54.75 *(978-1-4193-6026-8(4))* 2006. 132.75 *(978-1-4193-6022-0(1))* 2005. 56.75 *(978-1-4193-6024-4(8))* Recorded Bks., Inc.
—Artemis Fowl. 2009. (Artemis Fowl Ser.: 1). (J). (gr. 5-8). lib. bdg. 19.65 *(978-0-613-60637-0(X)*, Turtleback) Turtleback Bks.
—Artemis Fowl. Feldmann, Claudia, tr. (Artemis Fowl Ser.: Bk. 1). (GER.). pap. 24.95 *(978-3-548-60320-9(3))* Ullstein-Taschenbuch-Verlag DEU. Dist: Distribooks, Inc.
—Artemis Fowl: El Mundo Subterráneo. 2013. (Vintage Espanol Ser.: Bk. 1). (SPA.). 288p. (YA). (gr. 5). pap. 9.95 *(978-0-345-80418-1(X)*, Vintage Espanol) Knopf Doubleday Publishing Group.
—Encuentro en el Artico. 2013. (Vintage Espanol Ser.).Tr. of Arctic Incident. (SPA.). 320p. (YA). pap. 9.95 *(978-0-345-80535-5(6)*, Vintage Espanol) Knopf Doubleday Publishing Group.
—EL MUNDO SUBTERRÁNEO (ARTEMIS FOWL 1) (Artemis Fowl Ser.: Bk. 1). (SPA.). 288p. pap. *(978-84-8441-115-4(X)*, MO31567) Grijalbo Mondadori, S.A.-Montena.
—The Opal Deception. 2006. (Artemis Fowl Ser.: Bk. 4). 17.10 *(978-0-7569-6828-1(3))* Disney Pr.
—The Opal Deception. rev. ed. 2009. (Artemis Fowl Ser.). (ENG.). 368p. (J). (gr. 5-9). pap. 8.99 *(978-1-4231-2455-9(3))* Hyperion Pr.
—The Opal Deception. (Artemis Fowl Ser.: 4). (J). 2007. 1.25 *(978-1-4193-6041-1(8))* 2006. 72.75 *(978-1-4193-6045-9(0))* 2006. 69.75 *(978-1-4193-6047-3(7))* Recorded Bks., Inc.
Colfer, Eoin & Donkin, Andrew. Artemis Fowl. Rigano, Giovanni & Lamanna, Paolo, illus. 2007. (Artemis Fowl Ser.). (ENG.). 112p. (J). (gr. 5-9). 18.99 *(978-0-7868-4881-2(2))*; pap. 12.99 *(978-0-7868-4882-9(0))* Hyperion Pr.
Collins, David Paul. Shanghaied. 2011. 320p. 29.95 *(978-1-4620-3184-9(6))*; pap. 19.95 *(978-1-4620-3183-2(8))* iUniverse, Inc.
Columbus, Chris & Vizzini, Ned. Battle of the Beasts. 2014. (House of Secrets Ser.: 2). (ENG.). 480p. (J). (gr. 3-7). 17.99 *(978-0-06-219249-3(3))* HarperCollins Pubs.
Cooney, Caroline B. The Face on the Milk Carton. 2009. 9.14 *(978-0-7848-0397-4(8)*, Everbind) Marco Bk. Co.
—The Face on the Milk Carton. 2012. (Janie Bks.: 1). lib. bdg. 20.85 *(978-0-606-26368-9(3)*, Turtleback) Turtleback Bks.
—Hit the Road. rev. l.t. ed. 2007. (Thorndike Literacy Bridge Ser.). 259p. (YA). (gr. 7-12). 23.95 *(978-0-7862-9429-9(9))* Thorndike Pr.
—Janie Face to Face. 2013. (ENG.). 352p. (YA). (gr. 7). 17.99 *(978-0-385-74206-1(1)*, Delacorte Bks. for Young Readers) Random Hse. Children's Bks.
—What Janie Found. 2012. (ENG.). 208p. (YA). (gr. 7). pap. 9.99 *(978-0-385-74241-2(X)*, Ember) Random Hse. Children's Bks.
—What Janie Found. 2012. (Janie Bks.: 4). lib. bdg. 20.85 *(978-0-606-26370-2(5)*, Turtleback) Turtleback Bks.
—Whatever Happened to Janie? 2012. (ENG.). 224p. (YA). (gr. 7). pap. 9.99 *(978-0-385-74239-9(8)*, Ember) Random Hse. Children's Bks.
Coppel, Chris. Far from Burden Dell. 2005. 286p. (J). (gr. 6-16). per. 4.95 *(978-0-9746481-6-3(7))* Brown Barn Bks.
Corder, Zizou. Lionboy. 2004. (ENG., Illus.). 304p. (J). (gr. 3-7). reprint ed. pap. 8.99 *(978-0-14-240226-9(5)*, Puffin Books) Penguin Young Readers Group.
—Lionboy: The Truth. 2006. (ENG., Illus.). 240p. (J). (gr. 3-7). 7.99 *(978-0-14-240705-9(4)*, Puffin Books) Penguin Young Readers Group.
Côté, Denis. La Machination du Scorpion Noir. 2004. (Mon Roman Ser.). (FRE.). 160p. (J). (gr. 2). pap. *(978-2-89021-667-9(5))* Diffusion du livre Mirabel (DLM).
Cox, Judy. The Case of the Purloined Professor, 0 vols. Rayyan, Omar, illus. 2009. (Tails of Frederick & Ishbu Ser.: 0). (ENG.). 256p. (J). (gr. 5-7). 16.99 *(978-0-7614-5544-8(2)*, 9780761455448, Amazon Children's Publishing) Amazon Publishing.
Cross, Gillian. Where I Belong. 2011. (ENG., Illus.). 256p. (J). (gr. 5-18). 17.95 *(978-0-8234-2332-3(8))* Holiday Hse., Inc.
Crutcher, Chris. Period 8. 2013. 288p. (YA). (gr. 9). (ENG.). 17.99 *(978-0-06-191480-5(0))*; lib. bdg. 18.89 *(978-0-06-191481-2(9))* HarperCollins Pubs. (Greenwillow Bks.).
Dailey, Reid. Ross the Reader & the Adventure of the Pirate's Treasure. Edgerley, Ross, illus. 2009. 44p. pap. 16.95 *(978-1-59858-900-9(8))* Dog Ear Publishing, LLC.
Daneshvari, Gitty. The League of Unexceptional Children. 2015. (League of Unexceptional Children Ser.: 1). (ENG., Illus.). 240p. (J). (gr. 3-7). 17.00 *(978-0-316-40570-6(1))* Little Brown & Co.
—The League of Unexceptional Children. 2016. (League of Unexceptional Children Ser.: 1). (ENG., Illus.). 256p. (J). (gr. 3-7). pap. 6.99 *(978-0-316-40568-3(X))* Little, Brown Bks. for Young Readers.
Daniels, J. M. The Secret of the Little Dutch Doll. 2009. 68p. pap. 25.49 *(978-1-4343-9356-2(9))* AuthorHouse.
Darlison, Aleesah. Krystal's Choice. Brailsford, Jill, illus. 2016. (Unicorn Riders Ser.). (ENG.). 112p. (gr. 3-5). lib. bdg. 22.65 *(978-1-4795-6546-7(6))* Picture Window Bks.
—Krystal's Choice Cancelled. Brailsford, Jill, illus. 2017. (Unicorn Riders Ser.). (ENG.). 112p. (gr. 3-5). pap. 5.95 *(978-1-4795-6554-2(7))* Picture Window Bks.
—Quinn's Riddles. Brailsford, Jill, illus. 2016. (Unicorn Riders Ser.). (ENG.). 112p. (gr. 3-5). 22.65 *(978-1-4795-6544-3(X))* Picture Window Bks.
—Unicorn Riders. Brailsford, Jill, illus. 2017. (Unicorn Riders Ser.). (ENG.). 112p. (gr. 3-5). 181.20 *(978-1-5158-0821-3(1))* Picture Window Bks.
Darlison, Aleesha. Quinn's Riddles. Brailsford, Jill, illus. 2017. (Unicorn Riders Ser.). (ENG.). 112p. (gr. 3-5). pap. 5.95 *(978-1-4795-6552-8(0))* Picture Window Bks.
Davies, Stephen. Outlaw. 2011. (ENG.). 304p. (YA). (gr. 7). 16.99 *(978-0-547-39017-8(3))* Houghton Mifflin Harcourt Publishing Co.
Davis, Susan Page. Feather. 2006. (Illus.). 213p. (J). 8.99 *(978-1-59166-668-4(6))* BJU Pr.
de Brunhoff, Jean. Babar & Zephir. de Brunhoff, Jean, illus. 2005. (Illus.). 38p. (J). (gr. k-4). reprint ed. 16.00 *(978-0-7567-8935-0(4))* DIANE Publishing Co.
DeMatteis, J. M. Stardust Kid. Ploog, Mike, illus. 2008. (ENG.). 128p. pap. 14.99 *(978-1-934506-04-2(4))* Boom! Studios.
Derting, Kimberly. The Replaced. 2015. (Taking Ser.: 2). (ENG.). 368p. (YA). (gr. 9). 17.99 *(978-0-06-229363-3(X)*, HarperTeen) HarperCollins Pubs.
DeStefano, Lauren. Wither, 9 vols. (Chemical Garden Ser.: 1). (YA). 90.75 *(978-1-4561-2060-3(3))*; 1.25 *(978-1-4561-2064-1(6))*; 256.75 *(978-1-4561-2059-7(X))*; 2011. 120.75 *(978-1-4561-2063-4(8))*; 2011. 122.75 *(978-1-4561-2061-0(1))* Recorded Bks., Inc.
—Wither. 2011. (Chemical Garden Trilogy Ser.: 1). (ENG.). (YA). (gr. 9). 384p. pap. 10.99 *(978-1-4424-0906-4(1))*; 368p. 19.99 *(978-1-4424-0905-7(3))* Simon & Schuster Bks. For Young Readers. (Simon & Schuster Bks. For Young Readers).
Devlin, Calla. Right Where You Left Me. 2017. (ENG., Illus.). 256p. (YA). (gr. 9). 17.99 ***(978-1-4814-8699-6(3)***, Atheneum Bks. for Young Readers) Simon & Schuster Children's Publishing.
Diamand, Emily. Raiders' Ransom. 2009. (Raiders' Ransom Ser.: 1). (ENG.). 368p. (J). (gr. 3-7). 17.99 *(978-0-545-14297-7(0))* Scholastic, Inc.
Dickens, Charles. Oliver Twist. 2009. (Foundation Classics Ser.). (Illus.). 56p. (J). (gr. 5-9). lib. bdg. 27.95 *(978-1-60754-542-2(X))* Windmill Bks.
Disney Press Editors. Miles from Tomorrowland: Who Stole the Stellosphere? 2015. (World of Reading Ser.). (J). lib. bdg. 13.55 *(978-0-606-36902-2(3))* Turtleback Bks.
Dixon, Franklin W. Bound for Danger. 2016. (Hardy Boys Adventures Ser.: 13). (ENG., Illus.). 144p. (J). (gr. 3-7). pap. 6.99 *(978-1-4814-6831-2(6)*, Aladdin) Simon & Schuster Children's Publishing.
—Kidnapped at the Casino. 2007. (Hardy Boys Undercover Brothers: Super Mystery Ser.: 2). (ENG., Illus.). 240p. (J). (gr. 3-7). pap. 5.99 *(978-1-4169-3923-8(7)*, Aladdin) Simon & Schuster Children's Publishing.
Dixon, Ken. Cobweb Jack & the Sacred Khunjar. 2009. 210p. pap. 28.50 *(978-1-4092-8919-7(2))* Lulu Pr., Inc.
Doller, Trish. Where the Stars Still Shine. 2013. (ENG.). 352p. (YA). (gr. 9). 17.99 *(978-1-61963-144-1(X)*, 9781619631441, Bloomsbury USA Childrens) Bloomsbury Publishing USA.
Donbavand, Tommy. Terror of the Nightwatchman. 2014. (Scream Street Ser.: 9). (ENG.). 128p. (J). (gr. 3-7). pap. 5.99 *(978-0-7636-5761-1(1))* Candlewick Pr.
Doyle, Arthur Conan. A Desert Drama: Being the Tragedy of the Korosko. 2007. (ENG.). 160p. pap. 19.99 *(978-1-4346-4997-3(0))*; 172p. pap. 21.99 *(978-1-4346-4998-0(9))* Creative Media Partners, LLC.
Draper, Sharon M. Panic. 2013. (ENG., Illus.). 272p. (YA). (gr. 9). 17.99 *(978-1-4424-0896-8(0)*, Atheneum Bks. for Young Readers) Simon & Schuster Children's Publishing.
Ducharme, Huguette. Enquete Tres Speciale. Caron, Romi, illus. 2004. (Collection des 6 Ans: Vol. 32). (FRE.). 68p. (YA). 7.95 *(978-2-922565-94-2(7))* Editions de la Paix CAN. Dist: World of Reading, Ltd.
Duff, Hilary. Devoted. 2011. (Elixir Ser.). (ENG.). 368p. (YA). (gr. 9). 17.99 *(978-1-4424-0855-5(3)*, Simon & Schuster Bks. For Young Readers) Simon & Schuster Bks. For Young Readers.
—Devoted: An Elixir Novel. 2012. (Elixir Ser.). (ENG.). 368p. (YA). (gr. 9). pap. 9.99 *(978-1-4424-0856-2(1)*, Simon & Schuster Bks. For Young Readers) Simon & Schuster Bks. For Young Readers.
Duncan, Lois. The Third Eye. 2012. (ENG.). 288p. (YA). (gr. 7-17). pap. 10.99 *(978-0-316-09908-0(2))* Little, Brown Bks. for Young Readers.
Dunlop, Ed. Sherlock Jones: The Missing Diamond. 2005. (Sherlock Jones Ser.). 109p. (J). (gr. 3-7). per. 8.99 *(978-1-59166-316-4(4))* BJU Pr.
Durst, Sarah Beth. Chasing Power. 2014. (ENG.). 376p. (YA). (gr. 9). 17.99 *(978-0-8027-3755-7(2)*, 9780802737557, Bloomsbury USA Childrens) Walker & Co.
Ehrenhaft, Daniel. Drawing a Blank: Or How I Tried to Solve a Mystery, End a Feud, & Land the Girl of My Dreams. Ristow, Trevor, illus. 2009. (ENG.). 352p. (J). pap. 8.99 *(978-0-06-075254-5(8)*, HarperTeen) HarperCollins Pubs.
Ehrlich, Amy. Joyride. 2008. (ENG., Illus.). 256p. (YA). (gr. 7). pap. 8.99 *(978-0-7636-2321-0(0))* Candlewick Pr.
Eisenstein, Ann. Fallen Prey, a Sean Gray Junior Special Agent Mystery. Waugh, Leslie, ed. 2013. 190p. pap. 9.99 *(978-1-935711-31-5(8))* Peak City Publishing, LLC.
Epstein, Adam Jay & Jacobson, Andrew. The Familiars. Chiu, Bobby, illus. 2010. (Familiars Ser.: 1). (ENG.). 368p. (J). (gr. 3-7). 16.99 *(978-0-06-196108-3(6))* HarperCollins Pubs.
Erdrich, Louise. Chickadee. Erdrich, Louise, illus. (Birchbark House Ser.: 4). (Illus.). (J). (gr. 3-7). 2013. (ENG.). 224p. pap. 6.99 *(978-0-06-057792-6(4))* 2012. (ENG., 208p. 16.99 *(978-0-06-057790-2(8))* 2012. 208p. lib. bdg. 17.89 *(978-0-06-057791-9(6))* HarperCollins Pubs.
Erickson, John R. The Case of the Kidnapped Collie. Holmes, Gerald L., illus. 2011. (Hank the Cowdog Ser.). (ENG.). 113p. (J). (gr. 3-6). pap. 5.99 *(978-1-59188-126-1(9))* Maverick Bks., Inc.

J
K
L

Eustache, Harold. Shuswap Journey. 2004. (Shuswap Journey Ser.). (ENG.). 176p. pap. 15.95 *(978-1-894778-15-2(4))* Theytus Bks., Ltd. CAN. Dist: Univ. of Toronto Pr.

Evans, Richard. Hunt for Jade Dragon. 2015. (Michael Vey Ser.: 4). (ENG., Illus.). 336p. (YA). (gr. 7). pap. 11.99 *(978-1-4814-2439-4(4))* Simon & Schuster, Inc.

Evelyn Gill Hilton. Kidnapped by Pirates: Based on the true story of a fourteen year-old boy, Charles Tilton, who was kidnapped alone from an Amer. 2010. 124p. (gr. 1-2). pap. 11.95 *(978-1-4269-2017-2(2))* Trafford Publishing.

—Kidnapped by Pirates: Based on the true story of a fourteen year-old boy, Charles Tilton, who was kidnapped alone from an Amer. 2010. 124p. *(978-1-4269-2018-9(0))* Trafford Publishing (UK) Ltd.

Fahnestock, Todd. The Wishing World. 2016. (ENG.). 224p. (J). 17.99 *(978-0-7653-8588-8(0)*, 9780765385888, Starscape) Doherty, Tom Assocs., LLC.

Farshtey, Greg. Way of the Ninja. 2012. (Lego Ninjago Ser.). (ENG.). 32p. (J). (gr. -1-3). pap. 3.99 *(978-0-545-40113-5(5))* Scholastic, Inc.

Faunce-Brown, Michael. Slave Children. 2015. (ENG., Illus.). 140p. (J). pap. *(978-1-78222-422-8(X))* Paragon Publishing, Rothersthorpe.

Feinstein, John. Vanishing Act: Mystery at the U. S. Open. 2008. (Sports Beat Ser.). (ENG.). 304p. (J). (gr. 3-7). 7.99 *(978-0-440-42125-2(X)*, Yearling) Random Hse. Children's Bks.

Ferris, Jean. Thrice upon a Marigold: A Royal Kidnapping Caper. 2014. (ENG.). 256p. (J). (gr. 2-5). pap. 6.99 *(978-0-544-30262-4(1)*, HMH Books For Young Readers) Houghton Mifflin Harcourt Publishing Co.

Flanagan, John. The Icebound Land. 2007. (Ranger's Apprentice Ser.: Bk. 3). 260p. (J). 25.66 *(978-1-4287-4632-9(3)*, Follettbound) Follett School Solutions.

—The Icebound Land, Bk. 3. 2008. (Ranger's Apprentice Ser.: 3). (ENG.). 304p. (J). (gr. 5-18). 8.99 *(978-0-14-241075-2(6)*, Puffin Books) Penguin Young Readers Group.

—The Sorcerer of the North, 5 vols., Bk. 5. (Ranger's Apprentice Ser.: 5). (ENG.). (J). (gr. 5-18). 2009. 336p. pap. 8.99 *(978-0-14-241429-3(8)*, Puffin Books) 2008. 304p. 18.99 *(978-0-399-25032-3(8)*, Philomel Bks.) Penguin Young Readers Group.

—The Sorcerer of the North. 2009. (Ranger's Apprentice Ser.: 5). lib. bdg. 19.65 *(978-0-606-02237-8(6)*, Turtleback) Turtleback Bks.

Flannigan, Liz. Cara & the Wizard, 2 vols. Docampo, Valeria, illus. 2013. (Magic Stories Ser.). (ENG.). 48p. (J). (gr. 1-4). pap. 8.99 *(978-1-84686-780-4(0))* Barefoot Bks., Inc.

Fogg, K. L. Widow's Revenge: A Novel. 2007. 355p. (J). *(978-1-59811-319-8(4))* Covenant Communications.

Fox Mazer, Norma. Taking Terri Mueller. 2015. (ENG.). 224p. (J). (gr. 5). pap. 12.95 *(978-1-939601-38-4(X))* Ig Publishing, Inc.

Frances, Barbara. Lottie's Adventure: A Kidnapping Unraveled. 2007. 180p. pap. 12.95 *(978-0-615-16787-9(X))* Positive Imaging, LLC.

Frederick, Heather Vogel. Once upon a Toad. (ENG., Illus.). (J). (gr. 5-9). 2013. 288p. pap. 6.99 *(978-1-4169-8479-5(8))* 2012. 272p. 16.99 *(978-1-4169-8478-8(X))* Simon & Schuster Bks. For Young Readers. (Simon & Schuster Bks. For Young Readers).

Freeman, Martha. Who Stole Halloween? 2005. (Chickadee Court Mystery Ser.). (ENG.). 224p. (J). (gr. 3-7). 16.95 *(978-0-8234-1962-3(2))* Holiday Hse., Inc.

Frost, Andrew David. The Magician & the Priestess. 2010. 416p. pap. 17.99 *(978-1-4490-7830-0(3))* AuthorHouse.

Funke, Cornelia. Inkdeath. 2010. (Inkheart Trilogy Ser.).Tr. of Tintentod. (ENG.). 704p. (J). (gr. 3-7). 12.99 *(978-0-439-86629-3(4)*, Scholastic Paperbacks) Scholastic, Inc.

Furlong, C. T. Killer Strangelets. 2011. (Arctic6 Ser.). 208p. (J). pap. *(978-0-9562315-6-7(X))* Inside Pocket Publishing, Ltd.

Fussell, Sandy. Samurai Kids #4: Monkey Fist. James, Rhian Nest, illus. 2012. (Samurai Kids Ser.: 4). (ENG.). 272p. (J). (gr. 4-7). pap. 6.99 *(978-0-7636-5827-4(8))* Candlewick Pr.

Gagnon, Michelle & Gangsei, Jan. Zero Day. 2016. (ENG., Illus.). 364p. (YA). (gr. 7-12). 17.99 *(978-1-4847-2226-8(4))* Hyperion Bks. for Children.

Gaines, Pat. O. O. Octopus: Sheriff of Blue Ribbon Sound. 2008. (Illus.). 24p. (J). lib. bdg. *(978-0-9801376-4-4(0))*; per. *(978-0-9801376-5-1(9))* Dragonfly Publishing, Inc.

Gallo, Tina, adapted by. Master of Manners. 2016. (Kung Fu Panda TV Ser.). (ENG., Illus.). 24p. (J). (gr. -1-2). pap. 3.99 *(978-1-4814-6183-2(4)*, Simon Spotlight) Simon Spotlight.

Gangsei, Jan. Zero Day. 2016. (ENG., Illus.). 368p. (YA). (gr. 7-12). pap. 9.99 *(978-1-4847-2548-1(4))* Hyperion Bks. for Children.

Garber, Stephanie. Caraval. 2017. (SPA.). 432p. pap. 16.95 ***(978-607-07-4044-2(0))*** Editorial Planeta, S. A. ESP. Dist: Two Rivers Distribution.

—Caraval. 2017. (Caraval Ser.). (ENG.). (YA). 416p. 18.99 *(978-1-250-09525-1(5)*, 9781250095251); (gr. 8-12). pap. 11.99 ***(978-1-250-14149-1(4))*** Flatiron Bks.

Gentry, Brad. The Hollywood Princess. 2009. 40p. pap. 20.99 *(978-1-4490-3545-7(0))* AuthorHouse.

Giff, Patricia Reilly. Hunter Moran Hangs Out. (ENG.). 144p. (J). (gr. 3-7). 2014. pap. 6.99 *(978-0-8234-3189-2(4))* 2013. (Illus.). 16.95 *(978-0-8234-2859-5(1))* Holiday Hse., Inc.

Gioseffi, Anthony P. Mainframe. 2007. 144p. per. 11.95 *(978-0-595-44953-8(0))* iUniverse, Inc.

Girdner, Randall P. Mr. Ping's Almanac of the Twisted & Weird presents Boyd Mccloyd & the Perpetual Motion Machine. 2009. 473p. pap. 25.00 *(978-0-615-25755-6(0))* Acclimated Spooks, Light, & Power.

Goscinny, René. Asterix & the Vikings: The Book of the Film. Bell, Anthea, tr. Uderzo, Albert, illus. 2006. (ENG.). 72p. (gr. 4-7). 17.99 *(978-0-7528-8590-2(1)*, Orion) Orion Publishing Group, Ltd. GBR. Dist: Hachette Bk. Group.

Grainger, A. J. Captive. 2016. (ENG.). 272p. (YA). (gr. 7). pap. 11.99 *(978-1-4814-2904-7(3))* Simon & Schuster Children's Publishing.

Grant, Holly. The Dastardly Deed. Portillo, Josie, illus. 2016. (League of Beastly Dreadfuls Ser.: Bk. 2). (ENG.). 368p. (J). (gr. 3-7). 16.99 *(978-0-385-37025-7(3)*, Random Hse. Bks. for Young Readers) Random Hse. Children's Bks.

—The League of Beastly Dreadfuls. (League of Beastly Dreadfuls Ser.: Bk. 1). (ENG., Illus.). (J). (gr. 3-7). 2016. 336p. 7.99 *(978-0-385-37010-3(5)*, Yearling) 2015. 320p. 16.99 *(978-0-385-37007-3(5)*, Random Hse. Bks. for Young Readers) Random Hse. Children's Bks.

Grant, Katy. Hide & Seek, 1 vol. (ENG.). 240p. (J). 2012. pap. 7.95 *(978-1-56145-669-7(1))* 2010. (gr. 3-7). 15.95 *(978-1-56145-542-3(3))* Peachtree Pubs.

Grant, Vicki. Nine Doors, 1 vol. 2009. (Orca Currents Ser.). (ENG.). (J). (gr. 5-9). 112p. 16.95 *(978-1-55469-074-9(9))*; 128p. pap. 9.95 *(978-1-55469-073-2(0))* Orca Bk. Pubs. USA.

Grisham, John. The Abduction. 2009. (Theodore Boone Ser.: Bk. 2). 9.68 *(978-0-7848-3783-2(X)*, Everbind) Marco Bk. Co.

—The Abduction, 2 vols. (Theodore Boone Ser.: 2). (ENG.). 256p. (J). (gr. 3-7). 2012. pap. 8.99 *(978-0-14-242137-6(5)*, Puffin Books) 2011. 16.99 *(978-0-525-42557-1(8)*, Dutton Books for Young Readers) Penguin Young Readers Group.

—The Abduction. 2012. (Theodore Boone Ser.: 2). lib. bdg. 19.65 *(978-0-606-26079-4(X)*, Turtleback) Turtleback Bks.

Grove, S. E. The Glass Sentence. 2014. (Mapmakers Trilogy Ser.: 1). (ENG., Illus.). 512p. (J). (gr. 5). 17.99 *(978-0-670-78502-5(4)*, Viking Books for Young Readers) Penguin Young Readers Group.

Grover, Lorie Ann. Hold Me Tight. 2007. (ENG.). 352p. (J). (gr. 5-9). pap. 16.95 *(978-1-4169-6753-8(2)*, McElderry, Margaret K. Bks.) McElderry, Margaret K. Bks.

Haddix, Margaret Peterson. Escape from Memory. (ENG.). (YA). (gr. 7). 2012. 272p. pap. 8.99 *(978-1-4424-4602-1(1))* 2003. (Illus.). 224p. 17.99 *(978-0-689-85421-7(8))* Simon & Schuster Bks. For Young Readers. (Simon & Schuster Bks. For Young Readers).

—Revealed. 2015. (Missing Ser.: 7). lib. bdg. 19.65 *(978-0-606-37847-5(2))* Turtleback Bks.

Hall, Maggie. Map of Fates. 2016. (Conspiracy of Us Ser.). (ENG.). 320p. (YA). (gr. 7). 17.99 *(978-0-399-16651-8(3)*, G.P. Putnam's Sons Books for Young Readers) Penguin Young Readers Group.

Hamilton, Peter F. The Secret Throne. Eason, Rohan, illus. 2015. (Queen of Dreams Ser.: 1). (ENG.). 288p. (J). (gr. 4-7). pap. 11.99 *(978-1-4472-8865-7(3))* Pan Macmillan GBR. Dist: Independent Pubs. Group.

Hancocks, Helen. Penguin in Peril. Hancocks, Helen, illus. 2014. (ENG., Illus.). 32p. (J). (gr. -1-2). 15.99 *(978-0-7636-7159-4(2)*, Templar) Candlewick Pr.

Handwerk, Marina. Hey Cool, I've Never Seen a Teacher with His Head Cut off Before! 2007. 284p. per. 11.95 *(978-1-4327-0332-5(3))* Outskirts Pr., Inc.

Hardinge, Frances. Fly Trap. 2012. 592p. (J). (gr. 5). pap. 7.99 *(978-0-06-088046-0(5))* HarperCollins Pubs.

Harrison, Michelle. 13 Curses. 2011. (13 Treasures Trilogy Ser.: 2). (ENG.). 496p. (J). (gr. 5-9). 15.99 *(978-0-316-04150-8(5))* Little Brown & Co.

—13 Curses. 2012. (13 Treasures Trilogy Ser.: 2). (ENG.). 512p. (J). (gr. 5-9). pap. 8.99 *(978-0-316-04149-2(1))* Little, Brown Bks. for Young Readers.

—13 Curses. 2012. (13 Treasures Ser.: 2). (J). lib. bdg. 19.65 *(978-0-606-26160-9(5)*, Turtleback) Turtleback Bks.

Hartley, James. Berlina's Quest. Legge, Barbara, ed. Kelsey, Amanda, illus. 2013. 146p. (J). pap. 17.99 *(978-1-61572-948-7(8))* Damnation Bks.

Harvey, Sarah N. Deadly, 1 vol. 2013. (Orca Soundings Ser.). (ENG.). 128p. (YA). (gr. 8-12). 16.95 *(978-1-4598-0365-7(5))*; pap. 9.95 *(978-1-4598-0364-0(7))* Orca Bk. Pubs. USA.

Hautman, Pete & Logue, Mary. Snatched. 2007. (Bloodwater Mysteries Ser.). (ENG.). 224p. (J). (gr. 5-7). 7.99 *(978-0-14-240795-0(X)*, Puffin Books) Penguin Young Readers Group.

Hawkins, Mia K. The Broken Guild of Twelve Pirates, 1 vol. 2009. 201p. pap. 24.95 *(978-1-61546-333-6(X))* PublishAmerica, Inc.

Henry, April. Count All Her Bones. 2017. (Girl, Stolen Ser.). (ENG.). 240p. (YA). 17.99 *(978-1-62779-591-3(X)*, 9781627795913, Holt, Henry & Co. Bks. For Young Readers) Holt, Henry & Co.

—Girl, Stolen. 2010. (Girl, Stolen Ser.). (ENG.). 224p. (YA). (gr. 7-12). 18.99 *(978-0-8050-9005-5(3)*, 9780805090055, Holt, Henry & Co. Bks. For Young Readers) Holt, Henry & Co.

—The Night She Disappeared. 2013. (ENG.). 256p. (YA). (gr. 7-12). pap. 10.99 *(978-1-250-01674-4(6)*, 9781250016744) Square Fish.

Hicks, John. Divided World. 2003. 192p. (YA). per. 6.50 *(978-0-9742829-1-6(X))* Quiet Man Publishing.

Hoffman, Nina Kiriki. Meeting. 2011. (Magic Next Door Ser.). (ENG.). 336p. (J). (gr. 5). E-Book *(978-1-101-52934-8(2)*, Viking Books for Young Readers) Penguin Young Readers Group.

Hofland. Little Manuel, the Captive Boy. 2003. 63p. 88.00 *(978-0-7950-5545-4(5))* New Library Press LLC.

Holub, Joan & Williams, Suzanne. Zeus & the Thunderbolt of Doom. Phillips, Craig, illus. 2012. (Heroes in Training Ser.: 1). (ENG.). 112p. (J). (gr. 1-4). 16.99 *(978-1-4424-5787-4(2))*; pap. 5.99 *(978-1-4424-5263-3(3))* Simon & Schuster Children's Publishing. (Aladdin).

Hoover, Krystal Dawn. Tabby Town. 2011. 40p. pap. *(978-1-4269-7276-8(8))* Trafford Publishing (UK) Ltd.

Hopkins, Ellen. The You I've Never Known. 2017. (ENG., Illus.). 608p. (YA). (gr. 9). 18.99 *(978-1-4814-4290-9(2)*, McElderry, Margaret K. Bks.) McElderry, Margaret K. Bks.

Hopkins, Howard. The Nightmare Club #3: the Willow Witch. 2009. 104p. pap. 9.98 *(978-0-578-00361-0(9))* Golden Perils Pr.

Horvath, Polly. Mr. & Mrs. Bunny: Detectives Extraordinaire! Blackall, Sophie, illus. 2012. (ENG.). 256p. (J). (gr. 3-7). 16.99 *(978-0-375-86755-2(4)*, Schwartz & Wade Bks.) Random Hse. Children's Bks.

Houts, Michelle. Winterfrost. 2016. (ENG.). 272p. (J). (gr. 3-7). pap. 7.99 *(978-0-7636-9101-1(1))* Candlewick Pr.

Howard, Jenny. Bittersweet Voyage. 2012. 172p. pap. 12.95 *(978-1-4685-7573-6(2))* AuthorHouse.

Hubbard, Crystal. Alive & Unharmed. 2013. 164p. (J). pap. 12.95 *(978-1-60043-144-9(5))* Parker Publishing Inc.

Hunt, Bonnie. The Missing Chimp: A Grayson Twins Adventures, 1 vol. 2009. 100p. pap. 19.95 *(978-1-60813-481-6(4))* America Star Bks.

Hunt, Elizabeth Singer. The Secret of the Sacred Temple. Williamson, Brian, illus. 2008. (Secret Agent Jack Stalwart Ser.: 5). (ENG.). 128p. (J). (gr. 1-4). per. 5.99 *(978-1-60286-003-2(3)*, Weinstein Bks.) Perseus Bks. Group.

Hunt for Jade Dragon. 2014. (Michael Vey Ser.: No. 4). (ENG., Illus.). 336p. (YA). (gr. 7). 19.99 *(978-1-4814-2438-7(6)*, Simon Pulse/Mercury Ink) Simon Pulse/Mercury Ink.

Jacques, Brian. The Sable Quean, 21 vols. 2011. (Redwall Ser.: 21). (ENG.). 368p. (J). (gr. 5). 8.99 *(978-0-441-01998-4(6)*, Ace Bks.) Penguin Publishing Group.

—The Sable Quean, 21 vols. Elliot, David, illus. 2010. (Redwall Ser.: 21). (ENG.). 448p. (J). (gr. 5-18). 23.99 *(978-0-399-25164-1(2)*, Philomel Bks.) Penguin Young Readers Group.

—The Sable Quean. Elliot, David, illus. 2012. (Redwall Ser.: 21). lib. bdg. 19.65 *(978-0-606-23646-1(5)*, Turtleback) Turtleback Bks.

Jakobsen, Lars. The Santa Fe Jail. Jakobsen, Lars, illus. 2012. (Mortensen's Escapades Ser.: 2). (ENG., Illus.). 48p. (gr. 6-12). pap. 6.95 *(978-0-8225-9421-5(8))*; lib. bdg. 27.93 *(978-0-7613-7886-0(3))* Lerner Publishing Group. (Graphic Universe™).

Jasper, Elizabeth. The Golden Cuckoo. 2013. 102p. (J). pap. *(978-1-78299-195-3(6))* FeedARead.com.

Jenkins, Jerry B. & Fabry, Chris. Stolen Secrets. 2005. (Red Rock Mysteries Ser.: 2). (ENG., Illus.). 224p. (YA). (gr. -1-7). pap. 6.99 *(978-1-4143-0141-9(3)*, Tyndale Kids) Tyndale Hse. Pubs.

Jennings, Sharon. Batnapped. *(978-1-897039-30-4(1))* High Interest Publishing (HIP).

Jonell, Lynne. Emmy & the Home for Troubled Girls. Bean, Jonathan, illus. 2010. (Emmy & the Rat Ser.: 2). (ENG.). 384p. (J). (gr. 4-7). pap. 12.99 *(978-0-312-60873-6(X)*, 9780312608736) Square Fish.

Jones, Chris. Cameron Jack & the Key to the Universe. 2010. (Illus.). 136p. pap. 10.99 *(978-1-4490-6547-8(3))* AuthorHouse.

Jones, Diana Wynne. Castle in the Air. 2008. (World of Howl Ser.: 2). 400p. (J). (gr. 3-7). pap. 7.99 *(978-0-06-147877-2(6)*, Greenwillow Bks.) HarperCollins Pubs.

—Castle in the Air, 7 vols. 2009. (J). 91.75 *(978-1-4361-6121-3(5))*; 94.75 *(978-1-4361-6119-0(3))*; 1.25 *(978-1-4361-6112-1(6))*; 70.75 *(978-1-4361-6117-6(7))*; 73.75 *(978-1-4361-6115-2(0))*; 156.75 *(978-1-4361-6116-9(9))* Recorded Bks., Inc.

Jones, Ena. Clayton Stone, at Your Service. 2015. (ENG.). 224p. (J). (gr. 2-6). 16.95 *(978-0-8234-3389-6(7))* Holiday Hse., Inc.

Jordan, Devin. The Dragon's Pearl. Di Bartolo, Jim, illus. 2010. (ENG.). 352p. (YA). (gr. 5-9). pap. 8.99 *(978-1-4169-6411-7(8)*, Simon & Schuster Bks. For Young Readers) Simon & Schuster Bks. For Young Readers.

Kay, Alan. Breaking the Rules. 2007. (Young Heroes of History Ser.: 7). 149p. (J). pap. 7.95 *(978-1-57249-389-6(5)*, White Mane Kids) White Mane Publishing Co., Inc.

Kehret, Peg. Abduction! 2006. (ENG.). 224p. (J). (gr. 5-18). 6.99 *(978-0-14-240617-5(1)*, Puffin Books) Penguin Young Readers Group.

—Abduction! 2007. 215p. (gr. 3-7). 17.00 *(978-0-7569-8282-9(0))* Perfection Learning Corp.

—Deadly Stranger. 2012. (ENG.). 176p. (J). (gr. 3-7). pap. 9.99 *(978-1-4424-6044-7(X)*, Simon & Schuster/Paula Wiseman Bks.) Simon & Schuster/Paula Wiseman Bks.

—Desert Danger. 2008. (Frightmares Ser.). (ENG.). 128p. (J). (gr. 3-7). pap. 7.99 *(978-1-4169-9111-3(5)*, Simon & Schuster/Paula Wiseman Bks.) Simon & Schuster/Paula Wiseman Bks.

—Stolen Children. 2010. (ENG.). 176p. (J). (gr. 3-7). 6.99 *(978-0-14-241513-9(8)*, Puffin Books) Penguin Young Readers Group.

Kehret, Peg & the Cat, Pete. Spy Cat. 2008. (Pete the Cat Ser.). (ENG.). 192p. (J). (gr. 3-7). 5.99 *(978-0-14-241219-0(8)*, Puffin Books) Penguin Young Readers Group.

—Trapped! 2008. (Pete the Cat Ser.). (ENG.). 192p. (J). (gr. 3-7). 5.99 *(978-0-14-241189-6(2)*, Puffin Books) Penguin Young Readers Group.

Kennedy, Leo B. Devin & the Greedy Ferret. 2013. 86p. (gr. 4-6). pap. 9.99 *(978-1-4497-8429-4(1)*, WestBow Pr.) Author Solutions, Inc.

King, Wesley. The Vindico. 2013. (ENG.). 320p. (YA). (gr. 7). pap. 8.99 *(978-0-14-242656-2(3)*, Speak) Penguin Young Readers Group.

Korman, Gordon. The Abduction, Bk. 1. 2006. (Kidnapped Ser.: 1). (ENG.). (J). (gr. 3-7). audio compact disk 39.95 *(978-0-439-89847-8(1))* Scholastic, Inc.

—The Medusa Plot. 2011. (39 Clues: Cahills vs. Vespers Ser.: 1). (ENG., Illus.). 224p. (J). (gr. 3-7). 12.99 *(978-0-545-32409-0(2)*, Scholastic Pr.); 12.99 *(978-0-545-29839-1(3))* Scholastic, Inc.

Krause, Ute. Nick & the Nasty Knight. 2012. (ENG., Illus.). 32p. (J). (gr. -1-3). 17.95 *(978-0-7358-4091-1(1))* North-South Bks., Inc.

Lago-Weed, Melissa. The Hairys: Don't Talk to Strangers. 2004. 33p. pap. 24.95 *(978-1-4137-3223-8(2))* PublishAmerica, Inc.

Laurel Associates. Kidnapped Study Guide: The Complete Adventures of David Balfour. 2006. (Classics Ser.). (Illus.). 48p. (YA). per. 17.95 *(978-1-56254-874-2(3))* Saddleback Educational Publishing, Inc.

Law, Jerel. Spirit Fighter, 1 vol. 2012. (Son of Angels, Jonah Stone Ser.). (ENG.). 256p. (J). pap. 9.99 *(978-1-4003-1843-8(2))* Nelson, Thomas Inc.

Leet, Karen M. Sarah's Courage: A Kentucky Frontier Kidnapping. 2014. (ENG., Illus.). 144p. (gr. 4-7). 14.99 *(978-1-62619-477-9(7)*, History Pr., The) Arcadia Publishing.

Leicht, Martin & Neal, Isla. The World Forgot. 2015. 279p. (YA). pap. *(978-1-4424-2967-3(4)*, Simon & Schuster Bks. For Young Readers) Simon & Schuster Bks. For Young Readers.

Leray, Merrill. The Kidnapping. 2009. 58p. pap. 15.99 *(978-1-4415-4380-6(5))* Xlibris Corp.

Leszczynski, Diana. Fern Verdant & the Silver Rose. 2009. (Playaway Children Ser.). (J). 59.99 *(978-1-4332-7708-5(5))* Findaway World, LLC.

Leveen, Tom. Shackled: The Truth Doesn't Always Set You Free. 2015. (ENG., Illus.). 224p. (YA). (gr. 9). 17.99 *(978-1-4814-2249-9(9)*, Simon Pulse) Simon Pulse.

Lewis, Gill. Gorilla Dawn. Meyer, Susan, illus. 2017. (J). pap. ***(978-1-4814-8658-3(6))*** Simon & Schuster Children's Publishing.

Lewis, Micahel G. Battle for the Knotty List, 1 vol. Jaskiel, Stan, illus. 2016. (ENG.). 32p. (J). (gr. k-8). 16.99 *(978-1-4556-2133-0(1))* Pelican Publishing Co., Inc.

Lim, Rebecca. Mercy (Mercy, Book 1) 2016. (Mercy Ser.: 1). (ENG.). 288p. (J). pap. 9.99 *(978-0-00-816903-9(9)*, HarperCollins Children's Bks.) HarperCollins Pubs. Ltd. GBR. Dist: HarperCollins Pubs.

Lin, Grace. When the Sea Turned to Silver. (ENG.). (J). (gr. 3-7). 2017. 400p. pap. 9.99 ***(978-0-316-12594-9(6))*** 2016. (Illus.). 384p. 18.99 *(978-0-316-12592-5(X))* Little, Brown Bks. for Young Readers.

—When the Sea Turned to Silver. 2017. (J). lib. bdg. 20.85 ***(978-0-606-40629-1(8))*** Turtleback Bks.

Littke, Lael. Searching for Selene. 2003. 203p. (J). pap. 13.95 *(978-1-59038-179-3(3))* Deseret Bk. Co.

Littlewood, Kathryn. Bite-Sized Magic: A Bliss Novel. McGuire, Erin, illus. (Bliss Bakery Trilogy Ser.: 3). (ENG.). 432p. (J). (gr. 3-7). 2015. pap. 7.99 *(978-0-06-208427-9(5))* 2014. 16.99 *(978-0-06-208426-2(7))* HarperCollins Pubs. (Tegen, Katherine Bks).

Livingston, Lesley. The Valiant. 2017. (ENG.). 384p. (YA). (gr. 7). 17.99 *(978-0-448-49378-7(0)*, Razorbill) Penguin Young Readers Group.

Lo, Malinda. Inheritance. 2014. (ENG.). 480p. (YA). (gr. 10-17). pap. 25.99 *(978-0-316-19799-1(8))* Little, Brown Bks. for Young Readers.

Locke, Terry. Spencer Hurley & the Aliens: Book One: the Abduction, Vol. 1. Hucks, Robin, ed. Locke, Terry, illus. 2008. (Spencer Hurley & the Aliens Ser.: 1). (Illus.). 256p. (J). per. 8.99 *(978-0-9786940-1-2(5))* Dream Workshop Publishing Co., LLC, The.

Lockwood, Vicki. The Magnificent Lizzie Brown & the Fairy Child. Hans, Stephanie, illus. 2015. (Magnificent Lizzie Brown Ser.). (ENG.). 200p. (gr. 5-9). 10.95 *(978-1-62370-210-6(0))* Stone Arch Bks.

Long, Angela Pullam. Salvador the Spy in the Case of the Missing Cats. 2008. 32p. pap. 24.95 *(978-1-60672-724-9(9))* America Star Bks.

Lord, Gabrielle. Revenge. 2012. (Illus.). 193p. (J). *(978-1-61067-082-1(5))* Kane Miller.

Lovelady, W. f. The Adventures of Johnny Saturday: Back to the Drawing Board. 2012. 76p. pap. 12.95 *(978-1-4685-5286-7(4))* AuthorHouse.

Lynne, Kimberlee, illus. The Frog & the Mouse. 2011. (First Steps in Music Ser.). (ENG.). 32p. (J). (gr. k-2). 16.95 *(978-1-57999-802-8(X))* G I A Pubns., Inc.

Lyons, C. J. Watched. 2014. (ENG.). 320p. (YA). (gr. 8-12). 16.99 *(978-1-4022-8548-6(5)*, 9781402285486) Sourcebooks, Inc.

Mabbitt, Will. Mabel Jones & the Forbidden City. Collins, Ross, illus. 2016. (Mabel Jones Ser.). (ENG.). 304p. (J). (gr. 3-7). 16.99 *(978-0-451-47197-0(0)*, Viking Books for Young Readers) Penguin Young Readers Group.

—The Unlikely Adventures of Mabel Jones. Collins, Ross, illus. 2015. (Mabel Jones Ser.). (ENG.). 304p. (J). (gr. 3-7). 16.99 *(978-0-451-47196-3(2)*, Viking Books for Young Readers) Penguin Young Readers Group.

—The Unlikely Adventures of Mabel Jones. 2016. lib. bdg. 19.65 *(978-0-606-38422-3(7))* Turtleback Bks.

MacDonald, George. The Wise Woman. 2009. 128p. 23.95 *(978-1-60664-614-4(1))*; pap. 10.95 *(978-1-60664-352-5(5))* Rodgers, Alan Bks.

MacGregor, Roy. The Kindergarten Caper: The Screech Owls Prequel. 2008. (ENG.). 144p. (YA). (gr. 3-7). mass mkt. 6.99 *(978-0-7710-5608-6(7)*, Screech Owls) McClelland & Stewart CAN. Dist: Penguin Random Hse. LLC.

Mahoney, Karen. The Iron Witch. 2011. (Iron Witch Ser.: 1). (ENG.). 312p. (YA). (gr. 7-18). pap. 9.95 *(978-0-7387-2582-6(X)*, Flux) North Star Editions.

Mark, Yudel. The Jewish Pope: A Yiddish Tale. Goodman, Ruth Fisher, tr. from YID. Krupin, Connie G., illus. 2015. (ENG.). 100p. per. 14.95 *(978-1-56474-459-3(0)*, Fithian Pr) Daniel & Daniel, Pubs., Inc.

Marko, Cyndi. Heroes on the Side. Marko, Cyndi, illus. 2014. (Kung Pow Chicken Ser.: 4). (ENG., Illus.). 80p. (J). (gr. k-2). 15.99 *(978-0-545-61077-3(X))*; pap. 4.99 *(978-0-545-61074-2(5))* Scholastic, Inc.

—Heroes on the Side. 2014. (Kung Pow Chicken Ser.: 4). lib. bdg. 14.75 *(978-0-606-36049-4(2))* Turtleback Bks.

Martens, Kara. The Two Missing Kids. 2008. 80p. pap. 11.49 *(978-1-4343-8696-0(1))* AuthorHouse.

Martin, J. Marshall. The Bird. 2008. 88p. pap. 12.50 *(978-0-9801224-1-1(4))* Boys Read Bks.

Massey, David. Taken. 2014. 311p. (YA). *(978-0-545-66129-4(3))*; (ENG.). 320p. (J). (gr. 9). 18.99 *(978-0-545-66128-7(5)*, Chicken Hse., The) Scholastic, Inc.

Mathieu, Jennifer. Afterward. 2016. (ENG.). 320p. (YA). 17.99 *(978-1-62672-238-5(2)*, 9781626722385) Roaring Brook Pr.

—Afterward. 2017. (ENG.). 336p. (YA). pap. 9.99 ***(978-1-250-12962-8(1)***, 9781250129628) Square Fish.

—Afterward. 2017. (YA). lib. bdg. 20.85 ***(978-0-606-40590-4(9))*** Turtleback Bks.

Mazer, Norma Fox. The Missing Girl. 2010. (ENG.). 304p. (YA). (gr. 8). pap. 8.99 *(978-0-06-447365-1(1)*, HarperTeen) HarperCollins Pubs.

McBride, Kristina. The Tension of Opposites. 2011. (ENG.). 288p. (J). (gr. 9). pap. 8.99 *(978-1-60684-213-3(7)*, Carolrhoda Lab™) Lerner Publishing Group.

McCabe, James Dabney, Jr. Planting the Wilderness or, the Pioneer Boys: a Story of Frontier Life. 2007. pap. 27.95 *(978-1-4304-8187-4(0))* Kessinger Publishing, LLC.

McIsaac, Meaghan. The Boys of Fire & Ash. 2015. (ENG.). 336p. (J). (gr. 5). 19.99 *(978-0-375-99167-7(0)*, Delacorte Bks. for Young Readers) Random Hse. Children's Bks.

McKay, Sharon E. & Lafrance, Daniel. War Brothers: The Graphic Novel. Lafrance, Daniel, illus. 2013. (ENG., Illus.). 176p. (YA). (gr. 9-12). 2nd ed. 27.95 *(978-1-55451-489-2(4)*, 9781554514892) 3rd ed. pap. 18.95 *(978-1-55451-488-5(6)*,

9781554514885) Annick Pr., Ltd. CAN. Dist: Publishers Group West (PGW).
McMann, Lisa. Dead to You. 2012. (ENG.). (YA). (gr. 9). 272p. pap. 10.99 *(978-1-4424-0389-5(6))*; 256p. 16.99 *(978-1-4424-0388-8(8))* Simon Pulse. (Simon Pulse).
McNeil, Natalie. Wylli Nilly's Amazing Adventures. 2011. (Illus.). 56p. pap. 20.38 *(978-1-4567-7672-5(X))* AuthorHouse.
McQuestion, Karen. Favorite, 0 vols. unabr. ed. 2011. (ENG.). 172p. (gr. 7-9). pap. 9.95 *(978-1-935597-25-4(6)*, 9781935597254, Skyscape) Amazon Publishing.
Meade, L. T. Sue A Little Heroine. 2007. (ENG.). 222p. pap. 20.99 *(978-1-4346-3546-4(5))*; 244p. pap. 22.99 *(978-1-4346-3547-1(3))* Creative Media Partners, LLC.
Meadows, Daisy. Mara the Meerkat Fairy: A Rainbow Magic Book. 2015. (Baby Animal Rescue Fairies Ser.: 3). (ENG.). 80p. (J). (gr. 2-5). pap. 4.99 *(978-0-545-70850-0(8)*, Scholastic Paperbacks) Scholastic, Inc.
—Nora the Arctic Fox Fairy. 2015. (Baby Animal Rescue Fairies Ser.: 7). (ENG.). 80p. (J). (gr. 2-5). pap. 4.99 *(978-0-545-70856-2(7)*, Scholastic Paperbacks) Scholastic, Inc.
Mellon, David. Silent. 2017. (ENG.). 320p. (YA). (gr. 9-12). 17.99 *(978-1-5072-0168-8(0)*, Simon Pulse) Simon Pulse.
Merialdo, Lee K. Kidnapped. 2006. 112p. pap. 10.95 *(978-0-7414-3407-4(5))* Infinity Publishing.
Methods, Bryan. The Shanghai Incident. 2017. (Master Diplexito & Mr. Scant Ser.). (ENG.). 264p. (J). (gr. 5-8). 17.99 ***(978-1-5124-0580-4(9)***, Carolrhoda Bks.) Lerner Publishing Group.
Meyer, L. A. In the Belly of the Bloodhound: Being an Account of a Particularly Peculiar Adventure in the Life of Jacky Faber. 2008. (Bloody Jack Adventures Ser.: 4). (ENG., Illus.). 528p. (YA). (gr. 7-12). pap. 7.95 *(978-0-15-206166-1(5))* Houghton Mifflin Harcourt Publishing Co.
—Rapture of the Deep: Being an Account of the Further Adventures of Jacky Faber, Soldier, Sailor, Mermaid, Spy. (Bloody Jack Adventures Ser.: 7). (ENG.). 464p. (YA). (gr. 9). 2011. pap. 9.99 *(978-0-547-55120-3(7))* 2009. (Illus.). 17.00 *(978-0-15-206501-0(6))* Houghton Mifflin Harcourt Publishing Co.
Miller, Daniel, et al. A Miller Cousin Mystery. 2010. 120p. pap. 49.00 *(978-0-557-57235-9(5))*; pap. 17.80 *(978-0-557-57118-5(9))* Lulu Pr., Inc.
Millman, Selena. More Than a Hero. 2006. 92p. (YA). per. 11.37 *(978-1-4243-2351-7(7))* Independent Publisher Services.
Miranda, Megan. The Safest Lies. (ENG.). 368p. (YA). (gr. 9). 2017. pap. 9.99 ***(978-0-553-53754-3(7)***, Ember) 2016. 17.99 *(978-0-553-53751-2(2)*, Crown Books For Young Readers) Random Hse. Children's Bks.
Mohr, L. C. Krumbuckets. Musheno, Erica, illus. 2007. (ENG.). 144p. (J). (gr. 2-7). 13.95 *(978-0-9769417-6-7(7))* Blooming Tree Pr.
Moldavsky, Goldy. Kill the Boy Band. (ENG.). 320p. (J). (gr. 9). 2017. pap. 9.99 *(978-0-545-86750-4(9))* 2016. 17.99 *(978-0-545-86747-4(9))* Scholastic, Inc.
—Kill the Boy Band. 2017. lib. bdg. 20.85 ***(978-0-606-39701-8(9))*** Turtleback Bks.
Monaghan, Annabel. A Girl Named Digit: Under Cover, under Pressure, under Estimated. 2013. (ENG.). 192p. (YA). (gr. 7). pap. 8.99 *(978-0-544-02248-5(3))* Houghton Mifflin Harcourt Publishing Co.
Moser, Elise. Lily & Taylor. 2013. (ENG.). 224p. E-Book *(978-1-55498-336-0(3))* Groundwood Bks.
—Lily & Taylor, 1 vol. 2013. (ENG.). 224p. (J). (gr. 8). 16.95 *(978-1-55498-334-6(7))* Groundwood Bks. CAN. Dist: Publishers Group West (PGW).
Mulazzi, Paola, et al. Disney Fairies Graphic Novel #4: Tinker Bell to the Rescue. Urbano, Emilio et al, illus. 2010. (Disney Fairies Ser.: 4). (ENG.). 80p. (J). (gr. 1-6). 12.99 *(978-1-59707-230-4(3))*; pap. 7.99 *(978-1-59707-200-7(1)*, 9781597072007) Papercutz.
Napoli, Donna Jo. Lights on the Nile. 2011. (ENG.). 288p. (J). (gr. 3-7). 16.99 *(978-0-06-166793-0(5))* HarperCollins Pubs.
—Three Days. 2003. (ENG., Illus.). 160p. (J). (gr. 5-18). pap. 5.99 *(978-0-14-250025-5(9)*, Puffin Books) Penguin Young Readers Group.
—Three Days. 2003. 151p. (J). (gr. 5-9). 13.65 *(978-0-7569-6313-2(3))* Perfection Learning Corp.
Naylor, Phyllis Reynolds. Emily & Jackson Hiding Out. (ENG.). 176p. (J). (gr. 2-5). 2013. 6.99 *(978-0-375-87185-6(3)*, Yearling) 2012. (Illus.). 14.99 *(978-0-385-74097-5(2)*, Delacorte Bks. for Young Readers) Random Hse. Children's Bks.
Neff, Henry H. The Hound of Rowan. 2008. (Tapestry Ser.: 1). (ENG., Illus.). 448p. (J). (gr. 3-7). 7.99 *(978-0-375-83895-8(3)*, Yearling) Random Hse. Children's Bks.
Nelson, James Gary. Dientecito y la Placa Peligros. Bumstead, Debbie, illus. 2011. 16p. pap. 9.95 *(978-1-61633-132-0(1))* Guardian Angel Publishing, Inc.
—Smileytooth & Bushwack Plaque. Bumstead, Debbie, illus. 2009. 16p. pap. 9.95 *(978-1-61633-009-5(0))* Guardian Angel Publishing, Inc.
Nixon, Joan Lowery. The Kidnapping of Christina Lattimore. 2004. (ENG.). 320p. (YA). (gr. 7-12). pap. 8.99 *(978-0-15-205031-3(0))* Houghton Mifflin Harcourt Publishing Co.
O'Hart, Sinead. Eye of the North. 2017. (ENG.). 352p. (J). (gr. 3-7). 16.99 *(978-1-101-93503-3(0)*, Knopf Bks. for Young Readers) Random Hse. Children's Bks.
Panitch, Amanda. Never Missing, Never Found. 2016. (ENG.). 320p. (YA). (gr. 9). 17.99 *(978-0-553-50764-5(8)*, Random Hse. Bks. for Young Readers) Random Hse. Children's Bks.
Paquette, Jessica E. Sophie the Clown in Crinkle Town. 2013. 258p. (gr. 4-6). 26.95 *(978-1-4759-7322-8(5))*; pap. 16.95 *(978-1-4759-7321-1(7))* iUniverse, Inc.
Park, Linda Sue. Trust No One. 2012. (39 Clues: Cahills vs. Vespers Ser.: Bk. 5). (ENG.). 192p. (J). (gr. 3-7). 12.99 *(978-0-545-32415-1(7))* Scholastic, Inc.
Parker, Robert B. Chasing the Bear. 2010. (ENG.). 176p. (YA). (gr. 7-18). 8.99 *(978-0-14-241573-3(1)*, Speak) Penguin Young Readers Group.
Parrish, Emma. Lou. 2010. 106p. pap. 15.95 *(978-1-4452-6573-5(7))* Lulu Pr., Inc.
Patterson, James. The Dangerous Days of Daniel X. 2014. lthr. 79.00 *(978-1-62715-506-9(6))* Leatherbound Bestsellers.
—The Dangerous Days of Daniel X. (Daniel X Ser.: 1). (ENG.). 2010. 272p. (J). (gr. 3-7). pap. 8.00 *(978-0-316-11970-2(9)*, Jimmy Patterson) 2008. 304p. pap. 20.99 *(978-0-316-03025-0(2))* Little Brown & Co.
—The Dangerous Days of Daniel X. 2010. (Daniel X Ser.: 1). (J). lib. bdg. 18.45 *(978-0-606-14720-0(9)*, Turtleback) Turtleback Bks.
—Maximum Ride. 2010. (ENG.). 1392p. (YA). (gr. 5-17). pap., pap. 29.99 *(978-0-316-12825-4(2)*, Jimmy Patterson) Little Brown & Co.
Patterson, James & Ledwidge, Michael. The Dangerous Days of Daniel X. 2009. (Daniel X Ser.: 1). (ENG.). 288p. mass mkt. 7.99 *(978-0-446-50913-8(2)*, Jimmy Patterson) Little Brown & Co.
Patton, Jack. The Cobra Clash (Battle Bugs #5) 2015. (Battle Bugs Ser.: 5). (ENG.). 128p. (J). (gr. 2-5). pap. 4.99 *(978-0-545-79124-3(3)*, Scholastic Pr.) Scholastic, Inc.
Paulsen, Gary. Woods Runner. 2011. (ENG.). 176p. (YA). (gr. 7). pap. 7.99 *(978-0-375-85908-3(X)*, Lamb, Wendy Bks.) Random Hse. Children's Bks.
Paulson, Elizabeth. Dead upon a Time. 2015. (ENG.). 224p. (J). (gr. 7). 17.99 *(978-0-545-64046-6(6)*, Scholastic Pr.) Scholastic, Inc.
Paulson, Ingrid. Valkyrie Rising. 2012. (Valkyrie Rising Ser.). (ENG.). 352p. (YA). (gr. 8). 17.99 *(978-0-06-202572-2(4)*, HarperTeen) HarperCollins Pubs.
Pavanello, Roberto. The Midnight Witches, 1 vol. Zeni, Marco, tr. from ITA. Pisapia, Blasco & Brughera, Pamela, illus. 2012. (Echo & the Bat Pack Ser.). (ENG.). 128p. (gr. 2-3). 9.95 *(978-1-4342-4246-4(3))*; lib. bdg. 25.32 *(978-1-4342-3822-1(9)*, Echo & the Bat Pack) Stone Arch Bks.
Paver, Michelle. The Burning Shadow. 2015. (Gods & Warriors Ser.: 2). (ENG.). 320p. (J). (gr. 5). 7.99 *(978-0-14-242285-4(1)*, Puffin Books) Penguin Young Readers Group.
Perritano, John. The Snickerblooms & the Age Bug, 1 vol. Laughead, Mike, illus. 2014. (Kid Squad Saves the World Ser.). (ENG.). 112p. (J). (gr. 8-12). 27.07 *(978-1-62402-041-4(0))* Magic Wagon.
Peters, Tony. Kids on a Case: The Case of the Ten Grand Kidnapping. 2008. 84p. pap. 9.95 *(978-1-60693-173-8(3)*, Eloquent Bks.) Strategic Book Publishing & Rights Agency (SBPRA).
Phillips, Grant R. Jay Walker & the Case of the Missing Action Figure. 2004. (J). pap. 10.95 *(978-0-9749608-4-5(5))* Quiet Storm Publishing Group.
Pierce, Tamora. Mastiff. 2012. (Beka Cooper Ser.). (ENG.). 608p. (YA). (gr. 7-11). pap. 10.99 *(978-0-375-83818-7(X)*, Ember) Random Hse. Children's Bks.
Plum, Amy. Until the Beginning. 2016. (After the End Ser.: 2). 352p. (YA). (gr. 8). pap. 9.99 *(978-0-06-222564-1(2)*, HarperTeen) HarperCollins Pubs.
Plum-Ucci, Carol. The Body of Christopher Creed. 2011. 8.98 *(978-0-7848-3578-4(0)*, Everbind) Marco Bk. Co.
Pollock, Tom. The Glass Republic. 2016. (Skyscraper Throne Ser.: 2). (ENG.). 448p. (YA). (gr. 7-9). pap. 14.99 *(978-1-68144-348-5(1)*, Jo Fletcher Books) Quercus NA.
Poole, Richard. Jewel & Thorn. 2007. (Book of Lowmoor Ser.: 1). (ENG., Illus.). 400p. (J). (gr. 7-12). pap. 11.95 *(978-0-689-87290-7(9))* Simon & Schuster, Ltd. GBR. Dist: Simon & Schuster, Inc.
Porter, Kevin Don. Missing. 2013. 166p. pap. 11.99 *(978-0-9857014-7-5(1))* Artists' Orchard, LLC, The.
Prasad, Sunayna. Alyssa Mccarthy's Magical Missions: Book 1. 2013. 216p. pap. *(978-1-4602-0701-7(7))* FriesenPress.
Preston, Natasha. The Cellar. 2014. (ENG.). 368p. (YA). (gr. 10-12). pap. 9.99 *(978-1-4926-0097-8(0)*, 9781492600978) Sourcebooks, Inc.
Prophet, John M. Body in the Salt Marsh Boatyard: A Casey Miller Mystery. 2004. 162p. (YA). pap. 13.95 *(978-0-595-30991-7(7)*, Mystery & Suspense Pr.) iUniverse, Inc.
Pullman, Philip. Der goldene Kompass. (GER.). pap. 27.95 *(978-3-453-13744-8(2))* Verlag Wilhelm Heyne DEU. Dist: Distribooks, Inc.
Pyle, Howard. The Story of Jack Ballister's Fortunes: Being the Narrative of the Adventures of a Young Gentleman of Good Family, Who Was Kidnapped in the Year 1719 & Carried to the Plantations of the Continent of Virginia, Where He Fell in with That Famous Pirate Captain Edward Teach, or Blackbeard: of His Escape from the Pirates & the Rescue of a Young Lady from Out Their Hands. unabr. ed. 2012. (Illus.). 436p. 49.99 *(978-1-4622-8858-8(8))* Repressed Publishing LLC.
Raffa, Edwina & Rigsby, Annelle. Kidnapped in Key West. (Florida Historical Fiction for Youth Ser.). (ENG.). (J). 2012. 138p. pap. 9.95 *(978-1-56164-537-4(0))* 2008. (Illus.). 127p. (gr. 3-7). 14.95 *(978-1-56164-413-1(7))* Pineapple Pr., Inc.
Rainfield, Cheryl. Stained. 2013. (ENG.). 304p. (YA). (gr. 9). 16.99 *(978-0-547-94208-7(7))* Houghton Mifflin Harcourt Publishing Co.
Ramage, Rosalyn Rikel. The Windmill. 2013. 182p. (gr. 4-6). pap. 11.66 *(978-1-4907-0909-3(6))* Trafford Publishing.
Rapp, Adam. The Children & the Wolves. Ering, Timothy Basil, illus. 2012. (ENG.). 160p. (YA). (gr. 9). 16.99 *(978-0-7636-5337-8(3))* Candlewick Pr.
Rautenberg, Karen Rita. Lady Lucy's Gallant Knight. 2007. (ENG.). 156p. (J). (gr. 4-7). per. *(978-1-933255-22-4(6))* DNA Pr.
Redwine, C. J. Deliverance. 2014. (Defiance Trilogy Ser.: 3). (ENG.). 480p. (YA). (gr. 8). 17.99 *(978-0-06-211723-6(8))* HarperCollins Pubs.
Regan, Dian. Space Boy & the Space Pirate. Neubecker, Robert, illus. 2016. (Space Boy Ser.). (ENG.). 40p. (J). (gr. k-5). 16.95 *(978-1-59078-956-8(3))* Boyds Mills Pr.
Reiss, Kathryn. A Bundle of Trouble: A Rebecca Mystery. Giovine, Sergio, illus. 2011. (ENG.). 192p. (YA). (gr. 4-18). pap. 6.95 *(978-1-59369-754-9(6))* American Girl Publishing, Inc.
—The Strange Case of Baby H. 2009. (Mysteries Through Time Ser.). 144 - 176p. (YA). (gr. 4-8). 31.95 *(978-1-60754-423-4(7))*; pap. 15.25 *(978-1-60754-424-1(5))* Windmill Bks.
Revealed. 2014. (Missing Ser.: 7). (ENG., Illus.). 448p. (J). (gr. 3-7). 18.99 *(978-1-4169-8986-8(2)*, Simon & Schuster Bks. For Young Readers) Simon & Schuster Bks. For Young Readers.
Richard, Laurent. The Championship! Gauvin, Edward, tr. Ryser, Nicolas, illus. 2014. (ENG.). 64p. (J). (gr. 2-5). pap. 6.95 *(978-1-4677-4459-1(X))*; (Tao, the Little Samurai Ser.: 4). lib. bdg. 29.27 *(978-1-4677-2097-7(6))* Lerner Publishing Group. (Graphic Universe™).
Rifkin, L. (Lauren). The Nine Lives of Romeo Crumb: Life Two. 2010. 277p. (J). pap. 8.95 *(978-0-9743221-4-8(8))* Sunrise Publishing Co.
Rivera, Raquel. Orphan Ahwak, 1 vol. 2007. (ENG.). 144p. (J). (gr. 4-8). per. 7.95 *(978-1-55143-653-1(1))* Orca Bk. Pubs. USA.
Roberts, Willo Davis. Baby-Sitting Is a Dangerous Job. 2016. (ENG., Illus.). 224p. (J). (gr. 3-7). pap. 6.99 *(978-1-4814-3704-2(6)*, Aladdin) Simon & Schuster Children's Publishing.
—Baby-Sitting Is a Dangerous Job. 2016. (ENG., Illus.). 224p. (J). (gr. 3-7). 17.99 *(978-1-4814-3705-9(4)*, Simon & Schuster/Paula Wiseman Bks.) Simon & Schuster/Paula Wiseman Bks.
—Hostage. 2016. (ENG., Illus.). 176p. (J). (gr. 3-7). pap. 6.99 *(978-1-4814-5788-0(8)*, Aladdin) Simon & Schuster Children's Publishing.
—Hostage. 2016. (ENG., Illus.). 176p. (J). (gr. 3-7). 17.99 *(978-1-4814-5789-7(6)*, Simon & Schuster/Paula Wiseman Bks.) Simon & Schuster/Paula Wiseman Bks.
—The Kidnappers. 2016. (ENG., Illus.). 208p. (J). (gr. 3-7). pap. 6.99 *(978-1-4814-4904-5(4)*, Aladdin) Simon & Schuster Children's Publishing.
—The One Left Behind. 2007. (ENG., Illus.). 144p. (J). (gr. 3-7). pap. 7.99 *(978-0-689-85083-7(2)*, Aladdin) Simon & Schuster Children's Publishing.
—Scared Stiff. 2016. (ENG., Illus.). 256p. (J). (gr. 3-7). pap. 7.99 *(978-1-4814-4910-6(9)*, Aladdin) Simon & Schuster Children's Publishing.
Robinson, W. Heath. The Adventures of Uncle Lubin. 2013. (Dover Children's Classics Ser.). (ENG., Illus.). 128p. (J). (gr. 6-8). pap. 9.95 *(978-0-486-49821-8(2))* Dover Pubns., Inc.
Rocha, K. E. Mission to Moon Farm. 2016. (J). *(978-0-545-81316-7(6)*, Scholastic Pr.) Scholastic, Inc.
—Mission to Moon Farm (Secrets of Bearhaven #2) 2016. (Secrets of Bearhaven Ser.: 2). (ENG.). 224p. (J). (gr. 3-7). 14.99 *(978-0-545-81304-4(2)*, Scholastic Pr.) Scholastic, Inc.
Rodriguez, Angelica. Mia y Primos/Mia & Cousins: Yo grito,corro y grito / I scream, run & Scream. 2009. 24p. pap. 12.49 *(978-1-4389-7095-0(1))* AuthorHouse.
Roscoe, Charlie. The Red Prince. Cole, Tom Clohosy, illus. 2016. (ENG.). 32p. (J). (-k). 16.99 *(978-0-7636-8912-4(2)*, Templar) Candlewick Pr.
Round, J. The Catcher. 2008. 168p. pap. 14.95 *(978-1-4092-0372-8(7))* Lulu Pr., Inc.
Roy, Ron. Capital Mysteries #13: Trapped on the D. C. Train! Bush, Timothy, illus. 2011. (Capital Mysteries Ser.). (ENG.). 96p. (J). (gr. 1-4). 4.99 *(978-0-375-85926-7(8)*, Random Hse. Bks. for Young Readers) Random Hse. Children's Bks.
—White House White-Out. Gurney, John Steven, illus. 2008. (A to Z Mysteries Ser.: No. 3). 124p. (gr. 1-4). 15.00 *(978-0-7569-8799-2(7))* Perfection Learning Corp.
—White House White-Out. Gurney, John Steven, illus. 2008. (to Z Mysteries Ser.: 3). (ENG.). 144p. (J). (gr. 1-4). 5.99 *(978-0-375-84721-9(9)*, Random Hse. Bks. for Young Readers) Random Hse. Children's Bks.
Ruby, Laura. Bone Gap. 368p. (YA). (gr. 9). 2016. pap. 9.99 *(978-0-06-231762-9(8))* 2015. (ENG.). 17.99 *(978-0-06-231760-5(1))* HarperCollins Pubs.
—Bone Gap. 2016. (YA). lib. bdg. 20.85 *(978-0-606-38739-2(0))* Turtleback Bks.
Runholt, Susan. Rescuing Seneca Crane. 2009. (Kari & Lucas Mystery Ser.). (ENG.). 288p. (J). (gr. 5-18). 16.99 *(978-0-670-06291-1(X)*, Viking Books for Young Readers) Penguin Young Readers Group.
Ryan, Darlene & Fernández, Queta. De Nadie Mas, 1 vol. 2008. (Spanish Soundings Ser.). (SPA.). 112p. (YA). (gr. 8-12). pap. 9.95 *(978-1-55143-969-3(7))* Orca Bk. Pubs. USA.
Saddleback Educational Publishing Staff, ed. Ransom, 1 vol. 2013. (Heights Ser.). (ENG.). 52p. (gr. 5-8). 7.95 *(978-1-62250-047-5(4))* Saddleback Educational Publishing, Inc.
—Score, 1 vol. unabr. ed. 2011. (Heights Ser.). (ENG.). 50p. (gr. 5-8). 7.95 *(978-1-61651-624-6(0))* Saddleback Educational Publishing, Inc.
—Swamp, 1 vol. unabr. ed. 2011. (Heights Ser.). (ENG.). 49p. (gr. 5-8). 7.95 *(978-1-61651-625-3(9))* Saddleback Educational Publishing, Inc.
Saedi, Sara. Never Ever. 2016. (ENG.). 320p. (YA). (gr. 7). 17.99 *(978-0-451-47576-3(3)*, Viking Books for Young Readers) Penguin Young Readers Group.
Sage, Angie. Septimus Heap - Todhunter Moon. Zug, Mark, illus. 2014. (World of Septimus Heap Ser.: 1). (ENG.). 480p. (J). (gr. 3-7). 17.99 *(978-0-06-227245-4(4)*, Tegen, Katherine Bks) HarperCollins Pubs.
Samphire, Patrick. Secrets of the Dragon Tomb. Holmes, Jeremy, illus. 2016. (ENG.). 336p. (J). (gr. 5-8). 16.99 *(978-0-8050-9906-5(9)*, 9780805099065, Holt, Henry & Co. Bks. For Young Readers) Holt, Henry & Co.
—Secrets of the Dragon Tomb. 2017. (J). lib. bdg. 18.40 ***(978-0-606-39941-8(0))*** Turtleback Bks.
Sandler, Karen. Rebellion, 1 vol. 2014. (Tankborn Trilogy Ser.). (ENG.). 400p. (YA). 18.95 *(978-1-60060-984-8(8))* Lee & Low Bks., Inc.
Savage, Kim. After the Woods. 2016. (ENG.). 304p. (YA). 17.99 *(978-0-374-30055-5(0)*, 9780374300555, Farrar, Straus & Giroux (BYR)) Farrar, Straus & Giroux.
Schlitz, Laura Amy. Splendors & Glooms. (ENG.). 400p. (J). 2014. (gr. 5-9). pap. 8.99 *(978-0-7636-6926-3(1))* 2012. (Illus.). (gr. 4-7). 17.99 *(978-0-7636-5380-4(2))* Candlewick Pr.
—Splendors & Glooms. 2014. (ENG.). (J). (gr. 4-7). lib. bdg. 18.60 ***(978-1-62765-443-2(7))*** Perfection Learning Corp.
—Splendors & Glooms. 2014. lib. bdg. 18.40 *(978-0-606-35170-6(1))* Turtleback Bks.
Scholastic, Inc. Staff. Cahills vs Vespers, Pack. 2011. (39 Clues: Cahills vs. Vespers Ser.). (ENG.). 16p. (J). (gr. 3-7). 6.99 *(978-0-545-31640-8(5))* Scholastic, Inc.
Schroeder, Lisa. The Girl in the Tower. Ceccoli, Nicoletta, illus. 2016. (ENG.). 256p. (J). 16.99 *(978-0-8050-9513-5(6)*, 9780805095135, Holt, Henry & Co. Bks. For Young Readers) Holt, Henry & Co.
Sclafani, Terry. The Thompson Twins Cruise Adventure. 2007. 84p. per. 10.95 *(978-1-4327-1542-7(9))* Outskirts Pr., Inc.
Scott, Elizabeth. Living Dead Girl. 2009. (ENG.). 176p. (YA). (gr. 10). pap. 10.99 *(978-1-4169-6060-7(0)*, Simon Pulse) Simon Pulse.
Seifert, Brandon. Disney Kingdoms: Seekers of the Weird. 2014. (ENG., Illus.). 120p. (J). (gr. -1-17). 24.99 *(978-0-7851-5452-5(3))* Marvel Worldwide, Inc.
Service, Pamela F. Alien Encounter. Gorman, Mike, illus. (Alien Agent Ser.: 4). (ENG.). 152p. (J). (gr. 4-6). 2011. pap. 5.95 *(978-0-7613-5248-8(1))* 2010. 16.95 *(978-0-8225-8873-3(0)*, Carolrhoda Bks.) Lerner Publishing Group.
—Alien Expedition. 2010. pap. 33.92 *(978-0-7613-6958-5(9))* Lerner Publishing Group.
—Alien Expedition. Gorman, Mike, illus. (Alien Agent Ser.: 3). (ENG.). 160p. (J). (gr. 4-6). 2009. 16.95 *(978-0-8225-8870-2(6))*No. 3. 2010. pap. 5.95 *(978-0-7613-5249-5(X))* Lerner Publishing Group. (Carolrhoda Bks.).
—Escape from Planet Yastol. Gorman, Mike, illus. (Way-Too-Real Aliens Ser.: 1). (ENG.). 112p. (J). (gr. 4-6). 2015. 34.65 *(978-1-4677-5960-1(0)*, Lerner Digital)No. 1. 2011. 15.95 *(978-0-7613-7918-8(5)*, Darby Creek)No. 1. 2011. pap. 5.95 *(978-0-7613-7921-8(5)*, Darby Creek) Lerner Publishing Group.
—#4 Alien Encounter. Gorman, Mike, illus. 2011. (Alien Agent Ser.). 152p. (J). pap. 33.92 *(978-0-7613-7608-8(9)*, Darby Creek) Lerner Publishing Group.
Shackelford, Mary. Cinnamon's Quest. 2005. 115p. pap. 19.95 *(978-1-4137-6430-7(4))* America Star Bks.
Sheinmel, Courtney. Twinsanity. Bell, Jennifer A., illus. 2017. (Zacktastic Ser.). (ENG.). 272p. (J). (gr. 2-4). 11.99 ***(978-1-58536-936-2(5)***, 204319); pap. 6.99 ***(978-1-58536-937-9(3)***, 204333) Sleeping Bear Pr.
Sherrard, Valerie. Eyes of a Stalker. 2006. (ENG.). 180p. (YA). (gr. 6). pap. 12.99 *(978-1-55002-643-6(7)*, Boardwalk Bks.) Dundurn CAN. Dist: Ingram Publisher Services.
Shreve, Susan. The Search for Baby Ruby. 2015. 213p. (J). pap. *(978-0-545-41784-6(8))* Scholastic, Inc.
Skuse, C. J. Rockoholic. 2012. (YA). *(978-0-545-44251-0(6))*; (ENG.). 368p. (J). (gr. 9). 18.99 *(978-0-545-42960-3(9))* Scholastic, Inc.
Skye, Lucy. The Adventure of Maisie Voyager. 2012. (ENG.). 240p. (J). pap. 15.95 *(978-1-84905-287-0(5)*, 4927) Kingsley, Jessica Pubs. GBR. Dist: Macmillan Distribution Ltd.
Slade, Mark. A Week of Mushrooming Book One. 2013. 88p. pap. 8.00 *(978-1-927558-14-0(X))* Birch Tree Publishing.
Smith, Andrew. The Marbury Lens. 2010. (ENG.). 368p. (YA). (gr. 9-12). 17.99 *(978-0-312-61342-6(3)*, 9780312613426) Feiwel & Friends.
Smith, Cynthia Leitich. Feral Pride. 2015. (ENG.). 304p. (YA). (gr. 9). 17.99 *(978-0-7636-5911-0(8))* Candlewick Pr.
Smith, Dan. Boy X. 2017. (J). ***(978-1-338-17150-1(X))***; (ENG.). 288p. (gr. 3-7). 16.99 *(978-1-338-06564-0(5)*, Chicken Hse., The) Scholastic, Inc.
Smith, Greg Leitich. Chronal Engine. Henry, Blake, illus. 2013. (ENG.). 192p. (J). (gr. 5-7). pap. 6.99 *(978-0-544-02277-5(7))* Houghton Mifflin Harcourt Publishing Co.
Smith, Roland. Jack's Run. 2007. (ENG.). 256p. (J). (gr. 5-17). pap. 6.99 *(978-1-4231-0407-0(2))* Hyperion Pr.
Smith, Sherri L. The Toymaker's Apprentice. 2015. (ENG., Illus.). 400p. (J). (gr. 5). 16.99 *(978-0-399-25295-2(9)*, G.P. Putnam's Sons Books for Young Readers) Penguin Young Readers Group.
Snyder, Zilpha Keatley. The Famous Stanley Kidnapping Case. 2012. (Stanley Family Ser.). (ENG.). 216p. (J). (gr. 3-7). pap. 10.99 *(978-1-4424-8446-7(2)*, Atheneum Bks. for Young Readers) Simon & Schuster Children's Publishing.
Springer, Nancy. The Case of the Left-Handed Lady. 2008. (Enola Holmes Mystery Ser.: 2). (ENG.). 256p. (J). (gr. 5-7). 7.99 *(978-0-14-241190-2(6)*, Puffin Books) Penguin Young Readers Group.
—Somebody. 2009. (ENG.). 128p. (YA). (gr. 7-18). 16.95 *(978-0-8234-2099-5(X))* Holiday Hse., Inc.
Staunton, Ted. Coda, 1 vol. 2014. (Seven Sequels Ser.). (ENG., Illus.). 224p. (J). (gr. 5-10). pap. 10.95 *(978-1-4598-0549-1(6))* Orca Bk. Pubs. USA.
Stevenson, Robert Louis. Kidnapped. Kennedy, Cam, illus. 2007. (ENG.). 64p. (YA). (gr. 5). pap. 11.95 *(978-0-88776-843-9(1)*, Tundra Bks.) Tundra Bks. CAN. Dist: Penguin Random Hse. LLC.
—Kidnapped. 2006. (Classics Ser.). (Illus.). 80p. (YA). (gr. 4-7). per. 8.95 *(978-1-56254-873-5(5))* Saddleback Educational Publishing, Inc.
—Kidnapped & Catriona. 2007. (ENG.). 496p. per. *(978-1-84697-033-7(4))* Birlinn, Ltd.
—Secuestrado. 3rd ed. (Coleccion Clasicos en Accion).Tr. of Kidnapped. (SPA., Illus.). 80p. (YA). (gr. 5-8). 15.95 *(978-84-241-5781-4(8)*, EV1487) Everest Editora ESP. Dist: Lectorum Pubns., Inc.
Stewart, Dianne C. Season of the Cold Moon. 2011. (ENG.). 108p. (J). (gr. 2). pap. 8.95 *(978-0-9831032-0-2(8)*, BeanPole Bks.) Harren Communications, LLC.
Stewart, E. J. The Wayfaring Dolphin. 2010. 298p. pap. 16.95 *(978-0-557-33701-9(1))* Lulu Pr., Inc.
Stilton, Geronimo & Stilton, Thea. Thea Stilton & the Secret of the Old Castle. 2012. (Thea Stilton Ser.: 10). (ENG., Illus.). 176p. (J). (gr. 2-5). pap. 8.99 *(978-0-545-34107-3(8)*, Scholastic Paperbacks) Scholastic, Inc.
Stilton, Thea. Thea Stilton & the Journey to the Lion's Den. 2013. (Thea Stilton Ser.: 17). (ENG.). 176p. (J). (gr. 2-5). pap. 8.99 *(978-0-545-55627-9(9)*, Scholastic Paperbacks) Scholastic, Inc.
—Thea Stilton & the Secret of the Old Castle. 2012. (Thea Stilton Ser.: 10). lib. bdg. 19.65 *(978-0-606-23930-1(8)*, Turtleback) Turtleback Bks.
Stokes, Jonathan W. Addison Cooke & the Treasure of the Incas. 2016. (Addison Cooke Ser.). (ENG., Illus.). 336p. (J).

(gr. 3-7). 16.99 (978-0-399-17377-6(3), Philomel Bks.) Penguin Young Readers Group.
Strasser, Todd. Wish You Were Dead. (ENG.). 240p. (gr. 9). 2010. (J). pap. 8.99 (978-1-60684-138-9(6)) 2009. 16.99 (978-1-60684-007-8(X)) Lerner Publishing Group. (Carolrhoda Lab™).
Stratton, Allan. Chanda's Wars. 2009. (ENG.). 416p. (YA). (gr. 8). pap. 8.99 (978-0-06-087265-6(9), HarperTeen) HarperCollins Pubs.
—Chanda's Wars. 2011. 10.36 (978-0-7848-3486-2(5), Everbind) Marco Bk. Co.
Strickler, Ashley. Once upon A Time. 2007. 212p. pap. 12.95 (978-1-4327-0207-6(6)) Outskirts Pr., Inc.
Surrisi, C. M. The Maypop Kidnapping. 2016. (Quinnie Boyd Mysteries Ser.: 1). (ENG.). 304p. (gr. 4-8). 35.99 (978-1-4677-9560-9(7)); (Illus.). (J). 17.99 (978-1-4677-5789-8(6)) Lerner Publishing Group. (Carolrhoda Bks.).
Sutcliffe, William. Concentr8. 2016. (ENG.). 256p. (YA). 17.99 (978-1-61963-919-5(X), 9781619639195, Bloomsbury USA Childrens) Bloomsbury Publishing USA.
Sutton, Laurie S. Legend of the Gator Man. Neely, Scott, illus. 2016. (Scooby-Doo Comic Chapter Bks.). (ENG.). 88p. (gr. 3-7). lib. bdg. 27.32 (978-1-4965-3584-9(7)) Capstone Press of Coughlan Cos.
Sylvester, Kevin. Neil Flambé & the Aztec Abduction. Sylvester, Kevin, illus. 2012. (Neil Flambe Capers Ser.: 2). (ENG., Illus.). 320p. (J). (gr. 3-7). 14.99 (978-1-4424-4607-6(2), Simon & Schuster Bks. For Young Readers) Simon & Schuster Bks. For Young Readers.
Sylvester, Kevin, illus. Neil Flambé & the Aztec Abduction. 2010. (Neil Flambé Capers Ser.: No. 2). 304p. (J). (gr. 4-7). (978-1-55470-329-6(8)) Me to We.
Tanner, Lian. City of Lies. 2012. (Keepers Trilogy: Bk. 2). (ENG.). 288p. (J). (gr. 4-7). 6.99 (978-0-375-85979-3(9), Yearling) Random Hse. Children's Bks.
Taylor, G. P. The Secret of Indigo Moon. 2009. (Dopple Ganger Chronicles Ser.: 2). (ENG., Illus.). 304p. (J). (gr. 3-7). 19.99 (978-1-4143-1948-3(7), SaltRiver) Tyndale Hse. Pubs.
Telmosse, Gerard. The Curse of the Sourlands. 2008. 132p. pap. 14.51 (978-1-4357-0169-4(0)) Lulu Pr., Inc.
Thompson, Mary G. Amy Chelsea Stacie Dee. 2016. (ENG.). 304p. (YA). (gr. 9). 17.99 (978-1-101-99680-5(3), G.P. Putnam's Sons Books for Young Readers) Penguin Young Readers Group.
Titus, Eve. Basil of Baker Street. Galdone, Paul, illus. 2016. (Great Mouse Detective Ser.: 1). (ENG.). 112p. (J). (gr. 1-4). 16.99 (978-1-4814-6402-4(7)); pap. 5.99 (978-1-4814-6401-7(9)) Simon & Schuster Children's Publishing. (Aladdin).
Torres, J. Titans Together. 2014. (ENG., Illus.). 144p. (J). (gr. 2-5). pap. 12.99 (978-1-4012-5367-7(9)) DC Comics.
Town, Vicky. Mayhem in the Museum. 2013. 74p. pap. 9.99 (978-1-61720-974-1(0)) Wilder Pubns., Corp.
Townsend, Kari. Fused. 2010. (ENG.). 208p. (J). (gr. 5-7). pap. 7.99 (978-1-4022-4042-3(2), Sourcebooks Jabberwocky) Sourcebooks, Inc.
Tozier, Christopher. Olivia Brophie & the Sky Island. 2014. (ENG.). 304p. (J). pap. 12.95 (978-1-56164-680-7(6)) Pineapple Pr., Inc.
Trine, Greg. Invasion from Planet Dork. Montijo, Rhode, illus. 2010. (Melvin Beederman, Superhero Ser.: 8). (ENG.). 144p. (J). (gr. 2-7). pap. 8.99 (978-0-8050-8167-1(4), 9780805081671) Square Fish.
Trout, Richard. Eclipse of the Jaguar, 1 vol. 2011. (ENG., Illus.). 224p. (YA). (gr. 8-12). 16.99 (978-1-58980-872-0(X)) Pelican Publishing Co., Inc.
Turner, Henry. Ask the Dark. (ENG.). 256p. (YA). (gr. 9). 2016. pap. 9.99 (978-0-544-81353-3(7), HMH Books For Young Readers) 2015. 17.99 (978-0-544-30827-5(1), Clarion Bks.) Houghton Mifflin Harcourt Publishing Co.
Van Tol, Alex. Gravity Check, 1 vol. 2011. (Orca Sports Ser.). (ENG.). 176p. (YA). (gr. 6-10). pap. 9.95 (978-1-55469-349-8(7)) Orca Bk. Pubs. USA.
Varley, Dax. The Crow. Proctor, Jon, illus. 2016. (ENG.). 48p. (J). lib. bdg. (978-1-62402-160-2(3)) Magic Wagon.
—Graveyard Dirt. Proctor, Jon, illus. 2016. (ENG.). 48p. (J). lib. bdg. (978-1-62402-158-9(1)) Magic Wagon.
—Hideout. Proctor, Jon, illus. 2016. (ENG.). 48p. (J). lib. bdg. 28.50 (978-1-62402-157-2(3)) Magic Wagon.
—The Locket. Proctor, Jon, illus. 2016. (ENG.). 48p. (J). lib. bdg. (978-1-62402-159-6(X)) Magic Wagon.
Vaughan, M. M. Six. 2015. (ENG., Illus.). 368p. (J). (gr. 3-7). 16.99 (978-1-4814-2069-3(0), McElderry, Margaret K. Bks.) McElderry, Margaret K. Bks.
Villeneuve, Marie-Paule & Audet, Patrice. Qui a Enleve Polka? 2004. (FRE., Illus.). 122p. (J). 8.95 (978-2-922565-81-2(5)) Editions de la Paix CAN. Dist: World of Reading, Ltd.
Walden, Mark. Dreadnought. (H. I. V. E. Ser.: 4). (ENG.). (J). (gr. 3-7). 2012. 320p. pap. 8.99 (978-1-4424-1368-9(9)) 2011. 304p. 16.99 (978-1-4424-2186-8(X)) Simon & Schuster Bks. For Young Readers. (Simon & Schuster Bks. For Young Readers).
Walsh, Laurence & Walsh, Suella. In the Middle of the Night. 2006. (J). pap. (978-0-88092-473-3(X)) Royal Fireworks Publishing Co.
Wardale, David. Psico. 2013. 302p. (J). pap. (978-1-78299-172-4(7)) FeedARead.com.
Warman, Jessica. Beautiful Lies. 2014. (ENG.). 432p. (YA). (gr. 9). pap. 9.99 (978-0-8027-3543-0(6), 9780802735430, Bloomsbury USA Childrens) Bloomsbury Publishing USA.
—The Last Good Day of the Year. (ENG.). 288p. (YA). 2016. pap. 9.99 (978-0-8027-3663-5(7), 9780802736635) 2015. (gr. 9). 17.99 (978-0-8027-3662-8(9), 9780802736628) Bloomsbury Publishing USA. (Bloomsbury USA Childrens).
Watson, Jude. A King's Ransom. 2011. (39 Clues: Cahills vs. Vespers Ser.: 2). (ENG.). 192p. (J). (gr. 3-7). 12.99 (978-0-545-29840-7(7), Scholastic Pr.);Bk. 2. 12.99 (978-0-545-32410-6(6)) Scholastic, Inc.
Waxman, Rachel. The Crickhowell School for the Muses. 2013. (ENG.). 228p. (YA). pap. 14.95 (978-1-56474-541-5(4), Fithian Pr) Daniel & Daniel, Pubs., Inc.
Webb, Holly. Rose & the Lost Princess. 2011. (ENG.). 272p. (J). (gr. 4-6). pap. 8.99 (978-1-4083-0448-8(1)) Hodder & Stoughton GBR. Dist: Hachette Bk. Group.
—Rose & the Lost Princess. 2014. (Rose Ser.: 2). (ENG.). 256p. (J). (gr. 3-6). pap. 6.99 (978-1-4022-8584-4(1), Sourcebooks Jabberwocky) Sourcebooks, Inc.
—Rose & the Magician's Mask. 2014. (Rose Ser.: 3). (ENG.). 224p. (J). (gr. 3-6). pap. 6.99 (978-1-4926-0430-3(5), 9781492604303, Sourcebooks Jabberwocky) Sourcebooks, Inc.
Weiner, Ellis. The Templeton Twins Have an Idea. Holmes, Jeremy, illus. 2012. (ENG.). 232p. (J). (gr. 4-7). 16.99 (978-0-8118-6679-8(3)) Chronicle Bks. LLC.
—The Templeton Twins Have an Idea: Book 1. Holmes, Jeremy, illus. 2013. (Templeton Twins Ser.). (ENG.). 240p. (J). (gr. 3-7). pap. 6.99 (978-1-4521-2704-0(2)) Chronicle Bks. LLC.
West, Tracey. A Team Divided , Bk. 6. 2014. (Lego Ninjago Ser.). (ENG.). 80p. (J). (gr. 2-5). pap. 4.99 (978-0-545-74640-3(X)) Scholastic, Inc.
Whitehouse, Howard. The Faceless Fiend: Being the Tale of a Criminal Mastermind, His Masked Minions & a Princess with a Butter Knife, Involving Explosives & a Certain Amount of Pushing & Shoving. Slavin, Bill, illus. 2007. (Mad Misadventures of Emmaline & Rubberbones Ser.). (ENG.). 272p. (J). (gr. 4-7). 7.95 (978-1-55453-180-6(2)) Kids Can Pr., Ltd. CAN. Dist: Hachette Bk. Group.
—The Island of Mad Scientists: Being an Excursion to the Wilds of Scotland, Involving Many Marvels of Experimental Invention, Pirates, a Heroic Cat, a Mechanical Man & a Monkey. Slavin, Bill, illus. 2008. (Mad Misadventures of Emmaline & Rubberbones Ser.). (ENG.). 264p. (J). (gr. 4-7). pap. 7.95 (978-1-55453-237-7(X)) Kids Can Pr., Ltd. CAN. Dist: Hachette Bk. Group.
Wicke, Ed. Mattie & the Highwaymen. 2012. 216p. (J). per. 9.99 (978-0-9677652-1-1(8), BlacknBlue Pr. UK) Blacknblue Pr.
Wildavsky, Rachel. The Secret of Rover. Caparo, Antonio, illus. (ENG.). 368p. (J). (gr. 3-7). 2015. pap. 7.95 (978-1-4197-1968-4(8)) 2011. 17.95 (978-0-8109-9710-3(X)) Abrams, Inc. (Amulet Bks.).
Willey, Margaret. Four Secrets. Hauser, Bill, illus. 2012. (Carolrhoda YA Ser.). (ENG.). 288p. (YA). (gr. 7-12). 17.95 (978-0-7613-8535-6(5)) Lerner Publishing Group.
Williams, David Morgan. Ebony & Ivory. 2007. (ENG.). 136p. (J). pap. 11.95 (978-0-86243-972-9(8)) Y Lolfa GBR. Dist: Dufour Editions, Inc.
Williams, Mandi Tillotson. The Many Adventures of Mortimer Crump: Mortimer's Sweet Retreat. 2011. 28p. pap. 13.83 (978-1-4634-2637-8(2)) AuthorHouse.
Wilson, Heather Gemmen. Lydia Barnes & the Escape from Shark Bay. 2008. 160p. (J). 9.99 (978-0-89827-352-6(8)) Wesleyan Publishing Hse.
Wilson, Martin. We Now Return to Regular Life. 2017. (ENG.). 384p. (YA). (gr. 9). 17.99 **(978-0-7352-2782-8(9)**, Dial Bks) Penguin Young Readers Group.
Wofford, Delaney. For Courage. 2010. 229p. pap. 17.98 (978-0-557-17045-6(1)) Lulu Pr., Inc.
Wreggelsworth, Irene. Help, Children! - The Monsters Kidnapped Santa Claus: Bilingual Book in English & Spanish. Piccione, Dana, illus. 2010. (ENG.). 120p. pap. 26.99 (978-1-4537-1272-6(0)) CreateSpace Independent Publishing Platform.
Yaccarino, Dan. Los Cuatro Vientos. (SPA.). (J). 7.95 (978-958-04-7606-1(3)) Norma S.A. COL. Dist: Distribuidora Norma, Inc.
Yohalem, Eve. Escape under the Forever Sky. (ENG.). 2011. 219p. (YA). (gr. 4-7). pap. 7.99 (978-0-8118-7874-6(0)) 2009. 224p. (J). (gr. 5-17). 16.99 (978-0-8118-6653-8(X)) Chronicle Bks. LLC.
Young, Andrea. Finny & the Boy from Horse Mountain. 2013. (ENG.). 320p. (J). (gr. 6-8). 16.95 (978-1-62087-682-4(5), 620682, Sky Pony Pr.) Skyhorse Publishing Co., Inc.
Young, Moira. Blood Red Road. (Dust Lands Ser.: 1). (ENG.). (YA). (gr. 9). 2012. 480p. pap. 10.99 (978-1-4424-2999-4(2)) 2011. (Illus.). 464p. 17.99 (978-1-4424-2998-7(4)) McElderry, Margaret K. Bks. (McElderry, Margaret K. Bks.).
—Blood Red Road, 9 vols. 2011. (YA). 122.75 (978-1-4618-0629-5(1)); 286.75 (978-1-4618-0634-9(8)); 120.75 (978-1-4618-0633-2(X)); 1.25 (978-1-4640-2632-4(7)); 120.75 (978-1-4618-0630-1(5)) Recorded Bks., Inc.
—Rebel Heart. 2012. (Dust Lands Ser.: 2). (ENG., Illus.). 432p. (YA). (gr. 9). 17.99 (978-1-4424-3000-6(1), McElderry, Margaret K. Bks.) McElderry, Margaret K. Bks.
4RV Publishing LLC Staff. Case of the Missing Coach. 2007. (Illus.). 144p. (J). per. 18.99 (978-0-9797513-1-8(4)) 4RV Publishing, LLC.

KILLING, MERCY

see Euthanasia

KINDERGARTEN

Beck, Isabel L., et al. Trophies Kindergarten: The Party. 2003. (Trophies Ser.). (gr. k-6). 13.80 (978-0-15-329523-2(6)) Harcourt Schl. Pubs.
Dealey, Erin. K Is for Kindergarten. Cowman, Joseph, illus. 2017. (ENG.). 32p. (J). (gr. -1-1). 16.99 **(978-1-58536-995-9(0)**, 204326) Sleeping Bear Pr.
Hoffman, Joan. Kindergarten Basics. Boyer, Robin, illus. 2004. (ENG.). 32p. (J). pap. 2.99 (978-1-58947-436-9(8)) School Zone Publishing Co.
—Kindergarten Basics. 2003. (ENG.). 64p. (J). (gr. k). pap., wbk. ed. 3.99 (978-1-58947-036-1(2)) School Zone Publishing Co.
Johnson, Anne, et al. Shukalaka Shake: Songs for a Young Child's Day, 1 vol. 2011. (Songbooks Ser.). (ENG., Illus.). 64p. (J). pap. 24.95 incl. audio compact disk **(978-1-4081-4657-6(6))** HarperCollins Pubs. Ltd. GBR. Dist: Independent Pubs. Group.
Kannenberg, Stacey. Let's Get Ready for Kindergarten! rev. ed. 2006. (Let's Get Ready Ser.). (Illus.). 30p. (J). (gr. -1-1). per. 19.00 (978-1-933476-00-1(1)) Cedar Valley Publishing.
Leatherdale, Mary Beth & Leatherdale, Mary. My Class & Me: Kindergarten. Ritchie, Scot, illus. 2003. (Memory Scrapbook for Kids Ser.). (ENG.). 32p. (J). (gr. k-2). 5.95 (978-1-55337-129-8(1)) Kids Can Pr., Ltd. CAN. Dist: Hachette Bk. Group.
Munamarty, Lasya. Fun Days at School. 2012. 76p. (gr. 1-2). pap. 10.95 (978-1-4620-8347-3(1)) iUniverse, Inc.
Practice Power School Bus Book: Kindergarten. 2003. 24p. (J). spiral bd. (978-1-930355-42-2(4)) Bright of America.
School Zone Interactive Staff. Kindergarten. 2006. (ENG.). (J). cd-rom 24.99 (978-1-58947-682-0(4)) School Zone Publishing Co.
School Zone Publishing. Kindergarten. 2003. (Power Packs Ser.). (ENG., Illus.). (J). 24.99 (978-1-58947-530-4(5)) School Zone Publishing Co.

KINDERGARTEN—FICTION

Anderson, Patricia. It's Time for Kindergarten PJ & Parker. 2012. (Illus.). 26p. (J). 19.95 (978-1-61863-379-8(1)) Bookstand Publishing.
Argueta, Jorge. Moony Luna. Gómez, Elizabeth, illus. 2013.Tr. of Luna, Lunita Lunera. (ENG & SPA.). 32p. (J). pap. 9.95 (978-0-89239-306-0(8), Children's Book Press) Lee & Low Bks., Inc.
Bieber, Hartmut. Busy Bear Goes to Kindergarten. 2004. (Illus.). 14p. (J). 5.99 (978-1-59384-049-5(7)) Parklane Publishing.
Biro, Sharon. Snaggleloopus. 2008. (Illus.). 36p. pap. 24.95 (978-1-60474-118-6(X)) America Star Bks.
Borden, Louise. Kindergarten Luck. Godbout, Geneviève, illus. 2015. (ENG.). 32p. (J). (gr. -1-k). 16.99 (978-1-4521-1394-4(7)) Chronicle Bks. LLC.
Brown, Marc. Monkey: Not Ready for Kindergarten. 2015. (ENG., Illus.). 32p. (J). (gr. -1-2). 12.99 (978-0-553-49658-1(1), Knopf Bks. for Young Readers) Random Hse. Children's Bks.
Buzzeo, Toni. Adventure Annie Goes to Kindergarten. Wummer, Amy, illus. 2013. (ENG.). 32p. (J). (gr. -1-k). mass mkt. 7.99 (978-0-14-242695-1(4), Puffin Books) Penguin Young Readers Group.
Cardoza, Kristina. Pinky Bunny's First Day of Kindergarten. 2011. 16p. pap. 8.75 (978-1-4634-8753-9(3)) AuthorHouse.
Carlson, Nancy. Henry's 100 Days of Kindergarten. Carlson, Nancy, illus. 2007. (ENG., Illus.). 32p. (J). (gr. -1-1). pap. 5.99 (978-0-14-240758-5(5), Puffin Books) Penguin Young Readers Group.
—Henry's 100 Days of Kindergarten. 2007. 16.00 (978-1-4177-5983-5(6), Turtleback) Turtleback Bks.
—Henry's Amazing Imagination. 2010. (ENG.). 32p. (J). (gr. -1-1). pap. 6.99 (978-0-14-241605-1(3), Puffin Books) Penguin Young Readers Group.
—Henry's Show & Tell. Carlson, Nancy, illus. 2012. (Nancy Carlson Picture Bks). (Illus.). 32p. (J). (gr. k-2). (ENG.). 9.95 (978-0-7613-8953-8(9)); 56.72 (978-0-7613-9308-5(0)) Lerner Publishing Group. (Carolrhoda Bks.).
—Look Out, Kindergarten, Here I Come! Mlawer, Teresa, tr. Carlson, Nancy, illus. 2004.Tr. of Preparate, Kindergarten! Alla Voy! (SPA & ENG., Illus.). 32p. (J). (gr. -1-k). 15.99 (978-0-670-03673-8(0), Viking Books for Young Readers) Penguin Young Readers Group.
Cathcart Jr., George R. Ernie Goes to Kindergarten. 2013. 24p. pap. 24.95 (978-1-4626-9628-4(7)) America Star Bks.
Cerullo, Claudio V. Isabella Goes to Kindergarden, 1 vol. 2010. 24p. 24.95 (978-1-4489-2455-4(3)) PublishAmerica, Inc.
Chang, Hae-Kyung. Oh No, School! Bisaillon, Josée, illus. 2014. 30p. (J). (978-1-4338-1333-7(5), Magination Pr.) American Psychological Assn.
Cleary, Beverly. Ramona la Chinche, 1 vol. Darling, Louis et al, illus. 2006. (Ramona Ser.: 2).Tr. of Ramona the Pest. (SPA.). 192p. (J). (gr. 3-7). pap. 5.99 (978-0-688-14888-1(3), MR2295) HarperCollins Pubs.
—Ramona la Chinche. Palacios, Argentina, tr. Darling, Louis, illus. 2006. (Ramona Quimby Spanish Ser.: 2).Tr. of Ramona the Pest. (SPA.). 181p. (J). (gr. 4-7). lib. bdg. 16.00 (978-0-613-00464-0(7), Turtleback) Turtleback Bks.
—Ramona the Pest. Darling, Louis & Rogers, Jacqueline, illus. 2013. (Ramona Ser.: 2). (SPA & ENG.). 240p. (J). (gr. 3-7). pap. 6.99 (978-0-380-70954-0(6)) HarperCollins Pubs.
—Ramona the Pest. Darling, Louis et al, illus. 2013. (Ramona Ser.: 2). (ENG.). 240p. (J). (gr. 3-7). 16.99 (978-0-688-21721-1(4)) HarperCollins Pubs.
—Ramona the Pest. (Ramona Quimby Ser.). (J). (gr. 3-5). Random House Publishing Group.
—Ramona the Pest. (Ramona Quimby Ser.). 192p. (J). (gr. 3-5). pap. 4.99 (978-0-8072-1438-1(8), Listening Library) Random Hse. Audio Publishing Group.
Cohen, Jeff. Eva & Sadie & the Best Classroom Ever! Allen, Elanna, illus. 2015. (ENG.). 32p. (J). (gr. -1-3). 17.99 (978-0-06-224938-8(X)) HarperCollins Pubs.
Cole, Anjennetta. Cory's Classroom Rules. 2012. 28p. pap. 15.99 (978-1-4685-3652-2(4)) AuthorHouse.
Davis, Katie. Kindergarten Rocks! (ENG., Illus.). 32p. (J). (gr. -1-3). 2008. pap. 7.99 (978-0-15-206468-6(0)) 2005. 16.99 (978-0-15-204932-4(0)) Houghton Mifflin Harcourt Publishing Co.
dePaola, Tomie. Stagestruck. dePaola, Tomie, illus. 2007. (ENG., Illus.). 32p. (J). (gr. -1-3). pap. 6.99 (978-0-14-240899-5(9), Puffin Books) Penguin Young Readers Group.
—Stagestruck. dePaola, Tomie, illus. 2007. (Illus.). (gr. -1-3). 17.00 (978-0-7569-8159-4(X)) Perfection Learning Corp.
Dozier, Mike. Zack & the Bean Stalk. 2009. pap. 10.00 (978-1-61584-582-8(8)) Independent Pub.
Elliott, Laura Malone. Hunter's Best Friend at School. Munsinger, Lynn, illus. 2005. (gr. -1-2). 17.00 (978-0-7569-5786-5(9)) Perfection Learning Corp.
Friedman, Darlene. Star of the Week: A Story of Love, Adoption, & Brownies with Sprinkles. Roth, Roger, illus. 2009. (ENG.). 32p. (J). (gr. k-3). 17.99 (978-0-06-114136-2(4)) HarperCollins Pubs.
Ganz-Schmitt, Sue. Planet Kindergarten. Prigmore, Shane, illus. (ENG.). (J). (gr. -1-k). 2016. 36p. 7.99 (978-1-4521-5644-6(1)) 2014. 40p. 16.99 (978-1-4521-1893-2(0)) Chronicle Bks. LLC.
—Planet Kindergarten. Prigmore, Shane, illus. 2014. 37.75 (978-1-4906-3417-3(7)); 39.75 (978-1-4906-3418-0(5)); 1.25 (978-1-4906-3415-9(0)) Recorded Bks., Inc.
—Planet Kindergarten: 100 Days in Orbit. Prigmore, Shane, illus. 2016. (ENG.). 36p. (J). (gr. -1-k). 16.99 (978-1-4521-3776-6(5)) Chronicle Bks. LLC.
Hall, Rosemary. The Kids Knee Garden from the Adventures with Lamb E. Boy Series. 2008. (ENG.). 30p. pap. 9.13 (978-1-4196-8967-3(3)) CreateSpace Independent Publishing Platform.
Hays, Anna Jane. Kindergarten Countdown. Davick, Linda, illus. 2013. (ENG.). 24p. (J). (gr. -1-2). 6.99 (978-0-385-75371-5(3), Dragonfly Bks.) Random Hse. Children's Bks.
Himle, Lisa. Hands as Warm as Toast. Langton, Bruce, illus. 2006. 32p. (J). (gr. -1-3). 17.95 (978-1-58726-298-2(3), Mitten Pr.) Ann Arbor Editions LLC.
Houdek, Andi. Mice in My Tummy. 2006. (J). per. 16.95 (978-0-9771939-9-8(3), 012) New World Publishing.
Howard, Kate, illus. On Our Way to First Grade. 2015. 32p. (J). (978-0-545-82340-1(4)) Scholastic, Inc.
Huneke, Amanda. A Monster at School, 1 vol. Wolek, Guy, illus. 2013. (Monster on the Loose Ser.). (ENG.). 32p. (J). (gr. -1-4). 28.50 (978-1-61641-931-8(8)) Magic Wagon.
Huxman, K. D. Dragon Talk. 2007. (Illus.). 24p. (J). per. 11.99 (978-0-9797574-9-5(5)) Dragonfly Publishing, Inc.
Huxman, Karin (K. D.). Dragon Talk. 2006. (Illus.). 24p. (J). lib. bdg. 24.95 (978-0-9778651-7-8(7)) Dragonfly Publishing, Inc.
Kattan, Peter & Kattan, Nicola. More Kindergarten Sudoku: 4x4 Classic Sudoku Puzzles for Kids. 2008. 48p. pap. 7.50 (978-0-615-18718-1(8)) Kattan, Peter I.
Klein, Adria F. Max Goes to School. Gallagher-Cole, Mernie, illus. 2007. (Read-It! Readers: the Life of Max Ser.). (ENG.). 24p. (gr. -1-2). per. 3.95 (978-1-4048-3059-2(6), Easy Readers) Picture Window Bks.
—Max Va a la Escuela, 1 vol. Lozano, Clara, tr. Gallagher-Cole, Mernie, illus. 2007. (Read-It! Readers en Español: la Vida de Max Ser.). (SPA.). 24p. (gr. -1-3). per. 3.95 (978-1-4048-3037-0(5), Easy Readers) Picture Window Bks.
Kramer, Joyce. The Gingerbread Man Goes to Kindergarten. 2012. 71p. (gr. 2-2). 24.99 (978-1-4797-2374-4(6)); pap. 15.99 (978-1-4797-2373-7(8)) Xlibris Corp.
Labadie, Sally Zolkosky. The Schoolhouse Mouse. 2013. 32p. pap. (978-1-4602-3128-9(7)) FriesenPress.
Lloyd, Jennifer. The Best Thing about Kindergarten. Leng, Qin, illus. 2013. (ENG.). 36p. (J). (gr. -1-1). 16.95 (978-1-897476-82-6(5)) Simply Read Bks. CAN. Dist: Ingram Publisher Services.
Loewen, Nancy. The Last Day of Kindergarten, 0 vols. Yoshikawa, Sachiko, illus. 2011. (ENG.). 32p. (J). (gr. -1-1). 16.99 (978-0-7614-5807-4(7), 9780761458074, Amazon Children's Publishing) Amazon Publishing.
MacDowell, Maureen. Tomorrow Is the First Day of School. Hergenrother, Max, illus. 2007. 32p. (J). 15.95 (978-0-9791463-0-5(5)) Wading River Bks., LLC.
Mackall, Dandi Daley. Natalie: School's First Day of Me, 1 vol. Blakeslee, Lys, illus. 2009. (That's Nat! Ser.). (ENG.). 96p. (J). (gr. 1-4). pap. 4.99 (978-0-310-71568-9(7)) Zonderkidz.
—Natalie & the Downside-Up Birthday, 1 vol. Blakeslee, Lys, illus. 2009. (That's Nat! Ser.). (ENG.). 96p. (J). (gr. 1-4). pap. 4.99 (978-0-310-71569-6(5)) Zonderkidz.
Marie, Lynne. Hedgehog Goes to Kindergarten. Kennedy, Anne, illus. 2011. (J). pap. (978-0-545-29874-2(1)) Scholastic, Inc.
Marshall, Linda Elovitz. Kindergarten Is Cool! Chatterton, Chris, illus. 2016. (ENG.). 32p. (J). (gr. -1-1). 8.99 (978-0-545-65266-7(9), Cartwheel Bks.) Scholastic, Inc.
Mcghee, Alison. Countdown to Kindergarten. Bliss, Harry, illus. 2006. (ENG.). 32p. (J). (gr. -1-3). reprint ed. pap. 6.99 (978-0-15-205586-8(X)) Houghton Mifflin Harcourt Publishing Co.
—Countdown to Kindergarten. Bliss, Harry, illus. pap. incl. audio compact disk (978-1-59112-469-6(7)); pap. 39.95 incl. audio (978-1-59112-929-5(X)) Live Oak Media.
McGinty, Alice B. Eliza's Kindergarten Pet, 0 vols. Speir, Nancy, illus. 2010. (ENG.). 32p. (J). (gr. k-3). 15.99 (978-0-7614-5702-2(X), 9780761457022, Amazon Children's Publishing) Amazon Publishing.
McGowan, Joby. Bossy Bianc. 2011. 20p. pap. 24.95 (978-1-4626-2908-4(3)) America Star Bks.
McGrail-Gamble, Vicki. Kindergarten Colors. 2010. 28p. 15.99 (978-1-4520-4681-5(6)) AuthorHouse.
Minuto, Kristin. My First Day of Kindergarten. 2011. 28p. pap. 21.99 (978-1-4568-6470-5(X)) Xlibris Corp.
The Night Before Kindergarten. 2014. (Night Before Ser.). (ENG.). 32p. (J). (gr. 7-12). 8.24 (978-1-63245-263-4(4)) Lectorum Pubns., Inc.
Park, Barbara. Junie B. Jones Complete Kindergarten Collection, 17 vols. Brunkus, Denise, illus. 2014. (ENG.). 96p. (J). (gr. 1-4). 84.83 (978-0-385-37694-5(4), Random Hse. Bks. for Young Readers) Random Hse. Children's Bks.
—Junie B. Jones y Su Gran Bocota. Brunkus, Denise, illus. 2005. (Junie B. Jones Ser.).Tr. of Junie B. Jones & Her Big Fat Mouth. (SPA.). 80p. (J). (gr. 2-5). pap. 4.99 (978-0-439-42516-2(6), Scholastic en Espanol) Scholastic, Inc.
—Junie B. Jones's Third Boxed Set Ever!, 4 vols., Bks. 9-12. Brunkus, Denise, illus. 2003. (Junie B. Jones Ser.). (ENG.). (J). (gr. 1-4). 19.96 (978-0-375-82552-1(5), Random Hse. Bks. for Young Readers) Random Hse. Children's Bks.
Penn, Audrey. Un Beso en Mi Mano. Harper, Ruth E. & Leak, Nancy M., illus. 2006. (Kissing Hand Ser.). (SPA & ENG.). 32p. (J). (gr. -1-3). 16.95 (978-1-933718-01-9(3)) Tanglewood Pr.
—The Kissing Hand. Gibson, Barbara Leonard, illus. 2014. (Kissing Hand Ser.). (ENG.). 14p. (J). (-k). bds. 7.99 (978-1-933718-77-4(3)) Tanglewood Pr.
—The Kissing Hand. Harper, Ruth E. & Leak, Nancy M., illus. 2007. (Kissing Hand Ser.). (ENG.). 32p. (J). (gr. -1-3). 28.95 (978-1-933718-07-1(2)); 12.95 (978-1-933718-10-1(2)) Tanglewood Pr.
Penn, Audrey, et al, illus. The Kissing Hand. 2010. 23.05 (978-0-7569-9299-6(0)) Natl Bk. Network.
Plucker, Sheri. Me, Hailey. Fargo, Todd, illus. 2005. (Turtle Books). 32p. (J). (gr. k-3). pap. 9.95 (978-0-944727-49-2(2)); lib. bdg. 15.95 (978-0-944727-50-8(6), Turtle Bks.) Jason & Nordic Pubs.
Portis, Antoinette. Kindergarten Diary. Portis, Antoinette, illus. 2010. (Illus.). 32p. (J). (gr. -1-3). (ENG.). 12.99 (978-0-06-145691-6(8)); lib. bdg. 14.89 (978-0-06-145692-3(6)) HarperCollins Pubs.
Rabe, Tish. On the First Day of Kindergarten. Hughes, Laura, illus. 2016. 32p. (J). (gr. -1-3). 9.99 (978-0-06-234834-0(5)) HarperCollins Pubs.
Ransom, Candice. Amanda Panda Quits Kindergarten. Grove, Christine, illus. 2017. (ENG.). 32p. (J). (gr. -1-2). 17.99

(978-0-399-55455-1(6), Doubleday Bks. for Young Readers) Random Hse. Children's Bks.

Robbins, Jacqui. The New Girl... & Me. Phelan, Matt, illus. 2006. (ENG.). 32p. (J). (gr. -1-2). 17.99 *(978-0-689-86468-1(X),* Atheneum/Richard Jackson Bks.) Simon & Schuster Children's Publishing.

Rockwell, Anne F. Welcome to Kindergarten. Rockwell, Anne F., illus. 2004. (ENG., Illus.). 32p. (J). (gr. -1-1). pap. 7.99 *(978-0-8027-7664-8(7),* 9780802776648, Bloomsbury USA Childrens) Bloomsbury Publishing USA.

Rothenberg, B. Annye. I'm Getting Ready for Kindergarten. Bright, Bonnie04, illus. 2012. 48p. (J). pap. 9.95 *(978-0-9790420-5-8(4))* Perfecting Parenting Pr.

Rowlett, Dana. Treasures from a Kindergarten Room. 2012. 50p. pap. 15.99 *(978-1-4691-9849-1(5))* Xlibris Corp.

Rutland, Mirium. Miss Pistachios Big Day. 2007. (Illus.). 48p. pap. *(978-1-58690-063-2(3))* Mould, Paul Publishing.

Schmitt, H. D. Pee Wee Pickle Goes to Kinder-Garden. Spears, Sheri, illus. 2008. 20p. pap. 24.95 *(978-1-60672-731-7(1))* America Star Bks.

Shakespeare, Nancy. Benjamin the Bear Goes to Kindergarten. Clouette, Katie, illus. 2013. (Benjamin the Bear Ser.). (ENG.). (J). (gr. -1-k). 14.95 *(978-1-62086-320-6(0))* Mascot Bks., Inc.

Skarmeas, Nancy. My First Day of School. 2nd ed. 2010. (Illus.). 32p. (J). (gr. -1-1). 8.99 *(978-0-8249-5622-6(2),* Ideal Pubns.) Worthy Publishing.

Slate, Joseph. Miss Bindergarten & the Best Friends. Wolff, Ashley, illus. 2014. (Penguin Young Readers, Level 2 Ser.). (ENG.). 32p. (J). (gr. 1-2). pap. 3.99 *(978-0-448-48132-6(4),* Penguin Young Readers) Penguin Young Readers Group.

—Miss Bindergarten Celebrates the Last Day of Kindergarten. Wolff, Ashley, illus. 2008. (ENG.). 40p. (J). (gr. -1-k). pap. 7.99 *(978-0-14-241060-8(8),* Puffin Books) Penguin Young Readers Group.

—Miss Bindergarten Has a Wild Day in Kindergarten. Wolff, Ashley, illus. 2006. (ENG.). 40p. (J). (gr. -1-k). reprint ed. pap. 6.99 *(978-0-14-240709-7(7),* Puffin Books) Penguin Young Readers Group.

—Miss Bindergarten Stays Home from Kindergarten. Wolff, Ashley, illus. 2004. (ENG.). 48p. (J). (gr. -1-k). reprint ed. pap. 6.99 *(978-0-14-230127-2(2),* Puffin Books) Penguin Young Readers Group.

—Miss Bindergarten Takes a Field Trip with Kindergarten. Wolff, Ashley, illus. 2004. (ENG.). 40p. (J). (gr. -1-k). pap. 6.99 *(978-0-14-240139-2(0),* Puffin Books) Penguin Young Readers Group.

Smith, Jane. It's the First Day of Kindergarten, Chloe Zoe! Smith, Jane, illus. 2016. (Chloe Zoe Ser.). (ENG., Illus.). 32p. (J). (gr. -1-3). 12.99 *(978-0-8075-2458-9(1))* Whitman, Albert & Co.

St. Mark Kindergarten. Kindergarten Goes to Outer Space for the Day. 2009. 28p. pap. 12.49 *(978-1-4490-0587-0(X))* AuthorHouse.

Steinberg, D. J. Kindergarten, Here I Come! Chambers, Mark, illus. 2012. (ENG.). 32p. (J). (gr. -1-k). pap. 3.99 *(978-0-448-45624-9(9),* Grosset & Dunlap) Penguin Young Readers Group.

Sturges, Philemon. I Love School! Halpern, Shari, illus. 2014. 32p. pap. 7.00 *(978-1-61003-329-9(9))* Center for the Collaborative Classroom.

—I Love School! Halpern, Shari, illus. 2004. 32p. (J). (gr. -1-1). lib. bdg. 14.89 *(978-0-06-009285-6(8))* HarperCollins Pubs.

Underwood, Deborah. Super Saurus Saves Kindergarten. Young, Ned, illus. 2017. (ENG.). 40p. (J). (gr. -1-k). 16.99 *(978-1-4231-7568-1(9))* Disney Pr.

Urdahl, Catherine. Polka-Dot Fixes Kindergarten. Kemble, Mai S., illus. 2011. (ENG.). 32p. (J). (gr. -1-3). 16.95 *(978-1-57091-737-0(X));* pap. 7.95 *(978-1-57091-738-7(8))* Charlesbridge Publishing, Inc.

VanDenhoven, Godelieve. Louis in Kindergarten. 2009. 40p. pap. 14.50 *(978-1-60693-752-5(9),* Eloquent Bks.) Strategic Book Publishing & Rights Agency (SBPRA).

Vernick, Audrey. Is Your Buffalo Ready for Kindergarten? Jennewein, Daniel, illus. 2010. (ENG.). 32p. (J). (gr. -1-3). 16.99 *(978-0-06-176275-8(X))* HarperCollins Pubs.

Walton, Rick. Mr. President Goes to School, 1 vol. Sneed, Brad, illus. 2010. (ENG.). 32p. (J). (gr. -1-3). 15.95 *(978-1-56145-538-6(5))* Peachtree Pubs.

Wells, Rosemary. Hands Off, Harry! Wells, Rosemary, illus. 2011. (ENG., Illus.). 40p. (J). (gr. -1-1). 14.99 *(978-0-06-192112-4(2),* Tegen, Katherine Bks) HarperCollins Pubs.

—Miracle Melts Down. Wells, Rosemary, illus. 2012. (ENG., Illus.). 40p. (J). (gr. -1-3). 14.99 *(978-0-06-192115-5(7),* Tegen, Katherine Bks) HarperCollins Pubs.

Wing, Natasha. The Night Before Kindergarten. Durrell, Julie, illus. 2014. (Night Before Ser.). (ENG.). 32p. (J). (gr. -1-k). 12.99 *(978-0-448-48255-2(X),* Grosset & Dunlap) Penguin Young Readers Group.

Winget, Susan. Tucker's Four-Carrot School Day. Winget, Susan, illus. 2005. (ENG., Illus.). 40p. (J). (gr. -1-k). 12.99 *(978-0-06-054642-7(5))* HarperCollins Pubs.

Wolfgang, Jane. Art Today. 2013. (ENG., Illus.). 32p. (J). 14.95 *(978-1-56290-706-8(9))* Crystal Productions.

Yum, Hyewon. Mom, It's My First Day of Kindergarten!, 1 vol. Yum, Hyewon, illus. 2012. (ENG., Illus.). 36p. (J). (gr. -1-2). 16.99 *(978-0-374-35004-8(3),* 9780374350048, Farrar, Straus & Giroux (BYR)) Farrar, Straus & Giroux.

KINDNESS—FICTION

Alexander, Brooke. Little Mia's Big Heart. 2013. 72p. pap. *(978-1-4602-1670-5(9))* FriesenPress.

Allison, Teresa J. Bobble Stories: The Humbobble's Lost Hum. Allison, Charles T., illus. 2013. 48p. pap. 12.99 *(978-0-9887612-1-6(1))* Tawnsy Publishing.

Allred, Chris Ross. Sir E. Bobbo! 2004. 21p. pap. 24.95 *(978-1-4137-2785-2(9))* PublishAmerica, Inc.

Bakker, Merel. Maks & Mila on a Special Journey. Mini Pois Etc, illus. 2013. 54p. *(978-2-9700865-0-5(6))* Mila Publishing, Merel Bakker.

Banta, Sandra F. Fancy the Beautiful Little Dragon: Book Number Two Little One's Series. Hecker, Vera, illus. I.t. ed. 2006. 45p. per. 11.99 *(978-1-59879-157-0(5))* Lifevest Publishing, Inc.

Barnett, Brandi. Glamour. 2008. 231p. 19.95 *(978-1-930709-68-3(4))* HAWK Publishing Group.

Barnhouse Ms Ncc, Natalie. Shimmy Saves the Day: A Tale about Embracing Your Differences. 2012. 28p. pap. 19.99 *(978-1-4772-9933-3(5))* AuthorHouse.

Becq, Cecile. Once upon a Timeless Tale: Cinderella. 2016. (Once upon a Timeless Tale Ser.). (ENG.). 32p. (J). (gr. k-2). 9.99 *(978-1-74297-403-3(1))* Little Hare Bks. AUS. Dist: Independent Pubs. Group.

Belmore, Vickie J. Paul the Pack Rat: Helping Children Learn to Share. Claravino, Paul, illus. 2009. (Let's Talk Ser.). (ENG.). 48p. (J). (gr. -1-4). pap. 8.95 *(978-0-88282-307-2(8))* New Horizon Pr. Pubs., Inc.

Berenstain, Jan, et al. Kindness Counts, 1 vol. 2010. (Berenstain Bears/Living Lights Ser.). (ENG.). 32p. (J). (gr. -1-2). pap. 3.99 *(978-0-310-71257-2(2))* Zonderkidz.

Beverly-Barrier, Essie. Ouse the Mouse. Allen, Joshua, illus. 2009. 20p. pap. 12.99 *(978-1-4389-4518-7(3))* AuthorHouse.

Bilovsky, Stephanie. Great Grandpa Is Weird. Bishop, Tracy, illus. 2016. (Family Snaps Ser.). (ENG.). 32p. (gr. k-2). lib. bdg. 16.99 *(978-1-63440-042-8(9))* Red Chair Pr.

Bongiovanni, Debbie. Kindness Pays Off, 1 vol. 2010. 58p. pap. 16.95 *(978-1-4489-6320-1(6))* America Star Bks.

Brightwood, Laura, illus. Little Freddie & His Whistle. Brightwood, Laura, . 2007. (J). DVD *(978-1-934409-01-5(4))* 3-C Institute for Social Development.

Camcam, Princesse, creator. Fox's Garden. 2014. (Stories Without Words Ser.). (ENG., Illus.). 32p. (J). (gr. -1-3). 14.95 *(978-1-59270-167-4(1))* Enchanted Lion Bks., LLC.

Cerullo, Claudio V. A Thankful Day. Avila, Jesus Villicana, illus. 2008. 25p. pap. 24.95 *(978-1-60672-599-3(8))* America Star Bks.

Chrisagis, Shawn & Chrisagis, Brian. Prejudice in Mandi's Garden: Seeds of Kindness. 2006. 24p. (J). pap. 2.99 *(978-1-59958-009-8(8))* Journey Stone Creations, LLC.

Clark, Janice E. Roscoe Is a RAKster: You Can Be One Too. 2010. 24p. pap. 12.99 *(978-1-4520-9235-5(4))* AuthorHouse.

Costello, Judi. Gertrude & the Creature. Bouthyette, Valerie, illus. 2008. 28p. pap. 24.95 *(978-1-60672-737-9(0))* America Star Bks.

Cowen-Fletcher, Jane. Baby Be Kind. Cowen-Fletcher, Jane, illus. 2012. (ENG., Illus.). 18p. (J). (gr. k — 1). bds. 5.99 *(978-0-7636-5647-8(X))* Candlewick Pr.

Cummins, Maria S. The Lamplighter. 2011. 308p. pap. 16.99 *(978-1-61203-228-3(1))* Bottom of the Hill Publishing.

Cuyler, Margery. Kindness Is Cooler, Mrs. Ruler. Yoshikawa, Sachiko, illus. 2007. (ENG.). 48p. (J). (gr. k-5). 17.99 *(978-0-689-87344-7(1),* Simon & Schuster Bks. For Young Readers) Simon & Schuster Bks. For Young Readers.

Dahl, Michael. Be a Star, Wonder Woman! Lozano, Omar, illus. 2017. (DC Super Heroes Ser.). (ENG.). 32p. (J). (gr. -1-2). 15.95 ***(978-1-62370-875-7(3),*** DC Super Heroes) Stone Arch Bks.

Dharma Publishing Staff. A Wise Ape Teaches Kindness: A Story about the Power of Positive Actions. 2nd ed. 2013. (ENG.). 36p. (gr. -1-7). pap. 8.95 *(978-0-89800-519-6(1))* Dharma Publishing.

Ding, Sean. Monkey Ming & the Dream Team. 2013. 34p. pap. *(978-981-07-0631-9(6))* Lukano Publishing Pte, Ltd.

—Zedlogram. 2013. 118p. pap. *(978-981-07-5534-8(1))* Lukano Publishing Pte, Ltd.

Domogala, Sophia Z. Buzzin' with Kindness. 2012. 24p. pap. 15.99 *(978-1-4797-5023-8(9))* Xlibris Corp.

Dudley, Rebecca. Hank Finds an Egg. Dudley, Rebecca, photos by. 2013. (ENG., Illus.). 40p. (J). 16.99 *(978-1-4413-1158-0(0))* Peter Pauper Pr. Inc.

Early, Kelly. Something for Nothing. Sherman, Shandel, illus. I.t. ed. 2007. 13p. (J). per. 8.95 *(978-1-59879-100-6(1));* (gr. -1-3). 14.95 *(978-1-59879-131-0(1))* Lifevest Publishing, Inc.

Easton, Tom. Pirates Can Be Kind, 01 vols., 1. 2016. (Pirate Pals Ser.). (ENG.). 32p. (J). pap. 10.00 *(978-1-5081-9145-2(X),* Windmill Bks.) Rosen Publishing Group, Inc., The.

Edwards, M. J. Dontayan. 2008. 62p. pap. 19.95 *(978-1-60610-026-4(2))* America Star Bks.

Elk, Ronit. A Surprise at Dancing Fields. 2009. 76p. pap. 10.49 *(978-1-4490-2064-4(X))* AuthorHouse.

Fields, Terri. One Good Deed. Melmon, Deborah, illus. 2015. (ENG.). 24p. (J). (gr. -1-3). pap. 7.99 *(978-1-4677-3479-0(9),* Kar-Ben Publishing) Lerner Publishing Group.

—One Good Deed. Melmon, Deborah, illus. 2015. (ENG.). 24p. (J). (gr. -1-3). 17.99 *(978-1-4677-3478-3(0))* Lerner Publishing Group.

Freeman, Don. Fly High, Fly Low. Freeman, Don, illus. 50th anniv. ed. 2007. (ENG., Illus.). 64p. (J). (gr. -1-k). 7.99 *(978-0-14-240817-9(4),* Puffin Books) Penguin Young Readers Group.

—Fly High, Fly Low. Freeman, Don, illus. 2007. (Illus.). 56p. (gr. -1-3). 18.00 *(978-0-7569-8001-6(1))* Perfection Learning Corp.

French, Simon. My Cousin's Keeper. 2014. (ENG.). 240p. (J). (gr. 3-7). 16.99 *(978-0-7636-6279-0(8))* Candlewick Pr.

Friend, R. R. Friend - Hats off to Heroes. 2005. (Down on Friendly Acres Ser.: 3). (J). lib. bdg. *(978-0-9743627-5-5(1));* (Illus.). 90p. per. *(978-0-9743627-2-4(7))* Sunflower Seeds Pr.

Gales, Rick. Granny Puckerlips: Keepin' It Real with Kindness & Respect. 2013. 108p. (gr. 9-12). pap. 11.95 *(978-1-4908-0437-8(4),* WestBow Pr.) Author Solutions, Inc.

Galvin, Laura Gates & Studio Mouse Editorial. Cinderella & Belle: Kindness Counts. Williams, Tracee, ed. 2008. (ENG., Illus.). 24p. (J). (gr. -1). 4.99 *(978-1-59069-652-1(2))* Studio Mouse LLC.

Gates, Pat. The Apple Tree's Secret, 1 vol. Hoesselkus, Devin, illus. 2009. 47p. pap. 24.95 *(978-1-60836-637-8(5))* America Star Bks.

Gault, Linda Fulford. The Chosen Tree. 2011. 28p. pap. 12.95 *(978-1-4567-1561-8(5))* AuthorHouse.

Gillen, Lynea. Good People Everywhere. Swamer, Kristina, illus. 2012. (ENG.). 32p. (J). (gr. -1-2). 15.95 *(978-0-9799289-8-7(2))* Three Pebble Pr., LLC.

Gould, M&R. What Would Jesus Do? Purity of Intention. 2008. 35p. pap. 24.95 *(978-1-60672-675-4(7))* America Star Bks.

Graham, Judith A. The Didley-Doo's, 1 vol. 2009. 36p. pap. 24.95 *(978-1-60836-035-2(0))* America Star Bks.

Hall, S.C. Turns of Fortune & Other Tales. 2007. (ENG.). 116p. per. *(978-1-4065-1586-2(8))* Dodo Pr.

Hallinan, P. K. Let's Be Kind. Hallinan, P. K., illus. 2008. (ENG., Illus.). 24p. (J). (gr. -1-2). 8.99 *(978-0-8249-5605-9(2),* Ideal Pubns.) Worthy Publishing.

—Let's Be Kind. 2003. (ENG., Illus.). 24p. (J). bds. 7.95 *(978-0-8249-5477-2(7),* Ideal Pubns.) Worthy Publishing.

Hansen, Kate. Spike the Sewer Cat. Illustrations byVoigt, Karen S., illus. 2008. 27p. pap. 24.95 *(978-1-60474-094-3(9))* America Star Bks.

Harkrader, Lisa. No Place Like Space: Kindness. Warrick, Jessica, illus. 2017. (How to Be an Earthling (r) Ser.: 5). (ENG.). 64p. (gr. 1-3). 34.65 ***(978-1-57565-851-3(8))*** Kane Press, Inc.

Harpan, Gaile. The Ballad of Calvin the Cat. Reddy, Sneha, illus. 2008. 24p. pap. 12.95 *(978-0-9817572-6-1(X))* Peppertree Pr., The.

Harris, Dee. The Croaker Sack Bunny. Bohart, Lisa, illus. 2012. 24p. pap. 12.95 *(978-1-61493-043-3(0))* Peppertree Pr., The.

Harris, Patrice. Grandma Asks: Were You Good at School Today? Harrison, Nicholas, illus. 2013. 26p. pap. 10.00 *(978-0-9892358-5-3(8))* CLF Publishing.

Hendricks, Brenda K. What's Better Than That, Seren Dippity? Hendricks, Brenda K., illus. 2013. (Illus.). 32p. pap. 9.99 *(978-0-9826582-4-6(9))* Two Small Fish Pubns.

Henn, Sophy. Pass It On. Henn, Sophy, illus. 2017. (ENG., Illus.). 32p. (J). (gr. -1-2). 16.99 *(978-0-399-54775-1(4),* Philomel Bks.) Penguin Young Readers Group.

Hill, Meggan. Nico & Lola: Kindness shared between a boy & a dog. 2009. 32p. (J). *(978-0-615-23040-5(7))* Genuine Prints, LLC.

—Nico & Lola: Kindness Shared Between a Boy & a Dog. Graunke, Susan M., illus. 2010. (ENG.). 40p. (J). (gr. -1-3). 16.99 *(978-0-06-199043-4(4))* HarperCollins Pubs.

Hinkel, Patricia. Frog in My Bucket. 2012. 16p. pap. 15.99 *(978-1-4772-4815-7(3))* AuthorHouse.

Holling, Prudence. Grace Has a Secret. 2013. 32p. pap. 16.95 *(978-1-4525-7145-4(7),* Balboa Pr.) Author Solutions, Inc.

Hollis, Nicole Phillips. My Neighborhood Super Kids. 2012. 44p. pap. 21.99 *(978-1-4685-6169-2(3))* AuthorHouse.

Howell, Trisha Adelena. The Adventures of Melon & Turnip. Lopez, Paul, illus. 2004. 32p. 15.95 *(978-1-931210-04-1(7))* Howell Canyon Pr.

Irvin, Vanessa. Jack's Perfect World. 2011. 48p. pap. 31.99 *(978-1-4568-5502-4(6))* Xlibris Corp.

Jones, Julie. The Problem at Pepperpine Zoo. Jones, Julie, illus. I.t. ed. 2004. (Illus.). 24p. (J). pap. 7.95 *(978-0-9745553-0-0(4))* Greenwood Street Publishing. GSP.

Jorden, Edwin W. Cookie Paws/Spreadin' the Sweetness. Waywell, Valerie J., illus. 2008. 32p. (J). 12.95 *(978-0-9793483-1-0(5))* Gilded Dog Enterprises LLC.

Karol, Leslee. Sylvie the Littlest Guardian Angel: Cassie Makes a Friend. 2013. 48p. pap. 21.99 *(978-1-4817-0864-7(3))* AuthorHouse.

Kaye, Christian Thomas. Rachel the Homely Rabbit: A Story about Kindness. Albright, Audrey, illus. 2011. 30p. pap. 9.95 *(978-1-60844-763-3(4))* Dog Ear Publishing, LLC.

Kerwin, Betsy. The Adventures of Floret the Woodland Fairy: The Adventures Begin. 2008. 44p. pap. 18.49 *(978-1-4343-9426-2(3))* AuthorHouse.

Kim, Cecil. Nicknames. Han, SooJin, illus. 2014. (MySELF Bookshelf Ser.). (ENG.). 32p. (J). (gr. k-2). pap. 11.94 *(978-1-60357-699-4(1));* lib. bdg. 25.27 *(978-1-59953-664-4(1))* Norwood Hse. Pr.

Kretzer, Joyce B. Shane & the Jackadoo: A Butcher Hollow Fantasy. 2008. 24p. pap. 11.49 *(978-1-4389-1894-5(1))* AuthorHouse.

Laconi, Kristin. Karma the Kangaroo Takes the Court. 2010. 24p. pap. 12.99 *(978-1-4490-3227-2(3))* AuthorHouse.

Lampson, Rosalie. Give Mom a Minute. 2009. 32p. pap. 13.99 *(978-1-4490-1407-0(0))* AuthorHouse.

Lang, Andrew. The Queen & the Mouse: A Story about Friendship. Lohmann, Renate, illus. 2006. (J). *(978-1-59939-081-9(7),* Reader's Digest Young Families, Inc.) Studio Fun International.

Logan, Laura. Little Butterfly. Logan, Laura, illus. 2016. (Illus.). 32p. (J). (gr. -1-3). 14.99 *(978-0-06-228126-5(7))* HarperCollins Pubs.

Lord, Janet. Albert the Fix-It Man, 1 vol. Paschkis, Julie, illus. (ENG.). 32p. (J). 2015. (gr. 1-3). pap. 7.95 *(978-1-56145-830-1(9))* 2008. (gr. k-3). 15.95 *(978-1-56145-433-4(8))* Peachtree Pubs.

Love, Katie. Fruit to Live By..., 1 vol. 2009. 62p. pap. 16.95 *(978-1-60836-122-9(5))* PublishAmerica, Inc.

Madden, Michelle. The Butterfly Garden. 2008. 24p. pap. 24.95 *(978-1-60813-375-8(3))* America Star Bks.

Margulies, Julianna & Margulies, Paul. Three Magic Balloons. Shaffer, Grant, illus. 2016. (ENG.). 40p. (J). (gr. -1-2). 17.99 *(978-1-101-93523-1(5),* Random Hse. Bks. for Young Readers) Random Hse. Children's Bks.

Mayer, Mercer. Just a Teacher's Pet. Mayer, Mercer, illus. 2015. (My First I Can Read Ser.). (ENG., Illus.). 32p. (J). (gr. -1-3). pap. 3.99 *(978-0-06-147819-2(9))* HarperCollins Pubs.

Mazzafro, Howard. No Room for George. 2011. (Illus.). 24p. (gr. -1). pap. 14.93 *(978-1-4269-6782-5(9))* Trafford Publishing.

McBay, Bruce. Angels Inc., 1 vol. LaFave, Kim, illus. 2008. (ENG.). 71p. (J). (gr. 1-3). pap. 7.95 *(978-1-896580-30-2(0))* Tradewind Bks. CAN. Dist: Orca Bk. Pubs. USA.

McCloud, Carol, et al. Bucket Filling from a to Z: The Key to Being Happy. Zimmer, Glenn, illus. 2017. (ENG.). 32p. (J). (gr. -1-4). pap. 9.95 *(978-0-9974864-3-8(0))* Bucket Fillers, Inc.

McMurtrie, Kevin. The Very Thoughtful Turtle. 2013. 20p. pap. 13.77 *(978-1-4907-0940-6(1))* Trafford Publishing.

Meadows, Daisy. Esther the Kindness Fairy. 2017. (Rainbow Magic — Friendship Fairies Ser.: 1). lib. bdg. 14.75 ***(978-0-606-40175-3(X))*** Turtleback Bks.

—Esther the Kindness Fairy (Friendship Fairies #1) 2017. (Friendship Fairies Ser.: 1). (ENG.). 80p. (J). (gr. 2-5). pap. 4.99 ***(978-1-338-15767-3(1),*** Scholastic Paperbacks) Scholastic, Inc.

Mello, Roger. You Can't Be Too Careful! Hahn, Daniel, tr. from POR. Mello, Roger, illus. 2017. (ENG., Illus.). 36p. (J). (gr. k-3). 18.00 *(978-0-914671-64-0(2),* Elsewhere Editions) Steerforth Pr.

Metallinos, Sophia. The Heavenly Place. I.t. ed. 2016. (ENG., Illus.). (J). pap. 9.99 ***(978-1-58169-640-0(X),*** Axiom Pr.) Genesis Communications, Inc.

Mims, Melanie. Neeko's Angel: A Story about Kindness. Floyd, John, Jr., illus. 2006. (Fruit of the Spirit Ser.). 24p. (J). (gr. -1-1). 6.95 *(978-0-9752860-7-4(2))* OurRainbow Pr., LLC.

Mitchell, Laurence. Patty Liz & Kindness: Character Tales. 2009. 24p. pap. 12.00 *(978-1-4389-5408-0(5))* AuthorHouse.

Myracle, Lauren. The Life of Ty - Non-Random Acts of Kindness. Henry, Jed, illus. 2015. (Life of Ty Ser.: 2). (ENG.). 128p. (J). (gr. 1-4). 5.99 *(978-0-14-242319-6(X),* Puffin Books) Penguin Young Readers Group.

Nelson, Kadir. If You Plant a Seed. Nelson, Kadir, illus. 2015. (ENG., Illus.). 32p. (J). (gr. -1-3). 18.99 *(978-0-06-229889-8(5))* HarperCollins Pubs.

Nevers, Merri B. Lonely Lucille. 2012. 28p. pap. 16.95 *(978-1-4497-4246-1(7),* WestBow Pr.) Author Solutions, Inc.

Nevins, Mary. The Adventures of Molly. 2009. 20p. pap. 14.50 *(978-1-60693-919-2(X),* Eloquent Bks.) Strategic Book Publishing & Rights Agency (SBPRA).

Norton Kreider, Barbara. The Surprise Party. Dimbylow, Jube, illus. 2013. 30p. pap. *(978-1-921883-37-8(5),* MBS Pr.) Pick-a-Woo Woo Pubs.

Osborne, Amber & Osborne, Dwight. Puffy Buffy Jones Jones Osborne Dadoot Da Do. Osborne, Amber, illus. 2006. (Illus.). (J). pap. 11.99 *(978-0-9786431-0-2(0))* AAO Publishing.

Parker, Lucy. Acorn Meadow has a Secret. 2010. (ENG., Illus.). 80p. pap. *(978-1-84748-600-4(2))* Athena Pr.

Perrault, Charles. Cinderella. Innocenti, Roberto, illus. 2013. (ENG.). 32p. (J). (gr. 1-17). pap. 7.99 *(978-0-89812-828-4(5),* Creative Paperbacks) Creative Co., The.

Persaud, Sandhya S. One Day. Ahmad, Maryam & Ramotar, Alexandra, illus. 2009. 12p. pap. 12.99 *(978-1-4389-4437-1(3))* AuthorHouse.

Polacco, Patricia. Tucky Jo & Little Heart. Polacco, Patricia, illus. 2015. (ENG., Illus.). 48p. (J). (gr. -1-3). 17.99 *(978-1-4814-1584-2(0),* Simon & Schuster Bks. For Young Readers) Simon & Schuster Bks. For Young Readers.

Poole, Susie. All These Things: Based on 1 Corinthians 13:4-7. 2012. (ENG., Illus.). 26p. bds. 7.99 *(978-1-904637-27-1(2),* 1904637272, Pupfish) Authentic Media GBR. Dist: EMI CMG Distribution.

Porter, Jen. I Am Kind. Saunders, Katie, illus. 2016. (ENG.). 16p. (J). (-3). bds. 7.99 *(978-1-4926-4169-8(3),* 9781492641698, Sourcebooks Jabberwocky) Sourcebooks, Inc.

Price, Cheryl. The Golden Aspen. 2009. 36p. pap. 15.95 *(978-1-4490-2855-8(1))* AuthorHouse.

Qahhaar El-Amin, Mary M. Baby Ears: The Littlest Elephant. 2010. 37p. (J). pap. 20.95 *(978-1-4327-2369-9(3))* Outskirts Pr., Inc.

The Quest for Kindness. 2006. (Amazing Travels of Wannabe Ser.). (Illus.). 32p. (J). (gr. -1-3). 8.99 *(978-0-7847-1802-5(4),* 04128) Standard Publishing.

Regis-Etumnu, Anusjka. Sid the Kindest Kid: Sweets ... Sweets ... Sweets! 2012. (Illus.). 32p. pap. 21.35 *(978-1-4772-2283-6(9))* AuthorHouse.

Rice, Dona Herwick & Bradley, Kathleen. Molly Pitcher, 1 vol. 2009. (Building Fluency Through Reader's Theater Ser.). (ENG., Illus.). 24p. (J). (gr. 2-4). pap. 6.99 *(978-1-4333-0993-9(9))* Teacher Created Materials, Inc.

Richards, Laura Elizabeth Howe. Queen Hildegarde. 2007. 92p. per. *(978-1-4068-3867-1(5))* Echo Library.

Rosciti, Donna. The Birthday Train: Book 1. 2013. (ENG.). 48p. (J). 24.95 *(978-1-4787-2236-6(3))* Outskirts Pr., Inc.

Rosenthal, Amy Krouse. Plant a Kiss. Reynolds, Peter H., illus. 2015. (ENG.). 36p. (J). (gr. -1 — 1). bds. 7.99 *(978-0-06-241652-0(9),* HarperFestival) HarperCollins Pubs.

Rosenthal, Sally. Matzo Frogs. Sheldon, David, illus. 2014. (ENG.). 32p. (J). 17.95 *(978-1-58838-302-0(4),* NewSouth Bks.) NewSouth, Inc.

Rubel, David. The Carpenter's Gift: A Christmas Tale about the Rockefeller Center Tree. LaMarche, Jim, illus. 2011. (ENG.). 48p. (J). (gr. k-4). 17.99 *(978-0-375-86922-8(0),* Random Hse. Bks. for Young Readers) Random Hse. Children's Bks.

Schieber, Barry J. An Open Heart: A Story about Moritz. 2006. (Illus.). 32p. (J). 17.00 *(978-0-9721457-2-5(9))* Silent Moon Bks.

Schneider, Richard H. Why Christmas Trees Aren't Perfect. 2016. (ENG.). 32p. 12.99 *(978-1-5018-2583-5(6),* Cokesbury) Abingdon Pr.

Schulz, Charles M. Be Kind: Peanuts Wisdom to Carry You Through. 2013. (ENG., Illus.). 72p. (J). (gr. -1-17). 7.95 *(978-0-7624-4862-3(8),* Running Pr. Kids) Running Pr. Bk. Pubs.

Sewell, Anna. Black Beauty: And a Discussion of Kindness. Martin, Richard, illus. 2003. (Values in Action Illustrated Classics Ser.). 191p. (J). *(978-1-59203-028-6(9))* Learning Challenge, Inc.

Sheinmel, Courtney. The Kindness Club. 2016. (Kindness Club Ser.). (ENG.). 224p. (J). 15.99 *(978-1-68119-091-4(5),* 9781681190914, Bloomsbury USA Childrens) Bloomsbury Publishing USA.

Sherrard, Valerie. Random Acts. 2016. (ENG., Illus.). 272p. (J). (gr. 3-7). 6.99 *(978-0-14-319105-6(5),* Puffin Canada) Penguin Random House Canada Young Readers CAN. Dist: Penguin Random Hse. LLC.

Sherwood, Lance. Grandpa Tales. 2012. 54p. pap. 14.95 *(978-0-615-72525-3(2))* Spitzer, Lance.

Simon, Mary Manz. Kitty Shows Kindness. Clearwater, Linda, illus. 2006. (First Virtues for Toddlers Ser.). 20p. (J). 5.99 *(978-0-7847-1408-9(8),* 04036) Standard Publishing.

Simon, Tanya & Simon, Richard. Oskar & the Eight Blessings. Siegel, Mark, illus. 2015. (ENG.). 40p. (J). (gr. -1-3). 17.99 *(978-1-59643-949-8(1),* 9781596439498) Roaring Brook Pr.

Sparks, Favre. Agnes, the Eggless Quail. 2009. 28p. pap. 16.50 *(978-1-60693-491-3(0),* Strategic Bk. Publishing) Strategic Book Publishing & Rights Agency (SBPRA).

Speak, Steven. Skip & L, Guardian Angel. 2011. 20p. pap. 12.45 *(978-1-4525-3643-9(0))* Get Published.

Spurgeon, Charles. Queen Victoria's Request: A Story of Grace & Mercy. Anderson, Jeff, illus. 2008. (Story Time Ser.). (ENG.). 24p. (J). (gr. -1-3). 7.99 *(978-1-84550-325-3(2),* 0d42e451-d842-4279-bf70-b929d8508ca9) Christian Focus Pubns. GBR. Dist: Bookmasters Distribution.

J
K
L

Sschweiger-dmiel, Izhak. Hanna's Sabbath Dress. Eitan (tchernov), Ora, illus. 2012. (ENG.). 32p. (J). (gr. -1-3). 16.99 *(978-1-4424-7439-0(4),* Simon & Schuster Bks. For Young Readers) Simon & Schuster Bks. For Young Readers.

Stepp, Shirley. Pongo Penguin's Whale of a Tale. 2012. 24p. 24.95 *(978-1-4626-5478-9(9))* America Star Bks.

Sterling, L. E. True North. 2017. (True Born Ser.: 2). (ENG.). 304p. (YA). 16.99 *(978-1-63375-595-6(9),* 9781633755956) Entangled Publishing, LLC.

Stevens, Carla & Stevens, Chapman. Who's Knocking at the Door?, 1 vol. Chapman, Lee, illus. 2004. (ENG.). 32p. (J). 16.95 *(978-0-7614-5168-6(4))* Marshall Cavendish Corp.

Stoutland, Allison. What Can I Do Today? To Make This World a Happier Place. Hofner, Cathy, illus. 2005. 32p. (J). (gr. -1-3). 16.95 *(978-0-9670941-3-7(5))* Inch By Inch Pubns., LLC.

Studio Mouse, creator. Kindness Counts. rev. ed. 2008. (Learn-Aloud Bks.). (ENG., Illus.). (J). 12.99 *(978-1-59069-627-9(1))* Studio Mouse LLC.

Studio Mouse Staff. Kindness Counts. rev. ed. 2004. (Kindness Counts Ser.). (Illus.). 36p. (J). (gr. -1-3). 12.99 *(978-1-59069-364-3(7),* 1A500) Studio Mouse LLC.

Telle, Anita. Always Time for Kindness. 2012. (ENG.). (J). pap. *(978-1-4675-2560-2(X))* Independent Pub.

Tenney, Shawna J. C., illus. Brunhilda's Backwards Day. 2016. (ENG.). 32p. (J). (gr. -1-k). 16.99 *(978-1-63450-691-5(X),* Sky Pony Pr.) Skyhorse Publishing Co., Inc.

Theobald the Iron Hearted or Love to Ene. 2004. reprint ed. pap. 15.95 *(978-1-4191-8941-8(7))* Kessinger Publishing, LLC.

Theobald the Iron Hearted or Love to Enemies. 2004. reprint ed. pap. 1.99 *(978-1-4192-8941-5(1))* Kessinger Publishing, LLC.

Thompson, Don. Bunny World: Kindness Is the Key to Happiness. 2009. 28p. pap. 14.99 *(978-1-4389-5475-2(1))* AuthorHouse.

Thong, Roseanne Greenfield. Fly Free! Neilan, Eujin Kim, illus. 2010. (ENG.). 32p. (J). (gr. 2-4). 17.95 *(978-1-59078-550-8(9))* Boyds Mills Pr.

Tollefson, Carol. McTavich That Rascal Squirrel. 2015. (ENG., Illus.). 20p. pap. 12.00 *(978-1-62288-101-7(X))* Austin, Stephen F. State Univ. Pr.

Van Dusen, Ross, illus. How Crocka Dog Came to Be. 2015. (J). *(978-1-936744-39-8(2))* LPD Pr.

VanDenhoven, Godelieve. Louis in Kindergarten. 2009. 40p. pap. 14.50 *(978-1-60693-752-5(9),* Eloquent Bks.) Strategic Book Publishing & Rights Agency (SBPRA).

Vincent, Victoria. The City of Kind Words: A Story by Tory. l.t. ed. 2006. (Illus.). 56p. (J). per. 19.95 *(978-0-9788950-0-6(2))* All Over Creation.

Wainwright, Joann M. Winston, the Polite St Bernard. Ross, Adam, illus. 2009. 28p. pap. 14.99 *(978-1-4389-2704-6(5))* AuthorHouse.

Wallace, Nancy Elizabeth. The Kindness Quilt, 0 vols. 2006. (ENG., Illus.). 48p. (J). (gr. -1-k). 16.99 *(978-0-7614-5313-0(X),* 9780761453130, Amazon Children's Publishing) Amazon Publishing.

Wekelo, Kerry Alison. Audrey's Journey: Playful Namaste. 2012. 16p. pap. 15.99 *(978-1-4772-7207-7(0))* AuthorHouse.

Wheeler, Christine. Bella's Marigold Cake. 2008. 20p. pap. 18.50 *(978-1-60693-100-4(8),* Eloquent Bks.) Strategic Book Publishing & Rights Agency (SBPRA).

Wildsmith, Brian. Hunter & His Dog, 1 vol. Wildsmith, Brian, illus. 2008. (ENG., Illus.). 32p. (J). 16.95 *(978-1-59572-123-5(1))* Star Bright Bks., Inc.

Will, R. K. Harry's Flowers. 2012. 24p. 24.95 *(978-1-4626-5967-8(5))* America Star Bks.

Williamson, Pam. Sweet & Sour Milk. 2011. 24p. pap. 12.79 *(978-1-4634-0725-4(4))* AuthorHouse.

Woodson, Jacqueline. Each Kindness. Lewis, E. B., illus. 2012. (ENG.). 32p. (J). (gr. k-3). 17.99 *(978-0-399-24652-4(5),* Nancy Paulsen Books) Penguin Young Readers Group.

Yamada, Shale. Rainbow Kitty Saves the Day. Riedler, Amelia, ed. 2013. (Story Lines Ser.). (ENG.). 24p. (J). (gr. -1-3). 9.95 *(978-1-935414-92-6(5))* Compendium, Inc., Publishing & Communications.

Yamaguchi, Kristi. Cara's Kindness. Lee, John, illus. 2016. (ENG.). 32p. (J). (-4). 16.99 *(978-1-4926-1686-3(9),* 9781492616863, Sourcebooks Jabberwocky) Sourcebooks Inc.

KINDNESS TO ANIMALS

see Animals—Treatment

KINETICS

see Dynamics; Motion

KING, BILLIE JEAN, 1943-

Gitlin, Martin. Billie Jean King: Tennis Star & Social Activist, 1 vol. 2011. (Legendary Athletes Ser.). (ENG., Illus.). 112p. (YA). (gr. 7-12). 34.22 *(978-1-61714-757-9(5))* ABDO Publishing Co.

KING, CORETTA SCOTT, 1927-2006

Gelfand, Dale Evva. Coretta Scott King: Civil Rights Activist. 2nd rev. ed. 2006. (Black Americans of Achievement Legacy Edition Ser.). (Illus.). 137p. (YA). (gr. 7-12). lib. bdg. 35.00 *(978-0-7910-9522-5(3))* Facts On File, Inc.

Hally, Ashleigh. Coretta Scott King. 2012. (Illus.). 24p. (J). *(978-1-935884-78-1(6));* pap. *(978-1-935884-84-2(0))* State Standards Publishing, LLC.

Krull, Kathleen & Freeman, Laura. Coretta Scott King: I Kept on Marching. 2015. (Women Who Broke the Rules Ser.). (ENG., Illus.). 48p. (J). (gr. 1-4). pap. 6.99 *(978-0-8027-3827-1(3),* 9780802738271, Bloomsbury USA Childrens) Bloomsbury Publishing USA.

Mattern, Joanne. Coretta Scott King: Civil Rights Activist. (Women Who Shaped History Ser.). 24p. 2009. (gr. 2-3). 42.50 *(978-1-60854-816-3(3))* 2009. (gr. 2-3). 42.50 *(978-1-60854-816-3(3))* 2003. (Illus.). (J). lib. bdg. 19.95 *(978-0-8239-6504-5(X))* Rosen Publishing Group, Inc., The. (PowerKids Pr.).

McPherson, Stephanie Sammartino. Biography Coretta Scott King. 2007. (Biography Ser.). (Illus.). 112p. (YA). (gr. 7-12). lib. bdg. 29.27 *(978-0-8225-7156-8(0))* Twenty First Century Bks.

Mis, Melody S. Meet Coretta Scott King. 2008. (Civil Rights Leaders Ser.). (Illus.). 24p. (YA). (gr. 2-5). lib. bdg. 22.60 *(978-1-4042-4211-1(2))* Rosen Publishing Group, Inc., The.

Pingry, Patricia A. The Story of Coretta Scott King. Walker, Steven, illus. 2007. (ENG.). 26p. (J). (gr. 3-7). bds. 7.69 *(978-0-8249-6717-8(8),* Ideal Pubns.) Worthy Publishing.

Shange, Ntozake. Coretta Scott. Nelson, Kadir, illus. (ENG.). 32p. (J). (gr. -1-4). 2011. pap. 6.99 *(978-0-06-125366-9(9))* 2009. 17.99 *(978-0-06-125364-5(2))* HarperCollins Pubs. (Tegen, Katherine Bks).

Sharp, Anne Wallace. Coretta Scott King. 2008. (People in the News Ser.). (ENG., Illus.). 128p. (gr. 7-10). lib. bdg. 39.40 *(978-1-4205-0087-5(2),* LML02109-242091, Lucent Bks.) Cengage Gale.

Stanley, George E. Coretta Scott King: First Lady of Civil Rights. Madsen, Jim & Henderson, Meryl, illus. 2008. (Childhood of Famous Americans Ser.). (ENG.). 224p. (J). (gr. 3-7). pap. 7.99 *(978-1-4169-6800-9(8),* Simon & Schuster/Paula Wiseman Bks.) Simon & Schuster/Paula Wiseman Bks.

Waxman, Laura Hamilton. Coretta Scott King. 2008. pap. 52.95 *(978-0-8225-9387-4(4));* (ENG., Illus.). 48p. (gr. 3-6). lib. bdg. 27.93 *(978-0-8225-7168-1(4),* Lerner Pubns.) Lerner Publishing Group.

KING, MARTIN LUTHER, JR., 1929-1968

Adler, David A. Dr. Martin Luther King, Jr: A Historical Perspective. Bootman, Colin, illus. 2003. (ENG.). 48p. (J). (gr. k-3). pap. 7.99 *(978-0-8234-1803-9(0))* Holiday Hse., Inc.

—A Picture Book of Martin Luther King, Jr. Casilla, Robert, illus. 2004. (Picture Book Biography Ser.). (J). (gr. -1-3). pap. 18.95 incl. audio compact disk *(978-1-59112-773-4(4))* Live Oak Media.

Alexander, Florence. Dare to Be. . . Martin Luther King Jr. Whitmore, Yvette, illus. 2003. (ENG & SPA.). 17p. (J). 3.99 *(978-0-915960-65-1(6))* Ebon Research Systems Publishing, LLC.

Archer, Jules. They Had a Dream: The Struggles of Four of the Most Influential Leaders of the Civil Rights Movement, from Frederick Douglass to Marcus Garvey to Martin Luther King Jr. & Malcolm X. 2016. (Jules Archer History for Young Readers Ser.). (ENG., Illus.). 272p. (J). (gr. 6). 16.99 *(978-1-63450-194-1(2),* Sky Pony Pr.) Skyhorse Publishing Co., Inc.

Aretha, David. Martin Luther King Jr. & the 1963 March on Washington. 2014. (Illus.). 112p. (J). 28.95 *(978-1-59935-372-2(5))* Reynolds, Morgan Inc.

—Selma & the Voting Rights Act. 2007. (Civil Rights Movement Ser.). (Illus.). 128p. (J). (gr. 3-7). lib. bdg. 27.95 *(978-1-59935-056-1(4))* Reynolds, Morgan Inc.

Bader, Bonnie. Who Was Martin Luther King, Jr. ? Wolf, Elizabeth & Harrison, Nancy, illus. 2007. (Who Was? Ser.). (ENG.). 112p. (J). (gr. 3-7). pap. 5.99 *(978-0-448-44723-0(1),* Grosset & Dunlap) Penguin Young Readers Group.

—Who Was Martin Luther King, Jr. ? Wolf, Elizabeth, illus. 2008. (Who Was... ? Ser.). 105p. (J). (gr. 2-5). 12.65 *(978-0-7569-8935-4(3))* Perfection Learning Corp.

Bailey, Gerry & Foster, Karen. Martin Luther King Jr.'s Microphone. Radford, Karen & Noyes, Leighton, illus. 2008. (Stories of Great People Ser.). (ENG.). 40p. (J). (gr. 3-8). pap. *(978-0-7787-3711-7(X));* lib. bdg. *(978-0-7787-3689-9(X))* Crabtree Publishing Co.

Ball, Jacqueline A. Martin Luther King, Jr: I Have a Dream! 2005. (Defining Moments Ser.). (Illus.). 32p. (J). (gr. 2-5). lib. bdg. 25.27 *(978-1-59716-077-3(6))* Bearport Publishing Co., Inc.

Bauer, Marion Dane. Martin Luthur King, Jr. Smith, Jamie, illus. 2009. (My First Biography Ser.). (ENG.). 32p. (J). (gr. -1-3). pap. 3.99 *(978-0-545-14233-5(4))* Scholastic, Inc.

Bausum, Ann. Marching to the Mountaintop: How Poverty, Labor Fights, & Civil Rights Set the Stage for Martin Luther King Jr.'s Final Hours. 2012. (ENG., Illus.). 112p. (J). (gr. 5-9). lib. bdg. 28.90 *(978-1-4263-0940-3(6),* National Geographic Children's Bks.) National Geographic Society.

Bausum, Ann & National Geographic Kids Staff. Marching to the Mountaintop: How Poverty, Labor Fights, & Civil Rights Set the Stage for Martin Luther King Jr.'s Final Hours. 2012. (ENG., Illus.). 112p. (J). (gr. 5-9). 19.95 *(978-1-4263-0939-7(2),* National Geographic Children's Bks.) National Geographic Society.

Berlatsky, Noah. The Assassination of Martin Luther King Jr. 2011. (Perspectives on Modern World History Ser.). (ENG., Illus.). 224p. (gr. 12-12). lib. bdg. 47.80 *(978-0-7377-5259-5(9),* Greenhaven Pr., Inc.) Cengage Gale.

Bodden, Valerie. The Assassination of Martin Luther King Jr. 2016. (Illus.). 48p. (J). *(978-1-60818-747-8(0),* Creative Education) Creative Co., The.

Boerst, William J. Marching in Birmingham. 2007. (Civil Rights Movement Ser.). (Illus.). 112p. (J). (gr. 3-7). lib. bdg. 27.95 *(978-1-59935-055-4(6))* Reynolds, Morgan Inc.

Bolden, Tonya. M. L. K. The Journey of a King. Adelman, Bob, ed. 2007. (ENG., Illus.). 128p. (J). (gr. 5-9). 27.95 *(978-0-8109-5476-2(1),* Abrams Bks. for Young Readers) Abrams, Inc.

Boshier, Rosa. How to Analyze the Works of Martin Luther King Jr, 1 vol. 2013. (Essential Critiques Set 4 Ser.). (ENG., Illus.). 112p. (J). (gr. 6-12). lib. bdg. 35.64 *(978-1-61783-647-3(8),* Essential Library) ABDO Publishing Co.

Boyd, Herb. Martin Luther King, Jr. Marcos, Pablo, illus. 2005. (Heroes of America Ser.). 239p. (gr. 3-8). 27.07 *(978-1-59679-258-6(2),* Abdo & Daughters) ABDO Publishing Co.

Boyd, Herb. Martin Luther King Jr. 2006. (Heinle Reading Library: Biography Collection). (ENG.). 240p. pap. 16.95 ***(978-1-4240-0546-8(9))*** Cengage Heinle.

Brown, Jonatha A. Martin Luther King, Jr. 2005. (People We Should Know Ser.). (Illus.). 24p. (gr. 1-4). pap. 8.15 *(978-0-8368-4474-0(2));* (ENG & SPA., lib. bdg. 22.00 *(978-0-8368-4583-9(8));* lib. bdg. 22.00 *(978-0-8368-4467-2(X))* Stevens, Gareth Publishing LLLP. (Weekly Reader Leveled Readers).

Bull, Angela. The Story of Martin Luther King, Level 4. 2009. (DK Readers Ser.). (ENG.). 48p. (J). (gr. 3-7). 3.99 *(978-0-7566-5615-7(X),* DK Children) Dorling Kindersley Publishing, Inc.

Bunting, Eve. The Cart That Carried Martin. 2013. 32p. pap. 16.95 *(978-1-60734-601-2(X))* Charlesbridge Publishing, Inc.

—The Cart That Carried Martin. Tate, Don, illus. 2013. (ENG.). 32p. (J). (gr. 1-4). lib. bdg. 16.95 *(978-1-58089-387-9(2))* Charlesbridge Publishing, Inc.

Carson, Mary Kay. What Was Your Dream, Dr. King? And Other Questions About... Martin Luther King, Jr. Madsen, Jim, illus. 2013. (Good Question! Ser.). (ENG.). 32p. (J). (gr. 2). pap. 5.95 *(978-1-4027-9045-4(7))* Sterling Publishing Co., Inc.

Cella, Clara. Martin Luther King Jr. Day. 2012. (Let's Celebrate Ser.). (ENG.). 24p. (gr. k-1). pap. 41.70 *(978-1-4296-9389-9(4));* (Illus.). 26.65 *(978-1-4296-8733-1(9));* (Illus.). pap. 7.29 *(978-1-4296-9388-2(6))* Capstone Press of Coughlan Cos. (Pebble Plus).

Colbert, David. Martin Luther King Jr. 2008. (10 Days Ser.). (ENG.). 160p. (J). (gr. 3-8). pap. 7.99 *(978-1-4169-6805-4(9),* Aladdin) Simon & Schuster Children's Publishing.

Coleman, Wim & Perrin, Pat. Martin Luther King, Jr. National Historic Site: A MyReportLinks.com Book. 2005. (Virtual Field Trips Ser.). (Illus.). 48p. (J). (gr. 4-10). lib. bdg. 26.60 *(978-0-7660-5225-3(7),* MyReportLinks.com Bks.) Enslow Pubs., Inc.

Collins, Terry. The Assassination of Martin Luther King, Jr: April 4 1968, 1 vol. 2014. (24-Hour History Ser.). (ENG.). 48p. (gr. 3-5). pap. 8.95 *(978-1-4329-9302-3(X));* (Illus.). lib. bdg. 33.32 *(978-1-4329-9296-5(1))* Heinemann-Raintree. (NA-h).

Conklin, Wendy. Martin Luther King Jr, 1 vol. 2007. (Primary Source Readers Ser.). (ENG.). 32p. (J). (gr. 4-4). pap. 8.99 *(978-0-7439-0671-5(3))* Shell Educational Publishing.

Cooke, Tim. Martin Luther King Jr. 2016. (Meet the Greats Ser.). 00048p. (J). pap. 14.05 ***(978-1-4824-5952-4(3))*** Stevens, Gareth Publishing LLLP.

Darby, Jean. Martin Luther King Jr. 2005. (Just the Facts Biographies Ser.). (ENG., Illus.). 112p. (gr. 5-12). 27.93 *(978-0-8225-2471-7(6))* Lerner Publishing Group.

Dash, Meredith. Día de Martin Luther King Jr. 2015. (Días Festivos Ser.). (SPA., Illus.). 24p. (gr. k-1). pap. 7.95 *(978-1-4966-0423-1(7))* Capstone Classroom.

—MLK Jr. Day, 1 vol. 2014. (National Holidays Ser.). (ENG.). 24p. (J). (gr. 4-8). lib. bdg. 28.50 *(978-1-62970-045-8(2))* ABDO Publishing Co.

The Day Martin Luther King Jr Died, 6 vols. (Multicultural Programs Ser.). 16p. (gr. 1-6). 31.95 *(978-0-7802-8325-1(2))* Wright Group/McGraw-Hill.

Dayton, Connor. Martin Luther King Jr. Day. 2012. (American Holidays Ser.). (ENG.). 24p. (J). (gr. k-3). pap. 8.25 *(978-1-4488-6246-7(9));* lib. bdg. 22.60 *(978-1-4488-6144-6(6))* Rosen Publishing Group, Inc., The. (PowerKids Pr.).

—Martin Luther King Jr. Day: Natalicio de Martin Luther King Jr. Alamán, Eduardo, tr. from ENG. 2012. (American Holidays / Celebraciones en los Estados Unidos Ser.). (SPA & ENG.). 24p. (gr. k-3). lib. bdg. 22.60 *(978-1-4488-6710-3(X),* PowerKids Pr.) Rosen Publishing Group, Inc., The.

Dean, Sheri. Martin Luther King, Jr. Day. 2010. (Our Country's Holidays Ser.). (ENG.). 24p. (J). (gr. k-3). pap. 8.15 *(978-1-4339-3918-1(5));* lib. bdg. 22.60 *(978-1-4339-3917-4(7))* Stevens, Gareth Publishing LLLP.

deRubertis, Barbara. Let's Celebrate Martin Luther King, Jr. Day. Griffith, Gershom, illus. 2014. (Holidays & Heroes Ser.). 32p. (gr. 1-3). lib. bdg. 25.26 *(978-1-57565-724-0(4))* Kane Press, Inc.

—Let's Celebrate Martin Luther King, Jr. Day. 2013. 32p. pap. 16.95 *(978-1-57565-639-7(6))* Kane Press, Inc.

Dunn, Joeming W. Martin Luther King, Jr, 1 vol. Allen, Chris, illus. 2008. (Bio-Graphics Ser.). (ENG.). 32p. 28.50 *(978-1-60270-175-5(X),* Graphic Planet- Nonfiction) ABDO Publishing Co.

Fandel, Jennifer. Martin Luther King, Jr. 2005. (Genius Ser.). (Illus.). 48p. (J). (gr. 5-9). lib. bdg. 21.95 *(978-1-58341-329-6(4),* Creative Education) Creative Co., The.

—Martin Luther King, Jr: Great Civil Rights Leader, 1 vol. Bascle, Brian, illus. 2006. (Graphic Biographies Ser.). (ENG.). 32p. (gr. 3-4). 30.65 *(978-0-7368-6498-5(9),* Graphic Library) Capstone Press of Coughlan Cos.

Farris, Christine King. March On! The Day My Brother Martin Changed the World. Ladd, London, illus. 2011. (J). (gr. 2-7). 29.95 *(978-0-545-10689-4(3))* Weston Woods Studios, Inc.

—My Brother Martin: A Sister Remembers Growing up with the Rev. Dr. Martin Luther King Jr. Soentpiet, Chris K., illus. 2003. (ENG.). 32p. (J). (gr. 1-6). 19.99 *(978-0-689-84387-7(9),* Simon & Schuster Bks. For Young Readers) Simon & Schuster Bks. For Young Readers.

—My Brother Martin: A Sister Remembers Growing up with the Rev. Dr. Martin Luther King Jr. Soentpiet, Chris K., illus. 2006. (ENG.). 40p. (J). (gr. 1-6). 8.99 *(978-0-689-84388-4(7),* Aladdin) Simon & Schuster Children's Publishing.

Feinstein, Stephen. Read about Martin Luther King, Jr. 2004. (I Like Biographies! Ser.). (Illus.). 24p. (J). lib. bdg. 24.95 *(978-0-7660-2300-0(1))* Enslow Pubs., Inc.

Fine, Edith Hope. Martin Luther King, Jr: Champion of Civil Rights. 2006. (Heroes of American History Ser.). (Illus.). 32p. (J). (gr. 3-7). lib. bdg. 23.94 *(978-0-7660-2466-3(0),* Enslow Elementary) Enslow Pubs., Inc.

Fleming. Famous Americans Series: Martin Luther King. 2003. (Illus.). 32p. (J). pap. 9.95 *(978-0-590-53545-8(5))* Scholastic, Inc.

Fleming, Alice. Martin Luther King, Jr. A Dream of Hope. 2008. (Sterling Biographies(r) Ser.). (ENG., Illus.). 128p. (J). (gr. 5). pap. 5.95 *(978-1-4027-4439-6(0))* Sterling Publishing Co., Inc.

Flowers, Arthur. I See the Promised Land: A Life of Martin Luther King, Jr., 1 vol. Chitrakar, Manu, illus. rev. ed. 2013. (ENG.). 156p. (J). (gr. 6). 16.95 *(978-1-55498-328-5(2))* Groundwood Bks. CAN. Dist: Publishers Group West (PGW).

Flynn, Riley. Martin Luther King Jr, 1 vol. 2014. (Great African-Americans Ser.). (ENG.). 24p. (gr. k-1). lib. bdg. 21.99 *(978-1-4765-3953-9(7),* Pebble Bks.) Capstone Press of Coughlan Cos.

Foran, Jill. Martin Luther King Jr. Day. 2004. (American Holidays Ser.). (Illus.). 24p. (J). lib. bdg. 24.45 *(978-1-59036-107-8(5));* (gr. 1-3). per. 8.95 *(978-1-59036-167-2(9))* Weigl Pubs., Inc.

—Martin Luther King, Jr. Day. 2015. (Illus.). 24p. (J). *(978-1-5105-0112-6(6))* SmartBook Media, Inc.

—Martin Luther King, Jr. Day. 2010. (American Celebrations Ser.). (Illus.). 24p. (J). (gr. 3-5). pap. 11.95 *(978-1-60596-779-0(3));* lib. bdg. 25.70 *(978-1-60596-772-1(6))* Weigl Pubs., Inc.

Frey, Wendy. Citizen Heroes. 2007. (Illus.). 68p. (J). *(978-1-4105-0887-4(0)); (978-1-4105-0888-1(9))* Johnston, Don Inc.

Ganeri, Anita. I Have a Dream: Martin Luther King, Jr. & the Fight for Equal Rights. 2013. (Turning Points in History Ser.). (Illus.). 48p. (gr. 5-12). 37.10 *(978-1-59920-972-2(1))* Black Rabbit Bks.

—Martin Luther King's I Have a Dream Speech. 2013. (Turning Points in History Ser.). 48p. (gr. 5-9). 24.95 *(978-1-59920-772-8(9))* Black Rabbit Bks.

Gelfand, Dale Evva. Coretta Scott King: Civil Rights Activist. 2nd rev. ed. 2006. (Black Americans of Achievement Legacy Edition Ser.). (Illus.). 137p. (YA). (gr. 7-12). lib. bdg. 35.00 *(978-0-7910-9522-5(3))* Facts On File, Inc.

Gnojewski, Carol. El Dia de Martin Luther King, JR: Honramos a un Hombre de Paz. Jusid, Carolina, tr. from ENG. 2005. (Dias Festivos Ser.). (SPA., Illus.). 48p. (J). (gr. 3-4). lib. bdg. 25.27 *(978-0-7660-2617-9(5),* Enslow Elementary) Enslow Pubs., Inc.

Gosman, Gillian. Martin Luther King, Jr. 2011. (Life Stories Ser.). (Illus.). 24p. (J). pap. 8.25 *(978-1-4488-2755-8(8),* PowerKids Pr.); (gr. 1-4). lib. bdg. 22.60 *(978-1-4488-2583-7(0),* PowerKids Pr.); (ENG & SPA., (gr. 1-4). lib. bdg. 22.60 *(978-1-4488-3217-0(9))* Rosen Publishing Group, Inc., The.

Gotsch, Patrice. Martin Luther King, Jr: Changing Lives. Arreola, Gil, illus. 2006. 19p. pap. 6.30 *(978-1-55501-779-8(7))* Ballard & Tighe Pubs.

Graves, Kerry A. I Have a Dream: The Story Behind Martin Luther King JR. 's Most Famous Speech. 2003. (America in Words & Song Ser.). (Illus.). 32p. (gr. 4-6). lib. bdg. 23.00 *(978-0-7910-7335-3(1),* Chelsea Hse.) Facts On File, Inc.

Gregory, Josh. Martin Luther King Jr. 2015. (ENG., Illus.). 48p. (J). pap. 6.95 *(978-0-531-21208-0(4),* Orchard Bks.) Scholastic Library Publishing.

Haldy, Emma E. Martin Luther King, Jr. Bane, Jeff, illus. 2016. (My Early Library: My Itty-Bitty Bio Ser.). (ENG.). 24p. (J). (gr. k-1). 28.50 *(978-1-63470-477-9(0),* 207639) Cherry Lake Publishing.

Hall, M. C. Martin Luther King, Jr. Civil Rights Leader, 1 vol. Soud, illus. 2008. (Beginner Biographies Ser.). (ENG.). 32p. (gr. -1-3). 28.50 *(978-1-60270-251-6(9),* Looking Glass Library- Nonfiction) Magic Wagon.

Hally, Ashleigh. Coretta Scott King. 2012. (Illus.). 24p. (J). *(978-1-935884-78-1(6));* pap. *(978-1-935884-84-2(0))* State Standards Publishing, LLC.

Hansen, Grace. Martin Luther King, Jr. Civil Rights Leader, 1 vol. 2014. (History Maker Biographies Ser.). (ENG., Illus.). 24p. (J). (gr. 2-4). lib. bdg. 28.50 *(978-1-62970-704-4(X))* ABDO Publishing Co.

Hayes, Amy. Celebrate Martin Luther King Jr. Day. 2015. (Our Holidays Ser.). (ENG., Illus.). 24p. (J). (gr. 1-1). pap. 8.22 *(978-1-5026-0229-9(6))* Cavendish Square Publishing.

Helfand, Lewis & Teitelbaum, Michael. Martin Luther King. Banerjee, Sankha, illus. 2013. (Campfire Graphic Novels Ser.). (ENG.). 88p. (YA). (gr. 5). pap. 11.99 *(978-93-80028-69-9(5),* Campfire) Steerforth Pr.

Hinton, KaaVonia. Martin Luther King, Jr. 2008. (What's So Great About... ? Ser.). (Illus.). 32p. (YA). (gr. 2-4). lib. bdg. 25.70 *(978-1-58415-724-3(0))* Mitchell Lane Pubs., Inc.

Horender, Philip M. Homeward Bound: Civil Rights Mouse Leader, 1 vol. Wolek, Guy, illus. 2013. (Maximilian P. Mouse, Time Traveler Ser.). (ENG.). 112p. (J). (gr. 3-6). lib. bdg. 27.07 *(978-1-61641-962-2(8),* Calico Chapter Bks) Magic Wagon.

Jakoubek, Robert. Martin Luther King Jr. 2008. (Black Americans of Achievement: Legacy Edition Ser.). 112p. (gr. 6-12). pap. 11.95 *(978-1-60413-328-8(7),* Checkmark Bks.) Facts On File, Inc.

Jakoubek, Robert E. Martin Luther King, Jr. Civil Rights Leader. 2004. (Black Americans of Achievement Ser.). (Illus.). 112p. (gr. 6-12). 35.00 *(978-0-7910-8161-7(3),* Chelsea Hse.) Facts On File, Inc.

Jazynka, Kitson. National Geographic Readers: Martin Luther King, Jr. 2012. (Readers Bios Ser.). (ENG.). 48p. (J). (gr. k-3). pap. 3.99 *(978-1-4263-1087-4(0));* lib. bdg. 13.90 *(978-1-4263-1088-1(9))* National Geographic Society. (National Geographic Children's Bks.).

Jeffrey, Gary. Martin Luther King Jr: The Life of a Civil Rights Leader. 2009. (Graphic Nonfiction Biographies Ser.). (ENG.). 48p. (YA). (gr. 4-5). 58.50 *(978-1-61513-021-4(7),* Rosen Reference) Rosen Publishing Group, Inc., The.

—Martin Luther King Jr: The Life of a Civil Rights Leader. Forsey, Chris, illus. 2007. (Graphic Nonfiction Biographies Ser.). (ENG.). 48p. (YA). (gr. 4-7). lib. bdg. 31.95 *(978-1-4042-0858-2(5))* Rosen Publishing Group, Inc., The.

—Martin Luther King Jr: The Life of a Civil Rights Leader. Forsey, Christopher, illus. 2007. (Graphic Biographies Ser.). (ENG.). 48p. (gr. 5-8). pap. 14.05 *(978-1-4042-0921-3(2))* Rosen Publishing Group, Inc., The.

—Martin Luther King Jr. & the March on Washington. 2012. (Graphic History of the Civil Rights Movement Ser.). (Illus.). 24p. (J). (gr. 3-8). pap. 8.15 *(978-1-4339-7492-2(4));* lib. bdg. 23.95 *(978-1-4339-7491-5(6))* Stevens, Gareth Publishing LLLP.

Jeffrey, Laura S. Celebrate Martin Luther King, Jr. , Day. 2006. (Celebrate Holidays Ser.). (Illus.). 104p. (J). (gr. 5). lib. bdg. 33.27 *(978-0-7660-2492-2(X))* Enslow Pubs., Inc.

Jones, Rob Lloyd. Martin Luther King, Jr. 2006. (Illus.). 62p. (J). pap. *(978-0-439-02299-6(1))* Scholastic, Inc.

—Martin Luther King Jr. Le Rolland, Leonard, illus. 2006. (Usborne Famous Lives Gift Bks.). 64p. (J). (gr. 2-5). 8.99 *(978-0-7945-1260-6(7),* Usborne) EDC Publishing.

Kaplan, Leslie C. Martin Luther King Jr. Day. (Library of Holidays Ser.). 24p. 2009. (gr. 2-3). 42.50 *(978-1-60853-714-3(5))* 2004. (Illus.). (J). lib. bdg. 22.60

(978-0-8239-6661-5(5)) Rosen Publishing Group, Inc., The. (PowerKids Pr.).

Kelley, Kitty. Martin's Dream Day. Tretick, Stanley, photos by. 2017. (ENG., Illus.). 40p. (J). (gr. k). 17.99 *(978-1-4814-6766-7(2))* Simon & Schuster Children's Publishing.

King Farris, Christine. My Brother Martin: A Sister Remembers Growing up with the Rev. Dr. Martin Luther King Jr. Soentpiet, Chris K., illus. 2005. 35p. (J). (gr. 4-7). 15.65 *(978-0-7569-6552-5(7))* Perfection Learning Corp.

King, Martin Luther, Jr. I Have a Dream. 2007. (Illus.). 40p. (J). (gr. -1-3). 14.65 *(978-0-7569-8119-8(0))* Perfection Learning Corp.

King, Martin Luther, III. My Daddy, Dr. Martin Luther King, Jr. Ford, A. G., illus. 2013. 32p. (J). (gr. -1-3). (ENG.). 17.99 *(978-0-06-028075-8(1))*; 18.89 *(978-0-06-028076-5(X))* HarperCollins Pubs. (Amistad).

King, Meet Martin Luther, Jr. Meet Martin Luther King Jr. 2004. (ENG., Illus.). 32p. (J). 8.75 *(978-0-8249-5486-4(6)*, Ideal Pubns.) Worthy Publishing.

Krull, Kathleen & Freeman, Laura. Coretta Scott King: I Kept on Marching. 2015. (Women Who Broke the Rules Ser.). (ENG., Illus.). 48p. (J). (gr. 1-4). pap. 6.99 *(978-0-8027-3827-1(3)*, 9780802738271, Bloomsbury USA Childrens) Bloomsbury Publishing USA.

Kurtz, Jane. Martin's Dream. Bates, Amy June, illus. 2008. (Ready-To-Reads Ser.). (ENG.). 32p. (J). (gr. -1-1). pap. 3.99 *(978-1-4169-2774-7(3)*, Simon Spotlight) Simon Spotlight.

Lee, T. S. The Martin Luther King, Jr. Story: The Boy Who Broke Barriers with Faith. 2010. (J). pap. 14.95 *(978-0-9819542-4-0(3))* DASANBOOKS.

Linde, Barbara M. Martin Luther King Jr. 2011. (Civil Rights Crusaders Ser.). (Illus.). 24p. (gr. 2-5). (J). pap. 8.15 *(978-1-4339-5692-8(6)*, Gareth Stevens Learning Library); (YA). lib. bdg. 22.60 *(978-1-4339-5690-4(X))* Stevens, Gareth Publishing LLLP.

Linney, Susan. Martin Luther King, Jr: With a Discussion of Responsibility. 2004. (Values in Action Ser.). (J). *(978-1-59203-069-9(6))* Learning Challenge, Inc.

Lowery, Linda. Martin Luther King Jr. Day. Mitchell, Hetty, illus. rev. ed. 2003. (On My Own Holidays Ser.). (ENG.). 56p. (gr. 2-4). pap. 6.95 *(978-1-57505-709-5(3))* Lerner Publishing Group.

MacMillan, Dianne M. Martin Luther King, Jr. Day. rev. ed. 2008. (Best Holiday Bks.). (Illus.). 48p. (J). (gr. 3-7). lib. bdg. 25.27 *(978-0-7660-3043-5(1))* Enslow Pubs., Inc.

Malam, John. Martin Luther King. (Illus.). 24p. *(978-0-237-51919-3(4))* Evans Brothers, Ltd.

Maloof, Torrey. Martin Luther King Jr: Destined to Lead. 2016. (Primary Source Readers Ser.). (Illus.). 32p. (gr. 2-2). 8.99 *(978-1-4938-2559-2(3))* Teacher Created Materials, Inc.

—You Are There! March on Washington, August 28, 1963. 2nd ed. 2017. (TIME for KIDS(r) Nonfiction Readers Ser.). 32p. (gr. 8-8). 8.99 ***(978-1-4938-3929-2(2))*** Teacher Created Materials, Inc.

—You Are There! March on Washington, August 28 1963. 2017. (Time for Kids Nonfiction Readers Ser.). lib. bdg. 19.65 ***(978-0-606-40288-0(8))*** Turtleback Bks.

Manheimer, Ann S. Martin Luther King Jr: Dreaming of Equality. 2004. (Trailblazer Biographies Ser.). (ENG., Illus.). 112p. (gr. 5-9). 31.93 *(978-1-57505-627-2(5)*, Carolrhoda Bks.) Lerner Publishing Group.

Mara, Wil. Martin Luther King Jr. 2013. (Rookie Biographies(r) Ser.). (ENG.). 32p. (J). pap. 5.95 *(978-0-531-24704-4(X))*; lib. bdg. 23.00 *(978-0-531-24738-9(4))* Scholastic Library Publishing.

Martin Luther King Jr. (Illus.). 112p. pap. 9.95 *(978-0-8225-5316-8(3))* Lerner Publishing Group.

Martin Luther King, JR. 2007. (Illus.). 33p. (J). per. 6.95 *(978-0-9795887-0-9(7))* EZ Comics.

Marzollo, Jean. Happy Birthday, Martin Luther King. Pinkney, J. Brian, illus. 2006. (ENG.). 32p. (J). (gr. -1-3). per. 6.99 *(978-0-439-78224-1(4)*, Scholastic Paperbacks) Scholastic, Inc.

Mattern, Joanne. Coretta Scott King: Civil Rights Activist. (Women Who Shaped History Ser.). 24p. 2009. (gr. 2-3). 42.50 *(978-1-60854-816-3(3))* 2003. (Illus.). (J). lib. bdg. 19.95 *(978-0-8239-6504-5(X))* Rosen Publishing Group, Inc., The. (PowerKids Pr.).

McKissack, Fredrick L. & McKissack, Lisa Beringer. Martin Luther King, Jr. Count & Celebrate! 2009. (Holidays—Count & Celebrate! Ser.). (Illus.). 32p. (J). (gr. k-3). lib. bdg. 23.94 *(978-0-7660-3105-0(5))* Enslow Pubs., Inc.

McKissack, Patricia C. & McKissack, Fredrick L. Martin Luther King, Jr. Civil Rights Leader. 2013. (Famous African Americans Ser.). 24p. (J). (gr. k-3). pap. 7.95 *(978-1-4644-0203-6(5))*; (Illus.). 22.60 *(978-0-7660-4099-1(2))* Enslow Pubs., Inc. (Enslow Elementary).

McNeil, Niki, et al. HOCPP 1055 Martin Luther King Jr. 2006. spiral bd. 18.50 *(978-1-60308-055-2(4))* In the Hands of a Child.

McPherson, Stephanie Sammartino. Biography Coretta Scott King. 2007. (Biography Ser.). (Illus.). 112p. (YA). (gr. 7-12). lib. bdg. 29.27 *(978-0-8225-7156-8(0))* Twenty First Century Bks.

Meltzer, Brad. I Am Martin Luther King, Jr. Eliopoulos, Christopher, illus. 2016. (Ordinary People Change the World Ser.). (ENG.). 40p. (J). (gr. k-3). 14.99 *(978-0-525-42852-7(6)*, Dial Bks) Penguin Young Readers Group.

Michelson, Richard. As Good As Anybody. Colón, Raúl, illus. 2013. (ENG.). 40p. (J). (gr. 1-4). 7.99 *(978-0-385-75387-6(X)*, Dragonfly Bks.) Random Hse. Children's Bks.

Miller, Reagan. Martin Luther King, Jr. Day. 2009. (Celebrations in My World Ser.). (ENG., Illus.). 32p. (J). (gr. 1-3). pap. *(978-0-7787-4308-8(X))*; lib. bdg. *(978-0-7787-4290-6(3))* Crabtree Publishing Co.

Mis, Melody S. Meet Coretta Scott King. (Civil Rights Leaders Ser.). 24p. (gr. 2-3). 2009. 42.50 *(978-1-61511-851-9(9)*, PowerKids Pr.) 2008. (Illus.). (YA). lib. bdg. 22.60 *(978-1-4042-4211-1(2))* Rosen Publishing Group, Inc., The.

—Meet Martin Luther King Jr. 2009. (Civil Rights Leaders Ser.). 24p. (gr. 2-3). 42.50 *(978-1-61511-854-0(3)*, PowerKids Pr.) Rosen Publishing Group, Inc., The.

—Meet Martin Luther King Jr. 2008. (Civil Rights Leaders Ser.). (Illus.). 24p. (YA). (gr. 2-5). lib. bdg. 22.60 *(978-1-4042-4209-8(0))* Rosen Publishing Group, Inc., The.

Moore, Johnny Ray. The Story of Martin Luther King Jr. Wummer, Amy, illus. 2016. (J). *(978-0-8249-1974-0(2)*, Ideal Pubns.) Worthy Publishing.

Murcia, Rebecca Thatcher. The Civil Rights Movement. 2005. (Monumental Milestones Ser.). (Illus.). 48p. (YA). (gr. 4-7). lib. bdg. 29.95 *(978-1-58415-401-3(2))* Mitchell Lane Pubs., Inc.

Murray, Julie. Martin Luther King, Jr. Day. 1 vol. 2005. (Buddy Book Ser.). (ENG., Illus.). 24p. (gr. k-4). 25.65 *(978-1-59197-589-2(1)*, Buddy Bks.) ABDO Publishing Co.

Myers, Walter Dean. I've Seen the Promised Land: The Life of Dr. Martin Luther King, Jr. Jenkins, Leonard, illus. 2012. (ENG.). 40p. (J). (gr. -1-3). pap. 6.99 *(978-0-06-225002-5(7)*, Amistad) HarperCollins Pubs.

—I've Seen the Promised Land: The Life of Dr. Martin Luther King, Jr. Jenkins, Leonard, tr. Jenkins, Leonard, illus. 2003. (ENG.). 40p. (J). (gr. -1-3). 17.99 *(978-0-06-027703-1(3)*, Amistad) HarperCollins Pubs.

Nagelhout, Ryan. Martin Luther King Jr. 2015. (Heroes of Black History Ser.). (ENG.). 32p. (J). (gr. 3-4). 26.60 *(978-1-4824-2906-0(3))* Stevens, Gareth Publishing LLLP.

Nelson, Maria. Coretta Scott King. 2011. (Civil Rights Crusaders Ser.). 24p. (gr. 2-5). (J). pap. 8.15 *(978-1-4339-5680-5(2)*, Gareth Stevens Learning Library); (YA). lib. bdg. 22.60 *(978-1-4339-5678-2(0))* Stevens, Gareth Publishing LLLP.

Nelson, Robin. Martin Luther King, Jr. Day. 2003. (First Step Nonfiction Ser.). (Illus.). 24p. (J). (gr. k-2). lib. bdg. 18.60 *(978-0-8225-1282-0(3))* Lerner Publishing Group.

Nichols, Kaitlyn. Martin Luther King. 2009. pap. 13.25 *(978-1-60559-065-3(7))* Hameray Publishing Group, Inc.

Norwich, Grace. Martin Luther King, Jr. Alba, Elisabeth, illus. 2012. (I Am Ser.: 4). (ENG.). 128p. (J). (gr. 2-5). pap. 5.99 *(978-0-545-44780-5(1)*, Scholastic Paperbacks) Scholastic, Inc.

Pastan, Amy, et al. Martin Luther King, Jr. 2004. (DK Biography Ser.). (ENG., Illus.). 128p. (J). (gr. 5-12). pap. 6.99 *(978-0-7566-0342-7(0)*, DK Children) Dorling Kindersley Publishing, Inc.

Patrick, Denise Lewis. A Lesson for Martin Luther King, Jr. Pate, Rodney S., illus. 2003. (Ready-To-read COFA Ser.). (ENG.). 32p. (J). (gr. k-2). pap. 3.99 *(978-0-689-85397-5(1)*, Simon Spotlight) Simon Spotlight.

Pierce, Alan. Assasination of Martin Luther King, Jr. 1 vol. 2005. (American Moments Set Ii Ser.). (ENG.). 48p. (gr. 4-8). 27.07 *(978-1-59197-727-8(4)*, Abdo & Daughters) ABDO Publishing Co.

Pingry, Patricia A. The Story of Coretta Scott King. Walker, Steven, illus. 2007. (ENG.). 26p. (J). (gr. 3-7). bds. 7.69 *(978-0-8249-6717-8(8)*, Ideal Pubns.) Worthy Publishing.

Pinkney, Andrea Davis. Martin & Mahalia: His Words, Her Song. 2013. (ENG., Illus.). 40p. (J). (gr. 1-17). 18.99 *(978-0-316-07013-3(0))* Little Brown & Co.

Ponto, Joanna & Gnojewski, Carol. Martin Luther King Jr. Day. 2016. (Story of Our Holidays Ser.). (Illus.). 32p. (J). pap. 10.52 *(978-0-7660-8340-0(3))* Enslow Pubs., Inc.

Ridley, Sarah. Martin Luther King: ...And the Fight for Equality. 2013. (History Makers Ser.). (Illus.). 24p. (J). (gr. 2-4). 25.65 *(978-1-59771-389-4(9))* Sea-To-Sea Pubns.

Rivera, Sheila. Martin Luther King, Jr: A Life of Determination. 2006. (Illus.). 32p. (J). pap. 6.95 *(978-0-8225-5697-8(9))* Lerner Publishing Group.

—Martin Luther King Jr: A Life of Determination. 2006. (Pull Ahead Bks.). (Illus.). 32p. (J). (gr. 3-7). lib. bdg. 22.60 *(978-0-8225-3477-8(0)*, Lerner Pubns.) Lerner Publishing Group.

—Martin Luther King Jr: Una vida de determinación (A Life of Determination) 2006. (Libros para Avanzar-Biografías (Pull Ahead Books-Biographies Ser.). (Illus.). 32p. (J). (gr. 3-7). per. 6.95 *(978-0-8225-6556-7(0)*, Ediciones Lerner) Lerner Publishing Group.

Robert Sheldon Stradford. Dj's First Parade. 2009. 44p. pap. 19.99 *(978-1-4389-5864-4(1))* AuthorHouse.

Roop, Peter & Roop, Connie. Let's Dream, Martin Luther King, Jr.! 2004. (Scholastic Chapter Book Biography Ser.). (Illus.). 59p. (J). pap. *(978-0-439-55443-5(8))* Scholastic, Inc.

Ruffin, Frances E. Martin Luther King & the March on Washington. 2014. (Penguin Young Readers, L3 Ser.). (ENG.). 48p. (J). (gr. 1-2). 8.24 *(978-1-63245-254-2(5))* Lectorum Pubns., Inc.

Rustad, Martha E. H. & Leslie, Tonya. Martin Luther King, Jr: A Life of Fairness. 2007. (People of Character Ser.). (ENG., Illus.). 24p. (J). (gr. 2-5). lib. bdg. 25.95 *(978-1-60014-090-7(4))* Bellwether Media.

Saddleback Educational Publishing Staff, ed. Martin Luther King Jr., 1 vol. unabr. ed. 2008. (Graphic Biographies Ser.). (ENG., Illus.). 25p. (YA). (gr. 9-12). pap. 7.95 *(978-1-59905-227-4(X))* Saddleback Educational Publishing, Inc.

Schraff, Anne E. Martin Luther King, Jr: We Shall Overcome. 2005. (African-American Biography Library). (Illus.). 128p. (J). (gr. 6-13). lib. bdg. 33.27 *(978-0-7660-1774-0(5))* Enslow Pubs., Inc.

Schuldt, Lori Meek. Martin Luther King, Jr: With Profiles of Mohandas K. Gandhi & Nelson Mandela. 2006. (Biographical Connections Ser.). (Illus.). 112p. (J). *(978-0-7166-1822-5(2))* World Bk., Inc.

Schuman, Michael A. The Life of Martin Luther King, Jr: Leader for Civil Rights. 2014. (Legendary African Americans Ser.). (Illus.). 96p. (J). (gr. 6-12). 27.94 *(978-0-7660-6147-7(7))* Enslow Pubs., Inc.

Schuman, Michael A. & Schraff, Anne E. Martin Luther King Jr: Fighting for Civil Rights. 2017. (Rebels with a Cause Ser.). 128p. (gr. 8-8). lib. bdg. 37.27 ***(978-0-7660-8511-4(2))*** Enslow Pubs., Inc.

Schwartz, Heather E. The March on Washington: A Primary Source Exploration of the Pivotal Protest, 1 vol. 2014. (We Shall Overcome Ser.). (ENG.). 32p. (gr. 3-4). lib. bdg. 27.32 *(978-1-4914-0223-8(7))* Capstone Press of Coughlan Cos.

Shange, Ntozake. Coretta Scott. Nelson, Kadir, illus. (ENG.). 32p. (J). (gr. -1-4). 2011. pap. 6.99 *(978-0-06-125366-9(9))* 2009. 17.99 *(978-0-06-125364-5(2))* HarperCollins Pubs. (Tegen, Katherine Bks).

Spence, Kelly. Martin Luther King Jr. & Peaceful Protest. 2016. (Primary Sources of the Civil Rights Movement Ser.). (Illus.). 64p. (J). (gr. 6-6). 34.21 *(978-1-5026-1864-1(8))* Cavendish Square Publishing.

Staley, Erin. Martin Luther King Jr. & the Speech That Inspired the World. 2014. (Celebration of the Civil Rights Movement Ser.). 80p. (YA). (gr. 7-12). 34.25 *(978-1-4777-7745-9(8))* Rosen Publishing Group, Inc., The.

Stanmyre, Jackie F. Coretta Scott King & the Center for Nonviolent Social Change. 2016. (Primary Sources of the Civil Rights Movement Ser.). (Illus.). 64p. (J). (gr. 6-6). 34.21 *(978-1-5026-1876-4(1))* Cavendish Square Publishing.

Swain, Gwenyth. Riding to Washington. Geister, David, illus. 2007. (Tales of Young Americans Ser.). (ENG.). 32p. (YA). (gr. 6-12). 17.95 *(978-1-58536-324-7(3))* Sleeping Bear Pr.

Sweeney, Alyse. Easy Reader Biographies: Martin Luther King, Jr: A Man with a Dream. 2007. (ENG.). 16p. pap. 2.99 *(978-0-439-77419-2(5)*, Teaching Resources) Scholastic, Inc.

Tisdale, Rachel. The March on Washington, 1 vol., 1. 2014. (We Shall Overcome Ser.). (ENG.). 32p. (J). (gr. 3-6). 26.25 *(978-1-4777-6069-7(5)*, PowerKids Pr.) Rosen Publishing Group, Inc., The.

Trueit, Trudi Strain. Martin Luther King Jr. Day. 2006. (Rookie Read-About Holidays Ser.). (ENG., Illus.). 32p. (J). (gr. 1-2). lib. bdg. 20.50 *(978-0-531-12459-8(2))* Scholastic Library Publishing.

—Martin Luther King, Jr. Day. Snyder, Joel, illus. 2013. (Holidays & Celebrations Ser.). (ENG.). 32p. (J). (gr. k-3). 27.07 *(978-1-62323-509-3(X)*, 206283) Child's World, Inc., The.

Vaughn, Wally G. & Davis, Mattie Campbell, eds. The Selma Campaign, 1963-1965: The Decisive Battle of the Civil Rights Movement. 2006. (ENG., Illus.). 244p. pap. 19.95 *(978-0-912469-44-7(7))* Majority Pr., The.

Vietze, Andrew. The Life & Death of Martin Luther King Jr. 2017. (J). ***(978-1-5383-8038-3(2))***; pap. ***(978-1-5383-8039-0(0))*** Rosen Publishing Group, Inc., The.

Walker, Ida. The Assassination of Dr. Martin Luther King Jr, 1 vol. 2008. (Essential Events Set 2 Ser.). (ENG., Illus.). 112p. (J). (gr. 6-12). lib. bdg. 35.64 *(978-1-60453-044-5(8))* ABDO Publishing Co.

Ward, Jill. Martin Luther King, Jr: Georgia, My State Biographies. l.t. ed. 2008. (ENG., Illus.). 24p. (J). (gr. k-2). 22.60 *(978-1-935077-01-5(5))*; pap. 22.60 *(978-1-935077-08-4(2))* State Standards Publishing, LLC.

Watkins, Angela Farris. Love Will See You Through: Martin Luther King Jr.'s Six Guiding Beliefs. Comport, Sally Wern, illus. 2014. (ENG.). 32p. (J). (gr. 1-6). 17.99 *(978-1-4169-8693-5(6)*, Simon & Schuster Bks. For Young Readers) Simon & Schuster Bks. For Young Readers.

—My Uncle Martin's Big Heart. Velasquez, Eric, illus. 2010. (ENG.). 32p. (J). (gr. k-2). 19.95 *(978-0-8109-8975-7(1)*, Abrams Bks. for Young Readers) Abrams, Inc.

—My Uncle Martin's Words for America: Martin Luther King Jr. 's Niece Tells How He Made a Difference. Velasquez, Eric, illus. (ENG.). 40p. (J). (gr. 1-4). 2015. 9.95 *(978-1-4197-1836-6(3))* 2011. 21.95 *(978-1-4197-0022-4(7))* Abrams, Inc. (Abrams Bks. for Young Readers).

Waxman, Laura Hamilton. Coretta Scott King. 2008. pap. 52.95 *(978-0-8225-9387-4(4))*; (ENG., Illus.). 48p. (gr. 3-6). lib. bdg. 27.93 *(978-0-8225-7168-1(4)*, Lerner Pubns.) Lerner Publishing Group.

Weakland, Mark. When Martin Luther King Jr. Wore Roller Skates. Ballesteros, Patrick, illus. 2017. 31p. (J). *(978-1-5158-0141-2(1))* 2016. (ENG.). 32p. (gr. 2-3). lib. bdg. 27.99 *(978-1-4795-9685-0(X))* Picture Window Bks.

Weston Woods Staff, creator. March on! the Day My Brother Martin Changed the World. 2011. 38.75 *(978-0-545-31399-5(6))*; 18.95 *(978-0-545-31398-8(8))* Weston Woods Studios, Inc.

—Martin's Big Words. 2011. 38.75 *(978-0-545-15256-3(9))* 2011. 18.95 *(978-0-545-15251-8(8))* 2004. (J). 29.95 *(978-1-55592-133-0(7))* Weston Woods Studios, Inc.

Who Was Martin Luther King, Jr? (Guided Reading Levels Ser.). 28.56 *(978-0-7362-1055-3(5))* CENGAGE Learning.

Winget, Mary. Martin Luther King, Jr. 2004. (History Maker Bios Ser.). (Illus.). 48p. (J). pap. 8.95 *(978-0-8225-4804-1(6)*, Lerner Pubns.) Lerner Publishing Group.

KING PHILIP'S WAR, 1675-1676—FICTION

Smith, Mary P. Wells. The Young Puritans in King Philip's War. Bridgman, L. J., illus. 2011. 396p. 54.95 *(978-1-258-05550-9(3))* Literary Licensing, LLC.

KINGFISHERS—FICTION

Burns, Dal. The Kookaburra & Other Stories. 2007. (ENG.). 76p. per. 16.95 *(978-1-4241-1770-3(4))* PublishAmerica, Inc.

KINGS, QUEENS, RULERS, ETC.

see also Dictators; Prime Ministers

also names of countries with the subdivision Kings and Rulers, e.g. Great Britain—Kings and Rulers; also names of individual kings and rulers, e.g. Elizabeth I, Queen of England, 1533-1603

Abbott, Jacob. Nero. 2009. 202p. (J). pap. 12.00 *(978-1-59128-057-6(5))* Canon Pr.

Aldritt, Jeremy. Thomas Paine & the Power of Common Sense. 2015. (Spotlight on American History Ser.). (ENG., Illus.). 24p. (J). (gr. 4-6). pap. 10.00 *(978-1-4994-1765-4(9)*, PowerKids Pr.) Rosen Publishing Group, Inc., The.

Aller, Susan Bivin. Sitting Bull. 2004. (History Maker Bios Ser.). (J). pap. 6.95 *(978-0-8225-2072-6(9))* Lerner Publishing Group.

—Sitting Bull. Parlin, Tim, tr. Parlin, Tim, illus. 2004. (History Maker Bios Ser.). 47p. (J). 26.60 *(978-0-8225-0700-0(5)*, Carolrhoda Bks.) Lerner Publishing Group.

Aronin, Miriam. Merciless Monarchs & Ruthless Royalty. (ShockZone (tm) — Villains Ser.). (ENG., Illus.). 32p. (gr. 5-8). 2015. 21.32 *(978-1-4677-6003-4(X)*, Lerner Digital) 2013. pap. 8.95 *(978-1-4677-0898-2(4))* 2013. lib. bdg. 26.60 *(978-1-4677-0607-0(8)*, Lerner Pubns.) Lerner Publishing Group.

Bailey, Gerry & Foster, Karen. Queen Victoria's Diamond. Noyes, Leighton & Radford, Karen, illus. 2008. (Stories of Great People Ser.). (ENG.). 40p. (J). (gr. 3-6). lib. bdg. *(978-0-7787-3697-4(0))*; pap. *(978-0-7787-3719-3(5))* Crabtree Publishing Co.

—Sitting Bull's Tomahawk. Radford, Karen & Noyes, Leighton, illus. 2008. (Stories of Great People Ser.). (ENG.). 40p. (J). (gr. 3-8). pap. *(978-0-7787-3714-8(4))*; lib. bdg. *(978-0-7787-3692-9(X))* Crabtree Publishing Co.

Bankston, John. The Life & Times of Alexander the Great. 2004. (Biography of Ancient Civilizations Ser.). (Illus.). 48p. (J). lib. bdg. *(978-1-58415-235-4(4))* Mitchell Lane Pubs., Inc.

Barnes-Murphy, Rowan. Kings & Queens of Britain. 2003. (Illus.). 40p. (YA). *(978-1-84365-027-0(4)*, Pavilion Children's Books) Pavilion Bks.

Barnham, Kay. Crackpot Kings, Queens & Other Daft Royals. 2017. (Barmy Biogs Ser.). (ENG., Illus.). 96p. (J). (gr. 4-6). pap. 7.99 ***(978-0-7502-8377-9(7)***, Wayland) Hachette Children's Group GBR. Dist: Hachette Bk. Group.

Baum, Margaux & Forsyth, Fiona. Augustus. 2016. (Leaders of the Ancient World Ser.). 00112p. (J). (gr. 6-6). 37.10 *(978-1-5081-7242-0(0))* Rosen Publishing Group, Inc., The.

Baum, Margaux & Morgan, Julian. Constantine. 2016. (Leaders of the Ancient World Ser.). 00112p. (J). (gr. 6-6). 37.10 *(978-1-5081-7252-9(8))* Rosen Publishing Group, Inc., The.

Beaumont, Steve. How to Draw Magical Kings & Queens. 2007. (Drawing Fantasy Art Ser.: Vol. 2). (Illus.). 32p. (J). (gr. 4-7). lib. bdg. 26.50 *(978-1-4042-3860-2(3))* Rosen Publishing Group, Inc., The.

Behnke, Alison. The Conquests of Alexander the Great. 2007. (Pivotal Moments in History Ser.). (ENG., Illus.). 160p. (gr. 9-12). lib. bdg. 38.60 *(978-0-8225-5920-7(X))* Lerner Publishing Group.

Benson, Lyn. Who Were the Magi. Joshua, Benson Benson Joshua, illus. 2007. 56p. pap. 23.99 *(978-0-615-13524-3(2))* Benson, Lyn.

Bhote, Themina. Charlemagne: Life & Times of an Early Medieval Emperor. 2004. (Leaders of the Middle Ages Ser.). (Illus.). 112p. (YA). (gr. 5-9). lib. bdg. 34.60 *(978-1-4042-0161-3(0))* Rosen Publishing Group, Inc., The.

—Charlemagne: The Life & Times of an Early Medieval Emperor. 2009. (Leaders of the Middle Ages Ser.). 112p. (gr. 5-8). 66.50 *(978-1-61513-896-8(X)*, Rosen Reference) Rosen Publishing Group, Inc., The.

Bodden, Valerie. Conquistadors. 2017. (J). *(978-1-60818-812-3(4)*, Creative Education) Creative Co., The.

Brennan, Joseph K. What Is an Oligarchy? Crabtree Publishing Staff, ed. 2012. (Forms of Government Ser.: No. 5). (ENG.). 48p. (J). pap. *(978-0-7787-5327-8(1))* Crabtree Publishing Co.

Bridges, Shirin Yim. Agrippina: "Atrocious & Ferocious" Malone, Peter, illus. 2011. (Thinking Girl's Treasury of Dastardly Dames Ser.). (ENG.). 32p. (J). (gr. 3-8). 18.95 *(978-0-9834256-1-8(2))* Goosebottom Bks. LLC.

—Isabella of Castile. Nguyen, Albert, illus. 2010. (Thinking Girl's Treasury of Real Princesses Ser.). (ENG.). 24p. (J). (gr. 3-8). 18.95 *(978-0-9845098-4-3(4))* Goosebottom Bks. LLC.

Bridges, Shirin Yim & Yim Bridges, Shirin. Nur Jahan of India. Nguyen, Albert, illus. 2010. (Thinking Girl's Treasury of Real Princesses Ser.). (ENG.). 24p. (J). (gr. 3-8). 18.95 *(978-0-9845098-5-0(2))* Goosebottom Bks. LLC.

Brooks, E. s. & Brooks, E. S. Historic Boys. 2013. 208p. pap. *(978-3-95507-947-5(3))* DOGMA. in Europäischer Hochschulverlag GmbH & Co. KG.

Buchanan, Jane. Mary Tudor: Courageous Queen or Bloody Mary? 2008. (Wicked History Ser.). (ENG.). 128p. (J). (gr. 6-18). pap. 5.95 *(978-0-531-20502-0(9)*, Watts, Franklin) Scholastic Library Publishing.

Burgan, Michael. Dracula's Dark World. 2010. (HorrorScapes Ser.). (Illus.). 32p. (J). (gr. 4-7). lib. bdg. 25.27 *(978-1-936087-96-9(0))* Bearport Publishing Co., Inc.

Cachola, Jean Iwata, et al. O Kamehameha III: Kauikeaouli. 2004. (HAW & ENG., Illus.). xiv, 120p. (J). pap. *(978-0-87336-047-0(8))* Kamehameha Publishing.

Caravantes, Peggy. Cleopatra: Powerful Leader or Ruthless Pharaoh? 2015. (Perspectives on History Ser.). (ENG.). 32p. (gr. 3-4). lib. bdg. 27.32 *(978-1-4914-2042-3(1))* Capstone Press of Coughlan Cos.

Carton, Gerard. We Four Kings. 2009. (Illus.). 52p. pap. *(978-1-84748-474-1(3))* Athena Pr.

Cassidy, Tam. The White Lady Ghost. 2014. (Jr. Graphic Ghost Stories Ser.). 24p. (J). (gr. 3-6). lib. bdg. 26.25 *(978-1-4777-7125-9(5)*, PowerKids Pr.) Rosen Publishing Group, Inc., The.

Cawthorne, Nigel. Notorious Tyrants. 2012. (Great People in History Ser.). (ENG., Illus.). 128p. (YA). (gr. 8-12). lib. bdg. 34.60 *(978-1-4777-0406-6(X))* Rosen Publishing Group, Inc., The.

Chambers, Catherine. An Emperor's Guide. Pentney, Ryan, illus. 2017. (How-To Guides for Fiendish Rulers Ser.). (ENG.). 32p. (J). (gr. 3-6). 7.99 *(978-1-5124-3071-4(4))*; lib. bdg. 26.65 *(978-1-5124-1551-3(0))*; 7.99 ***(978-1-5124-3621-1(6))***; 39.99 ***(978-1-5124-2707-3(1))***; 39.99 ***(978-1-5124-3620-4(8))*** Lerner Publishing Group.

Clark, Connie. Who in the World Was the Unready King? The Story of Ethelred. Mickle, Jed, illus. 2005. (Who in the World Ser.: 0). (ENG.). 54p. (gr. 2-18). pap. 9.50 *(978-0-9728603-7-6(1)*, 86037) Well-Trained Mind Pr.

Collier, James Lincoln. The Tecumseh You Never Knew. Copeland, Greg, illus. 2004. (You Never Knew Ser.). (ENG.). (J). 25.50 *(978-0-516-24426-6(4)*, Children's Pr.) Scholastic Library Publishing.

Connors, Kathleen. The Life of Cleopatra, Vol. 1. 2014. (Famous Lives Ser.). (ENG.). 24p. (J). (gr. 1-2). 22.60 *(978-1-4824-0384-8(6))* Stevens, Gareth Publishing LLLP.

Daning, Tom. Mitología Romana: Rómulo y Remo. Obregón, José María, illus. 2009. (Historietas Juveniles: Mitologías (Jr. Graphic Mythologies) Ser.). (SPA.). 24p. (J). (gr. 3-6). lib. bdg. 25.25 *(978-1-4358-8570-7(8))* Rosen Publishing Group, Inc., The.

—Roman Mythology: Romulus & Remus. 2007. (Jr. Graphic Mythologies Ser.). (ENG., Illus.). 24p. (J). (gr. 2-5). lib. bdg. 25.25 *(978-1-4042-3397-3(0))*; (gr. 3-8). pap. 10.60 *(978-1-4042-2150-5(6)*, PowerKids Pr.) Rosen Publishing Group, Inc., The.

Daning, Tom & Obregón, José María. Mitología Romana: Rómulo y Remo. 2009. (Historietas Juveniles: Mitologías (Jr. Graphic Mythologies) Ser.). (SPA., Illus.). 24p. (gr. 3-8). pap. 10.60 *(978-1-4358-3334-0(1))* Rosen Publishing Group, Inc., The.

J
K
L

Davenport, John C. Saladin. 2003. (Ancient World Leaders Ser.). (Illus.). 112p. (gr. 6-12). 30.00 (978-0-7910-7223-3(1), Chelsea Hse.) Facts On File, Inc.

Davis, Kenneth C. Don't Know Much about the Kings & Queens of England. Date not set. 48p. (J). (gr. 1-4). pap. 5.99 (978-0-06-446229-7(3)) HarperCollins Pubs.

Day, Nick. Queens of England. 2016. (Uncommon Women Ser.). (ENG., Illus.). 48p. (gr. 3-8). 27.99 (978-1-62920-578-6(8)) Scobre Pr. Corp.

Dean, Arlan. With All My Might: Cochise & the Indian Wars. 2009. (Great Moments in American History Ser.). 32p. (gr. 3-3). 47.90 (978-1-61513-137-2(X)) Rosen Publishing Group, Inc., The.

DeFord, Diane. Chief Sitting Bull. 2009. pap. 13.25 (978-1-60559-070-7(3)) Hameray Publishing Group, Inc.

Dell, Pamela. Queen Noor. 2013. 128p. (YA). (gr. 7-12). 39.93 (978-0-7614-4958-4(2)); pap. 19.99 (978-1-62712-116-3(1)) Cavendish Square Publishing.

Demi Staff & Marshall Cavendish Corporation Staff. Alexander the Great, 0 vols. 2010. (ENG., Illus.). 64p. (J). (gr. 3-7). 19.99 (978-0-7614-5700-8(3), 9780761457008, Amazon Children's Publishing) Amazon Publishing.

Demirel, Ruhi, et al. Abu Bakr As-Siddiq. 2016. (Age of Bliss Ser.). (ENG.). vi, 89p. (J). (gr. 4-8). pap. 5.95 (978-1-59784-371-3(7)) Tughra Bks.

—Uthman Ibn Affan. 2016. (Age of Bliss Ser.). (ENG.). vi, 72p. (J). (gr. 4-8). pap. 5.95 (978-1-59784-373-7(3)) Tughra Bks.

Doyle, William. Napoleon Bonaparte: Emperor. 2016. (History Makers Ser.). 144p. (J). 45.64 (978-1-5026-2447-5(8)) Cavendish Square Publishing.

Dyan, Penelope. A Royal Residence — A Kid's Guide to Windsor Castle. Weigand, John D., photos by. 2011. (Illus.). 40p. pap. 12.95 (978-1-935630-65-4(2)) Bellissima Publishing, LLC.

Eastwood, Kay. Medieval Society. 2003. (Medieval World Ser.). (ENG., Illus.). 32p. (J). (gr. 5). pap. (978-0-7787-1377-7(6)) Crabtree Publishing Co.

Emperor Ashoka of India: What Makes a Ruler Legitimate? (NCHS) (YA). (gr. 6-9). spiral bd., tchr.'s planning gde. ed. 11.50 (978-0-382-44467-8(1)) Cobblestone Publishing Co.

Evento, Susan. Sitting Bull. 2005. (Rookie Biographies Ser.). (ENG., Illus.). 32p. (J). (gr. 1-2). pap. 4.95 (978-0-516-25829-4(X), Children's Pr.) Scholastic Library Publishing.

Forsyth, Fiona. Augustus: The First Emperor. (Ancient Leaders Ser.). 112p. (gr. 5-8). 2009. 66.50 (978-1-61511-419-1(X)) 2003. (Illus.). (YA). lib. bdg. 34.60 (978-0-8239-3588-8(4)) Rosen Publishing Group, Inc., The. (Rosen Reference).

Gamblin, Rose Tooley & Hernández, Oscar. The Queen of Sheba. 2008. (SPA & ENG.). (J). (978-0-8127-0482-2(7)) Autumn Hse. Publishing Co.

Ganeri, Anita. Kings & Queens: The History of the British Monarchy. 2011. (Haynes Pocket Manual Ser.). (ENG., Illus.). 128p. (J). (gr. 3-17). pap. 7.95 (978-1-84425-960-1(9), 1844259609) Haynes Publishing PLC GBR. Dist: Hachette Bk. Group.

George, Enzo. The Tomb of China's First Emperor. 2017. (Crypts, Tombs, & Secret Rooms Ser.). 48p. (gr. 4-5). pap. 84.30 **(978-1-5382-0645-4(5))** Stevens, Gareth Publishing LLLP.

Gibson, Karen Bush. The Life & Times of Catherine the Great. 2005. (Biography from Ancient Civilizations Ser.). (Illus.). 48p. (J). (gr. 4-7). lib. bdg. 29.95 (978-1-58415-347-4(4)) Mitchell Lane Pubs., Inc.

Goldberg, Jan. Napoleon Bonaparte. 2004. (ZB Reads Trio Books). 87p. (gr. 5-7). pap. 5.00 (978-0-7367-1799-1(4)) Zaner-Bloser, Inc.

Gorman, Jacqueline & Guy, John. British Kings & Queens: 1,000 Years of Intrigue, Struggle, Passion & Power. 2009. (ENG.). 128p. (J). (gr. 4-7). pap. 12.95 (978-1-84696-987-4(5), TickTock Books) Octopus Publishing Group GBR. Dist: Independent Pubs. Group.

Green, Richard L. A Salute to Historic African Kings & Queens. 2011. (Empak "Black History" Publication Ser.: Vol. 6). (J). (978-0-9616156-5-9(6)) Empak Publishing Co.

Greenblatt, Miriam. Napoleon Bonaparte & Imperial France. 2005. (Rulers & Their Times Ser.). (Illus.). 96p. (J). (gr. 3-7). lib. bdg. (978-0-7614-1837-5(7), Benchmark Bks.) Marshall Cavendish Corp.

Hardyman, Robyn. What Is a Monarchy?, Vol. 1. 2014. (Understanding Political Systems Ser.). 48p. (J). (gr. 6-8). 31.95 (978-1-4824-0314-5(5)); pap. 14.05 (978-1-4824-0315-2(3)) Stevens, Gareth Publishing LLLP.

Harrison, Paul. Boudicca: Rebelled Against the Romans. 2017. (History VIPs Ser.). (ENG., Illus.). 32p. (J). (gr. 4-6). pap. 12.99 (978-0-7502-9917-6(7), Wayland) Hachette Children's Group GBR. Dist: Hachette Bk. Group.

Harrison, Paul. Dastardly Dictators, Rulers & Other Loony Leaders. 2017. (Barmy Biogs Ser.). (ENG., Illus.). 96p. (J). (gr. 4-6). pap. 7.99 **(978-0-7502-8392-2(0)**, Wayland) Hachette Children's Group GBR. Dist: Hachette Bk. Group.

Havemeyer, Janie. Catherine de' Medici: "The Black Queen" Malone, Peter, illus. 2011. (Thinking Girl's Treasury of Dastardly Dames Ser.). (ENG.). 32p. (J). (gr. 3-8). 18.95 (978-0-9834256-3-2(9)) Goosebottom Bks. LLC.

—Njinga the Warrior Queen. Malone, Peter, illus. 2011. (Thinking Girl's Treasury of Dastardly Dames Ser.). (ENG.). 32p. (J). (gr. 3-8). 18.95 (978-0-9834256-6-3(3)) Goosebottom Bks. LLC.

Hayhurst, Chris. Sitting Bull: Sioux War Chief. 2009. (Primary Sources of Famous People in American History Ser.). 32p. (gr. 2-3). 47.90 (978-1-60851-724-4(1)) Rosen Publishing Group, Inc., The.

—Sitting Bull / Toro Sentado: Sioux War Chief / Jefe Sioux. 2009. (Famous People in American History/Grandes personajes en la historia de los Estados Unidos Ser.). (SPA.). 32p. (gr. 2-3). 47.90 (978-1-61512-555-5(8), Editorial Buenas Letras) Rosen Publishing Group, Inc., The.

—Toro Sentado: Jefe Sioux. 2004. (Grandes personajes en la historia de los Estados Unidos Ser.). (ENG & SPA.). 32p. (gr. 3-6). pap. 10.00 (978-0-8239-4238-1(4)) Rosen Publishing Group, Inc., The.

—Toro Sentado: Jefe sioux (Sitting Bull: Sioux War Chief) 2009. (Grandes personajes en la historia de los Estados Unidos (Famous People in American History) Ser.). (SPA.). 32p. (gr. 2-3). 47.90 (978-1-61512-809-9(3), Editorial Buenas Letras) Rosen Publishing Group, Inc., The.

Heuston, Kimberley. Napoleon I: Emperor & Conqueror. 2010. (Wicked History Ser.). (ENG.). 128p. (J). (gr. 6-12). pap. 5.95 (978-0-531-22823-4(1), Watts, Franklin) Scholastic Library Publishing.

Heyer, Carol, illus. & retold by. Excalibur. Heyer, Carol, retold by. (978-1-59093-022-9(3), Eager Minds Pr.) Warehousing & Fulfillment Specialists, LLC (WFS, LLC).

Hilliam, David. Eleanor of Aquitaine: The Richest Queen in Medieval Europe. (Leaders of the Middle Ages Ser.). 112p. 2009. (gr. 5-8). 66.50 (978-1-61513-897-5(8), Rosen Reference) 2004. (Illus.). (J). lib. bdg. 34.60 (978-1-4042-0162-0(9)) Rosen Publishing Group, Inc., The.

—Richard the Lionheart & the Third Crusade: The English King Confronts Saladin in AD 1191. 2009. (Library of the Middle Ages Ser.). 64p. (gr. 5-8). 58.50 (978-1-60853-902-4(4), Rosen Reference) Rosen Publishing Group, Inc., The.

—Richard the Lionhearted & the Third Crusade: The English King Confronts Saladin, AD 1191. 2004. (Library of the Middle Ages Ser.). (Illus.). 64p. (YA). (gr. 5-8). lib. bdg. 31.95 (978-0-8239-4213-8(9), Rosen Reference) Rosen Publishing Group, Inc., The.

Hilliam, Paul. Elizabeth I: Queen of England's Golden Age. 2009. (Rulers, Scholars, & Artists of the Renaissance Ser.). 112p. (gr. 5-8). 66.50 (978-1-60852-940-7(1), Rosen Reference) Rosen Publishing Group, Inc., The.

Hockinson, Liz. Marie Antoinette "Madame Deficit" Malone, Peter, illus. 2011. (Thinking Girl's Treasury of Dastardly Dames Ser.). (ENG.). 32p. (J). (gr. 3-8). 18.95 (978-0-9834256-4-9(7)) Goosebottom Bks. LLC.

Hoffman, Megan Mills. Napoleon Bonaparte. 2017. (J). **(978-1-5026-2782-7(5))** Cavendish Square Publishing.

Hollander, Barbara Gottfried. Elizabeth I: Queen of England. 2017. (Women Who Changed History Ser.). 48p. (gr. 10-12). lib. bdg. 26.85 **(978-1-68048-643-8(8)**, Britannica Educational Publishing) Rosen Publishing Group, Inc., The.

Hollihan, Kerrie Logan. Elizabeth I, the People's Queen: Her Life & Times, 21 Activities. 2011. (For Kids Ser.). (ENG., Illus.). 144p. (J). (gr. 4-18). pap. 16.95 (978-1-56976-349-0(6)) Chicago Review Pr., Inc.

Jeffrey, Gary. Sitting Bull: The Life of a Lakota Chief. 2009. (Graphic Nonfiction Biographies Ser.). (ENG.). 48p. (YA). (gr. 4-5). 58.50 (978-1-61513-027-6(6), Rosen Reference) Rosen Publishing Group, Inc., The.

Jeffrey, Gary & Petty, Kate. Sitting Bull: The Life of a Lakota Sioux Chief. 2005. (Graphic Nonfiction Biographies Ser.). (ENG., Illus.). 48p. (YA). (gr. 4-7). lib. bdg. 31.95 (978-1-4042-0247-4(1)) Rosen Publishing Group, Inc., The.

Kaplan, Arie. Dracula: The Life of Vlad the Impaler. 2011. (Illus.). 64p. (J). 77.70 (978-1-4488-2233-1(5), Rosen Reference); pap. 12.95 (978-1-4488-2232-4(7), Rosen Reference); (gr. 5-9). lib. bdg. 31.95 (978-1-4488-1229-5(1)) Rosen Publishing Group, Inc., The.

Kerrigan, Michael. The Untold History of the Roman Emperors. 2016. (History Exposed Ser.). (ENG.). 224p. (YA). (gr. 9-9). 55.00 (978-1-5026-1910-5(5)) Cavendish Square Publishing.

Kings Curriculum Binder: Absolute Monarchs Curriculum with Audio CD. 2006. 208p. (YA). ring bd. 135.00 (978-0-9791118-0-8(3)) History Jukebox, LLC.

Knox, Barbara. Forbidden City: China's Imperial Palace. 2006. (Castles, Palaces, & Tombs Ser.). (Illus.). 32p. (J). (gr. 2-5). lib. bdg. 25.27 (978-1-59716-070-4(9), 1251394) Bearport Publishing Co., Inc.

Koestler-Grack, Rachel A. Eleanor of Aquitaine: Heroine of the Middle Ages. 2005. (Makers of the Middle Ages & Renaissance Ser.). (Illus.). 168p. (gr. 5-8). lib. bdg. 32.95 (978-0-7910-8633-9(X), Chelsea Hse.) Facts On File, Inc.

Koh, Frederick. The 10 Mightiest Conquerors. 2008. (J). 14.99 (978-1-55448-517-8(7)) Scholastic Library Publishing.

Kramer, Ann. Eleanor of Aquitaine: The Queen Who Rode off to Battle. 2006. (National Geographic World History Biographies Ser.). (ENG., Illus.). 64p. (J). (gr. 4-7). 17.95 (978-0-7922-5895-7(9)); lib. bdg. 27.90 (978-0-7922-5896-4(7)) National Geographic Society. (National Geographic Children's Bks.).

Leaders of the Ancient World: Set 2. 2017. (Leaders of the Ancient World Ser.). 112p. (gr. 12-11). 296.80 **(978-1-4994-6629-4(3)**, Rosen Young Adult) Rosen Publishing Group, Inc., The.

Lee, Sally. Kings & Queens, 1 vol. 2013. (Royalty Ser.). (ENG., Illus.). 24p. (gr. k-1). lib. bdg. 26.65 (978-1-62065-123-0(8), Pebble Plus) Capstone Press of Coughlan Cos.

—Royalty. 2013. (Royalty Ser.). (ENG.). 24p. (gr. k-1). lib. bdg. 79.95 (978-1-62065-125-4(4), Pebble Plus) Capstone Press of Coughlan Cos.

Levin, Judith. Hammurabi. 2008. (Ancient World Leaders Ser.). (Illus.). 120p. (gr. 6-12). 30.00 (978-0-7910-9603-1(3), Chelsea Hse.) Facts On File, Inc.

Lowe, Ruby Hasegawa, et al. O Kamehameha IV: Alexander Liholiho. 2004. (HAW & ENG., Illus.). x, 115p. (J). pap. (978-0-87336-054-8(0)) Kamehameha Publishing.

Lowery, Zoe & Morgan, Julian. Cleopatra. 2016. (Leaders of the Ancient World Ser.). 00112p. (J). (gr. 6-6). 37.10 (978-1-5081-7254-3(4)) Rosen Publishing Group, Inc., The.

—Nero. 2016. (Leaders of the Ancient World Ser.). 00112p. (J). (gr. 6-6). 37.10 (978-1-5081-7256-7(0)) Rosen Publishing Group, Inc., The.

Lucks, Naomi. Makeda (Queen of Sheba) 2008. (Ancient World Leaders Ser.). 112p. (gr. 6-12). 30.00 (978-0-7910-9579-9(7), Chelsea Hse.) Facts On File, Inc.

Lunge-Larsen, Lise. The Race of the Birkebeiners. Azarian, Mary, illus. 2007. (ENG.). 32p. (J). (gr. k — 1). 7.99 (978-0-618-91599-6(0)) Houghton Mifflin Harcourt Publishing Co.

Macdonald, Fiona. Top 10 Worst Wicked Rulers. Antram, David, illus. 2012. (Top 10 Worst Ser.). (ENG.). 32p. (J). (gr. 3-6). pap. 10.50 (978-1-4339-6701-6(4)); lib. bdg. 26.60 (978-1-4339-6700-9(6)) Stevens, Gareth Publishing LLLP. (Gareth Stevens Learning Library).

MacLeod, Elizabeth. Royal Murder: The Deadly Intrigue of Ten Sovereigns. 2008. (ENG., Illus.). 128p. (J). (gr. 5-7). 24.95 (978-1-55451-128-0(3), 9781554511280); pap. 14.95 (978-1-55451-127-3(5), 9781554511273) Annick Pr., Ltd. CAN. Dist: Publishers Group West (PGW).

Madame M. Trauma Queens/Trauma Kings. l.t. ed. 2003. (Madame M Presents:). (Illus.). 68p. (YA). per. 15.95 (978-0-9704159-3-6(1), 0970415931) Creepy Little Productions.

Marsh, Carole. King George III. 2004. 12p. (gr. k-4). 2.95 (978-0-635-02364-3(4)) Gallopade International.

—Sitting Bull. 2003. 12p. (gr. k-4). 2.95 (978-0-635-02378-0(4)) Gallopade International.

Marsico, Katie. Alexander the Great: Ancient King & Conqueror, 1 vol. 2009. (Essential Lives Set 3 Ser.). (ENG., Illus.). 112p. (J). (gr. 6-12). lib. bdg. 35.64 (978-1-60453-520-4(2)) ABDO Publishing Co.

Maurer, Gretchen. Mary Tudor: "Bloody Mary" Malone, Peter, illus. 2011. (Thinking Girl's Treasury of Dastardly Dames Ser.). (ENG.). 32p. (J). (gr. 3-8). 18.95 (978-0-9834256-2-5(0)) Goosebottom Bks. LLC.

Mayfield, Christine & Quinn, Kristine M. Hammurabi: Babylonian Ruler, 1 vol. 2007. (Primary Source Readers Ser.). (ENG.). 32p. (J). (gr. 4-4). pap. 8.99 (978-0-7439-0441-4(9)) Shell Educational Publishing.

Miller, Reagan. What Is a Monarchy? Crabtree Publishing Staff, ed. 2012. (Forms of Government Ser.: No. 4). (ENG.). 48p. (J). (gr. 5-8). pap. (978-0-7787-5325-4(5)) Crabtree Publishing Co.

Miller, Reagan & Brennan, Joseph K. What Is an Oligarchy? 2012. (Forms of Government Ser.). (ENG.). 48p. (J). (gr. 5-9). lib. bdg. (978-0-7787-5320-9(4)) Crabtree Publishing Co.

Morgan, Julian. Constantine: Ruler of Christian Rome. 2009. (Ancient Leaders Ser.). 112p. (gr. 5-8). 66.50 (978-1-61511-422-1(X), Rosen Reference) Rosen Publishing Group, Inc., The.

—Hadrian: Consolidating the Empire. 2009. (Ancient Leaders Ser.). 112p. (gr. 5-8). 66.50 (978-1-61511-423-8(8), Rosen Reference) Rosen Publishing Group, Inc., The.

—Nero: Destroyer of Rome. 2009. (Ancient Leaders Ser.). 112p. (gr. 5-8). 66.50 (978-1-61511-426-9(2), Rosen Reference) Rosen Publishing Group, Inc., The.

Nagelhout, Ryan. Ivan the Terrible. 2016. (History's Most Murderous Villains Ser.). (Illus.). 32p. (J). (gr. 5-4). pap. 10.50 (978-1-4824-4794-1(0)) Stevens, Gareth Publishing LLLP.

Nardo, Don. Cleopatra. 2016. (ENG.). 80p. (J). 38.60 (978-1-60152-948-0(1)) ReferencePoint Pr., Inc.

Norwich, Grace. Cleopatra. 2014. (I Am Ser.: 10). (ENG., Illus.). 128p. (J). (gr. 2-5). pap. 5.99 (978-0-545-58753-2(0), Scholastic Paperbacks) Scholastic, Inc.

Pack, Mary Fisk. Cleopatra: "Serpent of the Nile" Malone, Peter, illus. 2011. (Thinking Girl's Treasury of Dastardly Dames Ser.). (ENG.). 32p. (J). (gr. 3-8). 18.95 (978-0-9834256-0-1(4)) Goosebottom Bks. LLC.

Pfeffer, Wendy. Mysterious Spinners. Kim, Julie J., illus. 2005. 48p. (J). (978-1-59336-315-4(X)); pap. (978-1-59336-316-1(8)) Mondo Publishing.

Phillips, Charles. Kings & Queens of Britain's Modern Age: From Hanover to Windsor - 1714-Today. 2009. (ENG., Illus.). 96p. pap. 14.99 (978-1-84476-520-1(2)) Anness Publishing GBR. Dist: National Bk. Network.

Phillips, Larissa. Cochise: Apache Chief. 2009. (Primary Sources of Famous People in American History Ser.). 32p. (gr. 2-3). 47.90 (978-1-60851-660-5(1)) Rosen Publishing Group, Inc., The.

—Cochise: Apache Chief / Cochise: Jefe Apache. 2009. (Famous People in American History/Grandes personajes en la historia de los Estados Unidos Ser.). (ENG & SPA.). 32p. (gr. 2-3). 47.90 (978-1-61512-540-1(X), Editorial Buenas Letras) Rosen Publishing Group, Inc., The.

—Cochise: Jefe Apache. de la Vega, Eida, tr. from ENG. 2004. (Grandes Personajes en la Historia de Los Estados Unidos Ser.). (ENG & SPA., Illus.). 32p. (gr. 3-6). pap. 10.00 (978-0-8239-4223-7(6)) Rosen Publishing Group, Inc., The.

—Cochise: Jefe apache (Cochise: Apache Chief) 2009. (Grandes personajes en la historia de los Estados Unidos (Famous People in American History) Ser.). (SPA.). 32p. (gr. 2-3). 47.90 (978-1-61512-792-4(5), Editorial Buenas Letras) Rosen Publishing Group, Inc., The.

Phillips, Robin. Who in the World Was the Acrobatic Empress? The Story of Theodora. unabr. ed. 2010. (ENG.). 1p. audio compact disk 12.95 (978-1-933339-39-9(X), 333939) Well-Trained Mind Pr.

Pipe, Jim. You Wouldn't Want to Be Cleopatra! (Revised Edition) 2017. (You Wouldn't Want to... Ancient Civilizations Ser.). (ENG., Illus.). 32p. (J). lib. bdg. 29.00 (978-0-531-23834-9(2), Watts, Franklin) Scholastic Library Publishing.

Plain, Nancy. Eleanor of Aquitaine & the High Middle Ages. 2005. (Rulers & Their Times Ser.). (Illus.). 80p. (gr. 6-7). lib. bdg. 23.95 (978-0-7614-1834-4(2), Benchmark Bks.) Marshall Cavendish Corp.

Poolos, J. Darius the Great. 2008. (Ancient World Leaders Ser.). (Illus.). 128p. (gr. 6-12). lib. bdg. 30.00 (978-0-7910-9633-8(5), Chelsea Hse.) Facts On File, Inc.

Poulakidas, Georgene. Black Hawk's War. (Primary Sources of American Wars Ser.). 24p. 2009. (gr. 3-4). 42.50 (978-1-60851-518-9(4), PowerKids Pr.) 2006. (Illus.). (YA). (gr. 4-7). lib. bdg. 22.60 (978-1-4042-2682-1(6)) Rosen Publishing Group, Inc., The.

Pratt, Mary K. Elizabeth I: English Renaissance Queen, 1 vol. 2011. (Essential Lives Set 7 Ser.). (ENG., Illus.). 112p. (J). (gr. 6-12). lib. bdg. 35.64 (978-1-61783-003-7(8)) ABDO Publishing Co.

Price, Sean. Ivan the Terrible: Tsar of Death. 2008. (Wicked History Ser.). (ENG., Illus.). 128p. (J). (gr. 3-7). 31.00 (978-0-531-12597-7(1), Children's Pr.) Scholastic Library Publishing.

Rau, Dana Meachen. Who Was Marie Antoinette? O'brien, John, illus. 2015. 106p. (J). (978-1-4806-9210-7(7), Grosset & Dunlap) Penguin Publishing Group.

Reed, Jennifer Bond. The Saudi Royal Family. 2nd rev. ed. 2007. (Modern World Leaders Ser.). (Illus.). 120p. (YA). (gr. 7-12). lib. bdg. 30.00 (978-0-7910-9218-7(6)) Facts On File, Inc.

Rice, Earle. The Life & Times of Clovis. 2009. (Biography from Ancient Civilizations Ser.). 48p. (J). (gr. 4-8). 29.95 (978-1-58415-742-7(9)) Mitchell Lane Pubs., Inc.

—The Life & Times of Eleanor of Aquitaine. 2009. (Biography of Ancient Civilizations Ser.). 48p. (J). (gr. 4-8). 29.95 (978-1-58415-743-4(7)) Mitchell Lane Pubs., Inc.

Robinson, Tony. Kings & Queens. 2014. (ENG., Illus.). 112p. (J). (gr. k-2). pap. 17.99 (978-1-78295-287-9(X), Red Fox) Random House Children's Books GBR. Dist: Independent Pubs. Group.

Rojo, Sara, illus. Why the Sea Is Salty. 2009. (First Reading Level 4 Ser.). 48p. (J). 6.99 (978-0-7945-2308-4(0), Usborne) EDC Publishing.

Roshell, Starshine. Real-Life Royalty. 2007. (Reading Rocks! Ser.). (ENG., Illus.). 32p. (J). (gr. 2-5). 28.50 (978-1-59296-869-5(4), 200749) Child's World, Inc., The.

Roumain, Maryse Noel. Anacaona, Ayiti's Taino Queen/Anacaona, la Reine Taino D'Ayiti. 2012. 36p. pap. 18.41 (978-1-4669-5199-0(0)) Trafford Publishing.

Rowe, Brooke. What Kind of Royalty Are You? 2016. (Best Quiz Ever Ser.). (ENG., Illus.). 32p. (J). (gr. 4-8). 29.93 (978-1-63471-107-4(6), 208539, 45th Parallel Press) Cherry Lake Publishing.

Rucker, Jeffrey A. La historia de Toro Sentado (the Story of Sitting Bull) 2009. (Reading Room Collection: Spanish Ser.). (SPA.). 24p. (gr. 3-4). 42.50 (978-1-60854-178-2(9), Editorial Buenas Letras) Rosen Publishing Group, Inc., The.

—The Story of Sitting Bull. (Reading Room Collection 2 Ser.). 24p. (gr. 3-4). 2009. 42.50 (978-1-60851-998-9(8), PowerKids Pr.) 2003. (ENG.). 43.95 (978-0-8239-8731-3(0)) Rosen Publishing Group, Inc., The.

Rulers & Their Times, 4 bks., Group 4. Incl. Eleanor of Aquitaine & the High Middle Ages. Plain, Nancy. 80p. (gr. 6-7). lib. bdg. 23.95 (978-0-7614-1834-4(2)); Han Wu Di & Ancient China. Greenblatt, Miriam. 80p. (J). (gr. 3-7). lib. bdg. 29.93 (978-0-7614-1835-1(0)); Julius Caesar & the Roman Republic. Greenblatt, Miriam. 96p. (J). (gr. 3-7). lib. bdg. 29.93 (978-0-7614-1836-8(9)); Napoleon Bonaparte & Imperial France. Greenblatt, Miriam. 96p. (J). (gr. 3-7). lib. bdg. (978-0-7614-1837-5(7)); (Illus.). 2005. (978-0-7614-1833-7(4), Benchmark Bks.) Marshall Cavendish Corp.

Rulers, Scholars, & Artists of the Renaissance, 6 bk. set. 2005. (YA). (gr. 5-8). lib. bdg. 191.70 (978-1-4042-0370-9(2)) Rosen Publishing Group, Inc., The.

Sanford, William R. Hunkpapa Lakota Chief Sitting Bull. 2013. (Native American Chiefs & Warriors Ser.). 48p. (J). (gr. 5-18). lib. bdg. 22.60 (978-0-7660-4097-7(6)) Enslow Pubs., Inc.

—Seminole Chief Osceola. 2013. (Native American Chiefs & Warriors Ser.). 48p. (J). (gr. 5-18). lib. bdg. 22.60 (978-0-7660-4117-2(4)) Enslow Pubs., Inc.

Santillian, Beatriz & Morgan, Julian. Hadrian: Emperor of Rome. 2017. (Leaders of the Ancient World Ser.). 112p. (J). (gr. 12-11). 37.10 **(978-1-5081-7484-4(9)**, Rosen Young Adult) Rosen Publishing Group, Inc., The.

Santillian, Beatriz & Morris, Ian Macgregor. Leonidas I: Warrior King of Sparta. 2017. (Leaders of the Ancient World Ser.). 112p. (J). (gr. 12-11). 37.10 **(978-1-5081-7520-9(9)**, Rosen Young Adult) Rosen Publishing Group, Inc., The.

Sapet, Kerrily. Eleanor of Aquitaine: Medieval Queen. 2006. (European Queens Ser.). (Illus.). 192p. (J). (gr. 6-12). lib. bdg. 26.95 (978-1-931798-90-7(7)) Reynolds, Morgan Inc.

Saxena, Shalini. Nero: Ruthless Roman Emperor. 2016. (History's Most Murderous Villains Ser.). (Illus.). 32p. (J). (gr. 5-4). pap. 10.50 (978-1-4824-4799-6(1)) Stevens, Gareth Publishing LLLP.

Schanzer, Rosalyn. George vs. George: The Revolutionary War as Seen by Both Sides. 2004. (ENG., Illus.). 64p. (J). (gr. 4-7). 16.95 (978-0-7922-7349-3(4), National Geographic Children's Bks.) National Geographic Society.

Schiel, Katy. Monarchy: A Primary Source Analysis. (Primary Sources of Political Systems Ser.). 64p. 2009. (gr. 5-8). 58.50 (978-1-60851-838-8(8)) 2003. (Illus.). (J). lib. bdg. 31.95 (978-0-8239-4520-7(0)) Rosen Publishing Group, Inc., The.

Serrano, Francisco. The Poet King of Tezcoco: A Great Leader of Ancient Mexico, 1 vol. Balch, Trudy & Engelbert, Jo Anne, trs. from SPA. Serrano, Pablo, illus. 2007. (ENG.). 48p. (J). (gr. 3-6). 18.95 (978-0-88899-787-6(6)) Groundwood Bks. CAN. Dist: Publishers Group West (PGW).

Shea, John M. Vlad the Impaler. 2016. (History's Most Murderous Villains Ser.). (Illus.). 32p. (J). (gr. 5-4). pap. 10.50 (978-1-4824-4804-7(1)) Stevens, Gareth Publishing LLLP.

Shecter, Vicky Alvear. Cleopatra Rules! The Amazing Life of the Original Teen Queen. 2013. (ENG., Illus.). 176p. (J). (gr. 6-9). pap. 9.95 (978-1-62091-032-0(2)) Boyds Mills Pr.

Shone, Rob. Elizabeth I: The Life of England's Renaissance Queen. 2009. (Graphic Nonfiction Biographies Ser.). (Illus.). 48p. (YA). (gr. 4-5). 58.50 (978-1-61513-016-0(0), Rosen Reference) Rosen Publishing Group, Inc., The.

Shone, Rob & Ganeri, Anita. Elizabeth I: The Life of England's Renaissance Queen. 2005. (Graphic Nonfiction Biographies Ser.). (Illus.). 48p. (YA). (gr. 4-7). lib. bdg. 31.95 (978-1-4042-0246-7(3)) Rosen Publishing Group, Inc., The.

Silate, Jennifer. Seeing the Future: The Final Vision of Sitting Bull. 2009. (Great Moments in American History Ser.). 32p. (gr. 3-3). 47.90 (978-1-61513-150-1(7)) Rosen Publishing Group, Inc., The.

Spilsbury, Richard. Geronimo, 1 vol. Faure, Florence, illus. 2013. (Hero Journals). (ENG.). 48p. (gr. 4-6). pap. 9.95 (978-1-4109-5367-4(X), NA-r) Heinemann-Raintree.

—Geronimo, 1 vol. 2013. (Hero Journals). (ENG., Illus.). 48p. (gr. 4-6). 33.32 (978-1-4109-5360-5(2), NA-r) Heinemann-Raintree.

Stathis, Roberta & Blanch, Gregory. Women Who Ruled. 2003. (Explore the Ages Ser.). (Illus.). 79p. 17.00 (978-1-55501-592-3(1)) Ballard & Tighe Pubs.

Stefoff, Rebecca. Faisal: World Leaders: Past & Present. 2008. (ENG., Illus.). 112p. pap. 18.95 (978-1-891785-10-8(9)) Fons Vitae of Kentucky, Inc.

Storrie, Paul D. Yu the Great. 2008. pap. 52.95 (978-0-8225-9464-2(1)) Lerner Publishing Group.

—Yu the Great: Conquering the Flood - A Chinese Legend. Carruthers, Sandy, illus. 2008. (Graphic Myths & Legends Ser.). (ENG.). 48p. (gr. 4-8). per. 8.95 (978-0-8225-6562-8(5)) Lerner Publishing Group.

Stuckey, Rachel. Your Guide to Medieval Society. 2017. (Destination: Middle Ages Ser.). (ENG., Illus.). 32p. (J). **(978-0-7787-2991-4(5))**; pap. **(978-0-7787-2997-6(4))** Crabtree Publishing Co.

Sutcliffe, Jane. Chief Joseph. 2004. (History Maker Bios Ser.). (J). pap. 6.95 (978-0-8225-2068-9(0)) Lerner Publishing Group.

—Chief Joseph. Parlin, Tim, tr. Parlin, Tim, illus. 2004. (History Maker Bios Ser.). 48p. (J). (gr. 3-5). lib. bdg. 26.60 *(978-0-8225-0696-6(3))* Lerner Publishing Group.

Tait, Leia. Queen Rania Al-Abdullah. 2007. (Remarkable People Ser.). (Illus.). 24p. (J). (gr. 3-7). pap. 8.95 *(978-1-59036-646-2(8))*; (gr. 4-7). lib. bdg. 24.45 *(978-1-59036-645-5(X))* Weigl Pubs., Inc.

Taykutgul, Selcuk & Akin, Ferruh. Uthman: Bearer of Two Pure Lights. 2012. (ENG.). 98p. (J). (gr. 8-12). pap. 7.50 *(978-1-59784-267-9(2))* Tughra Bks.

Thomas, Susanna. Akhenaten & Tutankhamen: The Religious Revolution. 2009. (Ancient Leaders Ser.). 112p. (gr. 5-8). 66.50 *(978-1-61511-417-7(3)*, Rosen Reference) Rosen Publishing Group, Inc., The.

—Snefru: The Pyramid Builder. (Ancient Leaders Ser.). 112p. (gr. 5-8). 2009. 66.50 *(978-1-61511-428-3(9))* 2003. (Illus.). (J). lib. bdg. 34.60 *(978-0-8239-3598-7(1))* Rosen Publishing Group, Inc., The. (Rosen Reference).

Trumbauer, Lisa. King Ludwig's Castle: Germany's Neuschwanstein. 2005. (Castles, Palaces, & Tombs Ser.). 32p. (J). lib. bdg. 25.27 *(978-1-59716-002-5(4))* Bearport Publishing Co., Inc.

Turner, Patrenia. A Christmas Carol For Keeng Troyius. 2016. (Illus.). pap. *(978-0-578-18261-2(0))* Royalty Patrenia Turner Publications.

Turner, Queen of England Patrenia. Queen Patrenialla - A Canadian Story Poem. Turner, Keeng of England Troyius, ed. 2015. (Illus.). pap. *(978-0-578-18000-7(6))* Royalty Patrenia Turner Publications.

Turner, Tracey. Hard As Nails Kings & Queens. 2015. (Hard As Nails in History Ser.). (ENG., Illus.). 64p. (J). (gr. 3-6). lib. bdg. *(978-0-7787-1519-1(1))* Crabtree Publishing Co.

Uhl, Xina M. Cleopatra: Queen of Egypt. 2017. (Women Who Changed History Ser.). 48p. (gr. 10-12). 26.85 ***(978-1-68048-639-1(X)***, Britannica Educational Publishing) Rosen Publishing Group, Inc., The.

Ulasl, Zekeriya, et al. Ali Ibn Abi Talib. 2016. (Age of Bliss Ser.). (ENG.). v, 69p. (J). (gr. 4-8). pap. 5.95 *(978-1-59784-374-4(1))* Tughra Bks.

—Umar Ibn Al-Khattab. 2016. (Age of Bliss Ser.). (ENG.). vi, 82p. (J). (gr. 4-8). pap. 5.95 *(978-1-59784-372-0(5))* Tughra Bks.

UNESCO. Njinga Mbandi: Queen of Ndonga & Matamba. 2016. (ENG., Illus.). 112p. (J). (gr. 3-7). 13.95 *(978-0-00-814937-6(2))* HarperCollins Pubs. Ltd. GBR. Dist: Independent Pubs. Group.

Wagner, Heather Lehr. King Abdullah II: King of Jordan. Schlesinger, Arthur M., Jr., ed. 2005. (Major World Leaders Ser.). (Illus.). 112p. (gr. 6-12). 30.00 *(978-0-7910-8259-1(6)*, Chelsea Hse.) Facts On File, Inc.

Watling, James, illus. Jehoshaphat: 2 Chronicles 20:1-30. 2005. (Little Learner Bible Story Books). 16p. (J). pap. 2.29 *(978-0-7586-0945-8(0))* Concordia Publishing Hse.

Webb, Sarah Powers. Marie Antoinette: Fashionable Queen or Greedy Royal? 2015. (Perspectives on History Ser.). (ENG.). 32p. (gr. 3-4). pap. 7.95 *(978-1-4914-2216-8(5))* Capstone Press of Coughlan Cos.

Weston Woods Staff, creator. Can't You Make Them Behave, King George? 2004. 29.95 *(978-1-55592-378-5(X))*; (J). 18.95 *(978-1-55592-377-8(1))*; (J). 38.75 *(978-1-55592-379-2(8))* Weston Woods Studios, Inc.

White-Thomson, Stephen. Elizabeth I. 2017. (Popcorn: People in History Ser.). (ENG., Illus.). 24p. (J). (gr. k-2). pap. 10.99 *(978-0-7502-8412-7(9)*, Wayland) Hachette Children's Group GBR. Dist: Hachette Bk. Group.

Whiting, Jim. The Life & Times of Augustus Caesar. 2005. (Biography from Ancient Civilizations Ser.). (Illus.). 48p. (J). (gr. -1-7). lib. bdg. 29.95 *(978-1-58415-336-8(9))* Mitchell Lane Pubs., Inc.

—The Life & Times of Nero. 2005. (Biography from Ancient Civilizations Ser.). (Illus.). 48p. (J). (gr. 5-8). lib. bdg. 29.95 *(978-1-58415-349-8(0))* Mitchell Lane Pubs., Inc.

Wilhelm, Doug. Alexander the Great: Master of the Ancient World. 2009. (Wicked History Ser.). (ENG.). 128p. (J). (gr. 5-9). 31.00 *(978-0-531-21275-2(0))* Scholastic Library Publishing.

Woodman, Ros. The Great Celebration: A Puzzle Book about Hezekiah. rev. ed. 2008. (Puzzle Ser.). (ENG.). 24p. (J). 4.99 *(978-1-84550-403-8(8)*, 5fdc83c5-dfb7-462d-aaa0-4a3833eba38b) Christian Focus Pubns. GBR. Dist: Bookmasters Distribution.

Zeiger, Jennifer. Queen Elizabeth II. 2015. (ENG., Illus.). 48p. (J). lib. bdg. *(978-0-531-21599-9(7)*, Orchard Bks.) Scholastic, Inc.

KINGS, QUEENS, RULERS, ETC.—FICTION

Abbott, Tony. The Riddle of Zorfendorf Castle. Merrell, David, illus. 2005. (Secrets of Droon Ser.: No. 25). 124p. (J). lib. bdg. 15.38 *(978-1-4242-0310-9(4))* Fitzgerald Bks.

Adeniyi, Bab. The Servant, the King, & the Princess. 2012. 28p. pap. 15.99 *(978-1-4691-4989-9(3))* Xlibris Corp.

Adler, David A. The Secret Service Mystery. Natti, Susanna, illus. 2008. (Cam Jansen Ser.: Bk. 26). 57p. (J). (gr. 2-5). 11.65 *(978-0-7569-8917-0(5))* Perfection Learning Corp.

Aguiar, Judy Lee. The Littlest Camel: And the Journey of the Three Kings. Rodriguez, Tom, illus. 2008. 176p. (J). per. *(978-0-9725231-2-7(X))* Turnapaige & Reed Moore.

Alexander, Lloyd. Dream-of-Jade: The Emperor's Cat. Burkett, D. Brent, illus. 2005. (ENG.). 48p. (J). (gr. 3-7). 17.95 *(978-0-8126-2736-7(9))* Cricket Bks.

—The Rope Trick. 2004. (ENG.). 208p. (J). (gr. 3-7). reprint ed. pap. 7.99 *(978-0-14-240119-4(6)*, Puffin Books) Penguin Young Readers Group.

Amery, H. & Cartwright, S. The Royal Broomstick. 2004. (First Stories Ser.). 16p. (J). lib. bdg. 12.95 *(978-1-58086-572-2(0))* EDC Publishing.

Andersen, D. R. Why the Moon Changes in the Night Sky. 2005. (J). pap. *(978-1-4108-4190-2(1))* Benchmark Education Co.

Andersen, Hans Christian. The Emperor's New Clothes. 2005. (SPA.). 12p. (J). pap. *(978-958-30-1782-7(5))* Panamericana Editorial.

—The Nightingale. Oleynikov, Igor, illus. 2007.Tr. of Nattergalen. (ENG.). 40p. (J). (gr. k). lib. bdg. 16.50 *(978-1-933327-31-0(6))*; (gr. 1). 15.95 *(978-1-933327-30-3(8))* Purple Bear Bks., Inc.

—Snezhnaya Koroleva - the Snow Queen. Pym, T., illus. 2013. 56p. *(978-1-909115-60-6(6))* Planet, The.

—The Snow Queen. Tatarnikov, Pavel, illus. 2006.Tr. of ??????? ???????? (ENG.). 48p. (J). (gr. 1). 15.95 *(978-1-933327-22-8(7))*; lib. bdg. 16.50 *(978-1-933327-23-5(5))* Purple Bear Bks., Inc.

—El Traje Nuevo del Emperador.Tr. of Emperor's New Clothes. (SPA., Illus.). 48p. (J). (gr. 3-5). *(978-84-241-5527-8(0)*, EV0621) Everest Editora ESP. Dist: Lectorum Pubns., Inc.

—El Traje Nuevo del Emperador.Tr. of Emperor's New Clothes. (SPA.). 64p. (J). 9.50 *(978-84-207-3349-4(0))* Grupo Anaya, S.A. ESP. Dist: AIMS International Bks., Inc.

Andersen, Hans Christian & Starbright Foundation Staff. The Emperor's New Clothes. Burton, Virginia Lee, illus. (Folk Tale Classics Ser.). (ENG.). 48p. (J). (gr. -1-3). 2014. 8.99 *(978-0-544-15952-5(7)*, HMH Books For Young Readers) 2004. pap. 6.95 *(978-0-618-34420-8(9))* Houghton Mifflin Harcourt Publishing Co.

Anderson, Brian & Anderson, Liam. Monster Chefs. Anderson, Brian, illus. 2014. (ENG., Illus.). 32p. (J). (gr. -1-2). 16.99 *(978-1-59643-808-8(8)*, 9781596438088) Roaring Brook Pr.

Anna, Jennifer. Year of the Dragon. 2nd ed. 2007. (Illus.). 56p. (J). pap. 24.99 *(978-1-59092-155-5(0))* Blue Forge Pr.

Anthony, David & David, Charles. Knightscares #5: (Knightscares) 2004. (Illus.). 200p. (J). per. 5.99 *(978-0-9728461-4-1(X)*, 1236107) Sigil Publishing.

Antony, Steve. The Queen's Handbag. 2017. (ENG.). 32p. (J). (gr. -1-k). 17.99 ***(978-1-338-03293-2(3)***, Scholastic Pr.) Scholastic, Inc.

Antony, Steve. The Queen's Hat. 2015. (ENG., Illus.). 32p. (J). (gr. -1-k). 16.99 *(978-0-545-83556-5(9)*, Scholastic Pr.) Scholastic, Inc.

Appel, Julie & Guglielmo, Amy. Find King Henry's Treasure. 2010. (Touch the Art Ser.). (ENG., Illus.). 24p. (J). (gr. -1-1). bds. 12.95 *(978-1-4027-6324-3(7))* Sterling Publishing Co., Inc.

Atwater-Rhodes, Amelia. Wolfcry. 2008. (Kiesha'ra Ser.: Bk. 4). (ENG.). 208p. (YA). (gr. 9-12). pap. 7.99 *(978-0-440-23886-7(2)*, Delacorte Pr.) Random Hse. Children's Bks.

Aumuller, Kimberly. Dragon's Hope: Tale of the Guardians. 2009. 224p. 25.95 *(978-0-595-50945-4(2))*; pap. 15.95 *(978-0-595-52209-5(2))* iUniverse, Inc.

Avi. The Player King. 2017. (J). pap. ***(978-1-4814-3769-1(0))*** Simon & Schuster Children's Publishing.

Bacon, Lee. Legendtopia Book #2: the Shadow Queen. 2017. (Legendtopia Ser.: 2). (ENG.). 272p. (J). (gr. 4-7). 16.99 ***(978-0-553-53406-1(8)***, Delacorte Bks. for Young Readers) Random Hse. Children's Bks.

The Bad Luck of King Fred: Individual Title Six-Packs. (Action Packs Ser.). 104p. (gr. 3-5). 44.00 *(978-0-7635-8408-5(8))* Rigby Education.

Barchers, Suzanne. The Shipwrecked Sailor: A Tale from Egypt. Hehenberger, Shelly, illus. 2015. (Tales of Honor Ser.). (ENG.). 32p. (gr. 1-3). lib. bdg. 26.60 *(978-1-939656-86-5(9))* Red Chair Pr.

Barchers, Suzanne I. The Tale of the Oki Islands: A Tale from Japan. Yokota, Hiromitsu, illus. 2013. (Tales of Honor Ser.). (ENG.). 32p. (gr. 1-3). pap. 8.95 *(978-1-937529-62-8(2))* Red Chair Pr.

Barnett, Mac. Mustache! Cornell, Kevin, illus. 2011. (ENG.). 40p. (J). (gr. -1-3). 16.99 *(978-1-4231-1671-4(2))* Hyperion Pr.

Barry, Rick. Kiriath's Quest. 2008. (J). 8.99 *(978-1-59166-905-0(7))* BJU Pr.

Base, Graeme. The Last King of Angkor Wat. 2014. (ENG., Illus.). 36p. (J). (gr. k-2). 17.95 *(978-1-4197-1354-5(X)*, Abrams Bks. for Young Readers) Abrams, Inc.

Bauer, Deidre. Silver Mountain. 2008. 38p. pap. 8.00 *(978-0-8059-7672-4(8))* Dorrance Publishing Co., Inc.

Baum, L. Frank. Glinda of Oz. 2007. 108p. 22.95 *(978-1-60312-591-8(4))* Aegypan.

Beaty, Noel. The Legend of Snowy the Shrew. 2007. 168p. per. *(978-0-7552-0295-9(3))* Authors OnLine, Ltd.

Becker, Aaron. Return. Becker, Aaron, illus. 2016. (ENG., Illus.). 40p. (J). (gr. -1-3). 15.99 *(978-0-7636-7730-5(2))* Candlewick Pr.

Beddor, Frank. ArchEnemy: The Looking Glass Wars, Book Three, 3 vols. 2010. (Looking Glass Wars Ser.: 3). (ENG.). 384p. (YA). (gr. 7-18). 9.99 *(978-0-14-241689-1(4)*, Speak) Penguin Young Readers Group.

—The Looking Glass Wars, 1 vol. 2007. (Looking Glass Wars Ser.: 1). (ENG., Illus.). 400p. (YA). (gr. 7-18). 9.99 *(978-0-14-240941-1(3)*, Speak) Penguin Young Readers Group.

—Seeing Redd. (Looking Glass Wars Ser.: 2). (ENG.). (YA). (gr. 7-18). 2008. 400p. 9.99 *(978-0-14-241209-1(0)*, Speak) 2007. (Illus.). 384p. 17.99 *(978-0-8037-3155-4(8)*, Dial Bks) Penguin Young Readers Group.

Beiler, Joyce. The Kingdom of Laughter. 2012. 30p. pap. 13.95 *(978-1-4497-6596-5(3)*, WestBow Pr.) Author Solutions, Inc.

Bell, Hilari. Crown of Earth. Willis, Drew, illus. 2010. (Shield, Sword, & Crown Ser.: 3). (ENG.). 272p. (J). (gr. 3-7). pap. 5.99 *(978-1-4169-0599-8(5)*, Aladdin) Simon & Schuster Children's Publishing.

—Crown of Earth. Willis, Drew, illus. 2009. (Shield, Sword, & Crown Ser.: 3). (ENG.). 272p. (J). (gr. 3-7). 16.99 *(978-1-4169-0598-1(7)*, Simon & Schuster/Paula Wiseman Bks.) Simon & Schuster/Paula Wiseman Bks.

—Shield of Stars, No. 1. 2008. (Shield, Sword, & Crown Ser.: 1). (ENG.). 288p. (J). (gr. 3-7). pap. 13.99 *(978-1-4169-0595-0(2)*, Simon & Schuster/Paula Wiseman Bks.) Simon & Schuster/Paula Wiseman Bks.

—Sword of Waters, No. 2. Willis, Drew, illus. 2008. (Shield, Sword, & Crown Ser.: 2). (ENG.). 368p. (J). (gr. 3-7). 16.99 *(978-1-4169-0596-7(0)*, Simon & Schuster/Paula Wiseman Bks.) Simon & Schuster/Paula Wiseman Bks.

Bently, Peter. King Jack & the Dragon. Oxenbury, Helen, illus. 2011. (ENG.). 32p. (J). (gr. -1-k). 17.99 *(978-0-8037-3698-6(3)*, Dial Bks) Penguin Young Readers Group.

Bernreuter, Bob J. The Gift. 2006. (Illus.). 25p. (J). *(978-1-4120-7546-6(7))* Trafford Publishing.

Besson, Luc. Arthur & the Forbidden City. Sowchek, Ellen, tr. 2006. (ENG., Illus.). 192p. (J). (gr. 3-7). pap., pap. 5.99 *(978-0-06-059628-6(7)*, Harper Trophy) HarperCollins Pubs.

—Arthur & the Forbidden City. 2005. (ENG., Illus.). 192p. (J). 15.99 *(978-0-06-059626-2(0))* HarperCollins Pubs.

Biachi, Kelvin K. Tortoise the King. 2010. 74p. pap. 21.50 *(978-1-60911-875-4(8)*, Eloquent Bks.) Strategic Book Publishing & Rights Agency (SBPRA).

Binder, Mark. Kings, Wolves, Princesses & Lions: 28 Illustrated Stories for Young Readers. 2012. (ENG., Illus.). 122p. (J). pap. 14.99 *(978-0-9824707-8-7(9))* Light Pubns.

Binus, Ari, illus. Izzy Hagbah. 2005. 37p. (J). (gr. 1-4). 16.95 *(978-1-932687-38-5(6))*; per. 9.95 *(978-1-932687-39-2(4))* Simcha Media Group. (Devora Publishing).

Bishop, Anne. Anne Bishop's Christmas Dram: The Gift of Three. 2013. 28p. pap. 24.95 *(978-1-4626-8276-8(6))* America Star Bks.

Bishop, Jennie. The Three Gifts of Christmas. McDaniels, Preston, illus. 2009. 32p. (J). (gr. 3-18). 15.99 incl. audio compact disk *(978-1-59317-378-4(4))* Warner Pr., Inc.

Blackaby, Susan. El Traje Nuevo Del Emperador. Abello, Patricia, tr. from ENG. Delage, Charlene, illus. 2006. (Read-It! Readers en Español: Cuentos de Hadas Ser.). (SPA.). 32p. (gr. k-3). 21.32 *(978-1-4048-1629-9(1)*, Easy Readers) Picture Window Bks.

Blackthorn, J. D. & Rinehart, J. D. Crown of Three. 2015. (Crown of Three Ser.: 1). (ENG.). 416p. (J). (gr. 4-8). 17.99 *(978-1-4814-2443-1(2)*, Aladdin) Simon & Schuster Children's Publishing.

Blake, Kendare. Three Dark Crowns. (YA). (gr. 9). 2018. (Three Dark Crowns Ser.: 1). 432p. pap. 10.99 ***(978-0-06-238544-4(5))*** 2016. (ENG.). 416p. 17.99 *(978-0-06-238543-7(7))* HarperCollins Pubs. (HarperTeen).

—Three Dark Crowns. 2018. lib. bdg. 22.10 ***(978-0-606-40404-4(X))*** Turtleback Bks.

Bogumill, Mark P. KingMaker: The Swamp Crusade, 4 vols. 2003. 310p. (YA). bds. 25.00 *(978-0-9744870-0-7(7))* KingMaker Bks. LLC.

Bolognese, Don. The Warhorse. Bolognese, Don, illus. 2010. (ENG., Illus.). 176p. (J). (gr. 5-9). pap. 9.99 *(978-1-4424-2942-0(9)*, Simon & Schuster Bks. For Young Readers) Simon & Schuster Bks. For Young Readers.

Bolton, Michael. The Secret of the Lost Kingdom. Jermann, David, illus. 2004. 36p. (J). (gr. k-4). reprint ed. *(978-0-7567-7849-1(2))* DIANE Publishing Co.

—El Secreto del Reino Perdido. Jermann, David, illus. (Buenas Noches Ser.). (SPA.). (J). (gr. 3). pap. 7.16 *(978-958-04-4904-1(X))* Norma S.A. COL. Dist: Lectorum Pubns., Inc.

Booth, Bradley. Esther: A Star Is Born. 2009. (J). pap. 12.99 *(978-0-8163-2359-3(3))* Pacific Pr. Publishing Assn.

Bower, Tamara. How the Amazon Queen Fought the Prince of Egypt. Bower, Tamara, illus. 2014. (ENG., Illus.). 36p. (J). (gr. 2-6). 16.99 *(978-1-4814-2526-1(9)*, Atheneum Bks. for Young Readers) Simon & Schuster Children's Publishing.

Boyce, Catherine & Boyce, Peter. Tea with the Queen. Sibert, Stephanie Grace, illus. 2006. 32p. (J). per. 16.95 net. incl. audio compact disk *(978-0-9778420-0-1(2)*, 10,000) Semper Studio.

Boyd, David. Hidden Message. Alward, Jeff, illus. 2007. 48p. (J). lib. bdg. 23.08 *(978-1-4242-1637-6(0))* Fitzgerald Bks.

Bracken, Beth & Fraser, Kay. Wish, 1 vol. Sawyer, Odessa, illus. 2013. (Faerieground Ser.). (ENG.). 304p. (gr. 4-8). 12.95 *(978-1-62370-003-4(5))* Stone Arch Bks.

Brazier, Yuvonne. Princess Jordan Saves Golden Tree. 2008. 20p. pap. 12.49 *(978-1-4389-3591-1(9))* AuthorHouse.

Brenner, Peter. King for One Day. Wyss, Manspeter, illus. 36p. (J). (gr. -1-3). 12.95 *(978-0-87592-027-6(6))* Scroll Pr., Inc.

Bret Harte, Harte & Bret Harte. The Queen of the Pirate Isle. Kate Greenaway, illus. 2010. 56p. pap. 3.49 *(978-1-60386-381-0(8)*, Watchmaker Publishing) Wexford College Pr.

Brightwood, Laura, illus. Debate in Sign Language. Brightwood, Laura, . 2006. (J). *(978-0-9779290-6-1(X))* 3-C Institute for Social Development.

—King's New Suit. Brightwood, Laura, . 2007. (J). DVD *(978-1-934409-05-3(7))* 3-C Institute for Social Development.

—Wise People of Helm. Brightwood, Laura, . 2006. (J). *(978-0-9779290-4-7(3))* 3-C Institute for Social Development.

Brown, Gladys. The Adventures of King Flapjack. 2005. 36p. pap. 13.95 *(978-1-4116-2694-2(X))* Lulu Pr., Inc.

Bruchac, Joseph. Dragon Castle. 2011. (ENG.). 352p. (J). (gr. 5-18). 16.99 *(978-0-8037-3376-3(3)*, Dial Bks) Penguin Young Readers Group.

Bucay, Jorge. The King & the Magician. Gusti, illus. 2014. (ENG.). 52p. (J). (gr. -1). 14.95 *(978-0-7892-1204-7(8)*, Abbeville Kids) Abbeville Pr., Inc.

Buckmaster, Heath L. The Dragons of Tamack. 2008. 142p. pap. 13.99 *(978-1-4357-4624-4(4))* Lulu Pr., Inc.

Bulla, Lynda. Freedom Rings: An American Parable. 2005. (Illus.). 32p. (J). lib. bdg. 14.99 *(978-0-9724272-3-4(6))* Katydid Publishing LLC.

Bunce, Elizabeth C. StarCrossed. 2011. (ENG.). 368p. (YA). pap. 9.99 *(978-0-545-13606-8(7)*, Levine, Arthur A. Bks.) Scholastic, Inc.

Burkart, Jeffrey. The Hidden Prince. 2011. (YA). 16.95 *(978-0-9825713-3-0(X))* Clifton Carriage House Pr.

Burkart, Jeffrey E., retold by. The Hidden Prince. 2003. (Illus.). 32p. (J). 9.99 incl. audio compact disk *(978-0-570-07174-7(7))* Concordia Publishing Hse.

Burks, David W. Full Circle: The Story of Outlaw-Prince Edwin, High King of England. 2007. 124p. 20.95 *(978-0-595-70485-9(9))*; per. 10.95 *(978-0-595-46753-2(9))* iUniverse, Inc.

Burnett, Frances Hodgson. The Land of Blue Flower. 2007. 76p. pap. 14.45 *(978-1-59462-742-2(8)*, Book Jungle) Standard Pubns., Inc.

—The Land of the Blue Flower. 2007. 76p. per. 9.45 *(978-1-59462-779-8(7)*, Book Jungle) Standard Pubns., Inc.

—The Lost Prince. (J). 25.95 *(978-0-8488-0691-0(3))* Amereon Ltd.

Burns, Dal. The Adventures of Phoo. 2006. 148p. pap. 24.95 *(978-1-4241-1773-4(9))* PublishAmerica, Inc.

Cadic, Olivier, et al. Queen Margot - The Bloody Wedding. 2007. (Queen Margot Ser.: 2). (ENG., Illus.). 48p. (J). (gr. -1-12). pap. 13.95 *(978-1-905460-19-9(8))* CineBook GBR. Dist: National Bk. Network.

Cadic, Olivier & Gheysens, Francois. Queen Margot - The Age of Innocence. Derenne, Juliette & Barroux, Sophie, illus. 2007. (Queen Margot Ser.: 1). (ENG.). 48p. (J). (gr. 4-7). per. 13.95 *(978-1-905460-10-6(4))* CineBook GBR. Dist: National Bk. Network.

Cahoon, Rebecca. The Magic Garden. 2012. 44p. pap. 9.99 *(978-0-9836771-3-0(1))* Mindstir Media.

Carey, Anna. Once. 2013. (Eve Ser.: 2). (ENG.). 384p. (YA). (gr. 8). pap. 9.99 *(978-0-06-204855-4(4))* HarperCollins Pubs.

—Rise. 2013. (Eve Ser.: 3). (ENG.). (YA). (gr. 8). 336p. pap. 9.99 *(978-0-06-204858-5(9))*; 320p. 17.99 *(978-0-06-204857-8(0))* HarperCollins Pubs.

—Rise: An Eve Novel. 2013. (Illus.). 320p. (YA). pap. 9.99 *(978-0-06-226273-8(4))* HarperCollins Pubs.

Carey, Janet Lee. Dragon's Keep. 2007. 302p. (J). *(978-1-4287-3929-1(7))* Harcourt Trade Pubs.

—Dragon's Keep. 2008. (ENG., Illus.). 320p. (YA). (gr. 7-18). pap. 7.95 *(978-0-15-206401-3(X))* Houghton Mifflin Harcourt Publishing Co.

—In the Time of Dragon Moon. 2015. (ENG.). 480p. (YA). (gr. 7). 17.99 *(978-0-8037-3810-2(2)*, Kathy Dawson Books) Penguin Young Readers Group.

Carpenter, Nancy, illus. Queen Victoria's Bathing Machine. 2014. (ENG.). 40p. (J). (gr. k-3). 17.99 *(978-1-4169-2753-2(0)*, Simon & Schuster/Paula Wiseman Bks.) Simon & Schuster/Paula Wiseman Bks.

Carson, Rae. The Crown of Embers. 2013. (Girl of Fire & Thorns Ser.: 2). (ENG.). 432p. (YA). (gr. 8). pap. 9.99 *(978-0-06-202653-8(4)*, Greenwillow Bks.) HarperCollins Pubs.

—The Girl of Fire & Thorns. (Girl of Fire & Thorns Ser.: 1). (ENG.). (YA). (gr. 8). 2012. 448p. pap. 9.99 *(978-0-06-202650-7(X))* 2011. 432p. 17.99 *(978-0-06-202648-4(8))* HarperCollins Pubs. (Greenwillow Bks.).

Carter, Grant Matthew. The Disaster Caster. Morling, Donovan, illus. 2012. 38p. pap. 16.00 *(978-1-4349-8432-6(X)*, RoseDog Bks.) Dorrance Publishing Co., Inc.

Carter, Todd. A Monarch Universe Package Set: Children's Picture Book. 2007. (Illus.). 34p. (J). pap. 32.95 incl. cd-rom *(978-0-9800222-3-0(1))* UPfirst.com Bks.

Casey, Dawn. The Great Race: The Story of the Chinese Zodiac. Wilson, Anne, illus. 2006. (ENG.). 32p. (J). (gr. -1-3). 16.99 *(978-1-905236-77-0(8))* Barefoot Bks., Inc.

Castor, H. M. VIII. (ENG., Illus.). 432p. (YA). (gr. 7). 2014. pap. 9.99 *(978-1-4424-7419-2(X))* 2013. 17.99 *(978-1-4424-7418-5(1))* Simon & Schuster Bks. For Young Readers. (Simon & Schuster Bks. For Young Readers).

Catchpool, Michael. The Cloud Spinner. Jay, Alison, illus. 2012. (ENG.). 32p. (J). (gr. k-3). 16.99 *(978-0-375-87011-8(3)*, Knopf Bks. for Young Readers) Random Hse. Children's Bks.

Cavendish, Grace. The Grace Mysteries: Assassin & Betrayal. 2011. (Grace Mysteries Ser.). (ENG.). 384p. (J). (gr. 3-7). pap. 6.99 *(978-0-385-74005-0(0)*, Delacorte Bks. for Young Readers) Random Hse. Children's Bks.

Chad, Jon. Leo Geo & His Miraculous Journey Through the Center of the Earth. Chad, Jon, illus. 2012. (ENG., Illus.). 36p. (J). (gr. 2-5). 15.99 *(978-1-59643-661-9(1)*, 9781596436619) Roaring Brook Pr.

Cherubini. Pinocchio in Africa. 2004. reprint ed. pap. 15.95 *(978-1-4191-4166-9(X))*; pap. 1.99 *(978-1-4192-4166-6(4))* Kessinger Publishing, LLC.

Chester, Laura. Hiding Glory. Lippincott, Gary A., illus. 2007. (ENG.). 160p. (J). (gr. 3-7). 18.95 *(978-1-59543-616-0(2))* Willow Creek Pr., Inc.

Chima, Cinda Williams. The Crimson Crown. (Seven Realms Novel Ser.). (ENG.). (J). (gr. 5-9). 2013. 624p. pap. 9.99 *(978-1-4231-5214-9(X))* 2012. 608p. 18.99 *(978-1-4231-4433-5(3))* Hyperion Pr.

Church, Alfred J. Three Greek Children. 2008. (Illus.). 160p. pap. 9.95 *(978-1-59915-081-9(6))* Yesterday's Classics.

Clinton, J. Noel. The Prince of Warwood & the King's Key. 2005. (YA). per. 9.99 *(978-0-9773115-1-4(1))* C2 (C squared) Publishing.

Coatsworth, Elizabeth. The White Horse. Sewell, Helen, illus. 2006. (Sally (Bethlehem Books) Ser.). 169p. (J). (gr. 5-7). per. 11.95 *(978-1-883937-86-7(8))* Bethlehem Bks.

Coe, Mary E. The Prince of Betherland. 2008. 117p. 24.95 *(978-0-557-03112-2(5))* Lulu Pr., Inc.

—The Prince of Betherland a Wonderful World of Fantasy. 2009. 112p. pap. 9.95 *(978-0-557-09297-0(3))* Lulu Pr., Inc.

Cole, Nikki. Princess Hope. 2012. 40p. pap. 14.95 *(978-1-886528-39-0(X))* ASA Publishing Corp.

Colfer, Chris. The Land of Stories: Queen Red Riding Hood's Guide to Royalty. 2017. (ENG.). 128p. (J). (gr. 3-7). 10.99 *(978-0-316-38336-3(8))* Little Brown & Co.

—Queen Red Riding Hood's Guide to Royalty. Dorman, Brandon, illus. 2015. 118p. (J). *(978-0-316-38339-4(2))* Little Brown & Co.

—Trollbella Throws a Party: A Tale from the Land of Stories. Dorman, Brandon, illus. 2017. (ENG.). 32p. (J). (gr. -1-3). 17.99 *(978-0-316-38340-0(6))* Little Brown & Co.

Colum, Padraic & Pogány, Willy. The Adventures of Odysseus & the Tale of Troy. 2008. 280p. per. 27.95 *(978-0-548-81877-0(0))* Kessinger Publishing, LLC.

Comrie, Margaret S. The Heroes of Castle Bretten. 2003. (Illus.). 229p. (J). *(978-1-894666-65-7(8))* Inheritance Pubns.

Conners, Beatrice. The VeryVery Enchanted Kingdom, 1 vol. 2010. 48p. pap. 16.95 *(978-1-4512-9112-4(4))* PublishAmerica, Inc.

Coonan, Candace N. Where Shadows Linger: Tales from Fadreama: Book 2. 2012. 304p. (gr. 2-4). pap. 18.30 *(978-1-4669-3541-9(3))* Trafford Publishing.

Cooney, Caroline B. Enter Three Witches: A Story of Macbeth. l.t. ed. 2007. (Thorndike Literacy Bridge Young Adult Ser.). 343p. (YA). (gr. 8-12). 22.95 *(978-0-7862-9889-1(8))* Thorndike Pr.

Cooney, Caroline B. & Shakespeare, William. Enter Three Witches: A Story of Macbeth. 2007. 281p. (YA). pap. *(978-0-545-01972-9(9))* Scholastic, Inc.

Cordero, Silvia Jaeger & Cordero, Silvia Jaegar. El Huevo Azul. Sunset Producciones & Producciones, Sunset, illus. rev. ed. 2005. (Castillo de la Lectura Verde Ser.). (SPA & ENG.). 136p. (J). (gr. -1-7). pap. 7.95 *(978-970-20-0127-0(7))* Castillo, Ediciones, S. A. de C. V. MEX. Dist: Macmillan.

J K L

Corvino, Lucy, illus. Arabian Nights. 2008. (Classic Starts(tm) Ser.). (ENG.). 160p. (J). (gr. 2-4). 6.95 (978-1-4027-4573-7(7)) Sterling Publishing Co., Inc.

Cotes, Everard. The Story of Sonny Sahib. 2004. reprint ed. pap. 1.99 (978-1-4192-8402-1(9)); pap. 15.95 (978-1-4191-8402-4(4)) Kessinger Publishing, LLC.

Courtney, Kateri. Welby & the Knobby King. 2003. pap. 14.95 (978-0-9743588-0-2(0)) Castlegate Pr.

Creech, Sharon. The Castle Corona. Diaz, David, illus. (J). 2013. (ENG.). 352p. (gr. 3-7). pap. 7.99 (978-0-06-206395-3(2)) 2007. 336p. (gr. 4-7). lib. bdg. 19.89 (978-0-06-084622-0(4), Cotler, Joanna Books) HarperCollins Pubs.

Crichton, Julie. The King & the Queen & the Jelly Bean. Swaim, illus. l.t. ed. 2005. (SPA.). 24p. (J). bds. 7.95 (978-0-9761990-0-7(9)) Bean Bk. Publishing.

—El rey y la reina y el frijolito de Goma. Swaim, Ramon, illus. l.t. ed. 2005. 24p. (J). bds. 7.95 (978-0-9761990-1-4(7)) Bean Bk. Publishing.

Cronin, Doreen. Bloom. Small, David, illus. 2016. (ENG.). 40p. (J). (gr. -1-3). 17.99 (978-1-4424-0620-9(8)) Simon & Schuster Children's Publishing.

Cronshaw, Joseph. Podge & Dodge. 2009. 32p. pap. 13.50 (978-1-60693-868-3(1), Strategic Bk. Publishing) Strategic Book Publishing & Rights Agency (SBPRA).

Cross, Frances. The Mystery of the Green Elephant. 2007. (Blobber Ser.). (ENG.). 84p. (J). per. (978-1-84167-559-6(8)) Ransom Publishing Ltd.

Crowl, Janice. Kili & the Singing Snails. Orme, Harinani, illus. 2011. (J). 16.95 (978-1-58178-104-5(0)) Bishop Museum Pr.

Cypess, Leah. Mistwood. 2010. (ENG.). 320p. (YA). (gr. 8-18). 16.99 (978-0-06-195699-7(6), Greenwillow Bks.) HarperCollins Pubs.

—Nightspell. 2011. (ENG.). 336p. (YA). (gr. 8-18). 16.99 (978-0-06-195702-4(X), Greenwillow Bks.) HarperCollins Pubs.

Dadey, Debbie. The Crook & the Crown. Avakyan, Tatevik, illus. 2015. (Mermaid Tales Ser.: 13). (ENG.). 128p. (J). (gr. 1-4). pap. 5.99 (978-1-4814-4075-2(6), Aladdin) Simon & Schuster Children's Publishing.

Daniel, Tony. The Amber Arrow. 2017. (Wulf's Saga Ser.: 2). (ENG.). 416p. (J). (gr. 8-8). 18.99 **(978-1-4814-8253-0(X))** Baen Bks.

Darden, Amy. Yesterday Once Again: Guenevere's Quest. 2003. (J). pap. 11.00 (978-0-8059-9238-0(3), RoseDog Bks.) Dorrance Publishing Co., Inc.

Dargaw, Kate. Who Came First. Oleynikov, Igor, illus. 2008. 32p. 15.95 (978-1-933327-45-7(6)) Purple Bear Bks., Inc.

David, Erica. All Hail the Queen. RH Disney Staff & Robinson, Bill, illus. 2015. (Stepping Stone Book(TM) Ser.: 1). (ENG.). 128p. (J). (gr. 1-4). lib. bdg. 12.99 (978-0-7364-8216-5(4), RH/Disney) Random Hse. Children's Bks.

—Anna & Elsa - A Warm Welcome. RH Disney Staff et al, illus. 2015. (Stepping Stone Book(TM) Ser.: 3). (ENG.). 128p. (J). (gr. 1-4). 9.99 (978-0-7364-3289-4(2), RH/Disney) Random Hse. Children's Bks.

—Anna & Elsa #5: the Polar Bear Piper (Disney Frozen) Robinson, William et al, illus. 2015. (Stepping Stone Book Ser.: 5). (ENG.). 128p. (J). (gr. 1-4). 9.99 (978-0-7364-3436-2(4), RH/Disney) Random Hse. Children's Bks.

—Anna & Elsa #6: the Arendelle Cup (Disney Frozen) RH Disney Staff et al, illus. 2015. (Stepping Stone Book(TM) Ser.: 6). (ENG.). 128p. (J). (gr. 1-4). 9.99 (978-0-7364-3437-9(2), RH/Disney) Random Hse. Children's Bks.

—A Warm Welcome, No. 3. RH Disney Staff et al, illus. 2015. (Stepping Stone Book(TM) Ser.: 3). (ENG.). 128p. (J). (gr. 1-4). lib. bdg. 12.99 (978-0-7364-8247-9(4), RH/Disney) Random Hse. Children's Bks.

De Boer, Joan. THE SULTAN AND THE MICE. 2007. (ENG., Illus.). 36p. (J). 18.95 (978-84-96788-84-8(9)) OQO, Editora ESP. Dist: Baker & Taylor Bks.

de Brunhoff, Laurent. Babar's USA. 2008. (ENG., Illus.). 64p. (J). (gr. -1-k). 17.95 (978-0-8109-7096-0(1), Abrams Bks. for Young Readers) Abrams, Inc.

de Brunhoff, Laurent & Rose, Phyllis. Babar Comes to America. 2008. (ENG., Illus.). 72p. (J). (gr. -1-k). 18.95 (978-0-8109-7244-5(1), Abrams Bks. for Young Readers) Abrams, Inc.

De la Cruz, Melissa. Ring & the Crown. 2017. (Ring & the Crown Ser.). (ENG.). 480p. (YA). (gr. 9-17). pap. 9.99 (978-1-4847-9925-3(9)) Hyperion Bks. for Children.

De La Ramee, Louise & Ouida. Bimbi. 2007. 152p. per. 13.95 (978-1-60312-344-0(X)); 24.95 (978-1-60312-682-3(1)) Aegypan.

Demi. The Empty Pot. Demi, illus. 2007. (ENG., Illus.). 32p. (J). (gr. -1-3). pap. 25.99 (978-0-8050-8227-2(1), 9780805082272, Holt, Henry & Co. Bks. For Young Readers) Holt, Henry & Co.

Dennis, Peter, illus. The Adventures of King Arthur. 2003. (Young Reading Ser.). 64p. (J). (gr. k-7). pap. 5.99 (978-0-7945-0447-2(7), Usborne) EDC Publishing.

—The Adventures of King Arthur. 2003. (Usborne Young Reading: Series Two Ser.). 64p. (J). (gr. k-7). 8.99 (978-0-7945-1871-4(0), Usborne) EDC Publishing.

dePaola, Tomie, illus. In a Small Kingdom. 2016. (J). (978-0-8234-3551-7(2)) Holiday Hse., Inc.

Derting, Kimberly. The Essence. 2013. (Pledge Trilogy Ser.). (ENG., Illus.). (YA). (gr. 9). 368p. pap. 9.99 (978-1-4424-4560-4(2)); 352p. 16.99 (978-1-4424-4559-8(9)) McElderry, Margaret K. Bks. (McElderry, Margaret K. Bks.).

—The Pledge. (Pledge Trilogy Ser.). (ENG., Illus.). (YA). (gr. 9). 2012. 352p. pap. 10.99 (978-1-4424-2202-5(5)) 2011. 336p. 16.99 (978-1-4424-2201-8(7)) McElderry, Margaret K. Bks. (McElderry, Margaret K. Bks.).

Dharma Publishing Staff. The King Who Understood Animals: A Story about Using Knowledge Wisely. 2nd ed. 2013. (ENG.). 36p. (gr. -1-7). pap. 8.95 (978-0-89800-520-2(5)) Dharma Publishing.

—Three Wise Birds: A Story about Wisdom & Leadership. 3rd ed. 2013. (ENG.). 36p. (gr. -1-7). pap. 8.95 (978-0-89800-521-9(3)) Dharma Publishing.

DiMarco, Carol & Bowman, Sharon. The Tale of Two Kingdoms. 2009. (ENG.). 88p. (J). pap. 10.99 (978-1-59092-170-8(4)) Blue Forge Pr.

Dines, Carol. The Queen's Soprano. 2007. (ENG., Illus.). 336p. (YA). (gr. 9). pap. 18.95 (978-0-15-206102-9(9)) Houghton Mifflin Harcourt Publishing Co.

Disney Book Group Staff. World of Reading: Sofia the First Riches to Rags: Level 1. Disney Storybook Art Team, illus. 2015. (World of Reading Ser.). (ENG.). 32p. (J). (gr. -1-k). pap. 3.99 (978-1-4847-0699-2(4)) Disney Pr.

Dixon, Heather. Entwined. (ENG.). 480p. (YA). (gr. 8). 2012. pap. 9.99 (978-0-06-200104-7(3)) 2011. 17.99 (978-0-06-200103-0(5)) HarperCollins Pubs. (Greenwillow Bks.).

—Illusionarium. 2015. (ENG.). 368p. (YA). (gr. 8). 17.99 (978-0-06-200105-4(1), Greenwillow Bks.) HarperCollins Pubs.

Do, Kim-Thu, tr. from ENG. Tang Monk Disciples Monkey King: English/Vietnamese. Ma, Wenhai, illus. 2005. (Adventures of Monkey King Ser.: No. 3). (ENG & VIE.). 32p. (J). 16.95 (978-1-57227-087-9(X)) Pan Asia Pubns. (USA), Inc.

Dokey, Cameron. The Storyteller's Daughter: A Retelling of the Arabian Nights. 2007. (Once upon a Time Ser.). (ENG.). 240p. (YA). (gr. 9). mass mkt. 7.99 (978-1-4169-3776-0(5), Simon Pulse) Simon Pulse.

Dougherty, John. Stinkbomb & Ketchup-Face & the Badness of Badgers. Ricks, Sam, illus. 2017. (Stinkbomb & Ketchup-Face Ser.). (ENG.). 144p. (J). (gr. 3-7). 15.99 (978-1-101-99662-1(5), G.P. Putnam's Sons Books for Young Readers) Penguin Young Readers Group.

Doyle, Malachy. King Donal's Secret. Watson, Richard, illus. 2005. (ENG.). 24p. (J). lib. bdg. 23.65 (978-1-59646-740-8(1)) Dingles & Co.

Duffy, Carol Ann. The Princess's Blankets. Hyde, Catherine Ryan, illus. 2009. (ENG.). 40p. (J). (gr. k-3). 18.99 (978-0-7636-4547-2(8), Templar) Candlewick Pr.

—Queen Munch & Queen Nibble. Monks, Lydia, illus. 2008. (ENG.). 64p. (J). (gr. -1-3). (978-1-59692-238-9(9)) MacAdam/Cage Publishing, Inc.

Dumas, Alexandre. The Three Musketeers. Tayal, Amit, illus. 2011. (Campfire Graphic Novels Ser.). (ENG.). 104p. (YA). (gr. 3-7). pap. 12.99 (978-93-80028-57-6(1), Campfire) Steerforth Pr.

Dunlap, Susanne. Anastasia's Secret. 2010. (ENG.). 352p. (YA). (gr. 7-18). 16.99 (978-1-59990-420-7(9), 9781599904207, Bloomsbury USA Childrens) Bloomsbury Publishing USA.

Dunn, Carolyn. A Pie Went By. Date not set. 32p. (J). (gr. -1-1). pap. 4.99 (978-0-06-443649-6(7)) HarperCollins Pubs.

Durkee, Noura. The King, the Prince & the Naughty Sheep. Durkee, Noura, illus. 2007. (ENG., Illus.). 24p. (J). (gr. k-5). 16.00 (978-1-879402-58-4(0)) Tahrike Tarsile Quran, Inc.

Dutta, Arup Kumar. The Boy Who Became King. Arya, Viki, illus. 2004. 122p. (J). (978-81-291-0405-2(9)) Rupa & Co.

Edgson, Alison, illus. The Emperor's New Clothes. 2007. (Flip-Up Fairy Tales Ser.). (ENG.). 24p. (J). (gr. -1-2). audio compact disk (978-1-84643-093-0(3)) Child's Play International Ltd.

Edwards, Meinir Wyn. Maelgwn, King of Gwynedd. Wade, Gini, illus. 2008. (ENG.). 24p. (J). pap. 4.95 (978-1-84771-024-6(7)) Y Lolfa GBR. Dist: Dufour Editions, Inc.

Edwards, R. Katie King's Journal. 2004. 376p. (YA). 31.95 (978-0-595-66890-8(9)) iUniverse, Inc.

Elerya. One Step Higher: Piano Paradise Book II, 1 vol. 2009. 79p. pap. 16.95 (978-1-60749-477-5(9)) PublishAmerica, Inc.

Ella, Sara. Unraveling, 1 vol. 2017. (Unblemished Trilogy Ser.). (ENG.). 368p. (YA). 15.99 **(978-0-7180-8103-4(X))** Nelson, Thomas Inc.

Essama, Molly Jane. The Prince & the Three Ugly Hags. 2010. 28p. pap. 16.95 (978-1-4490-5587-5(7)) AuthorHouse.

Evans, Richard. The Spyglass: A Book about Faith. Linton, Jonathan, illus. 2014. (ENG.). 32p. (J). (gr. -1-3). 16.99 (978-1-4814-3109-5(9), Simon & Schuster/Paula Wiseman Bks.) Simon & Schuster/Paula Wiseman Bks.

Eyre, David. Breaking the Blood. Kalahele, Imaikalani, illus. 2008. 40p. 14.95 (978-0-87336-162-0(8)) Kamehameha Publishing.

Fairchild, Simone. Queen Bee's Midnight Caper, 3 vols. Key, Pamela Marie, illus. 2006. 33p. (J). (gr. -1-3). per. 17.95 (978-0-9771971-4-9(X)) Brass Frog Bookworks.

Fan, Nancy Yi. Sword Mountain. 2012. (Swordbird Ser.: 3). (ENG., Illus.). 336p. (J). (gr. 3-7). 16.99 (978-0-06-165108-3(7)) HarperCollins Pubs.

Fantaskey, Beth. Jessica Rules the Dark Side. 2012. (ENG.). 320p. (YA). (gr. 9). 16.99 (978-0-547-39309-4(1)) Houghton Mifflin Harcourt Publishing Co.

—Jessica's Guide to Dating on the Dark Side. 2010. (ENG., Illus.). 384p. (YA). (gr. 9-18). pap. 8.99 (978-0-547-25940-6(9)) Houghton Mifflin Harcourt Publishing Co.

Farah, Barbara. Parabola O Jednom Mostu: Parable of the Bridge. 2005. (CRO., Illus.). 36p. pap. 15.00 (978-0-9769346-0-8(4)) Farah, Barbara.

Farooqi, Imran A. The Spell of the Witch-Queen. 2006. (Illus.). 60p. pap. (978-1-84401-816-1(4)) Athena Pr.

Farrey, Brian. The Secret of Dreadwillow Carse. 2016. (ENG.). 256p. (J). (gr. 3-7). 16.95 (978-1-61620-505-8(9)) Algonquin Bks. of Chapel Hill.

Farrow, G. e. & Farrow, G. E. The Wallypug in London. 2011. 106p. 23.95 (978-1-4638-9696-6(4)) Rodgers, Alan Bks.

Fast, David R. Doctor Dave's Dragon Tales. Ciesinska, Izabela, illus. 2007. 160p. (J). per. 13.95 (978-0-9793944-8-5(1)) Digi-Tall Media.

Ferguson, M. J. The Mirror in the Box: A Children's Story & a Parable. 2013. 66p. (gr. 4-6). pap. 9.99 (978-1-4497-7804-0(6), WestBow Pr.) Author Solutions, Inc.

Ferguson, Sarah. Tea for Ruby. Glasser, Robin Preiss, illus. 2008. (ENG.). 40p. (J). (gr. -1-3). 16.99 (978-1-4169-5419-4(8), Simon & Schuster/Paula Wiseman Bks.) Simon & Schuster/Paula Wiseman Bks.

Ferguson, The Duchess of York, Sarah, The Duchess of York. Tea for Ruby. Glasser, Robin Preiss, illus. 2012. (ENG.). 40p. (J). (gr. -1-3). pap. 7.99 (978-1-4169-5420-0(1), Simon & Schuster/Paula Wiseman Bks.) Simon & Schuster/Paula Wiseman Bks.

Ferris, Jean. Once upon a Marigold. 2004. 275p. (gr. 5). 17.00 (978-0-7569-3613-6(6)) Perfection Learning Corp.

—Thrice upon a Marigold: A Royal Kidnapping Caper. 2014. (ENG.). 256p. (J). (gr. 2-5). pap. 6.99 (978-0-544-30262-4(1), HMH Books For Young Readers) Houghton Mifflin Harcourt Publishing Co.

Feuti, Norm. The King of Kazoo. 2016. (ENG.). 208p. (J). (gr. 2-5). 22.99 (978-0-545-77088-0(2), Graphix) Scholastic, Inc.

Field, Brett. Screno Magic Medieval Collision. 2007. 52p. per. 10.00 (978-1-4257-4700-8(0)) Xlibris Corp.

Fine, Sarah. The Cursed Queen. 2017. (Impostor Queen Ser.: 2). (ENG., Illus.). 432p. (YA). (gr. 7). 17.99 (978-1-4814-4193-3(0), McElderry, Margaret K. Bks.) McElderry, Margaret K. Bks.

—The Impostor Queen. (ENG., Illus.). (YA). (gr. 7). 2017. (Impostor Queen Ser.: 1). 448p. pap. 11.99 (978-1-4814-4191-9(4)) 2016. 432p. 18.99 (978-1-4814-4190-2(6)) McElderry, Margaret K. Bks. (McElderry, Margaret K. Bks.).

Fischer, Lavanya Regunathan. One Tree, One King & the Open Road. 2015. 212p. 14.99 (978-93-5177-028-2(1)) HarperCollins Pubs.

Fisscher, Tiny. RUBY & the LION. 2008. (ENG.). 48p. (J). (gr. 1-7). 11.95 (978-1-60136-014-4(2)) Audio Holdings, LLC.

Flanagan, John. The Emperor of Nihon-Ja, 10 vols., Bk. 10. (Ranger's Apprentice Ser.: 10). (ENG.). (J). (gr. 5-18). 2012. 464p. 8.99 (978-0-14-241859-8(5), Puffin Books) 2011. 448p. 18.99 (978-0-399-25500-7(1), Philomel Bks.) Penguin Young Readers Group.

—The Emperor of Nihon-Ja. 2012. (Ranger's Apprentice Ser.: 10). lib. bdg. 19.65 (978-0-606-23641-6(4), Turtleback) Turtleback Bks.

—The Kings of Clonmel, Bk. 8. 2011. (Ranger's Apprentice Ser.: 8). (ENG.). 400p. (J). (gr. 5-18). 8.99 (978-0-14-241857-4(9), Puffin Books) Penguin Young Readers Group.

Fletcher, Susan. Flight of the Dragon Kyn. 2010. (Dragon Chronicles Ser.). (ENG.). 240p. (J). (gr. 3-7). pap. 10.99 (978-1-4169-9713-9(X), Atheneum Bks. for Young Readers) Simon & Schuster Children's Publishing.

Fontes, Ron. Sunjata: Warrior King of Mali: A West African Legend. Carruthers, Sandy, illus. 2008. (Graphic Myths & Legends Ser.). 48p. (J). (gr. 3-7). lib. bdg. 26.60 (978-0-8225-6758-5(X), Graphic Universe™) Lerner Publishing Group.

Fowles, Shelley. Climbing Rosa. 2009. (ENG., Illus.). 32p. (J). (gr. -1-2). pap. 7.95 (978-1-84507-595-8(1), Frances Lincoln) Quarto Publishing Group UK GBR. Dist: Hachette Bk. Group.

Foxlee, Karen. Ophelia & the Marvelous Boy. 2014. (ENG.). 240p. (J). (gr. 3-7). 16.99 (978-0-385-75354-8(3), Knopf Bks. for Young Readers) Random Hse. Children's Bks.

Friesner, Esther M. Deception's Pawn. 2015. (ENG.). 336p. (YA). (gr. 7). 17.99 (978-0-449-81867-1(5), Random Hse. Bks. for Young Readers) Random Hse. Children's Bks.

—Sphinx's Princess. 2010. (Princesses of Myth Ser.). (ENG.). 400p. (YA). (gr. 7). pap. 9.99 (978-0-375-85655-6(2), Random Hse. Bks. for Young Readers) Random Hse. Children's Bks.

—Sphinx's Queen. 2011. (Princesses of Myth Ser.). (ENG., Illus.). 368p. (YA). (gr. 7). pap. 9.99 (978-0-375-85658-7(7), Ember) Random Hse. Children's Bks.

Fujimoto, Yoshie. The Ninjas & Goblins. 2008. pap. 13.00 (978-0-8059-8638-9(3)) Dorrance Publishing Co., Inc.

Furgang, Kathy. A Throne for the King: Set Of 6. 2010. (Early Connections Ser.). (J). 37.00 net. (978-1-4108-1372-5(X)) Benchmark Education Co.

—A Throne for the King & un trono para el Rey: 6 English, 6 Spanish Adaptations. 2011. (ENG & SPA.). (J). 75.00 net. (978-1-4108-5657-9(7)) Benchmark Education Co.

Fussell, Sandy. Owl Ninja. James, Rhian Nest, illus. 2011. (Samurai Kids Ser.: 2). (ENG.). 272p. (J). (gr. 4-7). 15.99 (978-0-7636-5003-2(X)) Candlewick Pr.

Gallego Garcia, Laura & Bellm, Dan. The Legend of the Wandering King. 2005. (J). (978-0-439-58557-6(0), Levine, Arthur A. Bks.) Scholastic, Inc.

Galloway, Priscilla. Aleta y la Reina: Una Historia de la Antigua Grecia.Tr. of Aleta & the Queen: A Tale of Ancient Greece. (SPA.). (YA). (gr. 5-8). pap. (978-968-6582-27-7(4)) Samara, Ediciones, S. A. de C. V.

Gamble, Paul. The Monster's Daughter. 2017. (Ministry of SUITs Ser.: 2). (ENG.). 384p. (J). 16.99 (978-1-250-07683-0(8), 9781250076830) Feiwel & Friends.

George, Jessica Day. Dragon Flight. 2009. (Dragon Slippers Ser.). (ENG.). 288p. (YA). (gr. 5-8). pap. 8.99 (978-1-59990-359-0(8), 9781599903590, Bloomsbury USA Childrens) Bloomsbury Publishing USA.

—Dragon Spear. (Dragon Slippers Ser.). (ENG.). (YA). (gr. 5-8). 2010. 272p. pap. 8.99 (978-1-59990-516-7(7), 9781599905167) 2009. 256p. 16.99 (978-1-59990-369-9(5), 9781599903699) Bloomsbury Publishing USA. (Bloomsbury USA Childrens).

—Tuesdays at the Castle. 2011. (Tuesdays at the Castle Ser.: 1). (ENG.). 240p. (YA). (gr. 3-12). 16.99 (978-1-59990-644-7(9), 9781599906447, Bloomsbury USA Childrens) Bloomsbury Publishing USA.

—Wednesdays in the Tower. 2017. (Tuesdays at the Castle Ser.). (ENG.). 256p. (J). pap. 7.99 (978-1-68119-219-2(5), 9781681192192, Bloomsbury USA Childrens) 2014. (Tuesdays at the Castle Ser.: 2). (ENG.). 256p. (YA). (gr. 3-6). pap. 7.99 (978-1-61963-265-3(9), 9781619632653, Bloomsbury USA Childrens) 2013. 240p. E-Book 16.99 (978-1-61963-051-2(6)) 2013. (Tuesdays at the Castle Ser.: 2). (ENG.). 240p. (YA). (gr. 3-6). 16.99 (978-1-59990-645-4(7), 9781599906454, Bloomsbury USA Childrens) Bloomsbury Publishing USA.

Gerhardt, Barbara. I Am of Scram. 2007. (Illus.). pap. 12.95 (978-1-934246-15-3(8)) Peppertree Pr., The.

Gerhardt, Paul L. The Diversity King. 2007. 35p. 19.50 (978-0-615-16208-9(8)) Gerhardt, Paul L.

Gerstein, Mordicai. You Can't Have Too Many Friends! Gerstein, Mordicai, illus. 2014. (ENG., Illus.). 32p. (J). (gr. -1-2). 16.95 (978-0-8234-2393-4(X)) Holiday Hse., Inc.

Gilman, Phoebe. The Balloon Tree. 2004. (J). (gr. k-3). spiral bd. (978-0-616-01650-3(6)) Canadian National Institute for the Blind/Institut National Canadien pour les Aveugles.

Glynn, W. Celebrando a Diario con el Rey.Tr. of Daily with the King. (SPA.). 10.99 (978-958-9269-28-2(1), 490190) Editorial Unilit.

Gogonya, Carol. The African Mermaid & Other Stories. 2011. 40p. pap. 32.70 (978-1-4568-5416-4(X)) Xlibris Corp.

Goldblatt, Mark. Finding the Worm. 2015. (ENG.). 352p. (J). (gr. 4-7). 16.99 (978-0-385-39108-5(0), Random Hse. Bks. for Young Readers) Random Hse. Children's Bks.

—Finding the Worm (Twerp Sequel) 2016. (ENG.). 368p. (J). (gr. 4-7). 7.99 (978-0-385-39111-5(0), Yearling) Random Hse. Children's Bks.

Gooderham, Chris. More Wicked Rhymes. 2008. 68p. pap. 13.95 (978-1-4092-1663-6(2)) Lulu Pr., Inc.

Goodhart, Pippa. Cake Test. McCafferty, Jan, illus. 2007. (Blue Bananas Ser.). (ENG.). 48p. (J). (gr. k-2). pap. 5.99 (978-1-4052-2955-5(1)) Egmont Bks., Ltd. GBR. Dist: Independent Pubs. Group.

Goodrum, Smith. The Marble War: The game of chess as told to Steven. 2011. 28p. pap. 14.95 (978-1-4567-5690-1(7)) AuthorHouse.

Gordon, Mike, illus. The Emperor's New Clothes. 2006. 24p. (J). (gr. -1-3). 9.99 (978-0-7945-1350-4(6), Usborne) EDC Publishing.

Goss, Leon. King for a Day. Nichols, Chris, illus. 2005. (J). pap. (978-1-933156-09-5(0)); per. 16.99 (978-1-933156-01-9(5)) GSVQ Publishing. (VisionQuest Kids).

Graham, Baxter. Old King Stinky Toes. Martin, James R., illus. 2005. 32p. (J). 15.95 (978-0-9764791-0-9(9)) Drumstick Media.

Grandoit, Jean. In the Quest for Inshalla: Simbies of the Caribbean at the World Under. 2010. 68p. pap. 25.49 (978-1-4520-3900-8(3)) AuthorHouse.

Graudin, Ryan. All That Burns. 2015. (ENG.). 464p. (YA). (gr. 8). pap. 9.99 (978-0-06-218743-7(0), HarperTeen) HarperCollins Pubs.

—All That Glows. 2014. (ENG.). 480p. (YA). (gr. 8). pap. 9.99 (978-0-06-218741-3(4), HarperTeen) HarperCollins Pubs.

Green, Rich. Pearlsus. 2007. 140p. per. 10.95 (978-0-595-45166-1(7)) iUniverse, Inc.

Grindley, Sally. Queen Ella's Feet. Aguilar, Sandra, illus. 2011. (My Phonics Readers: Level 3 Ser.). 24p. (J). (gr. -1-1). 24.25 (978-1-84898-513-1(4)) Sea-To-Sea Pubns.

Gruffudd, Elena & Owen, Carys Eurwen. Clustiau March. 2005. (WEL., Illus.). 36p. pap. (978-0-86381-329-0(1)) Gwasg Carreg Gwalch.

Gunderson, Jessica. The King's Warrior: A Story of Ancient India, 1 vol. Hu, Caroline, illus. 2009. (Read-It! Chapter Books: Historical Tales Ser.). (ENG.). 64p. (gr. 2-4). 22.65 (978-1-4048-5228-0(X), Chapter Readers) Picture Window Bks.

Haan, Linda de & Nijland, Stern. King & King. Haan, Linda de & Nijland, Stern, illus. 2003. (ENG., Illus.). 32p. (J). (gr. k-3). 15.99 (978-1-58246-061-1(2), Tricycle Pr.) Random Hse. Children's Bks.

Haddix, Margaret Peterson. Risked. 2013. (Missing Ser.: Bk. 6). (ENG., Illus.). 320p. (J). (gr. 3-7). 16.99 (978-1-4169-8984-4(6), Simon & Schuster Bks. For Young Readers) Simon & Schuster Bks. For Young Readers.

—Sent. (Missing Ser.: 2). (YA). 2011. 82.75 (978-1-4407-2678-1(7)) 2009. 98.75 (978-1-4407-2675-0(2)) 2009. 218.75 (978-1-4407-2670-5(1)) 2009. 1.25 (978-1-4407-2679-8(5)) Recorded Bks., Inc.

—Sent. (Missing Ser.: 2). (ENG.). (J). (gr. 3-7). 2010. 336p. pap. 7.99 (978-1-4169-5423-1(6)) 2009. 320p. 16.99 (978-1-4169-5422-4(8)) Simon & Schuster Bks. For Young Readers. (Simon & Schuster Bks. For Young Readers).

—Sent. abr. ed. 2009. (978-1-4424-0767-1(0)) Simon & Schuster Children's Publishing.

—Sent. l.t. ed. 2010. (Missing Ser.: Bk. 2). (ENG.). 346p. 23.99 (978-1-4104-3245-2(9)) Thorndike Pr.

—Sent. 2010. (Missing Ser.: 2). lib. bdg. 18.40 (978-0-606-14699-9(7), Turtleback) Turtleback Bks.

Hale, Shannon. The Forgotten Sisters. 2015. (Princess Academy Ser.: 3). (ENG.). 336p. (YA). (gr. 5-8). 17.99 (978-1-61963-485-5(6), 9781619634855, Bloomsbury USA Childrens) Bloomsbury Publishing USA.

—Palace of Stone. (Princess Academy Ser.: 2). (ENG.). (YA). (gr. 5-8). 2015. 352p. pap. 7.99 (978-1-61963-257-8(8), 9781619632578) 2012. 336p. 17.99 (978-1-59990-873-1(5), 9781599908731) Bloomsbury Publishing USA. (Bloomsbury USA Childrens).

—Palace of Stone. 2015. (Princess Academy Ser.: 2). (YA). lib. bdg. 18.40 (978-0-606-36439-3(0)) Turtleback Bks.

—Princess Academy - The Forgotten Sisters. 2016. (Princess Academy Ser.: 3). (ENG.). 352p. (J). pap. 7.99 (978-1-61963-933-1(5), 9781619639331, Bloomsbury USA Childrens) Bloomsbury Publishing USA.

Hamilton, Peter F. The Hunting of the Princes. 2016. (Queen of Dreams Ser.: 2). (ENG., Illus.). 320p. (J). (gr. 4-7). pap. 11.99 (978-1-4472-9114-5(X)) Pan Macmillan GBR. Dist: Independent Pubs. Group.

Hancock, R. C. An Uncommon Blue. 2014. (Illus.). xi, 275p. (YA). pap. 16.99 (978-1-4621-1488-7(1)) Cedar Fort, Inc./CFI Distribution.

Hand, Cynthia, et al. My Lady Jane. 512p. (YA). (gr. 8). 2017. pap. 9.99 (978-0-06-239176-6(3)) 2016. 17.99 (978-0-06-239174-2(7)) HarperCollins Pubs. (HarperTeen).

Hannan, Peter. Freddy! Deep-Space Food Fighter. Hannan, Peter, illus. 2011. (Freddy! Ser.: 2). (ENG., Illus.). 144p. (J). (gr. 2-6). pap. 5.99 (978-0-06-128468-7(8)) HarperCollins Pubs.

—Freddy! Locked in Space. Hannan, Peter, illus. 2011. (Freddy! Ser.: 3). (ENG., Illus.). 160p. (J). (gr. 2-6). pap. 5.99 (978-0-06-128470-0(X)) HarperCollins Pubs.

Harrison, Christy Gremore. Once upon A Monday. 2010. 40p. pap. 16.99 (978-1-4490-5854-8(X)) AuthorHouse.

Harrison, Mette Ivie. The Princess & the Bear. 2010. (ENG.). 352p. (YA). (gr. 8). pap. 8.99 (978-0-06-155316-5(6), HarperTeen) HarperCollins Pubs.

—The Princess & the Hound. (YA). 2008. (ENG.). 432p. (gr. 8). pap. 8.99 (978-0-06-113189-9(X), HarperTeen) 2007. 410p. (gr. 7-18). lib. bdg. 18.89 (978-0-06-113188-2(1), Eos) HarperCollins Pubs.

Harvey, Damian. A Gift for the King. Remphry, Martin, illus. 2005. (Reading Corner Ser.). 24p. (J). (gr. k-3). lib. bdg. 22.80 (978-1-59771-013-8(X)) Sea-To-Sea Pubns.

Hatton, Fredrick D. Dusty & a Gift for a King, 1 vol. 2009. 23p. pap. 24.95 (978-1-61546-094-6(2)) America Star Bks.

Hausman, Gerald & Hausman, Loretta. Farewell, Josephine: The Romance of Josephine & Napoleon. 2013. 248p. pap. 13.95 *(978-1-61720-381-7(5))* Wilder Pubns., Corp.

Hawkins, Mia K. The Broken Guild of Twelve Pirates, 1 vol. 2009. 201p. pap. 24.95 *(978-1-61546-333-6(X))* PublishAmerica, Inc.

HB Staff. The King Who Loved to Dance. 97th ed. 2003. (Signatures Ser.). (gr. 1-18). pap. 16.50 *(978-0-15-308161-3(9))* Harcourt Schl. Pubs.

Headrick, Tammy Hill. That Famous Bird, Sir Thornton the Third. 2009. 24p. pap. 12.00 *(978-1-4269-0550-6(5))* Trafford Publishing.

Healey, Bruce. The Delightfully Dreadful Tale of King Drod, 1 vol. 2009. 48p. pap. 16.95 *(978-1-61582-545-5(2))* America Star Bks.

Heap, Bridgette. The Pursuit of Pizan, 1 vol. Chodagiri, Shanthi, illus. 2009. 35p. pap. 24.95 *(978-1-61546-994-9(X))* America Star Bks.

Hendrickson, Kevis. The Legend of Witch Bane. 2008. 348p. per. 11.95 *(978-1-4327-1298-3(5))* Outskirts Pr., Inc.

Hendry, Frances. Quest for a Queen: The Lark. 2006. (Illus.). 251p. pap. *(978-1-905665-04-4(0))* Pollinger In Print.

Henty, George Alfred. At Agincourt: A Tale of the White Hoods of Paris. 2011. 332p. pap. 19.95 *(978-1-61179-111-2(1))* Fireship Pr.

—A March on London: A Story of Wat Tyler's Insurrection. 2004. reprint ed. pap. 27.95 *(978-1-4191-0224-0(9))*; pap. 1.99 *(978-1-4192-0224-7(3))* Kessinger Publishing, LLC.

—A March on London: Being a Story of Wat Tyler's Insurrection. I.t. ed. 2007. 316p. pap. 24.99 *(978-1-4264-3096-1(5))* Creative Media Partners, LLC.

Heos, Bridget. Queen Dog. O'Keeffe, Alejandro, illus. 2017. (ENG.). 40p. (J). (gr. -1-k). 16.99 *(978-1-4847-2852-9(1))* Disney Pr.

Herbert, Bethany Zohner. The Perfect Fool. 2015. 279p. (YA). pap. 17.99 *(978-1-4621-1620-1(5))* Cedar Fort, Inc./CFI Distribution.

Hewins, Shirley, illus. Rainy Brown & the Seven Midgets. I.t. ed. 2006. (J). (gr. k-3). pap. 11.95 *(978-1-884242-24-3(3)*, RB1STED); 44p. lib. bdg. 19.95 *(978-1-884242-25-0(1)*, RB1STED) Multicultural Pubns.

Hockerman, Dennis, illus. The Little Seed: A Tale about Integrity. 2006. (J). *(978-1-59939-094-9(9)*, Reader's Digest Young Families, Inc.) Studio Fun International.

Hodge, Rosamund. Crimson Bound. 2016. 464p. (YA). (gr. 8). pap. 9.99 *(978-0-06-222477-4(8))* HarperCollins Pubs.

Hodgson, Karen J. The King Who Wanted More. Dina, Madalina, illus. 2010. (ENG.). 32p. (J). (gr. -1-4). pap. 9.99 *(978-1-907432-03-3(5))* Hogs Back Bks. GBR. Dist: Independent Pubs. Group.

Hollier, Jo. Roary O'Rourke Challenge of the Trolls, Bk. 3. 2004. pap. 9.95 *(978-1-59374-115-0(4))* Whiskey Creek Pr., LLC.

—Roary O'Rourke the Princess & Dooley Do, Bk. 2. 2004. (J). pap. 9.95 *(978-1-59374-091-7(3))* Whiskey Creek Pr., LLC.

—Roary O'Rourke Victorious Duo, Bk. 4. 2004. (J). pap. 9.95 *(978-1-59374-117-4(0))* Whiskey Creek Pr., LLC.

Holman, Nedra. Beautiful Queen. Velitchenko, Olga, illus. 2008. 40p. (J). *(978-1-4363-5461-5(7))* Xlibris Corp.

Homberg, Ruth. Across the Sea (Disney Frozen) Random House Disney Staff, illus. 2016. (Step into Reading Ser.). (ENG.). 24p. (J). (gr. -1-1). 4.99 *(978-0-7364-3398-3(8)*, RH/Disney) Random Hse. Children's Bks.

Hoobler, Dorothy & Hoobler, Thomas. The Sword That Cut the Burning Grass. 2006. 211p. (gr. 5-9). 17.00 *(978-0-7569-6907-3(7))* Perfection Learning Corp.

Hood, Ann. Queen Liliuokalani: Royal Prisoner. Altmann, Scott & Zilber, Denis, illus. 2013. (Treasure Chest Ser.: 6). (ENG.). 176p. (J). (gr. 3-7). 15.99 *(978-0-448-45739-0(3))*; pap. 6.99 *(978-0-448-45729-1(6))* Penguin Young Readers Group. (Grosset & Dunlap).

Hood, Douglas. The Stone Hat. Simonton, Tom, illus. 2005. (ENG.). 16p. (J). 5.75 *(978-1-57274-754-8(4)*, 2784, Bks. for Young Learners) Owen, Richard C. Pubs., Inc.

Horvath, Polly. Lord & Lady Bunny — Almost Royalty! Blackall, Sophie, illus. 2016. (ENG.). 304p. (J). (gr. 3-7). pap. 8.99 *(978-0-307-98068-7(5)*, Yearling) Random Hse. Children's Bks.

Hosford, Kate. How the Queen Found the Perfect Cup of Tea. Swiatkowska, Gabi, illus. 2017. (Carolrhoda Picture Bks.). (ENG.). 40p. (gr. k-3). (J). 9.99 ***(978-1-5124-3273-2(3))***; (J). 38.65 ***(978-1-5124-3272-5(5))***; 38.65 ***(978-1-4677-9563-0(1))*** Lerner Publishing Group. (Carolrhoda Bks.).

Hosford, Kate. The Perfect Cup of Tea. Swiatkowska, Gabi, illus. 2017. (ENG.). 40p. (gr. k-3). 18.99 *(978-1-4677-3904-7(9))* Lerner Publishing Group.

Howard, Annabelle. Hammurabi's Law & Order. 2005. (J). pap. *(978-1-4108-4233-6(9))* Benchmark Education Co.

Howell, Gill. Snow King. Cann, Helen, illus. 2005. (ENG.). 24p. (J). lib. bdg. 23.65 *(978-1-59646-742-2(8))* Dingles & Co.

Hunt, Elizabeth Singer. Secret Agent Jack Stalwart: Book 14: the Mission to Find Max: Egypt. 2011. (Secret Agent Jack Stalwart Ser.: 14). (ENG.). 144p. (J). (gr. 1-4). pap. 5.99 *(978-1-60286-152-7(8)*, Weinstein Bks.) Perseus Bks. Group.

James, Dalton. The Sneakiest Pirates. 2008. 20p. pap. 10.95 *(978-1-4327-2477-1(0))* Outskirts Pr., Inc.

James, Ian. Why the Sky Is Far Away: A Tale from Nigeria. 2006. (J). pap. *(978-1-4108-6172-6(4))* Benchmark Education Co.

Janer, Montserrat. El Rey Listo y el Rey Fuerte. (SPA.). (J). pap. *(978-84-236-3342-5(X))* Edebé ESP. Dist: Lectorum Pubns., Inc.

Janisch, Heinz. The King & the Sea. 2015.Tr. of Der Koenig und das Meer. (Illus.). 48p. (J). (gr. 2-4). 16.99 *(978-1-877579-94-3(7))* Gecko Pr. NZL. Dist: Lerner Publishing Group.

Jarvis, Robin. Dark Waters of Hagwood. 2013. (Hagwood Trilogy Ser.: 2). (ENG.). 318p. (J). (gr. 4-6). pap. 14.99 *(978-1-4532-9920-3(3)*, Open Road Media E-riginal) Open Road Integrated Media, Inc.

Jay, Stacey. Of Beast & Beauty. 2014. (ENG.). 400p. (YA). (gr. 9). pap. 9.99 *(978-0-385-74321-1(1)*, Ember) Random Hse. Children's Bks.

Jennewein, James & Parker, Tom S. Sword of Doom. 2009. (RuneWarriors Ser.: 2). (ENG.). 432p. (J). (gr. 3-7). 17.99 *(978-0-06-144939-0(3))* HarperCollins Pubs.

Jesus, Opal De. The Golden Apple Kingdom, 1 vol. 2009. 48p. pap. 16.95 *(978-1-60749-414-0(0))* America Star Bks.

Jinks, Catherine. Pagan in Exile. 2005. (Pagan Chronicles Ser.: 2). (ENG., Illus.). 336p. (YA). (gr. 7-18). reprint ed. pap. 6.99 *(978-0-7636-2691-4(0))* Candlewick Pr.

Johnson, Alaya Dawn. The Summer Prince. (ENG.). 304p. (J). (gr. 9). 2014. pap. 9.99 *(978-0-545-41780-8(5))* 2013. 17.99 *(978-0-545-41779-2(1))* Scholastic, Inc. (Levine, Arthur A. Bks.).

Johnston, Emily Kate. A Thousand Nights. 2015. (ENG.). 336p. (YA). (gr. 9-17). 18.99 *(978-1-4847-2227-5(2))* Hyperion Bks. for Children.

Jones, Carrie. Captivate. 2010. (Need Ser.). (ENG.). (YA). (gr. 7-12). 304p. pap. 9.99 *(978-1-59990-523-5(X)*, 9781599905235); 288p. 16.99 *(978-1-59990-342-2(3)*, 9781599903422) Bloomsbury Publishing USA. (Bloomsbury USA Childrens).

—Endure. 2012. (Need Ser.). (ENG.). 272p. (YA). 17.99 *(978-1-59990-554-9(X)*, 9781599905549, Bloomsbury USA Childrens) Bloomsbury Publishing USA.

—Entice. (Need Ser.). (ENG.). (YA). 2011. 288p. pap. 9.99 *(978-1-59990-693-5(7)*, 9781599906935) 2010. 272p. (gr. 7-12). 17.99 *(978-1-59990-553-2(1)*, 9781599905532) Bloomsbury Publishing USA. (Bloomsbury USA Childrens).

Jones, Christianne C. Chicken Little, 1 vol. Hermanson, Kyle, illus. 2010. (My First Classic Story Ser.). (ENG.). 32p. (gr. k-3). lib. bdg. 22.65 *(978-1-4048-6072-8(X)*, My First Classic Story) Picture Window Bks.

Jones, Katy Huth. Treachery & Truth: A Story of Sinners, Servants, & Saints. 2016. 163p. (YA). pap. *(978-0-8198-7535-8(X))* Pauline Bks. & Media.

Joslin. Minstrel's Tale. (J). pap. 8.95 *(978-0-7459-3966-7(X)*, Lion Books) Lion Hudson PLC GBR. Dist: Trafalgar Square Publishing.

Journey to see the King. 2006. (J). *(978-0-9791168-0-3(5))* Lighthouse Bk. Publishing.

Jovanovic, Katarina. The King Has Goat Ears, 1 vol. Beha, Philippe, illus. 2008. (ENG.). 32p. (J). (gr. k-2). 16.95 *(978-1-896580-22-7(X))* Tradewind Bks. CAN. Dist: Orca Bk. Pubs. USA.

Judybee. Queen Amina of Zari: Queens of Africa Book 1. LittlePinkPebble, illus. 2011. 28p. pap. *(978-1-908218-43-8(6))* MX Publishing, Ltd.

—Queen Esther: Queens of Africa Book 4. LittlePinkPebble, illus. 2011. 28p. pap. *(978-1-908218-52-0(5))* MX Publishing, Ltd.

—Queen Idi: Queens of Africa Book 5. LittlePinkPebble, illus. 2011. 24p. pap. *(978-1-908218-55-1(X))* MX Publishing, Ltd.

—Queen Maked: Queens of Africa Book 2. LittlePinkPebble, illus. 2011. 28p. pap. *(978-1-908218-46-9(0))* MX Publishing, Ltd.

—Queen Moremi: Queens of Africa Book 3. LittlePinkPebble, illus. 2011. 28p. pap. *(978-1-908218-49-0(5))* MX Publishing, Ltd.

Karandeev, Oleg. Dmitri II: The Kind Storyteller Book Two of Five. Ciesinska, Izabela, illus. 2007. 76p. (YA). per. 15.95 *(978-0-9793944-3-0(0))* Digi-Tall Media.

Kato, Etsuo. The King Who Saved the Dove. Yasui, Koji, illus. 2014. (J). 8.95 *(978-1-935523-68-0(6))* World Tribune Pr.

Kats, Jewel. Prince Preemie: A Tale of a Tiny Puppy Who Arrives Early. Lenart, Claudia, illus. 2016. (J). pap. ***(978-1-61599-306-2(1))*** Loving Healing Pr., Inc.

Katz, Welwyn Wilton. Beowulf, 1 vol. Gal, Laszlo, illus. 2nd ed. 2007. (ENG.). 96p. (J). (gr. 4-7). 17.95 *(978-0-88899-807-1(4))* Groundwood Bks. CAN. Dist: Publishers Group West (PGW).

Keegan, Shannon. Legend of the Sea Fairies. 2006. (Illus.). (J). per. 14.99 *(978-0-9773433-0-0(8))* Bixie Gate Publishing.

Keene, Carolyn. The Clue in the Jewel Box, No. 20. Tandy, Russell H., illus. 2005. (Nancy Drew Mystery Stories Ser.). (ENG.). 228p. (J). (gr. 5-9). 17.95 *(978-1-55709-277-9(X))* Applewood Bks.

Kilgore, Lee. Widga's Quest, 1 vol. 2009. 48p. pap. 16.95 *(978-1-4489-2517-9(7))* America Star Bks.

Kimmel, Eric A. Joha Makes a Wish: A Middle Eastern Tale, 0 vols. Rayyan, Omar, illus. 2013. (ENG.). 40p. (J). (gr. k-3). pap. 7.99 *(978-1-4778-1687-5(9)*, 9781477816875, Amazon Children's Publishing) Amazon Publishing.

Kindl, Patrice. Goose Chase. 2010. (ENG.). 240p. (J). (gr. 5-7). pap. 6.99 *(978-0-547-33164-5(9))* Houghton Mifflin Harcourt Publishing Co.

King of the Mountain. Date not set. 5.95 *(978-0-89868-357-8(2))*; lib. bdg. 10.95 *(978-0-89868-356-1(4))* ARO Publishing Co.

King Robert the First. 2004. per. 26.00 *(978-0-8059-9391-2(6))* Dorrance Publishing Co., Inc.

The King's Ring: KinderReaders Individual Title Six-Packs. (Kinderstarters Ser.). 8p. (gr. -1-1). 21.00 *(978-0-7635-8656-0(0))* Rigby Education.

Kingsley, Kaza. The Secret of Ashona. Ng, James, illus. 2012. (Erec Rex Ser.: 5). (ENG.). 528p. (J). (gr. 5-9). 16.99 *(978-1-4169-7992-0(1)*, Simon & Schuster Bks. For Young Readers) Simon & Schuster Bks. For Young Readers.

Koontz, Robin Michal. Lizzie Little, the Sky Is Falling! Koontz, Robin Michal, illus. 2011. (ENG., Illus.). 24p. (gr. 2-3). pap. 8.95 *(978-1-61236-029-4(7))* Rourke Educational Media.

Korczak, Janusz & Lourie, Richard. King Matt the First: A Novel. Lourie, Richard, tr. from POL. 2004. (ENG.). 344p. (J). pap. 23.99 *(978-1-56512-442-4(1)*, 72442) Algonquin Bks. of Chapel Hill.

Kraljic, Helena. Cleopatra. 2017. (SPA.). 32p. (J). (gr. 1-4). 16.95 ***(978-84-9145-008-5(4)***, Picarona Editorial) Ediciones Obelisco ESP. Dist: Spanish Pubs., LLC.

Krensky, Stephen. Mike Fink. Reeves, Jeni, illus. 2007. (On My Own Folklore Ser.). (ENG.). 48p. (gr. 2-4). per. 6.95 *(978-0-8225-6478-2(5)*, First Avenue Editions) Lerner Publishing Group.

Kulkarni, Suresh. The Wise King & Other Stories. 2011. 44p. pap. 21.99 *(978-1-4535-0463-5(X))* Xlibris Corp.

Kwarta, Darlene. Walking with King Tut. 2008. 48p. pap. 9.95 *(978-1-60693-040-3(0)*, Eloquent Bks.) Strategic Book Publishing & Rights Agency (SBPRA).

Laky, Esther. Just Fairy Tales. 2010. 95p. pap. 11.80 *(978-0-557-01926-7(5))* Lulu Pr., Inc.

Lamplighter Staff. True Princess. 2004. pap. 14.00 *(978-1-58474-051-3(5))* Cornerstone Family Ministries/Lamplighter Publishing.

The Land of the Blue Flower. 2006. 76p. pap. 7.45 *(978-1-59462-377-6(5)*, 413, Book Jungle) Standard Pubns., Inc.

Lang, Andrew. The Queen & the Mouse: A Story about Friendship. Lohmann, Renate, illus. 2006. (J). *(978-1-59939-081-9(7)*, Reader's Digest Young Families, Inc.) Studio Fun International.

Larson, Sara B. Endure. (Defy Trilogy: Bk. 3). (ENG.). 320p. (J). (gr. 7). 2016. pap. 9.99 *(978-1-338-09552-4(8))* 2015. 17.99 *(978-0-545-64490-7(9)*, Scholastic Pr.) Scholastic, Inc.

—Ignite. 2014. (Defy Trilogy: Bk. 2). (ENG.). 304p. (J). (gr. 7). 17.99 *(978-0-545-64474-7(7)*, Scholastic Pr.) Scholastic, Inc.

Lasky, Kathryn. Exile. 2008. (Guardians of Ga'hoole Ser.: 14). (ENG., Illus.). 224p. (J). (gr. 3-7). 6.99 *(978-0-439-88808-0(5)*, Scholastic Paperbacks) Scholastic, Inc.

—The Golden Tree. 2007. (Guardians of Ga'Hoole Ser.: 12). (Illus.). 192p. lib. bdg. 17.20 *(978-1-4177-8260-4(9)*, Turtleback) Turtleback Bks.

—To Be a King. 2006. (Guardians of Ga'hoole Ser.: 11). (ENG.). 224p. (J). (gr. 3-7). 6.99 *(978-0-439-79570-8(2)*, Scholastic Paperbacks) Scholastic, Inc.

Lawson, Barbara. Huff the Magicless Dragon, 1 vol. Swope, Brenda, illus. 2009. 35p. pap. 24.95 *(978-1-61546-419-7(0))* PublishAmerica, Inc.

Lay, Kathryn. Crown Me! 2004. (ENG.). 208p. (J). (gr. 4-6). tchr. ed. 17.95 *(978-0-8234-1845-9(6))* Holiday Hse., Inc.

Lendler, Ian. An Undone Fairy Tale. Martin, Whitney, illus. 2005. (ENG.). 32p. (J). (gr. 1-5). 18.99 *(978-0-689-86677-7(1)*, Simon & Schuster Bks. For Young Readers) Simon & Schuster Bks. For Young Readers.

Lepp, Bil. The King of Little Things, 1 vol. Wenzel, David T., illus. 2013. (ENG.). 32p. (J). (gr. -1-3). 16.95 *(978-1-56145-708-3(6))* Peachtree Pubs.

Lesler, Rebecca. The Magic Stone: Return of Two Kings. 2008. 73p. pap. 19.95 *(978-1-60610-101-8(3))* America Star Bks.

Levine, Gail Carson. A Tale of Two Castles. Call, Greg, illus. (ENG.). (J). (gr. 3-7). 2012. 352p. pap. 6.99 *(978-0-06-122967-1(9))* 2011. 336p. 16.99 *(978-0-06-122965-7(2))* HarperCollins Pubs.

Lewis, Jill. Don't Read This Book! Allwright, Deborah, illus. 2010. (ENG.). 32p. (J). (gr. -1-2). 15.95 *(978-1-58925-094-9(X))* Tiger Tales.

Liddiment, Carol, illus. The Wooden Sword: A Jewish Folktale from Afghanistan. 2012. (ENG.). 32p. (J). (gr. k-3). 16.99 *(978-0-8075-9201-4(3))* Whitman, Albert & Co.

Lindgren, Astrid. Mio, My Son. Morgan, Jill, tr. from SWE. Wikland, Ilon, illus. 2015.Tr. of Mio, Min Mio. (ENG.). 184p. (J). (gr. 3-7). 16.95 *(978-1-59017-870-6(X)*, NYR Children's Collection) New York Review of Bks., Inc., The.

—Mio, My Son. Wikland, Ilon, illus. 2003.Tr. of Mio, Min Mio. 179p. (J). 17.95 *(978-1-930900-23-3(6))* Purple Hse. Pr.

Liv‡n, Paco. THE THING THAT HURTS MOST IN THE WORLD. 2007. (ENG., Illus.). 36p. (J). 17.95 *(978-84-96788-89-3(X))* OQO, Editora ESP. Dist: Baker & Taylor Bks.

Long, Ruth Frances. The Treachery of Beautiful Things. 2013. (ENG.). 384p. (YA). (gr. 7). pap. 9.99 *(978-0-14-242606-7(7)*, Speak) Penguin Young Readers Group.

Longshore, Katherine. Gilt. (ENG.). (YA). (gr. 7). 2013. 432p. pap. 9.99 *(978-0-14-242619-7(9)*, Speak) 2012. 416p. 17.99 *(978-0-670-01399-9(4)*, Viking Books for Young Readers) Penguin Young Readers Group.

Lou, Cindy, illus. & text. The King of Ing Wants to Sing. Lou, Cindy, text. 2008. (J). 12.00 *(978-1-935332-00-8(7))* Kite Tales Publishing.

Low, Vicki. First Emperor. Mayhew, Sara E., illus. 2007. 48p. (J). lib. bdg. 23.08 *(978-1-4242-1626-0(5))* Fitzgerald Bks.

Lowery, Linda & Keep, Richard. The Chocolate Tree: [A Mayan Folktale]. Porter, Janice, illus. 2009. (On My Own Folklore Ser.). (ENG.). 48p. (gr. 2-4). pap. 6.95 *(978-1-58013-851-2(9)*, First Avenue Editions) Lerner Publishing Group.

Luberto, Bradley. Clide & Druce: A Repulsive Tale of Trolls & Tax Money. 2006. (ENG.). 48p. per. 16.95 *(978-1-4241-5012-0(4))* PublishAmerica, Inc.

Lucado, Max. The Song of the King. Gillies, Chuck, illus. 2014. 32p. (J). 17.99 *(978-1-4335-4290-9(0))* Crossway.

Lucio, Mick. Kings for a Day: A Western. 2012. 24p. 24.95 *(978-1-4626-5422-2(3))* America Star Bks.

Lynes, William. Pirates, Scoundrels, & Kings. 2013. 450p. (gr. 10-12). 33.95 *(978-1-4759-6562-9(1))*; pap. 23.95 *(978-1-4759-6561-2(3))* iUniverse, Inc.

Ma, Wenhai, illus. Tang Monk Disciples Monkey King. 2005. (Adventures of Monkey King Ser.: No. 3). 32p. (J). 16.95 *(978-1-57227-084-8(5))* Pan Asia Pubns. (USA), Inc.

—Tang Monk Disciples Monkey King: English/Chinese. 2005. (Adventures of Monkey King Ser.: No. 3). (ENG & CHI.). 32p. (J). 16.95 *(978-1-57227-086-2(1))* Pan Asia Pubns. (USA), Inc.

Maas, Sarah J. Crown of Midnight. (Throne of Glass Ser.: 2). (ENG.). (YA). (gr. 9). 2014. 448p. pap. 10.99 *(978-1-61963-064-2(8)*, 9781619630642) 2013. (Illus.). 432p. 18.99 *(978-1-61963-062-8(1)*, 9781619630628) Bloomsbury Publishing USA. (Bloomsbury USA Childrens).

—Crown of Midnight. 2014. (Throne of Glass Ser.: 2). (YA). lib. bdg. 22.10 *(978-0-606-36441-6(2))* Turtleback Bks.

—Empire of Storms. (Throne of Glass Ser.). (ENG.). (YA). 2017. 720p. pap. 10.99 ***(978-1-61963-609-5(3)***, 9781619636095) 2016. 704p. (gr. 9). 18.99 *(978-1-61963-607-1(7)*, 9781619636071) Bloomsbury Publishing USA. (Bloomsbury USA Childrens).

—Empire of Storms. 2017. (Throne of Glass Ser.: 5). (YA). lib. bdg. 22.10 ***(978-0-606-40598-0(4))*** Turtleback Bks.

Maas, Sarah J. Heir of Fire. 2015. (Throne of Glass Ser.: 3). (ENG.). 592p. (YA). (gr. 9). pap. 10.99 *(978-1-61963-067-3(2)*, 9781619630673, Bloomsbury USA Childrens) Bloomsbury Publishing USA.

MacColl, Michaela. Prisoners in the Palace: How Princess Victoria Became Queen with the Help of Her Maid, a Reporter, & a Scoundrel. 2013. (ENG.). 368p. (J). (gr. 8-17). pap. 9.99 *(978-1-4521-1958-8(9))* Chronicle Bks. LLC.

MacDonald, George. Light Princess. I.t. ed. 2006. pap. *(978-1-84702-350-6(9))* Echo Library.

—The Light Princess & Other Fairy Stories. 2007. 102p. pap. 18.99 *(978-1-4346-1408-7(5))* Creative Media Partners, LLC.

MacHado, Ana Maria. Un Buen Coro. (Torre de Papel Ser.). (SPA., Illus.). (J). 7.95 *(978-958-04-4525-8(7)*, NR30643) Norma S.A. COL. Dist: Distribuidora Norma, Inc., Lectorum Pubns., Inc.

—Del Otro Lado Hay Secretos. (SPA.). pap. 11.95 *(978-950-07-2221-6(6))* Editorial Sudamericana S.A. ARG. Dist: Distribooks, Inc.

Maddern, Eric. The King with Horse's Ears. Hess, Paul, illus. 2003. 36p. (J). *(978-0-7112-1957-1(5))* ReiseArt Buchhandlung GmbH.

The Magic King. 2003. (J). *(978-1-4120-3345-9(4))* Black Dot Pubns.

Magness, Vicki. Victor the Victorious: And the Tale of Two Cities. 2012. 40p. pap. 21.99 *(978-1-4797-1955-6(2))* Xlibris Corp.

Mahoney, Karen. The Stone Demon. 2013. (Iron Witch Ser.: 3). (ENG.). 336p. (YA). pap. 9.99 *(978-0-7387-3340-1(7)*, Flux) North Star Editions.

Major, Roberta Olsen. The Ice Cream Crone. 2007. (Royal Pains Ser.: 5). (YA). pap. 11.95 *(978-1-59705-801-8(7))* Wings ePress, Inc.

—The 24-Karat King. 2008. (Royal Pains Ser.: 7). (ENG.). (YA). pap. 11.95 *(978-1-59705-671-7(5))* Wings ePress, Inc.

Marchetta, Melina. Quintana of Charyn: The Lumatere Chronicles. (Lumatere Chronicles Ser.). (ENG.). 528p. (YA). (gr. 9). 2014. pap. 10.99 *(978-0-7636-6930-0(X))* 2013. 18.99 *(978-0-7636-5835-9(9))* Candlewick Pr.

Marr, Melissa. Fragile Eternity. 2010. (Wicked Lovely Ser.: 3). (ENG.). 448p. (YA). (gr. 8). pap. 8.99 *(978-0-06-121473-8(6))* HarperCollins Pubs.

—Fragile Eternity, 9 vols. 2009. (Wicked Lovely Ser.: 3). (YA). 110.75 *(978-1-4407-3038-2(5))*; 112.75 *(978-1-4407-3036-8(9))*; 132.75 *(978-1-4407-3040-5(7))*; 130.75 *(978-1-4407-3042-9(3))*; 1.25 *(978-1-4407-3044-3(X))*; 265.75 *(978-1-4407-3037-5(7))* Recorded Bks., Inc.

—Ink Exchange. (Wicked Lovely Ser.: 2). (ENG.). (YA). (gr. 8). 2009. 352p. pap. 9.99 *(978-0-06-121470-7(1))* 2008. 336p. 17.99 *(978-0-06-121468-4(X))* HarperCollins Pubs.

—Wicked Lovely. 2008. (Wicked Lovely Ser.: 1). (ENG.). 352p. (YA). (gr. 8-12). pap. 9.99 *(978-0-06-121467-7(1))* HarperCollins Pubs.

Martha Louise, Princess. Why Kings & Queens Don't Wear Crowns (with CD) Sevig-Fajardo, Mari Elise, tr. from NOR. Nyhus, Svein, illus. 2006. Orig. Title: Fvorfor de kongelige ikke har krone på Hodet. 32p. (J). 19.95 incl. audio compact disk *(978-1-57534-038-8(0)*, CSC 100C) Skandisk, Inc.

Martin, J. P. Uncle. Blake, Quentin, illus. 2017. (ENG.). 176p. (J). (gr. 4-7). pap. 9.99 ***(978-1-68137-185-6(5)***, NYRB Kids) New York Review of Bks., Inc., The.

Martin, J. P. Uncle Cleans Up. Blake, Quentin, illus. 2008. (ENG.). 184p. (J). (gr. 4-7). 17.95 *(978-1-59017-276-6(0)*, NYR Children's Collection) New York Review of Bks., Inc., The.

Martin, Sara Hines. Shakin' up the Kingdom: Princess Lucinda Becomes the Queen. 2012. 66p. pap. 27.95 *(978-1-4497-4922-4(4)*, WestBow Pr.) Author Solutions, Inc.

Martinez, Rene. The Journey of the Golden Sword. 2011. 64p. pap. 15.99 *(978-1-4535-9187-1(7))* Xlibris Corp.

Masters, Elaine. The Royal Waker-Upper. Leung, Andrew, illus. 2003. (ENG.). 39p. (J). *(978-0-89610-992-6(5))* Island Heritage Publishing.

Mastromonaco, Pina. King Bartholomew & the Jesters Riddle. Martin, David Lozell, illus. 2005. 32p. (J). (gr. -1-7). 15.95 *(978-0-9744307-1-3(4))* Merry Lane Pr.

Matthews, Rodney, illus. Tales of King Arthur. rev. ed. 2007. (Usborne Classics Retold Ser.). 139p. (J). (gr. 4-7). per. 4.99 *(978-0-7945-1483-9(9)*, Usborne) EDC Publishing.

Mayo, Frank, illus. King Midas & the Golden Touch: A Tale about Greed. 2006. (J). 6.99 *(978-1-59939-022-2(1))* Cornerstone Pr.

McCaughrean, Geraldine. Casting the Gods Adrift: A Tale of Ancient Egypt. Ludlow, Patricia D., illus. 2003. (ENG.). 112p. (J). (gr. 4-7). 15.95 *(978-0-8126-2684-1(2))* Cricket Bks.

McCaughrean, Geraldine. Stories from Shakespeare. 2017. (ENG.). 176p. (J). (gr. 4-6). pap. 7.99 ***(978-1-5101-0145-6(4)***, Orion Children's Bks.) Hachette Children's Group GBR. Dist: Hachette Bk. Group.

McCloskey, Larry. Murder Fit for a King. 2007. (ENG.). 168p. (J). (gr. 6). pap. 11.99 *(978-1-55002-669-6(0)*, Sandcastle Bks.) Dundurn CAN. Dist: Ingram Publisher Services.

McCullough, L. E. We Three Kings: A Christmas Story. Maxwell, Cassandre, illus. 2006. 24p. (J). 7.95 *(978-0-88271-010-5(9))* Regina Pr., Malhame & Co.

McDaniels, Preston, illus. The Prince of Ireland & the Three Magic Stallions. 2003. (ENG.). 32p. (J). (gr. k-3). tchr. ed. 16.95 *(978-0-8234-1573-1(2))* Holiday Hse., Inc.

McGinnis, Mindy. Given to the Sea. 2017. (Given Duet Ser.). (ENG.). 352p. (YA). (gr. 9). 17.99 *(978-0-399-54461-3(5)*, G.P. Putnam's Sons Books for Young Readers) Penguin Young Readers Group.

McGriff, Shawna A. Princess Pink: Princess Pink Saves the Girls of Lahappyville. 2010. 44p. pap. 18.49 *(978-1-4520-3936-7(4))* AuthorHouse.

McKibben, Marion A. Pearl the Rodeo Queen. 2006. 24p. (J). per. 12.00 *(978-1-59971-711-1(5))* Aardvark Global Publishing.

McKillip, Patricia A. The Changeling Sea. 2003. (ENG., Illus.). 144p. (YA). (gr. 7-7). 5.99 *(978-0-14-131262-0(9)*, Firebird) Penguin Young Readers Group.

McMullan, Kate. Pig Latin — Not Just for Pigs!, 1 vol. Basso, Bill, illus. 2006. (Dragon Slayers' Academy Ser.: No. 14). (ENG.). 112p. (gr. 1-7). 24.21 *(978-1-59961-127-3(9))* Spotlight.

McPhate, Paul J. The Puggle King. 2008. 52p. pap. 16.95 *(978-1-60703-709-5(2))* America Star Bks.

McRoberts, Eddison. Sneaking Treats. Gadra, Jessica, illus. 2013. 48p. pap. 9.95 *(978-1-62137-298-1(7))* Virtualbookworm.com Publishing, Inc.

Mead, Richelle. Vampire Academy. 2007. (Vampire Academy Ser.: Bk. 1). (ENG.). 336p. (J). (gr. 7-18). pap. 10.99

JKL

(978-1-59514-174-3(X), Razorbill) Penguin Publishing Group.

Menge, Dawn. Queen Vernita's Visitors. Switzer, Bobbi, illus. 2008. 36p. pap. 19.95 (978-1-59800-714-5(9)) Outskirts Pr., Inc.

Meredith, Susan Markowitz. The Royal Zookeeper. 2011. (Early Connections Ser.). (J). (978-1-61672-678-2(4)) Benchmark Education Co.

Meyer, Carolyn. The Bad Queen: Rules & Instructions for Marie-Antoinette. 2011. (Young Royals Ser.). (ENG.). 432p. (YA). (gr. 7). pap. 9.99 (978-0-547-48249-1(3)) Houghton Mifflin Harcourt Publishing Co.

—Beauty's Daughter: The Story of Hermione & Helen of Troy. 2013. (ENG., Illus.). 352p. (YA). (gr. 7). 16.99 (978-0-544-10862-2(0)) Houghton Mifflin Harcourt Publishing Co.

—Cleopatra Confesses. (ENG.). 304p. (YA). (gr. 7). 2012. pap. 11.99 (978-1-4169-8728-4(2)) 2011. 16.99 (978-1-4169-8727-7(4)) Simon & Schuster/Paula Wiseman Bks. (Simon & Schuster/Paula Wiseman Bks.).

—Doomed Queen Anne. 2004. (Young Royals Ser.: 3). (ENG., Illus.). 240p. (YA). (gr. 7-12). pap. 7.99 (978-0-15-205086-3(8)) Houghton Mifflin Harcourt Publishing Co.

—Duchessina: A Novel of Catherine de' Medici. 2009. (Young Royals Ser.). (ENG., Illus.). 272p. (J). (gr. 9). pap. 8.99 (978-0-15-206620-8(9)) Houghton Mifflin Harcourt Publishing Co.

—Patience, Princess Catherine: A Young Royals Book. 2009. (Young Royals Ser.: 4). (ENG., Illus.). 208p. (YA). (gr. 7-12). pap. 13.95 (978-0-15-205447-2(2)) Houghton Mifflin Harcourt Publishing Co.

—Victoria Rebels. (ENG., Illus.). 272p. (YA). (gr. 7). 2014. pap. 9.99 (978-1-4169-8730-7(4)) 2013. 16.99 (978-1-4169-8729-1(0)) Simon & Schuster/Paula Wiseman Bks. (Simon & Schuster/Paula Wiseman Bks.).

—The Wild Queen: The Days & Nights of Mary, Queen of Scots. 2013. (Young Royals Ser.). (ENG.). 432p. (YA). (gr. 7). pap. 8.99 (978-0-544-02219-5(X)) Houghton Mifflin Harcourt Publishing Co.

Meyer, Marissa. Cress. 2014. (YA). (Lunar Chronicles: Bk. 3). (ENG.). 560p. (gr. 7-12). 19.99 (978-0-312-64297-6(0), 9780312642976); 552p. (978-1-250-05632-0(2)) Feiwel & Friends.

—Fairest: Levana's Story. 2016. (Lunar Chronicles Ser.: 0). (YA). lib. bdg. 20.85 (978-0-606-38438-4(3)) Turtleback Bks.

—Fairest: The Lunar Chronicles: Levana's Story. 2015. (YA). 222p. (978-1-250-06959-7(9)); (ENG.). 272p. (gr. 7-12). 17.99 (978-1-250-06055-6(9), 9781250060556) Feiwel & Friends.

—Fairest: The Lunar Chronicles: Levana's Story. Barcellona, Christine, ed. 2016. (Lunar Chronicles Ser.). (ENG.). 288p. (YA). pap. 10.99 (978-1-250-07355-6(3), 9781250073556) Square Fish.

—Winter. 2015. (Lunar Chronicles Ser.: 4). (ENG.). 832p. (YA). (gr. 7-12). 22.99 (978-0-312-64298-3(9), 9780312642983) Feiwel & Friends.

Michaelides, M. Rainbow Angel. 2012. 120p. (gr. 4-6). 20.95 (978-1-4759-6249-9(5)); pap. 10.95 (978-1-4759-6248-2(7)) iUniverse, Inc.

Miller, Sarah. The Lost Crown. (ENG., Illus.). 448p. (gr. 7). 2012. (YA). pap. 9.99 (978-1-4169-8341-5(4)) 2011. (J). 17.99 (978-1-4169-8340-8(6)) Simon & Schuster Children's Publishing. (Atheneum Bks. for Young Readers).

Miller, Victoria, illus. Dora & the Unicorn King. 2011. (Dora the Explorer Ser.). (ENG.). 24p. (J). pap. 3.99 (978-1-4424-1312-2(3), Simon Spotlight/Nickelodeon) Simon Spotlight/Nickelodeon.

Millman, Selena. The Prince & Me. 2006. 146p. (YA). per. 11.20 (978-1-4243-2353-1(3)) Independent Publisher Services.

Mini Cuentos: Rey de los Sapos, Sapatillas Rojas.Tr. of Mini Fairy Tales: King & His Shoes. (SPA.). (J). (gr. k-4). 4.98 (978-970-607-619-9(0)) Larousse, Ediciones, S. A. de C. V. MEX. Dist: Continental Bk. Co., Inc.

Miura, Taro. The Tiny King. Miura, Taro, illus. 2013. (ENG., Illus.). 32p. (J). (-k). 14.99 (978-0-7636-6687-3(4)) Candlewick Pr.

Miyares, Daniel. Bring Me a Rock! Miyares, Daniel, illus. 2016. (ENG., Illus.). 40p. (J). (gr. -1-3). 17.99 (978-1-4814-4602-0(9), Simon & Schuster Bks. For Young Readers) Simon & Schuster Bks. For Young Readers.

Moore, Inga. Captain Cat. Moore, Inga, illus. 2013. (ENG., Illus.). 48p. (J). (gr. -1-2). 15.99 (978-0-7636-6151-9(1)) Candlewick Pr.

Moore, Raina. A Charming Princess. 2005. (Charming Classics). 256p. (J). pap. 6.99 (978-0-06-059604-0(X), HarperFestival) HarperCollins Pubs.

Morgan-Cole, Trudy J. Esther: Courage to Stand. 2010. 144p. (J). pap. 12.99 (978-0-8280-2430-3(8)) Review & Herald Publishing Assn.

Moss, Jenny. Shadow. 2010. (ENG.). 384p. (J). (gr. 7-18). 17.99 (978-0-545-03641-2(0), Scholastic Pr.) Scholastic, Inc.

Moss, Marissa. The Pharaoh's Secret. 2009. (ENG., Illus.). 320p. (J). (gr. 3-7). 16.95 (978-0-8109-8378-6(8), Amulet Bks.) Abrams, Inc.

Mrozek, Elizabeth. The Fifth Chair. Mrozek, Elizabeth, illus. 2013. (Illus.). 38p. 19.95 (978-1-935766-80-3(5)) Windy City Pubs.

Muhammad, Shahid. The Adventures of the Math Doctor: Book One: King Jafiz & the Evil Farmer Nimra. 2007. (J). per. 7.95 (978-1-59872-778-4(8)) Instant Pub.

mulholland, robin. Bolivia & the sunshine King. 2008. 147p. pap. 14.98 (978-0-557-01401-9(8)) Lulu Pr., Inc.

Munson, Kyle Lloyd. The King They Call Dumm. 2008. 32p. per. 24.95 (978-1-60441-215-4(1)) America Star Bks.

Murdock, Catherine Gilbert. Princess Ben. 2009. (ENG.). 352p. (YA). (gr. 7). pap. 9.99 (978-0-547-22325-4(0)) Houghton Mifflin Harcourt Publishing Co.

Muthu, Antony M. Athim. 2008. 48p. pap. 19.49 (978-1-4389-3074-9(7)) AuthorHouse.

Nelson, Brett Alan. The Magical Forest. Ueda, Kumiko, illus. 2003. 42p. (J). (978-0-9655078-7-5(4)) Windsong Publishing Co.

Neumeier, Rachel. The Keeper of the Mist. 2016. (ENG.). 400p. (YA). (gr. 7). lib. bdg. 20.99 (978-0-553-50929-8(2), Knopf Bks. for Young Readers) Random Hse. Children's Bks.

Neuschwander, Cindy. Sir Cumference & All the King's Tens. Geehan, Wayne, illus. 2009. (ENG.). 32p. (J). (gr. 3-7). 16.95 (978-1-57091-727-1(2)) Charlesbridge Publishing, Inc.

—Sir Cumference & the off-The-Charts Dessert. Geehan, Wayne, illus. 2013. (ENG.). 32p. (J). (gr. 3-7). pap. 7.95 (978-1-57091-199-6(1)) Charlesbridge Publishing, Inc.

—Sir Cumference & the off-The-Charts Dessert. 2013. (Sir Cumference Ser.). lib. bdg. 18.40 (978-0-606-34743-3(7), Turtleback) Turtleback Bks.

Nielsen, Amy. Victor & the Sun Orb. 2008. 144p. 21.95 (978-0-595-50307-0(1)); pap. 11.95 (978-0-595-51212-6(7)) iUniverse, Inc.

Nielsen, Jennifer A. The Runaway King. (Ascendance Trilogy Ser.: 2). (ENG.). 352p. (J). (gr. 4-7). 2014. pap. 7.99 (978-0-545-28416-5(3), Scholastic Paperbacks) 2013. (Illus.). 17.99 (978-0-545-28415-8(5), Scholastic Pr.) Scholastic, Inc.

—The Runaway King. 2014. (Ascendance Trilogy Ser.: 2). lib. bdg. 18.40 (978-0-606-35663-3(0)) Turtleback Bks.

—The Shadow Throne. (ENG.). 336p. (J). 2015. (Ascendance Trilogy Ser.: 3). (gr. 3-7). pap. 7.99 (978-0-545-28418-9(X), Scholastic Paperbacks) 2014. (Ascendance Trilogy: Bk. 3). (gr. 5-9). 17.99 (978-0-545-28417-2(1), Scholastic Pr.) Scholastic, Inc.

Niemann, Christoph. The Potato King. 2015. (ENG., Illus.). 32p. (J). (gr. k-4). 17.95 (978-1-77147-139-8(5)) Owlkids Bks. Inc. CAN. Dist: Publishers Group West (PGW).

Nobacon, Danbert. 3 Dead Princes: An Anarchist Fairy Tale. Cox, Alex, illus. 2010. (ENG.). 208p. (gr. 8-18). pap. 13.00 (978-1-935259-06-0(7)) Exterminating Angel Pr.

Nobisso, Josephine. El Peso de Una Misa: Un Relato de fe. Szegedi, Katalin, illus. 2003. Orig. Title: The Weight of a Mass a Tale of Faith. (SPA.). 32p. (J). (gr. k-2). pap. 9.95 (978-0-940112-17-9(5)) Gingerbread Hse.

—El Peso de Una Misa: Un Relato de Fe. Szegedi, Katalin, illus. 2003. Orig. Title: The Weight of a Mass a Tale of Faith. (SPA.). 32p. (J). (gr. k-2). 17.95 (978-0-940112-15-5(9)) Gingerbread Hse.

—Take It to the Queen. 2009. 32p. 17.95 (978-0-8146-3288-8(2), Liturgical Pr. Bks.) Liturgical Pr.

—Take It to the Queen: A Tale of Hope. Szegedi, Katalin, illus. 2008. (ENG.). 32p. (J). (gr. k-2). 17.95 (978-0-940112-19-3(1)); pap. 9.95 (978-0-940112-21-6(3)) Gingerbread Hse.

La Noche en Que Casi Vimos a los Reyes Magos. (SPA.). (J). (978-0-9710860-9-8(5)) Libros, Encouraging Cultural Literacy.

North, Laura. The Princess & the Frozen Peas. 2014. (ENG., Illus.). 32p. (J). (978-0-7787-0446-1(7)); pap. (978-0-7787-0481-2(5)) Crabtree Publishing Co.

Nussbaum, Ben & Studio Mouse Editorial. Snow White: A New Beginning. 2008. (ENG., Illus.). 36p. (J). (gr. -1). 7.99 (978-1-59069-437-4(6)) Studio Mouse LLC.

O'Callaghan, G. Slave Prince. 2007. 172p. per. (978-1-84693-031-7(6)) Best Global Publishing Ltd.

Ofori-Mankata. Dede Akai. 2012. 48p. pap. 21.88 (978-1-4669-1569-5(2)) Trafford Publishing.

Oh, Ellen. Prophecy. 2013. (Prophecy Ser.: 1). (ENG., Illus.). 320p. (YA). (gr. 8). 17.99 (978-0-06-209109-3(3), HarperTeen) HarperCollins Pubs.

—Warrior. 2015. (Prophecy Ser.: 2). (ENG.). 352p. (YA). (gr. 8). pap. 9.99 (978-0-06-209113-0(1), HarperTeen) HarperCollins Pubs.

Old King Cole: 6 Small Books. (gr. k-2). 23.00 (978-0-7635-8493-1(2)) Rigby Education.

Olsen, Kent L. Tales of Kalindia. 2004. 356p. (YA). 30.95 (978-0-595-65998-2(5)); pap. 20.95 (978-0-595-29426-8(X)) iUniverse, Inc.

Oppel, Kenneth. The King's Taster. Johnson, Steve & Fancher, Lou, illus. 2009. 32p. (J). (gr. -1-1). (ENG.). 17.99 (978-0-06-075372-6(2)); lib. bdg. 18.89 (978-0-06-075373-3(0)) HarperCollins Pubs.

Ortiz, Zirzeria. The Queen in Me & My Bumblebee. 2008. 48p. pap. 24.95 (978-1-60441-045-7(0)) America Star Bks.

Osterbach, Batya Kirshenbaum. Pini the Pitcher: A Story for Hanukkah. Eisby, Lizzy, illus. 2005. 32p. (J). (gr. 1-4). 16.95 (978-1-932687-50-7(5), Devora Publishing) Simcha Media Group.

Osterlund, Anne. Aurelia. 2008. (ENG.). 256p. (YA). (gr. 7-18). 8.99 (978-0-14-240579-6(5), Speak) Penguin Young Readers Group.

Otis, James. Calvert of Maryland: A Story of Lord Baltimore's Colony. 2007. 140p. per. 9.95 (978-0-9790876-6-0(X)) Living Bks. Pr.

Ovani, Germano, illus. The Monkey King. 2007. (Young Reading Series 1 Gift Bks). 47p. (J). (gr. -1-3). 8.99 (978-0-7945-1593-5(2), Usborne) EDC Publishing.

Owings, Lisa. The Constellation Cassiopeia: The Story of the Queen. Morrow, J. T., illus. 2013. (Constellations Ser.). (ENG.). 32p. (J). (gr. 2-5). 29.93 (978-1-62323-484-3(0), 206252) Child's World, Inc., The.

Packard, Mary. I Am King! Gore, Leonid, illus. 2003. (My First Reader Ser.). (ENG.). 32p. (J). 18.50 (978-0-516-22927-0(3), Children's Pr.) Scholastic Library Publishing.

Page, Nick & Page, Claire. The King of Spring. Robert, Yannick, illus. 2006. (Read with Me (Make Believe Ideas) Ser.). 31p. (J). (gr. k-2). (978-1-84610-169-4(7)) Make Believe Ideas.

Paige, Danielle. Stealing Snow. 2016. (Stealing Snow Ser.). (ENG.). 384p. (YA). (gr. 9-12). 18.99 (978-1-68119-076-1(1), 9781681190761, Bloomsbury USA Childrens) Bloomsbury Publishing USA.

—Stealing Snow. 2017. (SPA.). 384p. (YA). 18.95 (978-84-16700-68-4(0)) Roca Editorial ESP. Dist: Spanish Pubs., LLC.

Paige, Danielle. Yellow Brick War. 2016. (Dorothy Must Die Ser.: 3). (ENG.). 288p. (YA). (gr. 9-12). 18.99 (978-0-06-228073-2(2)) HarperCollins Pubs.

Paquette, Ammi-Joan. Princess Juniper of the Anju. 2016. (Princess Juniper Ser.). (ENG., Illus.). 272p. (J). (gr. 3-7). 16.99 (978-0-399-17152-9(5), Philomel Bks.) Penguin Young Readers Group.

Paquette, Ammi-Joan. Princess Juniper of Torr. 2017. (Princess Juniper Ser.). (ENG.). 256p. (J). (gr. 3-7). 16.99 (978-0-399-17153-6(3), Philomel Bks.) Penguin Young Readers Group.

Paquette, Ammi-Joan & Mack, Jeff. Princess Juniper of the Hourglass. 2015. (Princess Juniper Ser.). (ENG., Illus.). 288p. (J). (gr. 3-7). bds. 16.99 (978-0-399-17151-2(7), Philomel Bks.) Penguin Young Readers Group.

Park, Linda Sue. Archer's Quest. 2008. (ENG., Illus.). 176p. (J). (gr. 3-7). 6.99 (978-0-440-42204-4(3), Yearling) Random Hse. Children's Bks.

Parragon Staff. Lion King. 2010. (Disney Diecut Classics). 72p. (J). (gr. -1-1). (978-1-4075-8936-7(9)) Parragon, Inc.

Paulsen, Gary & Roberts, Esyllt Nest. Plygu Amser. 2005. (WEL.). 80p. pap. (978-0-86381-683-3(5)) Gwasg Carreg Gwalch.

Peck, Richard. The Mouse with the Question Mark Tail. Murphy, Kelly, illus. 2013. (ENG.). 240p. (J). (gr. 3-7). 16.99 (978-0-8037-3838-6(2), Dial Bks) Penguin Young Readers Group.

Percival, J. M., ed. Romanian Fairy Tales. 2008. 160p. 25.95 (978-1-60664-929-9(9)); pap. 14.95 (978-1-60664-049-4(6)) Aegypan.

Peschke, Marci. Kylie Jean, 4 vols., Set. Mourning, Tuesday, illus. Incl. Blueberry Queen. lib. bdg. 22.65 (978-1-4048-6756-7(2)); Drama Queen. lib. bdg. 22.65 (978-1-4048-6757-4(0)); Hoop Queen. lib. bdg. 22.65 (978-1-4048-5962-3(4)); Rodeo Queen. lib. bdg. 22.65 (978-1-4048-5961-6(6)); (gr. 2-3). (Kylie Jean Ser.). (ENG., Illus.). 112p. 2011. Set lib. bdg. 90.60 (978-1-4048-6645-4(0), Kylie Jean) Picture Window Bks.

Peterson, Mark. The Tater Tot King. 2011. 16p. 12.68 (978-1-4269-5395-8(X)) Trafford Publishing.

Philpot, Graham, illus. The Emperor & the Nightingale. 2007. (First Reading Level 4 Ser.). 48p. (J). (gr. -1-3). 8.99 (978-0-7945-1614-7(9), Usborne) EDC Publishing.

Pierce, Tamora. Mastiff. 2012. (Beka Cooper Ser.). (ENG.). 608p. (YA). (gr. 7-11). pap. 10.99 (978-0-375-83818-7(X), Ember) Random Hse. Children's Bks.

—Trickster's Queen. 2005. (Daughter of the Lioness Ser.: Bk. 2). (Illus.). 467p. (gr. 7-12). 20.00 (978-0-7569-5482-6(7)) Perfection Learning Corp.

Pilegard, Virginia. The Emperor's Army, 1 vol. Tans, Adrian, illus. 2010. (ENG.). 32p. (J). (gr. k-3). 16.99 (978-1-58980-690-0(5)) Pelican Publishing Co., Inc.

Pilegard, Virginia Walton. The Warlord's Messengers, 1 vol. Debon, Nicolas, illus. 2005. (Warlord's Ser.). (ENG.). 32p. (J). (gr. k-3). 16.99 (978-1-58980-271-1(3)) Pelican Publishing Co., Inc.

Pittar, Gill. Milly, Molly & What Was That? (book W/dolls) 2006. 28p. pap. (978-1-86972-105-3(5)) Milly Molly Bks.

Plumides, Damon & Boerke, Arthur Mark. The Adventures of Caterwaul the Cat: Feline Pie. 2011. (ENG., Illus.). 226p. (J). (gr. 4-7). pap. 17.95 (978-1-937084-19-6(1)) Boutique of Quality Books Publishing Co., Inc.

Princess Protection Program Staff. The Palace of Mystery, No. 4. 2010. (Princess Protection Program Ser.). 144p. pap. 4.99 (978-1-4231-2727-7(7)) Disney Pr.

Pugliano-Martin, Carol. The Very Mean King: Set Of 6. 2010. (Early Connections Ser.). (J). pap. 37.00 net. (978-1-4108-1365-7(7)) Benchmark Education Co.

—The Very Mean King & el rey Malo: 6 English, 6 Spanish Adaptations. 2011. (ENG & SPA.). (J). 75.00 net. (978-1-4108-5648-7(8)) Benchmark Education Co.

The Quest for Seven Castles. 2006. (J). per. 7.99 (978-0-9785523-1-2(8)) Cross & Crown Publishing.

Quinn, Jordan. Let the Games Begin! McPhillips, Robert, illus. 2015. (Kingdom of Wrenly Ser.: 7). (ENG.). 128p. (J). (gr. k-4). pap. 5.99 (978-1-4814-2379-3(7), Little Simon) Little Simon.

—The Lost Stone. McPhillips, Robert, illus. 2014. (Kingdom of Wrenly Ser.: 1). (ENG.). 128p. (J). (gr. k-4). pap. 5.99 (978-1-4424-9690-3(8), Little Simon) Little Simon.

—The Lost Stone. 2014. (Kingdom of Wrenly Ser.: 1). lib. bdg. 16.00 (978-0-606-35443-1(3)) Turtleback Bks.

—The Scarlet Dragon. McPhillips, Robert, illus. 2014. (Kingdom of Wrenly Ser.: 2). (ENG.). 128p. (J). (gr. k-4). pap. 5.99 (978-1-4424-9693-4(2), Little Simon) Little Simon.

—The Scarlet Dragon. 2014. (Kingdom of Wrenly Ser.: 2). lib. bdg. 16.00 (978-0-606-35444-8(1)) Turtleback Bks.

—Sea Monster! McPhillips, Robert, illus. 2014. (Kingdom of Wrenly Ser.: 3). (ENG.). 128p. (J). (gr. k-4). pap. 5.99 (978-1-4814-0072-5(X), Little Simon) Little Simon.

—The Secret World of Mermaids. McPhillips, Robert, illus. 2015. (Kingdom of Wrenly Ser.: 8). (ENG.). 128p. (J). (gr. k-4). pap. 5.99 (978-1-4814-3122-4(6), Little Simon) Little Simon.

Raghbeer, Anjali. A Royal Deck: Ganjifa Art. Modak, Tejas, illus. 2012. (Art Tales from India Ser.). (ENG.). 23p. 14.95 (978-81-8328-187-4(7)) Wisdom Tree IND. Dist: SCB Distributors.

Ramirez, Gamaliel, illus. The Night We Almost Saw the Three Kings. 32p. (J). (gr. 1-18). 16.00 (978-0-9710860-8-1(7)) Libros, Encouraging Cultural Literacy.

Ravin Lodding, Linda. The Queen Is Coming to Tea. von Kitzing, Constanze, illus. 2017. (ENG.). 32p. (J). (-4). 16.99 (978-1-4926-0757-1(6), 9781492607571, Sourcebooks Jabberwocky) Sourcebooks, Inc.

Redwine, C. J. The Shadow Queen. 2016. (YA). (gr. 8). (Ravenspire Ser.: 1). 416p. pap. 9.99 (978-0-06-236025-0(6)); (ENG., Illus.). 400p. 17.99 (978-0-06-236024-3(8)) HarperCollins Pubs.

—The Shadow Queen. 2016. (Ravenspire Ser.: 1). (YA). lib. bdg. 20.85 (978-0-606-39615-8(2)) Turtleback Bks.

Reese, Jacob. Copperweight. 2008. 231p. pap. 24.95 (978-1-60813-240-9(4)) America Star Bks.

Renner, Ellen. Castle of Shadows. 2013. (ENG., Illus.). 400p. (J). (gr. 5-7). pap. 7.99 (978-0-544-02270-6(X)) Houghton Mifflin Harcourt Publishing Co.

Reuker, Heidi. Queen of the Rats. 2007. 56p. per. 16.95 (978-1-4137-9801-2(2)) America Star Bks.

Rey, H. A. Curious George What Do You See? 2009. (Curious George Ser.). (ENG., Illus.). 10p. (J). (gr. -1 — 1). bds. 6.99 (978-0-547-18263-6(5)) Houghton Mifflin Harcourt Publishing Co.

Rice, Morgan. A Grant of Arms. 2013. 238p. pap. 14.99 (978-1-939416-61-2(2)) Morgan Rice Bks.

—A Land of Fire. 2014. 196p. 26.99 (978-1-939416-87-2(6)) Morgan Rice Bks.

—A Land of Fire (Book #12 in the Sorcerer's Ring) 2014. 196p. (YA). pap. 15.99 (978-1-939416-86-5(8), Morgan Rice) Morgan Rice Bks.

—Night of the Bold (Kings & Sorcerers — Book 6) 2016. (ENG., Illus.). 162p. (J). pap. 12.99 (978-1-63291-497-2(2), Morgan Rice) Morgan Rice Bks.

—A Reign of Steel (Book #11 in the Sorcerer's Ring) 2014. 216p. (YA). pap. 15.99 (978-1-939416-76-6(0), Morgan Rice) Morgan Rice Bks.

—A Rite of Swords. 2013. 266p. 25.99 (978-1-939416-58-2(2)); pap. 14.99 (978-1-939416-57-5(4)) Morgan Rice Bks.

—A Vow of Glory. 2013. (Sorcerer's Ring Ser.: Bk. 5). 274p. pap. 13.99 (978-1-939416-28-5(0)) Morgan Rice Bks.

Richey, Denise. The Handwriting on the Wall. 2012. 28p. pap. 19.99 (978-1-4772-6606-9(2)) AuthorHouse.

—The King's Bad Dream. 2009. 32p. pap. 12.99 (978-1-4490-1303-5(1)) AuthorHouse.

Riddle, Sharon Kay & Sanders, Nancy/Ida. The King's Silverware. Lowe, Frank Allen, illus. 2007. 32p. (J). pap. 15.00 (978-0-9761583-5-6(3)) Olive Leaf Pubns.

Rifkin, L. (Lauren). The Nine Lives of Romeo Crumb: Life Two. 2010. 277p. (J). pap. 8.95 (978-0-9743221-4-8(8)) Sunrise Publishing Co.

Rigby Education Staff. Queen of Hearts. (gr. k-2). 21.00 (978-0-7635-2406-7(9)) Rigby Education.

Riley, Andy. King Flashypants & the Evil Emperor. Riley, Andy, illus. 2017. (King Flashypants Ser.). (ENG., Illus.). 224p. (J). 13.99 (978-1-62779-809-9(9), 9781627798099, Holt, Henry & Co. Bks. For Young Readers) Holt, Henry & Co.

Riley, Lehman C. Meeting Dr. Martin Luther King. 2004. (Adventures of Papa Lemon's Little Wanderers Ser.: Bk. 1). 35p. (978-0-9760523-0-2(X)) Matter of Africa America Time.

Rinaldi, Ann. Nine Days a Queen: The Short Life & Reign of Lady Jane Grey. 2006. (ENG.). 240p. (J). (gr. 8-12). pap. 8.99 (978-0-06-054925-1(4), HarperTeen) HarperCollins Pubs.

—The Redheaded Princess. 2008. (ENG.). 224p. (J). (gr. 3-7). 15.99 (978-0-06-073374-2(8)) HarperCollins Pubs.

Rinehart, J. D. Crown of Three. 2016. (Crown of Three Ser.: 1). (ENG., Illus.). 432p. (J). (gr. 4-8). pap. 7.99 (978-1-4814-2444-8(0), Aladdin) Simon & Schuster Children's Publishing.

Rinehart, J. D. The Lost Realm. (Crown of Three Ser.: 2). (ENG., Illus.). (J). (gr. 4-8). 2017. 512p. pap. 8.99 (978-1-4814-2447-9(5)) 2016. 496p. 17.99 (978-1-4814-2446-2(7)) Simon & Schuster Children's Publishing. (Aladdin).

Risso, Eduardo. Mysteries of the Red Moon, Vol. 3. 2006. (SPA.). 48p. pap. 16.95 (978-1-59497-163-1(3)) Public Square Bks.

Risso, Eduardo & Trillo, Carlos. Los Misterios de la Luna Roja Vol. 2: El Ataque del Circo. 2006. (SPA., Illus.). 72p. (J). (gr. 1). per. 16.95 (978-1-59497-162-4(5)) Public Square Bks.

Roberts, Daniel. The Dragon, the Princess & the Peanut Butter Sandwiches. 2009. 36p. pap. 16.99 (978-1-4389-8277-9(1)) AuthorHouse.

Rodriguez, Artemio. The King of Things/el Rey de Las Cosas. Rodriguez, Artemio, illus. 2006. (SPA & ENG., Illus.). 32p. (J). (gr. -1-1). 12.95 (978-0-938317-97-5(0)) Cinco Puntos Pr.

Rose, Kathryn. Avalon Rising. 2015. (Metal & Lace Novel Ser.: 2). (ENG., Illus.). 360p. (YA). pap. 11.99 (978-0-7387-4489-6(1), Flux) North Star Editions.

Rose, Phyllis & de Brunhoff, Laurent. Babar's Lost & Found. 2013. (ENG., Illus.). 22p. (J). (gr. -1 — 1). bds. 7.95 (978-1-4197-0981-4(X), Abrams Appleseed) Abrams, Inc.

Ross, Joel. Beast & Crown. 2017. 384p. (J). (gr. 3-7). 16.99 **(978-0-06-248459-8(1))** HarperCollins Pubs.

Ross, Tony. I Want My Mom! Ross, Tony, illus. 2012. (Andersen Press Picture Bks). (ENG., Illus.). 32p. (J). (gr. -1-3). 16.95 (978-1-4677-0318-5(4)) Lerner Publishing Group.

Ross, Tony & Ross, Tony. I Want a Sister! 2013. (Illus.). 32p. (J). (gr. -1-3). 16.95 (978-1-4677-2047-2(X)) Andersen Pr. GBR. Dist: Lerner Publishing Group.

Rovetch, L. Bob & Whitman, Emily. Sir Henry, the Polite Knight. Barnard, Bryn, illus. 2006. (J). (978-1-58987-204-2(5)) Kindermusik International.

Rowe, W. W. The Wizard's Wayward Wand. 2010. (ENG.). 99p. (J). (gr. 3-7). pap. 12.95 (978-0-9843754-0-0(6)) Sanctuary Publishing, Inc.

Rowley, Melissa. The Falcon Shield. 2009. (J). 6.99 (978-1-60641-103-2(9)) Deseret Bk. Co.

Rowley, M'lin. The Silver Coat. 2009. (Knights of Right Ser.: Bk. 2). 71p. (J). (gr. 1-5). pap. 6.99 (978-1-60641-104-9(7), Shadow Mountain) Shadow Mountain Publishing.

Roy, Jennifer. Cordially Uninvited. 2012. (ENG., Illus.). 256p. (J). (gr. 3-7). 15.99 (978-1-4424-3920-7(3), Simon & Schuster Bks. For Young Readers) Simon & Schuster Bks. For Young Readers.

Roy, Jennifer Rozines. Cordially Uninvited. 2013. (ENG.). 272p. (J). (gr. 3-7). pap. 6.99 (978-1-4424-3921-4(1), Simon & Schuster Bks. For Young Readers) Simon & Schuster Bks. For Young Readers.

A Royal Tea. 2014. (Mermaid Tales Ser.: 9). (ENG., Illus.). 112p. (J). (gr. 1-4). pap. 5.99 (978-1-4814-0254-5(4), Aladdin) Simon & Schuster Children's Publishing.

Royde-Smith, N. G. Una and the Red Cross Knight & Other T. 2006. (Illus.). pap. 28.95 (978-1-4254-8407-1(7)) Kessinger Publishing, LLC.

Rutkoski, Marie. The Jewel of the Kalderash. 3rd ed. 2011. (Kronos Chronicles Ser.: 3). (ENG.). 336p. (J). (gr. 5-9). 16.99 (978-0-374-33678-3(4), 9780374336783, Farrar, Straus & Giroux (BYR)) Farrar, Straus & Giroux.

—The Jewel of the Kalderash. 2013. (Kronos Chronicles Ser.: 3). (ENG.). 336p. (J). (gr. 5-9). pap. 7.99 (978-1-250-01025-4(X), 9781250010254) Square Fish.

Ryan, Brittney. The Legend of Holly Claus. Long, Laurel, illus. 2004. (Julie Andrews Collection). 544p. (J). (gr. 4-18). 16.99 (978-0-06-058511-2(0)); lib. bdg. 17.89 (978-0-06-058514-3(5)) HarperCollins Pubs. (Julie Andrews Collection).

Sadi. The Careless King & Other Stories. 2005. (Illus.). 64p. (J). (978-969-542-068-3(0)) Children Pubns.

Salimena, Kathleen Elizabeth. The Royal Yacht. 2008. (Illus.). 24p. (J). (gr. 11-18). 15.95 *(978-0-9798624-0-3(X))* Royal Imprint Pr., Inc.

Salisbury, Melinda. The Sin Eater's Daughter. 2015. (ENG.). 320p. (J). (gr. 9). 17.99 *(978-0-545-81062-3(0),* Scholastic Pr.) Scholastic, Inc.

Sanders, Roy E. Land of Pink. Patzelt, Kasie, illus. 2007. (Not So Far Ago Ser.). 37p. (J). (gr. -1-3). 19.99 *(978-1-59879-327-7(6))* Lifevest Publishing, Inc.

Sanderson, Jeanette. Robin Hood Shoots for the Queen: A Legend from England. 2006. (J). pap. *(978-1-4108-7167-1(3))* Benchmark Education Co.

Sanderson, Ruth. A Castle Full of Cats. 2015. (ENG., Illus.). 40p. (J). (gr. -1-2). lib. bdg. 19.99 *(978-0-375-97154-9(8),* Random Hse. Bks. for Young Readers) Random Hse. Children's Bks.

Santillo, LuAnn. Dip & Sip. Santillo, LuAnn, ed. 2003. (Half-Pint Kids Readers Ser.). (Illus.). 7p. (J). (gr. -1-1). pap. 1.00 *(978-1-59256-051-6(2))* Half-Pint Kids, Inc.

—The King. Santillo, LuAnn, ed. 2003. (Half-Pint Kids Readers Ser.). (Illus.). 7p. (J). (gr. -1-1). pap. 1.00 *(978-1-59256-050-9(4))* Half-Pint Kids, Inc.

Santore, Charles, illus. William the Curious: Knight of the Water Lilies. 2012. (J). *(978-1-60464-034-2(0))* Appleseed Pr. Bk. Pub. LLC.

Sargent, Dave & Sargent, Pat. Whiskers: (Roan) Pride & Peace, 30 vols., Vol. 59. Lenoir, Jane, illus. 2003. (Saddle up Ser.: Vol. 59). 42p. (J). pap. 10.95 *(978-1-56763-806-6(6))* Ozark Publishing.

Saunders, Kate. The Little Secret. Carman, William, illus. 2012. (ENG.). 240p. (J). (gr. 3-6). pap. 10.99 *(978-0-312-67427-4(9),* 9780312674274) Square Fish.

Scam, Busta. The Kingdom of Nome. 2006. (Illus.). 44p. pap. 12.95 *(978-1-59663-516-6(9),* Castle Keep Pr.) Rock, James A. & Co. Pubs.

Schanback, Mindy. Princess from Another Planet. 2005. (ENG.). 254p. (J). (gr. 5-9). 16.95 *(978-0-8234-1847-3(2))* Holiday Hse., Inc.

Schitt, Jayme & Schitt, Ron. Rags, Riches & the Robe. 2010. 32p. 17.25 *(978-1-4269-4666-0(X))* Trafford Publishing.

Scieszka, Jon. Los Caballeros de la Mesa de la Cocina. Smith, Lane, illus. (SPA.). (J). (gr. 5-8). 7.95 *(978-958-04-3400-9(X),* NR4516) Norma S.A. COL. Dist: Distribuidora Norma, Inc., Lectorum Pubns., Inc.

Scotton, Rob. On with the Show. Scotton, Rob, illus. 2013. (Splat the Cat Ser.). (ENG., Illus.). 24p. (J). (gr. -1-3). pap. 3.99 *(978-0-06-209010-2(0),* HarperFestival) HarperCollins Pubs.

Seiss, Ellie & Random House Staff. Dora & the Unicorn King. 2013. (Dora the Explorer Step into Reading Ser.). lib. bdg. 13.55 *(978-0-606-32415-1(1),* Turtleback) Turtleback Bks.

Shahegh, Mahvash. The Green Musician. Ewart, Claire, illus. 2015. (ENG.). 36p. (J). (gr. k-3). 16.95 *(978-1-937786-42-7(0),* Wisdom Tales) World Wisdom, Inc.

Shakespeare, William. Macbeth. Deas, Robert, illus. 2008. (ENG.). 208p. (YA). (gr. 7-11). pap. 12.95 *(978-0-8109-7073-1(2),* Amulet Bks.) Abrams, Inc.

—Macbeth, 1 vol. Pérez, Daniel & Ferran, Daniel, illus. 2011. (Shakespeare Graphics Ser.). (ENG.). 88p. (gr. 2-3). pap. 7.15 *(978-1-4342-3447-6(9),* Shakespeare Graphics) Stone Arch Bks.

—Macbeth, 1 vol. Ferran, Daniel, illus. 2011. (Shakespeare Graphics Ser.). (ENG.). 88p. (gr. 2-3). lib. bdg. 27.99 *(978-1-4342-2506-1(2),* Shakespeare Graphics) Stone Arch Bks.

—Macbeth: The Graphic Novel. 2010. (Classic Graphic Novel Collection). 144p. (YA). (gr. 7-12). 34.80 *(978-1-4205-0373-9(1))* Cengage Gale.

Shakespeare, William & Appignanesi, Richard. Hamlet. Vieceli, Emma, illus. 2007. (ENG.). 204p. (J). (gr. 2-8). pap. 12.95 *(978-0-8109-9324-2(4),* Abrams Bks. for Young Readers) Abrams, Inc.

Sharp, Laura. The Key Prince. 2012. 24p. pap. 24.95 *(978-1-4626-8959-0(0))* America Star Bks.

Sharplin, Emory. Scrap. 2013. 352p. (J). pap. 10.95 *(978-1-938416-35-4(X))* River Grove Bks.

Sheldon, Dyan. The Moon Dragons. Blythe, Gary, illus. 2015. (J). 17.32 *(978-1-4677-6318-9(7))* Lerner Publishing Group.

—Moon Dragons. Blythe, Gary, illus. 2015. (ENG.). 32p. (J). (gr. -1-3). 16.95 *(978-1-4677-6314-1(4))* Lerner Publishing Group.

Shields, Gillian. Holly Takes a Risk. Turner, Helen, illus. 2008. (Mermaid S. O. S. Ser.: 4). (ENG.). 96p. (J). (gr. 1-4). pap. 4.50 *(978-1-59990-214-2(1),* 9781599902142, Bloomsbury USA Childrens) Bloomsbury Publishing USA.

—Sophie Makes a Splash. Turner, Helen, illus. 2008. (Mermaid S. O. S. Ser.: 3). (ENG.). 96p. (J). (gr. 1-4). pap. 4.50 *(978-1-59990-212-8(5),* 9781599902128, Bloomsbury USA Childrens) Bloomsbury Publishing USA.

Shulevitz, Uri. One Monday Morning. Shulevitz, Uri, illus. 2003. (ENG., Illus.). 48p. (J). (gr. -1-1). reprint ed. pap. 8.99 *(978-0-374-45648-1(8),* 9780374456481) Square Fish.

—One Monday Morning. 2003. (J). (gr. -1-2). lib. bdg. 18.40 *(978-0-613-71877-6(1),* Turtleback) Turtleback Bks.

Siegel, Pete. Light Switch to Heaven. 2012. (ENG.). 46p. (J). pap. 15.95 *(978-1-4327-8817-9(5));* pap. 22.95 *(978-1-4327-8818-6(3))* Outskirts Pr., Inc.

Signor Sr., S. Ernest. The Book of Esther. 2013. 28p. pap. 13.99 *(978-1-4525-7313-7(1))* Balboa Pr.

Simonson, Louise. Snow White & the Seven Robots. Sanchez, Jimena, illus. 2015. (Far Out Fairy Tales Ser.). (ENG.). 40p. (gr. 3-4). lib. bdg. 25.32 *(978-1-4342-9648-1(2))* Stone Arch Bks.

Sims, Lesley. Snow Queen. 2005. 24p. (J). 9.95 *(978-0-7945-1160-9(0),* Usborne) EDC Publishing.

Singleton, Debbie. The King Who Wouldn't Sleep. Swain, Holly, illus. 2012. (Andersen Press Picture Bks). (ENG.). 32p. (J). (gr. -1-3). 16.95 *(978-0-7613-8997-2(0))* Lerner Publishing Group.

Skidmore, Lauren. What Is Lost. 2015. 217p. (YA). pap. 16.99 *(978-1-4621-1621-8(3))* Cedar Fort, Inc./CFI Distribution.

Sklyar, Igor. King & the Star. 2005. (Illus.). 50p. pap. *(978-1-84401-048-6(1))* Athena Pr.

Skye, Evelyn. The Crown's Game. (Crown's Game Ser.: 1). (ENG.). (YA). (gr. 8). 2017. 432p. pap. 9.99 *(978-0-06-242259-0(6))* 2016. 416p. 17.99 *(978-0-06-242258-3(8))* HarperCollins Pubs.

—The Crown's Game. 2017. (Crown's Game Ser.: bk.1). (ENG.). (J). lib. bdg. 20.85 ***(978-0-606-39645-5(4))*** Turtleback Bks.

Sleigh, Barbara. Carbonel & Calidor: Being the Further Adventures of a Royal Cat. Front, Charles, illus. 2009. (ENG.). 224p. (J). (gr. 4-7). 17.95 *(978-1-59017-333-6(3),* NYR Children's Collection) New York Review of Bks., Inc., The.

Sloane, Richard. Back to the Dark Ages! 2013. 138p. (gr. 4-6). 22.95 *(978-1-4669-7401-2(X));* pap. 12.95 *(978-1-4669-7399-2(4))* Trafford Publishing.

Sluzhaev, Viktor, illus. The Lute Player: A Tale from Russia. 2013. (Tales of Honor Ser.). (ENG.). 32p. (J). (gr. 1-4). pap. 8.95 *(978-1-937529-59-8(2));* lib. bdg. 26.60 *(978-1-937529-75-8(4))* Red Chair Pr.

Smedman, Lisa. Sacrifice of the Widow. 2007. (Lady Penitent Ser.: Bk. 1). 311p. *(978-1-4287-1497-7(9))* Wizards of the Coast.

Smith, Peggy. The Kingdom of Nod: A Sweet Tale about an Unlucky Young Queen, & the Men Who Try to Win Her Hand, for the Barton Reading & Spelling System. 2003. (J). pap. 7.95 *(978-0-9744343-6-0(1),* SA-401) Bright Solutions for Dyslexia, LLC.

Snell, Gordon. The King of Quizzical Island. McKee, David, illus. 2009. (ENG.). 40p. (J). (gr. -1-3). 16.99 *(978-0-7636-3857-3(9))* Candlewick Pr.

Snelson, Brian & Sellars, Rodney. Shaturanga: The Story of Onus. 2003. 244p. pap. 16.95 *(978-0-595-29569-2(X))* iUniverse, Inc.

Sommer, Carl. The Great Royal Race. Westbrook, Dick, illus. 2014. (J). pap. *(978-1-57537-952-4(X))* Advance Publishing, Inc.

—The Great Royal Race. 2003. (Another Sommer-Time Story Ser.). (Illus.). 48p. (J). (gr. k-4). lib. bdg. 23.95 incl. audio *(978-1-57537-758-2(6))* Advance Publishing, Inc.

—The Great Royal Race. Westbrook, Dick, illus. 2003. (Another Sommer-Time Story Ser.). 48p. (J). (gr. k-4). lib. bdg. 23.95 incl. audio compact disk *(978-1-57537-708-7(X))* Advance Publishing, Inc.

—The Great Royal Race. 2003. (Another Sommer-Time Story Ser.). (Illus.). 48p. (J). (gr. 1-4). 16.95 incl. audio *(978-1-57537-557-1(5))* Advance Publishing, Inc.

—The Great Royal Race. Westbrook, Dick, illus. 2003. (Another Sommer-Time Story Ser.). 48p. (J). (gr. 1-4). 16.95 incl. audio compact disk *(978-1-57537-508-3(7))* Advance Publishing, Inc.

—The Great Royal Race(La Gran Carrera Real) Westbrook, Dick, illus. 2009. (Another Sommer-Time Story Bilingual Ser.). (SPA & ENG.). 48p. (J). lib. bdg. 16.95 *(978-1-57537-152-8(9))* Advance Publishing, Inc.

—The Race. Budwine, Greg, illus. 2009. (Quest for Success Ser.). (ENG.). 56p. (YA). lib. bdg. 12.95 *(978-1-57537-256-3(8))* Advance Publishing, Inc.

—The Race(La Carrera) Budwine, Greg, illus. 2009. (Quest for Success Bilingual Ser.). (SPA & ENG.). 104p. (YA). lib. bdg. 14.95 *(978-1-57537-230-3(4))* Advance Publishing, Inc.

—The Racing Fools. Budwine, Greg, illus. 2009. (Quest for Success Ser.). (ENG.). 56p. (YA). pap. 4.95 *(978-1-57537-281-5(9))* Advance Publishing, Inc.

Sorensen, Launa. The King's First Journey, Bk. 1. 2007. 280p. (YA). pap. 15.99 *(978-1-59092-572-0(6))* Blue Forge Pr.

Souhami, Jessica. Rama & the de Mon King: An Ancient Tale from India. 2006. (Illus.). 30p. (J). (gr. k-4). reprint ed. 15.00 *(978-0-7567-9813-0(2))* DIANE Publishing Co.

Spring, Manda. Emerald & the Withered Willow. 2007. 148p. pap. 18.00 *(978-1-4303-1353-3(6))* Lulu Pr., Inc.

Spurgeon, Charles. Queen Victoria's Request: A Story of Grace & Mercy. Anderson, Jeff, illus. 2008. (Story Time Ser.). (ENG.). 24p. (J). (gr. -1-3). 7.99 *(978-1-84550-325-3(2),* 0d42e451-d842-4279-bf70-b929d8508ca9) Christian Focus Pubns. GBR. Dist: Bookmasters Distribution.

Squatrito, J. Michael, Jr. The Talisman of Unification: The Overlords. 2007. (ENG., Illus.). 424p. (YA). per. 22.95 *(978-0-595-47343-4(1))* iUniverse, Inc.

Stanek, Robert, pseud. The Elf Queen & the King III. 2007. 232p. (YA). pap. 15.00 *(978-1-57545-086-5(0))* RP Media.

—The Elf Queen & the King IV. 2008. 238p. (YA). pap. 15.00 *(978-1-57545-087-2(9))* RP Media.

Stanley, Diane. Bella at Midnight. Ibatoulline, Bagram, illus. 2007. (ENG.). 304p. (J). (gr. 3-7). pap. 7.99 *(978-0-06-077575-9(0))* HarperCollins Pubs.

—The Cup & the Crown. 2013. (Silver Bowl Ser.: 2). (ENG.). 368p. (J). (gr. 3-7). pap. 6.99 *(978-0-06-196323-0(2))* HarperCollins Pubs.

—The Princess of Cortova. (J). 2015. (Silver Bowl Ser.: 3). (ENG.). 336p. (gr. 3-7). pap. 6.99 *(978-0-06-204732-8(9))* 2013. 311p. lib. bdg. *(978-0-06-204731-1(0))* HarperCollins Pubs.

—The Silver Bowl. (Silver Bowl Ser.: 1). (ENG.). (J). (gr. 5). 2012. 336p. pap. 6.99 *(978-0-06-157546-4(1))* 2011. 320p. 16.99 *(978-0-06-157543-3(7))* HarperCollins Pubs.

Staska, H. M. How George Became King. 2012. 40p. pap. 32.70 *(978-1-4771-1475-9(0))* Xlibris Corp.

Steel, Flora. The Adventures of Akbar. 2007. 116p. per. 9.95 *(978-1-60312-207-8(9))* Aegypan.

Stein, Evaleen. Our Little Crusader Cousin of Long Ago. Meister, Charles E., illus. 2007. 136p. per. 8.95 *(978-1-59915-243-1(6))* Yesterday's Classics.

—Our Little Frankish Cousin of Long Ago. Landau, Helena Von & Meister, Charles, illus. 2007. 92p. per. 8.95 *(978-1-59915-244-8(4))* Yesterday's Classics.

Stephaan, Kynza. Empress Kynza of Skrollz: You Are Special. 2012. 24p. pap. 17.99 *(978-1-4772-7239-8(9))* AuthorHouse.

Stevens, Dan. The Magic of the Brass Ring. 2009. 84p. pap. 19.95 *(978-1-4489-7759-8(2))* America Star Bks.

Stevenson, Steve. The King of Scotland's Sword. 2013. (Agatha Girl of Mystery Ser.: 3). lib. bdg. 16.00 *(978-0-606-31688-0(4),* Turtleback) Turtleback Bks.

Stewart, Dianne C. Longitude - Zero Degrees. 2009. (ENG.). 200p. pap. 8.95 *(978-0-9667359-4-9(3),* BeanPole Bks.) Harren Communications, LLC.

Stewig, John Warren. Nobody Asked the Pea. Van Wright, Cornelius, illus. 2013. (ENG.). 32p. (J). (gr. 1-5). 16.95 *(978-0-8234-2224-1(0))* Holiday Hse., Inc.

Streich, Michel. Grumpy Little King. Streich, Michel, illus. 2012. (ENG., Illus.). 32p. (J). (gr. k-3). 19.99 *(978-1-74237-572-4(3))* Allen & Unwin AUS. Dist: Independent Pubs. Group.

Sundberg, Norma J. An Odd Fable. Leiper, Esther M., illus. 2007. 32p. (J). pap. 13.95 *(978-0-9776958-5-0(9))* CyPress Pubns.

Surget, Alain & Yeardley, Glynne. Cleopatra Must Be Saved! Parme, Fabrice, illus. 2014. 95p. (J). *(978-1-4351-5329-5(4))* Barnes & Noble, Inc.

Sutcliff, Rosemary. The Mark of the Horse Lord. 2006. (ENG.). 289p. (YA). (gr. 12). per. 10.95 *(978-1-932425-62-8(4),* Lemniscaat) Boyds Mills Pr.

—The Mark of the Horse Lord. 2015. (Rediscovered Classics Ser.). (ENG.). 296p. (YA). (gr. 7). pap. 12.95 *(978-1-61373-154-3(X))* Chicago Review Pr., Inc.

Sutherland, Tui T. The Hidden Kingdom. 2013. (Wings of Fire Ser.: 3). (ENG., Illus.). 336p. (J). (gr. 3-7). 16.99 *(978-0-545-34920-8(6),* Scholastic Pr.) Scholastic, Inc.

Swiatkowska, Gabi. Queen on Wednesday. Swiatkowska, Gabi, illus. 2014. (ENG., Illus.). 36p. (J). (gr. -1-3). 17.99 *(978-0-374-37446-4(5),* 9780374374464, Farrar, Straus & Giroux (BYR)) Farrar, Straus & Giroux.

The Sword, the Ring, & the Parchment. 2006. (J). per. 7.99 *(978-0-9785523-0-5(X))* Cross & Crown Publishing.

Sypolt, Carl W. Adventures of David the Honeybee. 2003. 51p. pap. 9.95 *(978-0-7414-1526-4(7))* Infinity Publishing.

Tappan, Eva March. In the Days of Queen Victori. 2009. 160p. pap. 9.95 *(978-1-60459-620-5(1))* Wilder Pubns., Corp.

Terry, Will, illus. Little Rooster's Diamond Button. 2013. (ENG.). 32p. (J). (gr. -1-3). pap. 7.99 *(978-0-8075-4645-1(3))* Whitman, Albert & Co.

Thomas, Gwyn. King Arthur. Jones, Margaret, illus. 2006. (ENG.). 144p. (J). pap. 21.95 *(978-0-86243-798-5(9))* Y Lolfa GBR. Dist: Dufour Editions, Inc.

Thomas, Jane Resh. The Counterfeit Princess. 2005. 197p. (J). *(978-0-618-93780-6(3),* Clarion Bks.) Houghton Mifflin Harcourt Trade & Reference Pubs.

Thomas, Rhiannon. A Wicked Thing. 2015. (ENG.). 352p. (YA). (gr. 9). 17.99 *(978-0-06-230353-0(8),* HarperTeen) HarperCollins Pubs.

Thomas, Sherry. The Immortal Heights. 2015. (Elemental Trilogy Ser.: 3). (ENG.). 448p. (YA). (gr. 9). 17.99 *(978-0-06-220735-7(0))* HarperCollins Pubs.

Thompson, James A., Jr. The Amarna Experiment. 2003. 128p. (YA). 21.95 *(978-0-595-65753-7(2));* pap. 11.95 *(978-0-595-28296-8(2))* iUniverse, Inc.

Thompson, Lisa. In Search of the Egyptian Queen. Cantell, Brenda, illus. 2006. (Treasure Trackers Ser.). 80p. (J). (gr. 3-4). lib. bdg. 19.00 *(978-0-7910-8874-6(X))* Facts On File, Inc.

Thompson, Nina C. The Puzzle King. 2009. 56p. pap. 9.95 *(978-1-60860-149-3(8),* Eloquent Bks.) Strategic Book Publishing & Rights Agency (SBPRA).

Thurber, James. The Tiger Who Would Be King. Yoon, JooHee, illus. 2015. (ENG.). 40p. (J). (gr. k-4). 18.95 *(978-1-59270-182-7(5))* Enchanted Lion Bks., LLC.

Tillworth, Mary. King for a Day! (PAW Patrol) Jackson, Mike, illus. 2016. (Step into Reading Ser.). (ENG.). 24p. (J). (gr. -1-1). 4.99 *(978-1-101-93684-9(3),* Random Hse. Bks. for Young Readers) Random Hse. Children's Bks.

Timms, E. H. Ring of Nine. 2010. 156p. pap. 16.95 *(978-1-4452-4512-6(4))* Lulu Pr., Inc.

Tomlin, Chris & Barrett, Pat. Good Good Father, 1 vol. 2016. (ENG.). 32p. (J). 16.99 *(978-0-7180-8695-4(3))* Nelson, Thomas Inc.

Tort, Pep & Josep, Tort. El Rey Ignacio. Duran, Teresa, illus. 2006. (Montana Encantada Ser.). (SPA.). 47p. (J). per. *(978-84-241-8558-9(7))* Everest Editora.

Townsend, S. P. The Star of Persia. 2007. 120p. 33.50 *(978-1-84799-236-9(6))* Lulu Pr., Inc.

Turk, Cheri. The Stone Between Kings. Turk, Cheri, illus. 2012. (Illus.). 36p. pap. 12.99 *(978-0-9860024-0-3(2))* Specialty Greetings.

Turner, Megan Whalen. A Conspiracy of Kings. (Queen's Thief Ser.: 4). (ENG.). (YA). (gr. 8). 2017. 368p. pap. 9.99 *(978-0-06-264299-8(5))* 2011. 352p. pap. 7.99 *(978-0-06-187095-8(1))* 2010. 336p. 16.99 *(978-0-06-187093-4(5))* HarperCollins Pubs. (Greenwillow Bks.).

—A Conspiracy of Kings, 7 vols. 2010. (Queen's Thief Ser.: BK.4). (YA). (ENG.). 230.75 *(978-1-4498-4569-8(X));* (ENG.). 73.75 *(978-1-4498-4570-4(3));* 1.25 *(978-1-4498-4574-2(6));* 88.75 *(978-1-4498-4573-5(8));*No. 4. (ENG.). 90.75 *(978-1-4498-4571-1(1))* Recorded Bks., Inc.

—The King of Attolia. (Queen's Thief Ser.: 3). (ENG.). (YA). (gr. 8). 2017. 432p. pap. 9.99 *(978-0-06-264298-1(7))* 2007. 432p. pap. 7.99 *(978-0-06-083579-8(6))* 2006. 400p. 17.99 *(978-0-06-083577-4(X))* HarperCollins Pubs. (Greenwillow Bks.).

—The King of Attolia. 2007. (Queen's Thief Ser.: BK.3). 387p. (YA). 18.00 *(978-0-7569-8106-8(9))* Perfection Learning Corp.

—The King of Attolia. (YA). 2008. (Queen's Thief Ser.: BK.3). (ENG.). 84.49 *(978-1-4281-8027-7(3))* 2007. (Attolia Ser.: 3). 119.75 *(978-1-4281-1722-8(9))* 2007. (Queen's Thief Ser.: BK.3). (ENG.). 92.75 *(978-1-4281-1716-7(4))* 2006. (Queen's Thief Ser.: BK.3). (ENG.). 90.75 *(978-1-4281-1718-1(0))* 2006. (Queen's Thief Ser.: BK.3). (ENG.). 122.75 *(978-1-4281-1720-4(2))* 2006. (Queen's Thief Ser.: BK.3). (ENG.). 251.75 *(978-1-4281-1717-4(2))* 2006. (Queen's Thief Ser.: BK.3). 281.75 *(978-1-4281-1721-1(0))* 2006. (Queen's Thief Ser.: BK.3). (ENG.). 1.25 *(978-1-4281-1713-6(X))* Recorded Bks., Inc.

—The Queen of Attolia. (Queen's Thief Ser.: 2). (ENG.). (YA). (gr. 8). 2017. 416p. pap. 9.99 *(978-0-06-264297-4(9))* 2006. 368p. pap. 6.99 *(978-0-06-084182-9(6))* HarperCollins Pubs. (Greenwillow Bks.).

—The Queen of Attolia, 8 vols. (Attolia Ser.: 2). (J). 2013. 188.75 *(978-1-4281-5237-3(7))* 2009. 73.75 *(978-1-4361-6574-7(1))* 2008. 104.75 *(978-1-4281-5236-6(9))* 2008. 75.75 *(978-1-4281-5234-2(2))* 2007. 78.75 *(978-1-4281-5232-8(6))* 2007. 101.75 *(978-1-4281-5233-0(5))* 2007. 162.75 *(978-1-4281-5233-5(4))* 2007. 1.25 *(978-1-4281-5229-8(6))* Recorded Bks., Inc.

—The Queen of Attolia. 2017. (Queen's Thief Ser.: BK.2). (ENG.). (YA). lib. bdg. 20.85 ***(978-0-606-40331-3(0))*** Turtleback Bks.

Turner, Megan Whalen. Thick As Thieves. 2017. (Queen's Thief Ser.: 5). (ENG.). 352p. (YA). (gr. 8). 17.99 *(978-0-06-256824-3(8),* Greenwillow Bks.) HarperCollins Pubs.

Turner, Patrenia. Barbie In The Queen Patrenialla Fairy - Tale. Turner, Keeng Troyius, ed. 2014. (Illus.). 31p. pap. *(978-0-578-14812-0(9))* Patrenialla Turner, Queen .

Twist, Clint. Cleopatra: Queen of Egypt. Andrew, Ian, illus. 2012. (Historical Notebooks Ser.). (ENG.). 30p. (J). (gr. 3-7). 19.99 *(978-0-7636-6095-6(7),* Templar) Candlewick Pr.

Van Dusen, Chris. King Hugo's Huge Ego. 2011. (ENG., Illus.). 40p. (J). (gr. -1-2). 16.99 *(978-0-7636-5004-9(8))* Candlewick Pr.

Vaughn, J. D. Second Guard. 2015. (Second Guard Novel Ser.). (ENG., Illus.). 424p. (J). (gr. 5-9). 16.99 *(978-1-4231-6909-3(3))* Disney Pr.

—The Shadow Guard. 2016. (Second Guard Novel Ser.). (ENG.). 320p. (J). (gr. 5-9). 16.99 *(978-1-4231-7097-6(0))* Hyperion Bks. for Children.

Vines, Audrey. Miranda. 2010. 28p. 15.99 *(978-1-4520-1105-9(2))* AuthorHouse.

Vision, David. Who's That Crying! Alcantara, Ignacio, illus. 2009. 64p. 17.00 *(978-0-9659538-1-8(5))* Von Curtis Publishing.

Voigt, Cynthia. The Tale of Elske. 2015. (Tales of the Kingdom Ser.: 4). (ENG., Illus.). 368p. (YA). (gr. 7). 19.99 *(978-1-4814-2189-8(1),* Atheneum Bks. for Young Readers) Simon & Schuster Children's Publishing.

Volpe, Theresa. The King's Mapmaker. 2006. (Early Explorers Ser.). (J). pap. *(978-1-4108-6129-0(5))* Benchmark Education Co.

Wade, Kerry. A Page Turns Twelve & Comes of Age. 2006. 9.00 *(978-0-8059-9169-7(7))* Dorrance Publishing Co., Inc.

Wadham, Tim. The Queen of France. Denton, Kady MacDonald, illus. 2011. (ENG.). 32p. (J). (gr. -1-3). 16.99 *(978-0-7636-4102-3(2))* Candlewick Pr.

Wakefield, Beth. The Cleaner. 2010. 151p. pap. 14.50 *(978-1-4457-6809-0(7))* Lulu Pr., Inc.

Wallace, Karen & Chapman, Neil. Arthur the King. 2009. (Hopscotch Adventures Ser.). (Illus.). 31p. (J). (gr. 1). lib. bdg. 25.65 *(978-1-59771-173-9(X))* Sea-To-Sea Pubns.

Walsleben, Edda Brigitte. The Little Bee Who Would Be Queen. 2012. 224p. 45.00 *(978-1-937911-33-1(0));* pap. 33.00 *(978-1-937911-32-4(2))* Heavenly Realm Publishing.

Warner, Larry. Chocolate Island, 1 vol. 2010. 42p. pap. 24.95 *(978-1-4489-7372-9(4))* PublishAmerica, Inc.

Warner, Sally. EllRay Jakes the Recess King! 2015. (EllRay Jakes Ser.: 8). lib. bdg. 16.00 *(978-0-606-36777-6(2))* Turtleback Bks.

Wasserman, Mira. Too Much of a Good Thing. Carolan, Christine, illus. 2003. 32p. (J). (gr. -1-3). pap. 6.95 *(978-1-58013-066-0(6));* (ENG.). 15.95 *(978-1-58013-082-0(8))* Lerner Publishing Group. (Kar-Ben Publishing).

Webb, Beth. Fleabag Trilogy. 2005. 640p. (J). pap. 14.00 *(978-0-7459-4977-2(0),* Lion Books) Lion Hudson PLC GBR. Dist: Trafalgar Square Publishing.

Weinbrecht, William. Stories for Amand. 2009. 48p. pap. 15.50 *(978-1-60693-150-9(4),* Eloquent Bks.) Strategic Book Publishing & Rights Agency (SBPRA).

Weiss, Ellen. Babar: Four Stories to Read & Share. Gibert, Jean Claude & Gray, J. M. L., illus. 2006. (J). 9.99 *(978-0-8109-9308-2(2),* Abrams Bks. for Young Readers) Abrams, Inc.

Welch, Julie. Happy Hearts, 1 vol. 2009. 52p. pap. 16.95 *(978-1-4489-1971-0(1))* America Star Bks.

Wend, Arran. The King & the Fire Chanter. 2007. (Runes of Medarya Ser.). (Illus.). 373p. (J). 15.95 *(978-0-9793284-0-4(3))* Antiquity Publishing.

What Is Hidden. 2014. 281p. (YA). pap. 16.99 *(978-1-4621-1429-0(6))* Cedar Fort, Inc./CFI Distribution.

Wilde, Oscar. The House of Pomegranates. 2005. (ENG.). 81p. pap. *(978-1-4065-0242-8(1))* Dodo Pr.

Wilkinson, Kerry. Renegade. 2015. (Silver Blackthorn Trilogy Ser.: 2). (ENG.). 368p. (YA). (gr. 8-12). 18.99 *(978-1-250-06133-1(4),* 9781250061331, St. Martin's Griffin) St. Martin's Pr.

Williams, Brenda. The Real Princess. Fatus, Sophie, illus. 2008. (ENG.). 40p. (J). (gr. -1-3). 16.99 *(978-1-905236-88-6(3))* Barefoot Bks., Inc.

Williams, Brenda & Barefoot Books Staff. Una Princesa Real: Un Cuento Matemagico. Fatus, Sophie, illus. 2014. (SPA.). 40p. (J). (gr. k-4). pap. 8.99 *(978-1-78285-078-6(3))* Barefoot Bks., Inc.

Williams, Rozanne Lanczak. Fairy Tale Mail. Allen, Joy, illus. (Learn to Write Ser.). 16p. (J). 2007. pap. 8.99 *(978-1-59198-359-0(2))* 2006. pap. 3.49 *(978-1-59198-301-9(0),* 6195) Creative Teaching Pr., Inc.

Willsea, Hedley. The Heath of the Graves. 2009. 371p. pap. 31.50 *(978-1-4092-2226-2(8))* Lulu Pr., Inc.

Wilson, N. D. The Chestnut King. 2011. (100 Cupboards Ser.: 3). (ENG., Illus.). 512p. (J). (gr. 3-7). 8.99 *(978-0-375-83886-6(4),* Yearling) Random Hse. Children's Bks.

Wolfe, Robert Hewitt. The Goblin Crown: Billy Smith & the Goblins, Book 1. 2016. (Billy Smith & the Goblins Ser.: 1). (ENG.). 336p. (J). 31.95 *(978-1-68162-613-0(6));* pap. 16.95 *(978-1-68162-612-3(8))* Turner Publishing Co.

Wolfe, Sean Fay. The New Order. 2015. (Elementia Chronicles Ser.: 2). (ENG.). 496p. (J). (gr. 3-7). pap. 9.99 *(978-0-06-241634-6(0))* HarperCollins Pubs.

Wood, Audrey. King Bidgood's in the Bathtub. Wood, Don, illus. 2010. (ENG.). 32p. (J). (gr. -1-3). pap. 7.99 *(978-0-15-205435-9(9))* Houghton Mifflin Harcourt Publishing Co.

Woodford, Pamela. King Giggle. 2013. (Brighter Little Minds Ser.). (ENG., Illus.). 24p. (J). pap. 10.95 *(978-1-871305-80-7(2))* Orpen Pr. IRL. Dist: Dufour Editions, Inc.

Wrede, Patricia C. Calling on Dragons. unabr. ed. 2004. (Enchanted Forest Chronicles: Bk. 3). 244p. (J). (gr. 6-18). pap. 38.00 incl. audio *(978-0-8072-0792-5(6),* LYA 347 SP, Listening Library) Random Hse. Audio Publishing Group.

J
K
L

—Talking to Dragons. unabr. ed. 2004. (Enchanted Forest Chronicles: Bk. 4). 255p. (J). (gr. 6-18). pap. 38.00 incl. audio (978-0-8072-0983-7(X), S YA 385 SP, Listening Library) Random Hse. Audio Publishing Group.
Wyss, Tyan. The Solitaire Prince. 2006. 168p. (YA). per. 12.95 (978-1-58939-906-8(4)) Virtualbookworm.com Publishing, Inc.
Yerushalmi, Miriam. Gedalia the Goldfish Who Wanted Be Just Like the King. Weinberg, Devorah, illus. 2007. 26p. (J). (gr. -1-3). 16.50 (978-0-911643-36-7(2)) Aura Printing, Inc.
Yokota, Hiromitsu, illus. The Tale of the Oki Islands: A Tale from Japan. 2013. (Tales of Honor (Red Chair Press) Ser.). (ENG.). 32p. (J). (gr. 1-4). lib. bdg. 26.60 (978-1-937529-78-9(9)) Red Chair Pr.
Yolen, Jane. Sword of the Rightful King: A Novel of King Arthur. 2004. (ENG., Illus.). 384p. (YA). (gr. 7-12). reprint ed. pap. 7.99 (978-0-15-202533-5(2)) Houghton Mifflin Harcourt Publishing Co.
Yonge, Charlotte M. The Little Duke. 2005. 26.95 (978-1-4218-0318-0(6)); 164p. pap. 11.95 (978-1-4218-0418-7(2)) 1st World Publishing, Inc. (1st World Library - Literary Society).
—The Little Duke. 2004. reprint ed. pap. 15.95 (978-1-4179-9958-3(6)); pap. 1.99 (978-1-4179-9908-8(X)) Kessinger Publishing, LLC.
—The Little Duke. 2008. 112p. pap. 9.05 (978-1-60459-557-4(4)) Wilder Pubns., Corp.

KINGS AND RULERS

see Kings, Queens, Rulers, etc.

KINGS CANYON NATIONAL PARK (CALIF.)

Nicholas, Jeff D. Sequoia & Kings Canyon. 2004. (Illus.). per. 4.95 (978-1-58071-054-1(9), Wish You Were Here) Sierra Pr.

KINKAJOU

Lynette, Rachel. Kinkajous. 2013. (Jungle Babies of the Amazon Rain Forest Ser.). 24p. (J). (gr. -1-3). lib. bdg. 21.32 (978-1-61772-752-8(0)) Bearport Publishing Co., Inc.
Petrie, Kristin. Kinkajous, 1 vol. 2010. (Nocturnal Animals Ser.). (ENG.). 24p. (J). (gr. 3-6). 25.65 (978-1-60453-737-6(X)) ABDO Publishing Co.

KINKAJOU—FICTION

Parente, Peter. Peeper the Kinkajou. l.t. ed. 2004. (Peeper & Friends Ser.). (Illus.). 28p. (J). 15.95 (978-0-9745052-0-6(X), Peeper & Friends) Tree Of Life Publishing.

KIPLING, RUDYARD, 1865-1936

Saddleback Educational Publishing Staff, ed. Captains Courageous. 2011. (Timeless Classics Ser.). (ENG.). 48p. (YA). (gr. 9-12). pupil's gde. ed. 19.95 incl. cd-rom (978-1-61651-129-6(X)) Saddleback Educational Publishing, Inc.

KIPLING, RUDYARD, 1865-1936—FICTION

Kipling, Rudyard. Just So Comics: Tales of the World's Wildest Beasts. Rodríguez, Pedro, illus. 2013. (Graphic Spin Ser.). (ENG.). 144p. (gr. 3-6). pap. 12.95 (978-1-4342-4880-0(1)) Stone Arch Bks.
Spillebeen, Geert. Kipling's Choice. Edelstein, Terese, tr. 2007. (ENG.). 160p. (YA). (gr. 7-9). pap. 12.95 (978-0-618-80035-3(2)) Houghton Mifflin Harcourt Publishing Co.
—Kipling's Choice. Edelstein, Terese, tr. 2007. 147p. (YA). (gr. 7-9). 15.65 (978-0-7569-8061-0(5)) Perfection Learning Corp.

KIPPER (FICTITIOUS CHARACTER: INKPEN)—FICTION

Inkpen, Mick. Hide Me, Kipper. 2016. (Kipper Ser.). (ENG., Illus.). 32p. (J). (gr. -1-k). 7.99 (978-1-4449-2977-5(1)) Hachette Children's Group GBR. Dist: Hachette Bk. Group.
—Kipper. (ENG & FRE., Illus.). 32p. (J). (978-1-85430-330-1(9), 93450); (978-1-85430-333-2(3), 93451) Little Tiger Pr. Group.
—Kipper: Kipper's Christmas Eve. 2016. (Kipper Ser.). (ENG., Illus.). 26p. (J). (gr. -1-k). bds. 8.99 (978-1-4449-3029-0(X)) Hachette Children's Group GBR. Dist: Hachette Bk. Group.
—Kipper's Birthday. 2014. (ENG., Illus.). 32p. (J). (gr. -1-k). pap. 10.99 **(978-1-4449-1817-5(6))** Hachette Children's Group GBR. Dist: Hachette Bk. Group.
—Kipper's Monster. 2016. (Get Well Friends Ser.). (ENG., Illus.). 32p. (J). (gr. -1-k). pap. 7.99 (978-1-4449-2383-4(8)) Hachette Children's Group GBR. Dist: Hachette Bk. Group.
—Kipper's Monster. 2008. (ENG., Illus.). 32p. (J). (gr. -1-12). pap. 10.99 (978-0-340-93208-7(2)) Hodder & Stoughton GBR. Dist: Hachette Bk. Group.
—Kipper's New Pet. 2016. (Kipper Ser.). (ENG., Illus.). 32p. (J). (gr. -1-k). pap. 7.99 (978-1-4449-3048-1(6)) Hachette Children's Group GBR. Dist: Hachette Bk. Group.
—Kipper's Snowy Day. 2015. (Kipper Ser.). (ENG., Illus.). 32p. (J). (gr. -1-k). pap. 10.99 (978-1-4449-2409-1(5)) Hodder & Stoughton GBR. Dist: Hachette Bk. Group.
—Kipper's Toybox. (Illus.). 25p. (J). (CHI, ENG, URD, VIE & FRE.). (978-1-85430-350-9(3), 93452); (ENG, FRE, URD, VIE & CHI., (978-1-85430-351-6(1), 93453) Little Tiger Pr. Group.
Inkpen, Mick & Layton, Neal. Kipper's Toybox. 2015. (Kipper Ser.). (ENG., Illus.). 32p. (J). (gr. -1-k). pap. 10.99 (978-1-4449-2377-3(3)) Hodder & Stoughton GBR. Dist: Hachette Bk. Group.

KISSINGER, HENRY, 1923-

Wagner, Heather Lehr. Henry Kissinger: Ending the Vietnam War. 2007. (Modern Peacemakers Ser.). (Illus.). 111p. (YA). (gr. 9-12). lib. bdg. 30.00 (978-0-7910-9222-4(4)) Facts On File, Inc.

KITCHEN GARDENS

see Vegetable Gardening

KITCHEN UTENSILS

see Household Equipment and Supplies

KITCHENS

Bloom, Chrissa. In the Kitchen with Solids, Liquids, & Gases. 2009. (Real Life Readers Ser.). 12p. (gr. 1-2). pap. 5.90 (978-1-4042-7897-4(4), Rosen Classroom) Rosen Publishing Group, Inc., The.
La Cocina: Individual Title Two-Packs. (Chiquilibros Ser.). (SPA.). (gr. -1-1). 12.00 (978-0-7635-8560-0(2)) Rigby Education.
In the Kitchen, 6 Packs. (Bookweb Ser.). 32p. (gr. 3-18). 34.00 (978-0-7635-3951-1(1)) Rigby Education.
In the Kitchen. 2005. (J). (978-1-59564-720-7(1)) Steps To Literacy, LLC.

KITES

Amado, Elisa. Un Barrilete: Para el Dia de los Muertos. Hairs, Joya, photos by. 2012. (SPA & ENG., Illus.). 32p. (J). (gr. k-4). pap. 9.95 (978-1-55498-112-0(3)) Groundwood Bks. CAN. Dist: Publishers Group West (PGW).
Avett, Harper. Go Fly a Kite! Reason with Shapes & Their Attributes. 2014. (Rosen Common Core Math Readers Ser.). (ENG., Illus.). 24p. (J). (gr. 3-4). pap. 8.25 (978-1-4777-4881-7(4), Rosen Classroom) Rosen Publishing Group, Inc., The.
Benchmark Education Co., LLC. Play, Play, Play All Day Big Book. 2014. (Shared Reading Foundations Ser.). (J). (gr. -1). (978-1-4509-9434-7(2)) Benchmark Education Co.
Gumede, William. A Kite's Flight. Sereda, Maja, illus. 2011. (ENG.). 32p. (J). (gr. k-2). pap. 11.00 (978-1-77009-804-6(6)) Jacana Media ZAF. Dist: Independent Pubs. Group.
Hord, Colleen. How to Make a Kite. 2015. (ENG.). 24p. (gr. k-3). 28.50 (978-1-63430-355-2(5)) Rourke Educational Media.
Hosking, Wayne. Asian Kites. 2017. (Asian Arts & Crafts for Creative Kids Ser.). (ENG., Illus.). 64p. 9.95 (978-0-8048-4869-5(6)) Tuttle Publishing.
Kites. (Early Intervention Levels Ser.). 21.30 (978-0-7362-0368-5(0)) CENGAGE Learning.
Lafette, Jordan. Kites: Shapes in the Air: Reason with Shapes & Their Attributes, 1 vol. 2015. (InfoMax Common Core Math Readers Ser.). (ENG.). 24p. (J). pap. 8.25 (978-1-4777-4582-3(3), Rosen Classroom) Rosen Publishing Group, Inc., The.
Make a Kite: Individual Title Six-Packs. (Story Steps Ser.). (gr. k-2). 29.00 (978-0-7635-9588-3(8)) Rigby Education.
Mini Kites. 2004. (Formula Fun Ser.). (Illus.). 48p. (J). (978-1-84229-580-9(2)) Top That! Publishing PLC.
Nagle, Jeanne. Kite Surfing & Kite Skiing. 2015. (Sports to the Extreme Ser.). (ENG., Illus.). 48p. (J). (gr. 5-6). 30.25 (978-1-4994-3561-0(4), Rosen Central) Rosen Publishing Group, Inc., The.
Ostrovsky, Alexsandr. Paper Kite. Ostrovsky, Alexsandr, illus. (Childrens Ser.). (Illus.). (Orig.). (J). pap. 14.95 (978-0-934393-18-8(4)) Rector Pr., Ltd.
Packard, Mary. The Kite. Huang, Benrei, illus. 2003. (My First Reader Ser.). (ENG.). 32p. (J). 18.50 (978-0-516-22930-0(3), Children's Pr.) Scholastic Library Publishing.
Torrijos, Eduardo & Garcia, Gretel. Papalotes: Tecnicas de Armado y Vuelo. Torrijos, Eduardo, illus. 2004. (SPA., Illus.). 157p. (J). pap. (978-970-643-734-1(7)) Selector, S.A. de C.V. MEX. Dist: Lectorum Pubns., Inc.
Wardle, Sue & Porter, Eleanor H. Kites Funstation. 2014. (ENG.). 251p. 17.50 (978-1-872700-40-3(3)) Award Pubns. Ltd. GBR. Dist: Parkwest Pubns., Inc.

KITES—FICTION

Ayer, Jacqueline, creator. Nu Dang & His Kite. 2017. (ENG.). 40p. (J). (gr. -1-3). 16.95 (978-1-59270-231-2(7)) Enchanted Lion Bks., LLC.
Baumgart, Klaus. Laura's Secret. Waite, Judy, tr. from GER. 2003. (Illus.). 32p. (J). (gr. -1-2). tchr. ed. 16.95 (978-1-58925-031-4(1)) Tiger Tales.
Berenstain, Stan & Berenstain, Jan. We Like Kites. 2004. (Step into Reading Ser.). (ENG., Illus.). 32p. (J). (gr. -1-1). pap. 3.99 (978-0-679-89231-1(1), Random Hse. Bks. for Young Readers) Random Hse. Children's Bks.
—We Like Kites. 2004. (Step into Reading Level 1 Ser.). (gr. -1-2). lib. bdg. 13.55 (978-0-613-87779-4(9), Turtleback) Turtleback Bks.
Berenstain, Stan, et al. The Berenstain Bears Do Their Best, 1 vol. 2010. (Berenstain Bears/Living Lights Ser.). (ENG.). 40p. (J). (gr. -1-2). 6.99 (978-0-310-71937-3(2)) Zonderkidz.
Bickel, Karla. The Kite Who Was Afraid to Fly. Bickel, Karla, illus. l.t. ed. 2004. (Illus.). 16p. (J). (gr. -1-6). pap. 5.00 (978-1-891452-08-6(8), 6) Heart Arbor Bks.
Blanco, Alberto. Angel's Kite (La estrella de Angel) Bellm, Dan, tr. Morales, Rodolfo, illus. 2014. (ENG & SPA.). 32p. (J). (gr. 1-4). pap. 9.95 (978-0-89239-156-1(1)) Lee & Low Bks., Inc.
—La Estrella de Angel. 2004.Tr. of Angel's Kite. (ENG & SPA., Illus.). (J). (gr. k-3). spiral bd. (978-0-616-14604-0(3)) Canadian National Institute for the Blind/Institut National Canadien pour les Aveugles.
Bloser, Cheryl. Little Mouse & the Muddy Feet. 2012. 28p. pap. 9.99 (978-0-9836771-1-6(5)) Mindstir Media.
Brown, Adam. The Adventures of Wormie Wormington Book Two: Wormie & the Kite. Smart, Andy, illus. 2013. 48p. pap. (978-0-9919196-2-8(9)) Beckon Creative.
Burchard, Patti. Cows Really Do Fly Kites: Patti Burchard. 2012. 24p. pap. 15.00 (978-1-4685-7627-6(5)) AuthorHouse.
Clark, Katherine. Seagull Sam. Huntington, Amy, illus. 2007. (ENG.). 32p. (J). (gr. -1-3). 15.95 (978-0-89272-715-5(2)) Down East Bks.
Compestine, Ying. The Story of Kites: Amazing Chinese Inventions. Xuan, YongSheng, illus. 2016. (ENG & CHI.). 40p. (J). (gr. -1-3). 15.95 (978-1-59702-122-7(9)) Immedium.
Deubreau, Sharon. Heather & Avery & the Magic Kite. Pileggi, Steve, illus. l.t. ed. 2006. 23p. (J). per. 11.99 (978-1-59879-143-3(5)) Lifevest Publishing, Inc.
Engelman, Beth. The Kite Race. 2007. 7p. 10.95 (978-1-58117-593-6(0), Intervisual/Piggy Toes) Bendon, Inc.
Fenske, Jonathan. Love Is in the Air. Fenske, Jonathan, illus. 2012. (Penguin Young Readers, Level 2 Ser.). (ENG., Illus.). 32p. (J). (gr. 1-2). mass mkt. 3.99 (978-0-448-49647-4(X), Penguin Young Readers) Penguin Young Readers Group.
Flor Ada, Alma. The Kite. (Stories the Year 'Round Ser.). (Illus.). 16p. (J). (gr. k-3). pap. 8.95 (978-1-58105-206-0(5)) Santillana USA Publishing Co., Inc.
Fox, Paula. La Cometa Rota.Tr. of Eagle Kite. (SPA., Illus.). 120p. (YA). (gr. 5-8). (978-84-279-3213-5(8), NG7615) Noguer y Caralt Editores, S. A. ESP. Dist: Lectorum Pubns., Inc.
Greensall, Maxine. Keith the Kite. 2009. (Illus.). 16p. pap. 8.49 (978-1-4389-5768-5(8)) AuthorHouse.
Hall, Bruce Edward & Hall, Bruce. Henry & the Kite Dragon. Low, William, tr. Low, William, illus. 2004. (ENG.). 40p. (J). (gr. 1-4). 17.99 (978-0-399-23727-0(5), Philomel Bks.) Penguin Young Readers Group.
Harvey, Alex. Olivia & the Kite Party. Spaziante, Patrick, illus. 2012. (Olivia Ready-To-Read Level 1 Ser.). lib. bdg. 13.55 (978-0-606-26360-3(8), Turtleback) Turtleback Bks.
Highway, Tomson. Dragonfly Kites: Kiweeginapiseek. 2004. (Illus.). (J). (gr. k-3). spiral bd. (978-0-616-14619-4(1)) Canadian National Institute for the Blind/Institut National Canadien pour les Aveugles.
Hillenbrand, Will. Kite Day: A Bear & Mole Story. Hillenbrand, Will, illus. (ENG., Illus.). 32p. (J). 2013. pap. 6.99 (978-0-8234-2758-1(7)) 2012. 16.95 (978-0-8234-1603-5(8)) Holiday Hse., Inc.
Hillert, Margaret. Dear Dragon Flies a Kite. Pullan, Jack, illus. 2014. (BeginningtoRead Ser.). (ENG.). 32p. (J). (gr. k-2). pap. 11.94 (978-1-60357-709-0(2)); lib. bdg. 22.60 (978-1-59953-674-3(9)) Norwood Hse. Pr.
—The Funny Ride. Selivanova, Elena, illus. 2016. (BeginningtoRead Ser.). (ENG.). 32p. (J). (gr. -1-2). pap. 11.94 (978-1-60357-978-0(8)); (gr. k-2). 22.60 (978-1-59953-816-7(4)) Norwood Hse. Pr.
Hirschmann, Kris. Triple Trouble Time. 2014. (Tickety Toc Ser.). (ENG.). 32p. (J). (gr. -1-k). pap. 3.99 (978-0-545-61473-3(2)) Scholastic, Inc.
Holub, Joan. Be Careful, Icarus! Patricelli, Leslie, illus. 2015. (Mini Myths Ser.). (ENG.). 24p. (J). (gr. -1 — 1). bds. 6.95 (978-1-4197-1677-5(8)) Abrams, Inc.
Hong, Chen Jian. La Leyenda De la Cometa. (SPA.). 32p. (978-84-95150-29-5(8)); (978-84-95150-39-4(5)) Corimbo, Editorial S.L.
Jeffers, Oliver. Stuck. Jeffers, Oliver, illus. 2011. (ENG., Illus.). 32p. (J). (gr. -1-2). 17.99 (978-0-399-25737-7(3), Philomel Bks.) Penguin Young Readers Group.
Jiang, Ji-Li. Red Kite, Blue Kite. Ruth, Greg, illus. 2013. (ENG.). 32p. (J). (gr. 1-3). 17.99 (978-1-4231-2753-6(6)) Hyperion Pr.
Kann, Victoria. Cherry Blossom. Kann, Victoria, illus. 2015. (I Can Read Level 1 Ser.). (ENG., Illus.). 32p. (J). (gr. -1-3). 16.99 (978-0-06-224593-9(7)); pap. 3.99 (978-0-06-224594-6(5)) HarperCollins Pubs.
Khan, Rukhsana. King for a Day, 1 vol. Krömer, Christiane, illus. 2014. (ENG.). 32p. (J). 17.95 (978-1-60060-659-5(8)) Lee & Low Bks., Inc.
Klepeis, Alicia & Ventura, Gabriela Baeza. Francisco's Kites. Undercuffler, Gary, illus. 2015. (SPA & ENG.). (J). 17.95 (978-1-55885-804-6(0), Piñata Books) Arte Publico Pr.
Kohake, Beverly. The Red Dragon Kite. 2008. (Illus.). 48p. pap. 9.95 (978-1-4357-1568-4(3)) Lulu Pr., Inc.
Kuhn, Douglas Wolcik. Uncle Kyle's Magic Kite. Kuhn, Douglas Wolcik, illus. 2012. (Illus.). 28p. pap. 24.95 (978-1-4626-9699-4(6)) America Star Bks.
Lebost, Diana. Mr. Kite & the Perilous Flight: Izzy & Daisy. Ersoz, Sahin, illus. 2013. 88p. pap. 18.95 (978-0-9912023-5-5(X)) Pep & Olie Publishing.
L'Heureux, Christine. Caillou, Ma Maman. braille ed. 2004. (FRE., Illus.). (J). (gr. 1). spiral bd. (978-0-616-03083-7(5)) Canadian National Institute for the Blind/Institut National Canadien pour les Aveugles.
—Caillou, Mon Papa. braille ed. 2004. (FRE., Illus.). (J). (gr. 1). bds. (978-0-616-03084-4(3)) Canadian National Institute for the Blind/Institut National Canadien pour les Aveugles.
Lin, Grace. Kite Flying. 2004. (ENG., Illus.). 32p. (J). (gr. -1-2). pap. 7.99 (978-0-553-11254-2(6), Dragonfly Bks.) Random Hse. Children's Bks.
Lindsay, Maud. Mother Stories. 2005. 25.95 (978-1-4218-1492-6(7)); 120p. pap. 10.95 (978-1-4218-1592-3(3)) 1st World Publishing, Inc. (1st World Library - Literary Society).
Little Blue Kite & Friends Activity Book. 2005. (YA). per. (978-1-59872-122-5(4)) Instant Pub.
Little Boo Kite. 2005. (J). per. 9.25 (978-1-59872-032-7(5)) Instant Pub.
Lorenzi, Natalie Dias. Flying the Dragon. (ENG.). 240p. (J). (gr. 4-7). 2014. pap. 8.95 (978-1-58089-435-7(6)) 2012. 16.95 (978-1-58089-434-0(8)) Charlesbridge Publishing, Inc.
Maunder, Brian. Polly's Little Kite. Maunder, Brian, illus. 2014. (ENG., Illus.). 44p. (J). (gr. -1-3). pap. 11.95 (978-1-56548-528-0(9)) New City Press of the Focolare.
Mayer, Mercer. Just a Kite. Mayer, Mercer, illus. 2014. (My First I Can Read Ser.). (ENG., Illus.). 32p. (J). (gr. -1-3). 16.99 (978-0-06-207197-2(1)) HarperCollins Pubs.
—Little Critter: Just a Kite. Mayer, Mercer, illus. 2014. (My First I Can Read Ser.). (ENG., Illus.). 32p. (J). (gr. -1-3). pap. 3.99 (978-0-06-147814-7(8)) HarperCollins Pubs.
—Little Critter: Just a Kite 6c Clip Strip. 2014. (ENG.). 100p. (J). 23.94 (978-0-06-230135-2(7)) HarperCollins Pubs.
—Shibumi & the Kitemaker, 1 vol. 2003. (ENG., Illus.). 32p. (J). (gr. -1-3). pap. 5.95 (978-0-7614-5145-7(5)) Marshall Cavendish Corp.
McCaughrean, Geraldine. The Kite Rider. 2003. (Illus.). 320p. (YA). (gr. 8-18). pap. 8.99 (978-0-06-441091-5(9), HarperTeen) HarperCollins Pubs.
McCune, Susan. Anisa's Kite, 01 vols., 1. 2016. (Rosen REAL Readers: STEM & STEAM Collection). (ENG.). 12p. (J). pap. 6.33 (978-1-5081-1536-6(2), Rosen Classroom) Rosen Publishing Group, Inc., The.
McLaurin, Corey F. Larry, Lisa & the Missing Kite, 1 vol. Dixon, Corey, illus. 2009. 20p. pap. 24.95 (978-1-61546-590-3(1)) America Star Bks.
Moore, Sharon. The Runaway Kite. 2006. (Neighborhood Readers Ser.). (ENG.). 8p. (gr. -1-3). pap. 5.15 (978-1-4042-6714-5(X), Rosen Classroom) Rosen Publishing Group, Inc., The.
My Kite: KinderConcepts Individual Title Six-Packs. (Kinderstarters Ser.). 8p. (gr. -1-1). 21.00 (978-0-7635-8715-4(X)) Rigby Education.
Nicholls, Maureen. Sylvester. 2008. 120p. pap. (978-1-84923-016-2(1)) YouWriteOn.
O'Keefe, Lauren. Raindrop Flies a Kite. 2012. 16p. pap. 12.68 (978-1-4669-7000-7(6)) Trafford Publishing.
Okereke, Laurence. Barry & the Gombeys. 2007. (ENG., Illus.). 20p. (J). (978-0-9795739-2-7(0)) Dion's Pubn.
Packard, Mary. The Kite. 2004. (My First Reader Ser.). (ENG., Illus.). 32p. (J). (gr. k-1). pap. 3.95 (978-0-516-24632-1(1), Children's Pr.) Scholastic Library Publishing.
Park, Linda Sue. The Kite Fighters. 2010. (ENG., Illus.). 144p. (J). (gr. 2-5). pap. 7.99 (978-0-547-32863-8(X)) Houghton Mifflin Harcourt Publishing Co.
Parker, Danny. The Silk Lakes Rescue. Shield, Guy, illus. 2017. (Lola's Toy Box Ser.: 7). (ENG.). 96p. (J). (gr. k-2). pap. 9.99 **(978-1-76012-686-5(1))** Hardie Grant Egmont Pty, Ltd. AUS. Dist: Independent Pubs. Group.
Peet, Mal & Graham, Elspeth. Night Sky Dragons. Benson, Patrick, illus. 2014. (ENG.). 64p. (J). (gr. -1-3). 15.99 (978-0-7636-6144-1(9)) Candlewick Pr.
Pilegard, Virginia Walton. The Warlord's Kites, 1 vol. Debon, Nicolas, illus. 2004. (Warlord's Ser.). (ENG.). 32p. (J). (gr. k-3). 16.99 (978-1-58980-180-6(6)) Pelican Publishing Co., Inc.
Pohl, William L. The Amazing Flight of Daisy: A Runaway Kite Circles the World on the Back of the Wind. 2006. 72p. 20.00 (978-1-4257-0666-1(5)) Xlibris Corp.
Reinheimer, Melinda T. Little Blue Kite Makes A Friend: Another Adventure of the Little Blue Kite. 2005. 24p. (J). per. 9.95 (978-1-59196-908-2(5)) Instant Pub.
Rey, H. A. Curious George Flies a Kite. 2004. (J). (gr. k-3). spiral bd. (978-0-616-01771-5(5)); spiral bd. (978-0-616-01770-8(7)) Canadian National Institute for the Blind/Institut National Canadien pour les Aveugles.
Rey, H. A. & Rey, Margret. Curious George Flies a Kite, 1 vol. 2008. (Curious George Ser.). (ENG., Illus.). 80p. (J). (gr. -1-3). audio compact disk 10.99 (978-0-618-99884-5(5)) Houghton Mifflin Harcourt Publishing Co.
—Jorge el Curioso Vuela Una Cometa. 2012. (Curious George Ser.). (ENG & SPA., Illus.). 80p. (J). (gr. -1-3). pap. 7.99 (978-0-547-69162-6(9)) Houghton Mifflin Harcourt Publishing Co.
Rey, H. A., et al. The Kite. 2007. (Curious George Ser.). (ENG., Illus.). 24p. (J). (gr. -1-3). 3.99 (978-0-618-72396-6(X)) Houghton Mifflin Harcourt Publishing Co.
Reynolds, Aaron. Tiger Moth & the Dragon Kite Contest. Lervold, Erik, illus. 2006. (Tiger Moth Ser.). (ENG.). 40p. (gr. 1-3). per. 5.95 (978-1-59889-229-1(0), Graphic Sparks) Stone Arch Bks.
Roller, Pat Kellogg. Pink Hat's Adventure with Kites. Salazar, Riana, illus. Roller, John, photos by. 2009. 36p. pap. 10.95 (978-1-59858-957-3(1)) Dog Ear Publishing, LLC.
Sheard, Jean. A Chinese Fantasy - Cave in a Casket. 2007. 128p. 34.95 (978-1-84753-349-4(3)); (Illus.). pap. 10.50 (978-1-84753-249-7(7)) Lulu Pr., Inc.
Spaziante, Patrick, illus. OLIVIA & the Kite Party. 2012. (Olivia TV Tie-In Ser.). (ENG.). 24p. (J). (gr. -1-1). 16.99 (978-1-4424-4650-2(1), Simon Spotlight) Simon Spotlight.
Spurr, Elizabeth. In the Wind, 1 vol. Oliphant, Manelle, illus. 2016. (In the Weather Ser.). (ENG.). 22p. (J). (gr. -1-k). bds. 6.95 (978-1-56145-854-7(6)) Peachtree Pubs.
Thiessen, Andrea G. Little Kite & the Big Wind. 2013. 24p. (978-1-4602-1850-1(7)); pap. (978-1-4602-0803-8(X)) FriesenPress.
Top That! Playtime Shapes (large Version) Parry, Jo, illus. 2007. 10p. (J). (gr. -1). (978-1-84666-555-4(8), Tide Mill Pr.) Top That! Publishing PLC.
Watson, Myrtle. Kite Flying in the Village: A Guyanese Girl's Story. 2011. 20p. 10.03 (978-1-4520-8632-3(X)) AuthorHouse.
Wilcox, Michael. Colors Around Us. Barber, Julia, illus. 2004. 32p. (J). per. 19.95 (978-1-931780-32-2(3)) School of Color Publishing.
Williams, Laura E. The Best Winds. Neilan, Eujin Kim, illus. 2006. (ENG.). 32p. (J). (gr. -1-2). 16.95 (978-1-59078-274-3(7)) Boyds Mills Pr.
Yolen, Jane. The Emperor & the Kite. Young, Ed, illus. 2015. 32p. pap. 7.00 (978-1-61003-535-4(6)) Center for the Collaborative Classroom.

KKK

see Ku Klux Klan (1915-)

KLEE, PAUL, 1879-1940

Vry, Silke & Klee, Paul. Paul Klee for Children. 2011. (ENG., Illus.). 96p. (J). (gr. 3-7). 14.95 (978-3-7913-7077-4(4)) Prestel Verlag GmbH & Co KG. DEU. Dist: Penguin Random Hse. LLC.

KLONDIKE GOLD FIELDS

Berton, Pierre. The Golden Trail: The Story of the Klondike Rush, 1 vol. 2005. (ENG., Illus.). 144p. pap. (978-1-894856-04-1(X)) Fitzhenry & Whiteside, Ltd.

KLONDIKE GOLD FIELDS—FICTION

Dell, Pamela. Half-Breed: A Story of Two Boys During the Klondike Gold Rush. 2003. (Scrapbooks of America Ser.). (ENG., Illus.). 48p. (J). (gr. 3-6). 32.79 (978-1-59187-044-9(5), 200809) Child's World, Inc., The.
Duncan, Sandy Frances. Gold Rush Orphan. 2005. (ENG., Illus.). 280p. (J). pap. 10.95 (978-1-55380-012-5(5)) Ronsdale Pr. CAN. Dist: Literary Pr. Group of Canada.
Piotrowski, Robert. Gold Rush. Alward, Jeff, illus. 2007. 48p. (J). lib. bdg. 23.08 (978-1-4242-1628-4(1)) Fitzgerald Bks.

KNIGHTHOOD

see Knights and Knighthood

KNIGHTS AND KNIGHTHOOD

see also Heraldry

Arlon, Penelope & Gordon-Harris, Tory. Knights & Castles: A LEGO Adventure in the Real World. 2016. (Illus.). 64p. (J). **(978-1-4844-8524-8(6))** Scholastic, Inc.
Arnold, Tedd. Castles. 2017. (Fly Guy Presents Ser.). lib. bdg. 13.55 **(978-0-606-39716-2(7))** Turtleback Bks.
Barter, James. A Medieval Knight. 2005. (Working Life Ser.). (ENG., Illus.). 112p. (YA). (gr. 7-10). lib. bdg. 29.95 (978-1-59018-580-3(3), Lucent Bks.) Cengage Gale.
Baum, Margaux & Hopkins, Andrea. Jousts, Tournaments, & War Training. 2016. (Life in the Middle Ages Ser.). 00064p. (J). (gr. 5-5). 34.45 (978-1-4994-6474-0(6)) Rosen Publishing Group, Inc., The.
Bergin, Mark. Knights & Castles. 2011. (It's Fun to Draw Ser.). (ENG., Illus.). 32p. (J). (gr. k-3). lib. bdg. 26.50 (978-1-61533-352-3(5)) Windmill Bks.
Bodden, Valerie. Gladiators. 2017. (J). **(978-1-60818-813-0(2)**, Creative Education) Creative Co., The.
Butterfield, Moira. Knight. 2009. (Medieval Lives Ser.). (J). 32.80 (978-1-59920-168-9(2)) Black Rabbit Bks.
Chambers, Catherine. Why Why Why... Did Knights Wear Heavy Armor? 2010. (Why Why Why Ser.). (Illus.). 32p. (J). (gr. 1-3). lib. bdg. 18.95 (978-1-4222-1575-3(X)) Mason Crest.

Claybourne, Anna. Knight Survival Guide. 2011. (ENG.). 24p. (J). pap. *(978-0-7787-7877-6(0))*; (gr. 3-6). *(978-0-7787-7855-4(X))* Crabtree Publishing Co.

Coggins, Jack. The Illustrated Book of Knights. 2006. (Dover Children's Classics Ser.). (ENG., Illus.). 112p. (J). (gr. 3-8). per. 14.95 *(978-0-486-45134-3(8))* Dover Pubns., Inc.

Cohn, Jessica. 10 Fascinating Facts about Knights. 2017. (Rookie Star — Fact Finder Ser.). (ENG., Illus.). 32p. (J). lib. bdg. 25.00 *(978-0-531-22261-4(6),* Children's Pr.) Scholastic Library Publishing.

Cutler, U. Waldo. Stories of King Arthur & His Knights. 2011. 160p. 24.95 *(978-1-4638-9661-4(1))* Rodgers, Alan Bks.

Dargie, Richard. Knights & Castles. 2008. (Age of Castles Ser.). (Illus.). 48p. (J). (gr. 4-8). lib. bdg. 29.25 *(978-1-4042-4295-1(3),* PowerKids Pr.) Rosen Publishing Group, Inc., The.

Dixon, Philip. Knights & Castles. 2007. (Insiders Ser.). (ENG., Illus.). 64p. (J). (gr. 3-7). 17.99 *(978-1-4169-3864-4(8),* Simon & Schuster Bks. For Young Readers) Simon & Schuster Bks. For Young Readers.

Dorling Kindersley Publishing Staff. Castles & Knights. 2014. (Eye Wonder Ser.). (ENG.). 56p. (J). (gr. k-4). 10.99 *(978-1-4654-1562-2(9),* DK Children) Dorling Kindersley Publishing, Inc.

Dorling Kindersley Publishing Staff. Lego Nexo Knights Character Encyclopedia. 2017. (ENG.). 176p. (J). (gr. 1-4). lib. bdg. 19.99 ***(978-1-4654-6554-2(5),*** DK Children) Dorling Kindersley Publishing, Inc.

Dorling Kindersley Publishing Staff & Hugo, Simon. LEGO NEXO KNIGHTS Build Your Own Adventure. 2017. (ENG.). 80p. (J). (gr. 1-4). 24.99 ***(978-1-4654-6087-5(X),*** DK Children) Dorling Kindersley Publishing, Inc.

Dorling Kindersley Publishing Staff & March, Julia. The Book of Knights. 2016. (ENG., Illus.). 80p. (J). (gr. 1-4). lib. bdg. 19.99 *(978-1-4654-5478-2(0),* DK Children) Dorling Kindersley Publishing, Inc.

Dorling Kindersley Publishing Staff & Matthews, Rupert. Knights & Castles. 2016. (DK Readers Ser.). (ENG., Illus.). 64p. (J). (gr. 2-4). pap. 3.99 *(978-1-4654-5393-8(8),* DK Children) Dorling Kindersley Publishing, Inc.

Eastwood, Kay. The Life of a Knight. 2003. (Medieval World Ser.). (ENG., Illus.). 32p. (J). (gr. 5). pap. *(978-0-7787-1374-6(1))* Crabtree Publishing Co.

Editors of Kingfisher. Awesome Knights: Come Face to Face with These Fearsome Fighters. 2016. (Fast Facts Ser.). (ENG., Illus.). 32p. (J). pap. 6.99 *(978-0-7534-7247-7(3),* 9780753472477, Kingfisher) Roaring Brook Pr.

English Heritage Staff. My Life as a Knight. 2005. (Illus.). 32p. pap. 19.95 *(978-1-85074-985-1(X))* Historic England Publishing GBR. Dist: Casemate Academic.

Firth, Rachel. Knights. (Discovering History Ser.). 48p. 2009. (YA). (gr. 3-18). 8.99 *(978-0-7945-2388-6(9),* Usborne) 2004. (SPA & ENG., Illus.). (J). pap. 8.95 *(978-0-7945-0385-7(3),* Usborne) 2004. (SPA., Illus.). (J). lib. bdg. 16.95 *(978-1-58086-509-8(7))* EDC Publishing.

—Knights & Armor. Gaudenzi, Giacinto & Montgomery, Lee, illus. 2006. 95p. (J). (gr. 4-7). 17.99 *(978-0-7945-1279-8(8),* Usborne) EDC Publishing.

Foran, Racquel. Knights, 1 vol. 2013. (Great Warriors Ser.). (ENG.). 48p. (J). (gr. 3-6). lib. bdg. 32.79 *(978-1-61783-724-1(5))*; (Illus.). pap. 15.64 *(978-1-61783-774-6(1),* Core Library) ABDO Publishing Co.

Ganeri, Anita. How to Live Like a Medieval Knight. Epelbaum, Mariano, illus. 2015. (How to Live Like... Ser.). (ENG.). 32p. (J). (gr. 3-6). lib. bdg. 26.65 *(978-1-4677-6353-0(5))* Lerner Publishing Group.

Gigliotti, Jim. Knight Life. 2008. (Reading Rocks! Ser.). (ENG., Illus.). 32p. (J). (gr. 2-5). 28.50 *(978-1-60253-100-0(5),* 200761) Child's World, Inc., The.

Gilbert, Henry. King Arthur's Knights: The Tales Retold for Boys & Girls. 2004. reprint ed. pap. 27.95 *(978-1-4191-2865-3(5))*; pap. 1.99 *(978-1-4192-2865-0(X))* Kessinger Publishing, LLC.

Gravett, Christopher. DK Eyewitness Books: Knight. Knight. 2015. (DK Eyewitness Bks.). (ENG., Illus.). 72p. (J). (gr. 3-7). pap. 9.99 *(978-1-4654-3572-9(7),* DK Children) Dorling Kindersley Publishing, Inc.

—Knight. 2015. (DK Eyewitness Bks.). (ENG., Illus.). 72p. (J). (gr. 3-7). 19.99 *(978-1-4654-3574-3(3),* DK Children) Dorling Kindersley Publishing, Inc.

—Real Knights: Over 20 True Stories of Chivalrous Deeds. James, John, illus. 2005. (ENG.). 48p. (J). (gr. 3-9). 15.95 *(978-1-59270-034-9(9))* Enchanted Lion Bks., LLC.

Hamilton, John. Knights & Heroes, 1 vol. 2006. (Fantasy & Folklore Ser.). (ENG., Illus.). 32p. (gr. 5-8). 27.07 *(978-1-59679-336-1(8),* Abdo & Daughters) ABDO Publishing Co.

Hanel, Rachael. Life as a Knight: An Interactive History Adventure. 2010. (You Choose: Warriors Ser.). (ENG.). 112p. (gr. 3-4). pap. 41.70 *(978-1-4296-5098-4(2),* You Choose Bks.) Capstone Press of Coughlan Cos.

Hanel, Rachel. Knights. 2007. (Fearsome Fighters Ser.). (Illus.). 48p. (J). (gr. 3-6). lib. bdg. 31.35 *(978-1-58341-536-8(X))* Creative Co., The.

Hare, Christopher. Bayard the Good Knight Without Fear & Without Reproach. 2004. reprint ed. pap. 1.99 *(978-1-4192-0906-2(X))* Kessinger Publishing, LLC.

Helstrom, Kraig. Knights. 2011. (History's Greatest Warriors Ser.). (ENG., Illus.). 24p. (J). (gr. 3-7). lib. bdg. 25.95 *(978-1-60014-629-9(5),* Torque Bks.) Bellwether Media.

Hindley, J. Knights & Castles. rev. ed. 2004. (Time Traveler Ser.). (Illus.). 32p. (J). pap. 6.95 *(978-0-7945-0335-2(7))* EDC Publishing.

Hindley, Judy. Knights & Castles. Wheatley, Abigail, ed. Goffe, Toni, illus. 2006. (Time Traveler Ser.). 32p. (J). (gr. 3). lib. bdg. 14.95 *(978-1-58086-554-8(2))* EDC Publishing.

Hopkins, Andrea. A Day in the Life of a Knight. 2009. (Day in the Life Ser.). 32p. (gr. 4-5). 47.90 *(978-1-61511-004-9(6),* PowerKids Pr.) Rosen Publishing Group, Inc., The.

—A Day in the Life of a Knight. Firenze, Inklink, illus. 2007. (Day in the Life Ser.: Vol. 4). 32p. (J). (gr. 4-7). lib. bdg. 25.25 *(978-1-4042-3851-0(4))* Rosen Publishing Group, Inc., The.

Hubbard, Ben. Gladiators. 2016. (Conquerors & Combatants Ser.). 224p. (YA). lib. bdg. 55.00 *(978-1-5026-2457-4(5))* Cavendish Square Publishing.

Jeffrey, Gary. Knights. 2014. (ENG., Illus.). 48p. (J). *(978-0-7787-0398-3(3))*; pap. *(978-0-7787-0404-1(1))* Crabtree Publishing Co.

Jones, Molly. Medieval Knights. 2015. (Ancient Warriors Ser.). (ENG.). 32p. (J). (gr. 2-5). 28.50 *(978-1-63143-755-7(0),* 208587) Child's World, Inc., The.

Knights & Warriors. 2009. (FACT ATLAS Ser.). 72p. (J). pap. 13.99 *(978-0-8437-0859-2(X))* Hammond World Atlas Corp.

Lacey, Minna & Davidson, Susanna. Gladiators. Cerisier, Emmanuel, illus. 2006. (Usborne Young Reading Ser.). 64p. (J). (gr. 3-7). 8.99 *(978-0-7945-1268-2(2),* Usborne) EDC Publishing.

Lassieur, Allison. Medieval Knight Science: Armor, Weapons, & Siege Warfare. 2016. (Warrior Science Ser.). (ENG., Illus.). 32p. (gr. 3-4). 27.99 *(978-1-4914-8130-1(7))* Capstone Press of Coughlan Cos.

Lee, Adrienne. Knights, 1 vol. Martin, Cynthia, illus. 2013. (Legendary Warriors Ser.). (ENG.). 32p. (gr. 1-2). 26.65 *(978-1-4765-3115-1(3),* Blazers) Capstone Press of Coughlan Cos.

Limke, Jeff. El Rey Arturo: La Espada Excalibur Desenvainada; King Arthur: Excalibur Unsheathed. 2008. pap. 52.95 *(978-0-8225-9636-3(9))* Lerner Publishing Group.

Macdonald, Fiona. Do You Want to Be a Medieval Knight? 2015. (Do You Want to Be... Ser.). (Illus.). 32p. (gr. 3-6). 28.50 *(978-1-909645-35-6(4))* Book Hse. GBR. Dist: Black Rabbit Bks.

MacDonald, Fiona. Knights & Castles. 2009. (History Explorers Ser.). (ENG.). 24p. (J). (gr. k-2). pap. 5.95 *(978-1-84696-215-8(3),* TickTock Books) Octopus Publishing Group GBR. Dist: Independent Pubs. Group.

—Knights, Castles, & Warfare in the Middle Ages. 2005. (World Almanac Library of the Middle Ages). (Illus.). 48p. (gr. 5-12). lib. bdg. 31.00 *(978-0-8368-5895-2(6),* Gareth Stevens Secondary Library) Stevens, Gareth Publishing LLLP.

Macdonald, Fiona. The Medieval Chronicles: Vikings, Knights, & Castles. Antram, David, illus. 2013. 92p. (J). *(978-1-4351-5067-6(8))* Barnes & Noble, Inc.

—You Wouldn't Want to Be a Medieval Knight! Armor You'd Rather Not Wear. Antram, David, illus. 2013. (ENG.). (J). 40p. pap. 9.95 *(978-0-531-23851-6(2))*; 32p. 29.00 *(978-0-531-27100-1(5))* Scholastic Library Publishing. (Watts, Franklin).

MacDonald, Fiona & Bergin, Mark. How to Be a Medieval Knight. 2005. (How to Be Ser.). (ENG., Illus.). 32p. (J). (gr. 3-7). 14.95 *(978-0-7922-3619-1(X),* National Geographic Children's Bks.) National Geographic Society.

Mason, Paul. Want to Be a Knight? 2011. (ENG.). 24p. (J). pap. *(978-0-7787-7867-7(3))*; (gr. 3-6). *(978-0-7787-7845-5(2))* Crabtree Publishing Co.

Mayer, Cassie. Knights & Castles. 2012. (Illus.). 64p. (J). pap. 12.99 *(978-1-62267-007-9(8))* Bright Connections Media.

McLeese, Don. Knights. 2009. 32p. pap. 7.99 *(978-0-8249-1447-9(3),* Ideal Pubns.) Worthy Publishing.

Media, Cont. Knights & Castles. 2008. (ENG., Illus.). 48p. (YA). 12.99 *(978-1-931703-24-6(8))* Crosby Advanced Medical Systems Inc.

Murrell, Deborah Jane. Knights & Armor. 2008. (Medieval Warfare Ser.). 32p. (gr. 5-8). (J). lib. bdg. 26.00 *(978-0-8368-9210-9(0),* Gareth Stevens Secondary Library); pap. 10.50 *(978-0-8368-9337-3(9))* Stevens, Gareth Publishing LLLP.

Murrell, Deborah Jane & Dennis, Peter. Knight. 2012. (Illus.). 32p. (gr. 3-5). pap. 8.95 *(978-1-926853-54-3(7))* Saunders Bk. Co. CAN. Dist: RiverStream Publishing.

Nishida, Masaki. Drawing Manga Medieval Castles & Knights. 2007. (How to Draw Manga Ser.: Vol. 4). (Illus.). 24p. (J). (gr. 4-7). lib. bdg. 25.25 *(978-1-4042-3849-7(2))* Rosen Publishing Group, Inc., The.

O'Brian, Pliny. Knights: Warriors of the Middle Ages. 2015. (J). lib. bdg. *(978-1-62713-407-1(7))*; (ENG., Illus.). 48p. (gr. 4-4). 31.36 *(978-1-5026-0120-9(6))* Cavendish Square Publishing.

O'Brien, Cynthia. Your Guide to Knights & the Age of Chivalry. 2017. (Destination: Middle Ages Ser.). (ENG., Illus.). 32p. (J). ***(978-0-7787-2992-1(3))***; pap. ***(978-0-7787-2998-3(2))*** Crabtree Publishing Co.

Park, Louise & Love, Timothy. The Medieval Knights. 2009. (Ancient & Medieval People Ser.). 32p. (gr. 5). 28.50 *(978-0-7614-4444-2(0))* Marshall Cavendish GBR. Dist: Marshall Cavendish Corp.

Pratt, Leonie. Knights & Castles Things to Make & Do. Thompson, Josephine Et Al, illus. 2006. 32p. (J). pap. 6.99 *(978-0-7945-1355-9(7),* Usborne) EDC Publishing.

Pyle, Howard. The Story of the Champions of the Round Table. 2004. reprint ed. pap. 28.95 *(978-1-4191-8405-5(9))*; pap. 1.99 *(978-1-4192-8405-2(3))* Kessinger Publishing, LLC.

Riggs, Kate. Knights. 2011. (Great Warriors Ser.). 24p. (J). (ENG.). (gr. 1-3). pap. 9.99 *(978-0-89812-572-6(3),* Creative Paperbacks); (Illus.). (gr. k-2). 16.95 *(978-1-60818-001-1(8),* Creative Education) Creative Co., The.

Scholastic, Inc. Staff. Knights & Castles: A LEGO(r) Adventure in the Real World. 2016. (LEGO Nonfiction Ser.). (ENG., Illus.). 64p. (J). (gr. 1-3). pap. 8.99 *(978-0-545-94767-1(7))* Scholastic, Inc.

Shirley, Rebekah Joy. I Want to Be a Knight. 2011. (Let's Play Dress up Ser.). (ENG., Illus.). 24p. (J). (gr. k-3). pap. 10.60 *(978-1-61533-392-9(4))*; lib. bdg. 25.25 *(978-1-61533-354-7(1))* Windmill Bks.

Simon, Seymour. Knights & Castles. 2006. (SeeMore Readers Ser.: SEMR). (ENG., Illus.). 40p. (J). (gr. 3-5). pap. 3.95 *(978-0-8118-5409-2(4))* Chronicle Bks. LLC.

Stiefel, Chana. Sweaty Suits of Armor: Could You Survive Being a Knight? Kelley, Gerald, illus. 2011. (Ye Yucky Middle Ages Ser.). 48p. (J). (gr. 5-18). pap. 8.95 *(978-1-59845-376-8(9))*; (gr. 7-12). lib. bdg. 25.27 *(978-0-7660-3784-7(3))* Enslow Pubs., Inc.

Storey, Rita. Knights & Castles. 2013. (Have Fun with Arts & Crafts Ser.). 32p. (gr. 4-7). 31.35 *(978-1-59920-899-2(7))* Black Rabbit Bks.

Taylor, Barbara. The Amazing History of Castles & Knights. 2016. (ENG., Illus.). 64p. (J). (gr. -1-12). 12.99 *(978-1-86147-717-0(1),* Armadillo) Anness Publishing GBR. Dist: National Bk. Network.

Templeman, Henry. Knights: The Secrets of Medieval Warriors. 2015. (ENG., Illus.). 80p. (J). (gr. 3). pap. 16.95 *(978-1-78312-146-5(7))* Carlton Kids GBR. Dist: Sterling Publishing Co., Inc.

Walker, Jane. Knights & Castles. 2013. (Illus.). 48p. (J). *(978-1-4351-5093-5(7))* Barnes & Noble, Inc.

—100 Things You Should Know about Knights & Castles. 2008. (Illus.). 64p. *(978-1-84236-002-6(7))* Miles Kelly Publishing, Ltd.

Watson, Danielle. The Castle in Medieval Europe. 2016. (Life in Medieval Europe Ser.). (Illus.). 80p. (J). (gr. 6-6). 35.64 *(978-1-5026-1878-8(8))* Cavendish Square Publishing.

Weatherly, Myra. William Marshal: Medieval England's Greatest Knight. 2004. (British Heroes Ser.). (Illus.). 112p. (YA). (gr. 6-12). 23.95 *(978-1-883846-48-0(X),* First Biographies) Reynolds, Morgan Inc.

West, David. Lots of Things You Want to Know about Knights: ... & Some You Don't! 2015. (Lots of Things You Want to Know About Ser.). (Illus.). 24p. (J). 28.50 *(978-1-62588-091-8(X))* Black Rabbit Bks.

Williams, Colleen Madonna Flood. My Adventure with Knights. 2009. (ENG.). 44p. (J). 8.99 *(978-1-59092-456-3(8))* Blue Forge Pr.

Woog, Adam. A Medieval Knight. 2003. (Daily Life Ser.). (ENG., Illus.). 48p. (J). (gr. 4-6). pap. 27.00 *(978-0-7377-0992-6(8),* Kidhaven) Cengage Gale.

World Book, Inc Staff, contrib. by. The Age of Knights & Castles. 2011. (J). *(978-0-7166-1787-7(0))* World Bk., Inc.

KNIGHTS AND KNIGHTHOOD—FICTION

Amery, H. & Cartwright, S. The Tournament. 2004. (First Stories Ser.). 16p. (J). pap. 4.95 *(978-0-7945-0520-2(1))*; lib. bdg. 12.95 *(978-1-58086-571-5(2))* EDC Publishing.

Andrews, Julie & Hamilton, Emma Walton. Dragon. 2004. (Julie Andrews Collection). 192p. (J). (gr. 4-18). 16.99 *(978-0-06-057119-1(5),* Julie Andrews Collection) HarperCollins Pubs.

Anthony, David & David, Charles. Knightscares #4: (Knightscares) 2004. (Illus.). 208p. (J). per. 5.99 *(978-0-9728461-3-4(1))* Sigil Publishing.

Banerjee, Anjali. The Silver Spell. Fiegenshuh, Emily, illus. 2005. (Knights of the Silver Dragon Ser.: Bk. 8). 174p. (J). *(978-1-4156-1645-1(0),* Mirrorstone) Wizards of the Coast.

Banks, Kate. Max's Castle. Kulikov, Boris, illus. 2011. (Max's Words Ser.: 3). (ENG.). 40p. (J). (gr. -1-3). 18.99 *(978-0-374-39919-1(0),* 9780374399191, Farrar, Straus & Giroux (BYR)) Farrar, Straus & Giroux.

Banks, Steven. Lost in Time. The Artifact Group, illus. 2006. 22p. (J). lib. bdg. 15.00 *(978-1-4242-0977-4(3))* Fitzgerald Bks.

Barandela, Jeremy. United We Stand. 2007. 376p. per. 20.95 *(978-1-4327-1495-6(3))* Outskirts Pr., Inc.

Barnes, Charles. Knight Light. 2006. 48p. pap. 16.95 *(978-1-4241-3831-9(0))* PublishAmerica, Inc.

Beekman, Kelley Lee. Sir Eli & the Halloween Dragon: The Legend of the Toasted Marshmallow. 2006. 55p. pap. 16.95 *(978-1-4241-4047-3(1))* PublishAmerica, Inc.

Bell, Hilari. The Goblin Gate. (ENG.). (YA). (gr. 8). 2011. 400p. pap. 8.99 *(978-0-06-165104-5(4))* 2010. 384p. 16.99 *(978-0-06-165102-1(8))* HarperCollins Pubs. (HarperTeen).

—The Goblin Wood. 2004. (Illus.). 371p. (J). (gr. 5-9). 14.65 *(978-0-7569-3253-4(X))* Perfection Learning Corp.

—The Last Knight. 2007. (Knight & Rogue Ser.: 1). (ENG.). 368p. (YA). (gr. 8-12). 16.99 *(978-0-06-082503-4(0),* HarperTeen) HarperCollins Pubs.

—Player's Ruse. 2010. (Knight & Rogue Ser.: 3). (ENG.). 384p. (YA). (gr. 8-10). 17.99 *(978-0-06-082509-6(X),* HarperTeen) HarperCollins Pubs.

—Rogue's Home. 2008. (Knight & Rogue Ser.: 2). (ENG.). 432p. (YA). (gr. 8-18). 17.99 *(978-0-06-082506-5(5),* HarperTeen) HarperCollins Pubs.

Bellairs, John. The Secret of the Underground Room (A Johnny Dixon Mystery: Book Eight) 2011. 96p. pap. 14.95 *(978-1-61756-352-2(8))* Open Road Integrated Media, Inc.

Bess, Alex Marie. The Scrapper. 2011. 188p. (J). pap. 13.95 *(978-1-936184-85-9(0))* Kidpub Pr.

Bishop, Jennie. The Squire & the Scroll: A Tale of the Rewards of a Pure Heart. McDaniels, Preston, illus. 2009. (ENG.). 32p. (J). 15.99 *(978-1-59317-382-1(2))* Warner Pr., Inc.

Black, Chuck. Lady Carliss & the Waters of Moorue. 2010. (Knights of Arrethtrae Ser.). (ENG.). 208p. (YA). (gr. 5-7). pap. 9.99 *(978-1-60142-127-2(3),* Multnomah Bks.) Crown Publishing Group.

—Sir Bentley & Holbrook Court. 2009. (Knights of Arrethtrae Ser.). (ENG., Illus.). 208p. (YA). (gr. 5-7). pap. 9.99 *(978-1-60142-125-8(7),* Multnomah Bks.) Crown Publishing Group.

—Sir Dalton & the Shadow Heart. 2009. (Knights of Arrethtrae Ser.). (ENG., Illus.). 176p. (YA). (gr. 7-9). pap. 9.99 *(978-1-60142-126-5(5),* Multnomah Bks.) Crown Publishing Group.

—Sir Quinlan & the Swords of Valor. 2010. (Knights of Arrethtrae Ser.). (ENG., Illus.). 208p. (YA). (gr. 4-7). pap. 9.99 *(978-1-60142-128-9(1),* Multnomah) Doubleday Religious Publishing Group, The.

—Sir Rowan & the Camerian Conquest. 2010. (Knights of Arrethtrae Ser.). (ENG., Illus.). 192p. (J). (gr. 4-7). pap. 9.99 *(978-1-60142-129-6(X),* Multnomah Bks.) Crown Publishing Group.

Black, Kat. A Templar's Apprentice. 2009. (Book of Tormod Ser.: 1). (ENG.). 288p. (J). (gr. 7-18). 17.99 *(978-0-545-05654-0(3))* Scholastic, Inc.

—A Templar's Destiny. 2012. (Book of Tormod Ser.). (ENG.). 256p. (J). (gr. 7-7). 17.99 *(978-0-545-05677-9(2),* Scholastic Pr.) Scholastic, Inc.

—A Templar's Gifts. 2011. (Book of Tormod Ser.: 2). (ENG.). 272p. (J). (gr. 7-7). 17.99 *(978-0-545-05675-5(6),* Scholastic Pr.) Scholastic, Inc.

Blackburne, Livia. Midnight Thief. (Midnight Thief Ser.). (ENG., Illus.). (YA). (gr. 7-12). 2014. 380p. 16.99 *(978-1-4231-7638-1(3))*Bk. 1. 2015. 394p. pap. 9.99 *(978-1-4231-9461-3(6))* Hyperion Bks. for Children.

Bolger, Kevin. Sir Fartsalot Hunts the Booger. Gilpin, Stephen, illus. 2009. (ENG.). 224p. (J). (gr. 3-7). 7.99 *(978-1-59514-284-9(3),* Razorbill) Penguin Young Readers Group.

Bonneval, Gwen de & Smith, Owen. William & the Lost Spirit. Smith, Anne Collins, tr. from FRE. Bonhomme, Matthieu, illus. 2013. (ENG.). 160p. (J). (gr. 8-12). lib. bdg. 30.60 *(978-0-7613-8567-7(3),* Graphic Universe™) Lerner Publishing Group.

Bowler, Michael J. Children of the Knight [Library Edition]. 2013. 344p. pap. 17.99 *(978-1-62380-925-6(8),* Harmony Ink Pr.) Dreamspinner Pr.

Los Caballeros del Rey Arturo. (SPA., Illus.). (YA). 14.95 *(978-84-7281-107-2(7),* AF1107) Auriga, Ediciones S.A. ESP. Dist: Continental Bk. Co., Inc.

Callahan, Lauren & Callahan, Michael T. Hello, Knightro! Williams, Tim, illus. 2013. (ENG.). (J). (gr. 4-7). 14.95 *(978-1-62086-169-1(0))* Mascot Bks., Inc.

Cervantes, Miguel de & Brook, Henry. Don Quixote: From the Story by Miguel de Cervantes Saavedra. 2005. (Illus.). 144p. (J). pap. 4.95 *(978-0-7945-0955-2(X),* Usborne) EDC Publishing.

Comrie, Margaret S. The Heroes of Castle Bretten. 2003. (Illus.). 229p. (J). *(978-1-894666-65-7(8))* Inheritance Pubns.

Connolly, Kara. No Good Deed. 2017. (ENG.). 352p. (YA). (gr. 9). 17.99 ***(978-0-385-74393-8(9))***; lib. bdg. 20.99 ***(978-0-375-99140-0(9))*** Random Hse. Children's Bks. (Delacorte Pr.).

Coutinho, Lucy M. The Rangers of Andor: The Beginning. 2011. 278p. pap. 27.95 *(978-1-4626-1014-3(5))* America Star Bks.

Cremer, Andrea. Rift. 2013. (Nightshade Ser.). (ENG.). 480p. (YA). (gr. 9). pap. 9.99 *(978-0-14-242493-3(5),* Speak) Penguin Young Readers Group.

Davey, Owen. Night Knight. Davey, Owen, illus. 2012. (ENG., Illus.). 32p. (J). (gr. k-k). 15.99 *(978-0-7636-5838-0(3),* Templar) Candlewick Pr.

Davies, Katie. Knights Sticker Dressing. 2010. 24p. (J). 8.99 *(978-0-7945-2891-1(0))* EDC Publishing.

Davis, Toby K. The Ever Part of Always: Keely Tucker's First Adventure. 2012. 208p. (gr. 4-6). 24.95 *(978-1-4697-4592-3(5))*; pap. 14.95 *(978-1-4697-4591-6(7))* iUniverse, Inc.

Davis, Tony. Roland Wright: at the Joust. Rogers, Gregory, illus. 2011. (ENG.). 144p. (J). (gr. 1-4). 6.99 *(978-0-375-87328-7(7),* Yearling) Random Hse. Children's Bks.

—Roland Wright: Brand-New Page. Rogers, Gregory, illus. 2011. (Roland Wright Ser.). (ENG.). 144p. (J). (gr. 1-4). 6.99 *(978-0-385-73803-3(X),* Yearling) Random Hse. Children's Bks.

—Roland Wright: Future Knight. Rogers, Gregory, illus. 2010. (Roland Wright Ser.). (ENG.). 160p. (J). (gr. 1-4). 6.99 *(978-0-385-73801-9(3),* Yearling) Random Hse. Children's Bks.

De Bonneval, Gwen. William & the Lost Spirit. Smith, Anne, tr. Bonhomme, Matthieu, illus. 2013. (ENG.). 160p. (YA). (gr. 8-12). pap. 9.95 *(978-1-4677-0807-4(0),* Graphic Universe™) Lerner Publishing Group.

Dean, James, illus. Sir Pete the Brave. 2016. 32p. (J). ***(978-1-5182-0881-2(9))*** Harper & Row Ltd.

DiTerlizzi, Tony. Kenny & the Dragon. 2008. (Playaway Children Ser.). (J). (gr. 3-7). 39.99 *(978-1-60640-958-9(1))* Findaway World, LLC.

—Kenny & the Dragon. DiTerlizzi, Tony, illus. (ENG., Illus.). (J). (gr. 3-7). 2012. 176p. pap. 8.99 *(978-1-4424-3651-0(4))* 2008. 160p. 17.99 *(978-1-4169-3977-1(6))* Simon & Schuster Bks. For Young Readers. (Simon & Schuster Bks. For Young Readers).

—Kenny & the Dragon. DiTerlizzi, Tony, illus. 2008. (Illus.). 160p. (J). (gr. 3-7). 15.99 Simon & Schuster Children's Publishing.

Docherty, Helen. The Storybook Knight. Docherty, Thomas, illus. 2016. (ENG.). 32p. (J). (-4). 16.99 *(978-1-4926-3814-8(5),* 9781492638148, Sourcebooks Jabberwocky) Sourcebooks, Inc.

Donaldson, Julia. A Gold Star for Zog. Scheffler, Axel, illus. 2012. (ENG.). 32p. (J). (gr. -1-3). 17.99 *(978-0-545-41724-2(4),* Levine, Arthur A. Bks.) Scholastic, Inc.

Donnell, Annie Hamil. Three Young Knights. 2004. reprint ed. pap. 15.95 *(978-1-4191-8994-4(8))* Kessinger Publishing, LLC.

Donnell, Annie Hamilton. Three Young Knights. 2004. reprint ed. pap. 1.99 *(978-1-4192-8994-1(2))* Kessinger Publishing, LLC.

Dorling Kindersley Publishing Staff. LEGO Nexo Knights: Stop the Monsters! 2017. (DK Reader Level 1 Ser.). lib. bdg. 13.55 ***(978-0-606-39896-1(1))*** Turtleback Bks.

Dormer, Frank W. The Sword in the Stove. Dormer, Frank W., illus. 2016. (ENG., Illus.). 40p. (J). (gr. -1-3). 17.99 *(978-1-4814-3167-5(6))* Simon & Schuster, Inc.

Downey, Glen. Gladiators. 2007. (Illus.). 48p. (J). lib. bdg. 23.08 *(978-1-4242-1627-7(3))* Fitzgerald Bks.

Dragt, Tonke. The Letter for the King. 2015. (ENG., Illus.). 528p. (J). (gr. 7). 18.99 *(978-0-545-81978-7(4))* Scholastic, Inc.

Driscoll, Laura. My Brother, the Knight. Smath, Jerry, illus. 2004. (Social Studies Connects). 32p. (J). (gr. 1-3). pap. 5.95 *(978-1-57565-140-8(8))* Kane Press, Inc.

Dube, Pierrette. How to Become a Perfect Knight in Five Days. Hamel, Caroline, illus. 2009. (Rainy Day Readers Ser.). 32p. (J). (gr. -1-3). 22.60 *(978-1-60754-373-2(7))*; pap. 10.55 *(978-1-60754-374-9(5))* Windmill Bks.

Ebers, Georg. The Greylock. 2004. reprint ed. pap. 15.95 *(978-1-4191-6506-1(2))*; pap. 1.99 *(978-1-4192-6506-8(7))* Kessinger Publishing, LLC.

Ezirim, E. C. Jet Black & the Ebony Knights. 2010. 40p. 16.99 *(978-1-4520-7567-9(0))* AuthorHouse.

Fafoutakis, Anne. Enchanted Talisman & Other Stories for Children of All Ages. 2004. 132p. pap. 13.50 *(978-1-84426-296-0(0))* Upfront Publishing Ltd. GBR. Dist: Printondemand-worldwide.com.

Flanagan, John. The Icebound Land. 2007. (Ranger's Apprentice Ser.: Bk. 3). 260p. (J). 25.66 *(978-1-4287-4632-9(3),* Follettbound) Follett School Solutions.

—The Icebound Land, Bk. 3. 2008. (Ranger's Apprentice Ser.: 3). (ENG.). 304p. (J). (gr. 5-18). 8.99 *(978-0-14-241075-2(6),* Puffin Books) Penguin Young Readers Group.

Flinders, Benjamin. Excalibur: Traveling Trunk Adventure 3. 2011. (Traveling Trunk Adventure Ser.). (ENG.). 162p. (J). (gr. 2-4). 9.95 *(978-0-9843955-6-9(3))* Flinders Pr.

J
K
L

French, Jackie. My Dad the Dragon. King, Stephen Michael, illus. 2004. 128p. *(978-0-207-19950-9(7))* HarperCollins Pubs. Australia.

Funke, Cornelia. Ghost Knight. 2013.Tr. of Geisterritter. (ENG., Illus.). 352p. (J). (gr. 3-7). pap. 7.99 *(978-0-316-05616-8(2))* Little, Brown Bks. for Young Readers.

Gashler, Stephen. The Bent Sword. 2010. (YA). pap. 15.99 *(978-1-59955-401-3(1))* Cedar Fort, Inc./CFI Distribution.

Gilman, Laura Anne. The Camelot Spell. 2006. (Grail Quest Ser.: No. 1). 291p. (J). (gr. 5-9). 10.99 *(978-0-06-077279-6(4))* HarperCollins Pubs.

Graham, Denise R. Curse of the Lost Grove. 2005. (Knights of the Silver Dragon Ser.: Bk. 10). (Illus.). 177p. (J). *(978-1-4156-3841-5(1)*, Mirrorstone) Wizards of the Coast.

Grahame, Kenneth. The Reluctant Dragon (Illustrated Edition) 2015. (ENG., Illus.). 42p. pap. *(978-1-5154-0330-2(0)*, Illustrated Bks.) Jorge Pinto Bks.

Grant, K. M. Blood Red Horse. 2006. (DeGranville Trilogy Ser.). (ENG.). 320p. (YA). (gr. 5-9). per. 10.99 *(978-0-8027-7734-8(1)*, 9780802777348, Bloomsbury USA Childrens) Bloomsbury Publishing USA.

Green, Norman, illus. Knights of the Round Table. 2005. (Reader's Workshop Ser.). (ENG.). 112p. (C). pap. 19.95 *(978-0-7362-2786-5(5))* CENGAGE Learning.

Haberdasher, Violet. Knightley Academy. 2011. (ENG.). 512p. (J). (gr. 3-7). pap. 5.99 *(978-1-4169-9144-1(1)*, Aladdin) Simon & Schuster Children's Publishing.

—Knightley Academy. 2010. (ENG.). 480p. (J). (gr. 3-7). 16.99 *(978-1-4169-9143-4(3)*, Simon & Schuster/Paula Wiseman Bks.) Simon & Schuster/Paula Wiseman Bks.

—The Secret Prince. 2011. (ENG.). 512p. (J). (gr. 3-7). 16.99 *(978-1-4169-9145-8(X)*, Simon & Schuster/Paula Wiseman Bks.) Simon & Schuster/Paula Wiseman Bks.

—The Secret Prince: A Knightley Academy Book. 2012. (ENG.). 512p. (J). (gr. 3-7). pap. 7.99 *(978-1-4169-9146-5(8)*, Simon & Schuster/Paula Wiseman Bks.) Simon & Schuster/Paula Wiseman Bks.

Hall, Frank. The Prince Who Did Not Want to be King. 2011. 132p. 28.95 *(978-1-4497-1440-6(4))*; (J). pap. 11.95 *(978-1-4497-1438-3(2))* Author Solutions, Inc. (WestBow Pr.).

Harvey, Damian & Remphry, Martin. Robin & the Friar. 2009. (Hopscotch Adventures Ser.). (Illus.). 31p. (J). (gr. 1). lib. bdg. 25.65 *(978-1-59771-177-7(2))* Sea-To-Sea Pubns.

Hedlund, Jody. A Daring Sacrifice, 1 vol. 2016. (ENG.). 224p. (YA). pap. 12.99 *(978-0-310-74937-0(9))* Zondervan.

—An Uncertain Choice, 1 vol. 2015. (ENG.). 256p. (YA). pap. 12.99 *(978-0-310-74919-6(0))* Zondervan.

Hemingway, Mike. The Legend of Vysallimore. 2010. 72p. pap. 28.00 *(978-1-4520-5648-7(X))* AuthorHouse.

Hensley, Judith Victoria. Sir Thomas the Eggslayer. 2008. 156p. pap. 14.95 *(978-0-9795103-8-0(4))* Ascended Ideas.

Henty, George Alfred. At Agincourt: A Tale of the White Hoods of Paris. 2011. 332p. pap. 19.95 *(978-1-61179-111-2(1))* Fireship Pr.

Hightman, Jason. The Saint of Dragons. 2004. 304p. (J). (gr. 7-18). (ENG.). 16.99 *(978-0-06-054011-1(7))*; lib. bdg. 17.89 *(978-0-06-054012-8(5))* HarperCollins Pubs.

Hill, Kevin Kelvin. The Red Baron, the Knight of Many Talents. 2009. 40p. pap. 20.99 *(978-1-4490-0642-6(6))* AuthorHouse.

Hoffman, Mary. Women of Camelot: Queens & Enchantresses at the Court of King Arthur. Balit, Christina, illus. 2006. 69p. (YA). (gr. 5-9). 20.00 *(978-1-4223-5260-1(9))* DIANE Publishing Co.

Holub, Joan. The Knights Before Christmas. Magoon, Scott, illus. 2015. (ENG.). 32p. (J). (gr. k-3). 16.99 *(978-0-8050-9932-4(8)*, 9780805099324, Holt, Henry & Co. Bks. For Young Readers) Holt, Henry & Co.

Howard, Cheryl L. Mikhael the Mighty: Be True to Who You Are & You Can Never Go Wrong. 2009. 52p. pap. 18.50 *(978-1-60860-760-0(7)*, Strategic Bk. Publishing) Strategic Book Publishing & Rights Agency (SBPRA).

Howard, Kate, adapted by. Fright Knight! 2016. 71p. (J). ***(978-1-4844-8023-6(6))*** Scholastic, Inc.

Hulme-Cross, Benjamin. The Knight's Enemies. Rinaldi, Angelo, illus. 2015. (ENG.). 160p. (J). *(978-0-7787-1765-2(8))* Crabtree Publishing Co.

Impey, Rose. The Terribly Ugly Troll. McEwen, Katharine, illus. 2017. (Sir Lance-A-Little Ser.). (ENG.). 32p. (J). (gr. k-2). pap. 9.99 ***(978-1-4083-2529-2(2)***, Orchard Bks.) Hachette Children's Group GBR. Dist: Hachette Bk. Group.

Jenkins, Amanda & Reeves, Tara McClary. The Knight & the Firefly: A Boy, a Bug, & a Lesson in Bravery. Fernandez, Daniel, illus. 2017. (Firefly Chronicles Ser.). (ENG.). 32p. (J). (gr. -1-3). pap. 3.99 ***(978-1-4627-4519-7(9)***, B&H Kids) B&H Publishing Group.

Kander, Beth & Kenyon, Bret. Glubbery Gray, the Knight-Eating Beast, 1 vol. Labbé, Jesse, illus. 2010. (ENG.). 40p. (J). (gr. k-3). 17.99 *(978-1-58980-867-6(3))* Pelican Publishing Co., Inc.

Kingsbury, Karen. The Brave Young Knight, 1 vol. Grimard, Gabrielle, illus. 2011. (ENG.). 40p. (J). (gr. -1-2). 15.99 *(978-0-310-71645-7(4))* Zonderkidz.

—The Princess & the Three Knights, 1 vol. Grimard, Gabrielle, illus. 2009. (ENG.). 40p. (J). (gr. -1-2). 15.99 *(978-0-310-71641-9(1))* Zonderkidz.

Kirkman, Robert. Marvel Knights 2099. 2005. (Marvel Heroes Ser.). (Illus.). 120p. (YA). pap. 13.99 *(978-0-7851-1613-4(3))* Marvel Worldwide, Inc.

Knights. (Awesome Adventures Ser.). 16p. (J). *(978-2-7643-0120-3(0))* Phidal Publishing, Inc./Editions Phidal, Inc.

Koller, Jackie French & Koller. Horace the Horrible: A Knight Meets His Match, 1 vol. Urbanovic, Jackie, illus. 2003. (ENG.). 32p. (J). 16.95 *(978-0-7614-5150-1(1))* Marshall Cavendish Corp.

Kraegel, Kenneth. King Arthur's Very Great Grandson. Kraegel, Kenneth, illus. 2012. (ENG., Illus.). 40p. (J). (gr. k-3). 16.99 *(978-0-7636-5311-8(X))* Candlewick Pr.

Krause, Ute. Nick & the Nasty Knight. 2012. (ENG., Illus.). 32p. (J). (gr. -1-3). 17.95 *(978-0-7358-4091-1(1))* North-South Bks., Inc.

Lampard, Frank. Frankie vs. the Knight's Nasties. 2016. (Frankie's Magic Soccer Ball Ser.: 5). (ENG., Illus.). 112p. (J). (gr. 2-5). pap. 4.99 *(978-1-338-08907-3(2))* Scholastic, Inc.

Lang, Andrew. The Red Romance Book; Tales of Knights. 2006. 396p. per. *(978-1-84664-477-1(1)*, Obscure Pr.) Read Bks.

Lang, Andrew & Ford, H. J. The Tale of the Cid: And Other Stories of Knights & Chivalry. Ford, H. J., illus. 2007. (Dover Children's Classics Ser.). (ENG., Illus.). 208p. (J). (gr. 4-7). per. 9.95 *(978-0-486-45470-2(3))* Dover Pubns., Inc.

Larson, M. A. Pennyroyal Academy. 2014. (Pennyroyal Academy Ser.: 1). (ENG.). 320p. (J). (gr. 5). 16.99 *(978-0-399-16324-1(7)*, G.P. Putnam's Sons Books for Young Readers) Penguin Young Readers Group.

Lemke, Donald. Rat Trap. 2016. (Batman 8X8 Storybooks Ser.). (J). lib. bdg. 13.55 *(978-0-606-38768-2(4))* Turtleback Bks.

Leung, Julie. Mice of the Round Table #1: a Tail of Camelot. Carr, Lindsey, illus. 2017. (Mice of the Round Table Ser.: 1). 320p. (J). (gr. 3-7). pap. 6.99 ***(978-0-06-240400-8(8))*** HarperCollins Pubs.

Leung, Julie. A Tail of Camelot. Carr, Lindsey, illus. 2016. (Mice of the Round Table Ser.: 1). 304p. (J). (gr. 3-7). 16.99 *(978-0-06-240399-5(0))* HarperCollins Pubs.

Lewin, Betsy. Good Night, Knight. Lewin, Betsy, illus. 2015. (I Like to Read(r) Ser.). (ENG., Illus.). 24p. (J). (gr. -1-3). 14.95 *(978-0-8234-3206-6(8))*; 6.99 *(978-0-8234-3315-5(3))* Holiday Hse., Inc.

Limke, Jeff. King Arthur: Excalibur Unsheathed. Yeates, Thomas, illus. 2007. (Graphic Myths & Legends Ser.). (ENG.). 48p. (gr. 4-8). per. 8.95 *(978-0-8225-6483-6(1))* Lerner Publishing Group.

—El Rey Arturo: La Espada Excalibur Desenvainada: Una Leyenda Inglesa. Translations.com Staff, tr. from ENG. Yeates, Thomas, illus. 2007. (Mitos y leyendas en viñetas (Graphic Myths & Legends) Ser.).Tr. of King Arthur - Excalibur Unsheathed [An English Legend. (SPA.). 48p. (gr. 4-8). per. 8.95 *(978-0-8225-7968-7(5))* Lerner Publishing Group.

Lowenstein, Sallie, illus. Sir Kyle & Lady Madeline. Lowenstein, Sallie, . 2007. 32p. (J). 18.95 *(978-0-9658486-6-4(3))* Lion Stone Bks.

Lucado, Max. The Song of the King. Gillies, Chuck, illus. 2014. 32p. (J). 17.99 *(978-1-4335-4290-9(0))* Crossway.

Macgregor, Kinley, pseud & Furth, Robin. Knight of Darkness. 2010. (Lords of Avalon Ser.: Bk. 2). (Illus.). 144p. pap. 14.99 *(978-0-7851-2769-7(0))* Marvel Worldwide, Inc.

Maglia. EL LIBRO DE DON QUIJOTE PARA NIÑOS: NUEVA EDICIÓN) 2016. (SPA., Illus.). 114p. *(978-84-16075-98-0(0))* Ediciones B.

March, Julia. Meet the Knights. 2016. (DK Reader Level 2 Ser.). lib. bdg. 13.55 *(978-0-606-38227-4(5))* Turtleback Bks.

Marcotte, Jennifer. The Nightly Knight. 2009. 28p. pap. 14.99 *(978-1-4490-1943-3(9))* AuthorHouse.

Marks, Alan, illus. The Stories of Knights. 2004. (Young Reading Series One Ser.). 48p. (J). (gr. 2-18). pap. 5.95 *(978-0-7945-0755-8(7)*, Usborne) EDC Publishing.

Martin, George R. R. & Avery, Ben. The Sworn Sword, 0 vols. 2014. (Game of Thrones Ser.). (ENG., Illus.). 184p. (YA). pap. 14.95 *(978-1-4778-4929-3(7)*, 9781477849293, Jet City Comics) Amazon Publishing.

Matthews, John. The Barefoot Book of Knights. Manna, Giovanni, illus. 2009. (ENG.). 80p. (J). 19.99 *(978-1-84686-307-3(4))* Barefoot Bks., Inc.

—Knights. Manna, Giovanni, illus. 2014. (Barefoot Bks.). (ENG.). 79p. (J). (gr. 3-6). pap. 15.99 incl. audio compact disk *(978-1-78285-165-3(8))* Barefoot Bks., Inc.

Matthews, John & Matthe, John. Arthur of Albion. Tatarnikau, Pavel, illus. 2008. (ENG.). 96p. (J). (gr. 3-6). 24.99 *(978-1-84686-049-2(0))* Barefoot Bks., Inc.

Mayer, Mercer. The Bravest Knight. Mayer, Mercer, illus. 2007. (ENG., Illus.). 32p. (J). (gr. -1-3). 16.99 *(978-0-8037-3206-3(6)*, Dial Bks) Penguin Young Readers Group.

McKee, David. Mr Benn - Red Knight. 2011. (ENG., Illus.). 48p. (J). (gr. -1-3). 14.50 *(978-1-85437-990-0(9))* Tate Publishing, Ltd. GBR. Dist: Abrams, Inc.

McMullan, Kate. The Ghost of Sir Herbert Dungeonstone, 1 vol. Basso, Bill, illus. 2006. (Dragon Slayers' Academy Ser.: No. 12). (ENG.). 112p. (gr. 1-7). 24.21 *(978-1-59961-124-2(4))* Spotlight.

—Help! It's Parent's Day at DSA, 1 vol. Basso, Bill, illus. 2006. (Dragon Slayers' Academy Ser.: No. 10). (ENG.). 112p. (gr. 1-7). 24.21 *(978-1-59961-125-9(2))* Spotlight.

—Knight for a Day. Basso, Bill, illus. 2003. (Dragon Slayers' Academy Ser.: 5). (ENG.). 112p. (J). (gr. 2-5). mass mkt. 5.99 *(978-0-448-43277-9(3)*, Grosset & Dunlap) Penguin Young Readers Group.

—Pig Latin — Not Just for Pigs!, 1 vol. Basso, Bill, illus. 2006. (Dragon Slayers' Academy Ser.: No. 14). (ENG.). 112p. (gr. 1-7). 24.21 *(978-1-59961-127-3(9))* Spotlight.

—Sir Lancelot, Where Are You? Basso, Bill, illus. 2003. (Dragon Slayers' Academy Ser.: 6). (ENG.). 112p. (J). (gr. 2-5). pap. 5.99 *(978-0-448-43278-6(1)*, Grosset & Dunlap) Penguin Young Readers Group.

Meister, Cari. King Arthur & the Sword in the Stone, 1 vol. Erkocak, Sahin, illus. 2008. (Read-It! Readers: Legends Ser.). (ENG.). 32p. (gr. k-3). 21.32 *(978-1-4048-4837-5(1)*, Easy Readers) Picture Window Bks.

Melling, David. Good Knight Sleep Tight. Melling, David, illus. 2006. (ENG., Illus.). 32p. (J). (gr. -1-k). pap. 9.99 *(978-0-340-86093-9(6))* Hodder & Stoughton GBR. Dist: Hachette Bk. Group.

—The Three Wishes. Melling, David, illus. 2008. (ENG., Illus.). 32p. (J). (gr. -1-k). pap. 10.99 *(978-0-340-93153-0(1))* Hodder & Stoughton GBR. Dist: Hachette Bk. Group.

Memling, Carl. The Sword in the Stone (Disney) Random House Disney Staff, illus. 2015. (Little Golden Book Ser.). (ENG.). 24p. (J). (-k). 4.99 *(978-0-7364-3374-7(0)*, Golden/Disney) Random Hse. Children's Bks.

Milbourne, Anna. Stories of Knights & Castles. Doherty, Gillian, ed. Marks, Alan, illus. 2007. (Stories for Young Children Ser.). 96p. (J). 16.99 *(978-0-7945-1466-2(9)*, Usborne) EDC Publishing.

Miles, Colin. Naughty Nicky & the Good Ship Oggy. Miles, Gail, illus. 2013. 24p. pap. *(978-1-909202-16-0(9))* Little Acorns Publishing.

Mohler, Marie. The Knight & His Armored Heart. 2008. 40p. pap. 18.95 *(978-1-4357-4572-8(8))* Lulu Pr., Inc.

Moore, Shawn. Sam & the Tale of the Dragon Prints. Baker, David, illus. 2011. 28p. pap. 24.95 *(978-1-4560-7724-2(4))* America Star Bks.

Morris, Gerald. The Adventures of Sir Balin the Ill-Fated. Renier, Aaron, illus. 2013. (Knights' Tales Ser.: 4). (ENG.). 112p. (J). (gr. 1-4). pap. 5.99 *(978-0-544-10488-4(9))* Houghton Mifflin Harcourt Publishing Co.

—The Adventures of Sir Givret the Short. Renier, Aaron, illus. 2009. (Knights' Tales Ser.: 2). (ENG.). 112p. (J). (gr. 1-4). pap. 8.95 *(978-0-547-24818-9(0))* Houghton Mifflin Harcourt Publishing Co.

—The Ballad of Sir Dinadan. 2008. (Squire's Tales Ser.: 5). (ENG.). 256p. (J). (gr. 5-7). pap. 15.95 *(978-0-547-01473-9(2))* Houghton Mifflin Harcourt Publishing Co.

—The Lioness & Her Knight. 2008. (Squire's Tales Ser.: 7). (ENG.). 352p. (J). (gr. 5-7). pap. 7.99 *(978-0-547-01485-2(6))* Houghton Mifflin Harcourt Publishing Co.

—Parsifal's Page. 2008. (Squire's Tales Ser.: 4). (ENG.). 240p. (J). (gr. 5-7). pap. 7.99 *(978-0-547-01434-0(1))* Houghton Mifflin Harcourt Publishing Co.

—The Princess, the Crone, & the Dung-Cart Knight. 2008. (Squire's Tales Ser.: 6). (ENG.). 320p. (J). (gr. 5-7). pap. 7.99 *(978-0-547-01480-7(5))* Houghton Mifflin Harcourt Publishing Co.

—The Quest of the Fair Unknown. 2008. (Squire's Tales Ser.: 8). (ENG.). 272p. (J). (gr. 5-7). pap. 7.99 *(978-0-547-01484-5(8))* Houghton Mifflin Harcourt Publishing Co.

—The Savage Damsel & the Dwarf. 2008. (Squire's Tales Ser.: 3). (ENG.). 224p. (J). (gr. 5-7). pap. 7.99 *(978-0-547-01437-1(6))* Houghton Mifflin Harcourt Publishing Co.

—The Squire, His Knight, & His Lady. 2008. (Squire's Tales Ser.: 2). (ENG., Illus.). 240p. (J). (gr. 5-7). pap. 7.99 *(978-0-547-01438-8(4))* Houghton Mifflin Harcourt Publishing Co.

—The Squire's Tale. 2008. (Squire's Tales Ser.: 1). (ENG.). 224p. (J). (gr. 5-7). pap. 7.99 *(978-0-618-73743-7(X))* Houghton Mifflin Harcourt Publishing Co.

Mortensen, Erik. Sir Cook, the Knight? Harrison, Laura, illus. 2008. *(978-0-9782026-5-1(1))* Crackjaw Publishing.

Moss, Barbara E. The Adventures of Sir Goblin, the Feline Knight. Houx, Emily Marie Cornell du, illus. 2009. 336p. pap. 15.95 *(978-1-882190-03-4(3))* Porcupine Communications.

Moxilada, J. L. Jonty Jones Takes Guard. 2005. 242p. pap. 16.88 *(978-1-4116-4126-6(4))* Lulu Pr., Inc.

Muschla, Gary Robert. Crusader. 2006. (YA). pap. *(978-0-88092-491-7(8))* Royal Fireworks Publishing Co.

—The Sword & the Cross. 2009. (YA). lib. bdg. *(978-0-88092-471-9(3))* Royal Fireworks Publishing Co.

Namm, Diane. King Arthur & His Knights. Calo, Marcos, illus. 2014. (Silver Penny Stories Ser.). (ENG.). 48p. (J). (gr. -1-1). 4.95 *(978-1-4027-8432-3(5))* Sterling Publishing Co., Inc.

Nunes, Rachel Ann. The Secret of the King. Ward, Jay Bryant, illus. 2005. 32p. (J). (gr. -1-3). 17.95 *(978-1-59038-241-7(2)*, Shadow Mountain) Shadow Mountain Publishing.

Oceanak, Karla. Kerfuffle: An Aldo Zelnick Comic Novel. Spanjer, Kendra, illus. 2016. (Aldo Zelnick Comic Novel Ser.: 11). (ENG.). 160p. (J). (gr. 1-8). pap. 8.95 *(978-1-934649-75-6(9))* Bailiwick Pr.

Oladokun, Alexander. Acrux Manor: The Prodigal's Curse (Hardcover) 2013. 206p. 28.50 *(978-1-300-68651-4(0))* Lulu Pr., Inc.

Osborn, Kelly. The Green Knight. 2006. 64p. pap. 19.95 *(978-1-4241-1741-3(0))* America Star Bks.

Osborne, Mary Pope. El Caballero Del Alba. 2004. (Casa del Arbol Ser.: 2). (SPA.). (J). pap. 5.99 *(978-1-930332-50-8(5))* Lectorum Pubns., Inc.

—The Knight at Dawn. unabr. ed. 2004. (Magic Tree House Ser.: No. 2). 66p. (J). (gr. k-3). pap. 17.00 incl. audio *(978-0-8072-0331-6(9)*, Listening Library) Random Hse. Audio Publishing Group.

—The Knight at Dawn. Murdocca, Sal, illus. 20th anniv. ed. 2013. (Magic Tree House Ser.). (ENG.). 96p. (J). (gr. 1-4). 14.99 *(978-0-449-81822-0(5)*, Random Hse. Bks. for Young Readers) Random Hse. Children's Bks.

Perkins, John. Perceval: King Arthur's Knight of the Holy Grail, 1 vol. Spirin, Gennady, illus. 2007. (ENG.). 40p. (J). (gr. 3-7). 16.99 *(978-0-7614-5339-0(3))* Marshall Cavendish Corp.

Pierce, Tamora. In the Hand of the Goddess. (Song of the Lioness Ser.: 2). (ENG., Illus.). 272p. (YA). (gr. 7). 2014. 19.99 *(978-1-4814-3960-2(X))* 2011. pap. 10.99 *(978-1-4424-2764-8(7))* Simon & Schuster Children's Publishing. (Atheneum Bks. for Young Readers).

—Lioness Rampant. 2011. (Song of the Lioness Ser.: 4). (ENG., Illus.). 384p. (YA). (gr. 7). pap. 10.99 *(978-1-4424-2766-2(3)*, Atheneum Bks. for Young Readers) Simon & Schuster Children's Publishing.

—The Woman Who Rides Like a Man. (Song of the Lioness Ser.: 3). (ENG., Illus.). 288p. (YA). (gr. 7). 2014. 19.99 *(978-1-4814-3962-6(6))* 2011. pap. 10.99 *(978-1-4424-2765-5(5))* Simon & Schuster Children's Publishing. (Atheneum Bks. for Young Readers).

Pyle, Ernie Howard. Men of Iron. 2005. 272p. 28.95 *(978-1-4218-0617-4(7)*, 1st World Library - Literary Society) 1st World Publishing, Inc.

—Men of Iron. 2007. (ENG.). 198p. pap. 19.99 *(978-1-4346-1014-0(4))*; 218p. pap. 22.99 *(978-1-4346-1113-0(2))* Creative Media Partners, LLC.

Pyle, Howard. King Arthur & the Knights of the Round Table, 1 vol. Mullarkey, Lisa, illus. 2010. (Calico Illustrated Classics Ser.: No. 1). (ENG.). 112p. (YA). (gr. 3-6). 27.07 *(978-1-60270-707-8(3))* Magic Wagon.

—Men of Iron. unabr. ed. 2003. (Dover Children's Classics Ser.). (ENG.). 192p. (J). (gr. 3-8). pap. 10.95 *(978-0-486-42841-3(9))* Dover Pubns., Inc.

—The Story of King Arthur & His Knights. Pyle, Howard, illus. 2006. (ENG., Illus.). 416p. (gr. 12-18). 6.95 *(978-0-451-53024-0(1)*, Signet) Penguin Publishing Group.

—The Story of King Arthur & His Knights. McKowen, Scott, illus. 2005. (Sterling Unabridged Classics Ser.). (ENG.). 320p. (J). (gr. 5-9). 14.95 *(978-1-4027-2503-6(5)*, 1252056) Sterling Publishing Co., Inc.

—The Story of Sir Lancelot & His Companions. 2004. reprint ed. pap. 27.95 *(978-1-4179-5609-8(7))* Kessinger Publishing, LLC.

Quinn, Jordan. Let the Games Begin! McPhillips, Robert, illus. 2015. (Kingdom of Wrenly Ser.: 7). (ENG.). 128p. (J). (gr. k-4). pap. 5.99 *(978-1-4814-2379-3(7)*, Little Simon) Little Simon.

Quinn, Jordan. The Sorcerer's Shadow. McPhillips, Robert, illus. 2017. (Kingdom of Wrenly Ser.: 12). (ENG.). 128p. (J). (gr. k-4). 16.99 ***(978-1-5344-0000-9(1))***; pap. 5.99 ***(978-1-4814-9999-6(8))*** Little Simon. (Little Simon).

Ransom, Candice. Key to the Griffon's Lair. Fiegenshuh, Emily, illus. 2005. (Knights of the Silver Dragon Ser.: Bk. 9). 182p. (J). *(978-1-4156-3032-7(1)*, Mirrorstone) Wizards of the Coast.

Read, Leon. George the Knight. 2011. (Tadpoles Ser.: No. 32). (ENG., Illus.). 24p. (J). (gr. k-3). pap. *(978-0-7787-0589-5(7))* Crabtree Publishing Co.

The Red Knight, Level 3. 2016. (Ladybird Readers Ser.). (ENG.). 64p. (J). (gr. 2-4). pap. 9.99 *(978-0-241-25384-7(5))* Penguin Bks., Ltd. GBR. Dist: Independent Pubs. Group.

Reed, Janet. Brave Dave & the Dragons. Fraser, Kara-Anne, illus. 2009. 12p. (J). *(978-0-545-16142-8(8))* Scholastic, Inc.

REID, D. H. Fantasies & Dreams. 2008. 208p. pap. 18.95 *(978-0-557-01592-4(8))* Lulu Pr., Inc.

Remsburg, Rebecca. Night, Night, Knight, 1 vol. 2009. 19p. pap. 24.95 *(978-1-60836-942-3(0))* America Star Bks.

Rice, Morgan. A Grant of Arms. 2013. 238p. pap. 14.99 *(978-1-939416-61-2(2))* Morgan Rice Bks.

—A Land of Fire. 2014. 196p. 26.99 *(978-1-939416-87-2(6))* Morgan Rice Bks.

—A Land of Fire (Book #12 in the Sorcerer's Ring) 2014. 196p. (YA). pap. 15.99 *(978-1-939416-86-5(8)*, Morgan Rice) Morgan Rice Bks.

—Night of the Bold (Kings & Sorcerers — Book 6) 2016. (ENG., Illus.). 162p. (J). pap. 12.99 *(978-1-63291-497-2(2)*, Morgan Rice) Morgan Rice Bks.

—A Quest of Heroes. 2012. (Sorcerer's Ring Ser.: Bk. 1). (ENG.). 348p. (YA). 22.99 *(978-1-939416-21-6(3))*; pap. 10.99 *(978-1-939416-20-9(5))* Morgan Rice Bks.

—A Reign of Steel (Book #11 in the Sorcerer's Ring) 2014. 216p. (YA). pap. 15.99 *(978-1-939416-76-6(0)*, Morgan Rice) Morgan Rice Bks.

—A Rite of Swords. 2013. 266p. 25.99 *(978-1-939416-58-2(2))*; pap. 14.99 *(978-1-939416-57-5(4))* Morgan Rice Bks.

—A Rule of Queens (Book #13 in the Sorcerer's Ring) 2014. 238p. (YA). pap. 15.99 *(978-1-939416-92-6(2)*, Morgan Rice) Morgan Rice Bks.

—A Vow of Glory. 2013. (Sorcerer's Ring Ser.: Bk. 5). 274p. pap. 13.99 *(978-1-939416-28-5(0))* Morgan Rice Bks.

Richards, C. E., illus. King Arthur. 2010. (Classic Fiction Ser.). 72p. 4.75 *(978-1-4342-2603-7(4)*, Graphic Revolve) Stone Arch Bks.

Robinson, Michelle. The Forgetful Knight. Blunt, Fred, illus. 2016. (ENG.). 40p. (J). (gr. -1-3). 16.99 *(978-0-8037-4067-9(0)*, Dial Bks) Penguin Young Readers Group.

Roche, Art. The Knights of Boo'Gar. 2017. (ENG.). 176p. (J). pap. 9.99 *(978-1-4494-7987-9(1))* Andrews McMeel Publishing.

Rose, Kathryn. Avalon Rising. 2015. (Metal & Lace Novel Ser.: 2). (ENG., Illus.). 360p. (YA). pap. 11.99 *(978-0-7387-4489-6(1)*, Flux) North Star Editions.

Rovetch, L. Bob & Whitman, Emily. Sir Henry, the Polite Knight. Barnard, Bryn, illus. 2006. (J). *(978-1-58987-204-2(5))* Kindermusik International.

Rowley, Melissa. The Falcon Shield. 2009. (J). 6.99 *(978-1-60641-103-2(9))* Deseret Bk. Co.

Rowley, M'lin. Knights of Right, BK 4: The Fiery Gloves. 2010. 80p. (J). pap. 6.99 *(978-1-60641-241-1(8)*, Shadow Mountain) Shadow Mountain Publishing.

—The Silver Coat. 2009. (Knights of Right Ser.: Bk. 2). 71p. (J). (gr. 1-5). pap. 6.99 *(978-1-60641-104-9(7)*, Shadow Mountain) Shadow Mountain Publishing.

Rowleym'Lin. Knights of Right, BK 3: The Warrior's Guard. 2010. 80p. (J). pap. 6.99 *(978-1-60641-240-4(X)*, Shadow Mountain) Shadow Mountain Publishing.

Royde-Smith, N. G. Una and the Red Cross Knight & Other T. 2006. (Illus.). pap. 28.95 *(978-1-4254-8407-1(7))* Kessinger Publishing, LLC.

Rudden, Dave. Knights of the Borrowed Dark. (Knights of the Borrowed Dark Ser.: 1). (ENG.). (J). (gr. 5). 2017. 400p. 7.99 ***(978-0-553-52300-3(7)***, Yearling) 2016. 384p. 16.99 *(978-0-553-52297-6(3)*, Random Hse. Bks. for Young Readers) Random Hse. Children's Bks.

Russell, Christopher. Dogboy. 2006. 272p. (J). (gr. 5). 15.99 *(978-0-06-084116-4(8)*, Greenwillow Bks.) HarperCollins Pubs.

Santore, Charles. William the Curious: Knight of the Water Lilies. Santore, Charles, illus. 2014. (ENG., Illus.). 44p. (J). (gr. -1). 16.95 *(978-1-60433-474-6(6))* Cider Mill Pr. Bk. Pubs., LLC.

Scholastic. Macy & the King's Tournament. 2017. (LEGO NEXO Knights Ser.). (ENG.). 32p. (J). (gr. 1-3). pap. 3.99 *(978-1-338-05558-0(5))* Scholastic, Inc.

Scholastic & Howard, Kate. Fright Knight!, Bk. 2. 2016. (LEGO NEXO Knights Ser.). (ENG.). 80p. (J). (gr. 2-5). pap. 4.99 *(978-0-545-92555-6(X))* Scholastic, Inc.

Scholastic, Inc. Staff & Schmidt, Rebecca L. The Power of the Fortrex. 2016. (Scholastic Reader, Level 2 Ser.: 1). (ENG.). 32p. (J). (gr. 1-3). pap. 3.99 *(978-0-545-93338-4(2))* Scholastic, Inc.

Scholastic, Inc. Staff & West, Tracey. Graduation Day, Bk. 1. 2016. (LEGO NEXO Knights Ser.). (ENG.). 80p. (J). (gr. 2-5). pap. 4.99 *(978-0-545-92554-9(1))* Scholastic, Inc.

Schurch, Maylan. The Sword of Denis Anwyck. 2009. (J). pap. 10.99 *(978-0-8280-2425-9(1))* Review & Herald Publishing Assn.

Scieszka, Jon. Knights of the Kitchen Table. (Time Warp Trio Ser.: No. 1). 55p. (J). (gr. 2-4). pap. 3.99 *(978-0-8072-1301-8(2)*, Listening Library) Random Hse. Audio Publishing Group.

Scott, Walter, ed. Ivanhoe. (SPA., Illus.). 176p. (YA). 14.95 *(978-84-7281-096-9(8)*, AF1096) Auriga, Ediciones S.A. ESP. Dist: Continental Bk. Co., Inc.

—Ivanhoe. 2008. (Bring the Classics to Life Ser.). (Illus.). 72p. (gr. 5-12). pap., act. bk. ed. 10.95 *(978-1-55576-099-1(6),* EDN506B) EDCON Publishing Group.

Shapiro D., Brian. Plaquetooth. 2008. 28p. pap. 13.99 *(978-1-4343-8913-8(8))* AuthorHouse.

Simon, Elizabeth. Tyler Adams & the Adventures of Bravura: the First Quest. 2009. 49p. pap. 19.95 *(978-0-557-06290-4(X))* Lulu Pr., Inc.

Sleiman, Dina L. Chivalrous. 2015. (Valiant Hearts Ser.: 2). (ENG.). 368p. (YA). pap. 16.00 *(978-0-7642-1313-7(X))* Bethany Hse. Pubs.

—Courageous. 2016. (Valiant Hearts Ser.: 3). (ENG.). 368p. (YA). pap. 13.99 *(978-0-7642-1314-4(8))* Bethany Hse. Pubs.

The Song of the Lioness Quartet. 2014. (Song of the Lioness Ser.). (ENG., Illus.). 1168p. (YA). (gr. 7). pap. 42.99 *(978-1-4814-1649-8(9),* Atheneum Bks. for Young Readers) Simon & Schuster Children's Publishing.

Spinner, Stephanie. Damosel: In Which the Lady of the Lake Renders a Frank & Often Startling Account of Her Wondrous Life & Times. 2010. (ENG.). 208p. (YA). (gr. 7). pap. 8.99 *(978-0-553-49511-9(9),* Knopf Bks. for Young Readers) Random Hse. Children's Bks.

Spradlin, Michael. Orphan of Destiny: Book 3, 3 vols. 2011. (Youngest Templar Ser.: 3). (ENG.). 272p. (J). (gr. 5-18). 7.99 *(978-0-14-241959-5(1),* Puffin Books) Penguin Young Readers Group.

Spradlin, Michael P. Keeper of the Grail, Bk. 1. 2009. (Youngest Templar Ser.: 1). (ENG.). 272p. (J). (gr. 5-6). 7.99 *(978-0-14-241461-3(1),* Puffin Books) Penguin Young Readers Group.

—Trail of Fate, 2 vols., Bk. 2. 2010. (Youngest Templar Ser.: 2). (ENG.). 256p. (J). (gr. 5-7). 7.99 *(978-0-14-241707-2(6),* Puffin Books) Penguin Young Readers Group.

Stanley, Diane. Bella at Midnight. Ibatoulline, Bagram, illus. 2007. (ENG.). 304p. (J). (gr. 3-7). pap. 7.99 *(978-0-06-077575-9(0))* HarperCollins Pubs.

Steele, Philip. A Knight's City: With Amazing Pop-Ups & an Interactive Tour of Life in a Medieval City! 2008. (ENG.). 32p. (J). (gr. 1-5). 18.99 *(978-1-4169-6124-6(0),* Little Simon) Little Simon.

Stewart, Paul & Riddell, Chris. Dragon's Hoard. Riddell, Chris, illus. 2014. (Knight's Story Ser.: 3). (ENG., Illus.). 144p. (J). (gr. 2-6). pap. 13.99 *(978-1-4814-2890-3(X),* Atheneum Bks. for Young Readers) Simon & Schuster Children's Publishing.

—Edge Chronicles: the Winter Knights. 2010. (Edge Chronicles Ser.). (ENG.). 400p. (J). (gr. 3-7). 8.99 *(978-0-385-73612-1(6),* Yearling) Random Hse. Children's Bks.

—Joust of Honor. Riddell, Chris, illus. 2014. (Knight's Story Ser.: 2). (ENG., Illus.). 144p. (J). (gr. 2-6). pap. 13.99 *(978-1-4814-2889-7(6),* Atheneum Bks. for Young Readers) Simon & Schuster Children's Publishing.

—Lake of Skulls. Riddell, Chris, illus. 2014. (Knight's Story Ser.: 1). (ENG., Illus.). 144p. (J). (gr. 2-6). pap. 13.99 *(978-1-4814-2888-0(8),* Atheneum Bks. for Young Readers) Simon & Schuster Children's Publishing.

Stine, R. L. Fright Knight & the Ooze: Twice Terrifying Tales. 2010. (R. L. Stine's Ghosts of Fear Street Ser.). (ENG.). 240p. (J). (gr. 3-7). pap. 6.99 *(978-1-4169-9135-9(2),* Aladdin) Simon & Schuster Children's Publishing.

Streit, Jakob. Three Knight Tales, 1 vol. 2013. (ENG.). 76p. pap. 12.00 *(978-1-936367-24-5(6))* Waldorf Publications.

Sweet, Susan D. & Miles, Brenda. Jacqueline & the Beanstalk: A Tale of Facing Giant Fears. Docampo, Valeria, illus. 2017. 32p. (J). 15.95 ***(978-1-4338-2682-5(8),*** Magination Pr.) American Psychological Assn.

Taylor, Dereen. The Knight's First Tournament. Kavanagh, Peter, illus. 2012. (ENG.). 12p. (J). (gr. 1-6). 16.99 *(978-1-84322-760-1(6))* Anness Publishing GBR. Dist: National Bk. Network.

Thomas, Shelley Moore. Get Well, Good Knight. Plecas, Jennifer, illus. 2004. (Penguin Young Readers, Level 3 Ser.). (ENG.). 48p. (J). (gr. 1-3). 3.99 *(978-0-14-240050-0(5),* Penguin Young Readers) Penguin Young Readers Group.

—Get Well, Good Knight. Plecas, Jennifer, illus. 2004. (Easy-to-Read Ser.). 44p. (gr. k-3). 14.00 *(978-0-7569-2923-7(7))* Perfection Learning Corp.

—Get Well, Good Knight. 2004. (Penguin Young Readers Level 3 Ser.). 13.55 *(978-0-613-97291-8(0),* Turtleback) Turtleback Bks.

—Happy Birthday, Good Knight. 2014. (Penguin Young Readers Level 3 Ser.). lib. bdg. 13.55 *(978-0-606-35728-9(9))* Turtleback Bks.

Thomson, Sarah L. Dragon's Egg. 2007. (ENG.). 272p. (J). (gr. 3-7). 16.99 *(978-0-06-128848-7(9),* Greenwillow Bks.) HarperCollins Pubs.

Tompert, Ann. The Errant Knight. Keith, Doug, illus. 2003. 32p. 15.95 *(978-0-9701907-6-5(X))* Illumination Arts Publishing Co., Inc.

Tullen, Sean. The Not-So-Deadly Dragon. Cunyat, Pol, illus. 2016. (Thud & Blunder Ser.). (ENG.). 56p. (gr. 2-4). pap. 4.95 *(978-1-4965-3224-4(4));* lib. bdg. 23.99 *(978-1-4965-3220-6(1))* Stone Arch Bks.

—The Not-So-Evil Wizard. Cunyat, Pol, illus. 2016. (Thud & Blunder Ser.). (ENG.). 56p. (gr. 2-4). pap. 4.95 *(978-1-4965-3225-1(2));* lib. bdg. 23.99 *(978-1-4965-3221-3(X))* Stone Arch Bks.

—Thud & Blunder, 4 vols. Cunyat, Pol, illus. 2016. (Thud & Blunder Ser.). (ENG.). 56p. (gr. 2-4). pap. 19.80 *(978-1-4965-3369-2(0))* Stone Arch Bks.

Tullen, Sean & Hoena, Blake. The Not-So-Helpless Princess. Cunyat, Pol, illus. 2016. (Thud & Blunder Ser.). (ENG.). 56p. (gr. 2-4). pap. 4.95 *(978-1-4965-3222-0(8));* lib. bdg. 23.99 *(978-1-4965-3218-3(X))* Stone Arch Bks.

—The Not-So-Heroic Knight. Cunyat, Pol, illus. 2016. (Thud & Blunder Ser.). (ENG.). 56p. (gr. 2-4). pap. 4.95 *(978-1-4965-3223-7(6));* lib. bdg. 23.99 *(978-1-4965-3219-0(8))* Stone Arch Bks.

Twain, Mark, pseud. A Connecticut Yankee in King Arthur's Court. 2008. (Bring the Classics to Life Ser.). (ENG., Illus.). 72p. (gr. 3-12). pap., act. bk. ed. 10.95 *(978-1-55576-357-2(X),* EDCTR-309B) EDCON Publishing Group.

van Genechten, Guido. Knight Ricky. van Genechten, Guido, illus. 2010. (Ricky Ser.). (ENG., Illus.). 30p. (J). (gr. -1-k). 16.95 *(978-1-60537-059-0(2))* Cobblestone Publishing Co.

Vande Velde, Vivian & Bash, Barbara. The Book of Mordred. 2007. (ENG.). 352p. (YA). (gr. 7-12). pap. 8.99 *(978-0-618-80916-5(3))* Houghton Mifflin Harcourt Publishing Co.

Ventura, Marne. The Worry Warriors, 4 vols. Trinidad, Leo, illus. 2016. (Worry Warriors Ser.). (ENG.). 96p. (gr. 2-4). 103.96 *(978-1-4965-3665-5(7))* Stone Arch Bks.

Vernon, Ursula. Knight-Napped! 2015. (Dragonbreath Ser.: 10). (ENG.). 208p. (J). (gr. 3-7). 12.99 *(978-0-8037-3849-2(8),* Dial Bks) Penguin Young Readers Group.

Wallace, Karen & Chapman, Neil. The Round Table. 2009. (Hopscotch Adventures Ser.). (Illus.). 31p. (J). (gr. 1). lib. bdg. 25.65 *(978-1-59771-175-3(6))* Sea-To-Sea Pubns.

—Sir Lancelot & the Ice Castle. 2009. (Hopscotch Adventures Ser.). (Illus.). 31p. (J). (gr. 1). lib. bdg. 25.65 *(978-1-59771-174-6(8))* Sea-To-Sea Pubns.

Weyn, Suzanne. The Night Dance: A Retelling of the Twelve Dancing Princesses. 2008. (Once upon a Time Ser.). (ENG.). 224p. (YA). (gr. 7). mass mkt. 6.99 *(978-1-4169-6132-1(1),* Simon Pulse) Simon Pulse.

Wheeler, Lisa. Boogie Knights. Siegel, Mark, illus. 2008. (ENG.). 40p. (J). (gr. -1-3). 16.99 *(978-0-689-87639-4(4),* Atheneum/Richard Jackson Bks.) Simon & Schuster Children's Publishing.

Wright, Joshua. Hapless, Hopeless, Horrible. 2004. (ENG., Illus.). 192p. (J). (gr. 3-8). pap. 11.99 *(978-1-74114-082-8(X))* Allen & Unwin AUS. Dist: Independent Pubs. Group.

Yancey, Rick. Alfred Kropp: the Thirteenth Skull. 2015. (Alfred Kropp Ser.). (ENG.). 304p. (YA). (gr. 7). pap. 9.99 *(978-1-61963-918-8(1),* 9781619639188, Bloomsbury USA Childrens) Bloomsbury Publishing USA.

—The Thirteenth Skull. (Alfred Kropp Ser.). (ENG.). 304p. (YA). (gr. 7). 2009. mass mkt. 6.99 *(978-1-59990-363-7(6),* 9781599903637) 2008. 16.99 *(978-1-59990-114-5(5),* 9781599901145) Bloomsbury Publishing USA. (Bloomsbury USA Childrens).

KNIGHTS OF THE ROUND TABLE

see Arthur, King

KNITTING

Anderson, Susan B. Kids' Knitting Workshop: The Easiest & Most Effective Way to Learn to Knit! 2015. (ENG., Illus.). 200p. (J). (gr. 3). spiral bd. 17.95 *(978-1-57965-590-7(4))* Artisan.

Blanchette, Peg & Thibault, Terri. 12 Easy Knitting Projects. Martin-Jourdenais, Norma Jean, illus. (ENG.). 64p. (J). (gr. 3-7). 2008. 12.95 *(978-0-8249-6784-0(4))* 2006. pap. 8.95 *(978-0-8249-6785-7(2))* Worthy Publishing. (Ideal Pubns.).

Blaxland, Wendy. Sweaters. 2009. (How Are They Made? 2 Ser.). 32p. (gr. 4). lib. bdg. 18.56 *(978-0-7614-4756-6(3))* Marshall Cavendish GBR. Dist: Marshall Cavendish Corp.

Bradberry, Sarah. Kids Knit! Simple Steps to Nifty Projects. 2006. (ENG., Illus.). 96p. (J). (gr. 3-7). pap. 9.95 *(978-1-4027-4057-2(3))* Sterling Publishing Co., Inc.

Dorling Kindersley Publishing Staff. Let's Knit. 2015. (ENG., Illus.). 64p. (J). (gr. 3-7). 15.99 *(978-1-4654-3668-9(5),* DK Children) Dorling Kindersley Publishing, Inc.

DRG, D. R. G. Kids Learn to Knit, Quilt & Crochet, 1 vol. 2009. (Workshop Ser.). (ENG., Illus.). 128p. (J). spiral bd. 16.99 *(978-1-897477-13-7(9),* 9781897477137) Company's Coming Publishing, Ltd. CAN. Dist: Lone Pine Publishing USA.

Dupernex, Alison. Start to Knit. 2009. (Start to Ser.). (ENG., Illus.). 48p. (J). (gr. 4). pap. 10.95 *(978-1-84448-388-4(6))* Stone Ridge Publishing.

Dyer, Janice. Get into Knitting. 2016. (Get-Into-It Guides). (ENG.). 32p. (J). (gr. 3-6). *(978-0-7787-2641-8(X))* Crabtree Publishing Co.

Easy-To-Make Spool Knit Animals: Simple & Charming Projects to Make with Spool Knitting! 2013. (Craft Box Kids Ser.). (ENG., Illus.). 48p. (J). *(978-1-77132-025-2(7))* SpiceBox Products Ltd.

Eckman, Edie. I Can Knit. 2012. (I Can Ser.). (ENG., Illus.). 32p. (J). (gr. 4-7). pap. 7.95 *(978-1-59217-440-9(X),* Annie's) Annie's Publishing, LLC.

Edwards, Miriam. Start to Quilt. 2009. (Start to Ser.). (ENG., Illus.). 48p. (J). (gr. 4). pap. 10.95 *(978-1-84448-389-1(4))* Stone Ridge Publishing.

Falick, Melanie. Kids Knitting. Nicholas, Kristin, illus. Hartiove, Chris, photos by. 2003. (ENG.). 128p. (J). pap. 15.95 *(978-1-57965-241-8(7),* 85241) Artisan.

Fryer, Jane Eayre. The Mary Frances Knitting & Crocheting Book 100th Anniversary Edition: A Childrens Story-Instruction Book with Doll Clothes Patterns for American Girl & Other 18-Inch Dolls. 2011. (ENG., Illus.). 208p. (J). pap. 19.95 *(978-1-937564-05-6(3),* Classic Bookwrights) Lindaloo Enterprises.

Gildersleeve, Mary C. Great Yarns for the Close-Knit Family: Over Two Dozen Original Hand-Knit Designs Inspired by One Dozen Family Read-alouds. 2008. 157p. pap. 14.99 *(978-0-9798469-4-6(3))* Hillside Education.

Hayes, Amy. Turning Wool into Sweaters. 2015. (Step-By-Step Transformations Ser.). (ENG., Illus.). 24p. (J). (gr. 1-1). 24.21 *(978-1-5026-0455-2(8))* Cavendish Square Publishing.

Huff, Mary Scott. Creative Kids Complete Photo Guide to Knitting. 2015. (Creative Kids Ser.). (ENG., Illus.). 144p. pap. 24.99 *(978-1-58923-869-5(9),* 1387860, Creative Publishing International) Quarto Publishing Group USA.

Johnson, Anne Akers. Knitting: Learn to Knit Six Great Projects. 2004. (Illus.). 96p. (J). 24.95 *(978-1-57054-861-1(7))* Klutz.

—Knitting: Learn to Knit Six Great Projects. 2013. (ENG.). 96p. (J). (gr. 5). 24.99 *(978-0-545-56167-9(1))* Klutz.

Kallmeyer-Mehlhorn, Margarete. The Wondrous Ball of Yarn: A Facsimile of the Previously Unpublished Manuscript. 2008.Tr. of Wunderknaul. (ENG & GER., Illus.). 40p. 41.00 *(978-0-9745168-2-0(1))* Cotsen Occasional Pr.

Klutz Editors. Finger Knitting. 2015. (ENG.). 56p. (J). (gr. 3-7). 21.99 *(978-0-545-85845-8(3))* Klutz.

Kuskowski, Alex. Cool Knitting for Kids: A Fun & Creative Introduction to Fiber Art, 1 vol. 2014. (Cool Fiber Art Ser.). (ENG.). 32p. (gr. 8-12). lib. bdg. 28.50 *(978-1-62403-308-7(3),* Checkerboard Library) ABDO Publishing Co.

Nelson, Robin. From Sheep to Sweater. 2003. (Start to Finish Ser.). (Illus.). 24p. (J). 18.60 *(978-0-8225-0716-1(1),* Lerner Pubns.) Lerner Publishing Group.

Rau, Dana Meachen. Learning to Knit. 2012. (How-To Library). (ENG.). 32p. (gr. 3-6). 28.50 *(978-1-61080-477-6(5),* 202087); pap. 14.21 *(978-1-61080-651-0(4),* 202261) Cherry Lake Publishing.

Steege, Gwen W. & Hansen, Robin. Knit Mittens/Knit Hats. (ENG., Illus.). 119.60 *(978-1-58017-901-0(0),* 67901) Storey Publishing, LLC.

Switzer, Chris. Projects for Alpaca & Llama. 2004. 16.00 *(978-0-9642663-2-2(6))* Switzer Land Enterprises.

Thalacker, Karen & Dwyer, Mindy. Knitting with Gigi: Includes Step-By-Step Instructions & 8 Patterns. 2007. (J). pap. *(978-1-56477-799-7(5))* Martingale & Co.

Thalcker, Karen. Knitting with Gigi. Dwyer, Mindy, illus. 2007. (ENG.). 32p. 24.95 *(978-1-56477-816-1(9))* Martingale & Co.

Warwick, Ellen. Fully Woolly. Lum, Bernice, illus. 2007. (Planet Girl Ser.). (ENG.). 80p. (J). (gr. 5-9). 12.95 *(978-1-55337-798-6(2))* Kids Can Pr., Ltd. CAN. Dist: Hachette Bk. Group.

Watt, Fiona. How to Knit. Baggott, Stella, illus. Allman, Howard, photos by. 2007. (Art Ideas Ser.). 64p. (J). (gr. 4-7). pap. 14.99 *(978-0-7945-1577-5(0),* Usborne) EDC Publishing.

KNOTS AND SPLICES

Adkins, Jan. Line: Tying It up, Tying It Down. 2004. (ENG., Illus.). 48p. (J). (gr. 3-7). 12.95 *(978-0-937822-83-8(3))* WoodenBoat Pubns.

Chen, D. M. & Sun, Michelle. Tie a Wish with Bracelets: Easy & Fun Chinese Knotting. 2012. (ENG., Illus.). 71p. (J). (gr. 4). pap. 10.95 *(978-1-937489-01-4(9))* StoryRobin Co.

Graham, Oakley. I Can Tie My Own Shoelaces. Green, Barry, illus. 2014. (I Can Bks.). (ENG.). 12p. (J). (gr. -1). 7.99 *(978-1-78244-824-2(1))* Top That! Publishing PLC GBR. Dist: Independent Pubs. Group.

Groves. Knots & Knocks, Bk. 16. Date not set. (Illus.). 32p. (J). pap. 129.15 *(978-0-582-18059-8(7))* Addison-Wesley Longman, Ltd. GBR. Dist: Trans-Atlantic Pubns., Inc.

Klutz Editors. The Klutz Book of Knots. 2017. (ENG.). 22p. (J). (gr. 3-7). 14.99 *(978-1-338-10642-8(2))* Scholastic, Inc.

Mooney, Carla. Get All Tied Up: Tying Knots. 2010. (Creative Adventure Guides). 48p. (J). (gr. 3-6). lib. bdg. 26.60 *(978-1-59953-384-1(7))* Norwood Hse. Pr.

Rau, Dana Meachen. Making Knot Projects. Petelinsek, Kathleen, illus. 2016. (How-To Library). (ENG.). 32p. (J). (gr. 3-6). 29.93 *(978-1-63471-420-4(2),* 208459) Cherry Lake Publishing.

Sadler, Judy Ann & Sadler, Judy. Knotting: Make Your Own Basketball Nets, Guitar Straps, Sports Bags & More. Gagnon, Celeste & Gagnon, Celeste, illus. 2006. (Kids Can Do It Ser.). (ENG.). 40p. (J). (gr. 3-7). 6.95 *(978-1-55337-834-1(2))* Kids Can Pr., Ltd. CAN. Dist: Hachette Bk. Group.

Smith, A. G. Celtic Knotwork Stained Glass Colouring Book. 2006. (Dover Design Stained Glass Coloring Book Ser.). (ENG., Illus.). 32p. (gr. 3-8). 7.99 *(978-0-486-44816-9(9))* Dover Pubns., Inc.

Wilson, Patrick. Ropes & Knots for Survival. Carney, John, ed. 2014. (Extreme Survival in the Military Ser.: 12). 64p. (J). (gr. 7-18). lib. bdg. 23.95 *(978-1-4222-3083-1(X))* Mason Crest.

KNOWLEDGE, SOCIOLOGY OF

The Big Book of Knowledge. 2003. 384p. (J). 9.98 *(978-0-7525-8436-2(7))* Parragon, Inc.

KNOWLEDGE, THEORY OF

Here are entered works that treat the origin, nature, methods and limits of human knowledge.

see also Belief and Doubt; Intellect; Perception; Senses and Sensation

Baxter, Nicola. Kaleidoscope Book: My First Book of Learning. Elliott, Rebecca, illus. 2013. (ENG.). 16p. bds. 16.99 *(978-1-84322-930-8(7),* Armadillo) Anness Publishing GBR. Dist: National Bk. Network.

Carlson, Dale. The Teen Brain Book: Who & What Are You? Teasdale, Nancy, ed. Nicklaus, Carol, illus. 2004. (ENG.). 230p. (gr. 7-12). pap. 14.95 *(978-1-884158-29-2(3))* Team Kreskin Productions, LLC.

De Medeiros, Michael. Common Sense. 2009. (World of Wonder Ser.). (Illus.). 24p. (J). (gr. 2-4). pap. 8.95 *(978-1-60596-063-0(2));* lib. bdg. 24.45 *(978-1-60596-062-3(4))* Weigl Pubs., Inc.

Dorling Kindersley Publishing Staff. Knowledge Encyclopedia. 2013. (ENG.). 360p. (J). (gr. 3-7). 29.99 *(978-1-4654-1417-5(7),* DK Children) Dorling Kindersley Publishing, Inc.

Dwyer, Helen. Cognitive Development. 2011. (CC: Psychology Ser.). 112p. (gr. 6-12). lib. bdg. 42.80 *(978-1-936333-17-2(1))* Brown Bear Bks.

Dwyer, Helen, ed. Intellectual Development. 2011. (CC: Psychology Ser.). (Illus.). 112p. (gr. 6-12). lib. bdg. 42.80 *(978-1-936333-18-9(X))* Brown Bear Bks.

Hansen, Sharon A. The Executive Functioning Workbook for Teens: Help for Unprepared, Late, & Scattered Teens. 2013. (ENG.). 144p. (YA). (gr. 6-12). pap. 17.95 *(978-1-60882-656-8(2))* New Harbinger Pubns.

Higgins, Melissa. We All Have Different Abilities, 1 vol. 2012. (Celebrating Differences Ser.). (ENG.). 24p. (gr. k-1). 26.65 *(978-1-4296-7575-8(6));* pap. 41.70 *(978-1-4296-8321-0(X));* pap. 7.29 *(978-1-4296-7888-9(7))* Capstone Press of Coughlan Cos. (Pebble Plus).

Lo Bosco, Maryellen. David Hume & a Treatise of Human Nature. 2016. (J). lib. bdg. *(978-1-68048-547-9(4))* Windmill Bks.

Orr, Tamra B. Tracking an Epidemic. 2014. (Explorer Library: Follow the Clues Ser.). (ENG., Illus.). 32p. (J). (gr. 4-8). 28.50 *(978-1-62431-776-7(6),* 203300) Cherry Lake Publishing.

Porchetta, Renato L. Universal Methodology: UNIVERSAL SCIENTIFIC PROGRAMMING CONTROL-HUMAN INTELLIGENCE AMPLIFICATION MANAGEMENT-SCIENCE of the COMPOSITION of the SIGNIFICANCE,SEMANTICS-SCIENCE of MANAGEMENT-the Mosaic Thinking, 2 vols, Vol.1. 2nd ed. 2007. (ENG., Illus.). 490p. lib. bdg. 100.00 *(978-0-9769931-0-0(4))* Ce Code Efficiency, Inc.

Reade, Clara. La Intuicin: El Sexto Sentido / Intuition: the Sixth Sense, 1 vol., 1. De La Vega, Eida, ed. 2014. (Tus Cinco Sentidos y Tu Sexto Sentido / Your Five Senses & Your Sixth Sense Ser.). (SPA & BYN.). 24p. (J). (gr. k-2). 23.60 *(978-1-4777-3280-9(2),* PowerKids Pr.) Rosen Publishing Group, Inc., The.

KNOX, HENRY, 1750-1806

Kravitz, Danny. The Untold Story of Henry Knox: The Man Who Saved Boston. 2015. (What You Didn't Know about the American Revolution Ser.). (ENG., Illus.). 64p. (gr. 4-8). 34.65 *(978-0-7565-4972-5(8))* Compass Point Bks.

Strum, Richard. Henry Knox: Washington's Artilleryman. 2006. (Forgotten Heroes of the American Revolution Ser.). (Illus.). 88p. (J). (gr. 5-11). lib. bdg. 23.95 *(978-1-59556-013-1(0))* OTTN Publishing.

Strum, Richard M. Henry Knox: Washington's Artilleryman. 2006. (J). pap. *(978-1-59556-018-6(1))* OTTN Publishing.

KOALA

Barwood, Lee. Klassic Koalas: Ancient Aboriginal Tales in New Retellings, BW Edition. 2007. (ENG., Illus.). 24p. (J). pap. 14.99 *(978-0-9764698-6-5(3))* Koala Jo Publishing.

Bodden, Valerie. Amazing Animals - Koalas. 2009. (Amazing Animals Ser.). 24p. (J). (gr. 1-5). 24.25 *(978-1-58341-715-7(X),* Creative Education) Creative Co., The.

—Koalas. 2015. (J). *(978-1-62832-257-6(8),* Creative Paperbacks) Creative Co., The.

Borgert-Spaniol, Megan. Baby Koalas. 2015. (Super Cute! Ser.). (ENG., Illus.). 24p. (J). (gr. k-3). lib. bdg. 25.95 *(978-1-62617-219-7(6),* Blastoff! Readers) Bellwether Media.

Clark, Willow. Koalas. 2012. (Up a Tree Ser.). (ENG., Illus.). 24p. (J). (gr. k-3). lib. bdg. 22.60 *(978-1-4488-6185-9(3));* pap. 8.25 *(978-1-4488-6329-7(5),* PowerKids Pr.) Rosen Publishing Group, Inc., The.

Eckart, Edana. Koala. 2005. (Welcome Bks.). (ENG., Illus.). 24p. (J). (gr. -1-2). pap. 4.95 *(978-0-516-25164-6(3),* Children's Pr.) Scholastic Library Publishing.

Eszterhas, Suzi. Koala Hospital. 2015. (Wildlife Rescue Ser.: 1). (ENG., Illus.). 44p. (J). (gr. 2-5). 17.95 *(978-1-77147-140-4(9),* Owlkids) Owlkids Bks. Inc. CAN. Dist: Publishers Group West (PGW).

Fishman, Jon M. Meet a Baby Koala. 2017. (Lightning Bolt Books (tm) — Baby Australian Animals Ser.). (ENG.). (J). (gr. 1-3). pap. 6.99 ***(978-1-5124-5589-2(X))*** Lerner Publishing Group.

Fishman, Jon M. Meet a Baby Koala. 2017. (Lightning Bolt Books (tm) — Baby Australian Animals Ser.). (ENG.). 24p. (J). (gr. 1-3). 25.32 ***(978-1-5124-3383-8(7))*** Lerner Publishing Group.

Frisch, Aaron. Koalas. 2014. 24p. *(978-1-60818-455-2(2),* Creative Education) Creative Co., The.

Green, Carl R. The Koala: A MyReportLinks. Com Book. 2003. (Endangered & Threatened Animals Ser.). (Illus.). 48p. (J). (gr. 4-10). lib. bdg. 25.26 *(978-0-7660-5058-7(0),* MyReportLinks.com Bks.) Enslow Pubs., Inc.

Gregory, Josh. Koalas. 2016. (Nature's Children Ser.). (ENG., Illus.). 48p. (J). pap. 6.95 *(978-0-531-22518-9(6),* Children's Pr.) Scholastic Library Publishing.

Hanel, Rachael. Koalas. 2008. (Living Wild Ser.). (Illus.). 46p. 22.95 *(978-1-58341-655-6(2),* Creative Education) Creative Co., The.

Hendrix, Emilia. Koalas & Joeys. 2016. (Animal Family Ser.). (ENG., Illus.). 24p. (J). (gr. k-k). pap. 8.15 *(978-1-4824-3779-9(1))* Stevens, Gareth Publishing LLLP.

Hengel, Katherine. It's a Baby Koala!, 1 vol. 2010. (Baby Australian Animals Ser.). (ENG., Illus.). 24p. (J). (gr. k-3). lib. bdg. 24.21 *(978-1-60453-577-8(6),* SandCastle) ABDO Publishing Co.

Hewett, Richard, illus. & photos by. A Koala Joey Grows Up. Hewett, Richard, photos by. Hewett, Joan, photos by. 2004. (Baby Animals Ser.). 32p. (J). (gr. k-3). lib. bdg. 21.27 *(978-1-57505-198-7(2))* Lerner Publishing Group.

Hoff, Mary King. Koalas. 2005. (Wild World of Animals (Creative Education) Ser.). (Illus.). 32p. (J). (gr. 2-5). lib. bdg. 18.95 *(978-1-58341-351-7(0),* Creative Education) Creative Co., The.

Jacobs, Liza. Koalas. 2003. (Wild Wild World Ser.). (Illus.). 24p. (J). 23.70 *(978-1-4103-0049-2(8),* Blackbirch Pr., Inc.) Cengage Gale.

Kalman, Bobbie, et al. Les Koalas. 2005. (Petit Monde Vivant Ser.). (FRE., Illus.). 32p. (J). pap. 9.95 *(978-2-89579-033-4(7))* Bayard Canada Livres CAN. Dist: Crabtree Publishing Co.

Kawa, Katie. Baby Koalas. 2011. (Cute & Cuddly: Baby Animals Ser.). 24p. (gr. k-2). (J). pap. 8.15 *(978-1-4339-5528-0(8));* (J). lib. bdg. 22.60 *(978-1-4339-5526-6(1));* 69.20 *(978-1-4339-6892-1(4))* Stevens, Gareth Publishing LLLP.

Kissock, Heather. Heather Kissock. 2015. (Illus.). 24p. (J). *(978-1-4896-4113-7(0))* Weigl Pubs., Inc.

Latta, Jan. Koby el Koala. 2007. (Familias de animales salvajes (Wild Animal Families) Ser.). (SPA., Illus.). 24p. (gr. 1-4). pap. 8.15 *(978-0-8368-7975-9(9));* lib. bdg. 24.00 *(978-0-8368-7968-1(6))* Stevens, Gareth Publishing LLLP. (Gareth Stevens Learning Library).

Marsh, Laura. National Geographic Readers: Koalas. 2014. (Readers Ser.). (ENG., Illus.). 32p. (J). (gr. -1-1). lib. bdg. 13.90 *(978-1-4263-1467-4(1),* National Geographic Children's Bks.) National Geographic Society.

Marsico, Katie. Koala Bears. 2012. (21st Century Basic Skills Library: Baby Zoo Animals Ser.). (ENG.). 24p. (gr. k-3). 22.79 *(978-1-61080-457-8(0),* 202067); pap. 12.79 *(978-1-61080-631-2(X),* 202241) Cherry Lake Publishing.

Murray, Julie. Koalas, 1 vol. 2011. (Australian Animals Ser.). (ENG., Illus.). 32p. (J). (gr. 2-5). 28.50 *(978-1-61783-012-9(7))* ABDO Publishing Co.

Murray, Laura K. Koala. 2015. (Illus.). 32p. (J). *(978-1-60818-562-7(1),* Creative Education) Creative Co., The.

—Koala: Grow with Me. 2016. (Grow with Me Ser.). (ENG.). 32p. (J). (gr. 3-5). pap. 9.99 *(978-1-62832-163-0(6),* Creative Paperbacks) Creative Co., The.

Otfinoski, Steven. Koalas. 2007. (Animals Animals Ser.). (Illus.). 48p. (gr. 3-7). lib. bdg. 29.93 *(978-0-7614-2526-7(8),* Benchmark Bks.) Marshall Cavendish Corp.

Owen, Ruth. Koalas, 1. 2014. (Dr. Bob's Amazing World of Animals Ser.). (ENG.). 32p. (J). (gr. k-5). 27.50 *(978-1-4777-9024-3(1),* Windmill Bks.) Rosen Publishing Group, Inc., The.

JKL

Phillips, Dee. Koala. 2013. (Science Slam: Treed-Animal Life in the Trees Ser.). 24p. (J). (gr. -1-3). lib. bdg. 23.93 *(978-1-61772-916-4(7))* Bearport Publishing Co., Inc.

Pingry, Patricia A. Baby Koala. 2003. (San Diego Zoo Animal Library: Vol. 3). (ENG., Illus.). 24p. (J). bds. 6.95 *(978-0-8249-6528-0(0),* Ideal Pubns.) Worthy Publishing.

Pohl, Kathleen. Koalas. 2007. (Let's Read about Animals/ Conozcamos a los animales Ser.). (SPA., Illus.). 24p. (gr. k-3). lib. bdg. 22.00 *(978-0-8368-8007-6(2),* Weekly Reader Leveled Readers) Stevens, Gareth Publishing LLLP.

Riggs, Kate. Seedlings: Koalas. 2015. (Seedlings Ser.). (ENG.). 24p. (J). (gr. -1-1). pap. 7.99 *(978-1-62832-044-2(3),* Creative Paperbacks) Creative Co., The.

Riley, Joelle. Koalas. 2005. (Early Bird Nature Bks.). (ENG., Illus.). 48p. (gr. 2-5). lib. bdg. 26.60 *(978-0-8225-2870-8(3),* Lerner Pubns.) Lerner Publishing Group.

Rose, Deborah Lee. Jimmy the Joey: The True Story of an Amazing Koala Rescue. Rose, Deborah Lee, photos by. 2013. (ENG., Illus.). 32p. (J). (gr. -1-3). lib. bdg. 25.90 *(978-1-4263-1372-1(1),* National Geographic Children's Bks.) National Geographic Society.

Rose, Deborah Lee & Kelly, Susan. Jimmy the Joey: The True Story of an Amazing Koala Rescue. Kelly, Susan, photos by. 2013. (ENG., Illus.). 32p. (J). (gr. -1-3). 16.95 *(978-1-4263-1371-4(3),* National Geographic Children's Bks.) National Geographic Society.

Schuetz, Kari. Koalas. 2011. (Animal Safari Ser.). (ENG., Illus.). 24p. (J). (gr. k-3). lib. bdg. 25.95 *(978-1-60014-607-7(4),* Blastoff! Readers) Bellwether Media.

Szymanski, Jennifer. Climb, Koala! 2017. (Readers Ser.). (ENG., Illus.). 24p. (J). (-k). pap. 3.99 ***(978-1-4263-2784-1(6),*** National Geographic Children's Bks.) National Geographic Society.

—National Geographic Readers: Climb, Koala! 2017. (Readers Ser.). (ENG.). 24p. (J). (-k). lib. bdg. 13.90 ***(978-1-4263-2785-8(4),*** National Geographic Children's Bks.) National Geographic Society.

KOALA—FICTION

Angel, Ido. Vipo in Australia: The Koala & the Kangaroo. 2015. (AV2 Animated Storytime Ser.). (ENG.). (J). lib. bdg. 29.99 *(978-1-4896-3905-9(5),* AV2 by Weigl) Weigl Pubs., Inc.

Azman, Hacer. The Adventures of Kyle. 2011. (ENG.). 96p. (J). (gr. k-1). 14.95 *(978-1-59784-231-0(1))* Tughra Bks.

Bettinger, John & Kina. Koa Becomes a Friend. 2012. 32p. (-18). pap. 13.95 *(978-1-4497-6153-0(4),* WestBow Pr.) Author Solutions, Inc.

Book Buddy: Koala with Story Book. Orig. Title: Child's Play. (Illus.). 10p. (J). (gr. -1-4). reprint ed. *(978-1-881469-43-8(3))* Safari, Ltd.

Brown, Gina Bates. Zen & Bodhi's Snowy Day. Hinder, Sarah Jane, illus. 2014. (ENG.). 24p. (J). 15.95 *(978-1-61429-165-7(9))* Wisdom Pubns.

Craig, Bobby & Manifold, Delwyn. The Learning Adventures of Spot. 2011. 28p. pap. 24.95 *(978-1-4560-3110-7(4))* America Star Bks.

Dennard, Deborah. Koala Country: A Story of an Australian Eucalyptus Forest. 2005. (Soundprints' Wild Habitats Ser.). (ENG., Illus.). 32p. (J). (gr. 1-4). 8.95 *(978-1-59249-106-3(5),* SC7018) Soundprints.

Dennis, Jen. Snoozy Sam. 2013. 42p. pap. *(978-1-922204-78-3(1))* Vivid Publishing.

deRubertis, Barbara. Kylie Kangaroo's Karate Kickers. Alley, R. W., illus. 2011. (Animal Antics A to Z Ser.). 32p. (J). pap. 45.32 *(978-0-7613-7657-6(7));* (ENG.). lib. bdg. 22.60 *(978-1-57565-332-7(X));* (gr. -1-3). pap. 7.95 *(978-1-57565-323-5(0))* Kane Press, Inc.

deRubertis, Barbara & DeRubertis, Barbara. Kylie Kangaroo's Karate Kickers. Alley, R. W., illus. 2012. (Animal Antics A to Z Ser.). 32p. (J). (gr. 2 — 1). cd-rom 7.95 *(978-1-57565-404-1(0))* Kane Press, Inc.

Dodd, Emma. Everything. Dodd, Emma, illus. 2015. (Emma Dodd's Love You Bks.). (ENG., Illus.). 24p. (J). (-k). 12.99 *(978-0-7636-7128-0(2),* Templar) Candlewick Pr.

Earl, David G. Koala Koala, I'm Not a Bear, I'm a Koala. Gentry, T. Kyle, illus. 2009. 32p. pap. 12.95 *(978-1-936051-22-9(2))* Peppertree Pr., The.

Galvin, Laura. Baby Koala & Mommy. 2008. (Smithsonian Baby Animals Ser.). (ENG., Illus.). 16p. (gr. -1-k). 13.95 *(978-1-59249-791-1(8))* Soundprints.

Galvin, Laura Gates. Baby Koala & Mommy. 2007. (Baby Animals Ser.). (ENG., Illus.). 16p. (gr. -1-k). 6.95 *(978-1-59249-744-7(6))* Soundprints.

Gehl, Laura. Koala Challah. Mola, Maria, illus. 2017. (ENG.). 24p. (gr. -1-1). 17.99 ***(978-1-5124-2087-6(5));*** pap. 7.99 ***(978-1-5124-2088-3(3))*** Lerner Publishing Group. (Kar-Ben Publishing).

Goldhawk, Emma. Cuddly Koala. Lambert, Jonathan, illus. 2015. (Snuggle Puppet Ser.). (ENG.). 10p. bds. 14.95 *(978-1-62686-328-6(8),* Silver Dolphin Bks.) Readerlink Distribution Services, LLC.

Griffiths, Andy. Killer Koalas from Outer Space & Lots of Other Very Bad Stuff That Will Make Your Brain Explode! Denton, Terry, illus. 2012. (ENG.). 192p. (J). (gr. 3-7). pap. 7.99 *(978-1-250-01017-9(9),* 9781250010179) Square Fish.

Hamilton, Martha & Weiss, Mitch. Why Koala Has a Stumpy Tail. Wrenn, Tom, illus. 2007. (Story Cove Ser.). (ENG.). 24p. (J). (gr. -1-3). pap. 4.95 *(978-0-87483-879-4(7))* August Hse. Pubs., Inc.

Harrison, Paula. The Rainbow Opal. 2014. (Rescue Princesses Ser.: 11). lib. bdg. 14.75 *(978-0-606-35837-8(4))* Turtleback Bks.

Kylie's Concert: Evaluation Guide. 2006. (J). *(978-1-55942-413-4(3))* Witcher Productions.

Kylie's Song: Evaluation Guide. 2006. (J). *(978-1-55942-414-1(1))* Witcher Productions.

Lang, Valerie E. Jet's Day: A Whisker Team Story. 2011. 32p. pap. 13.00 *(978-1-61204-178-0(7),* Strategic Bk. Publishing) Strategic Book Publishing & Rights Agency (SBPRA).

Larson, Angela. Harry Hiccers: Friends of A Feether. 2012. pap. *(978-1-4507-7996-8(4))* Independent Pub.

Law, Felicia. Kimberly the Koala: A Tale of Independence. Danson, Lesley, illus. 2010. (Animal Fair Values Ser.). (ENG.). 32p. (J). (gr. -1-3). pap. 10.55 *(978-1-60754-909-3(3));* lib. bdg. 22.60 *(978-1-60754-902-4(6))* Windmill Bks.

McGee, Warner, illus. Run, Run, Koala! 2010. (Go, Diego, Go! Ser.). (ENG.). 24p. (J). (gr. -1-2). pap. 3.99 *(978-1-4169-9937-9(X),* Simon Spotlight/Nickelodeon) Simon Spotlight/Nickelodeon.

Meadows, Daisy. Kimberly the Koala Fairy. 2015. (Baby Animal Rescue Fairies Ser.: 5). (ENG.). 80p. (J). (gr. 2-5). pap. 4.99 *(978-0-545-70854-8(0),* Scholastic Paperbacks) Scholastic, Inc.

Sakmar-Sullivan, Eva M. Kangaroo's Out of This World Restaurant, 1 vol. Sakmar-Sullivan, Eva M., illus. 2013. (ENG., Illus.). 32p. (J). 14.99 *(978-0-7643-4519-7(2),* 9780764345197) Schiffer Publishing, Ltd.

Smith, Clara Batton. Elliott & Anastaci. Smith, Clara Batton, illus. 2012. (Illus.). 16p. pap. 9.95 *(978-1-61633-233-4(6))* Guardian Angel Publishing, Inc.

Storti, Jill. Keiko the Koala. 2011. 24p. (gr. -1 — 1). pap. 12.95 *(978-1-4567-3110-6(6))* AuthorHouse.

Tabernik, John. Ricky the Picky Koala. Wise, Catlin, illus. 2005. (J). 14.95 *(978-0-9773936-0-2(7))* Little Munchkin Bks.

Thompson, Michael. Los Otros Osos, 1 vol. Thompson, Michael, illus. 2013. (SPA., Illus.). 32p. (J). pap. 6.99 *(978-1-59572-664-3(0))* Star Bright Bks., Inc.

—Los Otros Osos / the Other Bears. Thompson, Michael, illus. 2013. (ENG & SPA., Illus.). (J). 16.99 *(978-1-59572-644-5(6))* Star Bright Bks., Inc.

—The Other Bears, 1 vol. Thompson, Michael, illus. 2013.Tr. of Os Outros Ursos. (ENG., Illus.). 32p. (J). 16.99 *(978-1-59572-638-4(1));* pap. 6.99 *(978-1-59572-639-1(X))* Star Bright Bks., Inc.

Wall, Dorothy. The Complete Adventures of Blinky Bill. 2011. (Illus.). 442p. *(978-1-84902-571-3(1))* Benediction Classics.

Wilt, Gerri Ann, et al. My Little One: A Mother's Lullaby. Sargent, Shannon Marie, illus. 2008. (J). *(978-0-87839-299-5(8))* North Star Pr. of St. Cloud.

KOBAYASHI, ISSA, 1763-1827

Gollub, Matthew. Cool Melons - Turn to Frogs! The Life & Poems of Issa. 2004. (Illus.). (J). (gr. k-3). spiral bd. *(978-0-616-03095-0(9))* Canadian National Institute for the Blind/Institut National Canadien pour les Aveugles.

KOCH, ROBERT, 1843-1910

Tracy, Kathleen. Robert Koch & the Study of Anthrax. 2004. (Uncharted, Unexplored, & Unexplained Ser.). (Illus.). 48p. (J). (gr. 4-8). lib. bdg. 29.95 *(978-1-58415-261-3(3))* Mitchell Lane Pubs., Inc.

KOREA

Behnke, Alison. Kim Jong Il's North Korea. 2007. (Dictatorships Ser.). (ENG., Illus.). 160p. (gr. 9-12). lib. bdg. 38.60 *(978-0-8225-7282-4(6),* Twenty-First Century Bks.) Lerner Publishing Group.

—North Korea in Pictures. 2nd ed. 2005. (Visual Geography Ser.). (Illus.). 80p. (YA). (gr. 7-12). 27.93 *(978-0-8225-1908-9(9))* Lerner Publishing Group.

Bowler, Ann Martin. All about Korea: Stories, Songs, Crafts & More. Barg, Soosoonam, illus. 2011. (ENG.). 64p. (J). (gr. k-4). 16.95 *(978-0-8048-4012-5(1))* Tuttle Publishing.

Brimson, Samuel. Korea, North-Nicaragua, 8 vols., Vol. 5. 2003. (Nations of the World Ser.: Vol. 5). (Illus.). 64p. (gr. 5-12). lib. bdg. 31.00 *(978-0-8368-5489-3(6),* Gareth Stevens Secondary Library) Stevens, Gareth Publishing LLLP.

Choi, Anne Soon. Korean Americans. 2007. (New Immigrants Ser.). (Illus.). 132p. (gr. 6-12). lib. bdg. 30.00 *(978-0-7910-8788-6(3),* Chelsea Hse.) Facts On File, Inc.

Gifford, Clive. North Korea. 2009. (Global Hotspots Ser.). 32p. (gr. 5-18). lib. bdg. 18.56 *(978-0-7614-4761-0(X))* Marshall Cavendish Corp.

Han, Suzanne C. Let's Color Korea-Traditional Lifestyles. 2006. (ENG., Illus.). 24p. (J). (gr. k-3). pap. 12.50 *(978-0-930878-94-8(9))* Hollym International Corp.

Harkrader, Lisa. South Korea: A MyReportLinks. com Book. 2004. (Top Ten Countries of Recent Immigrants Ser.). (Illus.). 48p. (J). lib. bdg. 26.60 *(978-0-7660-5181-2(1),* MyReportLinks.com Bks.) Enslow Pubs., Inc.

Hart, Joyce. Kim Jong Il: Leader of North Korea. 2009. (Newsmakers Ser.). 112p. (gr. 9-10). 63.90 *(978-1-60851-133-4(2))* Rosen Publishing Group, Inc., The.

Hill, Valerie. Korea. 2004. (Ask about Asia Ser.). (Illus.). 48p. (J). (gr. 4-18). lib. bdg. 19.95 *(978-1-59084-206-5(5))* Mason Crest.

Ingram, Scott. Korean Americans. 2006. (World Almanac Library of American Immigration). (Illus.). 48p. (gr. 5-12). pap. 14.05 *(978-0-8368-7328-3(9));* lib. bdg. 31.00 *(978-0-8368-7315-3(7))* Stevens, Gareth Publishing LLLP. (Gareth Stevens Secondary Library).

Jackson, Tom. South Korea. 2007. (Countries of the World Ser.). (ENG., Illus.). 64p. (J). (gr. 5-9). lib. bdg. 27.90 *(978-1-4263-0125-4(1),* National Geographic Children's Bks.) National Geographic Society.

Jones, B. J. Let's Color Korea - Everyday Life in Traditional. 2005. (ENG., Illus.). 26p. (J). (gr. k-3). pap. 12.50 *(978-0-930878-98-6(1))* Hollym International Corp.

Kjelle, Marylou Morano. Korea. 2009. (J). *(978-1-58415-790-8(9))* Mitchell Lane Pubs., Inc.

—Meet Our New Student from Korea. 2008. (Meet Our New Student Ser.). (Illus.). 48p. (YA). (gr. 2-5). lib. bdg. 29.95 *(978-1-58415-649-9(X))* Mitchell Lane Pubs., Inc.

Kwek, Karen & Massé, Johanna. South Korea. 2010. (Welcome to My Country Ser.). 48p. (gr. 3). 28.50 *(978-1-60870-159-9(X))* Marshall Cavendish Corp.

Martin, Jennifer C. The Korean Americans. 2003. (Immigrants in America Ser.). (ENG., Illus.). 112p. (J). (gr. 4-7). lib. bdg. 30.85 *(978-1-59018-079-2(8),* Lucent Bks.) Cengage Gale.

Matray, James Irving. Korea Divided: The Thirty-Eighth Parallel & the Demilitarized Zone. 2004. (Arbitrary Borders Ser.). (Illus.). 120p. (C). (gr. 9-13). 35.00 *(978-0-7910-7829-7(9),* Chelsea Hse.) Facts On File, Inc.

Mis, Melody S. How to Draw South Korea's Sights & Symbols. 2009. (Kid's Guide to Drawing the Countries of the World Ser.). 48p. (gr. 4-4). 53.00 *(978-1-61511-126-8(3),* PowerKids Pr.) Rosen Publishing Group, Inc., The.

Nahm, Andrew C. & Jones, B. J. I Love Korea! Lee, Gi-eun, ed. 2nd ed. 2004. (ENG., Illus.). 86p. (J). (gr. 1-5). 24.50 *(978-0-930878-87-0(6))* Hollym International Corp.

Peterson, Mark. Korea. 2009. (Brief History Ser.). (Illus.). 344p. (C). (gr. 9). 49.50 *(978-0-8160-5085-7(6))* Facts On File, Inc.

Piddock, Charles. North Korea. 2006. (Nations in the News Ser.). (Illus.). 48p. (gr. 5-12). pap. 14.05 *(978-0-8368-6716-9(5));* lib. bdg. 31.00 *(978-0-8368-6709-1(2))* Stevens, Gareth Publishing LLLP. (Gareth Stevens Secondary Library).

Pugliano-Martin, Carol. Discover Seoul. 2006. (J). pap. *(978-1-4108-6424-6(3))* Benchmark Education Co.

—Seoul, Korea. 2006. (J). pap. *(978-1-4108-6421-5(9))* Benchmark Education Co.

Salter, Christopher L. North Korea. 2nd rev. ed. 2007. (Modern World Nations Ser.). (Illus.). 125p. (YA). (gr. 7-12). lib. bdg. 35.00 *(978-0-7910-9513-3(4))* Facts On File, Inc.

—South Korea. 2005. (Modern World Nations Ser.). 150p. (gr. 6-12). 35.00 *(978-0-7910-8662-9(3),* Chelsea Hse.) Facts On File, Inc.

Senker, Cath. North & South Korea. 2012. (Our World Divided Ser.). (ENG., Illus.). 48p. (J). (gr. 5-8). 27.95 *(978-1-4488-6029-6(6),* Rosen Reference) Rosen Publishing Group, Inc., The.

Shalant, Phyllis. Look What We've Brought You from Korea: Crafts, Games, Recipes, Stories & Other Cultural Activities from Korean-Americans. Park, Soyoo H., illus. (J). (gr. 2-18). pap. 7.95 *(978-0-382-24994-5(1))* Silver, Burdett & Ginn, Inc.

Sheen, Barbara. Korea. 2010. (Taste of Culture Ser.). (ENG.). 64p. 30.45 *(978-0-7377-5115-4(0),* Kidhaven) Cengage Gale.

Stickler, John. Land of Morning Calm: Korean Culture Then & Now. Han, Soma, illus. 2003. (Land of Morning Calm Ser.). 32p. (J). (gr. 4-7). 16.95 *(978-1-885008-22-0(8),* Shen's Bks.) Lee & Low Bks., Inc.

—Land of Morning Calm: Korean Culture Then & Now. Han, Soma, illus. 2014. (ENG.). 32p. (J). pap. 8.95 *(978-1-885008-47-3(3),* Shen's Bks.) Lee & Low Bks., Inc.

Suyenaga, Ruth. Korean Children's Day. Kyong-Nan, Nani, illus. 2004. 23p. (J). (gr. 4-8). reprint ed. pap. 15.00 *(978-0-7567-7068-6(8))* DIANE Publishing Co.

Suyenaga, Ruth, et al. Korean Children's Day. Kyong-Nan, Nani, illus. 2005. (Multicultural Celebrations Ser.). 32p. (J). 4.95 *(978-1-59373-011-6(X))* Bunker Hill Publishing, Inc.

Tieck, Sarah. Psy: Gangnam Style Rapper, 1 vol. 2013. (Big Buddy Biographies Set 10 Ser.). (ENG.). 32p. (J). (gr. 2-5). lib. bdg. 28.50 *(978-1-61783-860-6(8),* Big Buddy Bks.) ABDO Publishing Co.

Walters, Tara. North Korea. 2008. (True Bks.). (ENG.). 48p. (J). pap. 6.95 *(978-0-531-20728-4(5));* (Illus.). (gr. 3-7). 29.00 *(978-0-531-16854-7(9))* Scholastic Library Publishing. (Children's Pr.).

—South Korea. 2008. (True Book(tm), A — Countries Ser.). (ENG., 48p. (J). Illus.). (gr. 3-7). 31.00 *(978-0-531-16855-4(7));* pap. 6.95 *(978-0-531-20729-1(3))* Scholastic Library Publishing. (Children's Pr.).

Weber, Valerie J. I Come from South Korea. 2006. (This Is My Story Ser.). (Illus.). 24p. (gr. 1-4). lib. bdg. 22.00 *(978-0-8368-7237-8(1),* Weekly Reader Leveled Readers) Stevens, Gareth Publishing LLLP.

Weber, Valerie J. & Weber, Valerie J. I Come from South Korea. 2006. (This Is My Story Ser.). (Illus.). 24p. (gr. 1-4). pap. 8.15 *(978-0-8368-7244-6(4),* Weekly Reader Leveled Readers) Stevens, Gareth Publishing LLLP.

KOREA—FICTION

Alexander, Carol. When My Name Was Keoko. Friedland, Joyce & Kessler, Rikki, eds. 2008. (Novel-Ties Ser.). 29p. pap. 16.95 *(978-0-7675-1520-7(X))* Learning Links Inc.

Bohmer, Kara Dale. Walking Sarah: First Day Out. 2013. 32p. *(978-1-4602-0076-6(4));* pap. *(978-1-4602-0077-3(2))* FriesenPress.

Choi, Sook Nyul. Echoes of the White Giraffe. 2007. (ENG., Illus.). 144p. (YA). (gr. 7). pap. 10.95 *(978-0-618-80917-2(1))* Houghton Mifflin Harcourt Publishing Co.

Clamp Staff, contrib. by. Legend of Chun Hyang, Vol. 1. 2004. (Illus.). 192p. (gr. 2-5). pap. 9.99 *(978-1-59182-763-4(9),* Tokyopop Adult) TOKYOPOP, Inc.

Farley, Christina. Gilded, 0 vols. 2014. (Gilded Ser.: 1). (ENG.). 352p. (YA). (gr. 7-13). pap. 9.99 *(978-1-4778-1097-2(8),* 9781477810972) Amazon Publishing.

Groot, De. Black Moon. Spear, Luke, tr. from FRE. Rodrigue, illus. 2007. (Clifton Ser.: 4). (ENG.). 48p. (J). (gr. 4-7). pap. 9.99 *(978-1-905460-30-4(9))* CineBook GBR. Dist: National Bk. Network.

Jolley, Dan. Pigling: A Cinderella Story [A Korean Tale]. Timmons, Anne, illus. 2009. (Graphic Myths & Legends Ser.). (ENG.). 48p. (gr. 4-8). pap. 8.95 *(978-1-58013-825-3(X))* Lerner Publishing Group.

Lee, Marie Myung-Ok. Somebody's Daughter. 2006. (ENG.). 280p. per. 21.00 *(978-0-8070-8389-5(5),* Beacon Pr.) Beacon Pr.

London, C. Alexander. Blood in the Water. 2014. (Tides of War Ser.: 1). (ENG.). 224p. (J). (gr. 5-9). pap. 5.99 *(978-0-545-66298-7(2),* Scholastic Paperbacks) Scholastic, Inc.

Made in Korea: Six-Pack. (Greetings Ser.: Vol. 3). (gr. 3-5). 31.00 *(978-0-7635-1824-0(7))* Rigby Education.

Moon, Young Sook. Across the Tumen: A North Korean Kkotjebi Boy's Quest. 2013.Tr. of 꽃제비 영대: 죽음을 넘어 희망을 찾아간 소년. (ENG.). 344p. (J). pap. 16.99 *(978-1-62412-009-1(1))* Seoul Selection.

Mounts, Samia. Frunk the Skunk. Matricardi, Luca, illus. 2008. (ENG.). 150p. (J). (gr. 4-6). pap. 9.95 *(978-0-9798841-0-8(1))* 4N Publishing LLC.

O'Brien, Anne Sibley. In the Shadow of the Sun. 2017. (ENG.). 304p. (J). (gr. 3-7). 17.99 ***(978-0-545-90574-9(5))*** Scholastic, Inc.

Park, Frances & Park, Ginger. My Freedom Trip: A Child's Escape from North Korea. Jenkins, Debra Reid, illus. 2010. (ENG.). 32p. (J). pap. 11.95 *(978-1-59078-826-4(5))* Boyds Mills Pr.

Park, Frances, et al. Where on Earth Is My Bagel? Lin, Grace, illus. 2003. (Avenues Ser.). (ENG.). 32p. (C). (gr. -1-4). pap. 22.95 *(978-1-58430-033-5(7))* National Geographic School Publishing, Inc.

Park, Linda Sue. Archer's Quest. 2008. (ENG., Illus.). 176p. (J). (gr. 3-7). 6.99 *(978-0-440-42204-4(3),* Yearling) Random Hse. Children's Bks.

—Bee-Bim Bop! Lee, Ho Baek, illus. 2005. (ENG.). 32p. (J). (gr. -1-3). 17.99 *(978-0-618-26511-4(2))* Houghton Mifflin Harcourt Publishing Co.

—The Firekeeper's Son. Downing, Julie, illus. 2009. (ENG.). 40p. (J). (gr. -1-3). pap. 7.99 *(978-0-547-23769-5(3))* Houghton Mifflin Harcourt Publishing Co.

—The Kite Fighters. 2010. (ENG., Illus.). 144p. (J). (gr. 2-5). pap. 7.99 *(978-0-547-32863-8(X))* Houghton Mifflin Harcourt Publishing Co.

—Seesaw Girl. Tseng, Mou-Sien & Tseng, Jean, illus. 2009. (ENG.). 96p. (J). (gr. 2-5). pap. 6.99 *(978-0-547-24888-2(1))* Houghton Mifflin Harcourt Publishing Co.

—A Single Shard. 2011. 9.00 *(978-0-7848-3611-8(6),* Everbind) Marco Bk. Co.

—A Single Shard. unabr. ed. 2004. (Middle Grade Cassette Librariestm Ser.). (J). (gr. 5-9). pap. 36.00 incl. audio *(978-0-8072-1760-3(3),* S YA 349 SP, Listening Library) Random Hse. Audio Publishing Group.

—A Single Shard. 2011. (gr. 5-8). lib. bdg. 18.40 *(978-0-613-57327-6(7),* Turtleback) Turtleback Bks.

—When My Name Was Keoko. 2004. 199p. (J). (gr. 5). 14.65 *(978-0-7569-2928-2(8))* Perfection Learning Corp.

—When My Name Was Keoko. 2012. lib. bdg. 18.40 *(978-0-606-24716-0(5),* Turtleback) Turtleback Bks.

Park, So Hee, creator. The Royal Palace. (Goong Ser.: 15). (ENG., Illus.). (gr. 8-17). 2014. 352p. pap. 25.00 *(978-0-7595-3159-8(5))* 2014. 368p. pap. 25.00 *(978-0-7595-3158-1(7))* Vol. 13. 2013. 384p. pap. 25.00 *(978-0-7595-3157-4(9))* Orbit. (Yen Pr.).

RIGBY. The Moneybag: a Tale from Korea: Third Grade Big Books. 2003. (Rigby on Our Way to English Ser.). (ENG.). 24p. (gr. 3-3). pap. 50.70 *(978-0-7578-4214-6(3))* Rigby Education.

Samson, Lucretia. Hungry Tiger & Clever Rabbit: A Tale from Korea. Bijloo, Adrian, illus. 2016. 24p. (J). pap. *(978-1-927244-58-6(7))* Clean Slate Pr. Ltd.

—Hungry Tiger & Clever Rabbit (Big Book Edition) A Tale from Korea. Bijloo, Adrian, illus. 2016. 24p. (J). pap. *(978-1-927244-68-5(4))* Flying Start Bks.

Schoettler, Joan. Good Fortune in a Wrapping Cloth. Lanan, Jessica, illus. 2011. (ENG.). (J). 17.95 *(978-1-885008-40-4(6),* Shen's Bks.) Lee & Low Bks., Inc.

Sherman, M. Zachary & Iligan, Marlon. Damage Control, 1 vol. Cage, Josef, illus. 2012. (Bloodlines Ser.). (ENG.). 88p. (gr. 4-8). pap. 6.95 *(978-1-4342-3875-7(X));* lib. bdg. 26.65 *(978-1-4342-3765-1(6))* Stone Arch Bks.

Stickler, John C. & Han, Soma. Maya & the Turtle: A Korean Fairy Tale. 2012. (ENG., Illus.). 32p. (J). (gr. -1-3). 14.95 *(978-0-8048-4277-8(9))* Tuttle Publishing.

Stout, Katie M. Hello, I Love You: A Novel. 2015. (ENG.). 304p. (YA). (gr. 7-12). 18.99 *(978-1-250-05259-9(9),* 9781250052599, St. Martin's Griffin) St. Martin's Pr.

Tabak, Lawrence. In Real Life. 2014. (ENG.). 288p. (J). (gr. 7-12). 16.99 *(978-0-8048-4478-9(X))* Tuttle Publishing.

Watkins, Yoko Kawashima & Watkins, Yoko K. So Far from the Bamboo Grove. 2008. (ENG., Illus.). 192p. (J). (gr. 3-7). reprint ed. pap. 5.99 *(978-0-688-13115-9(8))* HarperCollins Pubs.

KOREA (NORTH)

Berlatsky, Noah. North & South Korea. Greenhaven Press Editors, ed. 2013. (Opposing Viewpoints Ser.). (ENG.). 224p. (gr. 10-12). pap. 33.80 *(978-0-7377-6964-7(5));* lib. bdg. 48.80 *(978-0-7377-6963-0(7))* Cengage Gale. (Greenhaven Pr., Inc.).

Foran, Racquel. North Korea, 1 vol. 2013. (Countries of the World Set 2 Ser.). (ENG.). 144p. (J). (gr. 6-12). lib. bdg. 37.07 *(978-1-61783-632-9(X),* Essential Library) ABDO Publishing Co.

Lee, Sungju & McClelland, Susan Elizabeth. Every Falling Star: The True Story of How I Survived & Escaped North Korea. 2016. (ENG.). 336p. (J). (gr. 8-17). 16.95 *(978-1-4197-2132-8(1),* Amulet Bks.) Abrams, Inc.

Murray, Julie. North Korea, 1 vol. 2016. (Explore the Countries Set 3 Ser.). (ENG., Illus.). 40p. (J). (gr. 2-5). 29.93 *(978-1-68078-069-7(7))* ABDO Publishing Co.

Raum, Elizabeth. North Korea, 1 vol. 2012. (Countries Around the World Ser.). (ENG.). 48p. (gr. 3-6). lib. bdg. 33.32 *(978-1-4329-6107-7(1),* NA-h) Heinemann-Raintree.

Rice Jr., Earle. The Evolution of Government & Politics in North & South Korea. 2014. (gr. 4-8). 29.95 *(978-1-61228-588-7(0))* Mitchell Lane Pubs., Inc.

Sonneborn, Liz. North Korea. 2013. (ENG.). 144p. (J). 40.00 *(978-0-531-23678-9(1))* Scholastic Library Publishing.

Wyborny, Sheila. Kim Jong Il. 2009. (People in the News Ser.). (ENG., Illus.). 128p. (gr. 7-10). lib. bdg. 39.40 *(978-1-4205-0091-2(0),* LML02109-242095, Lucent Bks.) Cengage Gale.

KOREA (SOUTH)

Berlatsky, Noah. North & South Korea. Greenhaven Press Editors, ed. 2013. (Opposing Viewpoints Ser.). (ENG.). 224p. (gr. 10-12). pap. 33.80 *(978-0-7377-6964-7(5));* lib. bdg. 48.80 *(978-0-7377-6963-0(7))* Cengage Gale. (Greenhaven Pr., Inc.).

Dalrymple, Lisa. Cultural Traditions in South Korea. 2016. (ENG., Illus.). 32p. (J). lib. bdg. *(978-0-7787-8088-5(0))* Crabtree Publishing Co.

DuBois, Jill & Nevins, Debbie. South Korea. 2015. (J). lib. bdg. *(978-1-62713-369-2(0))* Cavendish Square Publishing.

Dubois, Jill & Nevins, Debbie. South Korea. 2015. (Cultures of the World Ser.). (ENG.). 144p. (J). (gr. 6-6). 47.07 *(978-1-5026-0079-0(X))* Cavendish Square Publishing.

Foran, Racquel. South Korea, 1 vol. 2013. (Countries of the World Set 2 Ser.). (ENG.). 144p. (J). (gr. 6-12). lib. bdg. 37.07 *(978-1-61783-636-7(2),* Essential Library) ABDO Publishing Co.

Kallen, Stuart A. K-Pop: Korea's Musical Explosion. 2014. (Illus.). 64p. (gr. 6-12). lib. bdg. 33.26 *(978-1-4677-2042-7(9),* Twenty-First Century Bks.) Lerner Publishing Group.

Kalman, Bobbie. Spotlight on South Korea. 2013. (ENG., Illus.). 32p. (J). pap. *(978-0-7787-0868-1(3))* Crabtree Publishing Co.

Murray, Julie. South Korea, 1 vol. 2016. (Explore the Countries Set 3 Ser.). (ENG., Illus.). 40p. (J). (gr. 2-5). 29.93 *(978-1-68078-070-3(0))* ABDO Publishing Co.

Raum, Elizabeth. South Korea, 1 vol. 2012. (Countries Around the World Ser.). (ENG.). 48p. (gr. 3-6). pap. 9.95 *(978-1-4329-6139-8(X));* lib. bdg. 33.32 *(978-1-4329-6113-8(6))* Heinemann-Raintree. (NA-h).

Rice Jr., Earle. The Evolution of Government & Politics in North & South Korea. 2014. (gr. 4-8). 29.95 *(978-1-61228-588-7(0))* Mitchell Lane Pubs., Inc.

Rudolph, Jessica. South Korea. 2015. (Countries We Come From Ser.). (ENG., Illus.). 32p. (J). (gr. k-3). lib. bdg. 26.60 *(978-1-62724-854-9(4))* Bearport Publishing Co., Inc.

Salter, Christopher L. South Korea. 2003. (Modern World Nations Ser.). (Illus.). 200p. (J). (gr. 6-12). lib. bdg. 24.95 *(978-0-7910-7050-5(6),* Chelsea Hse.) Facts On File, Inc.

Senker, Cath. Samsung: The Business Behind the Technology. 2016. (Big Brands Ser.). (ENG., Illus.). 32p. (J). (gr. 4-6). 26.65 *(978-1-5124-0591-0(4))* Lerner Publishing Group.

Sheafer, Silvia Anne. Roh Moo-Hyun. 2008. (Modern World Leaders Ser.). (Illus.). 136p. (YA). (gr. 7-12). 30.00 *(978-0-7910-9760-1(9))* Facts On File, Inc.

Somervill, Barbara A. South Korea. 2015. (ENG., Illus.). 144p. (J). lib. bdg. 40.00 *(978-0-531-21255-4(6),* Orchard Bks.) Scholastic Library Publishing.

Yasuda, Anita. South Korea. 2014. (J). *(978-1-4896-3066-7(X))* Weigl Pubs., Inc.

Zobel, Derek. South Korea. 2011. (Exploring Countries Ser.). (ENG., Illus.). 32p. (YA). (gr. 3-7). lib. bdg. 26.95 *(978-1-60014-624-4(4),* Blastoff! Readers) Bellwether Media.

KOREAN AMERICANS

Bryan, Nichol. Korean Americans, 1 vol. 2004. (One Nation Set 2 Ser.). (ENG.). 32p. (gr. k-6). 27.07 *(978-1-59197-530-4(1),* Checkerboard Library) ABDO Publishing Co.

Choi, Anne Soon. Korean Americans. 2007. (New Immigrants Ser.). (Illus.). 132p. (gr. 6-12). lib. bdg. 30.00 *(978-0-7910-8788-6(3),* Chelsea Hse.) Facts On File, Inc.

Harkrader, Lisa. South Korea: A MyReportLinks. com Book. 2004. (Top Ten Countries of Recent Immigrants Ser.). (Illus.). 48p. (J). lib. bdg. 26.60 *(978-0-7660-5181-2(1),* MyReportLinks.com Bks.) Enslow Pubs., Inc.

Ingram, Scott. Korean Americans. 2006. (World Almanac Library of American Immigration). (Illus.). 48p. (gr. 5-12). pap. 14.05 *(978-0-8368-7328-3(9))*; lib. bdg. 31.00 *(978-0-8368-7315-3(7))* Stevens, Gareth Publishing LLLP. (Gareth Stevens Secondary Library).

Martin, Jennifer C. The Korean Americans. 2003. (Immigrants in America Ser.). (ENG., Illus.). 112p. (J). (gr. 4-7). lib. bdg. 30.85 *(978-1-59018-079-2(8),* Lucent Bks.) Cengage Gale.

Moreno, Barry. The Korean Americans. (Major American Immigration Ser.). (YA). 2010. (Illus.). 64p. (gr. 9-12). 22.95 *(978-1-4222-0612-6(2))* 2007. pap. 9.95 *(978-1-4222-0679-9(3))* Mason Crest.

Noonan, Sheila Smith. Korean Immigration. 2005. (Changing Face of North America Ser.). (Illus.). 112p. (YA). lib. bdg. 24.95 *(978-1-59084-693-3(1))* Mason Crest.

Snyder, Gail. Korean Americans. (Successful Americans Ser.). 64p. (YA). 2009. (gr. 9-12). 22.95 *(978-1-4222-0518-1(5))* 2007. (gr. 7-18). pap. 9.95 *(978-1-4222-0864-9(8))* Mason Crest.

Taus-Bolstad, Stacy. Koreans in America. 2005. (In America Ser.). (ENG., Illus.). 80p. (gr. 5-8). lib. bdg. 27.93 *(978-0-8225-4874-4(7),* Lerner Pubns.) Lerner Publishing Group.

Thomas, William David. Korean Americans. 2009. (New Americans Ser.). 80p. (gr. 5). 35.64 *(978-0-7614-4306-3(1))* Marshall Cavendish Corp.

Weber, Valerie J. I Come from South Korea. 2006. (This Is My Story Ser.). (Illus.). 24p. (gr. 1-4). lib. bdg. 22.00 *(978-0-8368-7237-8(1),* Weekly Reader Leveled Readers) Stevens, Gareth Publishing LLLP.

Weber, Valerie J. & Weber, Valerie J. I Come from South Korea. 2006. (This Is My Story Ser.). (Illus.). 24p. (gr. 1-4). pap. 8.15 *(978-0-8368-7244-6(4),* Weekly Reader Leveled Readers) Stevens, Gareth Publishing LLLP.

KOREAN AMERICANS—FICTION

An, Na. A Step from Heaven. 2016. (ENG., Illus.). 160p. (YA). (gr. 7). 17.99 *(978-1-4814-4235-0(X))*; pap. 10.99 *(978-1-4814-4236-7(8))* Simon & Schuster Children's Publishing. (Atheneum/Caitlyn Dlouhy Books).

Avraham, Kate Aver. What Will You Be, Sara Mee? O'Brien, Anne Sibley, illus. 2010. (ENG.). 32p. (J). (gr. -1-3). 16.95 *(978-1-58089-210-0(8))* Charlesbridge Publishing, Inc.

Bahk, Jane. Juna's Jar. Hoshino, Felicia, illus. 2015. (ENG.). 32p. (J). 17.95 *(978-1-60060-853-7(1),* 9781600000000) Lee & Low Bks., Inc.

Balgassi, Haemi. Tae's Sonata. 2005. (Reader's Workshop Ser.). (ENG.). 164p. (C). pap. 19.95 *(978-0-7362-2801-5(2))* National Geographic School Publishing, Inc.

Bonin, Liane. Pretty on the Outside: Fame Unlimited. 2007. 288p. (YA). pap. 9.99 *(978-0-451-22122-3(2),* N A L Trade) Penguin Publishing Group.

Brandon, Anthony G. Moving Day. Yee, Wong Herbert, illus. 2005. (Green Light Readers Level 2 Ser.). (ENG.). 32p. (J). (gr. -1-3). pap. 3.95 *(978-0-15-205652-0(1))* Houghton Mifflin Harcourt Publishing Co.

Farley, Christina. Gilded, 0 vols. 2014. (Gilded Ser.: 1). (ENG.). 352p. (YA). (gr. 7-13). pap. 9.99 *(978-1-4778-1097-2(8),* 9781477810972) Amazon Publishing.

Goo, Maurene. I Believe in a Thing Called Love. 2017. (ENG.). 336p. (YA). 17.99 *(978-0-374-30404-1(1),* 9780374304041, Farrar, Straus & Giroux (BYR)) Farrar, Straus & Giroux.

—Since You Asked... 2013. (YA). pap. *(978-0-545-44822-2(0))*; (ENG.). 272p. (J). (gr. 7). 17.99 *(978-0-545-44821-5(2))* Scholastic, Inc. (Scholastic Pr.).

Han, Jenny. Clara Lee & the Apple Pie Dream. 2014. (ENG.). 160p. (J). (gr. 3-7). pap. 5.99 *(978-0-316-07037-9(8))* Little, Brown Bks. for Young Readers.

Heo, Yumi. Ten Days & Nine Nights: An Adoption Story. Heo, Yumi, illus. 2009. (Rise & Shine Ser.). (ENG., Illus.). 40p. (J). (gr. -1-3). 17.99 *(978-0-375-84718-9(9),* Schwartz & Wade Bks.) Random Hse. Children's Bks.

Jung, Mike. Unidentified Suburban Object. (ENG.). 272p. (J). (gr. 3-7). 2017. pap. 6.99 ***(978-0-545-78227-2(9))*** 2016. 16.99 *(978-0-545-78226-5(0),* Levine, Arthur A. Bks.) Scholastic, Inc.

Kelly, Keith. Peace Comes to Ajani. Kelly, Keith, illus. 2009. (Illus.). 56p. (J). pap. 9.95 *(978-0-932112-59-0(5))* Carolina Wren Pr.

Kent, Rose. Kimchi & Calamari. 2010. (ENG.). 240p. (J). (gr. 3-7). pap. 6.99 *(978-0-06-083771-6(3))* HarperCollins Pubs.

Kline, Suzy. Horrible Harry & the Dragon War. Remkiewicz, Frank, illus. 2003. (Horrible Harry Ser.). (ENG.). 64p. (J). (gr. 2-4). 4.99 *(978-0-14-250166-5(2),* Puffin Books) Penguin Young Readers Group.

—Horrible Harry & the Dragon War. 2003. (Horrible Harry Ser.: 14). lib. bdg. 14.75 *(978-0-613-92539-6(4),* Turtleback) Turtleback Bks.

Making Heaven (Koreans) 76p. (YA). (gr. 6-12). pap. 9.95 *(978-0-8224-3801-4(1))* Globe Fearon Educational Publishing.

Oh, Jina, reader. A Step from Heaven. 2004. 160p. (J). (gr. 6-18). pap. 36.00 incl. audio *(978-0-8072-2287-4(9),* Listening Library) Random Hse. Audio Publishing Group.

Pak, Jiyeon. My Grandpa's Chair. 2017. (ENG.). 32p. (J). (gr. -1-2). 17.99 ***(978-1-5247-0075-1(4))***; lib. bdg. 20.99 ***(978-1-5247-0076-8(2))*** Random Hse. Children's Bks. (Knopf Bks. for Young Readers).

Park, Linda Sue. Archer's Quest. 2008. (ENG., Illus.). 176p. (J). (gr. 3-7). 6.99 *(978-0-440-42204-4(3),* Yearling) Random Hse. Children's Bks.

—Project Mulberry. 2017. (ENG.). 272p. (J). (gr. 5-7). pap. 6.99 *(978-0-544-93521-1(7),* HMH Books For Young Readers) Houghton Mifflin Harcourt Publishing Co.

—Project Mulberry. 2007. 225p. (gr. 4-7). 17.00 *(978-0-7569-7921-8(8))* Perfection Learning Corp.

—Project Mulberry. 2007. (ENG.). 240p. (J). (gr. 3-7). 6.99 *(978-0-440-42163-4(2),* Yearling) Random Hse. Children's Bks.

Recorvits, Helen. My Name Is Yoon. Swiatkowska, Gabi, illus. 2003. (ENG.). 32p. (J). (gr. -1-3). 17.99 *(978-0-374-35114-4(7),* 9780374351144, Farrar, Straus & Giroux (BYR)) Farrar, Straus & Giroux.

—My Name Is Yoon. Swiatkowska, Gabi, illus. 2014. (ENG.). 32p. (J). (gr. -1-3). 6.99 *(978-1-250-05711-2(6),* 9781250057112) Square Fish.

Recorvits, Helen & Recorvits, H. Yoon & the Jade Bracelet. Swiatkowska, Gabi, illus. 2008. (ENG.). 32p. (J). (gr. -1-3). 18.99 *(978-0-374-38689-4(7),* 9780374386894, Farrar, Straus & Giroux (BYR)) Farrar, Straus & Giroux.

Shin, Sun Yung. Cooper's Lesson. Cogan, Kim & Paek, Min, trs. from ENG. Cogan, Kim, illus. 2004. (ENG & KOR.). 32p. (J). 16.95 *(978-0-89239-193-6(0))* Lee & Low Bks., Inc.

—Cooper's Lesson. Cogan, Kim, illus. 2015. (ENG & KOR.). 32p. (J). (gr. k-3). pap. 9.95 *(978-0-89239-361-9(0),* Children's Book Press) Lee & Low Bks., Inc.

Son, John. Finding My Hat. 2005. (First Person Fiction Ser.). (ENG.). 192p. (J). (gr. 7). reprint ed. pap. 6.99 *(978-0-439-43539-0(0),* Scholastic Paperbacks) Scholastic, Inc.

Stokes, Paula. Vicarious. 2016. (Vicarious Ser.). (ENG.). 336p. (YA). 17.99 *(978-0-7653-8094-4(3),* 9780765380944, Tor Teen) Doherty, Tom Assocs., LLC.

Sullivan, Maureen. Cabbages & Queens. Ferrando, Carol, illus. 2010. 57p. (J). pap. *(978-0-9820381-3-0(5))* MoJo InkWorks.

Wait for Me. 2007. 169p. (gr. 4-7). 18.00 *(978-0-7569-7959-1(5))* Perfection Learning Corp.

Williams, Laura E. Slant. 2008. (ENG.). 160p. (J). (gr. 2-8). pap. 6.95 *(978-1-57131-682-0(5))* Milkweed Editions.

Yangsook, Choi. The Name Jar. 2014. (ENG.). 40p. (J). (gr. k-2). 11.24 *(978-1-63245-313-6(4))* Lectorum Pubns., Inc.

Yoo, David. The Detention Club. (ENG.). 304p. (J). (gr. 5). 2012. pap. 6.99 *(978-0-06-178380-7(3))* 2011. 16.99 *(978-0-06-178378-4(1))* HarperCollins Pubs.

Yoo, Paula. Good Enough. 2012. (ENG.). 336p. (YA). (gr. 8). pap. 7.99 *(978-0-06-079090-5(3),* HarperTeen) HarperCollins Pubs.

KOREAN LANGUAGE

Beullens-Maoui, Nathalie, ed. Animals Habitats: Korean, 01 vols., 1. 2016. (Our Wonderful World Ser.). (ENG & SPA.). 8p. (J). pap. 9.35 *(978-1-5081-1239-6(8),* Rosen Classroom) Rosen Publishing Group, Inc., The.

Burke, David. GOLDILOCKS (Korean to English - Level 2) Learn ENGLISH Through Fairy Tales. 2007. (KOR & ENG.). (J). per. 14.95 incl. audio compact disk *(978-1-891888-10-6(2))* Slangman Publishing.

In Our Words. Korean Letter Story. 2012.Tr. of 한글나라; 이야기;. (KOR., Illus.). 66p. (J). 29.99 *(978-1-938040-00-9(7))* In Our Words Inc.

Karapetian, Marjam. Bilingual Content Dictionary: English to Korean. 2004. (KOR & ENG.). 13.95 *(978-0-9767958-0-3(9))*; 4.95 *(978-0-9764829-7-0(5))*; 4.95 *(978-0-9764829-6-3(7))*; 9.95 *(978-0-9764829-8-7(3))*; 15.95 *(978-0-9767958-1-0(7))* WizdomInc.

—Bilingual Content Dictionary: English to Korean: Social Studies - American History Through 1776. 2004. (KOR & ENG.). 14.95 *(978-0-9764829-9-4(1))* WizdomInc.

Kudela, Katy R. My First Book of Korean Words. Translations.com Staff, tr. 2011. (Bilingual Picture Dictionaries Ser.). (MUL.). 32p. (gr. 1-2). pap. 47.70 *(978-1-4296-6166-9(6),* Aplus Bks.) Capstone Press of Coughlan Cos.

Lee, Sungun, et al, creators. Korean Language I: Easy to Learn, 5 vols. 2nd ed. 2004. 152p. (C). pap. 15.00 *(978-0-9762990-1-1(1))* Korean Culture Research, Inc.

Mahoney, Judy. Teach Me Everyday Korean V. 1, Vol 1. 2008. (KOR & ENG., Illus.). 32p. (J). (gr. -1). 19.95 *(978-1-59972-110-1(4))* Teach Me Tapes, Inc.

Milet Publishing Staff. Animals. 2011. (My First Bilingual Book Ser.). (ENG., Illus.). 24p. (J). (gr. k — 1). bds. 8.99 *(978-1-84059-615-1(5))* Milet Publishing.

—Bilingual Visual Dictionary CD-ROM (English-Korean) 2011. (Milet Multimedia Ser.). (ENG & KOR., Illus.). 1p. (J). (gr. k-2). cd-rom 19.95 *(978-1-84059-587-1(6))* Milet Publishing.

—Colors - My First Bilingual Book. 2011. (My First Bilingual Book Ser.). (ENG.). 24p. (J). (gr. k — 1). bds. 7.99 *(978-1-84059-601-4(5))* Milet Publishing.

—My Bilingual Book-Hearing. 2014. (My Bilingual Book Ser.). (ENG & KOR., Illus.). 28p. (J). (gr. -1-k). 9.95 *(978-1-84059-779-0(8))* Milet Publishing.

—My Bilingual Book-Sight. 2014. (My Bilingual Book Ser.). (ENG & KOR., Illus.). 28p. (J). (gr. -1-k). 9.95 *(978-1-84059-795-0(X))* Milet Publishing.

—My Bilingual Book-Smell. 2014. (My Bilingual Book Ser.). (ENG & KOR., Illus.). 28p. (J). (gr. -1-k). 9.95 *(978-1-84059-811-7(5))* Milet Publishing.

—My Bilingual Book-Taste (English-Korean) 2014. (My Bilingual Book Ser.). (ENG & KOR., Illus.). 28p. (J). (gr. -1-k). 9.95 *(978-1-84059-827-8(1))* Milet Publishing.

—My Bilingual Book-Touch. 2014. (My Bilingual Book Ser.). (ENG & KOR., Illus.). 28p. (J). (gr. -1-k). 9.95 *(978-1-84059-843-8(3))* Milet Publishing.

—My First Bilingual Book - Fruit. 2011. (My First Bilingual Book Ser.). (ENG., Illus.). 24p. (J). (gr. k — 1). bds. 7.99 *(978-1-84059-631-1(7))* Milet Publishing.

—My First Bilingual Book - Home. 2011. (My First Bilingual Book Ser.). (ENG., Illus.). 24p. (J). (gr. k — 1). bds. 7.99 *(978-1-84059-647-2(3))* Milet Publishing.

—My First Bilingual Book-Jobs (English-Korean) 2012. (My First Bilingual Book Ser.). (ENG & KOR., Illus.). 24p. (J). (gr. k — 1). bds. 7.99 *(978-1-84059-707-3(0))* Milet Publishing.

—My First Bilingual Book-Music (English-Korean) 2012. (My First Bilingual Book Ser.). (ENG & KOR., Illus.). 24p. (J). (gr. k — 1). bds. 7.99 *(978-1-84059-723-3(2))* Milet Publishing.

—My First Bilingual Book-Opposites (English-Korean) 2012. (My First Bilingual Book Ser.). (ENG & KOR., Illus.). 24p. (J). (gr. k — 1). bds. 7.99 *(978-1-84059-739-4(9))* Milet Publishing.

—My First Bilingual Book-Sports (English-Korean) 2012. (My First Bilingual Book Ser.). (ENG & KOR., Illus.). 24p. (J). (gr. k — 1). bds. 7.99 *(978-1-84059-755-4(0))* Milet Publishing.

—My First Bilingual Book-Vegetables. 2011. (My First Bilingual Book Ser.). (ENG., Illus.). 24p. (J). (gr. k — 1). bds. 7.99 *(978-1-84059-663-2(5))* Milet Publishing.

Park, Kyubyong & Amen, Henry J. My First Book of Korean Words: An ABC Rhyming Book. Padron, Aya, illus. 2012. (ENG.). 26p. (J). (gr. -1-3). 12.95 *(978-0-8048-4273-0(6))* Tuttle Publishing.

Pihl, Marshall R. Korean Word Book. 2004. (KOR., Illus.). 112p. pap. 14.95 *(978-1-57306-197-1(2))* Bess Pr., Inc.

The Rosetta Stone Language Library: Korean Level 1. 2005. (J). (gr. 1-18). cd-rom 209.00 *(978-1-883972-78-3(7))* Rosetta Stone Ltd.

Turhan, Sedat. New Bilingual Visual Dictionary (English-Korean) 2017. (New Bilingual Visual Dictionary Ser.). (ENG & KOR., Illus.). 144p. (J). (gr. k-2). 19.95 ***(978-1-78508-888-9(2))*** Milet Publishing.

KOREAN WAR, 1950-1953

Blohm, Craig E. Cause & Effect: The Korean War. 2017. (ENG.). 80p. (YA). (gr. 5-12). ***(978-1-68282-164-0(1))*** ReferencePoint Pr., Inc.

Burgan, Michael. The Korean War: An Interactive Modern History Adventure, 1 vol. 2014. (You Choose: Modern History Ser.). (ENG.). 112p. (gr. 3-4). lib. bdg. 31.99 *(978-1-4914-0355-6(1),* You Choose Bks.) Capstone Press of Coughlan Cos.

Conway, John Richard. Primary Source Accounts of the Korean War. 2006. (America's Wars Through Primary Sources Ser.). (Illus.). 128p. (J). (gr. 4-7). lib. bdg. 34.60 *(978-1-59845-003-3(4),* MyReportLinks.com Bks.) Enslow Pubs., Inc.

Doak, Robin S. The Korean War. 2006. (Wars That Changed American History Ser.). (Illus.). 48p. (gr. 5-12). pap. 14.05 *(978-0-8368-7303-0(3),* Gareth Stevens Secondary Library) Stevens, Gareth Publishing LLLP.

Feldman, Ruth Tenzer. The Korean War. 2004. (Chronicle of America's Wars Ser.). (Illus.). 96p. (J). (gr. 5-12). 27.93 *(978-0-8225-4716-7(3))* Lerner Publishing Group.

George, Enzo. The Korean War: Showdown with China. 2014. (Voices of War Ser.). 48p. (J). (gr. 4-6). lib. bdg. 31.36 *(978-1-62712-870-4(0))* Cavendish Square Publishing.

Grant, Reg. The Korean War. 2004. (Atlas of Conflicts Ser.). (Illus.). 64p. (gr. 6-12). pap. 14.05 *(978-0-8368-5673-6(2))*; lib. bdg. 34.00 *(978-0-8368-5666-8(X))* Stevens, Gareth Publishing LLLP. (Gareth Stevens Secondary Library).

Gruenberg, Leif A. The Korean War. 2004. (Defining Moments Ser.). (Illus.). 265p. 55.00 *(978-0-7808-0766-2(9))* Omnigraphics, Inc.

Higgins, Melissa. Sgt. Reckless - The War Horse: Korean War Hero. Iglesias, Alvaro, illus. 2014. (Animal Heroes Ser.). (ENG.). 32p. (gr. k-2). 28.65 *(978-1-4795-5462-1(6))* Picture Window Bks.

Hosch, William L. Korean War & the Vietnam War: People, Politics, & Power. 2009. (America at War Ser.). (Illus.). 232p. (YA). (gr. 9-12). lib. bdg. 49.00 *(978-1-61530-011-2(2))* Rosen Publishing Group, Inc., The.

—The Korean War & the Vietnam War: People, Politics, & Power. 2009. (America at War Ser.). (ENG.). 232p. (YA). 98.00 *(978-1-61530-088-4(0))* Rosen Publishing Group, Inc., The.

Isserman, Maurice. Korean War. 3rd rev. ed. 2010. (America at War Ser.). (Illus.). 184p. (gr. 6-12). 45.00 *(978-0-8160-8186-8(7),* Chelsea Hse.) Facts On File, Inc.

Jeffrey, Gary & Riley, Terry, illus. The Korean War. 2013. (ENG.). 48p. (J). *(978-0-7787-1234-3(6))*; pap. *(978-0-7787-1238-1(9))* Crabtree Publishing Co.

MacCarald, Clara. The Battle of Inchon: Turning Point of the Korean War. 2017. (Major Battles in US History (hardcover) Ser.). (ENG., Illus.). 32p. (J). (gr. 4-7). lib. bdg. 28.50 ***(978-1-63517-019-1(2),*** Focus Readers) North Star Editions.

Malkasian, Carter. The Korean War. 2008. (Essential Histories: War & Conflict in Modern Times Ser.). (Illus.). 96p. (YA). (gr. 9-12). lib. bdg. 33.25 *(978-1-4042-1834-5(3))* Rosen Publishing Group, Inc., The.

McCormick, Patricia. Sergeant Reckless: The True Story of the Little Horse Who Became a Hero. Bruno, Iacopo, illus. 2017. 40p. (J). (gr. 1-5). 17.99 ***(978-0-06-229259-9(5))*** HarperCollins Pubs.

Miller, Derek L. Minority Soldiers Fighting in the Korean War. 2017. (J). ***(978-1-5026-2665-3(9))*** Cavendish Square Publishing.

Moore, Shannon Baker. Korean War, 1 vol. 2013. (Essential Library of American Wars Ser.). (ENG.). 112p. (J). (gr. 6-12). lib. bdg. 35.64 *(978-1-61783-878-1(0),* Essential Library) ABDO Publishing Co.

Perritano, John. Korean War. 2010. (America at War Ser.). 32p. (J). 27.00 *(978-0-531-23207-1(7),* Watts, Franklin) Scholastic Library Publishing.

Reece, Richard. The Korean War, 1 vol. 2011. (Essential Events Set 6 Ser.). (ENG., Illus.). 112p. (J). (gr. 6-12). lib. bdg. 35.64 *(978-1-61714-766-1(4))* ABDO Publishing Co.

Rice, Earle. Korea 1950: From Pusan to Chosin. 2003. (Great Battles Through the Ages Ser.). (Illus.). 112p. (gr. 6-12). 30.00 *(978-0-7910-7436-7(6),* Chelsea Hse.) Facts On File, Inc.

—Overview of the Korean War. 2008. (Monumental Milestones Ser.). (Illus.). 48p. (YA). (gr. 4-7). lib. bdg. 29.95 *(978-1-58415-695-6(3))* Mitchell Lane Pubs., Inc.

Seth, Shaun. Key Figures of the Korean War. 2015. (Biographies of War Ser.). (ENG., Illus.). 112p. (J). (gr. 7-8). 32.90 *(978-1-68048-060-3(X),* Britannica Educational Publishing) Rosen Publishing Group, Inc., The.

Seth, Shaun, ed. Key Figures of the Korean War. 2015. (Biographies of War Ser.). (ENG.). 112p. (YA). (gr. 7-8). 65.80 *(978-1-68048-061-0(8),* Britannica Educational Publishing) Rosen Publishing Group, Inc., The.

Small, Cathleen. Strategic Inventions of the Korean War. 2016. (Tech in the Trenches Ser.). 112p. (J). 42.79 *(978-1-5026-2345-4(5))* Cavendish Square Publishing.

Streissguth, Tom. The Korean War. 2015. (Wars in U. S. History Ser.). (ENG.). 32p. (J). (gr. 2-5). 28.50 *(978-1-63143-710-6(0),* 208538) Child's World, Inc., The.

Young, Jeff C. The Korean War: A MyReportLinks. Com Book. 2003. (U.S. Wars Ser.). (Illus.). 48p. (J). lib. bdg. 26.60 *(978-0-7660-5148-5(X))* Enslow Pubs., Inc.

Ziff, John. The Korean War, Vol. 11. Musteen, Jason R., ed. 2015. (Major U. S. Historical Wars Ser.). (Illus.). 64p. (J). (gr. 7). lib. bdg. 23.95 *(978-1-4222-3356-6(1))* Mason Crest.

KOREAN WAR, 1950-1953—FICTION

Sherman, M. Zachary. Blood Brotherhood, 1 vol. Casas, Fritz, illus. 2011. (Bloodlines Ser.). (ENG.). 88p. (gr. 4-8). pap. 6.95 *(978-1-4342-3098-0(8))*; 26.65 *(978-1-4342-2559-7(3))* Stone Arch Bks.

Sherman, M. Zachary & Iligan, Marlon. Damage Control, 1 vol. Cage, Josef, illus. 2012. (Bloodlines Ser.). (ENG.). 88p. (gr. 4-8). pap. 6.95 *(978-1-4342-3875-7(X))*; lib. bdg. 26.65 *(978-1-4342-3765-1(6))* Stone Arch Bks.

Williams, Annie Morris. Marianne's Secret Cousins. Oldham, Cindi, illus. 2005. (Family History Adventures for Young Readers Ser.: 2). 240p. (J). per. 10.00 *(978-0-9645272-8-7(6))* Field Stone Pubs.

KOREANS—UNITED STATES

Thomas, William David. Korean Americans. 2009. (New Americans Ser.). 80p. (gr. 5). 35.64 *(978-0-7614-4306-3(1))* Marshall Cavendish Corp.

Yoo, Paula. Sixteen Years in Sixteen Seconds: The Sammy Lee Story, 1 vol. Lee, Dom, illus. 2005. (ENG.). 32p. (J). (gr. 1-5). 16.95 *(978-1-58430-247-6(X))* Lee & Low Bks., Inc.

KOREANS—UNITED STATES—FICTION

Choi, Yangsook. The Name Jar. 2003. (gr. k-3). lib. bdg. 18.40 *(978-0-613-82979-3(4),* Turtleback) Turtleback Bks.

KOUFAX, SANDY, 1935-

Doeden, Matt. Sandy Koufax. 2007. (YA). pap. 9.95 *(978-0-8225-6692-2(3))* 2006. (Illus.). 106p. (J). (gr. 3-7). lib. bdg. 27.93 *(978-0-8225-5961-0(7),* Twenty-First Century Bks.) Lerner Publishing Group.

Giordano, Geraldine. Sandy Koufax. (Baseball Hall of Famers Ser.). 112p. (gr. 5-8). 2009. 63.90 *(978-1-61511-516-7(1))* 2003. (Illus.). lib. bdg. 34.60 *(978-0-8239-3603-8(1))* Rosen Publishing Group, Inc., The. (Rosen Reference).

Winter, Jonah. You Never Heard of Sandy Koufax?! Carrilho, Andre, illus. 2016. (ENG.). 40p. (J). (gr. -1-3). 7.99 *(978-0-553-49842-4(8),* Dragonfly Bks.) Random Hse. Children's Bks.

KU KLUX KLAN (1915-)

Bartoletti, Susan Campbell. They Called Themselves the K. K. K. The Birth of an American Terrorist Group. (ENG., Illus.). 176p. (YA). (gr. 7). 2014. pap. 12.99 *(978-0-544-22582-4(1),* HMH Books For Young Readers) 2010. 19.00 *(978-0-618-44033-7(X))* Houghton Mifflin Harcourt Publishing Co.

—They Called Themselves the K. K. K. The Birth of an American Terrorist Group. 2014. lib. bdg. 24.50 *(978-0-606-35334-2(8))* Turtleback Bks.

Bowers, Rick. Superman Versus the Ku Klux Klan: The True Story of How the Iconic Superhero Battled the Men of Hate. 2012. (Illus.). 160p. pap. *(978-0-545-43745-5(8))* Scholastic, Inc.

Brimner, Larry Dane. Birmingham Sunday. 2010. (ENG., Illus.). 48p. (J). (gr. 5-18). 17.95 *(978-1-59078-613-0(0),* Calkins Creek) Boyds Mills Pr.

KU KLUX KLAN (1915-)—FICTION

Coleman, Evelyn. Circle of Fire. 2009. (Mysteries Through Time Ser.). 160p. (YA). (gr. 4-8). 31.95 *(978-1-60754-191-2(2))*; pap. 15.25 *(978-1-60754-192-9(0))* Windmill Bks.

Crawford, Ann Fears. Keechee: The Witch of the Woods. 2005. (J). *(978-1-931823-21-0(9))* Halcyon Pr.

Hesse, Karen. Witness. 2004. 168p. (J). (gr. 5-9). pap. 29.00 incl. audio *(978-0-8072-2094-8(9),* Listening Library) Random Hse. Audio Publishing Group.

—Witness. 2003. (ENG., Illus.). 176p. (J). (gr. 3-7). pap. 7.99 *(978-0-439-27200-1(9),* Scholastic Paperbacks) Scholastic, Inc.

Shan, Darren, pseud. Zom-B, Vol. 8. 2014. (Zom-B Ser.: 8). (ENG., Illus.). 192p. (YA). (gr. 7-17). 15.99 *(978-0-316-21429-2(9))* Little, Brown Bks. for Young Readers.

Stanley, George E. Night Fires. 2009. (ENG.). 192p. (J). (gr. 3-7). 15.99 *(978-1-4169-7559-5(4),* Simon & Schuster/Paula Wiseman Bks.) Simon & Schuster/Paula Wiseman Bks.

Stanley, George Edward. Night Fires. 2011. (ENG.). 192p. (J). (gr. 3-7). pap. 6.99 *(978-1-4169-1250-7(9),* Simon & Schuster/Paula Wiseman Bks.) Simon & Schuster/Paula Wiseman Bks.

Vander Zee, Ruth. Mississippi Morning. Cooper, Floyd, illus. 2004. 32p. (J). 16.00 *(978-0-8028-5211-3(4))* Eerdmans, William B. Publishing Co.

KUBLAI KHAN, 1216-1294

Krull, Kathleen. Kubla Khan: The Emperor of Everything. Byrd, Robert, illus. 2010. (ENG.). 48p. (J). (gr. 3-7). 17.99 *(978-0-670-01114-8(2),* Viking Books for Young Readers) Penguin Young Readers Group.

Sepahban, Lois. Mongol Warriors. 2015. (Ancient Warriors Ser.). (ENG.). 32p. (J). (gr. 2-5). 28.50 *(978-1-63143-756-4(9),* 208588) Child's World, Inc., The.

KUBLAI KHAN, 1216-1294—FICTION

Jones Yang, Dori. Daughter of Xanadu. 2012. (ENG.). 352p. (YA). (gr. 7). pap. 9.99 *(978-0-385-73924-5(9)*, Ember) Random Hse. Children's Bks.

McCaughrean, Geraldine. The Kite Rider. 2003. (Illus.). 320p. (YA). (gr. 8-18). pap. 8.99 *(978-0-06-441091-5(9)*, HarperTeen) HarperCollins Pubs.

Scieszka, Jon. Marco? Polo!, No. 16. McCauley, Adam, illus. 2008. (Time Warp Trio Ser.: 16). (ENG.). 96p. (J). (gr. 2-4). 5.99 *(978-0-14-241177-3(9)*, Puffin Books) Penguin Young Readers Group.

—Marco? Polo! McCauley, Adam, illus. 2008. (Time Warp Trio Ser.: No. 16). 90p. (J). (gr. 4-6). 12.65 *(978-0-7569-8923-1(X))* Perfection Learning Corp.

KUNG FU

Casarella, Antonello & Ghetti, Roberto. A Complete Guide to Kung Fu. 2017. (Mastering Martial Arts Ser.). 128p. (J). (gr. 6-6). lib. bdg. 37.27 ***(978-0-7660-8541-1(4))*** Enslow Pubs., Inc.

Eng, Paul. Kungfu for Kids. Tok, Stephanie, illus. 2016. (Martial Arts for Kids Ser.). (ENG.). 48p. (J). (gr. k-3). 8.95 *(978-0-8048-4740-7(1))* Tuttle Publishing.

Howell, Brian. Kung Fu, 1 vol. 2014. (Inside Martial Arts Ser.). (ENG., Illus.). 48p. (J). (gr. 3-6). lib. bdg. 32.79 *(978-1-62403-604-0(X)*, SportsZone) ABDO Publishing Co.

Johnson, Nathan. Kung Fu: Winning Ways. James, Adam, ed. 2015. (Mastering Martial Arts Ser.). (Illus.). 96p. (J). (gr. 5). lib. bdg. 24.95 *(978-1-4222-3240-8(9))* Mason Crest.

Ollhoff, Jim. Kung Fu, 1 vol. 2008. (World of Martial Arts Ser.). (ENG.). 32p. (gr. 4-8). 27.07 *(978-1-59928-978-6(4)*, Abdo & Daughters) ABDO Publishing Co.

Smith, Tony. Shaolin Monks. 2012. (History's Greatest Warriors Ser.). (ENG., Illus.). 24p. (J). (gr. 3-7). lib. bdg. 25.95 *(978-1-60014-748-7(8)*, Torque Bks.) Bellwether Media.

Warr, Peter. The Kung Fu Handbook. 2008. (Martial Arts Ser.). (Illus.). 256p. (J). (gr. 3-7). lib. bdg. 39.95 *(978-1-4042-1392-0(9))* Rosen Publishing Group, Inc., The.

Wood, Alix. Kung Fu. 2013. (Kid's Guide to Martial Arts Ser.). (ENG., Illus.). 32p. (J). (gr. 3-6). pap. 11.75 *(978-1-4777-0360-1(8))*; lib. bdg. 26.50 *(978-1-4777-0319-9(5))* Rosen Publishing Group, Inc., The. (PowerKids Pr.).

Wouk, Henry & Colligan, Douglas. Kung Fu. 2010. (Martial Arts in Action Ser.). 48p. (gr. 6-7). lib. bdg. 29.93 *(978-0-7614-4937-9(X))* Marshall Cavendish GBR. Dist: Marshall Cavendish Corp.

KUWAIT

DiPiazza, Francesca Davis. Kuwait in Pictures. 2nd ed. 2007. (Visual Geography Series, Second Ser.). (ENG., Illus.). 80p. (gr. 5-12). lib. bdg. 31.93 *(978-0-8225-6589-5(7))* Lerner Publishing Group.

Marcovitz, Hal. Kuwait. 2010. (Major Muslim Nations Ser.). 112p. (YA). (gr. 5-18). lib. bdg. 25.95 *(978-1-4222-1386-5(2))* Mason Crest.

O'Shea, Maria & Spilling, Michael. Kuwait. 2nd rev. ed. 2009. (Cultures of the World 17 Ser.). 144p. (gr. 6). 42.79 *(978-0-7614-4479-4(3))* Marshall Cavendish GBR. Dist: Marshall Cavendish Corp.

Ray, Kurt. A Historical Atlas of Kuwait. (Historical Atlases of South Asia, Central Asia, & the Middle East Ser.). 64p. 2009. (gr. 6-6). 61.20 *(978-1-61513-323-9(2))* 2004. (Illus.). (gr. 7-12). lib. bdg. 31.95 *(978-0-8239-3981-7(2))* Rosen Publishing Group, Inc., The.

Sonnebom, Liz. Kuwait. 2014. (Enchantment of the World Ser.: 2). (ENG.). 144p. (J). lib. bdg. 40.00 *(978-0-531-22015-3(X))* Scholastic Library Publishing.

Tracy, Kathleen. We Visit Kuwait. 2011. (Your Land & My Land Ser.). (Illus.). 64p. (J). (gr. 4-7). lib. bdg. 33.95 *(978-1-58415-958-2(8))* Mitchell Lane Pubs., Inc.

KWANZAA

Aloian, Molly. Kwanzaa. 2008. (Celebrations in My World Ser.). (ENG., Illus.). 32p. (J). (gr. k-3). pap. *(978-0-7787-4302-6(0))* Crabtree Publishing Co.

Altman, Linda Jacobs. Celebrate Kwanzaa. 2008. (Celebrate Holidays Ser.). (Illus.). 104p. (J). (gr. 3-7). lib. bdg. 33.27 *(978-0-7660-2862-3(3))* Enslow Pubs., Inc.

Benn, Lisa. Leroy's Kwanza Lesson. 2009. pap. 16.95 *(978-1-61623-891-9(7))* Independent Pub.

Bullard, Lisa. Kevin's Kwanzaa. Basaluzzo, Constanza, illus. 2012. (Cloverleaf Books (tm) — Fall & Winter Holidays Ser.). (ENG.). 24p. (gr. k-2). 6.95 *(978-0-7613-8588-2(6))*; lib. bdg. 23.93 *(978-0-7613-5075-0(6))* Lerner Publishing Group. (Millbrook Pr.).

Cain, Marie Mowery. Celebrate Kwanzaa. 2013. (Big Books, Red Ser.). (ENG & SPA., Illus.). 16p. pap. 33.00 *(978-1-59246-223-0(5))* Big Books, by George!

Corwin, Judith Hoffman. Kwanzaa Crafts: A Holiday Craft Book. 2004. (Illus.). 48p. (J). (gr. k-4). reprint ed. pap. 6.00 *(978-0-7567-7711-1(9))* DIANE Publishing Co.

Felix, Rebecca. We Celebrate Kwanzaa in Winter. 2014. (21st Century Basic Skills Library: Let's Look at Winter Ser.). (ENG., Illus.). 24p. (J). (gr. k-3). 22.79 *(978-1-63137-611-5(X)*, 205227) Cherry Lake Publishing.

Freeman, Dorothy Rhodes & MacMillan, Dianne M. Kwanzaa. rev. ed. 2008. (Best Holiday Bks.). (Illus.). 48p. (J). (gr. 3-7). lib. bdg. 25.27 *(978-0-7660-3042-8(3))* Enslow Pubs., Inc.

Gnojewski, Carol. Kwanzaa: Seven Days of African-American Pride. 2004. (Finding Out about Holidays Ser.). (Illus.). 48p. (J). lib. bdg. 25.27 *(978-0-7660-2209-6(9))* Enslow Pubs., Inc.

—Kwanzaa Crafts. 2004. (Fun Holiday Crafts Kids Can Do! Ser.). (Illus.). 32p. (J). lib. bdg. 23.94 *(978-0-7660-2203-4(X))* Enslow Pubs., Inc.

Heller, Daryl. Kwanzaa. 2009. (My Library of Holidays Ser.). 24p. (gr. 1-1). 37.50 *(978-1-61514-696-3(2)*, PowerKids Pr.) Rosen Publishing Group, Inc., The.

—Kwanzaa. Gonzalez, Tomas, tr. from ENG. 2004. (My Library of Holidays). (ENG & SPA., Illus.). 24p. (J). (gr. k-1). lib. bdg. 16.00 *(978-1-4042-7528-7(2)*, PowerKids Pr.) Rosen Publishing Group, Inc., The.

—Kwanzaa / Kwanzaa. 2009. (My Library of Holidays / Mi biblioteca de celebraciones Ser.). (ENG & SPA.). 24p. (gr. 1-1). 37.50 *(978-1-61514-702-1(0)*, Editorial Buenas Letras) Rosen Publishing Group, Inc., The.

Herrington, Lisa M. Kwanzaa. 2013. (Rookie Read-About(tm) Holidays Ser.). (ENG.). 32p. (J). 25.00 *(978-0-531-27204-6(4))*; pap. 5.95 *(978-0-531-27354-8(7))* Scholastic Library Publishing.

Hull, Bunny. Happy, Happy Kwanzaa: Kwanzaa for the World. Saint-James, Synthia, illus. 2003. 24p. (J). (gr. k-5). pap. 16.95 incl. audio compact disk *(978-0-9721478-1-1(0)*, KCC/HHKCD810, Kid's Creative Classics) BrassHeart Music.

Johnson, Dolores. The Children's Book of Kwanzaa: A Guide to Celebrating the Holiday. 2007. (Illus.). 159p. (J). pap. 7.00 *(978-1-4223-6600-4(6))* DIANE Publishing Co.

Kwanzaa, 6 vols. (Multicultural Programs Ser.). 16p. (gr. 1-3). 24.95 *(978-0-7802-9208-6(1))* Wright Group/McGraw-Hill.

Marsh, Carole. Kwanzaa: Activities, Crafts, Recipes & More! 2003. 32p. (J). (gr. 1-6). pap. 6.95 *(978-0-635-02173-1(0))* Gallopade International.

McGee, Randel. Paper Crafts for Kwanzaa. (Paper Craft Fun for Holidays Ser.). (Illus.). 48p. (J). (gr. 3-4). 2012. pap. 8.95 *(978-1-4644-0327-9(9))* 2008. lib. bdg. 25.27 *(978-0-7660-2949-1(2))* Enslow Pubs., Inc. (Enslow Elementary).

McKissack, Fredrick L. & McKissack, Lisa Beringer. Kwanzaa-Count & Celebrate! 2009. (Holidays—Count & Celebrate! Ser.). (Illus.). 32p. (J). (gr. k-3). lib. bdg. 23.94 *(978-0-7660-3102-9(0))* Enslow Pubs., Inc.

Murray, Julie. Kwanzaa, 1 vol. 2003. (Holidays Ser.). (ENG.). 24p. (gr. k-4). 25.65 *(978-1-57765-955-6(4)*, Buddy Bks.) ABDO Publishing Co.

Otto, Carolyn B. Celebrate Kwanzaa: With Candles, Community, & the Fruits of the Harvest. 2008. (Holidays Around the World Ser.). (ENG., Illus.). 32p. (J). (gr. 1-4). 15.95 *(978-1-4263-0319-7(X))*; lib. bdg. 23.90 *(978-1-4263-0320-3(3))* National Geographic Society. (National Geographic Children's Bks.).

—Holidays Around the World: Celebrate Kwanzaa: With Candles, Community, & the Fruits of the Harvest. 2010. (Holidays Around the World Ser.). (ENG., Illus.). 32p. (J). (gr. 1-4). pap. 6.95 *(978-1-4263-0705-8(5)*, National Geographic Children's Bks.) National Geographic Society.

Pettiford, Rebecca. Kwanzaa. 2014. (Illus.). 24p. (J). lib. bdg. 25.65 *(978-1-62031-131-8(3)*, Bullfrog Bks.) Jump! Inc.

Ponto, Joanna & Gnojewski, Carol. Kwanzaa. 2016. (Story of Our Holidays Ser.). (Illus.). 32p. (J). (gr. 3-3). pap. 10.52 *(978-0-7660-7621-1(0))* Enslow Pubs., Inc.

Raabe, Emily. A Kwanzaa Holiday Cookbook. 2009. (Festive Foods for the Holidays Ser.). 24p. (gr. 3-3). 42.50 *(978-1-61512-596-8(5)*, PowerKids Pr.) Rosen Publishing Group, Inc., The.

Ross, Kathy. All New Crafts for Kwanzaa. Holm, Sharon Lane, illus. 2006. (All New Holiday Crafts for Kids Ser.). 48p. (J). (gr. -1-3). per. 7.95 *(978-0-8225-3435-8(5)*, First Avenue Editions) Lerner Publishing Group.

Zocchi, Judy. On Kwanzaa. Wallis, Rebecca, illus. 2006. (Global Adventures I Ser.). (J). pap. 10.95 *(978-1-59646-200-7(0))*; 32p. lib. bdg. 21.65 *(978-1-891997-49-5(1))*; 32p. per. 10.95 *(978-1-59646-201-4(9))* Dingles & Co.

—On Kwanzaa/la Kwanzaa. Wallis, Rebecca, illus. 2006. (Global Adventures I Ser.).Tr. of Kwanzaa. (ENG & SPA.). 32p. (J). pap. 10.95 *(978-1-59646-202-1(7))*; lib. bdg. 21.65 *(978-1-891997-50-1(5))*; per. 10.95 *(978-1-59646-203-8(5))* Dingles & Co.

KWANZAA—FICTION

Burden-Patmon, Denise. Imani's Gift at Kwanzaa. (J). 48.95 *(978-0-8136-2248-4(4))* Modern Curriculum Pr.

Flor Ada, Alma. Celebrate Kwanzaa with Boots & Her Kittens. Docampo, Valeria, illus. 2007. (Cuentos para Celebrar / Stories to Celebrate Ser.). 30p. (gr. k-6). per. 11.95 *(978-1-59820-135-2(2))* Santillana USA Publishing Co., Inc.

Katz, Karen. My First Kwanzaa. Katz, Karen, illus. 2014. (My First Holiday Ser.). (ENG., Illus.). 32p. (J). (gr. -1-k). 7.99 *(978-1-250-05046-5(4)*, 9781250050465) Square Fish.

Meachen Rau, Dana. Holiday Time. 2004. (Compass Point Early Reader Ser.). (J). 18.60 *(978-0-7565-0571-4(2))* Compass Point Bks.

Shea, Therese. The Kwanzaa Surprise. 2006. (Neighborhood Readers Ser.). (ENG.). 12p. (gr. -1-3). pap. 5.90 *(978-1-4042-6746-6(8)*, Rosen Classroom) Rosen Publishing Group, Inc., The.

Washington, Donna L. Li'l Rabbit's Kwanzaa. Evans, Shane W., illus. 2010. (ENG.). 32p. (J). (gr. -1-2). 12.99 *(978-0-06-072816-8(7)*, Tegen, Katherine Bks) HarperCollins Pubs.

L

LABOR

Here are entered works on the collective human activities involved in the production and distribution of goods and services. Works on the physical or mental exertion of individuals to produce or accomplish something are entered under Work.

see also Child Labor; Migrant Labor; Working Class

Arnold, Quinn M. Seedlings: Construction Workers. 2017. (Seedlings Ser.). (ENG.). 24p. (J). (gr. -1-1). pap. 7.99 ***(978-1-62832-486-0(4)***, Creative Paperbacks) Creative Co., The.

Barber, Nicola. Ancient Roman Jobs. 2010. (Ancient Communities: Roman Life Ser.). (Illus.). 32p. (J). pap. 10.60 *(978-1-61532-317-3(1))*; (gr. 3-6). lib. bdg. 26.50 *(978-1-61532-307-4(4))* Rosen Publishing Group, Inc., The. (PowerKids Pr.).

Boothroyd, Jennifer. From Assembly Lines to Home Offices: How Work Has Changed. 2011. (Comparing Past & Present Ser.). pap. 7.95 *(978-0-7613-7842-6(1))*; pap. 45.32 *(978-0-7613-8389-5(1))*; (ENG., Illus.). 32p. lib. bdg. 26.60 *(978-0-7613-6748-2(9))* Lerner Publishing Group.

Chambers, Mary & Meinking, Mary. Who Swings the Wrecking Ball? Working on a Construction Site. 2010. (Wild Work Ser.). (ENG.). 32p. (gr. 1-2). 29.99 *(978-1-4109-3854-1(9)*, Read Me!) Heinemann-Raintree.

Farrell, Mary Cronk. Fannie Never Flinched: One Woman's Courage in the Struggle for American Labor Union Rights. 2016. (ENG., Illus.). 56p. (J). (gr. 5-9). 19.95 *(978-1-4197-1884-7(3)*, Abrams Bks. for Young Readers) Abrams, Inc.

Hatton, Fran. Learning about Earning. 2015. (First-Glance Finance Ser.). (ENG.). 48p. (J). (gr. 4-4). 31.36 *(978-1-5026-0094-3(3))* Cavendish Square Publishing.

Horn, Geoffrey M. Construction Worker. 2008. (Cool Careers Ser.). 32p. (gr. 5-8). pap. 10.50 *(978-0-8368-9325-0(5))*; (YA). lib. bdg. 26.00 *(978-0-8368-9192-8(9))* Stevens, Gareth Publishing LLLP.

Kalman, Bobbie. Ayudantes de Mi Comunidad. 2010. (SPA.). 24p. (J). pap. *(978-0-7787-8589-7(0))*; lib. bdg. *(978-0-7787-8563-7(7))* Crabtree Publishing Co.

Macken, JoAnn Early. Sanitation Workers. 2010. (People in My Community Ser.). (ENG.). 24p. (J). (gr. k-3). pap. 8.15 *(978-1-4339-3810-8(3))*; lib. bdg. 22.60 *(978-1-4339-3809-2(X))* Stevens, Gareth Publishing LLLP.

Mara, Wil. The Silversmith. 2010. (Colonial People Ser.). 48p. (gr. 3-18). 29.93 *(978-0-7614-4804-4(7))* Marshall Cavendish Corp.

McGill, Jordan. Edificios. 2012. (SPA.). (J). *(978-1-61913-208-5(7))* Weigl Pubs., Inc.

—Medios de Transporte. 2012. (SPA.). (J). *(978-1-61913-213-9(3))* Weigl Pubs., Inc.

Meachen Rau, Dana. Builders/Los Contructores. 2007. (Tools We Use/Instrumentos de Trabajo Ser.). (SPA & ENG., Illus.). 32p. (gr. k-2). lib. bdg. 15.95 *(978-0-7614-2821-3(6)*, Benchmark Bks.) Marshall Cavendish Corp.

Omoth, Tyler. Oil Rig Workers in Action. 2017. (Dangerous Jobs in Action Ser.). (ENG.). 32p. (J). (gr. 3-6). lib. bdg. 27.07 *(978-1-5038-1631-2(1)*, 211147) Child's World, Inc., The.

Paige, Joy. Cool Careers Without College for People Who Love to Build Things. 2009. (Cool Careers Without College Ser.). 144p. (gr. 6-6). 66.50 *(978-1-61511-970-7(1))* Rosen Publishing Group, Inc., The.

Pearce, Q. L. Given Kachepa: Advocate for Human Trafficking Victims. 2007. (Young Heroes Ser.). (ENG., Illus.). 64p. (J). (gr. 4-8). lib. bdg. 35.70 *(978-0-7377-3668-7(2)*, Kidhaven) Cengage Gale.

Raum, Elizabeth. Work: From Plows to Robots. 2010. (Timeline History Ser.). (ENG., Illus.). 32p. (gr. 3-5). 29.99 *(978-1-4329-3806-2(1)*, NA-h) Heinemann-Raintree.

Roza, Greg. Why People Work. 2009. (Real Life Readers Ser.). 16p. (gr. 2-3). pap. 7.05 *(978-1-4358-0045-8(1)*, Rosen Classroom) Rosen Publishing Group, Inc., The.

Tafolla, Carmen & Teneyuca, Sharyll. That's Not Fair! - ¡No es Justo! Emma Tenayuca's Struggle for Justice - La Lucha de Emma Tenayuca Por la Justicia. Ybáñez, Terry, illus. 2008. (ENG & SPA.). 40p. (J). (gr. k-2). 19.95 *(978-0-916727-33-8(5))* Wings Pr.

Tol, Alex Van & National Geographic Learning Staff. Dolores Huerta: Voice for the Working Poor. 2010. (ENG., Illus.). 112p. (J). pap. *(978-0-7787-2545-9(6))* Crabtree Publishing Co.

Waldendorf, Kurt. Hooray for Construction Workers! 2016. (Bumba Books (tm) — Hooray for Community Helpers! Ser.). (ENG., Illus.). 24p. (J). (gr. -1-1). 25.32 *(978-1-5124-1441-7(7))* Lerner Publishing Group.

Waldendorf, Kurt. Que Vivan los Obreros de Construccion! (Hooray for Construction Workers!) 2017. (Bumba Books (tm) en Español — ¡Que Vivan Los Ayudantes Comunitarios! (Hooray for Community Helpers!) Ser.). (SPA.). (J). (gr. -1-1). pap. 6.99 ***(978-1-5124-5385-0(4))***; (Illus.). lib. bdg. 25.32 ***(978-1-5124-4136-9(8))*** Lerner Publishing Group.

Whelan, Gloria. Waiting for the Owl's Call. Milelli, Pascal, illus. 2009. (Tales of the World Ser.). (ENG.). 32p. (J). (gr. 1-5). 17.95 *(978-1-58536-418-3(5))* Sleeping Bear Pr.

LABOR—FICTION

Creech, Sharon. Ruby Holler. 2004. (Joanna Cotler Bks.). 310p. (gr. 3-7). 17.00 *(978-0-7569-1940-5(1))* Perfection Learning Corp.

Evans, Nate & Brown, Stephanie Gwyn. Bang! Boom! Roar! A Busy Crew of Dinosaurs. Santoro, Christopher, illus. 2012. (ENG.). 40p. (J). (gr. -1-2). 15.99 *(978-0-06-087960-0(2))* HarperCollins Pubs.

—Dinosaur ABC. Santoro, Christopher, illus. 2011. (J). lib. bdg. 16.89 *(978-0-06-087962-4(9))* HarperCollins Pubs.

Francesco, D'Adamo. Iqbal. 2014. (ENG.). 128p. (J). (gr. 3-7). 11.24 *(978-1-63245-261-0(8))* Lectorum Pubns., Inc.

Haddix, Margaret Peterson. Uprising: Three Young Women Caught in the Fire That Changed America. 2007. (ENG.). 352p. (YA). (gr. 7-18). 16.99 *(978-1-4169-1171-5(5)*, Simon & Schuster Bks. For Young Readers) Simon & Schuster Bks. For Young Readers.

Kipling, Rudyard. The Bridge Builders. 2005. pap. *(978-1-4065-0310-4(X))* Dodo Pr.

Laird, Elizabeth. Lost Riders, 1. unabr. ed. 2010. (ENG., Illus.). 304p. (J). (gr. 4-7). pap. 8.99 *(978-0-330-45209-0(6))* Macmillan Pubs., Ltd. GBR. Dist: Independent Pubs. Group.

Malaspina, Ann. Yasmin's Hammer. Chayka, Doug, illus. 2010. (ENG.). 40p. (J). (gr. k-6). 18.95 *(978-1-60060-359-4(9))* Lee & Low Bks., Inc.

Pugliano-Martin, Carol. John Henry: An American Tall Tale. 2006. (J). pap. *(978-1-4108-6170-2(8))* Benchmark Education Co.

Renner, Jodie, et al. Childhood Regained: Canadian Schools Edition. 2016. (ENG., Illus.). (J). pap. ***(978-0-9937004-7-7(0))*** Cobalt Bks.

Ryan, Pam Muñoz. Esperanza Rising. 2005. (Reader's Workshop Ser.). (ENG.). 264p. (C). pap. 19.95 *(978-0-7362-2817-6(9))* CENGAGE Learning.

Salkey, Andrew. Riot. 2011. (Caribbean Modern Classics Ser.). (ENG., Illus.). 176p. (J). (gr. 7). pap. 14.95 *(978-1-84523-181-1(3))* Peepal Tree Pr., Ltd. GBR. Dist: Independent Pubs. Group.

Sheth, Kashmira. Boys Without Names. 2011. (ENG.). 320p. (J). (gr. 4-7). pap. 6.99 *(978-0-06-185762-1(9))* HarperCollins Pubs.

Sinclair, Upton, et al. The Jungle. (Classics Illustrated Ser.). (Illus.). 52p. (YA). pap. 4.95 *(978-1-57209-025-5(1))* Classics International Entertainment, Inc.

Spradlin, Michael P. Prisoner of War. 2017. (ENG.). 272p. (J). (gr. 7). 17.99 ***(978-0-545-85783-3(X)***, Scholastic Pr.) Scholastic, Inc.

Stokes, Jordan & Belinkie, Matt. Gilded Delirium. 2007. (YA). pap. *(978-1-4114-9670-5(1)*, Spark Publishing Group) Sterling Publishing Co., Inc.

Sullivan, Paul. Breaker at Dawn. 2010. (J). pap. *(978-0-88092-705-5(4))* Royal Fireworks Publishing Co.

LABOR—UNITED STATES

Brill, Marlene Targ. Annie Shapiro & the Clothing Workers' Strike. Akib, Jamel, illus. 2010. (History Speaks: Picture Books Plus Reader's Theater Ser.). (ENG.). 48p. (gr. 2-4). pap. 9.95 *(978-0-7613-6132-9(4))* Lerner Publishing Group.

Broyles, Janell. The Triangle Shirtwaist Factory Fire Of 1911. 2009. (Tragic Fires Throughout History Ser.). 48p. (gr. 5-8). 53.00 *(978-1-60854-584-1(9)*, Rosen Reference) Rosen Publishing Group, Inc., The.

Casil, Amy Sterling. The Department of Labor. (This Is Your Government Ser.). 64p. 2009. (gr. 5-6). 58.50 *(978-1-60854-374-8(9)*, Rosen Reference) 2005. (Illus.). (J). (gr. k-3). lib. bdg. 31.95 *(978-1-4042-0210-8(2))* Rosen Publishing Group, Inc., The.

Crewe, Sabrina & Schaefer, Adam. The Triangle Shirtwaist Factory Fire. 2004. (Events That Shaped America Ser.). (Illus.). 32p. (gr. 3-6). lib. bdg. 26.00 *(978-0-8368-3402-4(X)*, Gareth Stevens Learning Library) Stevens, Gareth Publishing LLLP.

Edge, Laura Bufano. We Stand As One: The International Ladies Garment Workers' Strike, New York, 1909. 2010. (Civil Rights Struggles around the World Ser.). (ENG., Illus.). 160p. (gr. 9-12). lib. bdg. 38.60 *(978-0-7613-4609-8(0))* Lerner Publishing Group.

Gold, Susan Dudley. Taft-Hartley Act. 2011. (Landmark Legislation 2 Ser.). (Illus.). 128p. (J). (gr. 7). 39.93 *(978-1-60870-488-0(2))* Marshall Cavendish Corp.

Greene, Jacqueline Dembar. The Triangle Shirtwaist Factory Fire. 2007. (Code Red Ser.). (Illus.). 32p. (YA). (gr. 2-5). lib. bdg. 25.27 *(978-1-59716-359-0(7))* Bearport Publishing Co., Inc.

Gunderson, Jessica. The Triangle Shirtwaist Factory Fire. Miller, Phil & Barnett III, Charles, illus. 2006. (Disasters in History Ser.). (ENG.). 32p. (gr. 3-4). pap. 47.70 *(978-0-7368-6999-7(9)*, Graphic Library) Capstone Press of Coughlan Cos.

Gunderson, Jessica Sarah. The Triangle Shirtwaist Factory Fire. Miller, Phil & Barnett, Charles, III, illus. 2006. (Disasters in History Ser.). (ENG.). 32p. (gr. 3-4). per. 8.10 *(978-0-7368-6878-5(X)*, Graphic Library) Capstone Press of Coughlan Cos.

Heinrichs, Ann. The Shoemaker. 2010. (Colonial People Ser.). 48p. (gr. 3-18). 29.93 *(978-0-7614-4798-6(9))* Marshall Cavendish Corp.

Miklowitz, Gloria. Cesar Chavez. 2009. pap. 13.25 *(978-1-60559-056-1(8))* Hameray Publishing Group, Inc.

Sioux, Tracee. Immigrants, Migration, & the Industrial Revolution. 2004. (Primary Sources of Immigration & Migration in America Ser.). (Illus.). 24p. (J). lib. bdg. 22.60 *(978-0-8239-6826-8(X)*, PowerKids Pr.) Rosen Publishing Group, Inc., The.

Thompson, E. L. Cesar Chavez, with Profiles of Terence V. Powderly & Dolores Huerta. 2006. (Biographical Connections Ser.). (Illus.). 112p. (J). *(978-0-7166-1827-0(3))* World Bk., Inc.

Warren, Sarah E. Dolores Huerta: A Hero to Migrant Workers, 0 vols. Casilla, Robert, illus. 2012. (ENG.). 32p. (J). (gr. 2-5). 17.99 *(978-0-7614-6107-4(8)*, 9780761461074, Amazon Children's Publishing) Amazon Publishing.

LABOR AND LABORING CLASSES

see Labor; Working Class

LABOR DAY

Dash, Meredith. Dia Del Trabajo. 2015. (Días Festivos Ser.). (SPA & ENG., Illus.). 24p. (gr. k-1). pap. 7.95 *(978-1-4966-0425-5(3))* Capstone Classroom.

—Labor Day, 1 vol. 2014. (National Holidays Ser.). (ENG., Illus.). 24p. (J). (gr. 4-8). lib. bdg. 28.50 *(978-1-62970-044-1(4))* ABDO Publishing Co.

Dayton, Connor. Labor Day. 2012. (American Holidays Ser.). (ENG.). 24p. (J). (gr. k-3). pap. 8.25 *(978-1-4488-6252-8(3))*; lib. bdg. 22.60 *(978-1-4488-6147-7(0))* Rosen Publishing Group, Inc., The. (PowerKids Pr.).

—Labor Day: Día Del Trabajo. Alamán, Eduardo, tr. from ENG. 2012. (American Holidays / Celebraciones en los Estados Unidos Ser.). (ENG & SPA.). 24p. (gr. k-3). lib. bdg. 22.60 *(978-1-4488-6713-4(4)*, PowerKids Pr.) Rosen Publishing Group, Inc., The.

DeRubertis, Barbara. Let's Celebrate Labor Day. 2015. (ENG.). 32p. (J). (gr. 1-4). pap. 7.95 *(978-1-57565-816-2(X))* Kane Press, Inc.

Hamilton, Lynn. Labor Day. (American Celebrations Ser.). (Illus.). 24p. (J). 2010. (gr. 3-5). pap. 11.95 *(978-1-60596-777-6(7))* 2010. (gr. 3-5). lib. bdg. 25.70 *(978-1-60596-770-7(X))* 2004. (gr. -1-3). per. 8.95 *(978-1-59036-166-5(0))* 2004. lib. bdg. 24.45 *(978-1-59036-129-0(6))* Weigl Pubs., Inc.

McNeil, Niki, et al. Labor Day. 2007. (In the Hands of a Child: Project Pack Continent Study Ser.). (Illus.). 75p. spiral bd. 19.00 *(978-1-60308-104-7(6))* In the Hands of a Child.

Morrison, Jessica. Labour Day. 2010. (Illus.). 24p. *(978-1-55388-619-8(4))*; pap. *(978-1-55388-620-4(8))* Weigl Educational Pubs. Ltd.

Nelson, Robin. Labor Day. 2009. (First Step Nonfiction - American Holidays Ser.). (J). (gr. k-2). 19.93 *(978-0-7613-4933-4(2))* Lerner Publishing Group.

Shava, Ryder. Labor Day, 01 vols., 1. 2016. (Rosen REAL Readers: Social Studies Nonfiction / Fiction: Family, Community, & the World Ser.). (ENG.). 12p. (J). pap. 6.33 *(978-1-5081-1728-5(4)*, Rosen Classroom) Rosen Publishing Group, Inc., The.

Walker, Robert. Labor Day. 2010. (Celebrations in My World Ser.). (ENG.). 32p. (J). (gr. k-3). pap. *(978-0-7787-4936-3(3))*; lib. bdg. *(978-0-7787-4929-5(0))* Crabtree Publishing Co.

LABOR (OBSTETRICS)

see Childbirth

LABOR ORGANIZATIONS

see Guilds; Labor Unions

LABOR REPRESENTATION IN REGULATION OF INDUSTRY

see Management—Employee Participation

LABOR UNIONS

Adler, David A. & Adler, Michael S. A Picture Book of Cesar Chavez. Olofsdotter, Marie, illus. 2010. (ENG.). 32p. (J). (gr. -1-3). 17.95 *(978-0-8234-2202-9(X))* Holiday Hse., Inc.

Bridegam, Martha. Unions & Labor Laws. 2009. (Point/Counterpoint Ser.). (Illus.). 128p. (C). (gr. 9-18). 35.00 *(978-1-60413-511-4(5),* Chelsea Hse.) Facts On File, Inc.

Brown, Jonatha A. César Chávez. (People We Should Know Ser.). 2005. (SPA.). 24p. (gr. 1-4). pap. 8.15 *(978-0-8368-4766-6(0),* Weekly Reader Leveled Readers) 2005. (SPA., Illus.). 24p. (gr. 1-4). lib. bdg. 22.00 *(978-0-8368-4759-8(8),* Weekly Reader Leveled Readers) 2005. (Illus.). 24p. (gr. 1-4). lib. bdg. 22.00 *(978-0-8368-4745-1(8),* Weekly Reader Leveled Readers) 2004. (Illus.). 48p. (gr. 5-12). pap. 14.05 *(978-0-8368-5257-8(5),* Gareth Stevens Secondary Library) 2004. (Illus.). 48p. (gr. 5-12). lib. bdg. 31.00 *(978-0-8368-5097-0(1),* Gareth Stevens Secondary Library) Stevens, Gareth Publishing LLLP.

Cesar Chavez, Lider Laboral. 2003. pap. 48.95 *(978-0-8136-9205-0(9))* Modern Curriculum Pr.

Collins, David R. Cesar Chavez. 2005. (Just the Facts Biographies Ser.). (Illus.). 112p. (J). (gr. 6-12). 27.93 *(978-0-8225-2248-5(9))* Lerner Publishing Group.

Dunn, Joeming W. Cesar Chavez, 1 vol. Espinosa, Rod, illus. 2008. (Bio-Graphics Ser.). (ENG.). 32p. (gr. 3-5). 28.50 *(978-1-60270-172-4(5),* Graphic Planet- Nonfiction) ABDO Publishing Co.

Ebon Research Systems Staff. Dare to Be... A Hero Vol. 3: Cesar Chavez. l.t. ed. 2003.Tr. of Atrevete Ser... Un Heroe Cesar Chavez. (ENG & SPA., Illus.). 16p. (J). 3.99 *(978-0-9648313-6-0(8))* Ebon Research Systems Publishing, LLC.

Farrell, Mary Cronk. Fannie Never Flinched: One Woman's Courage in the Struggle for American Labor Union Rights. 2016. (ENG., Illus.). 56p. (J). (gr. 5-9). 19.95 *(978-1-4197-1884-7(3),* Abrams Bks. for Young Readers) Abrams, Inc.

Feinstein, Stephen. Read about Cesar Chavez. 2004. (I Like Biographies! Ser.). (Illus.). 24p. (J). lib. bdg. 22.60 *(978-0-7660-2296-6(X))* Enslow Pubs., Inc.

Frey, Wendy. Citizen Heroes. 2007. (Illus.). 68p. (J). *(978-1-4105-0887-4(0)); (978-1-4105-0888-1(9))* Johnston, Don Inc.

Gay, Kathlyn. César Chávez: Fighting for Migrant Farmworkers. 2017. (Rebels with a Cause Ser.). 128p. (J). (gr. 8-8). lib. bdg. 37.27 ***(978-0-7660-8951-8(7))*** Enslow Pubs., Inc.

Gay, Kathlyn. Mother Jones. 2006. (American Workers Ser.). (Illus.). 144p. (J). (gr. 3-7). lib. bdg. 28.95 *(978-1-59935-016-5(5))* Reynolds, Morgan Inc.

Gunderson, Megan M. Labor & Management, 1 vol. 2012. (Economy in Action! Ser.). (ENG.). 32p. (J). (gr. 3-6). lib. bdg. 27.07 *(978-1-61783-488-2(2),* Checkerboard Library) ABDO Publishing Co.

Krull, Kathleen. Cosechando Esperanza: La Historia de César Chávez. Campoy, F. Isabel & Flor Ada, Alma, trs. Morales, Yuyi, illus. 2004. (SPA & ENG.). 48p. (J). (gr. -1-3). pap. 7.99 *(978-0-15-205169-3(4))* Houghton Mifflin Harcourt Publishing Co.

—Harvesting Hope: The Story of Cesar Chavez. Morales, Yuyi, illus. 2003. (ENG.). 48p. (J). (gr. -1-3). 17.99 *(978-0-15-201437-7(3))* Houghton Mifflin Harcourt Publishing Co.

Lyon, George Ella. Which Side Are You On? The Story of a Song. Cardinale, Christopher, illus. 2011. (ENG.). 40p. (J). (gr. 2-4). 17.95 *(978-1-933693-96-5(7))* Cinco Puntos Pr.

Magoon, Kekla. Cesar Chavez: Crusader for Labor Rights, 1 vol. 2010. (Essential Lives Set 5 Ser.). (ENG., Illus.). 112p. (J). (gr. 6-12). lib. bdg. 35.64 *(978-1-61613-512-6(3))* ABDO Publishing Co.

McNeese, Tim. The Labor Movement: Unionizing America. 2007. (Reform Movements in American History Ser.). (Illus.). 168p. (YA). (gr. 7-12). lib. bdg. 32.50 *(978-0-7910-9503-4(7))* Facts On File, Inc.

Miklowitz, Gloria. Cesar Chavez. 2009. pap. 13.25 *(978-1-60559-056-1(8))* Hameray Publishing Group, Inc.

Miklowitz, Gloria D. César Chávez. 2004. (ENG., Illus.). 29p. (J). (gr. 2-5). pap. 5.97 net. *(978-0-7685-1215-1(8),* Dominie Elementary) Pearson Schl.

Miller, Calvin Craig. A. Philip Randolph & the African American Labor Movement. 2005. (Civil Rights Leaders Ser.). (Illus.). 160p. (YA). (gr. 6-12). 26.95 *(978-1-931798-50-1(8))* Reynolds, Morgan Inc.

Miller, Connie Colwell. Mother Jones: Labor Leader. Erwin, Steve & Barnett, Charles, III, illus. 2006. (Graphic Biographies Ser.). (ENG.). 32p. (gr. 3-4). 30.65 *(978-0-7368-5487-0(8),* Graphic Library) Capstone Press of Coughlan Cos.

—Mother Jones: Labor Leader, 1 vol. Erwin, Steve & Barnett, Charles, III, illus. 2006. (Graphic Biographies Ser.). (ENG.). 32p. (gr. 3-4). per. 8.10 *(978-0-7368-9662-7(7),* Graphic Library) Capstone Press of Coughlan Cos.

Roome, Anne Ross & Mattern, Joanne. Cesar Chavez. 2016. (Rookie Biographies(tm) Ser.). (ENG., Illus.). 32p. (J). lib. bdg. 25.00 *(978-0-531-22546-2(1),* Children's Pr.) Scholastic Library Publishing.

Ruby, Lois. Strike! Mother Jones & the Colorado Coal Field War. 2012. (Illus.). 224p. (J). pap. 8.95 *(978-0-86541-141-8(7))* Filter Pr., LLC.

Seidman, David. Cesar Chavez: Labor Leader. 2004. (Great Life Stories Ser.). (ENG., Illus.). 127p. (J). 30.50 *(978-0-531-12319-5(7),* Watts, Franklin) Scholastic Library Publishing.

Skurzynski, Gloria. Sweat & Blood: A History of U. S. Labor Unions. 2008. (People's History Ser.). (ENG.). 112p. (gr. 5-12). lib. bdg. 33.26 *(978-0-8225-7594-8(9))* Lerner Publishing Group.

Soto, Gary. Cesar Chavez: A Hero for Everyone. Lohstoeter, Lori, illus. 2003. (Milestone Ser.). (ENG.). 80p. (J). (gr. 2-5). pap. 6.99 *(978-0-689-85922-9(8),* Simon & Schuster/Paula Wiseman Bks.) Simon & Schuster/Paula Wiseman Bks.

Tol, Alex Van & National Geographic Learning Staff. Dolores Huerta: Voice for the Working Poor. 2010. (ENG., Illus.). 112p. (J). pap. *(978-0-7787-2545-9(6))* Crabtree Publishing Co.

Van Tol, Alex. Dolores Huerta: Voice for the Working Poor. 2010. (Crabtree Groundbreaker Biographies Ser.). (ENG., Illus.). 112p. (J). (gr. 5-8). lib. bdg. *(978-0-7787-2536-7(7))* Crabtree Publishing Co.

Wadsworth, Ginger. Cesar Chavez. Schroeder, Mark, illus. 2005. (Yo Solo - Biografías (on My Own - Biographies) Ser.). (SPA.). 48p. (J). (gr. 2-4). per. 6.95 *(978-0-8225-3125-8(9))* Lerner Publishing Group.

—Cesar Chavez. 2005. (On My Own Biography Ser.). (Illus.). 48p. (J). 25.26 *(978-1-57505-652-4(6),* Carolrhoda Bks.) Lerner Publishing Group.

—Cesar Chavez. Schroder, Mark, illus. 2005. (On My Own Biography Ser.). (ENG.). 48p. (gr. 2-4). pap. 6.95 *(978-1-57505-826-9(X))* Lerner Publishing Group.

—César Chávez. Fitzpatrick, Julia, tr. from ENG. Schroder, Mark, illus. 2005. (Yo Solo: Biografías (on My Own Biographies) Ser.). (SPA.). 48p. (gr. 2-4). lib. bdg. 25.26 *(978-0-8225-3124-1(0),* Ediciones Lerner) Lerner Publishing Group.

Wagner, Viqi. Labor Unions. 2007. (Opposing Viewpoints Ser.). (Illus.). 239p. (YA). (gr. 7-12). 29.45 *(978-0-7377-3823-0(5));* pap. 42.95 *(978-0-7377-3822-3(7))* Cengage Gale. (Greenhaven Pr., Inc.).

Warren, Sarah E. Dolores Huerta: A Hero to Migrant Workers, 0 vols. Casilla, Robert, illus. 2012. (ENG.). 32p. (J). (gr. 2-5). 17.99 *(978-0-7614-6107-4(8),* 9780761461074, Amazon Children's Publishing) Amazon Publishing.

Wheeler, Jill C. Cesar Chavez. 2003. (Breaking Barriers Ser.). 64p. (gr. 3-8). 27.07 *(978-1-57765-905-1(8),* Abdo & Daughters) ABDO Publishing Co.

LABORATORY ANIMALS

Cagno, Stefano. Lou, Buc & All the Others. 2012. 178p. pap. 7.99 *(978-1-61667-441-0(5))* Raider Publishing International.

Dunn, Joeming & Dunn, Ben. Albert II: The 1st Monkey in Space, 1 vol. 2011. (Famous Firsts: Animals Making History Ser.). (ENG., Illus.). 32p. (YA). (gr. 3-6). 28.50 *(978-1-61641-637-9(8))* Magic Wagon.

—Laika: The 1st Dog in Space, 1 vol. 2011. (Famous Firsts: Animals Making History Ser.). (ENG., Illus.). 32p. (YA). (gr. 3-6). 28.50 *(978-1-61641-641-6(6))* Magic Wagon.

Hartman, Eve & Meshbesher, Wendy. Do Scientists Care about Animal Welfare?, 1 vol. 2012. (Sci-Hi: Science Issues Ser.). (ENG., Illus.). 48p. (gr. 4-4). lib. bdg. 33.32 *(978-1-4109-4462-7(X),* Sci-Hi) Heinemann-Raintree.

Lubka, S. Ruth. Pupniks: The Story of Two Space Dogs, 1 vol. 2003. (ENG., Illus.). 32p. (J). (gr. k-3). 16.95 *(978-0-7614-5137-2(4))* Marshall Cavendish Corp.

Watson, Stephanie. Animal Testing: Issues & Ethics. 2009. (Science & Society Ser.). 64p. (gr. 5-6). 58.50 *(978-1-60853-006-9(X))* Rosen Publishing Group, Inc., The.

LABORERS

see Labor

LABOURE, CATHERINE, SAINT, 1806-1876

Trouvé, Marianne Lorraine. Saint Catherine Labouré: And Our Lady of the Miraculous Medal. 2011. (ENG.). (J). pap. 7.95 *(978-0-8198-7224-1(5))* Pauline Bks. & Media.

Windle, Margaret. St Catherine Laboure. 2007. (Illus.). 53p. (J). 11.99 *(978-0-9798889-2-2(1))* Growing with the Saints, Inc.

LADYBIRDS

see Ladybugs

LADYBUGS

Allen, Judy, et al. Are You a Ladybug? Humphries, Tudor, illus. 2003. (Backyard Bks.). (ENG.). 31p. (J). (gr. k-3). pap. 6.99 *(978-0-7534-5603-3(6),* 9780753456033, Kingfisher) Roaring Brook Pr.

Amstutz, Lisa J. Ladybugs. 2016. (Little Critters Ser.). (ENG.). 24p. (gr. k-1). lib. bdg. 21.99 *(978-1-5157-1937-3(5),* Pebble Bks.) Capstone Press of Coughlan Cos.

Anderson, Jo Marie. If I Were a Ladybug. 2017. (I'm a Bug! Ser.). 24p. (gr. 4-6). 23.60 ***(978-1-5081-5723-6(5),*** PowerKids Pr.) Rosen Publishing Group, Inc., The.

Appleby, Alex. I See a Ladybug. 2013. (In My Backyard Ser.). (Illus.). 24p. (J). (gr. k-2). 22.60 *(978-1-4339-8555-3(1));* pap. 8.15 *(978-1-4339-8556-0(X))* Stevens, Gareth Publishing LLLP.

—I See a Ladybug: Puedo Ver una Mariquita. 2013. (In My Backyard / en Mi Jardín Ser.). (SPA & ENG., Illus.). 24p. (J). (gr. k-2). lib. bdg. 22.60 *(978-1-4339-8798-4(8))* Stevens, Gareth Publishing LLLP.

Ashley, Susan. Ladybugs. (Incredible World of Insects Ser.). (Illus.). 24p. 2011. (J). (gr. 1-3). pap. 8.15 *(978-1-4339-4592-4(4))* 2011. (J). (gr. 1-3). lib. bdg. 22.60 *(978-1-4339-4591-5(6))* 2004. (gr. k-3). pap. 8.15 *(978-0-8368-4062-9(3),* Weekly Reader Leveled Readers) 2004. (gr. k-3). lib. bdg. 22.00 *(978-0-8368-4055-1(0),* Weekly Reader Leveled Readers) Stevens, Gareth Publishing LLLP.

Berger, Melvin & Berger, Gilda. De Larva a Mariquita: Grub to Ladybug. 2006. (ENG & SPA., Illus.). (J). pap. *(978-0-439-87985-9(X))* Scholastic, Inc.

—Ladybugs. 2011. (Illus.). 16p. (J). pap. *(978-0-545-24444-2(7))* Scholastic, Inc.

Black, Nessa. Ladybugs. 2017. (Spot Creepy Crawlies Ser.). (ENG.). 16p. (gr. k-3). 17.95 ***(978-1-68151-109-2(6))*** Amicus Publishing.

Carr, Aaron. Ladybugs. 2014. (J). *(978-1-4896-3208-1(5))* Weigl Pubs., Inc.

Cleland, JoAnn. Ladybug, Ladybug, What Are You Doing? 2008. (My First Science Discovery Library). (Illus.). 24p. (J). (gr. k-2). lib. bdg. 21.35 *(978-1-60472-537-7(0))* Rourke Educational Media.

Coughlan, Cheryl. Ladybugs. 2016. (Insects Ser.). (ENG.). 24p. (gr. k-1). pap. 5.95 *(978-1-5157-4227-2(X),* Pebble Bks.) Capstone Press of Coughlan Cos.

Dahl, Michael. Lots of Ladybugs! Counting by Fives, 1 vol. Ouren, Todd, illus. 2005. (Know Your Numbers Ser.). (ENG.). 24p. (gr. -1-2). 26.65 *(978-1-4048-0944-4(9))* Picture Window Bks.

—¡Montones de Mariquitas! Cuenta de Cinco en Cinco. Ouren, Todd, illus. 2010. (Apréndete Tus Números/Know Your Numbers Ser.).Tr. of Lots of Ladybugs! - Counting by Fives. (SPA & MUL.). 24p. (gr. -1-2). lib. bdg. 26.65 *(978-1-4048-6297-5(8))* Picture Window Bks.

Enslow, Brian. Counting Ladybugs 1-2-3. 2011. (All about Counting Bugs 1-2-3 Ser.). (Illus.). 24p. (J). (gr. -1-18). pap. 7.95 *(978-1-59845-251-8(7),* Enslow Elementary); (gr. k-3). lib. bdg. 22.60 *(978-0-7660-3922-3(6))* Enslow Pubs., Inc.

Feldman, Thea. Kingfisher Readers L1: Ladybugs. 2015. (Kingfisher Readers Ser.). (ENG., Illus.). 32p. (gr. k-3). 12.99 *(978-0-7534-7219-4(8),* 9780753472194, Kingfisher) Roaring Brook Pr.

Frisch, Aaron. Ladybugs. 2014. 24p. *(978-1-60818-459-0(5),* Creative Education) Creative Co., The.

—Seedlings: Ladybugs. 2015. (Seedlings Ser.). (ENG.). 24p. (J). (gr. -1-1). pap. 7.99 *(978-1-62832-045-9(1),* Creative Paperbacks) Creative Co., The.

Gallagher, Debbie. Ladybugs. 2011. (Mighty Minibeasts Ser.). 32p. (gr. 2). 28.50 *(978-1-60870-546-7(3))* Marshall Cavendish Corp.

Gervais, Bernadette, illus. The Ladybug. 2017. (ENG.). 16p. (J). (gr. -1-k). 12.99 *(978-1-78627-002-3(1))* King, Laurence Publishing GBR. Dist: Hachette Bk. Group.

Gibbons, Gail. Ladybugs. Gibbons, Gail, illus. 2013. (ENG., Illus.). 32p. (J). pap. 7.99 *(978-0-8234-2760-4(9))* Holiday Hse., Inc.

Guillain, Charlotte. Life Story of a Ladybug, 1 vol. 2014. (Animal Life Stories Ser.). (ENG., Illus.). 32p. (gr. 1-3). 27.32 *(978-1-4846-0488-5(1),* Heinemann First Library) Heinemann-Raintree.

Hall, Margaret. Ladybugs [Scholastic]. 2010. (Bugs, Bugs, Bugs! Ser.). 24p. pap. 0.52 *(978-1-4296-5053-3(2),* Pebble Plus) Capstone Press of Coughlan Cos.

Ho, Cammie. Ladybug Ladybug. 2016. (Life Cycle Bks.). (ENG., Illus.). 29p. (J). (gr. k-2). pap. 7.99 *(978-1-943241-02-6(3))* Phonic Monic.

Huliska-Beith, Laura, illus. Cinco Pequenas Mariquitas. 2005.Tr. of Five Little Ladybugs. (SPA & ENG.). 12p. (J). 4.95 *(978-1-58117-333-8(4),* Intervisual/Piggy Toes) Bendon, Inc.

Humphries, Tudor & Allen, Judy. Are You a Ladybug? 2003. (Backyard Bks.). (J). (gr. -1-2). lib. bdg. 17.20 *(978-0-613-90173-4(8),* Turtleback) Turtleback Bks.

Kenney, Karen Latchana. Hide with the Ladybugs, 1 vol. Hedicker, Lisa, illus. 2010. (Bug's World Ser.). (ENG.). 32p. 28.50 *(978-1-60270-785-6(5),* Looking Glass Library-Nonfiction) Magic Wagon.

Ladybug. 2003. (J). 36.95 *(978-0-8136-9269-2(5));* 38.95 *(978-0-8136-4166-9(7))* Modern Curriculum Pr.

Ladybugs: Red, Fiery, & Bright. 2007. 32p. (J). (gr. k-4). pap. 6.95 *(978-0-8225-6989-3(2),* First Avenue Editions) Lerner Publishing Group.

Leaf, Christina. Ladybugs. 2017. (Insects up Close Ser.). (ENG., Illus.). 24p. (J). (gr. k-3). lib. bdg. 25.95 ***(978-1-62617-667-6(1),*** Blastoff! Discovery) Bellwether Media.

Lewellyn, Claire. Ladybug. Mendez, Simon, illus. 2004. (Starting Life Ser.). (ENG.). 24p. (J). (gr. k-3). 16.95 *(978-1-55971-892-9(7))* Cooper Square Publishing Llc.

Marie, Christian. Little Ladybugs. 2006. (Born to Be Wild Ser.). (Illus.). 24p. (gr. k-3). lib. bdg. 23.00 *(978-0-8368-6168-6(X),* Gareth Stevens Learning Library) Stevens, Gareth Publishing LLLP.

Marsico, Katie. Cómo Crece una Mariquita. 2008. (Scholastic News Nonfiction Readers en Espanol Ser.). 24p. (J). pap. 6.95 *(978-0-531-20644-7(0))* Scholastic Library Publishing.

—A Ladybug Larva Grows Up. 2007. (Scholastic News Nonfiction Readers Ser.). (ENG., Illus.). 24p. (J). (gr. 1-2). pap. 6.95 *(978-0-531-18697-8(0))* Scholastic Library Publishing.

Mattern, Joanne. It's a Good Thing There Are Ladybugs. 2014. (Rookie Read-About(r) Science — It's a Good Thing... Ser.). (ENG., Illus.). 32p. (J). pap. 5.95 *(978-0-531-22830-2(4));* lib. bdg. *(978-0-531-22358-1(2))* Scholastic Library Publishing.

McLaughlin, Kari Massie. My Adventure with Ladybugs. 2009. (ENG.). 44p. (J). 8.99 *(978-1-59092-457-0(6))* Blue Forge Pr.

Meachen Rau, Dana. Crawl, Ladybug, Crawl! 2007. (Go, Critter, Go! Ser.). (Illus.). 24p. (gr. k-1). lib. bdg. 15.95 *(978-0-7614-2652-3(3),* Benchmark Bks.) Marshall Cavendish Corp.

—Crawl, Ladybug, Crawl!/Trepa Mariquita, Trepa! 2007. (Go, Critter, Go!/¡Vamos Criaturita, Vamos! Ser.). (SPA & ENG., Illus.). 24p. (gr. k-1). lib. bdg. 15.95 *(978-0-7614-2817-6(8),* Benchmark Bks.) Marshall Cavendish Corp.

—Trepa Mariquita, Trepa! 2007. (¡Vamos Criaturita, Vamos! Ser.). (SPA & ENG., Illus.). 24p. (gr. k-1). lib. bdg. 15.95 *(978-0-7614-2793-3(7),* Benchmark Bks.) Marshall Cavendish Corp.

Murray, Julie. Ladybugs, 1 vol. (Big Buddy Bks.). (ENG.). 2010. 32p. (J). (gr. 2-5). 28.50 *(978-1-61613-487-7(9))* 2003. 24p. (gr. k-4). 25.65 *(978-1-57765-721-7(7),* Buddy Bks.) ABDO Publishing Co.

Nosy Crow Staff. Where's the Ladybug? Arrhenius, Ingela P., illus. 2017. (ENG.). 10p. (J). (— 1). bds. 8.99 *(978-0-7636-9335-0(9),* Nosy Crow) Candlewick Pr.

O'Brien, Joan. Lucky Ladybug Stickers. 2004. (Dover Little Activity Books Stickers Ser.). (ENG., Illus.). 4p. (J). (gr. k-3). pap. 1.99 *(978-0-486-43008-9(1))* Dover Pubns., Inc.

Owens, L. L. The Life Cycle of a Ladybug. 2011. (Life Cycles Ser.). (ENG., Illus.). 32p. (J). (gr. k-3). lib. bdg. 29.93 *(978-1-60973-189-2(1),* 201175) Child's World, Inc., The.

Owings, Lisa. From Egg to Ladybug. 2016. (Start to Finish, Second Ser.). (ENG., Illus.). 24p. (J). (gr. k-3). 23.99 *(978-1-5124-0910-9(3))* Lerner Publishing Group.

Posada, Mia. Ladybugs: Red, Fiery & Bright. 2005. (Picture Bks.). (Illus.). 32p. (gr. k-2). 15.95 *(978-0-87614-334-6(6))* Lerner Publishing Group.

Reher, Matt. Ladybug Babies. 2015. (2G Bugs Ser.). (ENG., Illus.). 36p. (J). pap. 5.99 *(978-1-63437-089-9(9))* American Reading Co.

Riggs, Kate. Grow with Me: Ladybug. 2013. (Grow with Me Ser.). (ENG.). 32p. (J). (gr. 1-3). pap. 9.99 *(978-0-89812-770-6(X),* Creative Paperbacks) Creative Co., The.

—Ladybug. 2012. (Grow with Me Ser.). 32p. (gr. 3-8). 19.95 *(978-1-60818-217-6(7),* Creative Education) Creative Co., The.

Ross, Michael Elsohn. Ladybugology. Erickson, Darren, illus. Grogan, Brian, photos by. 2005. (Backyard Buddies Ser.). 48p. (gr. 3-6). 19.93 *(978-1-57505-435-3(3))* Lerner Publishing Group.

Rustad, Martha E. H. Ladybugs. 2007. (World of Insects Ser.). (ENG., Illus.). 24p. (J). (gr. k-3). lib. bdg. 25.95 *(978-1-60014-077-8(7))* Bellwether Media.

Salzmann, Mary Elizabeth. Lucky Ladybugs, 1 vol. 2012. (Bug Bks.). (ENG.). 24p. (J). (gr. k-3). lib. bdg. 24.21 *(978-1-61783-192-8(1),* SandCastle) ABDO Publishing Co.

Santos, Penelope. I See a Ladybug. 2015. (Rosen REAL Readers: STEM & STEAM Collection). (ENG.). 8p. pap. 5.46 *(978-1-4994-9664-2(8),* Rosen Classroom) Rosen Publishing Group, Inc., The.

Schuh, Mari. Ladybugs. 2013. (ENG., Illus.). 24p. (J). lib. bdg. 25.65 *(978-1-62031-055-7(4))* Jump! Inc.

Sexton, Colleen. The Life Cycle of a Ladybug. 2010. (Life Cycles Ser.). (ENG., Illus.). 24p. (J). (gr. k-3). lib. bdg. 25.95 *(978-1-60014-309-0(1),* Blastoff! Readers) Bellwether Media.

Slade, Suzanne. Ladybugs. (Under the Microscope: Backyard Bugs Ser.). 24p. 2009. (gr. 2-3). 42.50 *(978-1-60854-616-9(0),* PowerKids Pr.) 2007. (Illus.). (J). (gr. 3-7). lib. bdg. 22.60 *(978-1-4042-3818-3(2))* Rosen Publishing Group, Inc., The.

Smith, Molly. Helpful Ladybugs. (No Backbone! Insects Ser.). 24p. (J). (gr. k-3). 2016. (ENG.). pap. 7.95 *(978-1-944998-47-9(0))* 2008. (Illus.). lib. bdg. 21.28 *(978-1-59716-584-6(0))* Bearport Publishing Co., Inc.

Smith, Sian. Ladybugs, 1 vol. 2012. (Creepy Critters Ser.). (ENG.). 24p. (gr. -1-k). pap. 9.95 *(978-1-4109-4822-9(6))* Heinemann-Raintree.

Stewart, Melissa. Zoom in on Ladybugs. 2014. (Zoom in on Insects! Ser.). 24p. (J). 22.60 *(978-0-7660-4215-5(4));* pap. 7.95 *(978-1-4644-0373-6(2),* Enslow Elementary) Enslow Pubs., Inc.

Thomson, Ruth. The Life Cycle of a Ladybug. 2009. (Learning about Life Cycles Ser.). 24p. (J). (ENG., Illus.). (gr. k-5). pap. 8.25 *(978-1-4358-2885-8(2),* PowerKids Pr.); (gr. 2-5). lib. bdg. 22.60 *(978-1-4358-2835-3(6))* Rosen Publishing Group, Inc., The.

Tracqui, Valérie. Face-to-Face with the Ladybug: Little Garden Monster. Lorne, Patrick, photos by. 2004. (Face-to-Face Ser.). (Illus.). 28p. (J). (gr. -1-2). 9.95 *(978-1-57091-453-9(2))* Charlesbridge Publishing, Inc.

LADYBUGS—FICTION

Adams, Gary. The Ladybug Story. 2012. 76p. pap. 28.99 *(978-1-4772-5627-5(X))* AuthorHouse.

Adams, Wayne. Laci the Ladybug. Kern, Shelly, illus. 2012. 16p. pap. 24.95 *(978-1-4626-7615-6(4))* America Star Bks.

Anansi Helps a Friend, Level 1. 2016. (Ladybird Readers Ser.). (ENG., Illus.). 48p. (J). pap. 9.99 *(978-0-241-25409-7(4))* Penguin Bks., Ltd. GBR. Dist: Independent Pubs. Group.

Anna, Jennifer. The Best Thing: An Almost True Story of Ladybugs & Sisters. 2007. (Illus.). 64p. (Orig.). (J). pap. 14.99 *(978-1-59092-154-8(2))* Blue Forge Pr.

Arpaci, Halis. Eric & Derrick. 2011. (ENG.). 160p. (J). (gr. 3-7). 11.95 *(978-1-59784-232-7(X))* Tughra Bks.

Basha, Irena Canaj. The Birthday Party, It Was Saturday... 2013. 16p. pap. 24.95 *(978-1-62709-182-4(3))* America Star Bks.

Blankenship, Paula. We Both Read-Lulu's Wild Party. Reinhart, Larry, illus. 2009. (We Both Read Ser.). 44p. (J). 9.95 *(978-1-60115-231-2(0));* pap. 4.99 *(978-1-60115-232-9(9))* Treasure Bay, Inc.

Boazu, Elena & Balestrieri, Mauro. Lila's Quest. 2007. 48p. per. 13.95 *(978-1-4327-0985-3(2))* Outskirts Pr., Inc.

Brahney, Jenny. Spotty, 1 vol. 2010. 30p. pap. 24.95 *(978-1-4489-8497-8(1))* PublishAmerica, Inc.

Branford, Anna. Violet Mackerel's Natural Habitat. Allen, Elanna, illus. 2013. (Violet Mackerel Ser.). (ENG.). 112p. (J). (gr. 1-5). 15.99 *(978-1-4424-3594-0(1));* pap. 5.99 *(978-1-4424-3595-7(X))* Simon & Schuster Children's Publishing.

Chapman, Mary Beth & Chapman, Steven Curtis. Shaoey & Dot: A Trip to Dr. Betterbee. 2005. 20p. (J). 6.99 *(978-1-4003-0568-1(3))* Nelson, Thomas Inc.

—Shaoey & Dot: Thunder & Lightning Bugs. 2005. 20p. (J). 6.99 *(978-1-4003-0570-4(5))* Nelson, Thomas Inc.

Coccia, Mina. Mother Nature & Mz Bee. 2012. 36p. pap. 14.95 *(978-1-4575-0709-0(9))* Dog Ear Publishing, LLC.

Cross, Jenny. Sadie the Ladybug. Bohart, Lisa, illus. 2009. 44p. pap. 14.95 *(978-1-936051-39-7(7))* Peppertree Pr., The.

Cuartas, Jennifer M. The Adventures of Delilah Doodie: Mealy Bug Stew. 2012. 24p. pap. 24.95 *(978-1-4626-8147-1(6))* America Star Bks.

Cummings, Troy. The Eensy Weensy Spider Freaks Out! Big-Time! 2015. lib. bdg. 18.40 *(978-0-606-37713-3(1))* Turtleback Bks.

Cummins, Judi, creator. It's Raining Acorns & Ladybugs. 2005. (Illus.). 28p. (J). per. *(978-0-9760377-4-3(2))* Cummins, Judi.

Cunningham, Karen. I See a Bug, 1 vol. 2010. 16p. 24.95 *(978-1-4489-4181-0(4))* PublishAmerica, Inc.

Cureton-Heifner, Donna Lynn. The Adventures of Itsy & Willy Wabbit: In Search of Lillian the Ladybug. 2012. 16p. pap. 24.95 *(978-1-4626-8547-9(1))* America Star Bks.

Davis, Jacky. Ladybug Girl Ready for Snow. Soman, David, illus. 2014. (Ladybug Girl Ser.). (ENG.). 12p. (J). (gr. -1 — 1). bds. 5.99 *(978-0-8037-4137-9(5),* Dial Bks) Penguin Young Readers Group.

Davis, Jacky & Soman, David. Ladybug Girl Book & Doll Set. Soman, David, illus. 2011. (Ladybug Girl Ser.). (ENG., Illus.). 32p. (J). (gr. -1-k). 18.99 *(978-0-8037-3444-9(1),* Dial Bks) Penguin Young Readers Group.

—Ladybug Girl Says Good Night. Soman, David, illus. 2014. (Ladybug Girl Ser.). (ENG., Illus.). 12p. (J). (gr. -1 — 1). bds. 5.99 *(978-0-8037-3893-5(5),* Dial Bks) Penguin Young Readers Group.

—Ladybug Girl Visits the Farm. Soman, David, illus. 2011. (Ladybug Girl Ser.). (ENG., Illus.). 16p. (J). (gr. -1-k). pap. 6.99 *(978-0-448-45598-3(6),* Grosset & Dunlap) Penguin Young Readers Group.

Deal, Sarah E. The Spotless Ladybug. 2008. 31p. pap. 24.95 *(978-1-60672-964-9(0))* America Star Bks.

Devant, Jourdan. The Little Ladybug. 2006. (Illus.). 15p. (J). per. 10.99 *(978-1-59879-219-5(9))* Lifevest Publishing, Inc.

Donaldson, Julia. What the Ladybug Heard. Monks, Lydia, illus. 2010. (ENG.). 32p. (J). (gr. -1-1). 16.99 *(978-0-8050-9026-4(2),* 9780805090284, Holt, Henry & Co. Bks. For Young Readers) Holt, Henry & Co.

J
K
L

Eisele, Barbara. Miss Thistle & Friends. 2009. 48p. pap. 12.99 *(978-1-4490-2007-1(0))* AuthorHouse.

Finn, Isobel. The Very Lazy Ladybug. Tickle, Jack, illus. 2005. 16p. (J). bds. 6.95 *(978-1-58925-758-0(8))* Tiger Tales.

Finn, Isobel & Tickle, Jack. The Very Lazy Ladybug. 2003. (Illus.). (J). 16p. tchr. ed. 15.95 *(978-1-58925-714-6(6))*; 32p. pap. 6.95 *(978-1-58925-379-7(5))* Tiger Tales.

Fisher, Meaghan. I Love Ladybugs! Mathieu, Middy, illus. 2012. 16p. pap. 6.99 *(978-1-938768-00-2(0))* Gypsy Pubns.

Fleming, Maria. Six Cheers for Ladybug. Chambliss, Maxie, illus. 2005. (Number Tales Ser.). (ENG.). 16p. (J). (gr. -1-1). pap. 2.99 *(978-0-439-69016-4(1))* Scholastic, Inc.

Florie, Christine. Lara Ladybug. Dalby, Danny Brooks, illus. 2011. (Rookie Ready to Learn — Animals Ser.). 32p. (J). (gr. -1-k). lib. bdg. 25.00 *(978-0-531-26417-1(3)*, Children's Pr.) Scholastic Library Publishing.

Florie, Christine & Dalby, Danny Brooks. La Mariquita Lara. Dalby, Danny Brooks, illus. 2011. (Rookie Ready to Learn Español Ser.). (SPA., Illus.). 32p. (J). pap. 5.95 *(978-0-531-26783-7(0))*; lib. bdg. 23.00 *(978-0-531-26115-6(8))* Scholastic Library Publishing. (Children's Pr.).

Fox, Mem. Yoo-Hoo, Ladybug! Ljungkvist, Laura, illus. 2013. (ENG.). 32p. (J). (gr. -1-k). 16.99 *(978-1-4424-3400-4(7))* Simon & Schuster Children's Publishing.

Frances, Janie. Krissy the Littlest Ladybug. 2013. 32p. pap. 8.95 *(978-0-9837403-9-1(9))* JGracia Publishing.

French, Vivian. Ladybird Ladybird. Young, Selina, illus. 2003. 32p. pap. *(978-1-84255-284-1(8)*, Orion Children's Bks.) Hachette Children's Group.

Gaydos, Stellisa. Lulu the Lucky Ladybug. 2011. 20p. 11.00 *(978-1-4567-3826-6(7))* AuthorHouse.

Gerth, Melanie. Five Little Ladybugs with Hand Puppet. Beith, Laura Huliska, illus. 2009. (ENG.). 12p. 12.95 *(978-1-58117-889-0(1)*, Intervisual/Piggy Toes) Bendon, Inc.

—Ten Little Ladybugs. Huliska-Beith, Laura, illus. 2007. (ENG.). 22p. (J). (gr. -1-3). bds. 15.95 *(978-1-58117-578-3(7)*, Intervisual/Piggy Toes) Bendon, Inc.

Gillingham, Sara. On My Leaf. Siminovich, Lorena, illus. 2012. (ENG.). 12p. (J). (gr. -1 — 1). bds. 8.99 *(978-1-4521-0813-1(7))* Chronicle Bks. LLC.

Golden Books. The Little Grumpy Cat That Wouldn't (Grumpy Cat) Golden Books, illus. 2016. (Little Golden Book Ser.). (ENG., Illus.). 24p. (J). (gr. -1-1). 4.99 *(978-0-399-55354-7(1)*, Golden Bks.) Random Hse. Children's Bks.

Gopinath, Karin Ursula. Friends in the Garden. Sutanto, Tommy, illus. 2008. 34p. (J). per. 19.95 *(978-0-9800637-0-7(1))* Lotus Art Works Inc.

Greban, Quentin. Mommy, I Love You. Greban, Quentin, illus. 2005. (Illus.). 32p. *(978-0-689-03922-5(0)*, Milk & Cookies) ibooks, Inc.

Happy Books. Little Ladybug. 2013. (Mini-Creatures Ser.). (ENG., Illus.). 8p. (J). (gr. -1 — 1). bds. 4.99 *(978-0-7641-6595-5(X))* Barron's Educational Series, Inc.

Hooray for Boys & Girls! 2006. (J). 15.95 *(978-0-9776837-0-3(2))* West Woods Pr.

Jaramillo, J.C. Best Buggies, 1 vol. 2010. 16p. 24.95 *(978-1-4489-4928-1(9))* PublishAmerica, Inc.

Kayaalp, Suzan. Inch Worm Inch Worm. Merrifield, Monarca, illus. 2013. 20p. pap. 12.95 *(978-1-62838-072-9(1))* Page Publishing Inc.

Keene, Carolyn. Cupcake Chaos. Pamintuan, Macky, illus. 2013. (Nancy Drew & the Clue Crew Ser.: 34). (ENG.). 96p. (J). (gr. 1-4). pap. 5.99 *(978-1-4424-5351-7(6)*, Aladdin) Simon & Schuster Children's Publishing.

King-Chai, Sharon. Lucy Ladybug. 2016. (ENG., Illus.). 32p. (J). (gr. -1-2). 16.99 *(978-0-553-51005-8(3)*, Random Hse. Bks. for Young Readers) Random Hse. Children's Bks.

Ladybug, Ladybug: Individual Title Six-Pack. (Story Steps Ser.). (gr. k-2). 23.00 *(978-0-7635-9802-0(X))* Rigby Education.

Lenny's Lost Spots. 2005. (J). per. 8.95 *(978-1-59566-131-9(X))* QEB Publishing Inc.

Lotorto-Soroka, Mary. Who Needs Spots Anyways? 2009. 24p. pap. 12.99 *(978-1-4490-3947-9(2))* AuthorHouse.

Lurie, Craig. Butterflies, Ladybugs, & Bumble Bees & the wonderful world this could Be ... . 2011. 36p. (gr. -1). pap. 14.95 *(978-1-4567-6300-8(8))* AuthorHouse.

Marranzino, Sami. The Littlest Ladybug. Currey, Andrew K., illus. 2012. 32p. pap. 24.95 *(978-1-4626-7781-8(9))* America Star Bks.

Martin, Anne E. There's A Ladybug in My House. Martin, Anne E., illus. l.t. ed. 2006. (Illus.). 45p. (J). per. 12.99 *(978-1-59879-165-5(6))* Lifevest Publishing, Inc.

McCabe, Lauren A. How Many Spots Have I Got? Foulke, Nancy, illus. 2005. (J). 16.00 *(978-1-893516-02-1(4))* Our Child Pr.

Miller, Amanda K. Lily's Grand Adventures. 2011. 36p. pap. 24.95 *(978-1-4626-2493-5(6))* America Star Bks.

Moore, Roland D. Bugging in the City. 2011. 80p. pap. 32.26 *(978-1-4567-4130-3(6))* AuthorHouse.

Morrow, John. Lilly Lightbug. 2017. (ENG., Illus.). 32p. (J). (gr. -1-6). 19.95 *(978-0-9790832-0-4(6)*, Three Ring Circus Publishing Hse., Inc.) 405 Pubns.

Newton-Kowalsky, Jacqueline. Itsy Bitsy Stories for Itsy Bitsy Tigers. 2012. 32p. pap. *(978-1-77097-138-7(6))* FriesenPress.

Nielander, Amy. The Ladybug Race. Nielander, Amy, illus. 2015. (ENG., Illus.). 40p. (J). 19.95 *(978-0-7649-7187-7(5)*, POMEGRANATE KIDS) Pomegranate Communications, Inc.

Pantelides, Sherry. It's Blue Like You! A Story about Loyalty. Perez, Debi, illus. 2007. 32p. (J). 12.99 *(978-0-9771076-1-2(2))* Lacey Productions.

—It's Red Like Me! A Story about the Blood of Jesus. Perez, Debi, illus. 2007. (J). lib. bdg. 12.99 *(978-0-9771076-0-5(4))* Lacey Productions.

—Make A Choice to Rejoice! A Story about Being Cheerful. Perez, Debi, illus. 2007. 32p. (J). 12.99 *(978-0-9771076-2-9(0))* Lacey Productions.

Parrott, Darcie. Ladybug's Walk. 2007. (ENG.). 32p. (J). (gr. -1-k). 10.95 *(978-0-9772692-8-0(0))* Birch Island.

Pèrols, Sylvaine & De Bourgoing, Pascale. Ladybird. 2006. (ENG., Illus.). 36p. (J). (gr. k-3). pap. 11.99 *(978-1-85103-089-7(1))* Moonlight Publishing, Ltd. GBR. Dist: Independent Pubs. Group.

Perry, Tally. Saving Sunny Stream, a Wormie Wormald Adventure. 2009. 60p. pap. 22.00 *(978-1-60860-296-4(6)*, Eloquent Bks.) Strategic Book Publishing & Rights Agency (SBPRA).

Peterson, Mary. Snail Has Lunch. Peterson, Mary, illus. 2016. (Pix Ser.). (ENG., Illus.). 64p. (J). (gr. 1-4). 12.99 *(978-1-4814-5302-8(5)*, Aladdin) Simon & Schuster Children's Publishing.

Pova, Rosie. Ladybug & Caterpillar: The Way to Friendship. 2008. 16p. pap. 24.95 *(978-1-60474-950-2(4))* America Star Bks.

Puzzi, Jessica. Rosy & Simon's Front Yard Adventure, 1 vol. 2010. 18p. pap. 24.95 *(978-1-4489-2601-5(7))* PublishAmerica, Inc.

Quanty, Donna. Dottie's New Look. 2008. 28p. pap. 24.95 *(978-1-60474-211-4(9))* America Star Bks.

Rist, Stephen. Ladybirds Don't Like Scrambled Eggs. 2010. (Illus.). 36p. 15.49 *(978-1-4490-6614-7(3))* AuthorHouse.

Satterfield, April. Leah Bug & Her Flying Friends. Guthrie, Lewis, illus. 2011. 20p. pap. 24.95 *(978-1-4560-8422-6(4))* America Star Bks.

Seward, Toni Gibson. Kloey & the Ladybug. 2013. 24p. pap. *(978-1-4602-3066-4(3))* FriesenPress.

Simee. Giggles Feel Good, 1 vol. 2010. 18p. pap. 24.95 *(978-1-4489-4878-9(9))* PublishAmerica, Inc.

Small, Lily. Bella the Bunny. 2015. (Fairy Animals of Misty Wood Ser.: 2). (ENG., Illus.). 144p. (J). (gr. k-3). pap. 5.99 *(978-1-62779-142-7(6)*, 9781627791427, Holt, Henry & Co. Bks. For Young Readers) Holt, Henry & Co.

Soler, Michael. The Ladybug & Me. Eisenberg, Serge, illus. 2007. 24p. (J). per. 8.99 *(978-0-9795469-0-7(7))* Soler, Michael.

Soman, David & Davis, Jacky. Doodle All Day with Ladybug Girl. Soman, David, illus. 2014. (Ladybug Girl Ser.). (ENG., Illus.). 32p. (J). (gr. -1-k). 6.99 *(978-0-448-47859-3(5)*, Grosset & Dunlap) Penguin Young Readers Group.

—Happy Halloween, Ladybug Girl! Soman, David, illus. 2014. (Ladybug Girl Ser.). (ENG., Illus.). 16p. (J). (gr. -1-k). 6.99 *(978-0-448-47860-9(9)*, Grosset & Dunlap) Penguin Young Readers Group.

—Play All Day with Ladybug Girl. Soman, David, illus. 2013. (Ladybug Girl Ser.). (ENG., Illus.). 16p. (J). (gr. -1-k). 6.99 *(978-0-448-46686-6(4)*, Grosset & Dunlap) Penguin Young Readers Group.

Stanek, Robert, pseud. The Bugville Critters So Many Lessons to Learn. 2009. (Illus.). 68p. (J). pap. 18.95 *(978-1-57545-237-1(5)*, Reagent Pr. Bks. for Young Readers) RP Media.

—Have a Backyard Picnic. 2009. (Bugville Critters Ser.: No. 14). (ENG., Illus.). 52p. (J). 14.95 *(978-1-57545-210-4(3)*, Reagent Pr. Bks. for Young Readers) RP Media.

—Have a Bad Day. 2009. (Bugville Critters Ser.: No. 11). (ENG., Illus.). 52p. (J). 14.95 *(978-1-57545-207-4(3)*, Reagent Pr. Bks. for Young Readers) RP Media.

—Have a Surprise Party. 2009. (Bugville Critters Ser.: No. 13). (ENG., Illus.). 52p. (J). 14.95 *(978-1-57545-209-8(X)*, Reagent Pr. Bks. for Young Readers) RP Media.

—Have Trouble at School. 2009. (Illus.). 24p. pap. 9.99 *(978-1-57545-212-8(X))*; 52p. (J). pap. 14.95 *(978-1-57545-204-3(9))* RP Media. (Reagent Pr. Bks. for Young Readers).

—Stay after School. 2009. (Bugville Critters Ser.: No. 10). (ENG., Illus.). 52p. (J). 14.95 *(978-1-57545-206-7(5)*, Reagent Pr. Bks. for Young Readers) RP Media.

—Visit City Hall. 2009. (Bugville Critters Ser.: No. 12). (ENG., Illus.). 52p. (J). 14.95 *(978-1-57545-208-1(1)*, Reagent Pr. Bks. for Young Readers) RP Media.

Thomas, Jan. Can You Make a Scary Face? Thomas, Jan, illus. 2009. (ENG., Illus.). 40p. (J). (gr. -1-3). 15.99 *(978-1-4169-8581-5(6)*, Beach Lane Bks.) Beach Lane Bks.

Tickle, Jack. Look Out, Ladybug. 2013. (ENG., Illus.). 32p. (J). *(978-1-58925-128-1(8))* Tiger Tales.

Treviño, Hilda L. Ladybugs on a Mission. 2013. 70p. (gr. 4-6). pap. 8.95 *(978-1-4759-7762-2(X))* iUniverse, Inc.

Turner-Rahman, Gregory. Ellabug. 2009. 40p. pap. 12.95 *(978-1-935290-09-4(6))* Diversion Pr.

Walshaw, Sam. Lulu Ladybug. 2012. (Illus.). (J). *(978-1-4351-3863-6(5))* Barnes & Noble, Inc.

Watt, Fiona. Busy Bug Book. Mantle, Ben, illus. 2011. (Pull-Back Books Ser.). 10p. (J). ring bd. 24.99 *(978-0-7945-2941-3(0)*, Usborne) EDC Publishing.

Woodson, Vera. Lady Bug, Beetle Boy, & Friends: Bullies Be Gone! 2013. (ENG., Illus.). (J). 14.95 *(978-1-62086-049-6(X))* Mascot Bks., Inc.

Younger, Mary. You're Not A Ladybird You've Got No Spots. 2011. (Illus.). 24p. 14.09 *(978-1-4567-7082-2(9))* AuthorHouse.

Yurksaitis, Anne. Genevieve the Singing Ladybug. Yurksaitis, Stephanie, illus. 2013. 28p. pap. 24.95 *(978-1-63000-927-4(X))* America Star Bks.

Zoehfeld, Kathleen Weidner & Smithsonian Institution Staff. Ladybug at Orchard Avenue (Mariquite en la avenida Orchard) 2008. (MUL.). 16p. 14.95 *(978-1-59249-844-4(2))* Soundprints.

LAFAYETTE, MARIE JOSEPH PAUL YVES ROCH GILBERT DU MOTIER, MARQUIS DE, 1757-1834

Bishop, Claire Huchet. Lafayette: French-American Hero. Brevannes, Maurice, illus. 2011. 82p. 37.95 *(978-1-258-03539-6(1))* Literary Licensing, LLC.

Castrovilla, Selene. Revolutionary Friends: General George Washington & the Marquis de Lafayette. Kozjan, Drazen, illus. 2013. (ENG.). 40p. (J). (gr. 3). 16.95 *(978-1-59078-880-6(X)*, Calkins Creek) Boyds Mills Pr.

Collins, Kathleen. El Marques de Lafayette: Heroe Frances de la Guerra de Independencia. 2004. (Grandes personajes en la historia de los Estados Unidos Ser.). (SPA.). 32p. (gr. 3-6). pap. 10.00 *(978-0-8239-4233-6(3)*, Rosen Classroom) Rosen Publishing Group, Inc., The.

—Marquis de Lafayette: French Hero of the American Revolution. (Primary Sources of Famous People in American History Ser.). 32p. 2009. (gr. 2-3). 47.90 *(978-1-60851-703-9(0))* 2004. (ENG., Illus.). (gr. 4-8). pap. 10.00 *(978-0-8239-4187-2(6))* Rosen Publishing Group, Inc., The.

—Marquis de Lafayette / el Marques de Lafayette: French Hero of the American Revolution / Héroe francés de la Revolución Estadounidense. 2009. (Famous People in American History/Grandes personajes en la historia de los Estados Unidos Ser.). (ENG & SPA.). 32p. (gr. 2-3). 47.90 *(978-1-61512-550-0(7)*, Editorial Buenas Letras) Rosen Publishing Group, Inc., The.

Corporate Contributor Staff & Colozza Cocca, Lisa. Marquis de Lafayette: Fighting for America's Freedom. 2012. (ENG.). 48p. (J). *(978-0-7787-0807-5(0))*; pap. *(978-0-7787-0813-1(6))* Crabtree Publishing Co.

Dugan, Christine. Marquis de Lafayette & the French (Alexander Hamilton) 2017. (Primary Source Readers Focus On Ser.). (Illus.). 32p. (J). (gr. 4-8). pap. 8.99 ***(978-1-4258-6353-1(1))*** Teacher Created Materials, Inc.

Jensen, Dorothea. A Buss from Lafayette. 2016. (ENG.). 266p. (J). (gr. 5-9). pap. 16.95 *(978-1-939371-90-4(2))* Boutique of Quality Books Publishing Co., Inc.

Randolph, Joanne. The Call of Liberty: Marquis de Lafayette & the American Revolution. 2009. (Great Moments in American History Ser.). 32p. (gr. 3-3). 47.90 *(978-1-61513-152-5(3))* Rosen Publishing Group, Inc., The.

LAFITTE, JEAN, 1782-1854—FICTION

Webber, Jake. Lafitte's Black Box: Boit Noir. 2009. 228p. 32.95 *(978-1-60594-361-9(4))*; pap. 14.95 *(978-1-60594-360-2(6))* Aeon Publishing Inc. (Llumina Pr.).

LA GUARDIA, FIORELLO H. (FIORELLO HENRY), 1882-1947

Leoni, Cristiana. New York in the 1930s with La Guardia. 2008. (Come See My City Ser.). 48p. (gr. 4). 28.50 *(978-0-7614-4336-0(3))* Marshall Cavendish Corp.

LAKE MICHIGAN

see Michigan, Lake

LAKES

AZ Books Staff. Frog's Pond. Potapenko, Olga, ed. 2012. (Talking Plush Animals Ser.). (ENG.). 10p. (J). (gr. -1-k). bds. 10.95 *(978-1-61889-113-6(8))* AZ Bks. LLC.

Barnes, Julia. 101 Facts about Lakes. 2003. (One Hundred One Facts about Our World Ser.). (Illus.). 32p. (gr. 1-4). lib. bdg. 26.00 *(978-0-8368-3707-0(X)*, Gareth Stevens Learning Library) Stevens, Gareth Publishing LLLP.

Berne, Emma Carlson. Lakes. 2008. (Geography Zone: Landforms Ser.). (Illus.). 24p. (J). (gr. 2-5). lib. bdg. 22.60 *(978-1-4042-4208-1(2))* Rosen Publishing Group, Inc., The.

Best, B. J. How Are Lakes Formed? 2017. (J). pap. 16.95 ***(978-1-5026-2549-6(0))*** Cavendish Square Publishing.

Bond, Rebecca. Out of the Woods: A True Story of an Unforgettable Event. 2015. (ENG., Illus.). 40p. (J). (gr. k-4). 17.99 *(978-0-374-38077-9(5)*, 9780374380779, Farrar, Straus & Giroux (BYR)) Farrar, Straus & Giroux.

Byerly, Robbie. At the Lake. rev. ed. 2011. (1-3Y in My World Ser.). (ENG., Illus.). 16p. (J). (gr. k-1). pap. 5.99 *(978-1-61541-411-6(8))* American Reading Co.

Carlson Berne, Emma. Lakes. 2009. (Geography Zone: Landforms Ser.). 24p. (gr. 2-3). 42.50 *(978-1-61512-711-5(9)*, PowerKids Pr.) Rosen Publishing Group, Inc., The.

Casado, Dami & Casado, Alicia. Los Rios y Lagos. 2005. (Yo Te Hablare De... Ser.). (SPA., Illus.). 14p. (J). per., bds. 8.99 *(978-84-272-7387-0(8))* Molino, Editorial ESP. Dist: Santillana USA Publishing Co., Inc.

Day, Trevor. Lakes & Rivers. Garratt, Richard, illus. 2006. (Biomes of the Earth Ser.). 272p. (gr. 6-12). 39.50 *(978-0-8160-5328-5(6))* Facts On File, Inc.

Declus, Jennifer. What Might I Find on a Pond. Kalasea, illus. 2004. (J). *(978-0-9743690-2-0(0))* Britt Allcroft Productions.

Fleisher, Paul. Lake & Pond Food Webs in Action. 2013. (Searchlight Books What Is a Food Web Ser.). (ENG., Illus.). 40p. (gr. 3-5). pap. 8.95 *(978-1-4677-1555-3(7))* Lerner Publishing Group.

Frisch, Aaron. Lakes. 2008. (Our World Ser.). (Illus.). 24p. (J). (gr. -1-3). lib. bdg. 24.25 *(978-1-58341-571-9(8)*, Creative Education) Creative Co., The.

Gamble, Adam. Good Night Lake. Kelly, Cooper, illus. 2008. (Good Night Our World Ser.). (ENG.). 28p. (J). (gr. k — 1). bds. 9.95 *(978-1-60219-028-3(3))* Good Night Bks.

Gingold, Janet. My Adventure on a Lake: Advanced My Adventure. 2009. (ENG.). 72p. (J). pap. 9.99 *(978-1-59092-442-6(8))* Blue Forge Pr.

Gray, Leon. Rivers & Lakes. 2015. (Amazing Biomes Ser.). (Illus.). 32p. (gr. 3-6). 31.35 *(978-1-78121-244-8(9)*, 1389646) Brown Bear Bks.

Green, Emily K. Lakes. 2011. (Blastoff! Readers Ser.). 24p. (J). pap. 5.95 *(978-0-531-26030-2(5)*, Children's Pr.) Scholastic Library Publishing.

Hibbert, Adam. Life in a Pond. 2010. (Nature in Focus Ser.). (Illus.). 32p. (gr. 2-5). (J). pap. 10.50 *(978-1-4339-3412-4(4)*, Gareth Stevens Learning Library); (YA). lib. bdg. 26.00 *(978-1-4339-3411-7(6))* Stevens, Gareth Publishing LLLP.

Howard, Fran. Lakes & Ponds, 1 vol. 2006. (Habitats Ser.). (ENG., Illus.). 32p. (J). (gr. -1-3). lib. bdg. 27.07 *(978-1-59679-779-6(7)*, Buddy Bks.) ABDO Publishing Co.

Johnson, Rebecca L. A Journey into a Lake. Saroff, Phyllis V., illus. 2004. (Biomes of North America Ser.). (J). pap. 6.95 *(978-0-8225-2043-6(5))*; 48p. (gr. 3-6). lib. bdg. 23.93 *(978-1-57505-594-7(5))* Lerner Publishing Group.

Klepeis, Alicia. 24 Hours in a Lake. 2017. (J). ***(978-1-5026-2480-2(X))*** Cavendish Square Publishing.

Kochanoff, Peggy. Be a Pond Detective, 1 vol. 2016. (ENG., Illus.). 40p. (J). (gr. -1-4). pap. 14.95 *(978-1-77108-394-2(8))* Nimbus Publishing, Ltd. CAN. Dist: Orca Bk. Pubs. USA.

Lowrie, Paul. Hooray for Minnesota Lakes. 2008. 19.95 *(978-0-9755801-8-9(3))* Questmarc Publishing.

Lynch, Seth. There's a Lake in My Backyard! 2016. (Backyard Biomes Ser.). 00024p. (J). pap. 8.15 ***(978-1-4824-5563-2(3))*** Stevens, Gareth Publishing LLLP.

Macken, JoAnn Early. Lagos. 2006. (Conoces la Tierra? Geografia del mundo (Where on Earth? World Geography) Ser.). (ENG & SPA., Illus.). 24p. (gr. 1-4). pap. 8.15 *(978-0-8368-6550-9(2))*; lib. bdg. 22.00 *(978-0-8368-6543-1(X))* Stevens, Gareth Publishing LLLP. (Weekly Reader Leveled Readers).

—Lakes. (Where on Earth? World Geography Ser.). (Illus.). 24p. 2006. (gr. 1-4). pap. 8.15 *(978-0-8368-6401-4(8))* 2006. (gr. 1-4). lib. bdg. 22.00 *(978-0-8368-6394-9(1))* 2005. (gr. k-3). pap. 8.15 *(978-0-8368-4891-5(8))* 2005. (gr. k-3). lib. bdg. 22.00 *(978-0-8368-4884-7(5))* Stevens, Gareth Publishing LLLP. (Weekly Reader Leveled Readers).

—Lakes/Lagos. 2005. (Water Habitats/ Habitats acuaticos Ser.). (SPA., Illus.). 24p. (gr. k-3). pap. 8.15 *(978-0-8368-6036-8(5))*; lib. bdg. 22.00 *(978-0-8368-6029-0(2))* Stevens, Gareth Publishing LLLP. (Weekly Reader Leveled Readers).

Minden, Cecilia. Lakes. 2010. (21st Century Basic Skills Library: the World Around Us Ser.). (ENG.). 24p. (gr. k-3). lib. bdg. 22.79 *(978-1-60279-859-5(1)*, 200584) Cherry Lake Publishing.

Nadeau, Isaac. Water in Rivers & Lakes. (Water Cycle Ser.). 24p. 2009. (gr. 4-4). 42.50 *(978-1-60854-271-0(8))* 2003. (Illus.). (J). lib. bdg. 22.60 *(978-0-8239-6266-2(0))* Rosen Publishing Group, Inc., The. (PowerKids Pr.).

Nemeth, Jason D. Rivers, Lakes, & Oceans. 2012. (Our Changing Earth Ser.). (ENG.). 24p. (J). (gr. 3-6). pap. 8.25 *(978-1-4488-6300-6(7)*, PowerKids Pr.); lib. bdg. 22.60 *(978-1-4488-6171-2(3))* Rosen Publishing Group, Inc., The.

Ostopowich, Melanie. Oceans, Lakes, & Rivers. 2015. (Illus.). 24p. (J). *(978-1-5105-0052-5(9))* SmartBook Media, Inc.

—Oceans, Lakes, & Rivers. 2010. (Water Science Ser.). (Illus.). 24p. (gr. 3-5). (J). pap. 11.95 *(978-1-61690-007-6(5))*; (YA). lib. bdg. 25.70 *(978-1-61690-001-4(6))* Weigl Pubs., Inc.

—Oceans, Rivers, & Lakes. 2005. (Science Matters Ser.). (Illus.). 24p. (J). (gr. 3-7). lib. bdg. 24.45 *(978-1-59036-304-1(3))* Weigl Pubs., Inc.

Rice, William & Franklin, Yvonne. Ponds, 1 vol. 2009. (Science Readers: a Closer Look Ser.). (ENG.). 32p. (J). (gr. 2-2). pap. 8.99 *(978-1-4333-0318-0(3))* Teacher Created Materials, Inc.

Rivers, Lakes, & Oceans. 2008. (Restless Earth Ser.). 112p. (YA). (gr. 5-9). 35.00 *(978-0-7910-9797-7(8))* Facts On File, Inc.

Silverman, Buffy. Let's Visit the Lake. 2016. (Lightning Bolt Books (tm) — Biome Explorers Ser.). (ENG., Illus.). 32p. (J). (gr. 1-3). lib. bdg. 26.65 *(978-1-5124-1193-5(0))* Lerner Publishing Group.

Smith, Ben. How Are Oceans & Lakes Alike? 2014. (Little Books of Answers: Level F Ser.). (Illus.). 16p. (gr. k-2). pap. 7.95 *(978-1-927136-55-3(5))* Three Crows Media NZL. Dist: RiverStream Publishing.

Spilsbury, Richard & Spilsbury, Louise. At Home in Rivers & Lakes, 01 vols., 1. 2016. (Home in the Biome Ser.). (ENG.). 32p. (J). pap. 10.00 *(978-1-5081-4556-1(3)*, PowerKids Pr.) Rosen Publishing Group, Inc., The.

Taylor, Trace, et al. En el Lago. 2011. (2Y Lugares Adonde Voy Ser.).Tr. of At the Lake. (SPA.). 16p. (J). (gr. k-2). pap. 6.99 *(978-1-61541-413-0(4))* American Reading Co.

Tull, Mary. Rivers & Lakes. 2007. (Rise & Shine Ser.). (ENG., Illus.). 32p. (J). pap. 17.95 *(978-0-7922-4561-2(X))* CENGAGE Learning.

Zollman, Pam. Lake Tahoe. 2006. (Rookie Read-About Geography Ser.). (ENG., Illus.). 32p. (J). (gr. 1-2). lib. bdg. 20.50 *(978-0-516-25036-6(1)*, Children's Pr.) Scholastic Library Publishing.

LAMBS

see Sheep

LAMPS—FICTION

Diroma, Joseph. Pinuccio. Jones, Bob, illus. 2009. 24p. pap. 14.99 *(978-1-60844-036-8(2))* Dog Ear Publishing, LLC.

Ebbeler, Jeffrey. Click! 2015. (ENG., Illus.). 32p. (J). (gr. -1-1). 16.95 *(978-0-8234-3295-0(5))* Holiday Hse., Inc.

Heine, Theresa & Barefoot Books Staff. Chandra's Magic Light. Gueyfier, Judith, illus. 2013. (J). 16.99 *(978-1-84686-493-3(3))* Barefoot Bks., Inc.

Lawrence, C. H., illus. Aladdin or, the Wonderful Lamp. 2012. (Shape Bks.). (ENG.). 16p. pap. 9.95 *(978-1-59583-454-6(0)*, 9781595834546, Green Tiger Pr.) Laughing Elephant.

LANCASTER COUNTY (PA.)—FICTION

Brenneman, Lynette Leaman, photos by. Susanna's Surprise: A Day at the Hans Herr House. 2012. (Illus.). 32p. (J). *(978-0-9859737-0-4(6))* Brenneman, Lynette.

Hurst, Elva. Autumn Days: Based on a True Story. 2015. (Farm Life Ser.). (ENG., Illus.). 80p. (J). pap. 6.99 *(978-0-7369-6094-6(5))* Harvest Hse. Pubs.

LAND

see Land Use

LAND, RECLAMATION OF

see Reclamation of Land

LAND SURVEYING

see Surveying

LAND USE

Here are entered general works which cover such topics as types of land, the utilization, distribution and development of land and the economic factors which affect the value of land. Works which treat only of ownership of land are entered under Real Estate.

see also Agriculture; Farms; Feudalism; Reclamation of Land

Banting, Erinn. England - The Land. 2012. (ENG.). 32p. (J). pap. *(978-0-7787-9832-3(1))* Crabtree Publishing Co.

Casper, Julie Kerr. Lands: Taming the Wilds. 2007. (Natural Resources Ser.). (Illus.). 225p. (YA). (gr. 7-12). lib. bdg. 39.50 *(978-0-8160-6356-7(7))* Facts On File, Inc.

Crabtree Publishing Company Staff & Greil, Marlene. United States: The Land. 2012. (ENG.). 32p. (J). *(978-0-7787-9835-4(6))*; pap. *(978-0-7787-9838-5(0))* Crabtree Publishing Co.

Gagne, Tammy. Life on Reservations. 2013. (ENG.). 48p. (J). (gr. 4-8). lib. bdg. 29.95 *(978-1-61228-444-6(2))* Mitchell Lane Pubs., Inc.

Greene, Carol. I Love Our Land. 2012. (I Love Our Earth Ser.). (Illus.). 24p. (J). (gr. 3-4). 22.60 *(978-0-7660-4040-3(2)*, Enslow Elementary) Enslow Pubs., Inc.

Gregory, Helen. Changing the Land. 2011. (Wonder Readers Early Level Ser.). (ENG.). (gr. -1-1). 16p. pap. 35.94 *(978-1-4296-8076-9(8))*; 32p. pap. 5.99 *(978-1-4296-7800-1(3))* Capstone Press of Coughlan Cos. (Wonder Readers).

Holt, Rinehart and Winston Staff. Environmental Science Chptr. 14: Land. 4th ed. Date not set. pap. 11.20 *(978-0-03-068074-8(3))* Holt McDougal.

Hyde, Natalie. Population Patterns: What Factors Determine the Location & Growth of Human Settlements? 2010. (Investigating Human Migration & Settlement Ser.). (ENG.,

Illus.). 48p. (J). (gr. 5-8). (978-0-7787-5182-3(1)); pap. (978-0-7787-5197-7(X)) Crabtree Publishing Co.

Linde, Barbara M. Urban Sprawl, Vol. 1. 2014. (Habitat Havoc Ser.). 32p. (J). (gr. 3-4). (ENG.). pap. 10.50 (978-1-4339-9868-3(8)); 26.60 (978-1-4339-9866-9(1)) Stevens, Gareth Publishing LLLP.

MacLeod, Elizabeth. Secrets Underground: North America's Buried Past. 2014. (ENG., Illus.). 96p. (YA). (gr. 5-12). 24.95 (978-1-55451-631-5(5), 9781554516315); pap. 14.95 (978-1-55451-630-8(7), 9781554516308) Annick Pr., Ltd. CAN. Dist: Publishers Group West (PGW).

Malone, Bobbie. Learning from the Land: Wisconsin Land Use. 2nd ed. 2011. (New Badger History Ser.). (ENG.). 160p. (J). pap. 15.95 (978-0-87020-464-7(5)) Wisconsin Historical Society.

Morgan, Sally. Changing Planet: What Is the Environmental Impact of Human Migration & Settlement? 2010. (Investigating Human Migration & Settlement Ser.). (ENG., Illus.). 48p. (J). (gr. 5-8). (978-0-7787-5179-3(1)); pap. (978-0-7787-5194-6(5)) Crabtree Publishing Co.

Price, Jane. Underworld: Exploring the Secret World Beneath Your Feet, 0 vols. Hancock, James Gulliver, illus. 2014. (ENG.). 96p. (J). (gr. 3-7). 18.95 (978-1-894786-89-8(0)) Kids Can Pr., Ltd. CAN. Dist: Hachette Bk. Group.

Rice, Dona Herweck. Land, 1 vol. 2nd rev. ed. 2011. (Nonfiction Readers Ser.). (ENG.). 12p. (J). (gr. 1-1). pap. 4.99 (978-1-4333-3574-7(3)) Teacher Created Materials, Inc.

—Terreno, 1 vol. 2nd rev. ed. 2011. (Nonfiction Readers Ser.). (SPA.). 12p. (J). (gr. 1-1). pap. 4.99 (978-1-4333-4413-8(0)) Teacher Created Materials, Inc.

Roza, G. On Flat Land: Learning the FL Sound. 2009. (PowerPhonics Ser.). 24p. (gr. 1-1). 39.90 (978-1-60851-463-2(3), PowerKids Pr.) Rosen Publishing Group, Inc., The.

Stefoff, Rebecca. Managing Land Use. 2011. (Environment at Risk 2 Ser.). (Illus.). 112p. (YA). (gr. 7). 39.93 (978-1-60870-478-1(5)) Marshall Cavendish Corp.

Weber, Valerie & Redlin, Janice L. Land Use. 2017. (J). **(978-1-5105-2201-5(8))** SmartBook Media, Inc.

Ylvisake, Anne. Land & Water: World Rivers. (Fact Finders Ser.). (Illus.). (J). (gr. 3-4). lib. bdg. 90.40 (978-0-7368-2559-7(2)) Capstone Press of Coughlan Cos.

LANDFORMS

see also Sand Dunes; Wetlands

Anderson, Sheila. Landforms: Classroom Set. 2008. pap. 34.95 (978-0-8225-9941-8(4)) Lerner Publishing Group.

—Landforms: Complete Set. 2008. pap. 208.95 (978-0-8225-9269-3(X)) Lerner Publishing Group.

—Plains. (First Step Nonfiction - Landforms Ser.). (gr. k-2). 2015. (ENG., Illus.). 24p. 23.99 (978-1-5124-1044-0(6), Lerner Pubns.) 2008. pap. 34.95 (978-0-8225-9938-8(4)) Lerner Publishing Group.

—Plateaus. (First Step Nonfiction - Landforms Ser.). (gr. k-2). 2015. (ENG., Illus.). 24p. 23.99 (978-1-5124-1045-7(4), Lerner Pubns.) 2008. pap. 34.95 (978-0-8225-9939-5(2)) Lerner Publishing Group.

—Valleys. (First Step Nonfiction - Landforms Ser.). (gr. k-2). 2015. (ENG., Illus.). 24p. 23.99 (978-1-5124-1046-4(2), Lerner Pubns.) 2008. pap. 34.95 (978-0-8225-9940-1(6)) Lerner Publishing Group.

Baltzer, Rochelle. Landslides, 1 vol. 2011. (Natural Disasters Ser.). (ENG., Illus.). 32p. (J). (gr. 2-5). 28.50 (978-1-61783-033-4(X)) ABDO Publishing Co.

Behrens, Janice. Totally Cool Caves & Hot Volcanoes: + 10 More Epic Landforms! 2017. (Rookie Amazing America(tm) Ser.). (ENG., Illus.). 32p. (J). pap. 5.95 (978-0-531-22589-9(5), Children's Pr.) Scholastic Library Publishing.

Benchmark Education Company, LLC Staff, compiled by. Landforms. 2006. spiral bd. 610.00 (978-1-4108-6793-3(5)) Benchmark Education Co.

Benoit, Peter. Tundra. 2011. (True Bk Ser.). 48p. (J). (ENG.). pap. 6.95 (978-0-531-28102-4(7)); (gr. 3-5). 29.00 (978-0-531-20553-2(3)) Scholastic Library Publishing. (Children's Pr.).

Berne, Emma Carlson. Hills. 2008. (Geography Zone: Landforms Ser.). (Illus.). 24p. (J). (gr. 2-5). lib. bdg. 22.60 (978-1-4042-4207-4(4)) Rosen Publishing Group, Inc., The.

—Plains. 2008. (Geography Zone: Landforms Ser.). (Illus.). 24p. (J). (gr. 2-5). lib. bdg. 22.60 (978-1-4042-4204-3(X)) Rosen Publishing Group, Inc., The.

Bow, James. Tundras Inside Out. 2014. (ENG.). 32p. (J). (978-0-7787-0639-7(7)) Crabtree Publishing Co.

Brennan, Linda Crotta. U. S. Landforms: What You Need to Know. 2017. (Fact Files Ser.). (ENG.). 24p. (gr. 1-2). lib. bdg. 25.32 **(978-1-5157-8112-7(7)**, First Facts) Capstone Press of Coughlan Cos.

Burgan, Michael. Land & Water. 2004. (Discovery Channel School Science Ser.). (Illus.). 32p. (gr. 4-8). lib. bdg. 26.00 (978-0-8368-3381-2(3), Gareth Stevens Learning Library) Stevens, Gareth Publishing LLLP.

Carlson Berne, Emma. Plains. 2009. (Geography Zone: Landforms Ser.). 24p. (gr. 2-3). 42.50 (978-1-61512-712-2(7), PowerKids Pr.) Rosen Publishing Group, Inc., The.

Carlson-Berne, Emma. Valleys. 2008. (Geography Zone: Landforms Ser.). (Illus.). 24p. (J). (gr. 2-5). lib. bdg. 22.60 (978-1-4042-4203-6(1)) Rosen Publishing Group, Inc., The.

Carlson Berne, Emma. Valleys. 2009. (Geography Zone: Landforms Ser.). 24p. (gr. 2-3). 42.50 (978-1-61512-713-9(5), PowerKids Pr.) Rosen Publishing Group, Inc., The.

Casil, Amy Sterling. The Creation of Canyons. 2009. (Illus.). 64p. (J). 77.70 (978-1-4358-5591-5(4)); (ENG., (YA). pap. 12.95 (978-1-4358-5590-8(6)); (ENG., (YA). (gr. 5-9). lib. bdg. 31.95 (978-1-4358-5296-9(6)) Rosen Publishing Group, Inc., The.

Ciocchi, Catherine. This Land Is Your Land, 1 vol. Morrison, Cathy, illus. 2015. (ENG.). 32p. (J). (gr. 1-4). 17.95 (978-1-62855-557-8(2)) Arbordale Publishing.

Ciocchi, Catherine & Morrison, Cathy. Esta Tierra, Es Tu País. Morrison, Cathy, illus. 2015. (ENG & SPA., Illus.). 32p. (J). (gr. 1-4). pap. 9.95 (978-1-62855-575-2(0)) Arbordale Publishing.

Craats, Rennay. Natural Landmarks. 2004. (American Symbols Ser.). (Illus.). 24p. (J). (gr. 4-7). per. 8.95 (978-1-59036-177-1(6)); (gr. 1-3). lib. bdg. 24.45 (978-1-59036-133-7(4)) Weigl Pubs., Inc.

Frankston, Evan. Mountains & Valleys: What's the Difference? 2013. (InfoMax Readers Ser.). (ENG.). 24p. (J). (gr. 3-4). pap. 49.50 (978-1-4777-2464-4(8)); (Illus.). pap. 8.25 (978-1-4777-2463-7(X)) Rosen Publishing Group, Inc., The. (Rosen Classroom).

Geiger, Beth & National Geographic Learning (Firm) Staff. Earth's Changing Land. 2007. (Avenues Ser.). (ENG., Illus.). 36p. (J). pap. 18.95 (978-0-7922-5427-0(9)) CENGAGE Learning.

Gonzales, Doreen & Graham, Amy. What Are the 7 Wonders of the Natural World? 2013. (What Are the Seven Wonders of the World? Ser.). 48p. (J). (gr. 4-18). 25.27 (978-0-7660-4153-0(0)) Enslow Pubs., Inc.

Graham, Amy. What Are the 7 Wonders of the Natural World? 2013. (What Are the Seven Wonders of the World? Ser.). 48p. (J). (gr. 4-10). pap. 8.95 (978-1-4644-0232-6(9)) Enslow Pubs., Inc.

Granger, Ronald. Exploring Earth's Surface. 2012. (Exploring Earth & Space Ser.). (ENG., Illus.). 24p. (J). (gr. 1-3). 22.60 (978-1-4488-8570-1(1), PowerKids Pr.) Rosen Publishing Group, Inc., The.

Green, Jen. Life on the Tundra. 2010. (Nature in Focus Ser.). (Illus.). 32p. (gr. 2-5). (J). pap. 10.50 (978-1-4339-3418-6(3), Gareth Stevens Learning Library); (YA). lib. bdg. 26.00 (978-1-4339-3417-9(5), 1309292) Stevens, Gareth Publishing LLLP.

Heos, Bridget. The Creation of Peninsulas. 2009. (J). 77.70 (978-1-4358-5601-1(5)); (ENG.). 64p. (YA). pap. 12.95 (978-1-4358-5600-4(7)); (ENG., Illus.). 64p. (YA). (gr. 5-9). lib. bdg. 31.95 (978-1-4358-5301-0(6)) Rosen Publishing Group, Inc., The.

How Water Got to the Plains: Individual Title Six-Packs. (gr. k-1). 23.00 (978-0-7635-8843-4(1)) Rigby Education.

Hutmacher, Kimberly M. Deltas, 1 vol. (Natural Wonders Ser.). (ENG., 24p. (gr. k-1). 2011. Illus.). pap. 7.29 (978-1-4296-6220-8(4)) 2011. pap. 41.70 (978-1-4296-6389-2(8)) 2010. lib. bdg. 26.65 (978-1-4296-5322-0(1)) Capstone Press of Coughlan Cos. (Pebble Plus).

Kalman, Bobbie. Earth's Coasts. 2008. (Looking at Earth Ser.). (ENG., Illus.). 32p. (J). (gr. 1-4). pap. (978-0-7787-3216-7(9)) Crabtree Publishing Co.

—I Can Write a Book about Landforms. 2012. (ENG.). 32p. (J). (978-0-7787-7992-6(0)); pap. (978-0-7787-8001-4(5)) Crabtree Publishing Co.

—Introducción a los Accidentes Geográficos. 2009. (SPA.). 32p. (J). (978-0-7787-8242-1(5)); pap. (978-0-7787-8259-9(X)) Crabtree Publishing Co.

—What Are Natural Structures? 2008. (Looking at Nature Ser.). (ENG., Illus.). 24p. (J). (gr. -1-2). pap. (978-0-7787-3343-0(2)); lib. bdg. (978-0-7787-3323-2(8)) Crabtree Publishing Co.

Kalman, Bobbie & MacAulay, Kelley. Introducing Landforms. 2008. (Looking at Earth Ser.). (ENG., Illus.). 32p. (J). (gr. 3-7). pap. (978-0-7787-3213-6(4)) Crabtree Publishing Co.

Labrecque, Ellen. Arctic Tundra, 1 vol. 2014. (Earth's Last Frontiers Ser.). (ENG.). 32p. (gr. 1-3). lib. bdg. 29.99 (978-1-4109-6177-8(X), Read Me!) Heinemann-Raintree.

—Valleys, 1 vol. 2014. (Learning about Landforms Ser.). (ENG.). 32p. (gr. 1-3). lib. bdg. 27.32 (978-1-4329-9535-5(9), Heinemann First Library) Heinemann-Raintree.

Labrecque, Ellen & Oxlade, Chris. Learning about Landforms, 1 vol. 2014. (Learning about Landforms Ser.). (ENG.). 32p. (gr. 1-3). lib. bdg. 136.60 (978-1-4329-9538-6(3), Heinemann First Library) Heinemann-Raintree.

Leavitt, Amie Jane. The Science Behind Wonders of the Earth: Cave Crystals, Balancing Rocks, & Snow Donuts. 2016. (Science Behind Natural Phenomena Ser.). (ENG., Illus.). 32p. (gr. 3-4). lib. bdg. 27.99 (978-1-5157-0773-8(3), Edge Bks.) Capstone Press of Coughlan Cos.

LernerClassroom Editors, ed. Landforms. 2008. pap. 7.95 (978-0-8225-9221-1(5)) Lerner Publishing Group.

The Library of Landforms. (Illus.). (J). (gr. k-6). 127.50 (978-1-4042-3293-8(1)) Rosen Publishing Group, Inc., The.

Lindeen, Mary. Landforms. 2017. (BeginningtoRead Ser.). (ENG.). 32p. (J). (-2). 22.60 **(978-1-59953-874-7(1))**; pap. 11.94 **(978-1-68404-093-3(0))** Norwood Hse. Pr.

Looye, Juliette, text. I Live near a Canyon. 2004. (Illus.). 16p. (J). pap. (978-0-7367-1937-7(7)) Zaner-Bloser, Inc.

Macken, JoAnn Early. Plains. 2006. (Where on Earth? World Geography Ser.). (Illus.). 24p. (gr. 1-4). pap. 8.15 (978-0-8368-6403-8(4)); lib. bdg. 22.00 (978-0-8368-6396-3(8)) Stevens, Gareth Publishing LLLP. (Weekly Reader Leveled Readers).

Maloof, Torrey. Weathering & Erosion, 1 vol. rev. ed. 2014. (Science Readers: Content & Literacy Ser.). (ENG.). 32p. (gr. 2-2). pap. 8.99 (978-1-4807-4611-4(8)) Teacher Created Materials, Inc.

McClish, Bruce. New World Continents & Land Bridges: North & South America. 2016. (Continents Ser.). (ENG.). 32p. (gr. 4-6). pap. 8.99 (978-1-4846-3639-8(2), NA-h) Heinemann-Raintree.

Meachen Rau, Dana. Land. 2008. (Earth Matters Ser.). 32p. (gr. 1-2). lib. bdg. 15.95 (978-0-7614-3043-8(1), Benchmark Bks.) Marshall Cavendish Corp.

Michele, Tracey. Earth's Land & Water. 2011. (Learn-Abouts Ser.). (Illus.). 16p. (J). pap. 7.95 (978-1-59920-593-9(9)) Black Rabbit Bks.

Mills, Nathan & Granger, Ronald. Exploring Earth's Surface. 2012. (Rosen Readers Ser.). (ENG., Illus.). 24p. (J). (gr. 1-2). pap. 8.25 (978-1-4488-8839-9(5), Rosen Classroom) Rosen Publishing Group, Inc., The.

Mis, Melody S. Exploring Canyons. 2009. (Geography Zone: Landforms Ser.). 24p. (gr. 2-4). (Illus.). (J). pap. 8.25 (978-1-4358-3114-8(4)); 42.50 (978-1-61512-692-7(9)) Rosen Publishing Group, Inc., The. (PowerKids Pr.).

—Exploring Peninsulas. 2009. (Geography Zone: Landforms Ser.). 24p. (gr. 2-3). 42.50 (978-1-61512-707-8(0)); (Illus.). (J). lib. bdg. 22.60 (978-1-4358-2711-0(2)) Rosen Publishing Group, Inc., The. (PowerKids Pr.).

Mitten, Ellen. Looking at Landforms. 2009. (ENG., Illus.). 24p. (gr. k-2). pap. 8.95 (978-1-60694-537-7(8)) Rourke Educational Media.

Munro, Roxie. Desert Days, Desert Nights. 2010. (ENG.). 32p. (J). 17.95 (978-1-933979-77-9(1), 7eb1e541-2180-4d1b-847f-abe71cd7cdcd) Bright Sky Pr.

Nadeau, Isaac. Peninsulas. 2009. (Library of Landforms Ser.). 24p. (gr. 3-4). 42.50 (978-1-60853-728-0(5), PowerKids Pr.) Rosen Publishing Group, Inc., The.

—Water in Rivers & Lakes. 2009. (Water Cycle Ser.). 24p. (gr. 4-4). 42.50 (978-1-60854-271-0(8), PowerKids Pr.) Rosen Publishing Group, Inc., The.

Nagel, Rob. UXL Encyclopedia of Landforms & Other Geologic Features, 3 vols. 2003. (Illus.). xxviii, 314p. (J). (978-0-7876-7672-8(1)); (978-0-7876-7671-1(3)); (978-0-7876-7670-4(5)) Cengage Gale. (UXL).

Nelson, Robin. Land. 2005. (First Step Nonfiction - Geography Ser.). (ENG.). 8p. (gr. -1-1). pap. 4.95 (978-0-8225-5392-2(9)) Lerner Publishing Group.

Rau, Dana Meachen. U. S. Landforms. 2012. (True Book Ser.). (ENG., Illus.). 48p. (J). pap. 6.95 (978-0-531-28329-5(1)); lib. bdg. 29.00 (978-0-531-24854-6(2)) Scholastic Library Publishing. (Children's Pr.).

Rice, William B. Landforms, 1 vol. rev. ed. 2014. (Science Readers: Content & Literacy Ser.). (ENG.). 32p. (gr. 2-2). pap. 8.99 (978-1-4807-4608-4(8)) Teacher Created Materials, Inc.

Roza, G. On Flat Land: Learning the FL Sound. 2009. (PowerPhonics Ser.). 24p. (gr. 1-1). 39.90 (978-1-60851-463-2(3), PowerKids Pr.) Rosen Publishing Group, Inc., The.

Science stories foss spanish landforms ea Cr05. 2005. (J). (978-1-59242-597-6(6)) Delta Education, LLC.

Sexton, Colleen. Tundra. 2008. (Learning about the Earth Ser.). (ENG., Illus.). 24p. (J). (gr. k-3). lib. bdg. 25.95 (978-1-60014-229-1(X)) Bellwether Media.

Sohn, Emily & Harter, Adam. Landforms: The Ever-changing Earth. 2011. (IScience Readers Ser.). 48p. (J). (gr. 5-6). lib. bdg. 23.94 (978-1-59953-425-1(8)) Norwood Hse. Pr.

Somervill, Barbara A. Plains & Plateaus. 2009. (21st Century Skills Library: Real World Math Ser.). (ENG.). 32p. (gr. 4-8). lib. bdg. 28.50 (978-1-60279-493-1(6), 200318) Cherry Lake Publishing.

Spilsbury, Louise. What Is a Landform?, 1 vol., 1. 2014. (Let's Find Out! Ser.). (ENG.). 32p. (gr. 3-6). 23.45 (978-1-62275-256-0(2)) Rosen Publishing Group, Inc., The.

Sweeney, Alyse. Canyons. 2010. (Natural Wonders Ser.). (ENG.). 24p. (gr. k-1). pap. 41.70 (978-1-4296-5593-4(3), Pebble Plus) Capstone Press of Coughlan Cos.

Taylor, Barbara. Understanding Landforms. 2007. (Geography Skills/Watts Ser.). (Illus.). 46p. (J). (gr. 4-7). lib. bdg. 32.80 (978-1-59920-049-1(X)) Black Rabbit Bks.

Van Gorp, Lynn. Investigating Landforms, 1 vol. 2007. (Science Readers Ser.). (ENG., Illus.). 32p. (J). (gr. 4-4). pap. 8.99 (978-0-7439-0557-2(1)) Shell Educational Publishing.

Warhol, Tom. Tundra. 2006. (Earth's Biomes Ser.). (Illus.). 80p. (gr. 6-7). lib. bdg. 34.21 (978-0-7614-2193-1(9), Benchmark Bks.) Marshall Cavendish Corp.

Wilder, Nellie. On Land, 1 vol. (Science Readers: Content & Literacy Ser.). (ENG., Illus.). 24p. (gr. k-k). 2015. (J). 22.96 (978-1-4938-1142-7(8)) 2014. pap. 8.99 (978-1-4807-4532-2(4)) Teacher Created Materials, Inc.

Woods, Michael & Woods, Mary B. Seven Natural Wonders of Africa. 2009. (Seven Wonders Ser.). (ENG., Illus.). 80p. (gr. 5-8). lib. bdg. 33.26 (978-0-8225-9071-2(9)) Lerner Publishing Group.

—Seven Natural Wonders of Asia & the Middle East. 2009. (Seven Wonders Ser.). (ENG., Illus.). 80p. (gr. 5-8). 33.26 (978-0-8225-9073-6(5)) Lerner Publishing Group.

—Seven Natural Wonders of Australia & Oceania. 2009. (Seven Wonders Ser.). (ENG., Illus.). 80p. (gr. 5-8). 33.26 (978-0-8225-9074-3(3)) Lerner Publishing Group.

—Seven Natural Wonders of Central & South America. 2009. (Seven Wonders Ser.). (Illus.). 80p. (YA). (gr. 5-9). lib. bdg. 33.26 (978-0-8225-9070-5(0)) Twenty First Century Bks.

—Seven Natural Wonders of the Arctic, Antarctica, & the Oceans. 2009. (Seven Wonders Ser.). (ENG., Illus.). 80p. (gr. 5-8). 33.26 (978-0-8225-9075-0(1)) Lerner Publishing Group.

World Book, Inc Staff, contrib. by. Carved by Time. 2017. (J). **(978-0-7166-3365-5(5))** World Bk.-Childcraft International.

—Enchanted Landscapes. 2017. (J). **(978-0-7166-3366-2(3))** World Bk., Inc.

LANDMARKS, PRESERVATION OF

see Natural Monuments

LANDSCAPE ARCHITECTURE

see also Cemeteries; Landscape Gardening

Allaire, Caroline & Krawczyk, Sabine. Let's Look at the Hedge. Hugo, Pierre de, illus. 2012. (ENG.). 38p. (J). (gr. 1-4). pap. 11.99 (978-1-85103-339-3(4)) Moonlight Publishing, Ltd. GBR. Dist: Independent Pubs. Group.

Conklin, Wendy. On the Job: Landscape Architects: Perimeter (Grade 3) 2017. (Mathematics Readers Ser.). (Illus.). 32p. (gr. 3-3). 8.99 **(978-1-4807-5809-4(4))** Teacher Created Materials, Inc.

Dunlap, Julie & Olmsted, Frederick Law. Parks for the People: The Life of Frederick Law Olmsted. 2011. (ENG., Illus.). 112p. (J). (gr. 4-7). pap. 12.95 (978-1-55591-470-7(5)) Fulcrum Publishing.

Kjelle, Marylou Morano. A Kid's Guide to Landscape Design. 2008. (Gardening for Kids Ser.). (Illus.). 48p. (YA). (gr. 1-4). lib. bdg. 29.95 (978-1-58415-637-6(6)) Mitchell Lane Pubs., Inc.

Lewis, Anna M. Women of Steel & Stone: 22 Inspirational Architects, Engineers, & Landscape Designers. 2014. (Women of Action Ser.). (ENG., Illus.). 272p. (YA). (gr. 7). 19.95 (978-1-61374-508-3(7)) Chicago Review Pr., Inc.

Mason, Helen. Landscape Designer. 2014. (Creative Careers Ser.). 48p. (J). (gr. 4-8). pap. 84.30 (978-1-4824-1301-4(9)) Stevens, Gareth Publishing LLLP.

Wishinsky, Frieda. The Man Who Made Parks: The Story of Parkbuilder Frederick Law Olmsted. Zhang, Song Nan, illus. 2009. (ENG.). 32p. (J). (gr. k-12). pap. 10.95 (978-0-88776-902-3(0), Tundra Bks.) Tundra Bks. CAN. Dist: Penguin Random Hse. LLC.

LANDSCAPE GARDENING

see also Landscape Architecture; Shrubs; Trees

Avery, Sebastian. A Landscaper's Tools. 2015. (Community Helpers & Their Tools Ser.). (ENG.). 24p. (J). (gr. 2-3). 23.60 (978-1-4994-0899-7(4), PowerKids Pr.) Rosen Publishing Group, Inc., The.

Buchanan, Heather. Logan's Landscaping: Foundations for Multiplication. 2014. (Rosen Common Core Math Readers Ser.). 24p. (J). (gr. 2-3). (ENG.). pap. 49.50 (978-1-4777-4649-3(8)); (Illus.). 23.60 (978-1-4777-6400-8(3)); (ENG., Illus.). pap. 8.25 (978-1-4777-4648-6(X)) Rosen Publishing Group, Inc., The. (Rosen Classroom).

Gerber, Larry. Careers in Landscaping & Gardening. 2013. (Essential Careers Ser.). 80p. (YA). (gr. 7-12). lib. bdg. 33.25 (978-1-4488-9477-2(8)) Rosen Publishing Group, Inc., The.

LANDSCAPE PAINTING

Bodden, Valerie. Brushes with Greatness: Landscapes. 2013. (Brushes with Greatness Ser.). (ENG.). 48p. (J). (gr. 4-7). pap. 12.00 (978-0-89812-764-5(5), Creative Paperbacks) Creative Co., The.

Freedman, Jeri. Land Formation: The Shifting, Moving, Changing Earth: The Creation of Mountains. 2009. (J). 77.70 (978-1-4358-5599-1(X)) Rosen Publishing Group, Inc., The.

Thomson, Leo. Sense of Place: Landscapes. 2005. (Artventures Ser.). (Illus.). 32p. (YA). (gr. 3-6). lib. bdg. 27.10 (978-1-58340-622-9(0), 1247320) Black Rabbit Bks.

LANGUAGE AND LANGUAGES

Here are entered general works on the history, philosophy, origin, etc. of language. Comparative studies of languages are entered under Philology, Comparative.

see also Grammar; Phonetics; Rhetoric; Semantics; Speech; Voice; Writing

also names of languages or groups of cognate languages, e.g. English Language; etc.; also classes of people with the subdivision Language, e.g. Children—Language; etc.

Abondolo, Daniel. Colloquial Finnish: The Complete Course for Beginners. 2nd rev. ed. 2011. (Colloquial Ser.). (ENG & FIN., Illus.). 368p. pap. 43.95 (978-0-415-49966-8(6), 0415499666) Routledge.

Abondolo, Daniel Mario. Colloquial Finnish Mp3. 2nd ed. 2011. (FIN & ENG., Illus.). xiii, 354p. cd-rom 44.95 (978-0-415-49967-5(4)) Routledge.

Aigner-Clark, Julie. La Guarderia de Idiomas (The Guarderia Language) 2004. (Baby Einstein Ser.). (SPA., Illus.). 16p. (J). bds. (978-970-718-153-3(2), Silver Dolphin en Español) Advanced Marketing, S. de R. L. de C. V.

Amery, Heather, et al. First Hundred Words in Maori. 2008. (MAO., Illus.). 40p. pap. 14.00 (978-1-86969-304-6(3)) Huia Pubs. NZL. Dist: Univ. of Hawaii Pr.

Athans, Sandra K. & Parente, Robin W. Tips & Tricks for Determining Point of View & Purpose. 2014. (Common Core Readiness Guide to Reading Ser.). 80p. (J). (gr. 5-8). 32.95 (978-1-4777-7555-4(2), Rosen Reference) Rosen Publishing Group, Inc., The.

Bancroft, Bronwyn. Possum & Wattle: My Big Book of Australian Words. enl. ed. 2009. (ENG., Illus.). 48p. (J). (gr. k-2). 18.99 (978-1-921272-58-5(9)) Little Hare Bks. AUS. Dist: Independent Pubs. Group.

Bardakigian, K. D. & Thompson, Robert W. Western Armenian, 8 cass., Set. (ARM.). 319p. (YA). (gr. 10-12). pap. 185.00 incl. audio (978-0-88432-444-7(3), AFAR15) Pavilion Pubs.

Barfell, Judith A. Learn & Sign Funtime: Sign with God's Angels. 2005. (Beginnings Ser.). (J). per. 14.95 (978-0-9753717-0-1(3)) Learn & Sign Funtime Bks.

Batot, Yvonne & Gose, Senora. Flip Flop French: Ages 3-5: Level 1. 2007. (Illus.). 84p. (J). spiral bd. 25.00 (978-1-60402-967-3(6)) Flip n Flop Learning, LLC.

Beard, Adrian. Language Change. 2004. (Intertext Ser.). (ENG., Illus.). 128p. (C). 95.00 (978-0-415-32055-9(0)); per. 30.95 (978-0-415-32056-6(9)) Routledge.

Bell-Rehwoldt, Sheri. Speaking Secret Codes, 1 vol. 2010. (Making & Breaking Codes Ser.). (ENG.). 32p. (gr. 3-4). lib. bdg. 27.99 (978-1-4296-4569-0(5), Edge Bks.) Capstone Press of Coughlan Cos.

Benati, R., et al. Meine Freunde und ich. Sammelmappe für Kinder. Mit Audio-CD: Zum Sammeln der Übungsblätter. 2005. (GER.). pap. 10.95 (978-3-468-49503-8(X)) Langenscheidt Publishing Group.

Bilingual Picture Dictionary [Capstone Sole Source]. 2010. (Bilingual Picture Dictionaries Ser.). 32p. lib. bdg. 155.94 (978-1-4296-5847-8(9), Aplus Bks.) Capstone Press of Coughlan Cos.

Blaisdell, Bette. A Mouthful of Onomatopoeia, 1 vol. 2014. (Words I Know Ser.). (ENG.). 32p. (gr. 1-2). lib. bdg. 27.32 (978-1-4765-3939-3(1), Aplus Bks.) Capstone Press of Coughlan Cos.

Bluedorn, Johannah. Little Bitty Baby Learns Greek. Bluedorn, Johannah, illus. 2006. (GRE & ENG., Illus.). 30p. (J). bds. (978-1-933228-06-8(7)) Trivium Pursuit.

Bowers, Linda, et al. No Glamour Language & Reasoning. 2003. (J). per. 41.95 (978-0-7606-0500-4(9)) LinguiSystems, Inc.

Boyles, Peggy Palo & Prentice Hall Dictionary Editors. Realidades Vol. 2: Level 2, 2 vols. l.t. ed. 2003. (SPA & ENG.). 508p. (YA). (gr. 9-9). 254.00 (978-0-13-035951-3(3), Prentice Hall) Pearson Schl.

Boyles, Peggy Palo & Prentice Hall Direct Education Staff. Realidades: Level B, 2 vols. l.t. ed. 2003. (SPA & ENG.). 416p. (YA). (gr. 7-7). 208.00 (978-0-13-035967-4(X), Prentice Hall) Pearson Schl.

Boyles, Peggy Palo & Prentice Hall Directories Staff. Realidades: Level 1, 2 vols. l.t. ed. 2003. (ENG.). 564p. (YA). (gr. 8-9). stu. ed. 282.00 (978-0-13-101687-3(3), Prentice Hall) Pearson Schl.

—Realidades: Level A. l.t. ed. 2003. (SPA & ENG.). 322p. (YA). (gr. 7-7). stu. ed. 161.00 (978-0-13-035966-7(1), Prentice Hall) Pearson Schl.

Boyles, Peggy Palo, et al. Realidades, Level 3, 2 vols. l.t. ed. 2003. (SPA & ENG.). 614p. (YA). (gr. 10-10). 307.00 (978-0-13-035968-1(8), Prentice Hall) Pearson Schl.

Bridge to Communication Level C: Class Set. (Illus.). (J). (gr. 2-5). 275.00 (978-1-56014-777-0(6)) Santillana USA Publishing Co., Inc.

Bridge to Communication Level C: Student Language Book. (J). (gr. 2-5). 9.50 (978-1-56014-752-7(0)); (YA). (gr. 6-8).

9.50 *(978-1-56014-755-8(5))* Santillana USA Publishing Co., Inc.

Bridge to Communication Level A: Student Language Book. (J). (gr. 2-5). 9.50 *(978-1-56014-750-3(4))*; (YA). (gr. 6-8). 9.50 *(978-1-56014-753-4(9))* Santillana USA Publishing Co., Inc.

Bridge to Communication Level B: Student Language Book. (J). (gr. 2-5). 9.50 *(978-1-56014-751-0(2))*; (YA). (gr. 6-8). 9.50 *(978-1-56014-754-1(7))* Santillana USA Publishing Co., Inc.

Brocket, Jane. Stickiest, Fluffiest, Crunchiest: Super Superlatives. Brocket, Jane, photos by. 2015. (ENG., Illus.). 32p. (J). (gr. -1-2). 26.60 *(978-1-4677-9241-7(1)*, Millbrook Pr.) Lerner Publishing Group.

Bullard, Lisa. My Language, Your Language. 2015. (Cloverleaf Books (tm) — Alike & Different Ser.). (ENG., Illus.). 24p. (J). (gr. k-2). pap. 6.99 *(978-1-4677-6034-8(X))*; lib. bdg. 23.99 *(978-1-4677-4906-0(0))* Lerner Publishing Group. (Millbrook Pr.).

Burke, David. BEAUTY & the BEAST (English to Japanese - Level 3) Learn JAPANESE Through Fairy Tales. 2007. (ENG & JPN.). (J). per. 14.95 incl. audio compact disk *(978-1-891888-90-8(0))* Slangman Publishing.

—Cinderella: Level 1: Learn Japanese Through Fairy Tales. Bobrick, Julie, ed. Bird, Mariko, tr. Sandoval, Migs, illus. 2006. (Slangman Kids: Level 1 Ser.). (ENG & JPN.). 29p. pap. 14.95 incl. audio compact disk *(978-1-891888-78-6(1))* Slangman Publishing.

—Goldilocks & the 3 Bears: Level 2: Learn Japanese Through Fairy Tales. Sandoval, Migs, illus. 2006. (Slangman Kids: Level 2 Ser.). (ENG & JPN.). 29p. (J). (gr. -1-3). pap. 14.95 incl. audio compact disk *(978-1-891888-84-7(6))* Slangman Publishing.

—GOLDILOCKS (Japanese to English - Level 2) Learn ENGLISH Through Fairy Tales. 2007. (JPN & ENG.). (J). per. 14.95 incl. audio compact disk *(978-1-891888-04-5(8))* Slangman Publishing.

Burrill, Richard L. Somewhere Behind the Eyes: Language Treasures Aha! Date not set. (Illus.). 85p. (J). (gr. 4-12). 15.95 *(978-1-878464-16-3(7))* Anthro Co., The.

Carole Marsh. Ah,So! Japanese for Kids. 2004. (Little Linguist Ser.). 32p. (gr. 2-6). pap. 5.95 *(978-0-635-02434-3(9))* Gallopade International.

—It Really Is Greek to Me! Greek for Kids. 2004. (Little Linguist Ser.). 32p. (gr. 2-6). pap. 5.95 *(978-0-635-02432-9(2))* Gallopade International.

—Say What When You Sneeze? German for Kids. 2004. (Little Linguist Ser.). 32p. (gr. 2-6). pap. 5.95 *(978-0-635-02431-2(4))* Gallopade International.

Cleary, Brian P. Breezier, Cheesier, Newest, & Bluest: What Are Comparatives & Superlatives? Gable, Brian, illus. 2013. (Words Are CATegorical (r) Ser.). (ENG.). 32p. (gr. 2-5). lib. bdg. 16.95 *(978-0-7613-5362-1(3)*, Millbrook Pr.) Lerner Publishing Group.

DeCesare, Ruth. Songs for the German Class. (GER.). (J). 9.95 *(978-0-8442-2262-2(3)*, National Textbook Co.) McGraw-Hill/Contemporary.

Dual Language Add-On Package. 2003. 170.50 *(978-0-673-57714-6(7))* Celebration Pr.

Dual Language Classroom Library. 2003. 769.50 *(978-0-673-77836-9(3))* Celebration Pr.

Elwell, Maggie. My Mom, the Coconut MacHine. 2009. 24p. pap. 12.00 *(978-1-4389-2674-2(X))* AuthorHouse.

Epps, S. Emmanuel & Robateau, Lisa. Bubble Brain: Story Time Rhymes That Build the Mind. 2013. 34p. pap. 12.95 *(978-0-9911410-0-5(8))* Addi-Boo Bks.

Erdogan, Fatih. Ece Ve Efe Ile Türkçe. Hambleton, Laura, illus. 2007. (Abby & Zak Ser.). (ENG.). 48p. (J). (gr. k-2). pap. 16.95 *(978-1-84059-493-5(4))* Milet Publishing.

Fatus, Sophie & Couëlle, Jennifer. My Big Barefoot Book of French & English Words. 2016. (FRE & ENG.). (J). pap. *(978-1-78285-303-9(0))* Barefoot Bks., Inc.

Fatus, Sophie & París, Mertxe. My Big Barefoot Book of Spanish & English Words. 2016. (SPA & ENG.). (J). pap. *(978-1-78285-275-9(1))* Barefoot Bks., Inc.

Fremdwoerterbuch. (Duden-Schuelerduden Ser.). (GER.). 480p. (YA). 27.95 *(978-3-411-05143-4(4))* Bibliographisches Institut & F. A. Brockhaus AG DEU. Dist: International Bk. Import Service, Inc.

Froman, Craig. Passport to the World: Your a to z guided Tour. 2010. (YA). lib. bdg. 15.99 *(978-0-89051-595-2(6))* Master Bks.

Ganeri, Anita. Hindi, 1 vol. 2011. (Languages of the World Ser.). (ENG.). 32p. (gr. k-2). 27.32 *(978-1-4329-5081-1(9)*, Heinemann First Library) Heinemann-Raintree.

—I Can Write! 2013. (I Can Write Ser.). (ENG.). 32p. (gr. 1-3). pap. 47.94 *(978-1-4329-6946-2(3)*, Heinemann First Library) Heinemann-Raintree.

Gasmen, Imelda Fines. Tuttle Tagalog for Kids. 2008. (Tuttle Flash Cards Ser.). (ENG., Illus.). 1p. (J). (gr. 1-8). 19.95 *(978-0-8048-3957-0(3))* Tuttle Publishing.

Gigarjian, Ani & Avedikian, Linda. My Second Book of Armenian Words. 2nd ed. 2006. (J). 18.00 *(978-0-9717799-1-4(0))* Gigarjian, Ani & Linda Avedikian.

Gilbert, Keith & Schuh, Leesa. TEENAGERS: Your Essential Guide to the Weird World of... Adults 2nd Edition. 2009. 180p. pap. 15.95 *(978-1-4452-4859-2(X))* Lulu Pr., Inc.

Giulieri, Anne. Oral Language-Book A: Speaking & Listening in the Classroom. 2012. (Engage Literacy Ser.). (ENG.). 28p. (gr. k-2). 75.00 *(978-1-4296-9558-9(7)*, Engage Literacy) Capstone Press of Coughlan Cos.

—Oral Language-Book B: Speaking & Listening in the Classroom. 2012. (Engage Literacy Ser.). (ENG.). 28p. (gr. k-2). 75.00 *(978-1-4296-9559-6(5)*, Engage Literacy) Capstone Press of Coughlan Cos.

Greeley, August. Writing in Ancient Egypt. 2009. (Writing in the Ancient World Ser.). 24p. (gr. 3-3). 42.50 *(978-1-60854-905-4(4)*, PowerKids Pr.) Rosen Publishing Group, Inc., The.

—Writing in Ancient India. 2009. (Writing in the Ancient World Ser.). 24p. (gr. 3-3). 42.50 *(978-1-60854-906-1(2)*, PowerKids Pr.) Rosen Publishing Group, Inc., The.

—Writing in Ancient Mesopotamia. 2009. (Writing in the Ancient World Ser.). 24p. (gr. 3-3). 42.50 *(978-1-60854-907-8(0)*, PowerKids Pr.) Rosen Publishing Group, Inc., The.

—Writing in Ancient Phoenicia. 2009. (Writing in the Ancient World Ser.). 24p. (gr. 3-3). 42.50 *(978-1-60854-908-5(9)*, PowerKids Pr.) Rosen Publishing Group, Inc., The.

Gu, Licheng & Hambleton, Laura. Chinese with Lulu & Maomao. 2008. (Abby & Zak Ser.). (CHI & ENG., Illus.). 48p. (J). (gr. k-2). pap. 16.95 *(978-1-84059-514-7(0))* Milet Publishing.

Ham, Catherine. You Talking to Me? Discover the World of Words, Codes, Emojis, Signs, Slang, Smoke Signals, Barks, Babbles, Growls, Gestures, Hieroglyphics & More. Owsley, Anthony, illus. 2017. (ENG.). 96p. (J). (gr. 3-7). 14.95 *(978-1-63322-155-0(5)*, Moondance) Quarto Publishing Group USA.

Handicott, Ben. The Hello Atlas: Listen to 133 Different Languages! Pak, Kenard, illus. 2016. (ENG.). 80p. (J). (gr. 1-4). 27.99 *(978-1-84780-863-9(8)*, Wide Eyed Editions) Quarto Publishing Group UK GBR. Dist: Hachette Bk. Group.

Hanson, Tracie. New World Baby - the Collection. 2007. (ENG, FRE, SPA, ITA & GER., Illus.). 28p. (J). 48.00 *(978-0-9799185-4-4(5))* Hanson, Tracie.

Haskins, James & Benson, Kathleen. Count Your Way Through Afghanistan. Moore, Megan, illus. 2006. (Count Your Way Ser.). 40p. (J). (gr. -1-3). lib. bdg. 19.93 *(978-1-57505-880-1(4)*, Millbrook Pr.) Lerner Publishing Group.

—Count Your Way Through Egypt. Rama, Sue, illus. 2006. (Count Your Way Ser.). 24p. (J). (gr. -1-3). lib. bdg. 19.93 *(978-1-57505-882-5(0)*, Millbrook Pr.) Lerner Publishing Group.

—Count Your Way Through Iran. Zaman, Farida, illus. 2006. (Count Your Way Ser.). 40p. (J). (gr. -1-3). lib. bdg. 19.93 *(978-1-57505-881-8(2)*, Millbrook Pr.) Lerner Publishing Group.

—Count Your Way Through Kenya. Leveque, Lyne, illus. 2006. (Count Your Way Ser.). 24p. (J). (gr. -1-3). lib. bdg. 19.93 *(978-1-57505-884-9(7)*, Millbrook Pr.) Lerner Publishing Group.

Haskins, Jim & Benson, Kathleen. Count Your Way Through South Africa. Neibert, Alissa, illus. 2006. (Count Your Way Ser.). (ENG.). 24p. (gr. 2-5). lib. bdg. 19.93 *(978-1-57505-883-2(9)*, Millbrook Pr.) Lerner Publishing Group.

—Count Your Way Through Zimbabwe. Park, Janie Jaehyun, illus. 2006. (Count Your Way Ser.). (ENG.). 24p. (gr. 2-5). lib. bdg. 19.93 *(978-1-57505-885-6(5)*, Millbrook Pr.) Lerner Publishing Group.

Hibbs, Linda. Let's Learn Indonesian: A\Complete Language Learning Kit for Kids. 2017. (ENG., Illus.). (J). (gr. k-8). 14.95 *(978-0-8048-4598-4(0))* Tuttle Publishing.

—My First Book of Indonesian Words: An ABC Rhyming Book of Indonesian Language & Culture. Laud, Julia, illus. 2016. (ENG & IND.). 32p. (J). (gr. -1-3). 12.95 *(978-0-8048-4557-1(3))* Tuttle Publishing.

Hindi Level One: The Rosetta Stone Language Library. 2005. (J). (gr. 1-18). cd-rom 209.00 *(978-1-58022-043-9(6))* Rosetta Stone Ltd.

Hippocrene Books Staff. Children's Illustrated Czech Dictionary: English-Czech/Czech-English. 2003. (Hippocrene Children's Illustrated Foreign Language Dictionaries Ser.). (ENG., Illus.). 96p. pap. 11.95 *(978-0-7818-0987-0(8))* Hippocrene Bks., Inc.

Hippocrene Books Staff, ed. Bengali Children's Picture Dictionary: English-Bengali/Bengali-English. 2006. (ENG.). 114p. 14.95 *(978-0-7818-1128-6(7))* Hippocrene Bks., Inc.

Hobson, Mark, tr. Language Helper German: Helpin you speak more German. 2007. (GER & ENG., Illus.). 195p. (J). pap. 22.95 *(978-0-9789152-0-9(8))* Chou Chou Pr.

Holt, Rinehart and Winston Staff. Elements of Language: Developing Language Skills. 4th ed. Date not set. (Elements of Language Ser.). (YA). (gr. 10). pap. 17.20 *(978-0-03-070063-7(9))*; (YA). (gr. 11). pap. 17.20 *(978-0-03-070064-4(7))*; (YA). (gr. 12). pap. 17.20 *(978-0-03-070066-8(3))*; (J). (gr. 6). pap. 17.20 *(978-0-03-070058-3(2))*; (YA). (gr. 7). pap. 17.20 *(978-0-03-070059-0(0))*; (YA). (gr. 8). pap. 17.20 *(978-0-03-070061-3(2))*; (YA). (gr. 9). pap. 17.20 *(978-0-03-070062-0(0))* Holt McDougal.

—Elements of Language: Developing Language Skills Answer Key. 4th ed. Date not set. (J). (gr. 6). pap. 12.80 *(978-0-03-070067-5(1))*; (YA). (gr. 7). pap. 12.80 *(978-0-03-070068-2(X))*; (YA). (gr. 8). pap. 12.80 *(978-0-03-070069-9(8))* Holt McDougal.

Isabella, Jude. Chitchat: Celebrating the World's Languages. Boake, Kathy, illus. 2013. (ENG.). 44p. (J). (gr. 3-7). 17.95 *(978-1-55453-787-7(8))* Kids Can Pr., Ltd. CAN. Dist: Hachette Bk. Group.

Khare, Pratibha & Bekooy Khare, Catherine. Hindi Primer, Pt. 1. 2nd ed. 2004. (HIN & ENG.). 172p. spiral bd. *(978-0-9663831-3-3(3))* Mukund Pubns.

Kiraz, George. The Syriac Alphabet for Children. 2004. (J). 25.00 *(978-1-59333-113-9(4))*; pap. 15.00 *(978-1-59333-112-2(6))* Gorgias Pr., LLC.

Kumar, Monica & Kumar, Manisha. Diwali: A Festival of Lights & Fun. Sona & Jacob, illus. 2006.Tr. of Diwali: Khushiyon Ka Tyohaar. (ENG & HIN.). 32p. (J). 11.00 *(978-0-9773645-7-2(7))* MeeraMasi, Inc.

Lanza, Janet R., et al. Artic to Go. 2004. (J). per. 35.95 *(978-0-7606-0540-0(8))* LinguiSystems, Inc.

Learn Bangla 2004. 2004. (J). cd-rom 29.95 *(978-0-9748503-8-2(1))* Griha.

Level One - Workbook 2005. 2007. (J). pap. *(978-0-932416-14-8(4))* Papaloizos Pubns., Inc.

Litton, Jonathan. Hello World. L'Atelier Cartographik, illus. 2016. (360 Degrees Ser.). (ENG.). 16p. (J). (gr. 3-6). 19.99 *(978-1-944530-00-6(2)*, 360 Degrees) Tiger Tales.

LoGiudice, Carolyn & McConnell, Nancy. Room 28 a Social Language Program. 2004. (YA). per. 25.95 *(978-0-7606-0530-1(0))* LinguiSystems, Inc.

Losada, Basilio. Isabel la Catolica. (SPA., Illus.). 192p. (YA). 11.95 *(978-84-7281-122-5(0)*, AF1122) Auriga, Ediciones S.A. ESP. Dist: Continental Bk. Co., Inc.

Marsh, Carole. It Really Is Greek to Me! Greek for Kids. Beard, Chad, ed. 2004. (Little Linguist Ser.). (Illus.). 32p. (J). (gr. 2-9). 29.95 *(978-0-635-02440-4(3))* Gallopade International.

—Say What When You Sneeze?! German for Kids. Beard, Chad, ed. 2004. (Little Linguist Ser.). (Illus.). 31p. 29.95 *(978-0-635-02439-8(X))* Gallopade International.

McCurry, Kristen. Little Scribe, 1 vol. 2014. (Little Scribe Ser.). (ENG.). 32p. (gr. 1-2). pap. 31.80 *(978-1-4765-7913-9(X)*, Aplus Bks.) Capstone Press of Coughlan Cos.

Mcgraw, Caroline. Litsemamba! Litsemba! 2009. pap. 15.00 *(978-1-61584-004-5(4))* Independent Pub.

Metropolitan Museum of Art Staff & Roehrig, Catharine. Fun with Hieroglyphs. 2008. (ENG.). 48p. (J). (gr. 4-7). 24.99 *(978-1-4169-6114-7(3)*, Simon & Schuster Bks. For Young Readers) Simon & Schuster Bks. For Young Readers.

Milet Publishing Staff. Milet Interactive for Kids - Turkish for English Speakers. 2012. (Milet Interactive for Kids Ser.). (ENG., Illus.). 1p. (J). (gr. k-2). cd-rom 24.95 *(978-1-84059-679-3(1))* Milet Publishing.

—My Bilingual Book - Sight. 2014. (My Bilingual Book Ser.). (ENG & TUR., Illus.). 28p. (J). (gr. -1-k). 9.95 *(978-1-84059-801-8(8))* Milet Publishing.

—My Bilingual Book-Hearing. 2014. (My Bilingual Book Ser.). (ENG & TUR., Illus.). 28p. (J). (gr. -1-k). 9.95 *(978-1-84059-785-1(2))* Milet Publishing.

—My Bilingual Book-Hearing (English-Bengali) 2014. (My Bilingual Book Ser.). (ENG & BEN., Illus.). 28p. (J). (gr. -1-k). 9.95 *(978-1-84059-773-8(9))* Milet Publishing.

—My Bilingual Book-Hearing (English-Farsi) 2014. (My Bilingual Book Ser.). (ENG & PER., Illus.). 28p. (J). (gr. -1-k). 9.95 *(978-1-84059-775-2(5))* Milet Publishing.

—My Bilingual Book-Hearing (English-Somali) 2014. (My Bilingual Book Ser.). (ENG & SOM., Illus.). 28p. (J). (gr. -1-k). 9.95 *(978-1-84059-783-7(6))* Milet Publishing.

—My Bilingual Book-Hearing (English-Urdu) 2014. (My Bilingual Book Ser.). (ENG & URD., Illus.). 28p. (J). (gr. -1-k). 9.95 *(978-1-84059-786-8(0))* Milet Publishing.

—My Bilingual Book-Sight (English-Bengali) 2014. (My Bilingual Book Ser.). (ENG & BEN., Illus.). 28p. (J). (gr. -1-k). 9.95 *(978-1-84059-789-9(5))* Milet Publishing.

—My Bilingual Book-Sight (English-Farsi) 2014. (My Bilingual Book Ser.). (ENG & PER., Illus.). 28p. (J). (gr. -1-k). 9.95 *(978-1-84059-791-2(7))* Milet Publishing.

—My Bilingual Book-Sight (English-Somali) 2014. (My Bilingual Book Ser.). (ENG & SOM., Illus.). 28p. (J). (gr. -1-k). 9.95 *(978-1-84059-799-8(2))* Milet Publishing.

—My Bilingual Book-Sight (English-Urdu) 2014. (My Bilingual Book Ser.). (ENG & URD., Illus.). 28p. (J). (gr. -1-k). 9.95 *(978-1-84059-802-5(6))* Milet Publishing.

—My Bilingual Book-Smell (English-Bengali) 2014. (My Bilingual Book Ser.). (ENG & BEN., Illus.). 28p. (J). (gr. -1-k). 9.95 *(978-1-84059-805-6(0))* Milet Publishing.

—My Bilingual Book-Smell (English-Farsi) 2014. (My Bilingual Book Ser.). (ENG & PER., Illus.). 28p. (J). (gr. -1-k). 9.95 *(978-1-84059-807-0(7))* Milet Publishing.

—My Bilingual Book-Smell (English-Turkish) 2014. (My Bilingual Book Ser.). (ENG & TUR., Illus.). 28p. (J). (gr. -1-k). 9.95 *(978-1-84059-817-9(4))* Milet Publishing.

—My Bilingual Book-Smell (English-Urdu) 2014. (My Bilingual Book Ser.). (ENG & URD., Illus.). 28p. (J). (gr. -1-k). 9.95 *(978-1-84059-818-6(2))* Milet Publishing.

—My Bilingual Book-Taste (English-Bengali) 2014. (My Bilingual Book Ser.). (ENG & BEN., Illus.). 28p. (J). (gr. -1-k). 9.95 *(978-1-84059-821-6(2))* Milet Publishing.

—My Bilingual Book-Taste (English-Farsi) 2014. (My Bilingual Book Ser.). (ENG & PER., Illus.). 28p. (J). (gr. -1-k). 9.95 *(978-1-84059-823-0(9))* Milet Publishing.

—My Bilingual Book-Taste (English-Somali) 2014. (My Bilingual Book Ser.). (ENG & SOM., Illus.). 28p. (J). (gr. -1-k). 9.95 *(978-1-84059-831-5(X))* Milet Publishing.

—My Bilingual Book-Taste (English-Turkish) 2014. (My Bilingual Book Ser.). (ENG & TUR., Illus.). 28p. (J). (gr. -1-k). 9.95 *(978-1-84059-833-9(6))* Milet Publishing.

—My Bilingual Book-Taste (English-Urdu) 2014. (My Bilingual Book Ser.). (ENG & URD., Illus.). 28p. (J). (gr. -1-k). 9.95 *(978-1-84059-834-6(4))* Milet Publishing.

—My Bilingual Book-Taste (English-Vietnamese) 2014. (My Bilingual Book Ser.). (ENG & VIE., Illus.). 28p. (J). (gr. -1-k). 9.95 *(978-1-84059-835-3(2))* Milet Publishing.

—My Bilingual Book-Touch (English-Bengali) 2014. (My Bilingual Book Ser.). (ENG & BEN., Illus.). 28p. (J). (gr. -1-k). 9.95 *(978-1-84059-837-7(9))* Milet Publishing.

—My Bilingual Book-Touch (English-Farsi) 2014. (My Bilingual Book Ser.). (ENG & PER., Illus.). 28p. (J). (gr. -1-k). 9.95 *(978-1-84059-839-1(5))* Milet Publishing.

—My Bilingual Book-Touch (English-Somali) 2014. (My Bilingual Book Ser.). (ENG & SOM., Illus.). 28p. (J). (gr. -1-k). 9.95 *(978-1-84059-847-6(6))* Milet Publishing.

—My Bilingual Book-Touch (English-Turkish) 2014. (My Bilingual Book Ser.). (ENG & TUR., Illus.). 28p. (J). (gr. -1-k). 9.95 *(978-1-84059-849-0(2))* Milet Publishing.

—My Bilingual Book-Touch (English-Urdu) 2014. (My Bilingual Book Ser.). (ENG & URD., Illus.). 28p. (J). (gr. -1-k). 9.95 *(978-1-84059-850-6(6))* Milet Publishing.

Ministry of Education Staff, creator. Te Kete Kupu: 300 Essential Words in Maori. 2007. (Illus.). 43p. (J). (gr. 4-7). pap. 9.00 *(978-1-86969-174-5(1))* Univ. of Hawaii Pr.

Morris, Paul. 101 Language Activities. 2004. (J). per. 35.95 *(978-0-7606-0532-5(7))* LinguiSystems, Inc.

Moshi Moshi. 2004. (Yoroshiku Ser.: Stages 1 and 2). (JPN., Illus.). (gr. k-12). 152p. pap., tchr. ed. 32.95 *(978-1-86366-143-0(3))*; 148p. pap., stu. ed. 39.95 *(978-1-86366-146-1(8))* Education Services Australia Ltd. AUS. Dist: Cheng & Tsui Co.

Mullin, Rene. Aibitir. 2014. (ENG., Illus.). 40p. (J). 13.95 *(978-0-85640-917-2(0))* Blackstaff Pr., Ltd. GBR. Dist: Dufour Editions, Inc.

National Curriculum Development Centre Staff. Luo. 2004. Bk. 1. pap., pupil's gde. ed. *(978-0-521-78936-3(2))*Bk. 2. pap., pupil's gde. ed. *(978-0-521-78937-0(0))*Bk. 3. pap., pupil's gde. ed. *(978-0-521-78938-7(9))*Bk. 4. pap., pupil's gde. ed. *(978-0-521-78939-4(7))* Cambridge Univ. Pr.

National Indonesian Curriculum Project Staff. Suara Siswa: Indonesian Language, Stages 1-2. 2004. (IND.). 242p. pap., tchr. ed., ldr.'s hndbk. ed. 39.95 *(978-1-86366-125-6(5))* Education Services Australia Ltd. AUS. Dist: Cheng & Tsui Co.

National Japanese Curriculum Project Staff. Pera Pera. 2004. (Yoroshiku Ser.: Stages 3 and 4). (JPN.). 224p. (gr. k-12). pap., stu. ed. 45.95 *(978-1-86366-147-8(6))* Education Services Australia Ltd. AUS. Dist: Cheng & Tsui Co.

Nordstrom, Ursula. Secret Language. 167p. (J). (gr. 3-5). pap. 4.95 *(978-0-8072-1425-1(6)*, Listening Library) Random Hse. Audio Publishing Group.

Nunn, Daniel. Colors in German: Die Farben, 1 vol. 2012. (World Languages - Colors Ser.). (ENG, GER & MUL.). 24p. (gr. 1-3). pap. 6.29 *(978-1-4329-6660-7(X))*; lib. bdg. 22.65 *(978-1-4329-6653-9(7))* Heinemann-Raintree. (Acorn).

—World Languages - Families. 2013. (World Languages - Families Ser.). 24p. (gr. 1-3). (ENG & MUL.). pap. 35.94 *(978-1-4329-7185-4(9))*; (MUL.). lib. bdg. 113.25 *(978-1-4329-7178-6(6))* Heinemann-Raintree. (Acorn).

Omary, Rachel, illus. Animals in Pashto. l.t. ed. 2003. 4p. (J). spiral bd. 10.95 *(978-0-9740535-5-4(4))* Knight Publishing.

Palazzo-Craig, Janet. Language Development Variety Text. 2004. (BrainBuilders Ser.). (ENG.). 48p. (gr. k-4). pap. 5.25 *(978-1-4042-8562-0(8))*; pap. 5.25 *(978-1-4042-8567-5(9))* Rosen Publishing Group, Inc., The.

Papaloizos, Theodore C. Workbook for Learning Greek. 2003. (GRE & ENG.). 76p. (YA). pap. *(978-0-932416-32-2(2))* Papaloizos Pubns., Inc.

Pera Pera. 2004. (Yoroshiku Ser.: Stages 3 and 4). (JPN.). 136p. (gr. k-12). pap., tchr. ed., ldr.'s hndbk. ed. 45.95 *(978-1-86366-141-6(7))* Education Services Australia Ltd. AUS. Dist: Cheng & Tsui Co.

Peterson, Hiromi & Omizo, Naomi. Adventures in Japanese Level 1, 4 vols. Muronaka, Michael & Kaylor, Emiko, illus. 2nd ed. 2005. pap., stu. ed., wbk. ed. 24.95 *(978-0-88727-450-3(1))* Cheng & Tsui Co.

Phillips, Lori. Yapese Alphabet. 2006. (Island Alphabet Books). (Illus.). 52p. (J). (gr. -1-k). 4.95 *(978-1-57306-260-2(X))* Bess Pr., Inc.

Prior, Jennifer. Map Skills Grade 3. 2003. (Practice Makes Perfect Ser.). (ENG., Illus.). 48p. (gr. 3). pap. 5.99 *(978-0-7439-3728-3(7))* Teacher Created Resources, Inc.

El Recuerdo Egipcio. (SPA., Illus.). 70p. (YA). (gr. 7-9). pap. *(978-88-8148-446-1(3))* EMC/Paradigm Publishing.

Rembisz, Linda. Count with Balloons. Liebeck, Lisa, illus. 2009. 28p. pap. 12.49 *(978-1-4490-1989-1(7))* AuthorHouse.

Ristuccia, Christine. The Entire World of Attributes. 2003. (J). 29.99 *(978-0-9723457-7-4(9))* Say It Right.

Ristuccia, Christine & Ristuccia, James. The Entire World of S & Z Screening Kit. 2003. (Illus.). 20p. (J). pap. 9.99 *(978-0-9723457-6-7(0))* Say It Right.

Robertson, James. Katie's A tae Z: An Alphabet for Wee Folk. Sutherland, Karen, illus. 2014. (ENG.). 20p. (J). (-k). bds. 12.99 *(978-1-84502-754-4(X))* Black and White Publishing Ltd. GBR. Dist: Independent Pubs. Group.

Romero, Victor Eclar. Learn Filipino: Book One, Book One. Francisco, Manny, illus. 2004. 384p. per. 29.95 *(978-1-932956-41-2(7))* Magsimba Pr.

The Rosetta Stone Language Library: Dutch Level 2. 2005. (J). (gr. 1-18). cd-rom 239.00 *(978-1-58022-046-0(0))* Rosetta Stone Ltd.

The Rosetta Stone Language Library: Thai Level 1. 2005. (J). (gr. 1-18). cd-rom 209.00 *(978-1-883972-75-2(2))* Rosetta Stone Ltd.

Ruffenach, Jessie, ed. Baby Learns to Count. Thomas, Peter, tr. Blacksheep, Beverly, illus. l.t. ed. 2003. (NAV & ENG.). 16p. (J). (gr. -1-12). 7.95 *(978-1-893354-47-0(4))* Salina Bookshelf Inc.

Savage, Leah, et al. POW Wow: Niimiwin Everyone Dance. 2009. (J). *(978-0-9820870-6-0(3))* IGI Pr.

Schmitt, Conrad J. & Glencoe McGraw-Hill Staff. Invitation to Languages: Exploratory Program. 2006. (Invitation to Languages Ser.). (ENG., Illus.). 298p. (gr. 6-8). stu. ed. 60.96 *(978-0-07-874249-1(8)*, 0078742498) McGraw-Hill Higher Education.

Shah, Sapna Jaiswal. Sapna Aunty's Hindi Book of Colors: Rang. 2004. (HIN.). (J). 8.00 *(978-0-9741686-0-9(2))* 3N Media Group.

Singh, Rina. My First Book of Hindi Words: An ABC Rhyming Book of Hindi Language & Indian Culture. Zaman, Farida, illus. 2016. (ENG & HIN.). 32p. (J). (gr. -1-3). 12.95 *(978-0-8048-4562-5(X))* Tuttle Publishing.

Sona & Jacob, illus. Varnamala Geet. 2006. (HIN & ENG.). 3p. (J). 12.00 *(978-0-9773645-6-5(9))* MeeraMasi, Inc.

Suter, Janine. The Not So Super Skyscraper! Gunther, Richard, illus. 2009. 32p. (J). 10.99 *(978-0-89051-577-8(8))* Master Bks.

Takarai, Saori. Manga Moods: 40 Faces + 80 Phrases. 2010. (ENG., Illus.). 96p. (YA). 9.99 *(978-4-921205-13-3(2)*, 9784921205133) Japanime Co., Ltd. JPN. Dist: Diamond Comic Distributors, Inc.

Thomas, Susan & Hughes, Annie. Mini Flashcards Language Games. 2013. (Mini Flashcards Language Games Ser.). (ENG.). 32p. pap., tchr. ed. 31.99 *(978-1-907584-03-9(X))* HarperCollins Pubs. Ltd. GBR. Dist: Independent Pubs. Group.

Thompson, Richard & Thompson, Ofa. Ko 'Eku Tohi 'oe Fanga Manu. Slutz, Stephani, illus. l.t. ed. 2004. (TON.). 16p. (J). (gr. -1-18). 5.00 *(978-0-9678979-2-9(0))* Friendly Isles Pr.

Treadwell, Harriette Taylor & Free, Margaret. A Furst Readin Book in Ulster Scot. 2011. (Illus.). 124p. pap. *(978-1-904808-68-8(9))* Evertype.

Trim, John & Kohl, Katrin M. Deutsch Direkt! Textbook. (J). (gr. 9-12). 16.95 *(978-0-8219-0225-7(3)*, 45290) EMC/Paradigm Publishing.

Turhan, Sedat. New Bilingual Visual Dictionary (English-Bengali) 2nd ed. 2017. (New Bilingual Visual Dictionary Ser.). (ENG & BEN., Illus.). 144p. (J). (gr. k-2). 19.95 ***(978-1-78508-882-7(3))*** Milet Publishing.

—New Bilingual Visual Dictionary (English-Farsi) 2nd ed. 2017. (New Bilingual Visual Dictionary Ser.). (ENG & PER., Illus.). 144p. (J). (gr. k-2). 19.95 ***(978-1-78508-884-1(X))*** Milet Publishing.

Turhan, Sedat & Hagin, Sally. Milet Flashwords. 2005. (Milet Flashwords Ser.). (Illus.). 1p. (J). (gr. 4-7). (ENG & SPA.). 8.95 *(978-1-84059-418-8(7))*; (BEN & ENG., 8.95 *(978-1-84059-410-2(1))* Milet Publishing.

Verdick, Elizabeth. Words Are Not for Hurting. Heinlen, Marieka, illus. 2004. (Best Behavior Ser.). (ENG.). 40p. (J). (gr. -1-2). pap. 11.95 *(978-1-57542-156-8(9))* Free Spirit Publishing, Inc.

Walker, Kevin. Learning a Second Language, Yes or No. 2016. (Seeing Both Sides Ser.). (ENG.). 32p. (gr. 3-6). 32.79 *(978-1-68191-386-5(0))* Rourke Educational Media.
Wallace, Mary. An Inuksuk Means Welcome. 2015. (ENG., Illus.). 32p. (J). (gr. -1-2). 17.95 *(978-1-77147-137-4(9),* Owlkids) Owlkids Bks. Inc. CAN. Dist: Publishers Group West (PGW).
Webb, Mick. The Book of Languages: Talk Your Way Around the World. 2015. (ENG., Illus.). 64p. (J). (gr. 2-7). 17.95 *(978-1-77147-155-8(7))* Owlkids Bks. Inc. CAN. Dist: Publishers Group West (PGW).
Wilson, P. R. Readle the Reading Beetle: The Journey to Love Read Land. 2007. 26p. pap. 8.95 *(978-0-7414-4318-2(X))* Infinity Publishing.
Workbook - My First Book. 2007. (J). pap. 20.00 *(978-0-932416-13-1(6))* Papaloizos Pubns., Inc.

LANGUAGE AND LANGUAGES—VOCATIONAL GUIDANCE

Miller, Anne Meeker. Baby Sing & Sign: A Play-filled Language Development Program for Hearing Infants & Toddlers. 2004. (J). spiral bd. 14.95 *(978-0-9749924-0-2(2))* Love Language Pubns.

LANGUAGE ARTS

see Communication; English Language; Reading; Speech

LAOS

Doeden, Matt. Laos in Pictures. 2007. (Visual Geography Series, Second Ser.). (ENG., Illus.). 80p. (gr. 5-12). 31.93 *(978-0-8225-6590-1(0))* Lerner Publishing Group.
Oachs, Emily Rose. Laos. 2016. (Exploring Countries Ser.). (ENG., Illus.). 32p. (J). (gr. 3-7). 26.95 *(978-1-62617-404-7(0),* Blastoff! Readers) Bellwether Media.

LAOS—HISTORY

Mansfield, Stephen & Koh, Magdalene. Laos. 2nd rev. ed. 2008. (Cultures of the World Ser.). 144p. (gr. 6-18). lib. bdg. 42.79 *(978-0-7614-3035-3(0),* Benchmark Bks.) Marshall Cavendish Corp.

LAPLAND

Alatalo, Jaakko. Iina-Marja's Day: From Dawn to Dusk in Lapland. 2011. (Child's Day Ser.). (ENG., Illus.). 32p. (J). (gr. k-3). pap. 8.95 *(978-1-84507-993-2(0),* Frances Lincoln) Quarto Publishing Group UK GBR. Dist: Hachette Bk. Group.

LAPLAND—FICTION

D'Aulaire, Ingri & D'Aulaire, Edgar Parin. Children of the Northlights. 2012. (ENG., Illus.). 40p. 16.95 *(978-0-8166-7923-2(1))* Univ. of Minnesota Pr.
Penny, Anne. Scraper. 2006. (Illus.). 56p. pap. *(978-1-84401-921-2(7))* Athena Pr.

LARGE TYPE BOOKS

Aardvark, D. The Congraduation Fish. Aardvark, D., illus. l.t. ed. 2005. (Illus.). 48p. (J). per. 12.95 *(978-0-9755567-1-9(1))* Aardvark's Weedpatch Pr.
—Merry Kissmoose. Aardvark, D., illus. l.t. ed. 2005. (Illus.). 48p. (J). per. 12.95 *(978-0-9755567-2-6(X))* Aardvark's Weedpatch Pr.
—Punkin's upside down Day. l.t. ed. 2004. (Illus.). 40p. (J). per. 10.95 *(978-0-9755567-0-2(3))* Aardvark's Weedpatch Pr.
The Adventures of Chip Green the Forestry Kid l.t. ed. 2005. (Illus.). 34p. (J). per. *(978-0-9729753-8-4(1))* Really Big Coloring Bks., Inc.
The Adventures of Little Nina: Nina's First Trip. l.t. ed. 2005. (Illus.). 40p. (J). 16.95 *(978-0-9769662-0-3(4))* Strategies Publishing Co.
The Adventures of Marc John Jefferies: The Missing Princess. l.t. ed. 2004. (Illus.). 110p. (YA). per. *(978-0-9747218-3-5(2),* 100, Young Women Programming) Harper Kids Hse.
The Adventures of Pinocchio. l.t. ed. 2004. (Large Print Ser.). 229p. 25.00 *(978-1-58287-732-7(7))* North Bks.
The Adventures of the Original Pumpkin Patch Pals. l.t. ed. 2005. (Illus.). 32p. (J). 15.00 *(978-0-9770960-1-5(7))* 3 Pals Media, LLC.
Ahmad, Iftikhar. World Cultures: A Global Mosaic, 8 vols. l.t. ed. 2004. 2467p. (YA). (gr. 6-9). 1236.00 *(978-0-13-036895-9(4),* A-L00012-00) Prentice Hall Pr.
Albert, Toni Diana. Saving the Rain Forest with Cammie & Cooper. Bowles, Carol, illus. l.t. ed. 2003. 32p. (J). pap. 7.95 *(978-1-929432-02-8(X),* 800-353-2791) Trickle Creek Bks.
Albright, Thomas B. Universal English: Second Language for All. unabr. l.t. ed. 2003. (Languages: Universal English for All). (ENM.). 128p. pap. 7.00 *(978-1-888264-17-3(9))* Twenty-First Century Co., The.
Alex, N. L. Smile All the While. l.t. ed. 2005. (Illus.). 16p. (J). 4.99 *(978-0-9766080-0-4(6))* Joe Girl Ink.
Alexander, Florence & Alexander, Stanley. Come with Me & See... African People. l.t. ed. 2003. (ENG & SPA., Illus.). 13p. (J). 3.99 *(978-0-9648313-8-4(4))* Ebon Research Systems Publishing, LLC.
—Come with Me & See... Birds of the World. l.t. ed. 2003. (Illus.). 32p. (J). 7.99 net. *(978-0-915960-95-8(8))* Ebon Research Systems Publishing, LLC.
—Come with Me & See... Children of the World. l.t. ed. 2003. (ENG & SPA., Illus.). 32p. (J). 9.99 *(978-0-9648313-9-1(2))* Ebon Research Systems Publishing, LLC.
—Jesus Child Is Born: Dare to Be Great. l.t. ed. 2003. (Illus.). 32p. (YA). 7.99 net. *(978-0-915960-85-9(0))* Ebon Research Systems Publishing, LLC.
Alexander, Geoff. Toothbugs! Carole, Isaacs, illus. l.t. ed. 2005. 12p. (J). bds. 12.95 *(978-0-9760944-0-1(1))* Alexander-Marcus Publishing.
Alexander, Ian. Do You See a Dozen?, Vol. 2. l.t. ed. 2005. (Sadlier Phonics Reading Program). (Illus.). 8p. (gr. -1-1). 23.00 net. *(978-0-8215-7347-1(0))* Sadlier, William H. Inc.
Alexie, Sherman. The Absolutely True Diary of a Part-Time Indian. Forney, Ellen, illus. l.t. ed. 2008. (Thorndike Literacy Bridge Ser.). (ENG.). 302p. (YA). (gr. 7-12). 23.95 *(978-1-4104-0499-2(4))* Thorndike Pr.
Allen, Toi Lynn. Game Day/Test Day: Who's Keeping Score? l.t. ed. 2004. (Illus.). (YA). pap. 14.95 *(978-0-9753787-0-0(8))* Allen, Toi Operations.
Allende, Isabel. Forest of the Pygmies. l.t. ed. 2005. (City of the Beasts Ser.: Bk. 3).Tr. of Bosque de los Pigmeos. 304p. (J). (gr. 5-18). pap. 19.99 *(978-0-06-076200-1(4),* Rayo) HarperCollins Pubs.
Allgood, Jean. Come Follow Me Bk. 1: Understanding One's Worth: Color Orange. Smith, Sandra, illus. l.t. ed. 2004. 23p. (J). 14.95 *(978-0-9741627-3-7(6))* PricePoint+Publications.
Alston, E. B. The Last Voyage of the Dan-D. Garrett, Toni, illus. l.t. ed. 2003. 47p. (J). per. 8.00 *(978-0-9747735-0-6(6))* Righter Publishing Co., Inc.
Altsheler, Joseph A. The Forest of Swords: A Story of Paris & the Marne. l.t. ed. 2007. (World War I Ser.: Vol. 3). (ENG.). 252p. (J). pap. 23.99 *(978-1-4264-8960-0(9))* Creative Media Partners, LLC.
—The Forest Runners: A Story of the Great War Trail in Early Kentucky. l.t. ed. 2007. (Young Trailers Ser.: Vol. 2). 178p. (J). pap. 22.99 *(978-1-4264-8301-1(5))* Creative Media Partners, LLC.
—The Free Rangers: A Story of the Early Days along the Mississippi. l.t. ed. 2007. (Young Trailers Ser.: Vol. 5). (ENG.). 278p. (J). (gr. 4-7). reprint ed. pap. 23.99 *(978-1-4346-2560-1(5))* Creative Media Partners, LLC.
—The Guns of Shiloh. l.t. ed. 2007. (Civil War Ser.: Vol. 2). (ENG.). 260p. (J). per. 23.99 *(978-1-4346-7681-8(1))* Creative Media Partners, LLC.
—The Hosts of the Air: The Story of a Quest in the Great War. l.t. ed. 2007. (World War I Ser.: Vol. 2). 258p. (J). reprint ed. pap. 23.99 *(978-1-4264-9850-3(0))* Creative Media Partners, LLC.
—The Hunters of the Hills: A Story of the Great French & Indian War. l.t. ed. 2007. (French & Indian War Ser.). (ENG.). 282p. (J). pap. 23.99 *(978-1-4264-8308-0(2))* Creative Media Partners, LLC.
—The Rock of Chickamauga: A Story of the Western Crisis. l.t. ed. 2007. (Civil War Ser.: Vol. 6). (ENG.). 258p. (J). reprint ed. pap. 23.99 *(978-1-4346-2064-4(6))* Creative Media Partners, LLC.
—The Rulers of the Lakes: A Story of George & Champlain. l.t. ed. 2007. (ENG.). 268p. reprint ed. pap. 23.99 *(978-1-4264-8309-7(0))* Creative Media Partners, LLC.
—The Scouts of Stonewall: The Story of the Great Valley Campaign. l.t. ed. 2007. (Civil War Ser.: Vol. 3). (ENG.). 240p. (J). reprint ed. pap. 22.99 *(978-1-4264-1531-9(1))* Creative Media Partners, LLC.
—The Shades of the Wilderness: A Story of Lee's Great Stand. l.t. ed. 2006. (Civil War Ser.: Vol. 7). (ENG.). 278p. (J). reprint ed. pap. 23.99 *(978-1-4264-6220-7(4))* Creative Media Partners, LLC.
—The Shadow of the North: A Story of Old New York & a Lost Campaign. l.t. ed. 2007. (French & Indian War Ser.: Vol. 2). (ENG.). 290p. (J). reprint ed. pap. 23.99 *(978-1-4264-5705-0(7))* Creative Media Partners, LLC.
—The Star of Gettysburg: A Story of Southern High Tide. l.t. ed. 2007. (Civil War Ser.: Vol. 5). (ENG.). 290p. (J). reprint ed. per. 23.99 *(978-1-4346-7685-6(4))* Creative Media Partners, LLC.
—The Sun of Quebec: A Story of a Great Crisis. l.t. ed. 2007. (French & Indian War Ser.: Vol. 6). 296p. (J). reprint ed. pap. 23.99 *(978-1-4264-9822-0(5))* Creative Media Partners, LLC.
—The Sword of Antietam: A Story of the Nation's Crisis. l.t. ed. 2006. (Civil War Ser.: Vol. 4). 262p. (J). reprint ed. pap. 23.99 *(978-1-4264-2714-5(X))* Creative Media Partners, LLC.
—The Texan Scouts: A Story of the Alamo & Goliad. l.t. ed. 2007. (Texan Ser.: Vol. 2). (ENG.). 316p. (J). reprint ed. pap. 24.99 *(978-1-4264-3365-8(4))* Creative Media Partners, LLC.
—The Texan Star: The Story of a Great Fight for Liberty. l.t. ed. 2007. (Texan Ser.: Vol. 1). (ENG.). 328p. (J). pap. 24.99 *(978-1-4264-9137-5(9))* Creative Media Partners, LLC.
—The Tree of Appomattox: A Story of the Civil War's Close. l.t. ed. 2007. (Civil War Ser.: Vol. 8). (ENG.). 298p. (J). reprint ed. pap. 23.99 *(978-1-4346-1261-8(9))* Creative Media Partners, LLC.
—The Young Trailers: A Story of Early Kentucky. l.t. ed. 2007. (Young Trailers Ser.: Vol. 1). 222p. (J). reprint ed. pap. 22.99 *(978-1-4346-3289-0(X))* Creative Media Partners, LLC.
Andersen, Hans Christian, tr. Andersen's Fairy Tales. l.t. ed. 2004. (Large Print Ser.). 266p. 25.00 *(978-1-58287-629-0(0))* North Bks.
Anderson, Laurie Halse. Chains. l.t. ed. 2009. (ENG.). 390p. (YA). 23.95 *(978-1-4104-1425-0(6))* Thorndike Pr.
Andreu Iglesias, Cesar & Hernández, Juan A. A Mal Tiempo, Buena Cara: El Humor en el Periodismo Puertorriqueño. l.t. ed. 2003. (SPA., Illus.). 48p. pap. *(978-0-9743102-0-6(4))* Casa de Periodistas Editorial.
Andrews-McKinney, Joyce. Jentle & Jewel Fix Things Andrews-McKinney, Joyce, illus. l.t. ed. 2006. (Illus.). 17p. (J). pap. 8.00 *(978-0-9728975-4-9(2))* JA-M Pubs., LLC.
Appleby, Ellen. Les Trois Barbichu, Big Bk. l.t. ed. (FRE.). (J). ring bd. 29.99 *(978-0-590-71769-4(3))* Scholastic, Inc.
Aresty, Reecy. Getting into College & Paying for It: Solutions for High School & College Families Guaranteed to Cut the Cost! l.t. ed. 2003.Tr. of Sueno Americano: Como Ingresar a la Universidad Y Pagar Los Mas Bajos Costos! (SPA., Illus.). 258p. (YA). per. 27.95 *(978-0-9760251-1-5(6))* College Assistance, Inc.
Arlene, Sonday. The Sonday System - Let's Play Learn: Shapes & Numbers Book. Cindy, Breckman, ed. l.t. ed. 2004. (Illus.). 29p. (J). per. *(978-1-891602-12-2(8))* Winsor Learning, Inc.
Asner, Anne-Marie. Kvetchy Boy. Asner, Anne-Marie, illus. l.t. ed. 2006. (Illus.). 32p. (J). per. 6.95 *(978-0-9753629-3-8(3))* Matzah Ball Bks.
—Noshy Boy. Asner, Anne-Marie, illus. l.t. ed. 2004. (Illus.). 32p. (J). (gr. -1-3). per. 6.95 *(978-0-9753629-1-4(7))* Matzah Ball Bks.
—Shmutzy Girl. Asner, Anne-Marie, illus. l.t. ed. 2004. (Illus.). 32p. (J). (gr. -1-3). per. 6.95 *(978-0-9753629-0-7(9))* Matzah Ball Bks.
Auxier, Bryan. Where Have All the Unicorns Gone? Daniels, Regina, illus. l.t. ed. 2003. 16p. (J). 7.95 *(978-0-9719144-1-4(9))* Where? Pr., Inc.
Ayers, Linda. Tiger Goes Collecting. Hunt, Jane, illus. l.t. ed. 2004. 55p. (J). per. 7.95 *(978-0-9760505-2-0(8))* Blue Thistle Pr.
Azzopardi, Jeannie. Maricio & the Magic Suitcase. l.t. ed. 2004. (Illus.). 93p. (J). per. 14.00 incl. cd-rom *(978-0-9744391-3-6(4),* MAR-BKCD-1st, Once Upon A Time in a Classroom) Interactive Media Publishing.
Babineaux, Jim. Cody Cottontail Makes a Wise Choice! Babineaux, Jim, illus. l.t. ed. 2005. (Illus.). 18p. (J). *(978-0-9769769-0-5(0))* ALCAPS, LLC.
Baldwin, Christy. Remembering Wilma. Barnes, Sarah, illus. l.t. ed. 2005. 22p. (J). per. 9.95 *(978-0-9765072-0-8(X))* Tribute Bks.
Barr, Mabel. Hamster Huey & the Gooey Kablooie: The Renowned Hero's Most Famous Adventure. l.t. ed. 2004. (Illus.). 8p. (J). 6.95 *(978-0-9749090-0-4(9),* 214) Hamster Huey Pr.
Barrie, J. M. Peter Pan. l.t. ed. 2003. (Perennial Bestsellers Ser.). (ENG.). 248p. (J). 29.95 *(978-0-7862-5263-3(4))* Thorndike Pr.
Baum, L. Frank. Dorothy & the Wizard of Oz. l.t. ed. 2004. (Large Print Ser.). lib. bdg. 25.00 *(978-1-58287-769-3(6))* North Bks.
—The Enchanted Island of Yew. l.t. ed. 2007. (ENG.). 136p. pap. 19.99 *(978-1-4264-2723-7(9))* Creative Media Partners, LLC.
—The Enchanted Island of Yew. l.t. ed. 2005. 228p. pap. *(978-1-84637-102-8(3))* Echo Library.
—The Enchanted Island of Yew. l.t. ed. 2004. (Large Print Ser.). 207p. 25.00 *(978-1-58287-737-2(8))* North Bks.
—Glinda of Oz. l.t. ed. 2004. (Large Print Ser.). 210p. 25.00 *(978-1-58287-740-2(8))* North Bks.
—The Lost Princess of Oz. l.t. ed. 2004. (Large Print Ser.). 241p. 25.00 *(978-1-58287-739-6(4))* North Bks.
—The Magic of Oz. l.t. ed. 2004. (Large Print Ser.). lib. bdg. 25.00 *(978-1-58287-775-4(0))* North Bks.
—The Marvelous Land of Oz. l.t. ed. 2004. (Large Print Ser.). lib. bdg. 25.00 *(978-1-58287-768-6(8))* North Bks.
—Ozma of Oz. l.t. ed. 2004. (Large Print Ser.). 210p. 25.00 *(978-1-58287-736-5(X))* North Bks.
—The Patchwork Girl of OZ. l.t. ed. 2004. (Large Print Ser.). lib. bdg. 25.00 *(978-1-58287-771-6(8))* North Bks.
—Rinkitink in Oz. l.t. ed. 2004. (Large Print Ser.). lib. bdg. 25.00 *(978-1-58287-774-7(2))* North Bks.
—The Road to Oz. l.t. ed. 2004. (Large Print Ser.). lib. bdg. 25.00 *(978-1-58287-770-9(X))* North Bks.
—The Scarecrow of Oz. l.t. ed. 2004. (Large Print Ser.). lib. bdg. 25.00 *(978-1-58287-773-0(4))* North Bks.
—Sky Island. l.t. ed. 2004. (Large Print Ser.). lib. bdg. 25.00 *(978-1-58287-792-1(0))* North Bks.
—The Tin Woodman of Oz. l.t. ed. 2007. (ENG.). 156p. pap. 21.99 *(978-1-4346-5200-3(9))* Creative Media Partners, LLC.
—The Tin Woodman of Oz. l.t. ed. 2005. 256p. pap. *(978-1-84637-112-7(0))* Echo Library.
—The Tin Woodman of Oz. l.t. ed. 2004. (Large Print Ser.). 230p. 25.00 *(978-1-58287-741-9(6))* North Bks.
Beck, Randy. Teen Quest. l.t. ed. 2004. 80p. (YA). per. 12.95 *(978-1-59196-535-0(7))* Instant Pub.
Beckler, Bruce. My Daddy Is A Deputy Sheriff. Finney, Simone, illus. l.t. ed. 2004. 14p. (J). per. 5.59 *(978-0-9745210-4-6(3))* Myers Publishing Co.
—My Daddy Is A Fire Fighter: My Daddy Is A Fireman. Peek, Jeannette, illus. l.t. ed. 2004. 16p. (J). 5.59 *(978-0-9745210-8-4(6))* Myers Publishing Co.
—My Daddy Is a Police Officer: My Daddy Wears a Star. Finney, Simone, illus. l.t. ed. 2004. 14p. (J). per. 5.59 *(978-0-9745210-3-9(5))* Myers Publishing Co.
—My Daddy Is A Police Officer: Wears A Badge, 8 bks. Finney, Simone, illus. l.t. ed. 2004. 14p. (J). per. 5.59 *(978-0-9745210-2-2(7))* Myers Publishing Co.
—My Mommy Is A Deputy Sheriff. Finney, Simone, illus. l.t. ed. 2004. 14p. (J). 5.59 *(978-0-9745210-7-7(8))* Myers Publishing Co.
—My Mommy Is A Nurse. Peek, Jeannette, illus. l.t. ed. 2004. 20p. (J). 5.59 *(978-0-9745210-9-1(4))* Myers Publishing Co.
—My Mommy Is A Police Officer: My Mommy Wears A Badge. Finney, Simone, illus. l.t. ed. 2004. 14p. (J). per. 5.59 *(978-0-9745210-5-3(1))* Myers Publishing Co.
—My Mommy Is A Police Officer: My Mommy Wears A Star. Finney, Simone, illus. l.t. ed. 2004. 14p. (J). 5.59 *(978-0-9745210-6-0(X))* Myers Publishing Co.
—The Secret Tunnels of Spring Mountain. l.t. ed. 2004. (Illus.). 220p. (J). per. 13.99 *(978-0-9745210-0-8(0))* Myers Publishing Co.
—The Secrets of the Green Mansion. l.t. ed. 2004. (Illus.). 240p. (J). per. 13.99 *(978-0-9745210-1-5(9))* Myers Publishing Co.
Becoming a Girl of Faith: According to God's Word. l.t. ed. 2004. 90p. (YA). 12.95 *(978-0-9764304-2-1(8))* Girls of Faith.
Beeson, Lea Ann. A Leopard Is More Than His Spots. Popovich, Richard E., ed. Rockfield, Darryl, illus. l.t. ed. 2005. 51p. (J). lib. bdg. 19.95 *(978-0-9604876-1-5(1))* REP Pubs.
Beken, Robert A. Tijuana River Estuary & Border Field State Park: Land of diversity, land of Hope. l.t. ed. 2004. (Illus.). 260p. spiral bd. 34.95 *(978-0-9761726-0-4(7))* Tritium Pr.
Bell, N. Wayne. Childrens' Economics: A Book on Money & Finance. l.t. ed. 2004. (Illus.). 32p. (J). per. *(978-0-9729753-5-3(7))* Really Big Coloring Bks., Inc.
—The Really Big Book of Zoo Animals. l.t. ed. 2004. (Illus.). 32p. (J). per. *(978-0-9729753-6-0(5))* Really Big Coloring Bks., Inc.
Bell, Nasherrall, creator. Child Safety at Home, School & Play l.t. ed. 2004. (Illus.). 32p. (J). pap. *(978-0-9729753-3-9(0))* Really Big Coloring Bks., Inc.
Benevenia, Rose. Dolly & Babe. Benevenia, Rose, illus. l.t. ed. 2004. (Illus.). 9p. (J). (gr. k-2). pap. 9.00 *(978-0-9729044-0-7(9))* Cabbage Patch Pr.
Berg, Dick. Padunkapoo: The Hawaiian Kangaroo. Berg, Gary, ed. l.t. ed. 2005. (Illus.). 28p. (J). per. 6.99 *(978-0-9769985-1-8(3))* Grace Publishing.
Berggren, Jeff. Chicken Cherries. Hansen, Tammy A., ed. Berggren, Jeff, illus. l.t. ed. 2005. (Illus.). 32p. (J). per. 14.95 *(978-0-9755033-0-0(8))* Deep Dish Design.
Bernal, Mitchell. Skelanimals: Dead Animals Need Love Too Bernal, Mitchell, illus. l.t. ed. 2005. (Illus.). 22p. (J). per. 12.95 *(978-0-9766621-0-5(8),* 818 554-8965) Kreations.
Bernstein, Susan H. N. E. Pominonous Epstein & Change. l.t. ed. 2003. (E. Pominonous Epstein Ser.: No. 3). (Illus.). 20p. (Orig.). (J). (gr. k-3). pap. 8.95 *(978-0-9706596-2-0(8))* Bernstein, Susan.
Bersson, Robert & Shoup, Dolores. Stripes & Stars. Bersson, Robert & Trobaugh, Scott, illus. l.t. ed. 2003. 40p. (J). (gr. 1-4). per. 16.95 *(978-0-9740585-0-4(5))* Legacy Group Productions, LLC.
Bickel, Karla. The Animals' Debate. Bickel, Karla, illus. l.t. ed. 2004. (Illus.). 16p. (J). (gr. -1-6). pap. 5.00 *(978-1-891452-16-1(9),* 10) Heart Arbor Bks.
—Easter Lights. Bickel, Karla, illus. l.t. ed. 2004. (Illus.). 16p. (J). (gr. -1-6). pap. 5.00 *(978-1-891452-14-7(2),* 7) Heart Arbor Bks.
—Fishnet Valentine. Bickel, Karla, illus. l.t. ed. 2004. (Illus.). 16p. (J). (gr. -1-5). pap. 5.00 *(978-1-891452-13-0(4),* 4) Heart Arbor Bks.
—Handmade Necklace. Bickel, Karla, illus. l.t. ed. 2004. (Illus.). 16p. (J). (gr. -1-6). pap. 5.00 *(978-1-891452-11-6(8),* 1) Heart Arbor Bks.
—Heart Petals on the Hearth: A Collection of Children's Stories. Bickel, Karla, illus. 2004. (Illus.). 64p. (J). (gr. -1-6). 20.00 *(978-1-891452-00-0(2))* Heart Arbor Bks.
—The Kite Who Was Afraid to Fly. Bickel, Karla, illus. l.t. ed. 2004. (Illus.). 16p. (J). (gr. -1-6). pap. 5.00 *(978-1-891452-08-6(8),* 6) Heart Arbor Bks.
—Lilac Rose: A Flower's Lifetime. Bickel, Karla, illus. l.t. ed. 2004. (Illus.). 16p. (J). (gr. -1-6). pap. 5.00 *(978-1-891452-10-9(X),* 8) Heart Arbor Bks.
—The Reading Machine. Bickel, Karla, illus. l.t. ed. 2004. (Illus.). 16p. (J). (gr. -1-6). pap. 5.00 *(978-1-891452-15-4(0),* 9) Heart Arbor Bks.
—Surprise Christmas Birthday Party. Bickel, Karla, illus. l.t. ed. 2004. (Illus.). 16p. (J). (gr. -1-6). pap. 5.00 *(978-1-891452-12-3(6),* 3) Heart Arbor Bks.
—Teacher's Remarkable Secret. Bickel, Karla, illus. l.t. ed. 2004. (Illus.). 16p. (J). (gr. -1-6). pap. 5.00 *(978-1-891452-09-3(6),* 2) Heart Arbor Bks.
Billiot, Wendy Wilson. Before the Saltwater Came. l.t. ed. 2005. (Illus.). 32p. (J). 19.95 *(978-0-9762592-0-6(6))* Billiot, Wendy Wilson.
Birdsall, Jeanne. The Penderwicks: A Summer Tale of Four Sisters, Two Rabbits & a Very Interesting Boy. l.t. ed. 2006. (Penderwick Ser.). 304p. (J). (gr. 3-7). 23.95 *(978-0-7862-8897-7(3))* Thorndike Pr.
Blackburn, C. Edward. The Stories of Christmas: As Told by a Little Lamb. Bishop, Megan, illus. l.t. ed. 2005. 24p. (J). 9.95 *(978-0-9727440-3-4(7))* Redline Bks.
Bock, Suzanne, illus. Meet the Angels l.t. ed. 2004. 10p. (J). bds. 12.99 *(978-0-9758709-4-5(7),* 13401) Journey Stone Creations, LLC.
Bolme, Edward Sarah. Baby Bible Board Books Collection No. 1: Stories of Jesus, 4 vols. Gillette, Tim, illus. l.t. ed. 2003. 20p. (J). bds. 23.99 *(978-0-9725546-4-0(5))* CREST Pubns.
—Jesus Feeds the People. Gillette, Tim, illus. l.t. ed. 2003. 20p. (J). bds. 6.99 *(978-0-9725546-0-2(2))* CREST Pubns.
—Jesus Heals a Little Girl. Gillette, Tim, illus. l.t. ed. 2003. 20p. (J). bds. 6.99 *(978-0-9725546-1-9(0))* CREST Pubns.
—Jesus Helps a Blind Man. Gillette, Tim, illus. l.t. ed. 2003. 20p. (J). bds. 6.99 *(978-0-9725546-2-6(9))* CREST Pubns.
—Jesus Stops a Storm. Gillette, Tim, illus. l.t. ed. 2003. 20p. (J). bds. 6.99 *(978-0-9725546-3-3(7))* CREST Pubns.
Boone, Melvin, Jr. JD Mc Doil What's up with Oil. l.t. ed. 2003. (Illus.). 32p. (J). 19.95 *(978-0-9741750-0-3(5))* Never Stop Reading Never Stop Learning.
Boritzer, Etan. What Is Right? Sale, Graham, illus. l.t. ed. 2005. (What Is? Ser.). 40p. (J). (gr. k-5). pap. 6.95 *(978-0-9762743-0-8(2)); (978-0-9762743-1-5(0))* Lane, Veronica Bks.
Boye, B. D. Easy As 1, 2, 3. Boye, B. D., illus. l.t. ed. 2005. (Illus.). 22p. (J). per. 4.99 *(978-0-9768078-0-3(7))* Innerchild Publishing, Inc.
—The Look Book. Boye, B. D., illus. l.t. ed. 2004. (Illus.). 20p. (J). per. 4.99 *(978-0-9768078-1-0(5),* 100001) Innerchild Publishing, Inc.
—Our New Home. Boye, B. D., illus. l.t. ed. 2005. (Illus.). 18p. (J). per. 4.99 *(978-0-9768078-2-7(3))* Innerchild Publishing, Inc.
Boyles, Peggy Palo & Prentice Hall Dictionary Editors. Realidades Vol. 2: Level 2, 2 vols. l.t. ed. 2003. (SPA & ENG.). 508p. (YA). (gr. 9-9). 254.00 *(978-0-13-035951-3(3),* Prentice Hall) Pearson Schl.
Boyles, Peggy Palo & Prentice Hall Direct Education Staff. Realidades: Level B, 2 vols. l.t. ed. 2003. (SPA & ENG.). 416p. (YA). (gr. 7-7). 208.00 *(978-0-13-035967-4(X),* Prentice Hall) Pearson Schl.
Boyles, Peggy Palo & Prentice Hall Directories Staff. Realidades: Level 1, 2 vols. l.t. ed. 2003. (ENG.). 564p. (YA). (gr. 8-9). stu. ed. 282.00 *(978-0-13-101687-3(3),* Prentice Hall) Pearson Schl.
—Realidades: Level A. l.t. ed. 2003. (SPA & ENG.). 322p. (YA). (gr. 7-7). stu. ed. 161.00 *(978-0-13-035966-7(1),* Prentice Hall) Pearson Schl.
Boyles, Peggy Palo, et al. Realidades, Level 3, 2 vols. l.t. ed. 2003. (SPA & ENG.). 614p. (YA). (gr. 10-10). 307.00 *(978-0-13-035968-1(8),* Prentice Hall) Pearson Schl.
Boyne, John. The Boy in the Striped Pajamas. rev. l.t. ed. 2007. (Thorndike Literacy Bridge Ser.). 247p. (YA). (gr. 7-12). 23.95 *(978-0-7862-9425-1(6))* Thorndike Pr.
Brady, Bill. A Charm for Jo. Brady, Laurie, illus. l.t. ed. 2005. (Turtle Books). 32p. (J). (gr. 2-5). lib. bdg. 15.95 *(978-0-944727-48-5(4))* Jason & Nordic Pubs.
Brady, Karen. God Is Great: A Collection of 13 Story Book Poems, 1. l.t. ed. 2004. (Illus.). 20p. (J). 12.50 *(978-0-9754169-0-7(1))* Bradybooks.biz.
Breems, Beau A. La Gran Historia: The Illustrated Gospel from Creation to Resurrection Breems, Beau A., illus. l.t. ed. 2005.Tr. of His Story. (SPA., Illus.). 50p. (J). 19.95 *(978-0-9768680-1-9(6),* 1000); per. 14.95 *(978-0-9768680-3-3(2),* 3000) Burning Bush Creation.
—His Story: The Illustrated Gospel from Creation to Resurrection. Breems, Beau A., illus. l.t. ed. 2005.Tr. of Gran Historia. (Illus.). 50p. (J). 19.95 *(978-0-9768680-0-2(8),* 0-9768680-0-8)* Burning Bush Creation.
Brez, Lisa. Hickerdoodle Gets Lost. l.t. ed. 2003. (Illus.). 32p. (J). per. 6.99 *(978-0-9743758-4-7(5))* Red Engine Pr.
—Hickerdoodle Gets the Hiccups. l.t. ed. 2003. (Illus.). 32p. (J). per. 6.99 *(978-0-9743758-3-0(7))* Red Engine Pr.
—Hickerdoodle Meets a Chigger. l.t. ed. 2004. (Illus.). 40p. (J). per. 6.99 *(978-0-9743758-5-4(3))* Red Engine Pr.
Brown, Jane. Who Has Four Feet? l.t. ed. 2005. (Sadlier Phonics Reading Program: Vol. 1). (Illus.). 8p. (gr. -1-1). 23.00 net. *(978-0-8215-7340-2(3))* Sadlier, William H. Inc.

J
K
L

Brown, Mark. Tommy Books: Faith, 10 vols. Mekis, Pete, illus. l.t. ed. 2005. 24p. (J). 12.99 *(978-0-9762690-0-7(7))* Tommy Bks. Pubng.

—Tommy Books: Kings, 10 vols. Mekis, Pete, illus. l.t. ed. 2005. 24p. (J). 12.99 *(978-0-9762690-4-5(X))* Tommy Bks. Pubng.

—Tommy Books Vol. 4: Praise, 10 vols. Mekis, Pete, illus. l.t. ed. 2005. 20p. (J). 12.99 *(978-0-9762690-3-8(1))* Tommy Bks. Pubng.

Bryant, Louella. Two Tracks in the Snow. Fargo, Todd, illus. l.t. ed. 2004. (Turtle Bks.). 32p. (J). lib. bdg. 15.95 *(978-0-944727-46-1(8),* Turtle Bks.) Jason & Nordic Pubs.

Brzycki, M. L. & Krueger, S. L. It Came from the Freezer ... or Was it the Drapes? l.t. ed. 2004. (Illus.). 110p. (YA). per. 13.00 *(978-0-9747581-0-7(8))* StrangeDays Publishing.

Bucki, Jo Dee & O'Malley, John. Maya Visits a Hospital: Love Is the Best Medicine, 110 vols. Hicks, Mindy, ed. Matthews, Ashley, illus. l.t. ed. 2007. 32p. (J). per. 4.95 *(978-0-9769069-0-2(2))* TAOH Inspired Education, LLC.

Buckler, Carol. Feathered Tales from the Barnyard. l.t. ed. 2004. (J). per. 5.95 *(978-1-932496-20-8(3))* Penman Publishing, Inc.

Bucky Badger A Children's Story: Becky Gets a Brother, 4 vols. l.t. ed. 2005. (Illus.). (J). 9.99 *(978-0-9765510-0-3(4))* Badgerland Bks. LLC.

Burchett, Loni R. Bear & Katie in a Day at Nestlenook Farm. l.t. ed. 2004. (Illus.). 76p. (J). per. 11.95 *(978-0-9742815-1-3(4))* Black Lab Publishing LLC.

—Bear & Katie in a Day with Friends, Vol. 3. l.t. ed. 2005. (Illus.). 68p. (J). per. 11.95 *(978-0-9742815-2-0(2),* bk003) Black Lab Publishing LLC.

—Bear & Katie in the Great Searsport Caper. l.t. ed. 2004. (Illus.). 81p. (J). per. 12.95 *(978-0-9742815-0-6(6))* Black Lab Publishing LLC.

Burnett, Frances Hodgson. A Little Princess: Being the whole story of Sara Crewe now told for T. l.t. ed. 2007. (ENG.). 210p. per. 22.99 *(978-1-4346-7029-8(5))* Creative Media Partners, LLC.

—A Little Princess: The Story of Sara Crewe. l.t. ed. 2005. 376p. pap. *(978-1-84637-117-2(1))* Echo Library.

—A Little Princess: The Story of Sara Crewe. l.t. ed. 2005. (Large Print Ser.). lib. bdg. 26.00 *(978-1-58287-814-0(5))* North Bks.

—A Little Princess: The Story of Sara Crewe. l.t. ed. 2003. 342p. pap. 10.95 *(978-0-7862-6247-2(8))* Thorndike Pr.

Burnford, Sheila. The Incredible Journey. (J). (gr. 6-8). 18.95 *(978-0-88411-099-6(0))* Amereon Ltd.

Busic, Valerie. Jason's First Day. OI Foundation, ed. Meyers, Jeff, illus. l.t. ed. 2004. 48p. per. 8.50 *(978-0-9642189-4-9(1))* Osteogenesis Imperfecta Foundation.

Byars, Betsy. Trouble River. l.t. ed. 2004. (Beeler Mystery Ser.). 28.95 *(978-1-58118-120-3(5))* LRS.

Campbell, Ellen Langas. Will Stephanie Get the Story?, 3 bks., No. 1. 2004. (Girls Know How Ser.: #1 - Journalism). (ENG., Illus.). 112p. (J). pap. 4.95 *(978-0-9743604-0-9(6),* GIRLS KNOW HOW) NouSoma Communications, Inc.

Candy, Wolf. The Tree, the House & the Hurricane. l.t. ed. 2005. (Illus.). 24p. (J). 7.00 *(978-0-9762292-3-0(4))* New Global Publishing.

Carmine, Mary & Baynton, Martin. Daniel et Ses Dinosaures. l.t. ed.Tr. of Daniel et Ses Dinosaures. (FRE., Illus.). (J). bds. 29.99 *(978-0-590-74124-8(1))* Scholastic, Inc.

Casey, Bert. Acoustic Guitar Book 2 Deluxe Edition: Book/DVD/CD, vol. 2. l.t. ed. 2003. (Watch & Learn Ser.: 2). (ENG., Illus.). 80p. pap. 15.95 incl. audio compact disk *(978-1-893907-43-0(0),* 256-535) Watch & Learn, Inc.

Cast, P. C. & Cast, Kristin. Chosen. l.t. ed. 2009. (House of Night Ser.: Bk. 3). (ENG.). 406p. (YA). 23.95 *(978-1-4104-1608-7(9))* Thorndike Pr.

—Marked. l.t. ed. 2008. (House of Night Ser.: No. 1). (ENG.). 442p. (YA). 23.95 *(978-1-4104-1021-4(8))* Thorndike Pr.

—Untamed. l.t. ed. 2009. (House of Night Ser.: Bk. 4). (ENG.). 510p. (YA). 23.95 *(978-1-4104-1965-1(7))* Thorndike Pr.

Causton, Linda. Lester's Rainy Lake Pony. l.t. ed. 2004. (Illus.). 32p. (J). 12.00 *(978-1-930374-09-6(7))* DeForest Pr.

Chabon, Michael. Summerland. l.t. ed. 2003. 615p. (J). 25.95 *(978-0-7862-5143-8(3))* Thorndike Pr.

Chamberlain, Lyn. Quonby & the Tree Den. Weltner, Dave, illus. l.t. ed. 2004. 12p. (J). 7.95 *(978-0-9706654-8-5(2))* Sprite Pr.

Ching, Jerry Yu & Onghai, Mike. The Greatest King. Ching, Jerry Yu, illus. 2nd l.t. ed. 2003. (Illus.). 52p. *(978-0-9743215-0-9(8))* WebCartoons, LLC.

Christian, Reinar Carl, Sr. Nate: The New Bus on the Block! l.t. ed. 2005. (Illus.). 41p. (J). 16.99 *(978-0-9769866-0-7(4))* Meritage Publishing.

The Christmas Chair l.t. ed. 2004. (Illus.). 27p. (J). 12.95 *(978-0-9763633-1-6(3))* Williams, Thomas.

Cintron, Carlos Juan, Sr., ed. Mis Primeros Pasos: Red de Niños. deluxe l.t. ed. 2005. (SPA., Illus.). 85p. (J). 12.00 *(978-0-9765828-5-4(6))* Editorial Vida Abundante.

Cioffi, Dom, illus. Digby & the Lake Monster. l.t. ed. 2006. 36p. (J). per. *(978-0-9745931-0-4(9))* Vermont Bookworks.

Claire, Elizabeth. Help Your Buddy Learn English, Bk. 1. Nichols, Dave, illus. l.t. ed. 2003. 64p. 15.00 *(978-0-937630-04-4(7))* Eardley Pubns.

Clements, Andrew. No Talking. Elliott, Mark, illus. l.t. ed. 2007. (Literacy Bridge Middle Reader Ser.). 155p. (J). (gr. 3-7). 23.95 *(978-1-4104-0294-3(0))* Thorndike Pr.

Clyde, Addie M. Sophie the Sofa. l.t. ed. 2004. 40p. (J). per. *(978-1-59196-744-6(9))* Instant Pub.

Cofer, Amadeus. Friendship Rules: How to Make & Keep Friends, 1. l.t. ed. 2004. (Illus.). 36p. (J). 14.00 *(978-1-932957-00-6(6))* Legacy Pubs.

—Mystery of the Golden Pearls: A Halloween Adventure in Clarkesville, 1. l.t. ed. 2004. (Illus.). 36p. (J). 14.00 *(978-1-932957-02-0(2))* Legacy Pubs.

Cohen, Judith Love. You Can Be A Chemist. Katz, David A., illus. l.t. ed. 2005. Orig. Title: You Can Be A Woman Chemist. 40p. (J). per. 7.00 *(978-1-880599-71-6(6))* Cascade Pass, Inc.

—You Can Be A Woman Chemist. Katz, David A., illus. l.t. ed. 2005. 40p. (J). 13.95 *(978-1-880599-72-3(4))* Cascade Pass, Inc.

—You Can Be A Woman Video Game Producer. l.t. ed. 2005. (Illus.). 72p. (J). 17.95 *(978-1-880599-74-7(0));* pap. 12.95 *(978-1-880599-73-0(2))* Cascade Pass, Inc.

Cohen, Sonia. Gigi. l.t. ed. 2005. (Illus.). 34p. (J). 14.95 *(978-0-615-12926-6(9))* Gigi Enterprises.

Collins, Suzanne. The Hunger Games. l.t. ed. 2009. (Hunger Games Trilogy: Bk. 1). (ENG.). 486p. (YA). 23.95 *(978-1-4104-1986-6(X))* Thorndike Pr.

—Mockingjay. l.t. ed. 2010. (Hunger Games Trilogy: Bk. 3). (ENG.). 503p. (YA). 23.99 *(978-1-4104-2841-7(9))* Thorndike Pr.

Condie, Ally. Matched. l.t. ed. 2011. (Matched Trilogy: Bk. 1). (ENG.). 450p. 23.99 *(978-1-4104-3954-3(2))* Thorndike Pr.

Conquistadore, H. Omni Presents the Universe. West, Jeremy, illus. l.t. ed. 2003. 51p. per. 8.99 *(978-1-932338-14-0(4))* Lifevest Publishing, Inc.

Coolidge, Susan. What Katy Did. l.t. ed. 2007. (ENG.). 160p. pap. 21.99 *(978-1-4346-5944-6(5))* Creative Media Partners, LLC.

Cope-Robinson, Lyn. Cat Tails. Cope-Robinson, Lyn, illus. l.t. ed. 2003. (Illus.). 32p. (J). lib. bdg. *(978-1-887774-14-7(9),* Wynden) Canmore Pr.

Counce, Paula. A Journey Remembered. l.t. ed. 2004. (Illus.). 135p. (J). 19.95 *(978-0-9762776-0-6(3))* Counce, Paula.

A Cow Had a Wish. l.t. ed. Date not set. (Illus.). 32p. (J). (gr. 1-6). *(978-0-9653327-1-2(3))* BF Publishing.

Crawford, Ann Fears. Rosa: A German Woman on the Texas Frontier. Fain, Cheryl, illus. l.t. ed. 2003. 60p. (J). (gr. 3-8). 16.95 *(978-1-931823-09-8(X))* Halcyon Pr.

Crichton, Julie. The King & the Queen & the Jelly Bean. Swaim, illus. l.t. ed. 2005. (SPA.). 24p. (J). bds. 7.95 *(978-0-9761990-0-7(9))* Bean Bk. Publishing.

—El rey y la reina y el frijolito de Goma. Swaim, Ramon, illus. l.t. ed. 2005. 24p. (J). bds. 7.95 *(978-0-9761990-1-4(7))* Bean Bk. Publishing.

Crosby, Vernon H. The Adventures of Scurry Little: Lost in my Dream. l.t. ed. 2004. 40p. (J). per. 10.95 *(978-1-59196-819-1(4))* Instant Pub.

Cross, Linda B. Lines from Linda. l.t. ed. 2003. 104p. (YA). per. 7.00 *(978-0-9748591-2-5(5),* MSP) Main St Publishing, Inc.

Cruzan, Patricia & Solly, Gloria, illus. Molly's Mischievous Dog. l.t. ed. 2004. 121p. (J). per. *(978-0-9653543-3-2(4))* Clear Creek Pubs.

Curry, Casey. I Remember You Today: An Interactive Picturebook for Children Dealing with the Loss of a Sibling or Parent. 2003. (Illus.). 24p. (J). wbk. ed. *(978-1-884878-15-2(6))* Annapolis Publishing Co.

Curtiss, A. B. The Little Chapel That Stood Golino, Mirto, illus. l.t. ed. 2005. (ENG.). 36p. (J). (gr. -1-3). 18.95 *(978-0-932529-77-0(1))* Oldcastle Publishing.

Damon - Beyond the Glory. l.t. ed. 2003. (Illus.). 152p. per. 14.95 *(978-0-9724033-2-0(9))* Backroads Pr.

Danziger, Paula. This Place Has No Atmosphere. 2006. (ENG.). 240p. (J). (gr. 5-18). 8.99 *(978-0-14-240680-9(5),* Puffin Books) Penguin Young Readers Group.

Das, Christina. Coo Coo Duckling. l.t. ed. 2005. (Illus.). 32p. (J). 15.95 *(978-0-9763082-4-9(X),* A JuneOne Production) JuneOne Publishing Hub.

—Munchy Mouse. l.t. ed. 2005. (Illus.). 32p. (J). 15.95 *(978-0-9763082-0-1(7),* A JuneOne Production) JuneOne Publishing Hub.

—Oomph-Pa-Pa at the Circus. l.t. ed. 2005. (Illus.). 32p. (J). 15.95 *(978-0-9763082-2-5(3),* A JuneOne Production) JuneOne Publishing Hub.

—The Red Spotted Balloon. l.t. ed. 2005. (Illus.). 32p. (J). 15.95 *(978-0-9763082-3-2(1),* A JuneOne Production) JuneOne Publishing Hub.

—Swinging under the Stars. l.t. ed. 2005. (Illus.). 32p. (J). 15.95 *(978-0-9763082-1-8(5),* A JuneOne Production) JuneOne Publishing Hub.

Davis, Adda Leah. Caleb's Song. l.t. ed. 2003. (Illus.). 56p. (J). *(978-0-9747904-0-4(0))* Golden Harvest Publishing Co.

Davis, Darren & Davis, Darren G. ABC's for Superheroes. l.t. ed. 2006. (Atlas Ser.). (ENG., Illus.). 12p. (J). (gr. -1-12). 5.99 *(978-1-59559-110-4(9))* Bluewater Productions, Inc.

De Saint-Exupéry, Antoine. The Little Prince. l.t. ed. 2005.Tr. of Petit Prince. (ENG.). 168p. pap. 10.95 *(978-0-7862-7539-7(1))* Thorndike Pr.

de Trevino, Elizabeth Borton. I, Juan de Pareja. l.t. ed. 2005. 244p. 20.95 *(978-0-7862-7666-0(5))* Thorndike Pr.

Demers, Dave & Demers, Lee Ann. My Grandpa Loves Trains: A Storybook for Preschoolers. Demers, David, photos by. l.t. ed. 2005. (Illus.). 76p. (J). per. 19.95 *(978-0-922993-23-9(8))* Marquette Bks., LLC.

Denny, Joe. Triune: Jimmy's Escape. 2005. 80p. (J). pap. *(978-0-9772240-0-5(7))* JD Entertainment.

DeSantis, Debi. A Bunch of Giggles & Hugs. l.t. ed. 2005. (Illus.). 26p. (J). 12.95 *(978-0-9770043-0-0(9))* New Global Publishing.

DeVos, Janie. Path Winds Home. Marsh, Nancy, illus. l.t. ed. 2005. 32p. 16.95 *(978-0-9743758-0-9(2))* Red Engine Pr.

Diaz, T. Richard. Little Growler, Big Heart. l.t. ed. 2003. (Illus.). 12p. (J). lib. bdg. 11.95 *(978-1-932338-21-8(7))* Lifevest Publishing, Inc.

DiCamillo, Kate. The Tale of Despereaux: Being the Story of a Mouse, a Princess, Some Soup & a Spool of Thread. Ering, Timothy Basil, illus. l.t. ed. 2004. (Thorndike Literacy Bridge Ser.). (ENG.). 247p. (J). pap. 11.95 *(978-1-4104-1527-1(9))* Thorndike Pr.

Dicicco, Joe. Planet Baseball, Japanese Edition, Volume 1: Making the Play, Vol. 1. Jimenez, Ruben D., tr. Dicicco, Joe, illus. l.t. ed. 2009. (JPN & ENG., Illus.). 14p. (J). (gr. -1-3). 7.95 *(978-1-929528-03-5(5))* Punta Gorda Pr.

Dickens, Charles. The Cricket on the Hearth. l.t. ed. 2005. 128p. pap. 17.95 *(978-1-59688-048-1(1),* 1-59688-048-1) Large Print Bk. Co., The.

Dickman, Jean M. Santa in Space. l.t. ed. 2003. (Illus.). 32p. (J). per. 9.95 *(978-0-9743718-0-1(7))* Tintagel Publications.

DiSunno, Rebecca, et al. Jeremy Goes to Camp Good Grief. l.t. ed. 2004. (Illus.). 48p. (J). per. 14.95 *(978-0-9754932-0-5(5))* East End Hospice, Inc.

Dolphin Halloween & Elsie's Scrapbook. l.t. ed. 2004. (Illus.). 32p. (J). mass mkt. 4.99 *(978-0-9760868-0-2(8))* Pluegl Bks.

Doolin, Jimmy. The Day the Circus Came to My Backyard. l.t. ed. 2003. 39p. lib. bdg. *(978-0-9710432-4-4(8))* Children's Literacy Pubns.

Dozier, Kim. The Ear-Less Kingdom. Dozier, Ashlyn McCauley, illus. l.t. ed. 2003. (ENG.). 24p. (J). 7.50 *(978-0-9745839-1-4(X),* Fun to Read Bks. with Royally Good Morals) MKADesigns.

—The Forgetful Princess. Dozier, Ashlyn McCauley, illus. 2nd l.t. ed. 2003. (ENG.). 24p. (J). 10.00 *(978-0-9745839-0-7(1),* Fun to Read Bks. with Royally Good Morals) MKADesigns.

—Where's Dwight Dragon. Dozier, Ashlyn McCauley, illus. l.t. ed. 2004. (ENG.). 32p. (J). 10.00 *(978-0-9745839-2-1(8),* Fun to Read Bks. with Royally Good Morals) MKADesigns.

Duchene-Marshall, Michele A. Charley Finds A Family. Marshall, Alan David, ed. Ousley, Clayton Gerard, photos by. l.t. ed. 2004. Orig. Title: Charley finds a Home. (Illus.). 20p. (J). spiral bd. 10.00 *(978-0-9761675-2-5(2))* Storybook Acres.

—Shirley's Red Satin Shoes. Marshall, Alan David, ed. Ousley, Clayton Gerard, photos by. l.t. ed. 2003. (Illus.). 17p. (J). spiral bd. 10.00 *(978-0-9761675-1-8(4))* Storybook Acres.

Dunbar, Paula J. Ruby's Rainbow: A Story of Acadia National Park. l.t. ed. 2005. (Illus.). 32p. (J). *(978-1-931207-59-1(3))* Dilligaf Publishing.

Eagle, Golden. It's Good to Laugh at Yourself (Coyote Medicine. l.t. ed. 2004. (Illus.). 22p. (J). per. 12.99 *(978-1-932338-36-2(5))* Lifevest Publishing, Inc.

—It's Good to Shed Your Skin (Snake Medicine) l.t. ed. 2004. (Illus.). 20p. (J). per. 12.99 *(978-1-932338-38-6(1))* Lifevest Publishing, Inc.

—It's Okay to Cry (Frog Medicine) l.t. ed. 2004. (Illus.). 16p. (J). per. 12.99 *(978-1-932338-37-9(3))* Lifevest Publishing, Inc.

—The Owl Who Lives in My House. l.t. ed. 2003. (Illus.). 24p. (J). per. 12.99 *(978-1-932338-34-8(9))* Lifevest Publishing, Inc.

Ebon Research Systems Staff. Dare to Be: Roberto Clemente. l.t. ed. 2003.Tr. of Atrevete a Ser un Heroe. . . Roberto Clemente. (ENG & SPA., Illus.). 22p. 3.99 *(978-0-9648313-5-3(X))* Ebon Research Systems Publishing, LLC.

—Dare to Be Vol. 2: Lessons in the Life of Esperanza. l.t. ed. 2003.Tr. of Atrevete Ser... Un Heroe. (ENG & SPA., Illus.). 16p. (J). 3.99 *(978-0-9648313-4-6(1))* Ebon Research Systems Publishing, LLC.

—Dare to Be... A Hero Vol. 3: Cesar Chavez. l.t. ed. 2003.Tr. of Atrevete Ser... Un Heroe Cesar Chavez. (ENG & SPA., Illus.). 16p. (J). 3.99 *(978-0-9648313-6-0(8))* Ebon Research Systems Publishing, LLC.

Eckdahl, Judith & Eckdahl, Kathryn. A Collection of Street Games. O'Regan, Lucy, ed. Miranda, Pedro, illus. 2005. 42p. pupil's gde. ed. 13.95 *(978-0-9767200-0-3(0))* Lesen Pub.

Ehlin, Gina. Emma & Friends: Emma's Airport Adventure. Ayzenberg, Nina, illus. l.t. ed. 2005. 32p. (J). per. 10.99 *(978-1-59879-014-6(5))* Lifevest Publishing, Inc.

—Emma's Airport Adventure. Ayesenberg, Nina, illus. l.t. ed. 2005. (Emma & Friends Ser.). 34p. (J). 15.99 *(978-1-59879-015-3(3))* Lifevest Publishing, Inc.

Eifrig, Kate. I'll Be a Pirate: World of Discovery II. Graves, Dennis, illus. l.t. ed. 2006. (SPA & ENG.). 12p. (gr. k-2). pap. 7.95 *(978-1-57874-053-6(3),* Kaeden Bks.) Kaeden Corp.

Ellis, Marvie. Tacos Anyone? Bk. 2: An Autism Story Book. l.t. ed. 2005.Tr. of Alguien quiere Tacos? (SPA., Illus.). 32p. (J). per. 16.95 *(978-1-933319-01-8(1))* Speech Kids Texas Pr.

Epstein, Brad M. Arizona State University 101: My First Text-Board-Book. l.t. ed. 2003. (101 — My First Text-Board Books). (Illus.). 20p. (J). bds. *(978-0-9727702-3-1(2),* 101 Bk.) Michaelson Entertainment.

—Auburn University 101: My First Text Board Bks.). (Illus.). 20p. (J). bds. 2003. (My First Text Board Bks.). (Illus.). 20p. (J). bds. *(978-0-9727702-7-9(5))* Michaelson Entertainment.

—Clemson University 101: My First Text-Board-Book. l.t. ed. 2004. (101 — My First Text-Board Books). (ENG., Illus.). 20p. (J). bds. *(978-1-932530-06-3(1),* 101 Bk.) Michaelson Entertainment.

—Columbia University 101: My First Text-Board-Book. l.t. ed. 2005. (101 — My First Text-Board Books). (Illus.). 20p. (J). bds. *(978-0-9727702-1-7(6))* Michaelson Entertainment.

—Cornell University 101: My First Text-Board-Book. l.t. ed. 2004. (101 — My First Text-Board Books). (Illus.). 20p. (J). bds. *(978-1-932530-00-1(2))* Michaelson Entertainment.

—Dartmouth College 101. l.t. ed. 2003. (My First Text Board Bks.). (Illus.). 20p. (J). bds. *(978-0-9727702-5-5(9))* Michaelson Entertainment.

—Louisiana State University 101: My First Text-Board-Book. l.t. ed. 2004. (My First Text Board Bks.). (Illus.). 20p. (J). bds. *(978-1-932530-09-4(6))* Michaelson Entertainment.

—Penn State University 101: My First Text-Board-Book. l.t. ed. 2004. (101 — My First Text-Board Books). (Illus.). 20p. (J). bds. *(978-1-932530-04-9(5),* 101 Bk.) Michaelson Entertainment.

—Purdue University 101: My First Text-Board-Book. l.t. ed. 2004. (101 — My First Text-Board Books). (ENG., Illus.). 20p. (J). bds. *(978-1-932530-11-7(8),* 101 Bk.) Michaelson Entertainment.

—UCLA 101: My First Text-Board-Book. l.t. ed. 2004. (My First Text Board Bks.). (Illus.). 20p. (J). bds. *(978-1-932530-15-5(0),* 101 Bk.) Michaelson Entertainment.

—University of Florida 101: My First Text-Board-Book. l.t. ed. 2004. (101 — My First Text-Board Books). (Illus.). 20p. (J). bds. *(978-1-932530-21-6(5),* 101 Bk.) Michaelson Entertainment.

—University of Georgia 101: My First Text-Board-Book. l.t. ed. 2004. (101 — My First Text-Board Books). (ENG., Illus.). 20p. (J). bds. *(978-1-932530-08-7(8),* 101 Bk.) Michaelson Entertainment.

—University of Illinois 101: My First Text-Board-Book. l.t. ed. 2004. (101 — My First Text-Board Books). (ENG., Illus.). 20p. (J). bds. *(978-1-932530-17-9(7),* 101 Bk.) Michaelson Entertainment.

—Usc 101: My First Text-Board-Book. l.t. ed. 2004. (101 — My First Text-Board Books). (ENG., Illus.). 20p. (J). bds. *(978-0-9727702-0-0(8),* 101 Bk.) Michaelson Entertainment.

Evans, Mary. Cats! Cats! Cats!, 2. Kovalcik, Terry, illus. l.t. ed. 2005. (Sadlier Phonics Reading Program). 8p. (gr. -1-1). 23.00 net. *(978-0-8215-7348-8(9))* Sadlier, William H. Inc.

—Good Pets, Vol. 3. l.t. ed. 2005. (Sadlier Phonics Reading Program). (Illus.). 8p. (gr. -1-1). 23.00 net. *(978-0-8215-7350-1(0))* Sadlier, William H. Inc.

Fabris, Judith. Money...Cool! Brolin, Carol, illus. l.t. ed. 2003. 155p. (YA). pap. 9.95 *(978-1-893335-12-7(7))* Archipelago Pr.

Fabulas de Siempre. l.t. ed.Tr. of Traditional Fables. (SPA.). (J). 3.98 *(978-84-7630-901-8(5))* Selector, S.A. de C.V. MEX. Dist: AIMS International Bks., Inc.

Falkner, John Meade. Moonfleet. l.t. ed. 2004. (Large Print Ser.). 370p. 26.00 *(978-1-58287-658-0(4))* North Bks.

Farrow, Stephanie, ed. Blue Wolf & Friends Storybook, 1 Vol., Units 1-4. l.t. ed. 2004. (Illus.). 93p. *(978-0-9758759-2-6(2))* Progressive Language, Inc.

Faye, Joanne & Whaley, Stacey Lynn. Conversations with Kids Ages 3 to 6. l.t. ed. 2004. (Illus.). 24p. (J). 9.95 *(978-0-9747375-0-8(X))* Joanne Faye Pr.

Fetzer, Erin. The Sonday System Readers - 6a-10c, 1. Breckman, Cindy, ed. l.t. ed. 2004. (Illus.). 12p. (J). *(978-1-891602-14-6(4))* Winsor Learning, Inc.

Fey, Sid & Vitello, Kathy. The Being Game: For the Love of Your Life. l.t. ed. 2004. (Illus.). 66p. per. 14.95 *(978-0-9753530-5-9(5))* Fey, Sid Designs, Inc.

Feyh, Janelle. Does God Have a Remote Control? Feyh, Alexa & Deghand, Tim, illus. l.t. ed. 2003. 66p. (J). per. 11.95 *(978-1-932344-26-4(8))* Thornton Publishing, Inc.

A Fifty Year Affair: Living with Light Planes. l.t. ed. 2004. (Illus.). 208p. (YA). pap. 18.95 *(978-0-9746564-0-3(2))* Julson, D. K.

Fisher, Phyllis Mae Richardson, illus. Chrissy (#1 in the 1989 Family Friends Paper Doll Set) l.t. ed. 2004. 24p. (J). 10.00 *(978-0-9745615-5-4(X))* PJs Corner.

—Melly, #2 in the 1989 Family Friends Paper Doll Set, Vols. 3, Vol. 2. l.t. ed. 2004. 24p. (J). 10.00 *(978-0-9745615-6-1(8))* PJs Corner.

Foce, Natalia, tr. from ENG. Daniel, el Principe que Oraba Apps, Fred, illus. l.t. ed. 2009. (SPA & ENG.). 32p. (J). 3.49 *(978-1-932789-19-5(7))* Editorial Sendas Antiguas, LLC.

—La Historia de Pablo — Viajes de Aventura, 1. Apps, Fred, illus. l.t. ed. 2009. Orig. Title: Journeys of Adventure — the Story of Paul. (SPA & ENG.). 32p. (J). 3.49 *(978-1-932789-23-2(5))* Editorial Sendas Antiguas, LLC.

—Jesus el Milagroso. Anderson, Jeff, illus. l.t. ed. 2009. Orig. Title: Jesus the Miracle Worker. (SPA & ENG.). 24p. (J). 3.49 *(978-1-932789-28-7(6))* Editorial Sendas Antiguas, LLC.

—Jesus Maestro. Anderson, Jeff, illus. l.t. ed. 2009. Orig. Title: Jesus the Teacher. (SPA & ENG.). 24p. (J). 3.49 *(978-1-932789-26-3(X))* Editorial Sendas Antiguas, LLC.

—Jesus Narrador. Anderson, Jeff, illus. l.t. ed. 2009. Orig. Title: Jesus the Storyteller. (SPA & ENG.). 24p. (J). 3.49 *(978-1-932789-25-6(1))* Editorial Sendas Antiguas, LLC.

—Jesus Niño. Anderson, Jeff, illus. l.t. ed. 2009. Orig. Title: Jesus the Child. (SPA & ENG.). 24p. (J). 3.49 *(978-1-932789-24-9(3))* Editorial Sendas Antiguas, LLC.

—Jesus Salvador. Anderson, Jeff, illus. l.t. ed. 2009. Orig. Title: Jesus the Saviour. (SPA & ENG.). 24p. (J). 3.49 *(978-1-932789-29-4(4))* Editorial Sendas Antiguas, LLC.

—Jesus Sanador. Anderson, Jeff, illus. l.t. ed. 2009. Orig. Title: Jesus the Healer. (SPA & ENG.). 24p. (J). 3.49 *(978-1-932789-27-0(8))* Editorial Sendas Antiguas, LLC.

—El Nacimiento de Jesús: El Niño Prometido, 1. Apps, Fred, illus. l.t. ed. 2009. Orig. Title: The Birth of Jesus — the Promised Child. (SPA & ENG.). 32p. (J). 3.49 *(978-1-932789-20-1(0))* Editorial Sendas Antiguas, LLC.

—El Plan de Rescate: La Historia de Noe, 1. Apps, Fred, illus. l.t. ed. 2009. Orig. Title: The Rescue Plan. (SPA & ENG.). 32p. (J). 3.49 *(978-1-932789-15-7(4))* Editorial Sendas Antiguas, LLC.

—La Resurrección: Jesús Está Vivo, 1. Apps, Fred, illus. l.t. ed. 2009. Orig. Title: The Resurrection — Jesus Is Alive. (SPA & ENG.). 32p. (J). 3.49 *(978-1-932789-21-8(9))* Editorial Sendas Antiguas, LLC.

—Samuel, el Niño que Escuchaba. Apps, Fred, illus. l.t. ed. 2009. (SPA & ENG.). 32p. (J). 3.49 *(978-1-932789-17-1(0))* Editorial Sendas Antiguas, LLC.

—Saúl — el Milagro en el Camino, 1. Apps, Fred, illus. l.t. ed. 2009. Orig. Title: Saul — the Miracle on the Road. (SPA & ENG.). 32p. (J). 3.49 *(978-1-932789-22-5(7))* Editorial Sendas Antiguas, LLC.

Fontanez, Edwin. On This Beautiful Island. Fontanez, Edwin, illus. l.t. ed. 2004. (Illus.). 32p. (J). 16.95 *(978-0-9640868-6-9(7),* 1241077) Exit Studio.

Forbes, Esther Hoskins. Johnny Tremain Set: Illustrated American Classics, 2 vols., l.t. ed. (J). reprint ed. *(978-0-89064-029-6(7))* National Assn. for Visually Handicapped.

Foster, Kathryn Joy. Always Room for One More. l.t. ed. 2004. (Illus.). 12p. (J). spiral bd. 13.00 *(978-0-9728779-6-1(7),* TBK-21007) Read All Over Publishing.

Frazier, Janet. The Case of the Theme Park Cry. l.t. ed. 2004. 90p. (J). per. *(978-1-59196-737-8(6))* Instant Pub.

Frontiera, Deborah K. Eric & the Enchanted Leaf: The First Adventure Scott, Korey, illus. 2nd l.t. ed. 2004. 32p. (J). pap. 16.95 *(978-0-9753410-0-1(6))* Jade Enterprises.

—Eric & the Enchanted Leaf / Eric y la Hoja Encantada: A Visit with Canis Lupis / una Visita con Canis Lupis. Santillan-Cruz, Silvia R., tr. Scott, Korey, illus. 2nd l.t. ed. 2005. (SPA & ENG.). 32p. (J). lib. bdg. 16.95 *(978-0-9663629-8-5(5))* By Grace Enterprises.

Furbush, Helen. Lying Awake. McCroskey, Christine, illus. l.t. ed. 2004. 32p. (J). (gr. 1-6). 15.95 *(978-0-9741787-0-7(5),* 1239134) Harbor Island Bks.

Fussell, Bonnie. More Than a Stove. Sadler, Dale, illus. l.t. ed. 2004. 32p. (J). pap. 7.99 *(978-0-615-12702-6(9))* Blackberry Pubs.

Gardiner, John Reynolds. Stone Fox. Sewall, Marcia, illus. 25th anniv. ed. 2005. (ENG.). 96p. (J). (gr. 2-6). 16.99 *(978-0-690-03983-2(2))* HarperCollins Pubs.

Garrick, Lainie. Losing Papou: One Child's Journey Towards Understanding & Accepting Death. Mandarino, Gene, illus. l.t. ed. 2003. 32p. (J). *(978-0-9765725-0-3(8))* printONDEMANDpublisher.com.

George, Jean Craighead. Julie of the Wolves. l.t. ed. 2004. (Beeler Mystery Ser.). 32.95 *(978-1-58118-121-0(3))* LRS.

Gibbs, Dreene. Am I Pretty, Momma? 2nd l.t. ed. 2004. (Illus.). 32p. (J). bds. 12.95 *(978-0-9741406-1-2(9),* 0138) Cranberry Quill Publishing Co.

Giunta, Brian. The Seven Presidents. Chapin, Patrick O., illus. l.t. ed. 2003. 24p. (J). 8.95 *(978-1-58597-172-5(3))* Leathers Publishing.

Golden Eagle Productions Staff. Grandmother Moon & Sammy the Loon, 36 vols. l.t. ed. 2003. (Illus.). 24p. per. 12.99 *(978-1-932338-24-9(1))* Lifevest Publishing, Inc.

Goldish, Meish. How Many Are Here? Meyerhoff, Jill, illus. l.t. ed. 2005. (Sadlier Phonics Reading Program). 8p. (gr. -1-1). 23.00 net. *(978-0-8215-7344-0(6))* Sadlier, William H. Inc.

—Nice Vine, Quite Fine, Vol. 2. Sargent, Claudia Karabaic, illus. l.t. ed. 2005. (Little Books & Big Bks.: Vol. 7). 8p. (gr. k-2). 23.00 net. *(978-0-8215-7516-1(3))* Sadlier, William H. Inc.

—Zack Can Fix It!, Vol. 4. Scruton, Clive, illus. l.t. ed. 2005. (Sadlier Phonics Reading Program). 8p. (gr. -1-1). 23.00 net. *(978-0-8215-7359-4(4))* Sadlier, William H. Inc.

Gonzalez, David J. There Are No Space Aliens! 12 Biblical Points Disproving Space Aliens. l.t. ed. 2003. 48p. 9.95 *(978-0-9741561-0-1(8))* Gonzalez, David J. Ministries.

Goodwin, Carol. Does This Belong Here? A Twiggyleaf Adventure. McDaniel, Thomas, illus. l.t. ed. 2003. 32p. (J). 14.95 *(978-0-9741072-1-9(2))* CornerWind Media, L.L.C.

—The Great Acorn: A Twiggyleaf Adventure. McDaniel, Thomas, illus. l.t. ed. 2004. 32p. (J). 14.95 *(978-0-9741072-2-6(0))* CornerWind Media, L.L.C.

—Tippy Needs A Home: A Twiggyleaf Adventure. McDaniel, Thomas, illus. l.t. ed. 2003. 32p. (J). per. 14.95 *(978-0-09-741072-2(1))* CornerWind Media, L.L.C.

—What's the Hurry, Furry? A Twiggyleaf Adventure. McDaniel, Thomas, illus. l.t. ed. 2003. 32p. (J). 14.95 *(978-0-9741072-0-2(4))* CornerWind Media, L.L.C.

Gorgas, Paula Blais. Little Lost Leprechaun. Taylor, Chet, illus. l.t. ed. 2005. 20p. (J). 17.99 *(978-0-9755888-4-0(2))* Dragonfly Publishing, Inc.

Gould, Carol. My Native American School. Drzewiecki, Paul, illus. l.t. ed. 2003. (ENG.). 16p. (gr. k-2). pap. 7.95 *(978-1-879835-77-1(0),* Kaeden Bks.) Kaeden Corp.

Grandma Janet Mary. Grandma's Treasure Chest. Pennington, Craig, illus. l.t. ed. 2005. (Grandma Janet Mary Ser.). 50p. (J). 16.95 *(978-0-9742732-3-5(6))* My Grandma & Me Pubs.

Graziani, Maria. The Adventures of Valeria Veterinarian: Las Aventuras de Valeria Veterinaria, 1. Elejalde, Eliana, illus. l.t. ed. 2004. (SPA.). 23p. (J). 7.00 *(978-0-9762361-0-8(9))* Ed. Acespanish S.A.C.- Lima, Peru.

—A Black Cat on Halloween: Un Gato Negro en Dia de Brujas. Elejalde, Eliana, illus. l.t. ed. 2004. (SPA.). 23p. (J). 7.00 *(978-0-9762361-1-5(7))* Ed. Acespanish S.A.C.- Lima, Peru.

Greendyk, William, tr. from ENG. Las Doce Historias de la Tía Margarita. l.t. ed. 2004. Orig. Title: Aunt Margaret's Twelve Stories. (SPA.). 84p. (J). pap. 3.99 *(978-1-932789-00-3(6),* X001N) Editorial Sendas Antiguas, LLC.

—Los DOS Osos. l.t. ed. 2004. (SPA.). 152p. (J). pap. 5.99 *(978-1-932789-02-7(2),* R009N) Editorial Sendas Antiguas, LLC.

—La Hierba Mala. l.t. ed. 2004.Tr. of Hierba Mala. (SPA.). 156p. (J). pap. 5.99 *(978-1-932789-01-0(4),* X002N) Editorial Sendas Antiguas, LLC.

—El Hijo de la Viuda. l.t. ed. 2004. Orig. Title: The Widow's Son. (SPA., Illus.). 92p. (J). pap. *(978-1-932789-11-9(1))* Editorial Sendas Antiguas, LLC.

—Los Niños de la Biblia. l.t. ed. 2004. (SPA.). 94p. (J). pap. 3.99 *(978-1-932789-03-4(0),* X003N) Editorial Sendas Antiguas, LLC.

—Primeras Impresiones de Dios. l.t. ed. 2004.Tr. of Primeras Impresiones de Dios. (SPA.). 94p. (J). pap. 3.99 *(978-1-932789-04-1(9),* W001N) Editorial Sendas Antiguas, LLC.

Gremila, Elaine Demetri. Seasons of the Heart. l.t. ed. 2003. (Illus.). 140p. per. 11.95 *(978-1-932338-16-4(0))* Lifevest Publishing, Inc.

Grimm, Jacob & Grimm, Wilhelm K. Grimm's Fairy Tales. l.t. ed. 2004. (Large Print Ser.). 477p. 26.00 *(978-1-58287-627-6(4))* North Bks.

Hairston, Angelica. Did Noah Have Whales on the Ark? Ferguson, Tamara, illus. l.t. ed. 2004. 44p. (J). *(978-0-9716136-1-4(3))* Broadcast Quality Productions, Inc.

Hall / Waltz. Mortimer Jones: The Bubble Gum Nerd, 1. l.t. ed. 2003. (Illus.). 32p. 19.95 *(978-0-9741774-2-7(3))* D. W. Publishing.

Hall, Nancy R. My Grandparents Live in an RV Hall, Nancy R., illus. l.t. ed. 2005. (Illus.). 32p. (J). 16.95 *(978-0-9761759-0-2(8))* Jasnans Publishing Co.

Hamilton, Elizabeth L. Katie Kangaroo's Leap of Courage. l.t. ed. 2005. (Character Critters Ser.: No. 9). (Illus.). 32p. (J). per. 5.95 *(978-0-9754629-6-6(2),* Character-in-Action) Quiet Impact, Inc.

—Ricky Raccoon's Trustworthiness Tree. l.t. ed. 2005. (Character Critters Ser.: No. 11). (Illus.). 32p. (J). per. 5.95 *(978-0-9754629-8-0(9),* Character-in-Action) Quiet Impact, Inc.

Hamilton, Patricia Birdsong & Scripts Publishing Staff. What's Up: William Explains Ataxia to His New Friends. l.t. ed. 2005. (Ataxia: A Lifestyle Change). 44p. 18.95 *(978-1-889826-90-5(1))* Scripts Publishing.

Hamilton, Virginia. M. C. Higgins, the Great. 2006. 271p. (gr. 8-12). 18.00 *(978-0-7569-6809-0(7))* Perfection Learning Corp.

—M. C. Higgins, the Great. 2006. (ENG., Illus.). 288p. (J). (gr. 3-7). pap. 7.99 *(978-1-4169-1407-5(2),* Aladdin) Simon & Schuster Children's Publishing.

Hampton, Randall. A Christmas Kiss. l.t. ed. 2005. (Illus.). 48p. (J). per. 16.95 *(978-1-59879-048-1(X))* Lifevest Publishing, Inc.

Handford, S. A. Aesop's Fables. Winter, Nilo, illus. l.t. ed. Date not set. (J). (gr. 1-12). lib. bdg. 22.95 *(978-0-88411-991-3(2))* Amereon Ltd.

Hanna, James Milton, Sr. Once upon a Time in the South. l.t. ed. 2004. (Illus.). 235p. per. 12.95 *(978-1-930052-15-4(4))* Cherokee Bks.

Hanson, Paige & Hanson, Jon. Harry Spotter: The Incontinent Puppy Sellers, Amy, illus. l.t. ed. 2005. 44p. (J). per. 20.00 *(978-0-9721146-1-5(0))* Monroe Educational Media.

Harbo, Gary. The Northern Woods Adventure: Early Reader. Harbo, Gary, illus. l.t. ed. 2004. (If You Want to Succeed, You Need to Read! Ser.: 6). (Illus.). 33p. (J). 10.95 *(978-1-884149-16-0(2))* Kutie Kari Bks., Inc.

Harkes, Willy. Little Dutch Girl in World War II. Blair, Jocelyn, illus. l.t. ed. 2004. 22p. (J). pap. 13.95 *(978-0-9741627-1-3(X))* PricePoint+Publications.

Harper, Stephan J. The Black Sheep Beach. Mary FitzGerald, illus. l.t. ed. 2005. 32p. (J). lib. bdg. 16.95 *(978-0-9741800-1-4(7))* Inspire Press, Inc.

Haworth, Margaret. Jarry, Garry Palas: Cat Tail Stories. Haworth, Margaret, photos by. l.t. ed. 2003. (Books That Help Ser.: Vol. 3). (Illus.). 34p. (J). (gr. 1-6). pap. 9.95 *(978-0-9740313-5-4(6))* Haworth, Margaret.

Hawthorne, Nathaniel. A Wonder Book & Tanglewood Tales. l.t. ed. 2004. (Large Print Ser.). 563p. 26.00 *(978-1-58287-673-3(8))* North Bks.

Hazelton, Jack W. Charlie Duck. Hazelton, Jack W., illus. l.t. ed. 2003. (Illus.). 24p. (J). 12.95 *(978-1-928907-54-1(7))* Jack's Bookshelf, Inc.

Hein, Connie L. Toliver in Time; for a Journey West: History in a Nutshell. Theobald, Denise, illus. l.t. ed. 2005. 28p. (J). lib. bdg. 17.95 *(978-0-9740855-6-2(1));* per. 9.95 *(978-0-9740855-7-9(X))* Still Water Publishing.

Heller, Andrew. No Bones about It. Rene, Perez, illus. l.t. ed. 2003. 12p. (J). 7.99 *(978-0-9722038-5-2(0))* Mr Do It All, Inc.

Heller, Ruth. Nous Ne Sommes Pas Nes/Oeuf! l.t. ed. (FRE., Illus.). (J). bds. 29.99 *(978-0-590-73029-7(0))* Scholastic, Inc.

Henderson, Tim. Butterflies & Magic Dreams. Hansen, Melissa, illus. l.t. ed. 2003. 28p. (J). *(978-0-9728691-0-2(7))* Logan Bks.

Henny, Rose. Teddy Finds His Way: A Teddy Tale. Henny, Rose, illus. l.t. ed. 2005. (Illus.). 22p. (J). per. 17.95 *(978-0-9705458-7-9(8))* Royalty Bks. International, Inc.

Hensley, Sarah M. Caillou Visits the Circus. Storch, Ellen N., illus. l.t. ed. 2005. (HRL Board Book Ser.). (J). (gr. -1-k). pap. 10.95 *(978-1-57332-309-3(8),* HighReach Learning, Incorporated) Carson-Dellosa Publishing, LLC.

Herron, Carolivia, photos by & told to. Little Georgia & the Apples: A Retelling of Aunt Georgia's First Catalpa Tale Herron, Carolivia, told to. l.t. ed. 2004. (Illus.). 33p. (J). 10.00 *(978-0-9760222-0-6(6),* Catalpa01) Epicenter Literary Software.

Heyman, Carly. My Extra Special Brother: How to Love, Understand, & Celebrate Your Sibling with Special Needs. Conley, Stephanie, illus. l.t. ed. 2003. 112p. pap. 12.95 *(978-0-9727865-0-8(3),* 1003894) Fragile X Assn. of Georgia.

Hill, Grace Livingston. Cloudy Jewel. (J). reprint ed. lib. bdg. 24.95 *(978-0-89190-037-5(3),* Rivercity Pr.) Amereon Ltd.

Hiris, Monica. Just Like Dad. Drzewiecki, Paul, illus. l.t. ed. 2003. (ENG.). 8p. (gr. k-1). pap. 7.95 *(978-1-879835-76-4(2),* Kaeden Bks.) Kaeden Corp.

—Sleepy Polar Bear. Harston, Jerry, illus. l.t. ed. 2006. (ENG.). 24p. (gr. k-2). pap. 8.95 *(978-1-57874-072-7(X),* Kaeden Bks.) Kaeden Corp.

Hoban, Russell. A Bargain for Frances. Hoban, Lillian, illus. l.t. ed. 2003. (I Can Read Level 2 Ser.). (ENG.). 64p. (J). (gr. k-3). pap. 3.99 *(978-0-06-444001-1(X))* HarperCollins Pubs.

Hock, Dan. The Birthday Bash 2 vols. An Iggy & Igor Mystery (#2) Hock, Dan, illus. l.t. ed. 2004. (Illus.). 51p. (J). per. 4.99 *(978-0-9754046-1-4(X))* Anticipation Pr.

Hoenecke, Karen. Little Mouse. Gedeon, Gloria, illus. l.t. ed. 2005. (ENG.). 12p. (gr. k-2). pap. 7.95 *(978-1-57874-023-9(1),* Kaeden Bks.) Kaeden Corp.

—Snake Hunts for Lunch. Drzewiecki, Paul, illus. l.t. ed. 2005. (ENG.). 12p. (gr. k-2). pap. 7.95 *(978-1-57874-006-2(1),* Kaeden Bks.) Kaeden Corp.

Hollaway, David. Quigley Mccormick: And the Curse of the Polka Dotted Pig, 3 vols. l.t. ed. 2005. (Illus.). 156p. (J). (gr. -1-3). per. 15.95 *(978-1-933211-54-1(7))* Quackenworth Publishing.

Holofcener, Mark. Evan's Earthly Adventure. l.t. ed. 2003. (Illus.). 202p. (YA). mass mkt. 11.00 *(978-0-9718626-1-6(3))* Holofcener, Mark.

Hood, Karen Jean Matsko. Washington State: Activity & Coloring Book. l.t. ed. 2014. (Educational Activity & Coloring Book Ser.). (J). 19.95 *(978-1-930948-56-3(5))* Whispering Pine Pr. International, Inc.

Hooker, Karen. Camping. Biddle, Bruce, illus. l.t. ed. 2003. (ENG.). 16p. (gr. k-1). pap. 7.95 *(978-1-879835-32-0(0),* Kaeden Bks.) Kaeden Corp.

Hooker, Lou. The Year of the Fire. l.t. ed. 2004. (Illus.). 102p. (J). pap. 8.95 *(978-0-9755106-0-5(6))* Hooker, Lou.

Horowitz, Alena Netia. The Tlytiettlym Tree. Horowitz, Alena Netia & De La Fuente, Mary, illus. l.t. ed. 2003. 64p. (J). per. 12.95 *(978-0-923550-42-4(9))* Tetrahedron Publishing LLC.

Hortten, Jacqueline Faye. Pu Beach. l.t. ed. 2004. (Illus.). 27p. (J). pap. 14.95 *(978-0-9728393-0-3(5))* Children's Bookshoppe Stop, The.

House, Darrell. Miller the Green Caterpillar. Argoff, Patti, illus. l.t. ed. 2005. 32p. 16.95 *(978-0-9663276-9-4(1))* Red Engine Pr.

Howard-Parham, Pam. Caillou Finds Colors. Gillen, Lisa P., illus. l.t. ed. 2005. (HRL Board Book Ser.). (J). (gr. -1-k). bds. 10.95 *(978-1-57332-313-0(6),* HighReach Learning, Incorporated) Carson-Dellosa Publishing, LLC.

—This Is Farmer Greg. Coates, Jennifer, illus. l.t. ed. 2005. (HRL Board Book Ser.). (gr. -1-k). pap. 10.95 *(978-1-57332-305-5(5),* HighReach Learning, Incorporated) Carson-Dellosa Publishing, LLC.

Hugh Granville Tilley North Carolina House of Representatives 1887 And 1889, 1 book. l.t. ed. 2007. (ENG., Illus.). 50p. lib. bdg. 36.99 *(978-0-9722724-3-8(7))* Blackfoot Burkino Cherokee Publishing.

Hunter, Erin. The Quest Begins. l.t. ed. 2008. (Seekers Ser.: No. 1). 372p. (J). pap. 16.99 *(978-0-06-170951-7(4))* HarperCollins Pubs.

Hunter, Julius K. Absurd Alphabedtime Stories. Bauman, Todd, illus. 2nd rev. l.t. ed. 2004. 32p. (J). 16.95 *(978-0-9761422-0-1(1))* J.K.H. Enterprises.

The Incarnation of Christ: Immanuel l.t. ed. 2004. (CHI., Illus.). 52p. (J). *(978-0-9752775-0-8(2),* 0-9752775-0-2) Unitrust Design.

Jackson, Vicky, illus. Poepal's Purpose. l.t. ed. 2005. 20p. (J). 7.95 *(978-0-9718741-0-7(7))* Tawa Productions.

Jacques, Brian. Triss. l.t. ed. 2004. (Redwall Ser.). 596p. (J). 23.95 *(978-0-7862-6207-6(9))* Thorndike Pr.

Jarrell, Pamela R. Caillou's Musical Band. Gray, Stacy A., illus. l.t. ed. 2005. (HRL Board Book Ser.). (J). (gr. -1-k). 10.95 *(978-1-57332-311-6(X),* HighReach Learning, Incorporated) Carson-Dellosa Publishing, LLC.

Jauregui, Patricia. Sentimientos. Jauregui, Reginald, ed. Pineda, Jesus, illus. l.t. ed. 2004. (SPA.). 39p. (YA). pap. 19.95 *(978-1-931481-41-0(5))* LiArt-Literature & Art.

Jax, T. L. Fraidy-Frieda's Light Show. Jax, T. L., illus. l.t. ed. 2004. (Illus.). 30p. (J). 9.95 *(978-0-9743890-2-8(1))* Flaxenfluff Pr., LLC.

Johnson, Nevlynn L., Sr. Faith, Courage & Wisdom: A Journey to Manhood. 3rd rev. l.t. ed. 2003. Orig. Title: Finding My Way: a Journey to Manhood. 240p. per. 14.95 *(978-0-9741413-0-5(5))* Lone Cypress Pubs.

Johnson, Sandi & Fefie, Flora. Zemo to the Rescue: Dorp 7 Rock Band. l.t. ed. 2003. (Illus.). 15p. (J). (gr. k-5). spiral bd. 4.99 *(978-1-929063-25-3(3),* 327) Moons & Stars Publishing For Children.

Jones, David C. One Person to Another: Smoking, Chewing Tobacco & Young Peopole. l.t. ed. 2003. 20p. (YA). 4.00 *(978-1-878400-17-8(7))* Dolphin Publishing.

Jones, Julie. The Problem at Pepperpine Zoo. Jones, Julie, illus. l.t. ed. 2004. (Illus.). 24p. (J). pap. 7.95 *(978-0-9745553-0-0(4))* Greenwood Street Publishing. GSP.

Jougla, Frederic. Tricked on Halloween: Rina & Jax's Stories. Jougla, Karina, illus. l.t. ed. 2004. 36p. (J). bds. 14.99 *(978-0-9754287-0-2(5))* Imagery Pr.

Kassandra, ed. V antología nuevo Milenio: Narración (Cuentos) y Poesía. Ramírez, Antonio & Morrissey, Kay, photos by. l.t. ed. 2004. (SPA., Illus.). 100p. (YA). pap. 12.00 *(978-1-931481-86-1(5))* LiArt-Literature & Art.

Keaster, Diane W. Darby - the Cow Dog, 9 vols. Page, Debbie et al, illus. l.t. ed. 2005. (ZC Horses: 9). (ENG.). 68p. (J). per. 7.95 *(978-0-9721496-8-6(6))* ZC Horses Series of Children's Bks.

—Goldie - the Wise, 25 vols. Page, Debbie, illus. l.t. ed. 2004. (ZC Horses: 7). (ENG.). 87p. (J). per. 7.95 *(978-0-9721496-6-2(X))* ZC Horses Series of Children's Bks.

—Leroy - the Stallion, 25 vols. Page, Debbie, illus. l.t. ed. 2003. (ZC Horses: 6). (ENG.). 79p. (J). per. 7.95 *(978-0-9721496-5-5(1))* ZC Horses Series of Children's Bks.

Keller, Rebecca W. Real Science-4-kids Chemistry Level I Student Textbook. l.t. ed. 2005. (Real Science-4-Kids Ser.). (ENG., Illus.). 64p. (gr. 3-6). 32.95 *(978-0-9749149-0-9(8))* Gravitas Pubns., Inc.

Ketchum, Ron, illus. Rochestrivia: 2,000 Amazing questions & answers all about Rochester NY, it's people & surrounding Towns. l.t. ed. 2005. 250p. per. 19.95 *(978-0-930249-01-4(1))* Big Kids Productions (Publishing).

Keyes, Eric, 3rd, et al. The Light in the Dark, 1. Marie, Paula Braxton, illus. l.t. ed. 2004. (ENG.). 40p. (J). pap. 14.99 *(978-0-9722795-5-0(5),* Highest Good Pubns.) EbonyEnergy Publishing, Inc.

Kitze, Carrie A. We See the Moon. Jinshan Painting Academy, illus. l.t. ed. 2003. 32p. (J). (gr. -1-3). 16.95 *(978-0-9726244-0-4(6))* EMK Pr.

Knapp, Susan. Bells Goes to the Fair. Whitehurst, John et al, illus. l.t. ed. 2003. 40p. (J). (gr. -1-3). 12.95 *(978-1-888223-34-7(0))* McMillen Publishing.

Krinard, Susan. Dark of the Moon. l.t. ed. 2008. 475p. (J). 23.95 *(978-1-4104-0956-0(2))* Thorndike Pr.

Kurz, Ron. The Inner Music Experience. l.t. ed. 2003. 124p. (YA). 75.00 *(978-0-939829-07-1(X),* Item#3) Kurz, Ron.

Lang, Andrew, ed. The Lilac Fairy Book. l.t. ed. 2004. (Large Print Ser.). lib. bdg. 26.00 *(978-1-58287-778-5(5))* North Bks.

—The Pink Fairy Book. l.t. ed. 2004. (Large Print Ser.). lib. bdg. 26.00 *(978-1-58287-781-5(5))* North Bks.

Larson, Eric. How Did Carpet Get in This House? Burns, William G., ed. l.t. ed. 2003. (Illus.). 62p. (YA). (gr. 4-7). pap. *(978-0-9673696-2-4(2))* Caliber Pubns.

Lawrence, Ava. A Button for a Crown. Ford, Christina, illus. l.t. ed. 2003. 84p. (J). 14.95 *(978-0-9651048-4-5(2))* Papillon Publishing.

Layne, Carmela C. I See Many Colors Around My House: Los Colores que Veo Por Mi Casa. Layne, Carmela C., ed. Arevalo, Jose Daniel, illus. l.t. ed. 2005. (SPA.). 24p. (J). (gr. -1-3). pap. 6.95 *(978-0-9769538-0-7(3))* Pannycake Pubn.

Layos, Alexandra. An Almost True Horse Tale. Bauer, Dana, illus. l.t. ed. 2003. 20p. (J). (gr. 1-5). pap. 8.95 *(978-0-9655501-3-0(3))* Saddle & Bridle, Inc.

Lee, Betsy B. Whoa, Wiggle-Worm: A Little Lemon Book about an Overly Active Child, 1 bk. Varnedoe, Catharine E., illus. l.t. ed. 2003. 24p. (J). pap. 7.95 *(978-0-9720267-3-4(8))* Learning Abilities Bks.

LeGrand, Hank, 3rd. Paddle Tail. Merrison, Stacy, illus. l.t. ed. 2004. 63p. (J). per. 7.95 *(978-1-59466-020-7(4),* Growing Years) Port Town Publishing.

Levine, Gail Carson. Ella Enchanted. 2008. (J). 39.99 *(978-0-7393-7107-7(X))* Findaway World, LLC.

—Ever. 2011. (ENG.). 288p. (J). (gr. 3-7). pap. 6.99 *(978-0-06-122964-0(4))* HarperCollins Pubs.

Li, Deborah, illus. Tricia & the Blue Cap. l.t. ed. 2003. 28p. (J). 7.95 net. *(978-0-9706654-5-4(8))* Sprite Pr.

Likins, Kim. Charlie's Perfect Day. Magalinska, Ingrid, illus. l.t. ed. 2003. 32p. (J). bds. *(978-0-9729987-0-3(5))* Island Friends LLC.

Looper, Grace W. Molasses Making Time. l.t. ed. 2004. 152p. (YA). pap. 8.95 *(978-0-9747685-5-7(3))* Bella Rosa Bks.

Loper, Kathleen. Angelina Katrina: Bugs in My Backyard. Waltz, Dan, illus. l.t. ed. 2004. 24p. (J). 17.95 *(978-0-9741774-4-1(X))* D. W. Publishing.

—Angelina Katrina: Builds Troy Snowman. Waltz, Dan, illus. l.t. ed. 2004. 36p. (J). 17.95 *(978-0-9741774-5-8(8))* D. W. Publishing.

Louthain, J. A. Arne the Elephant: Terrorized by Evil Mice. Eberbach, Andrea, illus. 2nd l.t. ed. 2003. 48p. (J). 12.97 *(978-0-9679416-2-2(8),* 0-9679416-2-8) Alexie Bks.

Lowes, Tom, illus. Casey's Four Holiday Celebrations. l.t. ed. 2003. 38p. (J). 16.95 *(978-0-9722099-9-1(9),* C4HC) Caseys World Bks.

Lu, Marie. Champion. 2014. (Legend Ser.: 3). (ENG.). 416p. (YA). (gr. 7). pap. 9.99 *(978-0-14-751228-4(X),* Speak) Penguin Young Readers Group.

Lyford, Cabot. Arthur the Moose. Lyford, Cabot, illus. l.t. ed. 2004. (Illus.). 32p. (J). lib. bdg. *(978-0-9748145-0-6(4))* Castlebay, Inc.

Mabie, Hamilton Wright. Heroes Every Child Should Know. l.t. ed. 2006. (ENG.). 258p. pap. 23.99 *(978-1-4264-1445-9(5))* Creative Media Partners, LLC.

MacCoon, Nancy. Backyard Wonders. Watkins, Courtney, illus. l.t. ed. 2003. 38p. (J). pap. 14.95 *(978-0-9742495-0-6(5))* Vibatorium LLC.

Madame M. Trauma Queens/Trauma Kings. l.t. ed. 2003. (Madame M Presents:). (Illus.). 68p. (YA). per. 15.95 *(978-0-9704159-3-6(1),* 0970415931) Creepy Little Productions.

Mader, Jan. My Brother Wants to Be Like Me. Palmer, Kate Salley, illus. l.t. ed. 2005. (ENG.). 16p. (gr. k-2). pap. 7.95 *(978-1-879835-27-6(4),* Kaeden Bks.) Kaeden Corp.

Madison, Ron. Ned Learns to Say No: A Lesson about Drugs. Covolo, David, illus. l.t. ed. 2003. (Health & Safety Ser.). 24p. pap. 4.95 *(978-1-887206-23-5(X))* Ned's Head Productions.

Magi, Aria. The Lulilites: And the Star of Seven Rays. l.t. ed. 2005. (Illus.). 34p. (J). (gr. -1-3). 19.95 *(978-0-9759631-0-4(4))* Lulilite Productions.

Magnus, Kellie. Little Lion Goes to School. Robinson, Michael, illus. l.t. ed. 2003. 16p. (J). 9.99 *(978-0-9744211-0-0(3))* Media Magic New York.

Mandracchia, Charles, creator. A Wacky Wonder World. l.t. ed. 2005. (Illus.). 24p. (J). 13.95 *(978-0-9721957-1-3(8))* Mandracchia, Charles.

Mankamyer, Laura. The Adventures of the Stonycreek Gang. Mankamyer, Laura, illus. l.t. ed. 2003. (Illus.). 84p. (J). 12.99 *(978-0-9728431-4-0(0))* Mankamyer, Laura.

Marek, Catherine. Sara's 1st Haircut Mitchell, Hazel, illus. l.t. ed. 2007. (ENG.). 32p. (J). (gr. -1-3). per. *(978-0-9748251-3-7(1))* Zoe Life Publishing.

Marjorie, as told by. A Flower Unfolds: Inspirational Teachings in Verse from Kwan Yin, Bodhisattva of Mercy & Compassion. l.t. ed. 2003. (Illus.). 52p. 12.95 *(978-0-9745712-0-1(2))* Sun Sprite Publishing.

Markarian, Marianne. The Pesky Bird Wasielewski, Margaret M., illus. l.t. ed. 2005. 32p. (J). 16.00 *(978-0-9767377-0-4(1))* Pomegranate Publishing.

Marrero, Rafelito. Amar sin decir Nada. 1000th l.t. ed. 2003. 137p. per. 14.95 net. *(978-0-9747569-0-5(3))* Marrero, Rafael.

Marrs, Christie, creator. The Perfect Gift: I B Hoofinit's Horse Tales. l.t. ed. 2004. (Illus.). 57p. (J). mass mkt. 5.99 *(978-1-928890-19-5(9))* I. B. Hoofinit Co.

Martin, Ann M. Kristy's Great Idea. 2010. (Baby-Sitters Club Ser.: 1). (ENG.). 176p. (J). (gr. 3-7). 6.99 *(978-0-545-17475-6(9),* Scholastic Paperbacks) Scholastic, Inc.

Martin, Oscar, Jr., creator. Birth of Jesus l.t. ed. 2003. (Illus.). 25p. (J). E-Book 19.95 incl. cd-rom *(978-0-9748416-4-9(1))* Build Your Story.

—Civil Rights Leaders. l.t. ed. 2004. (Illus.). 25p. (J). E-Book 19.95 incl. cd-rom *(978-0-9748416-9-4(2))* Build Your Story.

—The Creation Story l.t. ed. 2003. (Illus.). 25p. (J). E-Book 19.95 incl. cd-rom *(978-0-9748416-0-1(9))* Build Your Story.

—David & Goliath l.t. ed. 2003. (Illus.). 25p. (J). E-Book 19.95 incl. cd-rom *(978-0-9748416-3-2(3))* Build Your Story.

—Doctors l.t. ed. 2003. (Illus.). 25p. (J). E-Book 19.95 incl. cd-rom *(978-0-9748416-5-6(X))* Build Your Story.

—Famous Women l.t. ed. 2003. (Illus.). 25p. (J). E-Book 19.95 incl. cd-rom *(978-0-9748416-8-7(4))* Build Your Story.

—History of Music l.t. ed. 2003. (Illus.). 25p. (J). E-Book 19.95 incl. cd-rom *(978-0-9748416-7-0(6))* Build Your Story.

—Noah l.t. ed. 2003. (Illus.). 25p. (J). E-Book 19.95 incl. cd-rom *(978-0-9748416-1-8(7))* Build Your Story.

—Sports Legends l.t. ed. 2003. (Illus.). 25p. (J). E-Book 19.95 incl. cd-rom *(978-0-9748416-6-3(8))* Build Your Story.

—The Story of Moses l.t. ed. 2003. (Illus.). 25p. (J). E-Book 19.95 incl. cd-rom *(978-0-9748416-2-5(5))* Build Your Story.

Martin, Tyler. I Have a Question, Vol. 4. Williams, Toby, illus. l.t. ed. 2005. (Sadlier Phonics Reading Program). 8p. (gr. -1-1). 23.00 net. *(978-0-8215-7356-3(X))* Sadlier, William H. Inc.

Martinucci, Suzanne. At Space Camp, Vol. 2. l.t. ed. 2005. (Little Books & Big Bks.: Vol. 6). (Illus.). 8p. (gr. k-2). 23.00 net. *(978-0-8215-7515-4(5))* Sadlier, William H. Inc.

Matson, Laurie. Jaz-O & 'G' in Key West. Matson, Laurie, illus. l.t. ed. 2003. (Illus.). (J). 4.95 *(978-0-9673704-5-3(0))* Seastory Pr.

McCloskey, Robert. Homer Price. l.t. ed. (J). (gr. 4-6). reprint ed. 10.00 *(978-0-89064-072-2(6))* National Assn. for Visually Handicapped.

McElroy, Bonnie & Mandala Publishing Staff. Jagannath Coloring Book. McElroy, Bonnie, illus. l.t. ed. 2007. (ENG., Illus.). 32p. (J). 6.95 *(978-0-945475-29-3(2),* 1203) Mandala Publishing.

McGovern, Sheila. The Entire World of S & Z Book of Stories: 58 Targeted S & Z Pure Stories to Remediate Frontal & Lateral Lisps. l.t. ed. 2003. (Illus.). 148p. per. 34.99 *(978-0-9723457-5-0(2))* Say It Right.

McHaney, Eric & McHaney, Mandy. Rich the Itch. Smith, Jordyn, illus. l.t. ed. 2005. 20p. (J). *(978-0-9769086-0-9(3))* RTI Publishing, LLC.

McKee, Ruby. The Land of Phonicia: An Enchanted Tale to Learn Phonics. Allen, Timothy, illus. l.t. ed. 2003. 52p. (J). per. 39.95 *(978-0-9744944-0-1(2))* Jewel Publishing.

Mears, Richard Chase. Saint Nick & the Space Nicks. Westerfield, William Stephen, illus. l.t. ed. 2004. 32p. (J). 16.95 *(978-0-9754056-0-4(8))* Tuxedo Blue, LLC.

Mecham, Janeal A. Christmas Gifts. Mecham, Janeal A., illus. l.t. unabr. ed. 2003. (Illus.). 32p. (J). (gr. k-3). 12.95 *(978-1-932280-16-6(2),* 80162) Granite Publishing & Distribution.

Messinger, Robert M. & Messinger, Laura M. Why Me? Why Did I Have to Get Diabetes? l.t. ed. 2004. (Illus.). 64p. 12.95 *(978-1-893237-02-5(8))* Little Mai Pr.

Meyer, Kay L. The Adventures of Billie & Annie — Baby Bison. Kirchoff, Arthur, illus. l.t. ed. 2004. 32p. (J). 6.00 *(978-0-9744536-0-6(9),* 9780974453606) Meyer, Tjaden.

Meyers, Susan A. Callie & the Stepmother. Gauss, Rose, illus. l.t. ed. 2005. (ENG.). 64p. (J). (gr. -1-3). pap. 6.95 *(978-0-9718348-0-4(6))* Blooming Tree Pr.

Michaels, David. Bye-Bye, Katy, Vol. 3. Platt, Pierre, illus. l.t. ed. 2005. (Sadlier Phonics Reading Program). 8p. (gr. -1-1). 23.00 net. *(978-0-8215-7354-9(3))* Sadlier, William H. Inc.

Michels, Dia L. Look What I See! Where Can I Be? With My Animal Friends. Bowles, Michael J. N., photos by. l.t. ed. 2005. (Look What I See! Where Can I Be? Ser.: Vol. 3). (ENG., Illus.). 32p. (J). (gr. -1-12). 9.95 *(978-1-930775-07-7(5))* Platypus Media, L.L.C.

Mike. Lemon Drop Rain: Poems & Drawings by Mr. Mike. Mike, illus. l.t. ed. 2003. (ENG., Illus.). 180p. (J). pap. 14.95 *(978-0-9658365-6-2(8))* Beetle Bug Bks.

—New Pet. Mike, illus. l.t. ed. 2005. (ENG., Illus.). 32p. (J). lib. bdg. 14.95 *(978-0-9658365-8-6(4))* Beetle Bug Bks.

J K L

Milano, Jacque. Stay-at-Home Hank: The Little Hummingbird That Couldn't Fly. Milano, Jacque, illus. l.t. ed. 2003. (Illus.). 30p. (J). 9.95 (978-0-9728432-0-1(5)) Milano, Jacque & Assocs.

Miller, Kyle Linda. Dillo - A Baby Armadillo's Adventure on Sanibel Island. Eddy, Randon T., illus. l.t. ed. 2005. (ENG.). 64p. (J). 16.95 (978-0-9769332-0-5(9)) Jungle Hse. Pubns.

Miller, Roger Carlton. The Ant & the Grasshopper l.t. ed. 2003. Orig. Title: Same. (Illus.). 14p. (978-0-9712104-2-4(X)) Texas Woman's Univ. Pr.

Miranda, Anne. The Best Place. l.t. ed. 2005. (Little Books & Big Bks.: Vol. 5). (Illus.). 8p. (gr. k-2). 23.00 net. (978-0-8215-7514-7(7)) Sadlier, William H. Inc.

—Looking at Lizards, Vol. 2. l.t. ed. 2005. (Sadlier Phonics Reading Program). (Illus.). 8p. (gr. -1-1). 23.00 net. (978-0-8215-7346-4(2)) Sadlier, William H. Inc.

—Peach Tree Street, Vol. 2. Lodge, Katherine, illus. l.t. ed. 2005. (Little Books & Big Bks.: Vol. 10). 8p. (gr. k-2). 23.00 net. (978-0-8215-7519-2(8)) Sadlier, William H. Inc.

—Weather Wise, Vol. 3. l.t. ed. 2005. (Sadlier Phonics Reading Program). (Illus.). 8p. (gr. -1-1). 23.00 net. (978-0-8215-7351-8(9)) Sadlier, William H. Inc.

Modica, Cathy & Van Eyck, Laura. Niik & Bling: The Friendship Begins. Modica, Cathy, photos by. l.t. ed. 2005. (Illus.). 40p. (J). 19.95 (978-0-9762466-0-2(0)) Wholesome Puppy Tales.

Moeckel, Christine. Dick the Duck. Moeckel, Christine, illus. l.t. ed. 2004. (Illus.). 31p. (J). spiral bd. 9.98 (978-0-9720350-2-6(8)) Duckpond Publishing, Inc.

Moller, Jonathan R. Bath Time: Picture Book. l.t. ed. 2003. (Illus.). 71p. pap. 19.95 (978-0-9740169-0-0(X)) Lemonflavor Productions.

Montgomery, L. M. Anne of Green Gables. l.t. ed. 2006. pap. (978-1-4068-3174-0(3)) Echo Library.

—Anne of the Island. l.t. ed. 2006. (ENG.). pap. (978-1-4068-3175-7(1)) Echo Library.

—Anne of the Island. l.t. ed. 2004. 396p. 26.00 (978-1-58287-640-5(1)) North Bks.

Moore, Jim. The All Animal Band. Hall, Norris, illus. l.t. ed. 2004. 36p. (J). 16.00 (978-0-9752619-0-3(8)) Animal Band Productions, Inc., The.

Mracek, Ann. Friendship Flies the Sun: The Ancient Egyptian Legend of Scarab Beetle. l.t. ed. 2005. (DAN., Illus.). 32p. (J). per. 15.99 (978-0-9766488-0-2(6)) Mracek, Ann.

Mucha Aydlott, Julie A. My Favorite Time of Year. Mucha-Sullivan, Kalie A. & Mucha-Sullivan, Emily V., illus. l.t. ed. 2004. 22p. (J). 5.95 (978-0-9746093-2-4(3)) San Diego Business Accounting Solutions a Non CPA Firm.

Mullican, Judy. My Toys. Bicking, Judith, illus. l.t. ed. 2005. (HRL Board Book Ser.). (J). (gr. -1-k). pap. 10.95 (978-1-57332-307-9(1), HighReach Learning, Incorporated) Carson-Dellosa Publishing, LLC.

Mullican, Judy & Crowell, Knox. Caillou Finds Shapes. Gillen, Lisa P., illus. l.t. ed. 2005. (HRL Board Book Ser.). (J). (gr. -1-k). bds. 10.95 (978-1-57332-312-3(8), HighReach Learning, Incorporated) Carson-Dellosa Publishing, LLC.

Murnaugh, Lene. Touch of Christmas. Skrbic, Melissa, illus. l.t. ed. 2003. 28p. per. 9.95 (978-1-932344-19-6(5)) Thornton Publishing, Inc.

Murdock, Kita Helmetag & Helmetag, Patricia. Cecily Cicada 2004th l.t. ed. 2004. (Illus.). 28p. (J). pap. 9.95 (978-0-615-12548-0(4)) Possum Products.

The Mysteries of Shapeville. l.t. ed. 2005. (Illus.). 48p. (J). 18.95 (978-0-9747509-1-0(3)) Del Gatto, Maria.

Nadimi, Suzan. The Hungry Cat Downie, Christopher, illus. l.t. ed. 2005. (PER.). 32p. 5.95 net. (978-0-9764947-0-6(1)) Nur Pubns.

Naji, Jamilla. Musical Storyland: A Sing-A-Long Book with Musical Disc. l.t. ed. 2004. (Illus.). 32p. (J). per. 19.99 (978-0-9745568-0-2(7)) Worlds In Ink Publishing, Inc.

Nelson, Holly. Ig's Apples. l.t. ed. 2003. (Illus.). 15p. (J). per. 9.99 (978-1-932338-17-1(9)) Lifevest Publishing, Inc.

Nesbit, E. Five Children & It. l.t. ed. 2005. 296p. pap. (978-1-84637-200-1(3)) Echo Library.

Nettrour, Nelani. Banshees Bk. 2: Dragon Lands. Nettrour, Heather, illus. l.t. ed. 2003. 114p. (J). pap. 11.95 (978-1-932657-03-6(7)) Third Millennium Pubns.

—The Dragonlands Bk. 3: The Village. l.t. ed. 2004. (Illus.). 148p. (J). pap. 19.95 (978-1-932657-12-8(6)) Third Millennium Pubns.

—Jodi & the Seasons. Nettrour, Heather, illus. l.t. ed. 2004. 88p. pap. 11.95 (978-1-932657-16-6(9)) Third Millennium Pubns.

—Jodi's Bugs. Nettrour, Heather, illus. l.t. ed. 2003. 66p. (J). pap. 11.95 (978-1-932657-04-3(5)) Third Millennium Pubns.

New Mexico School for the Deaf Staff, 2nd Grade. Too Many Hands??? l.t. ed. 2004. (Illus.). 32p. (J). 16.95 (978-1-929115-10-5(5)) Azro Pr., Inc.

Nicholas, Melissa. Pumpkin Days, Vol. 3. l.t. ed. 2005. (Sadlier Phonics Reading Program). (Illus.). 8p. (gr. -1-1). 23.00 net. (978-0-8215-7352-5(7)) Sadlier, William H. Inc.

—Stop by a Pond. Gram, Patrick, illus. l.t. ed. 2005. (Little Books & Big Bks.: Vol. 3). 8p. (gr. k-2). 23.00 net. (978-0-8215-7512-3(0)) Sadlier, William H. Inc.

—Who Is My Mom? Cassels, Jean, illus. l.t. ed. 2005. (Sadlier Phonics Reading Program). 8p. (gr. -1-1). 23.00 net. (978-0-8215-7341-9(1)) Sadlier, William H. Inc.

Nickles, Clay & Ayres, Ella. Ali's Treasure. l.t. ed. 2005. (Illus.). 38p. (J). per. 16.95 (978-1-59879-006-1(4)) Lifevest Publishing, Inc.

Norman, Dayle. Tre's Surprise the Move. l.t. ed. 2005. 35p. (J). per. 8.00 (978-1-59196-896-2(8)) Instant Pub.

O'Dell, Scott. Island of the Blue Dolphins. l.t. ed. 2005. (ENG.). 223p. pap. 10.95 (978-0-7862-7254-9(6), Large Print Pr.) Thorndike Pr.

O'Donnell, Sallie. Animals, Vegetables & Minerals from A to Z. Plumley, Alea, illus. l.t. ed. 2005. 60p. pap. 9.95 (978-0-9764982-5-4(1)) Legacy Publishing Services, Inc.

Olivares, Katie Lydon. ABC Book of Shadows. l.t. ed. 2005. (Illus.). 30p. (J). bds. 9.99 (978-0-9768573-0-3(8)) Itty Bitty Witch Works.

Olivia, Cynthia. In January & June, Vol. 4. l.t. ed. 2005. (Sadlier Phonics Reading Program: Vol. 16). (Illus.). 8p. (gr. -1-1). 23.00 net. (978-0-8215-7355-6(1)) Sadlier, William H. Inc.

Olker, Constance. The Punctuation Pals Go Snow Skiing. l.t. ed. 2005. (Illus.). (J). per. 17.95 (978-0-9761289-7-7(7)) Nightengale Pr.

—The Punctuation Pals Go to the Baseball Park. l.t. ed. 2005. (Illus.). 22p. (J). per. 17.95 (978-0-9761289-8-4(5)) Nightengale Pr.

—The Punctuation Pals Go to the Beach. l.t. ed. 2005. (Illus.). 22p. (J). per. 17.95 (978-0-9761289-5-3(0)) Nightengale Pr.

—The Punctuation Pals Go to the Moon. l.t. ed. 2005. (Illus.). (J). per. 19.95 (978-0-9761289-6-0(9)) Nightengale Pr.

—The Punctuation Pals Meet at School. l.t. ed. 2005. (Illus.). 18p. (J). per. 16.95 (978-0-9761289-4-6(2)) Nightengale Pr.

Omary, Rachel, illus. Animals in Dari. l.t. ed. 2003. 4p. (J). spiral bd. 10.95 (978-0-9740535-3-0(8)) Knight Publishing.

—Animals in Farsi. l.t. ed. 2003. 4p. (J). spiral bd. 10.95 (978-0-9740535-4-7(6)) Knight Publishing.

—Animals in Pashto. l.t. ed. 2003. 4p. (J). spiral bd. 10.95 (978-0-9740535-5-4(4)) Knight Publishing.

—Shapes & Colors in Farsi. l.t. ed. 2004. 5p. (J). spiral bd. 14.95 (978-0-9740535-6-1(2)) Knight Publishing.

—Shapes & Colors in Pashto. l.t. ed. 2004. 5p. (J). spiral bd. 14.95 (978-0-9740535-8-5(9)) Knight Publishing.

The Origin of Chinese, 1. l.t. ed. 2004. (CHI., Illus.). 60p. (J). (978-0-9752775-1-5(0), 0-9752775-1-0) Unitrust Design.

Owens, Katherine. Tree Seasons Ball, 1 bk. l.t. ed. 2004. (Illus.). 40p. (J). per. 19.99 (978-0-9760419-0-0(1), TREESEASONSBALL) ThatsMyLife Co.

Ozaki, Yei Theodora, ed. Japanese Fairy Tales. l.t. ed. 2004. (Large Print Ser.). 335p. 26.00 (978-1-58287-750-1(5)) North Bks.

Palmer, Catherine. Fatal Harvest. l.t. ed. 2004. (Matthew 25 Ser.). 496p. (YA). 28.95 (978-0-7862-6259-5(1)) Thorndike Pr.

Palmer, Edward G. Book of Edward Christian Mythology, 4 vols., Set. l.t. ed. 2005. (Illus.). 1306p. per. 123.80 (978-0-9768833-4-0(1), 0976883341) JVED Publishing.

—Book of Edward Christian Mythology: Itching Christian Ears, 4 vols., Vol. 3. l.t. ed. 2005. (Illus.). 616p. per. 39.95 (978-0-9768833-2-6(5), 0976883325) JVED Publishing.

—Book of Edward Christian Mythology Vol. II: God Does Not Change, 4 vols. l.t. ed. 2005. (Illus.). 356p. per. 27.95 (978-0-9768833-1-9(7), 0976883317) JVED Publishing.

—Book of Edward Christian Mythology Vol. IV: Appendixes Reference, 4 vols. l.t. ed. 2005. (Illus.). 208p. per. 27.95 (978-0-9768833-3-3(3), 0976883333) JVED Publishing.

Parente, Peter. Boomer to the Rescue. Ivanov, Aleksey, illus. l.t. ed. 2005. 28p. 15.95 (978-0-9745052-3-7(4), Peeper & Friends) Tree Of Life Publishing.

—Peeper the Kinkajou. l.t. ed. 2004. (Peeper & Friends Ser.). (Illus.). 28p. (J). 15.95 (978-0-9745052-0-6(X), Peeper & Friends) Tree Of Life Publishing.

Parker, Sandy. What Day Is Today? Hofher, Cathy, illus. l.t. ed. 2003. 24p. (gr. k-1). 13.95 (978-0-9643462-3-9(0), 10, Just Think Bks.) Canary Connect Pubns.

Patterson, James. The Dangerous Days of Daniel X. l.t. ed. 2008. (Daniel X Ser.: 1). (ENG.). 304p. pap. 20.99 (978-0-316-03025-0(2)) Little Brown & Co.

—Max. l.t. ed. 2009. (Maximum Ride Ser.: 5). (ENG.). 416p. (YA). (gr. 5-17). 23.99 (978-0-316-03759-4(1)) Little Brown & Co.

—Saving the World & Other Extreme Sports. l.t. ed. 2007. (Maximum Ride Ser.: No. 3). 489p. (J). (gr. 3-7). 23.95 (978-0-7862-9887-7(1)) Thorndike Pr.

Paul, Kate. The Best Ride, Vol. 2. l.t. ed. 2005. (Sadlier Phonics Reading Program). (Illus.). 8p. (gr. -1-1). 23.00 net. (978-0-8215-7345-7(4)) Sadlier, William H. Inc.

Paulsen, Gary. Foxman. l.t. ed. 2004. (YA). (gr. 6-12). 27.95 (978-1-58118-112-8(4)) LRS.

Paulson, Michael W. The Baker Street Bunch No. 1: A Double Mystery Book. l.t. ed. 2004. (Illus.). 154p. (J). per. (978-0-9754241-0-0(6)) MiMar Publishing.

—The Baker Street Bunch & the Missing Pig Mystery. l.t. ed. 2004. (Illus.). 90p. (J). per. 3.95 (978-0-9754241-1-7(4)) MiMar Publishing.

Peck, Richard. The Teacher's Funeral. 2006. (ENG.). 224p. (J). (gr. 3-7). reprint ed. 7.99 (978-0-14-240507-9(8), Puffin Books) Penguin Young Readers Group.

Perkins, Lynne Rae. Criss Cross. 2007. (ENG., Illus.). 368p. (J). (gr. 5-9). pap. 6.99 (978-0-06-009274-0(2), Greenwillow Bks.) HarperCollins Pubs.

Persinger, Eric. Plaid the Platypus. l.t. ed. 2004. (Illus.). 25p. (J). per. 8.99 (978-1-932338-54-6(3)) Lifevest Publishing, Inc.

Peters, Kathryn. A Pet for Elizabeth Rose. Peters, Kathryn, illus. l.t. ed. 2005. (Illus.). 42p. (J). 8.99 (978-0-9752647-9-9(6)) Proton Arts.

Phillips, Rachelle. Dinkey the Donkey. Randolph, Carolyn, illus. l.t. ed. 2004. 24p. (J). 7.50 (978-0-9748591-5-6(X), MSP) Main St Publishing, Inc.

Pintozzi, Nick. Bentley & the Great Fire. Pintozzi, Nick et al, illus. l.t. ed. 2004. 120p. per. 17.95 (978-0-9749465-1-1(6)) BentDaiSha, LLC.

Pipkin, Evelyn Ruth. The Pretty Little Red Bird. l.t. ed. 2004. 19p. (J). (gr. 1-3). 7.95 (978-0-9755789-0-2(1)) Two Seed Planters Inc.

Pohrte, Kathysue, et al. In the Land of Liviaann. Pohrte, Kathysue, ed. Pohrte, Olivia & Pohrte, Juliann, illus. l.t. ed. 2003. 36p. (J). pap. 17.95 (978-0-9722296-0-9(4), 872493) Pohrte, Dorey Publishing, Inc.

Portman, Michelle Eva. Compost, by Gosh! An Adventure with Vermicomposting. Portman, Michelle Eva, illus. l.t. ed. 2003. (ENG., Illus.). 42p. (J). 16.95 (978-0-942256-16-1(6), Falcon Guides) Globe Pequot Pr., The.

Poussin, Nichol. Still Spins the Spider of Rennes-le-Chateau. l.t. ed. 2004.Tr. of L' arraignee tisse sa toile a Rennes-le-Chateaua. (Illus.). 347p. pap. (978-0-9541527-1-0(9), http//www.keysofantiquity.com) DEK Publishing.

Priest, Saira, photos by & des. If We Were... Priest, Saira, des. l.t. ed. 2003. (Illus.). 20p. 12.95 (978-0-9726628-7-1(1)) Niche Publishing & Marketing.

Princess Aurora: A Special Day in Her Life. l.t. ed. 2005. (Illus.). 32p. (J). 5.95 (978-0-9766640-0-0(3), 212-279-3492) Attitudes in Dressing, Inc.

Pritchard, Herman S. The Nautical Road: A Straight Forward Approach to Learning the Navigation Rules. Helwig, Teresa L., ed. Sink, Cynthia, illus. 2nd rev. l.t. ed. 2004. 176p. (YA). 29.95 (978-0-9716479-3-0(3)) Selby Dean Ventures, Inc.

Progressive Langauge Staff, prod. Bluw Wolf & Friends, Units 1-4. l.t. ed. 2004. (Illus.). 53p. act. bk. ed. (978-0-9758759-3-3(0)) Progressive Language, Inc.

Purcell, John M. American City Flags Vols. 9&10: 146 Flags from Akron to Yonkers. Kaye, Edward B., ed. l.t. ed. 2004. (Illus.). 400p. per. 35.00 (978-0-9747728-0-6(1), 48) North American Vexillological Assoc. (NAVA).

Pyle, Howard. The Merry Adventures of Robin Hood. l.t. ed. 2004. (Large Print Ser.). 518p. 26.00 (978-1-58287-684-9(3)) North Bks.

Rainville, Doris I., creator. The Girl Who Never Let Her Mother Brush Her Hair. l.t. ed. 2003. (Illus.). 24p. (J). per. 7.95 (978-0-9744879-0-8(2)) Magical Creations.

—The Power of Love. l.t. ed. 2003. (Illus.). 24p. (J). per. 7.95 (978-0-9744879-1-5(0)) Magical Creations.

Ramona Quimby, Age 8. 2005. (J). (978-1-59564-976-8(X)) Steps To Literacy, LLC.

Ratway, Michael J. & Ratway, Virginia K. Fractured Femur Fable. l.t. ed. 2003. (Illus.). 24p. (J). spiral bd. 10.00 (978-0-9724698-1-4(8)) Ratway, Michael.

Really Big Coloring Books Staff. ABC 123 Learn My Letters & Numbers. l.t. ed. 2003. Orig. Title: 123-ABC Learn My Letters & Numbers. (Illus.). 321p. (J). (978-0-9729753-1-5(4)) Really Big Coloring Bks., Inc.

Redding, David Asbury. He Never Spoke Without a Parable: His Kingdom, Your Antagonist, It's up to You, 3 bks, 5 vols. l.t. ed. 2003. pap. 16.00 (978-0-9671701-3-8(3), 0-9671701-3-3) Redding, Marion T.

Renaud, Andrea. Sammy the Surfing Pelican Meets Steve the Surf Guru. l.t. ed. 2003. (Illus.). 32p. (J). per. (978-0-9717041-3-8(9)) A Happy Friend, Inc.

Richmond, Marianne. Love-U-Grams: Postcards, Notes & Coupons to Connect with Your Kids. l.t. ed. 2005. (ENG., Illus.). 44p. (J). pap. 9.95 (978-0-9753528-9-2(X), Marianne Richmond Studios, Inc.) Sourcebooks, Inc.

Riker, Richard K. Scary Days Daze. l.t. ed. 2005. (Illus.). 224p. (J). 15.95 (978-0-9760416-1-0(8), 3,000) Safe Harbor Pubns.

Riley, John B. Benjamin Franklin: A Photo Biography. l.t. ed. 2004. (First Biographies Ser.). (Illus.). 24p. (YA). (gr. 5-18). 16.95 (978-1-883846-64-0(1), First Biographies) Reynolds, Morgan Inc.

—George Washington Carver: A Photo Biography. l.t. ed. 2004. (First Biographies Ser.). (Illus.). 24p. (YA). (gr. 5-18). 16.95 (978-1-883846-62-6(5), First Biographies) Reynolds, Morgan Inc.

—Jane Addams: A Photo Biography. l.t. ed. 2004. (First Biographies Ser.). (Illus.). 24p. (YA). (gr. 5-18). 16.95 (978-1-883846-61-9(7), First Biographies) Reynolds, Morgan Inc.

—John Paul Jones: A Photo Biography. l.t. ed. 2004. (First Biographies Ser.). (Illus.). 24p. (YA). (gr. 5-18). 16.95 (978-1-883846-63-3(3), First Biographies) Reynolds, Morgan Inc.

Riordan, Rick. The Battle of the Labyrinth. l.t. ed. 2008. (Percy Jackson & the Olympians Ser.: Bk. 4). (ENG.). 462p. (J). (gr. 4-7). 23.95 (978-1-4104-1018-4(8)) Thorndike Pr.

—The Lightning Thief. rev. l.t. ed. 2006. (Percy Jackson & the Olympians Ser.: 1). (ENG.). 483p. (gr. 5-18). 22.95 (978-0-7862-8225-8(8)) Thorndike Pr.

—Percy Jackson & the Olympians. l.t. ed. 2009. (Percy Jackson & the Olympians Ser.). (ENG.). 485p. (YA). 23.95 (978-1-4104-1678-0(X)) Thorndike Pr.

—The Red Pyramid. l.t. ed. 2010. (Kane Chronicles: Bk. 1). (ENG.). 671p. 23.95 (978-1-4104-2536-2(3)) Thorndike Pr.

—The Son of Neptune. l.t. ed. 2011. (Heroes of Olympus Ser.: Bk. 2). (ENG.). 616p. 23.99 (978-1-4104-4122-5(9)) Thorndike Pr.

—The Throne of Fire. l.t. ed. 2011. (Kane Chronicles: Bk. 2). (ENG.). 591p. 23.99 (978-1-4104-3607-8(1)) Thorndike Pr.

Ristuccia, Christine & Ristuccia, James. The Entire World of S & Z Instructional Workbook: A Comprehensive Approach to Remediate Frontal & Lateral Lisps. l.t. ed. 2003. (Illus.). 208p. (J). per. 34.99 (978-0-9723457-4-3(4)) Say It Right.

Robinson, Kelley. The Magic of Lo: Book 1, lo Trilogy. l.t. ed. 2004. (Illus.). 160p. (YA). per. 9.95 (978-0-9745865-0-2(1), SarahRose Children's Bks.) SarahRose Publishing.

Rock, Maria. MiMi's Garden, It's a Kid Thing! A Guide for Beginning Gardeners. l.t. ed. 2003. (Illus.). 45p. (J). 12.95 (978-0-9726979-0-3(X)) Rock Ink.

Rose, John N. Direct Approach: Maya 5. l.t. ed. 2003. (Illus.). 302p. per. 49.95 (978-0-9742948-0-3(2), DA-Ma5) Platinum Rose Publishing.

Rothman, Cynthia Anne. Funny Bugs. Lester, Mike, illus. l.t. ed. 2005. (Little Books & Big Bks.: Vol. 4). 8p. (gr. k-2). 23.00 net. (978-0-8215-7513-0(9)) Sadlier, William H. Inc.

—I Love to Read, 3. l.t. ed. 2005. (Sadlier Phonics Reading Program). (Illus.). 8p. (gr. -1-1). 23.00 net. (978-0-8215-7353-2(5)) Sadlier, William H. Inc.

—A Party for Nine. l.t. ed. 2005. (Sadlier Phonics Reading Program). (Illus.). 8p. (gr. -1-1). 23.00 net. (978-0-8215-7349-5(7)) Sadlier, William H. Inc.

—Violets & Vegetables, Vol. 4. l.t. ed. 2005. (Sadlier Phonics Reading Program). (Illus.). 8p. (gr. -1-1). 23.00 net. (978-0-8215-7357-0(8)) Sadlier, William H. Inc.

—What Does Sam Sell? Alley, R. W., illus. l.t. ed. 2005. (Sadlier Phonics Reading Program). 8p. (gr. -1-1). 23.00 net. (978-0-8215-7342-6(X)) Sadlier, William H. Inc.

—Yes, You Can, Vol. 4. l.t. ed. 2005. (Sadlier Phonics Reading Program). (Illus.). 8p. (gr. -1-1). 23.00 net. (978-0-8215-7358-7(6)) Sadlier, William H. Inc.

Rowling, J. K. Harry Potter & the Chamber of Secrets. l.t. ed. 2003. (Harry Potter Ser.: Year 2). (ENG.). 466p. pap. 13.95 (978-1-59413-001-4(9)) Thorndike Pr.

—Harry Potter & the Deathly Hallows. l.t. ed. 2009. (ENG.). 970p. pap. 14.95 (978-1-59413-355-8(7), Large Print Pr.) 2007. (Harry Potter Ser.: Year 7). (Illus.). 969p. (J). (gr. 4-7). 34.95 (978-0-7862-9665-1(8)) Thorndike Pr.

—Harry Potter & the Half-Blood Prince. l.t. ed. 2005. (Harry Potter Ser.: Year 6). (Illus.). 831p. (J). (gr. 4-8). 29.95 (978-0-7862-7745-2(9), Large Print Pr.) Thorndike Pr.

—Harry Potter & the Order of the Phoenix. l.t. ed. 2003. (Harry Potter Ser.: Year 5). 1093p. 29.95 (978-0-7862-5778-2(4), Large Print Pr.) Thorndike Pr.

—Harry Potter & the Order of the Phoenix. GrandPré, Mary, illus. l.t. ed. 2003. (Thorndike Young Adult Ser.). (ENG.). 1232p. (J). (gr. 4-7). per. 14.95 (978-1-59413-112-7(0), Large Print Pr.) Thorndike Pr.

Royster, D. A. Adoption Is... l.t. ed. 2005. (Illus.). 30p. (J). bds. 15.99 (978-0-9761538-0-1(7)) Unspeakable Joy Pr.

Sabol, Elizabeth, illus. Day Is Done: A Lullaby l.t. ed. 2004. 26p. (J). pap. incl. audio compact disk (978-0-9747382-0-8(4)) LeDor Publishing.

Sanders, Stephanie. Q. T. Pie Meets Smart E. Pauling, Galen T., illus. l.t. ed. 2003. (Q.T. Pie Ser.). 36p. (J). mass mkt. 4.99 (978-0-9670875-4-2(6), 313-533-7383) SanPaul Group, LLC, The.

Sargent, Daina. Alaska: Be Brave, 4 vols. Lenoir, Jane, illus. l.t. ed. 2004. (Double Trouble Ser.: 4). 48p. (J). pap. 10.95 (978-1-59381-121-1(7)); lib. bdg. 23.60 (978-1-59381-120-4(9)) Ozark Publishing.

—Arkansas: Dream Big. Lenoir, Jane, illus. l.t. ed. 2004. (Double Trouble Ser.). 48p. (J). pap. 10.95 (978-1-59381-123-5(3)); lib. bdg. (978-1-59381-122-8(5)) Ozark Publishing.

—Colors & the Number 10, 11 vols. Lenoir, Jane, illus. l.t. ed. 2004. (Learn to Read Ser.). 24p. (J). lib. bdg. 20.95 (978-1-59381-048-1(2)) Ozark Publishing.

—Colors & the Number 2, 11 vols. Lenoir, Jane, illus. l.t. ed. 2004. (Learn to Read Ser.). 24p. (J). lib. bdg. 20.95 (978-1-59381-032-0(6)) Ozark Publishing.

—Colors & the Number 6, 11 vols. Lenoir, Jane, illus. l.t. ed. 2004. (Learn to Read Ser.). 24p. (J). lib. bdg. 20.95 (978-1-59381-040-5(7)) Ozark Publishing.

—Colors & the Number 7, 11 vols. Lenoir, Jane, illus. l.t. ed. 2004. (Learn to Read Ser.). 24p. (J). lib. bdg. 20.95 (978-1-59381-042-9(3)) Ozark Publishing.

—Colors & the Number 8, 11 vols. Lenoir, Jane, illus. l.t. ed. 2004. (Learn to Read Ser.). 24p. (J). lib. bdg. 20.95 (978-1-59381-044-3(X)) Ozark Publishing.

—Colors & the Number 9, 11 vols. Lenoir, Jane, illus. l.t. ed. 2004. (Learn to Read Ser.). 24p. (J). lib. bdg. 20.95 (978-1-59381-046-7(6)) Ozark Publishing.

—Introduction to Colors & Numbers, 11 vols. Lenoir, Jane, illus. l.t. ed. 2004. (Learn to Read Ser.: 11). 24p. (J). lib. bdg. 20.95 (978-1-59381-050-4(4)) Ozark Publishing.

—Introduction to Colors & Numbers/Introduccion a los Colores Numeros, 11 vols. Lenoir, Jane, illus. l.t. ed. 2005. (Learn to Read Ser.: 11). (SPA & ENG.). 24p. (J). pap. 10.95 (978-1-59381-149-5(7)) Ozark Publishing.

—Kansas: Conquer Fear. Lenoir, Jane, illus. l.t. ed. 2004. (Double Trouble Ser.). 48p. (J). pap. 10.95 (978-1-59381-125-9(X)); lib. bdg. 23.60 (978-1-59381-124-2(1)) Ozark Publishing.

—Missouri: Teamwork. Lenoir, Jane, illus. l.t. ed. 2004. (Double Trouble Ser.). 48p. (J). pap. 10.95 (978-1-59381-127-3(6)); lib. bdg. 23.60 (978-1-59381-126-6(8)) Ozark Publishing.

Sargent, Dave & Sargent, Pat. The Colorado Blizzard: Be Determined, 10 vols., Vol. 8. Lenoir, Jane, illus. l.t. ed. 2004. (Colorado Cowboys Ser.: 8). 32p. (J). (gr. 3-8). lib. bdg. 23.60 (978-1-59381-026-9(1)) Ozark Publishing.

Sargent, Dave, et al. Berry Picking Time Vol. 3: (Apache) Be Brave, 20 vols. Lenoir, Jane, illus. l.t. ed. 2003. (Story Keeper Ser.: 3). 42p. (J). Vol. 3. lib. bdg. 23.60 (978-1-56763-907-0(0), 1228136)vol. 3. pap. 6.95 (978-1-56763-908-7(9), 1228136) Ozark Publishing.

—The Bundle Keeper: (Pawnee) Be Responsible, 20 vols., Vol. 18. Lenoir, Jane, illus. l.t. ed. 2004. (Story Keeper Ser.: 18). 48p. (J). pap. 10.95 (978-1-56763-938-4(0)) Ozark Publishing.

—Counting Coup Vol. 4: (Cheyenee) Be Proud, 20 vols. Lenoir, Jane, illus. l.t. ed. 2003. (Story Keeper Ser.). 42p. (J). lib. bdg. 23.60 (978-1-56763-909-4(7)) Ozark Publishing.

—Fields of Golden Corn Vol. 6: (Navajo) Be Energetic, 20 vols. Lenoir, Jane, illus. l.t. ed. 2003. (Story Keeper Ser.: 6). 42p. (J). lib. bdg. 23.60 (978-1-56763-913-1(5)) Ozark Publishing.

—A Hole in the Sun: (Choctaw) Be Independent, 20, Vol. 1. Lenoir, Jane, illus. l.t. ed. 2003. (Story Keeper Ser.: 1). 42p. (J). pap. 6.95 (978-1-56763-904-9(6)) Ozark Publishing.

—Keeping Ghosts Away Vol. 8: (Creek) Be Respectful, 20 vols. Lenoir, Jane, illus. l.t. ed. 2003. (Story Keeper Ser.: Vol. 8). 42p. (J). pap. 10.95 (978-1-56763-918-6(6), 1228135) Ozark Publishing.

—Knocking the Rice Vol. 9: (Chippewa) Be Powerful, 20 vols. Lenoir, Jane, illus. l.t. ed. 2003. (Story Keeper Ser.: 9). 42p. (J). pap. 10.95 (978-1-56763-920-9(8)); lib. bdg. 23.60 (978-1-56763-919-3(4)) Ozark Publishing.

—Ladder at the Door Vol. 10: (Hopi) Be Curious, 20 vols. Lenoir, Jane, illus. l.t. ed. 2004. (Story Keeper Ser.: 10). 48p. (J). pap. 10.95 (978-1-56763-922-3(4)); lib. bdg. 23.60 (978-1-56763-921-6(6)) Ozark Publishing.

—Land of the Sun Vol. 11: (Ute) Respect Elders, 20 vols., Vol. 11. Lenoir, Jane, illus. l.t. ed. 2004. (Story Keeper Ser.: 11). 48p. (J). lib. bdg. 23.60 (978-1-56763-923-0(2)); pap. 10.95 (978-1-56763-924-7(0)) Ozark Publishing.

—Little One Vol. 12: (Cherokee) Be Inventive, 20 vols. Lenoir, Jane, illus. l.t. ed. 2003. (Story Keeper Ser.: Vol. 12). 42p. (J). pap. 10.95 (978-1-56763-926-1(7)) Ozark Publishing.

—On the Banks of the Wallowa River: (Nez Perce) Use Your Talent, 20 vols., Vol. 13. Lenoir, Jane, illus. l.t. ed. 2004. (Story Keeper Ser.: 13). 48p. (J). pap. 10.95 (978-1-56763-928-5(3)); lib. bdg. 23.60 (978-1-56763-927-8(5)) Ozark Publishing.

—Rays of the Sun Vol. 15: (shoshone) Learn Lessons, 20 vols. Lenoir, Jane, illus. l.t. ed. 2004. (Story Keeper Ser.: 15). 48p. (J). pap. 10.95 (978-1-56763-932-2(1)) Ozark Publishing.

—Rays of the Sun Vol. 15: (Shoshone) Learn Lessons, 20 vols. Lenoir, Jane, illus. l.t. ed. 2004. (Story Keeper Ser.: 15). 48p. (J). lib. bdg. 23.60 (978-1-56763-931-5(3)) Ozark Publishing.

—A Strand of Wampum Vol. 2: Be Honest, 20 vols. Lenoir, Sue, illus. l.t. ed. 2003. (Story Keeper Ser.: 2). 42p. (J). pap. 10.95 (978-1-56763-906-3(2)) Ozark Publishing.

—Summer Milky Way: (Blackfeet) Be Compassionate, 20 vols., Vol. 16. Lenoir, Jane, illus. l.t. ed. 2004. (Story Keeper Ser.). 48p. (J). lib. bdg. 23.60 (978-1-56763-933-9(X)); pap. 10.95 (978-1-56763-934-6(8)) Ozark Publishing.

—Tattoos of Honor Vol. 17: (Osage) Be Gentle & Giving, 20 vols. Lenoir, Jane, illus. l.t. ed. 2004. (Story Keeper Ser.: Vol. 17). 42p. (J). pap. 10.95 (978-1-56763-936-0(4)); lib. bdg. 23.60 (978-1-56763-935-3(6)) Ozark Publishing.

—Truth, Power & Freedom Vol. 19: (Sioux) Show Respect, 20 vols., Vol. 19. Lenoir, Jane, illus. l.t. ed. 2004. (Story Keeper Ser.: 19). 42p. (J). pap. 10.95 *(978-1-56763-940-7(2))* Ozark Publishing.
—Valley Oaks Acorns Vol. 20: (Maidu) Be Helpful, 20 vols. Lenoir, Jane, illus. l.t. ed. 2004. (Story Keeper Ser.: 20). 48p. (J). pap. 10.95 *(978-1-56763-942-1(9))* Ozark Publishing.
Sargent, Pat L. The Cheetah, 6 vols., Vol. 6. Lenoir, Jane, illus. l.t. ed. 2004. (Barney the Bear Killer Ser.: No. 6). 146p. (YA). pap. 10.95 *(978-1-56763-974-2(7))* Ozark Publishing.
Scalzo, Linda V. Carazona's Coloring Book. l.t. ed. 2004. (Illus.). 8p. (J). 2.99 *(978-0-9753724-3-2(2))* Carazona Creations LLC.
—El circo llega al Pueblo: Version de Lectura Temprana. Torres, Marcela H., tr. Spalinski, Amanda, illus. l.t. ed. 2005. (SPA.). 24p. per. 9.99 *(978-0-9753724-2-5(4))* Carazona Creations LLC.
—The Circus Is coming to Town: Early Reader Version. Spalinski, Amanda, illus. l.t. ed. 2005. 24p. (J). per. 9.99 *(978-0-9753724-1-8(6))* Carazona Creations LLC.
—The Circus Is Coming to Town: Full-Length Version. l.t. ed. 2004. (Illus.). 32p. (J). 9.99 *(978-0-9753724-0-1(8))* Carazona Creations LLC.
Scheber, George. Earl Joins the Circus. Spicer, Bridgett, illus. l.t. ed. 2005. (Adventures of Earl the Squirrel Ser.). 32p. (J). (gr. -1-3). 12.95 *(978-1-878847-01-0(5))* Make Me A Story Pr.
—Earl the Squirrel. Spicer, Bridgett, illus. l.t. ed. 2005. (Adventures of Earl the Squirrel Ser.). 32p. (J). (gr. -1-2). 12.95 *(978-1-878847-00-3(7))* Make Me A Story Pr.
Schneider, Stephen A. Color My Chess World. l.t. ed. 2004. (Illus.). 48p. (J). act. bk. ed. 19.50 incl. audio compact disk *(978-0-9729456-9-1(5))* Championship Chess.
Schuepbach, Lynnette. Froggy Hollow. Schuepbach, Lynnette, illus. l.t. ed. 2004. (Illus.). 32p. (J). 7.00 net. *(978-0-9759613-0-8(6))* Creative Sources.
—Shhhh!!! Schuepbach, Lynnette, illus. l.t. ed. 2004. (ENG., Illus.). 32p. (J). pap. 12.95 *(978-0-9759613-1-5(4))* Creative Sources.
Schumacher, Stef. Amazing Blue Animals, Vol. 2. l.t. ed. 2005. (Little Books & Big Bks.: Vol. 9). (Illus.). 8p. (gr. k-2). 23.00 net. *(978-0-8215-7518-5(X))* Sadlier, William H. Inc.
Schwiebert, Pat & DeKlyen, Chuck. Tear Soup: A Recipe for Healing after Loss. Bills, Taylor, illus. 2nd rev. l.t. ed. 2004. (ENG.). 56p. (gr. -1-12). reprint ed. 19.95 *(978-0-9615197-6-6(2),* 798) Grief Watch.
Scott, Michael. The Sorceress. 2010. (Secrets of the Immortal Nicholas Flamel Ser.: 3). (ENG.). 512p. (YA). (gr. 7-18). pap. 10.99 *(978-0-385-73530-8(8),* Ember) Random Hse. Children's Bks.
Seagreaves, Kelly E. The Best Pet. Zoller, Jayson D., illus. l.t. ed. 2004. 29p. (J). per. 8.99 *(978-1-932338-53-9(5))* Lifevest Publishing, Inc.
Sewell, Anna. Black Beauty, 2 vols., Set. l.t. ed. (YA). (gr. 8-18). reprint ed. 10.00 *(978-0-89064-017-3(3))* National Assn. for Visually Handicapped.
—Black Beauty. l.t. ed. 2004. (Large Print Ser.). 268p. 25.00 *(978-1-58287-619-1(3))* North Bks.
Shaffert, Charles. Googus, the Toothless Alligator. Stringer, Margaret, illus. l.t. ed. 2003. 30p. (J). per. 7.95 *(978-1-932338-27-0(6))* Lifevest Publishing, Inc.
Shams, K. The Piggle. Spears, Ashley E., illus. l.t. ed. 2004. 20p. (J). 9.99 *(978-0-9728872-9-8(6))* Trent's Prints.
Shaw, Mary. Brady Brady & the Puck on the Pond, 11 vols. Temple, Chuck, illus. l.t. ed. 2005. 32p. (J). per. *(978-1-897169-07-0(8))* Brady Brady, Inc.
Shemin, Craig. Families Are Forever McCoy, John, illus. l.t. ed. 2003. 34p. 9.95 *(978-0-9728666-0-6(4),* 1) As Simple As That Publishing.
Simpson, Matt, creator. Happy Heart: English Book 1. l.t. ed. 2003. (Illus.). 44p. (J). per. *(978-0-9727660-0-5(6))* Bks. by Matt.
Singer, Isaac Bashevis. Short Friday & Other Stories. l.t. ed. (YA). (gr. 10-12). reprint ed. 10.00 *(978-0-89064-057-9(2))* National Assn. for Visually Handicapped.
Sinke, Grandma Janet Mary. Grandma's Christmas Tree. Pennington, Craig, illus. l.t. ed. 2004. (Grandma Janet Mary Ser.). 50p. (J). *(978-0-9742732-1-1(X))* My Grandma & Me Pubs.
Slamp, Kathy. Little House in the Arctic: An Adventure Story. l.t. ed. 2004. Orig. Title: Our Little House in the Arctic. (Illus.). 228p. pap. 17.95 *(978-0-9713345-3-3(6))* Vessel Ministries.
Smith, Dianne M. Cyanne Rose & Sherbet Are Best Friends. l.t. ed. 2004. 22p. (YA). per. *(978-1-59196-678-4(7))* Instant Pub.
—Happy Birthday to You! l.t. ed. 2004. 24p. per. *(978-1-59196-679-1(5))* Instant Pub.
—I Don't Want To! l.t. ed. 2004. (YA). per. *(978-1-59196-683-8(3))* Instant Pub.
Solice, Deborah. The Eye of the Undead: The Hidden Channel: an Adventure Series in Time. l.t. ed. 2005. (ENG., Illus.). 100p. (J). per. 7.59 *(978-1-933300-01-6(9))* Wandering Sage Pubns., LLC.
Sonday, Arlene. The Sonday System - Let's Play Learn: Alphabet Book. Breckman, Cindy, ed. l.t. ed. 2004. (Illus.). 53p. (J). per. *(978-1-891602-11-5(X))* Winsor Learning, Inc.
Spellman, Rhonda J., as told by. When I Was a Little Boy, by Jesus: Written for Children, Illustrated by Children: Experience the Life Jesus Lived When Jesus Was a Little Boy. l.t. ed. 2003. (Illus.). 32p. (J). per. 19.95 *(978-0-9741009-0-6(0))* Creative Cranium Concept, The.
Spinelle, Nancy Louise. Moose's Loose Tooth. Gedeon, Gloria, illus. l.t. ed. 2005. (ENG.). 16p. (gr. k-2). pap. 7.95 *(978-1-57874-032-1(0),* Kaeden Bks.) Kaeden Corp.
Sportelli-Rehak, Angela. Moving Again Mom! Hinlicky, Gregg, illus. 2004. (Uncle Sam's Kids Ser.: Bk. 2). 40p. (J). (gr. -1-7). pap. 7.95 *(978-0-9714515-0-6(8))* Abidenme Bks.
Sprecher, John. Eric & the Angrrry Frog, Vol. 2. Forrest, James, illus. l.t. ed. Date not set. (Special Kids "Special Message" Book Ser.). 32p. (J). (gr. k-4). pap. 10.00 *(978-1-892186-01-0(2))* Anythings Possible, Inc.
—Tori & Cassandra & the Pelican in Peril. Forrest, James, illus. l.t. ed. Date not set. (Special Kids "Special Message" Book Ser.: Vol. 3). 32p. (J). (gr. k-4). pap. 10.00 *(978-1-892186-02-7(0))* Anythings Possible, Inc.
—Zoe & the Very Unmerry Bear. Forrest, James, illus. l.t. ed. Date not set. (Special Kids "Special Message" Book Ser.). 32p. (J). (gr. k-4). pap. 10.00 *(978-1-892186-03-4(9),* SKPB4) Anythings Possible, Inc.
Spyri, Johanna. Heidi. l.t. ed. 2004. (Large Print Ser.). 433p. 26.00 *(978-1-58287-666-5(5))* North Bks.
Squires, Mary L. Margaret Who Dared to Dream. l.t. ed. 2003. (Illus.). 45p. 12.95 *(978-0-9631547-3-6(7))* Popular Truth, Inc.
Staheli, Bee, ed. The Owl Who Couldn't Say Whoo. Clish, Lori, illus. l.t. ed. (J). (gr. k-5). pap. 7.95 *(978-1-928632-50-4(5))* Writers Marketplace:Consulting, Critiquing & Publishing.
Stanley, Charles. The Spirit-Filled Life: Discover the Joy of Surrendering to the Holy Spirit. l.t. ed. 2014. (ENG.). 304p. (gr. 12). E-Book *(978-0-529-10168-6(8),* HG50BG-I) Nelson, Thomas Inc.
StarKidz: I Am Who I Am. l.t. ed. 2003. (Illus.). 28p. (J). 16.95 *(978-0-9743964-1-5(9))* World of Angels, A.
Steele, James M. Sadie Listens: An Inward Journey. l.t. ed. 2003. (Inward Journey Ser.: Vol. 1). (Illus.). iv, 48p. 17.95 *(978-0-9716811-3-2(9))* Steele Studios.
Stephenson, Nancy. The Three Little Kittens. Faris, Eva, illus. l.t. ed. 2003. 30p. (J). per. 7.99 *(978-1-932338-13-3(6))* Lifevest Publishing, Inc.
Stokes, N. L. Mystery of the Missing Teacup. l.t. ed. 2003. (Illus.). 48p. per. 19.95 *(978-0-9729411-1-2(8))* Stylewriter Pubns.
Storie Tree Inc, Staff. A Pocket Pearl of Light: Twinkle & Shinmet Come Home. l.t. ed. 2003. (Illus.). 27p. pap. 6.00 *(978-0-9679014-9-7(9))* Storie Tree, Inc., The.
Stormer, Kate. Casey's Unexpected Friend. Lowes, Tom, illus. l.t. ed. 2003. 38p. (J). 16.95 *(978-0-9722099-7-7(2),* CUF) Caseys World Bks.
Stoutland, Allison. Take a Deep Breath: Little Lessons from Flowers for a Happier World. Hofher, Cathy, illus. l.t. ed. 2003. 32p. 14.95 *(978-0-9670941-2-0(7))* Inch By Inch Pubns., LLC.
Stuart, Matt. Who Can Run Fast? l.t. ed. 2005. (Little Books & Big Bks.: Vol. 1). (Illus.). 8p. (gr. k-2). 23.00 net. *(978-0-8215-7510-9(4))* Sadlier, William H. Inc.
Stuck in the MUD. l.t. ed. 2004. (Illus.). 20p. (J). cd-rom 19.95 *(978-0-9759370-0-6(6))* Brown&Matthews.
Sundance/Newbridge LLC Staff. Birds, Birds, Birds. 2004. (Reading PowerWorks Ser.). (gr. 1-3). 37.50 *(978-0-7608-9783-6(2))* Sundance/Newbridge Educational Publishing.
Sundberg, Peggy. Isabelle Lives a Dream. Wiles, Pat, illus. l.t. ed. 2003. (ENG.). 32p. (J). 11.95 *(978-0-9721057-1-2(9))* Cowgirl Peg Enterprises.
Sutryn, Barbara M. Heartstrings: A Biography of Wilmos Csehy. l.t. ed. 2004. (Illus.). 160p. (YA). 21.00 *(978-1-892135-33-9(7))* Lamp Post Publishing, Inc.
Tanner, Dawn Leasman. A Kitty Named Indra/Una Gata Llamada Indra. Leasman, Nancy Packard, illus. l.t. ed. 2003. (SPA & ENG.). 36p. (J). per. 6.95 *(978-0-9741725-0-7(2))* Leatherwood Publishing.
Tarazona, Oscar, illus. Volando con Alas Propias. l.t. ed. 2004. (SPA.). 116p. (YA). pap. 12.00 *(978-1-931481-88-5(1))* LiArt-Literature & Art.
Tarver, Monroe S. Little Light Shine Bright. Tarver, Monroe S., illus. l.t. ed. 2004. (Illus.). 32p. (J). 6.99 *(978-0-9743568-4-6(0))* Tarver, Monroe.
Tarver, S., 1st. Imaga & the Magic Pearls 2nd l.t. ed. 2003. (Illus.). 20p. (J). 6.99 *(978-0-9743568-0-8(8))* Tarver, Monroe.
Tate, Suzanne. Sandy Seal: A Tale of Sea Dogs. Melvin, James, illus. l.t. ed. 2004. (Suzanne Tate's Nature Ser.: No. 27). 28p. (J). pap. 4.95 *(978-1-878405-49-4(7))* Nags Head Art, Inc.
Taylor, Beth. Tina's Toys. l.t. ed. 2005. (Sadlier Phonics Reading Program). (Illus.). 8p. (gr. -1-1). 23.00 net. *(978-0-8215-7343-3(8))* Sadlier, William H. Inc.
Taylor, Chet. Last, but Not Least. Taylor, Chet, illus. l.t. ed. 2004. (Illus.). 20p. (J). lib. bdg. 22.99 *(978-0-9755888-1-9(8))* Dragonfly Publishing, Inc.
Tennyson, Patrick & Bickford, Nicole. Tarantula Tracks: Rosie's Wild Adventure. l.t. ed. 2004. (Illus.). 32p. (J). 2.95 *(978-0-9729000-1-0(2))* Butterfly Pavilion.
The Concerned Group, prod. See Baby Jesus. l.t. ed. 2012. (Illus.). 8p. (gr. 5). pap. 3.99 *(978-1-58938-004-2(5))* Concerned Communications.
Thistle, Louise. Dramatizando la Gallinita Roja: Un Cuento para Contar y Actuar. Packer, Emily, illus. l.t. ed. 2003.Tr. of Dramatizing the Little Red Hen. (SPA.). 32p. (J). (gr. k-2). pap. 10.00 *(978-0-9644186-4-6(9))* Literature Dramatization Pr.
—Dramatizing the Little Red Hen. Landes, William-Alan, ed. Packer, Emily, illus. l.t. ed. 2003. 32p. (J). (gr. k-2). pap. 10.00 *(978-0-9644186-5-3(7))* Literature Dramatization Pr.
Thomas, Dina M. & Thomas, Andy, eds. The Artful Journey: The Artwork of Andy Thomas. Thomas, Tria M., photos by. l.t. ed. 2003. (Illus.). 122p. 50.00 *(978-0-9742285-0-1(8))* Maze Creek Studio.
Thryce, Marc & Robinson, Tim. Look at the Pictures. l.t. ed. 2005. (Little Books & Big Bks.: Vol. 2). (Illus.). 8p. (gr. k-2). 23.00 net. *(978-0-8215-7511-6(2))* Sadlier, William H. Inc.
Tillman, Nancy. On the Night You Were Born, 1. l.t. ed. 2005. (Illus.). 32p. (J). 17.95 *(978-0-9765761-0-5(4))* Darling Pr. LLC.
Tinkler, David. Revenge of the Dinner Ladies. l.t. ed. 2005. (J). pap. *(978-0-7540-7804-3(3),* CLP 185) AudioGo.
Toews, Rita Y. The Bully: A Discussion & Activity Story. Ljungberg, Jon, illus. l.t. ed. 2004. (ENG.). 40p. (J). *(978-0-9736224-0-9(7))* Birds Hill Publishing.
Toledo, Leila J. Little Peter & Sela. Davis, Chad L., illus. l.t. ed. 2004. 17p. (J). pap. 8.95 *(978-0-9753118-0-6(8))* Bimini Bks.
Tommy Books: Fear, 10 vols. l.t. ed. 2005. (Illus.). 24p. (J). 12.99 *(978-0-9762690-5-2(8))* Tommy Bks. Pubng.
Tommy Books: Forgiveness, 10 vols. l.t. ed. 2005. (Illus.). 24p. (J). 12.99 *(978-0-9762690-6-9(6))* Tommy Bks. Pubng.
Tommy Books: Grace & Mercy, 10 Vols. l.t. ed. 2005. (Illus.). 24p. (J). 12.99 *(978-0-9762690-8-3(2))* Tommy Bks. Pubng.
Tommy Books: Thank You, 10 vols. l.t. ed. 2005. (Illus.). 24p. (J). 12.99 *(978-0-9762690-9-0(0))* Tommy Bks. Pubng.
Tommy Books: Who Am I, 10 vols. l.t. ed. 2005. (Illus.). 24p. (J). 12.99 *(978-0-9762690-7-6(4))* Tommy Bks. Pubng.
Tompkins, Robyn Lee. Miss Molly's Adventure in the Park: Another Great Adventure Brought to You by Miss Molly & Her Dog Reybum, 10 vols. Carson, Shawn K., illus. l.t. ed. 2005. (ENG.). 60p. (J). per. *(978-0-9741647-6-2(3))* NRG Pubns.
Torgerson, Scotty Delray. Jacob Goes to the Moon. 2nd l.t. ed. 2005. (Illus.). 32p. (J). 10.00 *(978-0-9767116-0-5(5))* Torgerson Meadows Publishing.
Torrel, Wendy. GUARDIAN of DREAMS (1st Edition) Klingbeil, Kendall, illus. l.t. ed. 2004. 32p. (J). 14.95 *(978-0-9746890-0-5(9));* pap. 10.95 *(978-0-9746890-1-2(7))* White Tulip Publishing.
Trogdon, Wendell. Who Killed Hoosier Hysteria? Sport Survives amid Fading Fervor. l.t. ed. 2004. (Illus.). 168p. (YA). pap. *(978-0-9724033-3-7(7))* Backroads Pr.
Turman, Evelyn. J. B. 's Christmas Presents. Turman, Adam, illus. l.t. ed. 2004. 28p. (J). 15.95 *(978-0-9753042-0-4(8))* Turman, E.
Turner, Barbara. A Day in San Francisco, Vol. 1. l.t. ed. 2003. (Illus.). 32p. (J). per. 14.95 *(978-0-9747019-0-5(4))* Turner, Barbara.
Ulmer, Louise. The Bible That Wouldn't Burn: How the Tyndale English Version of the Bible Came About. 2nd l.t. ed. 2003. (Illus.). 32p. 4.95 *(978-0-941367-01-1(0))* Peach Blossom Pubns.
VanDerTuuk-Perkins, Jennifer E. Life with Gabriel. VanDerTuuk-Perkins, Jennifer E. & Perkins, Rodney R., illus. l.t. ed. 2004. 22p. (J). per. 9.95 *(978-0-9749862-0-3(8))* Theragogy.com.
Vogel, Rob & Azarov, Max. Garry the Groundhog l.t. ed. 2005. (Illus.). 10p. (J). spiral bd. 19.95 incl. DVD *(978-0-9768455-0-8(4),* N/A) Vogel, Robert.
Voigt, Cynthia. A Solitary Blue. l.t. ed. 2005. (Tillerman Cycle Ser.: Bk. 3). 359p. (J). pap. 10.95 *(978-0-7862-7912-8(5))* Thorndike Pr.
Vonthron, Satanta C. Caillov Visits the Farmer's Market. Meier, Kerry L., illus. l.t. ed. 2005. (HRL Board Book Ser.). (J). (gr. -1-k). pap. 10.95 *(978-1-57332-310-9(1),* HighReach Learning, Incorporated) Carson-Dellosa Publishing, LLC.
—Down at the Shore. Storch, Ellen N., illus. l.t. ed. 2005. (HRL Board Book Ser.). (J). (gr. -1-k). pap. 10.95 *(978-1-57332-306-2(3),* HighReach Learning, Incorporated) Carson-Dellosa Publishing, LLC.
Vorndran, Judith Clay. Mr. Bear Lives There. l.t. ed. 2005. (Illus.). 11p. (J). pap. 7.98 *(978-0-9772439-0-7(7))* Vorndran, Judith Clay.
Vroom, Angela. Airplane Letters to God. l.t. ed. 2004. (Illus.). 24p. (J). pap. 8.50 *(978-0-9762935-0-7(1))* Perkins Crawford.
Wade, Linda R. Condoleezza Rice. 2004. (Illus.). 32p. (J). lib. bdg. 25.70 *(978-1-58415-332-0(6))* Mitchell Lane Pubs., Inc.
Wagner, Jeff. My Day... at the Zoo. Alvarado, Paulo, illus. 2004. 20p. (J). bds. *(978-0-9754515-0-2(2))* Wagner Entertainment.
Walling, Sandy Seeley. A Day at the Beach: A Seaside Counting Book from One to Ten. Walling, Sandy Seeley, illus. 2003. (Illus.). 28p. (J). 6.95 *(978-0-9741940-0-4(X))* Abernathy Hse. Publishing.
Walling, Sandy Seeley, illus. & text. ABC's at the Zoo! The Fun Way to Teach Your Child the Relationship between Upper Case & Lower Case Letters Walling, Sandy Seeley, text. l.t. ed. 2004. 36p. (J). per. 7.95 *(978-0-9741940-1-1(8))* Abernathy Hse. Publishing.
Waltz, Dan. Kornstalkers: Corn Maze Massacre. Waltz, Dan, illus. l.t. ed. 2005. (Chilled to the Bone! Ser.: No. 1). (Illus.). 120p. (J). per. 6.99 *(978-0-9741774-3-4(1))* D. W. Publishing.
Waltz, Dan Hall. Freckles the Frog: A Read-a-Long/Sing-a-Long Story Book. Waltz, Dan Hall, illus. l.t. ed. 2003. (Illus.). 24p. (J). 19.95 *(978-0-9741774-0-3(7))* D. W. Publishing.
Watkins, Albert. The Brothers Three. l.t. ed. 2004. (Illus.). 48p. (J). pap. 22.95 *(978-0-9629124-4-3(1))* Floppinfish Publishing Co., Ltd.
Watkins, Patricia. Boyd-Friend: His Yippie-Skippie Journey to a Forever Home. Watkins, Christopher, illus. l.t. ed. 2004. 44p. 10.95 *(978-0-9753397-0-1(2))* Frayed Pages Publishing.
Watson, Don. The Legend of Red Leaf. Robbins, Ashley, illus. l.t. ed. 2005. 125p. (J). pap. 9.95 *(978-0-9714358-6-5(3))* Longhorn Creek Pr.
Watson, Regal. The Ant That Can't, 1. l.t. ed. 2005. (Illus.). 50p. (J). per. 10.95 *(978-0-9763686-0-1(9))* Rapha Publishing.
Watson, W. Hamp, Jr. Frederick Wilson Still Speaks - Big Words for Our Time. Watson, W. Hamp, Jr., ed. l.t. ed. 2004. (J). per. 12.95 *(978-0-9746976-0-4(5))* Cambridge Way Publishing.
Weddington, Carole. D+Anger I'm Mad! Anger Management Teen Style. l.t. ed. 2003. (YA). 28.00 *(978-0-9638007-7-0(9))* J M Pubns.
Weeks, Timothy A. The Wise Mullet of Cook Bayou l.t. ed. 2004. (Illus.). 48p. (J). per. *(978-0-9713573-8-9(2))* Thomas Expressions, LLC.
Westerfeld, Scott. Leviathan. l.t. ed. 2010. (Leviathan Trilogy: Bk. 1). (ENG.). 526p. 23.95 *(978-1-4104-2572-0(X))* Thorndike Pr.
Wheeler, Karla. Heart-Shaped Pickles: Gentle Grief Support for Kids & Grownups. Wheeler, Jenny Lee, illus. l.t. ed. 2003. (ENG.). 36p. (J). 4.95 *(978-0-9675532-2-1(9))* Quality of Life Publishing Co.
White, Russ. Cat Got Your Tongue? A Book of Idioms. Cornelison, Reuel, illus. l.t. ed. 2004. 44p. (J). per. *(978-0-9742885-0-5(0),* 00) White, Russ.
White, T. H. The Sword in the Stone. l.t. ed. 2003. (Children's Large Print Ser.). 35.95 *(978-1-58118-110-4(8))* LRS.
Whitedove, Michelle. My Invisible Friends. Poynter, Linda, illus. l.t. ed. 2005. 30p. (gr. -1-3). spiral bd. 18.95 *(978-0-9714908-4-0(8))* Whitedove Pr.
Wilde, Oscar. The Happy Prince & Other Tales. l.t. ed. 2006. 92p. pap. *(978-1-84637-306-0(9))* Echo Library.
Wilder, Laura Ingalls. These Happy Golden Years. l.t. ed. (J). (gr. 3-6). 35.95 *(978-1-58118-102-9(7))* LRS.
Williams, Deborah. Little Rabbit Is Sad. Gedeon, Gloria, illus. l.t. ed. 2005. (ENG.). 12p. (Orig.). (gr. k-1). pap. 7.95 *(978-1-879835-99-3(1),* Kaeden Bks.) Kaeden Corp.
—Nickels & Pennies. Gedeon, Gloria, illus. l.t. ed. 2005. (ENG.). 12p. (gr. k-1). pap. 7.95 *(978-1-879835-87-0(8),* Kaeden Bks.) Kaeden Corp.
Williams, Heather L. & Muench-Williams, Heather. Caillov Learns about Space. Storch, Ellen N., illus. l.t. ed. 2005. (HRL Board Book Ser.). (J). (gr. -1-k). bds. 10.95 *(978-1-57332-308-6(X),* HighReach Learning, Incorporated) Carson-Dellosa Publishing, LLC.
Williams, Thomas. The Christmas Chair. l.t. ed. 2004. (Illus.). 27p. (J). audio compact disk 22.95 *(978-0-9763633-0-9(5))* Williams, Thomas.
Wilson, Rebekah. Grandmother's Hope Chest: Lucie's Snowflakes. l.t. ed. 2004. (Illus.). 80p. (J). 15.00 *(978-1-59565-003-0(2))* Hope Chest Legacy, Inc.
—Grandmother's Hope Chest: The Running Rooster. l.t. ed. 2004. (Illus.). 52p. (J). 15.00 *(978-1-59565-002-3(4))* Hope Chest Legacy, Inc.
Winter, Max. Did You Know?, Vol. 2. Rechin, Kevin, illus. l.t. ed. 2005. (Little Books & Big Bks.: Vol. 8). 8p. (gr. k-2). 23.00 net. *(978-0-8215-7517-8(1))* Sadlier, William H. Inc.
Wong, Benedict Norbert. Lo & Behold. Wong, Benedict Norbert, illus. l.t. ed. 2003. (Illus.). 38p. (gr. 1-18). 16.95 *(978-0-9728192-0-6(7),* LOBE) Taiji Arts Publishing.
—Lo & Behold: Good Enough to Eat. Wong, Benedict Norbert, illus. l.t. ed. 2003. (Illus.). 40p. (J). (gr. 1-12). 16.95 *(978-0-9728192-1-3(5),* 1002LB) Taiji Arts Publishing.
Wood, Debra. William Warrior Bear. Blake, Joshua Aaron, illus. l.t. ed. 2005. 30p. (J). per. 12.95 *(978-1-59879-001-6(3))* Lifevest Publishing, Inc.
Wooding, Sharon. Mark Twain in Nevada, a History Coloring Book for Children. l.t. ed. 2003. (Illus.). 25p. (J). (SPA.). pap. 5.95 *(978-0-9727757-1-7(4));* pap. 5.95 *(978-0-9727757-0-0(6))* Susy & Livy Pubns.
Wright, Mary H. Grandma Spoils Me. Megenhardt, Bill, illus. l.t. ed. 2005. 32p. (J). lib. bdg. 16.95 *(978-0-9645493-4-0(4))* Bluebonnets, Boots & Bks. Pr.
Yamada, Debbie Leung. Striking It Rich: Treasures from Gold Mountain. Tang, You-shan, illus. l.t. ed. 2004. 128p. (J). (gr. 4-8). pap. 13.95 *(978-1-879965-21-8(6))* Polychrome Publishing Corp.
Young, Patricia A. The Holy Monks of Mt. Athos. Young, Patricia A., illus. l.t. ed. 2005. (Illus.). 28p. (J). 20.00 *(978-0-913026-24-3(7));* 10.00 *(978-0-913026-49-6(2))* St. Nectarios Pr.
Young Scribes Staff. Unlock the Secrets of Exeter: The Young Scribes of Exeter, NH. l.t. ed. 2004. (Illus.). 172p. (J). pap. 15.00 *(978-0-9744803-9-8(8))* PublishingWorks.
Zabrosky, Joseph. Herbie Hanson, 1 vol., 4 bks. l.t. ed. 2005. (Illus.). 32p. (J). per. *(978-0-9768831-0-4(4))* Elohim Bks.
—Rudy Cazootie, 3 vols., 4 bks. l.t. ed. 2005. (Illus.). 32p. (J). per. *(978-0-9768831-2-8(0))* Elohim Bks.
—Sunny & Hunny, 2 vols., 4 bks. l.t. ed. 2005. (Illus.). 32p. (J). per. *(978-0-9768831-1-1(2))* Elohim Bks.
Zabrosky, Joseph & Jacobs, Nathaniel. The Christmas Tree, 4 vols., 4bks. l.t. ed. 2005. (Illus.). 32p. (J). per. *(978-0-9768831-3-5(9))* Elohim Bks.
Zoller, Jayson D. The Laziest Duck. l.t. ed. 2004. (Illus.). 13p. (J). per. 7.99 *(978-1-932338-52-2(7))* Lifevest Publishing, Inc.

LAS VEGAS (NEV.)

Davis, Alan S. The Fun Seeker's Las Vegas: The Ultimate Guide to One of the World's Hottest Cities. 2nd rev. ed. 2006. (Illus.). 224p. pap. 19.95 *(978-0-9759022-1-9(0))* Davis, A. S. Media Group.

LA SALLE, ROBERT CAVELIER, SIEUR DE, 1643-1687

Aretha, David. La Salle: French Explorer of the Mississippi. 2009. (Great Explorers of the World Ser.). (Illus.). 112p. (J). (gr. 7-12). lib. bdg. 33.27 *(978-1-59845-098-9(0))* Enslow Pubs., Inc.
Crompton, Samuel Willard. Robert de la Salle. 2009. (Great Explorers Ser.). (Illus.). 112p. (J). (gr. 6-12). 30.00 *(978-1-60413-419-3(4),* Chelsea Hse.) Facts On File, Inc.
Donaldson-Forbes, Jeff. La Salle. 2009. (Primary Source Library of Famous Explorers Ser.). 24p. (gr. 4-4). 42.50 *(978-1-60854-129-4(0),* PowerKids Pr.) Rosen Publishing Group, Inc., The.
Hazleton, Amie. Sieur de la Salle: An Explorer of the Great West. 2017. (World Explorers Ser.). (ENG., Illus.). 32p. (gr. 3-4). lib. bdg. 27.32 *(978-1-5157-4206-7(7))* Capstone Press of Coughlan Cos.
Herr, Melody. Exploring the New World: An Interactive History Adventure. 2016. (You Choose: History Ser.). (ENG.). 112p. (gr. 3-4). pap. 6.95 *(978-1-5157-4258-6(X),* You Choose Bks.) Capstone Press of Coughlan Cos.
Kuligowski, Stephanie. La Salle: Early Texas Explorer, 1 vol. 2012. (Primary Source Readers Ser.). (ENG.). 32p. (J). (gr. 3-3). pap. 8.99 *(978-1-4333-5043-6(2))* Teacher Created Materials, Inc.
Mitchell, Mark. Raising la Belle. Mitchell, Mark, illus. (Professor Wigglestix & the Weather Ser.). (Illus.). 112p. 10.95 *(978-1-57168-703-6(3))* Eakin Pr.
Molzahn, Arlene Bourgeois. La Salle: Explorer of the Mississippi. 2004. (Explorers! Ser.). (Illus.). 48p. (J). lib. bdg. 25.27 *(978-0-7660-2141-9(6))* Enslow Pubs., Inc.
Owens, L. L. A Journey with Sieur de la Salle. 2017. (Primary Source Explorers Ser.). (ENG.). 40p. (J). (gr. 3-5). 30.65 *(978-1-5124-0775-4(5))* Lerner Publishing Group.
Payment, Simone. La Salle: Claiming the Mississippi River for France. (Library of Explorers & Exploration Ser.). 112p. (gr. 5-8). 2009. 66.50 *(978-1-60853-610-8(6))* 2004. (Illus.). lib. bdg. 34.60 *(978-0-8239-3628-1(7))* Rosen Publishing Group, Inc., The. (Rosen Reference).
Petrie, Kristin. La Salle, 1 vol. 2007. (Explorers Set 2 Ser.). (ENG., Illus.). 32p. (gr. 4-7). 27.07 *(978-1-59679-750-5(9),* Checkerboard Library) ABDO Publishing Co.
Zronik, John Paul. Sieur de la Salle: New World Adventurer. 2005. (In the Footsteps of Explorers Ser.). (ENG., Illus.). 32p. (J). (gr. 4-5). pap. *(978-0-7787-2449-0(2))* Crabtree Publishing Co.

LASERS

Amazing Lasers: Fourth Grade Guided Comprehension Level K. (On Our Way to English Ser.). (gr. 4-18). 34.50 *(978-0-7578-7148-1(8))* Rigby Education.
Gregory, Daniel. Solid State Lasers for the Laser Enthusiast - Pulse Edition, 1. American LaserTechnic, ed. 2003. (Illus.). 352p. (YA). per. 89.99 *(978-0-9741805-0-2(5))* American LaserTechnic.
Kamberg, Mary-Lane. Fab Lab Creating with Laser Cutters & Engravers. 2016. (Getting Creative with Fab Lab Ser.). 00064p. (J). (gr. 6-6). 34.45 *(978-1-4994-6504-4(1))* Rosen Publishing Group, Inc., The.

J
K
L

Labrecque, Ellen. Patricia Bath & Laser Surgery. 2017. (21st Century Junior Library: Women Innovators Ser.). (ENG., Illus.). 24p. (J). (gr. 2-5). lib. bdg. 27.07 *(978-1-63472-180-6(2)*, 209292) Cherry Lake Publishing.

Laser-Sailing Starships: Meet NASA Inventor Philip Lubin & His Team's. 2017. (J). ***(978-0-7166-6159-7(4))*** World Bk., Inc.

Sarver, Amy. Science at the Grocery. 2007. (Reading Expeditions Ser.). (ENG., Illus.). 24p. (J). pap. 14.95 *(978-0-7922-4567-4(9))* CENGAGE Learning.

Wyckoff, Edwin Brit. Laser Man: Theodore H. Maiman & His Brilliant Invention. 2007. (Genius at Work! Great Inventor Biographies Ser.). (Illus.). 32p. (J). (gr. 3-7). lib. bdg. 23.94 *(978-0-7660-2848-7(8)*, Enslow Elementary) Enslow Pubs., Inc.

—The Man Who Invented the Laser: The Genius of Theodore H. Maiman. 2013. (Genius Inventors & Their Great Ideas Ser.). 48p. (J). (gr. 3-4). pap. 8.95 *(978-1-4644-0208-1(6))*; (Illus.). 25.27 *(978-0-7660-4138-7(7))* Enslow Pubs., Inc. (Enslow Elementary).

LATCHKEY CHILDREN—FICTION

Brenda Seabrooke. Jerry on the Line. 2010. 132p. pap. 10.95 *(978-1-4401-8766-7(5))* iUniverse, Inc.

Horowitz, Jeanine. Latch Key Kid. 2006. 75p. (YA). lib. bdg. 12.99 *(978-1-934190-10-4(1))* Ocean Front Bk. Publishing, Inc.

Mantell, Paul & Christopher, Matt. Mountain Bike Mania. l.t. ed. 2007. (New Matt Christopher Sports Library). 160p. (J). (gr. 4-6). lib. bdg. 26.60 *(978-1-59953-108-3(9))* Norwood Hse. Pr.

Ocean Front Books. Coloring Book. l.t. ed. 2006. (Illus.). (J). lib. bdg. *(978-1-934190-02-9(0))* Ocean Front Bk. Publishing, Inc.

Sizer, Ralph Robuck. Rashad & Rameen. 2011. 26p. pap. 16.95 *(978-1-4560-6459-4(2))* America Star Bks.

LATIN AMERICA

see also South America

Ancona, George. Mis Fiestas: My Celebrations. 2005. (Somos Latinos (We Are Latinos) Ser.).Tr. of My Celebrations. (ENG & SPA., Illus.). 32p. (J). (gr. 1-3). lib. bdg. 21.00 *(978-0-516-25290-2(9))* Scholastic Library Publishing.

Brimson, Samuel. Ecuador-Honduras, 8 vols., Vol. 3. 2003. (Nations of the World Ser.: Vol. 3). (Illus.). 64p. (gr. 5-12). lib. bdg. 31.00 *(978-0-8368-5487-9(X)*, Gareth Stevens Secondary Library) Stevens, Gareth Publishing LLLP.

DePietro, Frank. Latino American Cuisine. 2012. (Illus.). 64p. (J). pap. *(978-1-4222-2337-6(X))* Mason Crest.

—Latino American Cuisine. Limón, José E., ed. 2012. (Hispanic Americans: Major Minority Ser.). (Illus.). 64p. (J). (gr. 4). 22.95 *(978-1-4222-2320-8(5))* Mason Crest.

Doak, Robin Santos. Fighting for American Values: 1941-1985. Overmyer-Velazquez, Mark, ed. 2007. (Latino-American History Ser.). (Illus.). 106p. (YA). (gr. 5-9). lib. bdg. 35.00 *(978-0-8160-6444-1(X))* Facts On File, Inc.

Goring, Ruth. Dias Festivos y Celebraciones. Palacios, Argentina, tr. Date not set. (Vida Latina Ser.). (SPA., Illus.). 48p. (J). (gr. 4-8). lib. bdg. 18.95 *(978-0-86625-564-6(8))* Rourke Educational Media.

Gritzner, Charles F. Latin America. 2006. (Modern World Cultures Ser.). (Illus.). 120p. (gr. 6-12). lib. bdg. 30.00 *(978-0-7910-8142-6(7)*, Chelsea Hse.) Facts On File, Inc.

Schon, Isabel. The Best of Latino Heritage, 1996-2002: A Guide to the Best Juvenile Books about Latino People, Vol. 2003. (ENG., Illus.). 272p. 70.00 *(978-0-8108-4669-2(1))* Scarecrow Pr., Inc.

Thatcher Murcia, Rebecca. What It's Like to Be Shakira. de la Vega, Eida, tr. from SPA. 2010. (What It's Like to Be/Que se Siente al Ser Ser.). (ENG & SPA., Illus.). 32p. (J). (gr. -1-2). lib. bdg. 25.70 *(978-1-58415-851-6(4))* Mitchell Lane Pubs., Inc.

Thomas, Isabel. Latin Dance. 2011. (On the Radar: Dance Ser.). (ENG., Illus.). 32p. (gr. 4-8). lib. bdg. 26.60 *(978-0-7613-7762-7(X))* Lerner Publishing Group.

Walker, Kathryn. See How Cats Grow. 2009. (See How They Grow Ser.). (SPA & ENG., Illus.). 24p. (J). (gr. k-3). pap. 8.25 *(978-1-4358-2875-9(5)*, PowerKids Pr.) Rosen Publishing Group, Inc., The.

Williams, Zella. Llamas & Other Latin American Camels: Llamas y Otros Camélidos de Latinoamérica. 2009. (Animals of Latin America / Animales de Latinoamérica Ser.). (SPA & ENG.). 24p. pap. 8.25 *(978-1-4358-3388-3(0))*; (Illus.). (J). (gr. 1-3). lib. bdg. 22.60 *(978-1-4042-8128-8(2))* Rosen Publishing Group, Inc., The. (PowerKids Pr.).

Zaragoza, Gonzalo. America Latina: Epoca Colonial. (Biblioteca Iberoamericana Ser.). (SPA.). 96p. (YA). 16.50 *(978-84-7525-445-6(4)*, ANY454) Grupo Anaya, S.A. ESP. Dist: Continental Bk. Co., Inc.

LATIN AMERICA—BIOGRAPHY

Brown, Monica. My Name is Celia (Me Llamo Celia) The Life of Celia Cruz (La Vida de Celia Cruz) López, Rafael, illus. 2015. (ENG, MUL & SPA.). 32p. (J). (gr. k-3). pap. 7.95 *(978-1-58979-998-1(4))* Jaffe Book Solutions.

Celia Cruz. 2010. (Great Hispanic Heritage Ser.). (Illus.). 112p. (gr. 6-12). 35.00 *(978-1-60413-771-2(1)*, Chelsea Hse.) Facts On File, Inc.

Chambers, Veronica. Celia Cruz, Queen of Salsa. Maren, Julie, illus. 2008. (J). (gr. -1-3). 25.95 incl. audio *(978-1-4301-0281-6(0))*; 28.95 incl. audio compact disk *(978-1-4301-0284-7(5))*; pap. 16.95 incl. audio *(978-1-4301-0280-9(2))* Live Oak Media.

—Celia Cruz, Queen of Salsa. Maren, Julie, illus. 2007. (gr. 2-5). 17.00 *(978-0-7569-8153-2(0))* Perfection Learning Corp.

Crompton, Samuel. Che Guevara: The Making of a Revolutionary. 2009. (Life Portraits Ser.). (Illus.). 112p. (J). (gr. 7-12). lib. bdg. 36.00 *(978-1-4339-0053-2(X))* Stevens, Gareth Publishing LLLP.

Kallen, Stuart A. Che Guevara: You Win or You Die. 2012. (Single Titles Ser.). (ENG., Illus.). 88p. (gr. 6-12). lib. bdg. 33.27 *(978-0-8225-9035-4(2))* Lerner Publishing Group.

Krohn, Katherine. Biography Shakira. 2007. (Biography Ser.). (Illus.). 112p. (J). (gr. -1). lib. bdg. 30.60 *(978-0-8225-7159-9(5)*, Twenty-First Century Bks.) Lerner Publishing Group.

Murcia, Rebecca Thatcher. Shakira. 2007. (Blue Banner Biography Ser.). (Illus.). 32p. (YA). (gr. 4-7). lib. bdg. 25.70 *(978-1-58415-609-3(0))* Mitchell Lane Pubs., Inc.

Smith-Llera, Danielle. Che Guevara's Face: How a Cuban Photographer's Image Became a Cultural Icon. 2016. (Captured World History Ser.). (ENG., Illus.). 64p. (gr. 5-7). lib. bdg. 34.65 *(978-0-7565-5440-8(3)*, CPB Grades 4-8) Compass Point Bks.

Tieck, Sarah. Shakira: International Music Star, 1 vol. 2014. (Big Buddy Biographies Set 12 Ser.). (ENG.). 32p. (gr. 2-5). 28.50 *(978-1-62403-573-9(6))* ABDO Publishing Co.

Williams, Zella. Shakira: Star Singer. 2010. (Hispanic Headliners Ser.). (ENG.). 24p. (J). pap. 8.25 *(978-1-4488-1480-0(4))*; lib. bdg. 22.60 *(978-1-4488-1457-2(X))* Rosen Publishing Group, Inc., The. (PowerKids Pr.).

—Shakira: Star Singer - Estrella de la Canción. 2010. (Hispanic Headliners / Hispanos en Las Noticias Ser.). (SPA & ENG.). 24p. (J). (gr. 2-5). lib. bdg. 22.60 *(978-1-4488-0714-7(X))* Rosen Publishing Group, Inc., The.

LATIN AMERICA—FICTION

Baez, Josefina. Comrade, Bliss Ain't Playing: Un Cuento de la Republica Dominicana. Cortes, Paulina, illus. 2008. (Marisol Ser.: Vol. 1). (ENG.). 100p. (Orig.). (gr. k-3). pap. 12.95 *(978-1-882161-01-0(7))* I.Om.Be Pr.

Byers, Arlene. Rainbows for Rosa. Halverson, Randal, illus. 2016. 172p. ***(978-0-7399-2521-8(0))*** Rod & Staff Pubs., Inc.

Delacre, Lulu. Salsa Stories. Delacre, Lulu, illus. 2012. (ENG., Illus.). 112p. (J). (gr. 2-5). pap. 6.99 *(978-0-545-43098-2(4)*, Scholastic Pr.) Scholastic, Inc.

Delacre, Lulu. Us, in Progress: Short Stories about Young Latinos. Delacre, Lulu, illus. 2017. (Illus.). 256p. (J). (gr. 3-7). 16.99 ***(978-0-06-239214-5(X))*** HarperCollins Pubs.

Iturralde, Edna. Verde Fue Mi Selva. Arroba, Doris et al, eds. Cornejo, Eulalia, illus. 2008. (Alfaguara Infantil Ser.).Tr. of My Forest Was Green. 152p. (J). (gr. 5-8). pap. *(978-9978-07-097-0(4))* Ediciones Alfaguara.

LeapFrog Staff. Disney Princess Stories - Latin America. 2003. (Illus.). (J). spiral bd. 14.99 *(978-1-59319-001-9(8))* LeapFrog Enterprises, Inc.

Martínez, Rueben. Once upon a Time: Traditional Latin American Tales. Unger, David, tr. from SPA. Colón, Raúl, illus. 2010. (ENG & SPA.). 96p. (J). (gr. k-5). 19.99 *(978-0-06-146895-7(9)*, Rayo) HarperCollins Pubs.

Mulder, Michelle. Not a Chance, 1 vol. 2013. (ENG.). 160p. (J). (gr. 4-7). pap. 9.95 *(978-1-4598-0216-2(0))* Orca Bk. Pubs. USA.

Porras, Javier Fernando, illus. Historias de Amores y Desvarios en America. 2004. (Literatura Juvenil (Panamericana Editorial) Ser.). (SPA.). 179p. (J). (gr. -1-7). pap. *(978-958-30-0569-5(X)*, PV4378) Centro de Informacion y Desarrollo de la Comunicacion y la Literatura MEX. Dist: Lectorum Pubns., Inc.

Skármeta, Antonio. The Composition, 1 vol. Ruano, Alfonso, illus. 2003. (ENG.). 32p. (J). (gr. 3-18). pap. 7.95 *(978-0-88899-550-6(4))* Groundwood Bks. CAN. Dist: Publishers Group West (PGW).

LATIN AMERICA—HISTORY

Coletti, Sharon. Everything You Need to Teach Latin America. 2005. (YA). ring bd. 149.95 *(978-1-933558-03-5(2))* InspirEd Educators.

Crompton, Samuel. Che Guevara: The Making of a Revolutionary. 2009. (Life Portraits Ser.). (Illus.). 112p. (J). (gr. 7-12). lib. bdg. 36.00 *(978-1-4339-0053-2(X))* Stevens, Gareth Publishing LLLP.

DePietro, Frank. Spain Arrives in the Americas. Limón, José E., ed. 2012. (Hispanic Americans: Major Minority Ser.). 64p. (J). (gr. 4). 22.95 *(978-1-4222-2330-7(2))* Mason Crest.

Ernesto Che Guevara. 2010. (Great Hispanic Heritage Ser.). (Illus.). 128p. (gr. 6-12). 35.00 *(978-1-60413-732-3(0)*, Chelsea Hse.) Facts On File, Inc.

Exploring Latin America. 2017. (Exploring Latin America Ser.). 48p. (gr. 10-12). 107.40 ***(978-1-5081-0524-4(3))***; pap. 56.20 ***(978-1-5081-0526-8(X))*** Rosen Publishing Group, Inc., The. (Britannica Educational Publishing).

Gerdes, Louise. Latin America. 2009. (Opposing Viewpoints Ser.). (ENG., Illus.). 240p. (YA). (gr. 10-12). pap. 42.95 *(978-0-7377-4374-6(3)*, LML02109-245378, Greenhaven Pr., Inc.) Cengage Gale.

Gerdes, Louise, ed. Latin America. 2009. (Opposing Viewpoints Ser.). (ENG., Illus.). 224p. (gr. 10-12). pap. 33.80 *(978-0-7377-4373-9(5)*, LML02109-245360, Greenhaven Pr., Inc.) Cengage Gale.

Hirsch, E. D., Jr., ed. Independence for Latin America. Level 6. tchr. ed. 9.95 *(978-0-7690-5090-4(5))*; stu. ed. 49.95 *(978-0-7690-2855-2(1))* Pearson Learning.

Kallen, Stuart A. Che Guevara: You Win or You Die. 2012. (Single Titles Ser.). (ENG., Illus.). 88p. (gr. 6-12). lib. bdg. 33.27 *(978-0-8225-9035-4(2))* Lerner Publishing Group.

Kallen, Stuart A., ed. The History of Latin Music. 2013. (Music Library). (ENG., Illus.). 128p. (gr. 7-10). lib. bdg. 34.45 *(978-1-4205-0947-2(0)*, Lucent Bks.) Cengage Gale.

Miller, Calvin Craig. Che Guevara: In Search of Revolution. 2006. (World Leaders Ser.). (Illus.). 192p. (J). (gr. 6-12). lib. bdg. 26.95 *(978-1-931798-93-8(1))* Reynolds, Morgan Inc.

Mooney, Carla. The Economy of Latin America. 2017. (Exploring Latin America Ser.). 48p. (gr. 10-12). 84.30 ***(978-1-68048-678-0(0)***, Britannica Educational Publishing) Rosen Publishing Group, Inc., The.

Nichols, Susan. The History of Latin America. 2017. (Exploring Latin America Ser.). 48p. (gr. 10-12). pap. 14.05 ***(978-1-68048-681-0(0)***, Britannica Educational Publishing) Rosen Publishing Group, Inc., The.

—The People & Culture of Latin America. 2017. (Exploring Latin America Ser.). 48p. (J). (gr. 10-12). pap. 14.05 ***(978-1-68048-689-6(6)***, Britannica Educational Publishing) Rosen Publishing Group, Inc., The.

Ollhoff, Jim. Conflicts & Independence, 1 vol. 2011. (Hispanic American History Ser.). (ENG., Illus.). 32p. (YA). (gr. 5-9). 27.07 *(978-1-61783-054-9(2))* ABDO Publishing Co.

Overmyer-Velazquez, Mark, ed. Latino-American History, 6 vols., Set. 2007. (Latino-American History Ser.). 112p. (gr. 5-8). 175.00 *(978-0-8160-7055-8(5)*, Chelsea Hse.) Facts On File, Inc.

Pearce, Q. L. La Llorona. 2009. (Mysterious Encounters Ser.). (ENG., Illus.). 48p. (J). 29.00 *(978-0-7377-4571-9(1))* Cengage Gale.

Putumayo Kids Staff, creator. Latin America Sticker Coll. 2011. (J). 11.95 *(978-1-58759-285-0(1))* Putumayo World Music & Crafts.

Rice, Earle, Jr. A Brief Political & Geographic History of Latin America: Where Are... Gran Colombia, la Plata, & Dutch Guiana. 2007. (Places in Time Ser.). (Illus.). 112p. (YA). (gr. 5-9). lib. bdg. 37.10 *(978-1-58415-626-0(0))* Mitchell Lane Pubs., Inc.

Salinas, Eva. Lo Inventaron los Latinoamericanos: Innovaciones Asombrosas. 2012. (SPA & ENG., Illus.). 48p. (J). (gr. 3-7). 21.95 *(978-1-55451-379-6(0)*, 9781554513796) Annick Pr., Ltd. CAN. Dist: Publishers Group West (PGW).

—Lo Inventaron los Latinoamericanos: Innovaciones Asombrosas. 2016. (We Thought of It Ser.). (ENG & SPA., Illus.). 48p. (J). (gr. 3-7). pap. 9.95 *(978-1-55451-378-9(2))* Annick Pr., Ltd. CAN. Dist: Publishers Group West (PGW).

—Latin Americans Thought of It: Amazing Innovations. 2012. (We Thought of It Ser.). (ENG., Illus.). 48p. (J). (gr. 5-7). 21.95 *(978-1-55451-377-2(4)*, 9781554513772); pap. 11.95 *(978-1-55451-376-5(6)*, 9781554513765) Annick Pr., Ltd. CAN. Dist: Publishers Group West (PGW).

Sebastian, Emily. The Colonial & Postcolonial Experience in Latin America & the Caribbean. 2016. (Colonial & Postcolonial Experience Ser.). 00128p. (J). (gr. 10-10). 54.00 *(978-1-5081-0439-1(5))* Rosen Publishing Group, Inc., The.

Shea, Therese. The Land & Climate of Latin America. 2017. (Exploring Latin America Ser.). 48p. (J). (gr. 10-12). pap. 14.05 ***(978-1-68048-685-8(3)***, Britannica Educational Publishing) Rosen Publishing Group, Inc., The.

Stein, R. Conrad. The Conquistadors: Building a Spanish Empire in the Americas. 2004. (Proud Heritage: the Hispanic Library). (ENG., Illus.). 40p. (J). (gr. 3-6). 29.93 *(978-1-59296-144-3(4)*, 200016) Child's World, Inc., The.

Williams, Zella. Coqui Frogs & Other Latin American Frogs. 2009. (Animals of Latin America / Animales de Latinoamérica Ser.). (SPA & ENG., Illus.). 24p. pap. 8.25 *(978-1-4358-3382-1(1)*, PowerKids Pr.) Rosen Publishing Group, Inc., The.

—Coqui Frogs & Other Latin American Frogs/Coquíes y Otras Ranas de Latinoamerica. 2009. (Animals of Latin America / Animales de Latinoamérica Ser.). (SPA & ENG., Illus.). 24p. (J). (gr. 1-3). lib. bdg. 22.60 *(978-1-4042-8148-6(7)*, PowerKids Pr.) Rosen Publishing Group, Inc., The.

LATIN AMERICA—POLITICS AND GOVERNMENT

Day, Meredith, ed. Revolution & Independence in Latin America. 2015. (Age of Revolution Ser.). (ENG.). 128p. (YA). (gr. 9-10). 70.50 *(978-1-68048-030-6(8)*, Britannica Educational Publishing) Rosen Publishing Group, Inc., The.

Dunn, John M. Life in Castro's Cuba. 2004. (Way People Live Ser.). (ENG., Illus.). 112p. (J). (gr. 7-10). 30.85 *(978-1-59018-464-6(5))* Cengage Gale.

LATIN AMERICA—SOCIAL CONDITIONS

Arkham, Thomas. Latino Americans & Their Jobs. 2013. (Illus.). 64p. (J). pap. *(978-1-4222-2340-6(X))* Mason Crest.

—Latino Americans & Their Jobs. Limón, José E., ed. 2012. (Hispanic Americans: Major Minority Ser.). (Illus.). 64p. (J). (gr. 4). 22.95 *(978-1-4222-2323-9(X))* Mason Crest.

Dunn, John M. Life in Castro's Cuba. 2004. (Way People Live Ser.). (ENG., Illus.). 112p. (J). (gr. 7-10). 30.85 *(978-1-59018-464-6(5))* Cengage Gale.

Hollihan, Kerrie Logan. Christmas Traditions in Latin America: Tradiciones Navidenas en Latinoamérica. Sanz, Ma Pilar, tr. 2010. (Latin American Celebrations & Festivals / Celebraciones y Festivales en Latinoamérica Ser.). (SPA & ENG., Illus.). 24p. (J). (gr. 2-5). lib. bdg. 22.60 *(978-1-4358-9365-8(4))* Rosen Publishing Group, Inc., The.

Nichols, Susan. The People & Culture of Latin America. 2017. (Exploring Latin America Ser.). 48p. (J). (gr. 10-12). 26.85 ***(978-1-68048-691-9(8)***, Britannica Educational Publishing) Rosen Publishing Group, Inc., The.

Worth, Richard. 1950s to 1960s. 2009. (Hispanic America 2 Ser.). 80p. (gr. 5). 34.21 *(978-0-7614-4177-9(8))* Marshall Cavendish GBR. Dist: Marshall Cavendish Corp.

LATIN AMERICAN LITERATURE—HISTORY AND CRITICISM

Bloom, Harold, ed. Love in the Time of Cholera. 2005. (Modern Critical Interpretations Ser.). (Illus.). 144p. (C). (gr. 9-13). 45.00 *(978-0-7910-8120-4(6)*, Chelsea Hse.) Facts On File, Inc.

Hispanic-American Writers. 2010. (Multicultural Voices Ser.). (Illus.). 128p. (gr. 6-12). 35.00 *(978-1-60413-312-7(0)*, Chelsea Hse.) Facts On File, Inc.

LATIN AMERICANS

Here are entered works on citizens of Latin American countries. Works on citizens of Latin American countries in the United States are entered under Latin Americans—United States. Works on United States citizens of Latin American descent are entered under Hispanic Americans.

Engle, Margarita. Bravo! Poems About Amazing Hispanics. López, Rafael, illus. 2017. (ENG.). 48p. (J). 18.99 *(978-0-8050-9876-1(3)*, 9780805098761, Holt, Henry & Co. Bks. For Young Readers) Holt, Henry & Co.

Hispanic-American Writers. 2010. (Multicultural Voices Ser.). (Illus.). 128p. (gr. 6-12). 35.00 *(978-1-60413-312-7(0)*, Chelsea Hse.) Facts On File, Inc.

Juarez, Christine. Great Hispanic & Latino Americans. 2016. (Great Hispanic & Latino Americans Ser.). (ENG.). 24p. (gr. k-1). 131.94 *(978-1-5157-1931-1(6)*, Pebble Bks.) Capstone Press of Coughlan Cos.

LATIN AMERICANS—FICTION

Cuentos, Mitos y Leyendas para Ninos de America Latina (Stories, Myths & Legends for Latin American Children) (SPA., Illus.). 72p. (J). 9.95 *(978-958-04-0957-1(9)*, NOR9609) Norma S.A. COL. Dist: Distribuidora Norma, Inc.

Flor Ada, Alma & Campoy, F. Isabel. Yes! We Are Latinos. Diaz, David, illus. 2013. (SPA & ENG.). 96p. (J). (gr. 5). 18.95 *(978-1-58089-383-1(X))* Charlesbridge Publishing, Inc.

Pinkney, Sandra L. I Am Latino: the Beauty in Me. Pinkney, Myles C., photos by. 2013. (ENG., Illus.). 28p. (J). (gr. -1-1). bds. 6.99 *(978-0-316-23385-9(4))* Little, Brown Bks. for Young Readers.

Robleda, Margarita. Paco: A Latino Boy in the U.S. 2004. (Paco & Maria Ser.). (SPA.). 36p. (gr. 3-5). pap. 13.95 *(978-1-59437-560-6(7)*, Alfaguara) Santillana USA Publishing Co., Inc.

van Diepen, Allison. Light of Day. 2015. (ENG.). 320p. (YA). (gr. 9). 17.99 *(978-0-06-230347-9(3))* HarperCollins Pubs.

LATIN AMERICANS—UNITED STATES

Flor Ada, Alma & Campoy, F. Isabel. Yes! We Are Latinos. Diaz, David, illus. 2016. (ENG & SPA.). 96p. (J). (gr. 5). pap. 9.95 *(978-1-58089-549-1(2))* Charlesbridge Publishing, Inc.

Worth, Richard. The 1970s to the 1980s. 2009. (Hispanic America 2 Ser.). 80p. (gr. 5). 34.21 *(978-0-7614-4178-6(6))* Marshall Cavendish Corp.

LATIN LANGUAGE

Baddorf, Robert A. & Perrin, Christopher. Latin for Children, Primer a Activity Book! 2005. (Latin for Childred Ser.). (ENG.). 163p. (J). (gr. -1-3). pap., act. bk. ed. 16.95 *(978-1-60051-005-2(1))* Classical Academic Pr.

Bolchazy, Marie Carducci. Quis Me Amat?/Who Loves Me? 2003. (I Am Reading Latin Ser.). (ENG & LAT., Illus.). 64p. (J). (gr. k-3). 10.00 *(978-0-86516-541-0(6))* Bolchazy-Carducci Pubs.

Carole Marsh. Of All the Gaul! Latin for Kids. 2004. (Little Linguist Ser.). 32p. (gr. 2-6). pap. 5.95 *(978-0-635-02429-9(2))* Gallopade International.

Griffith, Timothy. Orbis Naturalis. 2012. (Illus.). (J). *(978-1-59128-116-0(4))* Canon Pr.

Henderson, Charles, Jr., et al. Latin for Americans, 2 vols. 9th ed. 2003. (Latin for Americans Ser.). (ENG., Illus.). 624p. (gr. 8-12). stu. ed. 109.72 *(978-0-07-828176-1(8)*, 0078281768) McGraw-Hill Education.

Latin Grammar Student Workbook. 2003. stu. ed., ring bd., wbk. ed. *(978-1-931680-42-4(6))* Teaching Point, Inc.

Lowe, Leigh. Prima Latina Student Book: Introduction to Christian Latin. 2nd ed. 2003. (Classical Trivium Core Ser.). 128p. (J). per. 14.00 *(978-1-930953-51-2(8)*, 002) Memoria Pr.

Lundquist, Joegil K. & Lundquist, Jeanne L. English from the Roots up, Volume II: Help for Reading, Writing, Spelling & S. A. T. Scores. 2003. (English from the Roots Up Ser.). (Illus.). 107p. (J). (gr. -1-3). 44.95 *(978-1-885942-30-2(3))* Cune Pr., LLC.

—English from the Roots up Volume II: Help for Reading, Writing, Spelling, & S. A. T. Scores, vols. 2, II. 2003. (Illus.). 125p. 29.95 net. *(978-1-885942-31-9(1))* Cune Pr., LLC.

Marsh, Carole. Of All the Gaul! Latin for Kids. Beard, Chad, ed. 2004. (Little Linguist Ser.). (Illus.). 32p. 29.95 *(978-0-635-02437-4(3))* Gallopade International.

McGraw-Hill-Glencoe Staff. Latin for Americans, Level 2. 9th ed. 2004. (Latin for Americans Ser.). (ENG.). (gr. 8-12). stu. ed. 104.64 *(978-0-07-861252-7(7)*, 0078612527) McGraw-Hill Education.

Minkova, Milena & Tunberg, Terence O. Lingua Latina Perennis: An Introductory Course to the Language of the Ages. 2008. tchr. ed. 99.00 *(978-0-86516-562-5(9))* Bolchazy-Carducci Pubs.

Osburn, LeaAnn. Latin Verbs Rock! Exercise Book. 2007. spiral bd. 18.00 *(978-0-9760046-6-0(6))* L & L Enterprises.

The Rosetta Stone Language Library: Latin Level 1. 2005. (J). (gr. 1-18). cd-rom 209.00 *(978-1-58022-026-2(6))* Rosetta Stone Ltd.

Sheikh-Miller, Jonathan. Latin Words Sticker Book. Cartwright, Stephen, illus. 2006. (Latin Words Sticker Book Ser.). 16p. (J). (gr. 1). pap. 8.99 *(978-0-7945-1145-6(7)*, Usborne) EDC Publishing.

LATIN LANGUAGE—READERS

Baddorf, Robert & Perrin, Christopher. Latin for Children. Baddorf, Robert, illus. 2006. (Latin for Childred Ser.). (ENG., Illus.). 162p. (J). (gr. 4-7). pap., act. bk. ed. 16.95 *(978-1-60051-017-5(5))* Classical Academic Pr.

—Latin for Children, Primer B Activity Book! Baddorf, Robert, illus. 2005. (Latin for Childred Ser.). (ENG., Illus.). 196p. (J). (gr. 4-7). pap., act. bk. ed. 16.95 *(978-1-60051-011-3(6))* Classical Academic Pr.

Bolchazy, Marie Carducci. Quo Colore Est?/What Color Is It? 2003. (I Am Reading Latin Ser.). (ENG & LAT., Illus.). 64p. (J). (gr. k-3). 10.00 *(978-0-86516-539-7(4))* Bolchazy-Carducci Pubs.

Larsen, Aaron & Perrin, Christopher. Latin for Children, Primer B. 2004. (Latin for Childred Ser.). (ENG., Illus.). 286p. (J). (gr. -1-12). pap. 24.95 *(978-1-60051-006-9(X))* Classical Academic Pr.

—Latin for Children, Primer B Answer Key. 2004. (Latin for Childred Ser.). (ENG.). 144p. (J). (gr. 4-7). pap. 14.95 *(978-1-60051-007-6(8))* Classical Academic Pr.

—Latin for Children, Primer C. 2005. (Latin for Childred Ser.). (ENG., Illus.). 310p. (J). (gr. 4-7). pap. 24.95 *(978-1-60051-012-0(4))* Classical Academic Pr.

—Latin for Children, Primer C Answer Key. 2005. (Latin for Childred Ser.). (ENG.). 142p. (J). (gr. 4-7). pap. 14.95 *(978-1-60051-013-7(2))* Classical Academic Pr.

MacLaren, Dorothy H. Esopus Hodie, Aesop Today, Vol. 1. (ENG & LAT.). 64p. (YA). (gr. 9-12). 9.75 *(978-0-939507-06-1(4)*, B20) American Classical League, The.

Moore, Karen. Latin for Children: A History Reader. 2005. (Latin for Childred Ser.). (ENG., Illus.). 56p. (J). (gr. 4-7). pap. 9.95 *(978-1-60051-004-5(3))* Classical Academic Pr.

Moore, Karen & Davis, Erin. Latin for Children, Primer B History Reader. 2005. (Latin for Childred Ser.). (ENG., Illus.). 154p. (J). (gr. 4-7). pap. 12.95 *(978-1-60051-010-6(8))* Classical Academic Pr.

—Latin for Children, Primer C History Reader: Libellus de Historia. 2005. (Latin for Childred Ser.). (ENG., Illus.). 188p. (J). (gr. 4-7). pap. 16.95 *(978-1-60051-016-8(7))* Classical Academic Pr.

Robinson, Lorna. Telling Tales in Latin: A New Course & Story Book for Children. De, Soham, illus. 2014. (ENG & LAT.). 112p. (J). (gr. 4-7). pap. 15.95 *(978-0-285-64179-2(4))* Souvenir Pr. Ltd. GBR. Dist: Independent Pubs. Group.

Rose, Williams. Octavus Octopus. James, Estes, illus. 2008. (LAT & ENG.). 20p. (J). pap. 10.00 *(978-0-86516-698-1(6))* Bolchazy-Carducci Pubs.

—Rena Rhinoceros. James, Estes, illus. 2008. (LAT & ENG.). 20p. (J). pap. 10.00 *(978-0-86516-699-8(4))* Bolchazy-Carducci Pubs.

—Taurus Rex. James, Estes, illus. 2008. (LAT & ENG.). 20p. (J). pap. 10.00 *(978-0-86516-700-1(1))* Bolchazy-Carducci Pubs.

—Ursus et Porcus. James, Estes, illus. 2008. (LAT & ENG.). 20p. (J). pap. 10.00 *(978-0-86516-701-8(X))* Bolchazy-Carducci Pubs.

Williams, Rose. The Young Romans. 2007. (LAT & ENG.). pap. 23.00 *(978-0-86516-670-7(6))* Bolchazy-Carducci Pubs.

LATIN LITERATURE

Kerrigan, Michael. Romans. 2010. (Ancients in Their Own Words Ser.). 64p. (gr. 5). 32.79 *(978-1-60870-067-7(4))* Marshall Cavendish Corp.

LATTER-DAY SAINTS

see Mormons and Mormonism

LATVIA

Aizpuriete, Amanda. Latvia. Hartgers, Katarina, tr. Bultje, Jan Willem, photos by. 2006. (Looking at Europe Ser.). (Illus.). 48p. (YA). (gr. 5-8). 22.95 *(978-1-881508-37-3(4))* Oliver Pr., Inc.

Barlas, Robert & Wong, Winnie. Latvia. 2nd rev. ed. 2009. (Cultures of the World 19 Ser.). 144p. (gr. 6). 42.79 *(978-0-7614-4857-0(8))* Marshall Cavendish Corp.

Docalavich, Heather & Indovino, Shaina Carmel. Latvia. 2012. (J). *(978-1-4222-2249-2(7))*; pap. *(978-1-4222-2280-5(2))* Mason Crest.

Throp, Claire. Latvia, 1 vol. 2011. (Countries Around the World Ser.). (ENG.). 48p. (gr. 3-6). pap. 9.95 *(978-1-4329-5236-5(6),* NA-h) Heinemann-Raintree.

LAVOISIER, ANTOINE LAURENT, 1743-1794

Van Gorp, Lynn. Antoine Lavoisier: Founder of Modern Chemistry, 1 vol. 2007. (Science Readers Ser.). (SPA & ENG.). 32p. (J). (gr. 3-3). pap. 8.99 *(978-0-7439-0582-4(2))* Shell Educational Publishing.

Yount, Lisa. Antoine Lavoisier: Founder of Modern Chemistry. rev. ed. 2008. (Great Minds of Science Ser.). (Illus.). 128p. (J). (gr. k-5). lib. bdg. 33.27 *(978-0-7660-3011-4(3))* Enslow Pubs., Inc.

—Antoine Lavoisier: Genius of Modern Chemistry. 2015. (Genius Scientists & Their Genius Ideas Ser.). 96p. (J). (gr. 5-12). 27.94 *(978-0-7660-6520-8(0))*; pap. 10.95 *(978-0-7660-6521-5(9))* Enslow Pubs., Inc.

LAW

see also Courts; Judges; Jury; Lawyers; Police

also special branches of law, e.g. International Law; For laws on special subjects see names of subjects with the subdivision Laws and Regulations, e.g. Automobiles—Laws and Regulations

Arbetman, Lee P., et al. Street Law: A Course in Practical Law. 7th ed. 2004. (Ntc: Street Law Ser.). (ENG., Illus.). 684p. (gr. 9-12). stu. ed. 114.44 *(978-0-07-860019-7(7),* 0078600197) McGraw-Hill Higher Education.

Bage, Grant. Crime & Punishment Through the Ages: Band 18/Pearl. 2017. (ENG., Illus.). 80p. (J). pap. 9.99 ***(978-0-00-820899-8(9))*** HarperCollins Pubs. Ltd. GBR. Dist: Independent Pubs. Group.

Bailey, Rachel A. The Triangle Shirtwaist Factory Fire. 2014. (Perspectives Library). (ENG., Illus.). 32p. (J). (gr. 4-8). 28.50 *(978-1-63137-620-7(9),* 205263) Cherry Lake Publishing.

Beel, Rory. The Second Informant. 2005. 65p. pap. 16.95 *(978-1-4137-8359-9(7))* PublishAmerica, Inc.

Boocock, Charles & Yu, Jennifer. The 10 Most Memorable Court Cases. 2008. 14.99 *(978-1-55448-548-2(7))* Scholastic Library Publishing.

Boothroyd, Jennifer. What Are Rules & Laws? 2015. (ENG., Illus.). 24p. (J). (gr. k-2). 23.99 *(978-1-4677-8572-3(5),* Lerner Pubns.) Lerner Publishing Group.

Brignall, Richard. Real Justice: a Police Mr. Big Sting Goes Wrong: The Story of Kyle Unger, 1 vol. 2015. (Lorimer Real Justice Ser.). (ENG., Illus.). 136p. (YA). (gr. 8-12). pap. 12.95 *(978-1-4594-0862-3(4),* 9781459408623) Lorimer, James & Co., Ltd., Pubs. CAN. Dist: Casemate Pubs. & Bk. Distributors, LLC.

Cane, Ella. The U. S. House of Representatives, 1 vol. 2014. (Our Government Ser.). (ENG.). 24p. (gr. 1-2). lib. bdg. 25.32 *(978-1-4765-4201-0(5),* First Facts) Capstone Press of Coughlan Cos.

—The U. S. Senate, 1 vol. 2014. (Our Government Ser.). (ENG.). 24p. (gr. 1-2). lib. bdg. 25.32 *(978-1-4765-4202-7(3),* First Facts) Capstone Press of Coughlan Cos.

De Capua, Sarah. Making a Law. 2004. (True Bks.). (ENG., Illus.). 48p. (J). (gr. 3-5). pap. 6.95 *(978-0-516-27941-1(6),* Children's Pr.) Scholastic Library Publishing.

Dosen, Anthony, et al. Investigating Legal Studies for Queensland. 2013. (ENG.). pap. *(978-1-107-65346-7(0))* Cambridge Univ. Pr.

—Investigating Legal Studies for Queensland Bundle. 2013. (ENG.). pap. *(978-1-107-67198-0(1))* Cambridge Univ. Pr.

Engdahl, Sylvia. Driving. Greenhaven Press Staff, ed. 2014. (Teen Rights & Freedoms Ser.). (ENG., Illus.). 176p. (gr. 10-12). lib. bdg. 42.00 *(978-0-7377-6997-5(1),* Greenhaven Pr., Inc.) Cengage Gale.

Fisher, Margaret E., et al. Street Law: A Course in Practical Law. 7th ed. 2004. (Ntc: Street Law Ser.). (ENG., Illus.). 112p. (gr. 9-12). per., wbk. ed. 11.52 *(978-0-07-861208-4(X),* 007861208X) McGraw-Hill Higher Education.

Fridell, Ron. Miranda Law: The Right to Remain Silent. 2005. (Supreme Court Milestones Ser.). (Illus.). 144p. (J). (gr. 4-7). lib. bdg. *(978-0-7614-1942-6(X),* Benchmark Bks.) Marshall Cavendish Corp.

Gagne, Tammy. Immigration in the United States. 2013. (My Guide to U.S. Citizenship Ser.). (ENG.). 48p. (J). (gr. 4-6). lib. bdg. 29.95 *(978-1-61228-446-0(9))* Mitchell Lane Pubs., Inc.

Glencoe McGraw-Hill Staff. Street Law, StudentWorks CD-ROM. 8th ed. 2009. (Ntc: Street Law Ser.). (ENG.). (gr. 9-12). cd-rom 120.36 *(978-0-07-889521-0(9),* 0078895219) McGraw-Hill Education.

Glencoe McGraw-Hill Staff & McGraw-Hill Education Staff. Street Law: A Course in Practical Law. 8th ed. 2009. (Ntc: Street Law Ser.). (ENG.). 144p. (gr. 9-12). pap., stu. ed., wbk. ed. 12.32 *(978-0-07-889518-0(9),* 0078895189) McGraw-Hill Education.

Goldman, Arnold J. Study Guide: Used with ... Goldman-Business Law: Principles & Practices. 6th ed. 2003. (YA). pap., stu. ed. 34.76 *(978-0-618-30295-6(6),* 319043) CENGAGE Learning.

Hall, Kevin. Montesquieu & the Spirit of Laws. 2016. (J). lib. bdg. *(978-1-68048-546-2(6))* Rosen Publishing Group, Inc., The.

Hernandez, Carlos. It's the Law! 2012. (InfoMax Readers Ser.). (ENG., Illus.). 24p. (J). (gr. 1-2). pap. 8.25 *(978-1-4488-9073-6(X),* Rosen Classroom) Rosen Publishing Group, Inc., The.

Higgins, Melissa. Night Dad Went to Jail: What to Expect When Someone You Love Goes to Jail. Kirwan, Wednesday, illus. 2013. (Life's Challenges Ser.). (ENG.). 24p. (gr. 2-3). 8.99 *(978-1-4795-2142-5(6))* Picture Window Bks.

Hitchcock, David. Patent Searching Made Easy: How to Do Patent Searches on the Internet & in the Library. 7th ed. 2017. (ENG., Illus.). 272p. pap. 39.99 *(978-1-4133-2409-9(6))* NOLO.

Hollander, Barbara Gottfried. Marriage Rights & Gay Rights: Interpreting the Constitution. 2014. (Understanding the United States Constitution Ser.). (Illus.). 112p. (J). (gr. 7-12). 35.60 *(978-1-4777-7514-1(5))* Rosen Publishing Group, Inc., The.

Kowalski, Kathiann M. Judges & Courts: A Look at the Judicial Branch. 2012. (Searchlight Books How Does Government Work Ser.). (ENG., Illus.). 40p. (gr. 3-5). pap. 51.01 *(978-0-7613-9233-0(5))*; pap. 8.95 *(978-0-7613-8562-2(2))* Lerner Publishing Group.

Landmark Supreme Court Cases, 35 bks., Set. (Illus.). (YA). (gr. 6-12). lib. bdg. 733.25 *(978-0-89490-572-8(4))* Enslow Pubs., Inc.

Law Enforcement & Intelligence Gathering. 2016. (Law Enforcement & Intelligence Gathering Ser.). 00104p. (YA). (gr. 8-8). 145.00 *(978-1-5081-0293-9(7),* Britannica Educational Publishing) Rosen Publishing Group, Inc., The.

Leavitt, Amie Jane. United States Immigration Services. 2013. (My Guide to U.S. Citizenship Ser.). (ENG.). 48p. (J). (gr. 4-6). lib. bdg. 29.95 *(978-1-61228-447-7(7))* Mitchell Lane Pubs., Inc.

LeVert, Suzanne. How States Make Laws. 2003. (Kaleidoscope Ser.). (Illus.). 48p. (gr. 3-18). lib. bdg. 20.95 *(978-0-7614-1595-4(5),* Benchmark Bks.) Marshall Cavendish Corp.

—State Courts. 2003. (Kaleidoscope Ser.). (Illus.). 48p. (gr. 3-18). lib. bdg. 20.95 *(978-0-7614-1594-7(7),* Benchmark Bks.) Marshall Cavendish Corp.

Lindeen, Carol K. Who Makes Our Laws?, 6 vols., Set. 2004. (Phonics Readers Books 37-72 Ser.). (ENG.). 8p. (gr. k-1). pap. 35.70 *(978-0-7368-4073-6(7),* Phonics Readers) Capstone Press of Coughlan Cos.

Luce, Pat & Joyner, Holly. How a Bill Becomes a Law: A Complete Tool Kit with Background Information, Primary Sources, & More to Help Students Build Reading & Writing Skills-And Deepen Their Understanding of How Our Government Works. 2008. (Easy Simulations Ser.). (ENG.). 64p. pap. 11.99 *(978-0-439-62573-9(4),* Teaching Resources) Scholastic, Inc.

Lüsted, Marcia Amidon. What You Need to Know about Your Status As an Immigrant under the Law. 2015. (Know Your Rights Ser.). (ENG., Illus.). 64p. (J). (gr. 6-6). 33.25 *(978-1-4777-8102-9(1),* Rosen Young Adult) Rosen Publishing Group, Inc., The.

Luthringer, Chelsea. So What Is Justice Anyway? 2009. (Student's Guide to American Civics Ser.). 48p. (gr. 5-8). 53.00 *(978-1-61511-239-5(1),* Rosen Reference) Rosen Publishing Group, Inc., The.

Marshall, Derek. What Is a Law? 2009. (Real Life Readers Ser.). 16p. (gr. 2-3). pap. 7.05 *(978-1-4358-0097-7(4),* Rosen Classroom) Rosen Publishing Group, Inc., The.

Marzilli, Alan, ed. Point/Counterpoint. (Illus.). (J). 155.70 *(978-0-7910-7368-1(8),* Chelsea Hse.) Facts On File, Inc.

Maybury, Richard J. Uncle Eric Talks about Personal, Career, & Financial Security. Williams, Jane A. & Daniels, Kathryn, eds. 2nd ed. 2004. ("Uncle Eric" Bk.: 1). (ENG., Illus.). 187p. pap. 14.95 *(978-0-942617-38-2(X))* Bluestocking Pr.

Merino, Noel. Emancipation. Greenhaven Press Staff, ed. 2014. (Teen Rights & Freedoms Ser.). (ENG., Illus.). 176p. (gr. 10-12). lib. bdg. 42.00 *(978-0-7377-6999-9(8),* Greenhaven Pr., Inc.) Cengage Gale.

Meyer, Susan. Understanding Digital Piracy. 2013. (Digital & Information Literacy Ser.). 48p. (J). (gr. 5-8). 29.25 *(978-1-4488-9514-4(6))* Rosen Publishing Group, Inc., The.

Meyer, Terry Teague. Know Your Rights: Set 2. 2015. (Know Your Rights Ser.). (ENG.). 64p. (J). (gr. 6-6). 199.50 *(978-1-4994-6191-6(7),* Rosen Young Adult) Rosen Publishing Group, Inc., The.

Mills, Nathan & Ripley, Ellen. What Are Rules & Laws? 2012. (Rosen Readers Ser.). (ENG., Illus.). 24p. (J). (gr. 1-2). pap. 8.25 *(978-1-4488-8860-3(3),* Rosen Classroom) Rosen Publishing Group, Inc., The.

Mooney, Carla. Online Privacy & Business. 2014. (Privacy in the Online World). (ENG., Illus.). 80p. (J). lib. bdg. *(978-1-60152-724-0(1))* ReferencePoint Pr., Inc.

Ogden, Charlie. Law & Justice. 2017. 32p. (J). ***(978-0-7787-3721-6(7))*** Crabtree Publishing Co.

Otfinoski, Steven. The Triangle Shirtwaist Factory Fire: Core Events of an Industrial Disaster, 1 vol. 2014. (What Went Wrong? Ser.). (ENG.). 32p. (gr. 3-4). lib. bdg. 27.32 *(978-1-4765-4183-9(3),* Fact Finders) Capstone Press of Coughlan Cos.

Payno, Manuel. Los Bandidos de Rio Frio. Camacho, Ricardo, illus. 2003. (SPA.). 91p. (J). pap. *(978-970-643-638-2(3))* Selector, S.A. de C.V. MEX. Dist: Lectorum Pubns., Inc.

Pegis, Jessica. Why Do We Need Rules & Laws? 2016. (Citizenship in Action Ser.). (ENG., Illus.). 24p. (J). (gr. 1-4). *(978-0-7787-2598-5(7))* Crabtree Publishing Co.

Peppas, Lynn. Workers' Rights. 2016. (Uncovering the Past: Analyzing Primary Sources Ser.). (ENG.). 48p. (J). (gr. 5-8). *(978-0-7787-2861-0(7))* Crabtree Publishing Co.

Porterfield, Jason. File Sharing: Rights & Risks. 2014. (Digital & Information Literacy Ser.). (Illus.). 48p. (J). (gr. 5-8). pap. 11.75 *(978-1-4777-7641-4(9),* Rosen Reference) Rosen Publishing Group, Inc., The.

Rabbat, Suzy. Citing Sources: Learning to Use the Copyright Page. 2013. (Explorer Junior Library: Information Explorer Junior Ser.). (ENG.). 24p. (gr. 1-4). 28.50 *(978-1-62431-023-2(0),* 202543); pap. 12.79 *(978-1-62431-047-8(8),* 202545) Cherry Lake Publishing.

Reid, David. The Honorable Fido Lincoln, Judge Teaches Property Law. 2014. (ENG.). 15.99 *(978-1-4951-0555-5(5))* Independent Pub.

Rodgers, Emily Puckett & Fontichiaro, Kristin. Creative Commons. 2013. (Explorer Library: Information Explorer Ser.). (ENG.). 32p. (J). (gr. 4-8). 28.50 *(978-1-62431-020-1(6),* 202531); pap. 14.21 *(978-1-62431-044-7(3),* 202533) Cherry Lake Publishing.

Schauer, Peter J. What You Need to Know about Violent Crimes, Felonies, & the Law, 1 vol. 2015. (ENG., Illus.). 64p. (J). 33.25 *(978-1-4777-8024-4(6),* Rosen Reference) Rosen Publishing Group, Inc., The.

Shea, Therese. What Are Community Rules & Laws? 2017. (Let's Find Out! Communities Ser.). 32p. (gr. 6-8). pap. 12.90 ***(978-1-68048-721-3(3),*** Britannica Educational Publishing) Rosen Publishing Group, Inc., The.

Trembinski, Donna. Medieval Law & Punishment. 2005. (Medieval World Ser.). (ENG., Illus.). 32p. (J). (gr. 5-9). lib. bdg. *(978-0-7787-1360-9(1))* Crabtree Publishing Co.

—Medieval Laws & Punishment. 2005. (Medieval World Ser.). (ENG., Illus.). 32p. (J). (gr. 5-9). pap. *(978-0-7787-1392-0(X))* Crabtree Publishing Co.

Zarate, Gustavo Azgad. Youth Law: A Practical Guide to Legal Issues That Affect Young Adults. 2nd ed. 2005. (YA). per. 25.00 *(978-0-9763167-9-4(X))* Living Ministry, Inc.

LAW, CONSTITUTIONAL

see Constitutional Law

LAW, INTERNATIONAL

see International Law

LAW—UNITED STATES

Axelrod-Contrada, Joan. Reno V. ACLU Internet Censorship. 2006. (Supreme Court Milestones Ser.). (Illus.). 128p. (gr. 7-7). lib. bdg. 42.79 *(978-0-7614-2144-3(0),* Benchmark Bks.) Marshall Cavendish Corp.

bjornlund, lydia. Marijuana. 2011. (Compact Research Ser.). 96p. (YA). (gr. 7-12). lib. bdg. 27.95 *(978-1-60152-160-6(X))* ReferencePoint Pr., Inc.

Bodden, Valerie. Environmental Law. 2010. (Earth Issues Ser.). 48p. (YA). (gr. 5-18). 23.95 *(978-1-58341-981-6(0),* Creative Education) Creative Co., The.

Bright-Moore, Susan & Bedesky, Baron. How Is a Law Passed? 2008. (Your Guide to Government Ser.). (ENG., Illus.). 32p. (J). (gr. k-5). pap. *(978-0-7787-4331-6(4))* Crabtree Publishing Co.

Burns, Kate & Sharp, Anne Wallace. The Right to Die. 2009. (Hot Topics Ser.). (ENG., Illus.). 128p. (YA). (gr. 7-12). lib. bdg. 33.95 *(978-1-59018-834-7(9),* LML02109-225086) Cengage Gale.

Byers, Ann. Immigration: Interpreting the Constitution. 2014. (Understanding the United States Constitution Ser.). 112p. (YA). (gr. 7-12). 35.60 *(978-1-4777-7512-7(9))* Rosen Publishing Group, Inc., The.

Castle, Caroline. For Every Child: The UN Convention on the Rights of the Child in Words & Pictures. 2004. (J). (gr. k-3). spiral bd. *(978-0-616-14617-0(5))*; spiral bd. *(978-0-616-14618-7(3))* Canadian National Institute for the Blind/Institut National Canadien pour les Aveugles.

Cefrey, Holly. The Interstate Commerce ACT: The Government Takes Control of Trade Between the States. 2004. (America's Industrial Society in the 19th Century Ser.). (ENG., Illus.). 32p. (gr. 5-8). pap. 10.00 *(978-0-8239-4282-4(1))* Rosen Publishing Group, Inc., The.

Cohen, Laura. The Gault Case & Young People's Rights: Debating Supreme Court Decisions. 2006. (Debating Supreme Court Decisions Ser.). (Illus.). 128p. (J). (gr. 7-12). lib. bdg. 27.94 *(978-0-7660-2476-2(8))* Enslow Pubs., Inc.

Crompton, Samuel Willard. McCulloch V. Maryland: Implied Powers of the Federal Government. 2007. (Great Supreme Court Decisions Ser.). (Illus.). 136p. (YA). (gr. 5-9). lib. bdg. 32.95 *(978-0-7910-9262-0(3))* Facts On File, Inc.

De Capua, Sarah. Making a Law. 2004. (True Bks.). (ENG., Illus.). 48p. (J). (gr. 3-5). pap. 6.95 *(978-0-516-27941-1(6),* Children's Pr.) Scholastic Library Publishing.

Donovan, Sandy. Making Laws: A Look at How a Bill Becomes a Law. 2004. (How Government Works Ser.). (Illus.). 56p. (J). (gr. 4-8). lib. bdg. 25.26 *(978-0-8225-1346-9(3))* Lerner Publishing Group.

Egan, Tracie. How a Bill Becomes a Law. 2009. (Primary Source Library of American Citizenship Ser.). 32p. (gr. 5-5). 47.90 *(978-1-61511-219-7(7),* Rosen Reference) Rosen Publishing Group, Inc., The.

Election Reform. 2nd rev. ed. 2010. (Point/Counterpoint Ser.). (Illus.). 128p. (C). (gr. 9). 35.00 *(978-1-60413-691-3(X),* Chelsea Hse.) Facts On File, Inc.

Engdahl, Sylvia. Medical Rights. 2008. (Issues on Trial Ser.). (ENG., Illus.). 240p. (gr. 10-12). 48.30 *(978-0-7377-4179-7(1),* Greenhaven Pr., Inc.) Cengage Gale.

Freedman, Jeri. Intellectual Property. 2008. (Cyber Citizenship & Cyber Safety Ser.). (Illus.). 48p. (YA). (gr. 5-9). lib. bdg. 29.25 *(978-1-4042-1348-7(1))* Rosen Publishing Group, Inc., The.

Friedman, Lauri S. The Patriot Act. 2008. (Introducing Issues with Opposing Viewpoints Ser.). (ENG., Illus.). 144p. (YA). (gr. 7-10). 36.95 *(978-0-7377-4172-8(4),* Greenhaven Pr., Inc.) Cengage Gale.

Gold, Susan Dudley. Saluting the Flag: West Virginia State Board of Education V. Barnette. 2012. (J). 42.79 *(978-1-60870-911-3(6))* Marshall Cavendish Corp.

Gordon, Sherri Mabry. Downloading Copyrighted Stuff from the Internet: Stealing or Fair Use? 2005. (Issues in Focus Today Ser.). (Illus.). 104p. (J). (gr. 6-12). lib. bdg. 33.27 *(978-0-7660-2164-8(5))* Enslow Pubs., Inc.

Gorman, Jacqueline Laks. ¿Por Qué Tenemos leyes? 2008. (Conoce tu gobierno (Know Your Government) Ser.). (SPA., Illus.). 24p. (gr. 1-4). lib. bdg. 22.00 *(978-0-8368-8853-9(7),* Weekly Reader Leveled Readers) Stevens, Gareth Publishing LLLP.

—Why Do We Have Laws? 2008. (Know Your Government Ser.). (Illus.). 24p. (gr. 1-4). pap. 8.15 *(978-0-8368-8848-5(0))*; lib. bdg. 22.00 *(978-0-8368-8843-0(X))* Stevens, Gareth Publishing LLLP. (Weekly Reader Leveled Readers).

Gorman, Jacqueline Laks, et al. Apor Qu Tenemos Leyes? 2008. (Conoce tu gobierno (Know Your Government) Ser.). (SPA., Illus.). 24p. (gr. 1-4). pap. 8.15 *(978-0-8368-8858-4(8),* Weekly Reader Leveled Readers) Stevens, Gareth Publishing LLLP.

Gunderson, Jessica Sarah. The Triangle Shirtwaist Factory Fire. Miller, Phil & Barnett, Charles, III, illus. 2006. (Disasters in History Ser.). (ENG.). 32p. (J). (gr. 3-4). per. 8.10 *(978-0-7368-6878-5(X),* Graphic Library) Capstone Press of Coughlan Cos.

Hanrahan, Clare. Legal System. 2007. (Opposing Viewpoints Ser.). (ENG., Illus.). 237p. (YA). (gr. 10-12). pap. 29.45 *(978-0-7377-3758-5(1),* LML02109-234418, Greenhaven Pr., Inc.) Cengage Gale.

Hanrahan, Clare M. Legal System. Hanrahan, Clare, ed. 2007. (Opposing Viewpoints Ser.). (ENG., Illus.). 224p. (gr. 10-12). 48.80 *(978-0-7377-3757-8(3),* LML02109-234427, Greenhaven Pr., Inc.) Cengage Gale.

Haugen, David M. Criminal Justice. 2008. (Opposing Viewpoints Ser.). (ENG., Illus.). 240p. (YA). (gr. 10-12). 29.45 *(978-0-7377-4199-5(6),* LML02109-243131); lib. bdg. 42.95 *(978-0-7377-4198-8(8),* LML02109-243098) Cengage Gale. (Greenhaven Pr., Inc.).

Howell, Sara. Immigrants' Rights, Citizens' Rights. 2014. (American Mosaic: Immigration Today Ser.). 24p. (J). (gr. 3-6). pap. 49.50 *(978-1-4777-6647-7(2),* PowerKids Pr.) Rosen Publishing Group, Inc., The.

—Los Derechos de Los Inmigrantes, Los Derechos de Los Ciudadanos. 2014. (Mosaico Americano: la Inmigración Hoy en día (the American Mosaic: Immigration Today) Ser.). (SPA., Illus.). 24p. (J). (gr. 3-6). lib. bdg. 23.60 *(978-1-4777-6819-8(X),* PowerKids Pr.) Rosen Publishing Group, Inc., The.

Jacobs, Thomas A. & Jacobs, Natalie. Every Vote Matters: The Power of Your Voice, from Student Elections to the Supreme Court. 2016. lib. bdg. 28.15 *(978-0-606-37931-1(2))* Turtleback Bks.

Jacobs, Tom & Jacobs, Natalie. Every Vote Matters: The Power of Your Voice, from Student Elections to the Supreme Court. 2016. (Teens & the Law Ser.). (ENG.). 208p. (gr. 8-12). pap. 15.99 *(978-1-63198-069-5(6))* Free Spirit Publishing, Inc.

Jones, Phill. Disability Rights. 2012. (J). *(978-1-61753-042-5(5),* Chelsea Hse.) Facts On File, Inc.

Kishel, Ann-Marie. Rules & Laws. 2007. (First Step Nonfiction Ser.). (Illus.). 23p. (J). (gr. 3-7). lib. bdg. 18.60 *(978-0-8225-6396-9(7),* Lerner Pubns.) Lerner Publishing Group.

Kowalski, Kathiann M. Judges & Courts: A Look at the Judicial Branch. 2012. (Searchlight Books How Does Government Work Ser.). (ENG., Illus.). 40p. (gr. 3-5). lib. bdg. 27.93 *(978-0-7613-6516-7(8))* Lerner Publishing Group.

Law. 2010. (Career Launcher Ser.). 160p. (C). (gr. 9-18). 34.95 *(978-0-8160-7970-4(6),* Ferguson Publishing Co.); pap. 14.95 *(978-0-8160-7992-6(7),* Checkmark Bks.) Facts On File, Inc.

Lawrence, Katherine. Labor Legislation: The Struggle to Gain Rights for America's Workforce. 2004. (Progressive Movement, 1900-1920 Ser.). (Illus.). 32p. (YA). (gr. 5-9). lib. bdg. 22.50 *(978-1-4042-0191-0(2))* Rosen Publishing Group, Inc., The.

Libal, Joyce. A House Between Homes: Youth in the Foster Care System. 2003. (Youth with Special Needs Ser.). (Illus.). 127p. (YA). pap. 14.95 *(978-1-4222-0419-1(7))* Mason Crest.

The Library of American Laws & Legal Principles. (Illus.). (YA). (gr. 5-8). 143.70 *(978-1-4042-0621-2(3),* Rosen Reference) Rosen Publishing Group, Inc., The.

Lieurance, Suzanne. The Triangle Shirtwaist Fire & Sweatshop Reform in American History. 2003. (In American History Ser.). (Illus.). 128p. (J). (gr. 5-12). lib. bdg. 27.94 *(978-0-7660-1839-6(3))* Enslow Pubs., Inc.

Marsh, Carole. Georgia Law: Make It, Don't Break It! (HC) Make It, Don't Break It! (HC) 2004. 28p. 29.95 *(978-0-635-02687-3(2))* Gallopade International.

—Georgia Law: Make It, Don't Break It! (PB) Make It, Don't Break It! (PB) 2004. 28p. pap. 5.95 *(978-0-635-02686-6(4))* Gallopade International.

Marzilli, Alan, ed. Point/Counterpoint: Issues in Contemporary American Society. (Illus.). (gr. 9-13). pap. *(978-0-7910-8046-7(3))*; lib. bdg. 519.00 *(978-0-7910-8468-7(X))* Facts On File, Inc. (Chelsea Hse.).

Morgan, J. Tom. Ignorance Is No Defense: A Teenager's Guide to Georgia Law. 2007. (Illus.). 212p. (YA). pap. 15.00 *(978-0-9796625-1-5(6))* GDG Publishing.

New, David W. The Ten Commandments for Beginners. 2004. 60p. (YA). per. 4.95 *(978-0-9721333-4-0(8))* Pocket Pubn., A.

Noble, William. Presidential Power on Trial: From Watergate to All the President's Men. 2009. (Famous Court Cases That Became Movies Ser.). (Illus.). 128p. (J). (gr. 7-12). lib. bdg. 33.27 *(978-0-7660-3058-9(X))* Enslow Pubs., Inc.

Orr, Tamra. Careers in the Courts. 2009. (Careers in Criminal Justice Ser.). (ENG., Illus.). 112p. (J). lib. bdg. 34.60 *(978-1-4358-5265-5(6))* Rosen Publishing Group, Inc., The.

Pierce, Alan. Brown vs the Board of Education, 1 vol. 2005. (American Moments Set Ii Ser.). (ENG.). 48p. (gr. 4-8). 27.07 *(978-1-59197-725-4(8),* Abdo & Daughters) ABDO Publishing Co.

Product Liability. 2010. (Point/Counterpoint Ser.). (Illus.). 152p. (C). (gr. 9-18). 35.00 *(978-1-60413-509-1(3),* Chelsea Hse.) Facts On File, Inc.

Riley, Gail Blasser. And Justice for All. 2003. (Illus.). 60p. (J). 11.60 net. *(978-0-7398-5175-3(6))* Steck-Vaughn.

Ripley, Ellen. What Are Rules & Laws? 2012. (I'm an American Citizen Ser.). (ENG., Illus.). 24p. (J). (gr. 1-3). 22.60 *(978-1-4488-8585-5(X),* PowerKids Pr.) Rosen Publishing Group, Inc., The.

Rodger, Ellen. What Is the Judicial Branch? 2013. (ENG.). 32p. (J). *(978-0-7787-0880-3(2))*; pap. *(978-0-7787-0906-0(X))* Crabtree Publishing Co.

Roensch, Greg. Furman V. Georgia: Cruel & Unusual Punishment. 2007. (Great Supreme Court Decisions Ser.). (Illus.). 112p. (YA). (gr. 5-9). lib. bdg. 32.95 *(978-0-7910-9382-5(4))* Facts On File, Inc.

Roland, James. Ruth Bader Ginsburg: Iconic Supreme Court Justice. 2016. (Gateway Biographies Ser.). (ENG., Illus.). 48p. (J). (gr. 4-8). 26.65 *(978-1-5124-0596-5(5))*; 39.99 *(978-1-5124-0597-2(3))* Lerner Publishing Group. (Lerner Pubns.).

J
K
L

Scheppler, Bill. How a Law Is Passed. 2007. (U. S. Government Ser.). (Illus.). 103p. (YA). (gr. 5-9). lib. bdg. 30.00 (978-0-7910-9466-2(9)) Facts On File, Inc.

Suen, Anastasia. The U. S. Supreme Court, 1 vol. Skeens, Matthew, illus. 2008. (American Symbols Ser.). (ENG.). 24p. (gr. 1-2). 26.65 (978-1-4048-4707-1(3)) Picture Window Bks.

Supreme Court Milestones - Group 5, 5 bks., Set. Incl. Plessy v. Ferguson: Separate but Unequal. Axelrod-Contrada, Joan. lib. bdg. 42.79 (978-0-7614-2951-7(4)); Roberts v. Jaycees: Women's Rights. Gold, Susan Dudley. lib. bdg. 42.79 (978-0-7614-2952-4(2)); U. S. v. Eichman: Flag-Burning & Free Speech. Fridell, Ron. lib. bdg. 42.79 (978-0-7614-2953-1(0)); U. S. v. Nixon: The Limits of Presidential Privilege. Stefoff, Rebecca. lib. bdg. 42.79 (978-0-7614-2955-5(7)); Worcester v. Georgia: Native American Rights. Gold, Susan Dudley. lib. bdg. 42.79 (978-0-7614-2956-2(5)); 128p. (gr. 7-18). (Supreme Court Milestones 5 Ser.). 2008. Set lib. bdg. 213.95 (978-0-7614-2949-4(2), Benchmark Bks.) Marshall Cavendish Corp.

Swain, Gwenyth. Dred & Harriet Scott: A Family's Struggle for Freedom. 2004. (ENG., Illus.). 112p. (J). 22.95 (978-0-87351-482-8(3)); pap. 14.95 (978-0-87351-483-5(1)) Minnesota Historical Society Pr. (Borealis Bk.).

Swann, Kristina. US Law - Student Text. 2005. (Illus.). 48p. (YA). 11.95 (978-1-58804-397-9(5)) P C I Education.

Taylor, Chad. The United States Has Rules & Laws. 2016. (Rosen REAL Readers: Social Studies Nonfiction / Fiction: Family, Community, & the World Ser.). 12p. (gr. 1-k). pap. 6.33 (978-1-5081-2329-3(2), Rosen Classroom) Rosen Publishing Group, Inc., The.

Troisi-Paton, Kimberly, ed. The Right to Due Process. 2005. (Bill of Rights Ser.). (ENG.). 138p. (YA). (gr. 9-12). lib. bdg. 37.90 (978-0-7377-1941-3(9)) Cengage Gale.

Walker, Ida. William Blackstone & Commentaries upon the Laws of England. 2016. (J). lib. bdg. (978-1-68048-552-3(0)) Rosen Publishing Group, Inc., The.

Whelan, Elaine P., narrated by. My Mom's Making History: The Story of Computer Software, Copyrights & Creativity, 1. 2nd ed. 2003. 80p. (J). per. 12.99 (978-0-9726871-0-2(6)) Mainstreet Systems & Software Inc.

Wilberforce, Bertram. Why We Need Laws. 2009. (Real Life Readers Ser.). 24p. (gr. 3-4). pap. 8.25 (978-1-4358-0135-6(0), Rosen Classroom); 42.50 (978-1-61512-342-1(3), PowerKids Pr.); (J). lib. bdg. 22.60 (978-1-4358-2977-0(8), PowerKids Pr.) Rosen Publishing Group, Inc., The.

Wittekind, Erika & Gerhardt, Michael J. The United States v. Nixon: The Watergate Scandal & Limits to Us Presidential Power, 1 vol. 2012. (Landmark Supreme Court Cases Ser.). (ENG., Illus.). 160p. (J). (gr. 6-12). 37.07 (978-1-61783-478-3(5)) ABDO Publishing Co.

Worth, Richard. Sherman Antitrust ACT. 2011. (Landmark Legislation 2 Ser.). (Illus.). 128p. (J). (gr. 7). 39.93 (978-1-60870-487-3(4)) Marshall Cavendish Corp.

Wroble, Lisa A. The Right to Counsel: From Gideon V. Wainwright to Gideon's Trumpet. 2009. (Famous Court Cases That Became Movies Ser.). (Illus.). 104p. (J). (gr. 7-12). lib. bdg. 33.27 (978-0-7660-3057-2(1)) Enslow Pubs., Inc.

LAW—VOCATIONAL GUIDANCE

Ferguson. Law. 3rd rev. ed. 2009. (Careers in Focus Ser.). 208p. (gr. 6-12). 32.95 (978-0-8160-7299-6(X), Ferguson Publishing Co.) Facts On File, Inc.

Furgang, Kathy. Getting a Job in the Legal Profession. 2016. (Job Basics: Getting the Job You Need Ser.). 80p. (J). (gr. 8-8). 35.75 (978-1-4777-8562-1(0)) Rosen Publishing Group, Inc., The.

Hayhurst, Chris. Jobs in Environmental Law. 2010. (Green Careers Ser.). 80p. (YA). (gr. 7-12). E-Book 61.20 (978-1-4488-0133-6(8)) Rosen Publishing Group, Inc., The.

Law. 2010. (Career Launcher Ser.). 160p. (C). (gr. 9-18). 34.95 (978-0-8160-7970-4(6), Ferguson Publishing Co.); 160p. (C). (gr. 9-18). pap. 14.95 (978-0-8160-7992-6(7), Checkmark Bks.); 208p. (gr. 6-12). 32.95 (978-0-8160-8074-8(7), Ferguson Publishing Co.) Facts On File, Inc.

Orr, Tamra. Careers in the Courts. 2009. (Careers in Criminal Justice Ser.). (ENG., Illus.). 112p. (J). lib. bdg. 34.60 (978-1-4358-5265-5(6)) Rosen Publishing Group, Inc., The.

Reeves, Diane Lindsey. Career Ideas for Teens in Law & Public Safety. 2006. (Career Ideas for Teens Ser.). (Illus.). 192p. (gr. 8-12). per. 16.95 (978-0-8160-6922-4(0), Checkmark Bks.) Facts On File, Inc.

Sterngass, Jon. Great Careers with a High School Diploma: Public Safety, Law, & Security. 2008. (Great Careers with a High School Diploma Ser.). 114p. (C). (gr. 9). 32.95 (978-0-8160-7049-7(0), Ferguson Publishing Co.) Facts On File, Inc.

LAW ENFORCEMENT

see also Police

Behnke, Alison Marie. Racial Profiling. 2017. (ENG., Illus.). 160p. (J). (gr. 8-12). 35.99 (978-1-5124-0268-1(0), Twenty-First Century Bks.) Lerner Publishing Group.

Behnke, Alison Marie. Racial Profiling: Everyday Inequality. 2017. (Nonfiction — Young Adult Ser.). (ENG.). 160p. (YA). (gr. 8-12). 19.99 **(978-1-5124-3920-5(7))**; 53.32 **(978-1-5124-3921-2(5))**; (Illus.). 53.32 **(978-1-5124-2851-3(5))** Lerner Publishing Group. (Twenty-First Century Bks.).

Blackwell, Amy Hackney. Law Enforcement & Public Safety. 2011. (Career Launcher Ser.). (Illus.). 144p. (C). (gr. 9). 34.95 (978-0-8160-7956-8(0), Ferguson Publishing Co.) Facts On File, Inc.

Butts, Edward. Behind the Badge: Crimefighters Thorough History. Williams, Gareth Glyn, illus. 2014. (ENG.). 168p. (J). (gr. 5-8). pap. 14.95 (978-1-55451-674-2(9), 9781554516742) Annick Pr., Ltd. CAN. Dist: Publishers Group West (PGW).

Chrismer, Melanie. Lone Star Legacy: The Texas Rangers Then & Now, 1 vol. 2016. (ENG., Illus.). 144p. (J). (gr. 4-7). pap. 16.95 (978-1-4556-2104-0(8)) Pelican Publishing Co., Inc.

Eggleton, Jill. The Eye of the Law. 2007. (Connectors Ser.). (gr. 2-5). pap. (978-1-877453-14-4(5)) Global Education Systems Ltd.

Emert, Phyllis Raybin. Attorneys General: Enforcing the Law. 2005. (In the Cabinet Ser.). (Illus.). 176p. (J). (gr. 7-18). lib. bdg. 24.95 (978-1-881508-66-3(8)) Oliver Pr., Inc.

Extreme Law Enforcement. 2013. (Extreme Law Enforcement Ser.). 112p. (YA). (gr. 7-12). 207.60 (978-1-4777-1720-2(X)) Rosen Publishing Group, Inc., The.

Green, Carl R. & Sanford, William R. Wild Bill Hickok. rev. ed. 2008. (Outlaws & Lawmen of the Wild West, Revised Edition Ser.). (Illus.). 48p. (J). (gr. 5-18). lib. bdg. 25.27 (978-0-7660-3177-7(2)) Enslow Pubs., Inc.

Hahn, Kathy. Racial Profiling. 2010. (At Issue Ser.). (ENG.). 128p. pap. 24.45 (978-0-7377-5094-2(4)); (gr. 10-12). 39.40 (978-0-7377-5093-5(6)) Cengage Gale. (Greenhaven Pr., Inc.).

Hand, Carol. Using Computer Science in High Tech Criminal Justice Careers. 2017. (Coding Your Passion Ser.). 80p. (J). (gr. 12-12). 35.75 **(978-1-5081-7511-7(X)**, Rosen Young Adult) Rosen Publishing Group, Inc., The.

Kamberg, Mary-Lane. Getting a Job in Law Enforcement, Security, & Corrections. 2013. 80p. (YA). (gr. 9-12). 33.25 (978-1-4488-9605-9(3)) Rosen Publishing Group, Inc., The.

Karlitz, Gail. Virtual Apprentice: FBI Agent. 2009. (Virtual Apprentice Ser.). 64p. (gr. 4-9). pap. 9.95 (978-0-8160-7894-3(7), Checkmark Bks.) Facts On File, Inc.

La Bella, Laura. Drones & Law Enforcement. 2016. (Inside the World of Drones Ser.). 00064p. (J). (gr. 7-7). 34.45 (978-1-5081-7343-4(5), Rosen Young Adult) Rosen Publishing Group, Inc., The.

Lansford, Tom. Justice, Policing, & the Rule of Law, Vol. 8. Lansford, Tom, ed. 2016. (Foundations of Democracy Ser.). (Illus.). 64p. (J). (gr. 7). 23.95 (978-1-4222-3630-7(7)) Mason Crest.

Lindeen, Mary. Law Enforcement Robots. 2017. (Cutting-Edge Robotics Ser.). (ENG.). 32p. (J). (gr. 3-6). 27.99 **(978-1-5124-4011-9(6))** Lerner Publishing Group.

Mara, Wil. FBI Special Agent. 2015. (21st Century Skills Library: Cool STEAM Careers Ser.). (ENG., Illus.). 32p. (J). (gr. 4-7). pap. 14.21 (978-1-63362-648-5(2), 1391909) Cherry Lake Publishing.

Marcovitz, Harold. Privacy Rights & the Patriot Act, 1 vol. 2008. (Essential Viewpoints Set 2 Ser.). (ENG., Illus.). 112p. (J). (gr. 6-12). lib. bdg. 35.64 (978-1-60453-059-9(6)) ABDO Publishing Co.

Meyer, Jared. Homeland Security Officers. 2009. (Extreme Careers Ser.). 64p. (gr. 5-5). 58.50 (978-1-61512-398-8(9), Rosen Reference) Rosen Publishing Group, Inc., The.

Murley, Leon. Working the Case: Law Enforcement, Police Work, & Police Organizations. 2016. (Law Enforcement & Intelligence Gathering Ser.). 00104p. (YA). (gr. 8-8). lib. bdg. 36.25 (978-1-5081-0380-6(1), Britannica Educational Publishing) Rosen Publishing Group, Inc., The.

Newcomb, Tim. FBI Agent, Vol. 12. 2015. (On a Mission Ser.). 48p. (J). (gr. 5). 20.95 (978-1-4222-3394-8(4)) Mason Crest.

Orr, Tamra. Racial Profiling, 1 vol. 2009. (Essential Viewpoints Set 4 Ser.). (ENG., Illus.). 112p. (J). (gr. 6-12). lib. bdg. 35.64 (978-1-60453-535-8(0)) ABDO Publishing Co.

Savage, Jeff. Quick-Draw Gunfighters: True Tales of the Wild West. 2012. (True Tales of the Wild West Ser.). (Illus.). 48p. (J). (gr. 5-18). pap. 8.95 (978-1-4644-0029-2(6)) Enslow Pubs., Inc.

Thomas, William David & Thomas, William David. Working in Law Enforcement. 2005. (My Future Career Ser.). 64p. (gr. 3-7). lib. bdg. 27.00 (978-0-8368-4775-8(X), Gareth Stevens Learning Library) Stevens, Gareth Publishing LLLP.

Woog, Adam. Careers in State, County, & City Police Forces. 2014. (Illus.). 96p. (J). (978-1-62712-425-6(X)) Cavendish Square Publishing.

—Careers in the ATF. 2014. 96p. 39.92 (978-1-62712-428-7(4)) Cavendish Square Publishing.

—Careers in the ATF. 2012. (J). 34.21 (978-1-60870-956-4(6)) Marshall Cavendish Corp.

—Careers in the Secret Service. 2014. 96p. 39.92 (978-1-62712-434-8(9)) Cavendish Square Publishing.

Worth, Richard. Los Angeles Police Department. 2011. (Law Enforcement Agencies Ser.). (Illus.). 128p. (J). (gr. 6-12). 35.00 (978-1-60413-656-2(1), Chelsea Hse.) Facts On File, Inc.

Wyatt Earp. 2010. (Legends of the Wild West Ser.). (Illus.). 112p. (gr. 6-12). 35.00 (978-1-60413-597-8(2), Chelsea Hse.) Facts On File, Inc.

LAW ENFORCEMENT—VOCATIONAL GUIDANCE

FBI Agent. 2009. (Virtual Apprentice Ser.). 64p. (gr. 4-9). 29.95 (978-0-8160-6758-9(9), Ferguson Publishing Co.) Facts On File, Inc.

Ferguson, creator. Public Safety. 3rd rev. ed. 2007. (Careers in Focus Ser.). (Illus.). 224p. (gr. 6-12). 32.95 (978-0-8160-6594-3(2), Ferguson Publishing Co.) Facts On File, Inc.

Harmon, Daniel E. Working As a Law Enforcement Officer in Your Community. 2015. (Careers in Your Community Ser.). (ENG., Illus.). 80p. (J). (gr. 7-8). 34.25 (978-1-4994-6115-2(1), Rosen Young Adult) Rosen Publishing Group, Inc., The.

Larson, Kirsten W. Federal Air Marshals. 2016. (Protecting Our People Ser.). (ENG., Illus.). 32p. (J). (gr. 1-4). 20.95 (978-1-60753-984-1(5)) Amicus Publishing.

Meyer, Jared. Homeland Security Officers. 2007. (Extreme Careers Ser.). (Illus.). 64p. (J). (gr. 3-7). lib. bdg. 31.95 (978-1-4042-0945-9(X)) Rosen Publishing Group, Inc., The.

Porterfield, Jason. Careers in Undercover Gang Investigation. 2013. (Extreme Law Enforcement Ser.). 112p. (YA). (gr. 7-12). 34.60 (978-1-4777-1712-7(9)) Rosen Publishing Group, Inc., The.

Roby, Cynthia A. A Career As an Atf Agent. 2015. (Federal Forces: Careers As Federal Agents Ser.). (ENG.). 32p. (J). (gr. 4-5). pap. 10.00 (978-1-4994-1053-2(0), PowerKids Pr.) Rosen Publishing Group, Inc., The.

Rogers, Kate. Air Marshals, 01 vols., 1. 2016. (Careers for Heroes Ser.). (ENG., Illus.). 24p. (J). pap. 8.25 (978-1-5081-4387-1(0), PowerKids Pr.) Rosen Publishing Group, Inc., The.

Safety & Security. 2nd rev. ed. 2007. (What Can I Do Now? Ser.). 200p. (YA). (gr. 7-12). 32.95 (978-0-8160-6030-6(4)) Facts On File, Inc.

Sanna, Ellyn. Homeland Security Officer. Riggs, Ernestine G. & Gholar, Cheryl, eds. 2013. (Careers with Character Ser.: 18). 96p. (J). (gr. 7-18). 22.95 (978-1-4222-2757-2(X)) Mason Crest.

Suen, Anastasia. Careers with Swat Teams. 2013. (Extreme Law Enforcement Ser.). (Illus.). 112p. (J). (gr. 7-12). 34.60 (978-1-4777-1708-0(0)) Rosen Publishing Group, Inc., The.

Thomas, William David. How to Become an FBI Agent. 2009. (FBI Story Ser.). 64p. (J). (gr. 4-7). lib. bdg. 22.95 (978-1-4222-0571-6(1)) Mason Crest.

Uschan, Michael V. Careers in Law Enforcement. 2017. (ENG.). 80p. (J). (gr. 5-12). **(978-1-68282-106-0(4))** ReferencePoint Pr., Inc.

Watson, Stephanie. A Career as a Police Officer. 2010. (Essential Careers Ser.). (ENG.). 80p. (YA). lib. bdg. 33.25 (978-1-4358-9469-3(3)) Rosen Publishing Group, Inc., The.

Woog, Adam. Careers in the Secret Service. 2013. (J). 34.21 (978-1-60870-960-1(4)) Marshall Cavendish Corp.

LAW OF NATIONS

see International Law

LAWN TENNIS

see Tennis

LAWRENCE, T. E. (THOMAS EDWARD), 1888-1935

Jeffrey, Gary. Lawrence of Arabia & the Middle East & Africa. 2013. (ENG., Illus.). 48p. (J). (978-0-7787-0912-1(4)); pap. (978-0-7787-0918-3(3)) Crabtree Publishing Co.

LAWS

see Law

LAWYERS

see also Judges; Law—Vocational Guidance

Cooper, Ann Goode & Bowlin, William Harrison. Lawyer Will: The Story of an Appalachian Lawyer. Jessee, Diana, illus. 2004. 36p. (J). 12.95 (978-1-887905-90-9(1)) Parkway Pubs., Inc.

Edwards, Roberta. Michelle Obama: Primera Dama y Primera Mama. Call, Ken, illus. 2010. (SPA.). 48p. (gr. 3-5). pap. 9.99 (978-1-60396-946-8(2)) Santillana USA Publishing Co., Inc.

Emert, Phyllis Raybin. Attorneys General: Enforcing the Law. 2005. (In the Cabinet Ser.). (Illus.). 176p. (J). (gr. 7-18). lib. bdg. 24.95 (978-1-881508-66-3(8)) Oliver Pr., Inc.

Gold, Susan Dudley. Engel V. Vitale: Prayer in the Schools. 2005. (Supreme Court Milestones Ser.). (Illus.). 160p. (J). (gr. 3-7). lib. bdg. (978-0-7614-1940-2(3), Benchmark Bks.) Marshall Cavendish Corp.

Harris, Nancy. What's the State Judicial Branch? 2016. (First Guide to Government Ser.). (ENG.). 32p. (gr. 1-3). pap. 8.29 (978-1-4846-3691-6(0), Heinemann First Library) Heinemann-Raintree.

Helfand, Lewis. Abraham Lincoln: From the Log Cabin to the White House - Campfire Heroes Line. Jones, K. L. & Manikandan, illus. 2013. (Campfire Graphic Novels Ser.). (ENG.). 108p. (YA). (gr. 5-12). pap. 12.99 (978-93-80741-21-5(9), Campfire) Steerforth Pr.

Horn, Geoffrey M. Thurgood Marshall. 2004. (Trailblazers of the Modern World Ser.). (Illus.). 48p. (gr. 5-12). pap. 14.05 (978-0-8368-5258-5(3)); lib. bdg. 31.00 (978-0-8368-5098-7(X)) Stevens, Gareth Publishing LLLP. (Gareth Stevens Secondary Library).

Lucas, Eileen. Mahatma Gandhi: Fighting for Indian Independence. 2017. (Rebels with a Cause Ser.). 128p. (J). (gr. 8-8). lib. bdg. 37.27 **(978-0-7660-8513-8(9))** Enslow Pubs., Inc.

Machajewski, Sarah. Michelle Obama. 2016. (Superwomen Role Models Ser.). (Illus.). 32p. (J). (gr. 4-3). 26.25 (978-1-5081-4812-8(0), PowerKids Pr.) Rosen Publishing Group, Inc., The.

Mara, Wil. Thurgood Marshall: Champion for Civil Rights. 2004. (Great Life Stories Ser.). (ENG., Illus.). 125p. (J). 30.50 (978-0-531-12058-3(9), Watts, Franklin) Scholastic Library Publishing.

Marcovitz, Hal. Michelle. 2007. (Obamas Ser.). 64p. (YA). (gr. 3-6). pap. 9.95 (978-1-4222-1485-5(0)); (gr. 4-7). lib. bdg. 19.95 (978-1-4222-1478-7(8)) Mason Crest.

Mattern, Joanne. What's So Great about Michelle Obama. 2009. (What's So Great About... ? Ser.). 32p. (J). (gr. 2-4). lib. bdg. 25.70 (978-1-58415-833-2(6)) Mitchell Lane Pubs., Inc.

Michelle Obama. 2009. (Political Profiles Ser.). 112p. (YA). (gr. 5-9). lib. bdg. 28.95 (978-1-59935-090-5(4)) Reynolds, Morgan Inc.

Nault, Jennifer. Michelle Obama. 2009. (Remarkable People Ser.). (Illus.). 24p. (J). (gr. 4-6). pap. 8.95 (978-1-60596-666-3(5)); lib. bdg. 24.45 (978-1-60596-665-6(7)) Weigl Pubs., Inc.

Norgren, Jill. Belva Lockwood: The Woman Who Would Be President. 2007. (ENG., Illus.). 311p. 89.00 (978-0-8147-5834-2(7)) New York Univ. Pr.

Rohan, Rebecca Carey. Thurgood Marshall: The First African-American Supreme Court Justice. 2016. (Great American Thinkers Ser.). 128p. (J). (gr. 9-9). 45.64 (978-1-5026-1932-7(6)) Cavendish Square Publishing.

Weatherford, Carole Boston. Great African-American Lawyers: Raising the Bar of Freedom. 2003. (Collective Biographies Ser.). (Illus.). 112p. (J). (gr. 6-12). lib. bdg. 27.94 (978-0-7660-1837-2(7)) Enslow Pubs., Inc.

Wheeler, Jill C. Thurgood Marshall. 2003. (Breaking Barriers Ser.). 64p. (gr. 3-8). 27.07 (978-1-57765-907-5(4), Abdo & Daughters) ABDO Publishing Co.

LAWYERS—FICTION

Bauer, Joan. Backwater. 2005. 185p. 18.00 (978-0-7569-5779-7(6)) Perfection Learning Corp.

Clifford, Ross. The Shiddakovich Adventure. 2009. 122p. pap. 12.88 (978-1-4092-3520-0(3)) Lulu Pr., Inc.

Grippando, James. Leapholes. 2006. (ENG.). 176p. (YA). (gr. 8-17). 15.95 (978-1-59031-666-5(5)) American Bar Assn.

Grisham, John. The Abduction. 2009. (Theodore Boone Ser.: Bk. 2). 9.68 (978-0-7848-3783-2(X), Everbind) Marco Bk. Co.

—The Abduction, 2 vols. (Theodore Boone Ser.: 2). (ENG.). 256p. (J). (gr. 3-7). 2012. pap. 8.99 (978-0-14-242137-6(5), Puffin Books) 2011. 16.99 (978-0-525-42557-1(8), Dutton Books for Young Readers) Penguin Young Readers Group.

—The Abduction. 2012. (Theodore Boone Ser.: 2). lib. bdg. 19.65 (978-0-606-26079-4(X), Turtleback) Turtleback Bks.

—The Accused. (Theodore Boone Ser.: 3). (ENG.). (J). (gr. 3-7). 2013. 304p. pap. 8.99 (978-0-14-242613-5(X), Puffin Books) 2012. 288p. 16.99 (978-0-525-42576-2(4), Dutton Books for Young Readers) Penguin Young Readers Group.

—The Accused. 2013. (Theodore Boone Ser.: 3). lib. bdg. 18.40 (978-0-606-31696-5(5), Turtleback) Turtleback Bks.

—The Activist. 2014. (Theodore Boone Ser.: Bk. 4). (ENG.). 304p. (J). (gr. 4). pap. 8.99 (978-0-14-242309-7(2), Puffin Books) Penguin Publishing Group.

—The Activist. 2013. (Theodore Boone Ser.: Bk. 4). (ENG.). 272p. (J). (gr. 3-7). 16.99 (978-0-525-42577-9(2), Dutton Books for Young Readers) Penguin Young Readers Group.

—The Fugitive. 2015. (Theodore Boone Ser.: 5). (ENG.). 256p. (J). (gr. 3-7). 17.99 (978-0-525-42638-7(8), Dutton Books for Young Readers) Penguin Young Readers Group.

—The Fugitive. 2016. (Theodore Boone Ser.: 5). 272p. lib. bdg. 18.40 (978-0-606-38847-4(8)) Turtleback Bks.

—Kid Lawyer. (Theodore Boone Ser.: 1). (ENG.). (J). (gr. 3-7). 2011. 288p. 8.99 (978-0-14-241722-5(X), Puffin Books) 2010. 272p. 16.99 (978-0-525-42384-3(2), Dutton Books for Young Readers) Penguin Young Readers Group.

—Kid Lawyer. l.t. ed. 2010. (Theodore Boone Ser.: Bk. 1). (ENG.). 278p. (J). 24.99 (978-1-4104-3050-2(2)) Thorndike Pr.

—Kid Lawyer. 2011. (Theodore Boone Ser.: 1). lib. bdg. 19.65 (978-0-606-23071-1(8), Turtleback) Turtleback Bks.

—The Scandal. 2016. (Theodore Boone Ser.: 6). (ENG.). 224p. (J). (gr. 3-7). 17.99 (978-0-525-42639-4(6), Dutton Books for Young Readers) Penguin Young Readers Group.

—Theodore Boone Box Set, 5 vols. 2013. (Theodore Boone Ser.). (ENG.). 816p. (J). (gr. 3-7). 50.97 (978-0-525-42637-0(X), Dutton Books for Young Readers) Penguin Young Readers Group.

Henry, O. One Thousand Dollars & Other Plays, Level 2. Oxford University Press Staff & West, Clare, eds. 2nd ed. 2008. (ENG., Illus.). 64p. 9.38 (978-0-19-423520-4(3)) Oxford Univ. Pr., Inc.

Justice, Joseph. Lawyer's Week Before Christmas, 1 vol. Alikhan, Salima, illus. 2010. (Night Before Christmas Ser.). (ENG.). 32p. (J). (gr. 4-8). 16.99 (978-1-58980-739-6(1)) Pelican Publishing Co., Inc.

Margolin, Phillip & Rome, Ami Margolin. Vanishing Acts. 2012. (ENG.). 176p. (J). (gr. 3-7). pap. 8.99 (978-0-06-188558-7(4)) HarperCollins Pubs.

Patron, Susan. Behind the Masks: The Diary of Angeline Reddy - Bodie, California 1880. 2012. (Dear America Ser.). (ENG.). 304p. (J). (gr. 3-7). 12.99 (978-0-545-30437-5(7)) Scholastic, Inc.

RealBuzz Studios Staff. Hits & Misses, No. 3. 2007. 128p. (YA). pap. 4.97 (978-1-59789-571-2(7), Barbour Bks.) Barbour Publishing, Inc.

Segal, Howard. My Daddy the Lawyer: Mommy-Daddy Books. 2009. 16p. pap. 9.49 (978-1-4343-0883-2(9)) AuthorHouse.

Tricarico, Mark. Zoe Pope: Unlicensed Lawyer. 2007. 80p. per. 8.95 (978-0-595-46943-7(4)) iUniverse, Inc.

LAYOUT AND TYPOGRAPHY

see Printing

LEAD MINES AND MINING—FICTION

Long, Susan Hill. Whistle in the Dark. (ENG.). 192p. (J). 2014. (gr. 3-7). pap. 6.99 (978-0-8234-3191-5(6)) 2013. 16.95 (978-0-8234-2839-7(7)) Holiday Hse., Inc.

LEADERSHIP

Addington, Judith. A-Z Leader Alphabook. 2012. (ENG.). (J). spiral bd. 14.95 (978-1-4675-3105-4(7)) Independent Pub.

—Building Blocks for Leaders. 2012. (ENG.). (J). spiral bd. 19.95 (978-1-4675-3106-1(5)) Independent Pub.

Army JROTC: Leadership Education & Training, Cadet Reference. 2nd ed. 2003. (Illus.). vi, 56p. (J). (978-0-536-74189-9(1), Dept. of the Army) United States Government Printing Office.

Asgedom, Mawi. Win the Inner Battle: The Ultimate Teen Leadership Journal. Berger, Dave, ed. 2003. 96p. (YA). spiral bd. 14.00 (978-0-9743901-8-5(6)) Mawi, Inc.

Auster, Michael A. They Led the Way. 2005. (Yellow Umbrella Fluent Level Ser.). (ENG.). 16p. (gr. k-1). pap. 35.70 (978-0-7368-5315-6(4), Yellow Umbrella Bks.) Capstone Press of Coughlan Cos.

Baptiste, Tracey & Banas, Sharon L. Being a Leader & Making Decisions. 2009. (Character Education Ser.). (Illus.). 136p. (gr. 6-12). 35.00 (978-1-60413-125-3(X), Chelsea Hse.) Facts On File, Inc.

Barraclough, Sue. Liderazgo, 1 vol. 2010. (Explorar el Civismo Ser.). (SPA.). 32p. (gr. 1-3). 27.32 (978-1-4329-4461-2(4)); pap. 8.29 (978-1-4329-4469-8(X)) Heinemann-Raintree.

Be a Community Leader. 2014. (Be a Community Leader Ser.). 32p. (J). (gr. 4-6). pap. 60.00 (978-1-4777-7215-7(4), PowerKids Pr.) Rosen Publishing Group, Inc., The.

Boyd, Bentley. George Washington Leads the Way. 2011. (Mount Vernon Comix Ser.). (Illus.). 24p. (J). (gr. 3-9). pap. 6.95 (978-1-933122-44-1(7)) Chester Comix, LLC.

Chapman, Kelly. Princess with a Purpose. Lyon, Tammie, illus. ldr.'s ed. 2009. pap. 12.99 (978-0-7369-2743-7(3)) Harvest Hse. Pubs.

Chatlien, Ruth Hull. Modern American Indian Chiefs. 2009. (Sharing the American Dream Ser.). (Illus.). 64p. (YA). (gr. 7-12). 22.95 (978-1-4222-0592-1(4)) Mason Crest.

Drayton, Bill, frwd. Be a Changemaker: How to Start Something That Matters. 2014. (ENG., Illus.). 240p. (YA). (gr. 7). pap. 14.99 (978-1-58270-464-7(3)) Simon Pulse/Beyond Words.

Duignan, Brian, ed. The Britannica Guide to the World's Most Influential People (Print/eBook Combo Set), 8 vols., Set. Incl. 100 Most Influential Philosophers of All Time. 368p. (YA). (gr. 9-12). 2009. E-Book 106.00 (978-1-61530-072-3(4)); (Britannica Guide to the World's Most Influential People Ser.). 384p. 2009. Set E-Book 848.00 (978-1-61530-165-2(8)) Rosen Publishing Group, Inc., The.

Durrie, Karen. Diversión. 2012. (SPA.). (J). 27.13 (978-1-61913-209-2(5)) Weigl Pubs., Inc.

Freedman, Jeri. Being a Leader: Organizing & Inspiring a Group. 2011. (Communicating with Confidence Ser.). (ENG., Illus.). 80p. (YA). (gr. 7-12). pap. 14.15 (978-1-4488-5631-2(0)); lib. bdg. 33.25 (978-1-4488-5521-6(7)) Rosen Publishing Group, Inc., The.

—Step-By-Step Guide to Becoming a Leader at School & on the Job. 2014. (Winning at Work Readiness Ser.). 64p. (YA). (gr. 9-12). 32.95 (978-1-4777-7778-7(4)) Rosen Publishing Group, Inc., The.

Furstinger, Nancy. Women & Leadership. 2012. (Young Woman's Guide to Contemporary Issues Ser.). (ENG., Illus.).

112p. (YA). (gr. 9-12). lib. bdg. 34.60 *(978-1-4488-8402-5(0))* Rosen Publishing Group, Inc., The.

Gane, Declan. So You Want to Be Captain? Top Tips from Sporting Heroes. 2012. (ENG., Illus.). 96p. (J). 14.95 *(978-1-4081-3183-1(8)*, 9781408131831, Bloomsbury Sport) Bloomsbury Publishing USA.

Ganeri, Anita. The Top Ten Leaders That Changed the World. 2009. (J). 60.00 *(978-1-4358-9166-1(X)*, PowerKids Pr.); (ENG., Illus.). 32p. (J). pap. 10.00 *(978-1-4358-9165-4(1)*, PowerKids Pr.); (Illus.). 32p. (YA). (gr. 3-6). 26.50 *(978-1-4358-9164-7(3))* Rosen Publishing Group, Inc., The.

Gerety, Ed. Combinations: Opening the Door to Student Leadership. 2003. 160p. (YA). per. 14.95 *(978-0-9725938-3-0(7))* Whaleback Publishing.

Goddu, Krystyna Poray. George Washington's Presidency. 2016. (Presidential Powerhouses Ser.). (ENG., Illus.). 104p. (J). (gr. 6-12). 35.99 *(978-1-4677-7924-1(5))*; 53.32 *(978-1-4677-8598-3(9)*, Lerner Pubns.) Lerner Publishing Group.

Gorman, Jacqueline Laks. Quiénes Gobiernan Nuestro País? 2008. (Conoce tu gobierno (Know Your Government) Ser.). (SPA.). 24p. (gr. 1-4). pap. 8.15 *(978-0-8368-8856-0(1)*, Weekly Reader Leveled Readers) Stevens, Gareth Publishing LLLP.

—Quienes Gobieman Nuestro Pais? 2008. (Conoce tu gobierno (Know Your Government) Ser.). (SPA., Illus.). 24p. (gr. 1-4). lib. bdg. 22.00 *(978-0-8368-8851-5(0)*, Weekly Reader Leveled Readers) Stevens, Gareth Publishing LLLP.

—Who Leads Our Country? 2008. (Know Your Government Ser.). 24p. (gr. 1-4). pap. 8.15 *(978-0-8368-8846-1(4))*; (Illus.). lib. bdg. 22.00 *(978-0-8368-8841-6(3))* Stevens, Gareth Publishing LLLP. (Weekly Reader Leveled Readers).

Gwartney, Becky, et al. Lead On: Destination Reality. 2003. (YA). pap. 14.99 *(978-0-89265-968-5(8))* Randall Hse. Pubns.

Harcourt School Publishers Staff. Leaders for Peace. 3rd ed. 2003. (Horizons Ser.). (Illus.). (J). (gr. 3). pap. 5.50 *(978-0-15-333278-4(6))* Harcourt Schl. Pubs.

Harris, Laurie Lanzen. Biography for Beginners: African-American Leaders. 2007. (J). lib. bdg. 30.00 *(978-1-931360-35-7(9))* Favorable Impressions.

Harris, Laurie Lanzen, ed. Biography for Beginners Vol. 2: African-American Leaders. 2008. 316p. (YA). (gr. 5-10). lib. bdg. 30.00 *(978-1-931360-36-4(7))* Favorable Impressions.

Hemingway, Al. Chuck Norris. 2007. (Sharing the American Dream Ser.). 64p. (YA). (gr. 7-18). pap. 9.95 *(978-1-4222-0758-1(7))* Mason Crest.

Hollar, Sherman, contrib. by. George Washington. 2012. (Pivotal Presidents: Profiles in Leadership Ser.). (ENG.). 80p. (YA). (gr. 7-12). lib. bdg. 32.90 *(978-1-61530-939-9(X))*; (Illus.). 65.80 *(978-1-61530-956-6(X))* Rosen Publishing Group, Inc., The.

Killcoyne, Hope Lourie & Wolny, Philip, eds. The 100 Most Influential Religious Leaders of All Time, 1 vol., 1. 2016. (Britannica Guide to the World's Most Influential People Ser.). (ENG.). 224p. (J). (gr. 10-10). 54.00 *(978-1-68048-277-5(7)*, Britannica Educational Publishing) Rosen Publishing Group, Inc., The.

Kishel, Ann-Marie. Our Leaders. 2007. (First Step Nonfiction - Government Ser.). (ENG., Illus.). 24p. (gr. k-2). lib. bdg. 23.93 *(978-0-8225-6395-2(9)*, Lerner Pubns.) Lerner Publishing Group.

Leaders of the Middle Ages, 6 Bks, Set. 2004. (J). 191.70 *(978-1-4042-0345-7(1))* Rosen Publishing Group, Inc., The.

Lee, George L. Worldwide Interesting People: 162 History Makers of African Descent, 1 vol. alt. ed. 2012. (ENG., Illus.). 144p. pap. 19.99 *(978-0-7864-6768-6(1)*, 5efb588e-8e35-4188-81bd-86ff635cdb1d) McFarland & Co., Inc. Pubs.

Lewers, Rob & Murphy, Ed. The Hidden Hurt: How to Beat Bullying in Schools. 96p. pap. *(978-1-876367-66-4(0))* Wizard Bks.

Lindeen, Mary. Leading the Way, 1 vol. (Wonder Readers: Social Studies). (ENG.). (gr. -1-2). 2012. 20p. lib. bdg. 22.65 *(978-1-4296-9615-9(X))* 2011. 32p. pap. 5.99 *(978-1-4296-7947-3(6))* 2011. 16p. pap. 35.94 *(978-1-4296-8099-8(7))* Capstone Press of Coughlan Cos. (Wonder Readers).

Linder, Nani Aki. All about Me Look at Me I'm a Star: Children's Workbook. 2003. 121p. pap. 97.00 *(978-0-7414-1677-3(8))* Infinity Publishing.

Making a Difference. 2014. (Making a Difference: Leaders Who Are Changing the World Ser.). 48p. (YA). (gr. 5-8). pap. 84.30 *(978-1-62275-765-7(3))* Rosen Publishing Group, Inc., The.

Making a Difference: Leaders Who Are Changing the World. 2014. (Making a Difference: Leaders Who Are Changing the World Ser.). 48p. (YA). (gr. 5-8). 310.20 *(978-1-62275-754-1(8))* Rosen Publishing Group, Inc., The.

Mayer, Cassie. Being a Leader, 1 vol. Beech, Mark, illus. 2007. (Citizenship Ser.). (ENG.). 24p. (gr. -1-3). pap. 6.29 *(978-1-4034-9494-8(0)*, Acorn) Heinemann-Raintree.

—Ser un Líder, 1 vol. 2007. (Civismo Ser.). (SPA., Illus.). 24p. (gr. -1-1). pap. 6.29 *(978-1-4329-0408-1(6)*, Bellota) Heinemann-Raintree.

McCabe, Matthew. 12 Business Leaders Who Changed the World. 2015. (Change Makers Ser.). (ENG., Illus.). 32p. (J). (gr. 3-5). *(978-1-63235-145-6(5)*, 12-Story Library) Pr. Room Editions LLC.

Miller, Amanda. What Does the President Do? 2009. (Scholastic News Nonfiction Readers Ser.). (Illus.). 24p. (J). (gr. 1-2). 22.00 *(978-0-531-21088-8(X))* Scholastic Library Publishing.

Mooney, Brian. Great Leaders. 2012. (Great People in History Ser.). (ENG., Illus.). 128p. (YA). (gr. 8-12). lib. bdg. 34.60 *(978-1-4777-0403-5(5))* Rosen Publishing Group, Inc., The.

Mr. Blue. From Underdog to Wonderdog: Top Ten Tricks to Lead Your Pack. 2012. (ENG., Illus.). 52p. (J). (gr. 1-5). pap. 14.95 *(978-1-936354-26-9(8)*, Tremendous Leadership) Tremendous Life Bks.

Myers, Jeff. Secrets of Everyday Leaders Student Text: Create Positive Change & Inspire Extraordinary Results. 2006. 112p. stu. ed., per. 17.99 *(978-0-8054-6886-1(2))* B&H Publishing Group.

—Secrets of Great Communicators Student Text: Simple, Powerful Strategies for Reaching the Heart of Your Audience, Student Textbook. 2006. 158p. stu. ed., per. 17.99 *(978-0-8054-6880-9(3))* B&H Publishing Group.

—Secrets of World Changers Student Text: How to Achieve Lasting Influence as a Leader. 2006. 75p. pap., stu. ed. 12.99 *(978-0-8054-6883-0(8))* B&H Publishing Group.

Nelson, Robin. Being a Leader. 2003. (First Step Nonfiction Ser.). (Illus.). 24p. (gr. k-2). (J). lib. bdg. 18.60 *(978-0-8225-1287-5(4))*; (ENG., pap. 6.99 *(978-0-8225-1324-7(2))* Lerner Publishing Group.

Photo-Illustrated Biographies. 2010. (Photo-Illustrated Biographies Ser.). (ENG.). 24p. (gr. 2-3). pap. 662.40 *(978-1-4296-5209-4(8)*, Bridgestone Bks.) Capstone Press of Coughlan Cos.

Rotberg, Robert I. Governance & Leadership in Africa. Rotberg, Robert I. & Ojakorotu, Victor, eds. 2013. (Africa: Progress & Problems Ser.: 13). (Illus.). 112p. (J). (gr. 7-18). 24.95 *(978-1-4222-2940-8(8))* Mason Crest.

Shames, Stephen. Transforming Lives: Turning Uganda's Forgotten Children into Leaders. Shames, Stephen, photos by. 2009. (Illus.). 40p. (YA). pap. 12.95 *(978-1-59572-213-3(0))* Star Bright Bks., Inc.

Strack, Jay & Edwards, David. Life: How to Get There from Here, 1 vol. 2006. (Student Leadership University Study Guide Ser.). (ENG.). 144p. pap. 9.99 *(978-1-4185-0599-8(4))* Nelson, Thomas Inc.

Strack, Jay & Lucado, Max. Leadership Rocks: Becoming a Student of Influence, 1 vol. 2006. (Student Leadership University Study Guide Ser.). (ENG.). 144p. pap. 9.99 *(978-1-4185-0593-6(5))* Nelson, Thomas Inc.

Thomas, Wendy Russell & Ruchman, Laura. Bliss Live It! Bliss Give It! Starmer, Anika & Wertz, Michael, illus. 2010. 60p. (YA). *(978-0-88441-754-5(9))* Girl Scouts of the USA.

Tibbs, Janet. Being A Leader, 8 vols., Vol. 7. 2004. (Illus.). (J). per. *(978-1-932062-33-5(5))* Hability Solution Services, Inc.

Witt, Marcos. Liderazgo al Extremo, 1 vol. 2004. (SPA.). 112p. pap. 9.99 *(978-0-88113-762-0(6))* Grupo Nelson.

Wolny, Philip, ed. The 100 Most Influential Religious Leaders of All Time. 2016. (Britannica Guide to the World's Most Influential People Ser.). 224p. (gr. 10-10). 108.00 *(978-1-68048-240-9(8)*, Britannica Educational Publishing) Rosen Publishing Group, Inc., The.

Wooster, Patricia. So, You Want to Be a Leader? An Awesome Guide to Becoming a Head Honcho. 2016. (Be What You Want Ser.). (ENG., Illus.). 192p. (J). (gr. 3-7). pap. 11.99 *(978-1-58270-547-7(X))* Aladdin/Beyond Words.

WorldVenture Guide for Leaders of Grades 1-6. 2003. pap. 8.99 *(978-1-56309-634-1(X))* Woman's Missionary Union.

LEARNING, ART OF

see Study Skills

LEARNING AND SCHOLARSHIP

see also Culture; Education; Humanism; Research

Cornell, Kari A. Classroom up Close. 2016. (Illus.). 24p. (J). *(978-0-87659-704-0(5))* Gryphon Hse., Inc.

Howell, Dusti & Howell, Deanne, prods. Dr. Wiley Makes Sense. 2005. (YA). pap. 249.95 incl. cd-rom *(978-0-9677328-9-3(1))* SolidA, Inc.

Perry, William G., Jr. Learn to Love to Learn. Date not set. 300p. (YA). (gr. 8-12). pap. *(978-1-887946-01-8(2))* Learning Net, The.

Reed, Avery. Who Were the Brothers Grimm? O'brien, John, illus. 2015. 105p. (J). *(978-1-4844-6177-8(0)*, Grosset & Dunlap) Penguin Publishing Group.

Scott, John, text. How to Financially Fund Your College Education. 2004. (YA). 30.00 *(978-1-879498-83-9(9))* SportAmerica.

Silva, Patricia. Modern Times. Baldanzi, Alessandro, illus. 2008. (Reading & Writing Ser.). 32p. (gr. 4-7). 28.50 *(978-0-7614-4322-3(3)*, Benchmark Bks.) Marshall Cavendish Corp.

Whamond, Dave, illus. Superbrain: The Insider's Guide to Getting Smart. 2015. (ENG.). 72p. (J). (gr. 4-6). pap. 9.95 *(978-1-55451-734-3(6)*, 9781554517343) Annick Pr., Ltd. CAN. Dist: Publishers Group West (PGW).

LEARNING DISABILITIES

Allen, William H., creator. TEH Learns to Read: (13 Volume Set). 13 Volume Set. 2004. (Illus.). 40p. (J). 399.95 *(978-0-9745938-0-7(X))* LD Coach, LLC.

Brinkerhoff, Shirley. Learning Disabilities. Albers, Lisa et al, eds. 2014. (Living with a Special Need Ser.: 16). 128p. (J). (gr. 7-18). 25.95 *(978-1-4222-3040-4(6))* Mason Crest.

—Why Can't I Learn Like Everyone Else? Youth with Learning Disabilities. (Youth with Special Needs Ser.). (Illus.). (YA). 2004. 128p. 24.95 *(978-1-59084-730-5(X))* 2003. 127p. (gr. 7). pap. 14.95 *(978-1-4222-0432-0(4))* Mason Crest.

Cooper, Barbara & Widdows, Nancy. The Social Success Workbook for Teens: Skill-Building Activities for Teens with Nonverbal Learning Disorder, Asperger's Disorder & Other Social-Skill Problems. 2008. (Instant Help Ser.). (ENG., Illus.). 144p. (YA). (gr. 6-12). pap. 15.95 *(978-1-57224-614-0(6)*, Instant Help Books) New Harbinger Pubns.

Cummings, Rhoda. The Survival Guide for Kids with LD. 3rd rev. ed. 2016. (ENG., Illus.). 128p. (J). (gr. 4-8). pap. 13.99 *(978-1-63198-031-2(9))* Free Spirit Publishing, Inc.

Cummings, Rhoda & Fisher, Gary. Supera Tus Dificultades de Aprendizaje: Itu Puedes! 2005. (SPA & ENG., Illus.). 136p. (J). (gr. 4-7). per. 11.95 *(978-968-860-453-3(4))* Editorial Pax MEX. Dist: Independent Pubs. Group.

Edwards, Nicola. My Friend Has Dyslexia. 2004. (J). lib. bdg. 27.10 *(978-1-59389-167-1(9))* Chrysalis Education.

—My Friend Has Dyspraxia. 2004. (J). lib. bdg. 27.10 *(978-1-59389-168-8(7))* Chrysalis Education.

Flath, Camden, told to. Kids with Special Needs: IDEA (Individuals with Disabilities Education Act), 11 vols., Set. Incl. Finding My Voice: Kids with Speech Impairment. Stewart, Sheila. pap. 7.95 *(978-1-4222-1925-6(9))*; Hidden Child: Kids with Autism. Stewart, Sheila. pap. 7.95 *(978-1-4222-1927-0(5))*; I Can Do It! Kids with Physical Challenges. Stewart, Sheila. pap. 7.95 *(978-1-4222-1926-3(7))*; Listening with Your Eyes: Kids Who Are Deaf & Hard of Hearing. Stewart, Sheila. pap. 7.95 *(978-1-4222-1920-1(8))*; My Name Is Not Slow: Kids with Intellectual Disabilities. Stewart, Sheila. pap. 7.95 *(978-1-4222-1921-8(6))*; Sick All the Time: Kids with Chronic Illness. Chastain, Zachary. pap. 7.95 *(978-1-4222-1922-5(4))*; Something's Wrong! Kids with Emotional Disturbance. Stewart, Sheila. pap. 7.95 *(978-1-4222-1923-2(2))*; Speed Racer: Kids with Attention-Deficit/Hyperactivity Disorder. Stewart, Sheila. pap. 7.95 *(978-1-4222-1924-9(0))*; What's Wrong with My Brain? Kids with Brain Injury. Stewart, Sheila. pap. 7.95 *(978-1-4222-1928-7(3))*; Why Can't I Learn Like Everyone Else? Kids with Learning Disabilities. Stewart, Sheila. pap. 7.95 *(978-1-4222-1929-4(1))*; 48p. (YA). (gr. 5-18). 2009. 2011. Set pap. 87.45 *(978-1-4222-1918-8(6))* Mason Crest.

Gillard, Arthur. Learning Disabilities. 2011. (Issues That Concern You Ser.). (ENG., Illus.). 144p. (gr. 7-10). 42.00 *(978-0-7377-5695-1(0))* Cengage Gale.

Gillen-Connell, Linda. Dumb Bunny. 2005. 67p. (J). (gr. 4-6). pap. 16.95 *(978-1-4137-8454-1(2))* PublishAmerica, Inc.

Gunton, Sharon, ed. Learning Disabilities. 2007. (Social Issues Firsthand Ser.). (ENG., Illus.). 122p. (YA). (gr. 10-12). lib. bdg. 33.75 *(978-0-7377-3840-7(5)*, LML02109-234579, Greenhaven Pr., Inc.) Cengage Gale.

Libal, Autumn. My Name Isn't Slow: Youth with Mental Retardation. 2004. (Youth with Special Needs Ser.). (Illus.). 128p. (YA). 24.95 *(978-1-59084-731-2(8))* Mason Crest.

McMurchie, Susan. Understanding My Learning Differences. 2003. 148p. (gr. 4-5). spiral bd. 29.00 incl. audio compact disk *(978-1-57861-497-4(X)*, IEP Resources) Attainment Co., Inc.

Miles, Brenda & Patterson, Colleen A. How I Learn: A Kid's Guide to Learning Disability. Heinrichs, Jane, illus. 2014. 32p. (J). *(978-1-4338-1660-4(1))*; pap. *(978-1-4338-1661-1(X))* American Psychological Assn.

Nelson, Sheila & Livingston, Phyllis. Youth Who Are Gifted: Integrating Talents & Intelligence. 2007. (Helping Youth with Mental, Physical, & Social Challenges Ser.). (Illus.). 128p. (YA). pap. 14.95 *(978-1-4222-0435-1(9))* Mason Crest.

Paquette, Penny Hutchins & Tuttle, Cheryl Gerson. Learning Disabilities: The Ultimate Teen Guide. rev. ed. 2006. (It Happened to Me Ser.: 1). (ENG., Illus.). 312p. per. 25.00 *(978-0-8108-5643-1(3))* Scarecrow Pr., Inc.

Parks, Peggy J. Learning Disabilities. 2009. (Compact Research Ser.). 96p. (YA). (gr. 7-12). lib. bdg. 25.95 *(978-1-60152-077-7(8))* ReferencePoint Pr., Inc.

Stern, Judith M. & Ben-Ami, Uzi. Many Ways to Learn: A Kid's Guide to LD. Chesworth, Michael, illus. 2nd rev. ed. 2010. 96p. (J). (gr. 3-8). 14.95 *(978-1-4338-0739-8(4))*; pap. 9.95 *(978-1-4338-0740-4(8))* American Psychological Assn. (Magination Pr.).

Stewart, Sheila. Why Can't I Learn Like Everyone Else? Kids with Learning Disabilities. 2009. (Kids with Special Needs Ser.). 48p. (YA). (gr. 5-18). pap. 7.95 *(978-1-4222-1929-4(1))* Mason Crest.

Stewart, Sheila & Flath, Camden. Why Can't I Learn Like Everyone Else? Kids with Learning Disabilities. 2010. (Kids with Special Needs Ser.). 48p. (YA). (gr. 5-18). lib. bdg. 19.95 *(978-1-4222-1726-9(4))* Mason Crest.

Tourville, Amanda Doering. My Friend Has Dyslexia, 1 vol. Sorra, Kristin, illus. 2010. (Friends with Disabilities Ser.). (ENG.). 24p. (gr. k-3). lib. bdg. 25.99 *(978-1-4048-5752-0(4))* Picture Window Bks.

LEARNING DISABILITIES—FICTION

Asher, Diana Harmon. Sidetracked. 2017. (ENG.). 240p. (J). (gr. 3-7). 16.99 ***(978-1-4197-2601-9(3)**, Amulet Bks.)* Abrams, Inc.

Butler, Dori Hillestad. Alexandra Hopewell, Labor Coach. 2005. 136p. (J). (gr. 3-6). 15.99 *(978-0-8075-0242-6(1))* Whitman, Albert & Co.

Delacre, Lulu & Swanson, Katharine. Jay & Ben. Delacre, Lulu, illus. 2013. (ENG., Illus.). 18p. (J). bds. 20.00 *(978-1-60060-460-7(9))* Lee & Low Bks., Inc.

Ellis, Mark & Campbell, Ruth. Words. 2006. (ENG., Illus.). 40p. 19.95 *(978-0-88982-227-6(1))* Oolichan Bks. CAN. Dist: Univ. of Toronto Pr.

Ellison, Elizabeth Stow. Flight. 2008. (ENG.). 192p. (YA). (gr. 3-7). 16.95 *(978-0-8234-2128-2(7))* Holiday Hse., Inc.

Flake, Sharon G. Pinned. 2014. (ENG.). 240p. (J). (gr. 9). pap. 9.99 *(978-0-545-05733-2(7)*, Scholastic Pr.) Scholastic, Inc.

Gehret, Jeanne. The Don't-Give-Up Kid: And Learning Disabilities. LaDuca, Michael, illus. 4th ed. 2009. (Coping Ser.). (ENG.). 32p. (J). (gr. 1-3). 17.95 *(978-0-9821982-0-9(5))* Verbal Images Pr.

Gramp's Magic Gift. 2011. 98p. 24.99 *(978-1-4628-2980-4(5))*; pap. 15.99 *(978-1-4628-2979-8(1))* Xlibris Corp.

Hansen, Joyce. Yellow Bird & Me. 2005. (ENG.). 160p. (J). (gr. 5-7). pap. 6.95 *(978-0-618-61116-4(9))* Houghton Mifflin Harcourt Publishing Co.

Holland, Nikki Richardson. Meet Lanceamus Jones: A Special Kid with Special Needs. 2011. 24p. (J). pap. 12.95 *(978-1-4520-7649-2(9))* AuthorHouse.

Janover, Caroline D. Josh: A Boy with Dyslexia. 2004. 108p. (J). pap. 9.95 *(978-0-595-31381-5(7)*, Backinprint.com) iUniverse, Inc.

McClintock, Norah. Watch Me, 1 vol. 2008. (Orca Currents Ser.). (ENG.). (J). (gr. 5-9). 112p. 16.95 *(978-1-55469-040-4(4))*; 128p. pap. 9.95 *(978-1-55469-039-8(0))* Orca Bk. Pubs. USA.

Nichol, Tim. Stephen Harris in Trouble: A Dyspraxic Drama in Several Clumsy Acts. 2003. (ENG.). 144p. (J). pap. 19.95 *(978-1-84310-134-5(3)*, 4267) Kingsley, Jessica Pubs. GBR. Dist: Macmillan Distribution Ltd.

Polacco, Patricia. The Art of Miss Chew. Polacco, Patricia, illus. 2012. (ENG., Illus.). 40p. (J). (gr. k-3). 17.99 *(978-0-399-25703-2(9)*, G.P. Putnam's Sons Books for Young Readers) Penguin Young Readers Group.

Schmatz, Pat. Bluefish. 2013. (ENG.). 240p. (YA). (gr. 7). pap. 6.99 *(978-0-7636-6341-4(7))* Candlewick Pr.

Vision, David & Vision, Mutiya Sahar. If Only I Could! Alcantara, Ignacio, illus. 2009. 32p. 17.00 *(978-0-9659538-8-7(2))* Von Curtis Publishing.

Walters, Eric. Ed Spécial, 1 vol. 2011. (FRE.). 144p. (J). (gr. 5-9). pap. 9.95 *(978-1-55469-857-8(X))* Orca Bk. Pubs. USA.

—Special Edward, 1 vol. 2009. (Orca Currents Ser.). (ENG.). (J). (gr. 5-9). 112p. 16.95 *(978-1-55469-096-1(X))*; 136p. pap. 9.95 *(978-1-55469-092-3(7))* Orca Bk. Pubs. USA.

Whitlow, Crystal K. Charles Gordon Willingham. Fisher, Bonnie & Wolski, Bobbi, illus. 2006. per. *(978-0-9777361-0-2(5))* Day3 Productions, Inc.

Winkler, Henry & Oliver, Lin. Barfing in the Backseat: How I Survived My Family Road Trip. Watson, Jesse Joshua, illus. 2007. (Hank Zipzer Ser.: No. 12). 152p. (gr. 4-7). 15.00 *(978-0-7569-8162-4(X))* Perfection Learning Corp.

—Bookmarks Are People Too! Garrett, Scott, illus. 2014. (Here's Hank Ser.: 1). (ENG.). 128p. (J). (gr. 1-3). 14.99 *(978-0-448-48239-2(8))*;No. 1. 5.99 *(978-0-448-47997-2(4))* Penguin Young Readers Group. (Grosset & Dunlap).

—Bookmarks Are People Too! 2014. (Here's Hank Ser.: 1). lib. bdg. 16.00 *(978-0-606-34142-4(0)*, Turtleback) Turtleback Bks.

—A Brand-New Me! Watson, Jesse Joshua & Heitz, Tim, illus. 2010. (Hank Zipzer Ser.: 17). (ENG.). 160p. (J). (gr. 3-7). pap. 5.99 *(978-0-448-45210-4(3)*, Grosset & Dunlap) Penguin Young Readers Group.

—The Curtain Went Up, My Pants Fell Down. Watson, Jesse Joshua, illus. 2007. (Hank Zipzer Ser.: 11). (ENG.). 160p. (J). (gr. 3-7). pap. 5.99 *(978-0-448-44267-9(1)*, Grosset & Dunlap) Penguin Young Readers Group.

—Fake Snakes & Weird Wizards. Garrett, Scott, illus. 2015. (Here's Hank Ser.: No. 4). (ENG.). 128p. (J). (gr. 1-3). 5.99 *(978-0-448-48252-1(5)*, Grosset & Dunlap) Penguin Young Readers Group.

—Holy Enchilada! Heyer, Carol et al, illus. 2004. (Hank Zipzer Ser.: 6). (ENG.). 160p. (J). (gr. 3-7). pap. 5.99 *(978-0-448-43353-0(2)*, Grosset & Dunlap) Penguin Young Readers Group.

—The Life of Me (Enter at Your Own Risk) 2008. (Hank Zipzer Ser.: No. 14). (Illus.). 186p. (gr. 3-7). 16.00 *(978-0-7569-8819-7(5))* Perfection Learning Corp.

—My Dog's a Scaredy-Cat, 10 vols. Watson, Jesse Joshua, illus. 2006. (Hank Zipzer Ser.: 10). (ENG.). 160p. (J). (gr. 3-7). pap. 5.99 *(978-0-448-43878-8(X)*, Grosset & Dunlap) Penguin Young Readers Group.

—Niagara Falls, or Does It? Watson, Jesse Joshua et al, illus. 2004. (Hank Zipzer Ser.: 1). (ENG.). 144p. (J). (gr. 3-7). pap. 5.99 *(978-0-448-43162-8(9)*, Grosset & Dunlap) Penguin Young Readers Group.

—Niagara Falls, or Does It? 2004. (Hank Zipzer Ser.: No. 1). 128p. (J). (gr. 2-6). pap. 29.00 incl. audio *(978-1-4000-9006-8(7)*, Listening Library) Random Hse. Audio Publishing Group.

—Summer School! What Genius Thought That Up? 2006. (Hank Zipzer Ser.: No. 8). (Illus.). 157p. (J). (gr. 3-9). lib. bdg. 24.21 *(978-1-59961-107-5(4))* Spotlight.

—The Zippity Zinger, 4 vols. Heitz, Tim, illus. 2004. (Hank Zipzer Ser.: 4). (ENG.). 160p. (J). (gr. 3-7). mass mkt. 5.99 *(978-0-448-43193-2(9)*, Grosset & Dunlap) Penguin Young Readers Group.

Winkler, Henry, et al. How to Hug an Elephant #6. Garrett, Scott, illus. 2015. (Here's Hank Ser.: 6). (ENG.). 128p. (J). (gr. 1-3). bds. 5.99 *(978-0-448-48656-7(3))*; bds. 14.99 *(978-0-448-48657-4(1))* Penguin Young Readers Group. (Grosset & Dunlap).

Zemach, Kaethe. Ms. McCaw Learns to Draw. (J). 2008. (ENG., Illus.). 32p. (gr. -1-3). 16.99 *(978-0-439-82914-4(3))* 2006. *(978-0-439-82915-1(1))* Scholastic, Inc. (Levine, Arthur A. Bks.).

LEATHERWORK

Eastman, Linda Sue. Leathercraft. 2008. (ENG., Illus.). 120p. (gr. 4-7). pap. 14.95 *(978-1-56523-370-6(0)*, 3706) Fox Chapel Publishing Co., Inc.

Felix, Rebecca. Cool Leatherworking Projects: Fun & Creative Workshop Activities. 2016. (ENG., Illus.). 32p. (J). *(978-1-68078-128-1(6))* ABDO Publishing Co.

LEAVES

Bishop, Celeste. ¿Por Qué Las Plantas Tienen Hojas? / Why Do Plants Have Leaves?, 01 vols., 1. 2016. (Partes de la Planta / Plant Parts Ser.). (ENG & SPA., Illus.). 24p. (J). 23.60 *(978-1-5081-4741-1(8)*, PowerKids Pr.) Rosen Publishing Group, Inc., The.

—Why Do Plants Have Leaves?, 01 vols., 1. 2016. (Plant Parts Ser.). (ENG., Illus.). 24p. (J). pap. 8.25 *(978-1-5081-4221-8(1)*, PowerKids Pr.) Rosen Publishing Group, Inc., The.

Blackaby, Susan. Catching Sunlight: A Book about Leaves, 1 vol. Delage, Charlene, illus. 2003. (Growing Things Ser.). (ENG.). 24p. (gr. -1-2). per. 8.95 *(978-1-4048-0387-9(4))* Picture Window Bks.

Bodach, Vijaya K. Leaves [Scholastic]. 2010. (Plant Parts Ser.). 24p. pap. 0.52 *(978-1-4296-5058-8(3)*, Pebble Plus) Capstone Press of Coughlan Cos.

Bodach, Vijaya Khisty. Leaves. 2016. (Plant Parts Ser.). (ENG.). 24p. (gr. k-1). pap. 7.29 *(978-1-5157-4244-9(X)*, Pebble Plus) Capstone Press of Coughlan Cos.

Brennan, Linda Crotta. Leaves Change Color. 2014. (Tell Me Why Library). (ENG., Illus.). 24p. (J). (gr. 2-5). 25.64 *(978-1-63188-008-7(X)*, 205439) Cherry Lake Publishing.

Bullard, Lisa. Leaves Fall Down: Learning about Autumn Leaves, 1 vol. Takvorian, Nadine, illus. 2010. (Autumn Ser.). (ENG.). 24p. (gr. 1-2). pap. 8.95 *(978-1-4048-6390-3(7))*; lib. bdg. 26.65 *(978-1-4048-6013-1(4))* Picture Window Bks.

Charman, Andrew. I Wonder Why Leaves Change Color: And Other Questions about Plants. 2012. (I Wonder Why Ser.). (ENG., Illus.). (J). (gr. k-3). pap. 6.99 *(978-0-7534-6697-1(X)*, 9780753466971, Kingfisher) Roaring Brook Pr.

Edwards, Nicola. Leaves. 2007. (See How Plants Grow Ser.). (Illus.). 24p. (J). (gr. 3-7). lib. bdg. 22.60 *(978-1-4042-3703-2(8)*, PowerKids Pr.) Rosen Publishing Group, Inc., The.

Felix, Rebecca. What Happens to Leaves in Fall? 2013. (J). *(978-1-61080-984-9(X))*; (ENG.). 24p. 22.79 *(978-1-61080-909-2(2)*, 202615); (ENG.). 24p. pap. 12.79 *(978-1-61080-934-4(3)*, 202617) Cherry Lake Publishing.

Figorito, Christine. How Leaves Change Color. 2009. (Reading Room Collection 2 Ser.). 24p. (gr. 3-4). 42.50 *(978-1-60851-971-2(6)*, PowerKids Pr.) Rosen Publishing Group, Inc., The.

Gerber, Carole. Leaf Jumpers. Evans, Leslie, illus. (ENG.). (J). 2017. 28p. (— 1). bds. 7.99 *(978-1-58089-782-2(7))* 2006. 32p. (gr. -1-2). per. 7.95 *(978-1-57091-498-0(2))* Charlesbridge Publishing, Inc.

Glaser, Rebecca. Leaves. 2012. (ENG., Illus.). 24p. (J). lib. bdg. 25.65 *(978-1-62031-025-0(2))* Jump! Inc.

Granger, Ronald. Know Your Leaves. 2013. (InfoMax Readers Ser.). (ENG.). 24p. (J). (gr. 2-3). pap. 8.25 *(978-1-4777-2422-4(2))*; pap. 49.50 *(978-1-4777-2425-5(7))* Rosen Publishing Group, Inc., The. (Rosen Classroom).

J
K
L

Harvey, Calvin. Let's Look at Leaves. 2016. (We Love Spring! Ser.). 00024p. (J). pap. 8.15 *(978-1-4824-5493-2(9))* Stevens, Gareth Publishing LLLP.

Hicks, Terry Allan. Why Do Leaves Change Color? 2010. (Tell Me Why, Tell Me How 4 Ser.). 32p. (gr. 3-5). 29.93 *(978-0-7614-4827-3(6))* Marshall Cavendish GBR. Dist: Marshall Cavendish Corp.

Lake, Darlene A. Leaf Collecting & Preserving Made Easy. 2nd ed. 2003. (Illus.). 49p. (J). 12.00 *(978-0-9747654-0-2(6),* Egap Gifa Bks.) Leafcollecting.com Publishing Co.

Lara, Enrique & Garcia, Luis. Leaves. 2004. (Illus.). (J). *(978-81-89020-07-1(2))* Katha.

Leaves. 2006. 10.95 *(978-1-933427-72-0(8))* teNeues Publishing Co.

Linden, Joanne. Fiddleheads to Fir Trees: Leaves in All Seasons, 1 vol. Laurie, Caple, illus. 2013. (ENG.). 32p. (J). 12.00 *(978-0-87842-606-5(X))* Mountain Pr. Publishing Co., Inc.

MacAulay, Kelley. What Are Leaves? 2013. (ENG., Illus.). 24p. (J). *(978-0-7787-1287-9(7));* pap. *(978-0-7787-0017-3(8))* Crabtree Publishing Co.

Mack, Steve. The Leaves Fall All Around. 2009. (Rookie Preschool Ser.). (ENG.). 24p. (J). (gr. -1). 23.00 *(978-0-531-24402-9(4))* Scholastic Library Publishing.

Maestro, Betsy. Why Do Leaves Change Color? Krupinski, Loretta, illus. 2015. (Let's-Read-And-Find-Out Science 2 Ser.). (ENG.). 32p. (J). (gr. -1-3). pap. 6.99 *(978-0-06-238201-6(2))* HarperCollins Pubs.

—Why Do Leaves Change Color? 2015. (Let's Read & Find Out Science Stage 2 Ser.). (J). lib. bdg. 17.20 *(978-0-606-37893-2(6))* Turtleback Bks.

Morgan, Sally. Under a Leaf in Forests & Jungles. 2006. (Hidden Habitats Ser.). (J). *(978-1-59389-284-5(5))* Chrysalis Education.

Owen, Ruth. Science & Craft Projects with Trees & Leaves. 2013. (Get Crafty Outdoors Ser.). (ENG., Illus.). 32p. (J). (gr. k-3). 26.50 *(978-1-4777-0248-2(2));* pap. 11.75 *(978-1-4777-0259-8(8))* Rosen Publishing Group, Inc., The. (PowerKids Pr.).

—What Do Roots, Stems, Leaves, & Flowers Do? 2014. (World of Plants Ser.). 32p. (J). (gr. 2-5). lib. bdg. 26.25 *(978-1-4777-7137-2(9),* PowerKids Pr.) Rosen Publishing Group, Inc., The.

Pearson Learning Staff, creator. Trees & Leaves. 2005. (IOpeners Ser.). (J). pap. 7.56 *(978-0-7652-5136-7(1))* Celebration Pr.

Pressberg, Dava. How Leaves Work. 2013. (Rosen Readers Ser.). (ENG.). 24p. (J). (gr. 2-3). pap. 8.25 *(978-1-4777-2272-5(6));* pap. 49.50 *(978-1-4777-2273-2(4))* Rosen Publishing Group, Inc., The. (Rosen Classroom).

Ren&apos, et al. Investigating Why Leaves Change Their Color. 2009. (Science Detectives Ser.). (Illus.). 24p. (J). (gr. 2-5). lib. bdg. 22.60 *(978-1-4042-4485-6(9))* Rosen Publishing Group, Inc., The.

René, Ellen. Investigating Why Leaves Change Their Color. 2009. (Science Detectives Ser.). 24p. (gr. 2-3). 42.50 *(978-1-60853-017-5(5),* PowerKids Pr.) Rosen Publishing Group, Inc., The.

Roza, G. Lots of Leaves: Learning the L Sound. 2009. (PowerPhonics Ser.). 24p. (gr. 1-1). 39.90 *(978-1-60851-457-1(9),* PowerKids Pr.) Rosen Publishing Group, Inc., The.

Rustad, Martha E. Las Hojas en Otoño. 2009. (Todo Acerca Del Otoño/All about Fall Ser.).Tr. of Leaves in Fall. (ENG, SPA & MUL.). 24p. (gr. k-1). 26.65 *(978-1-4296-3260-7(7))* Capstone Press of Coughlan Cos.

Rustad, Martha E. H. Fall Leaves: Colorful & Crunchy. Enright, Amanda, illus. 2011. (Fall's Here! Ser.). pap. 39.62 *(978-0-7613-8646-9(7),* Millbrook Pr.); (ENG.). 24p. pap. 6.95 *(978-0-7613-8505-9(3),* Millbrook Pr.); (ENG.). 24p. lib. bdg. 23.93 *(978-0-7613-5062-0(4))* Lerner Publishing Group.

Rustad, Martha E. H. & Rustad, Martha E. Leaves in Fall, 1 vol. Saunders-Smith, Gail, ed. 2007. (All about Fall Ser.). (ENG., Illus.). 24p. (gr. k-1). 26.65 *(978-1-4296-0024-8(1),* Pebble Plus) Capstone Press of Coughlan Cos.

Schuh, Mari. Leaves in Fall. 2013. (ENG., Illus.). 24p. (J). lib. bdg. 25.65 *(978-1-62031-059-5(7))* Jump! Inc.

Schuh, Mari C. I See Fall Leaves. 2016. (First Step Nonfiction — Observing Fall Ser.). (ENG., Illus.). 24p. (J). (gr. k-2). 23.99 *(978-1-5124-0795-2(X))* Lerner Publishing Group.

Shapiro, Sara. What Do You See? A Book about the Seasons. 2009. (Illus.). 16p. (J). pap. *(978-0-545-16154-1(1))* Scholastic, Inc.

Sheffield, S. When Leaves Turn: Learning the UR Sound. 2009. (PowerPhonics Ser.). 24p. (gr. 1-1). 39.90 *(978-1-60851-480-9(3),* PowerKids Pr.) Rosen Publishing Group, Inc., The.

Shores, Erika L. Leaves. 2015. (Celebrate Fall Ser.). (ENG., Illus.). 24p. (gr. k-1). lib. bdg. 21.99 *(978-1-4914-6003-0(2),* Pebble Bks.) Capstone Press of Coughlan Cos.

Snow, Virginia Brimhall. Fall Walk, 1 vol. 2013. (ENG., Illus.). 32p. (J). 16.99 *(978-1-4236-3261-0(3))* Gibbs Smith, Publisher.

Sterling, Kristin. Exploring Leaves. 2011. (First Step Nonfiction / Let's Look at Plants Ser.). pap. 33.92 *(978-0-7613-8615-5(7));* lib. bdg. 21.27 *(978-0-7613-5780-3(7));* (ENG.). 24p. pap. 6.95 *(978-0-7613-7833-4(2))* Lerner Publishing Group.

Stone, Lynn. Leaves. 2007. (Plant Parts Ser.). (Illus.). 24p. (J). (gr. 2-4). per. 7.95 *(978-1-60044-693-1(0))* Rourke Educational Media.

Thrup, Claire. All about Leaves. (All about Plants Ser.). (ENG.). 24p. (gr. -1-1). 2016. pap. 5.99 *(978-1-4846-3847-7(6))* 2014. 22.65 *(978-1-4846-0507-3(1))* Heinemann-Raintree. (Acorn).

Waldron, Melanie. Leaves, 1 vol. 2014. (Plant Parts Ser.). (ENG.). 32p. (gr. 2-4). lib. bdg. 30.65 *(978-1-4109-5421-3(8),* Raintree Perspectives) Heinemann-Raintree.

Whitehouse, Patricia. Las Hojas, 1 vol. 2nd ed. 2010. (Las Plantas Ser.). (ENG & SPA.). 24p. (gr. k-2). pap. 6.79 *(978-1-4329-4192-5(5))* Heinemann-Raintree.

LEBANON

Abirached, Zeina. I Remember Beirut. 2014. (ENG.). 96p. pap. 9.95 *(978-1-4677-4458-4(1),* Graphic Universe™) Lerner Publishing Group.

Aretha, David. Lebanon in the News: Past, Present, & Future. 2006. (Middle East Nations in the News Ser.). (Illus.). 128p. (J). (gr. 4-10). lib. bdg. 34.60 *(978-1-59845-023-1(9),* MyReportLinks.com Bks.) Enslow Pubs., Inc.

Boutros, Jill, et al. Lebanon A to Z: A Middle Eastern Mosaic. Sabbagh, Tatiana, illus. 2006. (ENG.). 40p. (J). (gr. -1-3). 25.00 *(978-0-9744803-4-3(7))* PublishingWorks.

Etheredge, Laura. Syria, Lebanon, & Jordan. 2011. (Middle East: Region in Transition Ser.). (Illus.). 248p. (YA). (gr. 9-12). lib. bdg. 40.00 *(978-1-61530-329-8(4))* Rosen Publishing Group, Inc., The.

Gauvin, Edward, tr. I Remember Beirut. 2014. (ENG., Illus.). 96p. (gr. 8-12). lib. bdg. 29.27 *(978-1-4677-3822-4(0),* Graphic Universe™) Lerner Publishing Group.

Malaspina, Ann. Lebanon. 2008. (Creation of the Modern Middle East Ser.). (Illus.). 128p. (gr. 6-12). 35.00 *(978-1-60413-057-7(1),* Chelsea Hse.) Facts On File, Inc.

McDaniel, Jan. Lebanon. 2010. (Major Muslim Nations Ser.). 128p. (YA). (gr. 5-18). lib. bdg. 25.95 *(978-1-4222-1387-2(0))* Mason Crest.

Mcdaniel, Jan. Lebanon, Vol. 13. 2015. (Major Nations of the Modern Middle East Ser.). (Illus.). 128p. (J). (gr. 7). lib. bdg. 25.95 *(978-1-4222-3446-4(0))* Mason Crest.

Owings, Lisa. Lebanon. 2015. (Exploring Countries Ser.). (ENG., Illus.). 32p. (J). (gr. 3-7). lib. bdg. 26.95 *(978-1-62617-176-3(9),* Blastoff! Readers) Bellwether Media.

Perdew, Laura. Understanding Lebanon Today. 2014. (Illus.). 63p. (J). (gr. 3-6). 33.95 *(978-1-61228-653-2(4))* Mitchell Lane Pubs., Inc.

Rice Jr., Earle. Hezbollah. 2017. lib. bdg. 29.95 ***(978-1-68020-053-9(4))*** Mitchell Lane Pubs., Inc.

Sheehan, Sean & Latif, Zawiah Abdul. Lebanon. 2nd rev. ed. 2007. (Cultures of the World Ser.). 144p. (gr. 6). lib. bdg. 42.79 *(978-0-7614-2081-1(9),* Benchmark Bks.) Marshall Cavendish Corp.

Sheehan, Sean, et al. Lebanon. 2017. ***(978-1-5026-2612-7(8))*** Cavendish Square Publishing.

Skahill, Carolyn. A Historical Atlas of Lebanon. 2004. (Historical Atlases of South Asia, Central Asia, & the Middle East Ser.). (Illus.). 64p. (gr. 7-12). lib. bdg. 31.95 *(978-0-8239-3982-4(0))* Rosen Publishing Group, Inc., The.

Skahill, Carolyn M. A Historical Atlas of Lebanon. 2009. (Historical Atlases of South Asia, Central Asia, & the Middle East Ser.). 64p. (gr. 6-6). 61.20 *(978-1-61513-325-3(9))* Rosen Publishing Group, Inc., The.

Willis, Terri. Lebanon. 2005. (Enchantment of the World Ser.). (ENG., Illus.). 144p. (YA). (gr. 5-9). 39.00 *(978-0-516-23685-8(7))* Scholastic Library Publishing.

LEBANON—FICTION

Laird, Elizabeth. Oranges in No Man's Land. 2008. (ENG., Illus.). 128p. (J). (gr. 2-5). pap. 9.95 *(978-1-931859-56-1(6))* Haymarket Bks.

Marston, Elsa. The Olive Tree. Ewart, Claire, illus. 2014. (ENG.). 32p. (J). (gr. -1-2). 16.95 *(978-1-937786-29-8(3),* Wisdom Tales) World Wisdom, Inc.

St. John, Patricia. Nothing Else Matters. 2003. 176p. 6.49 *(978-0-85421-972-8(2))* Scripture Union GBR. Dist: Gabriel Resources.

LEE, HENRY, 1756-1818

Bodie, Idella. Light-Horse Harry. 2004. (Illus.). 86p. (J). pap. 6.95 *(978-0-87844-172-3(7))* Sandlapper Publishing Co., Inc.

LEE, ROBERT E. (ROBERT EDWARD), 1807-1870

Anderson, Paul Christopher. Robert E. Lee: Legendary Commander of the Confederacy. (Library of American Lives & Times Ser.). 112p. 2009. (gr. 5-5). 69.20 *(978-1-60853-501-9(0))* 2005. (Illus.). (YA). (gr. 4-8). lib. bdg. 34.60 *(978-0-8239-5748-4(9))* Rosen Publishing Group, Inc., The.

Archer, Jules. A House Divided: The Lives of Ulysses S. Grant & Robert E. Lee. rev. ed. 2015. (Jules Archer History for Young Readers Ser.). (ENG., Illus.). 176p. (J). (gr. 6). 16.99 *(978-1-63220-604-6(8),* Sky Pony Pr.) Skyhorse Publishing Co., Inc.

Bader, Bonnie. Who Was Robert E. Lee? Harrison, Nancy & O'brien, John, illus. 2014. (Who Was? Ser.). (ENG.). 112p. (J). (gr. 3-7). 5.99 *(978-0-448-47909-5(5),* Grosset & Dunlap) Penguin Young Readers Group.

—Who Was Robert E. Lee? 2014. (Who Was... ? Ser.). lib. bdg. 16.00 *(978-0-606-35693-0(2))* Turtleback Bks.

Benoit, Peter. The Surrender at Appomattox. 2011. (Cornerstones of Freedom, Third Ser.). 64p. (J). (ENG.). pap. 8.95 *(978-0-531-26566-6(8));* lib. bdg. 30.00 *(978-0-531-25041-9(5))* Scholastic Library Publishing. (Children's Pr.).

Collins, Terry. Robert E. Lee: The Story of the Great Confederate General. Mallea, Cristian, illus. (American Graphic Ser.). (ENG.). 32p. (gr. 3-4). 2011. pap. 47.70 *(978-1-4296-6436-3(3))* 2010. lib. bdg. 30.65 *(978-1-4296-5475-3(9))* Capstone Press of Coughlan Cos. (Graphic Library).

Conklin, Wendy. Robert E. Lee, 1 vol. 2005. (Primary Source Readers Ser.). (ENG.). 24p. (J). (gr. 4-4). pap. 8.99 *(978-0-7439-8918-3(X))* Shell Educational Publishing.

Hale, Sarah Elder, ed. Robert E. Lee: Duty & Honor. 2005. (ENG., Illus.). 48p. (J). (gr. 3-9). 17.95 *(978-0-8126-7905-2(9))* Cobblestone Publishing Co.

Kantor, MacKinlay. Lee & Grant at Appomattox. 2015. (ENG.). 144p. pap. 9.95 *(978-0-9904604-0-4(1))* Flying Point Pr.

—Lee & Grant at Appomattox. (Great Leaders & Events Ser.). (ENG.). 208p. (J). (gr. 4-8). 2017. lib. bdg. 35.99 ***(978-1-942875-25-3(8))*** 2016. (Illus.). pap. 12.99 *(978-0-7603-5226-7(7))* Quarto Publishing Group USA. (Voyageur Pr.).

Kerby, Mona. Robert E. Lee: Commander of the Confederate Army. 2015. (Legendary American Biographies Ser.). 96p. (J). (gr. 6-12). 27.94 *(978-0-7660-6490-4(5));* pap. 10.95 *(978-0-7660-6491-1(3))* Enslow Pubs., Inc.

Marrin, Albert. Virginia's General: Robert E. Lee & the Civil War. 2003. (Illus.). 201p. (YA). pap. 14.95 *(978-1-893103-14-6(5))* Beautiful Feet Bks.

McNeese, Tim. Robert E. Lee. 2009. (Leaders of the Civil War Era Ser.). (Illus.). 152p. (gr. 6-12). lib. bdg. 35.00 *(978-1-60413-304-2(X),* Chelsea Hse.) Facts On File, Inc.

Pingry, Patricia A. Meet Robert E. Lee. Johnson, Meredith, illus. 2004. (J). 9.95 *(978-0-8249-5465-9(3),* Ideal Pubns.) Worthy Publishing.

—The Story of Robert E. Lee. Johnson, Meredith, illus. 2004. (ENG.). 26p. (J). (gr. -1-k). bds. 6.95 *(978-0-8249-6501-3(9),* Ideal Pubns.) Worthy Publishing.

Ransom, Candice. Robert E. Lee. 2006. (History Maker Bios Ser.). (Illus.). 48p. (J). (gr. 3-7). lib. bdg. 26.60 *(978-0-8225-2437-3(6),* Lerner Pubns.) Lerner Publishing Group.

—Willie McLean & the Civil War Surrender. Reeves, Jeni, illus. 2004. (On My Own History Ser.). (ENG.). 48p. (gr. 2-4). 25.26 *(978-1-57505-588-6(0));* pap. 6.95 *(978-1-57505-698-2(4))* Lerner Publishing Group.

Rice, Earle, Jr. Robert E. Lee: First Soldier of the Confederacy. 2005. (Civil War Leaders Ser.). (Illus.). 176p. (gr. 6-12). 28.95 *(978-1-931798-47-1(8))* Reynolds, Morgan Inc.

Robertson, James I., Jr. Robert E. Lee: Virginian Soldier, American Citizen. 2005. (ENG., Illus.). 176p. (YA). (gr. 7-12). 29.99 *(978-0-689-85731-7(4),* Atheneum Bks. for Young Readers) Simon & Schuster Children's Publishing.

Stark, Ken. Marching to Appomattox: The Footrace That Ended the Civil War. Stark, Ken & Stark, illus. 2009. (ENG.). 48p. (J). (gr. 4-7). 17.99 *(978-0-399-24212-0(0),* G.P. Putnam's Sons Books for Young Readers) Penguin Young Readers Group.

Vansant, Wayne. Grant vs. Lee: The Graphic History of the Civil War's Greatest Rivals During the Last Year of the War. Vansant, Wayne, illus. 2015. (Graphic Histories Ser.). (ENG., Illus.). 104p. (J). (gr. 8-12). 34.65 *(978-1-939581-78-5(8))* Quarto Publishing Group USA.

—Grant vs. Lee: The Graphic History of the Civil War's Greatest Rivals During the Last Year of the War. 2013. (Zenith Graphic Histories Ser.). (ENG., Illus.). 104p. pap. 19.99 *(978-0-7603-4531-3(7),* 0760345317, Zenith Pr.) Quarto Publishing Group USA.

LEE, ROBERT E. (ROBERT EDWARD), 1807-1870—FICTION

Altsheler, Joseph A. The Shades of the Wilderness: A Story of Lee's Great Stand. 2006. (Civil War Ser.: Vol. 7). 308p. (J). reprint ed. 29.95 *(978-1-4218-2336-2(5));* pap. 14.95 *(978-1-4218-2436-9(1))* 1st World Publishing, Inc. (1st World Library - Literary Society).

—The Shades of the Wilderness: A Story of Lee's Great Stand. (Civil War Ser.: Vol. 7). 312p. (J). reprint ed. lib. bdg. 25.95 *(978-0-88411-940-1(8))* Amereon Ltd.

—The Shades of the Wilderness: A Story of Lee's Great Stand. l.t. ed. (Civil War Ser.: Vol. 7). (J). reprint ed. 2006. (ENG.). 278p. pap. 23.99 *(978-1-4264-6220-7(4))* 2008. 280p. 25.99 *(978-0-554-33603-9(0))* 2008. 280p. 28.99 *(978-0-554-24300-9(8))* 2006. (ENG.). 250p. pap. 20.99 *(978-1-4264-6165-1(8))* Creative Media Partners, LLC.

—The Shades of the Wilderness: A Story of Lee's Great Stand. 2006. (Civil War Ser.: Vol. 7). (J). reprint ed. pap. *(978-1-4065-0822-2(5))* Dodo Pr.

—The Shades of the Wilderness: A Story of Lee's Great Stand. 2007. (Civil War Ser.: Vol. 7). 180p. (J). reprint ed. per. *(978-1-4068-1686-0(8))* Echo Library.

—The Shades of the Wilderness: A Story of Lee's Great Stand. 2010. (Civil War Ser.: Vol. 7). (Illus.). 162p. (J). (gr. 4-7). reprint ed. pap. 19.99 *(978-1-153-72059-5(0))* General Bks. LLC.

—The Shades of the Wilderness: A Story of Lee's Great Stand. (Civil War Ser.: Vol. 7). (J). reprint ed. 2011. (gr. 4-7). *(978-1-164-50265-4(4))* 2010. 324p. (gr. 4-7). pap. 24.76 *(978-1-163-19558-1(8))* 2008. 324p. 45.95 *(978-1-4366-8424-8(2))* 2007. 324p. per. 30.95 *(978-1-4325-9861-7(9))* Kessinger Publishing, LLC.

—The Shades of the Wilderness: A Story of Lee's Great Stand. 2007. (Civil War Ser.: Vol. 7). 308p. reprint ed. per. 16.45 *(978-1-60424-029-0(6),* Book Jungle) Standard Pubns., Inc.

—The Shades of the Wilderness: A Story of Lee's Great Stand. 2011. (Civil War Ser.: Vol. 7). 280p. (J). reprint ed. pap. *(978-3-8424-4396-9(X))* Tredition GmbH.

—The Tree of Appomattox: A Story of the Civil War's Close. 2006. (Civil War Ser.: Vol. 8). 324p. (J). reprint ed. 29.95 *(978-1-4218-2338-6(1));* pap. 14.95 *(978-1-4218-2438-3(8))* 1st World Publishing, Inc. (1st World Library - Literary Society).

—The Tree of Appomattox: A Story of the Civil War's Close. l.t. ed. (Civil War Ser.: Vol. 8). (J). reprint ed. 2007. (ENG.). 298p. pap. 23.99 *(978-1-4346-1261-8(9))* 2008. 300p. 28.99 *(978-0-554-26479-0(X))* 2008. 300p. 25.99 *(978-0-554-35782-9(8))* 2007. (ENG.). 266p. pap. 21.99 *(978-1-4346-1190-1(6))* Creative Media Partners, LLC.

—The Tree of Appomattox: A Story of the Civil War's Close. 2006. (Civil War Ser.: Vol. 8). (J). reprint ed. pap. *(978-1-4065-0828-4(4))* Dodo Pr.

—The Tree of Appomattox: A Story of the Civil War's Close. 2007. (Civil War Ser.: Vol. 8). 192p. (J). reprint ed. per. *(978-1-4068-1693-8(0))* Echo Library.

—The Tree of Appomattox: A Story of the Civil War's Close. 2010. (Civil War Ser.: Vol. 8). (Illus.). 174p. (J). (gr. 4-7). reprint ed. pap. 19.99 *(978-1-153-72402-9(2))* General Bks. LLC.

—The Tree of Appomattox: A Story of the Civil War's Close. Wrenn, Charles L., illus. (Civil War Ser.: Vol. 8). 332p. (J). (gr. 4-7). reprint ed. 2011. 45.95 *(978-1-169-88135-8(1))* 2010. 36.76 *(978-1-163-21361-2(6))* 2010. pap. 24.76 *(978-1-162-78752-7(X))* Kessinger Publishing, LLC.

—The Tree of Appomattox: A Story of the Civil War's Close. 2005. (Civil War Ser.: Vol. 8). (J). reprint ed. pap. 30.95 *(978-1-4179-2071-6(8))* Kessinger Publishing, LLC.

—The Tree of Appomattox: A Story of the Civil War's Close. Wrenn, Charles L., illus. 2005. (Civil War Ser.: Vol. 8). 332p. (J). reprint ed. 45.95 *(978-1-4326-1333-4(2))* Kessinger Publishing, LLC.

—The Tree of Appomattox: A Story of the Civil War's Close. 2011. (Civil War Ser.: Vol. 8). 294p. (J). (gr. 4-7). reprint ed. pap. *(978-3-8424-8485-6(2))* Tredition GmbH.

LEEUWENHOEK, ANTONI VAN, 1632-1723

Yount, Lisa. Antoni Van Leeuwenhoek: First to See Microscopic Life. rev. ed. 2008. (Great Minds of Science Ser.). (Illus.). 128p. (J). (gr. k-5). lib. bdg. 33.27 *(978-0-7660-3012-1(1))* Enslow Pubs., Inc.

—Antoni Van Leeuwenhoek: Genius Discoverer of Microscopic Life. 2015. (Genius Scientists & Their Genius Ideas Ser.). 96p. (J). (gr. 5-12). 27.94 *(978-0-7660-6525-3(1));* pap. 10.95 *(978-0-7660-6526-0(X))* Enslow Pubs., Inc.

LEFT (POLITICAL SCIENCE)

see Right and Left (Political Science)

LEFT- AND RIGHT-HANDEDNESS—FICTION

Barrett, Judi & Barrett, Ron. The Marshmallow Incident. Barrett, Ron, illus. 2009. (Illus.). (J). pap. *(978-0-545-04654-1(8),* Scholastic Pr.) Scholastic, Inc.

Ritter, John H. Choosing up Sides. 2004. 166p. (gr. 5-9). 16.00 *(978-0-7569-4094-2(X))* Perfection Learning Corp.

LEG

Brown, Jonatha A. Animal Feet & Legs. 2006. (Why Animals Look Different Ser.). (Illus.). 24p. (gr. 1-4). lib. bdg. 22.00 *(978-0-8368-6860-9(9),* Weekly Reader Leveled Readers) Stevens, Gareth Publishing LLLP.

—Las patas y los pies de los animales. 2006. (En que se diferencian los animales (Why Animals Look Different) Ser.). (SPA., Illus.). 24p. (J). (gr. 1-4). lib. bdg. 22.00 *(978-0-8368-7414-3(5),* Weekly Reader Leveled Readers) Stevens, Gareth Publishing LLLP.

Douglas, Lloyd G. My Legs & Feet. 2004. (Welcome Bks.). (ENG.). 24p. (J). (gr. -1-2). pap. 4.95 *(978-0-516-22130-4(2),* Children's Pr.) Scholastic Library Publishing.

Gill, Monica & Viegas, Jennifer. The Lower Limbs in 3D. 2015. (Human Body In 3D Ser.). (ENG., Illus.). 64p. (J). (gr. 5-6). 32.95 *(978-1-4994-3601-3(7),* Rosen Central) Rosen Publishing Group, Inc., The.

Holland, Mary. Animal Legs, 1 vol. 2016. (Animal Adaptations Ser.). (ENG., Illus.). 32p. (J). (gr. k-3). 17.95 *(978-1-62855-843-2(1))* Arbordale Publishing.

—Patas de Los Animales, 1 vol. 2016. (SPA., Illus.). 32p. (J). (gr. k-3). pap. 9.95 *(978-1-62855-845-6(8))* Arbordale Publishing.

Schaefer, Lola M. Some Kids Wear Leg Braces, 1 vol. 2007. (Understanding Differences Ser.). (ENG., Illus.). 24p. (gr. k-1). 21.99 *(978-1-4296-0813-8(7),* Pebble Bks.) Capstone Press of Coughlan Cos.

—Some Kids Wear Leg Braces. Saunders-Smith, Gail, ed. rev. ed. 2008. (Understanding Differences Ser.). (ENG., Illus.). 24p. (gr. k-1). pap. 6.29 *(978-1-4296-1777-2(2),* Pebble Bks.) Capstone Press of Coughlan Cos.

LEGAL HOLIDAYS

see Holidays

LEGAL PROFESSION

see Lawyers

LEGAL TENDER

see Paper Money

LEGENDS

see also Fables; Fairy Tales; Folklore; Mythology

Adil, Hajjah Amina & Sperling, Karima. My Little Lore of Light: A Child's Version of Lore of Light. 2005. (Illus.). x, 193p. (J). 22.00 *(978-1-930409-35-4(4))* Islamic Supreme Council of America.

American Mythology. 2013. (Mythology & Culture Worldwide Ser.). (ENG., Illus.). 128p. (J). (gr. 7-10). lib. bdg. 34.45 *(978-1-4205-0904-5(7),* Lucent Bks.) Cengage Gale.

Au, May Parker. Princess Huilua & Kamapuaa. 2007.Tr. of Ke Kamalii Wahine o Huilua a me Kamapuaa. (ENG & HAW.). (J). lib. bdg. *(978-0-9773495-4-8(3))* Na Kamalei Koolauloa Early Education Program.

Barber, Nicola. Lost Cities, 1 vol. 2013. (Treasure Hunters Ser.). (ENG., Illus.). 48p. (gr. 5-8). pap. 9.25 *(978-1-4109-4959-2(1));* lib. bdg. 29.99 *(978-1-4109-4952-3(4))* Heinemann-Raintree.

Benge, Janet & Benge, Geoffrey Francis. Heroes of History - Books 1-5 Gift Set, 5 vols. 2006. (ENG.). per. 44.95 *(978-1-883002-89-3(3))* Emerald Bks.

Biggs, Fiona, ed. Pocket Irish Legends. 2014. (ENG., Illus.). 256p. (J). 10.00 *(978-0-7171-5899-7(3))* M.H. Gill & Co. U. C. IRL. Dist: Dufour Editions, Inc.

Bingham, Jane. Classical Myth: A Treasury of Greek & Roman Legends, Art, & History. 2007. (Myth Ser.). (Illus.). 96p. (J). (gr. 4-7). pap. 7.99 *(978-0-7858-2350-6(6))* Book Sales, Inc.

—Classical Myth: A Treasury of Greek & Roman Legends, Art, & History. 2007. (ENG., Illus.). 96p. (C). (gr. 6-18). lib. bdg. 140.00 *(978-0-7656-8104-1(8),* Y181755) Routledge.

Blackwood, Gary L. Unsolved History, 4 bks., Set. Incl. Debatable Deaths. 80p. (gr. 6). lib. bdg. 23.95 *(978-0-7614-1888-7(1));* Enigmatic Events. 80p. (gr. 6-7). lib. bdg. 23.95 *(978-0-7614-1889-4(X));* Legends or Lies. 72p. lib. bdg. *(978-0-7614-1891-7(1));* Perplexing People. 80p. (gr. 6-7). lib. bdg. 23.95 *(978-0-7614-1890-0(3));* (Illus.). 2005. *(978-0-7614-1892-4(X),* Benchmark Bks.) Marshall Cavendish Corp.

Blackwood, Gary L. & Siburt, Ruth. Legends or Lies? 2009. (Benchmark Rockets: History's Mysteries Ser.). 32p. (gr. 3). 28.50 *(978-0-7614-4359-9(2))* Marshall Cavendish GBR. Dist: Marshall Cavendish Corp.

Bosco, Don. Island of Legends. 2016. (ENG., Illus.). 96p. pap. 12.99 *(978-981-4751-36-0(7))* Marshall Cavendish International (Asia) Private Ltd. SGP. Dist: National Bk. Network.

Braun, Eric & Bowman, James Cloyd. Pecos Bill Tames a Colossal Cyclone, 1 vol. Weber, Lisa K., illus. 2014. (American Folk Legends Ser.). (ENG.). 32p. (gr. k-2). lib. bdg. 27.32 *(978-1-4795-5429-4(4))* Picture Window Bks.

Brinkerhoff, Shirley. Contemporary Folklore. 2004. (North American Folklore Ser.). (Illus.). 112p. (J). (gr. 7-18). lib. bdg. 22.95 *(978-1-59084-331-4(2))* Mason Crest.

Burtinshaw, Julie. Romantic Ghost Stories, 1 vol., Vol. 1. Wangler, Chris, ed. rev. ed. 2003. (Ghost Stories Ser.). (ENG., Illus.). 224p. (gr. 4). pap. 12.95 *(978-1-894877-28-2(4),* 1894877284, Ghost Hse. Bks.) Lone Pine Publishing USA.

Carroll, Yvonne & Waters, Fiona, as told by. A Child's Treasury of Irish Stories & Poems. 2004. (ENG., Illus.). 194p. (J). 32.95 *(978-0-7171-3795-4(3))* M.H. Gill & Co. U. C. IRL. Dist: Dufour Editions, Inc.

Ceceri, Kathy. World Myths & Legends: 25 Projects You Can Build Yourself. Braley, Shawn, illus. 2010. (Build It Yourself Ser.). (ENG.). 128p. (J). (gr. 3-7). pap. 15.95 *(978-1-934670-43-9(X))* Octavio Publishing.

Clay, Kathryn & Vonne, Mira. Top 10 Urban Legends, 1 vol. 2012. (Top 10 Unexplained Ser.). (ENG.). 32p. (gr. 1-2).

26.65 *(978-1-4296-7638-0(8)*, Blazers) Capstone Press of Coughlan Cos.

Confederated Salish and Kootenai Tribes Staff. Bull Trout's Gift: By the Confederated Salish & Kootenai Tribes. 2011. (ENG., Illus.). 70p. 21.95 *(978-0-8032-3491-8(0))* Univ. of Nebraska Pr.

Cooper, Gilly Cameron. How the World Began: Creation in Myths & Legends. Ludlow, Patricia, illus. 2006. (ENG.). 48p. (J). (gr. 3-7). pap. 11.99 *(978-1-84476-246-0(7))* Anness Publishing GBR. Dist: National Bk. Network.

Daning, Tom. Chinese Mythology: The Four Dragons. 2007. (Jr. Graphic Mythologies Ser.). (ENG., Illus.). 24p. (J). (gr. 2-5). lib. bdg. 25.25 *(978-1-4042-3400-0(4))* Rosen Publishing Group, Inc., The.

—The Four Dragons: A Chinese Myth. 2007. (Graphic Myths (New York, N.Y.) Ser.). (ENG., Illus.). 24p. (gr. 3-8). pap. 10.60 *(978-1-4042-2153-6(0)*, PowerKids Pr.) Rosen Publishing Group, Inc., The.

de Las Casas, Dianne. Blue Frog: The Legend of Chocolate, 1 vol. Stone-Barker, Holly, illus. 2011. (ENG.). 32p. (J). (gr. k-3). 16.99 *(978-1-4556-1459-2(9))* Pelican Publishing Co., Inc.

Dias, Christina & Abreu, Aline. O Misterio Da Bola Castanho-Avermelhada. 2010. (POR.). (J). 12.00 *(978-1-58432-665-6(4))* Educa Vision Inc.

DuMont, Brianna. Famous Phonies: Legends, Fakes, & Phonies Who Changed History. 2014. (Changed History Ser.). (ENG., Illus.). 160p. (J). (gr. 4-9). 14.95 *(978-1-62914-645-4(5)*, Sky Pony Pr.) Skyhorse Publishing Co., Inc.

Encyclopaedia Britannica, Inc. Staff, compiled by. Legends, Myths & Folktales. 2003. (Illus.). 64p. 14.95 *(978-1-59339-037-2(8))* Encyclopaedia Britannica, Inc.

Famous Legends. 2015. (Famous Legends Ser.). (ENG.). 32p. (J). (gr. 2-3). 151.50 *(978-1-4824-2545-1(9))*; pap., pap., pap. 378.00 *(978-1-4824-3462-0(8))*; pap., pap., pap. 63.00 *(978-1-4824-3463-7(6))* Stevens, Gareth Publishing LLLP.

Famous Legends: Set 2. 2017. (Famous Legends Ser.). 32p. (gr. 2-3). pap. 63.00 ***(978-1-5382-0481-8(9))***; lib. bdg. 151.50 ***(978-1-5382-0466-5(5))*** Stevens, Gareth Publishing LLLP.

Ganeri, Anita & West, David. Heroes of Myths & Legends. 2012. (J). 70.50 *(978-1-4488-5239-0(0))*; pap. 11.75 *(978-1-4488-5238-3(2))*; lib. bdg. 26.50 *(978-1-4488-5200-0(5))* Rosen Publishing Group, Inc., The. (PowerKids Pr.).

Gitlin, Marty, et al. Legends in the Making, 1 vol. 2014. (Legends in the Making Ser.). (ENG.). 32p. (gr. 3-4). lib. bdg. 111.96 *(978-1-4765-6221-6(0))* Capstone Press of Coughlan Cos.

Guillain, Charlotte. Writing & Staging Myths & Legends. 2016. (Writing & Staging Plays Ser.). (ENG., Illus.). 48p. (gr. 4-6). lib. bdg. 33.32 *(978-1-4846-2772-3(5)*, Heinemann InfoSearch) Heinemann-Raintree.

Haberstroh, Marilyn & Panik, Sharon. A Quetzalcóatl Tale of Corn. Castle, Lynn, illus. 2014. (Quetzalcóatl Tales Ser.). (ENG.). 48p. (J). (gr. k-5). pap. 9.95 *(978-1-60732-345-7(1))* Univ. Pr. of Colorado.

Herdling, Glenn. African Mythology: Anansi. 2009. (Jr. Graphic Mythologies Ser.). (ENG.). 24p. (J). (gr. 2-3). 47.90 *(978-1-61513-855-5(2)*, PowerKids Pr.) Rosen Publishing Group, Inc., The.

Jacq, Christian. Cuentos y Leyendas de la Epoca de Las Pirámides. Corral, Mercedes, tr. from FRE. 6th ed. 2003. (Fables & Legends Ser.). (SPA., Illus.). 144p. (J). 9.95 *(978-84-239-8893-8(7))* Espasa Calpe, S.A. ESP. Dist: Planeta Publishing Corp.

Lassieur, Allison. Is the Loch Ness Monster Real? 2015. (Unexplained: What's the Evidence? Ser.). (ENG., Illus.). 32p. (J). (gr. 2-4). 19.95 *(978-1-60753-805-9(9))* Amicus Publishing.

Light, Kate. Mermaid Legends. 2017. (Famous Legends Ser.). 32p. (J). (gr. 2-3). pap. 10.50 ***(978-1-5382-0244-9(1))*** Stevens, Gareth Publishing LLLP.

Lynette, Rachel. Urban Legends. 2008. (Mysterious Encounters Ser.). (ENG., Illus.). 48p. (gr. 4-8). lib. bdg. 33.60 *(978-0-7377-4049-3(3)*, LML02109-240016, Kidhaven) Cengage Gale.

Mabie, Hamilton Wright. Legends That Every Child Should Know. 2004. reprint ed. pap. 22.95 *(978-1-4191-2963-6(5))*; pap. 1.99 *(978-1-4192-2963-3(X))* Kessinger Publishing, LLC.

—Legends That Every Child Should Know: A Selection of the Great Legends of All Times for Young People. 2007. (ENG.). 216p. pap. 20.99 *(978-1-4264-4960-4(7))*; 242p. pap. 22.99 *(978-1-4264-5261-1(6))* Creative Media Partners, LLC.

Massey, Eithne. Irish Legends: Newgrange, Tara & the Boyne Valley. Jackson, Lisa, illus. 2016. (ENG.). 64p. (J). 19.00 *(978-1-84717-683-7(6))* O'Brien Pr., Ltd., The IRL. Dist: Dufour Editions, Inc.

McCullum, Kenya. 12 Creepy Urban Legends. 2017. (Scary & Spooky Ser.). (ENG., Illus.). 32p. (J). (gr. 3-6). 21.95 *(978-1-63235-292-7(3))* Pr. Room Editions LLC.

McGinnis, Mark W. The Show-Off Monkey & Other Taoist Tales. 2017. (ENG.). 88p. (gr. k-4). 19.95 ***(978-1-61180-347-1(0))*** Shambhala Pubns., Inc.

Metaxas, Eric. King Midas & the Golden Touch, 1 vol. Prato, Rodica, illus. 2007. (Rabbit Ears: A Classic Tale Ser.). (ENG.). 36p. (gr. -1-3). 25.65 *(978-1-59961-309-3(3))* Spotlight.

Miller, Reagan & Stone, Janet. How to Tell a Legend. Crabtree Publishing Staff, ed. 2011. (Text Styles Ser.: No. 3). (ENG.). 32p. (J). (gr. 3-6). pap. *(978-0-7787-1637-2(6))* Crabtree Publishing Co.

—How to Tell a Legend. 2011. (Text Styles Ser.). (ENG.). 32p. (J). (gr. 3-6). lib. bdg. *(978-0-7787-1632-7(5))* Crabtree Publishing Co.

Mitchell, Chris. How Many Greeks Can You Fit Inside a Horse? Pinder, Andrew, illus. 2016. (Dr Dino's Learnatorium Ser.). (ENG.). 192p. (J). (gr. 4-7). pap. 8.99 *(978-1-78418-654-8(6))* Blake, John Publishing, Ltd. GBR. Dist: Independent Pubs. Group.

Montgomery, R. A. Journey under the Sea. Sundaravej, Sittisan, illus. 2006. (Choose Your Own Adventure Ser.: No. 2). 144p. (J). (gr. 4-8). per. 6.99 *(978-1-933390-02-4(6)*, CHCL02) Chooseco LLC.

—Journey under the Sea. 2006. (Choose Your Own Adventure Ser.: 2). 17.20 *(978-1-4177-6410-5(4)*, Turtleback) Turtleback Bks.

Morley, Jacqueline & Salariya, David. World of Myths & Legends. Franklin, Carolyn, illus. 2013. (Mythology Ser.). 64p. (gr. 3-6). 41.35 ***(978-1-908973-93-1(5))*** Book Hse. GBR. Dist: Black Rabbit Bks.

Morpurgo, Michael. Beowulf. Foreman, Michael, illus. 2015. (ENG.). 160p. (J). (gr. 3-7). pap. 6.99 *(978-0-7636-7297-3(1))* Candlewick Pr.

Oliveira, Jô de. Kuarup, a Festa DOS Mortos: Lendas DOS Povos Indigenas Do Xingu. 2010. (POR.). (J). 12.00 *(978-1-58432-661-8(1))* Educa Vision Inc.

Owings, Lisa. What Are Legends, Folktales, & Other Classic Stories? 2014. (Name That Text Type! Ser.). (Illus.). 32p. (gr. 2-4). pap. 7.95 *(978-1-4677-4518-5(9))*; lib. bdg. 26.60 *(978-1-4677-4061-6(6)*, Lerner Pubns.) Lerner Publishing Group.

Pearce, Q. L. La Llorona. 2009. (Mysterious Encounters Ser.). (ENG., Illus.). 48p. (J). 29.00 *(978-0-7377-4571-9(1))* Cengage Gale.

Pearson, Maggie. Magic & Misery: Traditional Tales from Around the World. Greenwood, Francesca, illus. 2016. (World of Stories Ser.). (ENG.). 176p. (J). (gr. 2-6). 26.65 *(978-1-5124-1319-9(4))* Lerner Publishing Group.

Randall, Ronne. The Children's Book of Myths & Legends. Howells, Graham, illus. 2012. (ENG.). 128p. (J). (gr. 2-7). pap. 11.99 *(978-1-84322-819-6(X))* Anness Publishing GBR. Dist: National Bk. Network.

Randall, Ronne. Children's Stories from Myths & Legends: Classic Tales from Around the World. Howells, Graham, illus. 2017. (ENG.). 128p. (J). (gr. 3-12). 16.99 ***(978-1-86147-852-8(6)***, Armadillo) Anness Publishing GBR. Dist: National Bk. Network.

Reed, Natasha. Mythical Creatures: Sticker Book. Kincaid, Angela, illus. 2005. (Stickertastic Ser.). 24p. (J). (gr. -1-7). pap. *(978-1-84510-119-0(7))* Top That! Publishing PLC.

Rosen Publishing Staff. Heroes & Legends, 1 vol. 2015. (Heroes & Legends Ser.). (ENG.). 80p. (YA). 213.60 *(978-1-4777-8171-5(4)*, Rosen Young Adult) Rosen Publishing Group, Inc., The.

Sanna, Ellyn. Folk Tales & Legends. 2004. (North American Folklore Ser.). (Illus.). 112p. (J). (gr. 7-18). lib. bdg. 22.95 *(978-1-59084-346-8(0))* Mason Crest.

Schulte, Mary. Dover Demon. 2009. (Mysterious Encounters Ser.). (ENG., Illus.). 48p. (J). 29.00 *(978-0-7377-4570-2(3)*, Greenhaven Pr., Inc.) Cengage Gale.

Sheppard, Si. Heroes & Legends: Set 2. 2015. (Heroes & Legends Ser.). (ENG.). 88p. (YA). (gr. 7-8). 178.00 *(978-1-4994-6193-0(3)*, Rosen Young Adult) Rosen Publishing Group, Inc., The.

Sinclair, Mehded Maryam. Miraculous Happenings in the Year of the Elephant. 2010. (ENG., Illus.). 28p. (J). (gr. 2-6). 14.95 *(978-0-86037-491-6(2))* Kube Publishing Ltd. GBR. Dist: Consortium Bk. Sales & Distribution.

Steele, Philip. Incredible Quests: Epic Journeys in Myth & Legend. Climpson, Sue, illus. 2006. (ENG.). 48p. (J). (gr. 3-7). pap. 11.99 *(978-1-84476-247-7(5))* Anness Publishing GBR. Dist: National Bk. Network.

Tappan, Eva March. The Children's Hour, Volume 4. Stories of Legendary Heroes. 2013. 514p. pap. 33.45 *(978-1-4733-1070-4(9))* Borah Pr.

Tonatiuh, Duncan. The Princess & the Warrior: A Tale of Two Volcanoes. 2016. (ENG., Illus.). 40p. (J). (gr. 1-4). 16.95 *(978-1-4197-2130-4(5)*, Abrams Bks. for Young Readers) Abrams, Inc.

Vickers, Roy Henry & Budd, Robert. Cloudwalker. Vickers, Roy Henry, illus. 2014. (ENG., Illus.). 40p. (J). 19.95 *(978-1-55017-619-3(6))* Harbour Publishing Co., Ltd. CAN. Dist: Midpoint Trade Bks., Inc.

—Orca Chief. Vickers, Roy Henry, illus. 2015. (ENG., Illus.). 40p. (J). 19.95 *(978-1-55017-693-3(5))* Harbour Publishing Co., Ltd. CAN. Dist: Midpoint Trade Bks., Inc.

—Peace Dancer. 2016. (ENG., Illus.). 40p. (J). 19.95 *(978-1-55017-739-8(7))* Harbour Publishing Co., Ltd. CAN. Dist: Midpoint Trade Bks., Inc.

—Raven Brings the Light: A Northwest Coast Legend. Vickers, Roy Henry, illus. 2013. (ENG., Illus.). 40p. (J). 19.95 *(978-1-55017-593-6(9))* Harbour Publishing Co., Ltd. CAN. Dist: Midpoint Trade Bks., Inc.

Whistler, Charles W. Havelok the Dane: A Legend of Old Grimsby & Lincoln. 2006. (ENG.). 248p. pap. 20.99 *(978-1-4264-6429-4(0))*; 280p. pap. 23.99 *(978-1-4264-6503-1(3))* Creative Media Partners, LLC.

Wildwood, Gretchen. Ancient Mesopotamian Civilization. Cantucci, Alessandro & Morandi, Andrea, illus. 2009. (Ancient Civilizations & Their Myths & Legends Ser.). (YA). (gr. 5-9). lib. bdg. 29.25 *(978-1-4042-8037-3(5))* Rosen Publishing Group, Inc., The.

Wilkinson, Philip. Chinese Myth: A Treasury of Legends, Art, & History. 2007. (Myth Ser.). (Illus.). 96p. (J). (gr. 4-7). pap. 7.99 *(978-0-7858-2348-3(4)*, Chartwell) Book Sales, Inc.

Williams, Rose. The Labors of Aeneas: What a Pain It Was to Found the Roman Race. 2003. (Illus.). (YA). 18.00 *(978-0-86516-556-4(4))* Bolchazy-Carducci Pubs.

World Book, Inc Staff, contrib. by. Tales Through Time: A Supplement to Childcraft-The How & Why Library. 2009. (Illus.). 204p. (J). *(978-0-7166-0622-2(4))* World Bk., Inc.

Yasuda, Anita. Dragon, the Phoenix, & the Beautiful Pearl: A Chinese Dragon Spirit Myth. 2014. (Short Tales Chinese Myths Ser.). 32p. (J). (gr. 3-6). lib. bdg. 24.21 *(978-1-62402-030-8(5)*, Short Tales) Magic Wagon.

—Jade Emperor: A Chinese Zodiac Myth. 2014. (Short Tales Chinese Myths Ser.). 32p. (J). (gr. 3-6). lib. bdg. 24.21 *(978-1-62402-031-5(3)*, Short Tales) Magic Wagon.

—The 12 Most Amazing American Myths & Legends. 2014. (ENG., Illus.). 32p. (J). *(978-1-63235-010-7(6))* Pr. Room Editions LLC.

—The 12 Most Amazing American Myths & Legends. 2015. (ENG., Illus.). 32p. (J). pap. 9.95 *(978-1-63235-070-1(X))* RiverStream Publishing.

LEGENDS—AFRICA

World Book, Inc Staff, contrib. by. Myths & Legends of Africa. 2015. (Illus.). 64p. (J). *(978-0-7166-2631-2(4))* World Bk., Inc.

LEGENDS—AUSTRALIA

Marshall, James Vance. Stories from the Billabong. Firebrace, Francis, illus. 2010. (ENG.). 64p. (J). (gr. k-3). pap. 12.99 *(978-1-84780-124-1(2)*, Frances Lincoln) Quarto Publishing Group UK GBR. Dist: Hachette Bk. Group.

LEGENDS, CELTIC

see Celts—Folklore; Legends—Ireland

LEGENDS—CHINA

Casey, Dawn. The Great Race: The Story of the Chinese Zodiac. Wilson, Anne, illus. 2006. (ENG.). 32p. (J). (gr. -1-3). 16.99 *(978-1-905236-77-0(8))* Barefoot Bks., Inc.

Daning, Tom. Chinese Mythology: The Four Dragons. 2009. (Jr. Graphic Mythologies Ser.). (ENG.). 24p. (J). (gr. 2-3). 47.90 *(978-1-61513-858-6(7)*, PowerKids Pr.) Rosen Publishing Group, Inc., The.

—Mitología China: Los Cuatro Dragones. 2009. (Historietas Juveniles: Mitologías (Jr. Graphic Mythologies) Ser.). (SPA., Illus.). 24p. (gr. 3-8). pap. 10.60 *(978-1-4358-3326-5(0))* Rosen Publishing Group, Inc., The.

Wilkinson, Philip. Chinese Myth: A Treasury of Legends, Art, & History. 2007. (ENG., Illus.). 96p. (C). (gr. 6-18). lib. bdg. 158.00 *(978-0-7656-8103-4(X)*, Y181705) Routledge.

LEGENDS—EGYPT

Kramer, Ann. Egyptian Myth: A Treasury of Legends, Art, & History. 2007. (Myth Ser.). (Illus.). 96p. (J). (gr. 4-7). pap. 7.99 *(978-0-7858-2347-6(6)*, Chartwell) Book Sales, Inc.

—Egyptian Myth: A Treasury of Legends, Art, & History. 2007. (ENG., Illus.). 96p. (C). (gr. 6-18). lib. bdg. 158.00 *(978-0-7656-8105-8(6)*, Y182128) Routledge.

World Book, Inc Staff, contrib. by. Myths & Legends of Ancient Egypt. 2015. (Illus.). 64p. (J). *(978-0-7166-2633-6(0))* World Bk., Inc.

LEGENDS—GERMANY

Bindrim, Hans-Wolfgang. Wilhelm Hauffs die Errettung Fatmes: Textanalyse und Interpretation. 2012. (Europaeische Hochschulschriften / European University Studies / Publications Universitaires Européennes Ser.: 2028). (GER.). 130p. pap. 32.95 *(978-3-631-63429-5(3)*, 263429) Lang, Peter GmbH, Internationaler Verlag der Wissenschaften DEU. Dist: Lang, Peter.

LEGENDS—HAWAII

Holokai, Ben W., Jr. Myths & Legends of Hawai'i Coloring Book. 2004. (Illus.). 32p. 5.95 *(978-1-57306-212-1(X))* Bess Pr., Inc.

Kaopio, Matthew. Hawaiian Family Legends. 2003. (Illus.). 55p. (J). *(978-1-56647-623-2(2))* Mutual Publishing LLC.

LEGENDS—INDIA

Adhikary, Qiron. Feminist Folktales from India. 2003. (Illus.). 97p. (YA). per. 9.95 *(978-0-9714127-3-6(1))* Masalai Pr.

Besant, Annie W. Legends & Tales Lotus Leaves for the Y. 2006. pap. 19.95 *(978-1-4286-2494-8(5))* Kessinger Publishing, LLC.

Husain, Shahrukh. Indian Myths. Willey, Bee, illus. 2007. (Stories from Ancient Civilisations Ser.). (ENG.). 32p. (J). pap. 10.99 *(978-0-237-53376-2(6))* Evans Brothers, Ltd. GBR. Dist: Independent Pubs. Group.

Novesky, Amy. The Elephant Prince: The Story of Ganesh. Wedman, Belgin K., illus. 2004. (ENG.). 32p. 16.95 *(978-1-886069-16-9(6)*, BK2304HB) Insight Editions.

Novesky, Amy & Wedman, Belgin K. The Elephant Prince: The Story of Ganesh. 2005. (Illus.). 32p. (J). 16.95 *(978-1-932771-16-9(6))* Mandala Publishing.

LEGENDS, INDIAN

see Indians of Mexico—Folklore; Indians of North America—Folklore; Indians of South America—Folklore

LEGENDS—IRELAND

Carroll, Yvonne. Great Irish Legends for Children. Lawrie, Robin, illus. 2005. (ENG.). 64p. (J). pap. 20.95 incl. audio compact disk *(978-0-7171-3872-2(0))* M.H. Gill & Co. U. C. IRL. Dist: Dufour Editions, Inc.

Milligan, Bryce. Brigid's Cloak: An Ancient Irish Story. Cann, Helen, illus. 2004. 32p. (J). (gr. k-18). 16.00 *(978-0-8028-5224-3(6))* Eerdmans, William B. Publishing Co.

LEGENDS, JEWISH

see Jewish Legends

LEGENDS—SCANDINAVIA

Rayner, Olivia, illus. World Book Myths & Legends Series, 8 vols., Vol. 8. 2007. (World Book Myths & Legends Ser.). 64p. (gr. 4-8). 239.00 *(978-0-7166-2613-8(6)*, 31020) World Bk., Inc.

LEGENDS—SPAIN

Leyendas Espanolas. (SPA., Illus.). (YA). 11.95 *(978-84-7281-212-3(X)*, AF0099) Aunga, Ediciones S.A. ESP. Dist: Continental Bk. Co., Inc.

LEGENDS—UNITED STATES

Asfar, Dan. Dear Liza, 1 vol., Vol. 1. Kubish, Shelagh, ed. rev. ed. 2003. (Ghost Stories Ser.). (ENG., Illus.). 216p. (gr. 4). pap. 12.95 *(978-1-894877-17-6(9)*, 1894877179, Ghost Hse. Bks.) Lone Pine Publishing USA.

Asfar, Dan, et al. Ghost Stories of America, 1 vol., Vol. 2. Kubish, Shelagh, ed. rev. ed. 2003. (Ghost Stories Ser.). (ENG., Illus.). 248p. (gr. 4). pap. 12.95 *(978-1-894877-31-2(4)*, 1894877314, Ghost Hse. Bks.) Lone Pine Publishing USA.

Cocca, Lisa Colozza. Sleepy Hollow. 2014. (Jr. Graphic Ghost Stories Ser.). (Illus.). 24p. (J). (gr. 3-6). lib. bdg. 26.25 *(978-1-4777-7084-9(4)*, PowerKids Pr.) Rosen Publishing Group, Inc., The.

Delano, Marfe Ferguson. American Heroes. 2005. (National Geographic Ser.). (ENG., Illus.). 240p. (J). (gr. 5-18). 24.95 *(978-0-7922-7208-3(0))*; 45.90 *(978-0-7922-7215-1(3))* National Geographic Society. (National Geographic Children's Bks.).

Dwyer, Mindy. Coyote in Love: The Story of Crater Lake. 2014. (ENG., Illus.). 32p. (J). (gr. -1-3). pap. 10.99 *(978-0-88240-997-9(2)*, 9780882409979, West Winds Pr.) Graphic Arts Ctr. Publishing Co.

Ferrell, David L. Pecos Bill. 2014. (Jr. Graphic American Legends Ser.). (Illus.). 24p. (J). (gr. 3-6). lib. bdg. 26.25 *(978-1-4777-7189-1(1)*, PowerKids Pr.) Rosen Publishing Group, Inc., The.

Ferut, Michael. Winchester Mystery House. 2014. (Scariest Places on Earth Ser.). (ENG., Illus.). 24p. (J). (gr. 3-7). lib. bdg. 25.95 *(978-1-60014-998-6(7)*, Torque Bks.) Bellwether Media.

Haley, Gail E., tr. & illus. Kokopelli, Drum in Belly. Haley, Gail E., illus. 2003. (J). pap. 12.95 *(978-0-86541-069-5(0))* Filter Pr., LLC.

Jameson, W. C. Buried Treasures of California. Hall, Wendell E., illus. 2006. (Buried Treasure Ser.). (ENG.). 175p. (Orig.). (J). (gr. 4-17). pap. 14.95 *(978-0-87483-406-2(6))* August Hse. Pubs., Inc.

Joseph, Frank. Legends & Lore of Ancient America, 1 vol., 1. 2014. (Discovering Ancient America Ser.). (ENG.). 296p. (YA). (gr. 7-12). lib. bdg. 38.25 *(978-1-4777-2807-9(4))* Rosen Publishing Group, Inc., The.

Jr. Graphic American Legends: Set 2. 2014. (Jr. Graphic American Legends Ser.). 24p. (J). (gr. 3-6). 157.50 *(978-1-4777-7096-2(8)*, PowerKids Pr.) Rosen Publishing Group, Inc., The.

Jr. Graphic American Legends: Sets 1-2. 2014. (Jr. Graphic American Legends Ser.). 24p. (J). (gr. 3-6). pap. 127.20 *(978-1-4777-7262-1(6)*, PowerKids Pr.) Rosen Publishing Group, Inc., The.

Mackall, Dandi Daley. The Legend of Ohio. LaFever, Greg, illus. 2005. (Legend Ser.). (ENG.). 40p. (J). (gr. k-5). 17.95 *(978-1-58536-244-8(1))* Sleeping Bear Pr.

Meister, Cari. Davy Crockett & the Great Mississippi Snag, 1 vol. George, Peter, illus. 2014. (American Folk Legends Ser.). (ENG.). 32p. (gr. k-2). lib. bdg. 27.32 *(978-1-4795-5431-7(6))* Picture Window Bks.

Petruccio, Steven James. American Legends & Tall Tales. 2011. (Dover Classic Stories Coloring Book Ser.). (ENG., Illus.). 32p. (J). (gr. 3-6). pap. 3.99 *(978-0-486-47786-2(X))* Dover Pubns., Inc.

Smitten, Susan. Ghost Stories of New England, 1 vol., Vol. 1. Wangler, Chris, ed. rev. ed. 2003. (Ghost Stories Ser.). (ENG., Illus.). 224p. (gr. 4). pap. 12.95 *(978-1-894877-12-1(8)*, 1894877128, Ghost Hse. Bks.) Lone Pine Publishing USA.

LEGERDEMAIN

see Magic

LEGISLATORS

Alexander, Heather & dePaola, Tomie. Who Is Hillary Clinton? Harrison, Nancy & Putra, Dede, illus. 2016. (Who Was? Ser.). (ENG.). 112p. (J). (gr. 3-7). lib. bdg. 15.99 *(978-0-399-54234-3(5)*, Grosset & Dunlap) Penguin Young Readers Group.

Benge, Janet & Benge, Geoff. William Wilberforce: Take up the Fight. 2015. (ENG.). 201p. (YA). pap. 9.99 *(978-1-62486-057-7(5))* Emerald Bks.

Blashfield, Jean F. Hillary Clinton. 2010. (Leading Women Ser.). 96p. (YA). (gr. 7-12). 39.93 *(978-0-7614-4954-6(X))* Marshall Cavendish Corp.

Brignall, Richard. Big Train: The Legendary Ironman of Sport, Lionel Conacher, 1 vol. 2009. (Lorimer Recordbooks Ser.). (ENG., Illus.). 168p. (YA). (gr. 6-12). 16.95 *(978-1-55277-451-9(1)*, 9781552774519); 9.95 *(978-1-55277-450-2(3)*, 9781552774502) Lorimer, James & Co., Ltd., Pubs. CAN. Dist: Casemate Pubs. & Bk. Distributors, LLC.

Brill, Marlene Targ. Barack Obama (Revised Edition) 2009. pap. 52.95 *(978-0-7613-5031-6(4))* Lerner Publishing Group.

Doeden, Matt. Michele Bachmann: Tea Party Champion. 2011. (Gateway Biographies Ser.). (YA). (gr. 4-7). lib. bdg. 26.60 *(978-0-7613-9074-9(X))* Lerner Publishing Group.

Espinosa, Rod. Patrick Henry, 1 vol. Espinosa, Rod, illus. 2007. (Bio-Graphics Ser.). (ENG., Illus.). 32p. (gr. 3-6). 28.50 *(978-1-60270-070-3(2)*, Graphic Planet- Nonfiction) ABDO Publishing Co.

Fitzgerald, Stephanie. Hillary Clinton. rev. ed. 2017. (Rookie Biographies(tm) Ser.). (ENG., Illus.). 32p. (J). lib. bdg. 25.00 ***(978-0-531-22931-6(9))*** Scholastic Library Publishing.

—Rookie Biographies: Hillary Clinton (Revised Edition) 2017. (Rookie Biographies Ser.). (ENG., Illus.). 32p. (J). pap. 5.95 ***(978-0-531-23406-8(1))*** Scholastic Library Publishing.

Furgang, Kathy. The Declaration of Independence & Richard Henry Lee of Virginia. 2009. (Framers of the Declaration of Independence Ser.). 24p. (gr. 3-3). 42.50 *(978-1-61512-630-9(9)*, PowerKids Pr.) Rosen Publishing Group, Inc., The.

—The Declaration of Independence & Roger Sherman of Connecticut. 2009. (Framers of the Declaration of Independence Ser.). 24p. (gr. 3-3). 42.50 *(978-1-61512-632-3(5)*, PowerKids Pr.) Rosen Publishing Group, Inc., The.

Gay, Oonagh & Leopold, Patricia, eds. Conduct Unbecoming? The Regulation of Parliamentary Behaviour. Gay, Oonagh & Leopold, Patricia, trs. 2004. vi, 378p. 39.95 *(978-1-84275-055-1(0))* Politico's Publishing Ltd. GBR. Dist: Consortium Bk. Sales & Distribution.

Haldy, Emma E. Davy Crockett. Bane, Jeff, illus. 2017. (My Early Library: My Itty-Bitty Bio Ser.). (ENG.). 24p. (J). (gr. k-1). lib. bdg. 28.50 *(978-1-63472-151-6(9)*, 209176) Cherry Lake Publishing.

Halfmann, Janet & Smith, Duane. Seven Miles to Freedom: The Robert Smalls Story, 1 vol. 2008. (ENG., Illus.). 40p. (J). pap. 10.95 *(978-1-60060-986-2(4))* Lee & Low Bks., Inc.

Haskins, Jim, et al. John Lewis in the Lead: A Story of the Civil Rights Movement, 1 vol. 2006. (ENG., Illus.). 40p. (J). pap. 11.95 *(978-1-60060-849-0(3))* Lee & Low Bks., Inc.

Hillstrom, Kevin. McCarthyism & the Communist Threat. 2011. (Defining Moments Ser.). 266p. 55.00 *(978-0-7808-1184-3(4))* Omnigraphics, Inc.

Immell, Myra. The McCarthy Era. Gale Editors, ed. 2011. (Perspectives on Modern World History Ser.). (ENG.). 224p. (gr. 12-12). lib. bdg. 47.80 *(978-0-7377-5260-1(2)*, Greenhaven Pr., Inc.) Cengage Gale.

Kunstler, James Howard. Davy Crockett, 1 vol. Brodner, Steve, illus. 2004. (Rabbit Ears-A Classic Tale Ser.). (ENG.). 36p. (gr. k-5). 25.65 *(978-1-59197-762-9(2))* Spotlight.

Marcovitz, Hal. Nancy Pelosi: Politician. 2009. (Women of Achievement Ser.). (Illus.). 160p. (gr. 6-12). 35.00 *(978-1-60413-075-1(X)*, Chelsea Hse.) Facts On File, Inc.

McElroy, Lisa Tucker. Ted Kennedy: A Remarkable Life in the Senate. 2009. (Gateway Biographies Ser.). (ENG.). 48p. (gr. 4-8). 26.60 *(978-0-7613-4457-5(8))* Lerner Publishing Group.

Moriarty, J. T. Davy Crockett: Defensor de la Frontera. 2004. (Grandes personajes en la historia de los Estados Unidos Ser.). (SPA.). 32p. (gr. 3-6). pap. 10.00

JKL

(978-0-8239-4226-8(0), Rosen Classroom) Rosen Publishing Group, Inc., The.

Nagelhout, Ryan. Standing in a Senator's Shoes. 2015. (My Government Ser.). (ENG.). 32p. (J). (gr. 4-4). pap. 10.58 (978-1-5026-0472-9(8)) Cavendish Square Publishing.

Raatma, Lucia. Shirley Chisholm. 2010. (Leading Women Ser.). 96p. (YA). (gr. 7-12). 39.93 (978-0-7614-4953-9(1)) Marshall Cavendish Corp.

Rose, Simon. House of Representatives. 2016. (J). **(978-1-5105-2245-9(X))** SmartBook Media, Inc.

Sapet, Kerrily. John Lewis. 2009. (Political Profiles Ser.). 100p. (YA). (gr. 5-9). 28.95 (978-1-59935-130-8(7)) Reynolds, Morgan Inc.

Silate, Jennifer. The Calhoun-Randolph Debate on the Eve of the War of 1812: A Primary Source Investigation. 2004. (Great Historic Debates & Speeches Ser.). (Illus.). 64p. (YA). (gr. 5-9). lib. bdg. 31.95 (978-1-4042-0150-7(5)) Rosen Publishing Group, Inc., The.

—The Calhoun-Randolph Debate on the Eve of the War Of 1812: A Primary Source Investigation. 2009. (Great Historic Debates & Speeches Ser.). 64p. (gr. 5-8). 58.50 (978-1-61513-124-2(8)) Rosen Publishing Group, Inc., The.

Slavicek, Louise Chipley. Daniel Inouye. 2nd ed. 2007. (Asian Americans of Achievement Ser.). (Illus.). 128p. (YA). (gr. 7-12). lib. bdg. 35.00 (978-0-7910-9271-2(2)) Facts On File, Inc.

Summers, Portia. Hillary Clinton: Politician & Activist. 2017. (Junior Biographies Ser.). 24p. (J). (gr. 3-4). lib. bdg. 22.60 **(978-0-7660-8670-8(4))** Enslow Pubs., Inc.

Turner, Carolyn. Sam Houston. 2010. pap. 9.95 (978-1-61690-066-3(0)); 24p. (J). (gr. 2-4). lib. bdg. 25.70 (978-1-61690-065-6(2)) Weigl Pubs., Inc.

Young, Jeff C. Joe Biden. 2009. (Political Profiles Ser.). 100p. (YA). (gr. 5-9). 28.95 (978-1-59935-131-5(5)) Reynolds, Morgan Inc.

LEGISLATORS—UNITED STATES

see also United States—Congress

ABDO Publishing Company Staff & Wheeler, Jill C. Barack Obama, 1 vol. 2009. (United States Presidents Ser.). (ENG., Illus.). 40p. (YA). (gr. 3-6). 27.07 (978-1-60453-481-8(8)) ABDO Publishing Co.

Abrams, Dennis. Hillary Rodham Clinton: Politician. 2009. (Women of Achievement Ser.). (Illus.). 144p. (gr. 6-12). 35.00 (978-1-60413-077-5(6), Chelsea Hse.) Facts On File, Inc.

Adler, David A. A Picture Book of Patrick Henry. Wallner, John et al, illus. 2005. (ENG.). 32p. (J). (gr. k-3). pap. 6.95 (978-0-8234-1678-3(X)) Holiday Hse., Inc.

Allen, Charles F. David Crockett: Scout, Small Boy, Pilgrim, Mountaineer, Soldier, Bear-Hunter, & Congressman, Defender of the Alamo. (Illus.). 308p. reprint ed. lib. bdg. 98.00 (978-0-7222-4856-0(3)) Library Reprints, Inc.

Asim, Jabari. Preaching to the Chickens: The Story of Young John Lewis. Lewis, E. B., illus. 2016. (ENG.). 32p. (J). (gr. k-3). 17.99 (978-0-399-16856-7(7), Nancy Paulsen Books) Penguin Young Readers Group.

Barack Obama. 2007. (Political Profiles Ser.). (Illus.). 128p. (YA). (gr. 5-9). lib. bdg. 27.95 (978-1-59935-045-5(9)) Reynolds, Morgan Inc.

Barbara Jordan. 2004. 12p. (gr. k-4). 2.95 (978-0-635-02616-3(3)) Gallopade International.

Barton, Chris. The Amazing Age of John Roy Lynch. Tate, Don, illus. 2015. (ENG.). 50p. (J). 17.00 (978-0-8028-5379-0(X), Eerdmans Bks For Young Readers) Eerdmans, William B. Publishing Co.

Benson, Kathleen & Haskins, Jim. John Lewis in the Lead: A Story of the Civil Rights Movement, 1 vol. Andrews, Benny, illus. 2006. (ENG.). 40p. (gr. 2-7). 17.95 (978-1-58430-250-6(X)) Lee & Low Bks., Inc.

Blumenthal, Karen. Hillary Rodham Clinton: A Woman Living History. 2016. (ENG., Illus.). 448p. (J). 18.99 (978-1-250-06014-3(1), 9781250060143) Feiwel & Friends.

Bodden, Valerie. Hillary Clinton: Historic Leader, 1 vol. 2009. (Essential Lives Set 4 Ser.). (ENG., Illus.). 112p. (J). (gr. 6-12). lib. bdg. 35.64 (978-1-60453-699-7(3)) ABDO Publishing Co.

—Samuel Houston: Army Leader & Historic Politician, 1 vol. 2010. (Military Heroes Ser.). (ENG.). 112p. (J). (gr. 6-12). lib. bdg. 35.64 (978-1-60453-962-2(3)) ABDO Publishing Co.

Boehme, Gerry. John Lewis & Desegregation. 2016. (Primary Sources of the Civil Rights Movement Ser.). (Illus.). 64p. (J). (gr. 6-6). 34.21 (978-1-5026-1868-9(0)) Cavendish Square Publishing.

Bourcier, Cammy S. Barack Obama. 2009. (Sharing the American Dream Ser.). (Illus.). 64p. (YA). (gr. 7-12). 22.95 (978-1-4222-0574-7(6)) Mason Crest.

Brager, Bruce L. John Kerry: Senator from Massachusetts. 2005. (Twentieth Century Leaders Ser.). (Illus.). 128p. (J). (gr. 6-12). lib. bdg. 23.95 (978-1-931798-64-8(8)) Reynolds, Morgan Inc.

Brill, Marlene Targ. Barack Obama: Working to Make a Difference. 2006. (J). pap. 6.95 (978-0-8225-6056-2(9), First Avenue Editions); (Illus.). 48p. 23.93 (978-0-8225-3417-4(7)) Lerner Publishing Group.

Buckley, James, Jr. Bill Bradley. 2009. (Basketball Hall of Famers Ser.). 112p. (gr. 5-8). 63.90 (978-1-61511-529-7(3), Rosen Reference) Rosen Publishing Group, Inc., The.

Burgan, Michael. Hillary Clinton, 1 vol. 2014. (Extraordinary Women Ser.). (ENG.). 48p. (gr. 6-6). lib. bdg. 32.65 (978-1-4109-5941-6(4)) Heinemann-Raintree.

Burlingame, Jeff. Hillary Clinton: A Life in Politics. 2008. (People to Know Today Ser.). (Illus.). 112p. (J). (gr. 3-7). lib. bdg. 33.27 (978-0-7660-2892-0(5)) Enslow Pubs., Inc.

Cane, Ella. The U. S. House of Representatives, 1 vol. 2014. (Our Government Ser.). (ENG.). 24p. (gr. 1-2). lib. bdg. 25.32 (978-1-4765-4201-0(5), First Facts) Capstone Press of Coughlan Cos.

—The U. S. Senate, 1 vol. 2014. (Our Government Ser.). (ENG.). 24p. (gr. 1-2). lib. bdg. 25.32 (978-1-4765-4202-7(3), First Facts) Capstone Press of Coughlan Cos.

Caravantes, Peggy. American in Texas: The Story of Sam Houston. 2004. (Notable Americans Ser.). (Illus.). 144p. (YA). (gr. 6-12). 23.95 (978-1-931798-19-8(2)) Reynolds, Morgan Inc.

Coddington, Andrew. Davy Crockett. Lapegüe, Matias, illus. 2016. (American Legends & Folktales Ser.). 32p. (J). 28.50 (978-1-5026-2193-1(2)) Cavendish Square Publishing.

Cohen, Sheila & Terman Cohen, Sheila. Gaylord Nelson: Champion for Our Earth. 2010. (Badger Biographies Ser.). (ENG., Illus.). 120p. (J). pap. 12.95 (978-0-87020-443-2(2)) Wisconsin Historical Society.

Collard, Sneed B., III. David Crockett: Fearless Frontiersman. 2006. (American Heroes Ser.). (Illus.). 40p. (J). (gr. 3-7). lib. bdg. 28.50 (978-0-7614-2160-3(2), Benchmark Bks.) Marshall Cavendish Corp.

—John Glenn: Hooked on Flying. 2008. (American Heroes Ser.). (Illus.). 48p. (J). (gr. 3-18). lib. bdg. 29.93 (978-0-7614-3066-7(0), Benchmark Bks.) Marshall Cavendish Corp.

Cooper, Ilene. A Woman in the House (and Senate) How Women Came to the United States Congress, Broke down Barriers, & Changed the Country. Baddeley, Elizabeth, illus. 2014. (ENG.). 144p. (J). (gr. 3-7). 24.95 (978-1-4197-1036-0(2), Abrams Bks. for Young Readers) Abrams, Inc.

Corey, Shana. Hillary Clinton: the Life of a Leader. Gustavson, Adam, illus. 2016. (Step into Reading Ser.). (ENG.). 48p. (J). (gr. k-3). 3.99 (978-1-101-93235-3(X), Random Hse. Bks. for Young Readers) Random Hse. Children's Bks.

Crawford, Ann Fears. Barbara Jordan: Breaking the Barriers. 2003. (Illus.). 90p. (J). (gr. 7-9). lib. bdg. 19.95 (978-1-931823-11-1(1)) Halcyon Pr., Ltd.

Davis, William Michael. Barack Obama: The Politics of Hope. 2007. (Illus.). 168p. (J). (gr. 10-18). lib. bdg. 25.95 (978-1-59556-024-7(6)); (YA). (gr. 8-18). pap. 16.99 (978-1-59556-032-2(7)) OTTN Publishing.

Davy Crockett. 2010. (Legends of the Wild West Ser.). (Illus.). 120p. (gr. 6-12). 35.00 (978-1-60413-592-3(1), Chelsea Hse.) Facts On File, Inc.

De Medeiros, James. Al Gore. 2008. (Remarkable People Ser.). (Illus.). 24p. (J). (gr. 4-6). pap. 8.95 (978-1-59036-993-7(9)); lib. bdg. 24.45 (978-1-59036-992-0(0)) Weigl Pubs., Inc.

De Medeiros, Michael. Barack Obama. (J). 2013. (978-1-62127-388-2(1)) 2008. (Illus.). 24p. (gr. 4-6). pap. 8.95 (978-1-59036-989-0(0)) 2008. (Illus.). 24p. (gr. 4-6). lib. bdg. 24.45 (978-1-59036-988-3(2)) Weigl Pubs., Inc.

Devaney, Sherri, et al. Barack Obama. 2009. (People in the News Ser.). (ENG.). 104p. (YA). (gr. 7-12). lib. bdg. 33.45 (978-1-4205-0206-0(9), LML02109-248525) Cengage Gale.

Doak, Robin S. Hillary Clinton. 2013. (True Book™—Biographies Ser.). (ENG., Illus.). 48p. (J). pap. 6.95 (978-0-531-23877-6(6)); lib. bdg. 29.00 (978-0-531-21906-5(2)) Scholastic Library Publishing.

Edwards, Roberta. Barack Obama: United States President. Call, Ken, illus. rev. exp. ed. 2009. (ENG.). 64p. (J). (gr. 1-3). mass mkt. 5.99 (978-0-448-45234-0(0), Grosset & Dunlap) Penguin Young Readers Group.

Epstein, Brad M. Barack Obama 101. l.t. ed. 2009. (My First Presidential Board Book Ser.). (Illus.). 28p. (J). (gr. -1-1). bds. (978-1-60730-044-1(3), 101 Bk.) Michaelson Entertainment.

Epstein, Dwayne. Hillary Clinton. 2010. (People in the News Ser.). (Illus.). 128p. (J). 33.95 (978-1-4205-0268-8(9), Lucent Bks.) Cengage Gale.

—Nancy Pelosi. 2008. (People in the News Ser.). (ENG., Illus.). 104p. (YA). (gr. 7-10). lib. bdg. 33.95 (978-1-4205-0057-8(0), LML02109-240045, Lucent Bks.) Cengage Gale.

Falk, Laine. Meet President Barack Obama. 2009. (Scholastic News Nonfiction Readers Ser.). (ENG.). 24p. (J). (gr. 1-2). 20.00 (978-0-531-23403-7(7), Children's Pr.) Scholastic Library Publishing.

—Meet President John McCain. 2009. (J). (978-0-531-23650-5(1)) Children's Pr., Ltd.

Feinstein, Stephen. Barack Obama. 2008. (African-American Heroes Ser.). (Illus.). 24p. (J). (gr. 1-3). lib. bdg. 22.60 (978-0-7660-2893-7(3), Enslow Elementary) Enslow Pubs., Inc.

Finley, Toiya Kristen. Russell Simmons. 2007. (Sharing the American Dream Ser.). 64p. (YA). (gr. 7-18). pap. 9.95 (978-1-4222-0762-8(5)) Mason Crest.

Flynn, Jean. Henry B. Gonzalez: Rebel with a Cause. 2003. (Illus.). v, 140p. (J). 16.95 (978-1-57168-780-7(7), Eakin Pr.) Eakin Pr.

Freedman, Jeri. Elizabeth Warren: Democratic Senator from Massachusetts. 2017. (J). **(978-1-5026-2699-8(3))** Cavendish Square Publishing.

Freedman, Jeri. Hillary Rodham Clinton: Profile of a Leading Democrat. (Career Profiles Ser.). 112p. 2009. (gr. 9-10). 63.90 (978-1-61511-794-9(6)) 2007. (YA). (gr. 7-12). lib. bdg. 34.60 (978-1-4042-1910-6(2)) Rosen Publishing Group, Inc., The.

Giblin, James Cross. The Rise & Fall of Senator Joe McCarthy. 2009. (ENG., Illus.). 304p. (YA). (gr. 7-18). 22.00 (978-0-618-61058-7(8)) Houghton Mifflin Harcourt Publishing Co.

Gibson, Karen Bush. The Historic Fight for the 2008 Democratic Presidential Nomination: The Obama View. 2009. (Monumental Milestones Ser.). (Illus.). 48p. (YA). (gr. 4-7). lib. bdg. 29.95 (978-1-58415-732-8(1)) Mitchell Lane Pubs., Inc.

Glaser, Jason. Patrick Henry: Liberty or Death. McDonnell, Peter, illus. 2005. (Graphic Biographies Ser.). (ENG.). 32p. (gr. 3-4). 30.65 (978-0-7368-4970-8(X), Graphic Library) Capstone Press of Coughlan Cos.

Goldsworthy, Kaite. Gabrielle Giffords. 2012. (J). (978-1-61913-535-2(3)); pap. (978-1-61913-590-1(6)) Weigl Pubs., Inc.

Goldsworthy, Steve. Edward Kennedy. 2010. (Remarkable People Ser.). (Illus.). 24p. (J). (gr. 4-6). pap. 11.95 (978-1-61690-170-7(5)); lib. bdg. 25.70 (978-1-61690-169-1(1)) Weigl Pubs., Inc.

Gorman, Jacqueline Laks. Miembro del Congreso (Member of Congress) 2009. (Conoce tu gobierno (Know Your Government) Ser.). (SPA.). 24p. (J). (gr. 2-4). lib. bdg. 22.00 (978-1-4339-0101-0(3), Weekly Reader Leveled Readers) Stevens, Gareth Publishing LLLP.

Gorman, Jacqueline Laks & Nations, Susan. Member of Congress. 2009. (Know Your Government Ser.). 24p. (J). (gr. 2-4). pap. 8.15 (978-1-4339-0122-5(6)); lib. bdg. 22.00 (978-1-4339-0094-5(7)) Stevens, Gareth Publishing LLLP. (Weekly Reader Leveled Readers).

Grimes, Nikki. Barack Obama: Son of Promise, Child of Hope. Collier, Bryan, illus. 2012. (ENG.). 48p. (J). (gr. k-3). pap. 9.99 (978-1-4424-5077-6(0), Little Simon) Little Simon.

—Barack Obama: Son of Promise, Child of Hope. Collier, Bryan, illus. (ENG.). 48p. (J). (gr. k-3). 2012. 9.99 (978-1-4424-4092-0(9)) 2008. 16.99 (978-1-4169-7144-3(0)) Simon & Schuster Bks. For Young Readers. (Simon & Schuster Bks. For Young Readers).

Guernsey, JoAnn B. Hillary Rodham Clinton. 2005. (Biography Ser.). (Illus.). 112p. (J). (gr. 6-18). pap. 7.95 (978-0-8225-9613-4(X)) Lerner Publishing Group.

Guernsey, Joann Bren. Hillary Rodham Clinton. 2005. (Biography Ser.). (Illus.). 112p. (J). (gr. 3-7). lib. bdg. 29.27 (978-0-8225-2372-7(8), Lerner Pubns.) Lerner Publishing Group.

Halfmann, Janet. Seven Miles to Freedom: The Robert Smalls Story. Smith, Duane, illus. 2008. 40p. (J). (gr. 1-6). 17.95 (978-1-60060-232-0(0)) Lee & Low Bks., Inc.

Harmon, Daniel E. Al Gore & Global Warming. 2009. (Celebrity Activists Ser.). 112p. (gr. 8-8). 66.50 (978-1-61511-826-7(8)) Rosen Publishing Group, Inc., The.

Harness, Cheryl. Hillary Clinton: American Woman of the World. 2016. (Real-Life Story Ser.). (ENG., Illus.). 192p. (J). (gr. 3-7). 17.99 (978-1-4814-6057-6(9), Aladdin) Simon & Schuster Children's Publishing.

Herman, Gail. Who Was Davy Crockett? Squier, Robert & Harrison, Nancy, illus. 2013. (Who Was? Ser.). (ENG.). 112p. (J). (gr. 3-7). 5.99 (978-0-448-46704-7(6), Grosset & Dunlap) Penguin Young Readers Group.

—Who Was Davy Crockett? 2013. (Who Was... ? Ser.). lib. bdg. 16.00 (978-0-606-32133-4(0), Turtleback) Turtleback Bks.

Hillstrom, Kevin & Hillstrom, Laurie Collier. Al Gore. 2008. (People in the News Ser.). (ENG., Illus.). 128p. (gr. 7-10). lib. bdg. 39.40 (978-1-4205-0086-8(4), LML02109-242090, Lucent Bks.) Cengage Gale.

Hiram Bingham & the Dream of Gold. 2014. (ENG.). 192p. (J). (gr. 3-7). pap. 13.95 (978-1-59077-350-5(0)) Evans, M. & Co., Inc.

Hoe, Susan. Rosa Parks. 2007. (Sharing the American Dream Ser.). 64p. (YA). (gr. 7-18). pap. 9.95 (978-1-4222-0760-4(9)) Mason Crest.

Holden, Henry M. Trailblazing Astronaut John Glenn: A MyReportLinks.com Book. 2004. (Space Flight Adventures & Disasters Ser.). (Illus.). 48p. (J). lib. bdg. 26.60 (978-0-7660-5166-9(8), MyReportLinks.com Bks.) Enslow Pubs., Inc.

Horn, Geoffrey M. John Mccain. 2009. (People We Should Know Ser.). 32p. (J). (gr. 3-5). pap. 10.50 (978-1-4339-0160-7(9), Gareth Stevens Learning Library) Stevens, Gareth Publishing LLLP.

—John McCain. 2009. (People We Should Know Ser.). 32p. (J). (gr. 3-5). lib. bdg. 31.00 (978-1-4339-0020-4(3), Gareth Stevens Learning Library) Stevens, Gareth Publishing LLLP.

—Nancy Pelosi. 2009. (People We Should Know Ser.). 32p. (J). (gr. 3-5). pap. 10.50 (978-1-4339-0162-1(5)); lib. bdg. 31.00 (978-1-4339-0021-1(1)) Stevens, Gareth Publishing LLLP. (Gareth Stevens Learning Library).

Iorio, Nicole. Joe Biden. 2009. (People We Should Know Ser.). 48p. (J). (gr. 3-5). pap. 10.50 (978-1-4339-2148-3(0)); lib. bdg. 31.00 (978-1-4339-1949-7(4)) Stevens, Gareth Publishing LLLP. (Gareth Stevens Learning Library).

Jackson, Garnet N. Shirley Chisholm, Congresswoman. 2012. (ENG., Illus.). (J). (gr. 1-4). pap. 7.47 net. (978-0-8136-5247-4(2), Modern Curriculum Pr.) Pearson Schl.

Jakubiak, David J. What Does a Congressional Representative Do? 2010. (How Our Government Works Ser.). 24p. (J). (gr. 3-6). lib. bdg., E-Book 42.50 (978-1-4488-0033-9(1)) Rosen Publishing Group, Inc., The.

—What Does a Senator Do? 2010. (How Our Government Works Ser.). 24p. (J). (gr. 3-6). lib. bdg., E-Book 42.50 (978-1-4488-0029-2(3)); (Illus.). pap. 8.25 (978-1-4358-9816-5(8), PowerKids Pr.); (Illus.). (gr. 3-6). lib. bdg. 22.60 (978-1-4358-9360-3(3), PowerKids Pr.) Rosen Publishing Group, Inc., The.

Jarnow, Jesse. Davy Crockett: Defensor de la frontera (Davy Crockett: Frontier Hero) 2009. (Grandes personajes en la historia de los Estados Unidos (Famous People in American History) Ser.). (SPA.). 32p. (gr. 2-3). 47.90 (978-1-61512-797-9(6), Editorial Buenas Letras) Rosen Publishing Group, Inc., The.

—Davy Crockett: Frontier Hero / Defensor de la Frontera. 2009. (Famous People in American History/Grandes personajes en la historia de los Estados Unidos Ser.). (ENG & SPA.). 32p. (gr. 2-3). 47.90 (978-1-61512-543-2(4), Editorial Buenas Letras) Rosen Publishing Group, Inc., The.

—Patrick Henry's Liberty or Death Speech: A Primary Source Investigation. (Great Historic Debates & Speeches Ser.). 64p. 2009. (gr. 5-8). 58.50 (978-1-61513-120-4(5)) 2004. (Illus.). (J). lib. bdg. 31.95 (978-1-4042-0152-1(1)) Rosen Publishing Group, Inc., The.

Johnston, Marianne. Davy Crockett. 2009. (American Legends Ser.). 24p. (gr. 3-3). 42.50 (978-1-61511-381-1(9), PowerKids Pr.) Rosen Publishing Group, Inc., The.

Kann, Bob. Belle & Bob la Follette: Partners in Politics. 2008. (Badger Biographies Ser.). (ENG., Illus.). 144p. (J). (gr. 3-7). pap. 12.95 (978-0-87020-407-4(6)) Wisconsin Historical Society.

Kennedy, Edward M. My Senator & Me: A Dog's-Eye View of Washington, D. C. Small, David, illus. 2011. (J). (gr. 2-5). 29.95 (978-0-545-04379-3(4)) Weston Woods Studios, Inc.

Klein, Adria F. Barack Obama. 2009. pap. 13.25 (978-1-60559-055-4(X)) Hameray Publishing Group, Inc.

Krull, Kathleen. The Brothers Kennedy: John, Robert, Edward. Bates, Amy June, illus. 2010. (ENG.). 40p. (J). (gr. -1-3). 16.99 (978-1-4169-9158-8(1), Simon & Schuster Bks. For Young Readers) Simon & Schuster Bks. For Young Readers.

Kunstler, James Howard. Davy Crockett, 1 vol. Brodner, Steve, illus. 2004. (Rabbit Ears-A Classic Tale Ser.). (ENG.). 36p. (gr. k-5). 25.65 (978-1-59197-762-9(2)) Spotlight.

Kupperberg, Paul. John Glenn. 2004. (Library of Astronaut Biographies Ser.). (Illus.). 112p. (J). (gr. 5-8). lib. bdg. 34.60 (978-0-8239-4460-6(3), Rosen Reference) Rosen Publishing Group, Inc., The.

Laks Gorman, Jacqueline. Miembro del Congreso (Member of Congress) 2009. (Conoce tu gobierno (Know Your Government) Ser.). (SPA.). 24p. (gr. 2-4). pap. 8.15 (978-1-4339-0129-4(3), Weekly Reader Leveled Readers) Stevens, Gareth Publishing LLLP.

Leavitt, Amie Jane. Nancy Pelosi. 2007. (Blue Banner Biography Ser.). (Illus.). 32p. (YA). (gr. 4-7). lib. bdg. 25.70 (978-1-58415-613-0(9)) Mitchell Lane Pubs., Inc.

Levinson, Cynthia. Hillary Rodham Clinton: Do All the Good You Can. 2016. (Illus.). 352p. (J). (gr. 3-7). pap. 6.99 (978-0-06-238729-5(4)) HarperCollins Pubs.

Mansfield, Cheryl. Barack Obama. 2016. (Premier Presidents Ser.). (ENG.). 24p. (J). (gr. 1-4). 27.07 (978-1-5038-0846-1(7), 210696) Child's World, Inc., The.

Mapua, Jeff. Hillary Clinton, 1 vol. 2015. (ENG., Illus.). 32p. (J). 23.45 (978-1-62275-689-6(4), Britannica Educational Publishing) Rosen Publishing Group, Inc., The.

Marcovitz, Hal. Barack. 2007. (Obamas Ser.). (Illus.). 64p. (YA). (gr. 3-6). pap. 9.95 (978-1-4222-1484-8(2)); (gr. 4-7). lib. bdg. 19.95 (978-1-4222-1477-0(X)) Mason Crest.

—Michelle. 2007. (Obamas Ser.). 64p. (YA). (gr. 3-6). pap. 9.95 (978-1-4222-1485-5(0)); (gr. 4-7). lib. bdg. 19.95 (978-1-4222-1478-7(8)) Mason Crest.

Marsh, Carole. Ben Nighthorse Campbell. 2003. 12p. (gr. k-4). 2.95 (978-0-635-02383-4(0)) Gallopade International.

—Carol Moseley Braun. 2003. 12p. (gr. k-4). 2.95 (978-0-635-02384-1(9)) Gallopade International.

Marx, Trish. Jeannette Rankin: First Lady of Congress. Andreasen, Dan, illus. 2013. (ENG.). 48p. (J). (gr. 2-5). 19.99 (978-1-4424-9618-7(5), McElderry, Margaret K. Bks.) McElderry, Margaret K. Bks.

Mattern, Joanne. Hillary Rodham Clinton, 1 vol. 2008. (First Ladies Set 1 Ser.). (ENG., Illus.). 32p. (YA). (gr. 1-4). 27.07 (978-1-59928-792-8(7)) ABDO Publishing Co.

McAuliffe, Bill. The U. S. House of Representatives. 2017. (By the People Ser.). (ENG., Illus.). 48p. (J). (gr. 7-11). pap. 12.00 (978-1-62832-271-2(3), Creative Paperbacks) Creative Co., The.

—The U.S. House of Representatives. 2016. (Illus.). 48p. (J). 39.95 (978-1-60818-675-4(X), Creative Education) Creative Co., The.

—The U.S. Senate. 2016. (Illus.). 48p. (J). 39.95 (978-1-60818-677-8(6), Creative Education) Creative Co., The.

McElroy, Lisa Tucker. Nancy Pelosi. 2008. pap. 52.95 (978-0-8225-9477-2(3)) Lerner Publishing Group.

—Nancy Pelosi: First Woman Speaker of the House. 2007. (Gateway Biographies Ser.). (ENG., Illus.). 48p. (gr. 4-8). lib. bdg. 26.60 (978-0-8225-8685-2(1), Lerner Pubns.) Lerner Publishing Group.

McGowan, Joe. Al Gore. 2009. (People We Should Know Ser.). (ENG.). 48p. (J). (gr. 3-5). pap. 10.50 (978-1-4339-2146-9(4), Gareth Stevens Learning Library) Stevens, Gareth Publishing LLLP.

McGowan, Joseph. Al Gore. 2009. (People We Should Know Ser.). (ENG.). 48p. (J). (gr. 3-5). lib. bdg. 31.00 (978-1-4339-1947-3(8), Gareth Stevens Learning Library) Stevens, Gareth Publishing LLLP.

Miller, Barbara Kiely. Sam Houston. 2007. (Great Americans Ser.). 24p. (gr. 1-4). pap. 8.15 (978-0-8368-8323-7(3)); (SPA.). pap. 8.15 (978-0-8368-8336-7(5)); lib. bdg. 22.00 (978-0-8368-8316-9(0)); (SPA., Illus.). lib. bdg. 22.00 (978-0-8368-8329-9(2)) Stevens, Gareth Publishing LLLP. (Weekly Reader Leveled Readers).

Modifica, Lisa. A Timeline of Congress. 2009. (Timelines of American History Ser.). 32p. (gr. 4-4). 47.90 (978-1-60854-380-9(3), Rosen Reference) Rosen Publishing Group, Inc., The.

Moriarty, J. T. Davy Crockett: Frontier Hero. 2009. (Primary Sources of Famous People in American History Ser.). 32p. (gr. 2-3). 47.90 (978-1-60851-670-4(9)) Rosen Publishing Group, Inc., The.

Nelson, Maria. Becoming a House Representative. 2016. (Who's Your Candidate? Choosing Government Leaders Ser.). (ENG., Illus.). 32p. (J). (gr. 3-4). pap. 10.50 (978-1-4824-4035-5(0)) Stevens, Gareth Publishing LLLP.

—Becoming a Senator. 2016. (Who's Your Candidate? Choosing Government Leaders Ser.). (ENG., Illus.). 32p. (J). (gr. 3-4). pap. 10.50 (978-1-4824-4043-0(1)) Stevens, Gareth Publishing LLLP.

Nichols, Kaitlyn. Davey Crockett. 2009. pap. 13.25 (978-1-60559-057-8(6)) Hameray Publishing Group, Inc.

Peppas, Lynn. Why Sam Houston Matters to Texas. 2014. (Illus.). 32p. (J). lib. bdg. 26.25 (978-1-4777-0912-2(6)) Rosen Publishing Group, Inc., The.

Raatma, Lucia. Barbara Jordan. 2013. 96p. (YA). (gr. 7-12). 39.93 (978-0-7614-4956-0(6)); pap. 19.99 (978-1-62712-114-9(5)) Cavendish Square Publishing.

Rice, Liz. Bill Richardson. (Sharing the American Dream Ser.). 64p. (YA). (gr. 7-12). 2009. 22.95 (978-1-4222-0589-1(4)) 2007. pap. 9.95 (978-1-4222-0761-1(7)) Mason Crest.

Riddolls, Tom & Wearing, Judy. Hillary Clinton. 2009. (Remarkable People Ser.). (Illus.). 24p. (J). (gr. 4-6). pap. 8.95 (978-1-60596-621-2(5)); lib. bdg. 24.45 (978-1-60596-620-5(7)) Weigl Pubs., Inc.

Robinson, Tom. Barack Obama: 44th U. S. President, 1 vol. 2009. (Essential Lives Set 3 Ser.). (ENG., Illus.). 112p. (J). (gr. 6-12). lib. bdg. 35.64 (978-1-60453-527-3(X)) ABDO Publishing Co.

—John McCain: POW & Statesman, 1 vol. 2010. (Military Heroes Ser.). (ENG.). 112p. (J). (gr. 6-12). lib. bdg. 35.64 (978-1-60453-963-9(1)) ABDO Publishing Co.

Rose, Simon. The House of Representatives. 2014. (J). (978-1-4896-1938-9(0)) Weigl Pubs., Inc.

Ryan, Bernard. Hillary Rodham Clinton: First Lady & Senator. 2004. (Ferguson Career Biographies Ser.). (Illus.). 160p. (gr. 6-12). 25.00 (978-0-8160-5544-9(0), Ferguson Publishing Co.) Facts On File, Inc.

Saddleback Educational Publishing Staff, ed. Davy Crockett, 1 vol. unabr. ed. 2008. (Graphic Biographies Ser.). (ENG., Illus.). 25p. (YA). (gr. 9-12). pap. 7.95 (978-1-59905-220-5(2)) Saddleback Educational Publishing, Inc.

Sanford, William R. & Green, Carl R. Davy Crockett: Courageous Hero of the Alamo. 2012. (Courageous Heroes of the American West Ser.). (Illus.). 48p. (J). pap. 8.95

(978-1-4644-0086-5(5)); (gr. 5-18). 22.60 *(978-0-7660-4005-2(4))* Enslow Pubs., Inc.
—Sam Houston: Courageous Texas Hero. 2012. (Courageous Heroes of the American West Ser.). (Illus.). 48p. (J). pap. 8.95 *(978-1-4644-0092-6(X))*; (gr. 5-18). lib. bdg. 22.60 *(978-0-7660-4009-0(7))* Enslow Pubs., Inc.
Sapet, Kerrily. Al Gore. 2007. (Political Profiles Ser.). (Illus.). 112p. (YA). (gr. 5-9). lib. bdg. 27.95 *(978-1-59935-070-7(X))* Reynolds, Morgan Inc.
Schuh, Mari C. The U. S. House of Representatives, 1 vol. 2012. (U. S. Government Ser.). (ENG.). 24p. (gr. k-1). lib. bdg. 26.65 *(978-1-4296-7565-9(9)*, Pebble Plus) Capstone Press of Coughlan Cos.
Schuman, Michael A. Barack Obama: We Are One People. 2008. (African-American Biography Library). (Illus.). 128p. (J). (gr. 3-7). lib. bdg. 33.27 *(978-0-7660-2891-3(7))* Enslow Pubs., Inc.
—Barack Obama: We Are One People, Revised & Expanded. rev. ed. 2009. (African-American Biography Library). (Illus.). 160p. (J). (gr. 6). lib. bdg. 33.27 *(978-0-7660-3649-9(9))* Enslow Pubs., Inc.
Shea, Therese. Meet the House of Representatives. 2012. (Guide to Your Government Ser.). (Illus.). 32p. (J). (gr. 4-6). 26.60 *(978-1-4339-7252-2(2))*; pap. 10.50 *(978-1-4339-7253-9(0))* Stevens, Gareth Publishing LLLP. (Gareth Stevens Learning Library).
Shichtman, Sandra H. Nancy Pelosi. 2008. (Political Profiles Ser.). (Illus.). 112p. (YA). (gr. 5-9). lib. bdg. 27.95 *(978-1-59935-049-3(1))* Reynolds, Morgan Inc.
Silate, Jennifer. The Calhoun-Randolph Debate on the Eve of the War of 1812: A Primary Source Investigation. 2004. (Great Historic Debates & Speeches Ser.). (Illus.). 64p. (YA). (gr. 5-9). lib. bdg. 31.95 *(978-1-4042-0150-7(5))* Rosen Publishing Group, Inc., The.
Smith, Andrea P. Davy Crockett. 2012. (Illus.). 24p. (J). 63.60 *(978-1-4488-5223-9(4))*; pap. 10.60 *(978-1-4488-5222-2(6))*; lib. bdg. 25.25 *(978-1-4488-5192-8(0))* Rosen Publishing Group, Inc., The. (PowerKids Pr.).
Stefoff, Rebecca. Al Gore: Fighting for a Greener Planet. rev. ed. 2008. (Gateway Biographies Ser.). (ENG.). 48p. (gr. 4-8). 26.60 *(978-1-57505-948-8(7))* Lerner Publishing Group.
Ted Kennedy. 2009. (Political Profiles Ser.). 144p. (YA). (gr. 5-9). 28.95 *(978-1-59935-089-9(0))* Reynolds, Morgan Inc.
Thomas, Garen. Yes We Can: A Biography of President Barack Obama. 2nd rev. ed. 2008. (ENG., Illus.). 256p. (J). (gr. 3-7). pap. 12.99 *(978-0-312-58639-3(6)*, 9780312586393) Feiwel & Friends.
Tieck, Sarah. Hillary Rodham Clinton, 1 vol. 2010. (First Biographies Set 6 Ser.). (ENG.). 32p. (J). (gr. 1-4). 27.07 *(978-1-60453-983-7(6))* ABDO Publishing Co.
Topinka, Joseph Baar. Just Judy: A Citizen & Leader for Illinois. 2017. (ENG.). (J). pap. 16.95 ***(978-0-9983282-2-5(7))*** Hilton Publishing Co.
Tracy, Kathleen. The Historic Fight for the 2008 Democratic Presidential Nomination: The Clinton View. 2009. (Monumental Milestones Ser.). (Illus.). 48p. (YA). (gr. 4-7). lib. bdg. 29.95 *(978-1-58415-731-1(3))* Mitchell Lane Pubs., Inc.
—The McCarthy Era. 2008. (Monumental Milestones Ser.). (Illus.). 48p. (YA). (gr. 4-7). lib. bdg. 29.95 *(978-1-58415-694-9(5))* Mitchell Lane Pubs., Inc.
Tukan, Jaytoe Anthony, Sr. United States Senators from North Carolina 1954 - 2008. 2003. per. 12.95 *(978-0-9665909-5-1(3))* Kalawantis Publishing Services, Inc.
Uschan, Michael V. Joe Biden. 2010. (People in the News Ser.). (Illus.). 128p. (J). 33.95 *(978-1-4205-0260-2(3)*, Lucent Bks.) Cengage Gale.
Wade, Mary Dodson. David Crockett: Creating a Legend. Hein, Joy Fisher, illus. 2009. (ENG.). 24p. (J). (gr. k-2). 16.95 *(978-1-933979-12-0(7)*, 9781933979120) Bright Sky Pr.
Wagner, Heather Lehr. Barack Obama. 2008. (Black Americans of Achievement: Legacy Edition Ser.). 104p. (gr. 6-12). pap. 11.95 *(978-1-60413-324-0(4)*, Checkmark Bks.) Facts On File, Inc.
—Barack Obama: Politician. 2008. (Black Americans of Achievement Ser.). (Illus.). 104p. (YA). (gr. 7-12). lib. bdg. 35.00 *(978-0-7910-9716-8(1))* Facts On File, Inc.
Watson, Marilyn Myrick. Barry Goldwater: State Greats Arizona. 2007. (Acacia Biographies Ser.). (Illus.). 28p. (J). (gr. 4-7). per. 6.95 *(978-0-9790826-0-3(9))* Acacia Publishing, Inc.
—Bary Goldwater: State Greats Arizona. 2007. (Acacia Biographies Ser.). (Illus.). 28p. (J). (gr. 3-7). lib. bdg. 16.95 *(978-0-9788283-4-9(8))* Acacia Publishing, Inc.
Welch, Catherine A. Patrick Henry. 2006. (History Maker Bios Ser.). (Illus.). 48p. (J). (gr. 3-6). lib. bdg. 26.60 *(978-0-8225-5941-2(2)*, Lerner Pubns.) Lerner Publishing Group.
Wells, Catherine. Hillary Clinton. 2007. (Political Profiles Ser.). (Illus.). 112p. (YA). (gr. 5-9). lib. bdg. 27.95 *(978-1-59935-047-9(5))* Reynolds, Morgan Inc.
—John McCain. 2008. (Political Profiles Ser.). (Illus.). 112p. (YA). (gr. 5-9). lib. bdg. 27.95 *(978-1-59935-046-2(7))* Reynolds, Morgan Inc.
Wheeler, Jill C. Hillary Rodham Clinton. 2003. (Breaking Barriers Ser.). 64p. (gr. 3-8). 27.07 *(978-1-57765-741-5(1)*, Abdo & Daughters) ABDO Publishing Co.
White, Carolyn. Standing in the Shoes of a Member of the House of Representatives. 2015. (My Government Ser.). (ENG., Illus.). 32p. (J). (gr. 4-4). lib. bdg. 28.50 *(978-1-5026-0470-5(1))* Cavendish Square Publishing.
Winders, Richard Bruce. Davy Crockett: The Legend of the Wild Frontier. 2009. (Library of American Lives & Times Ser.). 112p. (gr. 5-5). 69.20 *(978-1-60853-476-0(6))* Rosen Publishing Group, Inc., The.
Winget, Mary Mueller. Gerald R. Ford. 2007. (Presidential Leaders Ser.). (Illus.). 112p. (J). (gr. 3-7). lib. bdg. 29.27 *(978-0-8225-1509-8(1)*, Twenty-First Century Bks.) Lerner Publishing Group.
Winter, Jonah. Barack. Ford, A. G., illus. 2010. (ENG.). 32p. (J). (gr. -1-2). pap. 7.99 *(978-0-06-170396-6(6)*, Tegen, Katherine Bks) HarperCollins Pubs.
—Hillary. Colón, Raúl, illus. 2016. (ENG.). 40p. (J). (gr. -1-3). lib. bdg. 20.99 *(978-0-553-53389-7(4)*, Schwartz & Wade Bks.) Random Hse. Children's Bks.
Woodward, Mac. Sam Houston: For Texas & the Union. 2009. (Library of American Lives & Times Ser.). 112p. (gr. 5-5). 69.20 *(978-1-60853-504-0(5))* Rosen Publishing Group, Inc., The.

LEGUMES

Here are entered works on those plants belonging to the family Leguminosae, the pods or seeds of which are edible for man or domestic animals, e.g. peas, beans, lentils, etc. treated collectively.

Cleary, Brian P. Black Beans & Lamb, Poached Eggs & Ham: What Is in the Meat & Beans Group? Goneau, Martin, illus. 2011. (Food Is CATegorical Ser.). (ENG.). 32p. (gr. k-3). pap. 7.95 *(978-0-7613-6387-3(4))* Lerner Publishing Group.
Cleary, Brian P. & Goneau, Martin. Black Beans & Lamb, Poached Eggs & Ham: What Is in the Meat & Beans Group? 2011. (Food Is CATegorical Ser.). pap. 45.32 *(978-0-7613-8349-9(2)*, Millbrook Pr.) Lerner Publishing Group.
Dickmann, Nancy. La Vida del Frijol. 2011. (¡Mira Cómo Crece! Ser.). (Illus.). 24p. (gr. -1-1). (SPA & ENG.). 22.65 *(978-1-4329-5275-4(7))*; (ENG & SPA., pap. 6.29 *(978-1-4329-5287-7(0))* Heinemann-Raintree. (Bellota).
Dilkes, D. H. Beans, Nuts, & Oils. 2011. (All about Good Foods We Eat Ser.). (Illus.). 24p. (J). (gr. -1-18). pap. 7.95 *(978-1-59845-256-3(8)*, Enslow Elementary) Enslow Pubs., Inc.
Mitchell, Melanie S. Beans. (First Step Nonfiction Ser.). (Illus.). 24p. (gr. k-2). 2005. lib. bdg. 17.27 *(978-0-8225-4608-5(6))* 2003. (ENG., pap. 6.95 *(978-0-8225-4609-2(4)*, Lerner Pubns.) Lerner Publishing Group.
Murray, Julie. Beans, 1 vol. 2007. (Life Cycles Ser.). (ENG.). 24p. (gr. 4-7). 25.65 *(978-1-59928-702-7(1)*, Buddy Bks.) ABDO Publishing Co.
Murray, Laura K. Bean: Grow with Me. 2016. (Grow with Me Ser.). (ENG.). 32p. (J). (gr. 3-5). pap. 9.99 *(978-1-62832-161-6(X)*, Creative Paperbacks) Creative Co., The.
Royston, Angela. A Bean's Life. 2011. (ENG., Illus.). 24p. (J). pap. *(978-0-7787-7862-2(2))*; (gr. 3-6). *(978-0-7787-7840-0(1))* Crabtree Publishing Co.
Schwartz, David M. Bean. Kuhn, Dwight, photos by. (Life Cycles Ser.). (Illus.). 16p. (J). (gr. 1-3). pap. 2.99 *(978-1-57471-580-4(1)*, 3060) Creative Teaching Pr., Inc.
Shea, Therese. Watch Peas Grow. 2011. (Watch Plants Grow! Ser.). 24p. (gr. k-2). 69.20 *(978-1-4339-6157-1(1))* Stevens, Gareth Publishing LLLP.
Singer, Jane E. Soybeans. 2013. (Feeding the World Ser.: 8). (Illus.). 48p. (J). (gr. 4-18). 19.95 *(978-1-4222-2748-0(0))* Mason Crest.

LEIA, PRINCESS (FICTITIOUS CHARACTER)—FICTION

ABDO Publishing Company Staff & Wood, Brian. Star Wars: In the Shadow of Yavin. D'Anda, Carlos, illus. 2014. (Star Wars: in the Shadow of Yavin Ser.: 6). (ENG.). 24p. (J). (gr. 9-14). lib. bdg. 145.26 *(978-1-61479-285-7(2)*, Graphic Planet) Magic Wagon.
Barlow, Jeremy & Soriano, Carlo. Star Wars Adventures: Princess Leia & the Royal Ransom, 1 vol. 2012. (Star Wars Digests Ser.). (ENG., Illus.). 80p. (J). (gr. 4-7). 27.07 *(978-1-59961-902-6(4))* Spotlight.
Disney Book Group. Star Wars the Force Awakens. 2016. (Read-Along Storybook & CD Ser.). (ENG.). 32p. (J). (gr. 1-3). pap. 6.99 *(978-1-4847-3149-9(2))* Disney Pr.
Fry, Jason. Star Wars the Force Awakens Chapter Book. 2016. (ENG.). 128p. (J). (gr. 1-3). pap. 5.99 *(978-1-4847-7409-0(4)*, Disney Lucasfilm Press) Disney Publishing Worldwide.
Landers, Ace. The Empire Strikes Out. 2013. (Lego Star Wars Ser.). (ENG., Illus.). 48p. (J). (gr. 2-5). pap. 4.99 *(978-0-545-55224-0(9))* Math Solutions.
—Empire Strikes Out. 2013. (LEGO Star Wars Chapter Bks.). lib. bdg. 14.75 *(978-0-606-31554-8(3)*, Turtleback) Turtleback Bks.
Wang, Holman & Wang, Jack. Star Wars Epic Yarns: A New Hope. 2015. (ENG., Illus.). 24p. (J). (gr. -1 — 1). 9.95 *(978-1-4521-3393-5(X))* Chronicle Bks. LLC.
—Star Wars Epic Yarns: Return of the Jedi. 2015. (ENG., Illus.). 24p. (J). (gr. -1 — 1). 9.95 *(978-1-4521-3500-7(2))* Chronicle Bks. LLC.
—Star Wars Epic Yarns: The Empire Strikes Back. 2015. (ENG., Illus.). 24p. (J). (gr. -1 — 1). 9.95 *(978-1-4521-3499-4(5))* Chronicle Bks. LLC.

LEIF ERICSON, -APPROXIMATELY 1020

see Leiv Eiriksson, -approximately 1020

LEIGH-MALLORY, GEORGE HERBERT, 1886-1924

see Mallory, George, 1886-1924

LEISURE

see also Hobbies; Recreation

Barker, Geoff. Sports & Leisure Careers. 2010. (In the Workplace Ser.). 48p. (J). 35.65 *(978-1-60753-094-7(5))* Amicus Publishing.
Barker, Geoff & Savery, Annabel. Sports & Leisure Careers. 2011. (Been There! Ser.). 32p. (gr. 3-6). lib. bdg. 31.35 *(978-1-59920-474-1(6))* Black Rabbit Bks.
Diwrnod i'r Brenin: Chwaraeon, Hamdden a Thwristiaeth Er 1900. 2005. *(978-1-902346-01-4(7))* Addysg Y Cyfryngau Cymru.
Emlyn, Non ap. Hamddena. 2005. (WEL & ENG., Illus.). 20p. pap. *(978-1-86085-603-7(9))* ICA Video.
—Hamddena: Llawlyfr i Athrawon. 2005. (WEL.). 28p. pap. *(978-1-86085-604-4(7))* ICA Video.
—Hamddena - Llyfr 1 Lefel 3/4. 2005. (WEL & ENG., Illus.). 20p. pap. *(978-1-86085-600-6(4))* ICA Video.
—Hamddena - Llyfr 3 Lefel 5/6. 2005. (WEL & ENG., Illus.). 20p. pap. *(978-1-86085-602-0(0))* ICA Video.
Jupo, Frank. Time to Spare: The Story of Man's Leisure Hours. 2011. 66p. 36.95 *(978-1-258-07710-5(8))* Literary Licensing, LLC.
Knapman, Timothy & Collins UK Staff. Leisure & Entertainment since 1900. 2016. (ENG.). 32p. (J). (gr. 2-3). pap. 8.95 *(978-0-00-816382-2(0))* HarperCollins Pubs. Ltd. GBR. Dist: Independent Pubs. Group.
Nardo, Don. Arts, Leisure, & Sport in Ancient Egypt. 2005. (Lucent Library of Historical Eras Ser.). (ENG., Illus.). 112p. (YA). (gr. 7-12). lib. bdg. 33.45 *(978-1-59018-706-7(7))* Cengage Gale.
Whittaker, Helen. How Toys Slide. 2012. (Toys & Forces Ser.). 32p. (gr. 1-4). lib. bdg. 28.50 *(978-1-59920-466-6(5))* Black Rabbit Bks.
—Leisure. 2011. (Living Green Ser.). 32p. (gr. 3). 28.50 *(978-1-60870-575-7(7))* Marshall Cavendish GBR. Dist: Marshall Cavendish Corp.

LEIV EIRIKSSON, -APPROXIMATELY 1020

DeFries, Cheryl L. Leif Eriksson: Viking Explorer of the New World. 2010. (Great Explorers of the World Ser.). (Illus.). 112p. (J). (gr. 7-12). lib. bdg. 33.27 *(978-1-59845-126-9(X))* Enslow Pubs., Inc.
Hyde, Natalie. Explore with Leif Eriksson. 2014. (ENG., Illus.). 32p. (J). *(978-0-7787-1427-9(6))* Crabtree Publishing Co.
Knudsen, Shannon. Leif Eriksson. Oldroyd, Mark, illus. 2005. (On My Own Biography Ser.). (ENG.). 48p. (gr. 2-4). pap. 6.95 *(978-1-57505-828-3(6))*; lib. bdg. 25.26 *(978-1-57505-649-4(6)*, Carolrhoda Bks.) Lerner Publishing Group.
Mattern, Joanne. Leif Eriksson: Viking Explorer. 2004. (Explorers! Ser.). (Illus.). 48p. (J). lib. bdg. 25.27 *(978-0-7660-2146-4(7))* Enslow Pubs., Inc.

LEIV EIRIKSSON, -APPROXIMATELY 1020—FICTION

Wishinsky, Frieda. Yikes, Vikings! Griffiths, Dean & Owlkids Books Inc. Staff, illus. 2007. (Canadian Flyer Adventures Ser.: 4). (ENG.). 96p. (J). (gr. 1-4). per. 7.95 *(978-1-897066-97-3(X)*, Maple Tree Pr.) Owlkids Bks. Inc. CAN. Dist: Publishers Group West (PGW).

LEMMINGS

Phillips, Dee. Collared Lemming. 2015. (Arctic Animals: Life Outside the Igloo Ser.). (ENG.). 24p. (J). (gr. -1-3). lib. bdg. 23.93 *(978-1-62724-528-9(6))* Bearport Publishing Co., Inc.
Slade, Suzanne. What If There Were No Lemmings? A Book about the Tundra Ecosystem, 1 vol. Schwartz, Carol, illus. 2010. (Food Chain Reactions Ser.). (ENG.). 24p. (gr. 2-4). pap. 9.95 *(978-1-4048-6396-5(6))*; lib. bdg. 26.65 *(978-1-4048-6021-6(5))* Picture Window Bks.

LEMON

Royston, Angela. Experiments with a Lemon. 2016. (One-Stop Science Ser.). 32p. (gr. 2-5). 31.35 *(978-1-62588-140-3(1)*, Smart Apple Media) Black Rabbit Bks.

LEMURS

Aronin, Miriam. Aye-Aye: An Evil Omen. 2016. (Uncommon Animals Ser.). (ENG.). 32p. (J). (gr. 2-7). pap. 8.95 *(978-1-944998-60-8(8))* Bearport Publishing Co., Inc.
Baicker, Karen. Lemurs. 2007. (J). *(978-1-59939-132-8(5)*, Reader's Digest Young Families, Inc.) Studio Fun International.
Baicker, Karen, et al. Lemurs. 2009. (Amazing Animals Ser.). (ENG.). 48p. (J). (gr. 2-6). pap. 10.50 *(978-1-4339-2124-7(3)*, Gareth Stevens Learning Library); (gr. 3-6). lib. bdg. 28.00 *(978-0-8368-9120-1(1))* Stevens, Gareth Publishing LLLP.
Bell, Samantha S. Meet a Baby Lemur. 2015. (ENG., Illus.). 32p. (J). (gr. k-2). 26.65 *(978-1-4677-7972-2(5)*, Lerner Pubns.) Lerner Publishing Group.
Buckingham, Suzanne. Meet the Ring-Tailed Lemur. 2009. (Scales & Tails Ser.). 24p. (gr. 2-3). 42.50 *(978-1-60852-985-8(1)*, PowerKids Pr.) Rosen Publishing Group, Inc., The.
Carr, Aaron. Lemur. 2014. (J). *(978-1-4896-2633-2(6))* Weigl Pubs., Inc.
Costain, Meredith. Lemur. Jackson-Carter, Stuart, illus. 2016. (Wild World Ser.). 00032p. (J). (gr. 1-2). pap. 10.00 *(978-1-4994-8215-7(9)*, Windmill Bks.) Rosen Publishing Group, Inc., The.
Ganeri, Anita. Lemur, 1 vol. 2010. (Day in the Life: Rain Forest Animals Ser.). (ENG.). 24p. (gr. k-2). 23.32 *(978-1-4329-4111-6(9))*; pap. 6.79 *(978-1-4329-4122-2(4))* Heinemann-Raintree. (Heinemann Read & Learn).
Gish, Melissa. Lemurs. 2017. (J). ***(978-1-60818-830-7(2)***, Creative Education) Creative Co., The.
—Living Wild: Lemurs. 2017. (Living Wild Ser.). (ENG.). 48p. (J). (gr. 5-7). pap. 12.00 ***(978-1-62832-433-4(3)***, Creative Paperbacks) Creative Co., The.
Gregory, Josh. Lemurs. 2016. (Nature's Children Ser.). (ENG., Illus.). 48p. (J). pap. 6.95 *(978-0-531-21937-9(2)*, Children's Pr.) Scholastic Library Publishing.
Jolly, Alison. Ny Aiay Ako: Ako the Aye-Aye. Rasamimanana, Hantanirina, tr. Ross, Deborah, illus. 2005. (MLA & ENG.). (J). 20.00 *(978-0-9766009-0-9(0))* Lemur Conservation Foundation.
Kalman, Bobbie. Baby Lemurs. 2010. (Fun to Learn about Baby Animals Ser.). (ENG.). 24p. (J). (gr. k-3). *(978-0-7787-4893-9(6))*; pap. *(978-0-7787-4898-4(7))* Crabtree Publishing Co.
Marino, Angie. Lemurs! Greene's 29 after school art students, K., illus. 2013. 46p. pap. 11.99 *(978-0-9892732-0-6(2))* Illustrate to Educate.
Markovics, Joyce. My Tail Is Long & Striped (Lemur) 2014. (Zoo Clues Ser.). 24p. (J). (gr. -1-3). lib. bdg. 23.93 *(978-1-62724-107-6(8))* Bearport Publishing Co., Inc.
Markovics, Joyce L. Mi Cola Es Larga y Rayada. 2015. (Pistas de Animales Ser.). (SPA.). 24p. (J). (gr. -1-3). lib. bdg. 23.93 *(978-1-62724-586-9(3))* Bearport Publishing Co., Inc.
Owen, Ruth. Ring-Tailed Lemurs, 1. 2014. (Dr. Bob's Amazing World of Animals Ser.). (ENG.). 32p. (J). (gr. k-5). 27.50 *(978-1-4777-9040-3(3)*, Windmill Bks.) Rosen Publishing Group, Inc., The.
Owings, Lisa. Aye-Aye. 2014. (Extremely Weird Animals Ser.). (ENG., Illus.). 24p. (J). (gr. 3-8). lib. bdg. 25.95 *(978-1-62617-073-5(8)*, Pilot Bks.) Bellwether Media.
Phillips, Dee. Flying Lemur. 2013. (Science Slam: Treed-Animal Life in the Trees Ser.). 24p. (J). (gr. -1-3). lib. bdg. 23.93 *(978-1-61772-911-9(6))* Bearport Publishing Co., Inc.
Riley, Joelle. Ring-Tailed Lemurs. 2009. (Early Bird Nature Bks.). (ENG.). 48p. (gr. 2-5). 26.60 *(978-0-8225-9434-5(X)*, Lerner Pubns.) Lerner Publishing Group.
Schuetz, Kari. Lemurs. 2013. (Animal Safari Ser.). (ENG., Illus.). 24p. (J). (gr. k-3). lib. bdg. 25.95 *(978-1-60014-865-1(4)*, Blastoff! Readers) Bellwether Media.
Thomas, K. Clyde the Long Fingered Lemur. 2013. (ENG.). (J). pap. 9.99 *(978-1-4675-2874-0(9))* Independent Pub.
Throp, Claire. Lemurs, 1 vol. 2012. (Living in the Wild: Primates Ser.). (ENG.). 48p. (gr. 3-6). lib. bdg. 33.32 *(978-1-4329-5864-0(X)*, Heinemann InfoSearch) Heinemann-Raintree.

LEMURS—FICTION

Colfer, Eoin. The Time Paradox. 2009. (Artemis Fowl Ser.). (ENG.). 448p. (J). (gr. 5-9). pap. 8.99 *(978-1-4231-0837-5(X))* Hyperion Pr.
—The Time Paradox. 2009. (Artemis Fowl Ser.: 6). (J). lib. bdg. 19.65 *(978-0-606-10579-8(4)*, Turtleback) Turtleback Bks.
Cousins, Lucy. Jazzy in the Jungle. Cousins, Lucy, illus. 2013. (ENG., Illus.). 32p. (J). (-k). 14.99 *(978-0-7636-6806-8(0))* Candlewick Pr.
Dennard, Deborah. Lemur Landing: A Story of a Madagascan Dry Tropical Forest. Kest, Kristin, illus. 2005. (Wild Habitats Ser.). (ENG.). 32p. (J). (gr. 1-4). 19.95 *(978-1-56899-980-7(1))* Soundprints.
Dennard, Deborah & Kest, Kristin. Lemur Landing: A Story of a Madagascan Dry Tropical Forest. 2005. (Wild Habitats Ser.). (ENG., Illus.). 32p. (J). (gr. 1-4). pap. 6.95 *(978-1-56899-979-1(8)*, S7019) Soundprints.
Morrison Walton, Jeannie. The Little Lemur, a Fable of Pride. 2009. 32p. pap. 12.99 *(978-1-4389-8090-4(6))* AuthorHouse.
Preston-Gannon, Frann. How to Lose a Lemur. (ENG., Illus.). (J). (gr. -1 — 1). 2016. 30p. bds. 6.95 *(978-1-4549-2095-3(5))* 2014. 32p. 14.95 *(978-1-4549-1131-9(X))* Sterling Publishing Co., Inc.
Ryan, Candace. Ewe & Aye. Ruble, Stephanie, illus. 2014. (ENG.). 40p. (J). (gr. -1-k). 17.99 *(978-1-4231-7591-9(3))* Hyperion Bks. for Children.

LENIN, VLADIMIR ILICH, 1870-1924

Edwards, Judith & Schmermund, Elizabeth. Vladamir Lenin & the Russian Revolution. 2016. (People & Events That Changed the World Ser.). (ENG., Illus.). 128p. (J). (gr. 7-8). 37.27 *(978-0-7660-7414-9(5))* Enslow Pubs., Inc.
Goldstein, Margaret J. V. I. Lenin. 2007. (Biography Ser.). (Illus.). 112p. (J). (gr. 3-7). lib. bdg. 29.27 *(978-0-8225-5977-1(3)*, Twenty-First Century Bks.) Lerner Publishing Group.
Johnson, Robert, compiled by. Lenin, Stalin & Communist Russia: The Myth & Reality of Communism. 2003. (Studymates Ser.). (Illus.). 132p. (C). pap. 27.50 *(978-1-84285-039-8(3))* GLMP Ltd. GBR. Dist: Chicago Distribution Ctr.

LENINGRAD (RUSSIA)

see Saint Petersburg (Russia)

LENSES

I Spy! Individual Title Six-Packs. (Bookweb Ser.). 32p. (gr. 3-18). 34.00 *(978-0-7635-3948-1(1))* Rigby Education.
Roberts, Abigail B. Using Lenses. 2017. (Super Science Tools Ser.). 24p. (gr. 1-2). pap. 8.15 ***(978-1-4824-6389-7(X))*** Stevens, Gareth Publishing LLLP.
Sévigny, Eric, illus. The Jungle Explorer. 2010. (Clubhouse Ser.). (ENG.). 24p. (J). (gr. -1-1). pap. 3.95 *(978-2-89450-724-7(0))* Caillouet, Gerry.
Spilsbury, Louise & Spilsbury, Richard. Reflecting Light. 2015. (Exploring Light Ser.). (ENG., Illus.). 32p. (gr. 2-4). 30.65 *(978-1-4109-7943-8(1))* Heinemann-Raintree.
Williams, Brian. The Science of a Pair of Glasses: The Science of Light. 2009. (Science of... Ser.). (Illus.). 32p. (YA). (gr. 3-6). lib. bdg. 26.00 *(978-1-4339-0044-0(0))* Stevens, Gareth Publishing LLLP.

LEONARDO, DA VINCI, 1452-1519

Anderson, Maxine. Amazing Leonardo Da Vinci Inventions: You Can Build Yourself. 2006. (Build It Yourself Ser.). (ENG., Illus.). 128p. (J). (gr. 3-7). pap. 15.95 *(978-0-9749344-2-6(9))* Northern Trails Pr.
Bailey, Gerry & Foster, Karen. Leonardo's Pallete. Radford, Karen & Noyes, Leighton, illus. 2008. (Stories of Great People Ser.). (ENG.). 40p. (J). (gr. 3-8). lib. bdg. *(978-0-7787-3687-5(3))* Crabtree Publishing Co.
Barretta, Gene. Neo Leo: The Ageless Ideas of Leonardo da Vinci. Barretta, Gene, illus. 2009. (ENG., Illus.). 40p. (J). (gr. -1-4). 17.99 *(978-0-8050-8703-1(6)*, 9780805087031, Holt, Henry & Co. Bks. For Young Readers) Holt, Henry & Co.
Barsony, Piotr. The Stories of the Mona Lisa: An Imaginary Museum Tale about the History of Modern Art. 2012. (ENG., Illus.). 56p. (J). (gr. 3-6). 19.95 *(978-1-62087-228-4(5)*, 620228, Sky Pony Pr.) Skyhorse Publishing Co., Inc.
Brasch, Nicholas. Leonardo Da Vinci. 2013. (Discovery Education: Discoveries & Inventions Ser.). 32p. (J). (gr. 3-6). 25.25 *(978-1-4777-1330-3(1)*, PowerKids Pr.) Rosen Publishing Group, Inc., The.
—Leonardo Da Vinci: The Greatest Inventor. 2013. (Discovery Education: Discoveries & Inventions Ser.). 32p. (J). (gr. 3-6). pap. 60.00 *(978-1-4777-1503-1(7)*, PowerKids Pr.) Rosen Publishing Group, Inc., The.
Brasch, Nicolas. Leonardo Da Vinci: The Greatest Inventor. 2013. (Discovery Education: Discoveries & Inventions Ser.). (ENG., Illus.). 32p. (J). (gr. 3-6). pap. 10.00 *(978-1-4777-1502-4(9)*, PowerKids Pr.) Rosen Publishing Group, Inc., The.
Byrd, Robert. Leonardo, the Beautiful Dreamer. Byrd, Robert, illus. 2003. (ENG., Illus.). 48p. (J). (gr. 2-5). 17.99 *(978-0-525-47033-5(6)*, Dutton Books for Young Readers) Penguin Young Readers Group.
Cernak, Linda. Leonardo Da Vinci. Morrow, J. T., illus. 2014. (World's Greatest Artists Ser.). (ENG.). 24p. (J). (gr. 2-5). 28.50 *(978-1-62687-351-3(8)*, 207191) Child's World, Inc., The.
Ciovacco, Justine. Leonardo Da Vinci, 1 vol. 2015. (ENG., Illus.). 32p. (J). 23.45 *(978-1-62275-677-3(0)*, Britannica Educational Publishing) Rosen Publishing Group, Inc., The.
Conklin, Wendy. 16th Century Superstar: Da Vinci. 2017. (TIME for KIDS(r) Nonfiction Readers Ser.). (Illus.). 32p. (J). (gr. 7-7). pap. 8.99 *(978-1-4938-3630-7(7))* Teacher Created Materials, Inc.
—16th Century Superstar: Da Vinci. 2017. (Time for Kids Nonfiction Readers Ser.). lib. bdg. 19.65 ***(978-0-606-40291-0(8))*** Turtleback Bks.
Da Vinci, Leonardo & Benchmark Education Co. Staff. The Da Vinci Notebooks. 2014. (Text Connections Ser.). (J). (gr. 5). *(978-1-4900-1370-1(9))* Benchmark Education Co.
Dickins, Rosie & Ball, Karen. Leonardo Da Vinci. Unzner, Christa, illus. 2007. (Famous Lives Gift Bks). 63p. (J). (gr. 4-7). 8.99 *(978-0-7945-1594-2(0)*, Usborne) EDC Publishing.
Edwards, Roberta. Who Was Leonardo da Vinci? Kelley, True, illus. 2005. (Who Was... ? Ser.). 106p. (J). (gr. 2-6). 12.65 *(978-0-7569-6971-4(9))* Perfection Learning Corp.

J
K
L

Hall, M. C. Leonardo Da Vinci, 1 vol. 2007. (Essential Lives Set 1 Ser.). (ENG., Illus.). 112p. (J). (gr. 6-12). lib. bdg. 35.64 *(978-1-59928-844-4(3))* ABDO Publishing Co.

Harris, Godfrey, et al. The Life & Contributions of Leonardo Da Vinci. 2006. 58p. (J). pap. *(978-0-935047-60-8(3))* Americas Group, The.

January, Brendan. Leonardo Da Vinci: Renaissance Painter. 2013. (People of Importance Ser.: 21). (Illus.). 32p. (J). (gr. 4-18). 19.95 *(978-1-4222-2848-7(7))* Mason Crest.

Kalz, Jill. The Mona Lisa. 2004. (What in the World? Ser.). (Illus.). 48p. 19.95 *(978-1-58341-272-5(7)*, Creative Education) Creative Co., The.

Kennon, Caroline. Leonardo Da Vinci in His Own Words. 2016. (Eyewitness to History Ser.). (ENG.). 32p. (J). (gr. 4-5). pap. 10.50 *(978-1-4824-4074-4(1))* Stevens, Gareth Publishing LLLP.

Koestler-Grack, Rachel A. Leonardo Da Vinci: Artist, Inventor, & Renaissance Man. 2005. (Makers of the Middle Ages & Renaissance Ser.). (Illus.). 152p. (gr. 5-8). lib. bdg. 32.95 *(978-0-7910-8626-1(7)*, Chelsea Hse.) Facts On File, Inc.

Krull, Kathleen. Leonardo Da Vinci. Kulikov, Boris, illus. 2008. (Giants of Science Ser.). (ENG.). 128p. (J). (gr. 3-7). 7.99 *(978-0-14-240821-6(2)*, Puffin Books) Penguin Young Readers Group.

Kuligowski, Stephanie. Leonardo Da Vinci: Renaissance Artist & Inventor, 1 vol. 2012. (Primary Source Readers Ser.). (ENG.). 32p. (J). (gr. 4-4). pap. 8.99 *(978-1-4333-5008-5(4))* Teacher Created Materials, Inc.

Lebscky, Ibi. Leonardo. Cardoni, Paolo, illus. (Coleccion Seran Famosos).Tr. of Little Leonardo de Vinci. (SPA.). 28p. (J). (gr. 2-4). 10.36 *(978-84-233-1399-0(9))* Ediciones Destino ESP. Dist: Lectorum Pubns., Inc.

Leonardo & Harris, Godfrey. Leonardo's "Quotebook" Thoughts by & about Leonardo Da Vinci. 2006. 104p. (J). pap. *(978-0-935047-57-8(3))* Americas Group, The.

Leoni, Maria Teresa Zanobini. Leonardo Da Vinci. 2005. (Great Artists Ser.). (Illus.). 40p. (J). (gr. 5). per. 7.95 *(978-1-59270-048-6(9))* Enchanted Lion Bks., LLC.

Malam, John. Leonardo Da Vinci: El Genio Que Definio el Renacimiento. P. López, Wendy, tr. from ENG. 2007. (Altea Biografías Ser.).Tr. of Leonardo da Vinci. (SPA., Illus.). 64p. (J). (gr. -1-3). 17.99 *(978-84-372-2467-1(5))* Altea, Ediciones, S.A. - Grupo Santillana ESP. Dist: Santillana USA Publishing Co., Inc.

Mattern, Joanne. Leonardo Da Vinci, 1 vol. 2005. (Great Artists Set 1 Ser.). (ENG., Illus.). 32p. (gr. k-6). 27.07 *(978-1-59197-842-8(4)*, Checkerboard Library) ABDO Publishing Co.

Nardo, Don, ed. Leonardo da Vinci. 2012. (Eye on Art Ser.). (ENG., Illus.). 128p. (J). (gr. 7-10). lib. bdg. 34.80 *(978-1-4205-0735-5(4)*, Lucent Bks.) Cengage Gale.

Nichols, Catherine. Leonardo Da Vinci. 2006. (Primary Source Library of Famous Artists Ser.). (Illus.). 32p. (J). (gr. -1-3). lib. bdg. 23.95 *(978-1-4042-2762-0(8)*, PowerKids Pr.) Rosen Publishing Group, Inc., The.

—Leonardo da Vinci. 2009. (Primary Source Library of Famous Artists Ser.). 32p. (gr. 3-4). 42.50 *(978-1-60854-101-0(0)*, PowerKids Pr.) Rosen Publishing Group, Inc., The.

Noble, Marty & Da Vinci, Leonardo. Leonardo Da Vinci Stained Glass. 2006. (Dover Stained Glass Coloring Book Ser.). (ENG., Illus.). 32p. (gr. 3-8). 6.99 *(978-0-486-45059-9(7))* Dover Pubns., Inc.

Novelli, Luca. Leonardo Da Vinci & the Pen That Drew the Future. 2017. (Flashes of Genius Ser.). (ENG.). 112p. (J). (gr. 3). pap. 9.99 ***(978-1-61373-869-6(2))*** Chicago Review Pr., Inc.

Osborne, Mary Pope & Boyce, Natalie Pope. Leonardo Da Vinci: A Nonfiction Companion to Monday with a Mad Genius. Murdocca, Sal, illus. 2009. (Magic Tree House - Fact Tracker Ser.: 19). (ENG.). 128p. (J). (gr. 2-5). 6.99 *(978-0-375-84665-6(4)*, Random Hse. Bks. for Young Readers) Random Hse. Children's Bks.

—Leonardo Da Vinci: A Nonfiction Companion to Monday with a Mad Genius. 2009. (Magic Tree House Fact Tracker Ser.: 19). lib. bdg. 16.00 *(978-0-606-01834-0(4)*, Turtleback) Turtleback Bks.

Phillips, John & National Geographic Kids Staff. Leonardo Da Vinci: The Genius Who Defined the Renaissance. 2008. (National Geographic World History Biographies Ser.). (ENG., Illus.). 64p. (J). (gr. 3-7). pap. 7.99 *(978-1-4263-0248-0(7)*, National Geographic Children's Bks.) National Geographic Society.

Raynham, Alex. Factfiles Leonardo da Vinci. 3rd ed. 2013. (ENG., Illus.). 64p. pap. 10.00 *(978-0-19-423670-6(6))* Oxford Univ. Pr., Inc.

Reed, Jennifer. Leonardo da Vinci: Genius of Art & Science. 2005. (Great Minds of Science Ser.). (Illus.). 128p. (J). lib. bdg. 27.94 *(978-0-7660-2500-4(4))* Enslow Pubs., Inc.

Rinaldo, Denise. Leonardo Da Vinci: With a Discussion of Imagination. 2003. (Values in Action Ser.). (J). *(978-1-59203-066-8(1))* Learning Challenge, Inc.

Rockett, Paul. Leonardo Da Vinci, 01 vols., 1. 2016. (Inspiring Artists Ser.). (ENG.). 48p. (J). 30.25 *(978-1-5081-7054-9(1)*, Rosen Young Adult) Rosen Publishing Group, Inc., The.

Romeo, Francesca. Leonardo Da Vinci. 2008. (Art Masters Ser.). 64p. (YA). (gr. 6-18). lib. bdg. 24.95 net. *(978-1-934545-00-3(7))* Oliver Pr., Inc.

Rossi, Renzo. In Renaissance Florence with Leonardo. Baldanzi, Alessandro, illus. 2008. (Come See My City Ser.). 48p. (gr. 4-8). lib. bdg. 28.50 *(978-0-7614-4329-2(0)*, Benchmark Bks.) Marshall Cavendish Corp.

Stanley, George E. Leonardo Da Vinci: Young Artist, Writer, & Inventor. 2005. (Childhood of World Figures Ser.). (ENG.). 176p. (J). (gr. 3-7). pap. 5.99 *(978-1-4169-0570-7(7)*, Simon & Schuster/Paula Wiseman Bks.) Simon & Schuster/Paula Wiseman Bks.

Strom, Laura Layton. Leonardo Da Vinci. 2007. (Shockwave: Life Stories Ser.). (ENG., Illus.). 36p. (J). (gr. 3-5). 25.00 *(978-0-531-17771-6(8)*, Children's Pr.) Scholastic Library Publishing.

Sutcliffe, Jane. Leonardo's Monster, 1 vol. Leonhard, Herb & Leonard, Herb, illus. 2010. (ENG.). 32p. (J). (gr. k-3). 16.99 *(978-1-58980-838-6(X))* Pelican Publishing Co., Inc.

Tracy, Kathleen. Leonardo Da Vinci. 2008. (Art Profiles for Kids Ser.). (Illus.). 48p. (YA). (gr. 4-7). lib. bdg. 29.95 *(978-1-58415-711-3(9))* Mitchell Lane Pubs., Inc.

Venezia, Mike. Leonardo Davinci. Venezia, Mike, illus. rev. ed. 2015. (Getting to Know the World's Greatest Artists Ser.). (ENG., Illus.). 40p. (J). pap. 7.95 *(978-0-531-21289-9(0))* Scholastic Library Publishing.

Williams, Colleen Madonna Flood. My Adventure with Leonardo da Vinci. 2009. (ENG.). 44p. (J). 8.99 *(978-1-59092-458-7(4))* Blue Forge Pr.

Wood, Alix. Leonardo Da Vinci. 2013. (Artists Through the Ages Ser.). (ENG., Illus.). 32p. (J). (gr. 3-6). pap. 10.00 *(978-1-61533-629-6(X))*; lib. bdg. 25.25 *(978-1-61533-621-0(4))* Windmill Bks.

Zaczek, Iain. Leonardo Da Vinci. 2014. (Great Artists Ser.). 32p. (J). (gr. 3-6). pap. 10.50 *(978-1-4824-1214-7(4))* Stevens, Gareth Publishing LLLP.

Zanobini Leoni, Maria Teresa. Leonardo Da Vinci. 2003. (Great Artists Ser.). (Illus.). 40p. (J). 15.95 *(978-1-59270-007-3(1))* Enchanted Lion Bks., LLC.

LEONARDO, DA VINCI, 1452-1519—FICTION

Anholt, Laurence. Leonardo & the Flying Boy. 2007. (Anholt's Artists Books for Children Ser.). (ENG., Illus.). 36p. (J). (gr. -1-3). 8.99 *(978-0-7641-3851-5(0))* Barron's Educational Series, Inc.

Duey, Kathleen. Leonardo. Epstein, Eugene, illus. 2009. (Time Soldiers Ser.). (ENG.). (J). (gr. k-2). 95p. 9.95 *(978-1-929945-89-4(2))*;Bk. 8. 48p. 15.95 *(978-1-929945-88-7(4))* Big Guy Bks., Inc.

Elliott, L. M. Da Vinci's Tiger. (YA). (gr. 8). 2017. 320p. pap. 9.99 ***(978-0-06-074426-7(X))*** 2015. (ENG.). 304p. 17.99 *(978-0-06-074424-3(3))* HarperCollins Pubs. (Tegen, Katherine Bks).

Friedlander, Mark P., Jr. Innovators in Action! Leonardo Da Vinci Gets a Do-Over. Sakprayoonpong, Worachet Boon, illus. 2014. (Innovators in Action Ser.: 1). (ENG.). 208p. (J). (gr. 5-9). pap. 12.95 *(978-0-9678020-6-0(7))* Science, Naturally!

Grey, Christopher Peter & Grey, Christopher. Leonardo's Shadow: Or, My Astonishing Life As Leonardo Da Vinci's Servant. 2008. (ENG.). 400p. (YA). (gr. 7). pap. 12.99 *(978-1-4169-0544-8(8)*, Atheneum Bks. for Young Readers) Simon & Schuster Children's Publishing.

Konigsburg, E. L. The Second Mrs. Giaconda. 3rd ed. (J). pap. 4.95 *(978-0-13-800061-5(1))* Prentice Hall (Schl. Div.).

Lewis, J. Patrick. The Stolen Smile. Kelley, Gary, illus. 2nd ed. 2015. (ENG.). 40p. (J). (gr. 2-4). 16.99 *(978-1-56846-281-3(6)*, Creative Editions) Creative Co., The.

Mayhew, James. Katie & the Mona Lisa. 2016. (Katie Ser.). (ENG., Illus.). 32p. (J). (gr. -1-k). pap. 10.99 *(978-1-4083-3194-1(2)*, Orchard Bks.) Hachette Children's Group GBR. Dist: Hachette Bk. Group.

Napoli, Donna Jo. The Smile. 2009. (ENG.). 272p. (YA). (gr. 7-18). 7.99 *(978-0-14-241492-7(1)*, Speak) Penguin Young Readers Group.

Osborne, Mary Pope. Monday with a Mad Genius. Murdocca, Sal, illus. (Magic Tree House Merlin Mission Ser.: 10). (ENG.). (J). (gr. 2-5). 2009. 144p. 5.99 *(978-0-375-83730-2(2))* 2007. 128p. 11.99 *(978-0-375-83729-6(9))* Random Hse. Children's Bks. (Random Hse. Bks. for Young Readers).

—Monday with a Mad Genius. 2009. (Magic Tree House Merlin Missions Ser.: 10). lib. bdg. 16.00 *(978-0-606-01777-0(1)*, Turtleback) Turtleback Bks.

Pryor, Michael. Leo Da Vinci vs the Ice-Cream Domination League. Faber, Jules, illus. 2015. (Leo Da Vinci Ser.). (ENG.). 144p. (J). (gr. 4-7). 8.99 *(978-0-85798-837-9(9))* Random Hse. Australia AUS. Dist: Independent Pubs. Group.

Sabuda, Robert. Uh-Oh, Leonardo! The Adventures of Providence Traveler. Sabuda, Robert, illus. 2007. (ENG., Illus.). 48p. (J). (gr. k-3). 12.99 *(978-1-4169-6164-2(X)*, Aladdin) Simon & Schuster Children's Publishing.

Scieszka, Jon. Da Wild, Da Crazy, Da Vinci, No. 14. McCauley, Adam & Adam, Mccauley, illus. 2006. (Time Warp Trio Ser.: 14). (ENG.). 96p. (J). (gr. 2-4). 5.99 *(978-0-14-240465-2(9)*, Puffin Books) Penguin Young Readers Group.

—Da Wild, Da Crazy, Da Vinci. McCauley, Adam, illus. 2006. (Time Warp Trio Ser.: No. 14). 72p. (gr. 4-7). 15.00 *(978-0-7569-6677-5(9))* Perfection Learning Corp.

Wurge, B. B. The Last Notebook of Leonardo. 2010. (LeapKids Ser.). (ENG., Illus.). 154p. (J). (gr. 1-7). pap. 9.95 *(978-1-935248-14-9(6))* Leapfrog Pr.

LEOPARD

Archer, Claire. Leopards, 1 vol. 2014. (Big Cats Ser.). (ENG.). 24p. (J). (gr. 4-8). lib. bdg. 28.50 *(978-1-62970-003-8(7))* ABDO Publishing Co.

Archer, Claire, et al. Leopardos. 2015. (Grandes Felinos Ser.). (SPA., Illus.). 24p. (gr. k-1). pap. 7.95 *(978-1-4966-0463-7(6))* Capstone Classroom.

Borgert-Spaniol, Megan. Leopards. 2012. (Animal Safari Ser.). (ENG., Illus.). 24p. (J). (gr. k-3). lib. bdg. 25.95 *(978-1-60014-769-2(0)*, Blastoff! Readers) Bellwether Media.

—Snow Leopards. 2014. (Animal Safari Ser.). (ENG.). 24p. (J). (gr. k-3). lib. bdg. 25.95 *(978-1-60014-968-9(5)*, Blastoff! Readers) Bellwether Media.

Bowman, Donna H. Big Cats. Wald, Christina, illus. 2008. (ENG.). 24p. (J). (gr. 3-18). 19.95 *(978-1-58117-781-7(X)*, Intervisual/Piggy Toes) Bendon, Inc.

Carr, Aaron. Snow Leopard. 2014. (J). *(978-1-4896-2641-7(7))* Weigl Pubs., Inc.

Chottin, Ariane. Little Leopards. 2005. (Born to Be Wild Ser.). (Illus.). 24p. (gr. k-3). lib. bdg. 23.00 *(978-0-8368-4438-2(6)*, Gareth Stevens Learning Library) Stevens, Gareth Publishing LLLP.

Coffey, Michele. Let's Look at Leopards. 2003. (Real Readers - Upper Emergent Ser.). (ENG., Illus.). 12p. (gr. 1-2). pap. 5.90 *(978-0-8239-6362-1(4))* Rosen Publishing Group, Inc., The.

Dibble, Traci. Leopards. (Predator Animals Ser.). 16p. 2011. pap. 39.62 *(978-1-61541-372-0(3))* 2010. (ENG.). (J). pap. 5.99 *(978-1-61541-371-3(5))* American Reading Co.

Dibble, Traci & Sánchez, Lucía M. Leopardos: Leopards. 2011. (2Y Animales Depredador Ser.). (SPA.). 16p. (J). (gr. k-2). pap. 6.99 *(978-1-61541-373-7(1))* American Reading Co.

Dibble, Traci & Sanchez, Lucia M. Leopardos (Leopards) 2011. (Animales depredadores Ser.). (SPA.). 16p. pap. 39.62 *(978-1-61541-374-4(X))* American Reading Co.

Ellis, Carol. Leopards. 2010. (Endangered! 2 Ser.). 48p. (gr. 3). lib. bdg. 29.93 *(978-0-7614-4052-9(6))* Marshall Cavendish GBR. Dist: Marshall Cavendish Corp.

Esbaum, Jill. Explore My World Snow Leopards. 2014. (Explore My World Ser.). (ENG., Illus.). 32p. (J). (gr. -1-2). pap. 4.99 *(978-1-4263-1703-3(4)*, National Geographic Children's Bks.) National Geographic Society.

Fletcher, Marty & Scherer, Glenn. The Snow Leopard: Help Save This Endangered Species! 2007. (Saving Endangered Species Ser.). (Illus.). 128p. (J). (gr. 5). lib. bdg. 34.60 *(978-1-59845-040-8(9)*, MyReportLinks.com Bks.) Enslow Pubs., Inc.

Gish, Melissa. Leopards. 2011. (Living Wild Ser.). (ENG.). 48p. (J). (gr. 4-7). pap. 12.00 *(978-0-89812-555-9(3)*, Creative Paperbacks) Creative Co., The.

—Living Wild - Leopards. 2010. (Living Wild Ser.). 46p. (YA). (gr. 5-18). 23.95 *(978-1-58341-972-4(1)*, Creative Education) Creative Co., The.

—Snow Leopards. (Living Wild Ser.). (Illus.). (J). 2017. (ENG.). 48p. (gr. 4-7). pap. 12.00 *(978-1-62832-306-1(X)*, Creative Paperbacks) 2016. 46p. *(978-1-60818-710-2(1)*, Creative Education) Creative Co., The.

Goldsworthy, Steve. Leopards. 2014. (J). *(978-1-4896-0922-9(9))* Weigl Pubs., Inc.

Green, Jen. Leopards. 2009. (Illus.). 52p. (J). *(978-0-7172-8027-8(6))* Grolier, Ltd.

—Snow Leopards. 2014. (Collins Big Cat Progress Ser.). (ENG., Illus.). 32p. (J). (gr. 2-3). pap. 7.99 *(978-0-00-751932-3(X))* HarperCollins Pubs. Ltd. GBR. Dist: Independent Pubs. Group.

Group/McGraw-Hill, Wright. Leopard Level: Adventure Journal Set. (Wildcats Ser.). (gr. 2-8). 31.95 *(978-0-322-05792-0(2))* Wright Group/McGraw-Hill.

—Leopard Level: Wildcats Leopard Complete Kit. (Wildcats Ser.). (gr. 2-8). 599.95 *(978-0-322-06485-0(6))* Wright Group/McGraw-Hill.

Herrington, Lisa M. Cheetahs & Leopards. 2015. (Rookie Read-About(tm) Science: What's the Difference? Ser.). (ENG., Illus.). 32p. (J). lib. bdg. 25.00 *(978-0-531-21481-7(8)*, Children's Pr.) Scholastic Library Publishing.

Hutchison, Patricia. Snow Leopards. 2015. (Endangered Animals Ser.). (ENG.). 24p. (J). (gr. 1-4). 27.07 *(978-1-63143-974-2(X)*, 208809) Child's World, Inc., The.

Joubert, Dereck & Joubert, Beverly. Face to Face with Leopards. 2009. (Face to Face with Animals Ser.). (ENG.). 32p. (J). (gr. 2-5). 25.90 *(978-1-4263-0637-2(7)*, National Geographic Children's Bks.) National Geographic Society.

Joubert, Dereck, et al. Face to Face with Leopards. 2009. (Face to Face with Animals Ser.). (ENG., Illus.). 32p. (J). (gr. 2-5). 16.95 *(978-1-4263-0636-5(9)*, National Geographic Children's Bks.) National Geographic Society.

Kalman, Bobbie & Dyer, Hadley. Les Léopards. 2010. (Petit Monde Vivant Ser.). (FRE., Illus.). 32p. (J). pap. 9.95 *(978-2-89579-316-8(6))* Bayard Canada Livres CAN. Dist: Crabtree Publishing Co.

Landau, Elaine. Snow Leopards: Hunters of the Snow & Ice. 2010. (Animals of the Snow & Ice Ser.). (Illus.). 32p. (J). (gr. 1-3). 23.94 *(978-0-7660-3463-1(1))* Enslow Pubs., Inc.

Macheske, Felicia. Frosty Felines: Snow Leopard. 2017. (Guess What Ser.). (ENG., Illus.). 24p. (J). (gr. k-2). lib. bdg. 28.50 *(978-1-63472-174-5(8)*, 209268) Cherry Lake Publishing.

Maimone, Sofia. Snow Leopards in Danger. 2013. (Animals at Risk Ser.). 24p. (J). (gr. 2-5). pap. 8.15 *(978-1-4339-9175-2(6))*; pap. 48.90 *(978-1-4339-9176-9(4))*; (ENG., Illus.). lib. bdg. 22.60 *(978-1-4339-9174-5(8))* Stevens, Gareth Publishing LLLP.

Markle, Sandra. The Great Leopard Rescue: Saving the Amur Leopards. 2016. (ENG., Illus.). 48p. (J). (gr. 4-6). 46.65 *(978-1-4677-9755-9(3)*, Millbrook Pr.) Lerner Publishing Group.

—Snow School. Marks, Alan, illus. 2013. (ENG.). 32p. (J). (gr. -1-3). lib. bdg. 16.95 *(978-1-58089-410-4(0))* Charlesbridge Publishing, Inc.

Marks, Jennifer L. Clouded Leopards, 1 vol. 2010. (Wildcats Ser.). (ENG.). 24p. (gr. k-1). lib. bdg. 26.65 *(978-1-4296-4482-2(6)*, Pebble Plus) Capstone Press of Coughlan Cos.

Montgomery, Sy. Saving the Ghost of the Mountain: An Expedition among Snow Leopards in Mongolia. Bishop, Nic, illus. Bishop, Nic, photos by. (Scientists in the Field Ser.). (ENG.). 80p. (J). (gr. 5-7). 2012. pap. 9.99 *(978-0-547-72734-9(8))* 2009. 18.00 *(978-0-618-91645-0(8))* Houghton Mifflin Harcourt Publishing Co.

Newman, Aline Alexander. Lucky Leopards! 2014. (NGK Chapters Ser.). (ENG., Illus.). 112p. (J). (gr. 2-5). lib. bdg. 14.90 *(978-1-4263-1458-2(2)*, National Geographic Children's Bks.) National Geographic Society.

—Lucky Leopards! And More True Stories of Amazing Animal Rescues! 2014. (NGK Chapters Ser.). (ENG., Illus.). 112p. (J). (gr. 2-5). pap. 5.99 *(978-1-4263-1457-5(4)*, National Geographic Children's Bks.) National Geographic Society.

Nuzzolo, Deborah. Leopards. 2010. (African Animals Ser.). (ENG.). 24p. (gr. k-1). pap. 41.70 *(978-1-4296-5081-6(8)*, Pebble Plus) Capstone Press of Coughlan Cos.

Prebeg, Rick. Night Cat. Prebeg, Rick, photos by. 2005. (Illus.). (J). *(978-1-933248-15-8(7))* World Quest Learning.

Raatma, Lucia. Snow Leopards. 2013. (ENG.). 48p. (J). 28.00 *(978-0-531-23362-7(6))*; pap. 6.95 *(978-0-531-25160-7(8))* Scholastic Library Publishing.

Riggs, Kate. Amazing Animals: Leopards. 2012. (Amazing Animals Ser.). (ENG., Illus.). 24p. (J). (gr. 1-3). pap. 7.99 *(978-0-89812-695-2(9)*, Creative Paperbacks) Creative Co., The.

—Leopards. 2012. (Illus.). 24p. (J). 25.65 *(978-1-60818-110-0(3)*, Creative Education) Creative Co., The.

Rudolph, Jessica. Mi Pelambre es Gruesa y Moteada. 2015. (Pistas de Animales Ser.). (SPA.). 24p. (J). (gr. -1-3). lib. bdg. 23.93 *(978-1-62724-581-4(2))* Bearport Publishing Co., Inc.

—My Fur Is Thick & Spotted (Snow Leopard) 2014. (Zoo Clues Ser.). 24p. (J). (gr. -1-3). lib. bdg. 23.93 *(978-1-62724-113-7(2))* Bearport Publishing Co., Inc.

Ryndak, Rob. Leopard or Jaguar? 2015. (Animal Look-Alikes Ser.). (ENG., Illus.). 24p. (J). (gr. 1-2). pap. 8.15 *(978-1-4824-2720-2(6))* Stevens, Gareth Publishing LLLP.

Shores, Erika L. Snow Leopards, 1 vol. 2010. (Wildcats Ser.). (ENG.). 24p. (gr. k-1). lib. bdg. 26.65 *(978-1-4296-4483-9(4)*, Pebble Plus) Capstone Press of Coughlan Cos.

Silverman, Buffy. Can You Tell a Cheetah from a Leopard? 2011. (Animal Look-Alikes Ser.). pap. 45.32 *(978-0-7613-8384-0(0))*; (ENG.). 32p. pap. 7.95 *(978-0-7613-7847-1(2))*; (ENG., Illus.). 32p. lib. bdg. 26.60 *(978-0-7613-6735-2(7))* Lerner Publishing Group.

Simpson, Phillip. Life Cycle of a Leopard: A Sequence & Order Text, 1 vol. 2014. (Text Structures Ser.). (ENG.). 32p. (gr. 1-3). pap. 7.99 *(978-1-4846-0416-8(4)*, Heinemann First Library) Heinemann-Raintree.

Starbuck, Sara & The Born Free Foundation. Leopard Rescue: A True-Life Story. 2017. (Born Free... Bks.). (ENG.). 112p. (J). (gr. 2-6). pap. 6.99 *(978-1-4380-0988-9(7))* Barron's Educational Series, Inc.

Throp, Claire. Leopards, 1 vol. 2014. (Living in the Wild: Big Cats Ser.). (ENG.). 48p. (gr. 3-6). lib. bdg. 33.32 *(978-1-4329-8107-5(2)*, Heinemann InfoSearch) Heinemann-Raintree.

Vogel, Elizabeth. Leopards. 2009. (Big Cats (Powerkids Readers) Ser.). 24p. (gr. 1-1). 37.50 *(978-1-61511-569-3(2)*, PowerKids Pr.) Rosen Publishing Group, Inc., The.

Von Zumbusch, Amelie. Leopards: Silent Stalkers. 2007. (Dangerous Cats Ser.). (Illus.). 24p. (J). (gr. 3-7). lib. bdg. 22.60 *(978-1-4042-3633-2(3)*, PowerKids Pr.) Rosen Publishing Group, Inc., The.

von Zumbusch, Amelie. Leopards: Silent Stalkers. 2009. (Dangerous Cats Ser.). 24p. (gr. 2-3). 42.50 *(978-1-61512-128-1(5)*, PowerKids Pr.) Rosen Publishing Group, Inc., The.

Walden, Katherine. Leopards of the African Plains. 2009. (Safari Animals Ser.). (Illus.). 24p. (J). (gr. k-3). pap. 8.25 *(978-1-4358-3064-6(4))*; 24p. (gr. 1-1). 42.50 *(978-1-60852-953-7(3))*; (J). lib. bdg. 22.60 *(978-1-4358-2690-8(6))* Rosen Publishing Group, Inc., The. (PowerKids Pr.).

Zane, Dory. How to Track a Leopard, 1. 2014. (Scatalog: a Kid's Field Guide to Animal Poop Ser.). (ENG.). 24p. (J). (gr. k-5). 23.60 *(978-1-61533-885-6(3)*, Windmill Bks.) Rosen Publishing Group, Inc., The.

LEOPARD—FICTION

Achebe, Chinua & Iroaganachi, John. How the Leopard Got His Claws. GrandPré, Mary, illus. 2011. (ENG.). 32p. (J). (gr. 2-5). 16.99 *(978-0-7636-4805-3(1))* Candlewick Pr.

Anderson, Airlie, illus. A Very Spotty Flap Book. 2004. 10p. (J). bds. 5.95 *(978-1-58925-703-0(0))* Tiger Tales.

Basu, Anjana. Leopard in the Laboratory. 2016. (ENG., Illus.). 194p. pap. *(978-81-7993-370-1(9))* Energy and Resources Institute, The IND. Dist: Motilal (UK) Bks. of India.

Beeson, Lea Ann. A Leopard Is More Than His Spots. Popovich, Richard E., ed. Rockfield, Darryl, illus. l.t. ed. 2005. 51p. (J). lib. bdg. 19.95 *(978-0-9604876-1-5(1))* REP Pubs.

Burchett, Jan & Vogler, Sara. Avalanche Alert, 1 vol. Le Feyer, Diane, illus. 2013. (Wild Rescue Ser.). (ENG.). 152p. (gr. 3-6). 9.95 *(978-1-4342-4893-0(3))* Stone Arch Bks.

Castleton, Chaffee. Runty's Adventure: A Story of Love. Queen, Dana, illus. 2010. 97p. (J). pap. 17.95 *(978-0-578-06109-2(0))* Castleton, Julia J.

Cobb, Amelia. The Lucky Snow Leopard. 2016. (Zoe's Rescue Zoo Ser.: 4). (ENG.). 128p. (J). (gr. 2-5). pap. 4.99 *(978-0-545-84226-6(3)*, Scholastic Paperbacks) Scholastic, Inc.

Fox, Mem. Two Little Monkeys. Barton, Jill, illus. 2012. (ENG.). 32p. (J). (gr. -1-3). 16.99 *(978-1-4169-8687-4(1)*, Beach Lane Bks.) Beach Lane Bks.

Frampton, David. The Whole Night Through. Frampton, David, illus. Date not set. (Illus.). 32p. (J). (gr. -1-1). pap. 5.99 *(978-0-06-443652-6(7))* HarperCollins Pubs.

—The Whole Night Through: A Lullaby. Frampton, David, illus. 2004. (Illus.). 30p. (J). (gr. k-4). reprint ed. *(978-0-7567-7723-4(2))* DIANE Publishing Co.

Froggatt, Sarah H. E. Leopard Spots: How the Clouded Leopard Got Her Spots. 2012. 32p. pap. 32.70 *(978-1-4771-3891-5(9))* Xlibris Corp.

Harper, Kathryn. Leopard & His Spots Red Band. Mosedale, Julian, illus. 2016. (Cambridge Reading Adventures Ser.). (ENG.). 16p. pap. 6.56 *(978-1-316-50308-9(9))* Cambridge Univ. Pr.

Ipcar, Dahlov. Stripes & Spots, 1 vol. 2012. (ENG.). 42p. (J). 17.95 *(978-1-934031-70-4(4)*, 2e66d329-f317-4896-abd2-ae101e429c86) Islandport Pr., Inc.

Jaco, Paul. The Leopards of Sh'ong. 2010. 260p. pap. *(978-0-7981-4930-3(2))* NB Pubs. Ltd.

Kipling, Rudyard. How the Leopard Got His Spots, 1 vol. Lohstoeter, Lori, illus. 2005. (Rabbit Ears: A Classic Tale Ser.). (ENG.). 36p. (gr. 4-6). 25.65 *(978-1-59679-344-6(9))* Spotlight.

—How the Leopard Got His Spots. Rodriguez, Pedro, illus. 2012. (Graphic Spin Ser.). (ENG.). 40p. (gr. 1-3). lib. bdg. 23.99 *(978-1-4342-3223-6(9)*, Graphic Revolve) Stone Arch Bks.

—How the Leopard Got His Spots: The Graphic Novel, 1 vol. Rodriguez, Pedro, illus. 2012. (Graphic Spin Ser.). (ENG.). 40p. (gr. 1-3). pap. 5.95 *(978-1-4342-3881-8(4)*, Graphic Revolve) Stone Arch Bks.

Knutson, Barbara. Sungura & Leopard: A Swahili Trickster Tale. Knutson, Barbara, illus. 2007. (Illus.). 26p. (J). (gr. -1-3). per. 6.95 *(978-0-8225-6801-8(2)*, First Avenue Editions) Lerner Publishing Group.

Landau, Orna. Leopardpox! Sadie Is Having the Funniest Sick Day Ever! Hoffmann, Omer, illus. 2015. (ENG.). 40p. (J). (gr. -1-3). 16.99 *(978-0-544-29001-3(1))* Houghton Mifflin Harcourt Publishing Co.

Lodge, Ali, illus. The Leopard & the Sky God. 2007. (Usborne First Reading: Level 3 Ser.). 48p. (J). (gr. -1-3). 8.99 *(978-0-7945-1838-7(9)*, Usborne) EDC Publishing.

McGowan, Steve. The Adventures of Keke & the Golden Coconut. 2012. 48p. pap. 21.92 *(978-1-4251-4407-4(1))* Trafford Publishing.

McMaster, Alex. Giant George & Little Leo. 2012. 24p. pap. 14.95 *(978-1-4669-5080-1(3))* Trafford Publishing.

Nussbaum, Ben. Loli the Leopard. Wenzel, Gregory, illus. (ENG.). (J). (gr. -1-2). 2006. 32p. 9.95 *(978-1-59249-516-0(8)*, PS6556) 2006. 36p. 8.95 *(978-1-59249-514-6(1)*, SD6506) 2005. 36p. 14.95 *(978-1-59249-512-2(5)*, H6506) 2005. 36p. pap. 6.95 *(978-1-59249-513-9(3)*, S6506) Soundprints.

Nussbaum, Ben & Wenzell, Gregory. Loli Leopard. 2005. (ENG., Illus.). 36p. (J). (gr. -1-2). 2.95 (978-1-59249-515-3(X), S6556) Soundprints.

Parker, Vic, compiled by. How the Leopard Got His Spots & Other Silly Stories. 2016. (Silly Stories Ser.). (ENG.). 40p. (J). (gr. 2-3). pap. 14.05 (978-1-4824-4191-8(8)) Stevens, Gareth Publishing LLLP.

Sargent, Pat. The Black Panther, 6 vols., Vol. 2. Lenoir, Jane, illus. 2003. (Barney the Bear Killer Ser.: Vol. 2). 137p. (J). pap. 10.95 (978-1-56763-966-7(6)) Ozark Publishing.

Smith, Roland. The Edge. 2015. (Peak Marcello Adventure Ser.). (ENG.). 240p. (YA). (gr. 7). 17.99 (978-0-544-34122-7(8), HMH Books For Young Readers) Houghton Mifflin Harcourt Publishing Co.

St. John, Lauren. The Last Leopard. 2010. (ENG.). 224p. (J). (gr. 3-7). 6.99 (978-0-14-241515-3(4), Puffin Books) Penguin Young Readers Group.

Uncool!, 6 Packs. (Bookweb Ser.). 32p. (gr. 6-18). 34.00 (978-0-7578-0901-9(4)) Rigby Education.

White, Paul. Jungle Doctor Spots a Leopard. 2008. (Flamingo Fiction 9-13s Ser.). (ENG., Illus.). 176p. (J). (gr. 5-7). per. 8.99 (978-1-84550-301-7(5), 6c36bf51-d79e-4a21-bb4f-54dc3b30085b) Christian Focus Pubns. GBR. Dist: Bookmasters Distribution.

LEOPARDS

see Leopard

LEPIDOPTERA

see Butterflies; Moths

LEPROSY

Benge, Janet & Benge, Geoff. Paul Brand: Helping Hands. 2011. (ENG.). (YA). pap. 9.99 (978-1-57658-536-8(0)) YWAM Publishing.

Donnelly, Karen. Leprosy (Hansen's Disease) 2009. (Epidemics Ser.). 64p. (gr. 5-5). 58.50 (978-1-61512-290-5(7)) Rosen Publishing Group, Inc., The.

Leech, Bonnie Coulter. Prisms. 2006. (Exploring Shapes Ser.: Vol. 3). (Illus.). 24p. (J). (gr. 3-7). lib. bdg. 22.60 (978-1-4042-3498-7(5)) Rosen Publishing Group, Inc., The.

LEPROSY—FICTION

Durango, Julia. The Walls of Cartagena. Pohrt, Tom, illus. 2008. (ENG.). 160p. (J). (gr. 3-7). 15.99 (978-1-4169-4102-6(9), Simon & Schuster Bks. For Young Readers) Simon & Schuster Bks. For Young Readers.

Ellis, Deborah. No Ordinary Day, 1 vol. (ENG.). (J). (gr. 3-7). 2014. 160p. pap. 9.95 (978-1-55498-108-3(5)) 2011. 144p. 16.95 (978-1-55498-134-2(4)) Groundwood Bks. CAN. Dist: Publishers Group West (PGW).

—No Ordinary Day. 2013. 164p. pap. (978-1-4596-6451-7(5)) ReadHowYouWant.com, Ltd.

LETTER WRITING

see also Commercial Correspondence

Ashley, Susan. I Can Write a Letter. 2004. (I Can Do It! Ser.). (Illus.). 24p. (J). (gr. k-3). pap. 8.15 (978-0-8368-4335-4(5)); lib. bdg. 21.00 (978-0-8368-4328-6(2)) Stevens, Gareth Publishing LLLP. (Weekly Reader Leveled Readers).

Fields, Jan. You Can Write Great Letters & E-Mails, 1 vol. 2012. (You Can Write Ser.). (ENG.). 24p. (gr. 1-2). pap. 7.29 (978-1-4296-7963-3(8)); pap. 41.70 (978-1-4296-8385-2(6)); lib. bdg. 25.32 (978-1-4296-7613-7(2)) Capstone Press of Coughlan Cos. (First Facts).

Ganeri, Anita. I Can Write Letters & E-Mails, 1 vol. 2013. (I Can Write Ser.). (ENG., Illus.). 32p. (gr. 1-3). pap. 8.29 (978-1-4329-6942-4(0)); lib. bdg. 27.32 (978-1-4329-6935-6(8)) Heinemann-Raintree. (Heinemann First Library).

Leleu, Sinead & Greck-Ismair, Michaela. German Pen Pals Made Easy: A Fun Way to Write German & Make a New Friend. 2010. (Illus.). 57p. pap. (978-0-85747-144-4(9)) Brilliant Pubns.

Loewen, Nancy. Sincerely Yours: Writing Your Own Letter, 1 vol. Lyles, Christopher, illus. 2009. (Writer's Toolbox Ser.). (ENG.). 32p. (gr. 2-4). pap. 8.95 (978-1-4048-5339-3(1)) Picture Window Bks.

Lynette, Rachel. Leah & Leshawn Build a Letter. Cox, Steve, illus. 2012. (Writing Builders Ser.). 32p. (J). (gr. 2-4). pap. 11.94 (978-1-60357-390-0(9)); lib. bdg. 25.27 (978-1-59953-510-4(6)) Norwood Hse. Pr.

Minden, Cecilia & Roth, Kate. How to Write a Thank-You Letter. 2012. (Explorer Junior Library: Language Arts Explorer Junior Ser.). (ENG.). 24p. (gr. 1-4). 25.64 (978-1-61080-489-9(9), 202099); pap. 12.79 (978-1-61080-663-3(8), 202273) Cherry Lake Publishing.

—How to Write an E-Mail. 2011. (Explorer Junior Library: Language Arts Explorer Junior Ser.). (ENG.). 24p. (gr. 1-4). lib. bdg. 25.64 (978-1-60279-993-6(8), 200986) Cherry Lake Publishing.

Practice Power Bilingual Practice Book: Cursive Letters. 2003. (Illus.). 16p. (J). (gr. k-2). spiral bd. (978-1-930355-46-0(7)) Bright of America.

Practice Power Bilingual Practice Book: Manuscript Letters. 2003. (Illus.). 16p. (J). (gr. -1-1). spiral bd. (978-1-930355-45-3(9)) Bright of America.

Proudfit, Benjamin. Writing Letters. 2014. (Write Right! Ser.). 24p. (J). (gr. 2-5). 22.60 (978-1-4824-1132-4(6)) Stevens, Gareth Publishing LLLP.

Publications International Ltd. Staff, creator. Dora the Explorer Learn to Write. 2007. (Play-A-Sound Bks.). (Illus.). (J). (gr. -1-3). 19.98 (978-1-4127-6659-3(1)) Publications International, Ltd.

Sévigny, Eric, illus. Caillou Sends a Letter. 2012. (Clubhouse Ser.). (ENG.). 24p. (J). (gr. -1-1). pap. 3.99 (978-2-89450-866-4(2)) Caillouet, Gerry.

Summers, Jean. The Kids' Guide to Writing Great Thank-You Notes. 2010. (Illus.). 48p. (J). 9.95 (978-1-59411-125-9(1)) Writers' Collective, The.

Top That Publishing Staff, ed. Fairy Princess Letter Writing. 2004. (Letter Writing Kits Ser.). (Illus.). 24p. (J). pap. (978-1-84229-874-9(7)) Top That! Publishing PLC.

—Magical Horses Letter Writing. 2004. (Letter Writing Kits Ser.). (Illus.). 24p. (J). pap. (978-1-84510-015-5(8)) Top That! Publishing PLC.

—Princess Letter Writing. 2005. (Illus.). 24p. pap. (978-1-84510-762-8(4)) Top That! Publishing PLC.

LETTER WRITING—FICTION

Atwood, Megan. Molly Discovers Magic (Then Wants to un-Discover It) Fleming, Lucy, illus. 2016. (Dear Molly, Dear Olive Ser.). (ENG.). 96p. (gr. 1-3). lib. bdg. 21.99 (978-1-4795-8694-3(3)) Picture Window Bks.

—Olive Finds Treasure (of the Most Precious Kind) Fleming, Lucy, illus. (Dear Molly, Dear Olive Ser.). (ENG.). 96p. (gr. 1-3). 2017. pap. 5.95 (978-1-62370-615-9(7)) 2016. lib. bdg. 21.99 (978-1-4795-8693-6(5)) Picture Window Bks.

Borden, Louise & Borden, Louise W. Across the Blue Pacific: A World War II Story. Parker, Robert Andrew, illus. 2006. (ENG.). 48p. (J). (gr. -1-3). 17.00 (978-0-618-33922-8(1)) Houghton Mifflin Harcourt Publishing Co.

Borden, Louise W. Across the Blue Pacific: A World War II Story. Parker, Robert Andrew, illus. 2015. (ENG.). 48p. (J). (gr. -1-3). 7.99 (978-0-544-55552-5(X), HMH Books For Young Readers) Houghton Mifflin Harcourt Publishing Co.

Croteau, Marie-Danielle. Fred & the Mysterious Letter. St-Aubin, Bruno, illus. 2005. 61p. (J). lib. bdg. 12.00 (978-1-4242-1199-9(9)) Fitzgerald Bks.

Danziger, Paula & Martin, Ann M. P. S. Longer Letter Later. (Tara Starr & Elizabeth Ser.). 240p. (J). (gr. 3-5). pap. 4.99 (978-0-8072-1537-1(6), Listening Library) Random Hse. Audio Publishing Group.

Hesse, Karen. Letters from Rifka. 2009. 9.00 (978-0-7848-2599-0(8), Everbind) Marco Bk. Co.

—Letters from Rifka. 2008. (ENG.). 148p. 17.00 (978-1-60686-224-7(3)) Perfection Learning Corp.

—Letters from Rifka. 2009. (ENG.). 176p. (J). (gr. 5-9). pap. 6.99 (978-0-312-53561-2(9), 9780312535612) Square Fish.

Ives, David. Scrib. 2005. 208p. (J). (gr. 5-18). lib. bdg. 17.89 (978-0-06-059842-6(5)) HarperCollins Pubs.

Iwasa, Megumi. Yours Sincerely, Giraffe. Takabatake, Jun, illus. 2017. (ENG.). 104p. (gr. k-3). 16.99 (978-1-927271-88-9(6)) Gecko Pr. NZL. Dist: Lerner Publishing Group.

Jones, Christianne C. La Carta de Paula, 1 vol. Ruíz, Carlos, tr. from ENG. Trover, Zachary, illus. 2006. (Read-It! Readers en Español: Story Collection).Tr. of Paula's Letter. (SPA.). 24p. (gr. -1-3). 21.32 (978-1-4048-1687-9(9), Easy Readers) Picture Window Bks.

Koutsky, Jan Dale. My Grandma, My Pen Pal. Koutsky, Jan Dale, illus. 2003. (ENG., Illus.). 32p. (J). (gr. k-2). 15.95 (978-1-56397-118-1(6)) Boyds Mills Pr.

Manushkin, Fran. Sincerely, Katie: Writing a Letter with Katie Woo, 1 vol. Lyon, Tammie, illus. 2013. (Katie Woo: Star Writer Ser.). (ENG.). 32p. (gr. k-2). pap. 6.95 (978-1-4795-1921-7(9)); lib. bdg. 20.65 (978-1-4048-8126-6(3)) Picture Window Bks.

Nichol, Barbara. Beethoven Vive Arriba. 2003.Tr. of Beethoven Lives Upstairs. (SPA., Illus.). 48p. (J). (gr. 3-5). 10.95 (978-1-56014-619-3(2), SAN619) Santillana USA Publishing Co., Inc.

Orloff, Karen Kaufman. I Wanna New Room. Catrow, David, III, illus. 2010. (ENG.). 32p. (J). (gr. k-3). 16.99 (978-0-399-25405-5(6), G.P. Putnam's Sons Books for Young Readers) Penguin Young Readers Group.

Sís, Peter. Ice Cream Summer. 2015. (ENG., Illus.). 40p. (J). (gr. k-3). 17.99 (978-0-545-73161-4(5), Scholastic Pr.) Scholastic, Inc.

LETTERING

Bos, Samone. The Super Lettering Book: With 12 Bonus Stencils! 2017. (ENG.). 48p. (J). (gr. 3-7). pap. 10.99 **(978-1-4380-1097-7(4))** Barron's Educational Series, Inc.

Bukiet, Suzanne. Scripts of the World. 2nd ed. (Illus.). 91p. (YA). reprint ed. 19.95 (978-0-9656274-1-2(1)) Another Language Pr.

Doh, Jenny. Creative Lettering for Kids. 2017. (ENG., Illus.). 128p. (J). (gr. 3-8). pap. 16.95 (978-1-4549-2005-2(X)) Sterling Publishing Co., Inc.

Hanson, Anders. Cool Calligraphy: The Art of Creativity for Kids, 1 vol. 2009. (Cool Art Ser.). (ENG.). 32p. (gr. 3-6). 28.50 (978-1-60453-145-9(2), Checkerboard Library) ABDO Publishing Co.

Klutz Editors. Neon Chalk Lettering. 2016. (ENG.). 76p. (J). (gr. 3-7). 18.99 (978-1-338-03754-8(4)) Scholastic, Inc.

Mappin, Jennifer, text. The Lettering Book: A Totally Fun Approach to Lettering! 2004. (Illus.). 12p. (J). spiral bd. (978-1-74124-129-7(4)) Bonnier Publishing Australia.

Phillips, Karen. Lettering in Crazy, Cool, Quirky Style. 2006. (ENG., Illus.). 56p. (J). (gr. 3-7). 18.95 (978-1-57054-428-6(X)) Klutz.

Scott, Linda. My Monster Bubblewriter Book. 2013. (ENG., Illus.). 144p. (J). (gr. 3-6). pap. 16.95 (978-1-78067-102-4(4)) King, Laurence Publishing GBR. Dist: Hachette Bk. Group.

Top That Publishing Staff, ed. Create Your Own Lettering. 2005. (Illus.). 48p. (978-1-84510-304-0(1)) Top That! Publishing PLC.

Warnaar, Dawn. DIY Lettering. 2017. (DIY Ser.). (ENG., Illus.). (J). (gr. 3-8). lib. bdg. 34.65 **(978-1-942875-26-0(6)**, Walter Foster Jr) Quarto Publishing Group USA.

Warnaar, Dawn Nicole. Adventures in Lettering: 40 Exercises & Projects to Master Your Hand-Lettering Skills. 2016. (ENG.). 128p. (J). (gr. 3-7). pap. 12.95 (978-1-63322-173-4(3), Walter Foster Jr) Quarto Publishing Group USA.

LETTERS

Amazing Grace: Letters Alone My Journey. 2004. 160p. pap. 14.95 net. (978-0-9747983-0-1(4)) Lewis-Thornton, Rae.

Carson-Dellosa Publishing Staff. Mailboxes & Letters. 2009. (ENG.). 34p. (gr. -1-8). 6.99 (978-1-60418-612-3(7)) Carson-Dellosa Publishing, LLC.

Enea, Paul J. Letters to My Granddaughter. 2007. 64p. per. 9.95 (978-0-595-43781-8(8)) iUniverse, Inc.

Jakobsen, Kathy. My New York. Jakobsen, Kathy, illus. anniv. rev. ed. 2005. (Illus.). 54p. (J). (gr. k-4). 19.00 (978-0-7567-8588-8(X)) DIANE Publishing Co.

—My New York. Jakobsen, Kathy, illus. anniv. ed. 2003. (ENG., Illus.). 48p. (J). (gr. -1-3). 20.00 (978-0-316-92711-6(2)) Little, Brown Bks. for Young Readers.

Murray, Julie. Mail Carriers, 1 vol. 2015. (ENG., Illus.). 24p. (J). 27.07 (978-1-62970-915-4(8)) ABDO Publishing Co.

Reed, Gregory J. Dear Mrs. Parks: A Dialogue with Today's Youth. 2013. (ENG., Illus.). 111p. (J). (gr. 3-7). reprint ed. per. 16.95 (978-1-880000-61-8(X)) Lee & Low Bks., Inc.

Spence, Kelly & Burns, Kylie. Be a Diary Detective. 2017. (Be a Document Detective Ser.). (ENG., Illus.). 24p. (J). **(978-0-7787-3053-8(0))** Crabtree Publishing Co.

Stokes, Betty Southard. Postcards from George, 1763-1781: George Rogers Clark Writes Home to Virginia from the Kentucky Wilderness. Cable, Annette, illus. 2010. (J). (978-1-935497-12-7(X)) Butler Bk. Publishing.

Van Hoven, Constance. The Twelve Days of Christmas in Minnesota. Wohnoutka, Mike, illus. 2016. (Twelve Days of Christmas in America Ser.). (ENG.). 22p. (J). (— 1). bds. 7.95 (978-1-4549-2057-1(2)) Sterling Publishing Co., Inc.

Zourelias, Diana. Laugh Out Loud Letters for Boys: The Easy Way to Create Fast & Funny Notes! 2011. (Dover Children's Activity Bks.). (ENG., Illus.). 48p. (J). (gr. 2-5). pap. 5.99 (978-0-486-47788-6(6)) Dover Pubns., Inc.

—Laugh Out Loud Letters for Girls! The Easy Way to Create Fast & Funny Notes! 2011. (Dover Children's Activity Bks.). (ENG., Illus.). 48p. (J). (gr. 2-5). pap. 5.99 (978-0-486-47787-9(8)) Dover Pubns., Inc.

LETTERS—FICTION

Adams, Lisa. The Twelve Days of Christmas in New York City. Adams, Lisa, illus. 2009. (Twelve Days of Christmas in America Ser.). (ENG., Illus.). 40p. (J). (gr. k-3). 12.95 (978-1-4027-6440-0(5)) Sterling Publishing Co., Inc.

Alger Jr. Horatio Staff. Andy Grants Pluck. rev. ed. 2006. 312p. 29.95 (978-1-4218-1762-0(4)); pap. 14.95 (978-1-4218-1862-7(0)) 1st World Publishing, Inc. (1st World Library - Literary Society).

Amodeo, Darlene. Samantha & the Soldier: A Letter of Love. 2012. 40p. pap. 20.99 (978-1-4772-9263-1(2)) AuthorHouse.

Anderson, Jodi Lynn. Midnight at the Electric. 2017. 272p. (YA). (gr. 9). 17.99 (978-0-06-239354-8(5), HarperTeen) HarperCollins Pubs.

Andracki, Zenon. Dear Ashley: A Middle Grade Novel. 2006. (ENG.). 84p. per. 19.95 (978-1-4241-6168-3(1)) America Star Bks.

Anholt, Laurence & Coplestone, Jim. Seven for a Secret. 2006. (ENG., Illus.). 32p. (J). pap. (978-1-84507-590-3(0), Frances Lincoln) Quarto Publishing Group UK.

Anybody Shining. 2014. (ENG., Illus.). 240p. (J). (gr. 5-7). 16.99 (978-1-4424-3292-5(6), Atheneum Bks. for Young Readers) Simon & Schuster Children's Publishing.

Armstrong, Bill. Letters from Ozo, 1. 2005. (Illus.). 190p. (J). per. (978-0-9771676-0-9(7)) Rubicon Bks.

Arno, Ronni. Dear Poppy. 2016. (Mix Ser.). (ENG., Illus.). 256p. (J). (gr. 4-8). pap. 7.99 (978-1-4814-3759-2(3), Aladdin) Simon & Schuster Children's Publishing.

—Dear Poppy. 2016. (Mix Ser.). (ENG., Illus.). 256p. (J). (gr. 4-8). 17.99 (978-1-4814-3760-8(7), Simon & Schuster/Paula Wiseman Bks.) Simon & Schuster/Paula Wiseman Bks.

Ashman, Linda. The Twelve Days of Christmas in Colorado. 2011. (Twelve Days of Christmas in America Ser.). (ENG., Illus.). 40p. (J). (gr. k-3). 12.95 (978-1-4027-7463-8(X)) Sterling Publishing Co., Inc.

Asquith, Ros. Letters from an Alien Schoolboy. (ENG., Illus.). 192p. (J). (gr. 1-5). 2015. pap. 9.95 (978-1-62914-614-0(5)) 2013. 12.95 (978-1-62087-536-0(5), 620536) Skyhorse Publishing Co., Inc. (Sky Pony Pr.).

Axelrod, Amy. Your Friend in Fashion, Abby Shapiro. 2011. (ENG.). 288p. (J). (gr. 3-7). 17.95 (978-0-8234-2340-8(9)) Holiday Hse., Inc.

Baratz-Logsted, Lauren. I Love You, Michael Collins. 2017. (ENG.). 240p. (J). 16.99 (978-0-374-30385-3(1), 9780374303853, Farrar, Straus & Giroux (BYR)) Farrar, Straus & Giroux.

Bellisario, Gina. The Twelve Days of Christmas in Illinois. Ebbeler, Jeffrey, illus. 2012. (Twelve Days of Christmas in America Ser.). (ENG.). 40p. (J). (gr. k-3). 12.95 (978-1-4027-9733-0(8)) Sterling Publishing Co., Inc.

Bennett, Evelyn & Benson, Jenny, creators. Life Letters: Kid's Stuff. 2003. (J). 19.95 (978-0-9746022-2-6(1)) Life Letters Publishing.

Beverly, Cleary. Dear Mr. Henshaw. 2014. (Cleary Reissue Ser.). (ENG.). 160p. (J). (gr. 7-12). 10.24 (978-1-63245-195-8(6)) Lectorum Pubns., Inc.

Blackaby, Susan. The Twelve Days of Christmas in Oregon. Conahan, Carolyn Digby, illus. 2014. (Twelve Days of Christmas in America Ser.). (ENG.). 40p. (J). (gr. k). 12.95 (978-1-4549-0891-3(2)) Sterling Publishing Co., Inc.

Bond, Michael. Love from Paddington. Fortnum, Peggy & Alley, R. W., illus. 2016. (Paddington Ser.). 144p. (J). (gr. 3-7). pap. 5.99 (978-0-06-242526-3(9)) HarperCollins Pubs.

Boyd, Lizi. I Wrote You a Note. 2017. (ENG., Illus.). 36p. (J). 16.99 (978-1-4521-5957-7(2)) Chronicle Bks. LLC.

Bryant, Annie. Letters from the Heart. 2004. (Beacon Street Girls Ser.: No. 3). 224p. (J). 7.99 (978-0-9746587-8-0(2), Beacon Street Girls) B*tween Productions, Inc.

—Letters from the Heart. 2008. (Beacon Street Girls Ser.: 3). (ENG., Illus.). 256p. (J). (gr. 4-8). pap. 6.99 (978-1-4169-6426-1(6), Aladdin) Simon & Schuster Children's Publishing.

Bynum, Janie. The Twelve Days of Christmas in Texas. 2016. (Twelve Days of Christmas in America Ser.). (ENG., Illus.). 22p. (J). (— 1). bds. 7.95 (978-1-4549-2059-5(9)) Sterling Publishing Co., Inc.

—The Twelve Days of Christmas in Texas. Bynum, Janie, illus. 2009. (Twelve Days of Christmas in America Ser.). (ENG., Illus.). 40p. (J). (gr. k). 12.95 (978-1-4027-6350-2(6)) Sterling Publishing Co., Inc.

Callaghan, Cindy. Lost in Ireland. 2016. (Mix Ser.). (ENG., Illus.). 224p. (J). (gr. 4-8). pap. 7.99 (978-1-4814-6206-8(7), Aladdin) Simon & Schuster Children's Publishing.

—Lucky Me. 2014. (Mix Ser.). (ENG., Illus.). 224p. (J). (gr. 4-8). pap. 6.99 (978-1-4424-8950-9(2), Aladdin) Simon & Schuster Children's Publishing.

Candy, T. M. & Fisher, W. A. Dear Mister Mayor. 2010. 126p. pap. 15.54 (978-0-557-09733-3(9)) Lulu Pr., Inc.

Carroll, Emma. In Darkling Wood. 2017. (ENG.). 240p. (J). (gr. 5). 16.99 (978-0-399-55601-2(X), Delacorte Bks. for Young Readers) Random Hse. Children's Bks.

Cassidy, Yvonne. How Many Letters Are in Goodbye? 2016. (ENG.). 432p. (YA). pap. 11.99 (978-0-7387-4745-3(9), Flux) North Star Editions.

Chbosky, Stephen & Perez-Sauquillo, Vanesa. Las Ventajas de Ser Invisible. 2013. (SPA.). 272p. pap. 14.99 (978-1-4767-3245-9(0), MTV Bks.) MTV Books.

Clark, Anthony & Whybrow, Ian. Little Wolf's Book of Badness. 2008. (ENG.). 96p. (J). pap. 18.95 (978-1-84002-823-2(8)) Oberon Bks., Ltd. GBR. Dist: Consortium Bk. Sales & Distribution.

Clements, Andrew. Extra Credit. Elliott, Mark, illus. (ENG.). (J). (gr. 3-7). 2011. 224p. pap. 7.99 (978-1-4169-4931-2(3)) 2009. 192p. 16.99 (978-1-4169-4929-9(1)) Simon & Schuster Children's Publishing. (Atheneum Bks. for Young Readers).

Coffelt, Soraya Diase. It's Not about You Mr. Santa Claus: A Love Letter about the True Meaning of Christmas. 2014. (Love Letters Book Ser.). (ENG., Illus.). 34p. pap. 8.99 (978-1-63047-261-0(1)) Morgan James Publishing.

Cole, Barbara. Anna & Natalie, 1 vol. Himler, Ronald, illus. 2007. (ENG.). 32p. (J). 16.95 (978-1-59572-105-1(3)) Star Bright Bks., Inc.

Cole, Barbara H. Anna & Natalie, 1 vol. Himler, Ronald, illus. 2010. (ENG.). 32p. (J). pap. 6.95 (978-1-59572-211-9(4)) Star Bright Bks., Inc.

Cook, Danielle, illus. Letters from Pyggles, 1. 2003. 24p. 9.00 (978-0-9729914-0-7(9)) Oden, Rachel.

Cornelison, Sue F., illus. The Twelve Days of Christmas in Iowa. 2010. (Twelve Days of Christmas in America Ser.). (ENG.). 40p. (J). (gr. k). 12.95 (978-1-4027-6710-4(2)) Sterling Publishing Co., Inc.

Coyle, Carmela Lavigna. Thank You, Aunt Tallulah! MacPherson, Bruce, illus. 2006. (ENG.). 32p. (J). (gr. -1-3). 15.95 (978-0-87358-891-1(6)) Cooper Square Publishing Llc.

Cullen, Lynn. Dear Mr. Washington. Carpenter, Nancy, illus. 2015. (ENG.). 32p. (J). (gr. k-3). 16.99 (978-0-8037-3038-0(1), Dial Bks) Penguin Young Readers Group.

Cumyn, Alan. Dear Sylvia, 1 vol. 2009. (ENG.). 184p. (J). pap. 8.95 (978-0-88899-848-4(1)) Groundwood Bks. CAN. Dist: Publishers Group West (PGW).

Danneberg, Julie. First Year Letters. Love, Judy, illus. 2014. 32p. pap. 7.00 (978-1-61003-320-6(5)) Center for the Collaborative Classroom.

Dashner, James. The Journal of Curious Letters. Beus, Bryan, illus. 2008. (13th Reality Ser.: Bk. 1). 434p. (J). (gr. 4-7). 17.95 (978-1-59038-831-0(3), Shadow Mountain) Shadow Mountain Publishing.

—The Journal of Curious Letters. Beus, Bryan, illus. 2009. (13th Reality Ser.: 1). (ENG.). 528p. (J). (gr. 3-7). pap. 8.99 (978-1-4169-9152-6(2), Aladdin) Simon & Schuster Children's Publishing.

Daywalt, Drew. The Day the Crayons Quit. 2014. (CHI.). 32p. (J). (978-7-5448-3406-3(9)) Jieli Publishing Hse.

—The Day the Crayons Quit, 2 vols. Jeffers, Oliver, illus. (ENG.). (J). (gr. -1-2). 2016. 88p. 40.00 (978-0-399-54892-5(0)) 2013. 40p. 17.99 (978-0-399-25537-3(0)) Penguin Young Readers Group. (Philomel Bks.).

Dellaira, Ava. Love Letters to the Dead. 2014. (ENG.). 336p. (YA). (gr. 7). 17.99 (978-0-374-34667-6(4), 9780374346676, Farrar, Straus & Giroux (BYR)) Farrar, Straus & Giroux.

Donovan, Jane Monroe. Small, Medium & Large. Donovan, Jane Monroe, illus. 2010. (ENG., Illus.). 32p. (J). (gr. 1-4). 15.95 (978-1-58536-447-3(9), 202172) Sleeping Bear Pr.

Doughtie, Patrick & Doughtie, Heather. Letters to God, 1 vol. Lyon, Tammie, illus. 2016. (Letters to God Ser.). (ENG.). 32p. (J). 16.99 (978-0-310-75395-7(3)) Zonderkidz.

Dowell, Frances O'Roark. Anybody Shining. Wachter, Jill, photos by. 2015. (ENG., Illus.). 256p. (J). (gr. 5-7). pap. 7.99 (978-1-4424-3293-2(4), Atheneum Bks. for Young Readers) Simon & Schuster Children's Publishing.

Ewell, Katherine. Dear Killer. 2014. (ENG.). 368p. (YA). (gr. 8). 17.99 (978-0-06-225780-2(3)) HarperCollins Pubs.

Fishbone, Greg. The Penguins of Doom. 2007. (From the Desk of Septina Nash Ser.). (ENG., Illus.). 182p. (J). (gr. 2-7). 13.95 (978-1-933831-03-9(0)) Blooming Tree Pr.

Flor Ada, Alma & Zubizarreta, Gabriel M. Con Cariño, Amalia. 2013. (SPA., Illus.). 160p. (J). (gr. 3-7). pap. 6.99 (978-1-4424-2406-7(0)) Simon & Schuster Children's Publishing.

—Love, Amalia. (ENG., Illus.). (J). (gr. 3-7). 2013. 160p. pap. 6.99 (978-1-4424-2403-6(6)) 2012. 144p. 15.99 (978-1-4424-2402-9(8)) Simon & Schuster Children's Publishing. (Atheneum Bks. for Young Readers).

Fogelin, Adrian. The Sorta Sisters, 1 vol. 2007. (ENG., Illus.). 224p. (J). (gr. 3-7). 15.95 (978-1-56145-424-2(9)) Peachtree Pubs.

—Sorta Sisters, 1 vol. Fogelin, Adrian, illus. 2011. (ENG., Illus.). 288p. pap. 7.95 (978-1-56145-592-8(X), Peachtree Junior) Peachtree Pubs.

Frank, Hillary. I Can't Tell You. 2004. (ENG.). 208p. (YA). (gr. 7). pap. 7.99 (978-0-618-49491-0(X)) Houghton Mifflin Harcourt Publishing Co.

—I Can't Tell You. 2004. 208p. (YA). (gr. 7). 16.00 (978-0-618-41202-0(6)) Houghton Mifflin Harcourt Trade & Reference Pubs.

Gerber, Carole. The Twelve Days of Christmas in Ohio. Ebbeler, Jeffrey, illus. 2014. (Twelve Days of Christmas in America Ser.). (ENG.). 40p. (J). (gr. k). 12.95 (978-1-4549-0890-6(4)) Sterling Publishing Co., Inc.

Gil, Lydia. Letters from Heaven. 2014.Tr. of Cartas Del Cielo. (ENG & SPA.). 128p. (J). pap. 9.95 (978-1-55885-798-8(2), Piñata Books) Arte Publico Pr.

Goss, Matt. Bear Crimbo. 2010. (ENG., Illus.). 72p. (J). 17.95 (978-0-9815381-3-6(4)) Hilton Publishing Co.

Gray, Dianne & Gray, Dianne E. Holding up the Earth. 2006. (ENG.). 210p. (J). (gr. 5-7). pap. 12.95 (978-0-618-73747-5(2)) Houghton Mifflin Harcourt Publishing Co.

Griffin, Donna. The Twelve Days of Christmas in Indiana. Cummings, Troy, illus. 2014. (Twelve Days of Christmas in America Ser.). (ENG.). 40p. (J). (gr. k). 12.95 (978-1-4549-0888-3(2)) Sterling Publishing Co., Inc.

Grindley, Sally. Bravo, Max! Ross, Tony, illus. 2007. (ENG.). 160p. (J). (gr. 1-4). pap. 8.99 (978-1-4169-3645-9(9), Simon & Schuster/Paula Wiseman Bks.) Simon & Schuster/Paula Wiseman Bks.

Grindley, Sally & Lucas, D J. Dear Max. Ross, Tony, illus. 2007. (ENG.). 144p. (J). (gr. 1-4). pap. 7.99 (978-1-4169-3443-1(X), Simon & Schuster/Paula Wiseman Bks.) Simon & Schuster/Paula Wiseman Bks.

Haber, Melissa Glenn. Dear Anjali. 2010. (ENG.). 288p. (J). (gr. 4-8). 16.99 (978-1-4169-9599-9(4), Simon & Schuster/Paula Wiseman Bks.) Simon & Schuster/Paula Wiseman Bks.

—Your Best Friend, Meredith. 2011. (ENG.). 288p. (J). (gr. 4-8). pap. 6.99 (978-1-4169-9600-2(1), Aladdin) Simon & Schuster Children's Publishing.

Handler, Daniel. Why We Broke Up. Kalman, Maira, illus. 2011. (ENG.). 368p. (YA). (gr. 10-17). 20.00 (978-0-316-12725-7(6)) Little, Brown Bks. for Young Readers.

Harley, Bill. Dear Santa: The Letters of James B. Dobbins. Alley, R. W., illus. 2005. 32p. (J). (ENG.). 15.99 (978-0-06-623778-7(5)); lib. bdg. 16.89 (978-0-06-623779-4(3)) HarperCollins Pubs.

Harper, Suzanne. The Juliet Club. (YA). 2010. (ENG.). 416p. (gr. 8). pap. 9.99 (978-0-06-136693-2(5), Greenwillow Bks.) 2008. 402p. (gr. 7-18). lib. bdg. 18.89 (978-0-06-136692-5(7), HarperTeen) HarperCollins Pubs.

Harris, Christine. The Silver Path. (Illus.). (J). (ENG & VIE.). 26p. (978-1-85430-327-1(9), 93381); (CHI & ENG., 32p. (978-1-85430-323-3(6), 93425) Little Tiger Pr. Group.

Hedstrom-Page, Deborah. From Log Cabin to White House with Abraham Lincoln. Martinez, Sergio, illus. 2007. (My American Journey Ser.). 82p. (J). (gr. 3-9). 9.99 (978-0-8054-3269-5(8)) B&H Publishing Group.

Helmore, Jim & Wall, Karen. Letterbox Lil. (ENG., Illus.). 32p. (J). (gr. -1-1). 10.99 (978-0-19-279201-3(6)) Oxford Univ. Pr., Inc.

Hensley, Sarah M. Caillou's Trip to the Harbor. Gillen, Lisa P., illus. l.t. ed. 2004. (HRL Board Book Ser.). (J). (gr. -1-1). pap. 10.95 (978-1-57332-290-4(3), HighReach Learning, Incorporated) Carson-Dellosa Publishing, LLC.

—Helping Farmer Joe. Crowell, Knox, illus. l.t. ed. 2004. (HRL Little Book Ser.). (J). (gr. -1). pap. 10.95 (978-1-57332-296-6(2)); pap. 10.95 (978-1-57332-295-9(4)) Carson-Dellosa Publishing, LLC. (HighReach Learning, Incorporated).

Hest, Amy. Letters to Leo. Denos, Julia, illus. 2012. (ENG.). 160p. (J). (gr. 3-7). 14.99 (978-0-7636-3695-1(9)) Candlewick Pr.

—Letters to Leo. Denos, Julia, illus. 2014. (ENG.). 160p. (J). (gr. 3-7). pap. 6.99 (978-0-7636-7165-5(7)) Candlewick Pr.

Holland, Marci. The Birth Day Letter. 2005. 116p. 23.99 (978-1-4208-2920-4(3)) AuthorHouse.

—The Birth Day Letter: An Alzheimer's Story. 2005. 116p. pap. 14.95 (978-1-4208-2921-1(1)) AuthorHouse.

Holmes, Sara Lewis. Letters from Rapunzel. 2007. 184p. (J). (gr. 3-7). lib. bdg. 16.89 (978-0-06-078074-6(6)) HarperCollins Pubs.

Holt, Kimberly Willis. Dear Hank Williams. 2015. (ENG.). 224p. (J). (gr. 4-7). 16.99 (978-0-8050-8022-3(8), 9780805080223, Holt, Henry & Co. Bks. For Young Readers) Holt, Henry & Co.

Hopkinson, Deborah. A Letter to My Teacher. Carpenter, Nancy, illus. 2017. (ENG.). 40p. (J). (gr. -1-3). 17.99 (978-0-375-86845-0(3), Schwartz & Wade Bks.) Random Hse. Children's Bks.

Horse, Harry. The Last Gold Diggers: Being as It Were, an Account of a Small Dog's Adventures, down Under. Horse, Harry, illus. 2008. (ENG., Illus.). 128p. (J). (gr. 1-5). 12.95 (978-1-56145-435-8(4)) Peachtree Pubs.

—The Last Polar Bears. Horse, Harry, illus. 2007. (ENG., Illus.). 128p. (J). (gr. 1-5). 12.95 (978-1-56145-379-5(X), Peachtree Junior) Peachtree Pubs.

House, Silas & Vaswani, Neela. Same Sun Here. Schenker, Hilary, illus. (ENG.). (J). 2013. 304p. (gr. 4-7). pap. 7.99 (978-0-7636-6451-0(0)) 2012. 288p. (gr. 5). 15.99 (978-0-7636-5684-3(4)) Candlewick Pr.

Howard-Parham, Pam. Caillou Waits for Dinner. Crowell, Knox, illus. l.t. ed. 2004. (HRL Board Book Ser.). (J). (gr. -1-1). pap. 10.95 (978-1-57332-289-8(X), HighReach Learning, Incorporated) Carson-Dellosa Publishing, LLC.

—The Dinosaur Surprise. Neveu, Fred, illus. l.t. ed. 2004. (HRL Big Book Ser.). (J). (gr. -1-1). pap. 10.95 (978-1-57332-293-5(8)); pap. 10.95 (978-1-57332-294-2(6)) Carson-Dellosa Publishing, LLC. (HighReach Learning, Incorporated).

—Loving Our Country. Teeple, Jackie, illus. l.t. ed. 2004. (HRL Big Book Ser.). (J). (gr. -1-1). pap. 10.95 (978-1-57332-301-7(2)); pap. 10.95 (978-1-57332-302-4(0)) Carson-Dellosa Publishing, LLC. (HighReach Learning, Incorporated).

Iwasa, Megumi. Yours Sincerely, Giraffe. Takabatake, Jun, illus. 2017. (Gecko Press Titles Ser.). (ENG.). 104p. (gr. k-3). 9.99 **(978-1-77657-114-7(2))** Gecko Pr. NZL. Dist: Lerner Publishing Group.

Jarrell, Pamela R. Flitter, Flutter Butterfly. Middleton, Mikell, illus. l.t. ed. 2005. (HRL Board Book Ser.). 12p. (J). (gr. -1-1). pap. 10.95 (978-1-57332-286-7(5), HighReach Learning, Incorporated) Carson-Dellosa Publishing, LLC.

Johnson, Maureen. The Last Little Blue Envelope. 2012. (13 Little Blue Envelopes Ser.: 2). (ENG.). 288p. (YA). (gr. 8). pap. 9.99 (978-0-06-197681-0(4), HarperTeen) HarperCollins Pubs.

—The Last Little Blue Envelope. 2016. (13 Little Blue Envelopes Ser.: 2). (Illus.). 288p. (YA). (gr. 8). pap. 9.99 (978-0-06-243912-3(X), HarperTeen) HarperCollins Pubs.

—13 Little Blue Envelopes. (13 Little Blue Envelopes Ser.: 1). (ENG., Illus.). (YA). (gr. 8-18). 2005. 336p. 17.99 (978-0-06-054141-5(5)) 2010. 368p. reprint ed. pap. 9.99 (978-0-06-054143-9(1)) HarperCollins Pubs. (HarperTeen).

—13 Little Blue Envelopes. 2007. 317p. 20.00 (978-0-7569-7830-3(0)) Perfection Learning Corp.

Jones, Christianne C. La Carta de Paula, 1 vol. Ruíz, Carlos, tr. from ENG. Trover, Zachary, illus. 2006. (Read-It! Readers en Español: Story Collection).Tr. of Paula's Letter. (SPA.). 24p. (gr. -1-3). 21.32 (978-1-4048-1687-9(9), Easy Readers) Picture Window Bks.

Jones, Kelly. Unusual Chickens for the Exceptional Poultry Farmer. Kath, Katie, illus. 2015. (ENG.). 224p. (J). (gr. 3-7). 16.99 (978-0-385-75552-8(X), Knopf Bks. for Young Readers) Random Hse. Children's Bks.

Jones, Patrick. Outburst. 2014. (Alternative Ser.). (ENG.). 104p. (YA). (gr. 6-12). lib. bdg. 27.93 (978-1-4677-3901-6(4)) Lerner Publishing Group.

—Outburst. 2014. (Alternative Ser.). (ENG.). 104p. (YA). (gr. 6-12). pap. 7.95 (978-1-4677-4484-3(0), Darby Creek) Lerner Publishing Group.

Kelley, True. School Lunch. Kelley, True, illus. 2005. (ENG., Illus.). 32p. (J). (gr. -1-3). 16.95 (978-0-8234-1894-7(4)) Holiday Hse., Inc.

Kelly, Irene. A Small Dog's Big Life: Around the World with Owney. 2005. (ENG., Illus.). 32p. (J). 16.95 (978-0-8234-1863-3(4)) Holiday Hse., Inc.

Kemmerer, Brigid. Letters to the Lost. 2017. (ENG.). 400p. (YA). 17.99 (978-1-68119-008-2(7), 9781681190082, Bloomsbury USA Childrens) Bloomsbury Publishing USA.

Kephart, Beth. Undercover. 2009. (ENG.). 304p. (YA). (gr. 8). pap. 8.99 (978-0-06-123895-6(3), HarperTeen) HarperCollins Pubs.

Kieper, Rienhold Richard. Ten Letters for Our Children. 2004. 26p. (J). pap. 10.00 (978-0-9719284-1-1(X)) Blue Thunder One, Inc.

Klise, Kate. Dying to Meet You. Klise, M. Sarah, illus. (43 Old Cemetery Road Ser.: Bk. 1). (ENG.). 160p. (J). (gr. 2-5). 2010. pap. 6.99 (978-0-547-39848-8(4)) 2009. 16.99 (978-0-15-205727-5(7)) Houghton Mifflin Harcourt Publishing Co.

—Greetings from the Graveyard. Klise, M. Sarah, illus. (43 Old Cemetery Road Ser.). (ENG.). 160p. (J). (gr. 2-5). 2015. pap. 6.99 (978-0-544-54010-1(7)) 2014. 15.99 (978-0-544-10567-6(2)) Houghton Mifflin Harcourt Publishing Co. (HMH Books For Young Readers).

—Hollywood, Dead Ahead. Klise, M. Sarah, illus. (43 Old Cemetery Road Ser.: 5). (ENG.). 144p. (J). (gr. 2-5). 2014. pap. 6.99 (978-0-544-33661-2(5), HMH Books For Young Readers) 2013. 15.99 (978-0-547-85283-6(5)) Houghton Mifflin Harcourt Publishing Co.

—The Loch Ness Punster. Klise, M. Sarah, illus. 2016. (43 Old Cemetery Road Ser.: 7). (ENG.). 144p. (J). (gr. 2-5). pap. 6.99 (978-0-544-81085-3(6), HMH Books For Young Readers) Houghton Mifflin Harcourt Publishing Co.

—Over My Dead Body. Klise, M. Sarah, illus. 2009. (43 Old Cemetery Road Ser.: 2). (ENG.). 128p. (J). (gr. 2-5). 15.99 (978-0-15-205734-3(X)) Houghton Mifflin Harcourt Publishing Co.

—The Phantom of the Post Office. Klise, M. Sarah, illus. (43 Old Cemetery Road Ser.: 4). (ENG.). 160p. (J). (gr. 2-5). 2013. pap. 6.99 (978-0-544-02281-2(5)) 2012. 16.99 (978-0-547-51974-6(5)) Houghton Mifflin Harcourt Publishing Co.

—The Phantom of the Post Office. 2013. (43 Old Cemetery Road Ser.: 4). lib. bdg. 17.20 (978-0-606-31668-2(X), Turtleback) Turtleback Bks.

—Regarding the Sink: Where, Oh Where, Did Waters Go? Klise, M. Sarah, illus. 2006. (Regarding The ... Ser.: Bk. 2). (ENG.). 144p. (J). (gr. 2-5). pap. 6.99 (978-0-15-205544-8(4)) Houghton Mifflin Harcourt Publishing Co.

—Till Death Do Us Bark. 2012. (43 Old Cemetery Road Ser.: 3). lib. bdg. 17.20 (978-0-606-26543-0(0), Turtleback) Turtleback Bks.

Klise, Kate & Klise, Kate. Regarding the Bees: A Lesson, in Letters, on Honey, Dating, & Other Sticky Subjects. Klise, M. Sarah, illus. 2009. (Regarding The ... Ser.: Bk. 5). (ENG.). 144p. (J). (gr. 2-5). pap. 6.99 (978-0-15-206668-0(3)) Houghton Mifflin Harcourt Publishing Co.

Klise, Kate & Klise, M. Sarah. Regarding the Trees: A Splintered Saga Rooted in Secrets. 2007. (Regarding The ... Ser.: Bk. 3). (ENG., Illus.). 160p. (J). (gr. 2-5). pap. 7.99 (978-0-15-206090-9(1)) Houghton Mifflin Harcourt Publishing Co.

—Till Death Do Us Bark. Klise, Kate & Klise, M. Sarah, illus. 2011. (43 Old Cemetery Road Ser.: 3). (ENG., Illus.). 144p. (J). (gr. 2-5). 16.99 (978-0-547-40036-5(5)) Houghton Mifflin Harcourt Publishing Co.

Knaus, Patricia. Letters from Space. The Mousekins Staff, illus. 2004. 112p. (J). (gr. 3-4). pap. 8.50 (978-0-9758742-0-2(9), 10704) KnausWorks.

Kwan, James. Dear Yeti. 2015. (ENG., Illus.). 40p. (J). (gr. -1-2). 17.99 (978-0-374-30045-6(3), 9780374300456, Farrar, Straus & Giroux (BYR)) Farrar, Straus & Giroux.

Kyle, Sherry. Love, Lexi: Letters to God. 2016. (ENG.). 224p. (YA). pap. 12.99 (978-1-4964-0963-8(9)) Tyndale Hse. Pubs.

LaFleur, Suzanne. Love, Aubrey. 2011. (ENG.). 272p. (J). (gr. 3-7). pap. 7.99 (978-0-375-85159-9(3), Yearling) Random Hse. Children's Bks.

Lake, Nick. Whisper to Me. 2016. (ENG.). 544p. (YA). 17.99 (978-1-61963-456-5(2), 9781619634565, Bloomsbury USA Childrens) Bloomsbury Publishing USA.

Latimer, Miriam. Dear Panda. 2014. (ENG., Illus.). 32p. (J). (gr. -1-3). 17.95 (978-1-77147-078-0(X), Owlkids) Owlkids Bks. Inc. CAN. Dist: Publishers Group West (PGW).

LeSourd, Nancy. Adventures in Jamestown, 1 vol. 2008. (Liberty Letters Ser.). (ENG.). 240p. (J). pap. 7.99 (978-0-310-71392-0(7)) Zonderkidz.

—Attack at Pearl Harbor, 1 vol. 2008. (Liberty Letters Ser.). (ENG.). 224p. (J). pap. 7.99 (978-0-310-71389-0(7)) Zonderkidz.

—Escape on the Underground Railroad, 1 vol. 2008. (Liberty Letters Ser.). (ENG.). 224p. (J). pap. 7.99 (978-0-310-71391-3(9)) Zonderkidz.

—Secrets of Civil War Spies, 1 vol. 2008. (Liberty Letters Ser.). (ENG.). 224p. (J). pap. 7.99 (978-0-310-71390-6(0)) Zonderkidz.

Long, Melinda. The Twelve Days of Christmas in South Carolina. Mai-Wyss, Tatjana, illus. (Twelve Days of Christmas in America Ser.). (ENG.). (J). (—1). 2016. 22p. bds. 7.95 (978-1-4549-2058-8(0)) 2010. 40p. 12.95 (978-1-4027-6672-5(6)) Sterling Publishing Co., Inc.

Lucas, David. A Letter for Bear. 2013. (ENG., Illus.). 32p. (J). (gr. -1-2). 14.95 (978-1-909263-13-0(3)) Flying Eye Bks. GBR. Dist: Consortium Bk. Sales & Distribution.

Luthardt, Kevin. Larabee, 1 vol. Luthardt, Kevin, illus. 2009. (ENG., Illus.). 32p. (J). (gr. -1-1). pap. 7.95 (978-1-56145-482-2(6)) Peachtree Pubs.

Lyons, Mary E. Letters from a Slave Boy: The Story of Joseph Jacobs. 2009. (ENG.). 208p. (YA). (gr. 7). mass mkt. 7.99 (978-0-689-87868-8(0), Simon Pulse) Simon Pulse.

—Letters from a Slave Girl: The Story of Harriet Jacobs. 2008. (Illus.). 175p. (gr. 7-12). 16.00 (978-0-7569-8474-8(2)) Perfection Learning Corp.

—Letters from a Slave Girl: The Story of Harriet Jacobs. 2007. (ENG., Illus.). 192p. (YA). (gr. 7). mass mkt. 6.99 (978-1-4169-3637-4(8), Simon Pulse) Simon Pulse.

Mack, Jeff. Clueless Mcgee. Mack, Jeff, illus. 2012. (Clueless Mcgee Ser.: 1). (ENG., Illus.). 240p. (J). (gr. 3-7). 12.99 (978-0-399-25749-0(7), Philomel Bks.) Penguin Young Readers Group.

—Clueless McGee & the Inflatable Pants, Bk. 2. Mack, Jeff, illus. 2013. (Clueless Mcgee Ser.: 2). (ENG., Illus.). 256p. (J). (gr. 3-7). 12.99 (978-0-399-25750-6(0), Philomel Bks.) Penguin Young Readers Group.

Malcolm, Jahnna N. The Write Stuff. 2011. (Love Letters Ser.). (ENG.). 192p. (YA). (gr. 7). pap. 9.99 (978-1-4424-3100-3(8), Simon Pulse) Simon Pulse.

Mansbach, Adam & Zweibel, Alan. Benjamin Franklin: Huge Pain in My... 2015. (Benjamin Franklin Ser.). (ENG., Illus.). 208p. (J). (gr. 5-9). 12.99 (978-1-4847-1304-4(4)) Hyperion Bks. for Children.

Mansbach, Adam & Zwiebel, Alan. Benjamin Franklin: You've Got Mail. 2017. (Benjamin Franklin Ser.). (ENG.). 224p. (J). (gr. 5-9). 12.99 (978-1-4847-1305-1(2)) Hyperion Bks. for Children.

McDonald, Megan. Stink & the Incredible Super-Galactic Jawbreaker. Reynolds, Peter H., illus. 2013. (Stink Ser.: 2). (ENG.). (J). (gr. 1-4). 144p. pap. 4.99 (978-0-7636-6420-6(0));Bk. 2. 128p. 12.99 (978-0-7636-6389-6(1)) Candlewick Pr.

—Stink & the Incredible Super-Galactic Jawbreaker. Reynolds, Peter H., illus. 2010. (Stink Ser.: No. 2). 128p. (J). (gr. k-4). 24.21 (978-1-59961-684-1(X)) Spotlight.

—Stink & the Incredible Super-Galactic Jawbreaker. 2013. (Stink Ser.: 2). lib. bdg. 14.75 (978-0-606-31588-3(8), Turtleback) Turtleback Bks.

—Stink y el increíble Rompemuelas Supergaláctico. 2008. (SPA.). 207p. (J). (gr. 3-5). pap. 7.95 (978-1-60396-194-3(1)) Ediciones Alfaguara ESP. Dist: Two Rivers Distribution.

McElroy, Lisa Tucker. Love, Lizzie: Letters to a Military Mom. Paterson, Diane, illus. (ENG.). 32p. (J). (gr. 1-3). 2009. pap. 6.99 (978-0-8075-4778-6(6)) 2005. lib. bdg. 16.99 (978-0-8075-4777-9(8)) Whitman, Albert & Co.

Morris, Jennifer E. Please Write Back! Morris, Jennifer E., illus. 2010. (Scholastic Reader Level 1 Ser.). (ENG., Illus.). 32p. (J). (gr. -1-3). pap. 3.99 (978-0-545-11506-3(X), Cartwheel Bks.) Scholastic, Inc.

—Please Write Back! 2010. (Scholastic Reader Level 1 Ser.). lib. bdg. 13.55 (978-0-606-06822-2(8), Turtleback) Turtleback Bks.

Mullican, Judy. May We Go to the Zoo? Gray, Stacy A., illus. l.t. ed. 2004. (HRL Little Book Ser.). (J). (gr. -1-1). pap. 10.95 (978-1-57332-304-8(7)); pap. 10.95 (978-1-57332-303-1(9)) Carson-Dellosa Publishing, LLC. (HighReach Learning, Incorporated).

—Pretend. Meler, Kerry L., illus. l.t. ed. 2005. (HRL Board Book Ser.). 10p. (J). (gr. -1-1). pap. 10.95 (978-1-57332-283-6(0), HighReach Learning, Incorporated) Carson-Dellosa Publishing, LLC.

Nagus, Kari. Congratulations Q & U. 2010. 16p. 8.49 (978-1-4520-5153-6(4)) AuthorHouse.

Nobleman, Marc Tyler. Brave Like My Brother. 2016. (ENG.). 112p. (J). (gr. 2-5). 15.99 (978-0-545-88035-0(1), Scholastic Pr.) Scholastic, Inc.

Noël, Alyson. Forever Summer. 2011. (ENG.). 464p. (YA). (gr. 8-12). pap. 9.99 (978-0-312-60439-4(4), 9780312604394, St. Martin's Griffin) St. Martin's Pr.

Nolen, Jerdine & Keliher, Brian. Plantzilla. Catrow, David, illus. 2005. (ENG.). 32p. (J). (gr. -1-3). reprint ed. pap. 7.99 (978-0-15-205392-5(1)) Houghton Mifflin Harcourt Publishing Co.

O'Kelley, Jeff. Sharing Our Stories. 2006. (Early Explorers Ser.). (J). pap. (978-1-4108-6127-6(9)) Benchmark Education Co.

O'Neill, Karl. The Most Beautiful Letter in the World. Byrne, Emma, illus. 2007. (ENG.). 64p. (J). pap. 15.95 (978-1-84717-011-8(0)) O'Brien Pr., Ltd., The IRL. Dist: Dufour Editions, Inc.

Orloff, Karen Kaufman. I Wanna Go Home. Catrow, David, illus. 2014. (ENG.). 32p. (J). (gr. k-3). 16.99 (978-0-399-25407-9(2), G.P. Putnam's Sons Books for Young Readers) Penguin Young Readers Group.

—I Wanna Iguana. Catrow, David, illus. 2004. (ENG.). 32p. (J). (gr. -1-3). 16.99 (978-0-399-23717-1(8), G.P. Putnam's Sons Books for Young Readers) Penguin Young Readers Group.

Ouchley, Amy Griffin. Swamper: Letters from a Louisiana Swamp Rabbit. 2013. (ENG., Illus.). 72p. (gr. 4-7). 22.50 (978-0-8071-5074-0(6), 9780807150740) Louisiana State Univ. Pr.

Parham, Pam H. When I Take a Bath. Gillen, Lisa P., illus. l.t. ed. 2005. (HRL Board Book Ser.). 12p. (J). (gr. -1-1). pap. 10.95 (978-1-57332-284-3(9), HighReach Learning, Incorporated) Carson-Dellosa Publishing, LLC.

PeachMoon Publishing. The Lizard in the Mailbox. 2007. (J). pap. 9.95 (978-0-9795831-0-0(1)) PeachMoon Publishing.

Peaslee Levine, Martha. The Twelve Days of Christmas in Pennsylvania. Dougherty, Rachel, illus. 2014. (Twelve Days of Christmas in America Ser.). (ENG.). 40p. (J). (gr. k). 12.95 (978-1-4549-0889-0(0)) Sterling Publishing Co., Inc.

Pennypacker, Sara. Clementine's Letter. Frazee, Marla, illus. (Clementine Book Ser.). (ENG.). 160p. (J). (gr. 1-3). 2009. pap. 5.99 (978-0-7868-3885-1(X)) 2008. 16.99 (978-0-7868-3884-4(1)) Hyperion Pr.

Pichard, Alexandra. Pen Pals. Pichard, Alexandra, illus. 2017. (ENG., Illus.). 48p. (J). (gr. -1-2). 17.99 (978-1-4814-7247-0(X), Simon & Schuster/Paula Wiseman Bks.) Simon & Schuster/Paula Wiseman Bks.

Pingry, Patricia A. Dear Santa... Rasmussen, Wendy, illus. 2005. (ENG.). 24p. (J). (gr. -1-k). bds. 6.95 (978-0-8249-6618-8(X), Ideal Pubns.) Worthy Publishing.

Pitcher, Annabel. Ketchup Clouds. 2013. (ENG.). 272p. (YA). (gr. 7-17). 18.00 (978-0-316-24676-7(X)) Little Brown & Co.

—Yours Truly. 2014. (ENG., Illus.). 288p. (YA). (gr. 7-17). pap. 9.99 (978-0-316-24678-1(6)) Little, Brown Bks. for Young Readers.

PS, I Love You, Gramps: Individual Title, 6 packs. (Action Packs Ser.). 120p. (gr. 3-5). 44.00 (978-0-7635-8389-7(8)) Rigby Education.

Pung, Alice. Lucy & Linh. 2016. (ENG.). 352p. (YA). (gr. 7). 17.99 (978-0-399-55048-5(8), Knopf Bks. for Young Readers) Random Hse. Children's Bks.

Rader, Laura. The Twelve Days of Christmas in California. Rader, Laura, illus. 2009. (Twelve Days of Christmas in America Ser.). (ENG., Illus.). 40p. (J). (gr. k-3). 12.95 (978-1-4027-6247-5(X)) Sterling Publishing Co., Inc.

Radzinski, Kandy. What Cats Want for Christmas. Radzinski, Kandy, illus. rev. ed. 2007. (ENG., Illus.). 32p. (J). (gr. k-6). 16.95 (978-1-58536-340-7(5)) Sleeping Bear Pr.

Rakusin, Sudie. Dear Calla Roo... Love, Savannah Blue No. 2: A Letter about Getting Sick & Feeling Better. Rakusin, Sudie, illus. 2003. (Illus.). 32p. (J). (gr. -1-4). 16.95 (978-0-9664805-3-5(8)) Winged Willow Pr.

Ransom, Candice. The Twelve Days of Christmas in Washington, D. C. Hollander, Sarah, illus. 2010. (Twelve Days of Christmas in America Ser.). (ENG.). 40p. (J). (gr. k). 12.95 (978-1-4027-6394-6(8)) Sterling Publishing Co., Inc.

Rapp, Adam. Punkzilla. 2009. (ENG., Illus.). 256p. (YA). (gr. 9). 16.99 (978-0-7636-3031-7(4)) Candlewick Pr.

Remkiewicz, Frank, illus. The Twelve Days of Christmas in Florida. (Twelve Days of Christmas in America Ser.). (ENG.). (J). (—1). 2017. 22p. bds. 7.95 **(978-1-4549-2283-4(4))** 2008. 40p. 12.95 (978-1-4027-3817-3(X)) Sterling Publishing Co., Inc.

Rex, Adam. XO, OX: A Love Story. Campbell, Scott, illus. 2017. (ENG.). 40p. (J). 17.99 (978-1-62672-288-0(9), 9781626722880) Roaring Brook Pr.

Rissman, Angelica. Julius & the Lost Letter to Santa. 2003. (J). 7.99 (978-1-59384-019-8(5)) Parklane Publishing.

Rosenberg, Amye. A Surprise in the Mail! Salanitro, Robert, illus. 2009. (Discovery Ser.). (ENG.). 12p. (J). 7.99 (978-1-60436-018-9(6)) Educational Publishing LLC.

Ryan, Pam Muñoz. Tony Baloney: Pen Pal. Fotheringham, Ed, illus. 2014. 39p. (J). pap. (978-0-545-69227-4(X), Scholastic Pr.) Scholastic, Inc.

Sauer, Tammi. The Twelve Days of Christmas in Oklahoma. Hutto, Victoria, illus. 2012. (Twelve Days of Christmas in America Ser.). (ENG.). 40p. (J). (gr. k-3). 12.95 (978-1-4027-9224-3(7)) Sterling Publishing Co., Inc.

Scholastic, Inc. Staff. Dear Mrs. Larue. 2005. (ENG.). (J). pap. 550.00 (978-0-439-70787-9(0), Sidekicks TM) Scholastic, Inc.

Sedgwick, Chantele. Love, Lucas. 2015. (ENG.). 280p. (J). (gr. 6). 16.99 (978-1-63220-417-2(7), Sky Pony Pr.) Skyhorse Publishing Co., Inc.

Sís, Peter. Ice Cream Summer. 2015. (ENG., Illus.). 40p. (J). (gr. k-3). 17.99 (978-0-545-73161-4(5), Scholastic Pr.) Scholastic, Inc.

Smith, Yeardley. I, Lorelei. 2009. 352p. (J). (gr. 3-7). lib. bdg. 17.89 (978-0-06-149345-4(7), Geringer, Laura Book) HarperCollins Pubs.

Snicket, Lemony, pseud. The Beatrice Letters. Helquist, Brett, illus. 2006. (Series of Unfortunate Events Ser.). (ENG.). 72p. (J). (gr. 5-7). 22.99 (978-0-06-058658-4(3)) HarperCollins Pubs.

Spain, Susan Rosson. The Twelve Days of Christmas in Georgia. Dulemba, Elizabeth O., illus. 2010. (Twelve Days of Christmas in America Ser.). (ENG.). 40p. (J). (gr. k). 12.95 (978-1-4027-7008-1(1)) Sterling Publishing Co., Inc.

Spinelli, Jerry. Love, Stargirl. 2009. (ENG.). 288p. (YA). (gr. 7). pap. 9.99 (978-0-375-85644-0(7), Ember) Random Hse. Children's Bks.

Stanton, Melissa. My Pen Pal, Santa. Bell, Jennifer A., illus. 2013. (ENG.). 32p. (J). (gr. -1-2). 9.99 (978-0-375-86992-1(1), Random Hse. Bks. for Young Readers) Random Hse. Children's Bks.

Stead, Judy. The Twelve Days of Christmas in North Carolina. Stead, Judy, illus. 2009. (Twelve Days of Christmas in America Ser.). (ENG., Illus.). 40p. (J). (gr. k). 12.95 (978-1-4027-4467-9(6)) Sterling Publishing Co., Inc.

Stead, Judy, illus. The Twelve Days of Christmas in North Carolina. 2017. (Twelve Days of Christmas in America Ser.). (ENG.). 22p. (J). (—1). bds. 7.95 **(978-1-4549-2285-8(0))** Sterling Publishing Co., Inc.

Stein, David Ezra. Love, Mouserella. Stein, David Ezra, illus. 2011. (ENG., Illus.). 32p. (J). (gr. -1-k). 15.99 (978-0-399-25410-9(2), Nancy Paulsen Books) Penguin Young Readers Group.

Stewart, Jennifer J. The Twelve Days of Christmas in Arizona. Avril, Lynne, illus. 2010. (Twelve Days of Christmas in America Ser.). (ENG.). 40p. (J). (gr. k). 12.95 (978-1-4027-7036-4(7)) Sterling Publishing Co., Inc.

Stewart, Sarah. The Gardener. Small, David, illus. 2003. (J). (gr. -1-2). 28.95 incl. audio compact disk (978-1-59112-531-0(6)) Live Oak Media.

—The Gardener. Small, David, illus. 2007. (ENG.). 40p. (J). (gr. -1-2). per. 8.99 (978-0-312-36749-7(X), 9780312367497) Square Fish.

—The Quiet Place, 1 vol. Small, David, illus. 2012. (ENG.). 44p. (J). (gr. k-4). 17.99 (978-0-374-32565-7(0), 9780374325657, Farrar, Straus & Giroux (BYR)) Farrar, Straus & Giroux.

Stilton, Thea. Thea Stilton & the Lost Letters. 2015. (Thea Stilton Ser.: 21). (ENG., Illus.). 176p. (J). (gr. 2-5). pap. 8.99 (978-0-545-65602-3(8), Scholastic Paperbacks) Scholastic, Inc.

Strathie, Chae. Dear Dinosaur: With Real Letters to Read! O'Byrne, Nicola, illus. 2017. (ENG.). 28p. (J). (gr. -1-3). 11.99 **(978-0-7641-6898-7(3))** Barron's Educational Series, Inc.

Teague, Mark. Detective LaRue: Letters from the Investigation. Teague, Mark, illus. 2004. (LaRue Bks.). (ENG., Illus.). 32p. (J). (gr. -1-3). 17.99 (978-0-439-45868-9(4), Scholastic Pr.) Scholastic, Inc.

Tennant Iain Staff. Alby's Letters to Henry: Written from Isle of Mull. Smith, William, illus. 2007. (ENG.). 176p. (J). pap. 15.99 (978-1-903071-14-4(3)) Bene Factum Publishing, Ltd. GBR. Dist: Independent Pubs. Group.

Thomas, Leah. Because You'll Never Meet Me. 2015. (ENG.). 352p. (YA). (gr. 9-12). 17.99 (978-1-61963-590-6(9), 9781619635906, Bloomsbury USA Childrens) Bloomsbury Publishing USA.

—Nowhere near You. 2017. (ENG.). 400p. (YA). 17.99 (978-1-68119-178-2(4), 9781681191782, Bloomsbury USA Childrens) Bloomsbury Publishing USA.

Thoms, Susan Collins. The Twelve Days of Christmas in Michigan. Pilutti, Deb, illus. (Twelve Days of Christmas in

America Ser.). (ENG.). (J). (— 1). 2017. 22p. bds. 7.95 **(978-1-4549-2284-1(2))** 2010. 40p. 12.95 (978-1-4027-6351-9(4)) Sterling Publishing Co., Inc.

Tolkien, J. R. R. Letters from Father Christmas. Tolkien, Baillie, ed. 2004. (ENG., Illus.). 128p. pap. 23.99 (978-0-618-51265-2(9)) Houghton Mifflin Harcourt Publishing Co.

Vernon, Ursula. Nurk: The Strange, Surprising Adventures of a (Somewhat) Brave Shrew. 2008. (ENG., Illus.). 144p. (J). (gr. 3-7). 16.00 (978-0-15-206375-7(7)) Houghton Mifflin Harcourt Publishing Co.

Vonthron, Satanta C. Caillou's Dinosaur Day. Neveu, Fred, illus. l.t. ed. 2004. (HRL Board Book Ser.). (J). (gr. -1-1). pap. 10.95 (978-1-57332-288-1(1), HighReach Learning, Incorporated) Carson-Dellosa Publishing, LLC.

Wallace, Bill. Pick of the Litter. 2005. (ENG.). 160p. (J). (gr. 4-7). 16.95 (978-0-8234-1921-0(5)) Holiday Hse., Inc.

—Pick of the Litter. 2006. (ENG.). 176p. (J). (gr. 3-7). pap. 5.99 (978-1-4169-2511-8(2), Aladdin) Simon & Schuster Children's Publishing.

Warwick, Ellen. The Twelve Days of Christmas in Canada. Smith, Kimberly, illus. 2015. (Twelve Days of Christmas in America Ser.). (ENG.). 40p. (J). (gr. k). 12.95 (978-1-4549-1431-0(9)) Sterling Publishing Co., Inc.

Wells, Rosemary. Bunny Mail. Wells, Rosemary, illus. 2004. (Max & Ruby Ser.). (ENG., Illus.). 32p. (J). (gr. -1-k). 15.99 (978-0-670-03630-1(7), Viking Books for Young Readers) Penguin Young Readers Group.

Wells, Sheila Rae. Waiting for a Letter. 2004. 37p. (J). pap. 7.97 (978-1-4116-0908-2(5)) Lulu Pr., Inc.

Whitman, Sylvia. The Milk of Birds. (ENG., Illus.). 384p. (YA). (gr. 9). 2014. pap. 10.99 (978-1-4424-4683-0(8)) 2013. 16.99 (978-1-4424-4682-3(X), Atheneum Bks. for Young Readers) Simon & Schuster Children's Publishing.

Whybrow, Ian. Little Wolf, Terror of the Shivery Sea. Ross, Tony, illus. 2004. (Little Wolf Adventures Ser.). (ENG.). 144p. (J). (gr. 3-6). 14.95 (978-1-57505-629-6(1)) Lerner Publishing Group.

—Little Wolf's Diary of Daring Deeds. Ross, Tony, illus. (Middle Grade Fiction Ser.). 132p. (gr. 3-6). 2005. 14.95 (978-1-57505-411-7(6)) 2003. (J). pap. 6.95 (978-0-87614-536-4(5), Carolrhoda Bks.) Lerner Publishing Group.

—Lobito Aprende a Ser Malo. Azaola, Miguel, tr. from ENG. Ross, Tony, illus. 2007. (Ediciones Lerner Single Titles Ser.). (SPA.). 136p. (J). (gr. 3-6). per. 6.95 (978-0-8225-8644-9(4), Ediciones Lerner) Lerner Publishing Group.

Williams, Heather L. Caillou's Castle. Meier, Kerry L., illus. l.t. ed. 2005. (HRL Board Book Ser.). (J). (gr. -1-1). pap. 10.95 (978-1-57332-291-1(1), HighReach Learning, Incorporated) Carson-Dellosa Publishing, LLC.

Winthrop, Elizabeth. Franklin Delano Roosevelt: Letters from a Mill Town Girl. Winthrop, Elizabeth, illus. unabr. ed. 2003. (Illus.). (J). (gr. 4-7). 25.95 incl. audio (978-1-59112-213-5(9)) Live Oak Media.

Wittlinger, Ellen. Heart on My Sleeve. 2006. (ENG., Illus.). 240p. (YA). (gr. 7). reprint ed. pap. 10.99 (978-0-689-84999-2(0), Simon & Schuster Bks. For Young Readers) Simon & Schuster Bks. For Young Readers.

Wood, Francis Eusene. The Christmas Letter. Wood, Christine & Marken, Jon, eds. McDermott, Robert, illus. Wood, Christine, photos by. 2007. pap. 9.95 (978-0-9746372-6-6(2)) Tip-Of-The-Moon Publishing Co.

Woodson, Jacqueline. Peace, Locomotion. (ENG.). (J). 2010. 176p. (gr. 5-18). 8.99 (978-0-14-241512-2(X), Puffin Books) 2009. 144p. (gr. 4-7). 15.99 (978-0-399-24655-5(X), G.P. Putnam's Sons Books for Young Readers) Penguin Young Readers Group.

Woollatt, Margaret. The Twelve Days of Christmas in New Jersey. Rossi, Richard, illus. 2008. (Twelve Days of Christmas in America Ser.). (ENG.). 40p. (J). (gr. k). 12.95 (978-1-4027-3816-6(1)) Sterling Publishing Co., Inc.

Wrede, Patricia C. & Stevermer, Caroline. The Mislaid Magician or Ten Years After: Being the Private Correspondence Between Two Prominent Families Regarding a Scandal Touching the Highest Levels of Government & Thesecurity of the Realm. 2009. (ENG., Illus.). 336p. (J). (gr. 7). pap. 18.95 (978-0-15-206209-5(2)) Houghton Mifflin Harcourt Publishing Co.

Zweibel, Alan. Our Tree Named Steve. Catrow, David & David, Catrow, illus. 2007. (ENG.). 32p. (J). (gr. -1-k). pap. 5.99 (978-0-14-240743-1(7), Puffin Books) Penguin Young Readers Group.

—Our Tree Named Steve. 2007. 16.00 (978-1-4177-6974-2(2), Turtleback) Turtleback Bks.

LETTERS OF CREDIT

see Credit

LETTERS OF THE ALPHABET

see Alphabet

LEUKEMIA

Apel, Melanie Ann. Coping with Leukemia. 2009. (Coping Ser.). 192p. (gr. 7-12). 63.90 (978-1-61512-001-7(7)) Rosen Publishing Group, Inc., The.

Brent, Mary & Caitlin, Knutsson. Chemo to the Rescue: A Children's Book about Leukemia. 2008. 48p. pap. 17.49 (978-1-4343-9720-1(3)) AuthorHouse.

Chilman-Blair, Kim, et al. Medikidz Explain Leukaemia: What's up with Richard? 2009. (Illus.). 32p. (J). pap. (978-1-906935-05-4(X)) Medikidz Ltd.

Coerr, Eleanor. Sadako & the Thousand Paper Cranes. Himler, Ronald, illus. 2004. (Puffin Modern Classics Ser.). (ENG.). 80p. (J). (gr. 3-7). pap. 6.99 (978-0-14-240113-2(7), Puffin Books) Penguin Young Readers Group.

Goldsmith, Connie. Leukemia. 2011. (USA TODAY Health Reports: Diseases & Disorders Ser.). (ENG., Illus.). 128p. (gr. 6-12). lib. bdg. 34.60 (978-0-7613-6087-2(5)) Lerner Publishing Group.

Harmon, Daniel E. Leukemia. 2011. (Cancer & Modern Science Ser.). lib. bdg. 31.95 (978-1-4488-1311-7(5)) Rosen Publishing Group, Inc., The.

Klosterman, Lorrie. Leukemia. 2006. (Health Alert Ser.). (Illus.). 64p. (J). (gr. 3-7). lib. bdg. 32.79 (978-0-7614-1916-7(0), Benchmark Bks.) Marshall Cavendish Corp.

Lerner, Adrienne, ed. Leukemia. 2009. (Perspectives on Diseases & Disorders Ser.). (ENG., Illus.). 144p. (gr. 10-12). lib. bdg. 44.30 (978-0-7377-4247-3(X), LML02109-243159, Greenhaven Pr., Inc.) Cengage Gale.

Mack, Lorna B. Lorna's Whale. 2011. 56p. pap. 26.12 (978-1-4634-1610-2(5)) AuthorHouse.

Markle, Sandra. Leukemia. 2010. (Powerful Medicine Ser.). (ENG., Illus.). 48p. (gr. 5-8). lib. bdg. 27.93 (978-0-8225-8700-2(9)) Lerner Publishing Group.

Parks, Peggy J. Leukemia. 2010. (Compact Research Ser.). (YA). (gr. 7-12). 25.95 (978-1-60152-099-9(9)) ReferencePoint Pr., Inc.

LEUKEMIA—FICTION

Andrews, Jesse. Me & Earl & the Dying Girl. (ENG.). 304p. (YA). (gr. 9-17). 2012. 17.95 (978-1-4197-0176-4(2), Amulet Bks.) 2015. 17.95 (978-1-4197-2027-7(9)) 2015. 17.95 (978-1-4197-2013-0(9), Amulet Bks.) 2015. pap. 9.95 (978-1-4197-1960-8(2), Amulet Bks.) Abrams, Inc.

—Me & Earl & the Dying Girl. 2015. (CHI.). 320p. (YA). (gr. 9-17). pap. (978-986-344-282-0(8)) Rye Field Publishing, Co.

—Me & Earl & the Dying Girl. 2015. lib. bdg. 20.80 (978-0-606-37113-1(3)) Turtleback Bks.

Bryant, Cathy. The Doctor Said I Have Leukemi. Bunker, Thomas, illus. 2012. 24p. pap. 24.95 (978-1-4560-6929-2(2)) America Star Bks.

Devlin, Calla. Tell Me Something Real. 2016. (ENG., Illus.). 304p. (YA). (gr. 9). 17.99 (978-1-4814-6115-3(X), Atheneum Bks. for Young Readers) Simon & Schuster Children's Publishing.

Gilman, David. Monkey & Me. 2014. (ENG.). 240p. (J). (gr. 4-7). pap. 11.99 (978-1-84877-335-6(8)) Bonnier Publishing GBR. Dist: Independent Pubs. Group.

Gloster, Dean. Dessert First. 2016. (ENG.). 304p. (YA). 17.99 (978-1-4405-9454-0(6), Simon Pulse) Simon Pulse.

Johnston, Carol Shaw. Lily & Sophie: Sisters & Best Friends. 2010. 65p. pap. 26.99 (978-0-557-35894-6(9)) Lulu Pr., Inc.

Kantor, Melissa. Maybe One Day. 2014. (ENG.). 400p. (YA). (gr. 8). 17.99 (978-0-06-227920-0(3), HarperTeen) HarperCollins Pubs.

Murphy, Julie. Side Effects May Vary. (ENG.). (YA). (gr. 9). 2015. 352p. pap. 9.99 (978-0-06-224537-3(6)) 2014. 336p. 17.99 (978-0-06-224535-9(X)) HarperCollins Pubs.

Nicklas, Rita. The B-Liminator & I Fight Cancer. 2009. 40p. pap. 18.50 (978-0-557-04764-2(1)) Lulu Pr., Inc.

Novak, Ali. The Heartbreakers. 2015. (Heartbreak Chronicles Ser.: 1). (ENG.). 336p. (YA). (gr. 6-12). pap. 10.99 (978-1-4926-1256-8(1), 9781492612568) Sourcebooks, Inc.

O'Brien, Frances. Sheer Bliss: Confessions of a (Reluctant) Celebrity Spawn. 2006. (ENG.). 144p. (978-1-905886-32-6(2)) Troubador Publishing Ltd.

Rushford, Patricia H. Secrets of Ghost Island. 2007. (J). (978-88-02-46255-4(0)) Moody Pubs.

Sonnenblick, Jordan. Drums, Girls, & Dangerous Pie. 2005. (ENG.). 288p. (J). (gr. 7-12). 18.99 (978-0-439-75519-1(0), Scholastic Pr.) Scholastic, Inc.

Stimkorb, Patricia. All about Me! Regular Version. 2005. (Illus.). 12p. (J). bds. 12.99 (978-0-9758709-8-3(X), A.W.A. Gang) Journey Stone Creations, LLC.

Tucker, Seletha Marie Head. A Hat for Melinda: Fighting Leukemia Together. Lee, Anais, illus. 2013. (978-1-62086-164-6(X)) Mascot Bks., Inc.

Willner, Judy. How My Sun Got Its Smile: The Story of Deana Vega. 2010. 48p. pap. 20.99 (978-1-4520-7720-8(7)) AuthorHouse.

Wilson, Robert. Pippy: The Miracle of A Dream. 2011. 136p. 21.95 (978-1-4620-6634-6(8)); pap. 11.95 (978-1-4620-6633-9(X)) iUniverse, Inc.

LEVANT

see Middle East

LEWIS, C. S. (CLIVE STAPLES), 1898-1963

Bell, James Stuart, et al. Inside the Lion, the Witch & the Wardrobe: Myths, Mysteries, & Magic from the Chronicles of Narnia. 2005. (ENG., Illus.). 240p. (YA). (gr. 8-13). pap. 18.99 (978-0-312-34744-4(8), 9780312347444, St. Martin's Griffin) St. Martin's Pr.

Benge, Janet & Benge, Geoff. Christian Heroes - Then & Now - C. S. Lewis: Master Storyteller. 2007. (Christian Heroes Ser.). (ENG.). 192p. (YA). (gr. 3-7). pap. 9.99 (978-1-57658-385-2(6)) YWAM Publishing.

C. S. Lewis. 2nd rev. ed. 2010. (Who Wrote That? Ser.). (Illus.). 136p. (gr. 6-12). 35.00 (978-1-60413-725-5(8), Chelsea Hse.) Facts On File, Inc.

C. S. Lewis: Twentieth Century Pilgrim. 2011. (World Writers Ser.). 128p. (gr. 7-9). lib. bdg. 28.95 (978-1-59935-112-4(9)) Reynolds, Morgan Inc.

Coren, Michael. C. S. Lewis: The Man Who Created Narnia. 2006. (Illus.). 139p. per. 14.95 (978-1-58617-109-4(7)) Ignatius Pr.

Edwards, Anfrew & Edwards, Fleur. Footsteps of the past: C S Lewis: The story of one of the world's most famous authors who sold over a hundred million Books. 2007. (Footsteps of the Past Ser.). 32p. pap. 6.00 (978-1-84625-091-0(9)) DayOne Pubns. GBR. Dist: Send The Light Distribution LLC.

Gillespie, Natalie. Believing in Narnia: A Kid's Guide to Unlocking the Secret Symbols of Faith in C. S. Lewis' the Chronicles of Narnia, 1 vol. 2008. (ENG., Illus.). 192p. (gr. 2-6). pap. 12.99 (978-1-4003-1282-5(5)) Nelson, Thomas Inc.

Gormley, Beatrice. C. S. Lewis: The Man Behind Narnia. 2nd ed. 2005. (ENG., Illus.). 192p. (gr. 8-12). per. 14.00 (978-0-8028-5301-1(3), Eerdmans Bks For Young Readers) Eerdmans, William B. Publishing Co.

Lappi, Megan. C. S. Lewis. 2005. (My Favorite Writer Ser.). (Illus.). 32p. (J). (gr. 5-7). lib. bdg. 26.00 (978-1-59036-285-3(3)) Weigl Pubs., Inc.

Van Zee, Amy. How to Analyze the Works of C. S. Lewis, 1 vol. 2012. (Essential Critiques Set 3 Ser.). (ENG.). 112p. (J). (gr. 6-12). lib. bdg. 35.64 (978-1-61783-455-4(6), Essential Library) ABDO Publishing Co.

Wade, Mary Dodson. C. S. Lewis: The Chronicler of Narnia. 2005. (Authors Teens Love Ser.). (Illus.). 112p. (J). (gr. 7-12). lib. bdg. 27.94 (978-0-7660-2446-5(6)) Enslow Pubs., Inc.

Wheeler, Jill C. C. S. Lewis, 1 vol. 2009. (Children's Authors Set 5 Ser.). (ENG.). 24p. (YA). (gr. 2-5). 25.65 (978-1-60453-077-3(4)) ABDO Publishing Co.

LEWIS, JOHN LLEWELLYN, 1880-1969

Haskins, Jim, et al. John Lewis in the Lead: A Story of the Civil Rights Movement, 1 vol. 2006. (ENG., Illus.). 40p. (J). pap. 11.95 (978-1-60060-849-0(3)) Lee & Low Bks., Inc.

LEWIS, MERIWETHER, 1774-1809

Adler, David A. A Picture Book of Lewis & Clark. Himler, Ronald, illus. 2003. (ENG.). 32p. (J). (gr. k-3). tchr. ed. 17.95 (978-0-8234-1735-3(2)) Holiday Hse., Inc.

Bodden, Valerie. Through the American West. (Great Expeditions Ser.). (Illus.). 48p. (J). 2012. (ENG.). (gr. 4-7). pap. 12.00 (978-0-89812-663-1(0), Creative Paperbacks) 2011. 35.65 (978-1-60818-065-3(4), Creative Education) Creative Co., The.

Crompton, Samuel Willard. Lewis & Clark. 2009. (Great Explorers Ser.). (Illus.). 120p. (J). (gr. 6-12). 30.00 (978-1-60413-418-6(6), Chelsea Hse.) Facts On File, Inc.

Espinosa, Rod. Lewis & Clark, 1 vol. Espinosa, Rod, illus. 2007. (Bio-Graphics Ser.). (ENG., Illus.). 32p. (gr. 3-6). 28.50 (978-1-60270-069-7(9), Graphic Planet- Nonfiction) ABDO Publishing Co.

Fox, Suzanne G. Meriwether Lewis & William Clark: The Corp of Discovery & the Exploration of the American Frontier. 2009. (Library of American Lives & Times Ser.). 112p. (gr. 5-5). 69.20 (978-1-60853-493-7(6)) Rosen Publishing Group, Inc., The.

Fruge, William. Lewis & Clark: A Journey West. 2009. (Real Life Readers Ser.). 24p. (gr. 3-4). pap. 8.25 (978-1-4358-0040-3(0), Rosen Classroom) Rosen Publishing Group, Inc., The.

Ganeri, Anita. On Expedition with Lewis & Clark. 2010. (ENG.). 32p. (J). (gr. 3-5). (978-0-7787-9896-5(8)); (Crabtree Connections Ser.: No. 2). pap. (978-0-7787-9917-7(4)) Crabtree Publishing Co.

Gondosch, Linda. Where Did Sacagawea Join the Corps of Discovery? And Other Questions about the Lewis & Clark Expedition. 2011. (Six Questions of American History Ser.). (ENG.). 48p. (gr. 4-6). pap. 9.95 (978-0-7613-7131-1(1)); pap. 56.72 (978-0-7613-7644-6(5)); lib. bdg. 30.60 (978-0-7613-5226-6(0)) Lerner Publishing Group.

Hillstrom, Laurie Collier. The Lewis & Clark Expedition. 2015. (Defining Moments Ser.). (Illus.). 240p. (J). lib. bdg. 60.00 (978-0-7808-1417-2(7)) Omnigraphics, Inc.

Jeffrey, Gary. The Explorations of Lewis & Clark. Riley, Terry, illus. 2012. (Graphic History of the American West Ser.). (ENG.). 24p. (J). (gr. 3-8). pap. 8.15 (978-1-4339-6737-5(5), Gareth Stevens Learning Library); (gr. 4-7). lib. bdg. 23.95 (978-1-4339-6735-1(9)) Stevens, Gareth Publishing LLLP.

Keller, Susanna. The True Story of Lewis & Clark. 2013. (What Really Happened? Ser.). (ENG., Illus.). 24p. (J). (gr. 3-6). pap. 8.25 (978-1-4488-9846-6(3)); lib. bdg. 22.60 (978-1-4488-9694-3(0)) Rosen Publishing Group, Inc., The. (PowerKids Pr.).

Levy, Janey. Lewis & Clark in Their Own Words, Vol. 1. 2014. (Eyewitness to History Ser.). 32p. (J). (gr. 4-5). (ENG.). pap. 10.50 (978-1-4339-9930-7(7)); 26.60 (978-1-4339-9929-1(3)) Stevens, Gareth Publishing LLLP.

Lynette, Rachel. Meriwether Lewis & William Clark. 2013. (Pioneer Spirit: the Westward Expansion Ser.). 24p. (J). (gr. 3-6). 22.60 (978-1-4777-0783-8(2)); pap. 49.50 (978-1-4777-0900-9(2)); (ENG., Illus.). pap. 8.25 (978-1-4777-0899-6(5)) Rosen Publishing Group, Inc., The. (PowerKids Pr.).

Marsh, Carole. Meriwether Lewis & William Clark: Explorers of the Uncharted West: Explorers of the Uncharted West. 2003. 12p. (gr. k-4). 2.95 (978-0-635-02133-5(1)) Gallopade International.

Meloche, Renee Taft. Heroes of History for Young Readers - Meriwether Lewis: Journey Aross America. Pollard, Brian, illus. 2006. (Heroes of History Ser.). (ENG.). 32p. (gr. -1-3). 8.99 (978-1-932096-27-9(2)) Emerald Bks.

Molzahn, Arlene Bourgeois. Lewis & Clark: American Explorers. 2003. (Explorers! Ser.). (Illus.). 48p. (J). (gr. 1-4). lib. bdg. 25.27 (978-0-7660-2067-2(3)) Enslow Pubs., Inc.

Morley, Jacqueline. You Wouldn't Want to Explore with Lewis & Clark! An Epic Journey You'd Rather Not Make. Bergin, Mark, illus. 2013. (You Wouldn't Want to... Ser.). (ENG.). 32p. (J). 29.00 (978-0-531-25942-9(0)); pap. 9.95 (978-0-531-23039-8(2)) Scholastic Library Publishing. (Watts, Franklin).

—You Wouldn't Want to Explore with Lewis & Clark! An Epic Journey You'd Rather Not Make. 2013. (You Wouldn't Want To... Ser.). lib. bdg. 20.80 (978-0-606-31633-0(7), Turtleback) Turtleback Bks.

Mulhall, Jill K. Lewis & Clark. 2017. (Primary Source Readers Ser.). (Illus.). 32p. (J). (gr. 4-5). pap. 8.99 (978-1-4938-3886-8(5)) Teacher Created Materials, Inc.

Orr, Tamra. The Lewis & Clark Expedition: A Primary Source History of the Journey of the Corps of Discovery. (Primary Sources in American History Ser.). 64p. (gr. 5-8). 2009. 58.50 (978-1-60851-498-4(6)) 2004. (Illus.). lib. bdg. 31.95 (978-0-8239-4005-9(5), Rosen Reference) Rosen Publishing Group, Inc., The.

Perritano, John. The Lewis & Clark Expedition. 2010. (True Book Ser.). (ENG.). 48p. (J). (gr. 3-5). pap. 6.95 (978-0-531-21245-5(9), Children's Pr.); (Illus.). (gr. 2-5). 29.00 (978-0-531-20582-2(7)) Scholastic Library Publishing.

Petrie, Kristin. Lewis & Clark, 1 vol. 2007. (Explorers Set 2 Ser.). (ENG., Illus.). 32p. (gr. 4-7). 27.07 (978-1-59679-743-7(6), Checkerboard Library) ABDO Publishing Co.

Ransom, Candice. Lewis & Clark. 2003. (History Maker Bios Ser.). (Illus.). 48p. (J). (gr. 2-4). 26.60 (978-0-8225-0394-1(8), Lerner Pubns.) Lerner Publishing Group.

Robinson, Kate. Lewis & Clark: Exploring the American West. 2010. (Great Explorers of the World Ser.). (Illus.). 112p. (J). (gr. 7-12). 33.27 (978-1-59845-124-5(3)) Enslow Pubs., Inc.

Rodger, Ellen. Lewis & Clark: Opening the American West. 2005. (In the Footsteps of Explorers Ser.). (ENG., Illus.). 32p. (J). (gr. -1-9). pap. (978-0-7787-2446-9(8)); lib. bdg. (978-0-7787-2410-0(7)) Crabtree Publishing Co.

Sapp, Richard. Lewis & Clark on Their Journey to the Pacific. 2006. (In the Footsteps of American Heroes Ser.). (Illus.). 64p. (gr. 5-12). lib. bdg. 34.00 (978-0-8368-6429-8(8), Gareth Stevens Secondary Library) Stevens, Gareth Publishing LLLP.

Schanzer, Rosalyn. How We Crossed the West: The Adventures of Lewis & Clark. 2012. (ENG.). 48p. (J). (gr. 3-7). lib. bdg. 27.00 (978-1-4263-1328-8(4), National Geographic Children's Bks.) National Geographic Society.

Smalley, Carol Parenzan. Lewis & Clark. 2008. (What's So Great About...? Ser.). (Illus.). 32p. (YA). (gr. 2-4). lib. bdg. 25.70 (978-1-58415-725-0(9)) Mitchell Lane Pubs., Inc.

St. George, Judith. What Was the Lewis & Clark Expedition? Foley, Tim, illus. 2014. (What Was? Ser.). (ENG.). 112p. (J). (gr. 3-7). pap. 5.99 (978-0-448-47901-9(X), Penguin Workshop) Penguin Young Readers Group.

—What Was the Lewis & Clark Expedition? 2014. (What Was...? Ser.). lib. bdg. 16.00 (978-0-606-36185-9(5)) Turtleback Bks.

Stille, Darlene R. The Journals of Lewis & Clark, 1 vol. 2012. (Documenting U. S. History Ser.). (ENG.). 48p. (gr. 3-6). pap. 9.95 (978-1-4329-6763-5(0)); lib. bdg. 32.65 (978-1-4329-6754-3(1)) Heinemann-Raintree. (NA-h).

Stuckey, Rachel. Explore with Lewis & Clark. 2014. (ENG., Illus.). 32p. (J). (978-0-7787-1247-3(8)); pap. (978-0-7787-1259-6(1)) Crabtree Publishing Co.

Swanson, Jennifer. Lewis & Clark. 2016. (Spotlight on Explorers & Colonization Ser.). 00048p. (J). (gr. 6-6). pap. 11.75 (978-1-5081-7237-6(4)) Rosen Publishing Group, Inc., The.

LEWIS AND CLARK EXPEDITION (1804-1806)

Blashfield, Jean F. The Amazing Lewis & Clark Expedition. 2017. (Landmarks in U. S. History Ser.). (ENG.). 32p. (gr. 3-4). lib. bdg. 27.32 **(978-1-5157-7120-3(2)**, Fact Finders) Capstone Press of Coughlan Cos.

Blumberg, Rhoda. York's Adventures with Lewis & Clark: An African-American's Part in the Great Expedition. 2004. (ENG., Illus.). 96p. (J). (gr. 3-18). 17.99 (978-0-06-009111-8(8)) HarperCollins Pubs.

Bodden, Valerie. Through the American West. (Great Expeditions Ser.). (Illus.). 48p. (J). 2012. (ENG.). (gr. 4-7). pap. 12.00 (978-0-89812-663-1(0), Creative Paperbacks) 2011. 35.65 (978-1-60818-065-3(4), Creative Education) Creative Co., The.

Buffalohead, Julie, illus. Sacagawea. 2005. (Libros Ilustrados (Picture Bks.)). (SPA & ENG.). 40p. (J). (gr. 3-6). 16.95 (978-0-8225-3191-3(7), Ediciones Lerner) Lerner Publishing Group.

Buffalohead, Julie & Erdrich, Liselotte. Sacagawea. Buffalohead, Julie, illus. 2003. (ENG., Illus.). 40p. (J). (gr. 3-6). 17.95 (978-0-87614-646-0(9), Carolrhoda Bks.) Lerner Publishing Group.

Clifton, Chuck & Clifton, Joyce. A Daily Walk with Lewis & Clark - 1804. 2003. 308p. (J). spiral bd. 14.95 (978-0-9669760-3-8(7)) Maple Canyon Co.

—A Daily Walk with Lewis & Clark - 1805. 2003. 390p. (J). spiral bd. 14.95 (978-0-9669760-4-5(5)) Maple Canyon Co.

—A Daily Walk with Lewis & Clark - 1806. 2003. 292p. (J). spiral bd. 14.95 (978-0-9669760-5-2(3)) Maple Canyon Co.

Collard, Sneed B., III. Sacagawea: Brave Shoshone Girl. 2006. (American Heroes Ser.). (Illus.). 48p. (gr. 3-7). lib. bdg. 29.93 (978-0-7614-2166-5(1), Benchmark Bks.) Marshall Cavendish Corp.

Collins, Kathleen. On the Trail with Lewis & Clark: Learning to Use Line Graphs. 2004. (Math Big Bookstm Ser.). (ENG.). 16p. (gr. 2-3). 37.95 (978-0-8239-7639-3(4)) Rosen Publishing Group, Inc., The.

Conant, Susan Sens. Lewis & Clark's Journey of Discovery: A Guide for Young Explorers. Lynn, Rick, illus. 2004. 48p. (J). pap. (978-0-9725584-1-9(1)) Little Blue Pr.

Cosson, Jody. Sacagawea: Indian Guide, 1 vol. Soud, illus. 2008. (Beginner Biographies Ser.). (ENG.). 32p. (gr. -1-3). 28.50 (978-1-60270-252-3(7), Looking Glass Library-Nonfiction) Magic Wagon.

Crompton, Samuel Willard. Lewis & Clark. 2009. (Great Explorers Ser.). (Illus.). 120p. (J). (gr. 6-12). 30.00 (978-1-60413-418-6(6), Chelsea Hse.) Facts On File, Inc.

Crosby, Michael T. Sacagawea: Lewis & Clark's Pathfinder. 2007. 144p. (J). (gr. 6-18). 25.95 (978-1-59556-026-1(2)) OTTN Publishing.

Ditchfield, Christin. The Lewis & Clark Expedition. 2006. (True Bks.). (ENG., Illus.). 48p. (J). (gr. 3-7). pap. 6.95 (978-0-516-25222-3(4), Children's Pr.) Scholastic Library Publishing.

Domnauer, Teresa. Cornerstones of Freedom, Third Series: the Lewis & Clark Expedition. 2012. (ENG., Illus.). 64p. (J). lib. bdg. 30.00 (978-0-531-23059-6(7), Children's Pr.) Scholastic Library Publishing.

—The Lewis & Clark Expedition. 2012. (Cornerstones of Freedom, Third Ser.). (ENG., Illus.). 64p. (J). pap. 8.95 (978-0-531-28159-8(0)) Scholastic Library Publishing.

Dunn, Joeming W. Sacagawea, 1 vol. Espinosa, Rod, illus. 2008. (Bio-Graphics Ser.). (ENG.). 32p. 28.50 (978-1-60270-176-2(8), Graphic Planet- Nonfiction) ABDO Publishing Co.

Edwards, Judith. The Journey of Lewis & Clark in United States History. 2014. (In United States History Ser.). (Illus.). 96p. (J). (gr. 5-12). 27.94 (978-0-7660-6058-6(6)) Enslow Pubs., Inc.

Espinosa, Rod. Lewis & Clark, 1 vol. Espinosa, Rod, illus. 2007. (Bio-Graphics Ser.). (ENG., Illus.). 32p. (gr. 3-6). 28.50 (978-1-60270-069-7(9), Graphic Planet- Nonfiction) ABDO Publishing Co.

Feinstein, Stephen. Lee Sobre Sacagawea/Read about Sacagawea. 2006. (I Like Biographies! Bilingual Ser.). (ENG & SPA., Illus.). 24p. (J). (gr. 1-3). lib. bdg. 22.60 (978-0-7660-2674-2(4), Enslow Elementary) Enslow Pubs., Inc.

—Read about Sacagawea. 2004. (I Like Biographies! Ser.). (Illus.). 24p. (J). lib. bdg. 22.60 (978-0-7660-2297-3(8)) Enslow Pubs., Inc.

Fifer, Barbara. Going along with Lewis & Clark. 2004. (Illus.). 48p. (YA). (gr. 7-18). pap. 12.95 (978-1-56037-151-9(X)) Farcountry Pr.

Ford, Carin T. Sacagawea: Meet an American Legend. 2003. (Meeting Famous People Ser.). (Illus.). 32p. (J). lib. bdg. 22.60 (978-0-7660-2004-7(5)) Enslow Pubs., Inc.

Fox, Suzanne G. Meriwether Lewis & William Clark: The Corp of Discovery & the Exploration of the American Frontier. 2009. (Library of American Lives & Times Ser.). 112p. (gr. 5-5). 69.20 (978-1-60853-493-7(6)) Rosen Publishing Group, Inc., The.

Fradin, Judith Bloom & Fradin, Dennis Brindell. The Lewis & Clark Expedition. 2007. (Turning Points in U. S. History Ser.).

J

K

L

(Illus.). 48p. (gr. 3-7). lib. bdg. 31.36 *(978-0-7614-2044-6(4),* Benchmark Bks.) Marshall Cavendish Corp.

Franklin, Virgil. The Story of Sacagawea. 2009. (Reading Room Collection 2 Ser.). 24p. (gr. 3-4). 42.50 *(978-1-60851-997-2(X),* PowerKids Pr.) Rosen Publishing Group, Inc., The.

Frazier, Neta. Path to the Pacific: The Story of Sacagawea. 2017. (Great Leaders & Events Ser.). (ENG.). (J). (gr. 4-8). lib. bdg. 35.99 ***(978-1-942875-44-4(4))*** Quarto Publishing Group USA.

Frazier, Neta Lohnes. Path to the Pacific: The Story of Sacagawea. 2016. (Young Voyageur Ser.). (ENG., Illus.). 208p. (J). (gr. 4-9). pap. 12.99 *(978-0-7603-5227-4(5),* Voyageur Pr.) Quarto Publishing Group USA.

Fruge, William. Lewis & Clark: A Journey West. 2009. (Real Life Readers Ser.). 24p. (gr. 3-4). pap. 8.25 *(978-1-4358-0040-3(0),* Rosen Classroom) Rosen Publishing Group, Inc., The.

Ganeri, Anita. On Expedition with Lewis & Clark. 2010. (ENG.). 32p. (J). (gr. 3-5). *(978-0-7787-9896-5(8));* (Crabtree Connections Ser.: No. 2). pap. *(978-0-7787-9917-7(4))* Crabtree Publishing Co.

Gingrich, Callista. From Sea to Shining Sea. Arciero, Susan, illus. 2014. (Ellis the Elephant Ser.). (ENG.). 40p. (J). (gr. -1-3). 14.99 *(978-1-62157-253-4(6),* Regnery Kids) Regnery Publishing, Inc., An Eagle Publishing Co.

Gondosch, Linda. Where Did Sacagawea Join the Corps of Discovery? And Other Questions about the Lewis & Clark Expedition. 2011. (Six Questions of American History Ser.). (ENG.). 48p. (gr. 4-6). pap. 9.95 *(978-0-7613-7131-1(1));* pap. 56.72 *(978-0-7613-7644-6(5));* lib. bdg. 30.60 *(978-0-7613-5226-6(0))* Lerner Publishing Group.

Griffiths, Katie. Sacagawea. 2017. (J). ***(978-1-5026-2747-6(7))*** Cavendish Square Publishing.

Group/McGraw-Hill, Wright. Lewis & Clark: Mapping the West, 6 vols. (Book2WebTM Ser.). (gr. 4-8). 36.50 *(978-0-322-04460-9(X))* Wright Group/McGraw-Hill.

Gunderson, Jessica. Your Life As a Private on the Lewis & Clark Expedition, 1 vol. Madden, Colleen, illus. 2012. (Way It Was Ser.). (ENG.). 32p. (gr. 2-3). lib. bdg. 26.65 *(978-1-4048-7370-4(8))* Picture Window Bks.

Gunderson, Jessica Sarah. Sacagawea: Journey into the West, 1 vol. Martin, Cynthia & Schultz, Barbara, illus. 2006. (Graphic Biographies Ser.). (ENG.). 32p. (gr. 3-4). 30.65 *(978-0-7368-6499-2(7),* Graphic Library) Capstone Press of Coughlan Cos.

—Sacagawea: Journey into the West, 1 vol. Martin, Cynthia & Schulz, Barbara, illus. 2006. (Graphic Biographies Ser.). (ENG.). 32p. (gr. 3-4). per. 8.10 *(978-0-7368-9663-4(5),* Graphic Library) Capstone Press of Coughlan Cos.

—Your Life As a Private on the Lewis & Clark Expedition, 1 vol. Madden, Colleen, illus. 2012. (Way It Was Ser.). (ENG.). 32p. (gr. 2-3). pap. 8.95 *(978-1-4048-7746-7(0))* Picture Window Bks.

Haldy, Emma E. Sacagawea. Bane, Jeff, illus. 2016. (My Early Library: My Itty-Bitty Bio Ser.). (ENG.). 24p. (J). (gr. k-1). 28.50 *(978-1-63470-482-3(7),* 207659) Cherry Lake Publishing.

Hamen, Susan E. The Lewis & Clark Expedition, 1 vol. 2008. (Essential Events Set 2 Ser.). (ENG., Illus.). 112p. (J). (gr. 6-12). lib. bdg. 35.64 *(978-1-60453-048-3(0))* ABDO Publishing Co.

Hillstrom, Laurie Collier. The Lewis & Clark Expedition. 2015. (Defining Moments Ser.). (Illus.). 240p. (J). lib. bdg. 60.00 *(978-0-7808-1417-2(7))* Omnigraphics, Inc.

Isserman, Maurice. Across America: The Lewis & Clark Expedition, Revised Edition. 2nd rev. ed. 2009. (Discovery & Exploration Ser.). (Illus.). 128p. (gr. 5-8). 35.00 *(978-1-60413-192-5(6),* Chelsea Hse.) Facts On File, Inc.

Johmann, Carol A. The Lewis & Clark Expedition: Join the Corps of Discovery to Explore Uncharted Territory. 2008. (ENG., Illus.). 112p. (J). (gr. 4-6). pap. 14.25 *(978-1-885593-73-3(2),* Ideal Pubns.) Worthy Publishing.

Keller, Susanna. The True Story of Lewis & Clark. 2013. (What Really Happened? Ser.). (ENG., Illus.). 24p. (J). (gr. 3-6). pap. 8.25 *(978-1-4488-9846-6(3));* lib. bdg. 22.60 *(978-1-4488-9694-3(0))* Rosen Publishing Group, Inc., The. (PowerKids Pr.).

Kimmel, Elizabeth Cody. As Far as the Eye Can Reach: Lewis & Clark's Westward Quest. 2005. (Illus.). 119p. (YA). (gr. 4-8). reprint ed. 5.00 *(978-0-7567-9660-0(1))* DIANE Publishing Co.

King, Margaret. The Legacy & Legend of Sacagawea. 2017. (Primary Source Readers Ser.). (Illus.). 32p. (J). (gr. 4-5). pap. 8.99 *(978-1-4938-3793-9(1))* Teacher Created Materials, Inc.

Klepeis, Alicia. Lewis & Clark & Exploring the Louisiana Purchase. 2017. (J). ***(978-1-5026-2639-4(X))*** Cavendish Square Publishing.

Krull, Kathleen. Sacajawea. Collins, Matt, illus. 2015. (Women Who Broke the Rules Ser.). (ENG.). 48p. (J). (gr. 1-4). 16.99 *(978-0-8027-3799-1(4),* 9780802737991, Bloomsbury USA Childrens) Bloomsbury Publishing USA.

Labrecque, Ellen. What's Your Story, Sacagawea? 2015. (ENG., Illus.). 32p. (J). (gr. k-3). 26.65 *(978-1-4677-7966-1(0))* Lerner Publishing Group.

Levy, Janey. Lewis & Clark in Their Own Words, Vol. 1. 2014. (Eyewitness to History Ser.). (ENG.). 32p. (J). (gr. 4-5). pap. 10.50 *(978-1-4339-9930-7(7))* Stevens, Gareth Publishing LLLP.

Lewis & Clark Hands on Art And. 2004. (J). pap. 14.95 *(978-0-9715970-5-1(7))* Visual Manna.

Lynette, Rachel. Meriwether Lewis & William Clark. 2013. (Pioneer Spirit: the Westward Expansion Ser.). 24p. (J). (gr. 3-6). 22.60 *(978-1-4777-0783-8(2));* pap. 49.50 *(978-1-4777-0900-9(2));* (ENG., Illus.). pap. 8.25 *(978-1-4777-0899-6(5))* Rosen Publishing Group, Inc., The. (PowerKids Pr.).

Marsh, Carole. Lewis & Clark Go on a Hike. 2003. 32p. (J). (gr. 3-8). pap. 5.95 *(978-0-635-02122-9(6))* Gallopade International.

Maynard, Charles W. Fort Clatsop. 2009. (Famous Forts Throughout American History Ser.). 24p. (gr. 3-4). 42.50 *(978-1-61512-515-9(9),* PowerKids Pr.) Rosen Publishing Group, Inc., The.

McAneney, Caitie. The Life of Sacagawea. 2016. (Native American Biographies Ser.). (Illus.). 32p. (J). (gr. 5-4). 26.25 *(978-1-5081-4819-7(8),* PowerKids Pr.) Rosen Publishing Group, Inc., The.

Meinke, Amanda & Stegmann, Lisa. Lewis & Clark Famous Faces. Adams Marks, Elizabeth, illus. 2003. 2p. (J). pap. 2.99 *(978-1-56472-289-8(9))* Edupress, Inc.

Micklos, John, Jr. Discovering the West: The Expedition of Lewis & Clark, 1 vol. 2014. (Adventures on the American Frontier Ser.). (ENG.). 32p. (gr. 3-4). 27.32 *(978-1-4914-0185-9(0),* Fact Finders) Capstone Press of Coughlan Cos.

Molzahn, Arlene Bourgeois. Lewis & Clark: American Explorers. 2003. (Explorers! Ser.). (Illus.). 48p. (J). (gr. 1-4). lib. bdg. 25.27 *(978-0-7660-2067-2(3))* Enslow Pubs., Inc.

Moran, Margaret. Lewis & Clark: Set Of 6. 2011. (Navigators Ser.). (J). pap. 48.00 net. *(978-1-4108-0432-7(1))* Benchmark Education Co.

—Lewis & Clark & Lewis y Clark: 6 English, 6 Spanish Adaptations. 2011. (ENG & SPA.). (J). 97.00 net. *(978-1-4108-5712-5(3))* Benchmark Education Co.

Morley, Jacqueline. You Wouldn't Want to Explore with Lewis & Clark! An Epic Journey You'd Rather Not Make. Bergin, Mark, illus. 2013. (You Wouldn't Want to... Ser.). (ENG.). 32p. (J). 29.00 *(978-0-531-25942-9(0));* pap. 9.95 *(978-0-531-23039-8(2))* Scholastic Library Publishing. (Watts, Franklin).

Mulhall, Jill K. Lewis & Clark, 1 vol. 2005. (Primary Source Readers Ser.). (ENG.). 24p. (J). (gr. 4-4). pap. 8.99 *(978-0-7439-8906-0(6))* Shell Educational Publishing.

—Lewis & Clark. 2017. (Primary Source Readers Ser.). (Illus.). 32p. (J). (gr. 4-5). pap. 8.99 *(978-1-4938-3886-8(5))* Teacher Created Materials, Inc.

Nelson, Maria. The Life of Sacagawea. 2012. (Famous Lives Ser.). (ENG., Illus.). 24p. (J). (gr. k-3). lib. bdg. 22.60 *(978-1-4339-6357-5(4));* (gr. 1-4). pap. 8.15 *(978-1-4339-6359-9(0))* Stevens, Gareth Publishing LLLP.

On the Trail of Lewis & Clark Poster Map. 2004. (J). *(978-0-9759433-1-1(6))* Maps For Kids Inc.

On the Trail of Lewis & Clark Timeline/Fact Poster. 2004. (J). *(978-0-9759433-2-8(4))* Maps For Kids Inc.

Orr, Tamra. The Lewis & Clark Expedition: A Primary Source History of the Journey of the Corps of Discovery. (Primary Sources in American History Ser.). 64p. (gr. 5-8). 2009. 58.50 *(978-1-60851-498-4(6))* 2004. (Illus.). lib. bdg. 31.95 *(978-0-8239-4005-9(5),* Rosen Reference) Rosen Publishing Group, Inc., The.

Perritano, John. The Lewis & Clark Expedition. 2010. (True Book Ser.). (ENG., Illus.). 48p. (J). (gr. 2-5). 29.00 *(978-0-531-20582-2(7))* Scholastic Library Publishing.

Petrie, Kristin. Lewis & Clark, 1 vol. 2007. (Explorers Set 2 Ser.). (ENG., Illus.). 32p. (gr. 4-7). 27.07 *(978-1-59679-743-7(6),* Checkerboard Library) ABDO Publishing Co.

—Sacagawea, 1 vol. 2007. (Explorers Set 2 Ser.). (ENG., Illus.). 32p. (gr. 4-7). 27.07 *(978-1-59679-749-9(5),* Checkerboard Library) ABDO Publishing Co.

Pringle, Laurence. American Slave, American Hero: York of the Lewis & Clark Expedition. Van Wright, Cornelius & Hu, Ying-Hwa, illus. 2006. (ENG.). 40p. (J). (gr. 3-3). 19.95 *(978-1-59078-282-8(8))* Boyds Mills Pr.

—Dog of Discovery: A Newfoundland's Adventures with Lewis & Clark. 2004. (ENG., Illus.). 152p. (J). (gr. 3-7). pap. 10.95 *(978-1-59078-267-5(4))* Boyds Mills Pr.

Raabe, Emily. Thomas Jefferson & the Louisiana Purchase. 2009. (Westward Ho! Ser.). 24p. (gr. 2-3). 42.50 *(978-1-60854-763-0(9),* PowerKids Pr.) Rosen Publishing Group, Inc., The.

Ransom, Candice. Lewis & Clark. 2003. (History Maker Bios Ser.). (Illus.). 48p. (J). (gr. 2-4). 26.60 *(978-0-8225-0394-1(8),* Lerner Pubns.) Lerner Publishing Group.

Rausch, Monica. Sacagawea. 2007. (Grandes personajes (Spanish- Great Americans) Ser.). 24p. (gr. 1-4). (SPA.). pap. 8.15 *(978-0-8368-7991-9(0));* (Illus.). pap. 8.15 *(978-0-8368-7692-5(X));* (Illus.). lib. bdg. 22.00 *(978-0-8368-7685-7(7))* Stevens, Gareth Publishing LLLP. (Weekly Reader Leveled Readers).

Rausch, Monica L. Sacagawea. 2007. (Grandes personajes (Great Americans) Ser.). (SPA., Illus.). 24p. (gr. 1-4). lib. bdg. 22.00 *(978-0-8368-7984-1(8),* Weekly Reader Leveled Readers) Stevens, Gareth Publishing LLLP.

Redmond, Shirley Raye. Lewis & Clark: A Prairie Dog for the President. Manders, John, illus. 2003. (Step into Reading Ser.). 48p. 14.00 *(978-0-7569-1697-8(6))* Perfection Learning Corp.

—Lewis & Clark: A Prairie Dog for the President. Manders, John, illus. 2003. (Step into Reading Ser.: No. 3). (ENG.). 48p. (J). (gr. k-3). pap. 3.99 *(978-0-375-81120-3(6),* Random Hse. Bks. for Young Readers) Random Hse. Children's Bks.

Robinson, Kate. Lewis & Clark: Exploring the American West. 2010. (Great Explorers of the World Ser.). (Illus.). 112p. (J). (gr. 7-12). 33.27 *(978-1-59845-124-5(3))* Enslow Pubs., Inc.

Rodger, Ellen. Lewis & Clark: Opening the American West. 2005. (In the Footsteps of Explorers Ser.). (ENG., Illus.). 32p. (J). (gr. -1-9). pap. *(978-0-7787-2446-9(8));* lib. bdg. *(978-0-7787-2410-0(7))* Crabtree Publishing Co.

Ruffing, Faith Elizabeth. Lewis & Clark Bicentennial Corps of Discovery Journal & Record Book. 2003. (Illus.). 162p. spiral bd. 29.95 *(978-0-9763970-0-7(5))* Lewis & Clark Bicentennial Corps of Discovery Arch.

Sanford, William R. & Green, Carl R. Sacagawea: Courageous American Indian Guide. 2012. (Courageous Heroes of the American West Ser.). (Illus.). 48p. (J). (gr. 5-18). 22.60 *(978-0-7660-4006-9(2))* Enslow Pubs., Inc.

Sapp, Richard. Lewis & Clark on Their Journey to the Pacific. 2006. (In the Footsteps of American Heroes Ser.). (Illus.). 64p. (gr. 5-12). lib. bdg. 34.00 *(978-0-8368-6429-8(8),* Gareth Stevens Secondary Library) Stevens, Gareth Publishing LLLP.

Shea, Therese. The Louisiana Purchase & the Lewis & Clark Expedition. 2017. (J). pap. ***(978-1-68048-790-9(6),*** Britannica Educational Publishing) Rosen Publishing Group, Inc., The.

Sheely, Tiffany, illus. Captain William Clark's Great Montana Adventure. 2003. 32p. (J). mass mkt. 3.95 *(978-0-9711667-0-7(6))* Outlook Publishing, Inc.

Shepherd, Jodie. Sacagawea. 2015. (Rookie Biographies(tm) Ser.). (ENG., Illus.). 32p. (J). lib. bdg. 25.00 *(978-0-531-21414-5(1),* Children's Pr.) Scholastic Library Publishing.

Smalley, Carol Parenzan. Lewis & Clark. 2008. (What's So Great About... ? Ser.). (Illus.). 32p. (YA). (gr. 2-4). lib. bdg. 25.70 *(978-1-58415-725-0(9))* Mitchell Lane Pubs., Inc.

Smith, Jeff. William Clark: Explorer & Diplomat. 2016. (ENG., Illus.). 48p. (J). pap. 27.00 *(978-1-61248-178-4(7))* Truman State Univ. Pr.

St. George, Judith. Sacagawea. 2006. pap. 8.75 *(978-0-15-365175-5(X))* Harcourt Schl. Pubs.

—What Was the Lewis & Clark Expedition? Foley, Tim, illus. 2014. (What Was? Ser.). (ENG.). 112p. (J). (gr. 3-7). pap. 5.99 *(978-0-448-47901-9(X),* Penguin Workshop) Penguin Young Readers Group.

—What Was the Lewis & Clark Expedition? 2014. (What Was... ? Ser.). lib. bdg. 16.00 *(978-0-606-36185-9(5))* Turtleback Bks.

Stuckey, Rachel. Explore with Lewis & Clark. 2014. (ENG., Illus.). 32p. (J). *(978-0-7787-1247-3(8));* pap. *(978-0-7787-1259-6(1))* Crabtree Publishing Co.

Sullivan, Laura L. Life As an Explorer with Lewis & Clark. 2016. (Life As... Ser.). (ENG., Illus.). 32p. (J). (gr. 3-3). pap. 10.58 *(978-1-5026-1078-2(7))* Cavendish Square Publishing.

Sutcliffe, Jane. Sacagawea. 2009. (History Maker Biographies Ser.). (ENG.). 48p. (gr. 3-6). 27.93 *(978-0-7613-4222-9(2),* Lerner Pubns.) Lerner Publishing Group.

Swanson, Jennifer. Lewis & Clark. 2016. (Spotlight on Explorers & Colonization Ser.). 00048p. (J). (gr. 6-6). pap. 11.75 *(978-1-5081-7237-6(4))* Rosen Publishing Group, Inc., The.

Yomtov, Nel. Lewis & Clark Map the American West. 2015. (Extraordinary Explorers Ser.). (ENG., Illus.). 24p. (J). (gr. 3-7). lib. bdg. 29.95 *(978-1-62617-293-7(5),* Black Sheep) Bellwether Media.

LEWIS AND CLARK EXPEDITION (1804-1806)—FICTION

Bohner, Charles H. Bold Journey: West with Lewis & Clark. 2004. (ENG.). 192p. (J). (gr. 5-7). pap. 7.99 *(978-0-618-43718-4(5))* Houghton Mifflin Harcourt Publishing Co.

Bruchac, Joseph. Sacajawea. 2008. (ENG., Illus.). 208p. (YA). (gr. 7). pap. 7.99 *(978-0-15-206455-6(9))* Houghton Mifflin Harcourt Publishing Co.

—Sacajawea: The Story of Bird Woman & the Lewis & Clark Expedition. 2003. (Illus.). 199p. (J). (gr. 4-7). 12.65 *(978-0-7569-0732-7(2))* Perfection Learning Corp.

Eubank, Patricia Reeder. Seaman's Journal. 2010. 40p. (J). pap. 9.99 *(978-0-8249-5619-6(2),* Ideal Pubns.) Worthy Publishing.

Karwoski, Gail Langer. SeaMan: The Dog Who Explored the West with Lewis & Clark, 1 vol. Watling, James, illus. 2003. (Peachtree Junior Publication Ser.). (ENG.). 192p. (J). (gr. 3-7). 16.95 *(978-1-56145-276-7(9),* Q20194) Peachtree Pubs.

Munves, James. We Were There with Lewis & Clark. 2006. 128p. (J). pap. 13.95 *(978-0-9779000-0-8(2))* American Home-School Publishing, LLC.

Napoli, Donna Jo. The Crossing. Madsen, Jim, illus. 2011. (ENG.). 40p. (J). (gr. -1-3). 16.99 *(978-1-4169-9474-9(2),* Atheneum Bks. for Young Readers) Simon & Schuster Children's Publishing.

Oczkus, Lori. Close Reading with Paired Texts, Level 5. 2015. (Close Reading with Paired Texts). (ENG., Illus.). 128p. (gr. 5-5). pap. 19.99 *(978-1-4258-1361-1(5))* Shell Educational Publishing.

O'Dell, Scott. Streams to the River, River to the Sea. 2008. (ENG.). 208p. (J). (gr. 5-7). pap. 6.99 *(978-0-618-96642-4(0));* (Illus.). pap. 7.99 *(978-0-547-05316-5(9))* Houghton Mifflin Harcourt Publishing Co.

Olsen, Lauri. Pacific Bound: The Adventures of Lewis & Clark. Toonz Animation, ed. 2005. (Illus.). 44p. (J). 18.95 *(978-0-9742502-5-0(2))* Gossamer Bks., LLC.

—Pacific Bound: The Adventures of Lewis & Clark. 2004. (Illus.). 46p. (J). per. 15.95 *(978-0-9742502-4-3(4))* Gossamer Bks., LLC.

Rice, Dona Herwick & Bradley, Kathleen. Lewis & Clark, 1 vol. 2009. (Building Fluency Through Reader's Theater Ser.). (ENG., Illus.). 32p. (J). (gr. 3-5). pap. 7.99 *(978-1-4333-0540-5(2))* Teacher Created Materials, Inc.

Sargent, Dave & Sargent, Pat. Mack: (Medicine Hat Paint) Be a Leader, 30 vols., Vol. 39. Lenoir, Jane, illus. 2003. (Saddle up Ser.: Vol. 39). 42p. (J). pap. 10.95 *(978-1-56763-700-7(0))* Ozark Publishing.

Smith, Roland. The Captain's Dog: My Journey with the Lewis & Clark Tribe. 2008. (ENG., Illus.). 304p. (J). (gr. 5-7). pap. 7.99 *(978-0-15-202696-7(7))* Houghton Mifflin Harcourt Publishing Co.

Sneve, Virginia Driving Hawk. Bad River Boys. Farnsworth, Bill, illus. 2005. (ENG.). 32p. (YA). 16.95 *(978-0-8234-1856-5(1))* Holiday Hse., Inc.

Wolf, Allan. New Found Land: Lewis & Clark's Voyage of Discovery. 2007. (ENG., Illus.). 512p. (YA). (gr. 7-9). per. 14.99 *(978-0-7636-3288-5(0))* Candlewick Pr.

LEXINGTON, BATTLE OF, LEXINGTON, MASS., 1775

Brown, Don. Let It Begin Here! The Day the American Revolution Began April 19, 1775. Brown, Don, illus. 2010. (Actual Times Ser.: 1). (ENG., Illus.). 64p. (J). (gr. 1-5). pap. 9.99 *(978-1-59643-645-9(X),* 9781596436459) Roaring Brook Pr.

Crewe, Sabrina & Uschan, Michael V. Lexington & Concord. 2004. (Events That Shaped America Ser.). (Illus.). 32p. (gr. 3-6). lib. bdg. 26.00 *(978-0-8368-3398-0(8),* Gareth Stevens Learning Library) Stevens, Gareth Publishing LLLP.

—Lexington y Concord. 2006. (Hitos de la historia de Estados Unidos (Landmark Events in American History) Ser.). (SPA.). 48p. (gr. 5-12). pap. 11.70 *(978-0-8368-7474-7(9),* Gareth Stevens Learning Library) Stevens, Gareth Publishing LLLP.

Fradin, Dennis Brindell & Day, Larry. Let It Begin Here! Lexington & Concord - First Battles of the American Revolution. 2009. (ENG., Illus.). 40p. (J). (gr. 2-4). pap. 8.99 *(978-0-8027-9711-7(3),* 9780802797117, Bloomsbury USA Childrens) Bloomsbury Publishing USA.

Kallio, Jamie. 12 Questions about Paul Revere's Ride. 2016. (Examining Primary Sources Ser.). (ENG., Illus.). 32p. (J). pap. 9.95 *(978-1-63235-336-8(9),* 12-Story Library) Pr. Room Editions LLC.

—12 Questions about "Paul Revere's Ride" 2017. (Examining Primary Sources Ser.). (ENG., Illus.). 32p. (J). (gr. 3-6). 21.95 *(978-1-63235-286-6(9))* Pr. Room Editions LLC.

Mara, Wil. The Battles of Lexington & Concord: Start of the American Revolution. 2017. (Major Battles in US History (hardcover) Ser.). (ENG., Illus.). 32p. (J). (gr. 4-7). lib. bdg. 28.50 ***(978-1-63517-023-8(0),*** Focus Readers) North Star Editions.

Niz, Xavier & Niz, Xavier W. Paul Revere's Ride. Bascle, Brian, illus. 2005. (Graphic History Ser.). (ENG.). 32p. (gr. 3-4). 30.65 *(978-0-7368-4965-4(3),* Graphic Library) Capstone Press of Coughlan Cos.

Samuels, Charlie. The Battles of Lexington & Concord, Vol. 1. 2014. (Turning Points in US Military History Ser.). (ENG.). 48p. (J). (gr. 5-6). 31.95 *(978-1-4824-0417-3(6))* Stevens, Gareth Publishing LLLP.

Uschan, Michael V. Lexington & Concord. 2003. (Landmark Events in American History Ser.). (Illus.). 48p. (gr. 5-12). pap. 14.05 *(978-0-8368-5407-7(1),* Gareth Stevens Secondary Library) Stevens, Gareth Publishing LLLP.

Von Zumbusch, Amelie. The True Story of the Battle of Lexington & Concord. 2009. (What Really Happened? Ser.). (Illus.). 24p. (YA). (gr. 3-6). lib. bdg. 22.60 *(978-1-4042-4480-1(8))* Rosen Publishing Group, Inc., The.

von Zumbusch, Amelie. The True Story of the Battle of Lexington & Concord. 2009. (What Really Happened? Ser.). 24p. (gr. 2-3). 42.50 *(978-1-60854-767-8(1),* PowerKids Pr.) Rosen Publishing Group, Inc., The.

Waldman, Scott P. The Battle of Lexington & Concord. (Atlas of Famous Battles of the American Revolution Ser.). 24p. 2009. (gr. 3-3). 42.50 *(978-1-60853-328-2(X))* 2003. (Illus.). (J). lib. bdg. 22.60 *(978-0-8239-6328-7(4))* Rosen Publishing Group, Inc., The. (PowerKids Pr.).

Whitelaw, Nancy. The Shot Heard Round the World: The Battles of Lexington & Concord. 2004. (First Battles Ser.). (Illus.). 112p. (J). (gr. 6-12). 23.95 *(978-1-883846-75-6(7),* First Biographies) Reynolds, Morgan Inc.

Whitwell, Stephen. The Battles of Lexington & Concord: First Shots of the American Revolution. 2015. (Spotlight on American History Ser.). (ENG., Illus.). 24p. (J). (gr. 4-6). pap. 10.00 *(978-1-4994-1719-7(5),* PowerKids Pr.) Rosen Publishing Group, Inc., The.

LEYTE GULF, BATTLE OF, PHILIPPINES, 1944

Kevin, McDonald. Tin Can Sailors Save the Day. 2015. (J). pap. 10.95 *(978-1-55571-786-5(1),* Paloma Bks.) L & R Publishing, LLC.

LIBERIA

Baughan, Brian. Liberia. 2012. (J). pap. *(978-1-4222-2226-3(8))* Mason Crest.

—Liberia. Rotberg, Robert I., ed. (Evolution of Africa's Major Nations Ser.). (Illus.). 2012. 88p. (J). (gr. 7). 22.95 *(978-1-4222-2198-3(9))* 2009. 87p. (YA). (gr. 3-7). lib. bdg. 21.95 *(978-1-4222-0088-9(4))* Mason Crest.

Bjorklund, Ruth. Liberia. 2015. (ENG., Illus.). 144p. (J). lib. bdg. *(978-0-531-21695-8(0),* Orchard Bks.) Scholastic, Inc.

Doak, Robin S. Liberia, 1 vol. 2012. (Countries Around the World Ser.). (ENG.). 48p. (gr. 3-6). lib. bdg. 33.32 *(978-1-4329-6103-9(9),* NA-h) Heinemann-Raintree.

Hicks, Kyra E. Martha Ann's Quilt for Queen Victoria. Födi, Lee Edward, illus. 2012. 32p. (J). pap. 12.95 *(978-0-9824796-8-1(9))* Black Threads Pr.

Levy, Patricia & Spilling, Michael. Liberia: By Patricia Levy & Michael Spilling. 2nd rev. ed. 2008. (Cultures of the World Ser.). 144p. (gr. 6-18). lib. bdg. 42.79 *(978-0-7614-3414-6(3),* Benchmark Bks.) Marshall Cavendish Corp.

Ng, Yumi. Welcome to Liberia. 2004. (Welcome to My Country Ser.). (Illus.). 48p. (gr. 2-5). lib. bdg. 27.00 *(978-0-8368-2566-4(7))* Stevens, Gareth Publishing LLLP.

Rozario, Paul. Liberia. 2003. (Countries of the World Ser.). (Illus.). 96p. (gr. 5-12). lib. bdg. 31.00 *(978-0-8368-2366-0(4))* Stevens, Gareth Publishing LLLP.

Streissguth, Tom. Liberia in Pictures. 2006. (Visual Geography Series, Second Ser.). (ENG., Illus.). 80p. (gr. 5-12). lib. bdg. 31.93 *(978-0-8225-2465-6(1))* Lerner Publishing Group.

LIBERIA—FICTION

Allen, C. William. The African Interior Mission. Lee, Xiongpao, illus. 2006. 232p. (J). pap. 20.00 *(978-0-9653308-5-5(0))* Africana Homestead Legacy Pubs., Inc.

De Graaf, Anne. Son of a Gun. 2012. (ENG.). 125p. (YA). pap. 8.00 *(978-0-8028-5406-3(0),* Eerdmans Bks For Young Readers) Eerdmans, William B. Publishing Co.

Toh, Irene. Kumi the Bear. Hagan, Stacy, illus. 2008. (ENG.). 24p. pap. 12.75 *(978-1-4389-1368-1(0))* AuthorHouse.

Watkins, Samuel R. Ant-Bee Kingdom. 2011. 12p. (gr. -1). pap. 12.68 *(978-1-4269-5272-2(4))* Trafford Publishing.

—Precious Palm Tree. 2011. 32p. (gr. -1). pap. 17.25 *(978-1-4269-5267-8(8))* Trafford Publishing.

Wilson, Heather Gemmen. Lydia Barnes & the Blood Diamond Treasure. 2007. (Global Warning Ser.). 159p. (J). (gr. 3-7). per. 7.99 *(978-0-89827-350-2(1))* Wesleyan Publishing Hse.

LIBERTY

see also Anarchism; Assembly, Right of; Civil Rights; Equality; Freedom of Religion

Amnesty International Staff. Dreams of Freedom: In Words & Pictures. 2015. (ENG., Illus.). 48p. (J). (gr. 1-4). 18.99 *(978-1-84780-453-2(5),* Frances Lincoln) Quarto Publishing Group UK GBR. Dist: Hachette Bk. Group.

Aronson, Marc & Budhos, Marina Tamar. Sugar Changed the World: A Story of Magic, Spice, Slavery, Freedom, & Science. 2010. (ENG., Illus.). 176p. (YA). (gr. 7-18). 21.99 *(978-0-618-57492-6(1))* Houghton Mifflin Harcourt Publishing Co.

Beveridge, Amy. Let's Thank God for Freedom. 2006. 24p. (J). bds. 6.99 *(978-0-7847-1505-5(X),* 04384) Standard Publishing.

Bradley, Catherine. Freedom of Movement. 2005. (What Do We Mean by Human Rights? Ser.). (Illus.). 46p. (YA). (gr. 5-9). lib. bdg. 29.95 *(978-1-932889-64-2(7))* Sea-To-Sea Pubns.

Collins, Terry. Liberty, 1 vol. Bascle, Brian, illus. 2009. (Cartoon Nation Ser.). (ENG.). 32p. (gr. 3-4). lib. bdg. 30.65 *(978-1-4296-2340-7(3),* Graphic Library) Capstone Press of Coughlan Cos.

Golden, Nancy. The British Are Coming! The Midnight Ride of Paul Revere. 2009. (Great Moments in American History

Ser.). 32p. (gr. 3-3). 47.90 *(978-1-61513-136-5(1))* Rosen Publishing Group, Inc., The.

Hanson, Anders. Land of the Free: The Kids' Book of Freedom, 1 vol. 2014. (What We Stand For Ser.). (ENG.). 24p. (gr. 5-10). lib. bdg. 25.65 *(978-1-62403-295-0(8))*, Super SandCastle) ABDO Publishing Co.

Hess, Karl. Capitalism for Kids: Growing up to Be Your Own Boss. Williams, Jane A. & Daniels, Kathryn, eds. rev. ed. 2006. (ENG.). 196p. (YA). pap. 14.95 *(978-0-942617-35-1(5))* Bluestocking Pr.

King, Wilma. Children of the Emancipation. 2005. (Picture the American Past Ser.). (Illus.). 48p. (gr. 2-5). 22.60 *(978-1-57505-396-7(9))* Lerner Publishing Group.

Kukathas, Uma. Personal Liberty. 2009. (Issues on Trial Ser.). (ENG.). 240p. (gr. 10-12). 48.30 *(978-0-7377-4343-2(3)*, Greenhaven Pr., Inc.) Cengage Gale.

Lewison, Wendy Cheyette. L Is for Liberty. Hines, Laura Freeman, illus. 2003. (Reading Railroad Ser.). (ENG.). 24p. (J). (gr. -1-3). mass mkt. 3.99 *(978-0-448-43228-1(5)*, Grosset & Dunlap) Penguin Young Readers Group.

Lord, Jonathan. John Locke & the Second Treatise of Civil Government. 2016. (J). lib. bdg. *(978-1-68048-548-6(2))* Rosen Publishing Group, Inc., The.

Monk, Linda R. The Words We Live By: Your Annotated Guide to the Constitution. annot. rev. ed. 2004. (ENG., Illus.). 304p. (gr. -1-17). pap. 18.99 *(978-0-7868-8620-3(X))* Hyperion Pr.

Nelson, Kadir. Nelson Mandela. 2014. (SPA.). (J). (gr. 2-4). 21.99 *(978-84-261-4069-2(6))* Juventud, Editorial ESP. Dist: Lectorum Pubns., Inc.

Ogden, Charlie. Human Rights & Liberty. 2017. (Illus.). 32p. (J). ***(978-0-7787-3267-9(3))*** Crabtree Publishing Co.

Parker, Regina F. Let Freedom Ring. 2004. pap. 14.95 *(978-0-9754131-0-4(4))* Kids Donate, Inc.

Rees, Peter. Liberty: Blessing or Burden? 2007. (Shockwave: the Human Experience Ser.). (ENG., Illus.). 36p. (J). (gr. 3-5). 25.00 *(978-0-531-17760-0(2)*, Children's Pr.) Scholastic Library Publishing.

Rondeau, Amanda. Freedom. 2003. (United We Stand Ser.). (ENG., Illus.). 24p. (J). (gr. k-3). lib. bdg. 24.21 *(978-1-57765-878-8(7)*, SandCastle) ABDO Publishing Co.

Shamir, Ruby. What's the Big Deal about Freedom. Faulkner, Matt, illus. 2017. (What's the Big Deal About Ser.). (ENG.). 32p. (J). (gr. -1-3). 17.99 *(978-0-399-54728-7(2)*, Philomel Bks.) Penguin Young Readers Group.

Silate, Jennifer. Betsy Ross: Creadora de la bandera estadounidense (Betsy Ross: Creator of the American Flag) 2009. (Grandes personajes en la historia de los Estados Unidos (Famous People in American History) Ser.). (SPA.). 32p. (gr. 2-3). 47.90 *(978-1-61512-791-7(7)*, Editorial Buenas Letras) Rosen Publishing Group, Inc., The.

—Betsy Ross: Creator of the American Flag. 2009. (Primary Sources of Famous People in American History Ser.). 32p. (gr. 2-3). 47.90 *(978-1-60851-657-5(1))* Rosen Publishing Group, Inc., The.

—Betsy Ross: Creator of the American Flag / Creadora de la bandera Estadounidense. 2009. (Famous People in American History/Grandes personajes en la historia de los Estados Unidos Ser.). (ENG & SPA.). 32p. (gr. 2-3). 47.90 *(978-1-61512-539-5(6)*, Editorial Buenas Letras) Rosen Publishing Group, Inc., The.

To Be Free. 2003. (Illus.). pap. 5.60 *(978-0-7398-7507-0(8))* Steck-Vaughn.

Yoon, Nicola. Everything, Everything. 2017. (ENG.). 336p. (YA). (gr. 7). pap. 10.99 ***(978-1-5247-6960-4(6)***, Ember) Random Hse. Children's Bks.

York, Marion. Happy to Be Me. 2009. (ENG., Illus.). 26p. (J). pap. 15.95 *(978-0-9773738-9-5(4))* Bryson Taylor Publishing.

LIBERTY BELL

Ashley, Susan. The Liberty Bell. 2004. (Weekly Reader Early Learning Library). (Illus.). 24p. (YA). (gr. 1-4). lib. bdg. 22.00 *(978-0-8368-4141-1(7)*, Weekly Reader Leveled Readers) Stevens, Gareth Publishing LLLP.

Douglas, Lloyd G. The Liberty Bell. 2003. (Welcome Bks.). (Illus.). 24p. (J). 19.00 *(978-0-516-25852-2(4))*; (ENG., (gr. -1-2). pap. 4.95 *(978-0-516-27875-9(4))* Scholastic Library Publishing. (Children's Pr.).

Eldridge, Alison & Eldridge, Stephen. The Liberty Bell: An American Symbol. 2012. (All about American Symbols Ser.). 24p. (J). (gr. -1-1). (Illus.). pap. 7.95 *(978-1-4644-0048-3(2))*; 22.60 *(978-0-7660-4059-5(3))* Enslow Pubs., Inc. (Enslow Elementary).

Figley, Marty Rhodes. Salvar a la Campana de la Libertad. Lepp, Kevin, illus. 2005. (Yo Solo - Historia (on My Own - History) Ser.). (SPA.). 48p. (J). (gr. 3-7). lib. bdg. 25.26 *(978-0-8225-3094-7(5)*, Ediciones Lerner) Lerner Publishing Group.

—Salvar a la Campana de la Libertad; Saving the Liberty Bell. 2008. pap. 40.95 *(978-0-7613-3933-5(7))* Lerner Publishing Group.

—Saving the Liberty Bell. Lepp, Kevin, illus. 2005. (On My Own History Ser.). (ENG.). 48p. (gr. 2-4). pap. 6.95 *(978-1-57505-696-8(8))* Lerner Publishing Group.

—Saving the Liberty Bell. Lepp, Kevin, tr. Lepp, Kevin, illus. 2004. (On My Own History Ser.). (ENG.). 48p. (gr. 2-4). 25.26 *(978-1-57505-589-3(9))* Lerner Publishing Group.

Firestone, Mary. The Liberty Bell, 1 vol. Skeens, Matthew, illus. 2007. (American Symbols Ser.). (ENG.). 24p. (gr. 1-2). 9.95 *(978-1-4048-3467-5(2))* Picture Window Bks.

Firestone, Mary & Picture Window Books Staff. The Liberty Bell, 1 vol. Skeens, Matthew, illus. 2007. (American Symbols Ser.). (ENG.). 24p. (gr. 1-2). 26.65 *(978-1-4048-3101-8(0))* Picture Window Bks.

Francis, James. Visit the Liberty Bell. 2012. (Landmarks of Liberty Ser.). (ENG.). 24p. (J). (gr. 2-5). pap. 8.15 *(978-1-4339-6394-0(9)*, Gareth Stevens Learning Library); lib. bdg. 22.60 *(978-1-4339-6392-6(2))* Stevens, Gareth Publishing LLLP.

Gaspar, Joe. The Liberty Bell. 2013. (PowerKids Readers: American Symbols Ser.). 24p. (J). (gr. k-2). 22.60 *(978-1-4777-0739-5(5))*; pap. 49.50 *(978-1-4777-0820-0(0))*; (ENG., Illus.). pap. 8.25 *(978-1-4777-0819-4(7))* Rosen Publishing Group, Inc., The. (PowerKids Pr.).

—The Liberty Bell / la Campana de la Libertad. Alamn, Eduardo, ed. 2013. (PowerKids Readers: American Symbols / Smbolos de Amrica Ser.). (ENG & SPA.). 24p. (J). (gr. k-2). 22.60 *(978-1-4777-1207-8(0)*, PowerKids Pr.) Rosen Publishing Group, Inc., The.

Healy, Nick. The Liberty Bell. 2003. (J). pap. *(978-1-58417-119-5(7))*; lib. bdg. *(978-1-58417-057-0(3))* Lake Street Pubs.

Hess, Deborah. The Liberty Bell. 2007. (J). pap. 6.99 *(978-0-7614-3391-0(0))* Marshall Cavendish Corp.

Hicks, Terry Allan. Symbols of America Group 2, 6 bks., Set. Incl. Bald Eagle. (J). lib. bdg. 28.50 *(978-0-7614-2133-7(5))*; Capitol. lib. bdg. 20.95 *(978-0-7614-2132-0(7))*; Declaration of Independence. lib. bdg. 20.95 *(978-0-7614-2135-1(1))*; Ellis Island. lib. bdg. 20.95 *(978-0-7614-2134-4(3))*; Pledge of Allegiance. lib. bdg. 20.95 *(978-0-7614-2136-8(X))*; Uncle Sam. lib. bdg. 20.95 *(978-0-7614-2137-5(8))*; (Illus.). 40p. (gr. 3-7). 2006. 2007. Set lib. bdg. 171.00 *(978-0-7614-2130-6(0)*, Benchmark Bks.) Marshall Cavendish Corp.

Hopper, Whitney. I Visit the Liberty Bell. 2016. (Symbols of Our Country Ser.). 00024p. (J). (gr. 1-1). pap. 8.25 *(978-1-4994-2732-5(8)*, PowerKids Pr.) Rosen Publishing Group, Inc., The.

James, Lincoln. Making History: The Liberty Bell. 2006. (Tony Stead Nonfiction Independent Reading Collection). (ENG.). 24p. (gr. 3-6). pap. 8.85 *(978-1-4042-5587-6(7))* Rosen Publishing Group, Inc., The.

Jango-Cohen, Judith. La Campana de la Libertad. 2005. (Libros para Avanzar (Pull Ahead Bks.)). (SPA., Illus.). 32p. (J). (gr. k-3). per. 5.95 *(978-0-8225-3141-8(0)*, Ediciones Lerner) Lerner Publishing Group.

—The Liberty Bell. 2003. (Pull Ahead Books-American Symbols Ser.). (ENG.). 32p. (gr. k-3). pap. 7.95 *(978-0-8225-3754-0(0))*; (Illus.). lib. bdg. 22.60 *(978-0-8225-3803-5(2))* Lerner Publishing Group.

Kopp, Megan. La Campana de la Libertad. 2014. (SPA., Illus.). 24p. (J). *(978-1-62127-619-7(8))* Weigl Pubs., Inc.

—Liberty Bell with Code. 2012. (AV2 American Icons Ser.). (ENG., Illus.). 24p. (J). pap. 12.95 *(978-1-61913-301-3(6))*; lib. bdg. 27.13 *(978-1-61913-078-4(5))* Weigl Pubs., Inc. (AV2 by Weigl).

Magaziner, Henry Jonas. Our Liberty Bell. O'Brien, John A., illus. 2007. (ENG.). 32p. (J). (gr. 1-5). 15.95 *(978-0-8234-1892-3(8))* Holiday Hse., Inc.

—Our Liberty Bell. O'brien, John, illus. 2007. (ENG.). 32p. (J). (gr. 1-5). 5.95 *(978-0-8234-2081-0(7))* Holiday Hse., Inc.

McDonald, Megan. Saving the Liberty Bell. Carrington, Marsha Gray, illus. 2005. (ENG.). 32p. (J). (gr. k-3). 17.99 *(978-0-689-85167-4(7)*, Atheneum/Richard Jackson Bks.) Simon & Schuster Children's Publishing.

Meredith, Susan Markowitz. The Liberty Bell. 2016. (Spring Forward Ser.). (J). (gr. 1). *(978-1-4900-2233-8(3))* Benchmark Education Co.

Murray, Julie. Liberty Bell, 1 vol. 2005. (Buddy Book Ser.). (ENG., Illus.). 24p. (gr. k-4). 25.65 *(978-1-59197-507-6(7)*, Buddy Bks.) ABDO Publishing Co.

Nelson, Maria. The Liberty Bell. 2015. (Symbols of America Ser.). (ENG.). 24p. (J). (gr. 1-2). 22.60 *(978-1-4824-1870-5(3))* Stevens, Gareth Publishing LLLP.

Orr, Tamra B. The Liberty Bell: Introducing Primary Sources. 2016. (Introducing Primary Sources Ser.). (ENG., Illus.). 32p. (gr. 1-2). lib. bdg. 27.99 *(978-1-4914-8224-7(9))* Capstone Press of Coughlan Cos.

Reed, Cristie. Liberty Bell. 2014. (ENG.). 32p. (gr. 3-6). 32.79 *(978-1-62717-738-2(8))* Rourke Educational Media.

Rustad, Martha. Can We Ring the Liberty Bell? Poling, Kyle, illus. 2014. (Cloverleaf Books — Our American Symbols Ser.). 24p. (gr. k-2). (J). lib. bdg. 23.93 *(978-1-4677-2137-0(9))*; pap. 6.95 *(978-1-4677-4467-6(0))* Lerner Publishing Group. (Millbrook Pr.).

Shea, Therese. Zoom in on the Liberty Bell. 2016. (Zoom in on American Symbols Ser.). 24p. (J). pap. 9.35 *(978-0-7660-8454-4(X))* Enslow Pubs., Inc.

Silate, Jennifer. The Liberty Bell. (Primary Sources of American Symbols Ser.). 24p. 2009. (gr. 3-3). 42.50 *(978-1-60851-509-7(5)*, PowerKids Pr.) 2006. (Illus.). (J). (gr. -1-3). lib. bdg. 22.60 *(978-1-4042-2687-6(7))* Rosen Publishing Group, Inc., The.

LIBERTY OF SPEECH

see Freedom of Speech

LIBRARIANS

Alarcon, Roben. Librarians Then & Now, 1 vol. 2006. (Primary Source Readers Ser.). (ENG.). 32p. (J). (gr. 1-1). pap. 8.99 *(978-0-7439-9376-0(4))* Shell Educational Publishing.

Ames, Michelle. Librarians in Our Community. 2009. (On the Job Ser.). (Illus.). 24p. (J). (ENG.). pap. 8.25 *(978-1-4358-2458-4(X)*, 1300571); lib. bdg. 22.60 *(978-1-4042-8072-4(3)*, 1300571) Rosen Publishing Group, Inc., The. (PowerKids Pr.).

Austen, Mary. Librarians on the Job. 2017. (Jobs in Our Community Ser.). 24p. (J). (gr. 1-1). pap. 8.25 ***(978-1-5345-2145-2(3)***, KidHaven Publishing) Greenhaven Publishing LLC.

—Que Hacen Los Bibliotecarios? / What Do Librarians Do? 2015. (Ayudantes de la Comunidad / Helping the Community Ser.). (ENG & SPA.). 24p. (J). (gr. 1-1). 23.60 *(978-1-4994-0647-4(9)*, PowerKids Pr.) Rosen Publishing Group, Inc., The.

—What Do Librarians Do? 2015. (Helping the Community Ser.). (ENG., Illus.). 24p. (J). (gr. 1-1). pap. 8.25 *(978-1-4994-0640-5(1)*, PowerKids Pr.) Rosen Publishing Group, Inc., The.

Bellisario, Gina. Let's Meet a Librarian. Myer, Ed, illus. 2013. (Cloverleaf Books — Community Helpers Ser.). (ENG.). 24p. (gr. k-2). pap. 6.95 *(978-1-4677-0803-6(8))*; lib. bdg. 23.93 *(978-0-7613-9027-5(8))* Lerner Publishing Group. (Millbrook Pr.).

Carr, Aaron. The Library. 24p. 2014. (Illus.). (J). *(978-1-62127-346-2(6))* 2013. pap. 12.95 *(978-1-62127-351-6(2))* Weigl Pubs., Inc.

Crabtree, Marc. Meet My Neighbor, the Librarian. 2012. (ENG., Illus.). 24p. (J). *(978-0-7787-4559-4(7))*; pap. *(978-0-7787-4564-8(3))* Crabtree Publishing Co.

Davenport, Jefferson. Let's Help the Librarian! 2013. (InfoMax Math Readers Ser.). (ENG.). 24p. (J). (gr. 1-2). pap. 8.25 *(978-1-4777-2121-6(5)*, Rosen Classroom) Rosen Publishing Group, Inc., The.

—Let's Help the Librarian! Subtract Within 20. 2013. (InfoMax Math Readers Ser.). (ENG.). 24p. (J). (gr. 1-2). pap. 49.50 *(978-1-4777-2122-3(3)*, Rosen Classroom) Rosen Publishing Group, Inc., The.

Garrett, Winston. What Does a Library Media Specialist Do? 2014. (Jobs in My School Ser.). 24p. (J). (gr. k-2). lib. bdg. 23.60 *(978-1-4777-6546-3(8)*, PowerKids Pr.) Rosen Publishing Group, Inc., The.

—What Does a Library Media Specialist Do? / ¿Qué Hace el Especialista de Medios de la Biblioteca Escolar? de la Vega, Eida, ed. 2014. (Oficios en Mi Escuela / Jobs in My School Ser.). (SPA & ENG.). 24p. (J). (gr. k-2). lib. bdg. 23.60 *(978-1-4777-6796-2(7)*, PowerKids Pr.) Rosen Publishing Group, Inc., The.

Jango-Cohen, Judith. Librarians. 2005. (Pull Ahead Books: Community Helpers Ser.). 32p. (gr. k-3). (ENG.). pap. 7.95 *(978-0-8225-2533-2(X))*; (Illus.). (J). lib. bdg. 22.60 *(978-0-8225-1691-0(8))* Lerner Publishing Group.

Jeffries, Joyce. Meet the Librarian. 2013. (People Around Town Ser.). 24p. (J). (gr. k-2). pap. 48.90 *(978-1-4339-9374-9(0))*; pap. 8.15 *(978-1-4339-9373-2(2))*; (ENG., Illus.). lib. bdg. 22.60 *(978-1-4339-9372-5(4))* Stevens, Gareth Publishing LLLP.

—Meet the Librarian / Conoce a Los Bibliotecarios. 2013. (People Around Town / Gente de Mi Ciudad Ser.). (SPA.). 24p. (J). (gr. k-2). 22.60 *(978-1-4339-9468-5(2))* Stevens, Gareth Publishing LLLP.

Kawa, Katie. My First Trip to the Library: Mi Primera Visita a la Biblioteca. Livingston, Jessica, illus. 2012. (My First Adventures / Mis primeras aventuras Ser.). (ENG & SPA.). 24p. (J). (gr. k-2). lib. bdg. 22.60 *(978-1-4339-6631-6(X))* Stevens, Gareth Publishing LLLP.

Kenney, Karen Latchana. Librarians at Work, 1 vol. Dumm, Brian Caleb, illus. 2009. (Meet Your Community Workers Ser.). (ENG.). 32p. (J). (gr. -1-2). 28.50 *(978-1-60270-649-1(2))* Magic Wagon.

Laks Gorman, Jacqueline. Librarians. Andersen, Gregg, photos by. 2010. (People in My Community Ser.). (Illus.). 24p. (gr. k-3). pap. 8.15 *(978-1-4339-3342-4(X))* Stevens, Gareth Publishing LLLP.

—Librarians / Bibliotecarios. Andersen, Gregg, photos by. 2010. (People in My Community / Mi comunidad Ser.). (SPA., Illus.). 24p. (gr. k-3). pap. 8.15 *(978-1-4339-3760-6(3))* Stevens, Gareth Publishing LLLP.

Leone, Laura. Choosing a Career in Information Science. 2009. (World of Work Ser.). 64p. (gr. 5-5). 58.50 *(978-1-60854-332-8(3))* Rosen Publishing Group, Inc., The.

Library & Information Science. 2009. (Career Opportunities Ser.). 392p. (C). (gr. 9-18). pap. 18.95 *(978-0-8160-7547-8(6)*, Ferguson Publishing Co.) Facts On File, Inc.

Liebman, Dan. I Want to Be a Librarian. 2003. (I Want to Be Ser.). (ENG., Illus.). 24p. (J). (gr. -1-2). pap. 3.99 *(978-1-55297-689-0(0)*, 9781552976890) Firefly Bks., Ltd.

Liebman, Daniel & Liebman, Dan. I Want to Be a Librarian. 2003. (I Want to Be Ser.). (ENG., Illus.). 24p. (J). (gr. -1-2). 14.95 *(978-1-55297-691-3(2)*, 9781552976913) Firefly Bks., Ltd.

—Quiero Ser Bibliotecario. 2003. (Quiero Ser.). (SPA., Illus.). 24p. (J). (gr. -1-2). pap. 5.99 *(978-1-55297-726-2(9)*, 9781552977262) Firefly Bks., Ltd.

Marsico, Katie. Working at the Airport. 2009. (21st Century Junior Library: Careers Ser.). (ENG.). 24p. (gr. 2-5). lib. bdg. 25.64 *(978-1-60279-510-5(X)*, 200279) Cherry Lake Publishing.

—Working at the Library. 2009. (21st Century Junior Library: Careers Ser.). (ENG.). 24p. (gr. 2-5). lib. bdg. 25.64 *(978-1-60279-511-2(8)*, 200278) Cherry Lake Publishing.

Meachen Rau, Dana. Librarian. 2007. (J). *(978-0-7614-2621-9(3))* Marshall Cavendish.

—Librarians. 2007. (Tools We Use Ser.). (Illus.). 32p. (gr. k-2). lib. bdg. 15.95 *(978-0-7614-2662-2(0)*, Benchmark Bks.) Marshall Cavendish Corp.

—Librarians/Los Bibliotecarios. 2007. (Tools We Use/Instrumentos de Trabajo Ser.). (SPA., Illus.). 32p. (gr. k-2). lib. bdg. 15.95 *(978-0-7614-2826-8(7)*, Benchmark Bks.) Marshall Cavendish Corp.

—Los Bibliotecarios. 2007. (Instrumentos de Trabajo Ser.). (SPA., Illus.). 32p. (gr. k-2). lib. bdg. 15.95 *(978-0-7614-2802-2(X)*, Benchmark Bks.) Marshall Cavendish Corp.

Meister, Cari. Librarians. 2014. (ENG., Illus.). 24p. (J). lib. bdg. 25.65 *(978-1-62031-076-2(7))* Jump! Inc.

Monroe, Judy. A Day in the Life of a Librarian, 1 vol. 2004. (Community Helpers at Work Ser.). (ENG., Illus.). 24p. (gr. 1-2). 25.32 *(978-0-7368-2630-3(0)*, First Facts) Capstone Press of Coughlan Cos.

Murray, Julie. Bibliotecarios. 2016. (Trabajos en Mi Comunidad Ser.). (SPA.). 24p. (J). (gr. k-5). pap. 7.95 *(978-1-4966-0721-8(X))* Capstone Classroom.

—Librarians, 1 vol. (My Community: Jobs Ser.). (ENG.). (J). 2015. 24p. (gr. -1-1). 27.07 *(978-1-62970-914-7(X))* 2010. 32p. (gr. 2-5). 27.07 *(978-1-61613-506-5(9))* ABDO Publishing Co.

O'Brian, Virginia. A Librarian's Job. 2014. (Community Workers Ser.). 24p. (J). (gr. k-2). 24.21 *(978-1-62712-357-0(1))* Cavendish Square Publishing.

Oliver-Miles, Zelda. Amelia Gayle Gorgas: First Woman of Position. 2005. (Alabama Roots Biography Ser.). (Illus.). 100p. (J). pap. *(978-1-59421-017-4(9))* Seacoast Publishing, Inc.

Piehl, Janet. Explore the Library. 2013. (Library Smarts Ser.). (ENG., Illus.). 24p. (gr. -1-2). lib. bdg. 23.93 *(978-1-4677-1500-3(X)*, Lerner Pubns.) Lerner Publishing Group.

Rau, Dana Meachen. Librarians. 2007. (J). pap. 6.99 *(978-0-7614-3293-7(0))* Marshall Cavendish Corp.

Ready, Dee. Librarians Help, 1 vol. 2013. (Our Community Helpers Ser.). (ENG.). 24p. (gr. k-1). pap. 6.29 *(978-1-62065-847-5(X))*; pap. 35.70 *(978-1-62065-848-2(8))*; lib. bdg. 21.99 *(978-1-62065-084-4(3))* Capstone Press of Coughlan Cos. (Pebble Bks.).

Shepherd, Jodie. A Day with Librarians. 2012. (Rookie Read-About Community Ser.). (ENG.). 32p. (J). pap. 5.95 *(978-0-531-29252-5(5))*; lib. bdg. 23.00 *(978-0-531-28952-5(4))* Scholastic Library Publishing.

Sherman, Jill. Melvil Dewey: Library Genius, 1 vol. 2009. (Publishing Pioneers Ser.). (ENG., Illus.). 112p. (J). (gr. 6-12). lib. bdg. 35.64 *(978-1-60453-761-1(2)*, Essential Library) ABDO Publishing Co.

Siemens, Jared. Librarians. 2016. (J). ***(978-1-5105-2107-0(0))*** SmartBook Media, Inc.

—Librarians. 2015. 24p. (J). *(978-1-4896-3649-2(8))* Weigl Pubs., Inc.

Stamaty, Mark Alan. Alia's Mission: Saving the Books of Iraq. 2010. (ENG.). 32p. (J). (gr. k-3). pap. 7.99 *(978-0-375-85763-8(X)*, Dragonfly Bks.) Random Hse. Children's Bks.

—Alia's Mission: Saving the Books of Iraq: Inspired by a True Story. 2005. (Reader's Workshop Ser.). (ENG., Illus.). 32p. (C). pap. 21.95 *(978-0-7362-2802-2(0))* CENGAGE Learning.

—Muhimat Al Sayyda Alia: Inkaz Kuttub Al Irag. 2005.Tr. of Alia's Mission - Saving the Books of Iraq. 32p. pap. 12.00 *(978-977-6171-01-5(X)*, 706-001) Al-Balsam Pubng. Hse. EGY. Dist: Bookmasters Distribution.

Taylor, Allan & Parish, James Robert. Library & Information Science. 2009. (Career Opportunities Ser.). (Illus.). 364p. (C). (gr. 9-18). 49.50 *(978-0-8160-7546-1(8)*, Ferguson Publishing Co.) Facts On File, Inc.

Vasquez, Lidia. Damaged Friends: Sad but true stories about damaged Books. 2010. 28p. pap. 13.99 *(978-1-4520-1548-4(1))* AuthorHouse.

Vogel, Elizabeth. Meet the Librarian. 2009. (My School Ser.). 24p. (gr. 1-2). 37.50 *(978-1-61514-706-9(3)*, PowerKids Pr.) Rosen Publishing Group, Inc., The.

Winter, Jeanette. Biblioburro: A True Story from Colombia. Winter, Jeanette, illus. 2010. (ENG., Illus.). 32p. (J). (gr. 1-4). 17.99 *(978-1-4169-9778-8(4)*, Beach Lane Bks.) Beach Lane Bks.

—The Librarian of Basra: A True Story from Iraq. Winter, Jeanette, illus. 2005. (ENG., Illus.). 32p. (J). (gr. -1-3). 17.99 *(978-0-15-205445-8(6))* Houghton Mifflin Harcourt Publishing Co.

LIBRARIANS—FICTION

Arcane, Amicus. Tales from the Haunted Mansion: Volume I: The Fearsome Foursome. Jones, Kelley, illus. 2016. (Tales from the Haunted Mansion Ser.: 1). (ENG.). 240p. (J). (gr. 3-7). 14.99 *(978-1-4847-1329-7(X))* Disney Pr.

Aris, Mary. Bartholomew. 2010. 86p. pap. 36.95 *(978-1-4457-8958-3(2))*; pap. 36.50 *(978-1-4457-5351-5(0))* Lulu Pr., Inc.

As Orange As Marmalade: Tan naranja como Mermelada. 2007. (ENG & SPA.). (J). per. 10.00 *(978-0-9749876-8-2(9))* Journey of a Dream Pr.

Asher, Sandy. Chicken Story Time. Fearing, Mark, illus. 2016. (ENG.). 40p. (J). (-k). 17.99 *(978-0-8037-3944-4(3)*, Dial Bks) Penguin Young Readers Group.

Bancks, Tristan. Noob & the Librarian Supervillain. Gorissen, Dean, illus. 2015. (Legends in Their Own Lunchbox Ser.). (ENG.). 48p. (gr. 1-2). pap. 7.99 *(978-1-4966-0247-3(1)*, Legends in Their Own Lunchbox) Capstone Classroom.

—Noob, Crimebuster. Gorissen, Dean, illus. 2015. (Legends in Their Own Lunchbox Ser.). (ENG.). 48p. (gr. 1-2). pap. 7.99 *(978-1-4966-0241-1(2)*, Legends in Their Own Lunchbox) Capstone Classroom.

Barnett, Mac. The Case of the Case of Mistaken Identity. Rex, Adam, illus. (Brixton Brothers Ser.: 1). (ENG.). (J). (gr. 3-7). 2010. 208p. pap. 7.99 *(978-1-4169-7816-9(X))* 2009. 192p. 15.99 *(978-1-4169-7815-2(1))* Simon & Schuster Bks. For Young Readers. (Simon & Schuster Bks. For Young Readers).

—Mysterious Case of Cases: The Case of the Case of Mistaken Identity - The Ghostwriter Secret - It Happened on a Train - Danger Goes Berserk. Rex, Adam & Myers, Matthew, illus. 2013. (Brixton Brothers Ser.). (ENG.). 1024p. (J). (gr. 3-7). pap. 29.99 *(978-1-4424-9818-1(8)*, Simon & Schuster Bks. For Young Readers) Simon & Schuster Bks. For Young Readers.

Bellisario, Gina. Queen of the Spelling Bee. Von Innerebner, Jessika, illus. 2016. (Ellie Ultra Ser.). (ENG.). 128p. (gr. 2-3). lib. bdg. 25.99 *(978-1-4965-3141-4(8))* Stone Arch Bks.

Berg, Brook. What Marion Taught Willis. Alberg, Nathan, illus. 2005. (J). 16.95 *(978-1-932146-31-8(8)*, 1242215) Highsmith Inc.

Bernheimer, Kate. The Lonely Book. Sheban, Chris, illus. 2012. (ENG.). 40p. (J). (gr. -1-3). 17.99 *(978-0-375-86226-7(9)*, Schwartz & Wade Bks.) Random Hse. Children's Bks.

Biggs, Brian. Tinyville Town: I'm a Librarian. 2017. (Tinyville Town Ser.). (ENG., Illus.). 22p. (J). (gr. -1 — 1). bds. 7.95 *(978-1-4197-2322-3(7)*, Abrams Appleseed) Abrams, Inc.

Bottner, Barbara. Miss Brooks Loves Books! (And I Don't) Emberley, Michael, illus. 2010. (ENG.). 32p. (J). (gr. -1-2). 17.99 *(978-0-375-84682-3(4)*, Knopf Bks. for Young Readers) Random Hse. Children's Bks.

—Miss Brooks' Story Nook (where Tales Are Told & Ogres Are Welcome) Emberley, Michael, illus. 2014. (ENG.). 40p. (J). (gr. k-4). 16.99 *(978-0-449-81328-7(2)*, Knopf Bks. for Young Readers) Random Hse. Children's Bks.

Brouwer, Sigmund. Justine Mckeen, Pooper Scooper, 1 vol. Whamond, Dave, illus. 2012. (Orca Echoes Ser.). (ENG.). 64p. (J). (gr. 2-3). pap. 6.95 *(978-1-55469-931-5(2))* Orca Bk. Pubs. USA.

Buzzeo, Toni. Fire up with Reading! Yoshikawa, Sachiko, illus. 2007. 32p. 17.95 *(978-1-60213-019-7(1)*, Upstart Bks.) Highsmith Inc.

—The Great Dewey Hunt. Yoshikawa, Sachiko, illus. 2009. (Mrs. Skorupski Story Ser.). (J). 36p. (gr. -1-3). 17.95 *(978-1-60213-041-8(8))*; *(978-1-60213-029-6(9))* Highsmith Inc. (Upstart Bks.).

—The Library Doors. Westcott, Nadine Bernard, illus. 2008. (J). (gr. -1-3). 17.95 *(978-1-60213-037-1(X)*, Upstart Bks.) Highsmith Inc.

—Our Librarian Won't Tell Us Anything! Yoshikawa, Sachiko, illus. 2006. 32p. (J). (gr. -1-k). lib. bdg. 17.95 *(978-1-932146-73-8(3)*, Upstart Bks.) Highsmith Inc.

Casale, Karen. Never Let a Ghost Borrow Your Library Book: Book Care Guidelines from the Library Secret Service. Rebora, Cecilia, illus. 2012. 32p. (J). 17.75 *(978-1-60213-061-6(2)*, Upstart Bks.) Highsmith Inc.

Colfer, Eoin. The Legend of Spud Murphy. McCoy, Glenn, illus. 2005. (Eoin Colfer's Legend Of... Ser.). 95p. (gr. 2-6). 16.00 *(978-0-7569-6514-3(4))* Perfection Learning Corp.

J
K
L

Dahl, Michael. Blood in the Library, 1 vol. Kendall, Bradford, illus. 2011. (Return to the Library of Doom Ser.). (ENG.). 72p. (gr. 1-3). lib. bdg. 23.99 *(978-1-4342-3228-1(X)*, Zone Bks.) Stone Arch Bks.

—Cave of the Bookworms, 1 vol. Kendall, Bradford, illus. 2008. (Library of Doom Ser.). (ENG.). 40p. (gr. 1-3). pap. 6.25 *(978-1-4342-0549-0(5))*; lib. bdg. 23.99 *(978-1-4342-0489-9(8))* Stone Arch Bks. (Zone Bks.).

—The Creeping Bookends, 1 vol. Kendall, Bradford, illus. 2008. (Library of Doom Ser.). (ENG.). 40p. (gr. 1-3). pap. 6.25 *(978-1-4342-0546-9(0))*; lib. bdg. 23.99 *(978-1-4342-0486-8(3))* Stone Arch Bks. (Zone Bks.).

—Death Sentence. Evergreen, Nelson, illus. 2015. (Library of Doom: the Final Chapters Ser.). (ENG.). 40p. (gr. 1-3). 23.99 *(978-1-4342-9678-8(4))* Stone Arch Bks.

—Dictionary of 1,000 Rooms, 1 vol. Kendall, Bradford, illus. 2011. (Return to the Library of Doom Ser.). (ENG.). 72p. (gr. 1-3). lib. bdg. 23.99 *(978-1-4342-3229-8(8)*, Zone Bks.) Stone Arch Bks.

—Don't Open It! Kendall, Bradford, illus. 2016. 40p. (J). *(978-1-4747-1054-1(9))* Stone Arch Bks.

—Escape from the Pop-Up Prison. Kendall, Bradford, illus. 2008. (Library of Doom Ser.). (ENG.). 40p. (gr. 1-3). pap. 6.25 *(978-1-4342-0550-6(9))*; lib. bdg. 23.99 *(978-1-4342-0490-5(1))* Stone Arch Bks. (Zone Bks.).

—Ghost Writer, 1 vol. Kendall, Bradford, illus. 2011. (Return to the Library of Doom Ser.). (ENG.). 72p. (gr. 1-3). lib. bdg. 23.99 *(978-1-4342-3230-4(1)*, Zone Bks.) Stone Arch Bks.

—The Golden Book of Death. Souleiman, Serg, illus. 2008. (Library of Doom Ser.). (ENG.). 40p. (gr. 1-3). lib. bdg. 23.99 *(978-1-4342-0487-5(1))*; per. 6.25 *(978-1-4342-0547-6(9))* Stone Arch Bks. (Zone Bks.).

—Inkfoot, 1 vol. Kendall, Bradford, illus. 2010. (Return to the Library of Doom Ser.). (ENG.). 72p. (gr. 1-3). 23.99 *(978-1-4342-2146-9(6)*, Zone Bks.) Stone Arch Bks.

—Killer App, 1 vol. Kendall, Bradford, illus. 2011. (Return to the Library of Doom Ser.). (ENG.). 72p. (gr. 1-3). lib. bdg. 23.99 *(978-1-4342-3231-1(X)*, Zone Bks.) Stone Arch Bks.

—The Last Word. Kendall, Bradford, illus. 2016. 40p. (J). *(978-1-4747-1055-8(7))* Stone Arch Bks.

—The Lost Page. Evergreen, Nelson, illus. 2015. (Library of Doom: the Final Chapters Ser.). (ENG.). 40p. (gr. 1-3). 23.99 *(978-1-4342-9679-5(2))* Stone Arch Bks.

—Night of the Scrawler. Kendall, Bradford, illus. 2016. 40p. (J). *(978-1-4747-1056-5(5))* Stone Arch Bks.

—The Spine Tingler. Evergreen, Nelson, illus. 2015. (Library of Doom: the Final Chapters Ser.). (ENG.). 40p. (gr. 1-3). 23.99 *(978-1-4342-9680-1(6))* Stone Arch Bks.

—Thesaurus Rex. Kendall, Bradford, illus. 2016. 40p. (J). *(978-1-4747-1057-2(3))* Stone Arch Bks.

—Tome Raider. Evergreen, Nelson, illus. 2015. (Library of Doom: the Final Chapters Ser.). (ENG.). 40p. (gr. 1-3). 23.99 *(978-1-4342-9677-1(6))* Stone Arch Bks.

—The Twister Trap, 1 vol. Kendall, Bradford, illus. 2008. (Library of Doom Ser.). (ENG.). 40p. (gr. 1-3). pap. 6.25 *(978-1-4342-0548-3(7))*; lib. bdg. 23.99 *(978-1-4342-0488-2(X))* Stone Arch Bks. (Zone Bks.).

—The Word Eater, 1 vol. Kendall, Bradford, illus. 2008. (Library of Doom Ser.). (ENG.). 40p. (gr. 1-3). lib. bdg. 23.99 *(978-1-4342-0491-2(X))*; per. 6.25 *(978-1-4342-0551-3(7))* Stone Arch Bks. (Zone Bks.).

Dailey, Reid. The Legend of Ross the Reader: A Story of How a Smart Cowboy Saved the Prairie One Book at a Time. Edgerley, Ross, illus. 2007. 32p. per. 15.95 *(978-1-59858-483-7(9))* Dog Ear Publishing, LLC.

—Ross the Reader & the Adventure of the Pirate's Treasure. Edgerley, Ross, illus. 2009. 44p. pap. 16.95 *(978-1-59858-900-9(8))* Dog Ear Publishing, LLC.

Darden, Amy. Yesterday Once Again: Guenevere's Quest. 2003. (J). pap. 11.00 *(978-0-8059-9238-0(3)*, RoseDog Bks.) Dorrance Publishing Co., Inc.

Deedy, Carmen Agra. The Library Dragon, 1 vol. White, Michael P., illus. 2012. (ENG.). 32p. (J). 19.95 *(978-1-56145-639-0(X))* Peachtree Pubs.

—Return of the Library Dragon, 1 vol. White, Michael P., illus. 2012. (ENG.). 32p. (J). 16.95 *(978-1-56145-621-5(7))* Peachtree Pubs.

Dorling Kindersley Publishing Staff. Sophie la Girafe: Sophie's Little Library. 2015. (ENG., Illus.). 42p. (J). (— 1). bds. 19.99 *(978-1-4654-4013-6(5)*, DK Children) Dorling Kindersley Publishing, Inc.

Downey, Jen Swann. The Ninja Librarians: Sword in the Stacks. 2016. (Ninja Librarians Ser.: 2). (ENG.). 400p. (J). (gr. 5-8). 16.99 *(978-1-4022-8773-2(9)*, 9781402287732, Sourcebooks Jabberwocky) Sourcebooks, Inc.

—The Ninja Librarians: The Accidental Keyhand. 2015. (Ninja Librarians Ser.: 1). (ENG.). 400p. (J). (gr. 4-7). pap. 8.99 *(978-1-4926-0180-7(2)*, Sourcebooks Jabberwocky) Sourcebooks, Inc.

Farber, E. S. Fish Finelli (Book 1) Seagulls Don't Eat Pickles. Beene, Jason, illus. 2014. (Fish Finelli Ser.). (ENG.). 168p. (J). (gr. 3-7). pap. 6.99 *(978-1-4521-2853-5(7))* Chronicle Bks. LLC.

Farber, Erica. Fish Finelli: Seagulls Don't Eat Pickles. Beene, Jason, illus. 2013. (Fish Finelli Ser.). (ENG.). 155p. (J). (gr. 2-5). 15.99 *(978-1-4521-0820-9(X))* Chronicle Bks. LLC.

Garland, Michael. Miss Smith & the Haunted Library. 2012. (ENG.). 32p. (J). (gr. -1-2). 6.99 *(978-0-14-242122-2(7)*, Puffin Books) Penguin Young Readers Group.

—Miss Smith & the Haunted Library. Garland, Michael, illus. 2009. (ENG., Illus.). 32p. (J). (gr. -1-2). 16.99 *(978-0-525-42139-9(4)*, Dutton Books for Young Readers) Penguin Young Readers Group.

Gómez Cerda, Alfredo. Barro de Medellin/ Mud of Medellin. Lopez, Xan, illus. 2010. (SPA.). 146p. (YA). (gr. 5-8). *(978-84-263-6849-2(2))* Vives, Luis Editorial (Edelvives).

González, Lucía. The Storyteller's Candle: La Velita de Los Cuentos. Delacre, Lulu, illus. 2013. (ENG & SPA.). 32p. (J). pap. 9.95 *(978-0-89239-237-7(1)*, Children's Book Press) Lee & Low Bks., Inc.

Gonzalez, Lucia M. & Delacre, Lulu. The Storyteller's Candle. 2008.Tr. of La Velita de los Cuentos. (SPA & ENG., Illus.). 32p. (J). (gr. k-4). 16.95 *(978-0-89239-222-3(3))* Lee & Low Bks., Inc.

Henson, Heather. That Book Woman. Small, David, illus. 2008. (ENG.). 40p. (J). (gr. -1-3). 17.99 *(978-1-4169-0812-8(9)*, Atheneum Bks. for Young Readers) Simon & Schuster Children's Publishing.

—That Book Woman. Small, David, illus. 2011. (J). (gr. 2-4). 29.95 *(978-0-545-23715-4(7))* Weston Woods Studios, Inc.

Hopkins, Jackie Mims. Goldie Socks & the Three Libearians. Manders, John, illus. 2007. (J). *(978-1-932146-68-4(7)*, Upstart Bks.) Highsmith Inc.

Hubbell, Patricia. Check It Out! Reading, Finding, Helping, 0 vols. Speir, Nancy, illus. 2011. (ENG.). 32p. (J). (gr. -1-3). 16.99 *(978-0-7614-5803-6(4)*, 9780761458036, Amazon Children's Publishing) Amazon Publishing.

Jenkins, Emily. The Little Bit Scary People. Boiger, Alexandra, illus. 2008. (ENG.). 32p. (gr. -1-1). 16.99 *(978-1-4231-0075-1(1))* Hyperion Pr.

Knudsen, Michelle. Evil Librarian. 2014. (ENG.). 352p. (YA). (gr. 9). 16.99 *(978-0-7636-6038-3(8))* Candlewick Pr.

Luper, Eric. The Wizard's War (Key Hunters #4) 2017. (Key Hunters Ser.: 4). (ENG.). 128p. (J). (gr. 2-5). pap. 4.99 *(978-0-545-82213-8(0)*, Scholastic Paperbacks) Scholastic, Inc.

McQuinn, Anna. Lola at the Library. Beardshaw, Rosalind, illus. 2006. (ENG.). 32p. (J). (gr. -1-k). 6.95 *(978-1-58089-142-4(X))*; 15.95 *(978-1-58089-113-4(6))* Charlesbridge Publishing, Inc.

Miller, Nathan. The Official Librarian: Bessy's Back! 2009. 124p. pap. 12.49 *(978-1-4490-2391-1(6))* AuthorHouse.

Morris, Carla. The Boy Who Was Raised by Librarians, 1 vol. Sneed, Brad, illus. 2007. (ENG.). 32p. (J). (gr. k-3). 16.95 *(978-1-56145-391-7(9))* Peachtree Pubs.

Osborne, Mary Pope. The Mystery of the Enchanted Dog, 4 vols., Set. Murdocca, Sal, illus. 2009. (ENG.). 96p. (J). (gr. 1-4). 23.96 *(978-0-375-85811-6(3)*, Random Hse. Bks. for Young Readers) Random Hse. Children's Bks.

Peck, Richard. Here Lies the Librarian. 2007. (ENG.). 160p. (J). (gr. 5-18). 7.99 *(978-0-14-240908-4(1)*, Puffin Books) Penguin Young Readers Group.

—Here Lies the Librarian. 2007. 145p. (J). (gr. 4-7). 14.65 *(978-0-7569-8193-8(X))* Perfection Learning Corp.

—Here Lies the Librarian. rev. l.t. ed. 2007. (Thorndike Literacy Bridge Ser.). 173p. (J). (gr. 5-9). 23.95 *(978-0-7862-9183-0(4))* Thorndike Pr.

Rey, H. A. Librarian for a Day. 2012. (Curious George Ser.). (ENG., Illus.). 24p. (J). (gr. -1-3). pap. 3.99 *(978-0-547-85281-2(9))* Houghton Mifflin Harcourt Publishing Co.

Rey, H. A. & Rey, Margret. Librarian for a Day. 2012. (Curious George TV Tie-In Early Reader Ser.). lib. bdg. 13.55 *(978-0-606-26602-4(X)*, Turtleback) Turtleback Bks.

Ruurs, Margriet & Gooderham, Andrew. Ms. Bee's magical bookcase. 2004. (Illus.). 32p. (J). pap. 8.95 *(978-1-894601-10-8(6))* Chestnut Publishing Group CAN. Dist: Hushion Hse. Publishing, Ltd.

Sanderson, Brandon. Alcatraz Versus the Evil Librarians. Lazo, Hayley, illus. 2016. (Alcatraz Versus the Evil Librarians Ser.: 1). (ENG.). 320p. (J). 16.99 *(978-0-7653-7894-1(9)*, 9780765378941, Starscape) Doherty, Tom Assocs., LLC.

—Alcatraz Versus the Knights of Crystallia. 2016. (Alcatraz Versus the Evil Librarians Ser.: 3). (ENG.). 320p. (J). 16.99 *(978-0-7653-7898-9(1)*, 9780765378989, Starscape) Doherty, Tom Assocs., LLC.

—Alcatraz Versus the Shattered Lens. 2016. (Alcatraz Versus the Evil Librarians Ser.: 4). (ENG.). 336p. (J). 16.99 *(978-0-7653-7900-9(7)*, 9780765379009, Starscape) Doherty, Tom Assocs., LLC.

—The Scrivener's Bones. 2016. (Alcatraz Versus the Evil Librarians Ser.: 2). (ENG.). 368p. (J). 16.99 *(978-0-7653-7896-5(5)*, 9780765378965, Starscape) Doherty, Tom Assocs., LLC.

Shields, Gillian. Library Lily. Chessa, Francesca, illus. 2011. (ENG.). 26p. (YA). 16.00 *(978-0-8028-5401-8(X))* Eerdmans, William B. Publishing Co.

Sneed, Brad. The Boy Who Was Raised by Librarians. Sneed, Brad, illus. 2008. (Illus.). (J). (gr. k-3). 27.95 incl. audio *(978-0-8045-6965-1(7))* Spoken Arts, Inc.

Taylor, Laini. Strange the Dreamer. 2017. 536p. (YA). ***(978-0-316-43120-0(6))*** Little Brown & Co.

—Strange the Dreamer. 2017. (ENG.). (J). 544p. (gr. 10-17). 18.99 *(978-0-316-34168-4(1))*; 704p. (gr. 9-17). 20.99 *(978-0-316-46427-7(9))* Little, Brown Bks. for Young Readers.

Thaler, Mike. The Librarian from the Black Lagoon. Lee, Jared, illus. unabr. ed. 2007. (J). (gr. k-2). pap. 14.95 incl. audio *(978-0-439-02773-1(X))* Scholastic, Inc.

—The Librarian from the Black Lagoon, 1 vol. Lee, Jared, illus. 2011. (Black Lagoon Set 1 Ser.: No. 1). (ENG.). 32p. (gr. -1-2). lib. bdg. 24.21 *(978-1-59961-795-4(1))* Spotlight.

Time, Nicholas O. Stay a Spell. 2016. (In Due Time Ser.: 2). lib. bdg. 17.20 *(978-0-606-38986-0(5))* Turtleback Bks.

Weatherford, Carole Boston. The Library Ghost. White, Lee, illus. 2008. 22p. (J). (gr. -1-3). 17.95 *(978-1-60213-017-3(5)*, Upstart Bks.) Highsmith Inc.

LIBRARIANSHIP

see Library Science

LIBRARIES

see also School Libraries

ABDO. Essential Library of Cultural History, 1 vol. 2014. (Essential Library of Cultural History Ser.: 6). (ENG.). 112p. (J). (gr. 6-12). lib. bdg. 213.84 *(978-1-62403-550-0(7)*, Essential Library) ABDO Publishing Co.

Abdo Publishing. Library Resources, 1 vol. 2013. (Library Resources Ser.: 6). (ENG.). 32p. (J). (gr. k-4). lib. bdg. 162.42 *(978-1-61783-601-5(X)*, Super SandCastle) ABDO Publishing Co.

Ames, Michelle. Librarians in Our Community. 2009. (On the Job Ser.): (Illus.). 24p. (J). (ENG.). pap. 8.25 *(978-1-4358-2458-4(X)*, 1300571); lib. bdg. 22.60 *(978-1-4042-8072-4(3)*, 1300571) Rosen Publishing Group, Inc., The. (PowerKids Pr.).

Anderson, Sheila. Library. 2008. pap. 22.95 *(978-0-8225-9372-0(6))*; (ENG.). 8p. (gr. -1-1). pap. 4.95 *(978-0-8225-8839-9(0))* Lerner Publishing Group.

Austen, Mary. Librarians on the Job. 2017. (Jobs in Our Community Ser.). 24p. (J). (gr. 1-1). pap. 8.25 ***(978-1-5345-2145-2(3)***, KidHaven Publishing) Greenhaven Publishing LLC.

Balice, Mary Lee, ed. Information Science, 1 vol., 1. 2016. (Study of Science Ser.). (ENG.). 96p. (J). (gr. 8-8). 36.25 *(978-1-68048-232-4(7)*, Britannica Educational Publishing) Rosen Publishing Group, Inc., The.

Bellamy, Adam. This Is My Library. 2016. (All about My World Ser.). 24p. (J). pap. 9.35 *(978-0-7660-8089-8(7))* Enslow Pubs., Inc.

Bily, Cynthia A., ed. Banned Books. 2012. (Introducing Issues with Opposing Viewpoints Ser.). (ENG., Illus.). 144p. (J). (gr. 7-10). lib. bdg. 36.95 *(978-0-7377-5671-5(3)*, Greenhaven Pr., Inc.) Cengage Gale.

Bishop, Celeste. Craft Time at the Library. 2016. (Places in My Community Ser.). 00024p. (J). (gr. 1-1). 23.60 *(978-1-4994-3012-7(4))*; pap. 8.25 *(978-1-4994-2775-2(1))* Rosen Publishing Group, Inc., The. (PowerKids Pr.).

Bloom, Paul. Rules in the Library. 2015. (School Rules Ser.). (ENG., Illus.). 24p. (J). (gr. k-k). pap. 8.15 *(978-1-4824-2649-6(8))* Stevens, Gareth Publishing LLLP.

Bodden, Valerie. Navigating the Library. 2012. (Research for Writing Ser.). 48p. (gr. 5-12). 23.95 *(978-1-60818-206-0(1)*, Creative Education) Creative Co., The.

Buzzeo, Toni. Inside the Books: Readers & Libraries Around the World. Daly, Jude, illus. 2012. 32p. (J). 17.95 *(978-1-60213-058-6(2)*, Upstart Bks.) Highsmith Inc.

Carr, Aaron. The Library. 24p. 2014. (Illus.). (J). *(978-1-62127-346-2(6))* 2013. pap. 12.95 *(978-1-62127-351-6(2))* Weigl Pubs., Inc.

Colby, Jennifer. Library. 2016. (21st Century Junior Library: Explore a Workplace Ser.). (ENG., Illus.). 24p. (J). (gr. 2-5). 27.07 *(978-1-63471-075-6(4)*, 208379) Cherry Lake Publishing.

Coldwell, Lamar. The Library in My Town. 2016. (Rosen REAL Readers: Social Studies Nonfiction / Fiction: Family, Community, & the World Ser.). 8p. (gr. 1-k). pap. 5.46 *(978-1-5081-2260-9(1)*, Rosen Classroom) Rosen Publishing Group, Inc., The.

Dixon, Dale. Helping at the Library: Step by Step. 2017. (Computer Science for the Real World Ser.). 12p. (gr. 6-7). pap. 7.05 ***(978-1-5383-5144-4(7)***, Rosen Classroom) Rosen Publishing Group, Inc., The.

Donovan, Sandy. Bob the Alien Discovers the Dewey Decimal System, 1 vol. Haake, Martin, illus. 2010. (In the Library). (ENG.). 24p. (gr. k-4). lib. bdg. 26.65 *(978-1-4048-5757-5(5))* Picture Window Bks.

Dorling Kindersley Publishing Staff. My First Library. 2015. (ENG.). 36p. (J). (— 1). bds. 16.99 *(978-1-4654-4488-2(2)*, DK Children) Dorling Kindersley Publishing, Inc.

Farmer, Bonnie. Abc Letters in the Library. l.t. ed. 2012. 60p. (J). pap. *(978-1-4596-3446-6(2))* ReadHowYouWant.com, Ltd.

Finn, Carrie. Manners in the Library. Lensch, Chris, illus. (Way to Be!: Manners Ser.). 24p. (gr. -1-2). 2009. pap. 0.63 *(978-1-4048-5994-4(2)*, Nonfiction Picture Bks.) 2007. (ENG.). per. 7.95 *(978-1-4048-3557-3(1)*, 1265722) Picture Window Bks.

Flanagan, Alice K. & Dolbear, Emily J. Discovering Today's Library. 2006. (Reference Ser.). (Illus.). 64p. (gr. 2-6). lib. bdg. 30.00 *(978-0-8368-7426-6(9)*, Gareth Stevens Learning Library) Stevens, Gareth Publishing LLLP.

Gaines, Ann Graham. Master the Library & Media Center. 2009. (Ace It! Information Literacy Ser.). (Illus.). 48p. (J). (gr. 2-5). lib. bdg. 25.27 *(978-0-7660-3393-1(7))* Enslow Pubs., Inc.

Getting to Know the Library, Bk. A. (J). (gr. 1-2). suppl. ed. *(978-0-590-06374-6(X))* Scholastic, Inc.

Goldman, Phyllis, ed. Monkeyshines on the Library: For Your Information. 2003. (Illus.). 112p. (YA). per. 32.95 *(978-1-888325-28-7(3))* Allosaurus Pubs.

Gorman, Jacqueline Laks. La Biblioteca. 2005. (I Like to Visit Ser.).Tr. of Library. (ENG & SPA.). 24p. (gr. k-3). pap. 8.15 *(978-0-8368-4603-4(6)*, GHS33395, Weekly Reader Leveled Readers) Stevens, Gareth Publishing LLLP.

—The Library. 2005. (I Like to Visit Ser.). (Illus.). 24p. (gr. k-3). lib. bdg. 22.00 *(978-0-8368-4452-8(1)*, Weekly Reader Leveled Readers) Stevens, Gareth Publishing LLLP.

—The Library/La Biblioteca. Acosta, Tatiana & Gutiérrez, Guillermo, trs. from ENG. 2005. (I Like to Visit/Me Gusta Visitar Ser.). (ENG & SPA., Illus.). 24p. (J). (gr. k-3). lib. bdg. 22.00 *(978-0-8368-4596-9(X)*, Weekly Reader Leveled Readers) Stevens, Gareth Publishing LLLP.

Gorman, Jacqueline Laks & Laks Gorman, Jacqueline. Librarians. Andersen, Gregg, photos by. 2010. (People in My Community Ser.). (Illus.). 24p. (gr. k-3). 22.60 *(978-1-4339-3341-7(1))* Stevens, Gareth Publishing LLLP.

Graphic Library Collection. 2016. (Graphic Library). (ENG.). (gr. 3-4). lib. bdg. 1379.25 *(978-1-5157-4021-6(8)*, Graphic Library) Capstone Press of Coughlan Cos.

Green, Lyric & Graham Gaines, Ann. Future Ready Library & Media Center Mastery. 2017. (Future Ready Project Skills Ser.). 48p. (J). (gr. 3-4). pap. 11.70 ***(978-0-7660-8777-4(8))***; lib. bdg. 27.93 ***(978-0-7660-8657-9(7))*** Enslow Pubs., Inc.

Hamilton, John. Libraries & Reference Materials, 1 vol. 2005. (Straight to the Source Ser.). (ENG.). 32p. (gr. k-6). 27.07 *(978-1-59197-545-8(X)*, Checkerboard Library) ABDO Publishing Co.

Harasymiw, Therese. How Do I Use a Library? 2014. (Research Tools You Can Use Ser.). 32p. (J). (gr. 3-6). 23.45 *(978-1-62275-379-6(8))* Rosen Publishing Group, Inc., The.

Hill, Oriah. My Day at the Library. 2012. 16p. pap. 15.99 *(978-1-4772-7954-0(7))* AuthorHouse.

Jango-Cohen, Judith. Librarians. 2005. (Pull Ahead Books: Community Helpers Ser.). 32p. (gr. k-3). (ENG.). pap. 7.95 *(978-0-8225-2533-2(X))*; (Illus.). (J). lib. bdg. 22.60 *(978-0-8225-1691-0(8))* Lerner Publishing Group.

Kawa, Katie. My First Trip to the Library. Livingston, Jessica, illus. 2012. (My First Adventures Ser.). (ENG.). 24p. (J). (gr. k-2). pap. 8.15 *(978-1-4339-6251-6(9))*; lib. bdg. 22.60 *(978-1-4339-6249-3(7))* Stevens, Gareth Publishing LLLP.

—My First Trip to the Library: Mi Primera Visita a la Biblioteca. Livingston, Jessica, illus. 2012. (My First Adventures / Mis primeras aventuras Ser.). (ENG & SPA.). 24p. (J). (gr. k-2). lib. bdg. 22.60 *(978-1-4339-6631-6(X))* Stevens, Gareth Publishing LLLP.

Keogh, Josie. A Trip to the Library. 2012. (PowerKids Readers: My Community Ser.). (ENG., Illus.). 24p. (J). (gr. k-2). pap. 8.25 *(978-1-4488-7481-1(5))*; lib. bdg. 22.60 *(978-1-4488-7402-6(5))* Rosen Publishing Group, Inc., The. (PowerKids Pr.).

—A Trip to the Library: De Visita en la Biblioteca. 2012. (PowerKids Readers: My Community / Mi comunidad Ser.). (SPA & ENG., Illus.). 24p. (gr. k-2). lib. bdg. 22.60 *(978-1-4488-7833-8(0)*, PowerKids Pr.) Rosen Publishing Group, Inc., The.

King, M. G. Librarian on the Roof! A True Story. Gilpin, Stephen, illus. 2010. (ENG.). 32p. (J). (gr. 1-3). 16.99 *(978-0-8075-4512-6(0))* Whitman, Albert & Co.

—Librarian on the Roof: A True Story. Gilpin, Stephen, illus. 2012. (J). *(978-1-61913-147-7(1))* Weigl Pubs., Inc.

Kralovansky, Susan. What Would You Do in a Library?, 1 vol. 2013. (Library Resources Ser.). (ENG., Illus.). 32p. (J). (gr. k-4). lib. bdg. 27.07 *(978-1-61783-602-2(8)*, Super SandCastle) ABDO Publishing Co.

Kreisman, Rachelle. Places We Go: A Kids' Guide to Community Sites. Haggerty, Tim, illus. 2015. (Start Smart: Community Ser.). (ENG.). 32p. (gr. 1-3). 26.65 *(978-1-937529-36-9(3))* Red Chair Pr.

Laks Gorman, Jacqueline. Librarians. Andersen, Gregg, photos by. 2010. (People in My Community Ser.). (Illus.). 24p. (gr. k-3). pap. 8.15 *(978-1-4339-3342-4(X))* Stevens, Gareth Publishing LLLP.

—Librarians / Bibliotecarios. Andersen, Gregg, photos by. 2010. (People in My Community / Mi comunidad Ser.). (SPA., Illus.). 24p. (gr. k-3). pap. 8.15 *(978-1-4339-3760-6(3))* Stevens, Gareth Publishing LLLP.

Leone, Laura. Choosing a Career in Information Science. (World of Work Ser.). 64p. 2009. (gr. 5-5). 58.50 *(978-1-60854-332-8(3))* 2005. (Illus.). (YA). (gr. 7-12). lib. bdg. 31.95 *(978-0-8239-3569-7(8))* Rosen Publishing Group, Inc., The.

Libeary Skills. 125p. (gr. k-3). 11.99 *(978-0-513-02043-6(8)*, TSD20438) Denison, T. S. & Co., Inc.

Lindeen, Mary. A Visit to the Library. 2015. (BeginningtoRead Ser.). (ENG.). 32p. (J). (gr. k-2). pap. 11.94 *(978-1-60357-751-9(3))*; (Illus.). lib. bdg. 22.60 *(978-1-59953-691-0(9))* Norwood Hse. Pr.

Malam, John. Library: From Ancient Scrolls to the Worldwide Web: A Building Works Book. Malam, John, illus. 2006. (Illus.). 32p. (J). (gr. 4-18). reprint ed. 17.00 *(978-1-4223-5173-4(4))* DIANE Publishing Co.

Marsico, Katie. Working at the Airport. 2009. (21st Century Junior Library: Careers Ser.). (ENG.). 24p. (gr. 2-5). lib. bdg. 25.64 *(978-1-60279-510-5(X)*, 200279) Cherry Lake Publishing.

—Working at the Library. 2009. (21st Century Junior Library: Careers Ser.). (ENG.). 24p. (gr. 2-5). lib. bdg. 25.64 *(978-1-60279-511-2(8)*, 200278) Cherry Lake Publishing.

Martin, Isabel. A Library Field Trip. 2015. (Let's Take a Field Trip Ser.). (ENG.). 24p. (gr. k-1). pap. 6.95 *(978-1-4914-2315-8(3)*, Pebble Plus) Capstone Press of Coughlan Cos.

McClintock Miller, Shannon. Find a Book! Durst, Kathryn, illus. 2017. (Library Skills Ser.). (ENG.). 24p. (gr. 1-3). 33.99 ***(978-1-68410-027-9(5))*** Cantata Learning.

—Manners in the Library. Durst, Kathryn, illus. 2017. (Library Skills Ser.). (ENG.). 24p. (gr. 1-3). 33.99 ***(978-1-68410-039-2(9))*** Cantata Learning.

Meachen Rau, Dana. Librarian. 2007. (J). *(978-0-7614-2621-9(3))* Marshall Cavendish.

—Librarians. 2007. (Tools We Use Ser.). (Illus.). 32p. (gr. k-2). lib. bdg. 15.95 *(978-0-7614-2662-2(0)*, Benchmark Bks.) Marshall Cavendish Corp.

—Librarians/Los Bibliotecarios. 2007. (Tools We Use/Instrumentos de Trabajo Ser.). (SPA., Illus.). 32p. (gr. k-2). lib. bdg. 15.95 *(978-0-7614-2826-8(7)*, Benchmark Bks.) Marshall Cavendish Corp.

—Los Bibliotecarios. 2007. (Instrumentos de Trabajo Ser.). (SPA., Illus.). 32p. (gr. k-2). lib. bdg. 15.95 *(978-0-7614-2802-2(X)*, Benchmark Bks.) Marshall Cavendish Corp.

Meister, Cari. La Biblioteca Pública. 2016. (Los Primeros Viajes Escolares (First Field Trips)).Tr. of Public Library. (SPA.). 24p. (J). (gr. k-2). lib. bdg. 25.65 *(978-1-62031-327-5(8)*, Bullfrog Bks.) Jump! Inc.

—Librarians. 2014. (ENG., Illus.). 24p. (J). lib. bdg. 25.65 *(978-1-62031-076-2(7))* Jump! Inc.

—Public Library. Fretland VanVoorst, Jenny, ed. 2016. (First Field Trips). 24p. (J). (gr. k-2). lib. bdg. 25.65 *(978-1-62031-296-4(4)*, Bullfrog Bks.) Jump! Inc.

Miller, Connie Colwell. You Can Control Your Voice: Loud or Quiet? Victoria Assanelli, illus. 2017. (Making Good Choices Ser.). (ENG.). 24p. (J). (gr. 1-4). 20.95 ***(978-1-68151-167-2(3)***, Amicus Illustrated) Amicus Publishing.

Mortensen, Lori. Manners Matter in the Library. Hunt, Lisa, illus. (First Graphics: Manners Matter Ser.). (ENG.). 24p. (gr. 1-2). 2011. pap. 35.70 *(978-1-4296-6393-9(6))* 2010. lib. bdg. 23.99 *(978-1-4296-5330-5(2))* Capstone Press of Coughlan Cos.

Murray, Julie. Bibliotecarios. 2016. (Trabajos en Mi Comunidad Ser.). (SPA.). 24p. (J). (gr. k-5). pap. 7.95 *(978-1-4966-0721-8(X))* Capstone Classroom.

My First Library. Date not set. (Illus.). (J). bds. 7.98 *(978-0-7525-8724-0(2))* Parragon, Inc.

Myron, Vicki & Witter, Bret. Dewey: There's a Cat in the Library! James, Steve, illus. 2009. (ENG.). 40p. (J). (gr. -1-3). 16.99 *(978-0-316-06874-1(8))* Little, Brown Bks. for Young Readers.

The Need to Know Library. 2017. (Need to Know Library). 64p. (gr. 12-11). pap. 77.70 ***(978-1-4994-6642-3(0)***, Rosen Young Adult) Rosen Publishing Group, Inc., The.

The Need to Know Library: Set 1. 2017. (Need to Know Library). 64p. (gr. 12-11). 206.70 ***(978-1-4994-6640-9(4)***, Rosen Young Adult) Rosen Publishing Group, Inc., The.

Nugent, Samantha. Local Library Volunteer. 2016. (J). ***(978-1-4896-5857-9(2)***, AV2 by Weigl) Weigl Pubs., Inc.

O'Brian, Virginia. A Librarian's Job. 2014. (Community Workers Ser.). 24p. (J). (gr. k-2). 24.21 *(978-1-62712-357-0(1))* Cavendish Square Publishing.

Owings, Lisa. Learn about Authors & Illustrators. 2013. (Library Smarts Ser.). (ENG., Illus.). 24p. (gr. -1-2). lib. bdg. 23.93 *(978-1-4677-1502-7(6)*, Lerner Pubns.) Lerner Publishing Group.

Piehl, Janet. Explore the Library. 2013. (Library Smarts Ser.). (ENG., Illus.). 24p. (gr. -1-2). lib. bdg. 23.93

(978-1-4677-1500-3(X), Lerner Pubns.) Lerner Publishing Group.

Prieto, Anita C. B Is for Bookworm: A Library Alphabet. Graef, Renee, illus. 2007. (J). (gr. k-7). 16.10 *(978-0-7569-6657-7(4))* Perfection Learning Corp.

—B Is for Bookworm: A Library Alphabet. Graef, Renee, illus. 2007. (ENG.). 40p. (J). (gr. 1-4). per. 7.95 *(978-1-58536-326-1(X)*, 202290) Sleeping Bear Pr.

Publications International Ltd. Staff. My 1St Libraries Baby Enstein. 2011. 12p. 12.98 *(978-1-4508-1572-7(3))* Phoenix International Publications, Inc.

Rau, Dana Meachen. Librarians. 2007. (J). pap. 6.99 *(978-0-7614-3293-7(0))* Marshall Cavendish Corp.

Ready, Dee. Librarians Help, 1 vol. 2013. (Our Community Helpers Ser.). (ENG.). 24p. (gr. k-1). pap. 6.29 *(978-1-62065-847-5(X))*; pap. 35.70 *(978-1-62065-848-2(8))*; lib. bdg. 21.99 *(978-1-62065-084-4(3))* Capstone Press of Coughlan Cos. (Pebble Bks.).

Rissman, Rebecca. Going to a Library, 1 vol. 2012. (World of Field Trips Ser.). (ENG.). 24p. (gr. -1-1). lib. bdg. 22.65 *(978-1-4329-6071-1(7)*, Acorn) Heinemann-Raintree.

Rosenstock, Barb. Thomas Jefferson Builds a Library. O'brien, John, illus. 2013. (ENG.). 32p. (J). (gr. 3-6). 16.95 *(978-1-59078-932-2(6)*, Calkins Creek) Boyds Mills Pr.

Roth, Susan L. & Abouraya, Karen Leggett. Hands Around the Library: Protecting Egypt's Treasured Books. Roth, Susan L., illus. 2012. (ENG., Illus.). 32p. (J). (gr. -1-k). 16.99 *(978-0-8037-3747-1(5)*, Dial Bks) Penguin Young Readers Group.

Rudolph, Jessica. Spooky Libraries. 2017. (Tiptoe into Scary Places Ser.). (ENG.). 24p. (J). (gr. k-3). 18.95 ***(978-1-68402-049-2(2))*** Bearport Publishing Co., Inc.

Rustad, Martha. Sam Visits the School Library. Golden, Jess, illus. 2017. (Cloverleaf Books (tm) — off to School Ser.). (ENG.). (J). (gr. k-2). pap. 7.99 ***(978-1-5124-5578-6(4))***; lib. bdg. 25.32 ***(978-1-5124-3938-0(X))*** Lerner Publishing Group. (Millbrook Pr.).

Rustad, Martha E. H. Let's Go to the Library, 1 vol. 2013. (Wonderful World of Reading Ser.). (ENG.). 24p. (gr. k-1). lib. bdg. 26.65 *(978-1-62065-093-6(2)*, Pebble Plus) Capstone Press of Coughlan Cos.

Ruurs, Margriet. My Librarian Is a Camel: How Books Are Brought to Children Around the World. 2005. (ENG., Illus.). 32p. (J). (gr. 3-7). 16.95 *(978-1-59078-093-0(0))* Boyds Mills Pr.

Scholastic, Inc. Staff, contrib. by. Let's Go to the Library. 2012. (Rookie Toddler Ser.). (ENG.). 12p. (J). bds. 6.95 *(978-0-531-20853-3(2)*, Children's Pr.) Scholastic Library Publishing.

Shepherd, Jodie. A Day with Librarians. 2012. (Rookie Read-About Community Ser.). (ENG.). 32p. (J). pap. 5.95 *(978-0-531-29252-5(5))*; lib. bdg. 23.00 *(978-0-531-28952-5(4))* Scholastic Library Publishing.

Siemens, Jared. Librarians. 2016. (J). ***(978-1-5105-2107-0(0))*** SmartBook Media, Inc.

—Librarians. 2015. 24p. (J). *(978-1-4896-3649-2(8))* Weigl Pubs., Inc.

Stamaty, Mark Alan. Alia's Mission: Saving the Books of Iraq. 2010. (ENG.). 32p. (J). (gr. k-3). pap. 7.99 *(978-0-375-85763-8(X)*, Dragonfly Bks.) Random Hse. Children's Bks.

—Alia's Mission: Saving the Books of Iraq: Inspired by a True Story. 2005. (Reader's Workshop Ser.). (ENG., Illus.). 32p. (C). pap. 21.95 *(978-0-7362-2802-2(0))* CENGAGE Learning.

—Muhimat Al Sayyda Alia: Inkaz Kuttub Al Irag. 2005.Tr. of Alia's Mission - Saving the Books of Iraq. 32p. pap. 12.00 *(978-977-6171-01-5(X)*, 706-001) Al-Balsam Pubng. Hse. EGY. Dist: Bookmasters Distribution.

Taylor, Troy. Creepy Libraries. (Scary Places Ser.). (ENG.). 32p. (J). (gr. 4-8). 2017. 8.95 ***(978-1-68402-604-3(0))*** 2015. lib. bdg. 26.60 *(978-1-62724-862-4(5))* Bearport Publishing Co., Inc.

Vogel, Elizabeth. Meet the Librarian. 2009. (My School Ser.). 24p. (gr. 1-2). 37.50 *(978-1-61514-706-9(3)*, PowerKids Pr.) Rosen Publishing Group, Inc., The.

Vogel, Jennifer. A Library Story: Building a New Central Library. 2006. (Exceptional Social Studies Titles for Intermediate Grades). (ENG., Illus.). 64p. (gr. 4-6). lib. bdg. 26.60 *(978-0-8225-5916-0(1)*, Millbrook Pr.) Lerner Publishing Group.

Weatherford, Carole Boston. Schomburg: The Man Who Built a Library. Velasquez, Eric, illus. 2017. (ENG.). 48p. (J). (gr. 4-7). 16.99 ***(978-0-7636-8046-6(X))*** Candlewick Pr.

—Schomburg: The Man Who Built a Library. 2017. (J). 31.99 ***(978-1-5200-8717-7(9))***; 31.99 ***(978-1-5200-8716-0(0))*** Dreamscape Media, LLC.

Winter, Jeanette. The Librarian of Basra: A True Story from Iraq. Winter, Jeanette, illus. 2005. (ENG., Illus.). 32p. (J). (gr. -1-3). 17.99 *(978-0-15-205445-8(6))* Houghton Mifflin Harcourt Publishing Co.

Wohlrabe, Sarah C. A Visit to the Library. Thompson, Jeffrey, illus. (First Graphics: My Community Ser.). (ENG.). 24p. (gr. 1-2). 2011. pap. 35.70 *(978-1-4296-6404-2(5))* 2010. lib. bdg. 23.99 *(978-1-4296-5371-8(X))* Capstone Press of Coughlan Cos.

LIBRARIES, CHILDREN'S

see Children's Libraries; School Libraries

LIBRARIES—FICTION

Abdo Publishing. Abby & the Book Bunch, 1 vol. 2013. (Abby & the Book Bunch Ser.: 6). (ENG.). 80p. (J). (gr. 2-5). lib. bdg. 162.42 *(978-1-61641-911-0(3)*, Calico Chapter Bks) Magic Wagon.

Alexander, William. A Properly Unhaunted Place. Murphy, Kelly, illus. 2017. (ENG.). 192p. (J). (gr. 3-7). 16.99 ***(978-1-4814-6915-9(0)***, McElderry, Margaret K. Bks.) McElderry, Margaret K. Bks.

Arcane, Amicus. Tales from the Haunted Mansion: Volume I: The Fearsome Foursome. Jones, Kelley, illus. 2016. (Tales from the Haunted Mansion Ser.: 1). (ENG.). 240p. (J). (gr. 3-7). 14.99 *(978-1-4847-1329-7(X))* Disney Pr.

Beiko, S. M. The Lake & the Library. l.t. ed. 2013. 542p. pap. *(978-1-4596-6871-3(5))* ReadHowYouWant.com, Ltd.

Beinstein, Phoebe & Silverhardt, Lauryn. Dora's Little Library. 2009. (Dora the Explorer Ser.). (ENG.). 70p. (J). 6.99 *(978-1-4169-8029-2(6)*, Simon Spotlight/Nickelodeon) Simon Spotlight/Nickelodeon.

Bertram, Debbie & Bloom, Susan. The Best Book to Read. Garland, Michael, illus. 2011. (ENG.). 32p. (J). (gr. -1-2). pap. 7.99 *(978-0-375-87300-3(7)*, Dragonfly Bks.) Random Hse. Children's Bks.

Blue, Rose, et al. Ron's Big Mission. Tate, Don, illus. 2009. (ENG.). 32p. (J). (gr. 1-3). 16.99 *(978-0-525-47849-2(3)*, Dutton Books for Young Readers) Penguin Young Readers Group.

Brown, Marc. D W 's Library Card. 2003. (Arthur's Little Sister, DW Ser.: 7). (J). (gr. -1-2). lib. bdg. 17.20 *(978-0-613-71812-7(7)*, Turtleback) Turtleback Bks.

—D. W.'s Library Card. Brown, Marc, illus. 2003. (ENG., Illus.). 24p. (J). (gr. -1-3). pap. 7.00 *(978-0-316-73820-0(4))* Little, Brown Bks. for Young Readers.

Brown, Marc & Sarfatti, Esther. D. W. y el Carne de Biblioteca. 2004.Tr. of D.W.'s Library Card. (ENG & SPA., Illus.). (J). pap. 6.95 *(978-1-930332-47-8(5))* Lectorum Pubns., Inc.

Brown, Monica. Waiting for the Biblioburro. Parra, John, illus. 2011. (ENG.). 32p. (J). (gr. k-3). 16.99 *(978-1-58246-353-7(0)*, Tricycle Pr.) Random Hse. Children's Bks.

Browne, Anthony. Willy's Stories. Browne, Anthony, illus. 2015. (ENG., Illus.). 32p. (J). (gr. k-3). 16.99 *(978-0-7636-7761-9(2))* Candlewick Pr.

Bunting, Eve. Our Library. Smith, Maggie, illus. 2008. (ENG.). 32p. (J). (gr. -1-3). 16.00 *(978-0-618-49458-3(8))* Houghton Mifflin Harcourt Publishing Co.

Butler, Dori H. The Hide-And-Seek Ghost. 2016. (Haunted Library: 8). lib. bdg. 14.75 *(978-0-606-38838-2(9))* Turtleback Bks.

Butler, Dori Hillestad. The Case of the Library Monster. Tugeau, Jeremy, illus. 2012. (Buddy Files Ser.: 5). (J). lib. bdg. 16.00 *(978-0-606-23839-7(5)*, Turtleback) Turtleback Bks.

—The Haunted Library. 2014. (Haunted Library: 1). lib. bdg. 14.75 *(978-0-606-35702-9(5))* Turtleback Bks.

—The Haunted Library #1. Damant, Aurore, illus. 2014. (Haunted Library: 1). (ENG.). 128p. (J). (gr. 1-3). 5.99 *(978-0-448-46242-4(7)*, Grosset & Dunlap) Penguin Young Readers Group.

—The Hide-and-Seek Ghost. Damant, Aurore, illus. 2016. (Haunted Library: 8). (ENG.). 128p. (J). (gr. 1-3). 5.99 *(978-0-448-48942-1(2)*, Grosset & Dunlap) Penguin Young Readers Group.

Butler, Dori Hillestad & dePaola, Tomie. The Secret Room. Damant, Aurore, illus. 2015. (Haunted Library: 5). (ENG.). 128p. (J). (gr. 1-3). 5.99 *(978-0-448-48332-0(7)*, Grosset & Dunlap) Penguin Young Readers Group.

Buzbee, Lewis. Steinbeck's Ghost. 2010. (ENG.). 368p. (J). (gr. 5-9). pap. 18.99 *(978-0-312-60211-6(1)*, 9780312602116) Square Fish.

Buzzeo, Toni. Fire up with Reading! Yoshikawa, Sachiko, illus. 2007. 32p. 17.95 *(978-1-60213-019-7(1)*, Upstart Bks.) Highsmith Inc.

—The Great Dewey Hunt. Yoshikawa, Sachiko, illus. 2009. (Mrs. Skorupski Story Ser.). (J). 36p. (gr. -1-3). 17.95 *(978-1-60213-041-8(8))*; *(978-1-60213-029-6(9))* Highsmith Inc. (Upstart Bks.).

—The Library Doors. Westcott, Nadine Bernard, illus. 2008. (J). (gr. -1-3). 17.95 *(978-1-60213-037-1(X))*; *(978-1-60213-027-2(2))* Highsmith Inc. (Upstart Bks.).

—No T. Rex in the Library. Yoshikawa, Sachiko, illus. 2010. (ENG.). 32p. (J). (gr. -1-3). 17.99 *(978-1-4169-3927-6(X)*, McElderry, Margaret K. Bks.) McElderry, Margaret K. Bks.

—Our Librarian Won't Tell Us Anything! Yoshikawa, Sachiko, illus. 2006. 32p. (J). (gr. -1-k). lib. bdg. 17.95 *(978-1-932146-73-8(3)*, Upstart Bks.) Highsmith Inc.

—Penelope Popper, Book Doctor. Christy, Jana, illus. 2011. 32p. (J). 17.95 *(978-1-60213-054-8(X)*, Upstart Bks.) Highsmith Inc.

Caine, Rachel, pseud. Paper & Fire. (Great Library: 2). (ENG.). (YA). (gr. 9). 2017. 400p. pap. 9.99 ***(978-0-451-47314-1(0))*** 2016. 368p. 17.99 *(978-0-451-47240-3(3))* Penguin Publishing Group. (Berkley).

—Paper & Fire. 2017. (Great Library: 2). lib. bdg. 20.85 ***(978-0-606-40361-0(2))*** Turtleback Bks.

Capucilli, Alyssa Satin. Biscuit Loves the Library. Schories, Pat, illus. 2014. (My First I Can Read Ser.). (ENG.). 32p. (J). (gr. -1-3). 16.99 *(978-0-06-193507-7(7))*; pap. 3.99 *(978-0-06-193506-0(9))* HarperCollins Pubs.

Carle, Eric. My Very First Library, 5 vols. Carle, Eric, illus. 2006. (ENG., Illus.). 72p. (J). (gr. -1 — 1). bds. 23.99 *(978-0-399-24666-1(5)*, Philomel Bks.) Penguin Young Readers Group.

Carnavas, Peter. The Children Who Loved Books. Carnavas, Peter, illus. 2013. (ENG., Illus.). 32p. (J). 11.99 *(978-1-61067-145-3(7))* Kane Miller.

Casale, Karen. Never Let a Ghost Borrow Your Library Book: Book Care Guidelines from the Library Secret Service. Rebora, Cecilia, illus. 2012. 32p. (J). 17.75 *(978-1-60213-061-6(2)*, Upstart Bks.) Highsmith Inc.

Casanova, Mary. The Day Dirk Yeller Came to Town. Hoyt, Ard, illus. 2011. (ENG.). 36p. (J). (gr. -1-3). 16.99 *(978-0-374-31742-3(9)*, 9780374317423, Farrar, Straus & Giroux (BYR)) Farrar, Straus & Giroux.

Chapman, Susan Margaret. Too Much Noise in the Library. Carter, Abby, illus. 2010. 32p. (J). (gr. 1-4). 17.95 *(978-1-60213-026-5(4)*, Upstart Bks.) Highsmith Inc.

Child, Lauren. But Excuse Me That Is My Book. Child, Lauren, illus. 2006. (Charlie & Lola Ser.). (ENG., Illus.). 32p. (J). (gr. -1-3). 16.99 *(978-0-8037-3096-0(9)*, Dial Bks) Penguin Young Readers Group.

Clifford, Eth. Help! I'm a Prisoner in the Library. Hughes, George, illus. 2004. (Jo-Beth & Mary Rose Mystery Ser.). (ENG.). 112p. (J). (gr. 2-5). pap. 6.99 *(978-0-618-49482-8(0))* Houghton Mifflin Harcourt Publishing Co.

Colfer, Eoin. The Legend of Spud Murphy. McCoy, Glenn, illus. 2005. (Eoin Colfer's Legend Of... Ser.). 95p. (gr. 2-6). 16.00 *(978-0-7569-6514-3(4))* Perfection Learning Corp.

Colin, Thompson. How to Live Forever. 2008. 32p. 16.99 *(978-0-681-49757-3(2)*, State Street Pr.) Borders Pr.

Cotten, Cynthia. The Book Boat's In. Lessac, Frané, illus. 2013. (ENG.). 32p. (J). (gr. 1-5). 16.95 *(978-0-8234-2521-1(5))* Holiday Hse., Inc.

Cousins, Lucy. Maisy Goes to the Library. Cousins, Lucy, illus. 2009. (Maisy Ser.). (ENG., Illus.). 32p. (J). (gr. k-k). pap. 6.99 *(978-0-7636-4371-3(8))* Candlewick Pr.

—Maisy Goes to the Library. 2009. (Maisy First Experiences Ser.). lib. bdg. 17.20 *(978-0-606-06687-7(X)*, Turtleback) Turtleback Bks.

Dahl, Michael. Blood in the Library, 1 vol. Kendall, Bradford, illus. 2011. (Return to the Library of Doom Ser.). (ENG.). 72p. (gr. 1-3). lib. bdg. 23.99 *(978-1-4342-3228-1(X)*, Zone Bks.) Stone Arch Bks.

—Death Sentence. Evergreen, Nelson, illus. 2015. (Library of Doom: the Final Chapters Ser.). (ENG.). 40p. (gr. 1-3). 23.99 *(978-1-4342-9678-8(4))* Stone Arch Bks.

—Dictionary of 1,000 Rooms, 1 vol. Kendall, Bradford, illus. 2011. (Return to the Library of Doom Ser.). (ENG.). 72p. (gr. 1-3). lib. bdg. 23.99 *(978-1-4342-3229-8(8)*, Zone Bks.) Stone Arch Bks.

—Don't Open It! Kendall, Bradford, illus. 2016. 40p. (J). *(978-1-4747-1054-1(9))* Stone Arch Bks.

—Inkfoot, 1 vol. Kendall, Bradford, illus. 2010. (Return to the Library of Doom Ser.). (ENG.). 72p. (gr. 1-3). 23.99 *(978-1-4342-2146-9(6)*, Zone Bks.) Stone Arch Bks.

—The Last Word. Kendall, Bradford, illus. 2016. 40p. (J). *(978-1-4747-1055-8(7))* Stone Arch Bks.

—The Lost Page. Evergreen, Nelson, illus. 2015. (Library of Doom: the Final Chapters Ser.). (ENG.). 40p. (gr. 1-3). 23.99 *(978-1-4342-9679-5(2))* Stone Arch Bks.

—Night of the Scrawler. Kendall, Bradford, illus. 2016. 40p. (J). *(978-1-4747-1056-5(5))* Stone Arch Bks.

—The Spine Tingler. Evergreen, Nelson, illus. 2015. (Library of Doom: the Final Chapters Ser.). (ENG.). 40p. (gr. 1-3). 23.99 *(978-1-4342-9680-1(6))* Stone Arch Bks.

—Thesaurus Rex. Kendall, Bradford, illus. 2016. 40p. (J). *(978-1-4747-1057-2(3))* Stone Arch Bks.

—Tome Raider. Evergreen, Nelson, illus. 2015. (Library of Doom: the Final Chapters Ser.). (ENG.). 40p. (gr. 1-3). 23.99 *(978-1-4342-9677-1(6))* Stone Arch Bks.

—Zombie in the Library, 1 vol. Kendall, Bradford, illus. 2010. (Return to the Library of Doom Ser.). (ENG.). 72p. (gr. 1-3). lib. bdg. 23.99 *(978-1-4342-2145-2(8)*, Zone Bks.) Stone Arch Bks.

de Las Casas, Dianne. There's a Dragon in the Library, 1 vol. Gentry, Marita, illus. 2011. (ENG.). 32p. (J). (gr. k-3). 16.99 *(978-1-58980-844-7(4))* Pelican Publishing Co., Inc.

De Smet, Marian. Anna's Tight Squeeze. Meijer, Marja, illus. 2003. Orig. Title: Op Slot. 32p. (J). pap. 5.95 *(978-1-58925-378-0(7))* Tiger Tales.

Deedy, Carmen Agra. The Library Dragon, 1 vol. White, Michael P., illus. 2012. (ENG.). 32p. (J). 19.95 *(978-1-56145-639-0(X))* Peachtree Pubs.

—Return of the Library Dragon, 1 vol. White, Michael P., illus. 2012. (ENG.). 32p. (J). 16.95 *(978-1-56145-621-5(7))* Peachtree Pubs.

Dewdney, Anna. Llama Llama's Little Library. 2013. (Llama Llama Ser.). (ENG., Illus.). 56p. (J). (— 1). bds. 23.96 *(978-0-670-01648-8(9)*, Viking Books for Young Readers) Penguin Young Readers Group.

Downey, Lisa & Fox, Kathleen. The Pirates of Plagiarism. Downey, Lisa, illus. 2010. (Illus.). 32p. (J). (gr. 1-4). lib. bdg. 17.95 *(978-1-60213-053-1(1)*, Upstart Bks.) Highsmith Inc.

Eland, Lindsay. A Summer of Sundays. 2013. (ENG.). 336p. (J). (gr. 3-7). 16.99 *(978-1-60684-030-6(4)*, Carolrhoda Bks.) Lerner Publishing Group.

Emerson, Carl. Monster Boy at the Library, 1 vol. Levin, Lon, illus. 2008. (Monster Boy Ser.). (ENG.). 32p. (gr. -1-4). 28.50 *(978-1-60270-235-6(7)*, Looking Glass Library) ABDO Publishing Co.

Enderle, Dotti. The Library Gingerbread Man. Madden, Colleen M., illus. 2010. 32p. (J). (gr. -1). 17.95 *(978-1-60213-048-7(5)*, Upstart Bks.) Highsmith Inc.

Fairstein, Linda. Into the Lion's Den. 2016. (Devlin Quick Mysteries Ser.). (ENG.). 320p. (J). (gr. 3-7). 16.99 *(978-0-399-18643-1(3)*, Dial Bks) Penguin Young Readers Group.

Forte, Lauren. Olivia Goes to the Library. 2013. (Olivia Ready-To-Read Level 1 Ser.). lib. bdg. 13.55 *(978-0-606-35186-7(8))* Turtleback Bks.

Freeman, Don. Quiet! There's a Canary in the Library. 2009. (ENG.). 48p. (J). (gr. -1-k). pap. 7.99 *(978-0-14-241452-1(2)*, Puffin Books) Penguin Young Readers Group.

Garland, Michael. Miss Smith & the Haunted Library. 2012. (ENG.). 32p. (J). (gr. -1-2). 6.99 *(978-0-14-242122-2(7)*, Puffin Books) Penguin Young Readers Group.

—Miss Smith & the Haunted Library. Garland, Michael, illus. 2009. (ENG., Illus.). 32p. (J). (gr. -1-2). 16.99 *(978-0-525-42139-9(4)*, Dutton Books for Young Readers) Penguin Young Readers Group.

Gassman, Julie. Do Not Bring Your Dragon to the Library. Elkerton, Andy, illus. 2016. (Fiction Picture Bks.). (ENG.). 32p. (gr. -1-2). lib. bdg. 21.32 *(978-1-4795-9175-6(0)*, Fiction Picture Bks.) Picture Window Bks.

—Do Not Bring Your Dragon to the Library. Elkerton, Andy, illus. 2016. (ENG.). 32p. (gr. -1-2). 14.95 *(978-1-62370-651-7(3))* Capstone Young Readers of Coughlan Cos.

Gómez Cerdá, Alfredo. El Monstruo y la Bibliotecaria. 4th ed. (SPA., Illus.). 62p. (J). (gr. 3-5). *(978-84-279-3456-6(4)*, NG1580) Noguer y Caralt Editores, S. A. ESP. Dist: Lectorum Pubns., Inc.

González, Lucía. The Storyteller's Candle: La Velita de Los Cuentos. Delacre, Lulu, illus. 2013. (ENG & SPA.). 32p. (J). pap. 9.95 *(978-0-89239-237-7(1)*, Children's Book Press) Lee & Low Bks., Inc.

Grabenstein, Chris. Escape from Mr. Lemoncello's Library. (ENG.). (J). (gr. 3-7). 2014. 336p. 7.99 *(978-0-307-93147-4(1)*, Yearling) 2013. 304p. 17.99 *(978-0-375-87089-7(X)*, Random Hse. Bks. for Young Readers) 2013. 304p. lib. bdg. 19.99 *(978-0-375-97089-4(4)*, Random Hse. Bks. for Young Readers) 2017. 336p. 7.99 ***(978-0-525-58037-9(9)***, Yearling) Random Hse. Children's Bks.

—Escape from Mr. Lemoncello's Library. 2014. lib. bdg. 18.40 *(978-0-606-37114-8(1))* Turtleback Bks.

—Mr. Lemoncello's Library Olympics. (ENG., (J). (gr. 3-7). 2017. Illus.). 320p. 7.99 ***(978-0-553-51042-3(8)***, Yearling) 2016. 288p. 16.99 *(978-0-553-51040-9(1)*, Random Hse. Bks. for Young Readers) 2016. 288p. lib. bdg. 19.99 *(978-0-553-51041-6(X)*, Random Hse. Bks. for Young Readers) Random Hse. Children's Bks.

—Mr. Lemoncello's Library Olympics. 2017. lib. bdg. 18.40 ***(978-0-606-39875-6(9))*** Turtleback Bks.

Grambling, Lois G. Can I Bring Woolly to the Library, Ms. Reeder? Love, Judy, illus. 2012. (Prehistoric Pets Ser.). (ENG.). 32p. (J). (gr. k-3). pap. 7.95 *(978-1-58089-282-7(5))*; lib. bdg. 16.95 *(978-1-58089-281-0(7))* Charlesbridge Publishing, Inc.

Grau, Sheila & Sutphin, Joe. Gorilla Tactics. 2017. (Dr. Critchlore's School for Minions Ser.). (ENG., Illus.). 320p. (J). (gr. 3-7). pap. 7.95 *(978-1-4197-2645-3(5)*, Amulet Bks.) Abrams, Inc.

Greene, Rhonda Gowler. No Pirates Allowed! Said Library Lou. Ajhar, Brian, illus. 2013. (ENG.). 40p. (J). (gr. 1-3). 15.95 *(978-1-58536-796-2(6)*, 202364) Sleeping Bear Pr.

Gutman, Dan. Rappy Goes to the Library. Bowers, Tim, illus. 2017. (I Can Read Level 2 Ser.). 32p. (J). (gr. -1-3). pap. 3.99 *(978-0-06-225265-4(8))* HarperCollins Pubs.

Harper, Charise Mericle. A Big Surprise for Little Card. Raff, Anna, illus. 2016. (ENG.). 40p. (J). (gr. -1-3). 16.99 *(978-0-7636-7485-4(0))* Candlewick Pr.

Harris, Wendy. Daniel Visits the Library. 2015. (Daniel Tiger's Neighborhood Ready-To-Read Ser.). lib. bdg. 13.55 *(978-0-606-37875-8(8))* Turtleback Bks.

Harrison, Paul. Noisy Books. Fiorin, Fabiano, illus. 2009. (Get Ready (Windmill Books) Ser.). 32p. (J). (gr. k-2). lib. bdg. 22.60 *(978-1-60754-258-2(7))* Windmill Bks.

Hillert, Margaret. Dear Dragon Goes to the Library. Schimmell, David, illus. 2008. (BeginningtoRead Ser.). 32p. (J). (gr. k-2). lib. bdg. 22.60 *(978-1-59953-160-1(7))* Norwood Hse. Pr.

—Dear Dragon Goes to the Library (Querido Dragon Va a la Biblioteca) Del Risco, Eida, tr. from ENG. Schimmell, David, illus. 2010. (BeginningtoRead Ser.). (SPA & ENG.). 32p. (J). (gr. k-2). lib. bdg. 22.60 *(978-1-59953-361-2(8))* Norwood Hse. Pr.

—Querido Dragón Va a la Biblioteca/Dear Dragon Goes to the Library. del Risco, Eida, tr. Schimmell, David, illus. 2010. (BeginningtoRead Ser.). 32p. (J). (-2). pap. 11.94 *(978-1-60357-549-2(9))* Norwood Hse. Pr.

Hoffman, Mary. Special Powers. 200p. pap. *(978-0-340-62670-2(4))* Hodder & Stoughton.

Hopkins, Jackie Mims. Picture Book & Library Lessons. Thornburgh, Rebecca, illus. 2004. 32p. (gr. -1-2). 16.95 *(978-1-932146-27-1(X)*, K67-39703, Upstart Bks.) Highsmith Inc.

—The Shelf Elf. Thornburgh, Rebecca McKillip, illus. 2004. (J). (gr. k-3). 17.95 *(978-1-932146-16-5(4)*, 1237659) Highsmith Inc.

—The Shelf Elf Helps Out. Thornburgh, Rebecca McKillip, illus. 2006. (J). *(978-1-932146-45-5(8)*, Upstart Bks.) Highsmith Inc.

Hopkins, Lee Bennett. Jumping off Library Shelves. Manning, Jane, illus. 2015. (ENG.). 32p. (J). (gr. k). 17.95 *(978-1-59078-924-7(5)*, 1396014, Wordsong) Boyds Mills Pr.

Jennings, Sharon, et al. Franklin's Library Book. Gagnon, Céleste, illus. 2005. 32p. (J). *(978-0-439-82297-8(1))* Scholastic, Inc.

Johnson, Angela. Lottie Paris & the Best Place. Fischer, Scott M., illus. 2013. (ENG.). 32p. (J). (gr. k-4). 16.99 *(978-0-689-87378-2(6)*, Simon & Schuster Bks. For Young Readers) Simon & Schuster Bks. For Young Readers.

Joyce, William. The Fantastic Flying Books of Mr. Morris Lessmore. 2006. *(978-0-06-050838-8(8))* HarperCollins Canada, Ltd.

—The Fantastic Flying Books of Mr. Morris Lessmore. Joyce, William & Bluhm, Joe, illus. 2012. (ENG.). 56p. (J). (gr. -1-3). 18.99 *(978-1-4424-5702-7(3)*, Atheneum Bks. for Young Readers) Simon & Schuster Children's Publishing.

Just Mrs. Goose. 2004. (Illus.). 152p. 12.95 *(978-0-9746457-0-4(2))* Green Mansion Pr. LLC.

Kerrin, Jessica Scott. The Spotted Dog Last Seen, 1 vol. 2013. (ENG.). 196p. (J). 14.95 *(978-1-55498-387-2(8))* Groundwood Bks. CAN. Dist: Publishers Group West (PGW).

Kirby, Matthew J. Cave of Wonders. 2013. (Infinity Ring Ser.: 5). (ENG.). 192p. (J). (gr. 3-7). 16.99 *(978-0-545-48460-2(X))* Scholastic, Inc.

Kirk, Daniel. Library Mouse, No. 1. 2007. (ENG., Illus.). 32p. (J). (gr. 1-4). 17.95 *(978-0-8109-9346-4(5)*, Abrams Bks. for Young Readers) Abrams, Inc.

—Library Mouse. 2010. (ENG., Illus.). 32p. (J). (gr. 1-4). pap. 7.95 *(978-0-8109-8929-0(8))* UK Abrams Bks. for Young Readers.

—Library Mouse: A World to Explore. 2010. (ENG., Illus.). 32p. (J). (gr. 1-4). 17.95 *(978-0-8109-8968-9(9)*, Abrams Bks. for Young Readers) Abrams, Inc.

—Library Mouse: Home Sweet Home. 2013. (ENG., Illus.). 40p. (J). (gr. 1-4). 17.95 *(978-1-4197-0544-1(X)*, Abrams Bks. for Young Readers) Abrams, Inc.

—Library Mouse Bk. 2: A Friend's Tale. 2009. (ENG., Illus.). 32p. (J). (gr. 1-4). 17.95 *(978-0-8109-8927-6(1)*, Abrams Bks. for Young Readers) Abrams, Inc.

—Library Mouse No. 2: A Friend's Tale. 2010. (ENG., Illus.). 32p. (J). (gr. 1-4). pap. 7.95 *(978-0-8109-8930-6(1))* UK Abrams Bks. for Young Readers.

Klein, Adria F. Max Goes to the Library. Gallagher-Cole, Mernie, illus. (Read-It! Readers: the Life of Max Ser.). (ENG.). 24p. (gr. -1-2). 2007. per. 3.95 *(978-1-4048-3062-2(6))* 2005. lib. bdg. 21.32 *(978-1-4048-1182-9(6))* Picture Window Bks. (Easy Readers).

—Max Va a la Biblioteca, 1 vol. Lozano, Clara, tr. Gallagher-Cole, Mernie, illus. 2007. (Read-It! Readers en Español: la Vida de Max Ser.). (SPA.). 24p. (gr. -1-3). per. 3.95 *(978-1-4048-3036-3(7)*, Easy Readers) Picture Window Bks.

—Tia Tape Measure, 1 vol. Rowland, Andrew, illus. 2011. (Tool School Ser.). (ENG.). 32p. (gr. 1-2). pap. 6.25 *(978-1-4342-3388-2(X))*; lib. bdg. 22.65 *(978-1-4342-3046-1(5))* Stone Arch Bks.

Klimo, Kate. Dragon Keepers #3: the Dragon in the Library. Shroades, John, illus. 2011. (Dragon Keepers Ser.). (ENG.). 240p. (J). (gr. 3-7). 6.99 *(978-0-375-85592-4(0)*, Yearling) Random Hse. Children's Bks.

Knudsen, Michelle. Library Lion. Hawkes, Kevin, illus. 2006. (ENG.). 48p. (J). (gr. -1-3). 16.99 *(978-0-7636-2262-6(1))* Candlewick Pr.

—Library Lion. Hawkes, Kevin, illus. 2009. (ENG.). 48p. (J). (gr. -1-3). pap. 6.99 *(978-0-7636-3784-2(X))* Candlewick Pr.

—Library Lion. 2009. lib. bdg. 17.20 *(978-0-606-06666-2(7),* Turtleback) Turtleback Bks.

Kohara, Kazuno. The Midnight Library. Kohara, Kazuno, illus. 2014. (ENG., Illus.). 32p. (J). (gr. -1-1). 16.99 *(978-1-59643-985-6(8),* 9781596439856) Roaring Brook Pr.

Kuphal, Shirley M. Flavor's Wild Wish. 2008. 36p. pap. 21.99 *(978-1-4363-0656-0(6))* Xlibris Corp.

Lasky, Kathryn. Lost Tales of Ga'Hoole. Huang, Kathryn, illus. 2010. (Guardians of Ga'hoole Ser.). (ENG.). 192p. (J). (gr. 3-7). 6.99 *(978-0-545-10244-5(8),* Scholastic Paperbacks) Scholastic, Inc.

—Spiders on the Case. Gilpin, Stephen, illus. (Deadlies Ser.). (ENG.). 176p. (J). (gr. 2-5). 2012. pap. 5.99 *(978-0-545-11731-9(3))*Bk. 2. 2011. 15.99 *(978-0-545-11682-4(1))* Scholastic, Inc. (Scholastic Pr.).

Lies, Brian. Bats at the Library. 2014. (Bat Book Ser.). (ENG., Illus.). 32p. (J). (gr. -1-3). pap. 7.99 *(978-0-544-33920-0(7),* HMH Books For Young Readers) Houghton Mifflin Harcourt Publishing Co.

—Bats at the Library. Lies, Brian, illus. 2008. (Bat Book Ser.). (ENG., Illus.). 32p. (J). (gr. -1-3). 17.99 *(978-0-618-99923-1(X))* Houghton Mifflin Harcourt Publishing Co.

London, Jonathan. Froggy Goes to the Library. Remkiewicz, Frank, illus. 2016. (Froggy Ser.). (ENG.). 32p. (J). (gr. -1-k). 16.99 *(978-0-670-01573-3(3),* Viking Books for Young Readers) Penguin Young Readers Group.

Luper, Eric. The Haunted Howl. 2016. (Key Hunters Ser.: 3). (ENG., Illus.). 128p. (J). (gr. 2-5). pap. 4.99 *(978-0-545-82211-4(4),* Scholastic Paperbacks) Scholastic, Inc.

—The Mysterious Moonstone. 2016. (Key Hunters Ser.: 1). (ENG., Illus.). 128p. (J). (gr. 2-5). pap. 4.99 *(978-0-545-82204-6(1))* Scholastic, Inc.

—The Spy's Secret. 2016. (Key Hunters Ser.: 2). (ENG.). 128p. (J). (gr. 2-5). pap. 4.99 *(978-0-545-82206-0(8))* Scholastic, Inc.

—The Titanic Treasure. 2017. (Key Hunters Ser.: 5). (ENG.). 128p. (J). (gr. 2-5). pap. 4.99 ***(978-1-338-14926-5(1),*** Scholastic Paperbacks) Scholastic, Inc.

—The Titanic Treasure (Key Hunters #5) 2017. (Key Hunters Ser.: 5). (ENG.). 128p. (J). (gr. 2-5). lib. bdg. 16.99 ***(978-1-338-14927-2(X),*** Scholastic Paperbacks) Scholastic, Inc.

Luper, Eric. The Wizard's War (Key Hunters #4) 2017. (Key Hunters Ser.: 4). (ENG.). 128p. (J). (gr. 2-5). pap. 4.99 *(978-0-545-82213-8(0),* Scholastic Paperbacks) Scholastic, Inc.

Lynellen Sullivan & Bryan Castle. Poppers to the Rescue: Book 1 of the Popcorn Series. 2010. 72p. pap. 8.95 *(978-1-4401-9764-2(4))* iUniverse, Inc.

MacHale, D.j. Black Moon Rising. 2017. (J). pap. ***(978-1-101-93260-5(0))*** Random Hse., Inc.

Machale, D.j. The Library: Mysterious Messenger (Book 1) 2016. (Library: 1). (ENG.). 256p. (J). (gr. 3-7). 16.99 *(978-1-101-93253-7(8),* Random Hse. Bks. for Young Readers) Random Hse. Children's Bks.

Malaspina, Ann. Finding Lincoln. Bootman, Colin, illus. 2009. (ENG.). 32p. (J). (gr. 2-3). 16.99 *(978-0-8075-2435-0(2))* Whitman, Albert & Co.

Maloney, Peter & Zekausakas, Felicia. Late for the Library: Just Schoolin' Around Series. 2004. (Just Schoolin' Around Ser.). (Illus.). (J). *(978-0-439-55361-2(X))* Scholastic, Inc.

McDonald, Megan. When the Library Lights Go Out. Tillotson, Katherine, illus. 2009. (ENG.). 40p. (J). (gr. -1-1). 8.99 *(978-1-4169-8028-5(8),* Atheneum Bks. for Young Readers) Simon & Schuster Children's Publishing.

—When the Library Lights Go Out. Tillotson, Katherine, tr. Tillotson, Katherine, illus. 2005. (ENG.). 40p. (J). (gr. -1-3). 19.99 *(978-0-689-86170-3(2),* Atheneum/Richard Jackson Bks.) Simon & Schuster Children's Publishing.

McQuinn, Anna. Lola at the Library. Beardshaw, Rosalind, illus. 2007. 22p. (gr. -1). 16.95 *(978-0-7569-7931-7(5))* Perfection Learning Corp.

Meister, Cari. Shark in the Library!, 1 vol. Simard, Remy, illus. (My First Graphic Novel Ser.). (ENG.). 32p. (gr. k-2). 2011. pap. 6.25 *(978-1-4342-3104-8(6))* 2010. 24.65 *(978-1-4342-2058-5(3))* Stone Arch Bks. (My First Graphic Novel).

Miller, Amanda. The Library's Secret: A Hidden Adventure. 2010. 88p. pap. 10.49 *(978-1-4520-7012-4(1))* AuthorHouse.

Miller, Pat. We're Going on a Book Hunt. Bernard Westcott, Nadine, illus. 2008. (J). (gr. -1). 17.95 *(978-1-60213-034-0(5),* Upstart Bks.) Highsmith Inc.

Miller, William. Richard Wright y el Carne de Biblioteca. Christie, Gregory R., illus. 2003. (SPA.). (J). 32p. 16.95 *(978-1-58430-180-6(5));* pap. 6.95 *(978-1-58430-181-3(3))* Lee & Low Bks., Inc.

Montoya, Martha, creator. No, no a la Biblioteca! Take-Home. 2005. (Los Kitos Ser.). (SPA.). (YA). (gr. 1-3). 15.00 *(978-0-8215-8812-3(5))* Sadlier, William H. Inc.

Mora, Pat. Tomas & the Library Lady. Colón, Raúl, illus. 2007. (gr. k-3). 18.00 *(978-0-7569-7935-5(8))* Perfection Learning Corp.

—Tomas y la Senora de la Biblioteca. 2004. (SPA., Illus.). (J). (gr. k-3). spiral bd. *(978-0-616-03092-9(4))* Canadian National Institute for the Blind/Institut National Canadien pour les Aveugles.

Mörchen, Roland. Wir Gehen in Die Bibliothek - A Visit to the Library: Deutsch-Englische Ausgabe. Kiefer, Katja, illus. 2010. (ENG.). 40p. (J). (gr. 3-7). 19.99 *(978-3-487-08843-3(6))* Olms, Georg Verlag AG DEU. Dist: Independent Pubs. Group.

Morris, Carla. The Boy Who Was Raised by Librarians, 1 vol. Sneed, Brad, illus. 2007. (ENG.). 32p. (J). (gr. k-3). 16.95 *(978-1-56145-391-7(9))* Peachtree Pubs.

Morrison, Toni & Morrison, Slade. Please, Louise. Strickland, Shadra, illus. 2014. (ENG.). 32p. (J). (gr. -1-3). 17.99 *(978-1-4169-8338-5(4),* Simon & Schuster Bks. For Young Readers) Simon & Schuster Bks. For Young Readers.

Morton, Carlene. The Library Pages. Docampo, Valeria, illus. 2010. 32p. (J). (gr. k-4). 17.95 *(978-1-60213-045-6(0),* Upstart Bks.) Highsmith Inc.

Nickerson, Sara. How to Disappear Completely & Never Be Found. Comport, Sally Wern, illus. 2003. (ENG.). 288p. (J). (gr. 5-18). pap. 5.99 *(978-0-06-441027-4(7))* HarperCollins Pubs.

Numeroff, Laura Joffe. Beatrice Doesn't Want To. Munsinger, Lynn, illus. 2008. (ENG.). 32p. (J). (gr. -1-2). pap. 7.99 *(978-0-7636-3843-6(9))* Candlewick Pr.

OHora, Zachariah. The Not So Quiet Library. 2016. (ENG., Illus.). 40p. (J). (-k). 17.99 *(978-0-8037-4140-9(5),* Dial Bks) Penguin Young Readers Group.

Papp, Lisa. Madeline Finn & the Library Dog, 1 vol. Papp, Lisa, illus. 2016. (ENG., Illus.). 32p. (J). (gr. -1-3). 16.95 *(978-1-56145-910-0(0))* Peachtree Pubs.

Paratore, Coleen Murtagh. The Cupid Chronicles. 2008. (Wedding Planner's Daughter Ser.). (ENG.). 224p. (J). (gr. 4-8). pap. 6.99 *(978-1-4169-5484-2(8),* Aladdin) Simon & Schuster Children's Publishing.

Parish, Herman. Amelia Bedelia, Bookworm. Sweat, Lynn, illus. (I Can Read Level 2 Ser.). (ENG.). 64p. (J). (gr. k-3). 2005. pap. 3.99 *(978-0-06-051892-9(8))* 2003. 17.99 *(978-0-06-051890-5(1))* HarperCollins Pubs. (Greenwillow Bks.).

—Amelia Bedelia, Bookworm. Sweat, Lynn, illus. 2005. (I Can Read Bks.). 63p. (gr. -1-3). 14.00 *(978-0-7569-5766-7(4))* Perfection Learning Corp.

—Amelia Bedelia's Backpack Bundle. Sweat, Lynn, illus. 2012. 192p. (J). *(978-1-4351-4392-0(2),* Greenwillow Bks.) HarperCollins Pubs.

—Amelia Bedelia's First Library Card. Avril, Lynne, illus. 2013. (Amelia Bedelia Ser.). 32p. (J). (gr. -1-3). (ENG.). 17.99 *(978-0-06-209512-1(9));* lib. bdg. 18.89 *(978-0-06-209513-8(7))* HarperCollins Pubs. (Greenwillow Bks.).

Parsley, Elise. If You Ever Want to Bring a Circus to the Library, Don't! 2017. (Magnolia Says DON'T! Ser.). (ENG., Illus.). 40p. (J). (gr. -1-3). 17.99 *(978-0-316-37661-7(2))* Little Brown & Co.

Pauli, Lorenz. Fox in the Library. Schaerer, Kathrin, illus. 2013. (ENG.). 32p. (J). (gr. -1-3). 17.95 *(978-0-7358-4150-5(0))* North-South Bks., Inc.

—The Fox in the Library. Schärer, Kathrin, illus. 2015. (ENG.). 32p. (J). pap. 7.95 *(978-0-7358-4213-7(2))* North-South Bks., Inc.

Pearson, Mary E. I Can Do It All. Shelley, Jeff, illus. 2011. (Rookie Ready to Learn Ser.). (J). (gr. -1-k). (ENG.). 40p. pap. 5.95 *(978-0-531-26654-0(0));* 32p. lib. bdg. 23.00 *(978-0-531-26429-4(7),* Children's Pr.) Scholastic Library Publishing.

Pearson, Mary E. & Shelly, Jeff. Puedo Hacer de Todo. Shelly, Jeff, illus. 2011. (Rookie Ready to Learn Español Ser.).Tr. of I Can Do It All. (SPA., Illus.). 40p. (J). pap. 5.95 *(978-0-531-26787-5(3));* lib. bdg. 23.00 *(978-0-531-26119-4(0))* Scholastic Library Publishing. (Children's Pr.).

Phillips, Dee. Fright at the Freemont Library. 2016. (Cold Whispers II Ser.). (ENG.). 32p. (J). (gr. 2-6). 19.95 *(978-1-944102-36-4(1))* Bearport Publishing Co., Inc.

Plourde, Lynn. The Dump Man's Treasures. Owens, Mary Beth, illus. 2008. (ENG.). 32p. (J). (gr. -1-3). 15.95 *(978-0-89272-725-4(X))* Down East Bks.

Polacco, Patricia. The Mermaid's Purse. Polacco, Patricia, illus. 2016. (ENG., Illus.). 48p. (J). (gr. k-3). 17.99 *(978-0-399-16692-1(0),* G.P. Putnam's Sons Books for Young Readers) Penguin Young Readers Group.

Portman, Frank. Andromeda Klein. 2010. (ENG.). 432p. (YA). (gr. 9). pap. 9.99 *(978-0-385-73526-1(X),* Delacorte Bks. for Young Readers) Random Hse. Children's Bks.

Radlauer, Molly at the Library. 2007. (ENG.). 32p. (J). (gr. -1-2). 8.99 *(978-1-4169-6835-1(0),* Simon & Schuster/Paula Wiseman Bks.) Simon & Schuster/Paula Wiseman Bks.

Reed, M. K. Americus. Hill, Jonathan David, illus. 2011. (ENG.). 224p. (YA). (gr. 7). pap. 16.99 *(978-1-59643-601-5(8),* 9781596436015, First Second Bks.) Roaring Brook Pr.

Rey, H. A. Visits the Library / Jorge el Curioso Va a la Biblioteca. 2011. (Curious George Ser.). (ENG & SPA., Illus.). 24p. (J). (gr. -1-3). pap. 3.99 *(978-0-547-55075-6(8))* Houghton Mifflin Harcourt Publishing Co.

Rey, H. A. & Rey, Margret. Curious George Visits the Library. Weston, Martha, illus. 2013. (Curious George Ser.). (ENG.). 24p. (J). (gr. -1-3). pap. 4.99 *(978-0-544-11450-0(7))* Houghton Mifflin Harcourt Publishing Co.

—Librarian for a Day. 2012. (Curious George TV Tie-In Early Reader Ser.). lib. bdg. 13.55 *(978-0-606-26602-4(X),* Turtleback) Turtleback Bks.

RH Disney Staff, illus. Doc Mcstuffins Little Golden Book Library (Disney Junior: Doc Mcstuffins), 5 vols. 2015. (ENG.). 120p. (J). (-k). 24.95 *(978-0-7364-3407-2(0),* Golden/Disney) Random Hse. Children's Bks.

Robins, Eleanor. Library Book Mystery, 1 vol. unabr. ed. 2011. (Carter High Mysteries Ser.). (ENG.). 48p. (YA). (gr. 9-12). 7.95 *(978-1-61651-564-5(3))* Saddleback Educational Publishing, Inc.

Rockwell, Anne. Library Day. Rockwell, Lizzy, illus. 2016. (My First Experience Book Ser.). (ENG.). 32p. (J). (gr. -1-3). 16.99 *(978-1-4814-2731-9(8),* Aladdin) Simon & Schuster Children's Publishing.

Rockwell, Anne F. Library Day. 2017. lib. bdg. 18.40 ***(978-0-606-39759-9(0))*** Turtleback Bks.

Rylant, Cynthia. Mr. Putter & Tabby Turn the Page. Howard, Arthur, illus. (Mr. Putter & Tabby Ser.). (ENG.). 40p. (J). (gr. 1-4). 2015. pap. 5.99 *(978-0-544-58232-3(2))* 2014. 14.99 *(978-0-15-206063-3(4))* Houghton Mifflin Harcourt Publishing Co. (HMH Books For Young Readers).

—Mr. Putter & Tabby Turn the Page. 2015. (Mr. Putter & Tabby Ser.). lib. bdg. 16.00 *(978-0-606-37453-8(1))* Turtleback Bks.

Santos, Gloria. Good Manners at the Library. 2017. (Manners Matter Ser.). 24p. (gr. 4-6). 23.60 ***(978-1-5081-5728-1(6),*** PowerKids Pr.) Rosen Publishing Group, Inc., The.

Sateren, Shelley Swanson. Max & Zoe at the Library, 1 vol. Sullivan, Mary, illus. 2013. (Max & Zoe Ser.). (ENG.). 32p. (gr. k-2). pap. 5.19 *(978-1-4048-8058-0(5),* Max & Zoe) Picture Window Bks.

Sazaklis, John. Recess Is Ruined. Robinson, Lee, illus. 2016. (Billy Burger, Model Citizen Ser.). (ENG.). 96p. (gr. 2-3). lib. bdg. 22.65 *(978-1-4965-2588-8(4))* Stone Arch Bks.

Schwab, Victoria. The Archived. 2014. (Archived Ser.). (ENG., Illus.). 352p. (YA). (gr. 7-12). pap. 9.99 *(978-1-4231-7108-9(X))* Hyperion Bks. for Children.

Shea, Bob. Dinosaur vs. the Library. Shea, Bob, illus. 2011. (ENG., Illus.). 40p. (J). (gr. -1-1). 16.99 *(978-1-4231-3338-4(2))* Hyperion Pr.

Shulman, Polly. The Grimm Legacy. (ENG.). (J). (gr. 5-18). 2011. 352p. 8.99 *(978-0-14-241904-5(4),* Puffin Books) 2010. (Illus.). 336p. 16.99 *(978-0-399-25096-5(4),* G.P. Putnam's Sons Books for Young Readers) Penguin Young Readers Group.

Sierra, Judy. Mind Your Manners, B. B. Wolf. Seibold, J. Otto, illus. 2012. (ENG.). 40p. (J). (gr. -1-2). pap. 7.99 *(978-0-307-93101-6(3),* Dragonfly Bks.) Random Hse. Children's Bks.

—Mind Your Manners, B. B. Wolf. 2012. lib. bdg. 18.40 *(978-0-606-26784-7(0),* Turtleback) Turtleback Bks.

—Wild about Books. Brown, Marc, tr. Brown, Marc, illus. 2004. (ENG.). 40p. (J). (gr. -1-2). 16.95 *(978-0-375-82538-5(X),* Knopf Bks. for Young Readers) Random Hse. Children's Bks.

Silvestro, Annie. Bunny's Book Club. Mai-Wyss, Tatjana, illus. 2017. (ENG.). 40p. (J). (gr. -1-2). 17.99 *(978-0-553-53758-1(X),* Doubleday Bks. for Young Readers) Random Hse. Children's Bks.

Slater, David Michael. The Boy & the Book. Kolar, Bob, illus. 2015. (ENG.). 32p. (J). (-k). lib. bdg. 16.95 *(978-1-58089-562-0(X))* Charlesbridge Publishing, Inc.

Sneed, Brad. The Boy Who Was Raised by Librarians. Sneed, Brad, illus. 2008. (Illus.). (J). (gr. k-3). 27.95 incl. audio *(978-0-8045-6965-1(7))* Spoken Arts, Inc.

Stanek, Robert, pseud. Buguile Critters Visit the Library. 2011. (Illus.). 28p. pap. 4.99 *(978-1-57545-259-3(6),* Reagent Pr. Bks. for Young Readers) RP Media.

—Visit the Library. 2010. 28p. pap. 8.99 *(978-1-57545-176-3(X),* Reagent Pr. Bks. for Young Readers) RP Media.

StJohn, Amanda. How to Check Out a Book. Ostrom, Bob, illus. 2012. (Library Skills Ser.). (ENG.). 24p. (J). (gr. -1-2). 28.50 *(978-1-61473-249-5(3),* 204951) Child's World, Inc., The.

—How to Find a Book. Ostrom, Bob, illus. 2012. (Library Skills Ser.). (ENG.). 24p. (J). (gr. -1-2). 28.50 *(978-1-61473-250-1(7),* 204952) Child's World, Inc., The.

—How to Treat a Book. Ostrom, Bob, illus. 2012. (Library Skills Ser.). (ENG.). 24p. (J). (gr. -1-2). 28.50 *(978-1-61473-252-5(3),* 204954) Child's World, Inc., The.

Stoop, Naoko. Red Knit Cap Girl & the Reading Tree. 2014. (ENG., Illus.). 40p. (J). (gr. -1-3). 17.00 *(978-0-316-22886-2(9))* Little, Brown Bks. for Young Readers.

Tacang, Brian. Bully-Be-Gone: The Misadventures of Millicent Madding #1. 2006. (Illus.). 216p. (J). (gr. 3-7). 17.89 *(978-0-06-073912-6(6))* HarperCollins Pubs.

Terry, Sonya. L Is for Library. Wong, Nicole, illus. 2006. 32p. (J). (gr. -1-3). lib. bdg. 16.95 *(978-1-932146-44-8(X),* Upstart Bks.) Highsmith Inc.

Thielbar, Melinda. The Book Bandit: A Mystery with Geometry. Grandt, Eve et al, illus. 2010. (Manga Math Mysteries Ser.: 7). (ENG.). 48p. (gr. 3-5). 29.27 *(978-0-7613-4909-9(X))* Lerner Publishing Group.

—The Book Bandit No. 7: A Mystery with Geometry. Lee, Jenn Manley & Chow, Candice, illus. 2011. (Manga Math Mysteries Ser.: 7). (ENG.). 48p. (gr. 3-5). pap. 6.95 *(978-0-7613-8136-5(8),* Graphic Universe™) Lerner Publishing Group.

—#7 the Book Bandit: A Mystery with Geometry. Lee, Jenn Manley & Chow, Candice, illus. 2011. (Manga Math Mysteries Set II Ser.). pap. 39.62 *(978-0-7613-8364-2(6),* Graphic Universe™) Lerner Publishing Group.

Time, Nicholas O. Going, Going, Gone. 2016. (In Due Time Ser.: 1). (ENG., Illus.). 160p. (J). (gr. 3-7). pap. 6.99 *(978-1-4814-6729-2(8),* Simon Spotlight) Simon Spotlight.

—Going, Going, Gone. 2016. (In Due Time Ser.: 1). lib. bdg. 17.20 *(978-0-606-38985-3(7))* Turtleback Bks.

Twohy, Mike. Poindexter Makes a Friend. Twohy, Mike, illus. 2011. (ENG., Illus.). 32p. (J). (gr. -1-3). 15.99 *(978-1-4424-0965-1(7),* Simon & Schuster/Paula Wiseman Bks.) Simon & Schuster/Paula Wiseman Bks.

Vaughan, Grace. Annie & the Magic Book. 2012. 30p. pap. 19.99 *(978-1-4772-5498-1(6))* AuthorHouse.

Wallace, Nancy K. The Haunted Sleepover, 1 vol. Chronister, Amanda, illus. 2013. (Abby & the Book Bunch Ser.). (ENG.). 80p. (J). (gr. 2-5). 27.07 *(978-1-61641-913-4(X))* Magic Wagon.

—Movie Mishaps, 1 vol. Chronister, Amanda, illus. 2013. (Abby & the Book Bunch Ser.). (ENG.). 80p. (J). (gr. 2-5). 27.07 *(978-1-61641-914-1(8))* Magic Wagon.

—The Mystery of the Golden Key, 1 vol. Chronister, Amanda, illus. 2013. (Abby & the Book Bunch Ser.). (ENG.). 80p. (J). (gr. 2-5). 27.07 *(978-1-61641-915-8(6))* Magic Wagon.

—Out to Lunch, 1 vol. Chronister, Amanda, illus. 2013. (Abby & the Book Bunch Ser.). (ENG.). 80p. (J). (gr. 2-5). 27.07 *(978-1-61641-916-5(4))* Magic Wagon.

—Presumed Missing, 1 vol. Chronister, Amanda, illus. 2013. (Abby & the Book Bunch Ser.). (ENG.). 80p. (J). (gr. 2-5). 27.07 *(978-1-61641-917-2(2))* Magic Wagon.

Weatherford, Carole Boston. The Library Ghost. White, Lee, illus. 2008. 22p. (J). (gr. -1-3). 17.95 *(978-1-60213-017-3(5),* Upstart Bks.) Highsmith Inc.

Weston Woods Staff, creator. Wild about Books. 2011. 29.95 *(978-0-439-80485-1(X))* Weston Woods Studios, Inc.

Wexler, Django. The Forbidden Library. 2015. (ENG., Illus.). 400p. (J). (gr. 5). 8.99 *(978-0-14-242681-4(4),* Puffin Books) Penguin Young Readers Group.

—The Mad Apprentice. Jansson, Alexander, illus. 2015. (Forbidden Library). (ENG.). 352p. (J). (gr. 5). 16.99 *(978-0-8037-3976-5(1),* Kathy Dawson Books) Penguin Young Readers Group.

—The Palace of Glass: The Forbidden Library: Volume 3. 2016. (Forbidden Library). (ENG., Illus.). 368p. (J). (gr. 5). 16.99 *(978-0-8037-3978-9(8),* Kathy Dawson Books) Penguin Young Readers Group.

Williams, Zachary. Lions at the Library? 2006. (Neighborhood Readers Ser.). (ENG.). 12p. (gr. 1-3). pap. 5.90 *(978-1-4042-6863-0(4),* Rosen Classroom) Rosen Publishing Group, Inc., The.

Wilson, Sarah. La Mochila de Dora. Roper, Robert, illus. 2003. (Dora the Explorer Ser.).Tr. of Dora's Backpack. (SPA.). 24p. (J). pap. 3.99 *(978-0-689-86306-6(3),* Libros Para Ninos) Libros Para Ninos.

Yoo, Tae-Eun. The Little Red Fish. 2007. (Illus.). (J). *(978-1-4287-3601-6(8),* Dial) Penguin Publishing Group.

LIBRARIES—POETRY

Lewis, J. Patrick. Please Bury Me in the Library. Stone, Kyle M., illus. 2005. (ENG.). 32p. (J). (gr. -1-3). 16.99 *(978-0-15-216387-7(5))* Houghton Mifflin Harcourt Publishing Co.

LIBRARIES, SCHOOL

see School Libraries

LIBRARY ORIENTATION

Here are entered works dealing with the instruction of readers in library use.

Buzzeo, Toni. R Is for Research. Wong, Nicole, illus. 2008. 17.95 *(978-1-60213-032-6(9),* Upstart Bks.) Highsmith Inc.

Hannah, Eileen. Learning about the Library. 2008. (Rosen Real Readers: Upper Emergent Ser.). (ENG., Illus.). 12p. (gr. 1-2). pap. 5.90 *(978-0-8239-8130-4(4))* Rosen Publishing Group, Inc., The.

Harper, Leslie. Cómo Mantenerse Informado. 2014. (Sé un líder de la Comunidad (Be a Community Leader) Ser.). (SPA.). 32p. (J). (gr. 4-6). pap. 60.00 *(978-1-4777-6923-2(4),* PowerKids Pr.) Rosen Publishing Group, Inc., The.

—Cómo Mantenerse Informados. 2014. (Sé un líder de la Comunidad (Be a Community Leader) Ser.). (SPA.). 32p. (J). (gr. 4-6). lib. bdg. 26.25 *(978-1-4777-6921-8(8),* PowerKids Pr.) Rosen Publishing Group, Inc., The.

—How to Stay Informed. 2014. (Be a Community Leader Ser.). 32p. (J). (gr. 4-6). lib. bdg. 26.25 *(978-1-4777-6701-6(0),* PowerKids Pr.) Rosen Publishing Group, Inc., The.

StJohn, Amanda. How a Library Works. Ostrom, Bob, illus. 2012. (Library Skills Ser.). (ENG.). 24p. (J). (gr. -1-2). 28.50 *(978-1-61473-247-1(7),* 204949) Child's World, Inc., The.

Turrell, Linda. Complete Library Skills, Grade 5. rev. ed. 2004. (ENG., Illus.). 128p. (gr. 5-5). pap. 13.99 *(978-0-7424-1955-1(X),* IFG99136, Instructional Fair) Carson-Dellosa Publishing, LLC.

LIBRARY SCIENCE

Here are entered general works on the organization and administration of libraries. Works about services offered by libraries to patrons are entered under Library Service.

Bodden, Valerie. Doing Primary Research. 2012. (Research for Writing Ser.). 48p. (gr. 5-12). 23.95 *(978-1-60818-204-6(5),* Creative Education) Creative Co., The.

—Navigating the Library. 2012. (Research for Writing Ser.). 48p. (gr. 5-12). 23.95 *(978-1-60818-206-0(1),* Creative Education) Creative Co., The.

Carson-Dellosa Publishing Staff. Complete Library Skills. rev. ed. 2004. (ENG.). 128p. (gr. 4-4). pap. 13.99 *(978-0-7424-1954-4(1),* IFG99135); (gr. 6-6). pap. 13.99 *(978-0-7424-1956-8(8),* IFG99137) Carson-Dellosa Publishing, LLC.

—Complete Library Skills, Grades K - 2. rev. ed. 2004. (ENG.). 128p. (gr. k-2). pap. 13.99 *(978-0-7424-1952-0(5),* IFG99138) Carson-Dellosa Publishing, LLC.

Colby, Jennifer. Library. 2016. (21st Century Junior Library: Explore a Workplace Ser.). (ENG., Illus.). 24p. (J). (gr. 2-5). 27.07 *(978-1-63471-075-6(4),* 208379) Cherry Lake Publishing.

Crabtree, Marc. Meet My Neighbor, the Librarian. 2012. (ENG., Illus.). 24p. (J). *(978-0-7787-4559-4(7));* pap. *(978-0-7787-4564-8(3))* Crabtree Publishing Co.

Gaines, Ann Graham. Master the Library & Media Center. 2009. (Ace It! Information Literacy Ser.). (Illus.). 48p. (J). (gr. 2-5). lib. bdg. 25.27 *(978-0-7660-3393-1(7))* Enslow Pubs., Inc.

Gerber, Larry. The Distortion of Facts in the Digital Age. 2012. (Digital & Information Literacy Ser.). (ENG., Illus.). 48p. (YA). (gr. 5-8). 29.25 *(978-1-4488-8357-8(1));* pap. 11.75 *(978-1-4488-8368-4(7))* Rosen Publishing Group, Inc., The. (Rosen Reference).

Guillain, Charlotte. Reading & Writing, 1 vol. 2012. (Jobs If You Like... Ser.). (ENG.). 32p. (gr. 1-3). pap. 8.29 *(978-1-4329-6821-2(1));* lib. bdg. 27.32 *(978-1-4329-6810-6(6))* Heinemann-Raintree. (Heinemann First Library).

Jango-Cohen, Judith. Librarians. 2005. (Pull Ahead Books: Community Helpers Ser.). 32p. (gr. k-3). (ENG.). pap. 7.95 *(978-0-8225-2533-2(X));* (Illus.). (J). lib. bdg. 22.60 *(978-0-8225-1691-0(8))* Lerner Publishing Group.

Library & Information Science. 2nd rev. ed. 2011. (Careers in Focus Ser.). (Illus.). 212p. (gr. 6-12). 32.95 *(978-0-8160-8032-8(1),* Ferguson Publishing Co.) Facts On File, Inc.

LIBRARY SCIENCE—VOCATIONAL GUIDANCE

Ferguson. Discovering Careers for Your Future: Library & Information Science. 2008. (Discovering Careers for Your Future Ser.). 91p. (gr. 4-9). 21.95 *(978-0-8160-7282-8(5),* Ferguson Publishing Co.) Facts On File, Inc.

Kenney, Karen Latchana. Librarians at Work, 1 vol. Dumm, Brian Caleb, illus. 2009. (Meet Your Community Workers Ser.). (ENG.). 32p. (J). (gr. -1-2). 28.50 *(978-1-60270-649-1(2))* Magic Wagon.

Leone, Laura. Choosing a Career in Information Science. (World of Work Ser.). 64p. 2009. (gr. 5-5). 58.50 *(978-1-60854-332-8(3))* 2005. (Illus.). (YA). (gr. 7-12). lib. bdg. 31.95 *(978-0-8239-3569-7(8))* Rosen Publishing Group, Inc., The.

Library & Information Science. 2009. (Career Opportunities Ser.). 392p. (C). (gr. 9-18). pap. 18.95 *(978-0-8160-7547-8(6),* Ferguson Publishing Co.) Facts On File, Inc.

Murray, Julie. Librarians, 1 vol. 2010. (Buddy Bks.). (ENG.). 32p. (J). (gr. 2-5). 27.07 *(978-1-61613-506-5(9))* ABDO Publishing Co.

Taylor, Allan & Parish, James Robert. Library & Information Science. 2009. (Career Opportunities Ser.). (Illus.). 364p. (C). (gr. 9-18). 49.50 *(978-0-8160-7546-1(8),* Ferguson Publishing Co.) Facts On File, Inc.

LIBYA

DiPiazza, Francesca Davis. Libya in Pictures. 2005. (Visual Geography Series, Second Ser.). (Illus.). 80p. (YA). (gr. 7-12). lib. bdg. 27.93 *(978-0-8225-2549-3(6))* Lerner Publishing Group.

Harmon, Daniel E. Libya. 2010. (Major Muslim Nations Ser.). 119p. (YA). (gr. 5-18). lib. bdg. 25.95 *(978-1-4222-1388-9(9))* Mason Crest.

Hasday, Judy L. Libya. Rotberg, Robert I., ed. 2012. (Evolution of Africa's Major Nations Ser.). (Illus.). 80p. (J). (gr. 7). 22.95 *(978-1-4222-2181-5(4))* Mason Crest.

—Libya. 2011. (J). pap. *(978-1-4222-2209-6(8))* Mason Crest.

—Libya. Rotberg, Robert I., ed. 2009. (Africa Ser.). (Illus.). 79p. (YA). (gr. 3-7). lib. bdg. 21.95 *(978-1-4222-0083-4(3))* Mason Crest.

Hunter, Nick. Hoping for Peace in Libya. 2012. (Peace Pen Pals Ser.). (Illus.). 48p. (J). (gr. 6-8). 31.95 *(978-1-4339-7735-0(4))*; pap. 14.05 *(978-1-4339-7736-7(2))* Stevens, Gareth Publishing LLLP.

—Libya, 1 vol. 2012. (Countries Around the World Ser.). (ENG.). 48p. (gr. 3-6). lib. bdg. 33.32 *(978-1-4329-6104-6(7)*, NA-h) Heinemann-Raintree.

Lange, Brenda. Muammar Qaddafi: President of Libya. Schlesinger, Arthur M., Jr., ed. 2005. (Major World Leaders Ser.). (Illus.). 112p. (J). (gr. 6-12). 30.00 *(978-0-7910-8258-4(X)*, Chelsea Hse.) Facts On File, Inc.

Malcolm, Peter & Losienben, Elie. Libya. 2016. (ENG., Illus.). 144p. (J). lib. bdg. *(978-1-5026-0798-0(0))* Cavendish Square Publishing.

O'Neal, Claire. We Visit Libya. 2012. (J). lib. bdg. 33.95 *(978-1-61228-310-4(1))* Mitchell Lane Pubs., Inc.

Rozario, Paul. Libya. 2004. (Countries of the World Ser.). (Illus.). 96p. (gr. 5-12). lib. bdg. 31.00 *(978-0-8368-3111-5(X))* Stevens, Gareth Publishing LLLP.

Sullivan, Kimberly L. Muammar Al-Qaddafi's Libya. 2008. (Dictatorships Ser.). (YA). (gr. 7-12). lib. bdg. 38.60 *(978-0-8225-8666-1(5))* Twenty First Century Bks.

Willis, Terri. Libya. 2008. (Enchantment of the World Ser.). (ENG., Illus.). 144p. (J). (gr. 5-9). 40.00 *(978-0-531-12480-2(0))* Scholastic Library Publishing.

LIBYA—FICTION

Stolz, Joelle. The Shadows of Ghadames. Temerson, Catherine, tr. 2006. (ENG.). 128p. (J). (gr. 3-7). 5.99 *(978-0-440-41949-5(2)*, Yearling) Random Hse. Children's Bks.

LIFE

Bright, Michael. The Future of Life on Earth, 1 vol. 2012. (Web of Life Ser.). (ENG., Illus.). 48p. (gr. 6-10). pap. 9.49 *(978-1-4109-4406-1(9)*, Raintree Freestyle) Heinemann-Raintree.

Kansil, J. Q. Conversations with Opa: Sharing Wisdom about the Universe & Lesser Things. 2011. (ENG.). 168p. pap. 18.00 *(978-1-61614-497-5(1))* Prometheus Bks., Pubs.

Morrison, Matthew. Big Questions: Incredible Adventures in Thinking. Chalk, Gary, illus. 2007. (ENG.). 204p. (J). (gr. 4-8). pap. 7.95 *(978-1-84046-670-6(7))* Icon Bks., Ltd. GBR. Dist: Publishers Group Canada.

Mortensen, Lori. Cycle of Life. 2016. (Spring Forward Ser.). (J). (gr. 2). *(978-1-4900-9474-8(1))* Benchmark Education Co.

Pearce, Q. L. Reincarnation. 2009. (Mysterious Encounters Ser.). (ENG., Illus.). 48p. (gr. 4-8). lib. bdg. 33.60 *(978-0-7377-4412-5(X)*, LML02109-245413, Kidhaven) Cengage Gale.

Prentice-Hall Staff. Parade of Life: Animals. 2nd ed. (J). pap., act. bk. ed. *(978-0-13-400458-7(2))* Prentice Hall (Schl. Div.).

Real Life Issues, 6 vols., Set. Incl. Coping with Absent Parents. Colson, Mary. 32.65 *(978-1-4329-4760-6(5))*; Coping with Bullying. Guillain, Charlotte. 32.65 *(978-1-4329-4761-3(3))*; Coping with Moving Away. Guillain, Charlotte. 32.65 *(978-1-4329-4764-4(8))*; Coping with Unemployment. Colson, Mary. 32.65 *(978-1-4329-4765-1(6))*; (gr. 6-8). (Real Life Issues Ser.). (ENG., Illus.). 48p. 2011. Set lib. bdg. 130.60 *(978-1-4329-4766-8(4))* Heinemann-Raintree.

Steck-Vaughn Staff. Life on the Tallest Tree. 2003. pap. 4.10 *(978-0-7398-7636-7(8))* Steck-Vaughn.

You Choose: History. 2010. (You Choose: History Ser.). (ENG.). 112p. (gr. 3-4). pap. 13.90 *(978-1-4296-6274-1(3)*, You Choose Bks.) Capstone Press of Coughlan Cos.

LIFE (BIOLOGY)

see also Biology; Genetics; Old Age; Reproduction

Agnew, Kate, ed. Life & Death: A Collection of Classic Poetry & Prose. 2004. (ENG.). 208p. (YA). (gr. 7). per. 8.95 *(978-1-84046-567-9(0)*, Wizard Books) Icon Bks., Ltd. GBR. Dist: Publishers Group Canada.

Anderson, Michael. A Closer Look at Living Things. 2011. (J). lib. bdg. 31.70 *(978-1-61530-533-9(5))* Rosen Publishing Group, Inc., The.

Answers to Evolution Wall Chart. 2004. *(978-1-890947-87-3(3))* Rose Publishing.

Arbuthnott, Gill. Your Guide to Life on Earth. Mones, Marc, illus. 2016. (ENG.). 64p. (J). lib. bdg. *(978-0-7787-2243-4(0))* Crabtree Publishing Co.

Arlon, Penelope. Mirame Crecer. 2013. (Scholastic Explora Tu Mundo Ser.). (SPA.). 32p. (J). (gr. -1-3). 7.99 *(978-0-545-49084-9(7)*, Scholastic en Espanol) Scholastic, Inc.

Austen, Elizabeth. Living!, 1 vol. rev. ed. 2014. (Science Readers: Content & Literacy Ser.). (ENG., Illus.). 24p. (gr. k-k). pap. 22.96 *(978-1-4938-1130-4(4))*; pap. 8.99 *(978-1-4807-4520-9(0))* Teacher Created Materials, Inc.

—What Do Living Things Need?, 1 vol. rev. ed. 2014. (Science Readers: Content & Literacy Ser.). (ENG., Illus.). 24p. (gr. k-k). pap. 22.96 *(978-1-4938-1133-5(9))*; pap. 8.99 *(978-1-4807-4523-0(5))* Teacher Created Materials, Inc.

Banqueri, Eduardo. Life on Earth. 2005. (Our Planet Ser.). (Illus.). 32p. (gr. 4-6). lib. bdg. 28.00 *(978-0-7910-9010-7(8)*, Chelsea Clubhouse) Facts On File, Inc.

Benchmark Education Company, LLC Staff, compiled by. Life Science. 2006. spiral bd. 475.00 *(978-1-4108-6943-2(1))* 2006. spiral bd. 255.00 *(978-1-4108-6947-0(4))* 2006. spiral bd. 75.00 *(978-1-4108-6928-9(8))* 2006. spiral bd. 215.00 *(978-1-4108-6926-5(1))* 2005. spiral bd. 35.00 *(978-1-4108-3876-6(5))* 2005. spiral bd. 75.00 *(978-1-4108-3875-9(7))* 2005. spiral bd. 50.00 *(978-1-4108-3868-1(4))* 2005. spiral bd. 75.00 *(978-1-4108-3867-4(6))* 2005. spiral bd. 145.00 *(978-1-4108-3861-2(7))* 2005. spiral bd. 260.00 *(978-1-4108-3860-5(9))* 2005. spiral bd. 165.00 *(978-1-4108-3853-7(6))* 2005. spiral bd. 360.00 *(978-1-4108-3852-0(8))* 2005. spiral bd. 680.00 *(978-1-4108-4514-6(1))* 2005. spiral bd. 950.00 *(978-1-4108-5433-9(7))* 2005. spiral bd. 295.00 *(978-1-4108-5847-4(2))* 2005. spiral bd. 395.00 *(978-1-4108-5434-6(5))* 2005. spiral bd. 550.00 *(978-1-4108-5846-7(4))* 2005. spiral bd. 305.00 *(978-1-4108-3831-5(5))* 2005. spiral bd. 320.00 *(978-1-4108-3830-8(7))* Benchmark Education Co.

Braun, Eric. Gertrude & Reginald the Monsters Talk about Living & Nonliving, 1 vol. Bernardini, Cristian, illus. 2012. (In the Science Lab Ser.). (ENG.). 24p. (gr. 2-3). pap. 9.95 *(978-1-4048-7237-0(X))*; lib. bdg. 26.65 *(978-1-4048-7146-5(2))* Picture Window Bks.

Chapman, Joan. Living Things. 2008. (Real Readers - Upper Emergent Ser.). (ENG., Illus.). 12p. (gr. 1-2). pap. 5.90 *(978-0-8239-8190-8(8))* Rosen Publishing Group, Inc., The.

Claybourne, Anna. Life Processes, 1 vol. 2012. (Web of Life Ser.). (ENG.). 48p. (gr. 3-3). pap. 9.49 *(978-1-4109-4430-6(1)*, Raintree Freestyle Express); (gr. 3-3). lib. bdg. 34.65 *(978-1-4109-4423-8(9)*, Raintree Freestyle Express); (Illus.). (gr. 6-10). pap. 9.49 *(978-1-4109-4403-0(4)*, Raintree Freestyle); (Illus.). (gr. 6-10). lib. bdg. 34.65 *(978-1-4109-4396-5(8)*, Raintree Freestyle) Heinemann-Raintree.

—Living Things. 2017. (Mind Webs Ser.). (ENG., Illus.). 32p. (J). (gr. 4-6). pap. 11.99 *(978-0-7502-8960-3(0)*, Wayland) Hachette Children's Group GBR. Dist: Hachette Bk. Group.

Dartnell, Lewis. Astrobiology: Exploring Life in the Universe. 2011. (Contemporary Issues Ser.). (Illus.). 172p. (YA). (gr. 9-12). lib. bdg. 37.95 *(978-1-4488-1862-4(1))* Rosen Publishing Group, Inc., The.

Dickmann, Nancy. Life Cycles. 2016. (Earth Figured Out Ser.). (ENG., Illus.). 32p. (J). (gr. 4-4). pap. 10.58 *(978-1-5026-0862-8(6)*, 1399818) Cavendish Square Publishing.

Dorling Kindersley Publishing Staff. Life As We Know It. 2016. (Big Questions Ser.). (ENG., Illus.). 96p. (J). (gr. 2-5). pap. 9.99 *(978-1-4654-5138-5(2)*, DK Children) Dorling Kindersley Publishing, Inc.

Dunne, Abbie. Living or Nonliving? 2016. (Life Science Ser.). (ENG., Illus.). 24p. (gr. k-1). lib. bdg. 26.65 *(978-1-5157-0942-8(6)*, Pebble Plus) Capstone Press of Coughlan Cos.

Eggleton, Jill. The Right to Survive. 2007. (Connectors Ser.). (gr. 2-5). pap. *(978-1-877453-16-8(1))* Global Education Systems Ltd.

Evans, David & Williams, Claudette. Living Things. (Let's Explore Science Ser.). (Illus.). (J). 12.95 *(978-0-590-74945-9(5))* Scholastic, Inc.

Hartman, Eve & Meshbesher, Wendy. What Is the Threat of Invasive Species?, 1 vol. 2012. (Sci-Hi: Science Issues Ser.). (ENG.). 48p. (gr. 4-4). pap. 9.95 *(978-1-4109-4472-6(7))*; lib. bdg. 33.32 *(978-1-4109-4465-8(4))* Heinemann-Raintree. (Sci-Hi).

Herrington, Lisa M. Seed to Plant. 2014. (Rookie Read-About(tm) Science — Life Cycles Ser.). (ENG.). 32p. (J). lib. bdg. 25.00 *(978-0-531-21056-7(1))* Scholastic Library Publishing.

Higgins, Nadia. Life Science Through Infographics. Waananen, Lisa, illus. 2013. (Super Science Infographics Ser.). (ENG.). 32p. (gr. 3-5). lib. bdg. 26.60 *(978-1-4677-1288-0(4)*, Lerner Pubns.) Lerner Publishing Group.

Holland, Gini. Alive & Not Alive. 2007. (I Know Opposites Ser.). 16p. (gr. -1-2). pap. 5.30 *(978-0-8368-8298-8(9))*; lib. bdg. 19.00 *(978-0-8368-8293-3(8))* Stevens, Gareth Publishing LLLP. (Weekly Reader Leveled Readers).

—Alive & Not Alive (Vivo y no Vivo) 2007. (I Know Opposites/Conceptos Contrarios Ser.). (SPA & ENG., Illus.). 16p. (gr. -1-3). lib. bdg. 19.00 *(978-0-8368-8303-9(9)*, Weekly Reader Leveled Readers) Stevens, Gareth Publishing LLLP.

—Alive & Not Alive/Vivo y No Vivo. 2007. (I Know Opposites/Conceptos Contrarios Ser.). (SPA & ENG., Illus.). 16p. (gr. -1-3). pap. 5.30 *(978-0-8368-8308-4(X)*, Weekly Reader Leveled Readers) Stevens, Gareth Publishing LLLP.

Holt, Rinehart and Winston Staff. Holt Science & Technology. 4th ed. 2004. (Holt Science & Technology Ser.). (ENG., Illus.). 880p. (gr. 6-6). 96.80 *(978-0-03-073164-8(X))* Houghton Mifflin Harcourt Publishing Co.

How Life Science Works. 2017. (How Life Science Works). 24p. (gr. 7-8). 141.60 ***(978-1-5081-5582-9(8))***; pap. 49.50 ***(978-1-5081-5583-6(6))*** Rosen Publishing Group, Inc., The. (PowerKids Pr.).

Hunter, Rebecca. Living Organisms. 2010. (CC: 21st Century Science Ser.). 112p. (gr. 6-12). 42.80 *(978-1-933834-74-0(9))* Brown Bear Bks.

Jones, Phillip. Kingdoms of Life. 2011. (Science Foundations Ser.). (Illus.). 128p. (gr. 6-12). 35.00 *(978-1-60413-340-0(6)*, Chelsea Hse.) Facts On File, Inc.

Kalman, Bobbie. ¿Esto Es un Ser Vivo? 2008. (SPA.). 24p. (J). pap. *(978-0-7787-8689-4(7))* Crabtree Publishing Co.

—I Am a Living Thing. 2007. (Introducing Living Things Ser.). (ENG., Illus.). 24p. (J). (gr. k-4). lib. bdg. *(978-0-7787-3229-7(0))*; (gr. 1-4). pap. *(978-0-7787-3253-2(3))* Crabtree Publishing Co.

—Is It a Living Thing? 2007. (Introducing Living Things Ser.). (ENG., Illus.). 24p. (J). (gr. 1-4). pap. *(978-0-7787-3254-9(1))* Crabtree Publishing Co.

—Living Things Need Water. 2007. (Introducing Living Things Ser.). (ENG., Illus.). 24p. (J). (gr. 1-4). pap. *(978-0-7787-3256-3(8))* Crabtree Publishing Co.

—What Is a Bat, 32 bks. Incl. How Do Animals Move? Walker, Niki. 1999. lib. bdg. *(978-0-86505-981-8(0))*; What Is a Bear? Crossingham, John. 2000. lib. bdg. *(978-0-86505-983-2(7))*; What Is a Cat? Bishop, Amanda. 2002. lib. bdg. *(978-0-86505-990-0(X))*; What Is a Dog? Sotzek, Hannelore. 1999. lib. bdg. *(978-0-86505-979-5(9))*; What Is a Forest? Smithyman, Kathryn. 2002. lib. bdg. *(978-0-86505-992-4(6))*; What Is a Horse? Levigne, Heather. 2000. lib. bdg. *(978-0-86505-984-9(5))*; What Is an Arthropod? 2002. lib. bdg. *(978-0-86505-991-7(8))*; What Is an Elephant? Crossingham, John. 2001. lib. bdg. *(978-0-86505-989-4(6))*; (J). (gr. 2-3). (ENG., Illus.). 32p. *(978-0-86505-996-2(9))*; Set pap. *(978-0-86505-974-0(8))* Crabtree Publishing Co.

—What Kind of Living Thing Is It? 2010. (Introducing Living Things Ser.). (ENG.). 24p. (J). (gr. 1-4). pap. *(978-0-7787-3259-4(2))*; lib. bdg. *(978-0-7787-3235-8(5))* Crabtree Publishing Co.

Kalman, Bobbie & Sjonger, Rebecca. Animal Life Cycles: Growing & Changing. 2008. (ENG.). 32p. (J). *(978-0-7787-7723-6(5))* Crabtree Publishing Co.

—Metamorphosis: Changing Bodies. 2008. (ENG.). 32p. (J). *(978-0-7787-7714-4(6))* Crabtree Publishing Co.

Kim, Sue. How Does a Seed Grow? A Book with Foldout Pages. Tilde, photos by. 2010. (ENG., Illus.). 14p. (J). (gr. -1-1). bds. 8.99 *(978-1-4169-9435-0(1)*, Little Simon) Little Simon.

Latta, Sara L. Keep Out! Invasive Species, 1 vol. 2013. (Nature's Invaders Ser.). (ENG.). 32p. (gr. 3-4). lib. bdg. 27.99 *(978-1-4765-0140-6(8))* Capstone Press of Coughlan Cos.

Lomberg, Michelle. Animal Cells. 2016. (Illus.). 32p. (J). *(978-1-5105-1184-2(9))* SmartBook Media, Inc.

Mason, Helen. Weird Nature. 2013. (ENG.). 32p. (J). *(978-0-7787-1127-8(7))*; pap. *(978-0-7787-1131-5(5))* Crabtree Publishing Co.

McManus, Lori. Cell Systems, 1 vol. 2010. (Investigating Cells Ser.). (ENG., Illus.). 48p. (gr. 3-6). 33.32 *(978-1-4329-3879-6(7)*, Heinemann InfoSearch) Heinemann-Raintree.

Meachen Rau, Dana. Life. 2008. (Earth Matters/El Planeta Es Importante Ser.). 32p. (SPA & ENG.). (gr. k-1). lib. bdg. 15.95 *(978-0-7614-3491-7(7))*; (gr. 1-2). lib. bdg. 15.95 *(978-0-7614-3044-5(X))* Marshall Cavendish Corp. (Benchmark Bks.).

—La Vida. 2008. (Planeta Es Importante Ser.). (SPA.). 32p. (gr. 1-2). lib. bdg. 15.95 *(978-0-7614-3467-2(4)*, Benchmark Bks.) Marshall Cavendish Corp.

Parker, Steve. A Brief Illustrated History of Life on Earth. 2017. (Brief Illustrated History Ser.). (ENG.). 32p. (gr. 3-5). lib. bdg. 27.32 *(978-1-5157-2521-3(9)*, Fact Finders) Capstone Press of Coughlan Cos.

—Complete Guides Our World. 2012. (ENG.). 144p. (J). *(978-1-4351-4406-4(6))* Barnes & Noble, Inc.

Prior, Jennifer. The Human Life Cycle, 1 vol. 2nd rev. ed. 2014. (TIME for KIDS(r) Nonfiction Readers Ser.). (ENG., Illus.). 32p. (J). (gr. 3-3). pap. 25.96 *(978-1-4807-1087-0(3))* Shell Educational Publishing.

Rake, Matthew. The Dawn of Planet Earth. Minister, Peter, illus. 2015. (Prehistoric Field Guides). (ENG.). 32p. (J). (gr. 3-6). 26.65 *(978-1-4677-6348-6(9)*, Lerner Pubns.) Lerner Publishing Group.

Rau, Dana Meachen. Plants/Las Plantas. 2009. (Bookworms Ser.). (SPA & ENG.). 32p. (gr. 1-2). lib. bdg. 15.95 *(978-0-7614-4790-0(3))* Marshall Cavendish Corp.

Rice, David L. Lifetimes. Maydak, Michael S., illus. 2015. 32p. pap. 9.00 *(978-1-61003-549-1(6))* Center for the Collaborative Classroom.

Richards, Jon. The Natural World. Simkins, Ed, illus. 2013. (World in Infographics Ser.). (ENG.). 32p. (J). (gr. 3-7). 15.95 *(978-1-926973-74-6(7))* Owlkids Bks. Inc. CAN. Dist: Publishers Group West (PGW).

Rissman, Rebecca. Is It Living or Nonliving? 2013. (Is It Living or Nonliving? Ser.). (ENG.). 24p. (gr. k-2). pap. 38.94 *(978-1-4109-5393-3(9))*; lib. bdg. 139.92 *(978-1-4109-5386-5(6))* Heinemann-Raintree.

—Living & Nonliving in the Desert, 1 vol. 2013. (Is It Living or Nonliving? Ser.). (ENG.). 24p. (gr. k-2). 23.32 *(978-1-4109-5380-3(7))*; pap. 6.95 *(978-1-4109-5387-2(4))* Heinemann-Raintree.

—Living & Nonliving in the Grasslands, 1 vol. 2013. (Is It Living or Nonliving? Ser.). (ENG.). 24p. (gr. k-2). 23.32 *(978-1-4109-5384-1(X))*; pap. 6.95 *(978-1-4109-5391-9(2))* Heinemann-Raintree.

—Living & Nonliving in the Mountains, 1 vol. 2013. (Is It Living or Nonliving? Ser.). (ENG.). 24p. (gr. k-2). 23.32 *(978-1-4109-5385-8(8))*; pap. 6.95 *(978-1-4109-5392-6(0))* Heinemann-Raintree.

—Living & Nonliving in the Polar Regions, 1 vol. 2013. (Is It Living or Nonliving? Ser.). (ENG.). 24p. (gr. k-2). 23.32 *(978-1-4109-5383-4(1))*; pap. 6.95 *(978-1-4109-5390-2(4))* Heinemann-Raintree.

—Living & Nonliving in the Rain Forest, 1 vol. 2013. (Is It Living or Nonliving? Ser.). (ENG.). 24p. (gr. k-2). 23.32 *(978-1-4109-5382-7(3))*; pap. 6.95 *(978-1-4109-5389-6(0))* Heinemann-Raintree.

Rivera, Sheila. I Know It Is Living. 2006. (First Step Nonfiction - Living or Nonliving Ser.). (ENG., Illus.). 8p. (gr. -1-1). pap. 4.95 *(978-0-8225-5687-9(1)*, Lerner Pubns.) Lerner Publishing Group.

—I Know It Is Nonliving. 2006. (First Step Nonfiction - Living or Nonliving Ser.). (ENG., Illus.). 8p. (gr. -1-1). pap. 4.95 *(978-0-8225-5685-5(5)*, Lerner Pubns.) Lerner Publishing Group.

Rivera, Sheila & National Geographic Learning Staff. Is It Living or Nonliving? 2012. (ENG., Illus.). 8p. (C). (gr. -1-1). pap. 7.95 *(978-0-8225-5686-2(3))* National Geographic School Publishing, Inc.

Ross, Michael. Life Cycles. Moore, Gustav, illus. 2003. 32p. (J). (gr. 2-5). pap. 7.95 *(978-0-7613-1975-7(1)*, First Avenue Editions) Lerner Publishing Group.

Royston, Angela. Life Cycles. 2013. (Life Science Stories Ser.). (Illus.). 32p. (J). (gr. 3-5). pap. 10.50 *(978-1-4339-8712-0(0))*; lib. bdg. 26.60 *(978-1-4339-8711-3(2))* Stevens, Gareth Publishing LLLP.

—Looking at Life Cycles: How Do Plants & Animals Change? 2008. (Looking at Science: How Things Change Ser.). (Illus.). 32p. (J). (gr. 3-7). lib. bdg. 23.94 *(978-0-7660-3091-6(1)*, Enslow Elementary) Enslow Pubs., Inc.

Salas, Laura Purdie. Are You Living? A Song about Living & Nonliving Things, 1 vol. Garofoli, Viviana, illus. 2009. (Science Songs Ser.). (ENG.). 24p. (gr. 1-3). lib. bdg. 26.65 *(978-1-4048-5302-7(2))* Picture Window Bks.

Schutten, Jan Paul. The Mystery of Life: How Nothing Became Everything. Watkinson, Laura, tr. from DUT. Rieder, Floor, illus. 2015. (ENG.). 240p. (YA). (gr. 5-9). 15.99 *(978-1-58270-525-5(9)*, Simon & Schuster/Paula Wiseman Bks.) Simon & Schuster/Paula Wiseman Bks.

The Science of Life. 2016. (Illus.). 48p. (J). *(978-1-4222-3514-0(9))* Mason Crest.

Science Stories Foss Spanish Structures of Life EA CR05. 2005. (J). *(978-1-59242-589-1(5))* Delta Education, LLC.

Silverstein, Alvin & Silverstein, Virginia. Metamorphosis: Nature's Magical Transformations. unabr. ed. 2013. (Dover Children's Science Bks.). (ENG., Illus.). 80p. (J). (gr. 3-8). pap. 5.95 *(978-0-486-42396-8(4))* Dover Pubns., Inc.

Somervill, Barbara A. Animal Cells & Life Processes, 1 vol. 2010. (Investigating Cells Ser.). (ENG., Illus.). 48p. (gr. 3-6). 33.32 *(978-1-4329-3877-2(0)*, Heinemann InfoSearch) Heinemann-Raintree.

Spilsbury, Louise. What Are Living & Nonliving Things?, 1 vol., 1. 2014. (Let's Find Out! Ser.). (ENG.). 32p. (gr. 3-6). 23.45 *(978-1-62275-226-3(0))* Rosen Publishing Group, Inc., The.

—What Is a Life Cycle?, 1 vol., 1. 2014. (Let's Find Out! Ser.). (ENG.). 32p. (gr. 3-6). 23.45 *(978-1-62275-231-7(7))* Rosen Publishing Group, Inc., The.

Stoyles, Pennie & Pentland, Peter. Life on Earth. 2011. (Energy in Action Ser.). (Illus.). 32p. (J). (gr. 4). 28.50 *(978-1-60870-565-8(X))* Marshall Cavendish Corp.

Sundance/Newbridge LLC Staff. Animals & Their Babies. 2007. (Early Science Ser.). (gr. k-3). 18.95 *(978-1-4007-6215-6(4))*; pap. 6.10 *(978-1-4007-6211-8(1))* Sundance/Newbridge Educational Publishing.

—Is It Alive? 2007. (Early Science Ser.). (gr. k-3). 18.95 *(978-1-4007-6152-4(2))*; pap. 6.10 *(978-1-4007-6148-7(4))* Sundance/Newbridge Educational Publishing.

—What Is a Cycle? 2007. (Early Science Ser.). (gr. k-3). 18.95 *(978-1-4007-6242-2(1))*; pap. 6.10 *(978-1-4007-6238-5(3))* Sundance/Newbridge Educational Publishing.

Thomson, Ruth. Let's Look at Life Cycles, 4 vols., Set. Incl. Bee's Life Cycle. lib. bdg. 22.60 *(978-1-61532-216-9(7))*; Chicken's Life Cycle. lib. bdg. 22.60 *(978-1-61532-217-6(5))*; Frog's Life Cycle. lib. bdg. 22.60 *(978-1-61532-218-3(3))*; Sunflower's Life Cycle. lib. bdg. 22.60 *(978-1-61532-219-0(1))*; (J). (gr. k-2). (Illus.). 24p. 2010. Set lib. bdg. 85.00 *(978-1-4488-0281-4(4)*, PowerKids Pr.) Rosen Publishing Group, Inc., The.

Thornhill, Jan. I Am Josephine: (and I Am a Living Thing) Lee, Jacqui, illus. 2016. (ENG.). 32p. (J). (gr. -1-2). 16.95 *(978-1-77147-156-5(5)*, Owlkids) Owlkids Bks. Inc. CAN. Dist: Publishers Group West (PGW).

Troupe, Thomas Kingsley. Do Bees Poop? Learning about Living & Nonliving Things with the Garbage Gang, 1 vol. Toye, Derek, illus. 2014. (Garbage Gang's Super Science Questions Ser.). (ENG.). 24p. (gr. k-2). lib. bdg. 26.65 *(978-1-4795-5477-5(4))* Picture Window Bks.

Vogt, Gregory. The Biosphere: Realm of Life. 2007. (Earth's Spheres Ser.). (ENG., Illus.). 80p. (gr. 6-8). lib. bdg. 29.27 *(978-0-7613-2840-7(8))* Lerner Publishing Group.

Waldron, Melanie, et al. Essential Life Science. 2013. (Essential Life Science Ser.). (ENG.). 48p. (gr. 4-6). lib. bdg. 133.28 *(978-1-4329-7809-9(8)*, Heinemann InfoSearch) Heinemann-Raintree.

Weber, Belinda. I Wonder Why Caterpillars Eat So Much: And Other Questions about Life Cycles. 2012. (I Wonder Why Ser.). (ENG., Illus.). 32p. (J). (gr. k-3). pap. 6.99 *(978-0-7534-6707-7(0)*, 9780753467077, Kingfisher) Roaring Brook Pr.

Weber, Rebecca. El Ciclo de Tu Vida/the Cycle of Your Life, 1 vol. 2011. (Salud y Tu Cuerpo/Health & Your Body Ser.). (SPA, ENG & MUL.). 24p. (gr. k-1). 26.65 *(978-1-4296-6894-1(6))* Capstone Press of Coughlan Cos.

—The Cycle of Your Life, 1 vol. 2011. (Health & Your Body Ser.). (ENG.). 24p. (gr. k-1). pap. 7.29 *(978-1-4296-7126-2(2))*; pap. 41.70 *(978-1-4296-7132-3(7))* Capstone Press of Coughlan Cos. (Pebble Plus).

World Book Staff. The Circulatory System. 2014. 32p. *(978-0-7166-1841-6(9))* World Bk., Inc.

LIFE, CHRISTIAN

see Christian Life

LIFE, FUTURE

see Future Life

LIFE—ORIGIN

Bright, Michael. The Future of Life on Earth, 1 vol. 2012. (Web of Life Ser.). (ENG.). 48p. (gr. 3-3). pap. 9.49 *(978-1-4109-4433-7(6))*; lib. bdg. 34.65 *(978-1-4109-4426-9(3))* Heinemann-Raintree. (Raintree Freestyle Express).

Darwin, Charles. The Riverbank. Negrin, Fabian, illus. 2010. (ENG.). 32p. (J). (gr. 1-3). 17.95 *(978-1-56846-207-3(7)*, Creative Editions) Creative Co., The.

Gladstone, James. When Planet Earth Was New. Diemert, Katherine, illus. 2017. (ENG.). 40p. (J). (gr. -1-5). 18.95 ***(978-1-77147-203-6(0))*** Owlkids Bks. Inc. CAN. Dist: Publishers Group West (PGW).

Morgan, Jennifer. From Lava to Life: The Universe Tells Our Earth Story. Andersen, Dana Lynne, illus. (Sharing Nature with Children Book Ser.: Vol. 2). 48p. (YA). 2004. 19.95 *(978-1-58469-043-6(7))* 2003. (ENG.). pap. 9.95 *(978-1-58469-042-9(9))* Dawn Pubns.

Solway, Andrew. Why Is There Life on Earth?, 1 vol. 2011. (Earth, Space, & Beyond Ser.). (ENG., Illus.). 48p. (gr. 6-6). pap. 9.49 *(978-1-4109-4166-4(3))*; 34.65 *(978-1-4109-4160-2(4))* Heinemann-Raintree. (Raintree Freestyle).

Whitt, Stephen. The Turtle & the Universe. Hernandez, Stephanie, illus. 2008. (ENG.). 86p. (J). (gr. 3-7). pap. 14.99 *(978-1-59102-626-6(1))* Prometheus Bks., Pubs.

LIFE, SPIRITUAL

see Spiritual Life

LIFE AFTER DEATH

see Future Life

LIFE ON OTHER PLANETS

see also Interstellar Communication

Ames, Lee J. & Estrada, Ric. Draw 50 Aliens: The Step-by-Step Way to Draw UFOs, Galaxy Ghouls, Milky Way Marauders, & Other Extraterrestrial Creatures. 2013. (ENG., Illus.). 64p. pap. 9.99 *(978-0-8230-8616-0(X)*, Watson-Guptill) Potter/TenSpeed/Harmony.

Asimov, Isaac & Hantula, Richard. Is There Life in Outer Space? 2005. (Isaac Asimov's 21st Century Library of the Universe). (Illus.). 32p. (gr. 2-6). lib. bdg. 26.00 *(978-0-8368-3950-0(1)*, Gareth Stevens Learning Library) Stevens, Gareth Publishing LLLP.

J
K
L

Berkowitz, Jacob. Out of This World: The Amazing Search for an Alien Earth. 2009. (ENG., Illus.). 40p. (J). (gr. 3-7). 8.95 *(978-1-55453-198-1(5))*; 16.95 *(978-1-55453-197-4(7))* Kids Can Pr., Ltd. CAN. Dist: Hachette Bk. Group.

Bishop, Nic & Hughes, Jon. Is There Anybody Out There? Bishop, Nic, photos by. 2005. (Collins Big Cat Ser.). (ENG., Illus.). 352p. (J). (gr. 2-3). pap. 7.99 *(978-0-00-718635-8(5))* HarperCollins Pubs. Ltd. GBR. Dist: Independent Pubs. Group.

Bortz, Fred. Astrobiology. 2008. pap. 52.95 *(978-0-8225-9326-3(2))* 2007. (ENG., Illus.). 48p. (gr. 4-8). lib. bdg. 27.93 *(978-0-8225-6771-4(7)*, Lerner Pubns.) Lerner Publishing Group.

Coddington, Andrew. Aliens, UFOs, & Unexplained Encounters. 2017. (J). ***(978-1-5026-2845-9(7))*** Cavendish Square Publishing.

Cohen, Sheldon & Drawing Staff. How to Draw & Save Your Planet from Alien Invasion! 2011. (Dover How to Draw Ser.). (ENG.). 72p. (J). (gr. 3-5). pap. 4.99 *(978-0-486-47833-3(5))* Dover Pubns., Inc.

Culp, Jennifer. How We Find Other Earths: Technology & Strategies to Detect Planets Similar to Ours, 01 vols., 1. 2016. (Search for Other Earths Ser.). (ENG., Illus.). 112p. (J). 35.60 *(978-1-4994-6292-0(1)*, Rosen Young Adult) Rosen Publishing Group, Inc., The.

Dartnell, Lewis. Astrobiology: Exploring Life in the Universe. 2011. (Contemporary Issues Ser.). (Illus.). 172p. (YA). (gr. 9-12). lib. bdg. 37.95 *(978-1-4488-1862-4(1))* Rosen Publishing Group, Inc., The.

Donald, Rhonda Lucas. Life on Other Planets. 2004. (Watts Library). (ENG.). 64p. (J). (gr. 5-7). pap. 8.95 *(978-0-531-16374-0(1)*, Watts, Franklin) Scholastic Library Publishing.

Dorling Kindersley Publishing Staff & Kent, Lindsay. Ultimate Duels, Level 4. 2011. (DK Readers Ser.). (ENG.). 48p. (J). (gr. 3-7). 3.99 *(978-0-7566-8263-7(0)*, DK Children) Dorling Kindersley Publishing, Inc.

Firestone, Mary. Seti Science. 2005. (Weird Careers in Science Ser.). (Illus.). 88p. (gr. 5-8). lib. bdg. 25.00 *(978-0-7910-8701-5(8)*, Chelsea Hse.) Facts On File, Inc.

Gonzalez, David J. There Are No Space Aliens! 12 Biblical Points Disproving Space Aliens. l.t. ed. 2003. 48p. 9.95 *(978-0-9741561-0-1(8))* Gonzalez, David J. Ministries.

Hamilton, John. Aliens, 1 vol. 2006. (World of Science Fiction Ser.). (ENG., Illus.). 32p. (gr. 4-7). 27.07 *(978-1-59679-986-8(2)*, Abdo & Daughters) ABDO Publishing Co.

Hand, Carol. Is There Life Out There? The Likelihood of Alien Life & What It Would Look Like, 01 vols., 1. 2016. (Search for Other Earths Ser.). (ENG., Illus.). 112p. (J). 35.60 *(978-1-4994-6294-4(8)*, Rosen Young Adult) Rosen Publishing Group, Inc., The.

Herbst, Judith. Aliens. 2004. (Unexplained Ser.). (Illus.). 48p. (J). pap. 8.95 *(978-0-8225-2402-1(3)*, Lerner Pubns.); (ENG., (gr. 5-12). lib. bdg. 26.60 *(978-0-8225-0960-8(1))* Lerner Publishing Group.

Jedicke, Peter. Seti: The Search for Alien Intelligence. 2003. (Hot Science Ser.). (Illus.). 48p. (J). (gr. 6). lib. bdg. 28.50 *(978-1-58340-369-3(8))* Black Rabbit Bks.

Kallen, Stuart K. The search for extraterrestrial Life. 2011. (Extraterrestrial Life Ser.). (Illus.). 80p. (YA). (gr. 7-12). lib. bdg. 27.95 *(978-1-60152-171-2(5))* ReferencePoint Pr., Inc.

Kocienda, Genevieve. Aliens: Is Anybody Out There? Low Intermediate Book with Online Access. 2014. (ENG.). 24p. (J). pap. 9.50 *(978-1-107-66000-7(9))* Cambridge Univ. Pr.

Kortemeier, Todd. Searching for Alien Life. 2017. (Science Frontiers Ser.). (ENG., Illus.). 32p. (J). (gr. 3-6). 21.95 *(978-1-63235-380-1(6))* Pr. Room Editions LLC.

La Bella, Laura. The Goldilocks Zone: Conditions Necessary for Extraterrestrial Life, 01 vols., 1. 2016. (Search for Other Earths Ser.). (ENG., Illus.). 112p. (J). 35.60 *(978-1-4994-6298-2(0)*, Rosen Young Adult) Rosen Publishing Group, Inc., The.

McEvoy, Paul. The Alien Files. 2003. (Real Deal Ser.). (Illus.). 32p. (J). pap. *(978-0-7608-6691-7(0))* Sundance/Newbridge Educational Publishing.

Murray, Laura K. Aliens. 2017. (Illus.). 24p. (J). *(978-1-60818-759-1(4)*, Creative Education) Creative Co., The.

Murray, Laura K. Are They Real?: Aliens. 2017. (Are They Real? Ser.). (ENG., Illus.). 24p. (J). (gr. 1-3). pap. 8.99 ***(978-1-62832-367-2(1)***, Creative Paperbacks) Creative Co., The.

Netzley, Patricia D. Alien Encounters. 2011. (Extraterrestrial Life Ser.). 80p. (YA). (gr. 7-12). lib. bdg. 27.95 *(978-1-60152-169-9(3))* ReferencePoint Pr., Inc.

O'Brien, Patrick. You Are the First Kid on Mars. O'Brien, Patrick, illus. 2009. (ENG., Illus.). 32p. (J). (gr. k-3). 16.99 *(978-0-399-24634-0(7)*, G.P. Putnam's Sons Books for Young Readers) Penguin Young Readers Group.

Orme, Helen. Life in Space. Mongiovi, Jorge, illus. 2008. (Trailblazers Ser.). (ENG.). 36p. pap. *(978-1-84167-690-6(X))* Ransom Publishing Ltd.

Pipe, Jim. Aliens. 2013. (Twilight Realm Ser.). (Illus.). 32p. (J). (gr. 4-6). 26.60 *(978-1-4339-8747-2(3))*; pap. 10.50 *(978-1-4339-8748-9(1))* Stevens, Gareth Publishing LLLP. (Gareth Stevens Learning Library).

Porterfield, Jason. Aliens at Home: Studying Extreme Environment Species to Learn about Extraterrestrial Life, 01 vols., 1. 2016. (Search for Other Earths Ser.). (ENG.). 112p. (J). 35.60 *(978-1-4994-6297-5(2)*, Rosen Young Adult) Rosen Publishing Group, Inc., The.

Portman, Michael. Is There Life on Mars? 2013. (Space Mysteries Ser.). (Illus.). 32p. (J). (gr. 2-5). 25.25 *(978-1-4339-8272-9(2))*; pap. 10.50 *(978-1-4339-8273-6(0))* Stevens, Gareth Publishing LLLP. (Gareth Stevens Learning Library).

Rau, Dana Meachen. Aliens. 2010. (Bookworms Chapter Books: for Real? Ser.). 24p. (gr. 2-3). 22.79 *(978-0-7614-4861-7(6))* Marshall Cavendish Corp.

Roleff, Tamara L., ed. Alien Abductions. 2003. (Illus.). 160p. (J). lib. bdg. 32.45 *(978-0-7377-1589-7(8)*, Greenhaven Pr., Inc.) Cengage Gale.

Skurzynski, Gloria. Are We Alone? Scientist Search for Life in Space. 2004. (ENG., Illus.). 96p. (J). (gr. 5-9). lib. bdg. 28.90 *(978-0-7922-6967-0(5)*, National Geographic Children's Bks.) National Geographic Society.

—Are We Alone? Scientists Search for Life in Space. 2004. (ENG., Illus.). 96p. (J). (gr. 5-18). 18.95 *(978-0-7922-6567-2(X)*, National Geographic Children's Bks.) National Geographic Society.

Solway, Andrew. Why Is There Life on Earth?, 1 vol. 2011. (Earth, Space, & Beyond Ser.). (ENG.). 48p. (gr. 3-3). pap. 9.49 *(978-1-4109-4184-8(1)*, Raintree Freestyle Express); (Illus.). (gr. 6-6). pap. 9.49 *(978-1-4109-4166-4(3)*, Raintree Freestyle); (gr. 3-3). 34.65 *(978-1-4109-4178-7(7)*, Raintree Freestyle Express); (Illus.). (gr. 6-6). 34.65 *(978-1-4109-4160-2(4)*, Raintree Freestyle) Heinemann-Raintree.

Summers, Portia & Rau, Dana Meachen. Are Aliens Real? 2016. (I Want to Know Ser.). 32p. (J). pap. 10.52 *(978-0-7660-8228-1(8))* Enslow Pubs., Inc.

Surviving Alien Contact & Warfare. 2016. (Surviving Alien Contact & Warfare Ser.). 00048p. (J). (gr. 10-10). pap. 35.25 *(978-1-4994-6565-5(3)*, Rosen Young Adult) Rosen Publishing Group, Inc., The.

Turner, Pamela S. Life on Earth - & Beyond: An Astrobiologist's Quest. 2008. (ENG., Illus.). 112p. (J). (gr. 4-7). 19.95 *(978-1-58089-133-2(0))* Charlesbridge Publishing, Inc.

LIFE ON OTHER PLANETS—FICTION

Abdo Publishing. Star Wars Digests Set 2, 1 vol. 2013. (Star Wars Digests Set 2 Ser.: 4). (ENG.). 80p. (J). (gr. 4-8). lib. bdg. 108.28 *(978-1-61479-055-6(8)*, Essential Library) ABDO Publishing Co.

Adrien, Gilles & Broders, Alain. The Planet of the Giant. Élyum Studio, illus. 2013. (Little Prince Ser.: 9). (ENG.). 56p. (J). (gr. 4-8). lib. bdg. 26.60 *(978-0-7613-8759-6(5)*, Graphic Universe™) Lerner Publishing Group.

Agee, Jon. Life on Mars. 2017. (ENG., Illus.). 32p. (J). (gr. -1-3). 17.99 *(978-0-399-53852-0(6)*, Dial Bks) Penguin Young Readers Group.

Angleberger, Tom. Star Wars - Return of the Jedi: Beware the Power of the Dark Side! McCaig, Iain, illus. 2015. (ENG.). 432p. (J). (gr. 3-7). 17.99 *(978-1-4847-0913-9(6)*, Disney Lucasfilm Press) Disney Publishing Worldwide.

Appleton, Victor. Tom Swift & the Visitor from Planet X. 2006. pap. *(978-1-4068-0728-8(1))* Echo Library.

Arnett, Mindee. Avalon. 2014. (Avalon Ser.: 1). (ENG.). 432p. (YA). (gr. 8). 17.99 *(978-0-06-223559-6(1))* HarperCollins Pubs.

—Polaris. 2015. (Avalon Ser.: 2). (ENG.). 432p. (YA). (gr. 8). 17.99 *(978-0-06-223562-6(1))* HarperCollins Pubs.

Artifact Group, The. The Trash Planet. 2009. (Backyardigans Ser.: 12). (ENG.). 24p. (J). pap. 3.99 *(978-1-4169-6868-9(7)*, Simon Spotlight/Nickelodeon) Simon Spotlight/Nickelodeon.

Barichella, Thomas. The Star Snatcher's Planet. 2013. (Little Prince Ser.: 5). (ENG., Illus.). 56p. (J). (gr. 4-8). pap. 7.95 *(978-1-4677-0737-4(6)*, Graphic Universe™) Lerner Publishing Group.

Barrett, Judi. Cloudy with a Chance of Meatballs 3: Planet of the Pies. Mones, Isidre, illus. 2013. (ENG.). 32p. (J). (gr. -1-3). 17.99 *(978-1-4424-9027-7(6)*, Atheneum Bks. for Young Readers) Simon & Schuster Children's Publishing.

Blackman, Haden & Caldwell, Ben. Star Wars: Clone Wars Adventures, 1 vol. 2012. (Star Wars Digests Ser.). (ENG., Illus.). 96p. (J). (gr. 4-7). 27.07 *(978-1-59961-904-0(0))* Spotlight.

Blackman, Haden & The Fillbach Brothers. Star Wars: Clone Wars Adventures, 1 vol. 2012. (Star Wars Digests Ser.). (ENG., Illus.). 96p. (J). (gr. 4-7). 27.07 *(978-1-59961-905-7(9))*; 27.07 *(978-1-59961-906-4(7))* Spotlight.

Bracken, Alexandra. Star Wars - A New Hope: The Princess, the Scoundrel, & the Farm Boy. McCaig, Iain, illus. 2015. (ENG.). 336p. (J). (gr. 3-7). 17.99 *(978-1-4847-0912-2(8)*, 1384321, Disney Lucasfilm Press) Disney Publishing Worldwide.

Brackett, Leigh & Coppel, Jr., Alfred. Planet Stories - Summer 1949. 2008. 128p. (YA). pap. 14.95 *(978-1-59798-181-1(8))* Adventure Hse.

Brennan, Herbie. The Aliens Handbook. 2005. (ENG., Illus.). 144p. 9.95 *(978-0-571-22081-6(9))* Faber & Faber, Inc.

Calero, Dennis. You're Not the Captain of Me! 2011. (ENG.). 272p. (J). (gr. 4-7). pap. 9.95 *(978-1-59687-375-9(2))* IBks., Inc.

Capetta, Amy Rose. Entangled. (ENG.). (YA). (gr. 9). 2014. 352p. pap. 9.99 *(978-0-544-33624-7(0)*, HMH Books For Young Readers) 2013. 336p. 17.99 *(978-0-544-08744-6(5))* Houghton Mifflin Harcourt Publishing Co.

Carbone, Courtney. Star Wars: The Phantom Menace (Star Wars) Martinez, Heather, illus. 2015. (Little Golden Book Ser.). (ENG.). 24p. (J). (-k). 4.99 *(978-0-7364-3542-0(5)*, Golden Bks.) Random Hse. Children's Bks.

Cerasi, Chris. Star Wars Adventures: Chewbacca & the Slavers of the Shadowlands, 1 vol. 2013. (Star Wars Digests Set 2 Ser.). (ENG.). 80p. (J). (gr. 4-8). lib. bdg. 27.07 *(978-1-61479-057-0(4)*, Essential Library) ABDO Publishing Co.

Chase, Max. Deadly Mission. 2012. (Star Fighters Ser.). (ENG., Illus.). 128p. (YA). pap. 5.99 *(978-1-59990-851-9(4)*, 9781599908519, Bloomsbury USA Childrens) Bloomsbury Publishing USA.

Chatten, Vicky. Bonding. 2004. 173p. pap. 24.95 *(978-1-4137-5348-6(5))* America Star Bks.

Constantine, Clélia. The Planet of Ludokaa. Élyum Studio, illus. 2013. (Little Prince Ser.: 12). (ENG.). 48p. (J). (gr. 4-8). lib. bdg. 26.60 *(978-0-7613-8762-6(5)*, Graphic Universe™) Lerner Publishing Group.

Cooper, Lynne. Alien Invaders. Leick, Bonnie, illus. 2010. (ENG.). 32p. (J). (gr. 4-7). *(978-1-934960-83-7(7))* Continental Sales.

Delhohne, Jean-Philippe. Visit to Another Planet. 2004. (Illus.). 31p. (J). (gr. k-4). reprint ed. *(978-0-7567-7768-5(2))* DIANE Publishing Co.

Denofsky, Howard. Sillyishis, Beanie & the Hobblebobs. 2012. 32p. 24.95 *(978-1-4626-6211-1(0))* America Star Bks.

Disney Book Group. Star Wars: The Original Trilogy Stories. 2015. (Storybook Collection). (ENG.). 304p. (J). (gr. -1-k). 16.99 *(978-1-4847-0471-4(1)*, Disney Lucasfilm Press) Disney Publishing Worldwide.

Disney Book Group & Rucka, Greg. Guardians of the Whills. 2017. (ENG.). 240p. (J). (gr. 5-9). 12.99 *(978-1-4847-8081-7(7)*, Disney Lucasfilm Press) Disney Publishing Worldwide.

Disney Book Group Staff & Fry, Jason. Rebel in the Ranks. 2015. (ENG.). 176p. (J). (gr. 3-7). pap. 6.99 *(978-1-4847-1644-1(2)*, Disney Lucasfilm Press) Disney Publishing Worldwide.

Disney Book Group Staff & Heddle, Jennifer. World of Reading Star Wars Rebels. 2015. (World of Reading Ser.). (ENG.). 32p. (J). (gr. 1-3). pap. 3.99 *(978-1-4847-0491-2(6)*, Disney Lucasfilm Press) Disney Publishing Worldwide.

Disney Book Group Staff & Kogge, Michael. Ezra's Duel with Danger. 2015. (Star Wars Saga Chapter Book Ser.). (ENG., Illus.). 128p. (J). (gr. 1-3). pap. 5.99 *(978-1-4847-0469-1(X)*, Disney Lucasfilm Press) Disney Publishing Worldwide.

Disney Book Group Staff & Michaels, Kay. Star Wars Rebels. 2014. (Star Wars: World of Reading Ser.). (J). lib. bdg. 13.55 *(978-0-606-35282-6(1))* Turtleback Bks.

Dorling Kindersley Publishing Staff. Attack of the Clones. 2013. (LEGO Star Wars DK Reader Ser.). lib. bdg. 13.55 *(978-0-606-32111-2(X)*, Turtleback) Turtleback Bks.

Dorling Kindersley Publishing Staff & Fentiman, David. Fight the Empire. 2015. (DK Readers Ser.). (ENG.). 64p. (J). (gr. 2-4). 14.99 *(978-1-4654-1988-0(8)*, DK Children) Dorling Kindersley Publishing, Inc.

Dorling Kindersley Publishing Staff & Scott, Heather. Stand Aside - Bounty Hunters! 2009. (DK Readers Ser.). (ENG.). 32p. (J). (gr. 1-3). 3.99 *(978-0-7566-5775-8(X)*, DK Children) Dorling Kindersley Publishing, Inc.

Dorling Kindersley Publishing Staff, et al. The Clone Wars - Pirates... & Worse! 2009. (DK Readers Ser.). (ENG., Illus.). 32p. (J). (gr. k-2). 3.99 *(978-0-7566-5773-4(3)*, DK Children) Dorling Kindersley Publishing, Inc.

Duffett-Smith, James. A Curious Robot on Mars! Straker, Bethany, illus. 2013. (ENG.). 32p. (J). (gr. -1-k). 14.95 *(978-1-62087-994-8(8)*, 620994, Sky Pony Pr.) Skyhorse Publishing Co., Inc.

Echeverria-Bis, Olivia. The EGGbees. Echeverria Gyorkos, Charmaine, illus. 2009. (ENG & SPA.). 32p. (J). (gr. -1-3). 16.95 *(978-1-55885-529-8(7)*, Piñata Books) Arte Publico Pr.

Elizabeth, Lauren. Far from Forgotten. 2013. 112p. pap. 10.00 *(978-1-4575-2316-8(7))* Dog Ear Publishing, LLC.

—Looks of an Angel. 2012. 148p. (-18). pap. 12.00 *(978-1-4575-1445-6(7))* Dog Ear Publishing, LLC.

Epstein, Adam Jay & Jacobson, Andrew. Starbounders. McClellan, David, illus. 2013. (Starbounders Ser.: 1). (ENG.). 320p. (J). (gr. 3-7). 16.99 *(978-0-06-212022-9(0))* HarperCollins Pubs.

—Starbounders Vol. 2: Rebellion. 2014. (Starbounders Ser.: 2). (ENG.). 304p. (J). (gr. 3-7). 16.99 *(978-0-06-212027-4(1))* HarperCollins Pubs.

Fentiman, David. New Adventures. 2015. (Illus.). 47p. (J). ***(978-1-4806-9626-6(9))*** Dorling Kindersley Publishing, Inc.

Fillbach Brothers. Star Wars: Clone Wars Adventures, 1 vol. 2013. (Star Wars Digests Set 2 Ser.). (ENG.). 80p. (J). (gr. 4-8). lib. bdg. 27.07 *(978-1-61479-058-7(2))*; lib. bdg. 27.07 *(978-1-61479-059-4(0))* ABDO Publishing Co. (Essential Library).

Fillbach, Brothers & The Fillbach Brothers. Star Wars: Clone Wars Adventures, 1 vol. 2012. (Star Wars Digests Ser.). (ENG., Illus.). (J). (gr. 4-7). 88p. 27.07 *(978-1-59961-909-5(1))*; 96p. 27.07 *(978-1-59961-907-1(5))* Spotlight.

Gentry, Stephen. Journey to the Stars & Back. 2005. 52p. (J). pap. 16.49 *(978-1-4116-5985-8(6))* Lulu Pr., Inc.

Golden Books. Star Wars: Attack of the Clones (Star Wars) Beavers, Ethen, illus. 2015. (Little Golden Book Ser.). (ENG.). 24p. (J). (-k). 4.99 *(978-0-7364-3546-8(8)*, Golden Bks.) Random Hse. Children's Bks.

Golden Books, illus. The Star Wars Little Golden Book Library (Star Wars), 6 vols. 2015. (ENG.). 144p. (J). (-k). 29.94 *(978-0-7364-3470-6(4)*, Golden Bks.) Random Hse. Children's Bks.

Golden Books Staff. Star Wars: the Force Awakens (Star Wars) Golden Books Staff & Meurer, Caleb, illus. 2016. (Little Golden Book Ser.). (ENG.). 24p. (J). (-k). 4.99 *(978-0-7364-3491-1(7)*, Golden Bks.) Random Hse. Children's Bks.

Grahame, Howard. The Wishing Book 2 - Return to Mars. 2009. 102p. (J). pap. *(978-1-905809-80-6(8))* Pneuma Springs Publishing.

Grange, Emma. Lego Star Wars: The Return of the Jedi. 2014. (LEGO Star Wars DK Reader Ser.). lib. bdg. 13.55 *(978-0-606-35735-7(1))* Turtleback Bks.

Harper, Benjamin. Star Wars Rebels: the Secret Jedi: The Adventures of Kanan Jarrus: Rebel Leader & Jedi Master. 2015. (ENG.). 32p. (J). (gr. 2). 12.99 *(978-0-7944-3290-4(5)*, Reader's Digest Children's Bks.) Studio Fun International.

Hartley, Steve. Attack of the Alien Brain. Lum, Bernice, illus. unabr. ed. 2015. (Oliver Fibbs Ser.: 1). (ENG.). 192p. (J). (gr. 2-5). pap. 10.99 *(978-1-4472-2023-7(4))* Pan Macmillan GBR. Dist: Independent Pubs. Group.

Hatke, Ben. Zita the Spacegirl. Hatke, Ben, illus. 2011. (Zita the Spacegirl Ser.: 1). (ENG., Illus.). 192p. (J). (gr. 3-7). 19.99 *(978-1-59643-695-4(6)*, 9781596436954); pap. 12.99 *(978-1-59643-446-2(5)*, 9781596434462) Roaring Brook Pr. (First Second Bks.).

—Zita the Spacegirl. 2011. (Zita the Spacegirl Ser.: 1). (J). lib. bdg. 24.50 *(978-0-606-21623-4(5)*, Turtleback) Turtleback Bks.

Hayes, Vicki C. Home Planet, 1 vol. 2015. (Red Rhino Ser.). (ENG.). 72p. (J). (gr. 3-6). mass mkt. 7.95 *(978-1-62250-966-9(8))* Saddleback Educational Publishing, Inc.

Hirschfeld, Robert. Martians Are People, Too. 2011. (Navigators Ser.). (J). pap. *(978-1-61672-969-1(4))* Benchmark Education Co.

Howard, Grahame. The Wishing Book 3 - Extermination. 2010. 170p. (J). pap. *(978-1-905809-90-5(5))* Pneuma Springs Publishing.

Jeapes, Ben. His Majesty's Starship. 2013. 348p. pap. *(978-1-909016-18-7(7))* Monico.

Johnson, Mike. Galileo Seven Part 1, 1 vol. 2013. (Star Trek Ser.). (ENG.). 24p. (J). (gr. 6-12). lib. bdg. 24.21 *(978-1-61479-159-1(7))* Spotlight.

—Galileo Seven Part 2, 1 vol. 2013. (Star Trek Ser.). (ENG.). 24p. (J). (gr. 6-12). lib. bdg. 24.21 *(978-1-61479-160-7(0))* Spotlight.

—Star Trek. 2013. (Star Trek Ser.: 4). 24p. (J). (gr. 6-12). lib. bdg. 96.84 *(978-1-61479-158-4(9))* Spotlight.

—Where No Man Has Gone Before Part 1, 1 vol. 2013. (Star Trek Ser.). (ENG.). 24p. (J). (gr. 6-12). lib. bdg. 24.21 *(978-1-61479-161-4(9))* Spotlight.

—Where No Man Has Gone Before Part 2, 1 vol. 2013. (Star Trek Ser.). (ENG.). 24p. (J). (gr. 6-12). lib. bdg. 24.21 *(978-1-61479-162-1(7))* Spotlight.

Kogge, Michael. Ezra's Duel with Danger. 2015. (Illus.). 119p. (J). ***(978-1-4844-5079-6(5))*** Disney Publishing Worldwide.

Kogge, Michael. Rise of the Rebels. 2014. (Star Wars Rebels Chapter Bks.). (J). lib. bdg. 16.00 *(978-0-606-35281-9(3))* Turtleback Bks.

Landers, Ace. Anakin to the Rescue. 2012. (LEGO Star Wars 8X8 Ser.). lib. bdg. 13.55 *(978-0-606-26774-8(3)*, Turtleback) Turtleback Bks.

Lavoie, Rejean. Des Legumes Pour Frank Einstein. Begin, Jean-Guy, illus. 2004. (Des 9 Ans. Ser.: Vol. 44). (FRE.). 120p. (J). 8.95 *(978-2-89599-006-2(9))* Editions de la Paix CAN. Dist: World of Reading, Ltd.

Levine, Caroline Anne. Jay Grows an Alien. 2007. 73p. (J). (gr. 5-13). pap. 13.95 *(978-1-931282-29-1(3))* Autism Asperger Publishing Co.

LucasFilm Press. Star Wars Han & the Rebel Rescue. 2017. (ENG.). 24p. (J). (gr. 1-3). pap. 4.99 *(978-1-368-00352-0(4)*, Disney Lucasfilm Press) Disney Publishing Worldwide.

Manchee, William. Tarizon the Liberator: Tarizon Trilogy Vol 1. 2008. 340p. (YA). (gr. 7-18). lib. bdg. 24.00 *(978-1-929976-48-5(8)*, TOP) Top Pubns., Ltd.

McCliggott, Timothy M. A Report on Quibnoida. McCliggott, Timothy M., illus. 2007. (Illus.). 52p. (YA). pap. 17.00 *(978-0-8059-7289-4(7))* Dorrance Publishing Co., Inc.

McDougall, Sophia. Mars Evacuees. (J). (gr. 3-7). 2016. 432p. pap. 7.99 *(978-0-06-229400-5(8))* 2015. 416p. 16.99 *(978-0-06-229399-2(0))* HarperCollins Pubs.

Metzger, Joanna. The Space Program. Elizalde, Marcelo, illus. 2006. 142p. (J). *(978-1-59336-695-7(7))* Mondo Publishing.

Mordenga, Michael P. Spirit Box. 2007. 280p. per. 17.95 *(978-0-595-43785-6(0))* iUniverse, Inc.

My Teacher Flunked the Planet. 2014. (My Teacher Bks.: 4). (ENG., Illus.). 208p. (J). (gr. 3-7). 17.99 *(978-1-4814-0433-4(4)*, Simon & Schuster/Paula Wiseman Bks.) Simon & Schuster/Paula Wiseman Bks.

My Teacher Glows in the Dark. 2014. (My Teacher Bks.: 3). (ENG., Illus.). 192p. (J). (gr. 3-7). 17.99 *(978-1-4814-0432-7(6)*, Simon & Schuster/Paula Wiseman Bks.) Simon & Schuster/Paula Wiseman Bks.

Nivola, Claire A. Star Child. Nivola, Claire A., illus. 2014. (ENG., Illus.). 40p. (J). (gr. k-3). 16.99 *(978-0-374-37182-1(2)*, 9780374371821, Farrar, Straus & Giroux (BYR)) Farrar, Straus & Giroux.

N'Leh, Anne-Claire. The Planet of Trainiacs. Élyum Studio, illus. 2013. (Little Prince Ser.: 10). (ENG.). 56p. (J). (gr. 4-8). lib. bdg. 26.60 *(978-0-7613-8760-2(9)*, Graphic Universe™) Lerner Publishing Group.

North, Phoebe. Starbreak. 2014. (Starglass Sequence Ser.). (ENG., Illus.). 432p. (YA). (gr. 7). 17.99 *(978-1-4424-5956-4(5)*, Simon & Schuster Bks. For Young Readers) Simon & Schuster Bks. For Young Readers.

Park, Louise. New Girl. May, Kyla & Matthews, Melanie, illus. 2015. (Star Girl Ser.). (ENG.). 80p. (gr. 1-4). lib. bdg. 22.65 *(978-1-4795-8275-4(1))* Picture Window Bks.

—Odd One Out. May, Kyla & Matthews, Melanie, illus. 2015. (Star Girl Ser.). (ENG.). 80p. (gr. 1-4). lib. bdg. 22.65 *(978-1-4795-8276-1(X))* Picture Window Bks.

—Three's a Crowd. May, Kyla & Matthews, Melanie, illus. 2015. (Star Girl Ser.). (ENG.). 80p. (gr. 1-4). lib. bdg. 22.65 *(978-1-4795-8278-5(6))* Picture Window Bks.

—Winning Moves. May, Kyla & Matthews, Melanie, illus. 2015. (Star Girl Ser.). (ENG.). 80p. (gr. 1-4). lib. bdg. 22.65 *(978-1-4795-8277-8(8))* Picture Window Bks.

Peterson, Alyson. The Exiled Prince. 2017. (ENG.). (YA). (gr. 8-12). pap. 17.99 ***(978-1-4621-2035-2(0)***, Sweetwater Bks.) Cedar Fort, Inc./CFI Distribution.

Pike, Christopher, pseud. Aliens in the Sky. 2014. (Spooksville Ser.: 4). (ENG., Illus.). 128p. (J). (gr. 3-7). pap. 6.99 *(978-1-4814-1058-8(X)*, Aladdin) Simon & Schuster Children's Publishing.

Piper, Henry Beam. Little Fuzzy. 2007. (ENG.). 172p. per. 19.99 *(978-1-4346-2928-9(7))*; 188p. per. 21.99 *(978-1-4346-2952-4(X))* Creative Media Partners, LLC.

Pittman, Eddie. Red's Planet. 2016. (Red's Planet Ser.: 1). (J). lib. bdg. 20.80 *(978-0-606-38203-8(8))* Turtleback Bks.

Price, Michael & Howard, Kate. Droid Tales. 2015. (Lego Star Wars Ser.). (ENG.). 96p. (J). (gr. 2-5). pap. 7.99 *(978-0-545-87328-4(2))* Scholastic, Inc.

Pringle, Eric. Big George & the Winter King. Paine, Colin, illus. 2004. (ENG.). 208p. (J). pap. 12.99 *(978-0-7475-6341-9(1))* Bloomsbury Publishing Plc GBR. Dist: Independent Pubs. Group.

Richards, Barnaby. Blip! Toon Level 1. 2016. (ENG., Illus.). 40p. (J). (gr. -1-k). 12.95 *(978-1-935179-98-6(5))* TOON Books / RAW Junior, LLC.

Robinson, R. M. Death by Paradox. 2014. (Illus.). 320p. (YA). 29.95 *(978-1-939434-14-2(9))* Firefall Editions.

Rossignol, Manon Éléonor & Lecor, Tex. Isory Poutch et le Sortilege de Cacouna. 2004. (FRE., Illus.). 398p. (J). *(978-2-9807852-1-4(0)*, Spotlight Poets) Editions le Poutchoman.

Sachar, Louis. Marvin Redpost #6: a Flying Birthday Cake? Record, Adam, illus. 2015. (Marvin Redpost Ser.: 6). (ENG.). 96p. (J). (gr. 1-4). lib. bdg. 12.99 *(978-0-553-53544-0(7)*, Random Hse. Bks. for Young Readers) Random Hse. Children's Bks.

Schaefer, Elizabeth. The Force Awakens: Episode VII. White, Dave, illus. 2016. (LEGO Star Wars 8X8 Ser.). (ENG.). 24p. (J). (gr. -1-3). 13.55 *(978-0-606-39117-7(7))* Turtleback Bks.

Scholastic Editors & Fry, Jason. Darth Vader. 2017. (Backstories Ser.: Vol. 6). (ENG., Illus.). 128p. (J). (gr. 3-7). 16.00 *(978-0-606-39145-0(2))* Turtleback Bks.

Schoon, Christian. Zenn Scarlett. 2013. (ENG.). 304p. (J). (gr. 7). pap. 9.99 *(978-1-908844-55-2(8)*, Strange Chemistry) Watkins Media Limited GBR. Dist: Penguin Random Hse. LLC.

Scieszka, Jon. Baloney (Henry P.) Smith, Lane, illus. 2005. (gr. -1-3). 17.00 *(978-0-7569-5494-9(0))* Perfection Learning Corp.

Smith, Geof. A New Hope (Star Wars) Meurer, Caleb & Rose, Micky, illus. 2017. (Big Golden Book Ser.). (ENG.). 48p. (J). (gr. -1-2). 10.99 *(978-0-7364-3692-2(8),* Golden Bks.) Random Hse. Children's Bks.

—Star Wars: a New Hope (Star Wars) Meurer, Caleb, illus. 2015. (Little Golden Book Ser.). (ENG.). 24p. (J). (-k). 4.99 *(978-0-7364-3538-3(7),* Golden Bks.) Random Hse. Children's Bks.

—Star Wars: Revenge of the Sith (Star Wars) Spaziante, Patrick, illus. 2015. (Little Golden Book Ser.). (ENG.). 24p. (J). (-k). 4.99 *(978-0-7364-3540-6(9),* Golden Bks.) Random Hse. Children's Bks.

—Star Wars: the Empire Strikes Back (Star Wars) Kennett, Chris, illus. 2015. (Little Golden Book Ser.). (ENG.). 24p. (J). (-k). 4.99 *(978-0-7364-3544-4(1),* Golden Bks.) Random Hse. Children's Bks.

Stadler, Alexander. Trash Crisis on Earth, No. 1. 2009. (Julian Rodriguez Ser.: 1). (ENG.). 128p. (J). (gr. 2-5). 5.99 *(978-0-439-91970-8(3),* Scholastic Paperbacks) Scholastic, Inc.

Stock, Lisa. Battle for Naboo. 2012. (Star Wars DK Readers Level 3 Ser.). lib. bdg. 13.55 *(978-0-606-26564-5(3),* Turtleback) Turtleback Bks.

Strasser, Todd. The Beast of Cretacea. 2015. (ENG.). 432p. (J). (gr. 7). 18.99 *(978-0-7636-6901-0(6))* Candlewick Pr.

Trine, Greg. Willy Maykit in Space. Burks, James, illus. (ENG.). 208p. (J). (gr. 2-5). 2016. pap. 7.99 *(978-0-544-66848-5(0))* 2015. 13.99 *(978-0-544-31351-4(8))* Houghton Mifflin Harcourt Publishing Co. (HMH Books For Young Readers).

Victor, Pamela. Baj & the Word Launcher: Space Age Asperger Adventures in Communication. 2006. (ENG., Illus.). 112p. (J). (gr. 4-7). per. 19.95 *(978-1-84310-830-6(5),* 5281) Kingsley, Jessica Pubs. GBR. Dist: Macmillan Distribution Ltd.

Walsh, Jill Paton. The Green Book. Bloom, Lloyd, illus. 2012. (ENG.). 80p. (J). (gr. 3-7). pap. 6.99 *(978-0-312-64122-1(2),* 9780312641221) Square Fish.

Watson, Jude. Death on Naboo. 2006. (Star Wars Ser.: No. 4). 135p. (J). lib. bdg. 13.00 *(978-1-4242-0777-0(0))* Fitzgerald Bks.

—The Desperate Mission. 2005. (Star Wars Ser.: No. 1). 168p. (J). lib. bdg. 20.00 *(978-1-4242-0774-9(6))* Fitzgerald Bks.

—Underworld. 2005. (Star Wars Ser.: No. 3). 137p. (J). lib. bdg. 20.00 *(978-1-4242-0776-3(2))* Fitzgerald Bks.

Waugh, Sylvia. Carrera Espacial. (SPA.). (YA). 8.95 *(978-958-04-6028-2(0))* Norma S.A. COL. Dist: Distribuidora Norma, Inc.

Wells, H. G. The War of the Worlds. 2003. (Saddleback Classics Ser.). (Illus.). 79p. (YA). (gr. 8-12). per. 6.95 *(978-1-56254-533-8(7),* SP5337) Saddleback Educational Publishing, Inc.

—The War of the Worlds. 2008. 256p. (J). (gr. 3-7). 29.95 *(978-1-4344-6610-5(8));* pap. 14.95 *(978-1-4344-6609-9(4))* Wildside Pr., LLC.

White, Ruth. You'll Like It Here (Everybody Does) 2012. (ENG.). 272p. (J). (gr. 4-7). 7.99 *(978-0-375-86596-1(9),* Yearling) Random Hse. Children's Bks.

Williams, Suzanne. Human or Alien? Carter, Abby, illus. 2004. (Marvelous Mind of Matthew Mcghee Age 8 Ser.). 57p. (J). (gr. 1-4). 11.65 *(978-0-7569-5529-8(7))* Perfection Learning Corp.

Willis, Jeanne. Dr Xargle's Book of Earth Hounds. Ross, Tony, illus. 2012. (ENG.). 28p. (J). (gr. -1-k). pap. 13.99 *(978-1-84270-170-6(3))* Andersen Pr. GBR. Dist: Independent Pubs. Group.

—Dr Xargle's Book of Earth Relations. Ross, Tony, illus. (ENG.). 32p. (J). pap. 9.99 *(978-1-84270-307-6(2))* Andersen Pr. GBR. Dist: Trafalgar Square Publishing.

—Dr Xargle's Book of Earth Tiggers. Ross, Tony, illus. 2012. (ENG.). 28p. (J). (gr. -1-k). pap. 11.99 *(978-1-84939-297-6(8))* Andersen Pr. GBR. Dist: Independent Pubs. Group.

—Dr Xargle's Book of Earthlets. Ross, Tony, illus. 2012. (ENG.). 28p. (J). (gr. -1-k). pap. 12.99 *(978-1-84939-292-1(7))* Andersen Pr. GBR. Dist: Independent Pubs. Group.

Wilson, Eva Adriana. My Power Ball. 2013. 48p. pap. 17.45 *(978-1-4525-7676-3(9),* Balboa Pr.) Author Solutions, Inc.

Windham, Ryder. Ezra's Gamble. 2014. (Star Wars Rebels Chapter Bks.). 154p. (J). lib. bdg. 17.20 *(978-0-606-35283-3(X))* Turtleback Bks.

—Ezra's Gamble: An Original Novel. 2014. 154p. (J). ***(978-1-4242-6296-0(8))*** Disney Publishing Worldwide.

—Journey Through Space. rev. ed. 2015. (DK Readers Ser.). (ENG.). 48p. (J). (gr. 1-3). pap. 3.99 *(978-1-4654-3390-9(2),* DK Children) Dorling Kindersley Publishing, Inc.

—The Wrath of Darth Maul. 2012. 216p. (J). *(978-0-545-43367-9(3))* Scholastic, Inc.

LIFE SKILLS

Here are entered works that discuss a combination of the skills needed by an individual to exist in modern society, including skills related to education, employment, finance, health, housing, psychology, etc.

see also Conduct of Life

Adler, Mia Sharon. Essential Proteen-Student Journal: A Life Skills Program for Helping Teens Succeed: Student Journal. 2006. (ENG.). 48p. (YA). pap. 5.98 *(978-0-87822-582-8(X),* 5284) Research Pr.

Bailey, Annette Gentry & McGraw-Hill Education Staff. Discovering Life Skills. 9th ed. 2003. (Discovering Life Skills Ser.). (ENG., Illus.). 512p. (gr. 6-7). stu. ed. 76.28 *(978-0-07-829847-9(4),* 0078298474) McGraw-Hill Higher Education.

Barlow, C. E. Scary Man. Tharp, Lauren R., illus. 2009. 44p. pap. 18.99 *(978-1-4269-1060-9(6))* Trafford Publishing.

Berkley, Elizabeth. Ask Elizabeth: Real Answers to Everything You Secretly Wanted to Ask about Love, Friends, Your Body... & Life in General. 2011. (ENG., Illus.). 240p. (YA). (gr. 7-18). 16.99 *(978-0-399-25449-9(8),* G.P. Putnam's Sons Books for Young Readers) Penguin Young Readers Group.

Bernstein, Ben. Stressed Out! - For Teens: How to Be Calm, Confident, & Focused. 2014. (ENG., Illus.). 274p. (J). (gr. 8-12). pap. 18.95 *(978-1-939629-38-8(1),* 9781939629388) Familius LLC.

Berry, Joy. Get over it! Set, 6 vols. 2005. (Winning Skills Ser.). (ENG., Illus.). 1p. (J). pap. 19.95 *(978-1-57687-292-5(0),* PowerHouse Kids) powerHouse Cultural Entertainment, Inc.

Berry, Joy, contrib. by. Go for it! Set. 2005. (Winning skills series, go for It! Ser.). (ENG., Illus.). 48p. (J). pap. 19.95 *(978-1-57687-294-9(7),* PowerHouse Kids) powerHouse Cultural Entertainment, Inc.

Bizos, Erató-Nadia, et al. Life Skills Matters: Grade 3. 2003. (XHO & AFR.). 40p. pap., tchr. ed., wbk. ed. 2.05 *(978-0-521-53898-5(X))* Cambridge Univ. Pr.

—Life Skills Matters Grade 1. 2003. (AFR.). 32p. pap., wbk. ed. 1.85 *(978-0-521-53886-2(6))* Cambridge Univ. Pr.

—Life Skills Matters Grade 1 Sesotho Translation. 2003. (AFR.). 32p. pap., wbk. ed. 1.85 *(978-0-521-53884-8(X))* Cambridge Univ. Pr.

—Life Skills Matters Grade 1 Xitsonga Translation. 2003. (AFR.). 32p. pap., wbk. ed. 1.85 *(978-0-521-53885-5(8))* Cambridge Univ. Pr.

—Life Skills Matters Grade 2 isXhosa Translation. 2003. (XHO & AFR.). 32p. pap., tchr. ed., wbk. ed. 1.85 *(978-0-521-53892-3(0))* Cambridge Univ. Pr.

—Life Skills Matters Grade 2 Sesotho Translation. 2003. (AFR.). 32p. pap., wbk. ed. 1.85 *(978-0-521-53890-9(4))* Cambridge Univ. Pr.

—Life Skills Matters Grade 2 Xitsonga Translation. 2003. (AFR.). 32p. pap., wbk. ed. 1.85 *(978-0-521-53891-6(2))* Cambridge Univ. Pr.

—Life Skills Matters Grade 3 Workbook Sesotho Translation. 2003. (AFR.). 40p. pap. 2.05 *(978-0-521-53896-1(3))* Cambridge Univ. Pr.

—Life Skills Matters Grade 3 Workbook Xitsonga Translation. 2003. (AFR.). 40p. pap. 2.05 *(978-0-521-53897-8(1))* Cambridge Univ. Pr.

Borgenicht, David, et al. The Worst-Case Scenario Survival Handbook - Weird. 2010. (Worst Case Scenario Ser.). (ENG., Illus.). 128p. (J). (gr. 4-17). pap. 10.99 *(978-0-8118-7438-0(9))* Chronicle Bks. LLC.

Bostick, Nan. Consumer Spending. 2003. (Saddleback Lifeskills Ser.). (Illus.). 48p. pap., wbk. ed. 8.95 *(978-1-56254-568-0(X),* SP 568X) Saddleback Educational Publishing, Inc.

—Managing Money. 2003. (Saddleback Lifeskills Ser.). (Illus.). 47p. pap., wbk. ed. 8.95 *(978-1-56254-567-3(1),* SP 5671) Saddleback Educational Publishing, Inc.

Boyd, Ervin D., Sr. Help for the Hurting: Getting Beyond This Veil of Tears! 2003. (Illus.). 200p. (YA). spiral bd. 22.00 *(978-0-9744024-0-6(0))* Anointed Word Pubns.

Brown, Cherie. Love Doesn't Hurt: Life Lessons for Young Women. 2003. (YA). per. 19.95 *(978-0-9743676-0-6(5))* Avant-garde Bks.

Building a Culture of Life Leader's Manual. 2nd ed. 2004. (YA). per. 19.95 *(978-0-9764572-0-6(2))* Together, Inc.

Building a Culture of Life Study Guide. 2004. (YA). per. 17.95 *(978-0-9764572-1-3(0))* Together, Inc.

Cairney, Gemma. Open: a Toolkit for How Magic & Messed up Life Can Be. 2017. (ENG., Illus.). 320p. (YA). (gr. 9). 18.99 ***(978-1-5098-3611-6(X))*** Pan Macmillan GBR. Dist: Independent Pubs. Group.

Candell, Arianna. Mind Your Manners: In School. Curto, Rosa M., illus. 2005. (Mind Your Manners Ser.). (ENG.). 36p. (J). pap. 6.99 *(978-0-7641-3166-0(4))* Barron's Educational Series, Inc.

Capua, Sarah De. Life Skills Biographies. 2007. 48p. lib. bdg. 251.40 *(978-1-60279-110-7(4),* 200037) Cherry Lake Publishing.

Carle, Gilda. Teen Talk with Dr. Gilda: A Girl's Guide to Dating. 2003. (ENG.). 304p. pap. 13.99 *(978-0-06-095871-8(5),* William Morrow Paperbacks) HarperCollins Pubs.

Champion, Neil. Finding Food & Water. 2010. (Survive Alive Ser.). 32p. (J). (gr. 3-6). 28.50 *(978-1-60753-037-4(6))* Amicus Publishing.

—Fire & Cooking. 2010. (Survive Alive Ser.). 32p. (J). (gr. 3-6). 28.50 *(978-1-60753-039-8(2))* Amicus Publishing.

—In an Emergency. 2010. (Survive Alive Ser.). 32p. (J). (gr. 3-6). 28.50 *(978-1-60753-040-4(6))* Amicus Publishing.

—Tools & Crafts. 2010. (Survive Alive Ser.). 32p. (J). (gr. 3-6). 28.50 *(978-1-60753-042-8(2))* Amicus Publishing.

Champion, Neil & Ganeri, Anita. Fire & Cooking. 2011. (How the World Makes Music Ser.). 32p. (gr. 4-7). lib. bdg. 31.35 *(978-1-59920-480-2(0))* Black Rabbit Bks.

—In an Emergency. 2011. (How the World Makes Music Ser.). 32p. (gr. 4-7). lib. bdg. 31.35 *(978-1-59920-482-6(7))* Black Rabbit Bks.

—Tools & Crafts. 2011. (How the World Makes Music Ser.). 32p. (gr. 4-7). lib. bdg. 31.35 *(978-1-59920-481-9(9))* Black Rabbit Bks.

Chronicle Books Staff. 101 Things to Do While You Wait. (J). 15.95 *(978-0-8118-3922-8(2))* Chronicle Bks. LLC.

Coping. 2005. 192p. (gr. 7-12). lib. bdg. 1735.65 *(978-0-8239-3906-0(5))* Rosen Publishing Group, Inc., The.

Coping: Working Against the Odds, 8 bks. Incl. Coping When a Brother or Sister Is Autistic. Rosenberg, Marsha Sarah. 192p. 2005. lib. bdg. 34.60 *(978-0-8239-3194-1(3));* Coping When Someone in Your Family Has Cancer. Rocha, Toni L. 192p. 2005. lib. bdg. 34.60 *(978-0-8239-3195-8(1));* Coping with Dangers on the Internet. Rothman, Kevin F. 192p. 2005. lib. bdg. 34.60 *(978-0-8239-3201-6(X));* Coping with Leukemia. Apel, Melanie Ann. 106p. 2001. lib. bdg. 34.60 *(978-0-8239-3200-9(1));* Coping with Lyme Disease. Donnelly, Karen J. 192p. 2005. lib. bdg. 34.60 *(978-0-8239-3199-6(4));* Coping with Mental Illness. Moe, Barbara. 192p. 2005. lib. bdg. 34.60 *(978-0-8239-3205-4(2));* Coping with Schizophrenia. Kelly, Pat. 192p. 2005. lib. bdg. 34.60 *(978-0-8239-2853-8(5));* Coping with Vision Disorders. Stanley, Debbie. 192p. 2005. lib. bdg. 34.60 *(978-0-8239-3198-9(6));* (YA). (gr. 7-12). (Illus.). Set lib. bdg. 202.00 *(978-0-8239-9206-5(3))* Rosen Publishing Group, Inc., The.

Cosmic Debris Etc., Inc. Staff, et al. Middle School. 2009. (Worst Case Scenario Ser.). (ENG., Illus.). 128p. (J). (gr. 6-8). pap. 10.99 *(978-0-8118-6864-8(8))* Chronicle Bks. LLC.

Crow, Gary & Crow, Marissa. The Yes Bank. 2003. (Illus.). 73p. (J). pap. 9.95 *(978-0-9718758-7-6(1))* Koenisha Pubns.

Dewey D's Life Skills Curriculum. (J). ring bd. 95.00 *(978-1-56230-706-6(1))* Syndistar, Inc.

Do You Have What It Takes. 2007. (YA). per. 35.00 *(978-0-9661256-9-6(X))* Youth Communication - New York Center.

Earl, C. F. & Vanderhoof, Gabrielle. Army Rangers. 2010. (Special Forces Ser.). (Illus.). 64p. (YA). (gr. 7-18). lib. bdg. 22.95 *(978-1-4222-1838-9(4))* Mason Crest.

Earnhardt, Crystal. Race to Victory Lane. 2003. 75p. per. 2.49 *(978-0-8280-1775-6(1))* Review & Herald Publishing Assn.

Einenne, Arielle. The You Behind the Mascara: A Growing-up Guide for Teenage Girls. 2009. 41p. pap. 14.64 *(978-0-557-09624-4(3))* Lulu Pr., Inc.

Endres, Hollie J. The Letter Dd Set: Things I Can Do, 6 vols. 2004. (Letter Bks.). (ENG.). 8p. (gr. k-1). pap. 29.70 *(978-0-7368-4103-0(2),* Letter Bks.) Capstone Press of Coughlan Cos.

Everly, Nita. Early Social Behavior Books Can You Be a Helper? 2007. (J). spiral bd. 11.95 *(978-0-7606-0741-1(9))* LinguiSystems, Inc.

Falk, Emily. 78 Things they Didn't Teach You in School: But You Do Need to Know. 2004. (Illus.). 123p. (YA). pap. 10.95 *(978-1-58786-016-4(3),* Rabbit's Foot Pr.) Blue Mountain Arts Inc.

Fear Not My Child, I Am Here: Emerging from the Spiral of Fear the Practical Mystic's Guide for Embracing Your Heart's Desire. 2003rd ed. 2003. 240p. per. 15.95 *(978-0-9742213-0-4(9))* Community Works!

Fey, Sid & Vitello, Kathy. The Being Game: For the Love of Your Life. l.t. ed. 2004. (Illus.). 66p. per. 14.95 *(978-0-9753530-5-9(5))* Fey, Sid Designs, Inc.

Foster, John. Llinynnau. 2005. (WEL., Illus.). 78p. pap. *(978-1-85644-327-2(2))* CAA.

Foster, John & Stewart, Peter. Llinynnau. Isaac, Colin, tr. from ENG. 2005. (WEL., Illus.). 71p. pap. *(978-1-85644-328-9(0))* CAA.

Giddens, Sandra & Giddens, Owen. Coping with Grieving & Loss. 2003. (Coping Ser.). 124p. (YA). (gr. 7-12). lib. bdg. 34.60 *(978-0-8239-3758-5(5))* Rosen Publishing Group, Inc., The.

Glasser, Debbie & Schenck, Emily. New Kid, New Scene: A Guide to Moving & Switching Schools. 2011. (Illus.). 112p. (J). 14.95 *(978-1-4338-1039-8(5),* Magination Pr.) American Psychological Assn.

Gomez Seitz, M. Stella. The Master Cookie-Maker: A True Life Story for Children. 2003. 133p. (J). pap. 13.95 *(978-0-595-26314-1(3),* Writers Club Pr.) iUniverse, Inc.

Hansen, Mark & Ferber, Kevin S. Success 101 for Teens: Dollars & Sense for a Winning Financial Life. 2012. (ENG.). 176p. pap. 12.95 *(978-1-55778-901-3(0),* 4580c8ac-14b2-4d64-ae8a-be308d9302c6) Paragon Hse. Pubs.

Harrington, Paul. The Secret to Teen Power. 2010. (JPN., Illus.). 254p. (YA). *(978-4-04-791630-2(7))* Fukuinkan Shoten.

—The Secret to Teen Power. 2009. (ENG., Illus.). 192p. (YA). (gr. 7-18). 19.99 *(978-1-4169-9498-5(X))* Simon Pulse/Beyond Words.

Hawran, Mary. How to Be A Recycling Hero. 2004. (Illus.). 64p. 7.95 *(978-0-9753758-0-8(6))* Stourbridge Distributors, Inc.

Hipp, Earl. Fighting Invisible Tigers: Stress Management for Teens. 3rd rev. ed. 2008. (ENG., Illus.). 160p. (YA). (gr. 6-13). pap. 14.99 *(978-1-57542-282-4(4))* Free Spirit Publishing, Inc.

Hollis, Randy. Meet Sneazle, 1. Rahn, Jess, illus. 2004. 20p. (J). 6.95 *(978-0-9758815-0-7(7))* SNZ Publishing.

Holt, Rinehart and Winston Staff. A Lifetime of Health: Life Skills. 4th ed. Date not set. pap., wbk. ed. 11.20 *(978-0-03-068117-2(0))* Holt McDougal.

Hutchinson, Emily. Car & Driver. 2003. (Saddleback Lifeskills Ser.). (Illus.). 48p. pap., wbk. ed. 8.95 *(978-1-56254-573-4(6),* SP 5736) Saddleback Educational Publishing, Inc.

—Everyday Household Tasks. 2003. (Saddleback Lifeskills Ser.). (Illus.). 48p. pap., wbk. ed. 8.95 *(978-1-56254-565-9(5),* SP 5655) Saddleback Educational Publishing, Inc.

—Moving Out on Your Own. 2003. (Saddleback Lifeskills Ser.). (Illus.). 48p. wbk. ed. 8.95 *(978-1-56254-564-2(7),* SP 5647) Saddleback Educational Publishing, Inc.

Jane, Christy Gast, et al. Caring for Myself. 2007. (ENG., Illus.). 96p. pap. 24.95 ***(978-1-84310-887-0(9),*** 2643) Kingsley, Jessica Pubs. GBR. Dist: Macmillan Distribution Ltd.

Jeffrie, Sally. A Guide to Being a Goddess. 2009. (Best at Everything Ser.). (ENG.). 128p. (J). (gr. 3-7). 9.99 *(978-0-545-08537-3(3))* Scholastic, Inc.

Johnson, Leona. Strengthening Family & Self: Teaching Package Teacher's Annotated Edition. annot. ed. 845p. (gr. 9-12). tchr. ed. 69.00 *(978-1-59070-123-2(2))* Goodheart-Willcox Pub.

—Strengthening Family & Self: Teaching Package Teacher's Resource Guide. 424p. (gr. 9-12). tchr. ed. 64.00 *(978-1-59070-125-6(9))* Goodheart-Willcox Pub.

—Strengthening Family & Self: Teaching Package Teacher's Resource Portfolio. 460p. (gr. 9-12). tchr. ed. 136.00 *(978-1-59070-126-3(7))* Goodheart-Willcox Pub.

Jones, Steven. Journey to Excellence: An Introduction to E4. 2003. 75p. (YA). per. 19.99 *(978-0-9729798-0-1(8))* Keytochange Publishing, Inc.

King, Emily. Mrs. Twiggenbotham Goes to a Party. 2003. (Illus.). 32p. (J). 12.99 *(978-0-8254-3065-7(8))* Kregel Pubns.

Lindsey Reeves, Diane. Career Ideas for Teens in Education & Training. 2nd rev. ed. 2011. (Career Ideas for Teens Ser.). (Illus.). 182p. (gr. 6-12). 45.00 *(978-0-8160-8274-2(X))* Facts On File, Inc.

Machen Pritchard, M. Ann. Phil the Pill & Friends: Making Positive Choices. Machen Pritchard, M. Ann, illus. 2005. (Illus.). 75p. (J). per. 11.99 *(978-0-9772210-0-4(8),* Phil the Pill & Friends) MAMP Creations.

Mack, Cassandra. Cool, Confident & Strong: 52 Power Moves for Girls. 2007. 100p. per. 11.95 *(978-0-595-47560-5(4),* Authors Choice Pr.) iUniverse, Inc.

Magness, Valerie. A Special Book about Me! 2004. 40p. spiral bd. 10.00 *(978-1-4116-2500-6(5))* Lulu Pr., Inc.

Mahoney, Ellen Voelckers. Coping: A Specialized Title for Everyone, 6 bks. Rosen, Roger, ed. Incl. Coping: Now You've Got Your Period. rev. ed. (Illus.). 192p. (YA). (gr. 7-12). 1993. lib. bdg. 34.60 *(978-0-8239-1662-7(6),* COPERI); (Illus.). Set lib. bdg. 151.50 *(978-0-8239-9303-1(5))* Rosen Publishing Group, Inc., The.

Mathias, Adeline. How a Young Brave Survived. Hamilton, Penny, ed. Auld, Francis & Joseph, Debbie, illus. 2009. (ENG.). 30p. (J). pap. 5.95 *(978-1-934594-04-9(0))* Salish Kootenia College Pr.

McDougal, Anna. We Make Cookies: Working at the Same Time. 2017. (Computer Science for the Real World Ser.). 8p. (gr. 5-6). pap. 6.20 ***(978-1-5383-5099-7(8),*** Rosen Classroom) Rosen Publishing Group, Inc., The.

McGraw, Jay & Björkman, Manns. Life Strategies for Dealing with Bullies. Björkman, Steve, illus. 2008. (ENG.). 192p. (J). (gr. 4-8). 17.99 *(978-1-4169-7473-4(3),* Aladdin) Simon & Schuster Children's Publishing.

McTavish, Sandra. Life Skills: 225 Ready-to-Use Health Activities for Success & Well-Being (Grades 6-12) 2003. (ENG., Illus.). 284p. pap. 32.95 *(978-0-7879-6959-2(1),* Jossey-Bass) Wiley, John & Sons, Inc.

Michael O'Mara Books UK Staff. The Gift for Boys. 2010. (ENG., Illus.). 64p. (J). (gr. 1-7). 4.95 *(978-1-84317-423-3(5))* O'Mara, Michael Bks., Ltd. GBR. Dist: Independent Pubs. Group.

Mortimer, J. R. & Castaldo, Nancy F. This or That? 3: Even More Wacky Choices to Reveal the Hidden You. 2015. (ENG., Illus.). 176p. (J). (gr. 3-7). pap. 12.99 *(978-1-4263-1881-8(2),* National Geographic Children's Bks.) National Geographic Society.

Moss, Marissa. Bully Survival Guide. Moss, Marissa, illus. 2012. (Amelia Ser.). (ENG., Illus.). 40p. (J). (gr. 2-5). pap. 6.99 *(978-1-4169-1288-0(6),* Simon & Schuster/Paula Wiseman Bks.) Simon & Schuster/Paula Wiseman Bks.

Mulcahy, Lisa, et al. Bye Bye Boredom! The Girl's Life Big Book of Fun. 2003. (Illus.). 124p. (J). *(978-0-439-44976-2(6))* Scholastic, Inc.

Nagle, Jeanne. Great Lifelong Learning Skills. 2009. (Work Readiness Ser.). 64p. (gr. 6-6). 58.50 *(978-1-60854-825-5(2))* Rosen Publishing Group, Inc., The.

Nagle, Jeanne M. Great Lifelong Learning Skills. 2008. (Work Readiness Ser.). (Illus.). 64p. (YA). (gr. 8-12). lib. bdg. 31.95 *(978-1-4042-1424-8(0),* 1277025) Rosen Publishing Group, Inc., The.

Naik, Anita. Bras, Boys & Bad Hair Days: A Girl's Guide to Living with Style. 2008. (ENG., Illus.). 172p. (J). (gr. 7-17). pap. 7.99 *(978-0-340-97057-7(X))* Hodder & Stoughton GBR. Dist: Hachette Bk. Group.

Naish, Sarah & Jefferies, Rosie. William Wobbly & the Mysterious Holey Jumper: A Story about Fear & Coping. Evans, Megan, illus. 2017. (Therapeutic Parenting Bks.). (ENG.). 32p. (J). pap. 14.95 ***(978-1-78592-281-7(5),*** 9201) Kingsley, Jessica Pubs. GBR. Dist: Macmillan Distribution Ltd.

National Crime Prevention Council (U.S.) Staff, contrib. by. McGruff & Scruff(r)'s Stories & Activities for Children of Promise. 2004. (Illus.). 24p. (J). *(978-1-59686-001-8(4))* National Crime Prevention Council.

The Need to Know Library: Learning to Deal with Problems Facing Every Teen, 9 bks. Incl. Everything You Need to Know about Cancer. Massari, Francesca. lib. bdg. 31.95 *(978-0-8239-3164-4(1),* NTCANC); Everything You Need to Know about Dealing with Stalking. Wright, Cynthia. lib. bdg. 31.95 *(978-0-8239-2841-5(1),* NTSTAL); Everything You Need to Know about Drug Abuse. Herscovitch, Arthur. lib. bdg. 31.95 *(978-0-8239-3036-4(X),* NTGUGU); Everything You Need to Know about Eating Smart. Weintraub, Aileen. lib. bdg. 31.95 *(978-0-8239-3082-1(3),* NTEASM); Everything You Need to Know about Looking & Feeling Your Best: A Guide for Girls. Sommers, Annie Leah. lib. bdg. 31.95 *(978-0-8239-3079-1(3),* NTGUWO); Everything You Need to Know about Looking & Feeling Your Best: A Guide for Guys. Sommers, Michael A. lib. bdg. 31.95 *(978-0-8239-3080-7(7),* NTGUGU); Everything You Need to Know about Public Speaking. Blumstein, Rachel. lib. bdg. 31.95 *(978-0-8239-3087-6(4),* NTPUSP); Everything You Need to Know about Weapons in School & at Home. Schleifer, Jay. lib. bdg. 31.95 *(978-0-8239-3315-0(6));* 64p. (YA). (gr. 7-12). 2005. (Illus.). Set lib. bdg. 227.25 *(978-0-8239-9283-6(7))* Rosen Publishing Group, Inc., The.

The Need to Know Library: Overcoming Life's Obstacles, 8 bks. Incl. Everything You Need to Know about Bias Incidents. 2nd rev. ed. Osborn, Kevin. (gr. 7-12). 1997. lib. bdg. 31.95 *(978-0-8239-2600-8(1),* NTBIIN); Everything You Need to Know about Incest. rev. ed. Spies, Karen Bornemann. (gr. 4-6). 1997. lib. bdg. 27.95 *(978-0-8239-2607-7(9),* NTINCE); Everything You Need to Know about Your Parent's Divorce. rev. ed. Johnson, Linda Carlson. (gr. 7-12). 1998. lib. bdg. 31.95 *(978-0-8239-2876-7(4),* NTPDIV); Everything You Need to Know When a Parent Is Out of Work. rev. ed. St. Pierre, Stephanie. (gr. 7-12). 1997. lib. bdg. 31.95 *(978-0-8239-2608-4(7),* NTPAOU); 64p. (YA). (Illus.). Set lib. bdg. 202.00 *(978-0-8239-9441-0(4))* Rosen Publishing Group, Inc., The.

Neusom, Sherman. Big Fat Hunka Cheese's Quest Restored Svelte. 2003. (J). per. 799.00 *(978-0-9742811-6-2(6))* Professional Publishing Hse. LLC.

Nip It in the Bud. 2003. (Humble Heart Ser.). (J). spiral bd. *(978-0-9746148-3-0(1))* Common Courtesy.

Nunes, Bill. 284 Things a Bright Midwest Boy Should Know How to Do. 2010. 344p. pap. 19.95 *(978-0-9787994-7-2(X))* Nunes, H. William.

Olsen, Mary-Kate & Olsen, Ashley. The Ultimate Guide to Mary-Kate & Ashley. 2004. (Illus.). 93p. *(978-0-00-718136-0(1))* HarperCollins Pubs. Australia.

Outram, Richard. The Adventures of Exokid & the Teachings of Money. Kapatos, Elizabeth, illus. 2009. 36p. pap. 12.95 *(978-1-59858-898-9(2))* Dog Ear Publishing, LLC.

Pofahl, Jane. Everyday Life: Middle Ages. (Time Traveler Ser.). (Illus.). 32p. (gr. 3-6). 6.99 *(978-0-513-02194-5(9),* TSD21949) Denison, T. S. & Co., Inc.

Random House Australia Staff. Love You, Me. 2016. (ENG., Illus.). 96p. (YA). (gr. 8). 9.99 *(978-0-85798-585-9(X))* Random Hse. Australia AUS. Dist: Independent Pubs. Group.

Robinson, Matthew. Making Smart Choices about Relationships. 2008. (Making Smart Choices Ser.). (Illus.). 48p. (YA). (gr. 5-9). lib. bdg. 29.25 *(978-1-4042-1390-6(2))* Rosen Publishing Group, Inc., The.

Rush, Ryan. Home on Time: Life Management by the Book. 2003. 192p. per. 10.99 *(978-0-9728899-0-2(6))* 21st Century Pr.

Salas, Laura Purdie. Taking the Plunge. 2004. (Illus.). 250p. (J). pap. 12.95 *(978-1-58760-012-8(9))*, 10129, Child & Family Pr.) Child Welfare League of America, Inc.

Saul, "Aunt" Laya. You Don't Have to Learn Everything the Hard Way: What I Wish Someone Had Told Me. 2004. 214p. (YA). per. 14.95 net. *(978-0-9723229-4-2(9))* Kadima Pr.

Scholastic, Inc. Staff & Norton, Sally. The Girls' Book of Excellence: Even More Ways to Be the Best at Everything. 2009. (Best at Everything Ser.). (ENG.). 128p. (J). (gr. 3-7). 9.99 *(978-0-545-13409-5(9)*, Scholastic Nonfiction) Scholastic, Inc.

Scholastic, Inc. Staff & Oliver, Martin. The Boys' Book of Greatness: Even More Ways to Be the Best at Everything. 2009. (Best at Everything Ser.). (ENG.). 128p. (J). (gr. 3-7). 9.99 *(978-0-545-13408-8(0)*, Scholastic Nonfiction) Scholastic, Inc.

Scholastic News Nonfiction Readers: Kids Like Me (Global Awareness), 5 vols., Set. Incl. This Is the Way We Dress. Behrens, Janice. lib. bdg. 22.00 *(978-0-531-21338-4(2))*; This Is the Way We Eat Our Food. Falk, Laine. lib. bdg. 22.00 *(978-0-531-21339-1(0))*; This Is the Way We Go to School. Falk, Laine. lib. bdg. 22.00 *(978-0-531-21341-4(2))*; This Is the Way We Help at Home. Miller, Amanda. lib. bdg. 22.00 *(978-0-531-21340-7(4))*; This Is the Way We Play. Miller, Amanda. lib. bdg. 22.00 *(978-0-531-21342-1(0))*; 24p. (J). (gr. 1-2). 2009. Set lib. bdg. 110.00 *(978-0-531-21035-2(9)*, Children's Pr.) Scholastic Library Publishing.

Shapiro, Lawrence E. & Holmes, Julia. Let's Be Friends: A Workbook to Help Kids Learn Social Skills & Make Great Friends. 2008. (Instant Help Ser.). (ENG., Illus.). 144p. (J). (gr. k-5). pap. 16.95 *(978-1-57224-610-2(3)*, Instant Help Books) New Harbinger Pubns.

Staudacher, Carol. Getting Ahead at Work. 2003. (Saddleback Lifeskills Ser.). (Illus.). 48p. pap., wbk. ed. 8.95 *(978-1-56254-570-3(1)*, SP 5701) Saddleback Educational Publishing, Inc.

—Job Search. 2003. (Saddleback Lifeskills Ser.). (Illus.). 48p. pap., wbk. ed. 8.95 *(978-1-56254-569-7(8)*, SP 5698) Saddleback Educational Publishing, Inc.

Stewart, Jan. Knowing Yourself. 2004. (ENG., Illus.). 32p. (J). pap. 9.95 *(978-0-89793-311-7(7)*, Hunter Hse.) Turner Publishing Co.

Storeby, Jordan. A Boy's Book of Daily Thoughts: For Ages 8 To 12. 2004. 374p. (J). pap. 12.95 *(978-0-929636-20-7(1))* Syren Bk. Co.

Sullivan, James Kevin, illus. What Went Right Today? Journal: WWRT Journal. 2007. 72p. (J). spiral bd. 12.95 *(978-0-9766990-1-9(X))* Buz-Land Presentations, Inc.

Suter, Joanne. Community Resources. 2003. (Saddleback Lifeskills Ser.). (Illus.). 48p. pap., wbk. ed. 8.95 *(978-1-56254-571-0(X)*, SP 571X) Saddleback Educational Publishing, Inc.

—Health & Safety. 2003. (Saddleback Lifeskills Ser.). (Illus.). 48p. pap., wbk. ed. 8.95 *(978-1-56254-566-6(3)*, SP 5663) Saddleback Educational Publishing, Inc.

—Public Transportation & Travel. 2003. (Saddleback Lifeskills Ser.). (Illus.). 48p. pap., wbk. ed. 8.95 *(978-1-56254-572-7(8)*, SP 5728) Saddleback Educational Publishing, Inc.

Swain, Claudia. What's a Girl to Do? 2004. 128p. pap. 6.99 *(978-1-56309-440-8(1))* New Hope Pubs.

Taylor, Sally. On My Own: The Ultimate How-to Guide for Young Adults. 2nd ed. 2004. (Illus.). 640p. (YA). (gr. 11-12). reprint ed. per. 34.95 incl. cd-rom *(978-0-9711500-0-3(1))* Silly Goose Productions, LLC.

Tedesco, Ann & Alimonti, Frederick. Not Everyone Is Nice: Helping Children Learn Caution with Strangers. DePrince, Erik & Volinski, Jessica, illus. 2003. (Let's Talk Ser.). (ENG.). 48p. (J). pap. 9.95 *(978-0-88282-233-4(0))* New Horizon Pr. Pubs., Inc.

UFlipp. You & Your Military Hero: Building Positive Thinking Skills During Your Hero's Deployment. 2009. 72p. (J). pap. 19.95 *(978-1-59298-268-4(9))* Beaver's Pond Pr., Inc.

Understanding Catechesis. 2004. (Effective Dre Ser.). pap. *(978-0-8294-1054-9(6))* Loyola Pr.

Van Wagenen, Maya. Popular: A Memoir. 2014. (ENG., Illus.). 272p. (YA). (gr. 7). 18.99 *(978-0-525-42681-3(7)*, Dutton Books for Young Readers) Penguin Young Readers Group.

Vargas, Daraciela, adapted by. Refranero Popular de Puerto Rico. 2003. lib. bdg. 10.99 *(978-0-9702021-5-4(6))* Conexion Educativa.

Veillette, Sally M. Coming to Your Senses: Soaring with Your Soul. 2005. (ENG., Illus.). 251p. pap. 19.95 *(978-0-9741854-1-5(8)*, 9780974185415) Pop the Cork Publishing.

Wallace, Mary & Wallace, Jessica. Christmas: 20 Dreamy Ways to Relax & Feel Great. Smith, Scott McBride, ed. Dávila, Claudia, illus. 2009. (ENG.). 20p. (gr. 4-8). pap. 6.25 *(978-1-897379-47-9(1)*, 1897379471) Novus Via Music Group Inc. CAN. Dist: Leonard, Hal Corp.

Webster, Jeanne. If You Could Be Anything What Would You Be? A Teen's Guide to Mapping Out the Future. Nelson, Dianne, ed. 2004. (Illus.). 137p. (J). (gr. 5-18). pap. 19.95 *(978-0-9749199-0-4(X))* Dupuis North Publishing.

Weierbach, Jane & Phillips-Hershey, Elizabeth. Mind over Basketball: Coach Yourself to Handle Stress. Beyl, Charles, illus. 2007. (Coach Yourself to Handle Stress Ser.). 48p. (J). (gr. 3-7). 14.95 *(978-1-4338-0135-8(3)*, 4418006); per. 9.95 *(978-1-4338-0136-5(1)*, 4418007) American Psychological Assn. (Magination Pr.).

White, Kelly. The Girls' Life Guide to Being the Best You! Parett, Lisa, illus. 2003. 124p. (J). *(978-0-439-44978-6(2))* Scholastic, Inc.

Whitfield, Kate. The Empowered Gal's 9 Life Lessons: Keys, Tips, Strategies, Advice & Everything You Need to Know to be a Confident, Successful, in Control Gal. 2008. 236p. pap. 18.95 *(978-0-595-47829-3(8))* iUniverse, Inc.

Whitney, Brooks. How to Survive Almost Anything. 2004. (Illus.). 80p. (J). pap. *(978-0-439-57900-1(7))* Scholastic, Inc.

Williams, Anna Graf, et al. The Family Guide to the American Workplace. Williams, Anna Graf, ed. 2003. (Illus.). 272p. per. 31.00 *(978-0-9705790-4-1(7)*, 866/332-5905) Learnovation, LLC.

Wolny, Philip. Hurricane: True Stories of Survival. 2009. (Survivor Stories Ser.). 48p. (gr. 5-5). 53.00 *(978-1-60853-254-4(2)*, Rosen Reference) Rosen Publishing Group, Inc., The.

Zellmann, Anton Josef. I Read Minds: And So Do You! Lt. ed. 2005. (Illus.). 264p. 35.00 *(978-0-9763325-0-3(7))* Zellmann Publishing, LLC.

LIFE SUPPORT SYSTEMS (SPACE ENVIRONMENT)

see also Astronauts—Clothing; Project Apollo (U.S.)

Baker, David. Living in Space. 2008. (Exploring Space Ser.). (Illus.). 32p. (J). (gr. 4-6). lib. bdg. 26.00 *(978-1-59036-769-8(3))* Weigl Pubs., Inc.

Baker, David & Kissock, Heather. Living in Space. 2008. (Exploring Space Ser.). (Illus.). 32p. (J). (gr. 4-6). pap. 9.95 *(978-1-59036-770-4(7))* Weigl Pubs., Inc.

Clay, Kathryn. Living in Space. 2017. (Little Astronauts Ser.). (ENG., Illus.). 32p. (gr. 1-2). lib. bdg. 27.99 *(978-1-5157-3657-8(1))* Capstone Press of Coughlan Cos.

—Spacewalks. 2017. (Little Astronauts Ser.). (ENG., Illus.). 32p. (gr. 1-2). lib. bdg. 27.99 *(978-1-5157-3658-5(X))* Capstone Press of Coughlan Cos.

Hayden, Kate. Astronaut: Living in Space. 2013. (DK Reader Level 2 Ser.). (gr. k-3). lib. bdg. 13.55 *(978-0-613-24252-3(1)*, Turtleback) Turtleback Bks.

Littlejohn, Randy. Life in Outer Space. (Life in Extreme Environments Ser.). 64p. (gr. 5-8). 2009. 53.00 *(978-1-61514-269-9(X))* 2004. (Illus.). lib. bdg. 31.95 *(978-0-8239-3989-3(8))* Rosen Publishing Group, Inc., The. (Rosen Reference).

Lock, Deborah & Hayden, Kate. Astronaut Living in Space, Level 2. 2013. (DK Readers Ser.). (ENG.). 32p. (J). (gr. 1-4). pap. 3.99 *(978-1-4654-0241-7(1)*, DK Children) Dorling Kindersley Publishing, Inc.

Wishinsky, Frieda. Could We Live on the Moon? 2004. (ENG., Illus.). 24p. (J). (gr. 2-2). pap. 10.92 *(978-0-7652-5178-7(7)*, Celebration Pr.) Pearson Schl.

LIFESAVING

Gordon, Nick. Coast Guard Rescue Swimmer. 2012. (Dangerous Jobs Ser.). (ENG., Illus.). 24p. (J). (gr. 3-7). lib. bdg. 25.95 *(978-1-60014-778-4(X)*, Torque Bks.) Bellwether Media.

La Bella, Laura. Search & Rescue Swimmers. 2008. (Extreme Careers Ser.). (Illus.). 64p. (YA). (gr. 5-9). lib. bdg. 31.95 *(978-1-4042-1786-7(X))* Rosen Publishing Group, Inc., The.

—Search-and-rescue Swimmers. 2009. (Extreme Careers Ser.). 64p. (gr. 5-5). 58.50 *(978-1-61512-405-3(5)*, Rosen Reference) Rosen Publishing Group, Inc., The.

Oxlade, Chris. Rescue at Sea, 1 vol. 2012. (Heroic Jobs Ser.). (ENG., Illus.). 32p. (gr. 1-2). lib. bdg. 29.99 *(978-1-4109-4360-6(7)*, Read Me!) Heinemann-Raintree.

Perish, Patrick. Survive a Fire. 2017. (Survival Zone Ser.). (ENG., Illus.). 24p. (J). (gr. 3-7). lib. bdg. 25.95 *(978-1-62617-581-5(0)*, Torque Bks.) Bellwether Media.

Roza, Greg. Frequently Asked Questions about Emergency Lifesaving Techniques. 2009. (FAQ: Teen Life Ser.). (Illus.). 64p. (J). (gr. 5-6). lib. bdg. 31.95 *(978-1-4358-5327-0(X))* Rosen Publishing Group, Inc., The.

Staniford, Linda. Rescue at Sea Around the World. 2016. (To the Rescue! Ser.). (ENG., Illus.). 24p. (gr. k-2). lib. bdg. 23.32 *(978-1-4846-2753-2(9)*, Heinemann Read & Learn) Heinemann-Raintree.

Zullo, Allan. The Rescuers: Kids Who Risked Everything to Save Others. 2006. 135p. pap. *(978-0-439-85483-2(0))* Scholastic, Inc.

LIFTS

see Elevators; Hoisting Machinery

LIGHT

see also Color; Lasers; Optics; Radiation; Radioactivity; X-Rays

Aboff, Marcie. Light the Way. 2016. (Spring Forward Ser.). (J). (gr. 1). *(978-1-4900-9388-8(5))* Benchmark Education Co.

Adams, Alison. Light. 2011. (Early Connections Ser.). (J). *(978-1-61672-525-9(7))* Benchmark Education Co.

Anderson, Michael, ed. Light. 2012. (Introduction to Physics Ser.). (ENG., Illus.). 80p. (gr. 7-12). (J). 31.70 *(978-1-61530-840-8(7))*; (YA). 63.40 *(978-1-61530-847-7(4))* Rosen Publishing Group, Inc., The.

Ballard, Carol. Exploring Light. 2008. (How Does Science Work? Ser.). (Illus.). 32p. (J). (gr. 3-7). lib. bdg. 26.50 *(978-1-4042-4280-7(5))* Rosen Publishing Group, Inc., The.

Bang, Molly. My Light. Bang, Molly, illus. 2004. (ENG., Illus.). 40p. (J). (gr. -1-3). 18.99 *(978-0-439-48961-4(X))* Scholastic, Inc.

Bateman, Graham, ed. Light & Sound. 2011. (FAYFT: Introducing Physics Ser.). 64p. (gr. 4-10). lib. bdg. 39.95 *(978-1-936333-06-6(6))* Brown Bear Bks.

Benchmark Education Co., LLC Staff & Furgang, Kathy. The Light Around Us. 2015. (Content Connections Ser.). (J). (gr. 1). *(978-1-4900-0484-6(X))* Benchmark Education Co.

—The Light Around Us: Big Book Edition. 2015. (Content Connections Ser.). (J). (gr. 1). *(978-1-4900-0478-5(5))* Benchmark Education Co.

Benchmark Education Company, LLC Staff, compiled by. Light & Sound: Theme Set. 2006. (J). 215.00 *(978-1-4108-7121-3(5))* Benchmark Education Co.

Bodach, Vijaya Khisty. Reflection. 2008. (Discovering & Exploring Science Ser.). (Illus.). 16p. (J). (gr. -1-3). lib. bdg. 12.95 *(978-0-7569-8428-1(9))* Perfection Learning Corp.

Boothroyd, Jennifer. The Energy We See: A Look at Light. 2011. (Lightning Bolt Books Exploring Physical Science Ser.). 32p. pap. 45.32 *(978-0-7613-7648-4(8))*; (ENG.). pap. 7.95 *(978-0-7613-7104-5(4))*; (ENG.). lib. bdg. 26.60 *(978-0-7613-6092-6(1))* Lerner Publishing Group.

—Light Helps Me See. 2014. (First Step Nonfiction - Light & Sound Ser.). (Illus.). 24p. (gr. k-2). lib. bdg. 23.93 *(978-1-4677-3911-5(1)*, Lerner Pubns.) Lerner Publishing Group.

—Light Makes Colors. 2014. (First Step Nonfiction - Light & Sound Ser.). (ENG., Illus.). 24p. (gr. k-2). lib. bdg. 23.93 *(978-1-4677-3914-6(6)*, Lerner Pubns.) Lerner Publishing Group.

—Sending Messages with Light & Sound. 2014. (First Step Nonfiction - Light & Sound Ser.). (Illus.). 24p. (gr. k-2). pap. 6.95 *(978-1-4677-4504-8(9))*; (ENG.). lib. bdg. 23.93 *(978-1-4677-3913-9(8)*, Lerner Pubns.) Lerner Publishing Group.

—Sensing Light & Sound. 2014. (First Step Nonfiction - Light & Sound Ser.). (ENG., Illus.). 24p. (gr. k-2). lib. bdg. 23.93 *(978-1-4677-3915-3(4)*, Lerner Pubns.) Lerner Publishing Group.

Bortz, Alfred B. The Photon. 2004. (Library of Subatomic Particles Ser.). (Illus.). 64p. (gr. 7-12). lib. bdg. 31.95 *(978-0-8239-4531-3(6))* Rosen Publishing Group, Inc., The.

Bortz, Fred. The Photon. 2009. (Library of Subatomic Particles Ser.). 64p. (gr. 6-6). 58.50 *(978-1-60853-883-6(4))* Rosen Publishing Group, Inc., The.

Boulter, Carol & Wadsworth, Pamela. Golau. 2005. (WEL., Illus.). 24p. pap. *(978-1-85596-231-6(4))* Dref Wen.

—Rhagor Am Olau. 2005. (WEL., Illus.). 24p. pap. *(978-1-85596-232-3(2))* Dref Wen.

Brasch, Nicolas. Tricks of Sound & Light. 2010. (Science Behind Ser.). 32p. lib. bdg. 28.50 *(978-1-59920-564-9(5))* Black Rabbit Bks.

—Why Do Shadows Change? Level 5 Factbook. 2010. (Cambridge Young Readers Ser.). (ENG., Illus.). 24p. pap. 7.16 *(978-0-521-13731-7(4))* Cambridge Univ. Pr.

—Why Do Shadows Lengthen? 2010. (Solving Science Mysteries Ser.). (Illus.). 24p. (J). pap. 8.25 *(978-1-61531-913-8(1)*, PowerKids Pr.); (YA). (gr. 3-6). lib. bdg. 22.60 *(978-1-61531-891-9(7))* Rosen Publishing Group, Inc., The.

—Why Do Shadows Lengthen? All about Light. 2010. (Illus.). 24p. (J). 49.50 *(978-1-61531-914-5(X)*, PowerKids Pr.) Rosen Publishing Group, Inc., The.

Braun, Eric. Curious Pearl Investigates Light: 4D an Augmented Reality Science Experience. Dehennin, Stephanie, illus. 2017. (Curious Pearl, Science Girl 4D Ser.). (ENG.). 24p. (gr. k-2). lib. bdg. 20.65 ***(978-1-5158-1345-3(2))*** Picture Window Bks.

Braun, Eric. Lookin' for Light: Science Adventures with Manny the Origami Moth, 1 vol. Christoph, Jamey, illus. 2014. (Origami Science Adventures Ser.). (ENG.). 24p. (gr. 3-4). lib. bdg. 27.32 *(978-1-4795-2186-9(8))* Picture Window Bks.

Brent, Lynnette R. I've Discovered Light. 2008. (Eureka! Ser.). 32p. (gr. 4-18). lib. bdg. 28.50 *(978-0-7614-3198-5(5)*, Benchmark Bks.) Marshall Cavendish Corp.

Building Blocks of Science: Light Teacher's Guide. 2007. (Illus.). ring bd. *(978-0-89278-339-7(7))* Carolina Biological Supply Co.

Caes, Charles J. Discovering the Speed of Light. 2011. (Scientist's Guide to Physics Ser.). (Illus.). 112p. (YA). (gr. 7-12). lib. bdg. 34.60 *(978-1-4488-4699-3(4))* Rosen Publishing Group, Inc., The.

—How Do We Know the Speed of Light? 2009. (Great Scientific Questions & the Scientists Who Answered Them Ser.). 112p. (gr. 7-12). 63.90 *(978-1-61513-207-2(4))* Rosen Publishing Group, Inc., The.

Carlson Berne, Emma. Bright! Light Energy. 2013. (Energy Everywhere Ser.). (ENG., Illus.). 24p. (J). (gr. 3-6). 22.60 *(978-1-4488-9649-3(5))*; pap. 8.25 *(978-1-4488-9756-8(4))* Rosen Publishing Group, Inc., The. (PowerKids Pr.).

Cavell-Clarke, Steffi. Light. 2017. (First Science Ser.). (J). (gr. 1-1). 24p. pap. 8.25 ***(978-1-5345-2072-1(4))***; pap. 49.50 ***(978-1-5345-2073-8(2))***; 24p. lib. bdg. 24.60 ***(978-1-5345-2074-5(0))*** Greenhaven Publishing LLC. (KidHaven Publishing).

Chesborough, E. D. What Is Light Energy? 2017. (Let's Find Out! Forms of Energy Ser.). 32p. (gr. 6-8). pap. 12.90 ***(978-1-68048-705-3(1)***, Britannica Educational Publishing) Rosen Publishing Group, Inc., The.

Clark, John O. E. The Basics of Light. 2014. (Core Concepts Ser.). (Illus.). 96p. (YA). (gr. 7-12). 35.60 *(978-1-4777-7762-6(8))* Rosen Publishing Group, Inc., The.

Claybourne, Anna. Glaring Light & Other Eye-Burning Rays. 2013. (ENG., Illus.). 32p. (J). *(978-0-7787-0945-9(0))*; pap. *(978-0-7787-0955-8(8))* Crabtree Publishing Co.

—Light & Sound. 2017. (Mind Webs Ser.). (ENG., Illus.). 32p. (J). (gr. 4-6). pap. 11.99 *(978-0-7502-8959-7(7)*, Wayland) Hachette Children's Group GBR. Dist: Hachette Bk. Group.

—Secrets of Light. 2010. (Science Secrets Ser.). 32p. (gr. 4). 28.50 *(978-1-60870-139-1(5))* Marshall Cavendish Corp.

Coan, Sharon. Light Makes a Rainbow, 1 vol. (Science Readers: Content & Literacy Ser.). (ENG., Illus.). 24p. (gr. 1-1). 2015. (J). 22.96 *(978-1-4938-1153-3(3))* 2014. pap. 8.99 *(978-1-4807-4566-7(9))* Teacher Created Materials, Inc.

Colson, Mary. The Science of Light. 2016. (Flowchart Smart Ser.). (ENG.). 48p. (J). (gr. 4-5). pap. 14.05 *(978-1-4824-4143-7(8))* Stevens, Gareth Publishing LLLP.

Deeds, Christopher. Light & Color: What We See. 2013. (InfoMax Readers Ser.). (ENG.). 24p. (J). (gr. 3-4). pap. 49.50 *(978-1-4777-2638-9(1))*; (Illus.). pap. 8.25 *(978-1-4777-2637-2(3))* Rosen Publishing Group, Inc., The. (Rosen Classroom).

Dicker, Katie. Light. 2010. (Sherlock Bones Looks at Physical Science Ser.). (ENG.). 32p. (YA). (gr. 3-6). lib. bdg. 25.25 *(978-1-61533-212-0(X))* Windmill Bks.

Dodd, Emily & Collins UK Staff. Light. 2016. (ENG.). 56p. (J). (gr. 5-6). pap. 9.95 *(978-0-00-816399-0(5))* HarperCollins Pubs. Ltd. GBR. Dist: Independent Pubs. Group.

Duke, Shirley. Waves of Light & Sound. 2014. (ENG.). 48p. (gr. 4-6). 35.64 *(978-1-62717-749-8(3))* Rourke Educational Media.

Dunne, Abbie. Light. 2016. (Physical Science Ser.). (ENG., Illus.). 24p. (gr. k-1). lib. bdg. 26.65 *(978-1-5157-0937-4(X)*, Pebble Plus) Capstone Press of Coughlan Cos.

Ferrie, Chris. Optical Physics for Babies. 2017. (J). ***(978-1-4926-5606-7(2))***; (Baby University Ser.: 0). (ENG., Illus.). 24p. bds. 9.99 ***(978-1-4926-5621-0(6)***, Sourcebooks Jabberwocky) Sourcebooks, Inc.

Fields, B. H. & Bortz, Fred. Understanding Photons. 2015. (Exploring the Subatomic World Ser.). (ENG., Illus.). 64p. (YA). (gr. 8-8). lib. bdg. 34.21 *(978-1-5026-0544-3(9))* Cavendish Square Publishing.

Fink, Charles. Light Show: Reflection & Absorption. 2009. (Amazing Science Ser.). 24p. (gr. 3-3). 42.50 *(978-1-61511-329-3(0)*, PowerKids Pr.) Rosen Publishing Group, Inc., The.

Flynn, Claire E. Why Plants Need Light. 2009. (Real Life Readers Ser.). 12p. (gr. 1-2). pap. 5.90 *(978-1-4042-7919-3(9)*, Rosen Classroom) Rosen Publishing Group, Inc., The.

Frenkel, Karen A. Light & Sound Technology: Text Pairs. 2008. (Bridges/Navigators Ser.). (J). (gr. 4). 94.00 *(978-1-4108-8386-5(8))* Benchmark Education Co.

—Looking at Light: Set Of 6. 2011. (Navigators Ser.). (J). pap. 48.00 net. *(978-1-4108-6226-6(7))* Benchmark Education Co.

—Looking at Light: Text Pairs. 2008. (Bridges/Navigators Ser.). (J). (gr. 4). 89.00 *(978-1-4108-8388-9(4))* Benchmark Education Co.

Friesen, Helen Lepp. Uses of Light. 2011. (J). (gr. 4-6). pap. 12.95 *(978-1-61690-841-6(6)*, AV2 by Weigl); (Illus.). 24p. (gr. 3-6). 27.13 *(978-1-61690-837-9(8))* Weigl Pubs., Inc.

Gardner, Robert. Experiments with Light. 2017. (Science Whiz Experiments Ser.). 128p. (gr. 5-5). 37.27 ***(978-0-7660-8680-7(1))*** Enslow Pubs., Inc.

Gardner, Robert & Conklin, Joshua. A Kid's Book of Experiments about Light. 2016. (Surprising Science Experiments Ser.). (ENG., Illus.). 48p. (J). (gr. 4-4). 27.93 *(978-0-7660-7205-3(3))* Enslow Pubs., Inc.

—A Kid's Book of Experiments with Color. 2016. (Surprising Science Experiments Ser.). (ENG., Illus.). 48p. (J). (gr. 4-4). lib. bdg. 27.93 *(978-0-7660-7201-5(0))* Enslow Pubs., Inc.

Gish, Melissa. Light. 2005. (My First Look at Science Ser.). (Illus.). 24p. (J). (gr. k-3). lib. bdg. 15.95 *(978-1-58341-373-9(1)*, Creative Education) Creative Co., The.

Gorman, John. Light: An Investigation. 2008. (Science Investigations Ser.). (Illus.). 32p. (YA). (gr. 4-7). lib. bdg. 26.50 *(978-1-4042-4286-9(4))* Rosen Publishing Group, Inc., The.

Gray, Leon. Light. 2013. (Physical Science Ser.). 48p. (J). (gr. 4-6). pap. 14.05 *(978-1-4339-9513-2(1))*; pap. 84.30 *(978-1-4339-9514-9(X))*; (ENG., Illus.). lib. bdg. 31.95 *(978-1-4339-9512-5(3))* Stevens, Gareth Publishing LLLP.

Group/McGraw-Hill, Wright. Set 2: La Luz, 6 vols., Vol. 2. (First Explorers. Primeros Exploradores Nonfiction Sets Ser.). (SPA.). (gr. 1-2). 34.95 *(978-0-7699-1485-5(3))* Shortland Pubns. (U. S. A.) Inc.

Halpern, Monica. All about Light. 2006. (Science Chapters Ser.). (ENG., Illus.). 48p. (J). (gr. 1-4). lib. bdg. 17.90 *(978-0-7922-5942-8(4)*, National Geographic Children's Bks.) National Geographic Society.

Hamilton, Gina L. Light. 2016. (J). ***(978-1-5105-2239-8(5))*** SmartBook Media, Inc.

—Light. 2008. (Science Q & A Ser.). (Illus.). 48p. (YA). (gr. 5-8). pap. 10.95 *(978-1-59036-947-0(5))*; lib. bdg. 29.05 *(978-1-59036-946-3(7))* Weigl Pubs., Inc.

—Light Q & A. 2013. (J). *(978-1-62127-415-5(2))*; pap. *(978-1-62127-421-6(7))* Weigl Pubs., Inc.

Hartman, Eve & Meshbesher, Wendy. Light & Sound. 2016. (Sci-Hi: Physical Science Ser.). (ENG.). 48p. (gr. 4-4). pap. 8.99 *(978-1-4109-8536-1(9)*, Sci-Hi) Heinemann-Raintree.

Herold, Vickey. Discover Light. 2006. (J). pap. *(978-1-4108-6491-8(X))* Benchmark Education Co.

—Light & Color. 2006. (J). pap. *(978-1-4108-6488-8(X))* Benchmark Education Co.

Hewitt, Sally. Amazing Light. 2007. (Amazing Science Ser.). (ENG.). 32p. (J). pap. *(978-0-7787-3626-4(1))* Crabtree Publishing Co.

Holt, Rinehart and Winston Staff. Holt Science & Technology Chapter 22: Physical Science: The Nature of Light. 5th ed. 2004. (Illus.). pap. 12.86 *(978-0-03-030439-2(3))* Holt McDougal.

—Holt Science & Technology Chapter 23: Physical Science: Light & Our World. 5th ed. 2004. (Illus.). pap. 12.86 *(978-0-03-030441-5(5))* Holt McDougal.

Hotchkins, Dewayne. Darkness & Light. 2016. (Rosen REAL Readers: STEM & STEAM Collection). 8p. (gr. 1-k). pap. 5.46 *(978-1-5081-2407-8(8)*, Rosen Classroom) Rosen Publishing Group, Inc., The.

James, Emily. The Simple Science of Light. 2017. (Simply Science Ser.). (ENG.). 32p. (gr. 1-2). lib. bdg. 27.32 ***(978-1-5157-7082-4(6)***, Aplus Bks.) Capstone Press of Coughlan Cos.

Jankowski, Connie. All about Light & Sound, 1 vol. 2007. (Science Readers Ser.). (SPA & ENG.). 32p. (J). (gr. 4-4). pap. 8.99 *(978-0-7439-0579-4(2))* Shell Educational Publishing.

—Pioneers of Light & Sound, 1 vol. 2007. (Science Readers Ser.). (ENG.). 32p. (J). (gr. 3-3). pap. 8.99 *(978-0-7439-0580-0(6))* Shell Educational Publishing.

Jennings, Terry. Light & Dark. 2009. (Science Alive Ser.). (Illus.). 32p. (J). (gr. 4-7). pap. *(978-1-897563-56-4(6))* Saunders Bk. Co.

Jennings, Terry J. Light & Dark. 2009. (J). 28.50 *(978-1-59920-270-9(0))* Black Rabbit Bks.

Jensen Shaffer, Jody. Vampires & Light, 1 vol. Gervasio, illus. 2013. (Monster Science Ser.). (ENG.). 32p. (gr. 3-4). pap. 8.10 *(978-1-62065-820-8(8))*; 47.70 *(978-1-62065-821-5(6))* Capstone Press of Coughlan Cos. (Graphic Library).

Johnson, Rebecca L. & National Geographic Learning Staff. The Magic of Light & Sound. 2006. (Nonfiction Reading & Writing Workshops Ser.). (ENG., Illus.). 32p. (J). pap. 17.95 *(978-0-7922-8886-2(6))* CENGAGE Learning.

—Peering into Darkness. 2007. (Reading Expeditions Ser.). (ENG., Illus.). 32p. (J). pap. 17.95 *(978-0-7922-8451-2(8))* CENGAGE Learning.

Johnson, Robin. The Science of Light Waves. 2017. 32p. (J). ***(978-0-7787-2944-0(3))*** Crabtree Publishing Co.

—What Are Light Waves? 2014. (ENG., Illus.). 24p. (J). *(978-0-7787-0519-2(6))* Crabtree Publishing Co.

—What Are Shadows & Reflections? 2014. (ENG., Illus.). 24p. (J). *(978-0-7787-0521-5(8))* Crabtree Publishing Co.

Kelly, Lynne. Simple Concepts in Physics: Sound & Light. (Illus.). 88p. (J). (gr. 5-6). pap. *(978-1-875739-69-1(6))* Wizard Bks.

Kenney, Karen Latchana. The Science of Color: Investigating Light, 1 vol. 2016. (Science in Action Ser.). (ENG., Illus.). 32p. (J). (gr. 3-6). 27.07 *(978-1-62403-960-7(X))* ABDO Publishing Co.

Keranen, Rachel. The Big Bang Theory & Light Spectra. 2016. (Space Systems Ser.). 112p. (J). lib. bdg. 42.79 *(978-1-5026-2295-2(5))* Cavendish Square Publishing.

Kleiner, Mariela. Meet Einstein. Garofoli, Viviana, illus. 2011. 28p. (J). (gr. -1-1). lib. bdg. *(978-0-615-31579-9(8))* Meet Bks., LLC.

Koontz, Robin. Light in the Real World. 2013. (Science in the Real World EBook Ser.). (ENG.). 48p. (J). pap. 15.64 *(978-1-61783-791-3(1)*, Core Library); (gr. 3-6). lib. bdg. 32.79 *(978-1-61783-741-8(5))* ABDO Publishing Co.
Kopp, Megan. Light Works. 2011. (J). 27.13 *(978-1-61690-385-5(6))*; (J). (gr. 4-6). pap. 12.95 *(978-1-61690-839-3(4)*, AV2 by Weigl); (Illus.). 24p. (YA). (gr. 3-6). 27.13 *(978-1-61690-835-5(1))* Weigl Pubs., Inc.
Kukla, Lauren. Light at Work, 1 vol. 2016. (ENG., Illus.). 24p. (J). 24.21 *(978-1-68078-141-0(3))* ABDO Publishing Co.
Lauber, Patricia. What You Never Knew about Beds, Bedrooms, & Pajamas. Manders, John, illus. 2008. (ENG.). 40p. (J). (gr. 1-4). 6.99 *(978-1-4169-6738-5(9)*, Simon & Schuster Bks. For Young Readers) Simon & Schuster Bks. For Young Readers.
Lawrence, Ellen. Light. 2014. (Science Slam: FUN-Damentals Ser.). 24p. (J). (gr. -1-3). lib. bdg. 23.93 *(978-1-62724-093-2(4))* Bearport Publishing Co., Inc.
Light. (Jump Ser.). (Illus.). 32p. (J). (gr. 2-7). pap. *(978-1-882210-28-2(X))* Action Publishing, Inc.
Light. 2009. 67p. pap. 18.00 *(978-0-9841252-1-0(3))* Poet's Passage Pr., The.
Light & Sound. 2010. (Science Foundations Ser.). (Illus.). 128p. (gr. 6-12). 35.00 *(978-1-60413-344-8(9)*, Chelsea Hse.) Facts On File, Inc.
Lindeen, Mary. Light. 2017. (BeginningtoRead Ser.). (ENG.). 32p. (J). (-2). 22.60 ***(978-1-59953-881-5(4))***; pap. 11.94 ***(978-1-68404-100-8(7))*** Norwood Hse. Pr.
Lowery, Lawrence F. Dark As a Shadow. Goldsborough, June, illus. 2014. (I Wonder Why Ser.). (ENG.). 36p. (J). (gr. k-3). pap. 11.95 *(978-1-941316-06-1(9))* National Science Teachers Assn.
—Light & Color: I Wonder Why. Wood, Muriel, illus. 2014. (I Wonder Why Ser.). (ENG.). 36p. (J). (gr. k-3). pap. 11.95 *(978-1-938946-51-6(0))* National Science Teachers Assn.
Madgwick, Wendy. First Science Library: Light & Dark. 2014. (ENG., Illus.). 32p. (J). (gr. k-2). 8.99 *(978-1-86147-355-4(9)*, Armadillo) Anness Publishing GBR. Dist: National Bk. Network.
Mahaney, Ian F. Light. (Energy in Action Ser.). 24p. 2009. (gr. 3-3). 42.50 *(978-1-61512-259-2(1)*, PowerKids Pr.) 2007. (ENG.). (gr. 3-8). pap. 7.05 *(978-1-4042-2185-7(9)*, PowerKids Pr.) 2007. (Illus.). (YA). (gr. 4-7). lib. bdg. 22.60 *(978-1-4042-3476-5(4))* Rosen Publishing Group, Inc., The.
Matthews, John R. The Light Bulb. 2005. (Inventions That Shaped the World Ser.). (Illus.). 80p. (J). (gr. 5-8). 17.60 *(978-0-7569-6858-8(5))* Perfection Learning Corp.
Maurer, Daniel D. Do You Really Want to Walk in the Dark? A Book about Light. Alberini, Teresa, illus. 2016. (Adventures in Science Ser.). (ENG.). 24p. (J). (gr. k-3). 20.95 *(978-1-60753-960-5(8))* Amicus Publishing.
Monroe, Tilda. What Do You Know about Light? 2010. (20 Questions: Physical Science Ser.). (ENG.). 24p. (J). pap. 8.25 *(978-1-4488-1250-9(X)*, PowerKids Pr.); (gr. 2-5). lib. bdg. 22.60 *(978-1-4488-0672-0(0))* Rosen Publishing Group, Inc., The.
Murray, Julie. Light & Dark, 1 vol. 2006. (First Science Ser.). (ENG., Illus.). 24p. (J). (gr. k-4). 25.65 *(978-1-59679-826-7(2)*, Buddy Bks.) ABDO Publishing Co.
Nunn, Daniel. How Do We Use Light?, 1 vol. 2012. (Light All Around Us Ser.). (ENG.). 24p. (gr. -1-1). lib. bdg. 22.65 *(978-1-4329-6623-2(5)*, Acorn) Heinemann-Raintree.
—Light, 1 vol. 2012. (Why Living Things Need Ser.). (ENG.). 24p. (gr. -1-1). pap. 6.29 *(978-1-4329-5922-7(0))*; lib. bdg. 22.65 *(978-1-4329-5916-6(6))* Heinemann-Raintree. (Acorn).
—Light & Dark, 1 vol. 2012. (Light All Around Us Ser.). (ENG.). 24p. (gr. -1-1). pap. 6.29 *(978-1-4329-6627-0(8))*; lib. bdg. 22.65 *(978-1-4329-6622-5(7))* Heinemann-Raintree. (Acorn).
—Shadows & Reflections, 1 vol. 2012. (Light All Around Us Ser.). (ENG.). 24p. (gr. -1-1). pap. 6.29 *(978-1-4329-6629-4(4))*; lib. bdg. 22.65 *(978-1-4329-6624-9(3))* Heinemann-Raintree. (Acorn).
—Sources of Light, 1 vol. 2012. (Light All Around Us Ser.). (ENG.). 24p. (gr. -1-1). pap. 6.29 *(978-1-4329-6626-3(X))*; lib. bdg. 22.65 *(978-1-4329-6621-8(9))* Heinemann-Raintree. (Acorn).
O'DellKathryn. THE SCIENCE OF LIGHT LOW INTERMEDIATE BOOK WITH ONLINE ACCESS. 2014. (ENG., Illus.). 28p. (J). pap. 9.50 *(978-1-107-68198-9(7))* Cambridge Univ. Pr.
Peterson, Megan Cooley. Scooby-Doo! a Science of Light Mystery: The Angry Alien. Brizuela, Dario, illus. 2017. (Scooby-Doo Solves It with S. T. E. M. Ser.). (ENG.). 32p. (gr. 3-4). pap. 7.95 *(978-1-5157-3704-9(7))* Capstone Press of Coughlan Cos.
Pfeffer, Wendy. Light Is All Around Us. Meisel, Paul, illus. 2015. (Let's-Read-And-Find-Out Science 2 Ser.). (ENG.). 40p. (J). (gr. -1-3). pap. 6.99 *(978-0-06-238190-3(3))* HarperCollins Pubs.
—Light Is All Around Us. 2015. (Let's Read & Find Out Science Stage 2 Ser.). (J). lib. bdg. 17.20 *(978-0-606-37741-6(7))* Turtleback Bks.
Prentice-Hall Staff. Sound & Light. 2nd ed. (J). stu. ed. 7.97 *(978-0-13-400565-2(1))*; pap., act. bk. ed. *(978-0-13-400581-2(3))* Prentice Hall (Schl. Div.).
Pronnette, Veronica H. The Ancestors Anansi & the Light: A Delightful African Proverb Retold about How Light was Created by a Spider. 2009. 32p. pap. 14.49 *(978-1-4343-5430-3(X))* AuthorHouse.
Rajczak, Kristen. Rainbows. 2012. (Nature's Light Show Ser.). (Illus.). 24p. (J). (gr. 2-5). pap. 8.15 *(978-1-4339-7032-0(5))*; lib. bdg. 22.60 *(978-1-4339-7031-3(7))* Stevens, Gareth Publishing LLLP.
Randolph, Joane. Light in My World. 2009. (My World of Science Ser.). 24p. (gr. 2-2). 37.50 *(978-1-61514-725-0(X)*, PowerKids Pr.) Rosen Publishing Group, Inc., The.
Randolph, Joanne. Light in My World. (Journeys Ser.). 24p. 2007. (ENG.). (gr. k-8). pap. 7.05 *(978-1-4042-8420-3(6)*, Rosen Classroom) 2006. (Illus.). (J). (gr. 3-7). lib. bdg. 18.75 *(978-1-4042-3286-0(9)*, PowerKids Pr.) Rosen Publishing Group, Inc., The.
—Light in My World: La Luz en Mi Mundo. 2006. (My World of Science/ Mi mundo y la Ciencia Ser.). (ENG & SPA.). (J). (gr. k-3). 16.00 *(978-1-4042-3317-1(2))* Rosen Publishing Group, Inc., The.
—Light in My World/la luz en mi Mundo. 2009. (My World of Science/la ciencia en mi mundo Ser.). (ENG & SPA.). 48p. (gr. 2-2). 37.50 *(978-1-61514-737-3(3)*, Editorial Buenas Letras) Rosen Publishing Group, Inc., The.
Rea, Thelma. I Wonder Why the Sky Is Blue. 2009. (Reading Room Collection 2 Ser.). 24p. (gr. 3-4). 42.50 *(978-1-60851-973-6(2)*, PowerKids Pr.) Rosen Publishing Group, Inc., The.
Richards, Jon. Light & Sight. 2009. (Science Factory Ser.). 32p. (gr. 4-5). 50.50 *(978-1-60853-022-9(1)*, PowerKids Pr.) Rosen Publishing Group, Inc., The.
Riley, Peter. Light. 2016. (Moving up with Science Ser.). 00032p. (J). (gr. 3-4). pap. 10.00 *(978-1-4994-3145-2(7)*, PowerKids Pr.) Rosen Publishing Group, Inc., The.
—Light & Seeing. 2007. (Essential Science/Watts Ser.). (Illus.). 32p. (J). (gr. 4-7). lib. bdg. 28.50 *(978-1-59920-028-6(7))* Black Rabbit Bks.
Roberts, Abigail B. Using Lenses. 2017. (Super Science Tools Ser.). 24p. (gr. 1-2). pap. 8.15 ***(978-1-4824-6389-7(X))*** Stevens, Gareth Publishing LLLP.
Rogers, K. Light, Sound & Electricity. 2004. (Library of Science Ser.). 64p. (J). lib. bdg. 17.95 *(978-1-58086-376-6(0))* EDC Publishing.
Rondina, Catherine. Lighting Our World: A Year of Celebrations. Oakley, Jacqui, illus. 2012. (ENG.). 32p. (J). (gr. 2-5). 17.95 *(978-1-55453-594-1(8))* Kids Can Pr., Ltd. CAN. Dist: Hachette Bk. Group.
Rose, Simon. Sources of Light. 2011. (J). *(978-1-61690-386-2(4))*; (J). (gr. 4-6). pap. 12.95 *(978-1-61690-840-9(8)*, AV2 by Weigl); (Illus.). 24p. (YA). (gr. 3-6). 27.13 *(978-1-61690-836-2(X))* Weigl Pubs., Inc.
—What Is Light? 2011. (J). (gr. 4-6). pap. 12.95 *(978-1-61690-842-3(4)*, AV2 by Weigl); (Illus.). 24p. (YA). (gr. 3-6). 27.13 *(978-1-61690-838-6(6))* Weigl Pubs., Inc.
Royston, Angela. Light & Dark. 2012. (Science Corner Ser.). (Illus.). 24p. (J). (gr. 1-4). lib. bdg. 22.60 *(978-1-4488-5258-1(7))* Rosen Publishing Group, Inc., The.
Ruchlis, Hyman. The Wonder of Light: A Picture Story of How & Why We See. Hirsh, Alice, illus. 2011. 160p. 41.95 *(978-1-258-09816-2(4))* Literary Licensing, LLC.
Shaffer, Jody Jensen. Vampires & Light, 1 vol. Gervasio, illus. 2013. (Monster Science Ser.). (ENG.). 32p. (gr. 3-4). lib. bdg. 30.65 *(978-1-4296-9928-0(0)*, Graphic Library) Capstone Press of Coughlan Cos.
Silverman, Buffy. Let's Investigate Light. 2012. (ENG.). 24p. (gr. 4-5). pap. 8.95 *(978-1-61810-241-6(9))* Rourke Educational Media.
—Me & My Shadow: A Book about Light. 2011. (ENG., Illus.). 24p. (gr. 1-2). pap. 8.95 *(978-1-61741-943-0(5))* Rourke Educational Media.
Sohn, Emily. The Illuminating World of Light with Max Axiom, Super Scientist, 1 vol. Derrington, Nick, illus. 2008. (Graphic Science Ser.). (ENG.). 32p. (gr. 3-4). pap. 8.10 *(978-1-4296-1768-0(3)*, Graphic Library) Capstone Press of Coughlan Cos.
Spilsbury, Louise & Spilsbury, Richard. Light & Dark. 2015. (Exploring Light Ser.). (ENG., Illus.). 32p. (gr. 2-4). 30.65 *(978-1-4109-7942-1(3))* Heinemann-Raintree.
—Light & Sound, 1 vol. 2013. (Essential Physical Science Ser.). (ENG.). 48p. (gr. 4-6). 33.32 *(978-1-4329-8146-4(3)*, Heinemann InfoSearch) Heinemann-Raintree.
—Reflecting Light. 2015. (Exploring Light Ser.). (ENG., Illus.). 32p. (gr. 2-4). 30.65 *(978-1-4109-7943-8(1))* Heinemann-Raintree.
—Shadows. 2015. (Exploring Light Ser.). (ENG., Illus.). 32p. (gr. 2-4). 30.65 *(978-1-4109-7944-5(X))* Heinemann-Raintree.
—Sources of Light. 2015. (Exploring Light Ser.). (ENG., Illus.). 32p. (gr. 2-4). 30.65 *(978-1-4109-7945-2(8))* Heinemann-Raintree.
Spilsbury, Richard & Spilsbury, Louise. The Cave of Shadows. 2015. (Science Adventures Ser.). (ENG., Illus.). 32p. (J). (gr. 3-7). 31.35 *(978-1-62588-147-2(9))* Black Rabbit Bks.
—What Is Light? Exploring Science with Hands-on Activities. 2008. (In Touch with Basic Science Ser.). (Illus.). 32p. (J). (gr. 3-4). lib. bdg. 23.94 *(978-0-7660-3097-8(0)*, Enslow Elementary) Enslow Pubs., Inc.
Stephens, Catherine & Schifini, Alfredo. Looking at Light. 2007. (Avenues Ser.). (ENG., Illus.). 36p. (J). pap. 18.95 *(978-0-7922-5438-6(4))* CENGAGE Learning.
Sundance/Newbridge LLC Staff. Light. 2007. (Early Science Ser.). (gr. k-3). 18.95 *(978-1-4007-6314-6(2))*; pap. 6.10 *(978-1-4007-6310-8(X))* Sundance/Newbridge Educational Publishing.
Taylor, Kim. Light. (Illus.). 32p. (YA). (gr. 3-18). lib. bdg. 27.10 *(978-1-931983-75-4(5))* Chrysalis Education.
Top That Publishing Staff, ed. Light Science. 2004. (Top That! Labs Ser.). (Illus.). 24p. (J). *(978-1-84510-153-4(7))* Top That! Publishing PLC.
Torrence, Jack. Light Show: Reflection & Absorption. 2009. (Real Life Readers Ser.). 24p. (gr. 3-4). pap. 8.25 *(978-1-4358-0096-0(6)*, Rosen Classroom); (J). (gr. 2-5). lib. bdg. 22.60 *(978-1-4358-2974-9(3)*, PowerKids Pr.) Rosen Publishing Group, Inc., The.
Trumbauer, Lisa. All about Light. 2004. (Rookie Read-About Science Ser.). (ENG.). 32p. (J). (gr. 1-2). pap. 4.95 *(978-0-516-25842-3(7)*, Children's Pr.) Scholastic Library Publishing.
Twist, Clint. Light & Sound. 2010. (Science Everywhere! Ser.). 24p. 24.25 *(978-1-84898-297-0(6))* Black Rabbit Bks.
Upgrade kit dsm-3 Color&light. (J). 2004. *(978-1-59242-527-3(5))* 2003. *(978-1-59242-410-8(4))* Delta Education, LLC.
Wadsworth, Pamela. Golwg Gyntaf Ar Olau. 2005. (WEL., Illus.). 24p. pap. *(978-1-85596-249-1(7))* Dref Wen.
Walker, Sally M. Investigating Light. 2011. (Searchlight Books How Does Energy Work Ser.). (ENG., Illus.). (gr. 3-5). pap. 51.01 *(978-0-7613-8407-6(3))*; 40p. pap. 8.95 *(978-0-7613-7873-0(1))*; 40p. lib. bdg. 27.93 *(978-0-7613-5774-2(2))* Lerner Publishing Group.
—Light. 2006. (Illus.). 48p. (J). pap. 8.95 *(978-0-8225-2842-5(8))* Lerner Publishing Group.
—Light. King, Andy, photos by. 2005. (Early Bird Energy Ser.). (ENG., Illus.). 48p. (gr. 2-5). lib. bdg. 26.60 *(978-0-8225-2925-5(4)*, Lerner Pubns.) Lerner Publishing Group.
—La Luz. Translations.com Staff, tr. from ENG. King, Andy, photos by. 2007. (Libros de Energía para madrugadores (Early Bird Energy) Ser.). (SPA., Illus.). 48p. (gr. 2-5). lib. bdg. 26.60 *(978-0-8225-7719-5(4))* Lerner Publishing Group.
—La Luz; Light. 2008. pap. 52.95 *(978-0-8225-9869-5(8))* Lerner Publishing Group.
Way, Steve & Bailey, Gerry. Light & Color. 2008. (Simply Science Ser.). (Illus.). 32p. (YA). (gr. 3-6). lib. bdg. 26.00 *(978-0-8368-9229-1(1))* Stevens, Gareth Publishing LLLP.
Whitfield, David. Northern Lights. 2006. (Science Matters Ser.). (Illus.). 24p. (J). (gr. 3-7). lib. bdg. 24.45 *(978-1-59036-413-0(9))*; pap. 8.95 *(978-1-59036-419-2(8))* Weigl Pubs., Inc.
Whiting, Jim. Light. 2012. (Mysteries of the Universe Ser.). (Illus.). 48p. (J). (gr. 5-12). 23.95 *(978-1-60818-190-2(1)*, Creative Education) Creative Co., The.
—Mysteries of the Universe: Light. 2013. (Mysteries of the Universe Ser.). (ENG., Illus.). 48p. (J). (gr. 4-7). pap. 12.00 *(978-0-89812-915-1(X)*, Creative Paperbacks) Creative Co., The.
Winterberg, Jenna. Light & Its Effects. 2015. (Science Readers: Content & Literacy Ser.). (ENG., Illus.). 32p. (gr. 4-4). pap. 8.99 *(978-1-4807-4685-5(1))* Teacher Created Materials, Inc.
Woodford, Chris. Light: Investigating Visible & Invisible Electromagnetic Radiation. 2012. (Scientific Pathways Ser.). (ENG., Illus.). 48p. (J). (gr. 5-8). lib. bdg. 27.95 *(978-1-4488-7202-2(2)*, Rosen Reference) Rosen Publishing Group, Inc., The.
—Light & Radiation. 2004. (Routes of Science Ser.). (Illus.). 40p. (J). (gr. 4-7). 24.95 *(978-1-4103-0297-7(0)*, Blackbirch Pr., Inc.) Cengage Gale.
World Book, Inc Staff, contrib. by. Light. 2011. (J). *(978-0-7166-1426-5(X))* World Bk., Inc.
Wyatt, Katherine. The Science of Light & Color. 2013. (Rosen Readers Ser.). (ENG.). 24p. (J). (gr. 3-4). pap. 49.50 *(978-1-4777-2576-4(8))*; pap. 8.25 *(978-1-4777-2575-7(X))* Rosen Publishing Group, Inc., The. (Rosen Classroom).
Yasuda, Anita. Explore Light & Optics! With 25 Great Projects. Stone, Bryan, illus. 2016. (Explore Your World Ser.). (ENG.). 96p. (gr. 1-5). 19.95 *(978-1-61930-376-8(0))*; pap. 14.95 *(978-1-61930-380-5(9))* Open City Bks.

LIGHT—EXPERIMENTS

Angliss, Sarah, et al. Hands-On Science: Sound & Light. 2013. (Hands-On Science Ser.). (ENG., Illus.). 32p. (J). (gr. 2-5). pap. 7.99 *(978-0-7534-6974-3(X)*, 9780753469743, Kingfisher) Roaring Brook Pr.
Boothroyd, Jennifer. Light Makes Colors. 2014. (First Step Nonfiction - Light & Sound Ser.). (Illus.). 24p. (gr. k-2). pap. 6.95 *(978-1-4677-4502-4(2))*; (ENG.). lib. bdg. 23.93 *(978-1-4677-3914-6(6)*, Lerner Pubns.) Lerner Publishing Group.
—Playing with Light & Shadows. 2014. (First Step Nonfiction - Light & Sound Ser.). (Illus.). 24p. (gr. k-2). pap. 6.95 *(978-1-4677-4503-1(0))*; (ENG.). lib. bdg. 23.93 *(978-1-4677-3912-2(X)*, Lerner Pubns.) Lerner Publishing Group.
Canavan, Thomas. Super Experiments with Light & Sound. Linley, Adam, illus. 2017. (Mind-Blowing Science Experiments Ser.). 32p. (gr. 4-5). pap. 63.00 ***(978-1-5382-0733-8(8))*** Stevens, Gareth Publishing LLLP.
Clark, John & Walker, Richard. Light & Sound. 2006. (Real World Science Ser.). (Illus.). 32p. (gr. 2-6). lib. bdg. 26.00 *(978-0-8368-6306-2(2)*, Gareth Stevens Learning Library) Stevens, Gareth Publishing LLLP.
Claybourne, Anna. Light & Dark. 2012. (Illus.). 24p. (gr. k-4). pap. 7.95 *(978-1-926853-57-4(1))* Saunders Bk. Co. CAN. Dist: RiverStream Publishing.
—Make It Glow!, 1 vol. Scott, Kimberly & Dean, Venetia, illus. 2014. (Whiz Kid Science Ser.). (ENG.). 32p. (gr. 2-4). 29.99 *(978-1-4109-6747-3(6)*, Read Me!) Heinemann-Raintree.
Cobb, Allan B. Super Science Projects about Light & Optics. 2005. (Psyched for Science Ser.). (Illus.). 48p. (YA). (gr. 5-8). lib. bdg. 29.25 *(978-0-8239-3177-4(3)*, SCLIOP) Rosen Publishing Group, Inc., The.
Cook, Trevor. Experiments with Light & Sound. 2009. (Science Lab Ser.). (J). (ENG., Illus.). 32p. (gr. 4-6). pap. 10.00 *(978-1-4358-3221-3(3))*; lib. bdg. 26.50 *(978-1-4358-2808-7(9))* Rosen Publishing Group, Inc., The. (PowerKids Pr.).
Edom, H. Science Activities, Vol. 1. 2010. (Science Activities Ser.). 72p. (J). 13.99 *(978-0-7945-2752-5(3)*, Usborne) EDC Publishing.
Gardner, Robert. Dazzling Science Projects with Light & Color. LaBaff, Tom, illus. 2006. (Fantastic Physical Science Experiments Ser.). 48p. (J). (gr. 3-7). lib. bdg. 25.27 *(978-0-7660-2587-5(X)*, Enslow Elementary) Enslow Pubs., Inc.
—Easy Genius Science Projects with Light: Great Experiments & Ideas. 2008. (Easy Genius Science Projects Ser.). (Illus.). 128p. (J). (gr. 5-9). lib. bdg. 33.27 *(978-0-7660-2926-2(3))* Enslow Pubs., Inc.
—Light, Sound, & Waves Science Fair Projects: Using Sunglasses, Guitars, CDs, & Other Stuff. 2004. (Physics! Best Science Projects Ser.). (Illus.). 128p. (J). lib. bdg. 27.94 *(978-0-7660-2126-6(2))* Enslow Pubs., Inc.
—Light, Sound, & Waves Science Fair Projects, Revised & Expanded Using the Scientific Method. 2010. (Physics Science Projects Using the Scientific Method Ser.). (Illus.). 160p. (J). (gr. 5-18). 35.94 *(978-0-7660-3416-7(X))* Enslow Pubs., Inc.
Gardner, Robert & Conklin, Joshua. A Kid's Book of Experiments with Light. 2016. (Surprising Science Experiments Ser.). (ENG.). 48p. (J). (gr. 4-4). pap. 11.70 *(978-0-7660-7203-9(7))* Enslow Pubs., Inc.
Hawkins, Jay. Bright Ideas: The Science of Light. 2013. (Big Bang Science Experiments Ser.). (ENG., Illus.). 32p. (gr. 3-6). 26.50 *(978-1-4777-0320-5(9))*; pap. 11.75 *(978-1-4777-0362-5(4))* Windmill Bks.
Ives, Rob. Fun Experiments with Light: Periscopes, Kaleidoscopes, & More. Sassin, Eva, illus. 2017. (Amazing Science Experiments Ser.). (ENG.). (J). (gr. 3-6). lib. bdg. 26.65 ***(978-1-5124-3218-3(0))*** Lerner Publishing Group.
Jackson, Tom. Experiments with Light & Color. 2010. (Cool Science Ser.). (Illus.). 32p. (J). (gr. 5-6). pap. 10.50 *(978-1-4339-3454-4(X))*; lib. bdg. 28.00 *(978-1-4339-3453-7(1)*, 1309304) Stevens, Gareth Publishing LLLP. (Gareth Stevens Learning Library).
Jacobson, Ryan. Light & Vision. 2016. (J). *(978-1-4896-5283-6(3))* Weigl Pubs., Inc.
—Step-by-Step Experiments with Light & Vision. Ostrom, Bob, illus. 2012. (Step-By-Step Experiments Ser.). (ENG.). 32p. (J). (gr. 1-4). lib. bdg. 29.93 *(978-1-60973-588-3(9)*, 201233) Child's World, Inc., The.
Kessler, Colleen. A Project Guide to Light & Optics. 2011. (Physical Science Projects for Kids Ser.). (Illus.). 48p. (J). (gr. 3-6). lib. bdg. 29.95 *(978-1-58415-969-8(3)*, 1327831) Mitchell Lane Pubs., Inc.
Kuskowski, Alex. Science Experiments with Light, 1 vol. 2013. (More Super Simple Science Ser.). (ENG.). 32p. (gr. k-4). lib. bdg. 27.07 *(978-1-61783-851-4(9)*, Super SandCastle) ABDO Publishing Co.
Meiani, Antonella. Light. 2003. (Experimenting with Science Ser.). (Illus.). 40p. (J). (gr. 4-8). lib. bdg. 23.93 *(978-0-8225-0084-1(1))* Lerner Publishing Group.
Merrill, Amy French. Everyday Physical Science Experiments with Light. 2006. (Tony Stead Nonfiction Independent Reading Collection). (ENG.). 24p. (gr. 3-6). pap. 8.85 *(978-1-4042-5679-8(2))* Rosen Publishing Group, Inc., The.
—Everyday Physical Science Experiments with Light & Sound. 2009. (Science Surprises Ser.). 24p. (gr. 3-3). 42.50 *(978-1-60853-061-8(2)*, PowerKids Pr.) Rosen Publishing Group, Inc., The.
Oxlade, Chris. Experiments with Sound & Light, 1 vol. 2015. (ENG., Illus.). 32p. (J). lib. bdg. 27.50 *(978-1-4777-5965-3(4)*, PowerKids Pr.) Rosen Publishing Group, Inc., The.
Oxlade, Chris. Super Science Light & Sound Experiments: 10 Amazing Experiments with Step-By-Step Photographs. 2016. (ENG., Illus.). (J). pap. ***(978-1-78209-421-0(0))*** Miles Kelly Publishing, Ltd.
Parker, Steve. Tabletop Scientist — the Science of Light: Projects & Experiments with Light & Color. 2013. (ENG., Illus.). 32p. (J). (gr. 5). pap. 6.99 *(978-0-486-49264-3(8))* Dover Pubns., Inc.
Polinsky, Paige V. Super Simple Experiments with Light & Color: Fun & Innovative Science Projects. 2016. (ENG., Illus.). 32p. (J). *(978-1-68078-171-7(5))* ABDO Publishing Co.
Rau, Dana Meachen. Super Cool Science Experiments: Light. 2009. (Explorer Library: Science Explorer Ser.). (ENG., Illus.). 32p. (gr. 4-8). lib. bdg. 28.50 *(978-1-60279-531-0(2)*, 200285) Cherry Lake Publishing.
Richards, Jon. Light & Sight. Moores, Ian & Thompson, Ian, illus. 2008. (Science Factory Ser.). 32p. (YA). (gr. 4-7). lib. bdg. 26.50 *(978-1-4042-3904-3(9))* Rosen Publishing Group, Inc., The.
Riley, Peter D. Light. 2011. (Real Scientist Investigates Ser.). (Illus.). 32p. (J). (gr. 3-5). lib. bdg. 28.50 *(978-1-59771-281-1(7))* Sea-To-Sea Pubns.
Rompella, Natalie. Experiments in Light & Sound with Toys & Everyday Stuff. 2015. (Fun Science Ser.). (ENG., Illus.). 24p. (gr. 1-2). lib. bdg. 25.32 *(978-1-4914-5033-8(9))* Capstone Press of Coughlan Cos.
Royston, Angela. Experiments with a Flashlight. 2016. (One-Stop Science Ser.). 32p. (gr. 2-5). 31.35 *(978-1-62588-141-0(X)*, Smart Apple Media) Black Rabbit Bks.
Spilsbury, Louise & Spilsbury, Richard. Exploring Light. 2015. (Exploring Light Ser.). (ENG.). 32p. (gr. 2-4). lib. bdg. 122.60 *(978-1-4109-7946-9(6)*, Raintree Perspectives) Heinemann-Raintree.
Thomas, Isabel. Experiments with Light. 2015. (Read & Experiment Ser.). (ENG., Illus.). 32p. (gr. 2-4). 30.65 *(978-1-4109-6837-1(5)*, Raintree Perspectives) Heinemann-Raintree.

LIGHT AMPLIFICATION BY STIMULATED EMISSION OF RADIATION

see Lasers

LIGHT AND SHADE

see Shadows

LIGHT SHIPS

see Lightships

LIGHTHOUSES

see also Lightships

Batchelor, John. Lighthouses of the World. 2004. (Dover History Coloring Book Ser.). (ENG., Illus.). 32p. (J). (gr. 3-8). pap. 3.99 *(978-0-486-43685-2(3))* Dover Pubns., Inc.
Bissonette, Aimee. Miss Colfax's Light. Ewen, Eileen Ryan, illus. 2016. (ENG.). 32p. (J). (gr. 1-4). 16.99 *(978-1-58536-955-3(1)*, 204029) Sleeping Bear Pr.
Campbell, Marie L., illus. A Pocketful of Passage. 2007. (Great Lakes Books Ser.). (ENG.). 96p. (J). (gr. 3-7). per. 12.95 *(978-0-8143-3341-9(9)*, 20178) Wayne State Univ. Pr.
Clifford, Mary Louise & Clifford, J. Candace. Mind the Light, Katie: The History of Thirty-Three Female Lighthouse Keepers. 2006. (YA). per. 12.95 *(978-0-9636412-7-4(1))* Cypress Communications.
The Colors of the Lighthouse: A Children's History of Absecon Lighthouse. 2006. (J). 8.95 *(978-0-9779988-0-7(0))* Absecon Lighthouse.
DeWire, Elinor. Florida Lighthouses for Kids. 2004. (ENG., Illus.). 57p. (J). pap. 8.95 *(978-1-56164-323-3(8))* Pineapple Pr., Inc.
Glupker, Dianne & Delsi, Dawna. Great Lights of Michigan. Delsi, Dawna, illus. 2005. (Illus.). (J). per. 9.95 *(978-0-9769846-0-3(1)*, 318924) Harambee Pr.
Holden, Pam. About Lighthouses. 2015. (ENG., Illus.). 16p. (-1). pap. *(978-1-77654-077-8(8)*, Red Rocket Readers) Flying Start Bks.
House, Katherine L. Lighthouses for Kids: History, Science, & Lore with 21 Activities. 2008. (For Kids Ser.). (ENG., Illus.). 128p. (J). (gr. 4-7). pap. 16.95 *(978-1-55652-720-3(9))* Chicago Review Pr., Inc.
Keep the Lights Burning. 9.95 *(978-1-59112-293-7(7))* Live Oak Media.
Krebs, Laurie. A Day in the Life of a Colonial Lighthouse Keeper. (Library of Living & Working in Colonial Times Ser.). 24p. 2009. (gr. 3-3). 42.50 *(978-1-60853-733-4(1))* 2004. (Illus.). (J). lib. bdg. 22.60 *(978-0-8239-6226-6(1))* Rosen Publishing Group, Inc., The. (PowerKids Pr.).
Moss, Marissa. The Bravest Woman in America. U'Ren, Andrea, illus. 2011. (ENG.). 32p. (J). (gr. k-3). 16.99

J
K
L

(978-1-58246-369-8(7), Tricycle Pr.) Random Hse. Children's Bks.

Orr, Tamra B. How Did They Build That? Lighthouse. 2011. (Community Connections: How Did They Build That? Ser.). (ENG.). 24p. (gr. 2-5). lib. bdg. 25.64 *(978-1-61080-114-0(8)*, 201122) Cherry Lake Publishing.

PRESS, Celebration. Lighthouses: Beacons of the Past. 2003. (ENG.). (J). (gr. 2-5). pap., stu. ed. 34.95 *(978-0-673-62841-1(8)*, Celebration Pr.) Pearson Schl.

Roop, Connie & Roop, Peter. Keep the Lights Burning, Abbie. Hanson, Peter E., illus. 2016. (On My Own History Ser.). (ENG.). 40p. (J). (gr. 2-4). 38.65 *(978-1-5124-1862-0(5)*, Millbrook Pr.) Lerner Publishing Group.

Ruth, Angie. My Adventure at a Lighthouse. 2006. 44p. (J). 8.99 *(978-1-59092-316-0(2))* Blue Forge Pr.

Silcox, Diane. A Light to Keep. Moates, Carol Meetze, illus. 2013. 30p. pap. 14.95 *(978-1-938101-36-6(7))* Indigo Sea Pr., LLC.

Trumbauer, Lisa. Lighthouses of North America! Exploring Their History, Lore & Science. Kline, Michael, illus. 2007. (Kaleidoscope Kids Bks.). (ENG.). 96p. (J). (gr. 3-7). 16.99 *(978-0-8249-6791-8(7))*; pap. 12.99 *(978-0-8249-6790-1(9))* Worthy Publishing. (Ideal Pubns.).

Weintraub, Aileen. Alcatraz Island Light: The West Coast's First Lighthouse. (Great Lighthouses of North America Ser.). 24p. (gr. 3-3). 2009. 42.50 *(978-1-61513-127-3(2)*, PowerKids Pr.) 2003. (Illus.). (YA). 22.60 *(978-0-8239-6171-9(0))* Rosen Publishing Group, Inc., The.

—Boston Light: The First Lighthouse in North America. (Great Lighthouses of North America Ser.). 24p. (gr. 3-3). 2009. 42.50 *(978-1-61513-128-0(0)*, PowerKids Pr.) 2003. (Illus.). (YA). 22.60 *(978-0-8239-6170-2(2))* Rosen Publishing Group, Inc., The.

—Cape Disappointment Light: The First Lighthouse in the Pacific Northwest. (Great Lighthouses of North America Ser.). 24p. (gr. 3-3). 2009. 42.50 *(978-1-61513-129-7(9)*, PowerKids Pr.) 2003. (Illus.). (YA). 22.60 *(978-0-8239-6172-6(9))* Rosen Publishing Group, Inc., The.

—Cape Hatteras Light: The Tallest Lighthouse in the United States. 2009. (Great Lighthouses of North America Ser.). 24p. (gr. 3-3). 42.50 *(978-1-61513-130-3(2)*, PowerKids Pr.) Rosen Publishing Group, Inc., The.

—Navesink Twin Lights: The First U. S. Lighthouse to Use a Fresnel Lens. (Great Lighthouses of North America Ser.). 24p. 2009. (gr. 3-3). 42.50 *(978-1-61513-131-0(0))* 2003. (Illus.). (J). 22.60 *(978-0-8239-6169-6(9))* Rosen Publishing Group, Inc., The. (PowerKids Pr.).

—Point Pinos Light: The West Coast's Oldest Continuously Active Lighthouse. (Great Lighthouses of North America Ser.). 24p. 2009. (gr. 3-3). 42.50 *(978-1-61513-132-7(9))* 2003. (Illus.). (J). 22.60 *(978-0-8239-6173-3(7))* Rosen Publishing Group, Inc., The. (PowerKids Pr.).

Weintraub, Aileen, tr. Cape Hatteras Light: The Tallest Lighthouse in the United States. 2003. (Great Lighthouses of North America Ser.). (Illus.). 24p. (YA). (gr. 3-6). 22.60 *(978-0-8239-6168-9(0))* Rosen Publishing Group, Inc., The.

Wilbur, Helen L. B Is for Beacon: A Great Lakes Lighthouse Alphabet. Graef, Renee, illus. 2016. (ENG.). 32p. (J). (gr. 1-4). 16.99 *(978-1-58536-916-4(0)*, 204025) Sleeping Bear Pr.

Zepke, Terrance. Lighthouses of the Carolinas for Kids. 2009. (Carolinas for Kids Ser.). (ENG.). 64p. (J). (gr. 4-18). pap. 9.95 *(978-1-56164-429-2(3))* Pineapple Pr., Inc.

LIGHTHOUSES—FICTION

Acton, Vanessa. Skeleton Tower. 2016. (Atlas of Cursed Places Ser.). (ENG.). 104p. (YA). (gr. 6-12). lib. bdg. 26.65 *(978-1-5124-1322-9(4)*, Darby Creek) Lerner Publishing Group.

Armitage, Ronda & Armitage, Donald. Lighthouse Keeper's Lunch. Date not set. (ENG., Illus.). 32p. (J). pap. *(978-0-05-004387-5(0))* Addison-Wesley Longman, Inc.

Ballantyne, Robert Michael. The Lighthouse. 2007. (ENG.). 256p. pap. 21.99 *(978-1-4264-9381-2(9))*; 286p. pap. 23.99 *(978-1-4264-9762-9(8))* Creative Media Partners, LLC.

Brown, Ruth. Gracie, the Lighthouse Cat. Brown, Ruth, illus. 2011. (Andersen Press Picture Bks). (ENG., Illus.). 32p. (J). (gr. -1-3). 16.95 *(978-0-7613-7454-1(X))* Lerner Publishing Group.

Bunting, Eve. Ghost Cat. Barry, Kevin M., illus. 2017. (ENG.). 32p. (J). (gr. k-2). 16.99 ***(978-1-58536-993-5(4)***, 204323) Sleeping Bear Pr.

Butler, Gloria. Lighthouse Lindy. 2008. 16.95 *(978-0-9790469-6-4(3))* Arbor Bks.

Castro-Bran, Rose. The Adventures of Port Herman Lighthouse. 2008. 32p. pap. 14.95 *(978-1-4343-6547-7(6))* AuthorHouse.

Chakravorty, Amita. Rupadil's Lighthouse. 2011. 48p. pap. 19.67 *(978-1-4520-1904-8(5))* AuthorHouse.

Chase, Diana. The Light House Kids. 2003. (Illus.). 256p. (J). pap. 13.50 *(978-1-86368-346-3(1))* Fremantle Pr. AUS. Dist: Independent Pubs. Group.

Clark, Joyce. Katie. 2006. 196p. 27.43 *(978-1-4122-0067-7(9))* Trafford Publishing.

Coons, Susan. The Lighthouse Mouse. 2006. 19.99 *(978-0-9721410-1-7(4))* Vinland Pr.

Copeland, Cynthia L. Elin's Island. 2003. (Single Titles Ser.: up). (ENG.). 144p. (YA). (gr. 6-12). lib. bdg. 22.60 *(978-0-7613-2522-2(0)*, Millbrook Pr.) Lerner Publishing Group.

Corpus, Terrizita. The Grumpy Lighthouse Keeper. Prewett, Maggie, illus. 2017. (ENG.). 32p. (J). (gr. k-3). pap. 13.99 ***(978-1-925360-18-9(0))*** Magabala Bks. AUS. Dist: Independent Pubs. Group.

Crew, Gary. The Cat on the Island. Warden, Gillian, illus. 2008. 32p. *(978-0-207-20070-0(X))* HarperCollins Pubs. Australia.

Dilley, Ray. Brian's Lighthouse. 2013. 40p. pap. 19.99 *(978-1-4772-6663-2(1))* AuthorHouse.

Doyle, Patrick H. T. Edgar Font's Hunt for a House to Haunt: Adventure One: the Castle Tower Lighthouse. 2006. (Illus.). 213p. (J). (gr. -1). per. 6.99 *(978-0-9786132-0-4(1))* Armadillo Bks.

Dunn, Joeming. The Lighthouse Mystery. Dunn, Ben, illus. 2010. (Boxcar Children Graphic Novels Ser.: 14). (ENG.). 32p. (J). (gr. 2-5). pap. 6.99 *(978-0-8075-4547-8(3))* Whitman, Albert & Co.

Dunn, Joeming & Warner, Gertrude Chandler. The Lighthouse Mystery, 1 vol., Bk. 14. Dunn, Ben, illus. 2011. (Boxcar Children Graphic Novels Ser.). (ENG.). 32p. (J). (gr. 2-5). 28.50 *(978-1-61641-122-0(8))* ABDO Publishing Co.

Farren, Rick. Eliza's Wish. 2007. 154p. (J). per. 14.95 *(978-0-9794863-8-8(6))* Summerland Publishing.

—The Secret of the Lighthouse. 2004. (J). per. 12.95 *(978-0-9748087-3-4(3))* Journey Pubns., LLC.

—The Secret of the Lighthouse. 2007. 127p. (J). (gr. 1-7). per. 12.95 *(978-0-9794863-7-1(8))* Summerland Publishing.

Fletcher, Susan. Walk Across the Sea. Jakesevic, Nenad, illus. 2003. (ENG.). 224p. (J). (gr. 4-8). pap. 11.95 *(978-0-689-85707-2(1)*, Atheneum Bks. for Young Readers) Simon & Schuster Children's Publishing.

Gutzschhahn, Uwe-Michael. The Lighthouse under the Clouds. Docherty, Thomas, illus. 2008. (ENG.). 32p. (J). (gr. -1-k). 19.00 *(978-1-906367-03-9(5))* National Maritime Museum GBR. Dist: Independent Pubs. Group.

Herman, Gail. Scooby-Doo in the Lighthouse Mystery, 1 vol. 2016. (Scooby-Doo! Set 3 Ser.). (ENG., Illus.). 32p. (J). (gr. k-4). lib. bdg. 24.21 *(978-1-61479-410-3(3))* Spotlight.

Hernandez, Ruben. Elisa Escuchaba el Canto de las Ballenas. Corichi, Yadhira, illus. rev. ed. 2003. (Castillo de la Lectura Blanca Ser.). (SPA & ENG.). 48p. (J). (gr. 1-3). pap. 6.95 *(978-970-20-0141-6(2))* Castillo, Ediciones, S. A. de C. V. MEX. Dist: Macmillan.

Hunter, Sara Hoagland. The Lighthouse Santa. Miner, Julia, illus. 2011. 36p. (J). (gr. -1-3). 17.95 *(978-1-61168-006-5(9))* Univ. Pr. of New England.

Janis, Tim. Shine Like a Lighhouse. Steve, Lavigne, illus. 2nd ed. 2007. (J). 12.95 *(978-0-9773335-1-6(5))* Janis, Tim Ensemble, Inc.

Jansson, Tove. Moominpappa at Sea. Hart, Kingsley, tr. Jansson, Tove, illus. 2010. (Moomins Ser.: 7). (ENG., Illus.). 240p. (J). (gr. 4-7). pap. 7.99 *(978-0-312-60892-7(6)*, 9780312608927) Square Fish.

Kinkade, Thomas. Katherine's Story. 2004. (Girls of Lighthouse Lane Ser.). 176p. (J). (gr. 5-18). 13.89 *(978-0-06-054342-6(6))* HarperCollins Pubs.

Kinkade, Thomas & Tamar, Erika. Rose's Story. 2004. (Girls of Lighthouse Lane Ser.: No. 2). (Illus.). 192p. (J). (gr. 5-18). 12.99 *(978-0-06-054344-0(2))* HarperCollins Pubs.

Lasky, Kathryn. May. 2011. (Daughters of the Sea Ser.: 2). (ENG.). 336p. (J). (gr. 7-7). 17.99 *(978-0-439-78311-8(9)*, Scholastic Pr.) Scholastic, Inc.

Levy, Dana Alison. The Family Fletcher Takes Rock Island. (ENG.). 272p. (J). (gr. 4-7). 2017. 6.99 ***(978-0-553-52133-7(0)***, Yearling) 2016. 16.99 *(978-0-553-52130-6(6)*, Delacorte Bks. for Young Readers) Random Hse. Children's Bks.

Love, Pamela. Lighthouse Seeds. Warner, Linda, illus. 2004. (ENG.). 32p. (J). (gr. k-17). 15.95 *(978-0-89272-541-0(9))* Down East Bks.

Marsh, Carole. The Mystery on the Great Lakes. 2010. (Real Kids, Real Places Ser.). (Illus.). 158p. (J). 18.99 *(978-0-635-07449-2(4)*, Marsh, Carole Mysteries) Gallopade International.

Martin, Carol. The Lighthouse. 2011. 16p. 7.95 *(978-1-4497-0962-4(1)*, WestBow Pr.) Author Solutions, Inc.

Mason, Jane B. & Stephens, Sarah Hines. Bella Baxter & the Lighthouse Mystery. Shelley, John, illus. 2006. (Bella Baxter Ser.: 3). (ENG.). 80p. (J). (gr. 1-4). pap. 6.99 *(978-0-689-86282-3(2)*, Simon & Schuster/Paula Wiseman Bks.) Simon & Schuster/Paula Wiseman Bks.

McKinty, Adrian. The Lighthouse Land. 2006. (ENG., Illus.). 200p. (YA). (gr. 6-10). 16.95 *(978-0-8109-5480-9(X))* Abrams, Inc.

Messer, Celeste M. The Ghost of Piper's Landing. Hoeffner, Deb, illus. 2004. 82-92p. 4.95 *(978-0-9702171-7-2(X))* AshleyAlan Enterprises.

Panagopoulos, Janie Lynn. A Castle at the Straits. Evans, Laura, illus. 2003. 48p. (J). (gr. 1-6). *(978-0-911872-83-5(3))* Mackinac State Historic Parks.

Parsons, Carol. Mystery at Eagle Harbor Lighthouse. 2006. (J). pap. 11.95 *(978-1-59705-985-5(4))* Wings ePress, Inc.

Patterson, Nancy. May the Magnificent Lighthouse. Patterson, Nancy, illus. 2012. (Illus.). 24p. 18.95 *(978-0-615-61021-4(8))* Bayberry Cottage Gallery.

Pike, Christopher, pseud. The Howling Ghost. 2014. (Spooksville Ser.: 2). (ENG., Illus.). 128p. (J). (gr. 3-7). pap. 6.99 *(978-1-4814-1052-6(0)*, Aladdin) Simon & Schuster Children's Publishing.

Preus, Margi. Storm's Coming! Geister, David, illus. 2016. (ENG.). 32p. (J). 16.95 *(978-1-68134-018-0(6))* Minnesota Historical Society Pr.

Prior, Natalie Jane. Lily Quench & the Lighthouse of Skellig Mor, Vol. 4. 2004. (ENG., Illus.). 160p. (J). (gr. 3-7). 6.99 *(978-0-14-240059-3(9)*, Puffin Books) Penguin Young Readers Group.

Roy, James. Ichabod Hart & the Lighthouse Mystery. 2003. (Steampunk Ser.). (Illus.). 392p. pap. *(978-0-7022-3364-7(1))* Univ. of Queensland Pr.

Rylant, Cynthia. The Eagle. McDaniels, Preston, illus. 2004. (Lighthouse Family Ser.: 3). (ENG.). 64p. (J). (gr. 1-5). 15.99 *(978-0-689-86243-4(1)*, Simon & Schuster Bks. For Young Readers) Simon & Schuster Bks. For Young Readers.

—The Octopus. McDaniels, Preston, illus. 2005. (Lighthouse Family Ser.: 5). (ENG.). 64p. (J). (gr. 1-5). 15.99 *(978-0-689-86246-5(6)*, Simon & Schuster Bks. For Young Readers) Simon & Schuster Bks. For Young Readers.

—The Otter. McDaniels, Preston, illus. 2016. (Lighthouse Family Ser.: 6). (ENG.). 48p. (J). (gr. 1-5). 15.99 *(978-1-4814-6045-3(5)*, Beach Lane Bks.) Beach Lane Bks.

—The Sea Lion. McDaniels, Preston, illus. 2017. (Lighthouse Family Ser.: 7). (ENG.). 48p. (J). (gr. 1-5). 15.99 *(978-1-4814-6025-5(0)*, Beach Lane Bks.) Beach Lane Bks.

—The Turtle. McDaniels, Preston, illus. 2006. (Lighthouse Family Ser.). 47p. (J). (gr. -1-3). 11.65 *(978-0-7569-6611-9(6))* Perfection Learning Corp.

—The Turtle. McDaniels, Preston, illus. 2005. (Lighthouse Family Ser.: 4). (ENG.). 48p. (J). (gr. 1-5). 15.99 *(978-0-689-86244-1(X)*, Simon & Schuster Bks. For Young Readers) Simon & Schuster Bks. For Young Readers.

Schneider, Richard H. The Lighthouse Boy: A Story about Courage. Petrov, Anton, illus. 2007. (ENG.). 32p. (J). (gr. -1-3). pap. 8.99 *(978-0-8249-5557-1(9)*, Ideal Pubns.) Worthy Publishing.

Smith, Lauren E. Ashley Enright Investigations. 2006. 48p. pap. 16.95 *(978-1-4241-2963-8(X))* America Star Bks.

Smith, Ruth. Buddy Bear: Visits Michigan Lighthouses. 2010. 28p. pap. 13.99 *(978-1-4490-8363-2(3))* AuthorHouse.

Smucker, Anna Egan. To Keep the South Manitou Light. (Great Lakes Books Ser.). (ENG., Illus.). 144p. (J). 2006. (gr. 3-7). per. 15.99 *(978-0-8143-3236-8(6)*, 1147) 2004. 23.95 *(978-0-8143-3235-1(8)*, 1148, Painted Turtle) Wayne State Univ. Pr.

Snowman, Sally R. Sammy the Boston Lighthouse Dog. 2005. (J). (gr. 3-5). 15.00 *(978-0-9674666-2-0(8))* Snowman Learning Center, The.

Specter, Baron. The Lighthouse of Terror, 1 vol., Bk. 3. Evans, Dustin, illus. 2010. (Ghostly Graphic Adventures Ser.). (ENG.). 32p. (J). (gr. 3-6). 28.50 *(978-1-60270-772-6(3))* ABDO Publishing Co.

Stainton, Sue. The Lighthouse Cat. Mortimer, Anne, illus. 2004. (ENG.). 32p. (J). (gr. -1-2). 16.99 *(978-0-06-009604-5(7)*, Tegen, Katherine Bks) HarperCollins Pubs.

Stevenson, Charles. The Adventures of the Glo-Worm Family. 2012. (Illus.). 34p. pap. 9.99 *(978-1-78035-338-8(3)*, Fastprint Publishing) Upfront Publishing Ltd. GBR. Dist: Printondemand-worldwide.com.

Stonehouse, Frederick. My Summer at the Lighthouse: A Boy's Journal. 2003. (Illus.). 32p. (J). (gr. 3-9). *(978-1-892384-18-8(3))* Avery Color Studios, Inc.

Swift, Hildegarde H. The Little Red Lighthouse & the Great Gray Bridge: Restored Edition. Ward, Lynd, illus. 2003. (ENG.). 64p. (J). (gr. -1-3). pap. 8.99 *(978-0-15-204573-9(2))* Houghton Mifflin Harcourt Publishing Co.

Thiele, Colin. The Hammerhead Light. (Illus.). 196p. pap. *(978-0-7344-0401-5(8)*, Lothian Children's Bks.) Hachette Australia.

Valentine, Sally. The Ghost of the Charlotte Lighthouse. 2006. (J). *(978-1-59531-013-2(4))* North Country Bks., Inc.

VanRiper, Justin & VanRiper, Gary. The Lost Lighthouse. Gary, Glenn, illus. 2003. (Adirondack Kids Ser.: Vol. 3). 82p. (J). (gr. 2-7). pap. 9.95 *(978-0-9707044-2-9(9)*, ADK3) Adirondack Kids Pr.

Walton, O. F. Saved at Sea: A Young Boy in a Dramatic Rescue. 2007. (Classic Stories Ser.). (ENG., Illus.). 144p. (J). mass mkt. 7.99 *(978-1-85792-795-5(8)*, 9781857927955) Christian Focus Pubns. GBR. Dist: Bookmasters Distribution.

—Saved at Sea A Lighthouse Story. 2004. reprint ed. pap. 1.99 *(978-1-4192-4623-4(2))*; pap. 15.95 *(978-1-4191-4623-7(8))* Kessinger Publishing, LLC.

Weston Woods Staff, creator. Little Red Lighthouse & the Great Gray Bridge. 2011. 38.75 *(978-0-439-72751-8(0))*; 29.95 *(978-0-439-73487-5(8))*; 18.95 *(978-0-439-72750-1(2))* Weston Woods Studios, Inc.

Woodruff, Elvira. Fearless. 2011. (ENG.). 240p. (J). (gr. 3-7). pap. 6.99 *(978-0-439-67704-2(1)*, Scholastic Pr.) Scholastic, Inc.

LIGHTING

see also Candles

Bailer, Darice. Why Does It Thunder & Lightning? 2010. (Tell Me Why, Tell Me How 4 Ser.). 32p. (gr. 3-5). 29.93 *(978-0-7614-4825-9(X))* Marshall Cavendish Corp.

Cox-Cannons, Helen. Thunder & Lightning, 1 vol. 2014. (Weather Wise Ser.). (ENG., Illus.). 24p. (gr. -1-1). 22.65 *(978-1-4846-0548-6(9)*, Acorn) Heinemann-Raintree.

Edison, Erin. Lightning, 1 vol. 2011. (Weather Basics Ser.). (ENG.). 24p. (gr. k-1). pap. 7.29 *(978-1-4296-7078-4(9))*; pap. 41.70 *(978-1-4296-7085-2(1))*; lib. bdg. 26.65 *(978-1-4296-6058-7(9))* Capstone Press of Coughlan Cos. (Pebble Plus).

Hansen, Grace. Truenos y Relampagos. 2016. (Clima Ser.). (SPA.). 24p. (J). (gr. 1-6). pap. 7.95 *(978-1-4966-0695-2(7))* Capstone Classroom.

Hughes, Mónica & Zlatic, Tomislav. Lights. 2006. (Collins Big Cat Ser.). (ENG., Illus.). 136p. (J). (gr. 1-1). pap. 5.99 *(978-0-00-718680-8(0))* HarperCollins Pubs. Ltd. GBR. Dist: Independent Pubs. Group.

Kallio, Jamie. 12 Things to Know about Wild Weather. 2015. (ENG., Illus.). 32p. (J). *(978-1-63235-035-0(1))* Pr. Room Editions LLC.

Kenney, Karen Latchana. Cool Special Effects: How to Stage Your Very Own Show, 1 vol. 2010. (Cool Performances Ser.). (ENG., Illus.). 32p. (gr. 3-6). 28.50 *(978-1-60453-719-2(1)*, Checkerboard Library) ABDO Publishing Co.

Lay, Kathryn. Look Out for Lightning!, 1 vol., Vol. 2. Wolff, Jason, illus. 2011. (Wendy's Weather Warriors Ser.). (ENG.). 80p. (gr. 2-5). 27.07 *(978-1-60270-755-9(3)*, Calico Chapter Bks) Magic Wagon.

Mullins, Lisa. Inventing the Electric Light. 2007. (Breakthrough Inventions Ser.). (ENG., Illus.). 32p. (J). (gr. 3-7). lib. bdg. *(978-0-7787-2818-4(8))*; pap. *(978-0-7787-2840-5(4))* Crabtree Publishing Co.

Roland, James. How LEDs Work. 2016. (Connect with Electricity Ser.). (ENG., Illus.). 40p. (J). (gr. 4-6). 30.65 *(978-1-5124-0780-8(1))* Lerner Publishing Group.

Tolhurst, Marilyn. Lights & Candles. Date not set. (Sense of History Ser.). (Illus.). 24p. pap. 27.69 *(978-0-582-04026-7(4))* Addison-Wesley Longman, Ltd. GBR. Dist: Trans-Atlantic Pubns., Inc.

LIGHTNING

Bendick, Jeanne. Lightning. 2012. 62p. 36.95 *(978-1-258-22925-2(0))*; pap. 21.95 *(978-1-258-24664-8(3))* Literary Licensing, LLC.

Edison, Erin & Saunders-Smith, Gail. Relámpagos. Strictly Spanish LLC. Staff, tr. from ENG. 2013. (Lo Básico Sobre el Tiempo/Weather Basics Ser.).Tr. of Lightning. (SPA, MUL & ENG., Illus.). 24p. (gr. k-1). lib. bdg. 26.65 *(978-1-62065-163-6(7))* Capstone Press of Coughlan Cos.

Fleisher, Paul. Lightning, Hurricanes, & Blizzards: The Science of Storms. 2010. (Weatherwise Ser.). (ENG.). 48p. (gr. 4-8). lib. bdg. 29.27 *(978-0-8225-7536-8(1))* Lerner Publishing Group.

French, Cathy. Snap, Crackle, & Flow & Chasquea, cruje y Fluye: 6 English, 6 Spanish Adaptations. 2011. (ENG & SPA.). (J). 97.00 net. *(978-1-4108-5697-5(6))* Benchmark Education Co.

Galiano, Dean. Thunderstorms & Lightning. (Weather Watcher's Library). 48p. (gr. 5-8). 2009. 53.00 *(978-1-60854-275-8(0))* 2003. (Illus.). (YA). lib. bdg. 23.95 *(978-0-8239-3093-7(9)*, WETHLI) Rosen Publishing Group, Inc., The. (Rosen Reference).

Hamilton, John. Lightning, 1 vol. 2006. (Nature's Fury Ser.). (ENG., Illus.). 32p. (gr. 3-8). 27.07 *(978-1-59679-332-3(5)*, Abdo & Daughters) ABDO Publishing Co.

Hansen, Grace. Thunder & Lightning, 1 vol. 2015. (ENG., Illus.). 24p. (J). *(978-1-62970-934-5(4))* ABDO Publishing Co.

Herriges, Ann. Lightning. 2011. (Blastoff! Readers Ser.). 24p. (J). pap. 5.95 *(978-0-531-27621-1(X)*, Children's Pr.) Scholastic Library Publishing.

Hidalgo, Maria. Lightning. 2006. (My First Look at Weather Ser.). (Illus.). 24p. (J). (gr. -1-3). lib. bdg. 15.95 *(978-1-58341-450-7(9)*, Creative Education) Creative Co., The.

Lawrence, Ellen. What Is Lightning? 2015. (Weather Wise Ser.). (ENG., Illus.). 24p. (J). (gr. -1-3). lib. bdg. 23.93 *(978-1-62724-863-1(3))* Bearport Publishing Co., Inc.

Nagelhout, Ryan. When Lightning Strikes. 2015. (Eye on the Sky Ser.). (ENG., Illus.). 32p. (J). (gr. 3-4). pap. 10.50 *(978-1-4824-2892-6(X))* Stevens, Gareth Publishing LLLP.

Person, Stephen. Struck by Lightning! 2010. (Disaster Survivors Ser.). (Illus.). 32p. (YA). (gr. 4-7). lib. bdg. 25.27 *(978-1-936087-47-1(2))* Bearport Publishing Co., Inc.

Rajczak, Kristen. Lightning. 2012. (Nature's Light Show Ser.). (Illus.). 24p. (J). (gr. 2-5). pap. 8.15 *(978-1-4339-7024-5(4))*; lib. bdg. 22.60 *(978-1-4339-7023-8(6))* Stevens, Gareth Publishing LLLP.

Riley, Gail Blasser. Benjamin Franklin & Electricity. 2004. (Cornerstones of Freedom Ser.). (ENG., Illus.). 48p. (YA). (gr. 4-7). 26.00 *(978-0-516-24240-8(7))* Scholastic Library Publishing.

Roland, James. How LEDs Work. 2016. (Connect with Electricity Ser.). (ENG., Illus.). 40p. (J). (gr. 4-6). 46.65 *(978-1-5124-1009-9(8)*, Lerner Pubns.) Lerner Publishing Group.

Saunders-Smith, Gail. Lightning. 2016. (Weather Ser.). (ENG.). 24p. (gr. k-1). pap. 6.29 *(978-1-5157-3694-3(6)*, Pebble Bks.) Capstone Press of Coughlan Cos.

Simon, Seymour. Lightning. 2006. (ENG., Illus.). 32p. (J). (gr. k-4). pap. 6.99 *(978-0-06-088435-2(5)*, Collins) HarperCollins Pubs.

LIGHTSHIPS

Floca, Brian. Lightship. Floca, Brian, illus. 2007. (ENG., Illus.). 48p. (J). (gr. -1-3). 18.99 *(978-1-4169-2436-4(1)*, Atheneum/Richard Jackson Bks.) Simon & Schuster Children's Publishing.

—Lightship. 2007. (J). (gr. k-3). 29.95 incl. audio compact disk *(978-0-8045-4185-5(X))*; 27.95 incl. audio *(978-0-8045-6962-0(2))* Spoken Arts, Inc.

LIMERICKS

see also Nonsense Verses

Bodden, Valerie. Limericks. 2009. (Poetry Basics Ser.). (Illus.). 32p. (J). 19.95 *(978-1-58341-777-5(X)*, 1300263, Creative Education) Creative Co., The.

—Poetry Basics - Limericks. 2011. (Poetry Basics Ser.). (ENG.). 32p. (J). (gr. 5-17). pap. 8.99 *(978-1-926722-45-0(0)*, Creative Paperbacks) Creative Co., The.

Bumbalough, Jerry. Purple pup girls are grape Jelly. Bennett, Harry, Jr., illus. 2007. 16p. (J). 8.95 *(978-0-9797960-0-5(8))* Thirsty Sponge Publishing Co.

Cleary, Brian P. Limericks. Rowland, Andrew, illus. 2015. (Poetry Adventures Ser.). (ENG.). 32p. (J). (gr. 2-5). lib. bdg. 26.60 *(978-1-4677-2044-1(5)*, Millbrook Pr.) Lerner Publishing Group.

—Something Sure Smells Around Here: Limericks. Rowland, Andrew, illus. 2015. (Poetry Adventures Ser.). (ENG.). 32p. (J). (gr. 2-5). pap. 6.95 *(978-1-4677-6035-5(8)*, Millbrook Pr.) Lerner Publishing Group.

Early Macken, JoAnn. Read, Recite, & Write Limericks. 2014. (ENG., Illus.). 32p. (J). *(978-0-7787-0409-6(2))* Crabtree Publishing Co.

Foster, John, ed. Loopy Limericks. 2011. (ENG., Illus.). 96p. (J). (gr. k-4). pap. 5.99 *(978-0-00-711181-7(9))* HarperCollins Pubs. Ltd. GBR. Dist: HarperCollins Pubs.

Hubbell, Patricia & Hubbell. Boo! Halloween Poems & Limericks, 1 vol. Spackman, Jeff, illus. 2005. (ENG.). 32p. (YA). pap. 5.95 *(978-0-7614-5151-8(X))* Marshall Cavendish Corp.

Pearson, Yvonne. Limericks. Petelinsek, Kathleen, illus. 2015. (Poetry Party Ser.). (ENG.). 24p. (J). (gr. 2-5). 27.07 *(978-1-63143-696-3(1)*, 208532) Child's World, Inc., The.

Poffo, Lanny. Limericks from the Heart (and Lungs!) 2004. (Illus.). 180p. (J). pap. 14.00 *(978-1-888580-29-7(1))* White-Boucke Publishing.

LIMITATION OF ARMAMENT

see Disarmament

LIN, MAYA YING, 1959-

Harvey, Jeanne Walker. Maya Lin: Artist-Architect of Light & Lines. Phumiruk, Dow, illus. 2017. (ENG.). 32p. (J). 17.99 *(978-1-250-11249-1(4)*, 9781250112491, Holt, Henry & Co. Bks. For Young Readers) Holt, Henry & Co.

Lashnits, Tom. Maya Lin. 2007. (Asian Americans of Achievement Ser.). (Illus.). 128p. (J). (gr. 7-12). lib. bdg. 35.00 *(978-0-7910-9268-2(2))* Facts On File, Inc.

LINCOLN, ABRAHAM, 1809-1865

Abnett, Dan. Abraham Lincoln & the Civil War. (Jr. Graphic Biographies Ser.). (ENG.). 24p. 2009. (J). (gr. 2-3). 47.90 *(978-1-61513-807-4(2)*, PowerKids Pr.) 2007. (Illus.). (J). (gr. 2-5). lib. bdg. 25.25 *(978-1-4042-3392-8(X))* 2007. (Illus.). (gr. 3-8). pap. 10.60 *(978-1-4042-2145-1(X)*, PowerKids Pr.) Rosen Publishing Group, Inc., The.

—Abraham Lincoln y la Guerra Civil. 2009. (Historietas Juveniles: Biografías (Jr. Graphic Biographies) Ser.). (SPA., Illus.). 24p. (J). (gr. 2-5). 25.25 *(978-1-4358-8561-5(9))*; (gr. 3-8). pap. 10.60 *(978-1-4358-3316-6(3))* Rosen Publishing Group, Inc., The.

Abraham Lincoln: A Life of Respect. 2006. (J). pap. 6.95 *(978-0-8225-5700-5(2))* Lerner Publishing Group.

Abraham Lincoln & Slavery. 95p. (YA). (gr. 8-12). pap. 14.50 *(978-0-382-40942-4(6))*; spiral bd., tchr.'s planning gde. ed. 13.00 *(978-0-382-40941-7(8))* Cobblestone Publishing Co.

Abraham Lincoln's Shining Star: The Inspiring Story of Abraham Lincoln & Nebraska. 2010. (Illus.). 64p. 18.95 *(978-0-615-34265-8(5))* America's Great Stories.

Alexander, Carol. The Big Squeal: A True Story about a Homeless Pig's Search for Life, Liberty & the Pursuit of Happiness. 2013. (ENG., Illus.). 32p. (J). pap. 16.00 *(978-1-61009-112-1(4)*, Acorn) Oak Tree Publishing.

—The Big Squeal: A True Story about a Homeless Pig's Search for Life, Liberty & the Pursuit of Happiness. Kalpart Designs, illus. 2012. (ENG.). 24p. (J). 24.00 *(978-1-61009-036-0(5)*, Acorn) Oak Tree Publishing.

Algeo, Matthew. Abe & Fido: Lincoln's Love of Animals & the Touching Story of His Favorite Canine Companion. 2015. (ENG., Illus.). 176p. 22.95 *(978-1-55652-222-2(3))* Chicago Review Pr., Inc.

Allen, Thomas B. & Allen, Roger MacBride. Mr. Lincoln's High-Tech War: How the North Used the Telegraph, Railroads, Surveillance Balloons, Ironclads, High-Powered Weapons, & More to Win the Civil War. 2009. (ENG., Illus.). 144p. (J). (gr. 5-18). 18.95 *(978-1-4263-0379-1(3))*; lib. bdg. 25.90 *(978-1-4263-0380-7(7))* National Geographic Society. (National Geographic Children's Bks.).

Aloian, Molly. Emancipation. 2013. (ENG.). 48p. (J). *(978-0-7787-1100-1(5))*; pap. *(978-0-7787-1120-9(X))* Crabtree Publishing Co.

Andersen, Ron L. Ingenious Abe: Stories from the Life of Abraham Lincoln. 2016. (ENG.). (J). pap. 8.99 *(978-1-4621-1789-5(9))* Cedar Fort, Inc./CFI Distribution.

Anderson, AnnMarie. When I Grow up - Abraham Lincoln. Kelley, Gerald, illus. 2014. (Scholastic Reader Level 3 Ser.). (ENG.). 32p. (J). (gr. 1-2). pap. 3.99 *(978-0-545-60979-1(8)*, Scholastic Paperbacks) Scholastic, Inc.

Anderson, Michael, contrib. by. Abraham Lincoln. 2012. (Pivotal Presidents: Profiles in Leadership Ser.). (ENG., Illus.). 80p. (gr. 7-12). (J). lib. bdg. 32.90 *(978-1-61530-942-9(X))*; (YA). 65.80 *(978-1-61530-953-5(5))* Rosen Publishing Group, Inc., The.

Andronik, Catherine M. & Kenney, Karen Latchana. Abraham Lincoln's Presidency. 2016. (Presidential Powerhouses Ser.). (ENG., Illus.). 104p. (J). (gr. 6-12). 35.99 *(978-1-4677-7925-8(3)*, Lerner Pubns.) Lerner Publishing Group.

Armentrout, David & Armentrout, Patricia. The Emancipation Proclamation. 2005. (Documents that Shaped the Nation Ser.). (Illus.). 48p. (gr. 4-6). 20.95 *(978-1-59515-233-6(4))* Rourke Educational Media.

Aronson, Billy. Abraham Lincoln. 2008. (Presidents & Their Times Ser.). 96p. (gr. 6-18). lib. bdg. 34.21 *(978-0-7614-2839-8(9)*, Benchmark Bks.) Marshall Cavendish Corp.

Bader, Bonnie. My Little Golden Book about Abraham Lincoln. Garofoli, Viviana, illus. 2016. (Little Golden Book Ser.). (ENG.). 24p. (J). (-k). 4.99 *(978-1-101-93971-0(0)*, Golden Bks.) Random Hse. Children's Bks.

Baldwin, James. Four Great Americans. 2006. pap. *(978-1-4065-0509-2(9))* Dodo Pr.

Barretta, Gene. Lincoln & Kennedy: A Pair to Compare. Barretta, Gene, illus. 2016. (ENG., Illus.). 40p. (J). 17.99 *(978-0-8050-9945-4(X)*, 9780805099454, Holt, Henry & Co. Bks. For Young Readers) Holt, Henry & Co.

Benoit, Peter. Abraham Lincoln. 2011. (True Book(tm), a — Civil War Ser.). (J). (ENG., Illus.). 48p. lib. bdg. 31.00 *(978-0-531-26308-2(8))*; (ENG.). 64p. pap. 8.95 *(978-0-531-26550-5(1))*; 64p. lib. bdg. 30.00 *(978-0-531-25025-9(3))*; (Illus.). 48p. pap. 6.95 *(978-0-531-26621-2(4))* Scholastic Library Publishing. (Children's Pr.).

Berne, Emma Carlson. What's Your Story, Abraham Lincoln? 2015. (ENG., Illus.). 32p. (J). (gr. k-3). 26.65 *(978-1-4677-7969-2(5))* Lerner Publishing Group.

Best, B. J. Abraham Lincoln, the Emancipation Proclamation, & the 13th Amendment. 2015. (Primary Sources of the Abolitionist Movement Ser.). (ENG., Illus.). 64p. (J). (gr. 6-6). lib. bdg. 34.21 *(978-1-5026-0530-6(9))* Cavendish Square Publishing.

Bolden, Tonya. The Emancipation Proclamation: Lincoln & the Dawn of Liberty. 2013. (ENG., Illus.). 128p. (J). (gr. 3-7). 24.95 *(978-1-4197-0390-4(0)*, Abrams Bks. for Young Readers) Abrams, Inc.

Bowers, John. The Life of Abraham Lincoln. 2006. (ENG.). 68p. per. 16.95 *(978-1-4286-2279-1(9))* Kessinger Publishing, LLC.

Bozonelis, Helen Koutras. 200 Years with Abraham Lincoln: One Man's Life & Legacy. 2008. (Prime (Middle/Senior) Ser.). (Illus.). 64p. (J). (gr. 3-4). lib. bdg. 29.27 *(978-0-7660-3266-8(3))* Enslow Pubs., Inc.

Brandt, Keith & Macken, JoAnn Early. Abraham Lincoln: Road to the White House. Lawn, John, illus. 2007. 53p. (J). *(978-0-439-88005-3(X))* Scholastic, Inc.

Burleigh, Robert. Abraham Lincoln Comes Home. Minor, Wendell, illus. rev. ed. 2008. (ENG.). 40p. (J). (gr. 1-4). 16.95 *(978-0-8050-7529-8(1)*, 9780805075298, Holt, Henry & Co. Bks. For Young Readers) Holt, Henry & Co.

—Abraham Lincoln Comes Home. Minor, Wendell, illus. 2009. (J). (gr. 3-5). 27.95 incl. audio *(978-0-8045-6977-4(0))* Spoken Arts, Inc.

—Abraham Lincoln Comes Home. Minor, Wendell, illus. 2014. (ENG.). 40p. (J). (gr. 1-4). 6.99 *(978-1-250-03989-7(4)*, 9781250039897) Square Fish.

Carey, Charles W., Jr. The Emancipation Proclamation. 2009. (Journey to Freedom Ser.). (ENG., Illus.). 32p. (J). (gr. 4-7). 29.93 *(978-1-60253-137-6(4)*, 200403) Child's World, Inc., The.

Colbert, David. Abraham Lincoln. 2009. (10 Days Ser.). (ENG.). 160p. (J). (gr. 3-9). pap. 8.99 *(978-1-4169-6807-8(5)*, Simon & Schuster/Paula Wiseman Bks.) Simon & Schuster/Paula Wiseman Bks.

Collard, Sneed B., III. Abraham Lincoln: A Courageous Leader. 2006. (American Heroes Ser.). (Illus.). 48p. (gr. 3-7). lib. bdg. 29.93 *(978-0-7614-2162-7(9)*, Benchmark Bks.) Marshall Cavendish Corp.

D'Aulaire, Ingri & D'Aulaire, Edgar Parin. Abraham Lincoln. 2008. (Illus.). *(978-1-893103-27-6(7))*; pap. *(978-1-893103-26-9(9))* Beautiful Feet Bks.

D'Aulaire, Ingri & D'Aulaire, Edgar Parin, illus. Abraham Lincoln. 75th ed. 2015. (J). ***(978-1-893103-60-3(9))*** Beautiful Feet Bks.

Davis, Kenneth C. Don't Know Much about Abraham Lincoln, Vol. 4. Shepperson, Rob, illus. 2003. (Don't Know Much About Ser.). 144p. (J). (gr. 3-7). pap. 4.99 *(978-0-06-442127-0(9))* HarperCollins Pubs.

—Don't Know Much about Abraham Lincoln Abraham Lincoln, Vol. 4. Shepperson, Rob, illus. 2004. (Don't Know Much About Ser.). 144p. (J). (gr. 2-5). 15.89 *(978-0-06-028820-4(5))* HarperCollins Pubs.

Dayton, Connor. Presidents' Day. 2012. (American Holidays Ser.). (ENG., Illus.). 24p. (J). (gr. k-3). pap. 8.25 *(978-1-4488-6242-9(6))*; lib. bdg. 22.60 *(978-1-4488-6142-2(X))* Rosen Publishing Group, Inc., The. (PowerKids Pr.).

Dean, Sheri. Presidents Day/dia de los Presidentes. 2006. (Our Country's Holidays/ Las fiestas de nuestra nacion Ser.). (SPA., Illus.). 24p. (gr. k-3). lib. bdg. 22.00 *(978-0-8368-6522-6(7)*, Weekly Reader Leveled Readers) Stevens, Gareth Publishing LLLP.

Demers, Roxanna. The Rusty Bucket Kids, A Behind the Scenes Look at the Rusty Bucket Kids, Lincoln, Journey To 16. Eason, D. M., illus. 2010. (ENG.). 82p. (J). pap. 19.99 *(978-1-935711-04-9(0))* Peak City Publishing, LLC.

Demi. President Lincoln: From Log Cabin to White House. 2016. (ENG., Illus.). 32p. (J). (gr. k-3). 16.95 *(978-1-937786-50-2(1)*, Wisdom Tales) World Wisdom, Inc.

DeRubertis, Barbara. Let's Celebrate Presidents' Day: George Washington & Abraham Lincoln. Griffith, Gershom, illus. 2014. (Holidays & Heroes Ser.). 32p. (J). (gr. 1-3). pap. 7.95 *(978-1-57565-649-6(3))* Kane Press, Inc.

Diemer, Lauren & Cuthbert, Megan. Abraham Lincoln. 2014. (Illus.). 24p. (J). *(978-1-62127-308-0(3))* Weigl Pubs., Inc.

Duffield, Katy S. Abraham Lincoln. 2016. (Premier Presidents Ser.). (ENG.). 24p. (J). (gr. 1-4). 27.07 *(978-1-5038-0843-0(2)*, 210693) Child's World, Inc., The.

Dunn, Joe. Abraham Lincoln, 1 vol. Espinosa, Rod, illus. 2007. (Bio-Graphics Ser.). (ENG.). 32p. (gr. 3-6). 28.50 *(978-1-60270-064-2(8)*, Graphic Planet- Nonfiction) ABDO Publishing Co.

Dussling, Jennifer. Long, Tall Lincoln. Ko, Chin, illus. 2017. (I Can Read Level 2 Ser.). 32p. (J). (gr. -1-3). pap. 3.99 *(978-0-06-243255-1(9))* HarperCollins Pubs.

Dyan, Penelope. Abraham Lincoln Was Here! a Kid's Guide to Washington D C. Weigand, John D., photos by. 2009. (Illus.). 44p. pap. 11.95 *(978-1-935118-82-4(X))* Bellissima Publishing, LLC.

Edison, Erin. Abraham Lincoln, 1 vol. (Presidential Biographies Ser.). (ENG.). 24p. (gr. k-1). 2014. pap. 6.29 *(978-1-4765-9629-7(8)*, Pebble Bks.) 2012. (Illus.). lib. bdg. 26.65 *(978-1-4296-8735-5(5)*, Pebble Plus) Capstone Press of Coughlan Cos.

Edwards, Roberta. Hail to the Chiefs, 5 vols. 2013. (Who Was? Ser.). (ENG.). 560p. (J). (gr. 3-7). pap. 24.95 *(978-0-448-48122-7(7)*, Grosset & Dunlap) Penguin Young Readers Group.

The Emancipation Proclamation & the End of Slavery in America. 2014. (Celebration of the Civil Rights Movement Ser.). (Illus.). 80p. (J). (gr. 7-12). 34.25 *(978-1-4777-7749-7(0))* Rosen Publishing Group, Inc., The.

Erin, Audrey. Visit the Lincoln Memorial. 2012. (Landmarks of Liberty Ser.). (ENG.). 24p. (J). (gr. 2-5). pap. 8.15 *(978-1-4339-6398-8(1)*, Gareth Stevens Learning Library); lib. bdg. 22.60 *(978-1-4339-6396-4(5))* Stevens, Gareth Publishing LLLP.

Feinstein, Stephen. Lee Sobre Abraham Lincoln/Read about Abraham Lincoln. 2006. (I Like Biographies! Bilingual Ser.). (ENG & SPA., Illus.). 24p. (J). (gr. 1-3). lib. bdg. 22.60 *(978-0-7660-2672-8(8)*, Enslow Elementary) Enslow Pubs., Inc.

Figley, Marty Rhodes. President Lincoln, Willie Kettles, & the Telegraph Machine. 2010. pap. 56.72 *(978-0-7613-6929-5(5))* Lerner Publishing Group.

FitzGerald, Dawn. Vinnie & Abraham. Stock, Catherine, illus. 2007. (ENG.). 48p. (J). (gr. k-3). lib. bdg. 16.95 *(978-1-57091-658-8(6))* Charlesbridge Publishing, Inc.

Fleming, Candace. The Lincolns: A Scrapbook Look at Abraham & Mary. 2008. (ENG., Illus.). 200p. (J). (gr. 5-9). 24.99 *(978-0-375-83618-3(7)*, Schwartz & Wade Bks.) Random Hse. Children's Bks.

Fontes, Justine Korman & Fontes, Ron. Abraham Lincoln: Lawyer, Leader, Legend. 2009. (DK Readers Ser.). (ENG.). 48p. (J). (gr. 2-4). 3.99 *(978-0-7566-5689-8(3)*, DK Children) Dorling Kindersley Publishing, Inc.

Ford, Carin T. Abraham Lincoln: The 16th President. 2003. (Heroes of American History Ser.). (Illus.). 32p. (J). (gr. 1-4). lib. bdg. 22.60 *(978-0-7660-2000-9(2))* Enslow Pubs., Inc.

—The Emancipation Proclamation, Lincoln, & Slavery Through Primary Sources. 2013. (Civil War Through Primary Sources Ser.). 48p. (J). (gr. 4-10). pap. 8.95 *(978-1-4644-0187-9(X))*; lib. bdg. 25.27 *(978-0-7660-4129-5(8))* Enslow Pubs., Inc.

—Lincoln, Slavery, & the Emancipation Proclamation. 2004. (Civil War Library). (Illus.). 48p. (J). lib. bdg. 25.27 *(978-0-7660-2252-2(8))* Enslow Pubs., Inc.

Fradin, Dennis Brindell. The Emancipation Proclamation. 2007. (Turning Points in U. S. History Ser.). (J). lib. bdg. 31.36 *(978-0-7614-2038-5(X)*, Benchmark Bks.) Marshall Cavendish Corp.

Freedman, Russell. Abraham Lincoln & Frederick Douglass: The Story Behind an American Friendship. 2012. (ENG., Illus.). 128p. (J). (gr. 5-7). 18.99 *(978-0-547-38562-4(5))* Houghton Mifflin Harcourt Publishing Co.

Gilmore, Frederic. The Lincoln Memorial. 2014. (United States Landmarks Ser.). (ENG.). 24p. (J). (gr. 1-4). 27.07 *(978-1-62323-957-2(5)*, 206732) Child's World, Inc., The.

Gilpin, Caroline Crosson. National Geographic Readers: Abraham Lincoln. 2012. (Readers Bios Ser.). (ENG.). 32p. (J). (gr. k-3). pap. 3.99 *(978-1-4263-1085-0(4))*; lib. bdg. 13.90 *(978-1-4263-1086-7(2))* National Geographic Society. (National Geographic Children's Bks.).

Giovanni, Nikki. Lincoln & Douglass: An American Friendship. Collier, Bryan, illus. 2008. (ENG.). 40p. (J). (gr. 2-6). 16.95 *(978-0-8050-8264-7(6)*, 9780805082647, Holt, Henry & Co. Bks. For Young Readers) Holt, Henry & Co.

—Lincoln & Douglass: An American Friendship. Collier, Bryan, illus. 2013. (ENG.). 40p. (J). (gr. 2-6). 8.99 *(978-1-250-01869-4(2)*, 9781250018694) Square Fish.

—Lincoln & Douglass: An American Friendship. Collier, Bryan, illus. 2011. (J). (gr. -1-3). 29.95 *(978-0-545-13457-6(9))* Weston Woods Studios, Inc.

Gosman, Gillian. Abraham Lincoln. 2011. (Life Stories Ser.). (Illus.). 24p. (J). pap. 8.25 *(978-1-4488-2753-4(1)*, PowerKids Pr.); (SPA., (gr. 1-4). lib. bdg. 22.60 *(978-1-4488-3216-3(0))*; (gr. 1-4). lib. bdg. 22.60 *(978-1-4488-2582-0(2)*, PowerKids Pr.) Rosen Publishing Group, Inc., The.

Gregory, Josh. Abraham Lincoln: The 16th President. 2015. (First Look at America's Presidents Ser.). (ENG.). 24p. (J). (gr. -1-3). lib. bdg. 23.93 *(978-1-62724-554-8(5))* Bearport Publishing Co., Inc.

Group/McGraw-Hill, Wright. Abraham Lincoln: The Civil War President, 6 vols. (Book2WebTM Ser.). (gr. 4-8). 36.50 *(978-0-322-04462-3(6))* Wright Group/McGraw-Hill.

Gunderson, Jessica. The Election Of 1860: A Nation Divides on the Eve of War. 2016. (Presidential Politics Ser.). (ENG., Illus.). 48p. (gr. 3-4). lib. bdg. 29.32 *(978-1-4914-8240-7(0)*, Connect) Stone Arch Bks.

—Election of 1860: A Nation Divides on the Eve of War. 2016. (J). pap. *(978-1-4914-8737-2(2))* Capstone Press of Coughlan Cos.

Haldy, Emma E. Abraham Lincoln. Bane, Jeff, illus. 2016. (My Early Library: My Itty-Bitty Bio Ser.). (ENG.). 24p. (J). (gr. k-1). 28.50 *(978-1-63470-476-2(2)*, 207635) Cherry Lake Publishing.

Hall, Brianna. Freedom from Slavery: Causes & Effects of the Emancipation Proclamation, 1 vol. 2014. (Cause & Effect Ser.). (ENG.). 32p. (gr. 3-4). lib. bdg. 27.32 *(978-1-4765-3930-0(8)*, Fact Finders) Capstone Press of Coughlan Cos.

Hall, Margaret. Abraham Lincoln: 16th U. S. President, 1 vol. Soud, illus. 2008. (Beginner Biographies Ser.). (ENG.). 32p. (gr. -1-3). 28.50 *(978-1-60270-250-9(0)*, Looking Glass Library- Nonfiction) Magic Wagon.

Hally, Ashleigh. Abraham Lincoln. 2012. (Illus.). 24p. (J). *(978-1-935884-41-5(7))*; pap. *(978-1-935884-50-7(6))* State Standards Publishing, LLC.

Hamilton, Lynn. Presidents' Day. 2015. (Illus.). 24p. (J). *(978-1-5105-0116-4(9))* SmartBook Media, Inc.

—Presidents' Day. (American Celebrations Ser.). (Illus.). 24p. (J). 2010. (gr. 3-5). pap. 11.95 *(978-1-60596-931-2(1))* 2010. (gr. 3-5). lib. bdg. 18.99 *(978-1-60596-773-8(4))* 2004. (gr. 1-3). lib. bdg. 24.45 *(978-1-59036-108-5(3))* 2004. (gr. 1-3). per. 8.95 *(978-1-59036-169-6(5))* Weigl Pubs., Inc.

Hansen, Grace. Abraham Lincoln. 2015. (Biografías de Los Presidentes de Los Estados Unidos Ser.). (SPA., Illus.). 24p. (gr. k-1). pap. 7.95 *(978-1-4966-0401-9(6))* Capstone Classroom.

Harness, Cheryl. Abe Lincoln Goes to Washington: 1837-1865. 2nd ed. 2008. (ENG., Illus.). 48p. (J). (gr. 3-7). pap. 7.95 *(978-1-4263-0436-1(6)*, National Geographic Children's Bks.) National Geographic Society.

—Young Abe Lincoln: The Frontier Days: 1809-1837. 2nd ed. 2008. (ENG., Illus.). 32p. (J). (gr. 3-7). pap. 7.95 *(978-1-4263-0437-8(4)*, National Geographic Children's Bks.) National Geographic Society.

Harris, Laurie Lanzen. How to Analyze the Works of Abraham Lincoln, 1 vol. 2013. (Essential Critiques Set 4 Ser.). (ENG.). 112p. (J). (gr. 6-12). lib. bdg. 35.64 *(978-1-61783-642-8(7)*, Essential Library) ABDO Publishing Co.

Helfand, Lewis. Abraham Lincoln: From the Log Cabin to the White House - Campfire Heroes Line. Jones, K. L. & Manikandan, illus. 2013. (Campfire Graphic Novels Ser.). (ENG.). 108p. (YA). (gr. 5-12). pap. 12.99 *(978-93-80741-21-5(9)*, Campfire) Steerforth Pr.

Helwig, Laura. How Abraham Lincoln Fought the Civil War. 2017. (Presidents at War Ser.). 128p. (J). (gr. 8-8). lib. bdg. 37.27 ***(978-0-7660-8525-1(2))*** Enslow Pubs., Inc.

Herbert, Janis. Abraham Lincoln for Kids: His Life & Times with 21 Activities. 2007. (For Kids Ser.). (ENG., Illus.). 160p. (J). (gr. 4-7). pap. 16.95 *(978-1-55652-656-5(3))* Chicago Review Pr., Inc.

Herda, D. J. Slavery & Citizenship: The Dred Scott Case. 2016. (US Supreme Court Landmark Cases Ser.). 128p. (J). 37.27 *(978-0-7660-8426-1(4))* Enslow Pubs., Inc.

Holzer, Harold. Father Abraham: Lincoln & His Sons. 2011. (ENG., Illus.). 232p. (J). (gr. 5-18). 17.95 *(978-1-59078-303-0(4)*, Calkins Creek) Boyds Mills Pr.

—Lincoln: How Abraham Lincoln Ended Slavery in America - A Companion Book for Young Readers to the Steven Spielberg Film. 2012. (ENG.). 240p. 16.99 *(978-0-06-226509-8(1))* HarperCollins Pubs.

—Lincoln: How Abraham Lincoln Ended Slavery in America: A Companion Book for Young Readers to the Steven Spielberg Film. 2013. (ENG.). 240p. pap. 7.99 *(978-0-06-226511-1(3)*, Newmarket for It Bks.) HarperCollins Pubs.

Ingram Judson, Clara. Abraham Lincoln: Friend of the People. (Great Leaders & Events Ser.). (ENG.). (J). (gr. 4-8). 2017. 208p. lib. bdg. 35.99 ***(978-1-942875-22-2(3))*** 2016. (Illus.). 225p. pap. 12.99 *(978-0-7603-5225-0(9))* Quarto Publishing Group USA. (Voyageur Pr.).

Jeffery, Gary & Petty, Kate. Abraham Lincoln: The Life of America's Sixteenth President. Lacey, Mike, illus. 2005. (Graphic Biographies Ser.). (ENG.). 48p. (gr. 5-8). pap. 14.05 *(978-1-4042-5164-9(2))* Rosen Publishing Group, Inc., The.

Jeffrey, Gary. Abraham Lincoln: The Life of America's Sixteenth President. 2009. (Graphic Nonfiction Biographies Ser.). (ENG.). 48p. (YA). (gr. 4-5). 58.50 *(978-1-61513-011-5(X)*, Rosen Reference) Rosen Publishing Group, Inc., The.

Judson, Karen. Abraham Lincoln: This Nation Shall Have a New Birth of Freedom. rev. ed. 2008. (Americans—the Spirit of a Nation Ser.). (Illus.). 128p. (J). (gr. 3-7). lib. bdg. 33.27 *(978-0-7660-3170-8(5))* Enslow Pubs., Inc.

Kalman, Maira. Looking at Lincoln. Kalman, Maira, illus. 2012. (ENG., Illus.). 32p. (J). (gr. k-3). 17.99 *(978-0-399-24039-3(X)*, Nancy Paulsen Books) Penguin Young Readers Group.

Keating, Frank. Abraham. Wimmer, Mike, illus. 2017. (Mount Rushmore Presidential Ser.). (ENG.). 32p. (J). (gr. 1-4). 17.99 *(978-1-4424-9319-3(4)*, Simon & Schuster/Paula Wiseman Bks.) Simon & Schuster/Paula Wiseman Bks.

Kenison, Misti. Where's Your Hat, Abe Lincoln? 2017. (ENG.). 28p. (J). bds. 9.99 ***(978-1-4926-5250-2(4)***, Sourcebooks Jabberwocky) Sourcebooks, Inc.

Kenney, Karen Latchana & Andronik, Catherine M. Abraham Lincoln's Presidency. 2016. (Presidential Powerhouses Ser.). (ENG., Illus.). 104p. (J). (gr. 6-12). 53.32 *(978-1-4677-8547-1(4)*, Lerner Pubns.) Lerner Publishing Group.

Kirkman, Marissa. The Life & Times of Abraham Lincoln & the US Civil War. 2016. (Life & Times Ser.). (ENG., Illus.). 24p. (gr. 1-2). lib. bdg. 25.32 *(978-1-5157-2474-2(3)*, First Facts) Capstone Press of Coughlan Cos.

Knudsen, Shannon. When Were the First Slaves Set Free During the Civil War? And Other Questions about the Emancipation Proclamation. 2010. (Six Questions of American History Ser.). (ENG.). (gr. 4-6). pap. 56.72 *(978-0-7613-6948-6(1))*; (Illus.). 48p. lib. bdg. 30.60 *(978-1-58013-670-9(2))* Lerner Publishing Group.

—When Were the First Slaves Set Free During the Civil War? And Other Questions about the Emancipation Proclamation. 2010. (Six Questions of American History Ser.). (ENG.). 48p. (gr. 4-6). pap. 9.95 *(978-0-7613-6121-3(9))* Lerner Publishing Group.

Koestler-Grack, Rachel A. Abraham Lincoln. 2009. (Leaders of the Civil War Era Ser.). (Illus.). 144p. (gr. 6-12). 35.00 *(978-1-60413-298-4(1)*, Chelsea Hse.) Facts On File, Inc.

Krensky, Stephen. The Emancipaton Proclamation. 2011. (Documents of Democracy Ser.). 96p. (gr. 8). 34.21 *(978-0-7614-4915-7(9))* Marshall Cavendish Corp.

Krisher, Trudy. An Affectionate Farewell: the Story of Old Abe & Old Bob. Dodson, Bert, illus. 2015. (ENG.). 32p. (J). (gr. 1-2). 17.95 *(978-1-59373-155-7(8))* Bunker Hill Publishing, Inc.

Krull, Kathleen & Brewer, Paul. Lincoln Tells a Joke: How Laughter Saved the President (and the Country) Innerst, Stacy, illus. 2010. (ENG.). 40p. (J). (gr. 1-4). 17.99 *(978-0-15-206639-0(X))* Houghton Mifflin Harcourt Publishing Co.

Landau, Elaine. The Emancipation Proclamation: Would You Do What Lincoln Did? (What Would You Do? Ser.). (Illus.). 48p. (J). 2010. pap. 8.95 *(978-1-59845-194-8(4))* 2008. (gr. 3-7). lib. bdg. 25.27 *(978-0-7660-2899-9(2))* Enslow Pubs., Inc. (Enslow Elementary).

—Lincoln's Emancipation Proclamation: Would You Sign the Great Document? 2015. (What Would You Do? Ser.). 48p. (J). (gr. 3-4). 25.27 *(978-0-7660-6290-0(2))*; pap. 8.95 *(978-0-7660-6291-7(0)*, Enslow Elementary) Enslow Pubs., Inc.

Lee, T. S. The Lincoln Story: The Boy Who Embraced a Nation. 4th ed. 2010. (Great Heroes Ser.). 184p. (J). pap. 14.95 *(978-0-9819542-3-3(5))* DASANBOOKS.

Magoon, Kekla. Abraham Lincoln, 1 vol. 2007. (Essential Lives Set 1 Ser.). (ENG., Illus.). 112p. (J). (gr. 6-12). lib. bdg. 35.64 *(978-1-59928-839-0(7))* ABDO Publishing Co.

Maloof, Torrey. Abraham Lincoln: Addressing a Nation. 2017. (Primary Source Readers Ser.). 32p. (J). (gr. 4-5). pap. 8.99 *(978-1-4938-3805-9(9))* Teacher Created Materials, Inc.

Manolis, Kay & Leslie, Tonya. Abraham Lincoln: A Life of Honesty. 2007. (People of Character Ser.). (ENG., Illus.). 24p. (J). (gr. 2-5). lib. bdg. 25.95 *(978-1-60014-091-4(2))* Bellwether Media.

Mara, Wil. Abraham Lincoln. 2014. (Rookie Biographies(r) Ser.). (ENG.). 32p. (J). lib. bdg. 23.00 *(978-0-531-21058-1(8))* Scholastic Library Publishing.

Margaret, Amy. Presidents' Day. 2009. (Library of Holidays Ser.). 24p. (gr. 2-3). 42.50 *(978-1-60853-716-7(1)*, PowerKids Pr.) Rosen Publishing Group, Inc., The.

Mattern, Joanne. Mary Todd Lincoln, 1 vol. 2008. (First Ladies Set 1 Ser.). (ENG., Illus.). 32p. (YA). (gr. 1-4). 27.07 *(978-1-59928-797-3(8))* ABDO Publishing Co.

Meltzer, Brad. I Am Abraham Lincoln. Eliopoulos, Christopher, illus. 2014. (Ordinary People Change World Ser.). (ENG.). 40p. (J). (gr. k-3). 14.99 *(978-0-8037-4083-9(2)*, Dial Bks) Penguin Publishing Group.

Metzger, Steve & Kronheimer, Ann. Lincoln & Grace: Why Abraham Lincoln Grew a Beard. 2013. (ENG.). 40p. (J). (gr. 2-5). pap. 6.99 *(978-0-545-48432-9(4)*, Scholastic Paperbacks) Scholastic, Inc.

Moody, Dwight Lyman. President Lincoln Listened: A Story of Compassion. Bond, Bob, illus. 2006. (Story Time Ser.). (ENG.). 24p. (J). (gr. -1-4). 7.99 *(978-1-84550-115-0(2)*, 75397a47-48fa-498d-9c85-df9f190a384c) Christian Focus Pubns. GBR. Dist: Bookmasters Distribution.

Nagelhout, Ryan. Emancipation Proclamation. 2016. (Documents of American Democracy Ser.). (Illus.). 32p. (J). (gr. 5-5). pap. 10.00 *(978-1-4994-2081-4(1)*, PowerKids Pr.) Rosen Publishing Group, Inc., The.

Nardo, Don. The Presidency of Abraham Lincoln: The Triumph of Freedom & Unity, 1 vol. 2014. (Greatest U. S. Presidents Ser.). (ENG.). 64p. (gr. 5-7). lib. bdg. 33.99 *(978-0-7565-4926-8(4))* Compass Point Bks.

Nathan, Adele Gutman. Lincoln's Americ. 2011. 92p. 38.95 *(978-1-258-10382-8(6))* Literary Licensing, LLC.

Nelson, Maria. The Life of Abraham Lincoln. 2012. (Famous Lives Ser.). (ENG., Illus.). 24p. (J). (gr. k-3). lib. bdg. 22.60 *(978-1-4339-6341-4(8))*; (gr. 1-4). pap. 8.15 *(978-1-4339-6343-8(4))* Stevens, Gareth Publishing LLLP.

—The Life of Abraham Lincoln / la Vida de Abraham Lincoln. 2012. (Famous Lives / Vidas extraordinarias Ser.). (ENG & SPA., Illus.). 24p. (J). (gr. k-3). 22.60 *(978-1-4339-6651-4(4))* Stevens, Gareth Publishing LLLP.

Nicolay, Helen. The Boys' Life of Abraham Lincoln. 2007. 136p. per. *(978-1-4065-4046-8(3))* Dodo Pr.

—The Boys Life of Abraham Lincoln. 2005. 26.95 *(978-1-4218-0834-5(X))* 2004. 192p. pap. 11.95 *(978-1-59540-434-3(1))* 2004. 192p. per. 15.95 *(978-1-59540-991-1(2))* 1st World Publishing, Inc. (1st World Library - Literary Society).

—The Boys' Life of Abraham Lincoln. l.t. ed. 2007. (ENG.). 148p. pap. 18.99 *(978-1-4346-1638-8(X))* Creative Media Partners, LLC.

Olson, Kay Melchisedech & Melchisedech Olson, Kay. The Assassination of Abraham Lincoln, 1 vol. Lohse, Otha Zackariah Edward, illus. 2005. (Graphic History Ser.). (ENG.). 32p. (gr. 3-4). 30.65 *(978-0-7368-3831-3(7)*, Graphic Library) Capstone Press of Coughlan Cos.

Oney, Yannick. Abe Lincoln: President for the People. 2005. (World Discovery History Readers Ser.). (Illus.). 32p. (J). pap. *(978-0-439-66556-8(6))* Scholastic, Inc.

Osborne, Mary Pope. Abe Lincoln at Last! Murdocca, Sal, illus. 2013. (Magic Tree House Merlin Mission Ser.: 19). (ENG.). 144p. (J). (gr. 2-5). 5.99 *(978-0-375-86797-2(X),* Random Hse. Bks. for Young Readers) Random Hse. Children's Bks.

Osborne, Mary Pope & Boyce, Natalie Pope. Abraham Lincoln: A Nonfiction Companion to Magic Tree House No. 47 - Abe Lincoln at Last! Murdocca, Sal, illus. 2011. (Magic Tree House - Fact Tracker Ser.: No. 25). (ENG.). 128p. (J). (gr. 2-5). 6.99 *(978-0-375-87024-8(5),* Random Hse. Bks. for Young Readers) Random Hse. Children's Bks.

Pace, Betty. Abraham Lincoln. Walker, Bobbie H., illus. 2008. 32p. pap. 12.99 *(978-1-4343-7969-6(8))* AuthorHouse.

Parker, Christi E. Abraham Lincoln, 1 vol. 2005. (Primary Source Readers Ser.). (ENG.). 24p. (J). (gr. 4-4). pap. 8.99 *(978-0-7439-8916-9(3))* Shell Educational Publishing.

Pascal, Janet. Who Was Abraham Lincoln? Harrison, Nancy & O'brien, John, illus. 2008. (Who Was? Ser.). (ENG.). 112p. (J). (gr. 3-7). pap. 5.99 *(978-0-448-44886-2(6),* Grosset & Dunlap) Penguin Young Readers Group.

Patrick, Bethanne Kelly. Abraham Lincoln. 2004. (Childhoods of the Presidents Ser.). (Illus.). 48p. (J). (gr. 4-18). lib. bdg. 17.95 *(978-1-59084-275-1(8))* Mason Crest.

Petty, Kate. Abraham Lincoln: The Life of America's Sixteenth President. 2005. (Graphic Nonfiction Biographies Ser.). (ENG., Illus.). 48p. (YA). (gr. 4-7). lib. bdg. 31.95 *(978-1-4042-0237-5(4))* Rosen Publishing Group, Inc., The.

Pingry, Patricia A. Meet Abraham Lincoln. Britt, Stephanie McFetridge, illus. 2009. (ENG.). 32p. (J). pap. 7.99 *(978-0-8249-5613-4(3),* Ideal Pubns.) Worthy Publishing.

—The Story of Abraham Lincoln. Britt, Stephanie, illus. 2016. (J). *(978-0-8249-1972-6(6),* Ideal Pubns.) Worthy Publishing.

Porterfield, Jason. The Lincoln-Douglas Senatorial Debates of 1858: A Primary Source Investigation. 2004. (Great Historic Debates & Speeches Ser.). (ENG., Illus.). 64p. (YA). (gr. 5-8). lib. bdg. 31.95 *(978-1-4042-0153-8(X))* Rosen Publishing Group, Inc., The.

—The Lincoln-Douglas Senatorial Debates Of 1858: A Primary Source Investigation. 2009. (Great Historic Debates & Speeches Ser.). 64p. (gr. 5-8). 58.50 *(978-1-61513-126-6(4))* Rosen Publishing Group, Inc., The.

Prentzas, G. S. The Emancipation Proclamation. 2011. (Cornerstones of Freedom, Third Ser.). (Illus.). 64p. (J). (ENG.). pap. 8.95 *(978-0-531-26557-4(9));* lib. bdg. 30.00 *(978-0-531-25032-7(6))* Scholastic Library Publishing. (Children's Pr.).

Press, David P. Abraham Lincoln: The Great Emancipator. 2013. (ENG., Illus.). 64p. (J). *(978-0-7787-1061-5(0));* pap. *(978-0-7787-1064-6(5))* Crabtree Publishing Co.

Rabin, Staton. Mr. Lincoln's Boys. Ibatoulline, Bagram, illus. 2008. (ENG.). 36p. (J). (gr. k-3). 16.99 *(978-0-670-06169-3(7),* Viking Books for Young Readers) Penguin Young Readers Group.

Rappaport, Doreen. Abe's Honest Words. Nelson, Kadir, illus. 2009. (J). (gr. 2-4). 27.95 incl. audio *(978-0-8045-6984-2(3))* Spoken Arts, Inc.

—Abe's Honest Words: The Life of Abraham Lincoln. Nelson, Kadir, illus. 2016. (Big Words Ser.). (ENG.). 48p. (J). (gr. 1-3). pap. 8.99 *(978-1-4847-4958-6(8))* Hyperion Bks. for Children.

—Abe's Honest Words: The Life of Abraham Lincoln. Kelley, Gary & Nelson, Kadir, illus. 2008. (Big Words Ser.). (ENG.). 48p. (J). (gr. 3-7). 16.99 *(978-1-4231-0408-7(0))* Hyperion Pr.

Raum, Elizabeth. Abraham Lincoln, 1 vol. 2012. (American Biographies Ser.). (ENG.). 48p. (gr. 4-6). pap. 9.95 *(978-1-4329-6464-1(X),* NA-h) Heinemann-Raintree.

—Abraham Lincoln, 1 vol. Oxford Bible Staff, illus. 2012. (American Biographies Ser.). (ENG.). 48p. (gr. 4-6). lib. bdg. 32.65 *(978-1-4329-6453-5(4),* NA-h) Heinemann-Raintree.

Rivera, Sheila. Abraham Lincoln: A Life of Respect. 2006. (Pull Ahead Bks.). (Illus.). 32p. (J). (gr. 3-7). lib. bdg. 22.60 *(978-0-8225-3473-0(8),* Lerner Pubns.) Lerner Publishing Group.

—Abraham Lincoln: Una Vida de Respeto. 2006. (Libros para Avanzar Ser.). (ENG & SPA., Illus.). 32p. (J). (gr. 3-7). lib. bdg. 22.60 *(978-0-8225-6236-8(7))* Lerner Publishing Group.

—Abraham Lincoln: Una vida de respeto (A Life of Respect) 2006. (Libros para Avanzar-Biografías (Pull Ahead Books-Biographies Ser.). (Illus.). 32p. (J). (gr. 3-7). per. 6.95 *(978-0-8225-6559-8(5),* Ediciones Lerner) Lerner Publishing Group.

RJF Publishing Staff & Hankins, Chelsey. The Lincoln Memorial. 2009. (Symbols of American Freedom Ser.). 48p. (gr. 4-6). 30.00 *(978-1-60413-518-3(2),* Chelsea Clubhouse) Facts On File, Inc.

Roberts, Jeremy. Abraham Lincoln. 2004. (Presidential Leaders Ser.). (Illus.). 112p. (J). (gr. 6-12). lib. bdg. 29.27 *(978-0-8225-0817-5(6))* Lerner Publishing Group.

Roxburgh, Ellis. Abraham Lincoln vs. Jefferson Davis: Presidents of a Divided Nation. 2016. (History's Greatest Rivals Ser.). (ENG., Illus.). 48p. (J). (gr. 6-8). pap. 14.05 *(978-1-4824-4219-9(1))* Stevens, Gareth Publishing LLLP.

Ruffin, Frances & Phillips, Ellen Blue. Abraham Lincoln: From Pioneer to President. 2007. (Sterling Biographies(r) Ser.). (ENG., Illus.). 128p. (J). pap. 5.95 *(978-1-4027-3396-3(8))* Sterling Publishing Co., Inc.

Ruffin, Frances E. The Lincoln Memorial. 2006. (Places in American History Ser.). (Illus.). 24p. (gr. 1-4). pap. 8.15 *(978-0-8368-6418-2(2));* lib. bdg. 22.00 *(978-0-8368-6411-3(5))* Stevens, Gareth Publishing LLLP. (Weekly Reader Leveled Readers).

Rumsch, BreAnn. Abraham Lincoln, 1 vol. (ENG., Illus.). 40p. 2016. (J). *(978-1-68078-106-9(5))* 2009. (YA). (gr. 3-6). 27.07 *(978-1-60453-464-1(8))* ABDO Publishing Co.

Rustad, Martha. What Is Inside the Lincoln Memorial? Poling, Kyle, illus. 2014. (Cloverleaf Books — Our American Symbols Ser.). 24p. (gr. k-2). (J). lib. bdg. 23.93 *(978-1-4677-2135-6(2));* pap. 6.95 *(978-1-4677-4468-3(9))* Lerner Publishing Group. (Millbrook Pr.).

Saddleback Educational Publishing Staff, ed. Abraham Lincoln, 1 vol. unabr. ed. 2008. (Graphic Biographies Ser.). (ENG., Illus.). 25p. (YA). (gr. 9-12). per. 7.95 *(978-1-59905-211-3(3))* Saddleback Educational Publishing, Inc.

Sandburg, Carl. Abe Lincoln Grows Up. Daugherty, James, illus. 2009. (ENG.). 224p. (YA). (gr. 7-18). reprint ed. pap. 7.99 *(978-0-15-602615-4(5))* Houghton Mifflin Harcourt Publishing Co.

Schmidt, Roderic. How to Draw the Life & Times of Abraham Lincoln. (Kid's Guide to Drawing the Presidents of the United States of America Ser.). 2009. 32p. (gr. 4-4). 50.50 *(978-1-61511-130-5(1),* PowerKids Pr.) 2006. (YA). (gr. 2-5). 26.50 *(978-1-4042-2993-8(0))* Rosen Publishing Group, Inc., The.

Schott, Jane A. Abraham Lincoln. 2003. (History Maker Biographies Ser.). (ENG., Illus.). 48p. (gr. 3-6). pap. 8.95 *(978-0-8225-0381-1(6),* Lerner Pubns.) Lerner Publishing Group.

Schroeder, Alan. Abe Lincoln: His Wit & Wisdom from A to Z. O'brien, John, illus. 2015. (ENG.). 32p. (J). (gr. 1-5). 17.95 *(978-0-8234-2420-7(0))* Holiday Hse., Inc.

—Abe Lincoln: His Wit & Wisdom from A-Z. O'brien, John, illus. 2016. (ENG.). 32p. (J). 7.99 *(978-0-8234-3575-3(X))* Holiday Hse., Inc.

Sheinkin, Steve. Lincoln's Grave Robbers. 2013. (ENG.). 224p. (J). (gr. 5-9). 16.99 *(978-0-545-40572-0(6),* Scholastic Pr.) Scholastic, Inc.

Smith, Adam I. P. Abraham Lincoln. 2016. (History Makers Ser.). 144p. (J). (gr. 9-9). 45.64 *(978-1-5026-1912-9(1))* Cavendish Square Publishing.

St. George, Judith. Stand Tall, Abe Lincoln. Faulkner, Matt, illus. 2015. (ENG.). 48p. (J). (gr. 2-4). 8.99 *(978-0-14-751447-9(9),* Puffin Books) Penguin Young Readers Group.

Stewart, Whitney. Mr. Lincoln's Gift: A Civil War Story. Dunham Akiyama, Laine, illus. 2008. 32p. (J). 19.95 *(978-0-9754917-4-4(1))* Friends of Hildene, Inc.

Stock, Catherine. Vinnie & Abraham. unabr. ed. 2008. (J). (gr. 2-5). 27.95 incl. audio *(978-0-8045-6967-5(3));* 29.95 incl. audio compact disk *(978-0-8045-4190-9(6))* Spoken Arts, Inc.

Stone, Tanya Lee & Hamblyn, Richard. Abraham Lincoln: A Photographic Story of a Life. Dorling Kindersley Publishing Staff, ed. 2005. (DK Biography Ser.). (ENG., Illus.). 128p. (J). (gr. 5-12). pap. 6.99 *(978-0-7566-0834-7(1),* DK Children) Dorling Kindersley Publishing, Inc.

Tarbell, Ida M. Boy Scouts' Life of Lincoln. 2005. pap. 27.95 *(978-1-885529-53-4(8))* Stevens Publishing.

Thomson, Sarah L. What Lincoln Said. Ransome, James E., illus. 2009. 32p. (J). (gr. k-3). lib. bdg. 18.89 *(978-0-06-084820-0(0))* HarperCollins Pubs.

Tiwari, Saral. Abraham Lincoln: The Civil War President. Turner, Ginger, illus. 2004. 48p. (J). pap. 17.95 *(978-0-9742502-1-2(X))* Gossamer Bks., LLC.

Tiwari, Saral, illus. Abraham Lincoln: The Civil War President 2004. 48p. (J). 15.95 *(978-0-9742502-0-5(1))* Gossamer Bks., LLC.

Trumbauer, Lisa. Abraham Lincoln & the Civil War. 2016. (Life in the Time Of Ser.). (ENG.). 32p. pap. 8.29 *(978-1-4846-3822-4(0),* Heinemann First Library) Heinemann-Raintree.

Turner, Ann Warren. Abe Lincoln Remembers. Minor, Wendell, illus. 2003. (ENG.). 32p. (J). (gr. 1-4). pap. 6.99 *(978-0-06-051107-4(9))* HarperCollins Pubs.

Uglow, Loyd. Abraham Lincoln: Will You Ever Give Up?, 1bk. James, Kennon, illus. 2003. (Another Great Achiever Ser.). (J). lib. bdg. 23.95 incl. audio *(978-1-57537-790-2(X));* (ENG.). 48p. (YA). lib. bdg. 23.95 incl. audio compact disk *(978-1-57537-740-7(3))* Advance Publishing, Inc.

Vescia, Monique. The Emancipation Proclamation. 2016. (Let's Find Out! Primary Sources Ser.). 00032p. (J). (gr. 2-3). lib. bdg. 24.45 *(978-1-5081-0405-6(0))* Rosen Publishing Group, Inc., The.

Vierow, Wendy. The 1864 Presidential Election: A War-Weary Nation Reelects President Abraham Lincoln. (Headlines from History Ser.). 24p. 2009. (gr. 3-3). 42.50 *(978-1-61513-239-3(2),* PowerKids Pr.) 2004. (Illus.). (J). lib. bdg. 22.60 *(978-0-8239-6224-2(5))* Rosen Publishing Group, Inc., The.

Wade, Mary Dodson. Presidents' Day. 2016. (Story of Our Holidays Ser.). (Illus.). 32p. (J). pap. 10.52 *(978-0-7660-8345-5(4))* Enslow Pubs., Inc.

Waldman, Neil. Voyages: Reminiscences of Young Abe Lincoln. 2009. (ENG., Illus.). 32p. (J). (gr. 5-9). 16.95 *(978-1-59078-471-6(5),* Calkins Creek) Boyds Mills Pr.

Wearing, Judy. Abraham Lincoln. 2010. (My Life Ser.). 24p. (J). (gr. 2-4). lib. bdg. 25.70 *(978-1-61690-056-4(3))* Weigl Pubs., Inc.

—Abraham Lincoln: My Life. 2010. pap. 9.95 *(978-1-61690-057-1(1))* Weigl Pubs., Inc.

Winters, Kay. Abe Lincoln: The Boy Who Loved Books. Carpenter, Nancy, illus. 2004. 38p. (J). (gr. -1-3). reprint ed. 17.00 *(978-0-7567-7969-6(3))* DIANE Publishing Co.

—Abe Lincoln: The Boy Who Loved Books. Carpenter, Nancy, illus. 2006. (ENG.). 40p. (J). (gr. k-3). reprint ed. 7.99 *(978-1-4169-1268-2(1),* Aladdin) Simon & Schuster Children's Publishing.

Winters, Kay & Carpenter, Nancy. Abe Lincoln: The Boy Who Loved Books. 2003. (ENG., Illus.). 40p. (J). (gr. k-3). 17.99 *(978-0-689-82554-5(4),* Simon & Schuster Bks. For Young Readers) Simon & Schuster Bks. For Young Readers.

Woog, Adam. The Emancipation Proclamation: Ending Slavery in America. 2009. (Milestones in American History Ser.). (Illus.). 128p. (gr. 6-12). 35.00 *(978-1-60413-307-3(4),* Chelsea Hse.) Facts On File, Inc.

LINCOLN, ABRAHAM, 1809-1865—ANECDOTES

Adler, David A. Honest Abe Lincoln: Easy-to-Read Stories about Abraham Lincoln. Wallner, John C., illus. 2009. (Holiday House Reader Level 2 Ser.). (ENG.). 32p. (J). (gr. k-3). 15.95 *(978-0-8234-2057-5(4))* Holiday Hse., Inc.

Hansen, Grace. Abraham Lincoln, 1 vol. 2014. (United States President Biographies Ser.). (ENG.). 24p. (J). (gr. 4-8). lib. bdg. 28.50 *(978-1-62970-085-4(1))* ABDO Publishing Co.

LINCOLN, ABRAHAM, 1809-1865—ASSASSINATION

Brindell, Dennis Fradin. The Assassination of Abraham Lincoln. 2006. (Turning Points in U. S. History Ser.). (Illus.). 48p. (gr. 3-7). lib. bdg. 31.36 *(978-0-7614-2123-8(8),* Benchmark Bks.) Marshall Cavendish Corp.

Brown, Don. He Has Shot the President! April 14, 1865: the Day John Wilkes Booth Killed President Lincoln. Brown, Don, illus. 2014. (Actual Times Ser.: 5). (ENG., Illus.). 64p. (J). (gr. 1-5). 17.99 *(978-1-59643-224-6(1),* 9781596432246) Roaring Brook Pr.

Denenberg, Barry. Lincoln Shot: A President's Life Remembered. Bing, Christopher, illus. 2008. (ENG.). 40p. (J). (gr. 5-9). 24.95 *(978-0-312-37013-8(X),* 9780312370138) Feiwel & Friends.

—Lincoln Shot: A President's Life Remembered. Bing, Christopher, illus. 2011. (ENG.). 96p. (J). (gr. 5-9). pap. 14.99 *(978-0-312-60442-4(4),* 9780312604424) Square Fish.

Gunderson, Jessica. The Wound Is Mortal: The Story of the Assassination of Abraham Lincoln. 2015. (Tangled History Ser.). (ENG., Illus.). 112p. (gr. 3-4). pap. 6.95 *(978-1-4914-7080-0(1))* Capstone Press of Coughlan Cos.

Holzer, Harold. The President Is Shot! The Assassination of Abraham Lincoln. 2004. (ENG., Illus.). 184p. (J). (gr. 3-12). 17.95 *(978-1-56397-985-9(3))* Boyds Mills Pr.

Jones, Rebecca C. The Mystery of Mary Surratt: The Plot to Kill President Lincoln, 1 vol. 2009. (ENG., Illus.). 96p. (J). pap. 9.95 *(978-0-87033-560-0(X),* 9780870335600, Cornell Maritime Pr./Tidewater Pubs.) Schiffer Publishing, Ltd.

Langston-George, Rebecca. The Booth Brothers: Drama, Fame, & the Death of President Lincoln. 2017. (Encounter: Narrative Nonfiction Stories Ser.). (ENG.). 112p. (gr. 3-5). lib. bdg. 30.65 ***(978-1-5157-7338-2(8))*** Encounter Bks.

Marinelli, Deborah A. The Assassination of Abraham Lincoln. 2003. (Library of Political Assassinations Ser.). (Illus.). 64p. (YA). (gr. 7-12). lib. bdg. 31.95 *(978-0-8239-3539-0(6))* Rosen Publishing Group, Inc., The.

Marinelli, Debra A. The Assassination of Abraham Lincoln. 2009. (Library of Political Assassinations Ser.). 64p. (gr. 5-5). 58.50 *(978-1-60853-824-9(9))* Rosen Publishing Group, Inc., The.

Olson, Kay Melchisedech. The Assassination of Abraham Lincoln, 1 vol. Lohse, Otha Zackariah Edward, illus. 2005. (Graphic History Ser.). (ENG.). 32p. (gr. 3-4). per. 8.10 *(978-0-7368-5241-8(7),* Graphic Library) Capstone Press of Coughlan Cos.

O'Reilly, Bill & Zimmerman, Dwight Jon. Lincoln's Last Days. 2014. (ENG., Illus.). 352p. (J). (gr. 5). pap. 12.99 *(978-1-250-04429-7(4),* 9781250044297) Square Fish.

—Lincoln's Last Days. 2014. (J). lib. bdg. 24.50 *(978-0-606-35526-1(X))* Turtleback Bks.

—Lincoln's Last Days: The Shocking Assassination That Changed America Forever. 2012. (ENG., Illus.). 336p. (J). (gr. 5-10). 19.99 *(978-0-8050-9675-0(2),* 9780805096750, Holt, Henry & Co. Bks. For Young Readers) Holt, Henry & Co.

Swanson, James L. Chasing Lincoln's Killer: The Search for John Wilkes Booth. 2009. (ENG., Illus.). 208p. (J). (gr. 7-18). 16.99 *(978-0-439-90354-7(6),* Scholastic Pr.) Scholastic, Inc.

Van Steenwyk, Elizabeth. How Kate Warne Saved President Lincoln. Belloni, Valentina, illus. 2016. (ENG.). 32p. (J). (gr. -1-3). 16.99 *(978-0-8075-4117-3(6))* Whitman, Albert & Co.

Yomtov, Nelson. Tracking an Assassin! Nickolas Flux & the Assassination of Abraham Lincoln, 1 vol. Pinelli, Amerigo, illus. 2014. (Nickolas Flux History Chronicles Ser.). (ENG.). 32p. (gr. 3-4). lib. bdg. 30.65 *(978-1-4914-0252-8(0),* Graphic Library) Capstone Press of Coughlan Cos.

LINCOLN, ABRAHAM, 1809-1865—ASSASSINATION—FICTION

Blackwood, Gary L. Second Sight. 2007. (Illus.). 279p. (J). (gr. 5-9). 14.65 *(978-0-7569-8132-7(8))* Perfection Learning Corp.

Rinaldi, Ann. An Acquaintance with Darkness. 2005. (Great Episodes Ser.). (ENG.). 384p. (YA). (gr. 7-8). pap. 9.99 *(978-0-15-205387-1(5))* Houghton Mifflin Harcourt Publishing Co.

—An Acquaintance with Darkness. 2005. (Great Episodes Ser.). 374p. (gr. 7-12). 18.00 *(978-0-7569-5040-8(6))* Perfection Learning Corp.

LINCOLN, ABRAHAM, 1809-1865—FICTION

Biros, Florence W. Love & Loyalty: The Traits That Made Lincoln Great. 2005. (Illus.). 320p. pap. 14.95 *(978-0-936369-92-1(2))* Son-Rise Pubns. & Distribution Co.

Blackwood, Gary L. & Blackwood, Gary. Second Sight. 2007. (ENG.). 288p. (J). (gr. 5-18). 8.99 *(978-0-14-240747-9(X),* Speak) Penguin Young Readers Group.

Brandeis, Gayle. My Life with the Lincolns. 2010. (ENG.). 256p. (J). (gr. 5-9). 34.99 *(978-0-8050-9013-0(4),* 9780805090130, Holt, Henry & Co. Bks. For Young Readers) Holt, Henry & Co.

Brewer, Caroline. Kara & Friends Meet Abraham Lincoln. 2004. (Illus.). 40p. (J). 17.95 *(978-0-9717790-4-4(X))* Unchained Spirit Enterprises.

Cavanah, Frances. Abe Lincoln Gets His Chance. 2007. 72p. per. *(978-1-4068-4447-4(0))* Echo Library.

Hannigan, Kate. The Detective's Assistant. 2015. (ENG.). 368p. (J). (gr. 3-7). 17.00 *(978-0-316-40351-1(2))* Little Brown & Co.

Hedstrom-Page, Deborah. From Log Cabin to White House with Abraham Lincoln. Martinez, Sergio, illus. 2007. (My American Journey Ser.). 82p. (J). (gr. 3-9). 9.99 *(978-0-8054-3269-5(8))* B&H Publishing Group.

Hicks, Clifford B. Alvin Fernald's Incredible Buried Treasure. Bradfield, Roger, illus. 2009. (J). 17.95 *(978-1-930900-43-1(0))* Purple Hse. Pr.

Hopkinson, Deborah. Abe Lincoln Crosses a Creek: A Tall, Thin Tale (Introducing His Forgotten Frontier Friend) Hendrix, John, illus. (ENG.). 40p. (J). (gr. -1-3). 2016. 7.99 *(978-1-5247-0158-1(0),* Dragonfly Bks.) 2008. 17.99 *(978-0-375-83768-5(X),* Schwartz & Wade Bks.) Random Hse. Children's Bks.

Horender, Philip M. Yankee Mouse: Gettysburg Address Observer, 1 vol. Wolek, Guy, illus. 2013. (Maximilian P. Mouse, Time Traveler Ser.). (ENG.). 112p. (J). (gr. 3-6). lib. bdg. 27.07 *(978-1-61641-958-5(X),* Calico Chapter Bks) Magic Wagon.

Jackson, Ellen. Abe Lincoln Loved Animals. Ettlinger, Doris, illus. 2013. (AV2 Fiction Readalong Ser.: Vol. 56). (ENG.). 32p. (J). 34.28 *(978-1-62127-864-1(6),* AV2 by Weigl) Weigl Pubs., Inc.

Jakubowski, Michele. The Professor's Discovery. Pinelli, Amerigo, illus. 2016. (Sleuths of Somerville Ser.). (ENG.). 144p. (gr. 4-6). lib. bdg. 25.99 *(978-1-4965-3177-3(9))* Stone Arch Bks.

—The Professor's Discovery. Pinelli, Amerigo, illus. 2017. (Sleuths of Somerville Ser.). (ENG.). 144p. (gr. 4-6). pap. 6.95 *(978-1-4965-3181-0(7))* Stone Arch Bks.

Lyons, Kelly Starling. Hope's Gift. Tate, Don, illus. 2012. (ENG.). 32p. (J). (gr. 1-3). 16.99 *(978-0-399-16001-1(9),* G.P. Putnam's Sons Books for Young Readers) Penguin Young Readers Group.

Malaspina, Ann. Finding Lincoln. Bootman, Colin, illus. 2009. (ENG.). 32p. (J). (gr. 2-3). 16.99 *(978-0-8075-2435-0(2))* Whitman, Albert & Co.

Mazer, Harry. My Brother Abe: Sally Lincoln's Story. 2009. (ENG.). 208p. (J). (gr. 3-7). pap. 5.99 *(978-1-4169-3894-1(X));* 15.99 *(978-1-4169-3884-2(2))* Simon & Schuster Bks. For Young Readers. (Simon & Schuster Bks. For Young Readers).

Myers, Anna. Assassin. 2005. (J). *(978-978-080-278-3(9))* Walker & Co.

Osborne, Mary Pope. Abe Lincoln at Last! 2013. (Magic Tree House Merlin Missions Ser.: 19). lib. bdg. 16.00 *(978-0-606-35563-6(4))* Turtleback Bks.

Perry, Fred. Time Lincoln, Vol. 1. 2011. (ENG.). 122p. (YA). pap., pap. 19.95 *(978-0-9831823-7-5(X),* 9780983182375) Antarctic Pr., Inc.

Polacco, Patricia. Just in Time Abraham Lincoln. 2012. 29.95 *(978-0-8045-4240-1(6))* Spoken Arts, Inc.

Potter, David. The Left Behinds: Abe Lincoln & the Selfie That Saved the Union. 2016. (Left Behinds Ser.). (ENG.). 304p. (J). (gr. 3-7). 16.99 *(978-0-385-39060-6(2),* Crown Books For Young Readers) Random Hse. Children's Bks.

Rack, Charlene. The Adventures of Delaware Bear & Young Abraham Lincoln. 2011. 24p. (gr. -1). pap. 12.79 *(978-1-4567-5619-2(2))* AuthorHouse.

Schmidt, Bryan Thomas. Abraham Lincoln Dinosaur Hunter. 2013. 80p. pap. 5.99 *(978-1-61941-054-1(0))* Delabarre Publishing.

Strasser, Todd. Abe Lincoln for Class President. 2010. 144p. pap. 10.95 *(978-1-4502-1244-1(1))* iUniverse, Inc.

Strickland, James R. Lincoln's Lost Papers. 2008. 131p. (J). pap. 11.95 *(978-0-7414-4601-5(4))* Infinity Publishing.

Sullivan, Michael John & Petrone, Susan. The Sockkids Meet Lincoln. 2013. 42p. pap. 10.99 *(978-0-9727077-7-0(8))* Scribe Publishing.

Sun Edit and Book Design, ed. Abraham Lincoln & the Forest of Little Pigeon Creek. 2007. (Illus.). 56p. (J). 19.95 *(978-0-9798739-0-4(8))* AmeriTales Entertainment, LLC.

Tarbell, Ida M. Father Abraham. Campbell, Blendon, illus. 2004. reprint ed. pap. 15.95 *(978-1-4179-0070-1(9))* Kessinger Publishing, LLC.

Wells, Rosemary. Lincoln & His Boys. Lynch, P. J., illus. (ENG.). 96p. (J). (gr. 3-7). 2015. pap. 8.99 *(978-0-7636-8069-5(9))* 2008. 16.99 *(978-0-7636-3723-1(8))* Candlewick Pr.

LINCOLN, ABRAHAM, 1809-1865—GETTYSBURG ADDRESS

Armentrout, David & Armentrout, Patricia. The Gettysburg Address. 2004. (ENG.). 48p. (gr. 4-6). pap. 10.95 *(978-1-59515-333-3(0))* Rourke Educational Media.

Armentrout, David, et al. The Gettysburg Address. 2005. (Documents that Shaped the Nation Ser.). (Illus.). 48p. (gr. 4-6). 20.95 *(978-1-59515-232-9(6))* Rourke Educational Media.

Armstrong, Jennifer. A Three-Minute Speech: Lincoln's Remarks at Gettysburg. Lorenz, Albert, illus. 2003. (Milestone Ser.). (ENG.). 96p. (J). pap. 4.99 *(978-0-689-85622-8(9),* Simon & Schuster/Paula Wiseman Bks.) Simon & Schuster/Paula Wiseman Bks.

—The True Story Behind Lincoln's Gettysburg Address. Lorenz, Albert, illus. 2013. (ENG.). 96p. (J). (gr. 2-5). 15.99 *(978-1-4424-9388-9(7));* pap. 5.99 *(978-1-4424-9387-2(9))* Simon & Schuster/Paula Wiseman Bks. (Simon & Schuster/Paula Wiseman Bks.).

Butzer, C. M. The Gettysburg. Butzer, C. M., illus. (ENG., Illus.). 80p. 2009. (YA). (gr. 4-9). pap. 9.99 *(978-0-06-156175-7(4))* 2008. (J). (gr. 5-9). 16.99 *(978-0-06-156176-4(2))* HarperCollins Pubs.

Ford, Carin T. The Battle of Gettysburg & Lincoln's Gettysburg Address. 2004. (Civil War Library). (Illus.). 48p. (J). lib. bdg. 25.27 *(978-0-7660-2253-9(6))* Enslow Pubs., Inc.

—Lincoln's Gettysburg Address & the Battle of Gettysburg Through Primary Sources. 2013. (Civil War Through Primary Sources Ser.). 48p. (J). (gr. 4-18). lib. bdg. 25.27 *(978-0-7660-4126-4(3))* Enslow Pubs., Inc.

Gregory, Josh. The Gettysburg Address. 2013. (ENG.). 64p. (J). 30.00 *(978-0-531-28204-5(X));* pap. 8.95 *(978-0-531-27669-3(4))* Scholastic Library Publishing.

Kenison, Misti. Where's Your Hat, Abe Lincoln? 2017. (ENG.). 28p. (J). bds. 9.99 ***(978-1-4926-5250-2(4),*** Sourcebooks Jabberwocky) Sourcebooks, Inc.

Leavitt, Amie Jane, et al. Kids' Translations. 2017. (Kids' Translations Ser.). (ENG.). 32p. (gr. 3-4). pap. 40.50 ***(978-1-5157-9765-4(1),*** Fact Finders) Capstone Press of Coughlan Cos.

Miller, Mirella S. 12 Questions about the Gettysburg Address. 2017. (Examining Primary Sources Ser.). (ENG., Illus.). 32p. (J). (gr. 3-6). 21.95 *(978-1-63235-284-2(2))* Pr. Room Editions LLC.

Olson, Kay Melchisedech. The Gettysburg Address in Translation: What It Really Means. (Kids' Translations Ser.). (ENG.). 32p. (gr. 3-4). 2017. lib. bdg. 27.32 ***(978-1-5157-9136-2(X))*** 2016. pap. 8.10 *(978-1-5157-5168-7(6))* Capstone Press of Coughlan Cos. (Fact Finders).

Olson, Steve. Lincoln's Gettysburg Address: A Primary Source Investigation. 2009. 64p. (YA). (gr. 5-8). pap. 12.95 *(978-1-4358-3275-6(2))* Rosen Publishing Group, Inc., The.

Olson, Steven P. Lincoln's Gettysburg Address: A Primary Source Investigation. (Great Historic Debates & Speeches Ser.). 64p. 2009. (gr. 5-8). 58.50 *(978-1-61513-115-0(9))* 2004. (Illus.). (J). lib. bdg. 31.95 *(978-1-4042-0151-4(3))* Rosen Publishing Group, Inc., The.

Pingry, Patricia A. The Story of Gettysburg. Britt, Stephanie, illus. 2003. (ENG.). 26p. (J). (gr. -1-k). bds. 7.69 *(978-0-8249-6503-7(5),* Ideal Pubns.) Worthy Publishing.

Rivera, Sheila. Gettysburg Address, 1 vol. 2004. (American Moments Ser.). (ENG., Illus.). 48p. (gr. 4-8). 27.07 *(978-1-59197-285-3(X),* Abdo & Daughters) ABDO Publishing Co.

Tanaka, Shelley. Gettysburg: The Legendary Battle & the Address That Inspired a Nation. Craig, David, illus. 2003. (Day That Changed America Ser.). (ENG.). 48p. 16.99 *(978-0-7868-1922-5(7))* Hyperion Pr.

Warrick, Karen Clemens. Gettysburg National Military Park: A MyReportLinks.com Book. 2005. (Virtual Field Trips Ser.). (Illus.). 48p. (J). (gr. 4-10). lib. bdg. 26.60 (978-0-7660-5223-9(0), MyReportLinks.com Bks.) Enslow Pubs., Inc.

LINCOLN, ABRAHAM, 1809-1865—MONUMENTS

Carr, Aaron. Lincoln Memorial. 2013. (J). (978-1-62127-202-1(8)); pap. (978-1-62127-206-9(0)) Weigl Pubs., Inc.

Firestone, Mary. The Lincoln Memorial, 1 vol. Skeens, Matthew, illus. 2007. (American Symbols Ser.). (ENG.). 24p. (gr. 1-2). lib. bdg. 26.65 (978-1-4048-3718-8(3)) Picture Window Bks.

Kenney, Karen Latchana. The Lincoln Memorial, 1 vol. Hunt, Judith A., illus. 2011. (Our Nation's Pride Set 2 Ser.). (ENG.). 32p. (J). (gr. 1-4). 28.50 (978-1-61641-151-0(1)) Magic Wagon.

Marcovitz, Hal. Lincoln Memorial: Shrine to an American Hero. Moreno, Barry, ed. 2014. (Patriotic Symbols of America Ser.: 20). (Illus.). 48p. (J). (gr. 4-18). 20.95 (978-1-4222-3127-2(5)) Mason Crest.

Nelson, Kristin L. The Lincoln Memorial. (Lightning Bolt Bks.). (gr. k-2). 2010. (Illus.). 32p. (J). lib. bdg. 25.26 (978-0-7613-6018-6(2), Lerner Pubns.) 2010. pap. 45.32 (978-0-7613-6992-9(9)) 2010. (ENG.). 32p. pap. 7.95 (978-0-7613-6051-3(4)) 2003. (ENG., Illus.). 32p. pap. 7.95 (978-0-8225-3761-8(3)) Lerner Publishing Group.

RJF Publishing Staff & Hankins, Chelsey. The Lincoln Memorial. 2009. (Symbols of American Freedom Ser.). 48p. (gr. 4-6). 30.00 (978-1-60413-518-3(2), Chelsea Clubhouse) Facts On File, Inc.

LINCOLN, MARY TODD, 1818-1882

Hull, Mary. Mary Todd Lincoln: Civil War's First Lady. 2015. (Legendary American Biographies Ser.). 96p. (J). (gr. 6-12). pap. 10.95 (978-0-7660-6481-2(6)) Enslow Pubs., Inc.

Hull, Mary E. Mary Todd Lincoln: Civil War's First Lady. 2015. (Legendary American Biographies Ser.). 96p. (J). (gr. 6-12). 27.94 (978-0-7660-6480-5(8)) Enslow Pubs., Inc.

Jones, Lynda. Mrs. Lincoln's Dressmaker: The Unlikely Friendship of Elizabeth Keckley & Mary Todd Lincoln. 2009. (ENG., Illus.). 80p. (J). (gr. 5). lib. bdg. 27.90 (978-1-4263-0378-4(5)); 18.95 (978-1-4263-0377-7(7)) National Geographic Society. (National Geographic Children's Bks.).

Krull, Kathleen. Mary Todd Lincoln: I'm Usually the Smartest Person in the Room. Baddeley, Elizabeth, illus. 2015. (Women Who Broke the Rules Ser.). (ENG.). 48p. (J). (gr. 1-4). pap. 6.99 (978-0-8027-3825-7(7), 9780802738257, Bloomsbury USA Childrens) Bloomsbury Publishing USA.

Larkin, Tanya. What Was Cooking in Mary Todd Lincoln's White House? 2009. (Cooking Throughout American History Ser.). 24p. (gr. 3-3). 42.50 (978-1-61511-954-7(X), PowerKids Pr.) Rosen Publishing Group, Inc., The.

Mattern, Joanne. Mary Todd Lincoln, 1 vol. 2008. (First Ladies Set 1 Ser.). (ENG., Illus.). 32p. (YA). (gr. 1-4). 27.07 (978-1-59928-797-3(8)) ABDO Publishing Co.

LINCOLN, MARY TODD, 1818-1882—FICTION

Rinaldi, Ann. An Unlikely Friendship: A Novel of Mary Todd Lincoln & Elizabeth Keckley. 2008. (ENG., Illus.). 256p. (J). (gr. 5-7). pap. 7.99 (978-0-15-206398-6(6)) Houghton Mifflin Harcourt Publishing Co.

LINCOLN MEMORIAL (WASHINGTON, D.C.)

Carr, Aaron. Lincoln Memorial. 2013. (J). (978-1-62127-202-1(8)); pap. (978-1-62127-206-9(0)) Weigl Pubs., Inc.

Erin, Audrey. Visit the Lincoln Memorial. 2012. (Landmarks of Liberty Ser.). (ENG.). 24p. (J). (gr. 2-5). pap. 8.15 (978-1-4339-6398-8(1), Gareth Stevens Learning Library); lib. bdg. 22.60 (978-1-4339-6396-4(5)) Stevens, Gareth Publishing LLLP.

Firestone, Mary. The Lincoln Memorial, 1 vol. Skeens, Matthew, illus. 2007. (American Symbols Ser.). (ENG.). 24p. (gr. 1-2). lib. bdg. 26.65 (978-1-4048-3718-8(3)) Picture Window Bks.

Hopkinson, Deborah. Sweet Land of Liberty, 1 vol. Jenkins, Leonard, illus. 2007. (ENG.). 32p. (J). (gr. 1-5). 16.95 (978-1-56145-395-5(1)) Peachtree Pubs.

Marcovitz, Hal. Lincoln Memorial: Shrine to an American Hero. Moreno, Barry, ed. 2014. (Patriotic Symbols of America Ser.: 20). (Illus.). 48p. (J). (gr. 4-18). 20.95 (978-1-4222-3127-2(5)) Mason Crest.

Murray, Julie. Lincoln Memorial, 1 vol. 2003. (Buddy Book Ser.). (ENG., Illus.). 24p. (gr. k-4). 25.65 (978-1-57765-670-8(9), Buddy Bks.) ABDO Publishing Co.

Nelson, Kristin L. The Lincoln Memorial. (Lightning Bolt Bks.). (gr. k-2). 2010. (Illus.). 32p. (J). lib. bdg. 25.26 (978-0-7613-6018-6(2), Lerner Pubns.) 2010. pap. 45.32 (978-0-7613-6992-9(9)) 2010. (ENG.). 32p. pap. 7.95 (978-0-7613-6051-3(4)) 2003. (ENG., Illus.). 32p. pap. 7.95 (978-0-8225-3761-8(3)) Lerner Publishing Group.

—El Monumento a Lincoln. 2005. (Libros para Avanzar (Pull Ahead Bks.)). (SPA., Illus.). 32p. (J). (gr. k-3). per. 5.95 (978-0-8225-3143-2(7), Ediciones Lerner) Lerner Publishing Group.

Rustad, Martha. What Is Inside the Lincoln Memorial? Poling, Kyle, illus. 2014. (Cloverleaf Books — Our American Symbols Ser.). 24p. (gr. k-2). (J). lib. bdg. 23.93 (978-1-4677-2135-6(2)); pap. 6.95 (978-1-4677-4468-3(9)) Lerner Publishing Group. (Millbrook Pr.).

LINDBERGH, CHARLES A. (CHARLES AUGUSTUS), 1902-1974

Houran, Lori Haskins. The $25,000 Flight. Lowe, Wesley, illus. 2014. (Totally True Adventures Ser.). (ENG.). 112p. (J). (gr. 2-5). 4.99 (978-0-385-38284-7(7), Random Hse. Bks. for Young Readers) Random Hse. Children's Bks.

Koestler-Grack, Rachel A. Spirit of St. Louis, 1 vol. 2005. (American Moments Ser.). (ENG., Illus.). 48p. (gr. 4-8). 27.07 (978-1-59197-940-1(4), Abdo & Daughters) ABDO Publishing Co.

Lindbergh, Charles A., Jr. The Spirit of St Louis. 2003. 562p. pap. 29.00 (978-0-7581-3991-7(8)) Textbook Pubs.

Marsh, Carole. Charles Lindbergh. 2003. 12p. (gr. k-4). 2.95 (978-0-635-02130-4(7)) Gallopade International.

Rowell, Rebecca. Charles Lindbergh: Groundbreaking Aviator, 1 vol. 2010. (Essential Lives Set 5 Ser.). (ENG.). 112p. (J). (gr. 6-12). lib. bdg. 35.64 (978-1-61613-516-4(6)) ABDO Publishing Co.

Saddleback Educational Publishing Staff, ed. Charles Lindbergh, 1 vol. unabr. ed. 2008. (Graphic Biographies Ser.). (ENG., Illus.). 25p. (YA). (gr. 9-12). pap. 7.95 (978-1-59905-218-2(0)) Saddleback Educational Publishing, Inc.

Webber, Diane. Celebrity's Son Snatched: Can Handwriting Help Nab the Perp? 2011. (J). pap. (978-0-545-32810-4(1)) Scholastic, Inc.

LINE-ENGRAVING

see Engraving

LINGUISTICS

see Language and Languages

LINNAEUS, CAROLUS, 1707-1778

see Linne, Carl Von, 1707-1778

LINNE, CARL VON, 1707-1778

Anderson, Margaret J. Carl Linnaeus: Genius of Classification. 2015. (Genius Scientists & Their Genius Ideas Ser.). 96p. (J). (gr. 5-12). pap. 10.95 (978-0-7660-6541-3(3)) Enslow Pubs., Inc.

Anderson, Margaret Jean. Carl Linnaeus: Father of Classification. 2009. (Great Minds of Science Ser.). (Illus.). 128p. (J). (gr. 5). lib. bdg. 33.27 (978-0-7660-3009-1(1)) Enslow Pubs., Inc.

Stephens, Catherine. Classification Clues. 2007. (Nonfiction Reading & Writing Workshops Ser.). (ENG., Illus.). 32p. (J). pap. 17.95 (978-0-7922-4576-6(8)) CENGAGE Learning.

LION

Ackland, Nick. What Noise Does a Lion Make? Bee, Bella, illus. 2016. (What Noise Does A... . Ser.). (ENG.). 10p. (J). (gr. -1 — 1). bds. 6.99 (978-0-7641-6844-4(4)) Barron's Educational Series, Inc.

Albee, Sarah. Lions. 2006. (J). 7.99 (978-1-59939-035-2(3)) Cornerstone Pr.

—Lions. 2009. (Amazing Animals Ser.). 48p. (J). (gr. 2-6). pap. 10.50 (978-1-4339-2125-4(1), Gareth Stevens Learning Library); (ENG.). (YA). (gr. 3-6). lib. bdg. 28.00 (978-0-8368-9121-8(X)) Stevens, Gareth Publishing LLLP.

Amstutz, Lisa J. Lions Are Awesome! 2015. (Awesome African Animals! Ser.). (ENG.). 32p. (gr. 1-2). lib. bdg. 27.32 (978-1-4914-1762-1(5)) Capstone Press of Coughlan Cos.

Archer, Claire. Leones, 1 vol. 2014. (Grandes Felinos Ser.). (SPA.). 24p. (J). (gr. 4-8). lib. bdg. 28.50 (978-1-62970-298-8(6)) ABDO Publishing Co.

—Lions, 1 vol. 2014. (Big Cats Ser.). (ENG.). 24p. (J). (gr. 4-8). lib. bdg. 28.50 (978-1-62970-004-5(5)) ABDO Publishing Co.

Archer, Claire, et al. Leones. 2015. (Grandes Felinos Ser.). (SPA., Illus.). 24p. (gr. k-1). pap. 7.95 (978-1-4966-0461-3(X)) Capstone Classroom.

Barnes, Julia. 101 Facts about Lions. 2004. (One Hundred One Facts about Predators Ser.). (Illus.). 32p. (gr. 1-4). lib. bdg. 26.00 (978-0-8368-4037-7(2), Gareth Stevens Learning Library) Stevens, Gareth Publishing LLLP.

Bell, Samantha S. Meet a Baby Lion. 2015. (ENG., Illus.). 32p. (J). (gr. k-2). 26.65 (978-1-4677-7974-6(1), Lerner Pubns.) Lerner Publishing Group.

Bergeron, Alain M., et al. Les Lions. 2011. (FRE., Illus.). 64p. (J). pap. 8.95 (978-2-89435-510-7(6)) Quintin Pubs./Editions Michel Quintin CAN. Dist: Crabtree Publishing Co.

Big Cats. 2014. (Animal Q & A Ser.). (Illus.). 24p. (J). (gr. k-3). lib. bdg. 23.60 (978-1-4777-9182-0(5)) Windmill Bks.

Blewett, Ashlee Brown. Lion Rescue - National Geographic Kids Mission: All about Lions & How to Save Them. Raven-Ellison, Daniel, ed. 2014. (ENG., Illus.). 128p. (J). (gr. 5). pap. 12.99 (978-1-4263-1492-6(2), National Geographic Children's Bks.) National Geographic Society.

Bodden, Valerie. Amazing Animals - Lions. 2010. (Amazing Animals Ser.). 24p. (J). (gr. -1-3). 16.95 (978-1-58341-807-9(5), Creative Education) Creative Co., The.

—Amazing Animals: Lions. 2011. (Amazing Animals Ser.). (ENG.). 24p. (J). (gr. 1-3). pap. 8.99 (978-0-89812-747-8(5), Creative Paperbacks) Creative Co., The.

Books Are Fun 8 Title Animal Lives Set: Lions. 2006. (J). (978-1-59566-311-5(8)) QEB Publishing Inc.

Bowman, Donna H. Big Cats. Wald, Christina, illus. 2008. (ENG.). 24p. (J). (gr. 3-18). 19.95 (978-1-58117-781-7(X), Intervisual/Piggy Toes) Bendon, Inc.

Bredeson, Carmen. Lions up Close. (Zoom in on Animals! Ser.). (Illus.). 24p. (J). 2012. (gr. k-18). pap. 7.95 (978-1-59845-417-8(X)) 2008. (gr. 3-7). lib. bdg. 22.60 (978-0-7660-3080-0(6)) Enslow Pubs., Inc. (Enslow Elementary).

Browne, Philippa-Alys. "Lion roars" (African Animals ABC) (Illus.). 14.99 (978-1-84148-752-6(X)) Barefoot Bks., Inc.

Calhoun, Kelly. Ferocidad Felina (Fiercely Feline) León (Lion) 2016. (Adivina (Guess What) Ser.). (SPA., Illus.). 24p. (J). (gr. k-2). 28.50 (978-1-63471-448-8(2), 208855) Cherry Lake Publishing.

—Fiercely Feline: Lion. 2015. (Guess What Ser.). (ENG.). 24p. (J). (gr. k-2). pap. 12.79 (978-1-63362-713-0(6), 206673) Cherry Lake Publishing.

Clark, Willow. Lions: Life in the Pride. 2011. (Animal Families Ser.). 24p. (J). (ENG.). pap. 8.25 (978-1-4488-2612-4(8)); (Illus.). lib. bdg. 22.60 (978-1-4488-2513-4(X)) Rosen Publishing Group, Inc., The. (PowerKids Pr.).

Cline, Gina. Lions. Rupp, Kristina, illus. 2012. (1G Predator Animals Ser.). (ENG.). 24p. (J). pap. 5.99 (978-1-61406-320-9(6)) American Reading Co.

Cosmic Debris Etc., Inc. Staff, et al. Little Lion. 2009. (Little Finger Puppet Board Bks.). (ENG., Illus.). 12p. (J). (gr. -1 — 1). bds. 6.99 (978-0-8118-6788-7(9)) Chronicle Bks. LLC.

Daly, Ruth. Lions. 2014. (J). pap. (978-1-4896-0927-4(X)) Weigl Pubs., Inc.

Dineen, Jacqueline. Lions. (Amazing Animals Ser.). (Illus.). 24p. (J). 2009. (gr. 2-4). pap. 8.95 (978-1-60596-151-4(5)) 2009. (gr. 2-4). lib. bdg. 24.45 (978-1-60596-150-7(7)) 2003. lib. bdg. 21.35 (978-1-58340-230-6(6)) Weigl Pubs., Inc.

Doudna, Kelly. It's a Baby Lion!, 1 vol. 2009. (Baby African Animals Ser.). (ENG., Illus.). 24p. (J). (gr. k-3). lib. bdg. 24.21 (978-1-60453-156-5(8), SandCastle) ABDO Publishing Co.

Durrie, Karen. I Am a Lion. 2012. (J). (978-1-61913-228-3(1)); 27.13 (978-1-61913-227-6(3)) Weigl Pubs., Inc.

—León. 2013. (SPA.). (J). (978-1-62127-571-8(X)) Weigl Pubs., Inc.

Eszterhas, Suzi. Eye on the Wild: Lion. 2012. (Eye on the Wild Ser.: 3). (Illus.). 32p. (J). (978-1-84780-310-8(5), Frances Lincoln) Quarto Publishing Group UK.

Franks, Katie. Lions. 2014. (Zoo's Who's Who Ser.). (Illus.). 24p. (J). (gr. k-2). 23.60 (978-1-4777-6475-6(5), PowerKids Pr.) Rosen Publishing Group, Inc., The.

Frisch, Aaron. Lions. 2006. (Wild World of Animals Ser.). (Illus.). 31p. (J). 18.95 (978-1-58341-433-0(9), Creative Education) Creative Co., The.

Gagne, Tammy. Lions: Built for the Hunt. 2016. (Predator Profiles Ser.). (ENG., Illus.). 24p. (gr. 1-2). lib. bdg. 25.32 (978-1-4914-8260-5(5)) Capstone Press of Coughlan Cos.

Gareth Stevens Publishing Staff, contrib. by. Lions. 2004. (All about Wild Animals Ser.). (Illus.). 32p. (gr. k-4). lib. bdg. 26.00 (978-0-8368-4185-5(9), Gareth Stevens Learning Library) Stevens, Gareth Publishing LLLP.

Gish, Melissa. Lions. 2017. (J). **(978-1-60818-819-2(1)**, Creative Education) Creative Co., The.

Glaser, Rebecca Stromstad. Lions Roar. 2016. (ENG., Illus.). 16p. (J). (gr. -1 — 1). bds. 7.99 (978-1-68152-071-1(0)) Amicus.

Gordon, Sharon. Adivina Quien Ruge. 2006. (Bookworms Ser.). (SPA & ENG., Illus.). 32p. (gr. k-2). lib. bdg. 15.95 (978-0-7614-2386-7(9)) Marshall Cavendish Corp.

—Guess Who Roars. 2004. (Bookworms Ser.). (ENG & SPA., Illus.). 24p. (gr. k-2). lib. bdg. 15.95 (978-0-7614-1556-5(4), Benchmark Bks.) Marshall Cavendish Corp.

—Guess Who Roars/Adivina Quien Ruge. 2006. (Bookworms Ser.). (SPA & ENG., Illus.). 32p. (gr. k-2). lib. bdg. 15.95 (978-0-7614-2466-6(0)) Marshall Cavendish Corp.

—Roars. 2007. (J). pap. 6.99 (978-0-7614-3322-4(8)) Marshall Cavendish Corp.

Group/McGraw-Hill, Wright. Lion Level: Adventure Journal Set. (Wildcats Ser.). (gr. 2-8). 31.95 (978-0-322-05789-0(2)) Wright Group/McGraw-Hill.

—Lion Level: Wildcats Lion Complete Kit. (Wildcats Ser.). (gr. 2-8). 599.95 (978-0-322-06482-9(1)) Wright Group/McGraw-Hill.

Guillain, Charlotte. Mighty Lions, 1 vol. 2013. (Walk on the Wild Side Ser.). (ENG.). 32p. (gr. 1-3). 29.99 (978-1-4109-5215-8(0)); pap. 8.95 (978-1-4109-5222-6(3)) Heinemann-Raintree. (Read Me!).

Guillain, Charlotte, et al. Living in the Wild: Big Cats, 1 vol. 2014. (Living in the Wild: Big Cats Ser.). (ENG.). 48p. (gr. 3-6). lib. bdg. 199.92 (978-1-4329-8111-2(0), Heinemann InfoSearch) Heinemann-Raintree.

Hague, Bradley. Rise of the Lioness: Restoring a Habitat & its Pride on the Liuwa Plains. 2016. (ENG., Illus.). 56p. (J). (gr. 3-7). 18.99 (978-1-4263-2532-8(0), National Geographic Children's Bks.) National Geographic Society.

Hanel, Rachael. Lions. 2008. (Living Wild Ser.). (Illus.). 46p. 22.95 (978-1-58341-656-3(0), Creative Education) Creative Co., The.

Hansen, Sarah. When Mountain Lions Attack! 2006. (When Wild Animals Attack! Ser.). (Illus.). 48p. (J). (gr. 4-10). lib. bdg. 25.27 (978-0-7660-2668-1(X)) Enslow Pubs., Inc.

Harris, Tim, ed. Lions. 2012. (Animal Families Ser.). (ENG., Illus.). 32p. (gr. 2-5). 31.35 (978-1-78121-004-8(7), Brown Bear Bks.) Windmill Bks. Ltd. GBR. Dist: Black Rabbit Bks.

Hatkoff, Craig, et al. Cecil's Pride: The True Story of a Lion King. 2016. (ENG., Illus.). 40p. (J). (gr. -1-3). 17.99 (978-1-338-03445-5(6)) Scholastic, Inc.

Hern & Ez, Daniel. Endangered Lions. 2012. (ENG., Illus.). 24p. (J). pap. 5.99 (978-1-61406-169-4(6)) American Reading Co.

Hopgood, Sally & Graham, Oakley. Safari Wonders. Wood, Hannah, illus. 2012. (Sparkling Slide Nature Bks.). (ENG.). 12p. (J). (gr. -1-k). 9.99 (978-1-84956-676-6(3)) Top That! Publishing PLC GBR. Dist: Independent Pubs. Group.

Ipcizade, Catherine. Lions. 2010. (African Animals Ser.). (ENG.). 24p. (gr. k-1). pap. 41.70 (978-1-4296-5082-3(6), Pebble Plus) Capstone Press of Coughlan Cos.

—Lions [Scholastic]. 2010. (African Animals Ser.). 24p. pap. 0.49 (978-1-4296-5782-2(0), Pebble Plus) Capstone Press of Coughlan Cos.

Joubert, Beverly, et al. Face to Face with Lions. 2010. (Face to Face with Animals Ser.). (ENG., Illus.). 32p. (J). (gr. 2-5). pap. 6.95 (978-1-4263-0627-3(X), National Geographic Children's Bks.) National Geographic Society.

Joubert, Dereck. Face to Face with Lions. Joubert, Beverly, photos by. 2008. (Face to Face with Animals Ser.). (ENG., Illus.). 32p. (J). (gr. 2-5). 16.95 (978-1-4263-0207-7(X)); lib. bdg. 25.90 (978-1-4263-0208-4(8)) National Geographic Society. (National Geographic Children's Bks.).

Kalman, Bobbie. The Life Cycle of A Lion. 2007. (ENG.). 32p. (J). (978-0-7787-7703-8(0)) Crabtree Publishing Co.

Kalman, Bobbie & Bishop, Amanda. El Ciclo de Vida Del León. 2005. (Serie Ciclos de Vida Ser.). (SPA., Illus.). 32p. (J). lib. bdg. (978-0-7787-8664-1(1)); (gr. 1-4). pap. (978-0-7787-8710-5(9)) Crabtree Publishing Co.

Keller, Susanna. Meet the Lion. 2010. (At the Zoo Ser.). 24p. (J). (ENG.). pap. 8.25 (978-1-4358-9730-4(7)); (Illus.). (gr. -1-1). lib. bdg. 22.60 (978-1-4358-9309-2(3)) Rosen Publishing Group, Inc., The. (PowerKids Pr.).

Kjelle, Marylou Morano. Lion, 1 vol. 2013. (Great Predators Ser.). (ENG., Illus.). 48p. (J). (gr. 3-6). lib. bdg. 32.79 (978-1-61783-950-4(7)) ABDO Publishing Co.

—Lion Paperback. 2013. (Illus.). 48p. (J). pap. 15.64 (978-1-62403-015-4(7), Core Library) ABDO Publishing Co.

Klepeis, Alicia Z. Lions on the Hunt. 2017. (Searchlight Books (tm) — Predators Ser.). (ENG.). 32p. (J). (gr. 3-5). pap. 9.99 **(978-1-5124-5610-3(1))**; (Illus.). 30.65 **(978-1-5124-3395-1(0)**, Lerner Pubns.) Lerner Publishing Group.

Kopp, Megan. Gallinas/Megan Kopp. 2014. (SPA., Illus.). 24p. (J). (978-1-62127-861-0(1)) Weigl Pubs., Inc.

Kuskowski, Alex. Lions, 1 vol. 2014. (Zoo Animals Ser.). (ENG.). 24p. (J). (gr. k-3). lib. bdg. 24.21 (978-1-62403-272-1(9), SandCastle) ABDO Publishing Co.

Landau, Elaine. Fierce Cats. 2003. (Fearsome, Scary, & Creepy Animals Ser.). (Illus.). 48p. (J). (gr. 1-4). lib. bdg. 23.93 (978-0-7660-2062-7(2)) Enslow Pubs., Inc.

Latta, Jan. Leonor la leona (Lisa the Lion) 2007. (Familias de animales salvajes (Wild Animal Families) Ser.). (ENG & SPA., Illus.). 24p. (gr. 1-4). lib. bdg. 24.00 (978-0-8368-7969-8(4), Gareth Stevens Learning Library) Stevens, Gareth Publishing LLLP.

—Lisa the Lion. 2007. (Wild Animal Families Ser.). (Illus.). 24p. (gr. 1-4). pap. 8.15 (978-0-8368-7777-9(2)); lib. bdg. 24.00 (978-0-8368-7770-0(5)) Stevens, Gareth Publishing LLLP. (Gareth Stevens Learning Library).

Leaf, Christina. Baby Lions. 2014. (Super Cute! Ser.). (ENG., Illus.). 24p. (J). (gr. k-3). lib. bdg. 25.95 (978-1-60014-974-0(X), Blastoff! Readers) Bellwether Media.

Los Leones (Lions) 2006. (J). pap. 7.95 (978-0-8225-6628-1(1), Ediciones Lerner) Lerner Publishing Group.

Lindeen, Mary. Lions. 2013. (ENG., Illus.). 24p. (J). lib. bdg. 25.65 (978-1-62031-064-9(3)) Jump! Inc.

Lion: Killer King of the Plains. 2013. (Top of the Food Chain Ser.). 32p. (J). (gr. k-5). pap. 60.00 (978-1-61533-798-9(9), PowerKids Pr.) Rosen Publishing Group, Inc., The.

Lions, 6 bks. 2005. (Animal Predators Ser.). (Illus.). 40p. (J). (gr. 3-6). pap. 46.95 (978-0-8225-5491-2(7)) Lerner Publishing Group.

Markle, Sandra. Los Leones. 2006. (Animales Depredadores (Animal Predators) Ser.). (SPA., Illus.). 39p. (J). (gr. 3-7). lib. bdg. 25.26 (978-0-8225-6491-1(2), Ediciones Lerner) Lerner Publishing Group.

—Lions. 2005. (Animal Predators Ser.). (Illus.). 40p. (J). (gr. 4-6). pap. 7.95 (978-1-57505-744-6(1)); (gr. 3-6). lib. bdg. 25.26 (978-1-57505-727-9(1)) Lerner Publishing Group.

—Los Leones; Lions. 2008. pap. 46.95 (978-0-8225-7089-9(0)) Lerner Publishing Group.

Markle, Sandra. Ranger Rick: I Wish I Was a Lion. 2017. (I Can Read Level 1 Ser.). 32p. (J). (gr. -1-3). 16.99 **(978-0-06-243205-6(2))** HarperCollins Pubs.

Marsh, Laura. Lions. 2015. (Readers Ser.). (ENG., Illus.). 32p. (J). (gr. -1-1). pap. 3.99 (978-1-4263-1939-6(8), National Geographic Children's Bks.) National Geographic Society.

—National Geographic Readers: Lions. 2015. (Readers Ser.). (ENG., Illus.). 32p. (J). (gr. -1-1). lib. bdg. 13.90 (978-1-4263-1940-2(1), National Geographic Children's Bks.) National Geographic Society.

McCune, Jamie. Lion Cub Roars: Baby Animals. 2010. (ENG., Illus.). 16p. (J). (978-1-60727-203-8(2)) Soundprints.

Meachen Rau, Dana. El Leon en la Hierba. 2006. (Naturaleza Ser.). (SPA., Illus.). 24p. (gr. k-1). lib. bdg. 15.95 (978-0-7614-2411-6(3), Benchmark Bks.) Marshall Cavendish Corp.

Meinking, Mary. Lion vs. Gazelle, 1 vol. 2011. (Predator vs. Prey Ser.). (ENG., Illus.). 32p. (gr. 1-2). 29.99 (978-1-4109-3934-0(0)); pap. 8.29 (978-1-4109-3943-2(X)) Heinemann-Raintree. (Read Me!).

—Predator vs. Prey, 8 vols., Set. Incl. Crocodile vs. Wildebeest. (Illus.). pap. 8.29 (978-1-4109-3944-9(8)); Dolphin vs. Fish. (Illus.). pap. 8.29 (978-1-4109-3949-4(9)); Lion vs. Gazelle. (Illus.). pap. 8.29 (978-1-4109-3943-2(X)); Owl vs. Mouse. (Illus.). pap. 8.29 (978-1-4109-3945-6(6)); Polar Bear vs. Seal. (Illus.). pap. 8.29 (978-1-4109-3948-7(0)); Shark vs. Penguin. pap. 8.29 (978-1-4109-3946-3(4)); Tarantula vs. Bird. (Illus.). pap. 8.29 (978-1-4109-3947-0(2)); Wolf vs. Elk. (Illus.). pap. 8.29 (978-1-4109-3950-0(2)); (gr. 1-2). (Predator vs. Prey Ser.). (ENG.). 32p. 2011. Set pap. 63.92 (978-1-4109-3951-7(0)); Set lib. bdg. 119.96 (978-1-4109-3942-5(1)) Heinemann-Raintree. (Read Me!).

Meister, Cari. Do You Really Want to Meet a Lion? Fabbri, Daniele, illus. 2015. (Do You Really Want to Meet ... ? Ser.). (ENG.). 24p. (J). (gr. 1-3). 19.95 (978-1-60753-735-9(4)) Amicus Publishing.

Moldovo, Eustacia. Baby Lions at the Zoo. 2015. (J). (978-0-7660-6609-0(6)); (ENG., Illus.). 24p. (gr. -1-1). pap. 9.35 (978-0-7660-7085-1(9)) Enslow Pubs., Inc.

Morgan, Paul & Drewett, Jim. Toughest Test. 2005. (ENG., Illus.). 254p. 25.00 (978-1-905326-04-4(1)) Penguin Publishing Group.

Murray, Julie. Lions, 1 vol. (ENG.). 2012. 32p. 28.50 (978-1-61783-221-5(9), Big Buddy Bks.) 2003. 24p. 25.65 (978-1-57765-647-0(4), Buddy Bks.) ABDO Publishing Co.

National Geographic Kids Staff. Go, Cub! - National Geographic Kids. 2014. (ENG., Illus.). 24p. (J). pap. (978-1-4263-1794-1(8)) National Geographic Society.

Neuman, Susan B. National Geographic Readers: Go Cub! 2014. (Readers Ser.). (ENG.). 24p. (J). (-k). pap. 3.99 (978-1-4263-1512-1(0), National Geographic Children's Bks.) National Geographic Society.

Orme, Helen. Lions in Danger. 2006. (Wildlife Survival Ser.). (Illus.). 32p. (YA). (gr. 2-5). lib. bdg. 25.27 (978-1-59716-262-3(0)) Bearport Publishing Co., Inc.

Owen, Ruth. Lion Cubs. 2011. (Wild Baby Animals Ser.). 24p. (J). (gr. k-3). lib. bdg. 19.96 (978-1-61772-159-5(X)); lib. bdg., E-Book 39.93 (978-1-61772-240-0(5)) Bearport Publishing Co., Inc.

—Lions. 2012. (Dr. Bob's Amazing World of Animals Ser.). (Illus.). 32p. (J). (gr. k-5). pap. 11.75 (978-1-61533-554-1(4)); lib. bdg. 26.50 (978-1-61533-547-3(1)) Windmill Bks.

Owings, Lisa. The African Lion. 2012. (Nature's Deadliest Ser.). (ENG., Illus.). 24p. (J). (gr. 3-8). lib. bdg. 25.95 (978-1-60014-740-1(2), Pilot Bks.) Bellwether Media.

—The African Lion. 2012. (ENG., Illus.). 24p. 23.00 (978-0-531-20879-3(6), Children's Pr.) Scholastic Library Publishing.

Pallotta, Jerry. Lion vs. Tiger. Bolster, Rob, illus. 2016. (Who Would Win? Ser.). (ENG.). 32p. (J). (gr. 2-5). pap. 3.99 (978-0-545-17571-5(2)) Scholastic, Inc.

Patterson, John Henry. The Man-Eaters of Tsavo. 2011. 148p. pap. 7.49 (978-1-61382-001-8(1)) Simon & Brown.

Pelusey, Michael & Pelusey, Jane. Tigers & Lions. 2008. (Zoo Animals Ser.). 32p. (gr. 2-3). lib. bdg. 18.56 (978-0-7614-3151-0(9), Benchmark Bks.) Marshall Cavendish Corp.

Pingry, Patricia A. Cheetah. San Diego Zoo Staff, photos by. 2005. (San Diego Zoo Animal Library: Vol. 12). (ENG., Illus.). 24p. (J). bds. 6.95 (978-0-8249-6579-2(5), 1242115, Ideal Pubns.) Worthy Publishing.

Prebeg, Rick. Looking for Lions. Prebeg, Rick, photos by. 2005. (Illus.). (J). (978-1-933248-12-7(2)) World Quest Learning.

Quinton, Sasha. Yay-Hooray: A Phonics Reader. 2009. (Illus.). pap. (978-1-936199-07-5(6)) Book Shop, Ltd., The.

Reade, Clara. Lions. 2012. (PowerKids Readers: Safari Animals Ser.). (ENG., Illus.). 24p. (J). (gr. k-2). pap. 8.25

(978-1-4488-7470-5(X)); lib. bdg. 22.60 (978-1-4488-7391-3(6)) Rosen Publishing Group, Inc., The. (PowerKids Pr.).

Rennert, Violette. Little Lions. 2005. (Born to Be Wild Ser.). (Illus.). 24p. (gr. k-3). lib. bdg. 23.00 (978-0-8368-4737-6(7), Gareth Stevens Learning Library) Stevens, Gareth Publishing LLLP.

Riggs, Kate. Lions. 2012. (Seedlings Ser.). (Illus.). 24p. (J). (gr. -1-3). 15.95 (978-1-60818-277-0(0), Creative Education) Creative Co., The.

—Seedlings: Lions. 2013. (Seedlings Ser.). (ENG.). 24p. (J). (gr. -1-k). pap. 6.99 (978-0-89812-784-3(X), Creative Paperbacks) Creative Co., The.

Riley, Joelle. African Lions. 2009. pap. 40.95 (978-0-8225-9316-4(5)) 2007. (ENG., Illus.). 32p. lib. bdg. 22.60 (978-0-8225-6703-5(2), Lerner Pubns.) 2007. (ENG., Illus.). 32p. per. 7.95 (978-0-8225-6707-3(5), First Avenue Editions) Lerner Publishing Group.

Ringstad, Arnold. Leopards. 2014. (Illus.). 24p. (J). 27.10 (978-1-60753-602-4(1)) Amicus Publishing.

—Lions. 2014. (Wild Cats Ser.). 24p. (J). 27.10 (978-1-60753-603-1(X)) Amicus Publishing.

Ritchey, Kate & Bader, Bonnie. Lion, Tiger, & Bear, Level 4. 2015. (Penguin Young Readers, Level 4 Ser.). (ENG., Illus.). 48p. (J). (gr. 3-4). pap. 3.99 (978-0-448-48336-8(X), Penguin Young Readers) Penguin Young Readers Group.

Schafer, Susan & Meredith, Susan Markowitz. Lions. 2009. (Benchmark Rockets Ser.). 24p. (gr. 1-18). 24.21 (978-0-7614-4344-5(4)) Marshall Cavendish Corp.

Scott, Jonathan & Scott, Angela. Scarface: the Real Lion King Gold Band. 2016. (Cambridge Reading Adventures Ser.). (ENG.). 24p. pap. 7.19 (978-1-107-56047-5(0)) Cambridge Univ. Pr.

Server, Lee. Lions - Pb: A Portrait of the Animal World. 2013. (Portrait of the Animal World Ser.). (Illus.). 72p. pap. 9.95 (978-1-59764-331-3(9)) New Line Bks.

Shea, Mary Molly. Lions. 2010. (Animals That Live in the Grasslands Ser.). (ENG.). 24p. (J). (gr. -1-3). pap. 8.15 (978-1-4339-3873-3(1)); lib. bdg. 22.60 (978-1-4339-3872-6(3)) Stevens, Gareth Publishing LLLP.

Shea, Therese. Lions. 2012. (Killer Cats Ser.). (Illus.). 24p. (J). (gr. 2-5). pap. 8.15 (978-1-4339-7008-5(2)); lib. bdg. 22.60 (978-1-4339-7007-8(4)) Stevens, Gareth Publishing LLLP.

Simpson, Phillip. Lion Habitats under Threat: A Cause & Effect Text, 1 vol. 2014. (Text Structures Ser.). (ENG., Illus.). 32p. (gr. 1-3). pap. 7.99 (978-1-4846-0417-5(2), Heinemann First Library) Heinemann-Raintree.

Spilsbury, Louise. Lion. 2013. (Top of the Food Chain Ser.). 32p. (J). (gr. k-5). pap. 10.00 (978-1-61533-797-2(0), PowerKids Pr.) Rosen Publishing Group, Inc., The.

Starbuck, Sara & The Born Free Foundation. Lion Rescue: A True-Life Story. 2017. (Born Free... Bks.). (ENG.). 112p. (J). (gr. 2-6). pap. 6.99 (978-1-4380-0989-6(5)) Barron's Educational Series, Inc.

Stefoff, Rebecca. Lions. 2005. (Animalways Ser.). (Illus.). 104p. (gr. 6-7). lib. bdg. 24.95 (978-0-7614-1746-0(X), Benchmark Bks.) Marshall Cavendish Corp.

Taylor, Trace. African Lions. 2011. (ARC Press / Power 50 - Predators Ser.). pap. 45.32 (978-1-61541-030-9(9)) American Reading Co.

—Lions of Africa. Taylor, Trace, illus. 2007. (1-3Y Wild Animals Ser.). (ENG., Illus.). 24p. (J). (gr. k-2). pap. 5.99 (978-1-59301-654-8(9)) American Reading Co.

Taylor, Trace & SáNchez, LuciA M. Leones Africanos (African Lions) 2011. (ARC Press / el poder de 50 - Animales depredadores (Power 50 - Predators) Ser.). (SPA.). pap. 45.32 (978-1-61541-287-7(5)) American Reading Co.

Thomas, Isabel. Lion vs. Tiger. 2017. (Animal Rivals Ser.). (ENG.). 24p. (gr. k-2). lib. bdg. 23.32 **(978-1-4846-4073-9(X),** Heinemann Read & Learn) Heinemann-Raintree.

Throp, Claire. Lions, 1 vol. 2014. (Living in the Wild: Big Cats Ser.). (ENG., Illus.). 48p. (gr. 3-6). lib. bdg. 33.32 (978-1-4329-8108-2(0), Heinemann InfoSearch) Heinemann-Raintree.

Toufexis, George. Extreme Lions & Tigers Tattoos. 2011. (Dover Tattoos Ser.). (ENG.). 4p. (J). (gr. 1-4). pap. 1.50 (978-0-486-48184-5(0)) Dover Pubns., Inc.

Tourville, Amanda Doering. Lions Leaving: Counting from 10 To 1, 1 vol. Holm, Sharon Lane, illus. 2008. (Count the Critters Ser.). (ENG.). 24p. (J). (gr. k-3). 27.07 (978-1-60270-264-6(0)) Magic Wagon.

Troupe, Thomas Kingsley. I Want to Be a Lion. Beavers, Melinda, illus. 2015. (I Want to Be... Ser.). (ENG.). 24p. (gr. k-3). lib. bdg. 26.65 (978-1-4795-6860-4(0)) Capstone Press of Coughlan Cos.

Turnbull, Stephanie. Lion. 2015. (Big Beasts Ser.). (Illus.). 24p. (gr. k-3). 28.50 (978-1-62588-167-0(3)) Black Rabbit Bks.

—Lion. 2015. (ENG., Illus.). 24p. (J). pap. 8.95 (978-1-77092-216-7(4)) RiverStream Publishing.

Vogel, Elizabeth. Lions. 2009. (Big Cats (Powerkids Readers) Ser.). 24p. (gr. 1-1). 37.50 (978-1-61511-570-9(6), PowerKids Pr.) Rosen Publishing Group, Inc., The.

Von Zumbusch, Amelie. Lions. 2007. (Safari Animals Ser.). (Illus.). 24p. (J). (gr. 3-7). lib. bdg. 22.60 (978-1-4042-3612-7(0), PowerKids Pr.) Rosen Publishing Group, Inc., The.

von Zumbusch, Amelie. Lions. 2009. (Safari Animals Ser.). 24p. (gr. 1-1). 42.50 (978-1-60852-956-8(8), PowerKids Pr.) Rosen Publishing Group, Inc., The.

Von Zumbusch, Amelie. Lions: King of the Beasts. 2007. (Dangerous Cats Ser.). (Illus.). 24p. (J). (gr. 3-7). lib. bdg. 22.60 (978-1-4042-3631-8(7)) Rosen Publishing Group, Inc., The.

von Zumbusch, Amelie. Lions: King of the Beasts. 2009. (Dangerous Cats Ser.). 24p. (gr. 2-3). 42.50 (978-1-61512-129-8(3), PowerKids Pr.) Rosen Publishing Group, Inc., The.

Von Zumbusch, Amelie. Lions/Leones. 2007. (Safari Animals / Animales de Safari Ser.: Vol. 1). (ENG & SPA., Illus.). 24p. (J). (gr. k-3). lib. bdg. 22.60 (978-1-4042-7608-6(4)) Rosen Publishing Group, Inc., The.

von Zumbusch, Amelie. Lions/Leones. 2009. (Safari Animals/Animales de safari Ser.). (ENG & SPA.). 24p. (gr. 1-1). 42.50 (978-1-60852-978-0(9), Editorial Buenas Letras) Rosen Publishing Group, Inc., The.

Zane, Dory. How to Track a Lion, 1. 2014. (Scatalog: a Kid's Field Guide to Animal Poop Ser.). (ENG.). 24p. (J). (gr. k-5). 23.60 (978-1-61533-884-9(5), Windmill Bks.) Rosen Publishing Group, Inc., The.

Zeiger, Jennifer. Lions. 2012. (Nature's Children Ser.). (ENG., Illus.). 48p. (J). (gr. 3-5). lib. bdg. 28.00 (978-0-531-20903-5(2), Children's Pr.) Scholastic Library Publishing.

—Lions - Nature's Children. 2012. (Nature's Children Ser.). (ENG., Illus.). 48p. (J). pap. 6.95 (978-0-531-21078-9(2), Children's Pr.) Scholastic Library Publishing.

Zobel, Derek. Lions. 2011. (Animal Safari Ser.). (ENG., Illus.). 24p. (J). (gr. k-3). lib. bdg. 25.95 (978-1-60014-608-4(2), Blastoff! Readers) Bellwether Media.

Zorzi, Gina & Cline, Gina. The Lion Pride. Dibble, Traci, illus. 2010. (2G Predator Animals Ser.). (ENG.). 32p. (J). (gr. k-2). pap. 5.99 (978-1-61541-500-7(9)) American Reading Co.

Zorzi, Gina & Dibble, Traci. The Lion Pride. 2011. (ARC Press / Power 100 - Predator Animals Ser.). pap. 45.32 (978-1-61541-501-4(7)) American Reading Co.

Zubek, Adeline. Counting Lions. 2011. (Animal Math Ser.). 24p. (J). (gr. 1-3). pap. 8.15 (978-1-4339-5664-5(0)); lib. bdg. 22.60 (978-1-4339-5662-1(4)) Stevens, Gareth Publishing LLLP.

LION—FICTION

Abercrombie, Barbara. The Show-and-Tell Lion. Cravath, Lynne Avril & Avril, Lynne, illus. 2006. (ENG.). 32p. (J). (gr. -1-2). 17.99 (978-0-689-86408-7(6), McElderry, Margaret K. Bks.) McElderry, Margaret K. Bks.

Ackland, Nick. Little Lion in the Garden. Walshaw, Sam, illus. 2017. (Little Explorers Ser.). (ENG.). 10p. (J). (gr. -1 — 1). bds. 6.99 (978-0-7641-6895-6(9)) Barron's Educational Series, Inc.

Adams, Alison. Androcles & the Lion: Classic Tales Series. Greenhead, Bill, illus. 2011. (Classic Tales Ser.). (J). (978-1-936258-60-4(9)) Benchmark Education Co.

Aesop. The Lion & the Mouse. 2016. (ENG.). 79.82 **(978-1-367-86708-6(8))** Blurb, Inc.

—The Lion & the Mouse. 2017. (Let's Learn Aesop's Fables Ser.). 24p. (gr. 6-7). 24.60 **(978-1-4994-8369-7(4))**; pap. 8.25 **(978-1-4994-8374-1(0))** Rosen Publishing Group, Inc., The. (Windmill Bks.).

Aesop. The Lion & the Mouse Tuff Book. 2011. (ENG., Illus.). 28p. (J). 6.95 (978-0-7358-4028-7(8)) North-South Bks., Inc.

Aesop Enterprise Inc. Staff. The Lion & the Mouse. Watts, Bernadette, illus. 2007. (ENG.). 32p. (J). (gr. -1-3). pap. 8.95 (978-0-7358-2129-3(1)) North-South Bks., Inc.

Agee, Jon. Lion Lessons. 2016. (ENG., Illus.). 32p. (J). (gr. -1-3). 17.99 (978-0-8037-3908-6(7), Dial Bks) Penguin Young Readers Group.

Aina, Olaiya E. Ijapa, the Lion, & the Boar. 2010. 20p. 13.80 (978-1-4269-3183-3(2)) Trafford Publishing.

Andreae, Giles. Leo, the Lovable Lion. 2004. (Illus.). (978-0-439-65567-5(6)) Scholastic, Inc.

Anholt, Laurence. A Kiss Like This. Anholt, Catherine, illus. 2009. (ENG.). 32p. (J). (gr. -1-1). pap. 7.95 (978-1-84507-862-1(4), Frances Lincoln) Quarto Publishing Group UK GBR. Dist: Hachette Bk. Group.

Atxaga, Bernardo & Costa, Margaret Jull. Shola & the Lions. Valverde, Mikel, illus. 2016. (ENG.). 48p. (J). (gr. 2-5). pap. 9.99 (978-1-78269-064-1(6), Pushkin Press) Steerforth Pr.

Award, Anna & Aesop. The Lion & the Mouse with the Donkey & the Lapdog. Biro, Val, illus. 2014. (ENG.). 24p. (J). pap. 6.95 (978-1-84135-953-3(X)) Award Pubns. Ltd. GBR. Dist: Parkwest Pubns., Inc.

Award, Anna, et al. The Farmer & His Sons & the Donkey in the Lion's Den. 2014. (ENG.). 24p. (J). pap. 6.95 (978-1-84135-960-1(2)) Award Pubns. Ltd. GBR. Dist: Parkwest Pubns., Inc.

—The Sick Lion & Hare & the Tortoise. 2014. (ENG.). 24p. (J). pap. 6.95 (978-1-84135-954-0(8)) Award Pubns. Ltd. GBR. Dist: Parkwest Pubns., Inc.

Axtell, David. We're Going on a Lion Hunt. Axtell, David, illus. 2007. (ENG., Illus.). 32p. (J). (gr. -1-1). 8.99 (978-0-8050-8219-7(0), 9780805082197) Square Fish.

AZ Books, creator. Baby Lion Searches for His Dad. 2012. (Plush Baby Ser.). (ENG., Illus.). 10p. (J). (gr. -1 — 1). 11.95 (978-1-61889-217-1(7)) AZ Bks. LLC.

AZ Books Staff. Who Is the Lion Looking For? Shestakova, Anna, ed. 2012. (Who Is There Ser.). (ENG.). 10p. (J). (-k). bds. 11.95 (978-1-61889-041-2(7)) AZ Bks. LLC.

Barkow, Henriette. Buri & the Marrow. Finlay, Lizzie, illus. 2004. (ENG & FRE.). 24p. (J). pap. (978-1-85269-583-5(8)) Mantra Lingua.

Baron, Lindamichelle. The Lion & the Man: A Fable. Huggins, Carl, illus. 2009. 72p. pap. 15.95 (978-0-940938-25-0(1)) Harlin Jacque Pubns.

Baum, L. Frank. The Road to Oz. 2009. (Little Golden Book Ser.). (ENG., Illus.). 24p. (J). (gr. -1-2). 3.99 (978-0-375-84757-8(X), Golden Bks.) Random Hse. Children's Bks.

Baum, Roger S. The Oz Odyssey. Seitzinger, Victoria, illus. 2006. 176p. (J). 19.95 (978-1-57072-299-8(4)) Overmountain Pr.

Beeke, Joel R. & Kleyn, Diana. How God Used a Snowdrift. Anderson, Jeff, illus. 2013. (Building on the Rock Ser.). (ENG.). 176p. (J). pap. 8.99 (978-1-85792-817-4(2), 9781857928174, CF4Kids) Christian Focus Pubns. GBR. Dist: Bookmasters Distribution.

Bender, Chris. The Lion & the Lamb. 2011. 24p. 14.93 (978-1-4269-5732-1(7)) Trafford Publishing.

Bently, Peter. Look Out, Cub! A Lift-the-Flap Story about Lions. 2013. (ENG.). 20p. (J). (gr. -1-2). bds. 9.99 (978-1-4263-1096-6(X), National Geographic Children's Bks.) National Geographic Society.

Berry, Ron. Can You Roar Like a Lion? Sharp, Chris, illus. 2009. (ENG.). 14p. bds. 10.99 (978-0-8249-1433-2(3), Ideal Pubns.) Worthy Publishing.

Bewley, Elizabeth. The Moon Followed Me Home. Furukawa, Masumi, illus. 2007. (ENG.). 6p. (J). (gr. -1-3). 12.95 (978-1-58117-598-1(1), Intervisual/Piggy Toes) Bendon, Inc.

Binder, Mark. Kings, Wolves, Princesses & Lions: 28 Illustrated Stories for Young Readers. 2012. (ENG., Illus.). 122p. (J). pap. 14.99 (978-0-9824707-8-7(9)) Light Pubns.

Blair, Eric. The Donkey in the Lion's Skin: A Retelling of Aesop's Fable, 1 vol. Silverman, Dianne, illus. 2013. (My First Classic Story Ser.). (ENG.). 24p. (gr. k-3). pap. 7.10 (978-1-4795-1855-5(7), My First Classic Story) Picture Window Bks.

Blair, Eric & Aesop Enterprise Inc. Staff. The Donkey in the Lion's Skin: A Retelling of Aesop's Fable, 1 vol. Silverman, Dianne, illus. 2011. (My First Classic Story Ser.). (ENG.). 24p. (gr. k-3). lib. bdg. 22.65 (978-1-4048-6506-8(3), My First Classic Story) Picture Window Bks.

Brennan-Nelson, Denise. Leopold the Lion. Barshaw, Ruth McNally, illus. 2015. (ENG.). 32p. (J). (gr. 1-3). 16.99 (978-1-58536-828-0(8), 203951) Sleeping Bear Pr.

Bright, Rachel. The Lion Inside. Field, Jim, illus. 2016. (ENG.). 32p. (J). (gr. -1-k). 16.99 (978-0-545-87350-5(9), Scholastic Pr.) Scholastic, Inc.

Brightwood, Laura, illus. Lion & Mousie. Brightwood, Laura, . 2007. (J). DVD (978-1-934409-00-8(6)) 3-C Institute for Social Development.

Brooke, Susan Rich, adapted by. The Lion King. 2003. (Illus.). (J). (978-0-7853-9380-1(3)) Publications International, Ltd.

Broom, Jenny. The Lion & the Mouse: Turn-And-Tell Tales. Noj, Nahta, illus. 2014. (ENG.). 32p. (J). (gr. -1-2). 14.99 (978-0-7636-6619-4(X), Templar) Candlewick Pr.

Brown, J. A. Lion's Mane. Knight, Paula, illus. 2003. (Funny Faces Ser.). 10p. (J). 3.95 (978-1-58925-718-4(9)) Tiger Tales.

Brown, Ruth & Brown, Ken. Lion in the Long Grass. 2013. (Silver Tales Ser.). (ENG., Illus.). (J). (gr. -1-2). pap. (978-1-74352-445-9(5)) Hinkler Bks. Pty, Ltd.

Browne, Anthony. The Little Bear Book. Browne, Anthony, illus. 2014. (ENG., Illus.). 24p. (J). (gr. -1-2). 15.99 (978-0-7636-7007-8(3)) Candlewick Pr.

Buller, Ginny. Happy Misunderstanding: How Folly Gets his Name. Chettle, Julie, illus. 2012. (ENG.). 29p. (J). pap. 16.95 (978-1-4327-8234-4(7)) Outskirts Pr., Inc.

Burchett, Jan & Vogler, Sara. Desert Danger, 1 vol. Le Feyer, Diane, illus. 2013. (Wild Rescue Ser.). (ENG.). 152p. (gr. 3-6). 9.95 (978-1-4342-4892-3(5)) Stone Arch Bks.

—Desert Danger, 1 vol. Le Feyer, Diane & Kennedy, Sam, illus. 2012. (Wild Rescue Ser.). (ENG.). 152p. (gr. 3-6). lib. bdg. 25.32 (978-1-4342-3773-6(7)) Stone Arch Bks.

Burkert, Rand. Mouse & Lion. Burkert, Nancy Ekholm, illus. 2011. (ENG.). 32p. (J). (gr. -1-3). 18.99 (978-0-545-10147-9(6), Di Capua, Michael) Scholastic, Inc.

Busch, Miriam. Lion, Lion. Day, Larry, illus. 2014. (ENG.). 32p. (J). (gr. -1-3). 17.99 (978-0-06-227104-4(0)) HarperCollins Pubs.

Bushar, Carol. Robby the Lion Doesn't Eat Meat. 2006. 30p. 12.96 (978-1-4116-9113-1(X)) Lulu Pr., Inc.

Buzzeo, Toni. Just Like My Papa. Wohnoutka, Mike, illus. 2017. (ENG.). 32p. (J). (gr. -1 — 1). bds. 6.99 (978-1-4847-8795-3(1)) Hyperion Bks. for Children.

Byrne, Lex. Ever Met the Hooferjackal? 2009. 32p. pap. 14.95 (978-1-4490-4630-9(4)) AuthorHouse.

Cebollero, Julie. The Lion That Roared. 2012. (ENG.). 61p. pap. 9.95 (978-1-4327-8067-8(0)) Outskirts Pr., Inc.

Chalekian, Bobbie. The Legend of the Lamb & the Lion. 2011. 32p. (gr. 2-4). pap. 14.99 (978-1-4567-2713-0(3)) AuthorHouse.

Chidebelu-Eze / Dove Publishing, Chibueze Obi. The Lion That Finally Roared: Inspirational Story of Purpose & Destiny. Newborne, David / F., illus. 2008. 80p. (J). 17.99 (978-0-9766578-5-9(6)); pap. 11.99 (978-0-9766578-6-6(4)) Dove Publishing, Inc.

Cobb, Amelia. The Lonely Lion Cub. 2016. (Zoe's Rescue Zoo Ser.: 1). (ENG., Illus.). 128p. (J). (gr. 2-5). pap. 4.99 (978-0-545-84220-4(4), Scholastic Paperbacks) Scholastic, Inc.

Collingridge, Richard. Lionheart. 2016. (ENG., Illus.). 32p. (J). (gr. -1-k). 17.99 (978-0-545-83321-9(3)) Scholastic, Inc.

Cook, Gina J. Just a Little Lion: A Little Cheetah Learns the Truth about Little Lions As We Learn the Truth about Little Lies. 2012. 38p. pap. 13.95 (978-1-4497-6352-7(9), WestBow Pr.) Author Solutions, Inc.

Corder, Zizou. Lionboy. 2004. (ENG., Illus.). 304p. (J). (gr. 3-7). reprint ed. pap. 8.99 (978-0-14-240226-9(5), Puffin Books) Penguin Young Readers Group.

—Lionboy: The Truth. 2006. (ENG., Illus.). 240p. (J). (gr. 3-7). 7.99 (978-0-14-240705-9(4), Puffin Books) Penguin Young Readers Group.

Crowley, Jennifer Brasington. Lyndsay & Lainey Lion: E Is for Dragon. 2012. (ENG.). (J). pap. (978-1-4675-5417-6(0)) Independent Pub.

—Lyndsay & Lainey Lion: F Is for Dragon. 2012. (ENG.). (J). pap. (978-1-4675-5418-3(9)) Independent Pub.

Crowley, Jennifer Brasington, ed. Lyndsay & Lainey Lion: D Is for Dragon. 2012. (ENG.). (J). pap. (978-1-4675-5416-9(2)) Independent Pub.

Curry, Kenneth. Mandu & Minka. 2007. (Illus.). 22p. (J). 10.95 (978-0-9798364-7-3(6)) Curry Brothers Publishing Group.

Danby, Aaron. Jazzmin's Jamboree. Martin, M. J., illus. 2005. 40p. 13.95 (978-0-9730583-3-8(1)) Lion & Mouse Tales, Inc. CAN. Dist: Hushion Hse. Publishing, Ltd.

Davies, Nicola. The Lion Who Stole My Arm. Wright, Annabel, illus. 2014. (Heroes of the Wild Ser.). (ENG.). 96p. (J). (gr. 2-5). 14.99 (978-0-7636-6620-0(3)) Candlewick Pr.

Dean, Walter. How Leo the Lion Learned to Roar. 2013. 44p. pap. 12.95 (978-0-9844342-6-8(7)) C&K Publishing Co.

—How Leo the Lion Learned to Roar Student/ Teacher Workbook. 2013. 54p. pap. 14.95 (978-0-9844342-5-1(9)) C&K Publishing Co.

Debesay, Samson. Cubby, the Lionsheep: Son, you are a lion, live like One! 2011. (Illus.). 24p. pap. 14.89 (978-1-4567-7899-6(4)) AuthorHouse.

Del Riego, Erica. The Heart of Life. 2010. 36p. pap. 17.75 (978-1-4389-7572-6(4)) AuthorHouse.

Depken, Kristen L. & Jackson, Kathryn. Tawny Scrawny Lion. DiCicco, Sue, illus. 2016. (Step into Reading Ser.). (ENG.). 32p. (J). (gr. -1-1). pap. 3.99 (978-1-101-93424-1(7), Random Hse. Bks. for Young Readers) Random Hse. Children's Bks.

Dharma Publishing Staff. The Power of a Promise: A Story about the Power of Keeping Promises. 2010. (ENG.). 36p. (gr. -1-7). pap. 8.95 (978-0-89800-603-2(1)) Dharma Publishing.

—The Rabbit Who Overcame Fear: A Story about Wise Action. 2nd ed. 2013. (ENG.). 36p. (gr. -1-7). pap. 8.95 (978-0-89800-492-2(6)) Dharma Publishing.

—The Value of Friends: A Story about Helping Friends in Need. 2nd ed. 2015. (ENG.). 36p. (gr. -1-7). pap. 8.95 (978-0-89800-493-9(4)) Dharma Publishing.

Disney Book Group. The Lion Guard Adventures of the Lion Guard: Board Book Box Set. Disney Storybook Art Team, illus. 2017. (ENG.). 40p. (J). (gr. -1-k). 10.99 (978-1-4847-8250-7(X)) Disney Pr.

—The Lion Guard Babysitter Bunga. Disney Storybook Art Team, illus. 2017. (ENG.). 24p. (J). (gr. -1-k). pap. 4.99 (978-1-4847-8868-4(0)) Disney Pr.

—Lion Guard Bunga the Wise. Disney Storybook Art Team, illus. 2016. (World of Reading Ser.). (ENG.). 32p. (J). (gr. -1-k). pap. 3.99 (978-1-4847-1967-1(0)) Disney Pr.

—Lion Guard Can't Wait to Be Queen. Disney Storybook Art Team, illus. 2016. (ENG.). 24p. (J). (gr. -1-k). pap. 4.99 (978-1-4847-1912-1(3)) Disney Pr.

—The Lion Guard Finding a New Family. Disney Storybook Art Team, illus. 2016. (ENG.). 24p. (J). (gr. -1-k). pap. 4.99 (978-1-4847-5642-3(8)) Disney Pr.

—The Lion Guard Join the Lion Guard! Disney Storybook Art Team, illus. 2016. (ENG.). 10p. (J). (gr. -1-k). bds. 7.99 (978-1-4847-4678-3(3)) Disney Pr.

—Lion Guard Meet the New Guard. Disney Storybook Art Team, illus. 2016. (ENG.). 10p. (J). (gr. -1-k). bds. 8.99 (978-1-4847-1914-5(X)) Disney Pr.

—The Lion Guard Not So Different. Disney Storybook Art Team, illus. 2016. (World of Reading Ser.). (ENG.). 32p. (J). (gr. -1-k). pap. 3.99 (978-1-4847-5643-0(6)) Disney Pr.

—The Lion Guard Read-Along Storybook & CD the Power of the Roar. Disney Storybook Art Team, illus. 2017. (Read-Along Storybook & CD Ser.). (ENG.). 32p. (J). (gr. -1-k). pap. 6.99 (978-1-4847-2950-2(1)) Disney Pr.

—Lion Guard Return of the Roar. Disney Storybook Art Team, illus. 2015. (ENG.). 40p. (J). (gr. -1-k). 16.99 (978-1-4847-1551-2(9)) Disney Pr.

Disney Editors. Disney the Lion King Movie Comic. 2016. (ENG.). 64p. (J). (gr. 4-7). 18.40 (978-0-606-39084-2(7)) Turtleback Bks.

Disney Enterprises Inc. Staff, creator. Disney Caritas Felices: Simba. 2007. (Illus.). 8p. (J). (gr. -1). (978-970-718-392-6(6), Silver Dolphin en Español) Advanced Marketing, S. de R. L. de C. V.

Disney Press Staff & Disney Book Group Staff. The Lion King. 2011. (Read-Along Storybook & CD Ser.). (ENG.). 32p. (J). (gr. -1 — 1). pap. 6.99 (978-1-4231-3768-9(X)) Disney Pr.

Disney Storybook Artists Staff, et al, illus. Disney's the Lion King. 2007. (Play-A-Sound Ser.). 16p. (J). (gr. -1-3). 16.98 (978-1-4127-8776-5(9)) Publications International, Ltd.

Dony, John. Leah's Lions. 2nd ed. 2012. (ENG.). 62p. (J). 15.99 (978-0-9854076-6-7(2)) Dewberry Pr.

Douglas, Babette. The Lyon Bear. Johnson, John, illus. 2006. (Kiss a Me Teacher Creature Stories Ser.). (J). (gr. -1-3). 9.99 (978-1-890343-18-7(8)) Kiss A Me Productions, Inc.

Dubuc, Marianne, creator. The Lion & the Bird. 2014. (ENG., Illus.). 64p. (J). (gr. -1). 17.95 (978-1-59270-151-3(5)) Enchanted Lion Bks., LLC.

Duey, Kathleen. Leo: A Baby Lion's Story. Gurin, Lara, illus. 2008. (My Animal Family Ser.). 32p. (J). (gr. -1-3). 12.99 (978-0-8249-1817-0(7), Ideal Pubns.) Worthy Publishing.

—Leo the Lion - Book & Dvd. Gurin, Laura, illus. 2007. 32p. 14.99 (978-0-8249-6724-6(0), Ideal Pubns.) Worthy Publishing.

—Nanuq: A Baby Polar Bear's Story. Gurin, Lara, illus. 2008. (ENG.). 32p. (J). (gr. -1-3). 12.99 (978-0-8249-1818-7(5), Ideal Pubns.) Worthy Publishing.

Dynamo. Googly Eyes: Leo Lion's Noisy Roar! 2014. (ENG., Illus.). 12p. (J). (gr. -1-2). bds. 6.99 (978-1-84322-906-3(4), Armadillo) Anness Publishing GBR. Dist: National Bk. Network.

Easton, Marilyn. Eris to the Rescue. 2013. (LEGO Legends of Chima: Comic Reader Ser.: 3). lib. bdg. 13.55 (978-0-606-32398-7(8), Turtleback) Turtleback Bks.

Ebwelleson, Nelson. The Helpless King. 2012. 24p. pap. 17.99 (978-1-4772-8262-5(9)) AuthorHouse.

Edwards, Pamela Duncan. Roar! A Noisy Counting Book. Cole, Henry, illus. Date not set. 32p. (J). (gr. -1-2). pap. 5.99 (978-0-06-443572-7(5)) HarperCollins Pubs.

Emberley, Rebecca & Emberley, Ed. The Lion & the Mice. 2011. (I Like to Read(r) Ser.). (ENG., Illus.). 24p. (J). (gr. -1-2). 14.95 (978-0-8234-2357-6(3)) Holiday Hse., Inc.

Emberley, Rebecca & Emberley, Edward R. The Lion & the Mice. Emberley, Rebecca & Emberley, Edward R., illus. 2012. (I Like to Read(r) Ser.). (ENG., Illus.). 24p. (J). (gr. -1-2). pap. 6.99 (978-0-8234-2641-6(6)) Holiday Hse., Inc.

Esopo. EL LEÓN Y EL RATÓN. 2004. (Caballo Alado Clásicos-Al Galope Ser.). (SPA & ENG., Illus.). 24p. (J). (gr. k-2). 7.95 (978-84-7864-784-2(8)) Combel Editorial, S.A. ESP. Dist: Independent Pubs. Group.

Evans, Robert J. Dorothy's Mystical Adventures in Oz. 2004. reprint ed. pap. 1.99 (978-1-4192-1658-9(9)) Kessinger Publishing, LLC.

Everett, George W. G. W. Frog & the Circus Lion. 2010. 32p. 16.95 (978-1-4497-0443-8(3), WestBow Pr.) Author Solutions, Inc.

Farshtey, Greg. Beware of the Wolves. 2013. (LEGO Legends of Chima Chapter Bks.: 2). lib. bdg. 14.75 (978-0-606-32014-6(8), Turtleback) Turtleback Bks.

Fatio, Louise. The Happy Lion. Duvoisin, Roger, illus. (ENG.). 40p. (J). (gr. -1-2). 2015. 6.99 (978-0-553-50850-5(4), Dragonfly Bks.) 2010. pap. 7.99 (978-0-553-11364-8(X), Dragonfly Bks.) 2004. 16.99 (978-0-375-82759-4(5), Knopf Bks. for Young Readers) Random Hse. Children's Bks.

Fisher, Barbara. Nobody's Lion. Huismann, Duane, illus. 2004. (J). per. 16.95 (978-1-59571-049-9(3)) Word Association Pubs.

Fisscher, Tiny. RUBY & the LION. 2008. (ENG.). 48p. (J). (gr. 1-7). 11.95 (978-1-60136-014-4(2)) Audio Holdings, LLC.

Foley, Greg. Willoughby & the Lion. Foley, Greg, illus. 2009. (ENG., Illus.). 40p. (J). (gr. -1-2). 17.99 (978-0-06-154750-8(6)) HarperCollins Pubs.

Fontes, Justine & Korman, Justine. The Lion King. Golden Books Staff et al, illus. 2003. (Little Golden Book Ser.). (ENG.). 24p. (J). (gr. -1-2). 4.99 (978-0-7364-2095-2(9), Golden/Disney) Random Hse. Children's Bks.

Foust, Cindy. Louis Lion. 2008. (J). 12.94 (978-0-9749220-7-2(2)) Alpha-kidZ.

Franciosa, John F. Little Johnny Lion. 2009. 24p. pap. 11.99 (978-1-4389-8810-8(9)) AuthorHouse.

Fuerst, Jeff. The Lion & the Rabbit: A Fable from India. 2006. (J). pap. (978-1-4108-7156-5(8)) Benchmark Education Co.

Galvin, Laura Gates. Norman the Lion. Leeper, Christopher, illus. 2005. (African Wildlife Foundation Ser.). (ENG.). 36p. (J). (gr. -1-2). 2.95 *(978-1-59249-191-9(X)*, S6553) Soundprints.

—Norman the Lion. Leeper, Christopher J., tr. Leeper, Christopher J., illus. 2005. (African Wildlife Foundation Ser.). (ENG.). 36p. (J). (gr. -1-2). 14.95 *(978-1-59249-189-6(8)*, H6503); pap. 6.95 *(978-1-59249-190-2(1)*, S6503) Soundprints.

—Norman the Lion. Leeper, Christopher, illus. 2004. (ENG.). 36p. (J). (gr. -1-2). 9.95 *(978-1-59249-192-6(8)*, PS6553); 8.95 *(978-1-59249-208-4(8)*, SD6503) Soundprints.

Gerovasiliou, Oreanthy. Yuri the Lion: Three Stories. 2010. (Illus.). 48p. pap. 13.00 *(978-1-60888-069-0(9))* Nimble Bks. LLC.

Godley, Christina. Lion at the Gateway. 2010. 36p. pap. 16.99 *(978-1-4520-4508-5(9))* AuthorHouse.

Grant, Carrie and David. Lion's Speedy Sauce: Jump up & Join In. Busby, Ailie, illus. 2013. 32p. (J). pap. 7.99 *(978-1-61067-180-4(5))* Kane Miller.

Graves, Sue. Lion Is Worried. Dunton, Trevor, illus. 2016. (Behavior Matters Ser.). (ENG.). 32p. (J). (gr. 3-2). lib. bdg. 27.25 *(978-1-4994-8084-9(9)*, Windmill Bks.) Rosen Publishing Group, Inc., The.

Green, George & Brooke, Amy/ J. George Green's, the Lion Who Couldn't Roar. 2008. (Illus.). (J). per. 16.99 *(978-1-933156-14-9(7)*, Visikid Bks.) GSVQ Publishing.

Gregory, Steven. The Lion's Drum: A Retelling of an African Folk Tale. Obata, Claudia, illus. 2007. 32p. (J). 13.95 *(978-0-615-15540-1(5))* Words & Music.

Griffiths, Allen & Godinez, Mary. Rusty Finds a Home: A Christmas Miracle. Ulrich, Kelly, illus. 2012. 32p. pap. *(978-1-4602-0937-0(0))* FriesenPress.

Grover, Lorie Ann. Big Hug for Little Cub. Kightley, Rosalinda, illus. 2014. (ENG.). 18p. (J). (— 1). bds. 7.99 *(978-0-545-53091-0(1)*, Cartwheel Bks.) Scholastic, Inc.

Harrison, Paula. The Moonlight Mystery. 2013. (Rescue Princesses Ser.: 3). (ENG., Illus.). 128p. (J). (gr. 2-5). pap. 4.99 *(978-0-545-50915-2(7)*, Scholastic Paperbacks) Scholastic, Inc.

—The Moonlight Mystery. 2013. (Rescue Princesses Ser.: 3). lib. bdg. 14.75 *(978-0-606-31988-1(3)*, Turtleback) Turtleback Bks.

Hasan, K. A. Rufus' Big Scare. Primmasone, Bruce, illus. 2011. 48p. pap. 24.95 *(978-1-4626-0660-3(1))* America Star Bks.

Hiebert, Elfrieda H. & Juel, Connie. The Lion Roars. (Little Book Practice Reader Ser.). (J). *(978-0-8136-0895-2(3))* Modern Curriculum Pr.

Hockerman, Dennis, illus. The Lion & the Mouse: A Tale about Being Helpful. 2006. (J). 6.99 *(978-1-59939-007-9(8))* Cornerstone Pr.

Horácek, Petr. Silly Suzy Goose. Horácek, Petr, illus. 2009. (ENG., Illus.). 32p. (J). (— 1). bds. 7.99 *(978-0-7636-4141-2(3))* Candlewick Pr.

Howland, Leila. Nantucket Summer [Nantucket Blue & Nantucket Red Bind-Up]. 2017. (Nantucket Blue Ser.). (ENG.). 608p. (YA). (gr. 9-17). pap. 11.99 *(978-1-368-00212-7(9))* Hyperion Bks. for Children.

Huusmann, Thomas-Bo & Fables, Aesops. The Lion & the Mouse. 2013. 26p. pap. *(978-87-995724-4-1(3))* Huusmann, Thomas-Bo.

Ingram, Doreen. My Sanctuary: A Place I Call Home - Keepers of the Wild. Josh Green, illus. 2013. 54p. pap. 17.50 *(978-1-62516-273-1(1)*, Strategic Bk. Publishing) Strategic Book Publishing & Rights Agency (SBPRA).

Ismail, Yasmeen. Specs for Rex. 2015. (ENG., Illus.). 32p. (J). (gr. -1-3). 16.99 *(978-1-61963-710-8(3)*, 9781619637108, Bloomsbury USA Childrens) Bloomsbury Publishing USA.

Jackson, Kathryn. Tawney Scrawny Lion. Tenggren, Gustaf, illus. deluxe ed. Date not set. (J). (gr. -1-2). reprint ed. *(978-1-929566-61-7(1))* Cronies.

—Tawny Scrawny Lion: Classic Edition. Tenggren, Gustaf, illus. Date not set. 23p. (J). (gr. -1-1). reprint ed. *(978-1-929566-55-6(7))* Cronies.

Jarman, Julia. Lovely Old Lion. Varley, Susan, illus. 2015. (ENG.). 32p. (J). (gr. -1-3). 17.99 *(978-1-4677-9310-0(8))* Andersen Pr. GBR. Dist: Lerner Publishing Group.

—Lovely Old Lion. Varley, Susan, illus. 2015. (ENG.). 32p. (J). (gr. -1-3). 17.99 *(978-1-4677-9543-2(7))* Lerner Publishing Group.

Jenkins, Amanda. The Lion & the Mouse Shoot Hoops. 2006. (J). pap. *(978-1-4108-7173-2(8))* Benchmark Education Co.

Johnson, Sandi. The Peaceful Lion. Johnson, Britt, ed. Kraft, Lauri, illus. l.t. ed. 2014. (ENG.). 28p. (J). (gr. k-5). pap. 12.99 *(978-1-929063-95-6(4)*, 325) Moons & Stars Publishing For Children.

Jordan, Apple. Baboons! (Disney Junior: the Lion Guard) RH Disney, illus. 2017. (Little Golden Book Ser.). (ENG.). 24p. (J). (-k). 4.99 *(978-0-7364-3563-5(8)*, Golden/Disney) Random Hse. Children's Bks.

—Eye in the Sky (Disney Junior: the Lion Guard) RH Disney Staff et al, illus. 2016. (Little Golden Book Ser.). (ENG.). 24p. (J). (-k). 4.99 *(978-0-7364-3500-0(X)*, Golden/Disney) Random Hse. Children's Bks.

Joven, John, illus. The Wounded Lion: A Tale from Spain. 2013. (Tales of Honor (Red Chair Press) Ser.). (ENG.). 32p. (J). (gr. 1-4). lib. bdg. 26.60 *(978-1-937529-79-6(7))* Red Chair Pr.

Judith Anne Moody. Golden Eye & the Killer Cat. 2009. 248p. pap. 19.49 *(978-1-4251-7684-6(4))* Trafford Publishing.

Kasza, Keiko. The Mightiest. 2003. (ENG., Illus.). 32p. (J). (gr. -1-k). pap. 5.99 *(978-0-14-250185-6(9)*, Puffin Books) Penguin Young Readers Group.

Kellogg, Elijah. Lion Ben of Elm Island. 2005. pap. 27.95 *(978-1-4179-9427-4(4))* Kessinger Publishing, LLC.

Kerr, Valerie. The Adventures of Selwyn & Robert: Saving Whako the White Lion. 2013. 40p. pap. 16.46 *(978-1-4669-9252-8(2))* Trafford Publishing.

Kilimo, R. The, Donkey Who Wanted to Be a Lion. 2004. (Illus.). 16p. pap. *(978-9966-25-169-5(3))* Heinemann Kenya, Limited (East African Educational Publishers Ltd E.A.E.P.) KEN. Dist: Michigan State Univ. Pr.

King, Trey. The Legend Begins. 2013. (LEGO Legends of Chima: Comic Reader Ser.: 1). lib. bdg. 13.55 *(978-0-606-32012-2(1)*, Turtleback) Turtleback Bks.

Kinney, Kendall. Tiger Tails. 2004. 68p. (J). per. 10.95 *(978-1-932196-21-4(8))* WordWright.biz, Inc.

Knudsen, Michelle. Library Lion. Hawkes, Kevin, illus. 2006. (ENG.). 48p. (J). (gr. -1-3). 16.99 *(978-0-7636-2262-6(1))* Candlewick Pr.

—Library Lion. Hawkes, Kevin, illus. 2009. (ENG.). 48p. (J). (gr. -1-3). pap. 6.99 *(978-0-7636-3784-2(X))* Candlewick Pr.

—Library Lion. 2009. lib. bdg. 17.20 *(978-0-606-06666-2(7)*, Turtleback) Turtleback Bks.

Koffsky, Ann D., illus. Shabbat Shalom, Hey! 2015. (J). (ENG.). 24p. (gr. -1-k). lib. bdg. 16.95 *(978-1-4677-4917-6(6))*; 6.99 *(978-1-4677-6208-3(3))* Lerner Publishing Group. (Kar-Ben Publishing).

Kompelien, Tracy. Lion Manes, 1 vol. Haberstroh, Anne, illus. 2006. (Animal Tales Ser.). (ENG.). 24p. (J). (gr. k-3). lib. bdg. 24.21 *(978-1-59679-949-3(8)*, SandCastle) ABDO Publishing Co.

—Lion Manes. Nobens, C. A., illus. 2006. (Fact & Fiction Ser.). 24p. (J). pap. 48.42 *(978-1-59679-950-9(1))* ABDO Publishing Co.

Krensky, Stephen. The Lion & the Hare. Reeves, Jeni, illus. 2008. (On My Own Folklore Ser.). (ENG.). 48p. (gr. 2-4). lib. bdg. 25.26 *(978-0-8225-7546-7(9)*, Millbrook Pr.) Lerner Publishing Group.

La Coccinella. Here Comes Leo Lion. 2015. (Pull & Play Ser.). (ENG., Illus.). 12p. (J). (gr. -1-k). bds. 7.95 *(978-1-4549-1582-9(X))* Sterling Publishing Co., Inc.

Lamb, Jim. Ryan the Lion Finds His Roar. Schallmo, Carolyn, illus. 2011. 32p. 22.95 *(978-1-60844-880-7(0))*; pap. 12.95 *(978-1-60844-879-1(7))* Dog Ear Publishing, LLC.

Latimer, Alex. Lion vs Rabbit, 1 vol. Latimer, Alex, illus. 2013. (ENG., Illus.). 32p. (J). (gr. -1-3). 15.95 *(978-1-56145-709-0(4))* Peachtree Pubs.

Latimer, Alex. Lion vs. Rabbit, 1 vol. Latimer, Alex, illus. 2017. (ENG., Illus.). 32p. (J). (gr. -1-3). pap. 7.95 ***(978-1-56145-898-1(8))*** Peachtree Pubs.

Law, Felicia. Limpopo the Lion: A Tale of Laziness & Lethargy. Messina, Lilli, illus. 2010. (Animal Fair Values Ser.). 32p. (J). (gr. -1-3). pap. 10.55 *(978-1-60754-808-9(9))*; lib. bdg. 22.60 *(978-1-60754-804-1(6))* Windmill Bks.

LeapFrog Staff. Disney Lion King - U. K. 2003. (Illus.). spiral bd. 14.99 *(978-1-59319-006-4(9))* LeapFrog Enterprises, Inc.

Lewis, C. S. The Lion, the Witch & the Wardrobe. 2008. (Chronicles of Narnia Ser.: 2). (J). 18.40 *(978-0-613-94066-5(0)*, Turtleback) Turtleback Bks.

The Lion & the Hare: [an East African Folktale]. 2009. (On My Own Folklore Ser.). (gr. 3-5). pap. 6.95 *(978-1-58013-849-9(7)*, First Avenue Editions) Lerner Publishing Group.

Lion Country. 2003. (J). per. *(978-1-884907-38-8(5))*; per. *(978-1-884907-39-5(3))* Paradise Pr., Inc.

Lion King: Far from the Pridelands. (Read-Along Ser.). (J). 7.99 incl. audio *(978-1-55723-673-9(9))* Walt Disney Records.

Lion's Mane. Date not set. (Touch & Feel Ser.). (J). 4.98 *(978-0-7525-9569-6(5))* Parragon, Inc.

The Little Lion. (Early Intervention Levels Ser.). 21.30 *(978-0-7362-0367-8(2))* CENGAGE Learning.

Lochmandy, Sandy. Kids & Critters on an Adventure. 2009. 36p. pap. 14.95 *(978-1-60860-387-9(3)*, Eloquent Bks.) Strategic Book Publishing & Rights Agency (SBPRA).

Loesch, Joe. Lions, Lions Everywhere: The Story of Daniel as told by God's Animals. Hutchinson, Cheryl, ed. Cox, Brain T., illus. 2004. (Bible Stories for Kids Ser.). 56p. (J). bds. 16.95 incl. audio compact disk *(978-1-932332-24-7(3))* Toy Box Productions.

Long, Ethan. Lion & Tiger & Bear: Tag! You're It! 2016. (Lion & Tiger & Bear Ser.). (ENG., Illus.). 40p. (J). (gr. k-2). 14.95 *(978-1-4197-1896-0(7))* Abrams, Inc.

Mahy, Margaret. A Lion in the Meadow. 2013. (ENG., Illus.). 32p. (gr. 4-13). 17.95 *(978-1-4683-0665-1(0)*, 460665) Overlook Pr., The.

Martin, Janelle. Lexis, the Hiccupping Lion. 2013. 12p. pap. 7.95 *(978-1-4908-0545-0(1)*, WestBow Pr.) Author Solutions, Inc.

Marwood, Diane. The Lion & the Mouse. 2012. (ENG., Illus.). 24p. (J). *(978-0-7787-7893-6(2))*; pap. *(978-0-7787-7905-6(X))* Crabtree Publishing Co.

Mason, Charlene. Landon's Backyard Adventures. 2012. 24p. pap. 24.95 *(978-1-4626-7470-1(4))* America Star Bks.

Mason, Jane B. Attack of the Cheetah, 1 vol. Schoening, Dan, illus. 2013. (Wonder Woman Ser.). (ENG.). 56p. (gr. 2-3). pap. 4.95 *(978-1-4342-2254-1(3)*, DC Super Heroes) Stone Arch Bks.

Matteren, Joanne. The Old Lion & the Fox. 2005. (J). pap. *(978-1-4108-4206-0(1))* Benchmark Education Co.

McBrayer, Cassidy. You Can, Toucan! You Can. 2008. 20p. pap. 15.95 *(978-1-4327-1132-0(6))* Outskirts Pr., Inc.

McCall Smith, Alexander. The Mystery of the Missing Lion: A Precious Ramotswe Mystery for Young Readers. 2014. (Precious Ramotswe Mysteries for Young Readers Ser.: 3). (ENG., Illus.). 112p. (J). (gr. 2-5). pap. 6.99 *(978-0-8041-7327-8(3)*, Anchor) Knopf Doubleday Publishing Group.

McElligott, Matthew. The Lion's Share. McElligott, Matthew, illus. 2012. (ENG., Illus.). 40p. (J). (gr. k-8). pap. 8.99 *(978-0-8027-2360-4(8)*, 9780802723604, Bloomsbury USA Childrens) Bloomsbury Publishing USA.

—The Lion's Share: A Tale of Halving Cake & Eating It, Too. McElligott, Matthew, illus. 2009. (ENG., Illus.). 32p. (J). (gr. k-3). 16.99 *(978-0-8027-9768-1(7)*, 9780802797681, Bloomsbury USA Childrens) Bloomsbury Publishing USA.

McGonagle, Joanne L. The Tiniest Tiger. 2008. (ENG.). 52p. pap. 15.00 *(978-1-4196-8467-8(1))* CreateSpace Independent Publishing Platform.

McKayhan, Norma J. The Mighty King & the Small Creature. 2012. 24p. pap. 12.55 *(978-1-4669-1463-6(7))* Trafford Publishing.

McKendry, Sam. Are You Ticklish? Mitchell, Melanie, illus. 2006. (ENG.). 12p. (J). (gr. -1-18). bds. 10.95 *(978-1-58117-376-5(8)*, Intervisual/Piggy Toes) Bendon, Inc.

—Are You Ticklish? Mitchell, Melanie, illus. 2008. (ENG.). 12p. (J). bds. 5.95 *(978-1-58117-706-0(2)*, Intervisual/Piggy Toes) Bendon, Inc.

McKenzie, Larry. Leonardo the Lopsided Lion. 2012. 28p. pap. 16.09 *(978-1-4669-5979-8(7))* Trafford Publishing.

McOmber, Rachel B., ed. McOmber Phonics Storybooks: Chatsworth. rev. ed. (Illus.). (J). *(978-0-944991-74-9(2))* Swift Learning Resources.

McPhail, David. Pig Pig Meets the Lion. McPhail, David, illus. 2012. (Illus.). pap. 15.95 *(978-1-60734-080-5(1))*; (ENG., 32p. (J). (gr. -1-3). 15.95 *(978-1-58089-358-9(9))* Charlesbridge Publishing, Inc.

Meachen Rau, Dana. The Lion in the Grass. 2006. (Nature Ser.). (SPA., Illus.). 24p. (gr. k-1). lib. bdg. 15.95 *(978-0-7614-2305-8(2)*, Benchmark Bks.) Marshall Cavendish Corp.

Mehlhaff, Christine. Don't Talk to Strangers. Ember, Kathi, illus. 2007. (J). *(978-0-545-00103-8(X))* Scholastic, Inc.

Mejuto, Eva. Run Pumpkin, Run. 2007. (ENG., Illus.). 36p. (J). 17.95 *(978-84-96788-88-6(1))* OQO, Editora ESP. Dist: Baker & Taylor Bks.

Merlo, Maria. El Leon Ruge. Keeter, Susan, illus. 2012. (SPA.). 16p. (J). pap. 54.70 *(978-0-663-62198-9(4))* Silver, Burdett & Ginn, Inc.

Messimer, Wanda Fay. Tiny Teacup & Pot Belly Pig Go to Africa to Meet the 'Great Lion' 2013. 24p. pap. 24.95 *(978-1-4626-8736-7(9))* America Star Bks.

Millett, Peter & Wallace-Mitchell, Jane. Lions! 2008. (Rigby Focus Forward: Level G Ser.). (Illus.). 24p. (J). (gr. 4-7). pap. *(978-1-4190-3717-7(X)*, Rigby) Pearson Education Australia.

Modern Publishing Staff. ABCs! 2007. (Disney Bath Time Bubble Bks.). (Illus.). (J). (gr. -1-k). 4.99 *(978-0-7666-2551-8(6))* Modern Publishing.

Muller, Hildegard. Reach for the Moon, Little Lion. 2017. (ENG.). 32p. (J). (gr. -1-3). 16.95 *(978-0-8234-3777-1(9))* Holiday Hse., Inc.

Mullins, Rebecca. Tristan, 1 vol. 2009. 23p. pap. 24.95 *(978-1-60672-257-2(3))* America Star Bks.

Myers, Don. My Life with Roger. 2009. (Illus.). 49p. (J). pap. 12.95 *(978-1-4327-3873-0(9))* Outskirts Pr., Inc.

The Mystery of the Lion's Tail. 2014. (Greetings from Somewhere Ser.: 5). (ENG., Illus.). 128p. (J). (gr. -1-4). pap. 5.99 *(978-1-4814-1464-7(X)*, Little Simon) Little Simon.

The Mystery of the Missing Lion: A Precious Ramotswe Mystery for Young Readers. 2014. (Precious Ramotswe Mysteries for Young Readers Ser.: 3). (ENG., Illus.). 112p. (J). (gr. 2-5). 12.99 *(978-1-101-87202-4(0)*, Anchor) Knopf Doubleday Publishing Group.

Nayer, Judy. Androcles & the Lion: An Aesop's Fable. 2006. (J). pap. *(978-1-4108-6165-8(1))* Benchmark Education Co.

O'Donnell, Shannon. The Lion's Son. 2012. 42p. 24.95 *(978-1-4626-5013-2(9))* America Star Bks.

Orr, Wendy. Abandoned! - A Lion Called Kiki. Castelao, Patricia, illus. 2012. (Rainbow Street Shelter Ser.: 4). (ENG.). 128p. (J). (gr. 2-5). 15.99 *(978-0-8050-9501-2(2)*, 9780805095012, Holt, Henry & Co. Bks. For Young Readers) Holt, Henry & Co.

Osborn School Students. Paw-Sing for Positive Daily Affirmations: Lion Pride. Rosa, M. Nina & Perrien, Vicki, eds. 2003. (J). pap. 16.99 *(978-0-9740267-0-1(0))* Mz. Rosa Notions.

Osborne, Mary Pope. Lions at Lunchtime. unabr. ed. 2004. (Magic Tree House Ser.: No. 11). 70p. (J). (gr. k-3). pap. 17.00 incl. audio *(978-0-8072-0536-5(2)*, Listening Library) Random Hse. Audio Publishing Group.

Otukile, Mpho. The Lion's Deceit. Dow, S. B., illus. 2011. (ENG.). 32p. (J). pap. *(978-0-9867460-0-0(2))* Village Life Bks.

Papineau, Lucie. Leonardo le Lionceau. 2004. (FRE., Illus.). (J). (gr. k-3). spiral bd. *(978-0-616-07264-6(3))* Canadian National Institute for the Blind/Institut National Canadien pour les Aveugles.

Parker, Emma & Aesop. The Lion & the Mouse. 2010. (Illus.). pap. *(978-1-877547-45-4(X))* First Edition Ltd.

Parragon Staff. Lion King. 2010. (Disney Diecut Classics). 72p. (J). (gr. -1-1). *(978-1-4075-8936-7(9))* Parragon, Inc.

Paulus, Kristin Harkison. There's a Lion on the Dance Floor. 2010. (Illus.). 28p. pap. 12.98 *(978-1-4490-2692-9(3))* AuthorHouse.

Peters, Andrew Fusek. Rabbit Cooks up a Cunning Plan! Robert, Bruno, illus. 2007. (Traditional Tales with a Twist Ser.). (ENG.). 32p. (J). (gr. 2-2). pap. *(978-1-84643-097-8(6))* Child's Play International Ltd.

Pierce, Tamora. Lioness Rampant. unabr. ed. 2004. (Song of the Lioness Ser.: Bk. 4). 308p. (J). (gr. 6-18). pap. 38.00 incl. audio *(978-0-8072-0965-1(6)*, S YA 388 SP, Listening Library) Random Hse. Audio Publishing Group.

—Lioness Rampant. 2005. (Song of the Lioness Ser.: 4). (ENG.). 400p. (YA). (gr. 7). mass mkt. 7.99 *(978-0-689-87857-2(5)*, Simon Pulse) Simon Pulse.

Pistinier, Caroline. ThÃ(c)o et le Lion. 2010. (FRE.). 32p. pap. 17.95 *(978-1-4457-7871-6(8))* Lulu Pr., Inc.

pistinier, caroline. Théo & the Lion. 2010. 32p. pap. 17.95 *(978-1-4457-8804-3(7))* Lulu Pr., Inc.

Pogo the Clown. A Brave Little Lion: Harley's Great Adventures. Miller, Richard D., illus. 2005. (J). 12.95 *(978-0-9755253-5-7(2))* Chiliric Pubns.

Posner-Sanchez, Andrea. Follow That Hippo! (Disney Junior: the Lion Guard) Cortes, Mario & Colletti, Marco, illus. 2016. (Big Golden Book Ser.). (ENG.). 32p. (J). (-k). 9.99 *(978-0-7364-3391-4(0)*, Golden/Disney) Random Hse. Children's Bks.

Powell, Daniel M. King Grrr-egory & the Angel. 2010. 26p. 13.99 *(978-0-557-53182-0(9))* Lulu Pr., Inc.

Powell, Richard. Leo Lion. Rhodes, Katie, illus. 2004. (Fuzzy Friends Ser.). 10p. (J). 7.95 *(978-1-58925-719-1(7))* Tiger Tales.

Price, Olivia. Bible Stories: A Touch & Feel Book. Mitchell, Melanie, illus. 2008. (ENG.). 12p. (J). (gr. -1). 12.95 *(978-1-58117-802-9(6)*, Intervisual/Piggy Toes) Bendon, Inc.

Proimos, James, Jr. Apocalypse Meow Meow. Proimos, James, Jr., illus. 2015. (ENG., Illus.). 224p. (J). (gr. 3-6). 13.99 *(978-1-61963-472-5(4)*, 9781619634725, Bloomsbury USA Childrens) Bloomsbury Publishing USA.

Publications International Ltd. Staff, ed. Disney Lion King - We Can Share. 2011. 12p. (J). bds. *(978-1-4508-1383-9(6))* Publications International, Ltd.

Pugliano-Martin, Carol. Little Lion. 2011. (Early Connections Ser.). (J). *(978-1-61672-585-3(0))* Benchmark Education Co.

—Little Lion: Set Of 6. 2011. (Early Connections Ser.). (J). pap. 37.00 net. *(978-1-4108-1092-2(5))* Benchmark Education Co.

Ready Reader Staff. Glenda the Lion, 6 bks., set, Level 6, Bk. 25. 2003. (J). (gr. -1-3). pap. 33.50 *(978-0-8136-2051-0(1))* Modern Curriculum Pr.

Remey, Grace Anne. Lion's Pride: A Tail of Deployment. Remey, Grace Anne, illus. 2012. (ENG., Illus.). 38p. pap. 12.95 *(978-0-9855445-0-8(3))* Remey, Lisa.

Rempel, Jennifer, illus. Lavi the Lion Finds His Pride. 2005. (J). 15.95 *(978-0-9744715-2-5(6)*, Towers Maguire Publishing) Local History Co., The.

Rice, Dona Herwick. The Lion & the Mouse, 1 vol. 2008. (Building Fluency Through Reader's Theater Ser.). (ENG.). 24p. (J). (gr. 1-3). pap. 6.99 *(978-1-4333-0293-0(4))* Teacher Created Materials, Inc.

Richardson, Justin & Parnell, Peter. Christian, the Hugging Lion. Bates, Amy June, illus. 2010. (ENG.). 32p. (J). (gr. -1-3). 16.99 *(978-1-4169-8662-1(6)*, Simon & Schuster Bks. For Young Readers) Simon & Schuster Bks. For Young Readers.

Rigo, L. Little Lion. 2012. (Look at Me Bks.). (ENG., Illus.). 10p. (J). bds. 7.99 *(978-0-7641-6525-2(9))* Barron's Educational Series, Inc.

Robaard, Jedda. The Little Lion Who Lost Her Roar. 2014. (Illus.). 9p. (J). *(978-1-4351-5391-2(X))* Barnes & Noble, Inc.

Robertson, Rachel. When You Just Have to Roar! Prentice, Priscilla, illus. 2015. (ENG.). 32p. (J). (gr. -1-k). 15.95 *(978-1-60554-362-8(4))* Redleaf Pr.

Rock, Lois. The Lion First Book of Nursery Stories. Vagnozzi, Barbara, illus. 2013. (ENG.). 96p. (J). (gr. -1-k). 16.99 *(978-0-7459-6341-9(2))* Lion Hudson PLC GBR. Dist: Independent Pubs. Group.

Rogers, Terry, illus. Androcles & the Lion: A Roman Legend. 2003. (Dominie Collection of Myths & Legends). (SPA.). 20p. (J). lib. bdg. *(978-0-7685-2419-2(9))* Dominie Pr., Inc.

—Androcles & the Lion: A Roman Legend. 2004. (SPA & ENG.). 20p. (J). (gr. 3-3). pap. 6.47 net. *(978-0-7685-2122-1(X)*, Dominie Elementary) Pearson Schl.

Rose, Gerald. Horrible Melena. (SPA.). (J). 8.95 *(978-958-04-7343-5(9))* Norma S.A. COL. Dist: Distribuidora Norma, Inc.

Safari Press Staff, ed. Book Buddy - Lion with Story Book. (Illus.). 10p. (J). (gr. -1-3). pap. *(978-1-881469-84-1(0))* Safari, Ltd.

Schmidt, Troy. The Lion Tells His Side of the Story: Hey God, I'm Starving in This Den So Why Won't You Let Me Eat This Guy Named Daniel?! Jones, Cory, illus. 2014. (ENG.). 32p. (gr. -1-3). 9.99 *(978-1-4336-8310-7(5)*, B&H Kids) B&H Publishing Group.

Sendak, Maurice. Pierre Board Book: A Cautionary Tale in Five Chapters & a Prologue. Sendak, Maurice, illus. 2017. (Illus.). 38p. (J). (gr. -1-3). bds. 7.95 *(978-0-06-266810-3(2))* HarperCollins Pubs.

Senior, Patricia. Mischief on Mumpit Mountain. 2009. 36p. pap. 14.75 *(978-1-60693-661-0(1)*, Eloquent Bks.) Strategic Book Publishing & Rights Agency (SBPRA).

Shaw, Rebecca. Elisha's Great Mission. 2010. 32p. pap. 11.95 *(978-1-935268-43-7(0))* Halo Publishing International.

Shepherd, Keith D., illus. Kumba & Kambili: A Tale from Mali. 2013. (Tales of Honor Ser.). (ENG.). 32p. (J). (gr. 1-4). pap. 8.95 *(978-1-937529-58-1(4))* Red Chair Pr.

Shepherd, Keith D., illus. & retold by. Kumba & Kambili: A Tale from Mali. Shepherd, Keith D., retold by. 2013. (Tales of Honor (Red Chair Press) Ser.). (ENG.). 32p. (J). (gr. 1-4). lib. bdg. 26.60 *(978-1-937529-74-1(6))* Red Chair Pr.

Shirley, Alice. The Gentle Lion & the Little Owlet. Shirley, Alice, illus. 2013. Orig. Title: Owlet & Pussycat. (ENG., Illus.). 32p. (J). (gr. -1-k). pap. 8.99 *(978-1-84365-199-4(8)*, Pavilion) Pavilion Bks. GBR. Dist: Independent Pubs. Group.

Silverstein, Shel. Lafcadio, el Leon Que Disparo al Cazador. Rioja, Alberto Jimenez, tr. from ENG. 2011.Tr. of Lafcadio, the Lion Who Shot Back. (SPA., Illus.). 112p. (J). (gr. 2-3). pap. 16.99 *(978-1-933032-74-0(X))* Lectorum Pubns., Inc.

—Lafcadio, the Lion Who Shot Back. Silverstein, Shel, illus. 2013. (ENG., Illus.). 112p. (J). (gr. -1-3). 16.99 *(978-0-06-025675-3(3))* HarperCollins Pubs.

—Lafcadio, the Lion Who Shot Back. 2009. (CHI., Illus.). (J). *(978-7-5442-4521-0(7))* Nanhai Publishing Co.

Simon, Mary Manz. Lion Can Share. Harris, Phyllis & Clearwater, Linda, illus. 2006. (First Virtuestm for Toddlers Ser.). 20p. (J). 5.99 *(978-0-7847-1576-5(9)*, 04070) Standard Publishing.

Sleepytime Lion. 2005. (J). *(978-0-9767179-5-9(6))* ABC Development, Inc.

Smalley, Roger, adapted by. The Big-Hearted Monkey & the Lion. 2005. (J). *(978-1-933248-02-8(5))* World Quest Learning.

Smith, Alex T. Little Red & the Very Hungry Lion. 2016. (ENG., Illus.). 32p. (J). (gr. -1-k). 17.99 *(978-0-545-91438-3(8)*, Scholastic Pr.) Scholastic, Inc.

Smith, Carrie. The Lion & the Rabbit: Classic Tales Edition. Greenhead, Bill, illus. 2011. (Classic Tales Ser.). (J). *(978-1-936258-65-9(X))* Benchmark Education Co.

Smith, Crystal. The Lioness. 2010. 35p. (J). pap. 19.95 *(978-1-4327-3968-3(9))* Outskirts Pr., Inc.

Soffe, Caroline Dawn. The Burrows of Trother. 2011. 60p. pap. 19.95 *(978-1-4560-5202-7(0))* America Star Bks.

Sommer, Carl. I Am a Lion! Budwine, Greg, illus. 2014. (J). *(978-1-57537-403-1(X))* Advance Publishing, Inc.

—I Am a Lion! 2003. (Another Sommer-Time Story Ser.). (Illus.). 48p. (J). (gr. k-4). lib. bdg. 23.95 incl. audio *(978-1-57537-759-9(4))* Advance Publishing, Inc.

—I Am a Lion! Budwine, Greg, illus. 2003. (Another Sommer-Time Story Ser.). (ENG.). 48p. (J). (gr. k-4). lib. bdg. 23.95 incl. audio compact disk *(978-1-57537-709-4(8))* Advance Publishing, Inc.

—I Am a Lion! 2003. (Another Sommer-Time Story Ser.). (Illus.). 48p. (J). (gr. 1-4). 16.95 incl. audio *(978-1-57537-558-8(3))* Advance Publishing, Inc.

—I Am a Lion! Budwine, Greg, illus. 2003. (Another Sommer-Time Story Ser.). (ENG.). 48p. (J). (gr. 1-4). 16.95 incl. audio compact disk *(978-1-57537-509-0(5))* Advance Publishing, Inc.

—I Am a Lion!(Yo Soy un León!) Budwine, Greg, illus. 2009. (Another Sommer-Time Story Bilingual Ser.). (SPA & ENG.). 48p. (J). lib. bdg. 16.95 *(978-1-57537-153-5(7))* Advance Publishing, Inc.

—The Lion & the Mouse. Mercado, Jorge, illus. 2014. (Sommer-Time Story Classics Ser.). (ENG.). 32p. (J). (gr. k-4). 16.95 *(978-1-57537-082-8(4))* Advance Publishing, Inc.

—The Roar. Budwine, Greg, illus. 2009. (Quest for Success Ser.). (ENG.). 56p. (YA). pap. 4.95 *(978-1-57537-284-6(3))*;

J
K
L

lib. bdg. 12.95 *(978-1-57537-259-4(2))* Advance Publishing, Inc.

—The Roar(El Rugido) Budwine, Greg, illus. 2009. (Quest for Success Bilingual Ser.). (SPA & ENG.). 96p. (YA). lib. bdg. 14.95 *(978-1-57537-233-4(9))* Advance Publishing, Inc.

Spreng, Robert C. The Tahoe Tiger & the Lahontan Lion. 2008. 38p. pap. 14.50 *(978-0-557-02370-7(X))* Lulu Pr., Inc.

Stanbro, Heather. The Lion Without A Roar. 2011. 28p. pap. 12.95 *(978-1-4567-2768-0(0))* AuthorHouse.

Stegall, Kim. Mumsi Meets a Lion. Batti, Kimberly Rose, illus. 2008. (gr. -1-1). pap. 7.99 *(978-1-59166-871-8(9))* BJU Pr.

Stein, Kristen. The Vegetarian Lion. 2006. 36p. (J). pap. 13.28 *(978-1-4116-6459-3(0))* Lulu Pr., Inc.

Stephens, Helen. How to Hide a Lion. Stephens, Helen, illus. 2013. (ENG., Illus.). 32p. (J). (gr. -1-3). 16.99 *(978-0-8050-9834-1(8)*, 9780805098341, Holt, Henry & Co. Bks. For Young Readers) Holt, Henry & Co.

Stilton, Thea. Thea Stilton & the Journey to the Lion's Den. 2013. (Thea Stilton Ser.: 17). (ENG.). 176p. (J). (gr. 2-5). pap. 8.99 *(978-0-545-55627-9(9)*, Scholastic Paperbacks) Scholastic, Inc.

Stratten, Lou. Hello, I'm Sir Frettrick! Let's Say Hello to Our New Friends! Bennett, Judy, ed. Denaro, Sal, illus. 2006. (J). (gr. -1-2). pap. 6.95 incl. audio compact disk *(978-0-9747173-1-9(2))* Stratten, Lou.

Suritsch, Gina. Magical Tales from India: The Secret of the White Elephant & Mukti the Lion Finds Himself. 2013. 44p. pap. 22.99 *(978-1-4828-1435-4(8))* Partridge Pub.

Thomasson, Daniel E. The Lion & the Egg. 2012. 56p. pap. 24.20 *(978-1-4669-1303-5(7))* Trafford Publishing.

Tolstoi, Leo & Riordan, James. The Lion & the Puppy: And Other Stories for Children. Riordan, James, tr. from RUS. Sievert, Claus, illus. 2012. (ENG.). 76p. (J). (gr. 4-7). 16.95 *(978-1-61608-484-4(7)*, 608484, Sky Pony Pr.) Skyhorse Publishing Co., Inc.

Trent, Sandy Chase. Tommy's Amazing Journey: The Cat that Could Fly. 2011. 16p. pap. 24.95 *(978-1-4626-2363-1(8))* America Star Bks.

Vollmer, Cheryl. A Hungry Lion in My Tummy. Dimitriadis, Nick, illus. 2009. 24p. pap. 9.99 *(978-0-9825255-9-3(1)*, Epigraph Bks.) Monkfish Bk. Publishing Co.

Walsh, Sheila. Will, God's Mighty Warrior, 1 vol. Johnson, Meredith, illus. 2006. (Will, God's Mighty Warrior Ser.: 1). (ENG.). 32p. (gr. -1-3). 14.99 *(978-1-4003-0805-7(4))* Nelson, Thomas Inc.

Watt, F. & Wells, R. That's Not My Lion. 2004. (Touchy-Feely Board Bks.). (SPA.). 10p. (J). 7.99 *(978-0-7945-0047-4(1)*, Usborne) EDC Publishing.

Weaver, Amy Garrett. Zoe the Zebra. Schneider, Robin, illus. 2009. 33p. pap. 24.95 *(978-1-60749-552-9(X))* PublishAmerica, Inc.

Wehrmeijer, Annelien. Kato & Simba. van de Liejgraaf, Deborah, illus. 2015. (My Best Friend & Me Ser.). (ENG.). 10p. (J). (gr. -1-k). bds. 6.99 *(978-0-7641-6762-1(6))* Barron's Educational Series, Inc.

Weidensee, Ralph. The Cry'N Lion. 2010. 28p. pap. 21.99 *(978-1-4415-7923-2(0))* Xlibris Corp.

Weigl Publishers, creator. The Lion & the Mouse: Can Little Friends Be Great Friends? 2013. (AV2 Animated Storytime Ser.: Vol. 15). (ENG., Illus.). 32p. (J). (gr. -1-3). lib. bdg. 29.99 *(978-1-62127-919-8(7)*, AV2 by Weigl) Weigl Pubs., Inc.

Weiss, Ellen. Simba's Moon. Cuddy, Robin, illus. Date not set. (ENG.). 32p. (J). (gr. -1-2). 12.99 *(978-0-7868-3267-5(3))* Disney Pr.

White, Mark. El Leon y el Raton: Versión de la Fábula de Esopo. Abello, Patricia, tr. from ENG. Pérez, Sara Rojo, illus. 2006. (Read-It! Readers en Español: Fábulas Ser.).Tr. of Lion & the Mouse - A Retelling of Aesop's Fable. (SPA.). 24p. (gr. k-3). 21.32 *(978-1-4048-1623-7(2)*, Easy Readers) Picture Window Bks.

—The Lion & the Mouse: A Retelling of Aesop's Fable, 1 vol. Pérez, Sara Rojo, illus. 2010. (My First Classic Story Ser.). (ENG.). 24p. (gr. k-3). pap. 7.10 *(978-1-4048-7365-0(1)*, My First Classic Story) Picture Window Bks.

White, Mark & Aesop Enterprise Inc. Staff. The Lion & the Mouse: A Retelling of Aesop's Fable, 1 vol. Pérez, Sara Rojo, illus. 2010. (My First Classic Story Ser.). (ENG.). 24p. (gr. k-3). lib. bdg. 22.65 *(978-1-4048-6525-9(X)*, My First Classic Story) Picture Window Bks.

White, Paul. Jungle Doctor Meets a Lion. 2011. (Flamingo Fiction 9-13s Ser.). (ENG., Illus.). 176p. (J). 8.99 *(978-1-84550-392-5(9)*, 9781845503925) Christian Focus Pubns. GBR. Dist: Bookmasters Distribution.

White, Robb. The Lion's Paw. Ray, Ralph, illus. 2008. 243p. (J). (gr. 4-7). 29.95 *(978-0-9820932-0-7(9))* A. W. Ink, Inc.

Whitney, Elliott. The Blind Lion of the Congo. 2011. 128p. pap. 9.99 *(978-1-61203-066-1(1))* Bottom of the Hill Publishing.

William H. Sadlier Staff. The Lion & the Mouse, Vol. 2. 2005. (Fluent Library). (gr. 1-3). 29.34 *(978-0-8215-8968-7(7))* Sadlier, William H. Inc.

Williams, Zachary. Lions at the Library? 2006. (Neighborhood Readers Ser.). (ENG.). 12p. (gr. 1-3). pap. 5.90 *(978-1-4042-6863-0(4)*, Rosen Classroom) Rosen Publishing Group, Inc., The.

Wilson, Gerrard. Alice on Top of the World. 2009. 159p. pap. 17.50 *(978-0-9561553-0-6(8))* Wilson, Gerrard IRL. Dist: Lulu Pr., Inc.

Wolf, Gita. The Very Hungry Lion: A Folktale. Roy, Indrapramit, illus. 2006. (ENG.). 24p. 20.95 *(978-81-86211-02-1(0))* Tara Publishing IND. Dist: Consortium Bk. Sales & Distribution.

World of Lions. 2003. (J). per. *(978-1-884907-55-5(5))* Paradise Pr., Inc.

LION—HABITS AND BEHAVIOR

Jackson, Tom. Inside the Mind of a Fierce Lion. 2012. (Animal Instincts Ser.). (ENG.). 32p. (J). (gr. k-5). pap. 10.00 *(978-1-4488-7074-5(7))*; lib. bdg. 25.25 *(978-1-4488-7032-5(1))* Rosen Publishing Group, Inc., The. (PowerKids Pr.).

Spilsbury, Richard & Spilsbury, Louise. Lion Prides. 2013. (Animal Armies Ser.). (ENG., Illus.). 32p. (J). (gr. k-5). pap. 10.00 *(978-1-4777-0334-2(9))*; lib. bdg. 25.25 *(978-1-4777-0306-9(3))* Rosen Publishing Group, Inc., The. (PowerKids Pr.).

Troupe, Thomas Kingsley. I Want to Be... 2016. (I Want to Be... Ser.). (ENG.). 24p. (gr. k-3). 213.20 *(978-1-4795-8779-7(6))* Picture Window Bks.

LIONS

see Lion

LIQUID FUEL

see Gasoline; Petroleum As Fuel

LIQUIDS

Adamson, Thomas K. & Adamson, Heather. ¿Cómo Mides los Líquidos? 2011. (Mídelo/Measure It Ser.).Tr. of How Do You Measure Liquids? (MUL & SPA.). 32p. (gr. 1-2). 27.32 *(978-1-4296-6890-3(3)*, A+ Bilingue/Bilingual) Capstone Press of Coughlan Cos.

—How Do You Measure Liquids?, 1 vol. (Measure It! Ser.). (ENG.). 32p. (gr. 1-2). 2011. pap. 8.10 *(978-1-4296-6331-1(6))* 2010. lib. bdg. 27.32 *(978-1-4296-4457-0(5))* Capstone Press of Coughlan Cos. (Aplus Bks.).

Adamson, Thomas K. and Heather. How Do You Measure Liquids? 2011. (Measure It! Ser.). (ENG.). 32p. (gr. 1-2). pap. 47.70 *(978-1-4296-6458-5(4)*, Aplus Bks.) Capstone Press of Coughlan Cos.

Bentley, Joyce. Wet. 2006. (Things Around Us Ser.). (J). *(978-1-59389-279-1(9))* Chrysalis Education.

Bloom, Chrissa. In the Kitchen with Solids, Liquids, & Gases. 2009. (Real Life Readers Ser.). 12p. (gr. 1-2). pap. 5.90 *(978-1-4042-7897-4(4)*, Rosen Classroom) Rosen Publishing Group, Inc., The.

Boothroyd, Jennifer. What Floats? What Sinks? 2010. pap. 45.32 *(978-0-7613-6933-2(3))* Lerner Publishing Group.

—What Floats? What Sinks? A Look at Density. 2010. (Lightning Bolt Books (tm) — Exploring Physical Science Ser.). (ENG.). 32p. (gr. k-2). pap. 7.95 *(978-0-7613-6055-1(7))*; (Illus.). lib. bdg. 26.60 *(978-0-7613-5433-8(6))* Lerner Publishing Group.

—What Is a Liquid? 2007. (First Step Nonfiction - States of Matter Ser.). (ENG., Illus.). 24p. (gr. k-2). pap. 6.95 *(978-0-8225-6817-9(9)*, Carolrhoda Bks.); lib. bdg. 23.93 *(978-0-8225-6838-4(1)*, Lerner Pubns.) Lerner Publishing Group.

Brannon, Barbara. Discover Liquids. 2005. (J). pap. *(978-1-4108-5118-5(4))* Benchmark Education Co.

Braun, Eric. Joe-Joe the Wizard Brews up Solids, Liquids, & Gases, 1 vol. Boyden, Robin, illus. 2012. (In the Science Lab Ser.). (ENG.). 24p. (gr. 2-3). pap. 9.95 *(978-1-4048-7238-7(8))* Picture Window Bks.

Cardenas, Ernesto A. Liquid or Solid? 2009. 23.95 *(978-1-60698-041-5(6))*; pap. 4.95 *(978-1-60698-039-2(4))* Milo Educational Bks. & Resources.

Claybourne, Anna. Make It Splash!, 1 vol. Scott, Kimberly & Dean, Venetia, illus. 2014. (Whiz Kid Science Ser.). (ENG.). 32p. (gr. 2-4). 29.99 *(978-1-4109-6749-7(2)*, Read Me!) Heinemann-Raintree.

Doudna, Kelly. Let's Be Kids & Measure Liquids!, 1 vol. 2007. (Science Made Simple Ser.). (ENG., Illus.). 24p. (J). (gr. k-3). lib. bdg. 24.21 *(978-1-59928-610-5(6)*, SandCastle) ABDO Publishing Co.

Hoffmann, Sara. Liquids. 2012. (First Step Nonfiction - Kinds of Matter Ser.). (ENG., Illus.). 8p. (gr. -1-1). pap. 4.95 *(978-1-4677-0518-9(7))* Lerner Publishing Group.

Hurd, Will. Changing States: Solids, Liquids, & Gases. 2016. (Do It Yourself Ser.). (ENG.). 48p. (gr. 3-6). pap. 8.99 *(978-1-4846-3818-7(2)*, NA-h) Heinemann-Raintree.

Kjelle, Marylou Morano. The Properties of Liquids. (Library of Physical Science Ser.). 24p. (gr. 4-4). 2009. 42.50 *(978-1-60853-791-4(9)*, PowerKids Pr.) 2007. (ENG., Illus.). pap. 7.05 *(978-1-4042-2169-7(7)*, PowerKids Pr.) 2006. (Illus.). (YA). lib. bdg. 22.60 *(978-1-4042-3422-2(5))* Rosen Publishing Group, Inc., The.

Kuskowski, Alex. Science Experiments with Liquid, 1 vol. 2013. (More Super Simple Science Ser.). (ENG.). 32p. (gr. k-4). lib. bdg. 27.07 *(978-1-61783-852-1(7)*, Super SandCastle) ABDO Publishing Co.

Lawrence, Ellen. Liquids & Solids. 2014. (Science Slam: FUN-Damentals Ser.). (ENG., Illus.). 24p. (J). (gr. -1-3). lib. bdg. 23.93 *(978-1-62724-311-7(9))* Bearport Publishing Co., Inc.

Merrill, Amy French. Everyday Physical Science Experiments with Liquids. 2009. (Science Surprises Ser.). 24p. (gr. 3-3). 42.50 *(978-1-60853-062-5(0)*, PowerKids Pr.) Rosen Publishing Group, Inc., The.

Mezzanotte, Jim. Líquidos. 2006. (Estados de la materia (States of Matter) Ser.). (ENG & SPA.). 24p. (gr. 1-4). pap. 8.15 *(978-0-8368-7409-9(9)*, Weekly Reader Leveled Readers) Stevens, Gareth Publishing LLLP.

—Liquidos. 2006. (Estados de la materia (States of Matter) Ser.). (ENG & SPA., Illus.). 24p. (gr. 1-4). lib. bdg. 22.00 *(978-0-8368-7404-4(8)*, Weekly Reader Leveled Readers) Stevens, Gareth Publishing LLLP.

—Liquids. 2006. (States of Matter Ser.). (Illus.). 24p. (gr. 1-4). lib. bdg. 22.00 *(978-0-8368-6799-2(8)*, Weekly Reader Leveled Readers) Stevens, Gareth Publishing LLLP.

Montgomery, Anne. Solid or Liquid?, 1 vol. (Science Readers: Content & Literacy Ser.). (ENG., Illus.). 24p. (gr. k-k). 2015. (J). 22.96 *(978-1-4938-1137-3(1))* 2014. pap. 8.99 *(978-1-4807-4527-8(8))* Teacher Created Materials, Inc.

Mullins, Matt. Experiment with Liquids. 2010. (Explorer Junior Library: Science Explorer Junior Ser.). (ENG.). 32p. (gr. 3-6). lib. bdg. 28.50 *(978-1-60279-846-5(X)*, 200558) Cherry Lake Publishing.

Nelson, Robin. Freezing & Melting. 2003. (First Step Nonfiction Ser.). (Illus.). 24p. (gr. k-2). (J). lib. bdg. 18.60 *(978-0-8225-4590-3(X))*; (ENG., pap. 6.95 *(978-0-8225-4591-0(8))* Lerner Publishing Group.

Parker, Janice. The Science of Liquids & Solids. 2003. (Living Science Ser.). (Illus.). 32p. (J). (gr. 1-3). pap. 9.95 *(978-1-930954-11-3(5))* Weigl Pubs., Inc.

Peppas, Lynn. What Is a Liquid? 2012. (ENG.). 24p. (J). *(978-0-7787-0770-7(9))*; (Illus.). pap. *(978-0-7787-0777-6(6))* Crabtree Publishing Co.

Randolph, Joanne. Liquids in My World. (My World of Science Ser.). 24p. 2009. (gr. 2-2). 37.50 *(978-1-61514-726-7(8)*, PowerKids Pr.) 2007. (ENG.). (gr. k-8). pap. 7.05 *(978-1-4042-8421-0(4)*, Rosen Classroom) 2006. (Illus.). (J). (gr. 3-7). lib. bdg. 18.75 *(978-1-4042-3285-3(0)*, PowerKids Pr.) Rosen Publishing Group, Inc., The.

—Liquids in My World: Los Líquidos en Mi Mundo. 2006. (My World of Science/ Mi mundo y la Ciencia Ser.). (ENG & SPA.). (J). (gr. k-3). 16.00 *(978-1-4042-3316-4(4))* Rosen Publishing Group, Inc., The.

—Liquids in My World/Los líquidos en mi Mundo. 2009. (My World of Science/la ciencia en mi mundo Ser.). (ENG & SPA.). 48p. (gr. 2-2). 37.50 *(978-1-61514-738-0(1)*, Editorial Buenas Letras) Rosen Publishing Group, Inc., The.

Rodriguez, Cindy. Líquidos. 2013. (SPA.). (J). *(978-1-62127-603-6(1))* Weigl Pubs., Inc.

—Liquids, with Code. 2012. (What Is Matter? Ser.). (ENG., Illus.). 24p. (J). (gr. -1-3). pap. 12.95 *(978-1-61913-605-2(8)*, AV2 by Weigl) Weigl Pubs., Inc.

—Liquids with Code. 2012. (What Is Matter? Ser.). (ENG., Illus.). 24p. (J). (gr. -1-3). lib. bdg. 27.13 *(978-1-61913-603-8(1)*, AV2 by Weigl) Weigl Pubs., Inc.

Rodriguez, Cindy & Siemens, Jared. Liquid. 2016. (J). ***(978-1-4896-5746-6(0))*** Weigl Pubs., Inc.

Royston, Angela. Experiments with a Lemon. 2016. (One-Stop Science Ser.). 32p. (gr. 2-5). 31.35 *(978-1-62588-140-3(1)*, Smart Apple Media) Black Rabbit Bks.

—Experiments with Water. 2016. (One-Stop Science Ser.). 32p. (gr. 2-5). 31.35 *(978-1-62588-142-7(8)*, Smart Apple Media) Black Rabbit Bks.

Ryback, Carol & Mezzanotte, Jim. Liquids. 2006. (States of Matter Ser.). 24p. (gr. 1-4). pap. 8.15 *(978-0-8368-6804-3(8)*, Weekly Reader Leveled Readers) Stevens, Gareth Publishing LLLP.

Sohn, Emily & Gendler, Joel. Solids & Liquids: Who Messed up My Sand? 2011. (IScience Readers Ser.). 24p. (J). (gr. k-2). lib. bdg. 21.27 *(978-1-59953-410-7(X))* Norwood Hse. Pr.

Spilsbury, Louise & Spilsbury, Richard. Solids & Liquids. 2013. (Step up Science Ser.). (ENG., Illus.). 32p. (J). (gr. 2-6). pap. 12.99 *(978-0-237-54380-8(X))* Evans Brothers, Ltd. GBR. Dist: Independent Pubs. Group.

—Solids, Liquids, & Gases, 1 vol. (Essential Physical Science Ser.). (ENG., Illus.). 48p. (gr. 4-6). 2014. lib. bdg. 33.32 *(978-1-4329-8151-8(X))* 2013. pap. 9.95 *(978-1-4329-8160-0(9))* Heinemann-Raintree. (Heinemann InfoSearch).

Sullivan, Erin Ash. Liquids & Gases: Set Of 6. 2010. (Navigators Ser.). (J). pap. 44.00 net. *(978-1-4108-5071-3(4))* Benchmark Education Co.

—Liquids & Gases: Text Pairs. 2008. (Bridges/Navigators Ser.). (J). (gr. 3). 89.00 *(978-1-4108-8366-7(3))* Benchmark Education Co.

Taylor-Butler, Christine. Experiments with Liquids, 1 vol. 2011. (My Science Investigations Ser.). (ENG.). 32p. (gr. 1-3). 27.32 *(978-1-4329-5361-4(3)*, Heinemann First Library) Heinemann-Raintree.

Weakland, Mark. The Solid Truth about Matter. Lum, Bernice, illus. 2012. (LOL Physical Science Ser.). (ENG.). 32p. (gr. 3-4). pap. 47.70 *(978-1-4296-9303-5(7)*, Fact Finders) Capstone Press of Coughlan Cos.

Williams, Zella. Experiments with Solids, Liquids, & Gases. 2007. (Do-It-Yourself Science Ser.). (Illus.). 24p. (J). (gr. 2-5). lib. bdg. 25.25 *(978-1-4042-3658-5(9))* Rosen Publishing Group, Inc., The.

Wood, Ira. Water, Ice, & Steam. 2006. (Rosen Real Readers Big Bookstm Ser.). (ENG., Illus.). 12p. (gr. 1-2). 33.50 *(978-1-4042-6215-7(6))* Rosen Publishing Group, Inc., The.

Zoehfeld, Kathleen Weidner. What Is the World Made Of? Meisel, Paul, illus. 2015. (Let's-Read-And-Find-Out Science 2 Ser.). (ENG.). 32p. (J). (gr. -1-3). pap. 6.99 *(978-0-06-238195-8(4))* HarperCollins Pubs.

LISTER, JOSEPH, BARON, 1827-1912

Bankston, John. Joseph Lister & the Story of Antiseptics. 2004. (Uncharted, Unexplored, & Unexplained Ser.). (Illus.). 48p. (J). (gr. 4-8). lib. bdg. 29.95 *(978-1-58415-262-0(1))* Mitchell Lane Pubs., Inc.

LISZT, FRANZ, 1811-1886

Whiting, Jim. The Life & Times of Franz Liszt. 2004. (Masters of Music Ser.). (Illus.). 48p. (gr. 4-8). lib. bdg. 20.95 *(978-1-58415-280-4(X))* Mitchell Lane Pubs., Inc.

LITERACY

Digital & Information Literacy: Set 10. 2016. (Digital & Information Literacy Ser.). 00048p. (J). (gr. 6-6). 222.25 *(978-1-5081-7367-0(2)*, Rosen Central) Rosen Publishing Group, Inc., The.

Digital & Information Literacy: Set 8. 2016. (Digital & Information Literacy Ser.). 00048p. (J). (gr. 6-6). pap. 82.25 *(978-1-5081-7381-6(8)*, Rosen Central) Rosen Publishing Group, Inc., The.

Feldman, Jean & Karapetkova, Holly. ABC 123. unabr. ed. 2010. (ENG.). 16p. (gr. -1-k). 12.99 *(978-1-61741-589-0(8))* Rourke Educational Media.

McGill-Franzen, Anne. Kindergarten Literacy: Matching Assessment & Instruction in Kindergarten. 2006. (Teaching Resources Ser.). (ENG., Illus.). 288p. (gr. k-k). pap. 28.99 *(978-0-439-80034-1(X)*, Theory & Practice) Scholastic, Inc.

Nations, Susan & Alonso, Mellissa. Primary Literacy Responses: Core Tasks for Readers & Writers. 2014. (Maupin House Ser.). (ENG.). 224p. pap. 29.95 *(978-1-62521-520-8(7))* Capstone Press of Coughlan Cos.

Paxen Learning Staff. Career Pathways: Document Literacy. 2011. (Illus.). 218p. (YA). pap. 49.95 *(978-1-934350-38-6(9))* Paxen Publishing LLC.

richmond, keli. LIteracy Speaks 2. 2008. (J). pap. 197.00 *(978-0-9799245-5-2(3))* Northern Speech Services.

Skidmore, Sharon, et al. Balanced Literacy Grade 5. 2008. per. 34.00 *(978-1-879097-34-6(6))* Kagan Publishing.

LITERACY—FICTION

Battle-Lavert, Gwendolyn. Papa's Mark. Bootman, Colin, illus. 2003. (ENG.). 32p. (J). (gr. k-3). tchr. ed. 17.95 *(978-0-8234-1650-9(X))* Holiday Hse., Inc.

Breault, Christie Merriman. Logan West, Printer's Devil. Archembault, Matthew, illus. 2006. 142p. (J). pap. *(978-1-59336-762-6(7))* Mondo Publishing.

Crossley-Holland, Kevin. Crossing to Paradise. 2008. (J). pap. *(978-0-545-05868-1(6)*, Levine, Arthur A. Bks.) Scholastic, Inc.

Dean, Carolee. Take Me There. 2010. (ENG.). 336p. (YA). (gr. 9-18). pap. 8.99 *(978-1-4169-8950-9(1)*, Simon Pulse) Simon Pulse.

Ellison, Elizabeth Stow. Flight. 2008. (ENG.). 192p. (YA). (gr. 3-7). 16.95 *(978-0-8234-2128-2(7))* Holiday Hse., Inc.

Hest, Amy. Mr. George Baker. Muth, Jon J., illus. 2007. (Reading Rainbow Bks.). (ENG.). 32p. (J). (gr. k-3). 6.99 *(978-0-7636-3308-0(9))* Candlewick Pr.

—Mr. George Baker. 2007. lib. bdg. 17.20 *(978-1-4177-9067-8(9)*, Turtleback) Turtleback Bks.

Kinsey-Warnock, Natalie. Lumber Camp Library. Bernardin, James, illus. 2003. (ENG.). 96p. (J). (gr. 2-5). pap. 4.99 *(978-0-06-444292-3(6))* HarperCollins Pubs.

McKissack, Patricia C. A Picture of Freedom: The Diary of Clotee, a Slave Girl, Belmont Plantation, Virginia, 1859. 2011. (Dear America Ser.). (ENG.). 240p. (J). (gr. 3-7). 14.99 *(978-0-545-24253-0(3)*, Scholastic Pr.) Scholastic, Inc.

O'Donnell, Liam. Media Meltdown: A Graphic Guide Adventure, 1 vol. Deas, Mike, illus. 2009. (Graphic Guides). (ENG.). 64p. (J). (gr. 3-7). pap. 9.95 *(978-1-55469-065-7(X))* Orca Bk. Pubs. USA.

Paul, Ann Whitford. Word Builder. Cyrus, Kurt, illus. 2009. (ENG.). 32p. (J). (gr. k-2). 18.99 *(978-1-4169-3981-8(4)*, Simon & Schuster Bks. For Young Readers) Simon & Schuster Bks. For Young Readers.

Reedy, Trent. Words in the Dust. (ENG.). 272p. (J). 2013. (gr. 5-9). pap. 6.99 *(978-0-545-26126-5(0))* 2011. (gr. 4-7). 17.99 *(978-0-545-26125-8(2))* Scholastic, Inc. (Levine, Arthur A. Bks.).

Saint-Lot, Katia Novet & Tokunbo, Dimitrea. Amadi's Snowman. 2008. (ENG., Illus.). 32p. (gr. 1-6). 16.95 *(978-0-88448-298-7(7)*, 884298) Tilbury Hse. Pubs.

Schmatz, Pat. Bluefish. 2011. (ENG., Illus.). 240p. (YA). (gr. 7). 15.99 *(978-0-7636-5334-7(9))* Candlewick Pr.

Schurch, Maylan. The Sword of Denis Anwyck. 2009. (J). pap. 10.99 *(978-0-8280-2425-9(1))* Review & Herald Publishing Assn.

Shvarts, Andrew. Royal Bastards. 2017. (Royal Bastards Ser.). (ENG.). 352p. (YA). (gr. 9-17). 18.99 ***(978-1-4847-6765-8(9))*** Hyperion Bks. for Children.

Stanley, Diane. Raising Sweetness, 4 bks. Karas, G. Brian, illus. 2004. (J). pap. 39.95 incl. audio compact disk *(978-1-59112-524-2(3))* Live Oak Media.

—Raising Sweetness. 2003. (Illus.). (J). 28.95 incl. audio compact disk *(978-1-59112-516-7(2))*; 25.95 incl. audio *(978-1-59112-266-1(X))* Live Oak Media.

—Raising Sweetness, 4 bks. Stanley, Diane, illus. 2003. (Illus.). (J). pap. 37.95 incl. audio *(978-1-59112-267-8(8))* Live Oak Media.

Stolz, Joelle. The Shadows of Ghadames. Temerson, Catherine, tr. 2006. (ENG.). 128p. (J). (gr. 3-7). 5.99 *(978-0-440-41949-5(2)*, Yearling) Random Hse. Children's Bks.

LITERARY CHARACTERS

see Characters and Characteristics in Literature

LITERARY CRITICISM

see Criticism; Literature—History and Criticism

LITERARY STYLE

see Style, Literary

LITERATURE—BIOGRAPHY

see Authors

LITERATURE—CRITICISM

see Literature—History and Criticism

LITERATURE—EVALUATION

see Books and Reading; Criticism; Literature—History and Criticism

LITERATURE—HISTORY AND CRITICISM

see also Authors; Criticism

Beers. Elements of Literature. 5th ed. 2003. (Elements of Literature Ser.). (Illus.). 78.60 *(978-0-03-068373-2(4))*; tchr. ed. 134.46 *(978-0-03-068382-4(3))* Holt McDougal.

Bloom, Harold. Bloom's Modern Critical Views. Henry, W. & Berg, Albert A., eds. (J). 455.40 *(978-0-7910-7394-0(7)*, Chelsea Hse.) Facts On File, Inc.

Bloom, Harold, ed. Bloom's Literary Places. (gr. 9-13). (Illus.). pap. 41.85 *(978-0-7910-8391-8(8))*; (Illus.). lib. bdg. 95.85 *(978-0-7910-7835-8(3))*; 2005. 150p. (C). 240.00 *(978-0-7910-8719-0(0))* Facts On File, Inc. (Chelsea Hse.).

—Bloom's Major Literary Characters. 2005. (Major Literary Characters Ser.). 180p. (C). (gr. 9). 520.00 *(978-0-7910-8475-5(2)*, Chelsea Hse.) Facts On File, Inc.

—Bloom's Modern Critical Interpretations. (Illus.). (gr. 9-13). lib. bdg. 113.85 *(978-0-7910-8484-7(1)*, Chelsea Hse.) Facts On File, Inc.

—Bloom's Modern Critical Views. (Illus.). (gr. 9-13). pap. 39.90 *(978-0-7910-8479-3(5))*; lib. bdg. 189.75 *(978-0-7910-8487-8(6))* Facts On File, Inc. (Chelsea Hse.).

—Bloom's Notes. 2005. (Bloom's Notes Ser.). (C). (gr. 9). 240.00 *(978-0-7910-9137-1(6)*, Chelsea Hse.) Facts On File, Inc.

—Bloom's Period Studies. (gr. 9-13). (Illus.). lib. bdg. 379.50 *(978-0-7910-7893-8(0))*; (Illus.). lib. bdg. *(978-0-7910-8069-6(2))*; 2005. 350p. (C). 360.00 *(978-0-7910-8488-5(4))* Facts On File, Inc. (Chelsea Hse.).

—Carlos Fuentes' the Death of Artemio Cruz. 2006. (Bloom's Modern Critical Interpretations Ser.). 150p. (C). (gr. 9). lib. bdg. 45.00 *(978-0-7910-8587-5(2)*, Chelsea Hse.) Facts On File, Inc.

—Catch-22 - Joseph Heller. 2nd ed. 2007. (Modern Critical Interpretations Ser.). 281p. (C). (gr. 9-18). 45.00 *(978-0-7910-9617-8(3)*, Chelsea Hse.) Facts On File, Inc.

—Modern Critical Views. (Illus.). 144-300p. (J). 279.60 *(978-0-7910-5220-4(6)*, Chelsea Hse.) Facts On File, Inc.

Bodden, Valerie. What Are Nonfiction Genres? 2014. (Name That Text Type! Ser.). (Illus.). 32p. (gr. 2-4). pap. 7.95 *(978-1-4677-4519-2(7))* Lerner Publishing Group.

The Engaged Reader. 2005. (Engaged Reader Ser.). (Illus.). 64p. (gr. 5-8). 150.00 *(978-0-7910-9066-4(3)*, Chelsea Hse.) Facts On File, Inc.

Factor, Judith, ed. Pearl Workbook for 6th Grade: Mosdos Press Literature Series. 2003. (gr. 6-18). pap. 16.00 *(978-0-9671009-8-2(4))* Mosdos Pr.

Faulkner, Nicholas, ed. 101 Authors. 2016. (People You Should Know Ser.). 184p. (J). (gr. 8-8). lib. bdg. 36.25 *(978-1-68048-506-6(7))* Rosen Publishing Group, Inc., The.

Fernández de Moratín, Leandro. El Si de la Ninas. annot. ed. (SPA., Illus.). 176p. (J). 15.95 *(978-84-207-2634-2(6)*, ANY008) Grupo Anaya, S.A. ESP. Dist: Continental Bk. Co., Inc.

Fitzgerald, F. Scott. The Great Gatsby. Bloom, Harold Ron, ed. 2006. (Bloom's Guides). 80p. (YA). (gr. 9-12). lib. bdg. 30.00 *(978-0-7910-8580-6(5))* Facts On File, Inc.

Foster, Brett & Marcovitz, Hal. Rome. 2005. (Bloom's Literary Places Ser.). (Illus.). 150p. (C). (gr. 9-13). 40.00 *(978-0-7910-7839-6(6),* Chelsea Hse.) Facts On File, Inc.

García Márquez, Gabriel. Gabriel García Márquez's One Hundred Years of Solitude. Bloom, Harold, ed. annot. ed. 2006. (Bloom's Guides).Tr. of Cien Anos de Soledad. 80p. (YA). (gr. 9-12). 30.00 *(978-0-7910-8578-3(3))* Facts On File, Inc.

Guillain, Charlotte. Looking at Literature. 2015. (Connect with Text Ser.). (ENG.). 112p. (gr. 2-4). pap. 11.95 *(978-1-4109-6831-9(6),* Raintree Perspectives) Heinemann-Raintree.

Hacht, Anne Marie. Literary Themes for Students, 2 vols., Vol. 12. 2006. (Literary Themes for Students Ser.). (ENG., Illus.). 1200p. 285.00 *(978-1-4144-0271-0(6))* Cengage Gale.

Harper, Amelia. Literary Lessons from The Lord of the Rings. Howe, John, illus. 2004. 622p. (YA). (gr. 7-12). stu. ed., spiral bd. 50.00 *(978-0-9754934-1-0(8),* Literary Lessons) HomeScholar Bks.

Herron, Paul, ed. & contrib. by. A Cafe in Space: The Anais Nin Literary Journal, 8 vols., Vol. 2. Herron, Paul, contrib. by. 2004. (Illus.). 160p. pap. 15.00 *(978-0-9652364-9-2(8))* Sky Blue Pr.

Holt, Rinehart and Winston Staff. Elements of Literature: Family Involvement Activities. 5th ed. 2003. (SPA & ENG., Illus.). pap. 38.80 *(978-0-03-073853-1(9))* Holt McDougal.

—Elements of Literature: Holt Adapted Reader Answer Key. 5th ed. 2003. pap. 23.20 *(978-0-03-035911-8(2));* pap. 23.20 *(978-0-03-035909-5(0))* Holt McDougal.

—Elements of Literature: Holt Reader. 5th ed. 2003. (Elements of Literature Ser.). (ENG., Illus.). 424p. (gr. 9-9). pap. 17.15 *(978-0-03-068393-0(9))* Houghton Mifflin Harcourt Publishing Co.

—Elements of Literature: Holt Reader: Interactive Worktext - Georgia Edition. 3rd ed. 2003. (gr. 6). pap. 11.00 *(978-0-03-070197-9(X));* (gr. 7). pap. 11.00 *(978-0-03-070198-6(8));* (gr. 8). pap. 11.00 *(978-0-03-070199-3(6))* Holt McDougal.

—Elements of Literature: Holt Reader: Interactive Worktext - Mississippi Edition. 3rd ed. 2003. (YA). (gr. 10). pap. 11.00 *(978-0-03-071196-1(7));* (J). (gr. 6). pap. 11.00 *(978-0-03-071191-6(6));* (gr. 7). pap. 11.00 *(978-0-03-071192-3(4));* (gr. 8). pap. 11.00 *(978-0-03-071193-0(2))* Holt McDougal.

—Elements of Literature: Mississippi Edition. 3rd annot. ed. 2003. (gr. 6). tchr. ed. 121.60 *(978-0-03-071797-0(3))* Holt McDougal.

—Elements of Literature 2005 - The Holt Reader. 5th ed. 2003. (Elements of Literature Ser.). (ENG., Illus.). 400p. (gr. 11-11). pap. 17.15 *(978-0-03-068396-1(3))* Houghton Mifflin Harcourt Publishing Co.

—Holt Reader. 5th ed. 2003. (Elements of Literature Ser.). (ENG., Illus.). 392p. (gr. 12-12). pap. 17.15 *(978-0-03-068397-8(1));* 384p. (gr. 7-7). pap. 17.15 *(978-0-03-068391-6(2))* Houghton Mifflin Harcourt Publishing Co.

—The Holt Reader. 5th ed. 2003. (Elements of Literature Ser.). (ENG., Illus.). 368p. (gr. 8-8). pap. 17.15 *(978-0-03-068392-3(0))* Houghton Mifflin Harcourt Publishing Co.

—Reader Fourth Course. 4th ed. 2003. (Elements of Literature Ser.). (ENG., Illus.). 408p. (gr. 10-10). pap. 17.15 *(978-0-03-068394-7(7))* Houghton Mifflin Harcourt Publishing Co.

Kafer, Kathy & Benchmark Education Co. Staff. Opinions about Difficult Times Portrayed in Literature. 2014. (Text Connections Ser.). (J). (gr. 5). *(978-1-4900-1388-6(1))* Benchmark Education Co.

Kurian, George Thomas. Timetables of World Literature. 2003. 416p. (C). (gr. 9-18). 85.00 *(978-0-8160-4197-8(0))* Facts On File, Inc.

Lit Crit Guides: Set 3. 2016. (Lit Crit Guides). 176p. (J). lib. bdg. 239.58 *(978-0-7660-8397-4(7))* Enslow Pubs., Inc.

Lit Crit Guides: Set 4. 2017. (Lit Crit Guides). 160p. (gr. 8-8). lib. bdg. 239.58 ***(978-0-7660-8572-5(4))*** Enslow Pubs., Inc.

Mason, Antony. Literature. 2004. (Culture Encyclopedia Ser.). (Illus.). 40p. (YA). (gr. 5-18). lib. bdg. 19.95 *(978-1-59084-478-6(5))* Mason Crest.

Mirande, Jaqueline. Arturo y los Caballeros de la Tabla Redonda. 2003. (Advanced Reading Ser.). (SPA., Illus.). 134p. (J). 11.95 *(978-84-239-7072-8(8))* Espasa Calpe, S.A. ESP. Dist: Planeta Publishing Corp.

Nagle, Jeanne, ed. Great Authors of Classic Literature. 2013. (Essential Authors for Children & Teens Ser.). (YA). (gr. 7-12). 45.00 *(978-1-62275-084-9(5))* Rosen Publishing Group, Inc., The.

—Great Authors of Nonfiction. 2013. (Essential Authors for Children & Teens Ser.). (YA). (gr. 7-12). 45.00 *(978-1-62275-092-4(6))* Rosen Publishing Group, Inc., The.

—Great Poets & Playwrights. 2013. (Essential Authors for Children & Teens Ser.). (YA). (gr. 7-12). 45.00 *(978-1-62275-088-7(8))* Rosen Publishing Group, Inc., The.

Nardo, Don. Arts & Literature in Ancient Mesopotamia. 2008. (Lucent Library of Historical Eras Ser.). (ENG., Illus.). 104p. (YA). (gr. 7-12). lib. bdg. 37.45 *(978-1-4205-0099-8(6),* LML02109-244222) Cengage Gale.

Peacock, Scott. Beacham's Guide to Literature for Young Adults, Vol. 16. 2003. (Beacham's Literature for Young Adults Ser.). (ENG.). 608p. 183.00 *(978-0-7876-5836-6(7),* UXL) Cengage Gale.

Persky, Stan. The Short Version: An ABC Book. 2005. (ENG., Illus.). 352p. per. 21.00 *(978-1-55420-016-0(4))* New Star Bks., Ltd. CAN. Dist: SPD-Small Pr. Distribution.

Remarque, Erich Maria. All Quiet on the Western Front. Bloom, Harold, ed. annot. ed. 2008. (Bloom's Guides). 128p. (C). (gr. 9-18). 30.00 *(978-0-7910-9830-1(3),* Chelsea Hse.) Facts On File, Inc.

Responding to Literature. 912p. (YA). (gr. 8). 52.95 *(978-0-8219-1364-2(6),* 35456) EMC/Paradigm Publishing.

Saddleback Educational Publishing Staff, ed. Swiss Family Robinson. 2011. (Timeless Classics Ser.). (ENG.). 48p. (YA). (gr. 9-12). pupil's gde. ed. 19.95 incl. cd-rom *(978-1-61651-151-7(6))* Saddleback Educational Publishing, Inc.

—Treasure Island. 2011. (Timeless Classics Ser.). (ENG.). 48p. (YA). (gr. 9-12). pupil's gde. ed. 19.95 incl. cd-rom *(978-1-61651-155-5(9))* Saddleback Educational Publishing, Inc.

Schoenberg, Thomas J. & Trudeau, Lawrence J., eds. Twentieth-Century Literary Criticism, Volume 199, Vol. 199. annot. ed. 2008. (Twentieth-Century Literary Criticism Ser.: Vol. 199). (ENG.). 544p. 397.00 *(978-0-7876-9974-1(8))* Cengage Gale.

Smith, Kiley. Young Adult Literature: Dystopian Worlds (Grade 6) 2016. (TIME for KIDS(r) Nonfiction Readers Ser.). (Illus.). 48p. (J). (gr. 6-6). pap. 9.99 *(978-1-4938-3599-7(8))* Teacher Created Materials, Inc.

Spartz, Emerson & Schoen, Ben. Mugglenet. Com's Harry Potter Should Have Died: Controversial Views from the #1 Fan Site. 2009. (ENG.). 180p. (J). (gr. 3). pap. 14.95 *(978-1-56975-711-6(9))* Ulysses Pr.

Stobaugh, James. World Literature Student. 2005. (Broadman & Holman Literature Ser.). 272p. stu. ed. 24.99 *(978-0-8054-5892-3(1))* B&H Publishing Group.

Story Studio Vol. 2: Transmitting Stories Across the Curriculum. 2005. spiral bd. 39.95 *(978-1-56820-173-3(7))* Story Time Stories That Rhyme.

Wills, Adele. Texts Through History. 2004. (Routledge a Level English Guides). (ENG., Illus.). (C). 96p. 95.00 *(978-0-415-31909-6(9));* 94p. per. 25.95 *(978-0-415-31910-2(2),* RU26770) Routledge.

Zebrowski, Debra. World Literature Student Activity Book. Matthews, Douglas L., ed. 2003. (Illus.). stu. ed., per., wbk. ed. *(978-1-931680-53-0(1),* Expert Systems for Teachers) Teaching Point, Inc.

LITERATURE, MEDIEVAL

Kline, Daniel T., ed. Medieval Literature for Children. 2003. (ENG., Illus.). 366p. (C). 157.00 *(978-0-8153-3312-8(9),* RT7897) Routledge.

LITERATURE—STORIES, PLOTS, ETC.

Beck, Isabel L., et al. Julian's Glorious Summer. 2003. (Trophies Ser.). (gr. 3-18). 50.40 *(978-0-15-319277-7(1))* Harcourt Schl. Pubs.

Berne, Emma Carlson. What Are Graphic Novels? 2014. (Illus.). 32p. (gr. 2-4). lib. bdg. 26.60 *(978-1-4677-3666-4(X),* Lerner Pubns.) Lerner Publishing Group.

Holt, Rinehart and Winston Staff. Elemental Literature - Elements of Literature. 5th ed. 2003. (Elements of Literature Ser.). (ENG., Illus.). 160p. (gr. 6-6). pap. 17.15 *(978-0-03-035709-1(8))* Houghton Mifflin Harcourt Publishing Co.

—Elements of Literature: Adapted Reader. 5th ed. 2003. (Elements of Literature Ser.). (ENG., Illus.). 168p. (gr. 10-10). pap. 17.15 *(978-0-03-035458-8(7))* Houghton Mifflin Harcourt Publishing Co.

—Elements of Literature: Holt Adapted Reader. 5th ed. 2004. (Elements of Literature Ser.). (ENG.). 184p. (gr. 7-7). pap. 17.15 *(978-0-03-035711-4(X))* Houghton Mifflin Harcourt Publishing Co.

—Elements of Literature - Adapted Reader. 5th ed. 2003. (Elements of Literature Ser.). (ENG., Illus.). 184p. (gr. 12-12). pap. 17.15 *(978-0-03-035461-8(7))* Houghton Mifflin Harcourt Publishing Co.

—Elements of Literature - Holt Adapted Reader. 5th ed. 2003. (Elements of Literature Ser.). (ENG., Illus.). 208p. (gr. 11-11). pap. 17.15 *(978-0-03-035459-5(5));* (gr. 9-9). pap. 17.15 *(978-0-03-035454-0(4))* Houghton Mifflin Harcourt Publishing Co.

—Holt Adapted Reader. (Elements of Literature Ser.). (ENG.). 3rd ed. 2003. 216p. (gr. 9-9). pap. 15.60 *(978-0-03-067866-0(8))* 3rd ed. 2003. 224p. (gr. 12-12). pap. 15.60 *(978-0-03-067869-1(2))* 5th ed. 2004. (Illus.). 224p. (gr. 8-8). pap. 17.15 *(978-0-03-035712-1(8))* Houghton Mifflin Harcourt Publishing Co.

—Holt Adapted Reader 2003 - Elemental Literature. 3rd ed. 2003. (Elements of Literature Ser.). (ENG.). 176p. (gr. 10-10). pap. 15.60 *(978-0-03-067867-7(6))* Houghton Mifflin Harcourt Publishing Co.

Jaffe, Charlotte & Roberts, Barbara. A Day No Pigs Would Die: L-I-T Guide. Date not set. (J). (gr. 4-10). pap. 8.95 *(978-1-56644-005-9(X),* 005-XAP) Educational Impressions.

Loewen, Nancy. No Kidding, Mermaids Are a Joke! The Story of the Little Mermaid As Told by the Prince. Tayal, Amit, illus. 2013. (Other Side of the Story Ser.). (ENG.). 24p. (gr. 2-3). 9.95 *(978-1-4795-1947-7(2))* Picture Window Bks.

—No Kidding, Mermaids Are a Joke! The Story of the Little Mermaid As Told by the Prince. Tayal, Amit, illus. 2013. (Other Side of the Story Ser.). (ENG.). 24p. (gr. 2-3). 27.32 *(978-1-4048-8303-1(7))* Picture Window Bks.

LITERATURE AS A PROFESSION

see Authors; Authorship; Journalism; Journalists

LITHUANIA

Bultje, Jan Willem. Lithuania. Hoving, Wilma, tr. 2006. (Looking at Europe Ser.). 48p. (YA). (gr. 5-8). 22.95 *(978-1-881508-43-4(9))* Oliver Pr., Inc.

Docalavich, Heather & Indovino, Shaina Carmel. Lithuania. 2012. (J). *(978-1-4222-2260-8(0));* pap. *(978-1-4222-2281-2(0))* Mason Crest.

Kagda, Sakina & Latif, Zawiah Abdul. Lithuania. 2nd rev. ed. 2007. (Cultures of the World Ser.). 144p. (gr. 6). lib. bdg. 42.79 *(978-0-7614-2087-3(8),* Benchmark Bks.) Marshall Cavendish Corp.

Kagda, Sakina, et al. Lithuania. 2017. (Cultures of the World Ser.). ***(978-1-5026-2739-1(6))*** Cavendish Square Publishing.

Waldron, Melanie. Lithuania, 1 vol. 2011. (Countries Around the World Ser.). (ENG.). 48p. (gr. 3-6). pap. 9.95 *(978-1-4329-5237-2(4),* NA-h) Heinemann-Raintree.

LITTERING

see Refuse and Refuse Disposal

LITTLE, MALCOLM, 1925-1965

see X, Malcolm, 1925-1965

LITTLE, STUART (FICTITIOUS CHARACTER)—FICTION

Rubin, Bruce Joel & Michaels, Julie. Stuart Little 2 Vol. 2: El Libro de la Pelicula. 2003. (SPA., Illus.). 60p. (J). (gr. 3-5). 14.95 *(978-84-204-6503-6(8))* Santillana USA Publishing Co., Inc.

White, E. B. Le Avventure di Stuart Little.Tr. of Stuart Little. (ITA.). pap. 17.95 *(978-88-451-2736-6(2))* Fabbri Editori - RCS Libri ITA. Dist: Distribooks, Inc.

—Stuart Little. Date not set. 141p. 18.95 *(978-0-8488-2602-4(7))* Amereon Ltd.

—Stuart Little. 2008. (J). 34.99 *(978-0-7393-7101-5(0))* Findaway World, LLC.

—Stuart Little. Williams, Garth, illus. 60th anniv. ed. 2005. (Trophy Bk.). (ENG.). 144p. (J). (gr. 3-7). pap. 6.99 *(978-0-06-440056-5(5))* HarperCollins Pubs.

—Stuart Little. Williams, Garth & Wells, Rosemary, illus. 60th anniv. ed. 2005. (Stuart-Little Ser.). (ENG.). 144p. (J). (gr. 3-7). pap. 8.99 *(978-0-06-441092-2(7))* HarperCollins Pubs.

—Stuart Little. Williams, Garth, illus. 60th anniv. ed. 2005. (Stuart-Little Ser.). (ENG.). 144p. (J). (gr. 3-7). 16.99 *(978-0-06-026395-9(4))* HarperCollins Pubs.

—Stuart Little. 131p. (J). pap. 5.95 *(978-0-8072-8333-2(9));* 2004. (gr. 3-7). pap. 29.00 incl. audio *(978-0-8072-8332-5(0),* YA165SP) Random Hse. Audio Publishing Group. (Listening Library).

White, E. B. & White, E. Stuart Little. 2005. (J). (gr. 3-6). lib. bdg. 17.20 *(978-0-8085-3806-6(3),* Turtleback) Turtleback Bks.

LITTLE BEAR (FICTITIOUS CHARACTER: MINARIK)—FICTION

Little Bear. 2003. (Goodnight Mr. Moon Ser.). (Illus.). (J). bds. 2.98 *(978-0-7525-4740-4(2))* Parragon, Inc.

Minarik, Else Holmelund. Los Amigos de Osito. Benavides, Rosa, tr. Sendak, Maurice, illus. 2nd ed. (Infantil Alfaguara Ser.: 32).Tr. of Little Bear's Friends. (SPA.). 64p. (J). 7.95 *(978-84-204-3049-2(8))* Santillana USA Publishing Co., Inc.

—Un Beso para Osito. Benavides, Rosa, tr. Sendak, Maurice, illus. 2003. (Infantil Alfaguara Ser.: 31).Tr. of Kiss for Little Bear. (SPA.). 36p. (J). (gr. k-3). 11.95 *(978-84-204-3050-8(1),* AF1633) Ediciones Alfaguara ESP. Dist: Lectorum Pubns., Inc., Santillana USA Publishing Co., Inc.

—Un Beso para Osito. Sendak, Maurice, tr. Sendak, Maurice, illus.Tr. of Kiss for Little Bear. (SPA.). 34p. (J). (gr. k-3). pap. 8.95 *(978-84-204-4827-5(3))* Santillana USA Publishing Co., Inc.

—Little Bear. Sendak, Maurice, illus. 2003. (I Can Read Level 1 Ser.). (ENG.). 64p. (J). (gr. k-3). pap. 3.95 *(978-0-06-444004-2(4))* HarperCollins Pubs.

—Little Bear. 2003. (Little Bear: I Can Read! Ser.). (J). (gr. k-3). lib. bdg. 13.55 *(978-0-8085-2618-6(9),* Turtleback) Turtleback Bks.

—Little Bear's Visit. Sendak, Maurice, illus. (J). pap. 12.95 incl. audio Weston Woods Studios, Inc.

—Osito. Aguilar, Joaquina, tr. Sendak, Maurice, illus. 2003. (Infantil Alfaguara Ser.: 25).Tr. of Little Bear. (SPA.). 60p. (J). (gr. k-3). pap. 8.95 *(978-84-204-3044-7(7),* AF1346) Santillana USA Publishing Co., Inc.

—Papa Oso Vuelve a Casa. Benavides, Rosa, tr. Sendak, Maurice, illus. 2nd ed. 2003. (Infantil Alfaguara Ser.: 29).Tr. of Father Bear Comes Home. (SPA.). 63p. (J). (gr. -1-3). pap. *(978-84-204-3048-5(X),* AF1359) Ediciones Alfaguara ESP. Dist: Santillana USA Publishing Co., Inc.

—La Visita de Osito. Puncel, María, tr. Sendak, Maurice, illus. 2006. (Osito / Little Bear Ser.).Tr. of Little Bear's Visit. (SPA.). 64p. (gr. k-3). pap. 8.95 *(978-968-19-0623-8(3),* AF1060) Santillana USA Publishing Co., Inc.

Weston Woods Staff, creator. A Kiss for Little Bear. 2011. 29.95 *(978-0-439-73481-3(9));* 18.95 *(978-0-439-72735-8(9));* 38.75 *(978-0-439-72739-6(1))* Weston Woods Studios, Inc.

LITTLE BEAR (FICTITIOUS CHARACTER: WADDELL)—FICTION

Waddell, Martin. Can't You Sleep, Little Bear? (CHI & ENG., Illus.). 32p. (J). *(978-1-85430-315-8(5),* 93445) Little Tiger Pr. Group.

—Let's Go Home, Little Bear. 2004. (Illus.). (J). (gr. k-3). spiral bd. *(978-0-616-01804-0(5));* spiral bd. *(978-0-616-01805-7(3))* Canadian National Institute for the Blind/Institut National Canadien pour les Aveugles.

—You & Me, Little Bear. 2004. (Illus.). (J). (gr. -1-2). spiral bd. *(978-0-616-01802-6(9));* spiral bd. *(978-0-616-01803-3(7))* Canadian National Institute for the Blind/Institut National Canadien pour les Aveugles.

LITTLE BIGHORN, BATTLE OF THE, MONT., 1876

Abnett, Dan. Sitting Bull & the Battle of the Little Bighorn. (Jr. Graphic Biographies Ser.). (ENG.). 24p. 2009. (J). (gr. 2-3). 47.90 *(978-1-61513-822-7(6),* PowerKids Pr.) 2007. (Illus.). (J). (gr. 2-5). lib. bdg. 25.25 *(978-1-4042-3394-2(6))* 2007. (Illus.). (gr. 3-8). pap. 10.60 *(978-1-4042-2147-5(6),* PowerKids Pr.) Rosen Publishing Group, Inc., The.

—Toro Sentado y la Batalla de Little Bighorn. 2009. (Historietas Juveniles: Biografías (Jr. Graphic Biographies) Ser.). (SPA., Illus.). 24p. (J). (gr. 2-5). 25.25 *(978-1-4358-8562-2(7));* (gr. 3-8). pap. 10.60 *(978-1-4358-3318-0(X))* Rosen Publishing Group, Inc., The.

Aller, Susan Bivin. Sitting Bull. 2004. (History Maker Bios Ser.). (J). pap. 6.95 *(978-0-8225-2072-6(9))* Lerner Publishing Group.

—Sitting Bull. Parlin, Tim, tr. Parlin, Tim, illus. 2004. (History Maker Bios Ser.). 47p. (J). 26.60 *(978-0-8225-0700-0(5),* Carolrhoda Bks.) Lerner Publishing Group.

Anderson, Paul C. George Armstrong Custer: The Indian Wars & the Battle of the Little Bighorn. 2009. (Library of American Lives & Times Ser.). 112p. (gr. 5-5). 69.20 *(978-1-60853-483-8(9))* Rosen Publishing Group, Inc., The.

Collard, Sneed B., III. Sitting Bull: Tatanka-Iyotake. 2009. (American Heroes Ser.). 48p. (gr. 3-18). 29.93 *(978-0-7614-4059-8(3))* Marshall Cavendish Corp.

DeFord, Diane. Chief Sitting Bull. 2009. pap. 13.25 *(978-1-60559-070-7(3))* Hameray Publishing Group, Inc.

Duffield, Katy. The Battle of Little Bighorn: Legendary Battle of the Great Sioux War. 2017. (Major Battles in US History (paperback) Ser.). (ENG., Illus.). 32p. (J). (gr. 4-7). pap. 9.95 ***(978-1-63517-076-4(1),*** Focus Readers) North Star Editions.

Dunn, Joeming W. Custer's Last Stand, 1 vol. Smith, Tim, illus. 2008. (Graphic History Ser.). (ENG.). 32p. 28.50 *(978-1-60270-181-6(4),* Graphic Planet- Nonfiction) ABDO Publishing Co.

Evento, Susan. Sitting Bull. 2005. (Rookie Biographies Ser.). (ENG., Illus.). 32p. (J). (gr. 1-2). pap. 4.95 *(978-0-516-25829-4(X),* Children's Pr.) Scholastic Library Publishing.

Ferrell, Nancy Warren. The Battle of the Little Bighorn in United States History. 2014. (In United States History Ser.). (Illus.). 96p. (J). (gr. 5-12). 27.94 *(978-0-7660-6097-5(7));* pap. 10.95 *(978-0-7660-6098-2(5))* Enslow Pubs., Inc.

Fradin, Dennis Brindell. Custer's Last Stand. 2006. (Turning Points in U. S. History Ser.). (Illus.). 48p. (gr. 3-7). lib. bdg. 31.36 *(978-0-7614-2124-5(6),* Benchmark Bks.) Marshall Cavendish Corp.

Gitlin, Martin. The Battle of the Little Bighorn, 1 vol. 2008. (Essential Events Set 2 Ser.). (ENG., Illus.). 112p. (J). (gr. 6-12). lib. bdg. 35.64 *(978-1-60453-045-2(6))* ABDO Publishing Co.

Goble, Paul. Custer's Last Battle: Red Hawk's Account of the Battle of the Little Bighorn. 2013. (ENG., Illus.). 44p. (J). (gr. 2-4). 16.95 *(978-1-937786-11-3(0),* Wisdom Tales) World Wisdom, Inc.

Green, Carl R. Custer's Stunning Defeat by American Indians at the Little Bighorn. 2006. (Wild History of the American West Ser.). (Illus.). 128p. (J). (gr. 5-9). lib. bdg. 34.60 *(978-1-59845-020-0(4),* MyReportLinks.com Bks.) Enslow Pubs., Inc.

Higgins, Nadia. Last Stand: Causes & Effects of the Battle of the Little Bighorn. 2015. (Cause & Effect: American Indian History Ser.). (ENG.). 32p. (gr. 3-4). pap. 7.95 *(978-1-4914-2208-3(4))* Capstone Press of Coughlan Cos.

January, Brendan. Little Bighorn: June 25, 1876. 2004. (ENG., Illus.). 32p. (J). (gr. 3-8). 14.95 *(978-1-59270-028-8(4))* Enchanted Lion Bks., LLC.

Jeffrey, Gary. The Battle of the Little Bighorn. Spender, Nick, illus. 2012. (Graphic History of the American West Ser.). (ENG.). 24p. (J). (gr. 3-8). pap. 8.15 *(978-1-4339-6733-7(2),* Gareth Stevens Learning Library); (gr. 4-7). lib. bdg. 23.95 *(978-1-4339-6731-3(6))* Stevens, Gareth Publishing LLLP.

—Sitting Bull: The Life of a Lakota Chief. 2009. (Graphic Nonfiction Biographies Ser.). (ENG.). 48p. (YA). (gr. 4-5). 58.50 *(978-1-61513-027-6(6),* Rosen Reference) Rosen Publishing Group, Inc., The.

Jeffrey, Gary & Petty, Kate. Sitting Bull: The Life of a Lakota Sioux Chief. 2005. (Graphic Nonfiction Biographies Ser.). (ENG., Illus.). 48p. (YA). (gr. 4-7). lib. bdg. 31.95 *(978-1-4042-0247-4(1))* Rosen Publishing Group, Inc., The.

Josephson, Judith Pinkerton. Who Was Sitting Bull? And Other Questions about the Battle of Little Bighorn. 2011. (Six Questions of American History Ser.). (ENG.). 48p. (gr. 4-6). 30.60 *(978-0-7613-5230-3(9));* pap. 56.72 *(978-0-7613-7645-3(3));* pap. 9.95 *(978-0-7613-7125-0(7))* Lerner Publishing Group.

King, Zelda. The Battle of the Little Bighorn: Both Sides of the Story. 2009. (Real Life Readers Ser.). 32p. (gr. 5-6). pap. 10.00 *(978-1-4358-0197-4(0),* Rosen Classroom) Rosen Publishing Group, Inc., The.

Link, Theodore. George Armstrong Custer: General de la caballería Estadounidense. 2004. (Grandes personajes en la historia de los Estados Unidos Ser.). (SPA.). 32p. (gr. 3-6). pap. 10.00 *(978-0-8239-4228-2(7),* Rosen Classroom) Rosen Publishing Group, Inc., The.

—George Armstrong Custer: General de la caballería estadounidense (George Armstrong Custer: General of the U. S. Cavalry) 2009. (Grandes personajes en la historia de los Estados Unidos (Famous People in American History) Ser.). (SPA.). 32p. (gr. 2-3). 47.90 *(978-1-61512-799-3(2),* Editorial Buenas Letras) Rosen Publishing Group, Inc., The.

—George Armstrong Custer: General of the U. S. Cavalry. 2009. (Primary Sources of Famous People in American History Ser.).Tr. of George Armstrong Custer: General de la Caballería Estadounidense. 32p. (gr. 2-3). 47.90 *(978-1-60851-680-3(6))* Rosen Publishing Group, Inc., The.

—George Armstrong Custer: General of the U. S. Cavalry / General de la caballería Estadounidense. 2009. (Famous People in American History/Grandes personajes en la historia de los Estados Unidos Ser.). (ENG & SPA.). 32p. (gr. 2-3). 47.90 *(978-1-61512-545-6(0),* Editorial Buenas Letras) Rosen Publishing Group, Inc., The.

Mapua, Jeff. Sitting Bull, 01 vols., 1. 2016. (Britannica Beginner Bios Ser.). (ENG., Illus.). 32p. (J). pap. 12.90 *(978-1-5081-0062-1(4),* Britannica Educational Publishing) Rosen Publishing Group, Inc., The.

Rice, Earle. The Life & Times of the Brothers Custer: Galloping to Glory. 2008. (Profiles in American History Ser.). (Illus.). 48p. (J). (gr. 4-8). lib. bdg. 29.95 *(978-1-58415-665-9(1))* Mitchell Lane Pubs., Inc.

Roxburgh, Ellis. Sitting Bull vs. George Armstrong Custer: The Battle of the Little Bighorn. 2016. (History's Greatest Rivals Ser.). (ENG., Illus.). 48p. (J). (gr. 6-8). pap. 14.05 *(978-1-4824-4235-9(3))* Stevens, Gareth Publishing LLLP.

Sanford, William R. Hunkpapa Lakota Chief Sitting Bull. 2013. (Native American Chiefs & Warriors Ser.). 48p. (J). (gr. 5-18). lib. bdg. 22.60 *(978-0-7660-4097-7(6))* Enslow Pubs., Inc.

—Oglala Sioux Chief Crazy Horse. 2013. (Native American Chiefs & Warriors Ser.). 48p. (J). (gr. 5-18). 22.60 *(978-0-7660-4094-6(1));* pap. 8.95 *(978-1-4644-0261-6(2))* Enslow Pubs., Inc.

Silate, Jennifer. The Last Stand: The Final Military Campaign of General George Armstrong Custer. 2009. (Great Moments in American History Ser.). 32p. (gr. 3-3). 47.90 *(978-1-61513-154-9(X))* Rosen Publishing Group, Inc., The.

Sitting Bull. 2010. (Legends of the Wild West Ser.). (Illus.). 128p. (gr. 6-12). 35.00 *(978-1-60413-527-5(1),* Chelsea Hse.) Facts On File, Inc.

Snelson, Bob. Riding into Glory: An Introduction to the Battle of the Little Bighorn. 2004. (Illus.). 170p. (YA). per. 12.00 *(978-0-9723935-4-6(4))* Snelsonbks.com.

Theunissen, Steve. The Battle of the Little Bighorn. 2004. (History of the Old West Ser.). (Illus.). 64p. (YA). (gr. 5-18). lib. bdg. 19.95 *(978-1-59084-065-8(8))* Mason Crest.

Walker, Paul Robert. Remember Little Bighorn: Indians, Soldiers, & Scouts Tell Their Stories. (ENG., Illus.). 64p. (J). (gr. 5). 2015. pap. 7.99 *(978-1-4263-2246-4(1))* 2006. 17.95 *(978-0-7922-5521-5(6))* 2006. lib. bdg. 27.90 *(978-0-7922-5522-2(4))* National Geographic Society. (National Geographic Children's Bks.).

LITTLE LEAGUE BASEBALL—FICTION

Dixon, Franklin W. The Missing Playbook. David, Matt, illus. 2016. (Hardy Boys Clue Book Ser.: 2). (ENG.). 96p. (J). (gr. 1-4). 16.99 *(978-1-4814-5178-9(2),* Aladdin) Simon & Schuster Children's Publishing.

Green, Tim. Best of the Best. 2012. (Baseball Great Ser.: 3). (J). lib. bdg. 17.20 *(978-0-606-23590-7(6),* Turtleback) Turtleback Bks.

J
K
L

—Best of the Best: A Baseball Great Novel. 2011. (Playaway Children Ser.). (J). (gr. 5-8). 64.99 (978-1-61707-137-9(4)) Findaway World, LLC.

—Best of the Best: A Baseball Great Novel. (Baseball Great Ser.: 3). (ENG.). (J). (gr. 3-7). 2012. 288p. pap. 7.99 (978-0-06-168624-5(7)) 2011. 272p. 16.99 (978-0-06-168622-1(0)) HarperCollins Pubs.

Lupica, Mike. Heat. 2007. (ENG.). 256p. (J). (gr. 5-18). 7.99 (978-0-14-240757-8(7), Puffin Books) Penguin Young Readers Group.

—Heat. 2007. 220p. (gr. 5-9). 18.00 (978-0-7569-8131-0(X)) Perfection Learning Corp.

—Heat. 2007. 18.40 (978-1-4177-7264-3(6), Turtleback) Turtleback Bks.

Preller, James. Six Innings. 2010. (ENG.). 176p. (YA). (gr. 4-9). pap. 7.99 (978-0-312-60240-6(5), 9780312602406) Square Fish.

Tellier, Derek. Anderson's Heat. 2016. (What's Your Dream? Ser.). (ENG.). 96p. (gr. 3-4). lib. bdg. 25.32 (978-1-4965-3441-5(7)) Capstone Press of Coughlan Cos.

LIVERPOOL (ENGLAND)—FICTION

Boyce, Frank Cottrell. The Unforgotten Coat. Hunter, Carl & Heney, Clare, illus. Hunter, Carl & Heney, Clare, photos by. 2011. (ENG.). 112p. (J). (gr. 3-7). 16.99 (978-0-7636-5729-1(8)) Candlewick Pr.

—The Unforgotten Coat. 2011. (Playaway Children Ser.). (ENG.). (J). (gr. 4-7). 39.99 (978-1-4558-4539-2(6)) Findaway World, LLC.

Kristen, Judith. Once upon a Time in Liverpool. Cash, Eric, illus. 2012. 40p. pap. 15.95 (978-0-9849505-2-2(4)) Aquinas & Krone Publishing, LLC.

Naughton, Bill. Pony Boy. 2012. (ENG.). 256p. (YA). pap. 15.99 (978-1-4482-0327-7(9), 9781448203277, Bloomsbury Reader) Bloomsbury Publishing Plc GBR. Dist: Macmillan.

LIVESTOCK

see also Cattle; Cows; Dairying; Domestic Animals; Donkeys; Horses; Mules; Sheep; Veterinary Medicine

Award, Anna. My First Picture Book Farm Animals. 2012. (ENG., Illus.). 24p. (J). 6.50 (978-1-84135-554-2(2)) Award Pubns. Ltd. GBR. Dist: Parkwest Pubns., Inc.

Barghoorn, Linda. Temple Grandin: Pioneer for Animal Rights & Autism Awareness. 2016. (Remarkable Lives Revealed Ser.). (ENG., Illus.). 32p. (J). (gr. 2-5). (978-0-7787-2688-3(6)) Crabtree Publishing Co.

Barker, C. Penny. The Farm. 2004. 56p. spiral bd. 25.00 (978-1-4116-2501-3(3)) Lulu Pr., Inc.

Bauman, Amy. Farm Animal Sounds. 2010. 12p. (J). (gr. -1). 9.95 (978-1-60747-708-2(4), Pickwick Pr.) Phoenix Bks., Inc.

Becker, John E. Frenemies for Life: Cheetahs & Anatolian Shepherd Dogs. 2010. 56p. (YA). (gr. 5-8). pap. 8.95 (978-0-9841554-1-5(4)); lib. bdg. 18.95 (978-0-9841554-0-8(6)) Columbus Zoo & Aquarium, The.

Bergin, Mark. Farm Animals. 2012. (It's Fun to Draw Ser.). (Illus.). 32p. (J). (gr. k-3). lib. bdg. 26.50 (978-1-61533-599-2(4)) Windmill Bks.

Bodden, Valerie. Caring for Horses. 2013. (Horsing Around (Creative Education) Ser.). (ENG., Illus.). 24p. (J). (gr. -1-3). 25.65 (978-1-60818-470-5(6), Creative Education) Creative Co., The.

Diaz, Joanne Ruelos. Animals on the Farm, 1 vol. Mendez, Simon, illus. 2014. (Animals All Day! Ser.). (ENG.). 32p. (gr. k-2). 27.27 (978-1-4795-5699-1(8)) Picture Window Bks.

Dickmann, Nancy. Los Animales de la Granja. 2011. (Mundo de la Granja Ser.). 24p. (gr. -1-1). (SPA & ENG.). 22.65 (978-1-4329-5306-5(0)); (ENG & SPA.). pap. 6.29 (978-1-4329-5313-3(3)) Heinemann-Raintree. (Bellota).

—Farm Animals, 1 vol. 2010. (World of Farming Ser.). (ENG.). 24p. (gr. -1-1). pap. 6.29 (978-1-4329-3941-0(6), Acorn) Heinemann-Raintree.

Galvin, Laura Gates. First Look at Farm Animals. Fulcher, Roz, illus. 2009. (ENG.). 16p. bds. 6.95 (978-1-59249-999-1(6)) Soundprints.

Glaser, Rebecca Stromstad. Cows Moo. 2016. (ENG., Illus.). 14p. (J). (gr. -1 — 1). bds. 7.99 (978-1-68152-125-1(3)) Amicus.

—Horses Neigh. 2016. (ENG., Illus.). 14p. (J). (gr. -1 — 1). bds. 7.99 (978-1-68152-126-8(1)) Amicus.

Grimm, Sandra. Baby Farm Animals. Sodré, Julie, illus. 2012. (ENG.). 20p. (J). (gr. -1-1). 12.95 (978-1-61608-654-1(8), 608654, Sky Pony Pr.) Skyhorse Publishing Co., Inc.

Hengel, Katherine. Strong Siberian Huskies, 1 vol. Doucet, Bob, illus. 2009. (Dog Daze Ser.). (ENG.). 24p. 25.65 (978-1-60453-620-1(9), Super SandCastle) ABDO Publishing Co.

Holden, Pam. Farm Friends, 6 pack. Hawley, Kelvin, illus. 2009. (Red Rocket Readers Ser.). (ENG.). 16p. (gr. -1-1). pap. (978-1-877363-14-6(6), Red Rocket Readers) Flying Start Bks.

James, Diane. En la Granja. 2004. (Descubre los Animales Ser.).Tr. of On the Farm. (SPA., Illus.). 24p. (J). (gr. -1-2). 9.95 (978-1-58728-489-2(8), Two-Can Publishing) T&N Children's Publishing.

Kallen, Stuart A. Is Factory Farming Harming America? 2006. (At Issue Ser.). (ENG., Illus.). 149p. (YA). (gr. 9-12). pap. 34.45 (978-0-7377-3437-9(X)) Cengage Gale.

Kalman, Bobbie. Farm Animals. 2011. (ENG.). 16p. (J). pap. (978-0-7787-9577-3(2)); lib. bdg. (978-0-7787-9552-0(7)) Crabtree Publishing Co.

Kavanaugh, Missy & Gurman, Sarah, texts. Farm Animals. 2009. (Illus.). (J). (978-1-4351-1779-2(4)) Barnes & Noble, Inc.

Kawa, Katie. My First Trip to the Farm. 2012. (My First Adventures Ser.). (Illus.). 24p. (gr. k-2). 69.20 (978-1-4339-8050-3(9)); (J). pap. 8.15 (978-1-4339-7313-0(8)); (J). lib. bdg. 22.60 (978-1-4339-7312-3(X)) Stevens, Gareth Publishing LLLP.

—My First Trip to the Farm: Mi Primera Visita a una Granja. 2012. (My First Adventures / Mis primeras aventuras Ser.). (SPA & ENG., Illus.). 24p. (J). (gr. k-2). lib. bdg. 22.60 (978-1-4339-7378-9(2)) Stevens, Gareth Publishing LLLP.

Little & Large Sticker Activity on the Farm. 2008. 24p. pap. (978-1-84810-060-2(4)) Miles Kelly Publishing, Ltd.

Maher, Jack. Animal Instincts. 2011. (J). pap. (978-0-531-22560-8(7)) Scholastic, Inc.

Mattern, Joanne. Farm Animals. 2017. (Readers Ser.). (ENG., Illus.). 48p. (J). (-k). pap. 4.99 (978-1-4263-2687-5(4), National Geographic Children's Bks.) National Geographic Society.

Mickelson, Trina. Free-Range Farming. 2016. (Growing Green Ser.). (ENG., Illus.). 64p. (J). (gr. 6-8). 51.99 (978-1-4677-9710-8(3), Lerner Pubns.) Lerner Publishing Group.

Miles, Lisa. Origami Farm Animals. 2013. (Amazing Origami Ser.). 32p. (J). (gr. 2-5). pap. 63.00 (978-1-4339-9654-2(5)); pap. 10.50 (978-1-4339-9653-5(7)); (ENG., Illus.). lib. bdg. 26.60 (978-1-4339-9652-8(9)) Stevens, Gareth Publishing LLLP.

Montgomery, Sy & Grandin, Temple. Temple Grandin: How the Girl Who Loved Cows Embraced Autism & Changed the World. 2012. (ENG., Illus.). 160p. (J). (gr. 5-7). 18.99 (978-0-547-44315-7(3)) Houghton Mifflin Harcourt Publishing Co.

Nunn, Daniel. Farm Animals, 1 vol. 2013. (True or False? Ser.). (ENG.). 20p. (gr. -1-1). bds. 7.99 (978-1-4109-5084-0(0), NA-r) Heinemann-Raintree.

—The Farm Animals. 2013. (True or False? Ser.). (ENG.). 24p. (gr. -1-1). pap. 6.29 (978-1-4109-5073-4(5), NA-r) Heinemann-Raintree.

—True or False? 2013. (True or False? Ser.). (ENG.). 20p. (gr. -1-1). bds. 15.98 (978-1-4109-6296-6(2), NA-r) Heinemann-Raintree.

Paiva, Johannah Gilman, ed. Farm Find. Gardiner, Lisa M., illus. 2013. 20p. (J). (gr. -1-1). 8.99 (978-1-77093-688-1(2)) Flowerpot Children's Pr. Inc. CAN. Dist: Cardinal Pubs. Group.

PAN Macmillan, P. A. N. Baby Animals. Bos, Miriam, illus. 2015. (First Sticker Story Fun Ser.). (ENG.). 30p. (J). (gr. -1-k). pap. 9.99 **(978-1-4472-8658-5(8))** Pan Macmillan GBR. Dist: Independent Pubs. Group.

Priddy, Roger. My Big Farm Book. 2011. (My Big Board Bks.). (ENG., Illus.). 12p. (J). (gr. -1 — 1). bds. 8.99 (978-0-312-51082-4(9), 9780312510824, Priddy Bks.) St. Martin's Pr.

Regan, Lisa. Farm Animals. Thompson, Kim, illus. 2010. (I Love Animals Ser.). (ENG.). 24p. (J). (gr. 1-5). pap. 8.15 (978-1-61533-233-5(2)); lib. bdg. 22.60 (978-1-61533-227-4(8)) Windmill Bks.

Rotner, Shelley. I Like the Farm. 2017. (I Like to Read(r) Ser.). (ENG.). 32p. (J). (gr. -1-3). 14.95 **(978-0-8234-3833-4(3))** Holiday Hse., Inc.

Sanford, William R. & Green, Carl R. Richard King: Courageous Texas Cattleman. 2012. (Courageous Heroes of the American West Ser.). (Illus.). 48p. (J). pap. 8.95 (978-1-4644-0088-9(1)) Enslow Pubs., Inc.

Stanos, Dimi, et al. Taking Care of Farm Animals. 2007. (Windows on Literacy Ser.). (ENG., Illus.). 12p. (J). pap. 10.95 (978-0-7922-8482-6(8)) CENGAGE Learning.

Tatchell, Judy. On the Farm. Smith, Alastair, illus. 2004. (Lift-the-Flap Learners Ser.). (ENG.). 1p. (J). (gr. 1-18). pap. 8.95 (978-0-7460-2775-2(3)) EDC Publishing.

Tate, Nikki. Down to Earth: How Kids Help Feed the World, 1 vol. 2013. (Orca Footprints Ser.). (ENG., Illus.). 48p. (J). (gr. 3-7). 19.95 (978-1-4598-0423-4(6)) Orca Bk. Pubs. USA.

Walters, Eric. Bedtime 123, 1 vol. Bisaillon, Josée, illus. 2017. (ENG.). 26p. (J). (gr. -1-k). bds. 9.95 **(978-1-4598-1073-0(2))** Orca Bk. Pubs. USA.

Watt, Fiona & Wells, Rachel. Anifeiliaid y Fferm. 2005. (WEL., Illus.). 10p. (978-1-84512-000-9(0)) Cymdeithas Lyfrau Ceredigion.

West, David. Farm Animals. 2013. (Nora the Naturalist's Animals Ser.). 24p. (gr. k-3). 28.50 (978-1-62588-000-0(6)) Black Rabbit Bks.

Worek, Michael. What's on My Farm? 2013. (ENG., Illus.). 160p. (J). (gr. -1-k). 9.95 (978-1-77085-236-5(0), 9781770852365) Firefly Bks., Ltd.

LIVING FOSSILS

see also names of specific fossils, e.g Platypus

Hemstock, Annie Wendt. Living Fossils, 1 vol. 2015. (Living Fossils Ser.). (ENG.). 24p. (J). 49.50 (978-1-4994-0320-6(8), PowerKids Pr.) Rosen Publishing Group, Inc., The.

Rajczak, Kristen. Jellyfish, 1 vol. 2015. (ENG., Illus.). 24p. (J). pap. 8.25 (978-1-4777-5827-4(5), PowerKids Pr.) Rosen Publishing Group, Inc., The.

Rosen Publishing Staff. Living Fossils, 1 vol. 2015. (Living Fossils Ser.). (ENG.). 24p. (J). 141.60 (978-1-4777-5736-9(8), PowerKids Pr.) Rosen Publishing Group, Inc., The.

Shofner, Melissa Raé. Crocodiles Lived with the Dinosaurs! 2016. (Living with the Dinosaurs Ser.). 00024p. (J). pap. 8.15 **(978-1-4824-5645-5(1))** Stevens, Gareth Publishing LLLP.

LIVINGSTONE, DAVID, 1813-1873

Bodden, Valerie. To the Heart of Africa. (Great Expeditions Ser.). 48p. (J). 2012. (ENG.). (gr. 4-7). pap. 12.00 (978-0-89812-664-8(9), Creative Paperbacks) 2011. (Illus.). 35.65 (978-1-60818-066-0(2), Creative Education) Creative Co., The.

Mattews, Basil. Livingstone: The Pathfinder. 2003. (ENG.). 112p. (YA). pap. 9.95 (978-0-923309-86-2(1)) Hartland Pubns.

O'Brien, Cynthia. Explore with Stanley & Livingstone. 2016. (Travel with the Great Explorers Ser.). (ENG., Illus.). 32p. (J). (gr. 3-6). (978-0-7787-2848-1(X)) Crabtree Publishing Co.

Otfinoski, Steven. David Livingstone: Deep in the Heart of Africa. 2006. (Great Explorations Ser.). (Illus.). 79p. (J). (gr. 3-7). lib. bdg. 32.79 (978-0-7614-2226-6(9), Benchmark Bks.) Marshall Cavendish Corp.

LIZARDS

Ang, Karen. Collared Lizard. 2015. (Desert Animals Searchin' for Shade Ser.). (ENG.). 24p. (J). (gr. -1-3). lib. bdg. 23.93 (978-1-62724-537-1(5)) Bearport Publishing Co., Inc.

Arnosky, Jim. All about Lizards: Y Jim Arnosky. 2004. (J). 15.95 (978-0-590-48145-8(2)) Scholastic, Inc.

Aronson, Virginia & Szejko, Allyn. Iguana Invasion! Exotic Pets Gone Wild in Florida. 2010. (ENG.). 69p. (YA). (gr. 7-18). 16.95 (978-1-56164-468-1(4)); pap. 12.95 (978-1-56164-469-8(2)) Pineapple Pr., Inc.

Bach, Rachel. Geckos. 2017. (Spot Backyard Animals Ser.). (ENG.). 16p. (J). (gr. k-3). 17.95 **(978-1-68151-092-7(8))** Amicus Publishing.

—El Geco (Geckos) 2017. (Spot Backyard Animals Ser.). (ENG & SPA.). 16p. (J). (gr. k-3). 17.95 **(978-1-68151-272-3(6)**, Amicus Readers) Amicus Publishing.

Baer, T. H. Lagartijas Pequeitas / Itty Bitty Geckos, Vol. 1. 2014. (Animales Pequeñitos / Itty Bitty Animals Ser.). (SPA & BYN.). 24p. (J). (gr. k-2). 22.60 (978-1-4339-9905-5(6)) Stevens, Gareth Publishing LLLP.

Beer, Amy-Jane. Lizards. 2008. (Nature's Children Ser.). (Illus.). 52p. (J). (978-0-7172-6238-0(3)) Grolier, Ltd.

Belknap, Jodi P. & Montgomery, Tamara. Kraken Ka The Komodo Dragon. Dodd, Joseph D., illus. 2007. 32p. pap. 19.95 incl. audio compact disk (978-0-9723420-7-0(9)) Belknap Publishing & Design.

Betances, Roberto. Lizard Blood. 2015. (Nature's Grossest Ser.). (ENG., Illus.). 24p. (J). (gr. 1-2). 22.60 (978-1-4824-1843-9(6)) Stevens, Gareth Publishing LLLP.

Bishop, Nic. Lizard, Level 2. Bishop, Nic, illus. 2014. (Scholastic Reader Level 2 Ser.). (ENG., Illus.). 32p. (J). (gr. k-2). pap. 3.99 (978-0-545-60569-4(5), Scholastic Nonfiction) Scholastic, Inc.

Bjorklund, Ruth. Komodo Dragons. 2012. (Nature's Children Ser.). (ENG., Illus.). 48p. (J). (gr. 3-5). pap. 6.95 (978-0-531-21077-2(4)); lib. bdg. 28.00 (978-0-531-20902-8(4)) Scholastic Library Publishing. (Children's Pr.).

—Lizards. 2008. (Great Pets Ser.). 48p. (gr. 3-18). lib. bdg. 29.93 (978-0-7614-2997-5(2), Benchmark Bks.) Marshall Cavendish Corp.

Bodden, Valerie. Amazing Animals: Iguanas. 2017. (Amazing Animals Ser.). (ENG., Illus.). 24p. (J). (gr. 1-3). pap. 8.99 **(978-1-62832-362-7(0)**, Creative Paperbacks) Creative Co., The.

—Amazing Animals: Komodo Dragons. 2013. (Amazing Animals Ser.). (ENG.). 24p. (J). (gr. 1-3). pap. 8.99 (978-0-89812-789-8(0), Creative Paperbacks) Creative Co., The.

—Iguanas. 2017. (Illus.). 24p. (J). (978-1-60818-754-6(3), Creative Education) Creative Co., The.

—Komodo Dragons. 2013. (Illus.). 24p. (J). 25.65 (978-1-60818-087-5(5), Creative Education) Creative Co., The.

Borgert-Spaniol, Megan. Komodo Dragons. 2014. (Animal Safari Ser.). (ENG.). 24p. (J). (gr. k-3). lib. bdg. 25.95 (978-1-60014-967-2(7), Blastoff! Readers) Bellwether Media.

Bowman, Chris. Iguanas. 2015. (Illus.). 24p. (J). (978-0-531-20514-3(2)); (ENG., 25.95 (978-1-62617-164-0(5), Blastoff! Readers) Bellwether Media.

Bredeson, Carmen. Fun Facts about Lizards! 2007. (I Like Reptiles & Amphibians! Ser.). (Illus.). 24p. (J). (gr. 1-3). lib. bdg. 22.60 (978-0-7660-2789-3(9), Enslow Elementary) Enslow Pubs., Inc.

Brett, Flora. Get to Know Geckos. 2015. (Get to Know Reptiles Ser.). (ENG.). 24p. (gr. 1-2). lib. bdg. 25.32 (978-1-4914-2060-7(X)) Capstone Press of Coughlan Cos.

Buckingham, Suzanne. Meet the Iguana. 2009. (Scales & Tails Ser.). (Illus.). 24p. (J). lib. bdg. 22.60 (978-1-4042-4499-3(9), PowerKids Pr.) Rosen Publishing Group, Inc., The.

Carr, Aaron. Iguana. 2014. (Illus.). 24p. (J). (978-1-62127-295-3(8)) Weigl Pubs., Inc.

Chancellor, Deborah. Lizards. 2009. (Extreme Pets Ser.). (Illus.). 32p. (YA). (gr. 4-7). 28.50 (978-1-59920-239-6(5)) Black Rabbit Bks.

Cheshire, Gerard. Lizards. 2008. (Scary Creatures Ser.). (ENG., Illus.). 32p. (J). (gr. 2-4). pap. 8.95 (978-0-531-21007-9(3), Watts, Franklin) Scholastic Library Publishing.

—Lizards - Scary Creatures. 2008. (Scary Creatures Ser.). (ENG., Illus.). 32p. (J). (gr. 2-4). 27.00 (978-0-531-20448-1(0), Children's Pr.) Scholastic Library Publishing.

Clarke, Ginjer L. Giant Lizards. Rothman, Michael, illus. 2005. (Penguin Young Readers, Level 3 Ser.). (ENG.). 48p. (J). (gr. 1-3). mass mkt. 3.99 (978-0-448-43120-8(3), Penguin Young Readers) Penguin Young Readers Group.

Coates, Jennifer. Lizards. (J). 2009. (Illus.). 112p. 14.95 (978-1-932904-39-0(5)) 2008. (978-1-932904-31-4(X)) Eldorado Ink.

Collard, Sneed B. Sneed B. Collard III's Most Fun Book Ever about Lizards. 2012. (ENM & ENG., Illus.). 48p. (J). (gr. 4-7). pap. 7.95 (978-1-58089-325-1(2)) Charlesbridge Publishing, Inc.

Colson, Rob. Lizard. 2017. (Pet to Get Ser.). (ENG., Illus.). 32p. (J). (gr. 4-6). pap. 12.99 (978-0-7502-8930-6(9), Wayland) Hachette Children's Group GBR. Dist: Hachette Bk. Group.

Connors, Kathleen. Geckos. 2013. (Really Wild Reptiles Ser.). (Illus.). 24p. (J). (gr. 2-5). pap. 8.15 (978-1-4339-8365-8(6)); lib. bdg. 22.60 (978-1-4339-8364-1(8)) Stevens, Gareth Publishing LLLP.

—Gila Monsters. 2013. (Really Wild Reptiles Ser.). (Illus.). 24p. (J). (gr. 2-5). pap. 8.15 (978-1-4339-8370-2(2)); lib. bdg. 22.60 (978-1-4339-8369-6(9)) Stevens, Gareth Publishing LLLP.

—Iguanas. 2013. (Really Wild Reptiles Ser.). (Illus.). 24p. (J). (gr. 2-5). pap. 8.15 (978-1-4339-8375-7(3)); lib. bdg. 22.60 (978-1-4339-8374-0(5)) Stevens, Gareth Publishing LLLP.

—Komodo Dragons. 2013. (Really Wild Reptiles Ser.). (Illus.). 24p. (gr. 2-5). 22.60 (978-1-4339-8379-5(6)); pap. 8.15 (978-1-4339-8380-1(X)) Stevens, Gareth Publishing LLLP. (Gareth Stevens Learning Library).

Craats, Rennay. Gecko. 2009. (My Pet Ser.). (Illus.). 32p. (J). (gr. 3-5). pap. 9.95 (978-1-60596-099-9(3)); lib. bdg. 26.00 (978-1-60596-098-2(5)) Weigl Pubs., Inc.

Craats, Rennay & Gillespie, Katie. Gecko. 2015. (J). (978-1-4896-2958-6(0)) Weigl Pubs., Inc.

Davin, Rose. Lizards. 2017. (Meet Desert Animals Ser.). (ENG., Illus.). 24p. (gr. k-1). lib. bdg. 26.65 (978-1-5157-4599-0(6), Pebble Plus) Capstone Press of Coughlan Cos.

De la Bédoyère, Camilla. The Wild Life of Lizards, 1 vol. 2015. (ENG.). 24p. (J). lib. bdg. 23.60 (978-1-4777-5494-8(6), Windmill Bks.) Rosen Publishing Group, Inc., The.

Dennard, Deborah. Lizards. Dewey, Jennifer Owings, illus. 2003. (Our Wild World Ser.). (ENG.). 48p. (J). (gr. 2-5). 10.95 (978-1-55971-858-5(7)); pap. 8.95 (978-1-55971-857-8(9)) Cooper Square Publishing Llc.

Eidenbuller, Bernd & Reisinger, Manfred. Beaded Lizards & Gila Monsters: Captive Care & Husbandry. 2011. (Illus.). 157p. 79.50 (978-3-89973-498-0(X)) Edition Chimaira DEU. Dist: Serpent's Tale Natural History Bk. Distributors, Inc.

Everything Changes: Individual Title Six-Packs. (Discovery World Ser.). 16p. (gr. 1-2). 28.00 (978-0-7635-8461-0(4)) Rigby Education.

Flynn, James. From Egg to Lizard. 2003. (Grow up! Ser.). (J). (978-1-58417-173-7(1)); pap. (978-1-58417-179-9(0)) Lake Street Pubs.

Gagne, Tammy. Geckos, 1 vol. 2014. (Amazing Reptiles Ser.). (ENG.). 48p. (gr. 8-12). lib. bdg. 32.79 (978-1-62403-372-8(5)) ABDO Publishing Co.

Garcia, Alonso. How Do Chameleons Change Color? 2017. (How Life Science Works). 24p. (J). (gr. 7-8). 49.50 **(978-1-5081-5631-4(X)**, PowerKids Pr.) Rosen Publishing Group, Inc., The.

Gish, Melissa. Geckos. 2014. 46p. (978-1-60818-417-0(X), Creative Education) Creative Co., The.

—Iguanas. 2015. (Illus.). 46p. (J). (978-1-60818-567-2(2), Creative Education) Creative Co., The.

—Iguanas: Living Wild. 2016. (Living Wild Ser.). (ENG.). 48p. (J). (gr. 5-9). pap. 12.00 (978-1-62832-168-5(7), Creative Paperbacks) Creative Co., The.

—Living Wild: Geckos. 2015. (Living Wild Ser.). (ENG.). 48p. (J). (gr. 5-8). pap. 12.00 (978-1-62832-003-9(6), Creative Paperbacks) Creative Co., The.

Greenberg, Daniel A. Lizards. 2003. (Animalways Ser.). (Illus.). 104p. (gr. 6-18). lib. bdg. 24.95 (978-0-7614-1580-0(7), Benchmark Bks.) Marshall Cavendish Corp.

Gregory, Helen. All about Snakes & Lizards, 1 vol. 2011. (Wonder Readers Early Level Ser.). (ENG.). (gr. -1-1). 32p. pap. 5.99 (978-1-4296-7796-7(1)); 16p. pap. 35.94 (978-1-4296-8068-4(7)) Capstone Press of Coughlan Cos. (Wonder Readers).

Hamilton, S. L. Lizards. 2010. (Xtreme Predators Ser.). 32p. (gr. 3-9). 27.07 (978-1-60453-992-9(5), A&D Xtreme) ABDO Publishing Co.

Hansen, Grace. Iguanas, 1 vol. 2014. (Reptiles Ser.). (ENG.). 24p. (J). (gr. 4-8). lib. bdg. 28.50 (978-1-62970-059-5(2)) ABDO Publishing Co.

Hansen, Grace, et al. Iguanas. 2015. (Reptiles Ser.). (SPA., Illus.). 24p. (gr. k-1). pap. 7.95 (978-1-4966-0505-4(5)) Capstone Classroom.

Hanson, Anders. Lively Lizards, 1 vol. 2007. (Perfect Pets Ser.). (ENG., Illus.). 24p. (J). (gr. k-3). lib. bdg. 24.21 (978-1-59928-752-2(8), SandCastle) ABDO Publishing Co.

Harris, Tim. Lizards. 2010. (Slimy, Scaly, Deadly Reptiles & Amphibians Ser.). (Illus.). 32p. (J). (gr. 2-6). pap. 10.50 (978-1-4339-3427-8(2)); lib. bdg. 26.00 (978-1-4339-3426-1(4)) Stevens, Gareth Publishing LLLP. (Gareth Stevens Learning Library).

Heathcote, Peter. Lizards, 1 vol. 2nd ed. 2010. (Keeping Unusual Pets Ser.). (ENG., Illus.). 48p. (gr. 3-6). 32.65 (978-1-4329-3853-6(3), NA-h) Heinemann-Raintree.

Heos, Bridget. Do You Really Want a Lizard? Longhi, Katya, illus. 2015. (Do You Really Want a Pet? Ser.). (ENG.). 24p. (J). (gr. 1-3). 19.95 (978-1-60753-750-2(8)) Amicus Publishing.

Hernandez-Divers, Sonia. Geckos, 1 vol. 2nd ed. 2010. (Keeping Unusual Pets Ser.). (ENG., Illus.). 48p. (gr. 3-6). 32.65 (978-1-4329-3849-9(5), NA-h) Heinemann-Raintree.

Jango-Cohen, Judith. Let's Look at Iguanas. 2009. (Lightning Bolt Books — Animal Close-Ups Ser.). (ENG., Illus.). 32p. (gr. k-2). pap. 7.95 (978-0-7613-5005-7(5)); lib. bdg. 26.60 (978-0-7613-3888-8(8)) Lerner Publishing Group. (Lerner Pubns.).

Kalman, Bobbie. Les Dragons de Komodo. 2010. (Petit Monde Vivant Ser.). (FRE., Illus.). 32p. (J). pap. 9.95 (978-2-89579-315-1(8)) Bayard Canada Livres CAN. Dist: Crabtree Publishing Co.

—Endangered Komodo Dragons. 2004. (Earth's Endangered Animals Ser.). (ENG., Illus.). 32p. (J). pap. (978-0-7787-1903-8(0)); lib. bdg. (978-0-7787-1857-4(3)) Crabtree Publishing Co.

Kenan, Tessa. Es un Camaleón! 2017. (Bumba Books (tm) en Español — Animales de la Selva Tropical (Rain Forest Animals) Ser.). (SPA., Illus.). 24p. (J). (gr. -1-1). 25.32 **(978-1-5124-4127-7(9))** Lerner Publishing Group.

Kenney, Karen Latchana. Axolotls. 2017. (Weird & Unusual Animals Ser.). (ENG.). 24p. (gr. 1-4). 20.95 **(978-1-68151-154-2(1))** Amicus Publishing.

Komodo Dragons. 2006. (Ugly Animals Ser.). (Illus.). 24p. (J). (gr. 3-7). lib. bdg. 22.60 (978-1-4042-3530-4(2)) Rosen Publishing Group, Inc., The.

Kralovansky, Susan. Salamander or Lizard?, 1 vol. 2014. (This or That? Ser.). (ENG.). 24p. (gr. 5-10). lib. bdg. 25.65 (978-1-62403-289-9(3), Super SandCastle) ABDO Publishing Co.

Lawrence, Ellen. A Spiny Back & Green Scaly Skin (Iguana) 2015. (Whose Little Baby Are You? Ser.). (ENG.). 24p. (J). (gr. -1-3). lib. bdg. 23.93 (978-1-910549-22-3(3)) Bearport Publishing Co., Inc.

Lewis, Brenda Ralph. Lizards. 2006. (Nature's Monsters: Reptiles & Amphibians Ser.). (Illus.). 32p. (gr. 2-6). lib. bdg. 26.00 (978-0-8368-6173-0(6), Gareth Stevens Learning Library) Stevens, Gareth Publishing LLLP.

The Lizard Library. (Illus.). (J). (gr. k-5). 112.50 (978-0-8239-7274-6(7)) Rosen Publishing Group, Inc., The.

Lizards. (Eyes on Nature Ser.). 32p. (J). (gr. 1). pap. (978-1-882210-60-2(3)) Action Publishing, Inc.

Lizards: Level N, 6 vols. (Wonder Worldtm Ser.). 48p. 34.95 (978-0-7802-4583-9(0)) Wright Group/McGraw-Hill.

Lunis, Natalie. Black Spiny-Tailed Iguana: Lizard Lightning! 2010. (Blink of an Eye: Superfast Animals Ser.). 24p. (YA). (gr. k-3). lib. bdg. 22.61 (978-1-936087-91-4(X)) Bearport Publishing Co., Inc.

—Green Iguanas. 2009. (Peculiar Pets Ser.). (Illus.). 24p. (YA). (gr. 2-5). lib. bdg. 22.61 (978-1-59716-863-2(7)) Bearport Publishing Co., Inc.

—Komodo Dragon: The World's Biggest Lizard. 2007. (SuperSized! Ser.). (Illus.). 24p. (J). (gr. k-3). lib. bdg. 21.28 (978-1-59716-392-7(9), 1265937) Bearport Publishing Co., Inc.

Macken, JoAnn Early. Gila Monsters. 2nd rev. ed. 2009. (Animals That Live in the Desert Ser.). (ENG.). 24p. (J). (gr. -1-3). pap. 8.15 (978-1-4339-2449-1(8)); lib. bdg. 22.60 (978-1-4339-1951-0(6)) Stevens, Gareth Publishing LLLP. (Weekly Reader Leveled Readers).

—Gila Monsters;Monstruos de Gila. 2nd rev. ed. 2009. (Animals That Live in the Desert/Animales del desierto Ser.). (ENG & SPA.). 24p. (J). (gr. -1-3). pap. 8.15 (978-1-4339-2457-6(9)); lib. bdg. 22.60 (978-1-4339-2062-2(X)) Stevens, Gareth Publishing LLLP. (Weekly Reader Leveled Readers).

Magellan, Marta. Those Lively Lizards. Gersing, James & Weaver, Steve, illus. Gersing, James, photos by. 2008. (Those Amazing Animals Ser.). (ENG.). 55p. (J). (gr. k-4). pap. 9.95 (978-1-56164-427-8(7)) Pineapple Pr., Inc.

Maimone, Max Q. Hunting with Komodo Dragons, Vol. 1. 2014. (Animal Attack! Ser.). (ENG.). 32p. (J). (gr. 2-3). 22.60 (978-1-4824-0497-5(4)) Stevens, Gareth Publishing LLLP.

Mara, Wil. Bearded Dragons. 2017. (Real-Life Dragons Ser.). (ENG., Illus.). 32p. (gr. 3-4). pap. 7.95 (978-1-5157-5074-1(4), Edge Bks.) Capstone Press of Coughlan Cos.

—Flying Dragons. 2017. (Real-Life Dragons Ser.). (ENG., Illus.). 32p. (gr. 3-4). lib. bdg. 27.99 (978-1-5157-5071-0(X), Edge Bks.) Capstone Press of Coughlan Cos.

Marsh, Laura. National Geographic Readers: Lizards. 2012. (Readers Ser.). (ENG., Illus.). 32p. (J). (gr. k-3). lib. bdg. 13.90 (978-1-4263-0923-6(6), National Geographic Children's Bks.) National Geographic Society.

Marsico, Katie. Geckos. 2013. (ENG.). 48p. (J). 28.00 (978-0-531-23357-3(X)); pap. 6.95 (978-0-531-25155-3(1)) Scholastic Library Publishing.

—A Komodo Dragon Hatchling Grows Up. 2007. (Scholastic News Nonfiction Readers Ser.). (ENG., Illus.). 24p. (J). (gr. 1-2). 22.00 (978-0-531-17477-7(8)) Scholastic Library Publishing.

McFee, Shane. Deadly Lizards. (Poison! Ser.). 24p. (gr. 2-3). 2009. 42.50 (978-1-60851-322-2(X), PowerKids Pr.) 2007. (Illus.). (YA). lib. bdg. 22.60 (978-1-4042-3796-4(8)) Rosen Publishing Group, Inc., The.

Meister, Cari. Horned Lizards. 2015. (Illus.). 24p. (J). lib. bdg. (978-1-62031-196-7(8), Bullfrog Bks.) Jump! Inc.

—Komodo Dragons. 2015. (Illus.). 24p. (J). lib. bdg. (978-1-62031-197-4(6), Bullfrog Bks.) Jump! Inc.

Miller, Jake. The Bearded Dragon. (Lizard Library). 24p. 2009. (gr. 3-3). 42.50 (978-1-60854-009-9(X)) 2003. (Illus.). (J). lib. bdg. 21.25 (978-0-8239-6412-3(4)) Rosen Publishing Group, Inc., The. (PowerKids Pr.).

—The Gila Monster. 2009. (Lizard Library). 24p. (gr. 3-3). 42.50 (978-1-60854-013-6(8), PowerKids Pr.) Rosen Publishing Group, Inc., The.

—The Green Iguana. (Lizard Library). 24p. 2009. (gr. 3-3). 42.50 (978-1-60854-016-7(2)) 2003. (Illus.). (J). lib. bdg. 22.60 (978-0-8239-6415-4(9)) Rosen Publishing Group, Inc., The. (PowerKids Pr.).

—The Komodo Dragon. (Lizard Library). 24p. 2009. (gr. 3-3). 42.50 (978-1-60854-019-8(7)) 2003. (Illus.). (J). lib. bdg. 22.60 (978-0-8239-6416-1(7)) Rosen Publishing Group, Inc., The. (PowerKids Pr.).

—The Leopard Gecko. (Lizard Library). 24p. 2009. (gr. 3-3). 42.50 (978-1-60854-020-4(0)) 2003. (Illus.). (J). lib. bdg. 22.60 (978-0-8239-6413-0(2)) Rosen Publishing Group, Inc., The. (PowerKids Pr.).

Morey, Allan. Frilled Lizards. 2017. (Weird & Unusual Animals Ser.). (ENG.). 24p. (gr. 1-4). 20.95 **(978-1-68151-157-3(6))** Amicus Publishing.

Morgan, Sally. Lizards & Snakes. 2012. (Pets Plus Ser.). 32p. (gr. 3-6). lib. bdg. 31.35 (978-1-59920-704-9(4)) Black Rabbit Bks.

Murray, Julie. Iguanas, 1 vol. 2003. (Animal Kingdom Ser.). (ENG.). 24p. (gr. k-4). 25.65 (978-1-57765-727-9(6), Buddy Bks.) ABDO Publishing Co.

—Komodo Dragons, 1 vol. 2013. (Asian Animals Ser.). (ENG.). 32p. (J). (gr. 2-5). lib. bdg. 28.50 (978-1-61783-555-1(2), Big Buddy Bks.) ABDO Publishing Co.

—Lizards, 1 vol. 2005. (Animal Kingdom Set Ii Ser.). (ENG., Illus.). 24p. (gr. k-4). 25.65 (978-1-59197-325-6(2), Buddy Bks.) ABDO Publishing Co.

Olson, Amy. What's Bugging Camo the Chameleon. 2009. 32p. pap. 13.00 (978-1-60860-258-2(3), Strategic Bk. Publishing) Strategic Book Publishing & Rights Agency (SBPRA).

O'Shea, Mark. Exploring Nature: Incredible Lizards - Discover the Astonishing World of Chameleons, Geckos, Iguanas & More, with over 190 Pictures. 2013. (ENG., Illus.). 64p. (J). (gr. 3-7). 12.99 (978-1-84322-735-9(5), Armadillo) Anness Publishing GBR. Dist: National Bk. Network.

Owings, Lisa. Leaping Lizards! Teaching Alliteration. 2016. (Playing with Words Ser.). (ENG.). 16p. (J). (gr. -1-2). 25.64 (978-1-5038-0838-6(6), 210689) Child's World, Inc., The.

Pallotta, Jerry. Komodo Dragon vs. King Cobra. Bolster, Robert, illus. 2016. (Who Would Win? Ser.). (ENG.). 32p. (J). (gr. 1-3). pap. 3.99 (978-0-545-30171-8(8)) Scholastic, Inc.

Peterson, Megan Cooley & Rustad, Martha E. H. Iguanas, 1 vol. 2012. (Reptiles Ser.). (ENG., Illus.). 24p. (gr. k-1). lib. bdg. 26.65 (978-1-4296-5996-3(3), Pebble Plus) Capstone Press of Coughlan Cos.

Petrie, Kristin. Iguanas, 1 vol. 2012. (Unique Pets Ser.). (ENG.). 24p. (J). (gr. 3-6). lib. bdg. 25.65 (978-1-61783-440-0(8), Checkerboard Library) ABDO Publishing Co.

Phillips, Dee. Gila Monster's Burrow. 2015. (Illus.). 24p. (J). lib. bdg. (978-1-62724-309-4(7)) Bearport Publishing Co., Inc.

PRESS, Celebration. Looking at Lizards. 2003. (ENG.). (J). (gr. 2-5). pap., stu. ed. 34.95 (978-0-673-62835-0(3), Celebration Pr.) Pearson Schl.

Rake, Matthew. Scaly, Slippery Creatures. Mendez, Simon, illus. 2015. (Real-Life Monsters Ser.). (ENG.). 32p. (J). (gr. 3-6). pap. 7.99 (978-1-4677-7645-5(9), Lerner Pubns.) Lerner Publishing Group.

Randolph, Joanne. My Friend the Iguana. 2010. (Curious Pet Pals Ser.). (ENG., Illus.). 24p. (J). (gr. k-3). pap. 8.15 (978-1-60754-985-7(9)); lib. bdg. 22.60 (978-1-60754-977-2(8)) Windmill Bks.

Raum, Elizabeth. Geckos. 2015. (Lizards Ser.). (Illus.). 32p. (J). 28.50 (978-1-60753-485-3(1)) Amicus Publishing.

—Green Iguanas. 2015. (Illus.). 32p. (J). lib. bdg. 28.50 (978-1-60753-487-7(8)) Amicus Publishing.

Reid, Siuna Ann. Reptiles Are Cool- Understanding My Lizard. Lodge, Vivienne E., ed. 2013. (Illus.). 70p. pap. (978-0-9576568-3-3(1)) Siuna A Reid.

Riggs, Kate. Amazing Animals: Geckos. 2015. (Amazing Animals Ser.). (ENG.). 24p. (J). (gr. 1-3). pap. 8.99 (978-1-62832-089-3(3), Creative Paperbacks) Creative Co., The.

—Geckos. (J). 2017. **(978-1-60818-868-0(X))** 2015. (978-1-60818-489-7(7)) Creative Co., The. (Creative Education).

—Seedlings: Geckos. 2017. (Seedlings Ser.). (ENG.). 24p. (J). (gr. -1-1). pap. 7.99 **(978-1-62832-483-9(X)**, Creative Paperbacks) Creative Co., The.

Rudolph, Jessica. Gecko. 2016. (Weird but Cute Ser.). (ENG., Illus.). 24p. (J). (gr. -1-3). lib. bdg. 17.95 (978-1-62724-849-5(8)) Bearport Publishing Co., Inc.

—MIS Garras Son Largas y Curvas. 2015. (Pistas de Animales Ser.). (SPA., Illus.). 24p. (J). (gr. -1-3). lib. bdg. 23.93 (978-1-62724-578-4(2)) Bearport Publishing Co., Inc.

—My Claws Are Large & Curved (Komodo Dragon) 2014. (Zoo Clues Ser.). 24p. (J). (gr. -1-3). lib. bdg. 23.93 (978-1-62724-114-4(0)) Bearport Publishing Co., Inc.

Schuh, Mari. Iguanas. 2014. (Illus.). 24p. (J). lib. bdg. 25.65 (978-1-62031-110-3(0), Bullfrog Bks.) Jump! Inc.

Sherman, Jill. Komodo Dragons. 2017. (Real-Life Dragons Ser.). (ENG., Illus.). 32p. (gr. 3-4). lib. bdg. 27.99 (978-1-5157-5069-7(8), Edge Bks.) Capstone Press of Coughlan Cos.

Silverman, Buffy. Can You Tell a Gecko from a Salamander? 2012. (Lightning Bolt Books (tm) — Animal Look-Alikes Ser.). 32p. (gr. k-2). (ENG.). pap. 7.95 (978-0-7613-8552-3(5)); pap. 45.32 (978-0-7613-9255-2(6)) Lerner Publishing Group.

Silverstein, Alvin, et al. Iguanas: Cool Pets! Kelley, Gerald, illus. 2011. (Far-Out & Unusual Pets Ser.). 48p. (J). (gr. 2-5). lib. bdg. 25.27 (978-0-7660-3686-4(3)) Enslow Pubs., Inc.

Simon, Elizabeth. Iguana. 2010. pap. 9.95 (978-1-61690-077-9(6)); 32p. (J). (gr. 3-5). lib. bdg. 27.13 (978-1-61690-076-2(8)) Weigl Pubs., Inc.

Sokol, Dawn DeVries. Leapin' Lizards - Pet Palooza: A Lizards Primer, 1 vol. 2017. (ENG.). 22p. (J). bds. 9.99 **(978-1-4236-4737-9(8))** Gibbs Smith, Publisher.

Sovak, Jan. Lizards. 2006. (Dover Nature Coloring Book Ser.). (ENG., Illus.). 32p. (J). (gr. 1-5). 3.99 (978-0-486-44820-6(7)) Dover Pubns., Inc.

Stevens, Kathryn. Lizards. 2015. (Pet Care Ser.). (ENG.). 24p. (J). (gr. -1-2). 25.64 (978-1-63143-733-5(X), 208548) Child's World, Inc., The.

Stewart, Melissa. How Do Chameleons Change Color? 2008. (Tell Me Why, Tell Me How Ser.). (Illus.). 32p. (gr. 3-18). lib. bdg. 29.93 (978-0-7614-2922-7(0), Benchmark Bks.) Marshall Cavendish Corp.

—Salamander or Lizard? How Do You Know? 2011. (Which Animal Is Which? Ser.). (Illus.). 24p. (J). (gr. k-18). pap. 7.95 (978-1-59845-238-9(X), Enslow Elementary); lib. bdg. 22.60 (978-0-7660-3679-6(0)) Enslow Pubs., Inc.

Storad, Conrad J. Gila Monsters. 2008. (Early Bird Nature Books Ser.). (Illus.). 48p. (J). (gr. 3-7). lib. bdg. 26.60 (978-0-8225-7888-8(3), Lerner Pubns.) Lerner Publishing Group.

Thatcher, Henry. Komodo Dragons & Geckos, 1 vol., 1. 2014. (Big Animals, Small Animals Ser.). (ENG.). 32p. (J). (gr. k-5). 26.25 (978-1-4777-6106-9(3), PowerKids Pr.) Rosen Publishing Group, Inc., The.

Trueit, Trudi Strain. Lizards. 2003. (True Bks.). (ENG.). 48p. (gr. 3-5). pap. 6.95 (978-0-516-29351-6(6), Children's Pr.) Scholastic Library Publishing.

Truscott, Julia. Your Safari: In Search of the Real Komodo Dragon. White, Daniel, photos by. 2005. (Illus.). 48p. (J). 11.95 (978-1-59594-014-8(6), Wingspan Pr.) WingSpan Publishing.

Turnbull, Stephanie. Komodo Dragon. 2015. (Big Beasts Ser.). (Illus.). 24p. (J). (gr. k-3). 28.50 (978-1-62588-200-4(9)) Black Rabbit Bks.

World Book, Inc Staff, contrib. by. Green Anoles & Other Pet Lizards. 2009. (J). (978-0-7166-1368-8(9)) World Bk., Inc.

World Book, Inc. Staff, contrib. by. Iguanas & Other Lizards. 2005. (World Book's Animals of the World Ser.). (Illus.). 64p. (J). (978-0-7166-1268-1(2)) World Bk., Inc.

LIZARDS—FICTION

Abbott, Tony. The Hidden Stairs & the Magic Carpet. Jessell, Tim, illus. 2004. (Secrets of Droon Ser.: No. 1). 80p. (gr. 2-5). 15.00 (978-0-7569-3939-7(9)) Perfection Learning Corp.

ABDO Publishing Company Staff. Chet Gecko Mysteries - 10 Titles. 2008. (Chet Gecko Mystery Ser.). (J). 242.10 (978-1-59961-460-1(X)) Spotlight.

Abrams, Penny. The Calabash Tales. Mikki, illus. 2011. 66p. 28.00 (978-1-4349-1169-8(1)) Dorrance Publishing Co., Inc.

Ailes, Mark Cusco. The Snow Dargles: Book Two: the Chronicles of Weekland. 2010. 244p. pap. 16.95 (978-1-4327-5223-1(5)) Outskirts Pr., Inc.

Antony, Steve. Green Lizards vs. Red Rectangles. Antony, Steve, illus. 2015. (ENG., Illus.). 32p. (J). (gr. -1-k). 16.99 (978-0-545-84902-9(0), Scholastic Pr.) Scholastic, Inc.

Bennett, Steven. The Adventures of Super Dad: Colossal Encounters (Book #1) 2005. 98p. pap. 10.49 (978-1-4116-5947-6(3)) Lulu Pr., Inc.

Bentley, Dawn. Icky Sticky Chameleon. Mack, Jeff, illus. 2005. 18p. (J). 9.95 (978-1-58117-086-3(6), Intervisual/Piggy Toes) Bendon, Inc.

Berglund, Andrea Lloyd. A Good Little Horse: Thunder's Morning Stroll. 2009. 36p. (J). pap. 19.95 (978-1-4327-3822-8(4)) Outskirts Pr., Inc.

Blackshaw, Win. David's Dinosaur. 2009. 104p. pap. 17.55 (978-1-4092-3704-4(4)) Lulu Pr., Inc.

Bowler, Ann Martin & Bowler, Anna. Gecko's Complaint: A Balinese Folktale. Sukanada, I. Gusti Made, illus. 2009. (ENG & IND.). 32p. (J). (gr. k-3). 14.95 (978-0-7946-0484-4(6)) Tuttle Publishing.

Brecon, Connah. Frank! 2014. (ENG., Illus.). 32p. (J). (gr. -1-17). 16.95 (978-0-7624-5423-5(7), Running Pr. Kids) Running Pr. Bk. Pubs.

Brian, Janeen. The Adventures of Kingii the Frilled Lizard, 1 vol. rev. ed. 2013. (Fiction Readers Ser.). (ENG., Illus.). 28p. (J). (gr. 3-3). pap. 8.99 (978-1-4333-5607-0(4)) Shell Educational Publishing.

—The Adventures of Kingii the Frilled Lizard. rev. ed. 2013. (Fiction Readers Ser.). (ENG., Illus.). 28p. (gr. 3-3). pap. 19.96 (978-1-4807-1729-9(0)) Teacher Created Materials, Inc.

Brodhead, Kimberly Renee. The Seedling: The Osarian Tales. 2008. 232p. pap. 24.95 (978-1-60703-814-6(5)) America Star Bks.

Brodnax, Stephan. Dillwyn & the Purple Picnic Pack, 1 vol. 2009. 19p. pap. 24.95 (978-1-4241-9593-0(4)) America Star Bks.

Bush, Don. Magic Smith the Chameleon. 62p. (J). (gr. 3). 6.50 (978-0-943978-02-4(5)) Rolling Hills Pr.

Carter, Aubrey Smith. The Enchanted Lizard: La Lagartijita Mágica. Nelson, Esther Whitt, ed. Branton, Molly, illus. 2006. (ENG & SPA.). 96p. (J). 18.95 (978-1-893271-38-8(2), Maverick Bks.) Trinity Univ. Pr.

Chen, E. C. Bad Alphabet. 2013. 62p. 15.99 (978-0-9891510-0-9(X)) Zebra Ginkgo.

Clark, Kent & Snider, Brandon T. Peter Powers & the League of Lying Lizards! Bardin, Dave, illus. 2017. (Peter Powers Ser.: 4). (ENG.). 128p. (J). (gr. 1-5). 15.99 **(978-0-316-54640-9(2))** Little, Brown Bks. for Young Readers.

Conroe, Lindy. Rockafella Jones & the Hidden Treasure. Riette, Susanne, illus. 2011. 108p. (J). pap. 10.95 (978-1-935199-00-7(5)) Blue Mustang Pr.

Cook, Sherry & Johnson, Terri. Inquisitive Inman, 26 vols. Kuhn, Jesse, illus. l.t. ed. 2006. (Quirkles — Exploring Phonics through Science Ser.: 9). 32p. (J). 7.99 (978-1-933815-08-4(6), Quirkles, The) Creative 3, LLC.

Cowley, Joy. Friends: Snake & Lizard. Bishop, Gavin, illus. 2011. (Gecko Press Titles Ser.). (ENG.). 144p. 16.95 (978-1-877579-01-1(7)) Gecko Pr. NZL. Dist: Lerner Publishing Group.

Crane, Elizabeth J. Armando: The Case of the Missing Tail. 2011. 36p. pap. 15.95 (978-1-4490-8257-4(2)) AuthorHouse.

Crow, Melinda Melton. Little Lizards. Rowland, Andrew, illus. 2013. (Little Lizards Ser.). (ENG.). 32p. (gr. -1-1). 135.90 (978-1-4342-8840-0(4)) Stone Arch Bks.

—Little Lizard's Big Party, 1 vol. Rowland, Andrew, illus. 2010. (Little Lizards Ser.). (ENG.). 32p. (gr. -1-1). lib. bdg. 22.65 (978-1-4342-2007-3(9)) Stone Arch Bks.

—Little Lizard's Big Party. Rowland, Andrew & Rowlands, Andy, illus. 2010. (Little Lizards Ser.). (ENG.). 32p. (gr. -1-1). pap. 6.25 (978-1-4342-2791-1(X)) Stone Arch Bks.

—Little Lizard's Family Fun, 1 vol. Rowland, Andrew, illus. 2010. (Little Lizards Ser.). (ENG.). 32p. (gr. -1-1). lib. bdg. 22.65 (978-1-4342-2006-6(0)) Stone Arch Bks.

—Little Lizard's Family Fun. Rowland, Andrew & Rowlands, Andy, illus. 2010. (Little Lizards Ser.). (ENG.). 32p. (gr. -1-1). pap. 6.25 (978-1-4342-2790-4(1)) Stone Arch Bks.

—Little Lizard's First Day, 1 vol. Rowland, Andrew, illus. 2010. (Little Lizards Ser.). (ENG.). 32p. (gr. -1-1). lib. bdg. 22.65 (978-1-4342-2005-9(2)) Stone Arch Bks.

—Little Lizard's First Day. Rowland, Andrew & Rowlands, Andy, illus. 2010. (Little Lizards Ser.). (ENG.). 32p. (gr. -1-1). pap. 6.25 (978-1-4342-2789-8(8)) Stone Arch Bks.

—Little Lizard's New Baby, 1 vol. Rowland, Andrew, illus. 2011. (Little Lizards Ser.). (ENG.). 32p. (gr. -1-1). pap. 6.25 (978-1-4342-3047-8(3)) Stone Arch Bks.

—Little Lizard's New Bike, 1 vol. Rowland, Andrew, illus. 2010. (Little Lizards Ser.). (ENG.). 32p. (gr. -1-1). lib. bdg. 22.65 (978-1-4342-2008-0(7)) Stone Arch Bks.

—Little Lizard's New Bike. Rowland, Andrew & Rowlands, Andy, illus. 2010. (Little Lizards Ser.). (ENG.). 32p. (gr. -1-1). pap. 6.25 (978-1-4342-2792-8(8)) Stone Arch Bks.

—Little Lizard's New Friend, 1 vol. Rowland, Andrew, illus. 2011. (Little Lizards Ser.). (ENG.). 32p. (gr. -1-1). pap. 6.25 (978-1-4342-3048-5(1)) Stone Arch Bks.

—Little Lizard's New Pet, 1 vol. Rowland, Andrew, illus. 2011. (Little Lizards Ser.). (ENG.). 32p. (gr. -1-1). pap. 6.25 (978-1-4342-3049-2(X)); lib. bdg. 22.65 (978-1-4342-2508-5(9)) Stone Arch Bks.

—Little Lizard's New Shoes, 1 vol. Rowland, Andrew, illus. 2011. (Little Lizards Ser.). (ENG.). 32p. (gr. -1-1). pap. 6.25 (978-1-4342-3050-8(3)); lib. bdg. 22.65 (978-1-4342-2509-2(7)) Stone Arch Bks.

Crowe, Ellie. Go to Sleep, Hide & Seek. Wu, Julie, illus. 2009. 10p. (J). bds. 11.95 (978-1-59700-759-7(5)) Island Heritage Publishing.

Culici, Tonia. Kiku Gecko & Rainbow Girl. 2012. 44p. pap. 20.45 (978-1-4525-0584-8(5)) Balboa Pr.

Cummings, Pat. Harvey Moon, Museum Boy. Cummings, Pat, illus. 2008. (Illus.). 32p. (J). (gr. -1-3). lib. bdg. 18.89 (978-0-06-057861-9(0)) HarperCollins Pubs.

Cyr, Lynne G. Drako's ABC Adventures as an Iguana. 2006. (Illus.). 37p. (J). spiral bd. 21.95 (978-0-9774543-0-3(4)) Cyr Design Publishing.

Cyrus, Kurt. Invisible Lizard. Atkins, Andy, illus. 2017. (ENG.). 32p. (J). (gr. k-2). 16.99 **(978-1-58536-378-0(2)**, 204320) Sleeping Bear Pr.

De Serres, Michelle. The Gecko Ball. 2011. (Illus.). 28p. pap. (978-1-905553-78-5(1)) BookPublishingWorld.

Denise, Susan Denise. The Little Lazy Lizard. 2008. 16p. pap. 24.95 (978-1-60474-502-3(9)) America Star Bks.

Denucci, Sharon. Grammie & the Gecko. DeNucci, Corinne, illus. 2008. 40p. pap. 16.99 (978-1-4389-1790-0(2)) AuthorHouse.

Derenge, Garett. The Adventures of Iggy the Iguana. 2013. (ENG.). 30p. (J). pap. 13.95 (978-1-4787-1290-9(2)) Outskirts Pr., Inc.

DeSica, Melissa. Gecko & Mosquito. 2007. (Illus.). 32p. (J). 14.95 (978-0-9790647-6-0(7)) Watermark Publishing, LLC.

Dinardo, Jeff. The Sunrise Band: Cooperating. Palen, Debbie, illus. 2014. (Funny Bone Readers: Being a Friend Ser.). 24p. (gr. -1-1). pap. 4.99 (978-1-939656-06-3(0)) Red Chair Pr.

Donaldson, Julia. Superworm. Scheffler, Axel, illus. 2014. (ENG.). 32p. (J). (gr. -1-3). 16.99 (978-0-545-59176-8(7), Levine, Arthur A. Bks.) Scholastic, Inc.

Las Dos Iguanas.Tr. of Two Iguanas. (SPA.). (J). 9.95 (978-968-6044-78-2(7)) Corunda, Ediciones, S.A. de C.V. MEX. Dist: AIMS International Bks., Inc.

Eagle, Golden. Father Sun & Luis the Lizard. l.t. ed. 2005. (Illus.). 22p. (J). per. 12.99 (978-1-59879-026-9(9)) Lifevest Publishing, Inc.

Emanuel, Effie Ann. Charles Chameleon. 2007. 32p. per. 24.95 (978-1-4241-8621-1(8)) America Star Bks.

Escoffier, Michaël. Brief Thief. Di Giacomo, Kris, illus. 2013. (ENG.). 32p. (J). (gr. -1-3). 16.95 (978-1-59270-131-5(0)) Enchanted Lion Bks., LLC.

Escott, Maria. Green Anole Meets Brown Anole, a Love Story. Wigal, Mike, illus. 2010. 28p. pap. 12.95 (978-1-936051-82-3(6)) Peppertree Pr., The.

Fontenot, Mary Alice & Fontenot Landry, Julie. Clovis Crawfish & the Twin Sister, 1 vol. Butler, Julie Dupre & Buckner, Julie Dupre, illus. 2007. (Clovis Crawfish Ser.). (ENG.). 32p. (J). (gr. k-3). 16.99 (978-1-58980-467-8(8)) Pelican Publishing Co., Inc.

Giancamilli, Vanessa. Gecko Gathering. Kest, Kristin, illus. 2005. (Soundprints' Amazing Animal Adventures! Ser.). (ENG.). 32p. (J). (gr. -1-3). 19.95 (978-1-59249-321-0(1), BC7107) Soundprints.

Giuliani, Al. New Nanny. 2013. (Jessie Junior Novel Ser.). (ENG.). 128p. (J). (gr. 3-7). pap. 5.99 (978-1-4231-8369-3(X)) Disney Pr.

Goodyear-Brown, Paris. Gabby the Gecko. 2003. per. (978-1-932203-54-7(0)) Sundog, Ltd.

Grace, Phillip. The Lizard of Cupcake Lake. 2006. (J). pap. 15.95 (978-0-9601454-3-0(5), 06-2129LIZ) Stelucan Pr.

Gravett, Emily. Blue Chameleon. Gravett, Emily, illus. 2011. (ENG., Illus.). 32p. (J). (gr. -1-1). 16.99 (978-1-4424-1958-2(X), Simon & Schuster Bks. For Young Readers) Simon & Schuster Bks. For Young Readers.

Hale, Bruce. The Adventures of Space Gecko. (Illus.). (J). 8.95 (978-0-9621280-2-8(3)) Words & Pictures Publishing, Inc.

—The Big Nap. Hale, Bruce, illus. 2008. (Chet Gecko Mystery Ser.: No. 4). (ENG., Illus.). 128p. (gr. 1-5). 24.21 (978-1-59961-461-8(8)) Spotlight.

—Dial M for Mongoose: A Chet Gecko Mystery. 2010. (Chet Gecko Ser.: 15). (ENG., Illus.). 128p. (J). (gr. 2-5). pap. 5.99 (978-0-547-48079-4(2)) Houghton Mifflin Harcourt Publishing Co.

—The Malted Falcon. Hale, Bruce, illus. 2008. (Chet Gecko Mystery Ser.: No. 7). (ENG., Illus.). 128p. (gr. 1-5). 24.21 (978-1-59961-467-0(7)) Spotlight.

—Murder, My Tweet. 2005. (Chet Gecko Mystery Ser.). (Illus.). 117p. (gr. 3-7). 16.00 (978-0-7569-5248-8(4)) Perfection Learning Corp.

—Murder, My Tweet. Hale, Bruce, illus. 2008. (Chet Gecko Mystery Ser.: No. 10). (ENG., Illus.). 136p. (gr. 1-5). 24.21 (978-1-59961-468-7(5)) Spotlight.

—The Mystery of Mr. Nice. Hale, Bruce, illus. 2008. (Chet Gecko Mystery Ser.: No. 2). (ENG., Illus.). 112p. (gr. 1-5). 24.21 (978-1-59961-469-4(3)) Spotlight.

—This Gum for Hire. 2003. (Chet Gecko Ser.: 6). (ENG., Illus.). 144p. (J). (gr. 2-5). pap. 5.99 (978-0-15-202497-0(2)) Houghton Mifflin Harcourt Publishing Co.

—This Gum for Hire. Hale, Bruce, illus. 2008. (Chet Gecko Mystery Ser.: No. 6). (ENG., Illus.). 128p. (gr. 1-5). 24.21 (978-1-59961-471-7(5)) Spotlight.

—Trouble Is My Beeswax. 2004. (Chet Gecko Mystery Ser.). (Illus.). 111p. (gr. 3-7). 16.00 (978-0-7569-3488-0(5)) Perfection Learning Corp.

—Trouble Is My Beeswax. Hale, Bruce, illus. 2008. (Chet Gecko Mystery Ser.: No. 8). (ENG., Illus.). 128p. (gr. 1-5). 24.21 (978-1-59961-472-4(3)) Spotlight.

Hale, Mary. Karly & Sheila's Walk. 2012. (ENG.). 23p. (J). pap. 11.95 (978-1-4327-8647-2(4)) Outskirts Pr., Inc.

Halfmann, Janet. Little Skink's Tail, 1 vol. Klein, Laurie Allen, illus. 2007. (ENG.). 32p. (J). (gr. -1-3). 15.95 (978-0-9768823-8-1(8)) Arbordale Publishing.

Haneberg, Janet. Alamander, the Orange Salamander. 2006. 37p. (J). pap. 14.99 (978-1-4116-6678-8(X)) Lulu Pr., Inc.

Haselhuhn, Hugo & Cowdell, Luke. Lucas Lightfoot & the Fire Crystal. 2016. (ENG., Illus.). 180p. (J). pap. 12.95 (978-1-63047-783-7(4)) Morgan James Publishing.

Hilton, Marcel. The Magical Web. 2007. 38p. 19.50 (978-1-4303-2678-6(6)) Lulu Pr., Inc.

Irwin, Bindi & Kunz, Chris. Camouflage. 2011. (Bindi's Wildlife Adventures Ser.: 4). (ENG.). 112p. (gr. 3-6). pap. 4.99 (978-1-4022-5523-6(3), Sourcebooks Jabberwocky) Sourcebooks, Inc.

James, Shilah & James, Michael. Little Land Adventures - Little Iguan. Castles, Heather, illus. 2010. 24p. pap. (978-1-926635-34-7(5)) Adlibbed, Ltd.

Johnson, Regan. Hold on to Your Tail: Letters from Camp Lizard. Johnson, Regan, illus. 2008. (Letters From Camp Lizard Ser.). (ENG., Illus.). 112p. (J). (gr. 1-5). pap. 7.95 (978-1-933831-04-6(9)) Blooming Tree Pr.

Johnston, Cindy. Zip, Burp & Hula. 2006. (Illus.). 32p. (J). per. 10.95 (978-0-9787930-5-0(6)) Virtual Word Publishing.

Joyner, Andrew. Boris Gets a Lizard. 2013. (Boris Ser.: 2). (ENG., Illus.). 80p. (J). (gr. k-2). pap. 4.99 (978-0-545-48447-3(2)) Scholastic, Inc.

—Boris Gets a Lizard. 2013. (Boris Ser.: 2). lib. bdg. 14.75 (978-0-606-31975-1(1), Turtleback) Turtleback Bks.

Julie, Aunt. State Symbols of Texas - Paddleduck #8. 2012. 50p. pap. 5.95 (978-1-105-91163-7(2)) Lulu Pr., Inc.

Karre, Nancy. On Herman's Pond. 2005. 8.00 (978-1-933281-00-1(6), 2267) Battle Creek Area Mathematics & Science Ctr.

Kiker, Jean. Jumping Lizard Tales. 2005. pap. 12.95 (978-1-932196-51-1(X)) WordWright.biz, Inc.

Knight, Diedre. Beanie's Backyard. 2012. 28p. pap. 12.95 (978-1-62141-812-2(X)) Booklocker.com, Inc.

Koontz, Robin. The Three Billy Goats & Gruff. Koontz, Robin, illus. 2011. (ENG., Illus.). 24p. (gr. 2-3). pap. 8.95 (978-1-61236-030-0(0)) Rourke Educational Media.

Lambert, George J. 8 Boys & 8 Beasts, 1 vol. Lambert, Celeste, illus. 2010. 24p. 24.95 (978-1-4489-5901-3(2)) PublishAmerica, Inc.

Lemke, Donald B. Chameleon Cage Match! Eliopoulos, Chris, illus. 2013. (Lucha Lizards Ser.). (ENG.). 48p. (gr. 1-3). pap. 5.95 (978-1-4342-3874-0(1)); lib. bdg. 23.99 (978-1-4342-3285-4(9)) Stone Arch Bks.

Lingenfelser, Lynda L. The Adventures of Lizah Lizard: The Laughing, Lovable Lizard. 2006. 46p. (J). per. 22.98 (978-0-615-13290-7(1)) Lingenfelser, Lynda L.

—Lizah Lizard: Koco's Tale. 2008. 50p. pap. 22.98 (978-0-615-14072-8(6)) Lingenfelser, Lynda L.

Lionni, Leo. A Color of His Own: (Spanish-English Bilingual Edition) Lionni, Leo, illus. 2016. (ENG & SPA., Illus.). 32p. (J). (gr. -1-k). bds. 7.99 (978-0-553-53873-1(X), Knopf Bks. for Young Readers) Random Hse. Children's Bks.

Little, Celeste. Scales. Motz, Mike, illus. 2012. 24p. (J). 12.95 (978-1-60131-116-0(8)) Big Tent Bks.

Little, Jean. Emma's Strange Pet. Plecas, Jennifer, illus. (I Can Read Level 3 Ser.). 64p. (J). (gr. k-3). 2004. (ENG.). pap. 3.99 *(978-0-06-444259-6(4))* 2003. 15.99 *(978-0-06-028350-6(5))* HarperCollins Pubs.

Long, Ethan. Chamelia. 2011. (ENG., Illus.). 40p. (J). (gr. -1-3). 16.99 *(978-0-316-08612-7(6))* Little, Brown Bks. for Young Readers.

Mendenhall, Gaylee. My Teacher Is Bald! 2011. 28p. pap. 14.99 *(978-1-4634-5032-8(X))* AuthorHouse.

Milani, Joan. The Secret Society of the Palos Verdes Lizards. Schartup, Adam, illus. 2013. (ENG.). (J). 14.95 *(978-1-62086-346-6(4))* Mascot Bks., Inc.

Molchadsky, Yael. The Chameleon That Saved Noah's Ark. Bergman, Orit, illus. 2016. (ENG.). 32p. (J). (gr. k-3). 16.99 *(978-1-101-99676-8(5)*, Nancy Paulsen Books) Penguin Young Readers Group.

Moon, Alice. Lucky's Special Thanksgiving. 2007. (Illus.). (J). pap. 9.95 *(978-0-9795831-2-4(8))* PeachMoon Publishing.

Morin, Tara. There's an Iguana in My Bed. 2013. 28p. pap. 15.99 *(978-1-4817-1191-3(1))* AuthorHouse.

Murakami, Jon & BeachHouse Publishing. Geckos Surf. 2007. (ENG.). 16p. (J). (gr. -1-5). bds. 7.95 *(978-1-933067-22-3(5))* Beachhouse Publishing, LLC.

—Geckos up Geckos Down. 2010. (ENG.). 20p. (J). (gr. -1-1). bds. 7.95 *(978-1-933067-31-5(4))* Beachhouse Publishing, LLC.

My Special Place: Individual Title Six-Packs. (gr. -1-2). 23.00 *(978-0-7635-8811-3(3))* Rigby Education.

Nelson, Connie. The Lizard's Secret Door. Waller, Joyce, illus. 2014. 32p. (J). 19.95 *(978-1-59298-933-1(0))* Beaver's Pond Pr., Inc.

Oneto, Maria Teresa. Liliana, la Iguan. 2012. 52p. pap. 25.00 *(978-1-4389-8241-0(0))* AuthorHouse.

Orozco, Maria. Lizards on 41st Street. 2011. 28p. pap. 13.59 *(978-1-4567-2412-2(6))* AuthorHouse.

Osborn, D. W. Why Can't I Ribbit?, 1 vol. 2009. 48p. pap. 16.95 *(978-1-61582-641-4(6))* America Star Bks.

Paquette, Heather. Kammy the Chameleon Goes to School. Paquette Jr., Edward D., illus. 2012. 24p. pap. 24.95 *(978-1-62709-765-9(1))* America Star Bks.

Parker, Ty. The Golden Lizards. 2011. 20p. pap. 12.95 *(978-1-4670-2820-2(7))* AuthorHouse.

Patton, Jack. The Butterfly Rebellion. 2016. (Battle Bugs Ser.: 9). (ENG.). 128p. (J). (gr. 2-5). pap. 4.99 *(978-0-545-94515-8(1)*, Scholastic Paperbacks) Scholastic, Inc.

—The Lizard War. 2015. (Battle Bugs Ser.: 1). (ENG.). 128p. (J). (gr. 2-5). pap. 4.99 *(978-0-545-70741-1(2)*, Scholastic Paperbacks) Scholastic, Inc.

—The Poison Frog Assault (Battle Bugs #3) 2015. (Battle Bugs Ser.: 3). (ENG.). 128p. (J). (gr. 2-5). pap. 4.99 *(978-0-545-70744-2(7)*, Scholastic Paperbacks) Scholastic, Inc.

—The Spider Siege. 2015. (Battle Bugs Ser.: 2). (ENG.). 128p. (J). (gr. 2-5). pap. 4.99 *(978-0-545-70742-8(0)*, Scholastic Paperbacks) Scholastic, Inc.

Paul, Ann Whitford. Count on Culebra. Long, Ethan, illus. 2010. (ENG.). 40p. (J). (gr. -1-3). pap. 6.95 *(978-0-8234-2310-1(7))* Holiday Hse., Inc.

PeachMoon Publishing. The Adventures of Lucky the Lizard Las aventuras del lagarto Lucky. 2008. (ENG & SPA., Illus.). 100p. (J). pap. 19.95 *(978-0-9795831-4-8(4))* PeachMoon Publishing.

—The Lizard in the Mailbox. 2007. (J). pap. 9.95 *(978-0-9795831-0-0(1))* PeachMoon Publishing.

—Lucky Goes to School. 2007. (J). pap. 9.95 *(978-0-9795831-1-7(X))* PeachMoon Publishing.

Perlman, Janet. The Delicious Bug. Perlman, Janet, illus. 2009. (ENG., Illus.). 32p. (J). (gr. -1-2). 16.95 *(978-1-55337-996-6(9))* Kids Can Pr., Ltd. CAN. Dist: Hachette Bk. Group.

Phinn, Gervase. Who Am I? Phinn, Gervase, illus. 2012. (Andersen Press Picture Bks). (ENG., Illus.). 32p. (J). (gr. -1-3). 16.95 *(978-0-7613-8996-5(2))* Lerner Publishing Group.

Pickering, Jill. A Lizard Got into the Paint Pots. Wright, Petrina, illus. 2003. (ENG.). 220p. (J). (gr. -1-3). 14.95 *(978-0-333-98858-9(2))* Macmillan Caribbean GBR. Dist: Interlink Publishing Group, Inc.

Pinkwater, Daniel M. Lizard Music. Pinkwater, Daniel M., illus. 2017. (ENG., Illus.). 160p. (J). (gr. 4-7). pap. 9.99 ***(978-1-68137-184-9(7)***, NYRB Kids) New York Review of Bks., Inc., The.

—Lizard Music. 2011. (ENG., Illus.). 160p. (J). (gr. 4-7). 15.95 *(978-1-59017-387-9(2)*, NYR Children's Collection) New York Review of Bks., Inc., The.

Price, Allison W. A. The Dragons & the Words of Knowledge. 2009. 112p. pap. 14.98 *(978-0-557-05766-5(3))* Lulu Pr., Inc.

Ramirez, Iz. Bob the Lizard, 1 vol. Swope, Brenda, illus. 2009. 26p. pap. 24.95 *(978-1-60749-232-0(6))* America Star Bks.

Reich, Ashley. Izzy Lizzy. Reich, Ashley, illus. 2005. (Illus.). 32p. (J). per. 16.00 *(978-0-9754298-3-9(3)*, Ithaca Pr.) Authors & Artists Publishers of New York, Inc.

Richler, Mordecai. Jacob Two-Two & the Dinosaur. Petricic, Dusan, illus. 2009. (Jacob Two-Two Ser.). (ENG.). 104p. (J). (gr. 4-7). 10.95 *(978-0-88776-926-9(8))* Tundra Bks. CAN. Dist: Random Hse., Inc.

Roberts, Sarah E. Lunch with Sam & Max. 2012. 20p. pap. 17.99 *(978-1-4772-9053-8(2))* AuthorHouse.

Robertson, Elysia Hill. Dottie Goes to School. Robertson, Elysia Hill, illus. 2005. (Illus.). 30p. (J). per. 6.95 *(978-0-9764444-8-0(8))* E. J. Publishing.

Russell, Allyson. The Lizard Who Wanted to Be a Mouse. Bubp, Jennifer, illus. 2009. 28p. pap. 12.95 *(978-1-59858-938-2(5))* Dog Ear Publishing, LLC.

Salzmann, Mary Elizabeth. Leaping Lizards, 1 vol. Chawla, Neena, illus. 2007. (Critter Chronicles Ser.). (ENG.). 24p. (J). (gr. k-3). lib. bdg. 24.21 *(978-1-59928-450-7(2)*, SandCastle) ABDO Publishing Co.

Sands, Maria. Sanjee & Her Delightful Hats. 2008. 20p. pap. 24.95 *(978-1-60563-700-6(9))* America Star Bks.

Santillo, LuAnn. Liz. Santillo, LuAnn, ed. 2003. (Half-Pint Kids Readers Ser.). (Illus.). 7p. (J). (gr. -1-1). pap. 1.00 *(978-1-59256-083-7(0))* Half-Pint Kids, Inc.

Shamberger, Lindsey. I, I, I for Iguan. 2012. 44p. pap. 24.95 *(978-1-4626-7536-4(0))* America Star Bks.

Skelton, K. Magic from the Wishing Well. 2009. 28p. pap. 12.49 *(978-1-4389-8747-7(1))* AuthorHouse.

Smith, Rosemary. Lizard Tales: Lizzie Walks on the Wild Side. 2010. 28p. pap. 12.50 *(978-1-60911-082-6(X)*, Strategic Bk. Publishing) Strategic Book Publishing & Rights Agency (SBPRA).

—Lizzie Goes to Tea. 2013. 32p. pap. 12.50 *(978-1-62212-338-4(7)*, Strategic Bk. Publishing) Strategic Book Publishing & Rights Agency (SBPRA).

—Woody Gets Dunked. 2011. 28p. pap. 12.50 *(978-1-60976-628-3(8)*, Eloquent Bks.) Strategic Book Publishing & Rights Agency (SBPRA).

Sparkes, Ali. Chameleon Chaos. Collins, Ross, illus. 2014. (S. W. I. T. C. H. Ser.: 10). (ENG.). 112p. (J). (gr. 2-5). lib. bdg. 27.93 *(978-1-4677-2113-4(1)*, Darby Creek) Lerner Publishing Group.

—Gecko Gladiator. Collins, Ross, illus. 2014. (S. W. I. T. C. H. Ser.: 12). (ENG.). 104p. (J). (gr. 2-5). lib. bdg. 27.93 *(978-1-4677-2115-8(8)*, Darby Creek) Lerner Publishing Group.

—Lizard Loopy. Collins, Ross, illus. 2014. (S. W. I. T. C. H. Ser.: 9). (ENG.). 104p. (J). (gr. 2-5). lib. bdg. 27.93 *(978-1-4677-2112-7(3)*, Darby Creek) Lerner Publishing Group.

Stephens, Sarah Hines. Sleepy Time Crime, 1 vol. Baltazar, Art, illus. 2012. (DC Super-Pets Ser.). (ENG.). 56p. (gr. 2-2). pap. 4.95 *(978-1-4048-7215-8(9))*; lib. bdg. 23.99 *(978-1-4048-6485-6(7))* Picture Window Bks. (DC Super-Pets).

Stilton, Thea. Revenge of the Lizard Club. Cooper-McGuinness, Nanette, tr. from ITA. 2013. (Thea Stilton Graphic Novels Ser.). (ENG., Illus.). 56p. (J). (gr. 1-5). 9.99 *(978-1-59707-430-8(6)*, 9781597074308) Papercutz.

Stine, R. L. Lizard of Oz. 2016. (Goosebumps: Most Wanted Ser.: 10). (ENG.). 160p. (J). (gr. 3-7). pap. 6.99 *(978-0-545-82549-8(0)*, Scholastic Paperbacks) Scholastic, Inc.

Stockman, Hollie. Leon the Lizard. 2010. 36p. pap. 19.95 *(978-0-557-57889-4(2))* Lulu Pr., Inc.

Storad, Conrad J. Lizards for Lunch: A Roadrunner's Tale. 2009. (Sonoran Desert Tails Ser.). (Illus.). 32p. (J). (gr. k-4). 6.95 *(978-1-891795-00-8(7))* RGU Group, The.

Strunk, Peter, illus. & creator. Two Inch Hero: The Adventures of Lorenzo Lizard. Strunk, Peter, creator. 2006. (J). 17.95 *(978-0-9785961-0-1(2))* Smile Time Publishing.

TenNapel, Doug. Battle for Amphibopolis. 2017. (Nnewts Ser.: 3). (ENG.). 224p. (J). (gr. 3-7). 19.99 ***(978-0-545-67664-9(9))***; pap. 10.99 ***(978-0-545-67670-0(3))*** Scholastic, Inc. (Graphix).

TenNapel, Doug. The Rise of Herk. 2016. (Nnewts Ser.: 2). (ENG.). 208p. (J). (gr. 3-7). 19.99 *(978-0-545-67652-6(5)*, Graphix) Scholastic, Inc.

Trooboff, Rhoda. A Book for Elie. Radjou, Anna Nazaretz, illus. 2008. (ENG.). 31p. pap. 15.00 *(978-0-9773536-1-3(3))* Univ. of Toledo Pr.

Van Draanen, Wendelin. The Gecko & Sticky: the Power Potion. Gilpin, Stephen, illus. 2011. (Gecko & Sticky Ser.). (ENG.). 240p. (J). (gr. 3-7). 6.99 *(978-0-440-42245-7(0)*, Yearling) Random Hse. Children's Bks.

—The Greatest Power. Gilpin, Stephen, illus. 2011. (Gecko & Sticky Ser.: Bk. 1). (ENG.). 208p. (J). (gr. 3-7). 7.99 *(978-0-440-42243-3(4)*, Yearling) Random Hse. Children's Bks.

—Sinister Substitute. Gilpin, Stephen, illus. (Gecko & Sticky Ser.: Bk. 3). (ENG.). 224p. (J). (gr. 3-7). 2011. 7.99 *(978-0-440-42244-0(2)*, Yearling) 2010. 12.99 *(978-0-375-84378-5(7)*, Knopf Bks. for Young Readers) Random Hse. Children's Bks.

Vernon, Ursula. Curse of the Were-Wiener. 3rd ed. (Dragonbreath Ser.: 3). (ENG.). 208p. (J). (gr. 3-7). 2014. pap. 6.99 *(978-0-14-751321-2(9)*, Puffin Books) 2010. 12.99 *(978-0-8037-3469-2(7)*, Dial Bks) Penguin Young Readers Group.

—Curse of the Were-Wiener. 2014. (Dragonbreath Ser.: 3). lib. bdg. 17.20 *(978-0-606-35710-4(6))* Turtleback Bks.

—When Fairies Go Bad, No. 7. 7th ed. 2012. (Dragonbreath Ser.: 7). (ENG.). 208p. (J). (gr. 3-7). 12.99 *(978-0-8037-3678-8(9)*, Dial Bks) Penguin Young Readers Group.

Villata, Diane A. Louie the Lizard. 2010. 28p. 12.50 *(978-1-4389-6923-7(6))* AuthorHouse.

Wagstaff, Janiel. Stella & Class: Information Experts. 2015. (ENG.). pap. 7.95 *(978-1-63133-024-7(1))* Staff Development for Educators.

Wiebe, Trina. Lizards Don't Wear Lip Gloss. Sarrazin, Marisol, illus. 2004. (Abby & Tess Pet-Sitters Ser.). 91p. 15.95 *(978-0-7569-3425-5(7))* Perfection Learning Corp.

Wiesner, David. Art & Max. 2012. (CHI.). 37p. (J). *(978-7-5434-9586-9(4))* Hebei Jiaoyu Chubanshe.

—Art & Max. 2010. (ENG., Illus.). 40p. (J). (gr. -1-3). 17.99 *(978-0-618-75663-6(9)*, Clarion Bks.) Houghton Mifflin Harcourt Trade & Reference Pubs.

Williamson, Rose. Look at Me! Look at Me! Marts, Doreen, illus. 2014. (ENG.). 32p. (J). (gr. -1-k). 16.95 *(978-1-62914-617-1(X)*, Sky Pony Pr.) Skyhorse Publishing Co., Inc.

Wilson, A. c. & Wilson, A. C. Ambersil - the Legacy of Mr Harrison. 2011. 496p. pap. *(978-1-908105-45-5(3))* Grosvenor Hse. Publishing Ltd.

Winter, Barbara. Chameleon Capers. 2004. (Amazing Dictionary Ser.). (Illus.). 64p. pap. *(978-0-921156-97-0(9))* Rubicon Publishing, Inc.

Yates, Gene, illus. The Chameleon Colors Book. 2006. (J). *(978-1-58865-361-1(7))* Kidsbooks, LLC.

Zinsser, Kam. Turbo Fires Up! 2012. (ENG.). 28p. (J). 16.95 *(978-1-4787-1756-0(4))* Outskirts Pr., Inc.

LLAMAS

Aspen-Baxter, Linda & Kissock, Heather. Llamas. 2012. (SPA.). (J). *(978-1-61913-189-7(7))* Weigl Pubs., Inc.

Barnes, Julia. Camels & Llamas at Work. 2006. (Animals at Work Ser.). (Illus.). 32p. (gr. 3-6). lib. bdg. 26.00 *(978-0-8368-6222-5(8)*, Gareth Stevens Learning Library) Stevens, Gareth Publishing LLLP.

Dunn, Mary R. Llamas, 1 vol. 2012. (South American Animals Ser.). (ENG.). 24p. (gr. k-1). lib. bdg. 26.65 *(978-1-4296-7588-8(8)*, Pebble Plus) Capstone Press of Coughlan Cos.

Gish, Melissa. Living Wild: Llamas. 2017. (Living Wild Ser.). (ENG.). 48p. (J). (gr. 5-7). pap. 12.00 ***(978-1-62832-434-1(1)***, Creative Paperbacks) Creative Co., The.

—Llamas. 2017. (J). ***(978-1-60818-831-4(0)***, Creative Education) Creative Co., The.

Hudak, Heather C. Llamas. 2006. (Farm Animals Ser.). (Illus.). 24p. (J). (gr. 3-7). lib. bdg. 24.45 *(978-1-59036-427-7(9))*; per. 8.95 *(978-1-59036-434-5(1))* Weigl Pubs., Inc.

Kissock, Heather & Aspen-Baxter, Linda. Llamas. 2011. (J). 27.13 *(978-1-61690-930-7(7))* Weigl Pubs., Inc.

Marsico, Katie. Llama. 2011. (21st Century Junior Library: Farm Animals Ser.). (ENG.). 24p. (gr. 2-4). lib. bdg. 25.64 *(978-1-60279-977-6(6)*, 200944) Cherry Lake Publishing.

Murray, Julie. Llamas, 1 vol. 2003. (Animal Kingdom Ser.). (ENG.). 24p. (gr. k-4). 25.65 *(978-1-57765-724-8(1)*, Buddy Bks.) ABDO Publishing Co.

Stockland, Patricia M. In the Llama Yard, 1 vol. Ouren, Todd, illus. 2009. (Barnyard Buddies Set 2 Ser.). (ENG.). 24p. (gr. -1-2). 27.07 *(978-1-60270-644-6(1)*, Looking Glass Library-Nonfiction) Magic Wagon.

Williams, Zella. Llamas & Other Latin American Camels: Llamas y Otros Camélidos de Latinoamérica. 2009. (Animals of Latin America / Animales de Latinoamérica Ser.). (SPA & ENG.). 24p. pap. 8.25 *(978-1-4358-3388-3(0))*; (Illus.). (J). (gr. 1-3). lib. bdg. 22.60 *(978-1-4042-8128-8(2))* Rosen Publishing Group, Inc., The. (PowerKids Pr.).

LLAMAS—FICTION

Bishop, Sara. Luis the Llam. 2011. 16p. pap. 24.95 *(978-1-4560-7281-0(1))* America Star Bks.

Cangilla-McAdam, Claudia. Maria's Mysterious Mission. Crum, Anna-Maria, illus. 2007. 32p. (J). (gr. 3-7). 12.95 *(978-1-56579-588-4(1))* Fielder, John Publishing.

Chiappini, Lydia. A Llama's Tale: Freesia's Little Llama Farm. 2003. (Illus.). 64p. pap. 10.00 *(978-0-9669355-9-2(4))* Chiappini, Lydia .

Conroy, Christine. Mama Wants a Llam. 2012. 16p. pap. 15.99 *(978-1-4772-1605-7(7))* AuthorHouse.

deRubertis, Barbara. Lana Llama's Little Lamb. Alley, R. W., illus. 2011. (Animal Antics A to Z Ser.). 32p. (J). pap. 45.32 *(978-0-7613-7658-3(5))*; (ENG.). lib. bdg. 22.60 *(978-1-57565-333-4(8))*; (gr. -1-3). pap. 7.95 *(978-1-57565-324-2(9))* Kane Press, Inc.

deRubertis, Barbara & DeRubertis, Barbara. Lana Llama's Little Lamb. Alley, R. W., illus. 2012. (Animal Antics A to Z Ser.). 32p. (J). (gr. 2 — 1). cd-rom 7.95 *(978-1-57565-405-8(9))* Kane Press, Inc.

Dewdney, Anna. Llama Llama - Birthday Party! Dewdney, Anna, illus. 2013. (Llama Llama Ser.). (ENG., Illus.). 16p. (J). (gr. -1-k). 6.99 *(978-0-448-45880-9(2)*, Grosset & Dunlap) Penguin Young Readers Group.

—Llama Llama & the Bully Goat. 2013. (Llama Llama Ser.). (ENG., Illus.). 40p. (J). (gr. -1-k). 17.99 *(978-0-670-01395-1(1)*, Viking Books for Young Readers) Penguin Young Readers Group.

—Llama Llama Easter Egg. Dewdney, Anna, illus. 2015. (Llama Llama Ser.). (ENG., Illus.). 14p. (J). (— 1). bds. 5.99 *(978-0-451-46982-3(8)*, Viking Books for Young Readers) Penguin Publishing Group.

—Llama Llama Holiday Drama. 2010. (Llama Llama Ser.). (ENG.). 40p. (J). (gr. -1-k). 17.99 *(978-0-670-01161-2(4)*, Viking Books for Young Readers) Penguin Young Readers Group.

—Llama Llama Home with Mama. 2011. (Llama Llama Ser.). (ENG.). 32p. (J). (gr. -1-k). 17.99 *(978-0-670-01232-9(7)*, Viking Books for Young Readers) Penguin Young Readers Group.

—Llama Llama Hoppity-Hop! 2012. (Llama Llama Ser.). (ENG.). 14p. (J). (gr. -1 — 1). bds. 5.99 *(978-0-670-01329-6(3)*, Viking Books for Young Readers) Penguin Young Readers Group.

—Llama Llama I Love You. 2014. (Llama Llama Ser.). (ENG., Illus.). 14p. (J). (gr. -1 — 1). bds. 5.99 *(978-0-451-46981-6(X)*, Viking Books for Young Readers) Penguin Young Readers Group.

—Llama Llama Mad at Mama. Dewdney, Anna, illus. 2007. (Llama Llama Ser.). (ENG., Illus.). 40p. (J). (gr. -1-k). 17.99 *(978-0-670-06240-9(5)*, Viking Books for Young Readers) Penguin Young Readers Group.

—Llama Llama Mad at Mama. 2009. (Illus.). (J). *(978-0-545-15933-3(4))* Scholastic, Inc.

—Llama Llama Misses Mama. 2009. (Llama Llama Ser.). (ENG., Illus.). 40p. (J). (gr. -1-k). 17.99 *(978-0-670-06198-3(0)*, Viking Books for Young Readers) Penguin Young Readers Group.

—Llama Llama Nighty-Night. 2012. (Llama Llama Ser.). (ENG., Illus.). 14p. (J). bds. 5.99 *(978-0-670-01327-2(7)*, Viking Books for Young Readers) Penguin Young Readers Group.

—Llama Llama Red Pajama. Dewdney, Anna, illus. (Llama Llama Ser.). (ENG., Illus.). 40p. (J). (gr. -1-k). 2014. 25.00 *(978-0-451-46990-8(9))* 2005. 17.99 *(978-0-670-05983-6(8))* Penguin Young Readers Group. (Viking Books for Young Readers).

—Llama Llama Red Pajama, 6 vols., Pack. gif. ed. 2014. (ENG.). (J). 107.94 *(978-0-451-47544-2(5)*, Viking Books for Young Readers) Penguin Young Readers Group.

—Llama Llama Red Pajama. *(978-0-439-90665-4(2))*; 2006. lp *(978-0-439-90679-1(2))* Scholastic, Inc.

—Llama Llama Time to Share. 2012. (Llama Llama Ser.). (ENG.). 40p. (J). (gr. -1-k). 17.99 *(978-0-670-01233-6(5)*, Viking Books for Young Readers) Penguin Young Readers Group.

—Llama Llama Trick or Treat. Dewdney, Anna, illus. 2014. (Llama Llama Ser.). (ENG., Illus.). 14p. (J). (— 1). bds. 5.99 *(978-0-451-46978-6(X)*, Viking Books for Young Readers) Penguin Publishing Group.

—Llama Llama Wakey-Wake. 2012. (Llama Llama Ser.). (ENG.). 14p. (J). (— 1). bds. 5.99 *(978-0-670-01326-5(9)*, Viking Books for Young Readers) Penguin Young Readers Group.

—Llama Llama Zippity-Zoom! 2012. (Llama Llama Ser.). (ENG.). 14p. (J). (gr. -1 — 1). bds. 5.99 *(978-0-670-01328-9(5)*, Viking Books for Young Readers) Penguin Young Readers Group.

Dewdney, Anna & Wells, Rosemary. Llama Llama Gram & Grandpa. 2015. (Llama Llama Ser.). (ENG., Illus.). 40p. (J). (-k). bds. 17.99 *(978-0-670-01396-8(X)*, Viking Books for Young Readers) Penguin Young Readers Group.

Fraggolosch, Audrey. Land of the Wild Llama: A Story of the Patagonian Andes. 2005. (Soundprints' Wild Habitats Ser.). (ENG., Illus.). 32p. (J). (gr. 1-4). 8.95 *(978-1-59249-110-0(3)*, SC7022) Soundprints.

Guarino, Deborah. Is Your Mama a Llama? Kellogg, Steven, illus. 2010. (Rise & Shine Ser.). (ENG.). 32p. (C). (gr. -1-3). pap. 11.95 *(978-0-439-59842-2(7))* National Geographic School Publishing, Inc.

—Is Your Mama a Llama? Kellogg, Steven, illus. 2006. (ENG.). (J). (gr. -1-3). 18.95 incl. audio compact disk *(978-0-439-87594-3(3))*; 9.99 *(978-0-439-87588-2(9))* Scholastic, Inc.

Guarino, Deborah & Kellogg, Steven. Ta Maman Est-Elle un Lama? (FRE., Illus.). (J). pap. 7.99 *(978-0-590-74555-0(7))* Scholastic, Inc.

Hernandez, Elaine. Welcome to Humming Meadow Ranch. Hernandez, Stacy, illus. 2005. 28p. (J). lib. bdg. 16.95 *(978-0-9766431-0-4(3))* Humming Meadow Ranch.

Huy, Barbara. Llamas Need Pajamas. 2012. 36p. pap. 15.49 *(978-1-4669-5752-7(2))* Trafford Publishing.

Lakeshore Learning Materials Staff. Is Your Mama a Llama? Big Book Theme Packet. 2008. (J). pap. 44.50 *(978-1-60666-043-0(8))* Lakeshore Learning Materials.

Palacios, Argentina. El Secreto de la Llama - The Llama's Secret: Una Leyenda Peruana. 97th ed. 2003. (Leyendas del Mundo Ser.). (SPA., Illus.). 32p. (gr. 2-5). pap. 12.90 *(978-0-8167-3072-8(5))* Harcourt Schl. Pubs.

Punter, Russell. Llamas in Pajamas. 2015. (Phonics Readers (no Flaps) Ser.). (ENG.). 24p. (J). pap. 6.99 *(978-0-7945-2739-6(6)*, Usborne) EDC Publishing.

LOAN FUNDS, STUDENT

see Student Loan Funds

LOCKHART, SALLY (FICTITIOUS CHARACTER)—FICTION

Pullman, Philip. The Ruby in the Smoke. 2009. 9.84 *(978-0-7848-2919-6(5)*, Everbind) Marco Bk. Co.

—The Ruby in the Smoke. (Sally Lockhart Ser.: Bk. 1). (YA). 2008. (ENG.). 256p. (gr. 7). pap. 9.99 *(978-0-375-84516-1(X)*, Ember) 2003. (Illus.). pap. 9.95 *(978-0-375-82545-3(2)*, Knopf Bks. for Young Readers) Random Hse. Children's Bks.

—Sally y el Tigre en el Pozo. 2003. (SPA.). 512p. (YA). 16.95 *(978-84-95618-49-8(4)*, Umbriel) Ediciones Urano S. A. ESP. Dist: Spanish Pubs., LLC.

—Sally y la Sombra del Norte. 2003.Tr. of Shadow in the North. (SPA., Illus.). 352p. (YA). 14.95 *(978-84-95618-43-6(5)*, Umbriel) Ediciones Urano S. A. ESP. Dist: Spanish Pubs., LLC.

—The Shadow in the North. 2003. (Sally Lockhart Ser.: Bk. 2). (Illus.). (J). pap. 9.95 *(978-0-375-82546-0(0)*, Knopf Bks. for Young Readers) Random Hse. Children's Bks.

—The Tiger in the Well. 2003. (Sally Lockhart Ser.: Bk. 3). (Illus.). (J). pap. 9.95 *(978-0-375-82547-7(9))* Random Hse. Children's Bks.

LOBBYING

see also Political Corruption

Donovan, Sandy. Special Interests: From Lobbyists to Campaign Funding. 2015. (ENG., Illus.). 64p. (J). (gr. 6-8). 26.65 *(978-1-4677-7912-8(1)*, Lerner Pubns.) Lerner Publishing Group.

Herschbach, Elisabeth. Lobbyists & Special Interest Groups. 2016. (Illus.). 64p. (J). *(978-1-61900-090-2(3))* Eldorado Ink.

Horn, Geoffrey M. Political Parties, Interest Groups & the Media. 2003. (World Almanac Library of American Government). (Illus.). 48p. (gr. 5-12). pap. 14.05 *(978-0-8368-5483-1(7))*; lib. bdg. 31.00 *(978-0-8368-5478-7(0))* Stevens, Gareth Publishing LLLP. (Gareth Stevens Secondary Library).

LOBSTER FISHERIES

Volovar, Vivian. Lobster Lady. 2007. (Illus.). 32p. (J). pap. 14.95 *(978-0-9773725-8-4(8))* Flat Hammock Pr.

LOBSTER FISHERIES—FICTION

Baldwin, Robert F. The Fish House Door. Sheckels, Astrid, illus. 2010. (ENG.). 36p. (J). 16.95 *(978-1-934031-30-8(5)*, 10b511a5-c2dc-4bc7-8d33-85991c0a158b) Islandport Pr., Inc.

Hayes, Karel. The Amazing Journey of Lucky the Lobster Buoy. 2009. (ENG.). 32p. (J). (gr. -1-3). 16.95 *(978-0-89272-791-9(8))* Down East Bks.

LOBSTERS

Adamson, Heather. Lobsters. 2017. (Ocean Life up Close Ser.). (ENG., Illus.). 24p. (J). (gr. k-3). lib. bdg. 25.95 ***(978-1-62617-642-3(6)***, Blastoff! Readers) Bellwether Media.

Coldiron, Deborah. Lobsters, 1 vol. 2008. (Underwater World Set II Ser.). (ENG.). 32p. (gr. k-4). 27.07 *(978-1-60453-133-6(9)*, Buddy Bks.) ABDO Publishing Co.

Gordon, Sharon. Guess Who Snaps. 2004. (Bookworms: Guess Who Ser.). (SPA & ENG., Illus.). 31p. (J). (gr. 3-7). lib. bdg. 21.36 *(978-0-7614-1765-1(6)*, Benchmark Bks.) Marshall Cavendish Corp.

—Guess Who Snaps: Adivina Quién Tritura. 2007. (Bookworms — Spanish Editions: Adivina Quien 2 Ser.). (SPA & ENG.). 32p. (gr. k-2). 15.95 *(978-0-7614-2870-1(4))* Marshall Cavendish Corp.

—Guess Who Snaps: Adivina Quién Tritura. 2007. (Bookworms — Bilingual Editions: Guess Who/Adivina Quien 2 Ser.). (SPA & ENG.). 32p. (gr. k-2). 15.95 *(978-0-7614-2886-2(0))* Marshall Cavendish GBR. Dist: Marshall Cavendish Corp.

Hirschmann, Kris. Lobsters. 2004. (Creatures of the Sea Ser.). (ENG., Illus.). 48p. (J). (gr. 4-7). 29.15 *(978-0-7377-2343-4(2))* Cengage Gale.

Magby, Meryl. Lobsters. 2012. (Under the Sea Ser.). (ENG., Illus.). 24p. (J). (gr. k-5). pap. 8.25 *(978-1-4488-7475-0(0))*; lib. bdg. 22.60 *(978-1-4488-7396-8(7))* Rosen Publishing Group, Inc., The. (PowerKids Pr.).

Marsico, Katie. A Baby Lobster Grows Up. 2007. (Scholastic News Nonfiction Readers Ser.). (ENG., Illus.). 24p. (J). (gr. 1-2). pap. 6.95 *(978-0-531-18694-7(6))* Scholastic Library Publishing.

Meister, Cari. Lobsters. 2014. (Illus.). 24p. (J). lib. bdg. 25.65 *(978-1-62031-099-1(6)*, Bullfrog Bks.) Jump! Inc.

Pallotta, Jerry. Going Lobstering. Bolster, Rob, illus. 2008. (ENG.). 20p. (J). (gr. -1-3). bds. 7.95 (978-1-57091-623-6(3)) Charlesbridge Publishing, Inc.

—Lobster vs. Crab. Bolster, Rob, illus. 2014. 32p. (J). pap. (978-0-545-68121-6(9)) Scholastic, Inc.

Siemens, Jared. Lobster. 2016. (J). **(978-1-4896-5381-9(3))** Weigl Pubs., Inc.

Soundprints Staff, ed. Oceanic Collection III: Beluga Whale, Harp Seal, Walrus & Lobster Books, 4 micro bks. (Smithsonian Oceanic Collection). (Illus.). 128p. (J). (gr. -1-2). 18.95 (978-1-56899-633-2(0)) Soundprints.

Stone, Tanya Lee. Lobsters. 2003. (Wild Wild World Ser.). 24p. (YA). 24.94 (978-1-56711-816-2(X), Blackbirch Pr., Inc.) Cengage Gale.

World Book, Inc. Staff, contrib. by. Lobsters & Other Crustaceans. 2005. (World Book's Animals of the World Ser.). (Illus.). 64p. (J). (978-0-7166-1270-4(4)) World Bk., Inc.

LOBSTERS—FICTION

Aldrich, Sandra D. Lenny Lobster Saves the Day. 2012. 38p. 19.95 (978-1-4626-9817-2(4)) America Star Bks.

Chiarello, Robin Taylor. The Blue Lobster's Holiday! Bohart, Lisa, illus. 2012. 40p. pap. 16.95 (978-1-61493-053-2(8)) Peppertree Pr., The.

Ginn, Jennifer. Lobsters on the Loose, 1 vol. Krackow, Eric T., illus. 2011. (ENG.). 48p. (J). 16.99 (978-0-7643-3826-7(9), 9780764338267, Schiffer Publishing Ltd) Schiffer Publishing, Ltd.

Gist, Richard. Ayshus on the Inside. 2013. 104p. (978-1-4602-1899-0(X)); pap. (978-1-4602-1900-3(7)) FriesenPress.

Hollenbeck, Kathleen M. Lobster's Secret. Weiman, Jon, illus. 2011. (Smithsonian Oceanic Collection Ser.). (ENG.). 32p. (J). (gr. -1-3). 19.95 (978-1-60727-653-1(4)); 8.95 (978-1-60727-654-8(2)) Soundprints.

Lordon, Claire. Lorenzo, the Pizza-Loving Lobster. 2016. (ENG., Illus.). 32p. (J). (gr. -1-3). 16.99 (978-1-4998-0228-3(5)) Little Bee Books Inc.

Meister, Cari. The Grumpy Lobster, 1 vol. Harpster, Steve, illus. 2012. (Ocean Tales Ser.). (ENG.). 32p. (gr. 2-4). pap. 6.25 (978-1-4342-4230-3(7)); lib. bdg. 22.65 (978-1-4342-4025-5(8)) Stone Arch Bks.

Reilly, Antoinette. Mr. Lobster & the Mermaid. 2011. 24p. pap. 14.93 (978-1-4269-5683-6(5)) Trafford Publishing.

Schwarz, Viviane. Shark & Lobster's Amazing Undersea Adventure. Stewart, Joel, illus. 2006. 34p. (J). (978-1-4156-8140-4(6)) Candlewick Pr.

Stone, Summer. Lobster Trips. 2012. 24p. pap. 16.50 (978-1-4772-9130-6(X)) AuthorHouse.

Taylor-Chiarello, Robin. The Blue Lobster. Bohart, Lisa, illus. 2011. 36p. pap. 15.95 (978-1-936343-84-3(3)) Peppertree Pr., The.

Urbain, Catherine. Manuel & the Lobsterman. 2008. (ENG.). 214p. (J). (gr. 4-7). 16.95 (978-1-59078-516-4(9), Front Street) Boyds Mills Pr.

Verrier, Suzy. Titus Tidewater. 2005. (ENG.). 38p. (J). 15.95 (978-0-9763231-1-2(7), 9780976323112) Islandport Pr., Inc.

LOCAL GOVERNMENT

see also Cities and Towns; Public Administration

Benchmark Education Company. Local & State Government (Teacher Guide) 2005. (978-1-4108-4639-6(3)) Benchmark Education Co.

Benchmark Education Company, LLC Staff, compiled by. Social Studies Theme: GOVT & Citizenship. 2005. spiral bd. 115.00 (978-1-4108-5331-8(4)) Benchmark Education Co.

Brannon, Barbara. Discover Local & State Government. 2005. (J). pap. (978-1-4108-5145-1(1)) Benchmark Education Co.

Johnson, Etta. Local & State Government. 2005. (J). pap. (978-1-4108-4591-7(5)) Benchmark Education Co.

Kenney, Karen. Government in Your City or Town. 2014. (ENG.). 24p. (gr. 3-5). 28.50 (978-1-62717-684-2(5)) Rourke Educational Media.

Machajewski, Sarah. What Are State & Local Government? 2015. (Let's Find Out! Government Ser.). (ENG., Illus.). 32p. (J). (gr. 2-3). 23.45 (978-1-62275-986-6(9), Britannica Educational Publishing) Rosen Publishing Group, Inc., The.

Mara, Wil. Local Action. 2016. (21st Century Skills Library: a Citizen's Guide Ser.). (ENG., Illus.). 32p. (J). (gr. 4-7). 29.93 (978-1-63471-070-1(3), 208359) Cherry Lake Publishing.

McAuliffe, Bill. State & Local Government. (By the People Ser.). (Illus.). 48p. (J). 2017. (ENG.). (gr. 7-11). pap. 12.00 (978-1-62832-270-5(5), Creative Paperbacks) 2016. 39.95 (978-1-60818-674-7(1), Creative Education) Creative Co., The.

Miller, Jake. Who's Who in an Urban Community. 2005. (Communities at Work Ser.). (Illus.). 24p. (J). (gr. 2-4). lib. bdg. 22.60 (978-1-4042-2790-3(3), PowerKids Pr.) Rosen Publishing Group, Inc., The.

O'Nan, Denny. My Local Government. 2013. (Rosen Readers Ser.). (ENG.). 24p. (J). (gr. 3-4). pap. 8.25 (978-1-4777-2572-6(5)); pap. 49.50 (978-1-4777-2573-3(3)) Rosen Publishing Group, Inc., The. (Rosen Classroom).

Wiles, Jon. Landon's Local Government. 2013. (InfoMax Readers Ser.). (ENG.). 24p. (J). (gr. 3-4). pap. 49.50 (978-1-4777-2635-8(7)); (Illus.). pap. 8.25 (978-1-4777-2634-1(9)) Rosen Publishing Group, Inc., The. (Rosen Classroom).

LOCH NESS (SCOTLAND)

see Ness, Loch (Scotland)

LOCH NESS MONSTER

see also Ness, Loch (Scotland)

Bougie, Matt. Bigfoot, the Loch Ness Monster, & Unexplained Creatures. 2017. **(978-1-5026-2847-3(3))** Cavendish Square Publishing.

Brassey, Richard. Nessie the Loch Ness Monster. 2010. (ENG., Illus.). 24p. (gr. k-2). pap. 9.99 (978-1-4440-0056-6(X), Orion Children's Bks.) Hachette Children's Group GBR. Dist: Hachette Bk. Group.

Case, Nikki & Delrio, Martin. Searching for the Loch Ness Monster. 2011. (J). 77.70 (978-1-4488-4780-8(X)); pap. 12.95 (978-1-4488-4772-3(9)); lib. bdg. 31.95 (978-1-4488-4763-1(X)) Rosen Publishing Group, Inc., The.

Chambers, Catherine. The Loch Ness Monster. Billiau, Loic, illus. 2015. (Autobiographies You Never Thought You'd Read! Ser.). (ENG.). 32p. (gr. 1-3). 29.99 (978-1-4109-7962-9(8), Read Me!) Heinemann-Raintree.

DeMolay, Jack. The Loch Ness Monster: Scotland's Mystery Beast. (Jr. Graphic Mysteries Ser.). (ENG.). 24p. 2009. (J). (gr. 2-3). 47.90 (978-1-61513-849-4(8), PowerKids Pr.) 2007. (Illus.). (J). (gr. 2-5). lib. bdg. 25.25 (978-1-4042-3406-2(3)) 2007. (Illus.). (gr. 3-8). pap. 10.60 (978-1-4042-2159-8(X)) Rosen Publishing Group, Inc., The.

—Monstruo del Lago Ness: Una Misteriosa Bestia en Escocia. Obregón, José María, tr. from ENG. 2008. (Historietas Juveniles: Misterios (Jr. Graphic Mysteries) Ser.). (SPA., Illus.). 24p. (J). (gr. 2-5). lib. bdg. 25.25 (978-1-4358-2538-3(1)) Rosen Publishing Group, Inc., The.

Hile, Lori. The Loch Ness Monster, 1 vol. 2013. (Solving Mysteries with Science Ser.). (ENG., Illus.). 48p. (gr. 5-5). pap. 9.95 (978-1-4109-4992-9(3)) Heinemann-Raintree.

Hoffman, Mary Ann. Loch Ness Monster. 2006. (Tony Stead Independent Reading Collection). (ENG.). 24p. (gr. 3-6). pap. 8.85 (978-1-4042-5673-6(3)) Rosen Publishing Group, Inc., The.

Jeffrey, Gary. The Loch Ness Monster & Other Lake Mysteries. Moulder, Bob, illus. 2006. (Graphic Mysteries Ser.). (ENG.). 48p. (gr. 5-8). pap. 14.05 (978-1-4042-0807-0(0)) Rosen Publishing Group, Inc., The.

—The Loch Ness Monster & Other Lake Mysteries. Spender, Nik & Moulder, Bob, illus. 2006. (Graphic Mysteries Ser.). (ENG.). 48p. (YA). (gr. 5-8). lib. bdg. 31.95 (978-1-4042-0796-7(1)) Rosen Publishing Group, Inc., The.

—Loch Ness Monster & Other Lake Mysteries. 2009. (Graphic Mysteries Ser.). (ENG.). 48p. (YA). (gr. 5-5). 58.50 (978-1-61512-967-6(7), Rosen Reference) Rosen Publishing Group, Inc., The.

Kallen, Stuart A. The Loch Ness Monster. 2008. (Mysterious & Unknown Ser.). (YA). (gr. 7-12). 25.95 (978-1-60152-059-3(X)) ReferencePoint Pr., Inc.

Karst, Ken. Enduring Mysteries: Loch Ness Monster. 2015. (Enduring Mysteries Ser.). (ENG.). 48p. (J). (gr. 5-8). pap. 12.00 (978-1-62832-074-9(5), Creative Paperbacks) Creative Co., The.

—Loch Ness Monster. 2014. (Illus.). 48p. (J). (978-1-60818-403-3(X), Creative Education) Creative Co., The.

Lassieur, Allison. Is the Loch Ness Monster Real? 2015. (Unexplained: What's the Evidence? Ser.). (ENG., Illus.). 32p. (J). (gr. 2-4). 19.95 (978-1-60753-805-9(9)) Amicus Publishing.

McClellan, Ray. The Loch Ness Monster. 2014. (Unexplained Mysteries Ser.). (ENG., Illus.). 24p. (J). (gr. 3-7). lib. bdg. 25.95 (978-1-62617-106-0(8), Epic Bks.) Bellwether Media.

Murray, Laura K. Are They Real?: Loch Ness Monster. 2017. (Are They Real? Ser.). (ENG., Illus.). 24p. (J). (gr. 1-3). pap. 8.99 **(978-1-62832-372-6(8)**, Creative Paperbacks) Creative Co., The.

Murray, Laura K. Loch Ness Monster. 2017. (Illus.). 24p. (J). (978-1-60818-764-5(0), Creative Education) Creative Co., The.

Nagle, Frances. The Loch Ness Monster. 2016. (Monsters! Ser.). (Illus.). 32p. (J). (gr. 2-1). pap. 10.50 (978-1-4824-4863-4(7)) Stevens, Gareth Publishing LLLP.

Parks, Peggy J. The Loch Ness Monster. 2006. (Mysterious Encounters Ser.). (ENG., Illus.). 48p. (J). (gr. 3-7). lib. bdg. 27.50 (978-0-7377-3519-2(8), Kidhaven) Cengage Gale.

Peabody, Erin. The Loch Ness Monster. Rivas, Victor, illus. 2017. (Behind the Legend Ser.: 1). (ENG.). 128p. (J). (gr. 3-7). pap. 9.99 (978-1-4998-0423-2(7)) Little Bee Books Inc.

Rivkin, Jennifer. Searching for the Loch Ness Monster. 2014. (Mysterious Monsters Ser.). (Illus.). 32p. (J). (gr. 3-6). lib. bdg. 26.25 (978-1-4777-7101-3(8), PowerKids Pr.) Rosen Publishing Group, Inc., The.

Roberts, Steven. The Loch Ness Monster! 2012. (Jr. Graphic Monster Stories Ser.). (ENG., Illus.). 24p. (J). (gr. 3-6). 25.25 (978-1-4488-7904-5(3)); pap. 10.60 (978-1-4488-8004-1(1)) Rosen Publishing Group, Inc., The. (PowerKids Pr.).

Schach, David. The Loch Ness Monster. 2010. (Unexplained Ser.). (ENG., Illus.). 24p. (J). (gr. 3-7). lib. bdg. 25.95 (978-1-60014-502-5(7), Torque Bks.) Bellwether Media.

Sievert, Terri. The Unsolved Mystery of the Loch Ness Monster. 2013. (Unexplained Mysteries Ser.). (ENG.). 24p. (gr. 1-2). pap. 41.70 (978-1-62065-811-6(9), First Facts); pap. 7.95 (978-1-62065-810-9(0)); lib. bdg. 25.32 (978-1-62065-133-9(5)) Capstone Press of Coughlan Cos.

Troupe, Thomas Kingsley. The Legend of the Loch Ness Monster, 1 vol. Ice, D. C., illus. 2011. (Legend Has It Ser.). (ENG.). 32p. (gr. 2-4). lib. bdg. 27.32 (978-1-4048-6659-1(0)) Picture Window Bks.

LOCKS AND KEYS

Cruz-Martinez, George. The Wonder of Keys for Kids. Sturgeon, Brad, illus. 2006. 43p. (J). (978-1-55452-013-8(4)) Essence Publishing.

LOCKWOOD, BELVA ANN, 1830-1917

Bardhan-Quallen, Sudipta. Ballots for Belva: The True Story of a Woman's Race for the Presidency. Martin, Courtney A., illus. 2015. (ENG.). 32p. (J). (gr. k-2). 9.95 (978-1-4197-1627-0(1), Abrams Bks. for Young Readers) Abrams, Inc.

Norgren, Jill. Belva Lockwood: The Woman Who Would Be President. 2007. (ENG., Illus.). 311p. 89.00 (978-0-8147-5834-2(7)) New York Univ. Pr.

LOCOMOTION

see Aeronautics; Automobiles; Boats and Boating; Flight; Navigation; Transportation; Walking

LOCOMOTIVES

Bone, Emily & King, Colin. See Inside Trains. 2013. (Usborne Flap Book Ser.). (ENG., Illus.). 16p. (J). 13.99 (978-0-7945-3377-9(9), Usborne) EDC Publishing.

Daynes, Katie, et al. The Railway Revolution. 2016. (ENG.). 56p. (J). (gr. 4-5). pap. 9.95 (978-0-00-816395-2(2)) HarperCollins Pubs. Ltd. GBR. Dist: Independent Pubs. Group.

Farrington, Karen & Constable, Nick. Build Your Own Steam Locomotive: A Complete, Easy-to-Assemble Model. Osborne, Graham, illus. 2004. 34p. (J). (gr. 4-8). reprint ed. pap. 17.00 (978-0-7567-8261-0(9)) DIANE Publishing Co.

Floca, Brian. Locomotive. Floca, Brian, illus. 2013. (ENG., Illus.). 64p. (J). (gr. -1-5). 17.99 (978-1-4169-9415-2(7), Atheneum/Richard Jackson Bks.) Simon & Schuster Children's Publishing.

Hannon, Robert A. J. L. Cowen's Postwar Lionel Trains: O-Gauge Reference Manual II, Motorized Units, Rolling Stock & Accessories. 2003. (Illus.). 160p. per. 29.95 (978-0-9710225-2-2(6), 0-9710225-2-6) CrowsNest Publishing.

Mattern, Joanne. The Birth of the Locomotive (1780-1820) 2012. (Illus.). 47p. (J). (gr. 4-8). lib. bdg. 29.95 (978-1-61228-286-2(5)) Mitchell Lane Pubs., Inc.

Oxlade, Chris. Thomas the Tank Engine. 2015. (Owners' Workshop Manual Ser.). (ENG., Illus.). 40p. (J). (gr. -1-2). pap. 10.95 (978-0-85733-851-8(X)) Haynes Publishing PLC GBR. Dist: Hachette Bk. Group.

Ryan, Phillip. Passenger Trains. 2010. (All Aboard! Ser.). (ENG.). 24p. (J). pap. 8.25 (978-1-4488-1215-8(1)); lib. bdg. 22.60 (978-1-4488-0637-9(2)) Rosen Publishing Group, Inc., The. (PowerKids Pr.).

—Steam-Powered Trains. 2010. (All Aboard! Ser.). (ENG.). 24p. (J). pap. 8.25 (978-1-4488-1221-9(6)); lib. bdg. 22.60 (978-1-4488-0640-9(2)) Rosen Publishing Group, Inc., The. (PowerKids Pr.).

Trombello, William. Trains & Tow Boats. Tangen, Nick, illus. 2013. 34p. pap. (978-0-9842998-1-2(5)) Roxby Media Ltd.

Turnbull, S. Trains. 2004. (Discovery Program Ser.). (SPA., Illus.). 48p. (J). (gr. 3-18). lib. bdg. 16.95 (978-1-58086-410-7(4)) EDC Publishing.

Veitch, Catherine. Big Machines Ride Rails!, 1 vol. 2014. (Big Machines Ser.). (ENG.). 24p. (gr. k-1). 23.32 (978-1-4846-0589-9(6), Heinemann Read & Learn) Heinemann-Raintree.

Zimmermann, Karl. The Stourbridge Lion: America's First Locomotive. Walker, Steven, illus. 2012. (ENG.). 32p. (J). (gr. k). 16.95 (978-1-59078-859-2(1)) Boyds Mills Pr.

LOCOMOTIVES—FICTION

Amery, Heather. The Old Steam Train Kid Kit. Cartwright, Stephen, illus. rev. ed. 2007. (Kid Kits Ser.). (J). 16p. 13.99 (978-1-60130-038-6(7)); 14p. pap. 13.99 (978-1-60130-003-4(4)) EDC Publishing. (Usborne).

Awdry, W. Ride the Rails with Thomas (Thomas & Friends) Stubbs, Tommy, illus. 2015. (Pictureback(R) Ser.). (ENG.). 24p. (J). (gr. -1-2). 5.99 (978-0-385-38538-1(2), Random Hse. Bks. for Young Readers) Random Hse. Children's Bks.

—Secret of the Green Engine. 2012. (Thomas & Friends Step into Reading Ser.). lib. bdg. 13.55 (978-0-606-26804-2(9), Turtleback) Turtleback Bks.

—Sodor's Legend of the Lost Treasure. 2015. (Big Golden Book Ser.). (ENG., Illus.). 32p. (J). (gr. -1-2). 9.99 (978-0-553-52076-7(8), Golden Bks.) Random Hse. Children's Bks.

—A Valentine for Percy. 2015. (Thomas & Friends Step into Reading Ser.). lib. bdg. 14.75 (978-0-606-38471-1(5)) Turtleback Bks.

Burton, Virginia Lee. Choo Choo (with Full-Color Art) 2017. (ENG., Illus.). 48p. (J). (gr. -1-3). 17.99 **(978-0-544-74984-9(7)**, HMH Books For Young Readers) Houghton Mifflin Harcourt Publishing Co.

Fleming, Denise. Go, Shapes, Go! Fleming, Denise, illus. 2014. (ENG., Illus.). 40p. (J). (gr. -1-3). 17.99 (978-1-4424-8240-1(0), Beach Lane Bks.) Beach Lane Bks.

Gibbons, Faye. Full Steam Ahead. Meidell, Sherry, illus. 2003. (ENG.). 32p. (J). (gr. k-2). 15.95 (978-1-56397-858-6(X)) Boyds Mills Pr.

Horácek, Petr. Choo Choo. Horácek, Petr, illus. 2008. (ENG., Illus.). 16p. (J). (gr. k-k). bds. 5.99 (978-0-7636-3477-3(8)) Candlewick Pr.

Klein, Adria F. The Big Train. Cameron, Craig, illus. 2013. (Train Time Ser.). (ENG.). 32p. (gr. -1-1). pap. 5.95 (978-1-4342-4886-2(0)) Stone Arch Bks.

—The Big Train: Takes a Trip. Cameron, Craig, illus. 2013. (Train Time Ser.). (ENG.). 32p. (gr. -1-1). lib. bdg. 22.65 (978-1-4342-4191-7(2)) Stone Arch Bks.

—Big Train Takes a Trip, 1 vol. Cameron, Craig, illus. 2013. (Train Time Ser.). (ENG.). 32p. (gr. -1-1). pap. 5.95 (978-1-4342-6194-6(8)); pap. 29.70 (978-1-4342-6300-1(2)); lib. bdg. 22.65 (978-1-4342-4781-0(3)) Stone Arch Bks.

—City Train in Trouble, 1 vol. Cameron, Craig, illus. 2013. (Train Time Ser.). (ENG.). 32p. (gr. -1-1). pap. 5.95 (978-1-4342-6196-0(4)); pap. 29.70 (978-1-4342-6302-5(9)); lib. bdg. 22.65 (978-1-4342-4783-4(X)) Stone Arch Bks.

Lippman, Peter. Mini Express. (J). 119.40 (978-0-7611-2876-2(X), 22876); (ENG.). bds. 79.60 (978-0-7611-2883-0(2), 22883) Workman Publishing Co., Inc.

Little, Stephen R. The Mighty Locomotive. 2012. 40p. pap. 20.99 (978-1-4772-5936-8(8)) AuthorHouse.

Mlawer, Teresa, tr. On the Go!/a Moverse! Stockham, Jess, illus. 2013. (Just Like Me! Ser.). (ENG & SPA.). 12p. (J). (gr. -1). bds. (978-1-84643-563-8(3)) Child's Play International Ltd.

Mysak, Mary. Little Train! Stickley, Kelly, illus. 2004. 16p. (J). 7.50 (978-0-9762274-0-3(1)) Helping Hands Children's Bks.

Opie, David, illus. Monkey & the Engineer. 2007. 24p. (J). 14.95 (978-0-9793972-6-4(X)) JD Publishing.

Piper, Watty. The Little Engine That Could. Long, Loren, illus. 2005. (Little Engine That Could Ser.). (ENG.). 48p. (J). (gr. -1-2). 17.99 (978-0-399-24467-4(0), Philomel Bks.) Penguin Young Readers Group.

Publications International Ltd. Staff. Chuggington Little Lift & Listen. 2011. 12p. (J). bds. 10.98 (978-1-4508-0504-9(3)) Phoenix International Publications, Inc.

Publications International Ltd. Staff, ed. Cars. 2007. (J). 9.98 (978-1-4127-6514-5(5)) Phoenix International Publications, Inc.

—Chuggington Little Music Note Sound: Traintastic Tunes. 2011. 12p. (J). (gr. k-3). bds. 10.99 (978-1-4508-1141-5(8), dd98fbb4-eb4f-47f8-80b4-3d7a907afc5f) Phoenix International Publications, Inc.

Random House. Five Tank Engine Tales (Thomas & Friends) Courtney, Richard, illus. 2015. (Step into Reading Ser.). (ENG.). 160p. (J). (gr. -1-1). pap. 7.99 (978-0-385-38496-4(3), Random Hse. Bks. for Young Readers) Random Hse. Children's Bks.

Riley, Lehman C. Meeting Dr. Martin Luther King. 2004. (Adventures of Papa Lemon's Little Wanderers Ser.: Bk. 1). 35p. (978-0-9760523-0-2(X)) Matter of Africa America Time.

Sabo, J. Train Wrecker. 2011. 28p. pap. 24.95 (978-1-4626-4379-0(5)) America Star Bks.

Wondriska, William. Puff. 2015. (ENG., Illus.). 32p. (J). (gr. k-4). 16.95 (978-0-7893-2911-0(5)) Universe Publishing.

LOCUSTS

Alessi, Jolene. Zombie Grasshoppers. 2015. (Zombie Animals: Parasites Take Control! Ser.). (ENG.). 24p. (J). (gr. 2-3). 22.60 (978-1-4824-2846-9(6)) Stevens, Gareth Publishing LLLP.

Allen, Judy. Are You a Grasshopper? Humphries, Tudor, illus. 2004. (Backyard Bks.). (ENG.). 32p. (J). (gr. k-3). pap. 6.99 (978-0-7534-5806-8(3), 9780753458068, Kingfisher) Roaring Brook Pr.

Amstutz, Lisa J. Grasshoppers. 2017. (Little Critters Ser.). (ENG.). 24p. (gr. k-1). lib. bdg. 21.99 **(978-1-5157-7824-0(X))** Capstone Press of Coughlan Cos.

Ashley, Susan. Grasshoppers. (Incredible World of Insects Ser.). (Illus.). 24p. 2011. (J). (gr. 1-3). pap. 8.15 (978-1-4339-4588-5(6)) 2011. (J). (gr. 1-3). lib. bdg. 22.60 (978-1-4339-4587-8(8)) 2004. (gr. k-3). pap. 8.15 (978-0-8368-4061-2(5), Weekly Reader Leveled Readers) 2004. (gr. k-3). lib. bdg. 22.00 (978-0-8368-4054-4(2), Weekly Reader Leveled Readers) Stevens, Gareth Publishing LLLP.

Berger, Melvin & Berger, Gilda. Grasshoppers. 2011. (Illus.). 16p. (J). pap. (978-0-545-24445-9(5)) Scholastic, Inc.

Bodden, Valerie. Creepy Creatures: Grasshoppers. 2014. (Creepy Creatures Ser.). (ENG.). 24p. (J). (gr. 1-3). pap. 7.99 (978-0-89812-935-9(4), Creative Paperbacks) Creative Co., The.

—Grasshoppers. (Illus.). 24p. (J). 2014. (978-1-60818-356-2(4)) 2007. (gr. -1-3). lib. bdg. 24.25 (978-1-58341-544-3(0)) Creative Co., The. (Creative Education).

Bronson, Wilfrid S., illus. The Grasshopper Book. 2009. 136p. (J). pap. 22.95 (978-0-86534-690-1(9)) Sunstone Pr.

Carmichael, L. E. Locust Migration. 2012. (Animal Migrations Ser.). (ENG., Illus.). 32p. (J). (gr. 2-5). lib. bdg. 29.93 (978-1-60973-623-1(0), 201200) Child's World, Inc., The.

Goldish, Meish. Leaping Grasshoppers. 2008. (No Backbone! Ser.). (Illus.). 24p. (J). (gr. k-3). lib. bdg. 21.28 (978-1-59716-586-0(7)) Bearport Publishing Co., Inc.

Gray, Susan Heinrichs. Backyard Insects: Grasshoppers. 2015. (21st Century Junior Library: Creepy Crawly Critters Ser.). (ENG.). 24p. (J). (gr. k-3). 27.07 (978-1-63362-590-7(7), 206544) Cherry Lake Publishing.

Green, Emily K. Grasshoppers. 2006. (World of Insects Ser.). (ENG., Illus.). 24p. (J). (gr. k-3). lib. bdg. 25.95 (978-1-60014-014-3(9)) Bellwether Media.

Hall, Margaret. Grasshoppers [Scholastic]. 2010. (Bugs, Bugs, Bugs! Ser.). 24p. pap. 0.52 (978-1-4296-5052-6(4), Pebble Plus) Capstone Press of Coughlan Cos.

Halpert, Laine C. If I Were a Grasshopper. 2017. (I'm a Bug! Ser.). 24p. (gr. 4-6). 23.60 **(978-1-5081-5722-9(7)**, PowerKids Pr.) Rosen Publishing Group, Inc., The.

Haydon, Julie. Locust Plague, Vol. 107. 2014. (ENG.). 24p. spiral bd. 9.00 (978-1-4085-0155-9(4)) Oxford Univ. Pr., Inc.

Hudak, Heather C. Grasshoppers. 2008. (World of Wonder Ser.). (Illus.). 24p. (J). (gr. k-3). pap. 6.95 (978-1-59036-871-8(1)); lib. bdg. 24.45 (978-1-59036-870-1(3)) Weigl Pubs., Inc.

Kenney, Karen Latchana. Hop with the Grasshoppers, 1 vol. Hedicker, Lisa, illus. 2010. (Bug's World Ser.). (ENG.). 32p. 28.50 (978-1-60270-786-3(3), Looking Glass Library-Nonfiction) Magic Wagon.

Kravetz, Jonathan. Locusts. (Gross Bugs Ser.). 24p. 2009. (gr. 3-4). 42.50 (978-1-61513-228-7(7)) 2006. (Illus.). (J). (gr. -1-3). lib. bdg. 22.60 (978-1-4042-3042-2(4)) Rosen Publishing Group, Inc., The. (PowerKids Pr.).

Lockwood, Sophie. Grasshoppers. 2007. (World of Insects Ser.). (ENG., Illus.). 40p. (J). (gr. 3-6). 31.36 (978-1-59296-823-7(6), 200976) Child's World, Inc., The.

Lunis, Natalie. Giant Weta: The World's Biggest Grasshopper. 2013. (Even More SuperSized! Ser.). (Illus.). 24p. (J). (gr. k-3). lib. bdg. 23.93 (978-1-61772-731-3(8)) Bearport Publishing Co., Inc.

Markle, Sandra. Locusts. 2008. pap. 52.95 (978-1-58013-282-4(0)) Lerner Publishing Group.

—Locusts: Insects on the Move. 2008. (Insect World Ser.). (ENG., Illus.). 48p. (gr. 4-8). lib. bdg. 27.93 (978-0-8225-7298-5(2), Lerner Pubns.) Lerner Publishing Group.

Marwood, Diane. The Ant & the Grasshopper. 2012. (ENG., Illus.). 24p. (J). (978-0-7787-7889-9(4)); pap. (978-0-7787-7901-8(7)) Crabtree Publishing Co.

McAneney, Caitlin. Locusts. 2014. (Animals of Mass Destruction Ser.). 32p. (J). (gr. 2-5). 25.25 (978-1-4824-1051-8(6)); pap. 10.50 (978-1-4824-1052-5(4)) Stevens, Gareth Publishing LLLP.

Morris, Neil & Morris, Ting. Grasshopper. 2003. (Illus.). 32p. (J). lib. bdg. 27.10 (978-1-58340-381-5(7)) Black Rabbit Bks.

Murray, Julie. Grasshoppers, 1 vol. (Big Buddy Bks.). (ENG.). (J). 2010. 32p. (gr. 2-5). 28.50 (978-1-61613-486-0(0)) 2005. (Illus.). 24p. (gr. k-4). 25.65 (978-1-59197-317-1(1), Buddy Bks.) ABDO Publishing Co.

Nelson, Robin. Grasshoppers. 2009. pap. 34.95 (978-0-7613-4107-9(2)); (ENG.). 24p. 23.93 (978-0-7613-4063-8(7), Lerner Pubns.) Lerner Publishing Group.

Perish, Patrick. Grasshoppers. 2017. (Insects up Close Ser.). (ENG., Illus.). 24p. (J). (gr. k-3). lib. bdg. 25.95 **(978-1-62617-665-2(5)**, Blastoff! Readers) Bellwether Media.

Petrie, Kristin. Grasshoppers, 1 vol. 2009. (Bugs! Ser.). (ENG.). 32p. (gr. 3-6). 27.07 (978-1-60453-069-8(3), Checkerboard Library) ABDO Publishing Co.

Reher, Matt. Grasshoppers on the Go. 2015. (1G Bugs Ser.). (ENG., Illus.). 28p. (J). pap. 5.99 (978-1-63437-091-2(0)) American Reading Co.

Robbins, Lynette. Grasshoppers. 2012. (J). 49.50 (978-1-4488-5164-5(5), PowerKids Pr.); pap. 8.25 (978-1-4488-5163-8(7), PowerKids Pr.); lib. bdg. 22.60 (978-1-4488-5015-0(0)) Rosen Publishing Group, Inc., The.

Schuh, Mari. Grasshoppers. 2015. (J). lib. bdg. 25.65 (978-1-62031-162-2(3), Bullfrog Bks.) Jump! Inc.

Shusterman, Danielle. Grasshoppers & Crickets. 2015. (1G Bugs Ser.). (ENG., Illus.). 28p. (J). pap. 5.99 (978-1-63437-111-7(9)) American Reading Co.

Silverman, Buffy. Can You Tell a Cricket from a Grasshopper? 2012. (Animal Look-Alikes Ser.). 32p. (gr. k-2). pap. 45.32

(978-0-7613-9254-5(8)); (ENG.). pap. 7.95 (978-0-7613-8553-0(3)); (ENG.). lib. bdg. 26.60 (978-0-7613-6736-9(5), Lerner Pubns.) Lerner Publishing Group.

Slade, Suzanne. Grasshoppers. (Under the Microscope: Backyard Bugs Ser.). 24p. 2009. (gr. 2-3). 42.50 (978-1-60854-615-2(2), PowerKids Pr.) 2007. (Illus.). (J). (gr. 3-7). lib. bdg. 22.60 (978-1-4042-3820-6(4)) Rosen Publishing Group, Inc., The.

Smith, Sian. Grasshoppers, 1 vol. 2012. (Creepy Critters Ser.). (ENG.). 24p. (gr. -1-k). pap. 9.95 (978-1-4109-4821-2(8)); lib. bdg. 25.32 (978-1-4109-4808-3(0)) Heinemann-Raintree.

Squire, Ann O. Crickets & Grasshoppers. 2004. (True Bks.). (ENG.). 48p. (J). (gr. 3-5). pap. 6.95 (978-0-516-29357-8(5), Children's Pr.) Scholastic Library Publishing.

Stewart, Melissa. Zoom in on Grasshoppers. 2014. (Zoom in on Insects! Ser.). 24p. (J). 22.60 (978-0-7660-4214-8(6)); pap. 7.95 (978-1-4644-0371-2(6), Enslow Elementary) Enslow Pubs., Inc.

Trueit, Trudi Strain. Grasshoppers. 2013. (Backyard Safari 2 Ser.). 32p. (J). (gr. 6-9). pap. 10.58 (978-1-62712-029-6(7)) Cavendish Square Publishing.

—Grasshoppers. 2009. (Benchmark Rebus Ser.). 24p. (gr. k-1). 15.95 (978-0-7614-3964-6(1)) Marshall Cavendish Corp.

LOCUSTS—FICTION

Aesop. The Ant & the Grasshopper. 2012. (J). 29.99 (978-1-61913-106-4(4)) Weigl Pubs., Inc.

—The Grasshopper & the Ant: A Tale about Planning. Hockerman, Dennis, illus. 2006. (J). (978-1-59939-082-6(5), Reader's Digest Young Families, Inc.) Studio Fun International.

Aldrick, Shirley H. F. Gordon, the Great Gobbley Grasshopper. 2011. 32p. pap. 13.00 (978-1-60976-643-6(1), Strategic Bk. Publishing) Strategic Book Publishing & Rights Agency (SBPRA).

Bailer, Darice, et al. El Saltamontes y Las Hormigas. Bassa, illus. 2007. (SPA & ENG.). 28p. (J). (978-0-545-02965-0(1)) Scholastic, Inc.

Barkley, Roger C. Johnny Grasshopper. 2006. 52p. pap. 16.95 (978-1-4241-0221-1(9)) PublishAmerica, Inc.

Basha, Irena Canaj. The Birthday Party, It Was Saturday... 2013. 16p. pap. 24.95 (978-1-62709-182-4(3)) America Star Bks.

Berry, Jacqueline. Teeny Tiny Topper, the Grasshopper. 2007. 20p. per. 24.95 (978-1-4241-8338-8(3)) America Star Bks.

Binkley, Carolyn. The Errand: And Stinkbugs & Grasshoppers Green. 2012. 24p. pap. 15.99 (978-1-4691-6096-2(X)) Xlibris Corp.

Castle, Regina F. Henry Hopper. 2011. 20p. pap. 24.95 (978-1-4560-6563-8(7)) America Star Bks.

Christianson, Leslie Rose. Malinda Matters: And Priscilla the Praying Mantis. 2010. 36p. pap. 15.49 (978-1-4490-6914-8(2)) AuthorHouse.

Collier, Wayne Evans. Grumpy the Grasshopper. Goodman, Larry, illus. 2012. 20p. pap. 24.95 (978-1-4626-6844-1(5)) America Star Bks.

Emberley, Rebecca. The Ant & the Grasshopper. Emberley, Ed, illus. 2012. (ENG.). 28p. (J). (gr. -1-2). 18.99 (978-1-59643-493-6(7), 9781596434936) Roaring Brook Pr.

Eyckerman, Merel, illus. The Ant & the Grasshopper. 2013. (Usborne First Reading: Level 1 Ser.). (ENG.). 32p. (J). (gr. -1-3). 6.99 (978-0-7945-2257-5(2), Usborne) EDC Publishing.

Fleischman, Sid. La Maravillosa Granja de McBroom. Blake, Quentin, illus. 13th ed. 2003.Tr. of McBroom's Wonderful One-Acre Farm. (SPA.). 96p. (J). (gr. 3-5). 7.95 (978-84-204-4885-5(0)) Ediciones Alfaguara ESP. Dist: Santillana USA Publishing Co., Inc.

Grant, Judyann Ackerman. Chicken Said, "Cluck!" Truesdell, Sue, illus. 2010. (My First I Can Read Ser.). (ENG.). 32p. (J). (gr. -1-3). pap. 3.99 (978-0-06-444276-3(4)) HarperCollins Pubs.

Gray, Luli. Ant & Grasshopper. Ferri, Giuliano, illus. 2011. (ENG.). 32p. (J). (gr. -1-2). 17.99 (978-1-4169-5140-7(7), McElderry, Margaret K. Bks.) McElderry, Margaret K. Bks.

Hewitt, Hazel & Gillett, Chrissy. A Locust Ate My Daddy's Underwears. 2008. 24p. pap. 13.95 (978-1-84799-261-1(7)) Lulu Pr., Inc.

Johnston, Kathy. Get That Grasshopper! 2012. 24p. pap. 12.56 (978-1-4669-3743-7(2)) Trafford Publishing.

Jonell, Lynne. Grasshopper Magic. Dorman, Brandon, illus. 2013. (Magical Mix-Ups Ser.: 3). (ENG.). 112p. (J). (gr. 1-4). 12.99 (978-0-375-87084-2(9), Random Hse. Bks. for Young Readers) Random Hse. Children's Bks.

Lee, WonKyeong. The Chirping Band. Jang, EunJoo, illus. 2014. (MySELF Bookshelf Ser.). (ENG.). 32p. (J). (gr. k-2). pap. 11.94 (978-1-60357-698-7(3)); lib. bdg. 25.27 (978-1-59953-663-7(3)) Norwood Hse. Pr.

Mihalko, Ross, et al. Ant & the Grasshopper (Musical) 2012. (J). 8.95 (978-0-573-70112-2(1)) French, Samuel Inc.

Pinkney, Jerry. The Grasshopper & the Ants. 2015. (ENG., Illus.). 40p. (J). (gr. -1-3). 18.00 (978-0-316-40081-7(5)) Little, Brown Bks. for Young Readers.

Pryor, Bonnie. Perfect Percy. 2013. (ENG.). 28p. (J). (gr. -1-3). 12.99 (978-1-4424-8872-4(7), Atheneum Bks. for Young Readers) Simon & Schuster Children's Publishing.

Rice, Dona Herwick & Housel, Debra. The Grasshopper & the Ants, 1 vol. 2008. (Building Fluency Through Reader's Theater Ser.). (ENG., Illus.). 24p. (J). (gr. 1-3). pap. 6.99 (978-1-4333-0292-3(6)) Teacher Created Materials, Inc.

Salusso, S. T. Billy the Roly Poly Bug. 2012. 24p. pap. 13.00 (978-1-4269-6134-2(0)) Trafford Publishing.

Smith, Andrew. Grasshopper Jungle. 2015. lib. bdg. 22.10 (978-0-606-36795-0(0)) Turtleback Bks.

Smith, Michael & Oliva, Octavio. Grasshopper Buddy. Oliva, Octavio, illus. 2012. (SPA & ENG., Illus.). (J). (978-0-9856237-0-8(5)) East West Discovery Pr.

Sommer, Carl. The Ant & the Grasshopper. Noé, Ignacio, illus. 2016. (ENG.). 32p. (J). (gr. k-4). lib. bdg. 16.95 (978-1-57537-925-8(2), Another Sommer-Time Story) Advance Publishing, Inc.

Sparkes, Ali. Grasshopper Glitch. Collins, Ross, illus. 2013. (S. W. I. T. C. H. Ser.: 3). (ENG.). 104p. (J). (gr. 2-5). pap. 7.95 (978-1-4677-0712-1(0)) Lerner Publishing Group.

—Grasshopper Glitch. Collins, Ross, illus. 2013. (S. W. I. T. C. H. Ser.: 3). (ENG.). 104p. (J). (gr. 2-5). lib. bdg. 27.93 (978-0-7613-9201-9(7)) Lerner Publishing Group.

Stamps, Paula. Learning Makes Friends Fun, 1 vol. 2010. 22p. 24.95 (978-1-4512-8765-3(8)) PublishAmerica, Inc.

Stone, Forrest. The Ant & Grasshopper Show. 2006. (J). pap. (978-1-4108-6183-2(X)) Benchmark Education Co.

Walter, Jackie. The Ants & the Grasshopper. 2017. (Must Know Stories: Level 1 Ser.). (ENG., Illus.). 32p. (J). (gr. k-2). 4.99 **(978-1-4451-4454-2(9)**, Franklin Watts) Hachette Children's Group GBR. Dist: Hachette Bk. Group.

Zuggo, Violeta & Zuggo, Jutka. Story Time for Kids with Nlp by the English Sisters: The Little Grasshopper & the Big Ball of Dung. Kecskés, Anna, illus. 2013. 24p. pap. (978-1-78092-493-9(3)) MX Publishing, Ltd.

LOG CABINS

Meachen Rau, Dana. Bookworms: The Inside Story, 6 bks., Set. Incl. Castle. 32p. (gr. k-2). lib. bdg. 15.95 (978-0-7614-2272-3(2)); Igloo. 32p. (gr. k-2). lib. bdg. 15.95 (978-0-7614-2273-0(0)); Log Cabin. 31p. (J). (gr. -1-3). lib. bdg. 22.79 (978-0-7614-2274-7(9)); Pyramid. 32p. (gr. k-2). lib. bdg. 15.95 (978-0-7614-2275-4(7)); Skyscraper. 32p. (gr. k-2). lib. bdg. 15.95 (978-0-7614-2276-1(5)); Tepee. 31p. (J). (gr. -1-3). lib. bdg. 22.79 (978-0-7614-2277-8(3)); (Illus.). 2006. 2006. Set lib. bdg. 136.71 (978-0-7614-2271-6(4), Benchmark Bks.) Marshall Cavendish Corp.

—Log Cabin. 2006. (Bookworms Ser.). (Illus.). 31p. (J). (gr. -1-3). lib. bdg. 22.79 (978-0-7614-2274-7(9), Benchmark Bks.) Marshall Cavendish Corp.

Rae, Thelma. Pioneer Families. 2009. (Reading Room Collection 1 Ser.). 16p. (gr. 2-3). 37.50 (978-1-60851-948-4(1), PowerKids Pr.) Rosen Publishing Group, Inc., The.

Rau, Dana Meachen. Log Cabin. 2007. (J). pap. 6.99 (978-0-7614-3300-2(7)) Marshall Cavendish Corp.

Rubin, Donna. Log Cabin Kitty. Halbower, Susan J., illus. 2012. 56p. pap. 20.00 (978-0-87565-503-1(3)) Texas Christian Univ. Pr.

Skinner, Tina. Log & Timber Frame Homes, 1 vol. 2003. (ENG., Illus.). 224p. (gr. 10-13). 44.95 (978-0-7643-1754-5(7), 9780764317545) Schiffer Publishing, Ltd.

LOGGING

see Lumber and Lumbering

LOGIC

see also Knowledge, Theory of; Probabilities; Reasoning; Thought and Thinking

Boardworks Learning Centers: Figure It Out. 2006. (J). bds. (978-0-9755252-4-1(7)) Evergreen Pr. of Brainerd, LLC.

Brainy Baby Vertical Right/Left Tab Book. 2005. (Brainy Baby Ser.). (978-1-59394-450-6(0)) Bendon, Inc.

Carr, Mary Ann. The Great Chocolate Caper: A Mystery That Teaches Logic Skills. 2nd rev. ed. 2010. (ENG.). 88p. (gr. 5-8). pap. 16.95 (978-1-59363-499-5(4)) Prufrock Pr.

Harris, Patricia. Understanding Coding Using Boolean Logic. 2016. (Spotlight on Kids Can Code Ser.). 00024p. (J). (gr. 4-5). pap. 11.75 (978-1-4994-2806-3(5), PowerKids Pr.) Rosen Publishing Group, Inc., The.

Harris, Patricia. Understanding Coding Using Conditionals. 2017. (J). **(978-1-4994-2814-8(6)**, PowerKids Pr.) Rosen Publishing Group, Inc., The.

Heinrich, Erik. Survival Debate: A Rip-Roaring Game of Either-Or Questions. 2012. (This or That? Ser.). (ENG., Illus.). 32p. (gr. 3-4). lib. bdg. 27.99 (978-1-4296-8594-8(8)) Capstone Press of Coughlan Cos.

—This or That Survival Debate: A Rip-Roaring Game of Either - Or Questions. 2012. (This or That? Ser.). (ENG., Illus.). 32p. (gr. 3-4). pap. 8.29 (978-1-4296-9278-6(2)) Capstone Press of Coughlan Cos.

—This or That Survival Debate: A Rip-Roaring Game of Either/or Questions. 2012. (This or That? Ser.). (ENG.). 32p. (gr. 3-4). pap. 47.70 (978-1-4296-9279-3(0), Edge Bks.) Capstone Press of Coughlan Cos.

Kofman, Victoria. Guni-Pi Academy, Math & Logic: Hands-On Textbook for 4 - 7 Year Olds. 2006. spiral bd. (978-0-9777171-0-1(0)) VK Publishing, Inc.

—Guni-Pi Academy, Math & Logic: Hands-on Textbook for 4 - 7 Year Olds - Non-Laminated. 2006. spiral bd. (978-0-9777171-2-5(7)) VK Publishing, Inc.

Kreeft, Peter. Socratic Logic: A Logic Text Using Socratic Method, Platonic Questions, & Aristotelian Principles. 2004. (Illus.). x, 397p. (YA). 40.00 (978-1-890318-89-5(2)) St. Augustine's Pr., Inc.

Krieger, Emily. Just When You Thought You Knew What You Knew... Cocotos, Tom Nick, illus. 2013. (Myths Busted Ser.). (ENG.). 208p. (J). (gr. 4-7). pap. 7.95 (978-1-4263-1102-4(8)); lib. bdg. 16.90 (978-1-4263-1103-1(6)) National Geographic Society. (National Geographic Children's Bks.).

Krieger, Emily & National Geographic Kids Staff. Just When You Thought You Knew What You Knew... 2015. (Myths Busted Ser.). (ENG., Illus.). 208p. (J). (gr. 4-7). pap. 7.99 (978-1-4263-1883-2(9), National Geographic Children's Bks.) National Geographic Society.

Nance, James B. Intermediate Logic - Student (2nd Edition) 2nd ed. 2006. (ENG.). 209p. pap. 27.00 (978-1-59128-035-4(4)) Canon Pr.

Nance, James B. & Wilson, Douglas J. Introductory Logic - Student (4th Edition) 4th ed. 2006. (ENG.). 250p. pap. 29.00 (978-1-59128-033-0(8)) Canon Pr.

Pederson, Bridget. I Can Predict, I Wont Be Tricked!, 1 vol. 2007. (Science Made Simple Ser.). (ENG., Illus.). 24p. (J). (gr. k-3). lib. bdg. 24.21 (978-1-59928-582-5(7), SandCastle) ABDO Publishing Co.

Schultz-Ferrell, Karren, et al. Introduction to Reasoning & Proof, Grades 3-5. 2007. (ENG., Illus.). 160p. (C). (gr. 3-5). pap. 36.25 (978-0-325-01033-5(1), E01033) Heinemann.

Schulz, Charles. The Peanuts Guide to the Seasons: A Jumbo Activity Book. Bennett, Elizabeth, illus. 2003. (Peanuts Club with Charlie Brown & Friends Ser.). 144p. (J). (978-0-439-46826-8(4)) Scholastic, Inc.

Schulz, Charles & Bennett, Elizabeth. The Peanuts Guide to Sports: A Jumbo Activity Book. 2003. (Peanuts Club with Charlie Brown & Friends Ser.). (Illus.). 144p. (J). (978-0-439-46824-4(8)) Scholastic, Inc.

Somervill, Barbara A. Does This Make Sense? Constructing Explanations. 2009. (Think Like a Scientist Ser.). 24p. (gr. 2-3). 42.50 (978-1-60854-356-4(0), PowerKids Pr.) Rosen Publishing Group, Inc., The.

—What's the Big Idea? Forming Hypotheses. 2007. 24p. (gr. 3-5). pap. 8.25 (978-1-4358-2686-1(8), Rosen Classroom) Rosen Publishing Group, Inc., The.

LONDON, JACK, 1876-1916

Bankston, John. Jack London. 2004. (Classic Storytellers Ser.). (Illus.). 48p. (J). (gr. 4-8). lib. bdg. 29.95 (978-1-58415-263-7(X)) Mitchell Lane Pubs., Inc.

Buckwalter, Stephanie. Reading & Interpreting the Works of Jack London. 2017. (Lit Crit Guides). 160p. (J). (gr. 8-8). lib. bdg. 39.93 **(978-0-7660-8491-9(4))** Enslow Pubs., Inc.

Buckwalter, Stephanie. A Student's Guide to Jack London. 2007. (Understanding Literature Ser.). (Illus.). 160p. (YA). (gr. 8-12). lib. bdg. 29.27 (978-0-7660-2707-7(4)) Enslow Pubs., Inc.

Lourie, Peter. Jack London & the Klondike Gold Rush. Minor, Wendell, illus. 2017. (ENG.). 208p. (J). 18.99 (978-0-8050-9757-3(0), 9780805097573, Holt, Henry & Co. Bks. For Young Readers) Holt, Henry & Co.

Saddleback Educational Publishing Staff, ed. A Call of the Wild. 2011. (Timeless Classics Ser.). (ENG.). 48p. (YA). (gr. 9-12). pupil's gde. ed. 19.95 incl. cd-rom (978-1-61651-128-9(1)) Saddleback Educational Publishing, Inc.

—White Fang. 2011. (Timeless Classics Ser.). (ENG.). 48p. (YA). (gr. 9-12). pupil's gde. ed. 19.95 incl. cd-rom (978-1-61651-158-6(3)) Saddleback Educational Publishing, Inc.

Streissguth, Thomas. Jack London. 2005. (Biography Ser.). (Illus.). 112p. (gr. 6-12). lib. bdg. 27.93 (978-0-8225-4987-1(5)) Lerner Publishing Group.

LONDON (ENGLAND)

Adams, Jennifer. My Little Cities: London. Pizzoli, Greg, illus. 2017. (ENG.). 22p. (J). (gr. -1-k). bds. 9.99 (978-1-4521-5387-2(6)) Chronicle Bks. LLC.

Evanson, Ashley. London: A Book of Opposites. Evanson, Ashley, illus. 2015. (Hello, World Ser.). (ENG., Illus.). 14p. (J). (— 1). bds. 6.99 (978-0-448-48916-2(3), Grosset & Dunlap) Penguin Young Readers Group.

Holland, Simon. An Infographic Guide to London. 2017. (Infographic Guide To Ser.). (ENG., Illus.). 64p. (J). (gr. 4-6). pap. 9.99 **(978-0-7502-9954-1(1)**, Wayland) Hachette Children's Group GBR. Dist: Hachette Bk. Group.

Jones, Becky & Lewis, Clare. The Bumper Book of London: Everything You Need to Know about London & More... 2015. (ENG., Illus.). 280p. pap. 19.99 (978-0-7112-3736-0(0), Frances Lincoln) Quarto Publishing Group UK GBR. Dist: Littlehampton Bk Services, Ltd.

Mason, Paul. London. Bowden, Rob & Cooper, Adrian, photos by. 2006. (Global Cities Ser.). (Illus.). 61p. (gr. 5-8). 30.00 (978-0-7910-8852-4(9), Chelsea Hse.) Facts On File, Inc.

Mitchell, Arnold. Arnold's Dream. 2009. 32p. pap. 14.95 (978-1-4092-4776-0(7)) Lulu Pr., Inc.

Munro, Roxie. The Inside-Outside Book of London. 2015. (ENG., Illus.). 40p. (J). (gr. 2). 14.95 (978-0-7893-2913-4(1)) Universe Publishing.

Riley, Gail Blasser. Tower of London: England's Ghostly Castle. 2006. (Castles, Palaces, & Tombs Ser.). (Illus.). 32p. (YA). (gr. 2-5). lib. bdg. 25.27 (978-1-59716-249-4(3)) Bearport Publishing Co., Inc.

Rowe, Harriet. L Is for London. 2015. (Is for Alphabet Ser.). (ENG., Illus.). 32p. (J). (gr. -1-3). 10.99 (978-1-907432-08-8(6)) Hogs Back Bks. GBR. Dist: Independent Pubs. Group.

Sasek, Miroslav. This Is London. 2004. (This Is ... Ser.). (ENG., Illus.). 64p. (J). (gr. 2-12). 17.95 (978-0-7893-1062-0(7)) Universe Publishing.

Stacey, Gill. London. 2003. (Great Cities of the World Ser.). (Illus.). 48p. (gr. 5-12). lib. bdg. 31.00 (978-0-8368-5022-2(X), Gareth Stevens Secondary Library) Stevens, Gareth Publishing LLLP.

van der Meulen, Majel, illus. My London: Color, Draw, Explore. 2017. (ENG.). 40p. (J). (gr. 1-4). pap. 12.99 (978-1-78067-912-9(2)) King, Laurence Publishing GBR. Dist: Hachette Bk. Group.

LONDON (ENGLAND)—FICTION

Abbott, Jacob. Rollo in London. 2008. 124p. 23.95 (978-1-60664-942-8(6)); pap. 10.95 (978-1-60312-492-8(6)) Aegypan.

Ahern, Carolyn L. Tino Turtle Travels to London, England. Burt Sullivan, Neallia, illus. (J). 2007. 36p. 17.95 incl. audio compact disk (978-0-9793158-0-0(8)) 2008. (ENG.). 32p. 19.95 incl. audio compact disk (978-0-9816297-0-4(9)) Tino Turtle Travels, LLC.

Andrews, Julie. Little Bo: The Story of Bonnie Boadicea, No. 2. 2011. (Illus.). (J). lib. bdg. 18.89 (978-0-06-008912-2(1)) HarperCollins Pubs.

Angel, Ido. Vipo in London: The Ravens of the London Tower. 2015. (AV2 Animated Storytime Ser.). (ENG.). (J). lib. bdg. 29.99 (978-1-4896-3911-0(X), AV2 by Weigl) Weigl Pubs., Inc.

Anne-Marie-Mugwe. Cobjay's Summer Holiday & How to Catch a Squirrel. 2013. (Illus.). 36p. pap. 22.88 (978-1-4817-8223-4(1)) AuthorHouse.

Anstey, Cindy. Duels & Deception. 2017. (ENG.). 368p. (YA). pap. 10.99 (978-1-250-11909-4(X), 9781250119094) Feiwel & Friends.

Antony, Steve. The Queen's Hat. 2015. (ENG., Illus.). 32p. (J). (gr. -1-k). 16.99 (978-0-545-83556-5(9), Scholastic Pr.) Scholastic, Inc.

Arrigan, Mary. Rabbit Girl. 2011. (ENG.). 224p. (J). (gr. 4-7). pap. 8.95 (978-1-84780-156-2(0), Frances Lincoln) Quarto Publishing Group UK GBR. Dist: Hachette Bk. Group.

Ashley, Bernard. Aftershock. 2011. (ENG.). 144p. (J). (gr. 4-7). pap. 8.95 (978-1-84780-055-8(6), Frances Lincoln Children's Bks.) Quarto Publishing Group UK GBR. Dist: Hachette Bk. Group.

Ashley, Bernard & Morgan, Andrew. Dead End Kids. 2015. (Cordelia Codd Ser.). (ENG.). 224p. (J). (gr. 4-6). pap. 10.99 (978-1-4083-3895-7(5)) Hodder & Stoughton GBR. Dist: Hachette Bk. Group.

Atwarie, Rossi. The Adventures of Fox Brown. Bachan, Krystal Ann, illus. 2011. 62p. pap. 19.00 (978-1-60911-845-7(6), Eloquent Bks.) Strategic Book Publishing & Rights Agency (SBPRA).

Avery, Tom. My Brother's Shadow. 2014. (ENG.). 176p. (J). (gr. 4-7). 16.99 (978-0-385-38487-2(4), Schwartz & Wade Bks.) Random Hse. Children's Bks.

Avi. The Traitors' Gate. Raude, Karina, illus. 2010. (ENG.). 368p. (J). (gr. 5-8). pap. 7.99 (978-0-689-85336-4(X), Atheneum Bks. for Young Readers) Simon & Schuster Children's Publishing.

Axelsson, Carina. Model Undercover: London. 2016. (Model Undercover Ser.: 3). (ENG.). 368p. (J). (gr. 5-8). pap. 6.99 (978-1-4926-2088-4(2), Sourcebooks Jabberwocky) Sourcebooks, Inc.

Bachmann, Stefan. The Whatnot. (Peculiar Ser.: 2). (ENG.). 432p. (J). (gr. 3-7). 2014. pap. 8.99 (978-0-06-219522-7(0)) 2013. 16.99 (978-0-06-219521-0(2)) HarperCollins Pubs. (Greenwillow Bks.).

Ballantyne, Robert Michael. Life in the Red Brigade: London Fire Brigade. l.t. ed. 2007. 98p. pap. 18.99 (978-1-4346-3772-7(7)) Creative Media Partners, LLC.

Bankes, Liz. Undeniable. 2015. (ENG.). 256p. (YA). (gr. 9). 17.99 (978-0-8027-3623-9(8), 9780802736239, Bloomsbury USA Childrens) Bloomsbury Publishing USA.

Banks, Piper. Geek Abroad, 2 vols. 2008. (Geek High Ser.: 2). (ENG.). 256p. (YA). (gr. 9-18). 9.99 (978-0-451-22393-7(4), Berkley) Penguin Publishing Group.

—Revenge of the Geek. 2010. (Geek High Ser.: 4). (ENG.). 256p. (gr. 12-18). 9.99 (978-0-451-23134-5(1), Berkley) Penguin Publishing Group.

Barradell, Isabel. Even More Tales from the Toyshop. 2008. 380p. pap. 29.95 (978-1-60474-508-5(8)) America Star Bks.

Barrett, Tracy. The Case That Time Forgot. 2011. (Sherlock Files Ser.: 3). (ENG., Illus.). 176p. (J). (gr. 3-7). pap. 7.99 (978-0-312-56358-5(2), 9780312563585) Square Fish.

—The Missing Heir. 2012. (Sherlock Files Ser.: 4). (ENG., Illus.). 192p. (J). (gr. 3-7). pap. 8.99 (978-1-250-00480-2(2), 9781250004802) Square Fish.

—The Missing Heir. 2012. (Sherlock Files Ser.: 4). (J). lib. bdg. 19.65 (978-0-606-26131-9(1), Turtleback) Turtleback Bks.

Barrie, J. M. Peter Pan. (SPA.). 191p. 15.95 (978-84-206-3689-4(4)) Alianza Editorial, S. A. ESP. Dist: Distribooks, Inc.

—Peter Pan: Peter & Wendy & Peter Pan in Kensington Gardens. 2004. (ENG., Illus.). 352p. (gr. 12-18). 11.00 (978-0-14-243793-3(X), Penguin Classics) Penguin Publishing Group.

—Peter Pan in Kensington Gardens. 2006. pap. (978-1-4065-0950-2(7)) Dodo Pr.

Barrie, J. M. & Edens, Cooper. Peter Pan. (SPA.). 174p. 26.95 (978-84-666-0760-5(9)) Ediciones B ESP. Dist: Spanish Pubs., LLC.

Barry, Dave & Pearson, Ridley. Peter & the Sword of Mercy. Call, Greg, illus. 2011. (Peter & the Starcatchers Ser.: Bk. 4). (ENG.). 528p. (J). (gr. 5-9). pap. 9.99 (978-1-4231-3070-3(7)) Hyperion Pr.

Beecroft, Susan. Teddy Goes to Buckingham Palace. 2013. (Illus.). 24p. pap. 9.50 (978-1-78035-606-8(4), Fastprint Publishing) Upfront Publishing Ltd. GBR. Dist: Printondemand-worldwide.com.

Bennett, Sophia. The Look. 2013. (J). (ENG.). 336p. (gr. 7). 17.99 (978-0-545-46438-3(2)); (978-0-545-46439-0(0)) Scholastic, Inc. (Chicken Hse., The).

—Sequins, Secrets, & Silver Linings. 2011. (ENG.). 304p. (J). (gr. 7-11). 16.99 (978-0-545-24241-7(X), Chicken Hse., The) Scholastic, Inc.

Berk, Sheryl & Berk, Carrie. Royal Icing: The Cupcake Club. 2014. (Cupcake Club Ser.: 6). (ENG.). 144p. (J). (gr. 3-7). pap. 6.99 (978-1-4022-8333-8(4), Sourcebooks Jabberwocky) Sourcebooks, Inc.

Best, Rosie. Skulk. 2013. (ENG.). 400p. (J). pap. 9.99 (978-1-908844-70-5(1), Strange Chemistry) Watkins Media Limited GBR. Dist: Penguin Random Hse. LLC.

Blacker, Terence. The Angel Factory. 2012. (ENG., Illus.). 224p. (J). (gr. 5-9). pap. 10.99 (978-0-689-86413-1(2), Simon & Schuster/Paula Wiseman Bks.) Simon & Schuster/Paula Wiseman Bks.

Blyton, Enid. The Secret of the Lost Necklace: 3 Great Adventure Stories. Biro, Val, illus. 2013. (ENG.). 272p. (J). 16.50 (978-1-84135-587-0(9)) Award Pubns. Ltd. GBR. Dist: Parkwest Pubns., Inc.

Bond, Michael. Paddington & the Christmas Surprise. Alley, R. W., illus. 2015. (Paddington Ser.). (ENG.). 32p. (J). (gr. -1-3). 17.99 (978-0-06-231842-8(X)) HarperCollins Pubs.

Bond, Michael. Paddington's Day Off. 2017. (Paddington — I Can Read Ser.). (J). lib. bdg. 13.55 **(978-0-606-39636-3(5))** Turtleback Bks.

Botha, Ingrid. Chikin & Scrub. 2011. 108p. pap. 10.50 (978-1-60976-295-7(9), Strategic Bk. Publishing) Strategic Book Publishing & Rights Agency (SBPRA).

Boyne, John. Stay Where You Are & Then Leave. Jeffers, Oliver, illus. 2014. (ENG.). 256p. (J). (gr. 4-7). 16.99 (978-1-62779-031-4(4), 9781627790314, Holt, Henry & Co. Bks. For Young Readers) Holt, Henry & Co.

Bradbury, Jennifer. Wrapped. 2011. (ENG., Illus.). 320p. (YA). (gr. 7-18). 16.99 (978-1-4169-9007-9(0), Atheneum Bks. for Young Readers) Simon & Schuster Children's Publishing.

Braddock, Pauline. The long way Home. 2010. 156p. pap. 9.17 (978-1-4452-9248-9(3)) Lulu Pr., Inc.

Branson, Eve. Sarky Puddleboat. Lowe, Wes, illus. 2011. 44p. (J). 14.99 (978-1-4520-9754-1(2)) AuthorHouse.

Brundige, Patricia. Traveling with Aunt Patty: Aunt Patty Visits London. Wright, Cindy, ed. Hanlon, Leslie, illus. Date not set. (J). (gr. 1-4). 12.95 (978-0-9659668-0-1(1)) Aunt Patty's Travels-London.

Buckley-Archer, Linda. The Time Quake. 2009. (Gideon Trilogy Ser.: 3). (ENG.). 464p. (J). (gr. 5-9). 17.99 (978-1-4169-1529-4(X), Simon & Schuster Bks. For Young Readers) Simon & Schuster Bks. For Young Readers.

—The Time Thief. 2008. (Gideon Trilogy Ser.: 2). (ENG.). 512p. (J). (gr. 5-9). pap. 9.99 (978-1-4169-1528-7(1), Simon & Schuster Bks. For Young Readers) Simon & Schuster Bks. For Young Readers.

Burnett, Frances Hodgson. A Little Princess. 2008. 156p. 25.95 (978-1-60664-768-4(7)); pap. 13.95 (978-1-60664-141-5(7)) Aegypan.

—A Little Princess. 2008. 212p. (gr. 2-4). 27.99 *(978-0-554-29155-0(X))*; 24.99 *(978-0-554-38458-0(2))* Creative Media Partners, LLC.
—A Little Princess. Aldous, Kate, illus. 2005. 62p. (J). (gr. 4-7). 8.95 *(978-0-7945-1123-4(6)*, Usborne) EDC Publishing.
—A Little Princess. 2012. 212p. pap. 8.99 *(978-1-60796-454-4(6))* Meirovich, Igal.
—A Little Princess. 2012. (ENG., Illus.). 280p. *(978-1-905716-04-3(4)*, Collector's Library, The) Pan Macmillan.
—A Little Princess. 2012. (Puffin Classics Ser.). (ENG., Illus.). 320p. (J). (gr. 5-7). 16.99 *(978-0-14-134171-2(8)*, Puffin Books) Penguin Young Readers Group.
—A Little Princess. Gill, Margery, illus. 2008. (Puffin Classics Ser.). (ENG.). 320p. (J). (gr. 5-7). 5.99 *(978-0-14-132112-7(1)*, Puffin Books) Penguin Young Readers Group.
—A Little Princess. Betts, Ethel Franklin, illus. 2016. (Knickerbocker Children's Classics Ser.). (ENG.). 256p. (J). (gr. 4-7). 14.99 *(978-1-63106-250-6(6)*, Race Point Publishing) Quarto Publishing Group USA.
—A Little Princess. 2011. (ENG., Illus.). (J). 15.99 ***(978-1-61382-603-4(6))*** Simon & Brown.
—A Little Princess. 188p. 2009. pap. 13.95 *(978-1-4385-0876-4(X))* 2008. pap. 13.45 *(978-1-4385-0194-9(3))* Standard Pubns., Inc. (Book Jungle).
—A Little Princess. McKowen, Scott, illus. 2004. (Sterling Unabridged Classics Ser.). (ENG.). 208p. (J). (gr. 5). 9.95 *(978-1-4027-1454-2(8))* Sterling Publishing Co., Inc.
—A Little Princess. Engelbreit, Mary, illus. 2007. (Mary Engelbreit's Classic Library). (ENG.). 304p. (J). (gr. 3-7). 9.99 *(978-0-06-008137-9(6)*, HarperFestival) HarperCollins Pubs.
—A Little Princess. 2012. (Children's Classics Ser.). (ENG.). 186p. pap. 19.99 *(978-1-909438-52-1(9)*, Sovereign) Bollinger, Max GBR. Dist: Lightning Source UK, Ltd.
—A Little Princess. Kliros, Thea, illus. abr. ed. 2012. (Dover Children's Thrift Classics Ser.). (ENG.). 96p. (J). (gr. 3-8). pap. 3.00 *(978-0-486-29171-0(5))* Dover Pubns., Inc.
—A Little Princess: Being the whole story of Sara Crewe now told for T. 2007. 196p. per. 19.99 *(978-1-4346-7028-1(7))*; (ENG.). 210p. per. 22.99 *(978-1-4346-7029-8(5))* Creative Media Partners, LLC.
—A Little Princess: The Story of Sara Crewe. (J). 16.95 *(978-0-8488-1253-9(0))* Amereon Ltd.
—A Little Princess: The Story of Sara Crewe. Warren, Eliza, ed. Marcos, Pablo, illus. 2006. 239p. (YA). reprint ed. 10.00 *(978-0-7567-9835-2(3))* DIANE Publishing Co.
—A Little Princess: The Story of Sara Crewe. 2005. 112p. per. 4.95 *(978-1-4209-2529-6(6))* Digireads.com Publishing.
—A Little Princess: The Story of Sara Crewe. 2006. pap. *(978-1-4065-0559-7(5))* Dodo Pr.
—A Little Princess: The Story of Sara Crewe. l.t. ed. 2005. 376p. pap. *(978-1-84637-117-2(1))* Echo Library.
—A Little Princess: The Story of Sara Crewe. 2004. reprint ed. pap. 22.95 *(978-1-4191-0213-4(3))*; pap. 1.99 *(978-1-4192-0213-1(8))* Kessinger Publishing, LLC.
—A Little Princess: The Story of Sara Crewe. 2006. 204p. (YA). 19.95 *(978-1-934169-20-9(X))*; pap. 7.95 *(978-1-934169-21-6(8))* Norilana Bks.
—A Little Princess: The Story of Sara Crewe. 2005. (Twelve-Point Ser.). lib. bdg. 25.00 *(978-1-58287-320-6(8))*; lib. bdg. 26.00 *(978-1-58287-814-0(5))* North Bks.
—A Little Princess: The Story of Sara Crewe. Rust, Graham, illus. (J). pap. 22.95 *(978-0-590-24079-6(X))* Scholastic, Inc.
—A Little Princess: The Story of Sara Crewe. l.t. ed. 2003. 342p. pap. 10.95 *(978-0-7862-6247-2(8))* Thorndike Pr.
—A Little Princess: With a Discussion of Generosity. Gribbon, Sean & Jael, trs. Gribbon, Sean & Jael, illus. 2003. (Values in Action Illustrated Classics Ser.). (J). *(978-1-59203-050-7(5))* Learning Challenge, Inc.
—Petite Princess. pap. 19.95 *(978-2-07-051994-1(5))* Gallimard, Editions FRA. Dist: Distribooks, Inc.
—Sara Crewe. l.t. ed. 2006. 92p. pap. *(978-1-84637-263-6(1))* Echo Library.
—Sara Crewe. 2009. 68p. pap. 7.95 *(978-1-60664-388-4(6))* Rodgers, Alan Bks.
—Sara Crewe or What Happened at Miss Minc. 2005. pap. 20.95 *(978-0-7661-9708-4(5))* Kessinger Publishing, LLC.
—Sara Crewe or What Happened at Miss Minchin's. 2006. (ENG.). 88p. per. 8.95 *(978-1-59462-359-2(7)*, 395, Book Jungle) Standard Pubns., Inc.
—Sara Crewe, or What Happened at Miss Minchin's. 2007. 48p. per. *(978-1-4068-4489-4(6))* Echo Library.
Button, Timothy D. Matthew Mcsilly. 2012. 32p. pap. 17.95 *(978-1-4772-0817-5(8))* AuthorHouse.
Byrne, Michael. Lottery Boy. 2016. (ENG.). 304p. (YA). (gr. 7). 16.99 *(978-0-7636-7996-5(8))* Candlewick Pr.
Callaghan, Cindy. Lost in London. 2013. (Mix Ser.). (ENG., Illus.). 240p. (J). (gr. 4-8). pap. 7.99 *(978-1-4424-6653-1(7)*, Aladdin) Simon & Schuster Children's Publishing.
Calloway, Cassidy. Secrets of a First Daughter. 2010. (ENG.). 208p. (YA). (gr. 8-18). pap. 8.99 *(978-0-06-172442-8(4)*, HarperTeen) HarperCollins Pubs.
Carey, Edward. Heap House. 2014. (Iremonger Trilogy Ser.: 1). (ENG.). 416p. (gr. 4-13). 16.99 *(978-1-4683-0953-9(6)*, 460953) Overlook Pr., The.
—Lungdon: Book Three. 2016. (Iremonger Trilogy Ser.: 0). (ENG.). 512p. (YA). (gr. 5-12). pap. 11.99 *(978-1-4683-1306-2(1)*, 461306) Overlook Pr., The.
Carlson, Melody. Spotlight, 1 vol. 2014. (On the Runway Ser.). (ENG.). 224p. (YA). pap. 9.99 *(978-0-310-74821-2(6))* Zondervan.
Carmichael, Heather. Ellie Finds a New Home. McFarland, Shea, illus. 2008. (ENG.). 36p. pap. 16.99 *(978-1-4389-2976-7(5))* AuthorHouse.
Carter, Ally. Only the Good Spy Young. 2016. (Gallagher Girls Ser.: 4). (J). lib. bdg. 20.85 *(978-0-606-38298-4(4))* Turtleback Bks.
—Only the Good Spy Young (10th Anniversary Edition) 2016. (Gallagher Girls Ser.). (ENG.). 288p. (J). (gr. 5-9). pap. 9.99 *(978-1-4847-8506-5(1))* Hyperion Bks. for Children.
Casey, Jane. How to Fall. 2014. (Jess Tennant Mysteries Ser.: 1). (ENG.). 352p. (YA). (gr. 8-11). 18.99 *(978-1-250-04065-7(5)*, 9781250040657, St. Martin's Griffin) St. Martin's Pr.
Chadda, Sarwat. The City of Death. 2013. (J). pap. *(978-0-545-38519-0(9))*; (ENG.). 336p. (gr. 4-7). 16.99 *(978-0-545-38518-3(0)*, Levine, Arthur A. Bks.) Scholastic, Inc.
Cheshire, Simon. The Frankenstein Inheritance. 2012. 204p. pap. *(978-0-9565049-7-5(3))* Cheshire, Simon.
Chitty, Joan E. Charlie Macaffee: Search for the Genie's Body. 2005. 267p. pap. 27.95 *(978-1-4241-0007-1(0))* PublishAmerica, Inc.
Christen, Dennis H. Lundon's Bridge & the Three Keys. 2005. (YA). lib. bdg., act. bk. ed. 24.95 *(978-0-9718151-3-1(5))* 2006. (ENG.). (J). per. 12.95 *(978-0-9718151-2-4(7))* C-It Entertainment Group, LLC.
C.J. Eigert. The Elder Brothers & the Padstow Crystals. 2009. 284p. 27.95 *(978-1-4401-7678-4(7))*; pap. 17.95 *(978-1-4401-7676-0(0))* iUniverse, Inc.
Clare, Cassandra. Clockwork Prince. 2013. (Infernal Devices Graphic Novel Ser.: 2). lib. bdg. 24.55 *(978-0-606-32258-4(2)*, Turtleback) Turtleback Bks.
—The Infernal Devices: Clockwork Angel; Clockwork Prince; Clockwork Princess. 2013. (Infernal Devices Ser.: Bks. 1-3). (ENG.). 1520p. (YA). (gr. 9). 74.99 *(978-1-4424-8372-9(5)*, McElderry, Margaret K. Bks.) McElderry, Margaret K. Bks.
Clarke, E. J. Oakwing: A Fairy's Tale. 2017. (Oakwing Ser.: 1). (ENG., Illus.). 192p. (J). (gr. 2-6). 16.99 ***(978-1-4814-8191-5(6)***, Aladdin) Simon & Schuster Children's Publishing.
—Oakwing: A Fairy's Tale. 2017. (J). pap. ***(978-1-4814-8190-8(8)***, Simon & Schuster/Paula Wiseman Bks.) Simon & Schuster/Paula Wiseman Bks.
Clary, Julian. The Bolds. Roberts, David, illus. (Bolds Ser.). (ENG.). 272p. (J). (gr. 3-6). 2017. pap. 7.99 ***(978-1-5124-8174-7(2))*** 2016. 16.99 *(978-1-5124-0440-1(3))* Lerner Publishing Group. (Carolrhoda Bks.).
Clary, Julian. The Bolds to the Rescue. Roberts, David, illus. 2017. (Bolds Ser.: 2). (ENG.). 288p. (J). (gr. 3-6). 16.99 *(978-1-5124-1022-8(5)*, Carolrhoda Bks.) Lerner Publishing Group.
Cockcroft, Jason. Counter Clockwise. 2009. 208p. (J). lib. bdg. 16.89 *(978-0-06-125555-7(6))*; (ENG., Illus.). (gr. 5-18). 15.99 *(978-0-06-125554-0(8))* HarperCollins Pubs. (Tegen, Katherine Bks).
The Complete Gideon Trilogy: The Time Travelers; the Time Thief; the Time Quake. 2014. (Gideon Trilogy Ser.). (ENG., Illus.). 1424p. (J). (gr. 5-9). pap. 26.99 *(978-1-4814-2613-8(3)*, Simon & Schuster Bks. For Young Readers) Simon & Schuster Bks. For Young Readers.
Cook, Jacqueline. The Little Bear Who Worried Too Much: Suzie Bear Goes to London. 2011. 34p. (gr. 1-4). pap. 13.50 *(978-1-60976-875-1(2)*, Eloquent Bks.) Strategic Book Publishing & Rights Agency (SBPRA).
Cooney, Caroline B. The Terrorist. 2012. (ENG.). 144p. (YA). pap. 6.99 *(978-1-4532-7467-5(7))* Open Road Integrated Media, Inc.
Coppel, Chris. Far from Burden Dell. 2005. 286p. (J). (gr. 6-16). per. 4.95 *(978-0-9746481-6-3(7))* Brown Barn Bks.
Cousins, Lucy. Maisy Goes to London. Cousins, Lucy, illus. 2016. (Maisy Ser.). (ENG., Illus.). 32p. (J). (-k). 15.99 *(978-0-7636-8399-3(X))* Candlewick Pr.
Craig, Joe. Jimmy Coates: Assassin? 2005. 224p. (J). (gr. 5-18). 15.99 *(978-0-06-077263-5(8))* HarperCollins Pubs.
—Jimmy Coates: Assassin? 2006. 218p. (J). (gr. 5-9). per. 5.99 *(978-0-06-077265-9(4)*, Harper Trophy) HarperCollins Pubs.
Cross, Gillian. Where I Belong. 2011. (ENG., Illus.). 256p. (J). (gr. 5-18). 17.95 *(978-0-8234-2332-3(8))* Holiday Hse., Inc.
Cuffaro, Anna. Gatwick Bear & the Secret Plans. Anguissola, Anna, illus. 2009. (ENG.). 189p. (J). 18.00 *(978-1-907230-02-8(5))* Sparkling Bks. GBR. Dist: Silvermine International Bks., LLC.
Dalmatian Press Staff, adapted by. Oliver Twist. Date not set. (C). pap. *(978-0-7593-9612-8(4)*, Cengage Learning) CENGAGE Learning.
Daneshvari, Gitty, ed. Get Smart-Ish. 2016. (League of Unexceptional Children Ser.: 2). (ENG., Illus.). 240p. (J). (gr. 3-7). 16.99 *(978-0-316-40574-4(1))* Little, Brown Bks. for Young Readers.
Daniels, Darla. The Magic Ring: Summer Vacation in London. 2012. 30p. 16.95 *(978-1-4626-6252-4(8))* America Star Bks.
Danziger, Paula. Thames Doesn't Rhyme with James. (Remember Me to Harold Square Ser.: No. 2). 153p. (J). pap. 3.99 *(978-0-8072-1473-2(6)*, Listening Library) Random Hse. Audio Publishing Group.
—You Can't Eat Your Chicken Pox, Amber Brown. Ross, Tony, illus. 2006. (Amber Brown Ser.: No. 2). 100p. (gr. 2-5). 15.00 *(978-0-7569-6756-7(2))* Perfection Learning Corp.
—You Can't Eat Your Chicken Pox, Amber Brown. (Amber Brown Ser.: No. 2). 101p. (J). (gr. 3-6). pap. 3.50 *(978-0-8072-1290-5(3)*, Listening Library) Random Hse. Audio Publishing Group.
—You Can't Eat Your Chicken Pox, Amber Brown. Ross, Tony, illus. 2006. (Amber Brown Ser.: 2). (ENG.). 128p. (J). (gr. 2-5). 5.99 *(978-0-14-240629-8(5)*, Puffin Books) Penguin Young Readers Group.
Davis, Penny. Annabel's Yearnings. 2012. 274p. pap. *(978-1-78003-309-9(5))* Pen Pr. Pubs., Ltd.
Dawnay, Gabby. London Calls. Barrow, Alex, illus. 2015. (ENG.). 32p. (gr. k-3). 13.95 *(978-1-84976-230-4(9))* Tate Publishing, Ltd. GBR. Dist: Abrams, Inc.
Deekster, Deek. Ozzie Rozzie. 2005. 41p. (YA). pap. 7.85 *(978-1-4116-6420-3(5))* Lulu Pr., Inc.
Dickens, Charles. Great Expectations: The Graphic Novel. 2010. (Classic Graphic Novel Collection). (ENG.). 160p. (YA). (gr. 7-12). 34.80 *(978-1-4205-0372-2(3))* Cengage Gale.
—Oliver Twist. Andreasen, Dan, illus. 2006. (Classic Starts(tm) Ser.). (ENG.). 160p. (J). (gr. 2-4). 6.95 *(978-1-4027-2665-1(1))* Sterling Publishing Co., Inc.
—Oliver Twist. abr. ed. Date not set. (Nelson Readers Ser.). (J). pap. *(978-0-17-557020-1(5))* Addison-Wesley Longman, Inc.
—Oliver Twist. Ablett, Barry, illus. 2007. (Young Reading Series 3 Gift Bks.). 63p. (J). (gr. 3). 8.99 *(978-0-7945-1459-4(6)*, Usborne) EDC Publishing.
—Oliver Twist. 2008. (Bring the Classics to Life Ser.). (ENG., Illus.). 72p. (gr. 3-12). pap., act. bk. ed. 10.95 *(978-1-55576-325-1(1)*, EDCTR-308B) EDCON Publishing Group.
—Oliver Twist. abr. ed. (J). 9.95 *(978-1-56156-372-2(2))* Kidsbooks, LLC.
—Oliver Twist. 2007. (Oxford Bookworms Ser.). (Illus.). 120p. pap. 10.00 *(978-0-19-423763-5(X))* Oxford Univ. Pr., Inc.
—Oliver Twist. 2nd ed. 2008. (ENG.). 136p. pap. 11.99 *(978-1-4058-6525-8(3))* Pearson Education.
—Oliver Twist. 2008. (Puffin Classics Ser.). (ENG.). 416p. (J). (gr. 5-7). 5.99 *(978-0-14-132243-8(8)*, Puffin Books) Penguin Young Readers Group.
—Oliver Twist. 2006. 516p. (gr. 3-3). per. *(978-1-4067-9405-2(8)*, Hesperides Pr.) Read Bks.
—Oliver Twist. Johnson, Cynthia Brantley, ed. annot. ed. 2007. (Enriched Classics Ser.). (ENG.). 672p. (gr. 3). mass mkt. 4.95 *(978-1-4165-3475-4(X))* Simon & Schuster.
—Oliver Twist. Morgan, Richard & Fennell, Tracy, illus. 2008. 48p. (J). (gr. 4-7). pap. 10.00 *(978-1-4190-5075-6(3))* Steck-Vaughn.
—Oliver Twist. McKowen, Scott, illus. 2008. (Sterling Unabridged Classics Ser.). (ENG.). 464p. (J). 14.95 *(978-1-4027-5425-8(6))* Sterling Publishing Co., Inc.
—Oliver Twist, 3 cass.; set. 2004. (Masterpiece Theatre Ser.). (gr. 7-18). tchr. ed. 59.95 incl. VHS *(978-1-57807-576-8(9)*, WG1062) WGBH Boston Video.
—Oliver Twist. 2009. (Real Reads Ser.). (Illus.). 64p. (YA). (gr. 4-8). pap. 13.55 *(978-1-60754-153-0(X))* Windmill Bks.
—Oliver Twist: With a Discussion of Honesty. 2003. (Values in Action Illustrated Classics Ser.). (J). *(978-1-59203-051-4(3))* Learning Challenge, Inc.
Disney Book Group Staff & Lewis, Kevin. Hide & Hug Olaf: A Fun Family Experience! Disney Storybook Art Team & Mosqueda, Olga, illus. 2014. (ENG.). 48p. (J). (gr. -1-k). 26.99 *(978-1-4847-2150-6(0))* Disney Pr.
Doan, Lisa. The Alarming Career of Sir Richard Blackstone. 2017. (ENG.). 192p. (J). (gr. 2-7). 15.99 *(978-1-5107-1122-8(8)*, Sky Pony Pr.) Skyhorse Publishing Co., Inc.
Dolenz, Ami. Harold & Agatha: The Mysterious Jewel. 2013. 176p. *(978-1-4602-0520-4(0))*; pap. *(978-1-4602-0420-7(4))* FriesenPress.
Dolsingh, Kanisha. Once upon a Time: In London Town with Minnie Drew. 2011. 28p. pap. 16.99 *(978-1-4567-5731-1(8))* AuthorHouse.
Dowd, Siobhan. The London Eye Mystery. 2009. (ENG.). 336p. (J). (gr. 3-7). 7.99 *(978-0-385-75184-1(2)*, Yearling) Random Hse. Children's Bks.
—The London Eye Mystery. 2009. lib. bdg. 18.40 *(978-0-606-14413-1(7)*, Turtleback) Turtleback Bks.
Downey, Glen. Rebel Prince. Okum, David, illus. 2007. 48p. (J). lib. bdg. 23.08 *(978-1-4242-1642-0(7))* Fitzgerald Bks.
Doyle, Arthur Conan. #09 Sherlock Holmes & the Adventure of the Six Napoleons. Rohrbach, Sophie & Morrow, Jt, illus. 2011. (On the Case with Holmes & Watson Set II Ser.). pap. 39.62 *(978-0-7613-7611-8(9)*, Graphic Universe™) Lerner Publishing Group.
Dunbar, Fiona. The Truth Cookie. 2009. (Jinx,the Lulu Baker Trilogy Ser.: Bk. 1). (ENG.). 208p. (J). (gr. 4-6). pap. 9.99 *(978-1-4083-0744-1(8))* Hodder & Stoughton GBR. Dist: Hachette Bk. Group.
Eade, Oliver. The Terminus. 2013. 264p. pap. *(978-1-909411-26-5(4))* Mauve Square Publishing.
Edge, Christopher. The Black Crow Conspiracy. 2015. (Penelope Tredwell Mysteries Ser.: 3). (ENG.). 272p. (J). (gr. 3-7). 16.99 *(978-0-8075-0780-3(6))* Whitman, Albert & Co.
—Twelve Minutes to Midnight. 2014. (Penelope Tredwell Mysteries Ser.: Book 1). (ENG.). 256p. (J). (gr. 3-7). 16.99 *(978-0-8075-8133-9(X))* Whitman, Albert & Co.
Edwards, Julie Andrews. Little Bo in London, No. 2. Cole, Henry, illus. 2012. (ENG.). 112p. (J). (gr. 1-4). 19.99 *(978-0-06-008911-5(3))* HarperCollins Pubs.
Egan, Tim. Dodsworth in London. Egan, Tim, illus. (Dodsworth Book Ser.). (ENG., Illus.). 48p. (J). 2010. (gr. 2-5). pap. 3.99 *(978-0-547-41440-9(4))* 11th ed. 2009. (gr. 1-4). 15.00 *(978-0-547-13816-9(4))* Houghton Mifflin Harcourt Publishing Co.
Eigert, C. J. The Elder Brothers & the Padstow Crystals. 2013. 208p. *(978-1-4602-1788-7(8))*; pap. *(978-1-4602-1789-4(6))* FriesenPress.
Emerson, Kevin. Finding Abbey Road. 2017. 256p. (J). pap. 9.99 ***(978-0-06-213402-8(7))*** 2016. (Exile Ser.: 3). 240p. (YA). (gr. 9). 17.99 *(978-0-06-213401-1(9))* HarperCollins Pubs. (Tegen, Katherine Bks).
Eschberger, Beverly. The Elephants Visit London: An Elephant Family Adventure. Gower, Jim, illus. l.t. ed. 2007. 96p. (J). per. 3.99 *(978-1-932926-30-9(5)*, Kinkajou Pr.) Artemesia Publishing, LLC.
Ewell, Katherine. Dear Killer. 2014. (ENG.). 368p. (YA). (gr. 8). 17.99 *(978-0-06-225780-2(3))* HarperCollins Pubs.
Farrant, Natasha. After Iris. 2013. (ENG.). 272p. (J). (gr. 5). 16.99 *(978-0-8037-3982-6(6)*, Dial Bks) Penguin Young Readers Group.
Farrow, G. & Farrow, George. The Mysterious Shin Shira. 2007. 116p. per. 10.95 *(978-1-60312-225-2(7))* Aegypan.
Farrow, G. e. & Farrow, G. E. The Wallypug in London. 2011. 106p. 23.95 *(978-1-4638-9696-6(4))*; pap. 9.95 *(978-1-60664-480-5(7))* Rodgers, Alan Bks.
Feinstein, John. Rush for the Gold: Mystery at the Olympics. 2013. (Sports Beat Ser.). (ENG.). 336p. (J). (gr. 5). pap. 7.99 *(978-0-375-87168-9(3)*, Yearling) Random Hse. Children's Bks.
Fenn, G. Manville. Brownsmith's Boy. 2008. 260p. 29.95 *(978-1-60664-780-6(6))* Aegypan.
Foster, Darlene. Amanda in England. 2012. (Amanda Travels Ser.: 3). (ENG.). 118p. (J). (gr. 3-8). pap. 9.95 *(978-1-926760-77-3(8))* Central Avenue Publishing CAN. Dist: Independent Pubs. Group.
Foster, Matthew. The Gateway. 2010. 172p. pap. 16.95 *(978-1-4461-5024-5(0))* Lulu Pr., Inc.
Fougasse, J. Smith. Fougasse, illus. 2015. (ENG., Illus.). 152p. (J). (gr. 5). 25.00 *(978-0-7636-7763-3(9))* Candlewick Pr.
Frank, Hannah. If I Had Three Wishes. 2008. 56p. pap. 23.99 *(978-1-4343-7529-2(3))* AuthorHouse.
—The Train to Baker Street. 2008. 44p. pap. 19.49 *(978-1-4389-1026-0(6))* AuthorHouse.
Freeman, Hilary. The Boy from France. 2012. (ENG.). 192p. (YA). (gr. 8). pap. 11.99 *(978-1-84812-301-4(9))* Bonnier Publishing GBR. Dist: Independent Pubs. Group.
Gallico, Paul. The Abandoned. 2013. (ENG.). 320p. (J). (gr. 4-7). 15.95 *(978-1-59017-626-9(X)*, NYR Children's Collection) New York Review of Bks., Inc., The.
Gardner, Sally. The Door That Led to Where. 2016. (ENG.). 288p. (YA). (gr. 7). 17.99 *(978-0-399-54997-7(8)*, Delacorte Pr.) Random Hse. Children's Bks.
—I, Coriander. 2007. (Illus.). 280p. (J). (gr. 5-9). 14.65 *(978-0-7569-8130-3(1))* Perfection Learning Corp.
Gavin, Rohan. K-9. 2016. (Knightley & Son Ser.: 2). (ENG.). 320p. (J). pap. 7.99 *(978-1-61963-687-3(5)*, 9781619636873, Bloomsbury USA Childrens) Bloomsbury Publishing USA.
—Knightley & Son - K-9. 2015. (Knightley & Son Ser.: 2). (ENG., Illus.). 304p. (YA). (gr. 4-6). 16.99 *(978-1-61963-494-7(5)*, 9781619634947, Bloomsbury USA Childrens) Bloomsbury Publishing USA.
Gibbons, Alan. Renegade. 2010. (ENG., Illus.). 336p. (YA). (gr. 7-17). 8.99 *(978-1-4440-0079-5(9)*, Orion Children's Bks.) Hachette Children's Group GBR. Dist: Hachette Bk. Group.
—Scared to Death. 2010. (ENG., Illus.). 352p. (J). (gr. 4-6). pap. 8.99 *(978-1-4440-0143-3(4)*, Orion Children's Bks.) Hachette Children's Group GBR. Dist: Hachette Bk. Group.
Gier, Kerstin. Emerald Green. Bell, Anthea, tr. 2013. (Ruby Red Trilogy Ser.: Vol. 3). (ENG.). 464p. (YA). (gr. 7). 17.99 *(978-0-8050-9267-7(6)*, 9780805092677, Holt, Henry & Co. Bks. For Young Readers) Holt, Henry & Co.
—Sapphire Blue. Bell, Anthea, tr. from GER. 2012. (Ruby Red Trilogy Ser.: 2). (ENG.). 368p. (YA). (gr. 7). 18.99 *(978-0-8050-9266-0(8)*, 9780805092660, Holt, Henry & Co. Bks. For Young Readers) Holt, Henry & Co.
—Sapphire Blue. Bell, Anthea, tr. 2013. (Ruby Red Trilogy Ser.: 2). (ENG.). 384p. (YA). (gr. 7). pap. 10.99 *(978-1-250-03416-8(7)*, 9781250034168) Square Fish.
Gillanders, Ann. Fairy Fleur & Doug the Dragonfly's Adventures in London: Ann Gillanders. 2012. (Illus.). 36p. pap. 22.88 *(978-1-4772-4358-9(5))* AuthorHouse.
Gillott, C. M. Nelson 'n' Deck & Friends: How the Adventures Began. 2010. (Illus.). 48p. pap. 17.49 *(978-1-4490-9593-2(3))* AuthorHouse.
Gleason, Colleen. The Chess Queen Enigma: A Stoker & Holmes Novel. 2015. (Stoker & Holmes Ser.: 3). (ENG.). 360p. (YA). (gr. 7-12). 17.99 *(978-1-4521-4317-0(X))* Chronicle Bks. LLC.
—The Clockwork Scarab. 2013. (Stoker & Holmes Ser.: 1). (ENG.). 356p. (YA). (gr. 7-12). 17.99 *(978-1-4521-1070-7(0))* Chronicle Bks. LLC.
—The Spiritglass Charade: A Stoker & Holmes Novel. 2015. (Stoker & Holmes Ser.: 2). (ENG., Illus.). 368p. (YA). (gr. 7-12). pap. 9.99 *(978-1-4521-2885-6(5))* Chronicle Bks. LLC.
Goldman, Stanley M. The Doorway to Forever: September 2nd, 1666, the First Day of Forever. 2008. (ENG.). 186p. (J). (gr. 7). pap. 9.95 *(978-1-933255-46-0(3))* DNA Pr.
Gordon, Roderick. Closer. (Tunnels Ser.: 4). (J). 1.25 *(978-1-4498-2165-4(0))*; 121.75 *(978-1-4498-2159-3(6))*; 296.75 *(978-1-4498-2158-6(8))*; 2011. 132.75 *(978-1-4498-2163-0(4))*; 2011. 134.75 *(978-1-4498-2161-6(8))* Recorded Bks., Inc.
—Deeper, 15 vols. 2009. (J). 128.75 *(978-1-4361-3717-1(9))*; 134.75 *(978-1-4361-3721-8(7))*; 1.25 *(978-1-4361-3714-0(4))*; 126.75 *(978-1-4361-3719-5(5))*; 132.75 *(978-1-4361-3723-2(3))*; 301.75 *(978-1-4361-3718-8(7))* Recorded Bks., Inc.
Gordon, Roderick & Williams, Brian. The Tunnels. 2009. (Tunnels Ser.: 1). (ENG.). 496p. (J). (gr. 3-7). pap. 8.99 *(978-0-545-07881-8(4)*, Scholastic Paperbacks) Scholastic, Inc.
Gordon, Roderick & Williams, Brian James. Terminal. 2013. (J). *(978-0-545-47963-9(0))* Scholastic, Inc.
Gourlay, Candy. Tall Story. 2012. (ENG.). 304p. (J). (gr. 5). 6.99 *(978-0-385-75233-6(4)*, Yearling) Random Hse. Children's Bks.
Graudin, Ryan. All That Burns. 2015. (ENG.). 464p. (YA). (gr. 8). pap. 9.99 *(978-0-06-218743-7(0)*, HarperTeen) HarperCollins Pubs.
—All That Glows. 2014. (ENG.). 480p. (YA). (gr. 8). pap. 9.99 *(978-0-06-218741-3(4)*, HarperTeen) HarperCollins Pubs.
Greenhill, Ms Jane. Jolly Olde Teenage Alien. 2013. 258p. pap. *(978-0-9918766-2-4(8))* Greenhill, Jane.
Griffiths, Robert. Adventures of Clive. 2005. 45p. (J). pap. 10.01 *(978-1-4116-5332-0(7))*; 89p. pap. 8.81 *(978-1-4116-5191-3(X))* Lulu Pr., Inc.
Guillain, Adam. Bella Balistica & the Izta Warriors. 2012. (Bella Balistica Ser.). (ENG., Illus.). 170p. (J). (gr. 4-7). pap. 9.95 *(978-1-84059-771-4(2))* Milet Publishing.
Halsey, Jacqueline. Peggy's Letters, 1 vol. 2005. (Orca Young Readers Ser.). (ENG., Illus.). 132p. (J). (gr. 3-6). per. 5.95 *(978-1-55143-363-9(X))* Orca Bk. Pubs. USA.
Hampton, Sue. Pomp & Circumstances. 2012. (ENG.). 100p. (YA). pap. *(978-1-78228-181-8(9))* Pneuma Springs Publishing.
Hannibal, James R. The Lost Property Office. 2016. (Section 13 Ser.: 1). (ENG., Illus.). 400p. (J). (gr. 3-7). 16.99 *(978-1-4814-6709-4(3)*, Simon & Schuster Bks. For Young Readers) Simon & Schuster Bks. For Young Readers.
HarperCollins Publishers Ltd. Staff, et al. Paddington: Paddington in London. 2014. (Paddington Ser.). (ENG., Illus.). 24p. (J). (gr. -1-3). pap. 3.99 *(978-0-06-234995-8(3))* HarperCollins Pubs.
—Paddington: Paddington's World. 2014. (Paddington Ser.). (ENG., Illus.). 24p. (J). (gr. -1-3). pap. 3.99 *(978-0-06-234997-2(X))* HarperCollins Pubs.
Harris, Brooke. London Bridge. Boyer, Lyn, illus. 2010. (Rising Readers Ser.). (J). 3.49 *(978-1-60719-702-7(2))* Newmark Learning LLC.
Haslett, Katherine A. The Day Amy Met the Prime Minister & Mrs. Blair. 2007. (Illus.). 32p. (J). pap. 8.00 *(978-0-8059-7353-2(2))* Dorrance Publishing Co., Inc.
Hatton, Jenny. Finding Aunt Joan. Rankin, Joan, illus. 2012. (Lucy Bks.). (ENG.). 32p. (J). (gr. k-2). pap. 6.95 *(978-1-77009-803-9(8))* Jacana Media ZAF. Dist: Independent Pubs. Group.
Hayes, Rosemary. Payback. 2009. (ENG.). 208p. (J). (gr. 7-10). pap. 8.95 *(978-1-84507-935-2(3)*, Frances Lincoln)

Quarto Publishing Group UK GBR. Dist: Hachette Bk. Group.
Hendry, Frances. Quest for a Queen: The Jackdaw. 2006. pap. *(978-1-905665-05-1(9))* Pollinger In Print.
Henty, George Alfred. A March on London: Being a Story of Wat Tyler's Insurrection. l.t. ed. 2007. 316p. pap. 24.99 *(978-1-4264-3096-1(5))* Creative Media Partners, LLC.
—When London Burned: A Story of Restoration Times & the Great Fire. l.t. ed. 2005. 724p. pap. *(978-1-84637-212-4(7))* Echo Library.
Higgins, Jim. The Enchanted Nursery: Heather & Hamish, Fun in Florida, Reggie Rabbit at the Seaside, Percy Penguin's Friends. 2009. (Illus.). 36p. pap. 15.49 *(978-1-4389-9904-3(6))* AuthorHouse.
Higson, Charlie. The Dead (new Cover) (an Enemy Novel) 2014. (Enemy Novel Ser.). (ENG.). 512p. (YA). (gr. 9-17). pap. 9.99 *(978-1-4847-2145-2(4))* Hyperion Bks. for Children.
—The End (an Enemy Novel) (Enemy Novel Ser.). (ENG.). 512p. (YA). (gr. 9-17). 2017. pap. 9.99 **(978-1-4847-3291-5(X))** 2016. 17.99 *(978-1-4847-1695-3(7))* Hyperion Bks. for Children.
—The Enemy (new Cover) (an Enemy Novel) 2014. (Enemy Novel Ser.). (ENG.). 448p. (YA). (gr. 9-17). pap. 9.99 *(978-1-4847-2146-9(2))* Hyperion Bks. for Children.
—The Fallen (an Enemy Novel) 2014. (Enemy Novel Ser.). (ENG.). 544p. (YA). (gr. 9-17). 17.99 *(978-1-4231-6566-8(7))* Disney Pr.
—The Fallen (an Enemy Novel) 2015. (Enemy Novel Ser.). (ENG.). 560p. (YA). (gr. 9-17). pap. 9.99 *(978-1-4231-6636-8(1))* Hyperion Bks. for Children.
—The Fear (new Cover) (an Enemy Novel) 2014. (Enemy Novel Ser.). (ENG.). 496p. (YA). (gr. 9-17). pap. 9.99 *(978-1-4847-2144-5(6))* Hyperion Bks. for Children.
—The Hunted (an Enemy Novel) (Enemy Novel Ser.). (ENG.). (YA). (gr. 9-17). 2016. 480p. pap. 9.99 *(978-1-4231-6637-5(X))* 2015. 464p. 17.99 *(978-1-4231-6567-5(5))* Hyperion Bks. for Children.
—The Sacrifice. 2013. (Enemy Novel Ser.). (ENG.). 496p. (YA). (gr. 9-17). 17.99 *(978-1-4231-6565-1(9))* Hyperion Pr.
—The Sacrifice (an Enemy Novel) 2014. (Enemy Novel Ser.). (ENG.). 512p. (YA). (gr. 9-17). pap. 9.99 *(978-1-4231-6635-1(3))* Hyperion Bks. for Children.
Hildebrand, Jens. Team 002: The Abduction of the Queen. Garcia, Juan F., illus. 2013. 224p. pap. *(978-3-929892-46-8(4))* Hildebrand, Jutta Warped Tomato Publishing.
Hillan, Pamela & Dyan, Penelope. The Jewels of the Crown. Weigand, John, photos by. 2013. (Illus.). 128p. pap. 8.95 *(978-1-61477-111-1(1))* Bellissima Publishing, LLC.
Hobbs, Leigh. Mr Badger & the Big Surprise. l.t. ed. 2012. 120p. (J). pap. *(978-1-4596-3343-8(1))* ReadHowYouWant.com, Ltd.
—Mr Badger & the Missing Ape. l.t. ed. 2012. 120p. (J). pap. *(978-1-4596-3344-5(X))* ReadHowYouWant.com, Ltd.
Hood, Ann. Alexander Graham Bell: Master of Sound. Zilber, Denis, illus. 2013. (Treasure Chest Ser.: 7). (ENG.). 192p. (J). (gr. 3-7). 6.99 *(978-0-448-45730-7(X),* Grosset & Dunlap) Penguin Young Readers Group.
Horowitz, Anthony. The Devil & His Boy. 2007. (ENG.). 192p. (J). (gr. 3-7). 6.99 *(978-0-14-240797-4(6),* Puffin Books) Penguin Young Readers Group.
—Public Enemy Number Two. 2004. (Diamond Brothers Ser.). (ENG.). 208p. (J). (gr. 3-7). 16.99 *(978-0-399-24154-3(X),* Philomel Bks.); pap. 6.99 *(978-0-14-240218-4(4),* Puffin Books) Penguin Young Readers Group.
—Scorpia. (Alex Rider Ser.). (ENG.). (J). (gr. 5-18). 2006. 416p. pap. 8.99 *(978-0-14-240578-9(7),* Puffin Books) 2005. 336p. 17.99 *(978-0-399-24151-2(5),* Philomel Bks.) Penguin Young Readers Group.
—Scorpia Rising. (Alex Rider Ser.). (ENG.). (J). (gr. 5-18). 2012. 432p. 8.99 *(978-0-14-241985-4(0),* Puffin Books) 2011. 416p. 17.99 *(978-0-399-25057-6(3),* Philomel Bks.) Penguin Young Readers Group.
—Scorpia Rising, 9 vols. (J). 2012. 90.75 *(978-1-4561-3363-4(2))* 2012. 1.25 *(978-1-4640-0577-0(X))* 2012. 256.75 *(978-1-4561-3362-7(4))* 2011. 122.75 *(978-1-4561-3365-8(9))* 2011. 120.75 *(978-1-4561-3367-2(5))* Recorded Bks., Inc.
—Scorpia Rising. 2012. (Alex Rider Ser.: 9). lib. bdg. 19.65 *(978-0-606-23638-6(4),* Turtleback) Turtleback Bks.
—Three of Diamonds. 2005. (Diamond Brothers Ser.). (ENG.). 240p. (J). (gr. 3-7). 6.99 *(978-0-14-240298-6(2),* Puffin Books) Penguin Young Readers Group.
Hoyle, Tom. Thirteen. 2015. (ENG.). 224p. (J). (gr. 7-12). 16.95 *(978-0-8234-3294-3(7))* Holiday Hse., Inc.
Hunt, Elizabeth Singer. The Caper of the Crown Jewels, Bk. 4. 2008. (Secret Agent Jack Stalwart Ser.: 4). (ENG., Illus.). 144p. (J). (gr. 1-4). per. 5.99 *(978-1-60286-013-1(0),* Weinstein Bks.) Perseus Bks. Group.
Hutton, Sam. Countdown. 2011. (Special Agents Ser.: 3). (ENG.). 224p. (J). pap. 9.99 *(978-0-00-714843-1(7),* HarperCollins Children's Bks.) HarperCollins Pubs. Ltd. GBR. Dist: HarperCollins Pubs.
—Deep End. 2010. (Special Agents Ser.). (ENG.). 240p. (J). (gr. 5-7). pap. 9.99 *(978-0-00-714842-4(9))* HarperCollins Pubs. Ltd. GBR. Dist: HarperCollins Pubs.
—Meltdown. 2005. (Special Agents Ser.: 6). (ENG., Illus.). 224p. (J). pap. 9.99 *(978-0-00-714847-9(X),* HarperCollins Children's Bks.) HarperCollins Pubs. Ltd. GBR. Dist: HarperCollins Pubs.
Ibbotson, Eva. One Dog & His Boy. 2012. (ENG.). 288p. (J). (gr. 3-7). 16.99 *(978-0-545-35196-6(0),* Scholastic Pr.) Scholastic, Inc.
Imbernón, Maite & Dickens, Charles. Oliver Twist. 2003. (Timeless Classics Ser.). (SPA., Illus.). 92p. (J). pap. 10.95 *(978-84-204-5750-5(7))* Santillana USA Publishing Co., Inc.
Inglis, Lucy. City of Halves. 2015. (ENG.). 368p. (J). (gr. 7). 17.99 *(978-0-545-82958-8(5),* Chicken Hse., The) Scholastic, Inc.
Jarman, Julia. Time-Travelling Cat & the Great Victorian Stink. 2011. (Time-Travelling Cat Ser.: 6). (ENG.). 160p. (J). (gr. 4-7). pap. 12.99 *(978-1-84939-019-4(3))* Andersen Pr. GBR. Dist: Independent Pubs. Group.
Jinks, Catherine. The Last Bogler. 2017. (How to Catch a Bogle Ser.: 3). (ENG.). 336p. (J). (gr. 5-7). pap. 7.99 *(978-0-544-81309-0(X),* HMH Books For Young Readers) Houghton Mifflin Harcourt Publishing Co.
Johnson, Gillian. Thora & the Green Sea-Unicorn. Johnson, Gillian, illus. 2005. (Illus.). 272p. *(978-0-207-20016-8(5))* HarperCollins Pubs. Australia.
Johnson, Maureen. The Madness Underneath. 2013. (Shades of London Ser.: 2). (ENG.). 304p. (YA). (gr. 7). pap. 9.99 *(978-0-14-242754-5(3),* Speak) Penguin Young Readers Group.
—The Name of the Star. (Shades of London Ser.: 1). (ENG.). (YA). (gr. 7). 2012. 400p. pap. 10.99 *(978-0-14-242205-2(3),* Speak) 2011. 368p. 16.99 *(978-0-399-25660-8(1),* G.P. Putnam's Sons Books for Young Readers) Penguin Young Readers Group.
Kassel, Roger de. Mr P & the Silver Red Bag. 2013. (Illus.). 12p. pap. 7.00 *(978-1-78035-536-8(X),* Fastprint Publishing) Upfront Publishing Ltd. GBR. Dist: Printondemand-worldwide.com.
—Mr P & the Sticky Gum. 2013. (Illus.). 12p. pap. 7.00 *(978-1-78035-537-5(8),* Fastprint Publishing) Upfront Publishing Ltd. GBR. Dist: Printondemand-worldwide.com.
Kearns, Zannah & Quarto Generic Staff. No Use Crying. 2012. (ENG.). 320p. (J). (gr. 7-9). pap. 8.99 *(978-1-84780-214-9(1),* Frances Lincoln) Quarto Publishing Group UK GBR. Dist: Hachette Bk. Group.
Kelley, Ann. Inchworm. 2009. (Gussie Ser.). (ENG.). 224p. (YA). (gr. 7-12). pap. 12.95 *(978-1-906307-62-2(8))* Luath Pr. Ltd. GBR. Dist: Ingram Publisher Services.
Kingsley, Kate. Everything but the Truth. 2010. (Young, Loaded, & Fabulous Ser.: 2). (ENG.). 304p. (YA). (gr. 9-18). pap. 9.99 *(978-1-4169-9400-8(9),* Simon Pulse) Simon Pulse.
—Pretty on the Outside. 2010. (Young, Loaded, & Fabulous Ser.: 1). (ENG.). 320p. (YA). (gr. 9-18). pap. 9.99 *(978-1-4169-9399-5(1),* Simon Pulse) Simon Pulse.
Kirby, Matthew J. A Taste for Monsters. 2016. (ENG.). 352p. (YA). (gr. 7). 18.99 *(978-0-545-81784-4(6),* Scholastic Pr.) Scholastic, Inc.
Klein, Lisa. Love Disguised. 2013. (ENG., Illus.). 320p. (YA). (gr. 7). 17.99 *(978-1-59990-968-4(5),* 9781599909684, Bloomsbury USA Childrens) Bloomsbury Publishing USA.
Knight, Chris. Karen Bighead: The Story of a Little Girl with a Big Head. 2011. (Illus.). 24p. 12.12 *(978-1-4520-7730-7(4))* AuthorHouse.
Krulik, Nancy. Be Careful What You Sniff For, No. 1. Braun, Sebastien, illus. 2013. (Magic Bone Ser.: 1). (ENG.). 128p. (J). (gr. 1-3). pap. 5.99 *(978-0-448-46399-5(7),* Grosset & Dunlap) Penguin Young Readers Group.
—Be Careful What You Sniff For. 2013. (Magic Bone Ser.: 1). lib. bdg. 16.00 *(978-0-606-31680-4(9),* Turtleback) Turtleback Bks.
Lasky, Kathryn. Double Trouble Squared. 2008. (ENG., Illus.). 240p. (J). (gr. 2-5). pap. 14.99 *(978-0-15-205878-4(8))* Houghton Mifflin Harcourt Publishing Co.
Lebbon, Tim. Contagion. 2013. (Toxic City Ser.). (ENG.). 219p. (J). (gr. 7). 17.99 *(978-1-61614-821-8(7))* Prometheus Bks., Pubs.
Lee, Y. S. The Agency: the Traitor in the Tunnel. 2016. (Agency Ser.). (ENG.). 384p. (YA). (gr. 7). pap. 7.99 *(978-0-7636-8751-9(0))* Candlewick Pr.
Leonard, Niall. Crusher. 2013. (ENG.). 368p. (YA). (gr. 9). pap. 9.99 *(978-0-385-74362-4(9),* Ember) Random Hse. Children's Bks.
—Shredder. 2015. (ENG.). 384p. (YA). (gr. 9). 17.99 *(978-0-385-74365-5(3),* Delacorte Pr.) Random Hse. Children's Bks.
Levine, Phyllis. At the Skylight with Matilda. 2007. (ENG.). 160p. per. 12.95 *(978-1-60047-089-9(0))* Wasteland Pr.
—Matilda. 2007. (ENG.). 108p. per. 12.95 *(978-1-60047-079-0(3))* Wasteland Pr.
Lloyd, Saci. The Carbon Diaries 2017. (ENG.). (YA). (gr. 6). 2011. 384p. pap. 8.95 *(978-0-8234-2390-3(5))* 2010. 352p. 17.95 *(978-0-8234-2260-9(7))* Holiday Hse., Inc.
Lockwood, Vicki. The Magnificent Lizzie Brown & the Devil's Hound, 1 vol. 2014. (Magnificent Lizzie Brown Ser.). (ENG., Illus.). 200p. (gr. 5-9). lib. bdg. 26.65 *(978-1-4342-7941-5(3))* Stone Arch Bks.
—The Magnificent Lizzie Brown & the Mysterious Phantom, 1 vol. 2014. (Magnificent Lizzie Brown Ser.). (ENG., Illus.). 200p. (gr. 5-9). 10.95 *(978-1-62370-069-0(8));* lib. bdg. 26.65 *(978-1-4342-7940-8(5))* Stone Arch Bks.
—The Magnificent Lizzie Brown & the Mysterious Phantom, 1 vol. Hans, Stephanie, illus. 2014. (ENG.). 200p. (J). pap. *(978-1-4342-7942-2(1))* Stone Arch Bks.
London, Jack. Faith of Men. 2006. 116p. per. 9.95 *(978-1-59818-074-9(6))* Aegypan.
Macauley, Jo. Treason, 1 vol. 2014. (Secrets & Spies Ser.). (ENG., Illus.). 224p. (gr. 4-7). pap. 8.95 *(978-1-62370-052-2(3))* Capstone Young Readers of Coughlan Cos.
—Treason. 2014. (J). pap. *(978-1-4342-7944-6(8))* Stone Arch Bks.
MacDonald, George. The Elect Lady. 2008. 148p. 24.95 *(978-1-60664-792-9(X))* Aegypan.
Madonna, pseud. Friends for Life! Fulvimari, Jeffrey, illus. 2007. (English Roses Ser.: 1). (ENG.). 96p. (J). (gr. 3-7). 10.99 *(978-0-14-241114-8(0),* Puffin Books) Penguin Young Readers Group.
—Good-Bye, Grace?, No. 2. Fulvimari, Jeffrey, illus. 2007. (English Roses Ser.: 2). (ENG.). 144p. (J). (gr. 3-7). 10.99 *(978-0-14-240883-4(2),* Puffin Books) Penguin Young Readers Group.
—The New Girl, Vol. 3. Fulvimari, Jeffrey, illus. 2007. (English Roses Ser.: 3). (ENG.). 144p. (J). (gr. 3-7). 9.99 *(978-0-14-240884-1(0),* Puffin Books) Penguin Young Readers Group.
Malam, John, retold by. Oliver Twist. 2014. (Graphic Classics Ser.). 48p. (gr. 3-6). 37.10 *(978-1-908973-89-4(7))* Book Hse. GBR. Dist: Black Rabbit Bks.
Malloy, Chris. Wizard Academies - A Special Kind of Talent. 2008. 142p. pap. 19.95 *(978-0-615-18505-7(3))* Wizard Academies, LLC.
Mansfield, Keith. Battle for Earth. 2011. (Johnny Mackintosh Ser.). (ENG.). 336p. (J). (gr. 4-6). 8.99 *(978-1-84916-329-3(4))* Quercus GBR. Dist: Hachette Bk. Group.
Manzione, Lisa. Let's Visit London! Adventures of Bella & Harry. Lucco, Kristine, illus. 2011. (Adventures of Bella & Harry Ser.: 3). (ENG.). 35p. (J). (gr. k-3). 16.95 *(978-1-937616-03-8(7))* Bella & Harry, LLC.
Mark, Jan. Eyes Wide Open. 2003. (ENG., Illus.). 105p. *(978-0-7136-7648-8(5),* A&C Black) Bloomsbury Publishing Plc.
Marks, Alan, illus. A Christmas Carol. 2013. (ENG.). 24p. (J). 18.99 *(978-0-7945-2910-9(0),* Usborne) EDC Publishing.
Marsh, Carole. The Mystery at Big Ben. 2005. (Carole Marsh Mysteries Ser.). (Illus.). 129p. (J). (gr. 4-7). per. 7.99 *(978-0-635-03469-4(7))* Gallopade International.
Mayhew, James. Katie's London Christmas. 2016. (Katie Ser.). (ENG., Illus.). 32p. (J). (gr. -1-k). pap. 10.99 *(978-1-4083-2642-8(6),* Orchard Bks.) Hachette Children's Group GBR. Dist: Hachette Bk. Group.
Mayhew, James & MAYHEW, JAMES. Carlota Visita Londres. 2004. (SPA., Illus.). 36p. 16.99 *(978-84-8488-089-9(3))* Serres, Ediciones, S. L. ESP. Dist: Lectorum Pubns., Inc.
McDonald, Abby. Sophomore Switch. 2010. (ENG., Illus.). 304p. (YA). (gr. 9). pap. 8.99 *(978-0-7636-4774-2(8))* Candlewick Pr.
McKenzie, Sophie. Every Second Counts. 2016. 405p. (YA). pap. *(978-1-4814-3927-5(8))* Simon & Schuster Children's Publishing.
—In a Split Second. 2015. (ENG., Illus.). 368p. (YA). (gr. 7). 17.99 *(978-1-4814-1394-7(5))* Simon & Schuster Children's Publishing.
McKnight, Gillian. To Catch a Prince. 2010. (ENG.). 240p. (YA). (gr. 7). pap. 11.99 *(978-1-4424-2718-1(3),* Simon Pulse) Simon Pulse.
—To Catch a Prince: To Catch a Prince; the Frog Prince. 2011. (ENG., Illus.). 432p. (YA). (gr. 7). pap. 9.99 *(978-1-4424-3139-3(3),* Simon & Schuster Bks. For Young Readers) Simon & Schuster Bks. For Young Readers.
Meade, L. T. Sue A Little Heroine. 2007. (ENG.). 222p. pap. 20.99 *(978-1-4346-3546-4(5));* 244p. pap. 22.99 *(978-1-4346-3547-1(3))* Creative Media Partners, LLC.
Mechling, Lauren & Moser, Laura. Foreign Exposure: The Social Climber Abroad. 2007. (ENG.). 320p. (YA). (gr. 7-18). pap. 18.95 *(978-0-618-66379-8(7))* Houghton Mifflin Harcourt Publishing Co.
Meloy, Maile. The Apothecary. 2013. (Apothecary Ser.: 1). (ENG.). 368p. (J). (gr. 5). pap. 8.99 *(978-0-14-242206-9(1),* Puffin Books) Penguin Young Readers Group.
—The Apothecary. l.t. ed. 2012. (ENG.). 435p. (J). (gr. 4-7). 23.99 *(978-1-4104-4504-9(6))* Thorndike Pr.
Millar, Martin. Lonely Werewolf Girl. 2008. (ENG.). 560p. per. *(978-0-9796636-6-6(0))* CSA Telltapes, Ltd.
Montana, Hannah. Live from London. 2010. (Hannah Montana on Tour Ser.: No. 4). 80p. (gr. 2-5). pap. 3.99 *(978-1-4231-1815-2(4))* Disney Pr.
Morgan, Gloria. The Ducking Stool. 2013. (Illus.). 298p. pap. 24.99 *(978-1-78035-684-6(6),* Fastprint Publishing) Upfront Publishing Ltd. GBR. Dist: Printondemand-worldwide.com.
Morrill, Lauren. Meant to Be. (ENG.). 304p. (YA). (gr. 7). 2014. pap. 9.99 *(978-0-385-74178-1(2),* Ember) 2012. 17.99 *(978-0-385-74177-4(4),* Delacorte Pr.) 2012. E-Book *(978-0-375-98711-3(8),* Delacorte Pr.) Random Hse. Children's Bks.
Mudaly, Jessica. Cats Can Be So Cattish! 2013. 116p. pap. 10.95 *(978-1-62212-084-0(1),* Strategic Bk. Publishing) Strategic Book Publishing & Rights Agency (SBPRA).
Mullarkey, Lisa & Mullarkey, John. Shakespeare Saves the Globe, 1 vol. Bernard, Courtney, illus. 2015. (ENG.). 128p. (J). *(978-1-62402-090-2(9))* Magic Wagon.
Mumford, Martha. The Royal Baby's Big Red Bus Tour of London. Grey, Ada, illus. 2017. (ENG.). 32p. (J). 12.99 *(978-1-4088-6896-6(2),* 9781408886966, Bloomsbury USA Childrens) Bloomsbury Publishing USA.
Nadin, Joanna. Paradise. 2012. (ENG., Illus.). 272p. (YA). (gr. 9). 16.99 *(978-0-7636-5713-0(1))* Candlewick Pr.
Naidoo, Beverley. The Other Side of Truth. 2008. 252p. (gr. 5-9). 17.00 *(978-0-7569-8941-5(8))* Perfection Learning Corp.
Nesbit, E. Harding's Luck. 2006. 164p. (gr. 4-7). per. 13.95 *(978-1-59818-878-3(X))* Aegypan.
Newsome, Richard. The Billionaire's Curse. Duddle, Jonny, illus. 2011. (Archer Legacy Ser.). 384p. (J). (gr. 3-7). pap. 7.99 *(978-0-06-194491-8(2),* Waldon Pond Pr.) HarperCollins Pubs.
O'Connell, Tyne. A Royal Mess. 2011. (Calypso Chronicles Ser.). (ENG.). 512p. (YA). pap. 9.99 *(978-1-59990-888-5(3),* 9781599908885, Bloomsbury USA Childrens) Bloomsbury Publishing USA.
Odom, Mel. His Legacy Avenged. 2013. (Hunter's League Ser.: 4). (ENG.). 256p. (YA). (gr. 7). pap. 16.99 *(978-1-4814-0157-9(2),* Simon Pulse) Simon Pulse.
—The Secret Explodes. 2013. (Hunter's League Ser.: 3). (ENG.). 240p. (J). (gr. 7). pap. 15.99 *(978-1-4814-0156-2(4),* Simon Pulse) Simon Pulse.
Oliver & Company. (Read-Along Ser.). (J). 7.99 incl. audio *(978-1-55723-024-9(2))* Walt Disney Records.
Oliver, Helen. Ellen's First Swim. 2009. 32p. pap. 16.49 *(978-1-4389-9828-2(7))* AuthorHouse.
Osborne, Mary Pope. A Ghost Tale for Christmas Time. 2012. (Magic Tree House Merlin Missions Ser.: 16). lib. bdg. 16.00 *(978-0-606-26808-0(1),* Turtleback) Turtleback Bks.
Paling, Chris. The Adventures of Rumble, Tumble, & Titch: Uncertain Times. 2010. 62p. pap. 9.99 *(978-1-60911-263-9(6),* Eloquent Bks.) Strategic Book Publishing & Rights Agency (SBPRA).
Patterson, José. No Buts, Becky! 2013. (ENG., Illus.). 160p. pap. *(978-1-78088-438-7(9))* Troubador Publishing Ltd.
Peacock, Shane. Eye of the Crow: The Boy Sherlock Holmes, His 1st Case. 2007. (Boy Sherlock Holmes Ser.). (ENG.). 264p. (YA). (gr. 5-9). 19.95 *(978-0-88776-850-7(4),* Tundra Bks.) Tundra Bks. CAN. Dist: Penguin Random Hse. LLC.
—Vanishing Girl: The Boy Sherlock Holmes, His 3rd Case. 2010. (Boy Sherlock Holmes Ser.). (ENG., Illus.). 326p. (YA). (gr. 5-9). pap. 11.99 *(978-1-77049-234-9(8),* Tundra Bks.) Tundra Bks. CAN. Dist: Penguin Random Hse. LLC.
Penn, Audrey & Miller, Joshua. Blackbeard & the Gift of Silence. 2009. (ENG.). 350p. (J). (gr. 2-7). pap. 8.95 *(978-1-933718-32-3(3))* Tanglewood Pr.
Petty, Heather. Final Fall. 2017. (YA). pap. **(978-1-4814-2310-6(X),** Simon & Schuster Bks. For Young Readers) Simon & Schuster Bks. For Young Readers.
Petty, Heather. Lock & Mori. 2016. (Lock & Mori Ser.). (ENG.). 272p. (YA). (gr. 9). pap. 10.99 *(978-1-4814-2304-5(5))* Simon & Schuster, Inc.
Phillips, Dee. Terror in the Underground Tunnel. 2016. (Cold Whispers II Ser.). (ENG.). 32p. (J). (gr. 2-6). 19.95 *(978-1-944102-37-1(X))* Bearport Publishing Co., Inc.
Pitt, Darrell. The Monster Within. 2015. (Jack Mason Adventure Ser.). (ENG., Illus.). 264p. (J). (gr. 2-7). 7.99 *(978-1-922182-87-6(7))* Text Publishing Co. AUS. Dist: Consortium Bk. Sales & Distribution.
Plenge, Pete. Elephants Can't Hide Forever. 2012. 238p. pap. *(978-1-909039-88-9(8))* Legend Pr.
Podwitch. 2014. (ENG.). 304p. pap. *(978-1-78306-380-2(7))* Troubador Publishing Ltd.
Pollock, Tom. Our Lady of the Streets. 2017. (Skyscraper Throne Ser.: 3). (ENG.). 464p. (YA). (gr. 7-9). pap. 14.99 *(978-1-68144-381-2(3),* Jo Fletcher Books) Quercus NA.
Poulsen, David A. The Book of Vampire. 4th rev. ed. 2007. (Salt & Pepper Chronicles). (ENG., Illus.). 160p. (J). (gr. 4-7). 6.95 *(978-1-55263-805-7(7))* Leaf Storm Pr.
Powell, Laura. Burn Mark. (ENG.). (YA). (gr. 9). 2013. 432p. pap. 9.99 *(978-1-61963-119-9(9),* 9781619631199) 2012. 416p. 17.99 *(978-1-59990-843-4(3),* 9781599908434) Bloomsbury Publishing USA. (Bloomsbury USA Childrens).
—Witch Fire. 2013. (ENG.). 336p. (YA). (gr. 7). 17.99 *(978-1-61963-006-2(0),* 9781619630062, Bloomsbury USA Childrens) Bloomsbury Publishing USA.
Power, Barry. The First Ice Pigeon of London. 2009. 80p. pap. 10.49 *(978-1-4490-3070-4(X))* AuthorHouse.
Price, Robin. Threadneedle 01. McGrory, Paul, illus. 2016. (ENG.). 32p. (J). pap. *(978-1-906132-86-6(0))* Mogzilla.
Priestley, Chris. Death & the Arrow: A Gripping Tale of Murder & Revenge. 2007. (Tom Marlowe Ser.). (ENG., Illus.). 240p. (YA). (gr. 7). per. 12.95 *(978-0-552-55475-6(8))* Transworld Publishers Ltd. GBR. Dist: Independent Pubs. Group.
Prince, Maggie. The House on Hound Hill. 2003. (ENG.). 256p. (J). (gr. 5-7). pap. 15.95 *(978-0-618-33124-6(7))* Houghton Mifflin Harcourt Publishing Co.
Protobunker Studio Staff & Wells, H. G. La Guerra de los Mundos. Ruiz, Alfonso, illus. 2010. (Classic Fiction Ser.). (SPA.). 72p. (gr. 2-3). 27.99 *(978-1-4342-2322-7(1),* Graphic Revolve en Español) Stone Arch Bks.
Pullman, Philip. The Shadow in the North. 2008. (Sally Lockhart Ser.: Bk. 2). (ENG.). 384p. (J). (gr. 7). pap. 10.99 *(978-0-375-84515-4(1),* Ember) Random Hse. Children's Bks.
—The Shadow in the North. 2006. (Sally Lockhart Ser.: Bk. 2). 23.75 *(978-0-8446-7289-2(0))* Smith, Peter Pub., Inc.
—Spring-Heeled Jack. Mostyn, David, illus. 2004. (ENG.). 112p. (J). (gr. 3-7). per. 5.99 *(978-0-440-41881-6(X),* Yearling) Random Hse. Children's Bks.
—The Tiger in the Well. 2008. (Sally Lockhart Ser.: Bk. 3). (ENG.). 432p. (YA). (gr. 7). pap. 9.99 *(978-0-375-84517-8(8),* Ember) Random Hse. Children's Bks.
Raye, Marianna & Raye, Daniel. Olis & the Big Outside. 2011. (Illus.). 32p. pap. 14.09 *(978-1-4567-7157-7(4))* AuthorHouse.
Reeve, Philip. Fever Crumb. 2011. (Fever Crumb Ser.). (ENG.). 336p. (J). (gr. 7-7). pap. 9.99 *(978-0-545-22215-0(X),* Scholastic Pr.) Scholastic, Inc.
—Scrivener's Moon. 2012. (ENG.). 352p. (J). (gr. 7). 17.99 *(978-0-545-22218-1(4),* Scholastic Pr.) Scholastic, Inc.
Restivo, Andrea E. Arabella & the Perilous Pantheon. 2010. 28p. pap. 12.99 *(978-1-60693-790-7(1),* Strategic Bk. Publishing) Strategic Book Publishing & Rights Agency (SBPRA).
Richardson, Justin & Parnell, Peter. Christian, the Hugging Lion. Bates, Amy June, illus. 2010. (ENG.). 32p. (J). (gr. -1-3). 16.99 *(978-1-4169-8662-1(6),* Simon & Schuster Bks. For Young Readers) Simon & Schuster Bks. For Young Readers.
Rickett, Sally. Minky the Shoebox Monkey - a Little Monkey with a Long Way to Go. 2010. 54p. pap. 17.95 *(978-1-60860-625-2(2),* Strategic Bk. Publishing) Strategic Book Publishing & Rights Agency (SBPRA).
Riggs, Ransom. Hollow City. 2015. (Miss Peregrine's Peculiar Children Ser.: Bk. 2). (ENG., Illus.). 416p. (YA). pap. 10.99 *(978-1-59474-735-9(0))* Quirk Bks.
—Hollow City. Riggs, Ransom, illus. 2014. (ENG., Illus.). 352p. (YA). (gr. 9). 18.99 *(978-1-59474-612-3(5))* Quirk Bks.
—Hollow City. Riggs, Ransom, illus. 2015. (Miss Peregrine's Peculiar Children Ser.: 2). (Illus.). lib. bdg. 22.10 *(978-0-606-36394-5(7))* Turtleback Bks.
—Library of Souls. 2015. (Miss Peregrine's Peculiar Children Ser.: Bk. 3). (ENG., Illus.). 464p. (YA). (gr. 9). 18.99 *(978-1-59474-758-8(X))* Quirk Bks.
—Library of Souls. 2017. (Miss Peregrine's Peculiar Children Ser.: 3). (ENG.). (YA). (gr. 9). lib. bdg. 23.30 **(978-0-606-39808-4(2))** Turtleback Bks.
Riggs, Ransom & Jean, Cassandra. Hollow City: the Graphic Novel. 2016. (Miss Peregrine's Peculiar Children: the Graphic Novel Ser.: 2). (ENG., Illus.). 272p. (J). (gr. 8-17). 20.00 *(978-0-316-30679-9(7),* Yen Pr.) Orbit.
Ripley's Believe It or Not Editors & Ripley's Believe It Or Not! Staff. Wings of Fear. 2010. (Rbi Ser.: 5). (ENG.). 128p. (J). pap. 4.99 *(978-1-893951-56-3(1))* Ripley Entertainment, Inc.
Robert, Na'ima B. & Quarto Generic Staff. Far from Home. 2012. (ENG.). 352p. (J). (gr. 8-11). pap. 8.99 *(978-1-84780-006-0(8),* Frances Lincoln) Quarto Publishing Group UK GBR. Dist: Hachette Bk. Group.
Rochfort, Barry. The Adventures of Mortimer the Marmot. 2015. (ENG.). 107p. (J). (gr. 2-3). mass mkt. 11.95 *(978-1-78554-739-3(9),* dd7dabfb-8041-475e-8062-7133d7abcf1d) Austin, Stan AUS. Dist: Bookmasters Distribution.
Rodgers, Ilona. Musgrove in Kensington Gardens. 2007. (ENG.). 50p. 10.95 *(978-1-905299-49-2(4),* Stacey International) Stacey Publishing GBR. Dist: Casemate Pubs. & Bk. Distributors, LLC.
—Musgrove There's Something in My Shoe. 2006. (ENG., Illus.). 32p. 10.95 *(978-1-905299-19-5(2),* Stacey International) Stacey Publishing GBR. Dist: Casemate Pubs. & Bk. Distributors, LLC.

Rogers, Gregory. The Hero of Little Street. Rogers, Gregory, illus. 2012. (ENG., Illus.). 32p. (J). (gr. k-3). 17.99 *(978-1-59643-729-6(4)*, 9781596437296) Roaring Brook Pr.
Ross, Diana. The Little Red Engine Goes to Town. Wood, Leslie, illus. 2005. (Little Red Engine Ser.: 1). (ENG.). 32p. (J). (gr. k-2). pap. 8.99 *(978-0-233-00151-7(4))* Andre Deutsch GBR. Dist: Independent Pubs. Group.
Roy, Ron. The Castle Crime. 2014. (to Z Mysteries Ser.: 32). lib. bdg. 16.00 *(978-0-606-35190-4(6))* Turtleback Bks.
Rundell, Katherine. Cartwheeling in Thunderstorms. 2016. lib. bdg. 18.40 *(978-0-606-38273-1(9))* Turtleback Bks.
Saunders, Kate. The Curse of the Chocolate Phoenix: A Companion to the Whizz Pop Chocolate Shop. 2015. (ENG.). 272p. (J). (gr. 5). 19.99 *(978-0-375-99183-7(2)*, Delacorte Bks. for Young Readers) Random Hse. Children's Bks.
—The Whizz Pop Chocolate Shop. 2014. (ENG.). 304p. (J). (gr. 5). 7.99 *(978-0-385-74302-0(5)*, Yearling) Random Hse. Children's Bks.
Schemery, Beau. The 7th of London. 2016. (ENG., Illus.). (J). 32.99 ***(978-1-63477-960-9(6)***, Harmony Ink Pr.) Dreamspinner Pr.
Schroeder, Lisa. Sealed with a Secret. 2016. (ENG.). 224p. (J). (gr. 3-7). 16.99 *(978-0-545-90734-7(9)*, Scholastic Pr.) Scholastic, Inc.
Scott, Kate. Dick Whittington: Band 12/Copper. 2017. (Collins Big Cat Tales Ser.). (ENG., Illus.). 32p. (J). (gr. 2-3). pap. 7.99 ***(978-0-00-817932-8(8))*** HarperCollins Pubs. Ltd. GBR. Dist: Independent Pubs. Group.
Scott, Michael. The Necromancer. 2011. (Secrets of the Immortal Nicholas Flamel Ser.). (ENG.). 416p. (YA). (gr. 7). pap. 10.99 *(978-0-385-73532-2(4)*, Ember) Random Hse. Children's Bks.
—The Necromancer the Secrets of the Immortal Nicholas Flamel. l.t. ed. 2010. (Secrets of the Immortal Nicholas Flamel Ser.). (ENG.). 492p. 23.99 *(978-1-4104-2851-6(6))* Thorndike Pr.
Shan, Darren, pseud. Angels. 2013. (Zom-B Ser.: 4). (ENG.). 192p. (gr. 7-17). 15.00 *(978-0-316-21414-8(0))* Little, Brown Bks. for Young Readers.
—Gladiator. 2014. (Zom-B Ser.: 6). (ENG., Illus.). 176p. (YA). (gr. 7-17). 15.00 *(978-0-316-21407-0(8))* Little Brown & Co.
—Zom-B Baby. 2013. (Zom-B Ser.: 5). (ENG.). 176p. (YA). (gr. 7-17). 15.00 *(978-0-316-21420-9(5))* Little, Brown Bks. for Young Readers.
—Zom-B Chronicles. 2014. (Zom-B Ser.). (ENG.). 560p. (YA). (gr. 7-17). pap. 13.00 *(978-0-316-28489-9(0))* Little, Brown Bks. for Young Readers.
—Zom-B City. 2013. (Zom-B Ser.: 3). (ENG.). 176p. (YA). (gr. 7-17). 15.00 *(978-0-316-21436-0(1))* Little, Brown Bks. for Young Readers.
Sheldon, Dyan. I Conquer Britain. 2007. (ENG., Illus.). 208p. (YA). (gr. 7). 15.99 *(978-0-7636-3300-4(3))* Candlewick Pr.
Shepherd, Megan. Her Dark Curiosity. 2014. (Madman's Daughter Ser.: 2). (ENG.). 432p. (YA). (gr. 8). 17.99 *(978-0-06-212805-8(1))* HarperCollins Pubs.
Shevah, Emma. Dream on, Amber. Crawford-White, Helen, illus. 2016. (ENG.). 288p. (J). (gr. 3-7). pap. 7.99 *(978-1-4926-3592-5(8)*, 9781492635925, Sourcebooks Jabberwocky) Sourcebooks, Inc.
Siggins, Gerard. Rugby Flyer: Haunting History, Thrilling Tries. 2016. (ENG.). 176p. (J). 13.00 *(978-1-84717-819-0(7))* O'Brien Pr., Ltd., The IRL. Dist: Dufour Editions, Inc.
Siobhan, Dowd. The London Eye Mystery. 2014. (ENG.). 336p. (J). (gr. 3-7). 12.24 *(978-1-63245-320-4(7))* Lectorum Pubns., Inc.
Smith, Andrew. The Marbury Lens. 2010. (ENG.). 368p. (YA). (gr. 9-12). 17.99 *(978-0-312-61342-6(3)*, 9780312613426) Feiwel & Friends.
Smith, Charles. Out at First. 2010. 111p. pap. 11.95 *(978-0-557-60419-7(2))* Lulu Pr., Inc.
Smith, Jennifer E. The Statistical Probability of Love at First Sight. 2012. (ENG.). 256p. (YA). (gr. 7-17). 17.99 *(978-0-316-12238-2(6))* Little Brown & Co.
—The Statistical Probability of Love at First Sight. 2013. (ENG.). 272p. (YA). (gr. 7-17). pap. 10.00 *(978-0-316-12239-9(4)*, Poppy) Little, Brown Bks. for Young Readers.
Spinale, Wendy. Everland. (ENG.). (J). (gr. 7). 2017. (Everland Ser.: 1). 336p. pap. 9.99 *(978-1-338-09553-1(6)*, Scholastic Paperbacks) 2016. 320p. 17.99 *(978-0-545-83694-4(8)*, Scholastic Pr.) Scholastic, Inc.
Stevenson, Robert Louis. Dr. Jekyll & Mr. Hyde. 2008. (Bring the Classics to Life Ser.). (ENG., Illus.). 72p. (gr. 4-12). pap., act. bk. ed. 10.95 *(978-0-931334-50-4(0)*, EDCTR-402B) EDCON Publishing Group.
—Dr. Jekyll & Mr. Hyde, 1 vol. 2010. (Illustrated Classics Ser.). (ENG., Illus.). 64p. (YA). (gr. 9-12). per. 9.95 *(978-1-56254-894-0(8))* Saddleback Educational Publishing, Inc.
—The Strange Case of Dr. Jekyll & Mr. Hyde. (Classics Illustrated Ser.). (Illus.). 52p. (YA). pap. 4.95 *(978-1-57209-008-8(1))* Classics International Entertainment, Inc.
—The Strange Case of Dr. Jekyll & Mr. Hyde. Andrews, Gary, illus. 2008. (Fast Track Classics Ser.). (ENG.). 48p. pap. 10.00 *(978-1-4190-5082-4(6))* Steck-Vaughn.
—The Strange Case of Dr. Jekyll & Mr. Hyde. McKowen, Scott, illus. 2011. (Sterling Unabridged Classics Ser.). (ENG.). 96p. (J). 9.95 *(978-1-4027-8402-6(3))* Sterling Publishing Co., Inc.
—The Strange Case of Dr. Jekyll & Mr. Hyde. Akib, Jamel, illus. 2006. (Classic Starts(tm) Ser.). (ENG.). 160p. (J). (gr. 2-4). 6.95 *(978-1-4027-2667-5(8)*, 1252057) Sterling Publishing Co., Inc.
—Strange Case of Dr. Jekyll & Mr. Hyde. Kennedy, Cam, illus. 2008. (ENG.). 48p. (YA). (gr. 5). pap. 11.95 *(978-0-88776-882-8(2)*, Tundra Bks.) Tundra Bks. CAN. Dist: Penguin Random Hse. LLC.
—The Strange Case of Dr. Jekyll & Mr. Hyde (Quality Library Classics) 2008. (YA). pap. 14.95 *(978-1-57545-703-1(2))* RP Media.
Stevenson, Robert Louis & Venable, Alan. The Strange Case of Dr. Jekyll & Mr. Hyde. 2005. (Classic Literature Ser.). 108p. pap. 9.95 *(978-1-4105-0119-6(1))*; pap., E-Book 69.00 incl. audio compact disk *(978-1-4105-0117-2(5))* Johnston, Don Inc.
Stewart, Dianne C. Longitude - Zero Degrees. 2009. (ENG.). 200p. pap. 8.95 *(978-0-9667359-4-9(3)*, BeanPole Bks.) Harren Communications, LLC.
Stine, R. L. A Night in Terror Tower. 2009. (Classic Goosebumps Ser.: 12). (ENG.). 160p. (J). (gr. 3-7). 6.99 *(978-0-545-15887-9(7)*, Scholastic Paperbacks) Scholastic, Inc.
—A Night in Terror Tower. 2009. (Goosebumps Ser.: 11). lib. bdg. 17.20 *(978-0-606-00240-0(5)*, Turtleback) Turtleback Bks.
Stoker, Bram. Drácula. Schuler, Susan, tr. Ruiz, Alfonso, illus. 2010. (Classic Fiction Ser.). (ENG & SPA.). 72p. (gr. 2-3). pap. 7.15 *(978-1-4342-2277-0(2)*, Graphic Revolve en Español) Stone Arch Bks.
—Dracula. Schuler, Susan, tr. Ruiz, Alfonso, illus. 2010. (Classic Fiction Ser.). 72p. pap. 0.90 *(978-1-4342-2985-4(8)*, Graphic Revolve) Stone Arch Bks.
Stretton, Hesba. Jessica's First Prayer. 2004. reprint ed. pap. 1.99 *(978-1-4192-2751-6(3))*; pap. 15.95 *(978-1-4191-2751-9(9))* Kessinger Publishing, LLC.
Stroud, Jonathan. The Amulet of Samarkand, Bk. 1. 2003. (Bartimaeus Novel Ser.). (ENG., Illus.). 464p. (J). (gr. 5-9). 17.99 *(978-0-7868-1859-4(X))* Disney Publishing Worldwide.
—Bartimaeus, 3 vols., Set. 2010. (ENG.). 1552p. (J). (gr. 5-6). pap. 24.99 *(978-1-4231-3682-8(9))* Disney Pr.
—The Creeping Shadow. 2016. (Lockwood & Co Ser.). (ENG., Illus.). 464p. (J). (gr. 3-7). 16.99 *(978-1-4847-0967-2(5))* Hyperion Bks. for Children.
—The Golem's Eye, Bk. 2. 2nd rev. ed. 2006. (Bartimaeus Novel Ser.). (ENG.). 592p. (J). (gr. 5-9). reprint ed. per. 8.99 *(978-0-7868-3654-3(7))* Disney Publishing Worldwide.
—The Hollow Boy. 2015. (Lockwood & Co Ser.). (ENG.). 400p. (J). (gr. 3-7). 16.99 *(978-1-4847-0968-9(3))* Hyperion Bks. for Children.
—Lockwood & Co. Book Three the Hollow Boy. 2016. (Lockwood & Co Ser.). (ENG.). 416p. (J). (gr. 3-7). pap. 7.99 *(978-1-4847-1189-7(0))* Hyperion Bks. for Children.
—Lockwood & Co. the Screaming Staircase. 2014. (Lockwood & Co Ser.). (ENG., Illus.). 416p. (J). (gr. 3-7). pap. 7.99 *(978-1-4231-8692-2(3))* Hyperion Bks. for Children.
—The Screaming Staircase. 2013. (Lockwood & Co Ser.: Bk. 1). (ENG.). 400p. (J). (gr. 3-7). 16.99 *(978-1-4231-6491-3(1))* Hyperion Pr.
—The Whispering Skull. (ENG.). (J). (gr. 3-7). 2015. (Lockwood & Co Ser.). 464p. pap. 7.99 *(978-1-4231-9462-0(4))* 2014. (Lockwood & Co. Ser.: 2). 448p. 17.99 *(978-1-4231-6492-0(X))* Hyperion Bks. for Children.
Sutcliffe, William. Concentr8. 2016. (ENG.). 256p. (YA). 17.99 *(978-1-61963-919-5(X)*, 9781619639195, Bloomsbury USA Childrens) Bloomsbury Publishing USA.
A Tale of Two Cities. abr. ed. (ARA., Illus.). 48p. (J). 12.00 *(978-0-86685-627-0(7))* International Bk. Ctr., Inc.
Theobald, John Owen. What the Raven Brings. 2017. (Ravenmaster Trilogy Ser.: 2). (ENG., Illus.). 320p. (YA). (gr. 7-7). 9.99 ***(978-1-78497-440-4(4))***; 22.99 *(978-1-78497-438-1(2))* Head of Zeus GBR. Dist: Independent Pubs. Group.
Thompson, Lisa. The Goldfish Boy. 2017. (ENG.). 320p. (J). (gr. 3-7). 16.99 *(978-1-338-05392-0(2)*, Scholastic Pr.) Scholastic, Inc.
Toledano, Henry. The Turn in the Road: A Young Man on the Edge. 2017. (ENG.). 281p. pap. 14.95 ***(978-1-78629-094-6(4)***, 3a73d3c2-5e11-413b-a1f4-367ac0c75be4) Austin, Stan AUS. Dist: Bookmasters Distribution.
Trevayne, Emma. The Accidental Afterlife of Thomas Marsden. 2016. (ENG.). 272p. (J). (gr. 3-7). pap. 7.99 *(978-1-4424-9884-6(6)*, Simon & Schuster Bks. For Young Readers) Simon & Schuster Bks. For Young Readers.
Turnbull, Ann. Josie under Fire. 2009. (Historical House Ser.). 176p. (YA). (gr. 5-18). pap. 5.99 *(978-0-7945-2335-0(8)*, Usborne) EDC Publishing.
—Mary Ann & Miss Mozart. 2009. (Historical House Ser.). 166p. (YA). (gr. 5-18). pap. 5.99 *(978-0-7945-2332-9(3)*, Usborne) EDC Publishing.
Twain, Mark, pseud. The Prince & the Pauper. 2006. (Aladdin Classics Ser.). (ENG.). 352p. (J). pap. 7.99 *(978-1-4169-2805-8(7)*, Aladdin) Simon & Schuster Children's Publishing.
Twain, Mark, pseud & Clemens, Samuel L. The Prince & the Pauper. 2013. (Works of Mark Twain). 425p. reprint ed. lthr. 79.00 *(978-0-7812-1120-8(4))* Reprint Services Corp.
Valentine, Jenny. Broken Soup. 2009. (YA). 216p. 17.89 *(978-0-06-085072-2(8))*; 224p. (gr. 9-18). 16.99 *(978-0-06-085071-5(X))* HarperCollins Pubs. (HarperTeen).
—Me, the Missing, & the Dead. 2010. 224p. (YA). (gr. 9). pap. 8.99 *(978-0-06-085070-8(1)*, HarperTeen) HarperCollins Pubs.
Vidali, Valerio & Uman, Jennifer. Jemmy Button. Vidali, Valerio & Uman, Jennifer, illus. 2013. (ENG., Illus.). 48p. (J). (gr. k-12). 16.99 *(978-0-7636-6487-9(1)*, Templar) Candlewick Pr.
Walden, Mark. Earthfall. 2013. (Earthfall Trilogy Ser.: 1). (ENG., Illus.). 272p. (J). (gr. 3-7). 16.99 *(978-1-4424-9415-2(8)*, Simon & Schuster Bks. For Young Readers) Simon & Schuster Bks. For Young Readers.
Walker, Peter Lancaster. Space Travelers Land at Buckingham Palace. Dixit, Rama, illus. 2007. 275p. (J). 19.95 *(978-1-934138-12-0(6))* Bouncing Ball Bks., Inc.
Waller, Sharon Biggs. A Mad, Wicked Folly. 2014. (ENG.). 448p. (YA). (gr. 7). 17.99 *(978-0-670-01468-2(0)*, Viking Books for Young Readers) Penguin Young Readers Group.
Ward, Rachel. The Chaos. 2011. (Numbers Ser.: 2). (ENG.). 352p. (J). (gr. 9-9). 17.99 *(978-0-545-24269-1(X)*, Chicken Hse., The) Scholastic, Inc.
—Infinity: 2012. (Numbers Ser.: 3). (ENG.). 256p. (J). (gr. 9-9). 17.99 *(978-0-545-35092-1(1)*, Chicken Hse., The) Scholastic, Inc.
Watson, Sally. Linnet. 2004. (YA). pap. 12.95 *(978-1-59511-002-2(X)*, 800-691-7779) Image Cascade Publishing.
Webb, Catherine. The Extraordinary & Unusual Adventures of Horatio Lyle. 2006. (ENG.). 320p. (gr. 8). 9.95 *(978-1-904233-61-9(9))* Little, Brown Book Group Ltd. GBR. Dist: Hachette Bk. Group.
—The Obsidian Dagger: Being the Further Extraordinary Adventures of Horatio Lyle. 2007. (ENG.). 336p. (gr. 7). pap. 11.95 *(978-1-904233-79-4(1))* Little, Brown Book Group Ltd. GBR. Dist: Hachette Bk. Group.
Webb, Holly. The Case of the Feathered Mask. Lindsay, Marion, illus. 2016. (Mysteries of Maisie Hitchins Ser.: 4). (ENG.). 176p. (J). (gr. 2-5). 15.99 *(978-0-544-61993-7(5)*, HMH Books For Young Readers) Houghton Mifflin Harcourt Publishing Co.
Webb, Philip. Six Days. 2011. (ENG.). 352p. (J). (gr. 5-9). 17.99 *(978-0-545-31767-2(3)*, Chicken Hse., The) Scholastic, Inc.
Weinstein, Jacob Sager. Hyacinth & the Secrets Beneath. 2017. (Hyacinth Ser.: 1). (ENG.). 304p. (J). (gr. 3-7). 16.99 *(978-0-399-55317-2(7)*, Random Hse. Bks. for Young Readers) Random Hse. Children's Bks.
Wesson, Tim & Catlow, Nikalas. Pirates v. Ancient Egyptians in a Haunted Museum. Catlow, Nikalas, illus. 2012. (Mega Mash-Up Ser.). (ENG., Illus.). 96p. (J). (gr. 2-5). pap. 6.99 *(978-0-7636-5901-1(0)*, Nosy Crow) Candlewick Pr.
Westwood, Chris. Graveyard Shift. (Hauntings Ser.: bk.1). (ENG.). 304p. (J). (gr. 3-7). 2014. pap. 6.99 *(978-0-545-39920-3(3))* 2012. 17.99 *(978-0-545-39919-7(X))* Scholastic, Inc. (Scholastic Pr.).
Whelan, Gloria. Farewell to the Island. 2004. 200p. (J). (gr. 4-7). per. 7.95 *(978-1-882376-92-6(7))* Thunder Bay Pr.
White, Ellen Emerson. Voyage on the Great Titanic. 2010. (Dear America Ser.). (ENG., Illus.). 208p. (J). (gr. 3-7). 12.99 *(978-0-545-23834-2(X)*, Scholastic Pr.) Scholastic, Inc.
Whyman, Matt. Goldstrike: A Thriller. 2010. (ENG.). 272p. (YA). (gr. 7-18). 16.99 *(978-1-4169-9510-4(2)*, Atheneum Bks. for Young Readers) Simon & Schuster Children's Publishing.
Whytock, Cherry. My Scrumptious Scottish Dumplings: The Life of Angelica Cookson Potts. Whytock, Cherry, illus. 2006. (ENG., Illus.). 192p. (YA). mass mkt. 5.99 *(978-0-689-86552-7(X)*, Simon Pulse) Simon Pulse.
Wicke, Ed. Akayzia Adams & the Masterdragon's Secret. 2003. 280p. (J). per. 9.99 *(978-0-9677652-3-5(4)*, BlacknBlue Pr. UK) Blacknblue Pr.
Wilkins, Rose. So Super-Starry. 2004. (ENG.). 256p. (J). pap. *(978-0-330-42086-0(0)*, Macmillan Children's Bks.) Pan Macmillan.
The Windsor Caper. 2013. (Illus.). 258p. pap. *(978-0-9576554-0-9(1))* Good, Martin.
Wood, Maryrose. The Hidden Gallery. Klassen, Jon, illus. (J). (gr. 3-7). 2015. (Incorrigible Children of Ashton Place Ser.: 2). (ENG.). 336p. pap. 6.99 *(978-0-06-236694-8(7))* 2011. (Incorrigible Children of Ashton Place Ser.: 2). (ENG.). 320p. 16.99 *(978-0-06-179112-3(1))* 2011. (Incorrigible Children of Ashton Place Ser.: Bk. 2). 16.89 *(978-0-06-179114-7(8))* HarperCollins Pubs.
—The Unseen Guest. Klassen, Jon, illus. 2015. (Incorrigible Children of Ashton Place Ser.: 3). (ENG.). 352p. (J). (gr. 3-7). pap. 6.99 *(978-0-06-236695-5(5))* HarperCollins Pubs.
Woodruff, Elvira. The Ravenmaster's Secret. 2005. (Escape from the Tower of London Ser.). (Illus.). 225p. (gr. 3-7). 16.00 *(978-0-7569-4791-0(X))* Perfection Learning Corp.
Wyre, Yvonne. The Adventures of Cuthbert the Coal Lorry. 2005. 160p. pap. *(978-1-84401-500-9(9))* Athena Pr.
You Came for Me. 2013. (ENG.). 240p. pap. 14.99 *(978-1-60861-221-5(X))* Covenant Communications, Inc.
Zamorsky, Tania & Burnett, Frances Hodgson. A Little Princess. Corvino, Lucy, illus. 2005. (Classic Starts(tm) Ser.). (ENG.). 160p. (J). (gr. 2-4). 6.95 *(978-1-4027-1275-3(8))* Sterling Publishing Co., Inc.
Zettel, Sarah. Assassin's Masque. 2017. (Palace of Spies Ser.: 3). (ENG.). 432p. (YA). (gr. 7). pap. 8.99 *(978-0-544-81317-5(0)*, HMH Books For Young Readers) Houghton Mifflin Harcourt Publishing Co.
Zink, Michelle. A Temptation of Angels. 2013. (ENG.). 448p. (YA). (gr. 7). pap. 9.99 *(978-0-14-242423-0(4)*, Speak) Penguin Young Readers Group.
Zondervan Staff & Grant, Natalie. A London Art Chase, 1 vol. 2016. (Faithgirlz / Glimmer Girls Ser.). (ENG., Illus.). 208p. (J). pap. 8.99 *(978-0-310-75265-3(5))* Zonderkidz.

LONDON (ENGLAND)—FIRES AND FIRE PREVENTION

Baker, Chris & Ladybird Books Staff. The Great Fire of London. 2016. (Ladybird Histories Ser.). (ENG., Illus.). 48p. (J). (gr. 1-3). pap. 14.99 *(978-0-241-24821-8(3))* Penguin Bks., Ltd. GBR. Dist: Independent Pubs. Group.

LONDON (ENGLAND)—HISTORY

Adams, Emma. The Great Fire of London. Osborne, Fiz, ed. Lewis, James Weston, illus. 350th anniv. ed. 2016. (ENG.). 48p. (J). (gr. 2-4). 17.99 *(978-0-7502-9820-9(0)*, Wayland) Hachette Children's Group GBR. Dist: Hachette Bk. Group.
Alagna, Magdalena. The Great Fire of London of 1666. 2004. (Tragic Fires Throughout History Ser.). (Illus.). 48p. (gr. 5-8). lib. bdg. 29.25 *(978-0-8239-4485-9(9)*, Rosen Reference) Rosen Publishing Group, Inc., The.
—The Great Fire of London Of 1666. 2009. (Tragic Fires Throughout History Ser.). 48p. (gr. 5-8). 53.00 *(978-1-60854-583-4(0)*, Rosen Reference) Rosen Publishing Group, Inc., The.
Bailey, Ellen & Mosedale, Julian. The London Activity Book: With Palaces, Puzzles & Pictures to Colour. Pinder, Andrew, illus. 2013. (ENG.). 64p. (J). (gr. 2-4). pap. 8.99 *(978-1-78055-095-4(2)* O'Mara, Michael Bks., Ltd. GBR. Dist: Independent Pubs. Group.
Ball, Jacqueline A. Windsor Castle: England's Royal Fortress. 2005. (Castles, Palaces, & Tombs Ser.). (Illus.). 32p. (J). lib. bdg. 25.27 *(978-1-59716-005-6(9))* Bearport Publishing Co., Inc.
Barnham, Kay. London. 2017. (My Infographic Sticker Activity Book Ser.). (ENG.). 32p. (J). (gr. k-2). pap. 7.99 ***(978-0-7502-9943-5(6)***, Wayland) Hachette Children's Group GBR. Dist: Hachette Bk. Group.
Billet, Marion. My First London Bus. Billet, Marion, illus. 2015. (Whizzy Wheels Ser.). (ENG., Illus.). 10p. (J). (-k). bds. 9.99 *(978-0-230-76057-8(0))* Pan Macmillan GBR. Dist: Independent Pubs. Group.
—My First London Taxi. Billet, Marion, illus. 2015. (Whizzy Wheels Ser.). (ENG., Illus.). 10p. (J). (-k). bds. 11.99 *(978-0-230-76103-2(8))* Pan Macmillan GBR. Dist: Independent Pubs. Group.
Billet, Marion, illus. Hello! London. 2014. (Hello! Ser.). (ENG.). 10p. (J). (-k). bds. 15.99 *(978-1-4472-4682-4(9))* Pan Macmillan GBR. Dist: Independent Pubs. Group.
—London Bus. 2014. (ENG.). 12p. (J). (— 1). bds. 7.99 *(978-1-4472-5632-8(8))* Pan Macmillan GBR. Dist: Independent Pubs. Group.
—London Taxi. 2014. (ENG.). 12p. (J). (— 1). bds. 7.99 *(978-1-4472-5633-5(6))* Pan Macmillan GBR. Dist: Independent Pubs. Group.
—My First London Sticker Book. 2015. (ENG.). 32p. (J). (gr. k-3). pap. 10.99 *(978-1-4472-7617-3(5))* Pan Macmillan GBR. Dist: Independent Pubs. Group.
—My First London Whizzy Wheels: Four Vehicle-Shaped Board Books in a Carry Case, 4 vols. 2016. (ENG.). 40p. (J). (gr. -1-k). 19.99 *(978-1-5098-0459-7(5))* Pan Macmillan GBR. Dist: Independent Pubs. Group.
Bloom, Harold. London. 2005. (Bloom's Literary Places Ser.). (Illus.). 150p. (YA). (gr. 9-13). 40.00 *(978-0-7910-7841-9(8))* Facts On File, Inc.
Brook, Henry. True Stories of the Blitz. McNee, Ian, illus. 2006. (True Adventure Stories Ser.). 160p. (J). (gr. 4-7). per. 4.99 *(978-0-7945-1245-3(3)*, Usborne) EDC Publishing.
Clements, Gillian. Tudor Theatre. 2009. (Building History Ser.). (Illus.). 32p. (J). (gr. 3-5). 27.10 *(978-1-59771-147-0(0))* Sea-To-Sea Pubns.
Cottrell, Robert. London: From the Walled City to New Towns. 2006. (Arbitrary Borders Ser.). (Illus.). 144p. (C). (gr. 9-12). lib. bdg. 35.00 *(978-0-7910-8684-1(4)*, Chelsea Hse.) Facts On File, Inc.
Crisp, Dan, illus. London: A Colourful City. 2012. (ENG.). 20p. (J). (gr. -1 — 1). bds. 9.99 *(978-1-4052-6468-6(3))* Egmont Bks., Ltd. GBR. Dist: Independent Pubs. Group.
Dickins, Rosie. London Sticker Book. Clarke, Philip, ed. Lumley, Stef, photos by. 2006. (Usborne Sticker Bks.). (Illus.). 15p. (J). (gr. 2-5). pap. 8.99 *(978-0-7945-1284-2(4)*, Usborne) EDC Publishing.
Doder, Joshua. Time Traveler's Guide to Shakespeare's London. 2004. (Timetraveller's Guides). (ENG., Illus.). 96p. (J). pap. 8.99 *(978-1-904153-10-8(0))* Watling St., Ltd. GBR. Dist: Independent Pubs. Group.
—The Timetraveller's Guide to Saxon & Viking London. 2004. (Timetraveller's Guides). (ENG., Illus.). 96p. (J). (gr. 3-7). per. 8.99 *(978-1-904153-07-8(0))* Watling St., Ltd. GBR. Dist: Independent Pubs. Group.
Dunn, James & Quarto Generic Staff. ABC London. Slater, Kate, illus. rev. ed. 2014. (ENG.). 40p. (J). (gr. k-3). pap. 8.99 *(978-1-84780-495-2(0)*, Frances Lincoln) Quarto Publishing Group UK GBR. Dist: Hachette Bk. Group.
Dyan, Penelope. Where Is London Bridge? a Kid's Guide to London. Weigand, John D., photos by. 2009. (Illus.). 44p. pap. 11.95 *(978-1-935118-80-0(3))* Bellissima Publishing, LLC.
Elborough, Travis. Highwayman, Outlaws & Bandits of London. 2004. (. . . of London Ser.). (ENG., Illus.). 96p. pap. 8.99 *(978-1-904153-13-9(5))* Watling St., Ltd. GBR. Dist: Trafalgar Square Publishing.
—Rebels, Traitors & Turncoats of London. 2004. (Of London Ser.). (ENG., Illus.). 96p. (J). pap. 8.99 *(978-1-904153-15-3(1))* Tempus ESP. Dist: Independent Pubs. Group.
Ferreira, Rute Nieto & Alessandra, Amandine. The Big Letter Hunt: London: An Architectural a-Z Around the City. 2016. (ENG., Illus.). 64p. pap. 14.95 *(978-1-84994-366-6(4)*, Batsford) Pavilion Bks. GBR. Dist: Sterling Publishing Co., Inc.
Goldsworthy, Kaite. St. Paul's Cathedral. 2014. (J). *(978-1-4896-1154-3(1))* Weigl Pubs., Inc.
Goodrich, Olivia. Timetraveler's Guide to Roman London. 2004. (Timetraveller's Guides). (ENG., Illus.). 96p. (J). pap. 7.95 *(978-1-904153-06-1(2))* Watling St., Ltd. GBR. Dist: Independent Pubs. Group.
Holland, Simon. An Infographic Guide to London. 2016. (Infographic Guide To Ser.). (ENG., Illus.). 64p. (J). (gr. 4-6). 16.99 *(978-0-7502-9859-9(6)*, Wayland) Hachette Children's Group GBR. Dist: Hachette Bk. Group.
Howell, Izzi. Guy Fawkes & the Gunpowder Plot. 2016. (Why Do We Remember? Ser.). (ENG., Illus.). 32p. (J). (gr. 1-3). 17.99 *(978-1-4451-4850-2(1)*, Franklin Watts) Hachette Children's Group GBR. Dist: Hachette Bk. Group.
Jocelyn, Marthe. A Home for Foundlings. 2005. (Lord Museum Book Ser.). (ENG., Illus.). 120p. (J). (gr. k-12). pap. 16.95 *(978-0-88776-709-8(5)*, Tundra Bks.) Tundra Bks. CAN. Dist: Penguin Random Hse. LLC.
Kidney, Christine. Medieval London. 2004. (Timetraveller's Guide Ser.). (ENG., Illus.). 96p. (J). (gr. 4-7). pap. 8.99 *(978-1-904153-08-5(9))* Watling St., Ltd. GBR. Dist: Independent Pubs. Group.
Lamprell, Klay. Londres - Grandes Secretos para Pequenos Viajeros, 1 vol. 2012. (SPA & ENG.). 96p. (J). pap. 14.99 *(978-84-08-10913-6(8)*, 103551) Lonely Planet Pubns.
Lonely Planet & Mansfield, Andy. POP-UP LONDON, 1 vol. 2016. (Lonely Planet Kids Ser.). (ENG., Illus.). 16p. (J). 9.99 *(978-1-76034-339-2(0)*, 5339) Lonely Planet Pubns.
Lynch, Annabelle. London. 2017. (Let's Visit Ser.). (ENG., Illus.). 32p. (J). (gr. 1-3). 16.99 ***(978-1-4451-5365-0(3)***, Franklin Watts) Hachette Children's Group GBR. Dist: Hachette Bk. Group.
Machajewski, Sarah. El Gran Incendio de Londres (the Great Fire of London) Sarfatti, Esther, tr. from ENG. 2015. (Desastres Ser.). (SPA., Illus.). 32p. (J). (gr. 4-5). lib. bdg. 26.60 *(978-1-4824-3265-7(X))* Stevens, Gareth Publishing LLLP.
—The Great Fire of London. 2015. (Doomed! Ser.). (ENG., Illus.). 32p. (J). (gr. 4-5). pap. 10.50 *(978-1-4824-2932-9(2))* Stevens, Gareth Publishing LLLP.
Manning, Paul. The Thames. (River Adventures Ser.). 2014. (J). lib. bdg. 31.35 *(978-1-59920-918-0(7))* 2013. 48p. (gr. 5-11). lib. bdg. 37.10 *(978-1-59920-924-1(1))* Black Rabbit Bks.
—Thames River. 2015. (River Adventures Ser.). (Illus.). 32p. (gr. 4-7). 31.35 *(978-1-62588-588-3(1))* Black Rabbit Bks.
Martin, Claudia. The History Detective Investigates - London. 2017. (History Detective Investigates Ser.). (ENG., Illus.). 32p. (J). (gr. 4-6). pap. 12.99 ***(978-1-5263-0185-7(7)***, Wayland) Hachette Children's Group GBR. Dist: Hachette Bk. Group.
Martin, Claudia. London. 2016. (History Detective Investigates Ser.). (ENG., Illus.). 32p. (J). (gr. 4-6). 16.99 *(978-0-7502-9769-1(7)*, Wayland) Hachette Children's Group GBR. Dist: Hachette Bk. Group.

J
K
L

Mason Crest. London, Vol. 8. 2016. (Major World Cities Ser.: Vol. 8). (ENG., Illus.). 48p. (J). (gr. 5-8). 20.95 *(978-1-4222-3541-6(6))* Mason Crest.

McAllister, Angela. London Through Time. Maland, Nick, illus. 2015. (ENG.). 16p. (J). (gr. 1-4). 9.99 *(978-1-84780-689-5(9),* Frances Lincoln) Quarto Publishing Group UK GBR. Dist: Hachette Bk. Group.

Meyers, Haily & Meyers, Kevin. All Aboard: London, 1 vol. 2016. (ENG., Illus.). 22p. (J). bds. 9.99 *(978-1-4236-4242-8(2))* Gibbs Smith, Publisher.

Morgan, Sally Jane. Great Fire of London Activity Book. Lewis, James Weston, illus. 2017. (ENG.). 48p. (J). (gr. 1-3). pap. 9.99 ***(978-1-5263-0162-8(8),*** Wayland) Hachette Children's Group GBR. Dist: Hachette Bk. Group.

Narayan, Natasha. Black Death & Other Putrid Plagues of London. 2004. (... of London Ser.). (Illus.). 96p. 8.99 *(978-1-904153-01-6(1))* Watling St., Ltd. GBR. Dist: Independent Pubs. Group.

—Spies, Secret Agents & Spooks of London. 2004. (Of London Ser.). (ENG., Illus.). 96p. (J). pap. 8.99 *(978-1-904153-14-6(3))* Tempus ESP. Dist: Independent Pubs. Group.

—Time Traveler's Guide to Victorian London. 2004. (Timetraveller's Guides). (ENG., Illus.). 96p. (J). pap. 8.99 *(978-1-904153-11-5(9))* Watling St., Ltd. GBR. Dist: Independent Pubs. Group.

—Tudor London. 2004. (Timetraveller's Guides). (ENG., Illus.). 96p. (J). pap. 8.99 *(978-1-904153-09-2(7))* Watling St., Ltd. GBR. Dist: Independent Pubs. Group.

—Witches, Wizards & Warlocks of London. 2004. (Of London Ser.). (ENG., Illus.). 96p. (J). pap. 8.99 *(978-1-904153-12-2(7))* Watling St., Ltd. GBR. Dist: Independent Pubs. Group.

Nelson, Drew. Haunted! the Tower of London. 2013. 32p. (J). (gr. 3-6). 26.60 *(978-1-4339-9263-6(9));* pap. 63.00 *(978-1-4339-9265-0(5));* pap. 10.50 *(978-1-4339-9264-3(7))* Stevens, Gareth Publishing LLLP.

Pericoli, Matteo. London for Children. 2014. (ENG., Illus.). 64p. (J). (gr. -1). 16.99 *(978-1-4472-1313-0(0))* Pan Macmillan GBR. Dist: Independent Pubs. Group.

Rice, Dona & Rice, Dona Herweck. You Are There! London 1666. 2017. (TIME for KIDS(r) Nonfiction Readers Ser.). (Illus.). 32p. (J). (gr. 7-7). pap. 8.99 *(978-1-4938-3616-1(1))* Teacher Created Materials, Inc.

Rice, Dona Herweck. You Are There! London 1666. 2017. (Time for Kids Nonfiction Readers Ser.). lib. bdg. 19.65 ***(978-0-606-40263-7(2))*** Turtleback Bks.

RollasonJane. LONDON LEVEL 2 ELEMENTARY. 2014. (ENG.). 64p. pap. 12.00 *(978-1-107-61521-2(6))* Cambridge Univ. Pr.

Rossi, Renzo. In Nineteenth Century London with Dickens. Baldanzi, Alessandro, illus. 2008. (Come See My City Ser.). 48p. (gr. 4-8). lib. bdg. 28.50 *(978-0-7614-4333-9(9),* Benchmark Bks.) Marshall Cavendish Corp.

Rubbino, Salvatore. A Walk in London. Rubbino, Salvatore, illus. 2011. (ENG., Illus.). 40p. (J). (gr. k-3). 16.99 *(978-0-7636-5272-2(5))* Candlewick Pr.

Rudolph, Jessica. London. 2017. (Citified! Ser.). (ENG.). 24p. (J). (gr. k-3). 17.95 ***(978-1-68402-232-8(0))*** Bearport Publishing Co., Inc.

Shyam, Bhajju, illus. The London Jungle Book. 2nd ed. 2014. (ENG.). 48p. 19.95 *(978-81-923171-2-0(9))* Tara Books Agency IND. Dist: Publishers Group West (PGW).

Smith, Helen. Pirates, Swashbucklers & Buccaneers of London. 2004. (... of London Ser.). (ENG., Illus.). 96p. pap. 8.99 *(978-1-904153-17-7(8))* Watling St., Ltd. GBR. Dist: Trafalgar Square Publishing.

Sutherland, Adam. The Smell of Poo - Closed Parliment! The Fact or Fiction Behind London. 2017. (Truth or Busted Ser.). (ENG., Illus.). 96p. (J). (gr. 4-6). pap. 10.99 ***(978-1-5263-0066-9(4),*** Wayland) Hachette Children's Group GBR. Dist: Hachette Bk. Group.

Warren, Andrea. Charles Dickens & the Street Children of London. 2017. (ENG., Illus.). 160p. (J). (gr. 7). pap. 9.99 *(978-0-544-93260-9(9),* HMH Books For Young Readers) Houghton Mifflin Harcourt Publishing Co.

Watts, Franklin & Howell, Izzi. The Great Fire of London. 2017. (Why Do We Remember? Ser.). (ENG., Illus.). 32p. (J). (gr. 1-3). 17.99 *(978-1-4451-4824-3(2),* Franklin Watts) Hachette Children's Group GBR. Dist: Hachette Bk. Group.

Watts, Franklin & Miles, John. London on Fire: A Great City at the Time of the Great Fire. 2016. (ENG., Illus.). 48p. (J). (gr. 4-6). 18.99 *(978-1-4451-4691-1(6),* Franklin Watts) Hachette Children's Group GBR. Dist: Hachette Bk. Group.

LONDON (ENGLAND)—HISTORY—FICTION

Adler, Irene. The Mystery of the Scarlet Rose. McGuinness, Nanette, tr. from ITA. Bruno, Iacopo, illus. 2015. (Sherlock, Lupin, & Me Ser.). (ENG.). 256p. (gr. 4-8). lib. bdg. 26.65 *(978-1-4342-6524-1(2))* Stone Arch Bks.

—The Soprano's Last Song, 1 vol. Iacopo, Bruno & Bruno, Iacopo, illus. 2014. (Sherlock, Lupin, & Me Ser.). (ENG.). 240p. (gr. 4-8). lib. bdg. 26.65 *(978-1-4342-6522-7(6))* Stone Arch Bks.

Avi. The Traitors' Gate. Raude, Karina, illus. 2007. (ENG.). 368p. (J). (gr. 5-8). 17.99 *(978-0-689-85335-7(1),* Atheneum/Richard Jackson Bks.) Simon & Schuster Children's Publishing.

Bailey, Kristin. Legacy of the Clockwork Key. 2013. (Secret Order Ser.: 1). (ENG.). 416p. (YA). (gr. 9). 17.99 *(978-1-4424-4026-5(0),* Simon Pulse) Simon Pulse.

—Rise of the Arcane Fire. 2014. (Secret Order Ser.: 2). (ENG., Illus.). 464p. (YA). (gr. 9). 17.99 *(978-1-4424-6802-3(5),* Simon Pulse) Simon Pulse.

—Shadow of the War Machine. 2015. (Secret Order Ser.: 3). (ENG., Illus.). 448p. (YA). (gr. 9). 17.99 *(978-1-4424-6805-4(X),* Simon Pulse) Simon Pulse.

Baratz-Logsted, Lauren. The Twin's Daughter. 2014. (ENG.). 416p. (YA). (gr. 7-12). pap. 9.99 *(978-1-59990-661-4(9),* 9781599906614, Bloomsbury USA Childrens) Bloomsbury Publishing USA.

Bloor, Edward. London Calling. 2008. (ENG., Illus.). 304p. (YA). (gr. 7-9). per. 8.99 *(978-0-375-84363-1(9),* Ember) Random Hse. Children's Bks.

The Case of the Vanishing Emerald. 2015. (Mysteries of Maisie Hitchins Ser.: 2). (ENG., Illus.). 176p. (J). (gr. 2-5). 14.99 *(978-0-544-33927-9(4),* HMH Books For Young Readers) Houghton Mifflin Harcourt Publishing Co.

Clare, Cassandra. Clockwork Angel. (Infernal Devices Ser.: Bk. 1). (ENG., Illus.). (YA). (gr. 9). 2015. 544p. pap. 13.99 *(978-1-4814-5602-9(4))* 2010. 496p. 24.99 *(978-1-4169-7586-1(1))* McElderry, Margaret K. Bks. (McElderry, Margaret K. Bks.).

—Clockwork Angel. 2012. (Infernal Devices Ser.: 1). (ENG.). 240p. (gr. 8-17). pap. 13.00 *(978-0-316-20098-1(0),* Yen Pr.) Orbit.

—Clockwork Angel. 2015. (Infernal Devices Ser.: Bk. 1). 544p. (YA). lib. bdg. 25.75 *(978-0-606-37737-9(9))* 2012. (Infernal Devices Graphic Novel Ser.: 1). lib. bdg. 24.55 *(978-0-606-32257-7(4),* Turtleback) Turtleback Bks.

—Clockwork Prince. (Infernal Devices Ser.: Bk. 2). (YA). 2015. (ENG., Illus.). 560p. (gr. 9). pap. 13.99 *(978-1-4814-5601-2(6))* 2011. (ENG., Illus.). 528p. (gr. 9-18). 24.99 *(978-1-4169-7588-5(8))* 2011. 502p. *(978-1-4424-5174-2(2))* McElderry, Margaret K. Bks. (McElderry, Margaret K. Bks.).

—Clockwork Prince. 2013. (Infernal Devices Ser.: 2). (ENG., Illus.). 256p. (gr. 8-17). pap. 13.00 *(978-0-316-20096-7(4),* Yen Pr.) Orbit.

—Clockwork Prince. 2015. (Infernal Devices Ser.: Bk. 2). 560p. (YA). lib. bdg. 25.75 *(978-0-606-37895-6(2))* Turtleback Bks.

—Clockwork Princess. 2013. (YA). (Infernal Devices Ser.: 3). (ENG., Illus.). 592p. (gr. 9). 24.99 *(978-1-4169-7590-8(X));* 570p. *(978-1-4424-8541-9(8))* McElderry, Margaret K. Bks. (McElderry, Margaret K. Bks.).

Colfer, Eoin. The Hangman's Revolution. 2014. (W. A. R. P. Ser.: Bk. 2). (ENG.). 384p. (YA). (gr. 7-12). 17.99 *(978-1-4231-6163-9(7))* Disney Pr.

—The Hangman's Revolution. 2015. (Warp Ser.). (ENG.). 400p. (YA). (gr. 7-12). pap. 9.99 *(978-1-4231-6498-2(9))* Hyperion Bks. for Children.

Crilley, Paul. The Osiris Curse: A Tweed & Nightingale Adventure. 2013. (ENG.). 287p. (J). (gr. 7). 17.99 *(978-1-61614-857-7(8))* Prometheus Bks., Pubs.

Curry, Jane Louise. The Black Canary. 2005. (ENG., Illus.). 288p. (J). (gr. 5-9). 18.99 *(978-0-689-86478-0(7),* McElderry, Margaret K. Bks.) McElderry, Margaret K. Bks.

Dalton, Annie. Fogging Over: Mission - Take a Trip down Under. 2010. (Mel Beeby, Agent Angel Ser.: 5). (ENG.). 160p. (J). (gr. 4-7). pap. 7.99 *(978-0-00-720475-5(2))* HarperCollins Pubs. Ltd. GBR. Dist: HarperCollins Pubs.

Dickens, Charles. Oliver Twist. Volpari, Daniela, illus. 2014. (Big Picture Book Ser.). (ENG.). 48p. (J). (gr. 1). 16.95 *(978-2-7338-2529-7(1))* Auzou, Philippe Editions FRA. Dist: Consortium Bk. Sales & Distribution.

—Oliver Twist. 2014. (Graphic Classics Ser.). 48p. (gr. 2-7). pap. 8.95 *(978-1-905087-97-6(7))* Book Hse. GBR. Dist: Black Rabbit Bks.

—Oliver Twist. 2013. 274p. pap. 14.99 *(978-1-4837-0319-0(3))* Bottom of the Hill Publishing.

—Oliver Twist. Belli, Alfredo, illus. 2008. (Green Apple Step Two Ser.). (ENG.). 96p. (J). (gr. 5). pap. incl. audio compact disk *(978-88-530-0580-9(7))* Cideb.

—Oliver Twist. 2013. (ENG., Illus.). 722p. (J). (gr. 4-7). pap. 12.99 *(978-0-09-958263-2(5))* Random Hse. GBR. Dist: Independent Pubs. Group.

—A Tale of Two Cities: A Classic Retelling. 2006. (Classic Retelling Ser.). (Illus.). 240p. (YA). (gr. 8-12). *(978-0-618-03150-4(2),* 2-00144) Holt McDougal.

Dickens, Charles & Hawksley, L. Dickens. A Tale of Two Cities. 2004. (Paperback Classics Ser.). 144p. (J). pap. 4.95 *(978-0-7945-0390-1(X));* lib. bdg. 12.95 *(978-1-58086-515-9(1))* EDC Publishing.

Funaro, Gregory. Alistair Grim's Odditorium. 2015. (Alistair Grim Ser.). (ENG.). (J). (gr. 3-7). 448p. pap. 7.99 *(978-1-4847-0899-6(7));* (Illus.). 432p. 16.99 *(978-1-4847-0006-8(6))* Hyperion Bks. for Children.

—Alistair Grim's Odditorium. 2015. (J). lib. bdg. 18.40 *(978-0-606-37399-9(3))* Turtleback Bks.

Gardner, Sally. I, Coriander. 2007. (ENG., Illus.). 288p. (J). (gr. 5-18). 7.99 *(978-0-14-240763-9(1),* Puffin Books) Penguin Young Readers Group.

Garfield, Leon. John Diamond. 2015. (ENG., Illus.). 256p. (J). (gr. 4-6). 12.99 *(978-0-09-958327-1(5))* Random Hse. GBR. Dist: Independent Pubs. Group.

—Smith - The Story of a Pickpocket. 2013. (ENG.). 216p. (J). (gr. 4-7). 15.95 *(978-1-59017-675-7(8),* NYR Children's Collection) New York Review of Bks., Inc., The.

Gier, Kerstin. Ruby Red. Bell, Anthea, tr. from GER. 2011. (Ruby Red Trilogy Ser.: 1). (ENG.). 336p. (YA). (gr. 7-12). 18.99 *(978-0-8050-9252-3(8),* 9780805092523, Holt, Henry & Co. Bks. For Young Readers) Holt, Henry & Co.

—Ruby Red. Bell, Anthea, tr. 2012. (Ruby Red Trilogy Ser.: 1). (ENG.). 352p. (YA). (gr. 7-12). pap. 10.99 *(978-0-312-55151-3(7),* 9780312551513) Square Fish.

Gleason, Colleen. The Chess Queen Enigma: A Stoker & Holmes Novel. 2016. (ENG.). 360p. (YA). (gr. 7-12). pap. 9.99 *(978-1-4521-5649-1(2))* Chronicle Bks. LLC.

—The Clockwork Scarab. 2014. (Stoker & Holmes Ser.: 1). (ENG.). 384p. (YA). (gr. 7-12). pap. 11.99 *(978-1-4521-2873-3(1))* Chronicle Bks. LLC.

—The Spiritglass Charade. 2014. (Stoker & Holmes Ser.: 2). (ENG., Illus.). 360p. (YA). (gr. 7-12). 17.99 *(978-1-4521-1071-4(9))* Chronicle Bks. LLC.

Golding, Julia. The Diamond of Drury Lane. 2009. (Cat Royal Adventure Ser.: 1). (ENG., Illus.). 448p. (J). (gr. 5-9). pap. 11.99 *(978-0-312-56123-9(7),* 9780312561239) Square Fish.

Goodman, Alison. The Dark Days Club. 2016. (Lady Helen Novel Ser.: Bk. 1). (ENG.). 496p. (YA). (gr. 9). 18.99 *(978-0-670-78547-6(4),* Viking Books for Young Readers) Penguin Young Readers Group.

Harvey, Alyxandra. A Breath of Frost. 2014. (Lovegrove Legacy Ser.). (ENG.). 512p. (YA). (gr. 7). pap. 10.99 *(978-0-8027-3444-0(8),* 9780802734440, Bloomsbury USA Childrens) Bloomsbury Publishing USA.

—Whisper the Dead. 2014. (Lovegrove Legacy Ser.: Bk. 2). (ENG.). 408p. (YA). (gr. 7). 17.99 *(978-0-8027-3750-2(1),* 9780802737502, Bloomsbury USA Childrens) Bloomsbury Publishing USA.

Hayner, Linda K. Ellanor's Exchange. 2005. 195p. (YA). 8.99 *(978-1-59166-462-8(4))* BJU Pr.

Hearn, Julie. Hazel. 2009. (ENG.). 400p. (YA). (gr. 7-18). 17.99 *(978-1-4169-2504-0(X),* Atheneum Bks. for Young Readers) Simon & Schuster Children's Publishing.

—Ivy. 2008. (ENG.). 368p. (YA). (gr. 7-18). 17.99 *(978-1-4169-2506-4(6),* Atheneum Bks. for Young Readers) Simon & Schuster Children's Publishing.

Hehir, Tim. Julius & the Soul-Catcher. 2016. (ENG., Illus.). 368p. (J). (gr. 5-9). 9.95 *(978-1-925240-17-7(7))* Text Publishing Co. AUS. Dist: Consortium Bk. Sales & Distribution.

Hendry, Frances. Quest for a Queen: The Jackdaw. 2006. pap. *(978-1-905665-05-1(9))* Pollinger In Print.

Henty, George Alfred. A March on London: A Story of Wat Tyler's Insurrection. 2003. (YA). pap. *(978-1-887159-93-7(2))* Preston-Speed Pubns.

Hopkinson, Deborah. A Boy Called Dickens. Hendrix, John, illus. 2012. (ENG.). 40p. (J). (gr. -1-3). 17.99 *(978-0-375-86732-3(5),* Schwartz & Wade Bks.) Random Hse. Children's Bks.

—The Great Trouble: A Mystery of London, the Blue Death, & a Boy Called Eel. 2013. (ENG.). 256p. (J). (gr. 5). 16.99 *(978-0-375-84818-6(5),* Knopf Bks. for Young Readers) Random Hse. Children's Bks.

Jinks, Catherine. How to Catch a Bogle. Watts, Sarah, illus. 2014. (How to Catch a Bogle Ser.: 1). (ENG.). 336p. (J). (gr. 5-7). pap. 7.99 *(978-0-544-33627-8(5),* HMH Books For Young Readers) Houghton Mifflin Harcourt Publishing Co.

—A Plague of Bogles. 2015. (How to Catch a Bogle Ser.: 2). (ENG.). 336p. (J). (gr. 5-7). pap. 6.99 *(978-0-544-54067-5(0));* (Illus.). 16.99 *(978-0-544-08747-7(X))* Houghton Mifflin Harcourt Publishing Co. (HMH Books For Young Readers).

Jones, Gareth P. Constable & Toop. 2013. (ENG.). 416p. (J). (gr. 3-7). 17.95 *(978-1-4197-0782-7(5),* Amulet Bks.) Abrams, Inc.

Larwood, Kieran. Freaks. 2013. (J). (ENG.). 256p. (gr. 5-9). 16.99 *(978-0-545-47424-5(8)); (978-0-545-47425-2(6))* Scholastic, Inc. (Chicken Hse., The).

Lawrence, Iain. The Convicts. 2006. 15.10 *(978-0-7569-6901-1(8))* Random House Children's Books GBR. Dist: Perfection Learning Corp.

Lee, Y. S. The Agency: A Spy in the House. 2016. (Agency Ser.). (ENG.). 352p. (YA). (gr. 7). pap. 7.99 *(978-0-7636-8748-9(0))* Candlewick Pr.

—The Agency: the Body at the Tower. 2016. (Agency Ser.). (ENG.). 352p. (YA). (gr. 7). pap. 7.99 *(978-0-7636-8750-2(2))* Candlewick Pr.

—Rivals in the City. 2015. (Agency Ser.). (ENG.). 304p. (YA). (gr. 7). 16.99 *(978-0-7636-5914-1(2))* Candlewick Pr.

Macauley, Jo. Plague, 1 vol. 2014. (Secrets & Spies Ser.). (ENG.). 224p. (gr. 4-7). 26.65 *(978-1-4342-7947-7(2))* Stone Arch Bks.

—Treason, 1 vol. 2014. (Secrets & Spies Ser.). (ENG.). 224p. (gr. 4-7). 26.65 *(978-1-4342-7946-0(4))* Stone Arch Bks.

MacColl, Michaela. Prisoners in the Palace: How Princess Victoria Became Queen with the Help of Her Maid, a Reporter, & a Scoundrel. 2013. (ENG.). 368p. (J). (gr. 8-17). pap. 9.99 *(978-1-4521-1958-8(9))* Chronicle Bks. LLC.

MacLean, Sarah. The Season. 2010. (ENG.). 352p. (J). (gr. 7). 8.99 *(978-0-545-04887-3(7),* Orchard Bks.) Scholastic, Inc.

Maddison, Kate. The Incredible Charlotte Sycamore. 2013. (ENG.). 336p. (J). 17.95 *(978-0-8234-2737-6(4))* Holiday Hse., Inc.

Maniscalco, Kerri. Stalking Jack the Ripper. (ENG., Illus.). (YA). (gr. 10-17). 2017. 352p. pap. 10.99 ***(978-0-316-27351-0(1))*** 2016. 336p. 18.99 *(978-0-316-27349-7(X))* 2016. 464p. 20.99 *(978-0-316-46428-4(7))* Little Brown & Co. (Jimmy Patterson).

McKay, Hilary. Wishing for Tomorrow: The Sequel to a Little Princess. Maland, Nick, illus. 2011. (ENG.). 288p. (J). (gr. 3-7). pap. 6.99 *(978-1-4424-0170-9(2),* McElderry, Margaret K. Bks.) McElderry, Margaret K. Bks.

Meyer, L. A. The Mark of the Golden Dragon: Being an Account of the Further Adventures of Jacky Faber, Jewel of the East, Vexation of the West & Pearl of the South China Sea. (Bloody Jack Adventures Ser.: 9). (ENG.). (YA). (gr. 9). 2013. 400p. pap. 9.99 *(978-0-544-00328-6(4))* 2011. 384p. 16.99 *(978-0-547-51764-3(5))* Houghton Mifflin Harcourt Publishing Co.

Morpurgo, Michael. Kaspar the Titanic Cat. Foreman, Michael, illus. 2012. 208p. (J). (gr. 3-7). 16.99 *(978-0-06-200618-9(5))* HarperCollins Pubs.

Moss, Marissa, illus. Mira's Diary: Bombs over London. 2014. (ENG.). 190p. (J). (gr. 2-8). 12.99 *(978-1-939547-12-5(1))* Creston Bks.

Munch, Donna. Dark Tales of the Tower. 2005. (J). pap. 9.95 *(978-1-932196-71-9(4))* WordWright.biz, Inc.

Myers, Walter Dean. Juba! (Illus.). 208p. (YA). (gr. 8). 2016. pap. 9.99 *(978-0-06-211273-6(2))* 2015. (ENG.). 17.99 *(978-0-06-211271-2(6),* HarperTeen) HarperCollins Pubs.

Nix, Garth. Newt's Emerald. 2015. (ENG.). 304p. (YA). (gr. 8-12). 18.99 *(978-0-06-236004-5(3))* HarperCollins Pubs.

Orczy, Emmuska. The Old Man in the Corner. 2008. (J). 8.99 *(978-1-59166-952-4(9))* BJU Pr.

Orme, David. Blitz. 2004. (Shades Ser.). (ENG.). 54p. (J). pap. *(978-0-237-52624-5(7))* Evans Brothers, Ltd.

—Blitz. 2007. (Sharp Shades Ser.). (ENG., Illus.). 64p. (J). (gr. 6-8). pap. 8.99 *(978-0-237-53444-8(4))* Evans Brothers, Ltd. GBR. Dist: Independent Pubs. Group.

Pratchett, Terry. Dodger. 368p. (YA). (gr. 8). 2013. pap. 9.99 *(978-0-06-200951-7(6))* 2012. 17.99 *(978-0-06-200949-4(4))* 2012. lib. bdg. 18.89 *(978-0-06-200950-0(8))* HarperCollins Pubs.

Pullman, Philip. The Ruby in the Smoke. 2009. 9.84 *(978-0-7848-2919-6(5),* Everbind) Marco Bk. Co.

—The Ruby in the Smoke. (Sally Lockhart Ser.: Bk. 1). (YA). 2008. (ENG.). 256p. (gr. 7). pap. 9.99 *(978-0-375-84516-1(X),* Ember) 2003. (Illus.). pap. 9.95 *(978-0-375-82545-3(2),* Knopf Bks. for Young Readers) Random Hse. Children's Bks.

—Two Crafty Criminals! And How They Were Captured by the Daring Detectives of the New Cut Gang. (ENG.). 288p. (J). (gr. 3-7). 2013. 7.99 *(978-0-307-93035-4(1),* Yearling) 2012. (Illus.). 16.99 *(978-0-375-87029-3(6),* Knopf Bks. for Young Readers) Random Hse. Children's Bks.

Rees, Celia. The Fool's Girl. 2010. (ENG.). 304p. (YA). (gr. 7-18). 16.99 *(978-1-59990-486-3(1),* 9781599904863, Bloomsbury USA Childrens) Bloomsbury Publishing USA.

Reeves, Amy Carol. Resurrection. 2014. (Ripper Novel Ser.: 3). (ENG.). 336p. (YA). pap. 9.99 *(978-0-7387-3877-2(8),* Flux) North Star Editions.

—Ripper. 2012. (Ripper Novel Ser.: 1). (ENG., Illus.). 360p. (YA). pap. 9.95 *(978-0-7387-3072-1(6),* Flux) North Star Editions.

Richards, Justin. Rewind Assassin. 2007. (Time Runners Ser.: 2). (ENG.). 208p. (J). (gr. 4-7). pap. 8.99 *(978-1-4169-2643-6(7))* Simon & Schuster, Ltd. GBR. Dist: Simon & Schuster, Inc.

Sands, Kevin. The Blackthorn Key. (Blackthorn Key Ser.: 1). (ENG., Illus.). (J). (gr. 5-9). 2016. 400p. pap. 7.99 *(978-1-4814-4652-5(5))* 2015. 384p. 18.99 *(978-1-4814-4651-8(7))* Simon & Schuster Children's Publishing. (Aladdin).

—The Blackthorn Key. 2016. lib. bdg. 18.40 *(978-0-606-38966-2(0))* Turtleback Bks.

Schlitz, Laura Amy. Splendors & Glooms. (ENG.). 400p. (J). 2014. (gr. 5-9). pap. 8.99 *(978-0-7636-6926-3(1))* 2012. (Illus.). (gr. 4-7). 17.99 *(978-0-7636-5380-4(2))* Candlewick Pr.

—Splendors & Glooms. 2014. (ENG.). (J). (gr. 4-7). lib. bdg. 18.60 ***(978-1-62765-443-2(7))*** Perfection Learning Corp.

—Splendors & Glooms. 2014. lib. bdg. 18.40 *(978-0-606-35170-6(1))* Turtleback Bks.

Selznick, Brian. The Marvels. 2016. (CHI.). (J). ***(978-986-479-039-5(0))*** Commonwealth Publishing Co., Ltd.

—The Marvels. Selznick, Brian, illus. 2015. (ENG., Illus.). 672p. (J). (gr. 5-7). 32.99 *(978-0-545-44868-0(9),* Scholastic Pr.) Scholastic, Inc.

Slade, Arthur G. The Hunchback Assignments. 2010. (Hunchback Assignments Ser.). (ENG.). 288p. (YA). (gr. 7). pap. 8.99 *(978-0-375-85403-3(7),* Ember) Random Hse. Children's Bks.

Small Acts of Amazing Courage. 2013. (ENG., Illus.). 240p. (J). (gr. 4-7). pap. 6.99 *(978-1-4424-9495-4(6),* Simon & Schuster/Paula Wiseman Bks.) Simon & Schuster/Paula Wiseman Bks.

Springer, Nancy. The Case of the Bizarre Bouquets. 2009. (Enola Holmes Mystery Ser.: 3). (ENG.). 176p. (J). (gr. 3-7). pap. 6.99 *(978-0-14-241390-6(9),* Puffin Books) Penguin Young Readers Group.

—The Case of the Left-Handed Lady. 2008. (Enola Holmes Mystery Ser.: 2). (ENG.). 256p. (J). (gr. 5-7). 7.99 *(978-0-14-241190-2(6),* Puffin Books) Penguin Young Readers Group.

—The Case of the Missing Marquess. 2007. (Enola Holmes Mystery Ser.: 1). (ENG.). 240p. (J). (gr. 3-7). 7.99 *(978-0-14-240933-6(2),* Puffin Books) Penguin Young Readers Group.

Stewart, Paul & Riddell, Chris. Barnaby Grimes: Phantom of Blood Alley. 2013. (Barnaby Grimes Ser.). (ENG.). 208p. (J). (gr. 3-7). 6.99 *(978-0-385-73700-5(9),* Yearling) Random Hse. Children's Bks.

Stratford, Jordan. The Case of the Missing Moonstone. Murphy, Kelly, illus. 2015. (Wollstonecraft Detective Agency Ser.). (ENG.). 240p. (J). (gr. 3-7). 16.99 *(978-0-385-75440-8(X),* Knopf Bks. for Young Readers) Random Hse. Children's Bks.

Stretton, Hesba. Lost Gip. 2003. (Golden Inheritance Ser.: Vol. 7). (Illus.). 121p. (J). *(978-0-921100-93-5(0))* Inheritance Pubns.

Turnbull, Ann. Forged in the Fire. 2007. (ENG.). 320p. (YA). (gr. 7-12). 16.99 *(978-0-7636-3144-4(2))* Candlewick Pr.

Updale, Eleanor. Montmorency's Revenge. 2007. 289p. (J). 25.66 *(978-1-4287-3312-1(4),* Follettbound) Follett School Solutions.

Waller, Sharon Biggs. A Mad, Wicked Folly. 2015. (ENG.). 448p. (YA). (gr. 7). pap. 10.99 *(978-0-14-242790-3(X),* Speak) Penguin Young Readers Group.

Webb, Holly. The Case of the Feathered Mask: The Mysteries of Maisie Hitchins, Book 4. Lindsay, Marion, illus. 2017. (Mysteries of Maisie Hitchins Ser.: 4). (ENG.). 176p. (J). (gr. 2-5). pap. 5.99 *(978-0-544-94884-6(X),* HMH Books For Young Readers) Houghton Mifflin Harcourt Publishing Co.

—The Case of the Vanishing Emerald. Lindsay, Marion, illus. 2016. (Mysteries of Maisie Hitchins Ser.: 2). (ENG.). 176p. (J). (gr. 2-5). pap. 5.99 *(978-0-544-66851-5(0),* HMH Books For Young Readers) Houghton Mifflin Harcourt Publishing Co.

Wilde, Oscar & Fisher, Eric Scott. The Picture of Dorian Gray, 1 vol. 2012. (Calico Illustrated Classics Ser.: No. 4). (ENG., Illus.). 112p. (J). (gr. 3-6). 27.07 *(978-1-61641-618-8(1))* Magic Wagon.

Winterson, Jeanette. The Battle of the Sun. 2010. (ENG.). 400p. (YA). 17.99 *(978-1-4088-0042-3(X),* 9781408800423, Bloomsbury USA Childrens) Bloomsbury Publishing USA.

Zettel, Sarah. Palace of Spies. 2013. (Palace of Spies Ser.: 1). (ENG.). 368p. (YA). (gr. 7). 16.99 *(978-0-544-07411-8(4))* Houghton Mifflin Harcourt Publishing Co.

LONDON (ENGLAND)—TOWER OF LONDON

see Tower of London (London, England)

LONELINESS

Apel, Melanie Ann. Let's Talk about Feeling Lonely. 2009. (Let's Talk Library). 24p. (gr. 2-3). 42.50 *(978-1-60853-442-5(1),* PowerKids Pr.) Rosen Publishing Group, Inc., The.

Hill, Z. B. Loneliness. Croft, Cindy, ed. 2014. (Causes & Effects of Emotions Ser.: 13). 64p. (J). (gr. 7-18). 23.95 *(978-1-4222-3075-6(9))* Mason Crest.

Marcovitz, Hal. A Lonely Guy's Guide: How to Deal. 2014. (ENG.). 64p. (J). (gr. 5-12). 15.95 *(978-1-62293-025-8(8))* Enslow Pubs., Inc.

Marcovitz, Hal & Snyder, Gail. A Guys' Guide to Loneliness. 2008. (Flip-It-Over Guides to Teen Emotions Ser.). (Illus.). 128p. (J). (gr. k-5). lib. bdg. 33.27 *(978-0-7660-2856-2(9))* Enslow Pubs., Inc.

Snyder, Gail. Lonely Girl? Girls Dealing with Feelings. 2014. (ENG.). 64p. (J). (gr. 5-12). 15.95 *(978-1-62293-055-5(X))* Enslow Pubs., Inc.

LONELINESS—FICTION

Ackerman, Peter. The Lonely Phone Booth. Dalton, Max, illus. 2010. (ENG.). 32p. (J). (gr. k-2). 16.95 *(978-1-56792-414-5(X))* Godine, David R. Pub.

Ackerman, Peter & Dalton, Max. The Lonely Typewriter. 2014. (Illus.). 32p. (J). 16.95 *(978-1-56792-518-0(9))* Godine, David R. Pub.

Adler, Denise. Thank You for Looking for Me. 2010. 20p. 12.99 *(978-1-4520-2438-7(3))* AuthorHouse.

Ahlberg, Allan. The Pencil. Ingman, Bruce, illus. 2012. (ENG.). 48p. (J). (gr. -1-3). pap. 6.99 *(978-0-7636-6088-8(4))* Candlewick Pr.

—The Pencil. Ingman, Bruce, illus. 2012. lib. bdg. 17.20 *(978-0-606-26942-1(8),* Turtleback) Turtleback Bks.

Andrews, Andy. Henry Hodges Needs a Friend, 1 vol. 2015. (ENG., Illus.). 32p. (J). 14.99 *(978-0-529-11576-8(X))* Nelson, Thomas Inc.

Bauer, Marion Dane. Little Dog, Lost. Bell, Jennifer A., illus. (ENG.). 208p. (J). (gr. 3-7). 2013. pap. 6.99 *(978-1-4424-3424-0(4))* 2012. 16.99 *(978-1-4424-3423-3(6))* Simon & Schuster Children's Publishing. (Atheneum Bks. for Young Readers).

Bernheimer, Kate. The Lonely Book. Sheban, Chris, illus. 2012. (ENG.). 40p. (J). (gr. -1-3). 17.99 *(978-0-375-86226-7(9),* Schwartz & Wade Bks.) Random Hse. Children's Bks.

Brandes, Wendy L. MJ's Camp Crisis. Lorenzet, Eleonora, illus. 2016. (Summer Camp Ser.). (ENG.). 96p. (gr. 4-6). lib. bdg. 24.65 *(978-1-4965-2598-7(1))* Stone Arch Bks.

Brett, Jan. Gingerbread Friends. Brett, Jan, illus. 2008. (ENG., Illus.). 32p. (J). (gr. -1-k). 17.99 *(978-0-399-25161-0(8),* G.P. Putnam's Sons Books for Young Readers) Penguin Young Readers Group.

Brun-Cosme, Nadine. Big Wolf & Little Wolf. Bedrick, Claudia Z., tr. from FRE. Tallec, Olivier & Sorman, Joy, illus. 2009. (ENG.). 32p. (J). (gr. -1-2). 16.95 *(978-1-59270-084-4(5))* Enchanted Lion Bks., LLC.

—Big Wolf & Little Wolf: The Little Leaf That Wouldn't Fall. Tallec, Olivier & Sorman, Joy, illus. 2009. (ENG.). 32p. (J). (gr. -1-2). 16.95 *(978-1-59270-088-2(8))* Enchanted Lion Bks., LLC.

Bruno, Linette Arthurton. Three's No Crowd: Two's Company. 2011. 33p. (J). pap. 15.95 *(978-1-4327-7125-6(6))* Outskirts Pr., Inc.

Bucher, Charlotte. Cecil Learns to Smile. 2010. 26p. (J). pap. 19.95 *(978-1-4327-4992-7(7))* Outskirts Pr., Inc.

Chan, Janette Shipston. The Tiny Tiger. 2010. 24p. (J). 13.50 *(978-1-4520-4106-3(7))* AuthorHouse.

Chisolm, Melinda. Remembering to Breathe. Cross, Jo Ellen, illus. 2009. 31p. pap. 24.95 *(978-1-60703-914-3(1))* America Star Bks.

Collier, Kristen. Joy the Jellyfish. 2007. (Illus.). 24p. (J). per. *(978-0-9797574-7-1(9)); (978-0-9797574-6-4(0))* Dragonfly Publishing, Inc.

Conner, Wendy Simpson. Princess of the Moon. (Illus.). (J). 16.95 *(978-1-889599-20-5(4))* Interstellar Publishing Co.

Crowley, Cath. A Little Wanting Song. 2011. (ENG.). 288p. (YA). (gr. 9). pap. 8.99 *(978-0-375-85449-1(5),* Ember) Random Hse. Children's Bks.

Cuthand, Beth. Sikihpsis. Cuthand, Stan, tr. Longman, Mary, illus. ed. 2007. (Little Duck Ser.). (CRE & ENG.). 28p. 17.00 *(978-1-894778-44-2(8))* Theytus Bks., Ltd. CAN. Dist: Univ. of Toronto Pr.

Davies, Benji. The Storm Whale. Davies, Benji, illus. 2014. (ENG., Illus.). 32p. (J). (gr. -1-3). 17.99 *(978-0-8050-9967-6(0),* 9780805099676, Holt, Henry & Co. Bks. For Young Readers) Holt, Henry & Co.

DeFelice, Cynthia C. Signal. 2011. (ENG.). 176p. (J). (gr. 5-8). pap. 8.99 *(978-0-312-61776-9(3),* 9780312617769) Square Fish.

Elliott, Rebecca. Zoo Girl. Elliott, Rebecca, illus. 2012. (ENG., Illus.). 32p. (J). (gr. k-2). 14.99 *(978-0-7459-6323-5(4))* Lion Hudson PLC GBR. Dist: Independent Pubs. Group.

Emberley, Rebecca. Spare Parts. Emberley, Ed, illus. 2015. (ENG.). 32p. (J). (gr. -1-2). 17.99 *(978-1-59643-723-4(5),* 9781596437234) Roaring Brook Pr.

Everson, Chance. Beginnings Vol. 2: Tales of the Mandrasaurs, Volume the Second. Geary, Steve, illus. 2004. cd-rom 9.95 *(978-0-9760303-1-7(4))* R.A.R.E. TALES.

Floyd, Lucy. A Place for Nicholas. McPhail, David, illus. 2005. (Green Light Readers Level 2 Ser.). 18p. (gr. k-2). 13.95 *(978-0-7569-5243-3(3))* Perfection Learning Corp.

Fogg, K. L. Serpent Tide. 2006. 16.95 *(978-1-59156-861-2(7))* Covenant Communications, Inc.

Foreman, Jack. Say Hello. Foreman, Michael, illus. 2012. (ENG.). 40p. (J). (gr. -1-2). pap. 6.99 *(978-0-7636-6087-1(6))* Candlewick Pr.

Foreman, Jack & Foreman, Michael. Say Hello. 2015. 40p. pap. 7.00 *(978-1-61003-409-8(0))* Center for the Collaborative Classroom.

Foreman, Michael. El Lorito Pelon. Diego, Rapi & Flores, Martha, illus. 2008. (SPA.). 30p. (J). (gr. 1-3). 15.99 *(978-1-930332-56-0(4))* Lectorum Pubns., Inc.

Galliez, Roxane Marie. Farewell Sadness. Lhomme, Sandrine, illus. 2010. 24p. (J). 9.99 *(978-0-8416-7139-3(7))* Hammond World Atlas Corp.

A Gift for Roo. 2013. (Illus.). 24p. pap. 10.95 *(978-1-61633-441-3(X))* Guardian Angel Publishing, Inc.

Gil, Carmen. Un Fantasma con Asma. Webster, Sarah, illus. 2004. (Libros para Sonar Ser.). (SPA.). 40p. (J). 15.99 *(978-84-8464-186-5(4))* Kalandraka Editora, S.L. ESP. Dist: Lectorum Pubns., Inc.

Gonzalez, Rigoberto & González, Rigoberto. Soledad Sigh-Sighs. Ibarra, Rosa, illus. 2014.Tr. of Soledad Suspiros. (ENG & SPA.). 32p. (J). pap. 8.95 *(978-0-89239-309-1(2),* Children's Book Press) Lee & Low Bks., Inc.

Gordon, Gus. Herman & Rosie. Gordon, Gus, illus. 2013. (ENG., Illus.). 32p. (J). (gr. 2-5). 17.99 *(978-1-59643-856-9(8),* 9781596438569) Roaring Brook Pr.

Green, Andi. The Lonely Little Monster. 2007. (WorryWoo Monsters Ser.). (Illus.). 68p. (J). 14.99 *(978-0-9792860-0-1(X))* Monsters in My Head, LLC, The.

Hannigan, Katherine. Emmaline & the Bunny. Hannigan, Katherine, illus. 2009. (ENG., Illus.). 112p. (J). (gr. 2-7). 16.99 *(978-0-06-162654-8(6),* Greenwillow Bks.) HarperCollins Pubs.

Hanson, Anders. Lone Shark, 1 vol. Haberstroh, Anne, illus. 2007. (Critter Chronicles Ser.). (ENG.). 24p. (J). (gr. k-3). lib. bdg. 24.21 *(978-1-59928-452-1(9),* SandCastle) ABDO Publishing Co.

Harnett, Katie, illus. Archie Snufflekins Oliver Valentine Cupcake Tiberius Cat. 2016. (ENG.). 32p. (J). (gr. -1-k). 16.95 *(978-1-909263-37-6(0))* Flying Eye Bks. GBR. Dist: Consortium Bk. Sales & Distribution.

Harris, Isobel. Little Boy Brown. François, André, illus. 2013. (ENG.). 48p. (J). (gr. -1-3). 15.95 *(978-1-59270-135-3(3))* Enchanted Lion Bks., LLC.

Harris, Odis Clinton. Wee Willie & the Lonely Pine. 2008. 23p. pap. 24.95 *(978-1-60563-741-9(6))* America Star Bks.

Hartnett, Sonya. What the Birds See. 2007. (ENG., Illus.). 208p. (YA). (gr. 9). pap. 7.99 *(978-0-7636-3680-7(0))* Candlewick Pr.

Henkes, Kevin. All Alone. Henkes, Kevin, illus. 2003. (ENG., Illus.). 40p. (J). (gr. -1-3). 16.99 *(978-0-06-054115-6(6),* Greenwillow Bks.) HarperCollins Pubs.

Hest, Amy. The Dog Who Belonged to No One. Bates, Amy, illus. 2008. (ENG.). 32p. (J). (gr. k-2). 18.95 *(978-0-8109-9483-6(6),* Abrams Bks. for Young Readers) Abrams, Inc.

Jacques, Florence Page. There Once Was a Puffin. Halpern, Shari, illus. 2016. (ENG.). 32p. (J). 15.95 *(978-0-7358-4245-8(0))* North-South Bks., Inc.

Jean, Penny. Holding Grace. 2008. 28p. pap. 24.95 *(978-1-60441-692-3(0))* America Star Bks.

Jennerich, Douglas Todd. My Little Half-Moon. Berube, Kate, illus. 2017. (ENG.). 32p. (J). (gr. k-3). 16.99 *(978-0-399-16901-4(6),* G.P. Putnam's Sons Books for Young Readers) Penguin Young Readers Group.

Jiang, Ji-Li. Lotus & Feather. Downing, Julie, illus. 2016. (ENG.). 40p. (J). (gr. -1-k). 17.99 *(978-1-4231-2754-3(4))* Disney Pr.

Johnston, Tony. The Cat with Seven Names. Davenier, Christine, illus. 2013. (ENG.). 40p. (J). (gr. k-3). 16.95 *(978-1-58089-381-7(3))* Charlesbridge Publishing, Inc.

Judd, Christopher M. Bearable Moments. 2005. (J). 16.95 *(978-0-9766666-1-5(8))* Arcadian Hse.

Judge, Chris. The Lonely Beast. Judge, Chris, illus. 2011. (Andersen Press Picture Books Ser.). (Illus.). 32p. (J). (gr. -1-4). 16.95 *(978-0-7613-8097-9(3))* Andersen Pr. GBR. Dist: Lerner Publishing Group.

Kadono, Eiko. Grandpa's Soup. Ichikawa, Santomi, illus. 2009. (ENG.). 40p. (J). (gr. -1-3). pap. 9.00 *(978-0-8028-5347-9(1),* Eerdmans Bks For Young Readers) Eerdmans, William B. Publishing Co.

Lael, Anita. The Little Brick House. Gresham, Delia, illus. 2012. 30p. 24.95 *(978-1-4626-5972-2(1))* America Star Bks.

Lamar, Gail Renfroe. Moon of the Wishing Night. Mask, Cynthia, illus. 2004. 32p. (J). 17.95 *(978-1-57966-047-5(9),* River City Kids) River City Publishing.

LaReau, Kara. Ugly Fish. Magoon, Scott, illus. 2006. (ENG.). 40p. (J). (gr. -1-3). 16.99 *(978-0-15-205082-5(5))* Houghton Mifflin Harcourt Publishing Co.

Lescuyer, Moira. Little Life Reminders. 2010. 16p. 7.95 *(978-1-4525-0037-9(1))* Get Published.

Linden, Dianne. Peacekeepers. (J). 82p. stu. ed. 9.95 *(978-1-55050-297-8(2));* 2003. (ENG., Illus.). 208p. (gr. 3-6). pap. 7.95 *(978-1-55050-271-8(9))* Coteau Bks. CAN. Dist: Fitzhenry & Whiteside, Ltd., Orca Bk. Pubs. USA.

Marie, Carissa. The Lonely Puppy. 2011. 20p. 12.95 *(978-1-4490-8264-2(5))* AuthorHouse.

Martin, Ann M. Everything for a Dog. 2011. (ENG.). 240p. (J). (gr. 4-7). pap. 7.99 *(978-0-312-67484-7(8),* 9780312674847) Square Fish.

Mercado, Ariano. Soccer Shoes from Americ. 2011. 36p. pap. *(978-1-4269-8962-9(8))* Trafford Publishing (UK) Ltd.

Montijo, Rhode. Cloud Boy/Nino Nube. Mlawer, Teresa, tr. from ENG. 2006. (SPA & ENG., Illus.). 24p. (J). (gr. -1-3). 12.99 *(978-1-933032-06-1(5))* Lectorum Pubns., Inc.

Moskowitz, Hannah. Teeth. 2013. (ENG.). 288p. (YA). (gr. 9). 17.99 *(978-1-4424-6532-9(8),* Simon Pulse) Simon Pulse.

Mullarkey, Lisa. Kianna, 1 vol. Franco, Paula, illus. 2016. (Pony Girls Ser.). (ENG.). 112p. (J). (gr. 1-4). 27.07 *(978-1-62402-130-5(1))* Magic Wagon.

Murphy, Sally. Pearl Verses the World. Potter, Heather, illus. 2011. (ENG.). 80p. (J). (gr. 3-7). 14.99 *(978-0-7636-4821-3(3))* Candlewick Pr.

Nesselrode, Sandra. Princess Kelsie & Her Special Gifts. 2008. 28p. pap. 19.95 *(978-1-4327-1708-7(1))* Outskirts Pr., Inc.

Parpan, Justin, illus. Gwango's Lonesome Trail. 2006. 32p. (J). (gr. -1-3). 15.95 *(978-1-60108-004-2(2))* Red Cygnet Pr.

Perry, Sarah. Clara's Road. 2005. 64p. (J). per. *(978-1-55306-945-4(5),* Epic Pr.) Essence Publishing.

Peterson, John C. Adam Has No Brothers. 2009. 20p. pap. 10.99 *(978-1-4490-3207-4(9))* AuthorHouse.

Pugliano Martin, Carol. Lonely Pluto. 2005. (J). pap. *(978-1-4108-4194-0(4))* Benchmark Education Co.

Rex, Adam. Nothing Rhymes with Orange. 2017. (ENG., Illus.). 48p. (J). (gr. k-3). 16.99 ***(978-1-4521-5443-5(0))*** Chronicle Bks. LLC.

Rice, Clay. The Lonely Shadow. 2013. (ENG., Illus.). 64p. (J). (gr. k-4). 19.95 *(978-1-938301-08-7(0))* Familius LLC.

Root, Phyllis. Scrawny Cat. Friend, Alison, illus. 2011. (ENG.). 40p. (J). (gr. -1-3). 16.99 *(978-0-7636-4164-1(2))* Candlewick Pr.

Ross, Bakthi. Millipede Curl. 2007. 17.00 *(978-0-8059-8820-8(3))* Dorrance Publishing Co., Inc.

Ryan, Rob. The Invisible Kingdom. 2016. (ENG., Illus.). 64p. (J). 19.95 *(978-1-56656-077-1(2),* Crocodile Bks.) Interlink Publishing Group, Inc.

Samarasinghe, Sara. Dalaina. 2007. 352p. pap. 18.95 *(978-0-9796997-2-0(9))* iTeenBooks Inc.

Schraff, Anne. Just Another Name for Lonely. 2008. (Passages 2000 Ser.). 107p. (J). lib. bdg. 13.95 *(978-0-7569-8402-1(5))* Perfection Learning Corp.

Sedoti, Chelsea. The Hundred Lies of Lizzie Lovett. 2017. (ENG.). 400p. (YA). (gr. 8-12). 17.99 *(978-1-4926-3608-3(8),* 9781492636083) Sourcebooks, Inc.

Sherry, Kevin. Turtle Island. 2014. (ENG.). 40p. (J). (gr. -1-k). 16.99 *(978-0-8037-3391-6(7),* Dial Bks) Penguin Young Readers Group.

Sleator, William & Monticone, Ann. The Phantom Limb. 2011. (ENG.). 224p. (YA). (gr. 9-17). 16.95 *(978-0-8109-8428-8(8),* Amulet Bks.) Abrams, Inc.

Staake, Bob. Bluebird. Staake, Bob, illus. 2013. (ENG., Illus.). 40p. (J). (gr. -1-3). 17.99 *(978-0-375-87037-8(7),* Schwartz & Wade Bks.) Random Hse. Children's Bks.

Standiford, Natalie. The Only Girl in School. 2016. (ENG.). 224p. (J). (gr. 3-7). 16.99 *(978-0-545-82996-0(8),* Scholastic Pr.) Scholastic, Inc.

Strange, Jason. To Wake the Dead, 1 vol. Parks, Phil, illus. 2011. (Jason Strange Ser.). (ENG.). 72p. (gr. 2-3). pap. 6.25 *(978-1-4342-3094-2(5));* 25.32 *(978-1-4342-2963-2(7))* Stone Arch Bks.

Stren, Patti. Hug Me. Date not set. (Illus.). 40p. (J). pap. 5.99 *(978-0-06-443754-7(X))* HarperCollins Pubs.

Sutton, Kelsey. The Lonely Ones. 2016. (ENG.). 240p. (J). (gr. 5). 16.99 *(978-0-399-17289-2(0),* Philomel Bks.) Penguin Young Readers Group.

Syrstad, Suzi. Timmy the Tiny Troubled Turtle, 1 vol. Maki, Tab, illus. 2009. 13p. pap. 24.95 *(978-1-61546-455-5(7))* PublishAmerica, Inc.

Taylor, Theodore. The Boy Who Could Fly Without a Motor. 2004. (ENG., Illus.). 168p. (J). (gr. 2-5). pap. 11.95 *(978-0-15-204767-2(0))* Houghton Mifflin Harcourt Publishing Co.

Teckentrup, Britta. Grumpy Cat. 2013. (ENG., Illus.). 26p. (J). (— 1). bds. 6.95 *(978-1-907967-48-1(6))* Boxer Bks., Ltd. GBR. Dist: Sterling Publishing Co., Inc.

Thomas, Leah. Because You'll Never Meet Me. 2015. (ENG.). 352p. (YA). (gr. 9-12). 17.99 *(978-1-61963-590-6(9),* 9781619635906, Bloomsbury USA Childrens) Bloomsbury Publishing USA.

Tillworth, Mary. A Friend at the Zoo/un Amigo en el Zoologico (Bubble Guppies) Gomez, Yuliana, tr. Random House Editors, illus. 2014. (Pictureback(R) Ser.). (ENG.). 24p. (J). (gr. -1-2). 3.99 *(978-0-385-37928-1(5),* Random Hse. Bks. for Young Readers) Random Hse. Children's Bks.

Turnbull, Victoria. Pandora. 2017. (ENG., Illus.). 32p. (J). (gr. -1-3). 16.99 *(978-0-544-94733-7(9),* Clarion Bks.) Houghton Mifflin Harcourt Trade & Reference Pubs.

Ungureanu, Dan. Nara & the Island. Ungureanu, Dan, illus. 2016. (ENG., Illus.). 32p. (J). (gr. -1-3). 17.99 *(978-1-5124-1793-7(9))* Andersen Pr. GBR. Dist: Lerner Publishing Group.

Van Lieshout, Elle & Van Os, Erik. The Wish. 2007. (ENG., Illus.). 32p. (J). (gr. 1-3). 15.95 *(978-1-932425-91-8(8),* Lemniscaat) Boyds Mills Pr.

Wall, Laura. Goose. Wall, Laura, illus. 2015. (ENG., Illus.). 48p. (J). (gr. -1-3). 12.99 *(978-0-06-232435-1(7))* HarperCollins Pubs.

Ward, Joyce Claudine. Nanny the Goat. 2008. 22p. pap. 24.95 *(978-1-4241-9139-0(4))* America Star Bks.

Webster, Frank V. The Boys of Bellwood School. 2004. reprint ed. pap. 20.95 *(978-1-4191-5509-3(1));* pap. 1.99 *(978-1-4192-5509-0(6))* Kessinger Publishing, LLC.

Weston Woods Staff, creator. The Story about Ping. 2011. 18.95 *(978-0-439-72893-5(2));* 29.95 *(978-0-439-73519-3(X));* 38.75 *(978-0-439-72894-2(0))* Weston Woods Studios, Inc.

Whisler, Barbara. Shag Finds a Home. Jackson, Kay, illus. 2008. 24p. pap. 24.95 *(978-1-60703-730-9(0))* America Star Bks.

White, Amanda. Sand Sister. Morales, Yuyi, illus. 2004. 32p. (J). 16.99 *(978-1-84148-617-8(5))* Barefoot Bks., Inc.

Yerkes, Jennifer. A Funny Little Bird. 2013. (ENG., Illus.). 48p. (J). (-3). 15.99 *(978-1-4022-8013-9(0),* 9781402280139, Sourcebooks Jabberwocky) Sourcebooks, Inc.

Yolen, Jane. Elsie's Bird. Small, David, illus. 2010. (ENG.). 40p. (J). (gr. k-3). 17.99 *(978-0-399-25292-1(4),* Philomel Bks.) Penguin Young Readers Group.

Zolotow, Charlotte. A Tiger Called Thomas. 2017. (J). *(978-1-4926-0171-5(3))* Sourcebooks, Inc.

LONG ISLAND (N.Y.)—FICTION

Blume, Judy. Then Again, Maybe I Won't. (J). 125p. pap. 3.99 *(978-0-8072-1445-9(0));* 2004. 164p. (gr. 5-9). pap. 29.00 incl. audio *(978-0-8072-0796-3(9),* LYA 354 SP) Random Hse. Audio Publishing Group. (Listening Library).

Corbett, Sue. 12 Again. 2007. (ENG.). 240p. (J). (gr. 5-18). 6.99 *(978-0-14-240729-5(1),* Puffin Books) Penguin Young Readers Group.

Couloumbis, Audrey. Not Exactly a Love Story. 2014. (ENG.). 288p. (YA). (gr. 7). pap. 9.99 *(978-0-375-86606-7(X),* Ember) Random Hse. Children's Bks.

Edwards, Melvin Neal. Sticks & Stones. 2013. 114p. (gr. 2-4). 19.88 *(978-1-4669-8482-0(1));* pap. 9.88 *(978-1-4669-8480-6(5))* Trafford Publishing.

Falk, Elizabeth Sullivan. Freedom's Fire. Wang, Qi Z., illus. 2004. (J). *(978-1-59336-321-5(4));* pap. *(978-1-59336-322-2(2))* Mondo Publishing.

George, McKelle. Speak Easy, Speak Love. 2017. 432p. (YA). (gr. 8). 17.99 ***(978-0-06-256092-6(1),*** Greenwillow Bks.) HarperCollins Pubs.

Greenwald, Lisa. Reel Life Starring Us. (ENG.). (YA). (gr. 3-7). 2013. 320p. pap. 7.95 *(978-1-4197-0426-0(5))* 2011. 304p. 16.95 *(978-1-4197-0026-2(X))* Abrams, Inc. (Amulet Bks.).

Jacobellis, Michelle. Dachshund Tales: Adventures on the Great South Bay. 2012. 60p. pap. 17.95 *(978-1-62709-104-6(1))* America Star Bks.

Korman, Gordon. Zoobreak. (J). 2010. (ENG.). 240p. (gr. 3-7). pap. 6.99 *(978-0-545-12500-0(6),* Scholastic Paperbacks) 2009. 230p. *(978-0-545-20027-1(X),* Scholastic Pr.) Scholastic, Inc.

Kristina Learns about Fishing. 2007. (J). *(978-0-9792728-0-6(7))* Tracepaper Bks. Inc.

Lane, Nathan & Elliott, Devlin. Naughty Mabel. Krall, Dan, illus. 2015. (Naughty Mabel Ser.). (ENG.). 48p. (J). (gr. -1-3). 17.99 *(978-1-4814-3022-7(X),* Simon & Schuster Bks. For Young Readers) Simon & Schuster Bks. For Young Readers.

Marino, Nan. Neil Armstrong Is My Uncle & Other Lies Muscle Man McGinty Told Me. 2009. (ENG.). 160p. (J). (gr. 3-7). 16.95 *(978-1-59643-499-8(6),* 9781596434998) Roaring Brook Pr.

Miller, Meredith. Little Wrecks. 2017. 368p. (YA). (gr. 9). 17.99 ***(978-0-06-247425-4(1),*** HarperTeen) HarperCollins Pubs.

Murray, Caryn Eve. Philomena's Homecoming: The (mostly) true story of a New York prairie dog's search for a Family. 2010. 48p. pap. 8.95 *(978-1-4502-2769-8(4))* iUniverse, Inc.

Patterson, James & Grabenstein, Chris. I Even Funnier: A Middle School Story. Park, Laura, illus. 2013. (I Funny Ser.: 2). (ENG.). 368p. (J). (gr. 3-7). 13.99 *(978-0-316-20697-6(0),* Jimmy Patterson) Little Brown & Co.

—I Totally Funniest: A Middle School Story. Park, Laura, illus. 2015. (I Funny Ser.). (ENG.). 336p. (J). (gr. 3-7). 13.99 *(978-0-316-40593-5(0),* Jimmy Patterson) Little Brown & Co.

Preller, James. Bystander. 2011. (ENG.). 256p. (YA). (gr. 5-9). pap. 8.99 *(978-0-312-54796-7(X),* 9780312547967) Square Fish.

Schmidt, Gary D. The Wednesday Wars. (ENG.). 272p. (J). (gr. 5-7). 2009. pap. 7.99 *(978-0-547-23760-2(X))* 2007. 16.99 *(978-0-618-72483-3(4))* Houghton Mifflin Harcourt Publishing Co.

—The Wednesday Wars. 2008. *(978-0-545-10562-0(5))* Scholastic, Inc.

—The Wednesday Wars. 2009. lib. bdg. 18.40 *(978-0-606-10573-6(5),* Turtleback) Turtleback Bks.

Shoemaker, E. W. Mother Nature & the Tales of North Fork. 2009. 220p. pap. 18.75 *(978-1-4389-8604-3(1))* AuthorHouse.

Thimble Islands Storybook. 2005. (J). *(978-1-59872-094-5(5))* Instant Pub.

Worthington, Heather Hill. Miles of Smiles: The Story of Roxey, the Long Island Rail Road Dog. Farnsworth, Bill, illus. 2010. (J). *(978-0-9792918-4-5(4));* pap. *(978-0-9792918-8-3(7))* Blue Marlin Pubns.

LONG ISLAND (N.Y.)—HISTORY

Castrovilla, Selene. By the Sword. Farnsworth, Bill, illus. 2007. (ENG.). 40p. (J). (gr. 5-7). 17.95 *(978-1-59078-427-3(8))* Boyds Mills Pr.

Shodell, Elly, ed. Particles of the Past: Sandmining on Long Island, 1870s-1980s. 2nd ed. (Illus.). 43p. (YA). (gr. 9-12). reprint ed. pap. 8.95 *(978-0-9615059-0-5(7))* Port Washington Public Library.

LONG ISLAND, BATTLE OF, NEW YORK, N.Y., 1776

Castrovilla, Selene. By the Sword. Farnsworth, Bill, illus. 2007. (ENG.). 40p. (J). (gr. 5-7). 17.95 *(978-1-59078-427-3(8))* Boyds Mills Pr.

LONGEVITY

see Old Age

LONGFELLOW, HENRY WADSWORTH, 1807-1882

Cody, Sherwin. Four American Poets. 2009. 198p. pap. 14.14 *(978-0-217-47860-1(3))* General Bks. LLC.

Kallio, Jamie. 12 Questions about Paul Revere's Ride. 2016. (Examining Primary Sources Ser.). (ENG., Illus.). 32p. (J). pap. 9.95 *(978-1-63235-336-8(9),* 12-Story Library) Pr. Room Editions LLC.

—12 Questions about "Paul Revere's Ride" 2017. (Examining Primary Sources Ser.). (ENG., Illus.). 32p. (J). (gr. 3-6). 21.95 *(978-1-63235-286-6(9))* Pr. Room Editions LLC.

LONGSTOCKING, PIPPI (FICTITIOUS CHARACTER)—FICTION

Lindgren, Astrid. Pippa Mediaslargas. (Pippi Longstocking Ser.).Tr. of Pippi Longstocking. (SPA.). (J). (gr. 3-5). pap. 9.95 *(978-84-261-2304-6(X),* JV304X) Juventud, Editorial ESP. Dist: Continental Bk. Co., Inc.

—Pippi Goes on Board. (Pippi Longstocking Ser.). 140p. (J). (gr. 3-5). pap. 3.99 *(978-0-8072-1401-5(9),* Listening Library) Random Hse. Audio Publishing Group.

—Pippi in the South Seas. (Pippi Longstocking Ser.). 125p. (J). (gr. 3-5). pap. 3.99 *(978-0-8072-1392-6(6),* Listening Library) Random Hse. Audio Publishing Group.

—Pippi Longstocking. 2013. (Puffin Chalk Ser.). (ENG.). 160p. (J). (gr. 3-7). pap. 7.99 *(978-0-14-242752-1(7),* Puffin Books) Penguin Young Readers Group.

—Pippi Longstocking. Nunally, Tina, tr. Child, Lauren, illus. 2011. (Pippi Longstocking Ser.). (ENG.). 208p. (J). (gr. 2-5). pap. 15.99 *(978-0-670-01404-0(4),* Viking Books for Young Readers) Penguin Young Readers Group.

—Pippi Longstocking. Lamborn, Florence, tr. from SWE. Glanzman, Louis S., illus. 2005. (Puffin Modern Classics Ser.). (ENG.). 160p. (J). (gr. 3-7). pap. 6.99 *(978-0-14-240249-8(4),* Puffin Books) Penguin Young Readers Group.

—Pippi Longstocking. (Pippi Longstocking Ser.). 160p. (J). (gr. 3-5). pap. 4.99 *(978-0-8072-1431-2(0),* Listening Library) Random Hse. Audio Publishing Group.

LOOKING GLASSES

see Mirrors

LOONS

Griek, Susan Vande. Loon, 1 vol. Reczuch, Karen, illus. 2011. (ENG.). 48p. (J). (gr. -1-2). 18.95 *(978-1-55498-077-2(1))* Groundwood Bks. CAN. Dist: Publishers Group West (PGW).

Hodgkins, Fran. Little Loon. Hayes, Karel, illus. 2015. (ENG.). 32p. (J). (gr. -1-3). 16.95 *(978-1-60893-372-3(5))* Down East Bks.

Kalz, Jill. Loons. 2003. (Birds Ser.). (Illus.). 24p. (J). lib. bdg. 21.35 *(978-1-58340-133-0(4))* Black Rabbit Bks.

Love, Donna. Loons: Diving Birds of the North, Vol. 1. Turley, Joyce Mihran, tr. Turley, Joyce Mihran, illus. rev. ed. 64p. (J). (gr. 4). pap. 12.00 *(978-0-87842-482-5(2),* 340) Mountain Pr. Publishing Co., Inc.

Newman, Aline Alexander. Lucky Leopards! 2014. (NGK Chapters Ser.). (ENG., Illus.). 112p. (J). (gr. 2-5). lib. bdg. 14.90 *(978-1-4263-1458-2(2),* National Geographic Children's Bks.) National Geographic Society.

Ring, Elizabeth. Loon at Northwood Lake. Oughton, Taylor, illus. 2005. (Smith Sonian's Backyard Ser.). 32p. (J). (gr. -1-3). (ENG.). 6.95 *(978-1-59249-482-8(X),* S5017); pap. 8.95 incl. audio *(978-1-59249-491-0(9),* SC5013) Soundprints.

Woodward, John. Loons. 2008. (Nature's Children Ser.). (Illus.). 52p. (J). *(978-0-7172-6258-8(8))* Grolier, Ltd.

LOONS—FICTION

Banks, Kate. Dillon Dillon. 2005. 149p. (gr. 3-7). 18.00 *(978-0-7569-5767-4(2))* Perfection Learning Corp.

Bollendorf, Robert F. & Makely, William. Flight of the Loon: One Family's Battle with Recovery. Donlon, Eleanor, ed. 2007. 8.95 *(978-1-932514-15-5(5))* College of DuPage Pr.

Fuller, Sandy Fergus. Moon Loon. 2010. (ENG.). 32p. (J). (gr. k-17). 15.95 *(978-1-58979-453-5(2))* Taylor Trade Publishing.

Fuller, Sandy Ferguson. Moon Loon. 2010. (J). 7.95 *(978-1-58979-454-2(0));* (ENG.). 32p. pap. 7.95 *(978-1-58979-455-9(9))* Taylor Trade Publishing.

Holmes, Katherine L. The Wide Awake Loons. 2013. 188p. pap. 9.95 *(978-1-938083-18-1(0))* Silver Knight Publishing, LLC.

Lloyd, Jennifer & Wakelin, Kirsti Anne. Looking for Loons. 2007. (ENG., Illus.). 32p. (J). (gr. -1-3). 16.95 *(978-1-894965-54-5(X))* Simply Read Bks. CAN. Dist: Ingram Publisher Services.

Lowe, Tom. Louie the Loon & the Moon. Leadlove, Ben, illus. 2011. 28p. pap. 11.00 *(978-1-61170-030-5(2))* Robertson Publishing.

Trottier, Maxine. Loon Rock. Sylliboy, Helen, tr. Christmas, Dozay, illus. (ENG.). 22p. (J). (gr. k-2). pap. *(978-0-920336-84-7(1))* Cape Breton Univ. Pr.

LORD'S DAY

see Sabbath

LORD'S PRAYER

Bus, Sabrina. Our Father. Deneux, Xavier, illus. 2nd ed. 2006. (ENG.). 12p. (J). (gr. -1). 8.00 *(978-0-8028-5313-4(7),* Eerdmans Bks For Young Readers) Eerdmans, William B. Publishing Co.

David C. Cook Publishing Company Staff. The Lord's Prayer. 2008. (Pencil Fun Bks). 16p. (J). pap. 9.90 *(978-0-7814-4901-4(4))* Cook, David C.

DeVries, Catherine. Let's Learn about the Lord's Prayer. Jackson, Ryan, illus. 2015. (HeartSmart Ser.). (ENG.). 26p. (J). bds. 10.99 *(978-0-7814-1269-8(2))* Cook, David C.

Ladwig, Tim, illus. The Lord's Prayer. 2004. 32p. pap. 8.50 *(978-0-8028-5238-0(6));* (J). (gr. -1-3). 17.00 *(978-0-8028-5180-2(0))* Eerdmans, William B. Publishing Co.

M. A. Benjamin. When I Pray: The Lord's Prayer. 2009. 16p. pap. 9.99 *(978-1-4389-6317-4(3))* AuthorHouse.

Oberthür, Rainer. Our Father. Nascimbeni, Barbara, illus. 2016. (ENG.). 58p. (J). 16.00 *(978-0-8028-5468-1(0),* Eerdmans Bks For Young Readers) Eerdmans, William B. Publishing Co.

Our Father, 1 vol. 2014. (ENG., Illus.). 32p. (J). 9.99 *(978-1-78128-144-4(0),* Candle Bks.) Lion Hudson PLC GBR. Dist: Kregel Pubns.

Pingry, Patricia A. The Story of the Lord's Prayer. Garvin, Elaine, illus. (ENG.). (J). 2008. 24p. bds. 6.95 *(978-0-8249-6519-8(1))* 2008. 28p. (gr. -1-k). pap. 3.99 *(978-0-8249-5555-7(2))* 2005. 26p. (gr. -1-k). 9.95 *(978-0-8249-6637-9(6))* Worthy Publishing. (Ideal Pubns.).

Rock, Lois. Our Father in Heaven: The Lord's Prayer for Children. Rivers, Ruth, illus. 2004. (ENG.). 29p. (J). (gr. -1-2). 11.00 *(978-0-7459-4644-3(5),* Lion Books) Lion Hudson PLC GBR. Dist: Independent Pubs. Group.

Rock, Lois & Lush, Debbie. The Lord's Prayer & Ten Commandments: Bible Words to Know & Treasure. 2008. (ENG., Illus.). 64p. (J). (gr. -1-2). 5.99 *(978-0-7459-4941-3(X))* Lion Hudson PLC GBR. Dist: Independent Pubs. Group.

Walker, Joni. Follow & Do Books: The Lord's Prayer. Walker, Joni, illus. 2004. (Follow & Do Ser.). (Illus.). 32p. (J). 7.49 *(978-0-7586-0678-5(8))* Concordia Publishing Hse.

Warner Press, creator. Learning the Lord's Prayer: Coloring & Activity Book. 2008. (J). (gr. -1-3). pap. 11.34 *(978-1-59317-323-4(7))* Warner Pr., Inc.

Zondervan Staff & Warren, Rick. The Lord's Prayer, 1 vol. Watson, Richard Jesse, illus. 2011. (Illustrated Scripture Ser.). (ENG.). 40p. (J). (gr. -1-2). 16.99 *(978-0-310-71086-8(3))* Zonderkidz.

LOS ANGELES (CALIF.)

Andrade, Mary J. Uarhiri sapirhatiecheri Jukambekua: La velacion de los Angelitos. Murguia, Jose J., illus. Andrade, Mary J., photos by. 2005. Orig. Title: The Vigil of the Little Angels. 40p. (J). (gr. 3-6). pap. 9.95 *(978-0-9665876-8-5(5))* La Oferta Publishing Co.

Barber, Nicola. Los Angeles. Cooper, Adrian, photos by. 2007. (Global Cities Ser.). (Illus.). 64p. (gr. 5-8). lib. bdg. 30.00 *(978-0-7910-8847-0(2),* Chelsea Hse.) Facts On File, Inc.

Cohen, Judith L. & Friend, Robyn. Los Angeles' Water Future. Katz, David A., illus. 2015. 40p. (J). pap. 7.00 *(978-1-935999-11-9(7))* Cascade Pass, Inc.

Crewe, Sabrina. Los Angeles. 2004. (Great Cities of the World Ser.). (Illus.). 48p. (gr. 5-12). lib. bdg. 31.00 *(978-0-8368-5029-1(7),* Gareth Stevens Secondary Library) Stevens, Gareth Publishing LLLP.

Epstein, Brad M. Los Angeles 101: My First City-Board-book. l.t. ed. 2009. (Illus.). 24p. (J). *(978-1-60730-002-1(8),* 101 Bk.) Michaelson Entertainment.

Flatt, Lizann. Life in a Suburban City. 2010. (Learn about Urban Life Ser.). (ENG., Illus.). 32p. (J). (gr. 3-6). lib. bdg. *(978-0-7787-7394-8(9));* (gr. 4-9). pap. *(978-0-7787-7404-4(X))* Crabtree Publishing Co.

Friend, Robyn C. & Cohen, Judith Love. A Cleaner Port; A Brighter Future: The Greening of the Port of Los Angeles. Katz, David Arthur, illus. 2011. 46p. (J). 13.95 *(978-1-935999-01-0(X));* pap. 7.00 *(978-1-935999-00-3(1))* Cascade Pass, Inc.

Grabowski, John F. Alton Brown. 2012. (J). *(978-1-61900-007-0(5))* Eldorado Ink.

MacMillan, Dianne M. Los Angeles Area Missions. 2007. (Exploring California Missions Ser.). (Illus.). 64p. (J). lib. bdg. 27.93 *(978-0-8225-0898-4(2),* Lerner Pubns.) Lerner Publishing Group.

Ogintz, Eileen. Los Angeles County - Kid's Guide. 2013. (Kid's Guides Ser.). (ENG., Illus.). 160p. pap. 12.95 *(978-0-7627-9218-4(3))* Globe Pequot Pr., The.

Polsky, Cheryl. Libby & Her Friends Explore Los Angeles, Californi. 2012. 28p. pap. 17.99 *(978-1-4772-2125-9(5))* AuthorHouse.

Skewes, John & Mullin, Michael. Larry Gets Lost in Los Angeles. Skewes, John, illus. 2009. (Larry Gets Lost Ser.). (ENG., Illus.). 32p. (J). (gr. -1-2). 17.99 *(978-1-57061-568-9(3),* Little Bigfoot) Sasquatch Bks.

When Los Angeles Was Very Young 1849-1866. 2005. (YA). *(978-1-59872-140-9(2))* Instant Pub.

Worth, Richard. Los Angeles Police Department. 2011. (Law Enforcement Agencies Ser.). (Illus.). 128p. (J). (gr. 6-12). 35.00 *(978-1-60413-656-2(1),* Chelsea Hse.) Facts On File, Inc.

Zimmerman, Bill. City Doodles: Los Angles, 1 vol. 2013. (ENG., Illus.). 240p. (J). pap. 9.99 *(978-1-4236-3470-6(5))* Gibbs Smith, Publisher.

LOS ANGELES (CALIF.)—FICTION

Anderson, Dwayne. Partially Human. 2006. (YA). per. 12.00 *(978-0-9788612-0-9(5))* Capri Publishing.

Anderson, Laurie Halse. Acting Out, 14 vols. 2012. (Vet Volunteers Ser.: 14). (ENG.). 144p. (J). (gr. 3-7). pap. 6.99 *(978-0-14-241676-1(2),* Puffin Books) Penguin Young Readers Group.

Arcos, Carrie. There Will Come a Time. 2014. (ENG., Illus.). 320p. (YA). (gr. 9). 17.99 *(978-1-4424-9585-2(5),* Simon Pulse) Simon Pulse.

Arnold, Elana K. Infandous. 2015. (ENG.). 200p. (YA). (gr. 8-12). 18.99 *(978-1-4677-3849-1(2))* Lerner Publishing Group.

Aston, Dianna Hutts. Dream Something Big: The Story of the Watts Towers. Roth, Susan L., illus. 2011. (ENG.). 40p. (J). (gr. k-3). 17.99 *(978-0-8037-3245-2(7),* Dial Bks) Penguin Young Readers Group.

Barrett, Michellene. Englisha & David's Adventurous Vacation. 2009. 86p. (gr. 3-6). pap. 9.95 *(978-1-4401-2319-1(5))* iUniverse, Inc.

Bell, Taryn. In the Spotlight. 2010. (ENG.). 256p. pap. 8.99 *(978-0-545-21444-5(0))* Scholastic, Inc.

Bencastro, Mario. A Promise to Keep. Giersbach-Rascon, Susan, tr. from SPA. 2005. 134p. (J). (gr. 3-7). pap. 9.95 *(978-1-55885-457-4(6),* Piñata Books) Arte Publico Pr.

Block, Francesca Lia. Dangerous Angels. 2010. (Weetzie Bat Ser.). (ENG.). 496p. (YA). (gr. 9). pap. 9.99 *(978-0-06-200740-7(8),* HarperTeen) HarperCollins Pubs.

—Love in the Time of Global Warming. 2013. (ENG.). 240p. (YA). (gr. 9-13). 16.99 *(978-0-8050-9627-9(2),* 9780805096279, Holt, Henry & Co. Bks. For Young Readers) Holt, Henry & Co.

—Pink Smog: Becoming Weetzie Bat. 2012. (Weetzie Bat Ser.: 6). (ENG.). 208p. (YA). (gr. 9). 17.99 *(978-0-06-156598-4(9),* HarperTeen) HarperCollins Pubs.

—Pretty Dead. 2010. (ENG.). 224p. (YA). (gr. 9). pap. 8.99 *(978-0-06-154787-4(5),* HarperTeen) HarperCollins Pubs.

—Wasteland. 2003. (Illus.). 160p. (J). 16.89 *(978-0-06-028645-3(8),* Cotler, Joanna Books) HarperCollins Pubs.

—The Waters & the Wild. 2009. (ENG.). 128p. (YA). (gr. 9-18). 16.99 *(978-0-06-145244-4(0),* HarperTeen) HarperCollins Pubs.

—Weetzie Bat. 2004. (Weetzie Bat Ser.: 1). (ENG.). 128p. (YA). (gr. 9). pap. 8.99 *(978-0-06-073625-5(9),* HarperTeen) HarperCollins Pubs.

Bloom, M. Beth. Drain You. 2012. (ENG.). 400p. (YA). (gr. 8). pap. 8.99 *(978-0-06-203686-5(6),* HarperTeen) HarperCollins Pubs.

Bloom, Susan & Bertram, Debbie. City Hall: The Heart of Los Angeles. Leijten, Aileen, illus. 2015. (ENG.). 100p. (J). 9.95 *(978-1-931290-24-1(5),* Smallfellow Pr.) Tallfellow Pr.

Bowler, Michael J. Children of the Knight. 2016. (ENG., Illus.). (J). 29.99 ***(978-1-63477-952-4(5))*** 2013. 344p. pap. 17.99 *(978-1-62380-655-2(0))* Dreamspinner Pr. (Harmony Ink Pr.).

Brian, Kate, pseud. The Princess & the Pauper. 2004. 266p. (J). (gr. 5-9). 14.65 *(978-0-7569-3531-3(8))* Perfection Learning Corp.

—The Princess & the Pauper. 2004. (ENG., Illus.). 272p. (YA). reprint ed. mass mkt. 6.99 *(978-0-689-87042-2(6),* Simon Pulse) Simon Pulse.

Brightwood, Laura, illus. Growing up in East L. A. Brightwood, Laura, . 2006. (J). *(978-0-9779290-8-5(6))* 3-C Institute for Social Development.

Brody, Jessica. 52 Reasons to Hate My Father. 2013. (ENG.). 368p. (YA). (gr. 7-12). pap. 10.99 *(978-1-250-02459-6(5),* 9781250024596) Square Fish.

Bryan, Sabrina & DeVillers, Julia. Princess of Gossip. 2008. (ENG.). 384p. pap. 23.99 *(978-1-4165-7065-3(9),* MTV Bks.) MTV Books.

Buxbaum, Julie. Tell Me Three Things. (ENG.). (YA). (gr. 7). 2017. 352p. pap. 9.99 ***(978-0-553-53567-9(6),*** Ember) 2016. 336p. 17.99 *(978-0-553-53564-8(1),* Delacorte Pr.) 2016. 336p. lib. bdg. 20.99 *(978-0-553-53565-5(X),* Delacorte Pr.) Random Hse. Children's Bks.

Byng, Georgia. Molly Moon Stops the World. (J). 2004. (Illus.). 384p. 16.99 *(978-0-06-051410-5(8))* 2005. (Molly Moon Ser.: 2). (ENG.). 416p. (gr. 3-7). reprint ed. pap. 7.99 *(978-0-06-051415-0(9))* HarperCollins Pubs.

Castan, Mike. The Price of Loyalty. 2011. (ENG., Illus.). 256p. (YA). (gr. 7-18). 17.95 *(978-0-8234-2268-5(2))* Holiday Hse., Inc.

Castellucci, Cecil. Beige. (ENG., Illus.). 320p. (YA). (gr. 9). 2009. pap. 8.99 *(978-0-7636-4232-7(0))* 2007. 16.99 *(978-0-7636-3066-9(7))* Candlewick Pr.

—Boy Proof. (ENG.). 208p. (YA). (gr. 9-18). 2005. 15.99 *(978-0-7636-2333-3(4))* 2006. reprint ed. per. 8.99 *(978-0-7636-2796-6(8))* Candlewick Pr.

—Boy Proof, 4 vols. 2005. (YA). 62.75 *(978-1-4193-5131-0(1))* Recorded Bks., Inc.

—The Queen of Cool. 2007. (ENG., Illus.). 176p. (YA). (gr. 9-18). pap. 7.99 *(978-0-7636-3413-1(1))* Candlewick Pr.

Chambers, Veronica. The Go-Between. 2017. (ENG.). 208p. (YA). (gr. 7). 16.99 ***(978-1-101-93095-3(0),*** Delacorte Pr.) Random Hse. Children's Bks.

Chapman, Brenda. Trail of Secrets. 2009. (Jennifer Bannon Mystery Ser.: 4). (ENG.). 144p. (YA). (gr. 7-18). pap. 9.95 *(978-1-894917-76-6(6),* Napoleon & Co.) Dundurn CAN. Dist: Ingram Publisher Services.

Clare, Cassandra. Lady Midnight. 2016. (Dark Artifices Ser.: 1). (ENG., Illus.). 720p. (YA). (gr. 9-12). 24.99 *(978-1-4424-6835-1(1),* McElderry, Margaret K. Bks.) McElderry, Margaret K. Bks.

—Lady Midnight. 2017. lib. bdg. 26.95 ***(978-0-606-40535-5(6))*** Turtleback Bks.

Cocks, Heather & Morgan, Jessica. Messy. 2013. (ENG.). 368p. (YA). (gr. 7-17). pap. 9.00 *(978-0-316-09828-1(0),* Poppy) Little, Brown Bks. for Young Readers.

—Spoiled. 2012. (ENG.). 384p. (YA). (gr. 10-17). pap. 10.00 *(978-0-316-09827-4(2),* Poppy) Little, Brown Bks. for Young Readers.

Cohn, Diana. iSi, Se Puede! Delgado, Francisco, illus. 2009.Tr. of Yes, We Can! (SPA & ENG.). 32p. (J). (gr. k-2). pap. 7.95 *(978-0-938317-89-0(X))* Cinco Puntos Pr.

Coleman, Rowan. Shooting Star. 2011. (ENG.). 256p. (J). (gr. 6-9). pap. 9.99 *(978-0-00-725812-3(7))* HarperCollins Pubs. Ltd. GBR. Dist: HarperCollins Pubs.

Conrad, Lauren. The Fame Game. 2012. (YA). (Fame Game Ser.: 1). (ENG.). 336p. (gr. 9). pap. 10.99 *(978-0-06-207519-2(5));* 313p. 12.99 *(978-0-06-209271-7(5))* HarperCollins Pubs.

—Infamous. 2013. (Fame Game Ser.: 3). (ENG.). 288p. (YA). (gr. 9). 18.99 *(978-0-06-207984-8(0))* HarperCollins Pubs.

—Infamous. 2013. 277p. (J). 12.00 *(978-0-06-224756-8(5))* HarperCollins Pubs.

—L. A. Candy. (L. A. Candy Ser.: 1). (ENG.). (YA). (gr. 9-18). 2010. 352p. pap. 9.99 *(978-0-06-176759-3(X))* 2009. 336p. 17.99 *(978-0-06-176758-6(1))* HarperCollins Pubs.

—Sugar & Spice. (L. A. Candy Ser.: 3). (ENG.). 288p. (YA). (gr. 9). 2011. pap. 9.99 *(978-0-06-176763-0(8))* 2010. 17.99 *(978-0-06-176762-3(X))* HarperCollins Pubs.

—Sweet Little Lies. 2010. (L. A. Candy Ser.: 2). (YA). (ENG.). 336p. (gr. 9). pap. 9.99 *(978-0-06-176761-6(1));* 309p. 9.99 *(978-0-06-198572-0(4))* HarperCollins Pubs.

Currier, Katrina Saltonstall. Kai's Journey to Gold Mountain: An Angel Island Story. 2004. 40p. 16.95 *(978-0-9667352-7-7(7));* (Illus.). 44p. (J). pap. 10.95 *(978-0-9667352-4-6(2))* Angel Island Assoc.

Daswani, Kavita. Lovetorn. 2012. (ENG.). 256p. (YA). (gr. 8). 17.99 *(978-0-06-167311-5(0),* HarperTeen) HarperCollins Pubs.

De la Cruz, Melissa. Angels on Sunset Boulevard. 2008. (Angels on Sunset Boulevard Ser.: Bk. 1). (ENG.). 240p. (YA). (gr. 9-18). pap. 8.99 *(978-1-4169-3991-7(1),* Simon & Schuster Bks. For Young Readers) Simon & Schuster Bks. For Young Readers.

De la Peña, Matt. Ball Don't Lie. 2007. (ENG.). 288p. (YA). (gr. 9-12). pap. 9.99 *(978-0-385-73425-7(5),* Ember) Random Hse. Children's Bks.

Del Rio, Adam. Teo in Palo Verde/Teo en Palo Verde. III, Noel, illus. 2008. (ENG & SPA.). 32p. (J). (gr. k-3). pap. 8.95 *(978-1-60448-001-6(7))* Lectura Bks.

Divine, L. The Fight. 2008. (Drama High Ser.: Vol. 1). 202p. (gr. 8-12). 19.95 *(978-0-7569-8830-2(6))* Perfection Learning Corp.

—Hustlin' 2009. (Drama High Ser.: 7). lib. bdg. 26.95 *(978-0-606-00156-4(5),* Turtleback) Turtleback Bks.

—Keep It Movin' 2009. (Drama High Ser.: 8). lib. bdg. 20.80 *(978-0-606-00157-1(3),* Turtleback) Turtleback Bks.

Dixon, Franklin W. Top Ten Ways to Die. 2006. 169p. (J). lib. bdg. 16.92 *(978-1-4242-0390-1(2))* Fitzgerald Bks.

Dumas Lachtman, Ofelia. Looking for la Unica. 2004. (ENG & SPA., Illus.). 190p. (J). pap. 9.95 *(978-1-55885-412-3(6),* Piñata Books) Arte Publico Pr.

Ewing, Lynne. Daughters of the Moon, Vol. 1. 2010. (ENG.). 848p. (J). (gr. 7-17). pap. 9.99 *(978-1-4231-3450-3(8))* Disney Pr.

Fleischman, Paul. Breakout. 2003. (ENG.). 160p. (J). 15.95 *(978-0-8126-2696-4(6))* Cricket Bks.

—Breakout. 2005. (ENG.). 144p. (YA). (gr. 7). reprint ed. pap. 6.99 *(978-0-689-87189-4(9),* Simon Pulse) Simon Pulse.

Fowler, Elle & Fowler, Blair. Beneath the Glitter. 2013. (Sophia & Ava London Ser.: 1). (ENG.). 288p. (YA). (gr. 7). pap. 17.99 *(978-1-250-01715-4(7),* 9781250017154, St. Martin's Griffin) St. Martin's Pr.

—Where Beauty Lies. 2014. (Sophia & Ava London Ser.: 2). (ENG.). 272p. (YA). (gr. 7). pap. 9.99 *(978-1-250-01714-7(9),* 9781250017147, St. Martin's Griffin) St. Martin's Pr.

Francis, Pauline, retold by. The Mark of Zorro. 2010. (Essential Classics - Adventure Ser.). (Illus.). 48p. pap. *(978-0-237-54093-7(2))* Evans Brothers, Ltd.

Gallagher, Toni. Twist My Charm - The Popularity Spell. 2015. (Twist My Charm Ser.). (ENG.). 272p. (J). (gr. 3-7). 16.99 *(978-0-553-51115-4(7),* Random Hse. Bks. for Young Readers) Random Hse. Children's Bks.

—Twist My Charm: the Popularity Spell. 2016. (Twist My Charm Ser.). (ENG.). 288p. (J). (gr. 3-7). 6.99 *(978-0-553-51118-5(1),* Yearling) Random Hse. Children's Bks.

Gamble, Adam. Good Night Los Angeles. Kelly, Cooper, illus. 2007. (Good Night Our World Ser.). (ENG.). 20p. (J). (gr. k — 1). bds. 9.95 *(978-1-60219-009-2(7))* Good Night Bks.

Garfinkle, D. L. Stuck in the 70's. 2007. 182p. (YA). *(978-1-4287-4661-9(7))* Penguin Publishing Group.

Green, Tim. Pinch Hit. (ENG.). (J). (gr. 3-7). 2013. 336p. pap. 6.99 *(978-0-06-201247-0(9))* 2012. 320p. 16.99 *(978-0-06-201246-3(0))* HarperCollins Pubs.

Gurevich, Margaret. Made to Measure. Hagel, Brooke, illus. 2016. (Chloe by Design Ser.). (ENG.). 96p. (gr. 5-8). lib. bdg. 25.32 *(978-1-4965-3262-6(7))* Stone Arch Bks.

Haugaard, Kay. No Place. 2nd ed. 2007. (ENG., Illus.). 140p. (J). (gr. 2-8). per. 6.95 *(978-1-57131-675-2(2))* Milkweed Editions.

Howland, Leila. Hello, Sunshine. 2017. (ENG.). 368p. (YA). (gr. 9-17). 17.99 ***(978-1-4847-2545-0(X))*** Hyperion Bks. for Children.

Jacobs, Lily. The Littlest Bunny in Los Angeles: An Easter Adventure. 2015. (ENG.). 32p. (J). (-3). 9.99 *(978-1-4926-1102-8(6),* Sourcebooks Jabberwocky) Sourcebooks, Inc.

James, Eric. A Halloween Scare in Los Angeles. Le Ray, Marina, illus. 2015. (ENG.). 32p. (J). (-5). 9.99 *(978-1-4926-2379-3(2),* 9781492623793, Sourcebooks Jabberwocky) Sourcebooks, Inc.

—Santa's Sleigh Is on Its Way to Los Angeles: A Christmas Adventure. Dunn, Robert, illus. 2016. (ENG.). 32p. (J). (-2). 12.99 *(978-1-4926-4333-3(5),* 9781492643333, Sourcebooks Jabberwocky) Sourcebooks, Inc.

Johnston, Tony. Any Small Goodness. Colón, Raúl, illus. 2003. (Any Small Goodness Ser.). (ENG.). 128p. (J). (gr. 2-5). per. 6.99 *(978-0-439-23384-2(4),* Scholastic Paperbacks) Scholastic, Inc.

—Any Small Goodness: A Novel of the Barrio. Colón, Raúl, illus. 2005. (Reader's Workshop Ser.). (ENG.). 120p. (C). pap. 19.95 *(978-0-7362-2797-1(0))* CENGAGE Learning.

Kaplan, Isabel. Hancock Park. 2010. (ENG.). 272p. (YA). (gr. 9). pap. 8.99 *(978-0-06-137370-1(2),* HarperTeen) HarperCollins Pubs.

Kelly, David A. The L. A. Dodger. Meyers, Mark, illus. 2011. (Ballpark Mysteries Ser.: Bk. 3). (ENG.). 112p. (J). (gr. 1-4). 4.99 *(978-0-375-86885-6(2),* Random Hse. Bks. for Young Readers) Random Hse. Children's Bks.

Klingele, Lindsey. The Broken World. 2017. 432p. (YA). (gr. 8). 17.99 ***(978-0-06-238036-4(2),*** HarperTeen) HarperCollins Pubs.

Kogler, Jennifer Anne. Ruby Tuesday. 2005. (ENG.). 320p. (J). (gr. 7-18). 15.99 *(978-0-06-073956-0(8))* HarperCollins Pubs.

Lazebnik, Claire. Epic Fail. 2011. (ENG.). 304p. (YA). (gr. 8-18). pap. 9.99 *(978-0-06-192126-1(2),* HarperTeen) HarperCollins Pubs.

Lennon, Maria T. Confessions of a So-Called Middle Child. 2014. (ENG.). 304p. (J). (gr. 3-7). pap. 6.99 *(978-0-06-212691-7(1))* HarperCollins Pubs.

—Watch Out, Hollywood! More Confessions of a So-Called Middle Child. 2014. (ENG.). 224p. (J). (gr. 3-7). 16.99 *(978-0-06-212693-1(8))* HarperCollins Pubs.

Leray, Merrill. The Kidnapping. 2009. 58p. pap. 15.99 *(978-1-4415-4380-6(5))* Xlibris Corp.

Lewis, Stewart. The Secret Ingredient. 2013. (ENG.). 256p. (YA). (gr. 7). 17.99 *(978-0-385-74331-0(9),* Delacorte Bks. for Young Readers) Random Hse. Children's Bks.

Lopresti, Kirsten. Bright Coin Moon: A Novel. 2014. (ENG.). 272p. (J). (gr. 6). 16.95 *(978-1-62914-751-2(6),* Sky Pony Pr.) Skyhorse Publishing Co., Inc.

Markel, Michelle. Dream Town. Reese, Rick, illus. 2006. (J). 15.95 *(978-1-59714-022-5(8))* Heyday.

Matas, Carol. Rosie in Los Angeles: Action! 2004. (HEB & ENG., Illus.). 128p. (J). (gr. 4-7). pap. 9.95 *(978-0-689-85716-4(0),* Simon & Schuster/Paula Wiseman Bks.) Simon & Schuster/Paula Wiseman Bks.

Miklowitz, Gloria D. The Enemy Has a Face. 2004. 143p. (YA). pap. 8.00 *(978-0-8028-5261-8(0))* Eerdmans, William B. Publishing Co.

Mitchell, Saundra. The Elementals. 2014. (ENG.). 304p. (YA). (gr. 7). pap. 8.99 *(978-0-544-30239-6(7),* HMH Books For Young Readers) Houghton Mifflin Harcourt Publishing Co.

Noël, Alyson. Unrivaled. (Beautiful Idols Ser.: 1). (YA). (gr. 9). 2017. 448p. pap. 9.99 *(978-0-06-232453-5(5))* 2016. 432p. 17.99 *(978-0-06-232452-8(7))* HarperCollins Pubs. (Tegen, Katherine Bks).

Oliver, Lin. Secret of the Super-Small Superstar. Gilpin, Stephen, illus. 2010. (Who Shrunk Daniel Funk? Ser.: 4). (ENG.). 160p. (J). (gr. 3-7). 14.99 *(978-1-4169-0963-7(X),* Simon & Schuster Bks. For Young Readers) Simon & Schuster Bks. For Young Readers.

Paige, D. M. Size 0. 2013. (Opportunity Ser.). (ENG.). 120p. (YA). (gr. 6-12). pap. 7.95 *(978-1-4677-1497-6(6));* lib. bdg. 27.93 *(978-1-4677-1372-6(4))* Lerner Publishing Group. (Darby Creek).

Palmer, Robin. Cindy Ella. 2008. (ENG.). 336p. (YA). (gr. 7-18). 9.99 *(978-0-14-240392-1(X),* Speak) Penguin Young Readers Group.

Palund, Linda. The Little Black Dress. 2016. (ENG., Illus.). (J). 24.99 ***(978-1-63477-970-8(3),*** Harmony Ink Pr.) Dreamspinner Pr.

Pinkwater, Daniel M. The Neddiad: How Neddie Took the Train, Went to Hollywood, & Saved Civilization. Brown, Calef, illus. 2009. (ENG.). 320p. (J). (gr. 5-7). pap. 8.99 *(978-0-547-13367-6(7))* Houghton Mifflin Harcourt Publishing Co.

Politi, Leo. Juanita. 2009. (ENG., Illus.). 32p. 16.95 *(978-0-89236-991-1(4))* Oxford Univ. Pr., Inc.

Purcell, Kim. Trafficked. 2013. (ENG.). 400p. (YA). (gr. 7). pap. 9.99 *(978-0-14-242416-2(1),* Speak) Penguin Young Readers Group.

Rabin, Staton. Black Powder. 2005. (ENG.). 256p. (YA). (gr. 7-9). 16.95 *(978-0-689-86876-4(6),* McElderry, Margaret K. Bks.) McElderry, Margaret K. Bks.

Resnicoff, Stan. The BIG Parade: Los Angeles. 2012. (ENG.). (J). pap. *(978-1-4675-1540-5(X))* Independent Pub.

Reyes, M. G. Emancipated. 2015. (Emancipated Ser.: 1). (ENG.). 400p. (YA). (gr. 9). 17.99 *(978-0-06-228895-0(4),* Tegen, Katherine Bks) HarperCollins Pubs.

Rice, M. L. Who I Am. 2011. (ENG.). 264p. (J). (gr. 7). pap. 13.95 *(978-1-60282-231-3(X))* Bold Strokes Bks.

Richards, Linda L. Death Was in the Blood. 2013. (ENG.). 332p. 25.95 *(978-1-4328-2716-8(2),* Five Star Trade) Cengage Gale.

Rigby, Robert. Goal! The Dream Begins. 2006. (ENG., Illus.). 240p. (YA). (gr. 7-9). pap. 7.99 *(978-0-15-205798-5(6))* Houghton Mifflin Harcourt Publishing Co.

Roberts, Tina. Dream Watchman: Quest for the Missing Talisman Book I. 2011. 244p. pap. 15.95 *(978-1-60976-636-8(9),* Eloquent Bks.) Strategic Book Publishing & Rights Agency (SBPRA).

Ryan, Jessica. The Mystery of Arroyo Seco. Stone, David, illus. 2011. 186p. 42.95 *(978-1-258-08470-7(8))* Literary Licensing, LLC.

Salin-Pascual, Rafael. El espectro del seÑor Amok. 2008. 151p. pap. 20.49 *(978-1-4357-4508-7(6))* Lulu Pr., Inc.

Schraff, Anne. Leap of Faith, 1 vol. unabr. ed. 2011. (Urban Underground Ser.). (ENG.). 201p. (YA). (gr. 9-12). pap. 9.95 *(978-1-61651-588-1(0))* Saddleback Educational Publishing, Inc.

—The Lost, 1 vol. unabr. ed. 2011. (Urban Underground Ser.). (ENG.). 198p. (YA). (gr. 9-12). pap. 9.95 *(978-1-61651-585-0(6))* Saddleback Educational Publishing, Inc.

—The Unforgiven, 1 vol. unabr. ed. 2011. (Urban Underground Ser.). (ENG.). 198p. (YA). (gr. 9-12). pap. 9.95 *(978-1-61651-586-7(4))* Saddleback Educational Publishing, Inc.

—Waters Edge, 1 vol. unabr. ed. 2011. (Urban Underground Ser.). (ENG.). 197p. (YA). (gr. 9-12). pap. 9.95 *(978-1-61651-589-8(9))* Saddleback Educational Publishing, Inc.

Schraff, Anne E. Deliverance, 1 vol. unabr. ed. 2011. (Urban Underground Ser.). (ENG.). 198p. (YA). (gr. 9-12). pap. 9.95 *(978-1-61651-587-4(2))* Saddleback Educational Publishing, Inc.

—Second Chances. 2013. (Urban Underground — Harriet Tubman High School Ser.). (YA). lib. bdg. 20.80 *(978-0-606-31584-5(5),* Turtleback) Turtleback Bks.

Scieszka, Jon. Kat's Mystery Gift. Shannon, David et al, illus. 2013. (Jon Scieszka's Trucktown Ser.). (ENG.). 24p. (J). (gr. -1-1). 16.99 *(978-1-4814-1459-3(3),* Simon Spotlight) Simon Spotlight.

Shreve, Susan. The Search for Baby Ruby. 2015. 213p. (J). pap. *(978-0-545-41784-6(8))* Scholastic, Inc.

Silvano, Wendi. Love Is All Around Los Angeles. Czernichowska, Joanna, illus. 2016. (ENG.). 32p. (J). (-6). 12.99 *(978-1-4926-2929-0(4)*, Sourcebooks Jabberwocky) Sourcebooks, Inc.

Smallman, Steve. Santa Is Coming to Los Angeles. Dunn, Robert, illus. 2013. (ENG.). 32p. (J). (-3). 9.99 *(978-1-4022-8830-2(1)*, Sourcebooks Jabberwocky) Sourcebooks, Inc.

Smith, Charles R., Jr. Chameleon. 2010. (ENG., Illus.). 384p. (YA). (gr. 7). pap. 7.99 *(978-0-7636-4660-8(1))* Candlewick Pr.

Sones, Sonya. One of Those Hideous Books Where the Mother Dies. (ENG., (YA). (gr. 7). 2013. Illus.). 288p. pap. 9.99 *(978-1-4424-9383-4(6))* 2005. 272p. reprint ed. pap. 7.99 *(978-0-4169-0788-6(2))* Simon & Schuster Bks. For Young Readers. (Simon & Schuster Bks. For Young Readers).

Sonneborn, Scott. I for an Eye. Banks, Timothy, illus. 2014. (Frankenstein Journals). (ENG.). 80p. (gr. 2-3). 22.65 *(978-1-4342-9000-7(X))* Stone Arch Bks.

Soto, Gary. Chato & the Party Animals. Guevara, Susan, illus. (Chato Ser.). 28.95 incl. audio compact disk *(978-1-59112-920-2(6))*; 25.95 incl. audio *(978-1-59112-460-3(3))*; pap. 39.95 incl. audio compact disk *(978-1-59112-921-9(4))*; pap. 37.95 incl. audio *(978-1-59112-461-0(1))* Live Oak Media.

—Chato & the Party Animals. Guevara, Susan, illus. 2004. (Chato Ser.). (ENG.). 32p. (J). (gr. -1-3). reprint ed. pap. 7.99 *(978-0-14-240032-6(7)*, Puffin Books) Penguin Young Readers Group.

—Chato & the Party Animals. Guevara, Susan, illus. 2004. (Chato Ser.). (gr. -1-3). 17.00 *(978-0-7569-2921-3(0))* Perfection Learning Corp.

—Chato y los Amigos Pachangueros. Guevara, Susan, illus. 2004.Tr. of Chato & the Party Animals. (SPA & ENG.). 32p. (J). (gr. -1-3). reprint ed. pap. 7.99 *(978-0-14-240033-3(5)*, Puffin Books) Penguin Young Readers Group.

—Chato's Kitchen. Guevara, Susan, illus. 2003. (Chato Ser.). (J). (gr. -1-2). pap. 39.95 *(978-1-59112-527-3(8))* Live Oak Media.

Spalding, Amy. The Reece Malcolm List. 2013. (ENG.). 352p. (YA). (gr. 8). pap. 9.99 *(978-1-62061-240-8(2)*, 9781620612408) Entangled Publishing, LLC.

Stampler, Ann Redisch. Afterparty. 2013. (ENG., Illus.). 416p. (YA). (gr. 9). 17.99 *(978-1-4424-2324-4(2)*, Simon Pulse) Simon Pulse.

—Where It Began. 2013. (ENG.). 384p. (YA). (gr. 9). pap. 9.99 *(978-1-4424-2322-0(6)*, Simon Pulse) Simon Pulse.

Stohl, Margaret. Royce Rolls. 2017. (ENG.). 400p. (YA). (gr. 9-17). 18.99 *(978-1-4847-3233-5(2))* Disney Publishing Worldwide.

Summers, Gillian. The Tree Shepherd's Daughter. 2007. (Faire Folk Saga Ser.: 1). (ENG.). 336p. (YA). (gr. 7-12). per. 9.95 *(978-0-7387-1081-5(4)*, Flux) North Star Editions.

Tashjian, Janet. For What It's Worth. 2012. (ENG.). 288p. (YA). (gr. 7-12). 16.99 *(978-0-8050-9365-0(6)*, 9780805093650, Holt, Henry & Co. Bks. For Young Readers) Holt, Henry & Co.

—My Life As a Gamer. Tashjian, Jake, illus. 2015. (My Life Ser.: 5). (ENG.). 272p. (J). (gr. 4-7). 13.99 *(978-0-8050-9851-8(8)*, 9780805098518, Holt, Henry & Co. Bks. For Young Readers) Holt, Henry & Co.

—My Life As a Joke. Tashjian, Jake, illus. 2014. (My Life Ser.: 4). (ENG.). 272p. (J). (gr. 4-7). 13.99 *(978-0-8050-9850-1(X)*, 9780805098501, Holt, Henry & Co. Bks. For Young Readers) Holt, Henry & Co.

—My Life as a Stuntboy. Tashjian, Jake, illus. 2011. (My Life Ser.: 2). (ENG.). 272p. (J). (gr. 4-7). 15.99 *(978-0-8050-8904-2(7)*, 9780805089042, Holt, Henry & Co. Bks. For Young Readers) Holt, Henry & Co.

—My Life as a Stuntboy. Tashjian, Jake, illus. 2015. (My Life Ser.: 2). (ENG.). 288p. (J). (gr. 4-7). pap. 7.99 *(978-1-250-01038-4(1)*, 9781250010384) Square Fish.

Thomas, Jacquelin. Split Ends. 2010. (ENG.). 272p. pap. 17.99 *(978-1-4165-9879-4(0))* Pocket Books.

Toon, Paige. The Accidental Life of Jessie Jefferson. 2016. (Jessie Jefferson Novels Ser.: 1). (ENG.). 336p. (J). pap. 9.99 *(978-1-4711-4582-7(4)*, Simon & Schuster Children's) Simon & Schuster, Ltd. GBR. Dist: Simon & Schuster, Inc.

Trine, Greg. Attack of the Valley Girls. Montijo, Rhode, illus. 6th ed. 2008. (Melvin Beederman, Superhero Ser.: 6). (ENG.). 144p. (J). (gr. 2-5). pap. 8.99 *(978-0-8050-8161-9(5)*, 9780805081619) Square Fish.

—The Brotherhood of the Traveling Underpants. 2009. (Melvin Beederman Superhero Ser.: 7). (J). lib. bdg. 19.65 *(978-0-606-01751-0(8)*, Turtleback) Turtleback Bks.

—The Curse of the Bologna Sandwich. Montijo, Rhode, illus. 2006. (Melvin Beederman, Superhero Ser.: 1). (ENG.). 144p. (J). (gr. 2-5). pap. 8.99 *(978-0-8050-7836-7(3)*, 9780805078367) Square Fish.

—The Fake Cape Caper. Montijo, Rhode, illus. 5th rev. ed. 2007. (Melvin Beederman, Superhero Ser.: 5). (ENG.). 144p. (J). (gr. 2-5). pap. 8.99 *(978-0-8050-8159-6(3)*, 9780805081596) Square Fish.

—The Grateful Fred. Montijo, Rhode, illus. 3rd rev. ed. 2006. (Melvin Beederman, Superhero Ser.: 3). (ENG.). 144p. (J). (gr. 2-5). pap. 8.99 *(978-0-8050-7922-7(X)*, 9780805079227) Square Fish.

—Invasion from Planet Dork. Montijo, Rhode, illus. 2010. (Melvin Beederman, Superhero Ser.: 8). (ENG.). 144p. (J). (gr. 2-7). pap. 8.99 *(978-0-8050-8167-1(4)*, 9780805081671) Square Fish.

—Terror in Tights. Montijo, Rhode, illus. 4th rev. ed. 2007. (Melvin Beederman, Superhero Ser.: 4). (ENG.). 144p. (J). (gr. 2-5). pap. 8.99 *(978-0-8050-7924-1(6)*, 9780805079241) Square Fish.

Tyler, Bridget, et al. Keeping the Beat. 2017. (ENG.). 368p. (J). (gr. 8-17). 17.95 *(978-1-77138-730-9(0))* Kids Can Pr., Ltd. CAN. Dist: Hachette Bk. Group.

Umminger, Alison. American Girls. 2016. (ENG.). 304p. (YA). 17.99 *(978-1-250-07500-0(9)*, 9781250075000) Flatiron Bks.

Waid, Mark. City of Incredibles, Vol. 2. Takara, Marcio, illus. 2010. (Incredibles Ser.). (ENG.). 112p. (J). 24.99 *(978-1-60886-529-1(0))* Boom! Studios.

Wells, Dan. Bluescreen. 2016. (Mirador Ser.: 1). 352p. (J). (gr. 8). 17.99 *(978-0-06-234787-9(X))* HarperCollins Pubs.

Weston Woods Staff, creator. Chato & the Party Animals. 2011. 18.95 *(978-0-439-73984-9(5))* 2011. 38.75 *(978-0-439-84581-6(5))* 2004. 29.95 *(978-1-55592-703-5(3))* Weston Woods Studios, Inc.

—Chato's Kitchen. 2004. (J). 38.75 *(978-1-55592-388-4(7))*; 18.95 *(978-1-55592-386-0(0))* Weston Woods Studios, Inc.

Woods, Brenda. Emako Blue. 2005. (ENG.). 128p. (YA). (gr. 7-18). 6.99 *(978-0-14-240418-8(7)*, Speak) Penguin Young Readers Group.

—Emako Blue. 2005. 124p. (gr. 7). 16.00 *(978-0-7569-5495-6(9))* Perfection Learning Corp.

Yee, Lisa. Absolutely Maybe. 2009. (ENG.). 288p. (J). (gr. 7-18). 16.99 *(978-0-439-83844-3(4)*, Levine, Arthur A. Bks.) Scholastic, Inc.

LOS ANGELES (CALIF.)—RACE RELATIONS

Buckley, A. M. Racism, 1 vol. 2011. (Essential Issues Set 2 Ser.). (ENG., Illus.). 112p. (J). (gr. 6-12). lib. bdg. 35.64 *(978-1-61714-777-7(X)*, Essential Library) ABDO Publishing Co.

Gerdes, Louise I. 1992 Los Angeles Riots. Greenhaven Press Editors, ed. 2014. (Perspectives on Modern World History Ser.). (ENG., Illus.). 224p. (gr. 10-12). lib. bdg. 47.80 *(978-0-7377-7008-7(2)*, Greenhaven Pr., Inc.) Cengage Gale.

LOS ANGELES ANGELS OF ANAHEIM (BASEBALL TEAM)

Gilbert, Sara. Los Angeles Angels of Anaheim. 2013. (Illus.). 24p. (J). 25.65 *(978-1-60818-265-7(7)*, Creative Education) Creative Co., The.

—The Story of the Los Angeles Angels of Anaheim. (Illus.). 48p. 2011. (J). 35.65 *(978-1-60818-044-8(1)*, Creative Education) 2007. (YA). (gr. 4-7). lib. bdg. 32.80 *(978-1-58341-477-4(0))* Creative Co., The.

Sandler, Michael. Randy Johnson & the Arizona Diamondbacks: 2001 World Series. 2008. (World Series Superstars). (Illus.). 24p. (J). (gr. 1-4). lib. bdg. 22.61 *(978-1-59716-638-6(3))* Bearport Publishing Co., Inc.

—Troy Glaus & the Anaheim Angels: 2002 World Series. 2008. (World Series Superstars). (Illus.). 24p. (J). (gr. 1-4). lib. bdg. 22.61 *(978-1-59716-640-9(5))* Bearport Publishing Co., Inc.

Stewart, Mark. The Los Angeles Angels of Anaheim. 2012. (Team Spirit Ser.). 48p. (J). (gr. 3-6). lib. bdg. 29.27 *(978-1-59953-485-5(1))* Norwood Hse. Pr.

Wilson, Bernie. Los Angeles Angels, 1 vol. (Inside MLB Ser.). (ENG., Illus.). 48p. (J). (gr. 3-6). 2011. lib. bdg. 32.79 *(978-1-61714-047-1(3))* 2014. lib. bdg. 32.79 *(978-1-62403-473-2(X)*, SportsZone) ABDO Publishing Co.

LOS ANGELES DODGERS (BASEBALL TEAM)

Aretha, David. Dodger Blue: The Los Angeles Dodgers. 2007. (Sensational Sports Teams Ser.). (Illus.). 128p. (J). (gr. 5-9). lib. bdg. 34.60 *(978-1-59845-045-3(X)*, MyReportLinks.com Bks.) Enslow Pubs., Inc.

Friedman, Nick. Mike Piazza. 2007. (Baseball Superstars Ser.). (Illus.). 130p. (YA). (gr. 7-12). lib. bdg. 30.00 *(978-0-7910-9493-8(6))* Facts On File, Inc.

Frisch, Aaron. Los Angeles Dodgers. 2009. (World Series Champions Ser.). (Illus.). 23p. (J). (gr. 2-3). 24.25 *(978-1-58341-689-1(7)*, Creative Education) Creative Co., The.

Garcia, Tom & Naga, Karun. Daddy's Heroes: Gibby's Homer: the 1988 World Series. Donnelly, Jenifer, illus. 2007. (1988 World Ser.). 32p. (J). (gr. -1-3). pap. 9.95 *(978-0-9792111-0-2(7))* Daddy's Heroes, Inc.

Gilbert, Sara. Los Angeles Dodgers. 2013. (Illus.). 24p. (J). 25.65 *(978-1-60818-266-4(5)*, Creative Education) Creative Co., The.

—World Series Champs: Los Angeles Dodgers. 2013. (World Series Champions Ser.). (ENG.). 24p. (J). (gr. 1-3). pap. 7.99 *(978-0-89812-817-8(X)*, Creative Paperbacks) Creative Co., The.

Gitlin, Martin. Los Angeles Dodgers, 1 vol. 2011. (Inside MLB Ser.). (ENG., Illus.). 48p. (YA). (gr. 3-6). lib. bdg. 32.79 *(978-1-61714-048-8(1))* ABDO Publishing Co.

Gitlin, Marty. Los Angeles Dodgers, 1 vol. 2014. (Inside MLB Ser.). (ENG., Illus.). 48p. (J). (gr. 3-6). lib. bdg. 32.79 *(978-1-62403-474-9(8)*, SportsZone) ABDO Publishing Co.

Hammer, Max. Superstars of the Los Angeles Dodgers. 2014. (Pro Sports Superstars Ser.). 24p. (J). 27.10 *(978-1-60753-593-5(9))* Amicus Publishing.

Kennedy, Mike & Stewart, Mark. Meet the Dodgers. 2010. (Smart about Sports Ser.). 24p. (J). (gr. k-3). lib. bdg. 22.60 *(978-1-59953-371-1(5))* Norwood Hse. Pr.

LeBoutillier, Nate. The Story of the Los Angeles Dodgers. 2011. (Illus.). 48p. (J). 35.65 *(978-1-60818-045-5(X)*, Creative Education) Creative Co., The.

Nichols, John. The Story of the Los Angeles Dodgers. 2007. (Baseball, the Great American Game Ser.). (Illus.). 48p. (YA). (gr. 4-7). lib. bdg. 32.80 *(978-1-58341-491-0(6))* Creative Co., The.

Stewart, Mark. The Los Angeles Dodgers. 2012. (Team Spirit Ser.). 48p. (J). (gr. 3-6). lib. bdg. 29.27 *(978-1-59953-486-2(X))* Norwood Hse. Pr.

Winter, Jonah. You Never Heard of Sandy Koufax?! Carrilho, Andre, illus. 2016. (ENG.). 40p. (J). (gr. -1-3). 7.99 *(978-0-553-49842-4(8)*, Dragonfly Bks.) Random Hse. Children's Bks.

LOUIS XIV, KING OF FRANCE, 1638-1715

Mason, Anthony. Versailles. 2005. (Places in History Ser.). (Illus.). 48p. (gr. 5-12). lib. bdg. 31.00 *(978-0-8368-5815-0(8)*, World Almanac Library) Stevens, Gareth Publishing LLLP.

Rossi, Renzo. In the Sun King's Paris with Molière. Baldanzi, Alessandro, illus. 2008. (Come See My City Ser.). 48p. (gr. 4-8). lib. bdg. 28.50 *(978-0-7614-4332-2(0)*, Benchmark Bks.) Marshall Cavendish Corp.

Steinberg, D. J. King Louie's Shoes. Neubecker, Robert, illus. 2017. (ENG.). 48p. (J). (gr. -1-3). 17.99 ***(978-1-4814-2657-2(5)***, Beach Lane Bks.) Beach Lane Bks.

Tagliaferro, Linda. Palace of Versailles: France's Royal Jewel. 2005. (Castles, Palaces, & Tombs Ser.). 32p. (J). lib. bdg. 25.27 *(978-1-59716-003-2(2))* Bearport Publishing Co., Inc.

LOUISIANA

Bjorklund, Ruth. Louisiana. 2005. (It's My State! Ser.). (Illus.). 80p. (J). (gr. 4-7). lib. bdg. 27.07 *(978-0-7614-1863-4(6)*, Benchmark Bks.) Marshall Cavendish Corp.

Bjorklund, Ruth & Steinitz, Andy. Louisiana. 2014. (It's My State! (r) Ser.). 80p. (J). (gr. 4-8). lib. bdg. 34.21 *(978-1-62712-740-0(2))* Cavendish Square Publishing.

Bridges, Ruby. Ruby Bridges Goes to School: My True Story. 2009. (Scholastic Reader Level 2 Ser.). (ENG.). 32p. (J). (gr. -1-3). pap. 3.99 *(978-0-545-10855-3(1))* Scholastic, Inc.

Brown, Vanessa. Louisiana. 2009. (Bilingual Library of the United States of America Ser.). (ENG & SPA.). 32p. (gr. 2-2). 47.90 *(978-1-60853-363-3(8)*, Editorial Buenas Letras) Rosen Publishing Group, Inc., The.

—Louisiana/Luisiana. 2005. (Bilingual Library of the United States of America Ser.: Set 1). (ENG & SPA., Illus.). 32p. (J). (gr. 3-6). lib. bdg. 25.25 *(978-1-4042-3083-5(1))* Rosen Publishing Group, Inc., The.

Cassels, Jean. The Twelve Days of Christmas in Louisiana. Cravath, Lynne Avril, illus. 2007. (Twelve Days of Christmas in America Ser.). (ENG.). 40p. (J). (gr. k-3). 12.95 *(978-1-4027-3814-2(5))* Sterling Publishing Co., Inc.

Deinard, Jenny. How to Draw Louisiana's Sights & Symbols. 2009. (Kid's Guide to Drawing America Ser.). 32p. (gr. k-k). 50.50 *(978-1-61511-067-4(4)*, PowerKids Pr.) Rosen Publishing Group, Inc., The.

Downing, Johnette. Louisiana, the Jewel of the Deep South, 1 vol. Marshall, Julia, illus. 2015. (ENG.). 32p. (J). (gr. k-3). 16.99 *(978-1-4556-2096-8(3))* Pelican Publishing Co., Inc.

Hyde, Judith Jensen. Louisiana. 2007. (Rookie Read-About Geography Ser.). (ENG., Illus.). 32p. (J). (gr. 1-2). 20.50 *(978-0-516-21848-9(4)*, Children's Pr.) Scholastic Library Publishing.

Johnstone, Robb. Louisiana. 2011. (Guide to American States Ser.). (Illus.). 48p. (YA). (gr. 3-6). 29.99 *(978-1-61690-790-7(8))*; (J). *(978-1-61690-466-1(6))* Weigl Pubs., Inc.

Kadair, Deborah. I Spy in the Louisiana Sky, 1 vol. Kadair, Deborah, illus. 2011. (ENG., Illus.). 32p. (J). (gr. k-3). 16.99 *(978-1-58980-885-0(1))* Pelican Publishing Co., Inc.

Koontz, Robin. What Was Hurricane Katrina? 2015. (What Was... ? Ser.). lib. bdg. 16.00 *(978-0-606-36762-2(4))* Turtleback Bks.

LaDoux, Rita. Louisiana. 2012. (J). lib. bdg. 25.26 *(978-0-7613-4535-0(3)*, Lerner Pubns.) Lerner Publishing Group.

LaDoux, Rita C. Louisiana. 2nd rev. exp. ed. 2003. (Hello U. S. A. Ser.). (Illus.). 84p. (J). (gr. 3-6). pap. 6.95 *(978-0-8225-4145-5(9))* Lerner Publishing Group.

Lantier-Sampon, Patricia. Louisiana. 2006. (Portraits of the States Ser.). (Illus.). 32p. (gr. 2-6). pap. 10.50 *(978-0-8368-4686-7(9))*; lib. bdg. 26.00 *(978-0-8368-4667-6(2))* Stevens, Gareth Publishing LLLP. (Gareth Stevens Learning Library).

LeVert, Suzanne. Louisiana. 2nd rev. ed. 2005. (Celebrate the States Ser.). (Illus.). 144p. (gr. 6-7). lib. bdg. 42.79 *(978-0-7614-2021-7(5)*, Benchmark Bks.) Marshall Cavendish Corp.

Marsh, Carole. The Louisiana Coloring Book. 2004. (Louisiana Experience! Ser.). (Illus.). 32p. (J). (gr. k-2). pap. 3.95 *(978-0-7933-9551-4(8))* Gallopade International.

—Louisiana Current Events Projects: 30 Cool, Activities, Crafts, Experiments & More for Kids to Do to Learn about Your State! 2003. (Louisiana Experience Ser.). 32p. (gr. k-8). pap. 5.95 *(978-0-635-02037-6(8)*, Marsh, Carole Bks.) Gallopade International.

—The Louisiana Experience Pocket Guide. 2004. (Louisiana Experience! Ser.). (Illus.). 96p. (J). (gr. 3-8). pap. 6.95 *(978-0-7933-9546-0(1))* Gallopade International.

—Louisiana Geography Projects: 30 Cool, Activities, Crafts, Experiments & More for Kids to Do to Learn about Your State! 2003. (Louisiana Experience Ser.). 32p. (gr. k-5). pap. 5.95 *(978-0-635-01837-3(3)*, Marsh, Carole Bks.) Gallopade International.

—Louisiana Government Projects: 30 Cool, Activities, Crafts, Experiments & More for Kids to Do to Learn about Your State! 2003. (Louisiana Experience Ser.). 32p. (gr. k-5). pap. 5.95 *(978-0-635-01937-0(X)*, Marsh, Carole Bks.) Gallopade International.

—Louisiana Jeopardy. 2004. (Louisiana Experience! Ser.). (Illus.). 32p. (J). (gr. 3-8). pap. 7.95 *(978-0-7933-9548-4(8))* Gallopade International.

—Louisiana Jography. 2004. (Louisiana Experience! Ser.). (Illus.). 32p. (J). (gr. 3-8). pap. 7.95 *(978-0-7933-9549-1(6))* Gallopade International.

—Louisiana People Projects: 30 Cool, Activities, Crafts, Experiments & More for Kids to Do to Learn about Your State! 2003. (Louisiana Experience Ser.). 32p. (gr. k-5). pap. 5.95 *(978-0-635-01987-5(6)*, Marsh, Carole Bks.) Gallopade International.

—Louisiana Symbols & Facts Projects: 30 Cool, Activities, Crafts, Experiments & More for Kids to Do to Learn about Your State! 2003. (Louisiana Experience Ser.). 32p. (gr. k-5). pap. 5.95 *(978-0-635-01887-8(X)*, Marsh, Carole Bks.) Gallopade International.

—Louisiana's Big Activity Book. 2004. (Louisiana Experience! Ser.). (Illus.). 96p. (J). (gr. 2-6). pap. 9.95 *(978-0-7933-9550-7(X))* Gallopade International.

—My First Book about Louisiana. 2004. (Louisiana Experience! Ser.). (Illus.). 32p. (J). (gr. k-4). pap. 7.95 *(978-0-7933-9547-7(X))* Gallopade International.

Murray, Julie. Louisiana, 1 vol. 2006. (United States Ser.). (ENG., Illus.). 32p. (gr. 2-4). 27.07 *(978-1-59197-677-6(4)*, Buddy Bks.) ABDO Publishing Co.

O'Neill, Elizabeth. Alfred Visits Louisiana. 2007. 24p. (J). pap. 12.00 *(978-0-9790240-8-5(0))* Global Business Information Strategies, Inc.

Prieto, Anita C. P Is for Pelican: A Louisiana Alphabet. Knorr, Laura, illus. 2004. (Discover America State by State Ser.). (ENG.). 40p. (J). 17.95 *(978-1-58536-137-3(2))* Sleeping Bear Pr.

Reed, Jennifer. Louisiana: A MyReportLinks. Com Book. 2003. (States Ser.). (Illus.). 48p. (J). lib. bdg. 25.26 *(978-0-7660-5141-6(2)*, MyReportLinks.com Bks.) Enslow Pubs., Inc.

Scheunemann, Pam. Frenchy's Float: A Story about Louisiana, 1 vol. Doucet, Bob, illus. 2010. (Fact & Fable: State Stories Set 2 Ser.). (ENG.). 24p. (J). (gr. -1-2). 25.65 *(978-1-60453-922-6(4))* ABDO Publishing Co.

Shofner, Shawndra. Louisiana. 2008. (This Land Called America Ser.). (Illus.). 32p. (YA). (gr. 3-6). 22.95 *(978-1-58341-643-3(9))* Creative Co., The.

Smith, Rich. Louisiana, 1 vol. 2009. (United States Ser.). (ENG., Illus.). 48p. (YA). (gr. 2-5). 27.07 *(978-1-60453-653-9(5))* ABDO Publishing Co.

Zeiger, Jennifer. Louisiana. 2017. (True Book — My United States Ser.). (ENG.). 48p. (J). pap. 7.95 ***(978-0-531-23287-3(5)***, Children's Pr.) Scholastic Library Publishing.

LOUISIANA—FICTION

Allbritton, Stacy Demoran. The Diary of Marie Landry, Acadian Exile, 1 vol. Haynes, Joyce, illus. 2012. (ENG.). 160p. (J). (gr. 3-7). pap. 14.95 *(978-1-58980-865-2(7))* Pelican Publishing Co., Inc.

Ball, Marcia. Christmas Fais Do-Do. 2006. (Illus.). 36p. (J). per. 14.95 *(978-1-58939-972-3(2))* Virtualbookworm.com Publishing, Inc.

Boutte, Brock. Gris-Gris & the Cypress Tree: Louisiana. 2012. (ENG.). (J). pap. 17.95 *(978-1-4675-4497-9(3))* Independent Pub.

Bradley, John Ed. Call Me by My Name. (ENG.). (YA). (gr. 7). 2015. 288p. pap. 11.99 *(978-1-4424-9794-8(7))* 2014. (Illus.). 272p. 17.99 *(978-1-4424-9793-1(9)*, Atheneum Bks. for Young Readers) Simon & Schuster Children's Publishing.

Cochran, Thomas. Uncle Drew & the Bat Dodger, 1 vol. 2016. (ENG.). 248p. (J). (gr. 3-7). pap. 14.95 *(978-1-4556-2209-2(5))* Pelican Publishing Co., Inc.

Collins Morgan, Connie. Hercules on the Bayou, 1 vol. Leonhard, Herb, illus. 2016. (ENG.). 32p. (J). (gr. k-3). 16.99 *(978-1-4556-2185-9(4))* Pelican Publishing Co., Inc.

Connelly, Neil. Into the Hurricane. 2017. (ENG.). 240p. (J). (gr. 9). 17.99 ***(978-0-545-85381-1(8)***, Levine, Arthur A. Bks.) Scholastic, Inc.

Doucet, Sharon Arms. Fiddle Fever. 2007. (ENG.). 176p. (J). (gr. 5-7). pap. 12.95 *(978-0-618-77682-5(6))* Houghton Mifflin Harcourt Publishing Co.

Downing, Johnette. Down in Louisiana, 1 vol. Kadair, Deborah Ousley, illus. 2007. (ENG.). 32p. (J). (gr. k-3). 16.99 *(978-1-58980-451-7(1))* Pelican Publishing Co., Inc.

—The Fifolet, 1 vol. Lindsley, Jennifer, illus. 2015. (ENG.). 32p. (J). (gr. k-3). 16.99 *(978-1-4556-2036-4(X))* Pelican Publishing Co., Inc.

—Today Is Monday in Louisiana, 1 vol. Kadair, Deborah Ousley, illus. 2006. (ENG.). 32p. (J). (gr. k-k). 16.99 *(978-1-58980-406-7(6))* Pelican Publishing Co., Inc.

Duey, Kathleen & Bale, Karen A. Swamp: Louisiana 1851. 2016. (Survivors Ser.). (ENG., Illus.). 160p. (J). (gr. 3-7). pap. 6.99 *(978-1-4814-2783-8(0)*, Aladdin) Simon & Schuster Children's Publishing.

Dunham, Terri Hoover. The Legend of Papa Noel: A Cajun Christmas Story. Knorr, Laura, illus. 2006. (Legends Ser.). (ENG.). 32p. (J). (gr. -1-3). 17.95 *(978-1-58536-256-1(5))* Sleeping Bear Pr.

Elston, Ashley. The Rules for Breaking. 2014. (Rules Ser.). (ENG.). 320p. (YA). (gr. 7-12). 16.99 *(978-1-4231-6898-0(4))* Hyperion Bks. for Children.

—The Rules for Disappearing. 2014. (Rules Ser.). (ENG.). 336p. (YA). (gr. 7-12). pap. 8.99 *(978-1-4231-6926-0(3))* Hyperion Bks. for Children.

Fontenot, Mary Alice. Clovis Crawfish & Bertile's Bon Voyage, 1 vol. Blazek, Scott R., illus. 2008. (Clovis Crawfish Ser.). (ENG.). 32p. (J). (gr. k-3). 16.99 *(978-1-58980-541-5(0))* Pelican Publishing Co., Inc.

—Clovis Crawfish & Echo Gecko, 1 vol. Buckner, Julie Dupre, illus. 2003. (Clovis Crawfish Ser.). (ENG.). 32p. (J). (gr. k-3). 16.99 *(978-1-56554-708-7(X))* Pelican Publishing Co., Inc.

—Clovis Crawfish & His Friends, 1 vol. Graves, Keith, illus. 2009. (Clovis Crawfish Ser.). (ENG.). 32p. (J). (gr. k-3). 16.99 *(978-1-58980-762-4(6))* Pelican Publishing Co., Inc.

—Clovis Crawfish & Michelle Mantis, 1 vol. Blazek, Scott R., illus. 2008. (Clovis Crawfish Ser.). (ENG.). 32p. (J). (gr. k-3). 16.99 *(978-1-58980-540-8(2))* Pelican Publishing Co., Inc.

—Clovis Crawfish & Petit Papillon, 1 vol. Graves, Keith, illus. 2009. (Clovis Crawfish Ser.). (ENG.). 32p. (J). (gr. k-3). 16.99 *(978-1-58980-772-3(3))* Pelican Publishing Co., Inc.

—Clovis Crawfish & Silvie Sulphur, 1 vol. Buckner, Julie Dupre, illus. 2004. (Clovis Crawfish Ser.). (ENG & FRE.). 32p. (J). (gr. k-3). 16.99 *(978-1-56554-864-0(7))* Pelican Publishing Co., Inc.

Fontenot, Mary Alice & Fontenot Landry, Julie. Clovis Crawfish & the Twin Sister, 1 vol. Butler, Julie Dupre & Buckner, Julie Dupre, illus. 2007. (Clovis Crawfish Ser.). (ENG.). 32p. (J). (gr. k-3). 16.99 *(978-1-58980-467-8(8))* Pelican Publishing Co., Inc.

Gaines, Ernest J. The Autobiography of Miss Jane Pittman: And Related Readings. 2006. (McDougal Littell Literature Connections Ser.). (ENG.). 384p. (gr. 6-8). 16.90 *(978-0-395-86993-2(5)*, 2-70829) Great Source Education Group, Inc.

Gourley, Barbara. The Legacy of Tip: The Catahoula. 2012. 40p. pap. 20.95 *(978-1-4772-6337-2(3))* AuthorHouse.

Hébert-Collins, Sheila. Jean-Paul Hébert Was There/Jean-Paul Hébert Etait Là, 1 vol. Bergeron, John W., illus. 2004. (ENG & FRE.). 32p. (J). (gr. k-3). 16.99 *(978-1-56554-928-9(7))* Pelican Publishing Co., Inc.

Heflin, Ronald. Caddo Lake. 2011. 156p. pap. 24.95 *(978-1-4626-0093-9(X))* America Star Bks.

Holt, Kimberly Willis. Dear Hank Williams. 2015. (ENG.). 224p. (J). (gr. 4-7). 16.99 *(978-0-8050-8022-3(8)*, 9780805080223, Holt, Henry & Co. Bks. For Young Readers) Holt, Henry & Co.

—Dear Hank Williams. 2016. (J). lib. bdg. 18.40 *(978-0-606-38551-0(7))* Turtleback Bks.

—My Louisiana Sky. 208p. (gr. 5-18). (YA). 4.99 *(978-0-8072-8291-5(X))*; 2004. (J). pap. 36.00 incl. audio *(978-0-8072-8290-8(1)*, YA152SP) Random Hse. Audio Publishing Group. (Listening Library).

—Part of Me: Stories of a Louisiana Family. 2009. (ENG.). 240p. (J). (gr. 5-10). pap. 9.99 *(978-0-312-58145-9(9)*, 9780312581459) Square Fish.

—Part of Me: Stories of a Louisiana Family. rev. l.t. ed. 2007. (Thorndike Literacy Bridge Ser.). 223p. (J). (gr. 3-7). 23.95 *(978-0-7862-9184-7(2))* Thorndike Pr.

J
K
L

—Piper Reed, Rodeo Star. Davenier, Christine, illus. 2011. (Piper Reed Ser.: 5). (ENG.). 160p. (J). (gr. 3-6). 15.99 *(978-0-8050-9007-9(X)*, 9780805090079, Holt, Henry & Co. Bks. For Young Readers) Holt, Henry & Co.
—Piper Reed, Rodeo Star. Davenier, Christine, illus. 2012. (Piper Reed Ser.: 5). (ENG.). 176p. (J). (gr. 3-6). pap. 6.99 *(978-1-250-00409-3(8)*, 9781250004093) Square Fish.
Jacobs, Lily. The Littlest Bunny in Louisiana: An Easter Adventure. Dunn, Robert, illus. 2015. (ENG.). 32p. (J). (-3). 9.99 *(978-1-4926-1105-9(0)*, Sourcebooks Jabberwocky) Sourcebooks, Inc.
James, Eric. A Halloween Scare in Louisiana. Le Ray, Marina, illus. 2014. (ENG.). 32p. (J). (-5). 9.99 *(978-1-4926-0600-0(6)*, 9781492606000, Sourcebooks Jabberwocky) Sourcebooks, Inc.
—Santa's Sleigh Is on Its Way to Louisiana. Dunn, Robert, illus. 2015. (ENG.). 32p. (J). (-2). 12.99 *(978-1-4926-2762-3(3)*, Sourcebooks Jabberwocky) Sourcebooks, Inc.
Johnson, Temeka & Phillips, Quency. Decisions, Decisions, Decisions. 2010. 32p. 19.99 *(978-1-4520-5758-3(3))* AuthorHouse.
Jones, V. C. Anna Banana Goes to Louisiana. 2010. 16p. 8.49 *(978-1-4490-8390-8(0))* AuthorHouse.
Karwoski, Gail Langer. When Hurricane Katrina Hit Home. Marshall, Julia, illus. 2013. Orig. Title: When Hurricane Katrina Hit Home. (ENG.). 192p. (gr. 4-7). 15.99 *(978-1-62619-083-2(6)*, History Pr., The) Arcadia Publishing.
Kelly, Erin Entrada. The Land of Forgotten Girls. 2017. 320p. (J). (gr. 3-7). pap. 6.99 *(978-0-06-223865-8(5)*, Greenwillow Bks.) HarperCollins Pubs.
LaFaye, A. Nissa's Place. 2010. (ENG.). 256p. (J). (gr. 2-8). pap. 8.00 *(978-1-57131-697-4(3))* Milkweed Editions.
—The Year of the Sawdust Man. 2008. (ENG.). 224p. (J). (gr. 2-8). pap. 6.95 *(978-1-57131-679-0(5))* Milkweed Editions.
Lamana, Julie T. Three Little Bayou Fishermen. 2010. 28p. (J). pap. 17.95 *(978-1-4327-2056-8(2))* Outskirts Pr., Inc.
Lane, Alison Hoffman. Uncle Amel & the Awful, Angry Alligator. 2009. (Uncle Amel Ser.). (Illus.). 32p. (J). 15.95 *(978-1-58980-645-0(X))* Pelican Publishing Co., Inc.
Larson, Kirby. Liberty. 2016. (Dogs of World War II Ser.). (ENG.). 240p. (J). (gr. 3-7). 16.99 *(978-0-545-84071-2(6)*, Scholastic Pr.) Scholastic, Inc.
Little, Kimberley Griffiths. Circle of Secrets. 2011. 326p. (J). *(978-0-545-38523-7(7)*, Scholastic Pr.) Scholastic, Inc.
—The Healing Spell. 2010. (ENG.). 368p. (J). (gr. 3-7). 17.99 *(978-0-545-16559-4(8)*, Scholastic Pr.) Scholastic, Inc.
Lovett, Darrell F. Darrell's Lake Franklin. 2007. 13.00 *(978-0-8059-8807-9(6))* Dorrance Publishing Co., Inc.
Luvd, U. R. Camp Gumbo. 2007. 113p. pap. 7.52 *(978-1-4303-1322-9(6))* Lulu Pr., Inc.
Magaro, Dan. The Adventures of Fred & Daisymae. 2010. 48p. pap. 10.99 *(978-1-60957-407-9(9))* Salem Author Services.
Mason, Dianne. Danny's Ghost. 2007. 156p. pap. 9.39 *(978-1-4116-4937-8(0))* Lulu Pr., Inc.
Mayeux, Gertie. Jesse the Oil Patch Kid. 2012. 36p. pap. 20.99 *(978-1-4772-3691-8(0))* AuthorHouse.
Mc Daniel, Jessica & Morgan, Amanda. Goodnight Tigers. 2010. 32p. (J). 17.95 *(978-1-4507-0621-6(5))* Independent Pub.
Mock, Chara. The Cajun Nutcracker, 1 vol. Cassels, Jean, illus. 2011. (ENG.). 32p. (J). (gr. k-3). 16.99 *(978-1-58980-978-9(5))* Pelican Publishing Co., Inc.
Morrow, Dj. The Good Of Boys. 2012. 28p. pap. 24.95 *(978-1-4626-9533-1(7))* America Star Bks.
Moynihan, Lindsay. The Waiting Tree. 0 vols. 2013. (ENG.). 218p. (YA). (gr. 9-12). 17.99 *(978-1-4778-1634-9(8)*, 9781477816349, Amazon Children's Publishing) Amazon Publishing.
Napoli, Donna Jo. Alligator Bayou. 2010. (ENG.). 288p. (YA). (gr. 7). pap. 8.99 *(978-0-553-49417-4(1)*, Lamb, Wendy Bks.) Random Hse. Children's Bks.
Osborne, Erin. Spy Recruit, 1 vol. Simmons, Bethany, illus. 2010. (ENG.). 216p. (J). (gr. 3-6). pap. 8.95 *(978-1-58980-782-2(0))* Pelican Publishing Co., Inc.
Parker, Natalie C. Beware the Wild. 2014. (Beware the Wild Ser.: 1). (ENG.). 336p. (YA). (gr. 8). 17.99 *(978-0-06-224152-8(4)*, HarperTeen) HarperCollins Pubs.
Pellerin, Mona. Peetie & the Marsh Aliens, 1 vol. 2010. 58p. pap. 16.95 *(978-1-4489-7017-9(2))* America Star Bks.
Poole-Carter, Rosemary. Juliette Ascending. 2007. (YA). pap. 14.00 *(978-1-929976-41-6(0)*, TOP) Top Pubns., Ltd.
Preble, Laura. Lica's Angel. 2003. 142p. (YA). 21.95 *(978-0-595-74914-0(3))*; pap. 11.95 *(978-0-595-28253-1(9))* iUniverse, Inc.
Quinn, Spencer, pseud. ARF - A Bowser & Birdie Novel. 2016. (ENG.). 304p. (J). (gr. 3-7). 16.99 *(978-0-545-64334-4(1)*, Scholastic Pr.) Scholastic, Inc.
—Bow Wow: a Bowser & Birdie Novel. 2017. (ENG.). 304p. (J). (gr. 3-7). 16.99 ***(978-1-338-09134-2(4)***, Scholastic Pr.) Scholastic, Inc.
Quinn, Spencer, pseud. Woof. (Bowser & Birdie Mystery Ser.). (ENG.). 304p. (J). (gr. 3-7). 2016. pap. 7.99 *(978-0-545-64332-0(5))* 2015. 16.99 *(978-0-545-64331-3(7)*, Scholastic Pr.) Scholastic, Inc.
—Woof. 2016. lib. bdg. 18.40 *(978-0-606-39011-8(1))* Turtleback Bks.
Rhodes, Jewell Parker. Bayou Magic. 2015. (ENG., Illus.). 256p. (J). (gr. 3-7). 17.99 *(978-0-316-22484-0(7))* Little Brown & Co.
—Bayou Magic. 2016. (ENG.). 272p. (J). (gr. 3-7). pap. 7.99 *(978-0-316-22485-7(5))* Little, Brown Bks. for Young Readers.
—Sugar. (ENG.). 288p. (J). (gr. 3-7). 2014. pap. 7.99 *(978-0-316-04306-9(0))* 2013. 16.99 *(978-0-316-04305-2(2))* Little, Brown Bks. for Young Readers.
Ruby, Lois. The Secret of Laurel Oaks. 2009. (ENG.). 288p. (YA). (gr. 6-9). 5.99 *(978-0-7653-5229-3(X)*, 9780765352293, Starscape) Doherty, Tom Assocs., LLC.
Salley, Coleen. Epossumondas Plays Possum. Stevens, Janet, illus. 2009. (ENG.). 40p. (J). (gr. -1-3). 17.99 *(978-0-15-206420-4(6))* Houghton Mifflin Harcourt Publishing Co.
San Souci, Robert D. Six Foolish Fishermen, 1 vol. Kennedy, Doug, illus. 2011. (ENG.). 32p. (J). (gr. k-3). 16.99 *(978-1-4556-1473-8(4))* Pelican Publishing Co., Inc.
Savage, J. Scott. Making the Team. Holgate, Doug, illus. 2013. (Case File 13 Ser.: 2). (ENG.). 272p. (J). (gr. 3-7). 14.99 *(978-0-06-213331-1(4))* HarperCollins Pubs.
—Zombie Kid. Holgate, Doug, illus. 2013. (Case File 13 Ser.: 1). (ENG.). 304p. (J). (gr. 3-7). pap. 6.99 *(978-0-06-213327-4(6))* HarperCollins Pubs.
Schmitt, Nannette Toups. Remember Last Island. Gorman, Carolyn Portier, ed. Schmitt, Nannette Toups & Endres, Sharlene Duggan, illus. 2003. 206p. (YA). pap. 19.95 *(978-0-9740901-0-8(7)*, 11-May) Orage Publishing.
Silvano, Wendi. Love Is All Around Louisiana. Czernichowska, Joanna, illus. 2016. (ENG.). 32p. (J). (-6). 12.99 *(978-1-4926-2930-6(8)*, Sourcebooks Jabberwocky) Sourcebooks, Inc.
Simon, Margaret. Blessen. 2012. 120p. (J). pap. 15.00 *(978-0-9848915-2-8(8))* Border Pr.
Sinykin, Sheri. Giving up the Ghost, 1 vol. (ENG.). (YA). 2011. 240p. pap. 7.95 *(978-1-56145-572-0(5))* 2007. 224p. (gr. 4-7). pap. 14.95 *(978-1-56145-423-5(0))* Peachtree Pubs.
Smallman, Steve. Santa Is Coming to Louisiana. Dunn, Robert, illus. 2012. (ENG.). 32p. (J). (-3). 9.99 *(978-1-4022-7536-4(6)*, Sourcebooks Jabberwocky) Sourcebooks, Inc.
Smith, Rosemary. Lizard Tales: Lizzie Walks on the Wild Side. 2010. 28p. pap. 12.50 *(978-1-60911-082-6(X)*, Strategic Bk. Publishing) Strategic Book Publishing & Rights Agency (SBPRA).
Snyder, Sandy. There's Only One I in Charlie. Ferrenburg, Susie, illus. 2011. 48p. pap. 24.95 *(978-1-4626-4086-7(9))* America Star Bks.
St. Romain, Rose Anne. Monsieur Durand's Grosse Affaire, 1 vol. Waites, Joan, illus. 2011. (ENG.). 32p. (J). (gr. k-3). 16.99 *(978-1-58980-808-9(8))* Pelican Publishing Co., Inc.
Sullivan, Kiki. The Dolls. 2014. (Dolls Ser.: 1). (ENG.). 384p. (YA). (gr. 8). pap. 9.99 *(978-0-06-228148-7(8))* HarperCollins Pubs.
Thomas, Wes. Down the Crawfish Hole, 1 vol. Thomas, Wes, illus. 2004. (ENG., Illus.). 32p. (J). (gr. k-3). 16.99 *(978-1-58980-163-9(6))* Pelican Publishing Co., Inc.
Top Secret Tiaras. 2009. (Princess Protection Program Ser.: No. 3). (ENG.). 144p. (J). (gr. 3-7). pap. 4.99 *(978-1-4231-2392-7(1))* Disney Pr.
Watts, Jane & Nobel, DeAnna. The Adventures of Alligator Tater. 2007. 64p. per. 10.95 *(978-1-4327-0228-1(9))* Outskirts Pr., Inc.
Woods, Wendy. Welcome Home, Indigeaux: A Louisiana Adventure. Martin, Sherry, illus. 2013. (ENG.). (J). (gr. -1-3). 14.95 *(978-1-62086-246-9(8))* Mascot Bks., Inc.

LOUISIANA—HISTORY

Bailey, Tom. Jean Baptiste le Moyne, Sieur de Bienville: Father of Mobile. 2012. (Illus.). 112p. (J). *(978-1-59421-082-2(9)*, Blackbirch Pr., Inc.) Seacoast Publishing, Inc.
Bjorklund, Ruth & Steinitz, Andy. Louisiana. 2nd rev. ed. 2010. (It's My State! Ser.). 80p. (gr. 3-18). lib. bdg. 31.36 *(978-1-60870-051-6(8))* Marshall Cavendish Corp.
Cates, David & Armstrong, Margalynne. Plessy v. Ferguson: Segregation & the Separate but Equal Policy, 1 vol. 2012. (Landmark Supreme Court Cases Ser.). (ENG., Illus.). 160p. (J). (gr. 6-12). 37.07 *(978-1-61783-475-2(0))* ABDO Publishing Co.
Coleman, Miriam. Louisiana: The Pelican State. 2010. (Our Amazing States Ser.). (ENG.). 24p. (J). pap. 8.25 *(978-1-4488-0740-6(9))*; lib. bdg. 22.60 *(978-1-4488-0654-6(2))* Rosen Publishing Group, Inc., The. (PowerKids Pr.).
Downing, Johnette. Today Is Monday in Louisiana, 1 vol. Thomas, Deborah, illus. 2016. 8p. (J). bds. 9.95 *(978-1-4556-2306-8(7))* Pelican Publishing Co., Inc.
Eakin, Sue, et al. Louisiana: The Land & Its People, 1 vol. Culbertson, James Forrest, illus. 5th ed. 2006. (ENG.). 560p. 35.00 *(978-1-58980-303-9(5))* Pelican Publishing Co., Inc.
Faucheux, Guy N. & Faucheux, Wallace P. Cajun Comiques Historic Louisiana: An Illustrated History for Kids of All Ages. 2004. (Illus.). 56p. (YA). lib. bdg. 16.95 *(978-0-9718433-1-8(7))* St. Roux Pr.
Felix, Rebecca. What's Great about Louisiana? 2015. (ENG., Illus.). 32p. (J). (gr. 2-5). 26.65 *(978-1-4677-3879-8(4))* Lerner Publishing Group.
Freedman, Jeri. Louisiana: Past & Present. 2010. (United States: Past & Present Ser.). (ENG.). 48p. (YA). pap. 11.75 *(978-1-4358-9510-2(X))*; lib. bdg. 29.25 *(978-1-4358-9483-9(9))* Rosen Publishing Group, Inc., The. (Rosen Reference).
Jerome, Kate B. Lucky to Live in Louisiana. 2017. (Arcadia Kids Ser.). (ENG., Illus.). 32p. (J). 16.99 ***(978-0-7385-2792-5(0))*** Arcadia Publishing.
Johnstone, Robb. Louisiana: The Pelican State. 2016. (J). *(978-1-4896-4869-3(0))* Weigl Pubs., Inc.
Knudsen, Anders. Antoine de la Mothe Cadillac: French Settlements at Detroit & Louisiana. 2006. (In the Footsteps of Explorers Ser.). (ENG., Illus.). 32p. (J). (gr. 3-9). lib. bdg. *(978-0-7787-2429-2(8))*; (gr. 4-7). pap. *(978-0-7787-2465-0(4))* Crabtree Publishing Co.
Koestler-Grack, Rachel A. Daily Life in a Southern Trading Town: New Orleans. 2003. (J). *(978-1-58417-013-6(1))*; pap. *(978-1-58417-076-1(X))* Lake Street Pubs.
Kurtz, Jane. Celebrating Louisiana: 50 States to Celebrate. Canga, C. B., illus. 2016. (Green Light Readers Level 3 Ser.). (ENG.). 40p. (J). (gr. 1-4). pap. 3.99 *(978-0-544-51827-8(6)*, HMH Books For Young Readers) Houghton Mifflin Harcourt Publishing Co.
Lassieur, Allison. Louisiana. 2014. (America the Beautiful Ser.: 3). (ENG.). 144p. (J). lib. bdg. 40.00 *(978-0-531-24886-7(0)*, Children's Pr.) Scholastic Library Publishing.
Macaulay, Ellen. Louisiana. 2009. (From Sea to Shining Sea, Second Ser.). (ENG.). 80p. (J). pap. 7.95 *(978-0-531-21132-8(0)*, Children's Pr.) Scholastic Library Publishing.
Marsh, Carole. Exploring Louisiana Through Project-Based Learning. 2016. (Louisiana Experience Ser.). (ENG.). (J). pap. 9.99 *(978-0-635-12342-8(8))* Gallopade International.
—Let's Discover Louisiana! 2004. (J). (gr. 2-8). cd-rom 14.95 *(978-0-7933-9553-8(4))* Gallopade International.
—Louisiana History Projects: 30 Cool, Activities, Crafts, Experiments & More for Kids to Do to Learn about Your State! 2003. (Louisiana Experience Ser.). 32p. (gr. k-5). pap. 5.95 *(978-0-635-01787-1(3)*, Marsh, Carole Bks.) Gallopade International.
McGee, Randel. Paper Crafts for Mardi Gras. 2011. (Paper Craft Fun for Holidays Ser.). (Illus.). 48p. (J). (gr. 2-5). lib. bdg. 25.27 *(978-0-7660-3724-3(X))* Enslow Pubs., Inc.
Murray, Julie. Louisiana, 1 vol. 2012. (Explore the United States Ser.). (ENG., Illus.). 32p. (J). (gr. 2-5). lib. bdg. 28.50 *(978-1-61783-356-4(8)*, Big Buddy Bks.) ABDO Publishing Co.
Omoth, Tyler. The Story of the New Orleans Hornets. 2010. (NBA — A History of Hoops Ser.). 48p. (YA). (gr. 5-18). 23.95 *(978-1-58341-954-0(3)*, Creative Education) Creative Co., The.
Prieto, Anita C. Little Louisiana. Knorr, Laura, illus. 2011. (My Little State Ser.). (ENG.). 20p. 9.95 *(978-1-58536-184-7(4))* Sleeping Bear Pr.
Richard, Zachary, ed. The History of the Acadians of Louisiana. 2013. (ENG.). pap. 24.95 *(978-1-935754-29-9(7))* Univ. of Louisiana at Lafayette Pr.
Swanson, Angie. Louisiana. 2016. (States Ser.). (ENG., Illus.). 32p. (gr. 3-4). lib. bdg. 27.32 *(978-1-5157-0405-8(X))* Next Page Pr., The.
Vierow, Wendy. The Capture of New Orleans: Union Fleet Takes Control of the Lower Mississippi. 2009. (Headlines from History Ser.). 24p. (gr. 3-3). 42.50 *(978-1-61513-245-4(7)*, PowerKids Pr.) Rosen Publishing Group, Inc., The.
Worth, Richard. Louisiana, 1682-1803. 2006. (National Geographic Voices from ColonialAmerica Ser.). (ENG., Illus.). 112p. (J). (gr. 5-9). 21.95 *(978-0-7922-6544-3(0))*; lib. bdg. 32.90 *(978-0-7922-6850-5(4))* National Geographic Society. (National Geographic Children's Bks.).
Yasuda, Anita. Louisiana: The Pelican State. 2012. (J). *(978-1-61913-355-6(5))*; pap. *(978-1-61913-356-3(3))* Weigl Pubs., Inc.
Ziff, John. Gulf States: Alabama, Louisiana, Mississippi, Vol. 19. 2015. (Let's Explore the States Ser.). (Illus.). 64p. (J). (gr. 5). 23.95 *(978-1-4222-3324-5(3))* Mason Crest.

LOUISIANA PURCHASE

Alagna, Magdalena. The Louisiana Purchase: Expanding America's Boundaries. (Life in the New American Nation Ser.). 32p. 2009. (gr. 4-4). 47.90 *(978-1-61514-284-2(3))* 2004. (ENG., Illus.). (gr. 5-8). pap. 10.00 *(978-0-8239-4257-2(0))* Rosen Publishing Group, Inc., The.
Benoit, Peter. The Louisiana Purchase. 2012. (Cornerstones of Freedom, Third Ser.). (ENG., Illus.). 64p. (J). pap. 8.95 *(978-0-531-28160-4(4))*; (gr. 4-6). lib. bdg. 30.00 *(978-0-531-23060-2(0))* Scholastic Library Publishing. (Children's Pr.).
Burgan, Michael. The Louisiana Purchase. 2016. (Making a New Nation Ser.). (ENG.). 48p. (gr. 4-4). pap. 8.99 *(978-1-4846-3596-4(5)*, NA-h) Heinemann-Raintree.
Fradin, Dennis Brindell. The Louisiana Purchase. 2009. (Turning Points in U. S. History Ser.). 48p. (gr. 3-18). 31.36 *(978-0-7614-4257-8(X))* Marshall Cavendish Corp.
Harasymiw, Therese. The Louisiana Purchase. 2009. (American History Milestones Ser.). 32p. (gr. 5-5). 47.90 *(978-1-61511-374-3(6)*, PowerKids Pr.) Rosen Publishing Group, Inc., The.
Landau, Elaine. Jefferson's Louisiana Purchase: Would You Make the Deal of the Century? 2015. (What Would You Do? Ser.). 48p. (J). (gr. 3-4). 25.27 *(978-0-7660-6305-1(4))*; pap. 8.95 *(978-0-7660-6306-8(2)*, Enslow Elementary) Enslow Pubs., Inc.
—The Louisiana Purchase: Would You Close the Deal? (What Would You Do? Ser.). (Illus.). 48p. (J). 2010. pap. 8.95 *(978-1-59845-196-2(0))* 2008. (gr. 3-7). lib. bdg. 25.27 *(978-0-7660-2902-6(6))* Enslow Pubs., Inc. (Enslow Elementary).
Marsh, Carole. Louisiana Purchase. 2003. 12p. (gr. k-4). 2.95 *(978-0-635-02132-8(3))* Gallopade International.
—What a Deal! The Louisiana Purchase. 2003. 32p. (J). (gr. 3-8). pap. 5.95 *(978-0-635-02123-6(4))* Gallopade International.
McNeese, Tim. The Louisiana Purchase. 2008. (Milestones in American History Ser.). (Illus.). 144p. (YA). (gr. 7-12). 35.00 *(978-1-60413-052-2(0))* Facts On File, Inc.
Nelson, Sheila. Thomas Jefferson's America: The Louisiana Purchase (1800-1811) 2006. (How America Became America Ser.). (Illus.). 96p. (YA). lib. bdg. 22.95 *(978-1-59084-904-0(3))* Mason Crest.
Pierce, Alan. Louisiana Purchase, 1 vol. 2004. (American Moments Ser.). (ENG.). 48p. (gr. 4-8). 27.07 *(978-1-59197-287-7(6)*, Abdo & Daughters) ABDO Publishing Co.
Raabe, Emily. Thomas Jefferson & the Louisiana Purchase. (Westward Ho! Ser.). 24p. 2009. (gr. 2-3). 42.50 *(978-1-60854-763-0(9))* 2003. (Illus.). (J). lib. bdg. 22.60 *(978-0-8239-6499-4(X))* Rosen Publishing Group, Inc., The. (PowerKids Pr.).
Raum, Elizabeth. Expanding a Nation: Causes & Effects of the Louisiana Purchase, 1 vol. 2013. (Cause & Effect Ser.). (ENG.). 32p. (gr. 3-4). 27.32 *(978-1-4765-0236-6(6))*; pap. 8.95 *(978-1-4765-3402-2(0))* Capstone Press of Coughlan Cos. (Fact Finders).
Raum, Elizabeth, et al. Cause & Effect, 1 vol. (Cause & Effect Ser.). (ENG.). 32p. (gr. 3-4). 2014. lib. bdg. 163.92 *(978-1-4765-7825-5(7))* 2013. pap. 31.80 *(978-1-4765-3634-7(1))* 2013. lib. bdg. 109.28 *(978-1-4765-0371-4(0))* Capstone Press of Coughlan Cos. (Fact Finders).
Roop, Peter & Roop, Connie. Louisiana Purchase. Comport, Sally Wern, illus. 2004. 84p. (J). lib. bdg. 15.00 *(978-1-4242-0908-8(0))* Fitzgerald Bks.
Schaffer, David. The Louisiana Purchase: The Deal of the Century That Doubled the Nation. 2006. (Wild History of the American West Ser.). (Illus.). 128p. (J). (gr. 5-9). lib. bdg. 34.60 *(978-1-59845-018-7(2)*, MyReportLinks.com Bks.) Enslow Pubs., Inc.
Sharp, Constance. Thomas Jefferson & the Growing United States (1800-1811) 2012. (J). pap. *(978-1-4222-2414-4(7))* Mason Crest.
—Thomas Jefferson & the Growing United States (1800-1811) Rakove, Jack N., ed. 2012. (How America Became America Ser.). 48p. (J). (gr. 3-4). 19.95 *(978-1-4222-2400-7(7))* Mason Crest.
Shea, Therese. The Louisiana Purchase. 2009. (Real Life Readers Ser.). 32p. (J). (ENG., Illus.). (gr. 5-6). pap. 10.00 *(978-1-4358-0209-4(8))*; (gr. 4-6). lib. bdg. 25.25 *(978-1-4358-3017-2(2))* Rosen Publishing Group, Inc., The. (PowerKids Pr.).
Shea, Therese. The Louisiana Purchase & the Lewis & Clark Expedition. 2017. (J). ***(978-1-5383-0013-8(3))***; pap. ***(978-1-68048-790-9(6))*** Rosen Publishing Group, Inc., The. (Britannica Educational Publishing).
Steele, Christy. The Louisiana Purchase. 2005. (America's Westward Expansion Ser.). (Illus.). 48p. (gr. 5-12). lib. bdg. 31.00 *(978-0-8368-5789-4(5)*, Gareth Stevens Secondary Library) Stevens, Gareth Publishing LLLP.
Yasuda, Anita. 12 Incredible Facts about the Louisiana Purchase. 2015. (Turning Points in US History Ser.). (ENG., Illus.). 32p. (J). (gr. 3-5). *(978-1-63235-131-9(5)*, 12-Story Library) Pr. Room Editions LLC.
Zurn, Jon. The Louisiana Purchase, 1 vol. 2007. (Essential Events Set 1 Ser.). (ENG., Illus.). 112p. (J). (gr. 6-12). lib. bdg. 35.64 *(978-1-59928-853-6(2))* ABDO Publishing Co.

LOVE, NAT, 1854-1921

Cefrey, Holly. From Slave to Cowboy: The Nat Love Story. 2009. (Great Moments in American History Ser.). 32p. (gr. 3-3). 47.90 *(978-1-61513-142-6(6))* Rosen Publishing Group, Inc., The.
Nat Love. 2010. (Legends of the Wild West Ser.). (Illus.). 104p. (gr. 6-12). 35.00 *(978-1-60413-599-2(9)*, Chelsea Hse.) Facts On File, Inc.
Penn, Sarah. Nat Love: African American Cowboy. (Primary Sources of Famous People in American History Ser.). 32p. 2009. (gr. 2-3). 47.90 *(978-1-60851-706-0(3))* 2004. (ENG., Illus.). (gr. 4-8). pap. 10.00 *(978-0-8239-4188-9(4))* Rosen Publishing Group, Inc., The.
—Nat Love: African American Cowboy / Vaquero Afroamericano. 2009. (Famous People in American History/Grandes personajes en la historia de los Estados Unidos Ser.). (ENG & SPA.). 32p. (gr. 2-3). 47.90 *(978-1-61512-551-7(5)*, Editorial Buenas Letras) Rosen Publishing Group, Inc., The.
—Nat Love: Vaquero Afroamericano. 2004. (Grandes personajes en la historia de los Estados Unidos Ser.). (SPA.). 32p. (gr. 4-8). pap. 10.00 *(978-0-8239-4234-3(1)*, Rosen Classroom) Rosen Publishing Group, Inc., The.
—Nat Love: Vaquero afroamericano (Nat Love: African American Cowboy) 2009. (Grandes personajes en la historia de los Estados Unidos (Famous People in American History) Ser.). (SPA.). 32p. (gr. 2-3). 47.90 *(978-1-61512-804-4(2)*, Editorial Buenas Letras) Rosen Publishing Group, Inc., The.
Underwood, Deborah. Nat Love. 2008. pap. 52.95 *(978-0-8225-9395-9(5))*; (ENG., Illus.). 48p. (gr. 3-6). lib. bdg. 27.93 *(978-0-8225-7171-1(4)*, Lerner Pubns.) Lerner Publishing Group.

LOVE

see also Dating (Social Customs); Friendship; Marriage
Accord Publishing Staff. Where Does Love Come From? Kirkova, Milena, illus. 2012. (ENG.). 18p. (J). bds. 5.99 *(978-1-4494-2884-6(3))* Andrews McMeel Publishing.
Ashour, Monica. Every Body Is a Gift: God Made Us to Love. Kaminski, Karol, illus. 2015. (J). 12.95 *(978-0-8198-2376-2(7))* Pauline Bks. & Media.
Bloomsbury USA. I Love You. 2015. (ENG., Illus.). 10p. (J). (gr. -1-1). bds. 6.99 *(978-1-61963-802-0(9)*, 9781619638020, Bloomsbury USA Childrens) Bloomsbury Publishing USA.
Chidvilasananda. Good Night, Sweet Dreams, I Love You! 2004. (Illus.). (J). *(978-1-930939-01-1(9))* SYDA Foundation.
Chipman-Sullivan, Lois. What Does Love Mean, God? 2013. 36p. pap. 10.50 *(978-1-61286-141-8(5))* Avid Readers Publishing Group.
Clark, Chap. Next Time I Fall in Love: How to Handle Sex, Intimacy, & Feelings in Dating Relationships. 2004. 144p. pap. 20.00 *(978-1-59244-684-1(1)*, Wipf and Stock) Wipf & Stock Pubs.
Constantine, Robin. The Season of You & Me. 2016. 352p. (YA). (gr. 9). 17.99 *(978-0-06-243883-6(2))* HarperCollins Pubs.
Dean, James & Dean, Kimberly. Pete the Cat's Guide to Love. Dean, James, illus. 2015. (Pete the Cat Ser.). (ENG., Illus.). 48p. (J). (gr. -1-3). 12.99 *(978-0-06-243061-8(0))* HarperCollins Pubs.
Devadasan, Rashmi Ruth. Kumari Loves a Monster: Kumariyin Ratcaca Katalan. Shyam, illus. 2010. (TAM & ENG.). 52p. pap. 17.95 *(978-93-80636-01-6(6))* Blaft Pubns.
Eastham, Chad. The Truth about Breaking Up, Making Up, & Moving On, 1 vol. 2013. (ENG.). 240p. (YA). pap. 14.99 *(978-1-4003-2115-5(8))* Nelson, Thomas Inc.
Feldman, Rachel S. The Little Tree. 2010. 32p. pap. 14.99 *(978-1-4520-0033-6(6))* AuthorHouse.
Foldvary-Anderson, Carol. Hearts & Roses Stained Glass Coloring Book. 2009. (Dover Design Stained Glass Coloring Book Ser.). (ENG., Illus.). 32p. (gr. 3-8). pap. 6.99 *(978-0-486-47023-8(7))* Dover Pubns., Inc.
Garlick, Kim. Thank You. 2012. 20p. pap. 17.99 *(978-1-4772-0485-6(7))* AuthorHouse.
Greene, Kathy B. How I Love You!, 1 vol. 2009. 19p. pap. 24.95 *(978-1-60749-681-6(X))* America Star Bks.
Gynux, illus. Jesus Loves Me, 1 vol. 2017. (Sing-Along Book Ser.). (ENG.). 20p. (J). bds. 8.99 *(978-0-310-75894-5(7))* Zonderkidz.
Hamilton, Alice. Loving Hands of Grandma: A True Story. 2012. 24p. pap. 24.95 *(978-1-4626-7432-9(1))* PublishAmerica, Inc.
Hammonds, Theresa D. God's Invisible Fruit of Love. 2013. 24p. pap. 15.00 *(978-0-9824550-5-0(4))* Kingdom Kaught Publishing LLC.
Harper, Suzanne. The 10 Most Tragic Romances. 2008. (J). 14.99 *(978-1-55448-546-8(0))* Scholastic Library Publishing.
Hawkins Harris, Jennifer. Love: The Book of Love for Kids. Gray Mayo, Jo Ann, illus. 2003. 20p. (J). per. 7.00 *(978-0-9705458-2-4(7))* Royalty Bks. International, Inc.
Hinds, Sandra A. I Love You Every. 2012. 32p. pap. 19.99 *(978-1-4567-2418-4(5))* AuthorHouse.
Hudson, Sue. I Love You. Watanabe, Kaori, illus. 2004. (My First Taggies Book Ser.). (ENG.). 3p. (J). (gr. k — 1). 12.99 *(978-0-439-64947-6(1)*, Cartwheel Bks.) Scholastic, Inc.
I Love You Because You're. 2004. (J). pap. 6.99 *(978-0-439-57711-3(X))* Scholastic, Inc.

Kavanaugh, Dorothy. Feeling Unloved? Girls Dealing with Feelings. 2014. (ENG.). 64p. (J). (gr. 5-12). 15.95 *(978-1-62293-050-0(9))* Enslow Pubs., Inc.
Kid, Penelope. Teach Me to Love. Goffe, Toni, illus. 2004. (Teach Me Ser.). 24p. (gr. -1-2). 6.95 *(978-0-8294-1369-4(3))* Loyola Pr.
Lantos, James, ed. & compiled by. Love: Vintage Images of America's Living Past. Lantos, James, compiled by. 2010. (Applewood's Pictorial America Ser.). (ENG.). 56p. pap. 9.95 *(978-1-60889-008-8(2))* Applewood Bks.
Learn As You Grow. God Loves You So Much... Reuben, Borgen & Jenny, Lindley, photos by. 2010. (ENG., Illus.). 24p. (J). 12.95 *(978-0-9824652-3-3(8))* Learn As You Grow, L.L.C.
LeJeune, Shonda. Love Is... 2003. (Illus.). 30p. (gr. -1-3). pap. 11.50 *(978-0-87516-690-2(3))*; (gr. 2-18). 14.50 *(978-0-87516-691-9(1))* DeVorss & Co.
L'Heureux, Christine. Caillou: I Love You. Brignaud, Pierre, illus. 2012. (Hand in Hand Ser.). (ENG.). 24p. (J). (gr. -1-k). 5.95 *(978-2-89450-860-2(3))* Caillouet, Gerry.
—Caillou Meets a Princess. Brignaud, Pierre, illus. 2014. (ENG.). 24p. (J). (gr. -1-k). 5.99 *(978-2-89718-114-7(1))* Caillouet, Gerry.
Logan, John. An Unloved Guy's Guide: How to Deal. 2014. (ENG.). 64p. (J). (gr. 5-12). 15.95 *(978-1-62293-020-3(7))* Enslow Pubs., Inc.
Logan, John & Kavanaugh, Dorothy. A Guys' Guide to Love. 2008. (Flip-It-Over Guides to Teen Emotions Ser.). (Illus.). 128p. (J). (gr. k-5). lib. bdg. 33.27 *(978-0-7660-2855-5(0))* Enslow Pubs., Inc.
Mackall, Dandi Daley. God Made Polliwogs & Puppy Dogs. 2015. (ENG., Illus.). 32p. (J). 12.99 *(978-0-7369-5873-8(8))* Harvest Hse. Pubs.
Marsh, Carole. Someone I Love Went off to War. 2003. 24p. (gr. 1-8). pap. 5.95 *(978-0-635-02092-5(0))* Gallopade International.
Mayo, Jeanne. Uncensored: Dating, Friendship, & Sex. 2007. (Illus.). 237p. (YA). (gr. 7-12). per. 14.99 *(978-1-57794-821-6(1))* Harrison House Pubs.
McCloud, Carol & Wells, Karen. Will You Fill My Bucket? Daily Acts of Love Around the World. Weber, Penny, illus. 2012. (ENG.). 32p. (J). (-4). pap. 9.95 *(978-1-933916-97-2(4))* Bucket Fillers, Inc.
McKnight, Scot & McKnight Barringer, Laura. Sharing God's Love: The Jesus Creed for Children. Hill, David, illus. 2014. (ENG.). 32p. (J). pap. 15.99 *(978-1-61261-581-3(3))* Paraclete Pr., Inc.
Mcknight, Scot & McKnight Barringer, Laura. Sharing God's Love: the Jesus Creed for Children: Teacher Lesson & Activity Guide. 2014. (ENG., Illus.). 36p. (gr. 13). spiral bd. 19.95 *(978-1-61261-637-7(2))* Paraclete Pr., Inc.
Miles, Lisa & Chown, Xanna Eve. How to Survive Having a Crush. 2013. (Girl Talk Ser.). 48p. (J). (gr. 5-8). pap. 70.50 *(978-1-4777-0727-2(1),* Rosen Reference); (ENG., Illus.). pap. 11.75 *(978-1-4777-0720-3(4),* Rosen Reference); (ENG., Illus.). lib. bdg. 29.25 *(978-1-4777-0706-7(9),* Rosen Classroom) Rosen Publishing Group, Inc., The.
Miller, Eileen Rudisill. True Love Stained Glass Coloring Book. 2011. (Dover Stained Glass Coloring Book Ser.). (ENG., Illus.). 32p. (gr. 3-8). pap. 6.99 *(978-0-486-47835-7(1))* Dover Pubns., Inc.
óMeta, CéSar. Blue Dragonflies. 2011. 64p. (gr. 4-6). pap. 9.99 *(978-1-4634-4690-1(X))* AuthorHouse.
Pears, Alison. Gus & Oliver-A Family Tale. 2012. 30p. pap. 13.99 *(978-1-4525-5472-3(2))* Balboa Pr.
Poelman, Heidi. I Can Love Like Jesus. 2017. (ENG., Illus.). (J). (gr. -1-2). 14.99 ***(978-1-4621-1940-0(9))*** Cedar Fort, Inc./CFI Distribution.
Poulin, Andrée. The Magic Clothesline. Arbona, Marion, illus. 2012. 32p. (J). pap. 9.95 *(978-1-4338-1195-1(2),* Magination Pr.) American Psychological Assn.
Richardson, Joy K. A Helping Hand Series: I Love You. 2009. 16p. pap. 10.49 *(978-1-4389-9432-1(X))* AuthorHouse.
Rotner, Shelley. What's Love? 2013. (Shelley Rotner's World Ser.). (ENG.). 32p. (gr. 1-2). pap. 47.70 *(978-1-62065-757-7(0),* Aplus Bks.) Capstone Press of Coughlan Cos.
Rotner, Shelley & Kelly, Sheila M. What's Love?, 1 vol. Rotner, Shelley, photos by. 2013. (Shelley Rotner's World Ser.). (ENG., Illus.). 32p. (gr. 1-2). pap. 8.10 *(978-1-62065-756-0(2))*; lib. bdg. 27.32 *(978-1-62065-069-1(X))* Capstone Press of Coughlan Cos.
Rubow, Carol. God Loves You. 2010. (Illus.). 32p. (J). (gr. -1). 12.99 *(978-0-7586-1855-9(7))* Concordia Publishing Hse.
Sheriff, Marcia. God's Great Big Love. 2013. 24p. pap. 12.45 *(978-1-4497-9288-6(X),* WestBow Pr.) Author Solutions, Inc.
Shumway, Lindsey. I Chose You. 2005. (Illus.). 31p. (J). 15.99 *(978-1-55517-861-1(8))* Cedar Fort, Inc./CFI Distribution.
Solomon, Iris L. & Solomon, Ron. Friendz Pakz: Love. 2003. (YA). (gr. 3-18). 4.99 *(978-1-930680-07-4(4),* SSP-08LV) Swingset Pr., LLC.
Spencer, Lauren. Everything You Need to Know about Falling in Love. 2009. (Need to Know Library). 64p. (gr. 5-5). 58.50 *(978-1-60854-067-9(7))* Rosen Publishing Group, Inc., The.
Stewart, Ed & McDowell, Josh. Finding True Love. 2008. (Project 17:17 Ser.). (ENG.). 64p. (J). pap. 4.99 *(978-1-84550-356-7(2),* d5fc11fa-99e7-4d6c-b4b5-7793875db f44) Christian Focus Pubns. GBR. Dist: Bookmasters Distribution.
Stewart, Elizabeth. An Angel Named Love. 2005. 17.00 *(978-0-8059-9815-3(2))* Dorrance Publishing Co., Inc.
Stoop, Naoko, illus. Love Is Patient, Love Is Kind. 2017. (ENG.). 22p. (J). (— 1). bds. 6.95 *(978-1-4549-1767-0(9))* Sterling Publishing Co., Inc.
The True Love Waits Youth Bible. 2004. (Illus.). 1294p. pap. 19.99 *(978-1-55819-621-6(8))* B&H Publishing Group.
Twin Sisters(r) Staff, et al. Jesus Loves Me More Than... 2015. (Let's Share a Story Ser.). (ENG., Illus.). 10p. (J). (gr. -1-k). bds. 9.99 *(978-1-63058-896-0(2))* Barbour Publishing, Inc.
Welch, Ariel & Welch, Ashley. Waiting. 2003. 122p. (YA). pap. 13.95 *(978-0-595-27087-3(5))* iUniverse, Inc.
What Is... Love. (Illus.). 16p. (J). pap. 1.50 *(978-0-87162-827-5(9),* E6019) Warner Pr., Inc.
Wilcox, Christine. Understanding Family & Personal Relationships. 2017. (Understanding Psychology Ser.). (ENG.). 80p. (YA). (gr. 5-12). ***(978-1-68282-273-9(7))*** ReferencePoint Pr., Inc.
Yonezu, Yusuke, illus. We Love Each Other. 2013. (Yonezu Board Book Ser.). (ENG.). 28p. (J). (— 1). bds. 9.95 *(978-988-8240-56-2(0))* Neugebauer, Michael (Publishing) Limited HKG. Dist: Independent Pubs. Group.

LOVE—FICTION

A Caribbean Experience Con Amor. There's a Coqui in My Shoe! 2007. (Illus.). 66p. (J). 21.99 *(978-0-9797641-0-3(6))* Chi Chi Rodriguez Bks.
Abbaszadeh, Paul. One Love: A True Love Story. 2003. 466p. (YA). pap. 28.95 *(978-0-595-28878-6(2))* iUniverse, Inc.
Abbott, Hailey. Boy Crazy. 2009. (ENG.). 240p. (YA). (gr. 9). pap. 8.99 *(978-0-06-125385-0(5),* HarperTeen) HarperCollins Pubs.
—The Bridesmaid. 2005. (ENG.). 272p. (YA). (gr. 7). pap. 7.99 *(978-0-385-73220-8(1),* Delacorte Bks. for Young Readers) Random Hse. Children's Bks.
—Last Summer. 2007. (Summer Boys Ser.: 4). (ENG.). 240p. (J). (gr. 9-12). pap. 8.99 *(978-0-439-86725-2(8))* Scholastic, Inc.
Accord Publishing Staff. Where Does Love Come From? Kirkova, Milena, illus. 2011. (ENG.). 18p. (J). 9.99 *(978-1-4494-0839-8(7))* Andrews McMeel Publishing.
Acocella, Nunzio. Nunzu & His Best Friend. 2012. 32p. pap. 17.25 *(978-1-4669-1143-7(3))* Trafford Publishing.
Adams, Diane. Love Is. Keane, Claire, illus. 2017. (ENG.). 32p. (J). 15.99 *(978-1-4521-3997-5(0))* Chronicle Bks. LLC.
Adams, Kevin. A Stegosaurus Named Sam. Adams, Kevin & Price, Michael, illus. 2004. (J). per. 12.50 *(978-0-9740683-4-3(9))* Authors & Artists Publishers of New York, Inc.
Adams, Kylie. Bling Addiction: Fast Girls, Hot Boys Series. 2006. (Fast Girls, Hot Boys Ser.: 2). (ENG.). 240p. (gr. 10-13). pap. 15.99 *(978-1-4165-2041-2(4),* MTV Bks.) MTV Books.
Adams, L. Happy Memories: A Continuing Family Saga for Young Adults. 2003. 516p. pap. 26.95 *(978-0-595-29210-3(0))* iUniverse, Inc.
Adams, Michelle Medlock. How Much Does God Love You? Keiser, Paige, illus. 2010. 22p. (J). (gr. -1-k). 6.99 *(978-0-8249-1848-4(7),* Ideal Pubns.) Worthy Publishing.
Adkins, Jan. A Storm Without Rain. 2004. (ENG., Illus.). 179p. (YA). (gr. 7). 14.95 *(978-0-937822-80-7(9))* WoodenBoat Pubns.
Adler, Dahlia. Just Visiting. 2015. (ENG.). 348p. (YA). (gr. 10-12). pap. 9.95 *(978-1-63392-053-8(4),* 1396710, Spencer Hill Contemporary) Spencer Hill Pr.
Adornetto, Alexandra. Heaven. 2013. (Halo Trilogy Ser.: 3). (ENG.). 448p. (YA). (gr. 7-12). pap. 10.99 *(978-1-250-02941-6(4),* 9781250029416) Square Fish.
Agresti, Aimee. Illuminate: A Gilded Wings Novel, Book One. 2013. (ENG.). 544p. (YA). (gr. 7). pap. 9.99 *(978-0-544-02222-5(X))* Houghton Mifflin Harcourt Publishing Co.
—Infatuate: A Gilded Wings Novel, Book Two. (ENG.). 416p. (YA). (gr. 7). 2014. pap. 9.99 *(978-0-544-23291-4(7),* HMH Books For Young Readers) 2013. 17.99 *(978-0-547-62615-4(0))* Houghton Mifflin Harcourt Publishing Co.
Aguirre, Ann. Infinite Risk. 2016. (Immortal Game Ser.: 3). (ENG.). 384p. (YA). 17.99 *(978-1-250-02465-7(X),* 9781250024657) Feiwel & Friends.
—Vanguard. 2017. (Razorland Trilogy Ser.). (ENG.). 368p. (J). 17.99 *(978-1-250-08982-3(4),* 9781250089823) Feiwel & Friends.
Ahdieh, Renée. The Rose & the Dagger. (Wrath & the Dawn Ser.). (ENG., Illus.). (YA). (gr. 7). 2017. 448p. pap. 10.99 *(978-0-14-751386-1(3),* Speak) 2016. 432p. 17.99 *(978-0-399-17162-8(2),* G.P. Putnam's Sons Books for Young Readers) Penguin Young Readers Group.
—The Rose & the Dagger. 2017. (Wrath & the Dawn Ser.: 2). lib. bdg. 22.10 ***(978-0-606-40106-7(7))*** Turtleback Bks.
Ahdieh, Renée. The Wrath & the Dawn. 2016. (Wrath & the Dawn Ser.). (ENG.). 432p. (YA). (gr. 7). pap. 10.99 *(978-0-14-751385-4(5),* Speak) Penguin Young Readers Group.
—The Wrath & the Dawn. 2016. lib. bdg. 22.10 *(978-0-606-38849-8(4))* Turtleback Bks.
Ahdieh, Renée & McPike, Elizabeth. The Wrath & the Dawn. 2015. (Wrath & the Dawn Ser.). (ENG., Illus.). 416p. (YA). (gr. 7). 17.99 *(978-0-399-17161-1(4),* G.P. Putnam's Sons Books for Young Readers) Penguin Young Readers Group.
Ahmed, Naval. Blue Moon on Bandideau. 2008. 252p. pap. 15.50 *(978-1-4357-5458-4(1))* Lulu Pr., Inc.
Aker, Don. The Fifth Rule. 2014. 256p. (YA). (gr. 8). pap. 8.99 *(978-0-06-231348-5(7))* HarperCollins Pubs.
Albano, Lydia. Finding You. 2017. (ENG.). 320p. (YA). 17.99 ***(978-1-250-09858-0(0),*** 9781250098580) Feiwel & Friends.
Albert, Lisa. Mercy Lily. 2011. (ENG.). 240p. (YA). pap. 9.95 *(978-0-7387-2699-1(0),* Flux) North Star Editions.
Albert, Melissa & Gray, Lucinda. The Gilded Cage. 2016. (ENG.). 256p. (YA). (gr. 7). 17.99 *(978-1-62779-181-6(7),* 9781627791816, Holt, Henry & Co. Bks. For Young Readers) Holt, Henry & Co.
Alberts, Katharine O. Boo on the Loose. 2006. (J). 14.00 *(978-0-8059-7071-5(1))* Dorrance Publishing Co., Inc.
Alexander, Kwame. He Said, She Said. 2013. 330p. (YA). lib. bdg. *(978-0-06-211897-4(8))* Harper & Row Ltd.
—He Said, She Said. (ENG.). 336p. (YA). (gr. 9). 2014. pap. 9.99 *(978-0-06-211898-1(6))* 2013. 17.99 *(978-0-06-211896-7(X),* Amistad) HarperCollins Pubs.
Alexander, Sarah. The Art Of Not Breathing. 2016. (ENG.). 288p. (YA). (gr. 9). 17.99 *(978-0-544-63388-9(1),* HMH Books For Young Readers) Houghton Mifflin Harcourt Publishing Co.
Alexander, Shannon Lee. Love & Other Unknown Variables. 2014. (Entangled Teen Ser.). (ENG.). 352p. (YA). (gr. 7-12). 16.99 *(978-1-62266-467-2(1),* 9781622664672) Entangled Publishing, LLC.
Alford, Douglas J. & Alford, Pakaket. How Do Hedgehogs Hug? Anderson, Jane A., illus. 2013. 58p. pap. 11.99 *(978-1-62495-071-1(X))* Manufacturing Application Konsulting Engineering (MAKE)in.
Allison, Catherine. Dear Daddy, I Love You. McNicholas, Shelagh, illus. 2014. (ENG.). (J). (gr. -1-3). *(978-1-74363-284-0(3))* Hinkler Bks. Pty, Ltd.
Almond, David. A Song for Ella Grey. 2015. (ENG.). 272p. (YA). (gr. 7). 16.99 *(978-0-553-53359-0(2),* Delacorte Pr.) Random Hse. Children's Bks.
Alphen, Nick Van. One Day. 2012. 20p. pap. 24.95 *(978-1-4626-5524-3(6))* America Star Bks.
Ananda, Linda. Rainbow Childrenr-Magical Moving Stories: Stories with Movement, Dance, Yoga, & Song. 2012. 152p. pap. 47.95 *(978-1-4525-5475-4(7))* Balboa Pr.
Anderson, Jennifer. King of the Lake. 2013. 144p. (YA). pap. 10.99 *(978-1-62237-217-1(4))* Turquoise Morning Pr.
Anderson, Jodi Lynn. Tiger Lily. (ENG.). 304p. (YA). (gr. 9). 2013. pap. 9.99 *(978-0-06-200326-3(7))* 2012. 17.99 *(978-0-06-200325-6(9))* HarperCollins Pubs. (HarperTeen).
Anderson, Lily. The Only Thing Worse Than Me Is You. 2016. (ENG.). 352p. (YA). 18.99 *(978-1-250-07909-1(8),* 9781250079091, St. Martin's Griffin) St. Martin's Pr.
Anderson, Maree. Freaks in the City, Bk.2. 2015. (ENG., Illus.). 290p. pap. *(978-0-9941160-2-4(0))* Anderson, Maree.
Andreae, Giles. Heaven Is Having You. Cabban, Vanessa, illus. 2007. (Padded Board Bks.). 18p. (J). (gr. -1-1). bds. 7.95 *(978-1-58925-820-4(7))* Tiger Tales.
—Keep Love in Your Heart, Little One. Vulliamy, Clara, illus. 2007. 32p. (J). (gr. -1-3). 15.95 *(978-1-58925-066-6(4))* Tiger Tales.
—Love Is a Handful of Honey. Cabban, Vanessa, illus. 2004. 32p. (J). (gr. -1-k). 5.95 *(978-1-58925-353-7(1))* Tiger Tales.
Angelini, Josephine. Trail of Tears. 2015. (Worldwalker Trilogy Ser.: 2). (SPA & ENG.). 352p. (YA). (gr. 7). 17.99 *(978-1-250-05090-8(1),* 9781250050908) Feiwel & Friends.
Anne, Margo. Lily Rose. 2008. 194p. pap. 24.95 *(978-1-60703-847-4(1))* America Star Bks.
Anonuevo, Rechelle. The Moonlight Serenade. 2003. 140p. (YA). pap. 11.95 *(978-0-595-30627-5(6))* iUniverse, Inc.
Anstey, Cindy. Duels & Deception. 2017. (ENG.). 368p. (YA). pap. 10.99 *(978-1-250-11909-4(X),* 9781250119094) Feiwel & Friends.
Anstey, Cindy & Anstey, Cynthia. Love, Lies & Spies. 2016. (ENG.). 368p. (YA). pap. 10.99 *(978-1-250-08403-3(2),* 9781250084033) Feiwel & Friends.
Appelt, Kathi. Oh My Baby, Little One. Dyer, Jane, illus. 2006. (ENG.). 32p. (J). (gr. -1 — 1). pap. 3.99 *(978-0-15-206031-2(6))* Houghton Mifflin Harcourt Publishing Co.
Applegate, Katherine. Beach Blondes. 2008. (Summer Ser.: 1). (ENG.). 736p. (YA). (gr. 9). pap. 9.99 *(978-1-4169-6133-8(X),* Simon Pulse) Simon Pulse.
—Spring Break. 2010. (Summer Ser.). (ENG., Illus.). 240p. (YA). (gr. 9-18). pap. 8.99 *(978-1-4169-9094-9(1),* Simon Pulse) Simon Pulse.
—Sun-Kissed Christmas. 2010. (Summer Ser.). (ENG.). 208p. (YA). (gr. 9-18). pap. 8.99 *(978-1-4169-9397-1(5),* Simon Pulse) Simon Pulse.
—Tan Lines: Sand, Surf, & Secrets; Rays, Romance, & Rivalry; Beaches, Boys, & Betrayal. 2008. (Summer Ser.: 2). (ENG.). 544p. (YA). (gr. 9). pap. 9.99 *(978-1-4169-6134-5(8),* Simon Pulse) Simon Pulse.
Applegate, Katherine & Grant, Michael. The Islanders Vol. 2: Nina Won't Tell & Ben's in Love. 2015. (Islanders Ser.: 2). (ENG.). 464p. (YA). (gr. 8). pap. 9.99 *(978-0-06-234078-8(6),* HarperTeen) HarperCollins Pubs.
Archer, Jennifer. The Shadow Girl. 2013. (ENG.). 336p. (YA). (gr. 8). pap. 9.99 *(978-0-06-183460-8(2),* HarperTeen) HarperCollins Pubs.
Arcos, Carrie. Crazy Messy Beautiful. 2017. (ENG.). 320p. (YA). (gr. 7). 17.99 *(978-0-399-17553-4(9),* Philomel Bks.) Penguin Young Readers Group.
Arguello, Tito. A Dog in Love. 2005. 114p. (J). pap. 8.95 *(978-1-4116-2287-6(1))* Lulu Pr., Inc.
Argueta, Jorge. El Zipitio, 1 vol. Calderon, Gloria, illus. 2003. (SPA.). 32p. (J). 16.95 *(978-0-88899-539-1(3))* Groundwood Bks. CAN. Dist: Publishers Group West (PGW).
Armentrout, Jennifer L. Opposition. (ENG.). 2013. (Lux Ser.: Bk. 5). (J). pap. 9.99 *(978-1-62266-026-1(9),* Entangled Teen) 2014. (Lux Novel Ser.: 5). 500p. (YA). 19.99 *(978-1-62266-733-8(6),* 9781622667338) 2014. (Lux Novel Ser.: 5). 500p. (YA). (gr. 7-12). pap. 11.99 *(978-1-62266-264-7(4),* 9781622662647) Entangled Publishing, LLC.
—Origin. 2013. (ENG.). (Lux Ser.: Bk. 4). (J). pap. 9.99 *(978-1-62061-280-4(1))*; (Lux Novel Ser.: 4). 400p. (YA). (gr. 7-12). pap. 9.99 *(978-1-62266-075-9(7),* 9781622660759) Entangled Publishing, LLC.
—The Problem with Forever. 2016. (ENG.). 480p. 18.99 *(978-0-373-21205-7(4),* Harlequin Teen) Harlequin Enterprises, Ltd. CAN. Dist: HarperCollins Pubs.
Armstrong-Ellis, Carey F. I Love You More Than Moldy Ham. 2015. (ENG., Illus.). 32p. (J). (gr. -1-3). 14.95 *(978-1-4197-1646-1(8),* Abrams Bks. for Young Readers) Abrams, Inc.
Armstrong, Kelley. Forest of Ruin. 2016. (Age of Legends Trilogy Ser.: 3). 448p. (YA). (gr. 8). 17.99 *(978-0-06-207130-9(0))* HarperCollins Pubs.
Arnold, David. Kids of Appetite. (ENG.). (YA). (gr. 9). 2017. 368p. pap. 10.99 ***(978-0-14-751366-3(9),*** Speak) 2016. 352p. 18.99 *(978-0-451-47078-2(8),* Viking Books for Young Readers) Penguin Young Readers Group.
—Kids of Appetite. 2017. lib. bdg. 22.10 ***(978-0-606-40491-4(0))*** Turtleback Bks.
Arzave, Jose. Rabbit the Shepherd. 2013. 24p. pap. 10.99 *(978-1-62509-572-5(4))* Salem Author Services.
Asher, Jay. What Light. 2016. (ENG.). 272p. (YA). (gr. 7). 18.99 *(978-1-59514-551-2(6),* Razorbill) Penguin Young Readers Group.
—What Light. 2017. lib. bdg. 22.10 ***(978-0-606-40488-4(0))*** Turtleback Bks.
Ashton, Brodi. Diplomatic Immunity. 2016. 368p. (YA). (gr. 8). 17.99 *(978-0-06-236856-0(7))* HarperCollins Pubs.
—Everbound. 2013. (Everneath Ser.: 2). (ENG.). (YA). (gr. 8). 384p. pap. 9.99 *(978-0-06-207117-0(3))*; 368p. 17.99 *(978-0-06-207116-3(5))* HarperCollins Pubs.
—Everneath. 2012. (Everneath Ser.: 1). (ENG.). (YA). (gr. 9). 400p. pap. 9.99 *(978-0-06-207114-9(9))*; 384p. 17.99 *(978-0-06-207113-2(0))* HarperCollins Pubs.
Askew, Kim & Helmes, Amy. Anyone but You. 2014. (Twisted Lit Ser.). (ENG.). 224p. (YA). 17.99 *(978-1-4405-7001-8(9),* Simon Pulse) Simon Pulse.
Atwood, D. E. If We Shadows. 2016. (ENG., Illus.). (J). 24.99 ***(978-1-63533-033-5(5))*** 2014. 240p. pap. 14.99 *(978-1-62798-820-9(3))* Dreamspinner Pr. (Harmony Ink Pr.).
Audho, Gaitree. Moral Stories for Kids. 2011. 32p. pap. 12.77 *(978-1-4634-4709-0(4))* AuthorHouse.
Aulbach, Kathy. Flower Sprouts: Let's have a Fest! 2009. 29p. 15.95 *(978-0-615-21683-6(8))* Flower Sprouts.
Austen, Jane. Pride & Prejudice. Kronheimer, Ann, illus. 2013. (Jane Austen Ser.). (ENG.). 64p. pap. 6.95 *(978-1-906230-06-7(4))* Real Reads Ltd. GBR. Dist: Casemate Pubs. & Bk. Distributors, LLC.
—Pride & Prejudice. 2003. (Saddleback Classics Ser.). (Illus.). 48p. (J). stu. ed., per. 17.95 *(978-1-56254-530-7(2),* SP5302); 80p. (YA). (gr. 8-12). per. 6.95 *(978-1-56254-529-1(9),* SP5299) Saddleback Educational Publishing, Inc.
Authords, D. K. Being Alone. 2013. 120p. pap. 19.95 *(978-1-63000-114-8(7))* America Star Bks.
Averett, Edward. Cameron & the Girls. 2014. (ENG.). 224p. (YA). (gr. 9). pap. 8.99 *(978-0-544-30162-7(5),* HMH Books For Young Readers) Houghton Mifflin Harcourt Publishing Co.
Avery, Lara. The Memory Book. 2016. (ENG.). 368p. (YA). (gr. 10-17). 17.99 *(978-0-316-28374-8(6),* Poppy) Little, Brown Bks. for Young Readers.
—The Memory Book. 2017. (YA). lib. bdg. 20.85 ***(978-0-606-39907-4(0))*** Turtleback Bks.
Avery, Lara. A Million Miles Away. 2016. (ENG.). 336p. (YA). (gr. 10-17). pap. 9.99 *(978-0-316-28372-4(X),* Poppy) Little, Brown Bks. for Young Readers.
Babbitt, Natalie. The Eyes of the Amaryllis. 2007. (ENG.). 144p. (J). (gr. 5-8). per. 7.99 *(978-0-312-37008-4(3),* 9780312370084) Square Fish.
Babcock, Nabila. To You That Give. 2012. 24p. pap. 24.95 *(978-1-4626-5215-0(8))* PublishAmerica, Inc.
Bader, Arlys Elaine. The Adventures of Garth & Cloey. 2008. 40p. pap. 16.99 *(978-1-4389-2472-4(0))* AuthorHouse.
Bailey, J. Leigh. Do-Gooder. 2016. (ENG., Illus.). (YA). pap. 14.99 ***(978-1-63477-289-1(X))***; 24.99 ***(978-1-63533-003-8(3))*** Dreamspinner Pr. (Harmony Ink Pr.).
Bailey, Kristin. Legacy of the Clockwork Key. (Secret Order Ser.: 1). (ENG., (YA). (gr. 9). 2014. Illus.). 432p. pap. 9.99 *(978-1-4424-4027-2(9))* 2013. 416p. 17.99 *(978-1-4424-4026-5(0))* Simon Pulse. (Simon Pulse).
—Shadow of the War Machine. 2015. (Secret Order Ser.: 3). (ENG., Illus.). 448p. (YA). (gr. 9). 17.99 *(978-1-4424-6805-4(X),* Simon Pulse) Simon Pulse.
Baker, Chandler. Alive. 2017. (ENG.). 384p. (YA). (gr. 7-12). pap. 9.99 *(978-1-4847-0934-4(9))* Hyperion Bks. for Children.
—Alive. 2015. (ENG.). 368p. (YA). (gr. 7-12). 17.99 *(978-1-4847-0683-1(8))* Hyperion Pr.
—Alive. 2017. (YA). lib. bdg. 20.85 ***(978-0-606-39171-9(1))*** Turtleback Bks.
Baker, E. D. Dragon Kiss. 2nd ed. 2009. (Tales of the Frog Princess Ser.). (ENG.). 288p. (YA). (gr. 5-8). 16.99 *(978-1-59990-348-4(2),* 9781599903484, Bloomsbury USA Childrens) Bloomsbury Publishing USA.
Baker, Jason. People Are People. 2012. 80p. pap. 28.00 *(978-1-105-72519-7(7))* Lulu Pr., Inc.
Baker, Jennifer. Sworn to Silence. 2014. (ENG., Illus.). 192p. (YA). (gr. 7). pap. 13.99 *(978-1-4814-2877-4(2),* Simon Pulse) Simon Pulse.
Baker, Liza. I Love You Because You're You. McPhail, David, illus. 2008. (ENG.). 24p. (J). (gr. -1-k). bds. 8.99 *(978-0-545-02931-5(7),* Cartwheel Bks.) Scholastic, Inc.
—I Love You Because You're You (a StoryPlay Book) McPhail, David, illus. 2016. (ENG.). 32p. (J). (gr. -1-k). 5.99 *(978-0-545-94527-1(5),* Cartwheel Bks.) Scholastic, Inc.
Baker, Roe. What's Wrong with Gretel Goann. 2010. 24p. pap. 11.50 *(978-1-60976-050-2(6),* Eloquent Bks.) Strategic Book Publishing & Rights Agency (SBPRA).
Baldwin, James. The Story of Roland. 2013. pap. 31.93 *(978-1-4400-6789-1(9))* Forgotten Bks.
Baldwin, Kathleen. Refuge for Masterminds: A Stranje House Novel. 2017. (Stranje House Ser.: 3). (ENG.). 352p. (YA). 17.99 *(978-0-7653-7604-6(0),* 9780765376046, Tor Teen) Doherty, Tom Assocs., LLC.
—A School for Unusual Girls. 2015. (Stranje House Ser.: 1). (ENG.). 352p. (YA). (gr. 8-12). 17.99 *(978-0-7653-7600-8(8),* 9780765376008, Tor Teen) Doherty, Tom Assocs., LLC.
Bandeira, Isabel. Bookishly Ever After. 2016. (Ever After Ser.: 1). (ENG.). 350p. (YA). (gr. 10-12). pap. 9.95 *(978-1-63392-058-3(5),* Spencer Hill Contemporary) Spencer Hill Pr.
Banks, Anna. Of Neptune. 2014. (Syrena Legacy Ser.: 3). (ENG.). 336p. (YA). (gr. 8-12). 17.99 *(978-1-250-03960-6(6),* 9781250039606) Feiwel & Friends.
—Of Poseidon. 2013. (Syrena Legacy Ser.: 1). (ENG.). 384p. (YA). (gr. 8-12). pap. 10.99 *(978-1-250-02736-8(5),* 9781250027368) Square Fish.
—Of Triton. 2013. (Syrena Legacy Ser.: 2). (ENG.). 256p. (YA). (gr. 8-12). 17.99 *(978-1-250-00333-1(4),* 9781250003331) Feiwel & Friends.
—Of Triton. 2014. (Syrena Legacy Ser.: 2). (ENG., Illus.). 304p. (YA). (gr. 8-12). pap. 9.99 *(978-1-250-04431-0(6),* 9781250044310) Square Fish.
Banks, Jane Whelen. Loveable Liam: Affirmations for a Perfectly Imperfect Child. 2008. (ENG., Illus.). 32p. 12.95 *(978-1-84310-899-3(2),* 7171) Kingsley, Jessica Pubs. GBR. Dist: Macmillan Distribution Ltd.
Banks, Nancy. Shamoni & Noemi. 2013. 32p. pap. 24.95 *(978-1-4626-9627-7(9))* America Star Bks.
Barakiva, Michael. One Man Guy. 2014. (ENG.). 272p. (YA). (gr. 7). 17.99 *(978-0-374-35645-3(9),* Farrar, Straus & Giroux (BYR)) Farrar, Straus & Giroux.
Barcelona, Adrian. Little Derek's Dilemm. 2011. 28p. pap. 24.95 *(978-1-4560-7931-4(X))* America Star Bks.
Barchers, Suzanne I. One Last Wish: A Tale from India. Todd, Sue, illus. 2013. (Tales of Honor Ser.). (ENG.). 32p. (gr. 1-3). pap. 8.95 *(978-1-937529-60-4(6))* Red Chair Pr.
—The Tale of the Oki Islands: A Tale from Japan. Yokota, Hiromitsu, illus. 2013. (Tales of Honor Ser.). (ENG.). 32p. (gr. 1-3). pap. 8.95 *(978-1-937529-62-8(2))* Red Chair Pr.
—The Wounded Lion: A Tale from Spain. Joven, John, illus. 2013. (Tales of Honor Ser.). (ENG.). 32p. (gr. 1-3). pap. 8.95 *(978-1-937529-63-5(0))* Red Chair Pr.

JKL

Bardugo, Leigh. Ruin & Rising. 2014. (Grisha Trilogy: Vol. 3). (ENG., Illus.). 432p. (YA). (gr. 7-12). 19.99 *(978-0-8050-9461-9(X)*, 9780805094619, Holt, Henry & Co. Bks. For Young Readers) Holt, Henry & Co.

Barkley, Brad & Hepler, Heather. Dream Factory. 2009. (ENG.). 272p. (YA). (gr. 7-18). 8.99 *(978-0-14-241298-5(8)*, Speak) Penguin Young Readers Group.

Barnes, Jennifer Lynn. Nobody. 2014. (ENG.). 400p. (J). (gr. 7). pap. 9.99 *(978-1-60684-508-0(X)*, Carolrhoda Lab™) Lerner Publishing Group.

Barnes, Vivi. Olivia Twisted. 2013. (Olivia Twisted Ser.: 1). (ENG.). 352p. (J). (gr. 7-12). pap. 9.99 *(978-1-62266-028-5(5)*, 9781622660285) Entangled Publishing, LLC.

—Paper or Plastic. 2015. (Entangled Teen Ser.). (ENG.). 352p. (YA). pap. 9.99 *(978-1-62266-521-1(X)*, 9781622665211) Entangled Publishing, LLC.

Barnholdt, Lauren. Right of Way. (ENG., Illus.). (YA). (gr. 9). 2014. 336p. pap. 9.99 *(978-1-4424-5128-5(9))* 2013. 320p. 16.99 *(978-1-4424-5127-8(0))* Simon Pulse. (Simon Pulse).

—Through to You. 2014. (ENG., Illus.). 288p. (YA). (gr. 9). 17.99 *(978-1-4424-3463-9(5)*, Simon Pulse) Simon Pulse.

—Two-Way Street. 2007. (ENG.). 304p. (YA). (gr. 9-18). pap. 10.99 *(978-1-4169-1318-4(1)*, Simon Pulse) Simon Pulse.

Baron, Michael & Aronica, Lou. A Winter Discovery. 2011. (ENG.). 60p. pap. 4.99 *(978-1-61188-027-4(0))* Story Plant, The.

Barr, Emily. The One Memory of Flora Banks. 2017. (ENG.). 304p. (YA). (gr. 7). 15.99 *(978-0-399-54701-0(0)*, Philomel Bks.) Penguin Young Readers Group.

Barrett, John F. The Stories of Jake. 2008. 64p. pap. 31.99 *(978-1-4363-2010-8(0))* Xlibris Corp.

Barson, Kelly. 45 Pounds (More or Less) 2013. (ENG.). 272p. (YA). (gr. 7). 16.99 *(978-0-670-78482-0(6)*, Viking Books for Young Readers) Penguin Young Readers Group.

Baskin, Nora Raleigh. Subway Love. 2014. (ENG.). 224p. (YA). (gr. 9). 16.99 *(978-0-7636-6845-7(1))* Candlewick Pr.

Bass, Alexis. Love & Other Theories. 2014. (ENG.). 384p. (YA). (gr. 9). 17.99 *(978-0-06-227532-5(1)*, HarperTeen) HarperCollins Pubs.

Batchelor, Melanie. Remember Me. 2014. (ENG.). 208p. (J). (gr. 7). pap. 9.95 *(978-1-62639-184-0(X))* Bold Strokes Bks.

Batchelor, Rhonda. She Loves You. 2008. (ENG.). 136p. (YA). (gr. 7-8). pap. 11.99 *(978-1-55002-789-1(1)*, Sandcastle Bks.) Dundurn CAN. Dist: Ingram Publisher Services.

Bates, Marni. Awkwardly Ever After. 2014. (Smith High Ser.). (ENG.). 304p. (YA). (gr. 13). pap. 9.95 *(978-0-7582-9516-3(2)*, K-Teen) Kensington Publishing Corp.

Bauer, Joan. Thwonk. 2005. (ENG.). 224p. (YA). (gr. 7-7). pap. 7.99 *(978-0-14-240429-4(2)*, Speak) Penguin Young Readers Group.

—Thwonk. 2005. 215p. (gr. 7-12). 18.00 *(978-0-7569-5782-7(6))* Perfection Learning Corp.

Bauer, Marion Dane. How Do I Love You? / ¿Cómo Te Quiero? Church, Caroline Jayne, illus. 2014. (SPA & ENG.). 24p. (J). (gr. -1-k). bds. 8.99 *(978-0-545-66525-4(6)*, Scholastic en Espanol) Scholastic, Inc.

Beach, Rex. Heart of the Sunset. 2004. reprint ed. pap. 1.99 *(978-1-4192-2303-7(8))* Kessinger Publishing, LLC.

Beach, Rex E. Heart of the Sunset. 2004. reprint ed. pap. 33.95 *(978-1-4179-3787-5(4))* Kessinger Publishing, LLC.

Beard, Sarah. Beyond the Rising Tide. 2016. (YA). pap. 18.99 *(978-1-4621-1874-8(7))* Cedar Fort, Inc./CFI Distribution.

Beaty, Erin. The Traitor's Kiss. 2017. (Traitor's Trilogy Ser.: 1). (ENG.). 352p. (YA). 18.99 *(978-1-250-11794-6(1)*, 9781250117946) Imprint IND. Dist: Macmillan.

Beckford, Avril. I Love You 65 Bulldozers. 2009. 36p. pap. 15.49 *(978-1-4389-4048-9(3))* AuthorHouse.

Bedford, David. Mole's Babies. Beardshaw, Rosalind, illus. 2012. (ENG.). 32p. (J). *(978-1-58925-108-3(3))*; pap. *(978-1-58925-435-0(X))* Tiger Tales.

—Mole's in Love. Beardshaw, Rosalind, illus. 2009. 32p. (J). (gr. -1-2). 15.95 *(978-1-58925-084-0(2))*; pap. 6.95 *(978-1-58925-417-6(1))* Tiger Tales.

Bedford, L. B. Carefully Everywhere Descending. 2016. (ENG., Illus.). (YA). 24.99 ***(978-1-63477-946-3(0)***, Harmony Ink Pr.) Dreamspinner Pr.

Bedford, Martyn. Twenty Questions for Gloria. 2016. (ENG.). 288p. (YA). (gr. 9). 16.99 *(978-0-553-53939-4(6)*, Lamb, Wendy Bks.) Random Hse. Children's Bks.

Behl, Colin. Noüm. 2007. 108p. per. 16.95 *(978-1-4241-4518-8(X))* PublishAmerica, Inc.

Belasco, Sonia. Speak of Me As I Am. 2017. (ENG.). 272p. (YA). (gr. 7). 17.99 *(978-0-399-54676-1(6)*, Philomel Bks.) Penguin Young Readers Group.

Bell, Anthea. Frog in Love. Velthuijs, Max, illus. 2015. (J). *(978-1-4351-5750-7(8))* Barnes & Noble, Inc.

Bell, Cheryl. Boy Jesus. 2011. 24p. pap. 10.95 *(978-1-4497-1636-3(9)*, WestBow Pr.) Author Solutions, Inc.

Bell, Liz. Mohawk, Fro or Crew, It Is up to You. 2011. 24p. pap. 24.95 *(978-1-4626-3196-4(7))* America Star Bks.

Belonie, Shannon. Oliver Andrew Ostrich: My Full Name. 2008. 12p. pap. 8.74 *(978-1-4343-5849-3(6))* AuthorHouse.

Bennardo, Charlotte & Zaman, Natalie. Blonde Ops. 2014. (ENG.). 288p. (YA). (gr. 7). 17.99 *(978-1-250-03039-9(0)*, 9781250030399, St. Martin's Griffin) St. Martin's Pr.

Bennett-Boltinghouse, Jo Ann. Yolandababy: A Pooch Finds Her Purpose! an Adventure in Self-Esteem. Julich, Jenniffer, illus. 2007. (YolandaBaby Ser.). 28p. (J). (gr. -1-3). 16.00 *(978-0-9785151-0-2(2))* Ginger Pr., The.

Bennett, Jenn. The Anatomical Shape of a Heart. 2015. (ENG.). 304p. (YA). (gr. 7). 17.99 *(978-1-250-06645-9(X)*, 9781250066459) Feiwel & Friends.

Berenstain, Mike, illus. The Berenstain Bears Love One Another. 2016. (J). *(978-0-8249-1983-2(1)*, Ideal Pubns.) Worthy Publishing.

Bergren, Lisa T. God Gave Us Love. Bryant, Laura J., illus. 2011. (ENG.). 22p. (J). (gr. k — 1). bds. 6.99 *(978-0-307-73027-5(1)*, WaterBrook Pr.) Crown Publishing Group.

—God Gave Us Love. 2009. (ENG., Illus.). 40p. (gr. -1-2). 10.99 *(978-1-4000-7447-1(9)*, WaterBrook Pr.) Crown Publishing Group.

Berne, Emma Carlson. Never Let You Go. 2012. (ENG.). 256p. (YA). (gr. 9). pap. 9.99 *(978-1-4424-4017-3(1)*, Simon Pulse) Simon Pulse.

Bernet, Marti L. Remember... I Love You! 2010. 28p. 13.54 *(978-1-4269-4695-0(3))* Trafford Publishing.

Berry, Carolyn. Buster Tells It All: Stories from Pony Creek Ranch. Cash, Eric, illus. 2011. 24p. (J). 16.95 *(978-1-61254-011-5(2))* Brown Books Publishing Group.

Berry, Julie. All the Truth That's in Me. 2014. (ENG.). 304p. (YA). (gr. 7). pap. 9.99 *(978-0-14-242730-9(6)*, Speak) Penguin Young Readers Group.

Berry, Nina. Othermoon. 2013. (ENG.). 320p. (YA). (gr. 9). pap. 9.95 *(978-0-7582-7693-3(1)*, K-Teen) Kensington Publishing Corp.

Bickel, Karla. Heart Petals on the Hearth: A Collection of Children's Stories. Bickel, Karla, illus. 2004. (Illus.). 64p. (J). (gr. -1-6). 20.00 *(978-1-891452-00-0(2))* Heart Arbor Bks.

—Heart Petals on the Hearth: A Collection of Children's Stories. 2004. (Illus.). 64p. (J). (gr. -1-6). pap. 16.00 *(978-1-891452-01-7(0))* Heart Arbor Bks.

—Heart Petals on the Hearth II: A Collection of Children's Stories. 2004. (Illus.). 80p. (J). (gr. -1-6). 25.00 *(978-1-891452-04-8(5))*; pap. 20.00 *(978-1-891452-05-5(3))* Heart Arbor Bks.

Binks. The Girl with Chipmunk Hands. Begonia, Ruby, illus. 2013. 24p. (J). 15.95 *(978-1-935448-20-4(X))* Lost Coast Pr.

Biren, Sara. The Last Thing You Said. 2017. (ENG.). 320p. (YA). 17.95 *(978-1-4197-2304-9(9)*, Amulet Bks.) Abrams, Inc.

Bishop, Jennie. The Garden Wall: A Story of Love Based on I Corinthians 13. Stoddard, Jeff, illus. 2006. (ENG.). 32p. (J). (gr. 2-7). 12.99 *(978-1-59317-168-1(4))* Warner Pr., Inc.

Black, Cary & Schott, Gretchen Victoria. French Quarter Tori & the Red Owl. Travis, Caroline, illus. 2012. 38p. pap. 14.95 *(978-0-9754279-7-2(0))*; pap. 12.95 *(978-0-9754279-8-9(9))* Red Owl Pubns.

Black, Holly. Black Heart. (Curse Workers Ser.: 3). (ENG.). (YA). (gr. 9). 2013. 320p. pap. 11.99 *(978-1-4424-0347-5(0))* 2012. 304p. 17.99 *(978-1-4424-0346-8(2))* McElderry, Margaret K. Bks. (McElderry, Margaret K. Bks.).

—The Coldest Girl in Coldtown. 2013. 419p. (YA). *(978-0-316-27755-6(X))* Little Brown & Co.

—The Coldest Girl in Coldtown. (ENG.). (gr. 10-17). 2014. 448p. pap. 10.99 *(978-0-316-21309-7(8))* 2013. 432p. 19.00 *(978-0-316-21310-3(1))* Little, Brown Bks. for Young Readers.

—The Darkest Part of the Forest. 2015. (ENG.). 336p. (YA). (gr. 7-17). 18.00 *(978-0-316-21307-3(1))* Little Brown & Co.

—The Darkest Part of the Forest. 2016. (ENG.). 352p. (YA). (gr. 10-17). pap. 10.99 *(978-0-316-21308-0(X))* Little, Brown Bks. for Young Readers.

—The Darkest Part of the Forest. 2016. (YA). lib. bdg. 22.10 *(978-0-606-37533-7(3))* Turtleback Bks.

Black Ice. 2014. (ENG., Illus.). 400p. (YA). (gr. 9). 19.99 *(978-1-4424-7426-0(2)*, Simon & Schuster Bks. For Young Readers) Simon & Schuster Bks. For Young Readers.

Blackburne, Livia. Daughter of Dusk. 2015. (Midnight Thief Ser.). (ENG., Illus.). 380p. (YA). (gr. 7-12). 17.99 *(978-1-4847-2208-4(6))* Hyperion Bks. for Children.

Blackman, Malorie. Black & White. 2007. (ENG.). 512p. (YA). (gr. 9-12). pap. 12.99 *(978-1-4169-0017-7(9)*, Simon & Schuster Bks. For Young Readers) Simon & Schuster Bks. For Young Readers.

—Naughts & Crosses. 2005. (ENG., Illus.). 400p. (YA). (gr. 9-18). 18.99 *(978-1-4169-0016-0(0)*, Simon & Schuster Bks. For Young Readers) Simon & Schuster Bks. For Young Readers.

Blake, Ashley Herring. Suffer Love. (ENG.). 352p. (YA). (gr. 9). 2017. pap. 9.99 *(978-0-544-93689-8(2))* 2016. 17.99 *(978-0-544-59632-0(3))* Houghton Mifflin Harcourt Publishing Co. (HMH Books For Young Readers).

—Suffer Love. 2017. (ENG.). (YA). (gr. 9). lib. bdg. 20.85 ***(978-0-606-39817-6(1))*** Turtleback Bks.

Blakeslee, S. E. Once upon a Blue Moon: The Chronicles of the Blue Moon. Blakeslee, S. E., illus. 2007. (ENG., Illus.). 32p. (J). 17.95 *(978-0-9789031-0-7(2))* Blaumond Pr.

Blankman, Anne. Conspiracy of Blood & Smoke. 2015. (ENG.). 416p. (YA). (gr. 8). 17.99 *(978-0-06-227884-5(3))* HarperCollins Pubs.

—Prisoner of Night & Fog. (ENG.). (YA). (gr. 8). 2015. 432p. pap. 9.99 *(978-0-06-227882-1(7))* 2014. 416p. 17.99 *(978-0-06-227881-4(9))* HarperCollins Pubs.

Blaskovic, Eva A. Beyond the Precipice. 2013. 406p. (YA). pap. *(978-0-9881638-1-2(0))* Ashby-BP Publishing.

Bleed Like Me. 2014. (ENG., Illus.). 288p. (YA). (gr. 11). 17.99 *(978-1-4424-9890-7(0)*, Simon Pulse) Simon Pulse.

Bliss, Bryan. Meet Me Here. 2016. 272p. (YA). (gr. 9). 17.99 *(978-0-06-227538-7(0)*, Greenwillow Bks.) HarperCollins Pubs.

Block, Francesca Lia. The Island of Excess Love. 2014. (ENG.). 224p. (YA). (gr. 9). 16.99 *(978-0-8050-9631-6(0)*, 9780805096316, Holt, Henry & Co. Bks. For Young Readers) Holt, Henry & Co.

—Love in the Time of Global Warming. 2013. (ENG.). 240p. (YA). (gr. 9-13). 16.99 *(978-0-8050-9627-9(2)*, 9780805096279, Holt, Henry & Co. Bks. For Young Readers) Holt, Henry & Co.

—Psyche in a Dress. 2008. (ENG.). 128p. (YA). (gr. 9). pap. 8.99 *(978-0-06-076376-3(0)*, HarperTeen) HarperCollins Pubs.

Blount, Patty. Nothing Left to Burn. 2015. (ENG.). 368p. (YA). (gr. 8-12). pap. 9.99 *(978-1-4926-1329-9(0)*, 9781492613299) Sourcebooks, Inc.

—Some Boys. 2014. (ENG.). 352p. (YA). (gr. 7-12). pap. 9.99 *(978-1-4022-9856-1(0)*, 9781402298561) Sourcebooks, Inc.

Blume, Judy. Forever... 2007. (ENG.). 208p. (gr. 8-12). pap. *(978-1-4169-5391-3(4))* Gallery Pr., The.

Blumenthal, Deborah. The Lifeguard. (ENG.). 288p. (YA). (gr. 8-12). 2013. 9.99 *(978-0-8075-4536-2(8))* 2012. 16.99 *(978-0-8075-4535-5(X))* Whitman, Albert & Co.

Bochynek, Halina. A Beagle's Tale. 2008. 152p. pap. 14.99 *(978-1-4389-1960-7(3))* AuthorHouse.

Boecker, Virginia. The King Slayer. 2016. (Witch Hunter Ser.: 2). (ENG.). 368p. (YA). (gr. 10-17). 17.99 *(978-0-316-32723-7(9))* Little, Brown Bks. for Young Readers.

Bold, Emily. Breath of Yesterday. 0 vols. Bell, Katja, tr. from GER. 2014. (Curse Ser.: 2). (ENG.). 376p. (YA). (gr. 9-12). pap. 9.99 *(978-1-4778-4714-5(6)*, 9781477847145) Amazon Publishing.

Bolden, Tonya. Crossing Ebenezer Creek. 2017. (ENG.). 240p. (YA). 17.99 *(978-1-59990-319-4(9)*, 9781599903194, Bloomsbury USA Childrens) Bloomsbury Publishing USA.

Bonaste, Sophie. The Sacrifices We Make [Library Edition]. 2014. 190p. pap. 14.99 *(978-1-62798-187-3(X)*, Harmony Ink Pr.) Dreamspinner Pr.

Bonnell, Kris. We Love Pets. 2007. (J). pap. 5.95 *(978-1-933727-56-1(X))* Reading Reading Bks., LLC.

Boone, Martina. Illusion. 2016. (Heirs of Watson Island Ser.). (ENG., Illus.). 480p. (YA). (gr. 9). 17.99 *(978-1-4814-1128-8(4)*, Simon Pulse) Simon Pulse.

—Persuasion. 2015. (Heirs of Watson Island Ser.). (ENG., Illus.). 464p. (YA). (gr. 9). 17.99 *(978-1-4814-1125-7(X)*, Simon Pulse) Simon Pulse.

Boorman, Kate A. Darkthaw: A Winterkill Novel. 2015. (Winterkill Ser.). (ENG.). 336p. (YA). (gr. 7-17). 17.95 *(978-1-4197-1663-8(8)*, Amulet Bks.) Abrams, Inc.

—Heartfire: A Winterkill Novel. 2016. (Winterkill Ser.: 3). (ENG.). 336p. (YA). (gr. 7-17). 17.95 *(978-1-4197-2124-3(0)*, Amulet Bks.) Abrams, Inc.

—Winterkill. 2014. (Winterkill Ser.). (ENG.). 336p. (YA). (gr. 7-17). 17.95 *(978-1-4197-1235-7(7)*, Amulet Bks.) Abrams, Inc.

Boucher, Sarah E. Becoming Beauty: A Retelling of Beauty & the Beast. 2014. 249p. (YA). pap. 15.99 *(978-1-4621-1455-9(5))* Cedar Fort, Inc./CFI Distribution.

Bourgeois, Paulette. Un Nouvel Ami pour Benjamin. 2004.Tr. of Franklin's New Friend. (FRE., Illus.). (J). (gr. -1-2). spiral bd. *(978-0-616-01828-6(2))* Canadian National Institute for the Blind/Institut National Canadien pour les Aveugles.

Bower, Gary. Mommy Love. Bower, Jan, illus. 2012. (Little Lovable Board Bks.). (ENG.). 16p. (J). bds. 8.50 *(978-0-9845236-0-3(X))* Storybook Meadow Publishing.

The Boy I Love. 2014. (ENG., Illus.). 288p. (YA). (gr. 7). 17.99 *(978-1-4424-8056-8(4)*, Atheneum Bks. for Young Readers) Simon & Schuster Children's Publishing.

Boyd, Lizi. I Love Daddy: Super Sturdy Picture Books. Boyd, Lizi, illus. 2004. (Super Sturdy Picture Bks.). (ENG., Illus.). 24p. (J). (gr. -1 — 1). 8.99 *(978-0-7636-2217-6(6))* Candlewick Pr.

Boyle, Amanda N. The Dream. 2007. 59p. per. 8.95 *(978-1-59824-506-6(6))* E-BookTime LLC.

Boynton, Sandra. Snuggle Puppy! 2003. (ENG., Illus.). 24p. (J). (gr. k — 1). bds. 6.95 *(978-0-7611-3067-3(5)*, 13067) Workman Publishing Co., Inc.

Bracken, Alexandra. In the Afterlight. (Darkest Minds Novel Ser.). (ENG.). (YA). 2015. 592p. (gr. 9-17). pap. 9.99 *(978-1-4231-5934-6(9))* 2014. 544p. (gr. 7-12). 18.99 *(978-1-4231-5752-6(4))* Hyperion Bks. for Children.

—In the Afterlight. 2015. (Darkest Minds Ser.: 3). (YA). lib. bdg. 20.85 *(978-0-606-37505-4(8))* Turtleback Bks.

—Passenger. 2016. (Passenger Ser.). (ENG.). 512p. (YA). (gr. 9-17). pap. 9.99 *(978-1-4847-3279-3(0))* Disney Pr.

—Passenger. 2016. (Passenger Ser.). (ENG.). 496p. (YA). (gr. 9-12). 17.99 *(978-1-4847-1577-2(2))* Hyperion Bks. for Children.

—Wayfarer. 2017. (Passenger Ser.). (ENG.). 544p. (YA). (gr. 9-17). 17.99 *(978-1-4847-1576-5(4))* Hyperion Bks. for Children.

Bradbury, Jennifer. Wrapped. 2011. (ENG., Illus.). 320p. (YA). (gr. 7-18). 16.99 *(978-1-4169-9007-9(0)*, Atheneum Bks. for Young Readers) Simon & Schuster Children's Publishing.

Bradley, Carolyn. A Gingerbread Heart: Love... a Boy & a Gingerbread Boy with a Gingerbread Heart. 2012. 32p. pap. 21.99 *(978-1-4771-5730-5(1))* Xlibris Corp.

Brant, Wendy. Zenn Diagram. 2017. (ENG.). 328p. (J). (gr. 9-17). 17.95 *(978-1-77138-792-7(0))* Kids Can Pr., Ltd. CAN. Dist: Hachette Bk. Group.

Brashares, Ann. The Here & Now. 2015. lib. bdg. 22.10 *(978-0-606-37649-5(6))* Turtleback Bks.

Brassill, Amber M. My Greatest Mistake, 1 vol. 2010. 236p. pap. 24.95 *(978-1-4489-9143-3(9))* America Star Bks.

Braun, Sebastien. I Love You More. Braun, Sebastien, illus. 2013. (ENG., Illus.). 20p. (J). (gr. -1). bds. 8.95 *(978-1-58925-620-0(4))* Tiger Tales.

Brauning, Kate. How We Fall. 2014. (ENG.). 304p. (YA). 17.99 *(978-1-4405-8179-3(7)*, Simon Pulse) Simon Pulse.

Breese, K. Ryer. Past Continuous. 2011. (ENG.). 304p. (YA). (gr. 9-13). pap. 20.99 *(978-0-312-54772-1(2)*, 9780312547721, St. Martin's Griffin) St. Martin's Pr.

Brennan, Sarah Rees. Tell the Wind & Fire. 2016. (ENG.). 368p. (YA). (gr. 7). 17.99 *(978-0-544-31817-5(X))* Houghton Mifflin Harcourt Publishing Co.

—Unmade. 2014. (Lynburn Legacy Ser.: Bk. 3). (ENG., Illus.). 384p. (YA). (gr. 7). 17.99 *(978-0-375-87043-9(1)*, Random Hse. Bks. for Young Readers) Random Hse. Children's Bks.

Brents, Alan. Sheldon the Sheep. 2011. 24p. pap. 12.79 *(978-1-4634-8728-7(2))* AuthorHouse.

Brewer, Nancy B. Princess Bertha & the Goose. 2011. 32p. pap. 24.95 *(978-1-4560-7868-3(2))* America Star Bks.

Brewer, Zac. Madness. 2017. 304p. (YA). (gr. 9). 17.99 ***(978-0-06-245785-1(3))*** HarperCollins Pubs.

Brewis, Alan. Boris Returns A Hero! 2008. 72p. pap. 12.50 *(978-1-4357-4377-9(6))* Lulu Pr., Inc.

Brewster, Bobby. Layla the Ridgeless Rhodesian Ridgeback. 2011. 36p. (J). pap. 27.95 *(978-0-615-37153-5(1))* Brewster, Robert.

Brezenoff, Steve. Guy in Real Life. 2014. (ENG.). 400p. (YA). (gr. 9). 17.99 *(978-0-06-226683-5(7))* HarperCollins Pubs.

Brian, Kate. A Private Collection, 4 vols., Set; Vols. 1-4. 2007. (Private Ser.: Nos. 1-4). (ENG.). 1032p. (YA). (gr. 9). pap. 34.99 *(978-1-4169-5818-5(5)*, Simon & Schuster Bks. For Young Readers) Simon & Schuster Bks. For Young Readers.

Brian, Kate, pseud. Ex-Mas. 2009. (ENG., Illus.). 224p. (YA). (gr. 9-18). pap. 9.99 *(978-1-4169-9151-9(4)*, Simon & Schuster Bks. For Young Readers) Simon & Schuster Bks. For Young Readers.

—Lucky T. 2007. (ENG.). 304p. (YA). (gr. 9-12). pap. 9.99 *(978-1-4169-3545-2(2)*, Simon & Schuster Bks. For Young Readers) Simon & Schuster Bks. For Young Readers.

Briceno, Carole. Turtle's Journey, 1 vol. White, Tina Jorgenson, illus. 2009. 28p. pap. 24.95 *(978-1-60813-934-7(4))* America Star Bks.

Bright, Rachel. Love Monster. 2014. (ENG., Illus.). 32p. (J). (gr. -1 — 1). bds. 7.99 *(978-0-374-30186-6(7)*, 9780374301866, Farrar, Straus & Giroux (BYR)) Farrar, Straus & Giroux.

Brin, Susannah. A Summer Romance. 2003. (Illus.). 60p. (J). 3.95 *(978-1-58659-140-3(1))* Artesian Pr.

Brody, Jessica. Unchanged. 2015. (Unremembered Trilogy Ser.: 3). (ENG.). 432p. (YA). (gr. 7). 17.99 *(978-0-374-37989-6(0)*, 9780374379896, Farrar, Straus & Giroux (BYR)) Farrar, Straus & Giroux.

Brontë, Emily. Wuthering Heights. Bryant, Clive, ed. Burns, John M., illus. 2011. (ENG.). 160p. lib. bdg. 24.95 *(978-1-907127-80-9(1))* Classical Comics GBR. Dist: Publishers Group West (PGW).

Brooks, Kevin. Naked '76. 2016. (ENG.). 424p. (gr. 9-12). 18.99 *(978-1-5124-0418-0(7)*, Carolrhoda Bks.); (YA). 38.65 *(978-1-5124-0445-6(4)*, Carolrhoda Lab™) Lerner Publishing Group.

Bross, Lanie. Fates. (ENG.). (YA). (gr. 7). 2015. 354p. pap. 9.99 *(978-0-385-74283-2(5)*, Ember) 2014. 336p. 17.99 *(978-0-385-74282-5(7)*, Delacorte Pr.) Random Hse. Children's Bks.

Bross, Lee. Tangled Webs. 2015. (Tangled Webs Ser.). (ENG., Illus.). 304p. (YA). (gr. 9-17). 17.99 *(978-1-4231-8423-2(8))* Hyperion Bks. for Children.

Brown, Anne Greenwood. Deep Betrayal. 2013. (ENG.). 352p. (YA). (gr. 7). pap. 9.99 *(978-0-385-74204-7(5)*, Ember) Random Hse. Children's Bks.

—Lies Beneath. 2013. (ENG.). 320p. (YA). (gr. 7). pap. 8.99 *(978-0-385-74202-3(9)*, Ember) Random Hse. Children's Bks.

—Promise Bound. 2014. (ENG.). 368p. (YA). (gr. 7). 17.99 *(978-0-385-74383-9(1)*, Delacorte Pr.) Random Hse. Children's Bks.

Brown, Jaye Robin. No Place to Fall. 2016. 384p. (YA). (gr. 9). pap. 9.99 *(978-0-06-227096-2(6)*, HarperTeen) HarperCollins Pubs.

Brown, Jennifer. Thousand Words. 2014. (ENG.). 304p. (YA). (gr. 10-17). pap. 10.00 *(978-0-316-20970-0(8))* Little, Brown Bks. for Young Readers.

Brown, Marc. Who's in Love with Arthur?, Vol. 10. unabr. ed. 2004. (Arthur Chapter Bks.: Bk. 10). (Illus.). 57p. (J). (gr. 2-4). pap. 17.00 incl. audio *(978-0-8072-0407-8(2)*, Listening Library) Random Hse. Audio Publishing Group.

Brown, Tara. White Girl Problems. 2013. 266p. pap. *(978-1-927866-06-1(5))* Brown, Tara Publishing.

Brown, Teri. Born of Deception. 2014. (Born of Illusion Ser.: 2). (ENG.). 336p. (YA). (gr. 8). 17.99 *(978-0-06-218757-4(0))* HarperCollins Pubs.

Bruna, Dick. Miffy Says, I Love You! 2004. (Illus.). 12p. bds. 5.99 *(978-1-59226-187-1(6))* Big Tent Entertainment, Inc.

Brunner, Kym. Wanted - Dead or in Love. 2014. (ENG.). 288p. (YA). 17.99 *(978-1-4405-7057-5(4)*, Simon Pulse) Simon Pulse.

Bryan, Barbara. Starfish, Seashells, Coral & Gems. 2010. 47p. (J). pap. 27.95 *(978-1-4327-6265-0(6))*; pap. 21.95 *(978-1-4327-6009-0(2))* Outskirts Pr., Inc.

Bryant Sr., Lydia. I Love Lydia, 1 vol. 2009. 20p. pap. 24.95 *(978-1-60703-488-9(3))* America Star Bks.

Buchanan, Andrea J. Gift. 2012. (ENG.). 326p. (YA). (gr. 7-12). pap. 9.99 *(978-1-4532-2023-8(2)*, Open Road Media E-riginal) Open Road Integrated Media, Inc.

Buckley, Michael. Undertow. (Undertow Trilogy Ser.). (ENG.). (gr. 7). 2016. 400p. (YA). pap. 10.99 *(978-0-544-81319-9(7))* 2015. 384p. (J). 18.99 *(978-0-544-34825-7(7))* Houghton Mifflin Harcourt Publishing Co. (HMH Books For Young Readers).

Buehrlen, M. G. The Fifty-Seven Lives of Alex Wayfare. 2015. (ENG., Illus.). 324p. pap. 15.99 *(978-1-62681-872-9(X))* Diversion Publishing Corp.

Buggs, Matthews. Beach Party. 2006. (J). 10.00 *(978-0-9790515-3-1(3))* Pinkston, Anastasia.

Bulbring, Edyth. I Heart Beat. 2014. (ENG.). 224p. (YA). (gr. 8). 9.99 *(978-1-4714-0061-2(1))* Bonnier Publishing GBR. Dist: Independent Pubs. Group.

Bunting, Eve. The Pirate Captain's Daughter. 2012. (Pirate Captain's Daughter Ser.). (ENG.). 192p. (J). pap. 8.95 *(978-1-58536-790-0(7))*; lib. bdg. 15.95 *(978-1-58536-789-4(3))* Sleeping Bear Pr.

—You Were Loved Before You Were Born. Barbour, Karen, illus. 2008. (J). pap. *(978-0-439-04062-4(0)*, Blue Sky Pr., The) Scholastic, Inc.

Burkhart, Jessica. Wild Hearts. 2015. (If Only... Ser.). (ENG.). 368p. (YA). (gr. 7). 17.99 *(978-1-61963-258-5(6)*, 9781619632585, Bloomsbury USA Childrens) Bloomsbury Publishing USA.

Burnham, Niki. Scary Beautiful. 2006. (Romantic Comedies Ser.). (ENG.). 272p. (YA). (gr. 9-12). mass mkt. 6.99 *(978-0-689-87619-6(X)*, Simon Pulse) Simon Pulse.

—Spin Control. 2011. (Romantic Comedies Ser.). (ENG.). 256p. (YA). (gr. 9). pap. 12.99 *(978-1-4424-3112-6(1)*, Simon Pulse) Simon Pulse.

Burnham, Niki & Saidens, Amy. Royally Jacked. 2003. (Romantic Comedies Ser.). (ENG.). 208p. (YA). mass mkt. 6.99 *(978-0-689-86668-5(2)*, Simon Pulse) Simon Pulse.

Burns, Laura J. & Metz, Melinda. Sacrifice. 2011. (ENG.). 272p. (YA). (gr. 9). 17.99 *(978-1-4424-3900-9(9))*; pap. 9.99 *(978-1-4424-0818-0(9))* Simon & Schuster Bks. For Young Readers. (Simon & Schuster Bks. For Young Readers).

Burstein, Lisa. MIA & the Bad Boy. 2015. (ENG., Illus.). 220p. (J). pap. 14.99 *(978-1-943336-18-0(0))* Entangled Publishing, LLC.

Burton, Hallie. Tapestry. 2016. (ENG., Illus.). (J). 27.99 ***(978-1-63533-078-6(5))*** 2013. 276p. pap. 16.99 *(978-1-62380-355-1(1))* Dreamspinner Pr. (Harmony Ink Pr.).

Burton, Hallie. Tapestry [Library Edition]. 2013. 276p. pap. 16.99 *(978-1-62380-926-3(6)*, Harmony Ink Pr.) Dreamspinner Pr.

Burton, Sharon Ann. When I Grow Up. 2013. 28p. (J). 24.95 *(978-1-4575-1802-7(3))* Dog Ear Publishing, LLC.

Busby, Cylin. Blink Once. 2012. (ENG.). 304p. (YA). (gr. 7-12). 17.99 *(978-1-59990-818-2(2)*, 9781599908182, Bloomsbury USA Childrens) Bloomsbury Publishing USA.

The Butterpop Cafe. 2004. 26p. *(978-1-887654-08-1(9))* Premium Pr. America.

Butterworth, MyLinda. The Monster Run. Day, Linda S., ed. Mercer, Matthew, illus. l.t. ed. 2004. 32p. (J). (gr. -1-3). 14.95 *(978-1-890905-23-1(2)*, Writers Collective, The) Day to Day Enterprises.

Buxbaum, Julie. What to Say Next. 2017. (ENG.). 304p. (YA). (gr. 7). 18.99 *(978-0-553-53568-6(4)*, Delacorte Pr.) Random Hse. Children's Bks.

Buzo, Laura. Love & Other Perishable Items. (ENG.). 256p. (YA). (gr. 9). 2013. pap. 8.99 *(978-0-307-92974-7(4)*, Ember) 2012. 17.99 *(978-0-375-87000-2(8)*, Knopf Bks. for Young Readers) Random Hse. Children's Bks.

Byars, Betsy. A Blossom Promise. (Blossom Family Ser.: Bk. 4). 145p. (J). (gr. 4-6). pap. 4.50 *(978-0-8072-1444-2(2)*, Listening Library) Random Hse. Audio Publishing Group.

Byler, Linda. The Little Amish Matchmaker: A Christmas Romance. 2012. (ENG.). 187p. 14.95 *(978-1-56148-776-9(7)*, Good Bks.) Skyhorse Publishing Co., Inc.

—When Strawberries Bloom: A Novel Based on the True Experiences from an Amish Writer! 2010. (ENG.). 297p. pap. 13.99 *(978-1-56148-699-1(X)*, Good Bks.) Skyhorse Publishing Co., Inc.

Cabot, Meg. Awaken. 2013. (ENG.). 336p. (J). (gr. 9). 17.99 *(978-0-545-28412-7(0))* Scholastic, Inc.

—Princess in Love. Vol. 3. 2008. (Princess Diaries: 3). (ENG.). 256p. (YA). (gr. 8-12). pap. 9.99 *(978-0-06-147995-3(0)*, HarperTeen) HarperCollins Pubs.

—Princess in Love. 2004. (Princess Diaries: Vol. 3). 288p. (J). (gr. 7-18). pap. 38.00 incl. audio *(978-0-8072-2284-3(4)*, Listening Library) Random Hse. Audio Publishing Group.

Cahill, Katina. I Love You This Much. 2005. (Illus.). 24p. (J). 13.50 *(978-1-4120-4388-5(3))* Trafford Publishing.

Cain, Karen L. Squirrel's Curl. 2011. 24p. 13.00 *(978-1-4567-1466-6(X))* AuthorHouse.

Caletti, Deb. Essential Maps for the Lost. 2016. (ENG., Illus.). 336p. (YA). (gr. 9). 17.99 *(978-1-4814-1516-3(6)*, Simon Pulse) Simon Pulse.

—Honey, Baby, Sweetheart. 2008. (ENG.). 336p. (YA). (gr. 7-12). pap. 9.99 *(978-1-4169-5783-6(9)*, Simon Pulse) Simon Pulse.

—The Last Forever. 2014. (ENG., Illus.). 336p. (YA). (gr. 7-7). 17.99 *(978-1-4424-5000-4(2)*, Simon Pulse) Simon Pulse.

—The Last Forever. 2016. lib. bdg. 22.10 *(978-0-606-38271-7(2))* Turtleback Bks.

—Love Is All You Need: Wild Roses - The Nature of Jade. 2013. (ENG.). 608p. (YA). (gr. 7-7). pap. 11.99 *(978-1-4424-6636-4(7)*, Simon Pulse) Simon Pulse.

—The Queen of Everything. Greenberg, Anne, ed. 2008. (ENG.). 352p. (YA). (gr. 7-12). pap. 8.99 *(978-1-4169-5781-2(2)*, Simon Pulse) Simon Pulse.

—The Story of Us. 2012. (ENG.). 400p. (YA). (gr. 7). 16.99 *(978-1-4424-2346-6(3)*, Simon Pulse) Simon Pulse.

—Wild Roses. (ENG.). (YA). (gr. 7-12). 2008. 320p. pap. 8.99 *(978-1-4169-5782-9(0))* 2005. (Illus.). 304p. 15.95 *(978-0-689-86766-8(2))* Simon Pulse. (Simon Pulse).

Cali, Davide. When an Elephant Falls in Love. Lotti, Alice, illus. 2016. (ENG.). 32p. (J). (gr. k-3). 14.99 *(978-1-4521-4727-7(2))* Chronicle Bks. LLC.

Calin, Marisa. Between You & Me. 2012. (ENG.). 256p. (YA). (gr. 7-12). 16.99 *(978-1-59990-758-1(5)*, 9781599907581, Bloomsbury USA Childrens) Bloomsbury Publishing USA.

Camden, Steven. It's about Love. 2015. (ENG.). 448p. (J). 8.99 *(978-0-00-751124-2(8)*, HarperCollins Children's Bks.) HarperCollins Pubs. Ltd. GBR. Dist: HarperCollins Pubs.

Campbell, Wanda Gail. Little Buckets Full of Big Love. 2008. (Illus.). 48p. pap. 19.49 *(978-1-4389-0688-1(9))* AuthorHouse.

Capucilli, Alyssa Satin. Panda Kisses. Widdowson, Kay, illus. 2008. (Step into Reading Ser.). (ENG.). 32p. (J). (gr. -1-1). pap. 3.99 *(978-0-375-84562-8(3)*, Random Hse. Bks. for Young Readers) Random Hse. Children's Bks.

Caraballo, Samuel. Estas Manos: Manitas de Mi Familia. Costello, Shawn, illus. 2014.Tr. of These Hands: My Family's Hands. (ENG & SPA.). (J). 17.95 *(978-1-55885-795-7(8)*, Piñata Books) Arte Publico Pr.

Cardi, Annie. The Chance You Won't Return. 2014. (ENG.). 352p. (YA). (gr. 7). 16.99 *(978-0-7636-6292-9(5))* Candlewick Pr.

Carey, Anna. Once. 2013. (Eve Ser.: 2). (ENG.). 384p. (YA). (gr. 8). pap. 9.99 *(978-0-06-204855-4(4))* HarperCollins Pubs.

—Rise. 2013. (Eve Ser.: 3). (ENG.). (YA). (gr. 8). 336p. pap. 9.99 *(978-0-06-204858-5(9))*; 320p. 17.99 *(978-0-06-204857-8(0))* HarperCollins Pubs.

—Rise: An Eve Novel. 2013. (Illus.). 320p. (YA). pap. 9.99 *(978-0-06-226273-8(4))* HarperCollins Pubs.

Carle, Eric. Love from the Very Hungry Caterpillar. 2015. (ENG.). 32p. (J). (-k). 8.99 *(978-0-448-48932-2(5)*, Grosset & Dunlap) Penguin Young Readers Group.

Carrière, Francine. Comme un Conte d'Enfant et le Clochard de New Perry. 2012. 94p. pap. *(978-1-55483-933-9(5))* Insomniac Pr.

Carson, Diana Pastora. All the Muchos in the World: A Special Story about Love. Pruitt, Ginny, illus. 2006. 32p. (J). pap. 8.95 *(978-0-8198-0779-3(6))* Pauline Bks. & Media.

Carson, Rae. The Crown of Embers. 2013. (Girl of Fire & Thorns Ser.: 2). (ENG.). 432p. (YA). (gr. 8). pap. 9.99 *(978-0-06-202653-8(4)*, Greenwillow Bks.) HarperCollins Pubs.

Cart, Michael, et al. How Beautiful the Ordinary. 2009. (ENG.). 368p. (YA). (gr. 9-18). 17.99 *(978-0-06-115498-0(9)*, HarperTeen) HarperCollins Pubs.

Carter, Nikki. Get over It. 2013. (ENG., Illus.). 240p. (YA). (gr. 9). pap. 9.95 *(978-0-7582-7271-3(5)*, K-Teen/Dafina) Kensington Publishing Corp.

Carter, Rachel. So Close to You. 2012. (ENG.). 320p. (YA). (gr. 9). 17.99 *(978-0-06-208105-6(5)*, HarperTeen) HarperCollins Pubs.

Cash, John Carter. The Cat in the Rhinestone Suit. Nash, Scott, illus. 2012. (ENG.). 32p. (J). (gr. -1-3). 17.99 *(978-1-4169-7483-0(3)*, Little Simon Inspirations) Little Simon Inspirations.

—Daddy Loves His Little Girl. Burckhardt, Marc, illus. 2010. (ENG.). 32p. (J). (gr. -1-3). 16.99 *(978-1-4169-7482-6(2)*, Little Simon Inspirations) Little Simon Inspirations.

Cass, Kiera. The Elite. (Selection Ser.: 2). (ENG.). (YA). (gr. 8). 2014. 352p. pap. 9.99 *(978-0-06-205997-0(1))* 2013. 336p. 17.99 *(978-0-06-205996-3(3))* HarperCollins Pubs. (HarperTeen).

—LA ÉLITE. 2013. (SPA.). 224p. pap. 20.95 *(978-84-9918-613-9(0))* Roca Editorial ESP. Dist: Spanish Pubs., LLC.

—La Elite. 2017. (SPA.). 224p. (YA). (gr. 7-12). pap. 12.95 ***(978-84-16240-61-6(2))*** Roca Bolsillo ESP. Dist: Spanish Pubs., LLC.

—The Elite. 2014. (Selection Ser.: 2). (YA). lib. bdg. 20.85 *(978-0-606-35489-9(1))* Turtleback Bks.

—Happily Ever After. 2015. (Selection Novella Ser.). (ENG., Illus.). (YA). 416p. (gr. 8). 18.99 *(978-0-06-241408-3(9)*, HarperTeen); 320p. *(978-0-00-814366-4(8))* HarperCollins Pubs.

—The One. (Selection Ser.: 3). (ENG.). (gr. 8). 2015. 368p. (YA). pap. 9.99 *(978-0-06-206000-6(7))* 2014. 352p. (J). 17.99 *(978-0-06-205999-4(8))* HarperCollins Pubs. (HarperTeen).

—The Selection. (Selection Ser.: 1). (ENG.). (YA). (gr. 8). 2013. 352p. pap. 9.99 *(978-0-06-205994-9(7))* 2012. 336p. 17.99 *(978-0-06-205993-2(9))* HarperCollins Pubs. (HarperTeen).

—The Selection, 1. (ENG.). 272p. pap. *(978-0-00-746669-6(2)*, HarperCollins Children's Bks.) HarperCollins Pubs. Ltd.

—The Selection. 2013. (Selection Ser.: 1). (YA). lib. bdg. 20.85 *(978-0-606-35488-2(3))* Turtleback Bks.

—The Selection Stories: The Prince & the Guard. 2014. (Selection Ser.). (ENG.). 240p. (J). (gr. 8). pap. 9.99 *(978-0-06-231832-9(2))* HarperCollins Pubs.

—The Siren. (YA). 2017. 352p. (gr. 8). pap. 9.99 *(978-0-06-239200-8(X)*, HarperTeen) 2016. 327p. pap. *(978-0-06-244954-2(0))* 2016. 336p. (gr. 8-12). 18.99 *(978-0-06-239199-5(2)*, HarperTeen) HarperCollins Pubs.

—The Siren. 2017. lib. bdg. 20.85 ***(978-0-606-40073-2(7))*** Turtleback Bks.

—The Siren. 2009. 276p. pap. 16.95 *(978-1-4401-5423-2(6))* iUniverse, Inc.

Castle, Jennifer. The Beginning of After. 2013. (ENG.). 448p. (YA). (gr. 8). pap. 9.99 *(978-0-06-198580-5(5)*, HarperTeen) HarperCollins Pubs.

Castle, Lila. The Star Shack. 2010. (ENG., Illus.). 224p. (YA). (gr. 7-12). pap. 9.99 *(978-1-4022-4110-9(0))* Sourcebooks, Inc.

Castroman, Nicole. Blackhearts. 2016. (ENG., Illus.). 384p. (YA). (gr. 9). 17.99 *(978-1-4814-3269-6(9)*, Simon Pulse) Simon Pulse.

Castrovilla, Selene. The Girl Next Door. 2010. 240p. (YA). (gr. 9-12). 16.95 *(978-1-934813-15-7(X))* Westside Bks.

Cauvin, Raoul. Cedric 1 - High-Risk Class. Laudec, Calvinaoul, illus. 2008. (Cedric Ser.: 1). (ENG.). 48p. pap. 11.95 *(978-1-905460-68-7(6))* CineBook GBR. Dist: National Bk. Network.

Cavallaro, Brittany. A Study in Charlotte. (Charlotte Holmes Novel Ser.: 1). (YA). (gr. 8). 2017. 352p. pap. 9.99 *(978-0-06-239891-8(1))* 2016. 336p. 17.99 *(978-0-06-239890-1(3))* HarperCollins Pubs. (Tegen, Katherine Bks).

Cebollero, Julie. The Lion That Roared. 2012. (ENG.). 61p. pap. 9.95 *(978-1-4327-8067-8(0))* Outskirts Pr., Inc.

Cefalo, Andrea. The Fairytale Keeper: Avenging the Queen. 2012. (ENG., Illus.). 274p. pap. 11.99 *(978-0-9851678-1-3(5))* Scarlet Primrose Pr.

Centeio, Tara Jaye. Mommy Loves Her Baby. Date not set. 32p. (J). (gr. -1-1). pap. 5.99 *(978-0-06-443715-8(9))* HarperCollins Pubs.

Cestari, Crystal. The Best Kind of Magic. 2017. (Windy City Magic Ser.). (ENG.). 336p. (YA). (gr. 7-12). 17.99 *(978-1-4847-5272-2(4))* Hyperion Bks. for Children.

Chabot, Jason. Beyond: Broken Sky Chronicles, Book 3. 2017. (Broken Sky Chronicles Ser.: 3). (ENG.). 432p. (J). 35.99 ***(978-1-68162-608-6(X))***; (YA). pap. 19.99 *(978-1-68162-607-9(1))* Turner Publishing Co.

Chaffin, Dawn Marie. My Love. 2010. 20p. 11.99 *(978-1-4520-0031-2(X))* AuthorHouse.

Chambers, Aidan. Dying to Know You. 2012. (ENG.). 288p. (YA). (gr. 9-17). 16.95 *(978-1-4197-0165-8(7)*, Amulet Bks.) Abrams, Inc.

Chandler, Elizabeth. The Back Door of Midnight. 2004. (Dark Secrets Ser.: 5). (ENG.). 224p. (YA). mass mkt. 5.99 *(978-0-689-86642-5(9)*, Simon Pulse) Simon Pulse.

—Everafter. (Kissed by an Angel Ser.). (ENG., 272p. (YA). (gr. 9). 2014. Illus.). pap. 11.99 *(978-1-4424-0919-4(3))* 2013. 16.99 *(978-1-4424-0918-7(5))* Simon Pulse. (Simon Pulse).

—Evercrossed. (Kissed by an Angel Ser.). (ENG.). (YA). (gr. 7). 2012. 304p. pap. 9.99 *(978-1-4424-0915-6(0))* 2011. 288p. 16.99 *(978-1-4424-0914-9(2))* Simon Pulse. (Simon Pulse).

—Everlasting. (Kissed by an Angel Ser.). (ENG.). (YA). (gr. 7). 2013. 336p. pap. 9.99 *(978-1-4424-0917-0(7))* 2012. 320p. 16.99 *(978-1-4424-0921-7(5))* Simon Pulse. (Simon Pulse).

—Kissed by an Angel: Evercrossed; Everlasting; Everafter. 2014. (Kissed by an Angel Ser.). (ENG., Illus.). 912p. (YA). (gr. 9). pap. 29.99 *(978-1-4424-9494-7(8)*, Simon Pulse) Simon Pulse.

—Love at First Click. 2009. (First Kisses Ser.). (ENG.). 192p. (YA). (gr. 8-18). pap. 8.99 *(978-0-06-114311-3(1)*, HarperTeen) HarperCollins Pubs.

Chapman, Kelly. Princess with a Purpose. Lyon, Tammie, illus. 2010. (ENG.). 32p. (J). (gr. -1-4). 14.99 *(978-0-7369-2435-1(3))* Harvest Hse. Pubs.

Charbonneau, Joelle. Graduation Day. (ENG.). 304p. (gr. 7). 2015. (Testing Ser.: 3). (YA). pap. 9.99 *(978-0-544-54120-7(0))* 2014. (Testing Trilogy: Bk. 3). (J). 17.99 *(978-0-547-95921-4(4))* Houghton Mifflin Harcourt Publishing Co. (HMH Books For Young Readers).

—Independent Study. (ENG.). (YA). (gr. 7). 2015. (Testing Ser.: 2). 336p. pap. 9.99 *(978-0-544-43945-0(7)*, HMH Books For Young Readers) 2014. (Testing Trilogy: Bk. 2). 320p. 17.99 *(978-0-547-95920-7(6))* Houghton Mifflin Harcourt Publishing Co.

—Independent Study. 2015. (Testing Ser.: 2). lib. bdg. 20.85 *(978-0-606-36832-2(9))* Turtleback Bks.

Chastain, Emma. Confessions of a High School Disaster. 2017. (Chloe Snow's Diary Ser.). (ENG., Illus.). 352p. (YA). (gr. 7). 17.99 *(978-1-4814-8875-4(9)*, Simon Pulse) Simon Pulse.

Chen, Justina. Return to Me. 2013. (ENG.). 352p. (YA). (gr. 7-17). 17.99 *(978-0-316-10255-1(5))* Little Brown & Co.

Cherrington, Shamett Felicia. Bitter Sweet. 2005. (YA). per. 12.95 *(978-1-933570-70-9(9))* Aardvark Global Publishing.

Cherry, Alison. Look Both Ways. 2016. (ENG.). 304p. (YA). (gr. 7). 17.99 *(978-0-553-51186-4(6)*, Delacorte Pr.) Random Hse. Children's Bks.

Chichester Clark, Emma. Love Is My Favorite Thing. Chichester Clark, Emma, illus. 2015. (ENG., Illus.). 32p. (J). (gr. -1-k). 16.99 *(978-0-399-17503-9(2)*, Nancy Paulsen Books) Penguin Young Readers Group.

Childrens Books Staff & Williams, Avery. The Alchemy of Forever: An Incarnation Novel. 2012. (ENG.). 256p. (YA). (gr. 7). 16.99 *(978-1-4424-4316-7(2)*, Simon & Schuster Bks. For Young Readers) Simon & Schuster Bks. For Young Readers.

Childress, Story. Momma, What's Love?, 1 vol. 2010. 28p. 24.95 *(978-1-61546-067-0(5))* PublishAmerica, Inc.

Childs, Tera Lynn. Falling for the Girl Next Door. 2016. (ENG., Illus.). (YA). pap. 16.99 ***(978-1-68281-330-0(4))*** Entangled Publishing, LLC.

Chris, Jerry. Beau, the Story of a Horse. 2003. 317p. (J). pap. 9.99 *(978-0-88092-482-5(9))* Royal Fireworks Publishing Co.

Christopher, Nicholas. The True Adventures of Nicolo Zen: A Novel. 2015. (ENG.). 288p. (YA). (gr. 7). pap. 9.99 *(978-0-375-86492-6(X)*, Ember) Random Hse. Children's Bks.

Church, Caroline Jayne. I Love You! Church, Caroline Jayne, illus. 2012. (ENG., Illus.). 6p. (J). (— 1). 12.99 *(978-0-545-46140-5(5)*, Cartwheel Bks.) Scholastic, Inc.

Churchill, Vicky & Fuge, Charles. Butterfly Kiss. (Illus.). 28p. (J). pap. *(978-0-340-68614-0(6))* Hodder & Stoughton.

Ciocca, Gina. Last Year's Mistake. 2015. (ENG., Illus.). 320p. (YA). (gr. 9). 17.99 *(978-1-4814-3223-8(0)*, Simon Pulse) Simon Pulse.

Clark, Clara. Nellie Bishop. Shine, Andrea, illus. 2003. (ENG.). 128p. (YA). (gr. 4-6). pap. 12.95 *(978-1-56397-642-1(0))* Boyds Mills Pr.

Clark, K. M. Beautiful Disaster. 2013. 106p. 24.99 *(978-1-4797-6506-5(6))*; pap. 15.99 *(978-1-4797-6505-8(8))* Xlibris Corp.

Clark, M. H. T. L. C. 2015. 36p. 16.95 *(978-1-938298-42-4(X))* Compendium, Inc., Publishing & Communications.

Clark, Tracy. Deviate. 2015. (Light Key Trilogy Ser.: 2). (ENG.). 356p. (YA). pap. 9.99 *(978-1-62266-523-5(6)*, 9781622665235) Entangled Publishing, LLC.

—Mirage. 2016. (ENG.). 272p. (J). (gr. 9). 17.99 *(978-0-544-51790-5(3)*, HMH Books For Young Readers) Houghton Mifflin Harcourt Publishing Co.

Claypoole, Joann. The Gardener's Helpers. 2015. (ENG.). 106p. (J). pap. 14.95 *(978-1-63047-532-1(7))* Morgan James Publishing.

Cleary, Beverly & Cleary, B. The Luckiest Girl. 2007. (ENG., Illus.). 272p. (J). (gr. 5-18). pap. 6.99 *(978-0-380-72806-0(0))* HarperCollins Pubs.

Clemont, Lynn C. The Angel Children. 2011. 28p. pap. 13.59 *(978-1-4567-6610-8(4))* AuthorHouse.

Clifford, Leah. A Touch Morbid. 2012. (Touch Mortal Trilogy Ser.: 2). (ENG.). 304p. (YA). (gr. 9). 16.99 *(978-0-06-200502-1(2)*, Greenwillow Bks.) HarperCollins Pubs.

Clipston, Amy. Miles from Nowhere, 1 vol. 2015. (ENG.). 288p. (YA). pap. 9.99 *(978-0-310-73670-7(6))* Zondervan.

Cody, Paul. Love Is Both Wave & Particle. 2017. (ENG.). 320p. (YA). 17.99 *(978-1-62672-688-8(4)*, 9781626726888) Roaring Brook Pr.

Coe, Mary E. The Prince of Betherland a Wonderful World of Fantasy. 2009. 112p. pap. 9.95 *(978-0-557-09297-0(3))* Lulu Pr., Inc.

Cohn, Rachel. Beta. 2013. (Beta Novel Ser.). (ENG., Illus.). 336p. (YA). (gr. 9-17). pap. 9.99 *(978-1-4231-5734-2(6))* Hyperion Pr.

—Emergent. 2014. (Beta Novel Ser.). (ENG.). 288p. (YA). (gr. 9-17). 17.99 *(978-1-4231-5720-5(6))* Hyperion Bks. for Children.

Cohn, Rachel & Levithan, David. Nick & Norah's Infinite Playlist. 2009. 10.54 *(978-0-7848-2769-7(9)*, Everbind) Marco Bk. Co.

—Nick & Norah's Infinite Playlist. 2007. 183p. (gr. 9-12). 19.00 *(978-0-7569-7949-2(8))* Perfection Learning Corp.

—Nick & Norah's Infinite Playlist. (ENG.). 208p. (YA). (gr. 9-12). 2007. pap. 9.99 *(978-0-375-83533-9(4))* 2008. (Illus.). pap. 9.99 *(978-0-375-84614-4(X))* Random Hse. Children's Bks. (Ember).

—The Twelve Days of Dash & Lily. 2016. (ENG.). 224p. (YA). (gr. 7). 17.99 *(978-0-399-55380-6(0)*, Knopf Bks. for Young Readers) Random Hse. Children's Bks.

Coker, Lauren. The Phantom's Lullaby: A Novel. 2008. 332p. pap. 19.95 *(978-0-595-47695-4(3))* iUniverse, Inc.

Colasanti, Susane. All I Need. 2014. (ENG.). 240p. (YA). (gr. 7). pap. 9.99 *(978-0-14-242676-0(8)*, Speak) Penguin Young Readers Group.

—City Love. (City Love Ser.: 1). (YA). (gr. 9). 2016. 352p. pap. 9.99 *(978-0-06-230770-5(3))* 2015. (ENG.). 336p. 17.99 *(978-0-06-230768-2(1))* HarperCollins Pubs. (Tegen, Katherine Bks).

—Lost in Love. 2016. (City Love Ser.: 2). 352p. (YA). (gr. 9). 17.99 *(978-0-06-230773-6(8)*, Tegen, Katherine Bks) HarperCollins Pubs.

—Now & Forever. 2015. (ENG.). 304p. (YA). (gr. 7). pap. 9.99 *(978-0-14-751139-3(9)*, Speak) Penguin Young Readers Group.

Coley, Patrick. The Chronicles of Maxwell & His Runaways. 2012. 134p. 29.99 *(978-1-4797-0759-1(7))*; pap. 19.99 *(978-1-4797-0758-4(9))* Xlibris Corp.

Collie, Brenda Faye. College Freshman 101. 2014. (ENG.). 282p. pap. 9.99 *(978-0-9840220-2-1(3)*, 3c08c3a2-c1e2-4334-9d61-f48276aebfd9) Daylight Bks.

Collins, Amanda. Bff!!! or Not??? 2007. 168p. per. 20.99 *(978-1-4257-3370-4(0))* Xlibris Corp.

Collins, Amanda E. Bff!!! or Not??? 2007. 168p. 30.99 *(978-1-4257-3371-1(9))* Xlibris Corp.

Collins, Michael. Anu & the Blue. 2009. 166p. pap. 16.68 *(978-0-557-20316-1(3))* Lulu Pr., Inc.

Collins, Renee. Until We Meet Again. 2015. (ENG.). 336p. (YA). (gr. 8-12). 16.99 *(978-1-4926-2116-4(1)*, 9781492621164) Sourcebooks, Inc.

Collins, Tim. Notes from a Totally Lame Vampire: Because the Undead Have Feelings Too! Pinder, Andrew, illus. 2010. (ENG.). 336p. (J). (gr. 5-9). 12.99 *(978-1-4424-1183-8(X)*, Aladdin) Simon & Schuster Children's Publishing.

—Prince of Dorkness: More Notes from a Totally Lame Vampire. Pinder, Andrew, illus. 2011. (ENG.). 336p. (J). (gr. 5-9). 12.99 *(978-1-4424-3388-5(4)*, Aladdin) Simon & Schuster Children's Publishing.

Complete Nothing. 2014. (True Love Ser.: 2). (ENG., Illus.). 336p. (YA). (gr. 7). pap. 9.99 *(978-1-4424-7720-9(2)*, Simon & Schuster Bks. For Young Readers) Simon & Schuster Bks. For Young Readers.

Connor, Leslie. The Things You Kiss Goodbye. 2014. (ENG.). 368p. (YA). (gr. 9). 17.99 *(978-0-06-089091-9(6)*, Tegen, Katherine Bks) HarperCollins Pubs.

Conrad, Lauren. Infamous. 2013. (Fame Game Ser.: 3). (ENG.). 288p. (YA). (gr. 9). 18.99 *(978-0-06-207984-8(0))* HarperCollins Pubs.

Constantine, Robin. The Promise of Amazing. (ENG.). (YA). (gr. 9). 2015. 400p. pap. 9.99 *(978-0-06-227949-1(1))* 2013. 384p. 17.99 *(978-0-06-227948-4(3))* HarperCollins Pubs.

—The Secrets of Attraction. 2015. (ENG.). 384p. (YA). (gr. 9). 17.99 *(978-0-06-227951-4(3))* HarperCollins Pubs.

Conway, Celeste. Unlovely. 2015. (ENG.). 254p. (YA). 17.99 *(978-1-4405-8279-0(3)*, Simon Pulse) Simon Pulse.

Cook, Eileen. Remember. 2015. (ENG., Illus.). 320p. (YA). (gr. 9). 17.99 *(978-1-4814-1696-2(0)*, Simon Pulse) Simon Pulse.

—What Would Emma Do? 2008. (ENG.). 320p. (YA). (gr. 9-10). pap. 8.99 *(978-1-4169-7432-1(6)*, Simon Pulse) Simon Pulse.

Cook, Kristi. Eternal. (ENG., Illus.). (YA). (gr. 9). 2014. 432p. pap. 9.99 *(978-1-4424-8531-0(0))* 2013. 416p. 16.99 *(978-1-4424-8532-7(9))* Simon Pulse. (Simon Pulse).

—Magnolia. 2014. (ENG., Illus.). 336p. (YA). (gr. 9). 17.99 *(978-1-4424-8535-8(3))*; pap. 10.99 *(978-1-4424-8534-1(5))* Simon Pulse. (Simon Pulse).

Cooner, Donna. Skinny. 2012. (ENG.). 272p. (J). (gr. 7). 17.99 *(978-0-545-42763-0(0))* Scholastic, Inc.

Cooney, Caroline B. Janie Face to Face. 2013. (ENG.). 352p. (YA). (gr. 7). 17.99 *(978-0-385-74206-1(1)*, Delacorte Bks. for Young Readers) Random Hse. Children's Bks.

Cooper, Blayne. Blind Side of the Moon. 2016. (ENG.). 240p. (J). (gr. 7). pap. 16.95 *(978-1-59493-531-2(9))* Bella Bks., Inc.

Cooper, Jennifer. Guardian Angel. 2009. 155p. pap. 12.87 *(978-0-557-09330-4(9))* Lulu Pr., Inc.

Cooper, Mimi. Me Versus Cooties. 2006. 17p. 9.99 *(978-1-4116-8256-6(4))* Lulu Pr., Inc.

Cormier, Robert. Tenderness. 2004. (ENG.). 240p. (YA). (gr. 9). per. 8.99 *(978-0-385-73133-1(7)*, Ember) Random Hse. Children's Bks.

Cornwell, Betsy. Tides. 2014. (ENG.). 304p. (YA). (gr. 7). pap. 8.99 *(978-0-544-30296-9(6)*, HMH Books For Young Readers) Houghton Mifflin Harcourt Publishing Co.

Corp, Carey & Langdon, Lorie. Destined for Doon, 1 vol. (Doon Novel Ser.). (ENG.). (YA). 2015. 368p. pap. 12.99 *(978-0-310-74240-1(4))* 2014. 352p. 17.99 *(978-0-310-74233-3(1))* Blink.

Corthron, Kara Lee. The Truth of Right Now. 2017. (ENG., Illus.). 288p. (YA). (gr. 9). 17.99 *(978-1-4814-5947-1(3)*, Simon Pulse) Simon Pulse.

Cotugno, Katie. Fireworks. 2017. 336p. (YA). (gr. 8). 17.99 *(978-0-06-241827-2(0))* HarperCollins Pubs.

—How to Love. (ENG.). (YA). (gr. 9). 2015. 416p. pap. 9.99 *(978-0-06-221636-6(8))* 2013. 400p. 17.99 *(978-0-06-221635-9(X))* HarperCollins Pubs.

Cotugno, Katie. Top Ten. 2017. 368p. (YA). (gr. 8). 17.99 ***(978-0-06-241830-2(0))*** HarperCollins Pubs.

Coulthurst, Audrey. Of Fire & Stars. Saia, Jordan, illus. 2016. 400p. (YA). (gr. 8). 17.99 *(978-0-06-243325-1(3))* HarperCollins Pubs.

Courtenay, Christina. New England Rocks. 2013. (ENG.). 192p. pap. 6.95 *(978-1-78189-030-1(7))* Choc Lit Limited GBR. Dist: Casemate Pubs. & Bk. Distributors, LLC.

Covington, Jean. Nanny Planted Love. 2005. (J). lib. bdg. 19.95 *(978-0-9754728-9-7(5))* Big Ransom Studio.

Cox, Greg. Riese: Kingdom Falling. 2012. (ENG.). 288p. (YA). (gr. 7). 16.99 *(978-1-4424-2969-7(0)*, Simon & Schuster Bks. For Young Readers) Simon & Schuster Bks. For Young Readers.

Cozzo, Karole. The Truth about Happily Ever After. 2017. (ENG.). 320p. (YA). 17.99 *(978-1-250-12797-6(1)*, 9781250127976) Feiwel & Friends.

Craft, Elizabeth. Love Bytes. 2013. (@cafe Ser.: 1). (ENG., Illus.). 224p. (YA). (gr. 7). pap. 15.99 *(978-1-4814-2110-2(7)*, Simon Pulse) Simon Pulse.

—Make Mine to Go. 2013. (@cafe Ser.: 3). (ENG., Illus.). 192p. (YA). (gr. 7). pap. 13.99 *(978-1-4814-2112-6(3)*, Simon Pulse) Simon Pulse.

Craig-Kendall, Ruth. Bobby Pew, That's Who. 2008. 22p. pap. 24.95 *(978-1-60672-095-0(3))* America Star Bks.

Craver, Marcella Marino. Joey Daring, Caring, & Curious. Lew-Vriethoff, Joanne, illus. 2014. (J). *(978-1-4338-1652-9(0))*; pap. *(978-1-4338-1653-6(9))* American Psychological Assn. (Magination Pr.).

Creel, Ann Howard. Call Me the Canyon: A Love Story. 2006. 211p. (YA). per. 8.95 *(978-0-9768126-4-7(9))* Brown Barn Bks.

Cremer, Andrea. Bloodrose. 2012. (Nightshade Ser.: 3). (ENG.). 448p. (YA). (gr. 9). pap. 10.99 *(978-0-14-242370-7(X)*, Speak) Penguin Young Readers Group.

—Bloodrose. 2012. (Nightshade Ser.: 3). lib. bdg. 22.10 *(978-0-606-26635-2(6)*, Turtleback) Turtleback Bks.

—Snakeroot. 2014. (Nightshade Ser.: 4). (ENG.). 352p. (YA). (gr. 9). pap. 9.99 *(978-0-14-750860-7(6)*, Speak) Penguin Young Readers Group.

Crilley, Mark. Autumn. Crilley, Mark, illus. 2007. (Miki Falls Ser.: 3). (ENG., Illus.). 176p. (YA). (gr. 8-12). pap. 8.99 *(978-0-06-084618-3(6))* HarperCollins Pubs.

Cross, Julie. Timestorm: A Tempest Novel. 2014. (Tempest Trilogy Ser.: 3). (ENG.). 368p. (YA). (gr. 9-12). 18.99 *(978-0-312-56891-7(6)*, 9780312568917, St. Martin's Griffin) St. Martin's Pr.

—Vortex. 2013. (Tempest Trilogy Ser.: 2). (ENG.). 368p. (YA). (gr. 9-12). 18.99 *(978-0-312-56890-0(8)*, 9780312568900, St. Martin's Griffin) St. Martin's Pr.

—Vortex: A Tempest Novel. 2013. (Tempest Trilogy Ser.: 2). (ENG.). 384p. (YA). (gr. 9-12). pap. 9.99

(978-1-250-04478-5(2), 9781250044785, St. Martin's Griffin) St. Martin's Pr.
Cross, Julie & Perini, Mark. You Before Anyone Else. 2016. (ENG.). 400p. (YA). (gr. 8-12). pap. 10.99 *(978-1-4926-0492-1(5)*, 9781492604921) Sourcebooks, Inc.
Cross, Mimi. Before Goodbye, 0 vols. 2016. (ENG.). 389p. (YA). (gr. 8-12). pap. 9.99 *(978-1-5039-4972-0(9)*, 9781503949720, Skyscape) Amazon Publishing.
Cross, Sarah. Kill Me Softly. 2013. (ENG.). 336p. (J). (gr. 9). pap. 9.99 *(978-1-60684-495-3(4)*, Carolrhoda Lab™) Lerner Publishing Group.
—Tear You Apart. (ENG.). 384p. (gr. 9-12). 2016. pap. 9.99 *(978-1-5124-2628-1(8)*, Carolrhoda Bks.) 2015. 17.99 *(978-1-60684-591-2(8)*, Carolrhoda Lab™) Lerner Publishing Group.
Croteau, Marie-Danielle. Fred & the Mysterious Letter, 1 vol. Cummins, Sarah, tr. from FRE. St-Aubin, Bruno, illus. 2005. (Formac First Novels Ser.). (ENG.). 64p. (J). (gr. 2-5). 4.95 *(978-0-88780-688-9(0)*, 9780887806889) Formac Publishing Co., Ltd. CAN. Dist: Casemate Pubs. & Bk. Distributors, LLC.
Crowley, Cath. A Little Wanting Song. 2011. (ENG.). 288p. (YA). (gr. 9). pap. 8.99 *(978-0-375-85449-1(5)*, Ember) Random Hse. Children's Bks.
—Words in Deep Blue. 2017. (ENG.). 288p. (YA). (gr. 9). 17.99 *(978-1-101-93764-8(5))*; lib. bdg. 20.99 *(978-1-101-93765-5(3))* Random Hse. Children's Bks. (Knopf Bks. for Young Readers).
Crowley, Kieran Mark. Colm & the Lazarus Key. 2009. (ENG., Illus.). 224p. (J). pap. 14.95 *(978-1-85635-646-6(9))* Mercier Pr., Ltd., The IRL. Dist: Dufour Editions, Inc.
Crown Peak Publishing. Just Be You. Crown Peak Publishing, illus. 2008. (ENG., Illus.). 40p. (J). 19.95 *(978-0-9645663-5-4(4))* Crown Peak Publishing.
Crystal, Billy. I Already Know I Love You. Sayles, Elizabeth, illus. 2004. 40p. (J). (ENG.). 16.99 *(978-0-06-059391-9(1))*; lib. bdg. 17.89 *(978-0-06-059392-6(X))* HarperCollins Pubs.
Cuasay, Alison Taimanglo. Tasi & Matina: The Story of the First Clown Fish. 2010. 28p. pap. 12.99 *(978-1-4520-6672-1(8))* AuthorHouse.
Cuchna, Reid. Out of Love, 1 vol. 2009. 327p. pap. 29.95 *(978-1-60836-345-2(7))* America Star Bks.
Cummings, Lindsay. The Murder Complex. 2014. (Murder Complex Ser.: 1). (ENG.). 416p. (YA). (gr. 9). 17.99 *(978-0-06-222000-4(4)*, Greenwillow Bks.) HarperCollins Pubs.
Cumyn, Alan. Dear Sylvia, 1 vol. 2009. (ENG.). 184p. (J). pap. 8.95 *(978-0-88899-848-4(1))* Groundwood Bks. CAN. Dist: Publishers Group West (PGW).
Cunningham, P. E. Slayer for Hire. 2013. 204p. pap. *(978-1-77130-285-2(2))* Evernight Publishing.
Cupidity. 2014. (Romantic Comedies Ser.). (ENG., Illus.). 288p. (YA). (gr. 9). pap. 13.99 *(978-1-4814-2746-3(6)*, Simon Pulse) Simon Pulse.
Curham, Siobhan. Dark of the Moon. 2014. (Shipwrecked Ser.: 2). (ENG.). 288p. (J). (gr. 7). pap. 12.99 *(978-1-4052-6458-7(6))* Egmont Bks., Ltd. GBR. Dist: Independent Pubs. Group.
Curley, Marianne. Broken. 2014. (Avena Ser.). (ENG.). 384p. (YA). (gr. 7). 17.99 *(978-1-61963-168-7(7)*, 9781619631687, Bloomsbury USA Childrens) Bloomsbury Publishing USA.
—Fearless. 2015. (Avena Ser.). (ENG.). 384p. (YA). (gr. 7). pap. 13.99 *(978-1-4088-2264-7(4)*, 9781408822647, Bloomsbury USA Childrens) Bloomsbury Publishing USA.
Currie, Christopher. Clancy of the Undertow. 2016. (ENG., Illus.). 288p. (J). (gr. 8). 11.95 *(978-1-925240-40-5(1))* Text Publishing Co. AUS. Dist: Consortium Bk. Sales & Distribution.
Curry, Cicero. The Tickle Man. Ledbetter, John'el, illus. 2013. 44p. 24.95 *(978-1-63004-279-0(X))* America Star Bks.
Curtis, Jamie Lee. Tell Me Again about the Night I Was Born. 2004. (Illus.). (J). (gr. k-3). spiral bd. *(978-0-616-01623-7(9))* Canadian National Institute for the Blind/Institut National Canadien pour les Aveugles.
—Tell Me Again about the Night I Was Born. 2004. (Illus.). (J). (gr. k-3). spiral bd. *(978-0-616-01624-4(7))* Canadian National Institute for the Blind/Institut National Canadien pour les Aveugles.
Cypess, Leah. Death Marked. 2015. (ENG.). 400p. (YA). (gr. 8). 17.99 *(978-0-06-222124-7(8)*, Greenwillow Bks.) HarperCollins Pubs.
—Death Sworn. (ENG.). (YA). (gr. 8). 2015. 368p. pap. 9.99 *(978-0-06-222122-3(1))* 2014. 352p. 17.99 *(978-0-06-222121-6(3))* HarperCollins Pubs. (Greenwillow Bks.).
Dadey, Debbie & Jones, Marcia Thornton. Inside the Magic. 2009. (Keyholders Ser.: 3). (ENG.). 128p. (J). (gr. 2-5). 4.99 *(978-0-7653-5984-1(7)*, 9780765359841, Starscape) Doherty, Tom Assocs., LLC.
—The Wrong Side of Magic. 2009. (Keyholders Ser.: 4). (ENG.). 128p. (J). (gr. 2-5). pap. 4.99 *(978-0-7653-5985-8(5)*, 9780765359858, Starscape) Doherty, Tom Assocs., LLC.
Dahl, Regina. Love Is Not Selfish. 2013. 32p. pap. 13.95 *(978-1-4497-9289-3(8)*, WestBow Pr.) Author Solutions, Inc.
Daines, Julie. Unraveled: A Tale of True Love. 2014. 192p. (J). pap. 14.99 *(978-1-62108-627-7(5))* Covenant Communications, Inc.
Dalton, Michelle. Pulled Under. 2014. (Sixteenth Summer Ser.). (ENG., Illus.). 288p. (YA). (gr. 7). pap. 9.99 *(978-1-4814-0700-7(7)*, Simon Pulse) Simon Pulse.
—Sixteenth Summer. 2011. (Sixteenth Summer Ser.). (ENG.). 304p. (YA). (gr. 7-18). pap. 9.99 *(978-1-4424-2344-2(7)*, Simon Pulse) Simon Pulse.
—Swept Away. 2015. (Sixteenth Summer Ser.). (ENG., Illus.). 320p. (YA). (gr. 7). pap. 10.99 *(978-1-4814-3608-3(2)*, Simon Pulse) Simon Pulse.
Daly, Maureen. Seventeenth Summer. 2010. (ENG.). 384p. (YA). (gr. 7). pap. 9.99 *(978-1-4169-9463-3(7)*, Simon Pulse) Simon Pulse.
Daniel, Kashya. I Got the Terrible Twos Blues. 2010. 44p. 16.99 *(978-1-4490-9286-3(1))* AuthorHouse.
Dannenbring, McKinsey. A Lemon Without the Sour. 2009. 32p. pap. 14.49 *(978-1-4389-2367-3(8))* AuthorHouse.
Darling, Angela. Isabella's Spring Break Crush. 2014. (Crush Ser.: 6). (ENG., Illus.). 160p. (J). (gr. 3-7). pap. 5.99 *(978-1-4814-0493-8(8)*, Simon Spotlight) Simon Spotlight.
—Lauren Likes Charlie: Does He Like Her Too? 2013. (Crush Ser.: 1). (ENG., Illus.). 176p. (J). (gr. 3-7). 15.99 *(978-1-4424-8038-4(6)*, Simon Spotlight) Simon Spotlight.
—Lauren's Beach Crush. 2013. (Crush Ser.: 1). (ENG., Illus.). 176p. (J). (gr. 3-7). pap. 5.99 *(978-1-4424-8036-0(X)*, Simon Spotlight) Simon Spotlight.
—Lindsay Likes Nick Crush: Does He Like Her Too? 2013. (Crush Ser.: 3). (ENG., Illus.). 144p. (J). (gr. 3-7). 15.99 *(978-1-4424-8045-2(9)*, Simon Spotlight) Simon Spotlight.
—Lindsay's Surprise Crush. 2013. (Crush Ser.: 3). (ENG., Illus.). 144p. (J). (gr. 3-7). pap. 5.99 *(978-1-4424-8042-1(4)*, Simon Spotlight) Simon Spotlight.
—Maddie's Camp Crush. 2013. (Crush Ser.: 2). (ENG.). 160p. (J). (gr. 3-7). pap. 5.99 *(978-1-4424-8334-7(2))*; (Illus.). 15.99 *(978-1-4424-8335-4(0))* Simon Spotlight. (Simon Spotlight).
—Noelle's Christmas Crush. 2013. (Crush Ser.: 4). (ENG., Illus.). 160p. (J). (gr. 3-7). 15.99 *(978-1-4424-8338-5(5))*; pap. 5.99 *(978-1-4424-8337-8(7))* Simon Spotlight. (Simon Spotlight).
—Rachel's Valentine Crush. 2013. (Crush Ser.: 5). (ENG., Illus.). 160p. (J). (gr. 3-7). 15.99 *(978-1-4424-8641-6(4))*; pap. 5.99 *(978-1-4424-8640-9(6))* Simon Spotlight. (Simon Spotlight).
Darling, Tellulah. My Date from Hell. 2013. (Blooming Goddess Trilogy: 2). (ENG.). 388p. (YA). pap. *(978-0-9880540-6-6(X))* Te Da Media.
—My Life from Hell. 2014. (Blooming Goddess Trilogy: 3). (ENG.). 414p. (YA). pap. *(978-0-9880540-9-7(4))* Te Da Media.
Darwin, Florence Henrietta. The Lovers' Tasks. 2004. reprint ed. pap. 1.99 *(978-1-4192-7098-7(2))* Kessinger Publishing, LLC.
Daswani, Kavita. Lovetorn. 2012. (ENG.). 256p. (YA). (gr. 8). 17.99 *(978-0-06-167311-5(0)*, HarperTeen) HarperCollins Pubs.
David, Erica. Anna & Elsa No. 7: The Secret Admirer. Random House Disney Staff et al, illus. 2016. (Stepping Stone Book(TM) Ser.: 7). (ENG.). 128p. (J). (gr. 1-4). 9.99 *(978-0-7364-3475-1(5)*, RH/Disney) Random Hse. Children's Bks.
—The Secret Admirer. Random House Disney Staff et al, illus. 2016. (Stepping Stone Book(TM) Ser.: 7). (ENG.). 128p. (J). (gr. 1-4). lib. bdg. 12.99 *(978-0-7364-8210-3(5)*, RH/Disney) Random Hse. Children's Bks.
Davidowitz, Stacy. Crossing Over, Bk. 2. 2016. (Camp Rolling Hills Ser.: 2). (ENG., Illus.). 240p. (J). (gr. 3-7). pap. 8.95 *(978-1-4197-1880-9(0)*, Amulet Bks.) Abrams, Inc.
Davies, Jacqueline. The Candy Smash. (Lemonade War Ser.). (ENG., Illus.). 240p. (J). (gr. 2-5). 2014. pap. 7.99 *(978-0-544-22500-8(7)*, HMH Books For Young Readers) 2013. 15.99 *(978-0-544-02208-9(4))* Houghton Mifflin Harcourt Publishing Co.
Davis, Gene. Dromedarius & Camela. 2006. lib. bdg. 18.95 *(978-1-59094-115-7(2))* Jawbone Publishing Corp.
Davis, Lisa Selin. Lost Stars. 2016. (ENG.). 288p. (YA). (gr. 9). 17.99 *(978-0-544-78506-9(1)*, HMH Books For Young Readers) Houghton Mifflin Harcourt Publishing Co.
Davis, Terry. Vision Quest. 2015. (ENG., Illus.). 240p. (YA). (gr. 7). 19.99 *(978-1-4814-5636-4(9)*, Simon & Schuster Bks. For Young Readers) Simon & Schuster Bks. For Young Readers.
Dawn, Nyrae. Searching for Beautiful. 2014. (Entangled Teen Ser.). (ENG.). 304p. (YA). (gr. 7-12). pap. 9.99 *(978-1-62266-148-0(6)*, 9781622661480) Entangled Publishing, LLC.
de Angeli, Marguerite. Elin's Amerika. 3rd ed. 2007. (Illus.). 98p. (J). pap. 15.99 *(978-0-9800761-0-3(2))* American Swedish Historical Museum.
de Brunhoff, Laurent & Rose, Phyllis. Babar's Celesteville Games. 2011. (ENG., Illus.). 48p. (J). (gr. k-2). 18.95 *(978-1-4197-0006-4(5)*, Abrams Bks. for Young Readers) Abrams, Inc.
de Gramont, Nina. The Boy I Love. 2015. (ENG., Illus.). 288p. (YA). (gr. 7). pap. 10.99 *(978-1-4424-8057-5(2)*, Atheneum Bks. for Young Readers) Simon & Schuster Children's Publishing.
—Meet Me at the River. (ENG., Illus.). 384p. (YA). (gr. 9). 2014. pap. 11.99 *(978-1-4169-8016-2(4)*, Atheneum Bks. for Young Readers) 2013. 17.99 *(978-1-4169-8014-8(8))* Simon & Schuster Children's Publishing.
De la Cruz, Melissa. Alex & Eliza: A Love Story, 9 vols. 2017. (ENG.). (YA). 161.91 ***(978-0-525-48665-7(8))***; 368p. (gr. 7). 17.99 ***(978-1-5247-3962-1(6))*** Penguin Young Readers Group. (G.P. Putnam's Sons Books for Young Readers).
De la Cruz, Melissa. The Au Pairs. 2004. (Au Pairs Ser.: 1). (ENG.). 304p. (YA). 14.95 *(978-0-689-87066-8(3)*, Simon & Schuster Bks. For Young Readers) Simon & Schuster Bks. For Young Readers.
De la Cruz, Melissa & Johnston, Michael. Golden. 2016. (Heart of Dread Ser.: 3). (ENG.). 272p. (YA). (gr. 7). 17.99 *(978-0-399-25756-8(X)*, G.P. Putnam's Sons Books for Young Readers) Penguin Young Readers Group.
De Sena, Joseph. The Love Bug & the Light of Love. 2007. 64p. per. 19.95 *(978-1-4327-0737-8(X))* Outskirts Pr., Inc.
Delacre, Lulu. How Far Do You Love Me? Delacre, Lulu, illus. 2014. (ENG., Illus.). (J). pap. 8.95 *(978-1-62014-208-0(2))* Lee & Low Bks., Inc.
Dellaira, Ava. Love Letters to the Dead. 2015. (YA). lib. bdg. 20.85 *(978-0-606-37590-0(2))* Turtleback Bks.
DeLuca, Laura. Destiny. 2011. (ENG.). 276p. (YA). pap. 12.95 *(978-0-9826747-2-7(4))* Free Focus Publishing.
Demetrios, Heather. Bad Romance. 2017. (ENG.). 368p. (YA). 17.99 *(978-1-62779-772-6(6)*, 9781627797726, Holt, Henry & Co. Bks. For Young Readers) Holt, Henry & Co.
—Blood Passage. 2017. (Dark Caravan Cycle Ser.: 2). 512p. (YA). (gr. 8). pap. 9.99 *(978-0-06-231860-2(8))* HarperCollins Pubs.
—Exquisite Captive. 2014. (Dark Caravan Cycle Ser.: 1). (ENG., Illus.). 480p. (YA). (gr. 8). 17.99 *(978-0-06-231856-5(X))* HarperCollins Pubs.
—I'll Meet You There. 2015. (ENG.). 400p. (YA). (gr. 9). 17.99 *(978-0-8050-9795-5(3)*, 9780805097955, Holt, Henry & Co. Bks. For Young Readers) Holt, Henry & Co.
Dennard, Susan. Strange & Ever After. 2014. (Something Strange & Deadly Trilogy Ser.: 3). (ENG.). 400p. (YA). (gr. 9). 17.99 *(978-0-06-208332-6(5))* HarperCollins Pubs.
Derting, Kimberly. Desires of the Dead. 2012. (Body Finder Ser.: 2). (ENG.). 384p. (YA). (gr. 9). pap. 8.99 *(978-0-06-177986-2(5))* HarperCollins Pubs.
—The Last Echo. 2013. (Body Finder Ser.: 3). (ENG.). 384p. (YA). (gr. 9). pap. 9.99 *(978-0-06-208220-6(5))* HarperCollins Pubs.
—The Taking. 2014. (Taking Ser.: 1). (ENG.). 368p. (YA). (gr. 9). 17.99 *(978-0-06-229360-2(5)*, HarperTeen) HarperCollins Pubs.
Descoteaux, Chad. Once upon A Crime Syndicate: A mafia fairy Tale. 2006. 151p. pap. 24.95 *(978-1-4241-0893-0(4))* PublishAmerica, Inc.
Despain, Bree. The Eternity Key. 2015. (ENG.). 368p. (YA). (gr. 7). 18.99 *(978-1-60684-467-0(9))*; (Into the Dark Ser.: 2). 18.99 *(978-1-5124-0179-0(X))* Lerner Publishing Group. (Carolrhoda Lab™).
DeSpain, Bree. The Immortal Throne. 2016. (Into the Dark Ser.: 3). (ENG.). 344p. (YA). (gr. 7-12). 18.99 *(978-1-5124-0583-5(3)*, Carolrhoda Bks.) Lerner Publishing Group.
Despain, Bree. The Shadow Prince. (ENG.). 496p. (gr. 7). 2015. (Into the Dark Ser.: Bk. 1). pap. 9.99 *(978-1-60684-567-7(5))* 2014. (J). 18.99 *(978-1-60684-247-8(1))* Lerner Publishing Group. (Carolrhoda Lab™).
Desrochers, Lisa. Original Sin. 2011. (Personal Demons Ser.: 2). (ENG.). 400p. (YA). (gr. 9-18). pap. 25.99 *(978-0-7653-2809-0(7)*, 9780765328090, Tor Teen) Doherty, Tom Assocs., LLC.
Desrosiers, Sylvie. Qui Veut Entrer dans la Legende? Sylvestre, Daniel, illus. 2003. (Roman Jeunesse Ser.). (FRE.). 96p. (YA). (gr. 4-7). pap. *(978-2-89021-269-5(6))* Diffusion du livre Mirabel (DLM).
Dessen, Sarah. Once & for All. 2017. (ENG.). 368p. (YA). (gr. 7). 19.99 *(978-0-425-29033-0(6)*, Viking Books for Young Readers) Penguin Young Readers Group.
Destiny, A. & Hapka, Catherine. Virtually in Love. 2015. (Flirt Ser.). (ENG., Illus.). 240p. (YA). (gr. 7). pap. 9.99 *(978-1-4814-2118-8(2)*, Simon Pulse) Simon Pulse.
Destiny, A. & Kahler, A. R. Love Is in the Air. 2015. 221p. (YA). *(978-1-4814-2377-9(0)*, Simon Pulse) Simon Pulse.
Destiny, A. & Lenhard, Elizabeth. Our Song. 2015. 225p. (YA). *(978-1-4424-8407-8(1)*, Simon Pulse) Simon Pulse.
Deutsch, Stacia & Cohon, Rhody. In the Stars. 2012. (Romantic Comedies Ser.). (ENG.). 304p. (YA). (gr. 9). pap. 14.99 *(978-1-4424-8293-7(1)*, Simon Pulse) Simon Pulse.
Dewdney, Anna. Llama Llama I Love You. 2014. (Llama Llama Ser.). (ENG., Illus.). 14p. (J). (gr. -1 — 1). bds. 5.99 *(978-0-451-46981-6(X)*, Viking Books for Young Readers) Penguin Young Readers Group.
Diamond, Laura. Endure. 2013. 268p. pap. 11.99 *(978-1-940223-45-2(8))* Etopia Pr.
Diaz, Stephanie. Extraction. 2014. (Extraction Ser.: 1). (ENG.). 416p. (YA). (gr. 7-12). 18.99 *(978-1-250-04117-3(1)*, 9781250041173, St. Martin's Griffin) St. Martin's Pr.
—Rebellion. 2015. (Extraction Ser.: 2). (ENG.). 336p. (YA). (gr. 7). 19.99 *(978-1-250-04125-8(2)*, 9781250041258, St. Martin's Griffin) St. Martin's Pr.
DiCamillo, Kate. The Miraculous Journey of Edward Tulane. Ibatoulline, Bagram, illus. (ENG.). (J). 2015. 240p. (gr. 2-5). pap. 7.99 *(978-0-7636-8090-9(7))* 2009. 228p. (gr. 2-5). pap. 11.99 *(978-0-7636-4783-4(7))* 2006. 228p. (gr. 1-4). 19.99 *(978-0-7636-2589-4(2))* Candlewick Pr.
—The Miraculous Journey of Edward Tulane. 2012. 22.00 *(978-1-61383-813-6(1))* Perfection Learning Corp.
—The Miraculous Journey of Edward Tulane. 2015. lib. bdg. 17.20 *(978-0-606-37892-5(8))* Turtleback Bks.
—The Miraculous Journey of Edward Tulane. Ibatoulline, Bagram, illus. 2009. 198p. (gr. 8-12). 23.30 *(978-1-4178-0763-5(6)*, Turtleback) Turtleback Bks.
Dickerson, Melanie. The Golden Braid, 1 vol. 2015. (ENG.). 320p. (YA). 16.99 *(978-0-7180-2626-4(8))* Nelson, Thomas Inc.
—The Huntress of Thornbeck Forest, 1 vol. 2015. (Medieval Fairy Tale Ser.: 1). (ENG.). 320p. pap. 15.99 *(978-0-7180-2624-0(1))* Nelson, Thomas Inc.
—The Noble Servant, 1 vol. 2017. (ENG.). 336p. (J). 14.99 *(978-0-7180-2660-8(8))* Nelson, Thomas Inc.
—The Silent Songbird, 1 vol. 2016. (ENG.). 304p. (YA). 14.99 *(978-0-7180-2631-8(4))* Nelson, Thomas Inc.
Diesen, Deborah. Kiss, Kiss, Pout-Pout Fish. Hanna, Dan, illus. 2015. (Pout-Pout Fish Mini Adventure Ser.). (ENG.). 14p. (J). (gr. -1 — 1). 5.99 *(978-0-374-30190-3(5)*, 9780374301903, Farrar, Straus & Giroux (BYR)) Farrar, Straus & Giroux.
Dietrich, Cale. The Love Interest. 2017. (ENG.). 384p. (YA). 17.99 *(978-1-250-10713-8(X)*, 9781250107138) Feiwel & Friends.
Dillon, Elena. Crushing. 2013. 368p. (YA). pap. 13.99 *(978-0-9886353-4-0(8))* Dillon, Elena.
Dinnison, Kris. You & Me & Him. (ENG.). 288p. (YA). (gr. 9). 2016. pap. 8.99 *(978-0-544-67175-1(9))* 2015. 17.99 *(978-0-544-30112-2(9))* Houghton Mifflin Harcourt Publishing Co. (HMH Books For Young Readers).
Disney. A Mother's Love. 2012. (Disney Princess Step into Reading Ser.). lib. bdg. 13.55 *(978-0-606-26392-4(6)*, Turtleback) Turtleback Bks.
Disney Book Group Staff. Gravity Falls Pining Away. Disney Storybook Artists Staff & Disney Storybook Art Team, illus. 2014. (Gravity Falls Chapter Book Ser.: 1). (ENG.). 112p. (J). (gr. 1-3). pap. 4.99 *(978-1-4847-1139-2(4))* Disney Pr.
—I Love You! Disney Storybook Artists Staff, illus. 2012. (ENG.). 10p. (J). (gr. -1-k). pap. 7.99 *(978-1-4231-6571-2(3))* Disney Pr.
—The Little Mermaid Read-Along Storybook & CD. Disney Storybook Artists Staff, illus. 2013. (Read-Along Storybook & CD Ser.). (ENG.). 32p. (J). (gr. -1-k). pap. 6.99 *(978-1-4231-6889-8(5))* Disney Pr.
Divine, L. Holidaze. 2009. (ENG., Illus.). 256p. (YA). (gr. 9-18). pap. 9.95 *(978-0-7582-3109-3(1)*, K-Teen/Dafina) Kensington Publishing Corp.
—Hustlin' 2009. (ENG., Illus.). 256p. (YA). (gr. 9). pap. 15.00 *(978-0-7582-3105-5(9)*, K-Teen/Dafina) Kensington Publishing Corp.
Dodd, Emma. Love. Dodd, Emma, illus. 2016. (Emma Dodd's Love You Bks.). (ENG., Illus.). 24p. (J). (-k). 12.99 *(978-0-7636-8941-4(6)*, Nosy Crow) Candlewick Pr.
Dokey, Cameron. Beauty Sleep: A Retelling of Sleeping Beauty. 2006. (Once upon a Time Ser.). (ENG.). 208p. (YA). (gr. 9-12). mass mkt. 6.99 *(978-1-4169-4014-2(6)*, Simon Pulse) Simon Pulse.
—Before Midnight: A Retelling of Cinderella. 2007. (Once upon a Time Ser.). (ENG.). 208p. (YA). (gr. 7-12). mass mkt. 7.99 *(978-1-4169-3471-4(5)*, Simon Pulse) Simon Pulse.
—Belle: A Retelling of Beauty & the Beast. 2008. (Once upon a Time Ser.). (ENG.). 224p. (YA). (gr. 7-18). mass mkt. 6.99 *(978-1-4169-6131-4(3)*, Simon Pulse) Simon Pulse.
Doktorski, Jennifer Salvato. How My Summer Went up in Flames. 2013. (ENG.). 320p. (YA). (gr. 9). 17.99 *(978-1-4424-5940-3(9))*; pap. 10.99 *(978-1-4424-5939-7(5))* Simon Pulse. (Simon Pulse).
Doller, Trish. Something Like Normal. (ENG.). (YA). (gr. 9). 2013. 240p. pap. 9.99 *(978-1-61963-146-5(6)*, 9781619631465) 2012. 224p. 16.99 *(978-1-59990-844-1(1)*, 9781599908441) Bloomsbury Publishing USA. (Bloomsbury USA Childrens).
Dominy, Amy Fellner. Die for You. 2016. (ENG.). 304p. (YA). (gr. 7). 17.99 *(978-1-101-93619-1(3)*, Delacorte Pr.) Random Hse. Children's Bks.
Donovan, Rebecca. Reason to Breathe, 0 vols. 2013. (Breathing Ser.: 1). (ENG.). 466p. (YA). (gr. 10-12). pap. 9.99 *(978-1-4778-1714-8(X)*, 9781477817148, Amazon Children's Publishing) Amazon Publishing.
Dopirak, Kate. You're My Boo. Withrow, Lesley Breen, illus. 2016. (ENG.). 40p. (J). (gr. -1-3). 17.99 *(978-1-4424-4160-6(7)*, Beach Lane Bks.) Beach Lane Bks.
Doty, Mariel. A Different Kind of Princess: Pictures of You. 2010. 260p. 26.50 *(978-1-60911-318-6(7)*, Eloquent Bks.) Strategic Book Publishing & Rights Agency (SBPRA).
Doughty, Rebecca. Before You. 2016. (ENG., Illus.). 32p. (J). (gr. -1-3). 14.99 *(978-0-544-46317-2(X)*, HMH Books For Young Readers) Houghton Mifflin Harcourt Publishing Co.
Douglas, Babette. Kiss a Me: A Little Whale Watching. Rockwell, Barry, illus. 2006. (Kiss a Me Teacher Creature Stories Ser.). (J). (gr. 3-7). 9.99 *(978-1-890343-08-8(0))* Kiss A Me Productions, Inc.
Douglas, Helen. After Eden. 2013. (ENG.). 288p. (YA). (gr. 7). 17.99 *(978-1-61963-130-4(X)*, 9781619631304, Bloomsbury USA Childrens) Bloomsbury Publishing USA.
—Chasing Stars. 2016. (ENG.). 352p. (YA). 17.99 *(978-1-61963-410-7(4)*, 9781619634107, Bloomsbury USA Childrens) Bloomsbury Publishing USA.
Douglas, L. B. Looking for Moemoe: Love Is never far Away. 2010. 24p. pap. 12.99 *(978-1-4490-2768-1(7))* AuthorHouse.
Douglas, Ryke Leigh. Molly the Trolley & Bud. 2008. 24p. pap. 11.95 *(978-1-4327-2207-4(7))* Outskirts Pr., Inc.
Downes, Patrick. Ten Miles One Way. 2017. (ENG.). 208p. (YA). (gr. 9). 17.99 *(978-0-399-54499-6(2)*, Philomel Bks.) Penguin Young Readers Group.
Doxey, Heidi. The Jane Journals at Pemberley Prep: Liam Darcy, I Loathe You. 2015. 215p. (YA). pap. 14.99 *(978-1-4621-1682-9(5))* Cedar Fort, Inc./CFI Distribution.
Doyle, Catherine. Vendetta. 2015. (ENG.). 352p. (J). (gr. 9). 18.99 *(978-0-545-69982-2(7))* Scholastic, Inc.
Drake, Brenda. Cursing Fate. 2016. (ENG., Illus.). (YA). pap. 15.99 ***(978-1-68281-357-7(6))*** Entangled Publishing, LLC.
Drake, Brenda. Touching Fate. 2015. (ENG., Illus.). 236p. (YA). (gr. 7). pap. 15.99 *(978-1-943892-68-6(7))* Entangled Publishing, LLC.
Du Jardin, Rosamond. A Man for Marcy. 2003. (YA). pap. 12.95 *(978-1-930009-76-9(3)*, 800-691-7779) Image Cascade Publishing.
Duble, Kathleen Benner. Madame Tussaud's Apprentice: An Untold Story of Love in the French Revolution. 2014. (ENG.). 224p. (YA). 17.99 *(978-1-4405-8116-8(9)*, Simon Pulse) Simon Pulse.
Duffy, Jacqueline Ann. Dillon the Dog Finds His Family. 2008. 24p. pap. 24.95 *(978-1-60563-331-2(3))* America Star Bks.
DuJardin, Rosamond. Boy Trouble. 2003. (YA). pap. 12.95 *(978-1-930009-70-7(4)*, 800-691-7779) Image Cascade Publishing.
—The Real Thing. 2003. (YA). pap. 12.95 *(978-1-930009-71-4(2)*, 800-691-7779) Image Cascade Publishing.
—Someone to Count On. 2003. (YA). pap. 12.95 *(978-1-930009-78-3(X)*, 800-691-7779) Image Cascade Publishing.
Duksta, Laura. I Love You More. Keesler, Karen, illus. (ENG.). (J). 2009. 24p. bds. 6.99 *(978-1-4022-2460-7(5))* 2007. 34p. 16.99 *(978-1-4022-1126-3(0))* Sourcebooks, Inc. (Sourcebooks Jabberwocky).
—I Love You More Padded Board Book. Keesler, Karen, illus. 2013. (ENG.). 24p. (J). bds. 8.99 *(978-1-4022-9250-7(3)*, Sourcebooks Jabberwocky) Sourcebooks, Inc.
—I'll Hug You More. Iwai, Melissa, illus. 2017. (ENG.). 32p. (J). (-4). 16.99 *(978-1-4926-2618-3(X)*, 9781492626183, Sourcebooks Jabberwocky) Sourcebooks, Inc.
—Te Quiero Más. Keesler, Karen, illus. 2013. (ENG & SPA.). 24p. (J). bds. 6.99 *(978-1-4022-8177-8(3)*, Sourcebooks Jabberwocky) Sourcebooks, Inc.
Dumas, Alexandre & Dumas, Alexandre, eds. La Dama de las Camelias. (SPA.). (J). 9.00 *(978-958-04-7139-4(8))* Norma S.A. COL. Dist: Distribuidora Norma, Inc.
Duncan, Lois. Debutante Hill. 2013. (ENG., Illus.). 200p. (gr. 6). pap. 12.95 *(978-1-939601-00-1(2))* Ig Publishing, Inc.
Dunn, Gaby & Raskin, Allison. I Hate Everyone but You. 2017. (ENG.). 352p. (YA). 18.99 ***(978-1-250-12932-1(X)***, 9781250129321, Wednesday Bks.) St. Martin's Pr.
Dunne, Amy. Secret Lies. 2013. (ENG.). 288p. (gr. 7). pap. 11.95 *(978-1-60282-970-1(5))* Bold Strokes Bks.
Dyan, Penelope. Bunny Love! a Book about Home & Bunnies. Dyan, Penelope, illus. 2013. (Illus.). 34p. pap. 11.95 *(978-1-61477-084-8(0))* Bellissima Publishing, LLC.
—Mikey & Me & the Valentines — the Continuing Story of a Girl & Her Dog. Dyan, Penelope, illus. 2010. (Illus.). 50p. pap. 14.95 *(978-1-935118-96-1(X))* Bellissima Publishing, LLC.
—My Valentines. 2011. 34p. pap. 11.95 *(978-1-935630-52-4(0))* Bellissima Publishing, LLC.
—Some Bunny Loves You! 2013. 34p. pap. 11.95 *(978-1-61477-068-8(9))* Bellissima Publishing, LLC.

—The Warrior Mouse of Forest Hollow. Quinn, Courtney, illus. 2008. 108p. 17.95 *(978-1-935118-00-8(5))* Bellissima Publishing, LLC.

Eade, Oliver. The Terminus. 2013. 264p. pap. *(978-1-909411-26-5(4))* Mauve Square Publishing.

Earhardt, Ainsley & Cristaldi, Kathryn. Take Heart, My Child: A Mother's Dream. Kim, Jaime, illus. 2016. (ENG.). 32p. (J). (gr. -1-3). 18.99 *(978-1-4814-6622-6(4),* Aladdin) Simon & Schuster Children's Publishing.

Earnhardt, Heather L. The Wandering Goose: A Modern Fable of How Love Goes. Clements, Frida, illus. 2013. (ENG.). 64p. 15.95 *(978-1-57061-881-9(X))* Sasquatch Bks.

Ebner, Abra. Ladybird, Ladybird. 2011. 172p. (J). 16.99 *(978-0-9829505-4-8(3))* Crimson Oak Publishing LLC.

Echols, Jennifer. Love Story. 2011. (ENG.). 256p. pap. 11.00 *(978-1-4391-7832-4(1),* MTV Bks.) MTV Books.

—Most Likely to Succeed. 2015. (Superlatives Ser.). (ENG., Illus.). 352p. (YA). (gr. 9). 17.99 *(978-1-4424-7452-9(1),* Simon Pulse) Simon Pulse.

Eco, Umberto. The Story of the Betrothed. Lorenzetti, Marco, illus. 2017. (Save the Story Ser.). (ENG.). 104p. (J). (gr. 3-7). 19.95 *(978-1-78269-022-1(0),* Pushkin Press) Steerforth Pr.

Edwards, Jean Pearce. Little Jean's War. 2008. (Illus.). 208p. pap. 14.49 *(978-1-4343-9133-9(7))* AuthorHouse.

Edwards, Jo. Go Figure. 2007. (ENG.). 288p. (YA). (gr. 9-12). pap. 13.99 *(978-1-4169-2492-0(2),* Simon Pulse) Simon Pulse.

—Love Undercover. 2006. (Romantic Comedies Ser.). (ENG.). 288p. (YA). (gr. 9-12). mass mkt. 6.99 *(978-1-4169-2465-4(5),* Simon Pulse) Simon Pulse.

Edwards, Meinir Wyn. Rhys & Meinir. Wade, Gini, illus. 2007. (ENG.). 24p. (J). pap. 4.95 *(978-1-84771-020-8(4))* Y Lolfa GBR. Dist: Dufour Editions, Inc.

Ehlert, Lois. Heart to Heart. Ehlert, Lois, illus. 2017. (ENG., Illus.). 72p. (J). (gr. -1-3). 9.99 *(978-1-4814-8087-1(1),* Beach Lane Bks.) Beach Lane Bks.

Eliot, Stephanie. Sad Perfect. 2017. (ENG.). 320p. (YA). 17.99 *(978-0-374-30375-4(4),* 9780374303754, Farrar, Straus & Giroux (BYR)) Farrar, Straus & Giroux.

Elisabeth, Megan. A Star's Journey from Twinkle to Shine. 2012. 28p. pap. 24.95 *(978-1-62709-789-5(9))* America Star Bks.

Elkeles, Simone. Wild Cards. 2013. 352p. (YA). pap. *(978-0-8027-3738-0(2))* Walker & Co.

Ella, Sara. Unraveling, 1 vol. 2017. (Unblemished Trilogy Ser.). (ENG.). 368p. (YA). 15.99 ***(978-0-7180-8103-4(X))*** Nelson, Thomas Inc.

Ellen, Tom & Ivison, Lucy. A Totally Awkward Love Story. 2016. (ENG.). 320p. (YA). (gr. 9). 17.99 *(978-0-553-53732-1(6),* Delacorte Pr.) Random Hse. Children's Bks.

Elliott, Jenny. Save Me. 2015. (ENG.). 336p. (YA). (gr. 7-12). pap. 9.99 *(978-1-250-06147-8(4),* 9781250061478) Feiwel & Friends.

Elliott, Kate, pseud. Poisoned Blade. 2016. (Court of Fives Ser.: 2). (ENG., Illus.). 480p. (YA). (gr. 7-17). 17.99 *(978-0-316-34437-1(0))* Little, Brown Bks. for Young Readers.

Elston, Ashley. The Rules for Breaking. 2014. (Rules Ser.). (ENG.). 320p. (YA). (gr. 7-12). 16.99 *(978-1-4231-6898-0(4))* Hyperion Bks. for Children.

Emerson, Kevin. Encore to an Empty Room. (Exile Ser.: 2). (YA). (gr. 9). 2016. 336p. pap. 9.99 *(978-0-06-213399-1(3))* 2015. (ENG.). 320p. 17.99 *(978-0-06-213398-4(5))* HarperCollins Pubs. (Tegen, Katherine Bks).

—Finding Abbey Road. 2017. 256p. (J). pap. 9.99 ***(978-0-06-213402-8(7))*** 2016. (Exile Ser.: 3). 240p. (YA). (gr. 9). 17.99 *(978-0-06-213401-1(9))* HarperCollins Pubs. (Tegen, Katherine Bks).

Emery, Anne. Dinny Gordon Senior. 2004. (J). per. 9.95 *(978-1-59511-000-8(3))* Image Cascade Publishing.

Enderle, Dotti. Granny Gert & the Bunion Brothers, 1 vol. Kulka, Joe, illus. 2006. (ENG.). 32p. (J). (gr. k-3). 16.99 *(978-1-58980-373-2(6))* Pelican Publishing Co., Inc.

Engelbreit, Mary. Baby Booky: Honey Bunny. Engelbreit, Mary, illus. 2004. (ENG., Illus.). 14p. (J). (gr. -1-18). 6.99 *(978-0-06-008135-5(X),* HarperFestival) HarperCollins Pubs.

Engle, Dawn D. Ella's Golden Hearts. 2009. 40p. pap. 14.75 *(978-1-60860-218-6(4),* Strategic Bk. Publishing) Strategic Book Publishing & Rights Agency (SBPRA).

Epstein, Robin. Hear. 2015. (ENG., Illus.). 272p. (YA). (gr. 9). 18.99 *(978-1-61695-581-6(5),* Soho Teen) Soho Pr., Inc.

Erickson, Timothy Ronald. Death's Whisper Recoil, 2. Erickson, Timothy Ronald, illus. 2003. (Illus.). (YA). pap. 14.95 *(978-1-59492-001-1(X))* Erickson, Tim.

Escalante, Travis. The Story of Rocks & Balloons. 2013. 28p. 16.99 *(978-0-9897168-5-7(6))* Mindstir Media.

Escott, Maria. Green Anole Meets Brown Anole, a Love Story. Wigal, Mike, illus. 2010. 28p. pap. 12.95 *(978-1-936051-82-3(6))* Peppertree Pr., The.

Eshed, Tina. The Adventures of Bunzy: The Beginning. 2009. 60p. pap. 24.49 *(978-1-4389-2673-5(1))* AuthorHouse.

Estelle, Carrie. Molly Loves Her Sister. 2011. 20p. pap. 11.00 *(978-1-4567-6425-8(X))* AuthorHouse.

Esther Cravens Schwalger. Not Too Close. Eve Cravens Nawahine, illus. 2009. 16p. pap. 8.49 *(978-1-4389-6987-9(2))* AuthorHouse.

Ethington, Rebecca. Through Glass Omni 1: Omnibus Books 1-3. 2013. 324p. (YA). pap. 13.59 *(978-0-9884837-6-7(9))* Imdalind Pr.

Eulberg, Elizabeth. Better off Friends. 2014. (ENG.). 288p. (J). (gr. 7). 17.99 *(978-0-545-55145-8(5))* Scholastic, Inc.

Evangelista, Kate. No Holding Back. 2016. (Dodge Cove Trilogy Ser.). (ENG.). 256p. (YA). pap. 9.99 *(978-1-250-10062-7(3),* 9781250100627) Feiwel & Friends.

—No Love Allowed. 2016. (Dodge Cove Trilogy Ser.). (ENG.). 256p. (YA). pap. 9.99 *(978-1-250-07390-7(1),* 9781250073907) Feiwel & Friends.

Evans, Cordelia. Bet on It. Reel FX Inc. Staff, illus. 2014. (Book of Life Ser.). (ENG.). 16p. (J). (gr. -1-3). pap. 5.99 *(978-1-4814-2564-3(1),* Simon Spotlight) Simon Spotlight.

Evans, Janelle. Consequences: Rory's Choice - Book Two. 2017. (ENG., Illus.). (J). pap. 17.99 ***(978-1-941271-27-8(8),*** Ink & Quill Pubs.) Mystic Pubs., Inc.

—Thorns of Revenge: Rory's Choice - Book Three. 2017. (ENG., Illus.). (J). pap. 17.99 ***(978-1-941271-28-5(6),*** Ink & Quill Pubs.) Mystic Pubs., Inc.

Evans, Loralee. The King's Heir. 2006. 287p. (YA). (gr. 8-12). per. 18.99 *(978-1-55517-865-9(0),* Bonneville Bks.) Cedar Fort, Inc./CFI Distribution.

Evans, Mari. Trusting Love. 2014. (ENG., Illus.). 200p. (YA). pap. 14.99 *(978-1-62798-955-8(2))* Dreamspinner Pr.

Everett, Sarah. Everyone We've Been. 2016. (ENG., Illus.). 400p. (YA). (gr. 7). 17.99 *(978-0-553-53844-1(6),* Knopf Bks. for Young Readers) Random Hse. Children's Bks.

Ewing, Amy. The Jewel. (Lone City Trilogy Ser.: 1). (ENG.). (YA). (gr. 9). 2015. 400p. pap. 9.99 *(978-0-06-223578-7(8))* 2014. 368p. 17.99 *(978-0-06-223579-4(6))* HarperCollins Pubs. (HarperTeen).

Fairfield, J. S. Cunning Foe: Faulkil. 2009. 88p. pap. 19.95 *(978-1-61546-603-0(7))* America Star Bks.

Falkoff, Michelle. Pushing Perfect. 2016. 352p. (YA). (gr. 8). 17.99 *(978-0-06-231053-8(4),* HarperTeen) HarperCollins Pubs.

Falksen, G. D. The Transatlantic Conspiracy. Iwata, Nat, illus. 2016. (ENG.). 240p. (YA). (gr. 7). 18.99 *(978-1-61695-417-8(5),* Soho Teen) Soho Pr., Inc.

Fallon, Leigh. Carrier of the Mark. 2011. (Carrier of the Mark Ser.: 1). (ENG.). 352p. (YA). (gr. 8). pap. 8.99 *(978-0-06-202787-0(5),* HarperTeen) HarperCollins Pubs.

—Shadow of the Mark. 2013. (Carrier of the Mark Ser.: 2). (ENG.). 320p. (YA). (gr. 8). pap. 9.99 *(978-0-06-212800-3(0),* HarperTeen) HarperCollins Pubs.

Falter, Laury. Birthright. 2013. 310p. pap. 12.99 *(978-0-9855110-1-2(X))* Falter, Laury.

Fama, Elizabeth. Plus One. 2014. (ENG.). 384p. (YA). (gr. 7). 17.99 *(978-0-374-36007-8(3),* Farrar, Straus & Giroux (BYR)) Farrar, Straus & Giroux.

Farizan, Sara. If You Could Be Mine. (ENG.). (YA). (gr. 9-12). 2014. 272p. pap. 9.95 *(978-1-61620-455-6(9),* 73455) 2013. 256p. 16.95 *(978-1-61620-251-4(3),* 73251) Algonquin Bks. of Chapel Hill.

—Tell Me Again How a Crush Should Feel. 2014. (ENG.). 304p. (YA). (gr. 9-12). 16.95 *(978-1-61620-284-2(X),* 73284) Algonquin Bks. of Chapel Hill.

Farrant, Natasha. What We Did for Love: Resistance, Heartbreak, Betrayal. 2014. 208p. (Illus.). (YA). (gr. 6-12). pap. 10.95 *(978-1-62324-029-5(8));* 18.95 *(978-1-62324-028-8(X))* Enslow Pubs., Inc.

Farrington, Susan. What I Love about You. Farrington, Susan, illus. 2016. (Illus.). 32p. (J). (gr. -1-3). 17.99 *(978-0-06-239353-1(7))* HarperCollins Pubs.

Ferrer, Caridad. When the Stars Go Blue. 2010. (ENG.). 336p. (YA). (gr. 9-18). pap. 22.99 *(978-0-312-65004-9(3),* 9780312650049, St. Martin's Griffin) St. Martin's Pr.

Fine, Sarah. Of Dreams & Rust. 2016. (ENG.). 304p. (YA). (gr. 9). pap. 11.99 *(978-1-4424-8362-0(8),* McElderry, Margaret K. Bks.) McElderry, Margaret K. Bks.

—Of Metal & Wishes. 2015. (ENG., Illus.). 352p. (YA). (gr. 9). pap. 11.99 *(978-1-4424-8359-0(8),* McElderry, Margaret K. Bks.) McElderry, Margaret K. Bks.

Finn, Katie. Hearts, Fingers, & Other Things to Cross. 2016. (Broken Hearts & Revenge Novel Ser.: 3). (ENG.). 256p. (YA). 17.99 *(978-1-250-04526-3(6),* 9781250045263) Feiwel & Friends.

Finnegan, Amy. Not in the Script. 2014. (If Only... Ser.). (ENG.). 392p. (YA). (gr. 7). 17.99 *(978-1-61963-397-1(3),* 9781619633971, Bloomsbury USA Childrens) Bloomsbury Publishing USA.

Fiore, Kelly, et al. Just Like the Movies. (If Only... Ser.). (ENG.). (YA). (gr. 7-12). 2016. 304p. pap. 9.99 *(978-1-61963-356-8(6),* 9781619633568) 2014. 288p. 17.99 *(978-1-61963-354-4(X),* 9781619633544) Bloomsbury Publishing USA. (Bloomsbury USA Childrens).

Fiori, Natalie. Lobsters in Seacliff. 2009. 52p. pap. 20.99 *(978-1-4490-1811-5(4))* AuthorHouse.

Firestone, Carrie. The Loose Ends List. 2016. (ENG.). 352p. (YA). (gr. 9-17). 17.99 *(978-0-316-38282-3(5))* Little, Brown Bks. for Young Readers.

Fischer, Rusty. Vampire Book of the Month Club. 2016. (ENG.). 312p. (YA). (gr. 6). pap. 9.99 *(978-1-942546-38-2(6))* Nodin Pr.

Fitzpatrick, Becca. The Complete Hush, Hush Saga: Hush, Hush; Crescendo; Silence; Finale. 2012. (Hush, Hush Saga Ser.: Bks. 1-4). (ENG.). 1744p. (YA). (gr. 9). 74.99 *(978-1-4424-7372-0(X),* Simon & Schuster Bks. For Young Readers) Simon & Schuster Bks. For Young Readers.

—Dangerous Lies. 2015. (ENG., Illus.). 400p. (YA). (gr. 9). 18.99 *(978-1-4814-2491-2(2),* Simon & Schuster Bks. For Young Readers) Simon & Schuster Bks. For Young Readers.

—Silence. (Hush, Hush Saga Ser.: Bk. 3). (ENG.). (YA). (gr. 9). 2013. 464p. pap. 12.99 *(978-1-4424-2665-8(9))* 2011. 448p. 18.99 *(978-1-4424-2664-1(0))* Simon & Schuster Bks. For Young Readers. (Simon & Schuster Bks. For Young Readers).

Fitzpatrick, Heather. Chuck: The Chicken That Thought He Was a Duck. 2012. 24p. pap. 17.99 *(978-1-4772-6012-8(9))* AuthorHouse.

Fitzpatrick, Huntley. My Life Next Door. 2012. (ENG.). 400p. (YA). (gr. 7-18). 18.99 *(978-0-8037-3699-3(1),* Dial Bks) Penguin Young Readers Group.

—What I Thought Was True. 2015. (ENG.). 432p. (YA). (gr. 9). pap. 9.99 *(978-0-14-242395-0(5),* Speak) Penguin Young Readers Group.

Fleet, Katherine. The Secret to Letting Go. 2016. (ENG., Illus.). 334p. (J). pap. 14.99 *(978-1-68281-070-5(4))* Entangled Publishing, LLC.

Fleming, Meg. I Heart You. Wright, Sarah Jane, illus. 2016. (ENG.). 40p. (J). (gr. -1-3). 17.99 *(978-1-4424-8895-3(6),* Beach Lane Bks.) Beach Lane Bks.

Fleming, Theresa. Going Home with Jesus, 1 vol. Fleming, Yvonne B., illus. 2009. 22p. pap. 24.95 *(978-1-60813-703-9(1))* America Star Bks.

Fletcher, Erin. All Laced Up. 2016. (ENG., Illus.). (YA). (gr. 7). pap. 15.99 ***(978-1-68281-316-4(9))*** Entangled Publishing, LLC.

Fletcher, Susan E. A Little in Love. 2015. (ENG.). 288p. (J). (gr. 7). 17.99 *(978-0-545-82960-1(7),* Chicken Hse., The) Scholastic, Inc.

Foard, Judith P. Senior Year. 2013. 416p. pap. 16.95 *(978-1-4759-6552-0(4));* (gr. 10-12). 26.95 *(978-1-4759-6554-4(0))* iUniverse, Inc.

Fontaine, Catherine Silliman. Have a Not for Christmas ... & Always. 2006. (Illus.). 44p. (J). 11.95 *(978-0-9776958-0-5(8))* CyPress Pubns.

Fontaine, Nadine. More Than Anything in the World. 2008. 16p. per. 24.95 *(978-1-4241-9870-2(4))* America Star Bks.

Forbidden. 2014. (Forbidden Ser.: 1). (ENG.). 400p. (YA). (gr. 9). 17.99 *(978-0-06-219497-8(6))* HarperCollins Pubs.

Foreman, Michael. I Love You, Too! Foreman, Michael, illus. 2014. (ENG., Illus.). 32p. (J). (gr. -1-3). 16.95 *(978-1-4677-3451-6(9))* Lerner Publishing Group.

Forester, MaMa Eagle. Young Eagle, Pretty Flower. Spears, Ashley E., illus. 2004. 16p. (J). 7.95 *(978-0-9762389-4-2(2))* Trent's Prints.

Forian, Rosemary Talucci. My Own Angel. 2011. 28p. pap. 21.50 *(978-1-4583-3731-3(6))* Lulu Pr., Inc.

Forman, Gayle. Just One Day. 2013. (ENG.). (YA). (gr. 9). 416p. pap. 10.99 *(978-0-14-242295-3(9),* Speak); 384p. 17.99 *(978-0-525-42591-5(8),* Dutton Books for Young Readers) Penguin Young Readers Group.

—Just One Day. 2013. lib. bdg. 22.10 *(978-0-606-34405-0(5),* Turtleback) Turtleback Bks.

—Just One Year. (ENG.). (YA). (gr. 9). 2014. 352p. pap. 10.99 *(978-0-14-242296-0(7),* Speak) 2013. 336p. 17.99 *(978-0-525-42592-2(6),* Dutton Books for Young Readers) Penguin Young Readers Group.

—Just One Year. 2014. lib. bdg. 22.10 *(978-0-606-36190-3(1))* Turtleback Bks.

Foster, Jackie. Land of Anear, 1 vol. 2010. 27p. pap. 24.95 *(978-1-61546-634-4(7))* America Star Bks.

Foster, Jennifer L. The Puppy with the White Paw. 2011. 28p. pap. 12.99 *(978-1-4567-3912-6(3))* AuthorHouse.

Fox, Jeannine. Feeding Penny Pig. 2009. 32p. (J). 14.95 *(978-0-9841589-1-1(X))* Mincing Mockingbird, The.

Fox, Jennifer. My Little Pony: Hearts & Hooves. 2013. (Passport to Reading Level 1 Ser.). (ENG., Illus.). 32p. (J). (gr. -1-3). 4.99 *(978-0-316-24797-9(9))* Little, Brown Bks. for Young Readers.

Fox, Peter. April. 2004. 192p. (YA). per. *(978-0-9734848-2-3(9))* Coscom Entertainment.

Fraiberg, Jordanna. Our Song. 2014. (YA). pap. *(978-1-59514-625-0(3),* Razorbill) Penguin Publishing Group.

Frame, Andrew Graham. Ein Stein: The Chipmunk Who Succeeds by Brain Power. 2011. 52p. pap. 19.50 *(978-1-61204-416-3(6),* Strategic Bk. Publishing) Strategic Book Publishing & Rights Agency (SBPRA).

France, Emily. Signs of You. 2016. (ENG.). 240p. (YA). (gr. 9). 18.99 *(978-1-61695-657-8(7),* Soho Teen) Soho Pr., Inc.

Francis, Lilian. The Supper Dance. 2009. (Illus.). 56p. pap. *(978-1-84748-531-1(6))* Athena Pr.

Frazier, Angie. The Eternal Sea. 2011. (ENG.). 368p. (J). (gr. 7-7). 17.99 *(978-0-545-11475-2(6),* Scholastic Pr.) Scholastic, Inc.

Frederick, Heather Vogel. Wish You Were Eyre. 2012. (Mother-Daughter Book Club Ser.). (ENG.). 464p. (J). (gr. 4-9). 16.99 *(978-1-4424-3064-8(8),* Simon & Schuster Bks. For Young Readers) Simon & Schuster Bks. For Young Readers.

Fredericks, Mariah. Love. Watkins, Liselotte, illus. 2007. (In the Cards Ser.: No. 1). (ENG.). 288p. (YA). (gr. 4-8). pap. 5.99 *(978-0-689-87655-4(6),* Simon & Schuster/Paula Wiseman Bks.) Simon & Schuster/Paula Wiseman Bks.

Freedman, Claire. I Love You, Baby! Abbot, Judi, illus. 2017. (ENG.). 32p. (J). (gr. -1-3). 17.99 ***(978-1-4814-9904-0(1),*** Simon & Schuster/Paula Wiseman Bks.) Simon & Schuster/Paula Wiseman Bks.

Freeman, Shannon. Listed. 2014. (Port City High Ser.: 6). (YA). lib. bdg. 20.80 *(978-0-606-36618-2(0))* Turtleback Bks.

—A Port in Pieces. 2014. (Port City High Ser.: 8). (YA). lib. bdg. 20.80 *(978-0-606-36620-5(2))* Turtleback Bks.

French, Vivian. Pig in Love. Archbold, Tim, illus. 2005. 32p. (J). lib. bdg. 9.00 *(978-1-4242-0889-0(0))* Fitzgerald Bks.

Friedman, Aimee. A Novel Idea. 2006. (Romantic Comedies Ser.). (ENG., Illus.). 256p. (YA). (gr. 9-12). mass mkt. 7.99 *(978-1-4169-0785-5(8),* Simon Pulse) Simon Pulse.

Friedman, Laurie. Love, Ruby Valentine. Cravath, Lynne Avril, illus. 2006. (ENG.). 32p. (J). (gr. k-3). lib. bdg. 16.95 *(978-1-57505-899-3(5),* Carolrhoda Bks.) Lerner Publishing Group.

Friesen, Jonathan. Both of Me, 1 vol. 2016. (ENG.). 256p. (J). pap. 9.99 *(978-0-310-73187-0(9))* Blink.

Frost, Melissa. The Dating Tutor. 2013. 98p. pap. *(978-1-77130-562-4(2))* Evernight Publishing.

Fuchs, A. P. Magic Man. 2005. 50p. per. *(978-0-9734848-7-8(X))* Coscom Entertainment.

Fukuda, Andrew. The Trap. 2013. (Hunt Trilogy Ser.: 3). (ENG.). 320p. (YA). (gr. 7). 18.99 *(978-1-250-00512-0(4),* 9781250005120, St. Martin's Griffin) St. Martin's Pr.

Furman, A. L. Everygirls Romance Stories. Furman, A. L., ed. 2011. 224p. 44.95 *(978-1-258-07094-6(4))* Literary Licensing, LLC.

Gaertner, Connie. Wake-Up Calls. 2013. 154p. (gr. 10-12). pap. 12.95 *(978-1-4759-6646-6(6))* iUniverse, Inc.

Gagnon, Jilly. #famous. 2017. 384p. (YA). (gr. 8). 17.99 *(978-0-06-243003-8(3),* Tegen, Katherine Bks) HarperCollins Pubs.

Gale Editor, ed. Romeo & Juliet: The Graphic Novel. 2011. (Classic Graphic Novel Collection Ser.). (Illus.). 160p. (J). (gr. 7-12). lib. bdg. 34.80 *(978-1-4205-0631-0(5))* Cengage Gale.

Gallagher, Toni. Twist My Charm: Love Potion #11. 2016. (Twist My Charm Ser.). (ENG.). 272p. (J). (gr. 3-7). 16.99 *(978-0-553-51119-2(X),* Random Hse. Bks. for Young Readers) Random Hse. Children's Bks.

Galliez, Roxane Marie. Give Me Moon. Delanssay, Cathy, illus. 2009. 44p. (J). (gr. -1-3). 14.99 *(978-0-8416-7138-6(9))* Hammond World Atlas Corp.

Garcia, Kami. The Lovely Reckless. 2016. (ENG.). 384p. (YA). 18.99 *(978-1-250-07919-0(5),* 9781250079190) Imprint IND. Dist: Macmillan.

—Unbreakable. (Legion Ser.: 1). (ENG.). (YA). (gr. 7-17). 2014. 336p. pap. 10.00 *(978-0-316-21018-8(8))* 2013. 320p. 18.00 *(978-0-316-21017-1(X))* Little, Brown Bks. for Young Readers.

Garcia, Kami & Stohl, Margaret. Beautiful Chaos. (Beautiful Creatures Ser.: 3). (ENG.). 528p. (YA). (gr. 7-17). 2012. pap. 13.99 *(978-0-316-12351-8(X))* 2011. 18.99 *(978-0-316-12352-5(8))* Little, Brown Bks. for Young Readers.

—Beautiful Creatures. 2009. (Beautiful Creatures Ser.: 1). (ENG.). 576p. (YA). (gr. 7-17). 17.99 *(978-0-316-04267-3(6))* Little Brown & Co.

—Beautiful Creatures. (Beautiful Creatures Ser.: 1). (ENG.). 592p. (YA). (gr. 7-17). 2010. pap. 12.99 *(978-0-316-07703-3(8))* 2012. mass mkt. 7.99 *(978-0-316-23165-7(7))* 2012. pap. 10.99 *(978-0-316-23167-1(3))* Little, Brown Bks. for Young Readers.

—Beautiful Creatures. 2013. (ENG., Illus.). 240p. (gr. 8-17). 20.00 *(978-0-316-18271-3(0),* Yen Pr.) Orbit.

—Beautiful Creatures. 2010. (Beautiful Creatures Ser.: 1). (YA). lib. bdg. 23.30 *(978-0-606-26699-4(2),* Turtleback) Turtleback Bks.

—The Beautiful Creatures Complete Paperback Collection: Beautiful Creatures; Beautiful Darkness; Beautiful Chaos; Beautiful Redemption. 2013. (Beautiful Creatures Ser.: Bks. 1-4). (ENG.). 2272p. (YA). (gr. 7-17). pap. 50.00 *(978-0-316-25090-0(2))* Little, Brown Bks. for Young Readers.

—Beautiful Darkness. 2010. (Beautiful Creatures Ser.: Bk. 2). (YA). 59.99 *(978-1-60941-036-0(X))* Findaway World, LLC.

—Beautiful Darkness. (Beautiful Creatures Ser.: 2). 2011. (ENG.). 528p. (YA). (gr. 7-17). pap. 12.99 *(978-0-316-07704-0(6))* 2010. (ENG.). 512p. (YA). (gr. 7-17). 17.99 *(978-0-316-07705-7(4))* 2010. 512p. pap. 17.99 *(978-0-316-09861-8(2))* Little, Brown Bks. for Young Readers.

—Beautiful Darkness. 2011. (Beautiful Creatures Ser.: 2). (YA). lib. bdg. 24.50 *(978-0-606-26700-7(X),* Turtleback) Turtleback Bks.

—Beautiful Redemption. (Beautiful Creatures Ser.: 4). (ENG.). (YA). (gr. 7-17). 2013. 496p. pap. 13.99 *(978-0-316-12356-3(0))* 2012. 464p. 18.99 *(978-0-316-12353-2(6))* 2012. 576p. pap. 9.99 *(978-0-316-22519-9(3))* Little, Brown Bks. for Young Readers.

—Beautiful Redemption. 2013. (Beautiful Creatures Ser.: 4). (YA). lib. bdg. 24.50 *(978-0-606-32282-9(5),* Turtleback) Turtleback Bks.

—Dangerous Creatures. 2015. (ENG.). 400p. (J). (gr. 7-17). pap. 12.99 *(978-0-316-37032-5(0))* 2014. 327p. (YA). *(978-0-316-37626-6(4))* 2014. (Dangerous Creatures Ser.: Bk. 1). (ENG.). 384p. (YA). (gr. 7-17). 19.00 *(978-0-316-37031-8(2))* Little, Brown Bks. for Young Readers.

Garcia, Mary. Play with Me: Togetherness Time for Your Preschooler & You. (J). 2007. 16.95 *(978-0-9790931-2-8(0))* 2006. 16.95 *(978-0-9790931-0-4(4))* SMARTseeds Co., LLC, The.

—Play with Me: Togetherness Time for Your Preschooler & You: St. Valentine's Day. 2007. (J). *(978-0-9790931-1-1(2))* SMARTseeds Co., LLC, The.

Garcia, Mia. Even If the Sky Falls. 2016. 304p. (YA). (gr. 9). 17.99 *(978-0-06-241180-8(2),* Tegen, Katherine Bks) HarperCollins Pubs.

Gardner, Sheldon. The Converso Legacy. 2005. 264p. (J). 18.95 *(978-1-932687-18-7(1),* Devora Publishing) Simcha Media Group.

Garza, Amy Ammons. Sterlen: And a Mosaic of Mountain Women. Ammons, David F. & Ammons, Sherilyn, eds. Cain, Doreyl Ammons, illus. 2005. 308p. (YA). per. 16.00 *(978-0-9753023-2-3(9),* Catch the Spirit of Appalachia) Ammons Communications, Ltd.

Garza, Jenny. Beautiful. 2007. 56p. per. 8.95 *(978-0-595-46756-3(3))* iUniverse, Inc.

Gaskins, Terry & Treigle, Jimmy. The Very Big Storm: Created by Terry Gaskins Inspired by Jimmy Treigle. 2009. 28p. pap. 13.99 *(978-1-4389-4220-9(6))* AuthorHouse.

Gates, Pat. The Apple Tree's Secret, 1 vol. Hosselkus, Devin, illus. 2009. 47p. pap. 24.95 *(978-1-60836-637-8(5))* America Star Bks.

Gaughen, A. C. Lady Thief. 2015. (Scarlet Ser.: No. 2). (ENG.). 336p. (YA). (gr. 7). pap. 9.99 *(978-0-8027-3788-5(9),* 9780802737885, Bloomsbury USA Childrens) Bloomsbury Publishing USA.

—Lion Heart. 2015. (Scarlet Trilogy: No. 3). (ENG.). 352p. (YA). 17.99 *(978-0-8027-3616-1(5),* 9780802736161, Bloomsbury USA Childrens) Bloomsbury Publishing USA.

Gazdag, Adam. The Non Born Heir. 2010. 313p. pap. 19.27 *(978-0-557-17709-7(X))* Lulu Pr., Inc.

Geise, Brenda & Merkle, Blair Geise. Love Spot. 2008. 28p. pap. 12.99 *(978-1-4389-1102-1(5))* AuthorHouse.

Gensler, Sonia. The Dark Between. 2015. (ENG.). 352p. (YA). (gr. 7). pap. 9.99 *(978-0-375-86140-6(8),* Ember) Random Hse. Children's Bks.

George E. Keely, Jr. The Happy Day Fable. 2010. 20p. pap. 10.00 *(978-1-4269-0064-8(3))* Trafford Publishing.

George, Michele. The Rainbow of Love. 2004. (J). 5.00 *(978-0-9672049-1-8(7))* Grace & Mercy Publishing.

Geragotelis, Brittany. What the Spell. (Life's a Witch Ser.). (ENG., Illus.). (YA). (gr. 9). 2014. 352p. pap. 9.99 *(978-1-4424-6707-1(X))* 2013. 336p. 16.99 *(978-1-4424-6815-3(7))* Simon & Schuster Bks. For Young Readers. (Simon & Schuster Bks. For Young Readers).

Geras, Adèle. The Tower Room. 2005. (ENG.). 204p. (YA). (gr. 7-12). pap. 12.95 *(978-0-15-205537-0(1))* Houghton Mifflin Harcourt Publishing Co.

Gerhardt, Jake. Me & Miranda Mullaly. 2016. (ENG.). 256p. (J). (gr. 5). 16.99 *(978-0-451-47540-4(2),* Viking Books for Young Readers) Penguin Young Readers Group.

Gerver, Jane E. I Love You. Brown, Jo, illus. 2015. (ENG.). 14p. (J). (— 1). bds. 4.99 *(978-1-62979-416-7(3),* Highlights) Boyds Mills Pr.

Gessner, Kati. What Do You See When You Look at Me. 2012. 32p. pap. 19.99 *(978-1-4772-2106-8(9))* AuthorHouse.

Gessner, Marina, pseud. The Distance from Me to You. 2015. (ENG.). 352p. (YA). (gr. 7). 16.99 *(978-0-399-17323-3(4),* G.P. Putnam's Sons Books for Young Readers) Penguin Young Readers Group.

Gibaldi, Lauren. The Night We Said Yes. 2015. (ENG.). 304p. (YA). (gr. 9). 17.99 *(978-0-06-230219-9(1),* HarperTeen) HarperCollins Pubs.

J
K
L

Gibbs, Gretchen. The Book of Maggie Bradstreet. 2012. (Bradstreet Chronicles). (ENG.). 183p. (YA). pap. 9.99 (978-0-9852948-0-9(9)) Glenmere Pr.

Gibby, Bayne. You Mean the World to Me. Walker, David, illus. 2013. (ENG.). 16p. (J). (gr. -1-k). bds. 8.99 (978-0-545-40570-6(X), Cartwheel Bks.) Scholastic, Inc.

Gibsen, Cole. Katana. 2012. (Katana Novel Ser.: 1). (ENG.). 384p. (YA). pap. 9.95 (978-0-7387-3040-0(8), Flux) North Star Editions.

—Senshi. 2013. (Katana Novel Ser.: 2). (ENG.). 384p. (YA). pap. 9.99 (978-0-7387-3261-9(3), Flux) North Star Editions.

—Shinobi. 2014. (Katana Novel Ser.: 3). (ENG.). 288p. (YA). pap. 9.99 (978-0-7387-3911-3(1), Flux) North Star Editions.

Gier, Kerstin. Dream On. Bell, Anthea, tr. from GER. 2016. (Silver Trilogy Ser.: 2). (ENG.). 336p. (YA). 17.99 (978-1-62779-079-6(9), 9781627790796, Holt, Henry & Co. Bks. For Young Readers) Holt, Henry & Co.

—Emerald Green. Bell, Anthea, tr. 2013. (Ruby Red Trilogy Ser.: Vol. 3). (ENG.). 464p. (YA). (gr. 7). 17.99 (978-0-8050-9267-7(6), 9780805092677, Holt, Henry & Co. Bks. For Young Readers) Holt, Henry & Co.

—Just Dreaming. Bell, Anthea, tr. from GER. 2017. (Silver Trilogy Ser.). (ENG.). 368p. (YA). 18.99 (978-1-62779-080-2(2), 9781627790802, Holt, Henry & Co. Bks. For Young Readers) Holt, Henry & Co.

Gillmor, Don. Yuck, a Love Story. Gay, Marie-Louise, illus. 2004. (J). (gr. k-3). spiral bd. (978-0-616-07238-7(4)); spiral bd. (978-0-616-08494-6(3)) Canadian National Institute for the Blind/Institut National Canadien pour les Aveugles.

Gilmore, Jennifer. We Were Never Here. 2016. 320p. (YA). (gr. 9). 17.99 (978-0-06-239360-9(X), HarperTeen) HarperCollins Pubs.

Glass, Lisa. Blue. 2015. (Blue Ser.: 1). (ENG.). 352p. (J). (gr. 7-17). 16.99 (978-1-62365-414-6(9), Quercus) Quercus NA.

Gleason, Colleen. The Clockwork Scarab. 2014. (Stoker & Holmes Ser.: 1). (ENG.). 384p. (YA). (gr. 7-12). pap. 11.99 (978-1-4521-2873-3(1)) Chronicle Bks. LLC.

—The Spiritglass Charade. 2014. (Stoker & Holmes Ser.: 2). (ENG., Illus.). 360p. (YA). (gr. 7-12). 17.99 (978-1-4521-1071-4(9)) Chronicle Bks. LLC.

—The Spiritglass Charade: A Stoker & Holmes Novel. 2015. (Stoker & Holmes Ser.: 2). (ENG., Illus.). 368p. (YA). (gr. 7-12). pap. 9.99 (978-1-4521-2885-6(5)) Chronicle Bks. LLC.

Glines, Abbi. After the Game: A Field Party Novel. 2017. (YA). **(978-1-5344-0168-6(7)**, Simon Pulse) Simon Pulse.

—Bad for You. 2015. (Sea Breeze Ser.). (ENG., Illus.). 320p. (YA). (gr. 11). pap. 11.99 (978-1-4814-2074-7(7), Simon Pulse) Simon Pulse.

—Because of Low. 2013. (Sea Breeze Ser.). (ENG., Illus.). 320p. (YA). (gr. 11). 17.99 (978-1-4424-8864-9(6)); pap. 10.99 (978-1-4424-8863-2(8)) Simon Pulse. (Simon Pulse).

—Hold on Tight. 2015. (Sea Breeze Ser.). (ENG., Illus.). 288p. (YA). (gr. 11). pap. 11.99 (978-1-4814-2081-5(X), Simon Pulse) Simon Pulse.

—Just for Now. 2013. (Sea Breeze Ser.). (ENG., Illus.). 336p. (YA). (gr. 11). 17.99 (978-1-4424-8861-8(1)); pap. 9.99 (978-1-4424-8860-1(3)) Simon Pulse. (Simon Pulse).

—Misbehaving. 2014. (Sea Breeze Ser.). (ENG., Illus.). 352p. (YA). (gr. 11). 17.99 (978-1-4814-0674-1(4)); pap. 11.99 (978-1-4814-0673-4(6)) Simon Pulse. (Simon Pulse).

—The Sea Breeze Collection: Breathe; Because of Low; While It Lasts; Just for Now. 2013. (Sea Breeze Ser.). (ENG., Illus.). 1312p. (YA). (gr. 11-11). pap. 39.99 (978-1-4424-9608-8(8), Simon Pulse) Simon Pulse.

—Under the Lights. 2016. (Field Party Ser.: 2). (ENG., Illus.). 336p. (YA). (gr. 9). 17.99 (978-1-4814-3889-6(1), Simon Pulse) Simon Pulse.

—Until Friday Night. 2015. (Field Party Ser.: Bk. 1). (ENG.). 336p. (YA). pap. (978-1-4711-2502-7(5), Simon Pulse) Simon Pulse.

—While It Lasts. 2013. (Sea Breeze Ser.). (ENG., Illus.). 304p. (YA). (gr. 11). 18.99 (978-1-4424-8867-0(0)); pap. 9.99 (978-1-4424-8866-3(2)) Simon Pulse. (Simon Pulse).

Gliori, Debi. No Matter What. (ENG., Illus.). 24p. (J). (gr. -1 — 1). 2012. bds. 12.99 (978-0-547-71905-4(1)) 2008. bds. 6.99 (978-0-15-206343-6(9)) Houghton Mifflin Harcourt Publishing Co.

Globe-Fearon Staff, ed. Jane Eyre, Grades 5-12. pap., tchr. ed. 4.95 (978-0-8359-0109-3(2)) Globe Fearon Educational Publishing.

Godbersen, Anna. The Lucky Ones. 2013. (Bright Young Things Ser.: 3). (ENG.). 400p. (YA). (gr. 9). pap. 9.99 (978-0-06-196271-4(6)) HarperCollins Pubs.

—The Luxe. (ENG.). (YA). (gr. 9). 2008. (Luxe Ser.: 1). 464p. pap. 9.99 (978-0-06-134568-5(7)) 2007. (Luxe Ser.: No. 1). 448p. 17.99 (978-0-06-134566-1(0), HarperTeen) HarperCollins Pubs.

—Rumors. 2009. (Luxe Ser.: 2). (ENG.). 448p. (YA). (gr. 9). pap. 9.99 (978-0-06-134571-5(7)) HarperCollins Pubs.

—Splendor. 2010. (Luxe Ser.: 4). (ENG.). 416p. (YA). (gr. 9). pap. 9.99 (978-0-06-162633-3(3)) HarperCollins Pubs.

Gold, Willa. Stella & Tulip: A Home for Us. 2010. (ENG.). 36p. (J). (gr. k-2). 17.99 (978-0-930773-95-3(0)) Black Heron Pr.

Gonzalez, Jorge & Shakespeare, William. Romeo & Juliet, 1 vol. Cabrera, Eva, illus. 2011. (Shakespeare Graphics Ser.). (ENG.). 88p. (gr. 2-3). pap. 7.15 (978-1-4342-3448-3(7)); lib. bdg. 27.99 (978-1-4342-2563-4(1)) Stone Arch Bks. (Shakespeare Graphics).

Goo, Maurene. I Believe in a Thing Called Love. 2017. (ENG.). 336p. (YA). 17.99 (978-0-374-30404-1(1), 9780374304041, Farrar, Straus & Giroux (BYR)) Farrar, Straus & Giroux.

Goobie, Beth & Fernández, Queta. Ni un Día Más, 1 vol. 2009. (Spanish Soundings Ser.). (SPA.). 112p. (YA). (gr. 8-12). pap. 9.95 (978-1-55469-137-1(0)) Orca Bk. Pubs. USA.

Goode, Laura. Sister Mischief. 2013. (ENG.). 384p. (YA). (gr. 9). pap. 8.99 (978-0-7636-6456-5(1)) Candlewick Pr.

Goode, Molly. Mama Loves. McCue, Lisa, illus. 2015. (Step into Reading Ser.). (ENG.). 32p. (J). (gr. -1-1). 4.99 (978-0-553-53896-0(9), Random Hse. Bks. for Young Readers) Random Hse. Children's Bks.

Goodman, Carol. Blythewood. 2014. (Blythewood Novel Ser.). (ENG.). 512p. (YA). (gr. 7). pap. 9.99 (978-0-14-242251-9(7), Speak) Penguin Young Readers Group.

—Ravencliffe. 2015. (Blythewood Novel Ser.). (ENG.). 432p. (YA). (gr. 7). pap. 10.99 (978-0-14-242252-6(5), Speak) Penguin Young Readers Group.

Gormally, Eleanor. The Little One Asks. 2013. (ENG.). 32p. (J). pap. 12.95 (978-1-84730-407-0(9)) Veritas Pubns. IRL. Dist: Dufour Editions, Inc.

Gorman, Dl. Pudgy Wudgy: Pudgy Wudgy Meets a Friend. 2008. 32p. pap. 12.99 (978-1-4389-2151-8(9)) AuthorHouse.

Gornall, Louise. Under Rose-Tainted Skies. 2017. (ENG.). 336p. (YA). (gr. 7). 17.99 (978-0-544-73651-1(6), Clarion Bks.) Houghton Mifflin Harcourt Trade & Reference Pubs.

Gorzelanczyk, Melissa. Arrows. 2016. (ENG.). 240p. (YA). (gr. 9). 17.99 (978-0-553-51044-7(4), Delacorte Pr.) Random Hse. Children's Bks.

Gottesfeld, Jeff. Crush. 2014. (Campus Confessions Ser.: 4). (YA). lib. bdg. 20.80 (978-0-606-34001-4(7), Turtleback) Turtleback Bks.

—The Love Mints, 1 vol. 2015. (Red Rhino Ser.). (ENG.). 68p. (J). (gr. 4-6). pap. 7.95 (978-1-62250-963-8(3)) Saddleback Educational Publishing, Inc.

Gottfred, B. T. Forever for a Year. 2015. (ENG.). 432p. (YA). (gr. 9). 17.99 (978-1-62779-191-5(4), Holt, Henry & Co. Bks. For Young Readers) Holt, Henry & Co.

—The Nerdy & the Dirty. 2016. (ENG.). 304p. (YA). 17.99 (978-1-62779-850-1(1), 9781627798501, Holt, Henry & Co. Bks. For Young Readers) Holt, Henry & Co.

Grace, Amanda. The Truth about You & Me. 2013. (ENG.). 264p. (YA). pap. 9.99 (978-0-7387-3624-2(4), Flux) North Star Editions.

Grace, N. B. Rev It Up! 9th ed. 2010. (Wizards of Waverly Place Ser.: No. 9). 128p. (J). (gr. 3-7). pap. 4.99 (978-1-4231-2676-8(9)) Disney Pr.

Grady, Joi. I Like You & I Love You. 2012. 36p. pap. 20.99 (978-1-4670-3953-6(5)) AuthorHouse.

Graham, D. R. Put It Out There, 1. 2016. (Britannia Beach Ser.: 1). (ENG.). 212p. pap. 9.99 **(978-0-00-814519-4(9)**, HarperImpulse) HarperCollins Pubs. Ltd. GBR. Dist: HarperCollins Pubs.

Graham, Rosemary. Thou Shalt Not Dump the Skater Dude: And Other Commandments I Have Broken. 2008. (ENG.). 288p. (YA). (gr. 7-18). 8.99 (978-0-14-240851-3(4), Speak) Penguin Young Readers Group.

Granson, Steven. Zando. 2009. 124p. pap. 10.95 (978-1-4401-5658-8(1)) iUniverse, Inc.

Gratton, Tessa. Blood Magic. 2012. (Blood Journals). (ENG.). 432p. (YA). (gr. 9). pap. 9.99 (978-0-375-86485-8(7), Bluefire) Random Hse. Children's Bks.

Gray, Claudia. Afterlife. 2012. (Evernight Ser.: 4). (ENG.). 384p. (YA). (gr. 8). pap. 9.99 (978-0-06-128451-9(3), HarperTeen) HarperCollins Pubs.

—Balthazar. (Evernight Ser.: 5). (ENG.). (YA). (gr. 8). 2013. 400p. pap. 9.99 (978-0-06-196119-9(1)) 2012. 384p. 17.99 (978-0-06-196118-2(3)) HarperCollins Pubs. (HarperTeen).

—Evernight. 2009. (Evernight Ser.: 1). (ENG.). 352p. (YA). (gr. 8). pap. 8.99 (978-0-06-128444-1(0), HarperTeen) HarperCollins Pubs.

—Fateful. (ENG.). (YA). (gr. 9). 2012. 352p. pap. 9.99 (978-0-06-200621-9(5)) 2011. 336p. 17.99 (978-0-06-200620-2(7)) HarperCollins Pubs. (HarperTeen).

—Hourglass. 2011. (Evernight Ser.: 3). (ENG.). 368p. (YA). (gr. 8). pap. 8.99 (978-0-06-128448-9(3), HarperTeen) HarperCollins Pubs.

—Sorceress. 2016. (Spellcaster Ser.: 3). 368p. (YA). (gr. 8). pap. 9.99 (978-0-06-196125-0(6), HarperTeen) HarperCollins Pubs.

—Spellcaster. 2014. (Spellcaster Ser.: 1). (ENG., Illus.). 416p. (YA). (gr. 8). pap. 9.99 (978-0-06-196121-2(3), HarperTeen) HarperCollins Pubs.

—Ten Thousand Skies above You. (Firebird Ser.: 2). (YA). (gr. 9). 2016. 448p. pap. 9.99 (978-0-06-227900-2(9), HarperTeen) 2015. (ENG.). 432p. 17.99 (978-0-06-227899-9(1)) HarperCollins Pubs.

Gray, Lucinda. The Gilded Cage. 2017. (ENG., Illus.). 256p. (YA). pap. 9.99 (978-1-62779-182-3(5), 9781627791823) Square Fish.

Green, John. The Fault in Our Stars. 2013. (ENG & JPN.). 337p. (YA). (gr. 9-12). pap. (978-4-00-116405-3(1)) Iwanami Shoten.

—The Fault in Our Stars. 2013. (CHI & ENG.). 304p. (YA). (gr. 9-12). pap. (978-7-5448-3122-2(1)) Jieli Publishing Hse.

—The Fault in Our Stars. 2013. (ENG.). 336p. pap. (978-0-14-134565-9(9)) Penguin Bks., Ltd.

—The Fault in Our Stars. 2014. (ENG.). 336p. (YA). (gr. 9). pap. 12.99 (978-0-14-242417-9(X), Penguin Books) Penguin Publishing Group.

—The Fault in Our Stars. 2012. (978-0-525-42641-7(8)) 2012. (ENG., Illus.). 336p. (YA). (gr. 9-18). 19.99 (978-0-525-47881-2(7), Dutton Books for Young Readers) 2014. (ENG.). 352p. (YA). (gr. 9). reprint ed. pap. 12.99 (978-0-14-751373-1(1), Speak) Penguin Young Readers Group.

—The Fault in Our Stars. 2014. (ENG.). (YA). (gr. 9). lib. bdg. 23.60 **(978-1-62765-362-6(7))** Perfection Learning Corp.

—The Fault in Our Stars. l.t. ed. 2012. (ENG.). 364p. (J). (gr. 8-12). 23.99 (978-1-4104-5001-2(5)) Thorndike Pr.

—The Fault in Our Stars. 2014. lib. bdg. 24.50 (978-0-606-35633-6(9)) Turtleback Bks.

Green, Ken. Love in a Dustbin. 136p. pap. (978-0-340-58860-4(8)) Hodder & Stoughton.

Green, Margaret. Monster High: Why Do Ghouls Fall in Love? 2015. (ENG., Illus.). 24p. (J). (gr. -1-3). pap. 4.99 (978-0-316-30141-1(8)) Little, Brown Bks. for Young Readers.

Greenberg, Doris & Shandley, Pandré. The Legend of L'Esprit: Dance Legacy Series. 2011. 272p. pap. 15.95 (978-1-4634-1800-7(0)) AuthorHouse.

Greene, Bette. Morning Is a Long Time Coming. l.t. ed. 2004. (Beeler Mystery Ser.). 35.95 (978-1-58118-122-7(1)) LRS.

—Philip Hall Likes Me, I Reckon Maybe. l.t. ed. 2003. (Children's Large Print Ser.). (J). 28.95 (978-1-58118-107-4(8)) LRS.

Greene, Vivi. Sing. 2016. 288p. (YA). (gr. 8). 17.99 (978-0-06-245983-1(X), HarperTeen) HarperCollins Pubs.

Greenland, Shannon. Shadow of a Girl. 2016. (ENG., Illus.). (YA). (gr. 7). pap. 15.99 **(978-1-68281-303-4(7))** Entangled Publishing, LLC.

Gregory, Philippa. Fools' Gold. van Deelen, Fred, illus. 2014. (Order of Darkness Ser.: 3). (ENG.). 384p. (YA). (gr. 9). pap. 9.99 (978-1-4424-7691-2(5)); 19.99 (978-1-4424-7690-5(7)) Simon Pulse. (Simon Pulse).

Griffin, Adele. Loud Awake & Lost. (ENG.). 304p. (YA). (gr. 7). 2015. pap. 9.99 (978-0-385-75275-6(X), Ember) 2013. lib. bdg. 19.99 (978-0-385-75273-2(3), Knopf Bks. for Young Readers) Random Hse. Children's Bks.

Griffin, Bethany. Masque of the Red Death. 2013. (Masque of the Red Death Ser.: 1). (ENG.). 336p. (YA). (gr. 9). pap. 9.99 (978-0-06-210780-0(1), Greenwillow Bks.) HarperCollins Pubs.

Grime, L. L. Do You Love Me? 2008. 48p. pap. 22.95 (978-1-4357-1364-2(8)) Lulu Pr., Inc.

Grimm, J. & W. & Grimm, J. The Frog Prince: Or Iron Henry. Hager, Christian & Schroeder, Binette, illus. 2013. (ENG.). 32p. (J). (gr. -1-3). 17.95 (978-0-7358-4140-6(3)) North-South Bks., Inc.

Grogan, John. Marley Looks for Love. Cowdrey, Richard, illus. 2010. (Marley Ser.). (ENG.). 16p. (J). (gr. -1-1). pap. 6.99 (978-0-06-185590-0(1), HarperFestival) HarperCollins Pubs.

—Marley's Big Adventure. 2009. (Marley: I Can Read! Ser.). (J). lib. bdg. 13.55 (978-0-606-06942-7(9), Turtleback) Turtleback Bks.

Grossmann-Hensel, Katharina. How Mommy Met Daddy. Ward, Rachel, tr. from GER. 2008. (ENG., Illus.). 32p. (J). (gr. -1-3). 16.95 (978-0-7358-2176-7(3)) North-South Bks., Inc.

Grosso, Salvatore. The Butterfly & the Dinosaur: A true story of fiction Inspired by a Beautiful Butterfly. 2010. 32p. pap. 16.99 (978-1-4490-6603-1(8)) AuthorHouse.

Grover, Lorie Ann. Big Hug for Little Cub. Kightley, Rosalinda, illus. 2014. (ENG.). 18p. (J). (— 1). bds. 7.99 (978-0-545-53091-0(1), Cartwheel Bks.) Scholastic, Inc.

—Hit, 1 vol. 2015. (ENG.). 224p. (YA). pap. 8.99 (978-0-310-72938-9(6)) Blink.

Guertin, Chantel. The Rule of Thirds. 2013. (Pippa Greene Novel Ser.). (ENG., Illus.). 220p. (J). (gr. 7-11). pap. (978-1-77041-159-3(3)) Me to We.

Gupta, Jennifer. Love Shapes. 2009. 16p. pap. 8.49 (978-1-4343-9184-1(1)) AuthorHouse.

Gurtler, Janet. Who I Kissed. 2012. (ENG.). 320p. (YA). (gr. 8-12). pap. 9.99 (978-1-4022-7054-3(2), 1350501) Sourcebooks, Inc.

Gutman, Dan. Mr. Louie Is Screwy! Paillot, Jim, illus. 2007. (My Weird School Ser.: 20). (ENG.). 112p. (J). (gr. 1-5). pap. 4.99 (978-0-06-123479-8(6)) HarperCollins Pubs.

Habel, Lia. Dearly, Departed. 2012. (ENG.). 496p. (YA). (gr. 8-12). pap. 10.99 (978-0-345-52332-7(6), Del Rey) Random House Publishing Group.

Haber, Karen. Crossing Infinity. 2011. (ENG.). 256p. (J). (gr. -1-12). pap. 9.95 (978-1-59687-411-4(2)) IBks., Inc.

Hainsworth, Emily. Through to You. 2012. (ENG.). 272p. (YA). (gr. 8). 17.99 (978-0-06-209419-3(X)) HarperCollins Pubs.

Hale, Kathleen. Nothing Bad Is Going to Happen. 2016. (Kippy Bushman Ser.). 272p. (YA). (gr. 9). 17.99 (978-0-06-221121-7(8), HarperTeen) HarperCollins Pubs.

Hale, Shannon. Dangerous. (ENG.). 416p. (YA). (gr. 7). 2015. pap. 9.99 (978-1-61963-819-8(3), 9781619638198) 2014. 17.99 (978-1-59990-168-8(4), 9781599901688) Bloomsbury Publishing USA. (Bloomsbury USA Childrens).

Half a World Away. 2014. (ENG., Illus.). 240p. (J). (gr. 5-9). 17.99 (978-1-4424-1275-0(5), Atheneum Bks. for Young Readers) Simon & Schuster Children's Publishing.

Hall, Angela Marie. Priscilla Pennybrook: Hello World, I Have Arrived!, 1 vol. 2009. 55p. pap. 16.95 (978-1-61582-899-9(0)) America Star Bks.

Hall, Maggie. The Ends of the World. 2017. (Conspiracy of Us Ser.: 3). (ENG.). 320p. (YA). (gr. 7). 17.99 **(978-0-399-16652-5(1)**, G.P. Putnam's Sons Books for Young Readers) Penguin Young Readers Group.

Hall, Maggie. Map of Fates. 2016. (Conspiracy of Us Ser.). (ENG.). 320p. (YA). (gr. 7). 17.99 (978-0-399-16651-8(3), G.P. Putnam's Sons Books for Young Readers) Penguin Young Readers Group.

Hall, Sandy. A Little Something Different. 2014. (ENG.). 272p. (YA). (gr. 7-12). pap. 9.99 (978-1-250-06145-4(8), 9781250061454) Feiwel & Friends.

—Signs Point to Yes. 2015. (ENG.). 288p. (YA). (gr. 7). pap. 9.99 (978-1-250-06600-8(X), 9781250066008) Feiwel & Friends.

Hall, S.C. Turns of Fortune & Other Tales. 2007. (ENG.). 116p. per. (978-1-4065-1586-2(8)) Dodo Pr.

Hall, Traci. Wiccan Cool. 2010. (Rhiannon Godfrey Ser.). (ENG.). 264p. pap. 15.00 (978-1-60504-611-2(6)) Samhain Publishing, LTD.

Hallinan, P. K. ABC I Love You. 2003. (ENG., Illus.). 24p. (J). bds. 7.95 (978-0-8249-5458-1(0), Ideal Pubns.) Worthy Publishing.

—Grandma Loves You. 2008. (ENG., Illus.). 26p. (J). (gr. -1-k). bds. 7.99 (978-0-8249-6728-4(3), Ideal Pubns.) Worthy Publishing.

—Grandma Loves You! Kirkland, Katherine, illus. 2014. 22p. (J). bds. 8.99 (978-0-8249-1931-3(9), Ideal Pubns.) Worthy Publishing.

—Grandpa Loves You! Kirkland, Katherine, illus. 2014. 22p. (J). bds. 8.99 (978-0-8249-1932-0(7), Ideal Pubns.) Worthy Publishing.

—How Do I Love You? 24p. (J). pap. 5.95 (978-0-8249-5360-7(6), Ideal Pubns.) Worthy Publishing.

—How Do I Love You? Hallinan, P. K., illus. 2014. (Illus.). 24p. (J). bds. 8.99 (978-0-8249-1944-3(0), Ideal Pubns.) Worthy Publishing.

—How Do I Love You? 2005. (ENG., Illus.). (J). 32p. (gr. -1-k). pap. 4.35 (978-0-8249-5518-2(8)); 24p. 7.95 (978-0-8249-5359-1(2)) Worthy Publishing. (Ideal Pubns.).

—How Do I Love You/Como Te Amo. 2008. (SPA & ENG., Illus.). 30p. (J). pap. 4.35 (978-0-8249-5471-0(8), Ideal Pubns.) Worthy Publishing.

—I Know Jesus Loves Me. Hallinan, P. K., illus. 2014. (Illus.). 18p. (J). pap. 6.99 (978-0-8249-5663-9(X), Ideal Pubns.) Worthy Publishing.

—I Know Jesus Loves Me. 2007. (ENG., Illus.). 28p. (J). (gr. -1-3). 8.99 (978-0-8249-5553-3(6), Ideal Pubns.) Worthy Publishing.

Hamilton, Alwyn. Rebel of the Sands. (Rebel of the Sands Ser.). (ENG.). (YA). (gr. 7). 2017. 336p. pap. 10.99 (978-0-14-751797-5(4), Speak) 2016. 320p. 18.99 (978-0-451-47753-8(7), Viking Books for Young Readers) Penguin Young Readers Group.

Han, Jenny. Always & Forever, Lara Jean. 2017. (To All the Boys I've Loved Before Ser.: 3). (ENG., Illus.). 336p. (YA). (gr. 7). 17.99 (978-1-4814-3048-7(3), Simon & Schuster Bks. For Young Readers) Simon & Schuster Bks. For Young Readers.

—P.S. I Still Love You. 2015. (ENG., Illus.). 352p. (YA). (gr. 7). 17.99 (978-1-4424-2673-3(X)); (To All the Boys I've Loved Before Ser.: 2). E-Book (978-1-4424-2675-7(6)) Simon & Schuster Bks. For Young Readers. (Simon & Schuster Bks. For Young Readers).

—P.S. I Still Love You. 2017. (To All the Boys I've Loved Before Ser.: 2). (ENG.). 352p. (YA). (gr. 7). pap. 10.99 (978-1-4424-2674-0(8)) Simon & Schuster Children's Publishing.

—To All the Boys I've Loved Before. (ENG., Illus.). (YA). (gr. 7-10). 2016. 384p. pap. 10.99 (978-1-4424-2671-9(3)) 2014. 368p. 17.99 (978-1-4424-2670-2(5)) 2017. 1056p. 53.99 (978-1-4814-9536-3(4)) Simon & Schuster Bks. For Young Readers. (Simon & Schuster Bks. For Young Readers).

—To All the Boys I've Loved Before. 2016. lib. bdg. 22.10 (978-0-606-38270-0(4)) Turtleback Bks.

—We'll Always Have Summer. 2011. (YA). 1.25 (978-1-4640-1977-7(0)) Recorded Bks., Inc.

—We'll Always Have Summer. (Summer I Turned Pretty Ser.). (ENG.). (YA). (gr. 7). 2012. 320p. pap. 10.99 (978-1-4169-9559-3(5)) 2011. 304p. 17.99 (978-1-4169-9558-6(7)) Simon & Schuster Bks. For Young Readers. (Simon & Schuster Bks. For Young Readers).

Hannah, Martha. The Ghost of Hampton Court. Dowell, Larry, illus. 2006. 32p. (J). 17.95 (978-0-9779808-0-2(4)) CicadaSun.

Hannon, Rose. Finding Agate: An Epic Story of a Poodle's Heart & His Will to Survive. 2010. 268p. pap. 16.99 (978-1-4490-8986-3(0)) AuthorHouse.

Hansen, Lynne. The Change: Heritage of Horror Series. 2004. (Heritage of Horror Ser.: 2). 108p. (YA). pap. 9.00 (978-0-7599-4491-6(1)) Hard Shell Word Factory.

Hantz, Sara. Falling for the Wrong Guy. 2015. (ENG., Illus.). 170p. (YA). (gr. 7). pap. 12.99 (978-1-943892-67-9(9)) Entangled Publishing, LLC.

Hapgood, Harriet Reuter & Peppermint Frog Limited. The Square Root of Summer. 2016. (ENG.). 304p. (YA). 17.99 (978-1-62672-373-3(7), 9781626723733) Roaring Brook Pr.

Hapka, Catherine, pseud. Love on Cue. 2009. (Romantic Comedies Ser.). (ENG.). 288p. (YA). (gr. 7-18). mass mkt. 6.99 (978-1-4169-6857-3(1), Simon Pulse) Simon Pulse.

—Something Borrowed. 2008. (Romantic Comedies Ser.). (ENG.). 272p. (YA). (gr. 7-18). mass mkt. 6.99 (978-1-4169-5441-5(4), Simon Pulse) Simon Pulse.

Harber Freeman, Anna. Love You More Than Anything. Henry, Jed, illus. 2014. (Snuggle Time Stories Ser.). (ENG.). 24p. (J). (gr. -1-k). 9.95 (978-1-4549-0021-4(0)) Sterling Publishing Co., Inc.

Hardegree, Maureen. Hainted Love. 2011. 184p. pap. 12.95 (978-1-61194-014-5(1), Bell Bridge Bks.) BelleBks., Inc.

Hargrove, Jason. Looking Good, Cody Greer. 2006. 188p. pap. 24.95 (978-1-4241-4013-8(7)) PublishAmerica, Inc.

Harker, Jillian. I Love You, Daddy. 2008. (I Love... Ser.). 32p. (978-1-4075-0855-9(5)) Parragon, Inc.

Harris, Patrick. Where the Day Takes You volume One. 2010. 172p. pap. 10.00 (978-0-557-04401-6(4)) Lulu Pr., Inc.

Harris, Rachel. A Tale of Two Centuries. 2013. (Entangled Teen Ser.). (ENG.). 320p. (YA). (gr. 7-12). pap. 9.99 (978-1-62266-012-4(9), 9781622660124) Entangled Publishing, LLC.

Hart, Jeff. Undead with Benefits. 2014. (Eat, Brains, Love Ser.: 2). (ENG.). 416p. (YA). (gr. 8). pap. 9.99 (978-0-06-220036-5(4), HarperTeen) HarperCollins Pubs.

Harvey, Alyxandra. A Breath of Frost. 2014. (Lovegrove Legacy Ser.). (ENG.). 512p. (YA). (gr. 7). pap. 10.99 (978-0-8027-3444-0(8), 9780802734440, Bloomsbury USA Childrens) Bloomsbury Publishing USA.

—Whisper the Dead. 2014. (Lovegrove Legacy Ser.: Bk. 2). (ENG.). 408p. (YA). (gr. 7). 17.99 (978-0-8027-3750-2(1), 9780802737502, Bloomsbury USA Childrens) Bloomsbury Publishing USA.

Harvey, Sarah N. Shattered, 1 vol. 2011. (Orca Soundings Ser.). (ENG.). 128p. (YA). (gr. 8-12). pap. 9.95 (978-1-55469-845-5(6)); lib. bdg. 16.95 (978-1-55469-846-2(4)) Orca Bk. Pubs. USA.

Harward, Barnaby, ed. Romeo & Juliet: Interfact Shakespeare. 2006. 144p. (YA). (gr. 6-10). reprint ed. pap. 25.00 (978-1-4223-5004-1(5)) DIANE Publishing Co.

Hasan, Jamal I. A Journey to Remember. 2007. 64p. per. 8.95 (978-0-595-43375-9(8)) iUniverse, Inc.

Hastings, Avery. Feuds. 2014. (Feuds Ser.: 1). (ENG.). 272p. (YA). (gr. 7). 18.99 (978-1-250-05771-6(X), 9781250057716, St. Martin's Griffin) St. Martin's Pr.

Hauman, Carrie. Zoe the Magic Love Dog. 2003. (Illus.). 32p. (J). 16.00 (978-0-9746333-8-1(0)) Alma Pr.

Hawkins, Rachel. Lady Renegades: A Rebel Belle Novel. 2016. (Rebel Belle Ser.: 3). (ENG.). 272p. (YA). (gr. 7). 17.99 (978-0-399-25695-0(4), G.P. Putnam's Sons Books for Young Readers) Penguin Young Readers Group.

Hawley, Richard. Paul & Juliana: A Novel. 2003. 188p. (YA). 19.95 (978-1-890862-33-6(9)) Bancroft Pr.

Hawthorne, Rachel. Island Girls & Boys. 2005. (ENG.). 336p. (YA). (gr. 9). pap. 8.99 (978-0-06-075546-1(6), HarperTeen) HarperCollins Pubs.

—Love on the Lifts. 2005. (ENG.). 320p. (YA). (gr. 9-12). pap. 5.99 (978-0-06-081536-3(1), HarperTeen) HarperCollins Pubs.

—Moonlight. 2009. (Dark Guardian Ser.: No. 1). (ENG.). 272p. (YA). (gr. 9-18). pap. 8.99 (978-0-06-170955-5(7), HarperTeen) HarperCollins Pubs.

—One Perfect Summer: Labor of Love & Thrill Ride. 2015. (ENG.). 544p. (YA). (gr. 9). pap. 9.99 (978-0-06-232134-3(X), HarperTeen) HarperCollins Pubs.

Haydu, Corey Ann. The Careful Undressing of Love. 2017. (ENG.). 288p. (YA). (gr. 9). 17.99 (978-0-399-18673-8(5), Dutton Books for Young Readers) Penguin Young Readers Group.

—Life by Committee. 2014. (ENG.). 304p. (YA). (gr. 9). 17.99 (978-0-06-229405-0(9), Tegen, Katherine Bks) HarperCollins Pubs.

Hayes, Angela. The Mop Heads, 1 vol. Polly Jr., Jimmy Wayne, illus. 2009. 14p. pap. 24.95 *(978-1-61546-006-9(3))* America Star Bks.

Hayes, Gwen. Dreaming Awake. 2012. (ENG.). 332p. (YA). (gr. 7-18). 9.99 *(978-0-451-23554-1(1)*, Berkley) Penguin Publishing Group.

Hayes, Joe. Pajaro Verde. Castro L., Antonio, illus. 2005. (ENG & SPA.). 40p. (J). (gr. 4-6). pap. 8.95 *(978-0-938317-90-6(3))* Cinco Puntos Pr.

Headley, Maria Dahvana. Aerie. 2016. (Magonia Ser.: 2). 320p. (YA). (gr. 8). 17.99 *(978-0-06-232055-1(6))* HarperCollins Pubs.

—Magonia. (Magonia Ser.: 1). (YA). (gr. 8). 2016. 336p. pap. 9.99 *(978-0-06-232053-7(X))* 2015. (ENG.). 320p. 17.99 *(978-0-06-232052-0(1)*, HarperTeen) HarperCollins Pubs.

Heasley, Gwendolyn. Don't Call Me Baby. 2014. (ENG.). 304p. (YA). (gr. 8). pap. 9.99 *(978-0-06-220852-1(7)*, HarperTeen) HarperCollins Pubs.

Heckman, Ashley. The Last Three Words. 2013. 104p. pap. *(978-1-77130-651-5(3))* Evernight Publishing.

Hedlund, Jody. A Daring Sacrifice, 1 vol. 2016. (ENG.). 224p. (YA). pap. 12.99 *(978-0-310-74937-0(9))* Zondervan.

—An Uncertain Choice, 1 vol. 2015. (ENG.). 256p. (YA). pap. 12.99 *(978-0-310-74919-6(0))* Zondervan.

Heitritter, Laura. I Love You Just Because. Villim, Jim, illus. Date not set. 16p. (Orig.). (J). (gr. -1-18). pap. 6.95 *(978-1-885964-01-4(3))* P2 Educational Services, Inc.

Helean, April K. Love Can Build a Bridge. 2012. 24p. pap. 15.99 *(978-1-4691-5621-7(0))* Xlibris Corp.

Helgeson, Kat. Say No to the Bro. 2017. (ENG., Illus.). 272p. (YA). (gr. 9). 17.99 ***(978-1-4814-7193-0(7)***, Simon & Schuster Bks. For Young Readers) Simon & Schuster Bks. For Young Readers.

Helgeson, Kat & Moskowitz, Hannah. Gena/Finn. 2016. (ENG., Illus.). (YA). (gr. 7-12). 17.99 *(978-1-4521-3839-8(7))* Chronicle Bks. LLC.

Hemphill, Helen. Runaround. (ENG.). 117p. (J). (gr. 6-9). 2009. pap. 10.95 *(978-1-59078-777-9(3))* 2007. (Illus.). 16.95 *(978-1-932425-83-3(7))* Boyds Mills Pr. (Front Street).

Hemphill, Stephanie. Hideous Love: The Story of the Girl Who Wrote Frankenstein. 2013. (ENG.). 320p. (YA). (gr. 8). 17.99 *(978-0-06-185331-9(3))* HarperCollins Pubs.

—Sisters of Glass. 2013. (ENG.). 160p. (YA). (gr. 7). pap. 7.99 *(978-0-307-98141-7(X)*, Ember) Random Hse. Children's Bks.

Henry, April. Count All Her Bones. 2017. (Girl, Stolen Ser.). (ENG.). 240p. (YA). 17.99 *(978-1-62779-591-3(X)*, 9781627795913, Holt, Henry & Co. Bks. For Young Readers) Holt, Henry & Co.

Henry, Emily. The Love That Split the World. (ENG.). (YA). (gr. 7). 2017. 416p. pap. 9.99 *(978-1-59514-851-3(5))* 2016. 400p. 17.99 *(978-1-59514-850-6(7))* Penguin Young Readers Group. (Razorbill).

Henry, Sherrie. Last of the Summer Tomatoes. 2016. (ENG., Illus.). (YA). (gr. 8-12). 24.99 ***(978-1-63533-039-7(4))*** 2013. 246p. pap. 14.99 *(978-1-62380-959-1(2))* Dreamspinner Pr. (Harmony Ink Pr.).

Henry, Sherrie. Last of the Summer Tomatoes [Library Edition]. 2013. 246p. pap. 14.99 *(978-1-62380-931-7(2)*, Harmony Ink Pr.) Dreamspinner Pr.

Hepler, Heather. Love? Maybe. 2013. (ENG.). 288p. (YA). (gr. 7). pap. 8.99 *(978-0-14-242386-8(6)*, Speak) Penguin Young Readers Group.

Herbstritt, Rj. God Loves You More Than Rainbows & Butterflies! Herbstritt, T. J., illus. 2011. 40p. pap. 24.95 *(978-1-4560-6735-9(4))* America Star Bks.

Hermstad, Melanie. Bird, I Love You. Date not set. *(978-0-517-58561-0(8))* Random Hse. Value Publishing.

Herrick, Ann. The Perfect Guy. 2005. 120p. (YA). pap. 9.95 *(978-0-7599-3522-8(X))* Hard Shell Word Factory.

—Summer Replacement. 2004. (ENG.). 100p. (YA). per. 9.00 *(978-0-7599-4168-7(8))* Hard Shell Word Factory.

Herrick, Steven. Kissing Annabel: Love, Ghosts, & Facial Hair & a Place Like This. 2009. (ENG.). 272p. (YA). (gr. 9). pap. 7.99 *(978-1-4169-8287-6(6)*, Simon Pulse) Simon Pulse.

Hesik, Annameekee. Driving Lessons: A You Know Who Girls Novel. 2014. (You Know Who Girls Ser.: 2). (ENG.). 264p. (J). pap. 11.95 *(978-1-62639-228-1(5))* Bold Strokes Bks.

Hickman, Kirt. Purple. Olson, Julie, illus. 2012. 32p. pap. 15.99 *(978-0-9796330-8-9(7))* Quillrunner Publishing LLC.

Hicks, Constance. Florabelle Bunny & the Sparrow. 2011. 24p. pap. 12.99 *(978-1-4490-9969-5(6))* AuthorHouse.

Higgins, Wendy. Sweet Evil. 2012. (Sweet Evil Ser.: 1). (ENG.). 464p. (YA). (gr. 8). pap. 9.99 *(978-0-06-208561-0(1)*, HarperTeen) HarperCollins Pubs.

—Sweet Peril. 2013. (Sweet Evil Ser.: 2). (ENG.). 384p. (YA). (gr. 8). pap. 9.99 *(978-0-06-226594-4(6)*, HarperTeen) HarperCollins Pubs.

—Sweet Reckoning. 2014. (Sweet Evil Ser.: 3). (ENG.). 400p. (YA). (gr. 8). pap. 9.99 *(978-0-06-226597-5(0)*, HarperTeen) HarperCollins Pubs.

—Sweet Temptation. 2015. (Sweet Evil Ser.: 4). (ENG.). 512p. (YA). (gr. 8). pap. 9.99 *(978-0-06-238142-2(3)*, HarperTeen) HarperCollins Pubs.

Higginson, Sheila Sweeny. You're Getting a Baby Brother! Williams, Sam, illus. 2012. (ENG.). 24p. (J). (gr. -1-k). bds. 7.99 *(978-1-4424-2021-2(9)*, Little Simon) Little Simon.

—You're Getting a Baby Sister! Williams, Sam, illus. 2012. (ENG.). 24p. (J). (gr. -1-k). bds. 7.99 *(978-1-4424-2050-2(2)*, Little Simon) Little Simon.

Highley, Kendra C. The Bad Boy Bargain. 2016. (ENG., Illus.). (YA). pap. 16.99 ***(978-1-68281-335-5(5))*** Entangled Publishing, LLC.

Highley, Kendra C. Finding Perfect. 2015. (ENG., Illus.). 248p. (J). pap. 15.99 *(978-1-943892-43-3(1))* Entangled Publishing, LLC.

Hightman, J. P. Spirit. 2008. 224p. (gr. 7-18). (ENG.). (J). 16.99 *(978-0-06-085063-0(9))*; (YA). lib. bdg. 17.89 *(978-0-06-085064-7(7))* HarperCollins Pubs. (HarperTeen).

Hilburn, Dora. Between. 2015. 247p. (YA). pap. *(978-1-56825-175-2(0))* Rainbow Bks., Inc.

Hildebrand, Jens & Ridge, Sally. Cyberstalker. 2013. 242p. pap. *(978-3-929892-45-1(6))* Hildebrand, Jutta Warped Tomato Publishing.

Hill, Carolyn Swan. A Summer to Remember. 2013. 256p. (YA). (gr. 10-12). pap. 17.99 *(978-1-4624-0543-5(6)*, Inspiring Voices) Author Solutions, Inc.

Hill, Eric. Puppy Love. Hill, Eric, illus. 2016. (Spot Ser.). (ENG., Illus.). 40p. (J). (gr. -1-k). 6.99 *(978-0-399-20935-2(2)*, Warne) Penguin Young Readers Group.

Hill, Genita. My Very Special Brother. McCall, William L., illus. 2007. 40p. per. 24.95 *(978-1-4241-8852-9(0))* America Star Bks.

Hillhouse, Joanne C. Musical Youth. Aaron, Glenroy, illus. 2014. (ENG.). 275p. (J). pap. 9.99 *(978-0-9899305-1-2(3))* CaribbeanReads.

Hinds, Gareth. Romeo & Juliet. Hinds, Gareth, illus. 2013. (ENG., Illus.). 144p. (YA). (gr. 7). 21.99 *(978-0-7636-5948-6(7))*; pap. 12.99 *(978-0-7636-6807-5(9))* Candlewick Pr.

—Romeo & Juliet (Graphic Adaptation) 2013. lib. bdg. 24.50 *(978-0-606-32098-6(9)*, Turtleback) Turtleback Bks.

Hocking, Amanda. Ascend. 2012. (Trylle Novel Ser.: 3). (ENG.). 336p. (YA). (gr. 7). pap. 8.99 *(978-1-250-00633-2(3)*, 9781250006332, St. Martin's Griffin) St. Martin's Pr.

—Elegy. (Watersong Novel Ser.: 4). (ENG.). 560p. (YA). (gr. 7). 2014. pap. 10.99 *(978-1-250-00809-1(3)*, 9781250008091, St. Martin's Griffin) 2014. mass mkt. 9.99 *(978-1-250-05654-2(3)*, 9781250056542, St. Martin's Paperbacks) 2013. 17.99 *(978-1-250-00567-0(1)*, 9781250005670, St. Martin's Griffin) St. Martin's Pr.

—Switched. 2012. (Trylle Novel Ser.: 1). (ENG.). 336p. (YA). (gr. 7). pap. 8.99 *(978-1-250-00631-8(7)*, 9781250006318, St. Martin's Griffin) St. Martin's Pr.

—Tidal. (Watersong Novel Ser.: 3). (ENG.). 352p. (YA). (gr. 7). 2014. pap. 11.99 *(978-1-250-00566-3(3)*, 9781250005663, St. Martin's Griffin) 2014. mass mkt. 9.99 *(978-1-250-05657-3(8)*, 9781250056573, St. Martin's Paperbacks) 2013. 17.99 *(978-1-250-00811-4(5)*, 9781250008114, St. Martin's Griffin) St. Martin's Pr.

—Torn. 2012. (Trylle Novel Ser.: 2). (ENG.). 336p. (YA). (gr. 7-12). pap. 8.99 *(978-1-250-00632-5(5)*, 9781250006325, St. Martin's Griffin) St. Martin's Pr.

—Torn. l.t. ed. 2012. (Trylle Trilogy: Bk. 2). (ENG.). 450p. (J). (gr. 7-12). 23.99 *(978-1-4104-5013-5(9))* Thorndike Pr.

—Wake. 2013. (Watersong Novel Ser.: 1). (ENG.). 320p. (YA). (gr. 7). pap. 10.99 *(978-1-250-00564-9(7)*, 9781250005649, St. Martin's Griffin) St. Martin's Pr.

Hodge, Rosamund. Crimson Bound. 2016. 464p. (YA). (gr. 8). pap. 9.99 *(978-0-06-222477-4(8))* HarperCollins Pubs.

Hodkin, Michelle. The Evolution of Mara Dyer. (Mara Dyer Trilogy Ser.: 2). (ENG., Illus.). (YA). (gr. 9). 2013. 560p. pap. 12.99 *(978-1-4424-2180-6(0))* 2012. 544p. 19.99 *(978-1-4424-2179-0(7))* Simon & Schuster Bks. For Young Readers. (Simon & Schuster Bks. For Young Readers).

—The Retribution of Mara Dyer. 2014. (Mara Dyer Trilogy: Vol. 3). (ENG., Illus.). 480p. (YA). (gr. 9). 18.99 *(978-1-4424-8423-8(3)*, Simon & Schuster Bks. For Young Readers) Simon & Schuster Bks. For Young Readers.

Hoffman, Mary. The Falconer's Knot: A Story of Friars, Flirtation & Foul Play. (ENG., Illus.). 304p. (YA). (gr. 7). 2008. pap. 7.99 *(978-1-59990-229-6(X)*, 9781599902296) 2007. 16.95 *(978-1-59990-056-8(4)*, 9781599900568) Bloomsbury Publishing USA. (Bloomsbury USA Childrens).

Holder, Ramona V. Paco & Lexus Are Good Friends: Paco y Lexus son Buen Amigos. 2009. 24p. pap. 12.99 *(978-1-4389-5778-4(5))* AuthorHouse.

Holeman, Linda. Toxic Love. 2003. (ENG.). 184p. (J). (gr. 5-9). pap. 8.95 *(978-0-88776-647-3(1)*, Tundra Bks.) Tundra Bks. CAN. Dist: Penguin Random Hse. LLC.

Hollyer, Belinda & Brontë, Charlotte. Jane Eyre. 2003. (Illus.). 48p. *(978-0-7502-3668-3(X)*, Wayland) Hachette Children's Group.

Holm, Jennifer L. Wilderness Days. unabr. ed. 2004. (Boston Jane Ser.: No. 2). 288p. (J). (gr. 5-9). pap. 38.00 incl. audio *(978-0-8072-0787-1(X)*, S YA 307 SP, Listening Library) Random Hse. Audio Publishing Group.

Holub, Joan & Williams, Suzanne. Aphrodite the Beauty. (Goddess Girls Ser.: 3). (ENG.). 176p. (J). (gr. 3-7). 2013. 17.99 *(978-1-4424-5751-5(1))* 2010. pap. 7.99 *(978-1-4169-8273-9(6))* Simon & Schuster Children's Publishing. (Aladdin).

Homberg, Ruth. The Little Mermaid. 2013. (Disney Princess Step into Reading Ser.). lib. bdg. 13.55 *(978-0-606-32202-7(7)*, Turtleback) Turtleback Bks.

Honeybourn, Jennifer. Wesley James Ruined My Life. 2017. (ENG.). 256p. (YA). pap. 10.99 *(978-1-250-12373-2(9)*, 9781250123732) Feiwel & Friends.

Hoole, Elissa Janine. The Memory Jar. 2016. (ENG.). 336p. (YA). pap. 11.99 *(978-0-7387-4731-6(9)*, Flux) North Star Editions.

Hooper, Mary. Poppy. 2016. (ENG.). 288p. (YA). 17.99 *(978-1-61963-496-1(1)*, 9781619634961, Bloomsbury USA Childrens) Bloomsbury Publishing USA.

Hoover, P. J. Solstice. 2013. (ENG.). 384p. (YA). (gr. 8). 17.99 *(978-0-7653-3469-5(0)*, Tor Teen) Doherty, Tom Assocs., LLC.

Hopkins, Cathy. Love Lottery. 2012. (Truth or Dare Ser.). (ENG.). 208p. (YA). (gr. 7). pap. 11.99 *(978-1-4424-7176-4(X)*, Simon Pulse) Simon Pulse.

Hopkins, Cathy & Hopkins, Cathy. White Lies & Barefaced Truths. 2005. (Truth or Dare Ser.: No. 1). (ENG.). 176p. (YA). (gr. 7-12). mass mkt. 3.99 *(978-1-4169-1152-4(9)*, Simon Pulse) Simon Pulse.

Hopkins, Ellen. Tilt. (ENG., (YA). (gr. 9). 2014. Illus.). 624p. pap. 12.99 *(978-1-4169-8331-6(7))* 2012. 608p. 18.99 *(978-1-4169-8330-9(9))* McElderry, Margaret K. Bks. (McElderry, Margaret K. Bks.).

Hopkins, Ellen, ed. A New Dawn: Your Favorite Authors on Stephenie Meyer's Twilight Series. 2009. (ENG., Illus.). 200p. (J). (gr. 9-12). pap. 12.95 *(978-1-933771-93-9(3))* BenBella Bks.

Hoppey, Tim. Pedro, the Pirate. Bonder, Dianna, illus. 2012. (ENG & SPA.). 32p. (J). lib. bdg. 16.95 *(978-1-936299-18-8(6)*, Raven Tree Pr.,Csi) Continental Sales, Inc.

Houck, Colleen. Recreated. (Reawakened Ser.: 2). (ENG.). 416p. (YA). (gr. 9). 2017. pap. 10.99 ***(978-0-385-37663-1(4)***, Ember) 2016. 17.99 *(978-0-385-37660-0(X)*, Delacorte Pr.) Random Hse. Children's Bks.

Houde, Monique. Blinded by Love. 2004. (YA). pap. 14.95 *(978-0-9748689-0-5(6))* Choices For Tomorrow.

House, Catherine. Little Elephant. Whelan, Olwyn, illus. 2007. 32p. pap. 11.95 *(978-1-59325-093-5(2))* Word Among Us Pr.

Houston, Meradeth. Colors Like Memories. 2013. 178p. pap. *(978-1-77127-371-8(2))* MuseItUp Publishing.

Howard, A. G. Ensnared. 2015. (Splintered Ser.). (ENG.). 416p. (YA). (gr. 9-17). pap. 9.99 *(978-1-4197-1675-1(1))*; 17.95 *(978-1-4197-1229-6(2))* Abrams, Inc. (Amulet Bks.).

Howat, Irene. Adoniram Judson: Danger on the Streets of Gold. 2007. (Trailblazers Ser.). (ENG.). 160p. (J). mass mkt. 8.99 *(978-1-85792-660-6(9)*, aa09dd00-c28c-4172-8dee-7bb4c77f28dc) Christian Focus Pubns. GBR. Dist: Bookmasters Distribution.

Howe, James. Otter & Odder: A Love Story. Raschka, Chris, illus. 2012. (ENG.). 40p. (J). (gr. 1-4). 14.00 *(978-0-7636-4174-0(X))* Candlewick Pr.

Howe, Katherine. The Appearance of Annie Van Sinderen. 2015. (ENG.). 400p. (YA). (gr. 7). 18.99 *(978-0-399-16778-2(1)*, G.P. Putnam's Sons Books for Young Readers) Penguin Young Readers Group.

Howells, Amanda. The Summer of Skinny Dipping. 2010. (ENG.). 304p. (YA). (gr. 7-12). pap. 9.99 *(978-1-4022-3862-8(2)*, Sourcebooks Jabberwocky) Sourcebooks, Inc.

Howland, Leila. Nantucket Red. 2014. (Nantucket Blue Ser.). (ENG.). 288p. (YA). (gr. 9-17). 16.99 *(978-1-4231-6095-3(9))* Hyperion Bks. for Children.

Howson, Imogen. Linked. 2013. (ENG., Illus.). 368p. (YA). (gr. 7). 16.99 *(978-1-4424-4656-4(0)*, Simon & Schuster Bks. For Young Readers) Simon & Schuster Bks. For Young Readers.

—Unravel. 2014. (ENG., Illus.). 480p. (YA). (gr. 7). 17.99 *(978-1-4424-4658-8(7)*, Simon & Schuster Bks. For Young Readers) Simon & Schuster Bks. For Young Readers.

Howson, Imogen & Smith, Ali. Linked. 2014. (ENG., Illus.). 384p. (YA). (gr. 7). pap. 9.99 *(978-1-4424-4660-1(9)*, Simon & Schuster Bks. For Young Readers) Simon & Schuster Bks. For Young Readers.

Hubbard, Amanda & Hubbard, Mandy. Everything but the Truth. 2015. (If Only... Ser.). (ENG.). 288p. (YA). (gr. 7). 17.99 *(978-1-61963-659-0(X)*, 9781619636590, Bloomsbury USA Childrens) Bloomsbury Publishing USA.

Hubbard, Kirsten. Wanderlove. (ENG.). 352p. (YA). (gr. 9). 2013. pap. 9.99 *(978-0-385-73938-2(9)*, Ember) 2012. 17.99 *(978-0-385-73937-5(0)*, Delacorte Bks. for Young Readers) Random Hse. Children's Bks.

Hubbard, Mandy. Fool Me Twice. 2014. (If Only... Ser.). (ENG.). 272p. (YA). (gr. 7). 17.99 *(978-1-61963-229-5(2)*, 9781619632295, Bloomsbury USA Childrens) Bloomsbury Publishing USA.

—Fool Me Twice: An If Only Novel. 2014. (If Only... Ser.). (ENG.). 272p. (YA). (gr. 7). pap. 9.99 *(978-1-61963-230-1(6)*, 9781619632301, Bloomsbury USA Childrens) Bloomsbury Publishing USA.

Hubert. Adrian & the Tree of Secrets. 2014. (ENG., Illus.). 128p. (gr. 6). pap. 18.95 *(978-1-55152-556-3(9))* Arsenal Pulp Pr. CAN. Dist: Consortium Bk. Sales & Distribution.

Huffman, Jared. The Lost Piece. Huffman, Jared & Rampley, Leigh, illus. 2011. 36p. pap. 24.95 *(978-1-4626-1784-5(0))* America Star Bks.

Hugger, M. A. Danny Malloy & His Mississippi River Samurai. 2008. 132p. 21.95 *(978-0-595-49382-1(3))*; pap. 11.95 *(978-0-595-48462-1(X))* iUniverse, Inc.

Hughes, Lynn Gordon. To Live a Truer Life: A Story of the Hopedale Community. Lindro, illus. 2003. 32p. (J). 10.00 *(978-0-9725017-2-9(X))* Blackstone Editions.

Hughes, Mark Peter. I Am the Wallpaper. 2007. (Readers Circle Ser.). (ENG.). 256p. (YA). (gr. 7-11). pap. 8.99 *(978-0-440-42046-0(6)*, Delacorte Bks. for Young Readers) Random Hse. Children's Bks.

Hulslander, Dyan. I Just Love You So Much. Heaton, Jr., illus. 2009. 28p. pap. 14.49 *(978-1-4490-0454-5(7))* AuthorHouse.

Humphrey, Anna. Rhymes with Cupid. 2010. (ENG.). 240p. (YA). (gr. 8). pap. 7.99 *(978-0-06-193501-5(8)*, HarperTeen) HarperCollins Pubs.

Humphrey, Eleanor Cairns. Building Santa's Work Shop from Tales of the Crystal Cave. 2012. 268p. pap. 27.95 *(978-1-4626-7820-4(3))* America Star Bks.

Humphrey, T. Lewis. The Price of Love. 2003. 332p. (YA). pap. 18.95 *(978-0-595-27260-0(6)*, Writers Club Pr.) iUniverse, Inc.

Hunter, C. C. Chosen at Nightfall. 2013. (Shadow Falls Novel Ser.: 5). (ENG.). (YA). (gr. 7). 432p. mass mkt. 9.99 *(978-1-250-04765-6(X)*, 9781250047656, St. Martin's Paperbacks); 416p. pap. 10.99 *(978-1-250-01289-0(9)*, 9781250012890, St. Martin's Griffin) St. Martin's Pr.

—Eternal. 2014. (Shadow Falls: after Dark Ser.: 2). (ENG.). 400p. (YA). mass mkt. 9.99 *(978-1-250-07016-6(3)*, 9781250070166, St. Martin's Paperbacks); (gr. 7-12). 19.99 *(978-1-250-05630-6(6)*, St. Martin's Griffin) St. Martin's Pr.

—Eternal: Shadow Falls: After Dark. 2014. (Shadow Falls: after Dark Ser.: 2). (ENG.). 400p. (YA). (gr. 7-12). pap. 9.99 *(978-1-250-04461-7(8)*, 9781250044617, St. Martin's Griffin) St. Martin's Pr.

—Taken at Dusk. 2012. (Shadow Falls Novel Ser.: 3). (ENG.). 400p. (YA). (gr. 7-12). pap. 10.99 *(978-0-312-62469-9(7)*, 9780312624699, St. Martin's Griffin) St. Martin's Pr.

—Taken at Dusk: A Shadow Falls Novel. 2013. (Shadow Falls Novel Ser.: 3). (ENG.). 400p. (YA). (gr. 7-12). mass mkt. 9.99 *(978-1-250-04681-9(5)*, 9781250046819, St. Martin's Paperbacks) St. Martin's Pr.

—Whispers at Moonrise. 2013. (Shadow Falls Novel Ser.: 4). (ENG.). 400p. (YA). (gr. 7-12). mass mkt. 9.99 *(978-1-250-04682-6(3)*, 9781250046826, St. Martin's Paperbacks) St. Martin's Pr.

Hurley, Jeanette Clinger. The Crystal Prince: Love Is the Only Way. 2010. (Illus.). 77p. pap. 32.95 *(978-0-578-03963-3(X))* Outskirts Pr., Inc.

Hurley, Suzanne M. To the Stars. Josephsen, Laura, ed. Judson, Gemini, illus. 2016. (ENG.). 242p. (J). pap. 16.99 *(978-1-61160-891-5(0)*, Whiskey Creek Pr.) Whiskey Creek Pr., LLC.

Husby, Greg. The Zoebirds. 2008. 40p. pap. 21.99 *(978-1-4363-4941-3(9))* Xlibris Corp.

Huskins, Suzanne Hallier, illus. No Matter What! 2004. (J). *(978-1-887905-93-0(6))* Parkway Pubs., Inc.

Hutchinson, Shaun David. Fml. 2013. (ENG.). 304p. (YA). (gr. 9). pap. 9.99 *(978-1-4424-3287-1(X))*; (Illus.). 17.99 *(978-1-4424-8318-7(0))* Simon Pulse. (Simon Pulse).

I Love You, Mommy. 2008. (I Love... Ser.). 32p. *(978-1-4075-0856-6(3))* Parragon, Inc.

Ignatow, Amy. The Popularity Papers: Book Six: Love & Other Fiascos with Lydia Goldblatt & Julie Graham-Chang. 2015. (Popularity Papers). (ENG., Illus.). 208p. (J). (gr. 3-7). pap. 8.95 *(978-1-4197-1356-9(6)*, Amulet Bks.) Abrams, Inc.

Imes, Jarod. Age Ain't Nothing but a Number. 2007. 148p. (YA). pap. 10.99 *(978-1-934195-04-8(9))* Tinsley Phelps, LLC.

Imes, Jarold. Never Too Much - the Remix. 2007. (YA). per. 10.99 *(978-1-934195-07-9(3))* Tinsley Phelps, LLC.

Imes, Jarold, adapted by. U Can't Break Me. 2007. 148p. (YA). pap. 10.99 *(978-1-934195-03-1(0))* Tinsley Phelps, LLC.

Inglis, Lucy. Crow Mountain. 2016. (ENG.). 368p. (YA). (gr. 9). 17.99 *(978-0-545-90407-0(2)*, Chicken Hse., The) Scholastic, Inc.

Inoue, Kazurou. Midori Days. Inoue, Kazurou, illus. 2006. (Midori Days Ser.). (ENG., Illus.). 208p. Vol. 6. pap. 9.99 *(978-1-4215-0495-7(2))* Vol. 7. pap. 9.99 *(978-1-4215-0496-4(0))* Viz Media.

Ius, Dawn. Anne & Henry. Watcher, Jill, illus. 2015. (ENG.). 304p. (YA). (gr. 9). 18.99 *(978-1-4814-3941-1(3)*, Simon Pulse) Simon Pulse.

Jabaley, Jennifer. Crush Control. 2011. (ENG.). 336p. (YA). (gr. 7-18). 9.99 *(978-1-59514-424-9(2)*, Razorbill) Penguin Young Readers Group.

Jackson, Corrine. Ignited. 2014. (Sense Thieves Ser.). (ENG.). 368p. (YA). (gr. 13). pap. 9.95 *(978-0-7582-7335-2(5)*, K-Teen) Kensington Publishing Corp.

Jackson, G. A. Twelve Yellow Ducks. 2011. 28p. (gr. -1 — 1). pap. 13.59 *(978-1-4567-4268-3(X))* AuthorHouse.

Jacobson, Jennifer Richard. Andy Shane Is Not in Love. 2009. (Andy Shane Ser.: 4). lib. bdg. 14.75 *(978-0-606-06618-1(7)*, Turtleback) Turtleback Bks.

Jacobus, Ann. Romancing the Dark in the City of Light: A Novel. 2015. (ENG.). 288p. (YA). (gr. 7-12). 18.99 *(978-1-250-06443-1(0)*, 9781250064431) St. Martin's Pr.

James, Ellie. Shattered Dreams: A Midnight Dragonfly Novel. 2011. (Midnight Dragonfly Novel Ser.: 1). (ENG.). 352p. (YA). (gr. 7). pap. 22.99 *(978-0-312-64702-5(6)*, 9780312647025, St. Martin's Griffin) St. Martin's Pr.

James, Jenni. Pride & Popularity. 2011. (Jane Austen Diaries). (ENG.). 238p. (YA). (gr. 8-12). pap. 11.99 *(978-0-9838293-0-0(6))* Inkberry Pr.

James, Melody. Signs of Love: Destiny Date. 2013. (ENG.). 176p. (J). pap. 7.99 *(978-0-85707-328-0(1)*, Simon & Schuster Children's) Simon & Schuster, Ltd. GBR. Dist: Simon & Schuster, Inc.

Jansson, Tove. Moomin & the Golden Tail. 2014. (Moomin Ser.). (ENG., Illus.). 56p. (J). (gr. 4-7). pap. 9.95 *(978-1-77046-133-8(7)*, 9781770461338) Drawn & Quarterly Pubns. CAN. Dist: Macmillan.

Jarratt, Laura. Skin Deep. 2015. (ENG.). 384p. (YA). (gr. 7). pap. 12.99 *(978-1-4052-5672-8(9))* Egmont Bks., Ltd. GBR. Dist: Independent Pubs. Group.

Jaskulka, Marie. The Lost Marble Notebook of Forgotten Girl & Random Boy. 2015. (ENG.). 272p. (J). (gr. 6). 16.99 *(978-1-63220-426-4(6)*, Sky Pony Pr.) Skyhorse Publishing Co., Inc.

Jay, Stacey. Juliet Immortal. 2012. (ENG.). 324p. (YA). (gr. 9). pap. 9.99 *(978-0-385-74017-3(4)*, Ember) Random Hse. Children's Bks.

—Romeo Redeemed. 2013. (ENG.). 384p. (YA). (gr. 9). pap. 9.99 *(978-0-385-74019-7(0)*, Ember) Random Hse. Children's Bks.

Jaysree. Drama. 2004. 134p. (YA). pap. 11.95 *(978-0-595-29662-0(9))* iUniverse, Inc.

Jean, Emiko. We'll Never Be Apart. 2015. (ENG.). 288p. (YA). (gr. 9). 17.99 *(978-0-544-48200-5(X)*, HMH Books For Young Readers) Houghton Mifflin Harcourt Publishing Co.

Jeffers, Karen. Tosh. 2013. 26p. pap. 13.95 *(978-1-4787-0255-9(9))* Outskirts Pr., Inc.

Jefferson, Patti Brassard. How Long Will You Love Me? Jefferson, Patti Brassard, illus. 2013. (Illus.). 28p. pap. 12.95 *(978-1-61244-178-8(5))* Halo Publishing International.

Jeffrey, Sarah. Me & My Invisible Guy, 0 vols. 2013. (ENG.). 256p. (YA). (gr. 7-11). 15.99 *(978-1-4778-1636-3(4)*, 9781477816363, Amazon Children's Publishing) Amazon Publishing.

Jeffs, Dixie. A Baby to Love. 2012. 20p. pap. 24.95 *(978-1-4626-6780-2(5))* America Star Bks.

Jenisch, Betty. Rennie. 2007. 9.00 *(978-0-8059-8947-2(1))* Dorrance Publishing Co., Inc.

Jenkyns, Brenda. Ever After. 2012. pap. 11.95 *(978-0-7414-7620-3(7))* Infinity Publishing.

Jennings, Carol E. Marshall & Satchmo. 2008. 40p. pap. 21.32 *(978-1-4363-7117-9(1))* Xlibris Corp.

Jensen, Danielle L. Stolen Songbird. 2014. (Malediction Trilogy Ser.: 1). (ENG.). 480p. (YA). (gr. 9). pap. 9.99 *(978-1-908844-96-5(5)*, Angry Robot, Limited) Watkins Media Limited GBR. Dist: Penguin Random Hse. LLC.

Jensen, Kathryn. Splash! 2007. 193p. pap. 24.95 *(978-1-4241-9903-7(4))* America Star Bks.

Jitchotvisut, Donna M. Mittens for Christmas. 2009. 376p. 31.95 *(978-1-4401-0372-8(0))*; pap. 21.95 *(978-1-4401-0370-4(4))* iUniverse, Inc.

John, Antony. Imposter. 2015. (ENG.). 320p. (YA). (gr. 7). 17.99 *(978-0-8037-4124-9(3)*, Dial Bks) Penguin Young Readers Group.

Johnson, Alaya Dawn. The Summer Prince. (ENG.). 304p. (J). (gr. 9). 2014. pap. 9.99 *(978-0-545-41780-8(5))* 2013. 17.99 *(978-0-545-41779-2(1))* Scholastic, Inc. (Levine, Arthur A. Bks.).

Johnson, Christine. The Gathering Dark. (ENG., (YA). (gr. 9). 2014. Illus.). 528p. pap. 9.99 *(978-1-4424-3904-7(1))* 2013. 512p. 16.99 *(978-1-4424-3903-0(3))* Simon Pulse. (Simon Pulse).

Johnson, Elana. Abandon: A Possession Novel. 2013. (ENG.). 464p. (YA). (gr. 9). 17.99 *(978-1-4424-8482-5(9))*; (Illus.). pap. 9.99 *(978-1-4424-8481-8(0))* Simon Pulse. (Simon Pulse).

Johnson, Gerald J. J. Bessie's Little Mouse Day Care. Miltenberger, Dave & Miltenberger, Jeri, illus. 2012. 32p. pap. 24.95 *(978-1-62709-430-6(X))* America Star Bks.

—Buffy Bunny. Miltenberger, Jeri & Miltenberger, Dave, illus. 2011. 32p. pap. 24.95 *(978-1-4512-5292-7(7))* America Star Bks.

Jones, Carrie. Endure. 2012. (Need Ser.). (ENG.). 272p. (YA). 17.99 (978-1-59990-554-9(X), 9781599905549, Bloomsbury USA Childrens) Bloomsbury Publishing USA.

Jones, Jasmine. Head over Heels. 2004. 152p. (J). lib. bdg. 16.92 (978-1-4242-0677-3(4)) Fitzgerald Bks.

Jones, Jasmine, adapted by. Head over Heels. 2004. (Lizzie Mcguire Ser.). (Illus.). 152p. (J). 12.65 (978-0-7569-2723-3(4)) Perfection Learning Corp.

Jones, Patrick. Heart or Mind. 2016. (Unbarred Ser.). (ENG., Illus.). 120p. (YA). (gr. 6-12). lib. bdg. 27.99 (978-1-5124-0003-8(3), Darby Creek) Lerner Publishing Group.

—Heart or Mind. 2016. (Unbarred Ser.). (ENG.). 120p. (YA). (gr. 6-12). 42.65 (978-1-5124-0092-2(0), Darby Creek) Lerner Publishing Group.

Jones, Patrick & Clark, Marshunna. Duty or Desire. 2016. (Unbarred Ser.). (ENG.). 112p. (YA). (gr. 6-12). lib. bdg. 27.99 (978-1-5124-0002-1(5), Darby Creek) Lerner Publishing Group.

—Duty or Desire. 2016. (Unbarred Ser.). (ENG.). 112p. (YA). (gr. 6-12). pap. 7.99 (978-1-5124-0089-2(0), Darby Creek) Lerner Publishing Group.

—Duty or Desire. 2016. (Unbarred Ser.). (ENG.). 112p. (YA). (gr. 6-12). 42.65 (978-1-5124-0090-8(4), Darby Creek) Lerner Publishing Group.

Jones Yang, Dori. Daughter of Xanadu. 2012. (ENG.). 352p. (YA). (gr. 7). pap. 9.99 (978-0-385-73924-5(9), Ember) Random Hse. Children's Bks.

Joosse, Barbara M. & Lavallee, Barbara. Papa, Do You Love Me? Lavallee, Barbara, illus. 2005. (Mama Ser.: MAMA). (ENG., Illus.). 36p. (J). (gr. -1-7). 15.99 (978-0-8118-4265-5(7)) Chronicle Bks. LLC.

Jordan, Cat. The Leaving Season. 2016. 352p. (J). (gr. 8). 17.99 (978-0-06-235137-1(0), HarperTeen) HarperCollins Pubs.

Jordan, Deloris. Did I Tell You I Love You Today? Evans, Shane W., illus. 2004. (ENG.). 32p. (J). (gr. -1-3). 18.99 (978-0-689-85271-8(1), Simon & Schuster/Paula Wiseman Bks.) Simon & Schuster/Paula Wiseman Bks.

Jordan, Sophie. Hidden. (Firelight Ser.: 3). (ENG.). (YA). (gr. 8). 2013. 288p. pap. 9.99 (978-0-06-193513-8(1)) 2012. 272p. 17.99 (978-0-06-193512-1(3)) HarperCollins Pubs.

—Unleashed. (Uninvited Ser.: 2). (YA). (gr. 8). 2016. 384p. pap. 9.99 (978-0-06-223367-7(X)) 2015. (ENG.). 368p. 17.99 (978-0-06-223371-4(8)) HarperCollins Pubs. (HarperTeen).

Joseph, Lynn. Flowers in the Sky. 2013. (ENG.). 240p. (YA). (gr. 8). 17.99 (978-0-06-029794-7(8), HarperTeen) HarperCollins Pubs.

Joyce, Melanie. I Love You Because ... Lovsin, Polona, illus. 2016. (ENG.). 24p. (J). (gr. -1-1). 16.99 (978-1-4998-0212-2(9)) Little Bee Books Inc.

Jue, Thea. Remember the Love. Lenz, Mary, illus. 2013. 36p. pap. 13.95 (978-0-9827753-3-2(4)) Interdimensional Pr.

Justesen, Kim Williams. Kiss, Kiss, Bark! 2nd ed. 2012. (ENG.). 176p. (J). (gr. 4). pap. 8.95 (978-1-933718-76-7(5)) Tanglewood Pr.

Kade, Stacey. For This Life Only. 2016. (ENG., Illus.). 320p. (YA). (gr. 9). 17.99 (978-1-4814-3248-1(6), Simon & Schuster Bks. For Young Readers) Simon & Schuster Bks. For Young Readers.

Kadohata, Cynthia. Half a World Away. 2015. (ENG., Illus.). 256p. (J). (gr. 5-9). pap. 7.99 (978-1-4424-1276-7(3), Atheneum Bks. for Young Readers) Simon & Schuster Children's Publishing.

—Half a World Away. 2014. 240p. 16.99 (978-1-4814-1806-5(8)) Simon & Schuster, Inc.

Kagawa, Julie. The Iron King. 2010. (Iron Fey Ser.: 1). lib. bdg. 20.85 (978-0-606-14909-9(0), Turtleback) Turtleback Bks.

—The Iron Knight. 2011. (Iron Fey Ser.: 4). lib. bdg. 20.85 (978-0-606-23259-3(1), Turtleback) Turtleback Bks.

—The Iron Legends. 2012. (Iron Fey Ser.: 5). lib. bdg. 20.85 (978-0-606-26516-4(3), Turtleback) Turtleback Bks.

—The Iron Traitor. 2013. (Iron Fey Ser.: 6). lib. bdg. 20.85 (978-0-606-35037-2(3), Turtleback) Turtleback Bks.

Kahaney, Amelia. The Brokenhearted. (Brokenhearted Ser.: 1). (ENG.). (YA). (gr. 8). 2014. 368p. pap. 9.99 (978-0-06-223093-5(X)) 2013. 352p. 17.99 (978-0-06-223092-8(1)) HarperCollins Pubs. (HarperTeen).

—The Invisible. 2014. (Brokenhearted Ser.: 2). (ENG.). 304p. (YA). (gr. 8). 17.99 (978-0-06-223192-5(8), HarperTeen) HarperCollins Pubs.

Kala & Kol. Where Your Love Is: For Peace Is in This Place. 2012. 60p. pap. 31.99 (978-1-4691-5926-3(0)) Xlibris Corp.

Kamio, Yoko. Boys over Flowers, Vol. 18. Kamio, Yoko, illus. 2006. (Boys over Flowers Ser.). (ENG., Illus.). 208p. pap. 9.99 (978-1-4215-0532-9(0)) Viz Media.

Kang, Lydia & Carey, Janet Lee. Catalyst. 2015. (Control Duology Ser.). (ENG.). 400p. (YA). (gr. 7). 17.99 (978-0-8037-4093-8(X), Kathy Dawson Books) Penguin Young Readers Group.

Karalius, Kimberly. Love Charms & Other Catastrophes. 2016. (Grimbaud Ser.). (ENG.). 384p. (YA). pap. 10.99 (978-1-250-08404-0(0), 9781250084040) Feiwel & Friends.

—Love Fortunes & Other Disasters. 2015. (Grimbaud Ser.). (ENG.). 368p. (YA). (gr. 7). pap. 9.99 (978-1-250-04720-5(X), 9781250047205) Feiwel & Friends.

Karst, Patrice. The Invisible String. Stevenson, Geoff, illus. 2003. 36p. (J). 16.95 (978-0-87516-734-3(9), Devorss Pubns.) DeVorss & Co.

Kasza, Keiko. A Mother for Choco. 2003. (ENG.). 30p. (J). (gr. -1 — 1). bds. 7.99 (978-0-399-24191-8(4), G.P. Putnam's Sons Books for Young Readers) Penguin Young Readers Group.

Katcher, Brian. Deacon Locke Went to Prom. 2017. 400p. (YA). (gr. 8). 17.99 (978-0-06-242252-1(9), Tegen, Katherine Bks) HarperCollins Pubs.

Kate, Lauren. Atlántida. 2015. (SPA.). 368p. pap. 10.95 (978-1-101-91062-7(3), Vintage Espanol) Knopf Doubleday Publishing Group.

—Fallen. (Fallen Ser.: Bk. 1). (ENG.). (YA). (gr. 7). 2010. 480p. pap. 10.99 (978-0-385-73893-9(3), Ember) 2009. 464p. 17.99 (978-0-385-73893-4(5), Delacorte Pr.) Random Hse. Children's Bks.

—Fallen. 2010. (Fallen Ser.: 1). lib. bdg. 22.10 (978-0-606-15168-9(0), Turtleback) Turtleback Bks.

—Fallen in Love. 2012. (Fallen Ser.). (ENG.). (YA). (gr. 7). 224p. pap. 8.99 (978-0-385-74262-7(2), Ember); 256p. 15.99 (978-0-385-74261-0(4), Delacorte Pr.) Random Hse. Children's Bks.

—Oscuros. 2011. (Vintage Espanol Ser.: Bk. 1).Tr. of Fallen. (SPA.). 416p. (YA). (gr. 5). pap. 9.95 (978-0-307-74500-2(7), Vintage Espanol) Knopf Doubleday Publishing Group.

—Pasión. 2011. (Vintage Espanol Ser.: Bk. 3).Tr. of Passion. (SPA.). 384p. (YA). (gr. 7). pap. 9.95 (978-0-307-74523-1(6), Vintage Espanol) Knopf Doubleday Publishing Group.

—Passion. (Fallen Ser.: Bk. 3). (ENG.). (YA). (gr. 7). 2012. 448p. pap. 10.99 (978-0-385-73917-7(6), Ember) 2011. 432p. 17.99 (978-0-385-73916-0(8), Delacorte Pr.) Random Hse. Children's Bks.

—Passion. 2012. (Fallen Ser.: 3). lib. bdg. 22.10 (978-0-606-26410-5(8), Turtleback) Turtleback Bks.

—Rapture. (Fallen Ser.). (ENG.). (YA). (gr. 7). 2014. 480p. pap. 10.99 (978-0-385-73919-1(2), Ember) 2012. 464p. 17.99 (978-0-385-73918-4(4), Delacorte Pr.) Random Hse. Children's Bks.

—Teardrop. 2013. 441p. (YA). (978-0-385-38372-1(X)); (978-0-385-37491-0(7)) Random House Publishing Group. (Delacorte Pr).

—Teardrop. (Teardrop Ser.). (ENG.). (YA). (gr. 7). 2014. 480p. pap. 10.99 (978-0-385-74266-5(5), Ember) 2013. 464p. 18.99 (978-0-385-74265-8(7), Delacorte Pr.) Random Hse. Children's Bks.

—Torment. (Fallen Ser.: Bk. 2). (ENG.). (YA). (gr. 7). 2011. 480p. pap. 10.99 (978-0-385-73915-3(X), Ember) 2010. 464p. 17.99 (978-0-385-73914-6(1), Delacorte Pr.) Random Hse. Children's Bks.

—Torment. 2011. (Fallen Ser.: 2). lib. bdg. 22.10 (978-0-606-22247-1(2), Turtleback) Turtleback Bks.

—Tormento. 2011. (Vintage Espanol Ser.: Bk. 2).Tr. of Torment. (SPA.). 416p. (YA). (gr. 7). pap. 9.95 (978-0-307-74512-5(0), Vintage Espanol) Knopf Doubleday Publishing Group.

—Unforgiven. (Fallen Ser.). (ENG.). 368p. (YA). (gr. 7). 2016. pap. 10.99 (978-0-385-74264-1(9), Ember) 2015. 18.99 (978-0-385-74263-4(0), Delacorte Pr.) 2015. lib. bdg. 21.99 (978-0-375-99068-7(2), Delacorte Pr.) Random Hse. Children's Bks.

Katrana, Carol. Charlie, the Christmas Camel: A Christmas Story to Remember. 2012. 120p. (gr. 4-6). pap. 16.95 (978-1-4772-7710-2(2)) AuthorHouse.

Katschke, Judy. The Facts about Flirting. 2003. (Two of a Kind Ser.: Vol. 27). (Illus.). 112p. mass mkt. 4.99 (978-0-06-009323-5(4), Harper Entertainment) HarperCollins Pubs.

Katz, Karen. Mommy Hugs. Katz, Karen, illus. 2006. (ENG., Illus.). 32p. (J). (gr. -1-3). 17.99 (978-0-689-87772-8(2), McElderry, Margaret K. Bks.) McElderry, Margaret K. Bks.

Kaufman, Amie & Spooner, Meagan. Their Fractured Light. 2016. (Starbound Ser.). (ENG.). 432p. (YA). (gr. 7-12). pap. 9.99 (978-1-4847-4783-4(6)) Hyperion Pr.

—These Broken Stars. 2013. (Starbound Ser.). (ENG., Illus.). 382p. (YA). (gr. 7-12). 17.99 (978-1-4231-7102-7(0)) Hyperion Pr.

—This Shattered World. 2014. (Starbound Trilogy). (ENG.). 400p. (YA). (gr. 7-12). 17.99 (978-1-4231-7103-4(9)) Hyperion Bks. for Children.

Kay, L. M. Frederick's Birthday Surprise. 2009. 36p. pap. 24.95 (978-1-60836-944-7(7)) America Star Bks.

Keating, Lucy. Literally. 2017. 256p. (YA). (gr. 8). 17.99 (978-0-06-238004-3(4), HarperTeen) HarperCollins Pubs.

Keil, Melissa. The Incredible Adventures of Cinnamon Girl, 1 vol. Lawrence, Mike, illus. 2016. (ENG.). 300p. (YA). (gr. 7-10). 17.95 (978-1-56145-905-6(4)) Peachtree Pubs.

Keith, Donna. I Love You All the Same, 1 vol. Edgson, Allison, illus. 2014. (ENG.). 20p. (J). bds. 9.99 (978-0-529-10204-1(8)) Nelson, Thomas Inc.

Keith, Patty J. Will You Be My Friend? Even If I Am Different from You. Keith, Patty J., photos by. 2013. (Illus.). 36p. pap. 12.95 (978-0-615-78050-4(4)) Patty's Blooming Words.

Kelly, Allison Palmer. The Power of Words. 2013. 202p. 24.95 (978-1-4759-6745-6(4)); pap. 14.95 (978-1-4759-6743-2(8)) iUniverse, Inc.

Kelly, Tara. The Foxglove Killings. 2015. (ENG.). 320p. (J). 16.99 (978-1-63375-165-1(1), 9781633751651) Entangled Publishing, LLC.

Kemmerer, Brigid. Letters to the Lost. 2017. (ENG.). 400p. (YA). 17.99 (978-1-68119-008-2(7), 9781681190082, Bloomsbury USA Childrens) Bloomsbury Publishing USA.

Kenneally, Miranda. Breathe, Annie, Breathe. (Hundred Oaks Ser.: Bk. 5). (ENG.). (YA). (gr. 8-12). 2015. 336p. pap. 9.99 (978-1-4926-0866-0(1), 9781492608660) 2014. 320p. 16.99 (978-1-4022-8479-3(9), 9781402284793) Sourcebooks, Inc.

—Coming up for Air. 2017. (Hundred Oaks Ser.: Bk. 8). (ENG.). 304p. (YA). (gr. 8-12). pap. 10.99 (978-1-4926-3011-1(X)) Sourcebooks, Inc.

—Defending Taylor. 2016. (Hundred Oaks Ser.: Bk. 7). (ENG.). 304p. (YA). (gr. 8-12). pap. 10.99 (978-1-4926-3008-1(X), 9781492630081) Sourcebooks, Inc.

—Jesse's Girl. 2015. (Hundred Oaks Ser.: Bk. 6). (ENG.). 304p. (YA). (gr. 8-12). 16.99 (978-1-4022-8482-3(9), 9781402284823) Sourcebooks, Inc.

—Racing Savannah, 1 vol. unabr. ed. 2015. (Hundred Oaks Ser.: Bk. 4). (ENG.). (YA). (gr. 7-9). 14.99 (978-1-5012-1560-5(4), 9781501215605, Audible Studios on Brilliance Audio) Brilliance Publishing, Inc.

—Racing Savannah. 2013. (Hundred Oaks Ser.: Bk. 4). (ENG.). 304p. (YA). (gr. 7-12). pap. 9.99 (978-1-4022-8476-2(4), 9781402284762) Sourcebooks, Inc.

Kennedy, C. Slaying Isidore's Dragons. (ENG., Illus.). (J). 2016. 32.99 **(978-1-63533-073-1(4))** 2015. 350p. pap. 17.99 (978-1-63476-001-0(8)) Dreamspinner Pr. (Harmony Ink Pr.).

Kennedy, Katie. Learning to Swear in America. 2016. (ENG.). 352p. (YA). 17.99 (978-1-61963-909-6(2), 9781619639096, Bloomsbury USA Childrens) Bloomsbury Publishing USA.

Kennedy, Patricia Moran. The Loving Tree A Story of Love, Loss, & Transformation for All Ages. 2004. (Illus.). 64p. (YA). (gr. 5-18). per. 14.95 (978-0-9749848-0-3(9)) Dancer's Publishing.

Kennedy, Richard. Crazy in Love. Date not set. 48p. (J). (gr. -1-3). 14.99 (978-0-06-027213-5(9)); lib. bdg. 15.89 (978-0-06-027214-2(7)) HarperCollins Pubs. (Geringer, Laura Book).

Kenyon, Sherrilyn. Inferno. 2013. (Chronicles of Nick Ser.: 4). (ENG.). 464p. (YA). (gr. 7). 18.99 (978-1-250-00283-9(4), 9781250002839, St. Martin's Griffin) St. Martin's Pr.

Kephart, Beth. Undercover. 2009. (ENG.). 304p. (YA). (gr. 8). pap. 8.99 (978-0-06-123895-6(3), HarperTeen) HarperCollins Pubs.

Kiely, Brendan. The Last True Love Story. 2016. (ENG., Illus.). 288p. (YA). (gr. 9). 17.99 (978-1-4814-2988-7(4), McElderry, Margaret K. Bks.) McElderry, Margaret K. Bks.

—Last True Love Story. 2017. (ENG., Illus.). 288p. (YA). (gr. 9). pap. 11.99 (978-1-4814-2989-4(2), McElderry, Margaret K. Bks.) McElderry, Margaret K. Bks.

Kimaya. All the Flavours of Love. 2012. 40p. pap. 13.95 (978-1-4525-0649-4(3)) Balboa Pr.

Kimmelman, Leslie. How Do I Love You? McCue, Lisa, illus. 2005. 32p. (J). lib. bdg. 16.89 (978-0-06-001201-4(3)) HarperCollins Pubs.

King, A. S. Ask the Passengers. 2013. (ENG.). 336p. (YA). (gr. 10-17). pap. 10.99 (978-0-316-19467-9(0)) Little, Brown Bks. for Young Readers.

King, Deja. Ride Wit' Me: A Novel. 2009. 151p. (YA). pap. (978-0-9755811-9-3(8)) King Production, A.

Kirby, Jessi. Golden. (ENG.). 288p. (YA). (gr. 7). 2014. pap. 9.99 (978-1-4424-5218-3(8)) 2013. 16.99 (978-1-4424-5216-9(1)) Simon & Schuster Bks. For Young Readers. (Simon & Schuster Bks. For Young Readers).

—Things We Know by Heart. 304p. (YA). (gr. 9). 2016. pap. 9.99 (978-0-06-229944-4(1)) 2015. (ENG.). 17.99 (978-0-06-229943-7(3)) HarperCollins Pubs. (HarperTeen).

Kirchner, Janette. I Love You So Much. 2011. 20p. pap. 24.95 (978-1-4137-5952-5(1)) America Star Bks.

Kirkpatrick, Teresa. Roscoe's Forest Adventures. 2008. 177p. pap. 24.95 (978-1-60672-328-9(6)) America Star Bks.

Klein, Jen. Shuffle, Repeat. (ENG.). (YA). (gr. 7). 2017. 352p. pap. 9.99 **(978-0-553-50985-4(3)**, Ember) 2016. 336p. 17.99 (978-0-553-50982-3(9), Random Hse. Bks. for Young Readers) Random Hse. Children's Bks.

Klise, James. Love Drugged. 2010. (ENG.). 312p. (YA). (gr. 7-18). pap. 9.95 (978-0-7387-2175-0(1), Flux) North Star Editions.

Klocek-Lim, Christine. Disintegrate. 2013. 206p. pap. (978-1-77130-367-5(0)) Evernight Publishing.

Koehn, Wendel. Love Problematic: And Other Stories. 2012. 24p. pap. 14.93 (978-1-4669-1851-1(9)) Trafford Publishing.

Kollar, J. P. Three Tomato Brand. 2005. 127p. per. 12.95 (978-1-59879-076-4(5)) Lifevest Publishing, Inc.

Konen, Leah. The Romantics. 2016. (ENG.). 336p. (YA). (gr. 8-17). 18.95 (978-1-4197-2193-9(3), Amulet Bks.) Abrams, Inc.

Konigsburg, E. L. Journey to an 800 Number. 2008. (ENG.). 160p. (J). (gr. 4-8). pap. 6.99 (978-1-4169-5875-8(4), Atheneum Bks. for Young Readers) Simon & Schuster Children's Publishing.

Koops, Sheena. Voice of the Valley, 1 vol. 2006. (ENG.). 224p. (YA). (gr. 8-12). per. 8.95 (978-1-55143-514-5(4)) Orca Bk. Pubs. USA.

Kouga, Yun. Crown of Love, Vol. 1. 2010. (ENG., Illus.). 192p. pap. 9.99 (978-1-4215-3193-9(3)) Viz Media.

—Crown of Love, Vol. 2. 2010. (ENG., Illus.). 200p. pap. 9.99 (978-1-4215-3194-6(1)) Viz Media.

Krackow, Eric T. & Krackow, Krackow. Bill the Snowman, 1 vol. 2009. (ENG., Illus.). 64p. (J). 16.99 (978-0-7643-3219-7(8), 9780764332197) Schiffer Publishing, Ltd.

Kraevskaya, Tatiyana. Wings for Little Turtle. 2012. 16p. pap. 12.68 (978-1-4669-0733-1(9)) Trafford Publishing.

Kranz, Linda. Love You When. 2013. (ENG., Illus.). 32p. (J). (gr. -1-1). 7.95 (978-1-58979-907-3(0)) Taylor Trade Publishing.

Krauss, Ruth. Big & Little. Szilagyi, Mary, illus. 2003. (J). pap. 12.95 (978-0-590-40698-7(1)) Scholastic, Inc.

Krokos, Dan. False Future. 2014. (False Memory Novel Ser.). (ENG., Illus.). 320p. (YA). (gr. 9-17). 17.99 (978-1-4231-4987-3(4)) Hyperion Bks. for Children.

Krulik, Nancy. Puppy Love. 2011. (Romantic Comedies Ser.). (ENG.). 224p. (YA). (gr. 7). pap. 12.99 (978-1-4424-3079-2(6), Simon Pulse) Simon Pulse.

—Ripped at the Seams. 2004. (Romantic Comedies Ser.). (ENG.). 336p. (YA). (gr. 9). mass mkt. 6.99 (978-0-689-86771-2(9), Simon Pulse) Simon Pulse.

—She's Got the Beat. 2010. (Romantic Comedies Ser.). (ENG.). 320p. (YA). (gr. 9). pap. 14.99 (978-1-4424-1419-8(7), Simon Pulse) Simon Pulse.

Kuper, Tonya. Anomaly. 2014. (Schrodinger's Consortium Ser.: 1). (ENG.). 400p. (YA). (gr. 7-12). pap. 9.99 (978-1-62266-405-4(1), 9781622664054) Entangled Publishing, LLC.

Lacek, Carolyn. Destiny Awakened. 2009. 52p. pap. 18.25 (978-1-60860-736-5(4), Eloquent Bks.) Strategic Book Publishing & Rights Agency (SBPRA).

LaCour, Nina. Everything Leads to You. 2014. (ENG.). 272p. (YA). (gr. 9). 17.99 (978-0-525-42588-5(8), Dutton Books for Young Readers) Penguin Young Readers Group.

LaFevers, Robin. Dark Triumph. (His Fair Assassin Ser.: 2). (ENG.). 400p. (YA). (gr. 9). 2014. pap. 9.99 (978-0-544-22720-0(4), HMH Books For Young Readers) 2013. 17.99 (978-0-547-62838-7(2)) Houghton Mifflin Harcourt Publishing Co.

—Dark Triumph, 10 vols. 2013. (His Fair Assassin Ser.: 2). (YA). (978-1-4640-2397-2(2)) Recorded Bks., Inc.

LaFleur, John & Dubin, Shawn. Dreary & Naughty: Friday the 13th of February, 1 vol. 2013. (ENG., Illus.). 64p. (J). 14.99 (978-0-7643-4495-4(1), 9780764344954) Schiffer Publishing, Ltd.

Lake, Nick. Whisper to Me. 2016. (ENG.). 544p. (YA). 17.99 (978-1-61963-456-5(2), 9781619634565, Bloomsbury USA Childrens) Bloomsbury Publishing USA.

LaMarche, Una. Like No Other. 2015. (ENG.). 368p. (YA). (gr. 7). pap. 9.99 (978-1-59514-675-5(X), Razorbill) Penguin Young Readers Group.

—Like No Other. 2015. lib. bdg. 20.85 (978-0-606-36748-6(9)) Turtleback Bks.

Lambert, Jonny. Special You. Lambert, Jonny, illus. 2016. (ENG., Illus.). 24p. (J). (gr. -1-1). bds. 9.99 (978-1-58925-238-7(1)) Tiger Tales.

Lambert, Teres. Mommy, Do You Love Me? 2008. 20p. pap. 24.95 (978-1-60441-911-5(3)) America Star Bks.

Landers, Melissa. Invaded. 2015. (Alienated Ser.). (ENG.). 368p. (YA). (gr. 7-12). 17.99 (978-1-4231-6949-9(2)) Hyperion Bks. for Children.

—Starfall. 2017. (Starflight Ser.). (ENG.). 368p. (YA). (gr. 9-17). 17.99 (978-1-4847-5025-4(X)) Hyperion Bks. for Children.

—Starflight. 2016. (ENG., Illus.). 364p. (YA). (gr. 7-12). 17.99 (978-1-4847-2324-1(4)) Hyperion Pr.

Lane, Amy. Triane's Son Fighting. 2nd ed. 2016. (ENG., Illus.). (J). 32.99 **(978-1-63477-982-1(7))** 2014. (Bitter Moon Ser.: Bk. 3). 350p. pap. 17.99 (978-1-62798-340-2(6)) Dreamspinner Pr. (Harmony Ink Pr.).

Lane, Dakota. Orpheus Obsession. 2005. (Illus.). 288p. (J). lib. bdg. 17.89 (978-0-06-074174-7(0), HarperTeen) HarperCollins Pubs.

—The Orpheus Obsession. 2008. (ENG., Illus.). 288p. (YA). (gr. 9). pap. 8.99 (978-0-06-074175-4(9), HarperTeen) HarperCollins Pubs.

Lane, Ronald. Avina's Song: A Children's Story. 2007. (ENG.). 48p. per. 16.95 (978-1-4241-6252-9(1)) America Star Bks.

Lange, Sue. The Perpetual Motion Club. 2013. 208p. pap. 14.95 (978-0-9887488-6-6(X)) Perpetual Motion Machine Publishing.

Lara, Mike. A Boy & a Horse. 2011. 40p. pap. 21.99 (978-1-4628-8024-9(X)) Xlibris Corp.

Lark, Jane. I Found You. 2014. (ENG.). 392p. pap. 11.99 **(978-0-00-757776-7(1)**, HarperImpulse) HarperCollins Pubs. Ltd. GBR. Dist: HarperCollins Pubs.

Larkin, Susan. All the Ways I Love You. Trotter, Stuart, illus. 2012. 16p. (J). (978-1-4351-3857-5(0)) Barnes & Noble, Inc.

Larsen, Angela Sage. Broken Record, Bk. 4. 2013. (Fifties Chix Ser.: 4). (ENG., Illus.). 200p. (YA). pap. 9.95 (978-1-60746-446-4(2), Premiere) FastPrncl, Inc.

—Keeping Secrets, Bk. 2. 2012. (Fifties Chix Ser.: 2). (ENG.). 220p. (YA). pap. 9.95 (978-1-60746-367-2(9), Premiere) FastPrncl, Inc.

Larson, Angela. Anthony Smocchiano: First Loves. 2012. pap. (978-1-4507-7998-2(0)) Independent Pub.

Larson, Heidi. Love the Lord Your God! 2012. 32p. pap. 13.99 (978-1-4624-0295-3(X), Inspiring Voices) Author Solutions, Inc.

Laskin, Pamela L. Ronit & Jamil. 2017. 192p. (YA). (gr. 8). 17.99 (978-0-06-245854-4(X), Tegen, Katherine Bks) HarperCollins Pubs.

Laudati, Joe. Faela: A Fairy's Tale. 2008. 190p. pap. 14.50 (978-0-615-20324-9(8)) Laudati, Joe.

Laura Grey Wahl. The Magic Town of Stuart Easterly. 2009. 16p. pap. 15.00 (978-1-4389-4703-7(8)) AuthorHouse.

Laure, Estelle. This Raging Light. 2015. (ENG.). 288p. (YA). (gr. 9). 17.99 (978-0-544-53429-2(8), HMH Books For Young Readers) Houghton Mifflin Harcourt Publishing Co.

Laurens, Jennifer. Falling for Romeo. 2007. (YA). per. 12.95 (978-1-933963-94-5(8)) Grove Creek Publishing, LLC.

—Magic Hands. 2007. (YA). per. 12.95 (978-1-933963-97-6(2)) Grove Creek Publishing, LLC.

Laurie, Victoria. Forever, Again. 2016. (ENG.). 368p. (YA). (gr. 7-12). 17.99 (978-1-4847-0009-9(0)) Hyperion Bks. for Children.

Lawler, Janet. If Kisses Were Colors. Jay, Alison, illus. (ENG.). (J). (gr. -1 — 1). 2010. 22p. bds. 6.99 (978-0-8037-3530-9(8)) 2003. 32p. 16.99 (978-0-8037-2617-8(1)) Penguin Young Readers Group. (Dial Bks).

—Love Is Real. Brown, Anna, illus. 2013. (ENG.). 32p. (J). (gr. -1-3). 15.99 (978-0-06-224170-2(2)) HarperCollins Pubs.

Lawrence, Kelly. Unconditional. 2014. (ENG.). 162p. (YA). (gr. 8-17). pap. 11.95 (978-1-78279-394-6(1), Lodestone Bks.) Hunt, John Publishing Ltd. GBR. Dist: National Bk. Network.

Lawrence, Theo. Mystic City. (Mystic City Trilogy Ser.). (ENG.). 416p. (YA). (gr. 7). 2014. pap. 9.99 (978-0-385-74161-3(8), Ember) 2012. 17.99 (978-0-385-74160-6(X), Delacorte Pr.) Random Hse. Children's Bks.

Lawson, Shandy. The Loop. 2014. (ENG.). 208p. (YA). (gr. 7-12). pap. 8.99 (978-1-4231-6948-2(4)) Hyperion Bks. for Children.

Lazebnik, Claire. The Last Best Kiss. 2014. (ENG.). 384p. (YA). (gr. 8). pap. 9.99 (978-0-06-225228-9(3), HarperTeen) HarperCollins Pubs.

—Wrong about the Guy. 2015. (ENG.). 368p. (YA). (gr. 8). pap. 9.99 (978-0-06-225230-2(5), HarperTeen) HarperCollins Pubs.

Le Blanc, Lennie. The Minnesota Summer. 2011. 116p. (gr. 4-6). pap. 10.95 (978-1-4620-3887-9(5)) iUniverse, Inc.

Leathers, Rain. Purple Mountain. 2008. 36p. pap. 20.95 (978-1-4327-2685-0(4)) Outskirts Pr., Inc.

Leavitt, Martine. Keturah & Lord Death. (ENG.). (YA). 2012. 224p. (gr. 9-12). pap. 9.95 (978-1-59078-949-0(0)) 2006. 216p. (gr. 7-7). 16.95 (978-1-932425-29-1(2), Front Street) Boyds Mills Pr.

Leder, Meg. The Museum of Heartbreak. 2017. (ENG., Illus.). 288p. (YA). (gr. 7). pap. 10.99 (978-1-4814-3211-5(7), Simon Pulse) Simon Pulse.

—The Museum of Heartbreak. Wachter, Jill, photos by. 2016. (ENG., Illus.). 288p. (YA). (gr. 9). 17.99 (978-1-4814-3210-8(9), Simon Pulse) Simon Pulse.

Lee, Calee M. I Love You! Tharp, Tricia, illus. 2013. 32p. pap. 9.99 (978-1-62395-471-0(1)) Xist Publishing.

Lee, Darrien. 16 Going on 21. 2008. (ENG., Illus.). 288p. (YA). (gr. 9). 9.95 (978-1-933967-71-4(4), Urban Renaissance) Kensington Publishing Corp.

Lee, Edith. Romeo & Julie Square. 2012. 28p. pap. (978-0-9881235-0-2(9)) Bound Publishing.

Lee, M. C. You Don't Know Jack. 2016. (ENG., Illus.). (J). 24.99 **(978-1-63477-999-9(1)**, Harmony Ink Pr.) Dreamspinner Pr.

Lee, SangEun. 13th Boy, 12 vols., Vol. 5. 2010. (13th Boy Ser.: 5). (ENG., Illus.). 192p. (YA). (gr. 8-17). pap. 10.99 (978-0-7595-2998-4(1), Yen Pr.) Orbit.

Leech, Caroline. Wait for Me. 2017. 384p. (YA). (gr. 8). 17.99 (978-0-06-245988-6(0), HarperTeen) HarperCollins Pubs.

Lefall, Kathy. Stargaze. 2003. 346p. (YA). pap. 18.95 (978-0-595-26878-8(1)) iUniverse, Inc.

L'Engle, Madeleine. A House Like a Lotus. 2012. (ENG.). 336p. (YA). (gr. 7-12). pap. 11.99 (978-0-312-54798-1(6), 9780312547981) Square Fish.

Lenzi, Christy. Stone Field. 2016. (ENG.). 320p. (YA). 17.99 (978-1-62672-069-5(X), 9781626720695) Roaring Brook Pr.

Leonard, Niall. Shredder. 2015. (ENG.). 384p. (YA). (gr. 9). 17.99 *(978-0-385-74365-5(3),* Delacorte Pr.) Random Hse. Children's Bks.

LeRoye, Dee. Crossfire. 2003. 137p. (YA). per. 5.99 *(978-0-9727056-0-8(0))* Dakota Rose.

Leung, Helen. Toni. 2006. 251p. pap. 27.95 *(978-1-4137-8990-4(0))* PublishAmerica, Inc.

Levenseller, Tricia. Daughter of the Pirate King. 2017. (Daughter of the Pirate King Ser.). (ENG.). 320p. (YA). 17.99 *(978-1-250-09596-1(4),* 9781250095961) Feiwel & Friends.

Levithan, David. Another Day. 2015. (ENG.). 336p. (YA). (gr. 7). lib. bdg. 20.99 *(978-0-385-75621-1(6));* 17.99 *(978-0-385-75620-4(8))* Random Hse. Children's Bks. (Knopf Bks. for Young Readers).

—Every Day. 2015. (KOR.). 424p. (J). pap. *(978-89-374-3204-0(8))* Min-eumsa Publishing Co., Ltd.

—Every Day. (ENG.). (YA). (gr. 7). 2013. 400p. pap. 9.99 *(978-0-307-93189-4(7),* Ember) 2012. 336p. 17.99 *(978-0-307-93188-7(9),* Knopf Bks. for Young Readers) Random Hse. Children's Bks.

—Every Day. 2013. lib. bdg. 20.85 *(978-0-606-32238-6(8),* Turtleback) Turtleback Bks.

—Hold Me Closer: The Tiny Cooper Story. 2015. (ENG.). 208p. (YA). (gr. 9). 17.99 *(978-0-525-42884-8(4),* Dutton Books for Young Readers) Penguin Young Readers Group.

—Hold Me Closer: The Tiny Cooper Story. 2016. lib. bdg. 22.10 *(978-0-606-38390-5(5))* Turtleback Bks.

—How They Met & Other Stories. 2009. (ENG.). 256p. (YA). (gr. 9). pap. 9.99 *(978-0-375-84323-5(X),* Knopf Bks. for Young Readers) Random Hse. Children's Bks.

—Marly's Ghost. Selznick, Brian, illus. 2007. (ENG.). 208p. (YA). (gr. 7-18). 7.99 *(978-0-14-240912-1(X),* Speak) Penguin Young Readers Group.

—Two Boys Kissing. (ENG.). (YA). (gr. 9). 2015. 224p. pap. 9.99 *(978-0-307-93191-7(9),* Ember) 2013. 208p. 16.99 *(978-0-307-93190-0(0),* Knopf Bks. for Young Readers) Random Hse. Children's Bks.

—Two Boys Kissing. 2015. lib. bdg. 20.85 *(978-0-606-37273-2(3))* Turtleback Bks.

Levithan, David & LaCour, Nina. You Know Me Well. 2016. (ENG.). 256p. (YA). 18.99 *(978-1-250-09864-1(5),* 9781250098641, St. Martin's Griffin) St. Martin's Pr.

Levy, Michelle. Not after Everything. 2015. (ENG.). 336p. (YA). (gr. 9-12). 17.99 *(978-0-8037-4158-4(8),* Dial Bks) Penguin Publishing Group.

Lewis, Linda. All for the Love of That Boy. 2007. (ENG.). 224p. (YA). (gr. 7). pap. 12.95 *(978-1-4169-6142-0(9),* Simon Pulse) Simon Pulse.

—Loving Two Is Hard to Do. 2008. (ENG.). 160p. (YA). (gr. 7). pap. 8.95 *(978-1-4169-7534-2(9),* Simon Pulse) Simon Pulse.

—My Heart Belongs to That Boy. 2008. (ENG.). 176p. (Orig.). (YA). (gr. 7). pap. 9.95 *(978-1-4169-7536-6(5),* Simon Pulse) Simon Pulse.

—We Hate Everything but Boys. 2008. (ENG.). 160p. (YA). (gr. 7). pap. 8.95 *(978-1-4169-7537-3(3),* Simon Pulse) Simon Pulse.

—We Love Only Older Boys. 2008. (ENG.). 160p. (Orig.). (YA). (gr. 7). pap. 8.95 *(978-1-4169-7535-9(7),* Simon Pulse) Simon Pulse.

Lewis, Mark. Is There Life after Boys? 2007. (ENG.). 176p. (YA). (gr. 7). pap. 10.95 *(978-1-4169-6143-7(7),* Simon Pulse) Simon Pulse.

Lewis, Paeony. I'll Always Love You. Ives, Penny, illus. 2013. (ENG.). 32p. (J). pap. *(978-1-58925-441-1(4))* Tiger Tales.

Lewis, Stewart. You Have Seven Messages. 2012. (ENG.). 304p. (YA). (gr. 7). pap. 9.99 *(978-0-385-74029-6(8),* Ember) Random Hse. Children's Bks.

Lewman, David. Lovestruck! Fruchter, Jason, illus. 2004. (Fairly Oddparents Ser.). (J). (gr. -1-3). 11.15 *(978-0-7569-1992-4(4))* Perfection Learning Corp.

Liang, Kuan & Yung, Kao. Magic Lover's Tower, Vol. 1. 2008. (ENG., Illus.). 176p. (YA). pap. 9.95 *(978-1-59796-153-0(1))* DrMaster Pubns. Inc.

Liberty, Anita. The Center of the Universe: Yep, That Would Be Me. 2008. (ENG.). 304p. (YA). (gr. 7-18). pap. 9.99 *(978-1-4169-5789-8(8),* Simon Pulse) Simon Pulse.

Liggett, Kim. Blood & Salt. 2015. (ENG.). 352p. (YA). (gr. 9-12). 17.99 *(978-0-399-16648-8(3),* G.P. Putnam's Sons Books for Young Readers) Penguin Young Readers Group.

Lilly, Suzanne. Untellable. 2013. 158p. pap. 9.99 *(978-1-62237-218-8(2))* Turquoise Morning Pr.

Lim, Rebecca. Afterlight. 2016. (ENG., Illus.). 240p. (gr. 8). 11.95 *(978-1-925240-49-8(5))* Text Publishing Co. AUS. Dist: Consortium Bk. Sales & Distribution.

Limke, Jeff. Tristan & Isolde: The Warrior & the Princess [A British Legend]. Randall, Ron, illus. 2009. (Graphic Myths & Legends Ser.). (ENG.). 48p. (gr. 4-8). pap. 8.95 *(978-1-58013-889-5(6))* Lerner Publishing Group.

Lindner, April. Catherine. 2014. (ENG.). 336p. (YA). (gr. 10-17). pap. 10.00 *(978-0-316-19693-2(2),* Poppy) Little, Brown Bks. for Young Readers.

—Jane. 2011. (ENG.). 400p. (YA). (gr. 10-17). pap. 8.99 *(978-0-316-08419-2(0),* Poppy) Little, Brown Bks. for Young Readers.

—Love, Lucy. (ENG.). 304p. (YA). (gr. 10-17). 2016. pap. 9.99 *(978-0-316-40068-8(8))* 2015. 18.00 *(978-0-316-40069-5(6))* Little, Brown Bks. for Young Readers. (Poppy).

Lindquist, N. J. A Friend in Need. 2016. (Circle of Friends Ser.: Vol. 3). (ENG., Illus.). (YA). pap. ***(978-1-927692-06-6(7))*** That's Life! Communications.

—More Than a Friend. 2016. (Circle of Friends Ser.: Vol. 4). (ENG., Illus.). (YA). pap. ***(978-1-927692-07-3(5))*** That's Life! Communications.

Lindsey, Julie Anne. What She Wanted. 2016. (ENG., Illus.). 220p. (J). pap. 15.00 *(978-1-60183-489-8(6))* Kensington Publishing Corp.

Lindsey, Mary. Fragile Spirits. 2014. (ENG.). 320p. (YA). (gr. 7). 17.99 *(978-0-399-16186-5(4),* Philomel Bks.) Penguin Young Readers Group.

Lindstrom, Eric. A Tragic Kind of Wonderful. 2017. (ENG.). 288p. (YA). (gr. 10-17). 17.99 *(978-0-316-26006-0(1),* Poppy) Little, Brown Bks. for Young Readers.

Linka, Catherine. A Girl Called Fearless. 2014. (ENG.). 368p. (YA). (gr. 7). 18.99 *(978-1-250-03929-3(0),* 9781250039293, St. Martin's Griffin) St. Martin's Pr.

Little, Kimberley Griffiths. Returned. 2017. (Forbidden Ser.: 3). 384p. (YA). (gr. 9). 17.99 *(978-0-06-219504-3(2))* HarperCollins Pubs.

Livingston, Lesley. Starling, No. 1. 2012. (Starling Trilogy Ser.: 1). (ENG.). 352p. (YA). (gr. 8). 17.99 *(978-0-06-206307-6(3),* HarperTeen) HarperCollins Pubs.

Lloyd-Caldwell, Marian. Dancing Watermelon Babies & Mr Mouse's Good Deed. 2008. 44p. pap. 18.49 *(978-1-4343-9555-9(3))* AuthorHouse.

Lloyd-Jones, Emily. The Hearts We Sold. 2017. (ENG.). 400p. (YA). (gr. 10-17). 17.99 ***(978-0-316-31459-6(5))*** Little Brown & Co.

Lloyd-Jones, Sally. Just Because You're Mine. Endersby, Frank, illus. 2011. (ENG.). 32p. (J). (gr. -1-2). 16.99 *(978-0-06-201476-4(5))* HarperCollins Pubs.

Lo, Malinda. Adaptation. 2013. (ENG.). 416p. (YA). (gr. 10-17). pap. 10.00 *(978-0-316-19798-4(X))* Little, Brown Bks. for Young Readers.

—Ash. 2010. (ENG.). 272p. (gr. 10-17). pap. 10.99 *(978-0-316-04010-5(X))* Little, Brown Bks. for Young Readers.

—Huntress. 2012. (ENG.). 416p. (YA). (gr. 10-17). pap. 11.99 *(978-0-316-03999-4(3))* Little, Brown Bks. for Young Readers.

—Inheritance. 2014. (ENG.). 480p. (YA). (gr. 10-17). pap. 25.99 *(978-0-316-19799-1(8))* Little, Brown Bks. for Young Readers.

Lockhart, E. We Were Liars. 2014. (Illus.). 227p. (YA). *(978-0-385-39009-5(2),* Delacorte Pr) Random House Publishing Group.

—We Were Liars. (ENG., (YA). (gr. 7). 2014. Illus.). 240p. 17.99 *(978-0-385-74126-2(X))* 2017. 272p. 18.99 ***(978-1-5247-6458-6(2))*** Random Hse. Children's Bks. (Delacorte Pr.).

London, Kiara. Kiss Cam. 2016. (ENG.). 272p. (YA). pap. 9.99 *(978-1-250-07096-8(1),* 9781250070968) Feiwel & Friends.

Long, Ruth Frances. The Treachery of Beautiful Things. 2013. (ENG.). 384p. (YA). (gr. 7). pap. 9.99 *(978-0-14-242606-7(7),* Speak) Penguin Young Readers Group.

Lopez, Patricia A. Carly & Boey. 2009. 56p. pap. 16.95 *(978-1-61546-836-2(6))* America Star Bks.

Lord, Emery. The Names They Gave Us. 2017. (ENG.). 400p. (YA). 17.99 *(978-1-61963-958-4(0),* 9781619639584, Bloomsbury USA Childrens) Bloomsbury Publishing USA.

—Open Road Summer. 2015. (ENG.). 368p. (YA). (gr. 7). pap. 9.99 *(978-0-8027-3801-1(X),* 9780802738011, Bloomsbury USA Childrens) Bloomsbury Publishing USA.

—When We Collided. 2016. (ENG.). 352p. (YA). 17.99 *(978-1-61963-845-7(2),* 9781619638457, Bloomsbury USA Childrens) Bloomsbury Publishing USA.

Lore, Pittacus. I Am Number Four. (YA). (gr. 9). 2016. (Lorien Legacies: the Lost Files Ser.). 416p. pap. 9.99 *(978-0-06-238771-4(5))* 2011. (Lorien Legacies Ser.: 1). (ENG.). 496p. pap. 9.99 *(978-0-06-196957-7(5))* 2010. (Lorien Legacies Ser.: 1). (ENG.). 448p. 17.99 *(978-0-06-196955-3(9))* 2011. (Lorien Legacies Ser.: 1). (ENG.). 496p. pap. 9.99 *(978-0-06-211655-0(X))* 2011. (Lorien Legacies Ser.: 1). (ENG.). 480p. 17.99 *(978-0-06-202624-8(0))* HarperCollins Pubs.

—I Am Number Four. 2009. (Lorien Legacies Ser.: Bk. 1). 11.04 *(978-0-7848-3715-3(5),* Everbind) Marco Bk. Co.

—I Am Number Four. 2011. (I Am Number Four Ser.: Vol. 1). (ENG.). 440p. (gr. 9-12). 20.00 *(978-1-61383-207-3(9))* Perfection Learning Corp.

—I Am Number Four. 2011. (Lorien Legacies Ser.: 1). (YA). lib. bdg. 20.85 *(978-0-606-23545-7(0),* Turtleback) Turtleback Bks.

—I Am Number Four: The Lost Files: Rebel Allies. 2015. (Lorien Legacies: the Lost Files Ser.). (ENG.). 416p. (YA). (gr. 9). pap. 9.99 *(978-0-06-236404-3(9))* HarperCollins Pubs.

—I Am Number Four: The Lost Files: Secret Histories. 2013. (Lorien Legacies: the Lost Files Ser.). (ENG.). 416p. (YA). (gr. 9). pap. 9.99 *(978-0-06-222367-8(4))* HarperCollins Pubs.

—Secret Histories. 2013. (Lorien Legacies: the Lost Files Ser.). (YA). lib. bdg. 20.85 *(978-0-606-31823-5(2),* Turtleback) Turtleback Bks.

Lorentzen, Bent. Krona: Dragons of Nistala. 2009. 266p. (J). pap. 18.95 *(978-1-60619-091-3(1))* Twilight Times Bks.

Loughran, Kelley. A Crab Called Mouse. 2006. (Illus.). (J). (gr. -1-3). pap. 9.50 *(978-0-9787995-2-6(6))* High-Pitched Hum Inc.

Love in Bloom. 64p. (YA). (gr. 6-12). pap. *(978-0-8224-2380-5(4))* Globe Fearon Educational Publishing.

Love, Jessica. In Real Life: A Novel. 2016. (ENG.). 240p. (YA). 18.99 *(978-1-250-06471-4(6),* 9781250064714, St. Martin's Griffin) St. Martin's Pr.

Love, Katie. Fruit to Live By..., 1 vol. 2009. 62p. pap. 16.95 *(978-1-60836-122-9(5))* PublishAmerica, Inc.

Lu, Marie. Champion. 2013. (Legend Trilogy: 3). (ENG.). 384p. (YA). (gr. 7). 18.99 *(978-0-399-25677-6(6),* G.P. Putnam's Sons Books for Young Readers) Penguin Publishing Group.

—Champion. 2014. (Legend Ser.: 3). (ENG.). 416p. (YA). (gr. 7). pap. 9.99 *(978-0-14-751228-4(X),* Speak) Penguin Young Readers Group.

Luder, Doreen. Dax the Last Dragon. 2012. 24p. pap. 24.95 *(978-1-62709-988-2(3))* America Star Bks.

Lund, Fiauna. Indigo. 2013. 268p. pap. 13.99 *(978-1-936850-82-2(6))* Rhemalda Publishing.

Lundquist, Jenny. The Opal Crown. 2014. (ENG.). 368p. (YA). (gr. 2-17). pap. 9.95 *(978-0-7624-5422-8(9),* Running Pr. Kids) Running Pr. Bk. Pubs.

Luper, Eric. Seth Baumgartner's Love Manifesto. 2010. (ENG.). 304p. (YA). (gr. 8-18). 16.99 *(978-0-06-182753-2(3))* HarperCollins Pubs.

Lyles, Whitney. Love Off-Limits. 2009. (Romantic Comedies Ser.). (ENG.). 304p. (YA). (gr. 7-18). mass mkt. 6.99 *(978-1-4169-7508-3(X),* Simon Pulse) Simon Pulse.

Lynch, Janet Nichols. Addicted to Her. 2010. (ENG.). 256p. (YA). (gr. 7-18). pap. 17.95 *(978-0-8234-2186-2(4))* Holiday Hse., Inc.

Lynn, Kelly. The Princess Transformation, 1 vol. 2010. 132p. pap. 24.95 *(978-1-4512-1417-8(0))* America Star Bks.

Lynn, Tracy. Snow: A Retelling of Snow White & the Seven Dwarfs. 2006. (Once upon a Time Ser.). (ENG.). 272p. (YA). (gr. 9-12). mass mkt. 7.99 *(978-1-4169-4015-9(4),* Simon Pulse) Simon Pulse.

Lyons, C. J. Watched. 2014. (ENG.). 320p. (YA). (gr. 8-12). 16.99 *(978-1-4022-8548-6(5),* 9781402285486) Sourcebooks, Inc.

Lytton, Deborah. Silence. 2015. (ENG.). 320p. (YA). (gr. 7). 17.99 *(978-1-60907-945-1(0),* Shadow Mountain) Shadow Mountain Publishing.

Ma, Jyoti & Devi, Chandra. Sparkling Together: Starbright & His Earthling Friends. 2004. (ENG., Illus.). 96p. (J). pap. 19.95 *(978-0-932040-54-1(3),* 9780932040541) Integral Yoga Pubns.

Maas, Sarah J. A Court of Thorns & Roses. (Court of Thorns & Roses Ser.). (ENG.). (YA). 2017. 56.97 ***(978-1-68119-774-6(X),*** 9781681197746) 2016. 448p. (gr. 9). pap. 10.99 *(978-1-61963-518-0(6),* 9781619635180) 2015. 432p. (gr. 9). 18.99 *(978-1-61963-444-2(9),* 9781619634442) Bloomsbury Publishing USA. (Bloomsbury USA Childrens).

—A Court of Thorns & Roses. 2016. lib. bdg. 22.10 *(978-0-606-38548-0(7))* Turtleback Bks.

—Crown of Midnight. (Throne of Glass Ser.: 2). (ENG.). (YA). (gr. 9). 2014. 448p. pap. 10.99 *(978-1-61963-064-2(8),* 9781619630642) 2013. (Illus.). 432p. 18.99 *(978-1-61963-062-8(1),* 9781619630628) Bloomsbury Publishing USA. (Bloomsbury USA Childrens).

—Crown of Midnight. 2014. (Throne of Glass Ser.: 2). (YA). lib. bdg. 22.10 *(978-0-606-36441-6(2))* Turtleback Bks.

—Empire of Storms. (Throne of Glass Ser.). (ENG.). (YA). 2017. 720p. pap. 10.99 ***(978-1-61963-609-5(3),*** 9781619636095) 2016. 704p. (gr. 9). 18.99 *(978-1-61963-607-1(7),* 9781619636071) Bloomsbury Publishing USA. (Bloomsbury USA Childrens).

—Empire of Storms. 2017. (Throne of Glass Ser.: 5). (YA). lib. bdg. 22.10 ***(978-0-606-40598-0(4))*** Turtleback Bks.

Maberry, Jonathan. Mars One. 2017. (ENG., Illus.). 448p. (YA). (gr. 7). 17.99 *(978-1-4814-6161-0(3),* Simon & Schuster Bks. For Young Readers) Simon & Schuster Bks. For Young Readers.

Mabry, Samantha. A Fierce & Subtle Poison. 2016. (ENG.). 288p. (YA). (gr. 8-12). 17.95 *(978-1-61620-521-8(0))* Algonquin Bks. of Chapel Hill.

Mac, Carrie. Crush, 1 vol. 2006. (Orca Soundings Ser.). (ENG.). 136p. (YA). (gr. 8-12). per. 9.95 *(978-1-55143-526-8(8))* Orca Bk. Pubs. USA.

Macdangereuse, T. T. The Untamed Scoundrel. 2014. (Epic Tales from Adventure Time Ser.). lib. bdg. 17.20 *(978-0-606-35718-0(1))* Turtleback Bks.

MacDonald, George. Light Princess & Other Fairy Stories. 2006. 132p. per. 10.95 *(978-1-59818-618-5(3));* 24.95 *(978-1-59818-236-1(6))* Aegypan.

MacKenzie, Catherine. The Lonely Grey Dog at No. 6: Tammy & Jake Learn about Love & Loyalty. 2005. (Tales from Canterbury Place Ser.). (ENG., Illus.). 160p. (J). per. 6.99 *(978-1-84550-103-7(9),* bb65d1c0-1fc5-4a1a-8cb0-8c01c9ccdb70) Christian Focus Pubns. GBR. Dist: Bookmasters Distribution.

MacKenzie, Lachlan. The Duke's Daughter: A Story of Faith & Love. Anderson, Jeff, illus. 2008. (Story Time Ser.). (ENG.). 24p. (J). (gr. -1-3). 7.99 *(978-1-84550-326-0(0),* de5339b0-1f9f-400d-8814-ce3da22de27c) Christian Focus Pubns. GBR. Dist: Bookmasters Distribution.

Maetani, Valynne E. Ink & Ashes. 2015. (ENG.). 368p. (YA). 19.95 *(978-1-62014-211-0(2),* Tu Bks.) Lee & Low Bks., Inc.

Mafi, Tahereh. Ignite Me. 2014. (Shatter Me Ser.: 3). (ENG.). (gr. 9). 416p. (YA). pap. 9.99 *(978-0-06-208558-0(1));* 352p. (J). 17.99 *(978-0-06-208557-3(3))* HarperCollins Pubs.

—Shatter Me. (Shatter Me Ser.: 1). (ENG.). (YA). (gr. 9). 2012. 464p. pap. 9.99 *(978-0-06-208550-4(6))* 2011. 352p. 17.99 *(978-0-06-208548-1(4))* HarperCollins Pubs.

—Shatter Me. 2012. (Shatter Me Ser.: 1). (YA). lib. bdg. 20.85 *(978-0-606-26868-4(5),* Turtleback) Turtleback Bks.

—Unravel Me. 2013. (Shatter Me Ser.: 2). (ENG.). (YA). (gr. 9). 496p. pap. 9.99 *(978-0-06-208554-2(9));* 480p. 17.99 *(978-0-06-208553-5(0))* HarperCollins Pubs.

—Unravel Me. 2013. (Shatter Me Ser.: 2). (YA). lib. bdg. 20.85 *(978-0-606-35049-5(7),* Turtleback) Turtleback Bks.

Magnolia, B. Beautiful Wild Rose Girl. Hugel, William K., ed. Keba, Jamila, illus. 2012. 34p. pap. 7.95 *(978-0-9854289-0-7(2))* Mystic World Pr.

Magor, Dianne M. Ed. Lauren's Wish. 2012. 32p. (-18). pap. 21.99 *(978-1-4691-3986-9(3))* Xlibris Corp.

Maid of Deception. 2014. (Maids of Honor Ser.). (ENG., Illus.). 416p. (YA). (gr. 7). 17.99 *(978-1-4424-4141-5(0),* Simon & Schuster Bks. For Young Readers) Simon & Schuster Bks. For Young Readers.

Maizel, Rebecca. A Season for Fireflies. 2016. 256p. (YA). (gr. 9). 17.99 *(978-0-06-232764-2(X),* HarperTeen) HarperCollins Pubs.

—Stolen Nights. 2013. (Vampire Queen Ser.: 2). (ENG.). 320p. (YA). (gr. 7-18). pap. 9.99 *(978-0-312-64992-0(4),* 9780312649920, St. Martin's Griffin) St. Martin's Pr.

Malcolm, Jahnna N. The Write Stuff. 2011. (Love Letters Ser.). (ENG.). 192p. (YA). (gr. 7). pap. 9.99 *(978-1-4424-3100-3(8),* Simon Pulse) Simon Pulse.

Malkin, Nina. Swear. (ENG.). 480p. (YA). (gr. 11). 2012. pap. 9.99 *(978-1-4424-2111-0(8))* 2011. 17.99 *(978-1-4424-2110-3(X))* Simon Pulse. (Simon Pulse).

—Swoon. 2010. (ENG.). 432p. (YA). (gr. 11). pap. 9.99 *(978-1-4169-9801-3(2),* Simon Pulse) Simon Pulse.

Mallory, Alex. Wild. 2014. (ENG.). 448p. (YA). (gr. 8). 17.99 *(978-0-06-221874-2(3),* HarperTeen) HarperCollins Pubs.

Mancuso, Rudy. How to Be Famous in Six Seconds. 2016. (YA). pap. ***(978-1-5011-2767-0(5),*** Keywords Press) Atria Bks.

Mandelkorn, Carole. Grandma, Will You Clap! Phillips, Laverne, illus. 2013. 16p. pap. 10.95 *(978-1-61493-196-6(8))* Peppertree Pr., The.

Mannering, Rose. Feathers: The Tales Trilogy, Book 2. 2016. (Tales Trilogy Ser.). (ENG.). 288p. (YA). (gr. 6). 17.99 *(978-1-63450-165-1(9),* Sky Pony Pr.) Skyhorse Publishing Co., Inc.

Manners, Tyler. Continental Change of Heart. 2006. 65p. pap. 16.95 *(978-1-4137-9483-0(1))* PublishAmerica, Inc.

Manning, Sarra. Adorkable. 2013. (ENG.). 400p. (YA). (gr. 9). pap. 13.99 *(978-1-907411-00-7(3))* Little, Brown Book Group Ltd. GBR. Dist: Hachette Bk. Group.

—Guitar Girl. 2003. (ENG.). 256p. (YA). pap. *(978-0-340-86071-7(5))* Hodder & Stoughton.

—Guitar Girl. 2005. (ENG.). 240p. (YA). (gr. 7-9). reprint ed. pap. 6.99 *(978-0-14-240318-1(0),* Speak) Penguin Young Readers Group.

Manwiller, S. A. The Adventures of Jack & Max the Truliest Meaning of Christmas. Manwiller, S. A. & Overly, Kristen V., illus. 2013. (ACH & ENG.). 38p. 24.99 *(978-0-9838427-7-4(9))* SevenHorns Publishing.

Marquardt, Marie. Dream Things True. 2015. (ENG.). 352p. (YA). 18.99 *(978-1-250-07045-6(7),* 9781250070456, St. Martin's Griffin) St. Martin's Pr.

—The Radius of Us. 2017. (ENG., Illus.). 304p. (YA). 18.99 *(978-1-250-09689-0(8),* 9781250096890, St. Martin's Griffin) St. Martin's Pr.

Marr, Melissa, et al. Love Is Hell. 2008. (ENG.). 272p. (YA). (gr. 9-18). pap. 9.99 *(978-0-06-144304-6(2),* HarperTeen) HarperCollins Pubs.

Marsoli, Lisa Ann. Puppy Love. Durk, Jim, illus. 2003. pap. *(978-0-439-61116-9(4))* Scholastic, Inc.

Martin, Emily. The Year We Fell Apart. 2016. (ENG.). 320p. (YA). (gr. 9). 17.99 *(978-1-4814-3841-4(7),* Simon Pulse) Simon Pulse.

Martin, Jenny. Marked. 2016. (ENG.). 368p. (YA). (gr. 7). 17.99 *(978-0-525-42871-8(2),* Dial Bks) Penguin Young Readers Group.

Martin, LaJoyce. The Silver Ghost. 2004. (Illus.). 161p. (J). pap. 9.99 *(978-1-56722-643-0(4))* Word Aflame Pr.

Martin, Maggie Ann. The Big F. 2017. (ENG.). 304p. (YA). pap. 10.99 *(978-1-250-12321-3(6),* 9781250123213) Feiwel & Friends.

Martínez, Jessica. The Vow. (ENG., (YA). (gr. 9). 2014. Illus.). 448p. pap. 11.99 *(978-1-4424-5865-9(8))* 2013. 432p. 17.99 *(978-1-4424-5864-2(X))* Simon Pulse. (Simon Pulse).

Masciola, Carol. The Yearbook. 2015. (ENG.). 224p. (YA). 17.99 *(978-1-4405-8897-6(X),* Simon Pulse) Simon Pulse.

Maskame, Estelle. Did I Mention I Need You? 2016. (Did I Mention I Love You (DIMILY) Ser.: 2). (ENG.). 384p. (YA). (gr. 8-12). pap. 10.99 *(978-1-4926-3218-4(X),* 9781492632184) Sourcebooks, Inc.

Mason, Mimi Canda. Lola's Cane. 2009. 48p. pap. 19.95 *(978-1-4389-1464-0(4))* AuthorHouse.

Massini, Sarah, illus. Love Always Everywhere. 2014. (ENG.). 32p. (J). (gr. -1-2). 16.99 *(978-0-385-37552-8(2),* Random Hse. Bks. for Young Readers) Random Hse. Children's Bks.

—Love Always Everywhere. 2014. (J). *(978-0-385-37553-5(0))* Random Hse., Inc.

Masters, William H. Love & Sex. Cart, Michael, ed. 2003. (ENG.). 240p. (YA). (gr. 8). pap. 13.95 *(978-0-689-85668-6(7),* Simon Pulse) Simon Pulse.

Matson, Lynne. Nil. 2014. (Nil Ser.: 1). (ENG.). 384p. (YA). (gr. 9-13). 18.99 *(978-0-8050-9771-9(6),* 9780805097719, Holt, Henry & Co. Bks. For Young Readers) Holt, Henry & Co.

—Nil Unlocked. 2015. (Nil Ser.: 2). (ENG.). 432p. (YA). (gr. 9). 17.99 *(978-1-62779-293-6(7),* 9781627792936, Holt, Henry & Co. Bks. For Young Readers) Holt, Henry & Co.

Matson, Morgan. Second Chance Summer. (ENG.). (YA). (gr. 7). 2013. 496p. pap. 10.99 *(978-1-4169-9068-0(2))* 2012. 480p. 19.99 *(978-1-4169-9067-3(4))* Simon & Schuster Bks. For Young Readers. (Simon & Schuster Bks. For Young Readers).

—The Unexpected Everything. 2016. (ENG.). (YA). (gr. 7). pap. 12.99 *(978-1-4814-8207-3(6))* Simon & Schuster.

—The Unexpected Everything. (ENG., Illus.). (YA). (gr. 7). 2017. 560p. pap. 9.99 *(978-1-4814-0455-6(5))* 2016. 528p. 17.99 *(978-1-4814-0454-9(7))* Simon & Schuster Bks. For Young Readers. (Simon & Schuster Bks. For Young Readers).

Matsumoto, Reiko Odate. The Princess with the Magic Bowl: As retold from the Japanese folk tale By. 2008. 48p. pap. 22.49 *(978-1-4389-1225-7(0))* AuthorHouse.

Matthew-Barnes, David. Wonderland. 2013. (ENG.). 264p. (gr. 7). pap. 11.95 *(978-1-60282-788-2(5))* Bold Strokes Bks.

Maxwell, Lisa. Sweet Unrest. 2014. (ENG.). 336p. (YA). pap. 11.99 *(978-0-7387-4081-2(0),* Flux) North Star Editions.

Mayer, Mercer. Just a Little Love. Mayer, Mercer, illus. 2013. (My First I Can Read Ser.). (ENG., Illus.). 32p. (J). (gr. -1-3). 16.99 *(978-0-06-207196-5(3))* HarperCollins Pubs.

—Little Critter - Just a Little Love. Mayer, Mercer, illus. 2013. (My First I Can Read Ser.). (ENG., Illus.). 20p. (J). (gr. -1-3). pap. 3.99 *(978-0-06-147815-4(6))* HarperCollins Pubs.

Mazer, Norma Fox. When We First Met. 2015. (ENG., Illus.). 208p. (YA). (gr. 7). pap. 14.99 *(978-1-4814-5103-1(0),* Atheneum Bks. for Young Readers) Simon & Schuster Children's Publishing.

Mba, Ogochukwu. The Roaches, 1 vol. 2010. 20p. 24.95 *(978-1-4489-3951-0(8))* PublishAmerica, Inc.

McBay, Bruce & Heneghan, James. Waiting for Sarah. 2004. 170p. (gr. 7). 17.95 *(978-0-7569-4567-1(4))* Perfection Learning Corp.

McBratney, Sam. Guess How Much I Love You. Jeram, Anita, illus. 2005. 34p. (J). bds. 19.95 *(978-0-9769313-1-7(1))* BrailleInk.

—Guess How Much I Love You. Jeram, Anita, illus. (Guess How Much I Love You Ser.). (J). 2014. (ENG.). 30p. (gr. k-4). 9.99 *(978-0-7636-7446-5(X))* 2011. (ENG.). 16p. (gr. -1-2). 19.99 *(978-0-7636-5378-1(0))* 2011. (ENG.). (gr. -1-k). bds. 9.99 *(978-0-7636-4976-0(7))* 2006. 32p. (gr. -1-3). 15.99 *(978-0-7636-3503-9(0))* Candlewick Pr.

—Guess How Much I Love You 20th Anniversary Edition. Jeram, Anita, illus. 2014. (Guess How Much I Love You Ser.). (ENG.). 40p. (J). (gr. k-12). 16.99 *(978-0-7636-7448-9(6))* Candlewick Pr.

—Guess How Much I Love You: Baby Book. Jeram, Anita, illus. 2014. (Guess How Much I Love You Ser.). (ENG.). 64p. (J). (gr. k-12). 14.99 *(978-0-7636-7023-8(5))* Candlewick Pr.

—Guess How Much I Love You in the Winter: Deluxe Cut Paper Edition. Jeram, Anita, illus. 2016. (Guess How Much I Love You Ser.). (ENG.). 12p. (J). (-k). 18.99 *(978-0-7636-9057-1(0))* Candlewick Pr.

—Guess How Much I Love You Sweetheart Gift Edition. Jeram, Anita, illus. 2016. (Guess How Much I Love You Ser.). (ENG.). 32p. (J). (gr. k-12). 12.00 *(978-0-7636-9058-8(9))* Candlewick Pr.

—Tomhais Méid Mo Ghrá Duit (Guess How Much I Love You in Irish) Jeram, Anita, illus. 2013. (Guess How Much I Love

You Ser.). (ENG & GLE.). 32p. (J). (gr. -1-2). 9.99 *(978-0-7636-6570-8(3))* Candlewick Pr.

McBride, Martha J. And You Love Me. 2003. 346p. (YA). per. 5.99 *(978-1-59196-391-2(5))* Instant Pub.

McCafferty, Catherine. Rapunzel. Spong, Clive, illus. 2008. (Keepsake Stories Ser.). (ENG & SPA.). 32p. (gr. -1-3). pap. 3.99 *(978-0-7696-5418-8(5),* Brighter Child) Carson-Dellosa Publishing, LLC.

McCahan, Erin. Love & Other Foreign Words. (ENG., 336p. (YA). (gr. 7). 2015. Illus.). pap. 10.99 *(978-0-14-750959-8(9),* Speak) 2014. 17.99 *(978-0-8037-4051-8(4),* Dial Bks) Penguin Young Readers Group.

McCarry, Sarah. All Our Pretty Songs. 2013. (Metamorphoses Trilogy Ser.: 1). (ENG.). 240p. (YA). (gr. 8-12). pap. 9.99 *(978-1-250-02708-5(X),* 9781250027085, St. Martin's Griffin) St. Martin's Pr.

—Dirty Wings. 2014. (Metamorphoses Trilogy Ser.: 2). (ENG.). 288p. (YA). (gr. 8-12). 19.99 *(978-1-250-04938-4(5),* 9781250049384, St. Martin's Griffin) St. Martin's Pr.

McCarty, Peter. Henry in Love. McCarty, Peter, illus. 2009. (ENG., Illus.). 48p. (J). (gr. -1-1). 16.99 *(978-0-06-114288-8(3))* HarperCollins Pubs.

McClymer, Kelly. Getting to Third Date. 2006. (Romantic Comedies Ser.). (ENG., Illus.). 304p. (YA). (gr. 9-18). mass mkt. 6.99 *(978-1-4169-1479-2(X),* Simon Pulse) Simon Pulse.

McCourt, Lisa. I Love You, Stinky Face. Moore, Cyd, illus. 2009. (ENG.). (J). (gr. -1-3). 9.99 *(978-0-545-11757-9(7))* Scholastic, Inc.

McCreedy, J. L. The Orphan of Torundi. 2014. (ENG.). 300p. (YA). pap. 10.99 *(978-0-9882369-2-9(3))* Penelope Pipp Publishing.

McDaniel, Lurlene. As Long as We Both Shall Live. 2003. (ENG.). 416p. (YA). (gr. 7). mass mkt. 7.50 *(978-0-553-57108-0(7),* Laurel Leaf) Random Hse. Children's Bks.

—Kathleen's Story. 2006. (Angels in Pink Ser.). (ENG.). 256p. (YA). (gr. 7-12). mass mkt. 6.99 *(978-0-440-23865-2(X),* Laurel Leaf) Random Hse. Children's Bks.

—Losing Gabriel: a Love Story. 2017. (ENG.). 336p. (YA). (gr. 7). pap. 9.99 ***(978-0-385-74422-5(6),*** Ember) Random Hse. Children's Bks.

—My Secret Boyfriend. 2004. (ENG., Illus.). 128p. (YA). (gr. 7-12). pap. 4.99 *(978-1-58196-008-2(5))* Lerner Publishing Group.

—True Love. 2009. (ENG.). 672p. (YA). (gr. 7). pap. 10.99 *(978-0-375-86148-2(3),* Ember) Random Hse. Children's Bks.

—The Year of Chasing Dreams. (ENG.). 336p. (YA). (gr. 7). 2015. pap. 9.99 *(978-0-385-74174-3(X),* Ember) 2014. 16.99 *(978-0-385-74173-6(1),* Delacorte Pr.) Random Hse. Children's Bks.

—The Year of Luminous Love. 2013. (ENG.). 384p. (YA). (gr. 7). 16.99 *(978-0-385-74171-2(5),* Delacorte Bks. for Young Readers) Random Hse. Children's Bks.

McDonald, Abby. Getting over Garrett Delaney. 2012. (ENG.). 336p. (YA). (gr. 9). pap. 7.99 *(978-0-7636-6332-2(8));* (Illus.). 16.99 *(978-0-7636-5507-5(4))* Candlewick Pr.

—Jane Austen Goes to Hollywood. 2015. (ENG.). 336p. (YA). (gr. 9). pap. 8.99 *(978-0-7636-7669-8(1))* Candlewick Pr.

—Sophomore Switch. 2010. (ENG., Illus.). 304p. (YA). (gr. 9). pap. 8.99 *(978-0-7636-4774-2(8))* Candlewick Pr.

McDonald, Brenda. How Do You Love A Big Dog? 2007. 18.00 *(978-0-8059-7314-3(1))* Dorrance Publishing Co., Inc.

McEntire, K. D. Lightbringer. 2011. (ENG.). 319p. (YA). (gr. 7). 16.99 *(978-1-61614-539-2(0))* Prometheus Bks., Pubs.

McGarry, Katie. Pushing the Limits. 2013. (Pushing the Limits Ser.: 1). (ENG.). 416p. (YA). pap. 9.99 *(978-0-373-21086-2(8),* Harlequin Teen) Harlequin Enterprises, Ltd. CAN. Dist: HarperCollins Pubs.

McGee, Krista. Revolutionary, 1 vol. 2014. (Anomaly Ser.: 3). (ENG.). 320p. (YA). pap. 9.99 *(978-1-4016-8876-9(4))* Nelson, Thomas Inc.

Mcghee, Alison. All Rivers Flow to the Sea. 2005. (ENG.). 176p. (YA). (gr. 9-12). 15.99 *(978-0-7636-2591-7(4))* Candlewick Pr.

McGovern, Cammie. Say What You Will. (ENG.). (YA). (gr. 9). 2015. 368p. pap. 9.99 *(978-0-06-227111-2(3))* 2014. 352p. 17.99 *(978-0-06-227110-5(5))* HarperCollins Pubs. (HarperTeen).

McGowan, Jennifer. Maid of Secrets. (Maids of Honor Ser.). (ENG.). (YA). (gr. 7). 2014. 432p. pap. 9.99 *(978-1-4424-4139-2(9))* 2013. 416p. 17.99 *(978-1-4424-4138-5(0))* Simon & Schuster Bks. For Young Readers. (Simon & Schuster Bks. For Young Readers).

McGrath, Liz & Quick, Barbara. Even More/Todavía Más. de la Vega, Eida, tr. from ENG. McGrath, Liz, illus. 2004.Tr. of Todavía Más. (SPA & ENG., Illus.). 32p. (J). (gr. -1-3). 16.95 *(978-0-9720192-8-6(6),* 626999, Raven Tree Pr.,Csi) Continental Sales, Inc.

McGrellis, Barbara. Love Never Fails. 2013. 24p. pap. 10.99 *(978-1-4624-0745-3(5),* Inspiring Voices) Author Solutions, Inc.

McKellop, Holly R. To the Moon. 2012. 32p. pap. 24.95 *(978-1-4626-8034-4(8))* America Star Bks.

McKenney, M. W. Roosevelt Junior High. 2008. 73p. pap. 19.95 *(978-1-60672-157-5(7))* America Star Bks.

McLachlan, Jenny. Love Bomb. 2016. (Ladybirds Ser.: 2). (ENG.). 208p. (YA). 16.99 *(978-1-250-06149-2(0),* 9781250061492) Feiwel & Friends.

—Sunkissed. 2017. (Ladybirds Ser.: 3). (ENG.). 224p. (YA). 16.99 *(978-1-250-06150-8(4),* 9781250061508) Feiwel & Friends.

McLaren, Heather. Mythos. 2013. (ENG.). 260p. pap. 17.95 *(978-1-60619-093-7(8))* Twilight Times Bks.

McLaughlin, Emma & Kraus, Nicola. Over You. 2013. (ENG.). 304p. (YA). (gr. 9). pap. 9.99 *(978-0-06-172045-1(3),* HarperTeen) HarperCollins Pubs.

McLemore, Anna-Marie. The Weight of Feathers. 2015. (ENG.). 320p. (YA). 18.99 *(978-1-250-05865-2(1),* 9781250058652) St. Martin's Pr.

McMahon, Kara. Elmo's World: Love! Nelson, Mary Beth, illus. 2004. (Sesame Street(R) Elmos World(TM) Ser.). (ENG.). 12p. (J). (— 1). bds. 4.99 *(978-0-375-82843-0(5),* Random Hse. Bks. for Young Readers) Random Hse. Children's Bks.

McMann, Lisa. Bang. (Visions Ser.: 2). (ENG., (YA). (gr. 9). 2014. Illus.). 272p. pap. 9.99 *(978-1-4424-6628-9(6))* 2013. 256p. 16.99 *(978-1-4424-6625-8(1))* Simon Pulse. (Simon Pulse).

—Crash. 2013. (Visions Ser.: 1). (ENG.). 256p. (YA). (gr. 9). 16.99 *(978-1-4424-0391-8(8),* Simon Pulse) Simon Pulse.

—Gone. (Wake Ser.: Bk. 3). (ENG.). (YA). (gr. 9). 2011. 240p. pap. 9.99 *(978-1-4169-7921-0(2))* 2010. 224p. 17.99 *(978-1-4169-7918-0(2))* Simon Pulse. (Simon Pulse).

McNally, Janet. Girls in the Moon. 2016. 352p. (YA). (gr. 8). 17.99 *(978-0-06-243624-5(4),* HarperTeen) HarperCollins Pubs.

McNamara, Brian. Bottled up Secret. 2014. (ENG.). 264p. (J). (gr. 7). pap. 11.95 *(978-1-62639-209-0(9))* Bold Strokes Bks.

McNaughton, Janet. To Dance at the Palais Royale. 2006. (ENG.). 252p. (J). mass mkt. 6.99 *(978-0-00-639541-6(4),* Harper Trophy) HarperCollins Pubs.

McNeil, Gretchen. I'm Not Your Manic Pixie Dream Girl. 2016. 352p. (YA). (gr. 8). 17.99 *(978-0-06-240911-9(5))* HarperCollins Pubs.

McPhail, David. Brothers. 2014. (ENG., Illus.). 32p. (J). (gr. -1-3). 12.99 *(978-0-544-30200-6(1),* HMH Books For Young Readers) Houghton Mifflin Harcourt Publishing Co.

McStay, Moriah. Everything That Makes You. 2017. 352p. (YA). (gr. 8). pap. 9.99 *(978-0-06-229549-1(7),* Tegen, Katherine Bks) HarperCollins Pubs.

McVoy, Terra Elan. Criminal. (ENG., (YA). (gr. 9). 2014. Illus.). 304p. pap. 9.99 *(978-1-4424-2163-9(0))* 2013. 288p. 16.99 *(978-1-4424-2162-2(2))* Simon Pulse. (Simon Pulse).

Mead, Richelle. Midnight Jewel. 2017. (Glittering Court Ser.: 2). (ENG.). 416p. (YA). (gr. 7). 19.99 *(978-1-59514-843-8(4),* Razorbill) Penguin Young Readers Group.

—Silver Shadows. 2014. (Bloodlines Ser.: Bk. 5). (ENG.). 416p. (YA). (gr. 7). 18.99 *(978-1-59514-321-1(1),* Razorbill) Penguin Publishing Group.

—Silver Shadows. 2015. (Bloodlines Ser.: 5). (ENG.). 416p. (YA). (gr. 7). pap. 9.99 *(978-1-59514-632-8(6),* Razorbill) Penguin Young Readers Group.

—Soundless. l.t. ed. 2016. (ENG.). 352p. 25.99 *(978-1-4104-8817-6(9))* Cengage Gale.

—Soundless. 2015. (ENG.). 272p. (YA). (gr. 7-10). 19.99 *(978-1-59514-763-9(2),* Razorbill) Penguin Publishing Group.

Mead, Richelle & Loftin, Nikki. Soundless. 2016. (ENG.). 288p. (YA). (gr. 7). 10.99 *(978-1-59514-764-6(0),* Razorbill) Penguin Young Readers Group.

Mear, Shirley A. Feathers from Heaven. 2013. 24p. (J). pap. *(978-1-78148-567-5(4))* Grosvenor Hse. Publishing Ltd.

Mehta, Shyam. Stories for Children. 2009. 68p. pap. 8.47 *(978-1-4092-8990-6(7))* Lulu Pr., Inc.

Melean, Mary & Lascaris, Alexia. The Adventures of Don Quixote of la Mancha. 2011. 44p. pap. 18.46 *(978-1-4567-6131-8(5))* AuthorHouse.

Meléndez, Claudia. A Fighting Chance. 2015. (ENG.). 256p. (YA). (gr. 6). pap. 10.95 *(978-1-55885-818-3(0),* Piñata Books) Arte Publico Pr.

Melmed, Laura Krauss. Before We Met. Tsong, Jing Jing, illus. 2016. (ENG.). 32p. (J). (gr. -1-3). 17.99 *(978-1-4424-4156-9(9),* Beach Lane Bks.) Beach Lane Bks.

Mendelsohn, Jeffrey. Grumpalina. 2012. (ENG.). 30p. (J). 25.95 *(978-1-4327-7830-9(7))* Outskirts Pr., Inc.

Meredith, Christina. Red Velvet Crush. 2016. 304p. (YA). (gr. 9). 17.99 *(978-0-06-206227-7(1),* Greenwillow Bks.) HarperCollins Pubs.

Mesrobian, Carrie. Cut Both Ways. 2017. 368p. (YA). (gr. 9). pap. 9.99 *(978-0-06-234989-7(9))* HarperCollins Pubs.

Messenger, Shannon. Let the Storm Break. 2014. (Sky Fall Ser.: 2). (ENG., Illus.). 400p. (YA). (gr. 7). 17.99 *(978-1-4424-5044-8(4),* Simon Pulse) Simon Pulse.

—Let the Wind Rise. (Sky Fall Ser.: 3). (ENG., Illus.). (YA). (gr. 7). 2017. 432p. pap. 10.99 *(978-1-4814-4655-6(X))* 2016. 416p. 17.99 *(978-1-4814-4654-9(1))* Simon Pulse. (Simon Pulse).

Metallinos, Sophia. The Heavenly Place. l.t. ed. 2016. (ENG., Illus.). (J). pap. 9.99 ***(978-1-58169-640-0(X),*** Axiom Pr.) Genesis Communications, Inc.

Metzger, Lois. Change Places with Me. 2016. 224p. (YA). (gr. 9). 17.99 *(978-0-06-238553-6(4))* HarperCollins Pubs.

Mewburn, Kyle. Kiss! Kiss! Yuck! Yuck!, 1 vol. Teo, Ali & O'Reilly, John, illus. (ENG.). 32p. (J). (gr. -1-3). 2017. pap. 7.95 ***(978-1-56145-759-5(0))*** 2008. 16.95 *(978-1-56145-457-0(5))* Peachtree Pubs.

Meyer, Carolyn. Beauty's Daughter: The Story of Hermione & Helen of Troy. 2013. (ENG., Illus.). 352p. (YA). (gr. 7). 16.99 *(978-0-544-10862-2(0))* Houghton Mifflin Harcourt Publishing Co.

Meyer, Kai. Arcadia Falls. 2014. (Arcadia Ser.: 3). (ENG.). 480p. (YA). (gr. 9). 17.99 *(978-0-06-200610-3(X))* HarperCollins Pubs.

Meyer, L. A. Wild Rover No More: Being the Last Recorded Account of the Life & Times of Jacky Faber. (Bloody Jack Adventures Ser.). (ENG.). 368p. (YA). (gr. 9). 2016. pap. 9.99 *(978-0-544-66842-3(1))* 2014. 17.99 *(978-0-544-21777-5(2))* Houghton Mifflin Harcourt Publishing Co. (HMH Books For Young Readers).

Meyer, Marissa. Heartless. 2016. (ENG.). 464p. (YA). 19.99 *(978-1-250-04465-5(0),* 9781250044655) Feiwel & Friends.

—Heartless. 2016. (ENG.). (YA). (gr. 8-12). pap. 12.99 ***(978-1-250-11486-0(1))*** St. Martin's Pr.

—Heartless. 2017. 592p. (YA). pap. 17.99 ***(978-987-747-254-7(6))*** V&R Editoras.

Meyer, Stephenie. Amanecer. Pallarés, José Miguel & Sánchez, María Jesús, trs. 2008.Tr. of Breaking Dawn. (SPA.). 832p. (gr. 8-12). pap. 19.99 *(978-607-11-0033-7(X),* Alfaguara Juvenil) Santillana USA Publishing Co., Inc.

—Eclipse. 2009. (Twilight Saga Ser.: 3). (ENG.). 640p. (YA). (gr. 7-17). pap. 15.99 *(978-0-316-02765-6(0))* Little Brown & Co.

—Eclipse. 2007. (Twilight Saga Ser.: 3). (ENG.). 640p. (YA). (gr. 7-17). 19.99 *(978-0-316-16020-9(2))* Little, Brown Bks. for Young Readers.

—Eclipse. 2008. 576p. *(978-1-904233-91-6(0),* Atom Books) Little, Brown Book Group Ltd.

—Eclipse. 2011. (Twilight Saga: Bk. 3). 13.08 *(978-0-7848-3531-9(4),* Everbind) Marco Bk. Co.

—Eclipse. 2010. (Twilight Saga: Bk. 3). 629p. (YA). (gr. 9-12). 22.10 *(978-1-60686-303-9(7))* Perfection Learning Corp.

—Eclipse. Pallarés, José Miguel & Sánchez, María Jesús, trs. 2007. (SPA.). 870p. (YA). (gr. 8-12). pap. 15.99 *(978-1-60396-022-9(8),* Punto de Lectura) Santillana USA Publishing Co., Inc.

—Eclipse. 2007. (Twilight Saga Spanish Ser.: 3). (SPA.). 637p. (gr. 7-12). lib. bdg. 28.15 *(978-1-4177-9862-9(9),* Turtleback) Turtleback Bks.

—Life & Death: Twilight Reimagined. 2016. (ENG.). 400p. (YA). (gr. 7-17). pap. 9.99 *(978-0-316-50545-1(5))* Little, Brown Bks. for Young Readers.

—Luna Nueva. Pallares, Jose Miguel, tr. from ENG. 2009.Tr. of New Moon. (SPA.). 280p. (YA). (gr. 8-12). pap. 11.99 *(978-1-60396-698-6(6),* Punto de Lectura) Santillana USA Publishing Co., Inc.

—Luna Nueva. Pallarés, José Miguel & Sánchez, Maria Jesús, trs. from ENG. 2007.Tr. of New Moon. (SPA.). 696p. (YA). (gr. 8-12). per. 15.99 *(978-970-58-0023-8(5),* Alfaguara) Santillana USA Publishing Co., Inc.

—New Moon. (Twilight Saga Ser.: 2). (ENG.). 608p. (gr. 7-17). 2008. (YA). pap. 15.99 *(978-0-316-02496-9(1))* 2006. (J). 19.99 *(978-0-316-16019-3(9),* Tingley, Megan Bks.) Little, Brown Bks. for Young Readers.

—New Moon. 2011. (Twilight Saga: Bk. 2). 11.72 *(978-0-7848-3535-7(7),* Everbind) Marco Bk. Co.

—New Moon. 2008. (Twilight Saga: Bk. 2). 563p. (gr. 9-12). 21.00 *(978-1-60686-336-7(3))* Perfection Learning Corp.

—The Short Second Life of Bree Tanner. 2010. (Twilight Saga Ser.). (ENG.). 192p. (YA). (gr. 7-17). 16.00 *(978-0-316-12558-1(X))* Little, Brown Bks. for Young Readers.

—Twilight. 2008. (Twilight Saga: Bk. 1). (CHI.). 375p. (YA). pap. *(978-7-5448-0333-5(3))* Jieli Publishing Hse.

—Twilight. (ENG.). (YA). (gr. 7-17). 2005. (Twilight Saga Ser.: 1). 544p. 19.99 *(978-0-316-16017-9(2),* Tingley, Megan Bks.) 2006. (Twilight Saga Ser.: 1). 544p. reprint ed. pap. 15.99 *(978-0-316-01584-4(9),* Tingley, Megan Bks.) 10th anniv. ed. 2015. (Twilight Saga: Bk. 1). 1200p. pap. 23.99 *(978-0-316-35555-1(0))* Little, Brown Bks. for Young Readers.

—Twilight. 2008. 480p. pap. *(978-1-905654-34-5(0),* Atom Books) Little, Brown Book Group Ltd.

—Twilight. 2009. (Twilight Saga: Bk. 1). 11.72 *(978-0-7848-1934-0(3),* Everbind) Marco Bk. Co.

—Twilight. (Twilight Saga Ser.: 1). (ENG.). 2012. 224p. (gr. 7-17). pap. 14.99 *(978-0-316-20488-0(9))* 2011. (Illus.). 240p. (gr. 7-17). 19.99 *(978-0-316-13319-7(1))* 2010. (Illus.). 224p. 19.99 *(978-0-7595-2943-4(4))* Orbit. (Yen Pr.).

—Twilight. Kim, Young, illus. collector's ed. 2012. (Twilight Saga Ser.: 0). (ENG.). 464p. (gr. 7-17). 24.99 *(978-0-316-21717-0(4),* Yen Pr.) Orbit.

—Twilight. (Twilight Saga: Bk. 1). 2010. 498p. (YA). (gr. 9-12). 20.10 *(978-1-60686-352-7(5))* 2006. 21.00 *(978-0-7569-6825-0(9))* Perfection Learning Corp.

—Twilight. (Twilight Ser.: 1). (YA). 2007. 1.25 *(978-1-4193-9974-9(8))* 2006. 87.75 *(978-1-4193-9975-6(6))* Recorded Bks., Inc.

—Twilight. 2006. (Twilight Saga Ser.: 1). (Illus.). 498p. (YA). (gr. 9-12). lib. bdg. 28.15 *(978-1-4177-5591-2(1),* Turtleback) Turtleback Bks.

—Twilight / Life & Death. 10th anniv. ed. 2015. (Twilight Saga). (ENG.). 752p. (YA). (gr. 7-17). 21.99 *(978-0-316-26839-4(9))* Little, Brown Bks. for Young Readers.

—Twilight Tenth Anniversary / Life & Death Dual Edition. 2015. (Twilight Saga Ser.). (YA). lib. bdg. 35.50 *(978-0-606-37801-7(4))* Turtleback Bks.

Michaels, Robbie. Caught. 2016. (ENG., Illus.). (J). 24.99 ***(978-1-63477-950-0(9),*** Harmony Ink Pr.) Dreamspinner Pr.

—A Star Is Born. 2016. (ENG., Illus.). (J). 24.99 ***(978-1-63477-930-2(4))*** 2012. 200p. pap. 14.99 *(978-1-61372-730-0(5))* Dreamspinner Pr. (Harmony Ink Pr.).

Michelle, Sara. The Beginning: Book 5, 1 vol. unabr. ed. 2012. (My New Normal Ser.: 5). (ENG.). 97p. (YA). (gr. 9-12). pap. 8.95 *(978-1-61651-785-4(9))* Saddleback Educational Publishing, Inc.

Michot, Fabienne. Maki, I Love to Kiss You. braille ed. 2004. (J). (gr. 1). spiral bd., bds. *(978-0-616-07268-4(6))* Canadian National Institute for the Blind/Institut National Canadien pour les Aveugles.

Mifae. 2013. 200p. *(978-1-4602-2049-8(8))* FriesenPress.

Miller, Barnabas. The Girl with the Wrong Name. 2016. (ENG., Illus.). 272p. (YA). (gr. 9). pap. 10.99 *(978-1-61695-704-9(2),* Soho Teen) Soho Pr., Inc.

Miller, Jonathan. Kim's Introductions. 2009. 48p. pap. 21.99 *(978-1-4389-0856-4(3))* AuthorHouse.

Miller, Kirsten. The Eternal Ones: What If Love Refused to Die? 2011. (ENG.). 432p. (YA). (gr. 7-18). 9.99 *(978-1-59514-375-4(0),* Razorbill) Penguin Young Readers Group.

Miller, Lauren. Free to Fall. 2014. (ENG.). 480p. (YA). (gr. 8). 17.99 *(978-0-06-219980-5(3),* HarperTeen) HarperCollins Pubs.

Miller, Leah Rae. Romancing the Nerd. 2016. (ENG.). 352p. (YA). pap. 9.99 *(978-1-63375-225-2(9),* 9781633752252) Entangled Publishing, LLC.

Miller, Tiwana Mutch. Praying Time. 2008. (YA). per. 10.00 *(978-0-9788937-8-1(6))* Amani Publishing, LLC.

Miller, Whitney A. The Crimson Gate. 2015. (ENG.). 312p. (YA). pap. 9.99 *(978-0-7387-4204-5(X),* Flux) North Star Editions.

—The Violet Hour. 2014. (ENG.). 312p. (YA). pap. 9.99 *(978-0-7387-3721-8(6),* Flux) North Star Editions.

Millmann, Anita Sutherland. Zitta & Nelli. 2011. 24p. pap. 15.14 *(978-1-4634-0036-1(5))* AuthorHouse.

Mills, Wendy. All We Have Left. (ENG.). 368p. (YA). 2017. pap. 9.99 *(978-1-68119-432-5(5),* 9781681194325) 2016. 17.99 *(978-1-61963-343-8(4),* 9781619633438) Bloomsbury Publishing USA. (Bloomsbury USA Childrens).

Milord, Susan. If I Could. Denise, Christopher, illus. 2009. (ENG.). 32p. (J). (gr. k-k). 15.99 *(978-0-7636-4342-3(4))* Candlewick Pr.

Mirabelli, Eugene. The Queen of the Rain Was in Love with the Prince of the Sky. 2008. pap. 5.00 *(978-0-935891-08-9(0))* Spring Harbor Pr.

Mitchell, Melanie, illus. Who Do You Love? 2008. (ENG.). 6p. (J). bds. 5.95 *(978-1-58117-707-7(0),* Intervisual/Piggy Toes) Bendon, Inc.

Mitchell, Saundra. The Springsweet. 2013. (ENG.). 304p. (YA). (gr. 7). pap. 8.99 *(978-0-544-00327-9(6))* Houghton Mifflin Harcourt Publishing Co.

Mittal, Amitabh. The Heir Apparent. 2009. 32p. pap. 14.99 *(978-1-4389-7845-1(6))* AuthorHouse.

Miyasaka, Kaho. Kare First Love, 10 vols. Miyasaka, Kaho, illus. (Kare First Love Ser.). (ENG., Illus.). 2006. 208p. pap. 9.99 *(978-1-4215-0547-3(9))* 2006. 208p. pap. 9.99 *(978-1-4215-0546-6(0))* 2005. 192p. pap. 9.99 *(978-1-4215-0139-0(2))* Viz Media.

Mizutani, Fuka. Love at Fourteen. 2015. (Love at Fourteen Ser.: 3). (ENG., Illus.). 192p. (J). (gr. 8-17). pap. 15.00 *(978-0-316-29876-6(X),* Yen Pr.) Orbit.

Moffitt, Debra. Girls in Charge. 2011. (Pink Locker Society Novels Ser.: 4). (ENG.). 208p. (J). (gr. 3-7). pap. 18.99 *(978-0-312-64506-9(6),* 9780312645069, St. Martin's Griffin) St. Martin's Pr.

Molesworth. The Tapestry Room: A Child's Romance. l.t. ed. 2007. (ENG.). 160p. pap. 21.99 *(978-1-4346-0792-8(5))* Creative Media Partners, LLC.

Molesworth & Molesworth, Mary Louisa S. The Tapestry Room. 2008. 116p. 22.95 *(978-1-60664-990-9(6));* per. 9.95 *(978-1-60312-540-6(X))* Aegypan.

Monir, Alexandra. Timekeeper. (ENG.). (YA). (gr. 7). 2014. 304p. pap. 8.99 *(978-0-385-73841-5(2),* Ember) 2013. 288p. 16.99 *(978-0-385-73840-8(4),* Delacorte Bks. for Young Readers) Random Hse. Children's Bks.

—Timeless. 2012. (ENG.). 300p. (YA). (gr. 7). pap. 8.99 *(978-0-385-73839-2(0),* Ember) Random Hse. Children's Bks.

Montgomery, L. M. The Blue Castle. Date not set. (J). 22.95 *(978-0-8488-2370-2(2))* Amereon Ltd.

Moore, A. C. Always Room for Dessert. 2nd ed. 2004. 304p. (YA). per. 13.95 *(978-0-9744060-0-8(7))* Moore, Ammanuel.

Moore, Kelly, et al. Neverwas. 2014. (YA). pap. *(978-0-545-43419-5(X));* (Amber House Ser.: 2). (ENG.). 320p. (J). (gr. 9). 17.99 *(978-0-545-43418-8(1),* Levine, Arthur A. Bks.) Scholastic, Inc.

Moore, Stephen. Dancing in the Arms of Orion. 2004. 366p. (YA). 30.95 *(978-0-595-66335-4(4))* iUniverse, Inc.

Morrill, Lauren. My Unscripted Life. 2016. (ENG.). 288p. (YA). (gr. 7). 17.99 *(978-0-553-49801-1(0),* Delacorte Pr.) Random Hse. Children's Bks.

Mosher, Richard. Zazoo. 2004. (ENG.). 272p. (YA). (gr. 7-18). reprint ed. pap. 15.95 *(978-0-618-43904-1(8))* Houghton Mifflin Harcourt Publishing Co.

Moss, Marissa. Amelia's Summer Survival Guide: Amelia's Longest, Biggest, Most-Fights-Ever Family Reunion; Amelia's Itchy-Twitchy, Lovey-Dovey Summer at Camp Mosquito. Moss, Marissa, illus. 2011. (Amelia Ser.). (ENG., Illus.). 160p. (J). (gr. 5-8). 12.99 *(978-1-4424-2331-2(5),* Simon & Schuster/Paula Wiseman Bks.) Simon & Schuster/Paula Wiseman Bks.

Moulton, Courtney Allison. Shadows in the Silence. 2014. (Angelfire Ser.: 3). (ENG.). 480p. (YA). (gr. 9). pap. 9.99 *(978-0-06-200241-9(4),* Tegen, Katherine Bks) HarperCollins Pubs.

Moyer, Jenny. Flashfall. 2016. (Flashfall Ser.). (ENG.). 352p. (YA). 17.99 *(978-1-62779-481-7(6),* 9781627794817, Holt, Henry & Co. Bks. For Young Readers) Holt, Henry & Co.

Ms. G. Mommy, Why Can't I Be Rich? Dade, Raheem, illus. 2005. 20p. (J). 7.00 *(978-0-9724621-1-2(2))* Unlimited Possibilities Publishing, LLC.

Mullen, Susan & Kun, Michael. We Are Still Tornadoes. 2016. (ENG.). 304p. (YA). 18.99 *(978-1-250-09840-5(8),* 9781250098405, St. Martin's Griffin) St. Martin's Pr.

Munsch, Robert. Love You Forever Pop-Up Edition. McGraw, Sheila, illus. 2017. (ENG.). 14p. (J). (gr. -1-1). 24.95 ***(978-1-77085-965-4(9),*** 9781770859654) Firefly Bks., Ltd.

Munsch, Robert. Siempre Te Querre. 2004. (SPA., Illus.). (J). (gr. k-3). spiral bd. *(978-0-616-14608-8(6))* Canadian National Institute for the Blind/Institut National Canadien pour les Aveugles.

Murphy, Julie. Side Effects May Vary. (ENG.). (YA). (gr. 9). 2015. 352p. pap. 9.99 *(978-0-06-224537-3(6))* 2014. 336p. 17.99 *(978-0-06-224535-9(X))* HarperCollins Pubs.

Murphy, Lisa. Secret Smile. 2008. 52p. pap. 11.95 *(978-1-4092-2767-0(7))* Lulu Pr., Inc.

Murphy, Mary. Utterly Lovely One. 2012. (ENG., Illus.). 32p. (J). (gr. -1-k). 16.99 *(978-0-7636-5267-8(9))* Candlewick Pr.

Musgrave, Susan. Love You More, 1 vol. Melo, Esperança, illus. 2014. (ENG.). 24p. (J). (gr. -1-k). bds. 9.95 *(978-1-4598-0240-7(3))* Orca Bk. Pubs. USA.

Myers, Jason. Dead End. 2011. (ENG.). 384p. (YA). (gr. 10-18). pap. 9.99 *(978-1-4424-1430-3(8),* Simon Pulse) Simon Pulse.

—Exit Here. 2007. (ENG.). 464p. (YA). (gr. 10-12). pap. 9.99 *(978-1-4169-1748-9(9),* Simon Pulse) Simon Pulse.

—Run the Game: Play or Be Played. 2012. (ENG.). 544p. (YA). (gr. 10). pap. 9.99 *(978-1-4424-1432-7(4),* Simon Pulse) Simon Pulse.

Myers, Walter Dean. Street Love. (ENG.). 2007. 160p. (YA). (gr. 8-18). pap. 9.99 *(978-0-06-440732-8(2))* 2006. 144p. (J). (gr. 7-18). 15.99 *(978-0-06-028079-6(4))* HarperCollins Pubs. (Amistad).

—Street Love. 2007. 19.00 *(978-0-7569-8102-0(6))* Perfection Learning Corp.

—What They Found: Love on 145th Street. 2011. 10.54 *(978-0-7848-3386-5(9));* 10.54 *(978-0-7848-3499-2(7))* Marco Bk. Co. (Everbind).

—What They Found: Love on 145th Street. 2009. (ENG.). 256p. (YA). (gr. 9). pap. 8.99 *(978-0-375-84545-1(3),* Lamb, Wendy Bks.) Random Hse. Children's Bks.

Myracle, Lauren. The Infinite Moment of Us. (ENG.). 336p. (YA). (gr. 9-17). 2014. pap. 8.95 *(978-1-4197-1358-3(2))* 2013. 18.95 *(978-1-4197-0793-3(0))* Abrams, Inc. (Amulet Bks.).

Mystic. Talon Hawke: A Journey Through Darkness. 2007. 228p. per. 15.95 *(978-0-595-46386-2(X))* iUniverse, Inc.

Nadin, Joanna. Paradise. 2012. (ENG., Illus.). 272p. (YA). (gr. 9). 16.99 *(978-0-7636-5713-0(1))* Candlewick Pr.

Nahall Nikoo Fells. Drowning in the Mainstream: Confessions of a Sister. 2010. 284p. pap. 17.95 *(978-1-4502-0554-2(2))* iUniverse, Inc.

Nanette. Tootie the Green Kitten. 2004. (Life on Granny's Farm Ser.). (J). 12.95 *(978-0-9741269-7-5(7))* St. Bernard Publishing, LLC.

Napoli, Donna Jo. Skin, 0 vols. 2013. (ENG.). 352p. (YA). (gr. 9-12). pap. 9.99 *(978-1-4778-1690-5(9),* 9781477816905, Amazon Children's Publishing) Amazon Publishing.

Naraynan, Manjula. The Green Green Pear. 2009. (Illus.). 32p. pap. 14.49 *(978-1-4389-6957-2(0))* AuthorHouse.
Nayeri, Daniel. Straw House, Wood House, Brick House, Blow: Four Novellas by Daniel Nayeri. Weinberg, James, illus. 2011. (ENG.). 432p. (YA). (gr. 9). 19.99 *(978-0-7636-5526-6(0))* Candlewick Pr.
Naylor, Phyllis Reynolds. Achingly Alice. 2012. (Alice Ser.: 10). (ENG., Illus.). 176p. (J). (gr. 5-9). pap. 6.99 *(978-1-4424-3494-3(5)*, Atheneum Bks. for Young Readers) Simon & Schuster Children's Publishing.
—Alice in Rapture, Sort Of. 2011. (Alice Ser.: 2). (ENG.). 208p. (J). (gr. 5-9). pap. 6.99 *(978-1-4424-2362-6(5)*, Atheneum Bks. for Young Readers) Simon & Schuster Children's Publishing.
Nazemian, Abdi. The Authentics. 2017. 288p. (YA). (gr. 8). 17.99 *(978-0-06-248646-2(2))* HarperCollins Pubs.
Neal, Bethany. My Last Kiss. 2014. (ENG.). 368p. (YA). (gr. 7). 17.99 *(978-0-374-35128-1(7)*, Farrar, Straus & Giroux (BYR)) Farrar, Straus & Giroux.
Neely, Judith. And Even More. 2009. 24p. pap. 11.49 *(978-1-4389-5649-7(5))* AuthorHouse.
Neenan, Colin. Idiot! A Love Story with Drama, Betrayal & E-mail. 2004. (Illus.). 152p. (YA). (gr. 7-13). per. 8.95 *(978-0-9746481-1-8(6))* Brown Barn Bks.
Neighbour, Leona. Fairly Ballerina Princess. 2003. 26p. per. 10.95 *(978-1-932344-42-4(X))* Thornton Publishing, Inc.
Nelson, Jan. Signs of Love. Bohart, Lisa, illus. 2009. 24p. pap. 12.95 *(978-1-936051-54-0(0))* Peppertree Pr., The.
Nelson, Sarah. Just for You. 2012. 20p. (-18). pap. 10.95 *(978-1-4497-7017-4(7)*, WestBow Pr.) Author Solutions, Inc.
Nelson, Suzanne. Heart & Salsa. 2006. (S. A. S. S. Ser.). (ENG., Illus.). 224p. (YA). (gr. 7-18). 6.99 *(978-0-14-240647-2(3)*, Speak) Penguin Young Readers Group.
—You're Bacon Me Crazy: a Wish Novel. 2017. (ENG.). 256p. (J). (gr. 4-7). pap. 6.99 *(978-1-338-09919-5(1)*, Scholastic Paperbacks) Scholastic, Inc.
Neumann, A. C. The Drawer's Gift. 2010. 60p. pap. 25.95 *(978-1-935340-62-1(X))* Worthy Shorts.
Newland, Laura. Nicky Boy, I Love You. 2009. 24p. pap. 14.99 *(978-1-4389-2210-2(8))* AuthorHouse.
Nex, Anthony, photos by. Little Hands Love. 2009. (ENG., Illus.). 12p. (J). 8.95 *(978-1-58117-851-7(4)*, Intervisual/Piggy Toes) Bendon, Inc.
Nguyen, Jenn P. & Nguyen, Phuong Anh. The Way to Game the Walk of Shame. 2016. (ENG.). 336p. (YA). pap. 9.99 *(978-1-250-08407-1(5)*, 9781250084071) Feiwel & Friends.
Nickerson, Jane. The Mirk & Midnight Hour. 2014. (ENG.). 384p. (YA). (gr. 9). 16.99 *(978-0-385-75286-2(5)*, Knopf Bks. for Young Readers) Random Hse. Children's Bks.
Nielsen, Susin. Optimists Die First. 2017. (ENG.). 240p. (YA). (gr. 7). 17.99 *(978-0-553-49690-1(5)*, Lamb, Wendy Bks.) Random Hse. Children's Bks.
Night, P. J. Don't Drink the Punch! 2012. (You're Invited to a Creepover Ser.: 11). (ENG.). 160p. (J). (gr. 3-7). pap. 6.99 *(978-1-4424-5287-9(0)*, Simon Spotlight) Simon Spotlight.
Niven, Jennifer. Holding up the Universe. 2016. (ENG.). 400p. (YA). (gr. 9). 17.99 *(978-0-385-75592-4(9))*; lib. bdg. 20.99 *(978-0-385-75593-1(7))* Random Hse. Children's Bks. (Knopf Bks. for Young Readers).
Nix, Garth. Newt's Emerald. 2015. (ENG.). 304p. (YA). (gr. 8-12). 18.99 *(978-0-06-236004-5(3))* HarperCollins Pubs.
Noël, Alyson. The Beginning: Evermore + Blue Moon. 2013. (Immortals Ser.). (ENG.). 608p. (YA). (gr. 7-12). pap. 9.99 *(978-1-250-03728-2(X)*, 9781250037282, St. Martin's Griffin) St. Martin's Pr.
—Desafio: Quinto Libro de la Serie de Los Inmortales. 2012. (Vintage Espanol Ser.). (SPA.). 336p. (YA). (gr. 7). pap. 10.95 *(978-0-307-95147-2(2)*, Vintage Espanol) Knopf Doubleday Publishing Group.
—Echo. 2013. (Soul Seekers Ser.: 2). (ENG.). 352p. (YA). (gr. 7). mass mkt. 9.99 *(978-1-250-04689-5(0)*, 9781250046895, St. Martin's Paperbacks) St. Martin's Pr.
—Everlasting. 2013. (Immortals Ser.: 6). (ENG.). 352p. (YA). (gr. 7-12). mass mkt. 9.99 *(978-1-250-04685-7(8)*, 9781250046857, St. Martin's Paperbacks); pap. 10.99 *(978-1-250-02517-3(6)*, 9781250025173, St. Martin's Griffin) St. Martin's Pr.
—Horizon. 2013. (Soul Seekers Ser.: 4). (ENG.). 336p. (YA). (gr. 7). mass mkt. 9.99 *(978-1-250-05435-7(4)*, 9781250054357, St. Martin's Paperbacks) St. Martin's Pr.
—Keeping Secrets. 2012. (ENG.). 448p. (YA). (gr. 8-12). pap. 9.99 *(978-1-250-01862-5(5)*, 9781250018625, St. Martin's Griffin) St. Martin's Pr.
—Mystic. 2013. (Soul Seekers Ser.: 3). (ENG.). 320p. (YA). (gr. 7). mass mkt. 9.99 *(978-1-250-04818-9(4)*, 9781250048189, St. Martin's Paperbacks); 18.99 *(978-0-312-66488-6(5)*, 9780312664886, St. Martin's Griffin); pap. 9.99 *(978-0-312-57567-0(X)*, 9780312575670, St. Martin's Griffin) St. Martin's Pr.
—Night Star. (Immortals Ser.: 5). (ENG.). 320p. (YA). (gr. 7-12). 2013. mass mkt. 9.99 *(978-1-250-04688-8(2)*, 9781250046888, St. Martin's Paperbacks) 2010. 17.99 *(978-0-312-59098-7(9)*, 9780312590987, St. Martin's Griffin) St. Martin's Pr.
—Unrivaled. (Beautiful Idols Ser.: 1). (YA). (gr. 9). 2017. 448p. pap. 9.99 *(978-0-06-232453-5(5))* 2016. 432p. 17.99 *(978-0-06-232452-8(7))* HarperCollins Pubs. (Tegen, Katherine Bks).
Nolan, Allia Zobel. God's Rainbow. Chung, Chi, illus. 2007. 16p. (J). 12.99 *(978-0-8254-5537-7(5))* Kregel Pubns.
Norac, Carl. My Mummy Is Magic. Godon, Ingrid, illus. 2006. (ENG.). 32p. (J). (gr. 3-6). pap. 14.95 *(978-1-4050-9023-0(5)*, Macmillan) Pan Macmillan GBR. Dist: Trans-Atlantic Pubns., Inc.
—Las Palabras Dulces. 2003. (SPA., Illus.). 32p. (J). *(978-84-95150-05-9(0)*, COR1690) Corimbo, Editorial S.L. ESP. Dist: Lectorum Pubns., Inc.
North, Phoebe. Starbreak. 2014. (Starglass Sequence Ser.). (ENG., Illus.). 432p. (YA). (gr. 7). 17.99 *(978-1-4424-5956-4(5)*, Simon & Schuster Bks. For Young Readers) Simon & Schuster Bks. For Young Readers.
Nowlin, Laura. If He Had Been with Me. 2013. (ENG.). 336p. (YA). (gr. 7-12). pap. 9.99 *(978-1-4022-7782-5(2)*, 9781402277825) Sourcebooks, Inc.
—This Song Is (Not) for You. 2016. (ENG.). 240p. (YA). (gr. 8-12). pap. 9.99 *(978-1-4926-0290-3(6)*, 9781492602903) Sourcebooks, Inc.
Numeroff, Laura Joffe. Happy Valentine's Day, Mouse! Bond, Felicia, illus. 2009. (If You Give... Ser.). (ENG.). 24p. (J). (gr. -1-3). bds. 6.99 *(978-0-06-180432-8(0))* HarperCollins Pubs.
Nunes, Lygia Bojunga. El Sofa Estampado. (SPA.). 184p. (YA). (gr. 5-8). *(978-84-239-2748-7(2)*, EC2752) Espasa Calpe, S.A. ESP. Dist: Lectorum Pubns., Inc.
Oaklee, Mammy. Mailbox Kitten. 2012. 56p. pap. *(978-1-77097-643-6(4))* FriesenPress.
O'Brien, Caragh M. The Rule of Mirrors. 2016. (Vault of Dreamers Trilogy Ser.: 2). (ENG., Illus.). 432p. (YA). (gr. 7). 17.99 *(978-1-59643-940-5(8)*, 9781596439405) Roaring Brook Pr.
O'Brien, Lara. Chesca & the Spirit of Grace. 2013. 316p. pap. 13.99 *(978-0-9896752-0-8(3))* O'Brien, Lara Publishing.
Ockler, Sarah. The Book of Broken Hearts. (ENG., Illus.). (YA). (gr. 9). 2014. 384p. pap. 9.99 *(978-1-4424-3039-6(7))* 2013. 368p. 17.99 *(978-1-4424-3038-9(9))* Simon Pulse. (Simon Pulse).
—#scandal. 2014. (ENG., Illus.). 416p. (YA). (gr. 9). 17.99 *(978-1-4814-0124-1(6)*, Simon Pulse) Simon Pulse.
O'Dare, Helen. Love. O'Byrne, Nicola, illus. 2016. (ENG.). 26p. (J). bds. 6.99 *(978-1-62686-677-5(5)*, Silver Dolphin Bks.) Readerlink Distribution Services, LLC.
Ohlin, Nancy. Consent. 2015. (ENG., Illus.). 288p. (YA). (gr. 9). 17.99 *(978-1-4424-6490-2(9)*, Simon Pulse) Simon Pulse.
Olin, Sean. Wicked Games. 2014. (Wicked Games Ser.: 1). (ENG.). 352p. (YA). (gr. 9). 17.99 *(978-0-06-219237-0(X)*, Tegen, Katherine Bks) HarperCollins Pubs.
Oliver, Amanda Eaddy. Cheyenne the Cat. 2010. 28p. 13.99 *(978-1-4520-6218-1(8))* AuthorHouse.
Oliver, Lauren. Delirium. (Delirium Trilogy Ser.: 1). (ENG.). 480p. (YA). (gr. 9-18). 2016. pap. 9.99 *(978-0-06-172683-5(4))* 2011. 17.99 *(978-0-06-211243-9(0))* HarperCollins Pubs.
—Delirium. 2016. (Delirium Ser.: 1). (YA). lib. bdg. 20.85 *(978-0-606-23575-4(2)*, Turtleback) Turtleback Bks.
—Delirium Stories: Hana, Annabel, Raven & Alex. (Delirium Story Ser.). 224p. (YA). (gr. 9). 2016. pap. 9.99 *(978-0-06-248432-1(X))* 2013. (ENG.). pap. 9.99 *(978-0-06-226778-8(7))* HarperCollins Pubs.
—Delirium Stories: Hana, Annabel, Raven & Alex. (Delirium Ser.). (YA). 2016. lib. bdg. 20.85 *(978-0-606-38920-4(2))* 2013. lib. bdg. 20.85 *(978-0-606-31834-1(8)*, Turtleback) Turtleback Bks.
—Pandemonium. (YA). 2016. (Delirium Trilogy Ser.: 2). (ENG.). 400p. (gr. 9). pap. 9.99 *(978-0-06-197807-4(8))* 2012. (Delirium Trilogy Ser.: 2). (ENG.). 384p. (gr. 9-18). 17.99 *(978-0-06-197806-7(X))* 2012. (Delirium Trilogy: Bk. 2). 375p. *(978-0-06-213008-2(0))* HarperCollins Pubs.
—Pandemonium. 2016. (Delirium Ser.: 2). (YA). lib. bdg. 20.85 *(978-0-606-27141-7(4)*, Turtleback) Turtleback Bks.
—Requiem. 2013. (Delirium Trilogy: Bk. 3). (ENG.). 400p. (J). (gr. 9). 18.99 *(978-0-06-201453-5(6))* HarperCollins Pubs.
Olivieri, Laura. Where Are You: A Child's Book about Loss. 2007. 28p. 13.94 *(978-1-4357-0091-8(0))* Lulu Pr., Inc.
Olsen, Kaki. Swan & Shadow: A Swan Lake Story. 2016. (ENG.). 299p. (YA). pap. 18.99 *(978-1-4621-1814-4(3)*, Sweetwater Bks.) Cedar Fort, Inc./CFI Distribution.
Olsen, Mary-Kate & Olsen, Ashley. The Facts about Flirting. 2005. (ENG., Illus.). 112p. *(978-0-00-715883-6(1)*, HarperCollins Children's Bks.) HarperCollins Pubs. Ltd.
—Secret Crush. 2003. (ENG., Illus.). 128p. *(978-0-00-714452-5(0)*, HarperCollins Children's Bks.) HarperCollins Pubs. Ltd.
Olsen, Nora. Frenemy of the People. 2014. (ENG.). 264p. (J). (gr. 7). pap. 11.95 *(978-1-62639-063-8(0))* Bold Strokes Bks.
—Maxine Wore Black. 2014. (ENG.). 264p. (J). (gr. 7). pap. 11.95 *(978-1-62639-208-3(0))* Bold Strokes Bks.
—Swans & Klons. 2013. (ENG.). 192p. (gr. 7). pap. 11.95 *(978-1-60282-874-2(1))* Bold Strokes Bks.
Oppel, Kenneth. Every Hidden Thing. 2016. (ENG., Illus.). 368p. (YA). (gr. 9). 17.99 *(978-1-4814-6416-1(7)*, Simon & Schuster Bks. For Young Readers) Simon & Schuster Bks. For Young Readers.
Orczy, Emmuska. The Nest of the Sparrowhawk. 2008. 236p. pap. 15.95 *(978-1-60664-232-0(4))* Rodgers, Alan Bks.
—Unto Caesar. 2008. 260p. 29.95 *(978-1-60664-863-6(2))*; pap. 15.95 *(978-1-60664-110-1(7))* Aegypan.
Orlando, Kristen, et al. You Don't Know My Name. 2017. (Black Angel Chronicles Ser.). (ENG.). 304p. (YA). 16.99 *(978-1-250-08411-8(3)*, 9781250084118) Feiwel & Friends.
Ormand, Kate & Louise, Kate. Dark Days. 2014. (ENG.). 256p. (J). (gr. 6). 16.95 *(978-1-62873-594-9(5)*, Sky Pony Pr.) Skyhorse Publishing Co., Inc.
Ormsbee, Kathryn. Lucky Few. (ENG., Illus.). (YA). (gr. 9). 2017. 400p. pap. 10.99 *(978-1-4814-5529-9(X))* 2016. 384p. 17.99 *(978-1-4814-5528-2(1))* Simon & Schuster Bks. For Young Readers. (Simon & Schuster Bks. For Young Readers).
O'Rourke, Erica. Dissonance. 2014. (Dissonance Ser.). (ENG., Illus.). 496p. (YA). (gr. 7). 17.99 *(978-1-4424-6024-9(5)*, Simon & Schuster Bks. For Young Readers) Simon & Schuster Bks. For Young Readers.
—Resonance. 2015. (Dissonance Ser.). (ENG., Illus.). 448p. (YA). (gr. 7). 18.99 *(978-1-4424-6027-0(X)*, Simon & Schuster Bks. For Young Readers) Simon & Schuster Bks. For Young Readers.
Oseman, Alice. Solitaire. 2015. (ENG.). 368p. (YA). (gr. 8). 17.99 *(978-0-06-233568-5(5)*, HarperTeen) HarperCollins Pubs.
O'Shea, M.J. Blood Moon [Library Edition]. 3rd ed. 2014. 160p. pap. 14.99 *(978-1-62798-454-6(2)*, Harmony Ink Pr.) Dreamspinner Pr.
Owens, Robert. Butterfly Love. 2008. 34p. pap. 16.70 *(978-0-557-01168-1(X))* Lulu Pr., Inc.
Owens, Robert & Owens, Donna. The Misadventures of Our Son Henry. Bollinger, Carol, illus. 2007. 52p. per. 16.95 *(978-1-4241-8721-8(4))* America Star Bks.
Page, Nick & Claire. Snow White. 2006. (Read with Me (Make Believe Ideas) Ser.). (Illus.). 32p. (J). (gr. k-2). *(978-1-84610-163-2(8))* Make Believe Ideas.
Paige, Danielle. Stealing Snow. 2016. (Stealing Snow Ser.). (ENG.). 384p. (YA). (gr. 9-12). 18.99 *(978-1-68119-076-1(1)*, 9781681190761, Bloomsbury USA Childrens) Bloomsbury Publishing USA.
—Stealing Snow. 2017. (SPA.). 384p. (YA). 18.95 ***(978-84-16700-68-4(0))*** Roca Editorial ESP. Dist: Spanish Pubs., LLC.
Paige, Danielle. Yellow Brick War. 2017. (Dorothy Must Die Ser.: 3). 304p. (YA). (gr. 9). pap. 9.99 *(978-0-06-228074-9(0))* HarperCollins Pubs.
Panaitescu, Simona. The Unseen Paths of the Forest: 13 Tales about Love & Friendship. Moscal, Manuela, illus. 2012. (ENG.). 263p. pap. 14.95 *(978-1-4327-7908-5(7))* Outskirts Pr., Inc.
Pandell, Karen. Te Amo, Sol - Te Amo, Luna. dePaola, Tomie, illus. 2003.Tr. of I Love You, Sun - I Love You, Moon. (SPA & ENG.). 12p. (J). (gr. -1 — 1). bds. 7.99 *(978-0-399-24165-9(5)*, G.P. Putnam's Sons Books for Young Readers) Penguin Young Readers Group.
Parish, Herman. Amelia Bedelia Ties the Knot. 2016. (Amelia Bedelia Chapter Book Ser.: 10). (J). lib. bdg. 14.75 *(978-0-606-38762-0(5))* Turtleback Bks.
Parker, Amy Christine. Smash & Grab. 2016. (ENG.). 384p. (YA). (gr. 7). 17.99 *(978-0-553-53382-8(7)*, Random Hse. Bks. for Young Readers) Random Hse. Children's Bks.
Parker, Madison. Play Me, I'm Yours. 2016. (ENG., Illus.). (J). 24.99 ***(978-1-63533-062-5(9))*** 2013. 244p. pap. 14.99 *(978-1-62380-449-7(3))* Dreamspinner Pr. (Harmony Ink Pr.).
Parker, Madison. Play Me, I'm Yours [Library Edition]. 2013. 244p. pap. 14.99 *(978-1-62380-919-5(3)*, Harmony Ink Pr.) Dreamspinner Pr.
Parker, Marjorie Blain. I Love You near & Far. Henry, Jed, illus. 2015. (Snuggle Time Stories Ser.). (ENG.). 24p. (J). (gr. -1-1). 9.95 *(978-1-4549-0507-3(7))* Sterling Publishing Co., Inc.
Parker, Natalie C. Three Sides of a Heart: Stories about Love Triangles. 2017. 448p. (YA). (gr. 9). 17.99 ***(978-0-06-242447-1(5)***, HarperTeen) HarperCollins Pubs.
Parker, S. M. The Girl Who Fell. (ENG., Illus.). (YA). (gr. 11). 2017. 384p. pap. 10.99 *(978-1-4814-3724-0(0))* 2016. 368p. 17.99 *(978-1-4814-3725-7(9))* Simon Pulse. (Simon Pulse).
Parks, M. Elizabeth. The Sea Cow. 2013. (Illus.). 44p. pap. 16.95 *(978-0-9824565-2-1(2))* Sibyl Merritt.
Parr, Todd. The I Love You Book. 2013. (ENG., Illus.). 28p. (J). (gr. -1 — 1). bds. 6.99 *(978-0-316-24756-6(1))* Little, Brown Bks. for Young Readers.
—The I Love You Book. Parr, Todd, illus. 2009. (ENG., Illus.). 32p. (J). (gr. -1-1). 10.99 *(978-0-316-01985-9(2))* Little, Brown Bks. for Young Readers.
Parrish, Anya. Damage. 2011. (ENG.). 288p. (YA). pap. 9.95 *(978-0-7387-2700-4(8)*, Flux) North Star Editions.
Paschkis, Julie. Apple Cake: A Recipe for Love. 2012. (ENG., Illus.). 32p. (J). (gr. -1-3). 16.99 *(978-0-547-80745-4(7))* Houghton Mifflin Harcourt Publishing Co.
Patricelli, Leslie. Huggy Kissy. Patricelli, Leslie, illus. 2012. (Leslie Patricelli Board Bks.). (ENG., Illus.). 26p. (J). (gr. k — 1). bds. 6.99 *(978-0-7636-3246-5(5))* Candlewick Pr.
Patrick, J. Nelle. Tsarina. 2014. (ENG.). 336p. (YA). (gr. 7). 17.99 *(978-1-59514-693-9(8)*, Razorbill) Penguin Young Readers Group.
Patterson, Horace. Ernie the Ermine. Parker, Jack, illus. 2007. 28p. per. 7.99 *(978-1-58942-374-9(7))* R.H. Boyd Publishing Corp.
Patterson, James & Dembowski, Jill. The Kiss. 2013. (Witch & Wizard Ser.: 4). (ENG.). 384p. (YA). (gr. 7-17). pap. 10.00 *(978-0-316-10176-9(1)*, Jimmy Patterson) Little Brown & Co.
Patterson, James & Paetro, Maxine. Confessions: The Paris Mysteries. 2014. (Confessions Ser.). (ENG.). 320p. (YA). (gr. 7-17). 18.00 *(978-0-316-37084-4(3)*, Jimmy Patterson) Little Brown & Co.
—Confessions: The Private School Murders. 2013. 422p. (YA). *(978-0-316-24263-9(2))* Little Brown & Co.
—Confessions: the Murder of an Angel. 2015. (Confessions Ser.: 4). (ENG.). 304p. (YA). (gr. 7-12). 18.00 *(978-0-316-30102-2(7)*, Jimmy Patterson) Little Brown & Co.
—The Paris Mysteries. l.t. ed. 2014. (Confessions Ser.: 3). (ENG.). 352p. (YA). (gr. 7-17). 30.99 *(978-0-316-40963-6(4)*, Jimmy Patterson) Little Brown & Co.
—The Paris Mysteries. 2015. (Confessions Ser.: 3). (YA). lib. bdg. 20.85 *(978-0-606-37526-9(0))* Turtleback Bks.
—The Private School Murders. 2015. (Confessions Ser.: 2). (ENG.). 400p. mass mkt. 8.00 *(978-1-4555-5946-6(6)*, Jimmy Patterson) Grand Central Publishing.
—The Private School Murders. (Confessions Ser.: 2). (ENG.). (YA). (gr. 7-17). 2014. 448p. pap. 10.00 *(978-0-316-20764-5(0))* 2013. 448p. 18.00 *(978-0-316-20765-2(9))* 2013. 480p. 22.00 *(978-0-316-23992-9(5))* Little Brown & Co. (Jimmy Patterson).
—The Private School Murders. 2014. (Confessions Ser.: 2). (YA). lib. bdg. 20.85 *(978-0-606-35945-0(1))* Turtleback Bks.
Patterson, James & Raymond, Emily. First Love. 2017. (ENG., Illus.). 384p. mass mkt. 7.99 ***(978-1-4555-8500-7(9)***, Jimmy Patterson) Little Brown & Co.
—First Love. Illingworth, Sasha, photos by. 2015. (ENG., Illus.). 336p. (YA). (gr. 10-17). pap. 9.99 *(978-0-316-20703-4(9)*, Jimmy Patterson) Little Brown & Co.
—First Love. 2014. (ENG.). 560p. (YA). pap. 16.00 *(978-1-4555-8501-4(7)*, Jimmy Patterson) Little Brown & Co.
—First Love. 2014. (YA). lib. bdg. 28.20 *(978-0-606-35894-1(3))* Turtleback Bks.
Patterson, Shannon. The Princess & the Cheese. 2010. 43p. pap. 19.95 *(978-0-557-51615-5(3))* Lulu Pr., Inc.
Paulsen, Gary. Crush: The Theory, Practice & Destructive Properties of Love. (ENG.). 144p. (J). (gr. 4-7). 2013. pap. 6.99 *(978-0-385-74231-3(2)*, Yearling) 2012. 12.99 *(978-0-385-74230-6(4)*, Lamb, Wendy Bks.) Random Hse. Children's Bks.
Payne, K. E. Another 365 Days. 2013. (ENG.). 264p. (J). (gr. 7). pap. 11.95 *(978-1-60282-775-2(3))* Bold Strokes Bks.
—Before. 2016. (ENG.). 240p. (J). (gr. 7). pap. 11.95 *(978-1-62639-677-7(9))* Bold Strokes Bks.
—Me@You.com. 2012. (ENG.). 288p. (J). (gr. 7). pap. 13.95 *(978-1-60282-592-5(0))* Bold Strokes Bks.
Pearson, Mary E. The Beauty of Darkness. 2016. (Remnant Chronicles Ser.: 3). (ENG., Illus.). 688p. (YA). (gr. 9-12). 18.99 *(978-0-8050-9925-6(5)*, 9780805099256, Holt, Henry & Co. Bks. For Young Readers) Holt, Henry & Co.
—The Beauty of Darkness. 2017. (Remnant Chronicles Ser.: Bk. 3). (ENG.). 688p. (YA). pap. 10.99 *(978-1-250-11531-7(0)*, 9781250115317) Square Fish.
—The Heart of Betrayal. 2015. (Remnant Chronicles: Bk. 2). (ENG.). 480p. (YA). (gr. 9). 18.99 *(978-0-8050-9924-9(7)*, 9780805099249, Holt, Henry & Co. Bks. For Young Readers) Holt, Henry & Co.
—The Heart of Betrayal. 2016. (Remnant Chronicles Ser.: 2). (ENG.). 496p. (YA). pap. 10.99 *(978-1-250-08002-8(9)*, 9781250080028) Square Fish.
—The Kiss of Deception. 2014. (Remnant Chronicles Ser.: 1). (ENG.). 496p. (YA). (gr. 9-12). 18.99 *(978-0-8050-9923-2(9)*, 9780805099232); E-Book *(978-1-62779-218-9(X)*, 9781627792189) Holt, Henry & Co. (Holt, Henry & Co. Bks. For Young Readers).
—The Kiss of Deception. 2015. (Remnant Chronicles Ser.: 1). (ENG.). 512p. (YA). (gr. 9-12). pap. 10.99 *(978-1-250-06315-1(9)*, 9781250063151) Square Fish.
Pearson, Susan. Slugs in Love, 0 vols. O'Malley, Kevin, illus. 2012. (ENG.). 34p. (J). (gr. -1-3). pap. 7.99 *(978-0-7614-6248-4(1)*, 9780761462484, Amazon Children's Publishing) Amazon Publishing.
Pechero-Loewen, Mariella. I Want to Know How You Found Me. 2004. 39p. pap. 24.95 *(978-1-4137-2955-9(X))* PublishAmerica, Inc.
Peckham, Lori, ed. Guide's Greatest Animal Stories. 2006. 143p. (J). (gr. 5-9). per. 10.99 *(978-0-8280-1944-6(4))* Review & Herald Publishing Assn.
Pelton, Lisa. Logos & Adoption: Remi's Journey. 2012. 40p. pap. 14.95 *(978-1-4497-5378-8(7)*, WestBow Pr.) Author Solutions, Inc.
Penn, Audrey. A Pocket Full of Kisses. Gibson, Barbara Leonard, illus. 2004. (New Child & Family Press Titles Ser.). 32p. (gr. -1-1). 16.95 *(978-0-87868-894-4(3)*, 8943, Child & Family Pr.) Child Welfare League of America, Inc.
—A Pocket Full of Kisses. Gibson, Barbara Leonard, illus. 2006. (Kissing Hand Ser.). (ENG.). 32p. (J). (gr. -1-3). 16.95 *(978-1-933718-02-6(1))* Tanglewood Pr.
Pepper, Cally. Bird Without Wings: Faebles. 2013. (ENG.). 283p. (YA). (gr. 8-17). pap. 12.95 *(978-1-78099-902-9(X)*, Lodestone Bks.) Hunt, John Publishing Ltd. GBR. Dist: National Bk. Network.
Perini, Mark & Cross, Julie. Halfway Perfect. 2015. (ENG.). 384p. (YA). (gr. 8-12). pap. 9.99 *(978-1-4022-9719-9(X)*, 9781402297199) Sourcebooks, Inc.
Perkins, Kevin John. The Circlet. 2010. 316p. pap. *(978-1-907211-33-1(0))* Grosvenor Hse. Publishing Ltd.
Perkins, Stephanie. Isla & the Happily Ever After. 2015. (ENG.). 368p. (YA). (gr. 9-12). pap. 10.99 *(978-0-14-242627-2(X)*, Speak) Penguin Publishing Group.
—Isla & the Happily Ever After. 2014. (ENG.). 352p. (YA). (gr. 9). 17.99 *(978-0-525-42563-2(2)*, Dutton Books for Young Readers) Penguin Young Readers Group.
—My True Love Gave to Me: Twelve Holiday Stories. 2014. (ENG., Illus.). 336p. (YA). (gr. 8-12). 18.99 *(978-1-250-05930-7(5)*, 9781250059307, St. Martin's Griffin) St. Martin's Pr.
—Summer Days & Summer Nights: Twelve Love Stories. 2017. (ENG.). 400p. (YA). pap. 10.99 *(978-1-250-07913-8(6)*, 9781250079138, St. Martin's Griffin) St. Martin's Pr.
Perkins, Stephanie, ed. Summer Days & Summer Nights: Twelve Summer Romances. 2016. (ENG., Illus.). 400p. (YA). 19.99 *(978-1-250-07912-1(8)*, 9781250079121, St. Martin's Griffin) St. Martin's Pr.
Perrault, Charles. Cinderella. Innocenti, Roberto, illus. 2013. (ENG.). 32p. (J). (gr. 1-17). pap. 7.99 *(978-0-89812-828-4(5)*, Creative Paperbacks) Creative Co., The.
Perry, Jolene. The Next Door Boys. 2011. (YA). *(978-1-59955-910-0(2)*, Bonneville Bks.) Cedar Fort, Inc./CFI Distribution.
Perry, Laurie. Hello World, This Is Me!, 1 vol. 2009. 55p. pap. 16.95 *(978-1-4489-2013-6(2))* PublishAmerica, Inc.
Peter, Dawn. Mark the Remarkable & Can't Say Can't. 2012. 24p. pap. *(978-1-77067-033-4(5))* FriesenPress.
Peterfreund, Diana. For Darkness Shows the Stars. (Stars Ser.: 1). (ENG.). (YA). (gr. 8). 2013. 448p. pap. 9.99 *(978-0-06-200615-8(0))* 2012. 416p. 17.99 *(978-0-06-200614-1(2))* HarperCollins Pubs.
Peters, Julie Anne. Lies My Girlfriend Told Me. 2017. (ENG.). 256p. (YA). (gr. 10-17). pap. 9.99 ***(978-0-316-23495-5(8))*** Little, Brown Bks. for Young Readers.
Petersen, David. Snowy Valentine. Petersen, David, illus. 2011. (ENG., Illus.). 32p. (J). (gr. -1-3). 14.99 *(978-0-06-146378-5(7))* HarperCollins Pubs.
Petroff, Shani. Romeo & What's Her Name. 2017. (ENG.). 224p. (YA). pap. 9.99 *(978-1-250-11114-2(5)*, 9781250111142) Feiwel & Friends.
Petty, Heather. Final Fall. 2017. (YA). pap. ***(978-1-4814-2310-6(X)***, Simon & Schuster Bks. For Young Readers) Simon & Schuster Bks. For Young Readers.
Petty, Heather. Lock & Mori. 2016. (Lock & Mori Ser.). (ENG.). 272p. (YA). (gr. 9). pap. 10.99 *(978-1-4814-2304-5(5))* Simon & Schuster, Inc.
Petty, Heather W. Mind Games. 2016. (Lock & Mori Ser.). (ENG., Illus.). 304p. (YA). (gr. 9). 17.99 *(978-1-4814-2306-9(1)*, Simon & Schuster Bks. For Young Readers) Simon & Schuster Bks. For Young Readers.
Peyton, Km. Far from Home. 2014. (ENG., Illus.). 183p. (J). (gr. 4-7). pap. 5.99 *(978-0-7945-3292-5(6)*, Usborne) EDC Publishing.
Pham, LeUyen. All the Things I Love about You. Pham, LeUyen, illus. 2010. (ENG., Illus.). 40p. (J). (gr. -1-3). 14.99 *(978-0-06-199029-8(9))* HarperCollins Pubs.
Philbin, Joanna. Since Last Summer. 2014. (Rules of Summer Ser.: 2). (ENG.). 304p. (YA). (gr. 10-17). 18.00 *(978-0-316-21209-0(1)*, Poppy) Little, Brown Bks. for Young Readers.
Phillips, Rebecca. Any Other Girl. 2016. (ENG.). 272p. (J). (gr. 9). pap. 9.95 *(978-1-61773-882-1(4))* Kensington Publishing Corp.
Phipps, Alisha. Growing up with Allie: The Dance. 2005. 58p. pap. 16.95 *(978-1-4137-9713-8(X))* PublishAmerica, Inc.
Picoult, Jodi & van Leer, Samantha. Off the Page. Gilbert, Yvonne, illus. 2015. (YA). lib. bdg. *(978-0-553-53557-0(9)*, Delacorte Pr) Random House Publishing Group.

J K L

—Off the Page. Gilbert, Yvonne, illus. (ENG.). (YA). (gr. 7). 2016. 368p. pap. 9.99 *(978-0-553-53559-4(5),* Ember) 2015. 384p. 19.99 *(978-0-553-53556-3(0),* Delacorte Pr.) Random Hse. Children's Bks.

Pierce, Christa. Did You Know That I Love You? Pierce, Christa, illus. 2014. (ENG., Illus.). 32p. (J). (gr. -1-3). 17.99 *(978-0-06-229744-0(9))* HarperCollins Pubs.

Piggy Toes Press, creator. Five Little Kisses. 2007. (ENG., Illus.). 10p. (J). (gr. -1-3). 9.95 *(978-1-58117-683-4(X),* Intervisual/Piggy Toes) Bendon, Inc.

Pignataro, Anna. Our Love Grows. 2016. (ENG.). 24p. (J). (-4). 16.99 *(978-1-4926-3418-8(2),* 9781492634188, Sourcebooks Jabberwocky) Sourcebooks, Inc.

Pike, Christopher, pseud. Black Knight. 2014. (Witch World Ser.: 2). (ENG., Illus.). 464p. (YA). (gr. 9). 19.99 *(978-1-4424-6733-0(9));* pap. 11.99 *(978-1-4424-6734-7(7))* Simon Pulse. (Simon Pulse).

—Deepest Desires, Instant Remorse No. 2, Bk. 2. 2010. (Thirst Ser.: 2). (ENG.). 608p. (YA). (gr. 9). pap. 11.99 *(978-1-4169-8309-5(0),* Simon Pulse) Simon Pulse.

—The Eternal Dawn. 2010. (Thirst Ser.: 3). (ENG.). 512p. (YA). (gr. 9-18). pap. 11.99 *(978-1-4424-1317-7(4),* Simon Pulse) Simon Pulse.

—Human Urges, Fatal Consequences. 2009. (Thirst Ser.: 1). (ENG., Illus.). 624p. (YA). (gr. 9). pap. 12.99 *(978-1-4169-8308-8(2),* Simon Pulse) Simon Pulse.

—Red Queen. 2014. (Witch World Ser.: 1). (ENG., Illus.). 560p. (YA). (gr. 9). pap. 9.99 *(978-1-4424-3029-7(X),* Simon Pulse) Simon Pulse.

—The Shadow of Death. 2011. (Thirst Ser.: 4). (ENG., Illus.). 528p. (YA). (gr. 9). pap. 10.99 *(978-1-4424-1319-1(0),* Simon Pulse) Simon Pulse.

—Strange Girl. 2015. (ENG., Illus.). 432p. (YA). (gr. 9). pap. 12.99 *(978-1-4814-5058-4(1),* Simon Pulse) Simon Pulse.

—Thirst, 3 vols. 2013. (Thirst Ser.). (ENG.). 1744p. (YA). (gr. 9). pap. 30.99 *(978-1-4424-8375-0(X),* Simon Pulse) Simon Pulse.

—Witch World. 2012. (Witch World Ser.: 1). (ENG.). 528p. (YA). (gr. 9). 17.99 *(978-1-4424-3028-0(1),* Simon Pulse) Simon Pulse.

Pinto, Dan & Sutton, Benn. Hedgehug: A Sharp Lesson in Love. Pinto, Dan, illus. 2011. (ENG., Illus.). 40p. (J). (gr. -1-2). 9.99 *(978-0-06-196101-4(9))* HarperCollins Pubs.

Piper, Noël. Most of All, Jesus Loves You! Anderson, Debby, illus. 2004. 24p. (J). 11.99 *(978-1-58134-630-5(1))* Crossway.

Pisano, Maryann. The Decision. 2003. 66p. (YA). pap. 8.95 *(978-0-595-29262-2(3))* iUniverse, Inc.

Pitcher, Chelsea. The Last Faerie Queen. 2015. (ENG.). 408p. (YA). pap. 11.99 *(978-0-7387-4349-3(6),* Flux) North Star Editions.

Plank, Alex & Plank, Lisa. How Bad Could It Be? 2007. (ENG.). 64p. per. 19.95 *(978-1-4241-6217-8(3))* America Star Bks.

Platt, Cynthia. Little Bit of Love. Whitty, Hannah, illus. 2011. (ENG.). 32p. (J). (gr. -1-2). pap. 7.95 *(978-1-58925-426-8(0))* Tiger Tales.

—A Little Bit of Love. Whitty, Hannah, illus. 2011. (ENG.). 32p. (J). (gr. -1-2). 15.95 *(978-1-58925-095-6(8))* Tiger Tales.

Plum, Amy. Die for Me. (Die for Me Ser.: 1). (ENG.). (YA). (gr. 9). 2012. 368p. pap. 8.99 *(978-0-06-200402-4(6))* 2011. 352p. 17.99 *(978-0-06-200401-7(8))* HarperCollins Pubs. (HarperTeen).

—Until I Die. 2013. (Die for Me Ser.: 2). (ENG.). 384p. (YA). (gr. 9). pap. 9.99 *(978-0-06-200405-5(0),* HarperTeen) HarperCollins Pubs.

—Until the Beginning. 2015. (After the End Ser.: 2). (ENG.). 336p. (YA). (gr. 8). 17.99 *(978-0-06-222563-4(4),* HarperTeen) HarperCollins Pubs.

Polisner, Gae. The Memory of Things. 2016. (ENG.). 288p. (YA). 18.99 *(978-1-250-09552-7(2),* 9781250095527, St. Martin's Griffin) St. Martin's Pr.

—The Memory of Things. 2017. (YA). lib. bdg. 22.10 ***(978-0-606-40599-7(2))*** Turtleback Bks.

—The Memory of Things: A Novel. 2017. (ENG.). 288p. (YA). pap. 10.99 ***(978-1-250-14442-3(6),*** 9781250144423, Wednesday Bks.) St. Martin's Pr.

Ponti, Jamie. Sea of Love. 2008. (Romantic Comedies Ser.). (ENG.). 272p. (YA). (gr. 7-18). mass mkt. 6.99 *(978-1-4169-6791-0(5),* Simon Pulse) Simon Pulse.

Poole, Susie. All These Things: Based on 1 Corinthians 13:4-7. 2012. (ENG., Illus.). 26p. bds. 7.99 *(978-1-904637-27-1(2),* 1904637272, Pupfish) Authentic Media GBR. Dist: EMI CMG Distribution.

Porras, Javier Fernando, illus. Historias de Amores y Desvarios en America. 2004. (Literatura Juvenil (Panamericana Editorial) Ser.). (SPA.). 179p. (J). (gr. -1-7). pap. *(978-958-30-0569-5(X),* PV4378) Centro de Informacion y Desarrollo de la Comunicacion y la Literatura MEX. Dist: Lectorum Pubns., Inc.

Porter-Gaylord, Laurel. I Love My Mommy Because... Wolff, Ashley, illus. 2004. (ENG.). 22p. (J). (gr. -1 — 1). bds. 6.99 *(978-0-525-47247-6(9),* Dutton Books for Young Readers) Penguin Young Readers Group.

Porter, Sarah. Waking Storms. (Lost Voices Trilogy Ser.: 2). (ENG.). (YA). (gr. 7). 2013. 416p. pap. 8.99 *(978-0-547-48254-5(X))* 2012. 400p. 16.99 *(978-0-547-48251-4(5))* Houghton Mifflin Harcourt Publishing Co.

Prasadam-halls, Smriti. I Love You Night & Day. Brown, Alison, illus. 2014. (ENG.). 32p. (J). (gr. -1-1). 16.99 *(978-1-61963-222-6(5),* 9781619632226, Bloomsbury USA Childrens) Bloomsbury Publishing USA.

—I'll Never Let You Go. Brown, Alison, illus. 2015. (ENG.). 32p. (J). 16.99 *(978-1-61963-922-5(X),* 9781619639225, Bloomsbury USA Childrens) Bloomsbury Publishing USA.

Pratchett, Terry. Dodger. 368p. (YA). (gr. 8). 2013. pap. 9.99 *(978-0-06-200951-7(6))* 2012. 17.99 *(978-0-06-200949-4(4))* 2012. lib. bdg. 18.89 *(978-0-06-200950-0(8))* HarperCollins Pubs.

Preble, Joy. It Wasn't Always Like This. (ENG.). 256p. (YA). (gr. 9). 2017. pap. 10.99 *(978-1-61695-777-3(8))* 2016. 18.99 *(978-1-61695-588-5(0))* Soho Pr., Inc. (Soho Teen).

Prendergast, G. S. Zero Repeat Forever. 2017. (Nahx Invasions Ser.: 1). (ENG., Illus.). 496p. (YA). (gr. 9). 17.99 ***(978-1-4814-8184-7(3),*** Simon & Schuster Bks. For Young Readers) Simon & Schuster Bks. For Young Readers.

Prendergast, Gabrielle. Capricious, 1 vol. 2017. (ENG., Illus.). 352p. (YA). (gr. 8-12). pap. 14.95 *(978-1-4598-1428-8(2))* Orca Bk. Pubs. USA.

Prendergast, Gabrielle. Zero Repeat Forever. 2017. (YA). pap. ***(978-1-4814-8185-4(1),*** Simon & Schuster Bks. For Young Readers) Simon & Schuster Bks. For Young Readers.

Preston, Natasha. Awake. 2015. (ENG.). 336p. (YA). (gr. 9-12). pap. 9.99 *(978-1-4926-1852-2(7),* 9781492618522) Sourcebooks, Inc.

Price, David. Sly the Fox & Advice from la Princessa Roja. 2008. (Illus.). 34p. (J). 14.95 *(978-0-9779701-2-4(4))* Wishingstone Publishing.

Price, Jennifer L. Half Moon: Phases of the Moon: Book 2, 1 vol. 2009. 252p. pap. 27.95 *(978-1-4489-2193-5(7))* PublishAmerica, Inc.

Price, Kevin, ed. Fields of Wheat: And other Romance Stories. 2012. 200p. pap. *(978-0-9872559-4-5(0),* Crotchet Quaver) Logorythm.

—Ice Castles: A Born Storytellers Collection of Teen Fiction & Romance. 2013. (Illus.). 226p. pap. *(978-0-9872559-8-3(3),* Crotchet Quaver) Logorythm.

Priddy, Roger. Love You Always. 2016. (Shiny Shapes Ser.). (ENG.). 10p. (J). bds. 7.99 *(978-0-312-52053-3(0),* 9780312520533, Priddy Bks.) St. Martin's Pr.

Purtill, C. Leigh. FaceSpace Face-Off! 2010. 240p. pap. 5.95 *(978-1-60747-781-5(5),* Pickwick Pr.) Phoenix Bks., Inc.

Pyros, Andrea. My Year of Epic Rock: How to Survive 7th Grade: Make Some Noise. 2014. (ENG.). 208p. (J). (gr. 4-8). pap. 7.99 *(978-1-4022-9300-9(3),* 9781402293009, Sourcebooks Jabberwocky) Sourcebooks, Inc.

Qualey, Marsha. Come in from the Cold. 2008. (ENG.). 224p. (YA). (gr. 7). pap. 14.95 *(978-0-547-01439-5(2))* Houghton Mifflin Harcourt Publishing Co.

Quinn, Paul Michael. The Love Flute. 2013. 24p. pap. 24.95 *(978-1-63000-705-8(6))* America Star Bks.

Rabb, Margo. Kissing in America. 2015. (ENG.). 400p. (YA). (gr. 9). 17.99 *(978-0-06-232237-1(0))* HarperCollins Pubs.

Rae, Kristin. What You Always Wanted: An If Only Novel. 2016. (If Only... Ser.). (ENG.). 320p. (YA). pap. 9.99 *(978-1-61963-345-2(0),* 9781619633452, Bloomsbury USA Childrens) Bloomsbury Publishing USA.

—Wish You Were Italian. 2014. (If Only... Ser.). (ENG.). 352p. (YA). (gr. 7). 17.99 *(978-1-61963-285-1(3),* 9781619632851, Bloomsbury USA Childrens) Bloomsbury Publishing USA.

—Wish You Were Italian: An If Only Novel. 2014. (If Only... Ser.). (ENG.). 352p. (YA). (gr. 7). pap. 9.99 *(978-1-61963-286-8(1),* 9781619632868, Bloomsbury USA Childrens) Bloomsbury Publishing USA.

Rai, Bali. Kiss of Death. Gibbons, Alan, ed. 2014. (Read On Ser.). (ENG., Illus.). 48p. (J). (gr. 5). 9.99 *(978-0-00-746487-6(8))* HarperCollins Pubs. Ltd. GBR. Dist: Independent Pubs. Group.

Rajadel, Fernando López. False Love, True Love/Amor Falso, Amor Verdadero: The Alfambra Woman Buried Alive & the Lovers of Teruel. 2010.Tr. of Amor Falso, Amor Verdadero: La enterrada viva de Alfambra & Los amantes de Teruel. (SPA.). 164p. pap. 44.48 *(978-1-4251-8920-4(2))* Trafford Publishing.

Ramos, Maria Cristina. Del Amor Nacen Los Rios. (SPA.). pap. 9.95 *(978-950-07-1351-1(9))* Editorial Sudamericana S.A. ARG. Dist: Distribooks, Inc.

Ramos, Marielly. The Fast Getting Married Ugly Changing Bear. 2012. 24p. pap. 17.99 *(978-1-4772-8581-7(4))* AuthorHouse.

Ramsey, Jo. Ball Caps & Khakis. 2016. (ENG., Illus.). (YA). 24.99 ***(978-1-63477-938-8(X));*** 180p. (J). pap. 14.99 *(978-1-63477-034-7(X))* Dreamspinner Pr. (Harmony Ink Pr.).

Rasheed, Leila. Diamonds & Deceit. 2014. (At Somerton Ser.). (ENG.). 432p. (YA). (gr. 7-12). 17.99 *(978-1-4231-7118-8(7))* Hyperion Bks. for Children.

Rautenberg, Karen Rita. Ballerina Detective & the Missing Jeweled Tiara. 2009. (ENG.). 198p. (J). (gr. 5-8). pap. *(978-1-933255-47-7(1))* DNA Pr.

Rawls, Wilson. Where the Red Fern Grows. l.t. ed. 2017. (ENG.). 378p. 22.99 ***(978-1-4328-3845-4(8))*** Cengage Gale.

Rayburn, Tricia. Maggie Bean in Love. 2009. (ENG.). 288p. (J). (gr. 4-8). pap. 6.99 *(978-1-4169-8700-0(2),* Aladdin) Simon & Schuster Children's Publishing.

Raymond, Patrick. Daniel & Esther. 2007. (ENG.). 176p. (J). (gr. 3-7). pap. 9.95 *(978-1-4169-6798-9(2),* Simon & Schuster/Paula Wiseman Bks.) Simon & Schuster/Paula Wiseman Bks.

RealBuzz Studios Staff. Let There Be Lighten Up! 2007. (Goofyfoot Gurl Ser.: No. 1). 96p. (YA). pap. 4.97 *(978-1-59789-573-6(3),* Barbour Bks.) Barbour Publishing, Inc.

Reber, Deborah & Goode, Caroline. Love, Love, Love: Language of Love; Cupidity. 2010. (ENG.). 480p. (YA). (gr. 7-18). mass mkt. 9.99 *(978-1-4424-0313-0(6),* Simon Pulse) Simon Pulse.

Redwine, C. J. Defiance. (Defiance Trilogy Ser.: 1). (ENG.). (YA). (gr. 8). 2013. 432p. pap. 9.99 *(978-0-06-211717-5(3))* 2012. 416p. 17.99 *(978-0-06-211718-2(1))* HarperCollins Pubs.

—Deliverance. 2014. (Defiance Trilogy Ser.: 3). (ENG.). 480p. (YA). (gr. 8). 17.99 *(978-0-06-211723-6(8))* HarperCollins Pubs.

Reed, Amy. Invincible. 2015. (ENG.). 336p. (YA). (gr. 9). 17.99 *(978-0-06-229957-4(3),* Tegen, Katherine Bks) HarperCollins Pubs.

Reekles, Beth. The Kissing Booth. 2013. (ENG.). 448p. (YA). (gr. 9). pap. 8.99 *(978-0-385-37868-0(8),* Ember) Random Hse. Children's Bks.

Rees, Celia. This Is Not Forgiveness. 2012. (ENG.). 288p. (YA). (gr. 9-12). 17.99 *(978-1-59990-776-5(3),* 9781599907765, Bloomsbury USA Childrens) Bloomsbury Publishing USA.

Reese, Jacob. Copperweight. 2008. 231p. pap. 24.95 *(978-1-60813-240-9(4))* America Star Bks.

Reimer, Charlotte. Problems with Pies. 2006. 68p. (YA). pap. 13.50 *(978-1-4116-7646-6(7))* Lulu Pr., Inc.

Reisfeld, Randi. All Access. rev. ed. 2007. (ENG.). 288p. (gr. 7-12). pap. 8.99 *(978-1-4231-0503-9(6))* Hyperion Pr.

Rendina, Donna Rae. The Golden Leaf. Bronowski, Karen Kmetz, illus. 2011. 24p. 20.00 *(978-1-61170-014-5(0))* Robertson Publishing.

Rennison, Louise. Love Is a Many Trousered Thing. (Confessions of Georgia Nicolson Ser.: 8). (YA). 2008. (ENG.). 304p. (gr. 8). pap. 9.99 *(978-0-06-085389-1(1))* 2007. 256p. (gr. 7-12). 16.99 *(978-0-06-085387-7(5))* HarperCollins Pubs. (HarperTeen).

Rettig, Liz. Jumping to Confusions. 2010. (ENG.). 320p. (YA). (gr. 7-18). pap. 8.99 *(978-0-552-55757-3(9))* Transworld Publishers Ltd. GBR. Dist: Independent Pubs. Group.

—My Desperate Love Diary. 2007. (ENG.). 314p. (YA). (gr. 9-12). 16.95 *(978-0-8234-2033-9(7))* Holiday Hse., Inc.

Revis, Beth. Shades of Earth. 2013. (Across the Universe Trilogy: 3). lib. bdg. 20.85 *(978-0-606-32117-4(9),* Turtleback) Turtleback Bks.

—A World Without You. 2016. (ENG.). 384p. (YA). (gr. 7). 17.99 *(978-1-59514-715-8(2),* Razorbill) Penguin Young Readers Group.

Rex, Adam. XO, OX: A Love Story. Campbell, Scott, illus. 2017. (ENG.). 40p. (J). 17.99 *(978-1-62672-288-0(9),* 9781626722880) Roaring Brook Pr.

Reyes, M. G. Incriminated. 2016. (Emancipated Ser.: 2). 384p. (YA). (gr. 9). 17.99 *(978-0-06-228898-1(9),* Tegen, Katherine Bks) HarperCollins Pubs.

Reynolds, Alison. Why I Love My Dad. Geddes, Serena, illus. 2015. (ENG.). 22p. (J). (gr. -1-1). 9.99 *(978-1-4998-0035-7(5))* Little Bee Books Inc.

—Why I Love My Mom. Geddes, Serena, illus. 2015. (ENG.). 22p. (J). (gr. -1-1). 9.99 *(978-1-4998-0020-3(7))* Little Bee Books Inc.

Rhine, Linda H. The Ivory Buttons, 1 vol. 2010. 30p. 24.95 *(978-1-4512-1745-2(5))* PublishAmerica, Inc.

Ribar, Lindsay. Rocks Fall Everyone Dies. 2016. (ENG.). 336p. (YA). (gr. 7). 17.99 *(978-0-525-42868-8(2),* Kathy Dawson Books) Penguin Young Readers Group.

Rich, Jamie S. A Boy & a Girl. 2013. (ENG., Illus.). 168p. (YA). pap. 19.99 *(978-1-62010-089-9(4),* 9781620100899) Oni Pr., Inc.

—Love the Way You Love. Ellerby, Marc, illus. 2006. (J). *(978-1-932664-52-2(1))* Oni Pr., Inc.

Richmond, Marianne. Dear Sister: A Message of Love. 2008. (Illus.). 40p. (J). 15.95 *(978-1-934082-46-1(5),* Marianne Richmond Studios, Inc.) Sourcebooks, Inc.

—I Love You So... 2013. (ENG.). 24p. (J). bds. 7.99 *(978-1-4022-7953-9(1),* Sourcebooks Jabberwocky) Sourcebooks, Inc.

—Oh, the Things My Mom Will Do. 2013. (ENG., Illus.). 32p. (J). (-2). 9.99 *(978-1-4022-8215-7(X),* 9781402282157); 16.99 *(978-1-4022-8233-1(8))* Sourcebooks, Inc. (Sourcebooks Jabberwocky).

Rigaud, Debbie. Perfect Shot. 2009. (Romantic Comedies Ser.). (ENG.). 304p. (YA). (gr. 7-18). mass mkt. 6.99 *(978-1-4169-7835-0(6),* Simon Pulse) Simon Pulse.

Rikkers, Don. Jesus Loves Me. 2009. 16p. 6.95 *(978-1-60349-025-2(6),* Marimba Bks.) Hudson Publishing Group, The.

Rinaldi, Ann. Brooklyn Rose. 2006. (ENG., Illus.). 240p. (J). (gr. 5-7). reprint ed. pap. 15.95 *(978-0-15-205538-7(X))* Houghton Mifflin Harcourt Publishing Co.

Rivadeneira, Alexa. Confessions from the Heart of a Teenage Girl. 2007. 248p. per. 16.95 *(978-0-595-42432-0(5))* iUniverse, Inc.

Rivera, Jeff. Forever My Lady: Young Adult. 2005. (YA). per. 12.95 *(978-0-9762838-1-2(6))* Gumbo Multimedia Entertainment.

Rivera, Lilliam. The Education of Margot Sanchez. 2017. (ENG., Illus.). 304p. (YA). (gr. 9). 17.99 *(978-1-4814-7211-1(9),* Simon & Schuster Bks. For Young Readers) Simon & Schuster Bks. For Young Readers.

Rivers, Rae. Declan. 2014. (ENG.). 336p. pap. 11.99 ***(978-0-00-810443-6(3),*** HarperImpulse) HarperCollins Pubs. Ltd. GBR. Dist: HarperCollins Pubs.

Robert, Na'ima B. Black Sheep. 2014. (ENG., Illus.). 272p. (J). (gr. 8-11). pap. 8.99 *(978-1-84780-235-4(4),* Frances Lincoln) Quarto Publishing Group UK GBR. Dist: Hachette Bk. Group.

Roberts, Dina. Thirty Cats. 2003. 162p. (YA). pap. 12.95 *(978-0-595-29775-7(7))* iUniverse, Inc.

Roberts, Jeyn. When They Fade. 2016. (ENG.). 352p. (YA). (gr. 9). 17.99 *(978-0-385-75413-2(2),* Knopf Bks. for Young Readers) Random Hse. Children's Bks.

Roberts, Lisa Brown. Resisting the Rebel. 2016. (ENG., Illus.). 270p. (YA). pap. 14.99 *(978-1-68281-254-9(5))* Entangled Publishing, LLC.

Roberts, Pauline. Oh! I Wish. Bates, Lindsey E. & Wiggan, Desmond, illus. 2012. 24p. pap. 9.95 *(978-0-9848243-3-5(2))* Beckham Pubns. Group, Inc.

Rock, Brian. With All My Heart. Banta, Susan, illus. 2012. (ENG.). 24p. (J). *(978-1-58925-648-4(4))* Tiger Tales.

Rock, J. K. Camp Forget-Me-Not. 2014. (Camp Boyfriend Ser.: 3). (ENG.). 272p. (YA). (gr. 4-6). pap. 9.95 *(978-1-939392-30-5(6),* Spencer Hill Contemporary) Spencer Hill Pr.

Röder, Marlene. In the River Darkness. 2014. (Illus.). 224p. (YA). (gr. 9-12). pap. 10.95 *(978-1-62324-011-0(5))* Enslow Pubs., Inc.

—In the River Darkness. Reichel, Tammi, tr. 2014. 224p. 18.95 *(978-1-62324-010-3(7))* Enslow Pubs., Inc.

Rodriguez, A.J. Cycle of Life. 2009. 20p. pap. 12.49 *(978-1-4389-5528-5(6))* AuthorHouse.

Rodriguez, Bobbie. How I Love My Dad. 2013. 40p. 22.99 *(978-1-62697-112-7(9));* pap. 11.99 *(978-1-62509-995-2(9))* Salem Author Services.

Romano, Juliana. Summer in the Invisible City. 2016. (ENG.). 320p. (YA). (gr. 9). 17.99 *(978-0-525-42917-3(4),* Dial Bks) Penguin Young Readers Group.

Romanoff, Zan. Grace & the Fever. 2017. (ENG.). 352p. (YA). (gr. 7). 17.99 ***(978-1-5247-2084-1(4),*** Knopf Bks. for Young Readers) Random Hse. Children's Bks.

Romanoff, Zan. A Song to Take the World Apart. 2016. (ENG.). 320p. (YA). (gr. 7). 17.99 *(978-1-101-93879-9(X),* Knopf Bks. for Young Readers) Random Hse. Children's Bks.

Ron, Berry. Daddy Do You Love Me. 2009. (ENG.). 20p. bds. 5.99 *(978-0-8249-1423-3(6),* Ideal Pubns.) Worthy Publishing.

—Mommy Do You Love Me. 2009. (ENG.). 20p. bds. 5.99 *(978-0-8249-1422-6(8),* Ideal Pubns.) Worthy Publishing.

Ropal, Monica. When You Leave. 2015. (ENG.). 336p. (YA). (gr. 7). pap. 9.95 *(978-0-7624-5455-6(5),* Running Pr. Kids) Running Pr. Bk. Pubs.

Rosa-Mendoza, Gladys. Lola. 2007. (Englishspanish Story Book Ser.). (ENG & SPA., Illus.). 32p. (J). (gr. -1-3). 13.95 *(978-1-931398-51-0(8))* Me+Mi Publishing.

Rose, Nancy. The Secret Life of Squirrels: A Love Story. 2016. (ENG., Illus.). 32p. (J). (gr. -1-3). 16.99 *(978-0-316-27263-6(9))* Little, Brown Bks. for Young Readers.

Rose, R. M. Guardians or Demons. 2017. (ENG.). 419p. (YA). pap. 15.95 ***(978-1-78612-746-4(6),*** 9781786127464) Austin, Stan AUS. Dist: Bookmasters Distribution.

Rosenthal, Amy Krouse. Plant a Kiss. Reynolds, Peter H., illus. (ENG.). (J). (gr. -1 — 1). 2015. 36p. bds. 7.99 *(978-0-06-241652-0(9),* HarperFestival) 2011. 40p. 14.99 *(978-0-06-198675-8(5))* HarperCollins Pubs.

—Sugar Cookies: Sweet Little Lessons on Love. Dyer, Jane & Dyer, Brooke, illus. 2009. (ENG.). 40p. (J). (gr. k-5). 12.99 *(978-0-06-174072-5(1))* HarperCollins Pubs.

—That's Me Loving You. White, Teagan, illus. 2016. (ENG.). 40p. (J). (gr. -1-2). 16.99 *(978-1-101-93238-4(4),* Random Hse. Bks. for Young Readers) Random Hse. Children's Bks.

Rosland, Linsey. How Much Do I Love You? 2012. 20p. pap. 14.99 *(978-1-4567-4880-7(7))* AuthorHouse.

Rosoff, Meg. There Is No Dog. 2012. (ENG.). 288p. (YA). (gr. 7-18). 17.99 *(978-0-399-25764-3(0),* G.P. Putnam's Sons Books for Young Readers) Penguin Young Readers Group.

—There Is No Dog. l.t. ed. 2012. (ENG.). 392p. (J). (gr. 7-12). 23.99 *(978-1-4104-4707-4(3))* Thorndike Pr.

Ross, Leanna. Julie Simone. 2004. 194p. (YA). pap. 14.95 *(978-0-595-30376-2(5))* iUniverse, Inc.

Ross, Margaret Clark. Jumpy the Frog Learns the Meaning of Love, 1 vol. McNeely, William, illus. 2010. 20p. pap. 24.95 *(978-1-4489-8370-4(3))* PublishAmerica, Inc.

Ross, Marlene. The Adventures of Donny the Doorknob. Hallam, Colleen and Peggy, illus. 2009. 32p. pap. 24.95 *(978-1-61546-539-2(1))* America Star Bks.

Rossetti, Rinsai. The Girl with Borrowed Wings. 2012. (ENG.). 304p. (YA). (gr. 7). 17.99 *(978-0-8037-3566-8(9),* Dial Bks) Penguin Young Readers Group.

Rossetti-Shustak, Bernadette. I Love You Through & Through. Church, Caroline Jayne, illus. 2005. (ENG.). 24p. (J). (gr. k — 1). bds. 8.95 *(978-0-439-67363-1(1),* Cartwheel Bks.) Scholastic, Inc.

—I Love You Through & Through: Board Book & Plush. Church, Caroline Jayne, illus. 2014. (ENG.). 24p. (J). (— 1). 14.99 *(978-0-545-64792-2(4),* Cartwheel Bks.) Scholastic, Inc.

—I Love You Through & Through (Te Quiero, Yo Te Quiero) Church, Caroline Jayne, illus. 2013. (Caroline Jayne Church Ser.). (ENG & SPA.). 24p. (J). (— 1). bds. 8.95 *(978-0-545-58416-6(7))* Scholastic, Inc.

Rossi, Veronica. Through the Ever Night. 2013. 341p. (YA). *(978-0-06-224710-0(7))* Harper & Row Ltd.

Roth, Carol. Will You Still Love Me? Howarth, Daniel, illus. 2011. (ENG.). 16p. (J). (gr. -1 — 1). bds. 7.99 *(978-0-8075-9116-1(5))* Whitman, Albert & Co.

Roth, Susan L. Mi Amor Por Ti/My Love for You. 2003. (ENG & SPA., Illus.). 26p. (J). (gr. -1 — 1). bds. 6.99 *(978-0-8037-2944-5(8),* Dial Bks) Penguin Young Readers Group.

Rothenberg, Jess. The Catastrophic History of You & Me. 2013. (ENG.). 400p. (YA). (gr. 7). pap. 9.99 *(978-0-14-242390-5(4),* Speak) Penguin Young Readers Group.

Roy, Oscar. I Was Captured by Pirates. 2013. 110p. pap. 11.00 *(978-1-62212-790-0(0),* Strategic Bk. Publishing) Strategic Book Publishing & Rights Agency (SBPRA).

RR, Priscilla. 2008. 32p. pap. 24.95 *(978-1-60813-213-3(7))* America Star Bks.

Rubens, Michael. The Bad Decisions Playlist. (ENG.). 304p. (YA). (gr. 9). 2017. pap. 9.99 ***(978-1-328-74208-7(3),*** HMH Books For Young Readers) 2016. 17.99 *(978-0-544-09667-7(3))* Houghton Mifflin Harcourt Publishing Co.

Rudnick, Paul. Gorgeous. 2013. (ENG.). 336p. (J). (gr. 9). 18.99 *(978-0-545-46426-0(9),* Scholastic Pr.) Scholastic, Inc.

Rumbaugh, Melinda. Somebunny Loves You! Biscoe, Cee, illus. 2015. (ENG.). 16p. (J). 12.99 *(978-0-8249-1950-4(5),* Ideal Pubns.) Worthy Publishing.

Rusackas, Francesca. Daddy All Day Long. Burris, Priscilla, tr. Burris, Priscilla, illus. 2004. 32p. (J). (gr. -1-k). lib. bdg. 13.89 *(978-0-06-050285-0(1))* HarperCollins Pubs.

Russo, Meredith. If I Was Your Girl. 2016. (ENG.). 288p. (YA). 17.99 *(978-1-250-07840-7(7),* 9781250078407) Flatiron Bks.

Rutkoski, Marie. The Winner's Crime. 2015. (Winner's Trilogy: Vol. 2). (ENG., Illus.). 416p. (YA). (gr. 7-12). 18.99 *(978-0-374-38470-8(3),* 9780374384708, Farrar, Straus & Giroux (BYR)) Farrar, Straus & Giroux.

—The Winner's Curse. 2014. (Winner's Trilogy Ser.: 1). (ENG.). 368p. (YA). (gr. 7). 18.99 *(978-0-374-38467-8(3),* 9780374384678, Farrar, Straus & Giroux (BYR)) Farrar, Straus & Giroux.

—The Winner's Curse. 2015. (Winner's Trilogy Ser.: 1). (ENG.). 384p. (YA). (gr. 7). pap. 10.99 *(978-1-250-05697-9(7),* 9781250056979) Square Fish.

Rutland, J. I Love You No Matter What: A Prince Chirpio Story, 1 vol. 2013. (ENG.). 32p. (J). 9.99 *(978-1-4003-2195-7(6))* Nelson, Thomas Inc.

Ryan, Carrie. Daughter of Deep Silence. 2015. (ENG.). 384p. (YA). (gr. 9). 17.99 *(978-0-525-42650-9(7),* Dutton Books for Young Readers) Penguin Young Readers Group.

Ryan, Sara. Bad Houses. Hahn, Sierra, ed. 2013. (ENG., Illus.). 152p. pap. 19.99 *(978-1-59582-993-1(8))* Dark Horse Comics.

Ryder, Joanne. Won't You Be My Kissaroo? Sweet, Melissa, illus. 2008. (ENG.). 15p. (J). (gr. -1 — 1). bds. 6.95 *(978-0-15-206060-2(X))* Houghton Mifflin Harcourt Publishing Co.

Sabel, Lauren. Vivian Divine Is Dead. 2014. (ENG.). 288p. (YA). (gr. 8). 17.99 *(978-0-06-223195-6(2),* Tegen, Katherine Bks) HarperCollins Pubs.

Sacerdoti, Daniela. Spirit Bk. 3: The Sarah Midnight Trilogy. 2014. (Sarah Midnight Trilogy Ser.). (ENG.). 416p. (YA). (gr.

7). pap. 12.99 *(978-1-84502-540-3(7))* Black and White Publishing Ltd. GBR. Dist: Independent Pubs. Group.
Saedi, Sara. Never Ever. 2016. (ENG.). 320p. (YA). (gr. 7). 17.99 *(978-0-451-47576-3(3),* Viking Books for Young Readers) Penguin Young Readers Group.
Saeed, Aisha & Airgood, Ellen. Written in the Stars. 2015. (ENG.). 304p. (YA). (gr. 9). 17.99 *(978-0-399-17170-3(3),* Nancy Paulsen Books) Penguin Young Readers Group.
Sáenz, Benjamin Alire. Sammy & Juliana in Hollywood. 2004. (ENG.). 240p. (J). (gr. 10-12). 19.95 *(978-0-938317-81-4(4))* Cinco Puntos Pr.
Saiyo, Shinji. Iron Wok Jan!, Vol. 13. 2005. (Iron Wok Jan! Ser.). (ENG., Illus.). 200p. (YA). pap. 9.95 *(978-1-59796-031-1(4))* DrMaster Pubns. Inc.
Sainsbury, Adam. The Coin. 2005. 84p. (YA). pap. 9.96 *(978-1-4116-5358-0(0))* Lulu Pr., Inc.
Salemi, Dianne K. The Caged Graves. 2014. (ENG.). 336p. (YA). (gr. 7). pap. 8.99 *(978-0-544-33622-3(4),* HMH Books For Young Readers) Houghton Mifflin Harcourt Publishing Co.
Salisbury, Melinda. The Sin Eater's Daughter. 2015. (ENG.). 320p. (J). (gr. 9). 17.99 *(978-0-545-81062-3(0),* Scholastic Pr.) Scholastic, Inc.
Salzano, Tammi. I Love You Just the Way You Are. Grey, Ada, illus. 2014. (ENG.). 32p. (J). (gr. -1-3). 16.99 *(978-1-58925-161-8(X))* Tiger Tales.
Sama, Kent. Fruit of the Spirit - Love. Moody, Julie, illus. 2005. (J). bds. 9.99 *(978-1-4183-0060-9(8))* Christ Inspired, Inc.
Samples, Suzanne. Pivot. 2011. 208p. pap. 13.00 *(978-1-257-03969-2(5))* Lulu Pr., Inc.
Sanders, Russell J. Colors. 2016. (ENG., Illus.). (J). 24.99 ***(978-1-63477-956-2(8),*** Harmony Ink Pr.) Dreamspinner Pr.
—Special Effect. 2016. (ENG., Illus.). (J). 24.99 ***(978-1-63533-074-8(2),*** Harmony Ink Pr.) Dreamspinner Pr.
Sandoval, John. The Witches of Ruidoso. 2013. (ENG.). 120p. (YA). pap. 12.95 *(978-1-55885-766-7(4),* Piñata Books) Arte Publico Pr.
Sanrio. Merry Christmas, Hello Kitty! 2014. (ENG., Illus.). 24p. (J). (gr. k-2). 6.95 *(978-1-4197-1376-7(0),* Abrams Bks. for Young Readers) Abrams, Inc.
Santopolo, Jill. Summer Love. 2014. (Follow Your Heart Ser.: 1). (ENG.). 224p. (YA). (gr. 7). pap. 9.99 *(978-0-14-751092-1(9),* Speak) Penguin Young Readers Group.
Sarnella, Jeanette. Santini's Magic Castle. 2010. 28p. 15.49 *(978-1-4520-4908-3(4))* AuthorHouse.
Sauceda, Vickie. Doobie Kind & Mean Gene. 2013. 22p. pap. 9.99 *(978-1-62697-509-5(4))* Salem Author Services.
Sava, Scott Christian. Gary the Pirate. 2008. (Illus.). 112p. 12.95 *(978-0-9789168-5-5(9))* Blue Dream Studios.
Saxon, Lucy. The Almost King. 2016. (ENG., Illus.). 400p. (YA). (gr. 7-12). 17.99 *(978-1-61963-627-9(1),* 9781619636279, Bloomsbury USA Childrens) Bloomsbury Publishing USA.
—Take Back the Skies. 2014. (ENG.). 384p. (YA). (gr. 7). 17.99 *(978-1-61963-367-4(1),* 9781619633674, Bloomsbury USA Childrens) Bloomsbury Publishing USA.
Scaperrotta, Kirstyn. I Lost My Cracker to the Big Cheese: A Collection of Voices. 2003. 126p. (YA). pap. 10.95 *(978-0-595-26478-0(6),* Writers Club Pr.) iUniverse, Inc.
Scelsa, Kate. Fans of the Impossible Life. 2017. 368p. (YA). (gr. 9). pap. 9.99 *(978-0-06-233176-2(0))* HarperCollins Pubs.
Scheid, Petra Maria. DIARY for lovers: Tagebuch für Verliebte. 2011. (GER.). 120p. pap. 15.90 *(978-3-8423-7899-5(8))* Bks. on Demand.
Scheier, Leah. Your Voice Is All I Hear. 2015. (ENG.). 336p. (YA). (gr. 8-12). pap. 9.99 *(978-1-4926-1441-8(6))* Sourcebooks, Inc.
Schertle, Alice. When the Moon Is High. 2003. (Illus.). 32p. (J). 16.89 *(978-0-688-15144-7(2))* HarperCollins Pubs.
Schindler, Holly. Spark. 2016. 304p. (YA). (gr. 8). 17.99 *(978-0-06-222023-3(3),* HarperTeen) HarperCollins Pubs.
Schmidt, Tiffany. Break Me Like a Promise: Once upon a Crime Family. (ENG.). 416p. (YA). 2017. pap. 9.99 *(978-1-68119-404-2(X),* 9781681194042) 2016. 17.99 *(978-0-8027-3783-0(8),* 9780802737830) Bloomsbury Publishing USA. (Bloomsbury USA Childrens).
Schneider, Robyn. Extraordinary Means. (YA). (gr. 8). 2016. 352p. pap. 9.99 *(978-0-06-221717-2(8))* 2015. (ENG.). 336p. 17.99 *(978-0-06-221716-5(X))* HarperCollins Pubs. (Tegen, Katherine Bks).
Schombs, James. The Little Boy in a Dog Suit, 1 vol. Weidman, James, illus. 2010. 28p. pap. 24.95 *(978-1-61582-053-5(1))* PublishAmerica, Inc.
Schraff, Anne. A Matter of Trust. 2007. (Bluford High — Scholastic Ser.: 2). lib. bdg. 16.00 *(978-1-4177-7142-4(9),* Turtleback) Turtleback Bks.
—Please Don't Ask Me to Love You. 2008. (Passages Contemporary Ser.). 115p. (J). lib. bdg. 13.95 *(978-0-7569-8372-7(X))* Perfection Learning Corp.
—Secrets in the Shadows. 2007. (Bluford High — Scholastic Ser.: 3). lib. bdg. 16.00 *(978-1-4177-7149-3(6),* Turtleback) Turtleback Bks.
—Someone to Love Me. 2007. (Bluford High — Scholastic Ser.: 4). lib. bdg. 16.00 *(978-1-4177-7151-6(8),* Turtleback) Turtleback Bks.
Schraff, Anne E. Bad Blood. 2014. (Urban Underground — Cesar Chavez High School Ser.). (YA). lib. bdg. 20.80 *(978-0-606-35591-9(X))* Turtleback Bks.
—Misjudged. 2014. (Urban Underground — Cesar Chavez High School Ser.). (YA). lib. bdg. 20.80 *(978-0-606-35589-6(8))* Turtleback Bks.
Schreiber, Ellen. Immortal Hearts. 2013. (Vampire Kisses Ser.: 9). (ENG.). 272p. (YA). (gr. 8). pap. 9.99 *(978-0-06-207009-8(6),* Tegen, Katherine Bks) HarperCollins Pubs.
—Teenage Mermaid. 2003. 160p. (J). (gr. 4-18). lib. bdg. 16.89 *(978-0-06-008205-5(4))* HarperCollins Pubs.
Schroeder, Lisa. The Bridge from Me to You. 2014. (ENG.). 336p. (J). (gr. 7). 17.99 *(978-0-545-64601-7(4))* Scholastic, Inc.
—I Heart You, You Haunt Me. 2008. (ENG.). 240p. (YA). (gr. 9). pap. 10.99 *(978-1-4169-5520-7(8),* Simon Pulse) Simon Pulse.
Schulz, Charles. Love Is Walking Hand in Hand. 2012. (ENG.). 72p. 7.95 *(978-1-60433-302-2(2))* Cider Mill Pr. Bk. Pubs., LLC.
Schutz, Samantha. You Are Not Here. 2010. (ENG.). 304p. (J). (gr. 9-18). 17.99 *(978-0-545-16911-0(9),* PUSH) Scholastic, Inc.
Schwab, Victoria. This Savage Song. (Monsters of Verity Ser.: 1). (YA). (gr. 9). 2017. 480p. pap. 9.99 *(978-0-06-238086-9(9))* 2016. (ENG.). 464p. 17.99 *(978-0-06-238085-2(0))* HarperCollins Pubs. (Greenwillow Bks.).
—This Savage Song. 2017. (Monsters of Verity Ser.: 1). lib. bdg. 20.85 ***(978-0-606-40071-8(0))*** Turtleback Bks.
Schwarz, Larry & Palmer, Iva-Marie. Romeo, Juliet & Jim, Bk. 1. 2017. (ENG., Illus.). 288p. (YA). 17.99 *(978-1-62779-250-9(3),* 9781627792509, Holt, Henry & Co. Bks. For Young Readers) Holt, Henry & Co.
Scieszka, Jon. Melvin's Valentine. Shannon, David et al, illus. 2009. (Jon Scieszka's Trucktown Ser.). (ENG.). 24p. (J). (gr. -1-1). lib. bdg. 15.99 *(978-1-4169-4155-2(X),* Simon Spotlight) Simon Spotlight.
Scott, B. L. The Adventures of Babadoodle Kit Kit. 2008. 52p. pap. 22.99 *(978-1-4389-1812-9(7))* AuthorHouse.
Scott, Elizabeth. Bloom. 2007. (ENG.). 240p. (YA). (gr. 7-12). pap. 8.99 *(978-1-4169-2683-2(6),* Simon Pulse) Simon Pulse.
—Perfect You. 2008. (ENG.). 304p. (YA). (gr. 9-12). pap. 9.99 *(978-1-4169-5355-5(8),* Simon Pulse) Simon Pulse.
—Something, Maybe. 2010. (ENG.). 240p. (YA). (gr. 9). pap. 9.99 *(978-1-4169-5356-2(6),* Simon Pulse) Simon Pulse.
Scott, Kieran. A Non-Blonde Cheerleader in Love. 2008. (ENG.). 272p. (YA). (gr. 7-18). 8.99 *(978-0-14-241186-5(8),* Speak) Penguin Young Readers Group.
—Only Everything. 2014. (True Love Ser.: 1). (ENG., Illus.). 352p. (YA). (gr. 7). pap. 9.99 *(978-1-4424-7716-2(4),* Simon & Schuster Bks. For Young Readers) Simon & Schuster Bks. For Young Readers.
Scott, Shirley A. The Adventures of Jack & Dobbie: The Beginning. 2009. 32p. pap. 13.95 *(978-1-4389-4840-9(9))* AuthorHouse.
Second Look. 64p. (YA). (gr. 6-12). pap. *(978-0-8224-2385-0(5))* Globe Fearon Educational Publishing.
Sedgwick, Marcus. Blood Red, Snow White. 2016. (ENG.). 320p. (YA). 17.99 *(978-1-62672-547-8(0),* 9781626725478) Roaring Brook Pr.
—Midwinterblood. 2013. (ENG.). 272p. (YA). (gr. 7). 17.99 *(978-1-59643-800-2(2),* 9781596438002) Roaring Brook Pr.
—Midwinterblood. 2014. (ENG., Illus.). 288p. (YA). (gr. 7). pap. 9.99 *(978-1-250-04007-7(8),* 9781250040077) Square Fish.
—Midwinterblood. 2014. (YA). lib. bdg. 20.85 *(978-0-606-35221-5(X))* Turtleback Bks.
Seduction. 2014. (Legacy Ser.). (ENG., Illus.). 416p. (YA). (gr. 9). 17.99 *(978-1-4814-0023-7(1),* Simon & Schuster/Paula Wiseman Bks.) Simon & Schuster/Paula Wiseman Bks.
Selvadurai, Shyam. Swimming in the Monsoon Sea. 2007. (ENG.). 280p. (YA). (gr. 9-12). per. 12.95 *(978-0-88776-834-7(2),* Tundra Bks.) Tundra Bks. CAN. Dist: Penguin Random Hse. LLC.
Serle, Rebecca. Famous in Love. 2014. (ENG.). 336p. (YA). (gr. 7-17). 18.00 *(978-0-316-36632-8(3),* Poppy) Little, Brown Bks. for Young Readers.
—Truly Madly Famously. 2015. (Famous in Love Ser.: 2). (ENG.). 320p. (YA). (gr. 7-17). 18.00 *(978-0-316-36640-3(4),* Poppy) Little, Brown Bks. for Young Readers.
Shakespeare, William. A Midsummer Night's Dream. Bryant, Clive, ed. Nicholson, Kat & Cardy, Jason, illus. 2012. (ENG.). 144p. (gr. 6). lib. bdg. 24.95 *(978-1-907127-44-1(5))* Classical Comics GBR. Dist: Publishers Group West (PGW).
—Romeo & Juliet. Peluso, Martina, illus. 2013. (Big Picture Book Ser.). (ENG.). 40p. (J). (gr. 1). 14.95 *(978-2-7338-2119-0(9))* Auzou, Philippe Editions FRA. Dist: Consortium Bk. Sales & Distribution.
Shakespeare, William & Gabel, Claudia. Romeo & Juliet & Vampires. 2010. (ENG.). 256p. (YA). (gr. 9-18). pap. 8.99 *(978-0-06-197624-7(5),* HarperTeen) HarperCollins Pubs.
Shalant, Phyllis. Beware of Kissing Lizard Lips. 2010. 196p. pap. 13.95 *(978-1-4401-8339-3(2))* iUniverse, Inc.
Shalhout, Ahlam. For the Love of My Dreams, 1. 2004. 95p. per. 14.95 *(978-0-9668179-2-8(3))* Expressions Woven.
Shanker, Tarun & Zekas, Kelly. These Ruthless Deeds. 2017. (These Vicious Masks Ser.). (ENG.). 320p. (YA). pap. 10.99 *(978-1-250-12795-2(5),* 9781250127952) Feiwel & Friends.
—These Vicious Masks. 2016. (These Vicious Masks Ser.). (ENG.). 320p. (YA). pap. 9.99 *(978-1-250-07389-1(8),* 9781250073891) Feiwel & Friends.
Shankman, Adam & Sullivan, Laura L. Girl about Town. 2016. (ENG., Illus.). 336p. (YA). (gr. 9). 17.99 *(978-1-4814-4787-4(4),* Atheneum Bks. for Young Readers) Simon & Schuster Children's Publishing.
Shannon, George. Hands Say Love. Yoo, Taeeun, illus. 2014. (ENG.). 32p. (J). (gr. -1-1). 17.00 *(978-0-316-08479-6(4))* Little, Brown Bks. for Young Readers.
Shapiro, Jane. Daddy, What Is Love? Robinson, Don, illus. 2008. (ENG.). 28p. (J). (gr. -1-3). *(978-1-59700-244-8(5))* Island Heritage Publishing.
Sharp, Laura. The Key Prince. 2012. 24p. pap. 24.95 *(978-1-4626-8959-0(0))* America Star Bks.
Shaw, Tucker. Anxious Hearts. (ENG.). 272p. (YA). (gr. 7-17). 2011. pap. 6.95 *(978-0-8109-9711-0(8))* 2010. 16.95 *(978-0-8109-8718-0(X))* Abrams, Inc. (Amulet Bks.).
Shecter, Vicky Alvear. Curses & Smoke: A Novel of Pompeii. 2014. (ENG.). 336p. (J). (gr. 7). 17.99 *(978-0-545-50993-0(9),* Levine, Arthur A. Bks.) Scholastic, Inc.
Sheehan, Monica. Love Is You & Me. Sheehan, Monica, illus. (ENG., Illus.). (J). (gr. -1-3). 2013. 48p. 14.99 *(978-1-4424-3607-7(7))* 2010. 38p. bds. 7.99 *(978-1-4424-0765-7(4))* Little Simon. (Little Simon).
Sheldon, Dyan. One or Two Things I Learned about Love. (ENG.). 304p. (YA). (gr. 7). 2015. pap. 8.99 *(978-0-7636-7677-3(2))* 2013. 15.99 *(978-0-7636-6665-1(3))* Candlewick Pr.
Shepard, Sara. The Amateurs. 2016. (Amateurs Ser.). (ENG.). 320p. (YA). (gr. 9-17). 17.99 *(978-1-4847-4227-3(3))* Hyperion Bks. for Children.
—Pretty Little Liars. 2006. (Pretty Little Liars Ser.: No. 1). (ENG.). 304p. (YA). (gr. 9-12). 16.99 *(978-0-06-088730-8(3),* HarperTeen) HarperCollins Pubs.
Sherman, Paulette Kouffman. Shekhinah. Vine, Rachel Shana, illus. 2013. 26p. pap. 10.95 *(978-0-9852469-5-2(2))* Parachute Jump Publishing.
Shields, Breeana. Poison's Kiss. 2017. (Serpent's Promise Ser.). (ENG.). 304p. (YA). (gr. 7). 17.99 *(978-1-101-93782-2(3),* Random Hse. Bks. for Young Readers) Random Hse. Children's Bks.
Shields, Gillian. Eternal. (Immortal Ser.: 3). (ENG.). (YA). (gr. 8). 2012. 384p. pap. 9.99 *(978-0-06-200040-8(3))* 2011. 368p. 16.99 *(978-0-06-200039-2(X))* HarperCollins Pubs. (Tegen, Katherine Bks).
—Immortal. 2010. (Immortal Ser.: 1). (ENG.). 384p. (YA). (gr. 8). pap. 8.99 *(978-0-06-137583-5(7),* Tegen, Katherine Bks) HarperCollins Pubs.
Shifflett, Stephen. Josie Unlimited. 2007. 136p. (YA). per. 11.95 *(978-0-595-43013-0(9))* iUniverse, Inc.
Shimalla, Jen. Heaven Cent. 2013. 24p. pap. 10.95 *(978-1-4525-8042-5(1),* Balboa Pr.) Author Solutions, Inc.
Shine, Joe. I Become Shadow. 2015. (ENG.). 304p. (YA). (gr. 9). pap. 10.99 *(978-1-61695-537-3(6),* Soho Teen) Soho Pr., Inc.
Shirvington, Jessica. Corruption. 2017. (Disruption Ser.: 02). 448p. 9.99 *(978-1-4607-5219-7(8))* HarperCollins Pubs. Australia AUS. Dist: HarperCollins Pubs.
—Empower. 2014. (Embrace Ser.: 5). (ENG.). 496p. (YA). (gr. 7-12). 16.99 *(978-1-4022-9460-0(3))* Sourcebooks, Inc.
—Endless. 2014. (Embrace Ser.: 4). (ENG.). 480p. (YA). (gr. 7-12). pap. 9.99 *(978-1-4022-8945-3(6))* Sourcebooks, Inc.
—One Past Midnight. (ENG.). 352p. (YA). (gr. 9). 2015. pap. 9.99 *(978-0-8027-3707-6(2),* 9780802737076) 2014. 17.99 *(978-0-8027-3702-1(1),* 9780802737021) Bloomsbury Publishing USA. (Bloomsbury USA Childrens).
Short, Carol. Robert & the Princess. 2008. 16p. pap. 9.94 *(978-1-4389-2203-4(5))* AuthorHouse.
Shoshan, Beth. If You Can...we Can! Brown, Petra, illus. 2013. (J). *(978-1-4351-4800-0(2))* Barnes & Noble, Inc.
Shouoto, Aya. He's My Only Vampire, Vol. 4. 2015. (He's My Only Vampire Ser.: 4). (ENG., Illus.). 160p. (gr. 11-17). pap. 13.00 *(978-0-316-26168-5(8),* Yen Pr.) Orbit.
Showalter, Gena. Alice in Zombieland. 2013. lib. bdg. 20.85 *(978-0-606-31712-2(0),* Turtleback) Turtleback Bks.
Shubuck, Sheila. I Love You All Year Round. Padron, Alicia, illus. 2008. (ENG.). 16p. (J). (gr. -1). 10.95 *(978-1-58117-786-2(0),* Intervisual/Piggy Toes) Bendon, Inc.
Silva, Abbey. She Came to Heal. 2008. 136p. pap. 11.50 *(978-1-4389-1086-4(X))* AuthorHouse.
Silver, Ruth. Aberrant. 2013. 250p. pap. 14.99 *(978-0-9917897-8-8(4))* Patchwork Pr.
—Isaura. 2013. 242p. pap. 14.99 *(978-1-927940-02-0(8))* Patchwork Pr.
Silvera, Adam. History Is All You Left Me. 2017. (ENG.). 304p. (YA). (gr. 9). 18.99 *(978-1-61695-692-9(5),* Soho Teen) Soho Pr., Inc.
Silvera, Adam. They Both Die at the End. 2017. 384p. (YA). (gr. 9). 17.99 ***(978-0-06-245779-0(9))*** HarperCollins Pubs.
Silverstein, Shel. The Giving Tree. Silverstein, Shel, illus. gif. ed. 2007. (Illus.). 64p. 16.99 *(978-0-06-124001-0(X))* HarperCollins Pubs.
Simendinger, Ted. 12 Miles to Paradise: A People Story about Horses & Horseracing. 2nd ed. 2004. 364p. per. 12.95 *(978-0-9702405-4-5(6))* Airplane Reader Publishing.
Simon, Mary Manz. Bunny Loves Others. Stott, Dorothy, illus. 2006. (First Virtues for Toddlers Ser.). 20p. (J). 5.99 *(978-0-7847-1409-6(6),* 04037) Standard Publishing.
Simone, Ni-Ni & Abrams, Amir. Put Your Diamonds Up. 2014. (Hollywood High Ser.: 3). (ENG., Illus.). 256p. (YA). (gr. 13). pap. 16.00 *(978-0-7582-8852-3(2),* K-Teen) Kensington Publishing Corp.
Singh, Jay. Once upon a Time in a Forest Far Away. 2009. 394p. pap. 33.12 *(978-1-4251-9122-1(3))* Trafford Publishing.
Singleton, David & Martin, Loyce. Us Mail. 2008. 132p. pap. 11.95 *(978-0-595-52437-2(0))* iUniverse, Inc.
Skidmore, Lauren. What Is Lost. 2015. 217p. (YA). pap. 16.99 *(978-1-4621-1621-8(3))* Cedar Fort, Inc./CFI Distribution.
Skillchecks for Romance. 2005. (Double Fastback Ser.). (J). (gr. 6-12). 64p. pap. 5.95 *(978-0-13-024474-1(0));* 32p. pap. 5.95 *(978-0-13-024457-4(0))* Globe Fearon Educational Publishing.
Slater, Teddy. Beauty & the Beast. Dias, Ron et al, illus. 2004. (Little Golden Book Ser.). (ENG.). 24p. (J). (gr. -1-2). 4.99 *(978-0-7364-2197-3(1),* Golden/Disney) Random Hse. Children's Bks.
Sluzhaev, Viktor, illus. The Lute Player: A Tale from Russia. 2013. (Tales of Honor Ser.). (ENG.). 32p. (J). (gr. 1-4). pap. 8.95 *(978-1-937529-59-8(2));* lib. bdg. 26.60 *(978-1-937529-75-8(4))* Red Chair Pr.
Smith Annie, Laura. Whispers in the Wind. 2006. 144p. pap. 12.95 *(978-1-59113-914-0(7))* Booklocker.com, Inc.
Smith, Heather. Baygirl, 1 vol. 2013. (ENG.). 288p. (YA). (gr. 8-12). pap. 12.95 *(978-1-4598-0274-2(8))* Orca Bk. Pubs. USA.
Smith, Jennifer E. Hello, Goodbye, & Everything in Between. 2015. (ENG.). 256p. (YA). (gr. 7-17). 18.00 *(978-0-316-33442-6(1))* Little Brown & Co.
—The Statistical Probability of Love at First Sight. 2012. (ENG.). 256p. (YA). (gr. 7-17). 17.99 *(978-0-316-12238-2(6))* Little Brown & Co.
—The Statistical Probability of Love at First Sight. 2013. (ENG.). 272p. (YA). (gr. 7-17). pap. 10.00 *(978-0-316-12239-9(4),* Poppy) Little, Brown Bks. for Young Readers.
—This Is What Happy Looks Like. 2013. (ENG.). 432p. (YA). (gr. 7-17). pap. 10.99 *(978-0-316-21281-6(4),* Poppy) Little, Brown Bks. for Young Readers.
—Windfall. 2017. (ENG.). 432p. (YA). (gr. 7). 18.99 *(978-0-399-55937-2(X),* Delacorte Pr.) Random Hse. Children's Bks.
Smith, L. J. The Captive Part II & the Power. 2012. (Secret Circle Ser.: Vols. 1-2). (ENG.). 416p. (YA). (gr. 8). pap. 9.99 *(978-0-06-167135-7(5),* HarperTeen) HarperCollins Pubs.
—Dark Angel - The Chosen - Soulmate, 3 vols. 2008. (Night World Ser.: 2). (ENG.). 688p. (YA). (gr. 9). pap. 9.99 *(978-1-4169-7451-2(2),* Simon Pulse) Simon Pulse.
—The Divide, Vol. 4. 2013. (Secret Circle Ser.: 4). (ENG.). 320p. (YA). (gr. 8). pap. 10.99 *(978-0-06-213041-9(2),* HarperTeen) HarperCollins Pubs.
—The Hunt, Vol. 5. 2012. (Secret Circle Ser.: 5). (ENG.). 288p. (YA). (gr. 8). 17.99 *(978-0-06-213042-6(0),* HarperTeen) HarperCollins Pubs.
—Huntress, Black Dawn, Witchlight, 3 vols. 2009. (Night World Ser.: 3). (ENG., Illus.). 752p. (YA). (gr. 9). pap. 9.99 *(978-1-4169-7452-9(0),* Simon Pulse) Simon Pulse.
—The Initiation & the Captive. movie tie-in ed. 2011. (Secret Circle Ser.). (ENG.). 416p. (YA). (gr. 8). pap. 9.99 *(978-0-06-211900-1(1),* HarperTeen) HarperCollins Pubs.
—Moonsong. 2012. (Vampire Diaries: the Hunters Ser.: 2). (ENG.). 400p. (YA). (gr. 9). 17.99 *(978-0-06-201770-3(5),* HarperTeen) HarperCollins Pubs.
—Night World: Secret Vampire; Daughters of Darkness; Spellbinder. 2008. (Night World Ser.: 1). (ENG.). 752p. (YA). (gr. 9). pap. 9.99 *(978-1-4169-7450-5(4),* Simon Pulse) Simon Pulse.
—The Secret Circle Vol.4: The Divide. 2012. (Secret Circle Ser.: 4). (ENG.). 304p. (YA). (gr. 8). 17.99 *(978-0-06-213039-6(0),* HarperTeen) HarperCollins Pubs.
Smith-Ready, Jeri. Shine. 2012. (ENG.). 416p. (YA). (gr. 9). pap. 9.99 *(978-1-4424-3946-7(7),* Simon Pulse) Simon Pulse.
Smithern, Beth. Cocoa Bean & Squirt. 2010. 68p. pap. 10.49 *(978-1-4520-1929-1(0))* AuthorHouse.
Snadowsky, Daria. Anatomy of a Single Girl. 2014. (ENG.). 240p. (YA). (gr. 9). pap. 8.99 *(978-0-385-73799-9(8),* Ember) Random Hse. Children's Bks.
Sniegoski, Thomas E. The Fallen 5: Armageddon. 2013. (Fallen Ser.: 5). (ENG., Illus.). 592p. (YA). (gr. 9). pap. 9.99 *(978-1-4424-6005-8(9),* Simon Pulse) Simon Pulse.
—Forsaken. 2012. (Fallen Ser.: 4). (ENG.). 416p. (YA). (gr. 9). pap. 9.99 *(978-1-4424-4699-1(4),* Simon Pulse) Simon Pulse.
Snow, Carol. The Last Place on Earth. 2016. (ENG.). 304p. (YA). (gr. 7). 16.99 *(978-1-62779-039-0(X),* 9781627790390, Holt, Henry & Co. Bks. For Young Readers) Holt, Henry & Co.
Sobat, Gail Sidonie. Chance to Dance for You. 2011. (ENG.). 176p. pap. 14.95 *(978-1-926531-11-3(6),* Great Plains Teen Fiction) Great Plains Pubns. CAN. Dist: Publishers Group Canada.
Sones, Sonya. What My Girlfriend Doesn't Know. 2008. (ENG.). 320p. (YA). (gr. 7-18). pap. 8.99 *(978-0-689-87603-5(3),* Simon & Schuster Bks. For Young Readers) Simon & Schuster Bks. For Young Readers.
—What My Mother Doesn't Know. 2004. 259p. (gr. 7-12). 19.00 *(978-0-7569-4268-7(3))* Perfection Learning Corp.
—What My Mother Doesn't Know. (ENG., Illus.). (YA). 2013. 288p. (gr. 7). pap. 11.99 *(978-1-4424-9385-8(2))* 2003. 272p. pap. 8.99 *(978-0-689-85553-5(2))* Simon & Schuster Bks. For Young Readers. (Simon & Schuster Bks. For Young Readers).
Soto, Gary. Accidental Love. 2008. (ENG., Illus.). 192p. (YA). (gr. 7). pap. 9.99 *(978-0-15-206113-5(4))* Houghton Mifflin Harcourt Publishing Co.
Sowles, Joann I. Martin. Darkness (the Brookehaven Vampires Series #2) The Brookehaven Vampires. 2011. (YA). *(978-0-9844867-3-1(9))* Brookehaven Publishing.
Sparks, Favre. Agnes, the Eggless Quail. 2009. 28p. pap. 16.50 *(978-1-60693-491-3(0),* Strategic Bk. Publishing) Strategic Book Publishing & Rights Agency (SBPRA).
Spaziano, Layna. Shane & Molly's Magical Journey, 1 vol. 2010. 28p. pap. 24.95 *(978-1-4489-6261-7(7))* PublishAmerica, Inc.
Spears, Kat. Sway. 2014. (ENG.). 320p. (YA). (gr. 9-12). 18.99 *(978-1-250-05143-1(6),* 9781250051431, St. Martin's Griffin) St. Martin's Pr.
Speer, Scott. Battle Angel. 2014. (Immortal City Ser.: 3). (ENG.). 320p. (YA). (gr. 7). pap. 9.99 *(978-1-59514-598-7(2),* Razorbill) Penguin Young Readers Group.
Spinelli, Jerry. Love, Stargirl. 2009. (ENG.). 288p. (YA). (gr. 7). pap. 9.99 *(978-0-375-85644-0(7),* Ember) Random Hse. Children's Bks.
St. Aubin, Anne. Drafus the Daring Dragon. 2008. 24p. pap. 16.49 *(978-1-4343-8875-9(1))* AuthorHouse.
Staehli, Melissa. I Love You to the Moon. 2013. 28p. 15.95 *(978-1-61244-205-1(6))* Halo Publishing International.
Stamaty, Mark Alan. Who Needs Donuts? 2003. (ENG., Illus.). 40p. (J). (gr. -1-2). 16.95 *(978-0-375-82550-7(9),* Knopf Bks. for Young Readers) Random Hse. Children's Bks.
Stampler, Ann Redisch. How to Disappear. 2016. (ENG., Illus.). 416p. (YA). (gr. 9). 18.99 *(978-1-4814-4393-7(3),* Simon Pulse) Simon Pulse.
Staniszewski, Anna. Finders Reapers. 2016. (Switched at First Kiss Ser.: 2). (ENG.). 272p. (J). (gr. 5-8). pap. 7.99 *(978-1-4926-1549-1(8),* Sourcebooks Jabberwocky) Sourcebooks, Inc.
—I'm with Cupid. 2015. (Switched at First Kiss Ser.: 1). (ENG.). 240p. (J). (gr. 5-8). pap. 7.99 *(978-1-4926-1546-0(3),* 9781492615460, Sourcebooks Jabberwocky) Sourcebooks, Inc.
—Match Me If You Can. 2017. (Switched at First Kiss Ser.: 3). (ENG.). 240p. (J). (gr. 5-8). pap. 7.99 *(978-1-4926-1552-1(8),* 9781492615521, Sourcebooks Jabberwocky) Sourcebooks, Inc.
Stanley, Mandy. Who Do You Love? Stanley, Mandy, illus. 2007. (ENG., Illus.). 24p. (J). (gr. -1 — 1). bds. 8.99 *(978-1-4169-3929-0(6),* Little Simon) Little Simon.
Stanton, Angie. Snapshot. 2013. (Jamieson Brothers Ser.: 2). (ENG.). 416p. (YA). (gr. 9). pap. 9.99 *(978-0-06-227256-0(X),* HarperTeen) HarperCollins Pubs.
—Under the Spotlight. 2015. (Jamieson Brothers Ser.: 3). (ENG.). 400p. (YA). (gr. 8). pap. 9.99 *(978-0-06-227260-7(8),* HarperTeen) HarperCollins Pubs.
Stapleton, Rhonda. Pucker Up. 2010. (ENG.). 272p. (YA). (gr. 7-18). pap. 9.99 *(978-1-4169-7466-6(0),* Simon Pulse) Simon Pulse.
Steinkellner, Teddy. Two Roads from Here. 2017. (ENG., Illus.). 448p. (YA). (gr. 9). 17.99 ***(978-1-4814-3061-6(0),*** Simon & Schuster Bks. For Young Readers) Simon & Schuster Bks. For Young Readers.
Stephenson, Stone. Somewhere among the Stars & Snowflakes. 2013. 40p. pap. 20.99 *(978-1-4520-5629-6(3))* AuthorHouse.
Stepp, Shirley. Santa Lost His Cell Phone. 2012. 24p. 24.95 *(978-1-4626-5479-6(7))* America Star Bks.

J
K
L

Steven, Kenneth C. The Biggest Thing in the World. Mitchell, Melanie, illus. 2013. (ENG.). 32p. (J). (gr. -1-k). 6.99 (978-0-7459-6402-7(8)) Lion Hudson PLC GBR. Dist: Independent Pubs. Group.

Stevens, Jennifer. Love You More. 2013. 24p. pap. 24.95 (978-1-63004-655-2(8)) America Star Bks.

Stevenson, Peggy. Meet the Spencers & the Smart Knots. 2009. 48p. pap. 16.95 (978-1-60813-517-2(9)) America Star Bks.

Stewart, Kiera. How to Break a Heart. (ENG., Illus.). (J). (gr. 5-9). 2016. 304p. pap. 7.99 (978-1-4231-8531-4(5)) 2015. 316p. 16.99 (978-1-4231-7181-2(0)) Hyperion Bks. for Children.

Stiefvater, Maggie. Forever. 2014. (Shiver Ser.: 3). (ENG.). 416p. (J). (gr. 9). pap. 9.99 (978-0-545-68280-0(0)) Scholastic, Inc.

—Linger. 2014. (Shiver Ser.). (ENG.). (YA). (gr. 9). lib. bdg. 20.80 **(978-1-68065-091-4(2))** Perfection Learning Corp.

—Linger. (Shiver Ser.: 2). (ENG.). (J). (gr. 9). 2014. 384p. pap. 9.99 (978-0-545-68279-4(7)) 2010. 368p. 17.99 (978-0-545-12328-0(3), Scholastic Pr.) Scholastic, Inc.

—Linger. l.t. ed. 2011. (Shiver Trilogy: Bk. 2). (ENG.). 488p. 23.99 (978-1-4104-3447-0(8)) Thorndike Pr.

—The Raven King. 2016. (Raven Cycle Ser.: 4). (ENG.). 400p. (YA). (gr. 9). 18.99 (978-0-545-42498-1(4)); 439p. (J). **(978-0-605-90184-1(8))** Scholastic, Inc. (Scholastic Pr.).

—The Scorpio Races. 2011. (ENG.). 416p. (J). (gr. 9). 17.99 (978-0-545-22490-1(X), Scholastic Pr.) Scholastic, Inc.

Stilton, Geronimo. All Because of a Cup of Coffee. Wolf, Matt, illus. 2004. (Geronimo Stilton Ser.: 10). (ENG.). 128p. (J). (gr. 2-5). pap. 7.99 (978-0-439-55972-0(3), Scholastic Paperbacks) Scholastic, Inc.

Stine, R. L. The New Girl. 2006. (Fear Street Ser.: Bk. 1). (ENG., Illus.). 176p. (YA). (gr. 7-12). mass mkt. 7.99 (978-1-4169-1810-3(8), Simon Pulse) Simon Pulse.

Stockham, Jess, illus. Beauty & the Beast. 2007. (Flip-Up Fairy Tales Ser.). (ENG.). 24p. (J). (gr. 2-2). (978-1-84643-114-2(X)) Child's Play International Ltd.

Stoehr, Shelley. Tomorrow Wendy: A Love Story. 2003. 176p. (YA). pap. 14.95 (978-0-595-26954-9(0), Backinprint.com) iUniverse, Inc.

Stoffels, Karlijn. Heartsinger. 2009. (YA). pap. (978-0-545-06968-7(8), Levine, Arthur A. Bks.) Scholastic, Inc.

—Heartsinger. Watkinson, Laura, tr. from DUT. 2009. (ENG.). 144p. (J). (gr. 7-18). 16.99 (978-0-545-06929-8(7), Levine, Arthur A. Bks.) Scholastic, Inc.

Stone, Amy Wingrove. I Love You Every Minute. Lennhoff, Andrew, illus. 2006. pap. 18.00 (978-0-8059-9119-2(0), RoseDog Bks.) Dorrance Publishing Co., Inc.

Stone, Danika. Internet Famous. 2017. (ENG.). 336p. (YA). pap. 10.99 (978-1-250-11437-2(3), 9781250114372) Feiwel & Friends.

Stone, Danika & Goble, Karin. All the Feels. 2016. (ENG., Illus.). 336p. (YA). pap. 9.99 (978-1-250-08409-5(1), 9781250084095) Feiwel & Friends.

Stone, Juliana. Some Kind of Normal. 2015. (ENG.). 304p. (YA). (gr. 8-12). pap. 9.99 (978-1-4926-1871-3(3)) Sourcebooks, Inc.

Stone, Tamara Ireland. Every Last Word. 2015. (ENG.). 368p. (YA). (gr. 7-12). 17.99 (978-1-4847-0527-8(0)) Hyperion Bks. for Children.

—Every Last Word. 2017. (ENG.). (YA). (gr. 7-12). lib. bdg. 20.85 **(978-0-606-39885-5(6))** Turtleback Bks.

—Time after Time. 2014. (ENG.). 368p. (YA). (gr. 7-12). pap. 9.99 (978-1-4231-5981-0(0)) Hyperion Bks. for Children.

Stone, Tamara Ireland. Time & Time Again. 2017. (ENG.). 736p. (YA). (gr. 7-12). pap. 11.99 **(978-1-4847-8133-3(3))** Hyperion Bks. for Children.

Stott, Ann. Always. Phelan, Matt, illus. 2008. (ENG.). 32p. (J). (gr. k-k). 15.99 (978-0-7636-3232-8(5)) Candlewick Pr.

Stout, Katie M. Hello, I Love You. 2015. (ENG.). 304p. (YA). pap. (978-1-250-08195-7(5), St. Martin's Griffin) St. Martin's Pr.

—Hello, I Love You: A Novel. 2015. (ENG.). 304p. (YA). (gr. 7-12). 18.99 (978-1-250-05259-9(9), 9781250052599, St. Martin's Griffin) St. Martin's Pr.

Strange, Derek & Pearson Longman Staff. Girl Meets Boy. 2nd ed. 2008. (ENG., Illus.). 32p. pap. 11.99 (978-1-4058-6971-3(2)) Pearson Education.

Strasnick, Lauren. 16 Ways to Break a Heart. 2017. 208p. (YA). (gr. 9). 17.99 **(978-0-06-241872-2(6)**, Tegen, Katherine Bks) HarperCollins Pubs.

Strasser, Todd. For Money & Love. 2007. (Mob Princess Ser.: 1). (ENG.). 208p. (YA). (gr. 9-18). pap. 10.99 (978-1-4169-3533-9(9), Simon Pulse) Simon Pulse.

Strohmeyer, Sarah. The Secrets of Lily Graves. 2014. (ENG.). 304p. (YA). (gr. 8). pap. 9.99 (978-0-06-225960-8(1)) HarperCollins Pubs.

Studio Mouse Editorial. Belle: The Power of Love. 2008. (ENG., Illus.). 36p. (gr. -1-k). 7.99 (978-1-59069-435-0(X)) Studio Mouse LLC.

StVil, Lola. Girls Like Me. 2016. (ENG.). 320p. (YA). (gr. 7). 17.99 (978-0-544-70674-3(9), HMH Books For Young Readers) Houghton Mifflin Harcourt Publishing Co.

Style Guide, Style, illus. Lovely, Love My Family. 2011. (Yo Gabba Gabba! Ser.). (ENG.). 14p. (J). (gr. -1-1). bds. 5.99 (978-1-4424-2134-9(7), Simon Spotlight) Simon Spotlight.

Sublime. 2014. (ENG., Illus.). 336p. (YA). (gr. 9). 17.99 (978-1-4814-1368-8(6), Simon & Schuster Bks. For Young Readers) Simon & Schuster Bks. For Young Readers.

Sugar, Rebecca. The Answer. Ford, Tiffany & Michalka, Elle, illus. 2016. (Steven Universe Ser.). (ENG.). 32p. (J). (gr. 3-7). 9.99 (978-0-399-54170-4(5), Cartoon Network Books) Penguin Young Readers Group.

Sugg, Zoe "Zoella". Girl Online. 2014. (ENG.). 352p. 17.99 (978-1-4767-9745-8(5), Atria Bks.) Simon & Schuster.

Sullivan, Kiki. Midnight Dolls. 2015. (Dolls Ser.: 2). (ENG.). 336p. (YA). (gr. 8). pap. 9.99 (978-0-06-228150-0(X)) HarperCollins Pubs.

Sullivan, Laura L. Love by the Morning Star. 2014. (ENG.). 320p. (YA). (gr. 7-12). 17.99 (978-0-547-68951-7(9), HMH Books For Young Readers) Houghton Mifflin Harcourt Publishing Co.

Sullivan, Mary Jo. The Wonder of Us, 1 vol. 2010. 16p. 24.95 (978-1-4489-2600-8(9)) PublishAmerica, Inc.

Summers, Natalie. The Noweos: Neighbors One with Each Other. 2009. 20p. pap. 12.99 (978-1-4490-3710-9(0)) AuthorHouse.

Sundberg, Ingrid. All We Left Behind. 2015. (ENG.). 432p. (YA). (gr. 9). 17.99 (978-1-4814-3742-4(9), Simon Pulse) Simon Pulse.

Sunderland, Margot & Hancock, Nicky. The Day the Sea Went Out & Never Came Back, 2 vols. Armstrong, Nicky, tr. Armstrong, Nicky, illus. (ENG.). 32p. pap. (978-0-86388-463-4(6), 002-5147, Routledge) Taylor & Francis Group.

—The Frog Who Longed for the Moon to Smile, 2 vols. Armstrong, Nicky, tr. Armstrong, Nicky, illus. (ENG.). 28p. pap. (978-0-86388-495-5(4), 002-5066, Routledge) Taylor & Francis Group.

Sunseri, Heather. Mindsiege. 2013. (ENG.). 374p. (YA). pap. 14.00 (978-0-9887153-5-6(X)) Sunseri, Heather.

Surace, Joan. The Story of Lucia. Rockford, Nancy, illus. 2006. (YA). pap. 8.00 (978-0-8059-7062-3(2)) Dorrance Publishing Co., Inc.

Sutherland, Krystal. Our Chemical Hearts. (ENG.). (YA). (gr. 9). 2017. 336p. pap. 10.99 **(978-0-399-54657-0(X)**, Speak) 2016. 320p. 17.99 (978-0-399-54656-3(1), G.P. Putnam's Sons Books for Young Readers) Penguin Young Readers Group.

Suzuki, Mamoru. You Belong to Me. 2016. (ENG.). 32p. (J). (gr. -1-k). 12.99 (978-1-940842-12-7(3)) Museyon.

Swank, Denise Grover. One Paris Summer, 1 vol. 2016. (ENG.). 352p. (YA). pap. 14.99 (978-0-310-75516-6(6)) Blink.

Tahir, Sabaa. An Ember in the Ashes. l.t. ed. 2016. (Ember in the Ashes Ser.: 1). (ENG.). 648p. 25.99 (978-1-4104-8875-6(6)) Cengage Gale.

—An Ember in the Ashes. 2015. (ENG.). 464p. (YA). (gr. 9). 19.95 (978-1-59514-803-2(5), Razorbill) Penguin Publishing Group.

—An Ember in the Ashes. 2016. (Ember in the Ashes Ser.: Bk. 1). (ENG.). 464p. (YA). (gr. 7). pap. 11.99 (978-1-59514-804-9(3), Razorbill) Penguin Young Readers Group.

—An Ember in the Ashes. 2016. 464p. lib. bdg. 23.30 (978-0-606-38848-1(6)) Turtleback Bks.

Tahir, Sabaa. A Torch Against the Night. (Ember in the Ashes Ser.: 2). (ENG.). (YA). (gr. 9). 2017. 480p. pap. 11.99 **(978-1-101-99888-5(1))** 2016. 464p. 19.95 (978-1-101-99887-8(3)) Penguin Young Readers Group. (Razorbill).

—A Torch Against the Night. 2017. (Ember in the Ashes Ser.: 2). lib. bdg. 23.30 **(978-0-606-40085-5(0))** Turtleback Bks.

Take a Hike, Romeo. (Full House Ser.). 96p. (J). (gr. 4-6). pap. 3.95 (978-0-938753-75-9(4), PP4) Parachute Publishing, LLC.

Talbott, Shawn M. Springtime Robins. 2006. (J). lib. bdg. 19.95 (978-1-933732-05-3(9)) Big Ransom Studio.

Tara, Stephanie Lisa. Eliza's Forever Trees. Walton, Alex, illus. 2012. 290p. (J). pap. 9.99 net. (978-1-61254-067-2(8)) Brown Books Publishing Group.

Tash, Sarvenaz. The Geek's Guide to Unrequited Love. 2016. (ENG., Illus.). 256p. (YA). (gr. 9). 18.99 (978-1-4814-5653-1(9), Simon & Schuster Bks. For Young Readers) Simon & Schuster Bks. For Young Readers.

—Three Day Summer. 2016. (ENG.). 320p. (YA). (gr. 7). pap. 10.99 (978-1-4814-3932-9(4)) Simon & Schuster Children's Publishing.

Taylor, Janet B. Into the Dim. 2016. (ENG.). 432p. (YA). (gr. 9). 17.99 (978-0-544-60200-7(5), HMH Books For Young Readers) Houghton Mifflin Harcourt Publishing Co.

—Sparks of Light. 2017. (ENG.). 448p. (YA). (gr. 9). 16.99 (978-0-544-60957-0(3), HMH Books For Young Readers) Houghton Mifflin Harcourt Publishing Co.

Taylor, Jessica. A Map for Wrecked Girls. 2017. (ENG.). 368p. (YA). (gr. 9). 17.99 **(978-0-7352-2811-5(6)**, Dial Bks) Penguin Young Readers Group.

Taylor, Jessica. Wandering Wild. 2016. (ENG.). 368p. (YA). (gr. 8). 17.99 (978-1-5107-0400-8(0), Sky Pony Pr.) Skyhorse Publishing Co., Inc.

Taylor, Laini. Lips Touch: Three Times. Di Bartolo, Jim, illus. 2011. (ENG.). 288p. (J). (gr. 7-7). pap. 14.99 (978-0-545-05586-4(5), Levine, Arthur A. Bks.) Scholastic, Inc.

Taylor, Whitney. Definitions of Indefinable Things. 2017. (ENG.). 336p. (YA). (gr. 9). 17.99 (978-0-544-80504-0(6), HMH Books For Young Readers) Houghton Mifflin Harcourt Publishing Co.

Teis, Kyra, adapted by. The Magic Flute: An Opera by Mozart, 1 vol. 2008. (ENG., Illus.). 32p. (J). (gr. k-9). 17.95 (978-1-59572-058-0(8)) Star Bright Bks., Inc.

Telchin, Eric. See a Heart, Share a Heart. 2012. (ENG., Illus.). 48p. (J). (gr. -1-3). 12.99 (978-0-8037-3894-2(3), Dial Bks) Penguin Young Readers Group.

Telep, Trisha, ed. Kiss Me Deadly: 13 Tales of Paranormal Love. 2010. (ENG.). 432p. (YA). (gr. 9-17). pap. 9.95 (978-0-7624-3949-2(1)) Running Pr. Bk. Pubs.

Terrill, Cristin. All Our Yesterdays. 2014. (All Our Yesterdays Ser.). (ENG.). 368p. (YA). (gr. 7-12). pap. 9.99 (978-1-4231-8524-6(2)) Hyperion Bks. for Children.

—All Our Yesterdays. 2013. (All Our Yesterdays Ser.). (ENG.). 368p. (YA). (gr. 7-12). 17.99 (978-1-4231-7637-4(5)) Hyperion Pr.

Tetzlaff, Wendy Jo. A Girl Named Frannie. 2008. 28p. pap. 24.95 (978-1-60703-055-3(1)) America Star Bks.

Theobald the Iron Hearted or Love to Ene. 2004. reprint ed. pap. 15.95 (978-1-4191-8941-8(7)) Kessinger Publishing, LLC.

Theobald the Iron Hearted or Love to Enemies. 2004. reprint ed. pap. 1.99 (978-1-4192-8941-5(1)) Kessinger Publishing, LLC.

Thomas, Cynthia. Promise Ring: The Promise. 2013. (ENG.). 82p. (YA). pap. 12.95 (978-1-4787-1008-0(X)) Outskirts Pr., Inc.

Thomas, Isabel & Thomas, Marilyn. Stargazing from Nowhere. 2013. 448p. pap. (978-0-9880448-0-7(3)) Do Art Publishing.

Thomes, William Henry. The Bushrangers a Yankee's Adventures During His Second Visit to Australia by William H Thomes. 2006. 420p. per. 26.99 (978-1-4255-4567-3(X)) Michigan Publishing.

Thompson, Karri. Ascendancy. 2015. (ENG., Illus.). 248p. (YA). (gr. 7). pap. 15.99 (978-1-68281-024-8(0)) Entangled Publishing, LLC.

Thompson, Kelly. Lasting. 2005. 120p. pap. 19.95 (978-1-4137-9653-7(2)) PublishAmerica, Inc.

Thompson, Mary G. Flicker & Mist. 2017. (ENG.). 384p. (YA). (gr. 7). 17.99 (978-0-544-64840-1(4), Clarion Bks.) Houghton Mifflin Harcourt Trade & Reference Pubs.

Thomson, Celia. The Stolen. 2004. (Nine Lives of Chloe King Ser.: 2). (ENG.). 288p. (YA). (gr. 8). pap. 13.99 (978-0-689-86659-3(3), Simon Pulse) Simon Pulse.

Thomson, Celia & Braswell, Liz. The Nine Lives of Chloe King: The Fallen; the Stolen; the Chosen. 2011. (Nine Lives of Chloe King Ser.). (ENG.). 784p. (YA). (gr. 9). pap. 13.99 (978-1-4424-3570-4(4), Simon Pulse) Simon Pulse.

Thornburgh, Blair. Who's That Girl. 2017. 400p. (YA). (gr. 8). 17.99 **(978-0-06-244777-7(7)**, HarperTeen) HarperCollins Pubs.

Thorne, Bella. Autumn's Kiss. 2016. (ENG.). 256p. (YA). (gr. 7). pap. 9.99 (978-0-385-74436-2(6), Ember) Random Hse. Children's Bks.

Thorne, Jenn Marie. The Wrong Side of Right. 2016. (ENG.). 416p. (YA). (gr. 7). pap. 10.99 (978-0-14-750984-0(X), Speak) Penguin Young Readers Group.

Thornhorn. The Kestrel Waters: A Tale of Love & Devil. 2014. (ENG.). 33.39 (978-0-9916496-4-8(8)); pap. 19.95 (978-0-615-96746-2(9)) Rosasharn Pr.

Tiernan, Cate. Eternally Yours. 2013. (Immortal Beloved Ser.: 3). (ENG.). 464p. (YA). (gr. 7-17). pap. 10.00 (978-0-316-03595-8(5), Poppy) Little, Brown Bks. for Young Readers.

Tillit, L. B. 2 Days. 2012. (Gravel Road Ser.). (YA). lib. bdg. 20.80 (978-0-606-25252-2(5), Turtleback) Turtleback Bks.

Tillman, Nancy. The Spirit of Christmas. Tillman, Nancy, illus. 2009. (ENG., Illus.). 32p. (J). (gr. -1-3). 17.99 (978-0-312-54965-7(2), 9780312549657) Feiwel & Friends.

—Wherever You Are: My Love Will Find You. Tillman, Nancy, illus. (ENG., Illus.). 32p. (J). (gr. -1-3). 2012. bds. 7.99 (978-1-250-01797-0(1), 9781250017970) 2010. 16.99 (978-0-312-54966-4(0), 9780312549664) Feiwel & Friends.

Tinetti, Elizabeth Ordaz. Love Is Patient. 2012. 32p. pap. 16.99 (978-1-4634-3862-3(1)) AuthorHouse.

Tintera, Amy. Ruined. (Ruined Ser.: 1). (YA). (gr. 8). 2017. 384p. pap. 9.99 (978-0-06-239661-7(7)) 2016. 368p. 17.99 (978-0-06-239660-0(9)) HarperCollins Pubs. (HarperTeen).

Todd, Sue, illus. One Last Wish: A Tale from India. 2013. (Tales of Honor (Red Chair Press) Ser.). (ENG.). 32p. (J). (gr. 1-4). lib. bdg. 26.60 (978-1-937529-76-5(2)) Red Chair Pr.

Toliver, Wendy. Miss Match. 2009. (Romantic Comedies Ser.). (ENG.). 304p. (YA). (gr. 7-18). mass mkt. 6.99 (978-1-4169-6413-1(4), Simon Pulse) Simon Pulse.

—The Secret Life of a Teenage Siren. 2007. (Romantic Comedies Ser.). (ENG.). 304p. (YA). (gr. 7-12). mass mkt. 6.99 (978-1-4169-5065-3(6), Simon Pulse) Simon Pulse.

Tomlin, Chris & Barrett, Pat. Good Good Father, 1 vol. 2016. (ENG.). 32p. (J). 16.99 (978-0-7180-8695-4(3)) Nelson, Thomas Inc.

Toms, Kate. I Udderly Love You. 2009. (Kate Toms Ser.). (Illus.). 26p. (gr. -1). bds. 7.99 (978-1-84610-990-4(6)) Make Believe Ideas GBR. Dist: Nelson, Thomas Inc.

Tracy, Roseann. Do You Love Me When I Am Upside Down? 2008. 28p. pap. 12.99 (978-1-4389-0503-7(3)) AuthorHouse.

Tran, Tommy. Forever & a Day. 2010. 124p. 20.95 (978-1-4502-5125-9(0)); pap. 10.95 (978-1-4502-5124-2(2)) iUniverse, Inc.

Traver, N. K. & Traver, N. K. Duplicity. 2015. (ENG.). 256p. (YA). (gr. 9-12). 18.99 (978-1-250-05914-7(3), 9781250059147, Dunne, Thomas Bks.) St. Martin's Pr.

Tregay, Sarah. Fan Art. DeJesus, Melissa, illus. 2014. (ENG.). 368p. (YA). (gr. 8). 17.99 (978-0-06-224315-7(2), Tegen, Katherine Bks) HarperCollins Pubs.

Tremblay, Carole. Romeo, le Rat Romantique. 2004. (FRE., Illus.). (J). (gr. -1-3). spiral bd. (978-0-616-07266-0(X)) Canadian National Institute for the Blind/Institut National Canadien pour les Aveugles.

Triana, Gaby. Summer of Yesterday. 2014. (ENG., Illus.). 272p. (YA). (gr. 9). pap. 9.99 (978-1-4814-0130-2(0), Simon Pulse) Simon Pulse.

Tsahiridis, Van. Peree' & the Magic Fish: Fairy Tale from Pontos. 2010. 64p. pap. 10.16 (978-1-4269-2335-7(X)) Trafford Publishing.

Tucholke, April Genevieve. Between the Spark & the Burn. 2014. (ENG.). 336p. (YA). (gr. 7). 17.99 (978-0-8037-4047-1(6), Dial Bks) Penguin Young Readers Group.

Tuorto, Diana. Janie's New Legs. 2008. (ENG.). 48p. pap. 11.99 (978-1-4196-9142-3(2)) CreateSpace Independent Publishing Platform.

Two Lies & a Spy. 2014. (ENG., Illus.). 272p. (YA). (gr. 9). pap. 11.99 (978-1-4424-8173-2(0), Simon & Schuster Bks. For Young Readers) Simon & Schuster Bks. For Young Readers.

Tyrrell, Melissa. Beauty & the Beast. McMullen, Nigel, illus. 2005. (Fairytale Friends Ser.). 12p. (J). bds. 5.95 (978-1-58117-153-2(6), Intervisual/Piggy Toes) Bendon, Inc.

Ueda, Rinko. Tail of the Moon, Vol. 4. Ueda, Rinko, illus. 2007. (ENG., Illus.). 200p. (gr. 11). pap. 8.99 (978-1-4215-0816-0(8)) Viz Media.

Umansky, Kaye. The Romantic Giant. Weir, Doffy, illus. 2006. 29p. (J). (gr. k-2). pap. 6.95 (978-1-903015-25-4(1)) Barn Owl Bks, London GBR. Dist: Independent Pubs. Group.

Upperman, Katy. Kissing Max Holden. Brzozowski, Kat, ed. 2017. (ENG.). 304p. (YA). 17.99 (978-1-250-11116-6(1), 9781250111166) Feiwel & Friends.

Urbanek Reese, Dorothy. When Mice Sing — the Story of Mei & Yu. 2008. 138p. pap. 13.95 (978-1-4357-6104-9(9)) Lulu Pr., Inc.

Ure, Jean. Love & Kisses. 2009. (ENG.). 192p. (J). (gr. 4-7). pap. 9.99 (978-0-00-728172-5(2), HarperCollins Children's Bks.) HarperCollins Pubs. Ltd. GBR. Dist: HarperCollins Pubs.

—Strawberry Crush. 2016. (ENG.). 224p. (J). 6.99 (978-0-00-755396-9(X), HarperCollins Children's Bks.) HarperCollins Pubs. Ltd. GBR. Dist: HarperCollins Pubs.

Usera, Christian. The Ones. 2007. 35p. 17.00 (978-0-615-14645-4(7)) Usera, Christian.

Vail, Rachel. Kiss Me Again. 2013. (If We Kiss Ser.: 2). (ENG.). 272p. (YA). (gr. 8). pap. 9.99 (978-0-06-194719-3(9), HarperTeen) HarperCollins Pubs.

Valdes, Alisa. Perdition: A Kindred Novel. 2013. (YA). pap. (978-0-06-202421-3(3), HarperTeen) HarperCollins Pubs.

—The Temptation. 2012. (ENG.). 320p. (YA). (gr. 9). pap. 8.99 (978-0-06-202420-6(5), HarperTeen) HarperCollins Pubs.

Valdivia, Benjamin. The Cage of the Different People: A Story of Brotherly Love. 2012. 48p. pap. 21.99 (978-1-4771-0343-2(0)) Xlibris Corp.

Van Buren, David. I Love You As Big As the World. Warnes, Tim, illus. 2013. (ENG.). 22p. (J). bds. (978-1-58925-603-3(4)) Tiger Tales.

van Diepen, Allison. On the Edge. 2014. (ENG.). 304p. (YA). (gr. 9). 17.99 (978-0-06-230344-8(9)) HarperCollins Pubs.

—Raven. 2010. (ENG.). 304p. (YA). (gr. 9). pap. 8.99 (978-1-4169-7468-0(7), Simon Pulse) Simon Pulse.

—The Vampire Stalker. 2011. (ENG.). 272p. (J). (gr. 7-7). 17.99 (978-0-545-28375-5(2)) Scholastic, Inc.

Van Draanen, Wendelin. Flipped. 2003. (gr. 5-8). 20.85 (978-0-613-62948-5(5), Turtleback) Turtleback Bks.

Van Duzen, Fisher. Searching for Sand Dollars. 2013. 416p. 19.99 (978-0-9896335-0-5(0)) PoorHse. Publishing LLC.

Vandereyken, Leen. Loulou in Love. 2008. (Girls Only Ser.). (ENG.). 155p. (YA). (gr. 4-18). 16.95 (978-1-60537-025-5(8)) Clavis Publishing.

Vars, Elle Márjá. The Most Beautiful Dawn. Janda, Laura A., tr. Guttormsen, Trygve Lund, illus. 2013. 80p. (J). pap. 17.99 (978-0-9772714-6-7(3)) Nordic Studies Pr.

Vaught, Susan. Freaks Like Us. 2014. (ENG.). 256p. (YA). (gr. 7). pap. 9.99 (978-1-61963-163-2(6), 9781619631632, Bloomsbury USA Childrens) Bloomsbury Publishing USA.

Vaval, Fisepe. The Blueprint. Bubsy, Nancy, ed. 2003. 270p. (YA). pap. 15.00 (978-0-9743207-0-0(6)) Tayes Bks.

Verday, Jessica. The Haunted. (ENG.). (YA). (gr. 9). 2011. 496p. pap. 11.99 (978-1-4169-7896-1(8)) 2010. 480p. 17.99 (978-1-4169-7895-4(X)) Simon Pulse. (Simon Pulse).

Vernick, Shirley Reva. The Black Butterfly. 2014. (ENG.). 226p. (J). 19.95 (978-1-935955-79-5(9)) Cinco Puntos Pr.

—The Blood Lie. 2011. (ENG.). 144p. (J). (gr. 7). 15.95 (978-1-933693-84-2(3)) Cinco Puntos Pr.

Viguié, Debbie. Midnight Pearls: A Retelling of the Little Mermaid. 2006. (Once upon a Time Ser.). (ENG., Illus.). 208p. (YA). (gr. 9-12). mass mkt. 6.99 (978-1-4169-4016-6(2), Simon Pulse) Simon Pulse.

—The Summer of Cotton Candy, 1 vol. 2008. (Sweet Seasons Novel Ser.). (ENG., Illus.). 224p. (YA). (gr. 8-11). pap. 9.99 (978-0-310-71558-0(X)) Zondervan.

Villani, Donna. The Capture of Art. 2008. 244p. pap. 14.95 (978-1-60693-104-2(0), Eloquent Bks.) Strategic Book Publishing & Rights Agency (SBPRA).

Vincent, Rachel. Brave New Girl. 2017. (ENG.). 272p. (YA). (gr. 7). 17.99 **(978-0-399-55245-8(6)**, Delacorte Pr.) Random Hse. Children's Bks.

Vinesse, Cecilia. Seven Days of You. 2017. (ENG.). 336p. (YA). (gr. 10-17). 17.99 (978-0-316-39111-5(5)) Little Brown & Co.

Viselman, Kenn. I Love You Bunches. 2004. (Illus.). 28p. 14.98 (978-0-9722361-0-2(4)) Viselman, Kenn Presents...

Vision, David & Vision, Mutiya Sahar. Daddy Loves His Baby Girl. Vision, Mutiya Sahar, illus. 2009. (Illus.). 32p. 16.00 (978-0-9659538-7-0(4)) Visor Bks.

Vivian, Siobhan. The Last Boy & Girl in the World. 2016. (ENG., Illus.). 432p. (YA). (gr. 9). 17.99 (978-1-4814-5229-8(0), Simon & Schuster Bks. For Young Readers) Simon & Schuster Bks. For Young Readers.

Voss, Dawn. Avenging Aja. 2007. 50p. pap. 15.00 (978-0-615-15324-7(0)) Voss, Dawn L.

Vrabel, Beth. Pack of Dorks. 2016. (Pack of Dorks Ser.). (ENG.). 240p. (J). (gr. 2-7). 16.99 (978-1-63450-181-1(0), Sky Pony Pr.) Skyhorse Publishing Co., Inc.

Wagner, Paul. Just One Mo. 2003. 130p. (YA). pap. 10.95 (978-0-595-27223-5(1), Writers Club Pr.) iUniverse, Inc.

Wakefield, Beth. The Cleaner. 2010. 151p. pap. 14.50 (978-1-4457-6809-0(7)) Lulu Pr., Inc.

Wakefield, Nelida. Little Flathead & the Black Pearl. Smith, Nathan, illus. 2009. 36p. pap. 12.99 (978-1-59858-828-6(1)) Dog Ear Publishing, LLC.

Wakefield, Vikki. In-Between Days. 2016. (ENG., Illus.). 352p. (YA). (gr. 9). 17.99 (978-1-4424-8656-0(2), Simon & Schuster Bks. For Young Readers) Simon & Schuster Bks. For Young Readers.

Walker, Melissa. Ashes to Ashes. (ENG.). (YA). (gr. 8). 2015. 352p. pap. 9.99 (978-0-06-207735-6(X)) 2013. 336p. 17.99 (978-0-06-207734-9(1)) HarperCollins Pubs. (Tegen, Katherine Bks).

—Dust to Dust. 2016. 320p. (YA). (gr. 8). pap. 9.99 (978-0-06-207738-7(4), Tegen, Katherine Bks) HarperCollins Pubs.

Wallach, Tommy & Smith, Ali. Thanks for the Trouble. 2016. (ENG., Illus.). 288p. (YA). (gr. 9). 17.99 (978-1-4814-1880-5(7), Simon & Schuster Bks. For Young Readers) Simon & Schuster Bks. For Young Readers.

Waller, Sharon Biggs. A Mad, Wicked Folly. (ENG.). 448p. (YA). (gr. 7). 2015. pap. 10.99 (978-0-14-242790-3(X), Speak) 2014. 17.99 (978-0-670-01468-2(0), Viking Books for Young Readers) Penguin Young Readers Group.

Walsh, Joanna. The Biggest Kiss. Abbot, Judi, illus. 2011. (ENG.). 32p. (J). (gr. -1-3). 14.99 (978-1-4424-2769-3(8), Simon & Schuster/Paula Wiseman Bks.) Simon & Schuster/Paula Wiseman Bks.

Walsh, Meg. Mama, Won't You Play with Me? 2009. 28p. pap. 13.99 (978-1-4490-1424-7(0)) AuthorHouse.

Walton, A. E. What Should I Do with My Love for You? 2009. 24p. pap. 11.49 (978-1-4389-8532-9(0)) AuthorHouse.

Walton, Will. Anything Could Happen. 2015. (ENG.). 288p. (J). (gr. 7). 17.99 (978-0-545-70954-5(7), PUSH) Scholastic, Inc.

Wan, Joyce. Hug You, Kiss You, Love You. Wan, Joyce, illus. 2013. (ENG., Illus.). 14p. (J). (— 1). bds. 6.99 (978-0-545-54045-2(3), Cartwheel Bks.) Scholastic, Inc.

—My Lucky Little Dragon. Wan, Joyce, illus. 2014. (ENG., Illus.). 14p. (J). (— 1). bds. 6.99 (978-0-545-54046-9(1), Cartwheel Bks.) Scholastic, Inc.

—You Are My Cupcake. Wan, Joyce, illus. 2011. (ENG., Illus.). 14p. (J). (gr. k — 1). bds. 6.99 (978-0-545-30741-3(4)) Scholastic, Inc.

—You Are My Cupcake: a Cloth Book. 2016. (ENG.). 6p. (J). (— 1). 12.99 (978-1-338-02921-5(5), Cartwheel Bks.) Scholastic, Inc.

Wang, Dorothea DePrisco & Imperato, Teresa. All the Ways I Love You. Downing, Julie, illus. 2005. (ENG.). 10p. (J). bds. 8.95 (978-1-58117-190-7(0), Intervisual/Piggy Toes) Bendon, Inc.

Warburton, Carol. Edge of Night: A Novel. 2004. (Illus.). 278p. pap. 14.95 (978-1-59156-013-5(6)) Covenant Communications, Inc.

Warburton, Ruth. Witch Finder. 2014. (ENG.). 384p. (J). (gr. 7). pap. 10.99 (978-1-4449-1446-7(4)) Hodder & Stoughton GBR. Dist: Hachette Bk. Group.

—Witch Hunt. 2014. (ENG.). 400p. (J). (gr. 7-12). pap. 10.99 (978-1-4449-1448-1(0)) Hodder & Stoughton GBR. Dist: Hachette Bk. Group.

Ward, Heather P. I Promise I'll Find You. McGraw, Sheila, illus. 2005. (ENG.). 32p. (J). (gr. -1-2). pap. 6.95 (978-1-55209-094-7(9), 9781552090947) Firefly Bks., Ltd.

Ward, Nick. The Ice Child. Bailey, Peter, tr. Bailey, Peter, illus. 2003. 32p. (YA). (978-1-84365-004-1(5), Pavilion Children's Books) Pavilion Bks.

Wardell, Jenniffer. Fairy Godmothers, Inc. 2013. (ENG.). 304p. (YA). (gr. 7). pap. 15.99 (978-0-9886491-5-6(2), Jolly Fish Pr.) North Star Editions.

Wardlaw, Lee. Coreys Fire. 2006. pap. 12.95 (978-0-595-40170-3(8), Backinprint.com) iUniverse, Inc.

Watase, Yuu. Absolute Boyfriend, Vol. 3, 6 vols. 2007. (ENG., Illus.). 200p. pap. 9.99 (978-1-4215-1003-3(0)) Viz Media.

Watt, Fiona. I Love You, Baby. MacKinnon, Catherine-Anne, illus. 2008. (Snuggletime Touchy-Feely Ser.). 10p. (J). (gr. -1-k). bds. 8.99 (978-0-7945-2071-7(5), Usborne) EDC Publishing.

Watts, Frances. Kisses for Daddy. Legge, David, illus. 2008. 24p. (J). bds. (978-1-921272-56-1(2)) Little Hare Bks. AUS. Dist: HarperCollins Pubs. Australia.

Weatherly, L. A. Angel Burn. 2011. (Angel Ser.: 1). (ENG., Illus.). 464p. (YA). (gr. 9). pap. 9.99 (978-0-7636-5846-5(4)); 17.99 (978-0-7636-5652-2(6)) Candlewick Pr.

—Angel Fever. 2013. (Angel Ser.: 3). (ENG.). 496p. (J). (gr. 9). 17.99 (978-0-7636-5680-5(1)) Candlewick Pr.

—Angel Fire. 2012. (Angel Ser.: 2). (ENG., Illus.). (YA). (gr. 9). pap. 8.99 (978-0-7636-6064-2(7)); 17.99 (978-0-7636-5679-9(8)) Candlewick Pr.

Webster, Jean. Daddy-Long-Legs. 2004. reprint ed. pap. 1.99 (978-1-4192-1490-5(X)); pap. 19.95 (978-1-4191-1490-8(5)) Kessinger Publishing, LLC.

—Jerry Junior. 2005. pap. (978-1-4065-0014-1(3)) Dodo Pr.

Weil, Cynthia. I'm Glad I Did. 2015. (ENG., Illus.). 272p. (YA). (gr. 9). 18.99 (978-1-61695-356-0(X), Soho Teen) Soho Pr., Inc.

Weimer, Heidi. You're My Little Love Bug! 2013. (ENG., Illus.). 12p. (gr. -1). bds. 12.99 (978-1-891100-29-1(7), Smart Kids) Penton Overseas, Inc.

Weimer, Heidi R. Love from My Heart: To a Precious Sweet Little Girl. 2005. (ENG., Illus.). 14p. (J). (gr. -1-3). bds. 12.99 (978-0-8249-6655-3(4), Ideal Pubns.) Worthy Publishing.

—Love from My Heart: To a Snuggly Cuddly Little Boy. 2005. (Parent Love Letters Ser.). (ENG., Illus.). 14p. (J). (gr. -1-3). bds. 12.99 (978-0-8249-6654-6(6), Ideal Pubns.) Worthy Publishing.

Weinberg, Jennifer Liberts. Princess Hearts (Disney Princess) RH Disney Staff & Legramandi, Francesco, illus. 2012. (Step into Reading Ser.). (ENG.). 32p. (J). (gr. -1-1). pap. 3.99 (978-0-7364-3013-5(X), RH/Disney) Random Hse. Children's Bks.

Weingarten, Lynn. The Book of Love. 2013. (ENG.). 272p. (YA). (gr. 8). 17.99 (978-0-06-192620-4(5), HarperTeen) HarperCollins Pubs.

—The Secret Sisterhood of Heartbreakers. (ENG.). (YA). (gr. 8). 2013. 368p. pap. 9.99 (978-0-06-192619-8(1)) 2011. 352p. 17.99 (978-0-06-192618-1(3)) HarperCollins Pubs. (HarperTeen).

Weiss, Sonya. Reckoning. 2016. (ENG., Illus.). 210p. (J). pap. 15.00 (978-1-60183-730-1(5)) Kensington Publishing Corp.

Weiss, Sonya. Rising. 2017. (ENG., Illus.). (YA). pap. 15.00 **(978-1-5161-0028-6(X))** Kensington Publishing Corp.

Wekelo, Kerry Alison. Audrey's Journey: Playful Namaste. 2012. 16p. pap. 15.99 (978-1-4772-7207-7(0)) AuthorHouse.

Welch, Jenna Evans. Love & Gelato. (ENG., Illus.). 400p. (YA). (gr. 7). 2017. pap. 10.99 **(978-1-4814-3255-9(9))** 2016. 17.99 (978-1-4814-3254-2(0)) Simon Pulse. (Simon Pulse).

Welford, Sue. Secret Love. l.t. ed. 2006. pap. (978-1-905665-10-5(5)) Pollinger In Print.

Wells, Carolyn. Patty at Home. 2007. (ENG.). 204p. per. 12.95 (978-1-4218-3321-7(2)) 1st World Publishing, Inc.

Wells, Rosemary. Love Waves. Wells, Rosemary, illus. 2011. (ENG., Illus.). 32p. (J). (gr. -1-2). 15.99 (978-0-7636-4989-0(9)) Candlewick Pr.

—Love Waves: Midi Edition. Wells, Rosemary, illus. 2012. (ENG., Illus.). 32p. (J). (gr. k — 1). 8.99 (978-0-7636-6224-0(0)) Candlewick Pr.

West, Casey. To Nicole with Love. Miller, Fujiko, illus. 2003. (Romance Ser.). 60p. (J). pap. 4.95 (978-1-58659-188-5(6)) Artesian Pr.

West, Jacqueline. Dreamers Often Lie. 2016. (ENG.). 368p. (YA). (gr. 7). 17.99 (978-0-8037-3863-8(3), Dial Bks) Penguin Young Readers Group.

West, Kasie. By Your Side. 2017. 352p. (YA). (gr. 8). pap. 9.99 (978-0-06-245586-4(9), HarperTeen) HarperCollins Pubs.

—Pivot Point. 2013. (Pivot Point Ser.: Bk. 1). (ENG.). 352p. (YA). (gr. 8). 17.99 (978-0-06-211737-3(8), HarperTeen) HarperCollins Pubs.

—Split Second. 2015. (Pivot Point Ser.: Bk. 2). (ENG.). 384p. (YA). (gr. 8). pap. 9.99 (978-0-06-211739-7(4), HarperTeen) HarperCollins Pubs.

West, Temple. Velvet. 2015. (ENG.). 416p. (YA). (gr. 8). pap. 9.99 (978-1-250-05708-2(6), 9781250057082) Feiwel & Friends.

Westerfeld, Scott. Afterworlds. 2014. (ENG., Illus.). 608p. (YA). (gr. 9). 19.99 (978-1-4814-2234-5(0), Simon Pulse) Simon Pulse.

—Afterworlds. 2015. lib. bdg. 24.50 (978-0-606-37860-4(X)) Turtleback Bks.

Westover, Steve. A Nothing Named Silas. 2013. 304p. (J). 17.99 (978-1-4621-1165-7(3)) Cedar Fort, Inc./CFI Distribution.

Wettersten, Laura. My Faire Lady. 2014. (ENG., Illus.). 352p. (YA). (gr. 7). 17.99 (978-1-4424-8933-2(2), Simon & Schuster Bks. For Young Readers) Simon & Schuster Bks. For Young Readers.

Weyland, Jack. Brianna, My Brother, & the Blog. 2009. (YA). (978-1-60641-140-7(3)) Deseret Bk. Co.

Weyn, Suzanne & Gonzalez, Diana. South Beach Sizzle. 2005. (Romantic Comedies Ser.). (ENG.). 272p. (YA). (gr. 9). mass mkt. 5.99 (978-1-4169-0011-5(X), Simon Pulse) Simon Pulse.

What Is Hidden. 2014. 281p. (YA). pap. 16.99 (978-1-4621-1429-0(6)) Cedar Fort, Inc./CFI Distribution.

Whitcomb, Laura. Under the Light. 2014. (ENG.). 256p. (YA). (gr. 7). pap. 8.99 (978-0-544-30294-5(X), HMH Books For Young Readers) Houghton Mifflin Harcourt Publishing Co.

White Driscoll, Heather. He Calls Me Harp. 2013. 456p. 26.95 (978-1-4575-2229-1(2)); pap. 19.95 (978-1-4575-2086-0(9)) Dog Ear Publishing, LLC.

White, E. B. & DiCamillo, Kate. Charlotte's Web: a Harper Classic. Williams, Garth, illus. 2017. (Harper Classic Ser.). 208p. (J). (gr. 3-7). 16.99 **(978-0-06-265875-3(1))** HarperCollins Pubs.

White, Kiersten. Illusions of Fate. 2014. (ENG.). 288p. (YA). (gr. 8). 17.99 (978-0-06-213589-6(9), HarperTeen) HarperCollins Pubs.

Whitney, Daisy. The Fire Artist. 2014. (ENG.). 288p. (YA). (gr. 7). 17.99 (978-1-61963-132-8(6), 9781619631328, Bloomsbury USA Childrens) Bloomsbury Publishing USA.

—Starry Nights. (ENG.). (YA). (gr. 7). 2014. 304p. pap. 9.99 (978-1-61963-436-7(8), 9781619634367) 2013. 288p. 17.99 (978-1-61963-133-5(4), 9781619631335) Bloomsbury Publishing USA. (Bloomsbury USA Childrens).

Widmayer, Paul E. Bessie & Bo: The Story of a Mother's Love. 2013. 20p. pap. 12.45 (978-1-4908-0300-5(9), WestBow Pr.) Author Solutions, Inc.

Wiggin, Kate Douglas. The Old Peabody Pew. 2009. 60p. pap. 7.95 (978-1-60664-315-0(0)) Rodgers, Alan Bks.

Wilde, Jen. Queens of Geek. 2017. (ENG.). 288p. (YA). pap. 10.99 (978-1-250-11139-5(0), 9781250111395) Feiwel & Friends.

Wildsmith, Sarah. Princess Charming. Paramonova, Lea, illus. 2013. 32p. pap. 14.99 (978-1-62380-970-6(3), Harmony Ink Pr.) Dreamspinner Pr.

Wilhelm, Hans. Yo Siempre te Quierre. (SPA.). 296p. (J). 13.95 (978-84-261-2404-3(6)) Juventud, Editorial ESP. Dist: AIMS International Bks., Inc.

Wilkerson, L. Kobie, 3rd, reader. Fred & Mary. 2008. (Illus.). 32p. (J). 24.95 incl. DVD, audio compact disk (978-0-9796679-0-9(9)) Love II Learn Bks.

Wilkinson, Lili. Green Valentine. 2016. (ENG.). 288p. (YA). (gr. 9-12). 12.99 (978-1-76011-027-7(2)) Allen & Unwin AUS. Dist: Independent Pubs. Group.

Wilkinson, Sheena Maria. Still Falling. 2016. (ENG.). 256p. (YA). (gr. 10). pap. 12.99 (978-1-908195-92-0(4)) Little Island IRL. Dist: Independent Pubs. Group.

Wilkinson, Simon. Noah's Ark Black & White Visual Development Book for Babies. 2008. 34p. pap. 17.95 (978-1-4092-4702-9(3)) Lulu Pr., Inc.

Williams, Alison. Pink Cat Blue Cat. 2009. (Illus.). 32p. pap. 14.49 (978-1-4389-4623-8(6)) AuthorHouse.

Williams, Avery. The Alchemy of Forever. 2012. (ENG.). 368p. (YA). (gr. 7). pap. 9.99 (978-1-4424-4317-4(0), Simon & Schuster Bks. For Young Readers) Simon & Schuster Bks. For Young Readers.

Williams, C. B. Walkers. 2012. 118p. pap. 6.95 (978-0-9881814-0-3(1)) BRYN WILLIAMS LLC.

Williams, Erika. Through the Shattered Glass, 1 vol. 2010. 62p. pap. 19.95 (978-1-4489-5149-9(6)) America Star Bks.

Williams, Jamie L. Mommy's Little Helper, 1 vol. 2010. 26p. 24.95 (978-1-4512-9232-9(5)) PublishAmerica, Inc.

Williams, Nicole. Clash. 2012. (Crash Ser.: 2). (ENG.). 288p. (YA). (gr. 11). pap. 9.99 (978-0-06-226715-3(9)) HarperCollins Pubs.

—Crash. 2012. (Crash Ser.: 1). (ENG.). 384p. (YA). (gr. 11). pap. 9.99 (978-0-06-226714-6(0)) HarperCollins Pubs.

—Crush. 2013. (Crash Ser.: 3). (ENG.). 400p. (YA). (gr. 11). pap. 9.99 (978-0-06-226717-7(5)) HarperCollins Pubs.

Williams, Nicole. Trusting You & Other Lies. 2017. (ENG.). 304p. (YA). (gr. 9). 17.99 **(978-0-553-49877-6(0)**, Crown Books For Young Readers) Random Hse. Children's Bks.

Williams, Sam. That's Love. Moriuchi, Mique, illus. 2006. 24p. (J). (gr. -1-3). 16.95 (978-0-8234-2028-5(0)) Holiday Hse., Inc.

Willis, Jeanne. Never Too Little to Love. Fearnley, Jan, illus. 2013. (ENG.). 32p. (J). (gr. -1-2). 8.99 (978-0-7636-6656-9(4)) Candlewick Pr.

Wilson, Barbara Rogers. Deva & the Soul Snatcher an Environmental Fantasy. 2nd ed. 2013. 216p. pap. 11.95 (978-0-9834956-9-7(6), SpiritBooks) Portal Ctr. Pr.

Wilson, Budge. The Courtship, 1 vol. unabr. ed. 2003. (ENG.). 160p. (YA). (gr. 7-18). mass mkt. (978-0-7736-7456-1(X)) Fitzhenry & Whiteside, Ltd.

Wilson, Jacqueline. Kiss. 2010. (ENG., Illus.). 256p. (YA). (gr. 7-12). 32.99 (978-1-59643-242-0(X), 9781596432420) Roaring Brook Pr.

Wilson, Ricky Derail. Mirror of Hope Mirror of Fame. 2007. 32p. per. 12.95 (978-1-4327-1391-1(4)) Outskirts Pr., Inc.

Wilson, W. Shane. War for Ice. 2010. 158p. pap. 13.99 (978-0-557-23572-8(3)) Lulu Pr., Inc.

Wind, Chuck T. The Test of Love. 2011. 24p. pap. 24.95 (978-1-4626-2398-3(0)) America Star Bks.

Winegardner, Suze. Anya & the Shy Guy. 2015. (ENG., Illus.). 230p. (J). pap. 15.49 (978-1-943336-62-3(8)) Entangled Publishing, LLC.

Wise, Rachel. Breaking News. 2013. (Dear Know-It-All Ser.: 10). (ENG., Illus.). 160p. (J). (gr. 3-7). 15.99 (978-1-4424-8965-3(0)); pap. 6.99 (978-1-4424-8964-6(2)) Simon Spotlight. (Simon Spotlight).

—Cast Your Ballot! 2013. (Dear Know-It-All Ser.: 9). (ENG., Illus.). 160p. (J). (gr. 3-7). 15.99 (978-1-4424-8793-2(3)); pap. 5.99 (978-1-4424-8792-5(5)) Simon Spotlight. (Simon Spotlight).

Wittlinger, Ellen. Lombardo's Law. 2003. (ENG.). 144p. (J). (gr. 5-7). pap. 10.95 (978-0-618-31108-8(4)) Houghton Mifflin Harcourt Publishing Co.

—Razzle. 2003. (ENG.). 256p. (YA). (gr. 7). pap. 12.99 (978-0-689-85600-6(8), Simon & Schuster Bks. For Young Readers) Simon & Schuster Bks. For Young Readers.

Wolf, Ema. 18 Cuentos de Amor.Tr. of 18 Short Love Stories. (SPA.). (J). pap. (978-950-07-1107-4(9)) Editorial Sudamericana S.A.

Wolf, Jennifer Shaw. Breaking Beautiful. 2014. (ENG.). 384p. (YA). (gr. 9). pap. 9.99 (978-0-8027-3440-2(5), 9780802734402, Bloomsbury USA Childrens) Bloomsbury Publishing USA.

Wolf, Sara. Love Me Never. 2016. (Lovely Vicious Ser.: 1). (ENG.). 304p. (J). pap. 9.99 (978-1-63375-229-0(1), 9781633752290) Entangled Publishing, LLC.

Wood, Douglas. When a Dad Says "I Love You" Bell, Jennifer A., illus. 2013. (ENG.). 32p. (J). (gr. -1-3). 17.99 (978-0-689-87532-8(0), Simon & Schuster Bks. For Young Readers) Simon & Schuster Bks. For Young Readers.

—When a Grandpa Says I Love You. Bell, Jennifer A., illus. 2014. (ENG.). 32p. (J). (gr. -1-3). 16.99 (978-0-689-81512-6(3), Simon & Schuster Bks. For Young Readers) Simon & Schuster Bks. For Young Readers.

Woods, Darcy. Summer of Supernovas. (ENG.). 352p. (YA). (gr. 9). 2017. 9.99 **(978-0-553-53706-2(7)**, Ember) 2016. 17.99 (978-0-553-53704-8(0), Crown Books For Young Readers) Random Hse. Children's Bks.

Woodson, Jacqueline. If You Come Softly. 2010. (ENG.). 224p. (YA). (gr. 7-18). 7.99 (978-0-14-241522-1(7), Speak) Penguin Young Readers Group.

Woon, Yvonne. Love Reborn. 2014. (Dead Beautiful Novel Ser.). (ENG., Illus.). 368p. (YA). (gr. 7-12). 16.99 (978-1-4231-7120-1(9)) Hyperion Bks. for Children.

X, Sulayman & Sulayman, X. Tears of a Dragon. 2nd ed. 2016. (ENG., Illus.). (J). 29.99 **(978-1-63533-079-3(3)**, Harmony Ink Pr.) Dreamspinner Pr.

Yasko, Carmen R. Buddy & His Buddies. 2012. 40p. pap. 22.65 (978-1-4797-4710-8(6)) Xlibris Corp.

Yokota, Hiromitsu, illus. The Tale of the Oki Islands: A Tale from Japan. 2013. (Tales of Honor (Red Chair Press) Ser.). (ENG.). 32p. (J). (gr. 1-4). lib. bdg. 26.60 (978-1-937529-78-9(9)) Red Chair Pr.

Yolen, Jane. How Do Dinosaurs Say I Love You? Teague, Mark, illus. (J). 2011. pap. (978-0-545-33076-3(9)) 2009. (ENG.). 40p. 16.99 (978-0-545-14314-1(4), Blue Sky Pr., The) Scholastic, Inc.

Yoon, Nicola. Everything, Everything. (ENG.). (YA). (gr. 7). 2017. 352p. pap. 10.99 **(978-0-553-49667-3(0)**, Ember) 2015. (Illus.). 320p. 18.99 (978-0-553-49664-2(6), Delacorte Pr.) 2017. 336p. 18.99 **(978-1-5247-6980-2(0)**, Delacorte Pr.) Random Hse. Children's Bks.

—Everything, Everything. 2017. lib. bdg. 22.10 **(978-0-606-40341-2(8))** Turtleback Bks.

Yoon, Salina. Peek-a-Love. Yoon, Salina, illus. 2010. (ENG., Illus.). 14p. (J). (gr. -1 — 1). 6.99 (978-1-4424-0655-1(0), Little Simon) Little Simon.

—Penguin in Love. Yoon, Salina, illus. (Penguin Ser.). (ENG., Illus.). (J). (gr. -1-1). 2014. 34p. bds. 7.99 (978-0-8027-3758-8(7), 9780802737588) 2013. 40p. 14.99 (978-0-8027-3600-0(9), 9780802736000) Bloomsbury Publishing USA. (Bloomsbury USA Childrens).

Young, Ann Eastman. Once Blue. 2011. 108p. pap. 15.00 (978-0-557-71193-2(2)) Lulu Pr., Inc.

Young, Leslie. Plaid: A Tale of Compassion. 2006. (Illus.). 15p. 9.00 (978-1-4120-2793-9(4)) Trafford Publishing.

Young, Suzanne. The Adjustment. 2017. (Program Ser.: 5). (ENG., Illus.). 416p. (YA). (gr. 9). 17.99 (978-1-4814-7132-9(5), Simon Pulse) Simon Pulse.

—A Need So Beautiful. 2012. (Need So Beautiful Ser.: No. 1). (ENG.). 288p. (YA). (gr. 9). pap. 8.99 (978-0-06-200825-1(0)) HarperCollins Pubs.

—The Program. (Program Ser.: 1). (ENG., Illus.). (YA). (gr. 9). 2014. 432p. pap. 11.99 (978-1-4424-4581-9(5)) 2013. 416p. 17.99 (978-1-4424-4580-2(7)) Simon Pulse. (Simon Pulse).

—The Treatment. (ENG., Illus.). (YA). (gr. 9). 2015. (Program Ser.: 2). 368p. pap. 11.99 (978-1-4424-4584-0(X)) 2014. (Program Ser.). 352p. 18.99 (978-1-4424-4583-3(1)) Simon Pulse. (Simon Pulse).

Young, T. M. What's Love Got to Do with It. Vickie Washington and Carla Watts, ed. Cromwell, Danielle, illus. 2013. 32p. pap. 24.95 (978-1-4626-0889-8(2)) America Star Bks.

Young, Tonya. Here's to the Nights. 2011. 190p. pap. 19.99 (978-1-4628-8707-1(4)) Xlibris Corp.

Younge-Ullman, Danielle. Lola Carlyle's 12-Step Romance. 2015. (ENG.). 304p. (YA). pap. 9.99 (978-1-62266-785-7(9), 9781622667857) Entangled Publishing, LLC.

Youssef, Marcus. Jabber. 2015. (ENG.). 80p. (gr. 7). pap. 16.95 (978-0-88922-950-1(3)) Talonbooks, Ltd. CAN. Dist: Consortium Bk. Sales & Distribution.

Yovanoff, Brenna. The Space Between. 2012. (ENG., Illus.). 384p. (YA). (gr. 9). pap. 8.99 (978-1-59514-483-6(8), Razorbill) Penguin Young Readers Group.

Yung, Kao & Liang, Kuan. Magic Lover's Tower, Vol. 2. 2008. (Magic Lover's Tower Ser.). (ENG., Illus.). 176p. (YA). (gr. 8). pap. 9.95 (978-1-59796-154-7(X)) DrMaster Pubns. Inc.

Yunisa. Schoolaholic Princess 2: Romansa Singapura. 2008. 232p. pap. 14.88 (978-1-4357-6044-8(1)) Lulu Pr., Inc.

Zafón, Carlos Ruiz. Marina. 2014. (ENG.). 336p. (YA). (gr. 7-17). 19.00 (978-0-316-04471-4(7)) Little, Brown Bks. for Young Readers.

Zettel, Sarah. Palace of Spies. 2013. (Palace of Spies Ser.: 1). (ENG.). 368p. (YA). (gr. 7). 16.99 (978-0-544-07411-8(4)) Houghton Mifflin Harcourt Publishing Co.

Ziegesar, Cecily von. Dark Horses. 2016. (ENG.). 336p. (YA). (gr. 9). 18.99 (978-1-61695-517-5(1), Soho Teen) Soho Pr., Inc.

Zink, Michelle. A Walk in the Sun. 2016. 336p. (YA). (gr. 8). 17.99 (978-0-06-243446-3(2), HarperTeen) HarperCollins Pubs.

Zuckerman, Linda. I Will Hold You 'Til You Sleep. Muth, Jon J., illus. 2006. (J). (978-0-439-43421-8(1), Levine, Arthur A. Bks.) Scholastic, Inc.

LOVE (THEOLOGY)

Boynton, Jeannette. God Loves Variety. Boynton, Jeannette & Holdeen, Bonnie, illus. 2007. (J). per. 10.99 (978-1-59879-264-5(4)) Lifevest Publishing, Inc.

Cope, Dorothy. The Day Star: A Love Spirit, 1 vol. 2009. 30p. pap. 24.95 (978-1-60749-729-5(8)) America Star Bks.

Student Life Staff. 31 Verses - Love: Every Teenager Should Know. 2008. 76p. (YA). pap. 4.99 (978-1-935040-11-8(1)) NavPress Publishing Group.

LOVE POETRY

Berry, George B. The Compassionate Side of a Common Man: Love Poems from the Heart, Vol. 3. unabr. ed. 2004. 120p. (YA). pap. 12.99 (978-0-9720308-6-1(7)) Mindfull Publishing Co.

Berry, Ron. The 123s of How I Love You. Sharp, Chris, illus. 2012. 24p. (J). bds. 12.99 (978-0-8249-1601-5(8), Ideal Pubns.) Worthy Publishing.

Boynton, Sandra. Consider Love. Boynton, Sandra, illus. 2013. (ENG., Illus.). 32p. (J). (gr. -1-3). 14.99 (978-1-4424-9465-7(4), Little Simon) Little Simon.

Nino, Jairo Anibal. La Alegría de Querer: Poemas de Amor para Ninos. Acosta, Patricia, illus. 2010. (Literatura Juvenil (Panamericana Editorial) Ser.). (SPA.). 70p. (gr. 4-6). pap. 9.99 (978-958-30-0293-9(3), PV30142) Panamericana Editorial COL. Dist: Lectorum Pubns., Inc.

Prelutsky, Jack. It's Valentine's Day! 2013. (I Can Read! Level 3 Ser.). (J). lib. bdg. 13.55 (978-0-606-32174-7(8), Turtleback) Turtleback Bks.

Weeks, Sarah. Be Mine, Be Mine, Sweet Valentine. Kosaka, Fumi, illus. 2005. (ENG.). 20p. (J). (gr. -1-k). 9.99 (978-0-694-01514-6(8), HarperFestival) HarperCollins Pubs.

Young, Ed. Should You Be a River: A Poem about Love. 2015. (ENG.). 40p. (J). (gr. -1-3). 18.00 (978-0-316-23089-6(8)) Little, Brown Bks. for Young Readers.

LOW, JULIETTE GORDON, 1860-1927

Aller, Susan Bivin. Juliette Low. 2007. (History Maker Biographies Ser.). (Illus.). 48p. (J). (gr. 3-7). lib. bdg. 26.60 (978-0-8225-6580-2(3), Lerner Pubns.) Lerner Publishing Group.

Corey, Shana. Here Come the Girl Scouts! Hooper, Hadley, illus. 2012. (ENG.). 40p. (J). (gr. -1-3). 17.99 (978-0-545-34278-0(3), Scholastic Pr.) Scholastic, Inc.

Hally, Ashleigh. Juliette Gordon Low. 2012. (Illus.). 24p. (J). (978-1-935884-77-4(8)); pap. (978-1-935884-83-5(2)) State Standards Publishing, LLC.

LOW TEMPERATURES

Strazzabosco, John. Extreme Temperatures: Learning about Positive & Negative Numbers. (PowerMath Ser.). (ENG., 32p. (gr. 4-5). 2009. Illus.). pap. 10.00 (978-0-8239-8927-0(5), PowerKids Pr.) 2004. 47.50 (978-0-8239-7649-2(1)) Rosen Publishing Group, Inc., The.

LOWE, T. S. C. (THADDEUS SOBIESKIE COULINCOURT), 1832-1913

Jarrow, Gail. Lincoln's Flying Spies: Thaddeus Lowe & the Civil War Balloon Corps. 2010. (ENG., Illus.). 112p. (J). (gr. 4-12). 18.95 (978-1-59078-719-9(6), Calkins Creek) Boyds Mills Pr.

LOYALTY

Amoroso, Cynthia. Loyalty. 2013. (Values to Live By Ser.). (ENG.). 24p. (J). (gr. -1-2). 25.64 (978-1-62323-521-5(9), 206292) Child's World, Inc., The.

Raatma, Lucia. Loyalty. 2009. (21st Century Junior Library: Character Education Ser.). (ENG.). 24p. (gr. 2-5). lib. bdg. 25.64 (978-1-60279-326-2(3), 200222) Cherry Lake Publishing.

LOYALTY—FICTION

Barchers, Suzanne. The Wounded Lion: A Tale from Spain. 2013. pap. 26.60 (978-1-936163-89-2(6)) Red Chair Pr.

Bates, Michelle. Dream Pony. 2010. (Sandy Lane Stables Ser.). 100p. (J). pap. 4.99 (978-0-7945-2537-8(7), Usborne) EDC Publishing.

Bowser, Ken. Hal & Al. Bowser, Ken, illus. 2016. (Funny Bone Readers: Truck Pals on the Job Ser.). (ENG., Illus.). 24p. (gr. k-2). lib. bdg. 19.99 (978-1-63440-068-8(2)) Red Chair Pr.

—Hal & Al: Self-Esteem. Bowser, Ken, illus. 2016. (Funny Bone Readers: Truck Pals on the Job Ser.). (ENG., Illus.). 24p. (gr. k-2). 30.65 (978-1-63440-070-1(4)) Red Chair Pr.

Castner, K. D. Daughters of Ruin. 2017. (ENG.). 320p. (YA). (gr. 9). pap. 11.99 (978-1-4814-3666-3(X), McElderry, Margaret K. Bks.) McElderry, Margaret K. Bks.

Charbonneau, Joelle. Graduation Day. 2014. (Testing Trilogy: Bk. 3). (ENG.). 304p. (J). (gr. 7-12). 17.99 (978-0-547-95921-4(4), HMH Books For Young Readers) Houghton Mifflin Harcourt Publishing Co.

Charles, Rie. No More Dragons. 2010. (ENG., Illus.). 112p. (J). (gr. 5-7). pap. 9.95 (978-1-926607-12-2(0), Napoleon & Co.) Dundurn CAN. Dist: Ingram Publisher Services.

Choyce, Lesley. Sudden Impact, 1 vol. 2005. (Orca Currents Ser.). (ENG.). 128p. (J). (gr. 5-9). per. 9.95 (978-1-55143-476-6(8)) Orca Bk. Pubs. USA.

Clements, Andrew. Lost & Found. Elliott, Mark, illus. 2008. (ENG.). 176p. (J). (gr. 3-7). 16.99 (978-1-4169-0985-9(0), Atheneum Bks. for Young Readers) Simon & Schuster Children's Publishing.

Cleveland, Rob. The Bear, the Bat & the Dove: Three Stories from Aesop. Hoffmire, Baird, illus. 2006. (Story Cove Ser.). (ENG.). 32p. (J). (gr. -1-3). pap. 3.95 (978-0-87483-810-7(X)) August Hse. Pubs., Inc.

Cypess, Leah. Mistwood. 2010. (ENG.). 320p. (YA). (gr. 8-18). 16.99 (978-0-06-195699-7(6), Greenwillow Bks.) HarperCollins Pubs.

Daley, Pj. Roger & the Giant People: Roger meets Giant People. 2011. 20p. pap. (978-1-4269-6824-2(8)) Trafford Publishing (UK) Ltd.

Elliott, David. This Orq. (He Cave Boy.) Nichols, Lori, illus. 2014. (ENG.). 40p. (J). (gr. -1-2). 15.95 (978-1-62091-521-9(9)) Boyds Mills Pr.

Elliott, L. M. Suspect Red. 2017. (ENG.). 304p. (J). (gr. 5-9). 16.99 **(978-1-4231-5754-0(0))** Hyperion Bks. for Children.

Ellis, Deborah. The Breadwinner. 2015. (Breadwinner Ser.: 1). lib. bdg. 20.80 (978-0-606-37232-9(6)) Turtleback Bks.

Gallant, Mark D. Christmas at Wildwood Farm. 2010. 140p. 22.49 (978-1-4520-2808-8(7)); pap. 11.99 (978-1-4520-2807-1(9)) AuthorHouse.

Gunderson, Jessica & Gonzalez, Jorge. Full Court Pressure, 1 vol. Ruiz, Alfonso, illus. 2010. (Sports Illustrated Kids Graphic Novels Ser.). (ENG.). 56p. (gr. 2-3). pap. 7.19 (978-1-4342-2291-6(8)); 26.65 (978-1-4342-1911-4(9)) Stone Arch Bks.

Gunnery, Sylvia. Out of Bounds. 2004. (Sports Stories Ser.). (ENG.). 104p. (J). (gr. 3-8). (978-1-55028-827-8(X)) Lorimer,

J
K
L

James & Co., Ltd., Pubs. CAN. Dist: Casemate Pubs. & Bk. Distributors, LLC.

Han, Yu-Mei, illus. The Brave Servant: A Tale from China. 2013. (Tales of Honor Ser.). (ENG.). 32p. (J). (gr. 1-4). pap. 8.95 *(978-1-937529-57-4(6))* Red Chair Pr.

Hodge, Rosamund. Bright Smoke, Cold Fire. 2018. (Bright Smoke, Cold Fire Ser.: 1). (ENG.). 464p. (YA). (gr. 8). 9.99 ***(978-0-06-236942-0(3)**,* Balzer & Bray) HarperCollins Pubs.

Hunter, Erin. The Forgotten Warrior. Richardson, Owen & Douglas, Allen, illus. 2012. (Warriors: Omen of the Stars Ser.: 5). (ENG.). 384p. (J). (gr. 3-7). pap. 6.99 *(978-0-06-155526-8(6))* HarperCollins Pubs.

Jack, Gordon. The Boomerang Effect. 2016. 352p. (YA). (gr. 9). 17.99 *(978-0-06-239939-7(X),* HarperTeen) HarperCollins Pubs.

Jebiwool Art Museum Staff. Destination Blackbeard: Destinations in Time, Book 2, 1 vol. 2009. 101p. pap. 19.95 *(978-1-60749-626-7(7))* America Star Bks.

Keeble, Helen. Fang Girl. 2012. (ENG.). 352p. (YA). (gr. 8). pap. 9.99 *(978-0-06-208225-1(6),* HarperTeen) HarperCollins Pubs.

Kraatz, Jeramey. The Cloak Society. (Cloak Society Ser.: 1). (ENG.). (J). (gr. 3-7). 2013. 304p. pap. 6.99 *(978-0-06-209548-0(X))* 2012. 288p. 16.99 *(978-0-06-209547-3(1))* HarperCollins Pubs.

—Villains Rising. 2013. (Cloak Society Ser.: 2). (ENG.). 320p. (J). (gr. 3-7). 16.99 *(978-0-06-209550-3(1))* HarperCollins Pubs.

Lackey, Mercedes & Edghill, Rosemary. Shadow Grail #3: Sacrifices. 2013. (Shadow Grail Ser.: 3). (ENG.). 304p. (YA). (gr. 8-12). pap. 14.99 *(978-0-7653-1763-6(X),* 9780765317636, Tor Teen) Doherty, Tom Assocs., LLC.

Lavender, William. Just Jane: A Daughter of England Caught in the Struggle of the American Revolution. 2005. (Great Episodes Ser.). (ENG.). 336p. (YA). (gr. 7-12). pap. 15.95 *(978-0-15-205472-4(3))* Houghton Mifflin Harcourt Publishing Co.

Leibenkop, T. The Sovereign of the Northern Winds. 2009. 30p. pap. 13.50 *(978-1-60693-847-8(9),* Eloquent Bks.) Strategic Book Publishing & Rights Agency (SBPRA).

London, C. Alexander. Divided We Fall. 2014. (Dog Tags Ser.: 4). (ENG.). 192p. (J). (gr. 5-9). pap. 5.99 *(978-0-545-47707-9(7),* Scholastic Paperbacks) Scholastic, Inc.

MacKenzie, Catherine. The Lonely Grey Dog at No. 6: Tammy & Jake Learn about Love & Loyalty. 2005. (Tales from Canterbury Place Ser.). (ENG., Illus.). 160p. (J). per. 6.99 *(978-1-84550-103-7(9),* bb65d1c0-1fc5-4a1a-8cb0-8c01c9ccdb70) Christian Focus Pubns. GBR. Dist: Bookmasters Distribution.

Maddox, Jake. Taekwondo Clash. 2016. (Jake Maddox JV Ser.). (ENG.). 96p. (gr. 3-4). lib. bdg. 25.99 *(978-1-4965-3981-6(8))* Stone Arch Bks.

Marchetta, Melina. Quintana of Charyn: The Lumatere Chronicles. 2013. (Lumatere Chronicles Ser.: 3). (ENG.). 528p. (YA). (gr. 9). 18.99 *(978-0-7636-5835-9(9))* Candlewick Pr.

Orietta, Susan. The Day Tyson Became a Hero. 2011. 24p. pap. 15.99 *(978-1-4628-6823-0(1))* Xlibris Corp.

Pantelides, Sherry. It's Blue Like You! A Story about Loyalty. Perez, Debi, illus. 2007. 32p. (J). 12.99 *(978-0-9771076-1-2(2))* Lacey Productions.

Park, Linda Sue. When My Name Was Keoko. 2004. 199p. (J). (gr. 5). 14.65 *(978-0-7569-2928-2(8))* Perfection Learning Corp.

Porter, Pamela. The Crazy Man. 2013. 164p. pap. *(978-1-4596-6446-3(9))* ReadHowYouWant.com, Ltd.

Purday, Paul. The Two Lands. 2006. 310p. (J). pap. *(978-1-905809-11-0(5))* Pneuma Springs Publishing.

Schick, Joel, illus. The Jungle Book: A Story about Loyalty. 2006. (J). 6.99 *(978-1-59939-023-9(X))* Cornerstone Pr.

Shemtov, Yael. Sadie's Funny Feeling. 2009. 24p. pap. 16.99 *(978-1-4389-6023-4(9))* AuthorHouse.

Shultz, Charles M. & Bailer, Darice. Make a Trade, Charlie Brown!, 1 vol. Lo Bianco, Peter, illus. 2011. (Peanuts Ready-To-Reads Ser.). (ENG.). 32p. (gr. -1-2). lib. bdg. 24.21 *(978-1-59961-806-7(0))* Spotlight.

Soto, Gary. Chato Goes Cruisin' Guevara, Susan, illus. 2008. (Chato Ser.). (J). 25.95 incl. audio *(978-1-59519-906-5(3))* Live Oak Media.

—Chato Goes Cruisin' Guevara, Susan, illus. 2007. (Chato Ser.). (J). (gr. -1-3). 14.65 *(978-0-7569-8147-1(6))* Perfection Learning Corp.

Standish, Burt L. Frank Merriwell's Faith. Rudman, Jack, ed. 2003. (Frank Merriwell Ser.). 29.95 *(978-0-8373-9360-5(4));* pap. 9.95 *(978-0-8373-9060-4(5))* Merriwell, Frank Inc.

Turner, Megan Whalen. The King of Attolia. (Queen's Thief Ser.: 3). (ENG.). (YA). (gr. 8). 2017. 432p. pap. 9.99 *(978-0-06-264298-1(7))* 2007. 432p. pap. 7.99 *(978-0-06-083579-8(6))* 2006. 400p. 17.99 *(978-0-06-083577-4(X))* HarperCollins Pubs. (Greenwillow Bks.).

—The King of Attolia. 2007. (Queen's Thief Ser.: BK.3). 387p. (YA). 18.00 *(978-0-7569-8106-8(9))* Perfection Learning Corp.

—The King of Attolia. (YA). 2008. (Queen's Thief Ser.: BK.3). (ENG.). 84.49 *(978-1-4281-8027-7(3))* 2007. (Attolia Ser.: 3). 119.75 *(978-1-4281-1722-8(9))* 2007. (Queen's Thief Ser.: BK.3). (ENG.). 92.75 *(978-1-4281-1716-7(4))* 2006. (Queen's Thief Ser.: BK.3). (ENG.). 90.75 *(978-1-4281-1718-1(0))* 2006. (Queen's Thief Ser.: BK.3). (ENG.). 122.75 *(978-1-4281-1720-4(2))* 2006. (Queen's Thief Ser.: BK.3). (ENG.). 1.25 *(978-1-4281-1713-6(X))* 2006. (Queen's Thief Ser.: BK.3). 281.75 *(978-1-4281-1721-1(0))* 2006. (Queen's Thief Ser.: BK.3). (ENG.). 251.75 *(978-1-4281-1717-4(2))* Recorded Bks., Inc.

Van Gorder, Vivian Ezeife. Master Kofi & Friskey the Dog. 2012. 20p. pap. 17.99 *(978-1-4772-6817-9(0))* AuthorHouse.

Vrabel, Beth. Pack of Dorks. 2014. (ENG.). 240p. (J). (gr. 2-7). 15.95 *(978-1-62914-623-2(4),* Sky Pony Pr.) Skyhorse Publishing Co., Inc.

Wibberley, Leonard. Peter Treegate's War. 2009. 134p. (YA). pap. 12.95 *(978-1-932350-21-0(7))* Bethlehem Bks.

Yeamans Simrell, Elizabeth. Only Mr. Bromley Will Do. 2008. 26p. 14.25 *(978-0-615-22279-0(X))* Dash & Doodles Productions.

LOYOLA, IGNACIO DE, SAINT, 1491-1556

see Ignatius, of Loyola, Saint, 1491-1556

LSD (DRUG)

Petechuk, David. LSD. 2004. (Drug Education Library). (Illus.). 112p. (J). (gr. 7-10). 32.45 *(978-1-59018-417-2(3))* Cengage Gale.

LUDINGTON, SYBIL, 1761-1839

Schiffman, Jessica, illus. Sybil Ludington: Freedom's Brave Rider. 2005. 32p. (J). pap. *(978-0-7367-2931-4(3))* Zaner-Bloser, Inc.

LULLABIES

Aigner-Clark, Julie. Baby Einstein: Lullabies & Sweet Dreams. 2007. (Baby Einstein Ser.). (ENG.). (J). (gr. -1). *(978-0-7634-2151-9(0))* Walt Disney Records.

Baby's First Lullabies. 2008. (Nursery Rhyme Boards with CD Sliding Tray Ser.). 48p. *(978-1-4075-3201-1(4))* Parragon, Inc.

Balmer, Paul & Music Sales Corporation Staff. Lullaby Songbook. 2009. (ENG., Illus.). 104p. (J). 9.95 *(978-1-84772-582-0(1),* AM993861) Wise Pubns. GBR. Dist: Music Sales Corp.

Bang, Molly. Ten, Nine, Eight. Bang, Molly, illus. 2003. (ENG., Illus.). 24p. (J). (gr. -1-3). reprint ed. pap. 6.99 *(978-0-688-10480-1(0));* 20th ed. 16.99 *(978-0-688-00906-9(9))* HarperCollins Pubs. (Greenwillow Bks.).

Barber, Jill. Baby's Lullaby, 1 vol. HildaRose & Rose, Hilda, illus. 2011. (ENG.). 16p. (J). (gr. -1-k). bds. 8.95 *(978-1-55109-795-4(8))* Nimbus Publishing, Ltd. CAN. Dist: Orca Bk. Pubs. USA.

Baxter, Nicola. Bedtime Lullabies: Fall Asleep to Your Free Cd. Finn, Rebecca, illus. 2014. (ENG.). 12p. (J). (gr. -1-12). bds. 14.99 *(978-1-86147-360-8(5),* Armadillo) Anness Publishing GBR. Dist: National Bk. Network.

Beaton, Clare, illus. Mrs. Moon: Lullabies for Bedtime. 2003. 48p. (J). 19.99 incl. audio compact disk *(978-1-84148-176-0(9))* Barefoot Bks., Inc.

Bleck, Linda, illus. A Children's Treasury of Lullabies. 2014. (ENG.). 32p. (J). (-k). pap. 6.95 *(978-1-4549-1358-0(4))* Sterling Publishing Co., Inc.

Brown, Margaret Wise. Goodnight Songs: Illustrated by Twelve Award-Winning Picture Book Artists. 2014. (ENG., Illus.). 28p. (J). (gr. -1-k). 17.95 incl. audio compact disk *(978-1-4549-0446-5(1))* Sterling Publishing Co., Inc.

Brown, Petra, illus. Hush, Little Baby. 2007. (Padded Hardcover Ser.). 18p. (J). 8.95 *(978-1-58925-819-8(3))* Tiger Tales.

Chatelain, Jeremy. May the Stars Drip Down. McClure, Nikki, illus. 2014. (ENG.). 40p. (J). (gr. -1-k). 17.95 *(978-1-4197-1024-7(9),* Abrams Bks. for Young Readers) Abrams, Inc.

DaySpring Greeting Card Staff & Jensen, Bonnie Rickner. Really Woolly Nighttime Lullabies, 1 vol. 2015. (Really Woolly Ser.). (ENG.). 40p. (J). bds. 9.99 *(978-0-7180-2295-2(5))* Nelson, Thomas Inc.

Delacre, Lulu, illus. & compiled by. Arrorro Mi Nino: Latino Lullabies & Gentle Games, 1 vol. Delacre, Lulu, compiled by. 2004. (ENG & SPA.). 32p. (J). 16.95 *(978-1-58430-159-2(7))* Lee & Low Bks., Inc.

Dorrian, James G., contrib. by. Lullabys for Starry Nights. (J). pap. 10.98 *(978-0-9647786-1-0(0),* 3001-4) Baby Music Boom, Inc.

Downing, Julie, illus. Lullaby & Good Night: Songs for Sweet Dreams. 2014. (ENG.). 32p. (J). (gr. -1-3). 16.99 *(978-1-4814-2528-5(5),* Simon & Schuster Bks. For Young Readers) Simon & Schuster Bks. For Young Readers.

Geddes, Anne. Lullaby & Good Night. 2014. (ENG., Illus.). 24p. (J). bds. 8.99 *(978-1-4022-9823-3(4))* Sourcebooks, Inc.

God Is with You in Sleep. Date not set. 44p. (J). (gr. -1-5). 16.99 incl. audio compact disk *(978-0-9702219-0-2(8))* Bowden Music Co.

Heath, Beverly C. A Bedtime Lullaby. Floyd, John, Jr., illus. 2006. 9p. (J). (gr. -1). bds. 5.95 *(978-0-9752860-1-2(3))* OurRainbow Pr., LLC.

Ho, Minfong. Hush! A Thai Lullaby. 2004. (Illus.). (J). (gr. -1-1). spiral bd. *(978-0-616-08497-7(8))* Canadian National Institute for the Blind/Institut National Canadien pour les Aveugles.

Ho, Mingfong. Hush! A Thai Lullaby. Meade, Holly, illus. 2004. (J). (gr. -1-1). spiral bd. *(978-0-616-07255-4(4))* Canadian National Institute for the Blind/Institut National Canadien pour les Aveugles.

Hodges, Lynn & Buchanan, Sue. I Love You This Much, 1 vol. Bendall-Brunello, John, illus. 2010. (ENG.). 36p. (J). pap. 6.99 *(978-0-310-72265-6(9))* Zonderkidz.

Hodges, Lynn, et al. I Love You This Much, 1 vol. Bendall-Brunello, John, illus. 2005. (Songs of Gods Love Ser.). (ENG.). 16p. (J). (gr. -1). bds. 6.99 *(978-0-310-70961-9(X))* Zonderkidz.

Hogan, Micki. A Midnight's Lullaby: Volume One. Brown, Bobby, illus. 2011. 40p. pap. 24.95 *(978-1-4560-2090-3(0))* America Star Bks.

Hughes, Langston. Lullaby (for a Black Mother) Qualls, Sean, illus. 2013. (ENG.). 32p. (J). (gr. -1-3). 16.99 *(978-0-547-36265-6(X))* Houghton Mifflin Harcourt Publishing Co.

Keen, Sophie. Baby's First Lullabies. (Book of Rhymes & CD Ser.). 10p. bds. *(978-1-4054-9664-3(9))* Parragon, Inc.

Lacoursiere, Patrick. Dream Songs Night Songs: From Mali to Louisiana. Bourbonnière, Sylvie, illus. 2006. (ENG.). 36p. (J). (gr. -1-2). 16.95 *(978-2-923163-06-2(0))* La Montagne Secrete CAN. Dist: Independent Pubs. Group.

López, Oscar J., illus. Sing along with Abuelita Rosa: Hispanic Lullabies = Canciones de Cuna. 2006. (ENG & SPA.). 13p. (J). *(978-0-9788379-0-7(8))* Baby Abuelita Productions, Inc.

Myers, Stephanie L. Bedtime Lullaby for Baby. 2008. 16p. pap. 10.49 *(978-1-4389-0278-6(4))* AuthorHouse.

Nelson, Alexis Andria. Sing Mommie Sing: Lullabies from the Heart. 2010. 36p. 21.99 *(978-1-4490-9405-8(8))* AuthorHouse.

Our Time: Lullabies for those special Moments. 2010. 56p. pap. 23.99 *(978-1-4490-8172-0(X))* AuthorHouse.

Prelutsky, Jack. The Silver Moon: Lullabies & Cradle Songs. Ishida, Jui, illus. 2013. (ENG.). 48p. (J). (gr. -1-3). 17.99 *(978-0-06-201467-2(6),* Greenwillow Bks.) HarperCollins Pubs.

Seeger, Pete. One Grain of Sand: A Lullaby. Wingerter, Linda, illus. 2005. 30p. (J). (gr. -1-4). reprint ed. 16.00 *(978-0-7567-8586-4(3))* DIANE Publishing Co.

Sexton, Brenda, illus. Little Jackie Rabbit. 2008. (ENG.). 10p. (J). (gr. -1). 14.99 *(978-0-8249-6732-1(1),* Ideal Pubns.) Worthy Publishing.

—Little Sleepy Eyes. 2008. (ENG.). 10p. (J). 14.99 *(978-0-8249-6733-8(X),* Ideal Pubns.) Worthy Publishing.

Stohs, Anita Reith. Hush, Little One: A Lullaby for God's Children. Kanzler, John, tr. Kanzler, John, illus. 2004. 32p. (J). 12.99 *(978-0-570-07144-0(5))* Concordia Publishing Hse.

—Hush Little One: A Lullaby for God's Children. Kanzler, John, illus. 2006. 20p. (J). (gr. -1). bds. 5.49 *(978-0-7586-0861-1(6))* Concordia Publishing Hse.

Stuart, Kelly. Cancion de Cuna de la Virgen de Guadalupe. Caban, Carlos, tr. from ENG. Caban, Carlos, illus. 2003. (SPA.). 28p. (J). *(978-1-931721-18-9(1))* Bright Sky Pr.

Studio Mouse Staff. Mother Goose Lullabies. de La Cour, Gary et al, illus. rev. ed. 2007. (ENG.). 24p. (J). 4.99 *(978-1-59069-559-3(3))* Studio Mouse LLC.

Tiger Tales Staff, ed. Twinkle, Twinkle Little Star: And Other Favorite Bedtime Rhymes. Rescek, Sanja, illus. 2006. (ENG.). 22p. (J). bds. 7.95 *(978-1-58925-787-0(1))* Tiger Tales.

Tucker, Jill C. Dylan Rides the Sleepy Town Express, 1 vol. 2010. 43p. pap. 24.95 *(978-1-4489-2165-2(1))* PublishAmerica, Inc.

Van Camp, Richard. Welcome Song for Baby: A Lullaby for Newborns, 1 vol. 2007. (ENG., Illus.). 24p. (J). (gr. -1-k). bds. 9.95 *(978-1-55143-661-6(2))* Orca Bk. Pubs. USA.

Watt, Fiona. Baby's First Christmas. 2009. (Baby Board Books with CD Ser.). 10p. (J). (gr. -1). bds. 14.99 *(978-0-7945-1902-5(4),* Usborne) EDC Publishing.

Williams, Sarajane. Dreamtime: Lullabies for Lever & Pedal Harp, 1 vol. 2004. (ENG., Illus.). 32p. pap. 14.99 *(978-0-7866-7192-2(0))* Mel Bay Pubns., Inc.

Zoboli, Giovanna. The Big Book of Slumber. Mulazzani, Simona, illus. 2014. (ENG.). 26p. (J). 16.00 *(978-0-8028-5439-1(7),* Eerdmans Bks For Young Readers) Eerdmans, William B. Publishing Co.

LUMBER AND LUMBERING

see also Forests and Forestry; Trees; Wood

Cowan, Mary Morton. Timberrr! A History of Logging in New England. 2003. (Women at War Ser.). (Illus.). 128p. (gr. 5-18). lib. bdg. 25.90 *(978-0-7613-1866-8(6),* Twenty-First Century Bks.) Lerner Publishing Group.

Gordon, Nick. Lumberjack. 2012. (Dangerous Jobs Ser.). (ENG., Illus.). 24p. (J). (gr. 3-7). lib. bdg. 25.95 *(978-1-60014-780-7(1),* Torque Bks.) Bellwether Media.

Hamlin, John. Tales of an Old Lumber Camp: A Story of Early Days in A Great Industry. Bernard, C. E. B., illus. 2011. 188p. 42.95 *(978-1-258-04052-9(2))* Literary Licensing, LLC.

Johnston, Marianne. Paul Bunyan. 2009. (American Legends Ser.). 24p. (gr. 3-3). 42.50 *(978-1-61511-385-9(1),* PowerKids Pr.) Rosen Publishing Group, Inc., The.

Kostecki-Shaw, Jenny Sue. Luna & Me: The True Story of a Girl Who Lived in a Tree to Save a Forest. Kostecki-Shaw, Jenny Sue, illus. 2015. (ENG., Illus.). 40p. (J). (gr. k-4). 18.99 *(978-0-8050-9976-8(X),* 9780805099768, Holt, Henry & Co. Bks. For Young Readers) Holt, Henry & Co.

Marshall, Pam. From Tree to Paper. 2013. (Start to Finish, Second Series: Everyday Products Ser.). (ENG., Illus.). 24p. (gr. k-3). lib. bdg. 23.93 *(978-0-7613-9184-5(3),* Lerner Pubns.) Lerner Publishing Group.

Rae, Alison. Trees & Timber Products. 2010. (Development Without Damage Ser.). (YA). (gr. 5-9). 34.25 *(978-1-59920-247-1(6))* Black Rabbit Bks.

Thomas, Aaron. Logs & Lumber: From the Forest to Your Home. 2009. (Real Life Readers Ser.). 16p. (gr. 2-3). pap. 7.05 *(978-1-4358-0069-4(9),* Rosen Classroom) Rosen Publishing Group, Inc., The.

Zimm, John. John Nelligan: Wisconsin Lumberjack. 2015. (Badger Biographies Ser.). (ENG., Illus.). 80p. (J). (gr. 4-6). pap. 12.95 *(978-0-87020-698-6(2))* Wisconsin Historical Society.

LUMBER AND LUMBERING—FICTION

Briggs, Andy. The Savage Lands. 2013. (Tarzan Ser.). (ENG.). 212p. (J). (gr. 3-6). pap. 12.99 *(978-1-4804-0014-6(9),* Open Road Media E-riginal) Open Road Integrated Media, Inc.

—Tarzan: The Greystoke Legacy. 2011. (ENG.). 304p. pap. *(978-0-571-27238-9(X))* Faber & Faber, Ltd.

Brooks, Walter R. & Slayton-Mitchell, Joyce. Knuckleboom Loaders Load Logs: A Trip to the Sawmill. Wiese, Kurt & Borns, Steven, illus. 2003. (ENG.). 40p. (gr. 4-13). 16.95 *(978-1-58567-368-1(4),* 856368) Overlook Pr., The.

Burchett, Jan & Vogler, Sara. Rainforest Rescue, 1 vol. Le Feyer, Diane, illus. 2012. (Wild Rescue Ser.). (ENG.). 152p. (gr. 3-6). 9.95 *(978-1-4342-4595-3(0))* Stone Arch Bks.

Crossan, Sarah. Resist. 2013. (Breathe Ser.: 2). (ENG.). 368p. (YA). (gr. 8). 17.99 *(978-0-06-211872-1(2),* Greenwillow Bks.) HarperCollins Pubs.

Horne, Constance. The Tenth Pupil. 2005. (ENG., Illus.). 160p. (J). (gr. 3-9). pap., tchr. ed. 8.95 *(978-0-921870-86-9(8))* Ronsdale Pr. CAN. Dist: Literary Pr. Group of Canada.

Jennings, Patrick. Wish Riders. 2008. (ENG.). 288p. pap. 6.99 *(978-1-4231-0015-7(8))* Hyperion Pr.

Johnson, Lois Walfrid. Trouble at Wild River. 2009. (J). 8.99 *(978-0-88062-279-0(2))* Mott Media.

LUMINESCENCE, ANIMAL

see Bioluminescence

LUNAR EXPEDITIONS

see Space Flight to the Moon

LUNAR EXPLORATION

see Moon—Exploration

LUNAR PROBES

see also names of space projects, e.g. Mariner Project; etc.

Morey, Allan. Lunar Probes. 2017. (Space Tech Ser.). (ENG., Illus.). 24p. (J). (gr. 3-7). lib. bdg. 25.95 ***(978-1-62617-702-4(3)**,* Epic Bks.) Bellwether Media.

LUNCH ROOMS

see Restaurants

LUNCHEONS

Aunt Louisa Is coming for Lunch: Individual Title Six-Packs. (gr. 1-2). 25.00 *(978-0-7635-9128-1(9))* Rigby Education.

Franklin, Louise. Lunch Around the World. 2009. (Inside the USA Ser.). (ENG., Illus.). 16p. (C). pap. 13.95 *(978-0-7362-7060-1(4))* National Geographic School Publishing, Inc.

Greathouse, Lisa. What's for Lunch?, 1 vol. 2nd rev. ed. 2011. (Nonfiction Readers Ser.). (ENG., Illus.). 28p. (J). (gr. 2-2). pap. 6.99 *(978-1-4333-3639-3(1))* Teacher Created Materials, Inc.

Kalman, Bobbie. Lunch Munch: Step-by-Step Recipes. 2003. (Kid Power Ser.). (ENG., Illus.). 32p. (J). (gr. 3). pap. *(978-0-7787-1273-2(7));* lib. bdg. *(978-0-7787-1251-0(6))* Crabtree Publishing Co.

Llanas, Sheila Griffin. Easy Lunches from Around the World. 2011. (Easy Cookbooks for Kids Ser.). (Illus.). 48p. (J). lib. bdg. 25.27 *(978-0-7660-3708-3(8));* (gr. 3-18). pap. 8.95 *(978-1-59845-272-3(X))* Enslow Pubs., Inc. (Enslow Elementary).

Parker, Vic. Lunch: Healthy Food Choices, 1 vol. 2014. (Healthy Food Choices Ser.). (ENG.). 32p. (gr. 1-3). lib. bdg. 27.32 *(978-1-4329-9117-3(5),* Heinemann First Library) Heinemann-Raintree.

Thomson, Sarah L. What's for Lunch? Aye, Nila, illus. 2016. (Let's-Read-And-Find-Out Science 1 Ser.). 40p. (J). (gr. -1-3). pap. 6.99 *(978-0-06-233137-3(X))* HarperCollins Pubs.

Tuminelly, Nancy. Super Simple Lunches: Easy No-Bake Recipes for Kids, 1 vol. 2010. (Super Simple Cooking Ser.). (ENG.). 32p. (gr. k-4). 27.07 *(978-1-61613-387-0(2),* Super SandCastle) ABDO Publishing Co.

Vega, Ali. Tombstone Sandwiches & Other Horrifying Lunches. 2017. (Little Kitchen of Horrors Ser.). (ENG.). 32p. (J). (gr. 2-5). 12.99 ***(978-1-5124-3774-4(3)**,* Lerner Pubns.); 39.99 ***(978-1-5124-2807-0(8)**,* Lerner Pubns.); 39.99 ***(978-1-5124-3773-7(5)**,* Lerner Pubns.); (Illus.). 26.65 *(978-1-5124-2577-2(X))* Lerner Publishing Group.

LUTHER, MARTIN, 1483-1546

Baden, Marian. Martin Luther: Life & Legacy - Grade 3-4 Student Book. 2017. (ENG.). (J). pap. 5.25 ***(978-0-7586-5918-7(0))*** Concordia Publishing Hse.

—Martin Luther: Life & Legacy - Grade 5-6 Student Book. 2017. (ENG.). (J). pap. 5.25 ***(978-0-7586-5919-4(9))*** Concordia Publishing Hse.

—Martin Luther: Life & Legacy - Grade 7-8 Student Book. 2017. (ENG.). (J). pap. 5.25 ***(978-0-7586-5920-0(2))*** Concordia Publishing Hse.

—Martin Luther: Life & Legacy - K-2 Student Book. 2017. (ENG.). (J). pap. 5.25 ***(978-0-7586-5917-0(2))*** Concordia Publishing Hse.

Bodden, Valerie. The Assassination of Martin Luther King Jr. 2017. (Turning Points Ser.). (ENG., Illus.). 48p. (J). (gr. 7-12). pap. 12.00 *(978-1-62832-343-6(4),* Creative Paperbacks) Creative Co., The.

Hollingsworth, Tamara. Martin Luther: A Reforming Spirit, 1 vol. 2012. (Primary Source Readers Ser.). (ENG.). 32p. (J). (gr. 4-4). pap. 8.99 *(978-1-4333-5010-8(6))* Teacher Created Materials, Inc.

Nohl, Frederick. Martin Luther: Hero of Faith. Hook, Richard, illus. 2003. 160p. (YA). pap. 9.99 *(978-0-7586-0592-4(7))* Concordia Publishing Hse.

Rijswijk, Cor van. Martin Shows the Way. 2004. (Illus.). 43p. (J). *(978-1-894666-80-0(1))* Inheritance Pubns.

Roth-Beck, Meike. The Life & Times of Martin Luther. Ensikat, Klaus, illus. 2017. (ENG.). 44p. (J). ***(978-0-8028-5495-7(8)**,* Eerdmans Bks For Young Readers) Eerdmans, William B. Publishing Co.

LUTZ, FRANK EUGENE, 1879-1943

Pallister, John C. In the Steps of the Great American Entomologist. Elgin, Kathleen, illus. 2014. (ENG.). 128p. (J). (gr. 2-6). pap. 11.95 *(978-1-59077-364-2(0))* Evans, M. & Co., Inc.

LUXEMBOURG

Sheehan, Patricia & Dhilawala, Sakina. Luxembourg. 2nd rev. ed. 2007. (Cultures of the World Ser.). 144p. (gr. 6). lib. bdg. 42.79 *(978-0-7614-2088-0(6),* Benchmark Bks.) Marshall Cavendish Corp.

Simons, Rae. Luxembourg. 2007. (European Union Ser.). (Illus.). 88p. (YA). (gr. 3-7). lib. bdg. 21.95 *(978-1-4222-0055-1(8))* Mason Crest.

Simons, Rae & Indovino, Shaina Carmel. Luxembourg. 2012. (J). *(978-1-4222-2251-5(9));* pap. *(978-1-4222-2282-9(9))* Mason Crest.

LYING

see Truthfulness and Falsehood

LYME DISEASE

Donelly, Karen. Coping with Lyme Disease. 2009. (Coping Ser.). 192p. (gr. 7-12). 63.90 *(978-1-61512-002-4(5))* Rosen Publishing Group, Inc., The.

Donnelly, Karen J. Coping with Lyme Disease. 2005. (Coping Ser.). (Illus.). 192p. (YA). (gr. 7-12). lib. bdg. 34.60 *(978-0-8239-3199-6(4))* Rosen Publishing Group, Inc., The.

—Everything You Need to Know about Lyme Disease. 2005. (Need to Know Library). (Illus.). 64p. (YA). (gr. 7-12). 31.95 *(978-0-8239-3216-0(8),* NTLYDI) Rosen Publishing Group, Inc., The.

Fox, Nancy. Hide & Seek, No Ticks Please. Seward, Daniel, illus. 2014. (ENG.). 42p. (gr. k-6). pap. 9.95 *(978-1-61448-705-0(7))* Morgan James Publishing.

Kelly, Shannon, ed. Lyme Disease. 2011. (Diseases & Disorders Ser.). (Illus.). 128p. (YA). (gr. 9-12). lib. bdg. 34.95 *(978-1-4205-0635-8(8))* Cengage Gale.

Williams, Mary E., ed. Lyme Disease. 2011. (Perspectives on Diseases & Disorders Ser.). (Illus.). 144p. (YA). (gr. 9-12). 38.95 *(978-0-7377-5777-4(9))* Cengage Gale.

LYNX

Borgert-Spaniol, Megan. Canada Lynx. 2017. (North American Animals Ser.). (ENG., Illus.). 24p. (J). (gr. k-3). lib. bdg. 25.95 ***(978-1-62617-635-5(3)**,* Blastoff! Readers) Bellwether Media.

Doudna, Kelly. It's a Baby Lynx!, 1 vol. 2008. (Baby Mammals Ser.). (ENG., Illus.). 24p. (J). (gr. k-3). lib. bdg. 24.21 *(978-1-60453-025-4(1))* ABDO Publishing Co.

Haakonsen, Jens. Lynx Chase, Hares Dash. 2017. (Hunter & Hunted: Animal Survival Ser.). 24p. (J). (gr. 7-8). 23.60 ***(978-1-5081-5664-2(6)**,* PowerKids Pr.) Rosen Publishing Group, Inc., The.

Parker, Barbara Keevil & Parker, Duane F. Lynxes. 2005. (Early Bird Nature Bks.). (ENG., Illus.). 48p. (gr. 2-5). lib. bdg. 26.60 *(978-0-8225-2871-5(1),* Lerner Pubns.) Lerner Publishing Group.

Randall, Henry. Lynxes. 2011. (Cats of the Wild Ser.). (ENG.). 24p. (J). pap. 8.25 *(978-1-4488-2619-3(5));* lib. bdg. 22.60 *(978-1-4488-2517-2(2))* Rosen Publishing Group, Inc., The. (PowerKids Pr.).

—Lynxes: Linces. 2011. (Cats of the Wild / Felinos Salvajes Ser.). (SPA & ENG., Illus.). 24p. lib. bdg. 22.60 *(978-1-4488-3129-6(6),* PowerKids Pr.) Rosen Publishing Group, Inc., The.

LYNX—FICTION

Fox, L. B. The Adventures of Marky, Slash & Levy. 2006. (ENG.). 184p. per. 24.95 *(978-1-4241-4992-6(4))* PublishAmerica, Inc.

LYSERGIC ACID DIETHYLAMIDE

see LSD (Drug)

M

MACARTHUR, DOUGLAS, 1880-1964

Benge, Janet & Benge, Geoff. Heroes of History - Douglas MacArthur: What Greater Honor. 2005. (ENG., Illus.). 205p. (YA). pap. 9.99 *(978-1-932096-15-6(9))* Emerald Bks.

McPherson, Stephanie Sammartino. Douglas MacArthur. 2005. (History Maker Bios Ser.). (Illus.). 48p. (J). 26.60 *(978-0-8225-2434-2(1))* Lerner Publishing Group.

MACCABEES

Balsley, Tilda. Maccabee! The Story of Hanukkah. Harrington, David, illus. 2010. (Hanukkah Ser.). (ENG.). 32p. (J). (gr. -1-2). pap. 7.95 *(978-0-7613-4508-4(6));* lib. bdg. 7.95 *(978-0-7613-4507-7(8))* Lerner Publishing Group. (Kar-Ben Publishing).

Raabe, Emily. A Hanukkah Holiday Cookbook. 2009. (Festive Foods for the Holidays Ser.). 24p. (gr. 3-3). 42.50 *(978-1-61512-595-1(7),* PowerKids Pr.) Rosen Publishing Group, Inc., The.

MCCAIN, JOHN, 1936-

Falk, Laine. Meet President John McCain. 2009. (J). *(978-0-531-23650-5(1))* Children's Pr., Ltd.

Horn, Geoffrey M. John Mccain. 2009. (People We Should Know Ser.). 32p. (J). (gr. 3-5). pap. 10.50 *(978-1-4339-0160-7(9),* Gareth Stevens Learning Library) Stevens, Gareth Publishing LLLP.

—John McCain. 2009. (People We Should Know Ser.). 32p. (J). (gr. 3-5). lib. bdg. 31.00 *(978-1-4339-0020-4(3),* Gareth Stevens Learning Library) Stevens, Gareth Publishing LLLP.

Robinson, Tom. Barack Obama: 44th U. S. President, 1 vol. 2009. (Essential Lives Set 3 Ser.). (ENG., Illus.). 112p. (J). (gr. 6-12). lib. bdg. 35.64 *(978-1-60453-527-3(X))* ABDO Publishing Co.

—John McCain: POW & Statesman, 1 vol. 2010. (Military Heroes Ser.). (ENG.). 112p. (J). (gr. 6-12). lib. bdg. 35.64 *(978-1-60453-963-9(1))* ABDO Publishing Co.

Wells, Catherine. John McCain. 2008. (Political Profiles Ser.). (Illus.). 112p. (YA). (gr. 5-9). lib. bdg. 27.95 *(978-1-59935-046-2(7))* Reynolds, Morgan Inc.

Wizner, Kira. John Mccain: Profile of a Leading Republican. 2007. 116p. (gr. 3-7). pap. 31.95 *(978-1-4358-3790-4(8))* Rosen Publishing Group, Inc., The.

MCCARTHY, JOSEPH, 1908-1957

Cunningham, Jesse G., ed. The McCarthy Hearings. 2003. (At Issue in History Ser.). (Illus.). 144p. (YA). (gr. 7-10). pap. 18.70 *(978-0-7377-1347-3(X),* Greenhaven Pr., Inc.) Cengage Gale.

Giblin, James Cross. The Rise & Fall of Senator Joe McCarthy. 2009. (ENG., Illus.). 304p. (YA). (gr. 7-18). 22.00 *(978-0-618-61058-7(8))* Houghton Mifflin Harcourt Publishing Co.

Hillstrom, Kevin. McCarthyism & the Communist Threat. 2011. (Defining Moments Ser.). 266p. 55.00 *(978-0-7808-1184-3(4))* Omnigraphics, Inc.

Hudak, Heather C. McCarthyism & the Red Scare. 2017. 48p. (J). ***(978-0-7787-3939-5(2))*** Crabtree Publishing Co.

Immell, Myra. The McCarthy Era. Gale Editors, ed. 2011. (Perspectives on Modern World History Ser.). (ENG.). 224p. (gr. 12-12). lib. bdg. 47.80 *(978-0-7377-5260-1(2),* Greenhaven Pr., Inc.) Cengage Gale.

Tracy, Kathleen. The McCarthy Era. 2008. (Monumental Milestones Ser.). (Illus.). 48p. (YA). (gr. 4-7). lib. bdg. 29.95 *(978-1-58415-694-9(5))* Mitchell Lane Pubs., Inc.

Zeinert, Karen. McCarthyism & the Communist Scare in United States History. 2015. (In United States History Ser.). 96p. (J). (gr. 5-12). 27.94 *(978-0-7660-6345-7(3));* pap. 10.95 *(978-0-7660-6346-4(1))* Enslow Pubs., Inc.

MCCAULEY, MARY (LUDWIG) HAYS, 1754-1832

Marsh, Carole. Molly Pitcher. 2004. 12p. (gr. k-4). 2.95 *(978-0-635-02375-9(X))* Gallopade International.

MCCORMICK, CYRUS HALL, 1809-1884

Aldrich, Lisa J. Cyrus McCormick: And the Mechanical Reaper. 2004. (American Business Leaders Ser.). (Illus.). 112p. (YA). (gr. 6-12). 23.95 *(978-1-883846-91-6(9),* First Biographies) Reynolds, Morgan Inc.

Welch, Catherine A. Farmland Innovator: A Story about Cyrus Mccormick. Jones, Jan Naimo, illus. 2007. (Creative Minds Biographies Ser.). (ENG.). 64p. (gr. 4-8). lib. bdg. 22.60 *(978-0-8225-5988-7(9))* Lerner Publishing Group.

MCDUCK, SCROOGE (FICTITIOUS CHARACTER)—FICTION

Barks, Carl, et al. Uncle Scrooge #387. 2009. 64p. pap. 7.99 *(978-1-60360-087-3(6))* Gemstone Publishing, Inc.

—Uncle Scrooge #389. 2009. 64p. pap. 7.99 *(978-1-60360-089-7(2))* Gemstone Publishing, Inc.

—Walt Disney's Vacation Parade Volume 5. Clark, John, ed. 2008. (ENG., Illus.). 80p. pap. 9.95 *(978-1-60360-031-6(0),* 9781603600316) Gemstone Publishing, Inc.

Barosso, Abramo, et al. Uncle Scrooge #386. 2009. 64p. pap. 7.99 *(978-1-60360-086-6(8))* Gemstone Publishing, Inc.

Blum, Geoffrey & Barks, Carl. Uncle Scrooge #377. Clark, John, ed. 2008. (ENG., Illus.). 64p. pap. 7.99 *(978-1-60360-033-0(7),* 9781603600330) Gemstone Publishing, Inc.

McGreal, Pat & McGreal, Carol. Uncle Scrooge #385. 2008. 64p. pap. 7.99 *(978-1-60360-062-0(0))* Gemstone Publishing, Inc.

McGreal, Pat, et al. Uncle Scrooge #390. 2009. 64p. pap. 7.99 *(978-1-60360-090-3(6))* Gemstone Publishing, Inc.

Pujol, Miquel, et al. Uncle Scrooge #388. 2009. 64p. pap. 7.99 *(978-1-60360-088-0(4))* Gemstone Publishing, Inc.

—Uncle Scrooge: Timeless Tales Volume 1: Timeless Tales Volume 1. 2016. (Uncle Scrooge Ser.). (ENG., Illus.). 240p. 29.99 *(978-1-63140-566-2(7),* 9781631405662) Idea & Design Works, LLC.

Rosa, Don. Walt Disney Uncle Scrooge & Donald Duck: Treasure under Glass: The Don Rosa Library Vol. 3. 2015. (Don Rosa Library: 0). (ENG., Illus.). 192p. 29.99 *(978-1-60699-836-6(6),* 699836) Fantagraphics Bks.

Sarda, Bruno. Mickey & Donald: the Search for the Zodiac Stone. Vita, Massimo de & Valussi, Franco, illus. 2016. (Mickey Mouse Ser.). (ENG.). 368p. 39.99 *(978-1-63140-706-2(6),* 9781631407062) Idea & Design Works, LLC.

Scarpa, Romano, et al. Uncle Scrooge: the Eternal Knot: The Eternal Knot. 2016. (Uncle Scrooge Ser.). (ENG., Illus.). 120p. (J). (gr. 2-5). pap. 12.99 *(978-1-63140-639-3(6),* 9781631406393) Idea & Design Works, LLC.

MCGUIRE, LIZZIE (FICTITIOUS CHARACTER)—FICTION

Alfonsi, Alice. Lizzie for President. 2004. 149p. (J). lib. bdg. 16.92 *(978-1-4242-0681-0(2))* Fitzgerald Bks.

Alfonsi, Alice, adapted by. 'Rents: Lizzie Mcguire. 2005. 134p. (J). lib. bdg. 16.92 *(978-1-4242-0689-6(8))* Fitzgerald Bks.

Banim, Lisa. Hands off My Crush-Boy! 2004. 125p. (J). lib. bdg. 16.92 *(978-1-4242-0684-1(7))* Fitzgerald Bks.

—In the Doghouse. 2005. 124p. (J). lib. bdg. 16.92 *(978-1-4242-0685-8(5))* Fitzgerald Bks.

Banim, Lisa & Minsky, Terri. The Case of the Kate Haters. 2005. (Illus.). 124p. (J). *(978-1-4156-3927-6(2))* Disney Pr.

Jones, Jasmine, adapted by. The Importance of Being Gordo. 2005. (Illus.). 138p. (J). *(978-1-4155-7362-4(X))* Disney Pr.

—Importance of Being Gordo. 2005. 138p. (J). lib. bdg. 16.92 *(978-1-4242-0688-9(X))* Fitzgerald Bks.

—Just Like Lizzie. 2003. (Lizzie Mcguire Ser.). (Illus.). 153p. (J). 12.65 *(978-0-7569-2720-2(X))* Perfection Learning Corp.

—Oh, Brother! 2005. 146p. (J). lib. bdg. 16.92 *(978-1-4242-0682-7(0))* Fitzgerald Bks.

Jones, Jasmine & Alfonsi, Alice. My Second Way Cool, Set. 2nd gif. novel rev. ed. 2004. (ENG.). 144p. (gr. 3-7). 12.99 *(978-0-7868-4678-8(X))* Disney Pr.

Minsky, Terri. All over It! 2005. (Illus.). 138p. (J). *(978-1-4156-0271-3(9))* Disney Pr.

Minsky, Terri, creator. Lizzie McGuire Cine-Manga Vol. 2: Rumors & I've Got Rhythmic, 7 vols. 2003. (Lizzie McGuire Ser.: Vol. 2). (Illus.). 96p. (gr. 2-18). pap. 14.99 *(978-1-59182-148-9(7),* Tokyopop Kids) TOKYOPOP, Inc.

Papademetriou, Lisa. On the Job. 2005. (On the Job Ser.). (Illus.). 32p. (gr. 2-4). 138.00 *(978-0-7910-7408-4(0),* Chelsea Hse.) Facts On File, Inc.

Papademetriou, Lisa & Minsky, Terri. A Very Lizzie Summer. 2005. (Lizzie Mcguire Super Special Ser.). (Illus.). 265p. (J). *(978-1-4155-9625-8(5))* Disney Pr.

MCGWIRE, MARK, 1963-

Kirkpatrick, Rob. Mark Mcgwire: Record Breaker/Rompe Records. 2009. (Power Players / Deportistas de Poder Ser.). (ENG & SPA.). 24p. (gr. 1-2). 42.50 *(978-1-60851-332-1(7),* Editorial Buenas Letras) Rosen Publishing Group, Inc., The.

—Mark Mcgwire: Rompe Récords (Record Breaker) 2009. (Deportistas de Poder (Power Players) Ser.). (SPA.). 24p. (gr. 1-1). 42.50 *(978-1-61512-159-5(5),* Editorial Buenas Letras) Rosen Publishing Group, Inc., The.

—Mark Mcgwire: The Home Run King. 2009. (Great Record Breakers in Sports Ser.). 24p. (gr. 3-3). 42.50 *(978-1-61513-188-4(4),* PowerKids Pr.) Rosen Publishing Group, Inc., The.

Rains, Rob & Smith, Ozzie. Cardinals Sports Heroes Block: City Block St. Louis: Mark Mcgwire, Ozzie Smith. 2004. (Illus.). 5.98 *(978-1-58261-858-6(5))* Sports Publishing, LLC.

Savage, Jeff. Mark McGwire: Home Run King. 2003. (Sports Achievers Biographies Ser.). (Illus.). 64p. (YA). (gr. 4-9). pap. 5.95 *(978-0-8225-9845-9(0),* Carolrhoda Bks.) Lerner Publishing Group.

MACHINERY

see also Agricultural Machinery; Engines; Inventions; Locomotives; Mechanical Drawing; Mechanics; Steam-Engines

ABDO Publishing Company Staff. Mighty Movers. 2005. (Mighty Movers Ser.). (gr. k-4). 153.90 *(978-1-59197-824-4(6),* Buddy Bks.) ABDO Publishing Co.

Abramovitz, Melissa & Alpert, Barbara. Military Machines. 2012. (Military Machines Ser.). (ENG.). 24p. (gr. k-1). pap. 250.20 *(978-1-4296-8319-7(8),* Pebble Plus) Capstone Press of Coughlan Cos.

Adams, Simon, et al. Discover the Savage World. 2013. (Illus.). 224p. (J). *(978-1-4351-4990-8(4))* Barnes & Noble, Inc.

Addison, D. R. Diggers at Work. 2009. (Big Trucks Ser.). (Illus.). 24p. lib. bdg. 22.60 *(978-1-4358-2700-4(7))* Rosen Publishing Group, Inc., The.

Adkins, Jan. Moving Heavy Things. Adkins, Jan, illus. 2004. (ENG., Illus.). 48p. (J). (gr. -1-3). 13.95 *(978-0-937822-82-1(5))* WoodenBoat Pubns.

Adler, David A. Simple Machines: Wheels, Levers, & Pulleys. Raff, Anna, illus. (ENG.). 32p. (J). 2016. 7.99 *(978-0-8234-3572-2(5))* 2015. (gr. -1-3). 17.95 *(978-0-8234-3309-4(9))* Holiday Hse., Inc.

Alinas, Marv. Cranes. 2014. (Big Machines at Work Ser.). (ENG.). 24p. (J). (gr. -1-2). 25.64 *(978-1-62323-965-7(6),* 206740) Child's World, Inc., The.

—Diggers. 2014. (Big Machines at Work Ser.). (ENG.). 24p. (J). (gr. -1-2). 25.64 *(978-1-62323-966-4(4),* 206741) Child's World, Inc., The.

Alpert, Barbara & Abramovitz, Melissa. Military Machines. 2012. (Military Machines Ser.). (ENG.). 24p. (gr. k-1). lib. bdg. 159.90 *(978-1-4296-8112-4(8),* Pebble Plus) Capstone Press of Coughlan Cos.

Amazing Machines. 2004. (Sticker Timelines Ser.). (Illus.). 12p. (J). pap. *(978-1-84229-844-2(5))* Top That! Publishing PLC.

Ardagh, Philip. A Hole in the Road. (Illus.). 32p. (J). lib. bdg. 24.25 *(978-1-931983-02-0(X))* Chrysalis Education.

Armentrout, David & Armentrout, Patricia. Inclined Planes. 2009. (ENG., Illus.). 24p. (gr. 3-6). pap. 8.95 *(978-1-60694-519-3(X))* Rourke Educational Media.

—Levers. 2009. (ENG., Illus.). 24p. (gr. 3-6). pap. 8.95 *(978-1-60694-520-9(3))* Rourke Educational Media.

—Pulleys. 2009. (ENG., Illus.). 24p. (gr. 3-6). pap. 8.95 *(978-1-60694-521-6(1))* Rourke Educational Media.

—Wedges. 2009. (ENG., Illus.). 24p. (gr. 3-6). pap. 8.95 *(978-1-60694-523-0(8))* Rourke Educational Media.

Arnold, Quinn M. Krupp Digging Machine. 2016. (Illus.). 24p. (J). *(978-1-60818-713-3(6),* Creative Education) Creative Co., The.

—Overburden Conveyor Bridge F60. 2016. (Illus.). 24p. (J). *(978-1-60818-716-4(0),* Creative Education) Creative Co., The.

AZ Books, creator. Construction Machines. 2012. (Lively Machines Ser.). (ENG., Illus.). 10p. (J). (gr. -1-k). bds. 10.95 *(978-1-61889-324-6(6))* AZ Bks. LLC.

—Everyday Machines. 2012. (Peep Inside Ser.). (ENG.). 10p. (J). (gr. -1-k). 12.95 *(978-1-61889-099-3(9))* AZ Bks. LLC.

—Magic Machines. 2012. (Baby Book Ser.). (ENG., Illus.). 10p. (J). (gr. -1 — 1). bds. 4.95 *(978-1-61889-286-7(X))* AZ Bks. LLC.

—Powerful Machines. 2012. (Peep Inside Ser.). (ENG., Illus.). 10p. (J). (gr. -1-k). 12.95 *(978-1-61889-102-0(2))* AZ Bks. LLC.

—Rescue Machines. 2012. (Peep Inside Ser.). (ENG., Illus.). 10p. (J). (gr. -1-k). 12.95 *(978-1-61889-100-6(6))* AZ Bks. LLC.

Bailey, Gerry. Powerful Machines. 2009. (Simply Science Ser.). (Illus.). 32p. (YA). (gr. 3-6). lib. bdg. 26.00 *(978-1-4339-0035-8(1))* Stevens, Gareth Publishing LLLP.

—Pressing Down: The Lever. 2014. (ENG., Illus.). 32p. (J). *(978-0-7787-0416-4(5));* pap. *(978-0-7787-0422-5(X))* Crabtree Publishing Co.

—Pulling Up: The Pulley. 2014. (ENG., Illus.). 32p. (J). *(978-0-7787-0417-1(3));* pap. *(978-0-7787-0423-2(8))* Crabtree Publishing Co.

—Rolling Along: Wheels & Axles. 2014. (ENG., Illus.). 32p. (J). *(978-0-7787-0418-8(1));* pap. *(978-0-7787-0424-9(6))* Crabtree Publishing Co.

—Sloping up & Down: The Ramp. 2014. (ENG., Illus.). 32p. (J). *(978-0-7787-0419-5(X));* pap. *(978-0-7787-0425-6(4))* Crabtree Publishing Co.

—Splitting Apart: The Wedge. 2014. (ENG., Illus.). 32p. (J). *(978-0-7787-0420-1(3));* pap. *(978-0-7787-0426-3(2))* Crabtree Publishing Co.

—Winding Around: The Screw. 2014. (ENG., Illus.). 32p. (J). *(978-0-7787-0421-8(1));* pap. *(978-0-7787-0427-0(0))* Crabtree Publishing Co.

Baker, Wendy. Experimenta - Maquinas. (SPA.). 52p. (J). *(978-84-348-3997-7(0))* SM Ediciones.

Bender, Lionel. Diggers & Tractors. 2006. (J). *(978-1-59389-267-8(5))* Chrysalis Education.

Berendes, Mary. Las Máquinas. Petelinsek, Kathleen, illus. 2007. (WordBooks/Libros de Palabras Ser.).Tr. of Machines. (ENG.). 24p. (J). (gr. k-3). 25.64 *(978-1-59296-799-5(X),* 201095) Child's World, Inc., The.

Big Machines. 2016. (Big Machines Ser.). 32p. (gr. 2-1). 109.00 *(978-1-4994-8095-5(4));* pap. 40.00 *(978-1-5081-9269-5(3))* Rosen Publishing Group, Inc., The. (Windmill Bks.).

Bodden, Valerie. Inclined Planes. 2011. (Simple Machine Ser.). 24p. (J). (gr. 1-3). 24.25 *(978-1-60818-008-0(5));* (ENG.). pap. 8.99 *(978-0-89812-579-5(0),* Creative Paperbacks) Creative Co., The.

—Levers. 2011. (Simple Machine Ser.). 24p. (J). (gr. 1-3). 24.25 *(978-1-60818-009-7(3));* (ENG.). pap. 8.99 *(978-0-89812-580-1(4),* Creative Paperbacks) Creative Co., The.

—Pulleys. 2011. (Simple Machine Ser.). 24p. (J). (gr. 1-3). 24.25 *(978-1-60818-010-3(7));* (ENG.). pap. 8.99 *(978-0-89812-581-8(2),* Creative Paperbacks) Creative Co., The.

—Screws. 2011. (Simple Machine Ser.). 24p. (J). (gr. 1-3). 24.25 *(978-1-60818-011-0(5));* (ENG.). pap. 8.99 *(978-0-89812-582-5(0),* Creative Paperbacks) Creative Co., The.

—Wedges. 2011. (Simple Machine Ser.). 24p. (J). (gr. 1-3). 24.25 *(978-1-60818-012-7(3));* (ENG.). pap. 8.99 *(978-0-89812-583-2(9),* Creative Paperbacks) Creative Co., The.

Bonavista, Rufito & Beascoa, Santiago. Then & Now: A Journey Through the History of Things. Altarriba, Eduard, illus. 2016. (ENG.). 44p. (J). (gr. 1-5). 14.95 *(978-1-4549-1962-9(0))* Sterling Publishing Co., Inc.

Bowman, Chris. Backhoes. 2017. (Mighty Machines in Action Ser.). (ENG., Illus.). 24p. (J). (gr. k-3). lib. bdg. 25.95 *(978-1-62617-600-3(0),* Blastoff! Readers) Bellwether Media.

Brill, Marlene Targ. Concrete Mixers. 2006. (Pull Ahead Books-Mighty Movers Ser.). (ENG., Illus.). 32p. (gr. k-3). pap. 7.95 *(978-0-8225-5899-6(8),* First Avenue Editions) Lerner Publishing Group.

Brooks, Felicity. Diggers Lift-and-Look. 2005. (Illus.). 12p. (J). (gr. -1-k). per., bds. 9.95 *(978-0-7945-1067-1(1),* Usborne) EDC Publishing.

Bruning, Matt. Mighty Machines Picture Puzzles, 1 vol. 2009. (Look, Look Again Ser.). (ENG.). 32p. (gr. 1-2). lib. bdg. 27.32 *(978-1-4296-3289-8(5),* Aplus Bks.) Capstone Press of Coughlan Cos.

Bryant-Mole, Karen. Dot-to-Dot Machines. Tyler, Jenny, ed. Round, Graham, illus. rev. ed. 2006. (Dot to Dot Ser.). 22p. (J). (gr. -1-2). pap. 3.99 *(978-0-7945-1495-2(2),* Usborne) EDC Publishing.

Butterfield, Moira. Bulldozers & Other Construction Machines. Lyon, Chris & Biggin, Gary, illus. 32p. (J). mass mkt. 8.99 *(978-0-590-24556-2(2))* Scholastic, Inc.

Capici, Gaetano. What Does It Do? Cement Mixer. 2011. (Community Connections: What Does It Do? Ser.). (ENG.). 24p. (gr. 2-5). lib. bdg. 25.64 *(978-1-60279-973-8(3),* 200972) Cherry Lake Publishing.

Challen, Paul. Get to Know Screws. 2009. (Get to Know Simple Machines Ser.). (ENG., Illus.). 32p. (J). (gr. 2-4). pap. *(978-0-7787-4486-3(8));* lib. bdg. *(978-0-7787-4469-6(8))* Crabtree Publishing Co.

—Get to Know Wheels & Axles. 2009. (Get to Know Simple Machines Ser.). (ENG., Illus.). 32p. (J). (gr. 2-4). pap. *(978-0-7787-4488-7(4))* Crabtree Publishing Co.

Christiansen, Jennifer. Get to Know Inclined Planes. 2009. (Get to Know Simple Machines Ser.). (ENG., Illus.). 32p. (J). (gr. 2-4). pap. *(978-0-7787-4483-2(3))* Crabtree Publishing Co.

—Get to Know Wedges. 2009. (ENG.). 32p. (J). lib. bdg. *(978-0-7787-4470-2(1));* (gr. 2). pap. *(978-0-7787-4487-0(6))* Crabtree Publishing Co.

Clay, Kathryn. Backhoes. 2016. (Construction Vehicles at Work Ser.). (ENG.). 24p. (gr. k-1). lib. bdg. 21.99 *(978-1-5157-2527-5(8))* Capstone Press of Coughlan Cos.

—Construction Vehicles. 2015. (Wild about Wheels Ser.). (ENG.). 24p. (gr. k-1). lib. bdg. 26.65 *(978-1-4914-2117-8(7),* Pebble Plus) Capstone Press of Coughlan Cos.

—Construction Vehicles at Work. 2016. (Construction Vehicles at Work Ser.). (ENG.). 24p. (gr. k-1). 87.96 *(978-1-5157-2548-0(0),* Pebble Bks.) Capstone Press of Coughlan Cos.

—Cranes. 2016. (Construction Vehicles at Work Ser.). (ENG.). 24p. (gr. k-1). lib. bdg. 21.99 *(978-1-5157-2528-2(6))* Capstone Press of Coughlan Cos.

The Clean Machine: Individual Title Six-Packs. (gr. k-1). 23.00 *(978-0-7635-9077-2(0))* Rigby Education.

Close, Edward. Force & Motion, 1 vol., 1. 2014. (Discovery Education: How It Works). (ENG.). 32p. (gr. 3-6). 26.25 *(978-1-4777-6317-9(1),* PowerKids Pr.) Rosen Publishing Group, Inc., The.

Collander, Hope. Inclined Planes. 2013. (Simple Machine Science Ser.). (Illus.). 24p. (J). (gr. 1-3). pap. 8.15 *(978-1-4339-8132-6(7));* lib. bdg. 22.60 *(978-1-4339-8131-9(9))* Stevens, Gareth Publishing LLLP.

Community Connections: What Does It Do? 2011. 24p. lib. bdg. 143.60 *(978-1-60279-975-2(X),* 200928) Cherry Lake Publishing.

Community Connections: What Does It Do?, 10 vols., Set. Incl. What Does It Do? Ambulance. Gregory, Josh. lib. bdg. 25.64 *(978-1-60279-969-1(5),* 200970); What Does It Do? Bulldozer. Capici, Gaetano. lib. bdg. 25.64 *(978-1-60279-972-1(5),* 200966); What Does It Do? Cement Mixer. Capici, Gaetano. lib. bdg. 25.64 *(978-1-60279-973-8(3),* 200972); What Does It Do? Combine. Friedman, Mark. lib. bdg. 25.64 *(978-1-61080-117-1(2),* 201124); What Does It Do? Crane. Gregory, Josh. lib. bdg. 25.64 *(978-1-60279-967-7(9),* 200958); What Does It Do? Digger. Zeiger, Jennifer. lib. bdg. 25.64 *(978-1-60279-968-4(7),* 200968); What Does It Do? Dump Truck. Zeiger, Jennifer. lib. bdg. 25.64 *(978-1-60279-974-5(1),* 200962); What Does It Do? Fire Truck. Gregory, Josh. lib. bdg. 25.64 *(978-1-60279-971-4(7),* 200964); What Does It Do? Tractor. Gregory, Josh. lib. bdg. 25.64 *(978-1-60279-970-7(9),* 200960); What Does It Do? Windmill. Friedman, Mark. lib. bdg. 25.64 *(978-1-61080-118-8(0),* 201126); 24p. (gr. 2-5). 2011. Set lib. bdg. 256.40 *(978-1-61080-152-2(0))* Cherry Lake Publishing.

Conigliaro, Phil. Colossal Paper Machines: Make 10 Giant Models That Move! 2015. (ENG., Illus.). 128p. (J). (gr. 4-12). pap. 24.95 *(978-0-7611-7640-4(3))* Workman Publishing Co., Inc.

Corporate Contibutor & Snedden, Robert. Mechanical Engineering & Simple Machines. 2012. (ENG.). 32p. (J). *(978-0-7787-7498-3(8))* Crabtree Publishing Co.

Dahl, Michael. Pull, Lift, & Lower: A Book about Pulleys, 1 vol. Shea, Denise, illus. 2006. (Amazing Science: Simple Machines Ser.). (ENG.). 24p. (gr. k-4). lib. bdg. 26.65 *(978-1-4048-1305-2(5),* 1253208) Picture Window Bks.

Davis, Caroline. Diggers. Davis, Caroline, illus. 2010. (ENG., Illus.). 20p. (J). bds. *(978-1-4083-0785-4(5),* Orchard Bks.) Hachette Children's Group GBR. Dist: Hachette Bk. Group.

Dayton, Connor. Cherry Pickers. 2012. 24p. (J). 49.50 *(978-1-4488-5071-6(1));* pap. 8.25 *(978-1-4488-5070-9(3));* lib. bdg. 22.60 *(978-1-4488-4960-4(8))* Rosen Publishing Group, Inc., The. (PowerKids Pr.).

—Jackhammers. 2012. (J). 49.50 *(978-1-4488-5065-5(7));* pap. 8.25 *(978-1-4488-5064-8(9));* lib. bdg. 22.60 *(978-1-4488-4957-4(8))* Rosen Publishing Group, Inc., The. (PowerKids Pr.).

De Medeiros, J. Pulleys. 2009. (Science Matters Ser.). (Illus.). 24p. (J). (gr. 3-5). pap. 8.95 *(978-1-60596-042-5(X))* Weigl Pubs., Inc.

De Medeiros, James. Pulleys. (J). 2013. *(978-1-62127-426-1(8))* 2013. pap. *(978-1-62127-432-2(2))* 2009. (Illus.). 24p. (gr. 3-5). lib. bdg. 24.45 *(978-1-60596-041-8(1))* Weigl Pubs., Inc.

De Medeiros, M. Screws. 2009. (Science Matters Ser.). (Illus.). 24p. (J). (gr. 3-5). pap. 10.95 *(978-1-60596-040-1(3))* Weigl Pubs., Inc.

De Medeiros, Michael. Screws. (J). 2013. *(978-1-62127-427-8(6))* 2013. pap. *(978-1-62127-433-9(0))* 2009. (Illus.). 24p. (gr. 3-5). lib. bdg. 24.45 *(978-1-60596-039-5(X))* Weigl Pubs., Inc.

Deane-Pratt, Ade. Simple Machines. 2012. (How Things Work Ser.). (Illus.). 32p. (J). (gr. 3-6). lib. bdg. 26.50 *(978-1-4488-5279-6(X))* Rosen Publishing Group, Inc., The.

Doman, Mary Kate. Earthmovers & Diggers. 2011. (All about Big Machines Ser.). (Illus.). 24p. (J). (gr. -1-18). pap. 7.95 *(978-1-59845-245-7(2),* Enslow Elementary) Enslow Pubs., Inc.

Dorling Kindersley Publishing Staff. Noisy Digger Peekaboo! 2015. (ENG., Illus.). 12p. (J). (gr. -1 — 1). bds. 12.99 *(978-1-4654-3183-7(7),* DK Children) Dorling Kindersley Publishing, Inc.

Dorling Kindersley Publishing Staff, ed. Digger. 2009. (ENG.). 10p. (J). (gr. -1-k). bds. 8.99 *(978-0-7566-5229-6(4),* DK Children) Dorling Kindersley Publishing, Inc.

Dos Santos, Julie. Diggers. 2009. (Amazing Machines Ser.). 32p. (gr. 2). 28.50 *(978-0-7614-4402-2(5))* Marshall Cavendish Corp.

Doudna, Kelly. The Kids' Book of Simple Machines. 2015. (ENG., Illus.). 144p. (J). (gr. k-4). pap. 14.95 *(978-1-938063-59-6(7),* Mighty Media Kids) Mighty Media Pr.

MNO

—The Kids' Book of Simple Machines: Cool Projects & Activities That Make Science Fun! 2015. (Illus.). 144p. (J). (978-1-938063-60-2(0)) Mighty Media Pr.

Eggleton, Jill. The Amazing Machine. Kieley, Rob, illus. (Sails Literacy Ser.). 24p. (gr. 3-18). 27.00 (978-0-7578-6979-2(3));Pack. 57.00 (978-0-7578-6995-2(5)) Rigby Education.

—The Amazing Machine: 6 Small Books. Kieley, Rob, illus. (Sails Literacy Ser.). 24p. (gr. 3-18). 25.00 (978-0-7578-6987-7(4)) Rigby Education.

Eick, Jean. Concrete Mixers. 2014. (Big Machines at Work Ser.). (ENG.). 24p. (J). (gr. -1-2). 25.64 (978-1-62323-964-0(8), 206739) Child's World, Inc., The.

Enz, Tammy. Super Cool Mechanical Activities with Max Axiom. Baez, Marcelo, illus. 2015. (Max Axiom Science & Engineering Activities Ser.). (ENG.). 32p. (gr. 3-4). lib. bdg. 30.65 (978-1-4914-2080-5(4), Graphic Library) Capstone Press of Coughlan Cos.

—Zoom It: Invent New Machines That Move, 1 vol. 2012. (Invent It Ser.). (ENG.). 32p. (gr. 3-4). pap. 8.10 (978-1-4296-7984-8(0)); pap. 47.70 (978-1-4296-8458-3(5)); lib. bdg. 27.32 (978-1-4296-7634-2(5)) Capstone Press of Coughlan Cos. (Fact Finders).

Extreme Machines. 2015. (Extreme Machines Ser.). (ENG.). 32p. (J). (gr. 3-4). pap., pap., pap. 360.00 (978-1-4994-1369-4(6), PowerKids Pr.) Rosen Publishing Group, Inc., The.

Farndon, John. Stickmen's Guide to Gigantic Machines. Paul de Quay, John, illus. 2016. (Stickmen's Guides to How Everything Works). (ENG.). 32p. (J). (gr. 3-6). 30.65 (978-1-4677-9596-8(8)) Lerner Publishing Group.

Feldman, Roseann & Walker, Sally M. Put Inclined Planes to the Test. 2011. (Searchlight Books (tm) — How Do Simple Machines Work? Ser.). (ENG.). (gr. 3-5). pap. 51.01 (978-0-7613-8397-0(2)) Lerner Publishing Group.

—Put Levers to the Test. 2011. (Searchlight Books (tm) — How Do Simple Machines Work? Ser.). (ENG.). (gr. 3-5). pap. 51.01 (978-0-7613-8398-7(0)) Lerner Publishing Group.

—Put Pulleys to the Test. 2011. (Searchlight Books (tm) — How Do Simple Machines Work? Ser.). (ENG.). (gr. 3-5). pap. 51.01 (978-0-7613-8399-4(9)) Lerner Publishing Group.

—Put Screws to the Test. 2011. (Searchlight Books (tm) — How Do Simple Machines Work? Ser.). (ENG.). (gr. 3-5). pap. 51.01 (978-0-7613-8400-7(6)) Lerner Publishing Group.

—Put Wedges to the Test. 2011. (Searchlight Books (tm) — How Do Simple Machines Work? Ser.). (ENG.). (gr. 3-5). pap. 51.01 (978-0-7613-8401-4(4)) Lerner Publishing Group.

Feldman, Roseann, et al. Put Inclined Planes to the Test. 2011. (Searchlight Books (tm) — How Do Simple Machines Work? Ser.). (ENG.). 40p. (gr. 3-5). pap. 8.95 (978-0-7613-7865-5(0)) Lerner Publishing Group.

—Put Levers to the Test. 2011. (Searchlight Books (tm) — How Do Simple Machines Work? Ser.). (ENG.). 40p. (gr. 3-5). pap. 8.95 (978-0-7613-7866-2(9)) Lerner Publishing Group.

—Put Pulleys to the Test. 2011. (Searchlight Books (tm) — How Do Simple Machines Work? Ser.). (ENG.). 40p. (gr. 3-5). pap. 8.95 (978-0-7613-7867-9(7)) Lerner Publishing Group.

—Put Screws to the Test. 2011. (Searchlight Books (tm) — How Do Simple Machines Work? Ser.). (ENG.). 40p. (gr. 3-5). pap. 8.95 (978-0-7613-7868-6(5)) Lerner Publishing Group.

—Put Wedges to the Test. 2011. (Searchlight Books (tm) — How Do Simple Machines Work? Ser.). (ENG.). 40p. (gr. 3-5). pap. 8.95 (978-0-7613-7869-3(3)) Lerner Publishing Group.

Freed, Kira. Tools We Use. 2017. (Text Connections Guided Close Reading Ser.). (J). (gr. 2). (978-1-4900-1831-7(X)) Benchmark Education Co.

French, Cathy. From Axes to Zippers: Simple Machines & Del hacha al Cierre: 6 English, 6 Spanish Adaptations: Las máquinas Simples. 2011. (ENG & SPA.). (J). 89.00 net. (978-1-4108-5672-2(0)) Benchmark Education Co.

French, Kathy. From Axes to Zippers Simple Machines: Set Of 6. 2010. (Navigators Ser.). (J). pap. 44.00 net. (978-1-4108-0413-6(5)) Benchmark Education Co.

Frisch, Aaron. Diggers. 2013. 24p. 22.85 (978-1-60818-340-1(8)) Creative Co., The.

—Seedlings: Diggers. 2014. (Seedlings Ser.). (ENG.). 24p. (J). (gr. -1-k). pap. 7.99 (978-0-89812-885-7(4), Creative Paperbacks) Creative Co., The.

Gardner, Robert. Sensational Science Projects with Simple Machines. LaBaff, Tom, illus. 2006. (Fantastic Physical Science Experiments Ser.). 48p. (J). (gr. 3-4). lib. bdg. 25.27 (978-0-7660-2585-1(3), Enslow Elementary) Enslow Pubs., Inc.

—Simple Machine Experiments Using Seesaws, Wheels, Pulleys, & More: One Hour or Less Science Experiments. 2012. (Last-Minute Science Projects Ser.). 48p. (J). (gr. 5-18). 25.27 (978-0-7660-3957-5(9)) Enslow Pubs., Inc.

Gifford, Clive. Machines. 2017. (Record Busters Ser.). (ENG., Illus.). 32p. (J). (gr. 4-6). pap. 11.99 (978-0-7502-9979-4(7), Wayland) Hachette Children's Group GBR. Dist: Hachette Bk. Group.

Gilbert, Sara. Concrete Mixers. 2009. (Machines That Build Ser.). (J). (gr. 1-5). 24.25 (978-1-58341-726-3(5), Creative Education) Creative Co., The.

—Concrete Mixers: Machines That Build. 2011. (Machines That Build Ser.). (ENG.). 24p. (J). (gr. 1-17). pap. 7.99 (978-1-897563-71-7(X), Creative Paperbacks) Creative Co., The.

—Diggers. 2009. (Machines That Build Ser.). (J). (gr. 1-5). 24.25 (978-1-58341-728-7(1), Creative Education) Creative Co., The.

—Drilling Machines. (Machines That Build Ser.). (J). (gr. 1-17). 2011. (ENG.). 24p. pap. 7.99 (978-1-897563-74-8(4), Creative Paperbacks) 2009. 24.25 (978-1-58341-729-4(X), Creative Education) Creative Co., The.

—Dump Trucks. 2009. (Machines That Build Ser.). (J). (gr. 1-5). 24.25 (978-1-58341-730-0(3), Creative Education) Creative Co., The.

Gilpin, Daniel & Pang, Alex. Machines Close-Up, 6 vols., Set. Incl. Military Fighting Machines. 28.50 (978-1-60870-109-4(3)); Modern Military Aircraft. 28.50 (978-1-60870-108-7(5)); Modern Warships & Submarines. 28.50 (978-1-60870-110-0(7)); Record Breakers. 28.50 (978-1-60870-113-1(1)); Rescue Vehicles. 28.50 (978-1-60870-111-7(5)); Spacecraft. 28.50 (978-1-60870-112-4(3)); 32p. (J). (gr. 4-7). (Machines Close-up Ser.). 2010. Set lib. bdg. 171.00 o.p. (978-1-60870-107-0(7)) Marshall Cavendish Corp.

Glover, David & Barnes, Jon. Machines. (Make It Work! Ser.). (Illus.). 48p. (J). pap. 7.95 (978-0-590-24401-5(9)) Scholastic, Inc.

Glover, David & Glover, Penny. Digging Machines in Action. 2008. (On the Go Ser.). (Illus.). 24p. (J). (gr. 3-7). lib. bdg. 22.60 (978-1-4042-4307-1(0), PowerKids Pr.) Rosen Publishing Group, Inc., The.

Golden Books Staff. A Need for Speed! (Blaze & the Monster Machines) Golden Books Staff, illus. 2016. (Color Plus 1,000 Stickers Ser.). (ENG., Illus.). 64p. (J). (gr. -1-2). pap. 9.99 (978-0-553-53890-8(X), Golden Bks.) Random Hse. Children's Bks.

Good, Keith. Gear Up! Marvelous Machine Projects. 2008. (Design It! Ser.). pap. 6.95 (978-0-8225-9925-8(2)) Lerner Publishing Group.

Gordon, Nick. Monster Diggers. 2013. (Monster Machines Ser.). (ENG., Illus.). 24p. (J). (gr. k-3). lib. bdg. 25.95 (978-1-60014-937-5(5), Blastoff! Readers) Bellwether Media.

Gosman, Gillian. Inclined Planes in Action. 2010. (Simple Machines at Work Ser.). (ENG.). 24p. (J). pap. 8.25 (978-1-4488-1303-2(4)); lib. bdg. 22.60 (978-1-4488-0685-0(2)) Rosen Publishing Group, Inc., The. (PowerKids Pr.).

—Levers in Action. 2010. (Simple Machines at Work Ser.). (ENG.). 24p. (J). pap. 8.25 (978-1-4488-1297-4(6)); lib. bdg. 22.60 (978-1-4488-0682-9(8)) Rosen Publishing Group, Inc., The. (PowerKids Pr.).

—Pulleys in Action. 2010. (Simple Machines at Work Ser.). (ENG.). 24p. (J). pap. 8.25 (978-1-4488-1294-3(1)); lib. bdg. 22.60 (978-1-4488-0681-2(X)) Rosen Publishing Group, Inc., The. (PowerKids Pr.).

—Screws in Action. 2010. (Simple Machines at Work Ser.). (ENG.). 24p. (J). pap. 8.25 (978-1-4488-1305-6(0)); lib. bdg. 22.60 (978-1-4488-0686-7(0)) Rosen Publishing Group, Inc., The. (PowerKids Pr.).

—Simple Machines & Holidays. 2014. (Simple Machines Everywhere Ser.). 24p. (J). (gr. k-3). pap. 49.50 (978-1-4777-6643-9(X), PowerKids Pr.) Rosen Publishing Group, Inc., The.

—Simple Machines in Sports. 2014. (Simple Machines Everywhere Ser.). (Illus.). 24p. (J). (gr. k-3). 23.60 (978-1-4777-6829-7(7), PowerKids Pr.) Rosen Publishing Group, Inc., The.

—Simple Machines in the Great Outdoors. 2014. (Simple Machines Everywhere Ser.). (Illus.). 24p. (J). (gr. k-3). pap. 8.25 (978-1-4777-6838-9(6), PowerKids Pr.) Rosen Publishing Group, Inc., The.

—Simple Machines in the Military. 2014. (Simple Machines Everywhere Ser.). (Illus.). 24p. (J). (gr. k-3). pap. 8.25 (978-1-4777-6834-1(3), PowerKids Pr.) Rosen Publishing Group, Inc., The.

—Simple Machines in Your Home. 2014. (Simple Machines Everywhere Ser.). 24p. (J). (gr. k-3). pap. 49.50 (978-1-4777-6644-6(8), PowerKids Pr.) Rosen Publishing Group, Inc., The.

—Wedges in Action. 2010. (Simple Machines at Work Ser.). (ENG.). 24p. (J). pap. 8.25 (978-1-4488-1299-8(2)); lib. bdg. 22.60 (978-1-4488-0683-6(6)) Rosen Publishing Group, Inc., The. (PowerKids Pr.).

Graham, Ian. Building Machines: An Interactive Guide to Construction Machines. Ballestros, Carles, illus. 2016. (ENG.). 24p. (J). (gr. k-2). 17.95 (978-1-4197-2109-0(7), Abrams Bks. for Young Readers) Abrams, Inc.

—Emergency Vehicles. 2009. (How Machines Work Ser.). (Illus.). 32p. (J). pap. (978-1-897563-42-7(6)) Saunders Bk. Co.

—Machines & Inventions. Antram, David et al, illus. 2008. (World of Wonder Ser.). (ENG.). 32p. (J). (gr. 1-4). 29.00 (978-0-531-24027-4(4)); pap. 9.95 (978-0-531-23823-3(7)) Scholastic Library Publishing. (Children's Pr.).

—Mighty Machines. (Ripley Twists Ser.). (Illus.). 48p. (J). (gr. 3-18). 2010. lib. bdg. 19.95 (978-1-4222-1831-0(7), 1318260) 2009. pap. 8.95 (978-1-4222-2069-6(9), 1318260) Mason Crest.

—On the Water. 2006. (QEB Machines at Work Ser.). (Illus.). 36p. (J). lib. bdg. 16.95 (978-1-59566-190-6(5)) QEB Publishing Inc.

Graubart, Norman D. Cement Mixers, 1 vol. 2015. (ENG.). 24p. (J). lib. bdg. 23.60 (978-1-4994-0053-3(5), PowerKids Pr.) Rosen Publishing Group, Inc., The.

Greathead, Helen. Megamachines. 2016. (What Would You Choose? Ser.). 00032p. (J). pap. 10.50 (**978-1-4824-6079-7(3)**) Stevens, Gareth Publishing LLLP.

Gregory, Helen. How Things Move, 1 vol. (Wonder Readers Next Steps: Science Ser.). (ENG.). (gr. -1-1). 2013. 20p. 22.65 (978-1-4765-2372-9(X)) 2011. 32p. pap. 5.99 (978-1-4296-7814-8(3)) 2011. 16p. pap. 35.94 (978-1-4296-8096-7(2)) Capstone Press of Coughlan Cos. (Wonder Readers).

Gulkin, Sidney & Notkin, Jerome J. The How & Why Wonder Book of MacHines. Zaffo, George J., illus. 2011. 48p. pap. 35.95 (978-1-258-10533-4(0)) Literary Licensing, LLC.

Gunn, Richard. Monster Movers. 2006. (Cool Wheels Ser.). (Illus.). 32p. (gr. 2-6). lib. bdg. 26.00 (978-0-8368-6827-2(7), Gareth Stevens Learning Library) Stevens, Gareth Publishing LLLP.

Hankin, Rosie. Cut & Paste Trucks, Trains, & Big Machines. 2007. (Cut, Paste, & Create Ser.). (Illus.). 32p. (gr. k-3). lib. bdg. 26.00 (978-0-8368-7721-2(7), Gareth Stevens Learning Library) Stevens, Gareth Publishing LLLP.

Hansen, Grace. Machines to Thrill You!, 1 vol. 2014. (Seeing Is Believing Ser.). (ENG., Illus.). 24p. (J). (gr. 2-4). lib. bdg. 28.50 (978-1-62970-732-7(5)) ABDO Publishing Co.

Hanson, Anders. Drills, 1 vol. 2010. (Tools of the Trade Ser.). (ENG., Illus.). 24p. (J). (gr. k-3). lib. bdg. 24.21 (978-1-60453-581-5(4), SandCastle) ABDO Publishing Co.

Harris, Patricia. Understanding Coding with Lego Wedo(tm), 01 vols., 1. 2016. (Kids Can Code Ser.). (ENG., Illus.). 24p. (J). pap. 11.75 (978-1-5081-4466-3(4), PowerKids Pr.) Rosen Publishing Group, Inc., The.

Hawcock, David. Leonardo Da Vinci's Remarkable Machines. 2016. (ENG., Illus.). 14p. (J). (gr. 1). 24.95 (978-1-62686-517-4(5), Silver Dolphin Bks.) Readerlink Distribution Services, LLC.

Hayes, Amy. Big Diggers. 2015. (Machines That Work Ser.). (ENG., Illus.). 24p. (J). (gr. 1-1). pap. 8.22 (978-1-5026-0391-3(8)) Cavendish Square Publishing.

—Big Loaders. 2015. (Machines That Work Ser.). (ENG., Illus.). 24p. (J). (gr. 1-1). pap. 8.22 (978-1-5026-0397-5(7)) Cavendish Square Publishing.

Heitkamp, Kristina Lyn. Fab Lab Creating with Digital Sewing Machines. 2016. (Getting Creative with Fab Lab Ser.). 00064p. (J). (gr. 6-6). 34.45 (978-1-4994-6508-2(4)) Rosen Publishing Group, Inc., The.

Hill, Lee Sullivan. Earthmovers on the Move. 2010. (Lightning Bolt Books Vroom-Vroom Ser.). (ENG.). 32p. (gr. k-2). pap. 7.95 (978-0-7613-6116-9(2)) Lerner Publishing Group.

Hill, Lee Sullivan. Earthmovers on the Move. 2010. (Lightning Bolt Books Vroom-Vroom Ser.). (ENG., Illus.). 32p. (gr. k-2). lib. bdg. 26.60 (978-0-7613-3918-2(3)) Lerner Publishing Group.

—Palas Mecánicas. Translations.com Staff, tr. from ENG. 2006. (Libros para Avanzar-Potencia en Movimiento (Pull Ahead Books-Mighty Movers) Ser.). (ENG & SPA., Illus.). 32p. (gr. k-3). lib. bdg. 22.60 (978-0-8225-6230-6(8), Ediciones Lerner) Lerner Publishing Group.

Holzweiss, Kristina. Amazing Makerspace DIY Basic Machines. 2017. (True Book — MakerSpace Projects Ser.). (ENG.). 48p. (J). lib. bdg. 31.00 (**978-0-531-23844-8(X)**) Scholastic Library Publishing.

How Machines Help, 6 vols. (Sunshinetm Science Ser.). 24p. (gr. 1-2). 31.50 (978-0-7802-0301-3(1)); 36.95 (978-0-7802-0552-9(9)) Wright Group/McGraw-Hill.

Howse, Jennifer. Inclined Planes. (J). 2013. (978-1-62127-424-7(1)) 2013. pap. (978-1-62127-430-8(6)) 2009. (Illus.). 24p. (gr. 3-5). pap. 8.95 (978-1-60596-036-4(5)) 2009. (Illus.). 24p. (gr. 3-5). lib. bdg. 24.45 (978-1-60596-035-7(7)) Weigl Pubs., Inc.

—Levers. (J). 2013. 27.13 (978-1-62127-425-4(X)) 2013. pap. 12.95 (978-1-62127-431-5(4)) 2009. (Illus.). 24p. (gr. 3-5). pap. 8.95 (978-1-60596-032-6(2)) 2009. (Illus.). 24p. (gr. 3-5). lib. bdg. 24.45 (978-1-60596-031-9(4)) Weigl Pubs., Inc.

—Wedges. 2009. (Science Matters Ser.). (Illus.). 24p. (J). (gr. 3-5). lib. bdg. 24.45 (978-1-60596-037-1(3)) Weigl Pubs., Inc.

Huff, Regan A. Eli Whitney: The Cotton Gin & American Manufacturing. 2009. (Library of American Lives & Times Ser.). 112p. (gr. 5-5). 69.20 (978-1-60853-478-4(2)) Rosen Publishing Group, Inc., The.

Inside Machines. 2017. (Inside Machines Ser.). 24p. (gr. 8-8). 147.60 (**978-1-4994-8376-5(7)**); pap. 49.50 (**978-1-4994-8384-0(8)**) Rosen Publishing Group, Inc., The. (Windmill Bks.).

Jackson, Tom. Power & Energy. 2012. (FAYFT: Invention & Technology Ser.). 64p. (gr. 4-10). lib. bdg. 39.95 (978-1-936333-39-4(2)) Brown Bear Bks.

Jefferis, David. Extreme Structures: Mega-Constructions of the 21st Century. 2006. (Science Frontiers Ser.). (ENG., Illus.). 32p. (J). (gr. 3-7). pap. (978-0-7787-2872-6(2)) Crabtree Publishing Co.

—Micro Machines: Ultra-Small World of Nanotechnology. 2006. (Science Frontiers Ser.). (ENG., Illus.). 32p. (J). (gr. 4-7). pap. (978-0-7787-2873-3(0)) Crabtree Publishing Co.

Johnson, Rebecca L. Machines - Simple & Compound. 2007. (Language, Literacy, & Vocabulary - Reading Expeditions Ser.). (ENG., Illus.). 36p. (J). pap. 18.95 (978-0-7922-5439-3(2)) CENGAGE Learning.

Jones, Melanie Davis. Big Machines. Gay-Kassel, Doreen, illus. 2003. (Rookie Reader Español Ser.). (ENG.). (J). (gr. k-2). pap. 4.95 (978-0-516-27829-2(0), Children's Pr.) Scholastic Library Publishing.

Kalman, Bobbie & MacAulay, Kelley. Fantásticos Vehículos para la Construccion. 2007. (Vehículos en Acción Ser.). (SPA & ENG., Illus.). 32p. (J). lib. bdg. (978-0-7787-8304-6(9)) Crabtree Publishing Co.

Kawa, Katie. Loaders. 2011. (Big Machines Ser.). (Illus.). 24p. (J). (gr. k-2). pap. 8.15 (978-1-4339-5568-6(7)); lib. bdg. 22.60 (978-1-4339-5566-2(0)) Stevens, Gareth Publishing LLLP.

—Loaders: Palas Cargadoras. 2011. (Big Machines / Grandes MáQuinas Ser.). (SPA & ENG., Illus.). 24p. (J). (gr. k-3). lib. bdg. 22.60 (978-1-4339-5582-2(2)) Stevens, Gareth Publishing LLLP.

Kramer, Jon. Learning about Simple Machines with Graphic Organizers. 2009. (Graphic Organizers in Science Ser.). (ENG.). 24p. (J). (gr. 3-6). pap. 8.25 (978-1-4358-3277-0(9), PowerKids Pr.) Rosen Publishing Group, Inc., The.

Kulling, Monica. All Aboard! Elijah McCoy's Steam Engine. Slavin, Bill, illus. 2013. (ENG.). 32p. (C). (gr. k-3). pap. 12.95 (978-1-77049-514-2(2)) National Geographic School Publishing, Inc.

Lacey, Minna. Big Book of Big Machines. 2010. (Big Book of Big Machines Ser.). 14p. (J). 13.99 (978-0-7945-2764-8(7), Usborne) EDC Publishing.

LaMachia, Dawn. Inclined Planes at Work. 2015. (Zoom in on Simple Machines Ser.). (ENG.). 24p. (J). (gr. 2-2). pap. 9.35 (978-0-7660-6726-4(2)); (Illus.). 22.60 (978-0-7660-6728-8(9)) Enslow Pubs., Inc.

—Levers at Work. 2015. (Zoom in on Simple Machines Ser.). (ENG.). 24p. (J). (gr. 2-2). 22.60 (978-0-7660-6732-5(7)); pap. 9.35 (978-0-7660-6730-1(0)) Enslow Pubs., Inc.

—Pulleys at Work. 2015. (Zoom in on Simple Machines Ser.). (ENG.). 24p. (J). (gr. 2-2). pap. 9.35 (978-0-7660-6734-9(3)) Enslow Pubs., Inc.

—Screws at Work. 2015. (Zoom in on Simple Machines Ser.). (ENG.). 24p. (J). (gr. 2-2). 22.60 (978-0-7660-6740-0(8)); pap. 9.35 (978-0-7660-6738-7(6)) Enslow Pubs., Inc.

—Wedges at Work. 2015. (Zoom in on Simple Machines Ser.). (ENG.). 24p. (J). (gr. 2-2). 22.60 (978-0-7660-6744-8(0)); pap. 9.35 (978-0-7660-6742-4(4)) Enslow Pubs., Inc.

—Wheels & Axles. 2015. (Zoom in on Simple Machines Ser.). (ENG.). 24p. (J). (gr. 2-2). 22.60 (978-0-7660-6748-6(3)) Enslow Pubs., Inc.

—Wheels & Axles at Work. 2015. (Zoom in on Simple Machines Ser.). (ENG.). 24p. (J). (gr. 2-2). pap. 9.35 (978-0-7660-6746-2(7)) Enslow Pubs., Inc.

Lancaster, Juliana. PBIS- Building Big Things. 2005. pap., stu. ed. 8.00 (978-1-58591-565-1(3)) It's About Time, Herff Jones Education Div.

Langley, Andrew. Diggers. 2010. (Machines on the Move Ser.). 32p. (J). 28.50 (978-1-60753-058-9(9)) Amicus Publishing.

—Diggers. 2012. (Illus.). 32p. (gr. 1-3). pap. 8.95 (978-1-926722-68-9(X)) Saunders Bk. Co. CAN. Dist: RiverStream Publishing.

Latou, Pierre. Where Do Big Machines Work? 2014. (Little Books of Answers: Level B Ser.). (Illus.). 16p. (gr. k-2). pap. 7.95 (978-1-927136-12-6(1)) Three Crows Media NZL. Dist: RiverStream Publishing.

Law, Felicia. Simple Machines. 2015. (Stone Age Science Ser.). (ENG., Illus.). 32p. (J). lib. bdg. (978-0-7787-1890-1(5)) Crabtree Publishing Co.

Lawrence, Debbie & Lawrence, Richard. Machines & Motion: God's Design for the Physical World. 2005. (Illus.). 160p. per. (978-0-9725365-9-2(0)) Boarding House Publishing.

Lennie, Charles. Concrete Mixers, 1 vol. 2014. (Construction Machines Ser.). (ENG.). 24p. (J). (gr. 4-8). lib. bdg. 28.50 (978-1-62970-016-8(9)) ABDO Publishing Co.

—Excavators, 1 vol. 2014. (Construction Machines Ser.). (ENG.). 24p. (J). (gr. 4-8). lib. bdg. 28.50 (978-1-62970-019-9(3)) ABDO Publishing Co.

—Loaders, 1 vol. 2014. (Construction Machines Ser.). (ENG.). 24p. (J). (gr. 4-8). lib. bdg. 28.50 (978-1-62970-020-5(7)) ABDO Publishing Co.

Liddell, Mary. Little Machinery: A Critical Facsimile Edition. 2009. (Landscapes of Childhood Ser.). (ENG., Illus.). 120p. (J). pap. 34.99 (978-0-8143-3266-5(8), 2013) Wayne State Univ. Pr.

Lindeen, Mary. Graders. 2007. (Mighty Machines Ser.). (ENG., Illus.). 24p. (J). (gr. k-3). lib. bdg. 25.95 (978-1-60014-118-8(8)) Bellwether Media.

Litchfield, Jo & Brooks, Felicity. Diggers. 2004. (Chunky Board Bks.). (ENG., Illus.). 6p. (J). bds. 4.95 (978-0-7945-0350-5(0), Usborne) EDC Publishing.

Lock, Deborah. Mega Machines. 2014. (DK Readers Ser.). (ENG., Illus.). 32p. (J). (gr. k-4). 14.99 (978-1-4654-2000-8(2), DK Children) Dorling Kindersley Publishing, Inc.

Low, William & Cobalt Illustrations Studio Staff. Machines Go to Work. Low, William & Cobalt Illustrations Studio Staff, illus. 2009. (ENG., Illus.). 42p. (J). (gr. -1-1). 17.99 (978-0-8050-8759-8(1), 9780805087598, Holt, Henry & Co. Bks. For Young Readers) Holt, Henry & Co.

Lowery, Lawrence F. Michael's Racing Machine. Loehle, Richard, illus. 2014. (I Wonder Why Ser.). (ENG.). 36p. (J). (gr. k-3). pap. 11.95 (978-1-941316-05-4(0)) National Science Teachers Assn.

MacAulay, Kelley & Kalman, Bobbie. Cool Construction Vehicles. 2007. (Vehicles on the Move Ser.). (ENG., Illus.). 32p. (J). (gr. 3-7). lib. bdg. (978-0-7787-3042-2(5)); (gr. 1-5). pap. (978-0-7787-3056-9(5)) Crabtree Publishing Co.

—Fantasticos Vehiculos para la Construccion. 2007. (Vehículos en Acción Ser.). (SPA & ENG., Illus.). 32p. (J). (gr. 6-10). pap. (978-0-7787-8314-5(6)) Crabtree Publishing Co.

Machines. (Make it Work Ser.). 42p. (J). (gr. 4-8). pap. (978-1-882210-48-0(4)) Action Publishing, Inc.

Machines: Big Book: Level E. 8p. 20.95 (978-0-322-00344-6(X)) Wright Group/McGraw-Hill.

Machines at Sea. 2017. (Machines at Sea Ser.). 32p. (gr. 9-10). 131.25 (**978-1-4994-3401-9(4)**); pap. 50.00 (**978-1-5081-5429-7(5)**) Rosen Publishing Group, Inc., The. (PowerKids Pr.).

Machines in Motion. 2013. (Machines in Motion Ser.). 48p. (J). (gr. 3-5). 191.70 (978-1-4339-9685-6(5)); pap. 84.30 (978-1-4339-9817-1(3)); pap. 505.80 (978-1-4339-9818-8(1)) Stevens, Gareth Publishing LLLP.

Machines in the Home: Individual Title Six-Packs. (gr. k-1). 23.00 (978-0-7635-9075-8(4)) Rigby Education.

Machines That Work. 2015. (Machines That Work Ser.). (ENG.). 24p. (J). (gr. 1-1). 145.26 (978-1-5026-0350-0(0)); pap., pap., pap. 49.32 (978-1-5026-0693-8(3)) Cavendish Square Publishing.

Macken, JoAnn Early. Simple Machines. 2010. (Everyday Science Ser.). 24p. (J). (gr. k-3). 25.65 (978-1-60753-016-9(3)) Amicus Publishing.

Make Believe Ideas. My Best Ever: Things That Go. 2013. (ENG.). 16p. (J). bds. 12.99 (978-1-78235-609-7(6)) Make Believe Ideas GBR. Dist: Nelson, Thomas Inc.

—My Very First on the Move, 3 vols. 2011. 26p. bds. 12.99 (978-1-78065-103-3(1)) Make Believe Ideas GBR. Dist: Nelson, Thomas Inc.

Manolis, Kay. Levers. 2009. (Simple Machines Ser.). (ENG., Illus.). 24p. (J). (gr. 2-5). lib. bdg. 25.95 (978-1-60014-325-0(3), Blastoff! Readers) Bellwether Media.

—Pulleys. 2009. (Simple Machines Ser.). (ENG., Illus.). 24p. (J). (gr. 2-5). lib. bdg. 25.95 (978-1-60014-324-3(5), Blastoff! Readers) Bellwether Media.

—Skid Steer Loaders. 2008. (Mighty Machines Ser.). (ENG., Illus.). 24p. (J). (gr. k-3). lib. bdg. 25.95 (978-1-60014-181-2(1)) Bellwether Media.

Marsico, Katie. Inclined Planes. Butler, Reginald, illus. 2012. (Simple Machines Ser.). (ENG.). 24p. (J). (gr. -1-2). 27.07 (978-1-61473-273-0(6), 204978) Child's World, Inc., The.

—Levers. Butler, Reginald, illus. 2012. (Simple Machines Ser.). (ENG.). 24p. (J). (gr. -1-2). 27.07 (978-1-61473-274-7(4), 204979) Child's World, Inc., The.

—Pulleys. Butler, Reginald, illus. 2012. (Simple Machines Ser.). (ENG.). 24p. (J). (gr. -1-2). 27.07 (978-1-61473-275-4(2), 204980) Child's World, Inc., The.

—Wedges. Butler, Reginald, illus. 2012. (Simple Machines Ser.). (ENG.). 24p. (J). (gr. -1-2). 27.07 (978-1-61473-277-8(9), 204982) Child's World, Inc., The.

Martin, M. T. Earth Movers. 2006. (Mighty Machines Ser.). (ENG., Illus.). 24p. (J). (gr. k-3). lib. bdg. 25.95 (978-1-60014-047-1(5)) Bellwether Media.

Mason, Conrad. See Inside How Things Work. 2010. (See Inside Board Bks). 16p. (J). bds. 12.99 (978-0-7945-2406-7(0), Usborne) EDC Publishing.

Masters, Nancy Robinson. Heavy Equipment Operator. 2010. (21st Century Skills Library: Cool Careers Ser.). (ENG.). 32p. (gr. 4-8). lib. bdg. 28.50 (978-1-60279-941-7(5), 200627) Cherry Lake Publishing.

McBride, Carol. Making Magnificent Machines: Fun with Math, Science, & Engineering. 2008. (ENG.). 128p. (gr. k-8). pap. 19.95 *(978-1-59363-337-0(8))* Prufrock Pr.

McBride, Carol & Gonzales, Francisco L. Engineer This! 15 Amazing Projects for Young Mechanical Engineers. 2017. (Other Ser.). (ENG.). 150p. (J). (gr. 4-7). pap. 14.95 ***(978-1-61821-629-8(5))*** Prufrock Pr.

McClellan, Ray. Backhoes. 2006. (Mighty Machines Ser.). (ENG., Illus.). 24p. (J). (gr. k-3). lib. bdg. 25.95 *(978-1-60014-042-6(4))* Bellwether Media.

—Concrete Mixers. 2006. (Mighty Machines Ser.). (ENG., Illus.). 24p. (J). (gr. k-3). lib. bdg. 25.95 *(978-1-60014-044-0(0))* Bellwether Media.

Mega Machines. 2004. (Illus.). 64p. (J). pap. *(978-2-7643-0202-6(9))* Phidal Publishing, Inc./Editions Phidal, Inc.

Mezzanotte, Jim. Cargadores. 2005. (Vehiculos Gigantes (Giant Vehicles) Ser.). (SPA.). 24p. (gr. 1-4). lib. bdg. 23.00 *(978-0-8368-5987-4(1)*, Gareth Stevens Learning Library) Stevens, Gareth Publishing LLLP.

—Como Funcionan las Rampas, las Cunas y los Tornillos. 2006. (Como funcionan las maquinas simples (How Simple Machines Work) Ser.). (SPA., Illus.). 24p. (gr. 1-4). lib. bdg. 22.00 *(978-0-8368-7445-7(5)*, Weekly Reader Leveled Readers) Stevens, Gareth Publishing LLLP.

—Cómo Funcionan las Rampas, las Cuñas y los Tornillos. 2006. (Como funcionan las maquinas simples (How Simple Machines Work) Ser.). (SPA., Illus.). 24p. (gr. 1-4). pap. 8.15 *(978-0-8368-7450-1(1)*, Weekly Reader Leveled Readers) Stevens, Gareth Publishing LLLP.

—Cómo Funcionan Las Ruedas y Los Ejes. 2006. (Como funcionan las maquinas simples (How Simple Machines Work) Ser.). (SPA., Illus.). 24p. (gr. 1-4). pap. 8.15 *(978-0-8368-7451-8(X)*, Weekly Reader Leveled Readers) Stevens, Gareth Publishing LLLP.

—Cómo Funcionan las Ruedas y los Ejes. 2006. (Como funcionan las maquinas simples (How Simple Machines Work) Ser.). (SPA., Illus.). 24p. (gr. 1-4). lib. bdg. 22.00 *(978-0-8368-7446-4(3)*, Weekly Reader Leveled Readers) Stevens, Gareth Publishing LLLP.

—Excavadoras. Acosta, Tatiana & Gutierrez, Guillermo, trs. 2005. (Vehiculos Gigantes (Giant Vehicles) Ser.). (SPA., Illus.). 24p. (gr. 1-4). lib. bdg. 23.00 *(978-0-8368-5988-1(X)*, Gareth Stevens Learning Library) Stevens, Gareth Publishing LLLP.

—Giant Diggers. 2005. (Giant Vehicles Ser.). (Illus.). 24p. (gr. 1-4). pap. 8.15 *(978-0-8368-4918-9(3))*; lib. bdg. 23.00 *(978-0-8368-4911-0(6))* Stevens, Gareth Publishing LLLP. (Gareth Stevens Learning Library).

—Giant Loaders. 2005. (Giant Vehicles Ser.). (Illus.). 24p. (gr. 1-4). pap. 8.15 *(978-0-8368-4920-2(5))*; lib. bdg. 23.00 *(978-0-8368-4913-4(2))* Stevens, Gareth Publishing LLLP. (Gareth Stevens Learning Library).

—Giant Scrapers. 2005. (Giant Vehicles Ser.). (Illus.). 24p. (gr. 1-4). pap. 8.15 *(978-0-8368-4921-9(3))*; lib. bdg. 23.00 *(978-0-8368-4914-1(0))* Stevens, Gareth Publishing LLLP. (Gareth Stevens Learning Library).

—How Levers Work. 2006. (How Simple Machines Work Ser.). (Illus.). 24p. (gr. 1-4). pap. 8.15 *(978-0-8368-7352-8(1))*; lib. bdg. 22.00 *(978-0-8368-7347-4(5))* Stevens, Gareth Publishing LLLP. (Weekly Reader Leveled Readers).

—How Pulleys Work. 2006. (How Simple Machines Work Ser.). (Illus.). 24p. (gr. 1-4). lib. bdg. 22.00 *(978-0-8368-7348-1(3)*, Weekly Reader Leveled Readers) Stevens, Gareth Publishing LLLP.

—How Ramps, Wedges, & Screws Work. 2006. (How Simple Machines Work Ser.). (Illus.). 24p. (gr. 1-4). pap. 8.15 *(978-0-8368-7354-2(8))*; lib. bdg. 22.00 *(978-0-8368-7349-8(1))* Stevens, Gareth Publishing LLLP. (Weekly Reader Leveled Readers).

—Raspadores. 2005. (Vehiculos Gigantes (Giant Vehicles) Ser.). (SPA.). 24p. (gr. 1-4). lib. bdg. 23.00 *(978-0-8368-5990-4(1)*, Gareth Stevens Learning Library) Stevens, Gareth Publishing LLLP.

Michele, Tracey. Big Machines. 2011. (Learn-Abouts Ser.). (Illus.). 16p. (J). pap. 7.95 *(978-1-59920-610-3(2))* Black Rabbit Bks.

Mighty Machines. (Children's Reference Ser.). 224p. 18.35 *(978-1-4054-9925-5(7))* Parragon, Inc.

Mighty Machines (6 book Set) [NASCO]. 2012. (Mighty Machines Ser.). (ENG.). 24p. pap. 41.70 *(978-1-62065-473-6(3)*, Pebble Plus) Capstone Press of Coughlan Cos.

Miller, Jerry. Screws. 2013. (Simple Machine Science Ser.). (Illus.). 24p. (J). (gr. 1-3). pap. 8.15 *(978-1-4339-8147-0(5))*; lib. bdg. 22.60 *(978-1-4339-8146-3(7))* Stevens, Gareth Publishing LLLP.

Miller, Madison. Pulleys. 2013. (Simple Machine Science Ser.). (Illus.). 24p. (gr. 1-3). 22.60 *(978-1-4339-8141-8(6))*; pap. 8.15 *(978-1-4339-8142-5(4))* Stevens, Gareth Publishing LLLP.

Miller, Malinda. Modern Mechanics: Maintaining Tomorrow's Green Vehicles. 2010. (New Careers for the 21st Century Ser.). (Illus.). 64p. (YA). (gr. 7-18). lib. bdg. 22.95 *(978-1-4222-1818-1(X))* Mason Crest.

Miller, Tim. Levers in My Makerspace. 2017. (Simple Machines in My Makerspace Ser.). (ENG., Illus.). 32p. (J). pap. ***(978-0-7787-3377-5(7))*** Crabtree Publishing Co.

Mitton, Tony. My Amazing Machines Cool Cars Activity Book. Parker, Ant, illus. 2017. (Amazing Machines Ser.). (ENG.). 24p. pap. 5.99 *(978-0-7534-7296-5(1)*, 9780753472965, Kingfisher) Roaring Brook Pr.

—My Amazing Machines Roaring Rockets. Parker, Ant, illus. 2016. (Amazing Machines Ser.). (ENG.). 24p. pap., act. bk. ed. 4.99 *(978-0-7534-7257-6(0)*, 9780753472576, Kingfisher) Roaring Brook Pr.

—My Amazing Machines Terrific Trains Activity Book. Parker, Ant, illus. 2017. (Amazing Machines Ser.). (ENG.). 24p. (J). pap. 5.99 *(978-0-7534-7295-8(3)*, 9780753472958, Kingfisher) Roaring Brook Pr.

—Tough Trucks. Parker, Ant, illus. 2016. (Amazing Machines Ser.). (ENG.). 24p. pap., act. bk. ed. 4.99 *(978-0-7534-7254-5(6)*, 9780753472545, Kingfisher) Roaring Brook Pr.

Monroe, Tilda. What Do You Know about Simple Machines? 2010. (20 Questions: Physical Science Ser.). (ENG.). 24p. (J). pap. 8.25 *(978-1-4488-1257-8(7)*, PowerKids Pr.); (gr. 2-5). lib. bdg. 22.60 *(978-1-4488-0674-4(7))* Rosen Publishing Group, Inc., The.

El Mundo de las Maquinas. (Coleccion Lo Sabias?). (SPA., Illus.). 44p. (J). 12.95 *(978-950-11-0939-9(9)*, SGM9399) Sigmar ARG. Dist: Continental Bk. Co., Inc.

Murphy, Patricia J. Simple Machines. 2006. (Rosen Real Readers Big Bookstm Ser.). (ENG.). 16p. (gr. 2-3). 37.95 *(978-1-4042-6220-1(2))* Rosen Publishing Group, Inc., The.

Oliver, Simone G. Tools Make Work Easier. 2017. (Text Connections Guided Close Reading Ser.). (J). (gr. k). *(978-1-4900-1768-6(2))* Benchmark Education Co.

Oxlade, Chris. Find Out about Machines. 2013. (ENG., Illus.). 64p. (J). (gr. 3-7). 9.99 *(978-1-84322-973-5(0))* Anness Publishing GBR. Dist: National Bk. Network.

—Levers. 2009. (Simple Machines (Smart Apple Media Paperback) Ser.). (Illus.). 32p. (J). (gr. k-2). pap. 7.95 *(978-1-59920-200-6(X))* Black Rabbit Bks.

—Making Machines with Levers. 2015. (Simple Machine Projects Ser.). (ENG.). 32p. (gr. 2-4). 30.65 *(978-1-4109-6799-2(9)*, Raintree Perspectives) Heinemann-Raintree.

—Making Machines with Pulleys. 2015. (Simple Machine Projects Ser.). (ENG.). 32p. (gr. 2-4). 30.65 *(978-1-4109-6800-5(6)*, Raintree Perspectives) Heinemann-Raintree.

—Making Machines with Ramps & Wedges. 2015. (Simple Machine Projects Ser.). (ENG., Illus.). 32p. (gr. 2-4). 30.65 *(978-1-4109-6801-2(4)*, Raintree Perspectives) Heinemann-Raintree.

—Making Machines with Screws. 2015. (Simple Machine Projects Ser.). (ENG.). 32p. (gr. 2-4). 30.65 *(978-1-4109-6802-9(2)*, Raintree Perspectives) Heinemann-Raintree.

—Making Machines with Springs. 2015. (Simple Machine Projects Ser.). (ENG.). 32p. (gr. 2-4). 30.65 *(978-1-4109-6803-6(0)*, Raintree Perspectives) Heinemann-Raintree.

—Making Machines with Wheels & Axles. 2015. (Simple Machine Projects Ser.). (ENG.). 32p. (gr. 2-4). 30.65 *(978-1-4109-6804-3(9)*, Raintree Perspectives) Heinemann-Raintree.

—Pulleys. 2009. (Simple Machines (Smart Apple Media Paperback) Ser.). (Illus.). 32p. (J). (gr. k-2). pap. 7.95 *(978-1-59920-201-3(8))* Black Rabbit Bks.

—Screws. 2016. (Useful Machines Ser.). (ENG.). 32p. (gr. 1-3). pap. 8.29 *(978-1-4846-3637-4(6)*, Heinemann First Library) Heinemann-Raintree.

—Simple Experiments with Inclined Planes. 2013. (Science Experiments with Simple Machines Ser.). 32p. (J). (gr. k-3). 26.50 *(978-1-61533-752-1(0))*; pap. 11.75 *(978-1-61533-821-4(7))*; pap. 70.50 *(978-1-61533-822-1(5))* Windmill Bks.

—Simple Machine Projects. 2015. (Simple Machine Projects Ser.). (ENG.). 32p. (gr. 2-4). lib. bdg. 183.90 *(978-1-4109-6805-0(7)*, Raintree Perspectives) Heinemann-Raintree.

—This Is My Digger. Lalla, Christine, photos by. 2008. (Mega Machine Drivers Ser.). (Illus.). 30p. (J). (gr. k). lib. bdg. 28.50 *(978-1-59771-104-3(7))* Sea-To-Sea Pubns.

—This Is My Dump Truck. Crawford, Andy, photos by. 2008. (Mega Machine Drivers Ser.). (Illus.). 30p. (J). (gr. k). lib. bdg. 28.50 *(978-1-59771-105-0(5))* Sea-To-Sea Pubns.

—Wedges & Ramps. 2009. (Simple Machines (Smart Apple Media Paperback) Ser.). (Illus.). 32p. (J). (gr. 4-7). pap. 7.95 *(978-1-59920-203-7(4))* Black Rabbit Bks.

Oxlade, Chris & Farndon, John. Stickmen's Guide to Gigantic Machines. Pyke, Jerry & Quay, John Paul de, illus. 2016. (Stickmen's Guides to How Everything Works). (ENG.). 32p. (J). (gr. 3-6). lib. bdg. 26.65 *(978-1-4677-9361-2(2))* Lerner Publishing Group.

Oxlade, Chris & Peacock, Graham. Machines: Gears, Levers, Pulleys, Engine. 2016. (ENG., Illus.). 64p. 12.99 *(978-1-86147-490-2(3)*, Armadillo) Anness Publishing GBR. Dist: National Bk. Network.

Paes, Rob, illus. Mighty Machines. 2003. 12p. (J). (gr. k-3). 20.00 *(978-0-7567-6652-8(4))* DIANE Publishing Co.

Palas Mecánicas (Earthmovers) 2006. (J). pap. 6.95 *(978-0-8225-6644-1(3)*, Ediciones Lerner) Lerner Publishing Group.

Parker, Janice. Machines. 2016. (J). ***(978-1-5105-2241-1(7))*** SmartBook Media, Inc.

—Machines. 2008. (Science Q & A Ser.). (Illus.). 48p. (YA). (gr. 5-8). pap. 10.95 *(978-1-59036-951-7(3))*; lib. bdg. 29.05 *(978-1-59036-950-0(5))* Weigl Pubs., Inc.

—Machines Q & A. 2013. (J). *(978-1-62127-416-2(0))*; pap. *(978-1-62127-422-3(5))* Weigl Pubs., Inc.

Parker, Steve. Giant Machines. 2010. (How It Works Ser.). 40p. (J). (gr. 3-18). lib. bdg. 19.95 *(978-1-4222-1796-2(5))* Mason Crest.

—On the Building Site. 2010. (J). 28.50 *(978-1-59920-288-4(3))* Black Rabbit Bks.

Peppas, Lynn. Road Makers & Breakers. 2012. (ENG.). 32p. (J). *(978-0-7787-3020-0(4))*; pap. *(978-0-7787-3025-5(5))* Crabtree Publishing Co.

Perritano, John. The Revolution in Industry: How Machines Changed America. 2008. (Graphic America Ser.). (ENG., Illus.). 32p. (J). (gr. 3-6). lib. bdg. *(978-0-7787-4189-3(3))* Crabtree Publishing Co.

Petruccio, Steven. At the Construction Site (en el Sitio de Construccion) Gongora, Oscar, tr. 2011. (Dover Children's Bilingual Coloring Book Ser.). (ENG & SPA., Illus.). 32p. (J). (gr. k-6). pap. 3.99 *(978-0-486-46368-1(0))* Dover Pubns., Inc.

Pettiford, Rebecca. Concrete Mixers. 2017. (Mighty Machines in Action Ser.). (ENG., Illus.). 24p. (J). (gr. k-3). lib. bdg. 25.95 ***(978-1-62617-630-0(2)***, Blastoff! Readers) Bellwether Media.

—Earth Movers. 2017. (Mighty Machines in Action Ser.). (ENG., Illus.). 24p. (J). (gr. k-3). lib. bdg. 25.95 ***(978-1-62617-631-7(0)***, Blastoff! Readers) Bellwether Media.

Porterfield, Jason. Fab Lab Creating with Milling Machines. 2016. (Getting Creative with Fab Lab Ser.). 00064p. (J). (gr. 6-6). 34.45 *(978-1-4994-6506-8(8))* Rosen Publishing Group, Inc., The.

Priddy, Roger. Trucks & Things That Go. 2006. (First 100 Ser.). (ENG., Illus.). 14p. (J). (gr. -1 — 1). bds. 9.99 *(978-0-312-49806-1(3)*, 9780312498061, Priddy Bks.) St. Martin's Pr.

Professional Tools, 6 vols., Set. Incl. Archaeologist's Tools. Hanson, Anders. lib. bdg. 25.65 *(978-1-61613-577-5(8))*; Dentist's Tools. Salzmann, Mary Elizabeth. lib. bdg. 25.65 *(978-1-61613-578-2(6))*; Doctor's Tools. Salzmann, Mary Elizabeth. lib. bdg. 25.65 *(978-1-61613-579-9(4))*; Meteorologist's Tools. Hanson, Anders. lib. bdg. 25.65 *(978-1-61613-580-5(8))*; Scientist's Tools. Hanson, Anders. lib. bdg. 25.65 *(978-1-61613-581-2(6))*; Veterinarian's Tools. Salzmann, Mary Elizabeth. lib. bdg. 25.65 *(978-1-61613-582-9(4))*; (J). (gr. 3-5). (Professional Tools Ser.). (Illus.). 24p. 2011. 153.90 *(978-1-61613-576-8(X)*, Super SandCastle) ABDO Publishing Co.

Randolph, Joanne. Inclined Planes in My World. 2009. (My World of Science Ser.). 24p. (gr. 2-2). 37.50 *(978-1-61514-723-6(3)*, PowerKids Pr.) Rosen Publishing Group, Inc., The.

—Inclined Planes in My World/Planos inclinados en mi Mundo. 2009. (My World of Science/la ciencia en mi mundo Ser.). 48p. (gr. 2-2). 37.50 *(978-1-61514-735-9(7)*, Editorial Buenas Letras) Rosen Publishing Group, Inc., The.

—Levers in My World. (My World of Science Ser.). 24p. 2009. (gr. 2-2). 37.50 *(978-1-61514-724-3(1)*, PowerKids Pr.) 2007. (ENG.). (gr. k-8). pap. 7.05 *(978-1-4042-8424-1(9)*, Rosen Classroom) Rosen Publishing Group, Inc., The.

—Levers in My World/Palancas en mi Mundo. 2009. (My World of Science/la ciencia en mi mundo Ser.). 48p. (gr. 2-2). 37.50 *(978-1-61514-736-6(5)*, Editorial Buenas Letras) Rosen Publishing Group, Inc., The.

—Pulleys in My World. 2009. (My World of Science Ser.). 24p. (gr. 2-2). 37.50 *(978-1-61514-727-4(6)*, PowerKids Pr.) Rosen Publishing Group, Inc., The.

—Pulleys in My World/Poleas en mi Mundo. 2009. (My World of Science/la ciencia en mi mundo Ser.). (ENG & SPA.). 48p. (gr. 2-2). 37.50 *(978-1-61514-739-7(X)*, Editorial Buenas Letras) Rosen Publishing Group, Inc., The.

—Road Machines, 6 bks. Incl. Concrete Mixers. lib. bdg. 18.75 *(978-0-8239-6039-2(0))*; Road Milling Machines. lib. bdg. 18.75 *(978-0-8239-6041-5(2))*; Road Pavers. lib. bdg. 18.75 *(978-0-8239-6040-8(4))*; Road Rollers. lib. bdg. 18.75 *(978-0-8239-6037-8(4))*; Road Scrapers. lib. bdg. 18.75 *(978-0-8239-6042-2(0))*; Snowplows. lib. bdg. 18.75 *(978-0-8239-6038-5(2))*; 24p. (J). (gr. 1). 2002. (Illus.). Set lib. bdg. 88.50 *(978-0-8239-7115-2(5)*, PowerKids Pr.) Rosen Publishing Group, Inc., The.

—Wedges in My World. 2009. (My World of Science Ser.). 24p. (gr. 2-2). 37.50 *(978-1-61514-730-4(6)*, PowerKids Pr.) Rosen Publishing Group, Inc., The.

—Wedges in My World/Cunas en mi Mundo. 2009. (My World of Science/la ciencia en mi mundo Ser.). (ENG & SPA.). 48p. (gr. 2-2). 37.50 *(978-1-61514-742-7(X)*, Editorial Buenas Letras) Rosen Publishing Group, Inc., The.

—Wheel Loaders. 2009. (Earth Movers Ser.). 24p. (gr. k-1). 37.50 *(978-1-61512-237-0(0)*, PowerKids Pr.) Rosen Publishing Group, Inc., The.

—Wheels & Axels in My World/Ejes y ruedas en mi Mundo. 2009. (My World of Science/la ciencia en mi mundo Ser.). (ENG & SPA.). 48p. (gr. 2-2). 37.50 *(978-1-61514-743-4(8)*, Editorial Buenas Letras) Rosen Publishing Group, Inc., The.

—Wheels & Axles in My World. (My World of Science Ser.). 24p. 2009. (gr. 2-2). 37.50 *(978-1-61514-731-1(4)*, PowerKids Pr.) 2007. (ENG.). (gr. k-8). pap. 7.05 *(978-1-4042-8427-2(3)*, Rosen Classroom) 2006. (Illus.). (J). (gr. 3-7). lib. bdg. 18.75 *(978-1-4042-3313-3(X)*, PowerKids Pr.) Rosen Publishing Group, Inc., The.

—Wheels & Axles in My World: Ejes y Ruedas en Mi Mundo. 2006. (My World of Science/ Mi mundo y la Ciencia Ser.). (ENG & SPA.). (J). (gr. k-3). 16.00 *(978-1-4042-3325-6(3))* Rosen Publishing Group, Inc., The.

Rau, Dana Meachen. Simple Machines. 2011. (True Book(tm), a — Physical Science Ser.). (ENG., Illus.). 48p. (J). lib. bdg. 31.00 *(978-0-531-26324-2(X))*; pap. 6.95 *(978-0-531-26586-4(2))* Scholastic Library Publishing. (Children's Pr.).

Reinke, Beth Bence. Front Loaders Scoop! 2017. (Bumba Books (tm) — Construction Zone Ser.). (ENG.). 24p. (J). (gr. -1-1). 25.32 ***(978-1-5124-3360-9(8))*** Lerner Publishing Group.

Reynolds, Toby & Calver, Paul. Machines. 2017. (Visual Explorers Ser.). (ENG.). 32p. (J). (gr. 3-7). pap. 6.99 ***(978-1-4380-1083-0(4))*** Barron's Educational Series, Inc.

Richards, Jon. Forces & Simple Machines. (Science Factory Ser.). 32p. (gr. 4-5). 2009. 50.50 *(978-1-60853-021-2(3)*, PowerKids Pr.) 2008. (Illus.). (YA). lib. bdg. 26.50 *(978-1-4042-3908-1(1))* Rosen Publishing Group, Inc., The.

Richards, Mark & Creese, Sarah. Diggers & Dumpers. 2009. (Carry-Me Ser.). (ENG., Illus.). 12p. (gr. -1-k). 7.99 *(978-1-84610-870-9(5))* Make Believe Ideas GBR. Dist: Nelson, Thomas Inc.

Rigby Education Staff. Machines Around Your Home. (Illus.). 8p. (J). bds. 3.95 *(978-0-7635-6491-9(5)*, 764915C99) Rigby Education.

Rinkel, Ken, illus. Giant Machines. 2003. 12p. (J). (gr. k-3). 20.00 *(978-0-7567-6653-5(2))* DIANE Publishing Co.

Ripley's Believe It Or Not! Staff & Ripley's Believe It Or Not! Editors. Ripley Twists: Mighty Machines PORTRAIT EDN. 2014. (Twist Ser.). (ENG.). 48p. (J). 12.95 *(978-1-893951-85-3(5))* Ripley Entertainment, Inc.

Rissman, Rebecca. Simple Machines: Real Size Science, 1 vol. 2013. (Real Size Science Ser.). (ENG.). 24p. (gr. -1-1). 22.65 *(978-1-4329-7877-8(2))*; pap. 6.95 *(978-1-4329-7884-6(5))* Heinemann-Raintree. (Acorn).

Rogers, Hal. Cherry Pickers. 2014. (Big Machines at Work Ser.). (ENG.). 24p. (J). (gr. -1-2). 25.64 *(978-1-62323-963-3(X)*, 206738) Child's World, Inc., The.

Rooney, Anne. Mega Machine Record Breakers. 2014. (ENG., Illus.). 128p. (J). (gr. 3). pap. 14.95 *(978-1-78312-005-5(3))* Carlton Bks., Ltd. GBR. Dist: Sterling Publishing Co., Inc.

Royston, Angela. Levers. 2003. (Machines in Action Ser.). (ENG.). 32p. pap. 7.99 *(978-1-4034-4084-6(0)*, NA-h) Heinemann-Raintree.

Roza, Greg. Wedges. 2013. (Simple Machine Science Ser.). (Illus.). 24p. (gr. 1-3). 22.60 *(978-1-4339-8151-7(3))*; pap. 8.15 *(978-1-4339-8152-4(1))* Stevens, Gareth Publishing LLLP.

Ruck, Colleen. Diggers. 2011. (My Favorite Machines Ser.). 24p. (gr. 2-5). 28.50 *(978-1-59920-674-5(9))* Black Rabbit Bks.

Rushby, Pamela. Mysteries of the Fossil Dig: How Paleontologists Learn about Dinosaurs. 2006. (Science Chapters Ser.). (ENG., Illus.). 48p. (J). (gr. 2-5). 17.90 *(978-0-7922-5953-4(X)*, National Geographic Children's Bks.) National Geographic Society.

Saddleback, creator. Machines & Inventions. 2008. (Factoscope Ser.). (Illus.). 64p. (YA). (gr. 8-12). per. 10.95 *(978-1-59905-235-9(0))* Saddleback Educational Publishing, Inc.

Sadler, Wendy. Using Levers, 6 vols. 2005. (Raintree Perspectives Ser.). (Illus.). *(978-1-4109-1451-4(8))*; *(978-1-4109-1454-5(2))*; *(978-1-4109-1449-1(6))*; *(978-1-4109-1452-1(6))*; *(978-1-4109-1450-7(X))*; *(978-1-4109-1453-8(4))* Steck-Vaughn.

Samuels, Charlie. The Rise of Industry (1700-1800) 2010. (Science Highlights: A Gareth Stevens Timeline Ser.). (ENG.). 48p. (J). (gr. 6-8). pap. 14.05 *(978-1-4339-4146-7(5))*; lib. bdg. 31.95 *(978-1-4339-4145-0(7))* Stevens, Gareth Publishing LLLP. (Gareth Stevens Secondary Library).

Scheff, Matt. Speed Machines, 1 vol. 2014. (Speed Machines Ser.: 8). (ENG.). 32p. (gr. 3-6). lib. bdg. 216.56 *(978-1-62403-607-1(4)*, SportsZone) ABDO Publishing Co.

Scholastic & Arlon, Penelope. Mighty Machines (LEGO Nonfiction) 2017. (LEGO Nonfiction Ser.: 4). (ENG.). 32p. (J). (gr. -1-3). pap. 4.99 *(978-1-338-13020-1(X))* Scholastic, Inc.

Scholastic Clubs US Machines at Work Set #1: Machines at Work. 2006. (J). 39.80 *(978-1-59566-321-4(5))* QEB Publishing Inc.

Scholastic Clubs US Machines at Work Set #2: Machines at Work. 2006. 39.80 *(978-1-59566-322-1(3))* QEB Publishing Inc.

Scholastic, Inc. Staff, contrib. by. Counting Machines. 2015. (Rookie Toddler(tm) Ser.). (ENG., Illus.). 12p. (J). bds. 6.95 *(978-0-531-21268-4(8)*, Children's Pr.) Scholastic Library Publishing.

Schuh, Mari. Las Cargadoras (Loaders) 2017. (Spot Mighty Machines Ser.). (ENG & SPA.). 16p. (J). (gr. k-3). 17.95 ***(978-1-68151-269-3(6)***, Amicus Readers) Amicus Publishing.

—Las Excavadoras (Diggers) 2017. (Spot Mighty Machines Ser.). (ENG & SPA.). 16p. (J). (gr. k-3). 17.95 ***(978-1-68151-267-9(X)***, Amicus Readers) Amicus Publishing.

—Las Mezcladoras de Concreto (Concrete Mixers) 2017. (Spot Mighty Machines Ser.). (ENG & SPA.). 16p. (J). (gr. k-3). 17.95 ***(978-1-68151-265-5(3)***, Amicus Readers) Amicus Publishing.

Schuh, Mari C. Concrete Mixers. 2017. (Spot Mighty Machines Ser.). (ENG.). 16p. (gr. k-3). 17.95 ***(978-1-68151-098-9(7))*** Amicus Publishing.

—Diggers. 2017. (Spot Mighty Machines Ser.). (ENG.). 16p. (gr. k-3). 17.95 ***(978-1-68151-101-6(0))*** Amicus Publishing.

—Hauling a Pumpkin: Wheels & Axles vs. Lever. 2015. (ENG., Illus.). 24p. (J). (gr. k-2). pap. 6.99 *(978-1-4677-8304-0(8)*, Lerner Pubns.) Lerner Publishing Group.

—Holding a Door Open: Wedge vs. Wheels & Axles. 2015. (First Step Nonfiction - Simple Machines to the Rescue Ser.). (ENG., Illus.). 24p. (J). (gr. k-2). 23.99 *(978-1-4677-8303-3(X)*, Lerner Pubns.) Lerner Publishing Group.

—Loaders. 2017. (Spot Mighty Machines Ser.). (ENG.). 16p. (gr. k-3). 17.95 ***(978-1-68151-103-0(7))*** Amicus Publishing.

—Making a Salad: Wedge vs. Inclined Plane. 2015. (First Step Nonfiction - Simple Machines to the Rescue Ser.). (ENG., Illus.). 24p. (gr. k-2). 23.99 *(978-1-4677-8295-1(5)*, Lerner Pubns.) Lerner Publishing Group.

—Playing a Game: Inclined Plane vs. Lever. 2015. (ENG., Illus.). 24p. (J). (gr. k-2). 23.99 *(978-1-4677-8027-8(8)*, Lerner Pubns.) Lerner Publishing Group.

—Raising a Bag of Toys: Pulley vs. Inclined Plane. 2015. (ENG., Illus.). 24p. (J). (gr. k-2). 23.99 *(978-1-4677-8024-7(3)*, Lerner Pubns.) Lerner Publishing Group.

Science Experiments with Simple Machines. 2013. (Science Experiments with Simple Machines Ser.). 32p. (J). (gr. k-3). 159.00 *(978-1-61533-871-9(3))*; pap. 423.00 *(978-1-61533-879-5(9))* Windmill Bks.

Secrets of the Fun Park, 6 Packs. (gr. k-1). 23.00 *(978-0-7635-9080-2(0))* Rigby Education.

Selwyn, Josephine. Who Uses This Machine? 2014. (Little Books of Answers: Level C Ser.). (Illus.). 16p. (gr. k-2). pap. 7.95 *(978-1-927136-29-4(6))* Three Crows Media NZL. Dist: RiverStream Publishing.

Shand, Jennifer. Why Do Tractors Have Such Big Tires? Paiva, Johannah Gilman, ed. Fabbri, Daniele, illus. 2014. (ENG.). 20p. (J). (gr. k-4). 8.99 *(978-1-4867-0382-1(8))* Flowerpot Children's Pr. Inc. CAN. Dist: Cardinal Pubs. Group.

—Why Do Tractors Have Such Big Tires? 2015. (Why Do... ? Ser.). lib. bdg. 19.65 *(978-1-4867-0624-2(X))* Turtleback Bks.

Silverman, Buffy. I Use Simple Machines. 2011. (ENG., Illus.). 24p. (gr. k-1). pap. 8.95 *(978-1-61741-930-0(3))* Rourke Educational Media.

—Simple Machines: Forces in Action. 2016. (Do It Yourself Ser.). (ENG.). 48p. (gr. 3-6). pap. 8.99 *(978-1-4846-3640-4(6)*, NA-h) Heinemann-Raintree.

Simple Machines. 2004. (Illus.). lib. bdg. 7.95 *(978-0-8225-3352-8(9))*Set. 2006. (J). (gr. 2-4). 46.95 *(978-0-8225-3353-5(7))* Lerner Publishing Group.

Simple Machines - English Take Home Book. 2007. (Journeys Ser.). (J). pap. 20.00 *(978-1-4042-9493-6(7)*, Rosen Classroom) Rosen Publishing Group, Inc., The.

Simple Machines Everywhere. 2014. (Simple Machines Everywhere Ser.). 24p. (J). (gr. k-3). 141.60 *(978-1-4777-6646-0(4))*; pap. 49.50 *(978-1-4777-7246-1(4))* Rosen Publishing Group, Inc., The. (PowerKids Pr.).

Sirota, Lyn. Screws. Butler, Reginald, illus. 2012. (Simple Machines Ser.). (ENG.). 24p. (J). (gr. -1-2). 27.07 *(978-1-61473-276-1(0)*, 204981) Child's World, Inc., The.

Small, Cathleen. Fab Lab Creating with Vinyl Cutters. 2016. (Getting Creative with Fab Lab Ser.). 00064p. (J). (gr. 6-6). 34.45 *(978-1-5081-7350-2(8))* Rosen Publishing Group, Inc., The.

Small Machines Sets: 1 Each of 3 Big Books. (Sunshinetm Science Ser.). (gr. 1-2). 93.95 *(978-0-7802-0531-4(6))* Wright Group/McGraw-Hill.

Small Machines Sets: 1 Each of 3 Student Books. (Sunshinetm Science Ser.). (gr. 1-2). 17.95 *(978-0-7802-0272-6(4))* Wright Group/McGraw-Hill.
Smith, Sian. Machines at Work. 2013. (Machines at Work Ser.). (ENG.). 24p. (gr. 1-2). pap. 25.96 *(978-1-4329-7508-1(0))*; lib. bdg. 69.96 *(978-1-4329-7503-6(X))* Heinemann-Raintree. (Heinemann Read & Learn).
—Machines on the Road, 1 vol. 2013. (Machines at Work Ser.). (ENG.). 24p. (gr. 1-2). pap. 6.95 *(978-1-4329-7507-4(2))*; 23.32 *(978-1-4329-7502-9(1))* Heinemann-Raintree. (Heinemann Read & Learn).
Speed Machines Sticker Book. Date not set. (Illus.). 12p. (J). 3.98 *(978-1-4054-0499-0(X))* Parragon, Inc.
Stark, William N. Military Machines on Duty. 2016. (Military Machines on Duty Ser.). (ENG.). 24p. (gr. 1-2). 101.28 *(978-1-4914-8841-6(7)*, First Facts) Capstone Press of Coughlan Cos.
Stilwell, Dwayne. Levers. 2013. (Simple Machine Science Ser.). (Illus.). 24p. (gr. 1-3). 22.60 *(978-1-4339-8136-4(X))*; pap. 8.15 *(978-1-4339-8137-1(8))* Stevens, Gareth Publishing LLLP.
Stone, Tanya Lee. P Is for Passover. Lucas, Margeaux, illus. 2003. (ENG.). 32p. (J). (gr. -1-k). mass mkt. 5.99 *(978-0-8431-0238-3(1)*, Price Stern Sloan) Penguin Young Readers Group.
Sundance/Newbridge LLC Staff. Simple Machines. 2007. (Early Science Ser.). (gr. k-3). 18.95 *(978-1-4007-6612-3(5))*; pap. 6.10 *(978-1-4007-6608-6(7))* Sundance/Newbridge Educational Publishing.
—Six Simple Machines. 2004. (Reading PowerWorks Ser.). (gr. 1-3). 37.50 *(978-0-7608-9735-5(2))*; pap. 6.10 *(978-0-7608-9736-2(0))* Sundance/Newbridge Educational Publishing.
Super Explorers: Excavators & Diggers, 1 vol. 2016. (Super Explorers Ser.). (ENG., Illus.). 64p. (J). pap. 6.99 ***(978-1-926700-65-6(1)***, 9781926700656) Blue Bike Bks. CAN. Dist: Lone Pine Publishing USA.
Tango Books Staff. Digger: A Lift-the-Flap & Stand Up. Burton, Terry, illus. 2011. (Mini Trucks Ser.). (ENG.). 12p. (J). (gr. -1-k). 5.99 *(978-1-85707-751-3(2))* Tango Bks. GBR. Dist: Independent Pubs. Group.
Taylor, Trace. Earth Movers. Taylor, Trace, illus. 2008. (1-3Y Getting Around Ser.). (ENG., Illus.). 20p. (J). (gr. k-2). pap. 5.99 *(978-1-59301-466-7(X))* American Reading Co.
Thompson, Gare. Lever, Screw, & Inclined Plane: The Power of Simple Machines. 2006. (Science Chapters Ser.). (ENG., Illus.). 48p. (J). (gr. 1-4). lib. bdg. 17.90 *(978-0-7922-5949-7(1)*, National Geographic Children's Bks.) National Geographic Society.
Ticktock Media, Ltd. Staff. Extreme Machines. 2010. (Top Tens Ser.). (ENG.). 32p. (J). (gr. 1-3). pap. 6.95 *(978-1-84898-197-3(X)*, TickTock Books) Octopus Publishing Group GBR. Dist: Independent Pubs. Group.
Tieck, Sarah. Earthmovers. 2005. (Buddy Book Ser.). (Illus.). 24p. (gr. k-4). 25.65 *(978-1-59197-826-8(2)*, Buddy Bks.) ABDO Publishing Co.
—Inclined Planes, 1 vol. 2006. (Simple Machines Ser.). (ENG., Illus.). 24p. (gr. -1-3). 25.65 *(978-1-59679-818-2(1)*, Buddy Bks.) ABDO Publishing Co.
—Levers, 1 vol. 2006. (Simple Machines Ser.). (ENG., Illus.). 24p. (gr. -1-3). 25.65 *(978-1-59679-814-4(9)*, Buddy Bks.) ABDO Publishing Co.
—Pulleys, 1 vol. 2006. (Simple Machines Ser.). (ENG., Illus.). 24p. (gr. -1-3). 25.65 *(978-1-59679-815-1(7)*, Buddy Bks.) ABDO Publishing Co.
—Simple Machines, 6 vols., Set. Incl. Inclined Planes. 25.65 *(978-1-59679-818-2(1))*; Levers. 25.65 *(978-1-59679-814-4(9))*; Pulleys. 25.65 *(978-1-59679-815-1(7))*; Screws. 25.65 *(978-1-59679-817-5(3))*; Wedges. 25.65 *(978-1-59679-816-8(5))*; Wheels & Axles. 25.65 *(978-1-59679-819-9(X))*; (Illus.). 24p. (gr. -1-3). (Simple Machines Ser.). 2006. 153.90 *(978-1-59679-813-7(0)*, Buddy Bks.) ABDO Publishing Co.
—Wedges, 1 vol. 2006. (Simple Machines Ser.). (ENG., Illus.). 24p. (gr. -1-3). 25.65 *(978-1-59679-816-8(5)*, Buddy Bks.) ABDO Publishing Co.
Tiner, John Hudson. Levers. 2003. (Simple Machines Ser.). (Illus.). 24p. (J). lib. bdg. 21.35 *(978-1-58340-135-4(0))* Black Rabbit Bks.
—Pulleys. 2003. (Simple Machines Ser.). (Illus.). 23p. (J). lib. bdg. 21.35 *(978-1-58340-136-1(9))* Black Rabbit Bks.
Tomljanovic, Tatiana. Wedges. (J). 2013. *(978-1-62127-428-5(4))* 2013. pap. *(978-1-62127-434-6(9))* 2009. (Illus.). 24p. (gr. 3-5). pap. 8.59 *(978-1-60596-038-8(1))* Weigl Pubs., Inc.
Tools & Machines. 2010. (Experimenting with Everyday Science Ser.). (Illus.). 184p. (gr. 6-12). 35.00 *(978-1-60413-171-0(3)*, Chelsea Hse.) Facts On File, Inc.
Top That Publishing Staff, ed. Real Spies. 2004. (I-Quest Ser.). (Illus.). 48p. (J). per. *(978-1-84510-134-3(0))* Top That! Publishing PLC.
Troupe, Thomas Kingsley. Crush It!, 1 vol. 2013. (Destruction Ser.). (ENG.). 24p. (gr. k-1). lib. bdg. 26.65 *(978-1-4765-2088-9(7)*, Pebble Plus) Capstone Press of Coughlan Cos.
VanVoorst, Jenny Fretland. Bicycles. 2016. (Early Physics Fun). 24p. (J). (gr. 2-5). lib. bdg. 25.65 *(978-1-62031-314-5(6)*, Pogo) Jump! Inc.
Veitch, Catherine. Big Machines, 1 vol. 2014. (Big Machines Ser.). (ENG.). 24p. (gr. k-1). 139.92 *(978-1-4846-0590-5(X)*, Heinemann Read & Learn) Heinemann-Raintree.
—Big Machines Build!, 1 vol. 2014. (Big Machines Ser.). (ENG.). 24p. (gr. k-1). 23.32 *(978-1-4846-0584-4(5)*, Heinemann Read & Learn) Heinemann-Raintree.
—Big Machines Float!, 1 vol. 2014. (Big Machines Ser.). (ENG.). 24p. (gr. k-1). pap. 3.95 *(978-1-4846-0984-2(0))*; (Illus.). 23.32 *(978-1-4846-0587-5(X))* Heinemann-Raintree. (Heinemann Read & Learn).
Volpe, Karen. Get to Know Levers. 2009. (Get to Know Simple Machines Ser.). (ENG., Illus.). 32p. (J). (gr. 2-4). pap. *(978-0-7787-4484-9(1))*; lib. bdg. *(978-0-7787-4467-2(1))* Crabtree Publishing Co.
—Get to Know Pulleys. 2009. (Get to Know Simple Machines Ser.). (ENG., Illus.). 32p. (J). (gr. 2-4). pap. *(978-0-7787-4485-6(X))*; lib. bdg. *(978-0-7787-4468-9(X))* Crabtree Publishing Co.
Walker, Sally M. & Feldmann, Roseann. Levers. 2005. (Early Bird Physics Ser.). (Illus.). 48p. (gr. 3-6). lib. bdg. 25.26 *(978-0-8225-2218-8(7))* Lerner Publishing Group.
—Palancas. King, Andy, photos by. 2005. (Libros de Física para Madrugadores (Early Bird Physics) Ser.). (SPA & ENG., Illus.). 48p. (gr. 3-6). lib. bdg. 25.26 *(978-0-8225-2972-9(6)*, Ediciones Lerner) Lerner Publishing Group.
—Planos Inclinados. King, Andy, photos by. 2009. (Libros de Física para Madrugadores Ser.). (SPA., Illus.). 47p. (J). (gr. 3-7). pap. 11.95 *(978-0-8225-2971-2(8))* Lerner Publishing Group.
—Poleas. King, Andy, photos by. 2005. (Libros de Física para Madrugadores (Early Bird Physics) Ser.). (SPA & ENG., Illus.). 48p. (gr. 3-6). lib. bdg. 26.60 *(978-0-8225-2980-4(7)*, Ediciones Lerner) Lerner Publishing Group.
—Put Inclined Planes to the Test. 2011. (Searchlight Books (tm) — How Do Simple Machines Work? Ser.). (ENG., Illus.). 40p. (gr. 3-5). lib. bdg. 27.93 *(978-0-7613-5324-9(0))* Lerner Publishing Group.
—Put Wedges to the Test. 2011. (Searchlight Books (tm) — How Do Simple Machines Work? Ser.). (ENG., Illus.). 40p. (gr. 3-5). lib. bdg. 27.93 *(978-0-7613-5325-6(9))* Lerner Publishing Group.
—Tornillos. King, Andy, photos by. 2009. (Libros de Física para Madrugadores Ser.). (SPA., Illus.). 47p. (J). (gr. 3-7). pap. 11.95 *(978-0-8225-2979-8(3))* Lerner Publishing Group.
—Trabajo. King, Andy, photos by. 2005. (Libros de Física para Madrugadores (Early Bird Physics) Ser.). (SPA & ENG., Illus.). 48p. (gr. 3-6). lib. bdg. 26.60 *(978-0-8225-2984-2(X)*, Ediciones Lerner) Lerner Publishing Group.
Walker, Sally M., et al. Work. 2005. (Early Bird Physics Ser.). (Illus.). 48p. (gr. 3-6). lib. bdg. 25.26 *(978-0-8225-2217-1(9))* Lerner Publishing Group.
Walter Foster Creative Team. Mighty Machines. 2014. (Look, Read, Learn Ser.). (ENG., Illus.). 90p. (J). (gr. -1-1). 12.95 *(978-0-7603-4712-6(3)*, Walter Foster Jr) Quarto Publishing Group USA.
Ward, D. J. Simple Machines. Lowery, Mike, illus. 2015. (Let's-Read-And-Find-Out Science 2 Ser.). (ENG.). 40p. (J). (gr. -1-3). pap. 6.99 *(978-0-06-232147-3(1))* HarperCollins Pubs.
Watt, Fiona & Wells, Rachel. Diggers. 2004. (Ultimate Touchy-Feely Ser.). (Illus.). 10p. (J). 15.95 *(978-0-7945-0340-6(3)*, Usborne) EDC Publishing.
Way, Steve & Bailey, Gerry. Simple Machines. 2008. (Simply Science Ser.). (Illus.). 32p. (YA). (gr. 3-6). lib. bdg. 26.00 *(978-0-8368-9231-4(3))* Stevens, Gareth Publishing LLLP.
Weakland, Mark. Flintstones Explain Simple Machines. 2016. (Flintstones Explain Simple Machines Ser.). (ENG.). 24p. (gr. k-2). 163.92 *(978-1-4914-8485-2(3))* Capstone Press of Coughlan Cos.
—Fred Flintstone's Adventures with Inclined Planes: A Rampin' Good Time. Brown, Alan, illus. 2016. (Flintstones Explain Simple Machines Ser.). (ENG.). 24p. (gr. k-2). lib. bdg. 27.32 *(978-1-4914-8476-0(4))* Capstone Press of Coughlan Cos.
—Fred Flintstone's Adventures with Levers: Lift That Load! Cornia, Christian, illus. 2016. (Flintstones Explain Simple Machines Ser.). (ENG.). 24p. (gr. k-2). lib. bdg. 27.32 *(978-1-4914-8473-9(X))* Capstone Press of Coughlan Cos.
—Fred Flintstone's Adventures with Pulleys: Work Smarter, Not Harder. Sordo, Paco, illus. 2016. (Flintstones Explain Simple Machines Ser.). (ENG.). 24p. (gr. k-2). lib. bdg. 27.32 *(978-1-4914-8475-3(6))* Capstone Press of Coughlan Cos.
—Fred Flintstone's Adventures with Screws: Righty Tighty, Lefty Loosey. Billiau, Loic, illus. 2016. (Flintstones Explain Simple Machines Ser.). (ENG.). 24p. (gr. k-2). lib. bdg. 27.32 *(978-1-4914-8478-4(0))* Capstone Press of Coughlan Cos.
—Fred Flintstone's Adventures with Wedges: Just Split! 2016. (Flintstones Explain Simple Machines Ser.). (ENG., Illus.). 24p. (gr. k-2). lib. bdg. 27.32 *(978-1-4914-8477-7(2))* Capstone Press of Coughlan Cos.
—Fred Flintstone's Adventures with Wheels & Axles: Bedrock & Roll! Brown, Alan, illus. 2016. (Flintstones Explain Simple Machines Ser.). (ENG.). 24p. (gr. k-2). lib. bdg. 27.32 *(978-1-4914-8474-6(8))* Capstone Press of Coughlan Cos.
—Gears Go, Wheels Roll, 1 vol. 2011. (Science Starts Ser.). (ENG., Illus.). 32p. (gr. 1-2). pap. 8.10 *(978-1-4296-6143-0(7)*, Aplus Bks.) Capstone Press of Coughlan Cos.
—Smash! Wile E. Coyote Experiments with Simple Machines, 1 vol. Cornia, Christian, illus. 2014. (Wile E. Coyote, Physical Science Genius Ser.). (ENG.). 32p. (gr. 3-4). 30.65 *(978-1-4765-4222-5(8))* Capstone Press of Coughlan Cos.
Whitehouse, Patty. Moving Machines. 2006. (Construction Forces Discovery Library). (Illus.). 24p. (J). (gr. k-2). lib. bdg. 22.79 *(978-1-60044-192-9(0))* Rourke Educational Media.
—Pushes & Pulls. 2006. (Construction Forces Discovery Library). (Illus.). 24p. (J). (gr. k-2). lib. bdg. 22.79 *(978-1-60044-193-6(9))* Rourke Educational Media.
Woods, Bob. Massive Machines. 2007. (Reading Rocks! Ser.). (ENG., Illus.). 32p. (J). (gr. 2-5). 28.50 *(978-1-59296-858-9(9)*, 200745) Child's World, Inc., The.
The World's Most Powerful Machines. 2016. (World's Most Powerful Machines Ser.). 00224p. (YA). (gr. 9-9). 225.50 *(978-1-4994-6563-1(7)*, Rosen Young Adult) Rosen Publishing Group, Inc., The.
Wright, Nicola. Diggers. 2006. (Illus.). 24p. (YA). (gr. 1-18). lib. bdg. 22.80 *(978-1-931983-57-0(7))* Chrysalis Education.
Yasuda, Anita. Explore Simple Machines! With 25 Great Projects. 2011. (Explore Your World Ser.). (ENG., Illus.). 96p. (J). (gr. k-4). pap. 12.95 *(978-1-936313-82-2(0))* Open City Bks.
Young, Caroline & Castor, Harriet. The Usborne Book of Machines That Work. Lyon, Chris, illus. 2004. (Young MacHines Ser.). 95p. (J). (gr. k). lib. bdg. 22.95 *(978-1-58086-031-4(1)*, Usborne) EDC Publishing.
Zeiger, Jennifer. What Does It Do? Digger. 2011. (Community Connections: What Does It Do? Ser.). (ENG.). 24p. (gr. 2-5). lib. bdg. 25.64 *(978-1-60279-968-4(7)*, 200968) Cherry Lake Publishing.
Zobel, Derek. Blastoff! Readers - Mighty Machines, 4 vols., Set. Incl. Bucket Trucks. 20.00 *(978-0-531-21707-8(8))*; Diggers. 20.00 *(978-0-531-21708-5(6))*; Pickup Trucks. 20.00 *(978-0-531-21709-2(4))*; Wheel Loaders. 20.00 *(978-0-531-21710-8(8))*; (Illus.). 24p. (J). (gr. k-3). 2009. 2009. Set lib. bdg. 80.00 *(978-0-531-26127-9(1)*, Children's Pr.) Scholastic Library Publishing.
—Diggers. 2009. (Mighty Machines Ser.). (ENG., Illus.). 24p. (J). (gr. k-3). lib. bdg. 25.95 *(978-1-60014-235-2(4))* Bellwether Media.
—Diggers. 2009. (Blastoff! Readers Ser.). (ENG., Illus.). 24p. (J). (gr. k-3). 20.00 *(978-0-531-21708-5(6)*, Children's Pr.) Scholastic Library Publishing.
—Road Rollers. 2009. (Mighty Machines Ser.). (ENG., Illus.). 24p. (J). (gr. k-3). lib. bdg. 25.95 *(978-1-60014-266-6(4))* Bellwether Media.
—Scrapers. 2009. (Mighty Machines Ser.). (ENG., Illus.). 24p. (J). (gr. k-3). lib. bdg. 25.95 *(978-1-60014-271-0(0))* Bellwether Media.
—Wheel Loaders. 2009. (Blastoff! Readers Ser.). (ENG., Illus.). 24p. (J). (gr. k-3). 20.00 *(978-0-531-21710-8(8)*, Children's Pr.) Scholastic Library Publishing.
Zoom in on Simple Machines. 2015. (Zoom in on Simple Machines Ser.). (ENG.). 24p. (J). (gr. 2-2). 135.60 *(978-0-7660-6674-8(6))*; pap., pap., pap. 56.10 *(978-0-7660-7052-3(2))*; pap., pap., pap. 336.60 *(978-0-7660-6675-5(4))* Enslow Pubs., Inc.

MACHINERY, AUTOMATIC

see Automation

MACHINERY—FICTION

Angleberger, Tom. McToad Mows Tiny Island. Hendrix, John, illus. 2015. (ENG.). 40p. (J). (gr. -1-3). 16.95 *(978-1-4197-1650-8(6)*, Abrams Bks. for Young Readers) Abrams, Inc.
Auerbach, Annie. Junkyard Dig! Building from A to Z. Shannon, David et al, illus. 2010. (Jon Scieszka's Trucktown Ser.). (ENG.). 26p. (J). (gr. -1-k). bds. 5.99 *(978-1-4169-4187-3(8)*, Little Simon) Little Simon.
AZ Books Staff. Musical Machines. Tulup, Natalia, ed. 2012. (Tra-La-la Ser.). (ENG.). 14p. (J). (-k). bds. 10.95 *(978-1-61889-055-9(7))* AZ Bks. LLC.
Berrios, Frank. Big Monster Machines! (Blaze & the Monster Machines) Golden Books, illus. 2016. (Big Coloring Book Ser.). (ENG.). 48p. (J). (gr. -1-2). pap. 6.99 *(978-0-399-55691-3(5)*, Golden Bks.) Random Hse. Children's Bks.
—Blaze & the Monster Machines Little Golden Book. Foley, Niki, illus. 2016. (Little Golden Book Ser.). (ENG.). 24p. (J). (-k). 4.99 *(978-0-399-55351-6(7)*, Golden Bks.) Random Hse. Children's Bks.
—Blaze Takes the Lead! (Blaze & the Monster Machines) Golden Books, illus. 2017. (Color & Paint Plus Stickers Ser.). (ENG.). 128p. (J). (gr. -1-2). pap. 9.99 *(978-0-399-55794-1(6)*, Golden Bks.) Random Hse. Children's Bks.
—Stripes Roars down the Track! Random House & Aikins, Dave, illus. 2017. (Pictureback(R) Ser.). (ENG.). 16p. (J). (gr. -1-2). pap. 4.99 *(978-0-399-55840-5(3)*, Random Hse. Bks. for Young Readers) Random Hse. Children's Bks.
Castrataro, Kristen. Grandpa's Farm Has Lots of Saws. 2012. 32p. (-18). pap. 19.99 *(978-1-4772-8636-4(5))* AuthorHouse.
Cote, Genevieve & Côté, Geneviève. Mr. King's Machine. Cote, Genevieve & Côté, Geneviève, illus. 2016. (Mr. King Ser.). (ENG., Illus.). 32p. (J). (gr. -1-2). 16.95 *(978-1-77138-021-8(7))* Kids Can Pr., Ltd. CAN. Dist: Hachette Bk. Group.
Dover, Ilana. The Talking MacHine: The Story of Alexander Graham Bell. 2012. 36p. pap. 17.49 *(978-1-4691-8328-2(5))* Xlibris Corp.
Foofy the Friendly Crane. 2013. 24p. pap. *(978-965-550-219-0(8))* Contento De Semrik.
Goetz, Steve. Old MacDonald Had a Truck. Kaban, Eda, illus. 2016. (ENG.). 40p. (J). (gr. -1-k). 16.99 *(978-1-4521-3260-0(7))* Chronicle Bks. LLC.
Golden Books. Blaze & the Monster Machines Awesome Sticker Collection (Blaze & the Monster Machines) Golden Books, illus. 2017. (4 Color Plus 1,000 Stickers Ser.). (ENG., Illus.). 64p. (J). (gr. -1-2). pap. 12.99 ***(978-1-5247-1683-7(9)***, Golden Bks.) Random Hse. Children's Bks.
—Blaze & the Monster Machines Color Plus Cardstock & Stickers. Golden Books, illus. 2016. (Color Plus Cardstock & Stickers Ser.). (ENG., Illus.). 32p. (J). (gr. -1-2). pap. 5.99 *(978-0-399-55303-5(7)*, Golden Bks.) Random Hse. Children's Bks.
—Blaze Little Golden Book Favorites (Blaze & the Monster Machines) Golden Books, illus. 2017. (Little Golden Book Favorites Ser.). (ENG., Illus.). 80p. (J). (-k). 7.99 *(978-0-399-55891-7(8)*, Golden Bks.) Random Hse. Children's Bks.
Golden Books. Championship Colors! (Blaze & the Monster Machines) Golden Books, illus. 2017. (Jumbo Coloring Book Ser.). (ENG., Illus.). 224p. (J). (gr. -1-2). pap. 6.99 ***(978-1-5247-6558-3(9)***, Golden Bks.) Random Hse. Children's Bks.
Golden Books Staff. Rescue Team! Durk, Jim, illus. 2010. (Big Coloring Book Ser.). (ENG.). 48p. (J). (gr. -1-2). pap. 6.99 *(978-0-375-86160-4(2)*, Golden Bks.) Random Hse. Children's Bks.
Grant, Gavin J. & Link, Kelly, eds. Steampunk! an Anthology of Fantastically Rich & Strange Stories. 2013. (ENG.). 432p. (YA). (gr. 9). pap. 16.99 *(978-0-7636-5797-0(2))* Candlewick Pr.
Koehler, Lora. The Little Snowplow. Parker, Jake, illus. 2015. (ENG.). 32p. (J). (gr. -1-2). 15.99 *(978-0-7636-7074-0(X))* Candlewick Pr.
Langridge, Roger. Family Reunion. Langridge, Roger & Mebberson, Amy, illus. 2010. (Muppet Show Ser.). (ENG.). 112p. (J). pap. 9.99 *(978-1-60886-587-1(8))* Boom! Studios.
Letscher, Lance. The Perfect Machine. 2010. (ENG., Illus.). 56p. (J). 19.95 *(978-0-292-72338-2(5))* Univ. of Texas Pr.
Mangual, Cynthia Ines. Blaze's Biggest Race! (Blaze & the Monster Machines) Kobasic, Kevin, illus. 2017. (Step into Reading Ser.). (ENG.). 24p. (J). (gr. -1-1). pap. 4.99 ***(978-1-5247-1696-7(0))***; lib. bdg. 12.99 ***(978-1-5247-1697-4(9))*** Random Hse. Children's Bks. (Random Hse. Bks. for Young Readers).
Mattel & Sollinger, Emily. Bob the Builder: Sky-High Scoop. 2016. (ENG.). 24p. (J). (gr. -1-3). 12.99 *(978-0-316-39443-7(2))* Little, Brown Bks. for Young Readers.
Merry, Margaret. The Lonely Digger. 2009. 72p. pap. 21.50 *(978-1-60860-144-8(7)*, Strategic Bk. Publishing) Strategic Book Publishing & Rights Agency (SBPRA).
Publications International Ltd. Staff. Steering Wheel Sound Thomas the Tank. 2007. 12p. (J). bds. 17.98 *(978-1-4127-6811-5(X))* Phoenix International Publications, Inc.
Random House. Blazing Shapes! (Blaze & the Monster Machines) Dynamo Limited, illus. 2017. (ENG.). 24p. (J). (— 1). bds. 6.99 ***(978-1-5247-1716-2(9)***, Random Hse. Bks. for Young Readers) Random Hse. Children's Bks.
—Feel the Power (Blaze & the Monster Machines) Hechtenkopf, Omar, illus. 2016. (Touch-And-Feel Ser.). (ENG.). 10p. (J). (— 1). bds. 12.99 *(978-0-399-55372-1(X)*, Random Hse. Bks. for Young Readers) Random Hse. Children's Bks.
—Meet the Machines! (Blaze & the Monster Machines) Random House, illus. 2016. (Friendship Box Ser.). (ENG., Illus.). 48p. (J). (— 1). bds. 10.99 *(978-1-101-93678-8(9)*, Random Hse. Bks. for Young Readers) Random Hse. Children's Bks.
—A Monster Machine Treasury (Blaze & the Monster Machines) Random House, illus. 2016. (Padded Board Book Ser.). (ENG., Illus.). 30p. (J). (— 1). bds. 11.99 *(978-0-399-55594-7(3)*, Random Hse. Bks. for Young Readers) Random Hse. Children's Bks.
Random House Disney Staff. Catch Crusher! (Blaze & the Monster Machines) Random House Disney Staff & Dynamo Limited, illus. 2016. (Pictureback(R) Ser.). (ENG.). 24p. (J). (gr. -1-2). pap. 6.99 *(978-1-101-93683-2(5)*, Random Hse. Bks. for Young Readers) Random Hse. Children's Bks.
RH Disney. Cars 3 Big Golden Book (Disney/Pixar Cars 3) RH Disney, illus. 2017. (Big Golden Book Ser.). (ENG., Illus.). 48p. (J). (gr. -1-2). 9.99 ***(978-0-7364-3674-8(X)***, Golden/Disney) Random Hse. Children's Bks.
Roadbloc. Vending MacHine Lunch. 2012. 172p. pap. *(978-0-9570633-4-1(2))* Fragged Publishing.
Spangler, Lois. The Fort on Fourth Street, 1 vol. Wald, Christina, illus. 2013. (ENG.). 32p. (J). (gr. 1-4). 17.95 *(978-1-60718-620-5(9))*; pap. 9.95 *(978-1-60718-632-8(2))* Arbordale Publishing.
Swinburne, Minnie. Laz's Perfect State Machine. 2011. (Illus.). 52p. (gr. 4-6). pap. 11.76 *(978-1-4567-9293-0(8))* AuthorHouse.
Taplin, Sam. Noisy Diggers. 2012. (Noisy Bks). 10p. (J). bds. 18.99 *(978-0-7945-3264-2(0)*, Usborne) EDC Publishing.
Tillworth, Mary. Bubble Trouble! (Blaze & the Monster Machines) Kobasic, Kevin, illus. 2016. (Step into Reading Ser.). (ENG.). 24p. (J). (gr. -1-1). 4.99 *(978-1-101-93680-1(0)*, Random Hse. Bks. for Young Readers) Random Hse. Children's Bks.
—Dino Parade! (Blaze & the Monster Machines) Martinez, Heather, illus. 2017. (Little Golden Book Ser.). (ENG.). 24p. (J). (-k). 4.99 *(978-0-399-55795-8(4)*, Golden Bks.) Random Hse. Children's Bks.
—Zeg & the Egg (Blaze & the Monster Machines) Foley, Niki, illus. 2016. (Step into Reading Ser.). (ENG.). 24p. (J). (gr. -1-1). 4.99 *(978-0-553-53935-6(3)*, Random Hse. Bks. for Young Readers) Random Hse. Children's Bks.
Uribe, Denise. Queen MacHine. 2012. 24p. pap. 12.56 *(978-1-4669-6083-1(3))* Trafford Publishing.
Wojtowycz, David. Scoop, the Digger! 2003. (Illus.). (J). *(978-0-439-74269-6(2))* Scholastic, Inc.
Zimmerman, Andrea & Clemesha, David. Dig! Rosenthal, Marc, illus. 2014. (ENG.). 30p. (J). (— 1). bds. 7.99 *(978-0-544-17388-0(0)*, HMH Books For Young Readers) Houghton Mifflin Harcourt Publishing Co.

MACHINERY—HISTORY

The History of Machines: Individual Title Six-Packs. (gr. k-1). 23.00 *(978-0-7635-9079-6(7))* Rigby Education.
Perritano, John. The Revolution in Industry: How Machines Changed America. 2008. (Graphic America Ser.). (ENG., Illus.). 32p. (J). (gr. 3-6). pap. *(978-0-7787-4216-6(4))* Crabtree Publishing Co.
Woods, Michael & Woods, Mary B. Ancient Machines: From Wedges to Waterwheels. 2005. (Ancient Technology Ser.). (Illus.). 96p. (J). (gr. 6-12). 25.26 *(978-0-8225-2994-1(7))* Lerner Publishing Group.

MACHINERY—MODELS

see also Airplanes—Models; Automobiles—Models

Balmer, Alden J. Mousetrap Racers: The Complete Builder's Manual - Science Secrets You'll Need to Win. 2008. (ENG., Illus.). 144p. (gr. 7-18). pap. 14.95 *(978-1-56523-359-1(X)*, 3591D) Fox Chapel Publishing Co., Inc.

MACHINERY IN THE WORKPLACE

Addison, D. R. Cement Mixers at Work. 2009. (Big Trucks Ser.). 24p. (gr. 1-1). 42.50 *(978-1-61511-576-1(5)*, PowerKids Pr.) Rosen Publishing Group, Inc., The.

MACHINES

see Machinery

MACKENZIE RIVER (N.W.T.)

Harris, Tim. The Mackenzie River. 2003. (Rivers of North America Ser.). (Illus.). 32p. (gr. 2-6). lib. bdg. 26.00 *(978-0-8368-3756-8(8)*, Gareth Stevens Learning Library) Stevens, Gareth Publishing LLLP.

MACKINAC ISLAND (MICH.)—FICTION

Declercq, Al, et al. Bemida: A Michigan Sailing Legend. Miles, David, illus. 2014. (ENG.). 32p. (J). (gr. 1-4). 16.99 *(978-1-58536-904-1(7)*, 203553) Sleeping Bear Pr.
Hahn, Cathe. Step Up!, 1 vol. Artley, Bob, illus. 2005. (ENG.). 32p. (J). (gr. k-3). 16.99 *(978-1-58980-214-8(4))* Pelican Publishing Co., Inc.
Panagopoulos, Janie Lynn. A Castle at the Straits. Evans, Laura, illus. 2003. 48p. (J). (gr. 1-6). *(978-0-911872-83-5(3))* Mackinac State Historic Parks.

MCKINLEY, WILLIAM, 1843-1901

Amoroso, Cynthia. William Mckinley. 2008. (Presidents of the U. S. A. Ser.). (ENG., Illus.). 40p. (J). (gr. 3-6). 32.79 *(978-1-60253-053-9(X)*, 200692) Child's World, Inc., The.
Bailey, Diane & Nash, Philip. William McKinley, the 25th President. 2016. (First Look at America's Presidents Ser.). (ENG.). 24p. (J). (gr. -1-3). lib. bdg. 17.95 *(978-1-944102-68-5(X))* Bearport Publishing Co., Inc.
Edge, Laura Bufano. William Mckinley. 2007. (Presidential Leaders Ser.). (Illus.). 112p. (J). (gr. 3-7). lib. bdg. 29.27

(978-0-8225-1508-1(3), Twenty-First Century Bks.) Lerner Publishing Group.
Gunderson, Megan M. William McKinley, 1 vol. 2009. (United States Presidents Ser.). (ENG., Illus.). 40p. (YA). (gr. 3-6). 27.07 (978-1-60453-466-5(4)) ABDO Publishing Co.
Parker, Lewis. How to Draw the Life & Times of William Mckinley. 2009. (Kid's Guide to Drawing the Presidents of the United States of America Ser.). 32p. (gr. 4-4). 50.50 (978-1-61511-167-1(0), PowerKids Pr.) Rosen Publishing Group, Inc., The.
Parker, Lewis K. How to Draw the Life & Times of William McKinley. 2007. (Kid's Guide to Drawing the Presidents of the United States of America Ser.). (Illus.). 32p. (YA). (gr. 2-5). 26.50 (978-1-4042-3001-9(7)) Rosen Publishing Group, Inc., The.
Venezia, Mike. William McKinley. Venezia, Mike, illus. 2006. (Getting to Know the U. S. Presidents Ser.). (ENG., Illus.). 32p. (J). (gr. 3-7). lib. bdg. 28.00 (978-0-516-22629-3(0), Children's Pr.) Scholastic Library Publishing.
Wilson, Antoine. The Assassination of William McKinley. (Library of Political Assassinations Ser.). 64p. 2009. (gr. 5-5). 58.50 (978-1-60853-830-0(3)) 2003. (Illus.). (YA). (gr. 7-12). lib. bdg. 31.95 (978-0-8239-3546-8(9)) Rosen Publishing Group, Inc., The.

MCKINLEY, MOUNT (ALASKA)

Establishment of Mount McKinley Park. (Shorey Historical Ser.). (Illus.). 32p. (J). reprint ed. pap. 10.00 (978-0-8466-0015-2(3), S15) Shorey's Bookstore.
Gill, Shelley. Up on Denali: Alaska's Wild Mountain. Cartwright, Shannon, illus. 2006. (Paws IV Ser.). (ENG.). 32p. (J). (gr. -1-2). pap. 10.99 (978-1-57061-365-4(6), Little Bigfoot) Sasquatch Bks.

MACRAME

Boase, Petra. Friendship Bracelets & Beading Fun: 25 Knotty, Dotty, Stripey & Sparkly Designs to Make! 2014. (ENG., Illus.). 64p. (J). (gr. -1-6). 9.99 (978-1-84322-944-5(7), Armadillo) Anness Publishing GBR. Dist: National Bk. Network.
Hopping, Lucy. Friendship Bracelets: 35 Gorgeous Projects to Make & Give. 2014. (ENG., Illus.). 128p. (J). (gr. 5-11). pap. 14.95 (978-1-78249-107-1(4), CICO Books) Ryland Peters & Small GBR. Dist: WIPRO.
Johnson, Anne Akers. Pulseras Rusticas. 2005. (SPA., Illus.). 32p. (J). (gr. 1). 17.95 (978-968-5528-11-5(X)) Klutz Latino MEX. Dist: Independent Pubs. Group.
Rau, Dana Meachen. Making Knot Projects. Petelinsek, Kathleen, illus. 2016. (How-To Library). (ENG.). 32p. (J). (gr. 3-6). 29.93 (978-1-63471-420-4(2), 208459) Cherry Lake Publishing.
Torres, Laura. Brazaletes de la Amistad. 2005. (SPA., Illus.). 57p. (J). (gr. 3). 17.95 (978-968-5528-05-4(5)) Klutz Latino MEX. Dist: Independent Pubs. Group.

MACY, ANNE SULLIVAN, 1866-1936

see Sullivan, Annie, 1866-1936

MADAGASCAR

Aronin, Miriam. Aye-Aye: An Evil Omen. 2016. (Uncommon Animals Ser.). (ENG.). 32p. (J). (gr. 2-7). pap. 8.95 (978-1-944998-60-8(8)) Bearport Publishing Co., Inc.
Frazel, Ellen. Madagascar. 2013. (Exploring Countries Ser.). (ENG., Illus.). 32p. (J). (gr. 3-7). lib. bdg. 26.95 (978-1-60014-861-3(1), Blastoff! Readers) Bellwether Media.
Gagne, Tammy. We Visit Madagascar. 2012. (J). lib. bdg. 33.95 (978-1-61228-305-0(5)) Mitchell Lane Pubs., Inc.
Heale, Jay & Latif, Zawiah Abdul. Madagascar. 2nd rev. ed. 2008. (Cultures of the World Ser.). 144p. (gr. 6-18). lib. bdg. 42.79 (978-0-7614-3036-0(9), Benchmark Bks.) Marshall Cavendish Corp.
Kabana, Joni. Torina's World: A Child's Life in Madagascar. 2nd ed. 2007. (ENG., Illus.). 52p. (J). 14.95 (978-0-9794771-4-0(X)) ACS, LLC Amica Creative Services.
Kocienda, Genevieve. Madagascar Low Intermediate Book with Online Access. 2014. (ENG., Illus.). 24p. (J). pap. 9.50 (978-1-107-62940-0(3)) Cambridge Univ. Pr.
Oluonye, Mary N. Madagascar. (Country Explorers Ser.). (Illus.). 48p. (gr. 2-4). 2010. (ENG.). (J). pap. 9.95 (978-0-7613-5553-3(7), 1306314, Lerner Pubns.) 2010. (ENG., (J). lib. bdg. 29.27 (978-1-58013-601-3(X), 1306314) 2005. 22.60 (978-1-57505-145-1(1)) Lerner Publishing Group.
Orr, Tamra. Madagascar. 2017. (Enchantment of the World(tm) Ser.). (ENG., Illus.). 144p. (J). lib. bdg. 40.00 (978-0-531-22084-9(2), Children's Pr.) Scholastic Library Publishing.

MADAGASCAR—FICTION

Cunningham, Elaine. Missing in Madagascar. 2006. 32p. 4.50 (978-0-8341-2230-7(8)) Beacon Hill Pr. of Kansas City.
Dennard, Deborah. Lemur Landing: A Story of a Madagascan Dry Tropical Forest. Kest, Kristin, illus. 2005. (Wild Habitats Ser.). (ENG.). 32p. (J). (gr. 1-4). 19.95 (978-1-56899-980-7(1)) Soundprints.
Dennard, Deborah & Kest, Kristin. Lemur Landing: A Story of a Madagascan Dry Tropical Forest. 2005. (Wild Habitats Ser.). (ENG., Illus.). 32p. (J). (gr. 1-4). pap. 6.95 (978-1-56899-979-1(8), S7019) Soundprints.
Frolick, Billy. Madagascar. Golden Books, illus. 2017. (Little Golden Book Ser.). (ENG.). 24p. (J). (-k). 4.99 **(978-1-5247-6768-6(9)**, Golden Bks.) Random Hse. Children's Bks.
Gunby, Stephanie. The Clever Clouds. 2010. 56p. pap. 24.20 (978-1-4269-3902-0(7)) Trafford Publishing.
Lumry, Amanda & Hurwitz, Laura. Adventures of Riley: Mission to Madagascar. McIntyre, Sarah, illus. 2005. 36p. (gr. 2-3). 15.95 (978-0-9748411-2-0(9)) Eaglemont Pr.
Marcy Wirth's Second Grade Class, compiled by. A Journey to Madagascar. 2010. (Illus.). 38p. (YA). pap. 6.25 (978-0-9619407-8-2(6)) Country Messenger Pr. Publishing Group, LLC.
Meredith Books Staff, ed. Madagascar Activity Book & Floor Puzzle. 10p. (J). bds. 12.95 (978-0-696-22701-1(0)) Meredith Bks.
—Madagascar Stencil Activity Book with Stickers. 22p. (J). bds. 12.95 (978-0-696-22702-8(9)) Meredith Bks.

MADELINE (FICTITIOUS CHARACTER)—FICTION

Bemelmans, Ludwig. Madeline. (Madeline Ser.). (ENG.). (J). (gr. -1-k). 2012. 36p. bds. 9.99 (978-0-670-01407-1(9), Viking Books for Young Readers) 2007. (Illus.). 48p. 9.99 (978-0-14-240871-1(9), Puffin Books) Penguin Young Readers Group.
—Madeline: Activity Book with Stickers. 2012. (Madeline Ser.). (ENG.). 32p. (J). (gr. k-3). act. bk. ed. 7.99 (978-0-448-45903-5(5), Grosset & Dunlap) Penguin Young Readers Group.
—Madeline's Christmas, 1 vol. Bemelmans, Ludwig, illus. 2007. (Madeline Ser.). (ENG., Illus.). 15p. (J). (gr. -1-2). 9.99 (978-0-14-240897-1(2), Puffin Books) Penguin Young Readers Group.
Marciano, John Bemelmans. Madeline & the Cats of Rome. 2008. (Madeline Ser.). (ENG.). 48p. (J). (gr. 1-3). 17.99 (978-0-670-06297-3(9), Viking Books for Young Readers) Penguin Young Readers Group.
—Madeline at the White House. (Madeline Ser.). (ENG., (J). (gr. -1-2). 2016. Illus.). 48p. 8.99 (978-1-101-99780-2(X), Puffin Books) 2011. 45p. 17.99 (978-0-670-01228-2(9), Viking Books for Young Readers) Penguin Young Readers Group.
—Madeline at the White House. 2016. (Madeline Ser.). lib. bdg. 19.65 (978-0-606-38845-0(1)) Turtleback Bks.

MADISON, DOLLEY, 1768-1849

Brown, Don. Dolley Madison Saves George Washington. Brown, Don, illus. 2007. (ENG., Illus.). 32p. (J). (gr. -1-3). 16.00 (978-0-618-41199-3(2)) Houghton Mifflin Harcourt Publishing Co.
Carosella, Melissa. Dolley Madison: First Lady of the United States, 1 vol. 2011. (Primary Source Readers Ser.). (ENG.). 32p. (J). (gr. 4-4). pap. 8.99 (978-1-4333-1504-6(1)) Teacher Created Materials, Inc.
Figley, Marty Rhodes. Washington Is Burning. Orback, Craig, illus. (On My Own History Ser.). 48p. (gr. 2-4). 2007. (ENG.). per. 6.95 (978-0-8225-6050-0(X), First Avenue Editions) 2006. (J). lib. bdg. 25.26 (978-1-57505-875-7(8)) Lerner Publishing Group.
Kent, Zachary. Dolley Madison: The Enemy Cannot Frighten a Free People. 2010. (Americans—the Spirit of a Nation Ser.). (Illus.). 128p. (J). (gr. 7-12). lib. bdg. 33.27 (978-0-7660-3356-6(2)) Enslow Pubs., Inc.
Krull, Kathleen. Dolley Madison: Parties Can Be Patriotic! Fancher, Lou & Johnson, Steve, illus. 2015. (Women Who Broke the Rules Ser.). (ENG.). 48p. (J). (gr. 1-4). 16.99 (978-0-8027-3793-9(5), 9780802737939, Bloomsbury USA Childrens) Bloomsbury Publishing USA.
Larkin, Tanya. What Was Cooking in Dolley Madison's White House? 2009. (Cooking Throughout American History Ser.). 24p. (gr. 3-3). 42.50 (978-1-61511-950-9(7), PowerKids Pr.) Rosen Publishing Group, Inc., The.
Mattern, Joanne. Dolley Madison, 1 vol. 2008. (First Ladies Set 1 Ser.). (ENG., Illus.). 32p. (YA). (gr. 1-4). 27.07 (978-1-59928-798-0(6)) ABDO Publishing Co.
Shulman, Holly. Dolley Madison: Her Life, Letters, & Legacy. 2009. (Library of American Lives & Times Ser.). 112p. (gr. 5-5). 69.20 (978-1-60853-477-7(4)) Rosen Publishing Group, Inc., The.
Shulman, Holly Cowan & Mattern, David B. Dolley Madison: Her Life, Letters, & Legacy. 2005. (Library of American Lives & Times). (Illus.). 112p. (YA). (gr. 4-7). lib. bdg. 34.60 (978-0-8239-5749-1(7)) Rosen Publishing Group, Inc., The.
Weatherly, Myra. Dolley Madison: America's First Lady. 2004. (Notable Americans Ser.). (Illus.). 128p. (YA). (gr. 6-12). 23.95 (978-1-883846-95-4(1), First Biographies) Reynolds, Morgan Inc.

MADISON, JAMES, 1751-1836

Adler, David A. & Adler, Michael S. A Picture Book of Dolley & James Madison. Himler, Ronald, illus. 2009. (ENG.). 32p. (J). (gr. -1-3). 17.95 (978-0-8234-2009-4(4)) Holiday Hse., Inc.
Bramwell, Neil D. James Madison: A MyReportLinks. Com Book. 2003. (Presidents Ser.). (Illus.). 48p. (J). (gr. 4-10). lib. bdg. 25.26 (978-0-7660-5129-4(3), MyReportLinks.com Bks.) Enslow Pubs., Inc.
Britton, Arthur K. 20 Fun Facts about James Madison. 2017. (Fun Fact File: Founding Fathers Ser.). 32p. (gr. 2-3). pap. 63.00 **(978-1-5382-0273-9(5))** Stevens, Gareth Publishing LLLP.
Dooling, Sandra. James Madison. 2012. (Jr. Graphic Founding Fathers Ser.). (ENG., Illus.). 24p. (J). (gr. 3-6). pap. 10.60 (978-1-4488-7992-2(2)); lib. bdg. 25.25 (978-1-4488-7898-7(5)) Rosen Publishing Group, Inc., The. (PowerKids Pr.).
Elish, Dan. James Madison. 2007. (Presidents & Their Times Ser.). (Illus.). 96p. (gr. 6-7). lib. bdg. 34.21 (978-0-7614-2432-1(6), Benchmark Bks.) Marshall Cavendish Corp.
Gregory, Josh & Bose, Meenekshi. James Madison: The 4th President. 2015. (First Look at America's Presidents Ser.). (ENG.). 24p. (J). (gr. -1-3). lib. bdg. 23.93 (978-1-62724-559-3(6)) Bearport Publishing Co., Inc.
Gunderson, Megan M. James Madison, 1 vol. 2009. (United States Presidents Ser.). (ENG., Illus.). 40p. (YA). (gr. 3-6). 27.07 (978-1-60453-465-8(6)) ABDO Publishing Co.
Kent, Zachary. James Madison: Creating a Nation. 2004. (America's Founding Fathers Ser.). (Illus.). 128p. (J). lib. bdg. 26.60 (978-0-7660-2180-8(7)) Enslow Pubs., Inc.
Kozleski, Lisa. James Madison. 2004. (Childhoods of the Presidents Ser.). (Illus.). 48p. (J). (gr. 4-18). lib. bdg. 17.95 (978-1-59084-269-0(3)) Mason Crest.
Lusted, Marcia Amidon. Revolution & the New Nation: 1750-Early 1800s. 2007. (Presidents of the United States Ser.). (Illus.). 48p. (J). (gr. 4-7). lib. bdg. 29.05 (978-1-59036-739-1(1)); per. 10.95 (978-1-59036-740-7(5)) Weigl Pubs., Inc.
Maloof, Torrey. James Madison & the Making of the United States. 2017. (Primary Source Readers Ser.). (Illus.). 32p. (J). (gr. 4-5). pap. 8.99 (978-1-4938-3795-3(8)) Teacher Created Materials, Inc.
McDowell, Pamela. James Madison. 2015. (Padres Fundadores Ser.). (SPA.). (J). lib. bdg. 27.13 (978-1-48196-2796-4(0), AV2 by Weigl) Weigl Pubs., Inc.
Mitchell, Barbara. Father of the Constitution: A Story about James Madison. Tavoularis, Alex, illus. 2003. (Creative Minds Biographies Ser.). (ENG.). 64p. (gr. 4-8). 22.60 (978-1-57505-182-6(6), Carolrhoda Bks.); pap. 8.95 (978-1-57505-607-4(0)) Lerner Publishing Group.
Mulhall, Jill K. James Madison, 1 vol. 2005. (Primary Source Readers Ser.). (ENG.). 24p. (J). (gr. 4-4). pap. 8.99 (978-0-7439-8908-4(2)) Shell Educational Publishing.
Randolph, Ryan. Marbury V. Madison: The New Supreme Court Gets More Powers. 2009. (Life in the New American Nation Ser.). 32p. (gr. 4-4). 47.90 (978-1-61514-277-4(0)) Rosen Publishing Group, Inc., The.
Roberts, Jeremy. James Madison. 2004. (Presidential Leaders Ser.). (Illus.). 112p. (J). (gr. 6-12). lib. bdg. 29.27 (978-0-8225-0823-6(0)) Lerner Publishing Group.
Schmidt, Roderic. How to Draw the Life & Times of James Madison. (Kid's Guide to Drawing the Presidents of the United States of America Ser.). 2009. 32p. (gr. 4-4). 50.50 (978-1-61511-148-0(4), PowerKids Pr.) 2006. (YA). (gr. 2-5). 26.50 (978-1-4042-2981-5(7)) Rosen Publishing Group, Inc., The.
Somervill, Barbara A. The Life & Times of James Madison. 2008. (Profiles in American History Ser.). (Illus.). 48p. (J). (gr. 4-7). lib. bdg. 29.95 (978-1-58415-530-0(2)) Mitchell Lane Pubs., Inc.
Wittekind, Erika. James Madison's Presidency. 2016. (Presidential Powerhouses Ser.). (ENG., Illus.). 104p. (J). (gr. 6-12). 35.99 (978-1-4677-7929-6(6)); 53.32 (978-1-4677-8599-0(7), Lerner Pubns.) Lerner Publishing Group.

MADONNA

see Mary, Blessed Virgin, Saint

MAFIA

Bockmann, Melanie Scherencel. In the Shadow of the Mob/Melanie Scherencel Bockmann. 2011. (J). (978-0-8280-2583-6(5)) Review & Herald Publishing Assn.

MAFIA—FICTION

Blumenthal, Deborah. Mafia Girl. 2014. (ENG.). 272p. (YA). (gr. 8-12). 16.99 (978-0-8075-4911-7(8)) Whitman, Albert & Co.
Côté, Denis. La Machination du Scorpion Noir. 2004. (Mon Roman Ser.). (FRE.). 160p. (J). (gr. 2). pap. (978-2-89021-667-9(5)) Diffusion du livre Mirabel (DLM).
Cox, M. M. Accidental Mobster. 2012. 252p. pap. (978-1-927134-89-4(7)) Bluewood Publishing, Ltd.
Delany, Shannon. Destiny & Deception: A 13 to Life Novel. 2012. (13 to Life Ser.: 4). (ENG.). 304p. (YA). (gr. 7). pap. 17.99 (978-0-312-62446-0(8), 9780312624460, St. Martin's Griffin) St. Martin's Pr.
Delany, Shannon & Redgrave, Saoirse. Secrets & Shadows: A 13 to Life Novel. 2011. (13 to Life Ser.: 2). (ENG.). 320p. (YA). (gr. 7-18). pap. 9.99 (978-0-312-60915-3(9), 9780312609153, St. Martin's Griffin) St. Martin's Pr.
Doyle, Catherine. Vendetta. 2015. (ENG.). 352p. (J). (gr. 9). 18.99 (978-0-545-69982-2(7)) Scholastic, Inc.
Green, Tim. Football Hero. (Football Genius Ser.: 2). (ENG.). (J). (gr. 3-7). 2009. 320p. pap. 6.99 (978-0-06-112276-7(9)) 2008. (Illus.). 304p. 16.99 (978-0-06-112274-3(2)) HarperCollins Pubs.
—Football Hero. l.t. ed. 2008. (YA). 23.95 (978-1-4104-1116-7(8)) Thorndike Pr.
Shakespeare, William & Appignanesi, Richard. Romeo & Juliet. Leong, Sonia, illus. 2007. (ENG.). 208p. (J). (gr. 2-8). pap. 14.95 (978-0-8109-9325-9(2), Abrams Bks. for Young Readers) Abrams, Inc.
Trenchard, Robert. The Famous Frog Fiasco. 2008. 265p. (J). pap. 13.99 (978-0-615-20974-6(2)) Soxwings Publishing.

MAGALHAES, FERNAO DE, -1521

Burnett, Betty. Ferdinand Magellan: The First Voyage Around the World. (Library of Explorers & Exploration Ser.). 112p. (gr. 5-8). 2009. 66.50 (978-1-60853-602-3(5)) 2003. (Illus.). (J). lib. bdg. 34.60 (978-0-8239-3617-5(1)) Rosen Publishing Group, Inc., The. (Rosen Reference).
Crompton, Samuel Willard. Ferdinand Magellan & the Quest to Circle the Globe. Goetzmann, William H., ed. 2005. (Explorers of New Lands Ser.). (Illus.). 110p. (J). (gr. 5-8). lib. bdg. 30.00 (978-0-7910-8608-7(9)) Facts On File, Inc.
Fandel, Jennifer. Ferdinand Magellan. 2003. (Explorers of the Unknown Ser.). (J). (978-1-58417-036-5(0)); pap. (978-1-58417-099-0(9)) Lake Street Pubs.
Gould, Jane H. Ferdinand Magellan. 2013. (Jr. Graphic Famous Explorers Ser.). (ENG., Illus.). 24p. (J). (gr. 3-6). pap. 10.60 (978-1-4777-0123-2(0)); lib. bdg. 25.25 (978-1-4777-0069-3(2)) Rosen Publishing Group, Inc., The. (PowerKids Pr.).
Hoogenboom, Lynn. Ferdinand Magellan. 2009. (Primary Source Library of Famous Explorers Ser.). 24p. (gr. 4-4). 42.50 (978-1-60854-120-1(7), PowerKids Pr.) Rosen Publishing Group, Inc., The.
Koestler-Grack, Rachel A. Ferdinand Magellan. 2009. (Great Explorers Ser.). (Illus.). 112p. (gr. 6-12). 30.00 (978-1-60413-422-3(4), Chelsea Hse.) Facts On File, Inc.
Kramer, Sydelle. Who Was Ferdinand Magellan? Wolf, Elizabeth & Harrison, Nancy, illus. 2004. (Who Was? Ser.). (ENG.). 112p. (J). (gr. 3-7). pap. 5.99 (978-0-448-43105-5(X), Grosset & Dunlap) Penguin Young Readers Group.
—Who Was Ferdinand Magellan? Wolf, Elizabeth, illus. 2004. (Who Was... ? Ser.). 105p. (J). (gr. 3-7). 12.65 (978-0-7569-4615-9(8)) Perfection Learning Corp.
Landau, Elaine. Ferdinand Magellan. 2005. (History Maker Bios Ser.). (Illus.). 48p. (J). (gr. 3-7). lib. bdg. 26.60 (978-0-8225-2942-2(4), Lerner Pubns.) Lerner Publishing Group.
Marsh, Carole. Ferdinand Magellan, World Voyager. 2004. 12p. (gr. k-4). 2.95 (978-0-635-02373-5(3)) Gallopade International.
Meyer, Susan. Ferdinand Magellan. 2016. (Spotlight on Explorers & Colonization Ser.). 48p. (J). (gr. 6-6). pap. 11.75 (978-1-4777-8800-4(X)) Rosen Publishing Group, Inc., The.
Molzahn, Arlene Bourgeois. Ferdinand Magellan: First Explorer Around the World. 2003. (Illus.). 48p. (J). (gr. 1-4). lib. bdg. 23.93 (978-0-7660-2068-9(1)) Enslow Pubs., Inc.
Ollhoff, Jim. Ferdinand Magellan. 2013. (Great Explorers Ser.). 32p. (J). (gr. 5-9). lib. bdg. 27.07 (978-1-61783-967-2(1), Abdo & Daughters) ABDO Publishing Co.
Petrie, Kristin. Ferdinand Magellan, 1 vol. 2007. (Explorers Set 2 Ser.). (ENG., Illus.). 32p. (gr. 4-7). 27.07 (978-1-59679-744-4(4), Checkerboard Library) ABDO Publishing Co.
Powell, Marie. Explore with Ferdinand Magellan. 2014. (ENG., Illus.). 32p. (J). (978-0-7787-1425-5(X)) Crabtree Publishing Co.
Waldman, Stuart. Magellan's World. Manchess, Gregory, illus. 2007. (Great Explorers Ser.). (ENG.). 48p. (J). (gr. 4-8). 22.95 (978-1-931414-19-7(X), 9781931414197) Mikaya Pr.
Whiting, Jim. Ferdinand Magellan. 2006. (What's So Great About... ? Ser.). (Illus.). 32p. (J). (gr. 2-4). lib. bdg. 25.70 (978-1-58415-480-8(2)) Mitchell Lane Pubs., Inc.

MAGALHAES, FERNAO DE, -1521—FICTION

Johnson, Vargie. Ferdinand Magellan the Explorer: What Made Them Famous? 2006. 156p. (J). per. 15.00 (978-1-931195-92-8(7)) KiwE Publishing, Ltd.

MAGAZINES

see Periodicals

MAGELLAN, FERDINAND, -1521

see Magalhaes, Fernao de, -1521

MAGIC

Here are entered works on the use of charms, spells, etc., believed to have supernatural power to produce or prevent a particular result considered unobtainable by natural means. Works on performance of sleight of hand or tricks involving various types of illusion for purposes of entertainment are entered under Magic Tricks.

see also Card Tricks; Occultism

Andrews, Ted. Faerie Charms. 2005. (Young Person's School of Magic & Mystery Ser.: Vol. 6). (Illus.). 255p. (YA). (gr. 8-12). 18.95 (978-1-888767-42-1(1)) Dragonhawk Publishing.
Arnold, Laurie B. Hello There, We've Been Waiting for You! 2013. (ENG.). 176p. (J). (gr. 3-8). pap. 9.95 (978-1-935212-51-5(6), Prospecta Pr.) Easton Studio Pr., LLC.
Austin, John. Labcraft Wizards: Magical Projects & Experiments. 2016. (ENG., Illus.). 256p. (J). (gr. 4). pap. 16.99 (978-1-61373-621-0(5)) Chicago Review Pr., Inc.
Barnhart, Norm. Magic Manuals. 2011. (Magic Manuals Ser.). (ENG.). 32p. (gr. 3-4). lib. bdg. 111.96 (978-1-62065-972-4(7), Edge Bks.) Capstone Press of Coughlan Cos.
Beahm, George. The Whimsic Alley Book of Spells: Mythical Incantations for Wizards of All Ages. Goldin, Stan, ed. 2007. (ENG., Illus.). 192p. (YA). pap. 14.95 (978-1-57174-535-4(1)) Hampton Roads Publishing Co., Inc.
Blackstone, Gay. Around the House Magic. (Illus.). (J). (978-1-59093-000-7(2), Eager Minds Pr.) Warehousing & Fulfillment Specialists, LLC (WFS, LLC).
Blaine, Victor. Mi Trineo / My Sled, 1 vol. 2015. (¡Mírame, Ahí Voy! / Watch Me Go! Ser.). (ENG & SPA.). 24p. (J). 23.60 (978-1-4994-0284-1(8), PowerKids Pr.) Rosen Publishing Group, Inc., The.
Chorba, April & Klutz Editors. Prankster Magic: With Real Fake Gum. 2015. (ENG., Illus.). 60p. (J). (gr. 3). pap. 12.99 (978-0-545-80545-2(7)) Klutz.
Denne, Ben. Magia Para Todos. 2005. (Titles in Spanish Ser.). (SPA.). 32p. (J). pap. 8.95 (978-0-7460-6394-1(6), Usborne) EDC Publishing.
Dooling, Sandra. Sorcerers, Spells, & Magic!, 1 vol., 1. 2014. (Jr. Graphic Monster Stories Ser.). (ENG.). 24p. (J). (gr. 3-6). 26.25 (978-1-4777-6211-0(6), PowerKids Pr.) Rosen Publishing Group, Inc., The.
Dorling Kindersley Publishing Staff. Children's Book of Magic. 2014. (ENG.). 128p. (J). (gr. 2-5). 19.99 (978-1-4654-2459-4(8), DK Children) Dorling Kindersley Publishing, Inc.
Eldin, Peter. Great Box of Magic. 2008. 48p. (gr. 2-10). pap. 34.95 (978-1-905339-03-7(8), Red Kite Bks.) Haldane Mason, Ltd. GBR. Dist: Trans-Atlantic Pubns., Inc.
Hamilton, John. Magic Rings & Other Magical Things, 1 vol. 2006. (Fantasy & Folklore Ser.). (ENG., Illus.). 32p. (gr. 5-8). 27.07 (978-1-59679-337-8(6), Abdo & Daughters) ABDO Publishing Co.
—Witches, 1 vol. 2007. (World of Horror Ser.). (ENG., Illus.). 32p. (gr. 4-8). 27.07 (978-1-59928-776-8(5), Abdo & Daughters) ABDO Publishing Co.
Hayward, Mark Brauner. I'm a Magician's Helper. 2012. 24p. pap. 17.99 (978-1-4772-4107-3(8)) AuthorHouse.
Horsley, Kathryn. Investigating Magic. 2016. (Understanding the Paranormal Ser.). 48p. (J). (gr. 5-5). lib. bdg. 26.85 (978-1-68048-575-2(X), Britannica Educational Publishing) Rosen Publishing Group, Inc., The.
Kallmeyer-Mehlhorn, Margarete. The Wondrous Ball of Yarn: A Facsimile of the Previously Unpublished Manuscript. 2008.Tr. of Wunderknaul. (ENG & GER., Illus.). 40p. 41.00 (978-0-9745168-2-0(1)) Cotsen Occasional Pr.
Kiraithe, Jackie. Magic Links: Manual. Gonzales, Linda, ed. 200p. (J). 48.00 (978-0-942787-95-5(1)) Binet International.
Kronzek, Allan Zola & Kronzek, Elizabeth. Diccionario del Mago. Paula Vicens, Ines Belasategui, tr. 2005. (Escritura desatada Ser.). (SPA.). 368p. (J). 17.95 (978-970-710-056-5(7)) Ediciones B ESP. Dist: Independent Pubs. Group.
Marsico, Katie. Magic Monsters: From Witches to Goblins. 2017. (Monster Mania Ser.). (ENG.). 32p. (J). (gr. 2-5). 12.99 **(978-1-5124-3821-5(9)**, Lerner Pubns.); 39.99 **(978-1-5124-3822-2(7)**, Lerner Pubns.); 39.99 **(978-1-5124-2815-5(9)**, Lerner Pubns.); (Illus.). 26.65 (978-1-5124-2595-6(8)) Lerner Publishing Group.
Maurer, Tracy Nelson. Chilling Ancient Curses. 2017. (Searchlight Books (tm) — Fear Fest Ser.). (ENG.). 32p. (J). (gr. 3-5). pap. 9.99 **(978-1-5124-5603-5(9))**; (Illus.). 30.65 **(978-1-5124-3403-3(5)**, Lerner Pubns.) Lerner Publishing Group.
Merlin, Master. Wizardology: A Guide to Wizards of the World. Steer, Dugald A., ed. 2007. (Ologies Ser.). (ENG., Illus.). 40p. (J). (gr. 3-7). 14.99 (978-0-7636-3710-1(6)) Candlewick Pr.
Muten, Burleigh. Goddesses: A World of Myth & Magic. Guay, Rebecca, illus. 2003. (ENG.). 80p. (J). 19.99 (978-1-84148-075-6(4)) Barefoot Bks., Inc.
Orme, Helen. Magic. 2011. (Fact to Fiction Grafx Ser.). (ENG., Illus.). 36p. (J). (gr. 4-7). lib. bdg. 17.45 (978-1-61384-020-7(9)) Perfection Learning Corp.
Place, Robert M. Magic & Alchemy. 2009. (Mysteries, Legends, & Unexplained Phenomena Ser.). (Illus.). 144p.

MNO

(YA). (gr. 7-12). 29.95 (978-0-7910-9390-0(5)) Facts On File, Inc.

Price, Sean Stewart. Vanished! Magic Tricks & Great Escapes, 1 vol. 2010. (Culture in Action Ser.). (ENG.). 32p. (gr. 3-6). 30.65 (978-1-4109-3918-0(9), NA-r) Heinemann-Raintree.

Roleff, Tamara L., ed. Black Magic & Witches. 2003. (Illus.). 127p. (J). pap. 18.70 (978-0-7377-1319-0(4), Greenhaven Pr., Inc.) Cengage Gale.

Ross, Brad. Hocus Pocus Al I Mi Choo. Arnold, Michael, illus. 2012. 62p. pap. 19.95 (978-0-9834201-0-1(6)) Illusionary Magic LLC.

Savage, Candace & Savage, C. Wizards: An Amazing Journey Through the Last Great Age of Magic. 2003. (ENG., Illus.). 80p. (J). (gr. 4-7). 17.95 (978-1-55054-943-0(X)) Greystone Books Ltd. CAN. Dist: Publishers Group West (PGW).

Scott, Carey. Magic & Mystery. 2010. (Unpredictable Nature Ser.). (Illus.). 48p. (J). (gr. 3-18). lib. bdg. 19.95 (978-1-4222-2001-6(X)) Mason Crest.

Top That. Fun Kits Amazing Magic. 2008. (978-1-84666-592-9(2)) Top That! Publishing PLC.

Walton, Rick & Walton, Ann. Magical Mischief: Jokes That Shock & Amaze. Gable, Brian, illus. 2005. (Make Me Laugh! Ser.). 32p. (J). (gr. k-3). lib. bdg. 19.93 (978-1-57505-664-7(X)) Lerner Publishing Group.

Ytreeide, Arnold. Ishtar's Odyssey: A Storybook for Advent, 1 vol. 2015. 176p. (J). pap. 15.99 (978-0-8254-4393-0(8)) Kregel Pubns.

MAGIC—FICTION

Abbott, Tony. City in the Clouds. Jessell, Tim, illus. 2004. (Secrets of Droon Ser.: No. 4). 88p. 15.00 (978-0-7569-3930-4(5)) Perfection Learning Corp.

—The Hidden Stairs & the Magic Carpet. Jessell, Tim, illus. 2004. (Secrets of Droon Ser.: No. 1). 80p. (gr. 2-5). 15.00 (978-0-7569-3939-7(9)) Perfection Learning Corp.

—The Magic Escapes. Jessell, Tim, illus. 2004. (Secrets of Droon Ser.: No. 1). 161p. (gr. 2-5). 16.00 (978-0-7569-3944-1(5)) Perfection Learning Corp.

—The Moon Scroll. Jessell, Tim, illus. 2004. (Secrets of Droon Ser.: No. 15). 129p. (gr. 2-5). 15.00 (978-0-7569-3946-5(1)) Perfection Learning Corp.

—The Riddle of Zorfendorf Castle. Merrell, David, illus. 2005. (Secrets of Droon Ser.: No. 25). 124p. (J). lib. bdg. 15.38 (978-1-4242-0310-9(4)) Fitzgerald Bks.

ABDO Publishing Company Staff. Fairy Realm - 10 Titles. 2007. (Fairy Realm Ser.). (ENG., Illus.). 110p. 256.50 (978-1-59961-322-2(0)) Spotlight.

—Magic Readers. 2014. (Magic Readers Ser.: 18). (ENG.). 24p. (J). (gr. 5-9). lib. bdg. 435.78 (978-1-62402-053-7(4)) Magic Wagon.

—Meri's Mirror. 2014. (Meri's Mirror Ser.: 4). 80p. (J). (gr. 2-5). lib. bdg. 108.28 (978-1-62402-007-0(0), Calico Chapter Bks) Magic Wagon.

Abrahams, Peter. Outlaws of Sherwood Street: Stealing from the Rich. 2013. (ENG.). 320p. (J). (gr. 5). 7.99 (978-0-14-242438-4(2), Puffin Books) Penguin Young Readers Group.

Abrahamson, Jean. Manners Are Magic. 2005. (Illus.). 48p. 6.99 (978-1-57860-231-5(9)) Clerisy Pr.

Abrahamson, Ruth Ann. The Adventures of Magic Cookie Bean: A Precocious Calico Shares Christian-Principled Tales; Purrfect for Ages 5 & Up! 2010. 24p. pap. 10.95 (978-1-4497-0640-1(1), WestBow Pr.) Author Solutions, Inc.

—Paris & the Purple Purse: Continuing Adventures of Magic Cookie Bean. 2011. 40p. (gr. 1-2). pap. 13.95 (978-1-4497-1665-3(2), WestBow Pr.) Author Solutions, Inc.

Abromovitz, Jaime. Zazzy-Q Ding-A-Ling: Ding-A-Lings: the Magic Wand. 2004. (Illus.). (J). per. 9.95 (978-0-9762587-2-8(2)) StoryGirl Productions, LLC.

Abshire, Lisa D. Sam's Magical Day. 2006. 48p. pap. 16.95 (978-1-4241-1484-9(5)) PublishAmerica, Inc.

Adams, Alane. The Red Sun. 2015. (Legends of Orkney Ser.). (ENG., Illus.). 346p. (YA). pap. 17.00 (978-1-940716-24-4(1)) SparkPr. (a Bks.parks Imprint).

Adams, Jackie. Without a Blink. 2008. 40p. (J). 10.99 (978-0-9800327-0-3(9)) Speranza's Pr.

Addino, Victoria. Sadie's Wish: Three Little Elves. Garafalo, Beatrice, illus. 2012. 32p. (-18). pap. 24.95 (978-1-4626-9907-0(3)) America Star Bks.

Adler, David A. Young Cam Jansen & the Magic Bird Mystery. Natti, Susanna, illus. 2013. (Young Cam Jansen Ser.: 18). (ENG.). 32p. (J). (gr. 1-3). pap. 3.99 (978-0-448-46613-2(9), Penguin Young Readers) Penguin Young Readers Group.

Agee, Jon. Milo's Hat Trick. 2017. (ENG., Illus.). 40p. (J). (gr. k-3). 17.99 **(978-0-7352-2987-7(2)**, Dial Bks) Penguin Young Readers Group.

Agraso, Alberto & Dojeiji, Mony. Je Suis Heureuse. Agraso, Alberto, illus. 2013. (Illus.). 36p. pap. (978-1-927803-01-1(2)) Walking for Peace Publishing.

—Soy Feliz. 2012. 36p. pap. 14.95 (978-1-62141-690-6(9)) Booklocker.com, Inc.

Aguiar, Nadia. The Great Wave of Tamarind. 2017. (Book of Tamarind Ser.: 3). (ENG.). 384p. (J). 16.99 (978-0-312-38031-1(3), 9780312380311) Feiwel & Friends.

Ahdieh, Renée. The Rose & the Dagger. (Wrath & the Dawn Ser.). (ENG., Illus.). (YA). (gr. 7). 2017. 448p. pap. 10.99 (978-0-14-751386-1(3), Speak) 2016. 432p. 17.99 (978-0-399-17162-8(2), G.P. Putnam's Sons Books for Young Readers) Penguin Young Readers Group.

—The Rose & the Dagger. 2017. (Wrath & the Dawn Ser.: 2). lib. bdg. 22.10 **(978-0-606-40106-7(7))** Turtleback Bks.

Ahlers, Oly. Following My Magical Dream, 1 vol. 2010. 48p. pap. 16.95 (978-1-61582-758-9(7)) America Star Bks.

Ahour, Paravish. All Children of the World Smile in the Same Language: Iran, the Cradle of Civilization. 2006. (Illus.). 103p. (J). (gr. 4-7). per. 16.95 (978-1-60002-015-5(1), 3593) Mountain Valley Publishing, LLC.

Aiken, Joan. A Necklace of Raindrops & Other Stories. Hawkes, Kevin, illus. 2003. 84p. (J). (gr. 1-5). 13.15 (978-0-7569-5686-8(2)) Perfection Learning Corp.

—The Serial Garden. 2012. (ENG.). 320p. (J). (gr. 4). pap. 16.00 (978-1-931520-82-9(8), Big Mouth Hse.) Small Beer Pr.

Alcántara, Ricardo. Mauro Ojos Brillantes. 9th ed. 2003. (SPA., Illus.). 48p. (978-84-236-2865-0(5), ED6279) Edebé ESP. Dist: Lectorum Pubns., Inc.

Alcantara, Ricardo. Tomas y el Lapiz Magico. Gusti, illus. 2007. (SPA.). 46p. per. 10.50 (978-84-263-4829-6(7)) Vives, Luis Editorial (Edelvives) ESP. Dist: Lectorum Pubns., Inc.

Aldrick, Shirley H. F. Tobias & the Pale, Pale Leprechaun. 2009. 52p. pap. 19.50 (978-1-60693-959-8(9), Strategic Bk. Publishing) Strategic Book Publishing & Rights Agency (SBPRA).

Alexander, Alma. Gift of the Unmage. 2007. (Worldweavers Ser.: Bk. 1). (ENG.). 400p. (YA). (gr. 7-12). 16.99 (978-0-06-083955-0(4)) HarperCollins Pubs.

—Spellspam. 2008. (Worldweavers Ser.: Bk. 2). (YA). (gr. 7-18). (ENG.). 448p. 17.99 (978-0-06-083958-1(9)); 437p. lib. bdg. 18.89 (978-0-06-083959-8(7)) HarperCollins Pubs. (Eos).

Alexander, Annette M. Snow Magic & the Sad Little Christmas Tree. 2011. (Illus.). 32p. 14.66 (978-1-4567-7182-9(5)) AuthorHouse.

Alexander, Lloyd. The Black Cauldron 50th Anniversary Edition. 2015. (Chronicles of Prydain Ser.: 2). (ENG.). 224p. (J). (gr. 3-7). 25.99 (978-1-62779-323-0(2), 9781627793230, Holt, Henry & Co. Bks. For Young Readers) Holt, Henry & Co.

—The High King. 2006. (Chronicles of Prydain: Bk. 5). (Illus.). 253p. (gr. 3-7). 17.00 (978-0-7569-6816-8(X)) Perfection Learning Corp.

—The Rope Trick. 2004. (ENG.). 208p. (J). (gr. 3-7). reprint ed. pap. 7.99 (978-0-14-240119-4(6), Puffin Books) Penguin Young Readers Group.

Alexander, Michael. Until Wishes Are Fulfilled II: Alec's Story. 2007. 204p. per. 15.50 (978-1-84426-468-1(8)) Upfront Publishing Ltd. GBR. Dist: Printondemand-worldwide.com.

Alexander, R. C. Unfamiliar Magic. 2011. (ENG.). 368p. (J). (gr. 3-7). pap. 8.99 (978-0-375-85855-0(5), Yearling) Random Hse. Children's Bks.

Alexander, Susanne L. Adventures of the Pixies of Penny Brook Village: Reeza's Revenge. 2007. 174p. (J). pap. 12.95 (978-0-7414-4292-5(2)) Infinity Publishing.

Alexander, William. Goblin Secrets. (ENG., Illus.). (J). (gr. 3-7). 2013. 256p. pap. 7.99 (978-1-4424-2727-3(2)) 2012. 240p. 16.99 (978-1-4424-2726-6(4)) McElderry, Margaret K. Bks. (McElderry, Margaret K. Bks.).

Aliaga, Roberto. A Night Time Story. 2012. (ENG., Illus.). 24p. (J). (gr. k-2). (978-84-15241-98-0(4)) D P & G Military Pubs.

Alikhan, Salima. The Pied Piper of Austin, 1 vol. Alikhan, Salima, illus. 2009. (ENG., Illus.). 32p. (J). (gr. k-3). 16.99 (978-1-58980-629-0(8)) Pelican Publishing Co., Inc.

Allan, Delores. Magical Moments with Roy & Toni: Come on Lets Go. 2011. 24p. (gr. 1-2). pap. 12.79 (978-1-4634-0950-0(8)) AuthorHouse.

—Magical Moments with Roy & Toni: Do You Ever Wonder. 2012. 24p. pap. 17.99 (978-1-4772-8910-5(0)) AuthorHouse.

Allen, Elise & Stanford, Halle. Autumn's Secret Gift. Pooler, Paige, illus. 2014. (Enchanted Sisters Ser.). (ENG.). 128p. (J). (gr. 2-4). pap. 5.99 (978-1-61963-254-7(3), 9781619632547, Bloomsbury USA Childrens) Bloomsbury Publishing USA.

—Spring's Sparkle Sleepover. Pooler, Paige, illus. 2015. (Enchanted Sisters Ser.). (ENG.). 128p. (J). (gr. 2-4). 15.99 (978-1-61963-296-7(9), 9781619632967); pap. 5.99 (978-1-61963-269-1(1), 9781619632691) Bloomsbury Publishing USA. (Bloomsbury USA Childrens).

—Summer's Friendship Games. Pooler, Paige, illus. 2015. (Enchanted Sisters Ser.). (ENG.). 128p. (J). (gr. 2-4). 15.99 (978-1-61963-271-4(3), 9781619632714, Bloomsbury USA Childrens) Bloomsbury Publishing USA.

—Winter's Flurry Adventure. Pooler, Paige, illus. 2014. (Enchanted Sisters Ser.). (ENG.). 128p. (YA). (gr. 2-4). pap. 5.99 (978-1-61963-267-7(5), 9781619632677, Bloomsbury USA Childrens) Bloomsbury Publishing USA.

—Winter's Flurry Adventure. Pooler, Paige, illus. 2014. (Enchanted Sisters Ser.: 2). (YA). lib. bdg. 16.00 (978-0-606-36217-7(7)) Turtleback Bks.

Allen, F. M. Brayhard. 2009. 268p. pap. 30.95 (978-1-4092-7639-5(2)) Lulu Pr., Inc.

Allman, Joy. Hailey's Magic Stone. 2010. (ENG., Illus.). 32p. pap. 12.99 (978-1-4389-1264-6(1)) AuthorHouse.

Allman-Varty, Faye. The Kitten Tales of Pumpkin & Parsnip 'Fairy Fields. Knott, Stephen, illus. 2008. 20p. pap. (978-1-905553-28-0(5)) BookPublishingWorld.

Alloway, Kit. Dreamfever: A Novel. 2016. (Dream Walker Trilogy Ser.: 2). (ENG.). 320p. (J). 19.99 (978-1-250-07811-7(3), 9781250078117, St. Martin's Griffin) St. Martin's Pr.

Almhjell, Tone. Thornghost. 2016. (ENG., Illus.). 368p. (J). (gr. 5). 16.99 (978-0-8037-3897-3(8), Dial Bks) Penguin Young Readers Group.

—The Twistrose Key. Schoenherr, Ian, illus. 2014. (ENG.). 384p. (J). (gr. 5). pap. 8.99 (978-0-14-242345-5(9), Puffin Books) Penguin Young Readers Group.

Alton, Steve. The Firehills. 2005. (ENG.). 192p. (YA). (gr. 5-12). 15.95 (978-1-57505-798-9(0), Carolrhoda Bks.) Lerner Publishing Group.

—The Malifex. 2003. (Middle Readers Ser.). (Illus.). 182p. (J). (gr. 3-7). 14.95 (978-0-8225-0959-2(8)) Lerner Publishing Group.

Amara, Phil. The Treehouse Heroes: The Forgotten Beast. Chau, Alina, illus. 2012. (ENG.). 36p. (J). (gr. -1-3). 15.95 (978-1-59702-034-3(6)) Immedium.

Amato, Mary. The Word Eater. Ryniak, Christopher, illus. 2005. (ENG.). 151p. (J). (gr. 3-7). reprint ed. pap. 7.99 (978-0-8234-1940-1(1)) Holiday Hse., Inc.

Ambau, Getty. Desta & the Winds of Washaa Umera: The Winds of Washaa Umera, vols. 7, vol. 2. 2nd ed. 2013. (ENG., Illus.). 454p. (YA). pap. 15.95 (978-1-884459-03-0(X)) Falcon Pr. International.

Ameet Studio Staff. The Book of Monsters. 2016. (LEGO NEXO Knights Ser.). (ENG.). 96p. (J). (gr. 2-5). 12.99 (978-1-338-03488-2(X)) Scholastic, Inc.

Amestoy, Jennifer. Junkyard Junction: The Story of the Magic Microwave. 2008. 32p. pap. 14.75 (978-1-4389-1755-9(4)) AuthorHouse.

Amundson, Sandi. Zach & Dougie Dragonfly's Adventure. 2011. 55p. pap. 23.95 (978-1-4327-3536-4(5)) Outskirts Pr., Inc.

Ananda, Linda. Rainbow Childrenr-Magical Moving Stories: Stories with Movement, Dance, Yoga, & Song. 2012. 152p. pap. 47.95 (978-1-4525-5475-4(7)) Balboa Pr.

Andersen, Alan Lance. Wizard Academies - Rumpots, Crackpots, & Pooka-Mazed Halfwits. 2008. 174p. pap. 19.96 (978-0-615-18594-1(0)) Wizard Academies, LLC.

Andersen, Hans Christian & Capstone Press Staff. Jack y los Frijoles Magicos. Tercio, Ricardo, illus. 2010. (Graphic Spin en Español Ser.). (SPA.). 40p. (gr. 1-3). lib. bdg. 25.32 (978-1-4342-1902-2(X), Graphic Spin en Español) Stone Arch Bks.

Andersen, Hans Christian & Fowler, Gloria. The Red Shoes. Yung Yoo, Sun, illus. 2008. (ENG.). 32p. (J). (gr. -1-3). 16.95 (978-1-934429-06-8(6)) AMMO Bks., LLC.

Andersen, Hans Christian & Stone Arch Books Staff. Jack y los Frijoles Magicos. Tercio, Ricardo, illus. 2010. (Graphic Spin en Español Ser.). (SPA & ENG.). 40p. (gr. 1-3). pap. 5.95 (978-1-4342-2272-5(1), Graphic Spin en Español) Stone Arch Bks.

Anderson, Al. Adventures with Bingo Borden. Agora Publications Staff, tr. Kurzyca, Krystyna Emilia, illus. 2010. 77p. (J). pap. 9.50 (978-1-887250-46-7(8)) Agora Pubns., Inc.

Anderson, Jodi Lynn. Tiger Lily. (ENG.). 304p. (YA). (gr. 9). 2013. pap. 9.99 (978-0-06-200326-3(7)) 2012. 17.99 (978-0-06-200325-6(9)) HarperCollins Pubs. (HarperTeen).

Anderson, Matt & Lambert, Chad. Kung Fu Panda Vol. 2: It's Elemental & Other Stories. 2012. (ENG., Illus.). 24p. pap., pap. 6.95 (978-1-936340-56-9(9), 9781936340569) Ape Entertainment.

Anderson, R. J. A Little Taste of Poison. 2016. (ENG., Illus.). 368p. (J). (gr. 4-7). 17.99 (978-1-4814-3774-5(7), Atheneum Bks. for Young Readers) Simon & Schuster Children's Publishing.

—A Pocket Full of Murder. 2015. (ENG., Illus.). 352p. (J). (gr. 4-7). 18.99 (978-1-4814-3771-4(2)) Simon & Schuster Children's Publishing.

—Spell Hunter. 2009. (Faery Rebels Ser.). (ENG.). 336p. (J). (gr. 8-18). 16.99 (978-0-06-155474-2(X)) HarperCollins Pubs.

—Wayfarer. 2010. (ENG.). 304p. (J). (gr. 8-18). 16.99 (978-0-06-155477-3(4), HarperTeen) HarperCollins Pubs.

Andrew-Kollmann, Marcia. Blinky the Magical Elf. Dittus, Jade Moon, illus. 2012. 28p. pap. 24.95 (978-1-4626-5345-4(6)) America Star Bks.

Andrews, Kell. Mira Tells the Future. Marlin, Lissy, illus. 2016. (ENG.). 40p. (J). (gr. k-3). 14.95 (978-1-4549-1698-7(2)) Sterling Publishing Co., Inc.

Andrews, Randall. The Last Guardian of Magic. 2008. 448p. (YA). per. 23.95 (978-0-595-47345-8(8)) iUniverse, Inc.

Angeletti, Roberta, illus. The Golden Goose. 2010. (Flip-Up Fairy Tales Ser.). (ENG.). 24p. (J). (gr. -1-2). audio compact disk (978-1-84643-330-6(4)) Child's Play International Ltd.

Angelini, Josephine. Trail of Tears. 2015. (Worldwalker Trilogy Ser.: 2). (SPA & ENG.). 352p. (YA). (gr. 7). 17.99 (978-1-250-05090-8(1), 9781250050908) Feiwel & Friends.

Arbuthnott, Gill. The Chaos Clock, 1 vol. 2003. (Kelpies Ser.). (ENG.). 160p. 10.00 (978-0-86315-422-5(0)) Floris Bks. GBR. Dist: SteinerBooks, Inc.

Archer, Chris. Aftershock. 2010. (Mindwarp Ser.: 6). (ENG.). 144p. (YA). (gr. 11). pap. 8.99 (978-1-4424-1415-0(4), Simon Pulse) Simon Pulse.

Arevalo, Luis Paquime. Juan & the Magic Shoes. 2005. (J). per. 3.99 (978-0-9748598-1-1(8)) L. A. Eng Bks.

Arevamirp, Esile & Primavera, Elise. Fred & Anthony Meet the Demented Super-Degerm-O Zombie. Primavera, Elise, illus. 2007. (ENG., Illus.). 128p. (J). (gr. 2-6). pap. 4.99 (978-0-7868-3680-2(6)) Hyperion Pr.

Arias, Carlos Ballesteros. The Magic Forest. 2006. (J). pap. 8.00 (978-0-8059-7022-7(3)) Dorrance Publishing Co., Inc.

Arkin, Alan. Cosmo: A Cautionary Tale. Richards, Jon, illus. 2005. 40p. (J). 19.95 (978-1-929115-12-9(1)) Azro Pr., Inc.

Armenteros, Sarah. Emma & the Mashed Potato Monster. 2009. (ENG., Illus.). 44p. (J). 18.99 (978-1-59092-384-9(7)) Blue Forge Pr.

Armstrong, Kelley. The Awakening. (Darkest Powers Ser.: 2). (YA). (gr. 8). 2010. 384p. pap. 9.99 (978-0-06-145055-6(3)) 2009. 368p. 17.99 (978-0-06-166276-8(3)) HarperCollins Pubs.

—The Awakening, 7 vols. 2009. (Darkest Powers Ser.: 2). (YA). 133.75 (978-1-4407-3103-7(9)); 103.75 (978-1-4407-3099-3(7)) Recorded Bks., Inc.

—The Reckoning. 2011. (Darkest Powers Ser.: 3). 416p. (YA). (gr. 8). pap. 9.99 (978-0-06-145056-3(1)) HarperCollins Pubs.

Arnauld, D. S. Zertelo & the Road of Fire: Book Two. Scott, Sara, ed. 2007. 210p. (J). per. 9.95 (978-0-9801408-1-1(1)) Heroes & Leaders.

Arnett, Mindee. The Nightmare Charade. 2015. (Arkwell Academy Ser.: 3). (ENG.). 384p. (YA). (gr. 8-12). 18.99 (978-0-7653-3335-3(X), 9780765333353, Tor Teen) Doherty, Tom Assocs., LLC.

—The Nightmare Dilemma. 2015. (Arkwell Academy Ser.: 2). (ENG.). 400p. (YA). (gr. 8-12). pap. 10.99 (978-0-7653-3337-7(6), 9780765333377, Tor Teen) Doherty, Tom Assocs., LLC.

Arnold, Elizabeth. The Parsley Parcel. 2006. 212p. per. (978-1-904529-22-4(4), Back to Front) Solidus.

Aronson, Sarah. The Worst Fairy Godmother Ever! 2017. (Wish List Ser.: 1). (ENG.). 176p. (J). (gr. 3-7). 14.99 **(978-0-545-94151-8(2)**, Scholastic Pr.) Scholastic, Inc.

Aros, Angela. Aunt Emma's Secret Recipe, 1 vol. 2009. 15p. pap. 19.95 (978-1-60813-862-3(3)) PublishAmerica, Inc.

Arrathroon, Leigh A. Magical Adventures in Michigan. 2003. (Illus.). viii, 349p. (978-1-893047-10-5(5)) Archus Pr., LLC.

Artell, Mike. Jacques & de Beanstalk. Harris, Jim, illus. 2010. (ENG.). 32p. (J). (gr. k-3). 18.99 (978-0-8037-2816-5(6), Dial Bks) Penguin Young Readers Group.

Arthur, Jenny. Little Witch. Arthur, Jenny, illus. 2012. (Spooky Sounds Ser.). (ENG., Illus.). 10p. (J). (gr. k — 1). 7.99 (978-0-230-74487-5(7)) Macmillan Pubs., Ltd. GBR. Dist: Independent Pubs. Group.

Artz, D. M. Maggie & the Magic Sparkle Seed. 2007. 30p. 16.95 (978-1-4357-0152-6(6)) Lulu Pr., Inc.

Asphyxia. The Grimstones Collection. Asphyxia, illus. 2015. (Grimstones Ser.). (ENG., Illus.). 488p. (J). (gr. 3-7). pap. 17.99 (978-1-76011-391-9(3)) Allen & Unwin AUS. Dist: Independent Pubs. Group.

Atamer, Billie. The Magic Sleigh. 2013. 28p. pap. 13.95 (978-1-61244-213-6(7)) Halo Publishing International.

Atwater-Rhodes, Amelia. Wolfcry. 2008. (Kiesha'ra Ser.: Bk. 4). (ENG.). 208p. (YA). (gr. 9-12). pap. 7.99 (978-0-440-23886-7(2), Delacorte Pr.) Random Hse. Children's Bks.

Atwell, A. Erika Laura. 2008. 157p. pap. 24.95 (978-1-60703-006-5(3)) PublishAmerica, Inc.

Atwood, Megan. Molly Discovers Magic (Then Wants to un-Discover It) Fleming, Lucy, illus. 2016. (Dear Molly, Dear Olive Ser.). (ENG.). 96p. (gr. 1-3). lib. bdg. 21.99 (978-1-4795-8694-3(3)) Picture Window Bks.

—Molly Discovers Magic (Then Wants to Un-Discover It) Fleming, Lucy, illus. 2017. (Dear Molly, Dear Olive Ser.). (ENG.). 96p. (gr. 1-3). pap. 5.95 (978-1-62370-616-6(5)) Picture Window Bks.

Audouin-Mamikonian, H. R. H. Princess Sophie. Tara Duncan & the Forbidden Book. Rodarmor, William, tr. 2016. (Tara Duncan Ser.). (ENG.). 476p. (J). (gr. 2-7). pap. 9.99 (978-1-5107-0388-9(8), Sky Pony Pr.) Skyhorse Publishing Co., Inc.

—Tara Duncan & the Spellbinders. Rodarmor, William, tr. 2016. (Tara Duncan Ser.). (ENG.). 480p. (J). (gr. 2-7). pap. 9.99 (978-1-5107-0387-2(X), Sky Pony Pr.) Skyhorse Publishing Co., Inc.

Audouin-Mamikonian, Princess Sophie. Tara Duncan & the Forbidden Book. Rodarmor, William, tr. from FRE. 2013. (ENG.). 480p. (J). (gr. 2-7). 16.95 (978-1-61608-969-6(5), 608969, Sky Pony Pr.) Skyhorse Publishing Co., Inc.

—Tara Duncan & the Spellbinders. Rodarmor, Williams, tr. 2012. (ENG.). 480p. (J). (gr. 2-7). 16.95 (978-1-61608-733-3(1), 608733, Sky Pony Pr.) Skyhorse Publishing Co., Inc.

Augenstein, Marianne R. The Quest for Kair, 1 vol. 2009. 152p. pap. 24.95 (978-1-60813-899-9(2)) America Star Bks.

Aumuller, Kimberly. Dragon's Hope: Tale of the Guardians. 2009. 224p. 25.95 (978-0-595-50945-4(2)); pap. 15.95 (978-0-595-52209-5(2)) iUniverse, Inc.

Auxier, Jonathan. Peter Nimble & His Fantastic Eyes. (ENG.). 400p. (J). (gr. 3-7). 2012. pap. 9.95 (978-1-4197-0421-5(4)) 2011. 19.95 (978-1-4197-0025-5(1)) Abrams, Inc. (Amulet Bks.).

—Sophie Quire & the Last Storyguard. (ENG.). 464p. (gr. 3-7). 2017. (J). pap. 8.95 (978-1-4197-2202-8(6)) 2016. (YA). 18.95 (978-1-4197-1747-5(2)) Abrams, Inc. (Amulet Bks.).

Avi. Midnight Magic. 2004. (ENG.). 256p. (J). (gr. 3-7). 7.99 (978-0-439-24219-6(3), Scholastic Paperbacks) Scholastic, Inc.

AZ Books Staff. Cinderella. Zyl, Olga, ed. 2012. (Classic Fairy Tales Ser.). (ENG.). 10p. (J). (gr. -1-k). bds. 9.95 (978-1-61889-007-8(7)) AZ Bks. LLC.

—Horse's Farm. Potapenko, Olga, ed. 2012. (Talking Plush Animals Ser.). (ENG.). 10p. (J). (gr. -1-k). bds. 10.95 (978-1-61889-112-9(X)) AZ Bks. LLC.

—Little Thumb. Zyl, Olga, ed. 2012. (Classic Fairy Tales Ser.). (ENG.). 10p. (J). (gr. -1-k). bds. 9.95 (978-1-61889-008-5(5)) AZ Bks. LLC.

Babbitt, Natalie. Elsie Times Eight. Babbitt, Natalie, illus. 2005. (Illus.). 26p. (J). (gr. k-4). reprint ed. 16.00 (978-0-7567-9640-2(7)) DIANE Publishing Co.

Baccalario, P. D. Suitcase of Stars, 1 vol. Bruno, Iacopo, illus. 2014. (Enchanted Emporium Ser.). (ENG.). 240p. (gr. 4-8). pap. 9.25 (978-1-4342-6519-7(6)) Stone Arch Bks.

—Suitcase of Stars, 1 vol. Pernigotti, Chiara, tr. from ITA. Bruno, Iacopo, illus. 2014. (Enchanted Emporium Ser.). (ENG.). 240p. (gr. 4-8). 26.65 (978-1-4342-6516-6(1)) Stone Arch Bks.

Baccalario, Pierdomenico. Compass of Dreams, 1 vol. Pernigotti, Chiara, tr. from ITA. Bruno, Iacopo, illus. 2014. (Enchanted Emporium Ser.). (ENG.). 240p. (gr. 4-8). 26.65 (978-1-4342-6517-3(X)) Stone Arch Bks.

—Enchanted Emporium, 1 vol. Pernigotti, Chiara, tr. Bruno, Iacopo, illus. 2014. (Enchanted Emporium Ser.). (ENG.). 240p. (gr. 4-8). 53.30 (978-1-4342-9603-0(2)) Stone Arch Bks.

—Map of the Passages. McGuinness, Nanette, tr. from ITA. Bruno, Iacopo, illus. 2015. (Enchanted Emporium Ser.). (ENG.). 240p. (gr. 4-8). 12.95 (978-1-62370-204-5(6)) Stone Arch Bks.

—Suitcase of Stars, 1 vol. Bruno, Iacopo, illus. 2014. (Enchanted Emporium Ser.). (ENG.). 240p. (gr. 4-8). 12.95 (978-1-62370-039-3(6)) Capstone Young Readers of Coughlan Cos.

Baccalario, Pierdomenico & McGuinness, Nanette. The Thief of Mirrors. Pernigotti, Chiara, tr. from ITA. Bruno, Iacopo, illus. 2015. (Enchanted Emporium Ser.). (ENG.). 240p. (gr. 4-8). lib. bdg. 26.65 (978-1-4965-0516-3(6)) Stone Arch Bks.

Bach, Richard & Gardner, Sally. La Niña Más Pequeña del Mundo. Tapia, Sonia, tr. 2005. (Niños Mágicos Ser.).Tr. of One. (SPA & ENG., Illus.). 128p. (J). (gr. 2-4). pap. 7.95 (978-84-666-1339-2(0)) Ediciones B ESP. Dist: Independent Pubs. Group.

Bach, Shelby. Of Enemies & Endings. 2015. (Ever Afters Ser.: 4). (ENG., Illus.). 400p. (J). (gr. 3-7). 16.99 (978-1-4424-9787-0(4), Simon & Schuster Bks. For Young Readers) Simon & Schuster Bks. For Young Readers.

—Of Giants & Ice. Loftis, Cory, illus. 2013. (Ever Afters Ser.: 1). (ENG.). 368p. (J). (gr. 3-7). pap. 7.99 (978-1-4424-3147-8(4), Simon & Schuster Bks. For Young Readers) Simon & Schuster Bks. For Young Readers.

—Of Giants & Ice. 2012. (Ever Afters Ser.: 1). (ENG., Illus.). 352p. (J). (gr. 3-7). 15.99 (978-1-4424-3146-1(6), Simon & Schuster Bks. For Young Readers) Simon & Schuster Bks. For Young Readers.

—Of Sorcery & Snow. 2015. (Ever Afters Ser.: 3). (ENG., Illus.). 352p. (J). (gr. 3-7). pap. 8.99 (978-1-4424-9785-6(8), Simon & Schuster Bks. For Young Readers) Simon & Schuster Bks. For Young Readers.

—Of Witches & Wind. (Ever Afters Ser.: 2). (ENG., Illus.). (J). (gr. 3-7). 2014. 416p. pap. 8.99 (978-1-4424-3150-8(4)) 2013. 400p. 15.99 (978-1-4424-3149-2(0)) Simon & Schuster Bks. For Young Readers. (Simon & Schuster Bks. For Young Readers).

Bachmann, Stefan. The Peculiar. (Peculiar Ser.: 1). (ENG.). (J). (gr. 4). 2013. 400p. pap. 8.99 (978-0-06-219519-7(0)) 2012.

384p. 16.99 (978-0-06-219518-0(2)) HarperCollins Pubs. (Greenwillow Bks.).
—The Whatnot. 2013. 421p. (J). (978-0-06-228630-7(7), Collins Design) HarperCollins Pubs.
Backus, Leatha F. Annie & Timmy's Magic Pebbles. 2008. 32p. per. 24.95 (978-1-4241-9513-8(6)) America Star Bks.
Bacon, Lee. The Battle for Urth. 2016. (Legendtopia Ser.). (ENG., Illus.). 288p. (J). (gr. 4-7). 16.99 (978-0-553-53402-3(5), Delacorte Bks. for Young Readers) Random Hse. Children's Bks.
Bacon, Lee. Legendtopia Book #2: the Shadow Queen. 2017. (Legendtopia Ser.: 2). (ENG.). 272p. (J). (gr. 4-7). 16.99 **(978-0-553-53406-1(8)**, Delacorte Bks. for Young Readers) Random Hse. Children's Bks.
Badger, Meredith. Fairy School Dropout Undercover. 2011. (Fairy School Ser.: 2). (ENG., Illus.). 160p. (J). (gr. 2-4). pap. 14.99 (978-0-312-61951-0(0), 9780312619510) Square Fish.
Baeten, Lieve. Curious Little Witch Board Book. 2012. (ENG., Illus.). 14p. (J). (gr. -1 — 1). bds. 9.95 (978-0-7358-4102-4(0)) North-South Bks., Inc.
Bagley, Conor. Ziggy McFinster's Nantucket Adventure. Bernard Westcott, Nadine, illus. 2008. (ENG.). 40p. (J). (gr. -1-3). 16.95 (978-1-56625-315-4(2)) Bonus Bks., Inc.
Baird, Jeri. Tokens & Omens. 2016. (Tokens & Omens Ser.). (ENG.). 284p. (YA). (gr. 8). pap. 16.99 (978-1-63163-082-8(2), Jolly Fish Pr.) North Star Editions.
Baker, E. D. The Bravest Princess. 2014. (Wide-Awake Princess Ser.: 3). (ENG., Illus.). 272p. (YA). (gr. 5-8). 16.99 (978-1-61963-136-6(9), 9781619631366, Bloomsbury USA Childrens) Bloomsbury Publishing USA.
—Dragon Kiss. 2nd ed. 2009. (Tales of the Frog Princess Ser.). (ENG.). 288p. (YA). (gr. 5-8). 16.99 (978-1-59990-348-4(2), 9781599903484, Bloomsbury USA Childrens) Bloomsbury Publishing USA.
—The Dragon Princess. (Tales of the Frog Princess Ser.). (ENG.). (YA). 2010. 240p. (gr. 5-8). pap. 7.99 (978-1-59990-448-1(9), 9781599904481) 2008. (Illus.). 224p. (gr. 4-8). 16.99 (978-1-59990-194-7(3), 9781599901947) Bloomsbury Publishing USA. (Bloomsbury USA Childrens).
—Dragon's Breath: Read-Along/Homework Pack, 6 vols. unabr. ed. 2005. (Frog Princess Ser.: 2). (SPA.). (J). (gr. 5-8). 78.75 (978-1-4193-3563-1(4), 42041) Recorded Bks., Inc.
—Fairy Lies. (ENG., (YA). 2013. Illus.). 272p. (gr. 1-8). pap. 7.99 (978-1-61963-035-2(4), 9781619630352) 2012. 256p. (gr. 5-8). 16.99 (978-1-59990-550-1(7), 9781599905501) Bloomsbury Publishing USA. (Bloomsbury USA Childrens).
—The Flying Horse. Manuzak, Lisa, illus. 2017. (ENG.). 128p. (J). pap. 5.99 (978-1-68119-141-6(5), 9781681191416, Bloomsbury USA Childrens) Bloomsbury Publishing USA.
—Maggie & the Flying Horse. Manuzak, Lisa, illus. 2017. (ENG.). 128p. (J). 16.99 (978-1-68119-312-0(4), 9781681193120, Bloomsbury USA Childrens) Bloomsbury Publishing USA.
—Maggie & the Flying Pigs. 2017. (ENG., Illus.). 128p. (J). 16.99 **(978-1-68119-489-9(9)**, 9781681194899, Bloomsbury USA Childrens) Bloomsbury Publishing USA.
—Maggie & the Unicorn. 2017. (ENG., Illus.). 128p. (J). 16.99 **(978-1-68119-145-4(8)**, 9781681191454, Bloomsbury USA Childrens) Bloomsbury Publishing USA.
—Magic Animal Rescue 3: Maggie & the Unicorn. 2017. (ENG., Illus.). 128p. (J). pap. 5.99 **(978-1-68119-488-2(0)**, 9781681194882, Bloomsbury USA Childrens) Bloomsbury Publishing USA.
—Magic Animal Rescue 4: Maggie & the Flying Pigs. 2017. (ENG., Illus.). 128p. (J). pap. 5.99 **(978-1-68119-485-1(6)**, 9781681194851, Bloomsbury USA Childrens) Bloomsbury Publishing USA.
—A Prince among Frogs. 2nd ed. 2010. (Tales of the Frog Princess Ser.). (ENG.). 224p. (YA). (gr. 5-8). 16.99 (978-1-59990-349-1(0), 9781599903491, Bloomsbury USA Childrens) Bloomsbury Publishing USA.
—The Princess & the Pearl. 2017. (Wide-Awake Princess Ser.). (ENG.). 240p. (J). 16.99 (978-1-68119-135-5(0), 9781681191355, Bloomsbury USA Childrens) Bloomsbury Publishing USA.
—Princess Between Worlds: A Tale of the Wide-Awake Princess. 2016. (Wide-Awake Princess Ser.: 5). (ENG., Illus.). 224p. (J). 16.99 (978-1-61963-847-1(9), 9781619638471, Bloomsbury USA Childrens) Bloomsbury Publishing USA.
—Princess in Disguise. 2015. (Wide-Awake Princess Ser.: 4). (ENG.). 224p. (YA). (gr. 3-6). 16.99 (978-1-61963-573-9(9), 9781619635739, Bloomsbury USA Childrens) Bloomsbury Publishing USA.
—Princess in Disguise: A Tale of the Wide-Awake Princess. 2016. (Wide-Awake Princess Ser.: 4). (ENG., Illus.). 240p. (J). pap. 8.99 (978-1-61963-934-8(3), 9781619639348, Bloomsbury USA Childrens) Bloomsbury Publishing USA.
—A Question of Magic. 2015. (ENG.). 288p. (YA). (gr. 3-6). pap. 8.99 (978-1-61963-437-4(6), 9781619634374, Bloomsbury USA Childrens) Bloomsbury Publishing USA.
—Unlocking the Spell: A Tale of the Wide-Awake Princess. (Wide-Awake Princess Ser.: 2). (ENG.). (YA). 2014. 288p. (gr. 5-6). pap. 8.99 (978-1-61963-194-6(6), 9781619631946) 2012. 272p. (gr. 3-12). 16.99 (978-1-59990-841-0(7), 9781599908410) Bloomsbury Publishing USA. (Bloomsbury USA Childrens).
—The Wide-Awake Princess. (Wide-Awake Princess Ser.: 1). (ENG.). (YA). (gr. 5-14). 2012. 288p. pap. 8.99 (978-1-59990-658-4(9), 9781599906584) 2010. 272p. 16.99 (978-1-59990-487-0(X), 9781599904870) Bloomsbury Publishing USA. (Bloomsbury USA Childrens).
—The Wish Fish. Manuzak, Lisa, illus. 2017. (ENG.). 128p. (J). pap. 5.99 (978-1-68119-143-0(1), 9781681191430, Bloomsbury USA Childrens) Bloomsbury Publishing USA.
Baker, E. D. & Baker, E. No Place for Magic, Bk. 4. 2006. (Tales of the Frog Princess Ser.: 4). (ENG.). 256p. (YA). (gr. 4-6). 16.99 (978-1-58234-654-0(2), 9781582346540, Bloomsbury USA Childrens) Bloomsbury Publishing USA.
Baker, Keith. Cookies: A Mr. & Mrs. Green Adventure. 2012. (Green Light Readers Level 2 Ser.). (ENG., Illus.). 24p. (J). (gr. -1-3). pap. 3.99 (978-0-547-74561-9(3)) Houghton Mifflin Harcourt Publishing Co.
—On the Go with Mr. & Mrs. Green, 1 vol. Baker, Keith, illus. 2007. (Mr. & Mrs. Green Ser.). (ENG., Illus.). 72p. (gr. 2-4). 27.07 (978-1-59961-303-1(4)) Spotlight.
Baldacci, David. The Keeper. 2016. (Vega Jane Ser.: 2). (ENG.). 448p. (J). (gr. 4-7). pap. 9.99 (978-0-545-83195-6(4)) 2015. (Vega Jane Ser.: 2). (ENG.). 448p. (J). (gr. 5-9). 17.99 (978-0-545-83194-9(6)) 2015. 428p. (YA). (978-0-545-88230-9(3)) Scholastic, Inc. (Scholastic Pr.).
—The Keeper. 2016. (Vega Jane Ser.: 2). (ENG.). 428p. (J). (gr. 5-9). 20.85 (978-0-606-39127-6(4)) Turtleback Bks.
—The Keeper (Vega Jane, Book 2) 2017. (Vega Jane Ser.: 2). (ENG.). 464p. (J). (gr. 4-7). pap. 7.99 (978-1-338-05360-9(4)) Scholastic, Inc.
Baldwin, J. R. The Magic Jammies, 1 vol. 2010. 24p. 24.95 (978-1-4512-9442-2(5)) PublishAmerica, Inc.
Balfour, Melissa, et al. Yr Olion Traed Hud. 2005. (WEL., Illus.). 48p. pap. (978-1-85596-677-2(8)) Dref Wen.
Balian, Lorna. The Sweet Touch, 1 vol. Balian, Lecia, illus. 2005. (ENG.). 32p. (J). (gr. -1-3). 16.95 (978-1-59572-017-7(0)) Star Bright Bks., Inc.
Ball, Georgia & Disney Editors. Disney Frozen Comics Collection. 2016. (ENG.). 96p. (J). (gr. 4-7). 20.85 (978-0-606-39075-0(8)) Turtleback Bks.
Ballerina Magic Shoes. (Ballerina Charm Book Ser.). (Illus.). 32p. (J). (978-1-4054-1144-8(9)) Parragon, Inc.
Banda, Rey A. The Magical City of Northopolis; a Christmas Story. Patlan, Alyssa A., illus. 2012. 50p. (-18). pap. 16.95 (978-0-615-69125-1(0)) Northopolis.
Banks, Angelica. Finding Serendipity. Lewis, Stevie, illus. 2015. (Tuesday Mcgillycuddy Adventures Ser.). (ENG.). 288p. (J). (gr. 3-7). 16.99 (978-1-62779-154-0(X), 9781627791540, Holt, Henry & Co. Bks. For Young Readers) Holt, Henry & Co.
—Finding Serendipity. Lewis, Stevie, illus. 2016. (Tuesday Mcgillycuddy Adventures Ser.). (ENG.). 304p. (J). pap. 7.99 (978-1-250-07337-2(5), 9781250073372) Square Fish.
—A Week Without Tuesday. Lewis, Stevie, illus. 2016. (Tuesday Mcgillycuddy Adventures Ser.). (ENG.). 384p. (J). 16.99 (978-1-62779-155-7(8), 9781627791557, Holt, Henry & Co. Bks. For Young Readers) Holt, Henry & Co.
Banks, Lynne Reid. The Indian in the Cupboard. 2011. 9.14 (978-0-7848-3449-7(0), Everbind) Marco Bk. Co.
—The Indian in the Cupboard. 2010. (Indian in the Cupboard Ser.). (ENG.). 240p. (J). (gr. 3-7). 6.99 (978-0-375-84753-0(7), Yearling) Random Hse. Children's Bks.
—The Key to the Indian. 2004. (Indian in the Cupboard Ser.: 5). (J). (gr. 3-6). lib. bdg. 17.20 (978-0-613-23006-3(X), Turtleback) Turtleback Bks.
—The Mystery of the Cupboard. Newsom, Tom, illus. 2004. (Indian in the Cupboard Ser.: No. 4). (ENG.). 256p. (J). (gr. 4-18). pap. 6.99 (978-0-380-72013-2(2)) HarperCollins Pubs.
—The Return of the Indian. 2010. (Indian in the Cupboard Ser.). (ENG.). 208p. (J). (gr. 3-7). 6.99 (978-0-375-85523-8(8), Yearling) Random Hse. Children's Bks.
—The Secret of the Indian. 2010. (Indian in the Cupboard Ser.). (ENG.). 192p. (J). (gr. 3-7). 6.99 (978-0-375-85524-5(6), Yearling) Random Hse. Children's Bks.
—Secret of the Indian. 2003. (ENG., Illus.). 160p. pap. (978-0-00-714900-1(X), Collins) HarperCollins Pubs. Ltd.
Banks, Lynne Reid & Banks, L. The Return of the Indian. 2010. (Indian in the Cupboard Ser.: 2). (gr. 3-6). lib. bdg. 17.20 (978-0-8335-0902-4(0), Turtleback) Turtleback Bks.
Banks, Rosie. Enchanted Palace. 2014. (Secret Kingdom Ser.: 1). lib. bdg. 14.75 (978-0-606-35390-8(9)) Turtleback Bks.
—Glitter Beach. 2015. (Secret Kingdom Ser.: 6). lib. bdg. 14.75 (978-0-606-36349-5(1)) Turtleback Bks.
—Magic Mountain. 2014. (Secret Kingdom Ser.: 5). lib. bdg. 14.75 (978-0-606-36062-3(X)) Turtleback Bks.
—Mermaid Reef. 2014. (Secret Kingdom Ser.: 4). lib. bdg. 14.75 (978-0-606-35842-2(0)) Turtleback Bks.
—Secret Kingdom #3: Cloud Island. 2014. (Secret Kingdom Ser.: 3). (ENG.). 128p. (J). (gr. 2-5). pap. 4.99 (978-0-545-53555-7(7), Scholastic Paperbacks) Scholastic, Inc.
—Secret Kingdom #4: Mermaid Reef. 2014. (Secret Kingdom Ser.: 4). (ENG.). 128p. (J). (gr. 2-5). pap. 4.99 (978-0-545-53556-4(5), Scholastic Paperbacks) Scholastic, Inc.
—Secret Kingdom #6: Glitter Beach. 2015. (Secret Kingdom Ser.: 6). (ENG., Illus.). 128p. (J). (gr. 2-5). pap. 4.99 (978-0-545-53558-8(1), Scholastic Paperbacks) Scholastic, Inc.
Banks, Rosie. Starlight Adventure. 2017. (Secret Kingdom Ser.). (ENG., Illus.). 208p. (J). (gr. k-2). pap. 5.99 **(978-1-4083-2918-4(2)**, Orchard Bks.) Hachette Children's Group GBR. Dist: Hachette Bk. Group.
Banks, Tyra. Modelland. 2011. 569p. (YA). (gr. 7). 17.99 (978-0-375-97259-1(5), Delacorte Pr) Random House Publishing Group.
Baptiste, Tracey. The Jumbies. 2015. (ENG.). 240p. (J). (gr. 3-7). 15.95 (978-1-61620-414-3(1)) Algonquin Bks. of Chapel Hill.
Baratz-Logsted, Lauren, et al. The Final Battle... for Now Bk. 9. 2012. (Sisters Eight Ser.: 9). (ENG., Illus.). 160p. (J). (gr. 1-4). pap. 6.99 (978-0-547-55441-9(9)) Houghton Mifflin Harcourt Publishing Co.
Bardham-Quallen, Sudipta. The Fire Falls. Random House Disney Staff & Gurihiru Staff, illus. 2016. (Stepping Stone Book(TM) Ser.). (ENG.). 128p. (J). (gr. 1-4). 9.99 (978-0-7364-3291-7(4), RH/Disney) Random Hse. Children's Bks.
Bardhan-Quallen, Sudipta. Chasing Magic. Random House Disney Staff & Gurihiru Staff, illus. 2016. (Stepping Stone Book Ser.). (ENG.). 128p. (J). (gr. 1-4). 9.99 (978-0-7364-3290-0(6), RH/Disney) Random Hse. Children's Bks.
—The Fire Falls. Random House Disney Staff & Gurihiru, illus. 2016. (Stepping Stone Book(TM) Ser.). (ENG.). 128p. (J). (gr. 1-4). lib. bdg. 12.99 (978-0-7364-8249-3(0), RH/Disney) Random Hse. Children's Bks.
Bardugo, Leigh. The Language of Thorns: Midnight Tales & Dangerous Magic. Kipin, Sara, illus. 2017. (ENG.). 288p. (YA). 18.99 **(978-1-250-12252-0(X)**, 9781250122520) Imprint IND. Dist: Macmillan.
—Ruin & Rising. 2014. (Grisha Trilogy: Vol. 3). (ENG., Illus.). 432p. (YA). (gr. 7-12). 19.99 (978-0-8050-9461-9(X), 9780805094619, Holt, Henry & Co. Bks. For Young Readers) Holt, Henry & Co.
—Ruin & Rising. 2015. (Grisha Trilogy Ser.: 3). (YA). lib. bdg. 22.10 (978-0-606-37283-1(0)) Turtleback Bks.
—Shadow & Bone. 2012. (Shadow & Bone Trilogy Ser.: 1). (ENG.). 368p. (YA). (gr. 7-12). 19.99 (978-0-8050-9459-6(8), 9780805094596, Holt, Henry & Co. Bks. For Young Readers) Holt, Henry & Co.
—Shadow & Bone. 2013. (Shadow & Bone Trilogy Ser.: 1). (ENG.). 416p. (YA). (gr. 7-12). pap. 10.99 (978-1-250-02743-6(8), 9781250027436) Square Fish.
—Shadow & Bone. 2013. (Grisha Trilogy Ser.: 1). (YA). lib. bdg. 22.10 (978-0-606-31903-4(4), Turtleback) Turtleback Bks.
—Siege & Storm. 2013. (Shadow & Bone Trilogy Ser.: 2). (ENG., Illus.). 448p. (YA). (gr. 7). 19.99 (978-0-8050-9460-2(1), 9780805094602, Holt, Henry & Co. Bks. For Young Readers) Holt, Henry & Co.
—Siege & Storm. 2014. (Shadow & Bone Trilogy Ser.: 2). (ENG.). 496p. (YA). (gr. 7). pap. 10.99 (978-1-250-04443-3(X), 9781250044433) Square Fish.
Barker, Cicely Mary. Magical Doors: Discover the Doors to Fairyopolis. 2009. (Flower Fairies Ser.). (ENG.). 16p. (J). (gr. k-4). 22.99 (978-0-7232-6351-7(5), Warne) Penguin Young Readers Group.
Barker, Cicely Mary & Potter, Beatrix. Magical Secret Garden. 2010. (Flower Fairies Ser.). (ENG.). 24p. (J). (gr. k-3). 16.99 (978-0-7232-6440-8(6), Warne) Penguin Young Readers Group.
Barnard, Sarah. The Map & the Stone. 2nd ed. 2010. (Illus.). 142p. pap. 16.95 (978-0-9556887-2-0(8)) Ethics Trading GBR. Dist: Lulu Pr., Inc.
Barnett, Brandi. Glamour. 2008. 231p. 19.95 (978-1-930709-68-3(4)) HAWK Publishing Group.
Barnett, Mac. The Magic Word. Parsley, Elise, illus. 2016. 40p. (J). (gr. -1-3). 17.99 (978-0-06-235484-6(1)) HarperCollins Pubs.
Barnhill, Kelly. The Girl Who Drank the Moon. 2016. (ENG.). 400p. (J). (gr. 5-9). 17.95 (978-1-61620-567-6(9)) Algonquin Bks. of Chapel Hill.
—The Mostly True Story of Jack. 2012. (ENG.). 352p. (J). (gr. 3-7). pap. 8.99 (978-0-316-05672-4(3)) Little, Brown Bks. for Young Readers.
—The Witch's Boy. 2014. (ENG.). 384p. (J). (gr. 4). 17.95 (978-1-61620-351-1(X), 73351) Algonquin Bks. of Chapel Hill.
Barnholdt, Lauren. Hailey Twitch & the Campground Itch. Beaky, Suzanne, illus. 2011. (Hailey Twitch Ser.: 3). (ENG.). 144p. (J). (gr. 2-4). pap. 8.99 (978-1-4022-2446-1(X), Sourcebooks Jabberwocky) Sourcebooks, Inc.
—Hailey Twitch & the Wedding Glitch. Beaky, Suzanne, illus. 2011. (Hailey Twitch Ser.: 4). (ENG.). 144p. (J). (gr. 2-4). pap. 6.99 (978-1-4022-2447-8(8), Sourcebooks Jabberwocky) Sourcebooks, Inc.
Barr, Mary. The Trouble with Filly Tucker. 2010. 112p. (gr. 4-6). 20.95 (978-1-4502-3517-4(4)); pap. 10.95 (978-1-4502-3515-0(8)) iUniverse, Inc.
Barron, T. A. The Book of Magic, 12 vols., Bk. 12. Hall, August, illus. 2011. (Merlin Saga Ser.: 12). (ENG.). 160p. (J). (gr. 5-18). 17.99 (978-0-399-24741-5(6), Philomel Bks.) Penguin Young Readers Group.
—Child of the Dark Prophecy. 2004. (Merlin Saga Ser.: 9). (ENG.). 432p. (J). (gr. 5-18). 21.99 (978-0-399-23763-8(1), Philomel Bks.) Penguin Young Readers Group.
—Doomraga's Revenge. (Merlin Saga Ser.: 7). (ENG.). (J). (gr. 5-18). 2009. 256p. 19.99 (978-0-399-25212-9(6), Philomel Bks.)Bk. 7. 2011. 272p. 8.99 (978-0-14-241925-0(7), Puffin Books) Penguin Young Readers Group.
—The Eternal Flame: Book 11, 11 vols. 2011. (Merlin Saga Ser.: 11). (ENG.). 416p. (J). (gr. 5-18). 8.99 (978-0-14-241929-8(X), Puffin Books) Penguin Young Readers Group.
—The Great Tree of Avalon: Book 9, 9 vols. 2011. (Merlin Saga Ser.: 9). (ENG.). 464p. (J). (gr. 5-18). 8.99 (978-0-14-241927-4(3), Puffin Books) Penguin Young Readers Group.
—The Heartlight Saga. 2014. (Adventures of Kate Ser.). (ENG.). 864p. (J). pap. 10.99 (978-0-14-751032-7(5), Puffin Books) Penguin Young Readers Group.
—The Mirror of Fate, Bk. 4. 2011. (Merlin Saga Ser.: 4). (ENG.). 272p. (J). (gr. 5-18). 8.99 (978-0-14-241922-9(2), Puffin Books) Penguin Young Readers Group.
—Ultimate Magic, 8 vols., Bk. 8. 2011. (Merlin Saga Ser.: 8). (ENG.). 256p. (J). (gr. 5-18). 8.99 (978-0-14-241926-7(5), Puffin Books) Penguin Young Readers Group.
Barrowman, John & Barrowman, Carole E. Bone Quill. 2014. (Hollow Earth Ser.). (ENG., Illus.). 304p. (J). (gr. 3-7). pap. 8.99 (978-1-4424-8929-5(4), Aladdin) Simon & Schuster Children's Publishing.
—Book of Beasts. 2016. (Hollow Earth Ser.). (ENG.). 336p. (J). (gr. 3-7). pap. 7.99 (978-1-4814-4231-2(7), Simon & Schuster/Paula Wiseman Bks.) Simon & Schuster/Paula Wiseman Bks.
—Conjuror. 2016. (Orion Chronicles Ser.). (ENG.). 320p. (YA). (gr. 7). 16.99 (978-1-78185-637-6(0)) Head of Zeus GBR. Dist: Independent Pubs. Group.
—Hollow Earth. 2013. (Hollow Earth Ser.). (ENG., Illus.). 416p. (J). (gr. 3-7). pap. 7.99 (978-1-4424-5853-6(4), Aladdin) Simon & Schuster Children's Publishing.
Barrows, Annie. Magic in the Mix. (ENG.). 288p. (YA). (gr. 3-6). 2015. pap. 7.99 (978-1-61963-798-6(7), 9781619637986) 2014. 16.99 (978-1-61963-482-4(1), 9781619634824) Bloomsbury Publishing USA. (Bloomsbury USA Childrens).
Barry, Dave & Pearson, Ridley. Peter & the Starcatchers. Call, Greg, illus. rev. ed. 2006. (Peter & the Starcatchers Ser.). (ENG.). 480p. (J). (gr. 5-9). reprint ed. pap. 9.99 (978-0-7868-4907-9(X), Disney Editions) Disney Pr.
—Peter & the Sword of Mercy. Call, Greg, illus. 2011. (Peter & the Starcatchers Ser.: Bk. 4). (ENG.). 528p. (J). (gr. 5-9). pap. 9.99 (978-1-4231-3070-3(7)) Hyperion Pr.
Baruch, M. P. Spend the Day with Me. Arscott, Dean, illus. 2009. 20p. pap. 10.95 (978-1-936051-27-4(3)) Peppertree Pr., The.
Barulich-Liederbach, Terri & Liederbach, Tom. The Memory Chair. 2010. 48p. pap. 19.49 (978-1-4520-5672-2(2)) AuthorHouse.
Base, Graeme. Jungle Drums. 2004. (ENG., Illus.). 40p. (J). (gr. -1-3). 19.95 (978-0-8109-5044-3(8)) Abrams, Inc.
—Little Elephants. 2012. (ENG., Illus.). 40p. (J). (gr. k-2). 17.95 (978-1-4197-0463-5(X), Abrams Bks. for Young Readers) Abrams, Inc.
Bass, Patrik Henry. The Zero Degree Zombie Zone. Craft, Jerry, illus. 2014. (ENG.). 144p. (J). (gr. 3-7). 16.99 (978-0-545-13210-7(X), Scholastic Pr.) Scholastic, Inc.
Bassett, Alisa Cuthbertson. Threads of Time. 2013. 24p. pap. 24.95 (978-1-63000-063-9(9)) America Star Bks.
Bateson-Hill, Margaret. Chanda & the Mirror of Moonlight. Littlewood, Karin, illus. 2003. (Folk Tales Ser.). 32p. (J). (gr. 3-4). (978-1-84089-217-8(X)) Zero to Ten, Ltd.
Batham, Matthew. Lightsleep. 2006. 167p. pap. (978-1-904623-39-7(5)) WritersPrintShop.
Baucom, Ian. Through the Skylight. Gerard, Justin, illus. (ENG.). 400p. (J). (gr. 4-8). 2014. pap. 6.99 (978-1-4424-8167-1(6)) 2013. 17.99 (978-1-4169-1777-9(2)) Simon & Schuster Children's Publishing. (Atheneum Bks. for Young Readers).
Bauer, Deidre. Silver Mountain. 2008. 38p. pap. 8.00 (978-0-8059-7672-4(8)) Dorrance Publishing Co., Inc.
Baum, L. Frank. Adventures in Oz: Dorothy & the Wizard in Oz, the Road to Oz, the Emerald City of Oz. 2007. 296p. 24.95 (978-1-60459-017-3(3)); per. 12.95 (978-1-60459-016-6(5)) Wilder Pubns., Corp.
—Adventures in Oz: The Tin Woodman of Oz, the Magic of Oz, Glinda of Oz. 2007. 284p. 24.95 (978-1-60459-023-4(8)) Wilder Pubns., Corp.
—The Magic of Oz. 2007. 108p. (gr. 4-7). per. 9.95 (978-1-60312-334-1(2)); 22.95 (978-1-60312-671-7(6)) Aegypan.
—The Marvelous Land of Oz. 2007. 120p. per. 10.95 (978-1-60312-149-1(8)) Aegypan.
—Sky Island. 2007. 144p. (gr. 4-7). per. 11.95 (978-1-60312-253-5(2)) Aegypan.
—Sky Island. 2004. (Twelve-Point Ser.). lib. bdg. 24.00 (978-1-58287-280-3(5)); lib. bdg. 25.00 (978-1-58287-792-1(0)) North Bks.
Baum, L. Frank & Thompson, Ruth Plumly. The Royal Book of Oz. 2009. 112p. pap. 8.99 (978-1-60459-763-9(1)) Wilder Pubns., Corp.
Baum, L. Frank, et al. A Children's Treasury. 2007. 792p. per. 24.95 (978-1-60459-011-1(4)) Wilder Pubns., Corp.
Baxter, Nicola. Dreamland Fairies: Magical Bedtime Stories from Fairyland. Manson, Beverlie, illus. 2012. (ENG.). 80p. (J). (gr. k-4). pap. 9.99 (978-1-84322-806-6(8)) Anness Publishing GBR. Dist: National Bk. Network.
—My Treasury of Fairies & Elves: A Collection of 20 Magical Stories. Manson, Beverlie, illus. 2012. (ENG.). 240p. (J). (gr. k-4). 18.99 (978-1-84322-835-6(1)) Anness Publishing GBR. Dist: National Bk. Network.
—Witches, Wizards & Magicians. Morton, Ken, illus. 2012. (ENG.). 80p. (J). (gr. k-4). pap. 9.99 (978-1-84322-807-3(6)) Anness Publishing GBR. Dist: National Bk. Network.
Beamish, Diane. Grandma's Magic Button Necklace. 2006. 25p. 12.16 (978-1-4116-5487-7(0)) Lulu Pr., Inc.
Bear, F. T. Connor Finn: The Secret of Snow. 2013. 258p. pap. (978-0-646-91485-5(5)) F. T. Bear.
Beardslee, Nellie L. The Glenn's of Newberry Hills. 2008. 164p. pap. 24.95 (978-1-60703-471-1(9)) America Star Bks.
Beasley, Cassie. Circus Mirandus. 2016. (SPA.). 25.99 (978-84-246-5686-7(5)) La Galera, S.A. Editorial ESP. Dist: Lectorum Pubns., Inc.
—Circus Mirandus. (ENG., Illus.). 304p. (J). (gr. 4-7). 2016. pap. 8.99 (978-0-14-751554-4(8), Puffin Books) 2015. 17.99 (978-0-525-42843-5(7), Dial Bks) Penguin Young Readers Group.
—Circus Mirandus. 2016. (ENG.). 304p. (J). (gr. 3-7). 19.65 (978-0-606-39311-9(0)) Turtleback Bks.
Becker, Aaron. Return. Becker, Aaron, illus. 2016. (ENG., Illus.). 40p. (J). (gr. -1-3). 15.99 (978-0-7636-7730-5(2)) Candlewick Pr.
Becker, Bonny. The Magical Ms. Plum. Portnoy, Amy, illus. 2011. (ENG.). 112p. (J). (gr. 1-4). 6.99 (978-0-375-84760-8(X), Yearling) Random Hse. Children's Bks.
Becker, Jaqueline H. Listen, There Are More Than Seven Dwarfs. 2012. pap. 11.95 (978-0-7414-7037-9(3)) Infinity Publishing.
Begler, Peter. The Fearless Travelers' Guide to Wicked Places. 2017. (ENG., Illus.). 384p. (gr. 4-8). 14.95 (978-1-62370-799-6(4)) Capstone Young Readers of Coughlan Cos.
Belanger, Kathleen. Cooldog's Holiday Adventures. Baker, David, illus. 2012. 48p. 24.95 (978-1-4626-3045-5(6)) America Star Bks.
Bell, Anita & Bell, Belinda. 'Twas Ever. 2011. 208p. 28.99 (978-0-557-41894-7(1)); 210p. pap. 11.99 (978-1-257-00131-6(0)) Lulu Pr., Inc.
Bell, Braden. The Kindling. 2012. (YA). (978-1-4621-1027-8(4)) Cedar Fort, Inc./CFI Distribution.
—Luminescence. 2014. pap. 14.99 (978-1-4621-1405-4(9), Horizon Pubs.) Cedar Fort, Inc./CFI Distribution.
—Penumbras. 2013. (Middle School Magic Ser.). (ENG.). 305p. (J). (gr. 3-7). 14.99 (978-1-4621-1220-3(X), Sweetwater Bks.) Cedar Fort, Inc./CFI Distribution.
Bell, Frank. Ma Jong & the Magic Carpet. Seaman, Paul, illus. 2004. 24p. pap. 7.00 (978-1-84161-070-2(4)) Ravette Publishing, Ltd. GBR. Dist: Parkwest Pubns., Inc.
Bell, Hilari. Fall of a Kingdom. 2005. (Farsala Trilogy Ser.: 1). (ENG.). 448p. (YA). (gr. 7). pap. 6.99 (978-0-689-85414-9(5), Simon Pulse) Simon Pulse.
—The Goblin Gate. (ENG.). (YA). (gr. 8). 2011. 400p. pap. 8.99 (978-0-06-165104-5(4)) 2010. 384p. 16.99 (978-0-06-165102-1(8)) HarperCollins Pubs. (HarperTeen).
—The Goblin War. 2011. (ENG.). 304p. (J). (gr. 8). 17.99 (978-0-06-165105-2(2), HarperTeen) HarperCollins Pubs.
—The Goblin Wood. 2004. (Illus.). 371p. (J). (gr. 5-9). 14.65 (978-0-7569-3253-4(X)) Perfection Learning Corp.
—The Prophecy. 2006. (ENG., Illus.). 208p. (J). (gr. 5-9). 15.99 (978-0-06-059943-0(X)) HarperCollins Pubs.
—Trickster's Girl: The Raven Duet Book #1. 2011. (Raven Duet Ser.). (ENG.). 288p. (YA). (gr. 7). pap. 15.99

(978-0-547-57724-1(9)) Houghton Mifflin Harcourt Publishing Co.

Bell, Jennifer. The Crooked Sixpence. Helquist, Brett, illus. 2017. (Uncommoners Ser.: 1). (ENG.). 320p. (J). (gr. 3-7). 16.99 *(978-0-553-49843-1(6)*, Crown Books For Young Readers) Random Hse. Children's Bks.

Bell, Parker. Tale of the Hundred. 2012. (ENG.). pap. *(978-1-4675-2062-1(4))* Independent Pub.

Bellairs, John. The Chessmen of Doom (A Johnny Dixon Mystery: Book Seven) 2011. 114p. pap. 14.95 *(978-1-61756-348-5(X))* Open Road Integrated Media, Inc.

—The House with a Clock in Its Walls. Gorey, Edward, illus. 2004. (Lewis Barnavelt Ser.: Bk. 1). (ENG.). 192p. (J). (gr. 3-7). pap. 6.99 *(978-0-14-240257-3(5)*, Puffin Books) Penguin Young Readers Group.

—The House with a Clock in Its Walls. (Lewis Barnavelt Ser.: Bk. 1). 179p. (J). (gr. 4-6). pap. 4.50 *(978-0-8072-1423-7(X)*, Listening Library) Random Hse. Audio Publishing Group.

—The Spell of the Sorcerer's Skull. Gorey, Edward, illus. 2004. 170p. (J). (gr. 4-7). 13.65 *(978-0-7569-4965-5(3))* Perfection Learning Corp.

Belle, Trixie & Caruso-Scott, Melissa. Beauty & the Beast: Les Petits Fairytales. Lake, Oliver, illus. 2013. (Petits Fairytales Ser.). (ENG.). 26p. (J). (gr. -1 — 1). bds. 7.99 *(978-0-8050-9788-7(0)*, 9780805097887, Holt, Henry & Co. Bks. For Young Readers) Holt, Henry & Co.

—The Little Mermaid: Les Petits Fairytales. Lake, Oliver, illus. 2013. (Petits Fairytales Ser.). (ENG.). 26p. (J). (gr. -1 — 1). bds. 7.99 *(978-0-8050-9789-4(9)*, 9780805097894, Holt, Henry & Co. Bks. For Young Readers) Holt, Henry & Co.

—Rapunzel. Lake, Oliver, illus. 2013. (Petits Fairytales Ser.). (ENG.). 26p. (J). (gr. -1 — 1). bds. 7.99 *(978-0-8050-9790-0(2)*, 9780805097900, Holt, Henry & Co. Bks. For Young Readers) Holt, Henry & Co.

—Sleeping Beauty: Les Petits Fairytales. Lake, Oliver, illus. 2013. (Petits Fairytales Ser.). (ENG.). 26p. (J). (gr. -1 — 1). bds. 7.99 *(978-0-8050-9791-7(0)*, 9780805097917, Holt, Henry & Co. Bks. For Young Readers) Holt, Henry & Co.

Bennett, Jeffrey. El Mago Que Salvo el Mundo. Collier-Morales, Roberta, illus. 2011. (SPA.). 32p. (J). (gr. 2-4). 15.00 *(978-0-9721819-5-2(4))* Big Kid Science.

—The Wizard Who Saved the World. Collier-Morales, Roberta, illus. 2011. (ENG.). 32p. (J). (gr. 2-4). 15.00 *(978-0-9721819-4-5(6))* Big Kid Science.

Benoff-Nadel, Phyllis. The Magical Garden. 2013. 32p. pap. 16.99 *(978-1-4525-7445-5(6)*, Balboa Pr.) Author Solutions, Inc.

Bentley, Nancy Kaye. Mema's back Yard. 2010. 39p. pap. 17.95 *(978-0-557-68242-3(8))* Lulu Pr., Inc.

Bentley, Sue. Chocolate Wishes #1. Swan, Angela, illus. 2013. (Magic Bunny Ser.: 1). (ENG.). 128p. (J). (gr. 1-3). pap. 5.99 *(978-0-448-46727-6(5)*, Grosset & Dunlap) Penguin Young Readers Group.

—A Christmas Surprise. Swan, Angela & Farley, Andrew, illus. 2008. (Magic Kitten Ser.). (ENG.). 128p. (J). (gr. 1-3). pap. 5.99 *(978-0-448-45001-8(1)*, Grosset & Dunlap) Penguin Young Readers Group.

—Circus Surprise #7. Swan, Angela, illus. 2014. (Magic Ponies Ser.: 7). (ENG.). 128p. (J). (gr. 1-3). 4.99 *(978-0-448-46734-4(8)*, Grosset & Dunlap) Penguin Young Readers Group.

—A Circus Wish. 2009. (Magic Kitten Ser.: 6). lib. bdg. 14.75 *(978-0-606-06970-0(4)*, Turtleback) Turtleback Bks.

—A Circus Wish #6, 6 vols. Farley, Andrew & Swan, Angela, illus. 2009. (Magic Kitten Ser.: 6). (ENG.). 128p. (J). (gr. 1-3). pap. 5.99 *(978-0-448-45062-9(3)*, Grosset & Dunlap) Penguin Young Readers Group.

—Classroom Capers. 2014. (Magic Bunny Ser.: 4). lib. bdg. 14.75 *(978-0-606-34134-9(X)*, Turtleback) Turtleback Bks.

—Classroom Capers #4. Swan, Angela & Farley, Andrew, illus. 2014. (Magic Bunny Ser.: 4). (ENG.). 128p. (J). (gr. 1-3). 4.99 *(978-0-448-46792-4(5)*, Grosset & Dunlap) Penguin Young Readers Group.

—Classroom Chaos, 2 vols. Swan, Angela & Farley, Andrew, illus. 2008. (Magic Kitten Ser.: 2). (ENG.). 128p. (J). (gr. 1-3). pap. 5.99 *(978-0-448-44999-9(4)*, Grosset & Dunlap) Penguin Young Readers Group.

—Classroom Princess. 2013. (Magic Puppy Ser.: 9). lib. bdg. 16.00 *(978-0-606-32122-8(5)*, Turtleback) Turtleback Bks.

—Classroom Princess #9. Swan, Angela, illus. 2013. (Magic Puppy Ser.: 9). (ENG.). 128p. (J). (gr. 1-3). 5.99 *(978-0-448-46732-0(1)*, Grosset & Dunlap) Penguin Young Readers Group.

—Cloud Capers, 3 vols. Swan, Angela & Farley, Andrew, illus. 2009. (Magic Puppy Ser.: 3). (ENG.). 128p. (J). (gr. 1-3). pap. 5.99 *(978-0-448-45046-9(1)*, Grosset & Dunlap) Penguin Young Readers Group.

—Cloud Capers. 2009. (Magic Puppy Ser.: 3). lib. bdg. 14.75 *(978-0-606-06977-9(1)*, Turtleback) Turtleback Bks.

—Dancing Days. 2014. (Magic Bunny Ser.: 5). lib. bdg. 14.75 *(978-0-606-34135-6(8)*, Turtleback) Turtleback Bks.

—Dancing Days #5. Swan, Angela & Farley, Andrew, illus. 2014. (Magic Bunny Ser.: 5). (ENG.). 128p. (J). (gr. 1-3). 4.99 *(978-0-448-46793-1(3)*, Grosset & Dunlap) Penguin Young Readers Group.

—Double Trouble, 4 vols. Farley, Andrew & Swan, Angela, illus. 2009. (Magic Kitten Ser.: 4). (ENG.). 128p. (J). (gr. 1-3). pap. 5.99 *(978-0-448-45060-5(7)*, Grosset & Dunlap) Penguin Young Readers Group.

—Double Trouble. 2009. (Magic Kitten Ser.: 4). lib. bdg. 16.00 *(978-0-606-06004-2(9)*, Turtleback) Turtleback Bks.

—Firelight Friends. 2014. (Magic Kitten Ser.: 10). lib. bdg. 14.75 *(978-0-606-34136-3(6)*, Turtleback) Turtleback Bks.

—Firelight Friends #10. Swan, Angela, illus. 2014. (Magic Kitten Ser.: 10). (ENG.). 128p. (J). (gr. 1-3). 5.99 *(978-0-448-46788-7(7)*, Grosset & Dunlap) Penguin Young Readers Group.

—A Forest Charm. 2008. (ENG., Illus.). 128p. (J). pap. *(978-0-14-132380-0(9)*, Puffin) Penguin Bks., Ltd.

—Friendship Forever. 2013. (Magic Puppy Ser.: 10). lib. bdg. 14.75 *(978-0-606-32123-5(3)*, Turtleback) Turtleback Bks.

—Friendship Forever #10. Swan, Angela, illus. 2013. (Magic Puppy Ser.: 10). (ENG.). 128p. (J). (gr. 1-3). 5.99 *(978-0-448-46733-7(X)*, Grosset & Dunlap) Penguin Young Readers Group.

—A Glittering Gallop, No. 8. Swan, Angela, illus. 2013. (Magic Kitten Ser.: 8). (ENG.). 128p. (J). (gr. 1-3). 5.99 *(978-0-448-46730-6(5)*, Grosset & Dunlap) Penguin Young Readers Group.

—A Glittering Gallop. 2013. (Magic Kitten Ser.: 8). lib. bdg. 16.00 *(978-0-606-32120-4(9)*, Turtleback) Turtleback Bks.

—Magic Puppy - A New Beginning. 2009. (Magic Puppy Ser.: 1). lib. bdg. 16.00 *(978-0-606-06017-2(0)*, Turtleback) Turtleback Bks.

—Magic Puppy: Books 1-3. Swan, Angela & Farley, Andrew, illus. 2014. (Magic Puppy Ser.). (ENG.). 368p. (J). (gr. 1-3). 8.99 *(978-0-448-48460-0(9)*, Grosset & Dunlap) Penguin Young Readers Group.

—Moonlight Mischief. 2009. (Magic Kitten Ser.: 5). lib. bdg. 14.75 *(978-0-606-06016-5(2)*, Turtleback) Turtleback Bks.

—Muddy Paws, No. 2. Swan, Angela & Farley, Andrew, illus. 2009. (Magic Puppy Ser.: 2). (ENG.). 128p. (J). (gr. 1-3). pap. 5.99 *(978-0-448-45045-2(3)*, Grosset & Dunlap) Penguin Young Readers Group.

—Muddy Paws. 2009. (Magic Puppy Ser.: 2). lib. bdg. 14.75 *(978-0-606-06021-9(9)*, Turtleback) Turtleback Bks.

—New Beginning, No. 1. Swan, Angela & Farley, Andrew, illus. 2009. (Magic Puppy Ser.: 1). (ENG.). 128p. (J). (gr. 1-3). pap. 5.99 *(978-0-448-45044-5(5)*, Grosset & Dunlap) Penguin Young Readers Group.

—A New Friend, No. 1. Swan, Angela, illus. 2013. (Magic Ponies Ser.: 1). (ENG.). 128p. (J). (gr. 1-3). pap. 5.99 *(978-0-448-46205-9(2)*, Grosset & Dunlap) Penguin Young Readers Group.

—A New Friend. 2013. (Magic Ponies Ser.: 1). lib. bdg. 16.00 *(978-0-606-29584-0(4)*, Turtleback) Turtleback Bks.

—Party Dreams. 5th ed. 2008. (ENG., Illus.). 128p. (J). pap. *(978-0-14-132379-4(5)*, Puffin) Penguin Bks., Ltd.

—Party Dreams, 5 vols. Farley, Andrew & Swan, Angela, illus. 2010. (Magic Puppy Ser.: 5). (ENG.). 128p. (J). (gr. 1-3). pap. 5.99 *(978-0-448-45064-3(X)*, Grosset & Dunlap) Penguin Young Readers Group.

—The Perfect Secret. 2014. (Magic Puppy Ser.: 14). lib. bdg. 14.75 *(978-0-606-35686-2(X))* Turtleback Bks.

—The Perfect Secret #14. Swan, Angela & Farley, Andrew, illus. 2014. (Magic Puppy Ser.: 14). (ENG.). 128p. (J). (gr. 1-3). 5.99 *(978-0-448-46799-3(2)*, Grosset & Dunlap) Penguin Young Readers Group.

—Picture Perfect #13. Swan, Angela & Farley, Andrew, illus. 2014. (Magic Kitten Ser.: 13). (ENG.). 128p. (J). (gr. 1-3). 4.99 *(978-0-448-46796-2(8)*, Grosset & Dunlap) Penguin Young Readers Group.

—Pony Camp. 2014. (Magic Ponies Ser.: 8). lib. bdg. 16.00 *(978-0-606-34139-4(0)*, Turtleback) Turtleback Bks.

—Pony Camp #8. Swan, Angela, illus. 2014. (Magic Ponies Ser.: 8). (ENG.). 128p. (J). (gr. 1-3). 5.99 *(978-0-448-46787-0(9)*, Grosset & Dunlap) Penguin Young Readers Group.

—A Puzzle of Paws. 2014. (Magic Kitten Ser.: 12). lib. bdg. 14.75 *(978-0-606-35682-4(7))* Turtleback Bks.

—A Puzzle of Paws #12. Swan, Angela & Farley, Andrew, illus. 2014. (Magic Kitten Ser.: 12). (ENG.). 128p. (J). (gr. 1-3). 4.99 *(978-0-448-46795-5(X)*, Grosset & Dunlap) Penguin Young Readers Group.

—Riding Rescue #6. Swan, Angela, illus. 2013. (Magic Ponies Ser.: 6). (ENG.). 128p. (J). (gr. 1-3). 4.99 *(978-0-448-46735-1(6)*, Grosset & Dunlap) Penguin Young Readers Group.

—School of Mischief, 8 vols., No. 8. Farley, Andrew & Swan, Angela, illus. 2010. (Magic Puppy Ser.: 8). (ENG.). 128p. (J). (gr. 1-3). pap. 5.99 *(978-0-448-45067-4(4)*, Grosset & Dunlap) Penguin Young Readers Group.

—Seaside Mystery. 2013. (Magic Kitten Ser.: 9). lib. bdg. 16.00 *(978-0-606-32121-1(7)*, Turtleback) Turtleback Bks.

—Seaside Mystery #9. Swan, Angela, illus. 2013. (Magic Kitten Ser.: 9). (ENG.). 128p. (J). (gr. 1-3). 5.99 *(978-0-448-46731-3(3)*, Grosset & Dunlap) Penguin Young Readers Group.

—A Shimmering Splash. 2014. (Magic Kitten Ser.: 11). lib. bdg. 14.75 *(978-0-606-34137-0(4)*, Turtleback) Turtleback Bks.

—A Shimmering Splash #11. Swan, Angela & Farley, Andrew, illus. 2014. (Magic Kitten Ser.: 11). (ENG.). 128p. (J). (gr. 1-3). 4.99 *(978-0-448-46789-4(5)*, Grosset & Dunlap) Penguin Young Readers Group.

—Show-Jumping Dreams. 2013. (Magic Ponies Ser.: 4). lib. bdg. 14.75 *(978-0-606-31679-8(5)*, Turtleback) Turtleback Bks.

—Show-Jumping Dreams #4. Swan, Angela, illus. 2013. (Magic Ponies Ser.: 4). (ENG.). 128p. (J). (gr. 1-3). pap. 5.99 *(978-0-448-46208-0(7)*, Grosset & Dunlap) Penguin Young Readers Group.

—Snowy Wishes. Swan, Angela, illus. 2013. (Magic Puppy Ser.). (ENG.). 128p. (J). (gr. 1-3). 5.99 *(978-0-448-46737-5(2)*, Grosset & Dunlap) Penguin Young Readers Group.

—Snowy Wishes. 2013. (Magic Puppy Ser.). lib. bdg. 16.00 *(978-0-606-32124-2(1)*, Turtleback) Turtleback Bks.

—Sparkling Skates. 2014. (Magic Puppy Ser.: 13). lib. bdg. 14.75 *(978-0-606-35685-5(1))* Turtleback Bks.

—Sparkling Skates #13. Swan, Angela & Farley, Andrew, illus. 2014. (Magic Puppy Ser.: 13). (ENG.). 128p. (J). (gr. 1-3). 4.99 *(978-0-448-46798-6(4)*, Grosset & Dunlap) Penguin Young Readers Group.

—Sparkling Steps. 7th ed. 2007. (ENG., Illus.). 128p. (J). pap. *(978-0-14-132155-4(5)*, Puffin) Penguin Publishing Group.

—Sparkling Steps #7, 7 vols. Farley, Andrew & Swan, Angela, illus. 2009. (Magic Kitten Ser.: 7). (ENG.). 128p. (J). (gr. 1-3). pap. 5.99 *(978-0-448-45063-6(1)*, Grosset & Dunlap) Penguin Young Readers Group.

—A Special Wish, No. 2. Swan, Angela, illus. 2013. (Magic Ponies Ser.: 2). (ENG.). 128p. (J). (gr. 1-3). pap. 4.99 *(978-0-448-46206-6(0)*, Grosset & Dunlap) Penguin Young Readers Group.

—A Special Wish. 2013. (Magic Ponies Ser.: 2). lib. bdg. 14.75 *(978-0-606-29758-5(8)*, Turtleback) Turtleback Bks.

—Spellbound at School. 2014. (Magic Puppy Ser.: 11). lib. bdg. 16.00 *(978-0-606-34140-0(4)*, Turtleback) Turtleback Bks.

—Spellbound at School #11. Swan, Angela & Farley, Andrew, illus. 2014. (Magic Puppy Ser.: 11). (ENG.). 128p. (J). (gr. 1-3). 5.99 *(978-0-448-46790-0(9)*, Grosset & Dunlap) Penguin Young Readers Group.

—A Splash of Forever. 2014. (Magic Kitten Ser.: 14). lib. bdg. 16.00 *(978-0-606-35684-8(3))* Turtleback Bks.

—A Splash of Forever #14. Swan, Angela & Farley, Andrew, illus. 2014. (Magic Kitten Ser.: 14). (ENG.). 128p. (J). (gr. 1-3). 5.99 *(978-0-448-46797-9(6)*, Grosset & Dunlap) Penguin Young Readers Group.

—A Splash of Magic. 2013. (Magic Bunny Ser.: 3). lib. bdg. 14.75 *(978-0-606-31677-4(9)*, Turtleback) Turtleback Bks.

—A Splash of Magic #3. Swan, Angela, illus. 2013. (Magic Bunny Ser.: 3). (ENG.). 128p. (J). (gr. 1-3). pap. 5.99 *(978-0-448-46729-0(1)*, Grosset & Dunlap) Penguin Young Readers Group.

—Star Dreams, 3 vols. Swan, Angela & Farley, Andrew, illus. 2008. (Magic Kitten Ser.: 3). (ENG.). 128p. (J). (gr. 1-3). pap. 5.99 *(978-0-448-45000-1(3)*, Grosset & Dunlap) Penguin Young Readers Group.

—Star of the Show, 4 vols. Swan, Angela & Farley, Andrew, illus. 2009. (Magic Puppy Ser.: 4). (ENG.). 128p. (J). (gr. 1-3). pap. 5.99 *(978-0-448-45047-6(X)*, Grosset & Dunlap) Penguin Young Readers Group.

—Star of the Show. 2009. (Magic Puppy Ser.: 4). lib. bdg. 16.00 *(978-0-606-06978-6(X)*, Turtleback) Turtleback Bks.

—A Summer Spell. Swan, Angela & Farley, Andrew, illus. 2008. (Magic Kitten Ser.: 1). (ENG.). 128p. (J). (gr. 1-3). pap. 5.99 *(978-0-448-44998-2(6)*, Grosset & Dunlap) Penguin Young Readers Group.

—Sunshine Shimmers. 2014. (Magic Puppy Ser.: 12). lib. bdg. 14.75 *(978-0-606-34141-7(2)*, Turtleback) Turtleback Bks.

—A Twinkle of Hooves. 2013. (Magic Ponies Ser.: 3). lib. bdg. 14.75 *(978-0-606-31678-1(7)*, Turtleback) Turtleback Bks.

—A Twinkle of Hooves #3. Swan, Angela, illus. 2013. (Magic Ponies Ser.: 3). (ENG.). 128p. (J). (gr. 1-3). pap. 4.99 *(978-0-448-46207-3(9)*, Grosset & Dunlap) Penguin Young Readers Group.

—Twirling Tails, 7 vols. Farley, Andrew & Swan, Angela, illus. 2010. (Magic Puppy Ser.: 7). (ENG.). 128p. (J). (gr. 1-3). pap. 5.99 *(978-0-448-45066-7(6)*, Grosset & Dunlap) Penguin Young Readers Group.

—Vacation Dreams. 2013. (Magic Bunny Ser.: 2). lib. bdg. 16.00 *(978-0-606-31676-7(0)*, Turtleback) Turtleback Bks.

—Vacation Dreams #2. Swan, Angela, illus. 2013. (Magic Bunny Ser.: 2). (ENG.). 128p. (J). (gr. 1-3). pap. 5.99 *(978-0-448-46728-3(3)*, Grosset & Dunlap) Penguin Young Readers Group.

—Winter Wonderland. 2013. (Magic Ponies Ser.: 5). lib. bdg. 16.00 *(978-0-606-32118-1(7)*, Turtleback) Turtleback Bks.

—Winter Wonderland #5. Swan, Angela, illus. 2013. (Magic Ponies Ser.: 5). (ENG.). 128p. (J). (gr. 1-3). 5.99 *(978-0-448-46786-3(0)*, Grosset & Dunlap) Penguin Young Readers Group.

Benz, Derek & Lewis, J. S. The Brimstone Key. 2011. (Grey Griffins: the Clockwork Chronicles Ser.: 1). (ENG.). 400p. (J). (gr. 3-7). pap. 22.99 *(978-0-316-04521-6(7))* Little, Brown Bks. for Young Readers.

—The Brimstone Key Bk. 1. 2010. (Grey Griffins: the Clockwork Chronicles Ser.: 1). (ENG., Illus.). 384p. (J). (gr. 3-7). 15.99 *(978-0-316-04522-3(5))* Little, Brown Bks. for Young Readers.

—The Relic Hunters: Even Heroes Have to Go to School. 2012. (Grey Griffins: the Clockwork Chronicles Ser.: 2). (ENG.). 384p. (J). (gr. 3-7). pap. 7.99 *(978-0-316-04520-9(9))* Little, Brown Bks. for Young Readers.

—The Revenge of the Shadow King. unabr. ed. 2006. (Grey Griffins Ser.: 1). (ENG., Illus.). (J). (gr. 3-7). audio compact disk 39.95 *(978-0-439-87592-9(7)*, Scholastic) Scholastic, Inc.

Beobi & the Magic Coloring Book ABC First Words. 2005. (J). cd-rom 15.99 *(978-0-9743847-8-8(X))* Cohn, Tricia.

Beobi & the Magic Coloring Book at the Horse Stables. 2006. (J). 3.99 *(978-0-9743847-5-7(5))* Cohn, Tricia.

Beobi & the Magic Coloring Book Funland. 2006. (Illus.). 24p. (J). 3.99 *(978-0-9743847-7-1(1))* Cohn, Tricia.

Beobi & the Magic Coloring Book in the Universe. 2006. (J). 3.99 *(978-0-9743847-4-0(7))* Cohn, Tricia.

BEOBI & the Magic Coloring Book Our First Adventure. 2005. (J). cd-rom 15.99 *(978-0-9743847-9-5(8))* Cohn, Tricia.

Beobi & the Magic Coloring Book Our First Adventure. 2005. (J). 3.99 *(978-0-9743847-2-6(0))* Cohn, Tricia.

Bergsma, Jody. Wizard. 2nd ed. 2008. (Illus.). 32p. (J). 15.95 *(978-0-9740190-9-3(7))* Illumination Arts Publishing Co., Inc.

Bergstrom, Sarah. Desert Dwellers Born by Fire: The First Book in the Paintbrush Saga. 2015. (ENG.). 312p. (YA). (gr. 8-17). pap. 12.95 *(978-1-78279-587-2(1)*, Lodestone Bks.) Hunt, John Publishing Ltd. GBR. Dist: National Bk. Network.

Bergstrom, William. The Magic Telescope. 2006. 9.95 *(978-0-9787648-0-7(3))* Bergstrom Bks.

Berman, Ali. Misdirected: A Novel. 2014. (ENG., Illus.). 290p. (YA). (gr. 7). 18.95 *(978-1-60980-573-9(9)*, Triangle Square) Seven Stories Pr.

Bernatene, Poly, illus. The Sorcerer's Apprentice. 2007. (Usborne Young Reading: Series One Ser.). 47p. (J). (gr. -1-3). 8.99 *(978-0-7945-1589-8(4)*, Usborne) EDC Publishing.

Bernstein, Danielle V. The Magic in a Mermaid's Tear. 2013. 28p. pap. 24.95 *(978-1-62709-604-1(3))* America Star Bks.

Bernstein, David D. The Enchanted Rope. 2010. 25p. (J). pap. 13.95 *(978-1-4327-5175-3(1))* Outskirts Pr., Inc.

Bernstein, Nina. Magic by the Book, 4 vols. unabr. ed. 2005. (J). 65.75 *(978-1-4193-3607-2(X)*, 42048) Recorded Bks., Inc.

Berrow, G. M. My Little Pony: Equestria Girls: Through the Mirror. 2013. (Equestria Girls Ser.: 1). (ENG.). 240p. (J). (gr. 3-7). 9.99 *(978-0-316-24762-7(6))* Little, Brown Bks. for Young Readers.

Berry, Julie. The Emperor's Ostrich. 2017. (ENG.). 288p. (J). 16.99 *(978-1-59643-958-0(0)*, 9781596439580) Roaring Brook Pr.

Berry, Kit. Moondance of Stonewylde. 2011. (ENG.). 304p. (gr. 13-17). 10.99 *(978-0-575-09885-5(6)*, Gollancz) Orion Publishing Group, Ltd. GBR. Dist: Hachette Bk. Group.

—Solstice at Stonewylde. 2011. (ENG.). 400p. (gr. 13-17). 10.99 *(978-0-575-09887-9(2)*, Gollancz) Orion Publishing Group, Ltd. GBR. Dist: Hachette Bk. Group.

Berry, Nessa. Protectors of Little Africa. 2005. 108p. per. 9.99 *(978-1-58832-132-9(0))* Unlimited Publishing LLC.

Bessen, Luc. Arthur & the Minimoys. Sowchek, Ellen, tr. from FRE. 2005. (ENG.). 240p. (J). 15.99 *(978-0-06-059623-1(6))* HarperCollins Pubs.

Besson, Luc. Arthur & the Forbidden City. Sowchek, Ellen, tr. 2006. (ENG., Illus.). 192p. (J). (gr. 3-7). pap., pap. 5.99 *(978-0-06-059628-6(7)*, Harper Trophy) HarperCollins Pubs.

—Arthur & the Forbidden City. 2005. (ENG., Illus.). 192p. (J). 15.99 *(978-0-06-059626-2(0))* HarperCollins Pubs.

—Arthur & the Minimoys. 2005. (Illus.). 240p. (J). lib. bdg. 16.89 *(978-0-06-059624-8(4))* HarperCollins Pubs.

Bildner, Phil & Long, Loren. Game 3. Long, Loren, illus. 2008. (ENG., Illus.). 208p. (J). (gr. 2-5). 10.99 *(978-1-4169-1865-3(5)*, Simon & Schuster Bks. For Young Readers) Simon & Schuster Bks. For Young Readers.

Bingham, Laura. Álvor. 2009. pap. 17.99 *(978-1-59955-272-9(8))* Cedar Fort, Inc./CFI Distribution.

—Wings of Light. 2011. 240p. pap. 15.99 *(978-1-59955-492-1(5)*, Sweetwater Bks.) Cedar Fort, Inc./CFI Distribution.

Bird, Benjamin. Magic Monsters! Levins, Tim, illus. 2015. (Amazing Adventures of Superman! Ser.). (ENG.). 32p. (gr. k-2). pap. 3.95 *(978-1-4795-6525-2(3)*, DC Super Heroes) Stone Arch Bks.

Bishop, Helena Edwards. Lucille Tinderbox. 2012. (Illus.). 40p. pap. 18.95 *(978-1-4710-6053-3(5))* Lulu Pr., Inc.

Black, Holly. The Darkest Part of the Forest. 2015. (ENG.). 336p. (YA). (gr. 7-17). 18.00 *(978-0-316-21307-3(1))* Little Brown & Co.

—The Darkest Part of the Forest. 2016. (ENG.). 352p. (YA). (gr. 10-17). pap. 10.99 *(978-0-316-21308-0(X))* Little, Brown Bks. for Young Readers.

—The Darkest Part of the Forest. 2016. (YA). lib. bdg. 22.10 *(978-0-606-37533-7(3))* Turtleback Bks.

—The Iron Trial. 2014. (Magisterium Ser.: Bk. 1). pap. *(978-0-545-84067-5(8)*, Scholastic Pr.) Scholastic, Inc.

—Ironside: A Modern Faery's Tale. (ENG.). 336p. (YA). (gr. 9). 2008. pap. 10.99 *(978-0-689-86821-4(9))* 2007. 17.99 *(978-0-689-86820-7(0))* McElderry, Margaret K. Bks. (McElderry, Margaret K. Bks.).

—Kin. Naifeh, Ted, illus. 2008. (Good Neighbors Ser.: 1). (ENG.). 144p. (J). (gr. 7-18). 16.99 *(978-0-439-85562-4(4)*, Graphix) Scholastic, Inc.

—Kith. Naifeh, Ted, illus. 2010. (Good Neighbors Ser.: 2). (ENG.). 128p. (J). (gr. 3-7). pap. 12.99 *(978-0-439-85566-2(7)*, Graphix) Scholastic, Inc.

—Modern Faerie Tales: Tithe; Valiant; Ironside. 2010. (ENG.). 1040p. (YA). (gr. 9). pap. 24.99 *(978-1-4424-2020-5(0)*, McElderry, Margaret K. Bks.) McElderry, Margaret K. Bks.

—Red Glove. (Curse Workers Ser.: 2). (ENG.). (YA). (gr. 9). 2012. 352p. pap. 12.99 *(978-1-4424-0340-6(3))* 2011. 336p. 17.99 *(978-1-4424-0339-0(X))* McElderry, Margaret K. Bks. (McElderry, Margaret K. Bks.).

—Tithe: A Modern Faerie Tale. 2004. (ENG.). 336p. (YA). (gr. 8). reprint ed. pap. 10.99 *(978-0-689-86704-0(2)*, McElderry, Margaret K. Bks.) McElderry, Margaret K. Bks.

—Valiant: A Modern Faerie Tale. 2006. (ENG.). 320p. (YA). (gr. 8-12). pap. 10.99 *(978-0-689-86823-8(5)*, McElderry, Margaret K. Bks.) McElderry, Margaret K. Bks.

—White Cat. (Curse Workers Ser.: 1). (ENG.). (YA). (gr. 9). 2011. 336p. pap. 8.99 *(978-1-4169-6397-4(9))* 2010. 320p. 17.99 *(978-1-4169-6396-7(0))* McElderry, Margaret K. Bks. (McElderry, Margaret K. Bks.).

Black, Holly & Clare, Cassandra. The Bronze Key. 2016. (Magisterium Ser.: 3). (ENG., Illus.). 256p. (J). (gr. 3-7). 17.99 *(978-0-545-52231-1(5)*, Scholastic Pr.) Scholastic, Inc.

—The Copper Gauntlet. (Magisterium Ser.: 2). (ENG.). 272p. (J). 2016. (gr. 4-7). pap. 7.99 *(978-0-545-52229-8(3))* 2015. (gr. 3-7). 17.99 *(978-0-545-52228-1(5)*, Scholastic Pr.) Scholastic, Inc.

—The Copper Gauntlet. 2016. (Magisterium Ser.). (ENG.). (J). (gr. 4-7). lib. bdg. 18.40 ***(978-0-606-38811-5(7))*** Turtleback Bks.

—The Iron Trial. (ENG.). (J). 2015. (Magisterium Ser.: 1). 304p. (gr. 3-7). pap. 7.99 *(978-0-545-52226-7(9))* 2014. (Magisterium Ser.: 1). (Illus.). 304p. (gr. 3-7). 17.99 *(978-0-545-52225-0(0))* 2014. (Illus.). 320p. *(978-0-85753-250-3(2))* Scholastic, Inc. (Scholastic Pr.).

—The Iron Trial. 2015. (Magisterium Ser.: 1). lib. bdg. 18.40 *(978-0-606-37028-8(5))* Turtleback Bks.

—Magisterium. la Prueba de Hierro. 2015. (SPA & ENG.). 304p. (J). (gr. 8). pap. 13.95 *(978-607-07-2604-0(9))* Editorial Planeta, S. A. ESP. Dist: Two Rivers Distribution.

Black, Holly & DiTerlizzi, Tony. The Wrath of Mulgarath. DiTerlizzi, Tony, illus. 2013. (Spiderwick Chronicles Ser.: 5). (ENG., Illus.). (J). (gr. 1-5). 160p. 15.99 *(978-1-4424-8704-8(6))*; 176p. pap. 7.99 *(978-1-4424-8703-1(8))* Simon & Schuster Bks. For Young Readers. (Simon & Schuster Bks. For Young Readers).

—The Wrath of Mulgarath. l.t. ed. 2006. (Spiderwick Chronicles: Bk. 5). (Illus.). 183p. (J). (gr. 3-7). 23.95 *(978-0-7862-8579-2(6))* Thorndike Pr.

Blackburn, Sheila M. Stewie Scraps & the Super Sleigh. 2008. 72p. pap. *(978-1-903853-89-4(3))* Brilliant Pubns.

Blacker, Terence & Ross, Tony. Estrella de la Tele. 2003. (Serafina the Little Witch Ser.). (SPA.). 80p. (J). 7.95 *(978-84-8453-066-4(3))* Ediciones del Bronce ESP. Dist: Planeta Publishing Corp.

—Fuera de Control. 2003. (Serafina the Little Witch Ser.). (SPA., Illus.). 72p. (J). 7.95 *(978-84-8453-049-7(3))* Ediciones del Bronce ESP. Dist: Planeta Publishing Corp.

—Una Intrusa en el Hospital. 2003. (Serafina the Little Witch Ser.). (SPA., Illus.). 72p. (J). 7.95 *(978-84-8453-010-7(8))* Ediciones del Bronce ESP. Dist: Planeta Publishing Corp.

—Un Mundo de Problemas. 2003. (Serafina the Little Witch Ser.). (SPA.). 80p. (J). 7.95 *(978-84-8453-009-1(4))* Ediciones del Bronce ESP. Dist: Planeta Publishing Corp.

Blackford, Ami. Quest for the Dragon Stone: A Duncan Family Adventure. Blackford, Ami, illus. 2006. (Illus.). 48p. (J). (gr. 3-7). 16.95 *(978-1-60108-008-0(5))* Red Cygnet Pr.

—Quest for the Elfin Elixir: A Duncan Family Adventure Book 2. Blackford, Ami, illus. 2007. (Illus.). 79p. (J). (gr. 3-7). 16.95 *(978-1-60108-021-9(2))* Red Cygnet Pr.

Blackwood, Gary L. Second Sight. 2007. (Illus.). 279p. (J). (gr. 5-9). 14.65 *(978-0-7569-8132-7(8))* Perfection Learning Corp.

Blackwood, Sage. Jinx. (Jinx Ser.: 3). (J). (gr. 3-7). 2016. 400p. pap. 7.99 *(978-0-06-212997-0(X)*, Tegen, Katherine Bks) 2015. (ENG.). 400p. 16.99 *(978-0-06-212996-3(1)*, Tegen, Katherine Bks) 2014. (ENG.). 400p. 16.99 *(978-0-06-212993-2(7)*, Tegen, Katherine Bks) 2013.

(ENG.). 368p. 16.99 *(978-0-06-212990-1(2))* HarperCollins Pubs.

Blade, Adam. Sepron vs Narga. 2015. (Beast Quest Ser.: 3). (ENG., Illus.). 192p. (J). (gr. 2-4). pap. 5.99 *(978-1-4083-2409-7(1))* Hodder & Stoughton GBR. Dist: Hachette Bk. Group.

Blaha-Black, Caroline. Anika & the Magic Top. 2008. 60p. pap. 11.95 *(978-1-4357-1194-5(7))* Lulu Pr., Inc.

Blair, Eric. Rumpelstiltskin. Abello, Patricia, tr. from ENG. Shaw, David, illus. 2006. (Read-It! Readers en Español: Cuentos de Hadas Ser.). (SPA.). 32p. (gr. k-3). 21.32 *(978-1-4048-1637-4(2),* Easy Readers) Picture Window Bks.

Blair, Marion E. Just Beyond a Finger's Reach. 2013. (ENG.). 54p. (YA). pap. 21.95 *(978-1-4787-1396-8(8))* Outskirts Pr., Inc.

Blake, Drew. Engineer's Spell. 2007. 380p. per. 21.95 *(978-0-595-45249-1(3))* iUniverse, Inc.

Blake, Elly. Frostblood. 2017. (Frostblood Saga Ser.: 1). (ENG.). (YA). (gr. 7-17). 400p. pap. 9.99 ***(978-0-316-27318-3(X))***; 384p. 17.99 *(978-0-316-27325-1(2))* Little, Brown Bks. for Young Readers.

Blake, Kendare. Three Dark Crowns. (YA). (gr. 9). 2018. (Three Dark Crowns Ser.: 1). 432p. pap. 10.99 ***(978-0-06-238544-4(5))*** 2016. (ENG.). 416p. 17.99 *(978-0-06-238543-7(7))* HarperCollins Pubs. (HarperTeen).

—Three Dark Crowns. 2018. lib. bdg. 22.10 ***(978-0-606-40404-4(X))*** Turtleback Bks.

Blatchford, David. The Story of Mr Tomkins. 2012. (Illus.). 50p. pap. *(978-1-908773-29-6(4))* Ipoynmous Publishing, Ltd.

Bliss, Bob, illus. The Hardest Lessons: The Lost Babies Series #3. 2007. 118p. (J). per. 5.99 *(978-0-9792499-2-1(9))* Eagle Tree Pr.

—The Ruby Hind: The Lost Babies Series #1. 2007. 116p. (J). per. 5.99 *(978-0-9792499-0-7(2))* Eagle Tree Pr.

—Too Many Parents: The Lost Babies Series #2. 2007. 109p. (J). per. 5.99 *(978-0-9792499-1-4(0))* Eagle Tree Pr.

Bliss, Emily. Flash's Dash. Hanson, Sydney, illus. 2017. (Unicorn Princesses Ser.). (ENG.). 128p. (J). 15.99 *(978-1-68119-329-8(9),* 9781681193298, Bloomsbury USA Childrens) Bloomsbury Publishing USA.

—Sunbeam's Shine. Hanson, Sydney, illus. 2017. (Unicorn Princesses Ser.). (ENG.). 128p. (J). 15.99 *(978-1-68119-325-0(6),* 9781681193250, Bloomsbury USA Childrens) Bloomsbury Publishing USA.

Block, Betty Mitchell. The Magic Pork Chop Bone. 2013. (ENG.). 76p. (YA). pap. 8.95 *(978-1-4787-1482-8(4))* Outskirts Pr., Inc.

Bloomberg, Sandi. Ava & the Magic Tutu. 2008. 40p. per. 13.95 *(978-1-59800-248-5(1))* Outskirts Pr., Inc.

—Veronica & the Magic Fountain. 2010. (Illus.). 32p. (J). pap. 13.95 *(978-1-935268-66-6(X))* Halo Publishing International.

Bloomfield, Glynis. Jake's Secret. 2011. 194p. pap. 13.95 *(978-1-60976-615-3(6),* Strategic Bk. Publishing) Strategic Book Publishing & Rights Agency (SBPRA).

Blubaugh, Penny. Serendipity Market. 2011. (ENG.). 304p. (YA). (gr. 8). pap. 8.99 *(978-0-06-146877-3(0),* HarperTeen) HarperCollins Pubs.

Blueraven, Solaris. Mr. Sun & the Halloween Ball. 2010. 20p. 13.99 *(978-1-4520-0431-0(5))* AuthorHouse.

Blumer, J. Michael. The Book of Second Chances, Bk. 1. 2006. (Secret Books of Gabendoor Ser.). 284p. per. 14.99 *(978-1-59092-317-7(0))* Blue Forge Pr.

Blunden, Alan. Tommy & the Garden Shed. 2008. 104p. pap. *(978-1-84923-111-4(7))* YouWriteOn.

Blyton, Enid. The Goblin Aeroplane. (Illus.). 144p. (J). (gr. k-6). pap. 5.95 *(978-0-09-973590-8(3))* Random Hse. GBR. Dist: Trafalgar Square Publishing.

—Rag, Tag & Bobtail & Other Magical Stories. George, Hannah, illus. 2016. (ENG.). 224p. (J). (gr. 2-5). 9.99 *(978-1-5098-1084-0(5))* Pan Macmillan GBR. Dist: Independent Pubs. Group.

Bobet, Leah. Above. 2012. (ENG.). 368p. (J). (gr. 9). 17.99 *(978-0-545-29670-0(6),* Levine, Arthur A. Bks.) Scholastic, Inc.

Bobulski, Chelsea. The Wood. 2017. (ENG.). 320p. (YA). 17.99 *(978-1-250-09426-1(7),* 9781250094261) Feiwel & Friends.

Bode, N. E. The Anybodies. Ferguson, Peter, illus. 2005. (ENG.). 288p. (J). (gr. 5-8). reprint ed. pap. 6.99 *(978-0-06-055737-9(0))* HarperCollins Pubs.

Boehnert, Ernest. The Magic Christmas Train. 2010. 24p. 14.93 *(978-1-4269-4447-5(0))* Trafford Publishing.

Boelts, Maribeth. The Fairy Dogmother. 2017. (Step into Reading Ser.). (ENG.). 48p. (J). (gr. k-3). 3.99 *(978-1-101-93446-3(8),* Random Hse. Bks. for Young Readers) Random Hse. Children's Bks.

Boen, Sherry. The Fish Who Made a Magical Wish, 1 vol. 2009. 21p. pap. 24.95 *(978-1-61582-726-8(9))* America Star Bks.

Bolander, Sharon Miller. At the Stroke of Midnight. 2012. 40p. pap. 24.95 *(978-1-4626-8905-7(1))* America Star Bks.

Bond, Gwenda. Girl in the Shadows, 0 vols. 2016. (Cirque American Ser.: 2). (ENG.). 380p. (YA). (gr. 9-13). pap. 9.99 *(978-1-5039-5393-2(9),* 9781503953932, Skyscape) Amazon Publishing.

Bond, Michael. Paddington & the Magic Trick. Alley, R. W., illus. 2016. (I Can Read Level 1 Ser.). 32p. (J). (gr. -1-3). pap. 3.99 *(978-0-06-243067-0(X))* HarperCollins Pubs.

Bongiovanni, Debbie. It's All about Magic or Is It?, 1 vol. 2009. 55p. pap. 16.95 *(978-1-61546-875-1(7))* America Star Bks.

Booraem, Ellen. Small Persons with Wings. 2012. (ENG.). 304p. (J). (gr. 5-18). 7.99 *(978-0-14-242054-6(9),* Puffin Books) Penguin Young Readers Group.

Boos, Ben. Fantasy: An Artist's Realm. Boos, Ben, illus. 2010. (ENG., Illus.). 96p. (J). (gr. 5-9). 19.99 *(978-0-7636-4056-9(5))* Candlewick Pr.

Borchini, Ernest. Three Stories about Jonathan, the Computer, & Little Kitty: Three Short Stories about a Boy & His Magic Cat. 2013. 36p. (gr. -1). pap. 15.49 *(978-1-4669-6636-9(X))* Trafford Publishing.

Bosch, Pseudonymous. Bad Luck. (Bad Bks.: 2). (ENG., Illus.). (J). (gr. 3-7). 2017. 304p. pap. 7.99 *(978-0-316-32044-3(7))* 2016. 288p. 17.00 *(978-0-316-32042-9(0))* Little, Brown Bks. for Young Readers.

—Bad Luck. 2017. (Bad Bks.: 2). (J). lib. bdg. 18.40 *(978-0-606-39475-8(3))* Turtleback Bks.

—Bad Magic. 2014. (ENG.). (J). 384p. 153.00 *(978-0-316-37696-9(5))*; (Bad Bks.: 1). 400p. (gr. 3-7). 17.00 *(978-0-316-32038-2(2))* Little, Brown Bks. for Young Readers.

—Bad Magic. 2015. (Bad Bks.: 1). (J). lib. bdg. 18.45 *(978-0-606-37522-1(8))* Turtleback Bks.

—If You're Reading This, It's Too Late. 2009. (Secret Ser.: 2). (ENG.). 400p. (J). (gr. 3-7). pap. 8.99 *(978-0-316-11368-7(9))* Little, Brown Bks. for Young Readers.

—This Isn't What It Looks Like. (Secret Ser.: 4). (ENG.). (J). (gr. 3-7). 2011. 448p. pap. 8.99 *(978-0-316-07624-1(4))* 2010. 432p. 17.00 *(978-0-316-07625-8(2))* Little, Brown Bks. for Young Readers.

—You Have to Stop This. (Secret Ser.: 5). (ENG.). (J). (gr. 3-7). 2012. 368p. pap. 8.99 *(978-0-316-07627-2(9))* 2011. 352p. 16.99 *(978-0-316-07626-5(0))* Little, Brown Bks. for Young Readers.

—You Have to Stop This. 2012. (Secret Ser.: 5). (J). lib. bdg. 18.45 *(978-0-606-26695-6(X),* Turtleback) Turtleback Bks.

Boston, L. M. The Stones of Green Knowe. Boston, Peter, illus. 2006. (Green Knowe Ser.: 6). (ENG.). 144p. (J). (gr. 2-5). pap. 10.95 *(978-0-15-205566-0(5))* Houghton Mifflin Harcourt Publishing Co.

Botha, Si. Goosala Goop. 2009. 48p. pap. 16.50 *(978-1-60860-124-0(2),* Strategic Bk. Publishing) Strategic Book Publishing & Rights Agency (SBPRA).

Bottner, Barbara & Kruglik, Gerald. Pish & Posh. Bottner, Barbara, illus. 2004. (I Can Read Bks.). (Illus.). 48p. (J). (gr. k-3). pap. 15.99 *(978-0-06-051416-7(7))* HarperCollins Pubs.

—Pish & Posh Wish for Fairy Wings. Bottner, Barbara, illus. (I Can Read Level 2 Ser.). (Illus.). 48p. (J). 2007. (ENG.). (gr. k-3). pap. 3.99 *(978-0-06-051421-1(3),* Tegen, Katherine Bks) 2006. (gr. -1-3). lib. bdg. 16.89 *(978-0-06-051420-4(5))* HarperCollins Pubs.

Boukov, Lubima. The Magic Swing, 1 vol. 2009. 15p. pap. 24.95 *(978-1-60749-612-0(7))* America Star Bks.

Bover, Annie. Mooncorn. 2013. (Illus.). 20p. pap. *(978-1-909465-18-3(6))* Cloister Hse. Pr., The.

Bow, Erin. Plain Kate. (ENG.). 320p. (J). (gr. 7-7). 2012. pap. 9.99 *(978-0-545-16665-2(9))* 2010. 17.99 *(978-0-545-16664-5(0))* Scholastic, Inc. (Levine, Arthur A. Bks.).

—Sorrow's Knot. 2013. (ENG.). 352p. (J). (gr. 7). 17.99 *(978-0-545-16666-9(7),* Levine, Arthur A. Bks.) Scholastic, Inc.

Bow, Patricia. The Bone Flute, 1 vol. 2004. (ENG.). 144p. (J). (gr. 5-12). pap. 6.95 *(978-1-55143-301-1(X))* Orca Bk. Pubs. USA.

Bowers, Chuck. Leprechaun Legacy. 2009. 156p. pap. 12.95 *(978-1-4401-2248-4(2))* iUniverse, Inc.

Bowman, Mare. The Magic Shell. 2011. 108p. (gr. -1). 21.49 *(978-1-4520-5738-5(9))*; pap. 10.99 *(978-1-4520-5113-0(5))* AuthorHouse.

Bowser, D. M. The Enchanting Tales of Lilith. 2011. 54p. pap. 16.95 *(978-1-4560-9570-3(6))* America Star Bks.

Bowyer, Clifford B. The Darkness Within: The Imperium Saga: the Adventures of Kyria, 12 vols., Vol. 9. Brigman, June, illus. 2009. (Imperium Saga: 9). (ENG.). (J). 5.99 *(978-0-9787782-4-8(3))* Silver Leaf Bks., LLC.

The Boy Who Went to the North Wind: Individual Title Six-Packs. (Literatura 2000 Ser.). (gr. 2-3). 33.00 *(978-0-7635-0217-1(0))* Rigby Education.

Boyce, Frank Cottrell. Chitty Chitty Bang Bang & the Race Against Time. Berger, Joe, illus. (Chitty Chitty Bang Bang Ser.). (ENG.). 240p. (J). (gr. 4-7). 2014. pap. 6.99 *(978-0-7636-6931-7(8))* 2013. 15.99 *(978-0-7636-5982-0(7))* Candlewick Pr.

—Chitty Chitty Bang Bang Flies Again. Berger, Joe, illus. 2013. (Chitty Chitty Bang Bang Ser.). (ENG.). 224p. (J). (gr. 4-7). pap. 6.99 *(978-0-7636-6353-7(0))* Candlewick Pr.

—Desirable. 2012. (Stoke Books Titles Ser.). 64p. (J). (gr. 5-8). pap. 45.32 *(978-0-7613-9216-3(5))* Stoke Bks.

Boyd, Cathy. The Little Snowman's New Hat. 2011. 28p. pap. 24.95 *(978-1-4560-2751-3(4))* PublishAmerica, Inc.

Boyd, G. A. Alchemy Jones & the Source of Magic. 2011. 324p. (gr. -1). 29.95 *(978-1-4620-2234-2(0))*; pap. 19.95 *(978-1-4620-2232-8(4))* iUniverse, Inc.

Bozarth, Jan. The Fairy Godmother Academy #6: Trinity's Book. 2013. (Fairy Godmother Academy Ser.). (ENG., Illus.). 240p. (J). (gr. 3-7). 6.99 *(978-0-375-86576-3(4),* Yearling) Random Hse. Children's Bks.

—Lilu's Book. 2011. (Fairy Godmother Academy Ser.: No. 4). (ENG., Illus.). 192p. (J). (gr. 3-7). 6.99 *(978-0-375-85187-2(9),* Yearling) Random Hse. Children's Bks.

—Zally's Book. Burden, Andrea, illus. 2010. (Fairy Godmother Academy Ser.: No. 3). (ENG.). 208p. (J). (gr. 3-7). pap. 6.99 *(978-0-375-85185-8(2),* Yearling) Random Hse. Children's Bks.

Bracken, Beth & Fraser, Kay. Believe, 1 vol. Sawyer, Odessa, illus. 2014. (Faeriegound Ser.). (ENG.). 288p. (gr. 4-8). 12.95 *(978-1-62370-113-0(9))* Capstone Young Readers of Coughlan Cos.

—Fate of the Willow Queen. Sawyer, Odessa, illus. 2013. (Faeriegound Ser.). (ENG.). 96p. (gr. 1-3). 23.99 *(978-1-4342-4492-5(X),* Faeriegound) Stone Arch Bks.

—The Hidden Things, 1 vol. Sawyer, Odessa, illus. 2014. (Faeriegound Ser.). (ENG.). 96p. (gr. 1-3). 23.99 *(978-1-4342-9185-1(5),* Faeriegound) Stone Arch Bks.

—A Murder of Crows, 1 vol. Sawyer, Odessa, illus. 2013. (Faeriegound Ser.). (ENG.). 96p. (gr. 1-3). lib. bdg. 23.99 *(978-1-4342-4491-8(1))* Stone Arch Bks.

—The Seventh Kingdom, 1 vol. Sawyer, Odessa, illus. 2014. (Faeriegound Ser.). (ENG.). 96p. (gr. 1-3). 23.99 *(978-1-4342-9186-8(3),* Faeriegound) Stone Arch Bks.

—Two Mothers. Sawyer, Odessa, illus. 2013. (Faeriegound Ser.). (ENG.). 96p. (gr. 1-3). 23.99 *(978-1-4342-4490-1(3),* Faeriegound) Stone Arch Bks.

Bradfield, Jolly Roger. Benjamin Dilley's Thirsty Camel. Bradfield, Jolly Roger, illus. 2012. (ENG., Illus.). 64p. (J). (gr. 4-7). 18.95 *(978-1-930900-60-8(0))* Purple Hse. Pr.

Bradman, Tony. Flora the Fairy's Magic Spells. Carlow, Emma, illus. 2nd ed. 2016. (Reading Ladder Ser.). (ENG.). 48p. (J). (gr. k-2). 7.99 *(978-1-4052-8227-7(4))* Egmont Bks., Ltd. GBR. Dist: Independent Pubs. Group.

—Snow White & the Magic Mirror. Warburton, Sarah, illus. 2014. (After Happily Ever After Ser.). (ENG.). 56p. (gr. 2-3). pap. 5.05 *(978-1-4342-7956-9(1))*; lib. bdg. 25.32 *(978-1-4342-7950-7(2))* Stone Arch Bks. (After Happily Ever After).

Braithwaite, Lisa. Lucy Goes into the Wild. 2012. 28p. pap. 15.99 *(978-1-4771-4341-4(6))* Xlibris Corp.

Bramlett, Timothy A. Thomas in the Land of the Blips. 2012. 26p. pap. 19.99 *(978-1-4772-9576-2(3))* AuthorHouse.

Braswell, Liz. As Old As Time: A Twisted Tale. 2016. (Twisted Tale Ser.). (ENG.). 496p. (YA). (gr. 7-17). 17.99 *(978-1-4847-0728-9(1))* Disney Pr.

—A Whole New World. 2016. (Twisted Tale Ser.). (YA). lib. bdg. 20.85 *(978-0-606-38511-4(8))* Turtleback Bks.

—A Whole New World: A Twisted Tale. (Twisted Tale Ser.). (ENG.). (YA). (gr. 7-12). 2016. 400p. pap. 9.99 *(978-1-4847-0732-6(X))* 2015. 384p. 17.99 *(978-1-4847-0729-6(X))* Disney Pr.

Brauner, Barbara & Mattson, James Iver. The Glitter Trap. Halpin, Abigail, illus. 2014. (Oh My Godmother Ser.). (ENG.). 256p. (J). (gr. 3-7). pap. 6.99 *(978-1-4231-6474-6(1))* Hyperion Bks. for Children.

—Oh My Godmother the Magic Mistake. Halpin, Abigail, illus. 2014. (Oh My Godmother Ser.). (ENG.). 272p. (J). (gr. 3-7). pap. 6.99 *(978-1-4231-6479-1(2))* Hyperion Bks. for Children.

Bray, Libba. A Great & Terrible Beauty. 2005. (Gemma Doyle Trilogy Ser.: Bk. 1). (ENG.). 432p. (YA). (gr. 7). reprint ed. pap. 9.99 *(978-0-385-73231-4(7),* Ember) Random Hse. Children's Bks.

—Rebel Angels. 2006. (Gemma Doyle Trilogy Ser.: Bk. 2). (ENG.). 576p. (YA). (gr. 7-12). pap. 10.99 *(978-0-385-73341-0(0),* Ember) Random Hse. Children's Bks.

—The Sweet Far Thing. 2009. (Gemma Doyle Trilogy Ser.: Bk. 3). (ENG.). 848p. (YA). (gr. 7). pap. 10.99 *(978-0-440-23777-8(7),* Ember) Random Hse. Children's Bks.

Breece, Beverly. The Curwood Acorns. DeWeese, Susan, illus. 2012. 40p. pap. 24.95 *(978-1-4626-8202-7(2))* America Star Bks.

Brennan, Sarah Rees. The Demon's Covenant. (Demon's Lexicon Trilogy Ser.: 2). (ENG., Illus.). (YA). (gr. 9). 2011. 464p. pap. 12.99 *(978-1-4169-6382-0(0))* 2010. 448p. 17.99 *(978-1-4169-6381-3(2))* McElderry, Margaret K. Bks. (McElderry, Margaret K. Bks.).

—The Demon's Lexicon. (Demon's Lexicon Trilogy Ser.: 1). (ENG., Illus.). (YA). (gr. 9). 2010. 352p. pap. 12.99 *(978-1-4169-6380-6(4))* 2009. 336p. 18.99 *(978-1-4169-6379-0(0))* McElderry, Margaret K. Bks. (McElderry, Margaret K. Bks.).

—The Demon's Surrender. 2012. (Demon's Lexicon Trilogy Ser.: 3). (ENG., Illus.). 400p. (YA). (gr. 9). pap. 9.99 *(978-1-4169-6384-4(7),* McElderry, Margaret K. Bks.) McElderry, Margaret K. Bks.

—Tell the Wind & Fire. (ENG.). 368p. (YA). (gr. 7). 2017. pap. 9.99 *(978-0-544-93887-8(9),* HMH Books For Young Readers) 2016. 17.99 *(978-0-544-31817-5(X))* Houghton Mifflin Harcourt Publishing Co.

—Unmade. (Lynburn Legacy Ser.: Bk. 3). (ENG.). 384p. (YA). (gr. 7). 2015. pap. 9.99 *(978-0-375-87105-4(5),* Ember) 2014. (Illus.). 17.99 *(978-0-375-87043-9(1),* Random Hse. Bks. for Young Readers) Random Hse. Children's Bks.

—Unspoken. (Lynburn Legacy Ser.: Bk. 1). (ENG.). (YA). (gr. 7). 2012. 384p. 18.99 *(978-0-375-87041-5(5),* Random Hse. Bks. for Young Readers)Bk. 1. 2013. 400p. pap. 8.99 *(978-0-375-87103-0(9),* Ember) Random Hse. Children's Bks.

—Untold. Fochesato, Giorgio, illus. (Lynburn Legacy Ser.: Bk. 2). (ENG.). (YA). (gr. 7). 2014. 400p. pap. 9.99 *(978-0-375-87104-7(7),* Ember) 2013. 384p. 18.99 *(978-0-375-87042-2(3),* Random Hse. Bks. for Young Readers) Random Hse. Children's Bks.

Brent, Isabelle. The Christmas Horse & the Three Wise Men. 2016. (ENG., Illus.). 28p. (J). (gr. k-3). 17.95 *(978-1-937786-61-8(7),* Wisdom Tales) World Wisdom, Inc.

Breslin, Jayne. The Princess Jelly Tutu Adventures. 2011. (Illus.). 28p. (gr. -1). pap. 14.09 *(978-1-4567-7611-4(8))* AuthorHouse.

Brett, James. Infaeter. Englund, Jonathon, illus. 2nd ed. 2013. 238p. pap. *(978-1-908462-03-9(5))* New Dawn Pubs.

Brewin, Barbara. Sidney Snail's Wonderful World of Adventure. 2009. (Illus.). 32p. pap. 14.49 *(978-1-4389-4100-4(5))* AuthorHouse.

Bridge, George. Jack & the Beanstalk. Flowerpot Press, ed. 2012. (Illus.). 20p. (J). *(978-1-77093-127-5(9))* Flowerpot Children's Pr. Inc.

Bridgman, Rae. Kingdom of Trolls: A Middlegate Book. 2010. (Illus.). 287p. (J). pap. 15.00 *(978-0-9864974-1-4(X))* Sybertooth, Inc. CAN. Dist: Lightning Source, Inc.

Bright, J. E. The Joker's Magic Mayhem. Vecchio, Luciano, illus. 2016. (Batman & Robin Adventures Ser.). (ENG.). 88p. (gr. 2-3). lib. bdg. 26.65 *(978-1-4965-2538-3(8),* DC Super Heroes) Stone Arch Bks.

Bright, J. E. & Sutton, Laurie S. Wonder Woman vs. Circe, 1 vol. Vecchio, Luciano, illus. 2013. (DC Super Heroes Ser.). (ENG.). 56p. (gr. 2-3). lib. bdg. 26.65 *(978-1-4342-6014-7(3))* Stone Arch Bks.

Bright, Phoebe. Wish upon a Gift. 2012. (Lucky Stars Ser.: 6). (ENG.). 96p. (J). (gr. 2-5). pap. 5.99 *(978-0-545-42003-7(2),* Scholastic Paperbacks) Scholastic, Inc.

Brignole, Giancarla, tr. El Pulpo Campanero. Meconni, Beppe, illus. (Fabulas De Familia Ser.). (SPA.). 32p. *(978-970-20-0262-8(1))* Castillo, Ediciones, S. A. de C. V.

Brignull, Irena. The Hawkweed Prophecy. 2017. (Hawkweed Ser.: 1). (ENG.). 384p. (gr. 7-17). pap. 10.99 ***(978-1-60286-313-2(X),*** Weinstein Bks.) Perseus Bks. Group.

Brindle, I. J. Balthazar Fabuloso in the Lair of the Humbugs. Walker, Sholto, illus. 2016. (ENG.). 240p. (J). 16.95 *(978-0-8234-3577-7(6))* Holiday Hse., Inc.

Brittenham, Skip. Between Worlds. 2016. (ENG., Illus.). 256p. (YA). (gr. 7). 18.99 *(978-0-399-17689-0(6),* G.P. Putnam's Sons Books for Young Readers) Penguin Young Readers Group.

Brodhead, Kimberly. Gaden's Tower: Book One. 2007. 164p. per. 24.95 *(978-1-60441-038-9(8))* America Star Bks.

Brodien-Jones, Christine. The Owl Keeper. Kneen, Maggie, illus. 2011. (ENG.). 320p. (J). (gr. 3-7). 8.99 *(978-0-385-73815-6(3),* Yearling) Random Hse. Children's Bks.

Brody, Jessica. Addie Bell's Shortcut to Growing Up. 2017. (ENG.). 368p. (J). (gr. 5). 16.99 *(978-0-399-55510-7(2),* Delacorte Bks. for Young Readers) Random Hse. Children's Bks.

Brondos, Pam. The Last Remnant, 0 vols. 2016. (Fourline Trilogy Ser.: 3). (ENG.). 320p. (J). pap. 9.99 *(978-1-61218-470-8(7),* 9781612184708, Skyscape) Amazon Publishing.

—On the Meldon Plain, 0 vols. 2016. (Fourline Trilogy Ser.: 2). (ENG.). 356p. (YA). (gr. 9-13). pap. 9.99 *(978-1-5039-5320-8(3),* 9781503953208, Skyscape) Amazon Publishing.

Brooke, Jasmine. Jack & the Beanstalk: Chart Your Magic Bean's Life Cycle! 2017. (Fairy Tale Fixers: Fixing Fairy Tale Problems with STEM Ser.). 32p. (gr. 3-4). pap. 63.00 ***(978-1-5382-0666-9(8))*** Stevens, Gareth Publishing LLLP.

Brooks, Charlie. Greystone Valley. Grundy, Jessica, illus. 2013. 166p. 17.99 *(978-1-938821-33-2(5))*; 198p. pap. 9.99 *(978-1-938821-41-7(6))* Grey Gecko Pr.

Brooks, Donna. The Golden Spindle. 2010. 112p. pap. 30.00 *(978-1-60860-852-2(2),* Eloquent Bks.) Strategic Book Publishing & Rights Agency (SBPRA).

Brothers, Marilee. Moonstone. 2008. 236p. (YA). pap. 14.95 *(978-0-9802453-4-9(6),* Bell Bridge Bks.) BelleBks., Inc.

Brown, Alan James. Michael & the Monkey King. 2008. 180p. pap. 16.95 *(978-1-4092-0241-7(0))* Lulu Pr., Inc.

Brown, E.A. Gossamer. 2012. 24p. pap. 24.95 *(978-1-4626-5043-9(0))* America Star Bks.

Brown, Jason Robert. Tickety Tock. GrandPré, Mary, illus. 2008. 32p. (J). (gr. -1-3). lib. bdg. 18.89 *(978-0-06-078753-0(8),* Geringer, Laura Book) HarperCollins Pubs.

Brown, Jeff. Stanley & the Magic Lamp. Nash, Scott & Pamintuan, Macky, illus. 2009. (Flat Stanley Ser.). (ENG.). 128p. (J). (gr. 2-5). pap. 4.99 *(978-0-06-009793-6(0))* HarperCollins Pubs.

—Stanley & the Magic Lamp. 2009. (Flat Stanley Ser.). (J). (gr. k-3). lib. bdg. 14.75 *(978-0-613-68465-1(6),* Turtleback) Turtleback Bks.

Brown, Marc. D. W. the Big Boss. 2005. (ENG., Illus.). 24p. (J). (gr. -1-1). per. 3.99 *(978-0-316-73395-3(4))* Little, Brown Bks. for Young Readers.

Brownlow, Brooke. The Magic of Old Oak Hill. 2005. 48p. pap. 16.95 *(978-1-4241-0223-5(5))* PublishAmerica, Inc.

Bruckner, Tai. Lemon Path Encounter, 1 vol. Bruckner, Wes, illus. 2009. 15p. pap. 24.95 *(978-1-60836-407-7(0))* America Star Bks.

Bruno, Cristina. The Mother Store. 2009. 52p. pap. 30.00 *(978-1-4389-2875-3(0))* AuthorHouse.

Bryant, Anne. The Fantasy Soccer Wall. 2015. (Race Further with Reading Ser.). (ENG., Illus.). 48p. (J). *(978-0-7787-2061-4(6))* Crabtree Publishing Co.

Bubble Guppies Guess Who's Fin-Tastic! 2014. (Guess Who? Ser.: 1). (ENG.). 10p. (J). (gr. -1-k). bds. 10.99 *(978-0-7944-3254-6(9),* Reader's Digest Children's Bks.) Studio Fun International.

Buchanan, Johnny & Conway, Beth. Rachel & the Magic Beads. Bosak, Virginia, illus. 2007. 16p. (YA). pap. 7.99 *(978-0-9768772-9-5(5))* Wise Guides, LLC.

Buck, Alicia. Out of the Ashes. 2015. 281p. (YA). pap. 17.99 *(978-1-4621-1727-7(9))* Cedar Fort, Inc./CFI Distribution.

Buckley, Michael. The Council of Mirrors. Ferguson, Peter, illus. (Sisters Grimm Ser.). (ENG.). 352p. (gr. 3-7). 2013. (YA). pap. 7.95 *(978-1-4197-0538-0(5))* 2012. (J). 16.95 *(978-1-4197-0186-3(X))* Abrams, Inc. (Amulet Bks.).

—The Council of Mirrors. 2013. (Sisters Grimm Ser.: 9). (J). lib. bdg. 18.40 *(978-0-606-31650-7(7),* Turtleback) Turtleback Bks.

—The Everafter War. Ferguson, Peter, illus. (Sisters Grimm Ser.: Bk. 7). (ENG.). (J). (gr. 3-7). 2010. 336p. pap. 8.95 *(978-0-8109-8429-5(6))*Bk. 7. 2009. 320p. 16.95 *(978-0-8109-8355-7(9))* Abrams, Inc. (Amulet Bks.).

—The Everafter War. 2010. (Sisters Grimm Ser.: 7). (J). lib. bdg. 19.60 *(978-0-606-12500-0(0),* Turtleback) Turtleback Bks.

—The Inside Story. Ferguson, Peter, illus. 2011. (Sisters Grimm Ser.: 8). (ENG.). 288p. (J). (gr. 3-7). pap. 7.95 *(978-0-8109-9726-4(6),* Amulet Bks.) Abrams, Inc.

—The Inside Story, 6 vols. 2010. (Sisters Grimm Ser.: 8). (J). 89.75 *(978-1-4498-1969-9(9))*; 72.75 *(978-1-4498-1967-5(2))*; 219.75 *(978-1-4498-1966-8(4))*; 87.75 *(978-1-4498-1971-2(0))*; 1.25 *(978-1-4498-1973-6(7))* Recorded Bks., Inc.

—The Inside Story. 2011. (Sisters Grimm Ser.: 8). (J). lib. bdg. 18.40 *(978-0-606-23818-2(2),* Turtleback) Turtleback Bks.

—The Inside Story Bk. 8, Bk. 8. Ferguson, Peter, illus. 2010. (Sisters Grimm Ser.: Bk. 8). (ENG.). 288p. (J). (gr. 3-7). 16.95 *(978-0-8109-8430-1(X),* Amulet Bks.) Abrams, Inc.

—Magic & Other Misdemeanors. Ferguson, Peter, illus. 2007. (ENG.). 304p. (YA). (gr. 3-7). 16.95 *(978-0-8109-9358-7(9),* Amulet Bks.) Abrams, Inc.

—The Problem Child: The Sisters Grimm. 2007. (Sisters Grimm Ser.: 3). (YA). lib. bdg. 18.40 *(978-1-4178-0733-8(4),* Turtleback) Turtleback Bks.

—A Very Grimm Guide. Ferguson, Peter, illus. 2012. (Sisters Grimm Ser.). (ENG.). 128p. (J). (gr. 3-7). 16.95 *(978-1-4197-0201-3(7),* Amulet Bks.) Abrams, Inc.

Buckmaster, Heath L. Box of Hair: A Fairy Tale, 3 bks., Bk. 1. (Illus.). (YA). 2007. 102p. pap. 12.99 *(978-0-9771802-5-7(5))* 2008. 108p. lib. bdg. 25.00 *(978-0-9771802-4-0(7))* Transaltar Publishing.

—Box of Hair: A Fairy Tale. 2008. 104p. pap. 12.50 *(978-1-4357-2690-1(1))* Lulu Pr., Inc.

—The Venus Diary. 2008. 136p. pap. 13.50 *(978-0-615-20678-3(6))* Transaltar Publishing.

Budreau, Craig. Trail Map: Barton Creek Greenbelt — Loop 360 to Zilker Park. 2006. (J). per. 5.00 *(978-1-932196-26-9(9))* WordWright.biz, Inc.

Bugbird, Tim. Molly the Muffin Fairy. 2015. (ENG.). 32p. (J). 15.99 *(978-1-78393-466-9(2))* Make Believe Ideas GBR. Dist: Nelson, Thomas Inc.

Bugg, Ann T. Into the Forest & down the Tower. Kramin, Valerie, illus. 2012. 136p. pap. *(978-1-927044-24-7(3))* Writers AMuse Me.

Bullen, Alexandra. Wish. 2010. (ENG.). 336p. (J). (gr. 9). pap. 9.99 (978-0-545-13906-9(6)) Scholastic, Inc.
—Wishful Thinking. 2011. (ENG.). 256p. (J). (gr. 9-9). 17.99 (978-0-545-13907-6(4)) Scholastic, Inc.
Bunce, Elizabeth C. A Curse Dark as Gold. 2010. (ENG.). 400p. (J). (gr. 7). 9.99 (978-0-439-89577-4(4), Scholastic Paperbacks) Scholastic, Inc.
—Liar's Moon. 2011. (YA). pap. (978-0-545-13607-5(5)); (ENG.). 368p. (J). (gr. 7-7). 17.99 (978-0-545-13608-2(3)) Scholastic, Inc. (Levine, Arthur A. Bks.).
—StarCrossed. 2011. (ENG.). 368p. (YA). pap. 9.99 (978-0-545-13606-8(7), Levine, Arthur A. Bks.) Scholastic, Inc.
Bunn, Bill. Duck Boy. 2012. (ENG.). 246p. (gr. 6-8). pap. 16.99 (978-1-938463-60-0(9)) Bitingduck Pr.
Burden, Meg. The King Commands. 2010. (Tales of the Borderlands Ser.: Bk. 2). 312p. (YA). (gr. 7-18). pap. 8.95 (978-0-9798824-1-8(9)) Brown Barn Bks.
Burgess, Melvin. Lady: My Life as a Bitch. 2003. (Illus.). 272p. (J). pap. 6.99 (978-0-06-054033-3(8)) HarperCollins Pubs.
Burgess, V. L. The Mapmaker's Sons. 2012. (ENG.). 176p. (J). (gr. 4-7). 16.99 (978-0-9854810-0-1(5)) Move Bks., LLC.
Burgis, Stephanie. The Dragon with a Chocolate Heart. 2017. (ENG.). 256p. (J). 16.99 (978-1-68119-343-4(4), 9781681193434, Bloomsbury USA Childrens) Bloomsbury Publishing USA.
—Kat, Incorrigible. 2012. (Kat, Incorrigible Ser.: 1). (ENG., Illus.). 320p. (J). (gr. 5-9). pap. 7.99 (978-1-4169-9448-0(3), Atheneum Bks. for Young Readers) Simon & Schuster Children's Publishing.
—Renegade Magic. 2012. (Kat, Incorrigible Ser.: 2). (ENG., Illus.). 336p. (J). (gr. 5-9). 16.99 (978-1-4169-9449-7(1), Atheneum Bks. for Young Readers) Simon & Schuster Children's Publishing.
—Stolen Magic. (Kat, Incorrigible Ser.: 3). (ENG., Illus.). 400p. (YA). (gr. 5-8). 2014. pap. 7.99 (978-1-4169-9452-7(1)) 2013. 17.99 (978-1-4169-9451-0(3), Atheneum Bks. for Young Readers) Simon & Schuster Children's Publishing.
Burgis, Stephanie & Ward, Barnaby. Kat, Incorrigible. 2011. (Kat, Incorrigible Ser.: 1). (ENG., Illus.). 304p. (J). (gr. 5-9). 16.99 (978-1-4169-9447-3(5), Atheneum Bks. for Young Readers) Simon & Schuster Children's Publishing.
Burke, Ellinor Rozecki. Susana Worrywart & the Magical Teddy Bear Balloon. Perciopelo, illus. 2003. 32p. (J). 17.99 (978-0-9741586-3-1(1)) Comfort Tales, LLC.
—Susana Worrywart & the Magical Teddy Bear Balloon: With CD for Relaxation. Perciopelo, illus. 2003. 32p. (J). 27.00 incl. audio compact disk (978-0-9741586-0-0(7)) Comfort Tales, LLC.
Burns, Laura J. Bewitched in Oz. 1 vol. Peters, Liam, illus. 2014. (Bewitched in Oz Ser.). (ENG.). 256p. (gr. 4-8). 12.95 (978-1-62370-129-1(5)); lib. bdg. 30.65 (978-1-4342-9207-0(X)) Stone Arch Bks.
—Magic Below. 2016. (Bewitched in Oz Ser.). (ENG.). 240p. (gr. 4-8). lib. bdg. 30.65 (978-1-4965-2603-8(1)) Stone Arch Bks.
Burns, Mary Gore. The Magic Room: Mandy & the Lily Pond. 2011. 48p. pap. 17.30 (978-1-4634-2642-2(9)) AuthorHouse.
Burton, Elizabeth K. The Everdark Gate: The Everdark Wars Book 3. 2008. (ENG.). 280p. pap. 15.50 (978-1-934135-79-2(8), Zumaya Otherworlds) Zumaya Pubns. LLC.
Bush, Maureen. The Nexus Ring. 1 vol. 2007. (Veil of Magic Ser.: 1). (ENG.). 136p. (J). (gr. 3-6). per. 6.95 (978-1-55050-362-3(6)) Coteau Bks. CAN. Dist: Orca Bk. Pubs. USA.
Busiek, Kurt. Wizard's Tale. 2013. (ENG., Illus.). 144p. pap. 19.99 (978-1-61377-593-6(8), 9781613775936) Idea & Design Works, LLC.
Busse, R. R., adapted by. Meet Kubo. 2016. (Illus.). 32p. (J). **(978-1-5182-3471-2(2))** Little Brown & Co.
Bussell, Darcey. Christmas in Enchantia. 2010. (Magic Ballerina Ser.). (ENG., Illus.). 144p. (J). (gr. k-2). pap. 9.99 (978-0-00-734800-8(2), HarperCollins Children's Bks.) HarperCollins Pubs. Ltd. GBR. Dist: HarperCollins Pubs.
—Delphie & the Glass Slippers, 4. 2008. (Magic Ballerina Ser.: 4). (ENG., Illus.). 96p. (J). (gr. k-2). pap. 6.99 (978-0-00-728617-1(1), HarperCollins Children's Bks.) HarperCollins Pubs. Ltd. GBR. Dist: HarperCollins Pubs.
—Delphie & the Masked Ball, 3. 2008. (Magic Ballerina Ser.: 3). (ENG., Illus.). 96p. (J). (gr. k-2). pap. 6.99 (978-0-00-728610-2(4), HarperCollins Children's Bks.) HarperCollins Pubs. Ltd. GBR. Dist: HarperCollins Pubs.
—Summer in Enchantia. 2009. (Magic Ballerina Ser.). (ENG., Illus.). 144p. (J). (gr. k-2). pap. 9.99 (978-0-00-731721-9(2)) HarperCollins Pubs. Ltd. GBR. Dist: Independent Pubs. Group.
Butler, Kynora. Knowing Is Believing in Reading: Facing Your Fears. 2007. 48p. per. 16.95 (978-1-4241-7559-8(3)) America Star Bks.
Byrne, Jean Livingstone. Legends of Newgrange. 2014. 54p. pap. 12.99 (978-1-84386-818-7(0)) Vanguard Pr.
Cabell, Robert W. The Mermaid Adventures of Princess Miranda: Volume One. Cabell, Robert W., illus. 2013. (Illus.). 128p. pap. 7.95 (978-0-9890974-3-7(9), Oceanus Bks.) Warrington Pubns.
Cabrini, Joe. Chicco's Nicedream Van - Daniel's Winning Goal. Cabrini, Joe, illus. 2007. (Illus.). 32p. per. (978-0-7552-0300-0(3)) Authors OnLine, Ltd.
—Chicco's Nicedream Van - Jessica the Superstar. Cabrini, Joe, illus. 2007. (Illus.). 32p. per. (978-0-7552-0301-7(1)) Authors OnLine, Ltd.
Caine, Rachel, pseud, et al. Immortal: Love Stories with Bite. Cast, P. C., ed. 2009. (ENG., Illus.). 280p. (J). (gr. 9-12). pap. 8.95 (978-1-933771-92-2(5)) BenBella Bks.
Caldwell, Stella. Fairy World: Beautiful Maidens & Mischievous Sprites. Forshaw, Ryan, illus. 2016. (ENG.). 80p. (J). (gr. 4-8). 18.99 (978-0-7641-6820-8(7)) Barron's Educational Series, Inc.
Calhoun, Dia. Avielle of Rhia, 1 vol. 2006. (ENG.). 400p. (J). (gr. 6). 16.99 (978-0-7614-5320-8(2)) Marshall Cavendish Corp.
Calhoun, Megan. Oscar the Pig: Mommy Goes to Work. 2008. 32p. 18.50 (978-0-615-25193-6(5)) Silly String Media.
Callaghan, Cindy. Just Add Magic. 2010. (Just Add Magic Ser.: 1). (ENG., Illus.). 240p. (J). (gr. 4-8). pap. 7.99 (978-1-4424-0268-3(7), Aladdin) Simon & Schuster Children's Publishing.
Calmenson, Stephanie. The Frog Principal. Brunkus, Denise, illus. 2006. (ENG.). 32p. (J). pap. 5.99 (978-0-439-81217-7(8), Scholastic Paperbacks) Scholastic, Inc.
Calvert, Pam. The Multiplying Menace Divides! Geehan, Wayne, illus. 2011. (ENG.). 32p. (J). (gr. 2-5). pap. 7.95 (978-1-57091-782-0(5)) Charlesbridge Publishing, Inc.
Cameron, Anne. The Lightning Catcher. Jamieson, Victoria, illus. 2013. (Lightning Catcher Ser.: 1). (ENG.). 432p. (J). (gr. 3-7). 16.99 (978-0-06-211276-7(7), Greenwillow Bks.) HarperCollins Pubs.
Cammuso, Frank. Big Birthday Bash. 2014. (Misadventures of Salem Hyde Ser.). (ENG., Illus.). 96p. (J). (gr. 1-4). 14.95 (978-1-4197-1025-4(7), Amulet Bks.) Abrams, Inc.
—Cookie Catastrophe. 2014. (Misadventures of Salem Hyde Ser.: 3). (J). lib. bdg. 17.15 (978-0-606-36149-1(9)) Turtleback Bks.
—The Misadventures of Salem Hyde: Cookie Catastrophe. 2014. (Misadventures of Salem Hyde Ser.). (ENG., Illus.). 96p. (J). (gr. 1-4). 14.95 (978-1-4197-1198-5(9), Amulet Bks.) Abrams, Inc.
—The Misadventures of Salem Hyde: Spelling Trouble. 2013. (Misadventures of Salem Hyde Ser.: 1). (J). lib. bdg. 17.15 (978-0-606-33440-2(8), Turtleback) Turtleback Bks.
Campbell, Isaiah. AbrakaPOW. 2016. (ENG., Illus.). 400p. (J). (gr. 3-7). 16.99 (978-1-4814-2634-3(6), Simon & Schuster Bks. For Young Readers) Simon & Schuster Bks. For Young Readers.
Campbell, R. W. Merrick Tumbledorf: The Last Talcomite Dragon. 2013. (ENG.). 250p. (YA). pap. 15.95 (978-1-4787-1312-8(7)) Outskirts Pr., Inc.
Candlewick Press Staff. Magical Film Projections: Creatures. 2017. (J. K. Rowling's Wizarding World Ser.). (ENG.). 16p. (J). (gr. 2-5). 16.99 (978-0-7636-9585-9(8)) Candlewick Pr.
Caprin, K. F. The Adventures of the Little Savages. 2009. (ENG.). 167p. pap. 16.95 (978-1-4092-3379-4(0)) Lulu Pr., Inc.
Carbone, Courtney. Snow Day! 2014. (Step into Reading Level 2 Ser.). lib. bdg. 13.55 (978-0-606-36009-8(3)) Turtleback Bks.
Card, Melanie. Ward Against Darkness. 2013. (Necromancer Ser.: 2). (ENG.). 326p. (YA). (gr. 7). pap. 9.99 (978-1-62061-303-0(4), 9781620613030) Entangled Publishing, LLC.
Card, Orson Scott. Stonefather. Kidd, Tom, illus. 2008. 112p. 35.00 (978-1-59606-194-1(4)) Subterranean Pr.
Cardwell, Helen. Amber Janusson: Protector of the Magic Lands. 2003. 136p. pap. 11.95 (978-0-595-29436-7(7)) iUniverse, Inc.
Carlson, Caroline. The Buccaneers' Code. (Very Nearly Honorable League of Pirates Ser.: 3). 320p. (J). (gr. 3-7). 2016. pap. 6.99 (978-0-06-219440-4(2)) 2015. (ENG.). 16.99 (978-0-06-219439-8(9)) HarperCollins Pubs.
—Magic Marks the Spot. Phillips, Dave, illus. 2014. (Very Nearly Honorable League of Pirates Ser.: 1). (ENG.). 384p. (J). (gr. 3-7). pap. 6.99 (978-0-06-219435-0(6)) HarperCollins Pubs.
—The Terror of the Southlands. Phillips, Dave, illus. 2014. (ENG.). 336p. (J). pap. (978-0-06-236178-3(3)) Harper & Row Ltd.
—The Terror of the Southlands. Phillips, Dave, illus. 2015. (Very Nearly Honorable League of Pirates Ser.: 2). (ENG.). 352p. (J). (gr. 3-7). pap. 6.99 (978-0-06-219437-4(2)) HarperCollins Pubs.
—The Very Nearly Honorable League of Pirates - The Terror of the Southlands. Phillips, Dave, illus. 2014. (Very Nearly Honorable League of Pirates Ser.: 2). (ENG.). 336p. (J). (gr. 3-7). 16.99 (978-0-06-219436-7(4)) HarperCollins Pubs.
Carmody, Isobelle. A Mystery of Wolves. 2009. (Little Fur Ser.: Bk. 3). (ENG., Illus.). 256p. (J). (gr. 3-7). 6.99 (978-0-375-83859-0(7), Yearling) Random Hse. Children's Bks.
Carr, Lawrence. Under the Peach Tree. 2006. pap. 8.00 (978-0-8059-7019-7(3)) Dorrance Publishing Co., Inc.
Carris, Joan. Magic at the Bed & Biscuit. Jones, Noah Z., illus. 2012. (ENG.). 112p. (J). (gr. 1-4). pap. 5.99 (978-0-7636-5849-6(9)) Candlewick Pr.
Carris, Joan Davenport. Magic at the Bed & Biscuit. Meserve, Jessica & Jones, Noah Z., illus. 2011. (Daisy Dawson Ser.). (ENG.). 128p. (J). (gr. 1-4). 15.99 (978-0-7636-4306-5(8)) Candlewick Pr.
Carroll, D. L. Sir Licksalot & the Island Fools. 2012. 120p. pap. 19.95 (978-1-4626-8092-4(5)) America Star Bks.
Carroll, Emma. In Darkling Wood. 2017. (ENG.). 240p. (J). (gr. 5). 16.99 (978-0-399-55601-2(X), Delacorte Bks. for Young Readers) Random Hse. Children's Bks.
Carryl, Charles E. The Admiral's Caravan: A Tale Inspired by Lewis Carroll's Wonderland. 2011. 110p. pap. (978-1-904808-66-4(2)) Evertype.
Carson, Rae. The Crown of Embers. (Girl of Fire & Thorns Ser.: 2). (ENG.). (YA). (gr. 8). 2013. 432p. pap. 9.99 (978-0-06-202653-8(4)) 2012. 416p. 17.99 (978-0-06-202651-4(8)) HarperCollins Pubs. (Greenwillow Bks.).
—The Girl of Fire & Thorns. (Girl of Fire & Thorns Ser.: 1). (ENG.). (YA). (gr. 8). 2012. 448p. pap. 9.99 (978-0-06-202650-7(X)) 2011. 432p. 17.99 (978-0-06-202648-4(8)) HarperCollins Pubs. (Greenwillow Bks.).
—Like a River Glorious. Hendrix, John, illus. (Gold Seer Trilogy Ser.: 2). (YA). (gr. 8). 2017. (ENG.). 432p. pap. 9.99 **(978-0-06-224295-2(4))** 2016. 416p. 17.99 (978-0-06-224294-5(6)) HarperCollins Pubs. (Greenwillow Bks.).
Carson, Rae. Walk on Earth a Stranger. (Gold Seer Trilogy Ser.: 1). (YA). (gr. 8). 2016. 464p. pap. 9.99 (978-0-06-224292-1(X)) 2015. (ENG.). 448p. 17.99 (978-0-06-224291-4(1)) HarperCollins Pubs. (Greenwillow Bks.).
Carter, David. The Nutters of Pendle Forest - Part 1 the Enchanted Valley. 2012. (Illus.). 222p. pap. (978-1-908098-54-2(6)) 2QT, Ltd. (Publishing).
carter, robert bob. The Magic Eye. 2009. 106p. pap. 12.95 (978-0-557-05597-5(0)) Lulu Pr., Inc.
Carter, Scott William. Wooden Bones. (ENG., Illus.). 160p. (J). (gr. 3-7). 2013. pap. 6.99 (978-1-4424-2752-5(3)) 2012. 15.99 (978-1-4424-2751-8(5)) Simon & Schuster Bks. For Young Readers. (Simon & Schuster Bks. For Young Readers).
Cartmell, C. J. The Magic Mailbox. 2011. 28p. pap. 15.99 (978-1-4568-4525-4(X)) Xlibris Corp.
Cascone, Gina & Cascone, Annette. Little Magic Shop of Horrors. 2012. (Deadtime Stories Ser.: 5). (ENG.). 192p. (J). (gr. 3-7). 14.99 (978-0-7653-3075-8(X), 9780765330758, Starscape) Doherty, Tom Assocs., LLC.
Cash, M. A. Edward of Canterbury & the King of Red. Adams, Craig, illus. 2003. (J). (978-0-9772711-0-8(2)) Jama Kids.
Cashore, Kristin. Fire. November, S., ed. 2011. (ENG.). 528p. (YA). (gr. 7-18). pap. 10.99 (978-0-14-241591-7(X), Firebird) Penguin Young Readers Group.
—Fire. 2011. (Graceling Realm Ser.: 2). lib. bdg. 22.10 (978-0-606-23085-8(8), Turtleback) Turtleback Bks.
Caspian. The Magician in the Attic. 2014. (ENG., Illus.). 352p. (YA). pap. (978-1-908168-42-9(0), Eisewhen Pr.) Ainpete Ltd.
Cast, P. C. Moon Chosen. 2016. (Tales of a New World Ser.: 1). (ENG., Illus.). 608p. (YA). (gr. 7-12). 18.99 (978-1-250-10072-6(0), 9781250100726, St. Martin's Griffin) St. Martin's Pr.
Cast, P. C. & Cast, Kristin. Redeemed: A House of Night Novel. 2014. (YA). (978-1-250-05952-9(6)); (House of Night Ser.: Vol. 12). (ENG.). 320p. (gr. 7-12). 18.99 (978-0-312-59444-2(5), 9780312594442, St. Martin's Griffin) St. Martin's Pr.
Castle, Amber. Olivia the Otter Sister. Hall, Mary, illus. 2013. (ENG.). 160p. (J). (gr. 2-4). pap. 7.99 (978-0-85707-253-5(6), Simon & Schuster Children's) Simon & Schuster, Ltd. GBR. Dist: Simon & Schuster, Inc.
Castle, M. E. Fakespeare: Something Stinks in Hamlet. Jennewein, Daniel, illus. 2017. (J). pap. **(978-1-250-10157-0(3))** St. Martin's Pr.
—Fakespeare: Starcrossed in Romeo & Juliet. Jennewein, Daniel, illus. 2017. (J). pap. **(978-1-250-10160-0(3))** St. Martin's Pr.
—Fakespeare: Something Stinks in Hamlet. Jennewein, Daniel, illus. 2017. (Fakespeare Ser.: 1). (ENG.). 272p. (J). 13.99 (978-1-250-10159-4(X), 9781250101594) Imprint IND. Dist: Macmillan.
—Starcrossed in Romeo & Juliet. Jennewein, Daniel, illus. 2017. (Fakespeare Ser.: 2). (ENG.). 304p. (J). 13.99 (978-1-250-10162-4(X), 9781250101624) Imprint IND. Dist: Macmillan.
Castro, Adam-Troy & dePaola, Tomie. Gustav Gloom & the Cryptic Carousel #4. Margiotta, Kristen, illus. 2015. (Gustav Gloom Ser.: 4). (ENG.). 248p. (J). (gr. 3-7). 7.99 (978-0-448-48719-9(5), Grosset & Dunlap) Penguin Young Readers Group.
Catanese, P. W. Happenstance Found. 2009. (Books of Umber Ser.: 1). (ENG.). 352p. (J). (gr. 3-7). 16.99 (978-1-4169-7519-9(5), Simon & Schuster/Paula Wiseman Bks.) Simon & Schuster/Paula Wiseman Bks.
Cate, Annette LeBlanc. The Magic Rabbit. Cate, Annette LeBlanc, illus. 2013. (ENG., Illus.). 32p. (J). (gr. -1-3). 6.99 (978-0-7636-6685-9(8)) Candlewick Pr.
Caterer, Claire M. The Key & the Flame. (ENG.). (J). (gr. 3-7). 2015. 496p. pap. 7.99 (978-1-4424-5742-3(2)) 2013. 480p. 17.99 (978-1-4424-5741-6(4)) McElderry, Margaret K. Bks. (McElderry, Margaret K. Bks.).
Catipon, Atreyu. The Wizard's Magic Hat. 2012. 26p. 16.00 (978-1-61863-390-3(2)) Bookstand Publishing.
Catmull, Katherine. The Radiant Road. 2016. (ENG.). 368p. (YA). (gr. 7). 17.99 (978-0-525-95347-0(7), Dutton Books for Young Readers) Penguin Young Readers Group.
Caveney, Philip. Night on Terror Island. 2013. (ENG.). 240p. (J). (gr. 4-6). pap. 12.99 (978-1-84939-270-9(6)) Andersen Pr. GBR. Dist: Independent Pubs. Group.
—Spy Another Day. 2013. (ENG.). 240p. (J). (gr. 4-6). pap. 10.99 (978-1-84939-417-8(2)) Andersen Pr. GBR. Dist: Independent Pubs. Group.
Certain Signals. 2014. (Gift Ser.). (ENG.). 112p. (YA). (gr. 6-12). lib. bdg. 27.93 (978-1-4677-3511-7(6)) Lerner Publishing Group.
Cestari, Crystal. The Best Kind of Magic. 2017. (Windy City Magic Ser.). (ENG.). 336p. (YA). (gr. 7-12). 17.99 (978-1-4847-5272-2(4)) Hyperion Bks. for Children.
Chabon, Michael. Summerland. l.t. ed. 2003. 615p. (J). 25.95 (978-0-7862-5143-8(3)) Thorndike Pr.
Chad, Jon. Leo Geo & His Miraculous Journey Through the Center of the Earth. Chad, Jon, illus. 2012. (ENG., Illus.). 36p. (J). (gr. 2-5). 15.99 (978-1-59643-661-9(1), 9781596436619) Roaring Brook Pr.
—Leo Geo & the Cosmic Crisis. Chad, Jon, illus. 2013. (ENG., Illus.). 40p. (J). (gr. 2-6). 16.99 (978-1-59643-822-4(3), 9781596438224) Roaring Brook Pr.
Chadwick, J. R. Thomas & the Dragon's Pearl. 2008. (Illus.). v, 181p. pap. (978-0-7552-0430-4(1)) Authors OnLine, Ltd.
Chadwick, Jennie. The Peach Tree Kids: Circus Fleas. 2012. 96p. pap. 9.99 (978-1-61897-455-6(6), Strategic Bk. Publishing) Strategic Book Publishing & Rights Agency (SBPRA).
Chaisson, Kristen. Dreamland. 2013. 28p. pap. 24.95 (978-1-63000-664-8(5)) America Star Bks.
Chamberlain, Nick. The Adventures of Papillon. 2008. 176p. pap. 15.95 (978-1-60290-092-9(2)) OakTara Publishing Group LLC.
Chapman, Lara. Accidentally Evil. 2015. (Mix Ser.). (ENG., Illus.). 240p. (J). (gr. 4-8). pap. 7.99 (978-1-4814-0110-4(6), Aladdin) Simon & Schuster Children's Publishing.
—The XYZs of Being Wicked. 2014. (ENG., Illus.). 272p. (J). (gr. 4-8). pap. 6.99 (978-1-4814-0107-4(6), Aladdin) Simon & Schuster Children's Publishing.
—The XYZs of Being Wicked. 2014. (ENG., Illus.). 272p. (J). (gr. 4-8). 17.99 (978-1-4814-0108-1(4), Simon & Schuster/Paula Wiseman Bks.) Simon & Schuster/Paula Wiseman Bks.
Chapman, Linda. Max's Amazing Models. Jevons, Chris, illus. 2017. (Reading Ladder Ser.). (ENG.). 48p. (J). (gr. k-2). pap. 7.99 **(978-1-4052-7823-2(4))** Egmont Bks., Ltd. GBR. Dist: Independent Pubs. Group.
Chapman, Linda. Mr Monkey & the Fairy Tea Party. Hearn, Sam, illus. 2016. (Early Reader Ser.). (ENG.). 64p. (J). (gr. k-2). 6.99 (978-1-4440-1552-2(4), Orion Children's Bks.) Hachette Children's Group GBR. Dist: Hachette Bk. Group.
Charlesworth, Liza. Seven Magic Hats. Lewis, Stephen, illus. 2005. (Number Tales Ser.). (ENG.). 16p. (J). (gr. -1-1). pap. 2.99 (978-0-439-69018-8(8)) Scholastic, Inc.
Chartrand, Lili. Taming Horrible Harry. Ouriou, Susan, tr. from FRE. Rogé, illus. 2006. (ENG.). 32p. (J). (gr. -1-3). 16.95 (978-0-88776-772-2(9), Tundra Bks.) Tundra Bks. CAN. Dist: Penguin Random Hse. LLC.
Chase, Mary. Loretta Mason Potts. Berson, Harold, illus. 2014. (ENG.). 224p. (J). (gr. 3-7). 16.95 (978-1-59017-757-0(6), NYR Children's Collection) New York Review of Bks., Inc., The.
Chen, Wei Dong. Monkey King: The Sacred Tree. Peng, Chao, illus. 2012. (Monkey King Ser.: 6). (ENG.). 176p. (gr. 5-8). lib. bdg. 29.27 (978-89-94208-74-9(7)) JR Comics KOR. Dist: Lerner Publishing Group.
Cheverton, Mark. Herobrine's War: The Birth of Herobrine Book Three: a Gameknight999 Adventure: an Unofficial Minecrafter's Adventure. 2017. (Gameknight999 Ser.). (ENG.). 272p. (J). (gr. 3). pap. 9.99 (978-1-5107-0996-6(7), Sky Pony Pr.) Skyhorse Publishing Co., Inc.
Chew, Ruth. A Matter-of-Fact Magic Book: The Would-Be Witch. 2014. (Matter-Of-Fact Magic Book Ser.). (ENG., Illus.). 144p. (J). (gr. 2-5). 15.99 (978-0-449-81567-0(6), Random Hse. Bks. for Young Readers) Random Hse. Children's Bks.
—A Matter-Of-Fact Magic Book: Witch in the House. 2016. (Matter-Of-Fact Magic Book Ser.). (ENG., Illus.). 144p. (J). (gr. 2-5). 5.99 (978-0-449-81586-1(2), Random Hse. Bks. for Young Readers) Random Hse. Children's Bks.
—Witch's Broom. 2015. (Matter-Of-Fact Magic Book Ser.). (ENG., Illus.). 144p. (J). (gr. 2-5). pap. 5.99 (978-0-449-81578-6(1), Random Hse. Bks. for Young Readers) Random Hse. Children's Bks.
Chichester Clark, Emma. Amazing Mr. Zooty! Chichester Clark, Emma, illus. 2007. (ENG., Illus.). 32p. (J). (gr. k — 1). 15.99 (978-1-84270-480-6(X)) Andersen Pr. GBR. Dist: Independent Pubs. Group.
Chick, Bryan. Riddles & Danger. 2011. (Secret Zoo Ser.: 3). (ENG.). 288p. (J). (gr. 3-7). 16.99 (978-0-06-198927-8(4), Greenwillow Bks.) HarperCollins Pubs.
Child, Lydia Maria. The Magician's Show Box & Other Stories. 2007. (ENG.). 124p. per. (978-1-4065-1354-7(7)) Dodo Pr.
—The Magician's Show Box, & Other Stories by the Author of Rainbows for Children. 2006. 312p. per. 23.99 (978-1-4255-2973-4(9)) Michigan Publishing.
Chima, Cinda Williams. The Dragon Heir. 2009. (Heir Chronicles Ser.). (ENG., Illus.). 528p. (J). (gr. 5-9). pap. 9.99 (978-1-4231-1071-2(4)) Hyperion Pr.
—The Enchanter Heir. 2013. 464p. 18.99 (978-1-4231-8789-9(X)) Disney Pr.
—Flamecaster. (Shattered Realms Ser.: 1). (gr. 8). 2017. 560p. (YA). pap. 9.99 (978-0-06-238095-1(8)) 2016. 544p. (J). pap. 12.00 (978-0-06-245490-4(0)) 2016. (ENG.). 544p. (YA). 18.99 (978-0-06-238094-4(X)) HarperCollins Pubs. (HarperTeen).
—The Sorcerer Heir. (Heir Chronicles Ser.). (ENG.). 560p. 2016. (J). (gr. 5-9). pap. 9.99 (978-1-4231-9475-0(6)) 2014. (YA). (gr. 7-12). 18.99 (978-1-4231-4435-9(X)) Hyperion Bks. for Children.
—The Warrior Heir. 2007. (Heir Chronicles Ser.). (ENG.). 448p. (J). (gr. 5-9). pap. 9.99 (978-0-7868-3917-9(1)) Hyperion Pr.
—The Warrior Heir. 2006. (Heir Chronicles: No. 1). 1.00 (978-1-4294-0323-8(3)) Recorded Bks., Inc.
—The Wizard Heir. 2008. (Heir Chronicles Ser.). (ENG.). 480p. (J). (gr. 5-9). pap. 9.99 (978-1-4231-0488-9(9)) Hyperion Pr.
Chime, P. K. Moonrise. 2013. 452p. pap. (978-1-78299-644-6(3)) FeedARead.com.
Chipman, Laura. Dragonspeaker. 2005. 76p. pap. 19.95 (978-1-4241-0136-8(0)) America Star Bks.
Chizuru, Mio. The Pirate & the Princess Volume 1: the Timelight Stone: The Timelight Stone. 2007. 110p. (J). pap. 5.99 (978-1-933164-43-4(3)) Seven Seas Entertainment, LLC.
Chlebowski, Rachel. Magical Misadventures! (Shimmer & Shine) Golden Books, illus. 2017. (Color Plus 1,000 Stickers Ser.). (ENG.). 64p. (J). (gr. -1-2). pap. 9.99 (978-0-399-55890-0(X), Golden Bks.) Random Hse. Children's Bks.
The Chocolate Moose. 2007. (Illus.). 48p. (J). per. 13.00 (978-0-9767189-5-6(2)) Better Day Publishing LLC.
Chokshi, Roshani. The Star-Touched Queen. Rothschild, Eileen, ed. 2017. (Star-Touched Ser.). (ENG.). 368p. (YA). pap. 10.99 (978-1-250-10020-7(8), 9781250100207, St. Martin's Griffin) St. Martin's Pr.
—The Star-Touched Queen. 2016. (ENG.). 352p. (YA). (gr. 9). 18.99 (978-1-250-08547-4(0), 9781250085474, St. Martin's Griffin) St. Martin's Pr.
Christen, Dennis H. Lundon's Bridge & the Three Keys. 2008. 221p. (J). pap. 12.95 (978-0-9718151-5-5(1)) C-It Entertainment Group, LLC.
Christopher, Nicholas. The True Adventures of Nicolo Zen: A Novel. 2015. (ENG.). 288p. (YA). (gr. 7). pap. 9.99 (978-0-375-86492-6(X), Ember) Random Hse. Children's Bks.
Chubbs-Rogers, Shannon. Listen... Can You Hear It? 2013. 40p. pap. (978-1-4602-1960-5(5)) FriesenPress.
Ciccone, Tiziana. Tooth Fairy Trouble. 2013. 36p. pap. 13.95 (978-1-62857-176-9(4), Strategic Bk. Publishing) Strategic Book Publishing & Rights Agency (SBPRA).
Ciccone, Tiziana & Linardi, Franca. Lucinda, Queen of Everything. Cannavicci, Luigi A., illus. 2012. 36p. pap. 13.95 (978-1-61897-719-9(9), Strategic Bk. Publishing) Strategic Book Publishing & Rights Agency (SBPRA).
Ciddor, Anna. Runestone: The First Book about the Adventures of Oddo & Thora. 2007. (Viking Magic Ser.). (ENG., Illus.). 192p. (Orig.). (J). (gr. 4-7). pap. 11.99 (978-1-86508-689-7(4)) Allen & Unwin AUS. Dist: Independent Pubs. Group.
—Wolfspell. 2007. (Viking Magic Ser.). (ENG., Illus.). 192p. (J). (gr. 4-7). pap. 12.99 (978-1-74114-013-2(7)) Allen & Unwin AUS. Dist: Independent Pubs. Group.
Ciencin, Scott & Burge, Constance M. Luck Be a Lady. 2004. (Charmed Ser.). (ENG., Illus.). 224p. (YA). pap. 16.95 (978-0-689-85793-5(4), Gallery Bks.) Gallery Bks.

Cirrone, Dorian. The First Last Day. (ENG., Illus.). 240p. (J). (gr. 3-7). 2017. pap. 7.99 **(978-1-4814-5814-6(0))** 2016. 17.99 *(978-1-4814-5813-9(2))* Simon & Schuster Children's Publishing. (Aladdin).
C.J. Elgert. The Elder Brothers & the Padstow Crystals. 2009. 284p. 27.95 *(978-1-4401-7678-4(7))*; pap. 17.95 *(978-1-4401-7676-0(0))* iUniverse, Inc.
Clamp Staff. Cardcaptor Sakura, 4 vols., Bk. 4. Horn, Carl Gustav, ed. 2012. (ENG., Illus.). 592p. pap. 19.99 *(978-1-59582-889-7(3))* Dark Horse Comics.
—Cardcaptor Sakura, 4 vols., Vol. 1. 2010. (ENG., Illus.). 600p. pap. 19.99 *(978-1-59582-522-3(3))* Dark Horse Comics.
—Cardcaptor Sakura, 4 vols., Vol. 3. Clamp Staff, illus. 2012. (ENG., Illus.). 600p. pap. 19.99 *(978-1-59582-808-8(7))* Dark Horse Comics.
Clare, Cassandra. City of Ashes. 2008. (Mortal Instruments Ser.: Bk. 2). (YA). (gr. 9). 64.99 *(978-1-60640-964-0(6))* Findaway World, LLC.
—City of Ashes. 2008. (Mortal Instruments Ser.: 2). (ENG.). 464p. (YA). (gr. 9-12). 24.99 *(978-1-4169-1429-7(3),* McElderry, Margaret K. Bks.) McElderry, Margaret K. Bks.
—City of Fallen Angels. 2011. (Mortal Instruments Ser.: 4). (ENG.). 432p. (YA). (gr. 9-18). 24.99 *(978-1-4424-0354-3(3),* McElderry, Margaret K. Bks.) McElderry, Margaret K. Bks.
—City of Fallen Angels, 11 vols. (Mortal Instruments Ser.: 4). (YA). 2012. 133.75 *(978-1-4618-0638-7(0))* 2011. 135.75 *(978-1-4618-0637-0(2))* 2011. 1.25 *(978-1-4640-2483-2(9))* 2011. 317.75 *(978-1-4618-0642-4(9))* 2011. 133.75 *(978-1-4618-0641-7(0))* Recorded Bks., Inc.
—City of Glass. (Mortal Instruments Ser.: Bk. 3). (ENG., (YA). (gr. 9). 2015. Illus.). 592p. pap. 13.99 *(978-1-4814-5598-5(2))* 2009. 560p. 24.99 *(978-1-4169-1430-3(7))* McElderry, Margaret K. Bks. (McElderry, Margaret K. Bks.).
—City of Glass. 2010. 23.00 *(978-1-60686-827-0(6))* Perfection Learning Corp.
—City of Glass. 2009. pap. *(978-1-4424-9308-7(9))* Simon & Schuster.
—City of Glass. 2015. (Mortal Instruments Ser.: Bk. 3). 592p. (YA). lib. bdg. 25.75 *(978-0-606-37733-1(6))* Turtleback Bks.
—City of Heavenly Fire. 2014. (Mortal Instruments Ser.: No. 6). (ENG., Illus.). 752p. (YA). (gr. 9). 24.99 *(978-1-4424-1689-5(0),* McElderry, Margaret K. Bks.) McElderry, Margaret K. Bks.
—City of Lost Souls. (Mortal Instruments Ser.: Bk. 5). (ENG., (YA). (gr. 9). 2015. Illus.). 592p. pap. 13.99 *(978-1-4814-5600-5(8))* 2012. 544p. 21.99 *(978-1-4424-1686-4(6))* McElderry, Margaret K. Bks. (McElderry, Margaret K. Bks.).
—City of Lost Souls, 16 vols. 2012. (Mortal Instruments Ser.: Bk. 5). (YA). 133.75 *(978-1-4640-3948-5(8))*; 133.75 *(978-1-4640-3951-5(8))*; 133.75 *(978-1-4640-3952-2(6))*; 317.75 *(978-1-4640-3949-2(6))* Recorded Bks., Inc.
—City of Lost Souls. 2015. (Mortal Instruments Ser.: Bk. 5). 592p. (YA). lib. bdg. 25.75 *(978-0-606-37736-2(0))* Turtleback Bks.
—City of Lost Souls. 2012. 512p. pap. *(978-1-4063-3760-0(9))* Walker Bks., Ltd.
—Lady Midnight. 2016. (Dark Artifices Ser.: 1). (ENG., Illus.). 720p. (YA). (gr. 9-12). 24.99 *(978-1-4424-6835-1(1),* McElderry, Margaret K. Bks.) McElderry, Margaret K. Bks.
—Lady Midnight. 2017. lib. bdg. 26.95 **(978-0-606-40535-5(6))** Turtleback Bks.
Clare, Cassandra. Lord of Shadows. 2017. (Dark Artifices Ser.: 2). (ENG., Illus.). 720p. (YA). (gr. 9). 24.99 *(978-1-4424-6840-5(8),* McElderry, Margaret K. Bks.) McElderry, Margaret K. Bks.
Clare, Cassandra & Lewis, Joshua. The Shadowhunter's Codex. 2013. (Mortal Instruments Ser.). (ENG., Illus.). 288p. (YA). (gr. 9). 24.99 *(978-1-4424-1692-5(0))*; 49.99 *(978-1-4424-9682-8(7))* McElderry, Margaret K. Bks. (McElderry, Margaret K. Bks.).
Clare, Cassandra, et al. The Bane Chronicles. Clare, Cassandra, ed. 2014. (Bane Chronicles Ser.). (ENG., Illus.). 528p. (YA). (gr. 9). 22.99 *(978-1-4424-9599-9(5),* McElderry, Margaret K. Bks.) McElderry, Margaret K. Bks.
Clare, Cassandra, et al. Tales from the Shadowhunter Academy. (Tales from the Shadowhunter Academy Ser.). (ENG.). (YA). (gr. 9). 2017. 704p. pap. 14.99 **(978-1-4814-4326-5(7))** 2016. (Illus.). 672p. 23.99 *(978-1-4814-4325-8(9))* McElderry, Margaret K. Bks. (McElderry, Margaret K. Bks.).
Clarizio, Laura. If i Had a Magic Carpet. 2005. 48p. pap. 16.95 *(978-1-4137-8557-9(3))* America Star Bks.
—If I Had a Magic Carpet II: Key to Kindness. 2006. (ENG.). 48p. per. 16.95 *(978-1-4241-3985-9(6))* America Star Bks.
—If I Had a Magic Carpet III: Haunted Holidays. 2008. 73p. pap. 19.95 *(978-1-60563-240-7(6))* America Star Bks.
—Traveling Through Time: If I Had a Magic Carpet IV. 2012. 100p. 21.95 *(978-1-4489-3229-0(7))* 2010. 98p. pap. 16.95 *(978-1-4489-5428-5(2))* America Star Bks.
Clark, Chris Elliott. Hazel's Secret. 2008. 64p. pap. 19.95 *(978-1-60474-500-9(2))* America Star Bks.
Clark, Hannah L. Uncovering Cobbogoth. 2014. pap. 17.99 *(978-1-4621-1426-9(1))* Cedar Fort, Inc./CFI Distribution.
Clark, Isabelle. The Enchanted Forest of Hope. 2009. 44p. pap. 18.50 *(978-1-4389-7781-2(6))* AuthorHouse.
Clark, J. Metrognomes. 2007. 292p. per. 17.95 *(978-0-595-42973-8(4))* iUniverse, Inc.
Clark, Kristina. The Great Adventures of Ella: The Magic Desk. 2010. 28p. 12.95 *(978-1-4520-2412-7(X))* AuthorHouse.
Clark, Platte F. Bad Unicorn. (Bad Unicorn Trilogy Ser.: 1). (ENG., Illus.). (J). (gr. 3-7). 2014. 448p. pap. 7.99 *(978-1-4424-5013-4(4))* 2013. 432p. 15.99 *(978-1-4424-5012-7(6))* Simon & Schuster Children's Publishing. (Aladdin).
Clark, Simon P. Tell the Story to Its End. 2015. (ENG., Illus.). 208p. (YA). (gr. 7). 18.99 *(978-1-250-06675-6(1),* 9781250066756, St. Martin's Griffin) St. Martin's Pr.
Clark, William. Magic Raindrops. 2013. 24p. pap. 14.93 *(978-1-4669-7414-2(1))* Trafford Publishing.
Clarke, Christie. Star Spirit. 2013. 118p. pap. *(978-0-9917348-2-5(3))* RedemptionHse. Publishing.
Clarke, Lizzy. The Spirit of the Jaguar. 2013. 92p. pap. 11.38 *(978-1-4907-0600-9(3))*; (gr. -1). 21.38 *(978-1-4907-0602-3(X))* Trafford Publishing.
Clarkson, Kelly. River Rose & the Magical Lullaby. Hughes, Laura, illus. 2016. 32p. (J). (gr. -1-3). 18.99 *(978-0-06-242756-4(3))* HarperCollins Pubs.
Clement-Davies, David. The Telling Pool. Huebsch, Rand, illus. 2007. (ENG.). 382p. (YA). (gr. 7-17). per. 8.95 *(978-0-8109-9257-3(4))* Abrams, Inc.
—The Telling Pool. 2005. (ENG., Illus.). 376p. (J). (gr. 7-17). 19.95 *(978-0-8109-5758-9(2),* Abrams Bks. for Young Readers) Abrams, Inc.
—The Telling Pool. 2006. 1.00 *(978-1-4237-6417-5(X))* Recorded Bks., Inc.
Clement-Moore, Rosemary. Spirit & Dust. 2014. (ENG.). 400p. (YA). (gr. 7). pap. 9.99 *(978-0-385-74081-4(6),* Ember) Random Hse. Children's Bks.
Clickard, Carrie. Magic for Sale. Shelley, John, illus. 2017. (ENG.). 32p. (J). 16.95 *(978-0-8234-3559-3(8))* Holiday Hse., Inc.
Clifford, Leah. A Touch Morbid. 2012. (Touch Mortal Trilogy Ser.: 2). (ENG.). 304p. (YA). (gr. 9). 16.99 *(978-0-06-200502-1(2),* Greenwillow Bks.) HarperCollins Pubs.
Cluess, Jessica. A Poison Dark & Drowning (Kingdom on Fire, Book Two) 2017. (Kingdom on Fire Ser.: 2). (ENG.). 432p. (YA). (gr. 7). 17.99 **(978-0-553-53594-5(3),** Random Hse. Bks. for Young Readers) Random Hse. Children's Bks.
Cluess, Jessica. A Shadow Bright & Burning. 2016. (Kingdom on Fire Ser.: 1). (ENG.). 416p. (YA). (gr. 7). 17.99 *(978-0-553-53590-7(0))*; lib. bdg. 20.99 *(978-0-553-53591-4(9))* Random Hse. Children's Bks. (Random Hse. Bks. for Young Readers).
Cnockaert, Cindy. The Magical Stones. 2011. 36p. pap. 16.86 *(978-1-4389-8929-7(6))* AuthorHouse.
Cody, Matthew. The Peddler's Road. 2015. (Secrets of the Pied Piper Ser.: 1). (ENG., Illus.). 368p. (J). (gr. 3-7). 17.99 *(978-0-385-75522-1(8),* Knopf Bks. for Young Readers) Random Hse. Children's Bks.
—The Secrets of the Pied Piper 2: the Magician's Key. 2016. (Secrets of the Pied Piper Ser.: 2). (ENG., Illus.). 336p. (J). (gr. 3-7). 17.99 *(978-0-385-75526-9(0),* Knopf Bks. for Young Readers) Random Hse. Children's Bks.
Coe, Mary. The Prince of Betherland. 2007. 100p. pap. 9.95 *(978-1-4303-2521-5(6))* Lulu Pr., Inc.
Cofer, Amadeus. Aloha Adventure: The Magic of Imagination on a Rainy Day. l.t. ed. 2004. (Illus.). 36p. (J). 14.00 *(978-1-932957-01-3(4))* Legacy Pubs.
Cohen, Lawrence J. The Dragon's Familiar. 2008. 236p. (YA). pap. 15.95 *(978-0-595-51413-7(8))* iUniverse, Inc.
Cohen, Leah. The Magic Pond: How a Small Flock of Birds Brought Life & Cheer to a Lonely Pond. 2010. 36p. 15.49 *(978-1-4520-1082-3(X))* AuthorHouse.
Cohen, Lee. Find the Magic: A Rip Squeak Book. 2008. (Illus.). 32p. (J). 16.95 *(978-0-9747825-2-2(1),* Rip Squeak Pr.) Rip Squeak, Inc.
Cole, Myke. The Wildsidhe Chronicles Bk. 6: Car Trouble. 2003. (J). pap. 7.99 *(978-1-890096-18-2(0))* Padwolf Publishing, Inc.
Cole, Penelope Ann. Magical Matthew. Collier, Kevin Scott, illus. 2012. 24p. pap. 10.95 *(978-1-61633-326-3(X))* Guardian Angel Publishing, Inc.
Cole, Penelope Anne. Magical Matthew. Collier, Kevin Scott, illus. 2012. 24p. 19.95 *(978-1-61633-325-6(1))* Guardian Angel Publishing, Inc.
—Magical Mea. Collier, Kevin, illus. 2013. 24p. 19.95 *(978-1-61633-394-2(4))*; pap. 10.95 *(978-1-61633-395-9(2))* Guardian Angel Publishing, Inc.
Colebourn, Craig. The Knights of Videnland: Passing the Torch. 2007. 428p. per. 23.95 *(978-0-595-46989-5(2))* iUniverse, Inc.
Colfer, Chris. Adventures from the Land of Stories Boxed Set: The Mother Goose Diaries & Queen Red Riding Hood's Guide to Royalty. 2015. (Land of Stories Ser.). (ENG.). 256p. (J). (gr. 3-7). 22.00 *(978-0-316-26151-7(3))* Little, Brown Bks. for Young Readers.
—An Author's Odyssey. 2016. (Land of Stories Ser.: 5). (ENG.). (J). (gr. 3-7). 496p. pap. 11.99 *(978-0-316-27214-8(0))*; (Illus.). 464p. 19.99 *(978-0-316-38329-5(5))* Little, Brown Bks. for Young Readers.
—Beyond the Kingdoms. Dorman, Brandon, illus. 2015. (Land of Stories Ser.: Bk. 4). (ENG.). 432p. (J). (gr. 3-7). 19.99 *(978-0-316-40689-5(9))* Little, Brown Bks. for Young Readers.
—Beyond the Kingdoms. l.t. ed. 2015. (Land of Stories Ser.: No. 4). (ENG.). 624p. (J). (gr. 3-7). 28.99 *(978-0-316-33938-4(5))* Little, Brown Bks. for Young Readers.
—The Curvy Tree. Dorman, Brandon, illus. 2015. (ENG.). 32p. (J). (gr. -1-3). 17.00 *(978-0-316-40685-7(6))* Little Brown & Co.
—The Enchantress Returns. (Land of Stories Ser.: 2). (ENG.). (J). (gr. 3-7). 2014. 544p. pap. 9.99 *(978-0-316-20155-1(3))* 2013. (Illus.). 528p. 19.99 *(978-0-316-20154-4(5))* 2013. 832p. 43.99 *(978-0-316-24235-6(7))* Little, Brown Bks. for Young Readers.
—The Enchantress Returns. 2014. (Land of Stories Ser.: 2). (J). lib. bdg. 20.85 *(978-0-606-37229-9(6))* Turtleback Bks.
—A Grimm Warning. (Land of Stories Ser.: 3). (ENG.). (J). (gr. 3-7). 2015. 496p. pap. 9.99 *(978-0-316-40682-6(1))* 2014. 480p. 19.99 *(978-0-316-40681-9(3))* 2014. 768p. 32.99 *(978-0-316-40964-3(2))* Little, Brown Bks. for Young Readers.
—A Grimm Warning. 2015. (Land of Stories Ser.: 3). (J). lib. bdg. 20.85 *(978-0-606-37230-5(X))* Turtleback Bks.
—The Land of Stories: an Author's Odyssey. 2017. (Land of Stories Ser.: 5). (ENG., Illus.). 464p. (J). (gr. 3-7). pap. 9.99 **(978-0-316-38321-9(X))** Little, Brown Bks. for Young Readers.
—The Mother Goose Diaries. Dorman, Brandon et al, illus. 2015. 121p. (J). *(978-0-316-38332-5(5))* Little Brown & Co.
—Queen Red Riding Hood's Guide to Royalty. Dorman, Brandon, illus. 2015. 118p. (J). *(978-0-316-38339-4(2))* Little Brown & Co.
—The Wishing Spell. 2013. (Land of Stories Ser.: Bk. 1). (ENG.). 464p. (J). (gr. 3-7). pap. 9.99 *(978-0-316-20156-8(1))* Little, Brown Bks. for Young Readers.
—The Wishing Spell. Dorman, Brandon, illus. 2012. (Land of Stories Ser.: 1). (ENG.). 448p. (J). (gr. 3-7). 19.99 *(978-0-316-20157-5(X))* Little, Brown Bks. for Young Readers.
—The Wishing Spell. l.t. ed. 2013. (Land of Stories Ser.: 1). (ENG.). 672p. (J). (gr. 3-7). pap. 10.00 *(978-0-316-24236-3(5))* Little, Brown Bks. for Young Readers.
—The Wishing Spell. 2013. (Land of Stories Ser.: 1). (J). lib. bdg. 20.85 *(978-0-606-31746-7(5),* Turtleback) Turtleback Bks.
Colfer, Chris & Dorman, Brandon. The Land of Stories the Wishing Spell. 2013. pap. *(978-0-545-64793-9(2))* Scholastic, Inc.
Colfer, Eoin. The Arctic Incident. 2009. (Artemis Fowl Ser.). (ENG.). 304p. (J). (gr. 5-9). pap. 8.99 *(978-1-4231-2454-2(5))* Hyperion Pr.
—The Arctic Incident. 2003. (Artemis Fowl Ser.: 2). 277p. (J). (gr. 5-7). lib. bdg. 19.65 *(978-0-613-62927-0(2),* Turtleback) Turtleback Bks.
—Artemis Fowl, 3 vols., Set. 2010. (Artemis Fowl Ser.). (ENG.). 944p. (J). (gr. 5-17). pap. 19.99 *(978-1-4231-3681-1(0))* Disney Pr.
—Artemis Fowl. (Artemis Fowl Ser.: Bk. 1). (FRE.). pap. 34.95 *(978-2-07-054681-7(0))* Gallimard, Editions FRA. Dist: Distribooks, Inc.
—Artemis Fowl. rev. ed. 2009. (Artemis Fowl Ser.). (ENG.). 304p. (J). (gr. 5-9). pap. 8.99 *(978-1-4231-2452-8(9))* Hyperion Pr.
—Artemis Fowl. (Artemis Fowl Ser.: Bk. 1). pap. 34.95 *(978-88-04-49788-2(2))* Mondadori ITA. Dist: Distribooks, Inc.
—Artemis Fowl. (Artemis Fowl Ser.: 1). (YA). 2007. 1.25 *(978-1-4193-6020-6(5))* 2006. 52.75 *(978-1-4193-6023-7(X))* 2006. 54.75 *(978-1-4193-6021-3(3))* 2006. 54.75 *(978-1-4193-6026-8(4))* 2006. 132.75 *(978-1-4193-6022-0(1))* 2005. 56.75 *(978-1-4193-6024-4(8))* Recorded Bks., Inc.
—Artemis Fowl. 2009. (Artemis Fowl Ser.: 1). (J). (gr. 5-8). lib. bdg. 19.65 *(978-0-613-60637-0(X),* Turtleback) Turtleback Bks.
—Artemis Fowl. Feldmann, Claudia, tr. (Artemis Fowl Ser.: Bk. 1). (GER.). pap. 24.95 *(978-3-548-60320-9(3))* Ullstein-Taschenbuch-Verlag DEU. Dist: Distribooks, Inc.
—Artemis Fowl: El Mundo Subterráneo. 2013. (Vintage Espanol Ser.: Bk. 1). (SPA.). 288p. (YA). (gr. 5). pap. 9.95 *(978-0-345-80418-1(X),* Vintage Espanol) Knopf Doubleday Publishing Group.
—Artemis Fowl & the Atlantis Complex. 2012. (ENG.). 384p. (J). (gr. 5-9). pap. 8.99 *(978-1-4231-2972-1(5))* Hyperion Pr.
—The Atlantis Complex. 2010. (Artemis Fowl Ser.: 7). (ENG.). 368p. (J). (gr. 5-9). 17.99 *(978-1-4231-2819-9(2))* Hyperion Pr.
—The Atlantis Complex. 2012. (Artemis Fowl Ser.: 7). (J). lib. bdg. 19.65 *(978-0-606-23614-0(7),* Turtleback) Turtleback Bks.
—Encuentro en el Artico. 2013. (Vintage Espanol Ser.).Tr. of Arctic Incident. (SPA.). 320p. (YA). pap. 9.95 *(978-0-345-80535-5(6),* Vintage Espanol) Knopf Doubleday Publishing Group.
—The Eternity Code. rev. ed. 2009. (Artemis Fowl Ser.). (ENG.). 336p. (J). (gr. 5-9). pap. 8.99 *(978-1-4231-2453-5(7))* Hyperion Pr.
—The Last Guardian. 2012. (Artemis Fowl Ser.). (ENG.). 336p. (J). (gr. 5-9). 18.99 *(978-1-4231-6161-5(0))* Hyperion Pr.
—The Last Guardian. 2014. (Artemis Fowl Ser.: 8). (J). lib. bdg. 19.65 *(978-0-606-32288-1(4),* Turtleback) Turtleback Bks.
—The Lost Colony. rev. ed. 2009. (Artemis Fowl Ser.). (ENG.). 432p. (J). (gr. 5-9). pap. 8.99 *(978-1-4231-2494-8(4))* Hyperion Pr.
—EL MUNDO SUBTERRÁNEO (ARTEMIS FOWL 1) (Artemis Fowl Ser.: Bk. 1). (SPA.). 288p. pap. *(978-84-8441-115-4(X),* MO31567) Grijalbo Mondadori, S.A.-Montena.
—The Opal Deception. 2006. (Artemis Fowl Ser.: Bk. 4). 17.10 *(978-0-7569-6828-1(3))* Disney Pr.
—The Opal Deception. rev. ed. 2009. (Artemis Fowl Ser.). (ENG.). 368p. (J). (gr. 5-9). pap. 8.99 *(978-1-4231-2455-9(3))* Hyperion Pr.
—The Opal Deception. (Artemis Fowl Ser.: 4). (J). 2007. 1.25 *(978-1-4193-6041-1(8))* 2006. 69.75 *(978-1-4193-6047-3(7))* 2006. 72.75 *(978-1-4193-6045-9(0))* Recorded Bks., Inc.
—The Time Paradox. 2009. (Artemis Fowl Ser.). (ENG.). 448p. (J). (gr. 5-9). pap. 8.99 *(978-1-4231-0837-5(X))* Hyperion Pr.
—The Time Paradox. 2009. (Artemis Fowl Ser.: 6). (J). lib. bdg. 19.65 *(978-0-606-10579-8(4),* Turtleback) Turtleback Bks.
Colfer, Eoin & Donkin, Andrew. Artemis Fowl. Rigano, Giovanni & Lamanna, Paolo, illus. 2007. (Artemis Fowl Ser.). (ENG.). 112p. (J). (gr. 5-9). 18.99 *(978-0-7868-4881-2(2))*; pap. 12.99 *(978-0-7868-4882-9(0))* Hyperion Pr.
—Artemis Fowl the Opal Deception Graphic Novel. Rigano, Giovanni & Lamanna, Paolo, illus. 2014. (Artemis Fowl Ser.: 4). (ENG.). 112p. (J). (gr. 5-9). pap. 12.99 *(978-1-4231-4549-3(6))* Hyperion Bks. for Children.
—The Eternity Code. Rigano, Giovanni & Lamanna, Paolo, illus. 2013. (Artemis Fowl Ser.: 3). (ENG.). 112p. (J). (gr. 5-9). 19.99 *(978-1-4231-4527-1(5))* Hyperion Pr.
—Eternity Code. Rigano, Giovanni & Lamanna, Paolo, illus. 2013. (Artemis Fowl Ser.: 3). (ENG.). 112p. (J). (gr. 5-9). pap. 12.99 *(978-1-4231-4577-6(1))* Hyperion Pr.
Collar, Orpheus & Riordan, Rick. The Throne of Fire. Collar, Orpheus, illus. 2015. (Kane Chronicles Ser.). (ENG., Illus.). 160p. (J). (gr. 5-9). 21.99 *(978-1-4847-1490-4(3))* Hyperion Bks. for Children.
Compestine, Ying Chang. The Runaway Wok: A Chinese New Year Tale. Serra, Sebastia, illus. 2011. (ENG.). 32p. (J). (gr. 1-3). 16.99 *(978-0-525-42068-2(1),* Dutton Books for Young Readers) Penguin Young Readers Group.
Condenzio, John. Cocoa the Witch Cat. 2013. 20p. pap. 24.95 *(978-1-62709-264-7(1))* America Star Bks.
Conlon, Mara. Nutcracker Ballet: A Book, Theater, & Paper Doll Foldout Play Set. Gershman, Jo, illus. 2007. (Foldout Playset Ser.). 30p. (J). 17.99 *(978-1-59359-885-3(8))* Peter Pauper Pr. Inc.
Connolly, MarcyKate. Monstrous. Young, Skottie, illus. (J). (gr. 3-7). 2016. 448p. pap. 7.99 *(978-0-06-227272-0(1))* 2015. (ENG.). 432p. 16.99 *(978-0-06-227271-3(3))* HarperCollins Pubs.
—Monstrous. 2016. (J). lib. bdg. 18.40 *(978-0-606-38136-9(8))* Turtleback Bks.
—Ravenous. 2016. (Illus.). 416p. (J). (gr. 3-7). 16.99 *(978-0-06-227274-4(8))* HarperCollins Pubs.
Connolly, Tina. Seriously Wicked. 2016. (YA). lib. bdg. 20.85 *(978-0-606-38783-5(8))* Turtleback Bks.
Connor, Lexi. B Magical #5: the Chocolate Meltdown. 2011. (B Magical Ser.: 5). (ENG.). 144p. (J). (gr. 3-7). pap. 5.99 *(978-0-545-11740-1(2),* Scholastic Paperbacks) Scholastic, Inc.
—The Runaway Spell. 2011. (B Magical Ser.: 3). (ENG.). 144p. (J). (gr. 3-7). pap. 5.99 *(978-0-545-26552-2(5),* Scholastic Paperbacks) Scholastic, Inc.
Cook, Eileen. Gnome Invasion. 2011. (Fourth Grade Fairy Ser.: 3). (ENG.). 160p. (J). (gr. 3-7). pap. 6.99 *(978-1-4169-9813-6(6),* Aladdin) Simon & Schuster Children's Publishing.
Cook, Jeremy. Illusion Meets Reality. 2008. 116p. pap. 19.95 *(978-1-60813-059-7(2))* America Star Bks.
—The Illusion Stick. 2008. 115p. pap. 19.95 *(978-1-60474-705-8(6))* America Star Bks.
Cook, Katie. My Little Pony: Friendship Is Magic Part 1: Friendship Is Magic Part 1. Price, Andy, illus. 2013. (My Little Pony Ser.). (ENG.). 52p. (J). (gr. 2-5). pap. 6.99 *(978-1-61377-628-5(4),* 9781613776285) Idea & Design Works, LLC.
Cook, Maureen McNamee. Is There Magic in the Mountains, Mamma? Connell, Jacqueline, illus. 2008. 23p. pap. 24.95 *(978-1-60672-673-0(0))* America Star Bks.
Coomber, Suzanne. The Magic Sandcastle. 2011. 16p. 8.32 *(978-1-4520-9612-4(0))* AuthorHouse.
Coombs, Kate. The Runaway Princess. l.t. ed. 2007. (Literacy Bridge Middle Reader Ser.). 325p. (J). (gr. 3-7). 22.95 *(978-0-7862-9633-0(X))* Thorndike Pr.
Cooper, Catherine. The Golden Acorn. 2nd rev. ed. 2010. (Adventures of Jack Brenin Ser.). (ENG., Illus.). 376p. pap. 12.34 *(978-1-906821-65-4(8))* Infinite Ideas GBR. Dist: Sony Electronics.
Cooper, Diana. Tara & the Talking Kitten Meet a Unicorn. Shannon, Kate, illus. 2011. (Tara & Ash-ting Ser.). (ENG.). 80p. (J). (gr. k-4). 8.95 *(978-1-84409-557-5(6))* Innovation Pr., The.
—Tara & the Talking Kitten Meet Angels & Fairies. Shannon, Kate, illus. 2011. (Tara & Ash-ting Ser.). (ENG.). 80p. (J). (gr. k-4). 8.95 *(978-1-84409-551-3(7))* Innovation Pr., The.
Cooper, Susan. The Boggart. 2004. 196p. (gr. 3-7). 17.00 *(978-0-7569-3932-8(1))* Perfection Learning Corp.
—The Dark Is Rising. 2009. 7.64 *(978-0-7848-2212-8(3),* Everbind) Marco Bk. Co.
—The Dark Is Rising. 15.85 *(978-0-7569-8464-9(5))* Perfection Learning Corp.
—The Dark Is Rising. (Dark Is Rising Sequence Ser.). 244p. (YA). (gr. 5-18). pap. 4.99 *(978-0-8072-1533-3(3),* Listening Library) Random Hse. Audio Publishing Group.
—Over Sea, under Stone. 2013. (Dark Is Rising Sequence Ser.: 1). (ENG., Illus.). 288p. (J). (gr. 3-7). 17.99 *(978-1-4424-9592-0(8),* McElderry, Margaret K. Bks.) McElderry, Margaret K. Bks.
Coppock, Phil & Bower's 2008-2009 4th Grade Class. Rubber Tuesday. 2010. 70p. pap. 12.95 *(978-1-4327-5751-9(2))* Outskirts Pr., Inc.
Corbett, Sue. 12 Again. 2007. (ENG.). 240p. (J). (gr. 5-18). 6.99 *(978-0-14-240729-5(1),* Puffin Books) Penguin Young Readers Group.
Corderoy, Tracey. The Super-Spooky Fright Night! Hubble Bubble. Berger, Joe, illus. 2017. (ENG.). 128p. (J). (gr. 1-4). 14.99 *(978-0-7636-9502-6(5),* Nosy Crow) Candlewick Pr.
Córdova, Zoraida. Labyrinth Lost. (Brooklyn Brujas Ser.: 1). (ENG.). (YA). (gr. 8-12). 2017. 352p. pap. 10.99 *(978-1-4926-2316-8(4))* 2016. 336p. 17.99 *(978-1-4926-2094-5(7),* 9781492620945) Sourcebooks, Inc.
Corlett, William. The Door in the Tree. 2010. (Magician's House Quartet Ser.: 2). (ENG.). 304p. (YA). (gr. 5-8). pap. 13.99 *(978-1-4424-1414-3(6),* Simon Pulse) Simon Pulse.
—The Steps up the Chimney. 2011. (Magician's House Quartet Ser.: 1). (ENG.). 288p. (YA). (gr. 7). pap. 13.99 *(978-1-4424-2935-2(6),* Simon Pulse) Simon Pulse.
Cornwell, Betsy. Mechanica. (ENG.). 320p. (gr. 7). 2016. (YA). pap. 8.99 *(978-0-544-66868-3(5),* HMH Books For Young Readers) 2015. (J). 17.99 *(978-0-547-92771-8(1),* Clarion Bks.) Houghton Mifflin Harcourt Publishing Co.
—Mechanica. 2016. lib. bdg. 19.65 *(978-0-606-37999-1(1))* Turtleback Bks.
—Venturess. 2017. (ENG.). 320p. (J). (gr. 7). 17.99 *(978-0-544-31927-1(3),* Clarion Bks.) Houghton Mifflin Harcourt Trade & Reference Pubs.
Cossanteli, Veronica. The Extincts. Muradov, Roman, illus. 2016. (ENG.). 240p. (J). 16.99 *(978-1-62779-403-9(4),* 9781627794039, Holt, Henry & Co. Bks. For Young Readers) Holt, Henry & Co.
Coughlin, Jennie Rose. The Purple Scarf. Howes, Bryan Arthur, illus. 2008. 20p. per. 24.95 *(978-1-60441-733-3(1))* America Star Bks.
Courtauld, Sarah. Buckle & Squash: the Gigantic Giant Goof-Up. 2016. (Buckle & Squash Ser.). (ENG., Illus.). 192p. (J). 14.99 *(978-1-250-05279-7(3),* 9781250052797) Feiwel & Friends.
Coutinho, Lucy M. The Rangers of Andor: The Beginning. 2011. 278p. pap. 27.95 *(978-1-4626-1014-3(5))* America Star Bks.
Coven, Wanda. Heidi Heckelbeck & the Big Mix-Up. Burris, Priscilla, illus. 2016. (Heidi Heckelbeck Ser.: 18). (ENG.). 128p. (J). (gr. k-4). pap. 5.99 *(978-1-4814-7169-5(4),* Little Simon) Little Simon.
—Heidi Heckelbeck & the Christmas Surprise. Burris, Priscilla, illus. 2013. (Heidi Heckelbeck Ser.: 9). (ENG.). 128p. (J). (gr. k-2). 16.99 *(978-1-4424-8125-1(0))*; pap. 4.99 *(978-1-4424-8124-4(2))* Little Simon. (Little Simon).
—Heidi Heckelbeck & the Christmas Surprise. 2013. (Heidi Heckelbeck Ser.: 9). lib. bdg. 14.75 *(978-0-606-32325-3(2),* Turtleback) Turtleback Bks.
—Heidi Heckelbeck & the Cookie Contest. Burris, Priscilla, illus. 2012. (Heidi Heckelbeck Ser.: 3). (ENG.). 128p. (J). (gr. k-2). 16.99 *(978-1-4424-4166-8(6))*; pap. 5.99 *(978-1-4424-4165-1(8))* Little Simon. (Little Simon).

—Heidi Heckelbeck & the Cookie Contest. 2012. (Heidi Heckelbeck Ser.: 3). lib. bdg. 16.00 (978-0-606-26328-3(4), Turtleback) Turtleback Bks.

—Heidi Heckelbeck & the Magic Puppy. Burris, Priscilla, illus. 2017. (Heidi Heckelbeck Ser.: 20). (ENG.). 128p. (J). (gr. k-4). pap. 5.99 **(978-1-4814-9521-9(6)**, Little Simon) Little Simon.

—Heidi Heckelbeck & the Never-Ending Day. Burris, Priscilla, illus. 2017. (Heidi Heckelbeck Ser.: 21). (ENG.). 128p. (J). (gr. k-4). 16.99 **(978-1-4814-9525-7(9))**; pap. 5.99 **(978-1-4814-9524-0(0))** Little Simon. (Little Simon).

—Heidi Heckelbeck & the Tie-Dyed Bunny. 2014. (Heidi Heckelbeck Ser.: 10). lib. bdg. 16.00 (978-0-606-35429-5(8)) Turtleback Bks.

—Heidi Heckelbeck Goes to Camp! Burris, Priscilla, illus. 2013. (Heidi Heckelbeck Ser.: 8). (ENG.). 128p. (J). (gr. k-2). 15.99 (978-1-4424-6481-0(X)); pap. 5.99 (978-1-4424-6480-3(1)) Little Simon. (Little Simon).

—Heidi Heckelbeck Goes to Camp! 2013. (Heidi Heckelbeck Ser.: 8). lib. bdg. 16.00 (978-0-606-32031-3(8), Turtleback) Turtleback Bks.

—Heidi Heckelbeck Has a Secret - Heidi Heckelbeck Casts a Spell - Heidi Heckelbeck & the Cookie Contest. Burris, Priscilla, illus. 2014. (Heidi Heckelbeck Ser.). (ENG.). 384p. (J). (gr. k-4). pap. 8.99 (978-1-4814-2771-5(7), Little Simon) Little Simon.

—Heidi Heckelbeck in Disguise. Burris, Priscilla, illus. 2012. (Heidi Heckelbeck Ser.: 4). (ENG.). 128p. (J). (gr. k-2). 16.99 (978-1-4424-4169-9(0)); pap. 5.99 (978-1-4424-4168-2(2)) Little Simon. (Little Simon).

—Heidi Heckelbeck in Disguise. 2012. (Heidi Heckelbeck Ser.: 4). lib. bdg. 16.00 (978-0-606-26329-0(2), Turtleback) Turtleback Bks.

—Heidi Heckelbeck Is Not a Thief! Burris, Priscilla, illus. 2015. (Heidi Heckelbeck Ser.: 13). (ENG.). 128p. (J). (gr. k-4). pap. 5.99 (978-1-4814-2324-3(X), Little Simon) Little Simon.

—Heidi Heckelbeck Is the Bestest Babysitter! Burris, Priscilla, illus. 2015. (Heidi Heckelbeck Ser.: 16). (ENG.). 128p. (J). (gr. k-4). pap. 5.99 (978-1-4814-4630-3(4), Little Simon) Little Simon.

—Heidi Heckelbeck Makes a Wish. 2016. (Heidi Heckelbeck Ser.: 17). lib. bdg. 16.00 (978-0-606-38962-4(8)) Turtleback Bks.

—Heidi Heckelbeck Makes a Wish: Super Special! Burris, Priscilla, illus. 2016. (Heidi Heckelbeck Ser.: 17). (ENG.). 160p. (J). (gr. k-4). pap. 5.99 (978-1-4814-6613-4(5), Little Simon) Little Simon.

—Heidi Heckelbeck Says "Cheese!" Burris, Priscilla, illus. 2015. (Heidi Heckelbeck Ser.: 14). (ENG.). 128p. (J). (gr. k-4). pap. 5.99 (978-1-4814-2327-4(4), Little Simon) Little Simon.

—Heidi Heckelbeck Tries Out for the Team. Burris, Priscilla, illus. 2017. (Heidi Heckelbeck Ser.: 19). (ENG.). 128p. (J). (gr. k-4). pap. 5.99 (978-1-4814-7172-5(4), Little Simon) Little Simon.

Coville, Bruce. Cursed. 2016. (Enchanted Files Ser.: 1). lib. bdg. 17.20 (978-0-606-38460-5(X)) Turtleback Bks.

—Diary of a Mad Brownie. 2015. (Enchanted Files Ser.). (ENG., Illus.). 256p. (J). (gr. 3-7). lib. bdg. 19.99 (978-0-385-39248-8(6), Random Hse. Bks. for Young Readers) Random Hse. Children's Bks.

—Goblins in the Castle. Coville, Katherine, illus. 2015. (ENG.). 208p. (J). (gr. 3-7). 17.99 (978-1-4814-3900-8(6), Aladdin) Simon & Schuster Children's Publishing.

—Goblins on the Prowl. 2015. (ENG., Illus.). 272p. (J). (gr. 3-7). 17.99 (978-1-4169-1440-2(4), Aladdin) Simon & Schuster Children's Publishing.

—Jennifer Murdley's Toad. Lippincott, Gary A., illus. 2007. (Magic Shop Book Ser.: 3). (ENG.). 176p. (J). (gr. 5-7). pap. 7.99 (978-0-15-206246-0(7)) Houghton Mifflin Harcourt Publishing Co.

—The Monster's Ring. Coville, Katherine, illus. 2008. (Magic Shop Book Ser.: 1). (ENG.). 128p. (J). (gr. 5-7). pap. 6.99 (978-0-15-206442-6(7)) Houghton Mifflin Harcourt Publishing Co.

—The Skull of Truth. (Magic Shop Bks.). 208p. (J). (gr. 5-7). pap. 3.99 (978-0-8072-1538-8(4), Listening Library) Random Hse. Audio Publishing Group.

Coville, Bruce. Trolled. Kidby, Paul, illus. 2017. (Enchanted Files Ser.: 3). (ENG.). 288p. (J). (gr. 3-7). 16.99 **(978-0-385-39259-4(1)**, Random Hse. Bks. for Young Readers) Random Hse. Children's Bks.

Cowey, James. William Snottengrout - Gangor's Reign. 2006. 104p. per. (978-1-84667-006-0(3)) Derwent Pr., The.

—William Snottengrout - Quapta's Revenge. 2006. 104p. per. (978-1-84667-023-7(3)) Derwent Pr., The.

Cowsar, Susan. The Magic Flower. 2013. 58p. pap. 10.99 (978-1-62697-943-7(X)) Salem Author Services.

COX, Margaret. The Emerald-fire. 2010. 166p. pap. 11.50 (978-1-4461-3379-8(6)) Lulu Pr., Inc.

—The Soul-pearl. 2010. 169p. pap. 11.50 (978-1-4457-5679-0(X)) Lulu Pr., Inc.

Cox, R. The Lonely Wizard Named Wizzy: The Apprentice. 2009. 16p. pap. 8.49 (978-1-4490-2236-5(7)) AuthorHouse.

Crabtree, Julie. Discovering Pig Magic. 2008. (ENG.). 144p. (J). (gr. 2-8). 16.95 (978-1-57131-683-7(3)); pap. 6.95 (978-1-57131-684-4(1)) Milkweed Editions.

Craig, Barbara J. Santa's Magical Key. 2010. 20p. 10.49 (978-1-4520-4399-9(X)) AuthorHouse.

Crawford, Hannah. The Fight for Light by Hannah Crawford. 2012. (Illus.). 86p. pap. 8.50 (978-1-78035-335-7(9), Fastprint Publishing) Upfront Publishing Ltd. GBR. Dist: Printondemand-worldwide.com.

—The Fight with Darkness. 2013. (Illus.). 79p. pap. 8.49 (978-1-78035-586-3(6), Fastprint Publishing) Upfront Publishing Ltd. GBR. Dist: Printondemand-worldwide.com.

Creamer, Joan Klatil. The Magic Sceptre - the Legend of Blue Santa Claus. Creamer, Joan Klatil, illus. 2006. (Illus.). 32p. (J). 16.95 (978-0-9778476-3-1(2)) Silver Snowflake Publishing.

—The Magic Sceptre & Reginald the Rabbit. 2007. (Illus.). 32p. (J). 16.95 (978-0-9778476-5-5(9)) Silver Snowflake Publishing.

Croggon, Alison. The Riddle: Book Two of Pellinor. 2017. (Pellinor Ser.). (ENG.). 512p. (J). (gr. 7). pap. 9.99 (978-0-7636-9444-9(4)) Candlewick Pr.

—The Singing: Book Four of Pellinor. 2017. (Pellinor Ser.). (ENG.). 496p. (J). (gr. 7). pap. 9.99 (978-0-7636-9446-3(0)) Candlewick Pr.

Crommett, Lora. The Blue Witch Who Dared to Be Different. 2013. 64p. 14.99 (978-1-62951-025-5(4)) Mockingbird Lane Pr.

Cronin, Doreen. Bloom. Small, David, illus. 2016. (ENG.). 40p. (J). (gr. -1-3). 17.99 (978-1-4424-0620-9(8)) Simon & Schuster Children's Publishing.

Crossley-Holland, Kevin. At the Crossing-Places. 2004. (Arthur Trilogy). (Illus.). 394p. (YA). (gr. 7-12). 15.65 (978-0-7569-3182-7(7)) Perfection Learning Corp.

Crowder, Melanie. A Nearer Moon. (ENG., Illus.). (J). (gr. 3-7). 2016. 176p. pap. 7.99 (978-1-4814-4149-0(3), Atheneum Bks. for Young Readers) 2015. 160p. 16.99 (978-1-4814-4148-3(5)) Simon & Schuster Children's Publishing.

—A Nearer Moon. 2016. (ENG.). 176p. (J). (gr. 3-7). 18.40 (978-0-606-39238-9(6)) Turtleback Bks.

Crowl, M. Tara. Eden's Escape. (Eden of the Lamp Ser.). (ENG.). 320p. (J). (gr. 3-7). 2017. pap. 7.99 **(978-1-4847-4917-3(0))** 2016. 16.99 (978-1-4847-1186-6(6)) Hyperion Bks. for Children.

Cruz, Wilfredo. Charlie's Box: A Story about a Boy & His Magical Box. 2013. 24p. pap. 24.95 (978-1-63000-514-6(2)) America Star Bks.

Cullen, Seán. Hamish X & the Hollow Mountain. 2008. (ENG.). 288p. (J). (gr. 7-18). 9.99 (978-0-14-305312-5(4), Puffin Canada) Penguin Random House Canada Young Readers CAN. Dist: Penguin Random Hse. LLC.

Culpepper, R. B. W. Ellena & the Magic Lamp. 2011. 182p. pap. 24.95 (978-1-4626-2830-8(3)) America Star Bks.

Cummings, Lindsay. The Fires of Calderon. 2014. (Balance Keepers Ser.: 1). (ENG.). 352p. (J). (gr. 3-7). 16.99 (978-0-06-227518-9(6), Tegen, Katherine Bks) HarperCollins Pubs.

—The Pillars of Ponderay. 2015. (Balance Keepers Ser.: 2). (ENG.). 384p. (J). (gr. 3-7). 16.99 (978-0-06-227521-9(6), Tegen, Katherine Bks) HarperCollins Pubs.

Cumyn, Alan. After Sylvia. 2nd ed. 2008. (ENG.). 200p. (J). (gr. 3-7). pap. 8.95 (978-0-88899-868-2(6)) Groundwood Bks. CAN. Dist: Publishers Group West (PGW).

Cunningham, Mary. Cynthias Attic Magicians Castle. 2009. 158p. pap. 10.99 (978-1-59080-656-2(5)) Echelon Press Publishing.

Curnin, V. J. Millie's Magic Wellies. 2009. (Illus.). 20p. pap. 10.49 (978-1-4389-8258-8(5)) AuthorHouse.

Curry, Kenneth. The Legend of the Dancing Trees: An African American Folk Tale. 2007. 111p. (J). per. 14.95 (978-0-9798364-0-4(9)) Curry Brothers Publishing Group.

Curry, Kenneth, et al. The Legend of the Dancing Tees Teachers Resource: The Legend of the Dancing Trees. 2007.Tr. of Teachers Resource. per. 19.95 (978-0-9798364-1-1(7)) Curry Brothers Publishing Group.

Curtis, Jillian M. The Little Prince & His Magic Wand. 2005. (Illus.). 28p. (J). 24.95 (978-1-59858-015-0(9)); pap. 16.95 (978-1-59858-010-5(8)) Dog Ear Publishing, LLC.

Cushman, Karen. Grayling's Song. 2016. (ENG.). 224p. (J). (gr. 5-7). 16.99 (978-0-544-30180-1(3), Clarion Bks.) Houghton Mifflin Harcourt Trade & Reference Pubs.

Cussler, Clive. The Adventures of Hotsy Totsy. 2011. (ENG., Illus.). 176p. (J). (gr. 3-7). 6.99 (978-0-14-241873-4(0), Puffin Books) Penguin Young Readers Group.

Cyber. The Transdimensional War Series. 2006. 67p. pap. 16.95 (978-1-4241-2778-8(5)) PublishAmerica, Inc.

Cypess, Leah. Death Marked. 2015. (ENG.). 400p. (YA). (gr. 8). 17.99 (978-0-06-222124-7(8), Greenwillow Bks.) HarperCollins Pubs.

—Death Sworn. (ENG.). (YA). (gr. 8). 2015. 368p. pap. 9.99 (978-0-06-222122-3(1)) 2014. 352p. 17.99 (978-0-06-222121-6(3)) HarperCollins Pubs. (Greenwillow Bks.).

—Mistwood. 2010. (ENG.). 320p. (YA). (gr. 8-18). 16.99 (978-0-06-195699-7(6), Greenwillow Bks.) HarperCollins Pubs.

Da Vinci, Leonardo. Leonardo's Fables & Jests. 2003. 48p. per. 14.95 (978-0-9719898-9-4(3)) E & E Publishing.

Dadey, Debbie & Jones, Marcia Thornton. Inside the Magic. 2009. (Keyholders Ser.: 3). (ENG.). 128p. (J). (gr. 2-5). 4.99 (978-0-7653-5984-1(7), 9780765359841, Starscape) Doherty, Tom Assocs., LLC.

—The Wrong Side of Magic. 2009. (Keyholders Ser.: 4). (ENG.). 128p. (J). (gr. 2-5). pap. 4.99 (978-0-7653-5985-8(5), 9780765359858, Starscape) Doherty, Tom Assocs., LLC.

Daffern, Brian. Prince Albert Bk. 2: The Beast School. 2005. 160p. (YA). per. 10.95 (978-0-9709104-6-2(0)) Hickory Tales Publishing.

Dahl, Michael. The Assistant Vanishes!, 1 vol. Weber, Lisa K., illus. 2013. (Hocus Pocus Hotel Ser.). (ENG.). 112p. (gr. 2-3). lib. bdg. 25.32 (978-1-4342-4101-6(7)) Stone Arch Bks.

—Hocus Pocus Hotel, 1 vol. Weber, Lisa K., illus. 2014. (Hocus Pocus Hotel Ser.). (ENG.). 128p. (gr. 2-3). 50.64 (978-1-4342-8937-7(0)) Stone Arch Bks.

—Shadow Shoes: And Other Scary Tales. Bonet, Xavier, illus. 2017. (Michael Dahl's Really Scary Stories Ser.). (ENG.). 72p. (gr. 2-3). lib. bdg. 25.32 **(978-1-4965-4900-6(7))** Stone Arch Bks.

—The Thirteenth Mystery, 1 vol. Weber, Lisa K., illus. 2014. (Hocus Pocus Hotel Ser.). (ENG.). 224p. (gr. 2-3). 10.95 (978-1-4342-6509-8(9)) Stone Arch Bks.

—To Catch a Ghost, 1 vol. Weber, Lisa K., illus. 2012. (Hocus Pocus Hotel Ser.). (ENG.). 112p. (gr. 2-3). lib. bdg. 25.32 (978-1-4342-4100-9(9)) Stone Arch Bks.

—The Trouble with Abracadabra, 1 vol. Weber, Lisa K., illus. 2013. (Hocus Pocus Hotel Ser.). (ENG.). 112p. (gr. 2-3). lib. bdg. 25.32 (978-1-4342-4102-3(5)) Stone Arch Bks.

Dahl, Roald. El Dedo Magico. Marriot, Pat, illus.Tr. of Magic Finger. (SPA.). 74p. (J). (gr. 3-5). 9.95 (978-968-19-0621-4(7)) Aguilar Editorial MEX. Dist: Santillana USA Publishing Co., Inc.

—George's Marvelous Medicine. Blake, Quentin, illus. 2007. (ENG.). 112p. (J). (gr. 3-7). 7.99 (978-0-14-241035-6(7), Puffin Books) Penguin Young Readers Group.

—George's Marvelous Medicine. Blake, Quentin, illus. 2008. 88p. (gr. 4-7). 18.00 (978-0-7569-8777-0(6)) Perfection Learning Corp.

—George's Marvelous Medicine. 2007. lib. bdg. 18.40 (978-1-4177-8619-0(1), Turtleback) Turtleback Bks.

—James et la Grosse Peche.Tr. of James & the Giant Peach. (FRE.). (J). pap. 17.95 (978-2-07-051374-1(2)) Gallimard, Editions FRA. Dist: Distribooks, Inc.

—The Magic Finger. Blake, Quentin, illus. 2009. (ENG.). 96p. (J). (gr. 3-7). 7.99 (978-0-14-241385-2(2), Puffin Books) Penguin Young Readers Group.

—The Magic Finger. Blake, Quentin, illus. 2003. (CHI.). 133p. (J). pap. 11.70 (978-957-574-476-2(4)) Youth Cultural Publishing Co. CHN. Dist: Chinasprout, Inc.

Daily, Lorrie Ann. The Castlewood Twins, the Magic Begins. 2008. 196p. pap. 12.95 (978-0-9820479-8-9(3)) Peppertree Pr., The.

Daines, Julie. Unraveled: A Tale of True Love. 2014. 192p. (J). pap. 14.99 (978-1-62108-627-7(5)) Covenant Communications, Inc.

Dale, Anna. Magical Mischief. 2011. (ENG.). 304p. (YA). 16.99 (978-1-59990-629-4(5), 9781599906294, Bloomsbury USA Childrens) Bloomsbury Publishing USA.

Dalon, Phillip A. Clanwickie: Life High in the Kabalas. 2011. 232p. pap. 24.95 (978-1-4626-4033-1(8)) America Star Bks.

Dalton, Kippy. Nanna's Magic Globe. 2016. (Spring Forward Ser.). (J). (gr. k). (978-1-4900-2253-6(8)) Benchmark Education Co.

Dalton, Susan. The Magic Glasses. 2012. 36p. pap. 19.95 (978-1-4685-2586-1(7)) AuthorHouse.

Daly, Stuart. The Final Battle. 2016. (Brotherhood of Thieves Ser.: 3). (ENG.). 336p. (J). (gr. 4-7). pap. 9.99 (978-0-85798-538-5(8)) Random Hse. Australia AUS. Dist: Independent Pubs. Group.

Damitz, Charlie. Diving for el Corazon. Diefendorf, Cathy, illus. 2007. (ENG.). 101p. (J). pap. 7.95 (978-0-9744446-3-5(4)) All About Kids Publishing.

D'Angelo, Elaina R. The Magic Book of E, 1 vol. 2010. 48p. pap. 16.95 (978-1-4489-3949-7(6)) America Star Bks.

Daniels, Linda. The Magic Gazebo. 2012. 36p. pap. 18.41 (978-1-4669-6165-4(1)) Trafford Publishing.

Danielski, A. The Nick & Austin Chronicles: The Pirate Ship's Magic & a New Home. 2013. 28p. pap. 24.95 (978-1-4626-7709-2(6)) America Star Bks.

Darcy, Kate. Winnie Windmill: The Village Fete. 2012. (Illus.). 52p. pap. 24.40 (978-1-4678-8382-5(4)) AuthorHouse.

Dark, Gregory. Susie & the Snow-it-alls. 2011. (ENG.). 286p. pap. 24.95 (978-1-84694-881-7(9)) Hunt, John Publishing Ltd. GBR. Dist: National Bk. Network.

Darlison, Aleesah. Ellabeth's Light Cancelled. Brailsford, Jill, illus. 2017. (Unicorn Riders Ser.). (ENG.). 112p. (gr. 3-5). pap. 5.95 (978-1-4795-6559-7(8)) Picture Window Bks.

—Ellabeth's Test. Brailsford, Jill, illus. 2016. (Unicorn Riders Ser.). (ENG.). 112p. (gr. 3-5). lib. bdg. 22.65 (978-1-4795-6547-4(4)) Picture Window Bks.

—Ellabeth's Test Cancelled. Brailsford, Jill, illus. 2017. (Unicorn Riders Ser.). (ENG.). 112p. (gr. 3-5). pap. 5.95 (978-1-4795-6555-9(5)) Picture Window Bks.

—Krystal's Charge Cancelled. Brailsford, Jill, illus. 2017. (Unicorn Riders Ser.). (ENG.). 112p. (gr. 3-5). pap. 5.95 (978-1-4795-6558-0(X)) Picture Window Bks.

—Krystal's Choice. Brailsford, Jill, illus. 2016. (Unicorn Riders Ser.). (ENG.). 112p. (gr. 3-5). lib. bdg. 22.65 (978-1-4795-6546-7(6)) Picture Window Bks.

—Krystal's Choice Cancelled. Brailsford, Jill, illus. 2017. (Unicorn Riders Ser.). (ENG.). 112p. (gr. 3-5). pap. 5.95 (978-1-4795-6554-2(7)) Picture Window Bks.

—Quinn's Riddles. Brailsford, Jill, illus. 2016. (Unicorn Riders Ser.). (ENG.). 112p. (gr. 3-5). lib. bdg. 22.65 (978-1-4795-6544-3(X)) Picture Window Bks.

—Quinn's Truth Cancelled. Brailsford, Jill, illus. 2017. (Unicorn Riders Ser.). (ENG.). 112p. (gr. 3-5). pap. 5.95 (978-1-4795-6556-6(3)) Picture Window Bks.

—Willow's Challenge. Brailsford, Jill, illus. 2016. (Unicorn Riders Ser.). (ENG.). 112p. (gr. 3-5). lib. bdg. 22.65 (978-1-4795-6545-0(8)) Picture Window Bks.

—Willow's Victory Cancelled. Brailsford, Jill, illus. 2017. (Unicorn Riders Ser.). (ENG.). 112p. (gr. 3-5). pap. 5.95 (978-1-4795-6557-3(1)) Picture Window Bks.

Darlison, Aleesha. Quinn's Riddles. Brailsford, Jill, illus. 2017. (Unicorn Riders Ser.). (ENG.). 112p. (gr. 3-5). pap. 5.95 (978-1-4795-6552-8(0)) Picture Window Bks.

—Willow's Challenge. Brailsford, Jill, illus. 2017. (Unicorn Riders Ser.). (ENG.). 112p. (gr. 3-5). pap. 5.95 (978-1-4795-6553-5(9)) Picture Window Bks.

Dashney, John. The Adventures of Walter the Weremouse; the Adventures of Mishka the Mousewere. Somerville, Sheila, illus. 2005. 202p. (J). pap. (978-0-9633236-7-5(9)) Storm Peak Pr.

Davenport, Kelly. Do Hotdogs Grow on Trees? 2010. 32p. pap. 17.99 (978-1-4520-6636-3(1)) AuthorHouse.

David, Erica. All Hail the Queen. RH Disney Staff & Robinson, Bill, illus. 2015. (Stepping Stone Book(TM) Ser.: 1). (ENG.). 128p. (J). (gr. 1-4). lib. bdg. 12.99 (978-0-7364-8216-5(4), RH/Disney) Random Hse. Children's Bks.

—Anna & Elsa #6: the Arendelle Cup (Disney Frozen) RH Disney Staff et al, illus. 2015. (Stepping Stone Book(TM) Ser.: 6). (ENG.). 128p. (J). (gr. 1-4). 9.99 (978-0-7364-3437-9(2), RH/Disney) Random Hse. Children's Bks.

—Anna & Elsa: Books 1-4 (Disney Frozen), 4 vols. Random House Disney Staff, illus. 2015. (ENG.). 512p. (J). (gr. 1-4). 39.96 (978-0-7364-3459-1(3), RH/Disney) Random Hse. Children's Bks.

—Memory & Magic. RH Disney Staff & Robinson, William E., illus. 2015. (Stepping Stone Book(TM) Ser.: 2). (ENG.). 128p. (J). (gr. 1-4). 9.99 (978-0-7364-3285-6(X), RH/Disney) Random Hse. Children's Bks.

Davidson, Susanna. Stories of Dolls. Wanert, Amandine, illus. 2006. 48p. (J). (gr. 2-5). 8.99 (978-0-7945-1327-6(1), Usborne) EDC Publishing.

—Stories of Magic Ponies. Costa, Jana, illus. 2007. (Young Reading Series 1 Gift Bks). 48p. (J). 8.99 (978-0-7945-1790-8(0), Usborne) EDC Publishing.

Davies, Jacqueline. The Magic Trap. 2014. (Lemonade War Ser.: 5). (ENG., Illus.). 272p. (J). (gr. 2-5). 15.99 (978-0-544-05289-5(7), HMH Books For Young Readers) Houghton Mifflin Harcourt Publishing Co.

Davies, Peter. Molly's Magic Pencil: The Blue Genie. 2011. 28p. (gr. 1-2). 14.99 (978-1-4567-3018-5(5)) AuthorHouse.

—Molly's Magic Pencil: The Flying Carpet. 2010. 32p. 14.99 (978-1-4520-4830-7(4)) AuthorHouse.

Davis, Aubrey. Kishka for Koppel, 1 vol. Cohen, Sheldon, illus. 2011. (ENG.). 32p. (J). (gr. -1-3). 19.95 (978-1-55469-299-6(7)) Orca Bk. Pubs. USA.

Davis, Graeme. Re-Read Harry Potter & the Chamber of Secrets Today! an Unauthorized Guide. 2008. 112p. pap. 15.49 (978-1-934840-72-6(6)) Nimble Bks. LLC.

Davis, Kent. Riddle in Ruby - The Changer's Key. 2016. (Riddle in Ruby Ser.: 2). 448p. (J). (gr. 3-7). 17.99 (978-0-06-236837-9(0), Greenwillow Bks.) HarperCollins Pubs.

Davis, Kent. A Riddle in Ruby #2: the Changer's Key. 2017. (Riddle in Ruby Ser.: 2). 464p. (J). (gr. 3-7). pap. 7.99 **(978-0-06-236838-6(9)**, Greenwillow Bks.) HarperCollins Pubs.

Davis, Marshall L. Og the Magical Green Frog. 2012. (ENG.). (J). pap. (978-1-4675-4055-1(2)) Independent Pub.

Davis, Martine. There's a Red Hippo at My Door. 2012. 24p. pap. 13.99 (978-1-4772-8070-6(7)) AuthorHouse.

Dawley, Linda. The Tooth Fairy's Mistake. 2nd ed. 2014. (ENG.). 114p. (J). pap. (978-0-9941011-6-7(3), The Little Red Hen Community Pr.) CCB Publishing.

Day, K. The Silver Bullet: Tour of the Universe. 2010. 120p. pap. 12.49 (978-1-4490-6534-8(1)) AuthorHouse.

De Jesus, Opal. The Magical Purple-Blue Frog, 1 vol. Pagona, Aurora, illus. 2010. 16p. pap. 24.95 (978-1-4489-5925-9(X)) PublishAmerica, Inc.

De la Cruz, Melissa. Double Eclipse. 2016. (Summer on East End Ser.). (ENG.). 336p. (YA). (gr. 7). 17.99 (978-0-399-17356-1(0), G.P. Putnam's Sons Books for Young Readers) Penguin Young Readers Group.

—The Isle of the Lost. (Descendants Ser.). (ENG.). (J). 2017. 336p. (gr. 4-7). pap. 9.99 **(978-1-4847-2544-3(1))** 2015. 320p. (gr. 4-7). 17.99 (978-1-4847-2097-4(0))Set. 2017. 960p. (gr. 3-7). 47.99 **(978-1-368-01423-6(2))** Hyperion Bks. for Children.

—Return to the Isle of the Lost: A Descendants Novel. 2016. (Descendants Ser.). (ENG.). 320p. (J). (gr. 4-7). 17.99 (978-1-4847-8521-8(5)); 17.99 (978-1-4847-8522-5(3)); 17.99 (978-1-4847-8520-1(7)); (Illus.). 17.99 (978-1-4847-5071-1(3)) Hyperion Bks. for Children.

—Ring & the Crown. 2017. (Ring & the Crown Ser.). (ENG.). 480p. (YA). (gr. 9-17). pap. 9.99 (978-1-4847-9925-3(9)) Hyperion Bks. for Children.

De la Cruz, Melissa. Rise of the Isle of the Lost. 2017. (Descendants Ser.). (ENG.). 304p. (J). (gr. 4-7). 17.99 **(978-1-4847-8128-9(7))** Hyperion Bks. for Children.

De la Cruz, Melissa & Johnston, Michael. Frozen. 2014. (Heart of Dread Ser.: 1). (ENG.). 352p. (YA). (gr. 7). pap. 10.99 (978-0-14-751224-6(7), Speak) Penguin Young Readers Group.

—Golden. 2016. (Heart of Dread Ser.: 3). (ENG.). 272p. (YA). (gr. 7). 17.99 (978-0-399-25756-8(X), G.P. Putnam's Sons Books for Young Readers) Penguin Young Readers Group.

—Stolen Bk. 2: Heart of Dread. 2014. (Heart of Dread Ser.: 2). (ENG.). 304p. (YA). (gr. 7). 17.99 (978-0-399-25755-1(1), G.P. Putnam's Sons Books for Young Readers) Penguin Young Readers Group.

De Laurentiis, Giada. Hong Kong! #3. Gambatesa, Francesca, illus. 2014. (Recipe for Adventure Ser.: 3). (ENG.). 144p. (J). (gr. 2-5). 6.99 (978-0-448-46258-5(3)); 16.99 (978-0-448-48040-4(9)) Penguin Young Readers Group. (Grosset & Dunlap).

De Laurentiis, Giada, et al. Hawaii! #6. Gambatesa, Francesca, illus. 2015. (Recipe for Adventure Ser.: 6). (ENG.). 160p. (J). (gr. 2-4). bds. 6.99 (978-0-448-48391-7(2), Grosset & Dunlap) Penguin Young Readers Group.

—Rio de Janeiro! #5. Gambatesa, Francesca, illus. 2015. (Recipe for Adventure Ser.: 5). (ENG.). 160p. (J). (gr. 2-4). bds. 6.99 (978-0-448-48204-0(5), Grosset & Dunlap) Penguin Young Readers Group.

de Lint, Charles. The Cats of Tanglewood Forest. 2014. (J). lib. bdg. 22.10 (978-0-606-36532-1(X)) Turtleback Bks.

De Matos, Isabel Freire. El Pececito Magico. Torres, Walter, illus. 2004. (SPA.). 22p. (J). pap. 6.95 (978-1-57581-578-7(8)) Santillana USA Publishing Co., Inc.

De Valera, Sinead. The Magic Gifts: Classic Irish Fairytales. (Illus.). 224p. 16.95 (978-0-86327-822-8(1)) Wolfhound Pr. IRL. Dist: Irish Bks. & Media, Inc.

De Witt, Peter. Toaster Pond. 2006. (ENG.). 248p. (YA). (gr. 7-12). per. (978-1-933255-21-7(8)) DNA Pr.

Dean, James & Dean, Kimberly. Pete the Cat & His Magic Sunglasses. Dean, James, illus. 2013. (Pete the Cat Ser.). (Illus.). 40p. (J). (gr. -1-3). lib. bdg. 18.89 (978-0-06-227557-8(7)) HarperCollins Pubs.

Debono, Angelo. The Magic in You. 2011. 36p. pap. 13.95 (978-1-61204-783-6(1), Strategic Bk. Publishing) Strategic Book Publishing & Rights Agency (SBPRA).

Deep Trouble (Book 5) 2017. (Secret Mermaid Ser.). (ENG.). (J). pap. 4.99 **(978-0-7945-3685-5(9)**, Usborne) EDC Publishing.

Defabio, Richard Bryan. The Magic Spoon. 2011. 42p. pap. 21.99 (978-1-4568-1773-2(6)) Xlibris Corp.

Defilippis, Nunzio & Weir, Christina. The Avalon Chronicles, Vol. 2. 2013. (ENG., Illus.). 152p. (YA). 19.99 (978-1-934964-90-3(5), 9781934964903) Oni Pr., Inc.

Defreitas, Henrietta. Henratty Mortimer: The Meerville Myth. (Illus.). 2012. 84p. pap. 32.03 (978-1-4772-3867-7(0)) 2011. 88p. pap. 28.14 (978-1-4520-8237-0(5)) AuthorHouse.

DeGreeff, Davy. Tommy Bomani: Badru Rising, 1 vol. Brookins, Sam, illus. 2010. (Tommy Bomani: Teen Warrior Ser.: Bk. 3). (ENG.). 112p. (gr. 3-8). 27.07 (978-1-60270-699-6(9), Calico Chapter Bks) Magic Wagon.

—Tommy Bomani: Land of Legend, 1 vol. Brookins, Sam, illus. 2010. (Tommy Bomani: Teen Warrior Ser.: Bk. 2). (ENG.). 112p. (gr. 3-8). 27.07 (978-1-60270-698-9(0), Calico Chapter Bks) Magic Wagon.

—Tommy Bomani: Prophecy Fulfilled, 1 vol. Brookins, Sam, illus. 2010. (Tommy Bomani: Teen Warrior Ser.: Bk. 4). (ENG.). 112p. (gr. 3-8). 27.07 (978-1-60270-700-9(6), Calico Chapter Bks) Magic Wagon.

deGroat, Diane. Trick or Treat, Smell My Feet. deGroat, Diane, illus. 2008. (Illus.). (J). (gr. -1-7). pap. 16.95 incl. audio (978-1-4301-0425-4(2)) Live Oak Media.

DeKeyser, Stacy. The Brixen Witch. Nickle, John, illus. (ENG.). 208p. (J). (gr. 3-7). 2013. pap. 6.99 (978-1-4424-3329-8(9))

2012. 15.99 *(978-1-4424-3328-1(0))* McElderry, Margaret K. Bks. (McElderry, Margaret K. Bks.).

del Rio, Tania. Sabrina the Teenage Witch: the Magic Within 4. 2014. (Sabrina Manga Ser.: 4). (ENG., Illus.). 272p. (J). (gr. 4-7). pap. 10.99 *(978-1-936975-76-1(9),* Archie Comics) Archie Comic Pubns., Inc.

Delacre, Lulu. Rafi & Rosi. 2004. (Illus.). 64p. (J). lib. bdg. 13.85 *(978-1-4242-0596-7(4))* Fitzgerald Bks.

DeLaney, Edgar Azell. The Magical Hammock. DeLaney, Edgar Azell, illus. 2004. (ENG., Illus.). 83p. (J). 19.95 *(978-0-9759013-0-4(3))* Special Edition Studios, Inc.

Delaney, Joseph. Slither, Bk. 11. 2014. (Last Apprentice Ser.). (ENG.). 432p. (YA). (gr. 8). pap. 9.99 *(978-0-06-219235-6(3),* Greenwillow Bks.) HarperCollins Pubs.

Delporte, Peyo, et al. The Smurfs & the Howlibird. 2011. (Smurfs Graphic Novels Ser.). (ENG., Illus.). 56p. (J). (gr. 2-5). 10.99 *(978-1-59707-261-8(3),* 9781597072618) Papercutz.

Delporte, Yvan. The Smurfs & the Magic Flute. Peyo, illus. 2010. (Smurfs Graphic Novels Ser.). (ENG.). 64p. (J). (gr. 2-5). pap. 5.99 *(978-1-59707-208-3(7),* 9781597072083) Papercutz.

Delporte, Yvan & Peyo. The Smurfs & the Magic Flute. 2010. (Smurfs Graphic Novels Ser.). (ENG., Illus.). 64p. (J). (gr. 2-5). 10.99 *(978-1-59707-209-0(5),* 9781597072090) Papercutz.

Delrusso, Diana. Pages, the Book-Maker Elf. Schwab, Jordan, illus. 2008. 68p. pap. 23.49 *(978-1-4343-9844-4(7))* AuthorHouse.

Deluca, Alison. Christmas O'Clock: A Collection. Daly, Lisa, illus. 2013. 198p. pap. 9.99 *(978-1-939296-98-6(6))* Myrddin Publishing Group.

DeMatteis, J. M. Imaginalis. 2010. (ENG.). 256p. (J). (gr. 3-7). 16.99 *(978-0-06-173286-7(9),* Tegen, Katherine Bks) HarperCollins Pubs.

Dematteis, J. M. The Puppet, the Professor, & the Prophet. Ploog, Mike, illus. 3rd rev. ed. 2007. 144p. (J). (gr. 4-7). 9.99 *(978-1-4231-0063-8(8))* Hyperion Pr.

DeMatteis, J. M. Stardust Kid. Ploog, Mike, illus. 2008. (ENG.). 128p. pap. 14.99 *(978-1-934506-04-2(4))* Boom! Studios.

Demetrios, Heather. Blood Passage. 2016. (Dark Caravan Cycle Ser.: 2). (ENG.). 512p. (YA). (gr. 8). 17.99 *(978-0-06-231859-6(4))* HarperCollins Pubs.

—Exquisite Captive. 2014. (Dark Caravan Cycle Ser.: 1). (ENG., Illus.). 480p. (YA). (gr. 8). 17.99 *(978-0-06-231856-5(X))* HarperCollins Pubs.

Demi. The Magic Pillow. Demi, illus. 2008. (ENG., Illus.). 40p. (J). (gr. 2-5). 24.99 *(978-1-4169-2470-8(1),* McElderry, Margaret K. Bks.) McElderry, Margaret K. Bks.

Demolin, G. The Blaue Hexe. 2010. (Illus.). 44p. pap. 21.22 *(978-1-4520-5516-9(5))* AuthorHouse.

DeMonte, Joe. Lucy & the Magic Factory. 2008. 79p. pap. 19.95 *(978-1-60813-119-8(X))* America Star Bks.

Denman, K. L. Perfect Revenge, 1 vol. 2009. (Orca Currents Ser.). (ENG.). (J). (gr. 5-9). 112p. 16.95 *(978-1-55469-103-6(6));* 128p. pap. 9.95 *(978-1-55469-102-9(8))* Orca Bk. Pubs. USA.

—La Revanche Parfaite, 1 vol. 2011. (FRE.). 144p. (J). (gr. 5-9). pap. 9.95 *(978-1-55469-853-0(7))* Orca Bk. Pubs. USA.

Dennard, Susan. A Darkness Strange & Lovely. (Something Strange & Deadly Trilogy Ser.: 2). (ENG.). (YA). (gr. 9). 2014. 432p. pap. 9.99 *(978-0-06-208330-2(9))* 2013. 416p. 17.99 *(978-0-06-208329-6(5))* HarperCollins Pubs. (HarperTeen).

—Something Strange & Deadly. (Something Strange & Deadly Trilogy Ser.: 1). (ENG.). (YA). (gr. 9). 2013. 416p. pap. 9.99 *(978-0-06-208327-2(9))* 2012. 400p. 17.99 *(978-0-06-208326-5(0))* HarperCollins Pubs. (HarperTeen).

—Strange & Ever After. 2014. (Something Strange & Deadly Trilogy Ser.: 3). (ENG.). 400p. (YA). (gr. 9). 17.99 *(978-0-06-208332-6(5))* HarperCollins Pubs.

—Truthwitch. (ENG.). (YA). 2017. (Witchlands Ser.: 1). 432p. pap. 9.99 *(978-0-7653-7929-0(5),* 9780765379290) 2016. (Witchlands Ser.: Vol. 1). (gr. 8-12). pap. 12.99 ***(978-0-7653-9022-6(1))*** 2016. (Illus.). 416p. (gr. 9-12). 18.99 *(978-0-7653-7928-3(7),* 9780765379283) Doherty, Tom Assocs., LLC. (Tor Teen).

—Truthwitch. 2017. (Witchlands Ser.: 1). (YA). lib. bdg. 20.85 ***(978-0-606-39586-1(5))*** Turtleback Bks.

—Windwitch. 2017. (ENG., Illus.). (Witchlands Ser.). 380p. (J). (gr. 8-12). pap. 12.99 ***(978-0-7653-9579-5(7));*** (Witchlands Ser.: 2). 384p. (YA). 18.99 *(978-0-7653-7930-6(9),* 9780765379306) Doherty, Tom Assocs., LLC. (Tor Teen).

dePaola, Tomie. Strega Nona's Gift. dePaola, Tomie, illus. 2011. (ENG., Illus.). 32p. (J). (gr. -1-3). 17.99 *(978-0-399-25649-3(0),* Nancy Paulsen Books) Penguin Young Readers Group.

—Strega Nona's Harvest. dePaola, Tomie, illus. (ENG., Illus.). 32p. (J). (gr. -1-3). 2012. mass mkt. 7.99 *(978-0-14-242338-7(6),* Puffin Books) 2009. 16.99 *(978-0-399-25291-4(6),* G.P. Putnam's Sons Books for Young Readers) Penguin Young Readers Group.

Depken, Kristen L. Fairytale Magic. 2014. (Dora the Explorer Step into Reading Ser.). lib. bdg. 13.55 *(978-0-606-36011-1(5))* Turtleback Bks.

—Fairytale Magic (Dora the Explorer) Random House & Miller, Victoria, illus. 2014. (Step into Reading Ser.). (ENG.). 24p. (J). (gr. -1-1). 3.99 *(978-0-385-37503-0(4),* Random Hse. Bks. for Young Readers) Random Hse. Children's Bks.

—Monster Magic! (Shimmer & Shine) Aikins, David, illus. 2017. (Big Golden Book Ser.). (ENG.). 48p. (J). (gr. -1-2). 9.99 ***(978-1-5247-1671-4(5),*** Golden Bks.) Random Hse. Children's Bks.

Depken, Kristen L. Rubble's Big Wish (PAW Patrol) Moore, Harry, illus. 2017. (Step into Reading Ser.). (ENG.). 24p. (J). (gr. -1-1). pap. 4.99 *(978-0-399-55884-9(5),* Random Hse. Bks. for Young Readers) Random Hse. Children's Bks.

DeStefano, Lauren. The Glass Spare. 2017. (Glass Spare Ser.: 1). 416p. (YA). (gr. 8). 17.99 ***(978-0-06-249128-2(8))*** HarperCollins Pubs.

Deutsch, Stacia. Quest for the Keys. 2015. (LEGO Elves Chapter Book Ser.: 1). lib. bdg. 16.00 *(978-0-606-37769-0(7))* Turtleback Bks.

Dey, Frederic Van Re. The Magic Story. 2004. reprint ed. pap. 15.95 *(978-0-7661-8653-8(9))* Kessinger Publishing, LLC.

Dharma Publishing Staff. The King Who Understood Animals: A Story about Using Knowledge Wisely. 2nd ed. 2013. (ENG.). 36p. (gr. -1-7). pap. 8.95 *(978-0-89800-520-2(5))* Dharma Publishing.

Diamond, Kathryn. Rachel's Magic Swing. 2009. 80p. pap. 11.00 *(978-0-557-06497-7(X))* Lulu Pr., Inc.

Dickinson, Peter. The Ropemaker. Andrew, Ian, illus. 2004. 375p. (gr. 7). 17.95 *(978-0-7569-1935-1(5))* Perfection Learning Corp.

Dickson, Diane. 3 Things That Might Have Happened. 2010. 100p. pap. 15.50 *(978-1-4452-3414-4(9))* Lulu Pr., Inc.

DiGerolamo, Tony. The Wildsidhe Chronicles Bk. 5: The Undercover Dragon. 2003. (J). pap. 7.99 *(978-1-890096-17-5(2))* Padwolf Publishing, Inc.

DiMarco, Carol. The Magical Child. 3rd rev. ed. 2009. (ENG., Illus.). 44p. (J). 10.99 *(978-1-59092-273-6(5))* Blue Forge Pr.

DiMartino, Michael Dante. Rebel Genius. 2016. (Rebel Geniuses Ser.). (ENG., Illus.). 384p. (J). 16.99 *(978-1-62672-336-8(2),* 9781626723368) Roaring Brook Pr.

Disbro, Laura M. Adventures with Miss Lol: The Magic Paper Ride. 2011. 28p. pap. 15.99 *(978-1-4628-9072-9(5))* Xlibris Corp.

Disney. Frozen Cinestory, Volume 1. 2014. lib. bdg. 26.95 *(978-0-606-36645-8(8))* Turtleback Bks.

Disney Book Group. Beauty & the Beast: The Story of Belle. Disney Storybook Art Team, illus. 2016. (ENG.). 112p. (J). (gr. -1-k). 12.99 *(978-1-4847-6720-7(9))* Disney Pr.

—Frozen: The Story of Anna & Elsa. Disney Storybook Art Team, illus. 2016. (ENG.). 112p. (J). (gr. -1-k). 12.99 *(978-1-4847-6770-2(5))* Disney Pr.

—Frozen, Level 1. 2016. (World of Reading Ser.). (ENG.). 96p. (J). (gr. -1-k). pap. 7.99 *(978-1-4847-9032-8(4))* Disney Pr.

—Tangled: The Story of Rapunzel. Disney Storybook Art Team, illus. 2016. (ENG.). 112p. (J). (gr. -1-k). 12.99 *(978-1-4847-6727-6(6))* Disney Pr.

Disney Book Group & Brody, Jessica. CJ's Treasure Chase. No New Art Needed & Disney Storybook Art Team, illus. 2016. (School of Secrets Ser.: 1). (ENG.). 192p. (J). (gr. 3-7). 9.99 *(978-1-4847-7864-7(2))* Disney Pr.

Disney Book Group Staff. Cinderella. Disney Storybook Artists Staff, illus. 2nd ed. 2012. (Read-Along Storybook & CD Ser.). (ENG.). 32p. (J). (gr. -1 — 1). pap. 6.99 *(978-1-4231-6321-3(4))* Disney Pr.

—Frozen Read-Along Storybook & CD. Disney Storybook Artists Staff, illus. 2013. (Read-Along Storybook & CD Ser.). (ENG.). 32p. (J). (gr. -1-k). pap. 6.99 *(978-1-4231-7064-8(4))* Disney Pr.

—Sofia the First a Magical Match. Disney Storybook Art Team, illus. 2014. (ENG.). 24p. (J). (gr. -1-k). pap. 5.99 *(978-1-4847-2165-0(9))* Disney Pr.

—Sofia's Cup of Tea. Disney Storybook Art Team, illus. 2015. (ENG.). 10p. (J). (gr. -1-k). bds. 7.99 *(978-1-4847-0646-6(3))* Disney Pr.

—Tinker Bell & the Pirate Fairy. Disney Storybook Art Team, illus. 2014. (Read-Along Storybook & CD Ser.). (ENG.). 32p. (J). (gr. -1-k). pap. 6.99 *(978-1-4231-7407-3(0))* Disney Pr.

—World of Reading: Sofia the First Riches to Rags: Level 1. Disney Storybook Art Team, illus. 2015. (World of Reading Ser.). (ENG.). 32p. (J). (gr. -1-k). pap. 3.99 *(978-1-4847-0699-2(4))* Disney Pr.

Disney Book Group Staff & Hapka, Catherine. Sofia the First. Lee, Grace, illus. 2012. (ENG.). 40p. (J). (gr. -1-k). 15.99 *(978-1-4231-6986-4(7))* Disney Pr.

Disney Book Group Staff & Hicks, Barbara Jean. Frozen an Amazing Snowman. Disney Storybook Artists Staff & Mosqueda, Olga, illus. 2014. (ENG.). 40p. (J). (gr. -1-k). 16.99 *(978-1-4231-8514-7(5))* Disney Pr.

Disney Book Group Staff & Scollon, Bill. Sofia the First: a Royal Mouse in the House. Lee, Grace, illus. 2015. (ENG.). 40p. (J). (gr. -1-k). 8.99 *(978-1-4847-0643-5(9))* Disney Pr.

Disney Book Group Staff & Scollon, William. Mickey Mouse Clubhouse a Goofy Fairy Tale. Disney Storybook Art Team, illus. 2014. (ENG.). 24p. (J). (gr. -1-k). pap. 4.99 *(978-1-4231-8900-8(0))* Disney Pr.

Disney Editors. Beauty & the Beast Novelization. 2017. (J). lib. bdg. 19.65 ***(978-0-606-40201-9(2))*** Turtleback Bks.

—Disney Descendants Wicked World Cinestory Comic, Volume 3, 3. 2017. (J). lib. bdg. 20.85 ***(978-0-606-39833-6(3))*** Turtleback Bks.

—Disney Tangled Movie Comic. 2017. (ENG.). 64p. (J). (gr. 4-7). 18.40 *(978-0-606-39085-9(5))* Turtleback Bks.

—Frozen. 2013. lib. bdg. 14.75 *(978-0-606-32207-2(8),* Turtleback) Turtleback Bks.

—Frozen - Anna's Icy Adventure. 2013. lib. bdg. 14.75 *(978-0-606-32206-5(X),* Turtleback) Turtleback Bks.

Disney Frozen Melt My Heart. 2014. (Hugs Book Ser.). (ENG.). 10p. (J). (gr. -1-k). bds. 10.99 *(978-0-7944-3266-9(2),* Reader's Digest Children's Bks.) Studio Fun International.

Disney Junior, Disney. Disney Sofia the First Music Player Storybook. 2015. (Music Player Storybook Ser.: 1). (ENG.). 32p. (J). (gr. -1-2). 19.99 *(978-0-7944-3357-4(X),* Reader's Digest Children's Bks.) Studio Fun International.

Disney Press Editors. Riches to Rags. 2015. (Sofia the First World of Reading Ser.). (J). lib. bdg. 13.55 *(978-0-606-36901-5(5))* Turtleback Bks.

Distler, Christine A. Pegasus: The Introduction. 2005. 84p. pap. 11.95 *(978-1-59113-763-4(2))* Booklocker.com, Inc.

DiTerlizzi, Tony & Black, Holly. Care & Feeding of Sprites. DiTerlizzi, Tony, illus. 2006. (Spiderwick Chronicles Ser.). (ENG., Illus.). 48p. (J). (gr. 2-7). 18.99 *(978-1-4169-2757-0(3),* Simon & Schuster Bks. For Young Readers) Simon & Schuster Bks. For Young Readers.

—The Nixies Song - A Giant Problem - The Wyrm King Set, Set. DiTerlizzi, Tony, illus. 2009. (Beyond the Spiderwick Chronicles Ser.: Nos. 1-3). (ENG., Illus.). 528p. (J). (gr. 2-5). 33.99 *(978-1-4169-9011-6(9),* Simon & Schuster Bks. For Young Readers) Simon & Schuster Bks. For Young Readers.

Divakaruni, Chitra Banerjee. The Mirror of Fire & Dreaming. 2007. (ENG.). 336p. (J). (gr. 3-7). pap. 14.99 *(978-1-4169-1768-7(3),* Aladdin) Simon & Schuster Children's Publishing.

Dixon, Andy. Sword Quest. Brooks, Felicity, ed. Boni, Simone, illus. rev. ed. 2005. (Usborne Fantasy Puzzle Bks.). 31p. (J). (gr. 3-7). pap., pap. 7.95 *(978-0-7945-1096-1(5),* Usborne) EDC Publishing.

Dixon, Danielle. Project: Purest. 2012. 370p. pap. 19.99 *(978-1-4691-8247-6(5))* Xlibris Corp.

Dixon, Heather. Entwined. (ENG.). 480p. (YA). (gr. 8). 2012. pap. 9.99 *(978-0-06-200104-7(3))* 2011. 17.99 *(978-0-06-200103-0(5))* HarperCollins Pubs. (Greenwillow Bks.).

d'Lacey, Chris. The Fire Ascending. (ENG.). 576p. (J). (gr. 3-7). 2013. pap. 9.99 *(978-0-545-40293-4(X),* Scholastic Paperbacks) 2012. (Last Dragon Chronicles Ser.: 7). 18.99 *(978-0-545-40216-3(6),* Orchard Bks.) Scholastic, Inc.

—The Fire Ascending. 2013. (Last Dragon Chronicles Ser.: 7). lib. bdg. 20.85 *(978-0-606-31958-4(1),* Turtleback) Turtleback Bks.

—The Wearle. 2016. (Erth Dragons Ser.: 1). (ENG.). 320p. (J). (gr. 3-7). 16.99 *(978-0-545-90018-8(2),* Scholastic Pr.) Scholastic, Inc.

Dodd, Emma. Foxy. Dodd, Emma, illus. 2012. (ENG., Illus.). 40p. (J). (gr. -1-2). 14.99 *(978-0-06-201419-1(6))* HarperCollins Pubs.

—Foxy in Love. Dodd, Emma, illus. 2013. (ENG., Illus.). 40p. (J). (gr. -1-3). 17.99 *(978-0-06-201422-1(6))* HarperCollins Pubs.

—Foxy in Love. 2013. (Illus.). (J). lib. bdg. *(978-0-06-201423-8(4))* HarperCollins Pubs.

Dodd, Susan. Dreaming the Dreams That Only Cats Can Dream. 2013. 150p. pap. *(978-1-78148-654-2(9))* Grosvenor Hse. Publishing Ltd.

Doerrfeld, Cori. A Perfect View. Doerrfeld, Cori & Page, Tyler, illus. 2017. (Cici: a Fairy's Tale Ser.: 3). (ENG.). 48p. (J). (gr. 2-5). 26.65 *(978-1-4677-6154-3(0));* pap. 7.99 *(978-1-5124-3068-4(4));* E-Book 19.99 ***(978-1-5124-2700-4(4),*** 9781512427004) Lerner Publishing Group. (Graphic Universe™).

—Truth in Sight. Doerrfeld, Cori & Page, Tyler, illus. 2016. (Cici: a Fairy's Tale Ser.: 2). (ENG.). 48p. (J). (gr. 2-5). lib. bdg. 26.65 *(978-1-4677-6153-6(2),* Graphic Universe™) Lerner Publishing Group.

Doherty, Glen. The Magic Sucker or How Love Really Works. 2012. 24p. pap. 12.99 *(978-1-4797-0978-6(6))* Xlibris Corp.

Dokey, Cameron. Golden: A Retelling of Rapunzel. 2007. (Once upon a Time Ser.). (ENG.). 192p. (YA). (gr. 7-9). mass mkt. 7.99 *(978-1-4169-3926-9(1),* Simon Pulse) Simon Pulse.

Dolamore, Jaclyn. Dark Metropolis. 2014. (ENG., Illus.). 304p. (YA). (gr. 7-12). 17.99 *(978-1-4231-6332-9(X))* Hyperion Bks. for Children.

—Glittering Shadows. 2016. (Dark Metropolis Ser.). (ENG., Illus.). 442p. (YA). (gr. 7-12). pap. 9.99 *(978-1-4231-6477-7(5))* Hyperion Bks. for Children.

—Magic under Glass. (Magic under Glass Ser.). (ENG.). (YA). (gr. 7). 2011. 256p. pap. 8.99 *(978-1-59990-587-7(6),* 9781599905877) 2010. 240p. 16.99 *(978-1-59990-430-6(6),* 9781599904306) Bloomsbury Publishing USA. (Bloomsbury USA Childrens).

—Magic under Stone. 2012. (Magic under Glass Ser.). (ENG.). 304p. (YA). 16.99 *(978-1-59990-643-0(0),* 9781599906430, Bloomsbury USA Childrens) Bloomsbury Publishing USA.

Dolbeck, Andrew. Fever Jenny, Bk. 1. 2006. 120p. pap. 10.99 *(978-1-59092-324-5(3))* Blue Forge Pr.

Donaldson, Babette. Emma Lea's Magic Teapot. Van Dijk, Jerianne, illus. 2007. 32p. (J). lib. bdg. 16.95 *(978-0-9792612-1-3(X))* Blue Gate Bks.

Donfrancesco, Anna. Keepers of the Dream. 2007. (Illus.). 92p. per. *(978-1-84549-238-0(2))* arima publishing.

Donnelly, Jennifer. Deep Blue. 2014. (Waterfire Saga Novel Ser.: Bk. 1). (ENG., Illus.). 352p. (YA). (gr. 7-12). 17.99 *(978-1-4231-3316-2(1))* Disney Pr.

—Deep Blue. 2015. (Waterfire Saga Ser.: Bk. 1). (ENG.). 368p. (YA). (gr. 7-12). pap. 9.99 *(978-1-4847-1310-5(9))* Hyperion Bks. for Children.

—Rogue Wave. 2015. (Waterfire Saga Novel Ser.: Bk. 2). (ENG.). 320p. (YA). (gr. 7-12). 17.99 *(978-1-4231-8200-9(6))* Disney Pr.

—Rogue Wave. 2016. (Waterfire Saga Ser.: Bk. 2). (ENG.). 336p. (YA). (gr. 7-12). pap. 9.99 *(978-1-4847-1301-3(4))* Hyperion Bks. for Children.

Donnelly, Jennifer. Waterfire Saga, Book Four Sea Spell. 2017. (Waterfire Saga Ser.). (ENG.). 368p. (YA). (gr. 7-12). pap. 9.99 ***(978-1-4847-1303-7(6))*** Hyperion Bks. for Children.

Donovan, Dan. A Christmas Tail! 2008. 28p. pap. 14.50 *(978-1-4389-1220-2(X))* AuthorHouse.

Dora's Magical Adventures, Set. 2008. (Dora the Explorer Ser.). (ENG.). 144p. (J). pap. 10.99 *(978-1-4169-7583-0(7),* Simon Spotlight/Nickelodeon) Simon Spotlight/Nickelodeon.

Dorison, Xavier & Nury, Fabian. Century Club. Ross, C., illus. 2012. (Spooks Ser.: 2). (ENG.). 56p. (J). (gr. 10-12). pap. 13.95 *(978-1-84918-129-7(2))* CineBook GBR. Dist: National Bk. Network.

Dorothy, Grandma. Magic, Mystery, Adventure: Wild Animals Talk to Us. 2009. 196p. 24.99 *(978-1-4490-3578-5(7));* pap. 14.99 *(978-1-4490-3579-2(5))* AuthorHouse.

Doucette, Christina. Gordon's Treasure! A Sparkle Cove Adventure. 2011. 44p. (gr. 1-2). pap. 19.99 *(978-1-4634-0487-1(5))* AuthorHouse.

Dower, Laura. The Dessert Diaries, 4 vols. Lazuli, Lilly, illus. 2016. (Dessert Diaries). (ENG.). 160p. (gr. 4-5). 106.60 *(978-1-4965-3140-7(X))* Stone Arch Bks.

Downer, Ann. The Dragon of Never-Was. Rayyan, Omar, illus. 2008. (ENG.). 320p. (J). (gr. 3-6). pap. 14.99 *(978-1-4169-5453-8(8),* Atheneum Bks. for Young Readers) Simon & Schuster Children's Publishing.

—Hatching Magic. Rayyan, Omar, illus. 2004. 242p. 16.00 *(978-0-7569-3481-1(8))* Perfection Learning Corp.

—Hatching Magic. 2004. (ENG.). 256p. (J). (gr. 3-7). reprint ed. pap. 15.99 *(978-0-689-87057-6(4),* Atheneum Bks. for Young Readers) Simon & Schuster Children's Publishing.

Downes, Alice. Lucy & the Magic Loom: A Rainbow Loomer's Adventure Story. 2015. (ENG.). 112p. (gr. k-5). pap. 7.99 *(978-1-63450-137-8(3),* Sky Pony Pr.) Skyhorse Publishing Co., Inc.

Downes, Kit. Zal & Zara & the Great Race of Azamed. 2009. 1.00 *(978-1-4074-4352-2(6))* Recorded Bks., Inc.

Downest, Madeline. Lucy & the Magic Loom: the Daring Rescue: A Rainbow Loomer's Adventure Story. 2016. (ENG.). 112p. (J). (gr. k-5). pap. 7.99 *(978-1-63450-215-3(9),* Sky Pony Pr.) Skyhorse Publishing Co., Inc.

Doyle, Bill. Attack of the Shark-Headed Zombie. Altman, Scott, illus. 2011. (Stepping Stone Book Ser.). (ENG.). 112p. (J). (gr. 1-4). 4.99 *(978-0-375-86675-3(2),* Random Hse. Bks. for Young Readers) Random Hse. Children's Bks.

Doyle, Marissa. Betraying Season. 2010. (ENG.). 336p. (YA). (gr. 9-13). pap. 19.99 *(978-0-312-62916-8(8),* 9780312629168) Square Fish.

—Courtship & Curses. 2013. (ENG.). 368p. (YA). (gr. 9-13). pap. 10.99 *(978-1-250-02744-3(6))* Square Fish.

Doyle, Roddy. Brilliant. Hughes, Emily, illus. 2015. (ENG.). 192p. (J). (gr. 3-7). 16.95 *(978-1-4197-1479-5(1),* Amulet Bks.) Abrams, Inc.

Dragoon, Leigh. The Class of Classics. Sheron, Jessica, illus. 2017. (ENG.). 112p. (J). (gr. 3-7). pap. 9.99 *(978-0-316-33741-0(2))* Little Brown & Co.

Drake, Emily. The Curse of Arkady. (Magickers Ser.: 2). (ENG.). (gr. 12-18). Bk. 2. 2003. 384p. 6.99 *(978-0-7564-0103-0(8))* Vol. 1. 2010. (Illus.). 624p. 9.99 *(978-0-7564-0636-3(6))* DAW. (DAW).

Drischel, Candy L. Restless with the Dark Moon Rising. 2008. 105p. pap. 19.95 *(978-1-60610-421-7(7))* America Star Bks.

Driscoll, Roger K. Echo Mccool, Outlaw Through Time. 2011. 190p. pap. *(978-1-908105-26-4(7))* Grosvenor Hse. Publishing Ltd.

The Drums of Legenderry. 2006. (J). per. *(978-0-9776967-0-3(7))* Legenderry.com.

Duane, Diane. Games Wizards Play. (Young Wizards Ser.: 10). (ENG.). 640p. (YA). (gr. 7). 2017. pap. 8.99 *(978-0-544-81323-6(5))* 2016. 17.99 *(978-0-547-41806-3(X))* Houghton Mifflin Harcourt Publishing Co. (HMH Books For Young Readers).

Duce, Gillian. Magic & Mayhem. 2006. (ENG.). 212p. per. *(978-1-894936-64-4(7))* Saga Bks.

Due, Kirsten L. Bearen Bear & the Bunbury Tales. Berends, Jenny, illus. 2013. 194p. pap. *(978-0-9884916-3-2(X))* Roxby Media Ltd.

Duerr, Doug. The Adventures of Jazz & Elliott: Danielle goes to the Magical Land of Roop-E-Doo. 2010. 29p. (J). pap. 17.95 *(978-1-4327-5405-1(X))* Outskirts Pr., Inc.

Duey, Kathleen. Following Magic. Tang, Sandara, illus. 2010. (Faeries' Promise Ser.: 2). (ENG.). 128p. (J). (gr. 2-5). pap. 6.99 *(978-1-4169-8459-7(3),* Aladdin) Simon & Schuster Children's Publishing.

—Following Magic. Tang, Sandara, illus. 2010. (Faeries' Promise Ser.: 2). (ENG.). 128p. (J). (gr. 2-5). 15.99 *(978-1-4169-8458-0(5),* Simon & Schuster/Paula Wiseman Bks.) Simon & Schuster/Paula Wiseman Bks.

—The Full Moon. Tang, Sandara, illus. 2011. (Faeries' Promise Ser.: 4). (ENG.). 128p. (J). (gr. 2-5). pap. 4.99 *(978-1-4169-8463-4(1),* Aladdin) Simon & Schuster Children's Publishing.

—The Full Moon. Tang, Sandara, illus. 2011. (Faeries' Promise Ser.: 4). (ENG.). 128p. (J). (gr. 2-5). lib. bdg. 15.99 *(978-1-4169-8462-7(3),* Simon & Schuster/Paula Wiseman Bks.) Simon & Schuster/Paula Wiseman Bks.

—Sacred Scars, No. 2. Rayyan, Sheila, illus. 2009. (Resurrection of Magic Ser.: 2). (ENG.). 560p. (YA). (gr. 7-18). 18.99 *(978-0-689-84095-1(0),* Atheneum Bks. for Young Readers) Simon & Schuster Children's Publishing.

—Silence & Stone. Tang, Sandara, illus. 2010. (Faeries' Promise Ser.: 1). (ENG.). 128p. (J). (gr. 2-5). pap. 6.99 *(978-1-4169-8457-3(7),* Aladdin) Simon & Schuster Children's Publishing.

—Silence & Stone. Tang, Sandara, illus. 2010. (Faeries' Promise Ser.: 1). (ENG.). 128p. (J). (gr. 2-5). 15.99 *(978-1-4169-8456-6(9),* Simon & Schuster/Paula Wiseman Bks.) Simon & Schuster/Paula Wiseman Bks.

—Skin Hunger. 2008. (Resurrection of Magic Ser.: 1). (ENG.). 368p. (YA). (gr. 7-7). pap. 12.99 *(978-0-689-84094-4(2),* Atheneum Bks. for Young Readers) Simon & Schuster Children's Publishing.

—Wishes & Wings. Tang, Sandara, illus. 2011. (Faeries' Promise Ser.: 3). (ENG.). 128p. (J). (gr. 2-5). pap. 4.99 *(978-1-4169-8461-0(5),* Aladdin) Simon & Schuster Children's Publishing.

—Wishes & Wings. Tang, Sandara, illus. 2011. (Faeries' Promise Ser.: 3). (ENG.). 128p. (J). (gr. 2-5). 15.99 *(978-1-4169-8460-3(7),* Simon & Schuster/Paula Wiseman Bks.) Simon & Schuster/Paula Wiseman Bks.

DuFalla, Anita, illus. Sumac & the Magic Lake. 2004. (Reader's Theater Ser.). (J). pap. *(978-1-4108-2291-8(5),* A22915) Benchmark Education Co.

Dunbar, Fiona. The Truth Cookie. 2009. (Jinx,the Lulu Baker Trilogy Ser.: Bk. 1). (ENG.). 208p. (J). (gr. 4-6). pap. 9.99 *(978-1-4083-0744-1(8))* Hodder & Stoughton GBR. Dist: Hachette Bk. Group.

Duncan, Jasmin. The Unicorn Legacy. 2013. 100p. pap. *(978-1-909402-12-6(5));* pap. *(978-1-909402-11-9(7))* Vamptasy Publishing.

Dunkle, Clare B. Close Kin. 2nd rev. ed. 2006. (Hollow Kingdom Trilogy Ser.: 2). (ENG.). 224p. (J). (gr. 6-9). pap. 11.99 *(978-0-8050-8109-1(7),* 9780805081091, Holt, Henry & Co. Bks. For Young Readers) Holt, Henry & Co.

—The Hollow Kingdom. 2006. (Hollow Kingdom Trilogy Ser.: 1). (ENG.). 240p. (J). (gr. 6-9). reprint ed. pap. 10.99 *(978-0-8050-8108-4(9),* 9780805081084, Holt, Henry & Co. Bks. For Young Readers) Holt, Henry & Co.

—In the Coils of the Snake. 3rd rev. ed. 2006. (Hollow Kingdom Trilogy Ser.: 3). (ENG.). 240p. (J). (gr. 6-9). pap. 14.99 *(978-0-8050-8110-7(0),* 9780805081107, Holt, Henry & Co. Bks. For Young Readers) Holt, Henry & Co.

Dunseith, Peter. Bird of Heaven: The Story of a Swazi Sangoma. 2010. 257p. pap. *(978-0-624-04557-1(9))* NB Pubs. Ltd.

Dunston, Marc. The Magic of Giving, 1 vol. Cantrell, Katie, illus. 2010. (ENG.). 32p. (J). (gr. k-3). 16.99 *(978-1-58980-805-8(3))* Pelican Publishing Co., Inc.

Durst, Sarah Beth. Conjured. 2014. (ENG.). 384p. (YA). (gr. 9). pap. 9.99 *(978-0-8027-3749-6(8),* 9780802737496, Bloomsbury USA Childrens) Bloomsbury Publishing USA.

—Enchanted Ivy. (ENG.). (YA). (gr. 7). 2011. 336p. pap. 9.99 *(978-1-4169-8646-1(4))* 2010. 320p. 16.99 *(978-1-4169-8645-4(6))* McElderry, Margaret K. Bks. (McElderry, Margaret K. Bks.).

Dye, Troy & Kelesides, Tom. Goblin Chronicles 01A. 2008. (YA). 3.50 *(978-0-9801314-0-6(5))* Ape Entertainment.

—Goblin Chronicles #1B. 2008. (YA). 3.50 *(978-0-9801314-1-3(3))* Ape Entertainment.

MNO

—Goblin Chronicles #2A. 2008. (Illus.). 32p. (J). 3.50 *(978-0-9801314-2-0(1))* Ape Entertainment.
—Goblin Chronicles #2B. 2008. (Illus.). 32p. (J). 3.50 *(978-0-9801314-3-7(X))* Ape Entertainment.
Dyer, Heather. Magic in the City. Malyon, Serena, illus. 2017. (ENG.). 144p. (J). (gr. 2-5). 15.95 *(978-1-77138-203-8(1))* Kids Can Pr., Ltd. CAN. Dist: Hachette Bk. Group.
Eager, Edward. Half Magic. 192p. (J). (gr. 2-4). pap. 6.00 *(978-0-8072-1534-0(1),* Listening Library) Random Hse. Audio Publishing Group.
—Half Magic. l.t. ed. 2005. (ENG., Illus.). 216p. (J). (gr. 3-7). pap. 10.95 *(978-0-7862-7952-4(4))* Thorndike Pr.
—Magic by the Lake. Bodecker, N. M., illus. 2016. (Tales of Magic Ser.: 2). (ENG.). 224p. (J). (gr. 2-5). pap. 6.99 *(978-0-544-67170-6(8),* HMH Books For Young Readers) Houghton Mifflin Harcourt Publishing Co.
—The Well-Wishers. Bodecker, N. M., illus. 2016. (Tales of Magic Ser.: 6). (ENG.). 240p. (J). (gr. 2-5). pap. 7.99 *(978-0-544-67167-6(8),* HMH Books For Young Readers) Houghton Mifflin Harcourt Publishing Co.
Earhart, Kristin. Puppy Powers #2: Wag, You're It! 2014. (Puppy Powers Ser.: 2). (ENG., Illus.). 96p. (J). (gr. 2-5). pap. 4.99 *(978-0-545-61760-4(X),* Scholastic Paperbacks) Scholastic, Inc.
—Puppy Powers #3: Take a Bow-Wow. 2014. (Puppy Powers Ser.: 3). (ENG.). 96p. (J). (gr. 2-5). pap. 4.99 *(978-0-545-61761-1(8),* Scholastic Paperbacks) Scholastic, Inc.
Earle, Phil. Elsie & the Magic Biscuit Tin. Littler, Jamie, illus. 2016. (Early Reader Ser.). (ENG.). 64p. (J). (gr. k-2). 6.99 *(978-1-4440-1360-3(2),* Orion Children's Bks.) Hachette Children's Group GBR. Dist: Hachette Bk. Group.
Ebel, Sherry. Cassie's Magic Doors. 2008. 28p. pap. 15.99 *(978-1-4363-2970-5(1))* Xlibris Corp.
—Cassie's Magic Doors the Butterfly Garden. 2012. 36p. pap. 21.99 *(978-1-4797-0108-7(4))* Xlibris Corp.
Eberly, Chelsea. Magic Friends. 2014. (Step into Reading Ser.). (ENG., Illus.). 32p. (J). (gr. -1-1). 3.99 *(978-0-385-38296-0(0),* Random Hse. Bks. for Young Readers) Random Hse. Children's Bks.
—Magic Friends. 2014. (Barbie Step into Reading Level 2 Ser.). lib. bdg. 13.55 *(978-0-606-35991-7(5))* Turtleback Bks.
Ecton, Emily. Night of the Living Lawn Ornaments. 2009. (ENG.). 240p. (J). (gr. 3-7). pap. 5.99 *(978-1-4169-6451-3(7),* Aladdin) Simon & Schuster Children's Publishing.
EDCON Publishing Group Staff. Jack & the Beanstalk - The Stubborn Witch - Rapunzel - Betsy - The Magic Bus. l.t. ed. 2008. (Classic Children's Tales Ser.). 32p. (gr. k-4). pap. 8.95 *(978-1-55576-551-4(3))* EDCON Publishing Group.
—Little Toot - The Story of White Satin - Five Peas in a Pod - Rumpelstiltskin - The Little Magic Pot. l.t. ed. 2008. (Classic Children's Tales Ser.). 32p. (gr. k-4). pap. 8.95 *(978-1-55576-552-1(1))* EDCON Publishing Group.
Edgar, Amy. Bunny Surprise. Tejido, Jomike, illus. 2017. (Scholastic Reader, Level 2 Ser.). (ENG.). 32p. (J). (gr. k-2). pap. 5.99 *(978-1-338-04590-1(3))* Scholastic, Inc.
—Here, Kitty, Kitty. Tejido, Jomike, illus. 2017. (Scholastic Reader, Level 2 Ser.). (ENG.). 32p. (J). (gr. k-2). pap. 5.99 ***(978-1-338-04591-8(1))*** Scholastic, Inc.
Edgar, Amy. The Muddy Puppy (Scholastic Reader, Level 2: Pet Charms #1) Tejido, Jomike, illus. 2017. (Scholastic Reader, Level 2 Ser.: 1). (ENG.). 32p. (J). (gr. k-2). pap. 5.99 *(978-1-338-04589-5(X))* Scholastic, Inc.
Ediciones B (Firm) Staff & Outhwaite, Ida Rentoul. La Magia de las Hadas. 2005. (SPA & ENG., Illus.). 64p. (J). (gr. 2-4). 12.95 *(978-84-666-1610-2(1))* Ediciones B ESP. Dist: Independent Pubs. Group.
Edmondson, Frank. Mr. Frank's Magic School Bus: Rainbow's End Adventure. Edmondson, Brad, illus. 2007. 20p. per. 24.95 *(978-1-4241-8617-4(X))* America Star Bks.
—Mr. Frank's Magic School Bus: Rainbow's End Adventure, 1 vol. Edmondson, Brad, illus. 2010. 20p. 24.95 *(978-1-4512-1042-2(6))* PublishAmerica, Inc.
Edwards, Christine. The Charmed Enchanted Book. 2010. 24p. pap. 16.49 *(978-1-4490-7091-5(4))* AuthorHouse.
Edwards, Garth. The Magic Boots. Stasyuk, Max, illus. 2011. (Adventures of Titch & Mitch Ser.). (J). pap. *(978-0-9567449-8-2(2))* Inside Pocket Publishing, Ltd.
—The #04 Magic Boots. Stasyuk, Max, illus. 2011. (Adventures of Titch & Mitch, the Ser.). (J). pap. *(978-0-7613-8424-3(3))* Inside Pocket Publishing, Ltd.
Edwards, R. G. Eafin Lokdore & the Altar of the Sun Book II. 2007. 264p. pap. 19.96 *(978-0-615-17785-4(9))* Edwards, R. G. Publishing.
—Eafin Lokdore & the Magician's Lost Medallion: Book I of the Eafin Lokdore Trilogy. 2007. (Illus.). 268p. pap. 19.95 *(978-0-615-16739-8(X));* (J). 35.95 *(978-0-615-13336-2(3))* Edwards, R. G. Publishing.
Edwards, Wayne. Ali & the Magic Ball. Golden, Rayna, illus. 2009. 24p. pap. 12.50 *(978-1-60860-367-1(9),* Eloquent Bks.) Strategic Book Publishing & Rights Agency (SBPRA).
Egan, Catherine. The Unmaking, 1 vol. 2013. (Last Days of Tian Di Ser.: 2). (ENG.). 248p. (J). (gr. 4-6). pap. 12.95 *(978-1-55050-559-7(9))* Coteau Bks. CAN. Dist: Orca Bk. Pubs. USA.
Egan, Kate, adapted by. World's Apart. 2005. (W. I. T. C. H. Ser.: Bk. 14). 134p. (J). lib. bdg. 16.92 *(978-1-4242-0788-6(6))* Fitzgerald Bks.
Egan, Kate & Lane, Mike. The Great Escape. Wight, Eric, illus. 2014. (Magic Shop Ser.: 3). (ENG.). 176p. (J). (gr. 2-4). 14.99 *(978-1-250-02916-4(3),* 9781250029164) Feiwel & Friends.
Eldridge, Jim. The Final Showdown: Match Six. 2016. (Wrestling Trolls Ser.: 6). (ENG., Illus.). 176p. (J). (gr. k-3). pap. 9.99 *(978-1-4714-0269-2(X))* Bonnier Publishing GBR. Dist: Independent Pubs. Group.
Elfgren, Sara B. & Strandberg, Mats. The Circle: The Engelsfors Trilogy — Book 1. 2013. (Engelsfors Trilogy Ser.: 1). (ENG.). 608p. (gr. 9-13). 18.99 *(978-1-4683-0658-3(8),* 460658) Overlook Pr., The.
Elgert, C. J. The Elder Brothers & the Padstow Crystals. 2013. 208p. *(978-1-4602-1788-7(8));* pap. *(978-1-4602-1789-4(6))* FriesenPress.
Eliot, Ethel. The Little House in the Fairy Wood. 2006. 108p. per. 9.95 *(978-1-59818-097-8(5));* 22.95 *(978-1-59818-343-6(5))* Aegypan.
Elliott, Linda. When Little Pinkie Gets Her Wings. Switzer, Bobbi, illus. 2007. 28p. per. 11.95 *(978-1-59800-871-5(4))* Outskirts Pr., Inc.
Elliott, M. G. The Magic Wheel: And the Adventures of Ding-How, Ah-So, & Mi-Tu. 2011. 220p. (gr. 4-6). 33.95 *(978-1-4497-3050-5(7));* pap. 17.95 *(978-1-4497-3049-9(3))* Author Solutions, Inc. (WestBow Pr.).
Ellis, M. Henderson. Petra K & the Blackhearts: A Novel. 2014. (Young Europe Bks.). (ENG., Illus.). 202p. (J). (gr. 9). pap. 11.99 *(978-0-9850623-8-5(X))* New Europe Bks.
Ellsworth, Theo. Eyes of War. 2006. 385p. (YA). pap. 14.99 *(978-0-9776114-0-9(X))* Hidden Talent Pr.
Elovitz Marshall, Sylvia A. & Marshall, Linda. The Mitzvah Magician. Engel, Christiane, illus. 2012. (Kar-Ben Favorites Ser.). (ENG.). 24p. (J). (gr. -1-2). 7.95 *(978-0-7613-5656-1(8),* Kar-Ben Publishing) Lerner Publishing Group.
Else, Barbara. The Queen & the Nobody Boy. Broad, Sam, illus. 2013. (Tales of Fontania Ser.). (ENG.). 328p. (J). (gr. 4-7). *(978-1-877579-49-3(1))* Gecko Pr.
—The Traveling Restaurant: Jasper's Voyage in Three Parts. 2012. (Gecko Press Titles Ser.). (ENG.). 304p. (J). (gr. 5-8). 17.95 *(978-1-877579-03-5(3))* Gecko Pr. NZL. Dist: Lerner Publishing Group.
Emmett, Jonathan. The Conjuror's Cookbook Vol. I: Goblin Stew. (ENG., Illus.). 64p. (J). pap. 7.99 *(978-0-7475-4403-6(4))* Bloomsbury Publishing Plc GBR. Dist: Trafalgar Square Publishing.
—The Conjuror's Cookbook Vol. II: Serpent Soup. (ENG., Illus.). 64p. (J). pap. 7.99 *(978-0-7475-4408-1(5))* Bloomsbury Publishing Plc GBR. Dist: Trafalgar Square Publishing.
—The Conjuror's Cookbook Vol. III: Ghostly Goulash. (ENG., Illus.). 64p. (J). pap. 7.99 *(978-0-7475-4413-5(1))* Bloomsbury Publishing Plc GBR. Dist: Trafalgar Square Publishing.
Endacott, C. R. Afflatus. 2008. 232p. pap. 15.95 *(978-0-595-52418-1(4))* iUniverse, Inc.
Endicott, Megan. In the Hall of the Mountain King. 2013. 48p. pap. 20.95 *(978-1-4582-0789-0(7),* Abbott Pr.) Author Solutions, Inc.
Enyi, Patricia Nmukoso. Marcus the Magician: At the Beach. 2010. 38p. pap. 15.50 *(978-1-60911-447-3(7),* Eloquent Bks.) Strategic Book Publishing & Rights Agency (SBPRA).
Ephron, Amy. The Castle in the Mist. 2017. (ENG.). 192p. (J). (gr. 3-7). 16.99 *(978-0-399-54698-3(7),* Philomel Bks.) Penguin Young Readers Group.
Epner, Paul. Herbert Hilligan & His Magical Lunchbox. Kuon, Vuthy & Nguyen, Duke, illus. rev. ed. (Herbert Hilligan Ser.). 15.95 *(978-1-57168-549-0(9))* Eakin Pr.
—Herbert Hilligan's Lone Star Adventure. Kuon, Vuthy & Nguyen, Duke, illus. 2003. 32p. (J). 15.95 *(978-0-9743335-3-3(0))* Imaginative Publishing, Ltd.
—Herbert Hilligan's Tropical Adventure. Kuon, Vuthy & Nguyen, Duke, illus. 2003. 32p. (J). 15.95 *(978-0-9743335-2-6(2))* Imaginative Publishing, Ltd.
Epstein, Adam Jay & Jacobson, Andrew. Circle of Heroes. (Familiars Ser.: 3). (ENG.). 336p. (J). (gr. 3-7). 2013. pap. 6.99 *(978-0-06-196116-8(7))* 2012. (Illus.). 16.99 *(978-0-06-196114-4(0))* HarperCollins Pubs.
—The Familiars. 2011. (Familiars Ser.: 1). (ENG.). 384p. (J). (gr. 3-7). pap. 6.99 *(978-0-06-196110-6(8))* HarperCollins Pubs.
—The Familiars. Chiu, Bobby, illus. 2010. (Familiars Ser.: 1). (ENG.). 368p. (J). (gr. 3-7). 16.99 *(978-0-06-196108-3(6))* HarperCollins Pubs.
—Palace of Dreams. Phillips, Dave, illus. (Familiars Ser.: 4). (ENG.). 336p. (J). (gr. 3-7). 2015. pap. 6.99 *(978-0-06-212031-1(X))*No. 4. 2013. 16.99 *(978-0-06-212029-8(8))* HarperCollins Pubs.
—Secrets of the Crown. (Familiars Ser.: 2). (ENG.). (J). (gr. 3-7). 2012. 400p. pap. 6.99 *(978-0-06-196113-7(2))* 2011. 384p. 16.99 *(978-0-06-196111-3(6))* HarperCollins Pubs.
Epstein, Alex. The Circle Cast, 1 vol. 2011. (ENG., Illus.). 304p. (YA). (gr. 2-4). pap. 12.95 *(978-1-896580-63-0(7))* Tradewind Bks. CAN. Dist: Orca Bk. Pubs. USA.
Erich, James. Dreams of Fire & Gods: Dreams. 2016. (ENG., Illus.). (J). 27.99 ***(978-1-63533-005-2(X),*** Harmony Ink Pr.) Dreamspinner Pr.
—Dreams of Fire & Gods: Fire. 2016. (ENG., Illus.). (J). 24.99 ***(978-1-63533-006-9(8),*** Harmony Ink Pr.) Dreamspinner Pr.
—Dreams of Fire & Gods: Gods. 2016. (ENG., Illus.). (J). 24.99 ***(978-1-63533-007-6(6),*** Harmony Ink Pr.) Dreamspinner Pr.
Erickson, Melissa. When the Tooth Fairy Comes... Erickson, Melissa, illus. 2007. (Illus.). 15p. (J). (gr. -1-3). 10.99 *(978-1-59879-369-7(1))* Lifevest Publishing, Inc.
Errico, Jessica / C. Grandpa's Magical Accordion. Star, Brenda, illus. 2007. 28p. (J). pap. 17.95 incl. cd-rom *(978-0-9800577-0-6(1))* Three Part Harmony LLC.
Eschler, Linda. The Strawberry Fairies & the Secret of Mystery Island. 2008. 57p. pap. 16.95 *(978-1-60610-960-1(X))* America Star Bks.
Escondete y Grita, Vol. II. (Fantasmas de Fear Street Coleccion: No. 1). (SPA.). (J). (gr. 4-7). pap. 7.95 *(978-950-04-1999-4(8),* EM4474) Emecé Editores S.A. ARG. Dist: Planeta Publishing Corp., Lectorum Pubns., Inc.
Eshed, Tina. The Adventures of Bunzy: The Beginning. 2009. 60p. pap. 24.49 *(978-1-4389-2673-5(1))* AuthorHouse.
Estep, Jennifer. Bright Blaze of Magic. 2016. (Black Blade Ser.). (ENG.). 368p. (YA). (gr. 9). pap. 9.95 *(978-1-61773-828-9(X))* Kensington Publishing Corp.
—Touch of Frost. 2011. (ENG.). 336p. (YA). (gr. 9). 9.95 *(978-0-7582-6692-7(8),* K-Teen) Kensington Publishing Corp.
Eubank, Patricia Reeder. The Princess & the Snarls. Eubank, Patricia Reeder, illus. 2006. (ENG., Illus.). 32p. (J). (gr. k-3). 16.95 *(978-0-8249-5536-6(6),* Ideal Pubns.) Worthy Publishing.
Evans, Florence Adèle. Alice's Adventures in Pictureland: A Tale Inspired by Lewis Carroll's Wonderland. 2011. (Illus.). 152p. pap. *(978-1-904808-63-3(8))* Evertype.
Evans, Pamela. Tina Queen of the Dragons. 2006. 101p. pap. 16.95 *(978-1-4241-3356-7(4))* PublishAmerica, Inc.
Evans, Richard Paul. The Christmas Candle. Collins, Jacob, illus. (ENG.). 32p. (J). (gr. -1-3). 2007. 9.99 *(978-1-4169-5047-9(8))* 2006. 8.99 *(978-1-4169-2682-5(8))* Simon & Schuster Bks. For Young Readers. (Simon & Schuster Bks. For Young Readers).
Evans, Rosemary R. The Little Princesses Magical Party. Taylor, Erin, illus. 2012. 40p. (J). 16.95 *(978-1-60743-759-8(7))* Wink Publishing.
Eve, Laure. The Graces. 2016. (ENG.). 352p. (YA). (gr. 8-17). 18.95 *(978-1-4197-2123-6(2),* Amulet Bks.) Abrams, Inc.
Everburg, R. S. Audrika's Magic. 2011. 264p. 29.99 *(978-1-4628-5596-4(2));* pap. 19.99 *(978-1-4628-5595-7(4))* Xlibris Corp.
Everest, D. D. Archie Greene & the Magician's Secret. (Archie Greene Ser.: 1). (J). (gr. 3-7). 2016. 336p. pap. 6.99 *(978-0-06-231212-9(X))* 2015. (ENG.). 320p. 16.99 *(978-0-06-231211-2(1))* HarperCollins Pubs.
Eves, Rosalyn. Blood Rose Rebellion. 2017. (Blood Rose Rebellion Ser.). (ENG.). 416p. (YA). (gr. 7). 17.99 *(978-1-101-93599-6(5),* Knopf Bks. for Young Readers) Random Hse. Children's Bks.
Ewing, Amy. The Jewel. (Lone City Trilogy Ser.: 1). (ENG.). (YA). (gr. 9). 2015. 400p. pap. 9.99 *(978-0-06-223578-7(8))* 2014. 368p. 17.99 *(978-0-06-223579-4(6))* HarperCollins Pubs. (HarperTeen).
Faircloth, Sean. The Enchanted Globe. 2016. (ENG., Illus.). 224p. (J). (gr. 4-7). pap. 12.95 *(978-1-63431-101-4(9))* Pitchstone LLC.
Fairy Gardens Magic Painting Book. 2017. (Magic Painting Bks.). (ENG.). (J). pap. 9.99 ***(978-0-7945-3798-2(7),*** Usborne) EDC Publishing.
Fairy Palaces Magic Painting Book. 2017. (Magic Painting Bks.). (ENG.). (J). pap. 9.99 ***(978-0-7945-3876-7(2),*** Usborne) EDC Publishing.
Fairy Tale Fixers: Fixing Fairy Tale Problems with STEM. 2017. (Fairy Tale Fixers: Fixing Fairy Tale Problems with STEM Ser.). 32p. (gr. 3-4). pap. 42.00 ***(978-1-5382-0614-0(5));*** lib. bdg. 106.40 ***(978-1-5382-0616-4(1))*** Stevens, Gareth Publishing LLLP.
Fajardo, Alexis E. Kid Beowulf: The Song of Roland. 2017. lib. bdg. 24.50 ***(978-0-606-40301-6(9))*** Turtleback Bks.
Falcon Press International. Desta & King Solomon's Coin of Magic & Fortune: And king solomon's coinof of magic & Fortune, nos. 7, no. 2. 2nd ed. 2010. (ENG., Illus.). 430p. (YA). pap. 15.95 *(978-1-884459-01-6(3))* Falcon Pr. International.
Falkner, Brian. Maddy West & the Tongue Taker, 1 vol. Bixley, Donovan, illus. 2014. (ENG.). 256p. (gr. 4-8). 12.95 *(978-1-62370-084-3(1))* Capstone Young Readers of Coughlan Cos.
Falter, Laury. Residue. 2013. 306p. pap. 12.99 *(978-0-9855110-0-5(1))* Falter, Laury.
Farley, Christina. The Princess & the Page. 2017. (ENG.). 240p. (J). (gr. 3-7). 17.99 *(978-0-545-92409-2(X),* Scholastic Pr.) Scholastic, Inc.
Farooqi, Imran A. The Spell of the Witch-Queen. 2006. (Illus.). 60p. pap. *(978-1-84401-816-1(4))* Athena Pr.
Farr, Dan. Mr. Finnegan's Giving Chest. 2005. (Illus.). 32p. (J). (gr. -1-3). 19.95 incl. audio compact disk *(978-1-59038-555-5(1),* Shadow Mountain) Shadow Mountain Publishing.
Farrey, Brian. The Vengekeep Prophecies. Helquist, Brett, illus. (Vengekeep Prophecies Ser.: 1). (ENG.). (J). (gr. 3-7). 2013. 416p. pap. 7.99 *(978-0-06-204929-2(1))* 2012. 400p. 16.99 *(978-0-06-204928-5(3))* HarperCollins Pubs.
Farrow, G. & Farrow, George. The Mysterious Shin Shira. 2007. 116p. per. 10.95 *(978-0-60312-225-2(7))* Aegypan.
Faust, Lauren. The Magic Begins, Vol. 1. 2013. (My Little Pony Ser.). (ENG., Illus.). 112p. (J). (gr. 2-5). pap. 7.99 *(978-1-61377-754-1(X),* 9781613777541) Idea & Design Works, LLC.
Fayers, Claire. The Voyage to Magical North. 2016. (Accidental Pirates Ser.). (ENG.). 320p. (J). 16.99 *(978-1-62779-420-6(4),* 9781627794206, Holt, Henry & Co. Bks. For Young Readers) Holt, Henry & Co.
Feldman, Lowell S. Little Falabella the Magical Horse. 2006. 92p. (gr. 1-1). pap. 31.99 *(978-1-4257-1869-5(8))* Xlibris Corp.
Fénelon, Marie Jirlande. The Two Best Friends & the Old Lady. 2004. (Illus.). 28p. (J). bds. 19.00 *(978-1-58432-128-6(8))* Educa Vision Inc.
Ferguson, Sarah & Duchess of York Staff. Little Red's Autumn Adventure. Williams, Sam, illus. 2009. (ENG.). 40p. (J). (gr. -1-1). 16.99 *(978-0-689-84341-9(0),* Simon & Schuster/Paula Wiseman Bks.) Simon & Schuster/Paula Wiseman Bks.
Fernandez, David R. Lady Godiva & the Legend of the Black Rose. 2008. (Illus.). 32p. (J). pap. 8.99 *(978-0-9817521-4-3(4))* Mirror Publishing.
Fernandez, Eugenia. Astria & the Missing Prince. 2009. (Illus.). 39p. (J). 31.99 *(978-1-4363-7543-6(6))* Xlibris Corp.
Fernandez, Giselle. Gigi & the Birthday Ring. Petersen, Sheli, illus. 2005. (J). *(978-1-56492-358-5(4))* Laredo Publishing Co., Inc.
Fforde, Jasper. The Eye of Zoltar. 2014. (Chronicles of Kazam Ser.). (ENG.). 416p. (J). (gr. 5-7). 16.99 *(978-0-547-73849-9(8),* HMH Books For Young Readers) Houghton Mifflin Harcourt Publishing Co.
—The Last Dragonslayer. 2011. 352p. pap. *(978-1-4447-0720-5(5),* Hodder Faith) Hodder & Stoughton.
—The Last Dragonslayer. (Chronicles of Kazam Ser.). (ENG.). (gr. 5-9). 2013. 306p. (YA). pap. 7.99 *(978-0-544-10471-6(4))*Bk. 1. 2012. 296p. (J). 16.99 *(978-0-547-73847-5(1))* Houghton Mifflin Harcourt Publishing Co.
—The Song of the Quarkbeast. 2013. (Chronicles of Kazam Ser.: 2). (ENG.). 304p. (J). (gr. 5-7). 16.99 *(978-0-547-73848-2(X))* Houghton Mifflin Harcourt Publishing Co.
—The Song of the Quarkbeast: The Chronicles of Kazam, Book 2. 2014. (Chronicles of Kazam Ser.). (ENG.). 304p. (J). (gr. 5-7). pap. 7.99 *(978-0-544-33662-9(3),* HMH Books For Young Readers) Houghton Mifflin Harcourt Publishing Co.
Field, Brett. Screno Magic Medieval Collision. 2007. 52p. per. 10.00 *(978-1-4257-4700-8(0))* Xlibris Corp.
Fields, Jan. Facing a Frenemy, 1 vol. 2014. (Meri's Mirror Ser.). (ENG., Illus.). 80p. (J). (gr. 2-5). lib. bdg. 27.07 *(978-1-62402-008-7(9),* Calico Chapter Bks) Magic Wagon.
—Meri Mercer Doesn't Lie, Mostly, 1 vol. 2014. (Meri's Mirror Ser.). (ENG., Illus.). 80p. (J). (gr. 2-5). lib. bdg. 27.07 *(978-1-62402-009-4(7),* Calico Chapter Bks) Magic Wagon.
—Terrible Twin Mania, 1 vol. 2014. (Meri's Mirror Ser.). (ENG.). 80p. (J). (gr. 2-5). lib. bdg. 27.07 *(978-1-62402-011-7(9),* Calico Chapter Bks) Magic Wagon.
Fienberg, Anna & Fienberg, Barbara. Tashi & the Dancing Shoes. Gamble, Kim, illus. 8th ed. 2007. (Tashi Ser.). (ENG.). 64p. (Orig.). (J). (gr. k-2). pap. 8.99 *(978-1-74114-972-2(X))* Allen & Unwin AUS. Dist: Independent Pubs. Group.
—Tashi & the Royal Tomb. Gamble, Kim, illus. 10th ed. 2007. (Tashi Ser.: 10). (ENG.). 64p. (Orig.). (J). (gr. k-2). pap. 8.99 *(978-1-74114-973-9(8))* Allen & Unwin AUS. Dist: Independent Pubs. Group.
Fifford, Tanya. Robin & the Pocket Dragon. 2009. (Illus.). 24p. pap. 11.49 *(978-1-4389-9610-3(1))* AuthorHouse.
Figueroa, M. A. & Figueroa, P. A. Melissa & the Magic Pen. Barnoski, Karel, illus. 2004. 36p. pap. 24.95 *(978-1-4137-3441-6(3))* PublishAmerica, Inc.
Filaretos, William. The Potion of Time: A Story of Demetrios. 2006. per. 12.95 *(978-0-9724520-0-7(1))* Filaretos, William.
Findlay, Andrew. Roddy & the Magic Mattress. 2005. 54p. pap. 5.61 *(978-1-4116-3612-5(0))* Lulu Pr., Inc.
Fine, Sarah. The Cursed Queen. 2017. (Impostor Queen Ser.: 2). (ENG., Illus.). 432p. (YA). (gr. 7). 17.99 *(978-1-4814-4193-3(0),* McElderry, Margaret K. Bks.) McElderry, Margaret K. Bks.
—The Impostor Queen. (ENG., Illus.). (YA). (gr. 7). 2017. (Impostor Queen Ser.: 1). 448p. pap. 11.99 *(978-1-4814-4191-9(4))* 2016. 432p. 18.99 *(978-1-4814-4190-2(6))* McElderry, Margaret K. Bks. (McElderry, Margaret K. Bks.).
Finke, Margot. Ruthie & the Hippo's Fat Behind. Snider, K. C., illus. 2010. 16p. pap. 10.95 *(978-1-61633-059-0(7))* Guardian Angel Publishing, Inc.
Finley, Leah. The One & Only Mr C. 2009. 82p. pap. 8.95 *(978-1-935118-75-6(7))* Bellissima Publishing, LLC.
Finn McCool The Magic Leprechaun Cat. Irish Holiday Fairy Tales: Volume 1. 2012. 44p. pap. 19.95 *(978-1-4772-1331-5(7))* AuthorHouse.
Finn, Perdita. The Mane Event. 2014. (Equestria Girls Ser.: 3). (ENG.). 240p. (J). (gr. 3-7). 9.99 *(978-0-316-24777-1(4))* Little, Brown Bks. for Young Readers.
—Rainbow Rocks. 2014. (Equestria Girls Ser.: 2). (ENG.). 192p. (J). (gr. 3-7). 9.99 *(978-0-316-28486-8(6))* Little, Brown Bks. for Young Readers.
Finnegan, Delphine. Magic Carpet Race! (Shimmer & Shine) Fruchter, Jason, illus. 2017. (Step into Reading Ser.). (ENG.). 24p. (J). (gr. -1-1). pap. 4.99 ***(978-1-5247-1690-5(1));*** lib. bdg. 12.99 ***(978-1-5247-1691-2(X))*** Random Hse. Children's Bks. (Random Hse. Bks. for Young Readers).
Firtha, Gizella. Spookybrooke. 2011. 58p. pap. 16.95 *(978-1-4512-5822-6(4))* America Star Bks.
Fisch, Sholly. Wanted - The Super Friends. McKenny, Stewart & Moy, Philip, illus. 2012. (DC Super Friends Ser.). (ENG.). 32p. (gr. 1-2). lib. bdg. 22.60 *(978-1-4342-4543-4(8))* Stone Arch Bks.
Fisch, Sholly & Age, Heroic. Who Is the Mystery Bat-Squad?, 1 vol. Clugston, Chynna, illus. 2014. (DC Super Friends Ser.). (ENG.). 32p. (gr. 1-2). 22.60 *(978-1-4342-9224-7(X))* Stone Arch Bks.
Fischel, Ana. The Twelve Quests - Book 2, a Dragon's Tooth. 2009. 158p. pap. *(978-1-84923-874-8(X))* YouWriteOn.
—The Twelve Quests - Book 3, the Pied Piper's Flute. 2009. 158p. pap. *(978-1-84923-875-5(8))* YouWriteOn.
—The Twelve Quests - Book 5, a Firebird's Feather. 2009. 158p. pap. *(978-1-84923-877-9(4))* YouWriteOn.
—The Twelve Quests - Book 6, the Enchanted Harp. 2009. 158p. pap. *(978-1-84923-878-6(2))* YouWriteOn.
Fischer, David. Heir to Oswyn. 2011. 66p. pap. 19.95 *(978-1-4626-2581-9(9))* America Star Bks.
Fisher, Annabelle. Pixie Piper & the Matter of the Batter. 2017. (Pixie Piper Ser.: 2). 336p. (J). (gr. 3-7). 16.99 *(978-0-06-239380-7(4),* Greenwillow Bks.) HarperCollins Pubs.
Fisher, Catherine. Corbenic. 2006. 281p. (YA). (gr. 7). lib. bdg. 17.89 *(978-0-06-072471-9(4))* HarperCollins Pubs.
—Darkhenge. 2006. 340p. (YA). (gr. 7-12). 15.99 *(978-0-06-078582-6(9))* HarperCollins Pubs.
Fisher, Edward J. The Little Girl with the Magic Shoes: And Other Delights. 2008. 40p. 31.99 *(978-1-4363-4210-0(4))* Xlibris Corp.
Fisher, Maire & Beautement, Tiah, eds. Follow the Road. 2015. (ENG., Illus.). 154p. (J). pap. *(978-1-920590-98-7(6))* Modajaji Bks.
Fisher, Sam. The Midnight Door. 2015. (Scare Scape Ser.: 2). (ENG.). 352p. (J). (gr. 3-7). 12.99 *(978-0-545-52163-5(7),* Scholastic Pr.) Scholastic, Inc.
Fisscher, Tiny. RUBY & MAGIC TWIG. 2008. (ENG.). 48p. (J). (gr. 1-7). 11.95 *(978-1-60136-013-7(4))* Audio Holdings, LLC.
Fitzgerald, D. M. The True Story of the Big Red Onion. Cudd, Savannah, illus. 2013. 36p. 18.99 *(978-0-9890288-7-5(9));* pap. 10.99 *(978-0-9890288-5-1(2))* Mindstir Media.
Flaker, Tracey. Around the Corner: Gwenever's Quest. 2006. 55p. pap. 16.95 *(978-1-4241-1886-1(7))* PublishAmerica, Inc.
Flanagan, John. The Outcasts. 2011. (Brotherband Chronicles: Bk. 1). (ENG.). (J). (gr. 3-7). 54.99 *(978-1-61657-043-9(1))* Findaway World, LLC.
—The Outcasts. (Brotherband Chronicles Ser.: 1). (ENG.). (J). (gr. 5). 2012. 464p. pap. 8.99 *(978-0-14-242194-9(4),* Puffin Books) 2011. 448p. 18.99 *(978-0-399-25619-6(9),* Philomel Bks.) Penguin Young Readers Group.
—The Outcasts. 2012. (Brotherband Chronicles Ser.: 1). lib. bdg. 19.65 *(978-0-606-26636-9(4),* Turtleback) Turtleback Bks.
—The Royal Ranger. 2014. (Ranger's Apprentice Ser.: 12). (ENG.). 480p. (J). (gr. 5). pap. 8.99 *(978-0-14-242731-6(4),* Puffin Books) Penguin Young Readers Group.
—The Sorcerer of the North. 2009. (Ranger's Apprentice Ser.: 5). lib. bdg. 19.65 *(978-0-606-02237-8(6),* Turtleback) Turtleback Bks.
Flanagan, John A. The Tournament at Gorlan. 2016. (Ranger's Apprentice the Early Years Ser.: 1). lib. bdg. 19.65 *(978-0-606-39332-4(3))* Turtleback Bks.

Flavin, Teresa. The Blackhope Enigma. 2011. (ENG., Illus.). 304p. (J). (gr. 4-7). 15.99 (978-0-7636-5694-2(1), Templar) Candlewick Pr.
—The Crimson Shard. (ENG.). (J). (gr. 4-7). 2015. 288p. pap. 6.99 (978-0-7636-7172-3(X)) 2012. (Illus.). 256p. 15.99 (978-0-7636-6093-2(0)) Candlewick Pr. (Templar).
Fleming, Ian. Chitty Chitty Bang Bang. Berger, Joe, illus. 2013. (Chitty Chitty Bang Bang Ser.). (ENG.). 160p. (J). (gr. 4-7). pap. 6.99 (978-0-7636-6666-8(1)) Candlewick Pr.
Fliess, Sue. A Fairy Friend. Keane, Claire, illus. 2016. (ENG.). 32p. (J). 16.99 (978-1-62779-081-9(0), 9781627790819, Holt, Henry & Co. Bks. For Young Readers) Holt, Henry & Co.
Flinn, Alex. Beheld. 2017. 368p. (YA). (gr. 8). 17.99 (978-0-06-213455-4(8), HarperTeen) HarperCollins Pubs.
—Cloaked. (YA). 2012. (ENG.). 368p. (gr. 8). pap. 9.99 (978-0-06-087424-7(4)) 2011. 341p. lib. bdg. 17.89 (978-0-06-087423-0(6)) 2011. (ENG.). 352p. (gr. 8-18). 16.99 (978-0-06-087422-3(8)) HarperCollins Pubs. (HarperTeen).
—Towering. 2013. (YA). (Kendra Chronicles Ser.: 3). (ENG.). 304p. (gr. 9). 17.99 (978-0-06-202417-6(5), HarperTeen); (Kendra Chronicles Ser.: 3). 304p. (gr. 9). lib. bdg. 18.89 (978-0-06-202418-3(3), HarperTeen); 296p. (978-0-06-227632-2(8)) HarperCollins Pubs.
Flitcroft, Jean. The Loch Ness Monster. 2010. (Cryptid Files Ser.: No. 1). xii, 176p. (J). pap. (978-1-84840-940-8(0)) Little Island.
Fodi, Lee Edward. Kendra Kandlestar & the Crack in Kazah. 2011. (Illus.). 294p. (J). pap. 8.95 (978-1-61254-019-1(8)) Brown Books Publishing Group.
—Kendra Kandlestar & the Crack in Kazah. Fodi, Lee Edward, illus. 2011. (ENG., Illus.). 282p. (J). (gr. 4-7). 16.95 (978-1-61254-018-4(X)) Brown Books Publishing Group.
Foley, Greg. Willoughby & the Lion. Foley, Greg, illus. 2009. (ENG., Illus.). 40p. (J). (gr. -1-2). 17.99 (978-0-06-154750-8(6)) HarperCollins Pubs.
Folz, Alexandra. Indigo's Bracelet. 2010. 84p. pap. 9.95 (978-1-4525-0058-4(4)) Get Published.
Food Fight Frenzy. 2008. (ENG., Illus.). 32p. pap. 15.95 (978-1-933300-65-8(5)) Wandering Sage Pubns., LLC.
Forbes, Anne. The Underground City. 2008. (Contemporary Kelpies Ser.). (ENG.). 272p. (J). pap. (978-0-86315-637-3(1)) Floris Bks.
Ford, Adam B. The Six Sisters & Their Flying Carpets. Abbott, Kristin, illus. 2012. 34p. (-18). 20.95 (978-0-9794104-6-8(0)) H Bar Pr.
Ford, Laura. Buster Brown & Tige in Misfit Heroes. 2004. (Illus.). 320p. 19.95 (978-1-881554-28-8(7)) Skyward Publishing Co.
Ford, RoShawn T. Marty & the Magical Christmas Tree. 2012. 24p. pap. 17.99 (978-1-4772-3719-9(4)) AuthorHouse.
Fordham, Walter. Ilian. Krizmanic, Tatjana, illus. 2012. 42p. pap. (978-0-9813889-5-3(7)) Publish Yourself.
Forman, M. L. Adventurers Wanted, Book 1: Slathbog's Gold. 2011. 400p. mass mkt. 7.99 (978-1-60641-681-5(2)) Deseret Bk. Co.
—Adventurers Wanted, Book 2: The Horn of Moran. 2012. (J). pap. 7.99 (978-1-60908-911-5(1)) 2011. 400p. 39.99 (978-1-60641-255-8(8)) Deseret Bk. Co.
—Adventurers Wanted, Book 3: Albrek's Tomb. 2013. (Adventurers Wanted Ser.: 3). (ENG.). 504p. (J). (gr. 5). pap. 9.99 (978-1-60907-339-8(8), Shadow Mountain) Shadow Mountain Publishing.
—Adventurers Wanted, Book 4: Sands of Nezza. 2013. (Adventurers Wanted Ser.: 4). (ENG.). 400p. (J). (gr. 5). 19.99 (978-1-60907-329-9(0), Shadow Mountain) Shadow Mountain Publishing.
—Adventures Wanted, Book 3: Albrek's Tomb. 2012. (YA). 19.99 (978-1-60908-892-7(1)) Deseret Bk. Co.
Forman, Mark. The Horn of Moran. 2011. 400p. (YA). (gr. 3-18). 18.99 (978-1-60641-226-8(4), Shadow Mountain) Shadow Mountain Publishing.
Foster, D. S. The Stone Heart. Lewis, Jesse, illus. 2012. (J). pap. 12.99 (978-1-937331-14-6(8)) ShadeTree Publishing, LLC.
Foster, Emily. The Drowning Eyes. 2016. (ENG.). 144p. pap. 12.99 (978-0-7653-8768-4(9), 9780765387684, Tor Bks.) Doherty, Tom Assocs., LLC.
Fox, Alex. Windsock Wesley & His Wild & Wonderful Weather MacHine, Living in Cloud. Bazzoni, Lainie M. A., illus. 2010. 48p. pap. 16.50 (978-1-60911-873-0(1), Eloquent Bks.) Strategic Book Publishing & Rights Agency (SBPRA).
Fox, Janet. The Charmed Children of Rookskill Castle. 2016. (ENG., Illus.). 400p. (J). (gr. 5). 16.99 (978-0-451-47633-3(6), Viking Books for Young Readers) Penguin Young Readers Group.
—The Charmed Children of Rookskill Castle. 2017. lib. bdg. 19.65 **(978-0-606-39785-8(X))** Turtleback Bks.
Fox, Lucy. Keeper of the Enchanted Pool. 2009. 184p. pap. (978-1-84923-437-5(X)) YouWriteOn.
Fox, R. J. Stuart & His Incredibly Obnoxious Magical Book: Soccer, 1 vol. 2009. 86p. pap. 19.95 (978-1-4489-9833-3(6)) America Star Bks.
Foxlee, Karen. A Most Magical Girl. (ENG.). 304p. (J). (gr. 3-7). 2017. 7.99 **(978-0-553-51288-5(9)**, Yearling) 2016. 16.99 (978-0-553-51285-4(4), Knopf Bks. for Young Readers) 2016. lib. bdg. 19.99 (978-0-553-51286-1(2), Knopf Bks. for Young Readers) Random Hse. Children's Bks.
Foxlee, Karen. Ophelia & the Marvelous Boy. 2014. (ENG.). 240p. (J). (gr. 3-7). 16.99 (978-0-385-75354-8(3), Knopf Bks. for Young Readers) Random Hse. Children's Bks.
Frabetti, Carlo. La Magia Mas Poderosa. 11th ed. 2003. (SPA., Illus.). 120p. (J). 15.95 (978-84-204-4844-2(3)) Ediciones Alfaguara ESP. Dist: Santillana USA Publishing Co., Inc.
Francesca, Sieglinde De. A Donsy of Gnomes. 2009. pap. (978-1-61623-243-6(9)) Independent Pub.
Francis-Harris, Annabel. The Other Side of the Forest. 2006. pap. 19.95 (978-1-59526-458-9(2)) Aeon Publishing Inc.
Francis, Suzanne. Let It Glow (Disney Frozen: Northern Lights) The Disney Storybook Art Team, illus. 2017. (Big Golden Book Ser.). (ENG.). 48p. (J). (gr. -1-2). 9.99 **(978-0-7364-3678-6(2)**, Golden/Disney) Random Hse. Children's Bks.
Frank, Hannah. If I Had Three Wishes. 2008. 56p. pap. 23.99 (978-1-4343-7529-2(3)) AuthorHouse.
Franklin, Cathy. Pinta & Polly Go to the Moon, 1 vol. Poole, Tracy, illus. 2009. 27p. pap. 24.95 (978-1-60813-861-6(5)) America Star Bks.
Franks, Pam. The Magic Gingerbread House. 2015. (ENG.). 32p. (J). 19.95 (978-1-931721-10-3(6), 9781931721103) Bright Sky Pr.
Freeman, Faith L. Beyond the Magic Waterfall. 2006. 79p. pap. 26.38 (978-1-4116-8202-3(5)) Lulu Pr., Inc.
Freeman, Richard. The Legend of Booga Bearia. 2004. 117p. pap. 19.95 (978-1-4137-2016-7(1)) America Star Bks.
French, Vivian. The Bag of Bones: The Second Tale from the Five Kingdoms. Collins, Ross, illus. 2009. (Tales from the Five Kingdoms Ser.: 2). (ENG.). 256p. (J). (gr. 3-7). 14.99 (978-0-7636-4255-6(X)) Candlewick Pr.
—Princess Charlotte & the Enchanted Rose. Gibb, Sarah, illus. 2007. (Tiara Club Ser.: No. 7). 80p. (J). (gr. 1-4). pap. 3.99 (978-0-06-112441-9(9), Tegen, Katherine Bks) HarperCollins Pubs.
—Princess Katie & the Silver Pony. Gibb, Sarah, illus. 2007. (Tiara Club Ser.: No.2). 80p. (J). (gr. 1-4). 15.99 (978-0-06-112432-7(X), Tegen, Katherine Bks) HarperCollins Pubs.
—The Robe of Skulls: The First Tale from the Five Kingdoms. Collins, Ross, illus. 2009. (Tales from the Five Kingdoms Ser.: 1). (ENG.). 208p. (J). (gr. 3-7). pap. 5.99 (978-0-7636-4364-5(5)) Candlewick Pr.
Fridolfs, Derek. Darkseid & the Fires of Apokolips. Levins, Tim, illus. 2017. (Justice League Ser.). (ENG.). 88p. (gr. 2-3). lib. bdg. 26.65 **(978-1-4965-5157-3(5)**, DC Super Heroes) Stone Arch Bks.
Friedman, C. S. Dreamwalker. 2014. (Dreamwalker Ser.: 1). (ENG.). 320p. (gr. 12). 19.95 (978-0-7564-0888-6(1), DAW) DAW.
Friesner, Esther. Spirit's Chosen. 2013. (Princesses of Myth Ser.). (ENG., Illus.). 496p. (YA). (gr. 7). 17.99 (978-0-375-86908-2(5), Random Hse. Bks. for Young Readers) Random Hse. Children's Bks.
Friesner, Esther M. Spirit's Bride. 2014. (Princesses of Myth Ser.). (ENG., Illus.). 512p. (YA). (gr. 7). pap. 10.99 (978-0-375-87316-4(3), Ember) Random Hse. Children's Bks.
—Spirit's Princess. (Princesses of Myth Ser.). (ENG.). (YA). (gr. 7). 2013. 480p. pap. 10.99 (978-0-375-87314-0(7), Bluefire) 2012. 464p. 17.99 (978-0-375-86907-5(7), Random Hse. Bks. for Young Readers) Random Hse. Children's Bks.
—Spirit's Princess. 2012. 449p. (YA). (978-0-375-87315-7(5)) Random Hse., Inc.
Frost, C. Amethyst. Mourning under the Bridge. 2012. 280p. pap. 9.99 (978-0-9847236-2-1(5)) Frost, C. A.
Funaro, Gregory. Alistair Grim's Odd Aquaticum. 2016. (Alistair Grim Ser.). (ENG.). 448p. (J). (gr. 3-7). pap. 7.99 (978-1-4847-0900-9(4)) Hyperion Bks. for Children.
—Alistair Grim's Odd Aquaticum. 2016. (Alistair Grim Ser.). (ENG., Illus.). 448p. (J). (gr. 3-7). 16.99 (978-1-4847-0007-5(4)) Hyperion Pr.
—Alistair Grim's Odditorium. 2015. (Alistair Grim Ser.). (ENG.). (J). (gr. 3-7). 448p. pap. 7.99 (978-1-4847-0899-6(7)); (Illus.). 432p. 16.99 (978-1-4847-0006-8(6)) Hyperion Bks. for Children.
—Alistair Grim's Odditorium. 2015. (J). lib. bdg. 18.40 (978-0-606-37399-9(3)) Turtleback Bks.
Funke, Cornelia. Emma & the Blue Genie. Latsch, Oliver, tr. from GER. Meyer, Kerstin, illus. 2014. (ENG.). 96p. (J). (gr. 2-5). 9.99 (978-0-385-37540-5(9), Random Hse. Bks. for Young Readers) Random Hse. Children's Bks.
—Igraine the Brave. Bell, Anthea, tr. Funke, Cornelia, illus. l.t. ed. 2008. (Thorndike Literacy Bridge Middle Reader Ser.). (Illus.). 259p. (J). (gr. 4-7). 23.95 (978-1-4104-0341-4(6)) Thorndike Pr.
—Inkdeath. 2010. (Inkheart Trilogy Ser.).Tr. of Tintentod. (ENG.). 704p. (J). (gr. 3-7). 12.99 (978-0-439-86629-3(4), Scholastic Paperbacks) Scholastic, Inc.
—Inkheart. Bell, Anthea, tr. 2005. (Inkheart Trilogy Ser.: Bk. 1).Tr. of Tintenherz. (ENG., Illus.). 576p. (J). (gr. 3-7). pap. 10.99 (978-0-439-70910-1(5)) Scholastic, Inc.
—Inkheart Trilogy Boxed Set: Inkheart, Inkspell, Inkdeath. 2003. (Inkheart Trilogy: Bks. 1-3). 544p. (J). 60.00 (978-0-439-61671-3(9), Chicken Hse., The) Scholastic, Inc.
—Inkspell. Bell, Anthea, tr. from GER. 2007. (Illus.). 653p. (gr. 3-7). 21.00 (978-0-7569-7917-1(X)) Perfection Learning Corp.
—Inkspell. Bell, Anthea, tr. 2007. (Inkheart Trilogy Ser.: Bk. 2). (ENG., Illus.). 672p. (J). (gr. 3-7). pap. 10.99 (978-0-439-55401-5(2), Chicken Hse., The) Scholastic, Inc.
—Inkspell. 2007. (Inkheart Trilogy Ser.: 2). lib. bdg. 22.10 (978-1-4177-7471-5(1), Turtleback) Turtleback Bks.
Funny, Ania. The Power of Ania to Change the World of Bullying. 2012. 28p. pap. 15.99 (978-1-4797-4599-9(5)) Xlibris Corp.
Furman, Ben. Sam's Quest. 2008. 240p. pap. 8.95 (978-0-9778731-4-2(5)) Black Hawk Pr., Inc., The.
Furuya, Michael, illus. Keoni's Special Gift. 2009. (J). (978-1-56647-915-8(0)) Mutual Publishing LLC.
Gabriel, Thora. Chessie Bligh & the Scroll of Andelthor. 2006. 284p. (J). 27.95 (978-0-595-83579-9(1)) iUniverse, Inc.
Gaiman, NEil. The Graveyard Book: a Harper Classic. McKean, Dave, illus. 2017. (Harper Classic Ser.). 368p. (J). (gr. 3-7). 16.99 **(978-0-06-266703-8(3))** HarperCollins Pubs.
Gaiman, NEil, et al. Eternity's Wheel. (InterWorld Trilogy Ser.: 3). 288p. (YA). (gr. 8). 2016. pap. 9.99 (978-0-06-206800-2(8)) 2015. (ENG.). 17.99 (978-0-06-206799-9(0)) HarperCollins Pubs. (HarperTeen).
Gale, Audra. The Adventures of Buddy & Me. 2007. 32p. (YA). pap. 8.00 (978-0-8059-7277-1(3)) Dorrance Publishing Co., Inc.
Gale, Eric Kahn. The Wizard's Dog. 2017. (ENG., Illus.). 288p. (J). (gr. 3-7). 16.99 (978-0-553-53736-9(9), Crown Books For Young Readers) Random Hse. Children's Bks.
Gallagher, Toni. Twist My Charm: Love Potion #11. 2016. (Twist My Charm Ser.). (ENG.). 272p. (J). (gr. 3-7). 16.99 (978-0-553-51119-2(X), Random Hse. Bks. for Young Readers) Random Hse. Children's Bks.
Gallego Garcia, Laura & Peden, Margaret Sayers. The Valley of the Wolves. 2006. 247p. (J). pap. (978-0-439-58554-5(6), Levine, Arthur A. Bks.) Scholastic, Inc.
Galliez, Roxane Marie. Give Me Moon. Delanssay, Cathy, illus. 2009. 44p. (J). (gr. -1-3). 14.99 (978-0-8416-7138-6(9)) Hammond World Atlas Corp.
Gallo, Tina. Behold the Power of Gargamel! Riley, Kellee, illus. 2011. (Smurfs Movie Ser.). (ENG.). 24p. (J). (gr. -1-3). pap. 6.99 (978-1-4424-2395-4(1), Simon Spotlight) Simon Spotlight.
Garcia, Gloria. Magia. (SPA.). 8p. 9.95 (978-84-272-7275-0(8)) Molino, Editorial ESP. Dist: Distribooks, Inc.
Gardner, Lyn. Out of the Woods. 2011. (ENG., Illus.). 368p. (J). (gr. 3-7). 7.99 (978-0-385-75226-8(1), Yearling) Random Hse. Children's Bks.
Gardner, Sally. I, Coriander. 2007. (ENG., Illus.). 288p. (J). (gr. 5-18). 7.99 (978-0-14-240763-9(1), Puffin Books) Penguin Young Readers Group.
—Operation Bunny. Roberts, David, illus. 2014. (Wings & Co Ser.: 1). (ENG.). 192p. (J). (gr. 2-5). 12.99 (978-0-8050-9892-1(5), 9780805098921, Holt, Henry & Co. Bks. For Young Readers) Holt, Henry & Co.
—Operation Bunny. Roberts, David, illus. 2014. (Wings & Co Ser.: 1). (ENG.). 208p. (J). (gr. 2-5). pap. 6.99 (978-1-250-05053-3(7), 9781250050533) Square Fish.
—The Red Necklace. 2009. (ENG.). 400p. (YA). (gr. 7-18). 8.99 (978-0-14-241488-0(3), Speak) Penguin Young Readers Group.
—The Red Necklace: A Story of the French Revolution. l.t. ed. 2008. 583p. 23.95 (978-1-4104-1016-0(1)) Thorndike Pr.
—The Silver Blade. 2010. (ENG.). 384p. (YA). (gr. 7-18). 8.99 (978-0-14-241731-7(9), Speak) Penguin Young Readers Group.
—The Vanishing of Billy Buckle. Roberts, David, illus. 2015. (Wings & Co Ser.: 3). (ENG.). 240p. (J). (gr. 2-5). 13.99 (978-0-8050-9915-7(8), 9780805099157, Holt, Henry & Co. Bks. For Young Readers) Holt, Henry & Co.
Garis, Howard R. Umboo, the Elephant. 2008. 108p. pap. 9.95 (978-1-60664-156-9(5)) Aegypan.
Garland, Michael. Miss Smith & the Haunted Library. 2012. (ENG.). 32p. (J). (gr. -1-2). 6.99 (978-0-14-242122-2(7), Puffin Books) Penguin Young Readers Group.
—Miss Smith & the Haunted Library. Garland, Michael, illus. 2009. (ENG., Illus.). 32p. (J). (gr. -1-2). 16.99 (978-0-525-42139-9(4), Dutton Books for Young Readers) Penguin Young Readers Group.
—Miss Smith Reads Again! 2006. (Illus.). (J). (978-1-4156-8098-8(1), Dutton Juvenile) Penguin Publishing Group.
—Miss Smith Reads Again! Garland, Michael, illus. 2008. (ENG., Illus.). 32p. (J). (gr. -1-2). pap. 6.99 (978-0-14-241140-7(X), Puffin Books) Penguin Young Readers Group.
—Miss Smith under the Ocean. Garland, Michael, illus. 2011. (ENG., Illus.). 32p. (J). (gr. -1-2). 16.99 (978-0-525-42342-3(7), Dutton Books for Young Readers) Penguin Young Readers Group.
—Miss Smith's Incredible Storybook. Garland, Michael, illus. (ENG., Illus.). 32p. (J). (gr. -1-2). 2005. pap. 6.99 (978-0-14-240282-5(6), Puffin Books) 2003. 16.99 (978-0-525-47133-2(2), Dutton Books for Young Readers) Penguin Young Readers Group.
—Miss Smith's Incredible Storybook. 2007. 29.95 incl. audio compact disk (978-0-8045-4159-6(0)); 27.95 incl. audio (978-0-8045-6945-3(2)) Spoken Arts, Inc.
Garner, Alan. The Weirdstone of Brisingamen: A Tale of Alderley. 2006. (ENG., Illus.). 288p. (J). (gr. 4-8). pap. 16.95 (978-0-15-205636-0(X)) Houghton Mifflin Harcourt Publishing Co.
Garrido, Pedro Gelabert. El Libro del Abuelo: Un Mundo de Aventuras Entre la Realidad y la Fantasma. Velert, Miriam, illus. 2003. (Ficcion Interactiva Ser.). (SPA.). 160p. pap. 14.95 (978-84-89984-11-0(5)) Recursos, Ediciones ESP. Dist: Independent Pubs. Group.
Garvey, Amy. Glass Heart. 2012. (Cold Kiss Ser.: 2). (ENG.). 320p. (YA). (gr. 8). 17.99 (978-0-06-199624-5(6), HarperTeen) HarperCollins Pubs.
Gary R Kirby. Stories of Sunshine & Funtime of Wonder & Thunder of Mystery & Magic for the Young to Grow On. 2009. 404p. pap. 22.95 (978-1-4401-8640-0(5)) iUniverse, Inc.
Garza, Carmen Lomas, illus. Magic Windows: Ventanas Magicas. 2013. (ENG & SPA.). 32p. (J). pap. 9.95 (978-0-89239-183-7(9), Children's Book Press) Lee & Low Bks., Inc.
Gates, J. Gabriel & Keel, Charlene. Ghost Crown. 2012. (Tracks Ser.). (ENG.). 456p. (YA). (gr. 6-12). pap. 9.95 (978-0-7573-1594-7(1), HCI Teens) Health Communications, Inc.
Geiger, Kay. Treasure. 2010. 36p. pap. 19.95 (978-1-4457-6383-5(4)) Lulu Pr., Inc.
Gentry, Brad. The Hollywood Princess. 2009. 40p. pap. 20.99 (978-1-4490-3545-7(0)) AuthorHouse.
George, Jessica Day. Princess of Glass. (Twelve Dancing Princesses Ser.). (ENG.). 272p. (YA). (gr. 7). 2011. pap. 9.99 (978-1-59990-659-1(7), 9781599906591) 2010. 16.99 (978-1-59990-478-8(0), 9781599904788) Bloomsbury Publishing USA. (Bloomsbury USA Childrens).
—Princess of the Midnight Ball. 2010. (Twelve Dancing Princesses Ser.). (ENG.). 304p. (YA). (gr. 7-9). pap. 9.99 (978-1-59990-455-9(1), 9781599904559, Bloomsbury USA Childrens) Bloomsbury Publishing USA.
—Princess of the Silver Woods. (Twelve Dancing Princesses Ser.). (ENG.). (YA). (gr. 7). 2013. 352p. pap. 9.99 (978-1-61963-126-7(1), 9781619631267) 2012. 336p. 16.99 (978-1-59990-646-1(5), 9781599906461) Bloomsbury Publishing USA. (Bloomsbury USA Childrens).
—Saturdays at Sea. 2017. (Tuesdays at the Castle Ser.). (ENG.). 272p. (J). 16.99 (978-1-61963-957-7(2), 9781619639577, Bloomsbury USA Childrens) Bloomsbury Publishing USA.
George, Kallie. Clover's Luck. 2015. (Magical Animal Adoption Agency Ser.: 1). (J). lib. bdg. 16.00 (978-0-606-37504-7(X)) Turtleback Bks.
—The Enchanted Egg. Boiger, Alexandra, illus. 2015. (Magical Animal Adoption Agency Ser.). (ENG.). 138p. (J). (gr. 3-7). 14.99 (978-1-4231-8383-9(5)) Disney Pr.
—The Enchanted Egg. 2015. (Magical Animal Adoption Agency Ser.: 2). (J). lib. bdg. 26.95 (978-0-606-38337-0(9)) Turtleback Bks.
—The Magical Animal Adoption Agency - Clover's Luck. Boiger, Alexandra, illus. 2015. (Magical Animal Adoption Agency Ser.). (ENG.). 138p. (J). (gr. 2-5). 14.99 (978-1-4231-8382-2(7)) Hyperion Bks. for Children.
George, Kallie. The Missing Magic. 2017. (Magical Animal Adoption Agency Ser.: 3). (J). lib. bdg. 16.00 **(978-0-606-39973-9(9))** Turtleback Bks.
George, Kallie & Boiger, Alexandra. The Missing Magic. Boiger, Alexandra, illus. 2016. (Magical Animal Adoption Agency Ser.). (ENG., Illus.). 144p. (J). (gr. 2-5). 14.99 (978-1-4231-8384-6(3)) Hyperion Bks. for Children.
Geragotelis, Brittany. Life's a Witch. 2013. (Life's a Witch Ser.). (ENG., Illus.). 320p. (YA). (gr. 9). 16.99 (978-1-4424-6655-5(3), Simon & Schuster Bks. For Young Readers) Simon & Schuster Bks. For Young Readers.
—What the Spell. (Life's a Witch Ser.). (ENG., Illus.). (YA). (gr. 9). 2014. 352p. pap. 9.99 (978-1-4424-6707-1(X)) 2013. 336p. 16.99 (978-1-4424-6815-3(7)) Simon & Schuster Bks. For Young Readers. (Simon & Schuster Bks. For Young Readers).
—The Witch Is Back. 2014. (Life's a Witch Ser.). (ENG., Illus.). 352p. (YA). (gr. 9). 17.99 (978-1-4424-6688-3(X), Simon & Schuster Bks. For Young Readers) Simon & Schuster Bks. For Young Readers.
—The Witch Is Back: A Life's a Witch Book. 2015. (Life's a Witch Ser.). (ENG., Illus.). 352p. (YA). (gr. 9). pap. 11.99 (978-1-4424-6691-3(X)) Simon & Schuster Children's Publishing.
Geronimo Stilton Staff. The Wizard's Wand. 2016. (ENG.). 320p. (J). (gr. 2-5). 14.99 (978-1-338-03291-8(7), Scholastic Paperbacks) Scholastic, Inc.
Gianatti, Silvia, et al. Tinker Bell & Her Magical Arrival. Melaranci, Elisabetta & Urbano, Emilio, illus. 2012. (Disney Fairies Ser.: 9). (ENG.). 64p. (J). (gr. 1-6). 11.99 (978-1-59707-324-0(5), 9781597073240); pap. 7.99 (978-1-59707-323-3(7), 9781597073233) Papercutz.
Gibbins, Desiree. The Book Keeper's Oracle. 2008. 212p. pap. 14.49 (978-1-4389-0791-8(5)) AuthorHouse.
Gibson, Douglas. Tales of a Fifth-Grade Knight. Tuya, Jez, illus. 2015. (Middle-Grade Novels Ser.). (ENG.). 160p. (gr. 4-7). lib. bdg. 26.65 (978-1-4965-0488-3(7)) Stone Arch Bks.
Gibson, Julia Mary. Copper Magic. 2014. (ENG., Illus.). 336p. (J). (gr. 5-9). 16.99 (978-0-7653-3211-0(6), 9780765332110, Starscape) Doherty, Tom Assocs., LLC.
Gidali, Orit. Nora the Mind Reader. Gordon-Noy, Aya, illus. 2012. (ENG.). 32p. (J). (gr. -1-3). 15.95 (978-1-59270-120-9(5)) Enchanted Lion Bks., LLC.
Gidwitz, Adam. The Inquisitor's Tale: Or, the Three Magical Children & Their Holy Dog. Aly, Hatem, illus. 2016. (ENG.). 384p. (J). (gr. 5). 17.99 (978-0-525-42616-5(7), Dutton Books for Young Readers) Penguin Young Readers Group.
Giles, Chauncey. The Magic Spectacles: A Fairy Story. 2004. reprint ed. pap. 22.95 (978-0-7661-8731-3(4)) Kessinger Publishing, LLC.
Gill, Mehrnaz S. The Yellow Butterfly. Ward, Lindsay, illus. 2010. (ENG.). 24p. (J). (gr. k-2). 17.95 (978-1-933979-71-7(2), 45f00f36-ed1a-4633-929a-2bb04d2073f4) Bright Sky Pr.
Gillrie Fraser, Marg. The Dolphin Way. 2011. 156p. (gr. -1 — 1). 22.95 (978-1-4502-8225-3(3)); pap. 12.95 (978-1-4502-8224-6(5)) iUniverse, Inc.
Gilman, Laura Anne. The Camelot Spell. 2006. (Grail Quest Ser.: No. 1). 291p. (J). (gr. 5-9). 10.99 (978-0-06-077279-6(4)) HarperCollins Pubs.
Gilman, Phoebe. The Balloon Tree. 2011. (ENG., Illus.). 32p. (J). (gr. -1-k). 16.95 (978-1-61608-454-7(5), 608454, Sky Pony Pr.) Skyhorse Publishing Co., Inc.
Gilson. Melusine - Hocus Pocus. Clarke & Clarke, illus. 2007. (Melusine Ser.: 1). (ENG.). 48p. (J). (gr. -1-12). per. 9.99 (978-1-905460-20-5(1)) CineBook GBR. Dist: National Bk. Network.
Ginoschio De Osceola, Ibrahim. Enter the Corn Bunny, Vol. 1. 2007. 56p. per. 8.95 (978-0-595-45273-6(6)) iUniverse, Inc.
Giordano, Anne. Spencer, the Magic Rabbit. 2009. 40p. pap. 16.99 (978-1-4490-3296-8(6)) AuthorHouse.
Giorgio, Marg. Maxi's Magical Dream. 2011. 24p. pap. 12.79 (978-1-4634-4491-4(5)) AuthorHouse.
Glass, Calliope. Tiana: The Stolen Jewel. 2013. (Disney Princess Early Chapter Bks.). (J). lib. bdg. 14.75 (978-0-606-32291-1(4), Turtleback) Turtleback Bks.
Glennon, Michelle. My Big Green Teacher: Don't Rock the Boat: Saving Our Oceans. Glennon, Michelle, illus. 2008. (Illus.). 32p. (J). 19.95 (978-0-9796625-2-2(4)) GDG Publishing.
—My Big Green Teacher: Seven Generations from Now. Glennon, Michelle, illus. 2008. (Illus.). (J). 19.95 (978-0-9797952-1-3(4)) GDG Publishing.
—My Big Green Teacher: Take a Deep Breath: Saving Our Rainforests. Glennon, Michelle, illus. 2008. (ENG., Illus.). 32p. (J). 19.95 (978-0-9797952-0-6(6)) GDG Publishing.
Glessner, Gordon. Water Wars, Secrets Revealed. 2012. 24p. 12.00 (978-0-9859603-0-8(2)) Laughing Rhino Bks.
Glewwe, Eleanor. Sparkers. 2014. (ENG.). 336p. (J). (gr. 5-8). 16.99 (978-0-451-46876-5(7), Viking Books for Young Readers) Penguin Young Readers Group.
—Wildings. 2016. (ENG.). 336p. (J). (gr. 5). 16.99 (978-0-451-46885-7(6), Viking Books for Young Readers) Penguin Young Readers Group.
Gliori, Debi. Witch Baby & Me. 2010. (ENG., Illus.). 256p. (J). (gr. 2-4). pap. 12.99 (978-0-552-55676-7(9)) Transworld Publishers Ltd. GBR. Dist: Independent Pubs. Group.
Glover, Ruth E. The Lost Labyrinth. 2008. 239p. pap. 15.95 (978-1-4092-1076-4(6)) Lulu Pr., Inc.
Goebel, Jenny. Grave Images. 2013. (ENG.). 208p. (J). (gr. 3-7). 16.99 (978-0-545-51930-4(6), Scholastic Pr.) Scholastic, Inc.
Goelman, Ari. The Path of Names. 2013. (Illus.). 339p. (J). pap. (978-0-545-47431-3(0), Levine, Arthur A. Bks.) Scholastic, Inc.
Gogolewski, Kathe, illus. Tato. 2008. (J). (978-0-9800064-2-1(2)) Red Engine Pr.
Going, K. L. The Garden of Eve. 2009. (ENG., Illus.). 240p. (J). (gr. 2-5). pap. 14.95 (978-0-15-206614-7(4)) Houghton Mifflin Harcourt Publishing Co.
Gold, Gina. Minnie: Hocus Bow-Cus! 2014. (Mickey & Friends World of Reading Ser.). (J). lib. bdg. 13.55 (978-0-606-35270-3(8)) Turtleback Bks.

Golden Books. Christmas Magic! (Frosty the Snowman) Golden Books, illus. 2016. (Color & Paint Plus Stickers Ser.). (ENG., Illus.). 128p. (J). (gr. -1-2). pap. 9.99 *(978-0-399-55224-3(3)*, Golden Bks.) Random Hse. Children's Bks.

—Flying Colors! (Shimmer & Shine) Golden Books, illus. 2017. (Jumbo Coloring Book Ser.). (ENG., Illus.). 224p. (J). (gr. -1-2). pap. 6.99 ***(978-1-5247-6541-5(4)***, Golden Bks.) Random Hse. Children's Bks.

—Genie Magic! (Shimmer & Shine) Golden Books, illus. 2016. (Color Plus Crayons & Sticker Ser.). (ENG., Illus.). 48p. (J). (gr. -1-2). pap. 4.99 *(978-0-553-52205-1(1)*, Golden Bks.) Random Hse. Children's Bks.

—Shimmer & Shine Awesome Sticker Collection (Shimmer & Shine) Golden Books, illus. 2017. (4 Color Plus 1,000 Stickers Ser.). (ENG., Illus.). 64p. (J). (gr. -1-2). pap. 12.99 ***(978-1-5247-1680-6(4)***, Golden Bks.) Random Hse. Children's Bks.

Golden Books. A Stroke of Magic (Shimmer & Shine) Garcia, Segundo, illus. 2016. (Deluxe Paint Box Book Ser.). (ENG.). 128p. (J). (gr. -1-2). pap. 7.99 *(978-0-553-52363-8(5)*, Golden Bks.) Random Hse. Children's Bks.

Goldstein, Lori. Circle of Jinn. 2016. (Becoming Jinn Ser.: 2). (ENG.). 400p. (YA). 18.99 *(978-1-250-05540-8(7)*, 9781250055408) Feiwel & Friends.

Gollahon, Carleen Anderson. Sophie & the Mysterious Ring. 2012. 62p. (gr. 4-18). pap. 8.99 *(978-1-4624-0379-0(4)*, Inspiring Voices) Author Solutions, Inc.

Gollub, Matthew. The Twenty-Five Mixtec Cats. Martinez, Leovigildo, illus. 2004. (J). *(978-1-889910-30-7(9))* Tortuga Pr.

Goode, Suzi. The Lost Wizard Series Bk 1. 2007. pap. 11.95 *(978-1-59374-817-3(5))* Whiskey Creek Pr., LLC.

Gooderham, Chris. Even More Wicked Rhymes. 2008. 68p. pap. 13.95 *(978-1-4092-1753-4(1))* Lulu Pr., Inc.

Goodman, Alison. Eon: Dragoneye Reborn. 2010. (ENG.). 576p. (YA). (gr. 7-18). 10.99 *(978-0-14-241711-9(4)*, Firebird) Penguin Young Readers Group.

—Eon: Dragoneye Reborn. 2010. (Eon Ser.: 1). lib. bdg. 22.10 *(978-0-606-23647-8(3)*, Turtleback) Turtleback Bks.

—The Last Dragoneye. 2012. (ENG.). 672p. (YA). (gr. 7-18). 11.99 *(978-0-14-242093-5(X)*, Firebird) Penguin Young Readers Group.

—The Last Dragoneye. 2012. (Eon Ser.: 2). lib. bdg. 23.30 *(978-0-606-23648-5(1)*, Turtleback) Turtleback Bks.

Goodman, Carol & Wells, Rosemary. Hawthorn. 2015. (Blythewood Novel Ser.). (ENG.). 416p. (YA). (gr. 7). bds. 17.99 *(978-0-670-78478-3(8)*, Viking Books for Young Readers) Penguin Young Readers Group.

Goodman, John. Percy's Magical Adventures. 2005. (Illus.). 170p. pap. *(978-1-84401-556-6(4))* Athena Pr.

Goodnight, Lora. Ivy Tales: The First Irish Fairy. Goins, Heather Lea, illus. 2012. 28p. pap. 24.95 *(978-1-4626-9484-6(5))* America Star Bks.

Goodyear-Brown, Paris. Gabby the Gecko. 2003. per. *(978-1-932203-54-7(0))* Sundog, Ltd.

Gordon, Amy. The Shadow Collector's Apprentice. 2012. (ENG.). 208p. (J). 16.95 *(978-0-8234-2359-0(X))* Holiday Hse., Inc.

Gordon, Judy Ann. Grammie's Magical Garden: Beyond the Gate. 2012. 68p. pap. 28.99 *(978-1-4772-7973-1(3))* AuthorHouse.

Gordon, Mike & Gordon, Carl, illus. The Magic Porridge Pot. 2008. (Usborne First Reading: Level 3 Ser.). 48p. (J). (gr. -1-3). 8.99 *(978-0-7945-1883-7(4)*, Usborne) EDC Publishing.

Gordon, Sylvia. Further Adventures of the Potty Wizard & His Cat, Muddles. 2009. (Illus.). 60p. pap. 10.49 *(978-1-4389-6819-3(1))* AuthorHouse.

Gorin, Leslie. Elly & the Smelly Sneaker: A Riches to Rags Story. Vamos, Lesley, illus. 2017. (ENG.). 40p. (J). (gr. -1). 14.95 *(978-1-4549-1817-2(9))* Sterling Publishing Co., Inc.

Gormley, Greg. Grandad's Busy Day. 2007. (Fantastic Phones Ser.). (ENG., Illus.). 12p. (J). (gr. k-k). bds. 9.99 *(978-0-7475-8377-6(3))* Bloomsbury Publishing Plc GBR. Dist: Independent Pubs. Group.

Gormon: The Sentinel Awakes. 2004. per. 2.75 *(978-0-9762294-0-7(4))* Corbett Features.

Gos & Peyo. The Astrosmurf. 2011. (Smurfs Graphic Novels Ser.). (ENG., Illus.). 56p. (J). (gr. 2-5). 10.99 *(978-1-59707-251-9(6)*, 9781597072519) Papercutz.

Gos, Charles & Peyo. The Astrosmurf. 2011. (Smurfs Graphic Novels Ser.). (ENG., Illus.). 56p. (J). (gr. 2-5). pap. 5.99 *(978-1-59707-250-2(8)*, 9781597072502) Papercutz.

Goscinny, René. Asterix & the Vikings: The Book of the Film. Bell, Anthea, tr. Uderzo, Albert, illus. 2006. (ENG.). 72p. (gr. 4-7). 17.99 *(978-0-7528-8590-2(1)*, Orion) Orion Publishing Group, Ltd. GBR. Dist: Hachette Bk. Group.

Gosine, Aarti. The Magic Cave: A Cascade Children's Book. 2011. (Illus.). 100p. pap. 12.52 *(978-1-4567-7050-1(0))* AuthorHouse.

Goudge, Elizabeth. The Little White Horse. movie tie-in ed. 2008. (ENG., Illus.). 248p. (J). (gr. 4-7). pap. *(978-0-7459-6118-7(5))* Lion Hudson PLC GBR. Dist: Independent Pubs. Group.

Graegin, Stephanie. Little Fox in the Forest. 2017. (ENG., Illus.). 40p. (J). (gr. -1-3). 17.99 *(978-0-553-53789-5(X)*, Schwartz & Wade Bks.) Random Hse. Children's Bks.

Graff, Lisa. A Clatter of Jars. 2016. (ENG.). 224p. (J). (gr. 3-7). 16.99 *(978-0-399-17499-5(0)*, Philomel Bks.) Penguin Young Readers Group.

Graham, Deborah. The Magic Comes Back: A Max & Sam Adventure. 2012. 66p. (gr. 2-4). pap. 8.95 *(978-1-4759-4758-8(5))* iUniverse, Inc.

Graham-Larkin, Debbie. Magic in the Air. 2005. (Graham Cracker Kids Adventure Ser.). (Illus.). (J). pap. 12.95 *(978-0-9716475-1-0(8))* Graham Cracker Kids.

Grahame, Howard. The Wishing Book 2 - Return to Mars. 2009. 102p. (J). pap. *(978-1-905809-80-6(8))* Pneuma Springs Publishing.

Gramp's Magic Gift. 2011. 98p. 24.99 *(978-1-4628-2980-4(5))*; pap. 15.99 *(978-1-4628-2979-8(1))* Xlibris Corp.

Grandma's Magical Storybook. 2003. (Illus.). 256p. (J). 12.98 *(978-1-4054-0968-1(1))* Parragon, Inc.

Grant, John. Littlenose the Magician. Collins, Ross, illus. 2009. (ENG.). 112p. (J). (gr. k-12). pap. 5.99 *(978-1-84738-201-6(0)*, Simon & Schuster Children's) Simon & Schuster, Ltd. GBR. Dist: Simon & Schuster, Inc.

Gratton, Tessa. Blood Magic. 2011. (YA). pap. *(978-0-375-86486-5(5))* Random Hse. Children's Bks.

Grau, Sheila. The Boy with Seventeen Senses. 2016. (ENG.). 256p. (J). (gr. 3-7). 16.95 *(978-1-4197-2119-9(4)*, Amulet Bks.) Abrams, Inc.

Graudin, Ryan. All That Burns. 2015. (ENG.). 464p. (YA). (gr. 8). pap. 9.99 *(978-0-06-218743-7(0)*, HarperTeen) HarperCollins Pubs.

—All That Glows. 2014. (ENG.). 480p. (YA). (gr. 8). pap. 9.99 *(978-0-06-218741-3(4)*, HarperTeen) HarperCollins Pubs.

Graves, Annie. A Dog's Breakfast. McElhinney, Glenn, illus. 2015. (Nightmare Club Ser.: 1). (ENG.). 64p. (J). (gr. 2-5). pap. 6.99 *(978-1-4677-6042-3(0))*; lib. bdg. 25.32 *(978-1-4677-4350-1(X))* Lerner Publishing Group.

Graves, Jonathan. Isabella Propeller & the Magic Beanie. Haley, Gail E., illus. 2011. (J). 15.95 *(978-1-933251-74-5(3))* Parkway Pubs., Inc.

Graves, Peter, tr. from SWE. Nils Holgersson's Wonderful Journey Through Sweden, 2 vols. 2013. (ENG., Illus.). 382p. pap. 32.00 *(978-1-870041-97-3(6))*; 360p. pap. 32.00 *(978-1-870041-96-6(8))* Norvik Pr. GBR. Dist: Dufour Editions, Inc.

Graves, Sue. Harry & the Horse. 2011. (Tadpoles Ser.). (ENG., Illus.). 24p. (J). (gr. k-2). *(978-0-7787-0579-6(X))*; pap. *(978-0-7787-0590-1(0))* Crabtree Publishing Co.

Gravett, Emily. Spells. Gravett, Emily, illus. 2009. (ENG., Illus.). 32p. (J). (gr. -1-3). 16.99 *(978-1-4169-8270-8(1)*, Simon & Schuster Bks. For Young Readers) Simon & Schuster Bks. For Young Readers.

Gray, Betty. The Legend of CaseyRock. 2007. (Illus.). 40p. (J). per. 12.00 *(978-0-9779601-2-5(9))* BareBones Publishing.

Gray, Christopher. There Be Goblins in the Wood! 2012. 112p. (gr. 2-4). 23.99 *(978-1-4772-6994-7(0))*; pap. 14.95 *(978-1-4772-6995-4(9))* AuthorHouse.

Gray, Claudia. Sorceress. 2015. (Spellcaster Ser.: 3). (ENG.). 352p. (YA). (gr. 8). 17.99 *(978-0-06-196124-3(8)*, HarperTeen) HarperCollins Pubs.

—Spellcaster. 2013. (Spellcaster Ser.: 1). (ENG.). 400p. (YA). (gr. 8). 17.99 *(978-0-06-196120-5(5)*, HarperTeen) HarperCollins Pubs.

—Steadfast. (Spellcaster Ser.: 2). (ENG.). (YA). (gr. 8). 2015. 368p. pap. 9.99 *(978-0-06-196123-6(X))* 2014. 352p. 17.99 *(978-0-06-196122-9(1))* HarperCollins Pubs. (HarperTeen).

Graziani, Maria. A Black Cat on Halloween: Un Gato Negro en Dia de Brujas. Elejalde, Eliana, illus. l.t. ed. 2004. (SPA.). 23p. (J). 7.00 *(978-0-9762361-1-5(7))* Ed. Acespanish S.A.C.- Lima, Peru.

Greban, Tanguy. Sarah So Small. Greban, Quentin, illus. 2004. (ENG.). 32p. (J). (gr. 4-7). 16.95 *(978-1-59687-179-3(2))* IBks., Inc.

Green, Katie May. Seen & Not Heard. Green, Katie May, illus. 2015. (ENG., Illus.). 32p. (J). (gr. k-3). 15.99 *(978-0-7636-7612-4(8))* Candlewick Pr.

Green with Envy. 2014. (Unicorn Magic Ser.: 3). (ENG., Illus.). 144p. (J). (gr. 1-4). pap. 5.99 *(978-1-4424-9826-6(9)*, Aladdin) Simon & Schuster Children's Publishing.

Greene, Montrell. The Magic in Me Series #1: Magical Me. 2011. 16p. (gr. -1). pap. 12.95 *(978-1-4567-5785-4(7))* AuthorHouse.

Greene, Montrell & Greene, Robie. The Magic in Me Series #2: Imagine Me. 2011. 16p. (gr. -1). pap. 12.95 *(978-1-4567-5783-0(0))* AuthorHouse.

Greene, Stephanie. Princess Posey & the Christmas Magic. 2013. (Princess Posey, First Grader Ser.: 7). (ENG.). 96p. (J). (gr. k-3). pap. 4.99 *(978-0-14-242734-7(9)*, Puffin Books) Penguin Young Readers Group.

—Princess Posey & the Christmas Magic. Sisson, Stéphanie Roth, illus. 2013. (Princess Posey, First Grader Ser.: 7). (ENG.). 96p. (J). (gr. k-3). 13.99 *(978-0-399-16363-0(8)*, G.P. Putnam's Sons Books for Young Readers) Penguin Young Readers Group.

Greenfield, Amy Butler. Chantress Alchemy. 2015. (Chantress Ser.). (ENG., Illus.). 368p. (YA). (gr. 7). pap. 10.99 *(978-1-4424-5708-9(2)*, McElderry, Margaret K. Bks.) McElderry, Margaret K. Bks.

Greenspan, Deborah. Kids' Day. 2004. (J). pap. 10.95 *(978-1-59526-197-7(4))* Aeon Publishing Inc.

Greer, Hannah. The Castle Ivengless: The Velvet Bag Memoirs, Bk. 3. 2009. 145p. pap. 24.95 *(978-1-60749-105-7(2))* America Star Bks.

—The Velvet Bag Memoirs, Bk. 1. 2008. 132p. pap. 24.95 *(978-1-60672-190-2(9))* America Star Bks.

Grey, Melissa. The Savage Dawn. 2017. (Girl at Midnight Ser.: 3). (ENG.). 496p. (YA). (gr. 9). 17.99 ***(978-0-385-74469-0(2))***; lib. bdg. 20.99 ***(978-0-375-99181-3(6))*** Random Hse. Children's Bks. (Delacorte Pr.).

Griesmer, Russell. My Hometown. Wong, Priscilla, illus. 2015. (ENG.). 40p. (gr. 1-4). 15.95 *(978-1-62370-174-1(0))* Capstone Young Readers of Coughlan Cos.

Griffin, Lydia. BeBa & the Curious Creature Catchers. Lostimolo, Stephanie, illus. l.t. ed. 2006. 32p. (J). 16.95 *(978-0-9770516-0-1(9))* Laffin Minor Pr.

Griffith, Diane. Granny's Magic Garden. 2010. 66p. pap. 19.95 *(978-1-60693-925-3(4)*, Eloquent Bks.) Strategic Book Publishing & Rights Agency (SBPRA).

Griggs, Terry. Nieve. L'Hirondelle, Cheryl, illus. 2010. (ENG.). 264p. (J). (gr. 4-10). pap. 14.95 *(978-1-897231-87-6(3))* Biblioasis CAN. Dist: Consortium Bk. Sales & Distribution.

Grime, L. L. Do You Love Me? 2008. 48p. pap. 22.95 *(978-1-4357-1364-2(8))* Lulu Pr., Inc.

Grimm, J. & W. Sleeping Beauty. Dusikova, Maja, illus. 2012. (ENG.). 32p. (J). (gr. -1-3). 17.95 *(978-0-7358-4087-4(3))* North-South Bks., Inc.

Grinti, Mike & Grinti, Rachel. Claws. 2012. (J). *(978-0-545-43314-3(2))*; (ENG.). 256p. (gr. 5-9). 16.99 *(978-0-545-43313-6(4))* Scholastic, Inc. (Chicken Hse., The).

Gripari, Pierre. Le Gentil Petit Diable: Et Autres Contes de la Rue Broca. Rosado, Puig, illus. 2007. (Folio Junior Ser.). 142p. (J). per. *(978-2-07-061255-0(4))* National Round Table on the Environment & the Economy (NRTEE)/Table ronde nationale sur l'environnement et l'economie (TRNEE).

Gruber, Daveda. Castle of Ice. 2008. 51p. pap. 10.94 *(978-1-4357-3251-3(0))* Lulu Pr., Inc.

Guess, Catherine Ritch. Rudy & the Magic Sleigh. 2006. (Rudy the Red Pig Ser.). (ENG., Illus.). 32p. 14.95 *(978-1-933341-18-7(1))* CRM.

Guibord, Maurissa. Warped. 2012. (ENG.). 348p. (YA). (gr. 7). pap. 9.99 *(978-0-385-73892-7(7)*, Ember) Random Hse. Children's Bks.

Guillain, Adam. Bella Balistica & the Temple of Tikal. 2004. (Bella Balistica Ser.). (ENG., Illus.). 350p. (J). (gr. 4-7). pap. 9.95 *(978-1-84059-394-5(6))* Milet Publishing.

Gummelt, Donna & Melchiorre, Dondino. Michelina the Magical Musical Good Witch of the Forest. Wall, Randy Hugh, ed. Varela, Juan D., tr. Varela, Juan D., illus. 2006. (SPA.). 34p. (J). 14.95 *(978-0-9764798-6-4(9))* Story Store Collection Publishing.

Gwyer, Gillian K. Podnockery Forest - Owl & the Trickster. 2013. 40p. *(978-1-4602-3974-2(1))* FriesenPress.

Haesche, Richard Paul, Sr. The Magic of the Leprechaun. 2007. (ENG.). 182p. (YA). *(978-0-9798536-3-0(X))* Kreative X-Pressions Pubns.

Hagen, George. Gabriel Finley & the Raven's Riddle. Bakal, Scott, illus. 2014. (ENG.). 384p. (J). (gr. 4-7). 16.99 *(978-0-385-37103-2(9)*, Schwartz & Wade Bks.) Random Hse. Children's Bks.

Hahn, Rebecca. A Creature of Moonlight. 2014. (ENG.). 224p. (YA). (gr. 7-12). 17.99 *(978-0-544-10935-3(X)*, HMH Books For Young Readers) Houghton Mifflin Harcourt Publishing Co.

Hahner, Aaron. The Magic of Midnight. 2004. per. 8.95 *(978-1-932560-58-9(0))* Aeon Publishing Inc.

Hahnke. Through the Eyes of a Raptor. 2007. 424p. per. 19.95 *(978-0-595-42609-6(3))* iUniverse, Inc.

Haig, Matt. To Be a Cat. Curtis, Stacy, illus. (ENG.). 304p. (J). (gr. 3-7). 2014. pap. 8.99 *(978-1-4424-5406-4(7))* 2013. 16.99 *(978-1-4424-5405-7(9))* Simon & Schuster Children's Publishing.

Haile, Carol J. The Princess Tree: A Tale of Fairies, Elves & Magic. l.t. ed. 2005. (ESK., Illus.). 32p. (J). 19.95 *(978-0-9711236-1-8(6))* Firenze Pr.

Haining, Peter. Magicians' Circle. 2012. 348p. (-18). pap. *(978-1-4596-4365-9(8))* ReadHowYouWant.com, Ltd.

Haining, Peter, ed. Magician's Circle: More Spellbinding Stories of Wizards & Wizardry. 2004. (ENG., Illus.). 256p. (J). (gr. 5). 19.95 *(978-0-285-63681-1(2))* Souvenir Pr. Ltd. GBR. Dist: Independent Pubs. Group.

Haldane, Rachael. Nymphas' World. 2009. 392p. pap. 13.99 *(978-1-61667-003-0(7))* Raider Publishing International.

Hale, Bruce. Fat Cat of Underwhere. Hillman, Shane, illus. 2009. (Underwhere Ser.). 176p. (J). pap. 5.99 *(978-0-06-085135-4(X))* HarperCollins Pubs.

—Pirates of Underwhere. Hillman, Shane, illus. (Underwhere Ser.: 2). (J). (gr. 3-7). 2009. (ENG.). 176p. pap. 6.99 *(978-0-06-085129-3(5))* 2008. 164p. lib. bdg. 16.89 *(978-0-06-085128-6(7))* HarperCollins Pubs.

—Prince of Underwhere. Hillman, Shane, illus. 2009. (Underwhere Ser.: 1). (ENG.). 176p. (J). (gr. 3-7). pap. 5.99 *(978-0-06-085126-2(0))* HarperCollins Pubs.

Hale, Susan Elizabeth. Emma Oliver & the Song of Creation. 2016. (ENG.). 178p. (J). (gr. -1-12). pap. 11.95 *(978-1-78535-386-4(1)*, Our Street Bks.) Hunt, John Publishing Ltd. GBR. Dist: National Bk. Network.

Hall, J. Darroll. The Lollipop Club. 2011. (ENG.). 290p. pap. 4.99 *(978-0-615-56231-5(0))* Fantasy Island Bk. Publishing.

Hall, Kirsten. Revamp Your Room. 2005. (Illus.). 48p. pap. *(978-0-439-80296-3(2))* Scholastic, Inc.

Hall, Traci. Wiccan Cool. 2010. (Rhiannon Godfrey Ser.). (ENG.). 264p. pap. 15.00 *(978-1-60504-611-2(6))* Samhain Publishing, LTD.

Hamilton, C. After Ever Happily. 2006. 80p. pap. 16.95 *(978-1-4241-3190-7(1))* PublishAmerica, Inc.

Hamilton, John. Dog Friday. 2010. (Illus.). 60p. pap. 21.99 *(978-1-4490-9468-3(6))* AuthorHouse.

Hamilton, Kersten. Tyger Tyger. 2011. (ENG.). 336p. (YA). (gr. 7). pap. 18.99 *(978-0-547-57732-6(X))* Houghton Mifflin Harcourt Publishing Co.

—When the Stars Threw down Their Spears. (ENG.). 400p. (YA). (gr. 7). 2014. pap. 8.99 *(978-0-544-22771-2(9)*, HMH Books For Young Readers) 2013. 16.99 *(978-0-547-73964-9(8))* Houghton Mifflin Harcourt Publishing Co.

Hamilton, Peter F. The Hunting of the Princes. 2016. (Queen of Dreams Ser.: 2). (ENG., Illus.). 320p. (J). (gr. 4-7). pap. 11.99 *(978-1-4472-9114-5(X))* Pan Macmillan GBR. Dist: Independent Pubs. Group.

Hampton, Patrick. Down by the Mulberry Tree, 1 vol. 2009. 15p. pap. 24.95 *(978-1-60703-672-2(X))* America Star Bks.

Han, Jia. My Name Is Zedonk. 2017. (ENG.). 40p. (J). (gr. -1-2). 16.95 *(978-1-941529-53-9(4)*, Plum Blossom Bks.) Parallax Pr.

Hanna, Kevin & Fagan, Dave. Creature Academy GN. 2011. (Illus.). 80p. (YA). pap. 14.95 *(978-1-897548-53-0(2))* Arcana Studio, Inc.

Hannigan, Kate. Cupcake Cousins, Book 3 Winter Wonders. Hughes, Brooke Boynton, illus. 2017. (Cupcake Cousins Ser.). (ENG.). 240p. (J). (gr. 3-7). pap. 6.99 ***(978-1-4847-2363-0(5))*** Hyperion Bks. for Children.

Hao, K. T. The Magic Book. Ferri, Giuliano, illus. 2008. (ENG.). 32p. (J). (gr. -1). 16.50 *(978-1-933327-44-0(8))*; 15.95 *(978-1-933327-43-3(X))* Purple Bear Bks., Inc.

Hapka, Catherine, pseud. Don't Meddle with Miss Nettle. 2014. (Sofia the First Ser.). (J). lib. bdg. 24.50 *(978-0-606-34101-1(3)*, Turtleback) Turtleback Bks.

—Echo's Lucky Charm. Hibbert, Hollie, illus. 2016. (Dolphin School Ser.: 2). (ENG.). 112p. (J). (gr. 2-5). pap. 4.99 *(978-0-545-75025-7(3))* Scholastic, Inc.

Hapka, Catherine, pseud & Disney Book Group Staff. The Amulet & the Anthem. Disney Storybook Art Team, illus. 2013. (ENG.). 24p. (J). (gr. -1-k). pap. 4.99 *(978-1-4231-8023-4(2))* Disney Pr.

Hapka, Cathy, pseud & Disney Book Group Staff. Sofia Makes a Friend. Disney Storybook Artists Staff, illus. 2013. (World of Reading Ser.). (ENG.). 32p. (J). (gr. -1-k). pap. 3.99 *(978-1-4231-6408-1(3))* Disney Pr.

Hapka, Cathy, pseud, et al. The Royal Slumber Party. Disney Storybook Art Team, illus. 2013. (ENG.). 24p. (J). (gr. -1-k). pap. 3.99 *(978-1-4231-6410-4(5))* Disney Pr.

Haptie, Charlotte. Otto & the Bird Charmers: The Second Book of the Karmidee. 2005. (Illus.). 417p. (J). 17.95 *(978-0-8234-1883-1(9))* Holiday Hse., Inc.

—Otto & the Flying Twins. 2004. (Illus.). 320p. (J). (gr. 4-6). 17.95 *(978-0-8234-1826-8(X))* Holiday Hse., Inc.

Hardwell, Gary D. A Boo Bears' Story: Stormy Night. 2007. (Illus.). 36p. per. 10.00 *(978-0-9792016-9-1(1))* Professional Publishing Hse. LLC.

Hargreaves, Roger. Mr. Stingy. 2011. (Mr. Men & Little Miss Ser.). (ENG.). 32p. (J). (gr. -1-2). mass mkt. 4.99 *(978-0-8431-9959-8(8)*, Price Stern Sloan) Penguin Young Readers Group.

Harkey, Faith. Genuine Sweet. (ENG.). 288p. (J). (gr. 5-7). 2016. pap. 6.99 *(978-0-544-66853-9(7)*, HMH Books For Young Readers) 2015. 16.99 *(978-0-544-28366-4(X))* Houghton Mifflin Harcourt Publishing Co.

Harper, Charise Mericle. Dreamer, Wisher, Liar. 2014. (ENG.). 352p. (J). (gr. 3-7). 16.99 *(978-0-06-202675-0(5))* HarperCollins Pubs.

Harrington, Claudia. Book 3: Yum-Yum the Very Spoiled Fish. 2016. (Hank the Pet Sitter Ser.). (ENG.). (gr. -1-3). lib. bdg. 27.07 ***(978-1-62402-189-3(1))*** ABDO Publishing Co.

Harris, Patricia. Rosalina Becomes a Flower Fairy. 2017. (Rosalina's Flower Garden Ser.). 24p. (gr. 4-6). pap. 8.25 ***(978-1-5383-2109-6(2)***, PowerKids Pr.) Rosen Publishing Group, Inc., The.

—Rosalina Learns Magic Games. 2017. (Rosalina's Flower Garden Ser.). 24p. (gr. 4-6). pap. 8.25 ***(978-1-5383-2113-3(0)***, PowerKids Pr.) Rosen Publishing Group, Inc., The.

Harrison, Mette Ivie. The Princess & the Bear. 2010. (ENG.). 352p. (YA). (gr. 8). pap. 8.99 *(978-0-06-155316-5(6)*, HarperTeen) HarperCollins Pubs.

—The Princess & the Hound. (YA). 2008. (ENG.). 432p. (gr. 8). pap. 8.99 *(978-0-06-113189-9(X)*, HarperTeen) 2007. 410p. (gr. 7-18). lib. bdg. 18.89 *(978-0-06-113188-2(1)*, Eos) HarperCollins Pubs.

Harrison, Michelle. One Wish. 2016. (13 Treasures Trilogy Ser.: Prequel). (ENG.). 384p. (J). (gr. 3-7). 17.00 *(978-0-316-33529-4(0))* Little Brown & Co.

—13 Curses. 2011. (13 Treasures Trilogy Ser.: 2). (ENG.). 496p. (J). (gr. 5-9). 15.99 *(978-0-316-04150-8(5))* Little Brown & Co.

—13 Curses. 2012. (13 Treasures Trilogy Ser.: 2). (ENG.). 512p. (J). (gr. 5-9). pap. 8.99 *(978-0-316-04149-2(1))* Little, Brown Bks. for Young Readers.

—13 Curses. 2012. (13 Treasures Ser.: 2). (J). lib. bdg. 19.65 *(978-0-606-26160-9(5)*, Turtleback) Turtleback Bks.

Harrold, A. F. The Song from Somewhere Else. Pinfold, Levi, illus. 2017. (ENG.). 240p. (J). 16.99 *(978-1-68119-401-1(5)*, 9781681194011, Bloomsbury USA Childrens) Bloomsbury Publishing USA.

Hartwell, David G., ed. Christmas Magic. 2016. (ENG.). 496p. (Orig.). pap. 18.99 *(978-0-7653-1580-9(7)*, 9780765315809, Tor Bks.) Doherty, Tom Assocs., LLC.

Hartwright, Gianna. The Befana Drama. 2013. 352p. pap. *(978-0-9575697-6-8(9))* Gianna Della Luna Publishing.

Harvey, Alyxandra. A Breath of Frost. 2014. (Lovegrove Legacy Ser.). (ENG.). 512p. (YA). (gr. 7). pap. 10.99 *(978-0-8027-3444-0(8)*, 9780802734440, Bloomsbury USA Childrens) Bloomsbury Publishing USA.

—Whisper the Dead. 2014. (Lovegrove Legacy Ser.: Bk. 2). (ENG.). 408p. (YA). (gr. 7). 17.99 *(978-0-8027-3750-2(1)*, 9780802737502, Bloomsbury USA Childrens) Bloomsbury Publishing USA.

Harvey, Keith. Oscar & the Magic Table: A Story about a Little Boy Who For got His Table Manners. 2015. (ENG., Illus.). 24p. pap. 8.99 *(978-1-84135-922-9(X))* Award Pubns. Ltd. GBR. Dist: Parkwest Pubns., Inc.

Harwell, Andrew. The Spider Ring. 2015. (ENG.). 224p. (J). (gr. 3-7). 16.99 *(978-0-545-68290-9(8)*, Scholastic Pr.) Scholastic, Inc.

Hasbro. Gift of Maud Pie. 2016. (Passport to Reading Level 2 Ser.). (J). lib. bdg. 13.55 *(978-0-606-39194-8(0))* Turtleback Bks.

—My Little Pony: Chapter Book Bind-Up. 2016. (ENG., Illus.). 416p. (J). (gr. 3-7). pap. 12.99 *(978-0-316-27259-9(0))* Little, Brown Bks. for Young Readers.

Hasbro & Finn, Perdita. My Little Pony: Friendship Is Magic. 2016. (Equestria Girls Ser.: 6). (ENG., Illus.). 208p. (J). (gr. 3-7). 9.99 *(978-0-316-26699-4(X))* Little, Brown Bks. for Young Readers.

Haselhuhn, Hugo & Cowdell, Luke. Lucas Lightfoot & the Fire Crystal. 2016. (ENG., Illus.). 180p. (J). pap. 12.95 *(978-1-63047-783-7(4))* Morgan James Publishing.

Haskell, Merrie. The Princess Curse. (ENG.). (J). (gr. 3-7). 2013. 352p. pap. 6.99 *(978-0-06-200815-2(3))* 2011. 336p. 16.99 *(978-0-06-200813-8(7))* HarperCollins Pubs.

Hattan, Ann. Jake & Bobby's Magical Christmas. 2012. (Illus.). 16p. pap. 18.30 *(978-1-4772-2748-0(2))* AuthorHouse.

Hauman, Carrie. Zoe the Magic Love Dog. 2003. (Illus.). 32p. (J). 16.00 *(978-0-9746333-8-1(0))* Alma Pr.

Hawkins, Delta Michelle. Cassandra's Journey. 2012. 28p. pap. 24.95 *(978-1-4626-9566-9(3))* America Star Bks.

Hawkins, Elizabeth. Ben's Birthdays. Cemmick, Paul, illus. 2010. (ENG.). 40p. (J). (gr. k-2). pap. 10.99 *(978-1-84853-018-8(8))* Transworld Publishers Ltd. GBR. Dist: Independent Pubs. Group.

Hawkins, Rachel. Demonglass. 2012. (ENG.). 384p. (YA). (gr. 6-17). pap. 8.99 *(978-1-4231-2844-1(3))* Hyperion Pr.

—Hex Hall, Bk. 1. 2010. (ENG.). 336p. (J). (gr. 7-17). 16.99 *(978-1-4231-2130-5(9))* Hyperion Pr.

—Lady Renegades: A Rebel Belle Novel. 2016. (Rebel Belle Ser.: 3). (ENG.). 272p. (YA). (gr. 7). 17.99 *(978-0-399-25695-0(4)*, G.P. Putnam's Sons Books for Young Readers) Penguin Young Readers Group.

—Miss Mayhem. 2015. (Rebel Belle Ser.: 2). (ENG.). 288p. (YA). (gr. 7). 17.99 *(978-0-399-25694-3(6)*, G.P. Putnam's Sons Books for Young Readers) Penguin Young Readers Group.

—Rebel Belle. 2015. (Rebel Belle Ser.: 1). (ENG.). 368p. (YA). (gr. 7). pap. 9.99 *(978-0-14-751435-6(5)*, Speak) Penguin Young Readers Group.

—School Spirits. 2014. (Hex Hall Novel Ser.). (ENG.). 304p. (YA). (gr. 7-12). pap. 9.99 *(978-1-4231-4850-0(9))* Hyperion Bks. for Children.

—School Spirits. 2013. (Hex Hall Novel Ser.). (ENG.). 304p. (YA). (gr. 7-12). 17.99 *(978-1-4231-4849-4(5))* Hyperion Pr.
—Spell Bound (a Hex Hall Novel) 2013. (ENG.). 352p. (YA). (gr. 7-17). pap. 9.99 *(978-1-4231-2140-4(6))* Hyperion Pr.
Hawley, Bobby. Matt & the Wonder of Wishes, 1 vol. 2009. 165p. pap. 24.95 *(978-1-60836-743-6(6))* America Star Bks.
Hay, Sam. Knit-Knotters. Tran, Turine, illus. 2016. (Stella & the Night Sprites Ser.: 1). (ENG.). 96p. (J). (gr. 1-3). pap. 4.99 *(978-0-545-81998-5(9))* Scholastic, Inc.
—Tooth Bandits. Manuzak, Lisa, illus. 2016. (Stella & the Night Sprites Ser.: 2). (ENG.). 96p. (J). (gr. 1-3). 15.99 *(978-0-545-82001-1(4))* Scholastic, Inc.
Hayden, Jeanne. Last Minute Wilma & Her Toad Soup. 2009. 24p. pap. 14.95 *(978-1-4327-3857-0(7))* Outskirts Pr., Inc.
Haydu, Corey Ann. Rules for Stealing Stars. 2015. (ENG.). 336p. (J). (gr. 3-7). 16.99 *(978-0-06-235271-2(7)*, Tegen, Katherine Bks) HarperCollins Pubs.
Haydu, Corey Ann. The Someday Suitcase. 2017. 304p. (J). (gr. 3-7). 16.99 ***(978-0-06-235275-0(X)***, Tegen, Katherine Bks) HarperCollins Pubs.
Hayes, John C. Splurge & the Theatre of Magic. 2008. 348p. pap. 22.00 *(978-1-84426-500-8(5))* Upfront Publishing Ltd. GBR. Dist: Printondemand-worldwide.com.
Hayes, Kathryn. The Balloon Fairy. 2009. 30p. pap. 13.99 *(978-1-4389-6857-5(4))* AuthorHouse.
Heacock, David & Giles, Inga. Child of Oz. 2010. (J). pap. *(978-0-88092-479-5(9))* Royal Fireworks Publishing Co.
Heap, Sue. A Fabulous Fairy Feast. Heap, Sue, illus. 2009. (ENG., Illus.). 32p. (J). (gr. -1-k). pap. 8.99 *(978-1-4052-3644-7(2))* Egmont Bks., Ltd. GBR. Dist: Independent Pubs. Group.
Hearn, Lian. Heaven's Net Is Wide. unabr. ed. 2008. (Illus.). 592p. pap. *(978-0-330-45428-5(5)*, Macmillan Children's Bks.) Pan Macmillan.
Hearne, Betsy. Wishes, Kisses, & Pigs. 2003. (ENG.). 144p. (J). (gr. 3-7). pap. 6.99 *(978-0-689-86347-9(0)*, Simon & Schuster/Paula Wiseman Bks.) Simon & Schuster/Paula Wiseman Bks.
Heible, Beverly. A Christmas Party on River Row. 2012. 98p. 22.95 *(978-1-62709-018-6(5))*; pap. 17.95 *(978-1-4626-9575-1(2))* America Star Bks.
Heidi Heckelbeck Gets the Sniffles. 2014. (Heidi Heckelbeck Ser.: 12). (ENG., Illus.). 128p. (J). (gr. k-4). pap. 5.99 *(978-1-4814-1362-6(7)*, Little Simon) Little Simon.
Helgerson, Joseph. Horns & Wrinkles. Ceccoli, Nicoletta, illus. 2008. (ENG.). 240p. (J). (gr. 5-7). pap. 6.99 *(978-0-618-98178-6(0))* Houghton Mifflin Harcourt Publishing Co.
Heller, Donna & Payne, James. The Enchanted Tree. Zamboni, David, illus. 2007. 44p. per. 14.95 *(978-1-934246-72-6(7))* Peppertree Pr., The.
Helliwell, Sheila. Gammy. Hawthorn, Paul & Hopkins, Simon, illus. 2nd ed. 2013. 70p. pap. *(978-0-9560331-4-7(8))* Children' Story Pubs.
—Hoonraki Moon: The Murphy Stories. 2006. (J). pap. 9.00 *(978-0-8059-7027-2(4))* Dorrance Publishing Co., Inc.
Hemmings, Lisa & O'Keefe, Allan. Imagine Me with the Three Owls: Feeling Great. 2012. 32p. pap. 13.95 *(978-1-4525-0551-0(9))* Balboa Pr.
Hendesi, Roya. The Ancient Queendom. 2011. 52p. pap. 29.05 *(978-1-4568-2783-0(9))* Xlibris Corp.
Henighan, Tom. Mercury Man. 2004. (ENG.). 200p. (YA). (gr. 6). pap. 9.99 *(978-1-55002-508-8(2))* Dundurn CAN. Dist: Ingram Publisher Services.
Henry, Heather French. Claire's Magic Sades. Henry, Heather French, illus. 2004. (Claire's Everyday Adventures Ser.). (Illus.). 32p. (J). (gr. k-4). pap. 8.95 *(978-0-9706341-7-7(X)*, 1231609) Cubbie Blue Publishing.
Henry, James. The Cabinet of Curiosities. 2010. 240p. pap. 21.50 *(978-0-9559851-0-2(2))* Blue Cat GBR. Dist: Lulu Pr., Inc.
Henry, William. Tir na NOg: A New Adventure. Arnault, Delphine, illus. 2009. (ENG.). 128p. (J). pap. 25.95 *(978-1-85635-597-1(7))* Mercier Pr., Ltd., The IRL. Dist: Dufour Editions, Inc.
Heppermann, Christine & Koertge, Ron. Sadie's Story. Marcero, Deborah, illus. 2016. (Backyard Witch Ser.: 1). 176p. (J). (gr. 3-7). pap. 5.99 *(978-0-06-233839-6(0)*, Greenwillow Bks.) HarperCollins Pubs.
Herbert, Frances. Fran's Van & the Magic Box. Herbert, Frances, illus. 2013. (Illus.). 24p. pap. *(978-1-78222-085-5(2))* Paragon Publishing, Rothersthorpe.
Herbert Hilligan & His Magical Adventure Curriculum Guide. 2004. ring bd. 24.95 *(978-0-9743335-4-0(9))* Imaginative Publishing, Ltd.
Herbert Hilligan's Lone Star Adventure Curriculum Guide. 2004. ring bd. 24.95 *(978-0-9743335-7-1(3))* Imaginative Publishing, Ltd.
Herbert Hilligan's Tropical Adventure Curriculum Guide. 2004. ring bd. 24.95 *(978-0-9743335-6-4(5))* Imaginative Publishing, Ltd.
Herda, Frank A. The Cup of Death: Cronicles of the Dragons of the Magi. 2007. 180p. 16.95 *(978-1-4327-0922-8(4))*; 212p. per. 9.95 *(978-1-4327-1412-3(0))* Outskirts Pr., Inc.
Hernandez, Janice. Lisa & the Light Dancer. 2009. 48p. pap. 9.95 *(978-1-60860-243-8(5)*, Eloquent Bks.) Strategic Book Publishing & Rights Agency (SBPRA).
Herrera, Joaquin. Horris, Little Eli & the Lens of Truth. 2007. (DreamFever Chronicles Ser.: Bk. 1). 208p. *(978-1-59258-245-7(1))* Hylas Publishing.
Hess, Brian F. Lynquest & the Search for Greatness. 2006. (ENG.). 116p. per. 19.95 *(978-1-4241-4503-4(1))* PublishAmerica, Inc.
Hewett, Katherine. Magic Bubble Bath. 2012. 40p. pap. 25.10 *(978-0-578-09202-7(6))* Hewett, Katherine J.E.
Hibbett, Myles. Zephyr Spheres & the Lost Spell. 2004. 156p. (YA). 22.95 *(978-0-595-66307-1(9))*; pap. 12.95 *(978-0-595-31395-2(7))* iUniverse, Inc.
Higgins, Jim. The Enchanted Nursery: Heather & Hamish, Fun in Florida, Reggie Rabbit at the Seaside, Percy Penguin's Friends. 2009. (Illus.). 36p. pap. 15.49 *(978-1-4389-9904-3(6))* AuthorHouse.
Higgins, Nadia. Hansel & Gretel & the Cheddar Trail, 1 vol. Johnson, Meredith, illus. 2009. (Fiona & Frieda's Fairy-Tale Adventures Ser.). (ENG.). 80p. (J). (gr. 2-5). 27.07 *(978-1-60270-574-6(7))* Magic Wagon.
—Sleeping Beauty & the Snapdragons, 1 vol. Johnson, Meredith, illus. 2009. (Fiona & Frieda's Fairy-Tale Adventures Ser.). (ENG.). 80p. (J). (gr. 2-5). 27.07 *(978-1-60270-576-0(3))* Magic Wagon.
—Snow White & the Candy Apple, 1 vol. Johnson, Meredith, illus. 2009. (Fiona & Frieda's Fairy-Tale Adventures Ser.). (ENG.). 80p. (J). (gr. 2-5). 27.07 *(978-1-60270-577-7(1))* Magic Wagon.
Hildahl, Violetta R. Peacock of Taj Mahal. 2011. 28p. (gr. -1). pap. 13.59 *(978-1-4520-0259-0(2))* AuthorHouse.
Hill, C. J. Slayers. 2011. (Slayers Ser.: 1). (ENG.). 384p. (YA). (gr. 7). 16.99 *(978-0-312-61414-0(4))* Feiwel & Friends.
Hill, Sarah. Posie Pixie & the Lost Matchbox. O'Gorman, Sarah, ed. Mauchline, Sarah, illus. 2013. 60p. pap. *(978-1-909302-31-0(7))* Abela Publishing.
Hill, Tony. The Curse of the Crooked Spire & Other Fairy Tales. 2013. (Illus.). 230p. pap. *(978-0-9568409-3-6(0))* Northern Lights Lit.
Hillyer, Rhonda. Butterfly Magic. Wood, Steve, illus. 2013. 84p. pap. 12.00 *(978-1-62212-306-3(9)*, Strategic Bk. Publishing) Strategic Book Publishing & Rights Agency (SBPRA).
Hilton, Marcel. The Magical Web. 2007. 38p. 19.50 *(978-1-4303-2678-6(6))* Lulu Pr., Inc.
Hilton, N. E. The Spell. 2010. (Illus.). 216p. pap. 15.95 *(978-1-4452-7791-2(3))* Lulu Pr., Inc.
hines, j. Finding Raven. 2007. 101p. pap. 8.95 *(978-0-615-17723-6(9))* Hines, Jerry.
Hines-Stephens, Sarah & Harper, Benjamin. Bug Girl. Syed, Anoosha, illus. 2017. (Bug Girl Ser.). (ENG.). 304p. (J). 14.99 *(978-1-250-10661-2(3)*, 9781250106612) Imprint IND. Dist: Macmillan.
Hinkler Books, ed. Ghostly Glow in the Haunted House. 2012. (Glow & Learn Ser.). (Illus.). 16p. (J). bds. 12.99 *(978-1-74308-808-1(6))* Hinkler Bks. Pty, Ltd. AUS. Dist: Ideals Pubns.
Hitchcock, Fleur. Sunk! A Shrunk! Adventure. 2016. (Shrunk! Adventure Ser.: 4). (ENG., Illus.). 240p. (J). (gr. 3-7). pap. 9.99 *(978-1-84812-448-6(1))* Bonnier Publishing GBR. Dist: Independent Pubs. Group.
Hliva, Diana. My Pet Lunecat. 2010. 36p. pap. 18.41 *(978-1-4269-3208-3(1))* Trafford Publishing.
Hoban, Russell. Rosie's Magic Horse. Blake, Quentin, illus. 2013. (ENG.). 40p. (J). (gr. -1-3). 15.99 *(978-0-7636-6400-8(6))* Candlewick Pr.
Hobbs, Will. Kokopelli's Flute. 2005. 148p. (gr. 5-9). 17.00 *(978-0-7569-5503-8(3))* Perfection Learning Corp.
—Kokopelli's Flute. 2005. (ENG.). 160p. (J). (gr. 5-9). pap. 7.99 *(978-1-4169-0250-8(3)*, Simon & Schuster/Paula Wiseman Bks.) Simon & Schuster/Paula Wiseman Bks.
Hocking, Amanda. Tidal. 2013. (Watersong Novel Ser.: 3). (ENG.). 352p. (YA). (gr. 7). 17.99 *(978-1-250-00811-4(5)*, 9781250008114, St. Martin's Griffin) St. Martin's Pr.
Hodgson, Julie. Earth Child. 2008. 81p. pap. 6.95 *(978-1-4092-2764-9(2))* Lulu Pr., Inc.
Hodgson, Sandra. The Toof Fairies. 2011. (Illus.). 44p. (gr. -1). pap. 16.76 *(978-1-4567-7978-8(8))* AuthorHouse.
Hoena, Blake. Witch's Brew. Bardin, Dave, illus. 2016. (Monster Heroes Ser.). (ENG.). 32p. (gr. 1-2). lib. bdg. 21.32 *(978-1-4965-3756-0(4))* Stone Arch Bks.
Hoffman, Judy. The Art of Flying: A Novel. Graegin, Stephanie, illus. 2014. (ENG.). 320p. (J). (gr. 3-7). pap. 7.99 *(978-1-4231-5907-0(1))* Hyperion Bks. for Children.
Hoffman, Nina Kiriki. Meeting. 2011. (Magic Next Door Ser.). (ENG.). 336p. (J). (gr. 5). E-Book *(978-1-101-52934-8(2)*, Viking Books for Young Readers) Penguin Young Readers Group.
Holbrook, John Robert. Gingerbread Jimmi: Magical Storybook. Scott, Catherine, ed. Stensaas, Martin & Strasburg, Sunny, illus. 2004. (J). 19.95 *(978-0-9762440-0-4(4))* Holbrook Studios.
Holbrook, L. E. Victoria & the Door to Travarmis. 2007. 108p. per. 19.95 *(978-1-4241-6934-4(8))* America Star Bks.
Holder, Nancy. Spirited. 2004. (Once upon a Time Ser.). (ENG.). 272p. (YA). (gr. 9). pap. 13.95 *(978-0-689-87063-7(9)*, Simon Pulse) Simon Pulse.
Holder, Nancy & Viguié, Debbie. Legacy & Spellbound. 2008. (Wicked Ser.). (ENG.). 672p. (YA). (gr. 9). pap. 8.99 *(978-1-4169-7117-7(3)*, Simon Pulse) Simon Pulse.
—Resurrection. 2009. (Wicked Ser.). (ENG.). 416p. (YA). (gr. 9-18). pap. 9.99 *(978-1-4169-7227-3(7)*, Simon Pulse) Simon Pulse.
Holland, Dwayne K. Princess Laura & the Magic Waterfall. 2010. 42p. pap. 15.50 *(978-1-60860-744-0(5)*, Strategic Bk. Publishing) Strategic Book Publishing & Rights Agency (SBPRA).
Holley, M. E. Jonah & the Last Great Dragon: Legend of the Heart Eaters. 2012. (ENG.). 149p. pap. 13.95 *(978-1-78099-541-0(5)*, Our Street Bks.) Hunt, John Publishing Ltd. GBR. Dist: National Bk. Network.
Holmes, Anna. Emmet's Awesome Day. Scholastic, Inc. Staff, illus. 2014. (LEGO: the LEGO Movie Ser.). (ENG.). 32p. (J). (gr. 1-3). pap. 3.99 *(978-0-545-79539-5(7))* Scholastic, Inc.
Holmes-Merritt, Angela. LINK Fairflies & Fairies. 2008. 36p. 17.50 *(978-0-615-17415-0(9))* AnglesInk.
Holmes, Sara. The Wolf Hour. 2017. (J). pap. ***(978-0-545-10798-3(9)***, Levine, Arthur A. Bks.) Scholastic, Inc.
Holthaus, Abbey. The Treasures of Christmas. Downs, Braden, illus. 2008. 126p. pap. 19.95 *(978-1-60672-152-0(6))* America Star Bks.
Holub, Joan & Williams, Suzanne. Sleeping Beauty Dreams Big. 2015. (Grimmtastic Girls Ser.: 5). lib. bdg. 16.00 *(978-0-606-36358-7(0))* Turtleback Bks.
—Snow White Lucks Out. 2014. (Grimmtastic Girls Ser.: 3). lib. bdg. 16.00 *(978-0-606-35852-1(8))* Turtleback Bks.
Holyoak, Kathleen & Summers, Sherry. Flowers in Heaven. 2009. 32p. pap. 14.49 *(978-1-4389-4607-8(4))* AuthorHouse.
Homeyer, Henry. Wobar & the Quest for the Magic Calumet. Yunger, Joshua, illus. 2012. (ENG.). 144p. (YA). (gr. 3-4). 19.95 *(978-1-59373-108-3(6))* Bunker Hill Publishing, Inc.
Hong, Lily Toy, illus. & retold by. Two of Everything. Hong, Lily Toy, retold by. 2012. (J). *(978-1-61913-138-5(2))* Weigl Pubs., Inc.
Honigsberg, Peter Jan. Pillow of Dreams. Morse, Tony, illus. 2004. 32p. (gr. k-4). 17.95 *(978-1-57143-076-2(8))* RDR Bks.
Hood, Ann. Amelia Earhart: Lady Lindy. Zilber, Denis, illus. 2014. (Treasure Chest Ser.: 8). (ENG.). 176p. (J). (gr. 3-7). 6.99 *(978-0-448-45731-4(8)*, Grosset & Dunlap) Penguin Young Readers Group.
Hook, Derek. He Walked & He Walked & He Walked. 2012. 110p. 23.95 *(978-1-937902-08-7(0))* Karina Library Pr.
Hoover, Leighnne W. Festus & his Fest Favorites. 2010. pap. 11.99 *(978-0-578-05051-5(X))* Word of Mouth Pr.
Hoover, P. J. The Navel of the World. 2013. (ENG.). 304p. (J). (gr. 6-9). pap. 8.95 *(978-1-933767-20-8(0))* CBAY Bks.
Hope, Harry S. The Elements of Lore - Volume 1 of the Books of Lore. 2008. 272p. pap. *(978-1-906210-83-0(7))* Grosvenor Hse. Publishing Ltd.
Hopkins, Jeanette. The Juggler. 2011. (Illus.). 32p. (J). 16.95 *(978-1-888160-58-1(6))* Ice Cube Pr., LLC.
Hoppe, Bethany A. Molly B. Golly's Wonderful Dancing Debut. Ayotte, Andie C., illus. 2013. 32p. 28.00 *(978-1-937763-85-5(4))* Published by Westview, Inc.
Horn, Sandra. Silkie. (Illus.). 89p. pap. 7.95 *(978-0-340-67265-5(X))* Hodder & Stoughton GBR. Dist: Trafalgar Square Publishing.
Horowitz, Alena Netia. The Tlytiettlym Tree. Horowitz, Alena Netia & De La Fuente, Mary, illus. l.t. ed. 2003. 64p. (J). per. 12.95 *(978-0-923550-42-4(9))* Tetrahedron Publishing LLC.
Houghton Mifflin Harcourt Publishing Company Staff. Girl Power 5-Minute Stories. 2015. (5-Minute Stories Ser.). (ENG., Illus.). 224p. (J). (gr. -1-3). 12.99 *(978-0-544-33925-5(8)*, HMH Books For Young Readers) Houghton Mifflin Harcourt Publishing Co.
Houle, Kelly. Gracie's Gallery: A Magic Mirror Book. 2008. (ENG., Illus.). 28p. (J). (gr. -1). 14.95 *(978-1-58117-784-8(4)*, Intervisual/Piggy Toes) Bendon, Inc.
Hounam, Donald. A Dangerous Magic. 2017. (ENG.). 352p. (YA). (gr. 5-12). 17.99 ***(978-1-5124-3232-9(6))*** Lerner Publishing Group.
Howard, A. G. A Splintered Companion. 2015. (ENG.). 240p. (J). (gr. 9-17). pap. 7.95 *(978-1-4197-1926-4(2))* Abrams, Inc.
Howard, Cheryl L. Mikhael the Mighty: Be True to Who You Are & You Can Never Go Wrong. 2009. 52p. pap. 18.50 *(978-1-60860-760-0(7)*, Strategic Bk. Publishing) Strategic Book Publishing & Rights Agency (SBPRA).
Howard, Grahame. The Wishing Book 3 - Extermination. 2010. 170p. (J). pap. *(978-1-905809-90-5(5))* Pneuma Springs Publishing.
Howard, Peggy Ann. Zorees: Land of Dreams. 2007. (YA). per. 16.95 *(978-0-9795519-0-1(0))* Dream Scape Publishing, LLC.
Howell, Heather. Emily's Ballet Recital. 2010. 32p. pap. 12.99 *(978-1-4490-8457-8(5))* AuthorHouse.
Howells, Andrea. Finding Peace & the True Soul. 2006. 60p. (J). per. *(978-0-9765072-4-6(2))* Tribute Bks.
Howland, Naomi. Latkes, Latkes, Good to Eat: A Chanukah Story. 2004. (ENG., Illus.). 32p. (J). (gr. -1-3). pap. 6.99 *(978-0-618-49295-4(X))* Houghton Mifflin Harcourt Publishing Co.
—Latkes, Latkes, Good to Eat Send-A-Story. 2011. (Send a Story Ser.). (ENG., Illus.). 32p. (J). (gr. -1-3). pap. 4.99 *(978-0-547-56690-0(5))* Houghton Mifflin Harcourt Publishing Co.
Hoyle, K. B. The Enchanted. 2016. (ENG., Illus.). (J). 29.99 ***(978-1-61213-399-7(1))*** Writer's Coffee Shop, The.
Hoylie, Gerry. Byron Unleashed. 2005. 60p. pap. 14.95 *(978-1-59113-670-5(9))* Booklocker.com, Inc.
Hru, Dakari. Joshua's Masai Mask. Rich, Anna, illus. 2013. (ENG.). 32p. (J). (gr. -1-5). pap. 9.95 *(978-1-880000-32-8(6))* Lee & Low Bks., Inc.
Hubbard, L. Ron, contrib. by. If I Were You: Literature Guide for Teachers & Librarians, Based on Common Core ELA Standards for Classrooms 6-9. 2013. (Stories from the Golden Age Ser.). (ENG.). 35p. (gr. 6-9). pap., tchr. ed. 14.95 *(978-1-61986-201-2(8))* Galaxy Pr., LLC.
Hubbell, Mary A. The Miracle of Annie's Ring. 2010. 138p. pap. 11.50 *(978-1-60911-530-2(9)*, Eloquent Bks.) Strategic Book Publishing & Rights Agency (SBPRA).
Hudson, Margaret Parker. The Blue Umbrella. 2005. (Illus.). (J). 15.95 *(978-0-9771301-0-8(X))* FayRe Pr.
Hudson, Wade. Places I Love to Go. 2008. (Illus.). 24p. (J). (gr. -1-3). 3.99 *(978-1-60349-008-5(6)*, Marimba Bks.) Hudson Publishing Group, The.
Huggett, Christopher. The Magic Man. 2011. 216p. pap. 24.95 *(978-1-4560-6701-4(X))* America Star Bks.
Hughley-Edwards, Phyllis. Nana's Magical Closet: First Edition. 2012. 24p. pap. 15.99 *(978-1-4797-3573-0(6))* Xlibris Corp.
Hult, Robert William. Time Dancer. 2004. (Illus.). (YA). pap. 14.00 *(978-0-9754114-0-7(3))* Hegemony Pr.
Humphreys, Neil. Picking up a Penguin's Egg Really Got Me into Trouble. Cheng, Puay Koon, illus. 2014. (Abbie Rose & the Magic Suitcase Ser.). (ENG.). 24p. (J). (gr. -1-3). pap. 9.90 *(978-981-4484-18-3(0))* Marshall Cavendish International (Asia) Private Ltd. SGP. Dist: National Bk. Network.
Hunt, Leo. Eight Rivers of Shadow. (ENG.). 368p. (YA). (gr. 9). 2017. pap. 9.99 ***(978-0-7636-9457-9(6))*** 2016. 17.99 *(978-0-7636-8994-0(7))* Candlewick Pr.
Hunt, Zoe Paton. Azrael's Magical Moment. 2008. 24p. pap. 18.95 *(978-1-60693-070-0(2)*, Strategic Bk. Publishing) Strategic Book Publishing & Rights Agency (SBPRA).
Hunter, Erin. The Burning Horizon. 2016. (Seekers: Return to the Wild Ser.: 5). (J). lib. bdg. 18.40 *(978-0-606-38147-5(3))* Turtleback Bks.
—Moonrise. Richardson, Owen & Stevenson, Dave, illus. 2015. (Warriors: the New Prophecy Ser.: 2). (ENG.). 336p. (J). (gr. 3-7). pap. 7.99 *(978-0-06-236703-7(X))* HarperCollins Pubs.
—Shadows of the Clans. 2016. (Warriors Ser.). (J). lib. bdg. 18.40 *(978-0-606-38146-8(5))* Turtleback Bks.
—Thunder Rising. McLoughlin, Wayne & Douglas, Allen, illus. 2014. (Warriors: Dawn of the Clans Ser.: 2). (ENG.). 368p. (J). (gr. 3-7). pap. 7.99 *(978-0-06-206352-6(9))* HarperCollins Pubs.
Hunter, Erin & Jolley, Dan. Bramblestar's Storm. 2016. (Warriors Super Edition Ser.). (J). lib. bdg. 18.40 *(978-0-606-38180-2(5))* Turtleback Bks.
Huntley, Tex. Catch a Wishing Star (Shimmer & Shine) Cartobaleno, illus. 2017. (Little Golden Book Ser.). (ENG.). 24p. (J). (-k). 4.99 ***(978-1-5247-1667-7(7)***, Golden Bks.) Random Hse. Children's Bks.
Hurwitz, Johanna. Magical Monty. McGrory, Anik, illus. 2013. (Monty Ser.). (ENG.). 112p. (J). (gr. k-4). pap. 5.99 *(978-0-7636-6457-2(X))* Candlewick Pr.
Hyperion Staff. Walt Disney World: Where Magic Lives 2006. 2006. (ENG.). 96p. (gr. -1-17). pap. 9.95 *(978-1-4231-0257-1(6)*, Disney Editions) Disney Pr.
I Am a Wish. 2013. 36p. pap. 16.99 *(978-1-4808-0094-6(5))* Archway Publishing.
Ibbotson, Eva. The Ogre of Oglefort. 2012. (ENG.). 272p. (J). (gr. 3-7). pap. 6.99 *(978-0-14-242135-2(9)*, Puffin Books) Penguin Young Readers Group.
The Indian in the Cupboard. 2004. (J). *(978-1-59564-280-6(3))* Steps To Literacy, LLC.
Inglis, Lucy. City of Halves. 2015. (ENG.). 368p. (J). (gr. 7). 17.99 *(978-0-545-82958-8(5)*, Chicken Hse., The) Scholastic, Inc.
Irvine, Kitty. Mysterious Moorings with Mouse. 2017. (ENG.). 96p. (J). pap. 11.95 ***(978-1-78693-220-4(2)***, 2bcedaac-1c94-4640-ab5f-7088dc6903a6) Austin, Stan AUS. Dist: Bookmasters Distribution.
Isern, Susanna. The Magic Ball of Wool. 2013. (ENG., Illus.). 32p. (J). (gr. -1-k). 16.95 *(978-84-15619-89-5(8))* Eastern National.
Island, Fiona. Wishbone's Magic Garden. 2006. (Illus.). 120p. pap. *(978-1-84401-733-1(8))* Athena Pr.
Ivanoff, George. Gamers' Quest. 2009. (Gamers Ser.: Bk. 1). (ENG.). 208p. (YA). pap. *(978-1-876462-86-4(8)*, Ford Street Publishing) Hybrid Pubs.
Jackson, Corrine. Ignited. 2014. (Sense Thieves Ser.). (ENG.). 368p. (YA). (gr. 13). pap. 9.95 *(978-0-7582-7335-2(5)*, K-Teen) Kensington Publishing Corp.
Jackson, Ruth Montgomery. A Bit of Magic with Wee Willie & Double Trouble. 2011. 76p. pap. 27.50 *(978-1-4567-0050-8(2))* AuthorHouse.
Jackson, Shirley. Nine Magic Wishes. 2015. (ENG., Illus.). 48p. pap. 9.99 *(978-0-486-79808-0(9))* Dover Pubns., Inc.
Jackson, Stephen. Mundoespejo. 2005. (SPA., Illus.). 28p. (J). (gr. 2-4). 15.95 *(978-84-666-1495-5(8))* Ediciones B ESP. Dist: Independent Pubs. Group.
James, Bethany & Shady, Leigh. Matilda Turnip's Endless Belly Button. 2010. (Illus.). 32p. (J). 12.99 *(978-1-60706-187-8(2))* Image Comics.
James, J. Alison. Eucalyptus Wings. Demi, illus. 2012. (ENG.). 36p. (J). (gr. k-3). 17.99 *(978-1-4424-7484-0(X)*, Atheneum Bks. for Young Readers) Simon & Schuster Children's Publishing.
James, M. R. The Five Jars. 2008. 96p. pap. *(978-1-84830-112-2(X)*, Wildhern Pr.) Echo Library.
Janesh, Ron. Anela Aparecida E O Vale Da Neblina Da Cachoeir. Gonçalves da Silva, Fabio, illus. 2012. 56p. pap. 20.50 *(978-1-60976-925-3(2)*, Strategic Bk. Publishing) Strategic Book Publishing & Rights Agency (SBPRA).
Jardine, Kathy & Jardine, Ashley. The Durples: Go to School. 2010. 28p. pap. 17.99 *(978-1-4490-3405-4(5))* AuthorHouse.
Jarman, Julia. The Magic Backpack. Gon, Adriano, illus. 2003. (Flying Foxes Ser.). (ENG.). 48p. (J). lib. bdg. *(978-0-7787-1487-3(X))* Crabtree Publishing Co.
Jeffers, Susan. The Nutcracker. Jeffers, Susan, illus. 2007. (Illus.). 40p. (J). (gr. -1-3). 17.89 *(978-0-06-074387-1(5))*; (ENG.). 17.99 *(978-0-06-074386-4(7))* HarperCollins Pubs.
—The Twelve Days of Christmas. Jeffers, Susan, illus. 2013. (ENG., Illus.). 40p. (J). (gr. -1-3). 17.99 *(978-0-06-206615-2(3))* HarperCollins Pubs.
Jeffers, Susan, illus. The Twelve Days of Christmas. 2013. (J). *(978-0-06-206616-9(1))* Harper & Row Ltd.
Jefferson, Barbara. The Luck of the Dragonfly. Jefferson, Daniel E., illus. 2008. 31p. pap. 24.95 *(978-1-60672-283-1(2))* America Star Bks.
Jenkins, Gloria. Storm: The Peace Maker. 2006. (J). pap. 8.00 *(978-0-8059-7116-3(5))* Dorrance Publishing Co., Inc.
Jennings, Terry Catasús. Magnetic Magic, 1 vol. Gabriel, Andrea, illus. 2016. (ENG & SPA.). 32p. (J). (gr. k-3). 17.95 *(978-1-62855-861-6(X))* Arbordale Publishing.
Jensen, Michael R. & King, David Powers. Woven. 2015. (Illus.). 344p. (J). *(978-0-545-83117-8(2)*, Scholastic Pr.) Scholastic, Inc.
Jerome, Louie. Peter & the Black Dog. 2009. 120p. 22.50 *(978-1-60693-737-2(5)*, Strategic Bk. Publishing) Strategic Book Publishing & Rights Agency (SBPRA).
Jesperson, Per. Wonder & Magic: The David Tales. 2003. 50p. pap. *(978-1-84401-017-2(1))* Athena Pr.
Jobling, Curtis. The Beast of Bone Creek. 2016. (Max Helsing: Monster Hunter Ser.: 2). (ENG., Illus.). 304p. (J). (gr. 5). 16.99 *(978-0-451-47480-3(5)*, Viking Books for Young Readers) Penguin Young Readers Group.
Joe, O'Brien. Alfie Green & the Magical Gift. Jean, Texier, illus. 2007. (Alfie Green Ser.). (ENG.). 80p. (J). pap. 10.95 *(978-1-84717-041-5(2))* O'Brien Pr., Ltd., The IRL. Dist: Dufour Editions, Inc.
Joe Thomson-Swift. The Magic Stone. 2011. 92p. pap. *(978-1-908105-83-7(6))* Grosvenor Hse. Publishing Ltd.
Johnson, D. B. Magritte's Marvelous Hat. Johnson, D. B., illus. 2012. (ENG., Illus.). 32p. (J). (gr. -1-3). 17.99 *(978-0-547-55864-6(3))* Houghton Mifflin Harcourt Publishing Co.
Johnson, Gerald J. J. A Boy Called Tiny Tim. 2013. 20p. pap. 24.95 *(978-1-62709-865-6(8))* America Star Bks.
Johnson, Gillian. Thora. Johnson, Gillian, illus. 2003. (Illus.). 128p. *(978-0-207-19815-1(2))* HarperCollins Pubs. Australia.
Johnson, Jane. Legends of the Shadow World: The Secret Country; the Shadow World; Dragon's Fire. Stower, Adam, illus. 2010. (ENG.). 1120p. (J). (gr. 3-7). pap. 14.99 *(978-1-4169-9082-6(8)*, Simon & Schuster Bks. For Young Readers) Simon & Schuster Bks. For Young Readers.
—The Secret Country. Stower, Adam, illus. 2007. (Eidolon Chronicles Ser.: 1). (ENG.). 336p. (J). (gr. 3-7). per. 15.99 *(978-1-4169-3815-6(X)*, Simon & Schuster Bks. For Young Readers) Simon & Schuster Bks. For Young Readers.
Johnson, Sandi. Dittle's Christmas Wish. Durant, Sybrina, ed. Sturgen, Bobbi, illus. 2014. 40p. (J). (gr. k-5). pap. 12.99 *(978-1-929063-65-9(2)*, 164) Moons & Stars Publishing For Children.
Johnson, Sarah Blake. Crossings. 2017. (YA). pap. 17.99 ***(978-1-4621-1957-8(3))*** Cedar Fort, Inc./CFI Distribution.

M
N
O

Johnston, E. K. Spindle. 2016. (ENG.). 368p. (YA). (gr. 9-17). 18.99 (978-1-4847-2228-2(0)) Hyperion Bks. for Children.

Johnston, Emily Kate. A Thousand Nights. 2015. (ENG.). 336p. (YA). (gr. 9-17). 18.99 (978-1-4847-2227-5(2)) Hyperion Bks. for Children.

Johnston, Tony. The Spoon in the Bathroom Wall. 2006. (ENG., Illus.). 144p. (J). (gr. 2-5). pap. 10.95 (978-0-15-205625-4(4)) Houghton Mifflin Harcourt Publishing Co.

Johnstone, G. L. Sleep Tight Nancy... 2012. (Illus.). 12p. pap. 18.30 (978-1-4772-1517-3(4)) AuthorHouse.

Jonell, Lynne. Grasshopper Magic. Dorman, Brandon, illus. (Magical Mix-Ups Ser.: 3). (ENG.). 112p. (J). (gr. 1-4). 2014. pap. 4.99 (978-0-307-93123-8(4)) 2013. 12.99 (978-0-375-87084-2(9)) Random Hse. Children's Bks. (Random Hse. Bks. for Young Readers).

—Hamster Magic. Dorman, Brandon, illus. 2012. (Magical Mix-Ups Ser.: 1). (ENG.). 112p. (J). (gr. 1-4). pap. 4.99 (978-0-375-86616-6(7), Random Hse. Bks. for Young Readers) Random Hse. Children's Bks.

—Wild Water Magic. Dorman, Brandon, illus. 2014. (Magical Mix-Ups Ser.: 4). (ENG.). 112p. (J). (gr. 1-4). 12.99 (978-0-375-87085-9(7), Random Hse. Bks. for Young Readers) Random Hse. Children's Bks.

Jones, Alexandra. Moon Magic. 2012. 28p. pap. 21.99 (978-1-4771-3995-0(8)) Xlibris Corp.

Jones, Carrie. Quest for the Golden Arrow. 2017. (Time Stoppers Ser.). (ENG.). 464p. (J). 16.99 (978-1-61963-863-1(0), 9781619638631, Bloomsbury USA Childrens) Bloomsbury Publishing USA.

—Time Stoppers. (Time Stoppers Ser.). (ENG.). (J). 2017. 400p. pap. 7.99 (978-1-68119-437-0(6), 9781681194370) 2016. 384p. 16.99 (978-1-61963-861-7(4), 9781619638617) Bloomsbury Publishing USA. (Bloomsbury USA Childrens).

Jones, Christianne C. How the Camel Got Its Hump, 1 vol. Rooney, Ronnie, illus. 2011. (My First Classic Story Ser.). (ENG.). 32p. (gr. k-3). pap. 7.10 (978-1-4048-7358-2(9), My First Classic Story) Picture Window Bks.

Jones, Christianne C. & Kipling, Rudyard. How the Camel Got Its Hump, 1 vol. Rooney, Ronnie, illus. 2010. (My First Classic Story Ser.). (ENG.). 32p. (gr. k-3). lib. bdg. 22.65 (978-1-4048-6075-9(4), My First Classic Story) Picture Window Bks.

Jones, Diana Wynne. Castle in the Air. 2008. (World of Howl Ser.: 2). 400p. (J). (gr. 3-7). pap. 7.99 (978-0-06-147877-2(6), Greenwillow Bks.) HarperCollins Pubs.

—Castle in the Air, 7 vols. 2009. (J). 94.75 (978-1-4361-6119-0(3)); 91.75 (978-1-4361-6121-3(5)); 70.75 (978-1-4361-6117-6(7)); 156.75 (978-1-4361-6116-9(9)); 73.75 (978-1-4361-6115-2(0)); 1.25 (978-1-4361-6112-1(6)) Recorded Bks., Inc.

—The Chronicles of Chrestomanci. (Chronicles of Chrestomanci Ser.: Nos. 1-2). (YA). (gr. 8-12). Vol. 1. 2007. 608p. pap. 8.99 (978-0-06-447268-5(X)) Vol. 2. 2007. 560p. pap. 8.99 (978-0-06-447269-2(8)) Vol. 3. 2008. 688p. pap. 8.99 (978-0-06-114832-3(6)) HarperCollins Pubs. (Greenwillow Bks.).

—The Chronicles of Chrestomanci Vol. 1: Charmed Life; The Lives of Christopher Chant, Vol. 1. 2007. (Chrestomanci Ser.). (YA). (gr. 5-8). lib. bdg. 19.65 (978-0-613-31070-3(5), Turtleback) Turtleback Bks.

—Conrad's Fate. 2006. (ENG., Illus.). 352p. (978-0-00-719087-4(5)) HarperCollins Children's Bks.

—Conrad's Fate. (J). 2006. (Chronicles of Chrestomanci Ser.: 3). 400p. (gr. 3-7). per. 6.99 (978-0-06-074745-9(5), Greenwillow Bks.) 2005. (Chrestomanci Ser.: No. 5). 384p. (gr. k-17). lib. bdg. 17.89 (978-0-06-074744-2(7)) 2005. (Chrestomanci Ser.: No. 5). 384p. (gr. 5-18). 16.99 (978-0-06-074743-5(9)) HarperCollins Pubs.

—Conrad's Fate: Read-Along/Homework Pack, 6 vols. 2005. (Chrestomanci Ser.: No. 5). (J). (gr. 5-8). 86.75 (978-1-4193-3551-8(0), 42039) Recorded Bks., Inc.

—Earwig & the Witch. Zelinsky, Paul O., illus. 2012. 128p. (J). (gr. 3-7). 15.99 (978-0-06-207511-6(X), Greenwillow Bks.) HarperCollins Pubs.

—Enchanted Glass. 304p. (J). (gr. 3-7). 2011. pap. 6.99 (978-0-06-186685-2(7)) 2010. 16.99 (978-0-06-186684-5(9)) HarperCollins Pubs. (Greenwillow Bks.).

—House of Many Ways. 2008. 404p. (J). 9.99 (978-0-06-147798-0(2), Greenwillow Bks.) HarperCollins Pubs.

—House of Many Ways, 7 vols. 2009. (J). 245.75 (978-1-4361-6127-5(4)); 100.75 (978-1-4361-6132-9(0)); 79.75 (978-1-4361-6128-2(2)); 102.75 (978-1-4361-6130-5(4)); 1.25 (978-1-4361-6123-7(1)) Recorded Bks., Inc.

—The Merlin Conspiracy. 480p. (J). 2004. (Magids Ser.: 2). (gr. 3-7). pap. 9.99 (978-0-06-052320-6(4), Greenwillow Bks.) 2003. (gr. 5-18). 17.89 (978-0-06-052319-0(0)) HarperCollins Pubs.

—The Pinhoe Egg. (J). 2007. (Chronicles of Chrestomanci Ser.: 6). 480p. (gr. 3-7). per. 7.99 (978-0-06-113126-4(1), Greenwillow Bks.) 2006. (Chrestomanci Ser.: No. 6). 528p. lib. bdg. 18.89 (978-0-06-113125-7(3)) HarperCollins Pubs.

Jones, Diana Wynne & Jones, Ursula. The Islands of Chaldea. 368p. (J). (gr. 3-7). 2015. pap. 9.99 (978-0-06-229508-8(X)) 2014. 17.99 (978-0-06-229507-1(1)) HarperCollins Pubs. (Greenwillow Bks.).

Jones, Elwynn. Frank's Frantic Friday. 2010. 40p. pap. 16.95 (978-1-60911-750-4(6), Eloquent Bks.) Strategic Book Publishing & Rights Agency (SBPRA).

Jones, Frewin. Destiny's Path. 2009. (Warrior Princess Ser.: 2). (ENG.). 352p. (YA). (gr. 8-18). 16.99 (978-0-06-087146-8(6), HarperTeen) HarperCollins Pubs.

—The Emerald Flame. 2010. (Warrior Princess Ser.: 3). (ENG.). 352p. (YA). (gr. 8-18). 16.99 (978-0-06-087149-9(0), HarperTeen) HarperCollins Pubs.

—The Seventh Daughter. 2009. (Faerie Path Ser.: 3). (ENG.). 352p. (YA). (gr. 8). pap. 9.99 (978-0-06-087110-9(5), HarperTeen) HarperCollins Pubs.

—Warrior Princess. 2009. (YA). 346p. lib. bdg. 17.89 (978-0-06-087144-4(X)); (ENG.). 352p. (gr. 7-18). 16.99 (978-0-06-087143-7(1)) HarperCollins Pubs. (Eos).

—Warrior Princess #2: Destiny's Path. 2010. (Warrior Princess Ser.: 2). (ENG.). 352p. (YA). (gr. 8). pap. 8.99 (978-0-06-087148-2(2), HarperTeen) HarperCollins Pubs.

Jones, Marcia Thornton & Dadey, Debbie. This Side of Magic. Stower, Adam, illus. 2009. (Keyholders Ser.: 1). (ENG.). 144p. (J). (gr. 2-5). 3.99 (978-0-7653-5982-7(0), 9780765359827, Starscape) Doherty, Tom Assocs., LLC.

—Wizards Do Roast Turkeys. Dreidemy, Joëlle, illus. 2007. 64p. (J). pap. (978-0-545-00235-6(4)) Scholastic, Inc.

Jordan, Claire. Fanakapan & the Fairies - a Children's Fairy Story. Skou, Nick, illus. 2013. 52p. pap. (978-1-78148-648-1(4)) Grosvenor Hse. Publishing Ltd.

Juster, Norton. Casello Magico. pap. 19.95 (978-88-452-3854-3(7)) Fabbri Editori - RCS Libri ITA. Dist: Distribooks, Inc.

Kaaberbøl, Lene. Heartbreak Island. 2005. (W. I. T. C. H. Adventures Ser.: Bk. 3). (Illus.). 105p. (J). lib. bdg. 11.00 (978-1-4242-0786-2(X)) Fitzgerald Bks.

Kaczka, Fallon. What about Oysters. 2010. 24p. 13.00 (978-1-4520-2066-2(3)) AuthorHouse.

Kagawa, Julie. The Iron Legends. 2012. (Iron Fey Ser.: 5). lib. bdg. 20.85 (978-0-606-26516-4(3), Turtleback) Turtleback Bks.

Kagna, Barbara. Magic of Masara. Gonzalez, Ashley, illus. 2010. 24p. pap. 12.50 (978-1-4490-5651-3(2)) AuthorHouse.

Kamachi, Kazuma. A Certain Magical Index, Vol. 1. Haimura, Kiyotaka, illus. 2014. (Certain Magical Index Ser.: 1). (ENG.). 224p. (YA). (gr. 8-17). 14.00 (978-0-316-33912-4(1), Yen Pr.) Orbit.

Kamon. Hooty & the Magic Power. Krit, Joey, illus. 2011. 36p. pap. 14.39 (978-1-4634-1042-1(5)) AuthorHouse.

Kann, Victoria. Emeraldalicious. Kann, Victoria, illus. 2013. (Illus.). 40p. (J). (gr. -1-3). (ENG.). 17.99 (978-0-06-178126-1(6)); lib. bdg. 18.89 (978-0-06-178127-8(4)) HarperCollins Pubs.

Karalius, Kimberly. Love Charms & Other Catastrophes. 2016. (Grimbaud Ser.). (ENG.). 384p. (YA). pap. 10.99 (978-1-250-08404-0(0), 9781250084040) Feiwel & Friends.

—Love Fortunes & Other Disasters. 2015. (Grimbaud Ser.). (ENG.). 368p. (YA). (gr. 7). pap. 9.99 (978-1-250-04720-5(X), 9781250047205) Feiwel & Friends.

Karcz, Lauren. The Gallery of Unfinished Girls. 2017. 352p. (YA). (gr. 8). 17.99 (978-0-06-246777-5(8), HarperTeen) HarperCollins Pubs.

Karre, Elizabeth. All You Are. 2014. (Gift Ser.). 120p. (YA). (gr. 6-12). (ENG.). pap. 7.95 (978-1-4677-4477-5(8)); lib. bdg. 27.93 (978-1-4677-3510-0(8)) Lerner Publishing Group. (Darby Creek).

—Certain Signals. 2014. (Gift Ser.). (ENG.). 112p. (YA). (gr. 6-12). pap. 7.95 (978-1-4677-4479-9(4), Darby Creek) Lerner Publishing Group.

Kate, Lauren. Teardrop. 2013. 441p. (YA). (978-0-385-38372-1(X)); (978-0-385-37491-0(7)) Random House Publishing Group. (Delacorte Pr).

—Teardrop. (Teardrop Ser.). (ENG.). (YA). (gr. 7). 2014. 480p. pap. 10.99 (978-0-385-74266-5(5), Ember) 2013. 464p. 18.99 (978-0-385-74265-8(7), Delacorte Pr.) Random Hse. Children's Bks.

Kate Smith Designs, illus. Who's Playing on the Farm? 2011. (Magic Bath Bks.). (ENG.). 8p. (J). (gr. -1-3). 5.99 (978-1-4380-7179-4(5)) Barron's Educational Series, Inc.

Kats, Jewel. Cinderella's Magical Wheelchair: An Empowering Fairy Tale. Kinra, Richa, illus. 2012. (J). 24p. 29.95 (978-1-61599-113-6(1)); 20p. pap. 16.95 (978-1-61599-112-9(3)) Loving Healing Pr., Inc.

Katz, Bebe Weinberg. Princess Claudia & the Freckles. 2007. 48p. per. 16.95 (978-1-4241-6446-2(X)) America Star Bks.

Kauffman, Tracy. Gwendolyn's Wish. 2012. 24p. (-18). 24.95 (978-1-62709-555-6(1)) America Star Bks.

Kaylor, J. Garcia. Animal Magic Coloring Pages. 2012. (ENG.). pap. 11.99 (978-1-4675-2458-2(1)) Independent Pub.

Kelley, Jane. The Book of Dares for Lost Friends. 2015. (ENG.). 304p. (J). (gr. 3-7). 16.99 (978-1-250-05087-8(1), 9781250050878) Feiwel & Friends.

Kellogg, Steven. The Pied Piper's Magic. Kellogg, Steven, illus. 2009. (ENG., Illus.). 40p. (J). (gr. -1-3). 16.99 (978-0-8037-2818-9(2), Dial Bks) Penguin Young Readers Group.

Kelly, Diana. Tamla Bear & the Magic Goblin. Walker, Jack, illus. 2013. 30p. pap. (978-1-78148-182-0(2)) Grosvenor Hse. Publishing Ltd.

Kelly, Kevin Vincent. Hattie Mcdimple Makes a Wish. 2012. 20p. pap. 24.95 (978-1-4626-8310-9(X)) America Star Bks.

Kelly, Tess. Buko's Journey. 2004. 262p. (YA). 26.95 (978-0-595-66864-9(X)) iUniverse, Inc.

Kemler, Nancy. Dragon Box: The Key to Magic. 2005. 108p. pap. 19.95 (978-1-4137-8445-9(3)) America Star Bks.

Kendall, Jack. The Magic Apple Tree. Bostrom, Sally, illus. l.t. ed. 2006. (ENG.). 48p. (J). per. 9.95 (978-0-9787740-4-2(3)) Peppertree Pr., The.

Kennedy, Kim & Kennedy, Doug. Hee-Haw-Dini & the Great Zambini. 2009. (ENG., Illus.). 32p. (J). (gr. k-2). 15.95 (978-0-8109-7025-0(2), Abrams Bks. for Young Readers) Abrams, Inc.

Kent, Jaden. #1: the Cave of Aaaaah! Doom! Bodnaruk, Iryna, illus. 2017. (Ella & Owen Ser.: 1). (ENG.). 112p. (J). (gr. 1-3). pap. 5.99 (978-1-4998-0368-6(0)) Little Bee Books Inc.

—#2: Attack of the Stinky Fish Monster! Bodnaruk, Iryna, illus. 2017. (Ella & Owen Ser.: 2). (ENG.). 112p. (J). (gr. 1-3). pap. 5.99 (978-1-4998-0369-3(9)) Little Bee Books Inc.

Kerr, P. B., pseud. The Day of the Djinn Warriors. 2008. (Children of the Lamp Ser.: 4). (ENG.). 400p. (J). (gr. 3-7). 7.99 (978-0-439-93216-5(5), Scholastic Paperbacks) Scholastic, Inc.

—The Eye of the Forest. 2009. (Children of the Lamp Ser.: 5). (ENG.). 432p. (J). (gr. 3-7). 17.99 (978-0-439-93215-8(7), Orchard Bks.) Scholastic, Inc.

—The Five Fakirs of Faizabad. 2011. (Children of the Lamp Ser.: Vol. 6). (ENG.). 448p. (J). (gr. 3-7). pap. 8.99 (978-0-545-12659-5(2), Scholastic Paperbacks) Scholastic, Inc.

Kessler, Liz. Emily Windsnap: Six Swishy Tails of Land & Sea. 2016. (Emily Windsnap Ser.). (ENG.). (J). (gr. 3-7). pap. 34.99 (978-0-7636-9223-0(9)) Candlewick Pr.

—Philippa Fisher & the Dream-Maker's Daughter. 2015. (Philippa Fisher Ser.: 2). (ENG.). 288p. (J). (gr. 3-7). pap. 6.99 (978-0-7636-7460-1(5)) Candlewick Pr.

—Philippa Fisher & the Fairy Godsister. 2015. (Philippa Fisher Ser.: 1). (ENG.). 288p. (J). (gr. 3-7). pap. 6.99 (978-0-7636-7462-5(1)) Candlewick Pr.

—Philippa Fisher & the Fairy's Promise. (Philippa Fisher Ser.: 3). (ENG.). (J). (gr. 3-7). 2015. 288p. pap. 6.99 (978-0-7636-7461-8(3)) 2010. (Illus.). 274p. 15.99 (978-0-7636-5031-5(5)) Candlewick Pr.

—Philippa Fisher's Fairy Godsister. 2008. (Philippa Fisher Ser.: 1). (ENG., Illus.). 256p. (J). (gr. 3-7). 15.99 (978-0-7636-4070-5(0)) Candlewick Pr.

Khan, Joshua. Shadow Magic. Hibon, Ben, illus. (ENG.). (J). (gr. 3-7). 2017. 352p. pap. 6.99 (978-1-4847-3788-0(1)) 2016. 336p. 16.99 (978-1-4847-3272-4(3)) Hyperion Bks. for Children.

Kharbanda, Priya. Flumpa & Bosly Learn the Magic Three Rs: Reduce, Reuse & Recycle. 2010. 32p. pap. 23.50 (978-1-4461-3602-7(7)) Lulu Pr., Inc.

Khoury, Jessica. The Forbidden Wish. (ENG.). 352p. (YA). (gr. 7). 2017. pap. 9.99 (978-1-59514-768-4(3)) 2016. 17.99 (978-1-59514-767-7(5)) Penguin Young Readers Group. (Razorbill).

Kibuishi, Kazu. The Cloud Searchers. 2015. (Amulet Ser.: 3). (ENG.). 208p. (J). (gr. 3-7). 24.99 (978-0-545-20884-0(X), Graphix) Scholastic, Inc.

—Escape from Lucien. 2014. (Amulet Ser.: Bk. 6). (ENG., Illus.). 224p. (J). (gr. 3-7). pap. 12.99 (978-0-545-43315-0(0), Graphix) Scholastic, Inc.

—Firelight. 2016. (Amulet Ser.: 7). (ENG., Illus.). 208p. (J). (gr. 3-7). 24.99 (978-0-545-83966-2(1)); pap. 12.99 (978-0-545-43316-7(9)) Scholastic, Inc. (Graphix).

—Firelight. 2016. (Amulet Ser.: 7). (ENG., Illus.). 224p. (J). (gr. 3-7). lib. bdg. 24.50 (978-0-606-38070-6(1)) Turtleback Bks.

—The Last Council. 2015. (Amulet Ser.: 4). (ENG.). 224p. (J). (gr. 3-7). 24.99 (978-0-545-20886-4(6), Graphix) Scholastic, Inc.

—Prince of the Elves. 2015. (Amulet Ser.: 5). (ENG.). 208p. (J). (gr. 3-7). 24.99 (978-0-545-20888-8(2), Graphix) Scholastic, Inc.

Kibuishi, Kazu, illus. Firelight. 2016. 197p. (J). (978-1-4806-9909-0(8)) Baker & Taylor, CATS.

Kimmel, Eric A. Anansi & the Magic Stick. Stevens, Janet, illus. 2003. (J). 25.95 incl. audio (978-1-59112-482-5(4)); pap. 39.95 incl. audio compact disk (978-1-59112-519-8(7)); pap. 37.95 incl. audio (978-1-59112-483-2(2)) Live Oak Media.

Kimmons, Janet M. The Jewel in the Attic & the Adventures of Tiger. Farmer, Zoe, illus. 2007. 108p. (J). (gr. 1-3). pap. (978-1-58690-028-1(5)) Mould, Paul Publishing.

King, J. R. Arianna Kelt & the Renegades of Time: Signature Edition, Wizards of Skyhall Book 2. 2008. (ENG.). 256p. (J). 18.95 (978-1-57545-165-7(4), Reagent Pr. Echo) RP Media.

—Arianna Kelt & the Wizards of Skyhall: Deluxe Edition, Wizards of Skyhall Book 1. 2008. (ENG.). 200p. (YA). per. 14.95 (978-1-57545-170-1(0)) RP Media.

KING, R. O. N. S. The emerald Fire. 2010. 166p. pap. 11.50 (978-1-4461-3748-2(1)) Lulu Pr., Inc.

—The Soul-pearl. 2010. 169p. pap. 11.50 (978-1-4457-5542-7(4)) Lulu Pr., Inc.

King, Zach. Zach King: My Magical Life. 2017. 208p. (J). (gr. 3-7). 18.99 **(978-0-06-267718-1(7))** HarperCollins Pubs.

Kingsley, Kaza. The Dragon's Eye. 2007. (Erec Rex Ser.). (Illus.). 384p. (J). (gr. 3-7). per. 9.99 (978-0-9786555-3-2(2)) Firelight Press, Inc.

—The Dragon's Eye. Grant, Melvyn, illus. 2009. (Erec Rex Ser.: 1). (ENG.). 368p. (J). (gr. 5-9). pap. 12.99 (978-1-4169-7933-3(6), Simon & Schuster Bks. For Young Readers) Simon & Schuster Bks. For Young Readers.

—Erec Rex: The Dragon's Eye. Payne, John, ed. Grant, Melvyn, illus. 2006. 360p. (J). 17.99 (978-0-9786555-6-3(7)) Firelight Press, Inc.

Kinra, Richa, illus. The Princess Panda Tea Party: A Cerebral Palsy Fairy Tale. 2014. 45p. (J). pap. 14.95 (978-1-61599-219-5(7)) Loving Healing Pr., Inc.

Kintz, Elizabeth. The Magic Hose. 2012. 30p. 16.95 (978-1-4575-1087-8(1)); pap. 14.00 (978-1-4575-0948-3(2)) Dog Ear Publishing, LLC.

Kirk, Daniel. Elf Realm: The High Road. (ENG., Illus.). 576p. (YA). (gr. 7-17). 2010. pap. 8.95 (978-0-8109-8979-5(4)) 2009. 19.95 (978-0-8109-4075-8(2)) Abrams, Inc. (Amulet Bks.).

—Elf Realm: The Road's End. 2011. (Elf Realm Ser.). (ENG., Illus.). 496p. (YA). (gr. 7-17). 18.95 (978-0-8109-8978-8(6), Amulet Bks.) Abrams, Inc.

Kirov, Erica. The Chalice of Immortality. 2011. (ENG.). 208p. (J). (gr. 4-7). pap. 7.99 (978-1-4022-1503-2(7), Sourcebooks Jabberwocky) Sourcebooks, Inc.

—Magickeepers: The Eternal Hourglass. Fortune, Eric, illus. 2010. (ENG.). 256p. (J). (gr. 4-7). pap. 10.99 (978-1-4022-3855-0(X), Sourcebooks Jabberwocky) Sourcebooks, Inc.

Kisinger, E. Jean. Firebug & the Mind Spark. Marta, Diana M., illus. 2012. 42p. pap. 12.50 (978-0-615-58954-1(5)) Firebug Fairy Tales.

Kitamura, Satoshi. Me & My Cat? Kitamura, Satoshi, illus. 2009. (ENG., Illus.). 32p. (J). (gr. k-k). pap. 12.95 (978-1-84270-775-3(2)) Andersen Pr. GBR. Dist: Independent Pubs. Group.

Kittredge, Caitlin. The Iron Thorn. 2012. (Iron Codex Ser.). (ENG.). 512p. (YA). (gr. 7). pap. 10.99 (978-0-385-73830-9(7), Ember) Random Hse. Children's Bks.

—The Mirrored Shard: the Iron Codex Book Three. 2013. (Iron Codex Ser.). (ENG.). 304p. (YA). (gr. 7). 17.99 (978-0-385-73833-0(1), Delacorte Bks. for Young Readers) Random Hse. Children's Bks.

—The Nightmare Garden: the Iron Codex Book Two. 2013. (Iron Codex Ser.). (ENG.). 432p. (YA). (gr. 7). pap. 10.99 (978-0-385-73832-3(3), Ember) Random Hse. Children's Bks.

Klein Bernstein, Sandy. The Door in the Sky. 2012. 268p. pap. 12.95 (978-1-4575-1111-0(8)) Dog Ear Publishing, LLC.

Klimo, Kate. The Dragon in the Driveway. Shroades, John, illus. 2010. (Dragon Keepers Ser.). (ENG.). 176p. (J). (gr. 3-7). pap. 6.99 (978-0-375-85590-0(4), Yearling) Random Hse. Children's Bks.

—The Dragon in the Sea. Shroades, John, illus. 2013. (Dragon Keepers Ser.: 5). (ENG.). 224p. (J). (gr. 3-7). 6.99 (978-0-375-87116-0(0), Yearling) Random Hse. Children's Bks.

—Dragon Keepers #3: the Dragon in the Library. Shroades, John, illus. 2011. (Dragon Keepers Ser.). (ENG.). 240p. (J). (gr. 3-7). 6.99 (978-0-375-85592-4(0), Yearling) Random Hse. Children's Bks.

—Dragon Keepers #4: the Dragon in the Volcano. Shroades, John, illus. 2012. (Dragon Keepers Ser.). (ENG.). 256p. (J). (gr. 3-7). 6.99 (978-0-375-86688-3(4), Yearling) Random Hse. Children's Bks.

—Dragon Keepers #6: the Dragon at the North Pole. Shroades, John, illus. (Dragon Keepers Ser.). (ENG.). 176p. (J). (gr. 3-7). 2014. 6.99 (978-0-375-87117-7(9), Yearling) 2013. 15.99 (978-0-375-87066-8(0), Random Hse. Bks. for Young Readers) Random Hse. Children's Bks.

Kline, Lisa Williams. Write Before Your Eyes. 2010. (ENG.). 192p. (J). (gr. 3-7). 6.99 (978-0-440-42251-8(5), Yearling) Random Hse. Children's Bks.

Klingele, Lindsey. The Broken World. 2017. 432p. (YA). (gr. 8). 17.99 **(978-0-06-238036-4(2)**, HarperTeen) HarperCollins Pubs.

Kloczko, Edouard. The Magical World of Tolkien. Camprubi, Krystal, illus. 2012. (ENG.). 28p. (J). (gr. 2). 24.95 (978-2-7338-2151-0(2)) Auzou, Philippe Editions FRA. Dist: Consortium Bk. Sales & Distribution.

K.M. Mohr, John Kelley and. Waking Dalifi. 2005. 72p. pap. 9.95 (978-1-4116-6364-0(0)) Lulu Pr., Inc.

Knickerbocker, S. J. King of the Ball. 2008. 24p. pap. 13.50 (978-1-60693-215-5(2), Eloquent Bks.) Strategic Book Publishing & Rights Agency (SBPRA).

Knight, Aya. The Chronicles of Kale: Dawn of Retribution. 2012. 456p. 28.95 (978-1-938083-13-6(X)); pap. 15.95 (978-1-938083-12-9(1)) Silver Knight Publishing, LLC.

Knox, Elizabeth. Mortal Fire. 2013. (ENG.). 448p. (YA). (gr. 7). 17.99 (978-0-374-38829-4(6), 9780374388294, Farrar, Straus & Giroux (BYR)) Farrar, Straus & Giroux.

Knox nee Ramsamugh, Lorna. Fire the Wolf & His Magical Kingdom, 1 vol. 2010. 24p. pap. 24.95 (978-1-4489-6677-6(9)) PublishAmerica, Inc.

Knudsen, Michelle. The Dragon of Trelian. (Trelian Ser.: 1). (ENG.). 416p. (J). (gr. 5). 2017. pap. 9.99 (978-0-7636-9454-8(1)) 2011. (Illus.). pap. 8.99 (978-0-7636-4993-7(7)) 2009. (Illus.). 16.99 (978-0-7636-3455-1(7)) Candlewick Pr.

—Mage of Trelian. 2016. (Trelian Ser.). (ENG.). 432p. (J). (gr. 5). 17.99 (978-0-7636-7436-6(2)) Candlewick Pr.

—The Princess of Trelian. (Trelian Ser.: 2). (ENG.). 448p. (J). (gr. 5). 2017. pap. 9.99 (978-0-7636-9455-5(X)) 2014. pap. 8.99 (978-0-7636-6935-5(0)) 2012. (Illus.). 16.99 (978-0-7636-5062-9(5)) Candlewick Pr.

Koch, Claus. The Three Little Wolves & the Big Bad Boar. 2011. 68p. pap. 9.99 (978-1-4520-5321-9(9)) AuthorHouse.

Koehler, Hanne Lore & Laraya-Coutts, Corie. A Tale of a Malipayon Warrior. 2010. 128p. 21.95 (978-1-4502-1344-8(8)); pap. 11.95 (978-1-4502-1346-2(4)) iUniverse, Inc.

Kohl, T. Michelle. The Magical Adventures of Bailey Boo the Cockatoo: When the Family's Away, the Parrots Will Play! 2012. 24p. pap. 24.95 (978-1-4626-6215-9(3)) America Star Bks.

Kok, Gemma. Explore. 2008. 44p. pap. 18.50 (978-1-4092-2058-9(3)) Lulu Pr., Inc.

—Explore (Printed in black & White) 2008. 44p. pap. 8.00 (978-1-4092-2530-0(5)) Lulu Pr., Inc.

Koller, Jackie French. The Wizard's Scepter. 2012. (ENG., Illus.). 176p. (J). (gr. 3-7). pap. 9.99 (978-0-689-85593-1(1), Aladdin) Simon & Schuster Children's Publishing.

Komorn, Julie, adapted by. Out of the Dark. 2004. (W. I. T. C. H. Ser.: Bk. 8). (Illus.). 128p. (J). lib. bdg. 16.92 (978-1-4242-0789-3(4)) Fitzgerald Bks.

Komorn, Julie & Lenhard, Elizabeth, adapted by. The Light of Meridian. 2004. (W. I. T. C. H. Ser.: Bk. 7). (Illus.). 144p. (J). lib. bdg. 16.92 (978-1-4242-0794-7(0)) Fitzgerald Bks.

Kongyin. Gooby & the Dreamwalker. 2011. 296p. pap. (978-0-9869858-4-3(8)) Kima Global Pubs.

Kontis, Alethea. Dearest, Bk. 3. 2015. (Woodcutter Sisters Ser.: 3). (ENG.). 288p. (YA). (gr. 7). 17.99 (978-0-544-07407-1(6), HMH Books For Young Readers) Houghton Mifflin Harcourt Publishing Co.

Korczak, Janusz. Kaytek the Wizard. Lloyd-Jones, Antonia, tr. from POL. 2012. (ENG.). 272p. (J). (gr. 4-7). 17.95 (978-0-9838685-0-7(6)) Flashlight Pr.

Korelitz, Jean Hanff. Interference Powder, 0 vols. 2006. (ENG.). 146p. (J). (gr. 4-7). pap. 7.99 (978-0-7614-5275-1(3), 9780761452751, Amazon Children's Publishing) Amazon Publishing.

—Interference Powder, 1 vol. 2003. (ENG.). 300p. (J). 15.95 (978-0-7614-5139-6(0)) Marshall Cavendish Corp.

Korte, Steve. Mxy's Magical Mayhem. Levins, Tim, illus. 2013. (Man of Steel Ser.). (ENG.). 88p. (gr. 2-3). pap. 5.95 (978-1-4342-4826-8(7)); 26.65 (978-1-4342-4488-8(1)) Stone Arch Bks.

Kova, Elise. Water's Wrath (Air Awakens Series Book 4) 2016. (ENG., Illus.). 378p. pap. 14.99 (978-1-61984-425-4(7)) Price World Publishing.

Kovalkova-McKenna, Svetlana & McKenna, Konstantin. Oberon. 2009. 44p. pap. 7.26 (978-0-557-06114-3(8)) Lulu Pr., Inc.

Kozlowsky, M. P. The Dyerville Tales. Thompson, Brian, illus. 2014. (ENG.). 336p. (J). (gr. 3-7). 16.99 (978-0-06-199871-3(0), Waldon Pond Pr.) HarperCollins Pubs.

Krakower, Harold. Sugarland: Josh & his magic Bed. 2011. 24p. (gr. -1). pap. 11.32 (978-1-4567-2957-8(8)) AuthorHouse.

—Sugarland: Princess Sarafina. 2011. 32p. (gr. 1-2). pap. 12.77 (978-1-4634-0123-8(X)) AuthorHouse.

Kramer, Stacy & Thomas, Valerie. Karma Bites. 2010. (ENG.). 348p. (J). (gr. 5-7). pap. 18.99 (978-0-547-36301-1(X)) Houghton Mifflin Harcourt Publishing Co.

Kravitz, Cathy. The Art Box. 2012. 30p. pap. 11.95 (978-1-4575-1262-9(9)) Dog Ear Publishing, LLC.

Krensky, Stephen. The Magic Pomegranate: A Jewish Folktale. 2009. pap. 40.95 (978-0-7613-4818-4(2)) Lerner Publishing Group.

—Too Many Leprechauns: Or How That Pot O' Gold Got to the End of the Rainbow. Andreasen, Dan, illus. 2007. (ENG.).

32p. (J). (gr. -1-1). 12.99 *(978-0-689-85112-4(X)*, Simon & Schuster Bks. For Young Readers) Simon & Schuster Bks. For Young Readers.

Kretzer, Kimberly. The Mystic Valley Adventures of Kody & Kory: The Journey Begins. 2008. 25p. pap. 24.95 *(978-1-60610-692-1(9))* America Star Bks.

Krouskop, Adrienne. The Bakers Moon. 2013. 24p. pap. 10.50 *(978-1-938743-92-4(X))* Reimann Bks.

Krulik, Nancy. All's Fair. John and Wendy Staff, illus. 2013. (Katie Kazoo, Switcheroo Ser.). (ENG.). 144p. (J). (gr. 2-4). pap. 5.99 *(978-0-448-45682-9(6)*, Grosset & Dunlap) Penguin Young Readers Group.

—Any Way You Slice It. John and Wendy Staff, illus. 9th ed. 2003. (Katie Kazoo, Switcheroo Ser.: 9). (ENG.). 80p. (J). (gr. 2-4). pap. 4.99 *(978-0-448-43204-5(8)*, Grosset & Dunlap) Penguin Young Readers Group.

—Attack of the Tighty Whities! Blecha, Aaron, illus. 2012. (George Brown, Class Clown Ser.: 7). (ENG.). 128p. (J). (gr. 2-4). pap. 4.99 *(978-0-448-45575-4(7)*, Grosset & Dunlap) Penguin Young Readers Group.

—Attack of the Tighty Whities! 2012. (George Brown, Class Clown Ser.: 7). lib. bdg. 14.75 *(978-0-606-23651-5(1)*, Turtleback) Turtleback Bks.

—Be Careful What You Sniff For, No. 1. Braun, Sebastien, illus. 2013. (Magic Bone Ser.: 1). (ENG.). 128p. (J). (gr. 1-3). pap. 5.99 *(978-0-448-46399-5(7)*, Grosset & Dunlap) Penguin Young Readers Group.

—Be Careful What You Sniff For. 2013. (Magic Bone Ser.: 1). lib. bdg. 16.00 *(978-0-606-31680-4(9)*, Turtleback) Turtleback Bks.

—Be Nice to Mice!, No. 20. John and Wendy Staff, illus. 2006. (Katie Kazoo, Switcheroo Ser.: 20). (ENG.). 80p. (J). (gr. 2-4). pap. 4.99 *(978-0-448-44132-0(2)*, Grosset & Dunlap) Penguin Young Readers Group.

—Camp Rules! John and Wendy Staff, illus. 2007. (Katie Kazoo, Switcheroo Ser.: No. 5). (ENG.). 160p. (J). (gr. 2-4). pap. 5.99 *(978-0-448-44542-7(5)*, Grosset & Dunlap) Penguin Young Readers Group.

—Catch That Wave. Braun, Sebastien, illus. 2013. (Magic Bone Ser.: 2). (ENG.). 128p. (J). (gr. 1-3). pap. 5.99 *(978-0-448-46444-2(6)*, Grosset & Dunlap) Penguin Young Readers Group.

—Catch That Wave. 2013. (Magic Bone Ser.: 2). lib. bdg. 14.75 *(978-0-606-31681-1(7)*, Turtleback) Turtleback Bks.

—Dance Your Pants Off!, No. 9. Blecha, Aaron, illus. 2013. (George Brown, Class Clown Ser.: 9). (ENG.). 128p. (J). (gr. 2-4). pap. 5.99 *(978-0-448-45679-9(6)*, Grosset & Dunlap) Penguin Young Readers Group.

—Dance Your Pants Off! 2013. (George Brown, Class Clown Ser.: 9). lib. bdg. 14.75 *(978-0-606-29802-5(9)*, Turtleback) Turtleback Bks.

—Doggone It! John and Wendy Staff, illus. 8th ed. 2006. (Katie Kazoo, Switcheroo Ser.: 8). (ENG.). 80p. (J). (gr. 2-4). pap. 4.99 *(978-0-448-43172-7(6)*, Grosset & Dunlap) Penguin Young Readers Group.

—Don't Be Such a Turkey! John and Wendy Staff, illus. 2010. (Katie Kazoo, Switcheroo Ser.). (ENG.). 160p. (J). (gr. 2-4). pap. 4.99 *(978-0-448-45448-1(3)*, Grosset & Dunlap) Penguin Young Readers Group.

—Don't Mess with the Ninja Puppy!, No. 6. Braun, Sebastien, illus. 2014. (Magic Bone Ser.: 6). (ENG.). 128p. (J). (gr. 1-3). 5.99 *(978-0-448-48095-4(6)*, Grosset & Dunlap) Penguin Young Readers Group.

—Don't Mess with the Ninja Puppy! 2014. (Magic Bone Ser.: 6). lib. bdg. 14.75 *(978-0-606-36162-0(6))* Turtleback Bks.

—Eww! What's on My Shoe? 2013. (George Brown, Class Clown Ser.: 11). lib. bdg. 14.75 *(978-0-606-32126-6(8)*, Turtleback) Turtleback Bks.

—Flower Power. John and Wendy Staff, illus. 2008. (Katie Kazoo, Switcheroo Ser.: 27). (ENG.). 80p. (J). (gr. 2-4). pap. 4.99 *(978-0-448-44674-5(X)*, Grosset & Dunlap) Penguin Young Readers Group.

—Follow That Furball. 2013. (Magic Bone Ser.: 3). lib. bdg. 16.00 *(978-0-606-32127-3(6)*, Turtleback) Turtleback Bks.

—Free the Worms! John and Wendy Staff, illus. 2008. (Katie Kazoo, Switcheroo Ser.: 28). (ENG.). 80p. (J). (gr. 2-4). pap. 3.99 *(978-0-448-44675-2(8)*, Grosset & Dunlap) Penguin Young Readers Group.

—Free the Worms! John & Wendy, illus. 2008. (Katie Kazoo, Switcheroo Ser.). 78p. (J). 11.65 *(978-0-7569-8807-4(1))* Perfection Learning Corp.

—Friends for Never, 14 vols. John and Wendy Staff, illus. 2004. (Katie Kazoo, Switcheroo Ser.: 14). (ENG.). 80p. (J). (gr. 2-4). pap. 4.99 *(978-0-448-43606-7(X)*, Grosset & Dunlap) Penguin Young Readers Group.

—Get Lost!, 6 vols. John and Wendy Staff, illus. 2006. (Katie Kazoo, Switcheroo Ser.: 6). (ENG.). 80p. (J). (gr. 2-4). pap. 4.99 *(978-0-448-43101-7(7)*, Grosset & Dunlap) Penguin Young Readers Group.

—Go Fetch! Braun, Sebastien, illus. 2014. (Magic Bone Ser.: 5). (ENG.). 128p. (J). (gr. 1-3). 4.99 *(978-0-448-48094-7(8)*, Grosset & Dunlap) Penguin Young Readers Group.

—Go Fetch! 2014. (Magic Bone Ser.: 5). lib. bdg. 14.75 *(978-0-606-35701-2(7))* Turtleback Bks.

—Going Batty. John and Wendy Staff, illus. 2009. (Katie Kazoo, Switcheroo Ser.: 32). (ENG.). 80p. (J). (gr. 2-4). pap. 4.99 *(978-0-448-45042-1(9)*, Grosset & Dunlap) Penguin Young Readers Group.

—Going Overboard! John and Wendy Staff, illus. 2012. (Katie Kazoo, Switcheroo Ser.: No. 9). (ENG.). 144p. (J). (gr. 2-4). pap. 5.99 *(978-0-448-45681-2(8)*, Grosset & Dunlap) Penguin Young Readers Group.

—Hair Today, Gone Tomorrow!, 34 vols., No. 34. John and Wendy Staff, illus. 2010. (Katie Kazoo, Switcheroo Ser.: 34). (ENG.). 80p. (J). (gr. 2-4). pap. 3.99 *(978-0-448-45231-9(6)*, Grosset & Dunlap) Penguin Young Readers Group.

—Hey! Who Stole the Toilet?, 8 vols. Blecha, Aaron, illus. 2012. (George Brown, Class Clown Ser.: 8). (ENG.). 128p. (J). (gr. 2-4). pap. 5.99 *(978-0-448-45576-1(5)*, Grosset & Dunlap) Penguin Young Readers Group.

—Hey! Who Stole the Toilet? 2012. (George Brown, Class Clown Ser.: 8). lib. bdg. 14.75 *(978-0-606-26075-6(7)*, Turtleback) Turtleback Bks.

—Holly's Jolly Christmas. John and Wendy Staff, illus. 2009. (Katie Kazoo, Switcheroo Ser.: No. 8). (ENG.). 160p. (J). (gr. 2-4). pap. 4.99 *(978-0-448-45218-0(9)*, Grosset & Dunlap) Penguin Young Readers Group.

—I Hate Rules! John and Wendy Staff, illus. 2006. (Katie Kazoo, Switcheroo Ser.: 5). (ENG.). 80p. (J). (gr. 2-4). pap. 4.99 *(978-0-448-43100-0(9)*, Grosset & Dunlap) Penguin Young Readers Group.

—I'm Game!, No. 21. John and Wendy Staff, illus. 2006. (Katie Kazoo, Switcheroo Ser.: 21). (ENG.). 80p. (J). (gr. 2-4). pap. 3.99 *(978-0-448-44133-7(0)*, Grosset & Dunlap) Penguin Young Readers Group.

—It's Snow Joke. John and Wendy Staff, illus. 2006. (Katie Kazoo, Switcheroo Ser.: 22). (ENG.). 80p. (J). (gr. 2-4). pap. 3.99 *(978-0-448-44396-6(1)*, Grosset & Dunlap) Penguin Young Readers Group.

—Karate Katie, 18 vols. John and Wendy Staff, illus. 2006. (Katie Kazoo, Switcheroo Ser.: 18). (ENG.). 80p. (J). (gr. 2-4). pap. 4.99 *(978-0-448-43767-5(8)*, Grosset & Dunlap) Penguin Young Readers Group.

—Katie Kazoo, Switcheroo: A Collection of Katie. John and Wendy, illus. 2008. (Katie Kazoo, Switcheroo Ser.: Bks. 1-4). (ENG.). 320p. (J). (gr. 2-4). 10.99 *(978-0-448-44910-4(2)*, Grosset & Dunlap) Penguin Young Readers Group.

—Let the Burping Begin. Blecha, Aaron, illus. 2012. (George Brown, Class Clown Ser.: 6). (ENG.). 384p. (J). (gr. 2-4). pap. 8.99 *(978-0-448-46284-4(2)*, Grosset & Dunlap) Penguin Young Readers Group.

—Magic Bone: Two Tales, One Dog. Braun, Sebastien, illus. 2016. (Magic Bone Ser.: 12). (ENG.). 192p. (J). (gr. 1-3). 6.99 *(978-0-448-48877-6(9)*, Grosset & Dunlap) Penguin Young Readers Group.

—Never Box with a Kangaroo #11. Braun, Sebastien, illus. 2016. (Magic Bone Ser.: 11). (ENG.). 128p. (J). (gr. 1-3). 4.99 *(978-0-448-48876-9(0)*, Grosset & Dunlap) Penguin Young Readers Group.

—Nice Snowing You! Braun, Sebastien, illus. 2014. (Magic Bone Ser.: 4). (ENG.). 128p. (J). (gr. 1-3). 5.99 *(978-0-448-46446-6(2)*, Grosset & Dunlap) Penguin Young Readers Group.

—Nice Snowing You! 2014. (Magic Bone Ser.: 4). lib. bdg. 14.75 *(978-0-606-34145-5(5)*, Turtleback) Turtleback Bks.

—No Biz Like Show Biz. John and Wendy Staff, illus. 2007. (Katie Kazoo, Switcheroo Ser.: 24). (ENG.). 80p. (J). (gr. 2-4). pap. 4.99 *(978-0-448-44440-6(2)*, Grosset & Dunlap) Penguin Young Readers Group.

—On Thin Ice. John and Wendy Staff, illus. 2007. (Katie Kazoo, Switcheroo Ser.: No. 6). (ENG.). 160p. (J). (gr. 2-4). pap. 5.99 *(978-0-448-44447-5(X)*, Grosset & Dunlap) Penguin Young Readers Group.

—On Your Mark, Get Set, Laugh! John and Wendy Staff, illus. 2004. (Katie Kazoo, Switcheroo Ser.: 13). (ENG.). 80p. (J). (gr. 2-4). pap. 4.99 *(978-0-448-43605-0(1)*, Grosset & Dunlap) Penguin Young Readers Group.

—Open Wide. John and Wendy Staff, illus. 2007. (Katie Kazoo, Switcheroo Ser.: 23). (ENG.). 80p. (J). (gr. 2-4). pap. 3.99 *(978-0-448-44439-0(9)*, Grosset & Dunlap) Penguin Young Readers Group.

—Quiet on the Set! John and Wendy Staff, illus. 10th ed. 2003. (Katie Kazoo, Switcheroo Ser.: 10). (ENG.). 80p. (J). (gr. 2-4). pap. 4.99 *(978-0-448-43214-4(5)*, Grosset & Dunlap) Penguin Young Readers Group.

—Red, White, & - Achoo! John and Wendy Staff, illus. 2010. (Katie Kazoo, Switcheroo Ser.: 33). (ENG.). 80p. (J). (gr. 2-4). pap. 3.99 *(978-0-448-45230-2(8)*, Grosset & Dunlap) Penguin Young Readers Group.

—Something's Fishy, No. 26. John and Wendy Staff, illus. 2007. (Katie Kazoo, Switcheroo Ser.: 26). (ENG.). 80p. (J). (gr. 2-4). pap. 4.99 *(978-0-448-44442-0(9)*, Grosset & Dunlap) Penguin Young Readers Group.

—Super Burp!, No. 1. Blecha, Aaron, illus. 2010. (George Brown, Class Clown Ser.: 1). (ENG.). 128p. (J). (gr. 2-4). pap. 5.99 *(978-0-448-45367-5(3)*, Grosset & Dunlap) Penguin Young Readers Group.

—Three Cheers For... Who? John and Wendy Staff, illus. 2011. (Katie Kazoo, Switcheroo Ser.: 35). (ENG.). 80p. (J). (gr. 2-4). pap. 3.99 *(978-0-448-45449-8(1)*, Grosset & Dunlap) Penguin Young Readers Group.

—Tip-Top Tappin' Mom!, 31 vols. John and Wendy Staff, illus. 2009. (Katie Kazoo, Switcheroo Ser.: 31). (ENG.). 80p. (J). (gr. 2-4). pap. 4.99 *(978-0-448-45041-4(0)*, Grosset & Dunlap) Penguin Young Readers Group.

—Trouble Magnet. Blecha, Aaron, illus. 2010. (George Brown, Class Clown Ser.: 2). (ENG.). 128p. (J). (gr. 2-4). pap. 5.99 *(978-0-448-45368-2(1)*, Grosset & Dunlap) Penguin Young Readers Group.

—The Twelve Burps of Christmas. Blecha, Aaron, illus. 2012. (George Brown, Class Clown Ser.: No. 1). (ENG.). 192p. (J). (gr. 2-4). pap. 5.99 *(978-0-448-45680-5(X)*, Grosset & Dunlap) Penguin Young Readers Group.

—The Twelve Burps of Christmas. 2012. (George Brown, Class Clown Ser.: No. 1). lib. bdg. 16.00 *(978-0-606-26652-9(6)*, Turtleback) Turtleback Bks.

—Vote for Suzanne. John and Wendy Staff, illus. 2008. (Katie Kazoo, Switcheroo Ser.: No. 7). (ENG.). 160p. (J). (gr. 2-4). pap. 4.99 *(978-0-448-44678-3(2)*, Grosset & Dunlap) Penguin Young Readers Group.

—Wet & Wild! #5, 5 vols. Blecha, Aaron, illus. 2011. (George Brown, Class Clown Ser.: 5). (ENG.). 128p. (J). (gr. 2-4). pap. 4.99 *(978-0-448-45570-9(6)*, Grosset & Dunlap) Penguin Young Readers Group.

—What's Black & White & Stinks All Over? Blecha, Aaron, illus. 2011. (George Brown, Class Clown Ser.: 4). (ENG.). 128p. (J). (gr. 2-4). pap. 5.99 *(978-0-448-45370-5(3)*, Grosset & Dunlap) Penguin Young Readers Group.

—Witch Switch. John and Wendy, illus. 2006. (Katie Kazoo, Switcheroo Ser.: No. 4). (ENG.). 160p. (J). (gr. 2-4). pap. 4.99 *(978-0-448-44330-0(9)*, Grosset & Dunlap) Penguin Young Readers Group.

—World's Worst Wedgie. Blecha, Aaron, illus. 2010. (George Brown, Class Clown Ser.: 3). (ENG.). 128p. (J). (gr. 2-4). pap. 5.99 *(978-0-448-45369-9(X)*, Grosset & Dunlap) Penguin Young Readers Group.

Krulik, Nancy & dePaola, Tomie. Dogs Don't Have Webbed Feet. Braun, Sebastien, illus. 2015. (Magic Bone Ser.: 7). (ENG.). 128p. (J). (gr. 1-3). bds. 5.99 *(978-0-448-48096-1(4)*, Grosset & Dunlap) Penguin Young Readers Group.

—Rootin' Tootin' Cow Dog #8. Braun, Sebastien, illus. 2015. (Magic Bone Ser.: 8). (ENG.). 128p. (J). (gr. 1-3). bds. 4.99 *(978-0-448-48097-8(2)*, Grosset & Dunlap) Penguin Young Readers Group.

Krulik, Nancy E. Broadway Doggie. 2016. (Magic Bone Ser.: 10). lib. bdg. 14.75 *(978-0-606-38416-2(2))* Turtleback Bks.

—Flower Power. John and Wendy Staff, illus. 2008. (Katie Kazoo, Switcheroo Ser.). 78p. (gr. 2-5). 14.00 *(978-0-7569-8806-7(3))* Perfection Learning Corp.

—Something's Fishy. John & Wendy, illus. 2008. (Katie Kazoo, Switcheroo Ser.). 76p. 14.00 *(978-0-7569-8348-2(7))* Perfection Learning Corp.

Krumm, Brian & Kortenkamp, Steve. Exploring Space & Beyond. 2015. (Exploring Space & Beyond Ser.). (ENG.). (gr. 3-4). 114.61 *(978-1-4914-6659-9(6)*, Connect) Stone Arch Bks.

Krys, Michelle. Hexed. 2014. (ENG.). 384p. (YA). (gr. 7). 17.99 *(978-0-385-74337-2(8)*, Delacorte Pr.) Random Hse. Children's Bks.

Kuipers, Jennifer L. Lynn's Magic Trunk: An Adventure in King Arthur's Court. 2007. 76p. per. 19.95 *(978-1-4241-9860-3(7))* America Star Bks.

Kulick Triscila, Verne. Joel & the Magic Toy Tree. 2005. 36p. (J). 11.99 *(978-1-4116-6985-7(1))* Lulu Pr., Inc.

Kulka, Joe. The Rope, 1 vol. 2008. (ENG., Illus.). 32p. (J). (gr. k-3). 16.99 *(978-1-58980-487-6(2))* Pelican Publishing Co., Inc.

Kulper, Kendall. Drift & Dagger. 2015. (ENG.). 368p. (YA). (gr. 7-17). 18.00 *(978-0-316-40453-2(5))* Little, Brown Bks. for Young Readers.

—Salt & Storm. 2014. (YA). *(978-0-316-40456-3(X))* Little Brown & Co.

Kunkel, Mike. Billy Batson & the Magic. Kunkel, Mike, illus. 2015. (Billy Batson & the Magic of Shazam! Ser.). (ENG., Illus.). 32p. (gr. 2-3). 226.00 *(978-1-4965-0290-2(6))* Stone Arch Bks.

—Billy Batson & the Magic of Shazam!, 1 vol. Kunkel, Mike, illus. 2014. (Billy Batson & the Magic of Shazam! Ser.). (ENG., Illus.). 32p. (gr. 2-3). 90.40 *(978-1-4342-9524-8(9))* Stone Arch Bks.

—Brother vs. Brother!, 1 vol. Kunkel, Mike, illus. 2014. (Billy Batson & the Magic of Shazam! Ser.). (ENG., Illus.). 32p. (gr. 2-3). 22.60 *(978-1-4342-9228-5(2))* Stone Arch Bks.

—Magic Words!, 1 vol. Kunkel, Mike, illus. 2014. (Billy Batson & the Magic of Shazam! Ser.). (ENG., Illus.). 32p. (gr. 2-3). 22.60 *(978-1-4342-9209-4(6))* Stone Arch Bks.

—Perilous Peril!, 1 vol. Kunkel, Mike, illus. 2014. (Billy Batson & the Magic of Shazam! Ser.). (ENG., Illus.). 32p. (gr. 2-3). 22.60 *(978-1-4342-9227-8(4))* Stone Arch Bks.

—The World's Mightiest Mortal!, 1 vol. Kunkel, Mike, illus. 2014. (Billy Batson & the Magic of Shazam! Ser.). (ENG., Illus.). 32p. (gr. 2-3). 22.60 *(978-1-4342-9226-1(6))* Stone Arch Bks.

Kurzweil, Allen. Leon & the Champion Chip. Bertholf, Bret, illus. 2005. 352p. (J). lib. bdg. 16.89 *(978-0-06-053934-4(8))* HarperCollins Pubs.

—Leon & the Spitting Image. Bertholf, Bret, illus. (ENG.). 320p. (J). (gr. 3-18). 2005. pap. 7.99 *(978-0-06-053932-0(1)*, Greenwillow Bks.) 2003. 16.99 *(978-0-06-053930-6(5))* HarperCollins Pubs.

Lacamara, Laura. Dalia's Wondrous Hair / el Maravilloso Cabello de Dalia. Baeza Ventura, Gabriela, tr. from SPA. Lacamara, Laura, illus. 2014. (ENG & SPA., Illus.). (J). 17.95 *(978-1-55885-789-6(3)*, Piñata Books) Arte Publico Pr.

Lackey, Mercedes & Edghill, Rosemary. Conspiracies. 2011. (Shadow Grail Ser.: 2). (ENG.). 352p. (YA). (gr. 8-12). pap. 19.99 *(978-0-7653-1762-9(1)*, 9780765317629, Tor Teen) Doherty, Tom Assocs., LLC.

—Shadow Grail #3: Sacrifices. 2013. (Shadow Grail Ser.: 3). (ENG.). 304p. (YA). (gr. 8-12). pap. 14.99 *(978-0-7653-1763-6(X)*, 9780765317636, Tor Teen) Doherty, Tom Assocs., LLC.

—Shadow Grail #4: Victories. 2014. (Shadow Grail Ser.: 4). (ENG.). 256p. (YA). (gr. 8-12). pap. 11.99 *(978-0-7653-1764-3(8)*, 9780765317643, Tor Teen) Doherty, Tom Assocs., LLC.

LaFevers, R. L. Theodosia & the Eyes of Horus. Tanaka, Yoko, illus. 2011. (ENG.). 384p. (J). (gr. 2-5). pap. 7.99 *(978-0-547-55011-4(1))* Houghton Mifflin Harcourt Publishing Co.

—Theodosia & the Serpents of Chaos. Tanaka, Yoko, illus. 2008. (ENG.). 352p. (J). (gr. 2-5). pap. 7.99 *(978-0-618-99976-7(0))* Houghton Mifflin Harcourt Publishing Co.

Lagonegro, Melissa. Barbie in Princess Power - Saving the Day! 2015. (Step into Reading Ser.). (ENG., Illus.). 24p. (J). (gr. -1-1). 4.99 *(978-0-553-50890-1(3)*, Random Hse. Bks. for Young Readers) Random Hse. Children's Bks.

Lagrow, Victoria. The Adventures of the Magical Hubcap Kid. 2005. pap. 33.49 *(978-1-4208-7981-0(2))* AuthorHouse.

LAIKA & Rosen, Lucy. Kubo & the Two Strings: His Adventure Begins. 2016. (ENG.). 24p. (J). (gr. -1-3). pap. 5.99 *(978-0-316-36140-8(2))* Little, Brown Bks. for Young Readers.

Laird, Donivee M. Ula Li'i & the Magic Shark. Jossem, Carol, illus. 2003. 49p. (J). (gr. k-3). 9.95 *(978-0-940350-23-6(8))* Barnaby Bks., Inc.

Lake, A. J. The Book of the Sword. 2007. (Darkest Age Ser.). (ENG.). 240p. (YA). (gr. 4-7). 16.95 *(978-1-59990-039-1(4)*, 9781599900391, Bloomsbury USA Childrens) Bloomsbury Publishing USA.

—The Coming of Dragons: The Darkest Age. 2007. (Darkest Age Ser.). (ENG., Illus.). 256p. (YA). (gr. 4-7). per. 7.99 *(978-1-58234-902-2(9)*, 9781582349022, Bloomsbury USA Childrens) Bloomsbury Publishing USA.

Lalicki, Tom. Danger in the Dark: A Houdini & Nate Mystery. 2010. (Houdini & Nate Mysteries Ser.: 1). (ENG.). 208p. (J). (gr. 3-7). pap. 14.99 *(978-0-312-60214-7(6)*, 9780312602147) Square Fish.

Lallemand, Orianne & Strickland, Tessa. The Blue Bird's Palace. Hénaff, Carole, illus. 2016. (J). *(978-1-78285-308-4(1))* Barefoot Bks., Inc.

Lamb, Anne. Beat Bugs: Magical Mystery Tour. 2017. (Beat Bugs Ser.). 24p. (J). (gr. -1-3). pap. 3.99 *(978-0-06-264062-8(3)*, HarperFestival) HarperCollins Pubs.

Lamb, Charles & Lamb, Mary. Tales from Shakespeare: "A Midsummer Night's Dream" Strang, Kay, ed. Andrews, Gary, illus. rev. ed. 2005. 39p. pap. 4.95 *(978-0-9542905-3-5(4))* Capercaillie Bks., Ltd GBR. Dist: Wilson & Assocs.

Lambert, Shirley. Tales of Beaver Hollow: The Magic Flute, 1 vol. 2009. 31p. pap. 24.95 *(978-1-60836-705-4(3))* America Star Bks.

Lamere, Jill. The King's Crown. 2007. (Illus.). 5p. (J). (gr. -1). vinyl bd. 14.95 *(978-0-9772320-2-4(6))* Minikin Pr.

Lampard, Frank. Frankie vs. the Knight's Nasties. 2016. (Frankie's Magic Soccer Ball Ser.: 5). (ENG., Illus.). 112p. (J). (gr. 2-5). pap. 4.99 *(978-1-338-08907-3(2))* Scholastic, Inc.

Lanagan, Margo. The Brides of Rollrock Island. (ENG.). (YA). (gr. 9). 2013. 318p. pap. 9.99 *(978-0-375-87336-2(8)*, Ember) 2012. 320p. 17.99 *(978-0-375-86919-8(0)*, Knopf Bks. for Young Readers) Random Hse. Children's Bks.

Lancett, Peter. Dark Words. 2007. (Dark Man Ser.). (ENG.). 36p. pap. *(978-1-84167-602-9(0))* Ransom Publishing Ltd.

Landy, Derek. And He's the Good Guy. Percival, Tom, illus. 2007. (Skulduggery Pleasant Ser.: 1). (ENG.). 400p. (J). (gr. 5-7). 17.99 *(978-0-06-123115-5(0))* HarperCollins Pubs.

—The Faceless Ones. (Skulduggery Pleasant Ser.: 3). (ENG.). 432p. (J). (gr. 5). 2010. pap. 7.99 *(978-0-06-124093-5(1))* 2009. 16.99 *(978-0-06-124091-1(5))* HarperCollins Pubs.

—Playing with Fire. (Skulduggery Pleasant Ser.: 2). (ENG.). (J). (gr. 5). 2009. 416p. pap. 7.99 *(978-0-06-124090-4(7))* 2008. 400p. 16.99 *(978-0-06-124088-1(5))* HarperCollins Pubs.

—Scepter of the Ancients. Percival, Tom, illus. 2008. (Skulduggery Pleasant Ser.: 1). (ENG.). 416p. (J). (gr. 5). pap. 7.99 *(978-0-06-123117-9(7))* HarperCollins Pubs.

Lane, Jessica E. The Secret of the Swans. 2009. 52p. pap. 31.99 *(978-1-4415-5517-5(X))* Xlibris Corp.

Lane, Leonie. The Retford Witch Catchers. 2005. 144p. per. *(978-1-84667-002-2(0))* Derwent Pr., The.

Lane, Nickel. The Ferret Crusaders: Quest of the Wish A Pod. 2nd ed. 2004. 73p. (J). per. 8.49 *(978-1-4116-0459-9(8))* Lulu Pr., Inc.

Lang, Andrew. The Violet Fairy Book. 2005. 404p. pap. 16.95 *(978-1-4218-0107-0(8)*, 1st World Library - Literary Society) 1st World Publishing, Inc.

Langdo, Bryan. Tornado Slim & the Magic Cowboy Hat, 0 vols. 2011. (ENG.). 32p. (J). (gr. k-4). 17.99 *(978-0-7614-5962-0(6)*, 9780761459620, Amazon Children's Publishing) Amazon Publishing.

Langton, Jane. The Dragon Tree. 2008. (Hall Family Chronicles). 176p. (J). (gr. 3-7). lib. bdg. 16.89 *(978-0-06-082342-9(9))* HarperCollins Pubs.

Laplante, Carole. The Magic Is in You. Byrne-Walker, Mary Ann, illus. 2012. 36p. pap. 9.95 *(978-1-62006-055-1(8))* Sunbury Press, Inc.

Larbalestier, Justine. Magic's Child. 2007. (Magic or Madness Trilogy). 291p. (YA). *(978-1-4287-3603-0(4)*, Razorbill) Penguin Publishing Group.

Larsen, C. S. The Chronicles of Marvin Archibald Trekker: Boy Magician Book 1 - Penguins of Choice. l.t. ed. 2006. (Illus.). 163p. (YA). per. 5.99 *(978-0-9779844-1-1(9))* KnowledgeGain Inc.

Larson, Sara B. Dark Breaks the Dawn. 2017. (ENG.). 320p. (J). (gr. 7). 17.99 ***(978-1-338-06869-6(5)***, Scholastic Pr.) Scholastic, Inc.

—Defy. 2014. (Defy Trilogy: Bk. 1). (ENG.). 336p. (J). (gr. 7). 17.99 *(978-0-545-59758-6(7)*, Scholastic Pr.) Scholastic, Inc.

—Endure. (Defy Trilogy: Bk. 3). (ENG.). 320p. (J). (gr. 7). 2016. pap. 9.99 *(978-1-338-09552-4(8))* 2015. 17.99 *(978-0-545-64490-7(9)*, Scholastic Pr.) Scholastic, Inc.

—Ignite. 2014. (Defy Trilogy: Bk. 2). (ENG.). 304p. (J). (gr. 7). 17.99 *(978-0-545-64474-7(7)*, Scholastic Pr.) Scholastic, Inc.

Lasaracina, Barbara. Mermaid Tears: A Magical Sea Tale. Peer, Nancy, illus. 2010. 28p. pap. 11.99 *(978-1-60844-451-9(1))* Dog Ear Publishing, LLC.

Lasky, Kathryn. More Than Magic. 2016. (ENG.). 224p. (J). (gr. 3-7). 16.99 *(978-0-553-49891-2(6)*, Lamb, Wendy Bks.) Random Hse. Children's Bks.

Laura Beth. Two Girls 2 Cats: A Magical Mystery, 1 vol. 2010. 130p. pap. 24.95 *(978-1-4489-4235-0(7))* PublishAmerica, Inc.

Laura Grey Wahl. The Magic Town of Stuart Easterly. 2009. 16p. pap. 15.00 *(978-1-4389-4703-7(8))* AuthorHouse.

Laurence, Matthew. Freya. 2017. (Freya Ser.: 1). (ENG.). 352p. (YA). 17.99 *(978-1-250-08817-8(8)*, 9781250088178) Imprint IND. Dist: Macmillan.

Law, Ingrid. Savvy. 2011. 9.68 *(978-0-7848-3575-3(6)*, Everbind) Marco Bk. Co.

—Savvy. (ENG.). (J). (gr. 4-7). 2010. 368p. 7.99 *(978-0-14-241433-0(6)*, Puffin Books) 2008. (Illus.). 352p. 18.99 *(978-0-8037-3306-0(2)*, Dial Bks) Penguin Young Readers Group.

—Savvy. l.t. ed. 2011. (ENG.). 500p. 23.99 *(978-1-4104-3530-9(X))* Thorndike Pr.

—Savvy. 2010. lib. bdg. 18.40 *(978-0-606-14394-3(7)*, Turtleback) Turtleback Bks.

—Scumble. (ENG.). (J). (gr. 3-7). 2011. 432p. 8.99 *(978-0-14-241962-5(1)*, Puffin Books) 2010. 416p. 17.99 *(978-0-8037-3307-7(0)*, Dial Bks) Penguin Young Readers Group.

—Scumble. l.t. ed. 2011. (Companion to the Newberry Honor Winner Savvy Ser.). (ENG.). 575p. 23.99 *(978-1-4104-3531-6(8))* Thorndike Pr.

—Switch. 2015. (ENG.). 368p. (J). (gr. 3-7). 16.99 *(978-0-8037-3862-1(5)*, Dial Bks) Penguin Young Readers Group.

Lawhorn, Mary Joyce. When Annie Dreams. 2012. 74p. pap. 8.95 *(978-1-4697-8819-7(5))* iUniverse, Inc.

Lawlor, Ashley. Ashley & the First Day of School. 2012. 24p. pap. 24.95 *(978-1-4626-6518-1(7))* America Star Bks.

Lawrence, C. H., illus. Aladdin or, the Wonderful Lamp. 2012. (Shape Bks.). (ENG.). 16p. pap. 9.95 *(978-1-59583-454-6(0)*, 9781595834546, Green Tiger Pr.) Laughing Elephant.

Lawson, Barbara. Huff the Magicless Dragon, 1 vol. Swope, Brenda, illus. 2009. 35p. pap. 24.95 *(978-1-61546-419-7(0))* PublishAmerica, Inc.

Lay, Kathryn. Book 1: Time & Space. 2016. (Time Twisters Ser.). (ENG.). (J). (gr. 2-6). lib. bdg. 27.07 ***(978-1-62402-177-0(8))*** ABDO Publishing Co.

Layton, Roxanne A. Henry & His Amazing MacHine. 2012. 32p. pap. 24.95 *(978-1-4626-6550-1(0))* America Star Bks.

Lazear, Suzanne. Fragile Destiny. 2014. (Aether Chronicles Ser.: 3). (ENG.). 432p. (YA). pap. 9.99 *(978-0-7387-3986-1(3)*, Flux) North Star Editions.

—Innocent Darkness. 2012. (Aether Chronicles Ser.: 1). (ENG.). 408p. (YA). pap. 9.95 (978-0-7387-3248-0(6), Flux) North Star Editions.

Le Gallienne, Richard. The Book Bills of Narcissus. 2004. reprint ed. pap. 15.95 (978-1-4191-5479-9(6)); pap. 1.99 (978-1-4192-5479-6(0)) Kessinger Publishing, LLC.

Le Guin, Ursula K. Tehanu. 2012. (Earthsea Cycle Ser.: 4). (ENG., Illus.). 288p. (YA). (gr. 7). 16.99 (978-1-4424-5995-3(6), Atheneum Bks. for Young Readers) Simon & Schuster Children's Publishing.

Le Guin, Ursula K. A Wizard of Earthsea. 2012. (Earthsea Cycle Ser.: 1). (ENG.). (YA). (gr. 7). 240p. 17.99 (978-0-547-85139-6(1)); 264p. pap. 8.99 (978-0-547-72202-3(8)); 320p. mass mkt. 8.99 (978-0-547-77374-2(9)) Houghton Mifflin Harcourt Publishing Co.

—A Wizard of Earthsea. 2012. (Earthsea Cycle Ser.: Vol. 1). (ENG.). (YA). (gr. 7). lib. bdg. 19.60 **(978-1-68065-210-9(9))** Perfection Learning Corp.

—A Wizard of Earthsea. 2012. (Earthsea Ser.: 1). lib. bdg. 19.65 (978-0-606-26624-6(0), Turtleback) Turtleback Bks.

Ledford, Mary"Aunt Sissy"Ledlowtranette. Cowboy Will & the Magic Rope. 2012. 32p. pap. 19.99 (978-1-4772-5167-6(7)) AuthorHouse.

Ledger, Kate. Twin Magic: School Bully, Beware! 2013. (Scholastic Reader Level 2 Ser.). (Illus.). 32p. (J). lib. bdg. 13.55 (978-0-606-31972-0(7), Turtleback) Turtleback Bks.

Lee, Brian. Bouncey the Elf & Friends - Bedtime St. 2005. (ENG., Illus.). 53p. pap. (978-0-7552-1023-7(9)) Authors OnLine, Ltd.

Lee, Howard. Jamshid & the Lost Mountain of Light. 2008. (ENG.). 248p. pap. 14.99 (978-1-4196-8958-1(4)) CreateSpace Independent Publishing Platform.

Lee, Jihyeon. Pool. 2015. (ENG., Illus.). 56p. (J). (gr. -1-k). 16.99 (978-1-4521-4294-4(7)) Chronicle Bks. LLC.

Lee, Karin. Zangadoo Kangaroo & the Mysterious Boomerang. Porterfield, Scott, illus. 2012. 94p. pap. 6.99 (978-0-9847428-2-0(4)) Zangadoo Entertainment.

Lee, Shell. Teenie's Treehouse Adventures: The Magic Begins. 2004. 37p. pap. 24.95 (978-1-4137-2879-8(0)) PublishAmerica, Inc.

Lee, Stacey. The Secret of a Heart Note. 2016. 384p. (YA). (gr. 8). 17.99 (978-0-06-242832-5(2), Tegen, Katherine Bks) HarperCollins Pubs.

Lee, Stan. The Dragon's Return. Tong, Andie, illus. 2017. (Zodiac Ser.). (ENG.). 448p. (J). (gr. 3-7). pap. 9.99 (978-1-4847-5255-5(4)) Disney Pr.

—The Dragon's Return. 2017. (Zodiac Legacy Ser.: 2). (J). lib. bdg. 20.85 (978-0-606-39500-7(8)) Turtleback Bks.

Lee, Stan & Moore, Stuart. Convergence. Tong, Andie, illus. 2015. (Zodiac Ser.). (ENG.). 488p. (J). (gr. 3-7). 16.99 (978-1-4231-8085-2(2)) Disney Pr.

—The Dragon's Return. Tong, Andie, illus. 2016. (Zodiac Ser.: Bk. 2). (ENG.). 432p. (J). (gr. 3-7). 16.99 (978-1-4847-1352-5(4)) Disney Pr.

LeGette, M. L. The Unicorn Girl. 2008. (ENG.). 416p. pap. 10.00 (978-1-4196-8696-2(8)) CreateSpace Independent Publishing Platform.

Legrand, Claire. Foxheart. Zollars, Jaime, illus. 2016. 480p. (J). (gr. 3-7). 16.99 (978-0-06-242773-1(3), Greenwillow Bks.) HarperCollins Pubs.

Lehane, Pearse. The Train That Never Came. 2008. 328p. pap. (978-1-84923-249-4(0)) YouWriteOn.

Lehman, Seth. The Color Pets. 2006. (Illus.). 52p. (J). 7.00 net. (978-0-9787986-0-4(0)) 4All Ages LLC.

Lehrman, Maggie. The Cost of All Things. 2015. (ENG.). 416p. (YA). (gr. 9). 17.99 (978-0-06-232074-2(2)) HarperCollins Pubs.

Lemire, Lillie. A Young Witch's Magical Adventure. 2006. (ENG.). 48p. per. 16.95 (978-1-4241-5413-5(8)) America Star Bks.

Lemke, Donald. The Mightiest Magic. 2015. (Justice League Classic 8X8 Ser.). (J). lib. bdg. 13.55 (978-0-606-37619-8(4)) Turtleback Bks.

Lenhard, Elizabeth. A Bridge Between Worlds. 2004. (W. I. T. C. H. Ser.: Bk. 10). 158p. (J). lib. bdg. 16.92 (978-1-4242-0796-1(7)) Fitzgerald Bks.

—Different Path. 2004. (W. I. T. C. H. Ser.: Bk. 13). 158p. (J). lib. bdg. 16.92 (978-1-4242-0791-6(6)) Fitzgerald Bks.

—The Disappearance. 2004. (W. I. T. C. H. Ser.: Bk. 2). 158p. (J). lib. bdg. 16.92 (978-1-4242-0799-2(1)) Fitzgerald Bks.

—Finding Meridian. 2004. (W. I. T. C. H. Ser.: Bk. 3). 158p. (J). lib. bdg. 16.92 (978-1-4242-0801-2(7)) Fitzgerald Bks.

—Power of Five. 2004. 158p. (J). lib. bdg. 16.92 (978-1-4242-0795-4(9)) Fitzgerald Bks.

Lenhard, Elizabeth, adapted by. The Disappearance. 2004. (W. I. T. C. H. Ser.). (Illus.). 144p. (J). 12.65 (978-0-7569-4620-3(4)) Perfection Learning Corp.

—The Return of a Queen. 2004. (W. I. T. C. H. Ser.: Bk. 12). 152p. (J). lib. bdg. 16.92 (978-1-4242-0797-8(5)) Fitzgerald Bks.

Lerangis, Peter. Whoa! Amusement Park Gone Wild! Talbot, Jim, illus. 2003. (Abracadabra Ser.: No. 7). (ENG.). 112p. (J). pap. 3.99 (978-0-439-38938-9(0), Scholastic Paperbacks) Scholastic, Inc.

—Wow! Blast from the Past! Talbot, Jim, illus. 2003. (Abracadabra Ser.: No. 8). (ENG.). 112p. (J). pap. 3.99 (978-0-439-38939-6(9), Scholastic Paperbacks) Scholastic, Inc.

Lesler, Rebecca. The Magic Stone: Return of Two Kings. 2008. 73p. pap. 19.95 (978-1-60610-101-8(3)) America Star Bks.

—The Truth of the Magic Stone, 1 vol. 2009. 107p. pap. 19.95 (978-1-60836-422-0(4)) America Star Bks.

Lessing, Edeltraut B. Amber & Flax. 2009. (978-1-61623-777-6(5)) Independent Pub.

Lethcoe, Jason. Der Geheimnisvolle Mr. Spines - Wings. Altmann, Scott, illus. 2009. (Mysterious Mr. Spines Ser.: 1). (ENG.). 256p. (J). (gr. 5-18). pap. 7.99 (978-0-448-44653-0(7), Grosset & Dunlap) Penguin Young Readers Group.

Lethcoe, Jason, illus. You Wish. 2007. 215p. (J). (978-1-4287-1806-7(0), Grosset & Dunlap) Penguin Publishing Group.

Levine, Gail Carson. The Two Princesses of Bamarre. (J). 2012. (ENG.). 272p. (gr. 3-7). pap. 6.99 (978-0-06-440966-7(X)) 2004. (Illus.). 304p. (gr. 7-18). reprint ed. pap. 6.99 (978-0-06-057580-9(8)) HarperCollins Pubs.

Levinson, Marilyn. Rufus & Magic Run Amok, 1 vol. 2005. (ENG.). 32p. (YA). pap. 5.95 (978-0-7614-5176-1(5)) Marshall Cavendish Corp.

Levy, Carol L. Elphy Grey. 2012. 24p. pap. 17.99 (978-1-4772-6687-8(9)) AuthorHouse.

Lewis, Anne Margaret. Fly Blanky Fly. Chavarri, Elisa, illus. 2012. (ENG.). 40p. (J). (gr. -1-2). 16.99 (978-0-06-199996-3(2)) HarperCollins Pubs.

Lewis, C. S. Las Cronicas de Narnia, 1 vol. Baynes, Pauline, illus. 2006. (Cronicas de Narnia Ser.). (SPA.). 816p. (gr. 4-7). pap. 19.99 (978-0-06-119900-4(1)) HarperCollins Pubs.

Lewis, Regina N. The Smallest Schoolhouse. Moore, P. M., illus. 2007. 56p. (J). pap. 12.95 (978-0-9776958-3-6(2)) CyPress Pubns.

—The Smallest Toy Store, A Christmas Story. Moore, Phyllis M., illus. 2004. 44p. (J). per. 12.95 (978-0-9672585-8-4(8)) CyPress Pubns.

Lewman, David. A Tale of Two Genies (Shimmer & Shine) Aikins, David, illus. 2016. (Big Golden Book Ser.). (ENG.). 32p. (J). (gr. -1-2). 9.99 (978-0-553-52200-6(0), Golden Bks.) Random Hse. Children's Bks.

Leyva, Barbara. Henry & the Magic Window. Leyva, Barbara, illus. l.t. ed. 2003. (Illus.). 50p. (J). 3.50 (978-0-9729056-0-2(X), 0, Balticbard Publishing) Leyva, Barbara.

Liberto, Lorenzo. Matt the Rat & His Sister Maggie (Raton Mateo y Su Hermana Maggie) When I Grow Up (Cuando Yo Crezca) Gomez, Rocio, ed. Torres, Irving, illus. 2003. (Matt the Rat Ser. / La Serie de Ratón Mateo). (SPA & ENG.). 40p. (J). lib. bdg. 20.00 (978-0-9743668-1-4(1)) Harvest Sun Pr., LLC.

Liberts, Jennifer. The Cake Monster. VanTuyle, David, illus. 2015. (Step into Reading Ser.). (ENG.). 24p. (J). (gr. -1-1). 4.99 (978-0-553-52314-0(7), Random Hse. Bks. for Young Readers) Random Hse. Children's Bks.

Liess, Claudia Schmidt. Henry the Magical, Mythical Dragon. 2008. 74p. pap. 19.95 (978-1-60672-956-4(X)) America Star Bks.

Liggett, Kim. The Last Harvest. 2017. (ENG.). 352p. (YA). 17.99 (978-0-7653-8098-2(6), 9780765380982, Tor Teen) Doherty, Tom Assocs., LLC.

Limb, Lisa. The Wishing Wheelchair. 2009. 40p. pap. 16.99 (978-1-4389-4205-6(2)) AuthorHouse.

Lindsay, Elizabeth. Annie Saves the Day. Eastwood, John, illus. 2003. 92p. (J). (978-0-439-44651-8(1)) Scholastic, Inc.

—Unicorn Dreams (Book 1) 2011. (Silverlake Fairy School Ser.). 96p. (J). pap. 4.99 (978-0-7945-3062-4(1), Usborne) EDC Publishing.

Lindsey, Norman. The Magic Pudding. 2011. 126p. (978-1-84902-497-6(9)) Benediction Classics.

Link, Kelly. Pretty Monsters. 2010. (ENG., Illus.). 416p. (YA). (gr. 7-18). 9.99 (978-0-14-241672-3(X), Speak) Penguin Young Readers Group.

Lipinski, Maureen. Cleopatra Ascending. 2013. (Shadow's Edge Novel Ser.: 2). (ENG.). 240p. (YA). pap. 9.99 (978-0-7387-3193-3(5), Flux) North Star Editions.

Lipka, Francine. Balloon Babies Inside Our Rainbows. 2009. 32p. (gr. -1). pap. 14.49 (978-1-4490-3118-3(8)) AuthorHouse.

Litke, Erin. Crystal Shards. 2007. 528p. per. 16.95 (978-1-4327-1548-9(8)) Outskirts Pr., Inc.

Little Dragon & the Magic Wagon. 2008. (Little Dragon Storybooks Ser.). 32p. (978-1-4075-1289-1(7)) Parragon, Inc.

Little, Judy. Yody & Bippy the Boo: Friends for Life. 2010. 28p. pap. 12.49 (978-1-4389-7145-2(1)) AuthorHouse.

Littlewood, Kathryn. Bite-Sized Magic: A Bliss Novel. McGuire, Erin, illus. (Bliss Bakery Trilogy Ser.: 3). (ENG.). 432p. (J). (gr. 3-7). 2015. pap. 7.99 (978-0-06-208427-9(5)) 2014. 16.99 (978-0-06-208426-2(7)) HarperCollins Pubs. (Tegen, Katherine Bks).

—Bliss. (Bliss Bakery Trilogy Ser.: 1). (ENG.). (J). (gr. 3-7). 2013. 400p. pap. 7.99 (978-0-06-208424-8(0)) 2012. 384p. 16.99 (978-0-06-208423-1(2)) HarperCollins Pubs. (Tegen, Katherine Bks).

—A Dash of Magic: A Bliss Novel. McGuire, Erin, illus. 2013. (Bliss Bakery Trilogy Ser.: 2). (ENG.). 368p. (J). (gr. 3-7). 16.99 (978-0-06-208429-3(1), Tegen, Katherine Bks) HarperCollins Pubs.

Littman, Sarah Darer. Charmed, I'm Sure. 2016. (ENG., Illus.). 208p. (J). (gr. 3-7). 17.99 (978-1-4814-5127-7(8), Aladdin) Simon & Schuster Children's Publishing.

Livingston, Lesley. Starling, No. 1. 2012. (Starling Trilogy Ser.: 1). (ENG.). 352p. (YA). (gr. 8). 17.99 (978-0-06-206307-6(3), HarperTeen) HarperCollins Pubs.

Llewellyn, Sam. The Well Between the Worlds. 2010. (Lyonesse Ser.: 1). (ENG.). 368p. (J). (gr. 3-7). 7.99 (978-0-439-93470-1(2), Scholastic Paperbacks) Scholastic, Inc.

Lloyd, Natalie. A Snicker of Magic. (ENG.). 320p. (J). (gr. 3-7). 2015. pap. 6.99 (978-0-545-55273-8(7)) 2014. 16.99 (978-0-545-55270-7(2)) Scholastic, Inc. (Scholastic Pr.).

—A Snicker of Magic. 2015. lib. bdg. 17.20 (978-0-606-37089-9(7)) Turtleback Bks.

Lloyd, Natalie, et al. A Snicker of Magic. 2014. (ENG.). mass mkt. (978-0-545-68447-7(1)) Scholastic, Inc.

Locurto, Ian N. The Christmas Penny. 2010. 20p. 11.99 (978-1-4490-7100-4(7)) AuthorHouse.

Loehr, Mallory. Unicorn Wings. Silin-Palmer, Pamela, illus. 2006. (Step into Reading Ser.: Vol. 1). (ENG.). 32p. (J). (gr. -1-1). per. 3.99 (978-0-375-83117-1(7), Random Hse. Bks. for Young Readers) Random Hse. Children's Bks.

Loftin, Nikki. Nightingale's Nest. (ENG.). (J). (gr. 3-7). 2015. 272p. pap. 8.99 (978-1-59514-623-6(7)) 2014. 256p. 16.99 (978-1-59514-546-8(X)) Penguin Young Readers Group. (Razorbill).

Logan, Christopher. Daphne. 2008. 145p. pap. 18.95 (978-1-4357-5038-8(1)) Lulu Pr., Inc.

Loiske, Jennifer. Black Diamond. 2013. 246p. (J). pap. 13.61 (978-1-291-30145-8(3)) Lulu Pr., Inc.

Loiske, Jennifer, et al. Tales of an Old Wizard. 2013. 116p. pap. 10.58 (978-1-291-30601-9(3)) Lulu Pr., Inc.

Long, Loren & Bildner, Phil. Great Balls of Fire. Long, Loren, illus. 2009. (Sluggers Ser.: 3). (ENG., Illus.). 224p. (J). (gr. 3-7). pap. 7.99 (978-1-4169-1889-9(2), Simon & Schuster Bks. For Young Readers) Simon & Schuster Bks. For Young Readers.

Long, Matty. Super Happy Magic Forest. Long, Matty, illus. 2016. (ENG., Illus.). 32p. (J). (gr. -1-3). 17.99 (978-0-545-86059-8(8), Scholastic Pr.) Scholastic, Inc.

—Super Slug of Doom: A Super Happy Magic Forest Story. Long, Matty, illus. 2017. (ENG., Illus.). 32p. (J). (gr. -1-3). 17.99 (978-1-338-05435-4(X), Scholastic Pr.) Scholastic, Inc.

Long, Susan Hill. The Magic Mirror: Concerning a Lonely Princess, a Foundling Girl, a Scheming King & a Pickpocket Squirrel. 2016. (ENG., Illus.). 320p. (J). (gr. 3-7). 16.99 (978-0-553-51134-5(3), Knopf Bks. for Young Readers) Random Hse. Children's Bks.

Longus. The ADVENTURES of SILVANA & the MAGIC UNICORN. 2008. 48p. 18.95 (978-1-4357-1877-7(1)) Lulu Pr., Inc.

Look, Lenore. Ruby Lu, Brave & True. Wilsdorf, Anne, illus. 2006. (Ruby Lu Ser.). 105p. (J). (gr. 1-5). 11.65 (978-0-7569-6553-2(5)) Perfection Learning Corp.

Lopez, David Mark. Run Like a Fugitive. 2006. (J). (gr. 4-8). (978-0-9744097-2-6(3)) Lopez, David.

—Walk Like an Egyptian. 2006. (J). (gr. 3-7). (978-0-9744097-0-2(7)) Lopez, David.

Losure, Mary. Backwards Moon. 2014. (ENG.). 144p. (J). (gr. 2-5). 16.95 (978-0-8234-3160-1(6)) Holiday Hse., Inc.

Love, D. Anne. The Secret Prince. 2012. (ENG.). 240p. (J). (gr. 3-7). pap. 11.99 (978-1-4424-5931-1(X), McElderry, Margaret K. Bks.) McElderry, Margaret K. Bks.

Love, Emily. The Beginning of Freedom. 2010. 81p. pap. 9.00 (978-0-557-56598-6(7)) Lulu Pr., Inc.

Loveridge, Pamela. The Knife of Blood. 2012. 28p. pap. 32.70 (978-1-4797-4804-4(8)) Xlibris Corp.

Lovhaug, Lewis J. Angel Armor: The Cassandra Conflict. 2004. 188p. (YA). pap. 13.95 (978-0-595-30869-9(4)) iUniverse, Inc.

Lowe, Natasha. The Courage of Cat Campbell. 2015. (Poppy Pendle Ser.). (ENG., Illus.). 288p. (J). (gr. 3-7). 16.99 (978-1-4814-1870-6(X), Simon & Schuster/Paula Wiseman Bks.) Simon & Schuster/Paula Wiseman Bks.

—The Marvelous Magic of Miss Mabel. 2016. (Poppy Pendle Ser.). (ENG., Illus.). 288p. (J). (gr. 3-7). 16.99 (978-1-4814-6533-5(3), Simon & Schuster/Paula Wiseman Bks.) Simon & Schuster/Paula Wiseman Bks.

—The Power of Poppy Pendle. (Poppy Pendle Ser.). (ENG., 272p. (J). (gr. 3-7). 2013. Illus.). pap. 7.99 (978-1-4424-4926-8(8)) 2012. 16.99 (978-1-4424-4679-3(X)) Simon & Schuster/Paula Wiseman Bks. (Simon & Schuster/Paula Wiseman Bks.).

Lowe, Wesley. The Griffin's Gauntlet. 2003. (Illus.). (YA). per. 14.95 (978-0-9723011-2-1(7)) Helm Publishing.

Lowes, Sarah. The Snow Queen. Clara, Miss, illus. 2013. (ENG.). 64p. (J). 17.99 (978-1-84686-964-8(1)) Barefoot Bks., Inc.

Lubar, David. Dinosaur Disaster. Loveridge, Matt, illus. 2013. (Looniverse Ser.: 3). (ENG.). 96p. (J). (gr. 1-3). 15.99 (978-0-545-49605-6(5)); pap. 4.99 (978-0-545-49606-3(3)) Scholastic, Inc.

—Dinosaur Disaster. 2013. (Looniverse Ser.: 3). lib. bdg. 14.75 (978-0-606-32367-3(8), Turtleback) Turtleback Bks.

—Meltdown Madness. Loveridge, Matt, illus. 2013. (Looniverse Ser.: 2). (ENG.). 96p. (J). (gr. 1-3). 15.99 (978-0-545-49603-2(9)); pap. 4.99 (978-0-545-49604-9(7)) Scholastic, Inc.

—Meltdown Madness. 2013. (Looniverse Ser.: 2). lib. bdg. 14.75 (978-0-606-31983-6(2), Turtleback) Turtleback Bks.

—Stranger Things. Loveridge, Matt, illus. 2013. (Looniverse Ser.: 1). (ENG.). 96p. (J). (gr. 1-3). pap. 4.99 (978-0-545-49602-5(0)) Scholastic, Inc.

—Stranger Things. 2013. (Looniverse Ser.: 1). lib. bdg. 14.75 (978-0-606-31982-9(4), Turtleback) Turtleback Bks.

—Wizards of the Game. 2004. (ENG.). 176p. (J). (gr. 3-7). 6.99 (978-0-14-240215-3(X), Puffin Books) Penguin Young Readers Group.

Lucas, David. The Lying Carpet. Lucas, David, illus. 2011. (ENG., Illus.). 78p. (J). (gr. 4-7). 15.99 (978-1-84270-441-7(9)) Andersen Pr. GBR. Dist: Independent Pubs. Group.

Luciano, Sonia. Mr. I Forgot. 2009. 48p. pap. 16.95 (978-1-61582-765-7(X)) America Star Bks.

Lück, Stefanie. Carla's Worlds. 2010. 222p. pap. 20.90 (978-3-8391-4857-0(X)) Bks. on Demand.

Luiken, Nicole. In Truth & Ashes. 2016. (ENG., Illus.). (YA). pap. 19.99 **(978-1-68281-388-1(6))** Entangled Publishing, LLC.

Lundquist, Jenny. Seeing Cinderella. 2012. (Mix Ser.). (ENG.). 240p. (J). (gr. 4-8). pap. 6.99 (978-1-4424-2926-0(7), Aladdin) Simon & Schuster Children's Publishing.

—Seeing Cinderella. 2012. (ENG.). 240p. (J). (gr. 4-8). 16.99 (978-1-4424-4550-5(5), Simon & Schuster/Paula Wiseman Bks.) Simon & Schuster/Paula Wiseman Bks.

Lunetta, Demitria. Bad Blood. 2017. (ENG.). 272p. (YA). (gr. 7). 17.99 (978-1-101-93805-8(6), Delacorte Pr.) Random Hse. Children's Bks.

Luper, Eric. The Haunted Howl. 2016. (Key Hunters Ser.: 3). (ENG., Illus.). 128p. (J). (gr. 2-5). pap. 4.99 (978-0-545-82211-4(4), Scholastic Paperbacks) Scholastic, Inc.

—The Mysterious Moonstone. 2016. (Key Hunters Ser.: 1). (ENG., Illus.). 128p. (J). (gr. 2-5). pap. 4.99 (978-0-545-82204-6(1)) Scholastic, Inc.

—The Spy's Secret. 2016. (Key Hunters Ser.: 2). (ENG.). 128p. (J). (gr. 2-5). pap. 4.99 (978-0-545-82206-0(8)) Scholastic, Inc.

—The Titanic Treasure (Key Hunters #5) 2017. (Key Hunters Ser.: 5). (ENG.). 128p. (J). (gr. 2-5). lib. bdg. 16.99 **(978-1-338-14927-2(X)**, Scholastic Paperbacks) Scholastic, Inc.

Luper, Eric. The Wizard's War (Key Hunters #4) 2017. (Key Hunters Ser.: 4). (ENG.). 128p. (J). (gr. 2-5). pap. 4.99 (978-0-545-82213-8(0), Scholastic Paperbacks) Scholastic, Inc.

Lupton, Hugh & Barefoot Books. Tales of Mystery & Magic. Baruzzi, Agnese, illus. 2015. 64p. (J). (gr. -1-2). 16.99 (978-1-78285-254-4(9)) Barefoot Bks., Inc.

Lurie, Craig. Butterflies, Ladybugs, & Bumble Bees & the wonderful world this could Be ... . 2011. 36p. (gr. -1). pap. 14.95 (978-1-4567-6300-8(8)) AuthorHouse.

Lynn, Deidre. Treasure Delight: A Sweet Story about the Joy in Sharing. Morris, Jessica, illus. 2013. 36p. pap. 12.95 (978-0-9893181-0-5(9)) LoveLight Media.

Lyons Stroud, Patricia. The Seven Keys to Adventure. 2007. 148p. 23.00 (978-1-59048-252-0(2)) Long Riders' Guild Pr., The.

Maberry, Jonathan. The Orphan Army. 2015. (Nightsiders Ser.: 1). (ENG., Illus.). 400p. (J). (gr. 3-7). 16.99 (978-1-4814-1575-0(1), Simon & Schuster Bks. For Young Readers) Simon & Schuster Bks. For Young Readers.

—The Orphan Army. 2016. (Nightsiders Ser.: 1). lib. bdg. 18.40 (978-0-606-38959-4(8)) Turtleback Bks.

—Vault of Shadows. (Nightsiders Ser.: 2). (ENG.). 464p. (J). (gr. 3-7). 2017. pap. 8.99 (978-1-4814-1579-8(4)) 2016. (Illus.). 16.99 (978-1-4814-1578-1(6)) Simon & Schuster Bks. For Young Readers. (Simon & Schuster Bks. For Young Readers).

MacDonald, Betty Bard. Hello, Mrs. Piggle-Wiggle. Knight, Hilary & Boiger, Alexandra, illus. 2007. (ENG.). 176p. (J). (gr. 3-7). 16.99 (978-0-397-31715-8(8)); pap. 5.99 (978-0-06-440149-4(9)) HarperCollins Pubs.

—Mrs. Piggle-Wiggle's Magic. Knight, Hilary & Boiger, Alexandra, illus. 2007. (Trophy Bk.). (ENG.). 192p. (J). (gr. 3-7). pap. 5.99 (978-0-06-440151-7(0)) HarperCollins Pubs.

MacDonald, George. The Light Princess. 110p. (J). (gr. 4-5). pap. 5.95 (978-0-8072-1396-4(9), Listening Library) Random Hse. Audio Publishing Group.

—Light Princess. l.t. ed. 2006. pap. (978-1-84702-350-6(9)) Echo Library.

Macinnis, Katherine. Kelsar. 2006. pap. 12.95 (978-1-58939-876-4(9)) Virtualbookworm.com Publishing, Inc.

Mack, Karen. The Magical Adventures of Sun Beams. 2009. 42p. 31.99 (978-1-4415-3636-5(1)) Xlibris Corp.

Mack, Michele. Henry Fickle & the Secret Laboratory. 2005. (Illus.). 112p. (J). 18.00 (978-0-9667747-1-9(X), 1239658) Sorcerer's Pr., The.

MacKenzie, Ross. Zac & the Dream Stealers. (J). 2013. 297p. (978-0-545-40107-4(0)) 2012. (ENG.). 304p. (gr. 3-7). 16.99 (978-0-545-40106-7(2)) Scholastic, Inc. (Chicken Hse., The).

Madden, Michelle. The Butterfly Garden. 2008. 24p. pap. 24.95 (978-1-60813-375-8(3)) America Star Bks.

Madrid, Bo. The Lunar Express. 2010. (Illus.). 32p. 12.99 (978-1-4490-6949-0(5)) AuthorHouse.

Madsen, W. J. Arkeepers: Episode One. 2012. 142p. pap. 7.95 (978-0-9830487-0-1(3)) little m Bks.

—Arkeepers: Episode Two. 2012. 206p. pap. 9.30 (978-0-9830487-1-8(1)) little m Bks.

Mafi, Tahereh. Furthermore. 2016. (ENG.). 416p. (J). (gr. 4-7). 17.99 (978-1-101-99476-4(2), Dutton Books for Young Readers) Penguin Young Readers Group.

—Furthermore. 2017. lib. bdg. 19.65 **(978-0-606-40493-8(7))** Turtleback Bks.

Magaziner, Lauren. The Only Thing Worse Than Witches. 2014. (ENG.). 272p. (J). (gr. 3-7). 16.99 (978-0-8037-3918-5(4), Dial Bks) Penguin Young Readers Group.

Magic Box. (ARA., Illus.). 100p. (YA). pap. 5.95 (978-0-86685-743-7(5), LDL946) Librairie du Liban Pubns. FRA. Dist: International Bk. Ctr., Inc.

The Magic King. 2003. (J). (978-1-4120-3345-9(4)) Black Dot Pubns.

The Magic of Tobias Twissle. 2003. (J). lib. bdg. (978-0-9744923-0-8(2)) Purple Plume Pr.

Magic Painting Jungle. 2017. (Magic Painting Bks.). (ENG.). (J). pap. 9.99 **(978-0-7945-3982-5(3)**, Usborne) EDC Publishing.

The Magic Porridge Pot, Level 1. 2016. (Ladybird Readers Ser.). (ENG.). 48p. (J). pap. 9.99 (978-0-241-25406-6(X)) Penguin Bks., Ltd. GBR. Dist: Independent Pubs. Group.

Magic Wand Disney Princess. 2005. (Illus.). 10p. (J). bds. 16.98 (978-1-4127-3537-7(8), 7263500) Publications International, Ltd.

The Magical Horses Vol. 2000: A Fairy Tale for the Young & the Young at Heart. l.t. ed. 2005. (Illus.). 127p. (J). per. (978-0-9738625-0-8(5)) Blue Cat Publishing.

Magical Max Makes Friends. 2005. (Adventures of Magical Max, Scarlet Feather & Little Lilly Woo-Woo Ser.). (Illus.). 16p. (J). (gr. k-4). 14.95 (978-0-9762408-0-8(7)) Lead Life Pr., LLC.

Magness, Lee. Silver Dasher. 2003. 164p. pap. 12.95 (978-0-595-29043-7(4)) iUniverse, Inc.

Mahabeer, Rishen. Anna & Timothy. 2012. 20p. pap. 13.77 (978-1-4669-5509-7(0)) Trafford Publishing.

Mahon, Matthew. The Defenders of All Thats Fall. 2008. 56p. pap. 24.95 (978-1-4327-3169-4(6)) Outskirts Pr., Inc.

Mahoney, Jerry. My Stupid Stepbrother Ruined Aladdin. Bitskoff, Aleksei, illus. 2017. (J). lib. bdg. **(978-1-4965-4464-3(1))** Stone Arch Bks.

—My Stupid Stepbrother Ruined Beauty & the Beast. 2017. (J). lib. bdg. **(978-1-4965-4465-0(X))** Stone Arch Bks.

Mahoney, Jerry. My Stupid Stepbrother Ruined Cinderella. 2017. (J). lib. bdg. (978-1-4965-4466-7(8)) Stone Arch Bks.

Mahoney, Karen. The Iron Witch. 2011. (Iron Witch Ser.: 1). (ENG.). 312p. (YA). (gr. 7-18). pap. 9.95 (978-0-7387-2582-6(X), Flux) North Star Editions.

—The Stone Demon. 2013. (Iron Witch Ser.: 3). (ENG.). 336p. (YA). pap. 9.99 (978-0-7387-3340-1(7), Flux) North Star Editions.

Mahy, Margaret. Maddigan's Fantasia. 2012. (ENG.). 512p. (J). (gr. 5-9). pap. 22.99 (978-1-4424-6053-9(9), McElderry, Margaret K. Bks.) McElderry, Margaret K. Bks.

Make Believe Ideas. Molly the Muffin Fairy. 2015. (ENG.). 32p. (J). pap. 6.99 (978-1-78393-441-6(7)) Make Believe Ideas GBR. Dist: Nelson, Thomas Inc.

Mäkinen, Kirsti. The Kalevala: Tales of Magic & Adventure. Brooks, Kaarina, tr. from FIN. Surojegin, Pirkko-Liisa, illus. 2009. (ENG.). 214p. (YA). (gr. 4-18). 24.95 (978-1-897476-00-0(0)) Simply Read Bks. CAN. Dist: Ingram Publisher Services.

Malaspina, Ann. Feraj & the Magic Lute: An Arabian Folktale. Peluso, Martina, illus. 2013. (Folktales from Around the World Ser.). (ENG.). 24p. (J). (gr. k-3). 28.50 (978-1-62323-613-7(4), 206380) Child's World, Inc., The.

Malchow, Hal & Malchow, Alex. The Sword of Darrow. 2011. (ENG.). (gr. 3-7). 372p. pap. 12.99 (978-1-935618-47-8(4)); 532p. 17.99 (978-1-935618-46-1(6)) BenBella Bks.

Malloy, Chris. Wizard Academies - A Special Kind of Talent. 2008. 142p. pap. 19.95 *(978-0-615-18505-7(3))* Wizard Academies, LLC.

Malone, Marianne. The Pirate's Coin.. Call, Greg, illus. 2014. (Sixty-Eight Rooms Adventures Ser.). (ENG.). 240p. (J). (gr. 3-7). 7.99 *(978-0-307-97720-5(X)*, Yearling) Random Hse. Children's Bks.

—The Secret of the Key: a Sixty-Eight Rooms Adventure. 2015. (Sixty-Eight Rooms Adventures Ser.). (ENG., Illus.). 256p. (J). (gr. 3-7). 6.99 *(978-0-307-97724-3(2)*, Yearling) Random Hse. Children's Bks.

—The Sixty-Eight Rooms. Triplett, Gina & Call, Greg, illus. 2011. (Sixty-Eight Rooms Adventures Ser.). (ENG.). 288p. (J). (gr. 3-7). pap. 6.99 *(978-0-375-85711-9(7)*, Yearling) Random Hse. Children's Bks.

—Stealing Magic. Call, Greg, illus. (Sixty-Eight Rooms Adventures Ser.). (ENG.). (J). (gr. 3-7). 2013. 272p. pap. 6.99 *(978-0-375-86790-3(2)*, Yearling) 2012. 256p. 16.99 *(978-0-375-86819-1(4)*, Random Hse. Bks. for Young Readers) Random Hse. Children's Bks.

Malouf, Juman. The Trilogy of Two. 2015. (ENG.). 416p. (J). (gr. 5-7). 17.99 *(978-0-399-17114-7(2)*, G.P. Putnam's Sons Books for Young Readers) Penguin Young Readers Group.

Mama Doo. Zachary & the Magic Pumpkin Seeds, 1 vol. 2007. (ENG.). 35p. 24.95 *(978-1-4241-8579-5(3))* America Star Bks.

Man-Kong, Mary. Princess to the Rescue! 2015. (Pictureback(R) Ser.). (ENG., Illus.). 16p. (J). (gr. -1-2). 4.99 *(978-0-553-50737-9(0)*, Random Hse. Bks. for Young Readers) Random Hse. Children's Bks.

Mancil, Arlene. The Garden Fairy. 2008. 32p. pap. 24.95 *(978-1-60441-735-7(8))* PublishAmerica, Inc.

Manson, Beverlie, illus. The Mermaid's Secret Diaries. 2013. (ENG.). 96p. (J). (gr. -1-2). 9.95 *(978-1-907967-59-7(1))* Boxer Bks., Ltd. GBR. Dist: Sterling Publishing Co., Inc.

Mantchev, Lisa. Eyes Like Stars. 2010. (Theatre Illuminata Ser.: 1). (ENG.). 384p. (YA). (gr. 7-12). pap. 11.99 *(978-0-312-60866-8(7)*, 9780312608668) Square Fish.

—Perchance to Dream. 2011. (Theatre Illuminata Ser.: 2). (ENG.). 368p. (YA). (gr. 7-12). pap. 9.99 *(978-0-312-67510-3(0)*, 9780312675103) Square Fish.

Marciano, John Bemelmans. The All Powerful Ring. Blackall, Sophie, illus. 2016. (Witches of Benevento Ser.: 2). (ENG.). 144p. (J). (gr. 2-5). 13.99 *(978-0-451-47180-2(6)*, Viking Books for Young Readers) Penguin Young Readers Group.

—Mischief Season. Blackall, Sophie, illus. 2016. (Witches of Benevento Ser.: 1). (ENG.). 128p. (J). (gr. 2-5). 13.99 *(978-0-451-47181-9(4)*, Viking Books for Young Readers) Penguin Young Readers Group.

—Respect Your Ghosts. Blackall, Sophie, illus. 2017. (Witches of Benevento Ser.: 4). (ENG.). 128p. (J). (gr. 2-5). 13.99 *(978-0-451-47183-3(0)*, Viking Books for Young Readers) Penguin Young Readers Group.

Margolis, Leslie. If I Were You. 2015. (ENG.). 224p. (YA). (gr. 5-9). 15.99 *(978-0-374-30068-5(2)*, 9780374300685, Farrar, Straus & Giroux (BYR)) Farrar, Straus & Giroux.

Margo's Magic Trunk. 2006. (Illus.). 32p. (J). pap. 6.95 *(978-0-9789016-0-8(6))* Jodaviste Publishing.

Margulies, Julianna & Margulies, Paul. Three Magic Balloons. Shaffer, Grant, illus. 2016. (ENG.). 40p. (J). (gr. -1-2). 17.99 *(978-1-101-93523-1(5)*, Random Hse. Bks. for Young Readers) Random Hse. Children's Bks.

Mariconda, Barbara. The Voyage of Lucy P. Simmons. (ENG.). 256p. (J). (gr. 3-7). 2074. 6.99 *(978-0-06-211980-3(X))* 2012. (Voyage of Lucy P. Simmons Ser.: 1). 16.99 *(978-0-06-211979-7(6))* HarperCollins Pubs. (Tegen, Katherine Bks).

Marie, Jill Jana. Anna Lee Enis Bee. 2010. 24p. pap. 11.00 *(978-1-60860-907-9(3)*, Eloquent Bks.) Strategic Book Publishing & Rights Agency (SBPRA).

Marillier, Juliet. Cybele's Secret. 2011. (ENG.). 444p. (YA). (gr. 7). pap. 9.99 *(978-0-553-49486-0(4)*, Knopf Bks. for Young Readers) Random Hse. Children's Bks.

—Raven Flight. (ENG.). 416p. (YA). (gr. 7). 2014. pap. 9.99 *(978-0-375-87197-9(7)*, Ember) 2013. 16.99 *(978-0-375-86955-6(7)*, Knopf Bks. for Young Readers) Random Hse. Children's Bks.

—Shadowfell. 2013. (ENG.). 416p. (YA). (gr. 7). pap. 10.99 *(978-0-375-87196-2(9)*, Ember) Random Hse. Children's Bks.

—Wildwood Dancing. 2008. (ENG.). 432p. (YA). (gr. 7). pap. 10.99 *(978-0-375-84474-4(0)*, Knopf Bks. for Young Readers) Random Hse. Children's Bks.

Mariotte, Jeff. Dark Vengeance Vol. 1: Summer, Fall. 2011. (ENG.). 512p. (YA). (gr. 9). pap. 9.99 *(978-1-4424-2975-8(5)*, Simon Pulse) Simon Pulse.

Marr, Melissa. Carnival of Souls. 2012. (ENG.). 320p. (J). pap. 143.92 *(978-0-06-221668-7(6))* HarperCollins Pubs.

Marriott, Zoë. Swan Kingdom. 2009. (ENG., Illus.). 272p. (YA). (gr. 7). pap. 8.99 *(978-0-7636-4293-8(2))* Candlewick Pr.

Marrone, Amanda. Master of Mirrors. 2011. (Magic Repair Shop Ser.: 3). (ENG.). 192p. (J). (gr. 3-7). pap. 5.99 *(978-1-4169-9035-2(6)*, Aladdin) Simon & Schuster Children's Publishing.

—Revealers. 2008. (ENG.). 288p. (YA). (gr. 9-18). pap. 8.99 *(978-1-4169-5874-1(6)*, Simon Pulse) Simon Pulse.

Marsh, Richard Phillip. Mattress People Go to Bear Park. 2009. 44p. pap. 10.95 *(978-1-935125-39-6(7))* Robertson Publishing.

Marsh, Sarah Glenn. Fear the Drowning Deep. 2016. (ENG.). 312p. (YA). (gr. 6). 16.99 *(978-1-5107-0348-3(9)*, Sky Pony Pr.) Skyhorse Publishing Co., Inc.

Marshall, Heidi Amenda. Petra's Adventure in Nievenheim. Marshall, Heidi Amenda, illus. l.t. ed. 2003. (Illus.). 57p. (J). per. 7.99 *(978-0-9747445-0-6(6))* Landfall Co., The.

Marshall, Linda Elovitz. The Mitzvah Magician. Engel, Christiane, illus. 2012. (Kar-Ben Favorites Ser.). (ENG.). 24p. (J). (gr. -1-2). lib. bdg. 17.95 *(978-0-7613-5655-4(X)*, Kar-Ben Publishing) Lerner Publishing Group.

Marsham, Liz. Wonder Woman: Maze of Magic. 2017. (I Can Read! Level 2 Ser.). lib. bdg. 13.55 ***(978-0-606-40057-2(5))*** Turtleback Bks.

—Wonder Woman Classic: Maze of Magic. Ferguson, Lee, illus. 2017. (I Can Read Level 2 Ser.). 32p. (J). (gr. -1-3). pap. 3.99 ***(978-0-06-236093-9(0))*** HarperCollins Pubs.

Martin, Alison. Princess of Tabaria. 2004. (Illus.). 104p. pap. *(978-1-84401-151-3(8))* Athena Pr.

Martin, Ann M. & Parnell, Annie. Missy Piggle-Wiggle & the Won't-Walk-The-Dog Cure. Hatke, Ben, illus. 2017. (Missy Piggle-Wiggle Ser.). (ENG.). 240p. (J). 16.99 ***(978-1-250-07170-5(4)***, 9781250071705) Feiwel & Friends.

Martineck, Michael J. The Wrong Channel. 2005. 160p. (J). (gr. 4-8). 8.00 *(978-0-9720978-1-9(3))* Our Little Secret Pr.

Masessa, Ed. Scarecrow Magic. Myers, Matt, illus. 2015. (ENG.). 32p. (J). (gr. -1-k). 16.99 *(978-0-545-69109-3(5))* Scholastic, Inc.

—Wandmaker. 2016. (ENG.). 336p. (J). (gr. 3-7). 12.99 *(978-0-545-86174-8(8)*, Scholastic Pr.) Scholastic, Inc.

Masi, Sue. A Journey Through Fantasy Forest. 2012. 44p. pap. 21.99 *(978-1-4691-4837-3(4))* Xlibris Corp.

Mason, Alexis. Just an Ordinary Little Dog: Barnaby's Story. Bunch, Paul, illus. 2010. (J). *(978-0-9755280-4-4(1))* Insight Technical Education.

Mason-Black, Jennifer. Devil & the Bluebird. 2016. (ENG.). 336p. (J). (gr. 8-17). 17.95 *(978-1-4197-2000-0(7)*, Amulet Bks.) Abrams, Inc.

Mason, Conrad. The Watchmen of Port Fayt. 2015. (ENG.). 400p. (J). (gr. 3-7). 17.99 *(978-0-545-83308-0(6))* Scholastic, Inc.

Mass, Wendy. Graceful. 2015. (ENG.). 256p. (J). (gr. 3-7). 16.99 *(978-0-545-77313-3(X)*, Scholastic Pr.) Scholastic, Inc.

—The Last Present. 2015. (Willow Falls Ser.: 4). lib. bdg. 17.20 *(978-0-606-37015-8(3))* Turtleback Bks.

Mastro, M. L. Return to Baladah. 2011. 88p. (gr. 10-12). pap. 9.99 *(978-1-4520-7377-4(5))* AuthorHouse.

Matharu, Taran. The Battlemage. 2017. (Summoner Trilogy Ser.: bk.3). (ENG., Illus.). 384p. (YA). 18.99 ***(978-1-250-07632-8(3)***, 9781250076328) Feiwel & Friends.

Matharu, Taran. The Inquisition. 2016. (Summoner Trilogy: Bk. 2). (ENG.). 368p. (YA). (gr. 7). 17.99 *(978-1-250-07631-1(5)*, 9781250076311) Feiwel & Friends.

—The Inquisition. 2017. (Summoner Trilogy Ser.: Bk. 2). (ENG.). 384p. (YA). pap. 10.99 *(978-1-250-11521-8(3)*, 9781250115218) Square Fish.

—The Inquisition. 2017. (Summoner Ser.: 2). (YA). lib. bdg. 22.10 ***(978-0-606-39945-6(3))*** Turtleback Bks.

Matheos, George P. Pure Magic. 2011. 156p. (gr. 2-4). 22.95 *(978-1-4620-1619-8(7))*; pap. 12.95 *(978-1-4620-1617-4(0))* iUniverse, Inc.

Matheson, Christie. Tap the Magic Tree Board Book. Matheson, Christie, illus. 2016. (Illus.). 42p. (J). (gr. -1-3). bds. 7.99 *(978-0-06-227446-5(5)*, Greenwillow Bks.) HarperCollins Pubs.

Matthews, Caitlín, et al. Tales from Celtic Lands. Whelan, Olwyn, illus. 2008. (ENG.). 80p. (J). (gr. -1-3). 21.99 *(978-1-84686-213-7(2))* Barefoot Bks., Inc.

Matthews, John. The Barefoot Book of Giants, Ghosts, & Goblins. Manna, Giovanni, illus. 2008. (ENG.). 80p. (J). 21.99 *(978-1-84686-235-9(3))* Barefoot Bks., Inc.

Mawhinney, Art, illus. Olivia the Magnificent: A Lift-the-Flap Story. 2009. (Olivia TV Tie-In Ser.). (ENG.). 16p. (J). (gr. -1-2). pap. 6.99 *(978-1-4169-8297-5(3)*, Simon Spotlight) Simon Spotlight.

May, Elizabeth. The Fallen Kingdom: Book Three of the Falconer Trilogy. 2017. (Falconer Ser.: 3). (ENG.). 400p. (YA). 18.99 ***(978-1-4521-2883-2(9))*** Chronicle Bks. LLC.

Mazer, Anne. Violet Makes a Splash. Brown, Bill, illus. 2007. (Sister Magic Ser.: 2). (ENG.). 96p. (J). (gr. 2-5). 4.99 *(978-0-439-87247-8(2))* Scholastic, Inc.

Mcallister, Bruce. The Village Sang to the Sea. 2013. 172p. pap. *(978-0-9534784-9-1(1))* Aeon Pr.

McBride, Lish. Hold Me Closer, Necromancer. 2010. (Necromancer Ser.: 1). (ENG.). 352p. (YA). (gr. 9-13). 16.99 *(978-0-8050-9098-7(3)*, 9780805090987, Holt, Henry & Co. Bks. For Young Readers) Holt, Henry & Co.

—Necromancing the Stone. 2013. (Necromancer Ser.: 2). (ENG.). 368p. (YA). (gr. 9-13). pap. 9.99 *(978-1-250-03415-1(9)*, 9781250034151) Square Fish.

—Pyromantic. 2017. (Firebug Ser.). (ENG.). 336p. (YA). (gr. 9-17). 18.99 *(978-0-8050-9863-1(1)*, 9780805098631, Holt, Henry & Co. Bks. For Young Readers) Holt, Henry & Co.

McBrier, Page. Abracadabra Tut. 2014. (ENG.). (J). pap. 9.99 *(978-0-9960794-0-2(8))* Palm Canyon Pr.

McBroom, Danielle Loiselle. A Painted Dream. 2008. 20p. pap. 24.95 *(978-1-60441-694-7(7))* America Star Bks.

McCarthy, Jenna & Evans, Carolyn. Maggie Malone Makes a Splash. 2015. (Maggie Malone Ser.: 3). (ENG.). 192p. (J). (gr. 4-7). pap. 8.99 *(978-1-4022-9312-2(7)*, Sourcebooks Jabberwocky) Sourcebooks, Inc.

McCarthy, Jenna, et al. Maggie Malone & the Mostly Magical Boots. 2014. (Maggie Malone Ser.: 1). (ENG.). 224p. (J). (gr. 3-6). pap. 6.99 *(978-1-4022-9306-1(2)*, 9781402293061, Sourcebooks Jabberwocky) Sourcebooks, Inc.

McCaughrean, Geraldine. Peter Pan de Rojo Escarlata. Gonzalez-Gallarza, Isabel, tr. Wyatt, David, illus. 2006. 296p. (J). (gr. 5-8). 17.95 *(978-958-704-467-6(3))* Ediciones Alfaguara ESP. Dist: Santillana USA Publishing Co., Inc.

—Peter Pan in Scarlet. Fischer, Scott M., illus. 2008. (ENG.). 320p. (J). (gr. 4-9). pap. 6.99 *(978-1-4169-1809-7(4)*, McElderry, Margaret K. Bks.) McElderry, Margaret K. Bks.

McCorvie, D. Lawrence. Timothy Hunt: The Great Candy Caper. 2007. 232p. 30.00 *(978-1-4251-3618-5(4))* Trafford Publishing.

McDonagh, Christelle, et al. Mission Magic Bubble. 2009. (Illus.). 56p. pap. 23.99 *(978-1-4389-0640-9(4))* AuthorHouse.

McDonald, Ann-Eve. The Tale of the Black Square. 2004. (J). *(978-0-9770158-2-5(3))* BeachWalk Bks. Inc.

McDonald, Fiona. Ghost Doll & Jasper. 2012. (ENG., Illus.). 112p. (J). (gr. 2-7). 12.95 *(978-1-62087-174-4(2)*, 620174, Sky Pony Pr.) Skyhorse Publishing Co., Inc.

McDonald, Megan. Judy Moody, Mood Martian. 2015. (Judy Moody Ser.: 12). lib. bdg. 16.00 *(978-0-606-36876-6(0))* Turtleback Bks.

McFarland, Kim. A Refugee in Oz. 2010. 164p. pap. 11.95 *(978-0-557-48706-6(4))* Lulu Pr., Inc.

Mcfaul, Jason & Macdonald, Eric. What A Trip. 2007. pap. 77.53 *(978-0-7575-4014-1(7))* Kendall Hunt Publishing Co.

McGalliard, Julie. Waking up Naked in Strange Places. 2015. (YA). 24.99 *(978-1-941662-09-0(9))* Per Aspera Pr.

—Waking Up Naked in Strange Places. 2015. (YA). pap. 14.99 *(978-1-941662-10-6(2))* Per Aspera Pr.

McGaw, Wayne T. T-Boy of the Bayou. Crespo, George, illus. 2003. 32p. (J). (gr. -1-3). 15.95 *(978-0-87614-648-4(5)*, Carolrhoda Bks.) Lerner Publishing Group.

McGee, Helen. Ikky Dikky Dak: Magical Adventures with Googler! Book Two. Kaltenborn, Karl, illus. 2011. pap. 21.95 *(978-1-60494-573-7(7))* Wheatmark, Inc.

McGowan, Maureen. Cinderella: Ninja Warrior. 2010. 320p. pap. 8.95 *(978-1-60747-778-5(5)*, Pickwick Pr.) Phoenix Bks., Inc.

McGregor, Suzy. Moon Leopard. 2013. 40p. pap. 11.95 *(978-0-9824926-5-9(0))* Lollipop Media Productions, LP.

McGriff, Shawna A. Princess Pink: Princess Pink Saves the Girls of Lahappyville. 2010. 44p. pap. 18.49 *(978-1-4520-3936-7(4))* AuthorHouse.

McGuire, Jeremy. O'shaughnessey: Boy & His Leprechaun. 2007. 140p. per. 14.95 *(978-1-4327-0892-4(9))* Outskirts Pr., Inc.

McGuire Woods, Molly. Barbie Fall 2014 DVD Junior Novelization (Barbie) 2014. (Junior Novel Ser.). (ENG., Illus.). 128p. (J). (gr. 3-7). 5.99 *(978-0-385-38627-2(3)*, Random Hse. Bks. for Young Readers) Random Hse. Children's Bks.

McIntyre, Mel. Flutter Bunnies. Grady, Kit, illus. 2008. 24p. pap. 10.95 *(978-1-933090-68-9(5))* Guardian Angel Publishing, Inc.

McKay, Laurie. Quest Maker. 2016. (Last Dragon Charmer Ser.: 2). (Illus.). 352p. (J). (gr. 3-7). 16.99 *(978-0-06-230846-7(7))* HarperCollins Pubs.

—The Villain Keeper. 2015. (Last Dragon Charmer Ser.: 1). (ENG.). 352p. (J). (gr. 3-7). 16.99 *(978-0-06-230843-6(2))* HarperCollins Pubs.

Mckenzie, Riford. The Witches of Dredmoore Hollow, 0 vols. unabr. ed. 2013. (ENG.). 274p. (J). (gr. 5-7). pap. 9.99 *(978-1-4778-1702-5(6)*, 9781477817025, Amazon Children's Publishing) Amazon Publishing.

McKinley, Robin. Pegasus. 2010. (ENG.). 416p. (YA). (gr. 7-18). 18.99 *(978-0-399-24677-7(0)*, G.P. Putnam's Sons Books for Young Readers) Penguin Young Readers Group.

—Shadows. 2013. 356p. (YA). *(978-0-399-25625-7(3))* Penguin Publishing Group.

—Shadows. 2014. (ENG.). 384p. (YA). (gr. 7). pap. 9.99 *(978-0-14-751220-8(4)*, Speak) Penguin Young Readers Group.

McKinty, Adrian. The Lighthouse Keepers. 2008. (ENG.). 400p. (YA). (gr. 7-11). 17.95 *(978-0-8109-7070-0(8)*, Amulet Bks.) Abrams, Inc.

—The Lighthouse War. 2007. (ENG.). 414p. (J). (gr. 7-17). 16.95 *(978-0-8109-9354-9(6))* Abrams, Inc.

McLaren, Clemence. Aphrodite's Blessing. 2008. (ENG.). 208p. (YA). (gr. 7). pap. 10.99 *(978-1-4169-7860-2(7)*, Simon Pulse) Simon Pulse.

McLemore, Anna-Marie. When the Moon Was Ours. 2016. (ENG.). 288p. (YA). 18.99 *(978-1-250-05866-9(X)*, 9781250058669) St. Martin's Pr.

McMann, Lisa. Dragon Captives. 2017. (Unwanteds Quests Ser.: 1). (ENG., Illus.). 432p. (J). (gr. 3-7). 17.99 *(978-1-4814-5681-4(4)*, Simon & Schuster/Paula Wiseman Bks.) Simon & Schuster/Paula Wiseman Bks.

—Dragon Captives. 2018. (Unwanteds Quests Ser.: 1). lib. bdg. 18.40 ***(978-0-606-40846-2(0))*** Turtleback Bks.

—Island of Dragons. (Unwanteds Ser.: 7). (ENG., Illus.). 544p. (J). (gr. 3-7). 2017. pap. 8.99 *(978-1-4424-9338-4(0))* 2016. 17.99 *(978-1-4424-9337-7(2))* Simon & Schuster Children's Publishing. (Aladdin).

—Island of Graves. (Unwanteds Ser.: 6). (ENG., Illus.). (J). (gr. 3-7). 2016. 560p. pap. 8.99 *(978-1-4424-9335-3(6))* 2015. 528p. 18.99 *(978-1-4424-9334-6(8))* Simon & Schuster Children's Publishing. (Aladdin).

—Island of Graves. 2016. (Unwanteds Ser.: 6). lib. bdg. 19.65 *(978-0-606-38497-1(9))* Turtleback Bks.

—Island of Silence. (Unwanteds Ser.: 2). (ENG., (J). (gr. 3-7). 2013. Illus.). 432p. pap. 8.99 *(978-1-4424-0772-5(7))* 2012. 416p. 18.99 *(978-1-4424-0771-8(9))* Simon & Schuster Children's Publishing. (Aladdin).

—Island of Silence. 2013. (Unwanteds Ser.: 2). lib. bdg. 18.40 *(978-0-606-32044-3(X)*, Turtleback) Turtleback Bks.

—The Unwanteds, 6 vols. 2011. (Unwanteds Ser.: Bk. 1). (J). 88.75 *(978-1-4618-4117-3(8))*; 90.75 *(978-1-4618-4113-5(5))*; 88.75 *(978-1-4618-4116-6(X))*; 245.75 *(978-1-4618-4114-2(3))*; 1.25 *(978-1-4640-2489-4(8))* Recorded Bks., Inc.

—The Unwanteds. (Unwanteds Ser.: 1). (ENG., Illus.). (J). (gr. 3-7). 2012. 416p. pap. 7.99 *(978-1-4424-0769-5(7))* 2011. 400p. 18.99 *(978-1-4424-0768-8(9))* Simon & Schuster Children's Publishing. (Aladdin).

—The Unwanteds. 2012. (Unwanteds Ser.: 1). lib. bdg. 18.40 *(978-0-606-26953-7(3)*, Turtleback) Turtleback Bks.

—The Unwanteds Set: The Unwanteds; Island of Silence; Island of Fire. 2013. (Unwanteds Ser.). (ENG.). 1280p. (J). (gr. 3-7). 51.99 *(978-1-4424-9450-3(6)*, Aladdin) Simon & Schuster Children's Publishing.

McMullan, Kate. Danger! Wizard at Work, No. 11. Basso, Bill, illus. 2004. (Dragon Slayers' Academy Ser.: 11). (ENG.). 112p. (J). (gr. 2-5). pap. 4.99 *(978-0-448-43529-9(2)*, Grosset & Dunlap) Penguin Young Readers Group.

—The New Kid at School. Basso, Bill & Gilpin, Stephen, illus. 2003. (Dragon Slayers' Academy Ser.: 1). (ENG.). 112p. (J). (gr. 2-5). mass mkt. 5.99 *(978-0-448-43108-6(4)*, Grosset & Dunlap) Penguin Young Readers Group.

McNabb, Linda. Dragons' Bane. 2008. 208p. *(978-1-86950-655-1(3))* HarperCollins Pubs. Australia.

McNamara, Margaret. Clara & the Magical Charms. Denos, Julia, illus. 2013. (Fairy Bell Sisters Ser.: 4). (ENG.). 128p. (J). (gr. 1-5). 15.99 *(978-0-06-222811-6(0))*; pap. 4.99 *(978-0-06-222810-9(2))* HarperCollins Pubs.

—The Fairy Bell Sisters Vol. 5: Sylva & the Lost Treasure. Denos, Julia, illus. 2014. (Fairy Bell Sisters Ser.: 5). (ENG.). 144p. (J). (gr. 1-5). 15.99 *(978-0-06-226721-4(3))* HarperCollins Pubs.

—The Fairy Bell Sisters - Christmas Fairy Magic. 2014. (Fairy Bell Sisters Ser.: 6). (ENG.). 144p. (J). (gr. 1-5). pap. 4.99 *(978-0-06-226723-8(X))* HarperCollins Pubs.

—Sylva & the Lost Treasure. Denos, Julia, illus. 2014. (Fairy Bell Sisters Ser.: 5). (ENG.). 144p. (J). (gr. 1-5). pap. 4.99 *(978-0-06-226720-7(5))* HarperCollins Pubs.

McNiff, Dawn. Worry Magic. 2016. (ENG.). 256p. (J). (gr. 4-7). pap. 9.99 *(978-1-4714-0371-2(8))* Bonnier Publishing GBR. Dist: Independent Pubs. Group.

McOmber, Rachel B., ed. McOmber Phonics Storybooks: The Magic "E" rev. ed. (Illus.). (J). *(978-0-944991-37-4(8))* Swift Learning Resources.

—McOmber Phonics Storybooks: The Neat Trick. rev. ed. (Illus.). (J). *(978-0-944991-55-8(6))* Swift Learning Resources.

—McOmber Phonics Storybooks: The Prime Time Trick. rev. ed. (Illus.). (J). *(978-0-944991-56-5(4))* Swift Learning Resources.

McPhail, David. Water Boy. 2007. (ENG., Illus.). 32p. (J). (gr. -1-3). 16.95 *(978-0-8109-1784-2(X)*, Abrams Bks. for Young Readers) Abrams, Inc.

McPhate, Paul J. The Puggle King. 2008. 52p. pap. 16.95 *(978-1-60703-709-5(2))* America Star Bks.

McQuerry, Maureen Doyle. Time Out of Time. 2015. (Time Out of Time Ser.). (ENG., Illus.). 368p. (J). (gr. 5-9). 16.95 *(978-1-4197-1494-8(5)*, Amulet Bks.) Abrams, Inc.

—Time Out of Time: Book Two: the Telling Stone. 2016. (ENG., Illus.). 376p. (J). (gr. 3-7). pap. 8.95 *(978-1-4197-1916-5(5)*, Amulet Bks.) Abrams, Inc.

—Time Out of Time Bk. 1: Beyond the Door. 2014. (Time Out of Time Ser.). (ENG., Illus.). 384p. (J). (gr. 3-7). 16.95 *(978-1-4197-1016-2(8)*, Amulet Bks.) Abrams, Inc.

McQuestion, Karen. Secrets of the Magic Ring, 0 vols. unabr. ed. 2011. (ENG., Illus.). 156p. (J). (gr. 4-6). pap. 8.95 *(978-1-61218-142-4(2)*, 9781612181424, Amazon Children's Publishing) Amazon Publishing.

Mcshane, Pol. The Magic Elevator: The Adventures of Johnny & Joey. 2005. 129p. pap. 19.95 *(978-1-4241-0014-9(3))* PublishAmerica, Inc.

Mead, Richelle. Frostbite. 2008. (Vampire Academy Ser.: Bk. 2). (ENG.). 335p. (YA). (gr. 7-18). pap. 10.99 *(978-1-59514-175-0(8)*, Razorbill) Penguin Publishing Group.

—Frostbite. Vieceli, Emma, illus. 2012. (Vampire Academy Ser.: 2). (ENG.). 144p. (YA). (gr. 7-18). pap. 12.99 *(978-1-59514-430-0(7)*, Razorbill) Penguin Young Readers Group.

—Frostbite. 2012. (Vampire Academy (Graphic Novels) Ser.: 2). lib. bdg. 24.50 *(978-0-606-23631-7(7)*, Turtleback) Turtleback Bks.

—Shadow Kiss. 2013. (Vampire Academy (Graphic Novels) Ser.: 3). lib. bdg. 24.50 *(978-0-606-34129-5(3)*, Turtleback) Turtleback Bks.

—Vampire Academy. 2007. (Vampire Academy Ser.: Bk. 1). (ENG.). 336p. (J). (gr. 7-18). pap. 10.99 *(978-1-59514-174-3(X)*, Razorbill) Penguin Publishing Group.

—Vampire Academy. 2010. (SPA.). 256p. (gr. 8-12). pap. 16.99 *(978-607-11-0456-4(4)*, Alfaguara) Santillana USA Publishing Co., Inc.

—Vampire Academy. Vieceli, Emma, illus. 2011. (Vampire Academy Ser.: 1). (ENG.). 144p. (J). (gr. 7-18). pap. 12.99 *(978-1-59514-429-4(3)*, Razorbill) Penguin Young Readers Group.

—Vampire Academy 10th Anniversary Edition. 2016. (ENG.). 512p. (YA). (gr. 7). pap. 11.99 *(978-0-448-49429-6(9)*, Razorbill) Penguin Young Readers Group.

—Vampire Academy Box Set 1-3, 3 vols. 2013. (Vampire Academy Ser.). (ENG.). 1152p. (YA). (gr. 7). pap., pap., pap. 30.97 *(978-1-59514-775-2(6)*, Razorbill) Penguin Young Readers Group.

—Vampire Academy Box Set 1-6, 6 vols. 2013. (Vampire Academy Ser.). (ENG.). 2784p. (YA). (gr. 7). pap., pap., pap. 60.94 *(978-1-59514-758-5(6)*, Razorbill) Penguin Young Readers Group.

—Vampire Academy Box Set 4-6, 3 vols. 2013. (Vampire Academy Ser.). (ENG.). 1648p. (YA). (gr. 7). pap., pap., pap. 29.97 *(978-1-59514-787-5(X)*, Razorbill) Penguin Young Readers Group.

Meadows, Daisy. Abigail the Breeze Fairy. Ripper, Georgie, illus. 2006. (Weather Fairies Ser.: 2). (ENG.). 80p. (J). (gr. -1-3). 4.99 *(978-0-439-81386-0(7)*, Scholastic Paperbacks) Scholastic, Inc.

—Addison the April Fool's Day Fairy. 2014. (Rainbow Magic — Special Edition Ser.). lib. bdg. 17.20 *(978-0-606-35378-6(X))* Turtleback Bks.

—Adele the Voice Fairy. 2013. (Rainbow Magic — the Superstar Fairies Ser.: 2). lib. bdg. 14.75 *(978-0-606-31514-2(4)*, Turtleback) Turtleback Bks.

—Aisha the Princess & the Pea Fairy. 2016. (Illus.). (J). (Fairy Tale Fairies Ser.: 6). (ENG.). 80p. (gr. 2-5). pap. 4.99 *(978-0-545-85199-2(8)*, Scholastic Paperbacks); 62p. ***(978-0-545-88741-0(0))*** Scholastic, Inc.

—Alicia the Snow Queen Fairy. 2016. (Rainbow Magic — Special Edition Ser.). lib. bdg. 17.20 ***(978-0-606-39728-5(0))*** Turtleback Bks.

—Alyssa the Snow Queen Fairy. 2016. (Rainbow Magic Special Edition Ser.). (ENG.). 176p. (J). (gr. 2-5). pap. 6.99 *(978-0-545-85201-2(3)*, Scholastic Paperbacks) Scholastic, Inc.

—Alyssa the Star-Spotter Fairy. 2013. (Rainbow Magic — the Superstar Fairies Ser.: 6). lib. bdg. 14.75 *(978-0-606-31518-0(7)*, Turtleback) Turtleback Bks.

—Angelica the Angel Fairy (Rainbow Magic: Special Edition) 2015. (Rainbow Magic Special Edition Ser.). (ENG., Illus.). 176p. (J). (gr. 2-5). pap. 6.99 *(978-0-545-70828-9(1)*, Scholastic Paperbacks) Scholastic, Inc.

—Annabelle the Drawing Fairy. 2015. (Magical Crafts Fairies Ser.: 2). (ENG., Illus.). 80p. (J). (gr. 2-5). pap. 4.99 *(978-0-545-70830-2(3)*, Scholastic Paperbacks) Scholastic, Inc.

—Ashley the Dragon Fairy. 2012. (Illus.). (J). (Magical Animal Fairies Ser.: 1). (ENG.). 80p. (gr. 2-5). pap. 4.99 *(978-0-545-38417-9(6)*, Scholastic Paperbacks); 65p. *(978-0-545-42595-7(6))* Scholastic, Inc.

—Autumn the Falling Leaves Fairy. 2013. (Rainbow Magic — Special Edition Ser.). lib. bdg. 17.20 *(978-0-606-32370-3(8)*, Turtleback) Turtleback Bks.

—Ava the Sunset Fairy. 2011. (Illus.). 63p. (J). *(978-0-545-38040-9(5))* Scholastic, Inc.

—Belle the Birthday Fairy. 2012. (Rainbow Magic Ser.). (ENG., Illus.). 176p. (J). (gr. 2-5). pap. 6.99 *(978-0-545-27054-0(5)*, Scholastic Paperbacks) Scholastic, Inc.

M
N
O

—Belle the Birthday Fairy. 2012. (Rainbow Magic — Special Edition Ser.). lib. bdg. 17.20 (978-0-606-23726-0(7), Turtleback) Turtleback Bks.

—Best Friends in Fairyland. 2010. (Scholastic Reader Level 2 Ser.). (ENG.). 32p. (J). (gr. 1-3). pap. 3.99 (978-0-545-22293-8(1), Cartwheel Bks.) Scholastic, Inc.

—Blossom the Flower Girl Fairy. 2016. (Rainbow Magic: Special Edition Ser.). (ENG.). 176p. (J). (gr. 2-5). pap. 6.99 (978-0-545-85202-9(1), Scholastic Paperbacks) Scholastic, Inc.

—Brianna the Tooth Fairy. 2013. (Rainbow Magic — Special Edition Ser.). lib. bdg. 17.20 (978-0-606-31990-4(5), Turtleback) Turtleback Bks.

—Caitlin the Ice Bear Fairy. 2012. (Illus.). 65p. (J). (978-0-545-42602-2(2)) Scholastic, Inc.

—Cara the Camp Fairy. 2011. (Rainbow Magic Ser.). (Illus.). (J). (ENG.). 176p. (gr. 2-5). pap. 6.99 (978-0-545-30877-9(1), Scholastic Paperbacks); 165p. (978-0-545-31656-9(1)) Scholastic, Inc.

—Carmen the Cheerleading Fairy. 2017. (Rainbow Magic: Special Edition Ser.). (ENG.). 176p. (J). (gr. 2-5). pap. 6.99 **(978-1-338-05484-2(8)**, Scholastic Paperbacks) Scholastic, Inc.

—Cassidy the Costume Fairy. 2012. (Rainbow Magic — the Princess Fairies Ser.: 2). lib. bdg. 14.75 (978-0-606-26170-8(2), Turtleback) Turtleback Bks.

—Chloe Slipperside's Secret. 2016. (Magic Animal Friends Ser.: 11). (ENG., Illus.). 112p. (J). (gr. 2-5). pap. 4.99 (978-0-545-94078-8(8), Scholastic Paperbacks) Scholastic, Inc.

—Clara the Chocolate Fairy. 2014. (Sugar & Spice Fairies Ser.: 4). (ENG.). 80p. (J). (gr. 2-5). pap. 4.99 (978-0-545-60534-2(2), Scholastic Paperbacks) Scholastic, Inc.

—Coco the Cupcake Fairy. 2014. (Sugar & Spice Fairies Ser.: 3). (ENG.). 80p. (J). (gr. 2-5). pap. 4.99 (978-0-545-60533-5(4), Scholastic Paperbacks) Scholastic, Inc.

—Coral the Reef Fairy. 2014. (Rainbow Magic — the Earth Fairies Ser.). lib. bdg. 14.75 (978-0-606-35833-0(1)) Turtleback Bks.

—Courtney the Clownfish Fairy. 2011. (Illus.). 62p. (J). (978-0-545-28877-4(0)) Scholastic, Inc.

—Destiny the Rock Star Fairy. 2011. (Rainbow Magic Ser.). (ENG., Illus.). 176p. (J). (gr. 2-5). pap. 6.99 (978-0-545-27056-4(1), Scholastic Paperbacks) Scholastic, Inc.

—The Earth Fairies #5: Lily the Rain Forest Fairy. 2014. (Earth Fairies Ser.: 5). (ENG.). 80p. (J). (gr. 2-5). pap. 4.99 (978-0-545-60528-1(8), Scholastic Paperbacks) Scholastic, Inc.

—Edie the Garden Fairy. 2014. (Rainbow Magic — the Earth Fairies Ser.). lib. bdg. 14.75 (978-0-606-35832-3(3)) Turtleback Bks.

—Eleanor the Snow White Fairy. 2016. (Illus.). (J). (Fairy Tale Fairies Ser.: 2). (ENG.). 80p. (gr. 2-5). pap. 4.99 (978-0-545-85190-9(4), Scholastic Paperbacks); 65p. **(978-0-545-88738-0(0))** Scholastic, Inc.

—Elisa the Royal Adventure Fairy. 2012. (Rainbow Magic — the Princess Fairies Ser.: 4). lib. bdg. 14.75 (978-0-606-26172-2(9), Turtleback) Turtleback Bks.

—Elle the Thumbelina Fairy. 2017. (Storybook Fairies Ser.: 1). (ENG.). 80p. (J). (gr. 2-5). pap. 4.99 (978-1-338-05495-8(3), Scholastic Paperbacks) Scholastic, Inc.

—Ellie Featherbill All Alone. 2015. (Magic Animal Friends Ser.: 3). lib. bdg. 14.75 (978-0-606-37047-9(1)) Turtleback Bks.

—Emily, the Emerald Fairy. Ripper, Georgie, illus. 2005. 65p. (J). pap. (978-0-545-01190-7(6)) Scholastic, Inc.

—Emma the Easter Fairy. 2011. (Rainbow Magic Ser.). (ENG.). 192p. (J). (gr. 2-5). pap. 6.99 (978-0-545-27051-9(0), Scholastic Paperbacks) Scholastic, Inc.

—Erin the Phoenix Fairy. 2012. (Illus.). 64p. (J). (978-0-545-42597-1(2)) Scholastic, Inc.

—Esme the Ice Cream Fairy. 2014. (Sugar & Spice Fairies Ser.: 2). (ENG.). 80p. (J). (gr. 2-5). pap. 4.99 (978-0-545-60532-8(6), Scholastic Paperbacks) Scholastic, Inc.

—Eva the Enchanted Ball Fairy. 2012. (Rainbow Magic — the Princess Fairies Ser.: 7). lib. bdg. 14.75 (978-0-606-26175-3(3), Turtleback) Turtleback Bks.

—Evie Scruffypup's Big Surprise. 2016. (Magic Animal Friends Ser.: 1). (ENG., Illus.). 112p. (J). (gr. 2-5). pap. 4.99 (978-0-545-94077-1(X), Scholastic Paperbacks) Scholastic, Inc.

—Evie Scruffypup's Surprise. 2016. (Magic Animal Friends Ser.: 10). lib. bdg. 14.75 (978-0-606-38800-9(1)) Turtleback Bks.

—The Fairies' Birthday Surprise. 2010. (Scholastic Reader Level 2 Ser.). (ENG.). 32p. (J). (gr. 1-3). pap. 3.99 (978-0-545-22292-1(3), Cartwheel Bks.) Scholastic, Inc.

—A Fairy Ballet. 2011. (Scholastic Reader, Level 2 Ser.). (ENG.). 32p. (J). (gr. 1-3). pap. 3.99 (978-0-545-22294-5(X), Cartwheel Bks.) Scholastic, Inc.

—The Fairy Treasure Hunt. 2012. (Rainbow Magic — Scholastic Reader Ser.). lib. bdg. 13.55 (978-0-606-23912-7(X), Turtleback) Turtleback Bks.

—A Fairyland Costume Ball. 2012. (Scholastic Reader Level 2 Ser.). (ENG., Illus.). 32p. (J). (gr. 2-5). pap. 3.99 (978-0-545-43389-1(4), Scholastic Paperbacks) Scholastic, Inc.

—A Fairyland Costume Ball. 2012. (Rainbow Magic — Scholastic Reader Ser.). lib. bdg. 13.55 (978-0-606-26235-4(0), Turtleback) Turtleback Bks.

—Faith the Cinderella Fairy. 2016. (Fairy Tale Fairies Ser.: 3). (ENG., Illus.). 80p. (J). (gr. 2-5). pap. 4.99 (978-0-545-85195-4(5), Scholastic Paperbacks) Scholastic, Inc.

—Frankie the Makeup Fairy. 2013. (Rainbow Magic — the Superstar Fairies Ser.: 5). lib. bdg. 14.75 (978-0-606-31517-3(9), Turtleback) Turtleback Bks.

—Georgia the Guinea Pig Fairy. Ripper, Georgie, illus. 2008. (Rainbow Magic — the Pet Fairies Ser.). 65p. (gr. 3). lib. bdg. 14.75 (978-1-4178-2997-2(4), Turtleback) Turtleback Bks.

—Grace Woollyhop's Musical Mystery. 2016. (Magic Animal Friends Ser.: 12). lib. bdg. 14.75 (978-0-606-38802-3(8)) Turtleback Bks.

—Grace Woollyhop's Musical Mystery (Magic Animal Friends #12) 2016. (Magic Animal Friends Ser.: 12). (ENG., Illus.). 112p. (J). (gr. 2-5). pap. 4.99 (978-0-545-94079-5(6), Scholastic Paperbacks) Scholastic, Inc.

—Gwen the Beauty & the Beast Fairy. 2016. (Illus.). (J). (Fairy Tale Fairies Ser.: 5). (ENG.). 80p. (gr. 2-5). pap. 4.99 (978-0-545-85198-5(X), Scholastic Paperbacks); 67p. **(978-1-5182-1018-1(X))** Scholastic, Inc.

—Harriet the Hamster Fairy. Ripper, Georgie, illus. 2008. (Rainbow Magic — the Pet Fairies Ser.). 67p. (gr. -1-3). lib. bdg. 14.75 (978-1-4178-3007-7(7), Turtleback) Turtleback Bks.

—Inky the Indigo Fairy. Ripper, Georgie, illus. 2006. (Rainbow Magic Ser.: 6). (ENG.). 80p. (J). (gr. -1-3). per. 4.99 (978-0-439-74685-4(X), Scholastic Paperbacks) Scholastic, Inc.

—Isabella the Air Fairy. 2014. (Rainbow Magic — the Earth Fairies Ser.). lib. bdg. 14.75 (978-0-606-35831-6(5)) Turtleback Bks.

—Josie the Jewelry Fairy. 2015. (Magical Crafts Fairies Ser.: 4). (ENG., Illus.). 80p. (J). (gr. 2-5). pap. 4.99 (978-0-545-70832-6(X), Scholastic Paperbacks) Scholastic, Inc.

—Julia the Sleeping Beauty Fairy. 2016. (Illus.). (J). (Fairy Tale Fairies Ser.: 1). (ENG.). 80p. (gr. 2-5). pap. 4.99 (978-0-545-85189-3(0), Scholastic Paperbacks); 65p. **(978-0-545-88737-3(2))** Scholastic, Inc.

—Juliet the Valentine Fairy. 2009. (Rainbow Magic Ser.). (ENG., Illus.). 192p. (J). (gr. 2-5). pap. 6.99 (978-0-545-14886-3(3), Scholastic Paperbacks) Scholastic, Inc.

—Kathryn the Gym Fairy. 2016. (Rainbow Magic — the School Day Fairies Ser.: 4). lib. bdg. 14.75 (978-0-606-38792-7(7)) Turtleback Bks.

—Katie the Kitten Fairy. Ripper, Georgie, illus. 2008. (J). (Pet Fairies Ser.: 1). (ENG.). 80p. (gr. -1-3). pap. 4.99 (978-0-545-02816-5(7), Scholastic Paperbacks); 65p. pap. (978-0-545-13320-3(3)) Scholastic, Inc.

—Katie the Kitten Fairy. Ripper, Georgie, illus. 2008. (Rainbow Magic — the Pet Fairies Ser.). 65p. (gr. 1-4). lib. bdg. 14.75 (978-1-4178-2999-6(0), Turtleback) Turtleback Bks.

—Kayla the Pottery Fairy. 2015. (Magical Crafts Fairies Ser.: 1). (ENG., Illus.). 80p. (J). (gr. 2-5). pap. 4.99 (978-0-545-70829-6(X), Scholastic Paperbacks) Scholastic, Inc.

—Kimberly the Koala Fairy. 2015. (Baby Animal Rescue Fairies Ser.: 5). (ENG.). 80p. (J). (gr. 2-5). pap. 4.99 (978-0-545-70854-8(0), Scholastic Paperbacks) Scholastic, Inc.

—Kitty the Tiger Fairy. 2015. (Baby Animal Rescue Fairies Ser.: 2). (ENG.). 80p. (J). (gr. 2-5). pap. 4.99 (978-0-545-70846-3(X), Scholastic Paperbacks) Scholastic, Inc.

—Lacey the Little Mermaid Fairy. 2016. (Fairy Tale Fairies Ser.: 7). (ENG., Illus.). 80p. (J). (gr. 2-5). pap. 4.99 (978-0-545-85196-1(3), Scholastic Paperbacks) Scholastic, Inc.

—Lara the Black Cat Fairy. 2012. (Illus.). 65p. (J). (978-0-545-42596-4(4)) Scholastic, Inc.

—Layla the Cotton Candy Fairy. 2014. (Sugar & Spice Fairies Ser.: 6). (ENG.). 80p. (J). (gr. 2-5). pap. 4.99 (978-0-545-60536-6(9), Scholastic Paperbacks) Scholastic, Inc.

—Leona the Unicorn Fairy. 2012. (Illus.). 65p. (J). (978-0-545-42601-5(4)) Scholastic, Inc.

—Libby the Writing Fairy. (Illus.). (J). 2015. (Magical Crafts Fairies Ser.: 6). (ENG.). 80p. (gr. 2-5). pap. 4.99 (978-0-545-70834-0(6), Scholastic Paperbacks) 2014. 65p. (978-0-545-72414-2(7)) Scholastic, Inc.

—Lily the Rain Forest Fairy. 2014. (Rainbow Magic — the Earth Fairies Ser.). lib. bdg. 14.75 (978-0-606-35834-7(X)) Turtleback Bks.

—Lisa the Lollipop Fairy. 2014. (Sugar & Spice Fairies Ser.: 1). (ENG.). 80p. (J). (gr. 2-5). pap. 4.99 (978-0-545-60531-1(8), Scholastic Paperbacks) Scholastic, Inc.

—Lizzie the Sweet Treats Fairy. 2012. (Rainbow Magic — the Princess Fairies Ser.: 5). lib. bdg. 14.75 (978-0-606-26173-9(7), Turtleback) Turtleback Bks.

—Louise the Lily Fairy. 2009. (Petal Fairies Ser.: 3). (ENG., Illus.). 80p. (J). (gr. 2-5). pap. 4.99 (978-0-545-07092-8(9), Scholastic Paperbacks) Scholastic, Inc.

—Lucy Longwhiskers Gets Lost. 2015. (Magic Animal Friends Ser.: 1). lib. bdg. 14.75 (978-0-606-37045-5(5)) Turtleback Bks.

—Madeline the Cookie Fairy. 2014. (Sugar & Spice Fairies Ser.: 5). (ENG.). 80p. (J). (gr. 2-5). pap. 4.99 (978-0-545-60535-9(0), Scholastic Paperbacks) Scholastic, Inc.

—Mae the Panda Fairy. 2015. (Baby Animal Rescue Fairies Ser.: 1). (ENG.). 80p. (J). (gr. 2-5). pap. 4.99 (978-0-545-70844-9(3), Scholastic Paperbacks) Scholastic, Inc.

—Magic Animal Friends - Poppy Muddlepup's Daring Rescue. 2015. (Magic Animal Friends Ser.: 1). (ENG., Illus.). 176p. (J). (gr. 2-5). pap. 6.99 (978-0-545-90750-7(0)) Scholastic, Inc.

—Mariana the Goldilocks Fairy. 2017. (Storybook Fairies Ser.: 2). (ENG.). 80p. (J). (gr. 2-5). pap. 4.99 (978-1-338-05499-6(6), Scholastic Paperbacks) Scholastic, Inc.

—Mia the Bridesmaid Fairy. 2010. (Rainbow Magic Ser.). (ENG.). 176p. (J). (gr. 2-5). 6.99 (978-0-545-20251-0(5), Scholastic Paperbacks) Scholastic, Inc.

—Miley the Stylist Fairy. 2013. (Rainbow Magic — the Superstar Fairies Ser.: 4). lib. bdg. 14.75 (978-0-606-31516-6(0), Turtleback) Turtleback Bks.

—Milly the River Fairy. 2014. (Rainbow Magic — the Earth Fairies Ser.). lib. bdg. 14.75 (978-0-606-35835-4(8)) Turtleback Bks.

—Molly the Goldfish Fairy. Ripper, Georgie, illus. 2008. (Pet Fairies Ser.: 6). (ENG.). 80p. (J). (gr. -1-3). pap. 4.99 (978-0-545-04189-8(9), Scholastic Paperbacks) Scholastic, Inc.

—Molly Twinkletail Runs Away. 2015. (Magic Animal Friends Ser.: 2). lib. bdg. 14.75 (978-0-606-37046-2(3)) Turtleback Bks.

—Nicole the Beach Fairy. 2014. (Rainbow Magic — the Earth Fairies Ser.). lib. bdg. 14.75 (978-0-606-35830-9(7)) Turtleback Bks.

—Nina the Birthday Cake Fairy. 2014. (Sugar & Spice Fairies Ser.: 7). (ENG.). 80p. (J). (gr. 2-5). pap. 4.99 (978-0-545-60537-3(7), Scholastic Paperbacks) Scholastic, Inc.

—Olivia Nibblesqueak's Messy Mischief. 2016. (Magic Animal Friends Ser.: 9). (ENG., Illus.). 112p. (J). (gr. 2-5). pap. 4.99 (978-0-545-94076-4(1), Scholastic Paperbacks) Scholastic, Inc.

—Olympia the Games Fairy. 2012. (Rainbow Magic — Special Edition Ser.). lib. bdg. 17.20 (978-0-606-26541-6(4), Turtleback) Turtleback Bks.

—Paige the Christmas Play Fairy. 2010. (Rainbow Magic Ser.). (ENG.). 192p. (J). (gr. 2-5). pap. 6.99 (978-0-545-22177-1(3), Scholastic Paperbacks) Scholastic, Inc.

—Pia the Penguin Fairy. 2011. (Illus.). 63p. (J). (978-0-545-28873-6(8)) Scholastic, Inc.

—The Rainbow Fairies. 2010. (Scholastic Reader Level 2 Ser.). (ENG.). 32p. (J). (gr. 1-3). pap. 3.99 (978-0-545-22291-4(5), Cartwheel Bks.) Scholastic, Inc.

—Rainbow Magic Special Edition: Addison the April Fool's Day Fairy. 2014. (Rainbow Magic Special Edition Ser.). (ENG.). 176p. (J). (gr. 2-5). pap. 6.99 (978-0-545-60538-0(5), Scholastic Paperbacks) Scholastic, Inc.

—Rainbow Magic Special Edition: Autumn the Falling Leaves Fairy. 2013. (Rainbow Magic Special Edition Ser.). (ENG.). 176p. (J). (gr. 2-5). pap. 6.99 (978-0-545-48495-4(2), Scholastic Paperbacks) Scholastic, Inc.

—Rainbow Magic Special Edition: Brianna the Tooth Fairy. 2013. (Rainbow Magic Special Edition Ser.). (ENG.). 176p. (J). (gr. 2-5). pap. 6.99 (978-0-545-48494-7(4), Scholastic Paperbacks) Scholastic, Inc.

—Rainbow Magic Special Edition: Chelsea the Congratulations Fairy. 2015. (Rainbow Magic Special Edition Ser.). (ENG.). 176p. (J). (gr. 2-5). pap. 6.99 (978-0-545-70826-5(5), Scholastic Paperbacks) Scholastic, Inc.

—Rainbow Magic Special Edition: Cheryl the Christmas Tree Fairy. 2012. (Rainbow Magic Special Edition Ser.). (ENG.). 176p. (J). (gr. 2-5). pap. 6.99 (978-0-545-45571-8(5), Scholastic Paperbacks) Scholastic, Inc.

—Rainbow Magic Special Edition Collection. 2016. (Rainbow Magic Special Edition Ser.). (ENG.). 528p. (J). (gr. 2-5). pap. 9.99 (978-1-338-10243-7(5)) Scholastic, Inc.

—Rainbow Magic Special Edition: Olympia the Games Fairy. 2012. (Rainbow Magic Ser.). (ENG., Illus.). 176p. (J). (gr. 2-5). pap. 6.99 (978-0-545-45703-3(3)) Scholastic, Inc.

—Rihanna the Seahorse Fairy. 2012. (Illus.). 65p. (J). (978-0-545-42599-5(9)) Scholastic, Inc.

—Rita the Frog Princess Fairy. 2016. (Fairy Tale Fairies Ser.: 4). (ENG., Illus.). 80p. (J). (gr. 2-5). pap. 4.99 (978-0-545-85197-8(1), Scholastic Paperbacks) Scholastic, Inc.

—Rosalie the Rapunzel Fairy. 2017. (Storybook Fairies Ser.: 3). (ENG.). 80p. (J). (gr. 2-5). pap. 4.99 (978-1-338-05502-3(X), Scholastic Paperbacks) Scholastic, Inc.

—Rosie the Honey Bear Fairy. 2015. (Baby Animal Rescue Fairies Ser.: 6). (ENG.). 80p. (J). (gr. 2-5). pap. 4.99 (978-0-545-70855-5(9), Scholastic Paperbacks) Scholastic, Inc.

—Roxie the Baking Fairy. 2015. (Magical Crafts Fairies Ser.: 7). (ENG., Illus.). 80p. (J). (gr. 2-5). pap. 4.99 (978-0-545-70835-7(4), Scholastic Paperbacks) Scholastic, Inc.

—Ruby Fuzzybrush's Star Dance. 2016. (Magic Animal Friends Ser.: 7). (ENG., Illus.). 112p. (J). (gr. 2-5). pap. 4.99 (978-0-545-90745-3(4), Scholastic Paperbacks) Scholastic, Inc.

—Savannah the Zebra Fairy. 2015. (Baby Animal Rescue Fairies Ser.: 4). (ENG.). 80p. (J). (gr. 2-5). pap. 4.99 (978-0-545-70853-1(2), Scholastic Paperbacks) Scholastic, Inc.

—Scholastic Reader Level 2: Rainbow Magic: Pet Fairies to the Rescue! Artful Doodlers Ltd Staff, illus. 2013. (Scholastic Reader Level 2 Ser.). (ENG.). 32p. (J). (gr. -1-3). pap. 3.99 (978-0-545-46295-2(9), Scholastic Paperbacks) Scholastic, Inc.

—Shannon the Ocean Fairy. 2009. (Rainbow Magic Ser.). (ENG.). 176p. (J). (gr. 2-5). 6.99 (978-0-545-10576-7(5), Scholastic Paperbacks) Scholastic, Inc.

—Skyler the Fireworks Fairy (Rainbow Magic: Special Edition) 2016. (Rainbow Magic Ser.). (ENG., Illus.). 192p. (J). (gr. 2-5). pap. 6.99 (978-0-545-85204-3(8), Scholastic Paperbacks) Scholastic, Inc.

—Sophia the Snow Swan Fairy. 2012. (Illus.). 65p. (J). (978-0-545-42600-8(6)) Scholastic, Inc.

—Sophie Flufftail's Brave Plan. 2016. (Magic Animal Friends Ser.: 5). (ENG., Illus.). 112p. (J). (gr. 2-5). pap. 4.99 (978-0-545-90741-5(1), Scholastic Paperbacks) Scholastic, Inc.

—Stephanie the Starfish Fairy. 2011. (Illus.). 65p. (J). (978-0-545-28875-0(4)) Scholastic, Inc.

—Sunny the Yellow Fairy. Ripper, Georgie, illus. 2005. (Rainbow Magic Ser.: 3). (ENG.). 80p. (J). (gr. 2-5). pap. 4.99 (978-0-439-74466-9(0), Little Apple Bks) Scholastic Canada, Ltd. CAN. Dist: Scholastic, Inc.

—Tess the Sea Turtle Fairy. 2011. (Illus.). 65p. (J). (978-0-545-28874-3(6)) Scholastic, Inc.

—Vanessa the Choreography Fairy. 2013. (Rainbow Magic — the Superstar Fairies Ser.: 3). lib. bdg. 14.75 (978-0-606-31515-9(2), Turtleback) Turtleback Bks.

—Violet the Painting Fairy. 2015. (Illus.). (J). (Magical Crafts Fairies Ser.: 5). (ENG.). 80p. (gr. 2-5). pap. 4.99 (978-0-545-70833-3(8), Scholastic Paperbacks); 65p. (978-0-545-72413-5(9)) Scholastic, Inc.

—Whitney the Whale Fairy. 2011. (Illus.). 64p. (J). (978-0-545-28876-7(2)) Scholastic, Inc.

—Zadie the Sewing Fairy. 2015. (Illus.). (J). (Magical Crafts Fairies Ser.: 3). (ENG.). 80p. (gr. 2-5). pap. 4.99 (978-0-545-70831-9(1), Scholastic Paperbacks); 65p. (978-0-545-72411-1(2)) Scholastic, Inc.

Meadows, Jodi. Before She Ignites. 2017. (Fallen Isles Ser.: 1). 496p. (YA). (gr. 8). 17.99 **(978-0-06-246940-3(1)**, Tegen, Katherine Bks) HarperCollins Pubs.

Meadows, Melissa. What's the Word, Thunderbird? 2008. (ENG., Illus.). 80p. (J). (978-1-934517-01-7(1)) Firelight Press, Inc.

—What's the Word, Thunderbird? Book A: the Alamo. 2007. (Wishing Well Ser.). (Illus.). 81p. (J). (gr. k-3). per. 4.99 (978-1-934517-00-0(3)) Firelight Press, Inc.

Meeks, John R. Dugan's Magical Island. 2011. 28p. pap. 12.40 (978-1-4567-3947-8(6)) AuthorHouse.

Meer, Pippa Lee. Matilda's Marvellous Monday. 2008. 32p. pap. 14.49 (978-1-4389-0421-4(5)) AuthorHouse.

Megerdichian, Janet. Pine Needle Pedro. Adams, Allysa, illus. 2010. 36p. pap. 16.99 (978-1-4520-4422-4(8)) AuthorHouse.

Melling, O. R. The Book of Dreams. 2009. (Chronicles of Faerie Ser.). (ENG.). 720p. (J). (gr. 2-8). 19.95 (978-0-8109-8346-5(X), Amulet Bks.) Abrams, Inc.

—The Light-Bearer's Daughter. 2008. (ENG.). 368p. (YA). (gr. 2-8). pap. 9.95 (978-0-8109-7123-3(2), Amulet Bks.) Abrams, Inc.

Mello, Alondra. Alanora's Magic Tree: Alanora's Spirit Journey. 2007. 48p. per. 12.97 (978-1-932344-77-6(2)) Thornton Publishing, Inc.

Meloy, Maile. The Apprentices. Schoenherr, Ian, illus. 2013. (Apothecary Ser.: 2). (ENG.). 416p. (J). (gr. 5). 16.99 (978-0-399-16245-9(3), G.P. Putnam's Sons Books for Young Readers) Penguin Young Readers Group.

Meredith, Susan Markowitz. The Magical Simon & Roxie. 2016. (Spring Forward Ser.). (J). (gr. 2). (978-1-4900-9469-4(5)) Benchmark Education Co.

Merlin. Wizardology: The Book of the Secrets of Merlin. Steer, Dugald A., ed. gif. ed. 2005. (Ologies Ser.). (ENG., Illus.). 32p. (J). (gr. 3-7). 24.99 (978-0-7636-2895-6(6)) Candlewick Pr.

Merrick, M.R. Endure. 2013. 382p. pap. (978-0-9917862-4-4(6)) Merrick, M.R.

Meshach, Joanna. The Land of the Magical Mirrors. 2012. 32p. pap. 32.70 (978-1-4771-2595-3(7)) Xlibris Corp.

Mesibere, Ellen. The Magic Log. Naime, Sophie, ed. Joseph, Albert, illus. 2012. 24p. pap. (978-9980-945-68-6(0)) University of Papua New Guinea Press.

Messenger, Lois. Fairy Magic & the Healing Rainbow Colours. 2013. 36p. pap. 15.95 (978-1-4525-7663-3(7), Balboa Pr.) Author Solutions, Inc.

Messner, Kate. The Seventh Wish. (ENG.). (J). 2017. 256p. pap. 7.99 (978-1-68119-431-8(7), 9781681194318) 2016. 240p. 16.99 (978-1-61963-376-6(0), 9781619633766) Bloomsbury Publishing USA. (Bloomsbury USA Childrens).

Metcalf, Dan. The Egyptian Enchantment: A Lottie Lipton Adventure. Panagarry, Rachelle, illus. 2017. (Adventures of Lottie Lipton Ser.). (ENG.). (J). (gr. 2-5). 96p. pap. 6.99 **(978-1-5124-8188-4(2))**; lib. bdg. 25.32 **(978-1-5124-8182-2(3))** Lerner Publishing Group. (Darby Creek).

Metz, Diana. Brinn & the Dragons of Pallan Cliffs. 2003. 352p. (J). pap. (978-0-9718431-2-7(0)) M.O.T.H.E.R. Publishing Co., Inc., The.

Meyer, Kai. Dark Reflections: The Water Mirror - The Stone Light; the Glass Word. Crawford, Elizabeth D., tr. from GER. 2010. (Dark Reflections Trilogy Ser.). (ENG.). 896p. (YA). (gr. 7). pap. 9.99 (978-1-4424-0938-5(X), McElderry, Margaret K. Bks.) McElderry, Margaret K. Bks.

—The Glass Word. Crawford, Elizabeth D., tr. from GER. 2008. (ENG.). 288p. (YA). (gr. 7). (Dark Reflections Trilogy Ser.: 3). pap. 9.99 (978-0-689-87792-6(7)); (Dark Reflections Trilogy: Bk. 3). 16.99 (978-0-689-87791-9(9)) McElderry, Margaret K. Bks. (McElderry, Margaret K. Bks.).

—Pirate Wars. Crawford, Elizabeth D., tr. 2008. (Wave Walkers Ser.: 3). (ENG.). 384p. (J). (gr. 5-9). pap. 6.99 (978-1-4169-2477-7(9), McElderry, Margaret K. Bks.) McElderry, Margaret K. Bks.

—The Stone Light. Crawford, Elizabeth D., tr. 2007. (Dark Reflections Trilogy Ser.: 2). (ENG.). 384p. (YA). (gr. 7-12). pap. 8.99 (978-0-689-87790-2(0), McElderry, Margaret K. Bks.) McElderry, Margaret K. Bks.

Meyer, Linda Ross. The Recipe Box. 2010. 73p. pap. 7.99 (978-0-557-54210-9(3)) Lulu Pr., Inc.

Michael, Alexander. Until Wishes Are Fulfilled. 2007. (ENG.). 154p. per. 13.50 (978-1-84426-408-7(4)) Upfront Publishing Ltd. GBR. Dist: Printondemand-worldwide.com.

Michaelis, Antonia. The Dragons of Darkness. Bell, Anthea, tr. from GER. 2010. (ENG.). 566p. (YA). (gr. 7-11). 18.95 (978-0-8109-4074-1(4), Amulet Bks.) Abrams, Inc.

—Dragons of Darkness. Bell, Anthea, tr. 2011. (ENG.). 576p. (YA). (gr. 7-17). pap. 8.95 (978-1-4197-0085-9(5), Amulet Bks.) Abrams, Inc.

Miles, Cindy. Forevermore. 2013. (ENG.). 288p. (J). (gr. 7). pap. 9.99 (978-0-545-42622-0(7)) Scholastic, Inc.

Milford, Kate. Greenglass House. 2015. (CHI.). 352p. (J). (gr. 5-7). pap. (978-986-320-886-0(8)) Commonwealth Publishing Co., Ltd.

—Greenglass House. Zollars, Jaime, illus. (ENG.). (J). (gr. 5-7). 2016. 400p. pap. 7.99 (978-0-544-54028-6(X), HMH Books For Young Readers) 2014. 384p. 17.99 (978-0-544-05270-3(6)) Houghton Mifflin Harcourt Publishing Co.

—Greenglass House. 2016. lib. bdg. 18.40 (978-0-606-38908-2(3)) Turtleback Bks.

—The Left-Handed Fate. Wheeler, Eliza, illus. 2016. (ENG.). 384p. (J). 16.99 (978-0-8050-9800-6(3), 9780805098006, Holt, Henry & Co. Bks. For Young Readers) Holt, Henry & Co.

—The Left-Handed Fate. Wheeler, Eliza, illus. 2017. (ENG.). 384p. (J). pap. 7.99 (978-1-250-12183-7(3), 9781250121837) Square Fish.

Miller, Amanda. The Library's Secret: A Hidden Adventure. 2010. 88p. pap. 10.49 (978-1-4520-7012-4(1)) AuthorHouse.

Miller, Chris & Miller, Allan. Hunter Brown & the Consuming Fire, 3 bks., Bk.2. 2009. (ENG., Illus.). 352p. (J). pap. 13.99 (978-1-59317-357-9(1)) Warner Pr., Inc.

Miller, Christopher & Miller, Allan. Hunter Brown & the Eye of Ends, 3 bks., Bk.3. 2011. (J). pap. 13.99 (978-1-59317-400-2(4)) Warner Pr., Inc.

—Hunter Brown & the Secret of the Shadow, 3 bks., Bk.1. 2008. (ENG., Illus.). 384p. (J). (gr. 9-18). pap. 13.99 (978-1-59317-328-9(8)) Warner Pr., Inc.

Miller, Jennifer. Best Friends for Life. Choi Sung Hwan, Aragon Noel, illus. 2006. (Trollz Ser.). (ENG.). 120p. (J). pap. 4.99 (978-0-439-80311-3(X)) Scholastic, Inc.

Miller, Olive Beaupr. The Magic Garden of My Book House. 2005. reprint ed. pap. 24.95 (978-1-4191-4169-0(4)) Kessinger Publishing, LLC.

Miller, Sibley. Horse Magic - Or Not? Chang, Tara Larsen & Gershman, Jo, illus. 2011. (Wind Dancers Ser.: 12). (ENG.). 80p. (J). (gr. 1-4). pap. 16.99 (978-0-312-60545-2(5), 9780312605452) Feiwel & Friends.

—A Horse, of Course! Chang, Tara Larsen & Gershman, Jo, illus. 2009. (Wind Dancers Ser.: 7). (ENG.). 80p. (J). (gr. 1-4). pap. 16.99 (978-0-312-56402-5(3), 9780312564025) Feiwel & Friends.

—A Horse's Best Friend. Chang, Tara Larsen & Gershman, Jo, illus. 2011. (Wind Dancers Ser.: 9). (ENG.). 80p. (J). (gr. 1-4). pap. 6.99 (978-0-312-60542-1(0), 9780312605421) Feiwel & Friends.

—Horsey Trails. Chang, Tara Larsen & Gershman, Jo, illus. 2011. (Wind Dancers Ser.: 11). (ENG.). 80p. (J). (gr. 1-4). pap. 16.99 (978-0-312-60544-5(7), 9780312605445) Feiwel & Friends.

—Hungry as a Horse. 2009. (Wind Dancers Ser.: 8). (ENG., Illus.). 80p. (J). (gr. 1-4). pap. 6.99 (978-0-312-56403-2(1), 9780312564032) Feiwel & Friends.

—Merry-Go-Horses. Chang, Tara Larsen & Gershman, Jo, illus. 2011. (Wind Dancers Ser.: 10). (ENG.). 80p. (J). (gr. 1-4). pap. 6.99 (978-0-312-60543-8(9), 9780312605438) Feiwel & Friends.

Miller, Sibley & Lenhard, Elizabeth. The Horse Must Go On. Chang, Tara Larsen & Gershman, Jo, illus. 2008. (Wind Dancers Ser.: 3). (ENG.). 80p. (J). (gr. 1-4). pap. 11.99 (978-0-312-38282-7(0), 9780312382827) Feiwel & Friends.

—Horses' Night Out. Chang, Tara Larsen & Gershman, Jo, illus. 2008. (Wind Dancers Ser.: 4). (ENG.). 80p. (J). (gr. 1-4). pap. 16.99 (978-0-312-38283-4(9), 9780312382834) Feiwel & Friends.

—If Wishes Were Horses. Chang, Tara Larsen & Gershman, Jo, illus. 2008. (Wind Dancers Ser.: 1). (ENG.). 80p. (J). (gr. 1-4). pap. 7.99 (978-0-312-38280-3(4), 9780312382803) Feiwel & Friends.

Miller, Toby. The Magic Word. 2011. (Illus.). 24p. pap. 14.09 (978-1-4567-7793-7(9)) AuthorHouse.

Milligan, Domino. The Sandman. Spiller, Michael, illus. 2008. 16p. pap. 24.95 (978-1-60703-728-6(9)) America Star Bks.

Misra, Michelle. Birthday Surprise. Chaffey, Samantha, illus. 2016. (Angel Wings Ser.: 2). (ENG.). 128p. (J). (gr. 1-4). pap. 5.99 (978-1-4814-5800-9(0), Aladdin) Simon & Schuster Children's Publishing.

Miyazaki, Hayao. Ponyo Film Comic, Vol. 1. Miyazaki, Hayao, illus. movie tie-in ed. 2009. (ENG., Illus.). 172p. (J). pap. 9.99 (978-1-4215-3077-2(5)) Viz Media.

—Ponyo Film Comic, Vol. 2. Miyazaki, Hayao, illus. movie tie-in ed. 2009. (ENG., Illus.). 172p. (J). pap. 9.99 (978-1-4215-3078-9(3)) Viz Media.

—Ponyo Film Comic, Vol. 3. Miyazaki, Hayao, illus. movie tie-in ed. 2009. (ENG., Illus.). 172p. (J). pap. 9.99 (978-1-4215-3079-6(1)) Viz Media.

—Ponyo Film Comic, Vol. 4. Miyazaki, Hayao, illus. movie tie-in ed. 2009. (ENG., Illus.). 172p. (J). pap. 9.99 (978-1-4215-3080-2(5)) Viz Media.

—Ponyo Picture Book, Vol. 1. Miyazaki, Hayao, illus. 2009. (ENG., Illus.). 152p. (J). (gr. 2-7). 19.99 (978-1-4215-3065-9(1)) Viz Media.

Mlynowski, Sarah. Abby in Wonderland. 2017. (Whatever After Ser.). (ENG.). 256p. (J). (gr. 3-7). 16.99 **(978-0-545-74664-9(7)**, Scholastic Pr.) Scholastic, Inc.

—Bad Hair Day. 2014. (Whatever After Ser.: No. 5). (ENG.). 176p. (J). (gr. 3-7). 14.99 (978-0-545-62728-3(1), Scholastic Pr.) Scholastic, Inc.

—Beauty Queen. 2015. (Whatever After Ser.: 7). (ENG.). 176p. (J). (gr. 3-7). 14.99 (978-0-545-74654-0(X), Scholastic Pr.) Scholastic, Inc.

—Cold As Ice. 2015. (Whatever After Ser.: 6). (ENG.). 176p. (J). (gr. 3-7). pap. 5.99 (978-0-545-62736-8(2), Scholastic Pr.) Scholastic, Inc.

—Cold as Ice. 2014. (Whatever After Ser.: 6). (ENG.). 176p. (J). (gr. 3-7). 14.99 (978-0-545-62734-4(6), Scholastic Pr.) Scholastic, Inc.

—Dream On. (Whatever After Ser.: 4). (ENG.). 176p. (J). (gr. 3-7). 2014. pap. 5.99 (978-0-545-41572-9(1), Scholastic Paperbacks) 2013. 14.99 (978-0-545-41571-2(3), Scholastic Pr.) Scholastic, Inc.

—Fairest of All. (Whatever After Ser.: 1). (ENG.). 176p. (J). (gr. 3-7). 2013. pap. 5.99 (978-0-545-48571-5(1)) 2012. 14.99 (978-0-545-40330-6(8)) Scholastic, Inc. (Scholastic Pr.).

—Frogs & French Kisses. 2007. (Magic in Manhattan Ser.: No. 2). (ENG.). 304p. (YA). (gr. 7). pap. 8.99 (978-0-385-73185-0(X), Delacorte Pr.) Random Hse. Children's Bks.

—Genie in a Bottle (Whatever After #9) 2016. (Whatever After Ser.: 9). (ENG.). 176p. (J). (gr. 3-7). 14.99 (978-0-545-85102-2(5), Scholastic Pr.) Scholastic, Inc.

—If the Shoe Fits. 2013. 176p. (Whatever After Ser.: 2). (ENG.). (J). (gr. 3-7). pap. 5.99 (978-0-545-41568-2(3), Scholastic Pr.); 14.99 (978-0-545-50465-2(1)); (Whatever After Ser.: 2). (ENG.). (J). (gr. 3-7). 14.99 (978-0-545-41567-5(5), Scholastic Pr.) Scholastic, Inc.

—Magic in Manhattan: Bras & Broomsticks Frogs; French Kisses. 2012. (Magic in Manhattan Ser.). (ENG.). 608p. (YA). (gr. 7). pap. 10.99 (978-0-385-74232-0(0), Ember) Random Hse. Children's Bks.

—Sink or Swim. (Whatever After Ser.: 3). (J). 2014. (ENG.). 176p. (gr. 3-7). pap. 5.99 (978-0-545-41570-5(5)) 2013. 165p. (978-0-545-53316-4(3))Bk. 3. 2013. (ENG.). 176p. (gr. 3-7). 14.99 (978-0-545-41569-9(1)) Scholastic, Inc. (Scholastic Pr.).

—Sugar & Spice. 2016. (Whatever After Ser.: 10). (ENG.). 176p. (J). (gr. 3-7). 14.99 (978-0-545-85106-0(8), Scholastic Pr.) Scholastic, Inc.

—Whatever after Collection, Bks. 1-3. 2016. (Whatever After Ser.). (ENG.). 528p. (J). (gr. 3-7). pap. 9.99 (978-1-338-10175-1(7)) Scholastic, Inc.

Mlynowski, Sarah, et al. Showing Off. 2016. (Upside-down Magic Ser.: No. 3). (ENG.). 240p. (J). (gr. 3-7). 14.99 (978-0-545-80053-2(6), Scholastic Pr.) Scholastic, Inc.

—Sticks & Stones. (ENG.). 208p. (J). (gr. 3-7). 2017. (Upside-Down Magic Ser.: 2). pap. 5.99 **(978-0-545-80050-1(1))** 2016. (Upside-down Magic Ser.: No. 2). 14.99 (978-0-545-80049-5(8), Scholastic Pr.) Scholastic, Inc.

Mlynowski, Sarah, et al. Upside-Down Magic. (J). 2016. (Upside-Down Magic Ser.: 1). (ENG.). 208p. (gr. 3-7). pap. 5.99 (978-0-545-80046-4(3)) 2015. (Upside-down Magic Ser.: No. 1). (ENG.). 208p. (gr. 3-7). 14.99 (978-0-545-80045-7(5), Scholastic Pr.) 2015. 196p. pap. (978-0-545-90822-1(1), Scholastic Pr.) Scholastic, Inc.

Modesto, Michelle. Revenge & the Wild. 2016. 384p. (YA). (gr. 9). 17.99 (978-0-06-236615-3(7)) HarperCollins Pubs.

Moffit, Linda L. The Magic Mirror. 2003. (Illus.). 80p. (Orig.). (gr. k-7). 10.95 (978-0-87516-615-5(6), Devorss Pubns.) DeVorss & Co.

Molesworth. The Cuckoo Clock. 2007. (ENG.). 122p. pap. 18.99 (978-1-4346-4245-5(3)) Creative Media Partners, LLC.

—Cuckoo Clock. 2006. 216p. per. (978-1-4067-1668-9(5), Hesperides Pr.) Read Bks.

—The Cuckoo Clock. l.t. ed. 2007. 132p. pap. 19.99 (978-1-4346-4246-2(1)) Creative Media Partners, LLC.

Molesworth, Mary Louisa. The Cuckoo Clock. 2004. reprint ed. pap. 1.99 (978-1-4192-5839-8(7)); pap. 19.95 (978-1-4191-5839-1(2)) Kessinger Publishing, LLC.

Molesworth, Mary Louisa S. & Molesworth. The Palace in the Garden. 2011. 148p. 25.95 (978-1-4638-9525-9(9)) Rodgers, Alan Bks.

Monaghan, Joseph. The Boy Who Loved Trees. 2013. (Illus.). 24p. pap. 19.82 (978-1-4817-8225-8(8)) AuthorHouse.

Mongredien, Sue. Oliver Moon & the Dragon Disaster. 2011. (Oliver Moon Ser.). 94p. (J). pap. 4.99 (978-0-7945-3036-5(2), Usborne) EDC Publishing.

—Oliver Moon & the Monster Mystery. 2011. (Oliver Moon Ser.). 89p. (J). pap. 4.99 (978-0-7945-3095-2(8), Usborne) EDC Publishing.

—Oliver Moon & the Nipperbat Nightmare. 2011. (Oliver Moon Ser.). 94p. (J). pap. 4.99 (978-0-7945-3037-2(0), Usborne) EDC Publishing.

—Oliver Moon & the Spell Off. 2011. (Oliver Moon Ser.). 93p. (J). pap. 4.99 (978-0-7945-3093-8(1), Usborne) EDC Publishing.

Moone, Colin. Wonderful Adventures of the Margicans: The One Bad Apple. 2003. 164p. pap. (978-1-84426-189-5(1)) Upfront Publishing Ltd.

Moore, Clement C. Magie de Noel. pap. 16.95 (978-2-07-054886-6(4)) Gallimard, Editions FRA. Dist: Distribooks, Inc.

Moore, Rosey. Dreams. 2010. 228p. pap. 14.49 (978-1-4520-7485-6(2)) AuthorHouse.

Moore, Stuart, et al. The Dragon's Return. 2016. (978-1-4847-7415-1(9)) Disney Publishing Worldwide.

Moore, Victor L. The Pentacle of Northumbria. 2013. 432p. pap. (978-1-78222-073-2(9)) Paragon Publishing, Rothersthorpe.

Morales, Rebecca Lynn. Walter Plume & the Dehydrated Imagination. 2016. (ENG.). viii, 150p. (J). pap. 11.99 (978-1-4621-1780-2(5), Sweetwater Bks.) Cedar Fort, Inc./CFI Distribution.

Morgan, C. M. Silver Doorway #6: The Alchemist's Girl. 2008. 108p. pap. 6.99 (978-0-9771005-2-1(9)) Sabledrake Enterprises.

Morgan, Marlee. Soujon's Journey. 2010. 380p. (J). pap. 10.00 (978-0-9789247-6-8(2), INDI Best) INDI, LLC.

Morgan, Melissa J. Charmed Forces. 2008. (Camp Confidential Ser.: 19). (ENG.). 256p. (J). (gr. 3-7). pap. 5.99 (978-0-448-44722-3(3), Grosset & Dunlap) Penguin Young Readers Group.

Morgan, Nikki. Mithendrove: Escaping Callendae. 2003. 110p. (YA). pap. 9.95 (978-0-595-27138-2(3), Writer's Showcase Pr.) iUniverse, Inc.

Moriarty, Chris. The Inquisitor's Apprentice. Geyer, Mark Edward, illus. (ENG.). 352p. (J). (gr. 5-7). 2013. pap. 7.99 (978-0-547-85084-9(0)) 2011. 16.99 (978-0-547-58135-4(1)) Houghton Mifflin Harcourt Publishing Co.

—The Watcher in the Shadows. Geyer, Mark Edward, illus. (ENG.). 336p. (J). (gr. 5-7). 2014. pap. 7.99 (978-0-544-22776-7(X), HMH Books For Young Readers) 2013. 16.99 (978-0-547-46632-3(3)) Houghton Mifflin Harcourt Publishing Co.

Moriarty, Jaclyn. A Corner of White. 2013. (Colors of Madeleine Ser.: 1). (ENG.). 384p. (J). (gr. 7). 18.99 (978-0-545-39736-0(7), Levine, Arthur A. Bks.) Scholastic, Inc.

—The Cracks in the Kingdom. 2014. (Colors of Madeleine Ser.: 2). (ENG.). 480p. (J). (gr. 7). 18.99 (978-0-545-39738-4(3), Levine, Arthur A. Bks.) Scholastic, Inc.

—The Spell Book of Listen Taylor. 2007. (YA). (978-0-439-84679-0(X), Levine, Arthur A. Bks.) Scholastic, Inc.

—A Tangle of Gold. 2016. (Colors of Madeleine Ser.: 3). (ENG.). 480p. (YA). (gr. 7). 18.99 (978-0-545-39740-7(5), Levine, Arthur A. Bks.) Scholastic, Inc.

Morimoto, Sango. Taro & the Terror of Eats Street. Morimoto, Sango, illus. 2011. (Adventures of Taro Ser.). (ENG., Illus.). 96p. (J). (gr. 1-4). pap. 7.99 (978-1-4215-3525-8(4)) Viz Media.

Morlock, Theresa. Fairy & Leprechaun Legends. 2017. (Famous Legends Ser.). 32p. (J). (gr. 2-3). pap. 10.50 **(978-1-5382-0353-8(7))** Stevens, Gareth Publishing LLLP.

Morpurgo, Michael. Toto: The Dog-Gone Amazing Story of the Wizard of Oz. Chichester Clark, Emma, illus. 2017. (ENG.). 284p. (J). 17.99 **(978-0-00-825256-4(4)**, HarperCollins Children's Bks.) HarperCollins Pubs. Ltd. GBR. Dist: HarperCollins Pubs.

Morris, Gerald. The Savage Damsel & the Dwarf. 2008. (Squire's Tales Ser.: 3). (ENG.). 224p. (J). (gr. 5-7). pap. 7.99 (978-0-547-01437-1(6)) Houghton Mifflin Harcourt Publishing Co.

—The Squire, His Knight, & His Lady. 2008. (Squire's Tales Ser.: 2). (ENG., Illus.). 240p. (J). (gr. 5-7). pap. 7.99 (978-0-547-01438-8(4)) Houghton Mifflin Harcourt Publishing Co.

—The Squire's Tale. 2008. (Squire's Tales Ser.: 1). (ENG.). 224p. (J). (gr. 5-7). pap. 7.99 (978-0-618-73743-7(X)) Houghton Mifflin Harcourt Publishing Co.

Morris, J. S. The Jewel. 2007. 204p. pap. 22.95 (978-1-4357-0140-3(2)) Lulu Pr., Inc.

Morrisette, Sharon. Toads & Tessellations. O'Neill, Philomena, illus. 2012. (ENG.). 32p. (J). (gr. 2-5). 16.95 (978-1-58089-354-1(6)); pap. 7.95 (978-1-58089-355-8(4)) Charlesbridge Publishing, Inc.

Morrison, Megan. Disenchanted: The Trials of Cinderella. 2016. (Tyme Ser.: 2). (ENG., Illus.). 416p. (J). (gr. 3-7). 17.99 (978-0-545-64271-2(X), Levine, Arthur A. Bks.) Scholastic, Inc.

—Grounded: The Tale of Rapunzel. 2015. (Illus.). 374p. (J). (978-0-545-75468-2(2)) Scholastic, Inc.

Morrissey, Dean & Krensky, Stephen. The Wizard Mouse. Morrissey, Dean, illus. 2011. (ENG., Illus.). 32p. (J). (gr. k-4). 16.99 (978-0-06-008066-2(3)) HarperCollins Pubs.

Mosley, Walter. 47. 2006. (ENG., Illus.). 240p. (J). (gr. 7-17). reprint ed. per. 10.99 (978-0-316-01635-3(7)) Little, Brown Bks. for Young Readers.

Moss, J. P. The Kind Fairy Adventures: 3 Loving Fairy Tales from the Land of the Faye. 2010. (Illus.). 52p. pap. 22.99 (978-1-4520-3868-1(6)) AuthorHouse.

Moss, Ronald. The Wizard Next Door. 2009. 198p. pap. 14.95 (978-1-60911-077-2(3), Eloquent Bks.) Strategic Book Publishing & Rights Agency (SBPRA).

Mudenda, Duly & Nagunga, Kansi. Syankombo. 2004. (Illus.). 20p. 16.95 (978-1-77936-005-2(3)) Africa Community Publishing & Development Trust ZWE. Dist: Michigan State Univ. Pr.

Muir, Suzanne. The Magic Tile. 2007. (Illus.). 48p. (J). lib. bdg. 15.00 (978-1-4242-1619-2(2)) Dingles & Co.

Mulholland, Marie. A Study Guide for the Necklace of Terrersylvanous. 2007. 38p. (J). ring bd. 11.95 (978-0-9797715-0-7(1)) Sonic Sword Productions.

mulholland, robin. Bolivia & the sunshine King. 2008. 147p. pap. 14.98 (978-0-557-01401-9(8)) Lulu Pr., Inc.

Mull, Brandon. Arcade Catastrophe. 2012. (Candy Shop War Ser.: 2). (ENG.). 448p. (J). (gr. 5). 18.99 (978-1-60907-179-0(4), Shadow Mountain) Shadow Mountain Publishing.

—Arcade Catastrophe. 2014. (Candy Shop War Ser.: 2). lib. bdg. 18.40 (978-0-606-35795-1(5)) Turtleback Bks.

—The Candy Shop War. 2011. E-Book 6.64 (978-1-60641-649-5(9)) Deseret Bk. Co.

—The Candy Shop War. (Candy Shop War Ser.: Bk. 1). 2008. 368p. pap. 6.99 (978-1-59038-970-6(0)) 2007. (Illus.). 409p. (J). (gr. 3-7). 19.99 (978-1-59038-783-2(X)) Shadow Mountain Publishing. (Shadow Mountain).

—The Candy Shop War. 2014. (Candy Shop War Ser.: 1). lib. bdg. 18.40 (978-0-606-35794-4(7)) Turtleback Bks.

—Chasing the Prophecy. (Beyonders Ser.: 3). (ENG.). (J). (gr. 3-7). 2014. 528p. pap. 8.99 (978-1-4169-9797-9(0)) 2013. 512p. 19.99 (978-1-4169-9796-2(2)) Simon & Schuster Children's Publishing. (Aladdin).

—Crystal Keepers. (Five Kingdoms Ser.: 3). (ENG., Illus.). (J). (gr. 3-7). 2016. 512p. pap. 8.99 (978-1-4424-9707-8(6), Aladdin) 2015. 496p. 17.99 (978-1-4424-9706-1(8), Aladdin Library) Simon & Schuster Children's Publishing.

—Crystal Keepers. 2016. (Five Kingdoms Ser.: 3). lib. bdg. 18.40 (978-0-606-38253-3(4)) Turtleback Bks.

—Dragonwatch. 2017. (Dragonwatch Ser.: 1). (ENG., Illus.). 384p. (J). (gr. 3). 18.99 (978-1-62972-256-6(1), Shadow Mountain) Shadow Mountain Publishing.

—Dragonwatch. 2018. (Dragonwatch Ser.: 1). lib. bdg. 19.65 **(978-0-606-40838-7(X))** Turtleback Bks.

—Fablehaven. 2006. (ENG., Illus.). 351p. (J). lib. bdg. 20.00 (978-1-4242-4831-5(0)) Fitzgerald Bks.

—Fablehaven. 2009. (SPA.). 306p. (YA). (gr. 5-8). 24.95 (978-84-9918-033-5(7)) Roca Editorial ESP. Dist: Spanish Pubs., LLC.

—Fablehaven. 2006. (Fablehaven Ser.: 1). (ENG., Illus.). 368p. (J). (gr. 3-7). 19.99 (978-1-59038-581-4(0), Shadow Mountain) Shadow Mountain Publishing.

—Fablehaven. Dorman, Brandon, illus. 2007. (Fablehaven Ser.: 1). (ENG.). 384p. (J). (gr. 3-8). pap. 8.99 (978-1-4169-4720-2(5), Aladdin) Simon & Schuster Children's Publishing.

—Fablehaven. 2007. (Fablehaven Ser.: 01). lib. bdg. 18.40 (978-1-4177-9328-0(7), Turtleback) Turtleback Bks.

—Fablehaven: Las Llaves de la Prision de los Demonios. 2012. (SPA.). 466p. (YA). 24.95 (978-84-9918-438-8(3)) Roca Editorial ESP. Dist: Spanish Pubs., LLC.

—Fablehaven Vol. 5: The Complete Series Boxed Set. 2010. (Fablehaven Ser.: Bks. 1-3). 99.99 (978-1-60641-832-1(7), Shadow Mountain) Shadow Mountain Publishing.

—Fablehaven Collection Set. Dorman, Brandon, illus. 2011. (Fablehaven Ser.). (ENG.). 2512p. (J). (gr. 3-8). pap. 42.99 (978-1-4424-2977-2(1), Aladdin) Simon & Schuster Children's Publishing.

—Grip of the Shadow Plague. Dorman, Brandon, illus. 2008. (Fablehaven Ser.: 3). (ENG.). 480p. (J). (gr. 3-7). 19.99 (978-1-59038-898-3(4), Shadow Mountain) Shadow Mountain Publishing.

—Keys to the Demon Prison. Dorman, Brandon, illus. 2011. (Fablehaven Ser.: 5). (ENG.). 640p. (J). (gr. 3-8). pap. 8.99 (978-1-4169-9029-1(1), Aladdin) Simon & Schuster Children's Publishing.

—Rise of the Evening Star. Dorman, Brandon, illus. 2007. (Fablehaven Ser.: 2). (ENG.). 456p. (J). (gr. 3-7). 19.99 (978-1-59038-742-9(2), Shadow Mountain) Shadow Mountain Publishing.

—Rise of the Evening Star. Dorman, Brandon, illus. 2008. (Fablehaven Ser.: 2). (ENG.). 480p. (J). (gr. 3-8). pap. 7.99 (978-1-4169-5770-6(7), Aladdin) Simon & Schuster Children's Publishing.

—Rogue Knight. (Five Kingdoms Ser.: 2). (ENG., Illus.). (J). (gr. 3-7). 2015. 496p. pap. 8.99 (978-1-4424-9704-7(1)) 2014. 480p. 17.99 (978-1-4424-9703-0(3)) Simon & Schuster Children's Publishing. (Aladdin).

—Rogue Knight. 2015. (Five Kingdoms Ser.: 2). lib. bdg. 19.65 (978-0-606-38254-0(2)) Turtleback Bks.

—Secrets of the Dragon Sanctuary. Dorman, Brandon, illus. 2010. (Fablehaven Ser.: 4). (ENG.). 560p. (J). (gr. 3-8). pap. 8.99 (978-1-4169-9028-4(3), Aladdin) Simon & Schuster Children's Publishing.

—Secrets of the Dragon Sanctuary. 2010. (Fablehaven Ser.: 4). lib. bdg. 19.65 (978-0-606-10685-6(5), Turtleback) Turtleback Bks.

—Seeds of Rebellion. (Beyonders Ser.: 2). (ENG., Illus.). (J). (gr. 3-7). 2013. 528p. pap. 8.99 (978-1-4169-9795-5(4)) 2012. 512p. 19.99 (978-1-4169-9794-8(6)) Simon & Schuster Children's Publishing. (Aladdin).

—Seeds of Rebellion. 2012. (Beyonders Ser.: Bk. 2). (ENG., Illus.). 512p. (J). pap. 10.99 (978-1-4424-4965-7(9), Simon & Schuster/Paula Wiseman Bks.) Simon & Schuster/Paula Wiseman Bks.

—Seeds of Rebellion. 2013. (Beyonders Ser.: 2). lib. bdg. 19.65 (978-0-606-27030-4(2), Turtleback) Turtleback Bks.

—A World Without Heroes. (J). 2011. (Beyonders Ser.: 1). 1.25 (978-1-4640-0920-4(1)) (Beyonders Ser.: 1). 92.75 (978-1-4618-0338-6(1)) 2011. (Beyonders Ser.: 1). 124.75 (978-1-4618-0353-9(5)) 2011. 122.75 (978-1-4618-0363-8(2)) Recorded Bks., Inc.

—A World Without Heroes. (Beyonders Ser.: 1). (ENG.). (J). (gr. 3-7). 2012. 496p. pap. 8.99 (978-1-4169-9793-1(8)) 2011. 464p. 19.99 (978-1-4169-9792-4(X)) Simon & Schuster Children's Publishing. (Aladdin).

—A World Without Heroes. 2011. (Beyonders Ser.: Bk. 1). (ENG.). 464p. (J). pap. 10.99 (978-1-4424-3530-8(5), Simon & Schuster/Paula Wiseman Bks.) Simon & Schuster/Paula Wiseman Bks.

—A World Without Heroes. 2012. (Beyonders Ser.: 1). lib. bdg. 19.65 (978-0-606-23675-1(9), Turtleback) Turtleback Bks.

—A World Without Heroes; Seeds of Rebellion; Chasing the Prophecy, Set. 2013. (Beyonders Ser.). (ENG., Illus.). 1456p. (J). (gr. 3-7). 59.99 (978-1-4424-8593-8(0), Aladdin) Simon & Schuster Children's Publishing.

Muller, Rachel. When the Curtain Rises, 1 vol. 2007. (ENG.). 144p. (J). (gr. 3-7). per. 7.95 (978-1-55143-615-9(9)) Orca Bk. Pubs. USA.

Muneefa. My Tales for Children. 2006. 90p. (J). pap. 13.95 (978-1-58909-339-3(9)) Bookstand Publishing.

Munsch, Robert. MMM, Cookies. 2007. (J). 12.65 (978-0-7569-7657-6(X)) Perfection Learning Corp.

Murdock, Catherine Gilbert. Princess Ben. 2009. (ENG.). 352p. (YA). (gr. 7). pap. 9.99 (978-0-547-22325-4(0)) Houghton Mifflin Harcourt Publishing Co.

Murray, Martine. Molly & Pim & the Millions of Stars. 2017. (ENG., Illus.). 192p. (J). (gr. 3-7). 16.99 (978-0-399-55040-9(2), Knopf Bks. for Young Readers) Random Hse. Children's Bks.

Murtagh, Ciaran. Megastar. Wesson, Tim, illus. 2016. (Fincredible Diary of Fin Spencer Ser.: 2). (ENG.). 224p. (J). (gr. 4-7). pap. 7.99 (978-1-84812-447-9(3)) Bonnier Publishing GBR. Dist: Independent Pubs. Group.

Muscia, Marilena Carrubba. Misses Cowy to the Rescue. 2011. 24p. (gr. -1). 12.99 (978-1-4567-3582-1(9)) AuthorHouse.

Musgrove, Marianne. Forget-Me-Not Fairy Treasury. MacCarthy, Patricia, illus. 2013. (ENG.). 192p. (J). (gr. -1-3). (978-1-74308-536-3(2)) Hinkler Bks. Pty, Ltd.

My Amazing Pet Snail. 2013. (Illus.). (J). (978-1-4351-4755-3(3)) Barnes & Noble, Inc.

Myers, Tim J. Basho & the River Stones, 0 vols. Han, Oki, illus. 2013. (ENG.). 34p. (J). (gr. 1-4). pap. 9.99 (978-1-4778-1682-0(8), 9781477816820, Amazon Children's Publishing) Amazon Publishing.

!Myster?Ous M! & Courageous $Oul. The Lonely Flower. Courageous $oul, illus. 2011. 20p. pap. 24.95 (978-1-4560-6950-6(0)) America Star Bks.

Nagaraj, Josephine. The Big Magic Show! (Bubble Guppies) Jackson, Mike, illus. 2015. (Step into Reading Ser.). (ENG.). 24p. (J). (gr. -1-1). 4.99 (978-0-385-38457-5(2), Random Hse. Bks. for Young Readers) Random Hse. Children's Bks.

Na'Shae. The Magic Chronicles: Ice. 2008. 80p. pap. 9.99 (978-0-9814650-6-7(4)) G Publishing LLC.

Nathan, Sarah. Sofia's Magic Lesson. 2014. (Illus.). 32p. (J). (978-1-4844-2887-0(0)) Disney Pr.

—Sofia's Magic Lesson. 2014. (Sofia the First Ser.). (J). lib. bdg. 13.55 (978-0-606-35258-1(9)) Turtleback Bks.

Nathan, Sarah & Disney Book Group Staff. Sofia the First Sofia's Magic Lesson. 2014. (ENG.). 32p. (J). (gr. -1-k). pap. 3.99 (978-1-4231-9854-3(9)) Disney Pr.

Nation, Kaleb. The Specter Key. 2010. (ENG.). 352p. (J). (gr. 4-7). pap. 7.99 (978-1-4022-4059-1(7), Sourcebooks Jabberwocky) Sourcebooks, Inc.

Nazemi, Mary. Kaveh, Jolly & the Super Giant. 2006. (J). pap. 15.00 (978-0-8059-7001-2(0)) Dorrance Publishing Co., Inc.

Neff, Henry H. The Fiend & the Forge. 2011. (Tapestry Ser.). (ENG., Illus.). 560p. (J). (gr. 3-7). 7.99 (978-0-375-83899-6(6), Yearling) Random Hse. Children's Bks.

—The Hound of Rowan. 2008. (Tapestry Ser.: 1). (ENG., Illus.). 448p. (J). (gr. 3-7). 7.99 (978-0-375-83895-8(3), Yearling) Random Hse. Children's Bks.

—The Maelstrom: Book Four of the Tapestry. Neff, Henry H., illus. 2013. (Tapestry Ser.). (ENG., Illus.). 480p. (J). (gr. 3-7). 7.99 (978-0-375-87148-1(9), Yearling) Random Hse. Children's Bks.

—The Second Siege. 2010. (Tapestry Ser.). (ENG., Illus.). 512p. (J). (gr. 3-7). 7.99 (978-0-375-83897-2(X), Yearling) Random Hse. Children's Bks.

Negrin, Fabian, illus. Wizard Tales. 2003. 96p. 19.95 (978-1-55285-558-4(9)) Whitecap Bks., Ltd. CAN. Dist: Graphic Arts Ctr. Publishing Co.

Neill, Chloe. Charmfall. 2012. (Dark Elite Ser.: 3). (ENG.). 288p. (YA). (gr. 9). 9.99 (978-0-451-23080-5(9), Berkley) Penguin Publishing Group.

Neilson, G. E. F. Cosmic Aviators - Nathaniel's 1st Adventure. 2013. 332p. pap. (978-0-9576132-0-1(2)) Buzzword Pr.

Nelson, Brett Alan. The Magical Forest. Ueda, Kumiko, illus. 2003. 42p. (J). (978-0-9655078-7-5(4)) Windsong Publishing Co.

Nelson, S. D. Coyote Christmas: A Lakota Story. 2007. (ENG., Illus.). 40p. (J). (gr. 1-4). 18.95 (978-0-8109-9367-9(8), Abrams Bks. for Young Readers) Abrams, Inc.

Neno, Michael. The Children's Magical Adventure: 1 the Rescue. 2011. (Illus.). 48p. (gr. -1). pap. 19.59 (978-1-4567-7887-3(0)) AuthorHouse.

Nesbet, Anne. A Box of Gargoyles. 2013. (ENG.). 368p. (J). (gr. 3-7). 16.99 (978-0-06-210425-0(X)) HarperCollins Pubs.

—The Cabinet of Earths. 2013. (ENG.). 288p. (J). (gr. 3-7). pap. 6.99 (978-0-06-196319-3(4)) HarperCollins Pubs.

—The Wrinkled Crown. 2015. (ENG.). 400p. (J). (gr. 3-7). 17.99 (978-0-06-210429-8(2)) HarperCollins Pubs.

Nesbit, E. The Enchanted Castle. l.t. ed. 2005. 388p. pap. (978-1-84637-202-5(X)) Echo Library.

—Harding's Luck. 2006. 164p. (gr. 4-7). 25.95 (978-1-59818-170-8(X)) Aegypan.

—The House of Arden. 2006. 184p. (gr. 3-7). per. 14.95 (978-1-59818-967-4(0)); 26.95 (978-1-59818-181-4(5)) Aegypan.

—The House of Arden. 2006. (New York Review Children's Collection). (ENG.). 260p. (J). (gr. 4-7). 17.95 (978-1-59017-202-5(7), NYR Children's Collection) New York Review of Bks., Inc., The.

—The Magic City. 2008. 144p. (gr. 4-7). 24.95 (978-1-60664-925-1(6)); pap. 11.95 (978-1-60664-045-6(3)) Aegypan.

—The Magic World. 2006. 156p. (gr. -1-7). 24.95 (978-1-59818-176-0(9)) Aegypan.

—Magic World. 2006. 156p. (gr. -1-7). per. 12.95 (978-1-59818-966-7(2)) Aegypan.

—The Phoenix & the Carpet. 2009. 156p. pap. 4.95 (978-1-60459-693-9(7)) Wilder Pubns., Corp.

—The Red House. 2006. 140p. per. 11.95 (978-1-59818-965-0(4)) Aegypan.

—The Seven Dragons & Other Stories. 2006. 140p. 24.95 (978-1-59818-171-5(8)) Aegypan.

—The Story of the Amulet. 2009. 176p. (gr. -1-7). pap. 4.95 (978-1-60459-694-6(5)) Wilder Pubns., Corp.

—The Story of the Treasure Seekers. 2009. 128p. (gr. 4-7). pap. 5.50 (978-1-60459-695-3(3)) Wilder Pubns., Corp.

—Wet Magic. 2006. 200p. (gr. -1-7). per. (978-1-84350-095-7(7)) Soft Editions Ltd.

—7 Books in 1 - "The Railway Children", "Five Children & It", "The Phoenix & the Carpet", "The Story of the Amulet", "The Story of the Treasure-Seekers", "The Would-Be-Goods" & "The Enchanted Castle" 2004. 472p. pap. (978-0-9548401-0-5(0)) Shoes & Ships & Sealing Wax Ltd.

Nestell, Mark. Gordon & the Magic Fishbowl, 1 vol. Daley-Prado, M. J., illus. 2010. 26p. pap. 24.95 (978-1-4489-8495-4(5)) America Star Bks.

Neumeier, Rachel. The Floating Islands. 2012. (ENG.). 400p. (YA). (gr. 7). pap. 9.99 (978-0-440-24060-0(3)) Random Hse. Children's Bks.

—The Keeper of the Mist. 2016. (ENG.). 400p. (YA). (gr. 7). lib. bdg. 20.99 (978-0-553-50929-8(2), Knopf Bks. for Young Readers) Random Hse. Children's Bks.

Newcomb, Victoria. Gathering Grace. 2008. 250p. (YA). pap. 15.95 (978-1-59275-009-2(5)) Hanford Mead Pubs., Inc.

Newman, Samantha. Sammy Skizzors & the Rainbow Knight. 2010. 32p. 14.99 (978-1-4520-9976-7(6)) AuthorHouse.

Nickelodeon. Shimmer & Shine - Sleepover Wishes. 2016. (ENG.). 10p. (J). (gr. -1-2). bds. 9.99 (978-0-7944-3827-2(X)) Studio Fun International.

Nielsen, Amy. Victor & the Sun Orb. 2008. 144p. 21.95 (978-0-595-50307-0(1)); pap. 11.95 (978-0-595-51212-6(7)) iUniverse, Inc.

Nielsen, Jennifer A. Mark of the Thief. 2015. (Mark of the Thief Ser.: 1). (ENG.). 352p. (J). (gr. 4-7). pap. 7.99 (978-0-545-56155-6(8), Scholastic Paperbacks); 17.99 (978-0-545-56154-9(X), Scholastic Pr.) Scholastic, Inc.

—Rise of the Wolf. 2016. (Mark of the Thief Ser.: 2). (ENG.). 352p. (J). (gr. 4-7). pap. 7.99 (978-0-545-56205-8(8)); 17.99 (978-0-545-56204-1(X)) Scholastic, Inc. (Scholastic Pr.).

—Rise of the Wolf. 2016. (Mark of the Thief Ser.: 2). lib. bdg. 18.40 **(978-0-606-39707-0(8))** Turtleback Bks.

Nielsen, Jennifer A. Wrath of the Storm. 2017. (Mark of the Thief Ser.: 3). (ENG.). 352p. (J). (gr. 4-7). 16.99 (978-0-545-56207-2(4), Scholastic Pr.) Scholastic, Inc.

Nielson, Kelli S. Stone Mage Wars, Book 1: Journey to the Fringe. 2011. (YA). 17.99 (978-1-60908-833-0(6)) Deseret Bk. Co.

Niemi, Renee. Because Gage Believed. 2013. 20p. pap. 24.95 (978-1-62709-730-7(9)) America Star Bks.

Night, P. J. No Trick-Or-Treating!, 1 vol. 2013. (You're Invited to a Creepover Ser.). (ENG.). 192p. (J). (gr. 3-6). lib. bdg. 24.21 (978-1-61479-061-7(2), Essential Library) ABDO Publishing Co.

—No Trick-Or-Treating! 2012. (Creepover Ser.: 9). lib. bdg. 17.20 (978-0-606-26337-5(3), Turtleback) Turtleback Bks.

—Read It & Weep! 2013. (You're Invited to a Creepover Ser.: 13). (ENG., Illus.). 160p. (J). (gr. 3-7). pap. 5.99 (978-1-4424-5987-8(5), Simon Spotlight) Simon Spotlight.

—Read It & Weep! 2013. (Creepover Ser.: 13). lib. bdg. 16.00 (978-0-606-27039-7(6), Turtleback) Turtleback Bks.

Nimmo, Jenny. Chestnut Soldier. 2009. (Magician Trlogy Ser.). (ENG.). 208p. (J). (gr. 3-7). 5.99 (978-0-545-07127-7(5), Scholastic Paperbacks) Scholastic, Inc.

—Midnight for Charlie Bone. 2003. (Children of the Red King Ser.: Bk. 1). (J). (gr. 2-6). per. 4.99 (978-0-439-48839-6(7)) Scholastic, Inc.

—The Stones of Ravenglass. 2012. (Chronicles of the Red King Ser.). (ENG.). 272p. (J). (gr. 3-7). 16.99 (978-0-439-84674-5(9), Scholastic Pr.) Scholastic, Inc.

Nimmo, Jenny & Keating, John. The Snow Spider. 2006. (Magician Trlogy Ser.: Bk. 1). (ENG.). (J). (gr. 3-7). audio compact disk 39.95 (978-0-439-89844-7(7)) Scholastic, Inc.

Nishi, Yoshiyuki. Muhyo & Roji's Bureau of Supernatural Investigation, Vol. 18. Nishi, Yoshiyuki, illus. 2010. (ENG., Illus.). 192p. pap. 9.99 (978-1-4215-2840-3(1)) Viz Media.

Nix, Garth. Across the Wall: A Tale of the Abhorsen & Other Stories. 2006. (ENG.). 432p. (YA). (gr. 8-12). pap. 8.99 (978-0-06-074715-2(3), HarperTeen) HarperCollins Pubs.

—Clariel: The Lost Abhorsen. 2014. (Old Kingdom Ser.: Bk. 4). (ENG., Illus.). 400p. (YA). (gr. 8). 18.99 (978-0-06-156155-9(X)) HarperCollins Pubs.

—Frogkisser! 2017. (ENG.). 384p. (J). (gr. 7). 18.99 (978-1-338-05208-4(X), Scholastic Pr.) Scholastic, Inc.

—Goldenhand. 2016. (Old Kingdom Ser.: 5). (Illus.). 368p. (YA). (gr. 8). 19.99 (978-0-06-156158-0(4)) HarperCollins Pubs.

—Lirael. 2014. (Old Kingdom Ser.: 2). (ENG.). 512p. (YA). (gr. 8). pap. 9.99 (978-0-06-231556-4(0)) HarperCollins Pubs.

—Lirael, Daughter of the Clayr. 2009. 9.68 (978-0-7848-2612-6(9), Everbind) Marco Bk. Co.

—Newt's Emerald. 2015. (ENG.). 304p. (YA). (gr. 8-12). 18.99 (978-0-06-236004-5(3)) HarperCollins Pubs.

—Sir Thursday. 2007. (Keys to the Kingdom Ser.: No. 4). 344p. (gr. 4-7). 18.00 (978-0-7569-8121-1(2)) Perfection Learning Corp.

—Sir Thursday. 2007. (Keys to the Kingdom Ser.: 4). (ENG.). 352p. (J). (gr. 3-7). pap. 7.99 (978-0-439-43657-1(5), Scholastic Paperbacks) Scholastic, Inc.

—Superior Saturday. 2010. (Keys to the Kingdom Ser.: 6). (ENG.). 288p. (J). (gr. 3-7). 7.99 (978-0-439-43659-5(1), Scholastic Paperbacks) Scholastic, Inc.

—The Violet Keystone. 2004. (Seventh Tower Ser.: Bk. 6). 233p. (gr. 4-7). 17.00 (978-0-7569-3506-1(7)) Perfection Learning Corp.

Nix, Garth & Williams, Sean. The Magic, Bk. 1. 2012. (Troubletwisters Ser.: 1). (ENG.). 304p. (J). (gr. 3-7). pap. 7.99 (978-0-545-25903-3(7), Scholastic Paperbacks) Scholastic, Inc.

—The Missing. 2014. (Troubletwisters Ser.: 4). (ENG.). 320p. (J). (gr. 3-7). 17.99 (978-0-545-25900-2(2), Scholastic Pr.) Scholastic, Inc.

—The Monster. (Troubletwisters Ser.: 2). (ENG.). 304p. (J). (gr. 3-7). 2013. pap. 6.99 (978-0-545-25904-0(5), Scholastic Paperbacks) 2012. 16.99 (978-0-545-25898-2(7), Scholastic Pr.) Scholastic, Inc.

—The Mystery. (Troubletwisters Ser.: 3). (ENG.). 304p. (J). (gr. 3-7). 2014. pap. 6.99 (978-0-545-25905-7(3), Scholastic Paperbacks) 2013. 16.99 (978-0-545-25899-9(5)) Scholastic, Inc.

—Troubletwisters, Bk. 1. 2011. (Troubletwisters Ser.: 1). (ENG.). 304p. (J). (gr. 3-7). 16.99 (978-0-545-25897-5(9), Scholastic Pr.) Scholastic, Inc.

Nixon, Joan Lowery. A Deadly Game of Magic. 2004. (ENG.). 240p. (YA). (gr. 7-12). pap. 7.99 (978-0-15-205030-6(2)) Houghton Mifflin Harcourt Publishing Co.

—A Deadly Game of Magic. 2004. 228p. (YA). (gr. 7). 13.60 (978-0-7569-7230-1(2)) Perfection Learning Corp.

Noël, Alyson. Dark Flame. (Immortals Ser.: 4). (ENG.). 336p. (YA). (gr. 7-12). 2013. mass mkt. 9.99 (978-1-250-04687-1(4), 9781250046871, St. Martin's Paperbacks) 2012. pap. 10.99 (978-0-312-58375-0(3), 9780312583750, St. Martin's Griffin) 2010. 17.99 (978-0-312-59097-0(0), 9780312590970, St. Martin's Griffin) St. Martin's Pr.

Nolan, Lea. Allure. 2013. (Hoodoo Apprentice Ser.: 2). (ENG.). 304p. (YA). (gr. 7-12). pap. 9.99 (978-1-62266-022-3(6), 9781622660223) Entangled Publishing, LLC.

Nolan, Lucy. A Fairy in a Dairy, 0 vols. Bryant, Laura J., illus. 2013. (ENG.). 33p. (J). (gr. -1-2). pap. 9.99 (978-1-4778-1678-3(X), 9781477816783, Amazon Children's Publishing) Amazon Publishing.

Noland, Charles. The Adventures of Drew & Ellie: The Daring Rescue. Moyer, Tom, illus. 2nd ed. 2006. 92p. (J). per. 7.95 (978-0-9789297-2-5(1)) TMD Enterprises.

Norris, Christine. The Sword of Danu. 2012. (J). 268p. (gr. 3-7). pap. 14.99 (978-1-61271-095-2(6)); (978-1-61271-097-6(2)); (978-1-61271-096-9(4)) Zumaya Pubns. LLC.

—Talisman of Zandria, 1. Nagy, Robert, illus. 2005. 187p. (YA). pap. 14.95 (978-1-885093-44-8(6), LBF/Hadrosaur) Hadrosaur Pr.

—The Talisman of Zandria. 2013. 240p. pap. 14.99 (978-1-61271-220-8(7)) Zumaya Pubns. LLC.

North, Laura. The Boy with the Pudding Touch. Chapman, Neil, illus. 2014. (ENG.). 32p. (J). pap. (978-0-7787-1364-7(4)) Crabtree Publishing Co.

Northrop, Michael. Amulet Keepers. 2015. (TombQuest Ser.: 2). (ENG., Illus.). 192p. (J). (gr. 3-7). 12.99 (978-0-545-72339-8(6), Scholastic Pr.) Scholastic, Inc.

—Book of the Dead. 2015. (TombQuest Ser.: Bk. 1). (J). 197p. (978-1-76015-315-1(X)); 208p. pap. (978-1-74362-924-6(9)) Scholastic, Inc.

—The Final Kingdom. 2016. (TombQuest Ser.: 5). (ENG.). 192p. (J). (gr. 3-7). 12.99 (978-0-545-72342-8(6)); 16.99 (978-0-545-87111-2(5)) Scholastic, Inc. (Scholastic Pr.).

—The Stone Warriors. 2015. (TombQuest Ser.: 4). (ENG.). 192p. (J). (gr. 3-7). 16.99 (978-0-545-87108-2(5)); 12.99 (978-0-545-72341-1(8)) Scholastic, Inc. (Scholastic Pr.).

—Valley of Kings. 2015. (TombQuest Ser.: 3). (ENG.). 192p. (J). (gr. 3-7). 16.99 (978-0-545-87104-4(2)); 12.99 (978-0-545-72340-4(X), Scholastic Pr.) Scholastic, Inc.

Norton, Tamra. Shayla Witherwood: A Half-Faerie Tale. 2012. pap. 16.99 (978-1-59955-963-6(3)) Cedar Fort, Inc./CFI Distribution.

Nova, Jacy & Nova, Nick. City of the Lost Souls. 2008. (ENG., Illus.). 224p. (YA). (gr. 8-12). 9.99 (978-0-7582-2528-3(8), K-Teen) Kensington Publishing Corp.

Nowicki, Colin J. Lamia High: Moon of Destiny, 1 vol. 2010. 186p. pap. 24.95 (978-1-4512-8561-1(2)) America Star Bks.

Noyes, Deborah, ed. Sideshow: Ten Original Tales of Freaks, Illusionists, & Other Matters Odd & Magical. 2009. (ENG., Illus.). 240p. (YA). (gr. 9-18). 16.99 (978-0-7636-3752-1(1)) Candlewick Pr.

Nugent, Cynthia. Francesca & the Magic Bike. 2005. 4p. (J). pap., tchr. ed. (978-1-55192-825-8(6)) Raincoast Bk. Distribution CAN. Dist: Publishers Group West (PGW).

Nuño, Fran. The Great Magician of the World. 2012. (ENG., Illus.). 24p. (J). (gr. k-2). (978-84-15241-11-9(9)) D P & G Military Pubs.

Nye, Barry. Hannah & the Magic Blanket - Land of the Dinosaurs. 2009. 40p. pap. 18.50 (978-0-557-03682-0(8)) Lulu Pr., Inc.

Oakes, Colleen. Queen of Hearts. 2016. (Queen of Hearts Ser.: 1). 320p. (YA). (gr. 8). 17.99 (978-0-06-240972-0(7), HarperTeen) HarperCollins Pubs.

Oakes, Cory Putman. Witchtown. 2017. (ENG.). 320p. (YA). (gr. 7). 17.99 (978-0-544-76557-3(5), HMH Books For Young Readers) Houghton Mifflin Harcourt Publishing Co.

O'Brien, Joe. Alfie Green & the Bee-Bottle Gang. Texier, Jean, illus. 2nd rev. ed. 2007. (Alfie Green Ser.). (ENG.). 80p. (J). pap. 10.95 (978-1-84717-054-5(4)) O'Brien Pr., Ltd., The IRL. Dist: Dufour Editions, Inc.

—Alfie Green & the Conker King. Texier, Jean, illus. 2012. (Alfie Green Ser.). (ENG.). 80p. (J). pap. 10.95 (978-1-84717-283-9(0)) O'Brien Pr., Ltd., The IRL. Dist: Dufour Editions, Inc.

—Beyond the Cherry Tree. McGann, Oisín, illus. 2012. (ENG.). 224p. (J). pap. 12.95 (978-1-84717-212-9(1)) O'Brien Pr., Ltd., The IRL. Dist: Dufour Editions, Inc.

O'Callaghan, G. Sorcerers Apprentice. 2007. 244p. per. (978-1-84693-024-9(3)) Best Global Publishing Ltd.

—Tektite. 2007. 144p. per. (978-1-84693-025-6(1)) Best Global Publishing Ltd.

Ochse, Bobbie Colliton. Nana's Magic Closet. 2010. 40p. pap. 16.99 (978-1-4520-7663-8(4)) AuthorHouse.

O'Connor, Jane. Fancy Nancy: Jojo & the Magic Trick. Glasser, Robin Preiss, illus. 2017. (My First I Can Read Ser.). 32p. (J). (gr. -1-3). pap. 3.99 (978-0-06-237795-1(7)) HarperCollins Pubs.

O'connor, Jane. JoJo & the Magic Trick. 2017. (Fancy Nancy - I Can Read! Ser.). (J). lib. bdg. 13.55 **(978-0-606-39638-7(1))** Turtleback Bks.

O'Dell, Kathleen. The Aviary. 2012. (ENG.). 352p. (J). (gr. 3-7). 7.99 (978-0-375-85226-8(3), Yearling) Random Hse. Children's Bks.

Ogilvy, Ian. Measle & the Dragodon. 2006. 344p. (J). (gr. 3-8). per. 6.99 (978-0-06-058690-4(7), Harper Trophy) HarperCollins Pubs.

Oginga, Effua. Morgan Erika Pearl. 2012. 20p. pap. 16.20 (978-1-4670-4194-2(7)) AuthorHouse.

Okorafor, Nnedi. Akata Witch. (ENG.). (YA). (gr. 7). 2017. 384p. pap. 10.99 **(978-0-14-242091-1(3)**, Speak) 2011. 368p. 17.99 (978-0-670-01196-4(7), Viking Books for Young Readers) Penguin Young Readers Group.

Oladokun, Alexander. Acrux Manor: The Prodigal's Curse (Hardcover) 2013. 206p. 28.50 (978-1-300-68651-4(0)) Lulu Pr., Inc.

Older, Daniel José. Shadowhouse Fall. 2017. (Shadowshaper Cypher Ser.). (ENG.). 368p. (J). (gr. 7-7). 18.99 **(978-0-545-95282-8(4)**, Levine, Arthur A. Bks.) Scholastic, Inc.

Older, Daniel José. Shadowshaper. (ENG.). (J). 2016. 320p. (gr. 7). pap. 9.99 (978-1-338-03247-5(X)) 2015. 304p. (gr. 9). 17.99 (978-0-545-59161-4(9)) Scholastic, Inc.

Oldfield, Jenny. Dawn Light. Bright, Alasdair, illus. 2006. (ENG.). 144p. (J). (gr. 2-4). pap. 6.95 (978-0-340-91078-8(X)) Hachette Children's Group GBR. Dist: Hachette Bk. Group.

—Midnight Snow. Bright, Alasdair, illus. 2006. (ENG.). 144p. (J). (gr. 2-4). pap. 6.95 (978-0-340-91076-4(3)) Hachette Children's Group GBR. Dist: Hachette Bk. Group.

—New Beginnings. 2007. (ENG., Illus.). 144p. (J). (gr. 4-6). pap. 6.95 (978-0-340-93246-9(5)) Hachette Children's Group GBR. Dist: Hachette Bk. Group.

—Secret Whispers. 2007. (ENG., Illus.). 144p. (J). (gr. 4-6). pap. 6.95 (978-0-340-93245-2(7)) Hodder & Stoughton GBR. Dist: Hachette Bk. Group.

Olding, Lori. The Origami Nun. 2012. 80p. pap. (978-1-908505-74-3(5)) Vamptasy Publishing.

Oliver, Jana. Foretold. 2012. (Demon Trappers Ser.: 4). (ENG.). 368p. (YA). (gr. 7). pap. 9.99 (978-1-250-02184-7(7), 9781250021847, St. Martin's Griffin) St. Martin's Pr.

Oliver, Lauren. Liesl & Po. Acedera, Kei, illus. (ENG.). (J). (gr. 3-7). 2012. 336p. pap. 6.99 (978-0-06-201452-8(8)) 2011. 320p. 16.99 (978-0-06-201451-1(X)) HarperCollins Pubs.

—Liesl & Po. 2012. (J). lib. bdg. 17.20 (978-0-606-26853-0(7), Turtleback) Turtleback Bks.

Oliver, Lin. Beware! Shadows in the Night. Kallis, Samantha, illus. 2016. (Fantastic Frame Ser.: 3). (ENG.). 128p. (J). (gr. 2-4). 11.99 (978-0-448-48091-6(3), Grosset & Dunlap) Penguin Young Readers Group.

—Danger! Tiger Crossing. 2016. (Illus.). 115p. (J). pap. (978-0-448-48086-2(7), Grosset & Dunlap) Penguin Young Readers Group.

—Splat! Another Messy Sunday 2. 2016. (Fantastic Frame Ser.: 2). (ENG., Illus.). 128p. (J). (gr. 2-4). 11.99 (978-0-448-48089-3(1), Grosset & Dunlap) Penguin Young Readers Group.

Ollweiler, Angela Messina. The Strange Wish. Ollweiler, D. R., illus. 2010. 112p. pap. 10.95 (978-1-60844-274-4(8)) Dog Ear Publishing, LLC.

Olmstead, Kathleen. The Sorcerer's Apprentice. Olafsdottir, Linda, illus. 2015. (J). (978-1-4027-8350-0(7)) Sterling Publishing Co., Inc.

Olsen, Erik. Garden of the Lost Souls. 2012. (J). (978-1-4621-1010-0(X)) Cedar Fort, Inc./CFI Distribution.

Olsen, J. J. The Mystic Kingdom: A Jenny Dewberry Series. 2008. 400p. pap. 17.99 (978-1-4389-2598-1(0)) AuthorHouse.

O'Neal, Eilis. The False Princess. 2012. (ENG.). 336p. (J). (gr. 7). pap. 8.99 (978-1-60684-392-5(3), Carolrhoda Lab™) Lerner Publishing Group.

O'Neill, Richard & Quarmby, Katharine. Yokki & the Parno Gry. Nelissen, Marieke, illus. 2017. (Child's Play Library). (ENG.). 32p. (J). (978-1-84643-927-8(2)) Child's Play International Ltd.

Oracle of the Horses. 2005. (YA). per. (978-0-615-12836-8(X)) Miller, Don G.

O'Reilly, Avril. A Fairy in the Family. 2009. 32p. pap. 22.50 (978-1-4092-8061-3(6)) Lulu Pr., Inc.

Orford, Margie. The Magic Fish. Littlewort, Lizza, illus. 2012. (Best Loved Tales for Africa Ser.). (ENG.). 32p. (J). (gr. k-2). pap. 9.95 (978-1-77009-822-0(4)) Jacana Media ZAF. Dist: Independent Pubs. Group.

Ormondroyd, Edward. Time at the Top & All in Good Time: Two Novels. Ericksen, Barb et al, illus. 2011. (ENG.). 379p. (J). (gr. 4-7). pap. 12.95 (978-1-930900-55-4(4)) Purple Hse. Pr.

Ormsbee, K. E. The Doorway & the Deep. 2016. (ENG., Illus.). 480p. (J). (gr. 3-7). 16.99 (978-1-4521-3636-3(X)) Chronicle Bks. LLC.

—The Water & the Wild. Mora, Elsa, illus. 2015. (ENG.). 448p. (J). (gr. 3-7). 16.99 (978-1-4521-1386-9(6)) Chronicle Bks. LLC.

Orsi, Tea. Tinker Bell & the Legend of the NeverBeast. 2015. (Disney Fairies Graphic Novels Ser.: 17). (J). lib. bdg. 18.40 (978-0-606-37295-4(4)) Turtleback Bks.

Orsi, Tea & Panaro, Carlo. Tinker Bell & the Lost Treasure. Razzi, Manuela et al, illus. 2013. (Disney Fairies Ser.: 12). (ENG.). 64p. (J). (gr. 1-6). 11.99 (978-1-59707-429-2(2), 9781597074292) Papercutz.

Ortiz, Andrea. Snowflakes in June. Ortega, James, illus. 2013. 36p. 14.00 (978-0-9884237-9-4(0)) CLF Publishing.

Osborne, Mary A. Nonna's Book of Mysteries. 2010. (ENG., Illus.). 352p. (gr. 8-17). pap. 16.95 (978-1-936181-16-2(9)) Lake Street Pr.

Osborne, Mary Pope. Abe Lincoln at Last! Murdocca, Sal, illus. (Magic Tree House Merlin Mission Ser.: 19). (ENG.). (J). (gr. 2-5). 2013. 144p. 5.99 (978-0-375-86797-2(X)) 2011. 128p. 12.99 (978-0-375-86825-2(9)) Random Hse. Children's Bks. (Random Hse. Bks. for Young Readers).

—Abe Lincoln at Last! 2013. (Magic Tree House Merlin Missions Ser.: 19). lib. bdg. 16.00 (978-0-606-35563-6(4)) Turtleback Bks.

—Barcos Vikingos Al Amanecer. Brovelli, Marcela, tr. from ENG. Murdocca, Sal, illus. 2007. (Casa del Arbol Ser.: 15). (SPA.). 73p. (J). per. 5.99 (978-1-933032-21-4(9)) Lectorum Pubns., Inc.

—A Big Day for Baseball. Murdocca, Sal, illus. 2017. (Magic Tree House Ser.: 29). (ENG.). (J). (gr. 1-4). 80p. 13.99 **(978-1-5247-1308-9(2))**; 96p. lib. bdg. 16.99 **(978-1-5247-1309-6(0))** Random Hse. Children's Bks. (Random Hse. Bks. for Young Readers).

—Blizzard of the Blue Moon. Murdocca, Sal, illus. 2007. (Magic Tree House Merlin Mission Ser.: 8). (ENG.). 144p. (J). (gr. 2-5). 5.99 (978-0-375-83038-9(3), Random Hse. Bks. for Young Readers) Random Hse. Children's Bks.

—Buffalo Before Breakfast. 2004. (Magic Tree House Ser.: No. 18). 72p. (J). (gr. k-3). pap. 17.00 incl. audio (978-0-8072-0927-1(9), Listening Library) Random Hse. Audio Publishing Group.

—Carnival at Candlelight. Murdocca, Sal, illus. 2006. (Magic Tree House Merlin Mission Ser.: 5). (ENG.). 144p. (J). (gr. 2-5). 5.99 (978-0-375-83034-1(0), Random Hse. Bks. for Young Readers) Random Hse. Children's Bks.

—Christmas in Camelot. Murdocca, Sal, illus. 2009. (Magic Tree House Merlin Mission Ser.: 1). (ENG.). 144p. (J). (gr. 2-5). 5.99 (978-0-375-85812-3(1), Random Hse. Bks. for Young Readers) Random Hse. Children's Bks.

—Christmas in Camelot. 2009. (Magic Tree House Merlin Missions Ser.: 1). lib. bdg. 16.00 (978-0-606-06386-9(2), Turtleback) Turtleback Bks.

—Civil War on Sunday. unabr. ed. 2004. (Magic Tree House Ser.: No. 21). 76p. (J). (gr. k-3). pap. 17.00 incl. audio (978-0-8072-0930-1(9), S FTR 253 SP, Listening Library) Random Hse. Audio Publishing Group.

—A Crazy Day with Cobras. Murdocca, Sal, illus. (ENG.). (J). 2012. (Magic Tree House Merlin Missions Ser.: No. 17). 144p. (gr. 1-4). 5.99 (978-0-375-86795-8(3)) 2011. (Magic Tree House Merlin Mission Ser.: 45). 128p. (gr. 2-5). 12.99 (978-0-375-86823-8(2)) Random Hse. Children's Bks. (Random Hse. Bks. for Young Readers).

—A Crazy Day with Cobras. 2012. (Magic Tree House Merlin Missions Ser.: 17). lib. bdg. 16.00 (978-0-606-26997-1(5), Turtleback) Turtleback Bks.

—Danger in the Darkest Hour. Murdocca, Sal, illus. 2015. (Stepping Stone Book Ser.: No. 1). (ENG.). 192p. (J). (gr. 2-5). 14.99 (978-0-553-49772-4(3), Random Hse. Bks. for Young Readers) Random Hse. Children's Bks.

—Dark Day in the Deep Sea. 2009. (Magic Tree House Merlin Missions Ser.: 11). lib. bdg. 16.00 (978-0-606-01778-7(X), Turtleback) Turtleback Bks.

—Das magische Baumhaus 09. Der Ruf der Delfine. 18.95 (978-3-7855-4185-2(6)) Loewe Verlag GmbH DEU. Dist: Distribooks, Inc.

—Day of the Dragon King. unabr. ed. 2004. (Magic Tree House Ser.: No. 14). 68p. (J). (gr. k-3). pap. 17.00 incl. audio (978-0-8072-0783-3(7), S FTR 242 SP, Listening Library) Random Hse. Audio Publishing Group.

—Dinosaurs Before Dark. unabr. ed. 2004. (Magic Tree House Ser.: No. 1). 68p. (J). (gr. k-5). pap. 17.00 incl. audio (978-0-8072-0330-9(0), FTR208SP, Listening Library) Random Hse. Audio Publishing Group.

—Dinosaurs Before Dark. Murdocca, Sal, illus. 20th anniv. ed. 2012. (Magic Tree House Ser.: 1). (ENG.). 96p. (J). (gr. k-3). 14.99 (978-0-375-86988-4(3), Random Hse. Bks. for Young Readers) Random Hse. Children's Bks.

—Dogs in the Dead of Night. Murdocca, Sal, illus. 2013. (Magic Tree House (R) Merlin Mission Ser.: 18). (ENG.). 144p. (J). (gr. 2-5). 5.99 (978-0-375-86796-5(1), Random Hse. Bks. for Young Readers) Random Hse. Children's Bks.

—Dogs in the Dead of Night. 2013. (Magic Tree House Merlin Missions Ser.: 18). lib. bdg. 16.00 (978-0-606-31939-3(5), Turtleback) Turtleback Bks.

—Dragon of the Red Dawn. Murdocca, Sal, illus. 2008. (Magic Tree House Merlin Mission Ser.: 9). (ENG.). 144p. (J). (gr. 2-5). 5.99 (978-0-375-83728-9(0), Random Hse. Bks. for Young Readers) Random Hse. Children's Bks.

—Earthquake in the Early Morning. unabr. ed. 2004. (Magic Tree House Ser.: No. 24). 71p. (J). (gr. k-3). pap. 17.00 incl. audio (978-0-8072-0933-2(3), S FTR 256 SP, Listening Library) Random Hse. Audio Publishing Group.

—Eve of the Emperor Penguin. Murdocca, Sal, illus. 2009. (Magic Tree House Merlin Mission Ser.: No. 12). (ENG.). 144p. (J). (gr. 2-5). 5.99 (978-0-375-83734-0(5), Random Hse. Bks. for Young Readers) Random Hse. Children's Bks.

—A Ghost Tale for Christmas Time. Murdocca, Sal, illus. (Magic Tree House Merlin Mission Ser.: No. 16). (ENG.). (J). (gr. 2-5). 2012. 144p. pap. 5.99 (978-0-375-85653-2(6)) 2010. 128p. 12.99 (978-0-375-85652-5(8)) Random Hse. Children's Bks. (Random Hse. Bks. for Young Readers).

—A Ghost Tale for Christmas Time. 2012. (Magic Tree House Merlin Missions Ser.: 16). lib. bdg. 16.00 (978-0-606-26808-0(1), Turtleback) Turtleback Bks.

—Ghost Town at Sundown. unabr. ed. 2004. (Magic Tree House Ser.: No. 10). 73p. (J). (gr. k-3). pap. 17.00 incl. audio (978-0-8072-0535-8(4), Listening Library) Random Hse. Audio Publishing Group.

—A Good Night for Ghosts. 2010. (Magic Tree House Merlin Missions Ser.: No. 14). (Illus.). 157p. (J). pap. (978-4-8401-3411-8(1)) Fukuinkan Shoten.

—A Good Night for Ghosts. Murdocca, Sal, illus. (Magic Tree House Merlin Mission Ser.: 14). (ENG.). (J). (gr. 2-5). 2011. 144p. 5.99 (978-0-375-85649-5(8)) 2009. 128p. 12.99 (978-0-375-85648-8(X)) Random Hse. Children's Bks. (Random Hse. Bks. for Young Readers).

—Haunted Castle on Hallows Eve. Murdocca, Sal, illus. 2010. (Magic Tree House Merlin Mission Ser.: 2). (ENG.). 144p. (J). (gr. 2-5). pap. 5.99 (978-0-375-86090-4(8), Random Hse. Bks. for Young Readers) Random Hse. Children's Bks.

—Haunted Castle on Hallows Eve. 2010. (Magic Tree House Merlin Missions Ser.: 2). lib. bdg. 16.00 *(978-0-606-13992-2(3)*, Turtleback) Turtleback Bks.
—High Tide in Hawaii. Murdocca, Sal, illus. 2003. (Magic Tree House (R) Ser.: 28). (ENG.). 96p. (J). (gr. 1-4). pap. 5.99 *(978-0-375-80616-2(4)*, Random Hse. Bks. for Young Readers) Random Hse. Children's Bks.
—High Tide in Hawaii. 2003. (Magic Tree House Ser.: 28). (gr. k-3). lib. bdg. 16.00 *(978-0-613-62386-5(X)*, Turtleback) Turtleback Bks.
—La Hora de Los Juegos Olimpicos. Brovelli, Marcela, tr. Murdocca, Sal, illus. 2007. (Casa del Arbol Ser.: 16).Tr. of Hour of the Olympics Games. (ENG & SPA.). 68p. (J). per. 5.99 *(978-1-933032-22-1(7))* Lectorum Pubns., Inc.
—Hour of the Olympics. unabr. ed. 2004. (Magic Tree House Ser.: No. 16). 70p. (J). (gr. k-3). pap. 17.00 incl. audio *(978-0-8072-0785-7(3)*, LFTR 244 SP, Listening Library) Random Hse. Audio Publishing Group.
—Hurry up, Houdini! Murdocca, Sal, illus. 2013. (Magic Tree House Merlin Missions Ser.: No. 22). (ENG.). 128p. (J). (gr. 2-5). 12.99 *(978-0-307-98045-8(6)*, Random Hse. Bks. for Young Readers) Random Hse. Children's Bks.
—El Invierno Del Hechicero Del Hielo. 2015. (Casa De árbol Ser.: 32). (SPA., Illus.). 144p. (J). (gr. 2-4). pap. 5.99 *(978-1-63245-535-2(8))* Lectorum Pubns., Inc.
—The Knight at Dawn. unabr. ed. 2004. (Magic Tree House Ser.: No. 2). 66p. (J). (gr. k-3). pap. 17.00 incl. audio *(978-0-8072-0331-6(9)*, Listening Library) Random Hse. Audio Publishing Group.
—The Knight at Dawn. Murdocca, Sal, illus. 20th anniv. ed. 2013. (Magic Tree House Ser.). (ENG.). 96p. (J). (gr. 1-4). 14.99 *(978-0-449-81822-0(5)*, Random Hse. Bks. for Young Readers) Random Hse. Children's Bks.
—Leprechaun in Late Winter. Murdocca, Sal, illus. (Magic Tree House Merlin Mission Ser.: No. 15). (ENG.). 128p. (J). (gr. 2-5). 2012. 5.99 *(978-0-375-85651-8(X))* 2010. 12.99 *(978-0-375-85650-1(1))* Random Hse. Children's Bks. (Random Hse. Bks. for Young Readers).
—Leprechaun in Late Winter. 2012. (Magic Tree House Merlin Missions Ser.: 15). lib. bdg. 16.00 *(978-0-606-23860-1(3)*, Turtleback) Turtleback Bks.
—Midnight on the Moon. unabr. ed. 2004. (Magic Tree House Ser.: No. 8). 70p. (J). (gr. k-3). pap. 17.00 incl. audio *(978-0-8072-0341-5(6)*, Listening Library) Random Hse. Audio Publishing Group.
—Una Momia Al Amanecer. 2004. (Casa del Arbol Ser.: 3). (SPA.). (J). pap. 5.99 *(978-1-930332-51-5(3))* Lectorum Pubns., Inc.
—Una Momia en la Manana. 2003. (Magic Tree House Ser.: 3). (SPA.). (gr. 3-6). lib. bdg. 16.00 *(978-0-613-64609-3(6)*, Turtleback) Turtleback Bks.
—Monday with a Mad Genius. Murdocca, Sal, illus. (Magic Tree House Merlin Mission Ser.: 10). (ENG.). (J). (gr. 2-5). 2009. 144p. 5.99 *(978-0-375-83730-2(2))* 2007. 128p. 11.99 *(978-0-375-83729-6(9))* Random Hse. Children's Bks. (Random Hse. Bks. for Young Readers).
—Monday with a Mad Genius. 2009. (Magic Tree House Merlin Missions Ser.: 10). lib. bdg. 16.00 *(978-0-606-01777-0(1)*, Turtleback) Turtleback Bks.
—Moonlight on the Magic Flute. Murdocca, Sal, illus. 2010. (Magic Tree House Merlin Mission Ser.: No. 13). (ENG.). 144p. (J). (gr. 2-5). pap. 5.99 *(978-0-375-85647-1(1)*, Random Hse. Bks. for Young Readers) Random Hse. Children's Bks.
—The Mystery of the Enchanted Dog, 4 vols., Set. Murdocca, Sal, illus. 2009. (ENG.). 96p. (J). (gr. 1-4). 23.96 *(978-0-375-85811-6(3)*, Random Hse. Bks. for Young Readers) Random Hse. Children's Bks.
—Navidad en Camelot. 2015. (Casa De árbol Ser.: 29). (SPA., Illus.). 144p. (J). (gr. 2-4). pap. 5.99 *(978-1-63245-532-1(3))* Lectorum Pubns., Inc.
—Night of the New Magicians. 2007. (Magic Tree House Merlin Missions Ser.: 7). lib. bdg. 16.00 *(978-1-4177-9108-8(X)*, Turtleback) Turtleback Bks.
—Night of the Ninth Dragon. Murdocca, Sal, illus. 2016. (Magic Tree House Merlin Missions Ser.: No. 27). (ENG.). 144p. (J). (gr. 2-5). 13.99 *(978-0-553-51089-8(4)*, Random Hse. Bks. for Young Readers) Random Hse. Children's Bks.
—La Noche de los Ninjas. 2004. (Casa del Arbol Ser.: 5).Tr. of Night of the Ninjas. (SPA., Illus.). (J). pap. 5.99 *(978-1-930332-66-9(1))* Lectorum Pubns., Inc.
—Osos Polares Despues de la Medianoche. 2005. (Casa del Arbol Ser.: 12).Tr. of Polar Bears Past Bedtime. (SPA.). (J). pap. 5.99 *(978-1-930332-99-7(8))* Lectorum Pubns., Inc.
—A Perfect Time for Pandas. Murdocca, Sal, illus. 2014. (Magic Tree House Merlin Mission Ser.: No. 20). (ENG.). 144p. (J). (gr. 2-5). pap. 5.99 *(978-0-375-86798-9(8)*, Random Hse. Bks. for Young Readers) Random Hse. Children's Bks.
—A Perfect Time for Pandas. 2014. (Magic Tree House Merlin Missions Ser.: 20). lib. bdg. 16.00 *(978-0-606-35564-3(2))* Turtleback Bks.
—Revolutionary War on Wednesday. unabr. ed. 2004. (Magic Tree House Ser.: No. 22). 69p. (J). (gr. k-3). pap. 17.00 incl. audio *(978-0-8072-0931-8(7)*, S FTR 254 SP, Listening Library) Random Hse. Audio Publishing Group.
—Season of the Sandstorms. 2014. (Magic Tree House Merlin Missions Ser.: No. 6). 15.00 *(978-1-63419-681-9(3))* Perfection Learning Corp.
—Season of the Sandstorms. Murdocca, Sal, illus. 2006. (Magic Tree House Merlin Mission Ser.: No. 6). (ENG.). 144p. (J). (gr. 2-5). 5.99 *(978-0-375-83032-7(4)*, Random Hse. Bks. for Young Readers) Random Hse. Children's Bks.
—Shadow of the Shark. 2017. (Magic Tree House Merlin Mission Ser.: 25). (ENG., Illus.). 144p. (J). (gr. 2-5). 5.99 ***(978-0-553-51084-3(3)***, Random Hse. Bks. for Young Readers) Random Hse. Children's Bks.
—Shadow of the Shark. Murdocca, Sal, illus. 2015. (Magic Tree House Merlin Mission Ser.: No. 25). (ENG.). 144p. (J). (gr. 2-5). lib. bdg. 15.99 *(978-0-553-51082-9(7)*, Random Hse. Bks. for Young Readers) Random Hse. Children's Bks.
—Soccer on Sunday. Murdocca, Sal, illus. (Magic Tree House Merlin Missions Ser.: No. 24). (ENG.). (J). (gr. 2-5). 2016. 144p. 5.99 *(978-0-307-98056-4(1))* 2014. 128p. 12.99 *(978-0-307-98053-3(7))* Random Hse. Children's Bks. (Random Hse. Bks. for Young Readers).
—Stallion by Starlight. Murdocca, Sal, illus. (Magic Tree House Merlin Mission Ser.: No. 21). (ENG.). (J). (gr. 2-5). 2014. 144p. pap. 5.99 *(978-0-307-98044-1(8))* 2013. 128p. lib. bdg. 15.99 *(978-0-307-98042-7(1))* Random Hse. Children's Bks. (Random Hse. Bks. for Young Readers).
—Stallion by Starlight. 2014. (Magic Tree House Merlin Missions Ser.: 21). lib. bdg. 16.00 *(978-0-606-36411-9(0))* Turtleback Bks.
—Summer of the Sea Serpent. Murdocca, Sal, illus. 2011. (Magic Tree House Merlin Mission Ser.: No. 3). (ENG.). 144p. (J). (gr. 2-5). 5.99 *(978-0-375-86491-9(1)*, Random Hse. Bks. for Young Readers) Random Hse. Children's Bks.
—Una Tarde en el Amazonas. 2004. (Casa del Arbol Ser.: 6).Tr. of Afternoon on the Amazon. (SPA., Illus.). 66p. (J). pap. 5.99 *(978-1-930332-50-8(X))* Lectorum Pubns., Inc.
—Tigers at Twilight. unabr. ed. 2004. (Magic Tree House Ser.: No. 19). 72p. (J). (gr. k-3). pap. 17.00 incl. audio *(978-0-8072-0928-8(7)*, S FTR 251 SP, Listening Library) Random Hse. Audio Publishing Group.
—Un Tigre Dientes de Sable en el Ocaso. 2004. (Casa del Arbol Ser.: 7).Tr. of Sunset of the Sabretooth. (SPA., Illus.). (J). pap. 5.99 *(978-1-930332-68-3(8))* Lectorum Pubns., Inc.
—Tonight on the Titanic. unabr. ed. 2004. (Magic Tree House Ser.: No. 17). 71p. (J). (gr. k-3). pap. 17.00 incl. audio *(978-0-8072-0926-4(0)*, S FTR 249 SP, Listening Library) Random Hse. Audio Publishing Group.
—Twister on Tuesday. 2004. (Magic Tree House Ser.: No. 23). 70p. (J). (gr. k-3). pap. 17.00 incl. audio *(978-0-8072-9932-6(4)*, Listening Library) Random Hse. Audio Publishing Group.
—El Verano de la Serpiente Marina. 2015. (Casa De árbol Ser.: 31). (SPA., Illus.). 144p. (J). (gr. 2-4). pap. 5.99 *(978-1-63245-534-5(X))* Lectorum Pubns., Inc.
—Viking Ships at Sunrise. unabr. ed. 2004. (Magic Tree House Ser.: No. 15). 71p. (J). (gr. k-3). pap. 17.00 incl. audio *(978-0-8072-0784-0(5)*, LFTR 243 SP, Listening Library) Random Hse. Audio Publishing Group.
—Winter of the Ice Wizard. Murdocca, Sal, illus. 2011. (Magic Tree House Merlin Mission Ser.: 4). (ENG.). 144p. (J). (gr. 2-5). 5.99 *(978-0-375-87395-9(3)*, Random Hse. Bks. for Young Readers) Random Hse. Children's Bks.
Osborne, Mary Pope & Murdocca, Sal. Esta Noche en el Titanic. Murdocca, Sal, illus. 2008. (Casa del Arbol Ser.: 17).Tr. of Tonight on the Titanic. (SPA., Illus.). (J). (gr. 2-4). pap. 5.99 *(978-1-933032-47-4(2))* Lectorum Pubns., Inc.
Osborne, Mary Pope & Osborne, Magic Tree. Dark Day in the Deep Sea. Murdocca, Sal, illus. 2009. (Magic Tree House Merlin Mission Ser.: 11). (ENG.). 144p. (J). (gr. 2-5). 5.99 *(978-0-375-83732-6(9)*, Random Hse. Bks. for Young Readers) Random Hse. Children's Bks.
Osborne, Mary Pope & PLC Editors Staff. Carnival at Candlelight. Murdocca, Sal, illus. 2006. (Magic Tree House Merlin Missions Ser.: No. 5). 105p. (gr. 2-6). 15.00 *(978-0-7569-6690-4(6))* Perfection Learning Corp.
Osborne, Mary Pope, et al. Buenos Días, Gorilas. Murdocca, Sal, illus. 2014. 26. (SPA.). 88p. (J). (gr. 2-4). pap. 5.99 *(978-1-933032-93-1(6))* Lectorum Pubns., Inc.
—Búfalos Antes Del Desayuno. Murdocca, Sal, illus. 2008. (Casa del Arbol Ser.: 18).Tr. of Buffalo Before Breakfast. (SPA.). (J). (gr. 2-4). pap. 5.99 *(978-1-933032-48-1(0))* Lectorum Pubns., Inc.
—Carnaval a Media Luz. Murdocca, Sal, illus. 2016. (SPA.). (J). (gr. 2-4). pap. 5.99 ***(978-1-63245-643-4(5))*** Lectorum Pubns., Inc.
—La Estación de Las Tormentas de Arena. Murdocca, Sal, illus. 2016. (SPA.). (J). (gr. 2-4). pap. 5.99 ***(978-1-63245-644-1(3))*** Lectorum Pubns., Inc.
—Maremoto en Hawái. Murdocca, Sal, illus. 2014. 28. (SPA.). 88p. (J). (gr. 2-4). pap. 5.99 *(978-1-933032-95-5(2))* Lectorum Pubns., Inc.
—Miedo Escénico en una Noche de Verano. Murdocca, Sal, illus. 2014. 25. (SPA.). 86p. (J). (gr. 2-4). pap. 5.99 *(978-1-933032-92-4(8))* Lectorum Pubns., Inc.
—La Noche de los Nuevos Magos. Murdocca, Sal, illus. 2016. (SPA.). (J). (gr. 2-4). pap. 5.99 ***(978-1-63245-645-8(1))*** Lectorum Pubns., Inc.
—Perros Salvajes a la Hora de la Cena. Murdocca, Sal, illus. 2008. (Casa del Arbol Ser.: 20).Tr. of Dingoes at Dinnertime. (SPA.). (J). (gr. 2-4). pap. 5.99 *(978-1-933032-50-4(2))* Lectorum Pubns., Inc.
—Tigres Al Anochecer. Murdocca, Sal, illus. 2008. (Casa del Arbol Ser.: 19).Tr. of Tigers at Twilight. (SPA.). (J). (gr. 2-4). pap. 5.99 *(978-1-933032-49-8(9))* Lectorum Pubns., Inc.
Osborne, Mary Pope, et al. Tormenta de Nieve en Luna Azul. Murdocca, Sal, illus. 2016. (SPA.). (J). (gr. 2-4). pap. 5.99 ***(978-1-63245-646-5(X))*** Lectorum Pubns., Inc.
Osbourne, Ozzy, pseud & Zink, Michelle. Guardian of the Gate. 2011. (Prophecy of the Sisters Trilogy Ser.: 2). (ENG.). 368p. (YA). (gr. 7-17). pap. 8.99 *(978-0-316-02740-3(5))* Little, Brown Bks. for Young Readers.
Osterweil, Adam. The Amulet of Komondor. Thorpe, Peter, illus. 2003. (ENG.). 112p. (J). (gr. 4-6). 15.95 *(978-1-886910-81-2(2)*, Lemniscaat) Boyds Mills Pr.
O'Sullivan, Helen. The Magic Piano. Busutti, Conor, illus. 2013. 34p. pap. *(978-1-908773-36-4(7))* Iponymous Publishing, Ltd.
Ott, Alexandra. Rules for Thieves. 2017. (Rules for Thieves Ser.: 1). (ENG., Illus.). 320p. (J). (gr. 3-7). 17.99 ***(978-1-4814-7274-6(7)***, Aladdin) Simon & Schuster Children's Publishing.
—Rules for Thieves. 2017. (J). pap. ***(978-1-4814-7275-3(5)***, Simon & Schuster/Paula Wiseman Bks.) Simon & Schuster/Paula Wiseman Bks.
Outram, Evelyn. Sav & Josh O Lucky's Christmas Adventure & Magic Street. 2010. 56p. pap. 17.95 *(978-1-60911-876-1(6)*, Eloquent Bks.) Strategic Book Publishing & Rights Agency (SBPRA).
Ovani, Germano, illus. The Monkey King. 2007. (Young Reading Series 1 Gift Bks). 47p. (J). (gr. -1-3). 8.99 *(978-0-7945-1593-5(2)*, Usborne) EDC Publishing.
Pabbaraju, S. Adventures of Andreux: Book One - Aranya. 2008. 176p. 23.95 *(978-1-4401-0075-8(6))*; pap. 13.95 *(978-0-595-40964-8(4))* iUniverse, Inc.
Page, Lynda. Caley's Secret Garden. 2012. 28p. pap. 32.70 *(978-1-4771-0605-1(7))* Xlibris Corp.
Page, P. K. The Old Woman & the Hen. Westergard, Jim, illus. 2008. (ENG.). 32p. (J). pap. 10.95 *(978-0-88984-309-7(0))* Porcupine's Quill, Inc. CAN. Dist: Univ. of Toronto Pr.
Paige, Danielle. Stealing Snow. 2016. (Stealing Snow Ser.). (ENG.). 384p. (YA). (gr. 9-12). 18.99 *(978-1-68119-076-1(1)*, 9781681190761, Bloomsbury USA Childrens) Bloomsbury Publishing USA.
—Stealing Snow. 2017. (SPA.). 384p. (YA). 18.95 ***(978-84-16700-68-4(0))*** Roca Editorial ESP. Dist: Spanish Pubs., LLC.
Paige, Danielle. Yellow Brick War. 2016. *(978-0-06-245860-5(4))*; (Dorothy Must Die Ser.: 3). (ENG.). 288p. (YA). (gr. 9-12). 18.99 *(978-0-06-228073-2(2))* HarperCollins Pubs.
Panamkat, Matthew. Karan Quma & the Meluha Tree. 2007. 348p. per. 19.95 *(978-0-595-41816-9(3))* iUniverse, Inc.
Pandora. Ankh: Conquering the Seven Deadly Sins. 2013. 100p. pap. 10.95 *(978-1-62212-908-9(3)*, Strategic Bk. Publishing) Strategic Book Publishing & Rights Agency (SBPRA).
Pangalos, Carol B. Gabriella & the Magic Stars. 2011. 36p. (gr. -1). pap. 15.14 *(978-1-4634-1108-4(1))* AuthorHouse.
Paolini, Christopher. Eragon; Eldest. (Inheritance Cycle Ser.: Bks. 1-2). (ENG.). (YA). (gr. 7). 2008. 1216p. pap. 19.99 *(978-0-375-85704-1(4))*Set. 2005. 1232p. 39.95 *(978-0-375-83658-9(6))* Random Hse. Children's Bks. (Knopf Bks. for Young Readers).
Papademetriou, Lisa. A Tale of Highly Unusual Magic. (J). (gr. 3-7). 2017. 336p. pap. 6.99 *(978-0-06-237106-5(1))* 2015. (ENG.). 320p. 16.99 *(978-0-06-237121-8(5))* HarperCollins Pubs.
Paradise, Elizabeth. The Lost Dreamer. 2013. 192p. pap. 9.99 *(978-0-615-77563-0(2))* EJMP.
Park, Linda Sue. Archer's Quest. 2008. (ENG., Illus.). 176p. (J). (gr. 3-7). 6.99 *(978-0-440-42204-4(3)*, Yearling) Random Hse. Children's Bks.
—Cavern of Secrets. Madsen, Jim, illus. 2017. (Wing & Claw Ser.: 2). 320p. (J). (gr. 3-7). 16.99 *(978-0-06-232741-3(0))* HarperCollins Pubs.
—Forest of Wonders. Madsen, Jim, illus. 2017. (Wing & Claw Ser.: 1). 352p. (J). (gr. 3-7). pap. 6.99 *(978-0-06-232739-0(9))* HarperCollins Pubs.
Parker, Emma. The Magic Show. 2010. (Illus.). pap. *(978-1-877561-23-8(1))* First Edition Ltd.
—The Magic Snow Globe. 2010. (Illus.). pap. *(978-1-877561-30-6(4))* First Edition Ltd.
Parker, Patti. Book of Ominook: The Journey Begins. 2012. 28p. pap. 9.95 *(978-1-936587-98-8(X))* Brighton Publishing LLC.
Parkhouse, David. Lucy's Spoons. 2004. 52p. pap. *(978-1-84401-276-3(X))* Athena Pr.
Parsons, Julie. Julianne & the Jinn, the Evil Genie. 2008. 56p. pap. 16.95 *(978-1-60703-984-6(2))* America Star Bks.
Pasillo, Susan. The Perfect Pumpkin. 2006. (J). lib. bdg. 20.95 *(978-1-933732-14-5(8))* Big Ransom Studio.
Patrick, J. Nelle. Tsarina. 2014. (ENG.). 336p. (YA). (gr. 7). 17.99 *(978-1-59514-693-9(8)*, Razorbill) Penguin Young Readers Group.
Patrick, Ruthven. Prisoners under Glass. 2005. (YA). per. *(978-0-9735422-2-6(5))* Scroll Pr.
Patterson, Eric. Nature Boy. Wright, Christopher, illus. 2007. 112p. (J). pap. 6.95 *(978-0-9797106-0-5(X))* Avid Readers Publishing Group.
Patterson, James. The Gift. 2010. (Witch & Wizard Ser.: No. 2). (J). 59.99 *(978-1-60941-012-4(2))* Findaway World, LLC.
—The Gift. 2014. lthr. 79.00 *(978-1-62715-523-6(6))* Leatherbound Bestsellers.
—Nevermore: The Final Maximum Ride Adventure. 2012. (Maximum Ride Ser.: 8). (ENG.). 384p. (YA). (gr. 5-17). 17.99 *(978-0-316-10184-4(2)*, Jimmy Patterson) Little Brown & Co.
—SantaKid. Garland, Michael, illus. 2004. (ENG.). 48p. (J). (gr. -1-1). 17.99 *(978-0-316-00061-1(2)*, Jimmy Patterson) Little Brown & Co.
—Witch & Wizard. 2010. (Witch & Wizard Ser.: 1). (YA). lib. bdg. 20.85 *(978-0-606-15119-1(2)*, Turtleback) Turtleback Bks.
Patterson, James & Dembowski, Jill. The Fire. 2013. (Witch & Wizard Ser.: 3). (ENG.). 352p. (YA). (gr. 7-17). mass mkt. 8.00 *(978-1-4555-2152-4(3)*, Jimmy Patterson) Little Brown & Co.
—The Fire. 2012. (Witch & Wizard Ser.: 3). (YA). lib. bdg. 20.85 *(978-0-606-26698-7(4)*, Turtleback) Turtleback Bks.
Patterson, James & Raymond, Emily. The Lost. 2014. (YA). (Witch & Wizard Ser.: 5). (ENG.). 384p. (gr. 7-17). 18.00 *(978-0-316-20770-6(5)*, Jimmy Patterson); 355p. *(978-0-316-24266-0(7))* Little Brown & Co.
Patterson, James & Rust, Ned. The Gift. (Witch & Wizard Ser.: 2). (ENG.). 2012. 352p. mass mkt. 7.99 *(978-0-446-56245-4(9))* 2011. 400p. (gr. 5-17). pap. 9.99 *(978-0-316-03835-5(0))* 2010. 352p. (gr. 5-17). 17.99 *(978-0-316-03625-2(0))* Little Brown & Co. (Jimmy Patterson).
—The Gift. 2012. (Witch & Wizard Ser.: 2). lib. bdg. 18.40 *(978-0-606-26451-8(5)*, Turtleback) Turtleback Bks.
Patton, Chris. A Totally True Princess Story. Wellman, Mike, ed. St. Aubin, Claude, illus. 2009. 72p. 12.99 *(978-0-615-27602-1(4))* Atomic Basement.
Paulk, William. The Creatures of Vision City: Pokie's Party, Book One. 2009. 48p. pap. 10.99 *(978-1-4389-5659-6(2))* AuthorHouse.
Payton, Nicole. Dragon Savior. 2007. 212p. per. 24.95 *(978-1-4241-5498-2(7))* America Star Bks.
Peachey, Ted. The Adventures of Ryan & His Magic Carrot. 2010. 90p. pap. 9.99 *(978-1-60911-222-6(9)*, Eloquent Bks.) Strategic Book Publishing & Rights Agency (SBPRA).
Pearce, Jackson & Stiefvater, Maggie. Pip Bartlett's Guide to Magical Creatures. 2016. (Pip Bartlett Ser.: 1). (ENG.). 192p. (J). (gr. 3-7). 9.99 *(978-1-338-08815-1(7))* Scholastic, Inc.
Pearce, Philippa. A Finder's Magic. Craig, Helen, illus. 2009. (ENG.). 128p. (J). (gr. 2-4). 15.99 *(978-0-7636-4072-9(7))* Candlewick Pr.
—The Little Gentleman. Pohrt, Tom, illus. 2004. 208p. (J). (gr. 3-18). lib. bdg. 16.89 *(978-0-06-073161-8(3))* HarperCollins Pubs.
Pearl, Alexa. #2: Journey Beyond the Trees. Sordo, Paco, illus. 2017. (Tales of Sasha Ser.: 2). (ENG.). 112p. (J). (gr. 1-3). pap. 5.99 *(978-1-4998-0391-4(5))* Little Bee Books Inc.
Pearson, Kimberly Ann. Mystling Glen Book I: The Tale of A Prince. 2009. 207p. pap. 14.95 *(978-1-4327-4169-3(1))* Outskirts Pr., Inc.
Pearson, Luke, illus. Hilda & the Troll. 2013. (Hildafolk Ser.). (ENG.). 40p. (J). (gr. k). 18.95 *(978-1-909263-14-7(1))* Flying Eye Bks. GBR. Dist: Consortium Bk. Sales & Distribution.
Pearson, Maggie. Rumpelstiltskin Returns. 2014. (ENG., Illus.). 32p. (J). *(978-0-7787-1332-6(6))* Crabtree Publishing Co.
Pearson, Ridley. Legacy of Secrets. 2017. (Kingdom Keepers - the Return Ser.: 2). (J). lib. bdg. 19.65 *(978-0-606-39497-0(4))* Turtleback Bks.
—The Return: Legacy of Secrets. 2016. (Kingdom Keepers Ser.: Bk. 2). (ENG., Illus.). 394p. (J). (gr. 5-9). 17.99 *(978-1-4231-8432-4(7))* Hyperion Bks. for Children.
Pedersen, Peggy A. Jasmine & the Magic Squirrel. 2008. 12p. pap. 24.95 *(978-1-60474-052-3(3))* America Star Bks.
Peeler, Gail. Jackson's Magic Wishing Well. 2008. 25p. 35.50 *(978-1-4357-2950-6(1))* Lulu Pr., Inc.
Pendergrass, D. Louis, a Blue Dragon. 2009. 32p. pap. 15.00 *(978-1-4389-9036-1(7))* AuthorHouse.
Penick Phillips-Cermak, Mosetta. The Wishing Flower. 2007. 24p. 16.50 *(978-0-615-15573-9(1))* PM Moon Pubs., Ltd.
Pennypacker, Sara. Stuart Goes to School. Matje, Martin, illus. 2005. (ENG.). 64p. (J). (gr. -1-3). reprint ed. per. 5.99 *(978-0-439-30183-1(1)*, Scholastic Paperbacks) Scholastic, Inc.
Pentz, Jane A. Horatio's Magical Journeys - the Secret. 2007. 108p. pap. 10.00 *(978-1-892426-11-6(0))* LMA Publishing.
Percival, Tom. The Magic Looking Glass. 2017. (Little Legends Ser.: 4). (ENG.). 192p. (J). (gr. 2-5). 14.99 ***(978-1-4926-4667-9(9))***; pap. 5.99 ***(978-1-4926-4259-6(2))*** Sourcebooks, Inc. (Sourcebooks Jabberwocky).
Pereira, Chritine M. Madilynn Rose Rhyming Fairy: Volume 1, 1 vol. 2010. 44p. pap. 24.95 *(978-1-61546-591-0(X))* PublishAmerica, Inc.
Perelman, Helen. Gooey Goblins: Halloween Special. Waters, Erica-Jane, illus. 2011. (Candy Fairies Ser.). (ENG.). 176p. (J). (gr. 2-5). pap. 5.99 *(978-1-4424-2213-1(0)*, Aladdin) Simon & Schuster Children's Publishing.
—Gooey Goblins: Halloween Special. Waters, Erica-Jane, illus. 2013. (Candy Fairies Ser.). (ENG.). 176p. (J). (gr. 2-5). 15.99 *(978-1-4424-6495-7(X)*, Simon & Schuster/Paula Wiseman Bks.) Simon & Schuster/Paula Wiseman Bks.
—The Sugar Ball. Waters, Erica-Jane, illus. 2013. (Candy Fairies Ser.: 6). (ENG.). 128p. (J). (gr. 2-5). 15.99 *(978-1-4424-6498-8(4)*, Simon & Schuster/Paula Wiseman Bks.) Simon & Schuster/Paula Wiseman Bks.
Perkins, Kevin John. The Circlet. 2010. 316p. pap. *(978-1-907211-33-1(0))* Grosvenor Hse. Publishing Ltd.
Perone, S. P. Star of the Future. 2010. 176p. 23.95 *(978-1-4502-6861-5(7))*; pap. 13.95 *(978-1-4502-6859-2(5))* iUniverse, Inc.
Perrault, Charles. Cinderella. Innocenti, Roberto, illus. 2013. (ENG.). 32p. (J). (gr. 1-17). pap. 7.99 *(978-0-89812-828-4(5)*, Creative Paperbacks) Creative Co., The.
Perritano, John. Warlock Stone, 1 vol. 2014. (Kid Squad Saves the World Ser.). (ENG.). 112p. (J). (gr. 8-12). lib. bdg. 27.07 *(978-1-62402-042-1(9)*, Calico Chapter Bks) Magic Wagon.
Perry, Fred. Gold Digger Platinum, Vol. 4. 2012. (ENG., Illus.). 132p. (YA). pap. 14.95 *(978-0-9850925-0-4(5)*, 9780985092504) Antarctic Pr., Inc.
Perry, Valerie J. Trilby Learns a Lesson. 2011. 26p. pap. 14.00 *(978-1-60976-659-7(8)*, Eloquent Bks.) Strategic Book Publishing & Rights Agency (SBPRA).
Peters, Andrew J. Banished Sons of Poseidon. 2015. (ENG.). 240p. (J). (gr. 7). pap. 11.95 *(978-1-62639-441-4(5))* Bold Strokes Bks.
Peters, Jackie. Mary Maybelieve. 2011. (Illus.). 92p. pap. 30.63 *(978-1-4567-7283-3(X))* AuthorHouse.
Peters, Karen Lynn. If I Only Had a Horse. 2013. 36p. 16.99 *(978-0-9894748-4-9(4))* Mindstir Media.
Peters, Stephanie True. Sleeping Beauty, Magic Master: A Graphic Novel. Lopez, Alex, illus. 2016. (Far Out Fairy Tales Ser.). (ENG.). 40p. (gr. 3-4). lib. bdg. 25.32 *(978-1-4965-3784-3(X)*, Far Out Fairy Tales) Stone Arch Bks.
Peterson, Alyson. The Cursed Dagger. 2016. (YA). pap. *(978-1-4621-1865-6(8))* Cedar Fort, Inc./CFI Distribution.
—The Exiled Prince. 2017. (ENG.). (YA). (gr. 8-12). pap. 17.99 ***(978-1-4621-2035-2(0)***, Sweetwater Bks.) Cedar Fort, Inc./CFI Distribution.
Peterson, Alyson. Ian Quicksilver: The Warrior's Return. 2015. vii, 309p. (YA). pap. 17.99 *(978-1-4621-1629-4(9))* Cedar Fort, Inc./CFI Distribution.
Petrucha, Stefan. Harry Potty & the Deathly Boring. 2010. (Papercutz Slices Ser.). (ENG., Illus.). 64p. (J). (gr. 5-12). pap. 7.99 *(978-1-59707-217-5(6)*, 9781597072175) Papercutz.
Peyo. The Smurfs Apprentice. 2013. (Smurfs Classic Ser.). (ENG.). 24p. (J). (gr. -1-2). pap. 3.99 *(978-1-4424-7263-1(4)*, Simon Spotlight) Simon Spotlight.
Peyo & Delporte, Yvan. The Smurfs, 3 Vols., Set. 2011. (Smurfs Graphic Novels Ser.). (ENG., Illus.). 184p. (J). (gr. 2-5). 17.99 *(978-1-59707-273-1(7)*, 9781597072731) Papercutz.
—The Smurfs & the Egg. 2011. (Smurfs Graphic Novels Ser.). (ENG., Illus.). 64p. (J). (gr. 2-5). 10.99 *(978-1-59707-247-2(8)*, 9781597072472); pap. 5.99 *(978-1-59707-246-5(X)*, 9781597072465) Papercutz.
Peyo, et al. The Smurfs & the Howlibird. 2011. (Smurfs Graphic Novels Ser.). (ENG., Illus.). 56p. (J). (gr. 2-5). pap. 5.99 *(978-1-59707-260-1(5)*, 9781597072601) Papercutz.
Pfeiffer, Kathleen. Spartacus Sprout, Please Watch Out! 2011. 32p. pap. 15.99 *(978-1-257-50163-2(1))* Lulu Pr., Inc.
Phillips, Liam & Plumm, Gabi. Mumble & Jumble & the Great Corpsicle Conundrum. 2009. 278p. pap. 24.50 *(978-1-4092-5577-2(8))* Lulu Pr., Inc.
Phoenix International Staff, illus. Princess Sofia. 2012. 10p. (J). bds. 14.98 *(978-1-4508-6822-8(3)*, e41cac27-3be3-41b8-8dc5-7fb934c0ea6b) Phoenix International Publications, Inc.
Phoenix, Three. Daughter of the Sun. 2012. 36p. pap. 11.99 *(978-0-9830686-3-1(1))* Capital Apple Pr.

M
N
O

Picado, Gail. Magical Bandages. 2008. 32p. per. 24.95 *(978-1-4241-8851-2(2))* America Star Bks.

Pierce, Angelica. Wizard in Blue Jeans. 2007. 184p. pap. 10.95 *(978-1-4303-0647-4(5))* Lulu Pr., Inc.

Pierce, Meredith Ann. Treasure at the Heart of the Tanglewood. 2003. (Action Packs Ser.). (ENG., Illus.). 256p. (J). (gr. 7-7). 7.99 *(978-0-14-250013-2(5)*, Firebird) Penguin Young Readers Group.

Pierce, Tamora. Battle Magic. (ENG.). 464p. (J). (gr. 7). 2015. pap. 10.99 *(978-0-439-84298-3(0))* 2013. 17.99 *(978-0-439-84297-6(2)*, Scholastic Pr.) Scholastic, Inc.

—Cold Fire. 2003. (Circle Opens Ser.: 3). (ENG.). 384p. (J). (gr. 7). mass mkt. 7.99 *(978-0-590-39656-1(0)*, Scholastic Paperbacks) Scholastic, Inc.

—The Immortals Quartet: Wild Magic; Wolf-Speaker; Emperor Mage; the Realms of the Gods. 2015. (Immortals Ser.). (ENG., Illus.). 1440p. (YA). (gr. 7). pap. 43.99 *(978-1-4814-4030-1(6)*, Atheneum Bks. for Young Readers) Simon & Schuster Children's Publishing.

—Magic Steps. 2006. (Circle Opens Ser.: No. 1). 264p. 18.00 *(978-0-7569-6588-4(8))* Perfection Learning Corp.

—Shatterglass. 2004. (Circle Opens Ser.: 4). (ENG.). 368p. (J). (gr. 3-7). pap. 8.99 *(978-0-590-39696-7(X)*, Scholastic Paperbacks) Scholastic, Inc.

—Terrier. 2007. (Beka Cooper Ser.: Bk. 1). (ENG.). 608p. (YA). (gr. 7-11). pap. 10.99 *(978-0-375-83816-3(3)*, Ember) Random Hse. Children's Bks.

—Tortall & Other Lands: A Collection of Tales. 2012. (Beka Cooper Ser.). (ENG.). 400p. (YA). (gr. 7). pap. 10.99 *(978-0-375-86633-3(7)*, Bluefire) Random Hse. Children's Bks.

Pierce, Walter. Dreams Unseen: The Dragon of Mists. 2007. 260p. (YA). per. 16.95 *(978-0-595-45171-5(3))* iUniverse, Inc.

Pike, Christopher, pseud. Deepest Desires, Instant Remorse No. 2, Bk. 2. 2010. (Thirst Ser.: 2). (ENG.). 608p. (YA). (gr. 9). pap. 11.99 *(978-1-4169-8309-5(0)*, Simon Pulse) Simon Pulse.

—The Eternal Dawn. 2010. (Thirst Ser.: 3). (ENG.). 512p. (YA). (gr. 9-18). pap. 11.99 *(978-1-4424-1317-7(4)*, Simon Pulse) Simon Pulse.

—Human Urges, Fatal Consequences. 2009. (Thirst Ser.: 1). (ENG., Illus.). 624p. (YA). (gr. 9). pap. 12.99 *(978-1-4169-8308-8(2)*, Simon Pulse) Simon Pulse.

—The Shadow of Death. 2011. (Thirst Ser.: 4). (ENG., Illus.). 528p. (YA). (gr. 9). pap. 10.99 *(978-1-4424-1319-1(0)*, Simon Pulse) Simon Pulse.

—Thirst, 3 vols. 2013. (Thirst Ser.). (ENG.). 1744p. (YA). (gr. 9). pap. 30.99 *(978-1-4424-8375-0(X)*, Simon Pulse) Simon Pulse.

Pillsworth, Anne M. Summoned. 2014. (Redemption's Heir Ser.: 1). (ENG.). 320p. (YA). (gr. 8-7). 17.99 *(978-0-7653-3589-0(1)*, 9780765335890, Tor Teen) Doherty, Tom Assocs., LLC.

Pilumeli, Tanya. The Dragonfly Keeper. 2008. 264p. (J). per. 12.95 *(978-0-9801396-0-0(0))* FAVA Pr.

Plant, Marilyn. Trinka's Magic Bracelet. 2012. 40p. pap. *(978-1-77067-956-6(1))* FriesenPress.

Plotz, John. Time & the Tapestry. Saroff, Phyllis, illus. 2014. (ENG.). 192p. (YA). (gr. 4-6). 18.50 *(978-1-59373-145-8(0))* Bunker Hill Publishing, Inc.

Plourde, Lynn. The Blizzard Wizard. Aardema, John, illus. 2010. (ENG.). 32p. (J). (gr. -1-3). 16.95 *(978-0-89272-789-6(6))* Down East Bks.

Plourde, Paulette. My Magic Pillow. 2005. (Illus.). 40p. (J). per. 8.99 *(978-1-932338-76-8(4))* Lifevest Publishing, Inc.

Polanco, Amparo. The Magical Forest. 2016. (ENG., Illus.). (J). 16.95 ***(978-1-5069-0268-5(5))***; pap. 12.95 ***(978-1-5069-0269-2(3))*** First Edition Design eBook Publishing.

Poltera, Anne. Castle Magic & the Sinister Encroaching Fir Wood. 2012. (Illus.). 256p. (-18). pap. 19.76 *(978-1-4772-3943-8(X))* AuthorHouse.

Pool, Catherine. Catrina's Journey to Her Musical Friends, 1 vol. 2010. 18p. pap. 24.95 *(978-1-4489-7237-1(X))* PublishAmerica, Inc.

Poole, Philip. The Trouble with Time. 2012. (Illus.). 24p. pap. 19.82 *(978-1-4772-3459-4(4))* AuthorHouse.

Pope, Paul. Battling Boy. Pope, Paul, illus. 2013. (Battling Boy Ser.: 1). (ENG., Illus.). 208p. (J). (gr. 5-12). 24.99 *(978-1-59643-805-7(3)*, 9781596438057); pap. 16.99 *(978-1-59643-145-4(8)*, 9781596431454) Roaring Brook Pr. (First Second Bks.).

Popovic, Lana. Wicked Like a Wildfire. 2017. 416p. (YA). (gr. 9). 17.99 *(978-0-06-243683-2(X)*, Tegen, Katherine Bks) HarperCollins Pubs.

Porter, Sarah. Vassa in the Night. 2016. (ENG.). 304p. (YA). 17.99 *(978-0-7653-8054-8(4)*, 9780765380548, Tor Teen) Doherty, Tom Assocs., LLC.

Posner-Sanchez, Andrea. Bunny Magic! (Disney Junior: Sofia the First) RH Disney Staff, illus. 2014. (Little Golden Book Ser.). (ENG.). 24p. (J). (-k). 4.99 *(978-0-7364-3085-2(7)*, Golden/Disney) Random Hse. Children's Bks.

Potter, Beatrix. Mystery Thief! 2013. (Peter Rabbit Animation Ser.). (ENG.). 32p. (J). (gr. -1-k). 3.99 *(978-0-7232-8041-5(X)*, Warne) Penguin Young Readers Group.

Potter, Kay. I Hate Fairies! the Adventures of Katie James. 2013. 140p. pap. 13.97 *(978-1-62212-127-4(9)*, Strategic Bk. Publishing) Strategic Book Publishing & Rights Agency (SBPRA).

Potter, Tony, des. Finn & the Magic Harp. 2004. (Illus.). 12p. (J). 10.95 *(978-0-7171-3767-1(8))* M.H. Gill & Co. U. C. IRL. Dist: Dufour Editions, Inc.

Pounder, Sibéal. Witch Switch. Anderson, Laura Ellen, illus. 2017. (Witch Wars Ser.). (ENG.). 272p. (J). 16.99 *(978-1-61963-984-3(X)*, 9781619639843, Bloomsbury USA Childrens) Bloomsbury Publishing USA.

—Witch Wars. Anderson, Laura Ellen, illus. 2016. (Witch Wars Ser.). (ENG.). 272p. (J). 16.99 *(978-1-61963-925-6(4)*, 9781619639256, Bloomsbury USA Childrens) Bloomsbury Publishing USA.

—Witch Wars. Anderson, Laura Ellen, illus. 2017. (Witch Wars Ser.). (ENG.). 288p. (J). pap. 7.99 *(978-1-68119-296-3(9)*, 9781681192963, Bloomsbury USA Childrens) Bloomsbury Publishing USA.

Power, Nicholas D. Paudie's Magical Adventures. 2009. 236p. 24.75 *(978-1-60693-534-7(8)*, Strategic Bk. Publishing) Strategic Book Publishing & Rights Agency (SBPRA).

Prasad, Sunayna. Alyssa Mccarthy's Magical Missions: Book 1. 2013. 216p. pap. *(978-1-4602-0701-7(7))* FriesenPress.

Preble, Joy. Dreaming Anastasia. 2009. (ENG.). 320p. (YA). (gr. 7-12). pap. 13.99 *(978-1-4022-1817-0(6)*, Sourcebooks Jabberwocky) Sourcebooks, Inc.

—Haunted. 2011. (ENG.). 304p. (YA). (gr. 7-12). pap. 9.99 *(978-1-4022-4468-1(1))* Sourcebooks, Inc.

Preble, Laura. Lica's Angel. 2003. 142p. (YA). 21.95 *(978-0-595-74914-0(3))*; pap. 11.95 *(978-0-595-28253-1(9))* iUniverse, Inc.

Preussler, Otfried. The Little Witch. Bell, Anthea, tr. from GER. Gebhardt-Gayler, Winnie, illus. 2015. (ENG.). 144p. (J). (gr. k-4). 15.95 *(978-1-59017-934-5(X)*, NYR Children's Collection) New York Review of Bks., Inc., The.

Price, Ellen Ann. Gladiy's Magic. 2011. 160p. 27.50 *(978-0-557-71561-9(X))*; pap. 18.00 *(978-1-257-10561-8(2))*; pap. 55.00 *(978-1-4583-6372-5(4))* Lulu Pr., Inc.

The Princess & the Magic Locket. (My Tooth Is Loose!). (Illus.). 32p. (J). *(978-1-4054-1022-9(1))* Parragon, Inc.

Prineas, Sarah. Found. Caparo, Antonio Javier, illus. 2011. (Magic Thief Ser.: 3). (ENG.). 384p. (J). (gr. 5). pap. 7.99 *(978-0-06-137595-8(0))* HarperCollins Pubs.

—Lost. Caparo, Antonio Javier, illus. 2009. (Magic Thief Ser.: 2). (ENG.). 400p. (J). (gr. 5-18). 17.99 *(978-0-06-137589-7(6))* HarperCollins Pubs.

—Lost. 2009. (Magic Thief Ser.: 2). (J). 88.75 *(978-1-4407-3133-4(0))*; 130.75 *(978-1-4407-3129-7(2))*; 132.75 *(978-1-4407-3127-3(6))*; 1.25 *(978-1-4407-3131-0(4))*; 112.75 *(978-1-4407-3123-5(3))*; (SPA.). 265.75 *(978-1-4407-3124-2(1))*; 110.75 *(978-1-4407-3125-9(X))* Recorded Bks., Inc.

—The Magic Thief. Caparo, Antonio Javier, illus. (Magic Thief Ser.: 1). (ENG.). (J). (gr. 5). 2009. 448p. pap. 7.99 *(978-0-06-137590-3(X))* 2008. 432p. 16.99 *(978-0-06-137587-3(X))* HarperCollins Pubs.

—The Magic Thief - Found. Caparo, Antonio Javier, illus. 2010. (Magic Thief Ser.: 3). (ENG.). 368p. (J). (gr. 5-18). 16.99 *(978-0-06-137593-4(4))* HarperCollins Pubs.

—The Magic Thief - Home. Caparo, Antonio Javier, illus. 2015. (Magic Thief Ser.: 4). (ENG.). 416p. (J). (gr. 3-7). pap. 7.99 *(978-0-06-220956-6(6))* HarperCollins Pubs.

—The Magic Thief - Lost. Caparo, Antonio Javier, illus. 2010. (Magic Thief Ser.: 2). (ENG.). 416p. (J). (gr. 5). pap. 7.99 *(978-0-06-137592-7(6))* HarperCollins Pubs.

—The Magic Thief: Home. Caparo, Antonio Javier, illus. 2014. (Magic Thief Ser.: 4). (ENG.). 416p. (J). (gr. 3-7). 17.99 *(978-0-06-220954-2(X))* HarperCollins Pubs.

—Moonkind. (Summerlands Ser.: 3). (ENG.). 272p. (J). (gr. 3-7). 2014. pap. 6.99 *(978-0-06-192111-7(4))* 2013. 16.99 *(978-0-06-192109-4(2))* HarperCollins Pubs.

—Summerkin. 2013. (Summerlands Ser.: 2). (ENG.). (J). (gr. 3-7). 288p. pap. 6.99 *(978-0-06-192108-7(4))*; 272p. 16.99 *(978-0-06-192106-3(8))* HarperCollins Pubs.

—Winterling. (J). (gr. 5-7). 2013. (Summerlands Ser.: 1). (ENG.). 272p. pap. 6.99 *(978-0-06-192105-6(X))* 2012. 256p. lib. bdg. 17.89 *(978-0-06-192104-9(1))* 2012. (Summerlands Ser.: 1). (ENG.). 256p. 16.99 *(978-0-06-192103-2(3))* HarperCollins Pubs.

—Winterling, 5 vols. 2012. (Winterling Ser.: 1). (J). 75.75 *(978-1-4640-1032-3(3))*; 73.75 *(978-1-4640-1037-8(4))*; 73.75 *(978-1-4640-1036-1(6))*; 230.75 *(978-1-4640-1034-7(X))* Recorded Bks., Inc.

Pritchard, David. Ghost of Spring. 2010. 228p. pap. *(978-1-907652-11-0(6))* Grosvenor Hse. Publishing Ltd.

Promise, 1 vol. 2014. (Faerieground Ser.). (ENG., Illus.). 96p. (gr. 1-3). lib. bdg. 23.99 *(978-1-4342-9188-2(X))* Stone Arch Bks.

Provencher, Olga J. Joey & Mup. 2005. 134p. per. 9.95 *(978-1-59824-048-1(X))* E-BookTime LLC.

Pruitt, Lisa A. Savanna & the Magic Boots. 2011. 24p. (gr. 1-2). pap. 11.32 *(978-1-4634-0090-3(X))* AuthorHouse.

Pryce, Trevor. Amphibians' End. Greene, Sanford, illus. 2016. (Kulipari Ser.). (ENG.). 304p. (J). (gr. 3-7). pap. 8.95 *(978-1-4197-2194-6(1)*, Amulet Bks.) Abrams, Inc.

—An Army of Frogs. Greene, Sanford, illus. 2013. (Kulipari Ser.). (ENG.). 288p. (J). (gr. 3-7). 15.95 *(978-1-4197-0172-6(X)*, Amulet Bks.) Abrams, Inc.

Pryce, Trevor & Naftali, Joel. Amphibians' End. 2015. (Kulipari Ser.). (ENG., Illus.). 304p. (J). (gr. 3-7). 15.95 *(978-1-4197-1648-5(4)*, Amulet Bks.) Abrams, Inc.

—An Army of Frogs. Greene, Sanford, illus. 2014. (Kulipari Ser.). (ENG.). 304p. (J). (gr. 3-7). pap. 8.95 *(978-1-4197-1381-1(7)*, Amulet Bks.) Abrams, Inc.

—The Rainbow Serpent. Greene, Sanford, illus. 2014. (Kulipari Ser.). (ENG.). 304p. (J). (gr. 3-7). 15.95 *(978-1-4197-1309-5(4)*, Amulet Bks.) Abrams, Inc.

Psilopoulou, Koralia. The Magic Amulets. 2012. 24p. pap. 17.99 *(978-1-4389-6654-0(7))* AuthorHouse.

Publications International Ltd. Staff, creator. Fairy Tales: Keepsake Collection. 2007. (Illus.). 96p. 12.98 *(978-1-4127-7453-6(5))* Publications International, Ltd.

Publications International Ltd. Staff, ed. Disney Princess Storybook & Magic Bracelet. 2010. 12p. (J). bds. 12.98 *(978-1-4127-9912-6(0))* Phoenix International Publications, Inc.

—Princess Magic. 2010. (My First Look & Find Ser.). (Illus.). 12p. (gr. -1). bds. 7.98 *(978-1-4127-3074-7(0)*, 7227000) Phoenix International Publications, Inc.

Pullman, Philip. Das Magische Messer. (GER.). pap. 22.95 *(978-3-453-15227-4(1))* Verlag Wilhelm Heyne DEU. Dist: Distribooks, Inc.

—Lyra's Oxford. Lawrence, John, illus. 2007. (His Dark Materials Ser.). (ENG.). 64p. (J). (gr. 5-12). per. 6.99 *(978-0-375-84369-3(8)*, Knopf Bks. for Young Readers) Random Hse. Children's Bks.

Purday, Paul. The Two Lands. 2006. 310p. (J). pap. *(978-1-905809-11-0(5))* Pneuma Springs Publishing.

Purdie, Kathryn. Burning Glass. (Burning Glass Ser.: 1). (YA). (gr. 9). 2017. 528p. pap. 9.99 *(978-0-06-241237-9(X))* 2016. (Illus.). 512p. 17.99 *(978-0-06-241236-2(1))* HarperCollins Pubs. (Tegen, Katherine Bks).

—Crystal Blade. 2017. (Burning Glass Ser.: 2). 368p. (YA). (gr. 9). 17.99 *(978-0-06-241239-3(6)*, Tegen, Katherine Bks) HarperCollins Pubs.

Quest, Stacy. Sad Sam & the Magic Cookies. Wertheimer, Beverly & Ronsley, Jill, eds. Morris, Michael, illus. 2006. (ENG.). (J). 16.95 *(978-1-932367-01-0(2))* BookBound Publishing.

Quinlan, Nigel. The Weatherman. 2015. (ENG.). 320p. (J). (gr. 4-7). 16.99 *(978-1-62672-033-6(9)*, 9781626720336) Roaring Brook Pr.

Quinn, Jordan. The False Fairy. McPhillips, Robert, illus. 2016. (Kingdom of Wrenly Ser.: 11). (ENG.). 128p. (J). (gr. k-4). pap. 5.99 *(978-1-4814-8586-9(5)*, Little Simon) Little Simon.

—The Sorcerer's Shadow. McPhillips, Robert, illus. 2017. (Kingdom of Wrenly Ser.: 12). (ENG.). 128p. (J). (gr. k-4). 16.99 ***(978-1-5344-0000-9(1))***; pap. 5.99 ***(978-1-4814-9999-6(8))*** Little Simon. (Little Simon).

Quinn, Jordan. The Witch's Curse. McPhillips, Robert, illus. 2014. (Kingdom of Wrenly Ser.: 4). (ENG.). 128p. (J). (gr. k-4). pap. 5.99 *(978-1-4814-0075-6(4)*, Little Simon) Little Simon.

Raasch, Sara. Frost Like Night. (Snow Like Ashes Ser.: 3). (YA). (gr. 9). 2017. 512p. pap. 9.99 ***(978-0-06-228699-4(4))*** 2016. (Illus.). 496p. 17.99 *(978-0-06-228698-7(6))* HarperCollins Pubs.

Raasch, Sara. Ice Like Fire. (YA). 2016. (Snow Like Ashes Ser.: 2). 512p. (gr. 9). pap. 9.99 *(978-0-06-228696-3(X))* 2015. (Snow Like Ashes Ser.: Bk. 2). (ENG., Illus.). 496p. (gr. 9-12). 17.99 *(978-0-06-228695-6(1))* 2015. (Illus.). 496p. pap. ***(978-0-06-242793-9(8))*** HarperCollins Pubs.

Rabe, Tish. Frozen. 2013. (Disney Princess Step into Reading Ser.). lib. bdg. 13.55 *(978-0-606-32203-4(5)*, Turtleback) Turtleback Bks.

Racaniello, P. Marcella & the Magic Hat. 2012. 20p. pap. 9.99 *(978-1-105-02672-0(8))* Lulu Pr., Inc.

A Ragged Magic. 2014. (ENG.). (YA). 24.95 *(978-1-941662-03-8(X))* Per Aspera Pr.

Rallison, Janette. The Wrong Side of Magic. 2016. (ENG.). 336p. (J). 16.99 *(978-1-250-07428-7(2)*, 9781250074287) Feiwel & Friends.

Rand, Johnathan. Freddie Fernortner #8: Chippers Crazy Carnival. 2008. 96p. (J). pap. 4.99 *(978-1-893699-77-9(3))* AudioCraft Publishing, Inc.

Rand, Jonathan. Freddie Fernortner #7 Bk 7: Fearless First Grader: the Magical Wading Pool. 2007. pap. 4.99 *(978-1-893699-91-5(9))* AudioCraft Publishing, Inc.

Random House. Barbie Dreamtopia Step into Reading (Barbie) 2017. (Step into Reading Ser.). (ENG.). 24p. (J). (gr. -1-1). lib. bdg. 12.99 ***(978-1-5247-1639-4(1))***; (Illus.). pap. 4.99 ***(978-1-5247-1638-7(3))*** Random Hse. Children's Bks. (Random Hse. Bks. for Young Readers).

—Color Magic (Shimmer & Shine) Random House, illus. 2017. (ENG., Illus.). 24p. (J). (— 1). bds. 6.99 *(978-0-399-55789-7(X)*, Random Hse. Bks. for Young Readers) Random Hse. Children's Bks.

—Everything That Glitters Is Guy! Laguna, Fabio, illus. 2017. (Pictureback(R) Ser.). (ENG.). 16p. (J). (gr. -1-2). pap. 5.99 ***(978-1-5247-1732-2(0)***, Random Hse. Bks. for Young Readers) Random Hse. Children's Bks.

—Magical Mermaids! Random House, illus. 2017. (Step into Reading Ser.). (ENG., Illus.). 24p. (J). (gr. -1-1). pap. 4.99 *(978-0-399-55886-3(1)*, Random Hse. Bks. for Young Readers) Random Hse. Children's Bks.

—Make It Sparkle! (Shimmer & Shine) Random House, illus. 2016. (Glitter Board Book Ser.). (ENG., Illus.). 12p. (J). (— 1). bds. 8.99 *(978-1-5247-0159-8(9)*, Random Hse. Bks. for Young Readers) Random Hse. Children's Bks.

—Meet Shimmer & Shine! (Shimmer & Shine) Cardona, Jose Maria, illus. 2016. (Step into Reading Ser.). (ENG.). 24p. (J). (gr. -1-1). 4.99 *(978-0-553-52203-7(5)*, Random Hse. Bks. for Young Readers) Random Hse. Children's Bks.

Random House. 1, 2, 3, Tea! (Shimmer & Shine) Cespedes-Alicea, Marcela, illus. 2017. (ENG.). 24p. (J). (— 1). bds. 6.99 ***(978-1-5247-1719-3(3)***, Random Hse. Bks. for Young Readers) Random Hse. Children's Bks.

Random House Disney Staff. Skate This Way! (Shimmer & Shine) Random House Disney Staff & Aikins, Dave, illus. 2016. (Book & CD Ser.). (ENG.). 24p. (J). (gr. -1-2). pap. 6.99 *(978-1-101-93870-6(6)*, Random Hse. Bks. for Young Readers) Random Hse. Children's Bks.

Random House Disney Staff & Yuu, Kristen. Teeny Genies. Random House Disney Staff et al, illus. 2017. (Official Guide Ser.). (ENG.). 64p. (J). (gr. -1-1). pap. 8.99 *(978-1-5247-1919-7(6)*, Random Hse. Bks. for Young Readers) Random Hse. Children's Bks.

Random House Staff. Ballet Dreams. Random House Staff, illus. 2013. (Step into Reading Ser.). (ENG., Illus.). 32p. (J). (gr. -1-1). pap. 3.99 *(978-0-307-98115-8(0)*, Random Hse. Bks. for Young Readers) Random Hse. Children's Bks.

Ranjalkar, Shreyans. My Sunny British Days - Stories for Children by a Child. 2013. (Illus.). 70p. pap. *(978-1-78148-596-5(8))* Grosvenor Hse. Publishing Ltd.

Ranson, Erin. Woodland Fairies. Top That Publishing Staff, ed. Richards, Kirsten, illus. 2008. (Magnetic Story & Play Scene Ser.). 9p. (J). (gr. -1). bds. *(978-1-84666-440-3(3)*, Tide Mill Pr.) Top That! Publishing PLC.

Rao, Chatura. Amie & the Chawl of Colour. Pathak, Ashutosh, illus. 2004. 100p. pap. *(978-0-14-333592-4(8)*, Puffin) Penguin Publishing Group.

Rao, Lisa. Dora's Magic Watering Can. Miller, Victoria, illus. 2008. (Dora the Explorer Ser.). (ENG.). 16p. (J). (gr. -1-1). pap. 4.99 *(978-1-4169-4772-1(8)*, Simon Spotlight/Nickelodeon) Simon Spotlight/Nickelodeon.

Raynor, Michelle. A Magical World. 2011. 20p. pap. 11.99 *(978-1-257-65025-5(4))* Lulu Pr., Inc.

Reader, Gwendolin. The Life Cycle of A Snowman. 2010. 24p. pap. 12.50 *(978-1-4520-7686-7(3))* AuthorHouse.

Reader's Digest Staff. Rise of the Guardians: Worlds of Wonder. Primeau, Chuck, illus. deluxe ed. 2012. (ENG.). 24p. (J). (gr. k-2). 19.99 *(978-0-7944-2803-7(7))* Reader's Digest Assn., Inc., The.

Reardon, A. C. Galish: The adventure of Isabelle & Eva. 2011. 168p. pap. 14.69 *(978-1-4567-7818-7(8))* AuthorHouse.

Reaves, Esther R. Gammy's Snow Queen. 2011. 24p. pap. 12.79 *(978-1-4520-7158-9(6))* AuthorHouse.

The Rebel Princess. 2014. pap. 12.99 *(978-1-4621-1430-6(X))* Cedar Fort, Inc./CFI Distribution.

Redwine, C. J. The Shadow Queen. 2016. (YA). (gr. 8). (Ravenspire Ser.: 1). 416p. pap. 9.99 *(978-0-06-236025-0(6))*; (ENG., Illus.). 400p. 17.99 *(978-0-06-236024-3(8))* HarperCollins Pubs.

—The Shadow Queen. 2016. (Ravenspire Ser.: 1). (YA). lib. bdg. 20.85 *(978-0-606-39615-8(2))* Turtleback Bks.

Reef Rescue (Book 4) 2017. (Secret Mermaid Ser.). (ENG.). (J). pap. 4.99 ***(978-0-7945-3686-2(7)***, Usborne) EDC Publishing.

Rees, Gwyneth. Cosmo & the Great Witch Escape, 1. Hearn, Samuel, illus. 2nd unabr. ed. 2006. (Cosmo Ser.: 2). (ENG.). 256p. (J). (gr. 2-4). pap. 9.99 *(978-0-330-43733-2(X))* Macmillan Pubs., Ltd. GBR. Dist: Independent Pubs. Group.

—My Super Sister, 1. Monks, Lydia & Okstad, Ella, illus. unabr. ed. 2013. (ENG.). 176p. (J). (gr. 4). pap. 6.99 *(978-0-330-46114-6(1))* Pan Macmillan GBR. Dist: Independent Pubs. Group.

Reeve, Philip. Goblins. 2013. (ENG.). 352p. (J). (gr. 3-7). 17.99 *(978-0-545-22220-4(6)*, Scholastic Pr.) Scholastic, Inc.

—Here Lies Arthur. 2008. (ENG.). 352p. (J). (gr. 7-18). 17.99 *(978-0-545-09334-7(1)*, Scholastic Pr.) Scholastic, Inc.

—Here Lies Arthur. 2010. lib. bdg. 19.65 *(978-0-606-10557-6(3)*, Turtleback) Turtleback Bks.

—Pugs of the Frozen North. McIntyre, Sarah, illus. 2016. (Not-So-Impossible Tale Ser.). (ENG.). 224p. (J). (gr. 2-5). 12.99 *(978-0-385-38796-5(2)*, Random Hse. Bks. for Young Readers) Random Hse. Children's Bks.

Regan, Dian. The Dragon Stone, 0 vols. Curtis, Stacy, illus. 2013. (ENG.). 96p. (J). (gr. 2-4). pap. 9.99 *(978-1-4778-1632-5(1)*, 9781477816325, Amazon Children's Publishing) Amazon Publishing.

Reh, Rusalka. Pizzicato: The Abduction of the Magic Violin, 0 vols. Wilson, David Henry, tr. from GER. 2011. (ENG.). 132p. (J). (gr. 4-6). pap. 9.95 *(978-1-61109-004-8(0)*, 9781611090048) Amazon Publishing.

—The Secret of the Water Knight, 0 vols. Derbyshire, Katy, tr. unabr. ed. 2011. (ENG.). 100p. (J). (gr. 4-7). pap. 9.95 *(978-1-61109-006-2(7)*, 9781611090062) Amazon Publishing.

Reihs, Linda. The Adventures of Maddy Morphis. 2012. 34p. pap. 9.99 *(978-0-9819648-1-2(8))* Mindstir Media.

Reilly, Carmel & Hopkinson, Courtney. Magic Tricks. 2008. (Rigby Focus Forward: Level F Ser.). (Illus.). 24p. (J). (gr. 4-7). pap. *(978-1-4190-3697-2(1)*, Rigby) Pearson Education Australia.

—New Tricks. 2008. (Rigby Focus Forward: Level J Ser.). (Illus.). 24p. (J). (gr. 4-7). pap. *(978-1-4190-3766-5(8)*, Rigby) Pearson Education Australia.

Reiss, Kathryn. Paint by Magic. 2003. (ENG.). 288p. (J). (gr. 5-7). pap. 17.95 *(978-0-15-204925-6(8))* Houghton Mifflin Harcourt Publishing Co.

Return of the Dark Queen (Book 6) 2017. (Secret Mermaid Ser.). (ENG.). (J). pap. 4.99 ***(978-0-7945-3684-8(0)***, Usborne) EDC Publishing.

Return to the Crows, 1 vol. 2014. (Faeriground Ser.). (ENG., Illus.). 96p. (gr. 1-3). lib. bdg. 23.99 *(978-1-4342-9187-5(1))* Stone Arch Bks.

Reviejo, Carlos & Reviejo, Carlos. Dejame Que te Cuente: Cincuenta Cuentos de Animales para Ninos. 2003. (SPA., Illus.). 212p. *(978-84-348-7166-3(1)*, SM31147) SM Ediciones ESP. Dist: Lectorum Pubns., Inc.

Rex, Adam. Champions of Breakfast. 2014. (Cold Cereal Saga Ser.: 3). (ENG., Illus.). 368p. (J). (gr. 3-7). 16.99 *(978-0-06-206008-2(2))* HarperCollins Pubs.

—Cold Cereal. (Cold Cereal Saga Ser.: 1). (ENG.). (J). (gr. 3-7). 2013. 448p. pap. 7.99 *(978-0-06-206003-7(1))* 2012. 432p. 16.99 *(978-0-06-206002-0(3))* HarperCollins Pubs.

—Unlucky Charms. 2013. (Cold Cereal Saga Ser.: 2). (ENG., Illus.). 400p. (J). (gr. 3-7). 16.99 *(978-0-06-206005-1(8))* HarperCollins Pubs.

Reyes, Laurisa White. The Last Enchanter. 2013. (Celestine Chronicles Ser.: Bk. 2). (ENG.). 404p. (J). (gr. 2-7). 16.95 *(978-1-933718-93-4(5))* Tanglewood Pr.

—The Rock of Ivanore. 2012. (Celestine Chronicles Ser.: 1). (ENG., Illus.). 356p. (J). (gr. 2-7). 16.95 *(978-1-933718-60-6(9))* Tanglewood Pr.

Reynolds, Caroline. Bead Street-the Fable of Red Clover. 2009. 116p. 22.50 *(978-1-60693-579-8(8)*, Eloquent Bks.) Strategic Book Publishing & Rights Agency (SBPRA).

Reynolds, Mariem. The World in Between. 2008. 87p. pap. 16.95 *(978-1-60672-144-5(5))* PublishAmerica, Inc.

RH Disney Staff. Never Girls - In a Blink, 2 bks. in 1. Christy, Jana, illus. 2015. (Never Girls Ser.). (ENG.). 256p. (J). (gr. 1-4). 9.99 *(978-0-7364-3432-4(1)*, RH/Disney) Random Hse. Children's Bks.

—Welcome to Whisker Haven (Disney Palace Pets: Whisker Haven Tales) RH Disney Staff, illus. 2016. (Big Golden Book Ser.). (ENG., Illus.). 32p. (J). (gr. -1-2). 9.99 *(978-0-7364-3474-4(7)*, Golden/Disney) Random Hse. Children's Bks.

RH Disney Staff & Julius, Jessica. Anna's Birthday Surprise. RH Disney Staff, illus. 2015. (Pictureback(R) Ser.). (ENG., Illus.). 24p. (J). (gr. -1-2). 4.99 *(978-0-7364-3439-3(9)*, RH/Disney) Random Hse. Children's Bks.

Rhodes, Jewell Parker. Bayou Magic. 2015. (ENG., Illus.). 256p. (J). (gr. 3-7). 17.99 *(978-0-316-22484-0(7))* Little Brown & Co.

—Bayou Magic. 2016. (ENG.). 272p. (J). (gr. 3-7). pap. 7.99 *(978-0-316-22485-7(5))* Little, Brown Bks. for Young Readers.

Rhodes, Morgan. A Book of Spirits & Thieves. 2015. (Book of Spirits & Thieves Ser.: 1). (ENG.). 368p. (YA). (gr. 7). 18.99 *(978-1-59514-759-2(4)*, Razorbill) Penguin Young Readers Group.

—The Darkest Magic. 2016. (Book of Spirits & Thieves Ser.: 2). (ENG.). 368p. (YA). (gr. 7). 18.99 *(978-1-59514-761-5(6)*, Razorbill) Penguin Young Readers Group.

—Gathering Darkness. 2014. (Falling Kingdoms Ser.: 3). (ENG.). 430p. (YA). (gr. 7). 18.99 *(978-1-59514-705-9(5)*, Razorbill) Penguin Young Readers Group.

Ribar, Lindsay. The Art of Wishing. (ENG.). (YA). (gr. 7). 2014. 336p. pap. 9.99 *(978-0-14-242529-9(X)*, Speak) 2013. 320p. 17.99 *(978-0-8037-3827-0(7)*, Dial Bks) Penguin Young Readers Group.

—The Fourth Wish. 2014. (Art of Wishing Ser.). (ENG.). 368p. (YA). (gr. 7). 17.99 *(978-0-8037-3828-7(5)*, Kathy Dawson Books) Penguin Young Readers Group.

—Rocks Fall Everyone Dies. 2016. (ENG.). 336p. (YA). (gr. 7). 17.99 *(978-0-525-42868-8(2)*, Kathy Dawson Books) Penguin Young Readers Group.

Rice, Morgan. A Reign of Steel (Book #11 in the Sorcerer's Ring) 2014. 216p. (YA). pap. 15.99 *(978-1-939416-76-6(0)*, Morgan Rice) Morgan Rice Bks.

Richard Richtmyer. A Bit of Magic: A Novel. 2009. 116p. pap. 10.95 *(978-1-4401-5565-9(8))* iUniverse, Inc.

Richards, Chip & De Alessi, O. B. Flutes in the Garden. 2015. (ENG.). 68p. pap. 13.95 *(978-0-7387-4658-6(4))* Llewellyn Pubns.

Richards, Dawn. My Mommy Is Magic. Massey, Jane, illus. 2015. (ENG.). 32p. (J). (gr. -1-k). 8.99 *(978-0-7641-6757-7(X))* Barron's Educational Series, Inc.

Richemont, Enid. The Big Purple Wonderbook. Waldek, Kelly, illus. 2009. (Go! Readers Ser.). 48p. (J). (gr. 2-5). pap. 12.85 *(978-1-60754-279-7(X))*; lib. bdg. 29.25 *(978-1-60754-278-0(1))* Windmill Bks.

Rickis, Andrew. The Magic Oak: (A Baseball Story) A Novel for Young Adults. 2003. 114p. pap. 19.95 *(978-1-4137-0665-9(7))* America Star Bks.

Riggs, Mary L. Dragon Forge the Ballad of Beighn. 2009. 110p. pap. 9.95 *(978-1-60860-499-9(3)*, Strategic Bk. Publishing) Strategic Book Publishing & Rights Agency (SBPRA).

Riley, James. Secret Origins. 2017. (Story Thieves Ser.: 3). (ENG., Illus.). 384p. (J). (gr. 3-7). 17.99 *(978-1-4814-6125-2(7)*, Simon & Schuster/Paula Wiseman Bks.) Simon & Schuster/Paula Wiseman Bks.

—The Stolen Chapters. 2016. (Story Thieves Ser.: 2). (ENG., Illus.). 368p. (J). (gr. 3-7). 17.99 *(978-1-4814-0922-3(0)*, Aladdin) Simon & Schuster Children's Publishing.

—Story Thieves. 2015. (Story Thieves Ser.: 1). (ENG., Illus.). (J). (gr. 3-7). 416p. pap. 7.99 *(978-1-4814-0920-9(4))*; 400p. 17.99 *(978-1-4814-0919-3(0))* Simon & Schuster Children's Publishing. (Aladdin).

—Story Thieves. 2015. (Story Thieves Ser.: Vol. 1). (ENG.). (J). (gr. 3-7). lib. bdg. 18.40 ***(978-0-606-39444-4(3))*** Turtleback Bks.

Ringwald, Whitaker. The Secret Box. (Secret Box Ser.: 1). (ENG.). (J). (gr. 3-7). 2015. 320p. pap. 6.99 *(978-0-06-221615-1(5))* 2014. 304p. 16.99 *(978-0-06-221614-4(7))* HarperCollins Pubs. (Tegen, Katherine Bks).

—The Secret Cipher. 2016. (Secret Box Ser.: 2). 272p. (J). (gr. 3-7). pap. 6.99 *(978-0-06-221618-2(X)*, Tegen, Katherine Bks) HarperCollins Pubs.

—The Secret Cipher: A Secret Box Book. 2015. (Secret Box Ser.: 2). (ENG.). 256p. (J). (gr. 3-7). 16.99 *(978-0-06-221617-5(1)*, Tegen, Katherine Bks) HarperCollins Pubs.

Riordan, Rick. Demigods & Magicians: Percy & Annabeth Meet the Kanes. 2016. (ENG.). 224p. (J). (gr. 3-7). 14.99 *(978-1-4847-3278-6(2))* Hyperion Bks. for Children.

—The Kane Chronicles Box Set. Rocco, John, illus. 2013. (Kane Chronicles Ser.). (ENG.). 1472p. (J). (gr. 3-7). pap. 26.99 *(978-1-4231-9962-5(6))* Hyperion Bks. for Children.

—The Red Pyramid. 2011. (ENG.). 544p. (J). (gr. 5-17). pap. 9.99 *(978-1-4231-1345-4(4))* Disney Publishing Worldwide.

—The Red Pyramid. 2010. (Kane Chronicles Ser.). (ENG.). 528p. (J). (gr. 5-9). 17.99 *(978-1-4231-1338-6(1))* Hyperion Pr.

—The Red Pyramid, Bk. 1. Collar, Orpheus, illus. 2012. (Kane Chronicles Ser.). (ENG.). 192p. (J). (gr. 5-9). pap. 12.99 *(978-1-4231-5069-5(4))* Hyperion Pr.

—The Red Pyramid. 2009. (Kane Chronicles: Bk. 1). 11.04 *(978-0-7848-3733-7(3)*, Everbind) Marco Bk. Co.

—The Red Pyramid. 2012. 20.00 *(978-1-61383-660-6(0))* Perfection Learning Corp.

—The Red Pyramid. 2010. pap. *(978-0-545-40016-9(3))* Scholastic, Inc.

—The Red Pyramid. l.t. ed. 2010. (Kane Chronicles: Bk. 1). (ENG.). 671p. 23.95 *(978-1-4104-2536-2(3))* Thorndike Pr.

—The Red Pyramid. (Kane Chronicles Graphic Novels Ser.: 1). (J). 2012. lib. bdg. 24.50 *(978-0-606-37510-8(4))* 2011. lib. bdg. 20.85 *(978-0-606-39216-7(5))* Turtleback Bks.

—The Serpent's Shadow. (Kane Chronicles Ser.). (ENG.). (gr. 5-17). 2013. 464p. (J). pap. 9.99 *(978-1-4231-4202-7(0))*Bk. 3. 2012. 416p. (YA). 19.99 *(978-1-4231-4057-3(5))* Hyperion Pr.

—The Serpent's Shadow. 2012. 416p. *(978-0-14-133568-1(8)*, Puffin) Penguin Bks., Ltd.

—The Serpent's Shadow. l.t. ed. 2012. (Kane Chronicles: Bk. 3). (ENG.). 521p. (gr. 5-12). 23.99 *(978-1-4104-4789-0(8))* Thorndike Pr.

—The Throne of Fire. 2011. (Kane Chronicles: Bk. 2). 452p. (J). pap. *(978-1-4231-5059-6(7))* Disney Pr.

—The Throne of Fire. 2nd ed. 2012. (ENG.). 464p. (YA). (gr. 5-9). pap. 9.99 *(978-1-4231-6703-7(1))* Hyperion Bks. for Children.

—The Throne of Fire, Bk. 2. (ENG.). 464p. (gr. 5-17). 2012. (YA). pap. 9.99 *(978-1-4231-4201-0(2))* 2011. (J). 18.99 *(978-1-4231-4056-6(7))* Hyperion Pr.

—The Throne of Fire. 2011. (Kane Chronicles: Bk. 2). (ENG., Illus.). 451p. 28.25 *(978-0-85757-231-8(8))*; 2nd ed. 554p. pap. *(978-0-14-133566-7(1))* Penguin Publishing Group. (Puffin).

—The Throne of Fire. l.t. ed. 2011. (Kane Chronicles: Bk. 2). (ENG.). 591p. 23.99 *(978-1-4104-3607-8(1))* Thorndike Pr.

—The Throne of Fire. (Kane Chronicles Graphic Novels Ser.: 2). 2015. lib. bdg. 24.50 *(978-0-606-37509-2(0))* 2012. (YA). lib. bdg. 20.85 *(978-0-606-39217-4(3))* Turtleback Bks.

Rioux, Jo. The Golden Twine. Rioux, Jo, illus. 2012. (Cat's Cradle Ser.: 1). (ENG., Illus.). 112p. (J). (gr. 4-7). 9.95 *(978-1-55453-637-5(5))* Kids Can Pr., Ltd. CAN. Dist: Hachette Bk. Group.

Riva, Jim. Marvin Mallard & the Magic Medallion. Steinmark, Sharyl, illus. 2004. 64p. (YA). pap. 14.95 *(978-1-891262-03-6(3))* Soaring Sparrow Pr.

Rivers, Phoebe. Yesterday & Today. 2013. (Saranormal Ser.: 11). (ENG., Illus.). 160p. (J). (gr. 3-7). 15.99 *(978-1-4424-8962-2(6))*; pap. 5.99 *(978-1-4424-8961-5(8))* Simon Spotlight. (Simon Spotlight).

Robbins, Karen. Care for Our World Play Set. 2012. (ENG.). (J). 34.95 *(978-1-935414-63-6(1))* Casemate Pubs. & Bk. Distributors, LLC.

Roberts, Justin. The Great Henry Hopendower. Hocking, Deborah, illus. 2017. (ENG.). 32p. (J). (gr. k-3). 16.99 *(978-0-399-25744-5(6)*, G.P. Putnam's Sons Books for Young Readers) Penguin Young Readers Group.

Roberts, Rachel. All That Glitters. (gr. 3-6). 2008. (Avalon: Web of Magic Ser.: 2). (ENG., Illus.). 216p. (YA). pap. 6.95 *(978-1-933164-67-0(0)*, 9781933164670) 2007. (Avalon Ser.: Bk. 2). 175p. (J). 9.99 *(978-1-933164-65-6(4))* Seven Seas Entertainment, LLC.

—The Warlock Diaries Omnibus. Shiei, illus. 2010. (Avalon: Web of Magic Ser.). (ENG.). 304p. (J). (gr. 3-6). pap. 11.99 *(978-1-934876-88-6(7)*, 9781934876886) Seven Seas Entertainment, LLC.

Roberts, Roxanne. Angel Wings, Faery Dust & Other Magical Things: A Story about Witches, Warlocks & Such. 2011. 24p. pap. 11.50 *(978-1-61204-072-1(1)*, Eloquent Bks.) Strategic Book Publishing & Rights Agency (SBPRA).

Robichaud, Yves. Tomes of Tari: Kaylen's Rising. 2013. 240p. *(978-1-4602-0526-6(X))*; pap. *(978-1-4602-0524-2(3))* FriesenPress.

Robinson, Hilary. Cinderella & the Beanstalk. Sanfilippo, Simona, illus. 2013. (ENG.). 32p. (J). *(978-0-7787-1156-8(0))* Crabtree Publishing Co.

Robinson, Hilary & Catling, Andy. Aladdin & the Lamp. 2009. (Hopscotch Adventures Ser.). (Illus.). 31p. (J). (gr. 1). lib. bdg. 25.65 *(978-1-59771-181-4(0))* Sea-To-Sea Pubns.

Robinson, Kathleen Marie. The Magic Doorknob, 1 vol. 2009. 56p. pap. 16.95 *(978-1-60813-362-8(1))* America Star Bks.

Robinson, Steve. Tool Town. 2010. 85p. pap. 17.95 *(978-1-4452-4457-0(8))* Lulu Pr., Inc.

Rockwood, Roy. The Wizard of the Se. 2008. 124p. 23.95 *(978-1-60664-931-2(0))*; pap. 10.95 *(978-1-60664-051-7(8))* Aegypan.

Rodda, Emily. The Charm Bracelet. Vitale, Raoul, illus. 2003. (Fairy Realm Ser.). 128p. (J). (gr. 2-5). 8.99 *(978-0-06-009583-3(0))* HarperCollins Pubs.

—The Charm Bracelet Bk. 1. Vitale, Raoul, illus. 2009. (Fairy Realm Ser.: No. 1). (ENG.). 128p. (J). (gr. 2-5). pap. 4.99 *(978-0-06-009585-7(7))* HarperCollins Pubs.

—City of the Rats. 2012. (Deltora Quest Ser.). (ENG.). 160p. (J). (gr. 3-7). pap. 5.99 *(978-0-545-46022-4(0))* Scholastic, Inc.

—Deltora Quest 1. Niwano, Makoto, illus. 2011. (Deltora Quest Ser.). (ENG.). 202p. (gr. 8-12). pap. 10.99 *(978-1-935429-28-9(0))* Kodansha America, Inc.

—Deltora Quest 2. Niwano, Makoto, illus. 2011. (Deltora Quest Ser.). (ENG.). 206p. (gr. 8-12). pap. 10.99 *(978-1-935429-29-6(9))* Kodansha America, Inc.

—Deltora Quest #2: the Lake of Tears. 2012. (Deltora Quest Ser.). (ENG.). 160p. (J). (gr. 3-7). pap. 5.99 *(978-0-545-46021-7(2))* Scholastic, Inc.

—Deltora Quest 3. Niwano, Makoto, illus. 2011. (Deltora Quest Ser.). (ENG.). 208p. (gr. 8-12). pap. 10.99 *(978-1-935429-30-2(2))* Kodansha America, Inc.

—Deltora Quest #6: the Maze of the Beast. 2012. (Deltora Quest Ser.). (ENG.). 160p. (J). (gr. 3-7). pap. 5.99 *(978-0-545-46026-2(3))* Scholastic, Inc.

—Deltora Quest #7: the Valley of the Lost. 2012. (Deltora Quest Ser.). (ENG.). 160p. (J). (gr. 3-7). pap. 5.99 *(978-0-545-46027-9(1))* Scholastic, Inc.

—The Flower Fairies. Vitale, Raoul, illus. (Fairy Realm Ser.: No. 2). 128p. (J). 2009. (ENG.). (gr. 2-5). pap. 4.99 *(978-0-06-009588-8(1))* 2003. 8.99 *(978-0-06-009586-4(5))* HarperCollins Pubs.

—The Golden Door. 2012. (ENG.). 272p. (J). (gr. 3-7). 16.99 *(978-0-545-42990-0(0)*, Scholastic Pr.) Scholastic, Inc.

—Isle of the Dead. 2004. (Dragons of Deltora Ser.: No. 3). 195p. (J). lib. bdg. 16.92 *(978-1-4242-0273-7(6))* Fitzgerald Bks.

—The Rainbow Wand. Vitale, Raoul, illus. 2007. (Fairy Realm Ser.). 116p. (gr. 3-7). 25.65 *(978-1-59961-332-1(8))* Spotlight.

—Return to Del. 2012. (Deltora Quest Ser.). (ENG.). 160p. (J). (gr. 3-7). pap. 5.99 *(978-0-545-46028-6(X))* Scholastic, Inc.

—Shadowgate. 2004. (Dragons of Deltora Ser.: No. 2). 195p. (J). lib. bdg. 16.92 *(978-1-4242-0274-4(4))* Fitzgerald Bks.

—The Silver Door. 2013. (Illus.). (J). 278p. pap. *(978-0-545-42993-1(5))*; (ENG., 288p. (gr. 3-7). 16.99 *(978-0-545-42992-4(7))* Scholastic, Inc. (Scholastic Pr.).

—The Third Door. 2013. (J). pap. *(978-0-545-42995-5(1)*, Scholastic Pr.) Scholastic, Inc.

—The Wizard of Rondo. 2009. (ENG.). 400p. (J). (gr. 3-7). 16.99 *(978-0-545-11516-2(7)*, Scholastic Pr.) Scholastic, Inc.

Roderman, Anna Marie. Two Tales of Courage. 2004. 116p. (YA). pap. 7.95 *(978-0-87714-318-5(8))* i-5 Publishing LLC.

Rodriguez, AJ. A Cajun Crawfish Tale. 2009. 20p. pap. 12.49 *(978-1-4389-5529-2(4))* AuthorHouse.

Rodriguez, Sergio R. Little Santa & Snowboy: The Childhood Adventures of Santa Claus. 2007. (Illus.). 32p. (J). pap. 8.95 *(978-0-615-17411-2(6))* Little Santa Bks., Inc.

Rogers, Anne. The magic rainbow large Print. 2008. 332p. pap. 30.95 *(978-1-4092-3059-5(7))* Lulu Pr., Inc.

—The magic rainbow very large Print. 2008. 502p. pap. 39.50 *(978-1-4092-3065-6(1))* Lulu Pr., Inc.

Rogers, Bud & Martin, Gary. The Witch of Endor, 1 vol. Cariello, Sergio, illus. 2008. (Z Graphic Novels / Son of Samson Ser.). (ENG.). 160p. (J). pap. 6.99 *(978-0-310-71283-1(1))* Zonderkidz.

Rogers, Derek G. Monstrous Myths & Fabulous Fables. 2012. 184p. pap. *(978-1-78176-741-2(6))* FeedARead.com.

Rogers, John & Di Vito, Andrea. First Encounters, Vol. 2. Alcazar, Vicente et al, illus. 2012. (Dungeons & Dragons Ser.). (ENG.). 156p. pap. 19.99 *(978-1-61377-534-9(2)*, 9781613775349) Idea & Design Works, LLC.

Rogers, Suzanne J. Cody Meets A Butterfly. 2008. 72p. pap. 19.95 *(978-1-4327-2069-8(4))* Outskirts Pr., Inc.

Rohan, Julia K. Weaverworld: Grimsnipe's Revenge. 2012. 382p. 31.95 *(978-1-4697-0031-1(X))*; pap. 21.95 *(978-1-4697-0032-8(8))* iUniverse, Inc.

Rolly's Magic Pencil. 2005. (J). per. 6.99 *(978-0-9769985-0-1(5)*, 1-206-818-9769) Grace Publishing.

Roman, Javier. Adventures of Tinturu & Kumachan the M. 2007. (Illus.). 48p. pap. 16.95 *(978-1-4241-1626-3(0))* PublishAmerica, Inc.

Ronne, Susan. Webster the Spelling Dog. 2012. (ENG.). (J). pap. *(978-1-4675-1184-1(6))* Independent Pub.

Rooney-Freedman, Isabelle. Angus MacDream & the Roktopus Rogue. 2011. 206p. pap. 11.95 *(978-0-9843064-3-5(9))* Word with You Pr., A.

Roop, Peter. Houdini: Prince of Air. 2003. (ENG., Illus.). (J). spiral bd. 14.95 *(978-1-59319-023-1(9)*, LeapFrog Schl. Hse.) LeapFrog Enterprises, Inc.

Rosario, Joann. The Trick That Turned into Poop! Rosario, Joann, illus. 2004. (Illus.). 20p. (J). (gr. -1-13). pap. 10.00 *(978-0-9758746-5-3(9)*, 1246169) J.G.R. Enterprises.

Rosasco, Jose Luis. La Mariposa Negra y Otros Cuentos. 2003. (SPA.). pap. *(978-956-13-1661-4(7)*, AB12831) Bello, Andres CHL. Dist: Lectorum Pubns., Inc.

Rose, Kathryn. Avalon Rising. 2015. (Metal & Lace Novel Ser.: 2). (ENG., Illus.). 360p. (YA). pap. 11.99 *(978-0-7387-4489-6(1)*, Flux) North Star Editions.

Rose, Simon. The Alchemist's Portrait, 1 vol. 2003. (ENG., Illus.). 128p. (J). (gr. 4-6). per. 6.95 *(978-1-896580-29-6(7))* Tradewind Bks. CAN. Dist: Orca Bk. Pubs. USA.

Rosen, Lev Ac & Rosen, Ellis J. Woundabout. Rosen, Lev Ac & Rosen, Ellis J., illus. 2015. (ENG., Illus.). 288p. (J). (gr. 3-7). 17.00 *(978-0-316-37078-3(9))* Little Brown & Co.

Rosen, Lucy. My Little Pony - Meet the Princess of Friendship. 2014. (Passport to Reading Level 1 Ser.). (ENG., Illus.). 32p. (J). (gr. -1-3). pap. 4.99 *(978-0-316-28230-7(8))* Little, Brown Bks. for Young Readers.

Ross, Joel. Beast & Crown. 2017. 384p. (J). (gr. 3-7). 16.99 ***(978-0-06-248459-8(1))*** HarperCollins Pubs.

Ross, K. N. Daughters of the Lost World. 2012. 132p. 29.99 *(978-1-4653-8397-6(2))*; pap. 19.99 *(978-1-4653-8396-9(4))* Xlibris Corp.

Ross, Marlene. The Adventures of Donny the Doorknob. Hallam, Colleen and Peggy, illus. 2009. 32p. pap. 24.95 *(978-1-61546-539-2(1))* America Star Bks.

Rossell, Judith. Withering-By-Sea. Rossell, Judith, illus. 2017. (ENG., Illus.). 288p. (J). (gr. 3-7). pap. 7.99 *(978-1-4814-4368-5(2))* Simon & Schuster Children's Publishing.

Rossitto, Tamara. Alura. 2007. 127p. pap. 10.95 *(978-1-4357-0421-3(5))* Lulu Pr., Inc.

Rothenberger, Charlene. Kara's Kapers with Katy Pillar. Rothenberger, Boyd & Bays, Gail, illus. 2006. 64p. per. 9.99 *(978-0-9776260-6-9(7))* Bearhead Publishing, LLC.

Rouncville, Bibi. Bog Nymphs & Tiger Stones. 2008. 52p. pap. 15.50 *(978-1-4357-3966-6(3))* Lulu Pr., Inc.

—Trouble at Binka Bridge. 2010. 52p. pap. 9.50 *(978-0-557-16051-8(0))* Lulu Pr., Inc.

Round, Suzanne. The Dragonfire Crystal. 2011. 154p. pap. *(978-0-7552-1359-7(9))* Authors OnLine, Ltd.

Rounds, Harriet. The Magic Stairway, 1 vol. 2009. 48p. pap. 16.95 *(978-1-60749-707-3(7))* America Star Bks.

Rowe, W. W. The Wand Goes Wild. 2011. 120p. (gr. 3-7). pap. 12.95 *(978-0-9843754-4-8(9))* Sanctuary Publishing, Inc.

Rowling, J. K. Harrius Potter et Camera Secretorum. Needham, Peter, tr. from ENG. 2007. (Harry Potter Ser.).Tr. of Harry Potter & the Chamber of Secrets. (LAT & ENG., Illus.). 288p. (YA). (gr. 5). 23.95 *(978-1-59990-067-4(X)*, 9781599900674, Bloomsbury USA Childrens) Bloomsbury Publishing USA.

—Harrius Potter et Philosophi Lapis. Needham, Peter, tr. from ENG. 2003. (Harry Potter Ser.).Tr. of Harry Potter & the Philosopher's Stone. (LAT & ENG., Illus.). 256p. (YA). (gr. 7). 29.99 *(978-1-58234-825-4(1)*, 9781582348254, Bloomsbury USA Childrens) Bloomsbury Publishing USA.

—Harry Potter & the Chamber of Secrets. 2009. 9.64 *(978-0-7848-1444-4(9)*, Everbind) Marco Bk. Co.

—Harry Potter & the Chamber of Secrets. unabr. ed. 2004. (Harry Potter Ser.: Year 2). 352p. (J). (gr. 3-18). pap. 46.00 incl. audio *(978-0-8072-8207-6(3)*, S YA 137 SP, Listening Library) Random Hse. Audio Publishing Group.

—Harry Potter & the Chamber of Secrets. (Harry Potter Ser.: 2). (J). 2006. 1.25 *(978-1-4193-8079-2(6))* 2003. 78.75 *(978-1-4025-6698-1(0))* Recorded Bks., Inc.

—Harry Potter & the Chamber of Secrets. (Harry Potter Ser.: Year 2). (RUS., Illus.). 28.95 *(978-5-8451-0947-7(7))* Rosmen-Izdat RUS. Dist: Distribooks, Inc.

—Harry Potter & the Chamber of Secrets. Kay, Jim, illus. 2016. (Harry Potter Ser.: 2). (ENG.). 272p. (J). (gr. 3). 39.99 *(978-0-545-79132-8(4))*; 275.00 *(978-1-338-11986-2(9))* Scholastic, Inc. (Levine, Arthur A. Bks.).

—Harry Potter & the Chamber of Secrets. l.t. ed. 2003. (Harry Potter Ser.: Year 2). (ENG.). 466p. pap. 13.95 *(978-1-59413-001-4(9))* Thorndike Pr.

—Harry Potter & the Chamber of Secrets. 2013. (Harry Potter (Kazu Kibuishi Illustrations) Ser.: 2). lib. bdg. 24.50 *(978-0-606-32346-8(5)*, Turtleback) Turtleback Bks.

—Harry Potter & the Deathly Hallows. (Illus.). 2008. 832p. pap. *(978-0-7475-9586-1(0))* 2007. (ENG., 608p. *(978-0-7475-9106-1(7))* Bloomsbury Publishing Plc.

—Harry Potter & the Deathly Hallows. braille ed. 2007. (Harry Potter Ser.: Year 7). (J). (gr. 4-7). 34.99 *(978-0-939173-57-0(3))* National Braille Pr.

—Harry Potter & the Deathly Hallows. 2010. 25.00 *(978-1-60686-882-9(9))* Perfection Learning Corp.

—Harry Potter & the Deathly Hallows, 17 vols. 2007. (Harry Potter Ser.: 7). (YA). 129.79 *(978-1-4281-6654-7(8))*; 131.75 *(978-1-4281-6652-3(1))* Recorded Bks., Inc.

—Harry Potter & the Deathly Hallows. GrandPré, Mary, illus. (Harry Potter Ser.: 7). (ENG.). (J). 2009. 784p. (gr. 4-7). pap. 14.99 *(978-0-545-13970-0(8)*, Levine, Arthur A. Bks.) 2007. 784p. (gr. 5-9). 34.99 *(978-0-545-01022-1(5))* 2007. 816p. (gr. 4-7). 65.00 *(978-0-545-02937-7(6)*, Levine, Arthur A. Bks.) Scholastic, Inc.

—Harry Potter & the Deathly Hallows. l.t. ed. 2009. (ENG.). 970p. pap. 14.95 *(978-1-59413-355-8(7)*, Large Print Pr.) 2007. (Harry Potter Ser.: Year 7). (Illus.). 969p. (J). (gr. 4-7). 34.95 *(978-0-7862-9665-1(8))* Thorndike Pr.

—Harry Potter & the Deathly Hallows. (Harry Potter (Kazu Kibuishi Illustrations) Ser.: 7). 2013. lib. bdg. 29.40 *(978-0-606-32351-2(1))* 2009. lib. bdg. 26.95 *(978-0-606-00420-6(3))* Turtleback Bks. (Turtleback).

—Harry Potter & the Deathly Hallows. Bar-hillel, Gili, tr. from ENG. 2007. (Harry Potter Ser.: Year 7). (HEB., Illus.). 568p. (J). (gr. 4-7). pap. *(978-965-482-635-8(6))* Yediot Aharonot Bks., Miscal.

—Harry Potter & the Goblet of Fire. 2009. 10.24 *(978-0-7848-1587-8(9)*, Everbind) Marco Bk. Co.

—Harry Potter & the Goblet of Fire. (Harry Potter Ser.: 4). (J). 2006. 1.25 *(978-1-4193-8531-5(3))* 2003. 101.75 *(978-1-4025-6702-5(2))* Recorded Bks., Inc.

—Harry Potter & the Goblet of Fire. GrandPré, Mary, illus. l.t. ed. 2003. (Harry Potter Ser.: Vol. 4). (ENG.). 936p. pap. 11.66 *(978-1-59413-003-8(5))* Thorndike Pr.

—Harry Potter & the Goblet of Fire. 2013. (Harry Potter (Kazu Kibuishi Illustrations) Ser.: 4). lib. bdg. 26.95 *(978-0-606-32348-2(1)*, Turtleback) Turtleback Bks.

—Harry Potter & the Half-Blood Prince. 2005. (ENG.). cd-rom *(978-0-7475-8258-8(0))* Bloomsbury Publishing Plc.

—Harry Potter & the Half-Blood Prince, 9 vols. braille ed. 2005. (Harry Potter Ser.: Year 6). (J). (gr. 4-8). 29.99 *(978-0-939173-39-6(5)*, HALF) National Braille Pr.

—Harry Potter & the Half-Blood Prince. GrandPré, Mary, illus. 2006. (Harry Potter Ser.: Year 6). 652p. (gr. 4-8). 23.00 *(978-0-7569-6765-9(1))* Perfection Learning Corp.

—Harry Potter & the Half-Blood Prince. (Harry Potter Ser.: 6). (J). 2007. 1.25 *(978-1-4193-5430-4(2))* 2006. 110.75 *(978-1-4193-5436-6(1))* 2006. 193.75 *(978-1-4193-5432-8(9))* 2005. 113.75 *(978-1-4193-5434-2(5))* Recorded Bks., Inc.

—Harry Potter & the Half-Blood Prince. GrandPré, Mary, illus. (Harry Potter Ser.: 6). (ENG.). 672p. (J). (gr. 4-8). 2005. 29.99 *(978-0-439-78454-2(9))* 2006. reprint ed. per. 12.99 *(978-0-439-78596-9(0))* Scholastic, Inc. (Levine, Arthur A. Bks.).

—Harry Potter & the Half-Blood Prince. (Illus.). (J). (gr. 4-7). 2007. (ENG.). 832p. per. 14.95 *(978-1-59413-221-6(6))* 2005. (Harry Potter Ser.: Year 6). 831p. 29.95 *(978-0-7862-7745-2(9))* Thorndike Pr. (Large Print Pr.).

—Harry Potter & the Half-Blood Prince. 2013. (Harry Potter (Kazu Kibuishi Illustrations) Ser.: 6). lib. bdg. 26.95 *(978-0-606-32350-5(3)*, Turtleback) Turtleback Bks.

—Harry Potter & the Half Blood Prince - Chinese Language. 2005. (Harry Potter Ser.: Year 6). (CHI.). 496p. (YA). (gr. 4-8). pap. 28.95 *(978-7-02-005323-0(8)*, HAP06) People's Literature Publishing Hse. CHN. Dist: Chinasprout, Inc.

—Harry Potter & the Order of the Phoenix. (ENG.). 768p. (J). (gr. 6-10). pap. *(978-0-7475-6107-1(9))* Bloomsbury Publishing Plc.

—Harry Potter & the Order of the Phoenix, 13 vols. braille ed. 2003. (Harry Potter Ser.: Year 5). (YA). 29.99 *(978-0-939173-38-9(7))* National Braille Pr.

—Harry Potter & the Order of the Phoenix. 2003. (Harry Potter Ser.: Year 5). (CHI.). 575p. (YA). pap. 26.95 *(978-7-02-004327-9(5)*, HAP05) People's Literature Publishing Hse. CHN. Dist: Chinasprout, Inc.

—Harry Potter & the Order of the Phoenix. 2004. (Harry Potter Ser.). 870p. (gr. 4-6). 16.49 *(978-0-7569-4163-5(6))* Perfection Learning Corp.

—Harry Potter & the Order of the Phoenix. 2003. (ENG.). 768p. *(978-1-55192-570-7(2))* Raincoast Bk. Distribution.

—Harry Potter & the Order of the Phoenix. GrandPré, Mary, illus. (Harry Potter Ser.: 5). (ENG.). (J). (gr. 3-7). 2004. 896p. mass mkt. 12.99 *(978-0-439-35807-1(8)*, Scholastic Paperbacks) 2003. 870p. 29.99 *(978-0-439-35806-4(X))* Scholastic, Inc.

—Harry Potter & the Order of the Phoenix. l.t. ed. 2003. (Harry Potter Ser.: Year 5). 1093p. 29.95 *(978-0-7862-5778-2(4)*, Large Print Pr.) Thorndike Pr.

—Harry Potter & the Order of the Phoenix. GrandPré, Mary, illus. l.t. ed. 2003. (Thorndike Young Adult Ser.). (ENG.). 1232p. (J). (gr. 4-7). per. 14.95 *(978-1-59413-112-7(0)*, Large Print Pr.) Thorndike Pr.

—Harry Potter & the Order of the Phoenix. 2004. (Harry Potter Ser.: 5). lib. bdg. 24.50 *(978-0-613-99916-8(9)*, Turtleback) Turtleback Bks.

—Harry Potter & the Philosopher's Stone. 2014. (ENG., Illus.). 352p. *(978-1-4088-5589-8(5))* Bloomsbury Publishing Plc.

—Harry Potter & the Prisoner of Azkaban. 2009. 9.64 *(978-0-7848-1542-7(9)*, Everbind) Marco Bk. Co.

—Harry Potter & the Prisoner of Azkaban. 2005. (Harry Potter Ser.: Year 3). (CHI.). 260p. (YA). pap. 16.95 *(978-7-02-003345-4(8)*, HAP03) People's Literature Publishing Hse. CHN. Dist: Chinasprout, Inc.

—Harry Potter & the Prisoner of Azkaban, 10 vols. 2003. (Harry Potter Ser.: 3). (J). 84.75 *(978-1-4025-6700-1(6))* Recorded Bks., Inc.

—Harry Potter & the Prisoner of Azkaban. l.t. ed. 2003. (Harry Potter Ser.: Year 3). (ENG.). 592p. pap. 13.95 *(978-1-59413-002-1(7)*, Large Print Pr.) Thorndike Pr.

—Harry Potter & the Prisoner of Azkaban. 2013. (Harry Potter (Kazu Kibuishi Illustrations) Ser.: 3). lib. bdg. 24.50 *(978-0-606-32347-5(3)*, Turtleback) Turtleback Bks.

—Harry Potter & the Sorcerer's Stone. 2014. (ENG.). lthr. 79.00 *(978-1-62715-772-8(7))* Leatherbound Bestsellers.

—Harry Potter & the Sorcerer's Stone. 2009. 8.44 *(978-0-7848-2438-2(X))*; 10.84 *(978-0-7848-1357-7(4))* Marco Bk. Co. (Everbind).

—Harry Potter & the Sorcerer's Stone. 2003. (Harry Potter Ser.: Year 1). (CHI.). 191p. (YA). pap. 14.95 *(978-7-02-003343-0(1)*, HAP01) People's Literature Publishing Hse. CHN. Dist: Chinasprout, Inc.

—Harry Potter & the Sorcerer's Stone. (Harry Potter Ser.: 1). (J). 2004. 1.25 *(978-1-4025-6757-5(X))* 2003. 80.75 *(978-1-4025-6696-7(4))* Recorded Bks., Inc.

—Harry Potter & the Sorcerer's Stone. Kay, Jim, illus. 2015. (Harry Potter Ser.: 1). (ENG.). 256p. (J). (gr. 3). 39.99 *(978-0-545-79035-2(2)*, Levine, Arthur A. Bks.) Scholastic, Inc.

—Harry Potter & the Sorcerer's Stone, Bk. 1. 2013. (Harry Potter Ser.: 1). (ENG., Illus.). 336p. (J). (gr. 4). pap. 12.99 *(978-0-545-58288-9(1))* Scholastic, Inc.

—Harry Potter & the Sorcerer's Stone. 2013. (Harry Potter (Kazu Kibuishi Illustrations) Ser.: 1). lib. bdg. 24.50 *(978-0-606-32345-1(7)*, Turtleback) Turtleback Bks.

—Harry Potter e a Camara Secreta. (Harry Potter Ser.: Year 2).Tr. of Harry Potter & the Chamber of Secrets. (POR.). pap. 28.95 *(978-85-325-1166-9(X))* Rocco, Editora, Ltda BRA. Dist: Distribooks, Inc.

—Harry Potter y el Caliz de Fuego. 2004. (Harry Potter Ser.: Year 4).Tr. of Harry Potter & the Goblet of Fire. (SPA., Illus.). 240p. (YA). 19.95 *(978-84-7888-645-6(1)*, SAL30169) Emece Editores ESP. Dist: Lectorum Pubns., Inc.

—Harry Potter y el Prisionero de Azkaban. 2004. (Harry Potter Ser.: Year 3).Tr. of Harry Potter & the Prisoner of Azkaban.

M
N
O

(SPA., Illus.). 360p. (gr. 3-18). 17.95 *(978-84-7888-519-0(6),* SAL1889) Emece Editores ESP. Dist: Lectorum Pubns., Inc.

—Harry Potter y el Prisionero de Azkaban. 2015. (Harry Potter Spanish Ser.: 3).Tr. of Harry Potter & the Prisioner of Azkaban. (SPA.). (gr. 3-6). lib. bdg. 28.10 *(978-0-613-35958-0(5),* Turtleback) Turtleback Bks.

—Harry Potter y la Camara Secreta. 2004. (Harry Potter Ser.: Year 2).Tr. of Harry Potter & the Chamber of Secrets. (SPA., Illus.). 288p. (YA). (gr. 3-18). 15.95 *(978-84-7888-495-7(5),* SAL4595) Emece Editores ESP. Dist: Lectorum Pubns., Inc.

—Harry Potter Y la Orden del Fenix. 2004. (Harry Potter Ser.: Year 5).Tr. of Harry Potter & the Order of the Phoenix. (SPA.). 893p. (YA). 23.99 *(978-84-7888-901-3(9))* Emece Editores ESP. Dist: Lectorum Pubns., Inc.

—Harry Potter Y la Orden del Fenix. Ortega, Gemma Rovira, tr. from ENG. 2004. (Harry Potter Ser.: Year 5).Tr. of Harry Potter & the Order of the Phoenix. (SPA.). 893p. (YA). pap. 17.99 *(978-84-7888-884-9(5))* Emece Editores ESP. Dist: Lectorum Pubns., Inc.

—Harry Potter y la Piedra Filosofal. 2004. (Harry Potter Ser.: Year 1).Tr. of Harry Potter & the Sorcerer's Stone. (SPA., Illus.). 256p. (YA). (gr. 7-18). 15.95 *(978-84-7888-445-2(9),* SAL2819) Emece Editores ESP. Dist: Lectorum Pubns., Inc.

—The Tales of Beedle the Bard. GrandPré, Mary, illus. 2008. (ENG.). 128p. *(978-0-7475-9987-6(4))* Bloomsbury Publishing Plc.

—The Tales of Beedle the Bard. GrandPré, Mary, illus. collector's ed. 2008. 184p. *(978-0-9560109-0-2(3))* Children's High Level Group.

—The Tales of Beedle the Bard. 2017. (Harry Potter Ser.). (ENG.). 128p. (J). (gr. 3-3). 12.99 *(978-1-338-12568-9(0),* Levine, Arthur A. Bks.) Scholastic, Inc.

—The Tales of Beedle the Bard. 2017. (ENG.). (J). (gr. 3). lib. bdg. 24.50 ***(978-0-606-39695-0(0))*** Turtleback Bks.

Rowling, J. K. & Scholastic, Inc. Staff. Harry Potter. 2007. (Harry Potter Ser.: Years 1-7). (ENG.). (J). (gr. 3-7). 205.93 *(978-0-545-04425-7(1),* Levine, Arthur A. Bks.) Scholastic, Inc.

Rowling, J. K. & Xocuasvili, Cico. Hari Poteri Da Sikvdilis Sacukrebi. 2008. (GEO.). 636p. (J). *(978-9941-40-314-9(7))* Georgian Biographic Ctr., Ltd.

Rowntree, G. M. Wizards Spell Magic in the Legends of Mere Leander. 2010. 291p. pap. 32.50 *(978-1-4452-6812-5(4))* Lulu Pr., Inc.

—Wizards Spell Magic in the Legends of Mere Leander - US Trade Size. 2010. 291p. pap. 24.95 *(978-1-4452-9266-3(1))* Lulu Pr., Inc.

Rubens, Michael. Emily & the Spellstone. 2017. (ENG.). 288p. (J). (gr. 5-7). 16.99 *(978-0-544-79086-5(3))* Houghton Mifflin Harcourt Publishing Co.

Rubino-Bradway, Caitlen. Ordinary Magic. 2012. (ENG.). 288p. (YA). (gr. 3-12). 16.99 *(978-1-59990-725-3(9),* 9781599907253, Bloomsbury USA Childrens) Bloomsbury Publishing USA.

Rue, Ginger. Aleca Zamm Is a Wonder. Persico, Zoe, illus. 2017. (Aleca Zamm Ser.: 1). (ENG.). 160p. (J). (gr. 2-5). 16.99 ***(978-1-4814-7061-2(2),*** Aladdin) Simon & Schuster Children's Publishing.

—Aleca Zamm Is Ahead of Her Time. Persico, Zoe, illus. 2017. (Aleca Zamm Ser.: 2). (ENG.). 128p. (J). (gr. 2-5). pap. 6.99 ***(978-1-4814-7063-6(9),*** Aladdin) Simon & Schuster Children's Publishing.

Ruebush, McKenna. Enter a Glossy Web. Zollars, Jaime, illus. 2016. (ENG.). 400p. (YA). 16.99 *(978-1-62779-370-4(4),* 9781627793704, Holt, Henry & Co. Bks. For Young Readers) Holt, Henry & Co.

Ruiz Zafón, Carlos. The Prince of Mist. 2011. (ENG.). 256p. (YA). (gr. 7-17). pap., pap. 10.99 *(978-0-316-04480-6(6))* Little, Brown Bks. for Young Readers.

Rupp, Rebecca. The Dragon of Lonely Island. 2006. (Dragon of Lonely Island Ser.). (ENG.). 192p. (J). (gr. 4-7). 6.99 *(978-0-7636-2805-5(0))* Candlewick Pr.

Russell, Sharman Apt. Teresa of the New World. 2015. (ENG.). 192p. (gr. 6). 14.99 *(978-1-63158-042-0(6),* Yucca Publishing) Skyhorse Publishing Co., Inc.

Russo, Bud. The Magic Picture. 2007. 156p. pap. 10.95 *(978-1-4357-0110-6(0))* Lulu Pr., Inc.

Russon, Penni. Breathe. 2007. (ENG., Illus.). 368p. (YA). (gr. 9-18). 16.99 *(978-0-06-079393-7(7))* HarperCollins Pubs.

Rusu, Meredith. Charmer Girls Rock! 2016. (Scholastic Reader, Level 1 Ser.). (ENG.). 32p. (J). (gr. -1-1). pap. 5.99 *(978-1-338-03730-2(7))* Scholastic, Inc.

Ruth, Nick. The Breezes of Inspire. Concannon, Sue, illus. 2005. (Remin Chronicles: 2). (ENG.). 264p. (J). (gr. 3-7). 16.95 *(978-0-9745603-3-5(2))* Imaginator Pr.

Rutkoski, Marie. The Cabinet of Wonders. 2013. (Kronos Chronicles Ser.: 1). (ENG.). 288p. (J). (gr. 5-9). pap. 10.99 *(978-1-250-01804-5(8),* 9781250018045) Square Fish.

—The Celestial Globe. 2013. (Kronos Chronicles Ser.: 2). (ENG.). 320p. (J). (gr. 5-9). pap. 7.99 *(978-1-250-02732-0(2),* 9781250027320) Square Fish.

—The Jewel of the Kalderash. 3rd ed. 2011. (Kronos Chronicles Ser.: 3). (ENG.). 336p. (J). (gr. 5-9). 16.99 *(978-0-374-33678-3(4),* 9780374336783, Farrar, Straus & Giroux (BYR)) Farrar, Straus & Giroux.

—The Jewel of the Kalderash. 2013. (Kronos Chronicles Ser.: 3). (ENG.). 336p. (J). (gr. 5-9). pap. 7.99 *(978-1-250-01025-4(X),* 9781250010254) Square Fish.

Ryan, Brittney. The Legend of Holly Claus. Long, Laurel, illus. 2004. (Julie Andrews Collection). 544p. (J). (gr. 4-18). 16.99 *(978-0-06-058511-2(0));* lib. bdg. 17.89 *(978-0-06-058514-3(5))* HarperCollins Pubs. (Julie Andrews Collection).

Ryan, Carrie & Davis, John Parke. City of Thirst. (Map to Everywhere Ser.: 2). (ENG., Illus.). (J). (gr. 3-7). 2016. 416p. pap. 7.99 *(978-0-316-24082-6(6))* 2015. 400p. 17.00 *(978-0-316-24084-0(2))* Little, Brown Bks. for Young Readers.

—The Map to Everywhere. 2014. (Map to Everywhere Ser.: Bk. 1). (ENG., Illus.). 448p. (J). (gr. 3-7). 17.00 *(978-0-316-24077-2(X))* Little Brown & Co.

Ryder, Chloe. Best Friends Forever! 2015. (Princess Ponies Ser.). (ENG., Illus.). 128p. (YA). (gr. 2-4). pap. 5.99 *(978-1-61963-405-3(8),* 9781619634053, Bloomsbury USA Childrens) Bloomsbury Publishing USA.

—A Dream Come True. 2014. (Princess Ponies Ser.). (ENG., Illus.). 128p. (YA). (gr. 1-3). pap. 5.99 *(978-1-61963-167-0(9),* 9781619631670, Bloomsbury USA Childrens) Bloomsbury Publishing USA.

—A Magical Friend. 2014. (Princess Ponies Ser.). (ENG., Illus.). 128p. (J). (gr. 1-3). pap. 5.99 *(978-1-61963-165-6(2),* 9781619631656, Bloomsbury USA Childrens) Bloomsbury Publishing USA.

—Princess Ponies: An Amazing Rescue. 2015. (Princess Ponies Ser.). (ENG., Illus.). 128p. (YA). (gr. 2-4). pap. 5.99 *(978-1-61963-403-9(1),* 9781619634039, Bloomsbury USA Childrens) Bloomsbury Publishing USA.

—Princess Ponies 3: the Special Secret. 2014. (Princess Ponies Ser.). (ENG., Illus.). 128p. (J). (gr. 2-4). pap. 5.99 *(978-1-61963-237-0(3),* 9781619632370, Bloomsbury USA Childrens) Bloomsbury Publishing USA.

—Princess Ponies 4: a Unicorn Adventure! 2014. (Princess Ponies Ser.). (ENG., Illus.). 128p. (J). (gr. 2-4). pap. 5.99 *(978-1-61963-294-3(2),* 9781619632943, Bloomsbury USA Childrens) Bloomsbury Publishing USA.

—Princess Ponies 7: a Special Surprise. 2015. (Princess Ponies Ser.). (ENG., Illus.). 128p. (J). (gr. 2-4). pap. 5.99 *(978-1-61963-565-4(8),* 9781619635654, Bloomsbury USA Childrens) Bloomsbury Publishing USA.

—Princess Ponies 8: a Singing Star. 2015. (Princess Ponies Ser.). (ENG., Illus.). 128p. (J). (gr. 2-4). pap. 5.99 *(978-1-61963-567-8(4),* 9781619635678, Bloomsbury USA Childrens) Bloomsbury Publishing USA.

Rylant, Cynthia. The Van Gogh Cafe. 2006. (ENG., Illus.). 64p. (J). (gr. 2-5). pap. 6.99 *(978-0-15-205750-3(1))* Houghton Mifflin Harcourt Publishing Co.

—The Van Gogh Café. 2015. 64p. pap. 7.00 *(978-1-61003-500-2(3))* Center for the Collaborative Classroom.

Sabo-Western, Deborah. Peter Penny: Discovers the Gift. 2007. (ENG.). 46p. pap. 15.99 *(978-1-4196-8115-8(X))* CreateSpace Independent Publishing Platform.

Saccheri, Josephine. Magic on the Wall, 1 vol. Carrescia, Reid, illus. 2009. 11p. pap. 24.95 *(978-1-61546-374-9(7))* America Star Bks.

—The Secret to Easter Eggs. Saccheri, Briana, illus. 2008. 28p. pap. 24.95 *(978-1-60474-210-7(0))* America Star Bks.

Sachar, Louis. Marvin Redpost #8: a Magic Crystal? Record, Adam, illus. 2015. (Marvin Redpost Ser.: 8). (ENG.). 96p. (J). (gr. 1-4). lib. bdg. 12.99 *(978-0-553-53546-4(3),* Random Hse. Bks. for Young Readers) Random Hse. Children's Bks.

Sackett, Frances. The Misadventures of the Magician's Dog. 2013. (ENG.). 192p. (J). (gr. 2-7). 16.95 *(978-0-8234-2869-4(9))* Holiday Hse., Inc.

Saddleback Educational Publishing Staff, creator. Saddleback's Dark Man Full Set. 2010. (Illus.). (YA). pap. *(978-1-61651-257-6(1))* Saddleback Educational Publishing, Inc.

Sadler, Marilyn. P. J. Funnybunny's Bag of Tricks. Bollen, Roger, illus. 2005. (Step into Reading Ser.). 32p. 14.00 *(978-0-7569-5405-5(3))* Perfection Learning Corp.

—P. J. Funnybunny's Bag of Tricks. Bollen, Roger, illus. 2004. (Step into Reading Ser.). (ENG.). 32p. (J). (gr. -1-1). pap. 3.99 *(978-0-375-82444-9(8),* Random Hse. Bks. for Young Readers) Random Hse. Children's Bks.

—P. J. Funnybunny's Bag of Tricks. 2004. (Step into Reading Level 2 Ser.). (gr. -1-2). lib. bdg. 13.55 *(978-0-613-83535-0(2),* Turtleback) Turtleback Bks.

Safran, Sheri. The Magic Carousel: A Book & Removable 3-D Play Carousel. Safran, Sheri, illus. 2011. (ENG., Illus.). 6p. (J). (gr. -1-k). 24.99 *(978-1-85707-800-8(4))* Tango Bks. GBR. Dist: Independent Pubs. Group.

Sagar, Marie. Magical Snowman. 2009. 36p. pap. 16.99 *(978-1-4490-2194-8(8))* AuthorHouse.

Sage, Angie. Darke. Zug, Mark, illus. (Septimus Heap Ser.: 6). 656p. (J). (gr. 4). 2012. (ENG.). pap. 7.99 *(978-0-06-124244-1(6))* 2011. lib. bdg. 18.89 *(978-0-06-124243-4(8))*Bk. 6. 2011. (ENG.). 17.99 *(978-0-06-124242-7(X))* HarperCollins Pubs. (Tegen, Katherine Bks).

—Darke, 12 vols. (Septimus Heap Ser.: 6). (J). 131.75 *(978-1-4498-6218-3(7));* 1.25 *(978-1-4498-6226-8(8));* 297.75 *(978-1-4498-6217-6(9));* 2013. 92.75 *(978-1-4498-6225-1(X));* 2011. 133.75 *(978-1-4498-6220-6(9));* 2011. 131.75 *(978-1-4498-6222-0(5))* Recorded Bks., Inc.

—Darke. Zug, Mark, illus. 2012. (Septimus Heap Ser.: 6). (J). lib. bdg. 18.40 *(978-0-606-26264-4(4),* Turtleback) Turtleback Bks.

—Flyte. Zug, Mark, illus. (Septimus Heap Ser.: 2). (ENG.). 544p. (J). (gr. 4-7). 2007. pap. 7.99 *(978-0-06-057736-0(3))* 2006. 17.99 *(978-0-06-057734-6(7))* HarperCollins Pubs. (Tegen, Katherine Bks).

—Flyte. (Septimus Heap Ser.: 2). (J). 2009. 84.49 *(978-1-4361-5831-2(1))* 2008. 1.25 *(978-1-4193-9383-9(9))* 2006. 114.75 *(978-1-4193-9386-0(3))* 2006. 133.75 *(978-1-4193-9390-7(1))* 2006. 111.75 *(978-1-4193-9388-4(X))* 2006. 131.75 *(978-1-4193-9392-1(8))* 2006. 282.75 *(978-1-4193-9387-7(1))* Recorded Bks., Inc.

—Fyre. Zug, Mark, illus. 2013. (J). (Septimus Heap Ser.: 7). (ENG.). 720p. (gr. 3-7). 17.99 *(978-0-06-124245-8(4),* Tegen, Katherine Bks); 702p. *(978-0-06-224697-4(6))* HarperCollins Pubs.

—Fyre. 2014. (Septimus Heap Ser.: 7). (J). lib. bdg. 18.40 *(978-0-606-35067-9(5),* Turtleback) Turtleback Bks.

—Magyk. Zug, Mark, illus. (Septimus Heap Ser.: 1). (J). (gr. 4-18). 2005. (ENG.). 576p. 17.99 *(978-0-06-057731-5(2))* 2005. 576p. lib. bdg. 18.89 *(978-0-06-057732-2(0))* 2006. (ENG.). 608p. reprint ed. pap. 7.99 *(978-0-06-057733-9(9))* HarperCollins Pubs. (Tegen, Katherine Bks).

—Magyk. Zug, Mark, illus. 2007. (Septimus Heap Ser.: Bk. 1). 564p. (gr. 4-7). 18.00 *(978-0-7569-7760-3(6))* Perfection Learning Corp.

—Magyk. (Septimus Heap Ser.: 1). (J). 2008. 79.75 *(978-1-4361-0584-2(6))* 2007. 1.25 *(978-1-4193-2619-6(8))* 2006. 123.75 *(978-1-4193-3807-6(2))* 2005. 126.75 *(978-1-4193-3805-2(6))* 2005. 106.75 *(978-1-4193-2622-6(8))* 2005. 103.75 *(978-1-4193-2624-0(4))* Recorded Bks., Inc.

—Magyk. 2006. (Septimus Heap Ser.: 1). (J). lib. bdg. 18.40 *(978-1-4177-3321-7(7),* Turtleback) Turtleback Bks.

—Pathfinder. 2015. (Septimus Heap: TodHunter Moon Ser.: 1). (J). lib. bdg. 18.40 *(978-0-606-37612-9(7))* Turtleback Bks.

—Physik. Zug, Mark, illus. (Septimus Heap Ser.: 3). (ENG.). (J). (gr. 4-7). 2007. 560p. 17.99 *(978-0-06-057737-7(1))*Bk. 3. 2008. 576p. pap. 7.99 *(978-0-06-057739-1(8))* HarperCollins Pubs. (Tegen, Katherine Bks).

—Physik, 11 vols. 2007. (Septimus Heap Ser.: 3). (J). (SPA.). 131.75 *(978-1-4281-4582-5(6));* 133.75 *(978-1-4281-4580-1(X));* 113.75 *(978-1-4281-4576-4(1));* 111.75 *(978-1-4281-4578-8(8));* 1.25 *(978-1-4281-4573-3(7));* 277.75 *(978-1-4281-4577-1(X))* Recorded Bks., Inc.

—Physik. 2008. (Septimus Heap Ser.: 3). (J). lib. bdg. 18.40 *(978-1-4178-1565-4(5),* Turtleback) Turtleback Bks.

—Queste. Zug, Mark, illus. (Septimus Heap Ser.: 4). (ENG.). (J). (gr. 4). 2009. 624p. pap. 7.99 *(978-0-06-088209-9(3))* 2008. 608p. 17.99 *(978-0-06-088207-5(7))* HarperCollins Pubs. (Tegen, Katherine Bks).

—Queste. Zug, Mark, illus. 2009. (Septimus Heap Ser.: 4). 596p. (J). lib. bdg. 18.40 *(978-0-606-02607-9(X),* Turtleback) Turtleback Bks.

—Sandrider. 2015. (World of Septimus Heap Ser.: 2). (ENG., Illus.). 480p. (J). (gr. 3-7). 17.99 *(978-0-06-227248-5(9),* Tegen, Katherine Bks) HarperCollins Pubs.

—Septimus Heap, Set. Zug, Mark, illus. 2007. (Septimus Heap Ser.: Bks. 1-2). (J). (gr. 4). pap. 15.99 *(978-0-06-136195-1(X),* Tegen, Katherine Bks) HarperCollins Pubs.

—Septimus Heap - Todhunter Moon. Zug, Mark, illus. 2014. (World of Septimus Heap Ser.: 1). (ENG.). 480p. (J). (gr. 3-7). 17.99 *(978-0-06-227245-4(4),* Tegen, Katherine Bks) HarperCollins Pubs.

—Syren. Zug, Mark, illus. (Septimus Heap Ser.: 5). (J). (gr. 4). 2011. (ENG.). 656p. pap. 7.99 *(978-0-06-088212-9(3))* 2009. 640p. lib. bdg. 18.89 *(978-0-06-088211-2(5))* 2009. (ENG.). 640p. 17.99 *(978-0-06-088210-5(7))* HarperCollins Pubs. (Tegen, Katherine Bks).

—Todhunter Moon: Sandrider. Zug, Mark, illus. 2016. (Septimus Heap: TodHunter Moon Ser.: 2). (ENG.). 496p. (J). (gr. 3-7). 18.40 *(978-0-606-39255-6(6))* Turtleback Bks.

Sage, Angie. TodHunter Moon, Book Three: StarChaser. Zug, Mark, illus. 2017. (World of Septimus Heap Ser.: 3). 496p. (J). (gr. 3-7). pap. 7.99 ***(978-0-06-227252-2(7),*** Tegen, Katherine Bks) HarperCollins Pubs.

Saito, Taeko. Kiss the Frog. 2010. (Princess & the Frog Ser.). (JPN., Illus.). (J). bds. *(978-4-06-262548-7(2))* Kodansha America, Inc.

Salazar, L. J. Chin & the Magic Stones: Book One - Becoming Guardians. 2009. 108p. 20.95 *(978-0-595-63627-3(6));* pap. 10.95 *(978-0-595-53157-8(1))* iUniverse, Inc.

Salerni, Dianne K. The Eighth Day. McClellan, David, illus. (Eighth Day Ser.: 1). (ENG.). (J). (gr. 3-7). 2015. 336p. pap. 6.99 *(978-0-06-227216-4(0))* 2014. 320p. 16.99 *(978-0-06-227215-7(2))* HarperCollins Pubs.

—The Inquisitor's Mark. 2015. (Eighth Day Ser.: 2). (ENG.). 368p. (J). (gr. 3-7). pap. 6.99 *(978-0-06-227219-5(5))* HarperCollins Pubs.

—The Morrigan's Curse. 2016. (Eighth Day Ser.: 3). 400p. (J). (gr. 3-7). 16.99 *(978-0-06-227221-8(7))* HarperCollins Pubs.

Salsi, Lynn. Jack & the Giants. Young, James, illus. 2012. (ENG.). 32p. (J). 16.95 *(978-0-938467-52-6(2))* Headline Bks., Inc.

Sampson, Fay. The Sorcerer's Daughter. 2007. (ENG.). 224p. (J). (gr. 4-7). per. 9.95 *(978-0-7459-6072-2(3))* Lion Hudson PLC GBR. Dist: Independent Pubs. Group.

San Souci, Robert D. Cinderella Skeleton. Catrow, David, illus. 2004. (ENG.). 32p. (J). (gr. -1-3). reprint ed. pap. 6.99 *(978-0-15-205069-6(8))* Houghton Mifflin Harcourt Publishing Co.

Sanders, Stephanie S. Villain School: Good Curses Evil. 2011. (ENG.). 240p. (YA). (gr. 3-12). pap. 6.99 *(978-1-59990-848-9(4),* 9781599908489, Bloomsbury USA Childrens) Bloomsbury Publishing USA.

Sanders, Ted. The Box & the Dragonfly. Bruno, Iacopo, illus. 2015. (Keepers Ser.: No. 1). 534p. (J). *(978-0-06-239019-6(8))* Harper & Row Ltd.

—The Box & the Dragonfly. Bruno, Iacopo, illus. 2015. (Keepers Ser.: 1). (ENG.). 544p. (J). (gr. 3-7). 16.99 *(978-0-06-227582-0(8))* HarperCollins Pubs.

—The Harp & the Ravenvine. 2016. (Keepers Ser.: 2). (Illus.). 672p. (J). (gr. 3-7). 16.99 *(978-0-06-227585-1(2))* HarperCollins Pubs.

—The Keepers #3: the Portal & the Veil. 2017. (Keepers Ser.: 3). 592p. (J). (gr. 3-7). 16.99 ***(978-0-06-227588-2(7))*** HarperCollins Pubs.

Sanders, Ted. The Keepers: the Box & the Dragonfly. Bruno, Iacopo, illus. 2016. (Keepers Ser.: 1). 560p. (J). (gr. 3-7). pap. 7.99 *(978-0-06-227583-7(6))* HarperCollins Pubs.

Sanderson, Brandon. The Rithmatist. McSweeney, Ben, illus. 2014. (ENG.). 384p. (YA). (gr. 7). pap. 10.99 *(978-0-7653-3844-0(0),* 9780765338440, Tor Teen) Doherty, Tom Assocs., LLC.

—The Rithmatist. 2013. (ENG., Illus.). 384p. (YA). (gr. 7). 17.99 *(978-0-7653-2032-2(0),* 9780765320322, Tor Teen) Doherty, Tom Assocs., LLC.

—The Rithmatist. 2014. (YA). lib. bdg. 22.10 *(978-0-606-38512-1(6))* Turtleback Bks.

Santa the Chimney Sweep/the Candy Cane That Found a Home: Wee Voices Collection. 2005. (Illus.). 37p. per. 6.95 *(978-0-9764444-9-7(6))* E. J. Publishing.

Santiago, Shelly. The Fairies of Tythian. 2010. 40p. pap. 14.95 *(978-1-60976-143-1(X),* Eloquent Bks.) Strategic Book Publishing & Rights Agency (SBPRA).

Santillo, LuAnn. Look at Me. Santillo, LuAnn, ed. 2003. (Half-Pint Kids Readers Ser.). (Illus.). 7p. (J). (gr. -1-1). pap. 1.00 *(978-1-59256-052-3(0))* Half-Pint Kids, Inc.

Sarrasin, Alex. The Guardians of Neoegypti: Book One. 2007. 300p. per. 18.95 *(978-0-595-45710-6(X))* iUniverse, Inc.

Sataram, Nikita. Zatheria: The Hidden Realm. 2013. 194p. (gr. -1). 24.77 *(978-1-4907-0938-3(X));* pap. 14.77 *(978-1-4907-0936-9(3))* Trafford Publishing.

Saunders, George P. The Last Elf. 2007. 180p. per. 13.95 *(978-0-595-40843-6(5))* iUniverse, Inc.

Saunders, Kate. Beswitched. 2012. (ENG.). 272p. (J). (gr. 4-7). 7.99 *(978-0-375-87329-4(5),* Yearling) Random Hse. Children's Bks.

—The Curse of the Chocolate Phoenix. 2016. (ENG.). 272p. (J). (gr. 5). 6.99 *(978-0-385-39105-4(6),* Yearling) Random Hse. Children's Bks.

—The Curse of the Chocolate Phoenix: A Companion to the Whizz Pop Chocolate Shop. 2015. (ENG.). 272p. (J). (gr. 5). 19.99 *(978-0-375-99183-7(2),* Delacorte Bks. for Young Readers) Random Hse. Children's Bks.

—Magicalamity. 2013. (ENG.). 320p. (J). (gr. 4-7). 6.99 *(978-0-385-74078-4(6),* Yearling) Random Hse. Children's Bks.

—The Whizz Pop Chocolate Shop. (ENG.). 304p. (J). (gr. 5). 2014. 7.99 *(978-0-385-74302-0(5),* Yearling) 2013. 16.99 *(978-0-385-74301-3(7),* Delacorte Bks. for Young Readers) Random Hse. Children's Bks.

Sava, Scott Christian. Animal Crackers. 2011. (Illus.). 152p. pap. 11.99 *(978-1-60010-619-4(6))* Idea & Design Works, LLC.

—Magic Carpet. 2010. (Illus.). 110p. (J). pap. 11.99 *(978-1-60010-563-0(7))* Idea & Design Works, LLC.

Savage, J. Scott. Land Keep. 2009. (Farworld Ser.: Bk. 2). 432p. (YA). (gr. 5-18). 18.95 *(978-1-60641-164-3(0),* Shadow Mountain) Shadow Mountain Publishing.

Saveley, Barb. Dusky: The Lost Unicorn. 2008. 24p. pap. 24.95 *(978-1-60441-909-2(1))* America Star Bks.

Sawler, Kimberly. Rocket & the Magical Cosmic Candies. Walls, Ty, illus. 2006. 32p. (J). (gr. 4-7). 18.95 *(978-1-933285-51-1(6))* Brown Books Publishing Group.

Saxon, Victoria. Frozen (Disney Frozen) Lee, Grace & Cagol, Andrea, illus. 2015. (Little Golden Book Ser.). (ENG.). 24p. (J). (-k). 4.99 *(978-0-7364-3471-3(2),* Golden/Disney) Random Hse. Children's Bks.

Saxon, Victoria & RH Disney Staff. Frozen Fever. RH Disney Staff, illus. deluxe ed. 2015. (Junior Novel Ser.). (ENG., Illus.). 96p. (J). (gr. 3-7). 9.99 *(978-0-7364-3440-9(2),* RH/Disney) Random Hse. Children's Bks.

Sayre, Jill K. The Fairies of Turtle Creek. 2013. 322p. 22.17 *(978-0-9885066-4-0(5));* pap. 15.70 *(978-0-9885066-6-4(1))* Infinity Oak Bks.

Scaletta, Kurtis. Mudville. 2010. (ENG.). 272p. (J). (gr. 3-7). 8.99 *(978-0-375-84472-0(4),* Yearling) Random Hse. Children's Bks.

Schaefer, Lola M. & McCue, Lisa. Easter Surprises. 2009. (ENG., Illus.). 18p. (J). (gr. -1-1). 7.99 *(978-1-4169-6476-6(2),* Little Simon) Little Simon.

Scheunemann, Pam. Pelican's Pouch, 1 vol. 2007. (Critter Chronicles Ser.). (ENG., Illus.). 24p. (J). (gr. k-3). lib. bdg. 24.21 *(978-1-59928-462-0(6),* SandCastle) ABDO Publishing Co.

Schindler, Holly. Spark. 2016. 304p. (YA). (gr. 8). 17.99 *(978-0-06-222023-3(3),* HarperTeen) HarperCollins Pubs.

Schlesinger, Gretchen. Send Me the Soap #1: The Emerald Isle Adventure. Pietila, David, illus. 2006. (J). 11.95 *(978-0-9778536-0-1(8))* Eco-thumb Publishing Co.

—Send Me the Soap #1: The Emerald Isle Adventure (lib. Bdg.) Pietila, David, illus. 2006. (J). lib. bdg. *(978-0-9778536-1-8(6))* Eco-thumb Publishing Co.

Schlitz, Laura Amy. The Night Fairy. Barrett, Angela, illus. (ENG.). 128p. (J). (gr. 2-5). 2011. pap. 6.99 *(978-0-7636-5295-1(4))* 2010. 16.99 *(978-0-7636-3674-6(6))* Candlewick Pr.

—The Night Fairy, 2 vols. unabr. ed. 2010. (J). (gr. 1-4). 54.75 *(978-1-4407-6983-2(4))* Recorded Bks., Inc.

Schmid, Susan Maupin. Ghost of a Chance. Marlin, Lissy, illus. 2017. (100 Dresses Ser.: 2). (ENG.). 320p. (J). (gr. 3-7). 16.99 *(978-0-553-53373-6(8),* Random Hse. Bks. for Young Readers) Random Hse. Children's Bks.

—If the Magic Fits. (100 Dresses Ser.: 1). (ENG.). (J). (gr. 3-7). 2017. 320p. 7.99 ***(978-0-553-53369-9(X),*** Yearling) 2016. (Illus.). 304p. 16.99 *(978-0-553-53366-8(5),* Random Hse. Bks. for Young Readers) Random Hse. Children's Bks.

Schneller, Candace. Jayden's Magic Door. 2010. 60p. pap. 22.00 *(978-1-4269-4228-0(1))* Trafford Publishing.

Scholastic & Schmidt, Rebecca L. Movie Magic. Scholastic, Inc. Staff, illus. 2016. (LEGO NEXO Knights Ser.). (ENG.). 32p. (J). (gr. 2-5). pap. 3.99 *(978-1-338-03802-6(8))* Scholastic, Inc.

Scholastic, Inc. Staff. Ever after High: Yearbook. 2014. (ENG.). 96p. (J). (gr. 3-7). pap. 8.99 *(978-0-545-72368-8(X))* Scholastic, Inc.

—Friends Forever. 2012. (Lalaloopsy Ser.). (ENG.). 10p. (J). (gr. -1-k). bds. 12.99 *(978-0-545-46223-5(1))* Scholastic, Inc.

—Plan Your Destiny: A Spellbinding School Planner. 2014. (ENG.). 188p. (J). (gr. 3-7). 9.99 *(978-0-545-72365-7(5))* Scholastic, Inc.

Scholastic, Inc. Staff, contrib. by. A Day at Charm School. 2016. (ENG.). 32p. (J). (gr. -1-k). pap. 3.99 *(978-0-545-93224-0(6))* Scholastic, Inc.

Scholastic, Inc. Staff & Ameet Studio Staff. NEXO Powers Rule! 2016. (LEGO NEXO Knights Ser.). (ENG.). 32p. (J). (gr. 2-5). pap., act. bk. ed. 8.99 *(978-0-545-90584-8(2))* Scholastic, Inc.

Scholastic, Inc. Staff & Northrop, Michael. Book of the Dead. 2015. (TombQuest Ser.: 1). (ENG.). 208p. (J). (gr. 3-7). 12.99 *(978-0-545-72338-1(8))* Scholastic, Inc.

Schow, Betsy. Spelled. 2015. (Storymakers Ser.: 0). (ENG.). 352p. (YA). (gr. 6-12). pap. 9.99 *(978-1-4926-0871-4(8),* 9781492608714) Sourcebooks, Inc.

Schrader, Racheal. Doodlebugs: Trouble On Moss Farm. Schrader, Racheal, illus. 2008. (Illus.). 156p. (YA). per. 7.99 *(978-0-9815274-0-6(X))* Schrader, Racheal.

Schraff, Anne. The Magic Stone. 2015. (Red Rhino Ser.). (J). lib. bdg. 18.40 *(978-0-606-37207-7(5))* Turtleback Bks.

Schram, Kristina. The Chronicles of Anaedor. 2010. 416p. pap. 9.95 *(978-1-935142-10-2(0))* Variance Publishing, LLC.

Schram, Peninnah. The Magic Pomegranate. Hall, Melanie, illus. 2007. (On My Own Folklore Ser.). 48p. (J). lib. bdg. 17.95 *(978-0-8225-8856-6(0),* Kar-Ben Publishing) Lerner Publishing Group.

Schroeder, Lisa. Sealed with a Secret. 2016. (ENG.). 224p. (J). (gr. 3-7). 16.99 *(978-0-545-90734-7(9),* Scholastic Pr.) Scholastic, Inc.

Schuff, Nicolás & Fraticelli, Damin. Ana y la Maldicion de Las Pecas. Mey, illus. 2013. (Coleccion Heroinas Ser.).Tr. of Ana & the Cursed Freckles. (SPA.). 96p. (J). (gr. 4-7). pap. *(978-987-1710-84-3(4))* Ediciones Urano S. A.

Scieszka, Jon. Hey Kid, Want to Buy a Bridge? McCauley, Adam, illus. 2005. (Time Warp Trio Ser.: No. 11). 74p. (gr. 4-7). 15.00 *(978-0-7569-5988-3(8))* Perfection Learning Corp.

—Marco? Polo!, No. 16. McCauley, Adam, illus. 2008. (Time Warp Trio Ser.: 16). (ENG.). 96p. (J). (gr. 2-4). 5.99 (978-0-14-241177-3(9), Puffin Books) Penguin Young Readers Group.

—Marco? Polo! McCauley, Adam, illus. 2008. (Time Warp Trio Ser.: No. 16). 90p. (J). (gr. 4-6). 12.65 (978-0-7569-8923-1(X)) Perfection Learning Corp.

—Me Oh Maya. McCauley, Adam, illus. 2005. (Time Warp Trio Ser.: 13). (ENG.). 96p. (J). (gr. 2-4). 5.99 (978-0-14-240300-6(8), Puffin Books) Penguin Young Readers Group.

—Me Oh Maya. McCauley, Adam, illus. 2005. (Time Warp Trio Ser.: No. 13). 69p. (gr. 2-6). 15.00 (978-0-7569-5060-6(0)) Perfection Learning Corp.

—Summer Reading Is Killing Me! Smith, Lane, illus. 2004. (Time Warp Trio Ser.: 7). (ENG.). 80p. (J). (gr. 2-4). pap. 5.99 (978-0-14-240115-6(3), Puffin Books) Penguin Young Readers Group.

—Summer Reading Is Killing Me! Smith, Lane, illus. 2004. (Time Warp Trio Ser.: No. 7). 73p. (J). (gr. 4-7). 12.65 (978-0-7569-6781-9(3)) Perfection Learning Corp.

—Viking It & Liking It. McCauley, Adam, illus. 2004. (Time Warp Trio Ser.: No. 12). 73p. (gr. 2-6). 15.00 (978-0-7569-2589-5(4)) Perfection Learning Corp.

—Viking It & Liking It. 2004. (Time Warp Trio Ser.: 12). 16.00 (978-1-4176-3613-6(0), Turtleback) Turtleback Bks.

Scott, Michael. The Alchemyst. 2009. (ENG., Illus.). 375p. (gr. 6-10). 19.00 (978-1-60686-514-9(5)) Perfection Learning Corp.

—The Alchemyst. (Secrets of the Immortal Nicholas Flamel Ser.: Bk. 1). (ENG.). 400p. (YA). (gr. 7). 2008. pap. 10.99 (978-0-385-73600-8(2), Ember) 2007. (Illus.). 16.99 (978-0-385-73357-1(7), Delacorte Bks. for Young Readers) Random Hse. Children's Bks.

—The Enchantress. 2012. (Secrets of the Immortal Nicholas Flamel Ser.). (ENG.). 528p. (YA). (gr. 7). 18.99 (978-0-385-73535-3(9), Delacorte Bks. for Young Readers) Random Hse. Children's Bks.

—The Enchantress. 2013. (Secrets of the Immortal Nicholas Flamel Ser.: 6). (ENG.). 528p. (YA). (gr. 7). pap. 10.99 (978-0-385-73536-0(7), Ember) Random Hse. Children's Bks.

—The Enchantress. 2013. (Secrets of the Immortal Nicholas Flamel Ser.: 6). lib. bdg. 22.10 (978-0-606-31947-8(6), Turtleback) Turtleback Bks.

—The Magician. (Secrets of the Immortal Nicholas Flamel Ser.: Bk. 2). (ENG.). 496p. (YA). (gr. 7). 2009. pap. 10.99 (978-0-385-73728-9(9), Ember) 2008. 16.99 (978-0-385-73358-8(5), Delacorte Bks. for Young Readers) Random Hse. Children's Bks.

—The Necromancer. 2011. (Secrets of the Immortal Nicholas Flamel Ser.). (ENG.). 416p. (YA). (gr. 7). pap. 10.99 (978-0-385-73532-2(4), Ember) Random Hse. Children's Bks.

—The Necromancer the Secrets of the Immortal Nicholas Flamel. l.t. ed. 2010. (Secrets of the Immortal Nicholas Flamel Ser.). (ENG.). 492p. 23.99 (978-1-4104-2851-6(6)) Thorndike Pr.

—The Sorceress. (Secrets of the Immortal Nicholas Flamel Ser.: 3). (ENG.). 512p. (YA). (gr. 7-18). 2010. pap. 10.99 (978-0-385-73530-8(8), Ember) 2009. 17.99 (978-0-385-73529-2(4), Delacorte Bks. for Young Readers) Random Hse. Children's Bks.

—The Sorceress. 2010. (Secrets of the Immortal Nicholas Flamel Ser.: 3). lib. bdg. 22.10 (978-0-606-14133-8(2), Turtleback) Turtleback Bks.

—The Sorceress the Secrets of the Immortal Nicholas Flamel. l.t. ed. 2009. (Secrets of the Immortal Nicholas Flamel Ser.). (ENG.). 614p. (YA). 23.95 (978-1-4104-2092-3(2)) Thorndike Pr.

Scott, Molly. Broken Bones Are No Fun, but Broken Bones Won't Stop My Play! Baker, David, illus. 2012. 32p. pap. 24.95 (978-1-4626-7424-4(0)) America Star Bks.

Scotton, Rob. Russell's Christmas Magic. Scotton, Rob, illus. 2007. (Illus.). 32p. (J). (gr. -1-2). lib. bdg. 17.89 (978-0-06-059855-6(7)) HarperCollins Pubs.

Sealey, Philip. The Sorcerer's Tome. 2013. 254p. pap. (978-1-78407-199-8(4)) FeedARead.com.

Sedgwick, Julian. The Palace of Memory. Moffett, Patricia, illus. 2017. (Mysterium Ser.: 2). (ENG.). 352p. (J). (gr. 4-8). 18.99 (978-1-4677-7568-7(1), Carolrhoda Bks.) Lerner Publishing Group.

Sedgwick, Marcus. The Book of Dead Days. 2006. (ENG.). 288p. (YA). (gr. 5-12). reprint ed. per. 7.99 (978-0-385-74704-2(7), Lamb, Wendy Bks.) Random Hse. Children's Bks.

Segur, Sophie. Old French Fairy Tales. Sterrett, Virginia Frances, illus. 2010. (ENG.). 296p. (gr. -1-3). pap. 19.95 (978-1-4290-1186-0(6)) Applewood Bks.

Selfors, Suzanne. Ever after High: Science & Sorcery: a Destiny Do-Over Diary. 2015. (ENG., Illus.). 160p. (J). (gr. 3-7). 9.99 (978-0-316-40133-3(1)) Little, Brown Bks. for Young Readers.

—Kiss & Spell. 2015. (Ever after High Ser.: Bk. 2). (ENG., Illus.). 224p. (J). (gr. 3-7). 13.99 (978-0-316-40131-9(5)) Little, Brown Bks. for Young Readers.

Sellers, Kathy Lacey. Willie Chaff. 2010. pap. 10.95 (978-0-7414-6080-6(7)) Infinity Publishing.

Sexton, Shirley. Fairy with an Attitude. 2009. 142p. 22.50 (978-1-60860-616-0(3), Strategic Bk. Publishing) Strategic Book Publishing & Rights Agency (SBPRA).

Shah, Yasmin. Abby & the Feather Quest. 2010. (Illus.). 48p. pap. 10.49 (978-1-4343-9839-0(0)) AuthorHouse.

Shalant, Phyllis. When Pirates Came to Brooklyn. 2010. 224p. pap. 14.95 (978-1-4401-8338-6(4)) iUniverse, Inc.

Shan, Darren, pseud. Dark Calling. 2010. (ENG.). 224p. (YA). (gr. 10-17). pap. 10.00 (978-0-316-04872-9(0)) Little, Brown Bks. for Young Readers.

—Death's Shadow. 2009. (ENG.). 240p. (YA). (gr. 10-17). pap. 10.00 (978-0-316-00382-7(4)) Little Brown & Co.

—Slawter. 2007. (ENG.). 240p. (J). (gr. 10-17). pap. 10.99 (978-0-316-01388-8(9)) Little, Brown Bks. for Young Readers.

Shanghai Animation Studio Staff & Tang, Sanmu. Nezha Conquers the Dragon King. Yawtsong, Lee, tr. from CHI. 2010. (Favorite Children's Ser.). (ENG., Illus.). 32p. (J). (gr. -1-3). pap. 5.95 (978-1-60220-975-6(8)) BetterLink Pr., Inc.

Shannon, David. Alice the Fairy. Shannon, David, illus. 2009. (ENG., Illus.). (J). (gr. -1-k). pap. 9.95 incl. audio compact disk (978-0-545-11758-6(5)) Scholastic, Inc.

Sharkey, Niamh & Walker, Richard. Jack & the Beanstalk. Sharkey, Niamh, illus. 2006. (ENG., Illus.). 40p. (J). (gr. -1-2). 10.99 (978-1-905236-69-5(7)) Barefoot Bks., Inc.

Sharp, D. L. M. A Pocket of Magic on Beechwood Street. 2004. (J). pap. (978-0-9762626-0-2(6)) Sharp, Diana Consulting.

Sharp, Margery. The Rescuers. Williams, Garth, illus. 2016. (ENG.). 160p. (J). (gr. 4-7). pap. 9.99 (978-1-68137-007-1(7), NYRB Kids) New York Review of Bks., Inc., The.

Sharpe, Gerald. Parade of Lights. Moya, Patricia, illus. 2007. (What Lies Beneath the Bed Ser.). 487p. (J). per. 11.00 (978-1-933894-01-0(6)) IJN Publishing, Inc.

Sharpe, Leah Marinsky. The Goat-Faced Girl: A Classic Italian Folktale. Marinsky, Jane, illus. 2009. 32p. (J). (gr. 1-4). 16.95 (978-1-56792-393-3(3)) Godine, David R. Pub.

Sharplin, Emory. Scrap. 2013. 352p. (J). pap. 10.95 (978-1-938416-35-4(X)) River Grove Bks.

Shaughnessy, Adam. The Entirely True Story of the Unbelievable FIB. 2015. (Unbelievable FIB Ser.: 1). (ENG.). 272p. (J). (gr. 3-7). 16.95 (978-1-61620-498-3(2)) Algonquin Bks. of Chapel Hill.

—Over the Underworld. 2016. (Unbelievable FIB Ser.: 2). (ENG.). 304p. (J). (gr. 3-7). 16.95 (978-1-61620-499-0(0)) Algonquin Bks. of Chapel Hill.

Shepard, Aaron. The Mountain of Marvels: A Celtic Tale of Magic, Retold from the Mabinogion. 2007. (Ancient Fantasy Ser.: 1). 46p. (J). pap. 6.00 (978-0-938497-36-3(7)); lib. bdg. 15.00 (978-0-938497-34-9(0)) Shepard Pubns. (Skyhook Pr.).

—The Princess Mouse: A Tale of Finland. Gore, Leonid, illus. 2008. (ENG.). 40p. (J). (gr. -1-3). 13.99 (978-1-4169-8969-1(2), Atheneum Bks. for Young Readers) Simon & Schuster Children's Publishing.

—The Songs of Power: A Finnish Tale of Magic, Retold from the Kalevala. 2007. (Ancient Fantasy Ser.: 2). 54p. (J). lib. bdg. 15.00 (978-0-938497-35-6(9)); lib. bdg. 6.00 (978-0-938497-37-0(5)) Shepard Pubns. (Skyhook Pr.).

Shepherd, Anita. Easter Rabbit's Magic. 2013. 48p. pap. 7.95 (978-0-9882368-2-0(6)) New Eden Publishing.

Sherman, Delia. The Evil Wizard Smallbone. 2016. (ENG.). 416p. (J). (gr. 3-7). 17.99 (978-0-7636-8805-9(3)) Candlewick Pr.

Shire, Poppy. Jewel the Midnight Pony. Berg, Ron, illus. 2008. (Magic Pony Carousel Ser.: 4). (ENG.). 96p. (J). (gr. 2-5). pap. 3.99 (978-0-06-083788-4(8)) HarperCollins Pubs.

—Sparkle the Circus Pony. Berg, Ron, illus. 2007. (Magic Pony Carousel Ser.: 1). (ENG.). 96p. (J). (gr. 2-5). pap. 3.99 (978-0-06-083779-2(9)) HarperCollins Pubs.

—Star the Western Pony. Berg, Ron, illus. 2007. (Magic Pony Carousel Ser.: 3). (ENG.). 96p. (J). (gr. 2-5). pap. 3.99 (978-0-06-083785-3(3)) HarperCollins Pubs.

Shoesmith-Bateman, Amanda. The Magic Tree House, 1 vol. Beitz-Grant, Heather, illus. 2010. 22p. 24.95 (978-1-4489-3866-7(X)) PublishAmerica, Inc.

Shooter, Sam. The Goat in the Coat. 2012. 24p. pap. 15.99 (978-1-4691-8749-5(3)) Xlibris Corp.

Shorrock, Anne. The Secret Adventures of Amelia & Rainbow. 2008. 36p. pap. 15.95 (978-1-60693-011-3(7), Eloquent Bks.) Strategic Book Publishing & Rights Agency (SBPRA).

Shughart-Knecht, Kimberly. Princess Kiali & the Purple Box. 2010. 32p. pap. 12.99 (978-1-4490-0913-7(1)) AuthorHouse.

Shulda, Daron M. Dragon Boots. 2009. 40p. pap. 18.49 (978-1-4389-7022-6(6)) AuthorHouse.

Shulman, Polly. The Grimm Legacy. (ENG.). (J). (gr. 5-18). 2011. 352p. 8.99 (978-0-14-241904-5(4), Puffin Books) 2010. (Illus.). 336p. 16.99 (978-0-399-25096-5(4), G.P. Putnam's Sons Books for Young Readers) Penguin Young Readers Group.

Shultz, D. B. The World Adventures of Sahara the Mummy: The Magical Exploration of Ancient Egypt. 2012. 28p. pap. 17.99 (978-1-4772-3310-8(5)) AuthorHouse.

Shurtliff, Liesl. Rump: The True Story of Rumpelstiltskin. (ENG.). 272p. (J). (gr. 3-7). 2014. pap. 7.99 (978-0-307-97796-0(X), Yearling) 2013. 16.99 (978-0-307-97793-9(5), Knopf Bks. for Young Readers) 2013. lib. bdg. 19.99 (978-0-307-97794-6(3), Knopf Bks. for Young Readers) Random Hse. Children's Bks.

Shusterman, Neal. The Dark Side of Nowhere. unabr. ed. 2004. 192p. (J). (gr. 4-7). pap. 36.00 incl. audio (978-0-8072-8757-6(1), YA258SP, Listening Library) Random Hse. Audio Publishing Group.

—The Eyes of Kid Midas. 2009. (ENG.). 176p. (YA). (gr. 7). pap. 10.99 (978-1-4169-9750-4(4), Simon & Schuster Bks. For Young Readers) Simon & Schuster Bks. For Young Readers.

Shvarts, Andrew. Royal Bastards. 2017. (Royal Bastards Ser.). (ENG.). 352p. (YA). (gr. 9-17). 18.99 **(978-1-4847-6765-8(9))** Hyperion Bks. for Children.

Siegrist, Vicky. Our Magical House. 2008. 31p. 15.50 (978-0-615-21676-8(5)) Siegrist, Vicky.

Sierra, JulieAnn. Legacy & the Dark Prince, 1 vol. 2009. 209p. pap. 24.95 (978-1-61582-693-3(9)) America Star Bks.

Silberberg, Alan. The Awesome, Almost 100% True Adventures of Matt & Craz. Silberberg, Alan, illus. (ENG., Illus.). 336p. (J). (gr. 4-8). 2014. pap. 7.99 (978-1-4169-9433-6(5)) 2013. 16.99 (978-1-4169-9432-9(7)) Simon & Schuster Children's Publishing. (Aladdin).

Simard, Remy. La Bottine Magique de Pipo. 2004. (FRE., Illus.). (J). (gr. k-2). spiral bd. (978-0-616-01841-5(X)) Canadian National Institute for the Blind/Institut National Canadien pour les Aveugles.

Simko, Joe. The Sweet Rot Book 3: The Purple Meltdown, 1 vol. Simko, Joe, illus. 2012. (ENG., Illus.). 32p. (J). 19.99 (978-0-7643-3977-6(X), 9780764339776) Schiffer Publishing, Ltd.

Simner, Janni Lee. Bones of Faerie. (Bones of Faerie Trilogy Ser.). (YA). 2010. (ENG.). 256p. (gr. 7-11). pap. 9.99 (978-0-375-84565-9(8), Random Hse. Bks. for Young Readers) 2009. 247p. (978-0-375-84564-2(X)) Random Hse. Children's Bks.

—Faerie After. 2013. 264p. (YA). pap. (978-0-375-87118-4(7)) Random Hse., Inc.

Simon, Jenne. The Double Trouble. 2015. (ENG.). 32p. (J). (gr. -1-k). 8.99 (978-0-545-85023-0(1)) Scholastic, Inc.

—The Magic Charm Chase. 2016. (ENG.). 24p. (J). (gr. -1-k). 3.99 (978-0-545-94302-4(7)) Scholastic, Inc.

—Meet the Little Charmers (Little Charmers) 2015. (ENG.). 24p. (J). (gr. -1-k). 3.99 (978-0-545-85021-6(5)) Scholastic, Inc.

—Sparkle Bunny Day! (Little Charmers: 8x8) 2017. (Little Charmers Ser.: 5). (ENG.). 24p. (J). (gr. -1-k). pap. 3.99 (978-1-338-11279-5(1)) Scholastic, Inc.

—Spooky Pumpkin Moon Night. 2016. (ENG.). 24p. (J). (gr. -1-k). 3.99 (978-0-545-93225-7(4)) Scholastic, Inc.

Simon, Jenne & Rusu, Meredith. Santa Sparkle. 2016. (Little Charmers Ser.). (ENG.). 24p. (J). (gr. -1-1). pap. 4.99 (978-1-338-09764-1(4)) Scholastic, Inc.

Simonet, Evan, illus. Jake & the Sailing Tree. 2009. (J). (978-1-60108-019-6(0)) Red Cygnet Pr.

Sims, Lesley. The Enchanted Castle. Marks, Alan, illus. 2007. (Young Reading Series 2 Gift Bks). 62p. (J). (gr. 4-7). 8.99 (978-0-7945-1347-4(6), Usborne) EDC Publishing.

—The Magical Book. Tavares, Victor, illus. 2007. (Young Reading Series 2 Gift Bks). 64p. (J). (gr. 4-7). 8.99 (978-0-7945-1703-8(X), Usborne) EDC Publishing.

—Magical Stories for Little Children. 2012. (Picture Bks). 128p. (J). ring bd. 18.99 (978-0-7945-2919-2(4), Usborne) EDC Publishing.

Sinclair, Alison. Lightborn. 2011. (Darkborn Trilogy Ser.: 2). (ENG., Illus.). 312p. (gr. 12). 7.99 (978-0-451-46358-6(7), Ace Bks.) Penguin Publishing Group.

Singh, Rina. The Magic Braid. Zaman, Farida, illus. Date not set. 134p. (J). pap. (978-0-920813-25-6(9)) Sister Vision Pr.

Singleton, Linda Joy. Magician's Muse. 2010. (Seer Ser.: 6). (ENG.). 312p. (YA). (gr. 6-18). pap. 9.95 (978-0-7387-1957-3(9), Flux) Llewellyn Pubns.

Sire, Storma. Lessons in Magic. 2005. pap. (978-1-897242-11-7(5)) Aydy Pr.

Sisler, Celeste. Disney Fairies: Bedtime Fairy Stories: a Treasury. 2014. (ENG., Illus.). 272p. (J). (gr. -1-3). 11.99 (978-0-316-28339-7(8)) Little, Brown Bks. for Young Readers.

Sister Flowers. When Boo Boo Wakes Up!, 1 vol. Smith, Brenda, illus. 2009. 36p. pap. 24.95 (978-1-61546-250-6(3)) America Star Bks.

Skelton, K. Magic from the Wishing Well. 2009. 28p. pap. 12.49 (978-1-4389-8747-7(1)) AuthorHouse.

Skelton, Matthew. Endymion Spring. 2008. (ENG.). 416p. (YA). (gr. 7). pap. 9.99 (978-0-385-73456-1(5), Delacorte Bks. for Young Readers) Random Hse. Children's Bks.

Skye, Evelyn. The Crown's Fate. (Crown's Game Ser.: 2). (ENG.). 432p. (YA). (gr. 8). 2018. pap. 9.99 **(978-0-06-242262-0(6)**, Balzer & Bray) 2017. 17.99 (978-0-06-242261-3(8)) HarperCollins Pubs.

Skye, obert. Choke. 2010. (Pillage Ser.: 2). (ENG., Illus.). 336p. (YA). (gr. 7). 17.99 (978-1-60641-653-2(7), Shadow Mountain) Shadow Mountain Publishing.

—The Eyes of the Want. Sowards, Ben, illus. 2008. (Leven Thumps Ser.: 3). (ENG.). 464p. (J). (gr. 3-7). pap. 9.99 (978-1-4169-4719-6(1), Aladdin) Simon & Schuster Children's Publishing.

—The Gateway. Sowards, Ben, illus. 2006. (Leven Thumps Ser.: 1). (ENG.). 400p. (J). (gr. 3-7). pap. 9.99 (978-1-4169-2806-5(5), Aladdin) Simon & Schuster Children's Publishing.

—Leven Thumps 5 Volume Set. 2009. (ENG.). (J). (978-1-60641-220-6(5), Shadow Mountain) Shadow Mountain Publishing.

—Leven Thumps & the Gateway to Foo. (Leven Thumps Ser.: 1). (J). 2008. 74.75 (978-1-4361-1570-4(1)) 2007. 112.75 (978-1-4281-4622-8(9)) 2007. 85.75 (978-1-4281-4616-7(4)) 2007. 115.75 (978-1-4281-4620-4(2)) 2007. 1.25 (978-1-4281-4613-6(X)) 2007. 82.75 (978-1-4281-4618-1(0)) 2007. 178.75 (978-1-4281-4617-4(2)) Recorded Bks., Inc.

—Leven Thumps & the Gateway to Foo. 2005. (Leven Thumps Ser.: Bk. 1). (Illus.). 384p. (J). 17.95 (978-1-59038-369-8(9), Shadow Mountain) Shadow Mountain Publishing.

—Leven Thumps & the Wrath of Ezra. 2008. (Leven Thumps Ser.: Bk. 4). (Illus.). 388p. (J). 19.95 (978-1-59038-963-8(8), Shadow Mountain) Shadow Mountain Publishing.

—Pillage. (YA). 2010. (Pillage Ser.: 1). (ENG.). 320p. (gr. 7). mass mkt. 7.99 (978-1-60641-680-8(4)) 2008. (Illus.). 352p. 17.95 (978-1-59038-922-5(0)) Shadow Mountain Publishing. (Shadow Mountain).

—Pillagy: The Complete Trilogy. 2013. (ENG., Illus.). 712p. (YA). (gr. 6). pap. 17.99 (978-1-60907-706-8(7), Shadow Mountain) Shadow Mountain Publishing.

—The Ruins of Alder. Sowards, Ben, illus. 2010. (Leven Thumps Ser.: 5). (ENG.). 416p. (J). (gr. 4-9). pap. 9.99 (978-1-4169-9093-2(3), Aladdin) Simon & Schuster Children's Publishing.

—The Wrath of Ezra. Sowards, Ben, illus. 2009. (Leven Thumps Ser.: 4). (ENG.). 464p. (J). (gr. 4-9). pap. 9.99 (978-1-4169-9092-5(5), Aladdin) Simon & Schuster Children's Publishing.

Slayton, Shonna. Cinderella's Shoes. 2015. (ENG.). 400p. (YA). pap. 9.99 (978-1-63375-123-1(6), 9781633751231) Entangled Publishing, LLC.

Sleigh, Barbara. Carbonel: The King of the Cats. Drummond, V. H., illus. 2004. (ENG.). 216p. (J). (gr. 4-7). reprint ed. 16.95 (978-1-59017-126-4(8), NYR Children's Collection) New York Review of Bks., Inc., The.

Sloat, Teri & Huffmon, Betty. Berry Magic. 2015. (ENG., Illus.). 34p. (J). 21.99 (978-1-943328-12-3(9), Alaska Northwest Bks.) Graphic Arts Ctr. Publishing Co.

Smiletown's Upside Down. 2007. (J). per. 14.95 (978-0-9785132-3-8(1)) Smile-a-Lot, LLP.

Smith, Brian. The Intrepid EscapeGoat: Curse of the Buddha's Tooth. Conkling, Jon & DeVito, Michael A., eds. 2012. (ENG., Illus.). 96p. pap. 12.95 (978-0-9832161-3-1(4), 9780983216131) Th3rd World Studios.

Smith, Clete Barrett. Magic Delivery. Dziekan, Michal, illus. 2014. (ENG.). 288p. (J). (gr. 3-7). 16.99 (978-1-4231-6597-2(7)) Hyperion Bks. for Children.

Smith, Cliff. New Magical Holiday Stories. 2005. pap. 31.99 (978-1-4134-7971-3(5)) Xlibris Corp.

Smith, Debora Ann Baker. The Magnificent Fairy Party. 2010. (Illus.). 30p. pap. 13.00 (978-1-60911-404-6(3), Eloquent Bks.) Strategic Book Publishing & Rights Agency (SBPRA).

Smith, Jennifer E. The Storm Makers. Helquist, Brett, illus. 2013. (ENG.). 384p. (J). (gr. 3-7). pap. 8.00 (978-0-316-17959-1(0)) Little, Brown Bks. for Young Readers.

Smith, John C. Popee the Purple Pig-a-Saurus. 2010. 40p. pap. 16.99 (978-1-4490-9285-6(3)) AuthorHouse.

Smith, L. J. & Smith, Tom. The Night of the Solstice. 2008. (ENG.). 244p. (YA). pap. 11.99 (978-1-4169-8965-3(X), Simon & Schuster Bks. For Young Readers) Simon & Schuster Bks. For Young Readers.

Smith, Miss Diane Pearl. Princess S Magickal Christmas. 2012. 28p. pap. (978-0-9878503-0-0(X)) Rainbowchild.

Smith, Ronald L. Hoodoo. 2017. (ENG.). 224p. (J). (gr. 5-7). pap. 7.99 (978-0-544-93561-7(6), HMH Books For Young Readers) Houghton Mifflin Harcourt Publishing Co.

—Hoodoo. 2015. (ENG.). 224p. (J). (gr. 5-7). 16.99 (978-0-544-44525-3(2), Clarion Bks.) Houghton Mifflin Harcourt Trade & Reference Pubs.

—Hoodoo. 2017. (ENG.). (J). (gr. 5-7). lib. bdg. 18.40 **(978-0-606-39820-6(1))** Turtleback Bks.

Smyth, Jimmy. The Magic Garden. 2013. 36p. pap. (978-0-9569314-7-4(2)) Smith, Jimmy.

Snider, Brandon T. Doctor Strange: Mystery of the Dark Magic. 2016. (Mighty Marvel Chapter Bks.). (J). lib. bdg. 16.00 (978-0-606-39173-3(8)) Turtleback Bks.

Sniegoski, Thomas E. The Brimstone Network. 2008. (Brimstone Network Ser.: 1). (ENG.). 304p. (J). (gr. 4-8). pap. 14.99 (978-1-4169-5104-9(0), Simon & Schuster/Paula Wiseman Bks.) Simon & Schuster/Paula Wiseman Bks.

Sniegoski, Thomas E. & Golden, Christopher. Battle for Arcanum. 2013. (Magic Zero Ser.: 4). (ENG., Illus.). 240p. (J). (gr. 3-7). pap. 6.99 (978-1-4424-7315-7(0), Aladdin) Simon & Schuster Children's Publishing.

—Battle for Arcanum. 2013. (Magic Zero Ser.: 4). (ENG., Illus.). 240p. (J). (gr. 3-7). 17.99 (978-1-4424-7316-4(9), Simon & Schuster/Paula Wiseman Bks.) Simon & Schuster/Paula Wiseman Bks.

Sniegoski, Tom. Quest for the Spark. Smith, Jeff, illus. (Bone Ser.). (ENG.). (J). (gr. 3-7). 2012. 240p. pap. 10.99 (978-0-545-14104-8(4))Bk. 2. 2012. 240p. 26.99 (978-0-545-14103-1(6))Bk. 3. 2013. 288p. pap. 10.99 (978-0-545-14106-2(0))No. 3. 2013. 288p. 22.99 (978-0-545-14105-5(2)) Scholastic, Inc. (Graphix).

—Quest for the Spark. (Bone: Quest for the Spark Ser.: 3). 2013. lib. bdg. 22.10 (978-0-606-31497-8(0)) 2012. lib. bdg. 22.10 (978-0-606-23947-9(2)) Turtleback Bks. (Turtleback).

Sniegoski, Tom & Smith, Jeff. Quest for the Spark, Bk. 1. Smith, Jeff, illus. 2011. (BONE: Quest for the Spark Ser.: 1). (ENG., Illus.). 224p. (J). (gr. 3-7). 26.99 (978-0-545-14101-7(X), Graphix) Scholastic, Inc.

Snow, Carol. Snap. 2009. (ENG.). 224p. (YA). (gr. 8-18). 16.99 (978-0-06-145211-6(4), HarperTeen) HarperCollins Pubs.

Snowe, Olivia. Dandelion & the Witch, 1 vol. Lamoreaux, Michelle, illus. 2014. (Twicetold Tales Ser.). (ENG.). 128p. (gr. 3-4). 25.32 (978-1-4342-9147-9(2)) Stone Arch Bks.

—The Sealed-Up House, 1 vol. Lamoreaux, Michelle, illus. (Twicetold Tales Ser.). (ENG.). 128p. (gr. 3-4). 2014. pap. 5.95 (978-1-4342-9556-9(7)) 2013. 8.95 (978-1-4342-6281-3(2)) 2013. lib. bdg. 25.32 (978-1-4342-6019-2(4)) Stone Arch Bks.

Snyder, Laurel. Any Which Wall. Pham, LeUyen, illus. 2010. (ENG.). 256p. (J). (gr. 3-7). pap. 7.99 (978-0-375-85561-0(0), Yearling) Random Hse. Children's Bks.

Snyder, Maria V. Dawn Study. 2017. (Study Ser.: 6). (ENG.). 480p. pap. 16.99 (978-0-7783-1985-6(7), Mira Bks.) Harlequin Enterprises, Ltd. CAN. Dist: HarperCollins Pubs.

Snyder, Zilpha Keatley. The Bronze Pen. (ENG.). 208p. (J). (gr. 3-7). 2009. pap. 5.99 (978-1-4169-4208-5(4)) 2008. 16.99 (978-1-4169-4201-6(7)) Simon & Schuster Children's Publishing. (Atheneum Bks. for Young Readers).

—The Headless Cupid. Raible, Alton, illus. 2009. (Stanley Family Ser.). (ENG.). 224p. (J). (gr. 3-7). 16.99 (978-1-4169-9532-6(3), Atheneum Bks. for Young Readers) Simon & Schuster Children's Publishing.

—The Witches of Worm. 2009. 9.00 (978-0-7848-3612-5(4), Everbind) Marco Bk. Co.

—The Witches of Worm. Raible, Alton, illus. 2009. (ENG.). (J). (gr. 3-7). 192p. 16.99 (978-1-4169-9531-9(5)); 208p. pap. 7.99 (978-1-4169-9053-6(4)) Simon & Schuster Children's Publishing. (Atheneum Bks. for Young Readers).

—The Witches of Worm. 2006. 22.75 (978-0-8446-7290-8(4)) Smith, Peter Pub., Inc.

Sobat, Gail Sidonie. A Glass Darkly. 2006. (Ingamald Ser.: 3). (ENG., Illus.). 192p. (YA). (gr. 8-12). per. 14.95 (978-1-894283-69-4(4)) Great Plains Pubns. CAN. Dist: Publishers Group Canada.

—A Winter's Tale. 2004. (Ingamald Ser.: 2). (ENG.). 176p. pap. 16.95 (978-1-894283-45-8(7)) Great Plains Pubns. CAN. Dist: Publishers Group Canada.

Soderberg, Erin. The Quirks & the Freaky Field Trip. Jack, Colin, illus. 2015. (Quirks Ser.). (ENG.). 208p. (YA). (gr. 3-6). 13.99 (978-1-61963-668-2(9), 9781619636682, Bloomsbury USA Childrens) Bloomsbury Publishing USA.

—The Quirks & the Quirkalicious Birthday. Light, Kelly, illus. 2015. (Quirks Ser.). (ENG.). 208p. (YA). (gr. 3-6). 13.99 (978-1-61963-370-4(1), 9781619633704, Bloomsbury USA Childrens) Bloomsbury Publishing USA.

—The Quirks in Circus Quirkus. 2014. (Quirks Ser.). (ENG., Illus.). (YA). (gr. 3-6). 256p. pap. 7.99 (978-1-61963-663-7(8), 9781619636637); 240p. 13.99 (978-1-59990-790-1(9), 9781599907901) Bloomsbury Publishing USA. (Bloomsbury USA Childrens).

Soderberg, Erin & Munford, Rebecca. Welcome to Normal. 2013. (Quirks Ser.). (ENG., Illus.). 240p. (YA). (gr. 3-6). 13.99 (978-1-59990-789-5(5), 9781599907895, Bloomsbury USA Childrens) Bloomsbury Publishing USA.

Soontornvat, Christina. The Changelings. (Changelings Ser.: 1). (ENG.). (J). (gr. 5-8). 2017. 304p. pap. 7.99 **(978-1-4926-4795-9(0))** 2016. 288p. 16.99 (978-1-4926-3260-3(0), 9781492632603) Sourcebooks, Inc. (Sourcebooks Jabberwocky).

Spalding, Andrea. Dance of the Stones, 1 vol. 2003. (Summer of Magic Quartet Ser.: 2). (ENG., Illus.). 192p. (J). (gr. 3-7). pap. 7.95 (978-1-55143-268-7(4)) Orca Bk. Pubs. USA.

—Heart of the Hill, 1 vol. 2005. (Summer of Magic Quartet Ser.: 3). (ENG., Illus.). 192p. (J). (gr. 3-7). per. 7.95 (978-1-55143-486-5(5)) Orca Bk. Pubs. USA.

Spann, Bill. The Agents of Little Woods. 2005. 116p. pap. 19.95 (978-1-4137-6574-8(2)) America Star Bks.

Spanton, Elizabeth & Bright, Laren. Golden Voyages. 2013. 84p. pap. 27.99 (978-1-4525-7213-0(5), Balboa Pr.) Author Solutions, Inc.

Spaziano, Layna. Shane & Molly's Magical Journey, 1 vol. 2010. 28p. pap. 24.95 (978-1-4489-6261-7(7)) PublishAmerica, Inc.

Speakman, Peter & Galvin, Michael. Rebels of the Lamp, Book 1 Rebels of the Lamp. 2017. (Rebels of the Lamp Ser.). (ENG.). 304p. (J). (gr. 5-9). pap. 7.99 (978-1-4847-0847-7(4)) Hyperion Bks. for Children.

Speakman, Peter & Galvin, Michael M. B. Finders Keepers. 2017. (Rebels of the Lamp Ser.). (ENG.). 288p. (J). (gr. 5-9). 16.99 (978-1-4231-8040-1(2)) Disney Pr.

Speer, Cindy Lynn. Unbalanced. 2010. pap. (978-1-934841-90-7(0)) Zumaya Pubns. LLC.

Sperring, Mark. Max & the Won't Go to Bed Show. Warburton, Sarah, illus. 2014. (ENG.). 32p. (J). (gr. -1-k). 16.99 (978-0-545-70822-7(2), Scholastic Pr.) Scholastic, Inc.

Spicer, Lin. Faerie Baby. 2006. 148p. pap. 13.50 (978-1-84426-384-4(3)) Upfront Publishing Ltd. GBR. Dist: Printondemand-worldwide.com.

Spinner, Stephanie. Damosel: In Which the Lady of the Lake Renders a Frank & Often Startling Account of Her Wondrous Life & Times. 2010. (ENG.). 208p. (YA). (gr. 7). pap. 8.99 (978-0-553-49511-9(9), Knopf Bks. for Young Readers) Random Hse. Children's Bks.

—The Magic of Merlin. Sokolova, Valerie, illus. 2004. (Stepping Stones: A Chapter Book: Fantasy Ser.). 42p. (J). 11.65 (978-0-7569-0905-5(8)) Perfection Learning Corp.

Spooner, Meagan. Lark Ascending. 2014. (ENG.). 328p. (YA). 17.95 (978-0-7613-8867-8(2)) Lerner Publishing Group.

—Shadowlark. 2013. 327p. pap. 17.95 (978-1-4677-1664-2(2)); (ENG.). 336p. (YA). (gr. 7-12). 17.95 (978-0-7613-8866-1(4), Carolrhoda Lab™) Lerner Publishing Group.

—Skylark. 2012. (Skylark Trilogy Ser.). (ENG.). 344p. (YA). (gr. 7-12). 17.95 (978-0-7613-8865-4(6)) Lerner Publishing Group.

Spring, Manda. Emerald & the Magic of Raynon. 2004. 118p. pap. 19.95 (978-1-4137-3708-0(0)) America Star Bks.

St. Crow, Lili. Wayfarer. 2014. (Tales of Beauty & Madness Ser.). (ENG.). 352p. (YA). (gr. 7). pap. 9.99 (978-1-59514-620-5(2), Razorbill) Penguin Young Readers Group.

Stadelmann, Amy Marie. The Not-So Itty-Bitty Spiders. 2015. (Olive & Beatrix Ser.: 1). (ENG., Illus.). 80p. (J). (gr. k-2). pap. 4.99 (978-0-545-81480-5(4)) Scholastic, Inc.

—The Super-Smelly Moldy Blob. Stadelmann, Amy Marie, illus. 2016. (Olive & Beatrix Ser.: 2). (ENG., Illus.). 80p. (J). (gr. k-2). 15.99 (978-0-545-81485-0(5)) Scholastic, Inc.

Stainton, Sue. Christmas Magic. Melhuish, Eva, illus. 2007. 32p. (J). (gr. -1-1). lib. bdg. 16.89 (978-0-06-078572-7(1), Tegen, Katherine Bks) HarperCollins Pubs.

Stan, Adrianna. The Letters. 2012. 24p. pap. (978-1-4602-0045-2(4)) FriesenPress.

Stanek, Robert, pseud. In the Service of Dragons III: Keeper Martin's Tales, Book 7. 2005. (Keeper Martin's Tales Ser.). (Illus.). 240p. (J). (gr. 4-7). per. 14.00 (978-1-57545-093-3(3)) RP Media.

—In the Service of Dragons IV: Keeper Martin's Tales, Book 8. 2005. (Keeper Martin's Tales Ser.). (ENG., Illus.). 240p. (YA). (gr. 8-12). per. 14.00 (978-1-57545-094-0(1)) RP Media.

—Journey Beyond the Beyond. 2007. (ENG.). 156p. (J). per. 14.00 (978-1-57545-132-9(8)) RP Media.

—The Kingdoms & the Elves of the Reaches. Stanek, Robert, illus. alt. gif. ed. 2004. (Illus.). 176p. (YA). pap. 10.99 (978-1-57545-501-3(3), Reagent Pr. Echo) RP Media.

—The Kingdoms & the Elves of the Reaches: Keeper Martin's Tales, Book 1. deluxe ed. 2005. (Keeper Martin's Tales Ser.: Bk. 1). (Illus.). 240p. (J). pap. 14.00 (978-1-57545-059-9(3)) RP Media.

—The Kingdoms & the Elves of the Reaches: Signature, Keeper Martin's Tales, Bk. 1. 2007. (Illus.). 240p. (YA). 35.00 (978-1-57545-128-2(X)) RP Media.

—The Kingdoms & the Elves of the Reaches II. Stanek, Robert, illus. alt. gif. ed. 2004. (ENG., Illus.). 180p. (YA). pap. 10.99 (978-1-57545-502-0(1), Reagent Pr. Echo) RP Media.

—The Kingdoms & the Elves of the Reaches II: Keeper Martin's Tales, Book 2. deluxe ed. 2005. (Keeper Martin's Tales Ser.: Bk. 2). (Illus.). 240p. (J). pap. 14.00 (978-1-57545-060-5(7)) RP Media.

—The Kingdoms & the Elves of the Reaches Ii (Reader's Choice Edition, Keeper Martin's Tales Book 2) 2008. (Illus.). 244p. pap. 15.95 (978-1-57545-197-8(2)) RP Media.

—The Kingdoms & the Elves of the Reaches III. Stanek, Robert, illus. alt. gif. ed. 2004. (ENG., Illus.). 172p. (YA). pap. 10.99 (978-1-57545-503-7(X), Reagent Pr. Echo) RP Media.

—The Kingdoms & the Elves of the Reaches III: Keeper Martin's Tales, Book 3. deluxe ed. 2005. (Keeper Martin's Tales Ser.: Vol. 3). (Illus.). 240p. (J). pap. 14.00 (978-1-57545-063-6(1)) RP Media.

—The Kingdoms & the Elves of the Reaches Iii (Reader's Choice Edition, Keeper Martin's Tales Book 3) 2008. (Illus.). 244p. pap. 15.95 (978-1-57545-198-5(0)) RP Media.

—The Kingdoms & the Elves of the Reaches Iv. 2008. (Illus.). 244p. 35.00 (978-1-57545-131-2(X)) RP Media.

—The Kingdoms & the Elves of the Reaches IV. Stanek, Robert, illus. alt. gif. ed. 2005. (Illus.). 172p. (YA). pap. 10.99 (978-1-57545-504-4(8), Reagent Pr. Echo) RP Media.

—The Kingdoms & the Elves of the Reaches IV: Keeper Martin's Tales, Book 4. deluxe ed. 2005. (Keeper Martin's Tales Ser.: Vol. 4). (Illus.). 240p. (YA). pap. 14.00 (978-1-57545-065-0(8)) RP Media.

—The Kingdoms & the Elves of the Reaches Iv (Reader's Choice Edition, Keeper Martin's Tales Book 4) 2008. (Illus.). 244p. pap. 15.95 (978-1-57545-199-2(9)) RP Media.

—The Kingdoms & the Elves of the Reaches (Reader's Choice Edition, Keeper Martin's Tales Book 1) 2008. (Illus.). 240p. pap. 15.95 (978-1-57545-196-1(4)) RP Media.

Stanfield, Michael. Bucky & Becky - the Magic of Wigglepoo Mountain. 2009. 144p. pap. 14.96 (978-0-557-02614-2(8)) Lulu Pr., Inc.

Staniszewski, Anna. My Epic Fairy Tale Fail. 2013. (My Very Unfairy Tale Life Ser.: 2). (ENG.). 224p. (J). (gr. 4-7). pap. 6.99 (978-1-4022-7930-0(2), 9781402279300, Sourcebooks Jabberwocky) Sourcebooks, Inc.

—My Sort of Fairy Tale Ending. 2013. (My Very Unfairy Tale Life Ser.: 3). (ENG.). 224p. (J). (gr. 4-7). pap. 6.99 (978-1-4022-7933-1(7), Sourcebooks Jabberwocky) Sourcebooks, Inc.

Stanley, Diane. The Cup & the Crown. (Silver Bowl Ser.: 2). (ENG.). (J). (gr. 3-7). 2013. 368p. pap. 6.99 (978-0-06-196323-0(2)) 2012. 352p. 16.99 (978-0-06-196321-6(6)) HarperCollins Pubs.

—The Princess of Cortova. (J). 2015. (Silver Bowl Ser.: 3). (ENG.). 336p. (gr. 3-7). pap. 6.99 (978-0-06-204732-8(9)) 2013. 311p. lib. bdg. (978-0-06-204731-1(0)) HarperCollins Pubs.

—The Silver Bowl. (Silver Bowl Ser.: 1). (ENG.). (J). (gr. 5). 2012. 336p. pap. 6.99 (978-0-06-157546-4(1)) 2011. 320p. 16.99 (978-0-06-157543-3(7)) HarperCollins Pubs.

Stanley, Pauline. The Children & the Witches Magic. 2010. (Illus.). 48p. pap. 10.49 (978-1-4490-9544-4(5)) AuthorHouse.

Stapleton, Rhonda. Stupid Cupid. 2009. (ENG.). 272p. (YA). (gr. 7-18). pap. 9.99 (978-1-4169-7464-2(4), Simon Pulse) Simon Pulse.

Star Wars Staff, et al. Renegade. 2009. (Star Wars: Rebel For Ser.: 3). (ENG.). 176p. (J). (gr. 3-7). pap. 6.99 (978-0-545-11211-6(7)) Scholastic, Inc.

Starkey, R. Hawk. Mysterious Magical Circus Family Kids: The Chocolate Cake Turkey Lip Crumb Trail Mystery Adventure. 2008. 192p. pap. 13.95 (978-1-4327-3096-3(7)) Outskirts Pr., Inc.

Steig, William. Sylvester & the Magic Pebble. Steig, William, illus. 2012. (ENG., Illus.). 32p. (J). (gr. -1-2). pap. 9.99 (978-1-4424-3560-5(7), Little Simon) Little Simon.

—Sylvester & the Magic Pebble. Steig, William, illus. 2005. (ENG., Illus.). 42p. (J). (gr. -1-3). 17.99 (978-1-4169-0206-5(6), Simon & Schuster Bks. For Young Readers) Simon & Schuster Bks. For Young Readers.

—Sylvester & the Magic Pebble. Steig, William, illus. 2006. (Stories to Go! Ser.). (Illus.). 32p. (J). (gr. -1-3). 4.99 (978-1-4169-1857-8(4), Simon & Schuster/Paula Wiseman Bks.) Simon & Schuster/Paula Wiseman Bks.

Stein, A. K. EZEKIEL MAYHILL & the Crystal of God. 2007. 196p. pap. 16.96 (978-1-4303-2540-6(2)) Lulu Pr., Inc.

Stein, Mathilde. Brave Ben. Van Hout, Mies, illus. 2006. (ENG.). 32p. (J). (gr. 2-6). 15.95 (978-1-932425-64-2(0), Lemniscaat) Boyds Mills Pr.

Stein, Uriel Von. Gretta's & Graci's Bright, Bright, Moonlit Night. 2011. 24p. pap. 12.79 (978-1-4634-0225-9(2)) AuthorHouse.

Stephane, Nelly. Roland. François, André, illus. 2016. (ENG.). 36p. (J). (gr. -1-3). 17.95 (978-1-59270-204-6(X)) Enchanted Lion Bks., LLC.

Stephens, Helen. Witchety Sticks & the Magic Buttons. Stephens, Helen, illus. 2010. (ENG., Illus.). 32p. (J). (gr. -1-k). pap. 8.99 (978-1-4169-1107-4(3), Simon & Schuster Children's) Simon & Schuster, Ltd. GBR. Dist: Simon & Schuster, Inc.

Stephens, John. The Black Reckoning. 2015. (Books of Beginning Ser.). (ENG.). 432p. (J). (gr. 3-7). 17.99 (978-0-375-86872-6(0), Knopf Bks. for Young Readers) Random Hse. Children's Bks.

—The Emerald Atlas. (Books of Beginning Ser.). (ENG.). (J). (gr. 3-7). 2012. 448p. 7.99 (978-0-375-87271-6(X), Yearling) 2011. 432p. 17.99 (978-0-375-86870-2(4), Knopf Bks. for Young Readers) Random Hse. Children's Bks.

—The Emerald Atlas. l.t. ed. 2012. (Books of Beginning Ser.). (ENG.). 548p. (J). (gr. 4-7). 23.99 (978-1-4104-4234-5(9)) Thorndike Pr.

—The Fire Chronicle. 2012. (Illus.). 437p. (J). (978-0-449-81015-6(1)) Knopf, Alfred A. Inc.

—The Fire Chronicle. (Books of Beginning Ser.). (ENG.). 448p. (J). (gr. 3-7). 2013. 7.99 (978-0-375-87272-3(8), Yearling) 2012. (Illus.). 17.99 (978-0-375-86871-9(2), Knopf Bks. for Young Readers) Random Hse. Children's Bks.

Steps To Literacy Staff, compiled by. Eragon/Eldest Box Set: Variety Pack (2 Titles, 1 Each) 2010. (ENG.). (J). pap. 23.85 (978-1-61267-194-9(2)) Steps To Literacy, LLC.

Stevens, Janet & Crummel, Susan Stevens. Jackalope. 2003. (ENG., Illus.). 56p. (J). (gr. -1-3). 17.00 (978-0-15-216736-3(6)) Houghton Mifflin Harcourt Publishing Co.

Stevermer, Caroline. Magic below Stairs. 2011. (ENG.). 208p. (J). (gr. 3-7). 6.99 (978-0-14-241871-0(4), Puffin Books) Penguin Young Readers Group.

Stewart, Martin. Riverkeep. 2017. lib. bdg. 22.10 **(978-0-606-40100-5(8))** Turtleback Bks.

Stewart, Shawna. Amazing Tails of Zomber Doodles & Buttons, 1 vol. 2010. 30p. pap. 24.95 (978-1-4489-7913-4(7)) PublishAmerica, Inc.

Stewart, Trenton Lee. The Secret Keepers. Sudyka, Diana, illus. 2017. (ENG.). 512p. (J). (gr. 3-7). pap. 8.99 **(978-0-316-38954-9(4))** Little, Brown Bks. for Young Readers.

—The Secret Keepers. 2016. (ENG., Illus.). 512p. (J). (gr. 3-7). 18.99 (978-0-316-38955-6(2)) Little, Brown Bks. for Young Readers.

—The Secret Keepers. 2017. (J). lib. bdg. 19.65 **(978-0-606-40551-5(8))** Turtleback Bks.

Stiefvater, Maggie. Blue Lily, Lily Blue. (Raven Cycle Ser.: 3). (ENG.). 400p. (J). (gr. 9). 2015. pap. 9.99 (978-0-545-42497-4(6)) 2014. 18.99 (978-0-545-42496-7(8)) Scholastic, Inc. (Scholastic Pr.).

—Blue Lily, Lily Blue. 2015. (Raven Cycle Ser.: 3). lib. bdg. 20.85 (978-0-606-38004-1(3)) Turtleback Bks.

—The Dream Thieves. (Raven Cycle Ser.: 2). (ENG.). 448p. (J). (gr. 9). 2014. pap. 9.99 (978-0-545-42495-0(X), Scholastic Paperbacks) 2013. 18.99 (978-0-545-42494-3(1), Scholastic Pr.) Scholastic, Inc.

—The Dream Thieves. 2014. (Raven Cycle Ser.: 2). lib. bdg. 20.85 (978-0-606-36029-6(8)) Turtleback Bks.

—Lament: The Faerie Queen's Deception. 2008. (Lament Novel Ser.: 1). (ENG., Illus.). 336p. (YA). (gr. 8-18). pap. 9.95 (978-0-7387-1370-0(8), 1286181, Flux) North Star Editions.

—The Raven Boys. 2015. 50.87 (978-1-320-56337-6(6)) Blurb, Inc.

—The Raven Boys. 2013. (Raven Cycle Ser.: 1). 20.00 (978-1-62765-119-6(5)) Perfection Learning Corp.

—The Raven Boys. (Raven Cycle Ser.: 1). (ENG.). 416p. (J). (gr. 9). 2013. pap. 10.99 (978-0-545-42493-6(3), Scholastic Paperbacks) 2012. 18.99 (978-0-545-42492-9(5), Scholastic Pr.) 2012. E-Book (978-0-545-46979-1(1)) Scholastic, Inc.

—The Raven Boys. 2016. (CHI.). 448p. (YA). (gr. 7). pap. (978-986-361-180-6(8)) Sitak Group Holding, Ltd.

—The Raven Boys. 2013. (Raven Cycle Ser.: 1). lib. bdg. 20.85 (978-0-606-32028-3(8), Turtleback) Turtleback Bks.

Stiefvater, Maggie. The Raven King. 2016. (Raven Cycle Ser.: 4). (ENG.). 400p. (YA). (gr. 9). 18.99 (978-0-545-42498-1(4)); 439p. (J). **(978-0-605-90184-1(8))** Scholastic, Inc. (Scholastic Pr.).

Stiefvater, Maggie & Pearce, Jackson. Pip Bartlett's Guide to Magical Creatures. 2015. (Pip Bartlett Ser.: 1). (ENG.). 192p. (J). (gr. 3-7). 16.99 (978-0-545-70926-2(1), Scholastic Pr.) Scholastic, Inc.

Stilton, Geronimo. The Ship of Secrets (Geronimo Stilton & the Kingdom of Fantasy #10) 2017. (Geronimo Stilton & the Kingdom of Fantasy Ser.: 10). (ENG.). 320p. (J). (gr. 2-5). 14.99 **(978-1-338-08880-9(7)**, Scholastic Paperbacks) Scholastic, Inc.

Stilton, Geronimo & Dami, Elisabetta. The Phoenix of Destiny. 2015. (Geronimo Stilton & the Kingdom of Fantasy: Special Edition Ser.). (ENG.). 592p. (J). (gr. 2-5). 19.99 (978-0-545-82907-6(0)) Scholastic, Inc.

Stilton, Thea. The Journey to Atlantis. 2012. (Thea Stilton Special Edition Ser.). (ENG.). 320p. (J). (gr. 2-5). 14.99 (978-0-545-44020-2(3), Scholastic Paperbacks) Scholastic, Inc.

—The Treasure of the Sea. 5th ed. 2016. (Thea Stilton Special Edition Ser.: 5). (ENG.). 320p. (J). (gr. 2-5). 14.99 (978-1-338-03290-1(9), Scholastic Paperbacks) Scholastic, Inc.

Stine, Faye. The Magic Forest: The Magic of Childhood. 2009. 117p. (J). pap. 10.95 (978-1-4327-3617-0(5)) Outskirts Pr., Inc.

Stine, Megan, et al. Now You See Him, Now You Don't. 2004. (ENG., Illus.). 112p. (978-0-00-714446-4(6), HarperCollins Children's Bks.) HarperCollins Pubs. Ltd.

Stine, R. L. A Midsummer Night's Scream. 2013. (ENG.). 256p. (YA). (gr. 7). 17.99 (978-1-250-02434-3(X), 9781250024343) Feiwel & Friends.

—A Midsummer Night's Scream. 2014. (ENG.). 256p. (YA). (gr. 7-12). pap. 10.99 (978-1-250-04434-1(0), 9781250044341) Square Fish.

Stirling, Tricia. When My Heart Was Wicked. 2015. (ENG.). 192p. (J). (gr. 9). 17.99 (978-0-545-69573-2(2), Scholastic Pr.) Scholastic, Inc.

Stockham, Jess, illus. Beauty & the Beast. 2007. (Flip-Up Fairy Tales Ser.). (ENG.). 24p. (J). (gr. 2-2). (978-1-84643-114-2(X)) Child's Play International Ltd.

—The Frog Prince. 2007. (Flip-Up Fairy Tales Ser.). (ENG.). 24p. (J). audio compact disk (978-1-84643-143-2(3)) Child's Play International Ltd.

Stockham, Jess, et al, illus. The Frog Prince. 2007. (Flip-Up Fairy Tales Ser.). (ENG.). 24p. (J). (gr. 2-2). pap. (978-1-84643-077-0(1)) Child's Play International Ltd.

Stockton, Frank Richard. The Bee-Man of Orn & Other Fanciful Tales. 2007. (ENG.). 140p. pap. 18.99 (978-1-4264-5788-3(X)); 154p. pap. 21.99 (978-1-4264-5848-4(7)) Creative Media Partners, LLC.

—Ting-a-Ling Tales. 2008. 88p. pap. 8.95 (978-1-60664-056-2(9)) Aegypan.

Stolarz, Laurie Faria. Silver Is for Secrets. 2005. (Stolarz Ser.: 3). (ENG.). 288p. (YA). pap. 11.99 (978-0-7387-0631-3(0), Flux) North Star Editions.

—White Is for Magic. Karre, Andrew, ed. 2004. (Stolarz Ser.: 2). (ENG.). 312p. (YA). pap. 11.99 (978-0-7387-0443-2(1), Flux) North Star Editions.

Stone, Forrest. Loki & the Magic Hammer: A Norse Myth. 2006. (J). pap. (978-1-4108-6178-8(3)) Benchmark Education Co.

Stone, Kelsey. The Predahil Chronicles. 2005. (YA). per. 6.49 (978-1-59196-995-2(6)) Instant Pub.

Stones, Yvonne. Olivia's Magical Moment. 2010. 36p. pap. 16.99 (978-1-4490-8045-7(6)) AuthorHouse.

Storer, June. Kip, Brenda & Emong's Adventure. 2013. 164p. pap. (978-0-9923603-1-3(5)) BWM Bks.

Storm, Jeff. Petrified World, Determine Your Destiny No. 1: You Are the Hero of This Book! Chan, Harvey, illus. 2nd ed. 2014. 160p. pap. (978-1-77143-159-0(8), CCB Publishing) CCB Publishing.

Storr, Catherine. Marianne Dreams. 2014. (ENG., Illus.). 320p. pap. 9.95 (978-0-571-31327-3(2)) Faber & Faber, Inc.

Straffi, Iginio. Winx Club: Magic Collection. 2014. (ENG.). 832p. (J). pap. 19.99 (978-1-4215-7729-6(1)) Viz Media.

Strand, Kai. The Wishing Well. 2012. 104p. 19.95 (978-1-61633-301-0(4)); pap. 9.95 (978-1-61633-302-7(2)) Guardian Angel Publishing, Inc.

Strange, Jason. Faceless Friend, 1 vol. Parks, Phil, illus. 2011. (Jason Strange Ser.). (ENG.). 72p. (gr. 2-3). pap. 6.25 (978-1-4342-3431-5(2)); lib. bdg. 25.32 (978-1-4342-3232-8(8)) Stone Arch Bks.

—Strays, 1 vol. Evergreen, Nelson & Kendall, Bradford, illus. 2012. (Jason Strange Ser.). (ENG.). 72p. (gr. 2-3). pap. 6.25 (978-1-4342-3883-2(0)); lib. bdg. 25.32 (978-1-4342-3295-3(6)) Stone Arch Bks.

Strega Nona. 2005. (J). (978-1-59564-834-1(8)) Steps To Literacy, LLC.

Strickland, Brad. The House Where Nobody Lived. 2006. (Lewis Barnavelt Ser.). (ENG.). 176p. (J). (gr. 3-7). 16.99 (978-0-8037-3148-6(5), Dial Bks) Penguin Young Readers Group.

Strings Magazine Staff. The Wizard's Den: Spellbinding Stories of Magic & Magicians. Haining, Peter, ed. 2003. (ENG., Illus.). 320p. (J). (gr. 3-7). 22.95 (978-0-285-63628-6(6)) Souvenir Pr. Ltd. GBR. Dist: Independent Pubs. Group.

Stroud, Jonathan. The Amulet of Samarkand, Bk. 1. 2003. (Bartimaeus Novel Ser.). (ENG., Illus.). 464p. (J). (gr. 5-9). 17.99 (978-0-7868-1859-4(X)) Disney Publishing Worldwide.

—Bartimaeus, 3 vols., Set. 2010. (ENG.). 1552p. (J). (gr. 5-6). pap. 24.99 (978-1-4231-3682-8(9)) Disney Pr.

—The Golem's Eye, Bk. 2. 2nd rev. ed. 2006. (Bartimaeus Novel Ser.). (ENG.). 592p. (J). (gr. 5-9). reprint ed. per. 8.99 (978-0-7868-3654-3(7)) Disney Publishing Worldwide.

Studio Mouse Staff. Kindness Counts. rev. ed. 2004. (Kindness Counts Ser.). (Illus.). 36p. (J). (gr. -1-3). 12.99 (978-1-59069-364-3(7), 1A500) Studio Mouse LLC.

Stumpe, Jennifer. Aunt Jo Jo's Magical Gifts: Amazing Underwater Adventure. 2011. 32p. (gr. 1-2). pap. 14.95 (978-1-4567-3160-1(2)) AuthorHouse.

—Aunt Jo Jo's Magical Gifts: Ethan's Great African Journey. 2012. 32p. pap. 17.95 (978-1-4772-9097-2(4)) AuthorHouse.

Sturm, Ilana. The 13th Moon. 2013. 92p. pap. (978-1-936922-61-1(4)) Roxby Media Ltd.

Sturm, James, et al. Hocus Focus. 2017. (Adventures in Cartooning Ser.). (ENG., Illus.). 40p. (J). 14.99 (978-1-59643-654-1(9), 9781596436541, First Second Bks.) Roaring Brook Pr.

Stutzman, D. J. The Promise Ring. 2007. (J). pap. 9.00 (978-0-8059-7365-5(6)) Dorrance Publishing Co., Inc.

Suarez, Sergio Lopez. Huakala! a los Miedos. Suarez, Sergio Lopez, illus. 2003. (SPA., Illus.). 32p. (J). (gr. k-3). 9.95 (978-968-19-0556-9(3)) Aguilar, Altea, Taurus, Alfaguara, S.A. de C.V MEX. Dist: Santillana USA Publishing Co., Inc.

Suhay, Lisa. Our Fantasy Island: An Interactive Book. Hundley, Sam, illus. 2006. 30p. (J). pap. 8.00 (978-0-9766628-0-8(9)) Fantasy Island Pr.

Suits, Barbara Bradford. The Hidden Treasure. 2013. 48p. pap. 7.95 (978-1-61286-199-9(7)) Avid Readers Publishing Group.

Sullivan, Laura L. Delusion. 2014. (ENG.). 352p. (YA). (gr. 7). pap. 18.99 (978-0-544-10478-5(1)) Houghton Mifflin Harcourt Publishing Co.

Summerill, Erin. Ever the Hunted. 2016. (Clash of Kingdoms Novel Ser.). (ENG.). 400p. (YA). (gr. 7). 17.99 (978-0-544-66445-6(0), HMH Books For Young Readers) Houghton Mifflin Harcourt Publishing Co.

Summers, Gillian. The Goblin's Curse: The Scions of Shadow Trilogy, Book 3. 2012. (Faire Folk Saga Ser.: 6). (ENG.). 312p. (YA). pap. 9.95 (978-0-7387-1572-8(7), Flux) North Star Editions.

—Into the Wildewood. 2008. (Faire Folk Saga Ser.: 2). (ENG.). 312p. (YA). (gr. 7-14). pap. 9.95 (978-0-7387-1332-8(5), Flux) North Star Editions.

—The Quicksilver Faire: The Scions of Shadow Trilogy, Book 2. 2011. (Faire Folk Saga Ser.: 5). (ENG.). 336p. (YA). pap. 9.95 (978-0-7387-1571-1(9), Flux) North Star Editions.

—Shadows of the Redwood Bk. 1, Bk. 1. 2010. (Faire Folk Saga Ser.: 4). (ENG.). 336p. (YA). (gr. 7-18). pap. 9.95 (978-0-7387-1552-0(2), Flux) North Star Editions.

Sussman, Elissa. Stray. 2014. (Stray Ser.: 1). (ENG., Illus.). 384p. (YA). (gr. 8). 17.99 (978-0-06-227455-7(4), Greenwillow Bks.) HarperCollins Pubs.

Sutcliffe, Charlie. Zubert. 2014. (ENG., Illus.). 32p. (J). (gr. -1-3). 18.95 (978-1-84976-121-5(3)) Tate Publishing, Ltd. GBR. Dist: Abrams, Inc.

Sutherland, David, et al. Siriol Llywelyn A'r Salwch Chwyrlio Erchyll. Roberts, David, illus. 2005. (WEL.). 48p. pap. (978-1-85596-679-6(4)) Dref Wen.

Sutherland, Tui T. So This Is How It Ends. 2006. (Avatars Ser.: Bk. 1). 353p. (YA). (gr. 7-12). 16.99 (978-0-06-075024-4(3), Eos); lib. bdg. 17.89 (978-0-06-075028-2(6)) HarperCollins Pubs.

Sutherland, Tui T. & Sutherland, Kari H. The Menagerie. (Menagerie Ser.: 3). (J). (gr. 3-7). 2016. 368p. pap. 6.99 (978-0-06-078069-2(X)) 2015. (ENG.). 368p. 16.99 (978-0-06-078067-8(3)) 2013. (ENG., Illus.). 288p. 16.99 (978-0-06-078064-7(9)) HarperCollins Pubs.

Sutliff, Jamie. The Elves of Owl's Head Mountain. Blumberg, Christine A., ed. Evens, Kevin C., illus. 2007. 276p. pap. 10.95 (978-0-9712867-8-8(7)) Cold River Pubns.

—The Elves of Owl's Head Mountain. Blumberg, Christine A., ed. Evans, Kevin, illus. 2007. 280p. (gr. 8-12). 26.95 (978-0-9712867-7-1(9)) Cold River Pubns.

—The Land of Nen-Us-Yok. Blumberg, Christine A., ed. Evans, Kevin C., illus. 2007. 256p. pap. 10.95 (978-0-9712867-4-0(4)); 26.95 (978-0-9712867-6-4(0)) Cold River Pubns.

Sutton, Pamelina Jean'e. Bill Bill the Burger Boy. 2012. 24p. pap. 12.00 (978-1-61286-108-1(3)) Avid Readers Publishing Group.

Swanson, Stan. The Misadventures of Hobart Hucklebuck. 2007. (J). 16.95 (978-0-9787925-3-4(X)); per. 9.95 (978-0-9787925-2-7(1)) Stony Meadow Publishing.

Swendson, Shanna. Rebel Mechanics. 2015. (ENG.). 320p. (YA). (gr. 7). 18.99 (978-0-374-30009-8(7), 9780374300098, Farrar, Straus & Giroux (BYR)) Farrar, Straus & Giroux.

Swinney, Kay. Marty Moose & the Mystical Reunion, 1 vol. 2009. 73p. pap. 19.95 (978-1-61546-867-6(6)) America Star Bks.

Sykes, Tina . Elliot Makes a Friend. 2012. 26p. 24.95 (978-1-4626-5980-7(2)) America Star Bks.

Symes, Ruth. Bella Donna: Too Many Spells. Lindsay, Marion, illus. 2016. (ENG.). 192p. (J). (gr. 1-5). pap. 7.99 (978-1-63450-155-2(1), Sky Pony Pr.) Skyhorse Publishing Co., Inc.

Szpirglas, Jeff & Saint-Onge, Danielle. Messy Miranda, 1 vol. Whamond, Dave, illus. 2013. (Orca Echoes Ser.). (ENG.). 64p. (J). (gr. 2-3). pap. 6.95 (978-1-4598-0117-2(2)) Orca Bk. Pubs. USA.

Takahashi, Rumiko. Inuyasha, Vol. 44, Set. Takahashi, Rumiko, illus. 2003. (Inuyasha Ser.). (ENG., Illus.). 200p. (YA). pap. 39.98 (978-1-59116-235-3(1), Viz Comics) Viz Media.

The Tale of Jackie Berry. 2005. (J). per. 12.95 (978-0-9677047-5-3(8)) Marble Hse. Editions.

Tamura, Mitsuhisa & Fujita, Kazuhiro. BakéGyamon, Vol. 1. 2009. (ENG.). 200p. (J). pap. 7.99 (978-1-4215-1793-3(0)) Viz Media.

—BakéGyamon, Vol. 2. 2009. (ENG.). 200p. (J). pap. 7.99 (978-1-4215-1794-0(9)) Viz Media.

Tandi's World. 2006. (J). (978-0-9772634-0-0(1)) Hall, Monique P. Productions.

Tanguay, Dave. Come Together! Vaughns, Byron, illus. 2015. (Billy Batson & the Magic of Shazam! Ser.). (ENG.). 32p. (gr. 2-3). lib. bdg. 22.60 (978-1-4342-9744-0(6)) Stone Arch Bks.

—Deception Reception! Vaughns, Byron, illus. 2015. (Billy Batson & the Magic of Shazam! Ser.). (ENG.). 32p. (gr. 2-3). lib. bdg. 22.60 *(978-1-4342-9742-6(X))* Stone Arch Bks.
—Fire Fire Everywhere! Vaughns, Byron, illus. 2015. (Billy Batson & the Magic of Shazam! Ser.). (ENG.). 32p. (gr. 2-3). lib. bdg. 22.60 *(978-1-4342-9745-7(4))* Stone Arch Bks.
—The Legacy of Mr. Banjo! Vaughns, Byron, illus. 2015. (Billy Batson & the Magic of Shazam! Ser.). (ENG.). 32p. (gr. 2-3). lib. bdg. 22.60 *(978-1-4342-9746-4(2))* Stone Arch Bks.
—To Be King! DeStefano, Stephen, illus. 2015. (Billy Batson & the Magic of Shazam! Ser.). (ENG.). 32p. (gr. 2-3). lib. bdg. 22.60 *(978-1-4342-9657-3(1))* Stone Arch Bks.
Tanigawa, Nagaru. The Indignation of Haruhi Suzumiya. 2012. (Haruhi Suzumiya Ser.: 8). (ENG., Illus.). 224p. (YA). (gr. 10-17). 15.99 *(978-0-316-03900-0(4))*; pap. 18.00 *(978-0-316-03899-7(7))* Little, Brown Bks. for Young Readers.
Tanner, Matthew J. The Winds of Aragon. 2013. 40p. pap. 14.95 *(978-0-9885253-0-6(5))* Tanner, Matt J.
Tapia, Rayner. The Adventures of Tom Mcguire: Morkann's Revenge. 2010. (Illus.). 156p. pap. 11.99 *(978-1-4490-8183-6(5))* AuthorHouse.
Taranta, Mary. Shimmer & Burn. 2017. (YA). pap. ***(978-1-4814-7200-5(3)***, McElderry, Margaret K. Bks.) McElderry, Margaret K. Bks.
Tarnowska, Wafa'. The Seven Wise Princesses: A Medieval Persian Epic. Nilesh, Misty, illus. 2008. (ENG.). 96p. (J). (gr. 5-9). 19.99 *(978-1-84686-250-2(7))* Barefoot Bks., Inc.
Tarver, Monroe S. Tales from the Mapmaker: Imagia & the Magic Pearls. 2015. (ENG.). 100p. (J). (gr. k-4). pap. 6.99 *(978-0-9723936-5-2(X))* Wizarding World Pr.
Tarver, S., 1st. Imaga & the Magic Pearls 2nd l.t. ed. 2003. (Illus.). 20p. (J). 6.99 *(978-0-9743568-0-8(8))* Tarver, Monroe.
Tashjian, Janet. Sticker Girl. Wilmink, Inga, illus. 2016. (Sticker Girl Ser.). (ENG.). 176p. (J). 13.99 *(978-1-62779-335-3(6)*, 9781627793353, Holt, Henry & Co. Bks. For Young Readers) Holt, Henry & Co.
Tashlikowich, Natasha. The Secret of the Seven Stones. 2009. 117p. pap. 18.97 *(978-0-557-03747-6(6))* Lulu Pr., Inc.
Tate, Bernice & Andy. Funspell. 2009. 20p. pap. 14.95 *(978-1-4343-7103-4(4))* AuthorHouse.
Tatulli, Mark. Desmond Pucket Makes Monster Magic. (ENG.). 240p. (J). 2015. pap. 9.99 *(978-1-4494-7139-2(0))* 2013. (Desmond Pucket Ser.: 1). 13.99 *(978-1-4494-3548-6(3))* Andrews McMeel Publishing.
Tawa, Renee. Tink's Magical Day. 2011. (Illus.). (J). *(978-1-4508-1707-3(6))* Publications International, Ltd.
Taylor, Dereen. The Dragon's Magic Wish. Hutchinson, Tim, illus. 2012. (ENG.). 12p. (J). (gr. 1-6). 16.99 *(978-1-84322-856-1(4))* Anness Publishing GBR. Dist: National Bk. Network.
Taylor, G. P. Shadowmancer: What Can Stand Against an Ancient Evil... 2004. (ENG., Illus.). 275p. 16.99 *(978-1-59185-613-9(2)*, Charisma Hse.) Charisma Media.
—The Shadowmancer Returns: The Curse of Salamander Street. 2008. (ENG.). 256p. (gr. 7-12). pap. 17.99 *(978-1-59979-084-8(X)*, Realms) Charisma Media.
—The Shadowmancer Returns: The Curse of Salamander Street. 2007. (Shadowmancer; 04 Ser.). 240p. (J). *(978-1-4287-4670-1(6)*, Putnam Juvenile) Penguin Publishing Group.
Taylor, Phillip J. Brian, His Granddad & the Cup of Ages. 2012. 310p. pap. *(978-1-78003-422-5(9))* Pen Pr. Pubs., Ltd.
Taylor, Roy. Matilda's Magic Wand: Dreamland Adventure. 2008. 36p. (J). pap. 9.00 *(978-0-8059-7716-5(3))* Dorrance Publishing Co., Inc.
Taylor, Terry. Tim the Young Magician: Tim Discovers Magic. 2005. 48p. pap. 16.95 *(978-1-4137-6023-1(6))* America Star Bks.
Tea, Michelle. Mermaid in Chelsea Creek. Polan, Jason, illus. 2013. (ENG.). 240p. (gr. 5-11). 19.95 *(978-1-938073-36-6(3))* McSweeney's Publishing.
Teitelbaum, Michael. Tale of Zuko. Spaziante, Patrick, illus. 2008. (Avatar Ser.). (ENG.). 96p. (J). (gr. 2-6). pap. 5.99 *(978-1-4169-4984-8(4)*, Simon Spotlight/Nickelodeon) Simon Spotlight/Nickelodeon.
Tennapel, Doug. Cardboard. 2012. lib. bdg. 24.50 *(978-0-606-26212-5(1)*, Turtleback) Turtleback Bks.
Tercio, Ricardo, illus. Jack & the Beanstalk: The Graphic Novel. 2008. (Graphic Spin Ser.). (ENG.). 40p. (gr. 1-3). 25.32 *(978-1-4342-0766-1(8)*, Graphic Revolve) Stone Arch Bks.
Tewee, Laqaixit. Winterbloom & the Magical Swan: Book 1 Discovery of the Moon Treasure. 2012. 68p. pap. 31.99 *(978-1-4653-9933-5(X))* Xlibris Corp.
Thame, Val. Witches in Deed. l.t. ed. 2007. 100p. per. *(978-1-905665-25-9(3))* Pollinger In Print.
Thomas, Beth, Jack & the Richmond Bubble. 2012. pap. 11.95 *(978-0-7414-7495-7(6))* Infinity Publishing.
Thomas, Gerry. The Umbrella Race. 2010. 25p. (J). pap. 25.95 *(978-1-4327-6006-9(8))* Outskirts Pr., Inc.
Thomas, Joyce Carol. Christmas & the Magic Pie Pan. Date not set. 32p. (J). lib. bdg. 15.89 *(978-0-06-025386-8(X)*, Cotler, Joanna Books) HarperCollins Pubs.
Thomas, Rhiannon. A Wicked Thing. (YA). (gr. 9). 2016. 368p. pap. 9.99 *(978-0-06-230354-7(6))* 2015. (ENG.). 352p. 17.99 *(978-0-06-230353-0(8))* HarperCollins Pubs. (HarperTeen).
Thomas, Scarlett. Dragon's Green. 2017. (Worldquake Ser.: 1). (ENG., Illus.). 384p. (J). (gr. 4-7). 17.99 ***(978-1-4814-9784-8(7)***, Simon & Schuster Bks. For Young Readers) Simon & Schuster Bks. For Young Readers.
—Dragon's Green. 2017. (J). pap. ***(978-1-4814-9785-5(5)***, Simon & Schuster Bks. For Young Readers) Simon & Schuster Bks. For Young Readers.
Thomas, Sherry. The Burning Sky. 2013. (Elemental Trilogy Ser.: 1). (ENG.). 480p. (YA). (gr. 9). 17.99 *(978-0-06-220729-6(6))* HarperCollins Pubs.
—The Perilous Sea. 2015. (Elemental Trilogy Ser.: 2). (ENG.). 448p. (YA). (gr. 9). pap. 9.99 *(978-0-06-220733-3(4))* HarperCollins Pubs.
Thomasian, Sara. Charlie's Magical Night. Harrington, David, illus. 2007. (J). per. 11.99 *(978-1-59879-381-9(0))* Lifevest Publishing, Inc.
Thompson, Colin. The Floods #2: School Plot. Scrambly, Crab, illus. 2008. (Floods Ser.). (J). (ENG.). 224p. 15.99 *(978-0-06-113861-4(4))*; 256p. lib. bdg. 16.89 *(978-0-06-113855-3(X))* HarperCollins Pubs.
—Good Neighbors. Scrambly, Crab, illus. 2008. (Floods Ser.: No. 1). 214p. (J). (gr. 3-7). 15.99 *(978-0-06-113196-7(2))* HarperCollins Pubs.
Thompson, Jan & Sharpe, Jaime. Amara's Magical Playhouse: The Adventure Begins. 2010. 108p. pap. 37.99 *(978-1-4520-8284-4(7))* AuthorHouse.
Thompson, Jill. Magic Trixie & the Dragon. Thompson, Jill, illus. 2009. (ENG., Illus.). 96p. (J). (gr. 3-7). pap. 7.99 *(978-0-06-117050-8(X))* HarperCollins Pubs.
Thompson, John M. & Schultz, George M. Just Imagine. Wodin, illus. 2006. 32p. (J). (gr. -1-3). 16.95 *(978-0-9740190-6-2(2))* Illumination Arts Publishing Co., Inc.
Thompson, Lauren. The Christmas Magic. Muth, Jon J., illus. 2009. (ENG.). 40p. (J). (gr. -1-3). 16.99 *(978-0-439-77497-0(7)*, Scholastic Pr.) Scholastic, Inc.
Thompson, Paul B. The Battle for the Brightstone: Book III of the Brightstone Saga. 2013. (Brightstone Saga Ser.). 176p. (J). 18.95 *(978-0-7660-3984-1(6))* Enslow Pubs., Inc.
—The Brightworking, Bk. 1. 2012. (Brightstone Saga Ser.). (Illus.). 160p. (J). (gr. 5-18). 18.95 *(978-0-7660-3950-6(1))* Enslow Pubs., Inc.
—The Brightworking: Book I of the Brightstone Saga. 2013. (Brightstone Saga Ser.). 160p. (J). (gr. 5-12). pap. 10.95 *(978-1-4644-0169-5(1))* Enslow Pubs., Inc.
—The Fortune-Teller: Book II of the Brightstone Saga. 2013. (Brightstone Saga Ser.). 160p. (J). (gr. 5-12). pap. 10.95 *(978-1-4644-0265-4(5))*; 18.95 *(978-0-7660-3983-4(8))* Enslow Pubs., Inc.
Thompson-Swift, Joseph. The Adventures of Primrose Perfect. 2011. 248p. pap. *(978-1-907652-88-2(4))* Grosvenor Hse. Publishing Ltd.
Thomson-Swift, Joe. The Monkeyboy & the Gruffits. 2011. (Illus.). 44p. pap. *(978-1-908105-63-9(1))* Grosvenor Hse. Publishing Ltd.
—The Twig People of Mossdown Woods. 2011. (Illus.). 36p. pap. *(978-1-908105-35-6(6))* Grosvenor Hse. Publishing Ltd.
Thong, Roseanne Greenfield. Noodle Magic. So, Meilo, illus. 2014. (ENG.). 32p. (J). (gr. -1-3). 17.99 *(978-0-545-52167-3(X))* Scholastic, Inc.
Thorne, Bella. Autumn Falls. 2014. (ENG.). 224p. (YA). (gr. 7). lib. bdg. 21.99 *(978-0-375-99161-5(1)*, Delacorte Pr.) Random Hse. Children's Bks.
—Autumn's Kiss. 2015. (ENG.). 240p. (YA). (gr. 7). 18.99 *(978-0-385-74435-5(8)*, Delacorte Pr.) Random Hse. Children's Bks.
—Autumn's Wish. (ENG.). 320p. (YA). (gr. 7). 2017. pap. 9.99 ***(978-0-385-74438-6(2)***, Ember) 2016. 18.99 *(978-0-385-74437-9(4)*, Delacorte Pr.) Random Hse. Children's Bks.
Thorpe, Kiki. Before the Bell. RH Disney Staff & Christy, Jana, illus. 2015. (Never Girls Ser.: 9). (ENG.). 128p. (J). (gr. 1-4). lib. bdg. 12.99 *(978-0-7364-8167-0(2)*, RH/Disney) Random Hse. Children's Bks.
—Before the Bell. RH Disney Staff, illus. 2015. (Never Girls Ser.: No. 9). (ENG.). 128p. (J). (gr. 1-4). 5.99 *(978-0-7364-3304-4(X)*, RH/Disney) Random Hse. Children's Bks.
—A Dandelion Wish. Christy, Jana, illus. 2013. (Stepping Stone Book Series: No. 3). (ENG.). 128p. (J). (gr. 1-4). 5.99 *(978-0-7364-2796-8(1)*, RH/Disney) Random Hse. Children's Bks.
—A Dandelion Wish. Christy, Jana, illus. 2013. (Never Girls Ser.: 3). lib. bdg. 16.00 *(978-0-606-32199-0(3)*, Turtleback) Turtleback Bks.
—A Fairy's Gift (Disney: the Never Girls) Christy, Jana, illus. 2017. (Never Girls Ser.). (ENG.). 224p. (J). (gr. 1-4). 7.99 ***(978-0-7364-3773-8(8)***, RH/Disney) Random Hse. Children's Bks.
—A Fairy's Gift (Disney: the Never Girls) RH Disney Staff, illus. 2015. (Never Girls Ser.). (ENG.). 224p. (J). (gr. 1-4). 14.99 *(978-0-7364-3278-8(7)*, RH/Disney) Random Hse. Children's Bks.
—Far from Shore. RH Disney Staff & Christy, Jana, illus. 2015. (Never Girls Ser.: 8). (ENG.). 128p. (J). (gr. 1-4). lib. bdg. 12.99 *(978-0-7364-8166-3(4)*, RH/Disney) Random Hse. Children's Bks.
—From the Mist. Christy, Jana, illus. 2013. (Stepping Stone Book Ser.: No. 4). (ENG.). 128p. (J). (gr. 1-4). 5.99 *(978-0-7364-2797-5(X)*, RH/Disney) Random Hse. Children's Bks.
—In a Blink. Christy, Jana & Random House Disney Staff, illus. 2013. (Never Girls Ser.: 1). (ENG.). 128p. (J). (gr. 1-4). 5.99 *(978-0-7364-2794-4(5)*, RH/Disney) Random Hse. Children's Bks.
—In a Blink. Christy, Jana, illus. 2013. (Never Girls Ser.: 1). lib. bdg. 16.00 *(978-0-606-26977-3(0)*, Turtleback) Turtleback Bks.
—Into the Waves. Christy, Jana, illus. 2016. (Never Girls Ser.: 11). (ENG.). 128p. (J). (gr. 1-4). 5.99 *(978-0-7364-3525-3(5)*, RH/Disney) Random Hse. Children's Bks.
—Into the Waves. 2016. (Never Girls Ser.: 11). lib. bdg. 16.00 *(978-0-606-38467-4(7))* Turtleback Bks.
—Never Girls #12: in the Game (Disney: the Never Girls) Christy, Jana, illus. 2016. (Never Girls Ser.: 12). (ENG.). 128p. (J). (gr. 1-4). 5.99 *(978-0-7364-3527-7(1)*, RH/Disney) Random Hse. Children's Bks.
—On the Trail. Christy, Jana, illus. 2015. (Never Girls Ser.: No. 10). (ENG.). 128p. (J). (gr. 1-4). 5.99 *(978-0-7364-3306-8(6)*, RH/Disney) Random Hse. Children's Bks.
—A Pinch of Magic. Christy, Jana, illus. 2014. (Never Girls Ser.: No. 7). (ENG.). 128p. (J). (gr. 1-4). 5.99 *(978-0-7364-3097-5(0)*, RH/Disney) Random Hse. Children's Bks.
—A Pinch of Magic. 2014. (Never Girls Ser.: 7). lib. bdg. 16.00 *(978-0-606-36008-1(5))* Turtleback Bks.
—The Space Between. Christy, Jana & Random House Disney Staff, illus. 2013. (Never Girls Ser.: 2). (ENG.). 128p. (J). (gr. 1-4). 5.99 *(978-0-7364-2795-1(3)*, RH/Disney) Random Hse. Children's Bks.
—The Space Between. Christy, Jana, illus. 2013. (Never Girls Ser.: 2). lib. bdg. 16.00 *(978-0-606-26974-2(6)*, Turtleback) Turtleback Bks.
—Wedding Wings. Christy, Jana, illus. 2014. (Stepping Stone Book Series: No. 5). (ENG.). 128p. (J). (gr. 1-4). 5.99 *(978-0-7364-3077-7(6)*, RH/Disney) Random Hse. Children's Bks.
—Wedding Wings. 2014. (Never Girls Ser.: 5). lib. bdg. 16.00 *(978-0-606-35544-5(8))* Turtleback Bks.
—The Woods Beyond. Christy, Jana, illus. 2014. (ENG.). 128p. (J). (gr. 1-4). (Never Girls Ser.: 6). lib. bdg. 12.99 *(978-0-7364-8148-9(6))*; (Stepping Stone Book Ser.: No. 6). 5.99 *(978-0-7364-3096-8(2))* Random Hse. Children's Bks. (RH/Disney).
—The Woods Beyond. Christy, Jana, illus. 2014. (Never Girls Ser.: 6). lib. bdg. 16.00 *(978-0-606-35545-2(6))* Turtleback Bks.
Thrasher, Amanda M. Mischief in the Mushroom Patch. 2010. 174p. pap. 10.50 *(978-1-60911-165-6(6)*, Strategic Bk. Publishing) Strategic Book Publishing & Rights Agency (SBPRA).
Tiernan, Cate. A Chalice of Wind - A Circle of Ashes - A Feather of Stone - A Necklace of Water. 2011. (Balefire Ser.). (ENG.). 976p. (YA). (gr. 7-18). 9.99 *(978-1-59514-411-9(0)*, Razorbill) Penguin Young Readers Group.
—Book of Shadows - The Coven - Blood Witch. 2010. (Sweep Ser.: 1). (ENG.). 592p. (YA). (gr. 7-18). 8.99 *(978-0-14-241717-1(3)*, Speak) Penguin Young Readers Group.
—Eternally Yours. 2013. (Immortal Beloved Ser.: 3). (ENG.). 464p. (YA). (gr. 7-17). pap. 10.00 *(978-0-316-03595-8(5)*, Poppy) Little, Brown Bks. for Young Readers.
—Immortal Beloved. (Immortal Beloved Ser.: 1). (ENG.). (YA). (gr. 7-17). 2012. 432p. pap. 9.99 *(978-0-316-03591-0(2))* 2010. 416p. 16.99 *(978-0-316-03592-7(0))* Little, Brown Bks. for Young Readers.
—Sweep Vol. 3: The Calling - Changeling - Strife, 3 vols. 2011. (Sweep Ser.: 3). (ENG.). 576p. (YA). (gr. 7-18). 9.99 *(978-0-14-241955-7(9)*, Speak) Penguin Young Readers Group.
Tiki Machine, LLC Staff, creator. Deus Libris: An Illustrated Collection. 2011. (Illus.). 58p. 19.99 *(978-0-615-49510-1(9))* Tiki Machine, LLC.
Tilley, Laura. The Magic of the Morning. 2011. 36p. pap. 17.49 *(978-1-4568-6451-4(3))* Xlibris Corp.
Tillis, Dionne. Willameana Whitney White & the Magical Butterfly. 2012. 24p. pap. 17.99 *(978-1-4685-7286-5(5))* AuthorHouse.
Tillworth, Mary. All Bottled up! (Shimmer & Shine) Laviosa, Mattia Francesco, illus. 2017. (Pictureback(R) Ser.). (ENG.). 16p. (J). (gr. -1-2). pap. 5.99 ***(978-1-5247-1718-6(5)***, Random Hse. Bks. for Young Readers) Random Hse. Children's Bks.
—Barbie in Princess Power. 2015. (Little Golden Book Ser.). (ENG., Illus.). 24p. (J). (-k). 4.99 *(978-0-553-50741-6(9)*, Golden Bks.) Random Hse. Children's Bks.
—Dora in Magic Land (Dora & Friends) Haskett, Dan & Goddard, Brenda, illus. 2016. (Little Golden Book Ser.). (ENG.). 24p. (J). (gr. -1-2). 4.99 *(978-0-553-53840-3(3)*, Golden Bks.) Random Hse. Children's Bks.
—A Fairytale Adventure (Dora the Explorer) Jackson, Mike, illus. 2014. (Pictureback(R) Ser.). (ENG.). 24p. (J). (gr. -1-2). 3.99 *(978-0-385-37443-9(7)*, Random Hse. Bks. for Young Readers) Random Hse. Children's Bks.
—Leah's Dream Dollhouse (Shimmer & Shine) Yum, Heekyoung, illus. 2016. (Pictureback(R) Ser.). (ENG.). 16p. (J). (gr. -1-2). 4.99 *(978-1-101-93249-0(X)*, Random Hse. Bks. for Young Readers) Random Hse. Children's Bks.
—Mermaid Treasure Hunt (Dora & Friends) Aikins, David, illus. 2015. (Pictureback(R) Ser.). (ENG.). 24p. (J). (gr. -1-2). 3.99 *(978-0-553-51076-8(2)*, Random Hse. Bks. for Young Readers) Random Hse. Children's Bks.
—Nickelodeon 5-Minute Stories Collection. Random House, illus. 2016. (5-Minute Story Collection). (ENG.). 160p. (J). (gr. -1-2). 12.99 *(978-0-399-55314-1(2)*, Random Hse. Bks. for Young Readers) Random Hse. Children's Bks.
—Spark Bug Rescue! (Blaze & the Monster Machines) Aikins, Dave, illus. 2017. (Pictureback(R) Ser.). (ENG.). 16p. (J). (gr. -1-2). pap. 5.99 ***(978-1-5247-1717-9(7)***, Random Hse. Bks. for Young Readers) Random Hse. Children's Bks.
Tillworth, Mary. The Sweetest Cupcake (Shimmer & Shine) Cartobaleno, illus. 2016. (Pictureback(R) Ser.). (ENG.). 16p. (J). (gr. -1-2). 4.99 *(978-0-553-52201-3(9)*, Random Hse. Bks. for Young Readers) Random Hse. Children's Bks.
Timroth, Stephen. Dreamhawk. 2009. 24p. pap. 12.00 *(978-1-60860-501-9(9)*, Strategic Bk. Publishing) Strategic Book Publishing & Rights Agency (SBPRA).
Tobin, Irene. The Tidy Bunch. 2010. (Illus.). 58p. pap. *(978-1-84748-666-0(5))* Athena Pr.
Toby Forward Staff. Fireborn. 2013. (Dragonborn Ser.: 2). (ENG.). 432p. (YA). (gr. 5-6). 16.99 *(978-1-59990-889-2(1)*, 9781599908892, Bloomsbury USA Childrens) Bloomsbury Publishing USA.
Tomlinson, Heather. The Swan Maiden. 2008. (ENG.). 320p. (YA). (gr. 7-12). pap. 22.99 *(978-0-312-38447-0(5)*, 9780312384470) Square Fish.
Tooth, Lucy. Star the Tooth Fairy from Treasure Cloud Shares Secrets with You! 2010. 36p. 16.95 *(978-0-557-37985-9(7))* Lulu Pr., Inc.
—Star the Tooth Fairy Is Checking on You! 2010. 36p. 16.95 *(978-0-557-49450-7(8))* Lulu Pr., Inc.
—Star the Tooth Fairy Takes A Holiday to Visit Santa at the North Pole! 2010. 40p. 17.95 *(978-0-557-41623-3(X))* Lulu Pr., Inc.
—Star the Tooth Fairy Wants to Know If You Need Braces? 2010. 36p. 16.95 *(978-0-557-49455-2(9))* Lulu Pr., Inc.
Top That. Press Out & Play Magic Castle. 2008. *(978-1-84666-600-1(7))* Top That! Publishing PLC.
Torres, J. The Case of the Fractured Fairy Tale, 1 vol. Barberi, Carlo & Beatty, Terry, illus. 2013. (Batman: the Brave & the Bold Ser.). (ENG.). 32p. (gr. 2-3). 22.60 *(978-1-4342-4705-6(8))* Stone Arch Bks.
Torribio, Penelope. The Magic in You: From vacant lot to community Garden. 2011. 40p. pap. 16.46 *(978-1-4269-5723-9(8))* Trafford Publishing.
Touring Europe on a Magic Carpet. 2004. (J). ring bd. 4.50 *(978-0-9762740-9-4(4))* Smart Smiles Co., The.
Town, Nathan. Ned Stapleton & the Wrath of the Death Gods. 2006. 174p. (YA). *(978-0-9781040-0-9(5))* Emerald City Storytellers.
Townley, Roderick. A Bitter Magic. 2015. (ENG.). 304p. (J). (gr. 4-7). 16.99 *(978-0-449-81649-3(4)*, Knopf Bks. for Young Readers) Random Hse. Children's Bks.
Townsan, Judy. The Wishing Flower, 1 vol. Rosado, Michael, illus. 2009. 13p. pap. 24.95 *(978-1-61546-179-0(5))* America Star Bks.
Townsend, Tamela Ann. Finding Pumpkin, 1 vol. 2010. 48p. pap. 16.95 *(978-1-4489-5983-9(7))* America Star Bks.
Tozier, Christopher. Olivia Brophie & the Pearl of Tagelus. 2012. (ENG.). 208p. (J). pap. 12.95 *(978-1-56164-519-0(2))* Pineapple Pr., Inc.
—Olivia Brophie & the Sky Island. 2014. (ENG.). 304p. (J). pap. 12.95 *(978-1-56164-680-7(6))* Pineapple Pr., Inc.
Tracey, Andrée. Storyland: Poppy & Her Magic Hat: A Story Coloring Book. 2015. (Dover Coloring Bks.). (ENG., Illus.). 32p. (J). (gr. k-5). pap. 3.99 *(978-0-486-79403-7(2))* Dover Pubns., Inc.
Tracy, Judith. The Wildsidhe Chronicles Bk. 3: Dark Proposal. 2003. (J). pap. 7.99 *(978-1-890096-15-1(6))* Padwolf Publishing, Inc.
Travers, P. L. Mary Poppins. Shepard, Mary, illus. 2006. (Mary Poppins Ser.: No. 1). (ENG.). 224p. (J). (gr. 5-7). 16.99 *(978-0-15-205810-4(9))* Houghton Mifflin Harcourt Publishing Co.
—Mary Poppins in the Park. Shepard, Mary, illus. 2015. (Mary Poppins Ser.). (ENG.). 272p. (J). (gr. 5-7). pap. 6.99 *(978-0-544-51384-6(3)*, HMH Books For Young Readers) Houghton Mifflin Harcourt Publishing Co.
—Mary Poppins Opens the Door. Shepard, Mary & Sims, Agnes, illus. 2015. (Mary Poppins Ser.). (ENG.). 256p. (J). (gr. 5-7). pap. 6.99 *(978-0-544-43958-0(9)*, HMH Books For Young Readers) Houghton Mifflin Harcourt Publishing Co.
—Mary Poppins Vintage Boxed Set: Three Enchanting Classics: Mary Poppins, Mary Poppins Comes Back, & Mary Poppins Opens the Door. 2007. (Illus.). (J). 38.85 *(978-0-15-205858-6(3))* Harcourt Children's Bks.
Trevayne, Emma. The Accidental Afterlife of Thomas Marsden. 2016. (ENG.). 272p. (J). (gr. 3-7). pap. 7.99 *(978-1-4424-9884-6(6)*, Simon & Schuster Bks. For Young Readers) Simon & Schuster Bks. For Young Readers.
Trigg, Michael J. Greanwold & the Mystery Cave: Greanwold & the Minosaurs Story Books. 2013. 148p. pap. 12.97 *(978-1-61897-466-2(1)*, Strategic Bk. Publishing) Strategic Book Publishing & Rights Agency (SBPRA).
Trini Torres Carrion. The Magic of a Strawberry Lollipop. 2009. 16p. pap. 8.49 *(978-1-4389-7900-7(2))* AuthorHouse.
Tripp, Ben. The Accidental Highwayman: Being the Tale of Kit Bristol, His Horse Midnight, a Mysterious Princess, & Sundry Magical Persons Besides. 2014. (ENG., Illus.). 304p. (YA). (gr. 6). 17.99 *(978-0-7653-3549-4(2)*, Tor Teen) Doherty, Tom Assocs., LLC.
Trivas, Tracy. The Wish Stealers. 2010. (ENG.). 288p. (J). (gr. 3-7). 17.99 *(978-1-4169-8725-3(8)*, Simon & Schuster/Paula Wiseman Bks.) Simon & Schuster/Paula Wiseman Bks.
Trotter, Bob. The Curious Tale of Marmalade Tuttle. 2008. 116p. pap. 12.95 *(978-1-60693-014-4(1)*, Eloquent Bks.) Strategic Book Publishing & Rights Agency (SBPRA).
Troulis, Jennifer. Penelope & Priscilla: And the Enchanted House of Whispers. 2nd ed. 2004. (Illus.). 229p. per. 13.95 *(978-0-9768602-0-4(1))* Twin Monkeys Pr.
—Penelope & Priscilla & the City of the Banished. 2007. (J). per. 14.95 *(978-0-9768602-1-1(X))* Twin Monkeys Pr.
Trout, Jenny. Such Sweet Sorrow. 2014. (Entangled Teen Ser.). (ENG.). 304p. (YA). (gr. 8-12). pap. 9.99 *(978-1-62266-158-9(3)*, 9781622661589) Entangled Publishing, LLC.
Trowell, Michelle. Magical Mermaids. Top That Publishing Staff, ed. Richards, Kirsten, illus. 2008. (Magnetic Story & Play Scene Ser.). 9p. (J). (gr. -1). *(978-1-84666-442-7(X)*, Tide Mill Pr.) Top That! Publishing PLC.
Truax, Lois. Grandmothers Are Magic. 2010. 28p. pap. 5.95 *(978-1-935355-01-4(5))* New Shelves Bks.
Trudeau, Scott & Holzbauer, David. A Treasure to Share: Adventures in Social Skills. Trudeau, Scott, illus. 2003. (Illus.). 68p. (J). *(978-0-9743805-0-6(4))* Intellipop, LLC.
Tulien, Sean. The Not-So-Evil Wizard. Cunyat, Pol, illus. 2016. (Thud & Blunder Ser.). (ENG.). 56p. (gr. 2-4). pap. 4.95 *(978-1-4965-3225-1(2))*; lib. bdg. 23.99 *(978-1-4965-3221-3(X))* Stone Arch Bks.
Turetsky, Bianca. The Time-Traveling Fashionista at the Palace of Marie Antoinette. 2013. (Time-Traveling Fashionista Ser.: 2). (ENG., Illus.). 272p. (J). (gr. 3-7). pap. 9.00 *(978-0-316-10535-4(X)*, Poppy) Little, Brown Bks. for Young Readers.
Turner, Amber McRee. Circa Now. 2014. (ENG., Illus.). 288p. (J). (gr. 3-7). 16.99 *(978-1-4231-7639-8(1))* Hyperion Bks. for Children.
Turner, Megan Whalen. Instead of Three Wishes: Magical Short Stories. 2006. (ENG.). 160p. (J). (gr. 5-9). pap. 6.99 *(978-0-06-084231-4(8)*, Greenwillow Bks.) HarperCollins Pubs.
Tyrrell, Melissa. The Gingerbread Man. McMullen, Nigel, illus. 2005. (Fairytale Friends Ser.: Vol. 8). 12p. (J). (gr. -1-k). bds. 5.95 *(978-1-58117-154-9(4)*, Intervisual/Piggy Toes) Bendon, Inc.
Tzingoker, Lilach. Sonny's Adventure in Mystery Park. 2010. 44p. pap. 19.95 *(978-1-60911-927-0(4)*, Eloquent Bks.) Strategic Book Publishing & Rights Agency (SBPRA).
Ullman, Barb Bentler. Whistle Bright Magic: A Nutfolk Tale. 2010. 224p. (J). (gr. 3-7). 16.99 *(978-0-06-188286-9(0))* HarperCollins Pubs.
Umansky, Kaye. Clover Twig & the Perilous Path. Wright, Johanna, illus. 2013. (ENG.). 272p. (J). (gr. 3-7). pap. 7.99 *(978-1-250-02727-6(6)*, 9781250027276) Square Fish.
Uncle Bernie. Michaels Adventures in the Land of Nod Book: Michaels Trip to Orange County. 2008. 32p. pap. 12.99 *(978-1-4389-1097-0(5))* AuthorHouse.
Underwood, Kim. The Wonderful World of Sparkle Girl & Doobins. Goldman, Garnet, illus. 2009. 48p. (J). pap. 16.95 *(978-0-89587-373-6(7))* Blair, John F. Pub.
Upton, Robert Jesten. Milo & the Dragon Cross: A Novel. 2017. (YA). pap. ***(978-1-63293-177-1(X))*** Sunstone Pr.
Urban, Linda. Milo Speck, Accidental Agent. (ENG., Illus.). 272p. (J). (gr. 2-5). 2017. pap. 7.99 *(978-0-544-93523-5(3))* 2015. 16.99 *(978-0-544-41951-3(0))* Houghton Mifflin Harcourt Publishing Co. (HMH Books For Young Readers).

Ursu, Anne. Breadcrumbs. McGuire, Erin, illus. (ENG.). (J). (gr. 3-7). 2013. 336p. pap. 6.99 (978-0-06-201506-8(0)) 2011. 320p. 16.99 (978-0-06-201505-1(2)) HarperCollins Pubs. (Waldon Pond Pr.).

—Breadcrumbs. McGuire, Erin, illus. 2012. 320p. 55.00 (978-0-449-01400-4(2)) Random Hse., Inc.

—Breadcrumbs. 2013. (J). lib. bdg. 17.20 (978-0-606-27130-1(9), Turtleback) Turtleback Bks.

—The Immortal Fire. Fortune, Eric & Swaab, Neil, illus. 2009. (Cronus Chronicles Ser.: 3). (ENG.). 528p. (J). (gr. 3-7). 17.99 (978-1-4169-0591-2(X), Atheneum Bks. for Young Readers) Simon & Schuster Children's Publishing.

—The Real Boy. McGuire, Erin, illus. (ENG.). 352p. (J). (gr. 3-7). 2015. pap. 6.99 (978-0-06-201508-2(7)) 2013. 16.99 (978-0-06-201507-5(9)) HarperCollins Pubs. (Waldon Pond Pr.).

Usher, M. D. The Golden Ass of Lucius Apuleius. Motley, T., illus. 2011. (ENG.). 112p. (J). 17.95 (978-1-56792-418-3(2)) Godine, David R. Pub.

Uwuigiaren, Omoruyi. The Adventures of Nihu. Ayalomeh, Shedrach, illus. 2007. 158p. (J). (gr. 2-8). 16.95 (978-1-934138-15-1(0)) Bouncing Ball Bks., Inc.

Valente, Catherynne M. The Girl Who Fell Beneath Fairyland & Led the Revels There. Juan, Ana, illus. 2013. (Fairyland Ser.: 2). (ENG.). 304p. (YA). (gr. 5-9). pap. 7.99 (978-1-250-03412-0(4), 9781250034120) Square Fish.

Valentino, Serena. Poor Unfortunate Soul: A Tale of the Sea Witch. Disney Storybook Art Team, illus. 2016. (Villains Ser.: 3). (ENG.). 208p. (J). (gr. 5-9). 17.99 (978-1-4847-2405-7(4)) Disney Pr.

Valentino, Serena & Disney Book Group Staff. Fairest of All: A Tale of the Wicked Queen. Disney Storybook Artists Staff, illus. 2009. (Villains Ser.: 1). (ENG.). 256p. (J). (gr. 5-9). 15.99 (978-1-4231-0629-6(6)) Disney Pr.

Van Allsburg, Chris. Probuditi! 2009. 30p. (J). 19.00 (978-1-4379-6940-5(2)) DIANE Publishing Co.

—Probuditi! 2006. (ENG., Illus.). 32p. (J). (gr. 2-5). 18.95 (978-0-618-75502-8(0)) Houghton Mifflin Harcourt Publishing Co.

—The Sweetest Fig. 2014. 32p. pap. 9.00 (978-1-61003-223-0(3)) Center for the Collaborative Classroom.

Van Cleve, Kathleen. Drizzle. 2011. (ENG.). 368p. (J). (gr. 3-7). 7.99 (978-0-14-241113-1(2), Puffin Books) Penguin Young Readers Group.

Van Der Watt, Tony. Balthazar, the Wolf Who Reformed. 2010. 48p. pap. 12.50 (978-1-60911-125-0(7), Eloquent Bks.) Strategic Book Publishing & Rights Agency (SBPRA).

van Diepen, Allison. Raven. 2010. (ENG.). 304p. (YA). (gr. 9). pap. 8.99 (978-1-4169-7468-0(7), Simon Pulse) Simon Pulse.

Van Draanen, Wendelin. The Gecko & Sticky: the Power Potion. Gilpin, Stephen, illus. 2011. (Gecko & Sticky Ser.). (ENG.). 240p. (J). (gr. 3-7). 6.99 (978-0-440-42245-7(0), Yearling) Random Hse. Children's Bks.

—The Greatest Power. Gilpin, Stephen, illus. 2011. (Gecko & Sticky Ser.: Bk. 1). (ENG.). 208p. (J). (gr. 3-7). 7.99 (978-0-440-42243-3(4), Yearling) Random Hse. Children's Bks.

—Sinister Substitute. Gilpin, Stephen, illus. (Gecko & Sticky Ser.: Bk. 3). (ENG.). 224p. (J). (gr. 3-7). 2011. 7.99 (978-0-440-42244-0(2), Yearling) 2010. 12.99 (978-0-375-84378-5(7), Knopf Bks. for Young Readers) Random Hse. Children's Bks.

Vance, Alexander. Behind the Canvas. 2016. (ENG.). 336p. (J). 16.99 (978-1-250-02970-6(8), 9781250029706) Feiwel & Friends.

Vande Velde, Vivian. Curses, Inc. & Other Stories. 2007. (ENG., Illus.). 240p. (YA). (gr. 7-12). pap. 12.95 (978-0-15-206107-4(X)) Houghton Mifflin Harcourt Publishing Co.

—A Hidden Magic. 176p. (J). pap. 5.00 (978-0-8072-1519-7(8), Listening Library) Random Hse. Audio Publishing Group.

—Wizard at Work. 2004. (ENG., Illus.). 144p. (J). (gr. 5-7). pap. 10.95 (978-0-15-205309-3(3)) Houghton Mifflin Harcourt Publishing Co.

Varian, H. K. The Emerald Mask. 2016. (Hidden World of Changers Ser.: 2). (ENG., Illus.). 176p. (J). (gr. 3-7). pap. 6.99 (978-1-4814-6619-6(4), Simon Spotlight) Simon Spotlight.

Varveris, Ariana Eleni. The Adventures of Magic Island: Book I- Welcome to Magic Island. 2012. 122p. (gr. 2-2). pap. 9.95 (978-1-4620-5751-1(9)) iUniverse, Inc.

Vaughan, Grace. Annie & the Magic Book. 2012. 30p. pap. 19.99 (978-1-4772-5498-1(6)) AuthorHouse.

Venable, Alan. Take Me with You When You Go. Marshall, Laurie, illus. 2008. 112p. (J). 12.95 (978-0-9777082-7-7(6)) One Monkey Bks.

Vercz, Carol A. The Magic of Hidie. (J). 6.95 (978-0-910119-44-3(9)) S.O.C.O. Pubns.

Verhoosky, Michele. Molly Marie & the Amazing Jimmy. Verhoosky, Michele, illus. 2012. (Illus.). 34p. pap. 10.95 (978-1-937260-22-4(4)) Sleepytown Pr.

Vermazen, Eve. Dogtales: Sebastian & the Destiny Stone. 2012. 36p. pap. 32.70 (978-1-4797-4032-1(2)) Xlibris Corp.

Vernon, Ursula. Castle Hangnail. 2015. (ENG., Illus.). 384p. (J). (gr. 3-7). 16.99 (978-0-8037-4129-4(4), Dial Bks) Penguin Young Readers Group.

Vickers, Tamara. Mr. Green & the Animal Kingdom: (Imagine That!) You Draw the Picture! 2007. 228p. per. 24.95 (978-1-4241-8256-5(5)) America Star Bks.

Virant, Janice. T-Bone the Flying Horse. 2013. (ENG.). 26p. (J). pap. 10.95 (978-1-4327-5951-3(5)) Outskirts Pr., Inc.

Vivian Baron Cohen, Hyman. Joe & His Magic Snout. 2015. (ENG.). 106p. (J). (gr. 2-3). mass mkt. 11.95 (978-1-78554-195-7(1), d959877b-9c23-4fec-8095-a7a2baa8c006) Austin, Stan AUS. Dist: Bookmasters Distribution.

Viz Media. Fairy Dreams. 2013. (Winx Club Ser.: 5). lib. bdg. 17.20 (978-0-606-26987-2(8), Turtleback) Turtleback Bks.

—Time for Magic. 2013. (Winx Club Ser.: 6). lib. bdg. 17.20 (978-0-606-27022-9(1), Turtleback) Turtleback Bks.

VIZ Media, . & Straffi, Iginio. WINX Club, Vol. 7. 2013. (ENG.). 96p. (J). pap. 6.99 (978-1-4215-4204-1(8)) Viz Media.

—WINX Club, Vol. 8. 2013. (ENG.). 96p. (J). pap. 6.99 (978-1-4215-4205-8(6)) Viz Media.

VIZ Media Staff. WINX Club, Vol. 1. 2012. (ENG.). 96p. (J). pap. 6.99 (978-1-4215-4159-4(9)) Viz Media.

—WINX Club, Vol. 3. 2012. (ENG.). 96p. (J). pap. 6.99 (978-1-4215-4161-7(0)) Viz Media.

VIZ Media Staff & Staffi, Iginio. WINX Club, Vol. 5. 2013. (ENG.). 96p. (J). pap. 6.99 (978-1-4215-4163-1(7)) Viz Media.

VIZ Media Staff & Straffi, Iginio. WINX Club, Vol. 2. 2012. (ENG.). 96p. (J). pap. 6.99 (978-1-4215-4160-0(2)) Viz Media.

—WINX Club, Vol. 4. 2012. (ENG.). 96p. (J). pap. 6.99 (978-1-4215-4162-4(9)) Viz Media.

—WINX Club, Vol. 6. 2013. (ENG.). 96p. (J). pap. 6.99 (978-1-4215-4203-4(0)) Viz Media.

Volkov, Alexander. Tales of Magic Land 1. 2010. 360p. pap. 22.95 (978-0-557-44825-8(5)) Lulu Pr., Inc.

Vornholt, John. The Troll Treasure. 2003. (Troll King Trilogy). 185p. (J). (gr. 5-9). 12.65 (978-0-7569-3954-0(2)) Perfection Learning Corp.

Wagman, Diana. Extraordinary October. 2016. (ENG.). 264p. (YA). (gr. 6). 18.95 (978-1-63246-036-3(X)) Ig Publishing, Inc.

Wagner, Mckenzie. The Amulet Chase. 2017. (ENG.). (J). pap. 10.99 (978-1-4621-1983-7(2), Sweetwater Bks.) Cedar Fort, Inc./CFI Distribution.

—Casters of Doovik. 2015. 298p. (YA). pap. 17.99 (978-1-4621-1757-4(0)) Cedar Fort, Inc./CFI Distribution.

—Keys to the Dream World. 2014. pap. 8.99 (978-1-4621-1435-1(0)) Cedar Fort, Inc./CFI Distribution.

Wakem, Samantha. Milly's Magic Play House: The Hospital, 1 vol. Herridge, Debbie, illus. 2010. 20p. 24.95 (978-1-4489-5114-7(3)) PublishAmerica, Inc.

Waldman, Thomas. 1 ! 2 ! 3 ! 4 ! Saisons. 2005. 10p. 8.53 (978-1-4116-3332-2(6)) Lulu Pr., Inc.

Walker, Crystal. Maceys Magic Tree. 2009. 28p. pap. 12.49 (978-1-4490-4916-4(8)) AuthorHouse.

Walker-Renner, Christa. Santa's Magic. 2009. 20p. pap. 11.00 (978-1-4389-8206-9(2)) AuthorHouse.

Walker, Russell D. Michelle & the Magic Timepiece. 2006. 108p. pap. 19.95 (978-1-4241-3143-3(X)) PublishAmerica, Inc.

Walker, Victoria. The Winter of Enchantment. 2007. (Illus.). 152p. (YA). (gr. 8-12). 18.95 (978-1-930900-33-2(3)) Purple Hse. Pr.

Wallace, Becky. The Skylighter. 2017. (Keepers' Chronicles Ser.). (ENG.). 432p. (YA). (gr. 9). pap. 11.99 (978-1-4814-0569-0(1), McElderry, Margaret K. Bks.) McElderry, Margaret K. Bks.

—The Storyspinner. 2015. (Keepers' Chronicles Ser.). (ENG., Illus.). 432p. (YA). (gr. 9). 17.99 (978-1-4814-0565-2(9), McElderry, Margaret K. Bks.) McElderry, Margaret K. Bks.

Wallace, Kali. The Memory Trees. 2017. 432p. (YA). (gr. 9). 17.99 (978-0-06-236623-8(8), Tegen, Katherine Bks) HarperCollins Pubs.

Wallace, Karen. Where Are My Shoes? Allwright, Deborah, illus. 2005. (Reading Corner Ser.). 24p. (J). (gr. k-3). lib. bdg. 22.80 (978-1-59771-002-2(4)) Sea-To-Sea Pubns.

Wallace, William H. Santa's Magic Key. 2010. 20p. (J). 10.49 (978-1-4490-8924-5(0)) AuthorHouse.

Walsh, Pat. The Crowfield Curse. (ENG.). (J). (gr. 3-7). 2012. 352p. pap. 7.99 (978-0-545-23103-9(5)) 2010. 336p. 16.99 (978-0-545-22922-7(7)) Scholastic, Inc. (Chicken Hse., The).

—The Crowfield Demon. (J). 2013. 360p. (978-0-545-37350-0(6)) 2012. (ENG.). 368p. (gr. 3-7). 16.99 (978-0-545-31769-6(X), Chicken Hse., The) Scholastic, Inc.

Walsh, Sara. The Dark Light. (ENG., (YA). (gr. 9). 2013. Illus.). 512p. pap. 9.99 (978-1-4424-3458-5(9)) 2012. 496p. 16.99 (978-1-4424-3455-4(4)) Simon Pulse. (Simon Pulse).

Walter, Wendy D. & Walter, Wendy D. Return of the Dullaith: Ambri's Tale. 2012. (Illus.). 318p. (J). pap. 15.99 (978-0-9857147-1-0(9), Angry Bicycle) Walter, Wendy D.

Wampol, Pam & Woodard, Heather. Oscar's Dreamzz: The Story of Santa's First Elf. 2013. 40p. pap. (978-1-4602-0414-6(X)) FriesenPress.

Wandless, David. Natural Magic. 2010. 344p. pap. 27.50 (978-1-4461-4163-2(2)) Lulu Pr., Inc.

—Natural Magic Book 3 - the Milk Stone & the Tauren. 2010. 134p. pap. 20.95 (978-1-4461-5162-4(X)) Lulu Pr., Inc.

Wang, An. Anywhere but Here. 2006. 107p. (J). (gr. 6-8). per. 9.95 (978-0-88100-140-2(6)) National Writers Pr., The.

Wang, Gabrielle. The Wishbird. 2013. (ENG.). 200p. (YA). (gr. 7). 12.99 (978-0-14-330752-5(5)) Penguin Books Australia AUS. Dist: Independent Pubs. Group.

Ward, John. The Stone of Sorrow: The Revealer of Wonders. 2004. (Fate of the Stone Ser.: Pt. 2). 256p. (YA). pap. (978-1-55207-080-2(8)) Studio 9 Bks. and Music.

Warner, Michael N. The Titanic Game. Ordaz, Frank, illus. 2007. (ENG.). 208p. (J). pap. 11.95 (978-0-9744446-2-8(6)) All About Kids Publishing.

Warner, Sally. Ellray Jakes Is Magic. 2014. (EllRay Jakes Ser.: 6). lib. bdg. 16.00 (978-0-606-34215-5(X), Turtleback) Turtleback Bks.

Warren, Cindy. The Unicorn's Horn. 2011. 98p. pap. 19.95 (978-1-4560-6987-2(X)) America Star Bks.

Watase, Yuu & Caselman, Lance. Alice 19th, Vol. 1, 7 vols. Watase, Yuu, illus. 2003. (ENG., Illus.). 192p. pap. 9.95 (978-1-59116-215-5(7)) Viz Media.

—Alice 19th, Vol. 2, 7 vols. JN Productions Staff, tr. from JPN. Watase, Yuu, illus. 2003. (ENG., Illus.). 200p. pap. 9.95 (978-1-59116-229-2(7)) Viz Media.

Waterfield, Susan. Spunkie's Magical Garden. 2012. 32p. pap. 14.95 (978-1-257-77576-7(6)) Lulu Pr., Inc.

Watkins, Sam. Darcy Dolphin Is a Little Bit Magic! Barker, Vicky, illus. 2017. (Darcy Dolphin Ser.). (ENG.). 160p. (J). (gr. 1-3). pap. 9.99 (978-1-4052-8423-3(4)) Egmont Bks., Ltd. GBR. Dist: Independent Pubs. Group.

Watson, Heather M. J. L. Thistle Lodge: The Legendary Sidhe Saga. 2012. (ENG.). 224p. pap. (978-1-78088-181-2(9)) Troubador Publishing Ltd.

Watson, M. Desmond & the Challenge on Mudwig Mountain. 2005. 109p. pap. (978-1-84401-010-3(4)) Athena Pr.

Watson, Richard Jesse. The Magic Rabbit. Watson, Richard Jesse, illus. 2005. (ENG., Illus.). 40p. (J). (gr. -1-3). 16.99 (978-0-590-47964-6(4), Blue Sky Pr., The) Scholastic, Inc.

Weatherly, Lee. Pigwitchery. Reed, Nathan, illus. 2008. (ENG.). 32p. (J). (978-1-4050-9234-0(3), Macmillan Children's Bks.) Pan Macmillan.

Webb, Holly. Rose. 2013. (Rose Ser.: 1). (ENG.). 240p. (J). (gr. 3-6). pap. 6.99 (978-1-4022-8581-3(7), 9781402285813, Sourcebooks Jabberwocky) Sourcebooks, Inc.

—Rose & the Lost Princess. 2011. (ENG.). 272p. (J). (gr. 4-6). pap. 8.99 (978-1-4083-0448-8(1)) Hodder & Stoughton GBR. Dist: Hachette Bk. Group.

—Rose & the Lost Princess. 2014. (Rose Ser.: 2). (ENG.). 256p. (J). (gr. 3-6). pap. 6.99 (978-1-4022-8584-4(1), Sourcebooks Jabberwocky) Sourcebooks, Inc.

—Rose & the Magician's Mask. 2014. (Rose Ser.: 3). (ENG.). 224p. (J). (gr. 3-6). pap. 6.99 (978-1-4926-0430-3(5), 9781492604303, Sourcebooks Jabberwocky) Sourcebooks, Inc.

—Rose & the Silver Ghost. 2015. (Rose Ser.: 4). (ENG.). 224p. (J). (gr. 3-6). pap. 6.99 (978-1-4926-0433-4(X), Sourcebooks Jabberwocky) Sourcebooks, Inc.

Webster, Wendy. Magicus Perfecticum. 2009. (Illus.). 60p. pap. 11.49 (978-1-4490-0765-2(1)) AuthorHouse.

Weinberg, Jennifer. Surprise for a Princess. 2003. (Disney Princess Step into Reading Ser.). (gr. -1-2). 13.55 (978-0-613-73686-2(9), Turtleback) Turtleback Bks.

Weingarten, Lynn. The Book of Love. 2013. (ENG.). 272p. (YA). (gr. 8). 17.99 (978-0-06-192620-4(5), HarperTeen) HarperCollins Pubs.

—The Secret Sisterhood of Heartbreakers. (ENG.). (YA). (gr. 8). 2013. 368p. pap. 9.99 (978-0-06-192619-8(1)) 2011. 352p. 17.99 (978-0-06-192618-1(3)) HarperCollins Pubs. (HarperTeen).

Weinshall Liberman, Judith. The Little Fairy. 2013. 32p. 21.99 (978-1-4575-2351-9(5)) Dog Ear Publishing, LLC.

Weinstein, Jacob Sager. Hyacinth & the Secrets Beneath. 2017. (Hyacinth Ser.: 1). (ENG.). 304p. (J). (gr. 3-7). 16.99 (978-0-399-55317-2(7), Random Hse. Bks. for Young Readers) Random Hse. Children's Bks.

Welborn, Kathleen. The Cacklebeans, 1 vol. 2009. 33p. pap. 24.95 (978-1-4489-1933-8(9)) America Star Bks.

Welles, Lee. Enter the Earth. Hameister, Ann, illus. 2006. (Gaia Girls Ser.: 1). (ENG.). 336p. (YA). (gr. 4-7). 18.95 (978-1-933609-00-3(1)) Chelsea Green Publishing.

Welling, Martin. Guardian of the Stones: Nat & Mateo Discover the Two Forces of Magic Stones. 2012. (ENG.). 40p. (J). 29.95 (978-1-4327-7692-3(4)) Outskirts Pr., Inc.

Wells, Carolyn. Patty Fairfield. 2004. reprint ed. pap. 1.99 (978-1-4192-4033-1(1)); pap. 20.95 (978-1-4191-4033-4(7)) Kessinger Publishing, LLC.

Wells, J. & L. Antares & the Zodiac. 2012. (ENG.). 256p. pap. (978-1-78088-294-9(7)) Troubador Publishing Ltd.

Welsh, Kenneth Wilbur. Magic Chalk. 2011. 16p. pap. 12.00 (978-1-4520-6078-1(9)) AuthorHouse.

Wendling, Peter. The Magic of the Dark Ravine. Durie, Sally, illus. 2011. 36p. pap. 13.95 (978-1-60976-933-8(3), Eloquent Bks.) Strategic Book Publishing & Rights Agency (SBPRA).

Werlin, Nancy. Impossible. 2011. 11.04 (978-0-7848-3488-6(1), Everbind) Marco Bk. Co.

—Impossible. 2009. (ENG.). 384p. (YA). (gr. 7-18). 9.99 (978-0-14-241491-0(3), Speak) Penguin Young Readers Group.

—Unthinkable. 2014. (ENG.). 416p. (YA). (gr. 7). pap. 9.99 (978-0-14-242620-3(2), Speak) Penguin Young Readers Group.

Werner, Teresa O. A Quilt of Wishes. Tremlin, Nathan, illus. l.t. ed. 2005. 21p. (J). per. 9.99 (978-1-59879-037-5(4)) Lifevest Publishing, Inc.

Wert, Yijin, tr. The Little Monkey King's Journey: Retold in English & Chinese. Jian, Li, illus. 2012. (ENG & CHI.). 48p. (J). (gr. -1-3). 16.95 (978-1-60220-981-7(2)) BetterLink Pr., Inc.

West, Hilary. The Secret Kingdom. 2013. 76p. pap. 17.95 (978-1-62709-626-3(4)) America Star Bks.

West, Jacqueline. The Second Spy. Bernatene, Poly, illus. 2013. (Books of Elsewhere Ser.: 3). (ENG.). 320p. (J). (gr. 5). pap. 7.99 (978-0-14-242608-1(3), Puffin Books) Penguin Young Readers Group.

—The Second Spy. 2013. (Books of Elsewhere Ser.: 3). lib. bdg. 18.40 (978-0-606-31698-9(1), Turtleback) Turtleback Bks.

—The Second Spy, Vol. 3. Bernatene, Poly, illus. 2012. (Books of Elsewhere Ser.: 3). (ENG.). 304p. (J). (gr. 5-18). 16.99 (978-0-8037-3689-4(4), Dial Bks) Penguin Young Readers Group.

—The Shadows. 2011. (Books of Elsewhere Ser.: 1). (ENG.). 272p. (J). (gr. 5-7). 7.99 (978-0-14-241872-7(2), Puffin Books) Penguin Young Readers Group.

—The Shadows. Bernatene, Poly, illus. 2010. (Books of Elsewhere Ser.: 1). (ENG.). 256p. (J). (gr. 5-18). 16.99 (978-0-8037-3440-1(9), Dial Bks) Penguin Young Readers Group.

—The Shadows. l.t. ed. 2010. (Books of Elsewhere Ser.: Vol. 1). (ENG.). 268p. 23.99 (978-1-4104-3139-4(8)) Thorndike Pr.

—The Shadows. 2011. (Books of Elsewhere Ser.: 1). lib. bdg. 17.20 (978-0-606-23070-4(X), Turtleback) Turtleback Bks.

—Spellbound, 2 vols. (Books of Elsewhere Ser.: 2). (ENG.). (J). (gr. 5-18). 2012. 320p. pap. 7.99 (978-0-14-242102-4(2), Puffin Books) Vol. 2. 2011. (Illus.). 304p. 16.99 (978-0-8037-3441-8(7), Dial Bks) Penguin Young Readers Group.

—Spellbound. 2012. (Books of Elsewhere Ser.: 2). lib. bdg. 18.40 (978-0-606-26082-4(X), Turtleback) Turtleback Bks.

—Still Life. 2015. (Books of Elsewhere Ser.: 5). lib. bdg. 18.40 (978-0-606-36786-8(1)) Turtleback Bks.

—Still Life: The Books of Elsewhere: Volume 5. Bernatene, Poly, illus. 2015. (Books of Elsewhere Ser.: 5). (ENG.). 352p. (J). (gr. 5). 7.99 (978-0-14-242297-7(5), Puffin Books) Penguin Young Readers Group.

—The Strangers. Bernatene, Poly, illus. (Books of Elsewhere Ser.: 4). (ENG.). (J). (gr. 5). 2014. 336p. pap. 7.99 (978-0-14-242575-6(3), Puffin Books) 2013. 320p. 16.99 (978-0-8037-3690-0(8), Dial Bks) Penguin Young Readers Group.

—The Strangers. 2014. (Books of Elsewhere Ser.: 4). lib. bdg. 18.40 (978-0-606-35680-0(0)) Turtleback Bks.

West, Steve, reader. Island of Legends. 2014. (Unwanteds Ser.: 4). (ENG., Illus.). 496p. (J). (gr. 3-7). 18.99 (978-1-4424-9328-5(3), Aladdin) Simon & Schuster Children's Publishing.

West, Tracey. Flight of the Moon Dragon. Jones, Damien, illus. 2016. (Dragon Masters Ser.: 6). (ENG.). 96p. (J). (gr. 1-3). pap. 4.99 (978-0-545-91392-8(6)) Scholastic, Inc.

—Hermes & the Horse with Wings. 2017. (Heroes in Training Ser.: 13). lib. bdg. 16.00 (978-0-606-39738-4(8)) Turtleback Bks.

—Power of the Fire Dragon. Howells, Graham, illus. 2015. (Dragon Masters Ser.: No. 4). (ENG.). 96p. (J). (gr. 1-3). pap. 4.99 (978-0-545-64631-4(6)) Scholastic, Inc.

—Rise of the Earth Dragon. Howells, Graham, illus. 2014. (Dragon Masters Ser.: 1). (ENG.). 96p. (J). (gr. 1-3). 15.99 (978-0-545-64624-6(3)); pap. 4.99 (978-0-545-64623-9(5)) Scholastic, Inc.

—Rise of the Earth Dragon. 2014. (Dragon Masters Ser.: 1). lib. bdg. 14.75 (978-0-606-36050-0(6)) Turtleback Bks.

—Roar of the Thunder Dragon: a Branches Book. Jones, Damien, illus. 2017. (Dragon Masters Ser.: 8). (ENG.). 96p. (J). (gr. 1-3). lib. bdg. 15.99 (978-1-338-04293-1(9)); pap. 4.99 (978-1-338-04292-4(0)) Scholastic, Inc.

—Saving the Sun Dragon. Howells, Graham & Jones, Damien, illus. 2014. (Dragon Masters Ser.: 2). (ENG.). 96p. (J). (gr. 1-3). 15.99 (978-0-545-64626-0(X)); pap. 4.99 (978-0-545-64625-3(1)) Scholastic, Inc.

—Saving the Sun Dragon. 2014. (Dragon Masters Ser.: 2). lib. bdg. 14.75 (978-0-606-36051-7(4)) Turtleback Bks.

—Search for the Lightning Dragon: a Branches Book (Dragon Masters #7) Jones, Damien, illus. 2017. (Dragon Masters Ser.: 7). (ENG.). 96p. (J). (gr. 1-3). pap. 4.99 (978-1-338-04288-7(2)) Scholastic, Inc.

—Song of the Poison Dragon: a Branches Book (Dragon Masters #5) Jones, Damien, illus. 2016. (Dragon Masters Ser.: 5). (ENG.). 96p. (J). (gr. 1-3). pap. 4.99 (978-0-545-91387-4(X)) Scholastic, Inc.

West, Tracey, adapted by. Phantom Unmasked. 2006. (Illus.). 62p. (J). pap. (978-0-439-80000-6(5)) Scholastic, Inc.

Weston Woods Staff, creator. Harold & the Purple Crayon. 2011. 18.95 (978-0-439-72691-7(3)); 29.95 (978-0-439-73474-5(6)); 38.75 (978-0-439-72693-1(X)) Weston Woods Studios, Inc.

—James Marshall's Cinderella. 2011. 38.75 (978-0-439-84886-2(5)) Weston Woods Studios, Inc.

—Possum Magic. 2011. 18.95 (978-0-545-08634-9(5)); 38.75 (978-0-545-14784-2(0)) Weston Woods Studios, Inc.

—Sylvester & the Magic Pebble. 2011. 38.75 (978-0-439-72898-0(3)); 29.95 (978-0-439-73522-3(X)) Weston Woods Studios, Inc.

Westwood, Chris. Graveyard Shift. (Hauntings Ser.: bk.1). (ENG.). 304p. (J). (gr. 3-7). 2014. pap. 6.99 (978-0-545-39920-3(3)) 2012. 17.99 (978-0-545-39919-7(X)) Scholastic, Inc. (Scholastic Pr.).

Wexler, Django. The Forbidden Library. 2015. (ENG., Illus.). 400p. (J). (gr. 5). 8.99 (978-0-14-242681-4(4), Puffin Books) Penguin Young Readers Group.

—The Mad Apprentice. Jansson, Alexander, illus. 2015. (Forbidden Library). (ENG.). 352p. (J). (gr. 5). 16.99 (978-0-8037-3976-5(1), Kathy Dawson Books) Penguin Young Readers Group.

—The Palace of Glass: The Forbidden Library: Volume 3. 2016. (Forbidden Library). (ENG., Illus.). 368p. (J). (gr. 5). 16.99 (978-0-8037-3978-9(8), Kathy Dawson Books) Penguin Young Readers Group.

Weyn, Suzanne. Water Song: A Retelling of the Frog Prince. 2012. (Once upon a Time Ser.). (ENG.). 208p. (YA). (gr. 9). pap. 10.99 (978-1-4424-6052-2(0), Simon Pulse) Simon Pulse.

Wheeler, E. B. The Haunting of Springett Hall. 2015. (ENG.). 256p. (YA). (gr. 7-13). pap. 16.99 (978-1-4621-1672-0(8), Sweetwater Bks.) Cedar Fort, Inc./CFI Distribution.

Wheeler, Lisa. The Christmas Boot. Pinkney, Jerry, illus. 2016. (ENG.). 32p. (J). (gr. -1-3). 17.99 (978-0-8037-4134-8(0), Dial Bks) Penguin Young Readers Group.

Whelan, Olwyn. The Star Child. Maidment, Stella, illus. 2004. 40p. (J). 14.95 (978-1-84458-039-2(3)) Avalon Publishing Group.

Whirlwhim. The Baffelgagging Blundernagging Brothers: In Curse of the Bog Frog. 2008. (Illus.). 192p. (YA). 29.95 (978-0-9800274-0-2(3)) Whirlwhim.

White, Amanda. Sand Sister. Morales, Yuyi, illus. 2004. 32p. (J). 16.99 (978-1-84148-617-8(5)) Barefoot Bks., Inc.

White, Amy Brecount. Forget-Her-Nots. 2010. (ENG.). 384p. (YA). (gr. 8-18). 16.99 (978-0-06-167298-9(X), Greenwillow Bks.) HarperCollins Pubs.

White, Dorine. The Emerald Ring (Cleopatra's Legacy) 2013. 183p. (YA). pap. 13.99 (978-1-4621-1133-6(5), Horizon Pubs.) Cedar Fort, Inc./CFI Distribution.

White, J. A. The Thickety: a Path Begins. Offermann, Andrea, illus. 2017. (Thickety Ser.: 4). 512p. (J). (gr. 5). 16.99 (978-0-06-238139-2(3), Tegen, Katherine Bks) HarperCollins Pubs.

—Well of Witches. Offermann, Andrea, illus. 2016. (Thickety Ser.: 3). 512p. (J). (gr. 5). 16.99 (978-0-06-225732-1(3), Tegen, Katherine Bks) HarperCollins Pubs.

—The Whispering Trees. Offermann, Andrea, illus. 2015. (Thickety Ser.: 2). (ENG.). 528p. (J). (gr. 5). 16.99 (978-0-06-225729-1(3), Tegen, Katherine Bks) HarperCollins Pubs.

White, Kiersten. Illusions of Fate. 2014. (ENG.). 288p. (YA). (gr. 8). 17.99 (978-0-06-213589-6(9), HarperTeen) HarperCollins Pubs.

White, Paul. Jungle Doctor on the Hop. 2015. (Flamingo Fiction 9-13s Ser.). (ENG., Illus.). 160p. (J). (gr. 4-7). per. 8.99 (978-1-84550-297-3(3), 941c8ee3-121e-4dda-84ae-b6809a4d4b39) Christian Focus Pubns. GBR. Dist: Bookmasters Distribution.

White, Wade Albert. The Adventurer's Guide to Dragons (and Why They Keep Biting Me) 2017. (Adventurer's Guide Ser.: 2). (ENG.). 384p. (J). (gr. 3-7). 16.99 (978-0-316-30531-0(6)) Little, Brown Bks. for Young Readers.

Whitesides, Tyler. Heroes of the Dustbin. 2015. (Janitors Ser.: Bk. 5). (Illus.). vii, 408p. (J). 18.99 (978-1-62972-065-4(8), Shadow Mountain) Deseret Bk. Co.

—Strike of the Sweepers. 2014. (Janitors Ser.: 4). (ENG., Illus.). 400p. (J). (gr. 5). 18.99 (978-1-60907-907-9(8), Shadow Mountain) Shadow Mountain Publishing.

Whitney, Daisy. The Fire Artist. 2014. (ENG.). 288p. (YA). (gr. 7). 17.99 (978-1-61963-132-8(6), 9781619631328, Bloomsbury USA Childrens) Bloomsbury Publishing USA.

Whittle, J. Robert & Sandilands, Joyce. Leprechaun Magic. Galego, Ane M., illus. 2004. 64p. (J). *(978-0-9685061-2-7(7))* Whitlands Publishing, Ltd.
Whybrow, Ian. The Unvisibles. 2006. 184p. (J). (gr. 4-7). 16.95 *(978-0-8234-1972-2(X))* Holiday Hse., Inc.
Whyman, Matt. Street Runners. 2008. (ENG.). 272p. (J). (gr. 4-7). pap. 11.95 *(978-1-84738-282-5(7))* Simon & Schuster, Ltd. GBR. Dist: Simon & Schuster, Inc.
Wicke, Ed. Akayzia Adams & the Masterdragon's Secret. 2003. 280p. (J). per. 9.99 *(978-0-9677652-3-5(4),* BlacknBlue Pr. UK) Blacknblue Pr.
Wilce, Ysabeau S. Flora's Fury: How a Girl of Spirit & a Red Dog Confound Their Friends, Astound Their Enemies, & Learn the Importance of Packing Light. 2013. (ENG.). 528p. (YA). (gr. 7). pap. 7.99 *(978-0-15-205415-1(4))* Houghton Mifflin Harcourt Publishing Co.
Wiley, Melissa. The Prairie Thief. Madrid, Erwin, illus. (ENG.). 224p. (J). (gr. 3-7). 2013. pap. 6.99 *(978-1-4424-4057-9(0))* 2012. 15.99 *(978-1-4424-4056-2(2))* McElderry, Margaret K. Bks. (McElderry, Margaret K. Bks.).
Willett, Edward. The Cave Beneath the Sea: The Shards of Excalibur Book 4, 1 vol. 2015. (Shards of Excalibur Ser.: 4). (ENG.). 224p. (YA). (gr. 7-9). pap. 14.95 *(978-1-55050-639-6(0))* Coteau Bks. CAN. Dist: Orca Bk. Pubs. USA.
Williams, Alison. Pink Cat Blue Cat. 2009. (Illus.). 32p. pap. 14.49 *(978-1-4389-4623-8(6))* AuthorHouse.
Williams, Mandi Tillotson. The Many Adventures of Mortimer Crump: Mortimer's Sweet Retreat. 2011. 28p. pap. 13.83 *(978-1-4634-2637-8(2))* AuthorHouse.
Williams, Marie Sheppard. The Magic Stories. 2012. pap. 12.95 *(978-0-7414-7280-9(5))* Infinity Publishing.
Williams, Suzanne. The Gigantic, Genuine Genie. Gonzales, Chuck, illus. 2007. (Princess Power Ser.: No. 6). 128p. (J). 15.99 *(978-0-06-078309-9(5))* HarperCollins Pubs.
—The Mysterious, Mournful Maiden. Gonzales, Chuck, illus. 2007. 112p. (J). 15.99 *(978-0-06-078305-1(2))* HarperCollins Pubs.
Williams, T. D. Happy Village. 2010. 24p. 13.99 *(978-1-4269-3492-6(0))* Trafford Publishing.
Williamson, Hilary & Adams, Lynne. The Magic Pumpkin. 2008. 16p. 9.99 *(978-1-4357-0321-6(9))* Lulu Pr., Inc.
Williamson, Liza. Emily to the Rescue. Keddy, Brian, illus. 2011. 28p. pap. 24.95 *(978-1-4626-3342-5(0))* America Star Bks.
Willis, Jeanne. Shamanka. 2009. (J). pap. *(978-0-7636-3767-5(X))* Candlewick Pr.
Wilson, David Cramb. The Day that the Fairies stole Badger! 2008. 40p. pap. 9.95 *(978-0-557-00247-4(8))* Lulu Pr., Inc.
Wilson, Karma. Baby Cakes. Williams, Sam, illus. 2006. (ENG.). 32p. (J). (gr. -1 — 1). bds. 7.99 *(978-1-4169-0289-8(9),* Little Simon) Little Simon.
Wilson, Mary & Berrios, Frank. Disney Tales of Magic, 4 vols. 2004. (Illus.). (J). *(978-0-7364-2251-2(X)); (978-0-7364-2252-9(8)); (978-0-7364-2253-6(6)); (978-0-7364-2250-5(1))* Random Hse., Inc.
Wilson, N. D. The Chestnut King. 2011. (100 Cupboards Ser.: 3). (ENG., Illus.). 512p. (J). (gr. 3-7). 8.99 *(978-0-375-83886-6(4),* Yearling) Random Hse. Children's Bks.
—Dandelion Fire. 2009. (100 Cupboards Ser.: 2). (ENG.). 480p. (J). (gr. 3-7). 8.99 *(978-0-375-83884-2(8),* Yearling) Random Hse. Children's Bks.
—The Dragon's Tooth. (Ashtown Burials Ser.: Bk. 1). (ENG.). 496p. (J). (gr. 3-7). 2012. 8.99 *(978-0-375-86396-7(6),* Yearling) 2011. 16.99 *(978-0-375-86439-1(3),* Random Hse. Bks. for Young Readers) Random Hse. Children's Bks.
—The Drowned Vault. 2013. (Ashtown Burials Ser.: Bk. 2). (ENG.). 464p. (J). (gr. 3-7). 8.99 *(978-0-375-86397-4(4),* Yearling) Random Hse. Children's Bks.
—Outlaws of Time: the Legend of Sam Miracle. 2017. (Outlaws of Time Ser.: 1). 352p. (J). (gr. 3-7). pap. 6.99 *(978-0-06-232727-7(5),* Tegen, Katherine Bks) HarperCollins Pubs.
—100 Cupboards. 2008. (100 Cupboards Ser.: 1). (ENG.). 320p. (J). (gr. 3-7). 7.99 *(978-0-375-83882-8(1),* Yearling) Random Hse. Children's Bks.
Windsor, M. L. Jack Death. Ewald, Chris, illus. 2016. (ENG.). 165p. (J). (gr. 2-7). 12.99 *(978-1-939547-28-6(8))* Creston Bks.
Winkler, Ashley & Winkler, Michael. One Good Quest Deserves Another: A Crown of Amaranth Story. 2009. 292p. 28.95 *(978-0-595-71039-3(5));* pap. 18.95 *(978-0-595-47365-6(2))* iUniverse, Inc.
Winkler, Henry & Oliver, Lin. Fake Snakes & Weird Wizards. Garrett, Scott, illus. 2015. (Here's Hank Ser.: No. 4). (ENG.). 128p. (J). (gr. 1-3). 5.99 *(978-0-448-48252-1(5),* Grosset & Dunlap) Penguin Young Readers Group.
—Niagara Falls, or Does It? 2004. (Hank Zipzer Ser.: No. 1). 128p. (J). (gr. 2-6). pap. 29.00 incl. audio *(978-1-4000-9006-8(7),* Listening Library) Random Hse. Audio Publishing Group.
Winn, Sheridan. The Sprite Sisters: Magic at Drysdale's School (Vol 7) Winn, Christopher, illus. 2013. 256p. pap. *(978-0-9574231-2-1(8))* Winn, Sheridan.
Winslade, Jayn E. Emily & Jen Dance for Deeron. 2010. 352p. pap. *(978-1-907211-48-5(9))* Grosvenor Hse. Publishing Ltd.
Winstanley, Liz. The Adventures of Abra & His Magic Carpet. 2012. 32p. pap. 14.97 *(978-1-62212-406-0(5),* Strategic Bk. Publishing) Strategic Book Publishing & Rights Agency (SBPRA).
Winterspell. 2014. (ENG., Illus.). 464p. (YA). (gr. 9). 17.99 *(978-1-4424-6598-5(0),* Simon & Schuster Bks. For Young Readers) Simon & Schuster Bks. For Young Readers.
Wittner, Shirley. Kemira & the Ancient Book of Spells. 2006. 51p. pap. 16.95 *(978-1-4241-4840-0(5))* PublishAmerica, Inc.
Wizards of Waverly Place Insider's Guide. 2009. 128p. pap. 8.99 *(978-1-4231-2473-3(1))* Disney Pr.
Wolverton, Barry. The Vanishing Island. Stevenson, Dave, illus. (Chronicles of the Black Tulip Ser.: 1). (J). (gr. 3-7). 2016. 368p. pap. 6.99 *(978-0-06-222191-9(4))* 2015. (ENG.). 352p. 16.99 *(978-0-06-222190-2(6))* HarperCollins Pubs. (Walden Pond Pr.).
—The Vanishing Island. Stevenson, Dave, illus. 2016. (Chronicles of the Black Tulip Ser.: Vol. 1). (ENG.). 368p. (J). (gr. 3-7). 17.20 *(978-0-606-39260-0(2))* Turtleback Bks.
Wong, Carmen L. F. Written By... 2013. 252p. (gr. 4-6). 33.25 *(978-1-4669-3179-4(5));* pap. 18.85 *(978-1-4669-3178-7(7))* Trafford Publishing.
Wood, Audrey. Magic Shoelaces. Wood, Audrey, illus. 2005. (Child's Play Library). (ENG., Illus.). 32p. (J). (gr. 1-2). pap. *(978-1-904550-51-8(7))* Child's Play International Ltd.
Wood, Fiona. Cloudwish. 2016. (ENG.). 320p. (YA). (gr. 7-17). 17.99 *(978-0-316-24212-7(8),* Poppy) Little, Brown Bks. for Young Readers.
Woodward, Kay. Sleeping Handsome & the Princess Engineer. de Ruiter, Jo, illus. 2015. (Fairy Tales Today Ser.). (ENG.). 24p. (gr. 1-2). 23.99 *(978-1-4795-8615-8(3))* Picture Window Bks.
Worthington, Jennifer & Shoals, Melinda, illus. The Gift That Saved Christmas. 2008. 40p. (J). 17.00 *(978-0-9773460-1-1(3))* Spritelee Enterprises.
Worthington, Lisa & Moon, Susan. My Magic Bike. Harston, Jerry, illus. 2006. (ENG.). 16p. (gr. k-2). pap. 7.95 *(978-1-57874-039-0(8),* Kaeden Bks.) Kaeden Corp.
Worthington, Michelle. Noah Chases the Wind. Cowman, Joseph, illus. 2015. (ENG.). 32p. (J). (gr. -1-3). 16.95 *(978-1-60554-356-7(X))* Redleaf Pr.
Wrecks, Billy & Kaplan, Arie. Doctor Strange Little Golden Book (Marvel: Doctor Strange) Golden Books et al, illus. 2017. (Little Golden Book Ser.). (ENG.). 24p. (J). (-k). 4.99 *(978-1-101-93865-2(X),* Golden Bks.) Random Hse. Children's Bks.
Wrede, Patricia C. Book of Enchantments. 2005. (ENG., Illus.). 256p. (J). (gr. 5-7). pap. 14.95 *(978-0-15-205508-0(8))* Houghton Mifflin Harcourt Publishing Co.
—Calling on Dragons. unabr. ed. 2004. (Enchanted Forest Chronicles: Bk. 3). 244p. (J). (gr. 6-18). pap. 38.00 incl. audio *(978-0-8072-0792-5(6),* LYA 347 SP, Listening Library) Random Hse. Audio Publishing Group.
—The Far West. 2012. (ENG.). 384p. (J). (gr. 7-7). 17.99 *(978-0-545-03344-2(6),* Scholastic Pr.) Scholastic, Inc.
—Talking to Dragons. unabr. ed. 2004. (Enchanted Forest Chronicles: Bk. 4). 255p. (J). (gr. 6-18). pap. 38.00 incl. audio *(978-0-8072-0983-7(X),* S YA 385 SP, Listening Library) Random Hse. Audio Publishing Group.
Wrede, Patricia C. & Stevermer, Caroline. Sorcery & Cecelia or the Enchanted Chocolate Pot: Being the Correspondence of Two Young Ladies of Quality Regarding Various Magical Scandals in London & the Country. 2004. (ENG., Illus.). 336p. (YA). (gr. 7-12). pap. 7.99 *(978-0-15-205300-0(X))* Houghton Mifflin Harcourt Publishing Co.
Wurge, B. B. Squiggle. 2009. (LeapKids Ser.). (ENG., Illus.). 152p. (J). (gr. 2-7). pap. 9.95 *(978-0-9815148-9-5(8))* Leapfrog Pr.
Wyatt, Trina. Magical Mrs Mable Comes to Green Hills. 2008. 28p. pap. 12.50 *(978-1-4389-1015-4(0))* AuthorHouse.
Wyche, Wofford, Jane. Adventures at Hi-Lonesome Ranch: The Magic Cabin, Book Two. 2014. 194p. pap. 17.95 *(978-1-4908-1824-5(3),* WestBow Pr.) Author Solutions, Inc.
Wynne-Jones, Tim. Zoom, 1 vol. Beddows, Eric, illus. 2009. (ENG.). 96p. (J). (gr. -1-2). 25.00 *(978-0-88899-936-8(4))* Groundwood Bks. CAN. Dist: Publishers Group West (PGW).
Wynne, Rhys. The Magic Pencil, 1 vol. 2009. 13p. pap. 24.95 *(978-1-60749-089-0(7))* America Star Bks.
Xavier V, Sajjad. Baboonia. 2010. 191p. pap. 14.99 *(978-0-557-04174-9(0))* Lulu Pr., Inc.
Yager, Karen & Williams, Kiersten. Krickle Forest Adventures, Wizbet's Notebook. Walsh, Jennifer, illus. 2012. 60p. pap. 7.95 *(978-0-9855997-0-6(7))* Krickle Forest Adventures.
Yannuzzi, Frank M. The Magic Lacrosse Stick. 2011. 44p. pap. 21.99 *(978-1-4653-3930-0(2))* Xlibris Corp.
Yarrow, Peter & Lipton, Lenny. Puff, the Magic Dragon Pop-Up. Puybaret, Eric, illus. 2011. (ENG.). 14p. (J). (gr. 1). 26.95 *(978-1-4027-8711-9(1))* Sterling Publishing Co., Inc.
Yee, Wong Herbert. Abracadabra! Magic with Mouse & Mole. 2010. (Mouse & Mole Story Ser.). (ENG., Illus.). 48p. (J). (gr. -1-3). pap. 3.99 *(978-0-547-40621-3(5))* Houghton Mifflin Harcourt Publishing Co.
Yep, Laurence. The Magic Paintbrush. Wang, Suling, illus. 2003. (ENG.). 96p. (J). (gr. 3-7). pap. 6.99 *(978-0-06-440852-3(3))* HarperCollins Pubs.
—The Magic Paintbrush. Wang, Suling, illus. 2003. 89p. (J). (gr. 3-7). 12.65 *(978-0-7569-1444-8(2))* Perfection Learning Corp.
—The Tiger's Apprentice. 2005. (Tiger's Apprentice Ser.: Bk. 1). 184p. (J). lib. bdg. 24.62 *(978-1-4242-0449-6(6))* Fitzgerald Bks.
—The Tiger's Apprentice. 2005. (Tiger's Apprentice (Tandem Library) Ser.). 184p. (gr. 5-9). 17.00 *(978-0-7569-5074-3(0))* Perfection Learning Corp.
—Tiger's Blood. 2005. (Tiger's Apprentice Ser.: Bk. 2). (ENG.). 240p. (J). (gr. 5-18). 15.99 *(978-0-06-001016-4(9))* HarperCollins Pubs.
Yep, Laurence & Ryder, Joanne. A Dragon's Guide to Making Perfect Wishes. 2017. (Dragon's Guide Ser.: 3). (ENG.). 240p. (J). (gr. 3-7). 16.99 *(978-0-385-39236-5(2),* Crown Books For Young Readers) Random Hse. Children's Bks.
—A Dragon's Guide to Making Your Human Smarter. GrandPré, Mary, illus. 2016. (Dragon's Guide Ser.). (ENG.). 304p. (J). (gr. 3-7). 16.99 *(978-0-385-39232-7(X),* Crown Books For Young Readers) Random Hse. Children's Bks.
—A Dragon's Guide to the Care & Feeding of Humans. GrandPré, Mary, illus. 2015. (Dragon's Guide Ser.). (ENG.). 160p. (J). (gr. 3-7). 15.99 *(978-0-385-39228-0(1),* Crown Books For Young Readers) Random Hse. Children's Bks.
Yin, Aidi. Emily & Her Dolls. 2011. 28p. pap. 15.99 *(978-1-4628-5254-3(8))* Xlibris Corp.
Yolen, Jane. Curse of the Thirteenth Fey: The True Tale of Sleeping Beauty. 2013. (ENG.). 320p. (J). (gr. 5). pap. 7.99 *(978-0-14-242761-3(6),* Puffin Books) Penguin Young Readers Group.
—Snow in Summer. 2013. (ENG.). 272p. (J). (gr. 5). pap. 7.99 *(978-0-14-242197-0(9),* Puffin Books) Penguin Young Readers Group.
—Wizard's Hall. 144p. (J). (gr. 3-5). pap. 6.00 *(978-0-8072-1544-9(9),* Listening Library) Random Hse. Audio Publishing Group.
Yoo, Tae-Eun. The Little Red Fish. 2007. (Illus.). (J). *(978-1-4287-3601-6(8),* Dial) Penguin Publishing Group.
Young, Cleous. The Magical Rug. 2004. 25p. pap. 24.95 *(978-1-4137-3555-0(X))* PublishAmerica, Inc.
Young, Helen Ann. Hellie & the Sensational Magic Carpet. Young, Tim, illus. 2013. 106p. pap. *(978-1-908353-02-3(3))* Young Editions.
Young, Julie. Dragon Stone: Dragon Cliff Trilogy Book Two. 2011. 160p. (gr. 4-6). pap. 12.95 *(978-1-4620-0682-3(5))* iUniverse, Inc.
Yu, Li, et al. The Holy Spark; Rogel & the Goddess of Liberty. 2006. (J). *(978-1-931907-42-2(0))* Homa & Sekey Bks.
Yurksaitis, Anne. The Ingle Bingle. Yurksaitis, Stephanie, illus. 2012. 16p. pap. 24.95 *(978-1-4626-7687-3(1))* America Star Bks.
Zagarenski, Pamela. The Whisper. 2015. (ENG., Illus.). 40p. (J). (gr. -1-3). 17.99 *(978-0-544-41686-4(4),* HMH Books For Young Readers) Houghton Mifflin Harcourt Publishing Co.
Zahler, Diane. Baker's Magic. Price, Mina, illus. 2016. (Middle-Grade Novels Ser.). (ENG.). 336p. (gr. 4-7). lib. bdg. 26.65 *(978-1-4965-2724-0(0))* Stone Arch Bks.
—Sleeping Beauty's Daughters. 2013. 216p. (J). lib. bdg. *(978-0-06-200497-0(2))* Harper & Row Ltd.
—The Thirteenth Princess. 2011. (ENG.). 272p. (J). (gr. 3-7). pap. 6.99 *(978-0-06-182500-2(X))* HarperCollins Pubs.
Zales, S. R. Jenny & the Hummingbird Faeries. 2012. 152p. pap. 14.95 *(978-1-4575-1330-5(7))* Dog Ear Publishing, LLC.
Zellers, Michelle. Maya's Magic Carpet. 2006. (J). per. 11.95 *(978-1-889743-48-6(8))* Robbie Dean Pr.
Zettel, Sarah. Bad Luck Girl. 2014. (American Fairy Trilogy Ser.: Bk. 3). (ENG.). 368p. (YA). (gr. 7). 17.99 *(978-0-375-86940-2(9),* Random Hse. Bks. for Young Readers) Random Hse. Children's Bks.
—Dust Girl. (American Fairy Trilogy Ser.: Bk. 1). (ENG.). (YA). (gr. 7). 2013. 320p. pap. 9.99 *(978-0-375-87381-2(3),* Bluefire) 2012. 304p. 17.99 *(978-0-375-86938-9(7),* Random Hse. Bks. for Young Readers) Random Hse. Children's Bks.
—Golden Girl. 2013. (American Fairy Trilogy Ser.: Bk. 2). (ENG.). 320p. (YA). (gr. 7). 17.99 *(978-0-375-86939-6(5),* Random Hse. Bks. for Young Readers) Random Hse. Children's Bks.
Zimmerman, Virginia. The Rosemary Spell. (ENG.). (J). (gr. 5-7). 2017. 288p. pap. 7.99 *(978-0-544-93699-7(X),* HMH Books For Young Readers) 2015. 280p. 16.99 *(978-0-544-44537-6(6))* Houghton Mifflin Harcourt Publishing Co.
Zink, Michelle. Circle of Fire. 2012. (Prophecy of the Sisters Trilogy Ser.: 3). (ENG.). 368p. (YA). (gr. 7-17). pap. 22.99 *(978-0-316-03446-3(0))* Little, Brown Bks. for Young Readers.
Zinn, Bridget. Poison. 2014. (ENG.). 288p. (YA). (gr. 7-12). pap. 9.99 *(978-1-4231-5330-6(8))* Hyperion Bks. for Children.
123 Sesame Street, ed. Abby in Wonderland. 2009. (ENG.). 20p. 16.99 *(978-1-59069-834-1(7))* Studio Mouse LLC.

MAGIC—HISTORY

Bentley, Sue. Sunshine Shimmers #12. Swan, Angela & Farley, Andrew, illus. 2014. (Magic Puppy Ser.: 12). (ENG.). 128p. (J). (gr. 1-3). 5.99 *(978-0-448-46791-7(7),* Grosset & Dunlap) Penguin Young Readers Group.
Bosch, Pseudonymous. This Book Is Not Good for You. 2010. (Secret Ser.: 3). (ENG.). 416p. (J). (gr. 3-7). pap. 8.99 *(978-0-316-04085-3(1))* Little, Brown Bks. for Young Readers.
Dowswell, Paul. The Amazing History of Wizards & Witches: Discover a World of Magic & Mystery, with over 340 Exciting Pictures. 2016. (ENG., Illus.). 64p. (J). (gr. -1-12). 12.99 *(978-1-86147-731-6(7))* Anness Publishing, Inc.

MAGIC TRICKS

Here are entered works on performance of sleight of hand or tricks involving various types of illusion for purposes of entertainment. Works on the use of charms, spells, etc., believed to have supernatural power to produce or prevent a particular result considered unobtainable by natural means are entered under Magic.

Amazing Magic. 2004. (Fun Kits Ser.). (Illus.). 48p. (J). *(978-1-84229-859-6(3))* Top That! Publishing PLC.
Amazing Magic Tricks [Dollar General]: Apprentice Level. 2010. (Magic Tricks Ser.). 56p. pap. 0.75 *(978-1-4296-4633-8(0),* Edge Bks.) Capstone Press of Coughlan Cos.
Amery, Heather, et al. The Usborne Book of KnowHow. King, Colin, illus. 2008. (Usborne Book Of... Ser.). 127p. (J). (gr. 4-7). 19.99 *(978-0-7945-2040-3(5),* Usborne) EDC Publishing.
Anderson, James. The Science of Magic (Grade 6) 2016. (TIME for KIDS(r) Nonfiction Readers Ser.). (Illus.). 64p. (J). (gr. 6-6). pap. 10.99 *(978-1-4938-3606-2(4))* Teacher Created Materials, Inc.
Andrews, Ted. Faerie Charms. 2005. (Young Person's School of Magic & Mystery Ser.: Vol. 6). (Illus.). 255p. (YA). (gr. 8-12). 18.95 *(978-1-888767-42-1(1))* Dragonhawk Publishing.
Balloon Oriented Magic. 2004. (Illus.). 139p. (YA). spiral bd. 16.95 *(978-1-931084-01-7(7))* Balloon Magic.
Barnhart, Norm. Amazing Magic Tricks. 2008. (Magic Tricks Ser.). (ENG., Illus.). 32p. (gr. 3-4). 27.99 *(978-1-4296-1945-5(7),* Edge Bks.) Capstone Press of Coughlan Cos.
—Amazing Magic Tricks, Beginner Level, 1 vol. 2008. (Magic Tricks Ser.). (ENG., Illus.). 32p. (gr. 3-4). 27.99 *(978-1-4296-1942-4(2),* Edge Bks.) Capstone Press of Coughlan Cos.
—Amazing Magic Tricks [Home Design Alternatives]: Beginner Level. 2009. (Magic Tricks Ser.). 32p. (gr. 3-4). pap. 3.00 *(978-1-4296-3731-2(5),* Edge Bks.) Capstone Press of Coughlan Cos.
—Amazing Magic Tricks, Master Level, 1 vol. 2008. (Magic Tricks Ser.). (ENG., Illus.). 32p. (gr. 3-4). 27.99 *(978-1-4296-1944-8(9),* Edge Bks.) Capstone Press of Coughlan Cos.
Barnhart, Norm & Charney, Steve. My First Guide to Magic Tricks. 2015. (My First Guides). (ENG.). 24p. (gr. 1-2). lib. bdg. 25.32 *(978-1-4914-2048-5(0))* Capstone Press of Coughlan Cos.
Beak, Nick Huckleberry. Amazing Magic Tricks! 25 Fantastic Ideas for Crafty & Crazy Conjuring. 2016. (ENG., Illus.). 64p. 9.99 *(978-1-86147-634-0(5),* Armadillo) Anness Publishing GBR. Dist: National Bk. Network.
Becker, Helaine. Magic up Your Sleeve: Amazing Illusions, Tricks, & Science Facts You'll Never Believe. Dávila, Claudia, illus. 2010. (ENG.). 64p. (J). (gr. 3-6). pap. 10.95 *(978-1-897349-76-2(9),* Maple Tree Pr.) Owlkids Bks. Inc. CAN. Dist: Publishers Group West (PGW).
Bell-Rehwoldt, Sheri, et al. Kids' Guides. 2012. (Kids' Guides). (ENG.). 32p. (gr. 3-4). lib. bdg. 55.98 *(978-1-4296-9142-0(5),* Edge Bks.) Capstone Press of Coughlan Cos.
Blackstone, Bellamie. Everyday Magic. *(978-1-59093-002-1(9),* Eager Minds Pr.) Warehousing & Fulfillment Specialists, LLC (WFS, LLC).
Book of Magic Tricks Kid Kit. 2004. 64p. (J). 15.99 *(978-1-58086-454-1(6))* EDC Publishing.
Bree, Loris. Kids' Magic Secrets: Simple Magic Tricks & Why They Work. Bree, Marlin, illus. 2003. (ENG.). 112p. (J). (gr. 2-6). pap. 10.99 *(978-1-892147-08-0(4))* Marlor Pr., Inc.
Burgess, Ron. Kids Make Magic! The Complete Guide to Becoming an Amazing Magician. 2004. (ENG., Illus.). 128p. (J). pap. 12.95 *(978-1-885593-87-0(2),* Ideal Pubns.) Worthy Publishing.
Canavan, Thomas. Comedy Magic, 1. Mostyn, David, illus. 2014. (Miraculous Magic Tricks Ser.). (ENG.). 32p. (J). (gr. 3-6). 27.50 *(978-1-4777-9061-8(6),* Windmill Bks.) Rosen Publishing Group, Inc., The.
—Magical Escapes, 1. Mostyn, David, illus. 2014. (Miraculous Magic Tricks Ser.). (ENG.). 32p. (J). (gr. 3-6). 27.50 *(978-1-4777-9057-1(8),* Windmill Bks.) Rosen Publishing Group, Inc., The.
—Magical Illusions, 1. Mostyn, David, illus. 2014. (Miraculous Magic Tricks Ser.). (ENG.). 32p. (J). (gr. 3-6). 27.50 *(978-1-4777-9049-6(7),* Windmill Bks.) Rosen Publishing Group, Inc., The.
—Mental Magic, 1. Mostyn, David, illus. 2014. (Miraculous Magic Tricks Ser.). (ENG.). 32p. (J). (gr. 3-6). 27.50 *(978-1-4777-9065-6(9),* Windmill Bks.) Rosen Publishing Group, Inc., The.
—Number Magic, 1. Mostyn, David, illus. 2014. (Miraculous Magic Tricks Ser.). (ENG.). 32p. (J). (gr. 3-6). 27.50 *(978-1-4777-9069-4(1),* Windmill Bks.) Rosen Publishing Group, Inc., The.
—Table Magic, 1. Mostyn, David, illus. 2014. (Miraculous Magic Tricks Ser.). (ENG.). 32p. (J). (gr. 3-6). 27.50 *(978-1-4777-9053-3(5),* Windmill Bks.) Rosen Publishing Group, Inc., The.
Capstone Press. Easy Magic Tricks, 1 vol. 2010. (Easy Magic Tricks Ser.). (ENG.). 32p. lib. bdg. 95.96 *(978-1-4296-5933-8(5),* First Facts) Capstone Press of Coughlan Cos.
Carlson, Laurie M. Harry Houdini for Kids: His Life & Adventures with 21 Magic Tricks & Illusions. 2009. (For Kids Ser.). (ENG., Illus.). 144p. (J). (gr. 4-7). pap. 18.95 *(978-1-55652-782-1(9))* Chicago Review Pr., Inc.
Charney, Steve. Hocus-Jokus: 50 Funny Magic Tricks Complete with Jokes. 2003. (Illus.). ix, 132p. (J). *(978-0-88166-376-1(X))* Meadowbrook Pr.
—The Kids' Guide to Magic Tricks, 1 vol. 2012. (Kids' Guides). (ENG., Illus.). 32p. (gr. 3-4). lib. bdg. 27.99 *(978-1-4296-8452-1(6))* Capstone Press of Coughlan Cos.
Denne, B. Amazing Magic Tricks. 2004. (Illus.). 32p. (J). pap., act. bk. ed. 6.95 *(978-0-7945-0601-8(1))* EDC Publishing.
Denne, Ben. Amazing Magic Tricks Kid Kit. 2004. (Kid Kits Ser.). 32p. (J). 12.99 *(978-1-58086-736-8(7));* 12.99 *(978-1-58086-729-0(4))* EDC Publishing. (Usborne).
—Magic Tricks to Make & Do. 2009. (Activity Bks). 32p. (J). pap. 6.99 *(978-0-7945-2164-6(9),* Usborne) EDC Publishing.
Dorling Kindersley Publishing Staff. The Magic Show Book. 2016. (ENG., Illus.). 32p. (J). (gr. 3-7). 19.99 *(978-1-4654-5396-9(2),* DK Children) Dorling Kindersley Publishing, Inc.
Dunn, Anthony, illus. Completely Magi-CaLL: The TRUE Secrets of Magic: A Study of the Magician's Art. Gunther, Chat, photos by. 2009. 346p. (YA). pap. 29.95 *(978-0-9729546-8-6(6))* SMC Pubns., LLC.
Easy Magic Tricks, 1 vol. 2010. (Easy Magic Tricks Ser.). (ENG.). 24p. (gr. 1-2). lib. bdg. 50.64 *(978-1-4296-4518-8(0),* First Facts) Capstone Press of Coughlan Cos.
Einhorn, Nicholas. Abracadabra! Cool Magic Tricks with Cards. 2012. (Inside Magic Ser.). (ENG., Illus.). 64p. (YA). (gr. 5-8). lib. bdg. 31.95 *(978-1-4488-9219-8(8),* Rosen Reference) Rosen Publishing Group, Inc., The.
—Alakazam! Sensational Magic Tricks with Silk, Thimbles, Paper, & Money. 2012. (Inside Magic Ser.). (ENG., Illus.). 64p. (YA). (gr. 5-8). 31.95 *(978-1-4488-9221-1(X),* Rosen Reference) Rosen Publishing Group, Inc., The.
—Close-Up Magic. 2010. (Inside Magic Ser.). (ENG.). 64p. (YA). lib. bdg. 31.95 *(978-1-4358-9453-2(7),* Rosen Reference) Rosen Publishing Group, Inc., The.
—Presto Change-O! Jaw-Dropping Magic with Dinner Table Objects. 2012. (Inside Magic Ser.). (ENG., Illus.). 64p. (J). (gr. 5-8). 31.95 *(978-1-4488-9220-4(1),* Rosen Reference) Rosen Publishing Group, Inc., The.
—Stand-up Magic & Optical Illusions. 2010. (Inside Magic Ser.). (Illus.). 64p. (YA). 31.95 *(978-1-4358-9452-5(9),* Rosen Reference) Rosen Publishing Group, Inc., The.
—Stunts, Puzzles, & Stage Illusions. 2010. (Inside Magic Ser.). (ENG.). 64p. (YA). lib. bdg. 31.95 *(978-1-4358-9454-9(5),* Rosen Reference) Rosen Publishing Group, Inc., The.
Frederick, Guy. 101 Best Magic Tricks. Anderson, Doug, illus. 2012. 130p. 40.95 *(978-1-258-23095-1(X));* pap. 25.95 *(978-1-258-23889-6(6))* Literary Licensing, LLC.
Fullman, Joe. Mind Tricks. 2009. (Magic Handbook Ser.). (ENG., Illus.). 32p. (J). (gr. 3-12). pap. 6.95 *(978-1-55407-571-3(8),* 9781554075713) Firefly Bks., Ltd.
—Sleight of Hand. 2009. (Magic Handbook Ser.). (ENG., Illus.). 32p. (J). (gr. 3-12). pap. 6.95 *(978-1-55407-572-0(6),* 9781554075720) Firefly Bks., Ltd.
Gardner, Robert. The Science Behind Magic Science Projects. 2013. (Exploring Hands-On Science Projects Ser.). 128p. (J). (gr. 5-12). pap. 10.95 *(978-1-4644-0223-4(X));* 27.94 *(978-0-7660-4147-9(6))* Enslow Pubs., Inc.
Gross, Peter & Walter Foster Jr. Creative Team. 101 Ways to Amaze & Entertain: Amazing Magic & Hilarious Jokes to Try on Your Friends & Family. 2015. (101 Things Ser.). (ENG., Illus.). 144p. (J). (gr. 3-7). pap. 12.95 *(978-1-63322-042-3(7))* Quarto Publishing Group USA.
Harbo, Christopher L. Easy Magician Origami, 1 vol. 2011. (Easy Origami Ser.). (ENG.). 24p. (gr. 1-2). lib. bdg. 25.32

(978-1-4296-6000-6(7), First Facts) Capstone Press of Coughlan Cos.

Heos, Bridget. Do You Really Want to Visit Neptune? Fabbri, Daniele, illus. 2013. (Do You Really Want to Visit... ? Ser.). (ENG.). 24p. (gr. 1-4). 27.10 *(978-1-60753-201-9(8))* Amicus Publishing.

—Do You Really Want to Visit Uranus? Fabbri, Daniele, illus. 2013. (Do You Really Want to Visit... ? Ser.). (ENG.). 24p. (gr. 1-4). 27.10 *(978-1-60753-202-6(6))* Amicus Publishing.

Higginson, Sheila Sweeny. Pulling Back the Curtain on Magic! McClurkan, Rob, illus. 2015. (Science of Fun Stuff Ser.). (ENG.). 48p. (J). (gr. 1-3). 16.99 *(978-1-4814-3702-8(X)*, Simon Spotlight) Simon Spotlight.

Hunter, Nick. Fun Magic Tricks, 1 vol. 2013. (Try This at Home! Ser.). (ENG., Illus.). 32p. (gr. 1-2). pap. 8.29 *(978-1-4109-5012-3(3))*; lib. bdg. 29.99 *(978-1-4109-5005-5(0))* Heinemann-Raintree. (Read Me!).

Insight Editions. Harry Potter: Magical Film Projections: Patronus Charm. 2017. (J. K. Rowling's Wizarding World Ser.). (ENG.). 16p. (J). (gr. 2-5). 16.99 ***(978-0-7636-9586-6(6))*** Candlewick Pr.

Jacklin, Karl. It's Magic. (Illus.). (J). (gr. 3-6). pap. *(978-1-876367-03-9(2))* Wizard Bks.

Jay, Joshua. Big Magic for Little Hands: 25 Astounding Tricks for Young Magicians. 2014. (ENG., Illus.). 112p. (J). 19.95 *(978-0-7611-8009-8(5)*, 18009) Workman Publishing Co., Inc.

Kelly, Kristen & Kelly, Ken. Abracadabra! Fun Magic Tricks for Kids. Kelly, Colette, photos by. 2016. (ENG., Illus.). 96p. (J). (gr. 1). 14.99 *(978-1-5107-0296-7(2)*, Sky Pony Pr.) Skyhorse Publishing Co., Inc.

Khee, Seah Wee, et al. Chemagic. 2008. 148p. pap. *(978-981-283-707-3(8))* World Scientific Publishing Co. Pte Ltd.

King, Mac. Mac King's Campfire Magic: 50 Amazing, Easy-to-Learn Tricks & Mind-Blowing Stunts... King, Bill, illus. 2010. (ENG.). 176p. (J). (gr. -1-17). pap. 12.99 *(978-1-57912-829-6(7)*, 81829, Black Dog & Leventhal Pubs. Inc.) Hachette Bks.

Kole, Andre. Tricks & Twists. 2004. 168p. pap. *(978-0-9727279-7-6(3))* Pine Hill Graphics.

Kovacs, Vic. Get into Magic. 2017. (Get-Into-It Guides). (ENG., Illus.). 32p. (J). (gr. 3-6). ***(978-0-7787-3401-7(3))***; pap. ***(978-0-7787-3405-5(6))*** Crabtree Publishing Co.

Lane, Mike. Close-Up Magic. Mostyn, David, illus. 2012. (Miraculous Magic Tricks Ser.). (ENG.). 32p. (J). (gr. 3-6). pap. 11.75 *(978-1-4488-6737-0(1))*; lib. bdg. 26.50 *(978-1-61533-515-2(3))* Windmill Bks.

—Magic Tricks: Packed with Dozens of Dazzling Tricks to Learn in Simple Steps! 2012. (ENG., Illus.). 128p. (J). pap. 12.95 *(978-1-84837-914-5(5)*, 9781848379145) Arcturus Publishing GBR. Dist: Bookmasters Distribution.

—Mind Magic. Mostyn, David, illus. 2012. (Miraculous Magic Tricks Ser.). 32p. (J). (gr. 3-6). pap. 11.75 *(978-1-4488-6735-6(5))*; lib. bdg. 26.50 *(978-1-61533-514-5(5))* Windmill Bks.

Loh-Hagan, Virginia. Magic Show. 2016. (Illus.). 32p. (J). *(978-1-63470-493-9(2))* Cherry Lake Publishing.

Magic Card Tricks. 2004. (Whizz Kits Ser.). (Illus.). 48p. (J). *(978-1-84229-943-2(3))* Top That! Publishing PLC.

Martineau, Susan. Marvelous Magic. Ursell, Martin, illus. 2011. (Awesome Activities Ser.). (ENG.). 24p. (J). (gr. 3-6). pap. 10.60 *(978-1-61533-407-0(6))*; lib. bdg. 25.25 *(978-1-61533-368-4(1))* Windmill Bks.

Mason, Tom. Magic of the Masters: Learn Tricks by David Copperfield, Harry Houdini & More! 2007. (Illus.). 48p. (J). *(978-0-439-90716-3(0))* Scholastic, Inc.

Mason, Tom & Danko, Dan. Food Magic: How to Do Amazing Tricks with Ordinary Food! 2007. (Illus.). 48p. (J). *(978-0-439-90715-6(2))* Scholastic, Inc.

—Where Did It Go? Magic: How to Make Things Change Places! 2007. (Illus.). 48p. (J). *(978-0-439-90713-2(6))* Scholastic, Inc.

Mason, Tom, et al. Disappearing Magic: How to Make Things Vanish into Thin Air! 2007. (Illus.). 48p. (J). pap. *(978-0-439-90711-8(X))* Scholastic, Inc.

—Shape-Shifting Magic: How to Turn One Thing into Another. 2006. (Illus.). 48p. (J). *(978-0-439-90708-8(X))* Scholastic, Inc.

Mayne, Andrew. Handbook of Super Powers: Magic Tricks that Make It Look Like You Possess Super-human Abilities. 2004. (Illus.). 96p. (YA). per. 11.95 *(978-0-9715183-6-0(X))* Maynestream Pr.

Megram, Paul. My First Magic Book: 35 Fun Tricks & Illusions for Children Aged 7 Years + 2014. (ENG., Illus.). 112p. (J). (gr. 7-11). pap. 14.95 *(978-1-78249-158-3(9)*, CICO Books) Ryland Peters & Small GBR. Dist: WIPRO.

Mostyn, David, illus. Amazing Magic Tricks. 2014. (ENG.). 128p. (J). (gr. 2). 9.99 *(978-0-486-78034-4(1))* Dover Pubns., Inc.

Nightingale, Hugh. I Can Make Magic. 2016. (ENG., Illus.). 48p. 7.99 *(978-1-86147-482-7(2)*, Armadillo) Anness Publishing GBR. Dist: National Bk. Network.

Oliver, Claire. Marvellous Magic. 2008. (Factastic Journey Ser.). (Illus.). 32p. (J). (gr. k-7). pap. 8.95 *(978-1-59905-241-0(5))* Saddleback Educational Publishing, Inc.

Osborne, Mary Pope & Boyce, Natalie Pope. Magic Tricks from the Tree House. Murdocca, Sal & Vilela, Luiz, illus. 2013. (Magic Tree House Ser.). (ENG.). 128p. (J). (gr. 2-5). 5.99 *(978-0-449-81790-2(3)*, Random Hse. Bks. for Young Readers) Random Hse. Children's Bks.

—Magic Tricks from the Tree House: A Fun Companion to Magic Tree House 50: Hurry up, Houdini! 2013. (Magic Tree House Fact Tracker Ser.: 50). lib. bdg. 14.75 *(978-0-606-32476-2(3)*, Turtleback) Turtleback Bks.

Owen, Ruth. Kids Do Magic! 2016. (Creative Kids Ser.). (ENG.). 32p. (gr. 3-3). pap. 11.75 *(978-1-4994-8113-6(6)*, Windmill Bks.) Rosen Publishing Group, Inc., The.

Price, Sean Stewart. Vanished! Magic Tricks & Great Escapes, 1 vol. 2010. (Culture in Action Ser.). (ENG.). 32p. (gr. 3-6). 30.65 *(978-1-4109-3918-0(9)*, NA-r) Heinemann-Raintree.

Regan, Lisa. Magician. 2012. (Stage School Ser.). (ENG., Illus.). 32p. (J). (gr. 3-6). pap. 10.00 *(978-1-4488-8153-6(6))*; lib. bdg. 25.25 *(978-1-4488-8094-2(7))* Windmill Bks.

Sacks, Janet. A Mysterious Case of Magic & Trickery: Tricks & Tales from the Masters of Magic. 2013. (ENG.). 48p. (J). (gr. 3-7). 16.99 *(978-1-4380-7368-2(2))* Barron's Educational Series, Inc.

Schafer, Albert. Illusionology: The Secret Science of Magic. Wyatt, David & Pinfold, Levi, illus. 2012. (Ologies Ser.). (ENG.). 30p. (J). (gr. 3-7). 24.99 *(978-0-7636-5588-4(0))* Candlewick Pr.

Sherman, Patrice. The Secret, Mystifying, Unusual History of Magic, 1 vol. 2010. (Unusual Histories Ser.). (ENG.). 48p. (gr. 3-4). lib. bdg. 31.99 *(978-1-4296-4791-5(4))* Capstone Press of Coughlan Cos.

Stadler, Charlotte. Coin Magic. 2011. (Early Connections Ser.). (J). *(978-1-61672-611-9(3))* Benchmark Education Co.

Tilden, Thomasine E. Lewis. Mind Games! Can a Psychic Tell What You're Thinking? 2011. (J). pap. *(978-0-545-32943-9(4))* Scholastic, Inc.

Top That Publishing Editors, ed. Magical Mischief. Dahl, Roald, illus. 2005. 24p. (J). pap. *(978-1-905359-51-6(9))* Top That! Publishing PLC.

Tremaine, Jon. Magic with Numbers. 2012. (Illus.). 32p. (gr. 3-5). pap. 8.95 *(978-1-926853-82-6(2))* Saunders Bk. Co. CAN. Dist: RiverStream Publishing.

—Magical Illusions. 2012. (Illus.). 32p. (gr. 3-5). pap. 8.95 *(978-1-926853-83-3(0))* Saunders Bk. Co. CAN. Dist: RiverStream Publishing.

—Paper Tricks. 2012. (Illus.). 32p. (gr. 3-5). pap. 8.95 *(978-1-926853-84-0(9))* Saunders Bk. Co. CAN. Dist: RiverStream Publishing.

—Pocket Tricks. 2012. (Illus.). 32p. (gr. 3-5). pap. 8.95 *(978-1-926853-85-7(7))* Saunders Bk. Co. CAN. Dist: RiverStream Publishing.

Turnbull, Stephanie. Close-Up Tricks. 2011. (ENG., Illus.). 32p. (J). pap. 10.95 *(978-1-77092-042-2(0))* Saunders Bk. Co. CAN. Dist: RiverStream Publishing.

—Do You Really Want to Visit Neptune? 2011. (Secrets of Magic Ser.). 32p. (gr. 4-7). lib. bdg. 31.35 *(978-1-59920-499-4(1))* Black Rabbit Bks.

—Do You Really Want to Visit Uranus? 2011. (Secrets of Magic Ser.). 32p. (gr. 4-7). lib. bdg. 31.35 *(978-1-59920-498-7(3))* Black Rabbit Bks.

—Easy Dinner Table Tricks. 2014. (Beginner Magic Ser.). (ENG., Illus.). 24p. (J). (gr. 2-5). pap. 8.95 *(978-1-77092-156-6(7))* Saunders Bk. Co. CAN. Dist: RiverStream Publishing.

—Easy Mind & Body Tricks. 2014. (Beginner Magic Ser.). (ENG & FRE., Illus.). 24p. (J). (gr. 2-5). pap. 8.95 *(978-1-77092-157-3(5))* Saunders Bk. Co. CAN. Dist: RiverStream Publishing.

—Easy Pen & Paper Tricks. 2014. (Beginner Magic Ser.). (ENG., Illus.). 24p. (J). (gr. 2-5). pap. 8.95 *(978-1-77092-158-0(3))* Saunders Bk. Co. CAN. Dist: RiverStream Publishing.

—Incredible Illusions. 2011. (ENG., Illus.). 32p. (J). pap. 10.95 *(978-1-77092-043-9(9))* Saunders Bk. Co. CAN. Dist: RiverStream Publishing.

—Magic Skills. 2012. (Super Skills Ser.). (Illus.). 32p. (gr. 3-6). lib. bdg. 31.35 *(978-1-59920-801-5(6))* Black Rabbit Bks.

—A Magician. 2016. (How to Be... Ser.). 24p. (gr. 2-6). 28.50 *(978-1-62588-369-8(2)*, Smart Apple Media) Black Rabbit Bks.

—Mind-Reading Tricks. 2011. (ENG., Illus.). 32p. (J). pap. 10.95 *(978-1-77092-044-6(7))* Saunders Bk. Co. CAN. Dist: RiverStream Publishing.

—Prop Tricks. 2011. (ENG., Illus.). 32p. (J). pap. 10.95 *(978-1-77092-045-3(5))* Saunders Bk. Co. CAN. Dist: RiverStream Publishing.

—Transformation & Vanishing Tricks. 2011. (Secrets of Magic Ser.). 32p. (gr. 4-7). lib. bdg. 31.35 *(978-1-59920-500-7(9))* Black Rabbit Bks.

—Vanishing Tricks. 2011. (ENG., Illus.). 32p. (J). pap. 10.95 *(978-1-77092-046-0(3))* Saunders Bk. Co. CAN. Dist: RiverStream Publishing.

Zenon, Paul. Magic of the Mind: Tricks for the Master Magician. (Amazing Magic Ser.). (Illus.). 64p. (gr. 5-8). 2008. (ENG.). pap. 14.05 *(978-1-4042-1759-1(2)*, Rosen Reference) 2007. (YA). lib. bdg. 31.95 *(978-1-4042-1072-1(5))* Rosen Publishing Group, Inc., The.

—Paul Zenon's Practical Magic: Street Tricks, Sleight of Hand & Illusion. 2017. (ENG., Illus.). 144p. 12.95 *(978-1-78097-376-0(4))* Carlton Bks., Ltd. GBR. Dist: Sterling Publishing Co., Inc.

—Simple Sleight-of-Hand: Card & Coin Tricks for the Beginning Magician. (Amazing Magic Ser.). (Illus.). 64p. (gr. 5-8). 2008. (ENG.). per. 14.05 *(978-1-4042-1757-7(6)*, Rosen Reference) 2007. (YA). lib. bdg. 31.95 *(978-1-4042-1070-7(9))* Rosen Publishing Group, Inc., The.

MAGICIANS

see also Wizards

Adler, David A. & Adler, Michael S. A Picture Book of Harry Houdini. Matt, Collins, illus. 2010. (ENG.). 32p. (J). (gr. -1-3). pap. 7.99 *(978-0-8234-2302-6(6))* Holiday Hse., Inc.

—A Picture Book of Harry Houdini. Collins, Matt, illus. 2009. (ENG.). 32p. (J). (gr. -1-3). 17.95 *(978-0-8234-2059-9(0))* Holiday Hse., Inc.

Allen, John. Great Magicians & Illusionists. 2016. (ENG.). 80p. (J). (gr. 5-12). lib. bdg. *(978-1-60152-998-5(8))* ReferencePoint Pr., Inc.

Bednar, Chuck. David Blaine: Illusionist & Endurance Artist. (Transcending Race in America: Biographies of Biracial Achievers Ser.). (Illus.). 64p. (YA). (gr. 5-18). 2010. lib. bdg. 22.95 *(978-1-4222-1609-5(8))* 2009. pap. 9.95 *(978-1-4222-1623-1(3))* Mason Crest.

Biskup, Agnieszka. Houdini: The Life of the Great Escape Artist, 1 vol. Kinsella, Pat, illus. 2011. (American Graphic Ser.). (ENG.). 32p. (gr. 3-4). pap. 8.10 *(978-1-4296-6268-0(9))*; pap. 47.70 *(978-1-4296-6435-6(5))* Capstone Press of Coughlan Cos. (Graphic Library).

Carlson, Laurie M. Harry Houdini for Kids: His Life & Adventures with 21 Magic Tricks & Illusions. 2009. (For Kids Ser.). (ENG., Illus.). 144p. (J). (gr. 4-7). pap. 18.95 *(978-1-55652-782-1(9))* Chicago Review Pr., Inc.

Dillies, Lyn. Your Vote Is Magic! 2012. 184p. pap. 14.95 *(978-0-615-66530-6(6))* Dillies, Lyn.

Dooling, Sandra. Sorcerers, Spells, & Magic!, 1 vol., 1. 2014. (Jr. Graphic Monster Stories Ser.). (ENG.). 24p. (J). (gr. 3-6). 26.25 *(978-1-4777-6211-0(6)*, PowerKids Pr.) Rosen Publishing Group, Inc., The.

Fleischman, Sid. Escape! The Story of the Great Houdini. (Illus.). (J). 2008. (ENG.). 240p. (gr. 3-7). pap. 8.99 *(978-0-06-085096-8(5)*, Greenwillow Bks.) 2006. (ENG., 224p. (gr. 3-7). 19.99 *(978-0-06-085094-4(9)*, Greenwillow Bks.) 2006. 210p. (gr. 4-8). lib. bdg. 19.89 *(978-0-06-085095-1(7))* HarperCollins Pubs.

Higginson, Sheila Sweeny. Pulling Back the Curtain on Magic! McClurkan, Rob, illus. 2015. (Science of Fun Stuff Ser.). (ENG.). 48p. (J). (gr. 1-3). 16.99 *(978-1-4814-3702-8(X)*, Simon Spotlight) Simon Spotlight.

Hill, Douglas. Brujas y Magos. Wilson, Alex, illus. 2003. (SPA.). 64p. (J). 14.95 *(978-84-372-2321-6(0))* Altea, Ediciones, S.A. - Grupo Santillana ESP. Dist: Santillana USA Publishing Co., Inc.

Jarrow, Gail. The Amazing Harry Kellar: Great American Magician. 2012. (ENG., Illus.). 96p. (J). (gr. 3). 17.95 *(978-1-59078-865-3(6)*, Calkins Creek) Boyds Mills Pr.

Kacer, Kathy. The Magician of Auschwitz, 1 vol. Newland, Gillian, illus. 2014. (ENG.). 32p. (J). (gr. 3-5). 18.95 *(978-1-927583-46-3(2))* Second Story Pr. CAN. Dist: Orca Bk. Pubs. USA.

Kimmel, Eric A. A Spotlight for Harry. Madsen, Jim, illus. 2010. (Stepping Stone Book Ser.). (ENG.). 112p. (J). (gr. 2-5). pap. 4.99 *(978-0-375-85696-9(X)*, Random Hse. Bks. for Young Readers) Random Hse. Children's Bks.

Kraske, Robert. Harry Houdini. 2015. 72p. pap. 7.00 *(978-1-61003-493-7(7))* Center for the Collaborative Classroom.

MacLeod, Elizabeth. Harry Houdini. Mantha, John, illus. 2009. (Kids Can Read Ser.). (ENG.). 32p. (J). (gr. 1-3). 3.95 *(978-1-55453-299-5(X))*; 14.95 *(978-1-55453-298-8(1))* Kids Can Pr., Ltd. CAN. Dist: Hachette Bk. Group.

—Harry Houdini: A Magical Life. 2005. (Snapshots: Images of People & Places in History Ser.). (ENG., Illus.). 32p. (J). (gr. 3-7). 6.95 *(978-1-55337-770-2(2))* Kids Can Pr., Ltd. CAN. Dist: Hachette Bk. Group.

Noyes, Deborah. The Magician & the Spirits. 2017. (ENG., Illus.). 160p. (J). (gr. 5). 18.99 ***(978-0-8037-4018-1(2)***, Viking Books for Young Readers) Penguin Young Readers Group.

Piehl, Janet. Harry Houdini. 2009. (History Maker Biographies Ser.). (gr. 3-6). 26.60 *(978-1-58013-705-8(9)*, Lerner Pubns.) Lerner Publishing Group.

Price, Sean Stewart. Vanished! Magic Tricks & Great Escapes, 1 vol. 2010. (Culture in Action Ser.). (ENG.). 32p. (gr. 3-6). 30.65 *(978-1-4109-3918-0(9)*, NA-r) Heinemann-Raintree.

Regan, Lisa. Magician. 2012. (Stage School Ser.). (ENG., Illus.). 32p. (J). (gr. 3-6). pap. 10.00 *(978-1-4488-8153-6(6))*; lib. bdg. 25.25 *(978-1-4488-8094-2(7))* Windmill Bks.

Rockliff, Mara. Anything but Ordinary Addie: The True Story of Adelaide Herrmann, Queen of Magic. Bruno, Iacopo, illus. 2016. (ENG.). 48p. (J). (gr. 1-4). 17.99 *(978-0-7636-6841-9(9))* Candlewick Pr.

Saddleback Educational Publishing Staff, ed. Houdini, 1 vol. unabr. ed. 2008. (Graphic Biographies Ser.). (ENG., Illus.). 25p. (YA). (gr. 9-12). pap. 7.95 *(978-1-59905-224-3(5))* Saddleback Educational Publishing, Inc.

Sherman, Patrice. The Secret, Mystifying, Unusual History of Magic, 1 vol. 2010. (Unusual Histories Ser.). (ENG.). 48p. (gr. 3-4). lib. bdg. 31.99 *(978-1-4296-4791-5(4))* Capstone Press of Coughlan Cos.

Turnbull, Stephanie. A Magician. 2016. (How to Be... Ser.). 24p. (gr. 2-6). 28.50 *(978-1-62588-369-8(2)*, Smart Apple Media) Black Rabbit Bks.

MAGICIANS—FICTION

Afterglow. 2014. (ENG., Illus.). 336p. (YA). (gr. 9). pap. 11.99 *(978-1-4424-5038-7(X)*, Simon & Schuster Bks. For Young Readers) Simon & Schuster Bks. For Young Readers.

Agee, Jon. Milo's Hat Trick. 2017. (ENG., Illus.). 40p. (J). (gr. k-3). 17.99 ***(978-0-7352-2987-7(2)***, Dial Bks) Penguin Young Readers Group.

Akita, Yoshinobu. Orphen, Vol. 4. 2006. (Orphen Ser.). (Illus.). 168p. (YA). pap. 9.99 *(978-1-4139-0269-3(3))* ADV Manga.

Avi. Magia de Medianoche. 2004. (SPA.). 194p. (YA). 10.99 *(978-84-348-9112-8(3))* SM Ediciones ESP. Dist: Lectorum Pubns., Inc.

—Murder at Midnight. (ENG.). (J). (gr. 3-7). 2011. 256p. pap. 6.99 *(978-0-545-08091-0(6)*, Scholastic Paperbacks) 2009. 272p. 17.99 *(978-0-545-08090-3(8)*, Scholastic Pr.) Scholastic, Inc.

Axelrod, Amy & Axelrod, David. The Bullet Catch. 2015. (ENG.). 320p. (J). (gr. 5-9). 17.95 *(978-0-8234-2858-8(3))* Holiday Hse., Inc.

AZ Books, creator. Little Magician. 2012. (Millions of Inventions Ser.). (ENG., Illus.). 16p. (J). (gr. 1-3). pap. 5.95 *(978-1-61889-302-4(5))* AZ Bks. LLC.

Banks, Kate. The Magician's Apprentice. Sís, Peter, illus. 2012. (ENG.). 224p. (J). (gr. 5-9). 16.99 *(978-0-374-34716-1(6)*, 9780374347161, Farrar, Straus & Giroux (BYR)) Farrar, Straus & Giroux.

Barron, T. A. Doomraga's Revenge, 7 vols., Bk. 7. 2011. (Merlin Saga Ser.: 7). (ENG.). 272p. (J). (gr. 5-18). 8.99 *(978-0-14-241925-0(7)*, Puffin Books) Penguin Young Readers Group.

Base, Graeme, et al. Dinosaurs in Your Backyard: The Coolest, Scariest Creatures Ever Found in the USA! 2009. (ENG., Illus.). 32p. (J). (gr. 1-4). 16.95 *(978-0-8109-7099-1(6)*, Abrams Bks. for Young Readers) Abrams, Inc.

Beaty, Andrea. Dorko the Magnificent. (ENG.). (J). (gr. 3-7). 2014. 240p. pap. 7.95 *(978-1-4197-1019-3(2))* 2013. (Illus.). 224p. 17.95 *(978-1-4197-0638-7(1))* Abrams, Inc. (Amulet Bks.).

Bemelmans, Ludwig. Madeline Christmas Activity Book. 2013. (Madeline Ser.). (ENG.). 16p. (J). (gr. -1-2). pap. 7.99 *(978-0-670-01568-9(7)*, Viking Books for Young Readers) Penguin Young Readers Group.

—Madeline's Christmas, 1 vol. Bemelmans, Ludwig, illus. 2007. (Madeline Ser.). (ENG., Illus.). 15p. (J). (gr. -1-2). 9.99 *(978-0-14-240897-1(2)*, Puffin Books) Penguin Young Readers Group.

Benjamin, Sigalit. Garland of Stars. 2009. 26p. pap. 14.50 *(978-1-60860-345-9(8)*, Eloquent Bks.) Strategic Book Publishing & Rights Agency (SBPRA).

Bernatene, Poly, illus. The Sorcerer's Apprentice. 2007. (Usborne Young Reading: Series One Ser.). 47p. (J). (gr. -1-3). 8.99 *(978-0-7945-1589-8(4)*, Usborne) EDC Publishing.

Birney, Betty G. Humphrey's Mixed-Up Magic Trick. Burris, Priscilla, illus. 2016. (Humphrey's Tiny Tales Ser.: 5). (ENG.). 96p. (J). (gr. k-3). 4.99 *(978-0-14-751461-5(4)*, Puffin Books) Penguin Young Readers Group.

Bond, Gwenda. Girl in the Shadows, 0 vols. 2016. (Cirque American Ser.: 2). (ENG.). 380p. (YA). (gr. 9-13). pap. 9.99 *(978-1-5039-5393-2(9)*, 9781503953932, Skyscape) Amazon Publishing.

Brennan, Sarah Rees. Unmade. (Lynburn Legacy Ser.: Bk. 3). (ENG.). 384p. (YA). (gr. 7). 2015. pap. 9.99 *(978-0-375-87105-4(5)*, Ember) 2014. (Illus.). 17.99 *(978-0-375-87043-9(1)*, Random Hse. Bks. for Young Readers) Random Hse. Children's Bks.

—Unspoken. (Lynburn Legacy Ser.: Bk. 1). (ENG.). (YA). (gr. 7). 2012. 384p. 18.99 *(978-0-375-87041-5(5)*, Random Hse. Bks. for Young Readers)Bk. 1. 2013. 400p. pap. 8.99 *(978-0-375-87103-0(9)*, Ember) Random Hse. Children's Bks.

—Untold. Fochesato, Giorgio, illus. 2013. (Lynburn Legacy Ser.: Bk. 2). (ENG.). 384p. (YA). (gr. 7). 18.99 *(978-0-375-87042-2(3)*, Random Hse. Bks. for Young Readers) Random Hse. Children's Bks.

Brindle, I. J. Balthazar Fabuloso in the Lair of the Humbugs. Walker, Sholto, illus. 2016. (ENG.). 240p. (J). 16.95 *(978-0-8234-3577-7(6))* Holiday Hse., Inc.

Brooks, Walter R. Freddy the Magician. Wiese, Kurt, illus. 2011. (ENG.). 224p. (gr. 4-13). pap. 10.99 *(978-1-59020-481-8(6)*, 902481) Overlook Pr., The.

Brown, Teri. Born of Deception. 2014. (Born of Illusion Ser.: 2). (ENG.). 336p. (YA). (gr. 8). 17.99 *(978-0-06-218757-4(0))* HarperCollins Pubs.

—Born of Illusion. 2013. (ENG.). 384p. (YA). (Born of Illusion Ser.: 1). (gr. 8). 17.99 *(978-0-06-218754-3(6))*; pap. 9.99 *(978-0-06-227720-6(0))* HarperCollins Pubs.

Bryant, Annie. Out of Bounds. 2008. (Beacon Street Girls Ser.: 4). (ENG., Illus.). 288p. (J). (gr. 4-8). pap. 8.99 *(978-1-4169-6427-8(4)*, Aladdin) Simon & Schuster Children's Publishing.

Cate, Annette LeBlanc. The Magic Rabbit. 2013. lib. bdg. 17.20 *(978-0-606-31601-9(9)*, Turtleback) Turtleback Bks.

Cerda, Alfredo Gomez. Manolo Multon y el Mago Guason. Antonio & Covi, illus. 2004.Tr. of Manolo Citation & Boring the Magician. (SPA.). (J). pap. 7.99 *(978-84-236-6322-4(1))* Edebé ESP. Dist: Lectorum Pubns., Inc.

Child, Lydia Maria. The Magician's Show Box & Other Stories. 2007. 124p. pap. 18.99 *(978-1-4346-4663-7(7))*; (ENG.). 144p. pap. 19.99 *(978-1-4346-4664-4(5))* Creative Media Partners, LLC.

—The Magician's Show Box & Other Stories. 2007. (ENG.). 124p. per. *(978-1-4065-1354-7(7))* Dodo Pr.

—The Magician's Show Box & Other Stories. 2004. reprint ed. pap. 19.95 *(978-1-4191-7122-2(4))*; pap. 1.99 *(978-1-4192-7122-9(9))* Kessinger Publishing, LLC.

Clarke, Jane. G. E. M. Parsons, Garry, illus. 2008. (ENG.). 32p. (J). (gr. -1-k). pap. 9.95 *(978-0-09-948012-9(3)*, Red Fox) Random House Children's Books GBR. Dist: Independent Pubs. Group.

Cooper, Susan. The Magician's Boy. Riglietti, Serena, illus. 2006. (ENG.). 112p. (J). (gr. 3-7). pap. 9.99 *(978-1-4169-1555-3(9)*, McElderry, Margaret K. Bks.) McElderry, Margaret K. Bks.

Corlett, William. The Bridge in the Clouds. 2010. (Magician's House Quartet Ser.: 4). (ENG.). 352p. (YA). (gr. 5-8). pap. 15.99 *(978-1-4424-1412-9(X)*, Simon Pulse) Simon Pulse.

—The Door in the Tree. 2010. (Magician's House Quartet Ser.: 2). (ENG.). 304p. (YA). (gr. 5-8). pap. 13.99 *(978-1-4424-1414-3(6)*, Simon Pulse) Simon Pulse.

—The Steps up the Chimney. 2011. (Magician's House Quartet Ser.: 1). (ENG.). 288p. (YA). (gr. 7). pap. 13.99 *(978-1-4424-2935-2(6)*, Simon Pulse) Simon Pulse.

—The Tunnel Behind the Waterfall. 2010. (Magician's House Quartet Ser.: 3). (ENG.). 320p. (YA). (gr. 5-8). pap. 14.99 *(978-1-4424-1413-6(8)*, Simon Pulse) Simon Pulse.

Coville, Bruce. The Dragon of Doom. Coville, Katherine, illus. 2005. (Moongobble & Me Ser.: Bk. 1). (ENG.). 80p. (J). (gr. 1-5). pap. 5.99 *(978-0-689-85757-7(8)*, Aladdin) Simon & Schuster Children's Publishing.

—The Evil Elves. Coville, Katherine, illus. 2006. (Moongobble & Me Ser.: Bk. 3). (ENG.). 80p. (J). (gr. 1-5). pap. 6.99 *(978-0-689-85759-1(4)*, Simon & Schuster/Paula Wiseman Bks.) Simon & Schuster/Paula Wiseman Bks.

—The Mischief Monster. Coville, Katherine, illus. 2008. (Moongobble & Me Ser.: Bk. 4). (ENG.). 80p. (J). (gr. 1-5). pap. 5.99 *(978-1-4169-0808-1(0)*, Aladdin) Simon & Schuster Children's Publishing.

—The Naughty Nork. Coville, Katherine, illus. 2009. (Moongobble & Me Ser.). (ENG.). 128p. (J). (gr. 1-5). pap. 6.99 *(978-1-4169-0810-4(2)*, Aladdin) Simon & Schuster Children's Publishing.

—The Weeping Werewolf. Coville, Katherine, illus. 2006. (Moongobble & Me Ser.). 68p. (gr. 1-5). 16.00 *(978-0-7569-6582-2(9))* Perfection Learning Corp.

—The Weeping Werewolf. Coville, Katherine, illus. 2005. (Moongobble & Me Ser.: Bk. 2). (ENG.). 80p. (J). (gr. 1-5). pap. 5.99 *(978-0-689-85758-4(6)*, Aladdin) Simon & Schuster Children's Publishing.

Cross, Frances. Butternut Blobber & the Blue Jade. 2007. (Blobber Ser.). (ENG.). 84p. pap. *(978-1-84167-561-9(X))* Ransom Publishing Ltd.

Cunningham, Mary. Cynthias Attic Magicians Castle. 2009. 158p. pap. 10.99 *(978-1-59080-656-2(5))* Echelon Press Publishing.

Dahl, Michael. The Assistant Vanishes!, 1 vol. Weber, Lisa K., illus. 2013. (Hocus Pocus Hotel Ser.). (ENG.). 112p. (gr. 2-3). lib. bdg. 25.32 *(978-1-4342-4101-6(7))* Stone Arch Bks.

—Hocus Pocus Hotel, 1 vol. Weber, Lisa K., illus. 2014. (Hocus Pocus Hotel Ser.). (ENG.). 128p. (gr. 2-3). 50.64 *(978-1-4342-8937-7(0))* Stone Arch Bks.

—Hocus Pocus Hotel. 2013. (Hocus Pocus Hotel Ser.). (ENG.). 112p. (gr. 2-3). 101.28 *(978-1-4342-4821-3(6))*; 50.64 *(978-1-4342-4820-6(8))* Stone Arch Bks.

—Hocus Pocus Hotel, 1 vol. Weber, Lisa K., illus. 2012. (Hocus Pocus Hotel Ser.). (ENG.). 216p. (gr. 2-3). 10.95 *(978-1-4342-4253-2(6))* Stone Arch Bks.

—Out the Rear Window, 1 vol. Weber, Lisa K., illus. 2012. (Hocus Pocus Hotel Ser.). (ENG.). 112p. (gr. 2-3). lib. bdg. 25.32 *(978-1-4342-4038-5(X))* Stone Arch Bks.

—The Prisoners of the Thirteenth Floor, 1 vol. Weber, Lisa K., illus. 2014. (Hocus Pocus Hotel Ser.). (ENG.). 128p. (gr. 2-3). 25.32 *(978-1-4342-6508-1(0))* Stone Arch Bks.
—The Return of Abracadabra, 1 vol. Weber, Lisa K., illus. 2013. (Hocus Pocus Hotel Ser.). (ENG.). 208p. (gr. 2-3). 10.95 *(978-1-4342-4721-6(X))* Stone Arch Bks.
—The Thirteenth Mystery. Weber, Lisa K., illus. (Hocus Pocus Hotel Ser.). (ENG.). 224p. (gr. 2-3). 2016. pap. 7.95 *(978-1-4965-0755-6(X))* 2014. 10.95 *(978-1-4342-6509-8(9))* Stone Arch Bks.
—To Catch a Ghost, 1 vol. Weber, Lisa K., illus. 2012. (Hocus Pocus Hotel Ser.). (ENG.). 112p. (gr. 2-3). lib. bdg. 25.32 *(978-1-4342-4100-9(9))* Stone Arch Bks.
—The Trouble with Abracadabra, 1 vol. Weber, Lisa K., illus. 2013. (Hocus Pocus Hotel Ser.). (ENG.). 112p. (gr. 2-3). lib. bdg. 25.32 *(978-1-4342-4102-3(5))* Stone Arch Bks.
—The Wizard & the Wormhole, 1 vol. Weber, Lisa K., illus. 2014. (Hocus Pocus Hotel Ser.). (ENG.). 128p. (gr. 2-3). 25.32 *(978-1-4342-6507-4(2))* Stone Arch Bks.
Davies, Margaret, et al. Y Dewin Diog. 2005. (WEL., Illus.). 32p. pap. *(978-1-85596-219-4(5))* Dref Wen.
Delgado, Luis Cabrera. Catalina la Maga. (Torre de Papel Ser.). (J). (gr. 2). 7.95 *(978-958-04-4220-2(7))* Norma S.A. COL. Dist: Distribuidora Norma, Inc.
Dickson, Louise. The Disappearing Magician. Cupples, Pat, illus. 2007. (Kids Can Read Ser.). (ENG.). 32p. (J). (gr. 1-2). 3.95 *(978-1-55453-034-2(2))* Kids Can Pr., Ltd. CAN. Dist: Hachette Bk. Group.
Durrant, Geraldine. Twinbane: an Appalling True History. 2010. 142p. pap. 16.95 *(978-1-4457-7998-0(6))* Lulu Pr., Inc.
Duvall, Deborah L. Rabbit & the Fingerbone Necklace. Jacob, Murv, illus. 2009. (ENG.). 32p. (J). (gr. 1). 19.95 *(978-0-8263-4723-7(1))* Univ. of New Mexico Pr.
Edgson, Alison, illus. The Magician's Apprentice. 2011. (Flip-Up Fairy Tales Ser.). (ENG.). 24p. (J). audio compact disk *(978-1-84643-409-9(2))*; (gr. 2-2). *(978-1-84643-370-2(3))* Child's Play International Ltd.
Edwards, R. G. Eafin Lokdore & the Altar of the Sun Book II. 2007. 264p. pap. 19.96 *(978-0-615-17785-4(9))* Edwards, R. G. Publishing.
Egan, Kate & Lane, Mike. The Great Escape. Wight, Eric, illus. 2014. (Magic Shop Ser.: 3). (ENG.). 176p. (J). (gr. 2-4). 14.99 *(978-1-250-02916-4(3))*, 9781250029164) Feiwel & Friends.
Elmer, Robert. Trion Rising, 1 vol. 2008. (Shadowside Trilogy Ser.). (ENG.). 352p. (YA). (gr. 8-11). pap. 9.99 *(978-0-310-71421-7(4))* Zondervan.
Enderle, Dotti. Book 16: Abracadabra!, 1 vol. 2014. (Ghost Detectors Set 3 Ser.). (ENG., Illus.). 80p. (J). (gr. 2-5). lib. bdg. 27.07 *(978-1-62402-004-9(6)*, Calico Chapter Bks) Magic Wagon.
Enyi, Patricia Nmukoso. Marcus the Magician: At the Beach. 2010. 38p. pap. 15.50 *(978-1-60911-447-3(7)*, Eloquent Bks.) Strategic Book Publishing & Rights Agency (SBPRA).
Everson, Chance. Verlin's Magical Blunder: Tales of the Mandrasaurs, Volume the Seventh. Geary, Steve, illus. 2004. cd-rom 9.95 *(978-0-9760303-6-2(5))* R.A.R.E. TALES.
Fienberg, Anna, et al. Tashi & the Wicked Magician: And Other Stories. Kelly, Geoff, illus. 2017. (Tashi Ser.). (ENG.). 96p. (J). (gr. k-3). pap. 9.99 ***(978-1-76029-050-4(5))*** Allen & Unwin AUS. Dist: Independent Pubs. Group.
Frost, Andrew David. The Magician & the Priestess. 2010. 416p. pap. 17.99 *(978-1-4490-7830-0(3))* AuthorHouse.
Gauthier, Bertrand. Zunik dans le Grand Magicien. 2004. (FRE., Illus.). (J). (gr. -1-2). spiral bd. *(978-0-616-01831-6(2))* Canadian National Institute for the Blind/Institut National Canadien pour les Aveugles.
Giordano, Anne. Spencer, the Magic Rabbit. 2009. 40p. pap. 16.99 *(978-1-4490-3296-8(6))* AuthorHouse.
Gosling, Sharon. The Ruby Airship. 2015. (Diamond Thief Ser.). (ENG.). 496p. (gr. 9-12). 16.95 *(978-1-63079-004-2(4))* Switch Pr.
Hardinge, Frances. Cuckoo Song. (ENG.). (YA). (gr. 7-12). 2016. 432p. pap. 9.95 *(978-1-4197-1939-4(4))* 2015. 416p. 17.95 *(978-1-4197-1480-1(5))* Abrams, Inc. (Amulet Bks.).
Heneghan, Judith. The Magician's Apprentice. 2008. (Illus.). 168p. (J). (gr. 3-7). 16.95 *(978-0-8234-2150-3(3))* Holiday Hse., Inc.
Higgins, F. E. The Bone Magician. 2011. (ENG.). 304p. (J). (gr. 5-9). pap. 10.99 *(978-0-312-65944-8(X)*, 9780312659448) Square Fish.
Higgins, Lawrence. Demons & Dragons: Time, Space & Magic. 2010. (ENG., Illus.). 93p. pap. 20.99 *(978-1-906791-68-1(6))* Arena Bks. GBR. Dist: Lightning Source UK, Ltd.
Hood, Ann. Harry Houdini: Prince of Air. Altmann, Scott & Zilber, Denis, illus. 2012. (Treasure Chest Ser.: 4). (ENG.). 208p. (J). (gr. 3-7). pap. 6.99 *(978-0-448-45470-2(X)*, Grosset & Dunlap) Penguin Young Readers Group.
—Prince of Air, No. 4. Altmann, Scott & Zilber, Denis, illus. 2012. (Treasure Chest Ser.: 4). (ENG.). 208p. (J). (gr. 3-7). 15.99 *(978-0-448-45474-0(2)*, Grosset & Dunlap) Penguin Young Readers Group.
Horwitz, Sarah Jean. The Wingsnatchers. 2017. (Carmer & Grit Ser.: 1). (ENG.). 368p. (J). (gr. 5-9). 17.95 *(978-1-61620-663-5(2))* Algonquin Bks. of Chapel Hill.
Howe, James. Rabbit-Cadabra! Mack, Jeff, illus. (Bunnicula & Friends Ser.: 4). (ENG.). 48p. (J). (gr. 1-3). 2007. pap. 3.99 *(978-0-689-85752-2(7))* 2006. 16.99 *(978-0-689-85727-0(6))* Simon Spotlight. (Simon Spotlight).
Izzy, Joel Ben. Dreidels on the Brain. 2016. (ENG.). 320p. (J). (gr. 5-9). 17.99 *(978-0-8037-4097-6(2)*, Dial Bks) Penguin Young Readers Group.
Keene, Carolyn. The Magician's Secret. 2015. (Nancy Drew Diaries: 8). (ENG., Illus.). 176p. (J). (gr. 3-7). pap. 6.99 *(978-1-4814-1700-6(2)*, Aladdin) Simon & Schuster Children's Publishing.
Kennedy, Kim & Kennedy, Doug. Hee-Haw-Dini & the Great Zambini. 2009. (ENG., Illus.). 32p. (J). (gr. k-2). 15.95 *(978-0-8109-7025-0(2)*, Abrams Bks. for Young Readers) Abrams, Inc.
Kirov, Erica. The Chalice of Immortality. 2011. (ENG.). 208p. (J). (gr. 4-7). pap. 7.99 *(978-1-4022-1503-2(7)*, Sourcebooks Jabberwocky) Sourcebooks, Inc.
—Magickeepers: The Eternal Hourglass. Fortune, Eric, illus. 2010. (ENG.). 256p. (J). (gr. 4-7). pap. 10.99 *(978-1-4022-3855-0(X)*, Sourcebooks Jabberwocky) Sourcebooks, Inc.
Kova, Elise. Water's Wrath (Air Awakens Series Book 4) 2016. (ENG., Illus.). 378p. pap. 14.99 *(978-1-61984-425-4(7))* Price World Publishing.
Lalicki, Tom. Danger in the Dark: A Houdini & Nate Mystery. 2010. (Houdini & Nate Mysteries Ser.: 1). (ENG.). 208p. (J). (gr. 3-7). pap. 14.99 *(978-0-312-60214-7(6)*, 9780312602147) Square Fish.
—Shots at Sea: A Houdini & Nate Mystery. 2011. (Houdini & Nate Mysteries Ser.). 224p. (J). pap. 6.99 *(978-0-312-65920-2(2))* Square Fish.
Lawhorn, Mary Joyce. When Annie Dreams. 2012. 74p. pap. 8.95 *(978-1-4697-8819-7(5))* iUniverse, Inc.
Lee, Shell. Teenie's Treehouse Adventures: The Magic Begins. 2004. 37p. pap. 24.95 *(978-1-4137-2879-8(0))* PublishAmerica, Inc.
López, Diana. Nothing up My Sleeve. 2016. (ENG.). 400p. (J). (gr. 3-7). 16.99 *(978-0-316-34087-8(1))* Little, Brown Bks. for Young Readers.
Luciano, Sonia. Mr. I Forgot. 2009. 48p. pap. 16.95 *(978-1-61582-765-7(X))* America Star Bks.
Mahy, Margaret. The Magician of Hoad. (ENG.). 432p. (YA). (gr. 9). 2010. pap. 9.99 *(978-1-4169-7808-4(9))* 2009. 18.99 *(978-1-4169-7807-7(0))* McElderry, Margaret K. Bks. (McElderry, Margaret K. Bks.).
Mason, Adrienne. The Drop of Doom. Cupples, Pat, illus. 2007. (Kids Can Read Ser.). (ENG.). 32p. (J). (gr. 1-2). 3.95 *(978-1-55453-036-6(9))*; 14.95 *(978-1-55453-035-9(0))* Kids Can Pr., Ltd. CAN. Dist: Hachette Bk. Group.
Mawhinney, Art, illus. Olivia the Magnificent: A Lift-the-Flap Story. 2009. (Olivia TV Tie-In Ser.). (ENG.). 16p. (J). (gr. -1-2). pap. 6.99 *(978-1-4169-8297-5(3)*, Simon Spotlight) Simon Spotlight.
McDonald, Megan. Rocky Zang in the Amazing Mr. Magic. 2014. (Judy Moody & Friends Ser.). lib. bdg. 14.75 *(978-0-606-35163-8(9))* Turtleback Bks.
McLaren, Meg. Rabbit Magic. 2017. (ENG., Illus.). 40p. (J). (gr. -1-3). 16.99 *(978-0-544-78469-7(3))* Houghton Mifflin Harcourt Publishing Co.
McSkimming, Geoffrey. Phyllis Wong & the Waking of the Wizard. 2016. (Phyllis Wong Ser.). (ENG.). 400p. (J). (gr. 3-7). pap. 12.99 *(978-1-76011-338-4(7))* Allen & Unwin AUS. Dist: Independent Pubs. Group.
Merola, Caroline. Toni Biscotti's Magic Trick. Cummins, Sarah, tr. from FRE. Merola, Caroline, illus. 2006. (Formac First Novels Ser.: 60). (ENG., Illus.). 64p. (J). (gr. 2-5). 14.95 *(978-0-88780-719-0(4)*, 9780887807190); 4.95 *(978-0-88780-715-2(1)*, 9780887807152) Formac Publishing Co., Ltd. CAN. Dist: Casemate Pubs. & Bk. Distributors, LLC.
Morrisette, Sharon. Toads & Tessellations. O'Neill, Philomena, illus. 2012. (ENG.). 32p. (J). (gr. 2-5). 16.95 *(978-1-58089-354-1(6))*; pap. 7.95 *(978-1-58089-355-8(4))* Charlesbridge Publishing, Inc.
Nicholson, Simon. The Demon Curse. 2015. (Young Houdini Ser.: 2). (ENG.). 240p. (J). (gr. 5-8). 15.99 *(978-1-4926-0335-1(X)*, 9781492603351, Sourcebooks Jabberwocky) Sourcebooks, Inc.
—The Magician's Fire. (Young Houdini Ser.: 1). (ENG.). (J). 2015. 272p. (gr. 4-7). pap. 7.99 *(978-1-4926-0949-0(8))* 2014. (Illus.). 240p. (gr. 5-8). 15.99 *(978-1-4926-0332-0(5)*, 9781492603320, Sourcebooks Jabberwocky) Sourcebooks, Inc.
Nuño, Fran. The Great Magician of the World. 2012. (ENG., Illus.). 24p. (J). (gr. k-2). *(978-84-15241-11-9(9))* D P & G Military Pubs.
Osborne, Mary Pope. High Time for Heroes. Murdocca, Sal, illus. 2016. (Magic Tree House Merlin Mission Ser.: 23). (ENG.). 144p. (J). (gr. 2-5). 5.99 *(978-0-307-98052-6(9)*, Random Hse. Bks. for Young Readers) Random Hse. Children's Bks.
—Hurry up, Houdini! Murdocca, Sal, illus. 2013. (Magic Tree House Merlin Missions Ser.: No. 22). (ENG.). 128p. (J). (gr. 2-5). 12.99 *(978-0-307-98045-8(6)*, Random Hse. Bks. for Young Readers) Random Hse. Children's Bks.
—Hurry up, Houdini! 2015. (Magic Tree House Merlin Missions Ser.: 22). lib. bdg. 16.00 *(978-0-606-37718-8(2))* Turtleback Bks.
Parker, Emma. The Magic Show. 2010. (Illus.). pap. *(978-1-877561-23-8(1))* First Edition Ltd.
Paschkis, Julie. Magic Spell. Paschkis, Julie, illus. 2017. (ENG., Illus.). 32p. (J). (gr. -1-3). 17.99 *(978-1-4814-2210-9(3)*, Simon & Schuster Bks. For Young Readers) Simon & Schuster Bks. For Young Readers.
Paul, Ruth. Hedgehog's Magic Tricks. Paul, Ruth, illus. 2013. (ENG., Illus.). 32p. (J). (gr. -1-2). 12.99 *(978-0-7636-6385-8(9))* Candlewick Pr.
Peterson, Alyson. The Cursed Dagger. 2016. (YA). pap. *(978-1-4621-1865-6(8))* Cedar Fort, Inc./CFI Distribution.
—Ian Quicksilver: The Warrior's Return. 2015. vii, 309p. (YA). pap. 17.99 *(978-1-4621-1629-4(9))* Cedar Fort, Inc./CFI Distribution.
Petrucha, Stefan & Kinney, Sarah. High School Musical Mystery. 2010. (Nancy Drew Graphic Novels: Girl Detective Ser.). (ENG., Illus.). 96p. (J). (gr. 3-7). pap. 8.99 *(978-1-59707-178-9(1)*, 9781597071789) Papercutz.
Posner-Sanchez, Andrea. Bunny Magic! (Disney Junior: Sofia the First) RH Disney Staff, illus. 2014. (Little Golden Book Ser.). (ENG.). 24p. (J). (-k). 4.99 *(978-0-7364-3085-2(7)*, Golden/Disney) Random Hse. Children's Bks.
Prineas, Sarah. Found. Caparo, Antonio Javier, illus. 2011. (Magic Thief Ser.: 3). (ENG.). 384p. (J). (gr. 5). pap. 7.99 *(978-0-06-137595-8(0))* HarperCollins Pubs.
Risso, Eduardo. Mysteries of the Red Moon, Vol. 3. 2006. (SPA.). 48p. pap. 16.95 *(978-1-59497-163-1(3))* Public Square Bks.
Risso, Eduardo & Trillo, Carlos. Los Misterios de la Luna Roja Vol. 2: El Ataque del Circo. 2006. (SPA., Illus.). 72p. (J). (gr. 1). per. 16.95 *(978-1-59497-162-4(5))* Public Square Bks.
Roberts, Justin. The Great Henry Hopendower. Hocking, Deborah, illus. 2017. (ENG.). 32p. (J). (gr. k-3). 16.99 *(978-0-399-25744-5(6)*, G.P. Putnam's Sons Books for Young Readers) Penguin Young Readers Group.
Scheid, Petra Maria. Fairy Tales, Elves & Magicans. 2009. 82p. pap. *(978-3-8391-1065-2(3))* Books on Demand GmbH.
Scott, Michael. The Magician. 2008. (Secrets of the Immortal Nicholas Flamel Ser.: 2). (ENG.). 496p. (YA). (gr. 7). 16.99 *(978-0-385-73358-8(5)*, Delacorte Bks. for Young Readers) Random Hse. Children's Bks.
Sedgwick, Marcus. The Book of Dead Days. 2006. (ENG.). 288p. (YA). (gr. 5-12). reprint ed. per. 7.99 *(978-0-385-74704-2(7)*, Lamb, Wendy Bks.) Random Hse. Children's Bks.
Sheard, Jean. A Chinese Fantasy - Cave in a Casket. 2007. 128p. 34.95 *(978-1-84753-349-4(3))*; (Illus.). pap. 10.50 *(978-1-84753-249-7(7))* Lulu Pr., Inc.
Shehadeh, Y. i. The Legendary Heroes: The Beginning. 2011. 80p. pap. 13.00 *(978-1-4575-0372-6(7))* Dog Ear Publishing, LLC.
Singleton, Linda Joy. Magician's Muse. 2010. (Seer Ser.: 6). (ENG.). 312p. (YA). (gr. 6-18). pap. 9.95 *(978-0-7387-1957-3(9)*, Flux) Llewellyn Pubns.
Skye, Evelyn. The Crown's Game. (Crown's Game Ser.: 1). (ENG.). (YA). (gr. 8). 2017. 432p. pap. 9.99 *(978-0-06-242259-0(6))* 2016. 416p. 17.99 *(978-0-06-242258-3(8))* HarperCollins Pubs.
—The Crown's Game. 2017. (Crown's Game Ser.: bk.1). (ENG.). (J). lib. bdg. 20.85 ***(978-0-606-39645-5(4))*** Turtleback Bks.
Smith, Roy. Louphole Forest Tells Its Tale of Enchantment. Magpie, ed. Burnell Walsh, Avenda, illus. 2012. 38p. *(978-1-908000-18-7(X))* Pyjama Pr.
Soria, Destiny. Iron Cast. 2016. (ENG.). 384p. (YA). (gr. 8-17). 17.95 *(978-1-4197-2192-2(5)*, Amulet Bks.) Abrams, Inc.
Stephens, Juanita. Martha the Multiplying Magician. 2011. 48p. pap. 18.99 *(978-1-4634-2725-2(5))* AuthorHouse.
Stockton, Frank Richard. The Bee-Man of Orn & Other Fanciful Tales. 2004. reprint ed. pap. 1.99 *(978-1-4192-5383-6(2))*; pap. 20.95 *(978-1-4191-5383-9(8))* Kessinger Publishing, LLC.
Styles, Walker. Labra-Cadabra-dor's Revenge. Whitehouse, Ben, illus. 2017. (Rider Woofson Ser.: 7). (ENG.). 128p. (J). (gr. k-4). 16.99 *(978-1-4814-8593-7(8)*, Little Simon) Little Simon.
—Labra-Cadabra-Dor's Revenge. Whitehouse, Ben, illus. 2017. (Rider Woofson Ser.: 7). (ENG.). 128p. (J). (gr. k-4). pap. 5.99 *(978-1-4814-8592-0(X)*, Little Simon) Little Simon.
Sullivan, Laura L. Delusion. 2014. (ENG.). 352p. (YA). (gr. 7). pap. 18.99 *(978-0-544-10478-5(1))* Houghton Mifflin Harcourt Publishing Co.
Tait, Barbara. Timothy Toot… Finds A Hat. Margolis, Al, illus. 2011. 32p. (J). 24.95 *(978-1-58909-917-3(6))* Bookstand Publishing.
Taylor, Theodore. The Boy Who Could Fly Without a Motor. 2004. (ENG., Illus.). 168p. (J). (gr. 2-5). pap. 11.95 *(978-0-15-204767-2(0))* Houghton Mifflin Harcourt Publishing Co.
Thompson, Colin. The Great Montefiasco. Redlich, Ben, illus. 2004. 40p. (J). (gr. -1 — 1). 16.95 *(978-1-59572-008-5(1))* Star Bright Bks., Inc.
Thomson-Swift, Joseph & Thomson-Swift, Joe. The Giant, the Antman & the Mermaid. 2011. (Illus.). 30p. pap. *(978-1-908105-50-9(X))* Grosvenor Hse. Publishing Ltd.
The Three Magicians, 6 Packs. (Literatura 2000 Ser.). (gr. 2-3). 33.00 *(978-0-7635-0241-6(3))* Rigby Education.
Tiffany, Grace. Ariel. 2005. 240p. (J). 16.99 *(978-0-06-075327-6(7))* HarperCollins Pubs.
Tillworth, Mary. Dora in Magic Land (Dora & Friends) Haskett, Dan & Goddard, Brenda, illus. 2016. (Little Golden Book Ser.). (ENG.). 24p. (J). (gr. -1-2). 4.99 *(978-0-553-53840-3(3)*, Golden Bks.) Random Hse. Children's Bks.
Los tres Magos: Individual Title, 6 Packs. (Literatura 2000 Ser.). (SPA.). (gr. 2-3). 33.00 *(978-0-7635-1275-0(3))* Rigby Education.
Ursu, Anne. The Real Boy. McGuire, Erin, illus. 2013. (ENG.). 352p. (J). (gr. 3-7). 16.99 *(978-0-06-201507-5(9)*, Walden Pond Pr.) HarperCollins Pubs.
Villeneuve, Anne. The Red Scarf. 2010. (ENG., Illus.). 40p. (J). (gr. k-3). 17.95 *(978-0-88776-989-4(6)*, Tundra Bks.) Tundra Bks. CAN. Dist: Penguin Random Hse. LLC.
Warren, Cindy. The Unicorn's Horn. 2011. 98p. pap. 19.95 *(978-1-4560-6987-2(X))* America Star Bks.
Watson-Dubisch, Carolyn. Andy! & the Magician's Horn, 1. l.t. ed. 2006. (Illus.). 32p. (J). per. 9.95 *(978-0-9779295-0-4(7))* Medusa Road Pr.
Whited, Wayne & Burns, Robert David. The Adventures of Orie Alexander - the Story Thief (Paperback Edition) 2010. 70p. pap. 7.95 *(978-0-557-63433-0(4))* Lulu Pr., Inc.
Whittaker, Liz. Manawl's Treasure. 2005. (ENG.). 190p. (J). pap. 11.95 *(978-0-86243-785-5(7))* Y Lolfa GBR. Dist: Dufour Editions, Inc.
Wilson, Wendy. The First Book of Red. 2005. 99p. pap. 19.95 *(978-1-4137-5570-1(4))* America Star Bks.
Woodbridge, Nancy Garfield. A Bouquet of Fairy Tales. 2012. 108p. 24.99 *(978-1-4771-4493-0(5))*; pap. 15.99 *(978-1-4771-4492-3(7))* Xlibris Corp.
Yoyo Books Staff. Princess Charlotte Becomes a Magician. 2005. 32p. *(978-90-5843-459-3(1))* YoYo Bks.
Zucker, Jonny. Mission 6: Short Circuit. Woodman, Ned, illus. 2013. (Max Flash Ser.: 6). (ENG.). 144p. (J). (gr. 2-5). pap. 7.95 *(978-1-4677-1480-8(1))*; lib. bdg. 27.93 *(978-1-4677-1211-8(6))* Lerner Publishing Group. (Darby Creek).

MAGNA CARTA

Barrington, Richard. The Magna Carta. 2016. (J). lib. bdg. *(978-1-68048-549-3(0))* Windmill Bks.
Baxter, Roberta. The Magna Carta: Cornerstone of the Constitution, 1 vol. 2012. (Documenting U. S. History Ser.). (ENG.). 48p. (gr. 3-6). pap. 9.95 *(978-1-4329-6765-9(7))*; lib. bdg. 32.65 *(978-1-4329-6756-7(8))* Heinemann-Raintree. (NA-h).
Ladybird Books Staff & Du Garde Peach, L. King John & Magna Carta: A Ladybird Adventure from History Book. 2016. (Adventure from History Ser.). (ENG., Illus.). 56p. (J). (gr. 3-7). 9.99 *(978-0-7232-9402-3(X))* Penguin Bks., Ltd. GBR. Dist: Independent Pubs. Group.
Levy, Janey. The Magna Carta. 2013. 32p. (J). (gr. 4-6). 26.60 *(978-1-4339-9001-4(6))*; pap. 10.50 *(978-1-4339-9002-1(4))* Stevens, Gareth Publishing LLLP.
The Magna Carta. 2013. (Documents That Shaped America Ser.). 32p. (J). (gr. 4-6). pap. 63.00 *(978-1-4339-9003-8(2))* Stevens, Gareth Publishing LLLP.

MAGNET WINDING

see Electromagnets

MAGNETISM

see also Electricity; Electromagnetism; Electromagnets; Magnets

Adler, David A. Magnets Push, Magnets Pull. Raff, Anna, illus. 2017. (ENG.). 32p. (J). (gr. k-3). 17.95 *(978-0-8234-3669-9(1))* Holiday Hse., Inc.
Alpert, Barbara. A Look at Magnets, 1 vol. 2011. (Science Builders Ser.). (ENG.). 24p. (gr. k-1). pap. 7.29 *(978-1-4296-7109-5(2))*; lib. bdg. 26.65 *(978-1-4296-6069-3(4))* Capstone Press of Coughlan Cos. (Pebble Plus).
Arbuthnott, Gill. Your Guide to Electricity & Magnetism. 2017. (Illus.). 64p. (J). ***(978-0-7787-3398-0(X))*** Crabtree Publishing Co.
Beasley, Ava. My Magnet: Fixing a Problem. 2017. (Computer Science for the Real World Ser.). 12p. (gr. 6-7). pap. 7.05 ***(978-1-5383-5146-8(3)**, Rosen Classroom)* Rosen Publishing Group, Inc., The.
Benchmark Education Company, LLC Staff, compiled by. Electricity & Magnetism. 2006. (J). 91.00 *(978-1-4108-7035-3(9))* Benchmark Education Co.
—Electricity & Magnetism: Theme Set. 2006. (J). 131.00 *(978-1-4108-7136-7(3))* Benchmark Education Co.
Blevins, Wiley. Magnets, 6 vols., Set. 2003. (Phonics Readers 1-36 Ser.). (ENG.). 8p. (gr. k-1). pap. 29.70 *(978-0-7368-3195-6(9)*, Phonics Readers) Capstone Press of Coughlan Cos.
Boothroyd, Jennifer. Attract & Repel. 2010. pap. 45.32 *(978-0-7613-6930-1(9))* Lerner Publishing Group.
—Attract & Repel: A Look at Magnets. 2010. (Lightning Bolt Books (tm) — Exploring Physical Science Ser.). (ENG.). 32p. (gr. k-2). pap. 7.95 *(978-0-7613-6059-9(X))*; lib. bdg. 26.60 *(978-0-7613-5429-1(8))* Lerner Publishing Group.
Bryan, Dale-Marie. Experiments with Magnets. 2011. (True Bk Ser.). (Illus.). 48p. (J). (ENG.). pap. 6.95 *(978-0-531-26645-8(1))*; lib. bdg. 29.00 *(978-0-531-26345-7(2))* Scholastic Library Publishing. (Children's Pr.).
Canavan, Thomas. Excellent Experiments with Electricity & Magnetism. 2017. (Mind-Blowing Science Experiments Ser.). 32p. (gr. 4-5). pap. 63.00 ***(978-1-5382-0730-7(3))*** Stevens, Gareth Publishing LLLP.
Cavell-Clarke, Steffi. Magnets. 2017. (First Science Ser.). (J). (gr. 1-1). 24p. pap. 8.25 ***(978-1-5345-2076-9(7))***; pap. 49.50 ***(978-1-5345-2077-6(5))***; 24p. lib. bdg. 24.60 ***(978-1-5345-2078-3(3))*** Greenhaven Publishing LLC. (KidHaven Publishing).
Cheshire, Gerard. Electricity & Magnetism. 2006. (Fundamental Physics Ser.). (Illus.). 48p. (YA). (gr. 5-9). lib. bdg. 34.25 *(978-1-58340-994-7(7)*, 1262672) Black Rabbit Bks.
Claybourne, Anna. Electricity & Magnetism. 2016. (Mind Webs Ser.). (ENG., Illus.). 32p. (J). (gr. 4-6). pap. 11.99 *(978-0-7502-8971-9(6)*, Wayland) Hachette Children's Group GBR. Dist: Hachette Bk. Group.
Cobb, Vicki. Sources of Forces: Science Fun with Force Fields. Haefele, Steve, illus. 2007. (Science Fun with Vicki Cobb Ser.). 48p. (J). (gr. 4-7). per. 7.95 *(978-0-8225-7023-3(8)*, First Avenue Editions) Lerner Publishing Group.
Cook, Trevor M. Experiments with Electricity & Magnetism. 2009. (Science Lab Ser.). (J). (ENG., Illus.). 32p. (gr. 4-6). pap. 10.00 *(978-1-4358-3220-6(5))*; lib. bdg. 26.50 *(978-1-4358-2807-0(0))* Rosen Publishing Group, Inc., The. (PowerKids Pr.).
Cooper, Christopher. The Basics of Magnetism. 2014. (Core Concepts Ser.). (Illus.). 96p. (YA). (gr. 7-12). 35.60 *(978-1-4777-7760-2(1))* Rosen Publishing Group, Inc., The.
—Magnetism: From Pole to Pole. 2003. (Science Answers Ser.). (ENG., Illus.). 32p. pap. 7.99 *(978-1-4034-3551-4(0)*, Heinemann InfoSearch) Heinemann-Raintree.
Dunne, Abbie. Magnetism. 2016. (Physical Science Ser.). (ENG., Illus.). 24p. (gr. k-1). lib. bdg. 26.65 *(978-1-5157-0938-1(8)*, Pebble Plus) Capstone Press of Coughlan Cos.
Eboch, Chris. Magnets in the Real World. 2013. (Science in the Real World EBook Ser.). (ENG.). 48p. (J). pap. 15.64 *(978-1-61783-792-0(X)*, Core Library); (gr. 3-6). lib. bdg. 32.79 *(978-1-61783-742-5(3))* ABDO Publishing Co.
Electric & Magnetic Phenomena. 2011. (Science Made Simple Ser.). (ENG.). 64p. (YA). pap. 12.95 *(978-1-4488-2239-3(4)*, Rosen Reference) Rosen Publishing Group, Inc., The.
Fairley, Peter. Electricity & Magnetism. 2007. (Great Ideas of Science Ser.). (Illus.). 80p. (YA). (gr. 9-12). lib. bdg. 27.93 *(978-0-8225-6605-2(2))* Twenty First Century Bks.
Felix, Rebecca. Magnetism at Work. 2017. ***(978-1-68077-585-3(5))*** 2016. (ENG., Illus.). 24p. (J). *(978-1-68078-142-7(1))* ABDO Publishing Co.
Frisch-Schmoll, Joy. Magnetism. 2008. (Simple Science Ser.). (Illus.). 24p. (J). (gr. -1). lib. bdg. 24.25 *(978-1-58341-577-1(7)*, Creative Education) Creative Co., The.
Furgang, Kathy. Working with Electricity & Magnetism & Trabajar con la electricidad y el Magnetismo: 6 English, 6 Spanish Adaptations. 2011. (ENG & SPA.). (J). 97.00 net. *(978-1-4108-5719-4(0))* Benchmark Education Co.
Galiano, Dean. Electric & Magnetic Phenomena. 2011. (Science Made Simple Ser.). (Illus.). 64p. (YA). (gr. 5-8). lib. bdg. 31.95 *(978-1-4488-1231-8(3)*, Rosen Reference) Rosen Publishing Group, Inc., The.
Gardner, Robert. Easy Genius Science Projects with Electricity & Magnetism: Great Experiments & Ideas. 2009. (Easy Genius Science Projects Ser.). (Illus.). 128p. (J). (gr. 5-9). lib. bdg. 33.27 *(978-0-7660-2923-1(9))* Enslow Pubs., Inc.
—Electricity & Magnetism Science Fair Projects, Revised & Expanded Using the Scientific Method. LaBaff, Stephanie & LaBaff, Tom, illus. 2010. (Physics Science Projects Using the Scientific Method Ser.). 160p. (J). (gr. 5-18). 35.94 *(978-0-7660-3418-1(6))* Enslow Pubs., Inc.
Gardner, Robert. Experiments with Electricity & Magnetism. 2017. (Science Whiz Experiments Ser.). 128p. (gr. 5-5). 37.27 ***(978-0-7660-8678-4(X))*** Enslow Pubs., Inc.

M N O

Gianopoulos, Andrea. The Attractive Story of Magnetism with Max Axiom, Super Scientist. Martin, Cynthia & Schulz, Barbara, illus. 2008. (Graphic Science Ser.). (ENG.). 32p. (gr. 3-4). pap. 8.10 (978-1-4296-1769-7(1), Graphic Library) Capstone Press of Coughlan Cos.

—La Historia Atractiva del Magnetismo con Max Axiom, Supercientífico. Strictly Spanish, LLC., tr. from ENG. Martin, Cynthia & Schulz, Barbara, illus. 2012. (Ciencia Gráfica Ser.). (SPA.). 32p. (gr. 3-4). lib. bdg. 30.65 (978-1-4296-9239-7(1)) Capstone Press of Coughlan Cos.

Goldsworthy, Kaite. Magnetism. 2011. (J). (gr. 4-6). pap. 12.95 (978-1-61690-732-7(0), AV2 by Weigl); (Illus.). 24p. (YA). (gr. 3-6). 27.13 (978-1-61690-728-0(2)) Weigl Pubs., Inc.

—Studying Magnetism. 2016. (Illus.). 24p. (J). (978-1-5105-1126-2(1)) SmartBook Media, Inc.

Gray, Leon. Magnetism. 2013. (Physical Science Ser.). 48p. (J). (gr. 4-6). 31.95 (978-1-4339-9516-3(6)); pap. 14.05 (978-1-4339-9517-0(4)); pap. 84.30 (978-1-4339-9518-7(2)) Stevens, Gareth Publishing LLLP.

Hagler, Gina. Magnets. 2016. (J). (978-1-4896-5286-7(8)) Weigl Pubs., Inc.

Hantula, Richard. Electricity & Forces. 2006. (Real World Science Ser.). (Illus.). 32p. (gr. 2-6). lib. bdg. 26.00 (978-0-8368-6305-5(4), Gareth Stevens Learning Library) Stevens, Gareth Publishing LLLP.

Higgins, Nadia. Mighty Magnet CD+Book. Martinez Ricci, Andres, illus. 2010. (Science Rocks! Set 2 CD+Book Ser.). 32p. lib. bdg. 54.14 incl. cd-rom (978-1-60270-994-2(7)) ABDO Publishing Co.

—Mighty Magnets, 1 vol. Ricci, Andres Martinez, illus. 2008. (Science Rocks Ser.). (ENG.). 32p. (gr. -1-4). 28.50 (978-1-60270-279-0(9), 1287327, Looking Glass Library-Nonfiction) Magic Wagon.

Holt, Rinehart and Winston Staff. Holt Science & Technology Pt. N: Electricity & Magnetism. 3rd ed. 2003. (Holt Science & Technology Ser.). (SPA.). 18.60 (978-0-03-069329-8(2)) Holt McDougal.

James, Emily. The Simple Science of Magnets. 2017. (Simply Science Ser.). (ENG.). 32p. (gr. 1-2). lib. bdg. 27.32 **(978-1-5157-7083-1(4)**, Aplus Bks.) Capstone Press of Coughlan Cos.

Jennings, Terry. Electricidad y Magnetismo (Electricity & Magnetism) (SPA.). 32p. (J). 6.95 (978-84-348-1741-8(1)) SM Ediciones ESP. Dist: AIMS International Bks., Inc.

—Magnets. 2009. (Science Alive Ser.). (Illus.). 32p. (J). pap. (978-1-897563-57-1(4)) Saunders Bk. Co.

Kenney, Karen Latchana. Magnetism Investigations. 2017. (Key Questions in Physical Science Ser.). (ENG.). 32p. (J). (gr. 3-6). 27.99 **(978-1-5124-4005-8(1))** Lerner Publishing Group.

Kessler, Colleen. A Project Guide to Electricity & Magnetism. 2011. (Physical Science Projects for Kids Ser.). (Illus.). 48p. (J). (gr. 3-6). lib. bdg. 29.95 (978-1-58415-966-7(9), 1327821) Mitchell Lane Pubs., Inc.

Kuskowski, Alex. Science Experiments with Magnets, 1 vol. 2013. (More Super Simple Science Ser.). (ENG.). 32p. (gr. k-4). lib. bdg. 27.07 (978-1-61783-853-8(5), Super SandCastle) ABDO Publishing Co.

Lachner, Elizabeth. Magnetic Forces. 2009. (Real Life Readers Ser.). 32p. (gr. 4-5). pap. 10.00 (978-1-4358-0155-4(5), Rosen Classroom); 47.90 (978-1-60853-037-3(X), PowerKids Pr.) Rosen Publishing Group, Inc., The.

Lawrence, Ellen. Magnets. 2014. (Science Slam: FUN-Damentals Ser.). (ENG., Illus.). 24p. (J). (gr. -1-3). lib. bdg. 23.93 (978-1-62724-312-4(7)) Bearport Publishing Co., Inc.

Lew, Kristi. Electricity & Magnetism. 2011. (Science Foundations Ser.). (Illus.). 128p. (gr. 6-12). 35.00 (978-1-60413-293-9(0), Chelsea Hse.) Facts On File, Inc.

Loria, Laura. What Is Magnetism? 2014. (Let's Find Out! Ser.). 32p. (J). (gr. 3-6). 23.45 (978-1-62275-497-7(2)) Rosen Publishing Group, Inc., The.

Madgwick, Wendy. Magnets & Sparks: 16 Easy-to-Follow Experiments for Learning Fun - Find Out How Electricity & Magnetism Works! 2014. (ENG., Illus.). 270p. (J). (gr. -1-12). 8.99 (978-1-86147-352-3(4), Armadillo) Anness Publishing GBR. Dist: National Bk. Network.

Magnetic Magic. 2007. (J). pap. (978-1-59174-381-1(8)) Klutz.

Magnetism & Electricity. (Jump Ser.). (Illus.). 32p. (J). (gr. 2-7). pap. (978-1-882210-27-5(1)) Action Publishing, Inc.

McGregor, Harriet. Magnets & Springs. 2010. (Sherlock Bones Looks at Physical Science Ser.). (ENG.). 32p. (YA). (gr. 3-6). lib. bdg. 25.25 (978-1-61533-213-7(8)) Windmill Bks.

McKinnon, Elaine. Magnets Are Fun! 2013. (Rosen Readers Ser.). (ENG.). 24p. (J). (gr. 2-3). pap. 8.25 (978-1-4777-2240-4(8)); pap. 49.50 (978-1-4777-2241-1(6)) Rosen Publishing Group, Inc., The. (Rosen Classroom).

McMahon, Michael. Why Do Magnets Attract? Level 4 Factbook. 2010. (Cambridge Young Readers Ser.). (ENG., Illus.). 16p. pap. 6.00 (978-0-521-13721-8(7)) Cambridge Univ. Pr.

Meiani, Antonella. Magnetism. 2003. (Experimenting with Science Ser.). (Illus.). 40p. (J). (gr. 4-8). lib. bdg. 23.93 (978-0-8225-0085-8(X)) Lerner Publishing Group.

Murray, Julie. Magnets, 1 vol. 2006. (First Science - 12 Titles Ser.). (ENG., Illus.). 24p. (gr. k-4). 25.65 (978-1-59679-827-4(0), Buddy Bks.) ABDO Publishing Co.

National Geographic Learning Staff. Electricity & Magnetism. 2010. (ENG., Illus.). 32p. (C). (gr. 7-13). pap. 12.95 (978-0-7945-2217-9(3)) National Geographic School Publishing, Inc.

—Magnets, Level 3 - World Windows. 2011. (World Windows Ser.). (ENG., Illus.). 16p. (J). stu. ed. 9.95 (978-1-133-49266-5(5)) Cengage Heinle.

Navarro, Paula & Jimenez, Angels. Amazing Experiments with Electricity & Magnetism. Cuxart, Bernadette, illus. 2014. (Magic Science Ser.). (ENG.). 36p. (J). (gr. 1-6). pap. 7.99 (978-1-4380-0428-0(1)) Barron's Educational Series, Inc.

Nelson, Robin. Los Imanes; Magnets. 2008. pap. 34.95 (978-0-8225-9898-5(1)) Lerner Publishing Group.

—Magnets. 2005. (First Step Nonfiction Ser.). (Illus.). 24p. (J). (gr. k-2). lib. bdg. 18.60 (978-0-8225-5132-4(2)) Lerner Publishing Group.

Newson, Lesley & Wadsworth, Pamela. Trydan a Magnetedd. 2005. (WEL., Illus.). 24p. pap. (978-1-85596-225-5(X)) Dref Wen.

Oxlade, Chris. Experiments with Electricity & Magnets, 1 vol. 2015. (ENG., Illus.). 32p. (J). pap. 11.75 (978-1-4777-5962-2(X), PowerKids Pr.) Rosen Publishing Group, Inc., The.

Petersen, Kristen. Understanding Forces of Nature: Gravity, Electricity, & Magnetism. 2015. (J). lib. bdg. (978-1-62713-437-8(9)) Cavendish Square Publishing.

Peterson, Megan Cooley. Scooby-Doo! a Science of Magnetism Mystery: The Magnetic Monster. Cornia, Christian, illus. 2017. (Scooby-Doo Solves It with S. T. E. M. Ser.). (ENG.). 32p. (gr. 3-4). pap. 7.95 (978-1-5157-3703-2(9)) Capstone Press of Coughlan Cos.

Project Kit for Kids: Magnetism. 2004. (Illus.). 28p. pap. 19.99 (978-0-9724983-1-9(1)) Jazwares Distribution, Inc.

Randolph, Ryan P. Robotics. 2009. (Science Kaleidoscope Ser.). (J). lib. bdg. 25.25 (978-1-4358-2986-2(7), PowerKids Pr.) Rosen Publishing Group, Inc., The.

Rau, Dana Meachen. Electricity & Magnetism. 2009. (21st Century Skills Library: Real World Science Ser.). (ENG.). 32p. (gr. 4-8). lib. bdg. 28.50 (978-1-60279-459-7(6), 200236) Cherry Lake Publishing.

Riley, Peter. Forces & Magnets. 2016. (Moving up with Science Ser.). 00032p. (J). (gr. 3-4). pap. 10.00 (978-1-4994-3141-4(4), PowerKids Pr.) Rosen Publishing Group, Inc., The.

Rising, Trudy L. Is It Magnetic or Nonmagnetic? 2012. (ENG., Illus.). 24p. (J). (978-0-7787-2050-8(0)); pap. (978-0-7787-2057-7(8)) Crabtree Publishing Co.

Rosinsky, Natalie M. Imanes: Atraen y Rechazan, 1 vol. Robledo, Sol, tr. from ENG. Boyd, Sheree, illus. 2007. (Ciencia Asombrosa Ser.).Tr. of Magnets: Pulling Together & Pushing Apart. (SPA.). 24p. (gr. k-4). per. 8.19 (978-1-4048-2497-3(9)) Picture Window Bks.

Royston, Angela. All about Magnetism. 2016. (All about Science Ser.). (ENG., Illus.). 32p. (gr. 1-3). lib. bdg. 27.32 (978-1-4846-2690-0(7), Heinemann First Library) Heinemann-Raintree.

Schuh, Mari. Magnetism. 2007. (First Science Ser.). (ENG., Illus.). 24p. (J). (gr. 2-5). lib. bdg. 25.95 (978-1-60014-098-3(X)) Bellwether Media.

—Magnetism. 2011. (Blastoff! Readers Ser.). (ENG.). 24p. (J). pap. 5.95 (978-0-531-28456-8(5), Children's Pr.) Scholastic Library Publishing.

Sohn, Emily & Brennan, Joseph. Magnetism & Electricity: The Broken Toy Car. 2011. (IScience Readers Ser.). 32p. (J). (gr. 3-4). lib. bdg. 22.60 (978-1-59953-415-2(0)) Norwood Hse. Pr.

Solway, Andrew. Exploring Electricity & Magnetism. 2007. (Exploring Physical Science Ser.). (Illus.). 48p. (YA). (gr. 5-9). lib. bdg. 29.25 (978-1-4042-3749-0(6)) Rosen Publishing Group, Inc., The.

Spilsbury, Louise. The Science of Magnetism. 2016. (Flowchart Smart Ser.). (ENG.). 48p. (J). (gr. 4-5). pap. 14.05 (978-1-4824-4147-5(0)) Stevens, Gareth Publishing LLLP.

Spilsbury, Richard & Spilsbury, Louise. Magnetism, 1 vol. (Essential Physical Science Ser.). (ENG., 48p. (gr. 4-6). 2014. Illus.). 33.32 (978-1-4329-8148-8(X)) 2013. pap. 9.95 (978-1-4329-8157-0(9)) Heinemann-Raintree. (Heinemann InfoSearch).

—What Is Electricity & Magnetism? Exploring Science with Hands-on Activities. 2008. (In Touch with Basic Science Ser.). (Illus.). 32p. (J). (gr. 3-4). lib. bdg. 23.94 (978-0-7660-3096-1(2), Enslow Elementary) Enslow Pubs., Inc.

Stanley, Joseph. Magnet Magic! 2013. (InfoMax Readers Ser.). (ENG.). 24p. (J). (gr. 2-3). pap. 8.25 (978-1-4777-2341-8(2)); pap. 49.50 (978-1-4777-2343-2(9)) Rosen Publishing Group, Inc., The. (Rosen Classroom).

Stringer, John. Magnetism: An Investigation. 2008. (Science Investigations Ser.). (Illus.). 32p. (YA). (gr. 4-7). lib. bdg. 26.50 (978-1-4042-4288-3(0)) Rosen Publishing Group, Inc., The.

Sundance/Newbridge LLC Staff. The Mystery of Magnets. 2007. (Early Science Ser.). (gr. k-3). 18.95 (978-1-4007-6323-8(1)); pap. 6.10 (978-1-4007-6319-1(3)) Sundance/Newbridge Educational Publishing.

Swanson, Jennifer. The Attractive Truth about Magnetism. Lum, Bernice, illus. 2012. (LOL Physical Science Ser.). (ENG.). 32p. (gr. 3-4). pap. 47.70 (978-1-4296-9297-7(9), Fact Finders); pap. 8.10 (978-1-4296-9296-0(0)) Capstone Press of Coughlan Cos.

Taylor-Butler, Christine. Experiment with Magnets. 2010. (Explorer Junior Library: Science Explorer Junior Ser.). (ENG.). 32p. (gr. 3-6). lib. bdg. 28.50 (978-1-60279-844-1(3), 200554) Cherry Lake Publishing.

—Experiments with Magnets & Metals, 1 vol. 2011. (My Science Investigations Ser.). (ENG.). 32p. (gr. 1-3). pap. 8.29 (978-1-4329-5365-2(6), Heinemann First Library) Heinemann-Raintree.

Thomas, Isabel. Experiments with Magnets. 2015. (Read & Experiment Ser.). (ENG., Illus.). 32p. (gr. 2-4). 30.65 (978-1-4109-7922-3(9)) Heinemann-Raintree.

Top That Publishing Staff, ed. Magnet Science. 2004. (Top That! Labs Ser.). (Illus.). 24p. (J). (978-1-84510-154-1(5)) Top That! Publishing PLC.

Wadsworth, Pamela. Golwg Gyntaf Ar Drydan a Magnetau. 2005. (WEL., Illus.). 24p. pap. (978-1-85596-255-2(1)) Dref Wen.

Walker, Sally M. Investigating Magnetism. 2011. (Searchlight Books How Does Energy Work Ser.). (ENG., Illus.). (gr. 3-5). pap. 51.01 (978-0-7613-8408-3(1)); 40p. pap. 8.95 (978-0-7613-7874-7(X)); 40p. lib. bdg. 27.93 (978-0-7613-5775-9(0)) Lerner Publishing Group.

—Magnetism. 2006. (Illus.). 48p. (J). pap. 8.95 (978-0-8225-2843-2(6)) Lerner Publishing Group.

—Magnetism. King, Andy, photos by. 2005. (Early Bird Energy Ser.). (ENG., Illus.). 48p. (gr. 2-5). lib. bdg. 26.60 (978-0-8225-2932-3(7), Lerner Pubns.) Lerner Publishing Group.

—El Magnetismo. Translations.com Staff, tr. from ENG. King, Andy, photos by. 2007. (Libros de Energía para madrugadores (Early Bird Energy) Ser.). (SPA., Illus.). 48p. (gr. 2-5). lib. bdg. 26.60 (978-0-8225-7720-1(8)) Lerner Publishing Group.

—El Magnetismo; Magnetism. 2008. pap. 52.95 (978-0-8225-9778-0(0)) Lerner Publishing Group.

Weakland, Mark. Clang! Wile E. Coyote Experiments with Magnetism. Billiau, Loic, illus. 2017. (Wile E. Coyote, Physical Science Genius Ser.). (ENG.). 32p. (gr. 3-5). lib. bdg. 30.65 (978-1-5157-3731-5(4)) Capstone Press of Coughlan Cos.

—Gears Go, Wheels Roll, 1 vol. 2010. (Science Starts Ser.). (ENG.). 32p. (gr. 1-2). lib. bdg. 27.32 (978-1-4296-5253-7(5), Aplus Bks.) Capstone Press of Coughlan Cos.

—Magnets Push, Magnets Pull, 1 vol. 2011. (Science Starts Ser.). (ENG., 32p. (gr. 1-2). Illus.). pap. 8.10 (978-1-4296-6147-8(X)); pap. 47.70 (978-1-4296-6148-5(8)) Capstone Press of Coughlan Cos. (Aplus Bks.).

Woodford, Chris. Experiments with Electricity & Magnetism. 2010. (Cool Science Ser.). (Illus.). 32p. (J). (gr. 5-6). pap. 10.50 (978-1-4339-3445-2(0)); lib. bdg. 28.00 (978-1-4339-3444-5(2), 1309301) Stevens, Gareth Publishing LLLP. (Gareth Stevens Learning Library).

World Book, Inc Staff, contrib. by. Magnetism. 2011. (Illus.). 32p. (J). (978-0-7166-1427-2(8)) World Bk., Inc.

MAGNETS

see also Electromagnets

Adler, David A. Magnets Push, Magnets Pull. Raff, Anna, illus. 2017. (ENG.). 32p. (J). (gr. k-3). 17.95 (978-0-8234-3669-9(1)) Holiday Hse., Inc.

Alpert, Barbara. A Look at Magnets. 2011. (Science Builders Ser.). (ENG.). 24p. (gr. k-1). pap. 41.70 (978-1-4296-7115-6(7)); lib. bdg. 26.65 (978-1-4296-6069-3(4)) Capstone Press of Coughlan Cos. (Pebble Plus).

Anderson, Lynne. Fun with Magnets. 2011. (Early Connections Ser.). (J). (978-1-61672-622-5(9)) Benchmark Education Co.

Ballard, Carol. Exploring Magnets & Springs. 2008. (How Does Science Work? Ser.). (Illus.). 32p. (J). (gr. 3-7). lib. bdg. 26.50 (978-1-4042-4282-1(1)) Rosen Publishing Group, Inc., The.

Bliss, Pamela. The Mystery of Magnets. 2007. (Nonfiction Reading & Writing Workshops Ser.). (ENG., Illus.). 32p. (J). pap. 17.95 (978-0-7922-4581-0(4)) CENGAGE Learning.

Bodach, Vijaya Khisty. Magnets. 2008. (Discovering & Exploring Science Ser.). (Illus.). 16p. (J). (gr. -1-3). lib. bdg. 12.95 (978-0-7569-8429-8(7)) Perfection Learning Corp.

Bradley, Doug. Magnets in My World. 2009. (Real Life Readers Ser.). 16p. (gr. 2-3). pap. 7.05 (978-1-4358-0063-2(X), Rosen Classroom) Rosen Publishing Group, Inc., The.

Branley, Franklyn M. What Makes a Magnet? Kelley, True, illus. rev. ed. 2016. (Let's-Read-And-Find-Out Science 2 Ser.). 32p. (J). (gr. -1-3). pap. 6.99 (978-0-06-233801-3(3)) HarperCollins Pubs.

—What Makes a Magnet? 2016. (Let's Read & Find Out Science Stage 2 Ser.). (J). lib. bdg. 17.20 (978-0-606-38144-4(9)) Turtleback Bks.

Bryan, Dale-Marie. Experiments with Magnets. 2011. (True Bk Ser.). (Illus.). 48p. (J). (ENG.). pap. 6.95 (978-0-531-26645-8(1)); lib. bdg. 29.00 (978-0-531-26345-7(2)) Scholastic Library Publishing. (Children's Pr.).

Burton, Margie, et al. Using Magnets. 2011. (Early Connections Ser.). (J). (978-1-61672-311-8(4)) Benchmark Education Co.

Cavell-Clarke, Steffi. Magnets. 2017. (First Science Ser.). (J). (gr. 1-1). pap. 49.50 **(978-1-5345-2077-6(5))**; 24p. pap. 8.25 **(978-1-5345-2076-9(7))**; 24p. lib. bdg. 24.60 **(978-1-5345-2078-3(3))** Greenhaven Publishing LLC. (KidHaven Publishing).

Doherty, Paul & Cassidy, John. Magia Magnetica. 2005. (SPA., Illus.). 68p. (J). spiral bd. 15.95 (978-987-1078-40-0(4)) Klutz Latino MEX. Dist: Independent Pubs. Group.

Dunne, Abbie. Magnetism. 2016. (Physical Science Ser.). (ENG., Illus.). 24p. (gr. k-1). lib. bdg. 26.65 (978-1-5157-0938-1(8), Pebble Plus) Capstone Press of Coughlan Cos.

Edom, H. Science Activities, Vol. 1. 2010. (Science Activities Ser.). 72p. (J). 13.99 (978-0-7945-2752-5(3), Usborne) EDC Publishing.

Electricidad e Imanes. (Coleccion Jugando Con la Ciencia). (SPA., Illus.). 39p. (J). pap. 9.95 (978-950-11-0828-6(7), SGM309) Sigmar ARG. Dist: Continental Bk. Co., Inc.

Endres, Hollie J. The Letter Tt Set: Magnets, 6 vols. 2004. (Letter Bks.). (ENG.). 8p. (gr. k-1). pap. 29.70 (978-0-7368-4119-1(9), Letter Bks.) Capstone Press of Coughlan Cos.

French, Cathy. People Who Use Magnets at Work. 2011. (Early Connections Ser.). (J). (978-1-61672-241-8(X)) Benchmark Education Co.

Gianopoulos, Andrea. La Historia Atractiva del Magnetismo con Max Axiom, Supercientífico. Strictly Spanish, LLC., tr. from ENG. Martin, Cynthia & Schulz, Barbara, illus. 2012. (Ciencia Gráfica Ser.). (SPA.). 32p. (gr. 3-4). lib. bdg. 30.65 (978-1-4296-9239-7(1)) Capstone Press of Coughlan Cos.

Hagler, Gina. Magnets. 2016. (J). (978-1-4896-5286-7(8)) Weigl Pubs., Inc.

—Step-by-Step Experiments with Magnets. Ostrom, Bob, illus. 2012. (Step-By-Step Experiments Ser.). (ENG.). 32p. (J). (gr. 1-4). lib. bdg. 29.93 (978-1-60973-589-0(7), 201234) Child's World, Inc., The.

Hedde, Rebecca. Science with Magnets. rev. ed. 2008. (Science Activities Ser.). 24p. (J). pap. 5.99 (978-0-7945-1406-8(5), Usborne) EDC Publishing.

Higgins, Nadia. Mighty Magnet Site CD+Book. Martinez Ricci, Andres, illus. 2010. (Science Rocks! Set 2 Site CD+Book Ser.). 32p. lib. bdg. 84.14 incl. cd-rom (978-1-61641-011-7(6)) ABDO Publishing Co.

—Mighty Magnets, 1 vol. Ricci, Andres Martinez, illus. 2008. (Science Rocks Ser.). (ENG.). 32p. (gr. -1-4). 28.50 (978-1-60270-279-0(9), 1287327, Looking Glass Library-Nonfiction) Magic Wagon.

James, Emily. The Simple Science of Magnets. 2017. (Simply Science Ser.). (ENG.). 32p. (gr. 1-2). lib. bdg. 27.32 **(978-1-5157-7083-1(4)**, Aplus Bks.) Capstone Press of Coughlan Cos.

Jennings, Terry. Magnets. 2009. (Science Alive Ser.). (Illus.). 32p. (J). pap. (978-1-897563-57-1(4)) Saunders Bk. Co.

Kenney, Karen Lactchana. Magnets. 2010. (Everyday Science Ser.). 24p. (J). (gr. k-3). 25.65 (978-1-60753-019-0(8)) Amicus Publishing.

Kenney, Karen Latchana. Super Simple Magnets: Fun & Easy-to-Make Crafts for Kids, 1 vol. 2009. (Super Simple Crafts Ser.). (ENG., Illus.). 32p. (gr. k-4). 27.07 (978-1-60453-626-3(8), Super SandCastle) ABDO Publishing Co.

Kuskowski, Alex. Science Experiments with Magnets, 1 vol. 2013. (More Super Simple Science Ser.). (ENG.). 32p. (gr. k-4). lib. bdg. 27.07 (978-1-61783-853-8(5), Super SandCastle) ABDO Publishing Co.

Lawrence, Ellen. Magnets. 2014. (Science Slam: FUN-Damentals Ser.). (ENG., Illus.). 24p. (J). (gr. -1-3). lib. bdg. 23.93 (978-1-62724-312-4(7)) Bearport Publishing Co., Inc.

McGregor, Harriet. Magnets & Springs. 2010. (Sherlock Bones Looks at Physical Science Ser.). (ENG.). 32p. (YA). (gr. 3-6). lib. bdg. 25.25 (978-1-61533-213-7(8)) Windmill Bks.

McKinnon, Elaine. Magnets Are Fun! 2013. (Rosen Readers Ser.). (ENG.). 24p. (J). (gr. 2-3). pap. 49.50 (978-1-4777-2241-1(6)); pap. 8.25 (978-1-4777-2240-4(8)) Rosen Publishing Group, Inc., The. (Rosen Classroom).

Murray, Julie. Magnets, 1 vol. 2006. (First Science - 12 Titles Ser.). (ENG., Illus.). 24p. (gr. k-4). 25.65 (978-1-59679-827-4(0), Buddy Bks.) ABDO Publishing Co.

National Geographic Learning Staff. Magnets, Level 3 - World Windows. 2011. (World Windows Ser.). (ENG., Illus.). 16p. (J). stu. ed. 9.95 (978-1-133-49266-5(5)) Cengage Heinle.

Nelson, Robin. Los Imanes. Translations.com Staff, tr. from ENG. 2007. (Mi Primer Paso Al Mundo Real - Fuerzas y Movimiento (First Step Nonfiction - Forces & Motion) Ser.).Tr. of Magnets. (SPA., Illus.). 24p. (gr. k-2). lib. bdg. 23.93 (978-0-8225-7809-3(3), Ediciones Lerner) Lerner Publishing Group.

—Los Imanes; Magnets. 2008. pap. 34.95 (978-0-8225-9898-5(1)) Lerner Publishing Group.

—Magnets. 2005. (First Step Nonfiction Ser.). (Illus.). 24p. (J). (gr. k-2). lib. bdg. 18.60 (978-0-8225-5132-4(2)) Lerner Publishing Group.

Publications International Ltd. Staff, ed. Baby Faces. 2011. 10p. (J). bds. 12.98 (978-1-4508-1404-1(2)) Phoenix International Publications, Inc.

Roman, Nora. Using Magnets. 2017. (Super Science Tools Ser.). 24p. (gr. 1-2). pap. 8.15 **(978-1-4824-6393-4(8))** Stevens, Gareth Publishing LLLP.

Rosinsky, Natalie M. Imanes: Atraen y Rechazan, 1 vol. Robledo, Sol, tr. from ENG. Boyd, Sheree, illus. 2007. (Ciencia Asombrosa Ser.).Tr. of Magnets: Pulling Together & Pushing Apart. (SPA.). 24p. (gr. k-4). per. 8.19 (978-1-4048-2497-3(9)) Picture Window Bks.

Royston, Angela. All about Magnetism. 2016. (All about Science Ser.). (ENG., Illus.). 32p. (gr. 1-3). lib. bdg. 27.32 (978-1-4846-2690-0(7), Heinemann First Library) Heinemann-Raintree.

Schuh, Mari. Magnetism. 2011. (Blastoff! Readers Ser.). (ENG.). 24p. (J). pap. 5.95 (978-0-531-28456-8(5), Children's Pr.) Scholastic Library Publishing.

Science with Magnets Kid Kit. 2004. (Kid Kits Ser.). (Illus.). 24p. (J). 14.95 (978-1-58086-420-6(1)) EDC Publishing.

Selmes, Caroline. FridgeScapes: Polar Fridge Magnets. 2015. (ENG., Illus.). 44p. (J). (gr. -1-k). 15.95 (978-1-85669-970-9(6)) King, Laurence Publishing GBR. Dist: Hachette Bk. Group.

Sian Revision Magnet Magic. 2004. (Science in A Nutshell Ser.). (J). (978-1-59242-043-8(5)) Delta Education, LLC.

Stanley, Joseph. Magnet Magic! 2013. (InfoMax Readers Ser.). (ENG.). 24p. (J). (gr. 2-3). pap. 8.25 (978-1-4777-2341-8(2)); pap. 49.50 (978-1-4777-2343-2(9)) Rosen Publishing Group, Inc., The. (Rosen Classroom).

Stringer, John. Magnetism: An Investigation. 2008. (Science Investigations Ser.). (Illus.). 32p. (YA). (gr. 4-7). lib. bdg. 26.50 (978-1-4042-4288-3(0)) Rosen Publishing Group, Inc., The.

Sundance/Newbridge LLC Staff. The Mystery of Magnets. 2007. (Early Science Ser.). (gr. k-3). 18.95 (978-1-4007-6323-8(1)); pap. 6.10 (978-1-4007-6319-1(3)) Sundance/Newbridge Educational Publishing.

Swanson, Jennifer. The Attractive Truth about Magnetism, 1 vol. Lum, Bernice, illus. 2012. (LOL Physical Science Ser.). (ENG.). 32p. (gr. 3-4). pap. 8.10 (978-1-4296-9296-0(0)); pap. 47.70 (978-1-4296-9297-7(9), Fact Finders) Capstone Press of Coughlan Cos.

Taylor-Butler, Christine. Super Cool Science Experiments: Magnets. 2009. (Explorer Library: Science Explorer Ser.). (ENG., Illus.). 32p. (gr. 4-8). pap. 14.21 (978-1-60279-609-6(2), 200895); lib. bdg. 28.50 (978-1-60279-530-3(4), 200296) Cherry Lake Publishing.

Thomas, Isabel. Experiments with Magnets. 2015. (Read & Experiment Ser.). (ENG., Illus.). 32p. (gr. 2-4). 30.65 (978-1-4109-7922-3(9)) Heinemann-Raintree.

Troupe, Thomas Kingsley. Magnet Power! Science Adventures with MAG-3000 the Origami Robot, 1 vol. Christoph, Jamey, illus. 2013. (Origami Science Adventures Ser.). (ENG.). 24p. (gr. 3-4). pap. 6.95 (978-1-4048-8070-2(4)); lib. bdg. 27.32 (978-1-4048-7972-0(2)) Picture Window Bks.

Vogel, Julia. Discover Magnets. Yamada, Jane, illus. 2014. (Science Around Us Ser.). (ENG.). 24p. (J). (gr. -1-2). 25.64 (978-1-62687-304-9(6), 207145) Child's World, Inc., The.

Walker, Sally M. Investigating Magnetism. 2011. (Searchlight Books How Does Energy Work Ser.). (ENG., Illus.). (gr. 3-5). pap. 51.01 (978-0-7613-8408-3(1)); 40p. pap. 8.95 (978-0-7613-7874-7(X)); 40p. lib. bdg. 27.93 (978-0-7613-5775-9(0)) Lerner Publishing Group.

—Magnetism. King, Andy, photos by. 2005. (Early Bird Energy Ser.). (ENG., Illus.). 48p. (gr. 2-5). lib. bdg. 26.60 (978-0-8225-2932-3(7), Lerner Pubns.) Lerner Publishing Group.

—El Magnetismo. Translations.com Staff, tr. from ENG. King, Andy, photos by. 2007. (Libros de Energía para madrugadores (Early Bird Energy) Ser.). (SPA., Illus.). 48p. (gr. 2-5). lib. bdg. 26.60 (978-0-8225-7720-1(8)) Lerner Publishing Group.

—El Magnetismo; Magnetism. 2008. pap. 52.95 (978-0-8225-9778-0(0)) Lerner Publishing Group.

Weakland, Mark. Gears Go, Wheels Roll, 1 vol. 2010. (Science Starts Ser.). (ENG.). 32p. (gr. 1-2). lib. bdg. 27.32 (978-1-4296-5253-7(5), Aplus Bks.) Capstone Press of Coughlan Cos.

—Los Imanes Atraen, los Imanes Repelen. 2012. (Comienza la Ciencia/Science Starts Ser.).Tr. of Magnets Push, Magnets Pull. (SPA & MUL.). 32p. (gr. 1-2). lib. bdg. 27.32

(978-1-4296-8259-6(0), A+ Bilingue/Bilingual) Capstone Press of Coughlan Cos.

—Magnets Push, Magnets Pull, 1 vol. 2011. (Science Starts Ser.). (ENG., 32p. (gr. 1-2). Illus.). pap. 8.10 (978-1-4296-6147-8(X)); pap. 47.70 (978-1-4296-6148-5(8)) Capstone Press of Coughlan Cos. (Aplus Bks.).

MAGPIES—FICTION

Anholt, Laurence & Coplestone, Jim. Seven for a Secret. 2006. (ENG., Illus.). 32p. (J). pap. (978-1-84507-590-3(0), Frances Lincoln) Quarto Publishing Group UK.

Ferguson, Sarah & Duchess of York Staff. Little Red's Summer Adventure. Williams, Sam, illus. 2006. (ENG.). 40p. (J). (gr. -1-3). 17.99 (978-0-689-85562-7(1), Simon & Schuster/Paula Wiseman Bks.) Simon & Schuster/Paula Wiseman Bks.

Long, Jan. Azule & the White Hummingbird: The Birth of the White Hummingbird. 2014. (ENG., Illus.). 84p. (J). pap. 9.95 (978-1-63047-171-2(2)) Morgan James Publishing.

Restrepo, Bettina. Moose & Magpie, 1 vol. Rogers, Sherry, illus. 2009. (ENG.). 32p. (J). (gr. -1-3). pap. 8.95 (978-1-60718-042-5(1)) Arbordale Publishing.

Restrepo, Bettina & Rogers, Sherry. Moose & Magpie, 1 vol. 2009. (ENG., Illus.). 32p. (J). (gr. -1-3). 16.95 (978-1-934359-97-6(1)) Arbordale Publishing.

Slater, Kate. Magpie's Treasure. Slater, Kate, illus. 2012. (ENG., Illus.). 32p. (J). (gr. -1 — 1). pap. 10.99 (978-1-84939-075-0(4)) Andersen Pr. GBR. Dist: Independent Pubs. Group.

Springman, I. C. More. Lies, Brian, illus. 2012. (ENG.). 40p. (J). (gr. -1-3). 16.99 (978-0-547-61083-2(1)) Houghton Mifflin Harcourt Publishing Co.

Von Michaelis, Carol. Magpie Grows Up. 2012. 16p. pap. 15.99 (978-1-4772-6115-6(X)) AuthorHouse.

MAINE

Brown, Jonatha A. Maine. 2006. (Portraits of the States Ser.). 32p. (gr. 2-6). pap. 10.50 (978-0-8368-4718-5(0)); (Illus.). lib. bdg. 26.00 (978-0-8368-4701-7(6)) Stevens, Gareth Publishing LLLP. (Gareth Stevens Learning Library).

Craig, Janet. Maine: The Pine Tree State. 2003. (World Almanac Library of the States). (Illus.). 48p. (gr. 4-9). pap. 14.05 (978-0-8368-5322-3(9)); lib. bdg. 31.00 (978-0-8368-5151-9(X)) Stevens, Gareth Publishing LLLP. (Gareth Stevens Learning Library).

Dean, Carol. The Hen House: A True Story of Growing up on a Maine Farm. Dunn, Sandy, illus. 2003. (ENG.). 32p. (J). (gr. -1-17). 15.95 (978-0-89272-609-7(1)) Down East Bks.

Deinard, Jenny. How to Draw Maine's Sights & Symbols. 2009. (Kid's Guide to Drawing America Ser.). 32p. (gr. k-k). 50.50 (978-1-61511-068-1(2), PowerKids Pr.) Rosen Publishing Group, Inc., The.

Dornfeld, Margaret & Hart, Joyce. Maine. 2nd rev. ed. 2009. (Celebrate the States 10 Ser.). 144p. (gr. 6). 42.79 (978-0-7614-4726-9(1)) Marshall Cavendish Corp.

Engfer, LeeAnne. Maine. 2nd exp. rev. ed. 2003. (Hello U. S. A. Ser.). (Illus.). 84p. (J). (gr. 3-6). pap. 6.95 (978-0-8225-4138-7(6)) Lerner Publishing Group.

Exploring Acadia National Park: Solve Problems Involving the Four Operations. 2014. (Rosen Common Core Math Readers Ser.). (ENG., Illus.). 24p. (J). (gr. 3-4). pap. 8.25 (978-1-4777-4944-9(6), PowerKids Pr.) Rosen Publishing Group, Inc., The.

Fendler, Donn & Egan, Joseph. Lost on a Mountain in Maine. 2013. (ENG., Illus.). 112p. (J). (gr. 3-7). pap. 6.99 (978-0-688-11573-9(X)) HarperCollins Pubs.

Foran, Jill. Maine. 2011. (Guide to American States Ser.). (Illus.). 48p. (YA). (gr. 3-6). 29.99 (978-1-61690-791-4(6)); (J). 29.99 (978-1-61690-467-8(4)) Weigl Pubs., Inc.

Garry, J. W. Storm's Maine Vacation. 2011. 48p. pap. 17.50 (978-1-4567-2874-8(1)) AuthorHouse.

Heinrichs, Ann. Maine. 2014. (America the Beautiful Ser.: 3). (ENG.). 144p. (J). lib. bdg. 40.00 (978-0-531-24887-4(9)) Scholastic Library Publishing.

Hicks, Terry Allan. Maine. 2013. (It's My State 2nd Ed 4 Ser.). 80p. (J). (gr. 4-8). pap. 17.64 (978-1-62712-094-4(7)) Cavendish Square Publishing.

—Maine. 2006. (It's My State! Ser.). (Illus.). 80p. (J). (gr. 4-7). lib. bdg. (978-0-7614-1910-5(1), Benchmark Bks.) Marshall Cavendish Corp.

Jensen, Niels R. Maine, 1 vol. 2009. (United States Ser.). (ENG., Illus.). 48p. (YA). (gr. 2-5). 27.07 (978-1-60453-654-6(3)) ABDO Publishing Co.

Marsh, Carole. Maine Current Events Projects: 30 Cool, Activities, Crafts, Experiments & More for Kids to Do to Learn about Your State! 2003. (Maine Experience Ser.). 32p. (gr. k-8). pap. 5.95 (978-0-635-02038-3(6), Marsh, Carole Bks.) Gallopade International.

—Maine Geography Projects: 30 Cool, Activities, Crafts, Experiments & More for Kids to Do to Learn about Your State! 2003. (Maine Experience Ser.). 32p. (gr. k-5). pap. 5.95 (978-0-635-01838-0(1), Marsh, Carole Bks.) Gallopade International.

—Maine Government Projects: 30 Cool, Activities, Crafts, Experiments & More for Kids to Do to Learn about Your State! 2003. (Maine Experience Ser.). 32p. (gr. k-5). pap. 5.95 (978-0-635-01938-7(8), Marsh, Carole Bks.) Gallopade International.

—Maine People Projects: 30 Cool, Activities, Crafts, Experiments & More for Kids to Do to Learn about Your State! 2003. (Maine Experience Ser.). 32p. (gr. k-5). pap. 5.95 (978-0-635-01988-2(4), Marsh, Carole Bks.) Gallopade International.

—Maine Symbols & Facts Projects: 30 Cool, Activities, Crafts, Experiments & More for Kids to Do to Learn about Your State! 2003. (Maine Experience Ser.). 32p. (gr. k-5). pap. 5.95 (978-0-635-01888-5(8), Marsh, Carole Bks.) Gallopade International.

Murray, Julie. Maine, 1 vol. 2006. (United States Ser.). (ENG., Illus.). 32p. (gr. 2-4). 27.07 (978-1-59197-678-3(2), Buddy Bks.) ABDO Publishing Co.

Obregon, Jose Maria. Maine. Brusca, Maria Cristina, tr. 2005. (Bilingual Library of the United States of America Ser.: Set 1). (ENG & SPA., Illus.). 32p. (J). (gr. k-6). lib. bdg. 25.25 (978-1-4042-3084-2(X)) Rosen Publishing Group, Inc., The.

Obregón, José María. Maine. 2009. (Bilingual Library of the United States of America Ser.). (ENG & SPA.). 32p. (gr. 2-2). 47.90 (978-1-60853-364-0(6), Editorial Buenas Letras) Rosen Publishing Group, Inc., The.

Pelletier, Fran. Little Pine to King Spruce: A Franco-American Childhood, 1 vol. 2003. (ENG., Illus.). 192p. pap. 15.00 (978-0-88448-254-3(5), 884254) Tilbury Hse. Pubs.

Peterson, Sheryl. Maine. 2008. (This Land Called America Ser.). 32p. (YA). (gr. 3-6). 22.95 (978-1-58341-644-0(7)) Creative Co., The.

Reynolds, Cynthia Furlong. Fishing for Numbers: A Maine Number Book. Brett, Jeannie, illus. 2005. (Count Your Way Across the USA Ser.). (ENG.). 40p. (J). (gr. k-5). 16.95 (978-1-58536-035-2(X)) Sleeping Bear Pr.

Roop, Peter & Roop, Connie. Down East in the Ocean: A Maine Counting Book. 2011. (ENG., Illus.). 32p. (J). (gr. -1-3). 16.95 (978-0-89272-709-4(8)) Down East Bks.

—The Stormy Adventure of Abbie Burgess, Lighthouse Keeper. 2010. pap. 51.02 (978-0-7613-6922-6(8)) Lerner Publishing Group.

Walker, Cynthia. Maine. 2005. (Rookie Read-About Geography Ser.). (ENG., Illus.). 32p. (J). (gr. 1-2). lib. bdg. 20.50 (978-0-516-25255-1(0), Children's Pr.) Scholastic Library Publishing.

Zschock, Martha Day. Journey Around Maine from A to Z. 2007. (Journeys Ser.). (ENG., Illus.). 32p. (J). (gr. 1-6). 17.95 (978-1-933212-31-9(4), Commonwealth Editions) Applewood Bks.

MAINE—FICTION

Aldridge, Janet. The Meadow-Brook Girls in the Hills; Or the Missing Pilot of the White Mountains. 2006. pap. (978-1-4065-0694-5(X)) Dodo Pr.

Arenstam, Peter. Nicholas, a Maine Tale. Holman, Karen Busch, illus. 2015. (Nicholas Northeastern Ser.: 2). (ENG.). 166p. (J). (gr. k-7). pap. 8.95 (978-1-938170-67-6(9), Mitten Pr.) Ann Arbor Editions LLC.

Austin, Heather. Boatyard Ducklings. Austin, Heather, illus. 2008. (ENG., Illus.). 32p. (J). (gr. -1-3). 15.95 (978-0-89272-663-9(6)) Down East Bks.

Banghart, Tracy E. What the Sea Wants. Blum, Julia C., illus. 2006. 64p. (YA). kivar 16.00 (978-0-9779753-0-3(4)) LizStar Bks.

Beckhorn, Susan Williams. Moose Power! Muskeg Saves the Day. Huntington, Amy, illus. 2010. (ENG.). 40p. (J). (gr. -1-3). 16.95 (978-0-89272-762-9(4)) Down East Bks.

—Sarey by Lantern Light. 2003. (ENG., Illus.). 150p. (J). (gr. 4-17). pap. 9.95 (978-0-89272-612-7(1)) Down East Bks.

Beston, Henry. Chimney Farm Bedtime Stories. 2006. (Illus.). 80p. (J). pap. 13.95 (978-0-942396-93-5(6)) Blackberry Maine.

Birdsall, Jeanne. The Penderwicks at Point Mouette. 2011. (Playaway Children Ser.). (J). (gr. k). 44.99 (978-1-61707-434-9(9)) Findaway World, LLC.

—The Penderwicks at Point Mouette. (Penderwicks Ser.). (ENG.). (J). (gr. 3-7). 2012. 320p. 7.99 (978-0-375-85135-3(6), Yearling) 2011. 304p. 16.99 (978-0-375-85851-2(2), Knopf Bks. for Young Readers) Random Hse. Children's Bks.

Blakemore, Megan Frazer. The Water Castle. 2014. (ENG.). 368p. (YA). (gr. 3-8). pap. 7.99 (978-0-8027-3593-5(2), 9780802735935, Bloomsbury USA Childrens) Bloomsbury Publishing USA.

Blume, Judy. Fudge-a-Mania. 2007. (ENG.). 176p. (J). (gr. 3-7). 7.99 (978-0-14-240877-3(8), Puffin Books) Penguin Young Readers Group.

Blumstein, Amy Beth. Jamie & Tallulah. 2009. 16p. pap. 12.00 (978-1-4389-3997-1(3)) AuthorHouse.

Boat, Patty. A Disappointing Homecoming: (A Soldier's Story), 1 vol. 2009. 158p. pap. 24.95 (978-1-61546-997-0(4)) PublishAmerica, Inc.

Brewer, Sarah. Our New Garden. Brewer, Sarah & Brewer, Dean, illus. 2013. 20p. pap. 24.95 (978-1-63004-768-9(6)) America Star Bks.

Brown, Margaret Wise. The Little Island. Weisgard, Leonard, illus. 2003. (ENG.). 48p. (J). (gr. -1-2). 15.99 (978-0-385-74640-3(7), Doubleday Bks. for Young Readers) Random Hse. Children's Bks.

Carter, Herbert. The Boy Scouts on the Trail or Scouting. 2005. pap. 27.95 (978-1-885529-56-5(2)) Stevens Publishing.

Castonguay, Leo. Piper Peter. 2012. 44p. 24.95 (978-1-4626-8604-9(4)); pap. 24.95 (978-1-4626-8078-8(X)) America Star Bks.

Chenette, Roseanne V. Shellaby Willowbee. 2008. 13p. pap. 24.95 (978-1-60672-137-7(2)) America Star Bks.

Clark, Catherine. Maine Squeeze. 2004. (ENG.). 368p. (YA). (gr. 9-18). pap. 5.99 (978-0-06-056725-5(2), HarperTeen) HarperCollins Pubs.

Copeland, Cynthia L. Elin's Island. 2003. (Single Titles Ser.: up). (ENG.). 144p. (YA). (gr. 6-12). lib. bdg. 22.60 (978-0-7613-2522-2(0), Millbrook Pr.) Lerner Publishing Group.

Cornwell, Betsy. Tides. 2014. (ENG.). 304p. (YA). (gr. 7). pap. 8.99 (978-0-544-30296-9(6), HMH Books For Young Readers) Houghton Mifflin Harcourt Publishing Co.

Cotler, Steve. Cheesie Mack Is Cool in a Duel. McCauley, Adam, illus. (Cheesie Mack Ser.). (ENG.). 240p. (J). (gr. 3-7). 2013. 6.99 (978-0-375-86395-0(8), Yearling) 2012. 15.99 (978-0-375-86438-4(5), Random Hse. Bks. for Young Readers) Random Hse. Children's Bks.

Cowan, Charlotte. Moose with Loose Poops. Neal, Penelope, illus. 2008. (Dr. Hippo Ser.). (ENG.). 32p. (J). (gr. -1-2). 17.95 (978-0-9753516-5-9(6)) Hippocratic Pr., The.

Creech, Sharon. Moo. 288p. (J). (gr. 3-7). 2017. pap. 6.99 **(978-0-06-241526-4(3))** 2016. 16.99 (978-0-06-241524-0(7)) 2016. lib. bdg. 17.89 (978-0-06-241525-7(5)) HarperCollins Pubs.

—Moo. 2017. lib. bdg. 17.20 **(978-0-606-40402-0(3))** Turtleback Bks.

Cross, Mimi. Shining Sea, 0 vols. 2016. (ENG.). 432p. (YA). (gr. 9-12). pap. 9.99 (978-1-5039-3553-2(1), 9781503935532, Skyscape) Amazon Publishing.

Crossman, D. A. The Legend of Burial Island: A Bean & Ab Mystery. 2009. (J). pap. (978-0-89272-812-1(4)) Down East Bks.

Crossman, David. The Legend of Burial Island: A Bean & Ab Mystery. 2009. (ENG.). 201p. (J). (gr. 3-7). pap. 11.95 (978-0-89272-797-1(7)) Down East Bks.

Crowley, Peter. J T Seavey. 2012. (ENG.). 35p. (J). pap. 18.95 (978-1-4327-8712-7(8)) Outskirts Pr., Inc.

Day, Karen. A Million Miles from Boston. 2012. (ENG.). 224p. (J). (gr. 3-7). pap. 6.99 (978-0-375-85974-8(8), Yearling) Random Hse. Children's Bks.

Draper, Rochelle. The Stone Wall Dragon. Draper, Rochelle, illus. 2007. (ENG., Illus.). 32p. (J). (gr. 1-17). 15.95 (978-0-89272-690-5(3)) Down East Bks.

Eaton, Walter Prichard. Boy Scouts in the White Mountains: the Story of a Long Hike. Merrill, Frank T., illus. 2006. (ENG.). 316p. per. 30.95 (978-1-4286-4117-4(3)) Kessinger Publishing, LLC.

Edwards, Nicholas & White, Ellen Emerson. The Rescue. 2009. (Dog Whisperer Ser.: 1). (ENG.). 224p. (J). (gr. 3-7). pap. 9.99 (978-0-312-36768-8(6), 9780312367688) Square Fish.

Emerson, Alice B. Ruth Fielding on Cliff Island: Or the Old Hunter's Treasure Box. 2007. (ENG.). 136p. pap. 18.99 (978-1-4346-2493-2(5)); 148p. pap. 19.99 (978-1-4346-2535-9(4)) Creative Media Partners, LLC.

Farish, Terry. The Good Braider, 0 vols. 2014. (ENG.). 224p. (YA). (gr. 9-12). pap. 9.99 (978-1-4778-1628-8(3), 9781477816288, Amazon Children's Publishing) Amazon Publishing.

Fendler, Donn & Plourde, Lynn. Lost Trail: Nine Days Alone in the Wilderness, 1 vol. Bishop, Ben, illus. 2011. (ENG.). 72p. (J). (gr. 4-7). pap. 14.95 (978-0-89272-945-6(7)) Down East Bks.

Fields, Cassidy. Disaster Lake. 2011. 28p. pap. 16.09 (978-1-4269-6053-6(0)) Trafford Publishing.

Flint, Garrison. The Butler Did It! A Raymond Masrters Mystery. 2003. (Raymond Masters Mystery: 10). 206p. per. 13.99 (978-1-885631-72-5(3)) Hutchison, G.F. Pr.

Francis, Lee DeCora. Kunu's Basket: A Story of Indian Island, 1 vol. Drucker, Susan, illus. 2012. (ENG.). 32p. (J). 16.95 (978-0-88448-330-4(4)) Tilbury Hse. Pubs.

Frey, Hildegard G. The Camp Fire Girls in the Maine Woods: Or the Winnebagos Go Camping. 2007. (ENG.). 152p. pap. 19.99 (978-1-4264-9375-1(4)); 168p. pap. 21.99 (978-1-4264-9756-8(3)) Creative Media Partners, LLC.

Friedland, Joyce, ed. Lizzie Bright & the Buckminster Boy: Novel-Ties Study Guide. 2007. 36p. pap. 16.95 (978-0-7675-3558-8(8)) Learning Links Inc.

Fuller, Sandy Fergus. Moon Loon. 2010. (ENG.). 32p. (J). (gr. k-17). 15.95 (978-1-58979-453-5(2)) Taylor Trade Publishing.

Fuller, Sandy Ferguson. Moon Loon. 2010. (J). 7.95 (978-1-58979-454-2(0)); (ENG.). 32p. pap. 7.95 (978-1-58979-455-9(9)) Taylor Trade Publishing.

Gamble, Adam. Good Night Maine. Chan, Suwin, illus. 2007. (Good Night Our World Ser.). (ENG.). 18p. (J). (gr. k — 1). bds. 9.95 (978-1-60219-010-8(0)) Good Night Bks.

Garfield, Henry. My Father the Werewolf. 2016. (ENG.). 240p. (YA). (gr. 7). pap. 15.99 (978-1-4814-8808-2(2), Atheneum Bks. for Young Readers) Simon & Schuster Children's Publishing.

—Tartabull's Throw. 2015. (ENG., Illus.). 272p. (YA). (gr. 7). pap. 12.99 (978-1-4814-7510-5(X), Atheneum Bks. for Young Readers) Simon & Schuster Children's Publishing.

Gilbert, Julie. Into the Storm: A Mermaid's Journey. Fagan, Kirbi, illus. 2017. (Dark Waters Ser.). (ENG.). 160p. (gr. 2-4). pap. 6.95 (978-1-4965-4175-8(8)) Stone Arch Bks.

Goldsberry, Booty. Scaredy-Cat, I'm Not. 2007. (ENG., Illus.). 40p. (gr. 4-7). pap. 9.95 (978-0-9792875-0-3(2)) Goldsberry, Booty.

Griffin, N. The Whole Stupid Way We Are. (ENG., Illus.). 368p. (YA). (gr. 9). 2014. pap. 9.99 (978-1-4424-3156-0(3)) 2013. 16.99 (978-1-4424-3155-3(5)) Simon & Schuster Children's Publishing. (Atheneum Bks. for Young Readers).

Gutman, Dan. The Get Rich Quick Club. (ENG.). 128p. (J). 2006. (gr. 3-7). pap. 5.99 (978-0-06-053442-4(7)) 2004. 15.99 (978-0-06-053440-0(0)) HarperCollins Pubs.

Haesche, Richard Paul, Sr. The Treasure of Pirates Cave. 2007. (ENG.). 378p. (YA). 11.99 (978-0-9798536-7-8(2)) Kreative X-Pressions Pubns.

Hahn, Mary Downing. Look for Me by Moonlight. 2008. (ENG.). 208p. (YA). (gr. 7). pap. 7.99 (978-0-547-07616-4(9)) Houghton Mifflin Harcourt Publishing Co.

Harlow, Joan Hiatt. Shadows on the Sea. (ENG., Illus.). (J). (gr. 3-7). 2005. 272p. pap. 7.99 (978-0-689-84927-5(3)) 2003. 256p. 17.99 (978-0-689-84926-8(5)) McElderry, Margaret K. Bks. (McElderry, Margaret K. Bks.).

Harpan, Gaile. The Ballad of Omar the Cat. Reddy, Sneha, illus. 2008. 28p. pap. 12.95 (978-0-9820479-1-0(6)) Peppertree Pr., The.

Hawkes, Kevin. The Wicked Big Toddlah. 2010. (ENG.). 40p. (J). (gr. -1-2). pap. 7.99 (978-0-440-41788-0(0), Dragonfly Bks.) Random Hse. Children's Bks.

Hope, Lee Laura. Six Little Bunkers at Aunt Jo's. l.t. ed. 2007. (ENG.). 156p. pap. 21.99 (978-1-4346-3235-7(0)) Creative Media Partners, LLC.

Hopkins, Howard. The Nightmare Club #2: the Deadly Dragon. 2009. 104p. pap. 9.98 (978-0-578-00320-7(1)) Golden Perils Pr.

—The Nightmare Club #3: the Willow Witch. 2009. 104p. pap. 9.98 (978-0-578-00361-0(9)) Golden Perils Pr.

Horvath, Polly. The Canning Season. 2012. (ENG., Illus.). 224p. (YA). (gr. 7-12). pap. 11.99 (978-0-312-53564-3(3), 9780312535643) Square Fish.

Humphrey, Anna. Rhymes with Cupid. 2010. (ENG.). 240p. (YA). (gr. 8). pap. 7.99 (978-0-06-193501-5(8), HarperTeen) HarperCollins Pubs.

Jackson, Penny. Pepere's Little Girl. Jackson, Helston & Anderson, Betheny, illus. 2008. 27p. pap. 24.95 (978-1-60441-881-1(8)) America Star Bks.

Jacobs, Lily. The Littlest Bunny in Maine: An Easter Adventure. 2015. (ENG.). 32p. (J). (-3). 9.99 (978-1-4926-1108-0(5), Sourcebooks Jabberwocky) Sourcebooks, Inc.

—The Littlest Bunny in Portland: An Easter Adventure. Dunn, Robert, illus. 2015. (ENG.). 32p. (J). (-3). 9.99 (978-1-4926-1186-8(7), Sourcebooks Jabberwocky) Sourcebooks, Inc.

Jacobson, Jennifer Richard. The Complete History of Why I Hate Her. 2010. (ENG.). 192p. (YA). (gr. 7-18). 16.99 (978-0-689-87800-8(1), Atheneum/Richard Jackson Bks.) Simon & Schuster Children's Publishing.

Jahn-Clough, Lisa. Country Girl, City Girl. 2009. (ENG.). 192p. (YA). (gr. 7). pap. 12.95 (978-0-547-22322-3(6)) Houghton Mifflin Harcourt Publishing Co.

James, Eric. A Halloween Scare in Maine. Le Ray, Marina, illus. 2015. (ENG.). 32p. (J). (-5). 9.99 (978-1-4926-2380-9(6), 9781492623809, Sourcebooks Jabberwocky) Sourcebooks, Inc.

—A Halloween Scare in Portland. Le Ray, Marina, illus. 2015. (ENG.). 32p. (J). (-5). 9.99 (978-1-4926-2397-7(0), 9781492623977, Sourcebooks Jabberwocky) Sourcebooks, Inc.

—Santa's Sleigh Is on Its Way to Maine: A Christmas Adventure. Dunn, Robert, illus. 2016. (ENG.). 32p. (J). (-2). 12.99 (978-1-4926-4334-0(3), 9781492643340, Sourcebooks Jabberwocky) Sourcebooks, Inc.

Jones, Carrie. Captivate. 2010. (Need Ser.). (ENG.). (YA). (gr. 7-12). 304p. pap. 9.99 (978-1-59990-523-5(X), 9781599905235); 288p. 16.99 (978-1-59990-342-2(3), 9781599903422) Bloomsbury Publishing USA. (Bloomsbury USA Childrens).

—Endure. 2012. (Need Ser.). (ENG.). 272p. (YA). 17.99 (978-1-59990-554-9(X), 9781599905549, Bloomsbury USA Childrens) Bloomsbury Publishing USA.

—Entice. (Need Ser.). (ENG.). (YA). 2011. 288p. pap. 9.99 (978-1-59990-693-5(7), 9781599906935) 2010. 272p. (gr. 7-12). 17.99 (978-1-59990-553-2(1), 9781599905532) Bloomsbury Publishing USA. (Bloomsbury USA Childrens).

—Need. 2009. (Need Ser.). (ENG.). 336p. (YA). (gr. 7). pap. 9.99 (978-1-59990-453-5(5), 9781599904535, Bloomsbury USA Childrens) Bloomsbury Publishing USA.

Jones, Carrie, et al. After Obsession. 2012. (ENG.). 336p. (YA). (gr. 7-12). pap. 9.99 (978-1-59990-913-4(8), 9781599909134, Bloomsbury USA Childrens) Bloomsbury Publishing USA.

Jones, Kimberly K. Sand Dollar Summer. 2008. (ENG., Illus.). 224p. (J). (gr. 4-8). pap. 5.99 (978-1-4169-5834-5(7), McElderry, Margaret K. Bks.) McElderry, Margaret K. Bks.

Jones, Molly. The Choosing Tree. 2006. 126p. pap. 19.95 (978-1-4241-5076-2(0)) PublishAmerica, Inc.

Jordan, Evora. Annie Love: A Hannah Gray Dog Story. 2003. (Hannah Gray Mysteries). (J). per. (978-0-9725071-2-7(4)) EvoraBooks, LLC.

Keil, James. Tiger & the Poachers. 2010. 54p. pap. 15.52 (978-0-557-34105-4(1)) Lulu Pr., Inc.

LaFaye, A. The Keening. 2010. (ENG.). 224p. (J). (gr. 2-8). 17.00 (978-1-57131-692-9(2)); pap. 8.00 (978-1-57131-694-3(9)) Milkweed Editions.

LaFleur, Suzanne. Listening for Lucca. 2015. (ENG.). 240p. (J). (gr. 4-7). pap. 7.99 (978-0-307-98030-4(8), Yearling) Random Hse. Children's Bks.

Langer, Dana. Siren Sisters. 2017. (ENG., Illus.). 256p. (J). (gr. 4-8). 16.99 (978-1-4814-6686-8(0), Simon & Schuster/Paula Wiseman Bks.) Simon & Schuster/Paula Wiseman Bks.

Larbalestier, Justine & Brennan, Sarah Rees. Team Human. (ENG.). 352p. (YA). (gr. 8). 2013. pap. 9.99 (978-0-06-208965-6(X)) 2012. 17.99 (978-0-06-208964-9(1)) HarperCollins Pubs. (HarperTeen).

Lasky, Kathryn. Hannah. 2011. (Daughters of the Sea Ser.: 1). (ENG.). 320p. (J). (gr. 7-7). pap. 9.99 (978-0-545-23803-8(X)) Scholastic, Inc.

—Lucy. 2012. (Daughters of the Sea Ser.: 3). (ENG.). 320p. (J). (gr. 7). 17.99 (978-0-439-78312-5(7), Scholastic Pr.) Scholastic, Inc.

—May. (Daughters of the Sea Ser.). (ENG.). 336p. (J). (gr. 7-7). 2012. pap. 9.99 (978-0-545-24331-5(9)) 2011. 17.99 (978-0-439-78311-8(9)) Scholastic, Inc. (Scholastic Pr.).

Leach, Cheryl. Sally to the Rescue. 2012. 36p. pap. 20.99 (978-1-4772-9974-6(2)) AuthorHouse.

Les Becquets, Diane. Season of Ice. 2008. (ENG.). 288p. (YA). (gr. 9-13). 16.95 (978-1-59990-063-6(7), 9781599900636, Bloomsbury USA Childrens) Bloomsbury Publishing USA.

Lewis, Carolyn & DeVince, James. Hairy Beary Book Three: The Blue Ribbon Hero, 3 bks., Vol. 3. DeVince, James, ed. Porcheron, Tammy, illus. 2003. (Hairy Beary Ser.: 3). 46p. (J). pap. 9.95 (978-0-9712641-2-0(0)) J M D's Business Services.

Libhart, Virginia B. Carrie's Dream. 2005. (978-0-9652963-7-3(7)) Harborseal Publishing Co.

Lord, Cynthia. A Handful of Stars. 2015. (ENG.). 192p. (J). (gr. 3-7). 16.99 (978-0-545-70027-6(2), Scholastic Pr.) Scholastic, Inc.

—Touch Blue. 2012. (ENG.). 192p. (J). (gr. 3-7). pap. 6.99 (978-0-545-03532-3(5), Scholastic Pr.) Scholastic, Inc.

Mackinnon, Bernard. The Boy Who Turned Green. 2005. 119p. pap. 19.95 (978-1-4137-7262-3(5)) America Star Bks.

Mariconda, Barbara. The Voyage of Lucy P. Simmons. 2074. (ENG.). 256p. (J). (gr. 3-7). 6.99 (978-0-06-211980-3(X), Tegen, Katherine Bks) HarperCollins Pubs.

Marrone, Amanda. Slayed. 2010. (ENG., Illus.). 272p. (YA). (gr. 9-18). pap. 9.99 (978-1-4169-9487-9(4), Simon Pulse) Simon Pulse.

Martin, Ann M. Better to Wish. 2013. (Family Tree Ser.). (ENG.). 240p. (J). (gr. 3-7). 16.99 (978-0-545-35942-9(2), Scholastic Pr.) Scholastic, Inc.

—Family Tree Book One: Better to Wish. 2014. (Family Tree Ser.: 1). (ENG.). 240p. (J). (gr. 3-7). pap. 6.99 (978-0-545-67518-5(9)) Scholastic, Inc.

Martin-Fluet, Marie T. The Fairies' Century Celebration. 2011. 40p. pap. 18.62 (978-1-4567-2477-1(0)) AuthorHouse.

Martinez, David & Benchmark Education Co., LLC. My Whale of a Tale. 2014. (Text Connections Ser.). (J). (gr. 3). (978-1-4509-9651-8(5)) Benchmark Education Co.

McCloskey, Robert. Blueberries for Sal, 1 vol. 2010. (Puffin Storytime Ser.). (ENG.). 15p. (J). (gr. -1-k). 9.99 (978-0-14-241643-3(6), Puffin Books) Penguin Young Readers Group.

—Blueberries for Sal. (J). (gr. -1-k). pap. 12.95 incl. audio. 2004. 29.95 (978-1-55592-841-4(2)); 2004. (J). 18.95 (978-1-55592-799-8(8)); 2004. (J). 38.75 (978-1-55592-816-2(1)) Weston Woods Studios, Inc.

McCreight, Kimberly. The Outliers. (Outliers Ser.: 1). (YA). (gr. 9). 2017. 368p. pap. 9.99 (978-0-06-235910-0(X)) 2016. (ENG.). 352p. 18.99 (978-0-06-235909-4(6)) HarperCollins Pubs.

McKenzie, Lyn. Betsy, Girl Scout of Woodward Center 1935. 2007. 244p. (YA). pap. 17.95 net. (978-0-9722839-0-8(0)) Just Write Bks.

MNO

McKissack, Jenny & McKissack, Jennifer. Sanctuary. 2015. (ENG.). 320p. (J). (gr. 7). 17.99 *(978-0-545-58758-7(1),* Scholastic Pr.) Scholastic, Inc.
McTiernan, Deborah. Lilly Noble & Actual Magic. 2013. (ENG.). 318p. (YA). pap. 14.99 *(978-0-9891807-0-2(0))* Actual Magic Enterprises, LLC.
Merrill, Karen Grill. Oh, What a State I'm In: The USA in Rhyme & Riddle, 1 vol. Grill, Gerald, illus. 2010. 48p. pap. 24.95 *(978-1-4489-7979-0(X))* PublishAmerica, Inc.
Metzger, Steve. The Turkey Train. Paillot, Jim, illus. 2013. (ENG.). 32p. (J). (gr. -1-k). 6.99 *(978-0-545-49229-4(7),* Cartwheel Bks.) Scholastic, Inc.
Mitchell, Saundra. Mistwalker. 2014. (ENG.). 320p. (YA). (gr. 7). 16.99 *(978-0-547-85315-4(7))* Houghton Mifflin Harcourt Publishing Co.
Morgan, G. A. Chantarelle, 1 vol. 2015. (Five Stones Trilogy Ser.: 2). (ENG.). 316p. (J). pap. 18.95 *(978-1-939017-63-5(7),* a178678b-3da7-4c5c-96c5-09386c28787e) Islandport Pr., Inc.
Nana B. & Brittany. Forest Friends of Maine: The Chipmunks Have an Argument. 2010. 16p. pap. 8.49 *(978-1-4490-0647-1(7))* AuthorHouse.
Nolan, Han. Pregnant Pause. 2012. (ENG.). 352p. (YA). (gr. 9). pap. 8.99 *(978-0-547-85414-4(5))* Houghton Mifflin Harcourt Publishing Co.
Nugent, Matthew. Nightmares on Goose Rocks Beach in Kennebunkport, Maine: Book 4 of the Goose Rocks Tales. 2003. (Illus.). 204p. (J). per. 14.95 *(978-0-9705812-3-5(8))* CBI Pr.
O'Brien, Anne Sibley. A Path of Stars. O'Brien, Anne Sibley, illus. 2012. (ENG., Illus.). 40p. (J). (gr. k-3). 15.95 *(978-1-57091-735-6(3))* Charlesbridge Publishing, Inc.
O'Brien, Thomas E. The Magic of Finbar. 2011. 68p. pap. 19.95 *(978-1-4560-4235-6(1))* America Star Bks.
Ogilvie, Elizabeth. The Pigeon Pair. (J). reprint ed. lib. bdg. 19.95 *(978-0-88411-336-2(1))* Amereon Ltd.
Oliver, Lauren. Delirium. (Delirium Trilogy Ser.: 1). (ENG.). 480p. (YA). (gr. 9-18). 2016. pap. 9.99 *(978-0-06-172683-5(4))* 2011. 17.99 *(978-0-06-211243-9(0))* HarperCollins Pubs.
—Delirium. 2016. (Delirium Ser.: 1). (YA). lib. bdg. 20.85 *(978-0-606-23575-4(2),* Turtleback) Turtleback Bks.
—Delirium Stories: Hana, Annabel, Raven & Alex. (Delirium Story Ser.). 224p. (YA). (gr. 9). 2016. pap. 9.99 *(978-0-06-248432-1(X))* 2013. (ENG.). pap. 9.99 *(978-0-06-226778-8(7))* HarperCollins Pubs.
—Delirium Stories: Hana, Annabel, Raven & Alex. (Delirium Ser.). (YA). 2016. lib. bdg. 20.85 *(978-0-606-38920-4(2))* 2013. lib. bdg. 20.85 *(978-0-606-31834-1(8),* Turtleback) Turtleback Bks.
—Requiem. 2013. (Delirium Trilogy: Bk. 3). (ENG.). 400p. (J). (gr. 9). 18.99 *(978-0-06-201453-5(6))* HarperCollins Pubs.
O'Neill, Elizabeth. Alfred Visits Maine. 2008. (Illus.). 24p. (J). pap. 12.00 *(978-0-9799121-3-9(X))* Funny Bone Bks.
Padian, Maria. Brett McCarthy: Work in Progress. 2009. (ENG.). 288p. (YA). (gr. 7). pap. 8.99 *(978-0-440-24055-6(7),* Knopf Bks. for Young Readers) Random Hse. Children's Bks.
Pelletier, Cathie. The Summer Experiment. 2014. (ENG.). 288p. (J). (gr. 4-7). 16.99 *(978-1-4022-8578-3(7),* 9781402285783, Sourcebooks Jabberwocky) Sourcebooks, Inc.
Perkins, T. J. Wound Too Tight. 2006. (Illus.). 141p. (YA). 10.99 *(978-0-9777538-5-7(9))* GumShoe Press.
Poblocki, Dan. The House on Stone's Throw Island. 2015. (ENG.). 272p. (J). (gr. 5-9). 16.99 *(978-0-545-64556-0(5),* Scholastic Pr.) Scholastic, Inc.
Pochocki, Ethel. A Penny for a Hundred. Owens, Mary Beth, illus. 2005. 31p. (J). (gr. 2-5). pap. 9.95 *(978-1-883937-52-2(3))* Bethlehem Bks.
—A Penny for a Hundred. 2014. (ENG., Illus.). 32p. (J). (gr. -1-3). 15.95 *(978-1-60893-311-2(3))* Down East Bks.
Pohl, William L. The Amazing Flight of Daisy: A Runaway Kite Circles the World on the Back of the Wind. 2006. 72p. 20.00 *(978-1-4257-0666-1(5))* Xlibris Corp.
Potter, Ellen. Piper Green & the Fairy Tree: Pie Girl. Leng, Qin, illus. 2017. (Piper Green & the Fairy Tree Ser.: 5). (ENG.). 144p. (J). (gr. 2-4). pap. 5.99 ***(978-1-101-93968-0(0))***; lib. bdg. 17.99 ***(978-1-101-93966-6(4))*** Random Hse. Children's Bks. (Yearling).
Raabe, Emily. Lost Children of the Far Islands. 2014. (ENG.). 288p. (J). (gr. 3-7). 16.99 *(978-0-375-87091-0(1),* Knopf Bks. for Young Readers) Random Hse. Children's Bks.
Reynolds, Cynthia Furlong. Across the Reach. 2007. 269p. (J). (gr. 3-7). 16.95 *(978-1-58726-518-1(4),* Mitten Pr.) Ann Arbor Editions LLC.
Ross, Susan. Kiki & Jacques. 2015. (ENG.). 128p. (J). (gr. 3-7). 16.95 *(978-0-8234-3427-5(3))* Holiday Hse., Inc.
Roy, Ron. The White Wolf. Gurney, John Steven, tr. Gurney, John Steven, illus. 2004. (to Z Mysteries Ser.: No. 23). (ENG.). 96p. (J). (gr. 1-4). pap. 4.99 *(978-0-375-82480-7(4),* Random Hse. Bks. for Young Readers) Random Hse. Children's Bks.
Scaletta, Kurtis. The Tanglewood Terror. (ENG.). 272p. (J). 2012. (gr. 4-7). 7.99 *(978-0-375-86542-8(X),* Yearling) 2011. (gr. 3-7). 16.99 *(978-0-375-86758-3(9),* Knopf Bks. for Young Readers) Random Hse. Children's Bks.
Schmidt, Gary D. Lizzie Bright & the Buckminster Boy. 2013. (ENG.). 224p. (J). (gr. 5-7). pap. 7.99 *(978-0-544-02279-9(3))* Houghton Mifflin Harcourt Publishing Co.
Schmidt, Mollie. It Happened in Maine. Wood, Madeline, illus. 2013. (ENG.). 56p. (J). pap. 10.95 *(978-1-59713-137-7(7))* Goose River Pr.
Sedita, Francesco. Miss Popularity Goes Camping. 2009. (ENG.). 142p. (J). lib. bdg. 15.38 *(978-1-4242-4383-9(1))* Fitzgerald Bks.
Shankman, Ed. I Met a Moose in Maine One Day. O'Neill, Dave, illus. 2008. (Shankman & O'Neill Ser.). (ENG.). 32p. (J). (gr. -1-3). 14.95 *(978-1-933212-77-7(2),* Commonwealth Editions) Applewood Bks.
Shaw, Tucker. Anxious Hearts. (ENG.). 272p. (YA). (gr. 7-17). 2011. pap. 6.95 *(978-0-8109-9711-0(8))* 2010. 16.95 *(978-0-8109-8718-0(X))* Abrams, Inc. (Amulet Bks.).
Shue, Jenna. Animal Island. Herzog, Inge, illus. 2005. 27p. (J). (gr. -1-3). per. 14.95 *(978-1-4259-0039-7(9))* AuthorHouse.
Silvano, Wendi. Love Is All Around Maine. Czernichowska, Joanna, illus. 2016. (ENG.). 32p. (J). (-6). 12.99 *(978-1-4926-2931-3(6),* Sourcebooks Jabberwocky) Sourcebooks, Inc.
Simmons, Derek. Flash of Life. 2006. 85p. pap. 16.95 *(978-1-4241-3890-6(6))* PublishAmerica, Inc.
Skurzynski, Gloria & Ferguson, Alane. Out of the Deep. 2008. (Mysteries in Our National Park Ser.). (ENG., Illus.). 160p. (J). (gr. 3-7). pap. 4.99 *(978-1-4263-0251-0(7),* National Geographic Children's Bks.) National Geographic Society.
Smallman, Steve. Santa Is Coming to Maine. Dunn, Robert, illus. 2013. (ENG.). 32p. (J). (-3). 9.99 *(978-1-4022-9069-5(1),* Sourcebooks Jabberwocky) Sourcebooks, Inc.
Smith, Constance. Pea Soup Fog. Cart, Jen, illus. 2004. (ENG.). 32p. (J). (gr. -1-17). 15.95 *(978-0-89272-643-1(1))* Down East Bks.
Smith, George. The Journey of the Little Red Boat: A Story from the Coast of Maine. 2nd ed. 2004. (Illus.). 50p. (J). per. 7.99 *(978-0-9740434-1-8(9),* 255-3716) Smith, George Publishing.
Smith, Lauren. Ashley Enright & the Mystery at Miller's Pond. 2006. (ENG.). 60p. per. 16.95 *(978-1-4241-5268-1(2))* America Star Bks.
Smith, Lauren E. Ashley Enright & the Darnell Diamonds, 1 vol. 2009. 90p. pap. 19.95 *(978-1-60836-332-2(5))* America Star Bks.
—Ashley Enright Investigations. 2006. 48p. pap. 16.95 *(978-1-4241-2963-8(X))* America Star Bks.
Smith, Maggie. Counting Our Way to Maine. 2008. (ENG., Illus.). 32p. (J). (gr. -1-3). 15.95 *(978-0-89272-775-9(6))* Down East Bks.
Sockabasin, Allen & Raye, Rebekah. Thanks to the Animals, 1 vol. 2nd ed. 2014. (ENG., Illus.). 36p. (gr. 1-6). 17.95 *(978-0-88448-414-1(9),* 884414) Tilbury Hse. Pubs.
Speare, Elizabeth George. The Sign of the Beaver. 2011. (ENG.). 144p. (J). (gr. 5-7). pap. 7.99 *(978-0-547-57711-1(7))* Houghton Mifflin Harcourt Publishing Co.
—The Sign of the Beaver. 135p. (J). (gr. 4-6). pap. 4.99 *(978-0-8072-1517-3(1),* Listening Library) Random Hse. Audio Publishing Group.
Specter, Baron. The Spooky Short Sands Shipwreck: #4, 1 vol. Evans, Dustin, illus. 2010. (Ghostly Graphic Adventures Ser.). (ENG.). 32p. (J). (gr. 3-6). 28.50 *(978-1-60270-773-3(1))* ABDO Publishing Co.
Spencer, Jamie. The Train to Maine. Reed, Rebecca, illus. 2008. (ENG.). 32p. (J). (gr. -1-3). 15.95 *(978-0-89272-767-4(5))* Down East Bks.
Standish, Burt L. Frank Merriwell in Maine. Rudman, Jack, ed. 2003. (Frank Merriwell Ser.). (YA). (gr. 9-18). 29.95 *(978-0-8373-9328-5(0))*; pap. 9.95 *(978-0-8373-9028-4(1),* FM-028) Merriwell, Frank Inc.
Stephens, Charles Asbury. A Busy Year at the Old Squire's. 2007. 272p. pap. 21.99 *(978-1-4346-3560-0(0))*; (ENG.). 300p. pap. 23.99 *(978-1-4346-3561-7(9))* Creative Media Partners, LLC.
Sticks Stones & Stumped. 2006. (Illus.). 26p. (J). 19.95 *(978-0-9773738-0-2(0))* Bryson Taylor Publishing.
Stockwell, Jeff. Fandango: The Key to the Wind. Stockwell, Pel, illus. 2007. 58p. (YA). per. 22.50 *(978-0-9785594-0-3(1))* Stockwell Publishing.
Stone, Phoebe. Romeo Blue. (ENG.). 352p. (J). (gr. 3-7). 2015. pap. 7.99 *(978-0-545-44361-6(X))* 2013. 16.99 *(978-0-545-44360-9(1))* Scholastic, Inc. (Levine, Arthur A. Bks.).
Strohm, Stephanie Kate. Pilgrims Don't Wear Pink. 2012. (ENG.). 208p. (YA). (gr. 7). pap. 8.99 *(978-0-547-56459-3(7))* Houghton Mifflin Harcourt Publishing Co.
Strykowski, Marcia. Call Me Amy. 2013. (ENG.). 176p. (J). (gr. 3-10). 24.95 *(978-1-935462-76-7(8))*; pap. 14.95 *(978-1-935462-75-0(X))* Luminis Bks., Inc.
Surrisi, C. M. The Maypop Kidnapping. 2016. (Quinnie Boyd Mysteries Ser.: 1). (ENG.). 304p. (gr. 4-8). 35.99 *(978-1-4677-9560-9(7))*; (Illus.). (J). 17.99 *(978-1-4677-5789-8(6))* Lerner Publishing Group. (Carolrhoda Bks.).
Surrisi, Cynthia & Surrisi, C. M. Vampires on the Run: A Quinnie Boyd Mystery. 2017. (Quinnie Boyd Mysteries Ser.: 2). (ENG.). 296p. (J). (gr. 4-8). 16.99 *(978-1-5124-1150-8(7),* Carolrhoda Bks.) Lerner Publishing Group.
Tata, Cb. Ernie the Eagle Goes to Maine. Hanley, Zachary, illus. 2012. 42p. 24.95 *(978-1-4626-4545-9(3))* America Star Bks.
Urbain, Catherine. Manuel & the Lobsterman. 2008. (ENG.). 214p. (J). (gr. 4-7). 16.95 *(978-1-59078-516-4(9),* Front Street) Boyds Mills Pr.
Van Dusen, Chris. The Circus Ship. Van Dusen, Chris, illus. 2015. (ENG., Illus.). 40p. (J). (gr. -1-3). 6.99 *(978-0-7636-5592-1(9))* Candlewick Pr.
Vanderpool, Clare. Navigating Early. (ENG.). (J). (gr. 5). 2014. 336p. pap. 7.99 *(978-0-307-93065-1(3),* Yearling) 2013. 320p. 16.99 *(978-0-385-74209-2(6),* Delacorte Bks. for Young Readers) 2013. 320p. lib. bdg. 19.99 *(978-0-375-99040-3(2),* Delacorte Bks. for Young Readers) Random Hse. Children's Bks.
—Navigating Early. 2014. lib. bdg. 18.40 *(978-0-606-36420-1(X))* Turtleback Bks.
Vernick, Shirley Reva. The Black Butterfly. 2014. (ENG.). 226p. (J). 19.95 *(978-1-935955-79-5(9))* Cinco Puntos Pr.
Voigt, Cynthia. Angus & Sadie. Leigh, Tom, illus. (ENG.). 208p. (J). (gr. 3-7). 2008. pap. 6.99 *(978-0-06-074584-4(3))* 2005. 16.99 *(978-0-06-074582-0(7))* HarperCollins Pubs.
Wait, Lea. Stopping to Home. 2003. (ENG.). 160p. (J). (gr. 3-7). pap. 8.99 *(978-0-689-83849-1(2),* Simon & Schuster/Paula Wiseman Bks.) Simon & Schuster/Paula Wiseman Bks.
—Wintering Well. 2006. (ENG., Illus.). 192p. (J). (gr. 3-7). pap. 6.99 *(978-0-689-85647-1(4),* McElderry, Margaret K. Bks.) McElderry, Margaret K. Bks.
Walker, Brian F. Black Boy White School. 2012. (ENG.). 256p. (YA). (gr. 9). 17.99 *(978-0-06-191483-6(5),* HarperTeen) HarperCollins Pubs.
Weston Woods Staff, creator. Time of Wonder. 2011. 29.95 *(978-0-439-73525-4(4))*; 18.95 *(978-0-439-72905-5(X))*; 38.75 *(978-0-439-72906-2(8))* Weston Woods Studios, Inc.
White-Adams, Beverly. The Adventures of Rusty: Rusty Goes to Maine Vol. 3. 2012. 40p. pap. 19.57 *(978-1-4669-5442-7(6))* Trafford Publishing.
White, Kiersten & Di Bartolo, Jim. In the Shadows. Di Bartolo, Jim, illus. 2014. (ENG., Illus.). 384p. (J). (gr. 7). 21.99 *(978-0-545-56144-0(2),* Scholastic Pr.) Scholastic, Inc.
Whitten, A. J. The Well. 2009. (ENG., Illus.). 336p. (YA). (gr. 7-18). pap. 18.95 *(978-0-547-23229-4(2))* Houghton Mifflin Harcourt Publishing Co.
Wiggin, Kate Douglas. Homespun Tales. 2007. 240p. 26.95 *(978-1-60312-668-7(6))*; per. 14.95 *(978-1-60312-410-2(1))* Aegypan.
—Rose o' the River. 2004. reprint ed. pap. 15.95 *(978-1-4179-9998-9(5))*; pap. 1.99 *(978-1-4179-9948-4(9))* Kessinger Publishing, LLC.
Wigington, Patti. Summer's Ashes. 2007. (ENG.). 208p. (gr. 8-12). per. 15.00 *(978-0-9766805-9-8(9))* Keene Publishing.
Wolf, Elaine. Camp. 2012. (ENG.). 256p. (YA). (gr. 6-17). 16.95 *(978-1-61608-657-2(2),* 608657, Sky Pony Pr.) Skyhorse Publishing Co., Inc.
Wunder, Wendy. The Probability of Miracles. 2012. (ENG., Illus.). 336p. (YA). (gr. 9). pap. 9.99 *(978-1-59514-480-5(3),* Razorbill) Penguin Young Readers Group.

MAINE—HISTORY

Brett, Jeannie. Little Maine. Brett, Jeannie, illus. 2010. (My Little State Ser.). (ENG., Illus.). 22p. (J). 9.95 *(978-1-58536-497-8(5))* Sleeping Bear Pr.
Foran, Jill. Maine: The Pine Tree State. 2016. (J). *(978-1-4896-4872-3(0))* Weigl Pubs., Inc.
Hicks, Terry Allan, et al. Maine. 2015. (J). lib. bdg. *(978-1-62713-201-5(5))* Cavendish Square Publishing.
Hudson, Amanda & Hicks, Terry Allan. Maine. 2nd ed. 2013. 80p. (J). (gr. 4-8). 31.36 *(978-1-60870-881-9(0))* Cavendish Square Publishing.
Koontz, Robin Michal. Maine: The Pine Tree State. 2010. (Our Amazing States Ser.). (ENG.). 24p. (J). pap. 8.25 *(978-1-4488-0734-5(4))*; lib. bdg. 22.60 *(978-1-4488-0651-5(8))* Rosen Publishing Group, Inc., The. (PowerKids Pr.).
Marsh, Carole. Exploring Maine Through Project-Based Learning. 2016. (Maine Experience Ser.). (ENG.). (J). pap. 9.99 *(978-0-635-12343-5(6))* Gallopade International.
—I'm Reading about Maine. 2014. (Maine Experience Ser.). (ENG., Illus.). (J). pap., pap. 8.99 *(978-0-635-11294-1(9))* Gallopade International.
—Maine History Projects: 30 Cool, Activities, Crafts, Experiments & More for Kids to Do to Learn about Your State! 2003. (Maine Experience Ser.). 32p. (gr. k-5). pap. 5.95 *(978-0-635-01788-8(1),* Marsh, Carole Bks.) Gallopade International.
Perish, Patrick. Maine. 2013. (Exploring the States Ser.). (ENG., Illus.). 32p. (gr. 3-7). lib. bdg. 26.95 *(978-1-62617-018-6(5),* Blastoff! Readers) Bellwether Media.
Peterson, Judy Monroe. Maine: Past & Present. 2010. (United States: Past & Present Ser.). (ENG.). 48p. (YA). pap. 11.75 *(978-1-4358-9511-9(8))*; lib. bdg. 29.25 *(978-1-4358-9484-6(7))* Rosen Publishing Group, Inc., The. (Rosen Reference).
Ripley's Believe It Or Not! Staff, compiled by. The Mane Event! 2017. (Fun Facts Ser.: 4). (ENG.). 144p. (J). 18.95 ***(978-1-60991-184-3(9))*** Ripley Entertainment, Inc.
Schneider, Jack. Allagash River Towboat: A Maine Logging Adventure. 2003. (ENG., Illus.). 120p. (J). (gr. 4-17). pap. 10.95 *(978-0-89272-601-1(6))* Down East Bks.
Smolik, Jane Petrlik. The Great State of Maine Activity Book: Over 75 Puzzles about Life in Maine. rev. ed. 2006. (Illus.). 96p. (J). (gr. 2-7). per. 11.95 *(978-0-9664095-6-7(6))* MidRun Pr.
Swanson, Angie. Maine. 2016. (States Ser.). (ENG., Illus.). 32p. (gr. 3-4). lib. bdg. 27.32 *(978-1-5157-0406-5(8))* Next Page Pr., The.
Wang, Andrea. What's Great about Maine? 2015. (Our Great States Ser.). (ENG., Illus.). 32p. (J). (gr. 2-5). pap. 7.95 *(978-1-4677-6079-9(X))*; lib. bdg. 26.60 *(978-1-4677-3855-2(7))* Lerner Publishing Group. (Lerner Pubns.).
Webster, Christine. Maine. 2009. (Illus.). 80p. (J). pap. *(978-0-8312-0806-6(6))* Children's Pr., Ltd.
—Maine. 2008. (ENG.). 80p. (J). pap. 7.95 *(978-0-531-20806-9(0),* Children's Pr.) Scholastic Library Publishing.
Yasuda, Anita. Maine: The Pine Tree State. 2012. (J). *(978-1-61913-357-0(1))*; pap. *(978-1-61913-358-7(X))* Weigl Pubs., Inc.
Ziff, John. Northern New England: Maine, New Hampshire, Vermont, Vol. 19. 2015. (Let's Explore the States Ser.). (Illus.). 64p. (J). (gr. 5). 23.95 *(978-1-4222-3330-6(8))* Mason Crest.

MAINE—POETRY

Bull, Webster. A Kittery Kayaker. Decker, Jacqueline, illus. 2007. (Little Limericks Ser.). (ENG.). 24p. (J). (gr. k-3). 12.95 *(978-1-933212-36-4(5),* Commonwealth Editions) Applewood Bks.

MAINE (BATTLESHIP)

Crompton, Samuel Willard. The Sinking of the USS Maine. 2008. (Milestones in American History Ser.). (Illus.). 112p. (YA). (gr. 7-12). 35.00 *(978-1-60413-049-2(0))* Facts On File, Inc.
McNeese, Tim. Remember the Maine! The Spanish-American War Begins. 2004. (First Battles Ser.). (Illus.). 112p. (YA). (gr. 6-12). 23.95 *(978-1-883846-79-4(X),* First Biographies) Reynolds, Morgan Inc.

MAISY (FICTITIOUS CHARACTER: COUSINS)—FICTION

Cousins, Lucy. Beep, Beep, Maisy! Cousins, Lucy, illus. 2017. (Maisy Ser.). (ENG., Illus.). 16p. (J). (-k). bds. 12.99 ***(978-0-7636-9407-4(X))*** Candlewick Pr.
—Maisy Goes Camping. 2009. (Maisy First Experiences Ser.). lib. bdg. 17.20 *(978-0-606-06667-9(5),* Turtleback) Turtleback Bks.
—Maisy Goes on a Plane. Cousins, Lucy, illus. 2015. (Maisy Ser.). (ENG., Illus.). 32p. (J). (-k). 12.99 *(978-0-7636-7825-8(2))* Candlewick Pr.
—Maisy Goes to the Hospital. 2009. (Maisy First Experiences Ser.). lib. bdg. 17.20 *(978-0-606-06686-0(1),* Turtleback) Turtleback Bks.
—Maisy Goes to the Library. 2009. (Maisy First Experiences Ser.). lib. bdg. 17.20 *(978-0-606-06687-7(X),* Turtleback) Turtleback Bks.
—Maisy Goes to the Movies. 2014. (Maisy First Experiences Ser.). lib. bdg. 17.20 *(978-0-606-35156-0(6))* Turtleback Bks.
—Maisy Goes to the Museum. Cousins, Lucy, illus. 2009. (Maisy Ser.). (ENG., Illus.). 32p. (J). (gr. k-k). pap. 6.99 *(978-0-7636-4370-6(X))* Candlewick Pr.
—Maisy Learns to Swim. Cousins, Lucy, illus. 2015. (Maisy Ser.). (ENG., Illus.). 32p. (J). (-k). 6.99 *(978-0-7636-7749-7(3))* Candlewick Pr.
—Maisy Plays Soccer. 2014. (Maisy First Experiences Ser.). lib. bdg. 17.20 *(978-0-606-35155-3(8))* Turtleback Bks.
—Maisy's Birthday Party Sticker Book. Cousins, Lucy, illus. 2015. (Maisy Ser.). (ENG., Illus.). 16p. (J). (gr. -1-2). pap. 7.99 *(978-0-7636-7735-0(3))* Candlewick Pr.
—Maisy's Digger: A Go with Maisy Board Book. Cousins, Lucy, illus. 2015. (Maisy Ser.). (ENG., Illus.). 18p. (J). (— 1). bds. 5.99 *(978-0-7636-8010-7(9))* Candlewick Pr.
—Maisy's Pirate Ship: A Pop-Up-and-Play Book. Cousins, Lucy, illus. 2015. (Maisy Ser.). (ENG., Illus.). 10p. (J). (-k). 16.99 *(978-0-7636-7941-5(0))* Candlewick Pr.
—Maisy's Plane. Cousins, Lucy, illus. 2015. (Maisy Ser.). (ENG., Illus.). 18p. (J). (— 1). bds. 5.99 *(978-0-7636-7304-8(8))* Candlewick Pr.
—Maisy's Tractor. Cousins, Lucy, illus. 2015. (Maisy Ser.). (ENG., Illus.). 18p. (J). (— 1). bds. 5.99 *(978-0-7636-7305-5(6))* Candlewick Pr.
—Maisy's Wonderful Weather Book. Cousins, Lucy, illus. 2006. (Maisy Ser.). (ENG., Illus.). 14p. (J). (gr. -1). 11.99 *(978-0-7636-2987-8(1))* Candlewick Pr.
—Where Are Maisy's Friends? Cousins, Lucy, illus. 2010. (Maisy Ser.). (ENG., Illus.). 12p. (J). (-k). bds. 5.99 *(978-0-7636-4669-1(5))* Candlewick Pr.
—Where Does Maisy Live? 2010. 12p. bds. 4.99 *(978-976-3-64668-7(5))* Candlewick Pr.
—Where Does Maisy Live? Cousins, Lucy, illus. 2010. (Maisy Ser.). (ENG., Illus.). 12p. (J). (-k). bds. 5.99 *(978-0-7636-4668-4(7))* Candlewick Pr.

MAIZE

see Corn

MAKE-UP (COSMETICS)

see Cosmetics

MAKE-UP, THEATRICAL

see Theatrical Makeup

MALADJUSTED CHILDREN

see Problem Children

MALAGASY REPUBLIC

see Madagascar

MALARIA

Ciletti, Barbara. Malaria Parasites. 2017. (Awful, Disgusting Parasites Ser.). (ENG.). 32p. (gr. 3-7). 31.35 ***(978-1-68072-008-2(2))*** Black Rabbit Bks.
Donaldson, Olivia. Malaria. 2015. (Deadliest Diseases of All Time Ser.). (ENG.). 64p. (J). (gr. 7-7). 34.21 *(978-1-5026-0095-0(1))* Cavendish Square Publishing.
Dziedzic, Nancy & Naff, Clayton Farris. Malaria. 2009. (Perspectives on Diseases & Disorders Ser.). (ENG., Illus.). 144p. (gr. 10-12). 44.30 *(978-0-7377-4379-1(4),* Greenhaven Pr., Inc.) Cengage Gale.
Goldsmith, Connie. Battling Malaria: On the Front Lines against a Global Killer. 2010. (Exceptional Social Studies Titles for Upper Grades). (ENG., Illus.). 128p. (gr. 7-12). lib. bdg. 37.27 *(978-0-8225-8580-0(4))* Lerner Publishing Group.
Hardyman, Robyn. Fighting Malaria. 2014. (Tiny Battlefields Ser.). 48p. (YA). (gr. 6-8). pap. 84.30 *(978-1-4824-1310-6(8))* Stevens, Gareth Publishing LLLP.
Isle, Mick. Malaria. 2009. (Epidemics Ser.). 64p. (gr. 5-5). 58.50 *(978-1-61512-293-6(1))* Rosen Publishing Group, Inc., The.
Marcus, Bernard. Malaria, Second Edition. 2nd rev. ed. 2009. (Deadly Diseases & Epidemics Ser.). 128p. (C). (gr. 9-18). 34.95 *(978-1-60413-281-6(7),* Chelsea Hse.) Facts On File, Inc.
Mitchell, Kirstin. Madame Anopheles. 2008.Tr. of Seòora Anopheles. (Illus.). 26p. (J). pap. 20.00 *(978-0-9816301-0-6(3))* Alexander, Raine.
Ollhoff, Jim. Malaria, 1 vol. 2009. (History of Germs Ser.). (ENG., Illus.). 32p. (YA). (gr. 5-9). 27.07 *(978-1-60453-500-6(8))* ABDO Publishing Co.
Person, Stephen. Malaria: Super Killer! 2010. (Nightmare Plagues Ser.). 32p. (YA). (gr. 4-9). lib. bdg. 25.27 *(978-1-936088-07-2(X))* Bearport Publishing Co., Inc.

MALAWI

DeCapua, Sarah. Malawi in Pictures. 2009. (Visual Geography Series, Second Ser.). (ENG.). 80p. (gr. 5-12). 31.93 *(978-0-8225-8575-6(8))* Lerner Publishing Group.
Kamkwamba, William. The Boy Who Harnessed the Wind: Creating Currents of Electricity & Hope. 2009. 14.44 *(978-0-7848-3872-3(0),* Everbind) Marco Bk. Co.
—The Boy Who Harnessed the Wind: Creating Currents of Electricity & Hope. Hymas, Anna, illus. 2015. (ENG.). 304p. (J). (gr. 5). 18.99 *(978-0-8037-4080-8(6),* Dial Bks) Penguin Young Readers Group.
Kamkwamba, William & Mealer, Bryan. The Boy Who Harnessed the Wind: Young Readers Edition. Zunon, Elizabeth, illus. (ENG.). (J). 2016. 304p. (gr. 5). 8.99 *(978-0-14-751042-6(2),* Puffin Books) 2012. 32p. (gr. 1-3). 17.99 *(978-0-8037-3511-8(1),* Dial Bks) Penguin Young Readers Group.
Levete, Sarah. A Tale of One Well in Malawi. 2010. (Big Picture: Climate Ser.). (ENG.). 24p. (gr. 1-2). pap. 41.70 *(978-1-4296-5973-4(4),* First Facts) Capstone Press of Coughlan Cos.

MALAYSIA

Broadhead, Arp Raph. Mudley Explores Kuala Lumpur: An Amazing Adventure into Mudtown. 2017. (ENG., Illus.). 64p. pap. 16.50 *(978-981-4721-94-3(8))* Marshall Cavendish International (Asia) Private Ltd. SGP. Dist: National Bk. Network.
Burgan, Michael. Malaysia. 2015. (ENG., Illus.). 144p. (J). lib. bdg. *(978-0-531-21699-6(3),* Orchard Bks.) Scholastic, Inc.
Currie, Stephen. The Tallest Building. 2003. (Extreme Places Ser.). (ENG., Illus.). 48p. (J). (gr. 3-5). 27.50 *(978-0-7377-1374-9(7),* Kidhaven) Cengage Gale.

Di Piazza, Francesca. Malaysia in Pictures. 2006. (Visual Geography Series, Second Ser.). (ENG., Illus.). 80p. (gr. 5-12). 31.93 *(978-0-8225-2674-2(3))* Lerner Publishing Group.

Poisson, Barbara Aoki. Malaysia. 2010. (Major Muslim Nations Ser.). 128p. (YA). (gr. 5-18). lib. bdg. 25.95 *(978-1-4222-1409-1(5))* Mason Crest.

Pundyk, Grace & Radhakrishnan, Anand. Welcome to Malaysia. 2004. (Welcome to My Country Ser.). (Illus.). 48p. (gr. 2-5). lib. bdg. 27.00 *(978-0-8368-2560-2(8))* Stevens, Gareth Publishing LLLP.

Thomas, Mark. Las Torres Gemelas Petronas. 2004. (Estructuras extraordinarias (Record-Breaking Structures) Ser.). (SPA.). 24p. (J). (gr. 3-6). lib. bdg. 22.60 *(978-0-8239-6862-6(6)*, Editorial Buenas Letras) Rosen Publishing Group, Inc., The.

—The Petronas Twin Towers: World's Tallest Buildings. 2009. (Record-Breaking Structures Ser.). 24p. (gr. 1-2). 42.50 *(978-1-60852-457-0(4)*, PowerKids Pr.) Rosen Publishing Group, Inc., The.

Weil, Ann. Meet Our New Student from Malaysia. 2008. (Meet Our New Student Ser.). (Illus.). 48p. (J). (gr. 1-5). lib. bdg. 29.95 *(978-1-58415-654-3(6))* Mitchell Lane Pubs., Inc.

MALAYSIA—FICTION

Buchmann, Stephen & Cohn, Diana. The Bee Tree. 2012. (ENG., Illus.). 40p. (J). (gr. 1-6). pap. 8.95 *(978-1-935955-14-6(4))* Cinco Puntos Pr.

Cohn, Diana & Buchmann, Stephen. The Bee Tree. Mirocha, Paul, illus. 2007. (ENG.). 40p. (J). (gr. 4-6). 17.95 *(978-0-938317-98-2(9))* Cinco Puntos Pr.

Flint, Shamini. Ten: A Soccer Story. 2017. (ENG.). 176p. (J). (gr. 5-7). 16.99 *(978-0-544-85001-9(7)*, Clarion Bks.) Houghton Mifflin Harcourt Trade & Reference Pubs.

Lat. Kampung Boy. Lat, illus. rev. ed. 2006. Orig. Title: The Kampung Boy. (ENG., Illus.). 144p. (YA). (gr. 7-8). pap. 19.99 *(978-1-59643-121-8(0)*, 9781596431218, First Second Bks.) Roaring Brook Pr.

Zeiss, Joyce Burns. Out of the Dragon's Mouth. 2015. (ENG., Illus.). 240p. (YA). pap. 11.99 *(978-0-7387-4196-3(5)*, Flux) North Star Editions.

MALAYSIA—HISTORY

Choi, Eun-Mi. Where Are You, Sun Bear? Malaysia. Cowley, Joy, ed. Noh, Seong-bin, illus. 2015. (Global Kids Storybooks Ser.). (ENG.). 32p. (gr. 1-4). 7.99 *(978-1-925246-54-4(X))*; 26.65 *(978-1-925246-02-5(7))*; 26.65 *(978-1-925246-28-5(0))* ChoiceMaker Pty. Ltd., The AUS. (Big and SMALL). Dist: Lerner Publishing Group.

—Where Are You, Sun Bear? Malaysia. Cowley, Joy, ed. Noh, Seong-bin, illus. 2015. (Global Kids Storybooks Ser.). (ENG.). 32p. (J). (gr. 1-4). pap. 7.99 *(978-1-925233-45-2(6))* Lerner Publishing Group.

Munan, Heidi, et al. Malaysia. 3rd rev. ed. 2011. (Cultures of the World: 3rd Edition 1 Ser.). (Illus.). 144p. (J). (gr. 6). 47.07 *(978-1-60870-785-0(7))* Marshall Cavendish Corp.

Owings, Lisa. Malaysia. 2014. (Exploring Countries Ser.). (ENG., Illus.). 32p. (J). (gr. 3-7). lib. bdg. 26.95 *(978-1-62617-068-1(1)*, Blastoff! Readers) Bellwether Media.

Thomas, Mark. Las Torres Gemelas Petronas: Los Edificios Más Altos del Mundo (The Petronas Twin Towers: World'S Tallest Building) 2009. (Estructuras extraordinarias (Record-Breaking Structures) Ser.). (SPA.). 24p. (gr. 1-2). 42.50 *(978-1-61512-314-8(8)*, Editorial Buenas Letras) Rosen Publishing Group, Inc., The.

MALCOLM X, 1925-1965

see X, Malcolm, 1925-1965

MALI

Blauer, Ettagale & Lauré, Jason. Mali. 2007. (Cultures of the World Ser.). 144p. (gr. 6). lib. bdg. 42.79 *(978-0-7614-2568-7(3)*, Benchmark Bks.) Marshall Cavendish Corp.

Conrad, David C. Empires of Medieval West Africa, Revised Edition. 2nd rev. ed. 2009. (Great Empires of the Past Ser.). (Illus.). 152p. (gr. 6-12). 35.00 *(978-1-60413-164-2(0)*, Chelsea Hse.) Facts On File, Inc.

Diakite, Baba Wague. A Gift from Childhood: Memories of an African Boyhood, 1 vol. 2013. (ENG., Illus.). 136p. (J). (gr. 4). pap. 12.95 *(978-1-55498-421-3(1))* Groundwood Bks. CAN. Dist: Publishers Group West (PGW).

DiPiazza, Francesca Davis. Mali in Pictures. 2007. (Visual Geography Series, Second Ser.). (ENG., Illus.). 80p. (gr. 5-12). lib. bdg. 31.93 *(978-0-8225-6591-8(9))* Lerner Publishing Group.

Klobuchar, Lisa. Africans of the Ghana, Mali, & Songhai Empires. 2009. (J). *(978-0-7166-2134-8(7))* World Bk., Inc.

Krasner, Barbara. Mansa Musa. 2016. (Silk Road's Greatest Travelers Ser.). 112p. (J). (gr. 6-6). 37.10 *(978-1-5081-7151-5(3))* Rosen Publishing Group, Inc., The.

Ogunnaike, Oludamini. Meet Our New Student from Mali. 2009. (Meet Our New Student Ser.). (Illus.). 48p. (J). (gr. 2-5). lib. bdg. 25.70 *(978-1-58415-734-2(8))* Mitchell Lane Pubs., Inc.

Supples, Kevin & National Geographic Learning Staff. Mali. 2007. (Reading Expeditions Ser.). (ENG., Illus.). 24p. (J). pap. 14.95 *(978-0-7922-4539-1(3))* CENGAGE Learning.

Wolny, Philip. Discovering the Empire of Mali. 2013. (Exploring African Civilizations Ser.). 64p. (J). (gr. 5-8). 31.95 *(978-1-4777-1883-4(4)*, Rosen Reference) Rosen Publishing Group, Inc., The.

Zamosky, Lisa. Mansa Musa: Leader of Mali, 1 vol. 2007. (Primary Source Readers Ser.). (ENG.). 32p. (J). (gr. 4-4). pap. 8.99 *(978-0-7439-0439-1(7))* Shell Educational Publishing.

MALI—FICTION

Bowen, Carl & Fuentes, Benny. Sand Spider, 1 vol. Tortosa, Wilson, illus. 2014. (Shadow Squadron Ser.). (ENG.). 112p. (gr. 4-8). 26.65 *(978-1-4342-9169-1(3))* Stone Arch Bks.

Davies, Stephen. Blood & Ink. 2017. (ENG.). 224p. (YA). (gr. 7). lib. bdg. 17.99 ***(978-1-58089-790-7(8)***, Charlesbridge Teen) Charlesbridge Publishing, Inc.

Fontes, Justine & Fontes, Ron. Sunjata: Warrior King of Mali [A West African Legend]. Carruthers, Sandy, illus. 2009. (Graphic Myths & Legends Ser.). (ENG.). 48p. (gr. 4-8). pap. 8.95 *(978-1-58013-891-8(8))* Lerner Publishing Group.

McDowell, Josh & Hostetler, Bob. The Truth Twisters. 2006. (Illus.). 167p. (YA). (gr. 8-12). per. 11.99 *(978-1-932587-84-5(5))* Practical Christianity Foundation.

Shepherd, Keith D., illus. Kumba & Kambili: A Tale from Mali. 2013. (Tales of Honor Ser.). (ENG.). 32p. (J). (gr. 1-4). pap. 8.95 *(978-1-937529-58-1(4))* Red Chair Pr.

Shepherd, Keith D., illus. & retold by. Kumba & Kambili: A Tale from Mali. Shepherd, Keith D., retold by. 2013. (Tales of Honor (Red Chair Press) Ser.). (ENG.). 32p. (J). (gr. 1-4). lib. bdg. 26.60 *(978-1-937529-74-1(6))* Red Chair Pr.

Wingard, Lucinda. The Turn-Around Bird. 2012. 296p. pap. 16.00 *(978-0-9848400-1-4(X))* Plicata Pr. LLC.

MALLORY, GEORGE, 1886-1924

Herman, Gail & Amatrula, Michele. Climbing Everest (Totally True Adventures) 2015. (Totally True Adventures Ser.). (ENG., Illus.). 112p. (J). (gr. 2-5). 4.99 *(978-0-553-50986-1(1)*, Random Hse. Bks. for Young Readers) Random Hse. Children's Bks.

MALTA

Sheehan, Sean & Yong, Jui Lin. Malta. 2nd rev. ed. 2010. (Cultures of the World 20 Ser.). 144p. (gr. 6). 42.79 *(978-1-60870-024-0(0))* Marshall Cavendish Corp.

Stafford, James. Malta. 2007. (European Union Ser.). (Illus.). 88p. (YA). (gr. 3-7). lib. bdg. 21.95 *(978-1-4222-0056-8(6))* Mason Crest.

Stafford, James & Indovino, Shaina Carmel. Malta. 2012. (J). *(978-1-4222-2252-2(7))*; pap. *(978-1-4222-2283-6(7))* Mason Crest.

MALTA—FICTION

Brunson, Emma. Survivor Spirit Book: Megan's Ark. 2010. 204p. pap. 13.50 *(978-1-60911-834-1(0)*, Eloquent Bks.) Strategic Book Publishing & Rights Agency (SBPRA).

MAMMALS

see also Primates

also names of mammals, e.g. Bats

About Mammals: A Guide for Children / una Guía para Niños: a Guide for Children / Sobre Los Mamíferos: una Guía para Niños, 1 vol. 2014. (About... Ser.). (ENG & SPA., Illus.). 48p. (J). (gr. -1-2). 8.95 *(978-1-56145-800-4(7))* Peachtree Pubs.

Alden, Peter C. Mammals. Reid, Fiona, illus. 2nd ed. 2013. (Peterson Field Guide Color-In Bks.). (ENG.). 10p. (J). 8.95 *(978-0-544-03254-5(3))* Houghton Mifflin Harcourt Publishing Co.

Allman, Toney. Deadliest Mammals. 2016. (ENG.). 80p. (J). (gr. 5-12). lib. bdg. *(978-1-68282-050-6(5))* ReferencePoint Pr., Inc.

Alonso, Juan Carlos. Animal Journal: Land Mammals of the World: Notes, Drawings, & Observations about Animals That Live on Land. 2017. (834 Ser.). (ENG., Illus.). 128p. (J). (gr. 3-6). 19.95 *(978-1-63322-196-3(2)*, Walter Foster Jr) Quarto Publishing Group USA.

Amstutz, Lisa J. Mammals. 2017. (My First Animal Kingdom Encyclopedias Ser.). (ENG., Illus.). 32p. (gr. 1-2). lib. bdg. 27.32 *(978-1-5157-3930-2(9)*, Aplus Bks.) Capstone Press of Coughlan Cos.

—Meerkats Are Awesome! 2015. (Awesome African Animals! Ser.). (ENG.). 32p. (gr. 1-2). lib. bdg. 27.32 *(978-1-4914-1763-8(3))* Capstone Press of Coughlan Cos.

Anne McBride. Ferrets, Vol. 12. 2016. (Understanding & Caring for Your Pet Ser.: Vol. 12). (ENG., Illus.). 128p. (J). (gr. 5-8). 25.95 *(978-1-4222-3695-6(1))* Mason Crest.

Anteaters. 2014. (ENG.). 48p. (J). lib. bdg. 28.00 *(978-0-531-20667-6(X))* Scholastic Library Publishing.

Antill, Sara. Giant Anteater. 2010. (Unusual Animals Ser.). (Illus.). 24p. (J). (gr. k-3). (ENG.). pap. 8.15 *(978-1-61533-001-0(1))*; lib. bdg. 22.60 *(978-1-60754-993-2(X))* Windmill Bks.

—Okapi. 2010. (Unusual Animals Ser.). (Illus.). 24p. (J). (gr. k-3). (ENG.). pap. 8.15 *(978-1-61533-007-2(0))*; lib. bdg. 22.60 *(978-1-60754-996-3(4))* Windmill Bks.

Bailey, Diane. Saving Marine Mammals: Whales, Dolphins, Seals, & More. 2017. (J). ***(978-1-4222-3878-3(4))*** Mason Crest.

Batten, Mary. Who Has a Belly Button?, 1 vol. Bond, Higgins, illus. 2004. (ENG.). 32p. (J). (gr. 1-5). 15.95 *(978-1-56145-235-4(1))* Peachtree Pubs.

Beaumont, Holly. Why Do Monkeys & Other Mammals Have Fur? 2015. (Animal Body Coverings Ser.). (ENG., Illus.). 24p. (gr. 1-3). pap. 6.99 *(978-1-4846-2539-2(0)*, Heinemann Read & Learn) Heinemann-Raintree.

Bennett, Mia. Ferrets. 2017. (Our Weird Pets Ser.). 24p. (J). (gr. 7-8). 23.60 ***(978-1-5081-5416-7(3)***, PowerKids Pr.) Rosen Publishing Group, Inc., The.

Bloom & Ronzani, Maggie. Mammals: Grades 2 Through 4. (Illus.). (J). pap., wbk. ed. 4.99 *(978-0-88743-963-6(2))* School Zone Publishing Co.

Bodden, Valerie. Amazing Animals: Koalas. 2011. (Amazing Animals Ser.). (ENG.). 24p. (J). (gr. 1-3). pap. 8.99 *(978-0-89812-746-1(7)*, Creative Paperbacks) Creative Co., The.

Boothroyd, Jennifer. Endangered & Extinct Mammals. 2014. (Lightning Bolt Books Animals in Danger Ser.). (ENG., Illus.). 32p. (gr. k-2). lib. bdg. 26.60 *(978-1-4677-1329-0(5)*, Lerner Pubns.) Lerner Publishing Group.

Bowman, Chris. Pronghorn. 2015. (North American Animals Ser.). (ENG., Illus.). 24p. (J). (gr. k-3). lib. bdg. 25.95 *(978-1-62617-192-3(0)*, Blastoff! Readers) Bellwether Media.

Bredeson, Carmen. Fainting Goats & Other Weird Mammals. 2009. (I Like Weird Animals! Ser.). (Illus.). 24p. (J). (gr. 1-3). lib. bdg. 22.60 *(978-0-7660-3122-7(5)*, Enslow Elementary) Enslow Pubs., Inc.

Brewer, Duncan. 1000 Things You Should Know about Mammals. 2004. (1000 Things You Should Know about Ser.). (Illus.). 64p. (YA). (gr. 5-18). 19.95 *(978-1-59084-467-0(X))* Mason Crest.

Brown, Kathryn Keil. The Alpaca-Bet! Abc's of Alpacas. 2012. 48p. pap. 21.88 *(978-1-4669-7108-0(8))* Trafford Publishing.

Brown, Martin. Lesser Spotted Animals: The Coolest Creatures You've Never Heard Of. 2017. (J). ***(978-1-338-17148-8(8))*** Scholastic, Inc.

Buckingham, Suzanne. Meet the Ring-Tailed Lemur. 2009. (Scales & Tails Ser.). (Illus.). 24p. (J). lib. bdg. 22.60 *(978-1-4042-4501-3(4)*, PowerKids Pr.) Rosen Publishing Group, Inc., The.

Bulletpoints Mammals. 2005. (Illus.). (J). per. 4.99 *(978-1-933581-04-0(2))* Byeway Bks.

Burroughs, John. Squirrels & Other Fur-Bearers (Yesterday's Classics) 2006. (Illus.). 144p. (J). per. 8.95 *(978-1-59915-070-3(0))* Yesterday's Classics.

Caputo, Christine A. Mammals. 2012. (Illus.). 32p. (J). *(978-0-545-46699-8(7))* Scholastic, Inc.

Carper, Virginia. Animal Teachings: Mammals. 2005. ring bd., wbk. ed. 20.00 *(978-0-9788858-0-9(5))* Animal Teachers Enterprises.

Carr, Aaron. Ferret. 2014. (Illus.). 24p. (J). *(978-1-62127-292-2(3))* Weigl Pubs., Inc.

Carson, Janet. What Is a Mammal? 2008. (Real Readers - Upper Emergent Ser.). (ENG., Illus.). 12p. (gr. 1-2). pap. 5.90 *(978-0-8239-8191-5(6))* Rosen Publishing Group, Inc., The.

Ciovacco, Justine. Meerkats. 2008. (Amazing Animals Ser.). 48p. (YA). (gr. 3-6). lib. bdg. 28.00 *(978-0-8368-9098-3(1))* Stevens, Gareth Publishing LLLP.

Clark, Willow. Flying Lemurs. 2012. (Up a Tree Ser.). (ENG., Illus.). 24p. (J). (gr. k-3). lib. bdg. 22.60 *(978-1-4488-6184-2(5))*; pap. 8.25 *(978-1-4488-6327-3(9)*, PowerKids Pr.) Rosen Publishing Group, Inc., The.

—Meerkats: Life in the Mob. 2011. (Animal Families Ser.). 24p. (J). (ENG.). pap. 8.25 *(978-1-4488-2608-7(X))*; (Illus.). lib. bdg. 22.60 *(978-1-4488-2511-0(3))* Rosen Publishing Group, Inc., The. (PowerKids Pr.).

—Meerkats: Suricatas: Life in the Mob: Vida en la Colonia. 2011. (Animal Families / Familias de animales Ser.). (SPA & ENG., Illus.). 24p. lib. bdg. 22.60 *(978-1-4488-3125-8(3)*, PowerKids Pr.) Rosen Publishing Group, Inc., The.

Clarke, Ginjer L. Baby Otter. Cuddy, Robin, illus. 2009. (Penguin Young Readers, Level 3 Ser.). (ENG.). 48p. (J). (gr. 1-3). mass mkt. 3.99 *(978-0-448-45105-3(0)*, Penguin Young Readers) Penguin Young Readers Group.

Claybourne, Anna. A Pack of Wolves: And Other Canine Groups, 1 vol. 2012. (Animals in Groups Ser.). (ENG.). 48p. (gr. 4-6). pap. 9.95 *(978-1-4329-6489-4(5))*; lib. bdg. 33.32 *(978-1-4329-6482-5(8))* Heinemann-Raintree. (Heinemann InfoSearch).

Cleary, Brian P. Dolphin, Fox, Hippo, & Ox: What Is a Mammal? Goneau, Martin, illus. 2012. (Animal Groups Are CATegorical (tm) Ser.). (ENG.). 32p. (gr. k-3). (J). lib. bdg. 26.60 *(978-0-7613-6206-7(1))*; pap. 7.95 *(978-1-4677-0338-3(9))* Lerner Publishing Group. (Millbrook Pr.).

Coldiron, Deborah. Manatees, 1 vol. 2008. (Underwater World Set II Ser.). (ENG.). 32p. (gr. k-4). 27.07 *(978-1-60453-134-3(7)*, Buddy Bks.) ABDO Publishing Co.

Conklin, Wendy. Life Cycles, 1 vol. 2015. (Science Readers: Content & Literacy Ser.). (ENG., Illus.). 32p. (gr. 3-3). pap. 8.99 *(978-1-4807-4637-4(1))* Teacher Created Materials, Inc.

Costain, Meredith. Mammals Great & Small. 2014. (Discovery Education: Animals Ser.). 32p. (J). (gr. 3-6). 26.25 *(978-1-4777-6940-9(4))*; pap. 10.00 *(978-1-4777-6941-6(2))* Rosen Publishing Group, Inc., The. (PowerKids Pr.).

Dawson, Emily C. How Animals Find Water. 2010. (Our Animal World Ser.). 24p. (J). 25.65 *(978-1-60753-011-4(2))* Amicus Publishing.

De la Bédoyère, Camilla. Why Why Why Are Orang-Utans So Hairy? 2008. (Why Why Why Ser.). (Illus.). 32p. (J). (gr. 4-7). pap. *(978-1-84810-003-9(5))* Miles Kelly Publishing, Ltd.

—Why Why Why... Are Orangutans So Hairy? 2010. (Why Why Why Ser.). 32p. (J). (gr. 1-3). lib. bdg. 18.95 *(978-1-4222-1570-8(9))* Mason Crest.

Dorling Kindersley Publishing Staff. Mammals. 2013. (Pocket Genius Ser.). (ENG., Illus.). 160p. (J). (gr. 3-7). 7.99 *(978-1-4654-0884-6(3)*, DK Children) Dorling Kindersley Publishing, Inc.

—Pocket Genius: Mammals. 2016. (Pocket Genius Ser.). (ENG., Illus.). 160p. (J). (gr. 3-7). pap. 4.99 *(978-1-4654-4589-6(7)*, DK Children) Dorling Kindersley Publishing, Inc.

Doudna, Kelly. Frisky Ferrets, 1 vol. Craig, Diane, ed. 2007. (Perfect Pets Ser.). (ENG., Illus.). 24p. (J). (gr. k-3). lib. bdg. 24.21 *(978-1-59928-748-5(X)*, SandCastle) ABDO Publishing Co.

Drumlin, Sam. Manatees. 2013. (PowerKids Readers: Sea Friends Ser.). (ENG., Illus.). 24p. (J). (gr. k-2). pap. 8.25 *(978-1-4488-9746-9(7))*; lib. bdg. 22.60 *(978-1-4488-9644-8(4))* Rosen Publishing Group, Inc., The. (PowerKids Pr.).

—Manatees: Los Manatíes. Alamán, Eduardo, tr. from ENG. 2013. (PowerKids Readers: Sea Friends / Los Amigos Del Mar Ser.). (SPA & ENG., Illus.). 24p. (J). (gr. k-2). lib. bdg. 22.60 *(978-1-4488-9974-6(5)*, PowerKids Pr.) Rosen Publishing Group, Inc., The.

Editors of Kingfisher. Fantastic Mammals: Come Face to Face with Creatures Big & Small. 2016. (Fast Facts Ser.). (ENG.). 32p. 11.99 *(978-0-7534-7274-3(0)*, 9780753472743, Kingfisher) Roaring Brook Pr.

Encyclopaedia Britannica, Inc. Staff, compiled by. Britannica Illustrated Science Library: Mammals, 16 vols. 2008. (Illus.). (J). 29.95 *(978-1-59339-393-9(8))* Encyclopaedia Britannica, Inc.

—My First Britannica: Mammals. 2008. (gr. 7-12). *(978-1-59339-412-7(8))* Encyclopaedia Britannica, Inc.

Encyclopedia Britannica Staff, creator. Mammals. 2011. (Britannica Illustrated Science Library Ser.). 104p. (J). 37.44 *(978-1-61535-466-5(2))* Encyclopaedia Britannica, Inc.

Endangered Mammals - Africa: An Educational Coloring Book. (J). (gr. 3-18). pap. 1.99 *(978-0-86545-213-8(X))* Spizzirri Pr., Inc.

Endangered Mammals - Asia & China: An Educational Coloring Book. (J). (gr. 3-18). pap. 1.99 *(978-0-86545-214-5(8))* Spizzirri Pr., Inc.

Endangered Mammals - South America: An Educational Coloring Book. (J). pap. 1.99 *(978-0-86545-215-2(6))* Spizzirri Pr., Inc.

Falchetta, Drew. Mammals Love Their Babies. 2016. (1-3Y Animals Ser.). (ENG., Illus.). 20p. (J). pap. 5.99 ***(978-1-63437-623-5(4))*** American Reading Co.

Feldman, Thea. Animales Migratorios: Por Tierra. 2007. (En marcha: Migraciones animales (Spanish- on the Move: Animal Migration) Ser.). (SPA.). 24p. (gr. 1-4). pap. 8.15 *(978-0-8368-8433-3(7))*; (Illus.). lib. bdg. 22.00 *(978-0-8368-8428-9(0))* Stevens, Gareth Publishing LLLP. (Weekly Reader Leveled Readers).

—Migrating Animals of the Land. 2007. (On the Move: Animal Migration Ser.). 24p. (gr. 1-4). pap. 8.15 *(978-0-8368-8423-4(X))*; (Illus.). lib. bdg. 22.00 *(978-0-8368-8418-0(3))* Stevens, Gareth Publishing LLLP. (Weekly Reader Leveled Readers).

Furstinger, Nancy. 12 Mammals Back from the Brink. 2014. (ENG., Illus.). 32p. (J). *(978-1-63235-003-9(3))* Pr. Room Editions LLC.

Gagne, Tammy. The Most Adorable Animals in the World. 2015. (All about Animals Ser.). (ENG.). 24p. (gr. 1-2). pap. 6.95 *(978-1-4914-2239-7(4))* Capstone Press of Coughlan Cos.

Gaines, Ann. Kids Top 10 Small Mammal Pets. 2015. (American Humane Association Top 10 Pets for Kids Ser.). 48p. (J). (gr. 3-4). 25.27 *(978-0-7660-6650-2(9))* Enslow Pubs., Inc.

Gaines, Ann Graham. Kids Top 10 Small Mammal Pets. 2015. (American Humane Association Top 10 Pets for Kids Ser.). 48p. (J). (gr. 3-4). pap. 8.95 *(978-0-7660-6651-9(7)*, Enslow Elementary) Enslow Pubs., Inc.

—Top 10 Small Mammals for Kids. 2008. (Top Pets for Kids with American Humane Ser.). (Illus.). 48p. (J). (gr. 3-4). lib. bdg. 25.27 *(978-0-7660-3075-6(X)*, Enslow Elementary) Enslow Pubs., Inc.

Ganeri, Anita. Meerkat, 1 vol. 2011. (Day in the Life: Desert Animals Ser.). (ENG., Illus.). 24p. (J). (gr. k-2). 23.32 *(978-1-4329-4773-6(7)*, Heinemann Read & Learn) Heinemann-Raintree.

Gibbs, Maddie. Jackals. 2011. (Safari Animals Ser.). (ENG.). 24p. (J). pap. 8.25 *(978-1-4488-2596-7(2))*; lib. bdg. 22.60 *(978-1-4488-2505-9(9))* Rosen Publishing Group, Inc., The. (PowerKids Pr.).

—Jackals: Chacales. 2011. (Safari Animals / Animales de Safari Ser.). (ENG & SPA.). 24p. (J). (gr. -1-2). lib. bdg. 22.60 *(978-1-4488-3119-7(9))* Rosen Publishing Group, Inc., The.

Gilbert, Sara. Ice Age Mega Beasts: Giant Short-Faced Bears. 2017. (Ice Age Mega Beasts Ser.). (ENG., Illus.). 24p. (J). (gr. 1-3). pap. 8.99 ***(978-1-62832-374-0(4)***, Creative Paperbacks) Creative Co., The.

—Ice Age Mega Beasts: Stag-Moose. 2017. (Ice Age Mega Beasts Ser.). (ENG., Illus.). 24p. (J). (gr. 1-3). pap. 8.99 ***(978-1-62832-378-8(7)***, Creative Paperbacks) Creative Co., The.

Gish, Melissa. Bighorn Sheep. 2015. (Illus.). 46p. (J). *(978-1-60818-564-1(8)*, Creative Education) Creative Co., The.

—Bighorn Sheep: Living Wild. 2016. (Living Wild Ser.). (ENG.). 48p. (J). (gr. 5-9). pap. 12.00 *(978-1-62832-165-4(2)*, Creative Paperbacks) Creative Co., The.

—Manatees. 2017. (Living Wild Ser.). (ENG., Illus.). 48p. (J). (gr. 4-7). pap. 12.00 *(978-1-62832-301-6(9)*, Creative Paperbacks) Creative Co., The.

—Meerkats. 2015. (Illus.). 46p. (J). *(978-1-60818-569-6(9)*, Creative Education) Creative Co., The.

Goldish, Meish. Fossa: A Fearsome Predator. 2008. (Uncommon Animals Ser.). (Illus.). 32p. (J). (gr. 2-5). lib. bdg. 25.27 *(978-1-59716-732-1(0))* Bearport Publishing Co., Inc.

—Mammal Menu. 2009. (Extreme Cuisine Ser.). (Illus.). 24p. (J). (gr. 1-4). lib. bdg. 22.61 *(978-1-59716-760-4(6))* Bearport Publishing Co., Inc.

Gray, Susan H. The Life Cycle of Mammals, 1 vol. 2011. (Life Cycles Ser.). (ENG.). 48p. (gr. 3-5). pap. 9.95 *(978-1-4329-4988-4(8))*; 33.32 *(978-1-4329-4981-5(0))* Heinemann-Raintree. (Heinemann InfoSearch).

Gregory, Helen. All about Mammals, 1 vol. (Wonder Readers Next Steps: Science Ser.). (ENG.). (gr. -1-1). 2013. 20p. 22.65 *(978-1-4765-2371-2(1))* 2011. 16p. pap. 35.94 *(978-1-4296-8067-7(9))* 2011. 32p. pap. 5.99 *(978-1-4296-7795-0(3))* Capstone Press of Coughlan Cos. (Wonder Readers).

Grucella, Ann. Bobcats. 2012. (Killer Cats Ser.). (Illus.). 24p. (J). (gr. 2-5). pap. 8.15 *(978-1-4339-6996-6(3))*; lib. bdg. 22.60 *(978-1-4339-6995-9(5))* Stevens, Gareth Publishing LLLP.

Grzimek, Bernhard & McDade, Melissa C. Grzimek's Student Animal Life Resource. 2004. (J). *(978-0-7876-9234-6(4))*; *(978-0-7876-9188-2(7))*; *(978-0-7876-9187-5(9))*; *(978-0-7876-9184-4(4))*; (Illus.). *(978-0-7876-9185-1(2))* Cengage Gale. (UXL).

—Mammals, 5.0, Vol. 20. 2004. (Grzimek's Student Animal Life Resource Ser.). (ENG., Illus.). 1000p. (J). 458.00 *(978-0-7876-9183-7(6)*, UXL) Cengage Gale.

Gustafson, Sarah. Whales, Dolphins, & More Marine Mammals. 2005. (Illus.). 48p. (J). pap. *(978-0-439-71189-0(4))* Scholastic, Inc.

Hairy Little Critters: Individual Title Six-Packs. (Action Packs Ser.). 104p. (gr. 3-5). 44.00 *(978-0-7635-8404-7(5))* Rigby Education.

Hall, Katharine. Mamíferos: Un Libro de Comparación y Contraste, 1 vol. 2016. (SPA.). 32p. (J). (gr. k-3). pap. 9.95 *(978-1-62855-743-5(5))* Arbordale Publishing.

—Mammals: A Compare & Contrast Book, 1 vol. 2016. (Compare & Contrast Ser.). (ENG., Illus.). 32p. (J). (gr. k-3). 17.95 *(978-1-62855-729-9(X))* Arbordale Publishing.

Halls, Kelly Milner. Wild Horses: Galloping Through Time. Hallett, Mark, illus. 2008. (Darby Creek Exceptional Titles Ser.). 72p. (J). (gr. 1-7). 18.95 *(978-1-58196-065-5(4)*, Darby Creek) Lerner Publishing Group.

Hamilton, Lynn & Gillespie, Katie. Ferret. 2015. (J). *(978-1-4896-2954-8(8))* Weigl Pubs., Inc.

Hansen, Grace. Bonobos, 1 vol. 2015. (ENG., Illus.). 24p. (J). 28.50 *(978-1-62970-895-9(X))* ABDO Publishing Co.

Harris, Tim, ed. Mammals of the Northern Hemisphere. 2011. (FAYFT: Endangered Animals Ser.). 64p. (gr. 4-10). lib. bdg. 39.95 *(978-1-936333-34-9(1))* Brown Bear Bks.

Harvey, Jeanne Walker. Honey Girl: The Hawaiian Monk Seal. Bersani, Shennen, illus. 2017. (ENG.). 32p. (J). (gr. k-3). pap. 9.95 *(978-1-62855-922-4(5))* Arbordale Publishing.

Hay DeSimone, Corkey. Mammal Animal Board Book 2nd Edition. Hay DeSimone, Corkey, illus. 2007. (Illus.). 24p. (J). 7.95 *(978-0-9777394-2-4(2))* Gentle Giraffe Pr.

—Mammal Animal Coloring & Activity Book: What Is a mammal? You are a mammal Too! 2005. (Illus.). (J). pap. 4.95 *(978-0-9747921-2-5(6))* Gentle Giraffe Pr.

Haynes, Danielle. Mammal Fossils. 2016. (Fossil Files Ser.). 00032p. (J). (gr. 5-5). 26.25 *(978-1-4994-2859-9(6)*, PowerKids Pr.) Rosen Publishing Group, Inc., The.

Head, Honor. Amazing Mammals. 2008. (Amazing Life Cycles Ser.). (Illus.). 32p. (gr. 2-6). lib. bdg. 26.00 *(978-0-8368-8896-6(0)*, Gareth Stevens Learning Library) Stevens, Gareth Publishing LLLP.

Hengel, Katherine. It's a Baby Spiny Anteater!, 1 vol. 2010. (Baby Australian Animals Ser.). (ENG., Illus.). 24p. (J). (gr. k-3). lib. bdg. 24.21 *(978-1-60453-578-5(4),* SandCastle) ABDO Publishing Co.

—It's a Baby Tasmanian Devil!, 1 vol. 2010. (Baby Australian Animals Ser.). (ENG., Illus.). 24p. (J). (gr. k-3). lib. bdg. 24.21 *(978-1-60453-579-2(2),* SandCastle) ABDO Publishing Co.

Herriges, Ann. Manatees. 2006. (Oceans Alive Ser.). (ENG., Illus.). 24p. (J). (gr. k-3). lib. bdg. 25.95 *(978-1-60014-048-8(3))* Bellwether Media.

Herrington, Lisa M. Amazing Mammals. 2016. (Rookie Read-About Science(tm): Strange Animals Ser.). (ENG.). 32p. (J). lib. bdg. 25.00 *(978-0-531-22600-1(X),* Children's Pr.) Scholastic Library Publishing.

Higgins, Melissa. Woolly Mammoths. 2015. (Ice Age Animals Ser.). (ENG.). 24p. (gr. k-1). pap. 6.95 *(978-1-4914-2320-2(X),* Pebble Plus) Capstone Press of Coughlan Cos.

Holt, Rinehart and Winston Staff. Holt Science & Technology Chapter 17: Life Science: Birds & Mammals. 5th ed. 2004. (Illus.). pap. 12.86 *(978-0-03-030226-8(9))* Holt McDougal.

Housel, Debra J. Mamífero Manía. 2017. (TIME for Kids en Español - Level 3 Ser.). (SPA.). 32p. (gr. 3-3). lib. bdg. 31.99 ***(978-1-5157-5171-7(6))*** Time for Kids Inc AUS. Dist: Capstone Pub.

Housel, Debra J. Mammal Mania, 1 vol. 2nd rev. ed. 2013. (Nonfiction Readers Ser.). (ENG., Illus.). 28p. (J). (gr. 3-3). pap. 25.96 *(978-1-4807-1073-3(3))* Shell Educational Publishing.

—Mammal Mania, 1 vol. 2nd rev. ed. 2011. (Nonfiction Readers Ser.). (ENG.). 28p. (J). (gr. 3-3). pap. 8.99 *(978-1-4333-3658-4(8))* Teacher Created Materials, Inc.

Hudak, Heather C. Carnivores. 2011. (J). (gr. 4-6). pap. 12.95 *(978-1-61690-713-6(4),* AV2 by Weigl); (Illus.). 24p. (gr. 2-5). 27.13 *(978-1-61690-707-5(X))* Weigl Pubs., Inc.

—Land Mammals. 2005. (Animal Facts Ser.). (Illus.). 24p. (J). (gr. 2-3). per. 8.95 *(978-1-59036-245-7(4));* (gr. 4-7). lib. bdg. 24.45 *(978-1-59036-200-6(4))* Weigl Pubs., Inc.

Hunt, Santana. Name That Mammal! 2016. (Guess That Animal! Ser.). 24p. (J). (gr. 2-1). lib. bdg. 22.60 *(978-1-4824-4746-0(0))* Stevens, Gareth Publishing LLLP.

Inserra, Rose. Mammals. 2010. (Weird, Wild, & Wonderful Ser.). (Illus.). 24p. (J). (gr. 2-5). lib. bdg. 22.00 *(978-1-4339-3573-2(2),* Gareth Stevens Learning Library) Stevens, Gareth Publishing LLLP.

Jacobs, Daniel. Big Babies. 2005. (Yellow Umbrella Fluent Level Ser.). (ENG., Illus.). 16p. (gr. k-1). pap. 35.70 *(978-0-7368-5293-7(X),* Yellow Umbrella Bks.) Capstone Press of Coughlan Cos.

Jacobs, Pat. Why Do Mammals Have Fur? And Other Questions about Evolution & Classification. 2016. (Wildlife Wonders Ser.). 00032p. (J). (gr. 3-3). pap. 10.00 *(978-1-4994-3208-4(9),* PowerKids Pr.) Rosen Publishing Group, Inc., The.

Jeffrey, Laura S. Choosing a Hamster, Gerbil, Guinea Pig, Rabbit, Ferret, Mouse, or Rat: How to Choose & Care for a Small Mammal. 2013. (American Humane Association Pet Care Ser.). 48p. (J). (gr. 3-18). lib. bdg. 25.27 *(978-0-7660-4082-3(8));* pap. 8.95 *(978-1-4644-0217-3(5),* Enslow Elementary) Enslow Pubs., Inc.

—Hamsters, Gerbils, Guinea Pigs, Rabbits, Ferrets, Mice, & Rats: How to Choose & Care for a Small Mammal. 2004. (American Humane Pet Care Library). (Illus.). 48p. (J). lib. bdg. 25.27 *(978-0-7660-2518-9(7))* Enslow Pubs., Inc.

Jennings, Dorothy. Otters Smash, Crabs Pinch. 2017. (Hunter & Hunted: Animal Survival Ser.). 24p. (J). (gr. 7-8). 23.60 ***(978-1-5081-5662-8(X),*** PowerKids Pr.) Rosen Publishing Group, Inc., The.

Johnston, Coleen. Unusual Mammals from A to Z. 2009. 36p. pap. 19.95 *(978-1-4357-5566-6(9))* Lulu Pr., Inc.

Kalman, Bobbie. Baby Carnivores. 2013. (ENG., Illus.). 24p. (J). *(978-0-7787-1010-3(6));* pap. *(978-0-7787-1015-8(7))* Crabtree Publishing Co.

—Baby Mammals. 2013. (ENG., Illus.). 24p. (J). *(978-0-7787-1008-0(4));* pap. *(978-0-7787-1013-4(0))* Crabtree Publishing Co.

—Insect Eaters. 2008. (Big Science Ideas Ser.). (ENG., Illus.). 32p. (J). (gr. 1-4). pap. *(978-0-7787-3298-3(3));* lib. bdg. *(978-0-7787-3278-5(9))* Crabtree Publishing Co.

—What Is a Carnivore? 2008. (ENG., Illus.). 32p. (J). *(978-0-7787-7664-2(6))* Crabtree Publishing Co.

Kalman, Bobbie & Dyer, Hadley. Endangered Manatees. 2006. (Earth's Endangered Animals Ser.). (ENG., Illus.). 32p. (J). (gr. 3-7). lib. bdg. *(978-0-7787-1868-0(9))* Crabtree Publishing Co.

Kalman, Bobbie & Johnson, Robin. Koalas & Other Marsupials. 2005. (What Kind of Animal Is It? Ser.). (ENG., Illus.). 32p. (J). (gr. 1-2). lib. bdg. *(978-0-7787-2162-8(0))* Crabtree Publishing Co.

Kalman, Bobbie & Lundblad, Kristina. Animales Llamados Mamíferos. 2007. (Que Tipo de Animal Es? Ser.). (SPA., Illus.). 32p. (J). (gr. 1-2). lib. bdg. *(978-0-7787-8836-2(9));* (gr. k-4). pap. *(978-0-7787-8872-0(5))* Crabtree Publishing Co.

—Animals Called Mammals. 2005. (What Kind of Animal Is It? Ser.). (ENG., Illus.). 32p. (J). (gr. k-4). pap. *(978-0-7787-2215-1(5))* Crabtree Publishing Co.

Kaspar, Anna. What's a Mammal? 2012. (All about Animals Ser.). (ENG., Illus.). 24p. (J). (gr. k-3). pap. 8.25 *(978-1-4488-6232-0(9));* lib. bdg. 22.60 *(978-1-4488-6137-8(3))* Rosen Publishing Group, Inc., The. (PowerKids Pr.).

—What's a Mammal? Qué Es un Mamífero? 2012. (All about Animals / Todo sobre los animales Ser.). (SPA & ENG., Illus.). 24p. (J). (gr. k-3). lib. bdg. 22.60 *(978-1-4488-6703-5(7),* PowerKids Pr.) Rosen Publishing Group, Inc., The.

Katirgis, Jane & Reiter, Chris. Endangered Blue Whales. 2015. (Wildlife at Risk Ser.). (ENG., Illus.). 48p. (J). (gr. 6-6). 27.93 *(978-0-7660-6890-2(0))* Enslow Pubs., Inc.

King, Zelda. Manatees. 2012. (Illus.). 24p. (J). 49.50 *(978-1-4488-5136-2(X),* PowerKids Pr.); pap. 8.25 *(978-1-4488-5135-5(1),* PowerKids Pr.); lib. bdg. 22.60 *(978-1-4488-5002-0(9))* Rosen Publishing Group, Inc., The.

Kopp, Megan. Mammals. 2016. (Illus.). 32p. (J). *(978-1-5105-1116-3(4))* SmartBook Media, Inc.

Kuskowski, Alex. Miniature Mammals, 1 vol. 2014. (Mini Animal Marvels Ser.). (ENG., Illus.). 24p. (J). (gr. -1-3). lib. bdg. 24.21 *(978-1-62403-067-3(X))* ABDO Publishing Co.

Lee, David. Jackals. 2016. (Wild Canines Ser.). (Illus.). 24p. (J). (gr. 3-3). pap. 8.25 *(978-1-4994-2027-2(7),* PowerKids Pr.) Rosen Publishing Group, Inc., The.

Levine, Michelle. Mammals. 2015. (Illus.). 32p. (J). lib. bdg. 28.50 *(978-1-60753-475-4(4))* Amicus Publishing.

Levine, Sara. Tooth by Tooth. Spookytooth, T. S., illus. 2016. (ENG.). 32p. (J). (gr. k-4). 26.65 *(978-1-4677-5215-2(0),* Millbrook Pr.) Lerner Publishing Group.

—Tooth by Tooth: Comparing Fangs, Tusks, & Chompers. Spookytooth, T. S., illus. 2016. (ENG.). 32p. (gr. k-4). 39.99 *(978-1-4677-9727-6(8),* Millbrook Pr.) Lerner Publishing Group.

Levine, Sara C. Tooth by Tooth: Comparing Fangs, Tusks, & Chompers. Spookytooth, T. S., illus. 2016. (Millbrook Picture Bks). (ENG.). 32p. (gr. k-4). 39.99 *(978-1-5124-0732-7(1))* Lerner Publishing Group.

Levy, Janey. Really Strange Mammals. 2016. (Really Strange Adaptations Ser.). 00032p. (J). (gr. 5-5). pap. 10.00 *(978-1-4994-2789-9(1),* PowerKids Pr.) Rosen Publishing Group, Inc., The.

Lewis, Clare. Mammal Body Parts. 2015. (Animal Body Parts Ser.). (ENG., Illus.). 24p. (gr. k-2). 23.32 *(978-1-4846-2552-1(8))* Heinemann-Raintree.

Long, Olivia. Why Don't Cats Lay Eggs? Long, Olivia, illus. Date not set. (Our Precious Planet Ser.). (Illus.). 32p. (J). (gr. -1-4). *(978-1-880042-12-0(6))* Shelf-Life Bks.

Lundblad, Kristina. Les Mammifères. 2011. (FRE., Illus.). 32p. (J). pap. 9.95 *(978-2-89579-393-9(X))* Bayard Canada CAN. Dist: Crabtree Publishing Co.

Lunde, Darrin. Discovering a New Animal with a Scientist. 2007. (I Like Science! Ser.). (Illus.). 24p. (J). (gr. 1-3). lib. bdg. 22.60 *(978-0-7660-2815-9(1),* Enslow Elementary) Enslow Pubs., Inc.

—Meet the Meerkat. Wynne, Patricia J., illus. 2007. (gr. -1-1). 17.95 *(978-0-7569-8047-4(X))* Perfection Learning Corp.

Lynette, Rachel. South American Tapirs. 2013. (Jungle Babies of the Amazon Rain Forest Ser.). 24p. (J). (gr. -1-3). lib. bdg. 21.32 *(978-1-61772-759-7(8))* Bearport Publishing Co., Inc.

MacAulay, Kelley & Kalman, Bobbie. Dolphins & Other Marine Mammals. 2005. (What Kind of Animal Is It? Ser.). (ENG., Illus.). 32p. (J). (gr. 1-2). pap. *(978-0-7787-2222-9(8));* lib. bdg. *(978-0-7787-2164-2(7))* Crabtree Publishing Co.

Machajewski, Sarah. Life of a Honey Badger. 2013. (InfoMax Readers Ser.). (ENG.). 24p. (J). (gr. 3-4). pap. 8.25 *(978-1-4777-2515-3(6));* pap. 49.50 *(978-1-4777-2516-0(4))* Rosen Publishing Group, Inc., The. (Rosen Classroom).

Machajewski, Sarah. The Return of the Mountain Gorilla. 2017. (Bouncing Back from Extinction Ser.). 32p. (J). (gr. 9-10). 60.00 ***(978-1-5081-5603-1(4),*** PowerKids Pr.) Rosen Publishing Group, Inc., The.

Malam, John. Pinnipeds. 2009. (Scary Creatures Ser.). (ENG., Illus.). 32p. (J). (gr. 3-5). 27.00 *(978-0-531-21672-9(1),* Children's Pr.); pap. 8.95 *(978-0-531-21043-7(X),* Watts, Franklin) Scholastic Library Publishing.

Mamíferos Pequeños, 6 vols., Vol. 3. (Explorers. Exploradores Nonfiction Sets Ser.). (SPA.). (gr. 3-6). *(978-0-7699-0651-6(5))* Shortland Pubns. (U. S. A.) Inc.

Mamíferos de Gran TamanO, 6 vols., Vol. 2. (Explorers. Exploradores Nonfiction Sets Ser.). (SPA.). 32p. (gr. 3-6). 44.95 *(978-0-7699-0638-6(9))* Shortland Pubns. (U. S. A.) Inc.

Los Mamíferos Del Mar, 6 vols. (Explorers. Exploradores Nonfiction Sets Ser.). (SPA.). 32p. (gr. 3-6). 44.95 *(978-0-7699-0629-4(X))* Shortland Pubns. (U. S. A.) Inc.

Mammals Set 1: Mammals of North America. 2005. (J). spiral bd. 23.40 *(978-0-9770248-9-6(X))* Sidedoor Publishing LLC.

Markle, Sandra. Finding Home. Marks, Alan, illus. 2010. (ENG.). 32p. (J). (gr. -1-3). pap. 7.95 *(978-1-58089-123-3(3))* Charlesbridge Publishing, Inc.

—Finding Olinguito. 2017. (ENG., Illus.). 40p. (J). (gr. 3-6). 30.65 *(978-1-5124-1015-0(2),* Millbrook Pr.) Lerner Publishing Group.

—Jackals. 2005. (Animal Scavengers Ser.). (ENG., Illus.). 40p. (gr. 3-6). lib. bdg. 25.26 *(978-0-8225-3197-5(6),* Lerner Pubns.) Lerner Publishing Group.

—Los Demonios de Tasmania; Tasmanian Devils. 2008. pap. 46.95 *(978-0-8225-9452-9(8))* Lerner Publishing Group.

Markle, Sandra. The Search for Olinguito: Discovering a New Species. 2017. (Nonfiction — Grades 4-8 Ser.). (ENG.). 40p. (J). (gr. 3-6). 16.99 ***(978-1-5124-3875-8(8));*** 46.65 ***(978-1-5124-3876-5(6));*** (Illus.). 46.65 ***(978-1-5124-2842-1(6))*** Lerner Publishing Group. (Millbrook Pr.).

Markovics, Joyce. Mi Lengua Es Larga y Curva (Okapi) 2016. (Pistas de Animales 2 Ser.). (SPA.). 24p. (J). (gr. -1-3). 17.95 *(978-1-944102-77-7(9))* Bearport Publishing Co., Inc.

—My Nose Is Long & Fuzzy (Anteater) 2014. (Zoo Clues Ser.). 24p. (J). (gr. -1-3). lib. bdg. 23.93 *(978-1-62724-111-3(6))* Bearport Publishing Co., Inc.

Markovics, Joyce L. Ringtail: Miner's Cat. 2012. (America's Hidden Animal Treasures Ser.). 32p. (J). (gr. 2-7). lib. bdg. 26.60 *(978-1-61772-580-7(3))* Bearport Publishing Co., Inc.

—Warthog. 2016. (J). lib. bdg. *(978-1-62724-821-1(8))* Bearport Publishing Co., Inc.

Marsh, Laura. Meerkats. 2013. (Readers Ser.). (ENG., Illus.). 32p. (J). (gr. -1-1). pap. 3.99 *(978-1-4263-1342-4(X),* National Geographic Children's Bks.) National Geographic Society.

—National Geographic Readers: Meerkats. 2013. (Readers Ser.). (ENG., Illus.). 32p. (J). (gr. -1-1). lib. bdg. 13.90 *(978-1-4263-1343-1(8),* National Geographic Children's Bks.) National Geographic Society.

Marshall Cavendish Corporation Staff. Mammal Anatomy: An Illustrated Guide. 2009. (Illus.). 287p. (YA). (gr. 7-18). 99.93 *(978-0-7614-7882-9(5))* Marshall Cavendish Corp.

Marshall Cavendish Reference Staff, contrib. by. Mammals of the Northern Hemisphere. 2010. 208p. (J). 59.95 *(978-0-7614-7936-9(8),* Marshall Cavendish Reference Bks.) Marshall Cavendish Corp.

—Mammals of the Southern Hemisphere. 2010. 208p. (J). 59.95 *(978-0-7614-7937-6(6),* Marshall Cavendish Reference Bks.) Marshall Cavendish Corp.

Marsico, Katie. A Manatee Calf Grows Up. 2007. (Scholastic News Nonfiction Readers Ser.). (ENG., Illus.). 24p. (J). (gr. 1-2). 22.00 *(978-0-531-17479-1(4))* Scholastic Library Publishing.

Martin, Chia. Nos Gusta Amamantar / We Like to Nurse. Mithuna, Shukyu Linn, illus. 2nd alt. ed. 2016. (Family & World Health Ser.). (ENG.). 28p. bds. 12.95 *(978-1-942493-12-9(6))* Hohm Pr.

Martin, Isabel. Mammals: A Question & Answer Book, 1 vol. 2014. (Animal Kingdom Questions & Answers Ser.). (ENG.). 24p. (gr. k-1). 26.65 *(978-1-4914-0566-6(X));* (Illus.). pap. 6.95 *(978-1-4914-0634-2(8))* Capstone Press of Coughlan Cos. (Pebble Plus).

Martin-James, Kathleen. Gentle Manatees. 2005. (Pull Ahead Bks.). (J). 22.60 *(978-0-8225-2422-9(8),* Lerner Pubns.); (ENG., Illus.). 32p. pap. 7.95 *(978-0-8225-2441-0(4))* Lerner Publishing Group.

Matthews, Rupert. The Illustrated Encyclopedia of Mammals. 2008. (ENG., Illus.). 80p. (J). (gr. 3-18). 19.95 *(978-88-88166-59-9(9))* McRae Bks. Srl ITA. Dist: Independent Pubs. Group.

McGill, Jordan. Zarigüeyas. 2012. (SPA.). (J). *(978-1-61913-194-1(3))* Weigl Pubs., Inc.

McRae, Anne & Agosta, Loredana. Mammals. Dogi, Fiammetta, illus. 2007. (Back to Basics Ser.). 32p. (J). lib. bdg. *(978-88-6098-047-2(X))* McRae Bks. Srl.

Michele, Tracey. What Is a Mammal? 2011. (Learn-Abouts Ser.). (Illus.). 16p. (J). pap. 7.95 *(978-1-59920-643-1(9))* Black Rabbit Bks.

Michels, Dia L. If My Mom Were a Platypus: Mammal Babies & Their Mothers. 2006. (ENG & HEB., Illus.). 64p. (J). (gr. -1-12). 16.95 *(978-965-90219-6-3(8))* Platypus Media, L.L.C.

—If My Mom Were a Platypus: Mammal Babies & Their Mothers. Barthelmes, Andrew, illus. 4th ed. 2014. (SPA, DUT, ENG & HEB.). 64p. pap. 12.95 *(978-1-938492-11-2(0))* Science, Naturally!

—If My Mom Were A Platypus- Hebrew Language Edition. Barthelmes, Andrew, illus. 2006. Orig. Title: #1488;#1501; #1488;#1502;#1497; #1492;#1497;#1514;#1492; #1508;#1500;#1496;#1497;#1508;#1493;#1505;. 64p. (J). 29.95 *(978-0-9678020-9-1(1))* Science, Naturally!

—If My Mom Were a Platypus- Hebrew Language Edition. Barthelmes, Andrew, illus. 2006. Orig. Title: #1488;#1501; #1488;#1502;#1497; #1492;#1497;#1514;#1492; #1508;#1500;#1496;#1497;#1508;#1493;#1505;. (HEB.). 64p. (J). 19.95 *(978-0-9678020-8-4(3))* Science, Naturally!

Mighty Mammals: Level O, 6 vols., Vol. 2. (Explorers Ser.). 32p. (gr. 3-6). 44.95 *(978-0-7699-0602-7(8))* Shortland Pubns. (U. S. A.) Inc.

Miller, Sara Swan. Walruses of the Arctic. 2009. (Brrr! Polar Animals Ser.). (J). (gr. k-5). (ENG., Illus.). 24p. pap. 8.25 *(978-1-4358-3150-6(0),* 1291794, PowerKids Pr.); lib. bdg. 22.60 *(978-1-4358-2746-2(5))* Rosen Publishing Group, Inc., The.

Mini Mammals: Level P, 6 vols., Vol. 3. (Explorers Ser.). 32p. (gr. 3-6). 44.95 *(978-0-7699-0615-7(X))* Shortland Pubns. (U. S. A.) Inc.

Mitchell, Susan K. Biggest vs. Smallest Amazing Mammals. 2010. (Biggest vs. Smallest Animals Ser.). (Illus.). 24p. (J). 22.60 *(978-0-7660-3582-9(4),* Enslow Elementary) Enslow Pubs., Inc.

Moran, Paul. Where's the Meerkat? Journey Through Time. 2014. (ENG., Illus.). 48p. (J). (gr. 2-6). 14.99 *(978-1-84317-804-0(4))* O'Mara, Michael Bks., Ltd. GBR. Dist: Independent Pubs. Group.

—Where's the Meerkat? - Journey Through Time. 2014. (ENG., Illus.). 48p. (J). (gr. 2-6). pap. 7.99 *(978-1-84317-948-1(2))* O'Mara, Michael Bks., Ltd. GBR. Dist: Independent Pubs. Group.

Murray, Julie. Tasmanian Devils, 1 vol. 2011. (Australian Animals Ser.). (ENG., Illus.). 32p. (J). (gr. 2-5). 28.50 *(978-1-61783-014-3(3))* ABDO Publishing Co.

Mystifying Mammals. 2016. (Illus.). 32p. (J). *(978-1-4222-3523-2(8))* Mason Crest.

Nature Files. 2005. (Nature Files Ser.). (Illus.). 32p. (gr. 4-6). 168.00 *(978-0-7910-8446-5(9),* Chelsea Hse.) Facts On File, Inc.

Niver, Heather Moore. We Need Bats. 2015. (Creatures We Can't Live Without Ser.). (ENG., Illus.). 24p. (J). (gr. 3-4). pap. 8.25 *(978-1-4994-0979-6(6),* PowerKids Pr.) Rosen Publishing Group, Inc., The.

O'Connell, Kim A. The Wallaby: A MyReportLinks. com Book. 2005. (Endangered & Threatened Animals Ser.). (Illus.). 48p. (J). lib. bdg. 25.26 *(978-0-7660-5064-8(5),* MyReportLinks.com Bks.) Enslow Pubs., Inc.

O'Hare, Ted. Mammals. 2005. (What Is an Animal? Ser.). (Illus.). 24p. (J). (gr. 1-4). per. 5.45 *(978-1-59515-734-8(4));* lib. bdg. 14.95 *(978-1-59515-420-0(5))* Rourke Educational Media.

O'Reilly, Wenda. Go fish wildlife Mammals. 2007. n/ap. pap. 119.40 *(978-1-59960-016-1(1))* Birdcage Pr.

—Wild Cards. 2007. n/ap. pap. 119.40 *(978-1-59960-012-3(9))* Birdcage Pr.

Orr, Tamra. Care for a Pet Ferret. 2008. (How to Convince Your Parents You Can ... Ser.). (Illus.). 32p. (YA). (gr. 1-4). lib. bdg. 25.70 *(978-1-58415-660-4(0))* Mitchell Lane Pubs., Inc.

Owen, Ruth. Manatee Calves. 2012. (Water Babies Ser.). 24p. (J). (gr. -1-3). lib. bdg. 21.32 *(978-1-61772-599-9(4))* Bearport Publishing Co., Inc.

Parker, Steve. Mamiferos. 2nd ed. Date not set. (SPA., Illus.). 64p. 14.95 *(978-84-372-3714-5(9))* Santillana USA Publishing Co., Inc.

—Mammal. Dorling Kindersley Publishing Staff, ed. 2004. (DK Eyewitness Bks.). (ENG., Illus.). 72p. (J). (gr. 3-7). 16.99 *(978-0-7566-0703-6(5),* DK Children) Dorling Kindersley Publishing, Inc.

—Mammal: Eyewitness Books. Burton, Jane & King, Dave, photos by. 2004. (Illus.). 63p. (gr. 4-8). reprint ed. 16.00 *(978-0-7567-7286-4(9))* DIANE Publishing Co.

—Whales & Dolphins. 2010. (I Love Animals Ser.). (ENG., Illus.). 24p. (J). (gr. 1-5). pap. 8.15 *(978-1-61533-236-6(7));* lib. bdg. 22.60 *(978-1-61533-230-4(8))* Windmill Bks.

Pesta, K. My Ferret Dexter. 2008. 20p. per. 24.95 *(978-1-4241-9137-6(8))* America Star Bks.

Petersen, Christine. A Project Guide to Mammals. 2010. (Life Science Projects for Kids Ser.). (Illus.). 48p. (J). (gr. 4-8). lib. bdg. 29.95 *(978-1-58415-875-2(1))* Mitchell Lane Pubs., Inc.

Pettiford, Rebecca. Manatees. 2017. (Ocean Life up Close Ser.). (ENG., Illus.). 24p. (J). (gr. k-3). lib. bdg. 25.95 *(978-1-62617-570-9(5),* Blastoff! Readers) Bellwether Media.

Phillips, Dee. Mammals. 2006. (Blue Zoo Guides). (ENG., Illus.). 96p. (J). (gr. -1-2). 18.95 *(978-1-58728-519-6(3))* Cooper Square Publishing Llc.

—Meerkat's Burrow. 2014. (Science Slam: the Hole Truth Ser.). 24p. (J). (gr. -1-3). lib. bdg. 23.93 *(978-1-62724-092-5(6))* Bearport Publishing Co., Inc.

Rake, Jody Sullivan. Meerkats. 2010. (African Animals Ser.). (ENG.). 24p. (gr. k-1). pap. 41.70 *(978-1-4296-5083-0(4),* Pebble Plus) Capstone Press of Coughlan Cos.

—Star-Nosed Moles & Other Extreme Mammal Adaptations, 1 vol. 2014. (Extreme Adaptations Ser.). (ENG.). 32p. (gr. 3-4). lib. bdg. 27.32 *(978-1-4914-0167-5(2))* Capstone Press of Coughlan Cos.

Rake, Matthew. The Rise of Mammals. Minister, Peter, illus. 2015. (Prehistoric Field Guides). (ENG.). 32p. (J). (gr. 3-6). lib. bdg. 26.65 *(978-1-4677-6351-6(9))* Lerner Publishing Group.

Randall, Henry. Wildcats: Gatos Monteses. 2011. (Cats of the Wild / Felinos Salvajes Ser.). (SPA & ENG., Illus.). 24p. lib. bdg. 22.60 *(978-1-4488-3133-3(4),* PowerKids Pr.) Rosen Publishing Group, Inc., The.

Randolph, Joanne. My Friend the Ferret. 2010. (Curious Pet Pals Ser.). (ENG., Illus.). 24p. (J). (gr. k-3). pap. 8.15 *(978-1-60754-980-2(8));* lib. bdg. 22.60 *(978-1-60754-974-1(3))* Windmill Bks.

Reade, Clara. Warthogs. 2012. (PowerKids Readers: Safari Animals Ser.). (ENG., Illus.). 24p. (J). (gr. k-2). pap. 8.25 *(978-1-4488-7473-6(4));* lib. bdg. 22.60 *(978-1-4488-7393-7(2))* Rosen Publishing Group, Inc., The. (PowerKids Pr.).

Richardson, Joy. Mammals. 2005. (Variety of Life Ser.). (Illus.). 32p. (gr. 1-4). lib. bdg. 26.00 *(978-0-8368-4506-8(4),* Gareth Stevens Learning Library) Stevens, Gareth Publishing LLLP.

Rieger, Linda. How Are We Alike? Bianchi, John, illus. 2006. 20p. (J). *(978-0-9779427-0-1(8))* Pathways into Science.

Rodriguez, Ana María. The Secret of the Bird's Smart Brain... & More! 2017. (Animal Secrets Revealed! Ser.). 48p. (J). (gr. 4-4). pap. 11.70 ***(978-0-7660-8852-8(9));*** lib. bdg. 27.93 ***(978-0-7660-8623-4(2))*** Enslow Pubs., Inc.

—Secret of the Bloody Hippo ... & More! 2008. (Animal Secrets Revealed! Ser.). (Illus.). 48p. (J). (gr. 5-9). lib. bdg. 25.27 *(978-0-7660-2958-3(1))* Enslow Pubs., Inc.

Rodriguez, Ana María. The Secret of the Scorpion-Eating Meerkats... & More! 2017. (Animal Secrets Revealed! Ser.). 48p. (J). (gr. 4-4). pap. 11.70 ***(978-0-7660-8848-1(0));*** lib. bdg. 27.93 ***(978-0-7660-8627-2(5))*** Enslow Pubs., Inc.

Rodriguez, Ana Maria. Secret of the Singing Mice... & More! 2008. (Animal Secrets Revealed! Ser.). (Illus.). 48p. (J). (gr. 5-9). lib. bdg. 25.27 *(978-0-7660-2956-9(5))* Enslow Pubs., Inc.

Royston, Angela. Mammals. (Illus.). 32p. (YA). (gr. 2-18). lib. bdg. 27.10 *(978-1-932333-37-4(1))* Chrysalis Education.

—Mammals. 2015. (Animal Classifications Ser.). (ENG., Illus.). 32p. (gr. 1-3). 27.32 *(978-1-4846-0753-4(8),* Heinemann First Library) Heinemann-Raintree.

Rupp, Kristina. See the Mammals. 2015. (1-3Y Animals Ser.). (ENG., Illus.). 20p. (J). pap. 5.99 *(978-1-63437-152-0(6))* American Reading Co.

Sackett-Smith, Lucy. Hippos: Huge & Hungry. 2009. (Mighty Mammals Ser.). (Illus.). 24p. (J). (gr. k-3). 22.60 *(978-1-4042-8105-9(3))* Rosen Publishing Group, Inc., The.

Salzmann, Mary Elizabeth. What Has Horns?, 1 vol. 2007. (Creature Features Ser.). (ENG., Illus.). 24p. (gr. -1-3). 25.65 *(978-1-59928-868-0(0),* Super SandCastle) ABDO Publishing Co.

Savage, Stephen. Focus on Mammals. 2011. (Animal Watch Ser.). 32p. (YA). (gr. 3-6). lib. bdg. 26.60 *(978-1-4339-5990-5(9))* Stevens, Gareth Publishing LLLP.

School Zone Publishing Company Staff. Mammals. (Illus.). (J). 19.99 incl. audio compact disk *(978-0-88743-972-8(1))* School Zone Publishing Co.

Schuetz, Kari. Mammals. 2012. (Animal Classes Ser.). (ENG., Illus.). 24p. (J). (gr. k-3). lib. bdg. 25.95 *(978-1-60014-775-3(5),* Blastoff! Readers) Bellwether Media.

—Meerkats. 2012. (Animal Safari Ser.). (ENG., Illus.). 24p. (J). (gr. k-3). lib. bdg. 25.95 *(978-1-60014-718-0(6),* Blastoff! Readers) Bellwether Media.

Schuh, Mari. The World's Biggest Mammals. 2015. (Illus.). 24p. (J). lib. bdg. 25.65 *(978-1-62031-204-9(2))* Jump! Inc.

Sebastian, Emily. Moles. 2012. (Illus.). 24p. (J). 49.50 *(978-1-4488-5055-6(X),* PowerKids Pr.); pap. 8.25 *(978-1-4488-5054-9(1),* PowerKids Pr.); lib. bdg. 22.60 *(978-1-4488-4952-9(7))* Rosen Publishing Group, Inc., The.

—Mongooses. 2012. (Illus.). 24p. (J). 49.50 *(978-1-4488-5063-1(0),* PowerKids Pr.); pap. 8.25 *(978-1-4488-5062-4(2),* PowerKids Pr.); lib. bdg. 22.60 *(978-1-4488-4956-7(X))* Rosen Publishing Group, Inc., The.

Shaffer, Jody Jensen. Black-Footed Ferrets. 2015. (Endangered Animals Ser.). (ENG.). 24p. (J). (gr. 1-4). 27.07 *(978-1-63143-965-0(0),* 208800) Child's World, Inc., The.

Shea, Mary Molly. Being a Manatee. 2014. 32p. pap. 18.95 *(978-1-4824-6504-4(3))* Rosen Publishing Group, Inc., The.

Shea, Nicole. Creepy Mammals. 2012. (Nature's Creepiest Creatures Ser.). (ENG.). 24p. (J). (gr. 2-5). pap. 8.15 *(978-1-4339-6495-4(3));* lib. bdg. 22.60 *(978-1-4339-6493-0(7))* Stevens, Gareth Publishing LLLP. (Gareth Stevens Learning Library).

Sill, Cathryn. About Mammals: A Guide for Children, 1 vol. Sill, John, illus. rev. ed. 2014. (About ... Ser.). (ENG.). 48p. (J). (gr. -1-2). 16.95 *(978-1-56145-757-1(4))* Peachtree Pubs.

Silverman, Buffy. Do You Know about Mammals? 2009. (Lightning Bolt Books — Meet the Animal Groups Ser.). (ENG., Illus.). 32p. (gr. k-2). 26.60 *(978-0-8225-7539-9(6),* Lerner Pubns.); pap. 7.95 *(978-1-58013-860-4(8))* Lerner Publishing Group.

—¿Sabes Algo Sobre MamiFeros? (Do You Know about Mammals?) 2012. (Libros Rayo — Conoce Los Grupos de Animales (Lightning Bolt Books — Meet the Animal Groups) Ser.). (SPA., Illus.). 32p. (gr. k-2). lib. bdg. 26.60 *(978-0-7613-9331-3(5),* Ediciones Lerner) Lerner Publishing Group.

—¿Sabes Algo Sobre Mamíferos? (Do You Know about Mammals?) 2012. (Libros Rayo — Conoce Los Grupos de Animales (Lightning Bolt Books — Meet the Animal Groups)

Ser.). (ENG & SPA., Illus.). 32p. (gr. k-2). pap. 7.95 *(978-0-7613-9375-7(7)*, Ediciones Lerner) Lerner Publishing Group.

Simmons, Nancy B., ed. Exploring the World of Mammals, 6 vols. 2008. (Exploring the World of Mammals Ser.). (Illus.). 480p. (gr. 5-8). 210.00 *(978-0-7910-9651-2(3)*, Chelsea Hse.) Facts On File, Inc.

Smith, Lucy Sackett. Mighty Mammals, 6 vols., Set. Incl. Elephants: From Trunk to Tail. lib. bdg. 22.60 *(978-1-4042-8102-8(9))*; Tigers: Prowling Predators. lib. bdg. 22.60 *(978-1-4042-8107-3(X))*; (Illus.). 24p. (J). (gr. k-3). 2009. 2009. Set lib. bdg. 127.50 *(978-1-4358-3294-7(9)*, PowerKids Pr.) Rosen Publishing Group, Inc., The.

Snedden, Robert. Mammals. (Living Things Ser.). (Illus.). 32p. 2009. (J). (gr. -1-3). pap. 7.95 *(978-1-59920-198-6(4))* 2007. (YA). (gr. 3-6). lib. bdg. 28.50 *(978-1-59920-081-1(3))* Black Rabbit Bks.

Solway, Andrew. Classifying Mammals. 2016. (Classifying Living Things Ser.). (ENG.). 32p. (gr. 3-5). pap. 7.99 *(978-1-4846-3693-0(7)*, NA-h) Heinemann-Raintree.

Somervill, Barbara. Small Indian Mongoose. 2010. (21st Century Skills Library: Animal Invaders Ser.). (ENG.). 32p. (gr. 4-8). lib. bdg. 28.50 *(978-1-60279-630-0(0)*, 200336) Cherry Lake Publishing.

Spilsbury, Louise. A Mob of Meerkats: And Other Mammal Groups, 1 vol. 2012. (Animals in Groups Ser.). (ENG.). 48p. (gr. 4-6). pap. 9.95 *(978-1-4329-6488-7(7))*; lib. bdg. 33.32 *(978-1-4329-6481-8(X))* Heinemann-Raintree. (Heinemann InfoSearch).

—Superstar Mammals. 2014. (Nature's Got Talent Ser.). (Illus.). 32p. (J). (gr. k-5). 26.25 *(978-1-4777-7052-8(6)*, PowerKids Pr.) Rosen Publishing Group, Inc., The.

—Walruses, 1 vol. 2013. (Living in the Wild: Sea Mammals Ser.). (ENG.). 48p. (gr. 4-6). pap. 9.95 *(978-1-4329-7073-4(9))*; lib. bdg. 33.32 *(978-1-4329-7066-6(6))* Heinemann-Raintree. (Heinemann InfoSearch).

Spilsbury, Richard. A Pod of Dolphins: And Other Sea Mammal Groups, 1 vol. 2012. (Animals in Groups Ser.). (ENG.). 48p. (gr. 4-6). pap. 9.95 *(978-1-4329-6490-0(9))*; lib. bdg. 33.32 *(978-1-4329-6483-2(6))* Heinemann-Raintree. (Heinemann InfoSearch).

Squire, Ann O. Mammals. 2013. (ENG.). 48p. (J). 29.00 *(978-0-531-21754-2(X))*; pap. 6.95 *(978-0-531-22339-0(6))* Scholastic Library Publishing.

Stearns, Precious. Manatees. 2009. (ENG., Illus.). 24p. (gr. 3-6). pap. 8.95 *(978-1-60694-842-2(3))* Rourke Educational Media.

Steffora, Tracey. Skip Counting with Meerkats, 1 vol. 2013. (Animal Math Ser.). (ENG.). 24p. (gr. -1-1). 22.65 *(978-1-4329-7561-6(7))*; pap. 6.95 *(978-1-4329-7568-5(4))* Heinemann-Raintree. (NA-h).

Sterling Publishing Company Staff & Ward, Adam, contrib. by. Pocket Factfiles: Mammals. 2004. (Illus.). 256p. (J). 4.98 *(978-1-4027-1851-9(9))* Sterling Publishing Co., Inc.

Storad, Conrad J. Meerkats. 2007. (Early Bird Nature Books Ser.). (Illus.). 48p. (J). (gr. -1-3). lib. bdg. 25.26 *(978-0-8225-6466-9(1)*, Lerner Pubns.) Lerner Publishing Group.

Sullivant, Holly. Ferrets. 2009. (Illus.). 112p. (J). 14.95 *(978-1-932904-35-2(2))* Eldorado Ink.

Sullivant, Holly J. Ferrets. 2008. (J). *(978-1-932904-27-7(1))* Eldorado Ink.

Sweeney, Alyse & Rustad, Martha E. H. A Masked Mob Mystery: A Zoo Animal Mystery, 1 vol. 2010. (Zoo Animal Mysteries Ser.). (ENG.). 24p. (gr. k-1). lib. bdg. 26.65 *(978-1-4296-4497-6(4)*, Pebble Plus) Capstone Press of Coughlan Cos.

Swinburne, Stephen R. Saving Manatees. 2009. (ENG., Illus.). 40p. (J). (gr. 4-6). pap. 9.95 *(978-1-59078-785-4(4))* Boyds Mills Pr.

Thomas, Isabel. Marvelous Mammals, 1 vol. 2012. (Extreme Animals Ser.). (ENG.). 32p. (gr. 1-3). pap. 8.29 *(978-1-4109-4687-4(8)*, Read Me!) Heinemann-Raintree.

Thornhill, Jan. I Am Josephine: (and I Am a Living Thing) Lee, Jacqui, illus. 2016. (ENG.). 32p. (J). (gr. -1-2). 16.95 *(978-1-77147-156-5(5)*, Owlkids) Owlkids Bks. Inc. CAN. Dist: Publishers Group West (PGW).

Torre, Cristina de la. About Mammals: A Guide for Children = Sobre Los Mamíferos: Una Guía para Niños. Sill, Cathryn P. & Sill, John, illus. 2014. (SPA & ENG.). (J). *(978-1-56145-815-8(5)*, Peachtree Junior) Peachtree Pubs.

Urbigkit, Cat. The Path of the Pronghorn. Goeke, Mark, photos by. 2010. (ENG., Illus.). 32p. (J). (gr. 2-4). 17.95 *(978-1-59078-756-4(0))* Boyds Mills Pr.

Uttridge, Sarah. Mammals Around the World. 2014. (Animals Around the World Ser.). (Illus.). 32p. (J). (gr. 2-5). 31.35 *(978-1-62588-195-3(9))* Black Rabbit Bks.

Vastola, P. Huge Animals: Learning the Long U Sound. 2009. (PowerPhonics Ser.). 24p. (gr. 1-1). 39.90 *(978-1-60851-445-8(5)*, PowerKids Pr.) Rosen Publishing Group, Inc., The.

Veitch, Catherine. Mammal Babies, 1 vol. 2013. (Animal Babies Ser.). (ENG.). 24p. (gr. -1-1). 22.65 *(978-1-4329-7494-7(7))*; pap. 6.95 *(978-1-4329-8419-9(5))*; pap. 35.94 *(978-1-4329-8426-7(8))* Heinemann-Raintree. (Acorn).

Walden, Katherine. Meerkats. 2009. (Safari Animals Ser.). 24p. (Illus.). (J). (gr. k-3). pap. 8.25 *(978-1-4358-3065-3(2))*; (gr. 1-1). 42.50 *(978-1-60852-957-5(6))*; (J). (gr. -1-2). lib. bdg. 22.60 *(978-1-4358-2691-5(4))* Rosen Publishing Group, Inc., The. (PowerKids Pr.).

—Warthogs. 2009. (Safari Animals Ser.). (Illus.). 24p. (J). (gr. k-3). pap. 8.25 *(978-1-4358-3062-2(8)*, PowerKids Pr.) Rosen Publishing Group, Inc., The.

Weber, Valerie J. Manatees. 2008. (Animals That Live in the Ocean Ser.). (Illus.). 24p. (J). (gr. -1-3). lib. bdg. 22.60 *(978-0-8368-9241-3(0)*, Weekly Reader Leveled Readers) Stevens, Gareth Publishing LLLP.

—Manatees/Manatíes. 2008. (Animals That Live in the Ocean/Animales Que Viven en el Oceano Ser.). (SPA & ENG.). 24p. (gr. -1-3). pap. 8.15 *(978-0-8368-9346-5(8)*, Weekly Reader Leveled Readers) Stevens, Gareth Publishing LLLP.

—Manatees/Manatíes. 2008. (Animals That Live in the Ocean/Animales Que Viven en el Oceano Ser.). (SPA & ENG.). 24p. (J). (gr. -1-3). lib. bdg. 22.60 *(978-0-8368-9247-5(X)*, Weekly Reader Leveled Readers) Stevens, Gareth Publishing LLLP.

World Book, Inc Staff, contrib. by. Mammals. 2009. (J). *(978-0-7166-0406-8(X))* World Bk., Inc.

World Book, Inc. Staff, contrib. by. Mammals of the United States & Canada. 2004. (World Book's Science & Nature Guides Ser.). (Illus.). 80p. (J). *(978-0-7166-4215-2(8))* World Bk., Inc.

Wynne, Patricia J. Extreme Mammals. 2009. (Dover Nature Coloring Book Ser.). (ENG., Illus.). 32p. (J). (gr. 2-5). pap. 3.99 *(978-0-486-47286-7(8))* Dover Pubns., Inc.

Zabludoff, Marc. Basilosaurus. Bollinger, Peter, illus. 2009. (Prehistoric Beasts Ser.). 32p. (gr. 2). 29.93 *(978-0-7614-3999-8(4))* Marshall Cavendish Corp.

Zappa, Marcia. Echidnas, 1 vol. 2016. (ENG., Illus.). 32p. (J). *(978-1-62403-773-3(9))* ABDO Publishing Co.

—Elephant Shrews, 1 vol. 2016. (ENG., Illus.). 32p. (J). *(978-1-62403-774-0(7))* ABDO Publishing Co.

Zoehfeld, Kathleen Weidner. National Geographic Readers: Prehistoric Mammals. Tempesta, Franco, illus. 2015. (Readers Ser.). (ENG.). 32p. (J). (gr. k-3). pap. 3.99 *(978-1-4263-1951-8(7)*, National Geographic Children's Bks.) National Geographic Society.

MAMMALS—FICTION

Anderson, Laurie Halse. Manatee Blues, No. 4. 2008. (Vet Volunteers Ser.: 4). (ENG.). 144p. (J). (gr. 3-7). 7.99 *(978-0-14-241084-4(5)*, Puffin Books) Penguin Young Readers Group.

Asheida. Peach & Pun: The New Family Ferret. 2012. 28p. pap. 17.99 *(978-1-4685-8481-3(2))* AuthorHouse.

Bone, Thomas H. & LeTourneau, Anthony Alex, illus. Mama, Can Armadillos Swim? 2004. (J). 17.00 *(978-0-9674602-6-0(3))* Blue Marlin Pubns.

Brett, Jan. The 3 Little Dassies. Brett, Jan, illus. 2010. (ENG., Illus.). 32p. (J). (gr. -1-k). 17.99 *(978-0-399-25499-4(4)*, G.P. Putnam's Sons Books for Young Readers) Penguin Young Readers Group.

Clarke, Jane. Plodney Creeper, Supersloth. 2006. (Blue Bananas Ser.). (ENG., Illus.). 48p. (J). (gr. -1-3). *(978-0-7787-0896-4(9))* Crabtree Publishing Co.

Deal-Trainor, Carol. Marilee: A Manatee's First Journey to the Springs. 2008. 48p. pap. 16.95 *(978-1-60563-660-3(6))* America Star Bks.

Dewdney, Anna. Nelly Gnu & Daddy Too. (ENG., Illus.). (J). 2017. 36p. (-k). bds. 9.99 *(978-0-425-28977-8(X))* 2014. 40p. (gr. -1-k). 17.99 *(978-0-670-01227-5(0))* Penguin Young Readers Group. (Viking Books for Young Readers).

Dharma Publishing Staff. Golden Foot: A Story about Unselfish Love. 3rd ed. 2013. (ENG.). 36p. (gr. -1-7). pap. 8.95 *(978-0-89800-517-2(5))* Dharma Publishing.

Elsohn Ross, Michael. Mama's Milk. Wolff, Ashley, illus. 2007. (ENG.). 32p. (J). (gr. -1-2). 12.95 *(978-1-58246-181-6(3)*, Tricycle Pr.) Random Hse. Children's Bks.

—Mama's Milk / Mamá Me Alimenta. Wolff, Ashley, illus. 2016. (ENG & SPA.). 24p. (J). (-k). bds. 7.99 *(978-0-553-53874-8(8)*, Tricycle Pr.) Random Hse. Children's Bks.

Galvin, Laura Gates & Smithsonian Institution Staff. Armadillo at Riverside Road (Armadillo en la calle Riverside) 2008. (MUL.). 16p. 14.95 *(978-1-59249-842-0(6))* Soundprints.

The Girl Who Loved Meerkats. 2005. (J). *(978-1-933248-04-2(1))* World Quest Learning.

Hawkins, Wendy. Binky Goes to School. 2009. 20p. pap. 13.99 *(978-1-4389-6990-9(2))* AuthorHouse.

Hoffman, Peter. A ferret in a Garret. Olson, Cindy, illus. 2008. 36p. (J). 24.99 *(978-0-9790247-6-4(5))* Artpacks.

Hughes, Vicki Million. Growing up with Buck, 1 vol. 2009. 141p. pap. 24.95 *(978-1-61546-620-7(7))* America Star Bks.

Jones, Gareth P. Ninja Meerkats (#3): Escape from Ice Mountain. Finlayson, Luke, illus. 2013. (Ninja Meerkats Ser.: 3). (ENG.). 128p. (J). (gr. 2-4). pap. 5.99 *(978-1-250-02931-7(7)*, 9781250029317) Square Fish.

—Ninja Meerkats (#4): Hollywood Showdown. Finlayson, Luke, illus. 2013. (Ninja Meerkats Ser.: 4). (ENG.). 128p. (J). (gr. 2-4). pap. 5.99 *(978-1-250-02932-4(5)*, 9781250029324) Square Fish.

—Ninja Meerkats (#5): the Tomb of Doom. Finlayson, Luke, illus. 2013. (Ninja Meerkats Ser.: 5). (ENG.). 128p. (J). (gr. 2-4). pap. 8.99 *(978-1-250-03402-1(7)*, 9781250034021) Square Fish.

—Ninja Meerkats (#6): Big City Bust-Up. Finlayson, Luke, illus. 2013. (Ninja Meerkats Ser.: 6). (ENG.). 128p. (J). (gr. 2-4). pap. 5.99 *(978-1-250-03403-8(5)*, 9781250034038) Square Fish.

Julie, Aunt. State Symbols of Texas - Paddleduck #8. 2012. 50p. pap. 5.95 *(978-1-105-91163-7(2))* Lulu Pr., Inc.

Knesek, Marian. Zane & the Armadillo. Leipsic, Regina, illus. 2012. 26p. pap. 24.95 *(978-1-4626-6685-0(X))* America Star Bks.

Law, Felicia. Alice the Armadillo: A Tale of Self Discovery. Messina, Lilli, illus. 2010. (Animal Fair Values Ser.). 32p. (J). (gr. -1-3). pap. 10.55 *(978-1-60754-809-6(7))*; lib. bdg. 22.60 *(978-1-60754-805-8(4))* Windmill Bks.

Lee, Shari. Mandie's & Mindie's Adventure under the Sea, 1 vol. 2009. 63p. pap. 19.95 *(978-1-4489-9977-4(4))* America Star Bks.

Louie, Mary. Amazing Amand. 2009. 16p. pap. 13.49 *(978-1-4389-7903-8(7))* AuthorHouse.

McClure, Beverly Stowe. Frankie's Perfect Home. Morris, Alexander, illus. 2011. 16p. pap. 9.95 *(978-1-61633-162-7(3))* Guardian Angel Publishing, Inc.

Meadows, Daisy. Mara the Meerkat Fairy. 2015. (Rainbow Magic — Baby Animal Rescue Fairies Ser.: 3). lib. bdg. 14.75 *(978-0-606-37051-6(X))* Turtleback Bks.

Miller, Pat. Substitute Groundhog, 1 vol. Ember, Kathi, illus. 2010. (ENG.). 32p. (J). (gr. k-3). pap. 6.99 *(978-0-8075-7644-1(1))* Whitman, Albert & Co.

Ouchley, Amy Griffin. Swamper: Letters from a Louisiana Swamp Rabbit. 2013. (ENG., Illus.). 72p. (gr. 4-7). 22.50 *(978-0-8071-5074-0(6)*, 9780807150740) Louisiana State Univ. Pr.

Rabe, Tish. Wings & Paws & Fins & Claws. Ruiz, Aristides, illus. 2010. (Deluxe Coloring Book Ser.). (ENG.). 96p. (J). (gr. -1-2). pap. 3.99 *(978-0-375-85928-1(4)*, Golden Bks.) Random Hse. Children's Bks.

Random House Disney Staff. Big Trouble in Little Rodentia. Random House Disney Staff, illus. 2016. (Pictureback(R) Ser.). (ENG., Illus.). 24p. (J). (gr. -1-2). 4.99 *(978-0-7364-3531-4(X)*, RH/Disney) Random Hse. Children's Bks.

Ross, Michael Elsohn. Mama Me Alimenta. Wolff, Ashley, illus. 2008.Tr. of Mama's Milk. (ENG & SPA.). 32p. (J). (gr. -1-2). pap. 6.99 *(978-1-58246-245-5(3)*, Tricycle Pr.) Random Hse. Children's Bks.

Rostoker-Gruber, Karen. Ferret Fun, 0 vols. De Tagyos, Paul Rátz, illus. 2011. (ENG.). 32p. (J). (gr. k-3). 17.99 *(978-0-7614-5817-3(4)*, 9780761458173, Amazon Children's Publishing) Amazon Publishing.

Saxon, Victoria. Big Trouble in Little Rodentia. 2016. (Illus.). (J). ***(978-1-5182-0883-6(5))*** Random House Children's Books.

Thayer, Robert Scott. Kobee Manatee: Heading Home to Florida. Korman, Susan, ed. Gallegos, Lauren, illus. 2013. (Kobee Manatee Ser.). (ENG.). 32p. (J). (gr. k-2). 16.99 *(978-0-9883269-2-7(2))* Thompson Mill Pr.

Velástegui, Cecilia. Olinguito Speaks Up. 2013. (ENG., Illus.). 36p. (J). 19.99 *(978-0-9851769-7-6(0))* Libros Publishing.

Wallace, Nancy Elizabeth. Water! Water! Water!, 0 vols. 2014. (ENG.). 40p. (J). (gr. -1-k). 17.99 *(978-1-4778-4730-5(8)*, 9781477847305, Amazon Children's Publishing) Amazon Publishing.

Whybrow, Ian. Merry Meerkat Madness. 2013. (Awesome Animals Ser.). (ENG., Illus.). 192p. (J). (gr. 2-6). pap. 6.99 *(978-1-4380-0307-8(2))* Barron's Educational Series, Inc.

—More Meerkat Madness. 2013. (Awesome Animals Ser.). (ENG., Illus.). 192p. (J). (gr. 2-6). pap. 6.99 *(978-1-4380-0305-4(6))* Barron's Educational Series, Inc.

Young, Elizabeth. The ed up Platypus. Seabrooks, Lydia, illus. 2011. 20p. pap. 24.95 *(978-1-4560-7028-1(2))* America Star Bks.

Zamenhof, Robert. The Adventures of Armadillo Baby & Annabelli. Baker, Sara, illus. 2013. 56p. pap. 9.29 *(978-0-615-80196-4(X))* RGZ Consulting.

Zoehfeld, Kathleen Weidner. Manatee Winter. Petruccio, Steven James, illus. 2005. (ENG.). 32p. (J). (gr. -1-2). 8.95 *(978-1-59249-072-1(7)*, SC4003) Soundprints.

MAMMALS, FOSSIL

see also names of extinct animals, e.g. Mastodon; etc.

Brown, Charlotte Lewis. After the Dinosaurs: Mammoths & Fossil Mammals. Wilson, Phil, illus. 2006. (I Can Read Bks.). 32p. (J). (gr. -1-3). lib. bdg. 17.89 *(978-0-06-053054-9(5))* HarperCollins Pubs.

Brown, Charlotte Lewis & Brown, Charlotte L. After the Dinosaurs: Mammoths & Fossil Mammals. Wilson, Phil, illus. 2007. (I Can Read Level 2 Ser.). (ENG.). 32p. (J). (gr. -1-3). pap. 3.99 *(978-0-06-053055-6(3))* HarperCollins Pubs.

Clickard, Carrie. Thomas Jefferson & the Mammoth Hunt. Carpenter, Nancy, illus. 2017. (J). *(978-1-4814-4268-8(6)*, Beach Lane Bks.) Beach Lane Bks.

Colson, Rob Scott & de la Bédoyère, Camilla. Bone Collection: Skulls. Doyle, Sandra, illus. 2014. (ENG.). 96p. (J). (gr. 3-7). pap. 14.99 *(978-0-545-72457-9(0)*, Scholastic Paperbacks) Scholastic, Inc.

Gilbert, Sara. Giant Short-Faced Bears. 2017. (Illus.). 24p. (J). *(978-1-60818-766-9(7)*, Creative Education) Creative Co., The.

—Stag-Moose. 2017. (Illus.). 24p. (J). *(978-1-60818-770-6(5)*, Creative Education) Creative Co., The.

Holmes, Thom. Age of Mammals: The Oligocene & Miocene Periods. 2008. (Prehistoric Earth Ser.). (Illus.). 192p. (YA). (gr. 9-12). 35.00 *(978-0-8160-5964-5(0))* Facts On File, Inc.

Jeffrey, Gary. Giant Hunter. Poluzz, Alessandroi, illus. 2017. (Graphic Prehistoric Animals Ser.). 32p. (gr. 3-7). 31.35 ***(978-1-62588-408-4(7)***, Smart Apple Media) Black Rabbit Bks.

Mehling, Carl. Prehistoric Mammals. (Discovering Dinosaurs Ser.). (Illus.). 48p. (YA). 2010. (gr. 2-6). pap. 12.85 *(978-1-60754-787-7(2))* 2009. (gr. 4-7). 29.25 *(978-1-60754-779-2(1))* Windmill Bks.

Oard, Beverly & Oard, Michael. What Ever Happened to the Wooly Mammoth: Life at the End of the Great Ice Age. Looney, Bill, illus. 2007. 72p. (J). 15.99 *(978-0-89051-508-2(5))* Master Bks.

Parker, Steve. Ice Age Giants. 2011. (ENG., Illus.). 32p. (J). pap. 10.95 *(978-1-77092-012-5(9))* Saunders Bk. Co. CAN. Dist: RiverStream Publishing.

Rake, Matthew. The Rise of Mammals. Minister, Peter, illus. 2015. (Prehistoric Field Guides). (ENG.). 32p. (J). (gr. 3-6). lib. bdg. 26.65 *(978-1-4677-6351-6(9))* Lerner Publishing Group.

Staunton, Joseph & Flinthart, Dirk. Meat Eating Dinosaurs. Rey, Luis, illus. 2011. (Inside Crime Ser.). 48p. (YA). (gr. 5-9). 34.25 *(978-1-59920-395-9(2))* Black Rabbit Bks.

Thomson, Sarah L. Ancient Animals: Saber-Toothed Cat. Plant, Andrew, illus. 2014. (ENG.). 32p. (J). (gr. 1-4). pap. 5.95 *(978-1-58089-407-4(0))*; lib. bdg. 12.95 *(978-1-58089-400-5(3))* Charlesbridge Publishing, Inc.

West, David. Prehistoric Mammals, 01 vols., 1. 2016. (Prehistoric Animals Ser.). (ENG., Illus.). 24p. (J). pap. 8.25 *(978-1-5081-9041-7(0)*, 1397680, Windmill Bks.) Rosen Publishing Group, Inc., The.

—Sabertooth Tiger. Poluzzi, Alessandro, illus. 2017. (Graphic Prehistoric Animals Ser.). 32p. (gr. 3-7). lib. bdg. 31.35 *(978-1-62588-411-4(7))* Black Rabbit Bks.

—Woolly Mammoth. Poluzzi, Alessandro, illus. 2017. (Graphic Prehistoric Animals Ser.). 32p. (gr. 3-7). lib. bdg. 31.35 *(978-1-62588-414-5(1))* Black Rabbit Bks.

Worth, Bonnie. Once upon a Mastodon: All about Prehistoric Mammals. 2014. (Cat in the Hat's Learning Library). (ENG., Illus.). 48p. (J). (gr. k-3). 9.99 *(978-0-375-87075-0(X)*, Random Hse. Bks. for Young Readers) Random Hse. Children's Bks.

MAMMOTHS

Agenbroad, Larry D. & Nelson, Lisa W. Mammoths: Ice-Age Giants. 2003. (Illus.). 120p. (J). (gr. 7-12). pap. 7.95 *(978-0-8225-0470-2(7))* Lerner Publishing Group.

Bailey, Gerry. Woolly Mammoth. Carr, Karen, illus. 2011. (Smithsonian Prehistoric Zone Ser.). (ENG.). 32p. (J). (gr. k-3). *(978-0-7787-1808-6(5))*; pap. *(978-0-7787-1821-5(2))* Crabtree Publishing Co.

Bruce, Julia. Hunt! Can You Survive the Stone Age? Dennis, Peter, illus. 2009. (Step into History Ser.). 32p. (J). (gr. 2-5). lib. bdg. 23.94 *(978-0-7660-3476-1(3))* Enslow Pubs., Inc.

Clickard, Carrie. Thomas Jefferson & the Mammoth Hunt. Carpenter, Nancy, illus. 2017. (J). *(978-1-4814-4268-8(6)*, Beach Lane Bks.) Beach Lane Bks.

Frost, Helen. Woolly Mammoth [Scholastic]. Hughes, Jon, illus. 2009. (Dinosaurs & Prehistoric Animals Ser.). 24p. (gr. k-1). pap. 1.00 *(978-1-4296-4250-7(5)*, Pebble Plus) Capstone Press of Coughlan Cos.

Gilbert, Sara. Ice Age Mega Beasts: Mammoths. 2017. (Ice Age Mega Beasts Ser.). (ENG., Illus.). 24p. (J). (gr. 1-3). pap. 8.99 ***(978-1-62832-375-7(2)***, Creative Paperbacks) Creative Co., The.

Gilbert, Sara. Mammoths. 2017. (Illus.). 24p. (J). *(978-1-60818-767-6(5)*, Creative Education) Creative Co., The.

Goecke, Michael P. Woolly Mammoth, 1 vol. 2003. (Prehistoric Animals Ser.). (ENG.). 24p. (gr. k-4). 25.65 *(978-1-57765-971-6(6)*, Buddy Bks.) ABDO Publishing Co.

Higgins, Melissa. Woolly Mammoths. 2015. (Ice Age Animals Ser.). (ENG.). 24p. (gr. k-1). pap. 6.95 *(978-1-4914-2320-2(X)*, Pebble Plus) Capstone Press of Coughlan Cos.

Manning, Mick. Woolly Mammoth. Granstrom, Brita, illus. 2015. (ENG.). 32p. (J). (gr. -1-2). pap. 9.99 *(978-1-84780-664-2(3)*, Frances Lincoln) Quarto Publishing Group UK GBR. Dist: Hachette Bk. Group.

Miller, Debbie S. A Woolly Mammoth Journey. Van Zyle, Jon, illus. 2010. (ENG.). 32p. (J). pap. 9.95 *(978-1-60223-098-9(6))* Univ. of Alaska Pr.

Nelson, Lisa W. & Agenbroad, Larry D. Mammoths: Ice-Age Giants. Jansen, Paula, illus. Jansen, Paula, photos by. 2005. (Discovery! Ser.). 120p. (gr. 5-12). lib. bdg. 27.93 *(978-0-8225-2862-3(2))* Lerner Publishing Group.

Orr, Tamra B. Unearthing Fossils. 2014. (Explorer Library: Follow the Clues Ser.). (ENG., Illus.). 32p. (J). (gr. 4-8). 28.50 *(978-1-62431-781-1(2)*, 203320) Cherry Lake Publishing.

Philippo, Sophie. Meet the Woolly Mammoth. Dutertre, Charles, illus. 2005. (ENG.). 45p. (J). (gr. 4-7). 15.95 *(978-1-58728-521-9(5))* Cooper Square Publishing Llc.

Rober, Harold. Woolly Mammoth. 2017. (Bumba Books (tm) — Dinosaurs & Prehistoric Beasts Ser.). (ENG.). 24p. (J). (gr. -1-1). 12.99 ***(978-1-5124-3726-3(3))***; 38.65 ***(978-1-5124-2738-7(1))***; 38.65 ***(978-1-5124-3725-6(5))*** Lerner Publishing Group. (Lerner Pubns.).

Rober, Harold T. El Mamut Lanudo. 2017. (Bumba Books (tm) en Español — Dinosaurios y Bestias Prehistóricas (Dinosaurs & Prehistoric Beasts) Ser.). (SPA.). 24p. (J). (gr. -1-1). 25.32 ***(978-1-5124-4118-5(X))*** Lerner Publishing Group.

Rober, Harold T. Woolly Mammoth. 2017. (Bumba Books (tm) — Dinosaurs & Prehistoric Beasts Ser.). (ENG., Illus.). 24p. (J). (gr. -1-1). 25.32 *(978-1-5124-2644-1(X))* Lerner Publishing Group.

Sloan, Christopher. Baby Mammoth Mummy: Frozen in Time: A Prehistoric Animal's Journey into the 21st Century. 2011. (ENG., Illus.). 48p. (J). (gr. 3-7). 17.95 *(978-1-4263-0865-9(5))*; lib. bdg. 26.90 *(978-1-4263-0866-6(3))* National Geographic Society. (National Geographic Children's Bks.).

Wadsworth, Ginger. Woolly Mammoths. Zalewski, Todd, illus. (On My Own Science Ser.). (ENG.). 48p. (gr. 2-4). 2007. per. 6.95 *(978-0-8225-6447-8(5)*, First Avenue Editions) 2006. lib. bdg. 25.26 *(978-1-57505-879-5(0)*, Millbrook Pr.) Lerner Publishing Group.

Wheeler, Lisa. Mammoths on the Move. Cyrus, Kurt, illus. 2006. (ENG.). 32p. (J). (gr. -1-3). 17.99 *(978-0-15-204700-9(X))* Houghton Mifflin Harcourt Publishing Co.

Zabludoff, Marc. Woolly Mammoth. 2009. (Prehistoric Beasts Ser.). 32p. (gr. 2). 29.93 *(978-0-7614-3996-7(X))* Marshall Cavendish Corp.

Zeiger, Jennifer. Mammoth & Mastodon. 2015. (21st Century Junior Library: Dinosaurs & Prehistoric Creatures Ser.). (ENG., Illus.). 24p. (J). (gr. 2-5). lib. bdg. 27.07 *(978-1-63362-383-5(1)*, 206952) Cherry Lake Publishing.

MAMMOTHS—FICTION

Bentley, Dawn. Woolly Mammoth in Trouble. 2010. (Smithsonian's Prehistoric Pals Ser.). (Illus.). (J). 21.95 incl. audio compact disk *(978-1-59249-547-4(8))* Soundprints.

—Woolly Mammoth in Trouble. Carr, Karen, illus. (Smithsonian's Prehistoric Pals Ser.). (ENG.). 36p. (J). (gr. -1-2). 2005. 2.95 *(978-1-59249-367-8(X)*, S2454) 2005. 14.95 *(978-1-59249-364-7(5)*, H2404) 2005. pap. 6.95 *(978-1-59249-365-4(3)*, S2404) 2004. 9.95 *(978-1-59249-368-5(8)*, PS2454) 2004. 8.95 *(978-1-59249-366-1(1)*, SD2404) Soundprints.

Clark, Patricia Nikolina. In the Shadow of the Mammoth. LeTourneau, Anthony Alex, illus. (J). 2005. 14.99 *(978-0-9674602-8-4(X))* 2003. 190p. pap. 6.99 *(978-0-9674602-4-6(7))* Blue Marlin Pubns.

Elliott, David. This Orq. (He Say UGH!) Nichols, Lori, illus. 2015. (ENG.). 40p. (J). (gr. -1-3). 16.95 *(978-1-62091-789-3(0))* Boyds Mills Pr.

Escoffier, Michaël. A Mammoth in the Fridge. 2013. (ENG.). 36p. 16.95 *(978-1-877579-50-9(5))* 21st Century Publishing.

Fraser, Ian. Life with Mammoth, 0 vols. Fraser, Mary Ann, illus. (Ogg & Bob Ser.). (ENG.). 64p. (J). (gr. k-3). 2013. pap. 9.99 *(978-1-4778-1615-8(1)*, 9781477816158) 2010. 14.99 *(978-0-7614-5722-0(4)*, 9780761457220) Amazon Publishing. (Amazon Children's Publishing).

—Meet Mammoth, 0 vols. Fraser, Mary Ann, illus. 2013. (Ogg & Bob Ser.). (ENG.). 64p. (J). (gr. 1-3). pap. 9.99 *(978-1-4778-1617-2(8)*, 9781477816172, Amazon Children's Publishing) Amazon Publishing.

Gabriel, Andrea. Wandering Woolly, 1 vol. 2015. (ENG., Illus.). 32p. (J). (gr. 1-4). 17.95 *(978-1-62855-558-5(0))* Arbordale Publishing.

Layton, Neal. Hot Hot Hot. Layton, Neal, illus. 2004. (ENG., Illus.). 32p. (J). (gr. -1-3). 15.99 *(978-0-7636-2148-3(X))* Candlewick Pr.

little bee books, little bee, et al. Ice Age - Collision Course. 2016. (Ice Age: Collision Course Ser.). (ENG., Illus.). 144p. (J). (gr. 2-5). pap. 6.99 *(978-1-4998-0309-9(5))* Little Bee Books Inc.

Mayer, Kirsten. The Pack Is Back! 2012. (Ice Age Ser.). (ENG.). 24p. (J). (gr. -1-3). pap. 3.99 *(978-0-06-210479-3(9)*, HarperFestival) HarperCollins Pubs.

PaleoJoe & Caszatt-Allen, Wendy. Mysterious Mammoths. 2008. (ENG., Illus.). 200p. (J). (gr. 2-5). pap. 7.95 *(978-1-934133-43-9(4)*, Mackinac Island Press, Inc.) Charlesbridge Publishing, Inc.

Pavanello, Roberto. The Chilly Mammoth, 1 vol. Zeni, Marco, tr. from ITA. Pisapia, Blasco & Brughera, Pamela, illus. 2013. (Echo & the Bat Pack Ser.). (ENG.). 128p. (gr. 2-3). 9.95 *(978-1-4342-4889-3(5))* Stone Arch Bks.

Robinson, Michelle. How to Wash a Woolly Mammoth. Hindley, Kate, illus. 2014. (ENG.). 32p. (J). (gr. -1-3). 16.99 *(978-0-8050-9966-9(2)*, 9780805099669, Holt, Henry & Co. Bks. For Young Readers) Holt, Henry & Co.

Russell, Jesse & Cohn, Ronald, eds. Ice Age: Continental Drift. 2012. 158p. pap. *(978-5-512-74544-1(1))* Books on Demand.

Stead, Philip C. Samson in the Snow. 2016. (ENG., Illus.). 40p. (J). 17.99 *(978-1-62672-182-1(3)*, 9781626721821) Roaring Brook Pr.

Weston, Martha. Dr. Clock-Sicle: A Holiday House Reader, Level 1. (ENG., Illus.). 32p. (J). (gr. k-3). tchr. ed. 14.95 *(978-0-8234-1825-1(1))* Holiday Hse., Inc.

MAN

see Human Beings

MAN—COLOR

see Human Skin Color

MAN, PREHISTORIC

see Prehistoric Peoples

MAN IN SPACE

see Manned Space Flight

MANAGEMENT

see also Farm Management; Industrial Management

Aikins, Anne Marie. Authority: Deal with It Before It Deals with You, 1 vol. Murray, Steven, illus. 2005. (Lorimer Deal with It Ser.). (ENG.). 32p. (J). (gr. 4-6). 12.95 *(978-1-55028-869-8(5)*, 9781550288698) Lorimer, James & Co., Ltd., Pubs. CAN. Dist: Casemate Pubs. & Bk. Distributors, LLC.

Bailey, Rachel. Superstorm Sandy, 1 vol. 2013. (History's Greatest Disasters Ser.). (ENG., Illus.). 48p. (J). (gr. 3-6). lib. bdg. 32.79 *(978-1-61783-961-0(2)*, 1360926) ABDO Publishing Co.

Beasley, Ava. We Plant Vegetables: Working As a Team. 2017. (Computer Science for the Real World Ser.). 8p. (gr. 5-6). pap. 6.20 ***(978-1-5383-5063-8(7)***, Rosen Classroom) Rosen Publishing Group, Inc., The.

Bernstein, Daryl. Better Than a Lemonade Stand! Small Business Ideas for Kids. Husberg, Rob, illus. 2012. (ENG.). 224p. (J). (gr. 4-9). 19.99 *(978-1-58270-360-2(4))*; pap. 12.99 *(978-1-58270-330-5(2))* Aladdin/Beyond Words.

Broyles, Janell. Chemical Biological Incident Response Force. 2009. (Inside Special Operations Ser.). 64p. (gr. 6-6). 58.50 *(978-1-61513-551-6(0)*, Rosen Reference) Rosen Publishing Group, Inc., The.

Byers, Ann. Blackouts: A Practical Survival Guide. 2009. (Library of Emergency Preparedness Ser.). 64p. (gr. 6-6). 58.50 *(978-1-60853-591-0(6)*, Rosen Reference) Rosen Publishing Group, Inc., The.

Checkmark Books, creator. Organization Skills. 2nd rev. ed. 2007. (Mastering Career Skills Ser.). (Illus.). 144p. per. 12.95 *(978-0-8160-7116-6(0)*, Checkmark Bks.) Facts On File, Inc.

Cunningham, Kevin. Surviving Droughts & Famines, 1 vol. 2011. (Children's True Stories: Natural Disasters Ser.). (ENG.). 32p. (gr. 3-3). pap. 8.29 *(978-1-4109-4101-5(9))*; 30.65 *(978-1-4109-4094-0(2))* Heinemann-Raintree. (Raintree Perspectives).

—Surviving Tsunamis, 1 vol. 2011. (Children's True Stories: Natural Disasters Ser.). (ENG.). 32p. (gr. 3-3). pap. 8.29 *(978-1-4109-4102-2(7))*; 30.65 *(978-1-4109-4095-7(0))* Heinemann-Raintree. (Raintree Perspectives).

Donovan, Sandra. Teen Wise Guide to Time Management. 2012. (USA TODAY Teen Wise Guides: Time, Money, & Relationships Ser.). (ENG.). 64p. (gr. 8-12). lib. bdg. 31.93 *(978-0-7613-7019-2(6))* Lerner Publishing Group.

Ferguson. Business Managers. 2nd rev. ed. 2009. (Careers in Focus Ser.). 204p. (gr. 6-12). 32.95 *(978-0-8160-7296-5(5)*, Ferguson Publishing Co.) Facts On File, Inc.

Haugen, Hayley Mitchell. Disaster Relief. 2009. (Issues That Concern You Ser.). (ENG., Illus.). 144p. (gr. 10-12). 42.00 *(978-0-7377-4494-1(4))* Cengage Gale.

Hibbert, Clare. My Busy Day. Raga, Sylvia, illus. 2011. (Busy Times Ser.). (ENG.). 24p. (J). 19.99 *(978-0-237-54263-4(3))* Evans Brothers, Ltd. GBR. Dist: Independent Pubs. Group.

—My Busy Week. 2011. (Busy Times Ser.). (ENG., Illus.). 24p. (J). 19.99 *(978-0-237-54264-1(1))* Evans Brothers, Ltd. GBR. Dist: Independent Pubs. Group.

Jeffries, Corina. We Work Together for Equality! Working As a Team. 2017. (Computer Science for the Real World Ser.). 16p. (gr. 7-8). pap. 7.95 ***(978-1-5383-5212-0(5)***, Rosen Classroom) Rosen Publishing Group, Inc., The.

La Bella, Laura. Careers in Crisis Management & Hostage Negotiation. 2013. (Extreme Law Enforcement Ser.). (Illus.). 112p. (YA). (gr. 7-12). 34.60 *(978-1-4777-1709-7(9))* Rosen Publishing Group, Inc., The.

McCabe, Matthew. 12 Business Leaders Who Changed the World. 2015. (Change Makers Ser.). (ENG., Illus.). 32p. (J). (gr. 3-5). *(978-1-63235-145-6(5)*, 12-Story Library) Pr. Room Editions LLC.

Mooney, Carla. Bomb Disposal: Diffusing Danger. 2014. (ENG.). 32p. (gr. 4-8). 32.79 *(978-1-62717-657-6(8))* Rourke Educational Media.

—Fema: Prepare, Respond, & Recover. 2014. (ENG.). 32p. (gr. 4-8). 32.79 *(978-1-62717-656-9(X))* Rourke Educational Media.

Murdico, Suzanne. Earthquakes: A Practical Survival Guide. 2009. (Library of Emergency Preparedness Ser.). 64p. (gr. 6-6). 58.50 *(978-1-60853-593-4(2)*, Rosen Reference) Rosen Publishing Group, Inc., The.

Pelos, Rebecca & Greenberger, Robert. Cool Careers Without College for People Who Love Planning & Organizing. 2017. (Cool Careers Without College Ser.). 112p. (gr. 12-12). 38.45 ***(978-1-5081-7540-7(3)***, Rosen Young Adult) Rosen Publishing Group, Inc., The.

Plotkin, Robert. Computers in the Workplace. 2012. (Computers, Internet, & Society Ser.). (Illus.). xvii, 172p. (C). (gr. 9). 45.00 *(978-0-8160-7758-8(4))* Facts On File, Inc.

Raum, Elizabeth. Surviving Floods, 1 vol. 2011. (Children's True Stories: Natural Disasters Ser.). (ENG.). 32p. (gr. 3-3). pap. 8.29 *(978-1-4109-4098-8(5))*; 30.65 *(978-1-4109-4091-9(8))* Heinemann-Raintree. (Raintree Perspectives).

—Surviving Hurricanes, 1 vol. 2011. (Children's True Stories: Natural Disasters Ser.). (ENG.). 32p. (gr. 3-3). pap. 8.29 *(978-1-4109-4100-8(0))*; 30.65 *(978-1-4109-4093-3(4))* Heinemann-Raintree. (Raintree Perspectives).

—Surviving Tornadoes, 1 vol. 2011. (Children's True Stories: Natural Disasters Ser.). (ENG.). 32p. (gr. 3-3). pap. 8.29 *(978-1-4109-4099-5(3))*; 30.65 *(978-1-4109-4092-6(6))* Heinemann-Raintree. (Raintree Perspectives).

Suen, Anastasia. The Red Cross. 2009. (Helping Organizations Ser.). 24p. (gr. 2-2). 42.50 *(978-1-61513-262-1(7)*, PowerKids Pr.) Rosen Publishing Group, Inc., The.

MANAGEMENT—EMPLOYEE PARTICIPATION

Connolly, Sean. Rights at Work. 2005. (Campaigns for Change Ser.). (Illus.). 48p. (J). (gr. 6-9). lib. bdg. 29.95 *(978-1-58340-518-5(6)*, 1247340) Black Rabbit Bks.

MANAGEMENT, INDUSTRIAL

see Industrial Management

MANAGEMENT, SCIENTIFIC

see Management

MANAGEMENT OF CHILDREN

see Child Rearing

MANDELA, NELSON, 1918-2013

Baptiste, Tracey. Nelson Mandela: Nobel Peace Prize-Winning Champion for Hope & Harmony. 2015. (Britannica Beginner Bios Ser.). (ENG.). 32p. (J). (gr. 2-3). 46.90 *(978-1-62275-943-9(5)*, Britannica Educational Publishing) Rosen Publishing Group, Inc., The.

—Nelson Mandela: Nobel Peace Prize-Winning Warrior for Hope & Harmony. 2015. (Britannica Beginner Bios Ser.). (ENG., Illus.). 32p. (J). 23.45 *(978-1-62275-941-5(9)*, Britannica Educational Publishing) Rosen Publishing Group, Inc., The.

Barnham, Kay. Nelson Mandela: Revolutionary President. 2017. (Inspirational Lives Ser.). (ENG., Illus.). 32p. (J). (gr. 4-6). pap. 12.99 ***(978-0-7502-9311-2(X)***, Wayland) Hachette Children's Group GBR. Dist: Hachette Bk. Group.

Belviso, Meg & Pollack, Pam. Who Is Nelson Mandela? 2014. (Who Was... ? Ser.). lib. bdg. 16.00 *(978-0-606-34158-5(7)*, Turtleback) Turtleback Bks.

Belviso, Meg & Pollack, Pamela D. Who Was Nelson Mandela? Marchesi, Stephen, illus. 2014. (Who Was? Ser.). (ENG.). 112p. (J). (gr. 3-7). 5.99 *(978-0-448-47933-0(8)*, Grosset & Dunlap) Penguin Young Readers Group.

Boothroyd, Jennifer. Nelson Mandela: A Life of Persistence. (Pull Ahead Books-Biographies Ser.). (ENG., Illus.). 32p. (gr. k-3). 2007. pap. 7.95 *(978-0-8225-6434-8(3))* 2006. lib. bdg. 22.60 *(978-0-8225-6385-3(1))* Lerner Publishing Group. (Lerner Pubns.).

Bouma, Paddy, illus. Nelson Mandela: Long Walk to Freedom. 2009. (ENG.). 64p. (J). (gr. 2-6). 18.99 *(978-1-59643-566-7(6)*, 9781596435667) Roaring Brook Pr.

Capozzi, Suzy. Nelson Mandela: From Prisoner to President. Tadgell, Nicole, illus. 2016. (Step into Reading Ser.). (ENG.). 48p. (J). (gr. 2-4). 12.99 *(978-0-375-97467-0(9)*, Random Hse. Bks. for Young Readers) Random Hse. Children's Bks.

Crompton, Samuel Willard. Nelson Mandela: Ending Apartheid in South Africa. 2006. (Modern Peacemakers Ser.). (Illus.). 112p. (J). (gr. 9-12). 30.00 *(978-0-7910-8997-2(5))* Facts On File, Inc.

Dakers, Diane. Nelson Mandela: South Africa's Anti-Apartheid Revolutionary. 2014. (ENG., Illus.). 112p. (J). *(978-0-7787-1241-1(9))* Crabtree Publishing Co.

Denenberg, Barry. Nelson Mandela: No Easy Walk to Freedom. 2014. (ENG.). 240p. (J). (gr. 3-7). pap. 7.99 *(978-0-545-66911-5(1))* Scholastic, Inc.

Finlayson, Reggie. Nelson Mandela. pap. 9.95 *(978-0-8225-5743-2(6))*; 2005. (ENG., Illus.). 112p. (gr. 5-12). lib. bdg. 27.93 *(978-0-8225-2644-5(1)*, Lerner Pubns.) Lerner Publishing Group.

Gormley, Beatrice. Nelson Mandela: South African Revolutionary. 2015. (Real-Life Story Ser.). (ENG., Illus.). 256p. (J). (gr. 3-7). 17.99 *(978-1-4814-2059-4(3)*, Aladdin) Simon & Schuster Children's Publishing.

Grant, Karima. Nelson Mandela. 2006. (Rookie Biographies Ser.). (ENG., Illus.). 32p. (J). (gr. 1-2). per. 4.95 *(978-0-516-25537-8(1)*, Children's Pr.) Scholastic Library Publishing.

Holland, Gini & O'Hern, Kerri. Nelson Mandela. (Biografías Gráficas (Graphic Biographies) Ser.). (Illus.). 32p. (gr. 5-8). 2007. (ENG & SPA.). pap. 10.50 *(978-0-8368-7888-2(4))* 2007. (ENG & SPA., lib. bdg. 27.00 *(978-0-8368-7881-3(7))* 2006. pap. 10.50 *(978-0-8368-6249-2(X))* Stevens, Gareth Publishing LLLP.

—Nelson Mandela. McHargue, D., illus. 2006. (Graphic Biographies Ser.). 32p. (gr. 5-8). lib. bdg. 27.00 *(978-0-8368-6197-6(3))* Stevens, Gareth Publishing LLLP.

Hollingsworth, Tamara. Nelson Mandela: Leading the Way, 1 vol. 2nd rev. ed. 2013. (Nonfiction Readers Ser.). (ENG., Illus.). 48p. (J). (gr. 4-4). pap. 29.96 *(978-1-4807-1116-7(0))* Shell Educational Publishing.

—Nelson Mandela: Leading the Way, 1 vol. 2nd rev. ed. 2012. (Nonfiction Readers Ser.). (ENG., Illus.). 48p. (J). (gr. 4-4). pap. 9.99 *(978-1-4333-4864-8(0))* Teacher Created Materials, Inc.

—Nelson Mandela: Marcando el Camino. 2017. (TIME for Kids en Español - Level 4 Ser.). (SPA., Illus.). 48p. (gr. 4-4). lib. bdg. 31.99 *(978-1-5157-5145-8(7))* Time for Kids Inc AUS. Dist: Capstone Pub.

Hort, Lenny, et al. Nelson Mandela. 2006. (DK Biography Ser.). (ENG., Illus.). 128p. (J). (gr. 5-12). pap. 6.99 *(978-0-7566-2109-4(7)*, DK Children) Dorling Kindersley Publishing, Inc.

Josephson, Judith Pinkerton. Nelson Mandela. 2009. (History Maker Biographies Ser.). (ENG.). 48p. (gr. 3-6). 27.93 *(978-1-58013-703-4(2)*, Lerner Pubns.) Lerner Publishing Group.

Keller, Bill. Tree Shaker: The Life of Nelson Mandela. 2013. (New York Times Ser.). (ENG., Illus.). 128p. (J). (gr. 5-9). pap. 9.99 *(978-1-59643-533-9(X)*, 9781596435339) Square Fish.

—Tree Shaker: The Story of Nelson Mandela. 2013. (ENG., Illus.). 128p. (J). (gr. 7-12). 17.99 *(978-0-7534-7184-5(1)*, 9780753471845, Kingfisher) Roaring Brook Pr.

Kramer, Ann. Mandela: The Hero Who Led His Nation to Freedom. 2008. (National Geographic World History Biographies Ser.). (ENG., Illus.). 64p. (J). (gr. 3-7). pap. 7.99 *(978-1-4263-0173-5(1)*, National Geographic Children's Bks.) National Geographic Society.

—Mandela: The Rebel Who Led His Nation to Freedom. 2005. (National Geographic World History Biographies Ser.). (ENG., Illus.). 64p. (J). (gr. 3-7). 17.95 *(978-0-7922-3658-0(0))*; lib. bdg. 27.90 *(978-0-7922-3659-7(9))* National Geographic Society. (National Geographic Children's Bks.).

Magoon, Kekla. Nelson Mandela: A Leader for Freedom, 1 vol. 2008. (Essential Lives Set 2 Ser.). (ENG., Illus.). 112p. (J). (gr. 6-12). lib. bdg. 35.64 *(978-1-60453-038-4(3))* ABDO Publishing Co.

Malaspina, Ann. Nelson Mandela: Fighting to Dismantle Apartheid. 2017. (Rebels with a Cause Ser.). 128p. (YA). (gr. 8-8). lib. bdg. 37.27 ***(978-0-7660-8517-6(1))*** Enslow Pubs., Inc.

Meyer, Susan. Nelson Mandela: South African President & Anti-Apartheid Activist. 2017. (J). ***(978-1-5383-8089-5(7))***; pap. ***(978-1-5383-8088-8(9))*** Rosen Publishing Group, Inc., The. (Rosen Young Adult).

National Geographic Kids Staff & Kramer, Barbara. National Geographic Readers: Nelson Mandela. 2014. (Readers Bios Ser.). (ENG., Illus.). 48p. (J). (gr. 1-4). pap. 3.99 *(978-1-4263-1763-7(8)*, National Geographic Children's Bks.) National Geographic Society.

Nelson, Kadir. Nelson Mandela. Nelson, Kadir, illus. 2013. (Illus.). 40p. (J). (gr. -1-3). (ENG.). 17.99 *(978-0-06-178374-6(9))*; lib. bdg. 18.89 *(978-0-06-178376-0(5))* HarperCollins Pubs. (Tegen, Katherine Bks).

—Nelson Mandela. 2014. (SPA.). (J). (gr. 2-4). 21.99 *(978-84-261-4069-2(6))* Juventud, Editorial ESP. Dist: Lectorum Pubns., Inc.

Nelson Mandela: World Leader for Human Rights. 2014. (Gateway Biographies Ser.). (ENG.). 48p. (gr. 4-8). lib. bdg. 26.60 *(978-1-4677-5197-1(9)*, Lerner Pubns.) Lerner Publishing Group.

O'Neill, John R. Mahatma Gandhi, Nelson Mandela. 2011. (Readers' & Writers' Genre Workshop Ser.). (YA). pap. *(978-1-4509-3024-6(7))* Benchmark Education Co.

Rajczak, Kristen. Nelson Mandela. 2015. (Heroes of Black History Ser.). (ENG., Illus.). 32p. (J). (gr. 3-4). pap. 10.50 *(978-1-4824-2908-4(X))* Stevens, Gareth Publishing LLLP.

Riggs, Kate. The Release of Nelson Mandela. 2009. (Days of Change Ser.). (Illus.). 48p. (YA). (gr. 4-7). 22.95 *(978-1-58341-736-2(2))* Creative Co., The.

Rodriguez, Ann Graham Gaines. Nelson Mandela & the End of Apartheid. 2016. (People & Events That Changed the World Ser.). (ENG., Illus.). 128p. (J). (gr. 7-8). 37.27 *(978-0-7660-7300-5(9))* Enslow Pubs., Inc.

Rose, Simon. Nelson Mandela. 2010. (Remarkable People Ser.). (Illus.). 24p. (J). (gr. 3-5). lib. bdg. 25.70 *(978-1-61690-172-1(1))*; (gr. 4-6). pap. 11.95 *(978-1-61690-173-8(X))* Weigl Pubs., Inc.

Schuldt, Lori Meek. Martin Luther King, Jr: With Profiles of Mohandas K. Gandhi & Nelson Mandela. 2006. (Biographical Connections Ser.). (Illus.). 112p. (J). *(978-0-7166-1822-5(2))* World Bk., Inc.

Senker, Cath. Nelson Mandela. 2015. (Against the Odds Biographies Ser.). (ENG., Illus.). 48p. (gr. 3-6). 33.32 *(978-1-4846-2465-4(3))* Heinemann-Raintree.

Shone, Rob. Nelson Mandela: The Life of an African Statesman. 2009. (Graphic Nonfiction Biographies Ser.). (ENG.). 48p. (YA). (gr. 4-5). 58.50 *(978-1-61513-023-8(3)*, Rosen Reference) Rosen Publishing Group, Inc., The.

—Nelson Mandela: The Life of an African Statesman. Reed, Neil, illus. 2007. (Graphic Nonfiction Biographies Ser.). (ENG.). 48p. (J). (gr. 4-7). lib. bdg. 31.95 *(978-1-4042-0860-5(7))*; (gr. 5-8). pap. 14.05 *(978-1-4042-0923-7(9))* Rosen Publishing Group, Inc., The.

Stamper, G. C. Nelson Mandela. 2005. (Illus.). 32p. (J). pap. *(978-0-7367-2922-2(4))* Zaner-Bloser, Inc.

Toufexis, George. Nelson Mandela Coloring Book. 2014. (ENG.). 32p. (J). (gr. 3-8). pap. 3.99 *(978-0-486-78813-5(X))* Dover Pubns., Inc.

Trussell-Cullen, Alan. Nelson Mandela. 2009. pap. 13.25 *(978-1-60559-067-7(3))* Hameray Publishing Group, Inc.

Woll, Kris. Nelson Mandela: South African President & Civil Rights Activist, 1 vol. 2014. (Newsmakers Ser.). (ENG., Illus.). 48p. (J). (gr. 3-6). lib. bdg. 32.79 *(978-1-62403-643-9(0))* ABDO Publishing Co.

MANET, EDOUARD, 1832-1883

Mis, Melody S. Edouard Manet. (Meet the Artist Ser.). 24p. (gr. 2-3). 2009. 42.50 *(978-1-61514-629-1(6)*, PowerKids Pr.) 2007. (Illus.). (J). lib. bdg. 22.60 *(978-1-4042-3841-1(7))* Rosen Publishing Group, Inc., The.

Tracy, Kathleen. Edouard Manet. 2009. (Art Profiles for Kids Ser.). (Illus.). 48p. (YA). (gr. 4-7). lib. bdg. 29.95 *(978-1-58415-746-5(1))* Mitchell Lane Pubs., Inc.

Zaczek, Iain. Édouard Manet. 2014. (Great Artists Ser.). 32p. (J). (gr. 3-6). pap. 10.50 *(978-1-4824-1217-8(9))* Stevens, Gareth Publishing LLLP.

MANGROVE

Roth, Susan L. & Trumbore, Cindy. The Mangrove Tree: Planting Trees to Feed Families. Roth, Susan L., illus. 2011. (ENG., Illus.). 40p. (J). (gr. 1-6). 19.95 *(978-1-60060-459-1(5))* Lee & Low Bks., Inc.

MANNED SPACE FLIGHT

see also Astronauts; Outer Space—Exploration; Space Medicine

also names of projects, e.g. Gemini Project; etc.

Anderson, Rane. Stem: Mission to Mars: Problem Solving (Grade 3) 2017. (Mathematics Readers Ser.). (Illus.). 32p. (gr. 3-3). 8.99 ***(978-1-4807-5801-8(9))*** Teacher Created Materials, Inc.

Angelo, Joseph A., Jr. Human Spaceflight. 2007. (Frontiers in Space Ser.). (Illus.). 272p. (C). (gr. 9-10). 45.00 *(978-0-8160-5775-7(3))* Facts On File, Inc.

Barghoorn, Linda. Mae Jemison: Trailblazing Astronaut, Doctor, & Teacher. 2016. (Remarkable Lives Revealed Ser.). (ENG., Illus.). 32p. (J). (gr. 2-5). *(978-0-7787-2693-7(2))* Crabtree Publishing Co.

Brake, Mark & Lonely Planet Publications Staff. How to Be a Space Explorer: Your Out-of-This-World Adventure, 1 vol. 2014. (Lonely Planet Kids Ser.). (ENG., Illus.). 160p. (J). 17.99 *(978-1-74360-434-2(3)*, 4798) Lonely Planet Pubns.

Bredeson, Carmen & Dyson, Marianne. Astronauts Explore the Galaxy. 2015. (Launch into Space! Ser.). (ENG.). 32p. (J). (gr. 3-4). pap. 10.52 *(978-0-7660-6813-1(7))* Enslow Pubs., Inc.

Bredeson, Carmen, et al. Astronauts Explore the Galaxy. 2015. (Launch into Space! Ser.). (ENG., Illus.). 32p. (J). (gr. 3-4). 25.27 *(978-0-7660-6815-5(3))* Enslow Pubs., Inc.

Castaldo, Nancy F. Leap into Space: Exploring the Universe & Your Place in It. McRae, Patrick, illus. 2008. (ENG.). 128p. (J). (gr. 3-7). 16.99 *(978-0-8249-6815-1(8))*; pap. 12.99 *(978-0-8249-6816-8(6))*; pap. 12.99 *(978-0-8249-6816-8(6))* Worthy Publishing. (Ideal Pubns.).

Clay, Kathryn. Space Flights. 2017. (Little Astronauts Ser.). (ENG., Illus.). 32p. (gr. 1-2). lib. bdg. 27.99 *(978-1-5157-3659-2(8))* Capstone Press of Coughlan Cos.

—Spacewalks. 2017. (Little Astronauts Ser.). (ENG., Illus.). 32p. (gr. 1-2). lib. bdg. 27.99 *(978-1-5157-3658-5(X))* Capstone Press of Coughlan Cos.

Dickmann, Nancy. Exploring the Inner Planets. 2015. (Spectacular Space Science Ser.). (ENG., Illus.). 48p. (J). (gr. 5-6). 30.25 *(978-1-4994-3629-7(7)*, Rosen Central) Rosen Publishing Group, Inc., The.

Dugan, Christine. La Exploración Del Espacio. 2017. (TIME for Kids en Español - Level 3 Ser.). (SPA.). 32p. (gr. 3-3). lib. bdg. 31.99 ***(978-1-5157-5181-6(3))*** Time for Kids Inc AUS. Dist: Capstone Pub.

—Living in Space, 1 vol. 2nd rev. ed. 2014. (TIME for KIDS(r) Nonfiction Readers Ser.). (ENG., Illus.). 32p. (J). (gr. 3-3). pap. 25.96 *(978-1-4807-1084-9(9))* Shell Educational Publishing.

—Living in Space, 1 vol. 2nd rev. ed. 2012. (Nonfiction Readers Ser.). (ENG.). 32p. (J). (gr. 3-3). pap. 8.99 *(978-1-4333-3675-1(8))* Teacher Created Materials, Inc.

—Space Exploration, 1 vol. 2nd rev. ed. 2014. (TIME for KIDS(r) Nonfiction Readers Ser.). (ENG., Illus.). 32p. (J). (gr. 3-3). pap. 25.96 *(978-1-4807-1083-2(0))* Shell Educational Publishing.

Dugan, Christine. La Vida en el Espacio. 2017. (TIME for Kids en Español - Level 3 Ser.). (SPA.). 32p. (gr. 3-3). lib. bdg. 31.99 ***(978-1-5157-5182-3(1))*** Time for Kids Inc AUS. Dist: Capstone Pub.

Ertle-Rickard, Stephen. Astronaut. 2008. (321 Go! Ser.). (ENG., Illus.). 36p. pap. *(978-1-84167-781-1(7))* Ransom Publishing Ltd.

Furgang, Adam. Human Spaceflight. 2017. (From Earth to the Stars Ser.). 48p. (gr. 10-12). pap. 14.05 ***(978-1-68048-669-8(1)***, Britannica Educational Publishing) Rosen Publishing Group, Inc., The.

Goldstein, Margaret J. Astronauts: A Space Discovery Guide. 2017. (Space Discovery Guides). (ENG.). 48p. (J). (gr. 4-6). 16.99 ***(978-1-5124-3800-0(6)***, Lerner Pubns.); 47.99 ***(978-1-5124-2793-6(4)***, Lerner Pubns.); 47.99 ***(978-1-5124-3801-7(4)***, Lerner Pubns.); (Illus.). 31.99 *(978-1-5124-2588-8(5))* Lerner Publishing Group.

—Private Space Travel. 2017. (Space Discovery Guides). (ENG., Illus.). 48p. (J). (gr. 4-6). 31.99 *(978-1-5124-2589-5(3))* Lerner Publishing Group.

Goldstein, Margaret J. Private Space Travel: A Space Discovery Guide. 2017. (Space Discovery Guides). (ENG.). 48p. (J). (gr. 4-6). 16.99 ***(978-1-5124-3816-1(2))***; 47.99 ***(978-1-5124-3815-4(4))***; (Illus.). 47.99 ***(978-1-5124-2797-4(7))*** Lerner Publishing Group. (Lerner Pubns.).

Goodman, Susan E. How Do You Burp in Space? And Other Tips Every Space Tourist Needs to Know. Slack, Michael, illus. 2013. (ENG.). 80p. (J). (gr. 3-6). 17.89 *(978-1-59990-934-9(0)*, 9781599909349, Bloomsbury USA Childrens) Bloomsbury Publishing USA.

—How Do You Burp in Space? And Other Tips Every Space Tourist Needs to Know. Slack, Michael H., illus. 2013. (ENG.). 80p. (J). (gr. 3-6). 16.99 *(978-1-59990-068-1(8)*, 9781599900681, Bloomsbury USA Childrens) Bloomsbury Publishing USA.

Green, Carl R. The Gemini 4 Spacewalk Mission: A MyReportLinks. com Book. 2004. (Space Flight Adventures & Disasters Ser.). (Illus.). 48p. (J). lib. bdg. 26.60 *(978-0-7660-5163-8(3)*, MyReportLinks.com Bks.) Enslow Pubs., Inc.

Hamilton, S. L. Astronaut Firsts. 2011. (Xtreme Space Ser.). (Illus.). 32p. (gr. 3-9). 27.07 *(978-1-61714-736-4(2)*, A&D Xtreme) ABDO Publishing Co.

—Exploration. 2011. (Xtreme Space Ser.). (Illus.). 32p. (gr. 3-9). 27.07 *(978-1-61714-737-1(0)*, A&D Xtreme) ABDO Publishing Co.

Herrod, Robin & Kerrod, Robin. Space Pioneers. 2004. (History of Space Exploration Ser.). (Illus.). 48p. (gr. 5-12). lib. bdg. 31.00 *(978-0-8368-5707-8(0)*, Gareth Stevens Secondary Library) Stevens, Gareth Publishing LLLP.

Holden, Henry M. The Coolest Job in the Universe: Working Aboard the International Space Station. 2012. (American Space Missions — Astronauts, Exploration, & Discovery Ser.). (Illus.). 48p. (J). (gr. 5-18). lib. bdg. 25.27 *(978-0-7660-4074-8(7))* Enslow Pubs., Inc.

Hubbard, Ben. Yuri Gagarin & the Race to Space. 2015. (Adventures in Space Ser.). (ENG., Illus.). 48p. (gr. 4-6). 33.32 *(978-1-4846-2514-9(5))* Heinemann-Raintree.

Ingebretsen, Karen, et al. Human Space Exploration. 2006. (World Book's Solar System & Space Exploration Library). (Illus.). 63p. (J). *(978-0-7166-9509-7(X))* World Bk., Inc.

Jefferis, David & Irvine, Mat. Flight into Orbit. 2007. (Humans in Space Ser.). (ENG., Illus.). 32p. (J). (gr. 3-7). lib. bdg. *(978-0-7787-3101-6(4))*; pap. *(978-0-7787-3115-3(4))* Crabtree Publishing Co.

Jemison, Mae & Rau, Dana Meachen. The 100 Year Starship. 2013. (True Book™—Dr. Mae Jemison & 100 Year Starship™ Ser.). (ENG.). 48p. (J). 29.00 *(978-0-531-25500-1(X)*, Children's Pr.) Scholastic Library Publishing.

Kruesi, Liz. Discover Space Exploration. 2016. (Searchlight Books (tm) — What's Cool about Science? Ser.). (ENG., Illus.). 40p. (J). (gr. 3-5). 30.65 *(978-1-5124-0811-9(5))* Lerner Publishing Group.

Littlejohn, Randy. Life in Outer Space. 2004. (Life in Extreme Environments Ser.). (Illus.). 64p. (gr. 5-8). lib. bdg. 31.95

(978-0-8239-3989-3(8), Rosen Reference) Rosen Publishing Group, Inc., The.

Mallick, Nita. Space Exploration. 2016. (Study of Science Ser.). 00104p. (J). (gr. 8-8). lib. bdg. 36.25 *(978-1-5081-0427-8(1))* Rosen Publishing Group, Inc., The.

Nelson, Maria. Life on the International Space Station. 2013. (Extreme Jobs in Extreme Places Ser.). (Illus.). 32p. (gr. 3-6). 26.60 *(978-1-4339-8507-2(1));* pap. 10.50 *(978-1-4339-8508-9(X))* Stevens, Gareth Publishing LLLP. (Gareth Stevens Learning Library).

Newland, Sonya. Space Exploration: Triumphs & Tragedies. 2016. (ENG., Illus.). 48p. (J). pap. *(978-0-7787-2231-1(7))* Crabtree Publishing Co.

Parker, Steve. Space Pioneers. West, David, illus. 2015. (Story of Space Ser.). (ENG.). 32p. (J). (gr. 3-6). 31.35 *(978-1-62588-080-2(4),* 1389452) Black Rabbit Bks.

Parker, Steve & Snedding, Robert. A Brief Illustrated History of Space Exploration. 2017. (Brief Illustrated History Ser.). (ENG.). 32p. (gr. 3-5). lib. bdg. 27.32 *(978-1-5157-2519-0(7),* Fact Finders) Capstone Press of Coughlan Cos.

Peterson, Megan Cooley & Rustad, Martha E. H. The First Space Missions, 1 vol. 2014. (Famous Firsts Ser.). (ENG., Illus.). 24p. (gr. k-1). 26.65 *(978-1-4914-0576-5(7));* pap. 6.95 *(978-1-4914-0644-1(5))* Capstone Press of Coughlan Cos. (Pebble Plus).

Raketen und Raumfahrt. (GER.). 40p. *(978-3-411-08191-2(0))* Bibliographisches Institut & F. A. Brockhaus AG DEU. Dist: i. b. d., Ltd.

Rau, Dana Meachen & Jemison, Mae. The 100 Year Starship. 2013. (True Book™—Dr. Mae Jemison & 100 Year Starship™ Ser.). (ENG.). 48p. (J). pap. 6.95 *(978-0-531-24060-1(6),* Children's Pr.) Scholastic Library Publishing.

Rice, Dona Herweck & Rice, Dona. ¡Locos por Insectos y Arañas!, 1 vol. 2nd rev. ed. 2012. (Nonfiction Readers Ser.).Tr. of Going Buggy. (SPA.). 20p. (J). (gr. 1-1). pap. 4.99 *(978-1-4333-4424-4(6))* Teacher Created Materials, Inc.

Royston, Angela. Space Blog. 2010. (ENG., Illus.). 32p. (J). *(978-0-7787-9910-8(7));* pap. *(978-0-7787-9931-3(X))* Crabtree Publishing Co.

Sparrow, Giles. Astronauts. 2006. (Secrets of the Universe Ser.). (Illus.). 48p. (gr. 6-12). pap. 14.05 *(978-0-8368-7282-8(7));* lib. bdg. 31.00 *(978-0-8368-7275-0(4))* Stevens, Gareth Publishing LLLP. (Gareth Stevens Secondary Library).

Sparrow, Giles & John, Judith. Shuttles & Space Missions. 2016. (Discoveries in Space Science Ser.). (ENG., Illus.). 80p. (YA). (gr. 9-9). lib. bdg. 35.64 *(978-1-5026-1016-4(7),* 1398739) Cavendish Square Publishing.

Waxman, Laura Hamilton. Exploring Space Travel. 2011. (Searchlight Books Whats Amazing about Space Ser.). (ENG., Illus.). (gr. 3-5). pap. 51.01 *(978-0-7613-8418-2(9));* 40p. pap. 8.95 *(978-0-7613-7881-5(2));* 40p. lib. bdg. 27.93 *(978-0-7613-5447-5(6))* Lerner Publishing Group.

West, David. Lots of Things You Want to Know about Astronauts ...and Some You Don't! 2015. (Lots of Things You Want to Know About Ser.). (Illus.). 24p. (J). 28.50 *(978-1-62588-088-8(X))* Black Rabbit Bks.

World Book, contrib. by. Human Space Exploration. 2nd ed. 2006. (World Book's Solar System & Space Exploration Library). (Illus.). 64p. (J). *(978-0-7166-9514-1(6))* World Bk., Inc.

World Book, Inc Staff, contrib. by. Space Exploration. 2011. (J). *(978-0-7166-1792-1(7))* World Bk., Inc.

Zelon, Helen. The Endeavor Mission STS-61: Fixing the Hubble Space Telescope. 2009. (Space Missions Ser.). 24p. (gr. 3-4). 42.50 *(978-1-60853-117-2(1),* PowerKids Pr.) Rosen Publishing Group, Inc., The.

—The Gemini IV Mission: The First American Space Walk. 2009. (Space Missions Ser.). 24p. (gr. 3-4). 42.50 *(978-1-60853-119-6(8),* PowerKids Pr.) Rosen Publishing Group, Inc., The.

MANNED SPACE FLIGHT—FICTION

Hunt, Elizabeth Singer. The Deadly Race to Space: Russia. 2009. (Secret Agent Jack Stalwart Ser.: 9). (ENG.). 144p. (J). (gr. 1-4). pap. 5.99 *(978-1-60286-078-0(5),* Weinstein Bks.) Perseus Bks. Group.

Krasner, Nick. My Bed Is a Spaceship: The Globbus. White, Charlotte, illus. 2013. 122p. pap. *(978-1-909593-34-3(6))* Legend Pr.

Olivas, John D. Endeavour's Long Journey. Roski, Gayle Garner, illus. 2013. (J). *(978-0-9856237-2-2(1))* East West Discovery Pr.

—Endeavour's Long Journey: Celebrating 19 Years of Space Exploration. Roski, Gayle Garner, illus. 2013. (J). pap. *(978-0-9856237-3-9(X))* East West Discovery Pr.

Slivensky, Katie. The Countdown Conspiracy. 2017. 336p. (J). (gr. 3-7). 16.99 ***(978-0-06-246255-8(5))*** HarperCollins Pubs.

MANNERS

see Courtesy; Etiquette

MANNERS AND CUSTOMS

see also Chivalry; Clothing and Dress; Costume; Etiquette; Food Habits; Funeral Rites and Ceremonies; Holidays; Marriage Customs and Rites; Social Classes; Travel

Abramovitz, Melissa. The 100th Day of School. 2012. (Let's Celebrate Ser.). (ENG.). 24p. (gr. k-1). pap. 41.70 *(978-1-4296-9383-7(5),* Pebble Plus) Capstone Press of Coughlan Cos.

Ackerman, Jill. Please & Thank You! Berg, Michelle, illus. 2011. (Little Scholastic Ser.). (ENG.). 10p. (J). (gr. k — 1). bds. 6.99 *(978-0-545-27092-2(8),* Cartwheel Bks.) Scholastic, Inc.

Ajmera, Maya & Ivanko, John D. To Be a Kid. 2004. (ENG., Illus.). 26p. (J). (-k). bds. 7.95 *(978-1-57091-371-6(4))* Charlesbridge Publishing, Inc.

Alexander, Florence & Alexander, Stanley. Come with Me & See... Children of the World. I.t. ed. 2003. (ENG & SPA., Illus.). 32p. (J). 9.99 *(978-0-9648313-9-1(2))* Ebon Research Systems Publishing, LLC.

Aloian, Molly. What Does It Mean to Go Green? 2013. (ENG., Illus.). 24p. (J). *(978-0-7787-0275-7(8));* pap. *(978-0-7787-0286-3(3))* Crabtree Publishing Co.

Amery, Heather. Then & Now. Firmin, Peter, illus. 2008. (Then & Now Ser.). 24p. (J). (gr. -1-3). pap. 4.99 *(978-0-7945-2211-7(4),* Usborne) EDC Publishing.

Before You Say Yes to a Guest. 2003. (YA). *(978-0-9729586-0-8(6))* Imani-MCHS.

Berry, Joy. Bad Habits. 3rd ed. 2005. (Winning skills series, get over It! Ser.). (ENG., Illus.). 48p. (J). pap. 3.95 *(978-1-57687-280-2(7),* PowerHouse Kids) powerHouse Cultural Entertainment, Inc.

Bradford, Wade. Around the World in a Bathtub. Archer, Micha, illus. 2017. (ENG.). 32p. (J). (gr. -1-2). lib. bdg. 16.99 *(978-1-58089-544-6(1))* Charlesbridge Publishing, Inc.

Butterfield, Moira. Schools Around the World. 2016. (Children Like Us Ser.). (ENG., Illus.). 32p. (J). (gr. 3-3). pap. 10.58 *(978-1-5026-0846-8(4))* Cavendish Square Publishing.

Cain, Marie Mowery. Celebrate Cinco de Mayo. 2013. (Big Books, Red Ser.). (ENG & SPA., Illus.). 16p. pap. 33.00 *(978-1-59246-222-3(7))* Big Books, by George!

Chancellor, Deborah. Good Manners. 2009. (Now We Know About... Ser.). (ENG., Illus.). 24p. (J). (gr. k-3). pap. *(978-0-7787-4736-9(0));* lib. bdg. *(978-0-7787-4719-2(0))* Crabtree Publishing Co.

Cohen, Robert Z. Body Piercing & Tattooing: Making Smart Choices. 2013. 80p. (YA). (gr. 7-12). 33.25 *(978-1-4488-9451-2(4))* Rosen Publishing Group, Inc., The.

Coppendale, Jean. Life & Death. 2006. (Illus.). 32p. (YA). (gr. 1-18). lib. bdg. 27.10 *(978-1-931983-99-0(2))* Chrysalis Education.

Corrick, James A., et al. Disgusting History: The Smelliest, Dirtiest Eras of the Past 10,000 Years. 2014. (Disgusting History Ser.). (ENG.). 240p. pap. 12.95 *(978-1-4765-7745-6(5),* Fact Finders) Capstone Press of Coughlan Cos.

Cosson, M. J. Easter Traditions Around the World. Chavarri, Elisa, illus. 2013. (World Traditions Ser.). (ENG.). 32p. (J). (gr. k-3). 28.50 *(978-1-61473-426-0(7),* 205131) Child's World, Inc., The.

Cultures of the World - Group 14. 2nd rev. ed. Incl. Algeria. Kagda, Falaq & Latif, Zawiah Abdul. lib. bdg. 42.79 *(978-0-7614-2085-9(1),* Benchmark Bks.); Armenia. Dhilawala, Sakina. (Illus.). lib. bdg. 42.79 *(978-0-7614-2029-3(0));* Lithuania. Kagda, Sakina & Latif, Zawiah Abdul. lib. bdg. 42.79 *(978-0-7614-2087-3(8),* Benchmark Bks.); Luxembourg. Sheehan, Patricia & Dhilawala, Sakina. lib. bdg. 42.79 *(978-0-7614-2088-0(6),* Benchmark Bks.); Tahiti. NgCheong-Lum, Roseline. lib. bdg. 42.79 *(978-0-7614-2089-7(4),* Benchmark Bks.); Ukraine. Bassis, Volodymyr & Dhilawala, Sakina. lib. bdg. 42.79 *(978-0-7614-2090-3(8),* Benchmark Bks.); 144p. (gr. 6). (Cultures of the World 14 Ser.). 2007. Set lib. bdg. 256.74 *(978-0-7614-2084-2(3),* Benchmark Bks.) Marshall Cavendish Corp.

Delea, Pattie. Wisdom for Young Hearts Volume 1 Wisdom's Foundation. DeLea, Ray and Daniella, ed. Herman, Scott, illus. 2011. 114p. pap. 20.00 *(978-1-61286-030-5(3))* Avid Readers Publishing Group.

—Wisdom for Young Hearts Volume 2 - Applications of Wisdom. Gammage, Dana, illus. 2011. 126p. pap. 20.00 *(978-1-61286-058-9(3))* Avid Readers Publishing Group.

DiCicco, Sue, illus. Totally Monster: Manners. 2013. (Totally Monsters Ser.). (ENG.). 14p. (J). (gr. -1). 12.95 *(978-1-60710-645-6(0),* Silver Dolphin Bks.) Readerlink Distribution Services, LLC.

Do, Elisa Shipon-Blum. Understanding Katie: A Day in the Life Of. Salus, Diane, illus. 2003. 28p. (J). (gr. -1-18). pap. *(978-0-9714800-3-2(6))* Selective Mutism Anxiety Research & Treatment Ctr.

Doering Tourville, Amanda. Manners in the Lunchroom, 1 vol. Lensch, Chris, illus. 2009. (Way to Be!: Manners Ser.). (ENG.). 24p. (gr. -1-2). 26.65 *(978-1-4048-5308-9(1))* Picture Window Bks.

Doherty, Gillian & Claybourne, Anna. Peoples of the World. rev. ed. 2012. (World Cultures Ser.). 96p. (J). pap. 14.99 *(978-0-7945-3280-2(2),* Usborne) EDC Publishing.

Dorling Kindersley Publishing Staff. Sharing Is Caring. 2017. (Skills for Starting School Ser.). (ENG.). 18p. (J). (— 1). bds. 5.99 *(978-1-4654-5680-9(5),* DK Children) Dorling Kindersley Publishing, Inc.

Dover & Tattoos. Moustache Tattoos: For Your Face or Finger! 2013. (Dover Tattoos Ser.). (ENG., Illus.). 2p. (J). (gr. 3-4). pap. 1.99 *(978-0-486-49329-9(6))* Dover Pubns., Inc.

Dragon School. 2015. (Dragon School Ser.). (ENG.). 32p. (J). (gr. 1-2). pap., pap., pap. 240.00 *(978-1-4777-5689-8(2),* Windmill Bks.) Rosen Publishing Group, Inc., The.

Dyan, Penelope. Ladies First, Please! a Kid's Most Important & Fun Guide to Good Manners. Dyan, Penelope, illus. 2009. (Illus.). 106p. pap. 8.95 *(978-1-935118-67-1(6))* Bellissima Publishing, LLC.

East, Jacqueline, illus. Learn Good Habits with Jessica: Above All, Don't Behave Like Zoe! 2008. 28p. (J). (gr. -1-3). 6.95 *(978-1-59496-163-2(8))* Teora USA LLC.

—Learn Good Manners with Charles: Above All, Don't Behave Like Trevor! 2008. 28p. (J). (gr. -1-3). 6.95 *(978-1-59496-162-5(X))* Teora USA LLC.

Ever Wonder What to Do Manners. 2004. pap. 1.50 *(978-0-87162-918-0(6))* Warner Pr., Inc.

Flynn, Claire E. Running with the Bulls. 2013. (Thrill Seekers Ser.). (Illus.). 32p. (J). (gr. 3-6). pap. 10.50 *(978-1-4824-3294-7(3))* Rosen Publishing Group, Inc., The.

Fulcher, Roz. Mind Your Manners! 2013. (Dover Coloring Bks.). (ENG.). 48p. (J). (gr. 1-5). pap. 4.99 *(978-0-486-49883-6(2))* Dover Pubns., Inc.

Ganeri, Anita. Remembering the Dead Around the World. 2015. (Cultures & Customs Ser.). (ENG., Illus.). 32p. (gr. 3-3). 30.65 *(978-1-4109-8018-2(9))* Heinemann-Raintree.

Giles, Sophie, et al. The Children's Book of Manners. East, Jacqueline, illus. 2014. (ENG.). 32p. (J). pap. 10.00 *(978-1-84135-971-7(8))* Award Pubns. Ltd. GBR. Dist: Parkwest Pubns., Inc.

Gilmour, Barbara, et al. Cool Kind Kid Camp Kit 4-6: Social Skills Shaping Futures. 2007. (J). spiral bd. *(978-0-9743499-7-8(6))* CKK Educational, LLC.

Gordon, Sharon. We Are Kind. 2005. (Bookworms Ser.). (ENG & SPA., Illus.). 24p. (J). (gr. 3-7). lib. bdg. 22.79 *(978-0-7614-1992-1(6),* Benchmark Bks.) Marshall Cavendish Corp.

Gray, Carolyn. All about M. E. Manners & Etiquette for TWEENS & TEENS. 2007. 28p. (J). pap. 12.95 *(978-1-60131-010-1(2))* Big Tent Bks.

Greven, Alec. How to Talk to Dads. Acedera, Kei, illus. 2009. (ENG.). 48p. (J). (gr. 1-5). 9.99 *(978-0-06-172930-0(2),* Collins) HarperCollins Pubs.

Groves, Marsha. Manners & Customs in the Middle Ages. 2005. (Medieval World Ser.). (ENG., Illus.). 32p. (J). (gr. 5-9). pap. *(978-0-7787-1389-0(X))* Crabtree Publishing Co.

Gurkow, Malkie. Building a Better Me: Student's Workbook. 2005. 29p. pap., wbk. ed. 7.50 *(978-1-878895-44-8(3))* Torah Umesorah Pubns.

Gustafson, Angela. Imagine a House: A Journey to Fascinating Houses Around the World. 2003. (What a World We Live in Ser.). (Illus.). 32p. (J). (gr. k-6). lib. bdg. 16.95 *(978-0-9726849-0-3(5))* Out of the Box.

Guy, John. Victorian Life. 2004. (Illus.). 32p. (J). (gr. 4-7). pap. 5.95 *(978-1-86007-005-1(1),* TickTock Books) Octopus Publishing Group GBR. Dist: Independent Pubs. Group.

Harris, Lisa Delmedico. The Official Princess Handbook: A Little Girl's Guide to Beauty, Poise, & Righteousness. 2010. (ENG.). 96p. (J). pap. 9.99 *(978-1-60683-025-3(2))* Harrison House Pubs.

Harrison, Paul. Ancient Roman Clothes. 2010. (Ancient Communities: Roman Life Ser.). (Illus.). 32p. (J). (gr. 3-6). lib. bdg. 26.50 *(978-1-61532-304-3(X),* PowerKids Pr.) Rosen Publishing Group, Inc., The.

Haywood, John. Home, Family & Everyday Life Through the Ages: Compare the Food, Homes & Daily Lives of Ancient People from All the Major Civilizations. 2008. (ENG., Illus.). 64p. (J). (gr. 4-7). pap. 12.99 *(978-1-84476-602-4(0))* Anness Publishing GBR. Dist: National Bk. Network.

Hibbert, Clare. Our Busy Lives. Raga, Sylvia, illus. 2011. (Busy Times Ser.). (ENG.). 24p. (J). 19.99 *(978-0-237-54266-5(8))* Evans Brothers, Ltd. GBR. Dist: Independent Pubs. Group.

Hillstead, McKensy & Gonzales, Brittany. One Day. 2012. 28p. pap. 16.09 *(978-1-4669-5171-6(0))* Trafford Publishing.

Hogan, Wes. Balloons. Hogan, Wes & Hogan, Tom, illus. 2008. 24p. pap. 13.99 *(978-1-4389-0206-7(9))* AuthorHouse.

Holyoke, Nancy. A Smart Girl's Guide to Manners: The Secrets to Grace, Confidence, & Being Your Best. Watkins, Michelle, ed. Mingus, Cathi, illus. 2005. (ENG.). 120p. (J). (gr. 3). per. 9.95 *(978-1-58485-983-3(0),* American Girl) American Girl Publishing, Inc.

Howell, Des. The Abcs of Good Manners. 2009. 20p. pap. 13.00 *(978-1-4389-1837-2(2))* AuthorHouse.

Jackson, Abby. Fancy Feet. 2005. (Yellow Umbrella Fluent Level Ser.). (ENG.). 16p. (gr. k-1). pap. 35.70 *(978-0-7368-5313-2(8),* Yellow Umbrella Bks.) Capstone Press of Coughlan Cos.

Jacobs, Pat & Steele, Philip. I Wonder Why Countries Fly Flags. 2012. (I Wonder Why Ser.). (ENG., Illus.). 32p. (J). (gr. k-3). 6.99 *(978-0-7534-6793-0(3),* 9780753467930, Kingfisher) Roaring Brook Pr.

Jno-Lewis, Jason. The Thank You Book: A Thank-You Goes a Long Way. 2012. 28p. pap. 13.95 *(978-1-4582-0345-8(X),* Abbott Pr.) Author Solutions, Inc.

Jones, M. b. & Jones, M. B. Manners Are Free. 2011. 24p. pap. 11.95 *(978-1-4634-1307-1(6))* AuthorHouse.

Kenney, Karen Latchana. Cool Family Parties: Perfect Party Planning for Kids, 1 vol. 2012. (Cool Parties Ser.). (ENG., Illus.). 32p. (J). (gr. 3-6). 28.50 *(978-1-61714-973-3(X))* ABDO Publishing Co.

—Cool Holiday Parties: Perfect Party Planning for Kids, 1 vol. 2012. (Cool Parties Ser.). (ENG., Illus.). 32p. (J). (gr. 3-6). 28.50 *(978-1-61714-974-0(8))* ABDO Publishing Co.

Kids Talk, 12 vols. Incl. Do I Have To? Kids Talk about Responsibility. Loewen, Nancy. Wesley, Omarr, illus. 2002. 27.99 *(978-1-4048-0030-4(1));* Pitch In! Kids Talk about Cooperation. Nettleton, Pamela Hill. Muehlenhardt, Amy Bailey, illus. 2004. 27.99 *(978-1-4048-0621-4(0));* We Live Here Too! Kids Talk about Good Citizenship. Loewen, Nancy. Wesley, Omarr, illus. 2002. lib. bdg. 27.99 *(978-1-4048-0035-9(2));* (gr. 2-5). (Kids Talk Ser.). (ENG.). 32p. 2004. Set lib. bdg. 83.97 *(978-1-4048-0635-1(0))* Picture Window Bks.

King, Elizabeth. Quinceanera: Celebrating Fifteen. King, Elizabeth, photos by. 2006. (Illus.). 40p. (YA). (gr. 8-11). reprint ed. 17.00 *(978-1-4223-5728-6(7))* DIANE Publishing Co.

Krasner, Barbara. A Career As an Event Coordinator, 1 vol. 2015. (ENG., Illus.). 80p. (J). 34.25 *(978-1-4777-7878-4(0),* Rosen Young Adult) Rosen Publishing Group, Inc., The.

Leaf, Munro. How to Speak Politely & Why. 2005. (ENG., Illus.). 56p. (J). (gr. k-4). 14.95 *(978-0-7893-1352-2(9))* Universe Publishing.

Levete, Sarah & Randall, Ronne. Birth. 2016. (Journey of Life Ser.). (ENG., Illus.). 48p. (J). (gr. 4-6). pap. 11.99 *(978-0-7502-9637-3(2),* Wayland) Hachette Children's Group GBR. Dist: Hachette Bk. Group.

Lindeen, Mary. Where People Live. 2011. (Wonder Readers Fluent Level Ser.). (ENG.). (gr. -1-2). 16p. pap. 35.94 *(978-1-4296-8207-7(8));* 32p. pap. 5.99 *(978-1-4296-7975-6(1))* Capstone Press of Coughlan Cos. (Wonder Readers).

Love, Mary A. Learning Through Symbolism & Celebrations. Flournoy, L. Diana, illus. 2nd rev. ed. 2011. (ENG.). 168p. pap. 24.00 *(978-1-929548-00-2(1))* Love's Creative Resources.

MacDonald, Fiona. History of Culture. 2004. (Culture Encyclopedia Ser.). (Illus.). 40p. (YA). (gr. 5-18). lib. bdg. 19.95 *(978-1-59084-477-9(7))* Mason Crest.

Malaspina, Ann. Tooth Traditions Around the World. Chavarri, Elisa, illus. 2013. (World Traditions Ser.). (ENG.). 32p. (J). (gr. k-3). 28.50 *(978-1-61473-430-7(5),* 205135) Child's World, Inc., The.

Manners Matter. 2017. (Manners Matter Ser.). 24p. (gr. 4-6). 94.40 ***(978-1-5081-5788-5(X));*** pap. 33.00 ***(978-1-5081-5799-1(5))*** Rosen Publishing Group, Inc., The. (PowerKids Pr.).

Marsh, Carole. Christmas Traditions Around the World. 2003. 12p. (J). (gr. k-4). pap. 2.95 *(978-0-635-02154-0(4))* Gallopade International.

—Why Do We Hang Christmas Stockings. 2003. 12p. (J). (gr. k-4). pap. 2.95 *(978-0-635-02152-6(8))* Gallopade International.

Marshall, Shelley. Molly the Great Misses the Bus: A Book about Being on Time. Mahan, Ben, illus. 2010. (Character Education with Super Ben & Molly the Great Ser.). 24p. (J). pap. 7.95 *(978-0-7660-3743-4(6),* Enslow Elementary) Enslow Pubs., Inc.

Mattern, Joanne. Getting Ready for School (Me Preparo para Ir a la Escuela) 2006. (My Day at School/ Mi dia en la escuela Ser.). (ENG & SPA., Illus.). 24p. (gr. k-3). pap. 8.15 *(978-0-8368-7366-5(1),* Weekly Reader Leveled Readers) Stevens, Gareth Publishing LLLP.

—Me Preparo para IR a la Escuela (Getting Ready for School) 2006. (My Day at School/ Mi dia en la escuela Ser.). (ENG & SPA., Illus.). 24p. (gr. k-3). lib. bdg. 22.00 *(978-0-8368-7359-7(9),* Weekly Reader Leveled Readers) Stevens, Gareth Publishing LLLP.

Mauzy, Barbara E. Don't Be a Schwoe: Manners, 1 vol. Mauzy, Barbara E., illus. 2010. (ENG., Illus.). 64p. (J). 14.99 *(978-0-7643-3428-3(X),* 9780764334283) Schiffer Publishing, Ltd.

Meiners, Cheri J. Respect & Take Care of Things. 2015. (Learning to Get Along(r) Ser.). (ENG & SPA., Illus.). 48p. (J). (gr. -1-3). pap. 12.45 *(978-1-63198-036-7(X))* Free Spirit Publishing, Inc.

Miller, Connie Colwell. Monster Knows Manners, 1 vol. Chiodi, Maira, illus. 2014. (Monster Knows Manners Ser.). (ENG.). 24p. (gr. -1-2). lib. bdg. 98.60 *(978-1-4795-3346-6(7))* Picture Window Bks.

Montanari, Donata. Children Around the World. Montanari, Donata, illus. 2004. (Around the World Ser.). (ENG., Illus.). 32p. (J). (gr. -1-2). pap. 8.99 *(978-1-55337-684-2(6))* Kids Can Pr., Ltd. CAN. Dist: Hachette Bk. Group.

Morris, Taylor. Surviving a First Date. 2017. (J). ***(978-0-7660-9191-7(0))*** Enslow Pubs., Inc.

Mulcahy, William. Zach Makes Mistakes. McKee, Darren, illus. 2016. (Zach Rules Ser.). (ENG.). 32p. (J). 12.99 *(978-1-63198-110-4(2))* Free Spirit Publishing, Inc.

Mundy, Michaelene. Saying Good-Bye, Saying Hello... When Your Family Is Moving. Alley, R. W., illus. 2005. (Elf-Help Books for Kids). 32p. (J). (gr. -1-3). per. 7.95 *(978-0-87029-393-1(1))* Abbey Pr.

Neely, Judith. Never Too Big for Monkey Hugs. Joslin, Irene, illus. 2009. 16p. pap. 8.49 *(978-1-4389-7289-3(X))* AuthorHouse.

Newcomer, Ruth. Silly Songs for Little People. 2004. (Illus.). 42p. (J). spiral bd. 18.00 *(978-1-883911-63-8(X))* Brandylane Pubs., Inc.

Niven, Felicia Lowenstein. Fabulous Fashions of The 1920s. 2011. (Fabulous Fashions of the Decades Ser.). (Illus.). 48p. (J). (gr. 5-9). lib. bdg. 25.27 *(978-0-7660-3551-5(4))* Enslow Pubs., Inc.

—Fabulous Fashions of The 1930s. 2011. (Fabulous Fashions of the Decades Ser.). (Illus.). 48p. (J). (gr. 5-9). lib. bdg. 25.27 *(978-0-7660-3824-0(6))* Enslow Pubs., Inc.

—Fabulous Fashions of The 1940s. 2011. (Fabulous Fashions of the Decades Ser.). (Illus.). 48p. (J). (gr. 5-9). lib. bdg. 25.27 *(978-0-7660-3552-2(2))* Enslow Pubs., Inc.

—Fabulous Fashions of The 1950s. 2011. (Fabulous Fashions of the Decades Ser.). (Illus.). 48p. (J). (gr. 5-9). lib. bdg. 25.27 *(978-0-7660-3825-7(4))* Enslow Pubs., Inc.

—Fabulous Fashions of The 1960s. 2011. (Fabulous Fashions of the Decades Ser.). (Illus.). 48p. (J). (gr. 5-9). lib. bdg. 25.27 *(978-0-7660-3553-9(0))* Enslow Pubs., Inc.

—Fabulous Fashions of The 1970s. 2011. (Fabulous Fashions of the Decades Ser.). (Illus.). 48p. (J). (gr. 5-9). lib. bdg. 25.27 *(978-0-7660-3826-4(2))* Enslow Pubs., Inc.

—Fabulous Fashions of The 1980s. 2011. (Fabulous Fashions of the Decades Ser.). (Illus.). 48p. (J). (gr. 5-9). lib. bdg. 25.27 *(978-0-7660-3554-6(9))* Enslow Pubs., Inc.

—Fabulous Fashions of The 1990s. 2011. (Fabulous Fashions of the Decades Ser.). (Illus.). 48p. (J). (gr. 5-9). lib. bdg. 25.27 *(978-0-7660-3827-1(0))* Enslow Pubs., Inc.

Nunn, Daniel & Smith, Sian. Manners in the Community, 1 vol. 2012. (Oh, Behave! Ser.). (ENG.). 24p. (gr. -1-1). lib. bdg. 22.65 *(978-1-4329-6639-3(1),* Acorn) Heinemann-Raintree.

One City, One School, Many Foods: Six-Pack. (Greetings Ser.: Vol. 1). (gr. 3-5). 31.00 *(978-0-7635-1797-7(6))* Rigby Education.

Ornstein, Esther. Middos Man Book & CD. Judowitz, Yoel, illus. 2013. 33p. 19.95 *(978-1-60091-257-3(5))* Israel Bookshop Pubns.

Pacileo, Cindy, creator. The Virtues Activity & Coloring Book, Ages 5-7. 2005. (J). 4.50 *(978-0-9741930-0-7(3))* Changing-Times.net.

—The Virtues Activity & Coloring Book, Ages 8-10. 2005. (J). 4.50 *(978-0-9741930-1-4(1))* Changing-Times.net.

Padmanabhan, Manjula. I Am Different. 2011. (ENG., Illus.). 40p. (J). (gr. 1-4). 16.95 *(978-1-57091-639-7(X))* Charlesbridge Publishing, Inc.

Parish, Scott. Tiger at the Table. 2005. 14p. (J). 10.00 *(978-1-4116-4704-6(1))* Lulu Pr., Inc.

Petersen, Christine. The Smart Kid's Guide to Manners. Ronney, Ronnie, illus. 2014. (Smart Kid's Guide to Everyday Life Ser.). (ENG.). 32p. (J). (gr. 2-5). 28.50 *(978-1-62687-344-5(5),* 207184) Child's World, Inc., The.

PoliteKids 101. . . Social Skills Your Child Needs for Success in Life! 2004. (J). *(978-0-9729706-7-9(3));* wbk. ed. *(978-0-9729706-8-6(1))* Production 101, Inc.

Quarto Generic Staff & Wellfleet Press Editors. Thank You Notes for Kids. 2015. (ENG.). 32p. (J). (gr. 1-17). pap. 14.99 *(978-1-57715-111-1(9),* Wellfleet) Book Sales, Inc.

Ring, Susan. Places We Live. 2005. (Yellow Umbrella Fluent Level Ser.). (ENG.). 16p. (gr. k-1). pap. 35.70 *(978-0-7368-5316-3(2),* Yellow Umbrella Bks.) Capstone Press of Coughlan Cos.

Rosson, Denise & Tumblacer, Margaret. Tadpole Dreams Etiquette & Good Manners Program Handbook. 2005. 25p. (J). 12.95 *(978-0-9769320-1-7(6),* ss0002) Smith, S. Pubns.

Rotner, Shelley. Different Kinds of Good-Byes. 2013. (Shelley Rotner's World Ser.). (ENG.). 32p. (gr. 1-2). pap. 47.70 *(978-1-62065-751-5(1),* Aplus Bks.) Capstone Press of Coughlan Cos.

—Different Kinds of Good-Byes, 1 vol. Rotner, Shelley, photos by. 2013. (Shelley Rotner's World Ser.). (ENG., Illus.). 32p. (gr. 1-2). pap. 8.10 *(978-1-62065-750-8(3));* lib. bdg. 27.32 *(978-1-62065-066-0(5))* Capstone Press of Coughlan Cos.

Sato, Shozo. Tea Ceremony: Explore the Unique Japanese Tradition of Sharing Tea. 2004. (Asian Arts & Crafts for Creative Kids Ser.). (ENG., Illus.). 64p. (J). (gr. 2-6). 15.95 *(978-0-8048-3500-8(4))* Tuttle Publishing.

M
N
O

School Students, Tuttle Elementary. Respect, a Global Vision by the Students of Tuttle Elementary School. 2010. 32p. pap. 12.95 (978-1-936051-85-4(0)) Peppertree Pr., The.

Schwartz, Sara Leah. Let's Use Them Right: Social Skills for My Hands, Feet, & Mouth. David, Racheli, illus. 2013. 39p. 16.95 (978-1-60091-276-4(1)) Israel Bookshop Pubns.

Sesame Street Staff, creator. Sesame Street: My First Manners Boxed Set. 2011. 72p. (J). bds. 12.99 (978-1-60745-238-6(3)) Flying Frog Pubs.

Small, Mary. Being Respectful: A Book about Respectfulness, 1 vol. Previn, Stacey, illus. 2005. (Way to Be! Ser.). (ENG.). 24p. (gr. k-2). lib. bdg. 25.99 (978-1-4048-1053-2(6), Nonfiction Picture Bks.) Picture Window Bks.

Sonnier, Suzanne. Shinto, Spirits, & Shrines: Religion in Japan. 2007. (Lucent Library of Historical Eras:Twentieth-Century Japan Ser.). (ENG., Illus.). 96p. (J). (gr. 4-7). lib. bdg. 34.80 (978-1-4205-0029-5(5), Lucent Bks.) Cengage Gale.

Spangenburg, Ray & Moser, Kit. Teen Fads: Fun, Foolish, or Fatal? 2003. (Teen Issues Ser.). (Illus.). 64p. (J). (gr. 6-12). lib. bdg. 22.60 (978-0-7660-1665-1(X)) Enslow Pubs., Inc.

Stefoff, Rebecca. The Medieval World. 2004. (World Historical Atlases Ser.). (Illus.). 48p. (gr. 5). 26.95 (978-0-7614-1642-5(0), Benchmark Bks.) Marshall Cavendish Corp.

Stephens, Chris S. A Christmas Box. 2003. (ENG.). 48p. pap. 20.95 (978-1-84323-306-0(1)) Beekman Bks., Inc.

Summers, Jean. The Kids' Guide to Writing Great Thank-You Notes. 2010. (Illus.). 48p. (J). 9.95 (978-1-59411-125-9(1)) Writers' Collective, The.

Swain, Gwenyth. Bedtime! 2011. (Small World Ser.). (Illus.). 24p. bds. (978-1-84089-673-2(6)) Zero to Ten, Ltd.

—Celebrating. 2011. (Small World Ser.). (Illus.). 24p. bds. (978-1-84089-674-9(4)) Zero to Ten, Ltd.

Tadpole Dreams Etiquette & Good Manners Curriculum. 2005. (YA). ring bd. 249.95 (978-0-9769320-0-0(8), ss0001) Smith, S. Pubns.

Thomas, Pat. My Manners Matter: A First Look at Being Polite. Harker, Lesley, illus. 2006. (First Look AtÂÂ... Ser.). (ENG.). 32p. (J). pap. 7.99 (978-0-7641-3212-4(1)) Barron's Educational Series, Inc.

Tourville, Amanda Doering. Manners at a Friend's House, 1 vol. Lensch, Chris, illus. 2009. (Way to Be!: Manners Ser.). (ENG.). 24p. (gr. -1-2). pap. 7.95 (978-1-4048-5306-5(5)); lib. bdg. 26.65 (978-1-4048-5305-8(7)) Picture Window Bks.

—Manners with a Library Book, 1 vol. Lensch, Chris, illus. 2009. (Way to Be!: Manners Ser.). (ENG.). 24p. (gr. -1-2). lib. bdg. 26.65 (978-1-4048-5314-0(6)) Picture Window Bks.

Understanding Differences. 2010. (Understanding Differences Ser.). (ENG.). 24p. (gr. k-1). pap. 29.75 (978-1-4296-5770-9(7), Pebble Bks.) Capstone Press of Coughlan Cos.

Waddington, Emma. Why Do I Have to Say Please & Thank You? Big Issues for Little People about Behavior & Manners. Thomas, Louis & Thomas, Louis, illus. 2016. (Life & Soul Library). (ENG.). 32p. (J). (gr. -1-3). 12.99 **(978-1-84780-866-0(2)**, Frances Lincoln Children's Bks.) Quarto Publishing Group UK GBR. Dist: Hachette Bk. Group.

Washington, L. Manners First - G I F T S. 2007. 88p. pap. 14.99 (978-0-88144-273-1(9)) Yorkshire Publishing Group.

What Really Matters. 2007. (J). per. 10.00 (978-1-930052-35-2(9)) Cherokee Bks.

Whiteside, Doug. Thank You... No, Thank You! 2009. 80p. pap. 10.49 (978-1-4389-8173-4(2)) AuthorHouse.

Whyte, Daniel, III. Money under the Car Seat: And Other Things to Thank God For. 2008. (ENG., Illus.). 251p. per. 13.99 (978-0-9763487-0-2(5)) Torch Legacy Pubns.

World Book, Inc Staff, contrib. by. Cumulative Glossary & Index. 46p. (J). 2009. (978-0-7166-5051-5(7)) 2003. (978-0-7166-5017-1(7)) World Bk., Inc.

World Book, Inc. Staff, contrib. by. Everyday Celebrations & Rituals. 2003. (World Book's Celebrations & Rituals Around the World Ser.). (Illus.). 46p. (J). (978-0-7166-5016-4(9)) World Bk., Inc.

World Book, Inc Staff, contrib. by. Everyday Celebrations & Rituals. 2009. (Illus.). 46p. (J). (978-0-7166-5050-8(9)) World Bk., Inc.

—Marriage Celebrations. 2009. (Illus.). 46p. (J). (978-0-7166-5046-1(0)) World Bk., Inc.

Worthy of Honor. 2003. (Humble Heart Ser.). (J). spiral bd., wbk. ed. (978-0-9746148-2-3(3)) Common Courtesy.

MANNERS AND CUSTOMS—FICTION

Abraham, Holly. Good Manners at a Friend's House. 2017. (Manners Matter Ser.). 24p. (gr. 4-6). 23.60 **(978-1-5081-5731-1(6)**, PowerKids Pr.) Rosen Publishing Group, Inc., The.

Adler, David A. Cam Jansen & the Graduation Day Mystery. 2012. (Cam Jansen Ser.: 31). lib. bdg. 14.75 (978-0-606-26663-5(1), Turtleback) Turtleback Bks.

Alegria, Malin. Estrella's Quinceañera. 2006. (ENG., Illus.). 272p. (YA). (gr. 7). 15.99 (978-0-689-87809-1(5), Simon & Schuster Bks. For Young Readers) Simon & Schuster Bks. For Young Readers.

Alexander, Mary Helen. Please & Thank You. 2005. 23p. pap. 24.95 (978-1-4137-6240-2(9)) PublishAmerica, Inc.

Alimonti, Frederick & Tedesco, Ann. Tommy & the T-Tops: Helping Children Overcome Prejudice. Hazard, John, illus. 2009. (Let's Talk Ser.). (ENG.). 48p. (J). (gr. -1-4). pap. 8.95 (978-0-88282-305-8(1)) New Horizon Pr. Pubs., Inc.

Aunt Judy. Chickens on the Go! Chickens from different locations around the World. Aunt Judy, illus. 2nd ed. 2006. (Illus.). 40p. (J). pap. 7.00 (978-0-9780693-0-8(7)) McEwen, Judith A.

Barber, Elke & Barber, Alex. What Happened to Daddy's Body? Explaining What Happens after Death in Words Very Young Children Can Understand. 2016. (ENG., Illus.). 40p. (J). 18.95 (978-1-78592-107-0(X), 8559) Kingsley, Jessica Pubs. GBR. Dist: Macmillan Distribution Ltd.

Bauer, Joan. Best Foot Forward. 2006. 183p. (gr. 7-12). 18.00 (978-0-7569-6767-3(8)) Perfection Learning Corp.

Beek, Rosheena. Mommy Says! Maye, Warren L., illus. 2nd ed. 2013. (ENG.). 24p. pap. (978-1-927750-20-9(2)) Bermuda National Trust.

Beers, Gary. Pumpkinroo. 2013. 32p. pap. 24.95 (978-1-63004-258-5(7)) America Star Bks.

Belmore, Vickie J. Paul the Pack Rat: Helping Children Learn to Share. Ciaravino, Paul, illus. 2009. (Let's Talk Ser.). (ENG.). 48p. (J). (gr. -1-4). pap. 8.95 (978-0-88282-307-2(8)) New Horizon Pr. Pubs., Inc.

Binkow, Howard. Howard B. Wigglebottom Learns to Listen. Cornelison, Susan F., illus. 2006. (ENG.). 32p. (J). (gr. -1-k). 15.00 (978-0-9715390-1-3(4)) We Do Listen Foundation.

Birt, Pat. Ian Wakes Up. 2009. 28p. pap. 12.49 (978-1-4490-1213-7(2)) AuthorHouse.

Björkman, Steve. Dinosaurs Don't, Dinosaurs Do. Björkman, Steve, illus. 2012. (I Like to Read(r) Ser.). (ENG., Illus.). 24p. (J). (gr. -1-2). pap. 6.99 (978-0-8234-2640-9(8)) Holiday Hse., Inc.

Bland, Nick. The Runaway Hug. Blackwood, Freya, illus. 2013. (ENG.). 32p. (J). (gr. -1-2). 16.99 (978-0-449-81825-1(X), Random Hse. Bks. for Young Readers) Random Hse. Children's Bks.

Blessing, Victor. Santa Claus Got Sick Because. 2009. 24p. pap. 12.99 (978-1-4490-1126-0(8)) AuthorHouse.

Bloom, Becky. Leo & Lester. Biet, Pascal, illus. 2003. (J). 32p. 15.95 (978-1-59034-582-5(7)); 33p. pap. (978-1-59034-583-2(5)) Mondo Publishing.

Bowser, Ken. Homesick Penguin: Empathy/Caring for Others. Bowser, Ken, illus. 2014. (Funny Bone Readers: Being a Friend Ser.). (Illus.). 24p. (gr. -1-1). pap. 4.99 (978-1-939656-03-2(6)) Red Chair Pr.

Brown, Linnet. Keep Your Eyes on the Goal. 2013. 48p. pap. (978-1-4602-1828-0(0)) FriesenPress.

Bruce, David. Manners I. Care. Delehanty, Joan M., illus. 2006. 32p. (J). 16.95 (978-0-9771143-2-0(5)) Child LIfe Bks., LLC.

Buckley, Charlie. How to Wash Your Hands. 2007. (Show Jo Language Development Ser.). (Illus.). 16p. (J). (gr. -1-1). per., bds. 14.95 (978-1-933669-09-0(8)) Literary Architects, LLC.

Bunny, Hull. The Hidden Treasure. Fleming, Kye, illus. 2007. (Young Masters Ser.). (J). (gr. -1). 13.95 incl. audio compact disk (978-0-9721478-8-0(8)) BrassHeart Music.

Byrum, Isabel C. How John Became a Man Life Story of a Motherless Boy. 2005. reprint ed. pap. 15.95 (978-1-4179-0742-7(8)) Kessinger Publishing, LLC.

Catanzarite, Lisa. What the World Is Like to Bea Moore: The Treasure. Miller, Heidi, illus. 2009. 56p. pap. 17.26 (978-1-4251-6321-1(1)) Trafford Publishing.

Chambers, Robert W. The Purple Emperor. 2004. reprint ed. pap. 1.99 (978-1-4192-7947-8(5)); pap. 15.95 (978-1-4191-7947-1(0)) Kessinger Publishing, LLC.

Champier, Jacqueline. The Little Piggy Goes South. 2012. 28p. pap. 19.99 (978-1-4772-8976-1(3)) AuthorHouse.

Chi Omega - My First Board Book. 2006. (J). bds. 10.95 (978-0-9776627-1-5(3)) Captus, LLC.

Clark, Jeanne B. The Second Encounter: With the Snake Named Bully. 2012. 40p. pap. 24.99 (978-1-4772-1568-5(9)) AuthorHouse.

Coach B. Kingdom College. 2009. 48p. pap. 19.49 (978-1-4389-5181-2(7)) AuthorHouse.

Coates-Smith, Renee. Bobby's Secret Is Out. 2007. (Illus.). 43p. (J). 12.95 (978-0-615-14325-5(3)) Imani Productions.

Cochran, Jean M. Your Tummy's Talking! Gullens, Lee M., illus. 2008. (ENG.). 32p. (J). (gr. -1-k). 16.95 (978-0-9792035-3-4(8)) Pleasant St. Pr.

Consugar, Beth. Swanee Day. Rottinger, Amy, illus. 2013. 24p. pap. 12.95 (978-1-61244-176-4(9)) Halo Publishing International.

Crow, Marilee. A Pocketful of Manners. Snider, K. C., illus. 2011. 16p. pap. 9.95 (978-1-61633-176-4(3)) Guardian Angel Publishing, Inc.

Daly, Niki & Quarto Generic Staff. No More Kisses for Bernard! 2012. (ENG., Illus.). 32p. (J). (gr. -1-1). 17.99 (978-1-84780-105-0(6), Frances Lincoln) Quarto Publishing Group UK GBR. Dist: Hachette Bk. Group.

Davis, G. M. You Can Change Almost Anything! Go Challenge the Old Status Quo. 2013. 20p. pap. 12.45 (978-1-4908-0028-8(X), WestBow Pr.) Author Solutions, Inc.

Davis, Jacky & Soman, David. Super Catarina y los Super Insectos. Soman, David, illus. 2012. (Ladybug Girl Ser.).Tr. of Ladybug Girl & the Bug Squad. (ENG & SPA., Illus.). 40p. (J). (gr. -1-k). mass mkt. 6.99 (978-0-14-242582-4(6), Puffin Books) Penguin Young Readers Group.

Dean Van Scoyoc, Andrea. Graveyard katie & her Pals. 2008. 52p. pap. 20.00 (978-0-557-01337-1(2)) Lulu Pr., Inc.

Delta Delta Delta - My First Board Book. 2006. (J). bds. 10.95 (978-0-9776627-3-9(X)) Captus, LLC.

DiCicco, Sue. Manners. DiCicco, Sue, illus. 2010. (Illus.). 10p. 9.95 (978-1-60747-749-5(1), Pickwick Pr.) Phoenix Bks., Inc.

Dickens, Charles. Great Expectations. 2014. (Differentiated Timeless Classics Ser.). (ENG.). 80p. (YA). (gr. 9-12). 12.95 (978-1-62250-718-4(5)) Saddleback Educational Publishing, Inc.

Disney Sofia the First, Disney Sofia. Disney Sofia the First: Please & Thank You: Your Guide to Becoming the Perfect Princess! 2015. (ENG.). 32p. (J). (gr. -1-1). 10.99 (978-0-7944-3279-9(4), Reader's Digest Children's Bks.) Studio Fun International.

English, Karen. Nadia's Hands. Weiner, Jonathan, illus. 2009. (ENG.). 32p. (J). pap. 9.95 (978-1-59078-784-7(6)) Boyds Mills Pr.

Feder, Joel A. Kokomo Superhero. 2011. 32p. pap. 14.99 (978-1-4634-4748-9(5)) AuthorHouse.

Ferguson, Scott. The Itty Bitty It. Rudd, Benton, illus. 2012. 26p. pap. 9.99 (978-0-9858398-1-9(3)) Mindstir Media.

Fett, Ruth E. Goldilocks & the Three Bears: Baxter Bee Teaches about Respect. 2011. 24p. (gr. 1-2). 13.99 (978-1-4567-6192-9(7)) AuthorHouse.

Freeman, Emily. God Bless Your Way: A Christmas Journey. Burr, Dan, illus. 2007. 32p. (J). (gr. -1-3). 19.95 incl. audio compact disk (978-1-59038-806-8(2)) Deseret Bk. Co.

Galan, Ana. ¡Qué Cosas Dice Mi Abuela! 2013. (SPA.). 32p. (J). (gr. -1-3). 3.99 (978-0-545-32863-0(2), Scholastic en Espanol) Scholastic, Inc.

Gales, Rick. Granny Puckerlips: Keepin' It Real with Kindness & Respect. 2013. 108p. (gr. 9-12). 28.95 (978-1-4908-0438-5(2)); pap. 11.95 (978-1-4908-0437-8(4)) Author Solutions, Inc. (WestBow Pr.).

Gallegos, Eligio Stephen. Nothing Is Nothing. 2013. 144p. pap. 6.99 (978-0-944164-24-2(2)) Moon Bear Pr.

Gallo, Tina. Master of Manners. 2016. (Kung Fu Panda 8x8 Ser.). lib. bdg. 13.55 (978-0-606-38996-9(2)) Turtleback Bks.

Gilmore, Rachna. When-I-Was-a-Little-Girl, 1 vol. Benoit, Renne, illus. 2007. (ENG.). 24p. (J). (gr. -1-2). 14.95 (978-1-897187-12-8(2)) Second Story Pr. CAN. Dist: Orca Bk. Pubs. USA.

Goldberg, Barbara. Mindy's Passover Parsley. 2008. 24p. per. 24.95 (978-1-4241-9779-8(1)) America Star Bks.

Graham, Mary. Good Manners at the Table. 2017. (Manners Matter Ser.). 24p. (gr. 4-6). 23.60 **(978-1-5081-5730-4(8)**, PowerKids Pr.) Rosen Publishing Group, Inc., The.

Graham, Tamara. Little Miss Litterbug. 2008. 24p. pap. 12.99 (978-1-4389-2519-6(0)) AuthorHouse.

Greig, Elna. Bye-Bye! 2005. (Illus.). 16p. pap. 7.95 (978-1-932915-13-6(3)) Sandvik Publishing.

—Hello! 2005. (Illus.). 16p. pap. 7.95 (978-1-932915-12-9(5)) Sandvik Publishing.

Grimsdell, Jeremy. Bushbaby Night. 2006. (ENG., Illus.). 32p. per. 17.95 (978-1-77009-056-9(8)) Jacana Media ZAF. Dist: Independent Pubs. Group.

Hallinan, P. K. Let's Be Polite. (ENG., Illus.). (J). 2008. 24p. (gr. -1-3). lib. bdg. 8.99 (978-0-8249-5579-3(X)) 2004. 26p. bds. 8.75 (978-0-8249-6562-4(0)) Worthy Publishing. (Ideal Pubns.).

Hargreaves, Roger. Little Miss Quick. 2009. (Mr. Men & Little Miss Ser.). (ENG.). 32p. (J). (gr. -1-2). mass mkt. 3.99 (978-0-8431-8956-8(8), Price Stern Sloan) Penguin Young Readers Group.

—Mr. Nervous. 2009. (Mr. Men & Little Miss Ser.). (ENG.). 32p. (J). (gr. -1-2). mass mkt. 4.99 (978-0-8431-8957-5(6), Price Stern Sloan) Penguin Young Readers Group.

Harland, Richard. Worldshaker. 2010. (ENG.). 400p. (YA). (gr. 7-18). 16.99 (978-1-4169-9552-4(8), Simon & Schuster Bks. For Young Readers) Simon & Schuster Bks. For Young Readers.

Harris, Patrice. Grandma Asks: Were You Good at School Today? Harrison, Nicholas, illus. 2013. 26p. pap. 10.00 (978-0-9892358-5-3(8)) CLF Publishing.

Harvey, Keith. Oscar & the Magic Table: A Story about a Little Boy Who For got His Table Manners. 2015. (ENG., Illus.). 24p. pap. 8.99 (978-1-84135-922-9(X)) Award Pubns. Ltd. GBR. Dist: Parkwest Pubns., Inc.

Hawley, Richard And Elizabeth. There's a Monster in My Nose. Hawley, R. Spencer, illus. 2009. 36p. pap. 24.95 (978-1-61546-177-6(9)) America Star Bks.

Hickey, Barbara. Ms Sincerely Kind Goes Out & About: (Where Good Manners Matter) 2008. 76p. pap. 24.99 (978-1-4389-0851-9(2)) AuthorHouse.

Holliday, Anne. No More Puppet Shows. 2011. 20p. pap. 12.99 (978-1-4634-2354-4(3)) AuthorHouse.

Holm, Jennifer L. Wilderness Days. unabr. ed. 2004. (Boston Jane Ser.: No. 2). 288p. (J). (gr. 5-9). pap. 38.00 incl. audio (978-0-8072-0787-1(X), S YA 307 SP, Listening Library) Random Hse. Audio Publishing Group.

Jacober, Virginia. Trail Followers in India. 2013. pap. 12.95 (978-0-7414-8181-8(2)) Infinity Publishing.

Johnston, Annie Fellows. Mary Ware the Little Colonel's Chum. Barry, Etheldred B., illus. 2004. reprint ed. pap. 30.95 (978-1-4179-1704-4(0)) Kessinger Publishing, LLC.

Kappa Alpha Theta - My First Board Book. 2006. (J). bds. 10.95 (978-0-9776627-4-6(8)) Captus, LLC.

Kappa Delta - My First Board Book. 2006. (J). bds. 10.95 (978-0-9776627-5-3(6)) Captus, LLC.

Katz, Karin Jill. There's a Fly in My Soup. 2012. 16p. pap. 15.99 (978-1-4772-6331-0(4)) AuthorHouse.

Kimmelman, Leslie. Mind Your Manners, Alice Roosevelt!, 1 vol. Gustavson, Adam, illus. 2009. (ENG.). 32p. (J). (gr. -1-3). 16.95 (978-1-56145-492-1(3)) Peachtree Pubs.

Kirk, Katie. Eli, No! 2011. (ENG., Illus.). 32p. (J). (gr. -1-k). 14.95 (978-0-8109-8964-1(6), Abrams Bks. for Young Readers) Abrams, Inc.

Klempner, Rebecca. A Dozen Daises for Raizy: A Shavuos Story. Chava, illus. 2008. 30p. (J). (gr. -1-2). 10.95 (978-1-929628-41-4(2)) Hachai Publishing.

Krueger, T. W. Donkeys Are Special & So Are You! Bohart, Lisa, illus. 2013. (ENG.). 46p. (J). 12.99 (978-0-9887454-0-7(2)) Donkey Publishing.

Lagonegro, Melissa, et al. Sharing & Caring. RH Disney Staff et al, illus. 2014. (Pictureback(R) Ser.). (ENG.). 16p. (J). (gr. -1-2). 4.99 (978-0-7364-3334-1(1), RH/Disney) Random Hse. Children's Bks.

Lorraine, Loria. Wild about Manners. Bonnie, Spino, illus. 2013. 36p. 17.99 (978-0-9881889-1-4(0)) Piccolo Tales.

MacKey, Cindy. The Girl Who Blamed the World. Chiang, Shirley, illus. 2013. 50p. pap. 16.50 (978-0-9892699-0-2(6)) Cyrano Bks.

Madore, Michele. Rudee Goes Bananas for Manners. Gravitt, Bill, illus. 2006. (ENG.). 38p. (J). pap. 6.95 (978-0-615-17967-4(3)) Manners Toy Co., LLC.

Magi, Aria. The Lulilites: And the Star of Seven Rays. l.t. ed. 2005. (Illus.). 34p. (J). (gr. -1-3). 19.95 (978-0-9759631-0-4(4)) Lulilite Productions.

Manners I. Care. 2005. (J). pap. 5.99 (978-0-9771143-4-4(1)) Child LIfe Bks., LLC.

Marie, Tina. Isabella Learns Her Manners. 2011. 24p. 12.95 (978-1-4567-2000-1(7)) AuthorHouse.

Matchett, Gillian. The Adventures of Weston Super Cat with Activities. 2009. (Illus.). 92p. pap. 30.49 (978-1-4389-2241-6(8)) AuthorHouse.

Mcdoogle, Farrah. Thank You Day. 2014. (Daniel Tiger's Neighborhood Ready-To-Read Ser.). lib. bdg. 13.55 (978-0-606-35449-3(2)) Turtleback Bks.

McGuirk, Leslie & Von Bidder, Alex. Wiggens Learns His Manners at the Four Seasons Restaurant. McGuirk, Leslie, illus. 2009. (ENG., Illus.). 32p. (J). (gr. -1-2). 16.99 (978-0-7636-4014-9(X)) Candlewick Pr.

McLellan, Sean. The Red Booted Chicken. 2009. 48p. (J). pap. 17.49 (978-1-4389-5610-7(X)) AuthorHouse.

Meadows, Thomas. The Tales of Tommy Tucker: My Private Parts Are Private! 2013. 20p. pap. 13.77 (978-1-4669-8895-8(9)) Trafford Publishing.

Morel, John Henry. Is It True. 2009. 144p. 24.99 (978-1-935436-40-9(6)) Rodaian Pr.

Morrissey, Donna. What Beautiful Mistake Did You Make Today? 2012. 24p. pap. 13.95 (978-1-4772-5669-5(5)) AuthorHouse.

Mortensen, Lori. Dirty Gertie, 1 vol. Perry, Gina Marie, illus. 2009. (Read-It! Readers: Character Education Ser.). (ENG.). 32p. (gr. k-2). 21.32 (978-1-4048-4234-2(9), Easy Readers) Picture Window Bks.

Munson, Kyle Lloyd. The King They Call Dumm. 2008. 32p. per. 24.95 (978-1-60441-215-4(1)) America Star Bks.

Narsimhan, Mahtab. Mission Mumbai. 2016. (ENG.). 272p. (J). (gr. 4-7). 16.99 (978-0-545-74651-9(5), Scholastic Pr.) Scholastic, Inc.

Nicholson, Wanda. Mr Henry's Grass. Webb, Shamore, illus. 2008. 76p. pap. 20.95 (978-1-59800-665-0(7)) Outskirts Pr., Inc.

O'Connor, Jane. Apples Galore! 2013. (Fancy Nancy - I Can Read! Ser.). (J). lib. bdg. 13.55 (978-0-606-32150-1(0), Turtleback) Turtleback Bks.

—Fancy Nancy. Glasser, Robin Preiss, illus. 2005. (Fancy Nancy Ser.). 32p. (J). (gr. -1-3). 17.89 (978-0-06-054210-8(1)); (ENG.). 17.99 (978-0-06-054209-2(8)) HarperCollins Pubs.

—Fancy Nancy: Too Many Tutus. Glasser, Robin Preiss, illus. 2012. (I Can Read Level 1 Ser.). (ENG.). 32p. (J). (gr. -1-3). 16.99 (978-0-06-208308-1(2)) HarperCollins Pubs.

—Fancy Nancy & the Posh Puppy. Glasser, Robin Preiss, illus. 2007. (Fancy Nancy Ser.). 32p. (J). (gr. -1-2). (ENG.). 17.99 (978-0-06-054213-9(6)); lib. bdg. 18.89 (978-0-06-054215-3(2)) HarperCollins Pubs.

—Nancy la Elegante, 1 vol. Valenzuela, Liliana, tr. from ENG. Glasser, Robin Preiss, illus. 2008. (Fancy Nancy Ser.). (SPA.). 32p. (J). (gr. -1-2). 17.99 (978-0-06-143528-7(7)) HarperCollins Pubs.

—Too Many Tutus. Glasser, Robin Preiss, illus. 2012. (I Can Read Level 1 Ser.). (ENG.). 32p. (J). (gr. -1-3). pap. 3.99 (978-0-06-208307-4(4)) HarperCollins Pubs.

Olsen, Leigh & S. I. International. What Do You Say? A Book about Manners. 2009. (Playskool Ser.). (ENG.). 16p. (J). (gr. -1). pap. 6.99 (978-1-4169-8518-1(2), Simon Spotlight) Simon Spotlight.

Orozco, Maria. Lizards on 41st Street. 2011. 28p. pap. 13.59 (978-1-4567-2412-2(6)) AuthorHouse.

Parish, Scott. Tigre a la Mesa. 2005. 14p. (J). 10.00 (978-1-4116-6003-8(X)) Lulu Pr., Inc.

Pashilk, Meri. Pearl the Turtle. 2013. 32p. pap. 13.99 (978-1-4525-6658-0(5)) Balboa Pr.

Phillips, Dee. A Dream of America, 1 vol., Bk. 12. 2015. (Yesterday's Voices Ser.). (ENG.). 48p. (YA). (gr. 9-12). pap. 8.95 (978-1-62250-914-0(5)) Saddleback Educational Publishing, Inc.

Please! Thank You! (Book of Manners... Ser.). 32p. (978-1-4054-9481-6(6)) Parragon, Inc.

The Pledge of Allegiance. 2006. (J). bds. 7.95 (978-0-9776627-2-2(1)) Captus, LLC.

Prignano, Barbara. The Tiny Tomato & His Terrific Manners. Kalpart, illus. 2013. 32p. pap. 12.95 (978-1-62857-080-9(6), Strategic Bk. Publishing) Strategic Book Publishing & Rights Agency (SBPRA).

Racaniello, P. Emilia & Emma Say Please. 2011. 20p. pap. 9.99 (978-1-257-65455-0(1)) Lulu Pr., Inc.

—Emilia & Emma Say Sorry. 2012. 20p. pap. 9.99 (978-1-257-63118-6(7)) Lulu Pr., Inc.

—Emilia & Emma Say Thank You. 2012. 20p. pap. 9.99 (978-1-257-63119-3(5)) Lulu Pr., Inc.

Ricci, Christine. Dora's Book of Manners. Hall, Susan, illus. 2005. (Dora the Explorer Ser.: No. 7). 22p. (J). lib. bdg. 15.00 (978-1-59054-793-9(4)) Fitzgerald Bks.

Riddle, Sharon Kay & Sanders, Nancy/Ida. The King's Silverware. Lowe, Frank Allen, illus. 2007. 32p. (J). pap. 15.00 (978-0-9761583-5-6(3)) Olive Leaf Pubns.

Rodriguez, Emma Vera & Scogin, Connie. Blanca Rosa's Quinceaner. 2011. 34p. pap. 13.50 (978-1-60911-444-2(2), Eloquent Bks.) Strategic Book Publishing & Rights Agency (SBPRA).

Rose, Hayley. The Do's & Don'ts. 2013. 38p. 16.50 (978-1-939625-38-0(6)) Inkwell Books LLC.

Samoun, Abigail. How Penguin Says Please! Watts, Sarah, illus. 2015. (Little Traveler Ser.). (ENG & MUL.). 24p. (J). (gr. -1-k). bds. 6.95 (978-1-4549-1496-9(3)) Sterling Publishing Co., Inc.

—How Tiger Says Thank You! Watts, Sarah, illus. 2015. (Little Traveler Ser.). (ENG & MUL.). 22p. (J). (gr. -1-k). bds. 6.95 (978-1-4549-1497-6(1)) Sterling Publishing Co., Inc.

Santos, Gloria. Good Manners at the Library. 2017. (Manners Matter Ser.). 24p. (gr. 4-6). 23.60 **(978-1-5081-5728-1(6)**, PowerKids Pr.) Rosen Publishing Group, Inc., The.

Sateren, Shelley Swanson. Max & Zoe at the Library, 1 vol. Sullivan, Mary, illus. 2013. (Max & Zoe Ser.). (ENG.). 32p. (gr. k-2). pap. 5.19 (978-1-4048-8058-0(5), Max & Zoe) Picture Window Bks.

Scandora, Julie. Rules Are Rules. 2008. (ENG., Illus.). 32p. (gr. -1). 17.95 (978-1-887542-64-7(7)) Scandora.

Schaefer, Lola M. Please Pass the Manners! Mealtime Tips for Everyone. Lewis, Kellie, illus. 2009. (ENG.). 12p. (J). (gr. -1-1). 7.99 (978-1-4169-4826-1(0), Little Simon) Little Simon.

Shofner, Melissa Raé. Good Manners at the Playground. 2017. (Manners Matter Ser.). 24p. (gr. 4-6). 23.60 **(978-1-5081-5729-8(4)**, PowerKids Pr.) Rosen Publishing Group, Inc., The.

Sigma Kappa - My First Board Book. 2006. (J). bds. 10.95 (978-0-9776627-6-0(4)) Captus, LLC.

Smith, C. Michelle. Skeeter Uses Manners. Foreman, A., illus. 2010. 28p. pap. 17.36 (978-1-60888-017-1(6)) Nimble Bks. LLC.

Stanek, Robert, pseud. Bugville Critters Remember Their Manners. 2011. (Illus.). 46p. pap. 6.99 (978-1-57545-260-9(X), Reagent Pr. Bks. for Young Readers) RP Media.

—Remember Their Manners. 2010. 46p. pap. 11.99 (978-1-57545-177-0(8), Reagent Pr. Bks. for Young Readers) RP Media.

Taylor, Kyle. Friends That Care Always Share. 2012. 24p. pap. 14.93 (978-1-4669-4183-0(9)) Trafford Publishing.

Terrell, Andrea M. The Adventures of Sammy the Squirrel: Buying Shoes. Mitchell, Anthony W., illus. 2008. (ENG.). 28p. pap. 13.99 (978-1-4343-5608-6(6)) AuthorHouse.

Thaler, Mike. Earth Day from the Black Lagoon. Lee, Jared D., illus. 2013. 64p. (J). (978-0-545-47669-0(0)) Scholastic, Inc.

Tissot Lcsw, Jennifer. Grateful Gracie: A Story about Gratitude. Washburn, Cecilia, illus. 2013. 34p. pap. 14.95 (978-0-9882804-1-0(8)) Grateful Day Pr.

Toombs, Robert. Dottie the Bus Driver in Bicycle Safety. Barnett, Linda, illus. 2013. 24p. pap. 9.99 *(978-0-9885180-6-3(6))* Mindstir Media.

Tracy, Roseann. Do You Love Me When I Am Upside Down? 2008. 28p. pap. 12.99 *(978-1-4389-0503-7(3))* AuthorHouse.

Tym, Kate. Say Please. 2008. (Manners Ser.). (Illus.). 24p. (J). (gr. -1-1). lib. bdg. 16.95 *(978-1-59566-589-8(7))* QEB Publishing Inc.

VanDenhoven, Godelieve. Louis in Kindergarten. 2009. 40p. pap. 14.50 *(978-1-60693-752-5(9),* Eloquent Bks.) Strategic Book Publishing & Rights Agency (SBPRA).

Walton, Evangeline. The Misadventures of Rufus & Misha: Two Dogs Who Are Smart Enough to Go to School. 2013. 24p. pap. 14.93 *(978-1-4669-9970-1(5))* Trafford Publishing.

Weimer, Heidi R. How Do I Kiss You? Sharp, Chris, illus. 2008. (ENG.). 18p. (J). (gr. -1-k). bds. 12.99 *(978-0-8249-1814-9(2),* Ideal Pubns.) Worthy Publishing.

Williams, Felisha. I'm No Bully, Am I? 2012. 24p. (-18). pap. 15.99 *(978-1-4797-0973-1(5))* Xlibris Corp.

Wolek, Guy, illus. Dinner with OLIVIA. 2009. (Olivia TV Tie-In Ser.). (ENG.). 24p. (J). (gr. -1-2). pap. 3.99 *(978-1-4169-7187-0(4),* Simon Spotlight) Simon Spotlight.

Wong-Avery, Sally. Chinese Manners. 2007. (Illus.). (J). pap. *(978-0-9798874-0-6(2))* Tsui Wong-Avery, Sally.

Zima, Gordon. Sunbirds & Evergreens. 2006. (J). 16.00 *(978-0-9742894-5-8(0))* Hutton Electronic Publishing.

Zima, Gordon & Zima, Paula, illus. Sun Birds & Evergreens: The Nuk-Chuk Stories. 2005. (J). *(978-0-9742894-3-4(4))* Hutton Electronic Publishing.

MANPOWER POLICY

Canetti, Yanitzia. When Times Are Tough. Keating, Alison, tr. Willy, Romont, illus. 2009. 32p. (J). (gr. k-2). 8.99 *(978-1-59835-103-3(6))* Cambridge BrickHouse, Inc.

Haugen, David M. Unemployment. 2011. (Opposing Viewpoints Ser.). (ENG.). 224p. (gr. 12-12). lib. bdg. 48.80 *(978-0-7377-5247-2(5));* 240p. (J). pap. 29.45 *(978-0-7377-5248-9(3))* Cengage Gale. (Greenhaven Pr., Inc.)

Hill, Jeff. The WPA — Putting America to Work. 2013. (Defining Moments Ser.). (ENG.). 264p. lib. bdg. 55.00 *(978-0-7808-1331-1(6))* Omnigraphics, Inc.

Merino, Noël. Unemployment. Greenhaven Press Editors, ed. 2014. (Global Viewpoints Ser.). (ENG., Illus.). 224p. (gr. 10-12). lib. bdg. 46.20 *(978-0-7377-6916-6(5),* Greenhaven Pr., Inc.) Cengage Gale.

—Unemployment. Greenhaven Press Editors & Gale Editors, eds. 2014. (Global Viewpoints Ser.). (ENG., Illus.). 224p. (gr. 7-12). pap. 31.70 *(978-0-7377-6917-3(3),* Greenhaven Pr., Inc.) Cengage Gale.

Stewart, Sheila. When My Dad Lost His Job. (Kids Have Troubles Too Ser.). (Illus.). 48p. (YA). (gr. 5-18). 2010. lib. bdg. 19.95 *(978-1-4222-1703-0(5))* 2009. pap. 7.95 *(978-1-4222-1916-4(X))* Mason Crest.

MANTLE, MICKEY, 1931-1995

Marlin, John. Mickey Mantle. 2004. (Sports Heroes & Legends Ser.). (ENG., Illus.). 112p. (gr. 5-12). lib. bdg. 30.60 *(978-0-8225-1796-2(5))* Lerner Publishing Group.

Reis, Ronald A. Mickey Mantle. 2009. (Baseball Superstars Ser.). 136p. (gr. 6-12). pap. 11.95 *(978-0-7910-9900-1(8),* Checkmark Bks.) Facts On File, Inc.

Weinstein, Howard. Mickey Mantle. (Baseball Hall of Famers Ser.). 112p. (gr. 5-8). 2009. 63.90 *(978-1-61511-513-6(7))* 2004. (Illus.). lib. bdg. 34.60 *(978-0-8239-3782-0(8))* Rosen Publishing Group, Inc., The. (Rosen Reference).

Winter, Jonah. Mickey Mantle: The Commerce Comet. Payne, C. F., illus. 2017. (ENG.). 40p. (J). (gr. -1-3). 17.99 *(978-1-101-93352-7(6),* Schwartz & Wade Bks.) Random Hse. Children's Bks.

MANUFACTURES

see also Machinery; Waste Products

Abrams, Dennis. The Invention of the Moving Assembly Line. 2011. (Milestones in American History Ser.). (Illus.). 120p. (gr. 6-12). 35.00 *(978-1-60413-772-9(X),* Chelsea Hse.) Facts On File, Inc.

Andrews, Carolyn. What Are Goods & Services? 2008. (Economics in Action Ser.). (ENG., Illus.). 32p. (J). (gr. 3-7). pap. *(978-0-7787-4260-9(1))* Crabtree Publishing Co.

Bethea, Nikole Brooks. The Invention of the Assembly Line. 2017. (Engineering That Made America Ser.). (ENG.). 32p. (J). (gr. 3-6). lib. bdg. 28.50 *(978-1-5038-1636-7(2),* 211156) Child's World, Inc., The.

Cardenas, Ernesto A. Wholes & Parts. 2009. pap. 4.95 *(978-1-60698-078-1(5))* Milo Educational Bks. & Resources.

Carr, Aaron. Natural o Hecho Por el Hombre. 2013. (SPA., Illus.). 24p. (J). *(978-1-62127-607-4(4))* Weigl Pubs., Inc.

—Natural or Man-Made, with Code. 2012. (Science Kids Ser.). (ENG., Illus.). 24p. (J). (gr. -1-1). pap. 12.95 *(978-1-61913-757-8(7));* lib. bdg. 27.13 *(978-1-61913-087-6(4))* Weigl Pubs., Inc. (AV2 by Weigl).

CDs Super Glue & Salsa, 6 vols. 2004. (ENG.). 522.00 *(978-1-4144-0521-6(9),* UXL) Cengage Gale.

Gagne, Tammy. Teen Guide to Buying Goods & Services. 2014. (Illus.). 48p. (gr. 4-8). lib. bdg. 29.95 *(978-1-61228-472-9(8))* Mitchell Lane Pubs., Inc.

Giacobello, John. Choosing a Career in the Toy Industry. 2005. (World of Work Ser.). (Illus.). 64p. (YA). (gr. 7-12). lib. bdg. 31.95 *(978-0-8239-3438-6(1))* Rosen Publishing Group, Inc., The.

Greek, Joe. Incredible Projects Using 3D Printing, 1 vol. 2015. (ENG.). 48p. (YA). 30.25 *(978-1-4777-7946-0(9));* pap. 11.75 *(978-1-4777-7947-7(7))* Rosen Publishing Group, Inc., The. (Rosen Reference).

Houghton, Gillian. Goods & Services. 2009. (Invest Kids Ser.). 24p. (ENG., Illus.). (J). (gr. 2-5). pap. 8.25 *(978-1-4358-3210-7(8),* 1291654); (gr. 2-3). 42.50 *(978-1-61513-617-9(7));* (Illus.). (J). lib. bdg. 22.60 *(978-1-4358-2775-2(9),* 1291654) Rosen Publishing Group, Inc., The. (PowerKids Pr.).

Hustad, Douglas. How Can We Reduce Manufacturing Pollution? 2016. (Searchlight Books — What Can We Do about Pollution? Ser.). (ENG., Illus.). 40p. (J). (gr. 3-5). 30.65 *(978-1-4677-9518-0(6),* Lerner Pubns.) Lerner Publishing Group.

Johnson, Martin. Critical World Issues: Consumerism, Vol. 16. 2016. (Critical World Issues Ser.: Vol. 16). (ENG.). 112p. (J). (gr. 7-12). 25.95 *(978-1-4222-3650-5(1))* Mason Crest.

La Bella, Laura. What Are Goods & Services? 2016. (Let's Find Out! Ser.). (ENG.). 32p. (J). (gr. 3-2). lib. bdg. 24.45 *(978-1-68048-400-7(1))* Rosen Publishing Group, Inc., The.

Lafferty, Peter. How Things Are Made. 2004. (Knowledge Masters Plus Ser.). (Illus.). 32p. (YA). pap. incl. cd-rom *(978-1-903954-42-3(8),* Pavilion Children's Books) Pavilion Bks.

Manufacturing TCG. 3rd rev. ed. 2004. 48p. pap. *(978-0-86657-513-3(8))* Lab-Volt Systems, Inc.

Marsico, Katie. Working at a Factory. 2008. (21st Century Junior Library: Careers Ser.). (ENG., Illus.). 24p. (gr. 2-5). lib. bdg. 25.64 *(978-1-60279-268-5(2),* 200173) Cherry Lake Publishing.

Miller, Raymond H. Milton Bradley. 2004. (Inventors & Creators Ser.). (ENG., Illus.). 48p. (J). (gr. 4-7). lib. bdg. 27.50 *(978-0-7377-2613-8(X),* Greenhaven Pr., Inc.) Cengage Gale.

Mitten, Ellen. Consumers & Producers. 2011. (ENG., Illus.). 24p. (gr. k-2). pap. 8.95 *(978-1-61741-992-8(3))* Rourke Educational Media.

Nelson, Robin. What Do We Buy? A Look at Goods & Services. 2010. (Lightning Bolt Books — Exploring Economics Ser.). (ENG., Illus.). 32p. (gr. k-2). pap. 7.95 *(978-0-7613-5667-7(3));* lib. bdg. 26.60 *(978-0-7613-3913-7(2))* Lerner Publishing Group.

Prentzas, Scott. Gps. 2009. (21st Century Skills Library: Global Products Ser.). (ENG.). 32p. (gr. 4-8). lib. bdg. 28.50 *(978-1-60279-506-8(1),* 200321) Cherry Lake Publishing.

Reeves, Diane Lindsey. Career Ideas for Teens in Manufacturing. 2005. (Career Ideas for Teens Ser.). (Illus.). 192p. (gr. 6-12). 40.00 *(978-0-8160-5294-3(8),* Ferguson Publishing Co.) Facts On File, Inc.

—Manufacturing. 2017. (Bright Futures Press: World of Work Ser.). (ENG., Illus.). 32p. (J). (gr. 4-7). lib. bdg. 29.93 *(978-1-63472-627-6(8),* 209542) Cherry Lake Publishing.

Royston, Angela. Pencil. 2005. (How Are Things Made? Ser.). (Illus.). 32p. (J). *(978-0-431-05052-2(X));* tchr. ed. *(978-0-431-05045-4(7))* Steck-Vaughn.

Slavin, Bill. Transformed: How Everyday Things Are Made. Slavin, Bill, illus. (ENG., Illus.). 160p. (J). (gr. 3-7). 2007. pap. 18.95 *(978-1-55453-244-5(2))* 2005. 24.95 *(978-1-55337-179-3(8))* Kids Can Pr., Ltd. CAN. Dist: Hachette Bk. Group.

Turner, Donald R. & Tillema, Juliana O. Production of Goods & Services. 2011. (J). 244.80 *(978-1-4488-4860-7(1));* (J). pap. 12.95 *(978-1-4488-4721-1(4));* (YA). (gr. 5-9). lib. bdg. 31.95 *(978-1-4488-4711-2(7))* Rosen Publishing Group, Inc., The.

World Book, Inc Staff, contrib. by. Consumable Goods. 2008. (J). *(978-0-7166-1407-4(3))* World Bk., Inc.

MAO, TSE-TUNG, 1893-1976

see Mao, Zedong, 1893-1976

MAO, ZEDONG, 1893-1976

Gardner, April B. Mao: Boy of Stone. 2012. 24p. 24.95 *(978-1-4626-9867-7(0));* pap. 24.95 *(978-1-4626-8244-7(8))* America Star Bks.

Gay, Kathlyn. Mao Zedong's China. 2007. (Dictatorships Ser.). (ENG., Illus.). 160p. (gr. 9-12). lib. bdg. 38.60 *(978-0-8225-7285-5(0),* Twenty-First Century Bks.) Lerner Publishing Group.

Geyer, Flora. Mao Zedong: The Rebel Who Led a Revolution. 2007. (National Geographic World History Biographies Ser.). (ENG., Illus.). 64p. (J). (gr. 3-7). lib. bdg. 27.90 *(978-1-4263-0063-9(8),* National Geographic Children's Bks.) National Geographic Society.

Heuston, Kimberley. Mao Zedong. 2010. (Wicked History Ser.). (ENG.). 128p. (J). (gr. 6-12). pap. 5.95 *(978-0-531-22356-7(6),* Watts, Franklin) Scholastic Library Publishing.

Heuston, Kimberley Burton. Mao Zedong. 2010. (Wicked History Ser.). (ENG., Illus.). 128p. (J). (gr. 5-8). 31.00 *(978-0-531-20756-7(0))* Scholastic Library Publishing.

MacDonald, Fiona & Geyer, Flora. Mao Zedong: The Rebel Who Led a Revolution. 2007. (National Geographic World History Biographies Ser.). (ENG., Illus.). 64p. (J). (gr. 3-7). 17.95 *(978-1-4263-0062-2(X),* National Geographic Children's Bks.) National Geographic Society.

Malaspina, Ann. Mao Zedong & the Chinese Revolution. 2016. (People & Events That Changed the World Ser.). (ENG., Illus.). 128p. (J). (gr. 7-8). lib. bdg. 37.27 *(978-0-7660-7292-3(4))* Enslow Pubs., Inc.

MAORI (NEW ZEALAND PEOPLE)

Amery, Heather, et al. First Hundred Words in Maori. 2008. (MAO., Illus.). 40p. pap. 14.00 *(978-1-86969-304-6(3))* Huia Pubs. NZL. Dist: Univ. of Hawaii Pr.

Bekkering, Annalise. Great Lakes. 2012. (J). *(978-1-61913-526-0(4));* (Illus.). 32p. pap. *(978-1-61913-440-9(3))* Weigl Pubs., Inc.

Calman, Ross. The Treaty of Waitangi. 2014. (Illus.). 32p. pap. 20.00 *(978-1-877514-34-0(9))* Oratia Media NZL. Dist: Casemate Pubs. & Bk. Distributors, LLC.

McClellan, Ray. Maori Warriors. 2012. (History's Greatest Warriors Ser.). (ENG., Illus.). 24p. (J). (gr. 3-7). lib. bdg. 25.95 *(978-1-60014-745-6(3),* Torque Bks.) Bellwether Media.

Strudwick, Leslie. Maori. 32p. 2012. (Illus.). (J). *(978-1-61913-095-1(5))* 2005. pap. 9.95 *(978-1-59036-256-3(X))* 2004. (Illus.). (J). lib. bdg. 24.45 *(978-1-59036-221-1(7))* Weigl Pubs., Inc.

—Maori with Code. 2012. (World Cultures Ser.). (ENG., Illus.). 32p. (J). (gr. 3-7). pap. 13.95 *(978-1-61913-532-1(9),* AV2 by Weigl) Weigl Pubs., Inc.

Theunissen, Steve. The Maori of New Zealand. 2005. (First Peoples Ser.). (Illus.). 48p. (gr. 4-8). lib. bdg. 23.95 *(978-0-8225-0665-2(3))* Lerner Publishing Group.

World Book, Inc Staff, contrib. by. The Maori. 2009. (J). *(978-0-7166-2143-0(6))* World Bk., Inc.

MAORI (NEW ZEALAND PEOPLE)—FICTION

Alden, Raymond MacDonald. Once There Was a King: A Tournament of Stories. Copelman, Evelyn, illus. 2011. 194p. 42.95 *(978-1-258-08031-0(1))* Literary Licensing, LLC.

Barker, Stephen Elliot. The Secret of Spirits Bay. 2008. (Illus.). 224p. *(978-1-86950-725-1(8))* HarperCollins Pubs. Australia.

Dauphin, Vaya. The Greenstone Garden: The Elementals of Aotearoa, Vol. 2. 2013. viii, 297p. pap. *(978-1-74284-346-9(8))* ReadOnTime.

Dawe, Ted. Into the River. 2016. (ENG.). 304p. (J). (gr. 7). 17.99 *(978-1-943818-19-8(3))* Polis Bks.

Hollyer, Belinda. River Song. 2008. (ENG.). 198p. (J). (gr. 3-7). 16.95 *(978-0-8234-2149-7(X))* Holiday Hse., Inc.

Kapai, Tommy. Cuzzies Find the Rainbow's End. Henry, Mike, illus. 2004. (Cuzzies Adventures Ser.). (MAO & ENG.). 32p. (J). (gr. -1-3). pap. 9.00 *(978-0-9582517-0-9(3),* Kina) Huia Pubs. NZL. Dist: Univ. of Hawaii Pr.

—Cuzzies Meet the Motuhoa Shark. Henry, Mike, illus. 2006. (Cuzzies Adventures Ser.). (MAO & ENG.). 32p. (J). (gr. -1-3). pap. 9.00 *(978-1-86969-100-4(8))* Huia Pubs. NZL. Dist: Univ. of Hawaii Pr.

McConchie, Lyn. Winter of Waiting. 2015. (YA). (gr. 5-18). pap. 15.00 *(978-1-936021-55-0(2),* Banana Oil Bks.) Cyberwizard Productions.

Rolleston-Cummins, Toni. The Seven Stars of Matariki. Slade-Robinson, Nikki, illus. 28p. pap. 12.00 *(978-1-86969-327-5(2))* Huia Pubs. NZL. Dist: Univ. of Hawaii Pr.

Summer of Dreaming. 2010. (Illus.). 157p. (YA). pap. *(978-1-936021-22-2(6),* Banana Oil Bks.) Cyberwizard Productions.

Waerea, James. Pukunui. FireHydrant Creative Studios, ed. Waerea, James & Waerea, Mitch, illus. 2010. (ENG & MAO.). 26p. (J). pap. 14.95 *(978-0-9826066-0-5(5))* FireHydrant Creative Studios, Inc.

MAORI (NEW ZEALAND PEOPLE)—FOLKLORE

Croy, Anita. Myths & Legends of Australia, New Zealand, & Pacific Islands. 2015. (Illus.). 64p. (J). *(978-0-7166-2629-9(2))* World Bk., Inc.

MAP DRAWING

see also Atlases

Bandrova, Temenoujka, et al. Children Map the World Vol. 2: Selections from the Barbara Petchenik Children's World Map Competition. 2009. (ENG., Illus.). 136p. (J). pap. 29.95 *(978-1-58948-246-3(8),* ESRI Pr.) ESRI, Inc.

Burstein, John. Making Maps: Where's the Party? 2003. (Weekly Reader Early Learning Library). (Illus.). 24p. (J). (gr. k-4). pap. 8.15 *(978-0-8368-3826-8(2),* Weekly Reader Leveled Readers) Stevens, Gareth Publishing LLLP.

Green, Jen. A Village. 2016. (Mapping Ser.). (ENG., Illus.). 32p. (J). (gr. k-2). pap. 12.99 *(978-0-7502-9926-8(6),* Wayland) Hachette Children's Group GBR. Dist: Hachette Bk. Group.

Quinlan, Julia J. How to Draw a Map. 2012. (How to Use Maps Ser.). (ENG.). 24p. (J). (gr. 3-6). pap. 8.25 *(978-1-4488-6274-0(4),* PowerKids Pr.); lib. bdg. 22.60 *(978-1-4488-6158-3(6))* Rosen Publishing Group, Inc., The.

Torpie, Kate. Drawing Maps. 2008. (ENG., Illus.). 32p. (J). (gr. 1-4). pap. *(978-0-7787-4272-2(5))* Crabtree Publishing Co.

MAP-MAKING

see Cartography

MAPLE

George, Gale. The Life Cycle of a Maple Tree. 2015. (Watch Them Grow! Ser.). (ENG.). 24p. (J). (gr. 1-1). pap. 8.25 *(978-1-4994-0677-1(0),* PowerKids Pr.) Rosen Publishing Group, Inc., The.

Glaser, Rebecca. Maple Tree. 2012. (ENG., Illus.). 24p. (J). lib. bdg. 25.65 *(978-1-62031-026-7(0))* Jump! Inc.

Mitchell, Melanie. From Maple Tree to Syrup. (gr. k-3). 2012. (Start to Finish, Second Series: Food Ser.: No. 2). (ENG., Illus.). 24p. (J). lib. bdg. 23.93 *(978-0-7613-9181-4(9),* Lerner Pubns.) 2012. (Start to Finish, Second Series: Food Ser.: No. 2). (ENG., Illus.). 24p. pap. 6.95 *(978-1-58013-967-0(1))* 2004. pap. 5.95 *(978-0-8225-2144-0(X))* Lerner Publishing Group.

Moore, Elizabeth. Making Maple Syrup. 2011. (Wonder Readers Emergent Level Ser.). (ENG.). (gr. -1-1). 16p. pap. 35.94 *(978-1-4296-8124-7(1));* 32p. pap. 5.99 *(978-1-4296-7866-7(6))* Capstone Press of Coughlan Cos. (Wonder Readers).

Morgan, Emily R. Next Time You See a Maple Seed. 2014. (Next Time You See Ser.). (ENG.). 32p. (J). (gr. k-5). 12.95 *(978-1-938946-35-6(9))* National Science Teachers Assn.

Stockland, Patricia M. Look at a Maple Tree. 2012. (First Step Nonfiction - Look at Trees Ser.). (ENG., Illus.). 8p. (gr. -1-1). pap. 4.95 *(978-1-4677-0522-6(5),* Lerner Pubns.) Lerner Publishing Group.

MAPS

Here are entered works about maps. Works on the mapping of small areas and the drawing of maps in elementary schools are entered under Map Drawing. Works on the general science of map-making, including map projection and the mapping of large areas are entered under Cartography.

Aberg, Rebecca. Claves de Mapas. 2005. (Rookie Espanaol Geografia Ser.). (SPA & ENG., Illus.). 32p. (J). (gr. k-2). lib. bdg. 19.50 *(978-0-516-25242-1(9),* Children's Pr.) Scholastic Library Publishing.

Anderson, Wendy. Expeditions. 2007. (Action Numeracy Middle Primary Ser.). 32p. pap. 9.95 *(978-0-86431-646-2(1))* ACER Pr. AUS. Dist: ISBS Publisher Services.

Ashcroft, Minnie. Marvelous Map Activities for Young Learners. 2003. (ENG.). 64p. pap. 11.95 *(978-0-439-17887-7(6))* Scholastic, Inc.

The Atlas of the Seven Continents. (Illus.). (J). (gr. k-5). 148.75 *(978-0-8239-6996-8(7))* Rosen Publishing Group, Inc., The.

Autumn Publishing Staff, illus. World Map. 2004. (Wall Charts Ser.). (J). pap. 4.99 *(978-1-85997-235-9(7))* Byeway Bks.

Ball, Jacqueline A. & Ball, Jacqueline A. Mapping Earth. 2004. (Discovery Channel School Science Ser.). (Illus.). 32p. (gr. 4-8). lib. bdg. 26.00 *(978-0-8368-3382-9(1),* Gareth Stevens Learning Library) Stevens, Gareth Publishing LLLP.

Besel, Jennifer M. Compass Roses & Directions, 1 vol. 2013. (Maps Ser.). (ENG.). 24p. (gr. k-1). pap. 6.95 *(978-1-4765-3524-1(8),* Pebble Bks.); lib. bdg. 26.65 *(978-1-4765-3084-0(X),* Pebble Plus) Capstone Press of Coughlan Cos.

—Maps. 2013. (Maps Ser.). (ENG.). 24p. (gr. k-1). pap. 29.75 *(978-1-4765-3711-5(9),* Pebble Bks.); lib. bdg. 133.25 *(978-1-4765-3705-4(4),* Pebble Plus) Capstone Press of Coughlan Cos.

—Symbols & Keys, 1 vol. 2013. (Maps Ser.). (ENG.). 24p. (gr. k-1). 26.65 *(978-1-4765-3082-6(3),* Pebble Plus); pap. 6.95 *(978-1-4765-3522-7(1),* Pebble Bks.) Capstone Press of Coughlan Cos.

—Types of Maps, 1 vol. 2013. (Maps Ser.). (ENG.). 24p. (gr. k-1). 26.65 *(978-1-4765-3124-3(2),* Pebble Plus); pap. 6.95 *(978-1-4765-3525-8(6),* Pebble Bks.) Capstone Press of Coughlan Cos.

—What Is a Map?, 1 vol. 2013. (Maps Ser.). (ENG.). 24p. (gr. k-1). 26.65 *(978-1-4765-3081-9(5),* Pebble Plus); pap. 6.95 *(978-1-4765-3521-0(3),* Pebble Bks.) Capstone Press of Coughlan Cos.

Bluthenthal, Todd. The Equator. 2017. (Where on Earth? Mapping Parts of the World Ser.). 24p. (gr. 1-2). pap. 8.15 ***(978-1-4824-6421-4(7))*** Stevens, Gareth Publishing LLLP.

—Making Maps. 2017. (Where on Earth? Mapping Parts of the World Ser.). 24p. (gr. 1-2). pap. 8.15 ***(978-1-4824-6425-2(X))*** Stevens, Gareth Publishing LLLP.

Boothroyd, Jennifer. Map My Continent. 2013. (First Step Nonfiction - Map It Out Ser.). (ENG., Illus.). 24p. (gr. k-2). pap. 6.95 *(978-1-4677-1529-4(8));* lib. bdg. 23.93 *(978-1-4677-1114-2(4),* Lerner Pubns.) Lerner Publishing Group.

—Map My Country. 2013. (First Step Nonfiction - Map It Out Ser.). (ENG., Illus.). 24p. (gr. k-2). lib. bdg. 23.93 *(978-1-4677-1113-5(6),* Lerner Pubns.) Lerner Publishing Group.

—Map My Home. 2013. (First Step Nonfiction - Map It Out Ser.). (ENG., Illus.). 24p. (gr. k-2). pap. 6.95 *(978-1-4677-1530-0(1));* lib. bdg. 23.93 *(978-1-4677-1110-4(1),* Lerner Pubns.) Lerner Publishing Group.

—Map My Neighborhood. 2013. (First Step Nonfiction - Map It Out Ser.). (ENG., Illus.). 24p. (gr. k-2). pap. 6.95 *(978-1-4677-1531-7(X));* lib. bdg. 23.93 *(978-1-4677-1111-1(X),* Lerner Pubns.) Lerner Publishing Group.

—Map My Room. 2013. (First Step Nonfiction - Map It Out Ser.). (ENG., Illus.). 24p. (gr. k-2). pap. 6.95 *(978-1-4677-1532-4(8));* lib. bdg. 23.93 *(978-1-4677-1109-8(8),* Lerner Pubns.) Lerner Publishing Group.

—Map My State. 2013. (First Step Nonfiction - Map It Out Ser.). (ENG., Illus.). 24p. (gr. k-2). lib. bdg. 23.93 *(978-1-4677-1112-8(8),* Lerner Pubns.) Lerner Publishing Group.

Boswell, Kelly. Maps, Maps, Maps!, 1 vol. 2013. (Displaying Information Ser.). (ENG.). 32p. (gr. 1-2). 27.32 *(978-1-4765-0262-5(5));* pap. 8.95 *(978-1-4765-3339-1(3))* Capstone Press of Coughlan Cos. (Aplus Bks.).

Bredeson, Carmen. Mapas y Globos Terraqueos. 2005. (Rookie Espanaol Geografia Ser.). (ENG & SPA., Illus.). 32p. (J). (gr. k-2). lib. bdg. 19.50 *(978-0-516-25241-4(0),* Children's Pr.) Scholastic Library Publishing.

Brennan, Linda Crotta. Maps: What You Need to Know. 2017. (Fact Files Ser.). (ENG.). 24p. (gr. 1-2). lib. bdg. 25.32 ***(978-1-5157-8109-7(7),*** First Facts) Capstone Press of Coughlan Cos.

Cator, David. Map Symbols. 2009. (Real Life Readers Ser.). 16p. (gr. 2-3). pap. 7.05 *(978-1-4358-0075-5(3),* Rosen Classroom) Rosen Publishing Group, Inc., The.

Chancellor, Deborah. Maps & Mapping. 2011. (Discover Science Ser.). (ENG., Illus.). 56p. (J). (gr. k-3). pap. 7.99 *(978-0-7534-6718-3(6),* 9780753467183, Kingfisher) Roaring Brook Pr.

Chapman, Joan. Maps, Maps, Maps. 2006. (Rosen Real Readers Big Bookstm Ser.). (ENG.). 8p. (gr. k-1). 29.95 *(978-1-4042-6211-9(3))* Rosen Publishing Group, Inc., The.

Collins Maps Staff. United Kingdom: Wall Map. 2014. (ENG.). 448p. (J). (gr. -1). pap. 12.99 ***(978-0-00-753612-2(7))*** HarperCollins Pubs. Ltd. GBR. Dist: Independent Pubs. Group.

Comire, S. Joshua & Porter, Malcolm. Atlas of Australia & the Pacific. 2009. (Atlases of the World Ser.). (Illus.). 48p. (YA). (gr. 5-8). 29.25 *(978-1-4358-8456-4(6),* Rosen Reference) Rosen Publishing Group, Inc., The.

Como Ser un Experto en Mapas. (Coleccion Ciencia y Proyectos). (SPA., Illus.). (YA). (gr. 5-8). pap. *(978-950-724-562-6(6),* LMA8239) Lumen ARG. Dist: Lectorum Pubns., Inc.

Cooke, Tim. The Changing Face of Maps. 2017. 32p. (J). ***(978-0-7787-3221-1(5))*** Crabtree Publishing Co.

Cooke, Tim. Maps Today. 2010. (Understanding Maps of Our World Ser.). 48p. (YA). (gr. 4-7). lib. bdg. 31.00 *(978-1-4339-3521-3(X));* (Illus.). (J). (gr. 6-8). pap. 14.05 *(978-1-4339-3522-0(8),* Gareth Stevens Secondary Library) Stevens, Gareth Publishing LLLP.

Cooper, Alison & McRae, Anne. The Children's Pictorial Atlas of the World. De Luca, Daniela, illus. 2008. (ENG.). 45p. (J). (gr. -1-3). 17.95 *(978-88-88166-05-6(X))* McRae Bks. Srl ITA. Dist: Independent Pubs. Group.

Corporate Contributor Staff & O'Brien, Cynthia. Climate Maps. 2012. (ENG.). 32p. (J). pap. *(978-0-7787-4496-2(5));* lib. bdg. *(978-0-7787-4491-7(4))* Crabtree Publishing Co.

Corporate Contributor Staff & Pegis, Jessica. Political Maps. 2012. (ENG.). 32p. (J). pap. *(978-0-7787-4498-6(1));* lib. bdg. *(978-0-7787-4493-1(0))* Crabtree Publishing Co.

Corporate Contributor Staff & Rodger, Ellen. Physical Maps. 2012. (ENG.). 32p. (J). pap. *(978-0-7787-4497-9(3));* lib. bdg. *(978-0-7787-4492-4(2))* Crabtree Publishing Co.

Cunningham, Kevin. Reading Maps. 2012. (True Book(tm), a — Information Literacy Ser.). (ENG., Illus.). 48p. (J). lib. bdg. 31.00 *(978-0-531-26006-7(2));* pap. 6.95 *(978-0-531-26237-5(5))* Scholastic Library Publishing.

—Types of Maps. 2012. (True Book(tm), a — Information Literacy Ser.). (ENG.). 48p. (J). lib. bdg. 31.00 *(978-0-531-26007-4(0));* pap. 6.95 *(978-0-531-26238-2(3))* Scholastic Library Publishing.

Dispenzio, Michael A. Map Mania: Discovering Where You Are & Getting to Where You Aren't. Garbot, Dave, illus. 2006. 80p. (J). (gr. 4-8). reprint ed. 20.00 *(978-0-7567-9893-2(0))* DIANE Publishing Co.

Edson, Ann & Insel, Eunice. Reading Maps, Globes, Charts, Graphs. (J). (gr. 4-6). stu. ed., instr.'s gde. ed. 39.00 incl. audio *(978-0-89525-175-6(2),* AKC 356) Educational Activities, Inc.

Endres, Hollie J. The Letter Rr Set, 6 vols. Maps. 2004. (Letter Bks.). (ENG.). 8p. (gr. k-1). pap. 29.70 (978-0-7368-4117-7(2), Letter Bks.) Capstone Press of Coughlan Cos.

Facts on File, Inc. Staff. Maps on File. 2nd rev. ed. 2012. (Maps on File Ser.). (gr. 6-12). 250.00 (978-0-8160-8478-4(5)) Facts On File, Inc.

Fun with Map Skills. 2014. (Fun with Map Skills Ser.). 32p. (J). (gr. 3-6). 157.50 (978-1-4777-6985-0(4), PowerKids Pr.) Rosen Publishing Group, Inc., The.

Furgang, Kathy. Zoom in on Physical Maps. 2017. (J). **(978-0-7660-9219-8(4))** Enslow Pubs., Inc.

—Zoom in on Political Maps. 2017. (J). **(978-0-7660-9220-4(8))** Enslow Pubs., Inc.

—Zoom in on Road Maps. 2017. (J). **(978-0-7660-9223-5(2))** Enslow Pubs., Inc.

—Zoom in on Topographic Maps. 2017. (J). **(978-0-7660-9221-1(6))** Enslow Pubs., Inc.

George, Bobby, et al. Montessori: Map Work. 2014. (Montessori Ser.). (ENG., Illus.). 20p. (J). (gr. -1-k). bds. 9.95 (978-1-4197-0934-0(8), Abrams Appleseed) Abrams, Inc.

Gillis, Jennifer B. You Are Here. 2006. (My Neighborhood Ser.). (Illus.). 24p. (gr. k-2). 18.00 (978-0-7569-6931-8(X)) Perfection Learning Corp.

Gillis, Jennifer Blizin. Estas Aqui/You Are Here. Duque, Olga, tr. 2006. (My Neighborhood Discovery Library). (SPA & ENG., Illus.). 24p. (J). (gr. 3-7). lib. bdg. 22.79 (978-1-60044-294-0(3)) Rourke Educational Media.

Gonzales, Doreen. Up North & down South: Using Map Directions. 2016. (Map Mania Ser.). (ENG.). 24p. (gr. 1-2). pap. 7.29 (978-1-5157-4219-7(9), First Facts) Capstone Press of Coughlan Cos.

Greve, Meg. Keys & Symbols on Maps. 2009. (ENG., Illus.). 24p. (gr. k-2). pap. 8.95 (978-1-60694-535-3(1)) Rourke Educational Media.

—Maps Are Flat, Globes Are Round. 2009. (ENG., Illus.). 24p. (gr. k-2). pap. 8.95 (978-1-60694-533-9(5)) Rourke Educational Media.

Hammond World Atlas Corporation Staff, ed. Globes in a Box. 2008. (Hammond Ser.). 64p. (J). (gr. 5-18). 19.95 (978-0-8437-1825-6(0)) Hammond World Atlas Corp.

—Planet Earth: Our Planet as You've Never Seen It Before. 2008. 168p. (J). (gr. 3-7). 19.99 (978-0-8437-1834-8(X)) Hammond World Atlas Corp.

Henzel, Cynthia Kennedy. Classifying Maps, 1 vol. 2008. (On the Map Ser.). (ENG.). 32p. (gr. k-6). 27.07 (978-1-59928-948-9(2), Checkerboard Library) ABDO Publishing Co.

—Reading Maps, 1 vol. 2008. (On the Map Ser.). (ENG.). 32p. (gr. k-6). 27.07 (978-1-59928-953-3(9), Checkerboard Library) ABDO Publishing Co.

Hewitt, Sally. Maps. 2010. (Starting Geography Ser.). 32p. (J). (gr. 2-5). 28.50 (978-1-60753-126-5(7)) Amicus Publishing.

—Maps. 2012. (Deadly & Incredible Animals Ser.). 32p. (gr. 2-6). 27.10 (978-1-59920-412-3(6)) Black Rabbit Bks.

Hibbert, Clare. Around the World in 80 Maps. 2017. (ENG., Illus.). 96p. (J). (gr. 3-7). 19.95 **(978-0-2281-0010-2(0)**, 9780228100102) Firefly Bks., Ltd.

Hicer, Nancy. Maps & New York City. 2011. (My Community Ser.). 12p. (gr. 2-2). pap. 6.95 (978-1-4488-5732-6(5)) Rosen Publishing Group, Inc., The.

Hirsch, Rebecca E. Using Climate Maps. 2016. (Searchlight Books (tm) — What Do You Know about Maps? Ser.). (ENG., Illus.). 40p. (J). (gr. 3-5). 30.65 (978-1-5124-0950-5(2)) Lerner Publishing Group.

—Using Physical Maps. 2016. (Searchlight Books (tm) — What Do You Know about Maps? Ser.). (ENG., Illus.). 40p. (J). (gr. 3-5). 30.65 (978-1-5124-0949-9(9)) Lerner Publishing Group.

—Using Political Maps. 2016. (Searchlight Books (tm) — What Do You Know about Maps? Ser.). (ENG., Illus.). 40p. (J). (gr. 3-5). 30.65 (978-1-5124-0947-5(2)) Lerner Publishing Group.

Hoe, Susan C. Environments. 2008. (Maps & Mapping Ser.). 32p. (gr. 1-5). pap. 10.50 (978-0-8368-9331-1(X), Gareth Stevens Learning Library) Stevens, Gareth Publishing LLLP.

—Habitats. 2008. (Maps & Mapping Ser.). 32p. (gr. 1-5). (J). lib. bdg. 26.00 (978-0-8368-9205-5(4)); pap. 10.50 (978-0-8368-9332-8(8)) Stevens, Gareth Publishing LLLP. (Gareth Stevens Learning Library).

—Resources. 2008. (Maps & Mapping Ser.). 32p. (gr. 1-5). (J). lib. bdg. 26.00 (978-0-8368-9206-2(2)); pap. 10.50 (978-0-8368-9333-5(6)) Stevens, Gareth Publishing LLLP. (Gareth Stevens Learning Library).

—Where We Live. 2008. (Maps & Mapping Ser.). 32p. (gr. 1-5). pap. 10.50 (978-0-8368-9334-2(4), Gareth Stevens Learning Library) Stevens, Gareth Publishing LLLP.

Hoe, Susan C. & Hoe, Susan C. Environments. 2008. (Maps & Mapping Ser.). 32p. (J). (gr. 1-5). lib. bdg. 26.00 (978-0-8368-9204-8(6), Gareth Stevens Learning Library) Stevens, Gareth Publishing LLLP.

—Where We Live. 2008. (Maps & Mapping Ser.). 32p. (J). (gr. 1-5). lib. bdg. 26.00 (978-0-8368-9207-9(0), Gareth Stevens Learning Library) Stevens, Gareth Publishing LLLP.

Hollingum, Ben. Travel Maps. 2010. (Understanding Maps of Our World Ser.). (Illus.). 48p. (YA). (gr. 4-7). lib. bdg. 31.00 (978-1-4339-3506-0(6)); (J). (gr. 6-8). pap. 14.05 (978-1-4339-3507-7(4), Gareth Stevens Secondary Library) Stevens, Gareth Publishing LLLP.

—Understanding Maps of Our World: Maps & Mapping the World. 2010. (Understanding Maps of Our World Ser.). 48p. (YA). (gr. 4-7). lib. bdg. 31.00 (978-1-4339-3498-8(1)); (Illus.). (gr. 6-8). pap. 14.05 (978-1-4339-3501-5(5), Gareth Stevens Secondary Library) Stevens, Gareth Publishing LLLP.

Home & School. (J). (gr. k-1). (978-84-342-2416-2(X), PR30570) Parramon Ediciones S.A. ESP. Dist: Lectorum Pubns., Inc.

Home & School. (J). (gr. 1). 3.80 (978-0-8374-1450-8(4), 401) Weekly Reader Corp.

Hudak, Heather C. Mapping. 2007. (Social Studies Essential Skills Ser.). (Illus.). 24p. (J). (gr. 4-7). lib. bdg. 24.45 (978-1-59036-761-2(8)); per. 8.95 (978-1-59036-762-9(6)) Weigl Pubs., Inc.

In the World. (J). (gr. 6). 3.80 (978-0-8374-1455-3(5), 406) Weekly Reader Corp.

Jennings, Ken. Maps & Geography. Lowery, Mike, illus. 2014. (Ken Jennings' Junior Genius Guides). (ENG.). 160p. (J). (gr. 3-5). pap. 7.99 (978-1-4424-7328-7(2), Little Simon) Little Simon.

Kachur, Matthew. Making Maps: Set Of 6. 2011. (Navigators Ser.). (J). pap. 48.00 net. (978-1-4108-0416-7(X)) Benchmark Education Co.

Kalman, Bobbie. Rapping about Directions on Earth. 2012. (ENG.). 24p. (J). (978-0-7787-2796-5(3)); pap. (978-0-7787-2803-0(X)) Crabtree Publishing Co.

Kalz, Jill. Farm Adventure. Cerato, Mattia, illus. 2010. (A-MAZE-Ing Adventures Ser.). (ENG.). 32p. (gr. 1-2). lib. bdg. 26.65 (978-1-4048-6038-4(X)) Picture Window Bks.

—School Adventure. Cerato, Mattia, illus. 2010. (A-MAZE-Ing Adventures Ser.). (ENG.). 32p. (gr. 1-2). lib. bdg. 26.65 (978-1-4048-6039-1(8)) Picture Window Bks.

—Zoo Adventure. Cerato, Mattia, illus. 2010. (A-MAZE-Ing Adventures Ser.). (ENG.). 32p. (gr. 1-2). lib. bdg. 26.65 (978-1-4048-6024-7(X)) Picture Window Bks.

Klimchuk, Karen. Manuel Makes a Map! 2013. (Rosen Readers Ser.). (ENG.). 24p. (J). (gr. 2-3). pap. 8.25 (978-1-4777-2319-7(6)); pap. 49.50 (978-1-4777-2320-3(X)) Rosen Publishing Group, Inc., The. (Rosen Classroom).

Lawson, Barbara Spilman. Maps Show Where to Go. 2016. (Spring Forward Ser.). (J). (gr. 2). (978-1-4900-2245-1(7)) Benchmark Education Co.

Leithauser, Jessica. Maps Show Us the Way. 2006. (Rosen Real Readers Big Bookstm Ser.). (ENG., Illus.). 12p. (gr. 1-2). 33.50 (978-1-4042-6218-8(0)) Rosen Publishing Group, Inc., The.

Leithauser, Jessica & National Geographic Learning Staff. Maps Show Us the Way. 2012. (ENG., Illus.). 12p. (C). (gr. 1-2). pap. 9.95 (978-0-8239-6357-7(8)) National Geographic School Publishing, Inc.

Levy, Janey. Mapping Australia. 2013. 24p. (J). (gr. 2-5). 22.60 (978-1-4339-9104-2(7)) Stevens, Gareth Publishing LLLP.

—The Silk Road: Using a Map Scale to Measure Distances. 2009. (PowerMath Ser.). (ENG., Illus.). 32p. (gr. 5-6). pap. 10.00 (978-1-4042-5140-3(5)) Rosen Publishing Group, Inc., The.

—The Silk Road: Using A Map Scale to Measure Distances. 2005. (PowerMath Ser.). (Illus.). 32p. (J). (gr. 3-6). lib. bdg. 23.95 (978-1-4042-2938-9(8), PowerKids Pr.) Rosen Publishing Group, Inc., The.

Lierman, Jane. Standards-Based Map Activities: Easy & Engaging Lessons, Activities, & Practice Pages That Build Key Map & Geography Skills. 2005. (ENG., Illus.). 64p. (gr. 3-5). per. 14.99 (978-0-439-51774-4(5), Teaching Resources) Scholastic, Inc.

Linde, Barbara. Mapping Europe. 2013. (Mapping the World Ser.). 24p. (J). (gr. 2-5). pap. 48.90 (978-1-4339-9111-0(X)); (ENG., Illus.). pap. 8.15 (978-1-4339-9110-3(1)) Stevens, Gareth Publishing LLLP.

Linde, Barbara & Linde, Barbara M. Mapping Europe. 2013. 24p. (J). (gr. 2-5). 22.60 (978-1-4339-9109-7(8)) Stevens, Gareth Publishing LLLP.

Linde, Barbara M. Mapping Africa. 2013. (Mapping the World Ser.). 24p. (J). (gr. 2-5). pap. 48.90 (978-1-4339-9091-5(1)); (Illus.). 22.60 (978-1-4339-9089-2(X)); (Illus.). pap. 8.15 (978-1-4339-9090-8(3)) Stevens, Gareth Publishing LLLP.

—Mapping Asia. 2013. 24p. (J). (gr. 2-5). 22.60 (978-1-4339-9099-1(7)); pap. 8.15 (978-1-4339-9100-4(4)); pap. 48.90 (978-1-4339-9101-1(2)) Stevens, Gareth Publishing LLLP.

Lonely Planet, et al. MY FAMILY TRAVEL MAP, 1 vol. 2016. (Lonely Planet Kids Ser.). (ENG., Illus.). 16p. (J). pap. 14.99 (978-1-76034-101-5(0), 5185) Lonely Planet Pubns.

Lucas, Bruce. North America on the Map. 2013. (InfoMax Readers Ser.). (ENG.). 24p. (J). (gr. 2-3). pap. 49.50 (978-1-4777-2432-3(X)); (Illus.). pap. 8.25 (978-1-4777-2431-6(1)) Rosen Publishing Group, Inc., The. (Rosen Classroom).

MacReady, R. J. We Can Use a Map. 2012. (InfoMax Readers Ser.). (ENG., Illus.). 16 pp.p. (J). (gr. k-1). pap. 7.00 (978-1-4488-8935-8(9), Rosen Classroom) Rosen Publishing Group, Inc., The.

Mahaney, Ian F. Climate Maps. 2009. (Map It! Ser.). 24p. (gr. 3-4). 42.50 (978-1-61514-354-2(8), PowerKids Pr.) Rosen Publishing Group, Inc., The.

—Physical Maps. (Map It! Ser.). 24p. 2009. (gr. 3-4). 42.50 (978-1-61514-355-9(6), PowerKids Pr.) 2006. (Illus.). (YA). (gr. 2-5). lib. bdg. 22.60 (978-1-4042-3054-5(8)) Rosen Publishing Group, Inc., The.

—Political Maps. (Map It! Ser.). 24p. 2009. (gr. 3-4). 42.50 (978-1-61514-356-6(4), PowerKids Pr.) 2006. (Illus.). (YA). (gr. 2-5). lib. bdg. 22.60 (978-1-4042-3055-2(6)) Rosen Publishing Group, Inc., The.

—Road Maps. 2009. (Map It! Ser.). 24p. (gr. 3-4). 42.50 (978-1-61514-357-3(2), PowerKids Pr.) Rosen Publishing Group, Inc., The.

—Topographic Maps. (Map It! Ser.). 24p. 2009. (gr. 3-4). 42.50 (978-1-61514-358-0(0), PowerKids Pr.) 2006. (Illus.). (YA). (gr. 2-5). lib. bdg. 22.60 (978-1-4042-3053-8(X)) Rosen Publishing Group, Inc., The.

—Weather Maps. 2009. (Map It! Ser.). 24p. (gr. 3-4). 42.50 (978-1-61514-359-7(9), PowerKids Pr.) Rosen Publishing Group, Inc., The.

Make It Work Geography, 4 vol. set. 2003. (gr. 4-8). 59.00 (978-0-7166-5124-6(6)) World Bk., Inc.

Map Basics. 2014. (Map Basics Ser.). 24p. (J). (gr. 2-5). 135.60 (978-1-4824-1062-4(1)); pap. 48.90 (978-1-4824-1573-5(9)) Stevens, Gareth Publishing LLLP.

Map Mysteries, 6 vols., Pack. (gr. k-1). 23.00 (978-0-7635-9071-0(1)) Rigby Education.

Map Skills for Today Gr. 1 -revised 2003- rev. ed. 2003. (YA). (978-0-8374-0000-6(7)) Weekly Reader Corp.

Mapping Antarctica. 2013. (Mapping the World Ser.). 24p. (J). (gr. 2-5). pap. 48.90 (978-1-4339-9096-0(2)) Stevens, Gareth Publishing LLLP.

Mapping Australia. 2013. (Mapping the World Ser.). 24p. (J). (gr. 2-5). pap. 48.90 (978-1-4339-9106-6(3)) Stevens, Gareth Publishing LLLP.

Mapping Specialists. US & World Map Outlines, Vol. 8305. 2004. (Power Practice Ser.). (Illus.). 128p. (J). pap. 12.99 (978-1-59198-075-9(5), 8305) Creative Teaching Pr., Inc.

Mapping the World. 2013. (Mapping the World Ser.). 24p. (J). (gr. 2-5). 158.20 (978-1-4339-9674-0(X)); pap. 342.30 (978-1-4339-9760-0(6)); pap. 57.05 (978-1-4339-9759-4(2)) Stevens, Gareth Publishing LLLP.

Matteson, Adrienne. Using Digital Maps. Petelinsek, Kathleen, illus. 2013. (Explorer Library: Information Explorer Ser.). (ENG.). 32p. (J). (gr. 4-8). 28.50 (978-1-62431-129-1(6), 202836); pap. 14.21 (978-1-62431-261-8(6), 202838) Cherry Lake Publishing.

Maurer, Tracy Nelson. Using Economic & Resource Maps. 2016. (Searchlight Books (tm) — What Do You Know about Maps? Ser.). (ENG., Illus.). 40p. (J). (gr. 3-5). 30.65 (978-1-5124-0951-2(0)) Lerner Publishing Group.

—Using Road Maps & GPS. 2016. (Searchlight Books (tm) — What Do You Know about Maps? Ser.). (ENG., Illus.). 40p. (J). (gr. 3-5). 30.65 (978-1-5124-0952-9(9)) Lerner Publishing Group.

—Using Topographic Maps. 2016. (Searchlight Books (tm) — What Do You Know about Maps? Ser.). (ENG., Illus.). 40p. (J). (gr. 3-5). 30.65 (978-1-5124-0948-2(0)) Lerner Publishing Group.

McAneney, Caitlin. The Compass Rose & Cardinal Directions. 2014. (Map Basics Ser.). 24p. (J). (gr. 2-5). 22.60 (978-1-4824-1083-9(4)) Stevens, Gareth Publishing LLLP.

McKay, Sindy. We Both Read-My Town. Johnson, Meredith, illus. 2007. (We Both Read Ser.). 44p. (J). (gr. -1-2). 9.95 (978-1-60115-001-1(6)); pap. 4.99 (978-1-60115-002-8(4)) Treasure Bay, Inc.

McRae, Anne. The Animal Atlas. De Luca, Daniela, illus. 2008. (ENG.). 29p. (J). (gr. -1-3). 16.95 (978-88-88166-38-4(6)) McRae Bks. Srl ITA. Dist: Independent Pubs. Group.

Meachen Rau, Dana. Los Mapas. 2008. (Planeta Es Importante Ser.). (SPA.). 32p. (gr. 1-2). lib. bdg. 15.95 (978-0-7614-3468-9(2), Benchmark Bks.) Marshall Cavendish Corp.

—Maps. 2008. (Earth Matters Ser.). 32p. (gr. 1-2). lib. bdg. 15.95 (978-0-7614-3046-9(6), Benchmark Bks.) Marshall Cavendish Corp.

—Maps/Los Mapas. 2008. (Earth Matters/El Planeta Es Importante Ser.). (SPA & ENG.). 32p. (gr. k-1). lib. bdg. 15.95 (978-0-7614-3493-1(3), Benchmark Bks.) Marshall Cavendish Corp.

Meister, Cari. Lost Treasure of Larry Longfoot: Learning to Use a Map. Record, Adam, illus. 2013. (Take It Outside Ser.). (ENG.). 24p. (gr. k-2). 27.32 (978-1-4048-8305-5(3)); pap. 8.95 (978-1-4795-1935-4(9)) Picture Window Bks.

Meredith, Susan Markowitz. Maps Are Useful. 2016. (Spring Forward Ser.). (J). (gr. 2). (978-1-4900-9431-1(8)) Benchmark Education Co.

Michele, Tracey. Follow the Road Map. 2011. (Learn-Abouts Ser.). (Illus.). 16p. (J). pap. 7.95 (978-1-59920-638-7(2)) Black Rabbit Bks.

Miles, Justin. Ultimate Mapping Guide for Kids. 2016. (ENG., Illus.). 96p. (J). (gr. 5-8). pap. 9.95 (978-1-77085-741-4(9), 9781770857414) Firefly Bks., Ltd.

Mizielinska, Aleksandra & Mizielinski, Daniel. Maps. 2013. (ENG.). 112p. (J). (gr. k-12). 35.00 (978-0-7636-6896-9(6), Big Picture Press) Candlewick Pr.

—Maps Activity Book. 2015. (ENG., Illus.). 72p. (J). (gr. 2-5). 14.99 (978-0-7636-7771-8(X), Big Picture Press) Candlewick Pr.

—Maps Poster Book. 2016. (ENG.). 56p. (J). (gr. 2-4). 22.00 (978-0-7636-8835-6(5), Big Picture Press) Candlewick Pr.

Morris, Neil. The Atlas of Ancient Civilizations. De Luca, Daniela, illus. 2008. (ENG.). 28p. (J). (gr. -1-3). 17.95 (978-88-900466-0-5(0)) McRae Bks. Srl ITA. Dist: Independent Pubs. Group.

Neighborhood. (J). (gr. 2). 3.80 (978-0-8374-1451-5(2), 402) Weekly Reader Corp.

Nelson, Robin & National Geographic Learning Staff. Maps. 2012. (ENG.). 8p. (C). (gr. -1-1). pap. 7.95 (978-0-8225-5393-9(7)) National Geographic School Publishing, Inc.

Oleksy, Walter. Maps in History. 2003. (Watts Library). (ENG., Illus.). 64p. (J). (gr. 5-7). pap. 8.95 (978-0-531-16633-8(3), Watts, Franklin) Scholastic Library Publishing.

Olien, Rebecca. Looking at Maps & Globes. 2012. (Rookie Read-About(tm) Geography — Map Skills Ser.). (ENG., Illus.). 32p. (J). lib. bdg. 25.00 (978-0-531-28964-8(8)); (gr. -1-1). pap. 5.95 (978-0-531-29288-4(6)) Scholastic Library Publishing.

—Map Keys. 2012. (Rookie Read-About(tm) Geography — Map Skills Ser.). (ENG.). 32p. (J). lib. bdg. 25.00 (978-0-531-28965-5(6)); pap. 5.95 (978-0-531-29289-1(4)) Scholastic Library Publishing.

On the Right Track, 6, Pack. (gr. k-1). 23.00 (978-0-7635-9070-3(3)) Rigby Education.

Our Book of Maps: Individual Title Six-Packs. (Discovery World Ser.). 24p. (gr. 1-2). 33.00 (978-0-7635-8470-2(3)) Rigby Education.

Owen, James A. & Owen, Jeremy. Lost Treasures of the Pirates of the Caribbean. Owen, James A., illus. 2011. (ENG., Illus.). 32p. (J). (gr. 3-7). pap. 16.99 (978-1-4424-3093-8(1), Simon & Schuster Bks. For Young Readers) Simon & Schuster Bks. For Young Readers.

Panchyk, Richard. Charting the World: Geography & Maps from Cave Paintings to GPS with 21 Activities. 2011. (For Kids Ser.). (ENG.). 144p. (J). (gr. 4). pap. 18.95 (978-1-56976-344-5(5)) Chicago Review Pr., Inc.

Pearson, Claudia. This Way, Watson! A Map & Directions Primer, 1 vol. 2017. (ENG.). 32p. (J). 12.99 **(978-1-4236-4765-2(3))** Gibbs Smith, Publisher.

Petersen, David & Petersen, Christine A. Maps & Globes. 2004. (True Bks.). (Illus.). (J). lib. bdg. 24.00 (978-0-516-22044-4(6), Children's Pr.) Scholastic Library Publishing.

Phillips, Larissa. A Historical Atlas of Iraq. 2003. (Historical Atlases of South Asia, Central Asia, & the Middle East Ser.). (Illus.). 64p. (YA). lib. bdg. 31.95 (978-0-8239-3865-0(4)) Rosen Publishing Group, Inc., The.

Phoenix Learning Resources Staff, ed. Exploring Maps Volume 1. 2009. (ENG.). pap., stu. ed. 11.95 (978-0-7915-1539-6(7)) Phoenix Learning Resources, LLC.

Prior, Jennifer Overend. Map Skills, Grade 4. 2003. (Practice Makes Perfect Ser.). (ENG., Illus.). 48p. (gr. 4). pap. 5.99 (978-0-7439-3729-0(5)) Teacher Created Resources, Inc.

Quinlan, Julia J. Different Kinds of Maps. 2012. (How to Use Maps Ser.). (ENG.). 24p. (J). (gr. 3-6). pap. 8.25 (978-1-4488-6268-9(X), PowerKids Pr.); lib. bdg. 22.60 (978-1-4488-6155-2(1)) Rosen Publishing Group, Inc., The.

—Keys, Legends, & Symbols in Maps. 2012. (How to Use Maps Ser.). (ENG.). 24p. (J). (gr. 3-6). pap. 8.25 (978-1-4488-6266-5(3), PowerKids Pr.); lib. bdg. 22.60 (978-1-4488-6154-5(3)) Rosen Publishing Group, Inc., The.

—Scale & Distance in Maps. 2012. (How to Use Maps Ser.). (ENG.). 24p. (J). (gr. 3-6). pap. 8.25 (978-1-4488-6270-2(1), PowerKids Pr.); lib. bdg. 22.60 (978-1-4488-6156-9(X)) Rosen Publishing Group, Inc., The.

Rajczak, Kristen. The Climate Zones. 2014. (Map Basics Ser.). (Illus.). 24p. (J). (gr. 2-5). 22.60 (978-1-4824-0800-3(7)) Stevens, Gareth Publishing LLLP.

—Latitude & Longitude. 2014. (Map Basics Ser.). (Illus.). 24p. (J). (gr. 2-5). 22.60 (978-1-4824-1078-5(8)) Stevens, Gareth Publishing LLLP.

—Types of Maps. 2014. (Map Basics Ser.). (Illus.). 24p. (J). (gr. 2-5). 22.60 (978-1-4824-1063-1(X)) Stevens, Gareth Publishing LLLP.

Rand McNally Staff. Atlas Schoolhouse Beginner's Workbook. 2005. 128p. (J). pap. 7.95 (978-0-528-93469-8(4)) Rand McNally.

—Atlas Schoolhouse Illustrated World Atlas. 2005. 112p. (J). 9.95 (978-0-528-93458-2(9)) Rand McNally.

—Atlas Schoolhouse Intermediate World Atlas. 2005. 128p. (J). pap. 6.95 (978-0-528-93460-5(0)) Rand McNally.

—Atlas Scoolhouse Beginner's World Atlas. 2005. 48p. (J). pap. 5.95 (978-0-528-93463-6(5)) Rand McNally.

Rand McNally Staff, creator. Intermediate Geography & Map Activities. 2005. (Rand Mcnally Schoolhouse Ser.). (Illus.). 128p. per. 7.95 (978-0-528-93470-4(8)) Rand McNally.

Ray, Kurt. A Historical Atlas of Kuwait. 2004. (Historical Atlases of South Asia, Central Asia, & the Middle East Ser.). (Illus.). 64p. (gr. 7-12). lib. bdg. 31.95 (978-0-8239-3981-7(2)) Rosen Publishing Group, Inc., The.

Ritchie, Scot. Follow That Map! Ritchie, Scot, illus. 2009. (ENG., Illus.). 32p. (J). (gr. -1-2). 16.95 (978-1-55453-274-2(4)) Kids Can Pr., Ltd. CAN. Dist: Hachette Bk. Group.

Roza, Greg. Mapping Antarctica. 2013. 24p. (J). (gr. 2-5). 22.60 (978-1-4339-9094-6(6)); pap. 8.15 (978-1-4339-9095-3(4)) Stevens, Gareth Publishing LLLP.

—Tony Stewart. 2007. (NASCAR Champions Ser.). (Illus.). 24p. (J). (gr. 1-3). lib. bdg. 22.60 (978-1-4042-3456-7(X)) Rosen Publishing Group, Inc., The.

Rudgers, Stephanie. How We Use Maps. 2009. (Real Life Readers Ser.). 12p. (gr. 1-2). pap. 5.90 (978-1-4042-7907-0(5), Rosen Classroom) Rosen Publishing Group, Inc., The.

Rusinek, Catherine. So Many Maps! Reading Different Kinds of Maps. 2009. (Real Life Readers Ser.). 24p. (gr. 3-4). pap. 8.25 (978-1-4358-0133-2(4), Rosen Classroom) Rosen Publishing Group, Inc., The.

Schuette, Sarah L. Spot It. 2012. (Spot It Ser.). (ENG.). 32p. (gr. 1-2). lib. bdg. 54.64 (978-1-4296-8101-8(2), Aplus Bks.) Capstone Press of Coughlan Cos.

Segal Block, Marta & Block, Daniel R. Mapping the World. 2016. (First Guides to Maps Ser.). (ENG.). 32p. (gr. 1-3). pap. 8.29 (978-1-4846-3687-9(2), Heinemann First Library) Heinemann-Raintree.

Shannon, Terry Miller. The Key to City Maps. 2016. (Spring Forward Ser.). (J). (gr. 2). (978-1-4900-9450-2(4)) Benchmark Education Co.

—Maps & More Maps. 2016. (Spring Forward Ser.). (J). (gr. 1). (978-1-4900-9381-9(8)) Benchmark Education Co.

Shea, Therese. Reading Map Keys. 2014. (Map Basics Ser.). 24p. (J). (gr. 2-5). 22.60 (978-1-4824-1073-0(7)) Stevens, Gareth Publishing LLLP.

Silver, Donald M. & Wynne, Patricia J. Interactive 3-D Maps - American History: Easy-to-Assemble 3-D Maps That Students Make & Manipulate to Learn Key Facts & Concepts - In a Kinesthetic Way! 2005. (ENG.). 112p. (gr. 4-8). pap. 15.99 (978-0-439-24114-4(6), Teaching Resources) Scholastic, Inc.

Somervill, Barbara A. The Story Behind Maps, 1 vol. 2011. (True Stories Ser.). (ENG.). 32p. (gr. 3-3). 30.65 (978-1-4329-5443-7(1), NA-h) Heinemann-Raintree.

Sundance/Newbridge LLC Staff. Maps & Globes. 2004. (Reading PowerWorks Ser.). (gr. 1-3). 37.50 (978-0-7608-9747-8(6)); pap. 6.10 (978-0-7608-9748-5(4)) Sundance/Newbridge Educational Publishing.

Taylor, Barbara. Looking at Maps. 2007. (Geography Skills/Watts Ser.). (Illus.). 46p. (J). (gr. 4-7). lib. bdg. 32.80 (978-1-59920-050-7(3)) Black Rabbit Bks.

Thomas, Isabel. You Are Here. 2017. (ENG., Illus.). 32p. (J). pap. 7.99 **(978-0-00-820874-5(3))** HarperCollins Pubs. Ltd. GBR. Dist: Independent Pubs. Group.

Thompson, Sharon. Map Skills: Grade 1. Poitras, Tara & Brooks, Whitney, eds. 2003. (Basic Skills & Beyond Ser.). 48p. (gr. 1-1). pap. 7.99 (978-0-88724-959-4(0), CD-4700) Carson-Dellosa Publishing, LLC.

—Map Skills: Grade 3. Poitras, Tara & Brooks, Whitney, eds. 2003. (Basic Skills & Beyond Ser.). 48p. (gr. 3-3). pap. 7.99 (978-0-88724-961-7(2), CD-4702) Carson-Dellosa Publishing, LLC.

—Map Skills: Grade 5. Poitras, Tara & Brooks, Whitney, eds. 2003. (Basic Skills & Beyond Ser.). 48p. (gr. 5-5). pap. 7.99 (978-0-88724-963-1(9), CD-4704) Carson-Dellosa Publishing, LLC.

Torpie, Kate. Map Parts. 2008. (ENG., Illus.). 32p. (J). (gr. 1-4). pap. (978-0-7787-4273-9(3)) Crabtree Publishing Co.

Torpie, Kate & Becker, Ann. Map Types. 2008. (ENG., Illus.). 32p. (J). (gr. 1-4). pap. (978-0-7787-4274-6(1)) Crabtree Publishing Co.

Torpie, Kate & Sandvold, Rolf. Reading Maps. 2008. (All over the Map Ser.). (ENG., Illus.). 32p. (J). (gr. 1-4). pap. (978-0-7787-4275-3(X)) Crabtree Publishing Co.

Vierow, Wendy. Africa. 2004. (Atlas of the Seven Continents Ser.). (Illus.). 24p. (YA). (gr. 3-6). lib. bdg. 22.60 (978-0-8239-6687-5(9)) Rosen Publishing Group, Inc., The.

—Asia. 2004. (Atlas of the Seven Continents Ser.). (Illus.). 24p. (YA). (gr. 3-6). lib. bdg. 22.60 (978-0-8239-6689-9(5)) Rosen Publishing Group, Inc., The.

—Australia. 2004. (Atlas of the Seven Continents Ser.). (Illus.). 24p. (YA). (gr. 3-6). lib. bdg. 22.60 (978-0-8239-6690-5(9)) Rosen Publishing Group, Inc., The.

—North America. 2009. (Atlas of the Seven Continents Ser.). 24p. (gr. 3-3). 42.50 (978-1-61511-481-8(5), PowerKids Pr.) Rosen Publishing Group, Inc., The.

Wade, Mary Dodson. Map Scales. 2012. (Rookie Read-About(tm) Geography — Map Skills Ser.). (ENG., Illus.). 32p. (J). lib. bdg. 25.00 *(978-0-531-28966-2(4))*; pap. 5.95 *(978-0-531-29290-7(8))* Scholastic Library Publishing.

—Tipos de Mapas. DelRisco, Eida, tr. from ENG. 2005. (Rookie Espanol Geografia Ser.). (ENG & SPA., Illus.). 32p. (J). (gr. k-2). lib. bdg. 19.50 *(978-0-516-25243-8(7)*, Children's Pr.) Scholastic Library Publishing.

—Types of Maps. 2003. (Rookie Read-About Geography Ser.). (ENG.). 32p. (J). (gr. 1-2). pap. 5.95 *(978-0-516-27768-4(5)*, Children's Pr.) Scholastic Library Publishing.

Waldron, Melanie. Let's Get Mapping! 2013. (Let's Get Mapping! Ser.). (ENG.). 32p. (gr. 2-4). pap. 47.94 *(978-1-4109-4912-7(5))*; lib. bdg. 183.90 *(978-1-4109-4905-9(2))* Heinemann-Raintree. (Raintree Perspectives).

—Mapping Information, 1 vol. 2013. (Let's Get Mapping! Ser.). (ENG., Illus.). 32p. (gr. 2-4). 30.65 *(978-1-4109-4901-1(X))*; pap. 8.29 *(978-1-4109-4908-0(7))* Heinemann-Raintree. (Raintree Perspectives).

—Mapping the World, 1 vol. 2013. (Let's Get Mapping! Ser.). (ENG., Illus.). 32p. (gr. 2-4). 30.65 *(978-1-4109-4903-5(6))*; pap. 8.29 *(978-1-4109-4910-3(9))* Heinemann-Raintree. (Raintree Perspectives).

—Types of Maps, 1 vol. 2013. (Let's Get Mapping! Ser.). (ENG., Illus.). 32p. (gr. 2-4). 30.65 *(978-1-4109-4904-2(4))*; pap. 8.29 *(978-1-4109-4911-0(7))* Heinemann-Raintree. (Raintree Perspectives).

Walker, Rob. Mapping Towns & Cities. 2010. (Mapping Our World Ser.). 32p. (gr. 4). 28.50 *(978-1-60870-120-9(4))* Marshall Cavendish Corp.

Waxman, Malcolm & Porter, Malcolm. Atlas of South America & Antarctica. 2009. (Atlases of the World Ser.). (Illus.). 48p. (YA). (gr. 5-8). 29.25 *(978-1-4358-8459-5(0)*, Rosen Reference) Rosen Publishing Group, Inc., The.

The Western Hemisphere Through the Five Themes of Geography Map Activities Book plus 5 Transparencies. 2005. (Western Hemisphere Through the Five Themes of Geography Ser.). 16p. 55.95 *(978-1-4042-5159-5(6)*, Rosen Classroom) Rosen Publishing Group, Inc., The.

Where on Earth? Mapping Parts of the World. 2017. (Where on Earth? Mapping Parts of the World Ser.). 24p. (gr. 1-2). pap. 48.90 ***(978-1-5382-0239-5(5))***; lib. bdg. 135.60 ***(978-1-5382-0238-8(7))*** Stevens, Gareth Publishing LLLP.

The Whole World in Your Hands. (Discovery Readers Ser.). 48p. (J). pap. 3.95 *(978-0-8249-5315-7(0)*, Ideal Pubns.) Worthy Publishing.

Wood, Alix. Dinosaurs on the Map. 2014. (Fun with Map Skills Ser.). (Illus.). 32p. (J). (gr. 3-6). lib. bdg. 26.25 *(978-1-4777-6960-7(9)*, PowerKids Pr.) Rosen Publishing Group, Inc., The.

—Disasters on the Map. 2014. (Fun with Map Skills Ser.). (Illus.). 32p. (J). (gr. 3-6). lib. bdg. 26.25 *(978-1-4777-6976-8(5)*, PowerKids Pr.) Rosen Publishing Group, Inc., The.

—Hunting on the Map. 2014. (Fun with Map Skills Ser.). (Illus.). 32p. (J). (gr. 3-6). lib. bdg. 26.25 *(978-1-4777-6980-5(3)*, PowerKids Pr.) Rosen Publishing Group, Inc., The.

—The Military on the Map. 2014. (Fun with Map Skills Ser.). (Illus.). 32p. (J). (gr. 3-6). lib. bdg. 26.25 *(978-1-4777-6968-3(4)*, PowerKids Pr.) Rosen Publishing Group, Inc., The.

—Pirates on the Map. 2014. (Fun with Map Skills Ser.). 32p. (J). (gr. 3-6). lib. bdg. 26.25 *(978-1-4777-6964-5(1)*, PowerKids Pr.) Rosen Publishing Group, Inc., The.

—Sports on the Map. 2014. (Fun with Map Skills Ser.). (Illus.). 32p. (J). (gr. 3-6). lib. bdg. 26.25 *(978-1-4777-6972-0(2)*, PowerKids Pr.) Rosen Publishing Group, Inc., The.

X Marks the Spot, 6 Packs. (gr. k-1). 23.00 *(978-0-7635-9064-2(9))* Rigby Education.

Your Community. (J). (gr. 3). 3.80 *(978-0-8374-1452-2(0)*, 403) Weekly Reader Corp.

Zelon, Helen. The Endeavor SRTM: Mapping the Earth. 2009. (Space Missions Ser.). 24p. (gr. 3-4). 42.50 *(978-1-60853-118-9(X)*, PowerKids Pr.) Rosen Publishing Group, Inc., The.

Zuravicky, Orli. Map Math: Learning about Latitude & Longitude Using Coordinate Systems. 2009. (PowerMath Ser.). (ENG.). 32p. (gr. 5-6). pap. 10.00 *(978-1-4042-5133-5(2)*, PowerKids Pr.) Rosen Publishing Group, Inc., The.

MAPS, HISTORICAL

see Historical Geography—Maps

MARATHON, BATTLE OF, GREECE, 490 B.C.

Rice, Earle, Jr. Battle of Marathon. 2011. (Technologies & Strategies in Battle Ser.). (Illus.). 48p. (J). (gr. 4-7). lib. bdg. 29.95 *(978-1-61228-077-6(3))* Mitchell Lane Pubs., Inc.

MARCH FAMILY (FICTITIOUS CHARACTERS)—FICTION

Alcott, Louisa May. The Annotated Little Women. Matteson, John, ed. 2015. (Annotated Bks.: 0). (ENG., Illus.). 736p. (gr. 11-17). 39.95 *(978-0-393-07219-8(3)*, 7219) Norton, W. W. & Co., Inc.

—Good Wives. 2013. (ENG.). 464p. (J). (gr. 4-7). pap. 11.99 *(978-0-09-957369-2(5))* Random Hse. GBR. Dist: Independent Pubs. Group.

—Jo's Boys. abr. ed. 2011. (Dover Children's Thrift Classics Ser.). (ENG., Illus.). 112p. (J). (gr. 3-8). pap. 4.00 *(978-0-486-40789-0(6))* Dover Pubns., Inc.

—Jo's Boys. 2013. (Works of Louisa May Alcott). 366p. reprint ed. lthr. 79.00 *(978-0-7812-1642-5(7))* Reprint Services Corp.

—Little Women. 2007. 264p. (YA). 11.95 *(978-1-933486-01-7(5))* Core Knowledge Foundation.

—Little Women. 2015. (ENG.). 408p. (J). (gr. 2-4). 14.99 *(978-1-4052-7179-0(5))* Egmont Bks., Ltd. GBR. Dist: Independent Pubs. Group.

—Little Women. unabr. ed. 2004. (Chrysalis Childrens Classics Ser.). (Illus.). 190p. (YA). pap. *(978-1-84365-049-2(5)*, Pavilion Children's Books) Pavilion Bks.

—Little Women. 2013. (ENG., Illus.). 426p. (J). (gr. 4-7). pap. 10.99 *(978-0-09-957296-1(6))* Random Hse. GBR. Dist: Independent Pubs. Group.

—Little Women. 2013. (Works of Louisa May Alcott). 451p. reprint ed. lthr. 79.00 *(978-0-7812-1627-2(3))* Reprint Services Corp.

—Little Women. 2008. (Puffin Classics Ser.). (gr. k-3). lib. bdg. 19.65 *(978-0-613-86261-5(9)*, Turtleback) Turtleback Bks.

—Little Women: Bring the Classics to Life. 2008. (Bring the Classics to Life Ser.). (Illus.). 72p. (gr. 1-12). pap., act. bk. ed. 10.95 *(978-1-55576-047-2(3)*, EDCTR-103B) EDCON Publishing Group.

—Mujercitas.Tr. of Little Women. (SPA., Illus.). 192p. (YA). 11.95 *(978-84-7281-101-0(8)*, AF1101) Auriga, Ediciones S.A. ESP. Dist: Continental Bk. Co., Inc.

—Mujercitas. 2004.Tr. of Little Women. (SPA.). lib. bdg. *(978-1-4135-2067-5(7))* El Cid Editor Incorporated.

—Mujercitas. (Coleccion Estrella).Tr. of Little Women. (SPA., Illus.). 64p. (J). 14.95 *(978-950-11-0010-5(3)*, SGM010) Sigmar ARG. Dist: Continental Bk. Co., Inc.

Alcott, Louisa May, et al. Little Women. 2003. (Norton Critical Editions Ser.: 0). (ENG., Illus.). 665p. (C). pap. 13.00 *(978-0-393-97614-4(9)*, 97614) Norton, W. W. & Co., Inc.

Francis, Pauline & Alcott, Louisa May. Little Women. 2003. (Fast Track Classics Ser.). (Illus.). 48p. (YA). pap. *(978-0-237-52533-0(X))* Evans Brothers, Ltd.

Lauter, Richard, illus. Little Women. (Young Collector's Illustrated Classics Ser.). 192p. (J). 9.95 *(978-1-56156-371-5(4))* Kidsbooks, LLC.

Lindskoog, Kathryn, ed. Little Women. Chitouras, Barbara, illus. 2003. (Classics for Young Readers Ser.). 432p. (J). per. 12.99 *(978-0-87552-734-5(5))* P & R Publishing.

Rawsthorne, Paul, et al. Little Women. Selivanova, Elena, illus. 2016. (ENG.). 80p. (J). pap. 9.95 *(978-0-00-814737-2(X))* HarperCollins Pubs. Ltd. GBR. Dist: Independent Pubs. Group.

MARCONI, GUGLIELMO, 1874-1937

Auch, Allison. Electrifying Personalities & Personalidades Electrizantes: 6 English, 6 Spanish Adaptations. 2011. (ENG & SPA.). (J). 97.00 net. *(978-1-4108-5713-2(1))* Benchmark Education Co.

Kulling, Monica. Making Contact! Marconi Goes Wireless. 2016. (Great Idea Ser.). (ENG., Illus.). 32p. (J). (gr. k-3). pap. 6.99 *(978-1-101-91842-5(X)*, Tundra Bks.) Tundra Bks. CAN. Dist: Penguin Random Hse. LLC.

—Making Contact! Marconi Goes Wireless. Rudnicki, Richard, illus. 2013. (Great Idea Ser.). (ENG.). 32p. (J). (gr. k-3). 17.95 *(978-1-77049-378-0(6)*, Tundra Bks.) Tundra Bks. CAN. Dist: Penguin Random Hse. LLC.

O'Shei, Tim. Marconi & Tesla: Pioneers of Radio Communication. 2008. (Inventors Who Changed the World Ser.). (Illus.). 128p. (J). (gr. 3-7). lib. bdg. 34.60 *(978-1-59845-076-7(X)*, MyReportLinks.com Bks.) Enslow Pubs., Inc.

Sherrow, Victoria. Guglielmo Marconi: Inventor of Radio & Wireless Communication. 2004. (Nobel Prize-Winning Scientists Ser.). (Illus.). 112p. (J). lib. bdg. 27.94 *(978-0-7660-2280-5(3))* Enslow Pubs., Inc.

Zannos, Susan. Guglielmo Marconi & Radio Waves. 2004. (Uncharted, Unexplored, & Unexplained Ser.). (Illus.). 48p. (J). (gr. 4-8). lib. bdg. 29.95 *(978-1-58415-265-1(6))* Mitchell Lane Pubs., Inc.

MARFAN SYNDROME

Mitchell, Lori, illus. & compiled by. Marfan Syndrome A-Z. Mitchell, Lori, compiled by. 2007. 36p. (J). pap. *(978-0-918335-14-2(0))* National Marfan Foundation, The.

MARIE ANTOINETTE, QUEEN, CONSORT OF LOUIS XVI, KING OF FRANCE, 1755-1793

Daynes, Katie. Marie Antoinette. Mistry, Nilesh, illus. 2005. 64p. (J). 8.95 *(978-0-7945-1049-7(3)*, Usborne) EDC Publishing.

Hockinson, Liz. Marie Antoinette "Madame Deficit" Malone, Peter, illus. 2011. (Thinking Girl's Treasury of Dastardly Dames Ser.). (ENG.). 32p. (J). (gr. 3-8). 18.95 *(978-0-9834256-4-9(7))* Goosebottom Bks. LLC.

Lotz, Nancy & Phillips, Carlene. Marie Antoinette & the Decline of French Monarchy. 2004. (World Leaders Ser.). (Illus.). 160p. (YA). (gr. 6-12). lib. bdg. 26.95 *(978-1-931798-28-0(1))* Reynolds, Morgan Inc.

Rau, Dana Meachen. Who Was Marie Antoinette? O'brien, John, illus. 2015. 106p. (J). *(978-1-4806-9210-7(7)*, Grosset & Dunlap) Penguin Publishing Group.

—Who Was Marie Antoinette? 2015. (Who Was... ? Ser.). lib. bdg. 16.00 *(978-0-606-37554-2(6))* Turtleback Bks.

Rau, Dana Meachen & dePaola, Tomie. Who Was Marie Antoinette? O'brien, John, illus. 2015. (Who Was? Ser.). (ENG.). 112p. (J). (gr. 3-7). 5.99 *(978-0-448-48310-8(6)*, Grosset & Dunlap) Penguin Young Readers Group.

Schwartz, Heather. Marie Antoinette: The Controversial Queen of France, 1 vol. 2012. (Primary Source Readers Ser.). (ENG.). 32p. (J). (gr. 4-4). pap. 8.99 *(978-1-4333-5012-2(2))* Teacher Created Materials, Inc.

Webb, Sarah Powers. Marie Antoinette: Fashionable Queen or Greedy Royal? 2015. (Perspectives on History Ser.). (ENG.). 32p. (gr. 3-4). pap. 7.95 *(978-1-4914-2216-8(5))* Capstone Press of Coughlan Cos.

MARIE ANTOINETTE, QUEEN, CONSORT OF LOUIS XVI, KING OF FRANCE, 1755-1793—FICTION

Alender, Katie. Marie Antoinette, Serial Killer. 2014. (ENG.). 304p. (J). (gr. 7). pap. 9.99 *(978-0-545-46810-7(8)*, Scholastic Paperbacks) Scholastic, Inc.

Meyer, Carolyn. The Bad Queen: Rules & Instructions for Marie-Antoinette. 2011. (Young Royals Ser.). (ENG.). 432p. (YA). (gr. 7). pap. 9.99 *(978-0-547-48249-1(3))* Houghton Mifflin Harcourt Publishing Co.

Turetsky, Bianca. The Time-Traveling Fashionista at the Palace of Marie Antoinette. 2013. (Time-Traveling Fashionista Ser.: 2). (ENG., Illus.). 272p. (J). (gr. 3-7). pap. 9.00 *(978-0-316-10535-4(X)*, Poppy) Little, Brown Bks. for Young Readers.

MARIJUANA

Allen, John. Thinking Critically: Legalizing Marijuana. 2015. (ENG., Illus.). 80p. (J). lib. bdg. *(978-1-60152-782-0(9))* ReferencePoint Pr., Inc.

Barbour, Scott. Should Marijuana Be Legalized? 2010. (In Controversy Ser.). 96p. (YA). (gr. 7-12). 27.95 *(978-1-60152-106-4(5))* ReferencePoint Pr., Inc.

Benjamin, Daniel. Marijuana. 2013. 64p. (J). (gr. 6-9). 34.21 *(978-1-60870-825-3(X))*; pap. 15.28 *(978-1-62712-061-6(0))* Cavendish Square Publishing.

bjornlund, lydia. Marijuana. 2011. (Compact Research Ser.). 96p. (YA). (gr. 7-12). lib. bdg. 27.95 *(978-1-60152-160-6(X))* ReferencePoint Pr., Inc.

Collins, Anna & Marcovitz, Hal. Marijuana: Abuse & Legalization. 2017. (Drug Education Library). 104p. (YA). (gr. 7-7). lib. bdg. 37.45 ***(978-1-5345-6001-7(7)***, Lucent Pr.) Greenhaven Publishing LLC.

Connolly, Sean. Marijuana. 2009. (Straight Talking Ser.). (Illus.). 46p. (YA). (gr. 8-12). pap. *(978-1-895058-54-3(6))* Saunders Bk. Co.

Cunningham, Anne C. Critical Perspectives on Legalizing Marijuana. 2016. (Analyzing the Issues Ser.). 208p. (J). (gr. 8-8). 47.93 *(978-0-7660-7669-3(5))* Enslow Pubs., Inc.

Gillard, Arthur. Marijuana. 2009. (At Issue Ser.). (ENG., Illus.). 128p. (gr. 10-12). 39.40 *(978-0-7377-4432-3(4))*;No. 9. (J). 24.45 *(978-0-7377-4433-0(2))* Cengage Gale. (Greenhaven Pr., Inc.).

—Medical Marijuana. Greenhaven Press Editors, ed. 2013. (Issues That Concern You Ser.). (ENG., Illus.). 144p. (gr. 7-10). lib. bdg. 42.00 *(978-0-7377-6297-6(7)*, Greenhaven Pr., Inc.) Cengage Gale.

Goldstein, Margaret. Legalizing Marijuana: Promises & Pitfalls. 2016. (ENG., Illus.). 104p. (YA). (gr. 7-12). 35.99 *(978-1-4677-9243-1(8)*, Twenty-First Century Bks.) Lerner Publishing Group.

Goldstein, Margaret J. Legalizing Marijuana: Promises & Pitfalls. 2016. (ENG., Illus.). 104p. (YA). (gr. 7-12). 53.32 *(978-1-5124-1144-7(2)*, Twenty-First Century Bks.) Lerner Publishing Group.

Gottfried, Ted & Harkrader, Lisa. Marijuana. 2009. (Benchmark Rockets Ser.). 32p. (YA). (gr. 5-9). 28.50 *(978-0-7614-4351-3(7))* Marshall Cavendish Corp.

Gross, Frederick C. & Chace, Reeve. The Truth about Marijuana. 2011. (Drugs & Consequences Ser.). (YA). (gr. 7-12). lib. bdg. 31.95 *(978-1-4488-4639-9(0))* Rosen Publishing Group, Inc., The.

Harrison Adams, Troon & Harrison, Troon. Marijuana. 2011. (ENG.). 48p. (J). pap. *(978-0-7787-5516-6(9))*; (gr. 4-7). lib. bdg. *(978-0-7787-5509-8(6))* Crabtree Publishing Co.

Hillstrom, Kevin. Medical Marijuana. Gale, G., ed. 2014. (Hot Topics Ser.). (ENG., Illus.). 128p. (gr. 7-10). lib. bdg. 39.40 *(978-1-4205-0871-0(7)*, Lucent Bks.) Cengage Gale.

Ingram, W. Scott. Marijuana. 2008. (Junior Drug Awareness Ser.). (Illus.). 110p. (gr. 5-8). lib. bdg. 30.00 *(978-0-7910-9695-6(5)*, Chelsea Hse.) Facts On File, Inc.

Morgan, Kayla. Legalizing Marijuana, 1 vol. 2010. (Essential Viewpoints Set 5 Ser.). (ENG.). 112p. (J). (gr. 6-12). lib. bdg. 35.64 *(978-1-61613-523-2(9)*, Essential Library) ABDO Publishing Co.

Netzley, Patricia D. Is Legalized Marijuana Good for Society? 2015. (ENG., Illus.). 96p. (J). lib. bdg. *(978-1-60152-774-5(8))* ReferencePoint Pr., Inc.

Perritano, John. Marijuana & Synthetics, Vol. 13. Becker, Sara, ed. 2016. (Drug Addiction & Recovery Ser.). (Illus.). 64p. (J). (gr. 7). 23.95 *(978-1-4222-3606-2(4))* Mason Crest.

Sanna, E. J. Marijuana: Mind-Altering Weed. Henningfield, Jack E., ed. 2012. (Illicit & Misused Drugs Ser.). 128p. (J). (gr. 7). 24.95 *(978-1-4222-2435-9(X))*; pap. 14.95 *(978-1-4222-2454-0(6))* Mason Crest.

—Marijuana: Mind-Altering Weed. 2009. (Illicit & Misused Drugs Ser.). (Illus.). 128p. (YA). (gr. 7-18). lib. bdg. 24.95 *(978-1-4222-0158-9(9))* Mason Crest.

Steffens, Bradley. Is Marijuana Harmful? 2016. (ENG.). 80p. (J). (gr. 5-12). lib. bdg. *(978-1-68282-097-1(1))* ReferencePoint Pr., Inc.

Tardiff, Joseph C., ed. Marijuana. 2007. (Contemporary Issues Companion Ser.). (ENG., Illus.). 211p. (YA). (gr. 9-12). pap. 39.70 *(978-0-7377-2775-3(6))* Cengage Gale.

Waters, Rosa. Legal & Developmental Consequences. Borus, Joshua, ed. 2014. (Downside of Drugs Ser.). 48p. (J). (gr. 5-18). pap. 10.95 *(978-1-4222-3192-0(5))* Mason Crest.

—Marijuana: Legal & Developmental Consequences. Borus, Joshua, ed. 2014. (Downside of Drugs Ser.). (ENG., Illus.). 48p. (J). (gr. 5-18). lib. bdg. 20.95 *(978-1-4222-3022-0(8))* Mason Crest.

MARIJUANA—FICTION

Bussereth, Bianca. Sky Rod. 2010. 80p. pap. 6.95 *(978-1-60594-391-6(6)*, Llumina Pr.) Aeon Publishing Inc.

Cortés, Ricardo, illus. It's Just a Plant: A Children's Story about Marijuana. 2013. (ENG.). 48p. (J). 20.00 *(978-1-61775-186-8(3))* Akashic Bks.

Dirkes, Craig. Sucktown, Alaska. 2017. (ENG.). 352p. (gr. 9-12). 17.95 *(978-1-63079-055-4(9))* Switch Pr.

It's Just a Plant: A Children's Story about Marijuana. 2nd rev. ed. 2006.Tr. of Www. justaplant. com. (J). per. 20.00 *(978-0-9760117-2-9(7))* Magic Propaganda Mill.

Rivers, Karen. What Is Real, 1 vol. 2011. (ENG.). 304p. (YA). (gr. 7-12). pap. 12.95 *(978-1-55469-356-6(X))* Orca Bk. Pubs. USA.

Stone, Heather Duffy. Over the Tracks. 2015. (ENG.). 96p. (YA). (gr. 6-12). 27.99 *(978-1-4677-5711-9(X))* Lerner Publishing Group.

MARINE ANIMALS

see also Corals; Fishes; Freshwater Animals

Abbott, Simon. Pop & Play: under the Sea. 2014. (ENG., Illus.). 10p. (J). (gr. -1-k). bds. 7.99 *(978-0-7534-7155-5(8)*, 9780753471555, Kingfisher) Roaring Brook Pr.

Allen, Francesca, illus. Under the Sea. 2005. 10p. (J). 4.99 *(978-0-7945-0857-9(X)*, Usborne) EDC Publishing.

Allen, Nancy Kelly. What Sea Creature Is This? Brown, Gloria, illus. 2012. (J). *(978-1-933176-41-3(5))* Red Rock Pr., Inc.

Allgor, Marie. Endangered Ocean Animals. 2012. (Save Earth's Animals! Ser.). (ENG., Illus.). 24p. (J). (gr. k-5). pap. 8.25 *(978-1-4488-7493-4(9)*, PowerKids Pr.) Rosen Publishing Group, Inc., The.

American Museum of Natural History Staff. ABC Oceans. 2014. (AMNH ABC Board Bks.). (ENG., Illus.). 18p. (J). (gr. -1-k). bds. 7.95 *(978-1-4549-1195-1(6))* Sterling Publishing Co., Inc.

Anastasio, Dina. Hiding in the Sea & Escondidos en el Mar: 6 English, 6 Spanish Adaptations. 2011. (ENG & SPA.). (J). 75.00 net. *(978-1-4108-5643-2(7))* Benchmark Education Co.

Anderson, Sheila. What Can Live in the Ocean? 2010. pap. 33.92 *(978-0-7613-6906-6(0))*; (ENG.). 24p. pap. 6.95 *(978-0-7613-5673-8(8))*; (ENG., Illus.). 24p. (J). lib. bdg. 23.93 *(978-0-7613-4569-5(8))* Lerner Publishing Group.

Animales Marinos, 6 vols. (Explorers. Exploradores Nonfiction Sets Ser.).Tr. of Marine Animals. (SPA.). 32p. (gr. 3-6). 44.95 *(978-0-7699-0627-0(3))* Shortland Pubns. (U. S. A.) Inc.

Animales Marinos. 2005. (Collection Abre Tus Ojos, Collection Eye Openers Ser.).Tr. of Marine Animals. (SPA.). (J). (gr. k-2). 6.95 *(978-950-11-0966-5(6))* Sigmar ARG. Dist: Iaconi, Mariuccia Bk. Imports.

Animals of the Ocean Series (Illus.). (J). (gr. 2-6). lib. bdg. 44.85 *(978-1-56674-947-3(6))* Forest Hse. Publishing Co., Inc.

Arlon, Penelope. Really? Ocean. 2015. (ENG.). 64p. (J). (gr. 2-5). pap. 8.99 *(978-0-545-80650-3(X)*, Scholastic Nonfiction) Scholastic, Inc.

Arnosky, Jim. All about Manatees. Arnosky, Jim, illus. 2008. (All About Ser.). (ENG., Illus.). 32p. (J). (gr. -1-3). pap. 6.99 *(978-0-439-90361-5(0))* Scholastic, Inc.

—Shimmer & Splash: The Sparkling World of Sea Life. 2013. (ENG., Illus.). 40p. (J). (gr. 1-5). 14.95 *(978-1-4027-8623-5(9))* Sterling Publishing Co., Inc.

AZ Books, creator. Lake Animals Moving & Talking. 2012. (Funny Trails Ser.). (ENG., Illus.). 10p. (J). (gr. -1-k). bds. 9.95 *(978-1-61889-216-4(9))* AZ Bks. LLC.

—Water Animals. 2013. (Sounds Around Us Ser.). (ENG., Illus.). 16p. (J). (gr. 1-3). bds. 17.95 *(978-1-61889-283-6(5))* AZ Bks. LLC.

—Who Lives in the Ocean? 2012. (Funny Animals Ser.). (ENG., Illus.). 10p. (J). (gr. -1-k). bds. 8.95 *(978-1-61889-210-2(X))* AZ Bks. LLC.

AZ Books Staff. Exploring the Ocean. Vasilkova, Elena, ed. 2012. (Wild Theater Ser.). (ENG.). 8p. (J). (gr. -1-3). bds. 17.95 *(978-1-61889-020-7(4))* AZ Bks. LLC.

—In the Sea & Ocean. Efimova, Tatiana, ed. 2012. (Animal Sounds Ser.). (ENG.). 14p. (J). (-k). bds. 7.95 *(978-1-61889-127-3(8))* AZ Bks. LLC.

—Living Book of the Ocean. Aksinovich, Natalia, ed. 2012. (Our Amazing World Ser.). (ENG.). 12p. (J). (gr. 1-3). bds. 19.95 *(978-1-61889-021-4(2))* AZ Bks. LLC.

—Ocean Animals. Gorojan, Elena, ed. 2012. (My First Library). (ENG.). 12p. (J). (gr. -1-k). bds. 8.95 *(978-1-61889-119-8(7))* AZ Bks. LLC.

—Visiting the Ocean. Lukjanenko, Anna, ed. 2012. (Lively Pictures Ser.). (ENG.). 10p. (J). (gr. -1-1). bds. 9.95 *(978-1-61889-180-8(4))* AZ Bks. LLC.

Baggott, Stella. Glug, Glug, Glug. Cartwright, Mary, illus. 2007. (Bath Bks). 5p. (J). (gr. -1-k). 14.99 *(978-0-7945-1784-7(6)*, Usborne) EDC Publishing.

Baillie, Marilyn. Whoosh! A Watery World of Wonderful Creatures, 0 vols. Mitchell, Susan & Owlkids Books Inc. Staff, illus. 2014. (ENG.). 32p. (J). (gr. -1-2). 16.95 *(978-1-926973-98-2(4)*, Owlkids) Owlkids Bks. Inc. CAN. Dist: Publishers Group West (PGW).

Barner, Bob. Sea Bones. 2015. (ENG., Illus.). 32p. (J). (gr. k-3). 16.99 *(978-1-4521-2500-8(7))* Chronicle Bks. LLC.

Barraclough, Susan. Sharks & Other Creatures of the Deep. 2007. (Illus.). 192p. (J). *(978-0-7607-9143-1(0))* Barnes & Noble, Inc.

Beaton, Kathryn. Moray Eels. 2015. (21st Century Basic Skills Library: Splash! Ser.). (ENG., Illus.). 24p. (J). (gr. 2-4). 24.21 *(978-1-63362-601-0(6)*, 206588) Cherry Lake Publishing.

Beck, W. H. Glow: Animals with Their Own Night-Lights. 2015. (ENG., Illus.). 32p. (J). (gr. -1-3). 17.99 *(978-0-544-41666-6(X)*, HMH Books For Young Readers) Houghton Mifflin Harcourt Publishing Co.

Bedoyere, Camilla. Monsters of the Deep. 2014. (ENG., Illus.). 80p. (J). (gr. 3-6). pap. 9.95 *(978-1-77085-465-9(7)*, 9781770854659) Firefly Bks., Ltd.

Benchmark Education Company, LLC Staff, compiled by. Watery World & Animal Adaptations. 2005. spiral bd. 225.00 *(978-1-4108-5814-6(6))* Benchmark Education Co.

Bennett, Doraine. Atlantic Ocean. 2009. (J). *(978-1-935077-34-3(1))*; pap. *(978-1-935077-39-8(2))* State Standards Publishing, LLC.

Berger, Melvin & Berger, Gilda. Manta Rays. 2003. (Illus.). (J). pap. *(978-0-439-47393-4(4))* Scholastic, Inc.

Bessesen, Brooke. Look Who Lives in the Ocean: Splashing & Dashing, Nibbling & Quibbling, Blending & Fending. 2009. (Illus.). 48p. (J). (gr. k-4). 19.95 *(978-1-932082-82-1(4))* Arizona Highways.

Bishop, Celeste. Wandering Woodlice. 2015. (Icky Animals! Small & Gross Ser.). (ENG.). 24p. (J). (gr. 1-1). pap. 8.25 *(978-1-4994-0724-2(6)*, PowerKids Pr.) Rosen Publishing Group, Inc., The.

Blocksma, Mary. What's on the Beach? A Great Lakes Treasure Hunt. 2012. (ENG., Illus.). 48p. (gr. 3-8). pap. 12.50 *(978-0-9708575-2-1(7))* Beaver Island Arts.

—What's on the Beach? A Great Lakes Treasure Hunt. Blocksma, Mary, illus. 2003. (Great Lakes Treasure Hunts Ser.: No. 1). (Illus.). 48p. (J). pap. 9.95 *(978-0-9708575-1-4(9))* Beaver Island Arts.

Blyton, Enid, et al. Under the Sea. 2013. (ENG.). 10p. (J). bds. 9.95 *(978-1-84135-723-2(5))* Parkwest Pubns., Inc.

Boelts, Maribeth. Amazing Ocean Animals. 2016. (Spring Forward Ser.). (J). (gr. 1). *(978-1-4900-2244-4(9))* Benchmark Education Co.

Borin & Rin, Bo. What Lives in the Sea? Marine Life. Cowley, Joy, ed. Park, Yeong Jin, illus. 2015. (Science Storybooks Ser.). (ENG.). 32p. (J). (gr. k-3). 26.65 *(978-1-925233-63-6(4))* Lerner Publishing Group.

Bradley, Timothy. Demonios de la Profundidad. 2016. (TIME for Kids en Español - Level 5 Ser.). (SPA.). 64p. (gr. 5-5). lib. bdg. 31.99 *(978-1-5157-2941-9(9))* Time for Kids Inc AUS. Dist: Capstone Pub.

Bradley, Timothy J. Demons of the Deep, 1 vol. 2nd rev. ed. 2013. (Nonfiction Readers Ser.). (ENG., Illus.). 64p. (J). (gr. 5-5). pap. 31.96 *(978-1-4333-7419-7(6))*; pap. 10.99 *(978-1-4333-4896-9(9))* Teacher Created Materials, Inc.

Brecke, Nicole & Stockland, Patricia M. Sea Creatures You Can Draw. Brecke, Nicole, illus. 2010. (Ready, Set, Draw! Ser.). (ENG., Illus.). 32p. (gr. 2-4). lib. bdg. 25.26 *(978-0-7613-4168-0(4)*, Millbrook Pr.) Lerner Publishing Group.

Bredeson, Carmen. Baby Animals of the Ocean. (Nature's Baby Animals Ser.). (Illus.). 24p. (J). 2012. (gr. k-18). pap. 7.95 *(978-1-59845-407-9(2)*, Enslow Elementary) 2009. (gr. 1-3). lib. bdg. 22.60 *(978-0-7660-3003-9(2))* Enslow Pubs., Inc.

—Leafy Sea Dragons & Other Weird Sea Creatures. 2009. (I Like Weird Animals! Ser.). (Illus.). 24p. (J). (gr. 1-3). lib. bdg. 22.60 *(978-0-7660-3125-8(X)*, Enslow Elementary) Enslow Pubs., Inc.

Brewster, Joy. Animals of the Sea & Animales del Mar: 6 English, 6 Spanish Adaptations, 122 vols., Vol. 2. 2011. (SPA.). (J). instr.'s gde. ed. 97.00 net. *(978-1-4108-2397-7(0)*, 23970) Benchmark Education Co.

Brookes, Olivia. A Shark & Other Sea Creatures. 2009. (Ask Ser.). (Illus.). 32p. (J). lib. bdg. 26.50 *(978-1-4358-2515-4(2)*, PowerKids Pr.) Rosen Publishing Group, Inc., The.

Brown Bear Books (Firm) Staff, contrib. by. Ocean Life. 2007. (J). *(978-1-933834-16-0(1))* Brown Bear Books.

Brown, Laaren. Sea Creatures. 2017. (Scholastic Reader, Level 2 Ser.). (ENG.). 32p. (J). (gr. 1-3). pap. 4.99 *(978-1-338-14416-1(2))* Scholastic, Inc.

Buchanan, Shelly. The Powerful Ocean. 2015. (Science Readers: Content & Literacy Ser.). (Illus.). 32p. (J). (gr. 5-5). pap. 8.99 *(978-1-4807-4726-5(2))* Teacher Created Materials, Inc.

Bull, Peter, illus. Under the Sea. 2004. (Out & about Ser.). 12p. (J). bds. 4.99 *(978-1-85997-806-1(1))* Byeway Bks.

—Under the Sea. (Puzzle Shapes Ser.). (J). 10p. bds. *(978-2-89393-938-4(4))*; 8p. bds. *(978-2-7643-0146-3(4))* Phidal Publishing, Inc./Editions Phidal, Inc.

Buxton, Jane H. Undersea Animals: A Dramatic Dimensional Visit to Strange Underwater Realms. Pinkney, Jerry, illus. 2008. (ENG.). 12p. (J). (gr. -1-3). 14.95 *(978-1-4263-0334-0(3)*, National Geographic Children's Bks.) National Geographic Society.

Cando, Kinder. Creatures under the Sea Take Home. (J). 7.95 *(978-0-8136-0667-5(5))* Modern Curriculum Pr.

Castellano, Peter. Sea Creatures. 2016. (Monsters! Ser.). (ENG., Illus.). 32p. (J). (gr. 1-2). pap. 10.50 *(978-1-4824-4091-1(1))* Stevens, Gareth Publishing LLLP.

Cecchini, Marie E. Under the Sea: A Cross-Curricular Unit for Grades 1-3. Mitchell, Judy & Lindeen, Mary, eds. Armbrust, Janet & Skiles, Janet, illus. 2007. 32p. (J). pap. 6.95 *(978-1-57310-529-3(5))* Teaching & Learning Co.

Centore, Michael. Saving Ocean Animals: Sharks, Turtles, Coral, & Fish. 2017. (J). ***(978-1-4222-3879-0(2))*** Mason Crest.

Cerullo, Mary M. & Curtsinger, Bill. Life under Ice, 1 vol. 2003. (ENG., Illus.). 40p. (gr. 4-7). 16.95 *(978-0-88448-246-8(4)*, 884246) Tilbury Hse. Pubs.

Cerullo, Mary M. & Simmons, Beth E. Sea Secrets. Carlson, Kirsten, illus. 2015. (Long Term Ecological Research Ser.). (ENG.). 32p. (J). (gr. 1-5). pap. 9.95 *(978-1-63076-075-5(7))* Taylor Trade Publishing.

Chorkung, illus. Sea Creatures. 2017. (First Explorers Ser.). (ENG.). 10p. (J). (— 1). bds. 8.95 ***(978-1-4549-2658-0(9))*** Sterling Publishing Co., Inc.

Christiansen, Per. Terrifying & Ugly Sea Creatures. 2008. (Nature's Monsters Ser.). (Illus.). 32p. (YA). (gr. 3-6). lib. bdg. 26.00 *(978-0-8368-9221-5(6))* Stevens, Gareth Publishing LLLP.

Clark, Willow. Asian Dolphins & Other Marine Mammals. 2012. (Animals of Asia Ser.). (ENG., Illus.). 24p. (J). (gr. 1-5). 22.60 *(978-1-4488-7419-4(X))*; pap. 8.25 *(978-1-4488-7492-7(0))* Rosen Publishing Group, Inc., The. (PowerKids Pr.).

Clarke, Phillip. Seas & Oceans Sticker Atlas. Le Rolland, Leonard, illus. 2006. 24p. (J). pap. 8.95 *(978-0-7945-1218-7(6)*, Usborne) EDC Publishing.

Claybourne, Anna & Ganeri, Anita. Seas & Oceans. 2014. (First Animal Encyclopedia Ser.). (ENG., Illus.). 64p. (J). (gr. -1-3). 13.99 *(978-1-4088-4305-5(6)*, 9781408843055, Bloomsbury USA Childrens) Bloomsbury Publishing USA.

Claybourne, Anna, et al. Living in the Wild: Sea Mammals. 2013. (Living in the Wild: Sea Mammals Ser.). (ENG.). 48p. (gr. 4-6). pap. 53.94 *(978-1-4329-7074-1(7))*; lib. bdg. 166.60 *(978-1-4329-7067-3(4))* Heinemann-Raintree. (Heinemann InfoSearch).

Clemson, Wendy & Clemson, David. Ocean Giants. 2007. (Math Adventures Ser.). (Illus.). 32p. (gr. 1-4). pap. 10.50 *(978-0-8368-8139-4(7))*; lib. bdg. 26.00 *(978-0-8368-7840-0(X))* Stevens, Gareth Publishing LLLP. (Gareth Stevens Learning Library).

Cocoretto, illus. In the Ocean. 2016. (Peekaboo! Ser.: 4). (ENG.). 12p. (J). bds. *(978-1-84643-867-7(5))* Child's Play International Ltd.

Cole, Joanna. On the Ocean Floor. Degen, Bruce, illus. 2010. (Magic School Bus Ser.). (ENG.). (J). (gr. 2-5). 9.99 *(978-0-545-22751-3(8))* Scholastic, Inc.

—Sea Creatures. 2014. (Magic School Bus Presents Ser.). lib. bdg. 17.20 *(978-0-606-35814-9(5))* Turtleback Bks.

Cole, Joanna & Jackson, Tom. Sea Creatures. Degen, Bruce & Bracken, Carolyn, illus. 2014. (Magic School Bus Presents Ser.). (ENG.). 32p. (J). (gr. 1-3). pap. 6.99 *(978-0-545-68366-1(1)*, Scholastic Paperbacks) Scholastic, Inc.

Coleman, Miriam. Swimming with Manatees. 2009. (Flippers & Fins Ser.). (Illus.). 24p. (J). (ENG.). pap. 8.25 *(978-1-4358-3241-1(8)*, PowerKids Pr.); (gr. 1-3). lib. bdg. 22.60 *(978-1-4042-8092-2(8))* Rosen Publishing Group, Inc., The.

Collard, Sneed B., III. The Deep-Sea Floor. Wenzel, Gregory, illus. 2003. (ENG.). 32p. (J). (gr. 1-4). pap. 7.95 *(978-1-57091-403-4(6))* Charlesbridge Publishing, Inc.

—One Night in the Coral Sea. Brickman, Robin, illus. 2006. (ENG.). 32p. (J). (gr. 1-4). pap. 7.95 *(978-1-57091-390-7(0))* Charlesbridge Publishing, Inc.

—One Night in the Coral Sea. Brickman, Robin, illus. 2006. 32p. (gr. 3-7). 17.95 *(978-0-7569-6969-1(7))* Perfection Learning Corp.

Collins. Collins Fascinating Facts - Oceans. 2016. (Collins Fascinating Facts Ser.). (ENG.). 72p. (J). (gr. 1-3). pap. 10.99 *(978-0-00-816924-4(1))* HarperCollins Pubs. Ltd. GBR. Dist: Independent Pubs. Group.

Confalone, Nick & Confalone, Chelsea. Ocean Monsters. 2013. (Penguin Young Readers, Level 4 Ser.). (ENG.). 48p. (J). (gr. 3-4). pap. 3.99 *(978-0-448-46723-8(2)*, Penguin Young Readers) Penguin Young Readers Group.

Craig, Diane. Manatee, 1 vol. 2014. (Giant Animals Ser.). (ENG., Illus.). 24p. (J). (gr. -1-3). 24.21 *(978-1-62403-059-8(9))* ABDO Publishing Co.

Crenson, Victoria. Horseshoe Crabs & Shorebirds: The Story of a Foodweb, 0 vols. Cannon, Annie, illus. unabr. ed. 2009. (ENG.). 42p. (J). (gr. 3-5). pap. 9.99 *(978-0-7614-5552-3(3)*, 9780761455523, Amazon Children's Publishing) Amazon Publishing.

Crow, Marilee. Down by the Shore. Roberts, Mary Sue, photos by. 2011. (Illus.). 30p. 19.95 *(978-1-61633-087-3(2))* Guardian Angel Publishing, Inc.

Cryan, Mary Beth. Easy-to-Make Sea Animals Finger Puppets. 2012. (Dover Children's Activity Bks.). (ENG., Illus.). 16p. (J). (gr. 2-5). 9.99 *(978-0-486-48845-5(4))* Dover Pubns., Inc.

Dahl, Michael & Jensen, Brian. Profundo, Más Profundo, Muy Profundo: Animales Que Van a Grandes Profundidades. Translations.com Staff, tr. from ENG. Dahl, Michael & Jensen, Brian, illus. 2012. (Los Extremos y Los Animales/Animal Extremes Ser.).Tr. of Deep, Deeper, Deepest - Animals That Go to Great Depths. (ENG, SPA & MUL., Illus.). 24p. (gr. k-2). lib. bdg. 26.65 *(978-1-4048-7319-3(8))* Picture Window Bks.

Dawson, Emily C. Ocean Animals. 2010. (Our Animal World Ser.). 24p. (J). 25.65 *(978-1-60753-013-8(9))* Amicus Publishing.

Day, Nancy. Way down below Deep, 1 vol. Sheldon, David, illus. 2014. (ENG.). 32p. (J). (gr. k-3). 16.99 *(978-1-4556-1945-0(0))* Pelican Publishing Co., Inc.

Daynes, Katie. 1001 Things to Spot in the Sea. Gower, Teri, illus. 2009. (1001 Things to Spot Ser.). 32p. (J). (gr. 1). 9.99 *(978-0-7945-2615-3(2)*, Usborne) EDC Publishing.

—1001 Things to Spot in the Sea. 2004. (1001 Things to Spot Ser.). 32p. (J). pap. 6.95 *(978-0-7945-0229-4(6))* EDC Publishing.

De la Bédoyère, Camilla. Deep Ocean. 2010. (Unpredictable Nature Ser.). (Illus.). 48p. (J). (gr. 3-18). lib. bdg. 19.95 *(978-1-4222-1997-3(6))* Mason Crest.

—Fry to Sea Horse. 2011. (LifeCycles Ser.). (ENG.). 24p. (J). (gr. -1-k). lib. bdg. 15.99 *(978-1-60992-049-4(X))* QEB Publishing Inc.

de Lambilly-Bresson, Elisabeth. Animales de la Charca. 2007. (Los animales nos cuentan su vida (Animal Show & Tell) Ser.). (SPA., Illus.). 16p. (gr. -1-3). lib. bdg. 19.00 *(978-0-8368-8103-5(6)*, Gareth Stevens Learning Library) Stevens, Gareth Publishing LLLP.

—Animales de la Granja. 2007. (Los animales nos cuentan su vida (Animal Show & Tell) Ser.). (SPA., Illus.). 16p. (gr. -1-3). lib. bdg. 19.00 *(978-0-8368-8104-2(4)*, Gareth Stevens Learning Library) Stevens, Gareth Publishing LLLP.

—Animales Marinos. 2007. (Los animales nos cuentan su vida (Animal Show & Tell) Ser.). (SPA., Illus.). 16p. (gr. -1-3). lib. bdg. 19.00 *(978-0-8368-8162-2(1)*, Gareth Stevens Learning Library) Stevens, Gareth Publishing LLLP.

—Animals at the Pond. 2007. (Animal Show & Tell Ser.). (Illus.). 16p. (gr. -1-3). lib. bdg. 19.00 *(978-0-8368-7830-1(2)*, Gareth Stevens Learning Library) Stevens, Gareth Publishing LLLP.

—Sea Animals. 2007. (Animal Show & Tell Ser.). (Illus.). 16p. (gr. -1-3). lib. bdg. 19.00 *(978-0-8368-8160-8(5)*, Gareth Stevens Learning Library) Stevens, Gareth Publishing LLLP.

Delano, Marfé Ferguson & National Geographic Society Staff. Sea Monsters: A Prehistoric Adventure. 2007. (National Geographic Kids Ser.). (ENG., Illus.). 32p. (J). (gr. 3-7). pap. 6.95 *(978-1-4263-0162-9(6)*, National Geographic Children's Bks.) National Geographic Society.

Dembicki, Matt, ed. Wild Ocean: Sharks, Whales, Rays, & Other Endangered Sea Creatures. 2014. (ENG., Illus.). 156p. (YA). (gr. 7). pap. 19.95 *(978-1-938486-38-8(2))* Fulcrum Publishing.

Denne, B. First Encyclopedia of Seas & Oceans II. rev. ed. 2011. (First Encyclopedias Ser.). 64p. (J). pap. 9.99 *(978-0-7945-3048-8(6)*, Usborne) EDC Publishing.

Diamond, Claudia. What's under the Sea? 2009. (Reading Room Collection 2 Ser.). 24p. (gr. 3-4). 42.50 *(978-1-60852-002-2(1)*, PowerKids Pr.) Rosen Publishing Group, Inc., The.

Diaz, Joanne Ruelos. Animals by the Seashore, 1 vol. Mendez, Simon, illus. 2014. (Animals All Day! Ser.). (ENG.). 32p. (gr. k-2). 27.27 *(978-1-4795-5700-4(5))* Picture Window Bks.

DiCicco, Sue. 1, 2, 3 in the Sea. DiCicco, Sue, illus. 2012. (ENG., Illus.). 10p. (J). (— 1). bds. 6.99 *(978-0-545-43238-2(3))* Scholastic, Inc.

Dils, Tracey E. Under the Sea 1,2,3: An Ocean Counting Book. 2015. (1, 2, 3... Count with Me Ser.). (ENG., Illus.). 24p. (J). (gr. k-2). 19.95 *(978-1-60753-717-5(6))* Amicus Publishing.

Dorling Kindersley Publishing Staff. Amazing Giant Sea Creatures. 2014. (Amazing Giant Ser.). (ENG.). 16p. (J). (gr. -1-1). 19.99 *(978-1-4654-1901-9(2)*, DK Children) Dorling Kindersley Publishing, Inc.

—Ocean Glow in the Dark. 2003. (Ultimate Sticker Bks.). (ENG., Illus.). 16p. (J). (gr. k-3). pap. 6.99 *(978-0-7894-9277-7(6)*, DK Children) Dorling Kindersley Publishing, Inc.

—Oceans. 2015. (Eye Wonder Ser.). (ENG., Illus.). 56p. (J). (gr. k-4). 10.99 *(978-1-4654-1852-4(0)*, DK Children) Dorling Kindersley Publishing, Inc.

—Sharks & Other Deadly Ocean Creatures. 2016. (ENG., Illus.). 208p. (J). (gr. 4-7). 16.99 *(978-1-4654-5084-5(X)*, DK Children) Dorling Kindersley Publishing, Inc.

Dorling Kindersley Publishing Staff & Lock, Deborah. DK Adventures: Terrors of the Deep: Terrors of the Deep. 2013. (DK Adventures Ser.). (ENG.). 128p. (J). (gr. 3-7). 16.99 *(978-1-4654-1812-8(1)*, DK Children) Dorling Kindersley Publishing, Inc.

Dunn, Joeming & Denham, Brian. Shamu: The 1st Killer Whale in Captivity, 1 vol. 2011. (Famous Firsts: Animals Making History Ser.). (ENG., Illus.). 32p. (YA). (gr. 3-6). 28.50 *(978-1-61641-642-3(4))* Magic Wagon.

Duopress Labs Staff. Hello, Ocean Friends. 2015. (ENG., Illus.). 20p. (J). (-k). bds. 7.95 *(978-1-938093-41-8(0))* Duo Pr. LLC.

Eggleton, Jill. The Deep Ocean. 2007. (Connectors Ser.). (gr. 2-5). pap. *(978-1-877453-02-1(1))* Global Education Systems Ltd.

Encyclopaedia Britannica Publishers, Inc. Staff. Creatures of the Waters. 2003. (Illus.). 64p. 14.95 *(978-1-59339-014-3(9))* Encyclopaedia Britannica, Inc.

Erickson, Paul. The Pier at the End of the World, 1 vol. Martinez, Andrew, photos by. 2014. (Tilbury House Nature Book Ser.: 0). (ENG., Illus.). 36p. (gr. 3-7). 17.95 *(978-0-88448-382-3(7)*, 884382) Tilbury Hse. Pubs.

Evans, Topper. 200-Year-Old Red Sea Urchins! 2016. (World's Longest-Living Animals Ser.). 00024p. (J). lib. bdg. 22.60 ***(978-1-4824-5597-7(8))*** Stevens, Gareth Publishing LLLP.

Familius Staff & Miles, David. Slide-N-Seek: Ocean. 2017. (ENG., Illus.). 10p. (J). 15.95 *(978-1-944822-46-0(1))* Familius LLC.

Farndon, John. Marine Superstars. Portolano, Cristina, illus. 2016. (Animal Bests Ser.). (ENG.). 32p. (J). (gr. 3-6). lib. bdg. 26.65 *(978-1-5124-0625-2(2))* Lerner Publishing Group.

Farrell, Russell & Fisher, Diana, illus. All about Drawing Sea Creatures & Animals. 2010. (All about Drawing Ser.). 80p. (J). 34.25 *(978-1-936309-08-5(4))* Quarto Publishing Group USA.

Faundez, Anne. Sea Ceatures. 2004. (QEB Start Reading Ser.). (Illus.). 24p. (J). lib. bdg. 15.95 *(978-1-59566-008-4(9))* QEB Publishing Inc.

Ferri, Francesca. Peek-A-Boo Sea. 2014. (ENG., Illus.). 12p. (J). (gr. -1 — 1). 8.99 *(978-0-7641-6724-9(3))* Barron's Educational Series, Inc.

Fiedler, Heidi. Sea Swimmers: A Close-Up Photographic Look Inside Your World. 2017. (Up Close Ser.). (ENG., Illus.). (J). (gr. k-6). lib. bdg. 27.99 ***(978-1-942875-34-5(7)***, Walter Foster Jr) Quarto Publishing Group USA.

Firth, Alex & Lacey, Minna. Big Book of Big Sea Creatures. 2012. (Big Bks). 16p. (J). ring bd. 14.99 *(978-0-7945-3244-4(6)*, Usborne) EDC Publishing.

Fish, Lori Flying. One Shining Starfish. Fish, Lori Flying, illus. 2010. (Illus.). 16p. pap. 9.95 *(978-1-936343-12-6(6))* Peppertree Pr., The.

Fleisher, Paul. Ocean Food Webs in Action. 2013. (Searchlight Books What Is a Food Web Ser.). (ENG., Illus.). 40p. (gr. 3-5). pap. 8.95 *(978-1-4677-1556-0(5))*; lib. bdg. 27.93 *(978-1-4677-1255-2(8)*, Lerner Pubns.) Lerner Publishing Group.

Fokina, N. N., et al. Lipidnyi Sostav Midii Mytilus Edulis L. Belogo Moria: Vliianie Nekotorykh Faktorov Sredy Obitaniia. 2010. (RUS., Illus.). 241p. pap. *(978-5-9274-0405-6(7))* Karel'skij naucnyj centr Rossijskoj akademii nauk.

Franco, Betsy. A Spectacular Selection of Sea Critters: Concrete Poems. Wertz, Michael, illus. 2015. (ENG.). 32p. (J). (gr. 2-5). 19.99 *(978-1-4677-2152-3(2)*, Millbrook Pr.) Lerner Publishing Group.

Franklin, Carolyn. Ocean Life. Franklin, Carolyn, illus. 2013. (World of Wonder Ser.). (Illus.). 32p. (gr. 1-3). 31.35 ***(978-1-904642-63-3(2))*** Book Hse. GBR. Dist: Black Rabbit Bks.

Franklin, Carolyn & Stewart, David. Ocean Life. Franklin, Carolyn, illus. 2008. (World of Wonder Ser.). (ENG., Illus.). 32p. (J). (gr. 1-4). 29.00 *(978-0-531-20451-1(0)*, Children's Pr.) Scholastic Library Publishing.

Furstinger, Nancy. 12 Marine Animals Back from the Brink. 2014. (ENG., Illus.). 32p. (J). *(978-1-63235-004-6(1))* Pr. Room Editions LLC.

Gaarder-Juntti, Oona. What Lives in Coral Reefs?, 1 vol. 2008. (Animal Habitats Ser.). (ENG., Illus.). 24p. (J). (gr. k-3). 25.65 *(978-1-60453-170-1(3))* ABDO Publishing Co.

—What Lives in Streams & Rivers?, 1 vol. 2008. (Animal Habitats Ser.). (ENG., Illus.). 24p. (J). (gr. k-3). 25.65 *(978-1-60453-171-8(1))* ABDO Publishing Co.

—What Lives in the Ocean?, 1 vol. 2008. (Animal Habitats Ser.). (ENG., Illus.). 24p. (J). (gr. k-3). 25.65 *(978-1-60453-175-6(4))* ABDO Publishing Co.

Galvin, Laura Gates. Alphabet of Ocean Animals. Petruccio, Steven James et al, illus. 2009. (ENG.). 40p. 9.95 *(978-1-60727-024-9(2))* Soundprints.

—Alphabet of Ocean Animals. Petruccio, Steven James et al, illus. 2007. (ENG.). 40p. (J). (gr. k-2). 15.95 *(978-1-59249-690-7(3))* Soundprints.

Ganeri, Anita. I Wonder Why the Sea Is Salty. 2014. 32p. pap. 7.00 *(978-1-61003-352-7(3))* Center for the Collaborative Classroom.

—I Wonder Why the Sea Is Salty: And Other Questions about the Oceans. 2011. (I Wonder Why Ser.). (ENG., Illus.). 32p. (J). (gr. k-3). pap. 6.99 *(978-0-7534-6521-9(3)*, 9780753465219, Kingfisher) Roaring Brook Pr.

—Lifesize: Ocean. Jackson-Carter, Stuart, illus. 2014. (ENG.). 32p. (J). (gr. k-4). 16.99 *(978-0-7534-7096-1(9)*, 9780753470961, Kingfisher) Roaring Brook Pr.

Gardeski, Christina Mia. All about Oceans. 2017. (Habitats Ser.). (ENG.). 24p. (gr. k-1). lib. bdg. 21.99 ***(978-1-5157-7644-4(1)***, Pebble Bks.) Capstone Press of Coughlan Cos.

Garrett, Ann & Higney, Gene-Michael. Fins & Flippers, Scales & Nippers. 2003. (Illus.). 32p. (J). pap. *(978-1-59034-871-0(0))*; 15.95 *(978-1-59034-869-7(9))* Mondo Publishing.

Gibbs, Edward. I Spy under the Sea. Gibbs, Edward, illus. 2012. (ENG., Illus.). 32p. (J). (gr. k-k). 14.99 *(978-0-7636-5952-3(5)*, Templar) Candlewick Pr.

Gigantes marinos de la época de los dinosaurios (Sea Giants of Dinosaur Time) 2006. (J). pap. 6.95 *(978-0-8225-6638-0(9)*, Ediciones Lerner) Lerner Publishing Group.

Gish, Melissa. Manatees. 2016. (Illus.). 46p. (J). *(978-1-60818-705-8(5)*, Creative Education) Creative Co., The.

Golding, Elizabeth. Moonlight Ocean. Lodge, Ali, illus. 2012. (ENG.). 12p. (J). (gr. -1-3). 12.95 *(978-0-7624-4486-1(X))* Running Pr. Bk. Pubs.

Goldish, Meish. Florida Manatees: Warm Water Miracles. 2007. (America's Animal Comebacks Ser.). (Illus.). 32p. (YA). (gr. 2-5). lib. bdg. 25.27 *(978-1-59716-507-5(7))* Bearport Publishing Co., Inc.

Goldsack, Gaby. Ocean Animals. Bampton, Bob, illus. (J). *(978-1-57755-508-7(2))* Flying Frog Publishing, Inc.

Gordon, Sharon. Adivina Quien Atrapa. 2006. (Bookworms Ser.). (SPA & ENG., Illus.). 32p. (gr. k-2). lib. bdg. 15.95 *(978-0-7614-2383-6(4))* Marshall Cavendish Corp.

—Animales del Mar. Victory Productions, Inc. Staff, tr. from ENG. 2008. (Animales Salvajes Ser.). (SPA.). 24p. (gr. k-1). lib. bdg. 15.95 *(978-0-7614-3431-3(3)*, Benchmark Bks.) Marshall Cavendish Corp.

—Ocean Animals. 2008. (Animals in the Wild Ser.). 24p. (gr. k-1). lib. bdg. 15.95 *(978-0-7614-2903-6(4)*, Benchmark Bks.) Marshall Cavendish Corp.

Gowen, Fiona, illus. Incredible Sharks & Other Ocean Giants. 2016. (How to Draw Ser.). (ENG.). 32p. (J). (gr. 2-6). pap. 4.99 *(978-1-4380-0853-0(8))* Barron's Educational Series, Inc.

Greenaway, Theresa, ed. Ocean: A Foldout Book & Wall Chart. 2005. (Illus.). 12p. (J). (gr. k-4). reprint ed. 10.00 *(978-0-7567-8533-8(2))* DIANE Publishing Co.

Gross, Miriam J. The Moray Eel. 2006. (Weird Sea Creatures Ser.). (Illus.). 24p. (J). (gr. 3-7). lib. bdg. 22.60 *(978-1-4042-3189-4(7))* Rosen Publishing Group, Inc., The.

—The Octopus. 2006. (Weird Sea Creatures Ser.). (Illus.). 23p. (J). lib. bdg. 22.60 *(978-1-4042-3188-7(9)*, PowerKids Pr.) Rosen Publishing Group, Inc., The.

—The Sea Slug: Nudibranchs. 2006. (Weird Sea Creatures Ser.). (Illus.). 24p. (J). (gr. 3-7). lib. bdg. 22.60 *(978-1-4042-3191-7(9)*, PowerKids Pr.) Rosen Publishing Group, Inc., The.

—The Stingray. 2006. (Weird Sea Creatures Ser.). (Illus.). 24p. (J). (gr. 3-7). lib. bdg. 22.60 *(978-1-4042-3190-0(0)*, PowerKids Pr.) Rosen Publishing Group, Inc., The.

Group/McGraw-Hill, Wright. Under the Sea, 6 vols. (Wildcats Ser.). 32p. (gr. 2-8). *(978-0-322-05862-0(7))* Wright Group/McGraw-Hill.

Guiberson, Brenda Z. The Most Amazing Creature in the Sea. Spirin, Gennady, illus. 2015. (ENG.). 32p. (J). (gr. -1-3). 17.99 *(978-0-8050-9961-4(1)*, 9780805099614, Holt, Henry & Co. Bks. For Young Readers) Holt, Henry & Co.

Hall, Howard. The Secrets of Kelp Forests: Life's Ebb & Flow in the Sea's Richest Habitat. Leon, Vicki, ed. 2nd ed. 2007. (Jean-Michel Cousteau Presents Ser.). (ENG., Illus.). 48p. (J). (gr. 3-9). pap. 9.95 *(978-0-9766134-9-7(2))* London Town Pr.

Hall, Stephen. Exploring the Oceans. 2012. (ENG., Illus.). 48p. (J). 15.00 *(978-1-899762-79-8(5))* Award Pubns. Ltd. GBR. Dist: Parkwest Pubns., Inc.

Hansen, Judith. Seashells in My Pocket: AMC's Family Guide to Exploring the Coast from Maine to Florida. Sabaka, Donna, illus. 3rd ed. 2008. (ENG.). 160p. (gr. 3-7). per. 14.95 *(978-1-929173-61-7(X))* Appalachian Mountain Club Bks.

Hardy, A. S. Sea Stories for Wonder Eyes. 2005. reprint ed. pap. 21.95 *(978-1-4191-0670-5(8))* Kessinger Publishing, LLC.

Harris, Nicholas, text. Panoramas: Ocean Life. 2006. (Illus.). 23p. (J). *(978-0-7607-8156-2(7))* backpackbook.

Harrison, Paul. Sea Monsters. (Up Close Ser.). 24p. (gr. 3-3). 2009. 47.90 *(978-1-60854-701-2(9))* 2008. (Illus.). (J). lib. bdg. 25.25 *(978-1-4042-4224-1(4))* Rosen Publishing Group, Inc., The. (PowerKids Pr.).

Harrod-Eagles, Cynthia, et al. Curious about Fishes. 2015. (Smithsonian Ser.). (ENG., Illus.). 32p. (J). (gr. 1-3). bds. 3.99 *(978-0-448-48462-4(5)*, Grosset & Dunlap) Penguin Young Readers Group.

Harvey, Jeanne Walker. Astro: The Steller Sea Lion, 1 vol. Bersani, Shennen, illus. 2010. (ENG.). 32p. (J). (gr. -1-4). pap. 9.95 *(978-1-60718-874-2(0))* Arbordale Publishing.

Heos, Bridget. Do You Really Want a Hamster? Longhi, Katya, illus. 2013. (Do You Really Want a Pet? Ser.). (ENG.). 24p. (gr. 1-4). 27.10 *(978-1-60753-206-4(9))* Amicus Publishing.

Herndon, Ryan, compiled by. 3-D Deep-Sea Creatures! 2007. (Illus.). 31p. (J). *(978-0-439-02696-3(2))* Scholastic, Inc.

Hibbert, Clare. Seaside Plants & Animals. 2016. (Beside the Seaside Ser.). (ENG., Illus.). 24p. (J). (gr. k-2). 16.99 *(978-1-4451-3766-7(6)*, Franklin Watts) Hachette Children's Group GBR. Dist: Hachette Bk. Group.

Hirschi, Ron. Winter Is for Whales: A Book of Hawaiian Seasons. Green, Yuko, illus. 2007. (ENG.). 36p. (J). (gr. -1-3). *(978-1-59700-504-3(5))* Island Heritage Publishing.

Hogan, Martina, illus. 123 under the Sea. 2016. (Early Birds Ser.). (ENG.). 12p. (J). (gr. -1 — 1). bds. 6.99 *(978-1-4998-0208-5(0))* Little Bee Books Inc.

Holden, Pam. Watch Me Swim, 6 pack. Hansen, Christine, illus. 2009. (Red Rocket Readers Ser.). (ENG.). 16p. (gr. -1-1). pap. *(978-1-877363-31-3(6)*, Red Rocket Readers) Flying Start Bks.

Hopgood, Sally. Let's Find Ocean Animals. Hinton, Steph, illus. 2017. (Let's Find Pull-The-Tab Bks.). (ENG.). 12p. (J). (gr. -1-k). bds. 9.99 ***(978-1-78700-058-2(3))*** Top That! Publishing PLC GBR. Dist: Independent Pubs. Group.

Hopkins, Therese. Underwater Homes. 2009. (Home Sweet Home Ser.). (J). (gr. k-2). (Illus.). 24p. pap. 8.25 *(978-1-4358-3068-4(7)*, PowerKids Pr.); lib. bdg. 22.60 *(978-1-4358-2694-6(9))* Rosen Publishing Group, Inc., The.

Horsman, Paul. Out of the Blue: A Journey Through the World's Oceans. Seapics.com Staff, photos by. 2005. (ENG., Illus.). 160p. (gr. 17). 32.95 *(978-0-262-08341-6(8)*, 0262083418) MIT Pr.

Hoyt, Erich. Weird Sea Creatures. 2013. (ENG., Illus.). 64p. (J). (gr. 5-12). 19.95 *(978-1-77085-197-9(6)*, 9781770851979); pap. 9.95 *(978-1-77085-191-7(7)*, 9781770851917) Firefly Bks., Ltd.

Hubbell, Patricia. Papa Fish's Lullaby. Eaddy, Susan, illus. 2007. (ENG.). 32p. (J). (gr. -1-1). 16.95 *(978-1-55971-965-0(6))* Cooper Square Publishing Llc.

Hudak, Heather C. Marine Mammals. (Animal Facts Ser.). (Illus.). 24p. (J). 2005. (gr. 2-3). per. 8.95 *(978-1-59036-247-1(0))* 2004. lib. bdg. 24.45 *(978-1-59036-201-3(2))* Weigl Pubs., Inc.

Hughes, Mónica. Swimming Giants. 2007. (I Love Reading Ser.). (Illus.). 24p. (J). (gr. -1-2). lib. bdg. 19.96 *(978-1-59716-542-6(5))* Bearport Publishing Co., Inc.

Hugo, Pierre de, illus. The Seashore. 2012. (My First Discoveries Ser.: 13). (ENG.). 38p. (J). (gr. -1-k). spiral bd. 14.99 *(978-1-85103-394-2(7))* Moonlight Publishing, Ltd. GBR. Dist: Independent Pubs. Group.

Hyde, Natalie. Deep Sea Extremes. 2008. (Extreme Nature Ser.). (ENG., Illus.). 32p. (J). (gr. 2-3). pap. *(978-0-7787-4518-1(X))*; lib. bdg. *(978-0-7787-4501-3(5))* Crabtree Publishing Co.

Ipcar, Dahlov. Deep Sea Farm. 2014. (ENG., Illus.). 40p. (J). (gr. -1-3). 17.95 *(978-1-60893-317-4(2))* Down East Bks.

Jackson, Tom. Scary Sea Monsters. 2010. (Dangerous Animals Ser.). (ENG.). 32p. (J). (gr. 2-6). pap. 10.50 *(978-1-4339-4047-7(7)*, Gareth Stevens Learning Library); (YA). (gr. 3-6). lib. bdg. 26.60 *(978-1-4339-4046-0(9))* Stevens, Gareth Publishing LLLP.

Jango-Cohen, Judith. Real-Life Sea Monsters. 2009. pap. 40.95 *(978-0-7613-4820-7(4))* Lerner Publishing Group.

—Real-Life Sea Monsters. Burney, Ryan, illus. 2007. (On My Own Science Ser.). 48p. (J). (gr. 3-7). lib. bdg. 25.26

The check digit for ISBN-10 appears in parentheses after the full ISBN-13.

(978-0-8225-6747-9(4), Millbrook Pr.) Lerner Publishing Group.
—Real-life Sea Monsters. 2008. 48p. (J). pap. 6.95 (978-0-8225-6750-9(4), First Avenue Editions) Lerner Publishing Group.
Jenkins, Steve. Down, Down, Down: A Journey to the Bottom of the Sea. Jenkins, Steve, illus. 2009. (ENG., Illus.). 40p. (J). (gr. -1-3). 17.99 (978-0-618-96636-3(6)) Houghton Mifflin Harcourt Publishing Co.
Jenkins, Steve & Page, Robin. Flying Frogs & Walking Fish: Leaping Lemurs, Tumbling Toads, Jet-Propelled Jellyfish, & More Surprising Ways That Animals Move. 2016. (ENG., Illus.). 40p. (J). (gr. -1-3). 17.99 (978-0-544-63090-1(4), HMH Books For Young Readers) Houghton Mifflin Harcourt Publishing Co.
Jennings, Dorothy. Otters Smash, Crabs Pinch. 2017. (Hunter & Hunted: Animal Survival Ser.). 24p. (J). (gr. 7-8). 23.60 **(978-1-5081-5662-8(X)**, PowerKids Pr.) Rosen Publishing Group, Inc., The.
Jerome, Kate Boehm. Science at the Aquarium. 2006. (Reading Expeditions Ser.). (ENG., Illus.). 24p. (J). pap. 14.95 (978-0-7922-8625-7(1)) CENGAGE Learning.
Johnson, Gee. Orcas. 2011. (Power 100 - Marine Life Ser.). 24p. (J). (gr. k-2). pap. 6.95 (978-1-61541-403-1(7)) American Reading Co.
Johnson, Jinny. Coral Reef Life. 2011. (Watery Worlds Ser.). 32p. (gr. 3-6). 31.35 (978-1-59920-502-1(5)) Black Rabbit Bks.
—Deep Sea Life. 2011. (Watery Worlds Ser.). 32p. (gr. 3-6). 31.35 (978-1-59920-503-8(3)) Black Rabbit Bks.
—Ocean Life. 2011. (Watery Worlds Ser.). 32p. (gr. 3-6). 31.35 (978-1-59920-504-5(1)) Black Rabbit Bks.
—Seashore Life. 2011. (Watery Worlds Ser.). 32p. (gr. 3-6). lib. bdg. 31.35 (978-1-59920-501-4(7)) Black Rabbit Bks.
Johnson, Rebecca L. Journey into the Deep: Discovering New Ocean Creatures. 2010. (Exceptional Science Titles for Intermediate Grades Ser.). (ENG.). 64p. (gr. 4-8). lib. bdg. 31.93 (978-0-7613-4148-2(X)) Lerner Publishing Group.
Kainen, Dan. Ocean: A Photicular Book. 2014. (ENG., Illus.). 12p. 25.95 (978-0-7611-8051-7(6), 18051) Workman Publishing Co., Inc.
Kalman, Bobbie. Baby Animals in Ocean Habitats. 2011. (Habitats of Baby Animals Ser.). (ENG.). 24p. (J). (gr. k-3). (978-0-7787-7729-8(4)); pap. (978-0-7787-7742-7(1)) Crabtree Publishing Co.
Kalman, Bobbie & Dyer, Hadley. Endangered Manatees. 2006. (Earth's Endangered Animals Ser.). (ENG., Illus.). 32p. (J). (gr. 3-7). pap. (978-0-7787-1914-4(6)) Crabtree Publishing Co.
Kalman, Bobbie & Langille, Jacqueline. Les Mammiferes Marins. 2003. (Petit Monde Vivant Ser.). (FRE., Illus.). 32p. (J). pap. 9.95 (978-2-920660-97-7(7)) Bayard Canada Livres CAN. Dist: Crabtree Publishing Co.
Karwoski, Gail Langer. Water Beds: Sleeping in the Ocean, 1 vol. McLennan, Connie, illus. 2005. (ENG.). 32p. (J). (gr. -1-3). 15.95 (978-0-9764943-1-7(0)); pap. 8.95 (978-1-934359-01-3(7), 9781934359013) Arbordale Publishing.
Kavanagh, James. My First Seashores Nature. Leung, Raymond, illus. 2011. (Nature Activity Book Ser.). (ENG.). 32p. (J). (gr. 2-4). act. bk. ed. 6.95 (978-1-58355-590-3(0)) Western National Parks Assn.
—Seashore Wildlife. Leung, Raymond, illus. 2nd ed. 2011. (Nature Activity Book Ser.). (ENG.). 32p. (J). (gr. 4-7). act. bk. ed. 6.95 (978-1-58355-584-2(6)) Western National Parks Assn.
Kavanaugh, Missy & Gurman, Sarah, texts. Sea Creatures. 2009. (Illus.). (J). (978-1-4351-1785-3(9)) Barnes & Noble, Inc.
Kenan, Tessa. ¡Mira, una Raya! (Look, a Ray!) 2017. (Bumba Books (tm) en Español — Veo Animales Marinos (I See Ocean Animals) Ser.). (SPA., Illus.). 24p. (J). (gr. -1-1). 25.32 (978-1-5124-2867-4(1)) Lerner Publishing Group.
Kidpressions! Sea Creature Creations: A Hand Print Discovery Book. Uting, Justin, illus. 2008. 32p. pap. 24.95 (978-1-60610-853-6(0)) America Star Bks.
Kingfisher Editors. Animal Babies in Seas. 2006. (Animal Babies Ser.). (ENG., Illus.). 10p. (J). (gr. -1-k). bds. 6.99 (978-0-7534-5945-4(0), 9780753459454, Kingfisher) Roaring Brook Pr.
—Baby Animals - In the Sea. 2012. (Baby Animals Ser.). (ENG., Illus.). 14p. (J). (gr. -1-k). bds. 5.99 (978-0-7534-6689-6(9), 9780753466896, Kingfisher) Roaring Brook Pr.
Kingfisher Publications, Inc. Staff, creator. Animal Babies in Ponds & Rivers. 2007. (Animal Babies Ser.). (ENG., Illus.). 24p. (J). (gr. -1-k). bds. 6.99 (978-0-7534-6059-7(9), 9780753460597, Kingfisher) Roaring Brook Pr.
Kingsley, Charles. Glaucus: The Wonders of the Shore. 2006. (ENG.). 122p. pap. 18.99 (978-1-4264-0318-7(6)); 116p. pap. 19.99 (978-1-4264-0369-9(0)) Creative Media Partners, LLC.
Kralovansky, Susan. Whale or Fish?, 1 vol. 2014. (This or That? Ser.). (ENG.). 24p. (J). (gr. 5-10). lib. bdg. 25.65 (978-1-62403-290-5(7), Super SandCastle) ABDO Publishing Co.
Kranking, Kathy & Carrano, Matthew T. Swimming with Saurs. 2006. 32p. (J). (978-0-439-83875-7(4)) Scholastic, Inc.
Kravetz, Jonathan. Ticks. 2006. (Gross Bugs Ser.). (Illus.). 24p. (J). (gr. 3-7). lib. bdg. 22.60 (978-1-4042-3046-0(7), PowerKids Pr.) Rosen Publishing Group, Inc., The.
Kroll, Jennifer. Mighty Micros: Little Things Big Results, 1 vol. 2nd rev. ed. 2013. (Nonfiction Readers Ser.). (ENG., Illus.). 64p. (J). (gr. 5-5). pap. 31.96 (978-1-4333-7447-0(1)) Teacher Created Materials, Inc.
Kronstadt, Jonathan. Ocean Extremes: Life in the Darkest Depths & under the Ice. 2005. (Illus.). 48p. (J). (978-0-439-71190-6(8)) Scholastic, Inc.
Krusinski, Anna. Ocean Friends: A Journey Beneath the Sea. 2016. (Kubu Ser.). (ENG., Illus.). 32p. (J). (gr. -1-2). pap. 5.99 (978-1-57826-468-1(5), Hatherleigh Pr.) Hatherleigh Co., Ltd., The.
Kulavis, Allyson. Sea-Sational. 2013. (Science with Stuff Ser.: 5). (ENG.). 48p. (J). (gr. 1). 11.99 (978-1-935703-55-6(2)) Downtown Bookworks.
Kurtz, Kevin. A Day in the Deep, 1 vol. Hunter, Erin E., illus. 2013. (Day in the Habitat Ser.). (ENG.). 32p. (J). (gr. 1-4). 17.95 (978-1-60718-617-5(9)); pap. 9.95 (978-1-60718-629-8(2)) Arbordale Publishing.
—Un Día en la Profundidad, 1 vol. Hunter, Erin E., illus. 2013. (SPA.). 32p. (J). (gr. 1-4). 17.95 (978-1-60718-715-8(9)) Arbordale Publishing.
—Sharks & Dolphins: A Compare & Contrast Book, 1 vol. 2016. (Compare & Contrast Ser.). (ENG., Illus.). 32p. (J). (gr. k-3). 17.95 (978-1-62855-732-9(X)) Arbordale Publishing.
—Tiburones y Delfines: Un Libro de Comparación y Contraste, 1 vol. 2016. (SPA., Illus.). 32p. (J). (gr. k-3). pap. 9.95 (978-1-62855-746-6(X)) Arbordale Publishing.
Kuskowski, Alex. A School of Fish: Animal Groups in the Ocean, 1 vol. 2012. (Animal Groups Ser.). (ENG.). 24p. (J). (gr. k-3). lib. bdg. 24.21 (978-1-61783-541-4(2), SandCastle) ABDO Publishing Co.
Labella, Susan. Animales Migratorios: En el Agua. 2007. (En marcha: Migraciones animales (Spanish- on the Move: Animal Migration) Ser.). (SPA., Illus.). 24p. (gr. 1-4). pap. 8.15 (978-0-8368-8431-9(0)); lib. bdg. 22.00 (978-0-8368-8426-5(4)) Stevens, Gareth Publishing LLLP. (Weekly Reader Leveled Readers).
—Migrating Animals of the Water. 2007. (On the Move Ser.). (Illus.). 24p. (gr. 1-4). lib. bdg. 22.00 (978-0-8368-8419-7(1), Weekly Reader Leveled Readers) Stevens, Gareth Publishing LLLP.
LaBella, Susan & Labella, Susan. Migrating Animals of the Water. 2007. (On the Move: Animal Migration Ser.). 24p. (gr. 1-4). pap. 8.15 (978-0-8368-8424-1(8), Weekly Reader Leveled Readers) Stevens, Gareth Publishing LLLP.
Lambert, Nat. Sharks & Other Predators. Top That Publishing Staff, ed. 2004. (ENG., Illus.). 1p. (J). (gr. 2-4). pap. 5.99 (978-1-84510-117-6(0)) Top That! Publishing PLC GBR. Dist: Independent Pubs. Group.
Lantz, Peggy Sias & Hale, Wendy A. The Oceans of Florida. 2014. (Florida Water Story Ser.). (ENG., Illus.). 34p. (J). (gr. 4). pap. 6.95 (978-1-56164-704-0(7)) Pineapple Pr., Inc.
Laplante, Walter. Sea Anemones. 2015. (Things That Sting Ser.). (ENG., Illus.). 24p. (J). (gr. 2-3). lib. bdg. 22.60 (978-1-4824-1710-4(3)) Stevens, Gareth Publishing LLLP.
Lassen, Christian Riese, illus. Moon Dance. 2005. 16p. (J). (gr. -1-3). bds. 8.95 (978-1-74047-591-4(7), Penton Kids) Penton Overseas, Inc.
Laval, Thierry, et al. Look & Find - Oceans. 2016. (Look & Find Ser.). (ENG., Illus.). 14p. (J). 18.99 (978-0-531-22236-2(5), Children's Pr.) Scholastic Library Publishing.
Lawler, Janet. Ocean Counting. Skerry, Brian, photos by. 2013. (ENG., Illus.). 32p. (J). (-k). 16.95 (978-1-4263-1116-1(8)); lib. bdg. 25.90 (978-1-4263-1117-8(6)) National Geographic Society. (National Geographic Children's Bks.).
Leardi, Jeanette. Southern Sea Otters: Fur-Tastrophe Avoided. 2007. (America's Animal Comebacks Ser.). (Illus.). 32p. (YA). (gr. 2-5). lib. bdg. 25.27 (978-1-59716-534-1(4)) Bearport Publishing Co., Inc.
Lensch, Chris, illus. Coral Reef: Hide & Seek. 2005. (ENG.). 10p. (J). bds. 7.95 (978-1-58117-362-8(8), Intervisual/Piggy Toes) Bendon, Inc.
Leon, Vicki. A Raft of Sea Otters: The Playful Life of a Furry Survivor. 2nd ed. 2005. (Jean-Michel Cousteau Presents Ser.). (ENG., Illus.). 48p. (J). pap. 9.95 (978-0-9666490-4-8(4)) London Town Pr.
—The Secrets of Tidepools: The Bright World of the Rocky Shoreline. 2nd ed. 2006. (Jean-Michel Cousteau Presents Ser.). (ENG., Illus.). 48p. (J). (gr. 4). pap. 9.95 (978-0-9766134-6-6(8)) London Town Pr.
Lessem, Don. Sea Giants of Dinosaur Time. Bindon, John, illus. 2005. 32p. (J). (gr. 2-5). pap. 6.95 (978-0-8225-2623-0(9)); (gr. 3-7). lib. bdg. 23.93 (978-0-8225-1425-1(7)) Lerner Publishing Group.
Let's Find Out! Marine Life. 2016. (Let's Find Out! Marine Life Ser.). 00032p. (J). (gr. 2-3). 146.70 (978-1-5081-0284-7(8), Britannica Educational Publishing) Rosen Publishing Group, Inc., The.
Levine, Michelle & Waxman, Laura. Let's Look at Sea Otters. 2010. (Lightning Bolt Books — Animal Close-Ups Ser.). (ENG., Illus.). 32p. (gr. k-2). pap. 7.95 (978-1-58013-864-2(0)) Lerner Publishing Group.
Lindeen, Carol K. & Sullivan, Jody. Under the Sea (8 book Set) [NASCO]. 2012. (Under the Sea Ser.). (ENG.). 24p. (gr. k-1). pap. 55.60 (978-1-62065-475-0(X), Pebble Plus) Capstone Press of Coughlan Cos.
Llewellyn, Claire. In the Sea Red Band. Belcher, Andy, photos by. 2016. (Cambridge Reading Adventures Ser.). (ENG., Illus.). 16p. pap. 6.56 (978-1-107-57578-3(8)) Cambridge Univ. Pr.
—Sea Animals. 2005. (I Know That! Ser.). (Illus.). 24p. (J). (gr. 1-3). lib. bdg. 22.80 (978-1-932889-32-1(9)) Sea-To-Sea Pubns.
Louisy, Patrick. My Encyclopedia of the Sea. 2016. (My Encyclopedia Ser.). (ENG., Illus.). 128p. (J). lib. bdg. 34.00 (978-0-531-22473-1(2), Children's Pr.) Scholastic Library Publishing.
Lourie, Peter. The Manatee Scientists: Saving Vulnerable Species. 2016. (Scientists in the Field Ser.). (ENG., Illus.). 80p. (J). (gr. 5-7). pap. 9.99 (978-0-544-22529-9(5), HMH Books For Young Readers) Houghton Mifflin Harcourt Publishing Co.
Lunis, Natalie. Slimy Sea Slugs. 2007. (No Backbone! Ser.). (Illus.). 24p. (J). (gr. k-3). lib. bdg. 21.28 (978-1-59716-511-2(5)) Bearport Publishing Co., Inc.
Macken, JoAnn Early. Rivers: Rios. 2005. (Water Habitats/ Habitats acuaticos Ser.). (SPA.). 24p. (gr. k-3). pap. 8.15 (978-0-8368-6038-2(1), Weekly Reader Leveled Readers) Stevens, Gareth Publishing LLLP.
—Sea Lions/los Leones Marinos. 2004. (Animals I See at the Zoo/ Animales que veo en el zoologico Ser.). (ENG & SPA., Illus.). 24p. (gr. k-3). lib. bdg. 22.00 (978-0-8368-4384-2(3), Weekly Reader Leveled Readers) Stevens, Gareth Publishing LLLP.
MacQuitty, Miranda. DK Eyewitness Books: Ocean: Ocean. 2014. (DK Eyewitness Bks.). (ENG., Illus.). 72p. (J). (gr. 3-7). pap. 9.99 (978-1-4654-2054-1(1), DK Children) Dorling Kindersley Publishing, Inc.
Magby, Meryl. Sea Urchins. 2012. (Under the Sea Ser.). (ENG., Illus.). 24p. (J). (gr. k-5). pap. 8.25 (978-1-4488-7479-8(3)); lib. bdg. 22.60 (978-1-4488-7400-2(9)) Rosen Publishing Group, Inc., The. (PowerKids Pr.).
Makowski, Robin Lee, illus. Sea Creatures. 2004. (J). (978-1-59203-090-3(4)) Learning Challenge, Inc.
Mammals of the Sea: Level N, 6 vols. (Explorers Ser.). 32p. (gr. 3-6). 44.95 (978-0-7699-0593-8(5)) Shortland Pubns. (U. S. A.) Inc.
Marine Debris Program (U.S.), Office of Response and Restoration, ed. Understanding Marine Debris: Games & Activities for Kids of All Ages: Marine Debris 101: Games & Activities for Kids of All Ages: Marine Debris 101. 2012. (ENG.). 23p. 7.00 (978-0-16-091362-4(4), National Marine Fisheries Service) United States Government Printing Office.
Marsh, Laura. National Geographic Readers: Manatees. 2014. (Readers Ser.). (ENG., Illus.). 32p. (J). (gr. k-3). pap. 3.99 (978-1-4263-1472-8(8), National Geographic Children's Bks.) National Geographic Society.
Marsico, Katie. A Baby Lobster Grows Up. Marsico, Katie, illus. 2007. (Scholastic News Nonfiction Readers Ser.). (ENG., Illus.). 24p. (J). (gr. 1-2). 22.00 (978-0-531-17475-3(1)) Scholastic Library Publishing.
—Manatees. 2012. (Nature's Children Ser.). (ENG., Illus.). 48p. (J). pap. 6.95 (978-0-531-25480-6(1)); lib. bdg. 28.00 (978-0-531-26835-3(7)) Scholastic Library Publishing.
Martin, Claudia. Complete Guides Ocean Life. 2012. (ENG.). 144p. (J). (978-1-4351-4408-8(2)) Barnes & Noble, Inc.
Martin, Justin McCory. Deep-Sea Creatures. 2011. (Illus.). 16p. (J). (978-0-545-24789-4(6)) Scholastic, Inc.
Marx, Christy. Life in the Ocean Depths. 2009. 64p. (gr. 5-8). (YA). pap. 12.95 (978-1-4358-3265-7(5)); 53.00 (978-1-61514-272-9(X)) Rosen Publishing Group, Inc., The. (Rosen Reference).
Mason, Janeen. Ocean Commotion: Life on the Reef, 1 vol. Mason, Janeen, illus. 2010. (ENG., Illus.). 32p. (J). (gr. k-3). 16.99 (978-1-58980-783-9(9)) Pelican Publishing Co., Inc.
Massey, Kay. What Do You See in the Sea? Canals, Sonia & O'Toole, Jeanette, illus. 2009. (Little Green Footprints Ser.). 12p. (J). (gr. -1-k). bds. 11.40 (978-1-60754-698-6(1)) Windmill Bks.
Mattern, Joanne. What River Animals Eat (¿Qué comen los animales de los Ríos?) 2006. (Nature's Food Chains/ Las cadenas alimentarias en la naturaleza Ser.). (Illus.). 24p. (gr. k-3). (ENG & SPA.). pap. 8.15 (978-0-8368-7382-5(3)); (SPA., lib. bdg. 22.00 (978-0-8368-7375-7(0)) Stevens, Gareth Publishing LLLP. (Weekly Reader Leveled Readers).
—What Sea Animals Eat. 2006. (Nature's Food Chains Ser.). (Illus.). 24p. (gr. k-3). lib. bdg. 22.00 (978-0-8368-6875-3(7), Weekly Reader Leveled Readers) Stevens, Gareth Publishing LLLP.
—What Sea Animals Eat: Qué Comen los Animales del Mar? 2006. (Nature's Food Chains/ Las cadenas alimentarias en la naturaleza Ser.). (ENG & SPA., Illus.). 24p. (gr. k-3). pap. 8.15 (978-0-8368-7383-2(1), Weekly Reader Leveled Readers) Stevens, Gareth Publishing LLLP.
McAneney, Caitie. Freaky Stories from Beneath the Sea. 2015. (Freaky True Science Ser.). (ENG.). 32p. (J). (gr. 4-5). pap. 10.50 (978-1-4824-2964-0(0)); lib. bdg. 26.60 (978-1-4824-2966-4(7)) Stevens, Gareth Publishing LLLP.
—Really Strange Marine Animals. 2016. (Really Strange Adaptations Ser.). 00032p. (J). (gr. 5-5). 26.25 (978-1-4994-2853-7(7)); pap. 10.00 (978-1-4994-2738-7(7)) Rosen Publishing Group, Inc., The. (PowerKids Pr.).
McCall, Gerrie. Fierce Water Creatures. 2006. (Nature's Monsters Ser.). (Illus.). 32p. (gr. 2-6). lib. bdg. 26.00 (978-0-8368-6177-8(9), Gareth Stevens Learning Library) Stevens, Gareth Publishing LLLP.
McCune, Jamie. First Look at Ocean Animals. 2010. (First Look At Ser.). (ENG.). 16p. (J). (gr. -1). 6.95 (978-1-60727-138-3(9)) Soundprints.
McCurry, Kristen & Jackson, Aimee. Ocean Babies. NorthWord Books for Young Readers Staff, ed. 2004. (Animal Babies Ser.). (ENG., Illus.). 22p. (J). (gr. -1 — 1). bds. 9.95 (978-1-55971-898-1(6)) Cooper Square Publishing Llc.
McGinlay, Richard. My First Encyclopedia of Fish: A Great Big Book of Amazing Aquatic Creatures to Discover. 2017. (ENG., Illus.). 24p. (J). (gr. -1-12). pap. 7.99 **(978-1-86147-824-5(0)**, Armadillo) Anness Publishing GBR. Dist: National Bk. Network.
McKissack, Fredrick L. & McKissack, Lisa Beringer. Counting in the Oceans. 2009. (Counting in the Biomes Ser.). (Illus.). 32p. (J). (gr. 1-3). lib. bdg. 23.94 (978-0-7660-2994-1(8), Enslow Elementary) Enslow Pubs., Inc.
McKnight, Diane. The Lost Seal. Emerling, Dorothy, illus. 2006. (Long Term Ecological Research Ser.). (ENG.). 40p. (J). (gr. 4-7). 19.95 (978-0-9723422-7-8(3)) Taylor Trade Publishing.
McNeil, Niki, et al. HOCPP 1077 Predators of the Deep. 2006. spiral bd. 16.50 (978-1-60308-077-4(5)) In the Hands of a Child.
Mead, Brian. Creatures of the Deep Coloring Book. 2003. 32p. (J). (gr. -1-3). pap. 3.99 (978-0-9717509-3-7(9)) Mead, Brian Publishing.
Mehing, Carl. Prehistoric Creatures of the Sea & Skies. 2009. (Discovering Dinosaurs Ser.). (Illus.). 48p. (YA). (gr. 2-6). pap. 12.85 (978-1-60754-781-5(3)); (gr. 4-7). 29.25 (978-1-60754-773-0(2)) Windmill Bks.
Meister, Cari. Sea Dragons. 2014. (Illus.). 24p. (J). lib. bdg. 25.65 (978-1-62031-101-1(1), Bullfrog Bks.) Jump! Inc.
—Totally Wacky Facts about Sea Animals. 2015. (Mind Benders Ser.). (ENG., Illus.). 112p. (gr. 1-3). lib. bdg. 23.32 (978-1-4914-6521-9(2)) Capstone Press of Coughlan Cos.
Merlino, Kim. Ocean Life: Grades 2 Through 4. (Illus.). (J). pap., wbk. ed. 4.99 (978-0-88743-966-7(7)) School Zone Publishing Co.
Mihaltchev, Atanas. Kid-Agami — Sea Life: Kiragami for Kids: Easy-To-Make Paper Toys. 2013. (Dover Children's Activity Bks.). (ENG.). 24p. (J). (gr. 1-5). pap. 9.99 (978-0-486-49744-0(5)) Dover Pubns., Inc.
Milbourne, Anna. Under the Sea. Shimmen, Cathy, illus. 2007. (Picture Bks). 32p. (J). 9.99 (978-0-7945-1801-1(X), Usborne) EDC Publishing.
Miles, Lisa. Origami Sea Creatures. 2013. (Amazing Origami Ser.). 32p. (J). (gr. 2-5). pap. 63.00 (978-1-4339-9662-7(6)); pap. 10.50 (978-1-4339-9661-0(8)); (ENG., Illus.). lib. bdg. 26.60 (978-1-4339-9660-3(X)) Stevens, Gareth Publishing LLLP.
Miles, Liz. Sea Monsters. 2012. (Prehistoric Safari Ser.). (ENG., Illus.). 32p. (J). (gr. 3-6). lib. bdg. 28.50 (978-1-84858-570-6(5), North Light Bks.) F&W Media, Inc.
Miller, Sara Swan. Secret Lives of Deep Sea Creatures. 2010. (Secret Lives Ser.). 48p. (gr. 4). 29.93 (978-0-7614-4226-4(X)) Marshall Cavendish Corp.
Miller, Tori. Eels. 2009. (Freaky Fish Ser.). 24p. (J). (gr. 1-4). lib. bdg. 22.60 (978-1-4358-2754-7(6)) Rosen Publishing Group, Inc., The.
Mineo, Ella. Sea Otters in Danger. 2013. (Animals at Risk Ser.). 24p. (J). (gr. 2-5). pap. 8.15 (978-1-4339-9170-7(5)); pap. 48.90 (978-1-4339-9171-4(3)); (ENG., Illus.). lib. bdg. 22.60 (978-1-4339-9169-1(1)) Stevens, Gareth Publishing LLLP.
Moore, David. Expl on Your Own Watch Out! 2007. (Explore on Your Own Ser.). (ENG.). 16p. (C). pap. 7.95 (978-0-7362-5372-7(6)) National Geographic School Publishing, Inc.
Moore, Heidi. Giant Tube Worms & Other Interesting Invertebrates, 1 vol. 2011. (Creatures of the Deep Ser.). (ENG., Illus.). 32p. (gr. 3-5). pap. 8.95 (978-1-4109-4206-7(6)); 30.65 (978-1-4109-4199-2(X)) Heinemann-Raintree. (NA-r).
Moore, Heidi, et al. Creatures of the Deep. 2011. (Creatures of the Deep Ser.). (ENG.). 32p. (gr. 3-5). lib. bdg. 122.60 (978-1-4109-4200-5(7), NA-r) Heinemann-Raintree.
Morgan, Sally. Encyclopedia of Ocean Life. 2012. (Illus.). 224p. (J). (978-1-4351-4351-7(5)) Barnes & Noble, Inc.
Mumme, Sarah. Guess Who's under the Sea. Samuel, Janet, illus. 2015. (Guess Who's... Bks.). (ENG.). 10p. (J). (gr. -1 — 1). 5.99 (978-0-7641-6803-1(7)) Barron's Educational Series, Inc.
Munro, Fiona. Under the Sea. 2013. (My First Creativity Activity Bks.). (ENG.). 66p. (J). (gr. -1-2). pap. 9.99 (978-1-4380-0240-8(8)) Barron's Educational Series, Inc.
Munson, Victoria. British Seashore. 2016. (Nature Detective Ser.). (ENG., Illus.). 64p. (J). (gr. 2-4). pap. 9.99 (978-0-7502-9323-5(3), Wayland) Hachette Children's Group GBR. Dist: Hachette Bk. Group.
Murphy, Julie. Ocean Animal Adaptations, 1 vol. 2011. (Amazing Animal Adaptations Ser.). (ENG.). 32p. (gr. 1-2). pap. 8.10 (978-1-4296-7029-6(0)); pap. 47.70 (978-1-4296-7036-4(3)); lib. bdg. 27.32 (978-1-4296-6029-7(5)) Capstone Press of Coughlan Cos. (Aplus Bks.).
Murphy, Patricia J. Discovering Underwater Secrets with a Nature Photographer. 2007. (I Like Science! Ser.). (Illus.). 24p. (J). (gr. 1-3). lib. bdg. 22.60 (978-0-7660-2816-6(X), Enslow Elementary) Enslow Pubs., Inc.
Murray, Aaron R. Counting in the Oceans 1-2-3. 2012. (All about Counting in the Biomes Ser.). (Illus.). 24p. (J). (gr. -1-1). 22.60 (978-0-7660-4052-6(6)) Enslow Pubs., Inc.
Murray, Julie. Underwater, 1 vol. 2009. (That's Gross! A Look at Science Ser.). (ENG., Illus.). 32p. (J). (gr. 2-5). 28.50 (978-1-60453-558-7(X)) ABDO Publishing Co.
Nagle, Kerry. Marine Creatures. 2010. (Weird, Wild, & Wonderful Ser.). (Illus.). 24p. (J). (gr. 2-5). lib. bdg. 22.00 (978-1-4339-3581-7(3), Gareth Stevens Learning Library) Stevens, Gareth Publishing LLLP.
—Marine Minibeasts. 2010. (Weird, Wild, & Wonderful Ser.). 24p. (J). (gr. 2-5). lib. bdg. 22.00 (978-1-4339-3571-8(6), Gareth Stevens Learning Library) Stevens, Gareth Publishing LLLP.
National Geographic Kids. National Geographic Kids Beach Day Sticker Activity Book. 2017. (NG Sticker Activity Bks.). (ENG.). 56p. (J). (gr. -1-3). pap. 6.99 (978-1-4263-2776-6(5), National Geographic Children's Bks.) National Geographic Society.
—National Geographic Readers: Ocean Animals Collection. 2015. (Readers Ser.). (ENG., Illus.). 128p. (J). (gr. -1-1). pap. 7.99 (978-1-4263-2273-0(9), National Geographic Children's Bks.) National Geographic Society.
National Geographic Kids Staff. Ocean Animals: Over 1,000 Stickers! 2016. (NG Sticker Activity Bks.). (ENG.). 56p. (J). (gr. -1-3). pap., act. bk. ed. 6.99 (978-1-4263-2424-6(3), National Geographic Children's Bks.) National Geographic Society.
—Ocean Creatures. 2015. (Look & Learn Ser.). (ENG., Illus.). 24p. (J). (-k). bds. 6.99 (978-1-4263-2063-7(9), National Geographic Children's Bks.) National Geographic Society.
Natural History Museum. Sticker Art Ocean. Craig & Karl, illus. 2017. (Sticker Art Ser.). (ENG.). 24p. (J). (gr. -1-k). pap. 7.99 **(978-1-78603-005-4(5)**, Frances Lincoln Children's Bks.) Quarto Publishing Group UK GBR. Dist: Hachette Bk. Group.
Nature Series Books 25 & 26: Activities. 2004. (J). pap., instr.'s gde. ed. 2.95 (978-1-878405-48-7(9)) Nags Head Art, Inc.
Needham, Kate. Usborne the Great Undersea Search. Brooks, Felicity, ed. Jackson, Ian, illus. rev. ed. 2006. (Great Searches Ser.). 32p. (J). (gr. -1-3). per. 7.99 (978-0-7945-1228-6(3), Usborne) EDC Publishing.
Nelson, Robert Lyn. Ocean Friends. 2003. (ENG., Illus.). 32p. (J). (gr. -1-3). 15.95 (978-1-55971-840-0(4)) Cooper Square Publishing Llc.
Newland, Sonya. Ocean Animals. 2011. (Saving Wildlife Ser.). 32p. (YA). (gr. 3-6). lib. bdg. 28.50 (978-1-59920-658-5(7)) Black Rabbit Bks.
Niver, Heather Moore. 20 Fun Facts about Moray Eels. 2012. (Fun Fact File: Fierce Fish! Ser.). (Illus.). 32p. (J). (gr. 2-5). pap. 10.50 (978-1-4339-6984-3(X)); lib. bdg. 25.25 (978-1-4339-6983-6(1)) Stevens, Gareth Publishing LLLP.
NorthWord Books for Young Readers Editors. Ocean Babies. 2005. (SPA.). (J). bds. 5.95 (978-1-55971-908-7(7), NorthWord Bks. for Young Readers) T&N Children's Publishing.
Ocean Animals. 2004. (Illus.). lib. bdg. 7.95 (978-0-8225-4511-8(X)) Lerner Publishing Group.
Ocean Animals. Date not set. (Illus.). 16p. (J). 5.98 (978-0-7525-7698-5(4)); 2.98 (978-0-7525-9762-1(0)) Parragon, Inc.
Octopuses & Squids: Level N, 6 vols. (Wonder Worldtm Ser.). 48p. 34.95 (978-0-7802-2902-0(9)) Wright Group/McGraw-Hill.
O'Donnell, Kerri. Ugly Sea Creatures. 2009. (Ugly Animals Ser.). 24p. (gr. 2-3). 42.50 (978-1-60854-604-6(7), PowerKids Pr.) Rosen Publishing Group, Inc., The.
Oliver, Claire. Terror under the Sea. 2008. (Factastic Journey Ser.). (Illus.). 32p. (J). (gr. k-7). pap. 8.95 (978-1-59905-244-1(X)) Saddleback Educational Publishing, Inc.

O'Reilly, Wenda. Go fish wildlife sea Creatures. 2007. n/ap. pap. 119.40 (978-1-59960-020-8(X)) Birdcage Pr.

Osborne, Mary Pope & Boyce, Natalie Pope. Sea Monsters: A Nonfiction Companion to Dark Day in the Deep Sea. Murdocca, Sal, illus. 2008. (Magic Tree House Research Guides: No. 17). 121p. (J). (gr. 1-5). 12.65 (978-0-7569-8809-8(8)) Perfection Learning Corp.

—Sea Monsters: A Nonfiction Companion to Dark Day in the Deep Sea. Murdocca, Sal, illus. 2008. (Magic Tree House - Fact Tracker Ser.: 17). (ENG.). 128p. (J). (gr. 2-5). 6.99 (978-0-375-84663-2(8), Random Hse. Bks. for Young Readers) Random Hse. Children's Bks.

O'Sullivan, Robyn. Weedy Sea Dragons, Spitting Cobras: And Other Wild & Amazing Animals. 2006. (Science Chapters Ser.). (ENG., Illus.). 48p. (J). (gr. 1-4). lib. bdg. 17.90 (978-0-7922-5941-1(6), National Geographic Children's Bks.) National Geographic Society.

Otfinoski, Steven. Manatees. 2010. (Animals Animals 11 Ser.). 48p. (gr. 3). 23.95 (978-0-7614-4842-6(X)) Marshall Cavendish Corp.

Ottina, Laura. In the Sea. Ranchetti, Sebastiano, illus. 2009. (Learn with Animals Ser.). (ENG.). 24p. (J). (gr. -1-2). pap. 8.15 (978-1-4339-2091-2(3)); lib. bdg. 22.00 (978-1-4339-1914-5(1)) Stevens, Gareth Publishing LLLP. (Weekly Reader Leveled Readers).

Owen, Ruth. Marvelous Marine Mammals. 2012. (Eye to Eye with Animals Ser.). (ENG., Illus.). 32p. (J). (gr. k-5). 25.25 (978-1-4488-8070-6(X)); pap. 10.00 (978-1-4488-8106-2(4)) Windmill Bks.

—Sea Otter Pups. 2012. (Water Babies Ser.). 24p. (J). (gr. -1-3). lib. bdg. 21.32 (978-1-61772-601-9(X)) Bearport Publishing Co., Inc.

Paiva, Johannah Gilman, ed. The Awesome Book of Monsters of the Deep. Various, illus. 2013. (World of Wonder: the Awesome Book Of Ser.). (ENG.). 32p. (J). (gr. 3-7). 7.99 (978-1-77093-777-2(3)) Flowerpot Pr.

Pallotta, Jerry. The Ocean Alphabet Board Book. Mazzola, Frank, Jr., illus. 2003. (ENG.). 28p. (J). (-k). bds. 7.95 (978-1-57091-524-6(5)) Charlesbridge Publishing, Inc.

—Sea Mammal Alphabet Book. 2012. (ENG.). (J). 16.95 (978-0-9852032-5-2(0)) Bald Eagle Bks.

—Ultimate Ocean Rumble. Bolster, Rob, illus. 2015. 32p. (J). (978-0-545-68118-6(9)) Scholastic, Inc.

Parker, Steve. Sea Monsters. 2011. (ENG., Illus.). 32p. (J). pap. 10.95 (978-1-77092-014-9(5)) Saunders Bk. Co. CAN. Dist: RiverStream Publishing.

Patterson, Caroline. Fish Do WHAT in the Water? The Secret Lives of Marine Animals. Rath, Robert, illus. 2012. 48p. (J). 14.95 (978-1-56037-519-7(1)) Farcountry Pr.

Perkins, Wendy. Sea Cucumbers. 2017. (Weird & Unusual Animals Ser.). (ENG.). 24p. (gr. 1-4). 20.95 **(978-1-68151-160-3(6))** Amicus Publishing.

Person, Stephen. The Coral Reef: A Giant City under the Sea. 2009. (Spectacular Animal Towns Ser.). (Illus.). 32p. (J). (gr. 2-7). lib. bdg. 25.27 (978-1-59716-869-4(6)) Bearport Publishing Co., Inc.

Pettiford, Rebecca. Ocean Food Chains. 2016. (Who Eats What?). 24p. (J). (gr. 2-5). lib. bdg. 25.65 (978-1-62031-302-2(2), Pogo) Jump! Inc.

Phillips, Dee. Find It at the Beach. 2006. (Can You Find It? Ser.). (Illus.). 24p. (gr. k-3). lib. bdg. 23.00 (978-0-8368-6298-0(8), Gareth Stevens Learning Library) Stevens, Gareth Publishing LLLP.

Piddock, Charles. Creeps of the Deep: Explore the Ocean's Strangest Creatures. 2009. (Current Science Ser.). (ENG.). 48p. (gr. 4-7). (YA). lib. bdg. 31.00 (978-1-4339-2059-2(X)); (J). pap. 8.95 (978-1-4339-2130-8(8), Gareth Stevens Learning Library) Stevens, Gareth Publishing LLLP.

Pierce, Terry & Kofsky, Kristen. Dangerous Sea Creatures A to Z Coloring Book. 2004. (Illus.). 24p. pap. 4.95 (978-1-57306-177-3(8)) Bess Pr., Inc.

Pingry, Patricia A. Baby Manatee. Rose, Drew, illus. 2006. (SeaWorld Library: Vol. 5). 24p. (J). (gr. -1-k). bds. 6.95 (978-0-8249-6644-7(9), Ideal Pubns.) Worthy Publishing.

Pipe, Jim. Scary Creatures of the Deep. Bergin, Mark et al, illus. 2009. (Scary Creatures Ser.). (ENG.). 32p. (J). (gr. 2-4). 27.00 (978-0-531-21822-8(8), Watts, Franklin) Scholastic Library Publishing.

Pohl, Kathleen. Animals of the Ocean. 2007. (Animal Show & Tell Ser.). (Illus.). 16p. (gr. -1-3). lib. bdg. 19.00 (978-0-8368-8208-7(3), Gareth Stevens Learning Library) Stevens, Gareth Publishing LLLP.

Prager, Ellen. Sea Slime: It's Eeuwy, Gooey & under the Sea, 1 vol. Bersani, Shennen, illus. 2014. (ENG.). 32p. (J). (gr. 1-4). 17.95 (978-1-62855-210-2(7)) Arbordale Publishing.

—Sea Slime: It's Eeuwy, Gooey & under the Sea, 1 vol. Bersani, Shennen, illus. 2014. (SPA.). 32p. (J). (gr. 1-4). pap. 9.95 (978-1-62855-228-7(X)) Arbordale Publishing.

Pratt Serafini, Kristin Joy, illus. A Swim Through the Sea, 1 vol. 2006. (Simply Nature Bks.). (ENG.). 26p. (J). (gr. -1). bds. 7.95 (978-1-58469-080-1(1)) Dawn Pubns.

Press, Judy. Little Hands Sea Life Art & Activities: Creative Learning Experiences for 3-7-Year Olds. 2004. (Williamson's Little Hands Book Ser.). (Illus.). 128p. (J). pap. 12.95 (978-1-885593-94-8(5), Ideal Pubns.) Worthy Publishing.

Priddy, Roger. Coral Reef. 2014. (Smart Kids Ser.). (ENG.). 30p. (J). (gr. -1-2). 9.99 (978-0-312-51677-2(0), 9780312516772, Priddy Bks.) St. Martin's Pr.

—Ocean: Amazing Photo Pop-Ups Like You've Never Seen Before! 2005. (Picture Pops Ser.). (ENG., Illus.). 18p. (J). (gr. -1-1). 12.95 (978-0-312-49465-0(3), 9780312494650, Priddy Bks.) St. Martin's Pr.

Prince, Savannah. Manny the Mol. 2012. 40p. pap. 19.57 (978-1-4669-2968-5(5)) Trafford Publishing.

QEB Start Reading Together National Book Stores Edition: Sea Creatures. 2006. (J). per. (978-1-59566-258-3(8)) QEB Publishing Inc.

Quinlan, Julia J. What Are Sea Invertebrates? 2016. (Let's Find Out! Marine Life Ser.). (J). 00032p. (gr. 2-3). 24.45 (978-1-5081-0389-9(5), Britannica Educational Publishing); lib. bdg. (978-1-5081-0460-5(3)) Rosen Publishing Group, Inc., The.

Rajczak, Michael. Sea Urchins. 2015. (Things That Sting Ser.). (ENG., Illus.). 24p. (J). (gr. 2-3). pap. 8.15 (978-1-4824-1719-7(7)) Stevens, Gareth Publishing LLLP.

Rake, Jody S. Faceless, Spineless, & Brainless Ocean Animals. 2016. (Faceless, Spineless, & Brainless Ocean Animals Ser.). (ENG.). 24p. (gr. 1-2). 101.28 (978-1-5157-2164-2(7), First Facts) Capstone Press of Coughlan Cos.

—Kings of the Oceans. 2017. (Animal Rulers Ser.). (ENG.). 24p. (gr. 1-2). lib. bdg. 25.32 **(978-1-5157-8066-3(X)**, First Facts) Capstone Press of Coughlan Cos.

Rake, Jody S. Sea Urchins. 2016. (Faceless, Spineless, & Brainless Ocean Animals Ser.). (ENG.). 24p. (gr. 1-2). lib. bdg. 25.32 (978-1-5157-2142-0(6), First Facts) Capstone Press of Coughlan Cos.

Rake, Jody Sullivan. Sea Anemones. 2016. (Faceless, Spineless, & Brainless Ocean Animals Ser.). (ENG., Illus.). 24p. (gr. 1-2). 25.32 (978-1-5157-2139-0(6)) Capstone Press of Coughlan Cos.

—Sea Cucumbers. 2016. (Faceless, Spineless, & Brainless Ocean Animals Ser.). (ENG., Illus.). 24p. (gr. 1-2). 25.32 (978-1-5157-2140-6(X)) Capstone Press of Coughlan Cos.

Rake, Jody Sullivan, et al. Marine Mammals. 2012. (Marine Mammals Ser.). (ENG.). 24p. (gr. k-1). lib. bdg. 106.60 (978-1-4296-9170-3(0), Pebble Plus) Capstone Press of Coughlan Cos.

Rake, Matthew. Creatures of the Deep. Mendez, Simon, illus. 2015. (Real-Life Monsters Ser.). (ENG.). 32p. (J). (gr. 3-6). 26.65 (978-1-4677-6360-8(8)) Lerner Publishing Group.

—Prehistoric Sea Beasts. Mendez, Simon, illus. 2017. (If Extinct Beasts Came to Life Ser.). (ENG.). 32p. (J). (gr. 3-6). 7.99 (978-1-5124-1158-4(2)); 7.99 **(978-1-5124-3618-1(6))**; 39.99 **(978-1-5124-0909-3(X))**; 39.99 **(978-1-5124-3617-4(8))** Lerner Publishing Group.

Ranson, Erin. Fuzzy Ocean. Green, Barry, illus. 2017. (Soft Felt Play Bks.). (ENG.). 10p. (J). (gr. -1-k). 12.99 **(978-1-78700-084-1(2))** Top That! Publishing PLC GBR. Dist: Independent Pubs. Group.

Redmond, Shirley Raye. Tentacles! Tales of the Giant Squid. Barnard, Bryn, illus. 2003. (Step into Reading Ser.). (ENG.). 48p. (J). (gr. k-3). pap. 3.99 (978-0-375-81307-8(1), Random Hse. Bks. for Young Readers) Random Hse. Children's Bks.

Reinhart, Matthew & Sabuda, Robert. Encyclopedia Prehistorica Sharks & Other Sea Monsters. Reinhart, Matthew & Sabuda, Robert, illus. 2006. (Encyclopedia Prehistorica Ser.: 2). (ENG., Illus.). 12p. (J). (gr. k-4). 34.99 (978-0-7636-2229-9(X)) Candlewick Pr.

Reyes, Blanca Matilde. Sea Animals. 2006. (Illus.). 16p. (J). 0.75 (978-1-933984-03-2(1)) Two Lands.

Reynolds, Toby & Calver, Paul. Ocean Life. 2015. (Visual Explorers Ser.). (ENG.). 32p. (J). (gr. 3-7). pap. 6.99 (978-1-4380-0579-9(2)) Barron's Educational Series, Inc.

Rhodes, Mary Jo & Hall, David. Dolphins, Seals, & Other Sea Mammals. 2006. (Undersea Encounters Ser.). (ENG., Illus.). 48p. (J). (gr. 3-7). 27.00 (978-0-516-24392-4(6), Children's Pr.) Scholastic Library Publishing.

—Partners in the Sea. Hall, David, photos by. 2006. (Undersea Encounters Ser.). (ENG., Illus.). 48p. (J). (gr. 3-7). per. 6.95 (978-0-516-25492-0(8), Children's Pr.) Scholastic Library Publishing.

—Predators of the Sea. Hall, David, photos by. 2007. (Undersea Encounters Ser.). (ENG., Illus.). 48p. (J). (gr. 3-7). pap. 6.95 (978-0-516-25465-4(0), Children's Pr.) Scholastic Library Publishing.

—Predators of the Sea. 2006. (Undersea Encounters Ser.). (ENG., Illus.). 48p. (J). (gr. 3-7). lib. bdg. 27.00 (978-0-516-24399-3(3), Children's Pr.) Scholastic Library Publishing.

—Sea Turtles. Hall, David, photos by. 2006. (Undersea Encounters Ser.). (ENG., Illus.). 48p. (J). (gr. 3-7). per. 6.95 (978-0-516-25353-4(0), Children's Pr.) Scholastic Library Publishing.

Rice, Dona Herweck. Sea Life, 1 vol. 2nd rev. ed. 2013. (Nonfiction Readers Ser.). (ENG., Illus.). 20p. (J). (gr. 1-1). pap. 19.96 (978-1-4807-1023-8(7)) Shell Educational Publishing.

Rice, William. Animales Del Mar en Peligro. 2016. (TIME for Kids en Español - Level 5 Ser.). (SPA & ENG.). 64p. (gr. 5-5). lib. bdg. 31.99 (978-1-5157-2935-8(4)) Time for Kids Inc AUS. Dist: Capstone Pub.

Rice, William B. Endangered Animals of the Sea, 1 vol. 2nd rev. ed. 2013. (Nonfiction Readers Ser.). (ENG.). 64p. (J). (gr. 5-5). pap. 10.99 (978-1-4333-4935-5(3)); (Illus.). pap. 31.96 (978-1-4333-7434-0(X)) Teacher Created Materials, Inc.

Richards, Mose & Ferguson, Marfe Delano. Sea Monsters: A Prehistoric Adventure. 2007. (Sea Monsters Ser.). (ENG., Illus.). 32p. (J). (gr. 3-7). lib. bdg. 22.90 (978-1-4263-0119-3(7), National Geographic Children's Bks.) National Geographic Society.

Richards, Mose, et al. Sea Monsters: A Prehistoric Adventure. 2008. (ENG., Illus.). 12p. (J). (gr. 3-7). 24.95 (978-1-4263-0176-6(6), National Geographic Children's Bks.) National Geographic Society.

Richmond, Benjamin. Why Is the Sea Salty? And Other Questions about the Ocean. Azhderian, Cecelia, illus. 2014. (Good Question! Ser.). (ENG.). 32p. (J). (gr. 1). pap. 5.95 (978-1-4549-0677-3(4)) Sterling Publishing Co., Inc.

—Why Is the Sea Salty? And Other Questions about the Oceans. Azhderian, Cecelia, illus. 2014. (Good Question! Ser.). (ENG.). 40p. (J). (gr. 1). 12.95 (978-1-4549-0676-6(6)) Sterling Publishing Co., Inc.

Riggs, Kate. Under the Sea. Leonard, Tom, illus. 2017. (ENG.). 14p. (J). (gr. -1 — 1). bds. 7.99 (978-1-56846-302-5(2), Creative Editions) Creative Co., The.

Ripley's Believe It or Not Editors & Ripley's Believe It Or Not! Staff. Sharks: And Other Scary Sea Creatures. 2013. (Twist Ser.: 10). (ENG.). 48p. (J). (gr. 1-4). 12.95 (978-1-60991-083-9(4)) Ripley Entertainment, Inc.

Rissman, Rebecca. Counting in the Ocean, 1 vol. 2012. (I Can Count! Ser.). (ENG.). 24p. (gr. -1-k). pap. 9.95 (978-1-4329-6701-7(0)); lib. bdg. 25.32 (978-1-4329-6696-6(0)) Heinemann-Raintree.

—Living & Nonliving in the Ocean, 1 vol. 2013. (Is It Living or Nonliving? Ser.). (ENG., Illus.). 24p. (gr. k-2). 23.32 (978-1-4109-5381-0(5)); pap. 6.95 (978-1-4109-5388-9(2)) Heinemann-Raintree.

Rivera, Sheila. Ocean. 2005. (Illus.). 24p. (J). pap. 5.95 (978-0-8225-5372-4(4)); (ENG., lib. bdg. 23.93 (978-0-8225-2795-4(2), Lerner Pubns.) Lerner Publishing Group.

Rizzo, Johnna & National Geographic Kids Staff. Ocean Animals: Who's Who in the Deep Blue. 2016. (ENG., Illus.). 112p. (J). (gr. 3-7). pap. 12.99 (978-1-4263-2506-9(1), National Geographic Children's Bks.) National Geographic Society.

Roderick, Stacey. Ocean Animals from Head to Tail. Moriya, Kwanchai, illus. 2016. (Head to Tail Ser.). (ENG.). 36p. (J). (gr. -1-2). 16.95 (978-1-77138-345-5(3)) Kids Can Pr., Ltd. CAN. Dist: Hachette Bk. Group.

RodríGuez, Ana María. Leatherback Turtles, Giant Squids, & Other Mysterious Animals of the Deepest Seas. 2012. (Extreme Animals in Extreme Environments Ser.). (Illus.). 48p. (J). (gr. 5-18). pap. 8.95 (978-1-4644-0019-3(9)) Enslow Pubs., Inc.

Rodríguez, Ana María. Leatherback Turtles, Giant Squids, & Other Mysterious Animals of the Deepest Seas. 2012. (Extreme Animals in Extreme Environments Ser.). (Illus.). 48p. (J). (gr. 5-18). 25.27 (978-0-7660-3696-3(0)) Enslow Pubs., Inc.

—Secret of the Sleepless Whales... & More! 2008. (Animal Secrets Revealed! Ser.). (Illus.). 48p. (J). (gr. 5-9). lib. bdg. 25.27 (978-0-7660-2957-6(3)) Enslow Pubs., Inc.

Rodríguez, Ana María. The Secret of the Squiggly Green Bombers... & More! 2017. (Animal Secrets Revealed! Ser.). 48p. (gr. 4-4). lib. bdg. 27.93 **(978-0-7660-8631-9(3))** Enslow Pubs., Inc.

Rogan, Bernie. Creatures of the Sea: Can You Guess Me. 2012. 52p. pap. 10.99 (978-1-61904-758-7(6)) Salem Author Services.

Rogers, Kirsteen. Under the Sea Jigsaw Book. Scott, Peter, illus. 2007. (Luxury Jigsaw Bks.). 14p. (J). bds. 14.99 (978-0-7945-1330-6(1), Usborne) EDC Publishing.

Rose, Deborah Lee. Ocean Babies. Nakata, Hiroe, illus. 2005. (ENG.). 32p. (J). (gr. -1-3). 25.90 (978-0-7922-8312-6(0)); 16.95 (978-0-7922-6669-3(2)) National Geographic Society. (National Geographic Children's Bks.).

Royston, Angela. Ocean Food Chains, 1 vol. 2014. (Food Chains & Webs Ser.). (ENG., Illus.). 32p. (gr. 1-3). 27.32 (978-1-4846-0517-2(9), Heinemann First Library) Heinemann-Raintree.

Rudolph, Jessica. Mi Cuerpo Es Rayado y Parece Lleno de Hojas. 2015. (Pistas de Animales Ser.). (SPA.). 24p. (J). (gr. -1-3). lib. bdg. 23.93 (978-1-62724-577-7(4)) Bearport Publishing Co., Inc.

Rustad, Martha E. H. Sea Anemones. 2007. (Oceans Alive Ser.). (ENG., Illus.). 24p. (J). (gr. k-3). lib. bdg. 25.95 (978-1-60014-081-5(5)) Bellwether Media.

—Sea Urchins. 2007. (Oceans Alive Ser.). (ENG., Illus.). 24p. (J). (gr. k-3). lib. bdg. 25.95 (978-1-60014-109-6(9)) Bellwether Media.

—Stingrays. 2007. (Oceans Alive Ser.). (ENG., Illus.). 24p. (J). (gr. k-3). lib. bdg. 25.95 (978-1-60014-080-8(7)) Bellwether Media.

Sakanakun. Gensundai Suizokukan. Matsuzawa, Yoji, photos by. 2010. (JPN., Illus.). 48p. (J). (978-4-09-217253-1(2)) Shogakukan.

Samuel, Nigel. Creatures of the Deep. 2007. (Steck-Vaughn BOLDPRINT Anthologies Ser.). (ENG., Illus.). 48p. (gr. 4-7). pap. 16.90 (978-1-4190-4021-4(9)) Houghton Mifflin Harcourt Publishing Co.

Santillo, LuAnn. Under the Sea, 6 vols. Santillo, LuAnn, ed. 2003. (Half-Pint Kids Readers Ser.). (Illus.). 42p. (J). (gr. -1-1). pap. 6.95 (978-1-59256-091-2(1)) Half-Pint Kids, Inc.

Sayre, Jeff & Sayre, April Pulley. One Is a Snail, Ten Is a Crab Big Book: A Counting by Feet Book. Cecil, Randy, illus. 2010. (ENG.). 40p. (J). (gr. k-3). pap. 24.99 (978-0-7636-4790-2(X)) Candlewick Pr.

Schach, David. Sea Dragons. 2007. (Oceans Alive Ser.). (ENG., Illus.). 24p. (J). (gr. k-3). lib. bdg. 25.95 (978-1-60014-055-6(6)) Bellwether Media.

Schoeller, Jen. Biggest, Baddest Book of Sea Creatures, 1 vol. 2014. (Biggest, Baddest Books Set 2 Ser.). (ENG.). 24p. (gr. k-4). 25.65 (978-1-62403-517-3(5)) ABDO Publishing Co.

Schuh, Mari. Manatees. 2015. (Illus.). 24p. (J). lib. bdg. (978-1-62031-189-9(5), Bullfrog Bks.) Jump! Inc.

—Sea Anemones. 2017. (Ocean Life up Close Ser.). (ENG., Illus.). 24p. (J). (gr. k-3). lib. bdg. 25.95 (978-1-62617-573-0(X), Blastoff! Readers) Bellwether Media.

—Sea Slugs. 2015. (Illus.). 24p. (J). lib. bdg. (978-1-62031-192-9(5), Bullfrog Bks.) Jump! Inc.

Scott, Janine. An Ocean of Animals, 1 vol. 2011. (Habitats Around the World Ser.). (ENG.). 24p. (gr. k-1). pap. 7.29 (978-1-4296-7151-4(3)); pap. 41.70 (978-1-4296-7155-2(6)) Capstone Press of Coughlan Cos. (Pebble Plus).

Sea Creatures Pack [Scholastic]. 2011. (Under the Sea Ser.). pap. 3.00 (978-1-4296-6304-5(9), Pebble Plus) Capstone Press of Coughlan Cos.

Sea Mammals. (Illus.). (J). (gr. -1-6). pap., act. bk. ed. 2.95 (978-0-565-00974-8(5)) Natural History Museum Pubns. GBR. Dist: Parkwest Pubns., Inc.

Sea Shapes. (Illus.). 12p. (J). (978-2-7643-0150-0(2)) Phidal Publishing, Inc./Editions Phidal, Inc.

Sea Splash. (My Animal Library). (Illus.). 10p. (J). (978-2-7643-0103-6(0)) Phidal Publishing, Inc./Editions Phidal, Inc.

Sexton, Colleen. Blastoff! Readers - Oceans Alive, 6 vols., Set. Incl. Angelfish. 20.00 (978-0-531-21711-5(6)); Frogfish. 20.00 (978-0-531-21712-2(4)); Lionfish. 20.00 (978-0-531-21713-9(2)); Puffins. 20.00 (978-0-531-21714-6(0)); Shrimp. 20.00 (978-0-531-21716-0(7)); Swordfish. 20.00 (978-0-531-21715-3(9)); (Illus.). 24p. (J). (gr. k-3). 2009. 2009. Set lib. bdg. 120.00 (978-0-531-26128-6(X), Children's Pr.) Scholastic Library Publishing.

—Coral Reefs. 2011. (Blastoff! Readers Ser.). 24p. (J). pap. 5.95 (978-0-531-26026-5(7), Children's Pr.) Scholastic Library Publishing.

—Cuttlefish. 2009. (Oceans Alive Ser.). (ENG., Illus.). 24p. (J). (gr. k-3). lib. bdg. 25.95 (978-1-60014-273-4(7)) Bellwether Media.

—Sponges. 2009. (Oceans Alive Ser.). (ENG., Illus.). 24p. (J). (gr. k-3). lib. bdg. 25.95 (978-1-60014-268-0(0)) Bellwether Media.

Shea, Mary Molly. Being a Manatee, Vol. 1. 2014. (Can You Imagine? Ser.). (ENG., Illus.). 32p. (J). (gr. 2-3). 25.25 (978-1-4824-0127-1(4)) Stevens, Gareth Publishing LLLP.

Shea, Nicole. Creepy Sea Creatures. 2012. (Nature's Creepiest Creatures Ser.). (ENG., Illus.). 24p. (J). (gr. 2-5). pap. 8.15 (978-1-4339-6503-6(8)); lib. bdg. 22.60 (978-1-4339-6501-2(1)) Stevens, Gareth Publishing LLLP. (Gareth Stevens Learning Library).

Shea, Therese. What Are Crustaceans? 2016. (Let's Find Out! Marine Life Ser.). 00032p. (J). (gr. 2-3). pap. 12.90 (978-1-5081-0386-8(0), Britannica Educational Publishing) Rosen Publishing Group, Inc., The.

Shively, Julie. Baby Orca. Sharp, Chris, illus. Seaworld, photos by. 2005. (Seaworld Animal Library: Vol. 1). 24p. (J). (gr. -1-3). bds. 6.95 (978-0-8249-6615-7(5), Ideal Pubns.) Worthy Publishing.

Shocking Sea Creatures. 2016. (Illus.). 32p. (J). (978-1-4222-3528-7(9)) Mason Crest.

Sill, Cathryn. About Crustaceans: A Guide for Children, 1 vol. Sill, John, illus. 2007. (ENG.). 40p. (J). (gr. k-3). pap. 7.95 (978-1-56145-405-1(2)) Peachtree Pubs.

—About Crustaceans: A Guide for Children, 1 vol. Sill, John & Sill, John, illus. 2004. (ENG.). 40p. (J). (gr. k-3). 16.95 (978-1-56145-301-6(3)) Peachtree Pubs.

—About Marine Mammals: A Guide for Children, 1 vol. Sill, John, illus. 2016. (About... Ser.). (ENG.). 48p. (J). (gr. -1-2). 16.95 (978-1-56145-906-3(2)) Peachtree Pubs.

Silver Dolphin en Espanol Editors. El Mundo a Mi Alrededor: El Oceano. Zaidi, Nadeem, illus. 2007. (Baby Einstein Ser.). (SPA.). 12p. (J). (gr. -1). bds. (978-970-718-457-2(4), Silver Dolphin en Español) Advanced Marketing, S. de R. L. de C. V.

Simon, Seymour. Under the Sea. 2008. (Illus.). 24p. (J). (978-0-439-86656-9(1)) Scholastic, Inc.

Skerry, Brian. Face to Face with Manatees. 2010. (Face to Face with Animals Ser.). (ENG., Illus.). 32p. (J). (gr. 1-4). 16.95 (978-1-4263-0616-7(4)); 25.90 (978-1-4263-0617-4(2)) National Geographic Society. (National Geographic Children's Bks.).

—The Whale Who Stole Hearts: And More True Stories of Amazing Animal Adventures. 2014. (NGK Chapters Ser.). (ENG., Illus.). 112p. (J). (gr. 2-5). pap. 5.99 (978-1-4263-1520-6(1), National Geographic Children's Bks.) National Geographic Society.

Skerry, Brian & Zoehfeld, Kathleen Weidner. The Whale Who Won Hearts. 2014. (NGK Chapters Ser.). (ENG., Illus.). 112p. (J). (gr. 2-5). lib. bdg. 14.90 (978-1-4263-1521-3(X), National Geographic Children's Bks.) National Geographic Society.

Skewes, John & Ode, Eric. Larry Gets Lost under the Sea. Skewes, John, illus. 2015. (Larry Gets Lost Ser.). (ENG., Illus.). 32p. (J). (gr. -1-2). 16.99 (978-1-57061-925-0(5), Little Bigfoot) Sasquatch Bks.

Slade, Suzanne. What Eats What in an Ocean Food Chain, 1 vol. McLaughlin, Zack, illus. 2012. (Food Chains Ser.). (ENG.). 24p. (gr. 2-3). pap. 8.95 (978-1-4048-7696-5(0)) Picture Window Bks.

Smith, Alastair & Howell, Laura. On the Beach. 2004. (Lift-the-Flap Learners Ser.). (Illus.). 16p. (J). (gr. 1-18). pap. 8.95 (978-0-7945-0213-3(X), Usborne) EDC Publishing.

Smith, Alastair & Tachell, Judy. Under the Sea. Scott, Peter David, illus. 2007. (J). (978-0-545-03305-3(5)) Scholastic, Inc.

Smith, Carrie & Swain, Cameron. Life at the Beach. 2006. (Early Explorers Ser.). (J). pap. (978-1-4108-6020-0(5)) Benchmark Education Co.

Sovak, Jan. Let's Explore! Sea Animals. 2011. (Dover Nature Coloring Book Ser.). (ENG.). 32p. (J). (gr. 1-5). pap. 5.99 (978-0-486-47895-1(5)) Dover Pubns., Inc.

—Manatees Coloring Book. 2010. (Dover Nature Coloring Book Ser.). (ENG., Illus.). 32p. (J). (gr. 2-5). pap. 3.99 (978-0-486-47390-1(2)) Dover Pubns., Inc.

Spilsbury, Louise. Octopus Set. Incl. Dolphin. pap. 6.79 (978-1-4329-4006-5(6)); Jellyfish. pap. 6.79 (978-1-4329-4007-2(4)); Octopus. pap. 6.79 (978-1-4329-4011-9(2)); Sea Turtle. pap. 6.79 (978-1-4329-4008-9(2)); Seal. pap. 6.79 (978-1-4329-4009-6(0)); Shark. pap. 6.79 (978-1-4329-4010-2(4)); (gr. k-2). (Day in the Life: Sea Animals Ser.). (ENG.). 24p. 2010. Set pap. 40.74 (978-1-4329-4012-6(0), Heinemann Read & Learn) Heinemann-Raintree.

Spilsbury, Richard & Spilsbury, Louise. At Home in the Ocean, 01 vols., 1. 2016. (Home in the Biome Ser.). (ENG.). 32p. (J). 26.25 (978-1-5081-4567-7(9), PowerKids Pr.) Rosen Publishing Group, Inc., The.

Spizzirri, Linda, ed. Prehistoric Sea Life. Kohn, Arnie, illus. 32p. (J). (gr. 1-8). pap. 4.98 incl. audio (978-0-86545-020-2(X)) Spizzirri Pr., Inc.

Staunton, Joseph. Dinosaurs in the Sea. 2010. (Discover the Dinosaurs Ser.). 32p. (J). (gr. 2-5). 28.50 (978-1-60753-107-4(0)) Amicus Publishing.

Staunton, Joseph & Flinthart, Dirk. Dinosaurs in the Sea. Rey, Luis, illus. 2011. (Inside Crime Ser.). 48p. (YA). (gr. 5-9). 34.25 (978-1-59920-393-5(6)) Black Rabbit Bks.

Stefoff, Rebecca. Sea Mammals. 2008. (Family Trees Ser.). 96p. (gr. 6-18). lib. bdg. 34.21 (978-0-7614-3072-8(5), Benchmark Bks.) Marshall Cavendish Corp.

Stewart, Melissa. Extreme Coral Reef! 2008. (Smithsonian Q & A Ser.). (Illus.). 48p. (J). (gr. k-4). 16.99 (978-0-06-111577-6(0)) Smithsonian Institution Pr.

Stierle, Cynthia & Crawley, Annie. Ocean Life: From A to Z. 2007. (Readers Book & DVD Ser.). (ENG., Illus.). 32p. (J). (gr. -1-3). bds. 17.99 (978-0-7944-1222-7(X)) Reader's Digest Assn., Inc., The.

Stone, Lynn. How Do Animals Use Their Flippers? 2007. (How Do Animals Use (Discovery Library) Ser.). (Illus.). 24p. (J). (gr. -1-3). lib. bdg. 22.79 (978-1-60044-505-7(5)) Rourke Educational Media.

Sullivan, Laura. Saltwater & Freshwater Creatures Explained. 2016. (Distinctions in Nature Ser.). 32p. (J). pap. 10.58 (978-1-5026-2185-6(1)) Cavendish Square Publishing.

Summers, Portia & Grady, Colin. The Ocean Biome. 2016. (Zoom in on Biomes Ser.). 24p. (J). (gr. 2-2). pap. 9.35 (978-0-7660-7785-0(3)) Enslow Pubs., Inc.

Swanson, Diane. Safari Beneath the Sea: The Wonder World of the North Pacific Coast, 1 vol. Royal British Columbia Museum Staff, photos by. (ENG., Illus.). 64p. (J). pap. 12.95 (978-1-55110-441-6(5)) Whitecap Bks., Ltd. CAN. Dist: Graphic Arts Ctr. Publishing Co.

Swanson, Maggie. SPARK Sea Life Designs Coloring Book. 2016. (Dover Coloring Bks.). (ENG.). 64p. (J). (gr. 1-4). pap. 5.99 *(978-0-486-81025-6(9))* Dover Pubns., Inc.
Taylor, Trace, et al. In the Ocean. Reese, Jonathan, illus. 2006. (1-3Y Ecosystems Ser.). (ENG.). 16p. (J). (gr. k-1). pap. 5.99 *(978-1-59301-438-4(4))* American Reading Co.
Teora, creator. Sea Animals. 2007. (My First Sticker Encyclopedia Ser.). (Illus.). 18p. (J). (gr. -1-3). pap. 5.95 *(978-1-59496-148-9(4))* Teora USA LLC.
Toufexis, George. River Monsters of the World. 2014. (ENG., Illus.). 32p. (J). (gr. 3-8). pap. 3.99 *(978-0-486-49627-6(9))* Dover Pubns., Inc.
Twist, Clint. 1000 Things You Should Know about Oceans. 2008. (1000 Things You Should Know about (Miles Kelley) Ser.). (Illus.). 61p. (J). pap. *(978-1-84236-852-7(4))* Miles Kelly Publishing, Ltd.
U. S. National Geographic Society Staff & Marsh, Laura. National Geographic Readers: Weird Sea Creatures. 2012. (Readers Ser.). (ENG., Illus.). 32p. (J). (gr. k-3). lib. bdg. 13.90 *(978-1-4263-1048-5(X)*, National Geographic Children's Bks.) National Geographic Society.
—Weird Sea Creatures. 2012. (Readers Ser.). (ENG., Illus.). 32p. (J). (gr. k-3). pap. 3.99 *(978-1-4263-1047-8(1)*, National Geographic Children's Bks.) National Geographic Society.
Ugly Sea Creatures. 2006. (Ugly Animals Ser.). (Illus.). 24p. (J). (gr. 3-7). lib. bdg. 22.60 *(978-1-4042-3528-1(0))* Rosen Publishing Group, Inc., The.
Under the Sea [Scholastic]. 2010. (Under the Sea Ser.). pap. 3.12 *(978-1-4296-5068-7(0)*, Pebble Plus) Capstone Press of Coughlan Cos.
Underwater Animals: Level O, 6 vols. (Explorers Ser.). 32p. (gr. 3-6). 44.95 *(978-0-7699-0591-4(9))* Shortland Pubns. (U. S. A.) Inc.
Underwood, Deborah. Hiding in Oceans, 1 vol. 2010. (Creature Camouflage Ser.). (ENG., Illus.). 32p. (J). (gr. 1-3). 27.32 *(978-1-4329-4020-1(1))*; pap. 8.29 *(978-1-4329-4029-4(5))* Heinemann-Raintree. (Heinemann First Library).
Uttridge, Sarah. Ocean Animals Around the World. 2014. (Animals Around the World Ser.). (Illus.). 32p. (gr. 2-5). 31.35 *(978-1-62588-199-1(1))* Black Rabbit Bks.
—Sharks & Sea Creatures Around the World. 2014. (Animals Around the World Ser.). (Illus.). 32p. (gr. 2-5). 31.35 *(978-1-62588-196-0(7))* Black Rabbit Bks.
Van Zandt, Steve. River Song: With the Banana Slug String Band. Zecca, Katherine, illus. 2007. (Sharing Nature with Children Book Ser.). 32p. (J). (gr. -1-5). pap. 9.95 incl. audio compact disk *(978-1-58469-094-8(1)*, 1268621) Dawn Pubns.
—River Song: With the Banana Slug String Band (Includes Music CD) Zecca, Katherine, illus. 2007. 32p. (J). (gr. k-4). 17.95 *(978-1-58469-093-1(3)*, 1268621) Dawn Pubns.
Wade, Laura. Sea & Sealife. 2003. (Knowledge Masters Ser.). (Illus.). 32p. (YA). pap. incl. cd-rom *(978-1-903954-10-2(X)*, Pavilion Children's Books) Pavilion Bks.
Wagner, Karen. Mosasaurus: Mighty Ruler of the Sea. 2008. (ENG., Illus.). 36p. (J). (gr. k-2). pap. 6.95 *(978-1-59249-781-2(0))* Soundprints.
—Mosasaurus: Mighty Ruler of the Sea. Carr, Karen, illus. 2008. (ENG.). 36p. (J). (gr. k-2). 9.95 *(978-1-59249-784-3(5))*; 2.95 *(978-1-59249-783-6(7))*; 8.95 *(978-1-59249-782-9(9))*; 14.95 *(978-1-59249-780-5(2))* Soundprints.
Walker, Pam & Wood, Elaine. The Open Ocean. 2005. (Life in the Sea Ser.). (Illus.). 144p. (YA). (gr. 7-12). 35.00 *(978-0-8160-5705-4(2))* Facts On File, Inc.
Wallace, Karen. Think of an Eel. Bostock, Mike, illus. 2009. (Read, Listen, & Wonder Ser.). (ENG.). 32p. (J). (gr. -1-3). pap. 8.99 *(978-0-7636-3994-5(X))* Candlewick Pr.
Walter Foster Creative Team. Sea Creatures: Step-by-Step Insructions for 25 Ocean Animals. Farrell, Russell, illus. 2011. (Learn to Draw Ser.). 32p. (J). (gr. 1-4). 28.50 *(978-1-936309-19-1(X))* Quarto Publishing Group USA.
Walter Foster Jr. Creative Team & Fiedler, Heidi. Sea Life: A Close-up Photographic Look Inside Your World. 2015. (Up Close Ser.). (ENG.). 64p. (J). (gr. 1-3). 14.95 *(978-1-63322-045-4(1)*, Walter Foster Jr) Quarto Publishing Group USA.
Walters, Peter. The Hungriest Mouth in the Sea, 1 vol. 2015. (ENG., Illus.). 32p. (J). (gr. k-3). pap. 9.95 *(978-1-62855-636-0(6))* Arbordale Publishing.
Waters, Kate. Ocean Giants. 2009. (Illus.). 32p. (J). pap. *(978-0-545-07233-5(6))* Scholastic, Inc.
Watt, Fiona. Under the Sea Baby Jigsaw Book. 2010. (Baby Jigsaw Bks.). (Illus.). 10p. (J). bds. 9.99 *(978-0-7945-1314-6(X)*, Usborne) EDC Publishing.
Wearing, Judy. World of Wonder: Underwater Life, 4 vols., Set. Incl. Jellyfish. (gr. k-3). lib. bdg. 24.45 *(978-1-60596-100-2(0))*; Manta Rays. (gr. 2-4). lib. bdg. 24.45 *(978-1-60596-104-0(3))*; Sea Turtles. (gr. 2-4). lib. bdg. 24.45 *(978-1-60596-106-4(X))*; Seahorses. (gr. 2-4). lib. bdg. 24.45 *(978-1-60596-102-6(7))*; (Illus.). 24p. (J). 2009. 2010. Set lib. bdg. 97.80 *(978-1-60596-669-4(X))* Weigl Pubs., Inc.
Webb, Sophie. Far from Shore: Chronicles of an Open Ocean Voyage. 2011. (ENG., Illus.). 80p. (J). (gr. 5-7). 17.99 *(978-0-618-59729-1(8))* Houghton Mifflin Harcourt Publishing Co.
Weber, Valerie J. Manatees/Manaties. 2008. (Animals That Live in the Ocean/Animales Que Viven en el Oceano Ser.). (SPA & ENG.). 24p. (J). (gr. -1-3). lib. bdg. 22.60 *(978-0-8368-9247-5(X)*, Weekly Reader Leveled Readers) Stevens, Gareth Publishing LLLP.
—Sea Slugs. 2005. (Weird Wonders of the Deep Ser.). (Illus.). 24p. (gr. 1-4). lib. bdg. 23.00 *(978-0-8368-4563-1(3)*, Gareth Stevens Learning Library) Stevens, Gareth Publishing LLLP.
—Squids. 2005. (Weird Wonders of the Deep Ser.). (Illus.). 24p. (gr. 1-4). lib. bdg. 23.00 *(978-0-8368-4564-8(1)*, Gareth Stevens Learning Library) Stevens, Gareth Publishing LLLP.
Weird Sea Creatures. (Illus.). (J). (gr. k-6). 112.50 *(978-1-4042-3298-3(2))* Rosen Publishing Group, Inc., The.
West, David. Mega Shark: Graphic Prehistoric Animals. Poluzzi, Alessandro, illus. 2017. (Graphic Prehistoric Animals Ser.). 32p. (gr. 3-7). lib. bdg. 31.35 *(978-1-62588-410-7(9))* Black Rabbit Bks.
—Ocean Animals. 2016. (Safari Sam's Wild Animals Ser.). 24p. (gr. k-3). 28.50 *(978-1-62588-075-8(8)*, Smart Apple Media) Black Rabbit Bks.
—Tide Pool Animals. 2014. (Nora the Naturalist's Animals Ser.). 24p. (gr. k-3). pap. 8.95 *(978-1-62588-054-3(5))* Black Rabbit Bks.
Westerskov, Kim, photos by. Friends in the Sea. 2004. (Illus.). 32p. (J). *(978-0-7685-2112-2(2))* Dominie Pr., Inc.
—Ocean Travelers. 2004. (ENG., Illus.). 32p. (J). (gr. 5-5). pap. 7.47 net. *(978-0-7685-2118-4(1)*, Dominie Elementary) Pearson Schl.
Who Lives in the Coral Reef. 2004. (J). 6.95 *(978-0-931548-12-3(8))* Island Heritage Publishing.
Wicker, Jan L. Those Magical Manatees. Weaver, Steve, illus. 2008. (Those Amazing Animals Ser.). (ENG.). 55p. (J). (gr. k-4). pap. 9.95 *(978-1-56164-383-7(1))* Pineapple Pr., Inc.
Wicker, Jan Lee. Those Magical Manatees. Weaver, Steve, illus. 2008. (Those Amazing Animals Ser.). (ENG.). 55p. (J). (gr. k-4). lib. bdg. 14.95 *(978-1-56164-382-0(3))* Pineapple Pr., Inc.
Wilkes, Angela, contrib. by. Bajo el Mar: Under the Sea. 2004. (Ladders Ser.). (SPA & ENG., Illus.). 32p. (J). (gr. -1-3). 12.95 *(978-1-58728-475-5(8))* Cooper Square Publishing Llc.
Wilkins, John-Paul. What Can Live at the Beach?, 1 vol. 2014. (What Can Live There? Ser.). (ENG., Illus.). 24p. (gr. -1-1). 22.65 *(978-1-4846-0578-3(0)*, Heinemann Read & Learn) Heinemann-Raintree.
—What Can Live in the River?, 1 vol. 2014. (What Can Live There? Ser.). (ENG., Illus.). 24p. (gr. -1-1). 22.65 *(978-1-4846-0575-2(6)*, Heinemann Read & Learn) Heinemann-Raintree.
Wilkins, Mary-Jane. Deep Sea. 2017. (Fast Track: Who Lives Here? Ser.). (Illus.). 24p. (gr. k-3). 28.50 ***(978-1-78121-345-2(3))*** Brown Bear Bks.
Williams, Lily. If Sharks Disappeared. Williams, Lily, illus. 2017. (ENG., Illus.). 40p. (J). 17.99 *(978-1-62672-413-6(X)*, 9781626724136) Roaring Brook Pr.
Winkelman, Barbara Gaines. Puffer's Surprise. Petruccio, Steven James, illus. 2003. (Smithsonian Oceanic Collection). (ENG.). 32p. (J). (gr. -1-3). 8.95 *(978-1-59249-062-2(X)*, SC4024) Soundprints.
World Book, Inc Staff, contrib. by. Endangered Animals of the Oceans. 2014. (J). *(978-0-7166-5627-2(2))* World Bk., Inc.
—Mollusks & Similar Sea Creatures. 2009. (J). *(978-0-7166-0407-5(8))* World Bk., Inc.
—Oceans. 2012. (J). *(978-0-7166-0447-1(7))* World Bk., Inc.
—The Sea & Its Marvels. 2011. (J). *(978-0-7166-1791-4(9))* World Bk., Inc.
—Under the Sea. 2007. (J). *(978-0-7166-7731-4(8))* World Bk., Inc.
Wright, Craig, ed. In the Ocean. 2010. (ENG., Illus.). 16p. act. bk. ed. 4.06 *(978-0-19-440174-6(X))* Oxford Univ. Pr., Inc.
Wunderlich, Rick. Math on the Job: Caring for Marine Animals. 2016. (ENG., Illus.). 32p. (J). *(978-0-7787-2358-5(5))* Crabtree Publishing Co.
Wyland: Ocean Life. 2010. (Illus.). 24p. (J). pap. 6.95 *(978-1-884840-91-3(4))* Wyland Worldwide, LLC.
Wymarra, Elizabeth & Wymarra, Wandihnu. Wandihnu & the Old Dugong. Hodges, Benjamin, illus. 2007. (ENG.). 28p. (J). (gr. k-7). pap. 13.95 *(978-1-921248-18-4(1))* Magabala Bks. AUS. Dist: Independent Pubs. Group.
Yelagalawadi, Jyoti. Deep Sea Creatures. Nagaraju, Harsha, illus. 2004. 32p. (J). 14.99 *(978-0-9725901-2-9(9))* Lekha Pubs., LLC.
Yoon, Salina. Deep Sea Dive. 2012. (Lift-The-Flap Adventures Ser.). (ENG., Illus.). 12p. (J). (gr. -1-2). bds. 8.95 *(978-1-4027-8525-2(9))* Sterling Publishing Co., Inc.
Yoon, Salina, creator. Sea Creatures: A Sparkling Little Colors Book, 4 vols. 2005. (ENG., Illus.). 12p. (J). bds. 5.95 *(978-1-58117-169-3(2)*, Intervisual/Piggy Toes) Bendon, Inc.
Young, Mary. We Like to Nurse Too. Parker, Zac, illus. 2015. (ENG.). 32p. (J). (gr. -1). pap. 9.95 *(978-1-890772-98-7(4))* Hohm Pr.
Young, Mary & Parker, Zac. Tambian a Nosotros Nos Gusta Amamantar: We Like to Nurse Too. 2009. (ENG & SPA.). 32p. (J). pap. 10.95 *(978-1-890772-99-4(2))* Hohm Pr.
Young, Sarah & Candlewick Press Staff. Ocean Creatures: a 3D Pocket Guide. Young, Sarah, illus. 2014. (Panorama Pops Ser.). (ENG., Illus.). 30p. (J). (gr. k-4). 8.99 *(978-0-7636-6802-0(8))* Candlewick Pr.
Zeiger, Jennifer. Stingrays. 2012. (Nature's Children Ser.). (ENG., Illus.). 48p. (J). pap. 6.95 *(978-0-531-25483-7(6))*; lib. bdg. 28.00 *(978-0-531-26838-4(1))* Scholastic Library Publishing.
Zondervan Staff. Sea Creatures, 1 vol. 2011. (I Can Read! / Made by God Ser.). (ENG., Illus.). 32p. (J). (gr. -1-2). pap. 3.99 *(978-0-310-72183-3(0))* Zonderkidz.
199 Things under the Sea. 2017. (199 Things to Spot Ser.). (ENG.). (J). bds. 8.99 ***(978-0-7945-3998-6(X)***, Usborne) EDC Publishing.

MARINE ANIMALS—FICTION

Adams, Pam, illus. There Was an Old Lady Who Swallowed the Sea. 2007. (Classic Books with Holes Board Book Ser.). (ENG.). 14p. (J). (gr. -1-k). bds. *(978-1-84643-073-2(9))* Child's Play International Ltd.
Aldrich, Sandra D. Danny Dolphin. 2012. 30p. 19.95 *(978-1-4626-6594-5(2))* America Star Bks.
Allen, Elaine Ann. Olly's Treasure, 1 vol. Nash, Kelli, illus. 2011. (ENG.). 40p. (J). 16.99 *(978-0-7643-3772-7(6)*, 9780764337727, Schiffer Publishing Ltd) Schiffer Publishing, Ltd.
Altbacker, E. J. Kingdom of the Deep. 2012. (Shark Wars Ser.: 4). (ENG.). 240p. (J). (gr. 3-7). 12.99 *(978-1-59514-509-3(5)*, Razorbill) Penguin Young Readers Group.
Americo, Tiago. Under the Sea. 2016. (First Sticker Story Fun Ser.). (ENG.). 30p. (J). (gr. -1-k). pap. 9.99 ***(978-1-5098-0672-0(5))*** Pan Macmillan GBR. Dist: Independent Pubs. Group.
Anthony, Roger. Rindin the Puffer. 2007. (Crocponds Ser.). (Illus.). 32p. (J). (gr. -1-3). 19.95 *(978-0-9798297-0-3(4))* Crocodiles Not Waterlilies Entertainment.
Arone, Cathleen. Seababies Come Ashore. Date not set. (J). (gr. -1-3). 15.95 *(978-0-915009-60-2(9))* World Leisure Marketing Ltd GBR. Dist: Midpoint Trade Bks., Inc.
Artifact Group Staff & Artifact Group, The. Atlantis SquarePantis. 2007. (SpongeBob SquarePants Ser.). (ENG., Illus.). 24p. (J). (gr. k-3). pap. 3.99 *(978-1-4169-3799-9(4)*, Simon Spotlight/Nickelodeon) Simon Spotlight/Nickelodeon.
Auerbach, Annie. Spongebob Superstar, Vol. 5. 2004. 64p. (J). (gr. 2-5). pap. 17.00 incl. audio *(978-1-4000-8628-3(0)*, Listening Library) Random Hse. Audio Publishing Group.
Baker, Deirdre. Becca at Sea, 1 vol. 2009. (ENG.). 168p. (J). (gr. 3-7). pap. 8.95 *(978-0-88899-738-8(8))* Groundwood Bks. CAN. Dist: Publishers Group West (PGW).
Baltazar, Art. Starro & the Space Dolphins, 1 vol. Baltazar, Art, illus. 2012. (DC Super-Pets Ser.). (ENG., Illus.). 56p. (gr. 2-2). pap. 4.95 *(978-1-4048-7217-2(5))*; lib. bdg. 23.99 *(978-1-4048-6487-0(3))* Picture Window Bks. (DC Super-Pets).
Banks, Steven. The Big Halloween Scare. Martinez, Heather, illus. 2003. (SpongeBob SquarePants Ser.: Vol. 1). (ENG.). 32p. (J). (gr. k-2). pap. 3.99 *(978-0-689-84196-5(5)*, Simon Spotlight/Nickelodeon) Simon Spotlight/Nickelodeon.
—Lost in Time. The Artifact Group, illus. 2006. 22p. (J). lib. bdg. 15.00 *(978-1-4242-0977-4(3))* Fitzgerald Bks.
—Show Me the Bunny! Greenblatt, C. H. & Reiss, William, illus. 2004. (Spongebob Squarepants Ser.). 32p. (J). 11.65 *(978-0-7569-5643-1(9))* Perfection Learning Corp.
—Show Me the Bunny! Random House, illus. 2014. (Step into Reading Ser.). (ENG.). 24p. (J). (gr. -1-1). 4.99 *(978-0-385-37608-2(1)*, Random Hse. Bks. for Young Readers) Random Hse. Children's Bks.
—Special Delivery! DePorter, Vince, illus. 2003. (SpongeBob SquarePants Ser.: Vol. 2). (ENG.). 32p. (J). pap. 3.99 *(978-0-689-85887-1(6)*, Simon Spotlight/Nickelodeon) Simon Spotlight/Nickelodeon.
—Spongebob Goes to the Doctor. Saunders, Zina, illus. 2005. 22p. (J). lib. bdg. 15.00 *(978-1-4242-0976-7(5))* Fitzgerald Bks.
—Stop the Presses! DePorter, Vince, illus. 2005. 22p. (J). lib. bdg. 15.00 *(978-1-4242-0973-6(0))* Fitzgerald Bks.
Banks, Steven & Hillenburg, Stephen. Show Me the Bunny! Greenblatt, C. H. & Reiss, William, illus. 2004. (SpongeBob SquarePants Ser.: 3). (ENG.). 32p. (J). pap. 3.99 *(978-0-689-86485-8(X)*, Simon Spotlight/Nickelodeon) Simon Spotlight/Nickelodeon.
Banks, Steven, et al. For the Love of Bubbles. Osterhold, Jared, illus. 2006. (SpongeBob SquarePants Ser.: 12). (ENG.). 64p. (J). pap. 4.99 *(978-1-4169-1633-8(4)*, Simon Spotlight/Nickelodeon) Simon Spotlight/Nickelodeon.
Barefoot Books Staff. Out of the Blue. Alison, Jay & Jay, Alison, illus. 2014. 32p. (J). (gr. -1-k). 14.99 *(978-1-78285-042-7(2))* Barefoot Bks., Inc.
Barland, Dj. The Little Ray's Big Rescue. 2013. 40p. pap. 15.99 *(978-1-4808-0284-1(0))* Archway Publishing.
Barroux. Starfish, Where Are You? 2016. (ENG., Illus.). 40p. (J). (gr. -1-1). 17.99 *(978-1-4998-0258-0(7))* Little Bee Books Inc.
Baum, L. Frank. The Sea Fairies. l.t. ed. 2004. (Large Print Ser.). lib. bdg. 25.00 *(978-1-58287-793-8(9))* North Bks.
Berenstain, Mike. The Berenstain Bears under the Sea. 2016. (Illus.). (J). ***(978-1-5182-2637-3(X))*** Baker & Taylor, CATS.
Berk, Ari. The Secret History of Mermaids & Creatures of the Deep. Anderson, Wayne, illus. 2009. (ENG.). 48p. (J). (gr. 3-7). 17.99 *(978-0-7636-4515-1(X))* Candlewick Pr.
Blackstone, Stella. Secret Seahorse. Beaton, Clare, illus. 2005. (J). (gr. -1-2). 24p. bds. 7.99 *(978-1-905236-15-2(8))*; 24p. 15.99 *(978-1-84148-704-5(X))*; 32p. pap. 7.99 *(978-1-84148-937-7(9))* Barefoot Bks., Inc.
Bolam, Emily, illus. Under the Sea. 2013. (Peekabooks Ser.). (ENG.). 8p. (J). (gr. -1 — 1). bds. 5.99 *(978-0-7641-6630-3(1))* Barron's Educational Series, Inc.
Bonnell, Kris. Down in the Sea. 2006. (J). pap. 5.95 *(978-1-933727-38-7(1))* Reading Reading Bks., LLC.
—Mudskipper & the Water. 2006. (J). pap. 3.95 *(978-1-933727-21-9(7))* Reading Reading Bks., LLC.
Book Company Staff. Ocean Friends. Lassen, Christian R., illus. 2003. (Puzzles Ser.). (J). bds. 14.95 *(978-1-74047-381-1(7))* Book Co. Publishing Pty, Ltd., The AUS. Dist: Penton Overseas, Inc.
—Treasures of the Sea: Birthday & Address Book. Lassen, Christian R., illus. 2003. (Stationery Ser.). (J). 14.95 *(978-1-86309-793-2(7))* Book Co. Publishing Pty, Ltd., The AUS. Dist: Penton Overseas, Inc.
Botterill, Ron E. Big, Green & Mean, Ogie, the Misunderstood Monster. 2009. 28p. pap. 13.00 *(978-1-60860-712-9(7)*, Eloquent Bks.) Strategic Book Publishing & Rights Agency (SBPRA).
Bright, J. E. Heroes of the High Seas, 1 vol. Baltazar, Art, illus. 2011. (DC Super-Pets Ser.). (ENG.). 56p. (gr. 2-2). 23.99 *(978-1-4048-6263-0(3))*; pap. 4.95 *(978-1-4048-6621-8(3))* Picture Window Bks. (DC Super-Pets).
Bringsvaerd, Tor Age. Ruffen: The Sea Serpent Who Couldn't Swim. Hansen, Thore, illus. 2008. (Ruffen Ser.). 64p. (J). (gr. -1-3). 16.95 *(978-0-9790347-9-4(5))* Mackenzie Smiles, LLC.
Brooks, David. You Can Count at the Ocean. 2005. (You Can Count Ser.). (ENG., Illus.). 24p. (J). (gr. -1 — 1). bds. 7.95 *(978-1-55971-930-8(3))* Cooper Square Publishing Llc.
Brooks, Felicity. Under the Sea Lift & Look. 2010. (Lift & Look Board Bks). 12p. (J). bds. 9.99 *(978-0-7945-2576-7(8)*, Usborne) EDC Publishing.
Brooks, John. Balloons, Sea Creatures, & Me. 2006. 34p. (J). 14.58 *(978-0-9661789-3-7(9))* Lulu Pr., Inc.
Burns, Joanne. Ollie Oyster's Ouch. 2005. 21p. 8.99 *(978-1-4116-5337-5(8))* Lulu Pr., Inc.
Cafaro, Phyllis. The Legend of Captain McFinn & Friends. 2012. (ENG.). 24p. (J). 17.99 *(978-0-9799283-3-8(8)*, 9780979928338) Cold River Pubns.
Carle, Eric. A House for Hermit Crab. Carle, Eric, illus. 2013. (World of Eric Carle Ser.). (ENG., Illus.). 32p. (J). (gr. -1-2). pap. 9.99 *(978-1-4424-7224-2(3)*, Little Simon) Little Simon.
—A House for Hermit Crab. Carle, Eric, illus. 2014. (World of Eric Carle Ser.). (ENG., Illus.). 32p. (J). (gr. k-2). pap. 3.99 *(978-1-4814-0915-5(8)*, Simon Spotlight) Simon Spotlight.
Carpenter, L. J. Out of the Tank. 2012. 24p. pap. 15.99 *(978-1-4685-9633-5(0))* AuthorHouse.
Chaisson, Samuel Jam. Larry & Joe's Detective Agency. 2005. pap. 26.50 *(978-1-4184-6878-1(9))* AuthorHouse.
Chanda, J-P. Happy Birthday, SpongeBob! Martinez, Heather, illus. 2005. (SpongeBob SquarePants Ser.). (ENG.). 24p. (J). pap. 3.99 *(978-0-689-87674-5(2)*, Simon Spotlight/Nickelodeon) Simon Spotlight/Nickelodeon.
Chipponeri, Kelli. SpongeBob Rocks! Martinez, Heather, illus. 2006. (SpongeBob SquarePants Ser.: 9). (ENG.). 32p. (J). (gr. -1-3). pap. 3.99 *(978-1-4169-1314-6(9)*, Simon Spotlight/Nickelodeon) Simon Spotlight/Nickelodeon.
Clanton, Ben. Narwhal: Unicorn of the Sea! 2016. (Narwhal & Jelly Book Ser.). (ENG., Illus.). 64p. (J). (gr. 1-4). pap. 7.99 *(978-1-101-91871-5(3)*, Tundra Bks.) Tundra Bks. CAN. Dist: Penguin Random Hse. LLC.
Collins, Terry. Tea at the Treedome. 2004. 64p. (J). (gr. 2-5). pap. 17.00 incl. audio *(978-0-8072-1986-7(X)*, Listening Library) Random Hse. Audio Publishing Group.
Conrique, Samantha. The Pod-Poppers. 2007. (J). pap. 8.00 *(978-0-8059-7200-9(5))* Dorrance Publishing Co., Inc.
Corpus, Terrizita. The Grumpy Lighthouse Keeper. Prewett, Maggie, illus. 2017. (ENG.). 32p. (J). (gr. k-3). pap. 13.99 ***(978-1-925360-18-9(0))*** Magabala Bks. AUS. Dist: Independent Pubs. Group.
Craipeau, Jean-Lou & Dutrieux, Brigitte. Half & Half-Giants of the Ocean: Great Story & Cool Facts. Hyman, Miles & Alibert, Eric, illus. 2009. 56p. (J). pap. 4.99 *(978-1-60115-212-1(4))* Treasure Bay, Inc.
Craipeau, Jean-Lou & Dutrieux, Julien. Half & Half-Giants of the Ocean: Great Story & Cool Facts. Hyman, Miles & Alibert, Eric, illus. 2009. 56p. (J). 9.95 *(978-1-60115-211-4(6))* Treasure Bay, Inc.
Crow, Marilee. Down by the Shore. Roberts, MarySue, photos by. 2008. (Illus.). 28p. pap. 10.95 *(978-1-933090-39-9(1))* Guardian Angel Publishing, Inc.
Cuasay, Alison Taimanglo. Tasi & Matina: The Story of the First Clown Fish. 2010. 28p. pap. 12.99 *(978-1-4520-6672-1(8))* AuthorHouse.
Cyrus, Kurt. The Voyage of Turtle Rex. 2011. (ENG., Illus.). 40p. (J). (gr. -1-3). 16.99 *(978-0-547-42924-3(X))* Houghton Mifflin Harcourt Publishing Co.
Davies, Nicola. Manatee Rescue. Wright, Annabel, illus. 2016. (Heroes of the Wild Ser.). (ENG.). 112p. (J). (gr. 2-5). 14.99 *(978-0-7636-7830-2(9))* Candlewick Pr.
Davis, Caroline. Animals in the Water. 2009. (My First Noisy Bath Bks.). (ENG.). 8p. (J). (gr. -1). 4.99 *(978-0-7641-9591-4(3))* Barron's Educational Series, Inc.
Dean, James. Pete the Cat: Scuba-Cat. Dean, James, illus. 2016. (My First I Can Read Ser.). (Illus.). 32p. (J). (gr. -1-3). pap. 3.99 *(978-0-06-230388-2(0))* HarperCollins Pubs.
Dean, James, illus. Pete the Cat: Scuba-Cat. 2016. 31p. (J). *(978-1-4844-7052-7(4))* Harper & Row Ltd.
DePrisco, Dorothea. Who's in the Ocean? Gilvan-Cartwright, Chris, illus. 2006. (ENG.). 10p. (gr. -1-k). bds. 4.95 *(978-1-58117-509-7(4)*, Intervisual/Piggy Toes) Bendon, Inc.
Derrick, David G., Jr. Sid the Squid: And the Search for the Perfect Job. 2010. (ENG., Illus.). 36p. (J). (gr. -1-3). 15.95 *(978-1-59702-021-3(4))* Immedium.
Diesen, Deborah. The Not Very Merry Pout-Pout Fish. Hanna, Dan, illus. (Pout-Pout Fish Adventure Ser.). (ENG.). (J). 2017. 34p. bds. 7.99 *(978-0-374-30459-1(9)*, 9780374304591) 2015. 32p. (gr. -1-1). 16.99 *(978-0-374-35549-4(5)*, 9780374355494) Farrar, Straus & Giroux. (Farrar, Straus & Giroux (BYR)).
—The Pout-Pout Fish. Hanna, Dan, illus. (Pout-Pout Fish Adventure Ser.: 1). (ENG.). (J). (gr. -1 — 1). 2013. 36p. bds. 7.99 *(978-0-374-36097-9(9)*, 9780374360979) 2008. 32p. 16.99 *(978-0-374-36096-2(0)*, 9780374360962) Farrar, Straus & Giroux. (Farrar, Straus & Giroux (BYR)).
—The Pout-Pout Fish in the Big-Big Dark. Hanna, Dan, illus. (Pout-Pout Fish Adventure Ser.: 2). (ENG.). (J). (gr. -1-1). 2015. 34p. bds. 7.99 *(978-0-374-30189-7(1)*, 9780374301897) 2010. 32p. 16.99 *(978-0-374-30798-1(9)*, 9780374307981) Farrar, Straus & Giroux. (Farrar, Straus & Giroux (BYR)).
—Smile, Pout-Pout Fish. Hanna, Dan, illus. 2014. (Pout-Pout Fish Mini Adventure Ser.). (ENG.). 12p. (J). (gr. -1 — 1). bds. 5.99 *(978-0-374-37084-8(2)*, 9780374370848, Farrar, Straus & Giroux (BYR)) Farrar, Straus & Giroux.
DiPerna, Kaitlyn. Who's Hiding? in the Ocean. Capizzi, Giusi, illus. 2016. (Who's Hiding? Ser.). (ENG.). 16p. (J). (gr. -1). bds. 12.99 *(978-1-62686-745-1(3)*, Silver Dolphin Bks.) Readerlink Distribution Services, LLC.
Dobell, Darcy. The Oyster Who Looked at the Sky. 2008. (ENG., Illus.). 32p. 16.95 *(978-0-88982-250-4(6))* Oolichan Bks. CAN. Dist: Univ. of Toronto Pr.
Dombek, Jeff. How the Oysters Saved the Bay, 1 vol. 2013. (ENG., Illus.). 32p. (J). 16.99 *(978-0-7643-4283-7(5)*, 9780764342837) Schiffer Publishing, Ltd.
Donovan, Gail. !Listos... Ya! Clar, David Austin, illus. 2003. (Rainbow Fish & Friends Ser.). 24p. (J). mass mkt. 3.99 *(978-1-59014-123-6(7))* Night Sky Bks.
Downer, Ann. Shark Baby, 1 vol. Bersani, Shennen, illus. 2013. (SPA & ENG.). 32p. (J). (gr. -1-3). 17.95 *(978-1-60718-622-9(5))*; pap. 9.95 *(978-1-60718-634-2(9))*; pap. 9.95 *(978-1-62855-351-2(0))* Arbordale Publishing.
—Tiburoncito, 1 vol. Bersani, Shennen, illus. 2013. (SPA.). 32p. (J). (gr. -1-3). 17.95 *(978-1-60718-709-7(4))* Arbordale Publishing.
Downing, Johnette. Why the Oyster Has the Pearl, 1 vol. Hill, Bethanne, illus. 2011. (ENG.). 32p. (J). (gr. k-3). 16.99 *(978-1-4556-1460-8(2))* Pelican Publishing Co., Inc.
Dunn, Catherine. Oscar & Solomon. 2008. 40p. pap. 21.99 *(978-1-4363-6977-0(0))* Xlibris Corp.
Edgemon, Darcie. Seamore, the Very Forgetful Porpoise. Seibold, J. Otto, illus. 2008. 48p. (J). (gr. -1-3). lib. bdg. 17.89 *(978-0-06-085076-0(0))* HarperCollins Pubs.
Egmont UK, Egmont. Peekaboo! Sea. 2014. (Animaru Ser.). (ENG., Illus.). 12p. (J). (— 1). bds. 9.99 *(978-1-4052-6778-6(X))* Egmont Bks., Ltd. GBR. Dist: Independent Pubs. Group.
Ferris, Aimee. Girl Overboard. 2007. (S. A. S. S. Ser.). (ENG., Illus.). 224p. (YA). (gr. 7-18). 7.99 *(978-0-14-240799-8(2)*, Speak) Penguin Young Readers Group.
Fletcher, Corina. Playbook Pirates. Teckentrup, Britta, illus. 2013. (ENG.). 12p. (J). (gr. -1-2). 24.00 *(978-0-7636-6606-4(8)*, Nosy Crow) Candlewick Pr.
Fogle, Llynda, et al. A Pond Full of Feelings. Bicking, Judy, illus. 2005. (SPA.). (J). *(978-0-9760282-9-1(8))* RAPC - Sparkle & Shine Project.
Fry, Sonali. Under the Sea. Blanco, Migy, illus. 2014. (Dream Doodle Draw! Ser.). (ENG.). 96p. (J). (gr. -1-2). pap. 7.99 *(978-1-4814-0453-2(9)*, Little Simon) Little Simon.
Galloway, Ruth. Smiley Shark. Galloway, Ruth, illus. (Illus.). 32p. (J). 2005. 6.95 *(978-1-58925-391-9(4))* 2003. tchr. ed. 15.95 *(978-1-58925-028-4(1))* Tiger Tales.

M
N
O

Gantry, Chris. The Underwater Orchestra. Burns, Theresa, illus. 2013. 38p. 16.98 *(978-1-940224-19-0(5))* Taylor and Seale Publishing, LLC.

Garton, Sam. Otter: Hello, Sea Friends! Garton, Sam, illus. 2016. (My First I Can Read Ser.). (Illus.). 32p. (J). (gr. -1-3). pap. 3.99 *(978-0-06-236660-3(2))* HarperCollins Pubs.

Gelin, Antoinette. Captain Underfish: Superhero for the Underworld. 2011. 40p. pap. 25.95 *(978-1-4634-2662-0(3))* AuthorHouse.

Gladwell, Michael. Slappers Maui Vacation. 2008. 32p. pap. 6.95 *(978-0-615-21549-5(1))* Hawaii Fine Art Studio.

Golden Books. SpongeBob Squarepants Movie Tie-In. Golden Books & Meurer, Caleb, illus. 2015. (Little Golden Book Ser.). (ENG.). 24p. (J). (-k). 4.99 *(978-0-553-49775-5(8),* Golden Bks.) Random Hse. Children's Bks.

Goodrich, Carter. The Hermit Crab. Goodrich, Carter, illus. 2009. (ENG., Illus.). 40p. (J). (gr. 1-5). 16.99 *(978-1-4169-3892-7(3),* Simon & Schuster Bks. For Young Readers) Simon & Schuster Bks. For Young Readers.

Gould, Robert. Sea Creatures. 2005. (Big Stuff Ser.: 8). (ENG., Illus.). 16p. (J). bds. 7.95 *(978-1-929945-59-7(0))* Big Guy Bks., Inc.

Grant, Richard E. & Bently, Peter. The Wah-Wah Diaries: The Making of a Film. 3 CDs. Cort, Ben, illus. 2008. (ENG.). 32p. (J). (gr. 2-6). 23.95 *(978-0-230-01598-2(0),* Macmillan) Pan Macmillan GBR. Dist: Trans-Atlantic Pubns., Inc.

Greenburg, J. C. In the Deep. Gerardi, Jan, illus. 2004. (Andrew Lost Ser.: 8). (ENG.). 96p. (J). (gr. 1-4). 3.99 *(978-0-375-82526-2(6),* Random Hse. Bks. for Young Readers) Random Hse. Children's Bks.

—On the Reef. Reed, Mike, tr. Reed, Mike & Gerardi, Jan, illus. 2004. (Andrew Lost Ser.: 7). (ENG.). 96p. (J). (gr. 1-4). 3.99 *(978-0-375-82525-5(8),* Random Hse. Bks. for Young Readers) Random Hse. Children's Bks.

—Under Water. Reed, Mike, illus. 2003. (Andrew Lost Ser.: 5). (ENG.). 96p. (J). (gr. 1-4). mass mkt. 3.99 *(978-0-375-82523-1(1),* Random Hse. Bks. for Young Readers) Random Hse. Children's Bks.

Grindley, Sally & Foreman, Michael. La Playa de Pedro. 2003.Tr. of Peter's Place. (SPA., Illus.). 32p. (J). (gr. 1-3). 19.99 *(978-84-261-3314-4(2))* Juventud, Editorial ESP. Dist: Lectorum Pubns., Inc.

Gulliver, Amanda, illus. Underwater. 2011. (Baby Rattle Bks.). 12p. (J). (gr. -1-k). 6.99 *(978-0-7641-6393-7(0))* Barron's Educational Series, Inc.

Hale, Bruce. Afraid of the Dark. Francis, Guy, illus. 2015. (Clark the Shark Ser.). (ENG.). 32p. (J). (gr. -1-3). 17.99 *(978-0-06-237450-9(8))* HarperCollins Pubs.

—Clark the Shark. Francis, Guy, illus. 2013. (Clark the Shark Ser.). (ENG.). 32p. (J). (gr. -1-3). 17.99 *(978-0-06-219226-4(4))* HarperCollins Pubs.

—Clark the Shark - Tooth Trouble. Francis, Guy, illus. 2014. (I Can Read Level 1 Ser.). (ENG.). 32p. (J). (gr. -1-3). 16.99 *(978-0-06-227908-8(4));* pap. 3.99 *(978-0-06-227906-4(8))* HarperCollins Pubs.

—Clark the Shark Dares to Share. Francis, Guy, illus. 2013. (Clark the Shark Ser.). (ENG.). 32p. (J). (gr. -1-3). 17.99 *(978-0-06-227905-7(X))* HarperCollins Pubs.

—Clark the Shark Takes Heart. Francis, Guy, illus. 2014. (Clark the Shark Ser.). (ENG.). 32p. (J). (gr. -1-3). 17.99 *(978-0-06-219227-1(2))* HarperCollins Pubs.

Halter, Loretta. Lacy's Journey: The Life of a Decorator Crab. 2010. (ENG.). 64p. (J). 19.95 *(978-0-9822942-1-5(2))* Nature's Hopes & Heroes.

Hawk, J. L. If I Were a Creature under the Seaà. 2008. 12p. pap. 24.95 *(978-1-60703-378-3(X))* America Star Bks.

Haydon, Elizabeth. The Tree of Water. Dorman, Brandon, illus. 2014. (Lost Journals of Ven Polypheme Ser.: 4). (ENG.). 400p. (J). (gr. 5-9). 17.99 *(978-0-7653-2059-9(2),* 9780765320599, Starscape) Doherty, Tom Assocs., LLC.

Herz, Henry, et al. Little Red Cuttlefish, 1 vol. Gotfredson, Kate, illus. 2016. (ENG.). 32p. (J). (gr. k-3). 16.99 *(978-1-4556-2146-0(3))* Pelican Publishing Co., Inc.

Higginson, Sheila Sweeny. Diego rescata al bebé manatí (Diego's Manatee Rescue) McGee, Warner, illus. 2009. (Go, Diego, Go! Ser.). (SPA.). 24p. (J). pap. 3.99 *(978-1-4169-7983-8(2),* Libros Para Ninos) Libros Para Ninos.

Hogan, Barbora. How Ryan & Aiden Saved the Ocean. 2013. 36p. pap. 16.99 *(978-1-4525-7776-0(5),* Balboa Pr.) Author Solutions, Inc.

Holden, Pam, et al. Mira Como Nado. Hansen, Christine, illus. 2012.Tr. of Watch Me Swim. (SPA.). 16p. (gr. -1-1). pap. *(978-1-877506-90-1(7),* Red Rocket Readers) Flying Start Bks.

Holmes, Steve, illus. Animales Marinos: Mezcla y Diviertete. 2005. (Mezcla y Diviertete Ser.). (SPA.). 5p. (J). (gr. -1-7). *(978-970-718-291-2(1),* Silver Dolphin en Español) Advanced Marketing, S. de R. L. de C. V.

Jarkins, Sheila. The Adventures of Marco Flamingo in the Jungle. Jarkins, Sheila, illus. 2012. (Illus.). 32p. (J). 1.99 *(978-1-936299-31-7(3),* Raven Tree Pr.) Delta Systems Company, Inc.

Jarman, Julia. Class Three at Sea. Chapman, Lynne, illus. 2008. (ENG.). 32p. (J). (gr. k-3). 16.95 *(978-0-8225-7617-4(1),* Carolrhoda Bks.) Lerner Publishing Group.

Jefferson, E. Louis. Terry-The Little Tadpole-Making New Friends. 2013. 90p. pap. 35.00 *(978-1-300-61843-0(4))* Lulu Pr., Inc.

Kaplan, Osman. Animal Wonders of the Water. Kalender, Oznur, illus. 2009. (Amazing Animals Ser.). (ENG.). 56p. (J). (gr. 2-4). 9.95 *(978-1-59784-200-6(1))* Tughra Bks.

Kimmel, Eric A. Moby Dick: Chasing the Great White Whale. Glass, Andrew, illus. 2012. (ENG.). 40p. (J). (gr. k-1). 16.99 *(978-0-312-66297-4(1),* 9780312662974) Feiwel & Friends.

King, Kerrigan. At the Aquarium. 2006. (Neighborhood Readers Ser.). (ENG., Illus.). 12p. (gr. -1-3). pap. 5.90 *(978-1-4042-6726-8(3),* Rosen Classroom) Rosen Publishing Group, Inc., The.

Knife & Packer, creator. Deep-Sea Dash. 2016. (Illus.). 93p. (J). pap. 6.99 *(978-1-61067-398-3(0))* Kane Miller.

Korman, Susan. Swordfish Returns. Stegos, Daniel J., illus. 2011. (Smithsonian Oceanic Collection Ser.). (ENG.). 32p. (J). (gr. -1-3). 19.95 *(978-1-60727-665-4(8));* 8.95 *(978-1-60727-666-1(6))* Soundprints.

—Swordfish Returns. Stegos, Daniel, illus. (ENG.). 32p. (J). 2005. (gr. -1-2). 9.95 *(978-1-59249-132-2(4),* PB4075) 2005. (gr. -1-2). 4.95 *(978-1-59249-126-1(X),* B4075) 2004. (gr. 2-2). pap. 6.95 *(978-1-59249-127-8(8),* S4025) 2003. (gr. -1-2). 8.95 *(978-1-59249-129-2(4),* SC4025) 2003. (gr. -1-2). 19.95 *(978-1-59249-128-5(6),* BC4025) Soundprints.

—Swordfish Returns. Stegos, Daniel J., illus. 2003. (Smithsonian Oceanic Collection). (ENG.). 32p. (J). (gr. 2-2). 15.95 *(978-1-59249-125-4(1),* B4025) Soundprints.

Kuperman, Marina. Turtle Feet, Surfer's Beat. 2007. 164p. (J). pap. 9.99 *(978-0-9801109-0-6(4))* Kuperman, Marina.

Landrón, Rafael & Landrón, José Rafael. Beba y la Isla Nena: Beba & the Little Island. Ordóñez, María Antonia, illus. 2010. (SPA & ENG.). 32p. (J). *(978-1-934370-05-6(3),* Campanita Bks.) Editorial Campana.

Larsen, Kirsten. Dora & the Baby Crab. Roper, Robert, illus. 2008. (Dora the Explorer Ser.: 17). (ENG.). 24p. (J). (gr. -1-1). pap. 3.99 *(978-1-4169-5451-4(1),* Simon Spotlight/Nickelodeon) Simon Spotlight/Nickelodeon.

Lavin, Christine & Franco-Feeney, Betsy. Hole in the Bottom of the Sea. McHugh, Patricia & Feeney, Kathryn, eds. Franco-Feeney, Betsy, illus. 2012. (ENG., Illus.). 32p. (J). 18.95 incl. audio compact disk *(978-0-9726487-8-3(X))* Puddle Jump Pr., Ltd.

Leaf, Autumn. Coto, Child of the Ocean. 2008. 122p. pap. 19.95 *(978-1-60703-843-6(9))* America Star Bks.

Leopold, Nikia Speliakos Clark. Adam's Crayons. Nemett, Barry & Nemett, Laini, illus. 2011. (J). *(978-0-9817519-1-7(1))* Galileo Pr.

Lewman, David & Gomez, Yuliana. Batter up!/¡a Batear!(SpongeBob SquarePants) Random House, illus. 2014. (Pictureback Ser.). (ENG.). 24p. (J). (gr. -1-2). 3.99 *(978-0-385-38436-0(X),* Random Hse. Bks. for Young Readers) Random Hse. Children's Bks.

Lionni, Leo. Swimmy. 2013. (ENG., Illus.). 32p. (J). (gr. -1-2). 17.99 *(978-0-385-75358-6(6));* lib. bdg. 20.99 *(978-0-385-75366-1(7))* Random Hse. Children's Bks. (Knopf Bks. for Young Readers).

little bee books, little bee. Dive into the Sea! Llewhellin, Gareth, illus. 2016. (ENG.). 12p. (J). (gr. -1 — 1). bds. 7.99 *(978-1-4998-0297-9(8))* Little Bee Books Inc.

Litton, Jonathan. Planet Pop-Up: Shark Makes a Splash! Anderson, Nicola, illus. 2015. (Planet Pop-Up Ser.). (ENG.). 12p. (J). (gr. -1). 12.95 *(978-1-62686-353-8(9),* Silver Dolphin Bks.) Readerlink Distribution Services, LLC.

—Splish Splash: Pop-Up Fun. Galloway, Fhiona, illus. 2016. (Little Snappers Ser.). (ENG.). 10p. (J). (gr. -1-k). 9.99 *(978-1-58925-259-2(4))* Tiger Tales.

Long, Ethan. Clara & Clem under the Sea. Long, Ethan, illus. 2014. (Penguin Young Readers, Level 1 Ser.). (ENG., Illus.). 32p. (J). (gr. k-1). pap. 3.99 *(978-0-448-47812-8(9),* Penguin Young Readers) Penguin Young Readers Group.

Lucas, Nancy T. Peppy's Coral Kingdom. 2008. (ENG.). 24p. pap. 12.99 *(978-1-4196-9046-4(9))* CreateSpace Independent Publishing Platform.

Lumry, Amanda & Hurwitz, Laura. Adventures of Riley: Dolphins in Danger. McIntyre, Sarah, illus. 2005. 36p. 15.95 *(978-0-9748411-3-0(0))* Eaglemont Pr.

MacGregor, Doug, creator. Ochre the Smoker: A fantastic Fable. 2007. (Illus.). 48p. (J). per. 14.95 *(978-0-9654843-2-9(7))* MacGregor, Doug.

Macveety, Sue Maney. Singing Sea/el Mar Que Canta. Zantay, Valerie, tr. 2005. (SPA., Illus.). 33p. per. 15.99 *(978-1-4134-7275-2(3))* Xlibris Corp.

Mae, Darcie. Sammy & Robert Discover the Ocean, 1 vol. 2009. 39p. pap. 24.95 *(978-1-61546-827-0(7))* America Star Bks.

A Manatee Christmas. 2007. (Illus.). 32p. (J). lib. bdg. 15.99 *(978-0-9771059-7-7(0))* Thomas Expressions, LLC.

Marston, Hope Irvin. My Little Book of Manatees. Mirocha, Stephanie, illus. 2007. 32p. (J). (gr. k-5). pap. 7.95 *(978-0-89317-065-3(8),* Windward Publishing) Finney Co., Inc.

Mayer, Mercer. Going to the Sea Park. 2009. (Little Critter: I Can Read! Ser.). (J). lib. bdg. 13.55 *(978-0-606-06964-9(X),* Turtleback) Turtleback Bks.

—Just Critters Who Care. Mayer, Mercer, illus. 2010. (My First I Can Read Ser.). (ENG., Illus.). 32p. (J). (gr. -1-3). 16.99 *(978-0-06-083560-6(5));* pap. 3.99 *(978-0-06-083559-0(1))* HarperCollins Pubs.

Mayfield, Sue. Under the Sea. Hendra, Sue, illus. (Green Bananas Ser.). (ENG.). 48p. (J). 2013. (gr. 1-2). pap. 5.99 *(978-1-4052-5676-6(1))* 2nd ed. 2016. (gr. k-2). 7.99 *(978-1-4052-8230-7(4))* Egmont Bks., Ltd. GBR. Dist: Independent Pubs. Group.

McClure, Nikki. Waiting for High Tide. 2016. (ENG., Illus.). 48p. (J). (gr. k-2). 19.95 *(978-1-4197-1656-0(5),* Abrams Bks. for Young Readers) Abrams, Inc.

McDonnell, Patrick. Shine! 2017. (ENG., Illus.). 40p. (J). (gr. -1-3). 16.99 *(978-0-316-26278-1(1))* Little Brown & Co.

McDuffie, Linda. The Underwater Adventures of Little Ki. 2008. 26p. per. 21.99 *(978-1-4257-8392-1(9))* Xlibris Corp.

McGee, Warner, illus. Ariel's Song. 2007. (Play a Tune Tale Ser.). 16p. (gr. -1-k). 12.98 *(978-1-4127-8829-8(3))* Publications International, Ltd.

McGuinness, Elle J. & Caron, Romi. Baby Turtle's Tale. 2011. (ENG.). 12p. (J). 9.99 *(978-1-4494-0354-6(9))* Andrews McMeel Publishing.

Meadows, Daisy. Courtney the Clownfish Fairy. 2011. (Illus.). 62p. (J). *(978-0-545-28877-4(0))* Scholastic, Inc.

—Tess the Sea Turtle Fairy. 2011. (Illus.). 65p. (J). *(978-0-545-28874-3(6))* Scholastic, Inc.

—Whitney the Whale Fairy. 2011. (Illus.). 64p. (J). *(978-0-545-28876-7(2))* Scholastic, Inc.

Meister, Cari. Shark in the Library!, 1 vol. Simard, Remy, illus. (My First Graphic Novel Ser.). (ENG.). 32p. (gr. k-2). 2011. pap. 6.25 *(978-1-4342-3104-8(6))* 2010. 24.65 *(978-1-4342-2058-5(3))* Stone Arch Bks. (My First Graphic Novel).

Meng, Cece. Always Remember. Jago, Alison, illus. 2016. (ENG.). 32p. (J). (gr. -1-2). 17.99 *(978-0-399-16809-3(5),* Philomel Bks.) Penguin Young Readers Group.

Meyer, Bryce L. Dolphin & Manatee Friends End to End: Formerly Grant's Book of Manatees & Dolphins. 2009. 32p. pap. 16.99 *(978-1-4269-1678-6(7))* Trafford Publishing.

Milbourne, Anna. How Deep Is the Sea? Riglietti, Serena, illus. 2010. (Picture Bks). 24p. (J). 10.99 *(978-0-7945-2311-4(0))* EDC Publishing.

Mitton, Tony. Ocean Adventure. 2015. (Amazing Animals Ser.). (ENG., Illus.). 24p. (J). (gr. -1-1). pap. 4.99 *(978-0-7534-7228-6(7),* 9780753472286, Kingfisher) Roaring Brook Pr.

Moore, Angel. Squinky the Squid, 1 vol. 2010. 26p. pap. 24.95 *(978-1-4489-8111-3(5))* PublishAmerica, Inc.

Moore, Carol Hair. Busy Bumble Bee Rides the Waves. Harrell, Michael, illus. 2009. (I Wish You Ice Cream & Cake Ser.: 2). (ENG.). 32p. (J). lib. bdg. 15.95 *(978-1-935083-06-1(6))* CyPress Pubns.

Mora, Ebie. Kai: The Honu Didn't Know He Was Brave. Tackett, Mike, illus. 2005. 24p. (J). 12.95 *(978-1-56647-755-0(7))* Mutual Publishing LLC.

Napoli, Donna Jo. Fish Girl. 2017. (ENG.). (J). (gr. 5-7). lib. bdg. 30.60 ***(978-0-606-39824-4(4))*** Turtleback Bks.

Napoli, Donna Jo & Wiesner, David. Fish Girl. Wiesner, David, illus. 2017. (ENG., Illus.). 192p. (J). (gr. 5-7). 25.00 *(978-0-544-81512-4(2));* pap. 17.99 *(978-0-547-48393-1(7))* Houghton Mifflin Harcourt Trade & Reference Pubs. (Clarion Bks.).

Narvick, the Whark (or a Shwale) 2003. (J). 8.95 *(978-0-9729703-1-0(2))* Kidderature Publishing.

Nickelodeon. SpongeBob SquarePants: Goodnight Lagoon. 2014. (ENG.). 32p. (J). (-3). 15.99 *(978-1-4926-1669-6(9),* Sourcebooks Jabberwocky) Sourcebooks, Inc.

Nickelodeon Staff. Party Time! 2013. (Spongebob Squarepants Step into Reading Ser.). lib. bdg. 13.55 *(978-0-606-32221-8(3),* Turtleback) Turtleback Bks.

Nickelodeon Staff & Nickelodeon / LeapFrog. Go Diego Go! Underwater Mystery. 2008. (J). 13.99 *(978-1-59319-925-8(2))* LeapFrog Enterprises, Inc.

Norris, Eryl. What's That in the Water? Mansfield, Andy, illus. 2015. (ENG.). 18p. (J). (gr. -1-1). 9.99 *(978-1-4998-0139-2(4))* Little Bee Books Inc.

October the Octopus: A Huggable Concept Book about the Months of the Year. 2014. (ENG., Illus.). 28p. (J). (gr. -1-k). 24.99 *(978-1-4814-2047-1(X),* Simon & Schuster/Paula Wiseman Bks.) Simon & Schuster/Paula Wiseman Bks.

O'Neill, Michael Patrick. Fishy Friends: A Journey Through the Coral Kingdom. O'Neill, Michael Patrick, photos by. 2003. (Illus.). 64p. (J). 19.95 *(978-0-9728653-0-2(6))* Batfish Bks.

Osborne, Mary Pope. Das magische Baumhaus 09. Der Ruf der Delfine. 18.95 *(978-3-7855-4185-2(6))* Loewe Verlag GmbH DEU. Dist: Distribooks, Inc.

Packer. Deep-Sea Dash. Knife, illus. 2016. 93p. (J). *(978-1-61067-478-2(2))* Kane Miller.

Pallotta, Jerry. Dory Story. Biedrzycki, David, illus. 2006. (ENG.). 32p. (J). (gr. -1-3). pap. 7.95 *(978-0-88106-076-8(3))* Charlesbridge Publishing, Inc.

Pallotta, Jerry, et al. Dory Story. Biedrzycki, David, illus. 2003. (Avenues Ser.). (ENG.). 32p. (C). (gr. -1-3). pap. 27.95 *(978-0-88106-075-1(5))* National Geographic School Publishing, Inc.

Paquette, Ammi-Joan. The Tiptoe Guide to Tracking Mermaids. LeTourneau, Marie, illus. 2012. (ENG.). 32p. (J). (gr. -1-3). 16.95 *(978-1-933718-59-0(5))* Tanglewood Pr.

Pass, Erica. Hooray for Dads! 2014. (SpongeBob Squarepants 8X8 Ser.). lib. bdg. 14.75 *(978-0-606-35560-5(X))* Turtleback Bks.

Pass, Erica & Artifact Group Staff. Hooray for Dads! 2007. (SpongeBob SquarePants Ser.: 14). (ENG., Illus.). 24p. (J). (gr. k-2). pap. 3.99 *(978-1-4169-2782-2(4),* Simon Spotlight/Nickelodeon) Simon Spotlight/Nickelodeon.

Patterson, James. Max. 2009. (Maximum Ride Ser.: 5). (ENG.). (YA). (gr. 5-17). 352p. pap. 9.99 *(978-0-316-00290-5(9),* Jimmy Patterson); 416p. 23.99 *(978-0-316-03759-4(1))* Little Brown & Co.

—Saving the World: And Other Extreme Sports. 3rd rev. ed. 2008. (Maximum Ride Ser.: 3). (ENG.). 432p. (YA). (gr. 5-17). pap. 10.00 *(978-0-316-15427-7(X),* Jimmy Patterson) Little Brown & Co.

—Saving the World & Other Extreme Sports. l.t. ed. 2007. (Maximum Ride Ser.: No. 3). 489p. (J). (gr. 3-7). 23.95 *(978-0-7862-9887-7(1))* Thorndike Pr.

Peck, Jan. Way down Deep in the Deep Blue Sea. Petrone, Valeria, illus. 2004. (ENG.). 32p. (J). (gr. -1-3). 17.99 *(978-0-689-85110-0(3),* Simon & Schuster Bks. For Young Readers) Simon & Schuster Bks. For Young Readers.

Perrin, Martine. Look Who's There! Martens, Marianne, tr. from FRE. Perrin, Martine, illus. 2011. (ENG., Illus.). 16p. (J). (gr. -1-k). bds. 8.99 *(978-0-8075-7676-2(X))* Whitman, Albert & Co.

Pfister, Marcus. Rainbow Fish & the Big Blue Whale. (Rainbow Fish Ser.: 1). Orig. Title: Regenbogenfisch und Grosser Blauer Wal. (ENG., Illus.). 2017. 12p. (J). (gr. -1-k). 9.95 ***(978-0-7358-4286-1(8))*** 2012. 32p. pap. 9.95 *(978-3-314-01669-1(7))* North-South Bks., Inc.

Piggy Toes Press, creator. Crayola Sea Life: Counting Sea Life. 2011. (Crayola (Piggy Toes Press) Ser.). (ENG., Illus.). 6p. (gr. -1). bds. 5.95 *(978-1-61524-289-4(9),* Intervisual/Piggy Toes) Bendon, Inc.

Pledger, Maurice, illus. Dottie Dolphin Plays Hide-And-Seek. 2015. (Friendship Tales Ser.). (ENG.). 16p. (gr. -1). bds. 10.95 *(978-1-62686-344-6(X),* Silver Dolphin Bks.) Readerlink Distribution Services, LLC.

—Noisy Nature: in the Ocean. 2015. (Noisy Nature Ser.). (ENG.). 12p. (J). (gr. -1). 16.95 *(978-1-62686-105-3(6),* Silver Dolphin Bks.) Readerlink Distribution Services, LLC.

Poitier, Anton. Flippy Floppy Ocean Animals. Touliatou, Sophia, illus. 2015. 10p. (J). 12.99 *(978-1-61067-346-4(8))* Kane Miller.

Posner-Sanchez, Andrea. Ariel's Dolphin Adventure - Snow White's New Friend, 2 bks. in 1. Random House Disney Staff, illus. 2010. (Pictureback(R) Ser.). (ENG.). 32p. (J). (gr. -1-2). pap. 4.99 *(978-0-7364-2654-1(X),* RH/Disney) Random Hse. Children's Bks.

Prager, Ellen. The Shark Whisperer. Caparo, Antonio Javier, illus. 2014. (Tristan Hunt & the Sea Guardians Ser.). (ENG.). 288p. (J). (gr. 3-7). pap. 9.95 *(978-1-938063-44-2(9),* Mighty Media Junior Readers) Mighty Media Pr.

—Stingray City. Caparo, Antonio Javier, illus. 2016. (Tristan Hunt & the Sea Guardians Ser.: 3). (ENG.). 292p. (J). (gr. 2-7). pap. 9.95 *(978-1-938063-70-1(8),* Mighty Media Junior Readers) Mighty Media Pr.

R, J. Ff: The Weedy Sea Dragon Coloring Book (Standard Version) 2013. 38p. (J). pap. 9.95 *(978-1-935734-53-6(9))* Kitanie Bks.

Random House. Five Undersea Stories (SpongeBob SquarePants) Random House, illus. 2015. (Step into Reading Ser.). (ENG., Illus.). 160p. (J). (gr. -1-1). 7.99 *(978-0-553-50860-4(1),* Random Hse. Bks. for Young Readers) Random Hse. Children's Bks.

—The Great Train Mystery. 2013. (Spongebob Squarepants Step into Reading Ser.). lib. bdg. 13.55 *(978-0-606-35116-4(7))* Turtleback Bks.

—Hooray for Dads! (SpongeBob SquarePants) Random House, illus. 2014. (Pictureback(R) Ser.). (ENG., Illus.). 24p. (J). (gr. -1-2). 4.99 *(978-0-385-37607-5(3),* Random Hse. Bks. for Young Readers) Random Hse. Children's Bks.

Random House Dictionary Staff. You're Fired! (SpongeBob SquarePants) Random House Dictionary Staff & Aikins, Dave, illus. 2014. (Pictureback(R) Ser.). (ENG.). 24p. (J). (gr. -1-2). 3.99 *(978-0-385-37431-6(3),* Random Hse. Bks. for Young Readers) Random Hse. Children's Bks.

Random House Staff. The Great Train Mystery (SpongeBob SquarePants) Random House Staff, illus. 2013. (Step into Reading Ser.). (ENG., Illus.). 32p. (J). (gr. -1-1). pap. 3.99 *(978-0-449-81441-3(6),* Random Hse. Bks. for Young Readers) Random Hse. Children's Bks.

—SpongeBob's Easter Parade (SpongeBob SquarePants) Random House Staff, illus. 2013. (Pictureback(R) Ser.). (ENG., Illus.). 24p. (J). (gr. -1-2). pap. 3.99 *(978-0-449-81444-4(0),* Random Hse. Bks. for Young Readers) Random Hse. Children's Bks.

—You're Fired! 2014. (SpongeBob Squarepants 8X8 Ser.). lib. bdg. 13.55 *(978-0-606-35204-8(X))* Turtleback Bks.

Ranson, Erin. Ocean Wonders. Top That! Staff, ed. Mahoney, Daniel & Wood, Hannah, illus. 2007. (Sparkling Slide Nature Bks.). (ENG.). 12p. (J). (gr. -1). 9.99 *(978-1-84666-167-9(6))* Top That! Publishing PLC GBR. Dist: Independent Pubs. Group.

Raschka, Chris. Clammy Clam. Raschka, Chris, illus. 2014. (Thingy Things Ser.). (ENG., Illus.). 24p. (J). (gr. -1-k). 6.95 *(978-1-4197-1201-2(2),* Abrams Appleseed) Abrams, Inc.

Rash, Andy. Archie the Daredevil Penguin. Rash, Andy, illus. 2015. (ENG., Illus.). 34p. (J). (gr. -1-3). 16.99 *(978-0-451-47123-9(7),* Viking Books for Young Readers) Penguin Young Readers Group.

Rathmell, Donna & Rathmell, Doreen. Octavia & Her Purple Ink Cloud, 1 vol. McLennan, Connie, illus. 2006. (ENG.). 32p. (J). (gr. -1-2). 15.95 *(978-0-9764943-5-5(3))* Arbordale Publishing.

Reasoner, Charles. Ocean Tails. Nelson, Judy, illus. 2011. (Tail Spin Bks.). (ENG.). 14p. (J). (gr. -1-3). bds. 9.99 *(978-1-934650-92-9(7))* Just For Kids Pr., LLC.

Reeve, Philip. Oliver & the Sea Monkeys. McIntyre, Sarah, illus. 2016. (Not-So-Impossible Tale Ser.). (ENG.). 224p. (J). (gr. 2-5). pap. 6.99 *(978-0-385-38789-7(X),* Yearling) Random Hse. Children's Bks.

Reid, James. Ready, Set, Go!, 1 vol. rev. ed. 2013. (Fiction Readers Ser.). (ENG., Illus.). 20p. (J). (gr. 1-1). 4.99 *(978-1-4333-5488-5(8));* pap. 15.96 *(978-1-4807-1144-0(6))* Shell Educational Publishing.

Rey, H. A. Curious George Discovers the Ocean (Science Storybook) 2015. (Curious George Ser.). (ENG., Illus.). 32p. (J). (gr. -1-3). 6.99 *(978-0-544-43065-5(4),* HMH Books For Young Readers) Houghton Mifflin Harcourt Publishing Co.

—Jorge el Curioso Visita el Acuario. 2010. (Curious George Ser.).Tr. of Curious George at the Aquarium. (ENG & SPA., Illus.). 24p. (J). (gr. -1-3). pap. 4.99 *(978-0-547-29963-1(X))* Houghton Mifflin Harcourt Publishing Co.

Rey, H. A. & Rey, Margret. Curious George at the Aquarium. Hines, Anna Grossnickle, illus. 2007. (Curious George Ser.). (ENG.). 24p. (J). (gr. -1-3). 13.99 *(978-0-618-80067-4(0))* Houghton Mifflin Harcourt Publishing Co.

—Curious George at the Aquarium. 2014. (Curious George Ser.). (ENG., Illus.). 24p. (J). (gr. -1-3). pap. 4.99 *(978-0-544-17674-4(X))* Houghton Mifflin Harcourt Publishing Co.

RH Disney. Dory's Sea of Wonders. RH Disney, illus. 2016. (Pictureback(R) Ser.). (ENG., Illus.). 24p. (J). (gr. -1-2). 4.99 *(978-0-7364-3507-9(7),* RH/Disney) Random Hse. Children's Bks.

—Dory's Story. RH Disney, illus. 2016. (Step into Reading Ser.). (ENG., Illus.). 24p. (J). (gr. -1-1). 4.99 *(978-0-7364-3498-0(4),* RH/Disney) Random Hse. Children's Bks.

—Finding Dory. RH Disney, illus. 2016. (Junior Novel Ser.). (ENG., Illus.). 144p. (J). (gr. 2-5). 6.99 *(978-0-7364-3486-7(0),* RH/Disney) Random Hse. Children's Bks.

—Finding Dory Big Golden Book (Disney/Pixar Finding Dory) RH Disney, illus. 2016. (Big Golden Book Ser.). (ENG., Illus.). 48p. (J). (gr. -1-2). 9.99 *(978-0-7364-3506-2(9),* Golden/Disney) Random Hse. Children's Bks.

—Finding Dory Little Golden Book (Disney/Pixar Finding Dory) RH Disney, illus. 2016. (Little Golden Book Ser.). (ENG., Illus.). 24p. (J). (-k). 4.99 *(978-0-7364-3511-6(5),* Golden/Disney) Random Hse. Children's Bks.

—Finding Dory: the Deluxe Junior Novelization (Disney/Pixar Finding Dory) RH Disney, illus. 2016. (Deluxe Junior Novel Ser.). (ENG., Illus.). 144p. (J). (gr. 2-5). 9.99 *(978-0-7364-3573-4(5),* RH/Disney) Random Hse. Children's Bks.

—Hank the Septopus. RH Disney, illus. deluxe ed. 2016. (Pictureback(R) Ser.). (ENG., Illus.). 24p. (J). (gr. -1-2). 4.99 *(978-0-7364-3510-9(7),* RH/Disney) Random Hse. Children's Bks.

—Hello, Dory! RH Disney, illus. 2016. (Tabbed Board Book Ser.). (ENG., Illus.). 16p. (J). (— 1). bds. 7.99 *(978-0-7364-3625-0(1),* RH/Disney) Random Hse. Children's Bks.

RH Disney Staff & Scollon, Bill. Ocean of Color. RH Disney Staff & The Disney Storybook Art Team, illus. 2016. (Step into Reading Ser.). (ENG.). 24p. (J). (gr. -1-1). 4.99 *(978-0-7364-3519-2(0),* RH/Disney) Random Hse. Children's Bks.

Riddle, Jamie. Beach Bum Babies & Sand Sisters Stormy. 2006. 48p. pap. 16.95 *(978-1-4241-3600-1(8))* PublishAmerica, Inc.

Robinson, Fiona. Whale Shines: An Artistic Tale. 2013. (ENG., Illus.). 32p. (J). (gr. k-2). 18.95 (978-1-4197-0848-0(1), Abrams Bks. for Young Readers) Abrams, Inc.

Romeu, Emma. My Manatee Friend. Vigil, Luis Gerardo Sanchez & Broeck, Fabricio Vanden, illus. 2004. (Colección Animales de América / Animals of the Americas Ser.). (SPA.). 24p. (gr. 3-5). pap. 11.95 (978-1-59437-845-4(2)) Santillana USA Publishing Co., Inc.

Rovetch, L. Bob. 1,2,3 Octopus & Me. Gévry, Claudine, illus. 2006. (J). (978-1-58987-011-6(5)) Kindermusik International.

Roy, James. Chaz at the Fish Market. Gorissen, Dean, illus. 2015. (J). pap. (978-1-4966-0251-0(X)) Capstone Classroom.

Salton, Liz. Eelfish, a Rock & Roll King. Hathaway, Karen, illus. 2004. 38p. pap. 24.95 (978-1-4137-1847-8(7)) PublishAmerica, Inc.

Saunders, Zina, illus. Trouble at the Krusty Krab! 2004. (SpongeBob SquarePants Ser.). (ENG.). 32p. (J). pap. 3.99 (978-0-689-86838-2(3), Simon Spotlight/Nickelodeon) Simon Spotlight/Nickelodeon.

Schlegl, Stacey Lynn & Schlegl, Abigail. MerMountain. 2012. 84p. (J). pap. 11.95 (978-0-9850272-2-3(3)) Jan-Carol Publishing, INC.

Schwarz, Viviane. Shark & Lobster's Amazing Undersea Adventure. Stewart, Joel, illus. 2006. 34p. (J). (978-1-4156-8140-4(6)) Candlewick Pr.

Seven, John. The Ocean Story, 1 vol. Christy, Jana, illus. 2011. (Fiction Picture Bks.). (ENG.). 32p. (gr. k-2). lib. bdg. 23.99 (978-1-4048-6785-7(6), Fiction Picture Bks.) Picture Window Bks.

Shepherd, Jodie. Ocean Friends. Ovresat, Laura, illus. 2007. (Guess Who Ser.). (ENG.). 12p. (J). (gr. -1-k). bds. 8.99 (978-0-7944-1122-0(3), Reader's Digest Children's Bks.) Studio Fun International.

Sherry, Kevin. I'm the Best Artist in the Ocean! 2008. (ENG.). 24p. (J). (gr. -1-3). 16.99 (978-0-8037-3255-1(4), Dial Bks) Penguin Young Readers Group.

—I'm the Biggest Thing in the Ocean. 2007. (ENG., Illus.). 32p. (J). (gr. -1-3). 17.99 (978-0-8037-3192-9(2), Dial Bks) Penguin Young Readers Group.

—I'm the Biggest Thing in the Ocean! 2010. (ENG.). 28p. (J). (gr. k — 1). bds. 6.99 (978-0-8037-3529-3(4), Dial Bks) Penguin Young Readers Group.

Sierra, Judy. Ballyhoo Bay. Anderson, Derek, illus. 2009. (ENG.). 40p. (J). (gr. -1-3). 16.99 (978-1-4169-5888-8(6), Simon & Schuster/Paula Wiseman Bks.) Simon & Schuster/Paula Wiseman Bks.

Silver Dolphin en Español Editors. Amigos del Mar. 2006. (Magnets on the Move Ser.). (Illus.). 8p. (J). (gr. -1). bds. (978-970-718-368-1(3), Silver Dolphin en Español) Advanced Marketing, S. de R. L. de C. V.

Siminovich, Lorena, illus. You Are My Baby: Ocean. 2014. (ENG.). 10p. (J). (gr. -1 — 1). bds. 8.99 (978-1-4521-2650-0(X)) Chronicle Bks. LLC.

Slack, Michael. Turtle Tug to the Rescue. Slack, Michael, illus. 2017. (ENG., Illus.). 40p. (J). 16.99 (978-1-62779-194-6(9), 9781627791946, Holt, Henry & Co. Bks. For Young Readers) Holt, Henry & Co.

Slate, Jenny & Fleischer-Camp, Dean. Marcel the Shell with Shoes On: Things about Me, 1 vol. 2011. (Marcel the Shell Ser.: 1). (ENG.). 42p. (J). (gr. k-3). 18.99 (978-1-59514-455-3(2), Razorbill) Penguin Young Readers Group.

Slezak, Roy E. Marsha the Manatee. 2012. 32p. (-18). pap. 24.95 (978-1-4626-9465-5(9)) America Star Bks.

Smith, Danna. Swallow the Leader. Sherry, Kevin, illus. 2016. (ENG.). 32p. (J). (gr. -1-3). 16.99 (978-0-544-10518-8(4), Clarion Bks.) Houghton Mifflin Harcourt Trade & Reference Pubs.

Soileau, Hodges, illus. The Great Shark Mystery. 2003. (Boxcar Children Special Ser.). 130p. (gr. 4-7). 15.50 (978-0-7569-1616-9(X)) Perfection Learning Corp.

Sollinger, Emily. Diego's Ocean Adventure: A Book of Facts about Ocean Animals. Mawhinney, Art, illus. 2008. (Go, Diego, Go! Ser.). (ENG.). 16p. (J). (gr. -1-2). pap. 6.99 (978-1-4169-4781-3(7), Simon Spotlight/Nickelodeon) Simon Spotlight/Nickelodeon.

Soundprints Staff. Ocean Adventures: Story-Time Treasury. 2005. (Smithsonian Institution Story-Time Treasures Ser.). (Illus.). 256p. (J). (gr. -1-2). 14.95 (978-1-59069-226-4(8), HT1001) Studio Mouse LLC.

Srinivasan, Divya. Octopus Alone. 2013. (ENG., Illus.). 40p. (J). (gr. -1-k). 16.99 (978-0-670-78515-5(6), Viking Books for Young Readers) Penguin Young Readers Group.

St. Pierre, Stephanie. What the Sea Saw, 1 vol. Doyle, Beverly, illus. 2006. (ENG.). 48p. (J). (gr. k-3). 16.95 (978-1-56145-359-7(5)) Peachtree Pubs.

Steele, Kathleen Marie. The Legend of the Angel Wing Shell. Chylak, Jolie Catherine, illus. 2009. 20p. pap. 24.95 (978-1-60749-134-7(6)) America Star Bks.

Stine, R. L. The Good, the Bad & the Very Slimy. Park, Trip, illus. 2008. (Rotten School Ser.: 3). (ENG.). 128p. (J). (gr. 3-7). pap. 5.99 (978-0-06-078594-9(2)) HarperCollins Pubs.

Strasser, Todd. The Beast of Cretacea. 2015. (ENG.). 432p. (J). (gr. 7). 18.99 (978-0-7636-6901-0(6)) Candlewick Pr.

Swift, Ginger. Little Blue Boat. Persico, Zoe, illus. 2016. (ENG.). 10p. (J). bds. 0.00 (978-1-68052-077-4(6)) Cottage Door Pr.

Tate, Suzanne. Sandy Seal: A Tale of Sea Dogs. Melvin, James, illus. l.t. ed. 2004. (Suzanne Tate's Nature Ser.: No. 27). 28p. (J). pap. 4.95 (978-1-878405-49-4(7)) Nags Head Art, Inc.

Teevee, Ningeokuluk. Alego, 1 vol. Manning-Toonoo, Nina, tr. 2009. (ENG., Illus.). 24p. (J). (gr. -1-2). 17.95 (978-0-88899-943-6(7)) Groundwood Bks. CAN. Dist: Publishers Group West (PGW).

Ticktock Media, Ltd. Staff. Ocean. 2009. (Animal Fun Touch & Feel Ser.). (ENG.). 10p. (J). (gr. -1-k). bds. 4.95 (978-1-84696-830-3(5), TickTock Books) Octopus Publishing Group GBR. Dist: Independent Pubs. Group.

Todd-Stanton, Joe, illus. The Secret of Black Rock. 2017. (ENG.). 40p. (J). (gr. -1-2). 16.95 (978-1-911171-25-6(9)) Flying Eye Bks. GBR. Dist: Consortium Bk. Sales & Distribution.

Tunks, Karyn. Jubilee!, 1 vol. Buckner, Julie, illus. 2012. (ENG.). 32p. (J). (gr. k-3). 16.99 (978-1-58980-880-5(0)) Pelican Publishing Co., Inc.

Van Tassel, Mary A. Beach Ball's Discovery. 2013. 24p. pap. 24.95 (978-1-4626-9698-7(8)) America Star Bks.

Vanier, Jolie. Puwaii Adventures with Joliea & Friends. 2006. 16.95 (978-0-9787949-1-0(5)) Puwaii International, LLC.

Vernon, Ursula. Dragonbreath. Vernon, Ursula, illus. (Dragonbreath Ser.: 1). (ENG., Illus.). 160p. (J). (gr. 3-7). 2012. pap. 6.99 (978-0-14-242095-9(6), Puffin Books) 2009. 12.99 (978-0-8037-3363-3(1), Dial Bks) Penguin Young Readers Group.

—Dragonbreath. 2012. (Dragonbreath Ser.: 1). lib. bdg. 17.20 (978-0-606-26665-9(8), Turtleback) Turtleback Bks.

The Water Park, 6 Pack. (Sails Literacy Ser.). 16p. (gr. k-18). 27.00 (978-0-7635-4415-7(9)) Rigby Education.

Watt, Fiona. Baby's Very First Slide & See under the Sea. 2015. (Baby's Very First Slide & See Board Bks.). (ENG.). 10p. (J). 14.99 (978-0-7945-3482-0(1), Usborne) EDC Publishing.

Webster, Christy. Big Fish, Little Fish. 2016. (Illus.). 24p. (J). E-Book **(978-0-7364-3705-9(3))** Random Hse., Inc.

Whitehead, Jenny. You're a Crab! A Moody Day Book. Whitehead, Jenny, illus. 2015. (ENG., Illus.). 32p. (J). (gr. -1-2). 16.99 (978-0-8050-9361-2(3), 9780805093612, Holt, Henry & Co. Bks. For Young Readers) Holt, Henry & Co.

Whiteley, Jason. Tales from the Tacklebox: Escape from the Crooked Tree. 2012. 48p. 23.99 (978-1-4575-1152-3(5)); pap. 14.99 (978-1-4575-1150-9(9)) Dog Ear Publishing, LLC.

Wilson, Sarah. Moms Are the Best! 2014. (Spongebob Squarepants Step into Reading Ser.). lib. bdg. 13.55 (978-0-606-35203-1(1)) Turtleback Bks.

MARINE ARCHITECTURE

see Shipbuilding

MARINE BIOLOGY

see also Freshwater Biology; Marine Animals; Marine Ecology; Marine Plants; Marine Resources

Baker, Beth. Sylvia Earle. 2006. (Just the Facts Biographies Ser.). (ENG., Illus.). 112p. (gr. 5-12). 27.93 (978-0-8225-3422-8(3), Lerner Pubns.) Lerner Publishing Group.

Bennett, Paul. Ocean Habitats. 2006. (Exploring Habitats Ser.). (Illus.). 36p. (gr. 3-7). lib. bdg. 26.00 (978-0-8368-7255-2(X), Gareth Stevens Learning Library) Stevens, Gareth Publishing LLLP.

Bensinger, Lou. Tiny Invaders in the Water. 2010. (Tiny Invaders Ser.). (Illus.). 24p. (J). pap. 8.25 (978-1-4358-9852-3(4)); (gr. 1-5). lib. bdg. 22.60 (978-1-4358-9380-1(8)) Rosen Publishing Group, Inc., The. (PowerKids Pr.).

Bush Gibson, Karen. Marine Biology: Cool Women Who Dive. Chandhok, Lena, illus. 2016. (Girls in Science Ser.). (ENG.). 112p. (gr. 3-7). 19.95 (978-1-61930-431-4(7)) Open City Bks.

Chambers, Catherine. Stickmen's Guide to Oceans in Layers. Dean, Venitia & De Quay, John Paul, illus. 2016. (Stickmen's Guides to This Incredible Earth Ser.). (ENG.). 32p. (J). (gr. 3-6). 26.65 (978-1-5124-0619-1(8)) Lerner Publishing Group.

Childrens Ocean Life Encyclopedia. 2008. (1st Encyclopedia Ser.). 224p. (978-1-4075-1309-6(5)) Parragon, Inc.

Coss, Lauren. Life in Oceans. 2014. (Life in Water Biomes Ser.). (ENG.). 24p. (J). (gr. 2-5). 28.50 (978-1-62687-297-4(X), 207138) Child's World, Inc., The.

Crowson, Andrew. Flip Flap Ocean. 2003. (Illus.). 12p. bds. (978-1-85602-431-0(8), Pavilion Children's Books) Pavilion Bks.

Cummings, Priscilla. The Chadwick Coloring Book, 1 vol. Cohen, A. R., illus. 2009. (ENG.). 32p. (J). (gr. k-4). pap. 3.95 (978-0-87033-389-7(5), 9780870333897, Cornell Maritime Pr./Tidewater Pubs.) Schiffer Publishing, Ltd.

Davies, Kate. See under the Sea. 2008. (See Inside Board Bks). 16p. (J). (gr. 2). bds. 12.99 (978-0-7945-2238-4(6), Usborne) EDC Publishing.

Dorling Kindersley Publishing Staff. Sharkpedia. 2008. (ENG., Illus.). 128p. (J). (gr. 3-7). 12.99 (978-0-7566-3761-3(9), DK Children) Dorling Kindersley Publishing, Inc.

—Sharks, Dolphins, & Other Sea Creatures. 2015. (ENG.). 96p. (J). (gr. 2-4). pap. 12.99 (978-1-4654-2928-5(X), DK Children) Dorling Kindersley Publishing, Inc.

Evans, Topper. 100-Year-Old Tuataras! 2016. (World's Longest-Living Animals Ser.). 00024p. (J). pap. 8.15 **(978-1-4824-5624-0(9))** Stevens, Gareth Publishing LLLP.

Exploring Creation Marine Biology. 2006. cd-rom 58.50 (978-1-932012-66-8(4)) Apologia Educational Ministries, Inc.

Exploring Creation Marine Biology Companion CD-ROM. 2006. cd-rom 13.50 (978-1-932012-67-5(2)) Apologia Educational Ministries, Inc.

Field, Conrad. Alaska Ocean ABCs. Field, Conrad, illus. 2008. (Illus.). 32p. (J). pap. 9.95 (978-0-9797442-2-8(9)) Alaska Independent Pubs.

Field, Nancy H. Discovering Sharks & Rays. Maydak, Michael S., illus. 2003. (Discovering Nature Library). 40p. (J). (gr. 2-6). pap. 7.95 (978-0-941042-33-8(2)) Dog-Eared Pubns.

Ganeri, Anita. Protecting Ocean Habitats. 2005. (Protecting Habitats Ser.). (Illus.). 32p. (gr. 4-7). lib. bdg. 26.00 (978-0-8368-4992-9(2), Gareth Stevens Learning Library) Stevens, Gareth Publishing LLLP.

Gilpin, Daniel. Life-Size Sharks & Other Underwater Creatures. Knowelden, Martin, illus. 2005. (Life-Size Ser.). (ENG.). 28p. (J). (gr. 2-7). 9.95 (978-1-4027-2537-1(X)) Sterling Publishing Co., Inc.

Gilvan-Cartwright, Chris, illus. Who's in the Ocean? 2005. (Lift-The-Flap 'n' Learn Ser.). 10p. (J). 9.95 (978-1-58117-213-3(3), Intervisual/Piggy Toes) Bendon, Inc.

Hemmel, David Lee & Knutson, Janette C. Alexis' Island: Growing up in the Tropical Paradise of Key West. 2006. (J). per. 14.95 (978-0-9745637-2-5(2)) Duval Publishing.

Hopkins, Therese. Underwater Homes. 2009. (Home Sweet Home Ser.). 24p. (gr. 1-1). 42.50 (978-1-61513-408-3(5), PowerKids Pr.) Rosen Publishing Group, Inc., The.

Howard, Fran. Oceans, 1 vol. 2006. (Habitats Ser.). (ENG., Illus.). 32p. (gr. -1-3). 27.07 (978-1-59679-781-9(9), Buddy Bks.) ABDO Publishing Co.

Johnson, Elizabeth R. Sea Life. 2016. (Sea Life Ser.). (ENG.). 24p. (gr. k-1). lib. bdg. 213.20 (978-1-5157-2095-9(0), Pebble Plus) Capstone Press of Coughlan Cos.

Johnson, Rebecca L. & National Geographic Learning Staff. Sylvia Earle: Protecting the Seas. 2007. (Nonfiction Reading & Writing Workshops Ser.). (ENG., Illus.). 32p. (J). pap. 17.95 (978-0-7922-8879-4(3)) CENGAGE Learning.

Johnson, Rebecca L., et al. Ocean Exploration. 2007. (Avenues Ser.). (ENG., Illus.). 36p. (J). pap. 18.95 (978-0-7922-5430-0(9)) CENGAGE Learning.

Kalman, Bobbie. Le Biome Marin. 2012. (FRE.). 32p. (J). pap. 10.95 (978-2-89579-478-3(2)) Bayard Canada CAN. Dist: Crabtree Publishing Co.

—Los Océanos de la Tierra. 2009. (SPA.). 32p. (J). (978-0-7787-8243-8(3)); pap. (978-0-7787-8260-5(3)) Crabtree Publishing Co.

Kalman, Bobbie & Aloian, Molly. Les Océans Polaires. 2009. (FRE., Illus.). 32p. (J). pap. 9.95 (978-2-89579-248-2(8)) Bayard Canada Livres CAN. Dist: Crabtree Publishing Co.

Kalman, Bobbie & Macaulay, Kelly. Les Mers Tropicales. Briere, Marie-Josee, tr. from ENG. 2008. (Petit Monde Vivant Ser.). (FRE., Illus.). 32p. (J). (gr. 3-7). pap. 9.95 (978-2-89579-182-9(1)) Bayard Canada Livres CAN. Dist: Crabtree Publishing Co.

Kelley, K. C. Marine Biologists!, Vol. 10. 2015. (Scientists in Action Ser.). (Illus.). 48p. (J). (gr. 5). 20.95 (978-1-4222-3425-9(8)) Mason Crest.

Lantz, Peggy Sias & Hale, Wendy A. The Coral Reefs of Florida. 2014. (Florida Water Story Ser.). (ENG., Illus.). 34p. (J). (gr. 4). pap. 6.95 (978-1-56164-703-3(9), 9781561647033) Pineapple Pr., Inc.

Leardi, Jeanette. Protecting Our Oceans: Text Pairs. 2008. (Bridges/Navigators Ser.). (J). (gr. 6). 89.00 (978-1-4108-8447-3(3)) Benchmark Education Co.

Look Who's Popping Up: Under the Sea. 2003. (J). (gr. -1-k). 4.98 (978-0-7525-8904-6(0)) Parragon, Inc.

MacAulay, Kelley & Kalman, Bobbie. Tropical Oceans. 2005. (Living Ocean Ser.). (ENG., Illus.). 32p. (J). (gr. 3-4). lib. bdg. (978-0-7787-1300-5(8)) Crabtree Publishing Co.

Malnig, Anita. Tide Pools: Life at the Edge of the Sea. rev. ed. 2009. (Nature Watch Ser.). (YA). (gr. 3-6). 27.93 (978-1-58013-945-8(0)) Lerner Publishing Group.

Martin, Claudia. Complete Guides Ocean Life. 2012. (ENG.). 144p. (J). (978-1-4351-4408-8(2)) Barnes & Noble, Inc.

Marx, Christy. Life in the Ocean Depths. 2009. 64p. (YA). (gr. 5-8). pap. 12.95 (978-1-4358-3265-7(5), Rosen Reference) Rosen Publishing Group, Inc., The.

Morrison, Marianne. Mysteries of the Sea: How Divers Explore the Ocean Depths. 2006. (Science Chapters Ser.). (ENG., Illus.). 48p. (J). (gr. 1-4). lib. bdg. 17.90 (978-0-7922-5954-1(8), National Geographic Children's Bks.) National Geographic Society.

National Geographic Editors & Rizzo, Johnna. Oceans: Dolphins, Sharks, Penguins, & More! 2010. (ENG., Illus.). 64p. (J). (gr. 3-7). 24.90 (978-1-4263-0724-9(1), National Geographic Children's Bks.) National Geographic Society.

National Geographic Kids Staff & Rizzo, Johnna. Oceans: Dolphins, Sharks, Penguins, & More! 2010. (ENG., Illus.). 64p. (J). (gr. 3-7). 14.95 (978-1-4263-0686-0(5), National Geographic Children's Bks.) National Geographic Society.

Ocean Life: Level Q, 6 vols., Vol. 2. (Explorers Ser.). 32p. (gr. 3-6). 44.95 (978-0-7699-0604-1(4)) Shortland Pubns. (U. S. A.) Inc.

A Ocean Life, Set. 2005. (Ocean Life Ser.). (YA). (gr. k-3). 267.30 (978-0-7368-4214-3(4), Pebble Bks.) Capstone Press of Coughlan Cos.

Ocean Life, Set B. 2005. (Ocean Life Ser.). (YA). (gr. k-3). 267.30 (978-0-7368-4215-0(2), Pebble Bks.) Capstone Press of Coughlan Cos.

Owen, Ruth. Marine Biologists. 2013. (Out of the Lab: Extreme Jobs in Science Ser.). 32p. (J). (gr. 3-6). pap. 10.00 (978-1-4777-1381-5(6)); pap. 60.00 (978-1-4777-1386-0(7)); lib. bdg. 25.25 (978-1-4777-1291-7(7)) Rosen Publishing Group, Inc., The. (PowerKids Pr.).

Patchett, Fiona. Under the Sea. Kushii, Tetsuo & Wray, Zoe, illus. 2006. (Beginners Nature: Level 1 Ser.). 32p. (J). (gr. k-2). 4.99 (978-0-7945-1336-8(0), Usborne) EDC Publishing.

—Under the Sea. Kushii, Tetsuo, illus. 2006. (Usborne Beginners Ser.). 32p. (J). (gr. 1). lib. bdg. 12.99 (978-1-58086-931-7(9), Usborne) EDC Publishing.

Pebble Books: Ocean Life. 2005. (YA). (gr. k-3). 534.60 (978-0-7368-4223-5(3), Pebble Bks.) Capstone Press of Coughlan Cos.

Peterson, Judy Monroe. Underwater Explorers: Marine Biologists. 2009. (Extreme Scientists Ser.). 24p. (gr. 2-3). 42.50 (978-1-61512-453-4(5), PowerKids Pr.); (Illus.). (YA). lib. bdg. 22.60 (978-1-4042-4526-6(X)) Rosen Publishing Group, Inc., The.

Piano, Maureen. My Adventure with Tidepools. 2009. (ENG.). 44p. (J). 8.99 (978-1-59092-473-0(8)) Blue Forge Pr.

Priddy, Roger. Coral Reef. 2014. (Smart Kids Ser.). (ENG.). 30p. (J). (gr. -1-2). 9.99 (978-0-312-51677-2(0), 9780312516772, Priddy Bks.) St. Martin's Pr.

Read, Nicholas. The Great Bear Sea: Exploring the Marine Life of a Pacific Paradise, 1 vol. McAllister, Ian, photos by. 2013. (ENG., Illus.). 128p. (J). (gr. 3-9). pap. 19.95 (978-1-4598-0019-9(2)) Orca Bk. Pubs. USA.

Reid, Emily. Underwater Claymation. 2016. (Claymation Sensation Ser.). 32p. (gr. 3-3). pap. 11.75 (978-1-4994-8108-2(X), Windmill Bks.) Rosen Publishing Group, Inc., The.

Rice, Dona Herweck. Sea Life, 1 vol. 2nd rev. ed. 2013. (Nonfiction Readers Ser.). (ENG., Illus.). 20p. (J). (gr. 1-1). pap. 19.96 (978-1-4807-1023-8(7)) Shell Educational Publishing.

Roumanis, Alexis. Oceans. 2014. (Illus.). 24p. (J). (978-1-4896-3014-8(7)) Weigl Pubs., Inc.

Salas, Laura Purdie. Océanos: Mundos Submarinos. Abello, Patricia, tr. from ENG. Yesh, Jeff, illus. 2008. (Ciencia Asombrosa: Ecosistemas Ser.). (SPA.). 24p. (gr. k-4). lib. bdg. 26.65 (978-1-4048-3864-2(3)) Picture Window Bks.

Schuh, Mari. Sea Life. 2015. (Sea Life Ser.). (ENG.). 24p. (gr. k-1). 106.60 (978-1-4914-6937-8(4), Pebble Plus) Capstone Press of Coughlan Cos.

Seligson, Sherri. Exploring Creation with Marine Biology. Wile, Jay L., ed. 2005. stu. ed., per. 20.00 (978-1-932012-59-0(1));Set. 85.00 (978-1-932012-60-6(5)) Apologia Educational Ministries, Inc.

—Exploring Creation with Marine Biology: Student Text. Wile, Jay L., ed. 2005. 65.00 (978-1-932012-58-3(3)) Apologia Educational Ministries, Inc.

Sexton, Colleen. Blastoff! Readers - Oceans Alive, 6 vols., Set. Incl. Angelfish. 20.00 (978-0-531-21711-5(6)); Frogfish. 20.00 (978-0-531-21712-2(4)); Lionfish. 20.00 (978-0-531-21713-9(2)); Puffins. 20.00 (978-0-531-21714-6(0)); Shrimp. 20.00 (978-0-531-21716-0(7)); Swordfish. 20.00 (978-0-531-21715-3(9)); (Illus.). 24p. (J). (gr. k-3). 2009. 2009. Set lib. bdg. 120.00 (978-0-531-26128-6(X), Children's Pr.) Scholastic Library Publishing.

Smith, Marie & Smith, Roland. W Is for Waves: An Ocean Alphabet. Megahan, John & Rose, Melanie, illus. 2008. (ENG.). 32p. (J). (gr. k-6). 17.95 (978-1-58536-254-7(9)) Sleeping Bear Pr.

Smithyman, Kathryn & Kalman, Bobbie. El Bioma Marino. 2006. (Libro de Bobbie Kalman Ser.). (SPA., Illus.). 32p. (J). (gr. 3-7). pap. (978-0-7787-8414-2(2)); lib. bdg. (978-0-7787-8400-5(2)) Crabtree Publishing Co.

Somervill, Barbara. Marine Biologist. 2009. (21st Century Skills Library: Cool Science Careers Ser.). (ENG.). 32p. (gr. 4-8). lib. bdg. 28.50 (978-1-60279-504-4(5), 200306) Cherry Lake Publishing.

Spilsbury, Richard & Spilsbury, Louise. At Home in the Ocean, 01 vols., 1. 2016. (Home in the Biome Ser.). (ENG.). 32p. (J). 26.25 (978-1-5081-4567-7(9), PowerKids Pr.) Rosen Publishing Group, Inc., The.

Stern, Leonard, et al. Under the Sea Mad Libs Junior. 2005. (Mad Libs Junior Ser.). (ENG.). 48p. (J). (gr. k-3). mass mkt. 4.99 (978-0-8431-1350-1(2), Mad Libs) Penguin Young Readers Group.

Swanson, Diane. Safari Beneath the Sea: The Wonder World of the North Pacific Coast, 1 vol. Royal British Columbia Museum Staff, photos by. (ENG., Illus.). 64p. (J). pap. 12.95 (978-1-55110-441-6(5)) Whitecap Bks., Ltd. CAN. Dist: Graphic Arts Ctr. Publishing Co.

Tahta, Sophie. What's under the Sea? Trotter, Stuart, illus. rev. ed. 2006. (Starting Point Science Ser.). 24p. (J). (gr. 4-7). pap. 4.99 (978-0-7945-1409-9(X), Usborne) EDC Publishing.

Tejido, Jomike, illus. Under the Sea. 2017. (Jumbo Stickers for Little Hands Ser.). (ENG.). 24p. (J). (gr. -1-k). pap. 7.95 (978-1-63322-156-7(3), Moondance) Quarto Publishing Group USA.

Thomas, William David. Marine Biologist. 2009. (Cool Careers: Cutting Edge Ser.). 32p. (J). (gr. 5-8). pap. 10.50 (978-1-4339-2156-8(1)); lib. bdg. 26.00 (978-1-4339-1957-2(5)) Stevens, Gareth Publishing LLLP.

Vogel, Carole G. Savage Waters. 2003. (Restless Sea Ser.). (ENG., Illus.). 80p. (gr. 5-8). pap. 12.95 (978-0-531-16682-6(1), Watts, Franklin) Scholastic Library Publishing.

Walker, Pam & Wood, Elaine. The Continental Shelf. 2005. (Life in the Sea Ser.). (Illus.). 160p. (YA). (gr. 7-12). 35.00 (978-0-8160-5704-7(4)) Facts On File, Inc.

Westerskov, Kim, photos by. Life in a Frozen Sea. 2004. (Illus.). 32p. (J). pap. (978-0-7685-2114-6(9)) Dominie Pr., Inc.

Woodward, John. Under the Waves. 2010. (Oceans Alive! Ser.). lib. bdg. 28.50 (978-1-933834-62-7(5)) Brown Bear Bks.

MARINE BIOLOGY—FICTION

Baldwin, Robert F. The Fish House Door. Sheckels, Astrid, illus. 2010. (ENG.). 36p. (J). 16.95 (978-1-934031-30-8(5), 10b511a5-c2dc-4bc7-8d33-85991c0a158b) Islandport Pr., Inc.

Crowley, Peter. J T Seavey. 2012. (ENG.). 35p. (J). pap. 18.95 (978-1-4327-8712-7(8)) Outskirts Pr., Inc.

Mihalek, Alex, et al. The Adventures of Captain Fishhook Waterflea: the Invasion of Lake Champlain. 2009. 34p. pap. 13.98 (978-0-557-12868-6(4)) Lulu Pr., Inc.

Pittau, Francesco & Gervais, Bernadette. The Open Ocean. 2014. (ENG., Illus.). 12p. (J). (gr. k-3). 24.99 (978-1-4521-2701-9(8)) Chronicle Bks. LLC.

small world creations ltd. Splish Splash. 2017. (Magic Bath Bks.). (ENG.). 8p. (J). (gr. -1 — 1). 5.99 **(978-1-4380-7844-1(7))** Barron's Educational Series, Inc.

Stilton, Geronimo & Stilton, Thea. Thea Stilton & the Ghost of the Shipwreck. 2010. (Thea Stilton Ser.: 3). (ENG., Illus.). 176p. (J). (gr. 2-5). mass mkt. 8.99 (978-0-545-15059-0(0), Scholastic Paperbacks) Scholastic, Inc.

Treasures of the Barrier Reef. 2005. (J). audio, cd-rom 24.95 (978-0-9771381-7-3(8)) Williams, Geoffrey T.

MARINE ECOLOGY

Aitken, Stephen. Ocean Life. 2013. (Climate Crisis Ser.). (Illus.). 64p. (J). (gr. 5-8). 31.36 (978-1-60870-460-6(2)); pap. 15.28 (978-1-62712-040-1(8)) Cavendish Square Publishing.

Aloian, Molly & Kalman, Bobbie. Habitats Acuaticos. 2007. (Introduction a Los Habitats Ser.). (SPA., Illus.). 32p. (J). (gr. 3-7). lib. bdg. (978-0-7787-8325-1(1)); (gr. k-3). pap. (978-0-7787-8349-7(9)) Crabtree Publishing Co.

—Water Habitats. 2006. (Introducing Habitats Ser.). (ENG., Illus.). 32p. (J). (gr. 3-7). pap. (978-0-7787-2977-8(X)) Crabtree Publishing Co.

Anderson, Sheila. Coasts. 2015. (First Step Nonfiction - Landforms Ser.). (ENG., Illus.). 24p. (gr. k-2). 23.99 (978-1-5124-1041-9(1), Lerner Pubns.) Lerner Publishing Group.

Animals of the Ocean Series (Illus.). (J). (gr. 2-6). lib. bdg. 44.85 (978-1-56674-947-3(6)) Forest Hse. Publishing Co., Inc.

Arlon, Penelope. Really? Ocean. 2015. (ENG.). 64p. (J). (gr. 2-5). pap. 8.99 (978-0-545-80650-3(X), Scholastic Nonfiction) Scholastic, Inc.

Basher, Simon & Green, Dan. Oceans: Making Waves! Basher, Simon, illus. 2012. (Basher Science Ser.). (ENG., Illus.). 128p. (J). (gr. 5-9). pap. 8.99 (978-0-7534-6822-7(0), 9780753468227, Kingfisher) Roaring Brook Pr.

Bayrock, Fiona. The Ocean Explorer's Handbook. 2005. (Undersea University Ser.). (Illus.). 48p. (J). pap. (978-0-439-71184-5(3)) Scholastic, Inc.

Bennett, Doraine. Atlantic Ocean. 2009. (J). (978-1-935077-34-3(1)) State Standards Publishing, LLC.

—Coast. 2009. (J). (978-1-935077-35-0(X)); pap. (978-1-935077-40-4(6)) State Standards Publishing, LLC.

—Coastal Plain. 2009. (J). (978-1-935077-51-0(1)); pap. (978-1-935077-52-7(X)) State Standards Publishing, LLC.

Blocksma, Mary. What's on the Beach? A Great Lakes Treasure Hunt. 2012. (ENG., Illus.). 48p. (gr. 3-8). pap. 12.50 (978-0-9708575-2-1(7)) Beaver Island Arts.

—What's on the Beach? A Great Lakes Treasure Hunt. Blocksma, Mary, illus. 2003. (Great Lakes Treasure Hunts Ser.: No. 1). (Illus.). 48p. (J). pap. 9.95 (978-0-9708575-1-4(9)) Beaver Island Arts.

Bodden, Valerie. Great Barrier Reef. 2010. (Big Outdoors Ser.). 24p. (J). (gr. k-3). 16.95 (978-1-58341-816-1(4)) Creative Co., The.

Boothroyd, Jennifer. Let's Visit the Ocean. 2016. (Lightning Bolt Books (tm) — Biome Explorers Ser.). (ENG., Illus.). 32p. (J). (gr. 1-3). 26.65 (978-1-5124-1194-2(9)) Lerner Publishing Group.

Brown, Carron. Secrets of the Seashore. Nassner, Alyssa, illus. 2014. (ENG.). 36p. (J). 12.99 (978-1-61067-309-9(3)) Kane Miller.

Butterfield, Moira. Who Eats Who at the Seashore? 2006. (Food Chains in Action Ser.). (Illus.). 32p. (YA). (gr. 4-7). lib. bdg. 28.50 (978-1-58340-963-3(7), 1262631) Black Rabbit Bks.

Buxton, Jane H. Undersea Animals: A Dramatic Dimensional Visit to Strange Underwater Realms. Pinkney, Jerry, illus. 2008. (ENG.). 12p. (J). (gr. -1-3). 14.95 (978-1-4263-0334-0(3), National Geographic Children's Bks.) National Geographic Society.

Cain, Marie Mowery. Under the Waves. 2013. (Big Books, Blue Ser.). (ENG & SPA., Illus.). 16p. pap. 33.00 (978-1-59246-005-2(4)) Big Books, by George!

Cefrey, Holly. Oceans. (Biomes Ser.). 24p. 2009. (gr. 2-3). 42.50 (978-1-61511-592-1(7)) 2003. (Illus.). (J). lib. bdg. 22.60 (978-0-8239-6453-6(1)) Rosen Publishing Group, Inc., The. (PowerKids Pr.).

Centore, Michael. Saving Ocean Animals: Sharks, Turtles, Coral, & Fish. 2017. (J). **(978-1-4222-3879-0(2))** Mason Crest.

Cerullo, Mary M. & Simmons, Beth E. Sea Secrets. Carlson, Kirsten, illus. 2015. (Long Term Ecological Research Ser.). (ENG.). 32p. (J). (gr. 1-5). pap. 9.95 (978-1-63076-075-5(7)) Taylor Trade Publishing.

Channing, Margot. Seas & Oceans. 2014. (Closer Look At... Ser.). (Illus.). 32p. (gr. 3-6). 31.35 (978-1-905087-07-5(1)) Book Hse. GBR. Dist: Black Rabbit Bks.

Charles, Patrick. Ocean Food Chains. 2009. (Real Life Readers Ser.). 16p. (gr. 2-3). pap. 7.05 (978-1-4358-0065-6(6), Rosen Classroom) Rosen Publishing Group, Inc., The.

Crenson, Victoria. Horseshoe Crabs & Shorebirds: The Story of a Foodweb, 0 vols. Cannon, Annie, illus. unabr. ed. 2009. (ENG.). 42p. (J). (gr. 3-5). pap. 9.99 (978-0-7614-5552-3(3), 9780761455523, Amazon Children's Publishing) Amazon Publishing.

Crossingham, John & Kalman, Bobbie. Cadenas Alimentarias de la Costa Marina. 2006. (Cadenas Alimentarias Ser.). (SPA., Illus.). 32p. (J). (gr. 3-7). lib. bdg. (978-0-7787-8531-6(9)) Crabtree Publishing Co.

Davies, Nicola. Discover Science: Oceans & Seas. 2013. (Discover Science Ser.). (ENG., Illus.). 56p. (J). (gr. k-3). 7.99 (978-0-7534-6776-3(3), 9780753467763, Kingfisher) Roaring Brook Pr.

—Oceans & Seas. 2014. 48p. pap. 7.00 (978-1-61003-360-2(4)) Center for the Collaborative Classroom.

Day, Nancy. Way down below Deep, 1 vol. Sheldon, David, illus. 2014. (ENG.). 32p. (J). (gr. k-3). 16.99 (978-1-4556-1945-0(0)) Pelican Publishing Co., Inc.

Encyclopaedia Britannica, Inc. Staff, compiled by. Beginning of the Food Chain. 2008. 49.95 (978-1-59339-555-1(8)) Encyclopaedia Britannica, Inc.

Fleisher, Paul. Lake & Pond Food Webs. 2008. pap. 52.95 (978-0-8225-9352-2(1)) Lerner Publishing Group.

—Ocean Food Webs. 2008. pap. 52.95 (978-0-8225-9353-9(X)) Lerner Publishing Group.

—Ocean Food Webs in Action. 2013. (Searchlight Books What Is a Food Web Ser.). (ENG., Illus.). 40p. (gr. 3-5). pap. 8.95 (978-1-4677-1556-0(5)); lib. bdg. 27.93 (978-1-4677-1255-2(8), Lerner Pubns.) Lerner Publishing Group.

Franklin, Carolyn. Ocean Life. Franklin, Carolyn, illus. 2013. (World of Wonder Ser.). (Illus.). 32p. (gr. 1-3). 31.35 **(978-1-904642-63-3(2))** Book Hse. GBR. Dist: Black Rabbit Bks.

Gaarder-Juntti, Oona. What Lives in Coral Reefs?, 1 vol. 2008. (Animal Habitats Ser.). (ENG., Illus.). 24p. (J). (gr. k-3). 25.65 (978-1-60453-170-1(3)) ABDO Publishing Co.

—What Lives in Streams & Rivers?, 1 vol. 2008. (Animal Habitats Ser.). (ENG., Illus.). 24p. (J). (gr. k-3). 25.65 (978-1-60453-171-8(1)) ABDO Publishing Co.

—What Lives in the Ocean?, 1 vol. 2008. (Animal Habitats Ser.). (ENG., Illus.). 24p. (J). (gr. k-3). 25.65 (978-1-60453-175-6(4)) ABDO Publishing Co.

Gagne, Tammy. Marine Ecosystems. 2018. (ENG.). 32p. (gr. 3-6). **(978-1-63235-458-7(6)**, 12-Story Library) Pr. Room Editions LLC.

Ganeri, Anita. I Wonder Why the Sea Is Salty. 2014. 32p. pap. 7.00 (978-1-61003-352-7(3)) Center for the Collaborative Classroom.

—I Wonder Why the Sea Is Salty: And Other Questions about the Oceans. 2011. (I Wonder Why Ser.). (ENG., Illus.). 32p. (J). (gr. k-3). pap. 6.99 (978-0-7534-6521-9(3), 9780753465219, Kingfisher) Roaring Brook Pr.

Gardeski, Christina Mia. All about Oceans. 2017. (Habitats Ser.). (ENG.). 24p. (gr. k-1). lib. bdg. 21.99 **(978-1-5157-7644-4(1)**, Pebble Bks.) Capstone Press of Coughlan Cos.

George, Lynn. Coral: Reef Builders. 2010. (Animal Architects Ser.). (ENG.). 24p. (J). pap. 8.25 (978-1-4488-1349-0(2)); lib. bdg. 22.60 (978-1-4488-0694-2(1)) Rosen Publishing Group, Inc., The. (PowerKids Pr.).

Goldsmith, Mike. Under the Sea. Daubney, Kate, illus. 2015. (I Explore Ser.). (ENG.). 12p. (J). (gr. -1-k). bds. 6.95 (978-1-4549-1502-7(1)) Sterling Publishing Co., Inc.

Gottlieb. Water Life. 2004. (Wonders of Science Ser.). (ENG., Illus.). 144p. (gr. 7-12). pap. 24.55 (978-0-7398-9178-0(2)) Houghton Mifflin Harcourt Publishing Co.

Gray, Leon. Oceans. 2015. (Amazing Biomes Ser.). (Illus.). 32p. (gr. 3-6). 31.35 (978-1-78121-243-1(0), 1389630) Brown Bear Bks.

Green, Jen. Life in a Coral Reef. 2010. (Nature in Focus Ser.). (Illus.). 32p. (gr. 2-5). (J). pap. 10.50 (978-1-4339-3424-7(8), Gareth Stevens Learning Library); (YA). lib. bdg. 26.00 (978-1-4339-3423-0(X)) Stevens, Gareth Publishing LLLP.

Group/McGraw-Hill, Wright. La Vida en el Oceano, 6 vols., Vol. 2. (Explorers. Exploradores Nonfiction Sets Ser.). (SPA.). 32p. (gr. 3-6). 44.95 (978-0-7699-0740-6(7)) Shortland Pubns. (U. S. A.) Inc.

Haugen, Hayley Mitchell. Life in a Coral Reef. 2003. (Ecosystems Library). (Illus.). 48p. (J). 23.70 (978-0-7377-1370-1(4), Greenhaven Pr., Inc.) Cengage Gale.

Henzel, Cynthia Kennedy. Great Barrier Reef, 1 vol. 2011. (Troubled Treasures: World Heritage Sites Ser.). (ENG., Illus.). 32p. (YA). (gr. 3-6). 27.07 (978-1-61613-564-5(6)) ABDO Publishing Co.

Hibbert, Clare. Seaside Plants & Animals. 2016. (Beside the Seaside Ser.). (ENG., Illus.). 24p. (J). (gr. k-2). 16.99 (978-1-4451-3766-7(6), Franklin Watts) Hachette Children's Group GBR. Dist: Hachette Bk. Group.

Hidden World: Level P, 6 vols., Vol. 3. (Explorers Ser.). 32p. (gr. 3-6). 44.95 (978-0-7699-0616-4(8)) Shortland Pubns. (U. S. A.) Inc.

Hirschi, Ron. Ocean Seasons, 1 vol. Carlson, Kirsten, illus. 2007. (ENG.). 32p. (J). (gr. k-4). 15.95 (978-0-9777423-2-5(6)); pap. 9.95 (978-1-60718-863-6(5)) Arbordale Publishing.

Hudak, Heather C. Oceans. (Illus.). 32p. (J). 2017. **(978-1-5105-0878-1(3))** 2016. (978-1-5105-0876-7(7)) SmartBook Media, Inc.

—Oceans. 2005. (Biomes Ser.). (Illus.). 32p. (J). (gr. 4-6). lib. bdg. 24.45 (978-1-59036-348-5(5)) Weigl Pubs., Inc.

Hyde, Natalie. Deep Sea Extremes. 2008. (Extreme Nature Ser.). (ENG., Illus.). 32p. (J). (gr. 2-3). pap. (978-0-7787-4518-1(X)); lib. bdg. (978-0-7787-4501-3(5)) Crabtree Publishing Co.

Hyde, Natalie. Great Barrier Reef Research Journal. 2017. (Illus.). 32p. (J). **(978-0-7787-3470-3(6))**; pap. **(978-0-7787-3495-6(1))** Crabtree Publishing Co.

Inskipp, Carol. Healthy Seas. 2006. (Sustainable Futures Ser.). (Illus.). 48p. (YA). (gr. 5-9). lib. bdg. 31.35 (978-1-58340-980-0(7), 1262623) Black Rabbit Bks.

Johnson, Jinny. Deep Sea Life. 2011. (Watery Worlds Ser.). 32p. (gr. 3-6). 31.35 (978-1-59920-503-8(3)) Black Rabbit Bks.

Johnson, Rebecca L. Journey into the Deep: Discovering New Ocean Creatures. 2010. (Exceptional Science Titles for Intermediate Grades Ser.). (ENG.). 64p. (gr. 4-8). lib. bdg. 31.93 (978-0-7613-4148-2(X)) Lerner Publishing Group.

—A Journey into the Ocean. Saroff, Phyllis V., illus. 2004. (Biomes of North America Ser.). (ENG.). 48p. (gr. 3-6). pap. 8.95 (978-0-8225-2046-7(X), I); lib. bdg. 23.93 (978-1-57505-591-6(0)) Lerner Publishing Group.

Johnson, Robin. Oceans Inside Out. 2014. (ENG.). 32p. (J). (978-0-7787-0635-9(4)) Crabtree Publishing Co.

Joyce, John. Black John the Bogus Pirate - Cartoon Workbook of Marine Beasts. Joyce, John, illus. 2012. (ENG., Illus.). 20p. (J). (978-0-9557637-8-6(9)) Sprindrift Pr.

Kalman, Bobbie. Le Biome Marin. 2012. (FRE.). 32p. (J). pap. 10.95 (978-2-89579-478-3(2)) Bayard Canada CAN. Dist: Crabtree Publishing Co.

Kalman, Bobbie & Aloian, Molly. Les Océans Polaires. 2009. (FRE., Illus.). 32p. (J). pap. 9.95 (978-2-89579-248-2(8)) Bayard Canada Livres CAN. Dist: Crabtree Publishing Co.

King, Zelda. Examining Tide Pool Habitats. 2009. (Graphic Organizers: Habitats Ser.). 24p. (gr. 2-3). 42.50 (978-1-61513-103-7(5), PowerKids Pr.) Rosen Publishing Group, Inc., The.

Kortemeier, Todd. Exploring the Depths of the Ocean. 2017. (Science Frontiers Ser.). (ENG., Illus.). 32p. (J). (gr. 3-6). 21.95 (978-1-63235-377-1(6)) Pr. Room Editions LLC.

Kurtz, Kevin. A Day in the Salt Marsh, 1 vol. Powell, Consie, illus. 2007. (Day in the Habitat Ser.). (ENG.). 32p. (J). (gr. -1-3). pap. 8.95 (978-1-934359-19-8(X)) Arbordale Publishing.

Lantz, Peggy Sias & Hale, Wendy A. The Coral Reefs of Florida. 2014. (Florida Water Story Ser.). (ENG., Illus.). 34p. (J). (gr. 4). pap. 6.95 (978-1-56164-703-3(9), 9781561647033) Pineapple Pr., Inc.

—The Oceans of Florida. 2014. (Florida Water Story Ser.). (ENG., Illus.). 34p. (J). (gr. 4). pap. 6.95 (978-1-56164-704-0(7)) Pineapple Pr., Inc.

Lawrence, Ellen. Polluted Oceans. 2014. (Science Slam: Green World, Clean World Ser.). 24p. (J). (gr. -1-3). lib. bdg. 23.93 (978-1-62724-236-3(8)) Bearport Publishing Co., Inc.

Levy, Janey. Discovering Coral Reefs. 2009. (World Habitats Ser.). 32p. (gr. 4-5). 47.90 (978-1-60854-834-7(1), PowerKids Pr.) Rosen Publishing Group, Inc., The.

Lindop, Laurie. Venturing the Deep Sea. 2005. (Science on the Edge Ser.). (ENG., Illus.). 80p. (gr. 5-12). 27.93 (978-0-7613-2701-1(0)) Lerner Publishing Group.

Littlefield, Cindy A. Awesome Ocean Science: Investigating the Secrets of the Underwater World. 2004. (Kids Can Bks.). (Illus.). 120p. (J). (gr. 3-5). pap. 12.95 (978-1-885593-71-9(6), Ideal Pubns.) Worthy Publishing.

Llewellyn, Claire. In the Sea Red Band. Belcher, Andy, photos by. 2016. (Cambridge Reading Adventures Ser.). (ENG., Illus.). 16p. pap. 6.56 (978-1-107-57578-3(8)) Cambridge Univ. Pr.

Louisy, Patrick. My Encyclopedia of the Sea. 2016. (My Encyclopedia Ser.). (ENG., Illus.). 128p. (J). lib. bdg. 34.00 (978-0-531-22473-1(2), Children's Pr.) Scholastic Library Publishing.

Lynch, Seth. There's an Ocean in My Backyard! 2016. (Backyard Biomes Ser.). 00024p. (J). pap. 8.15 **(978-1-4824-5567-0(6))** Stevens, Gareth Publishing LLLP.

Mason, Janeen. Ocean Commotion: Life on the Reef, 1 vol. Mason, Janeen, illus. 2010. (ENG., Illus.). 32p. (J). (gr. k-3). 16.99 (978-1-58980-783-9(9)) Pelican Publishing Co., Inc.

Mataya, Marybeth. Deep Ocean Food Chains, 1 vol. Adams, Hazel, illus. 2010. (Fascinating Food Chains Ser.). (ENG.). 32p. 28.50 (978-1-60270-793-1(6), Looking Glass Library-Nonfiction) Magic Wagon.

Matsen, Bradford. The Incredible Submersible Alvin Discovers a Strange Deep-Sea World. 2003. (Incredible Deep-Sea Adventures Ser.). (Illus.). 48p. (J). (gr. 4-10). lib. bdg. 23.93 (978-0-7660-2189-1(0)) Enslow Pubs., Inc.

McFadzean, Lesley. Ocean Habitats. 2013. (Discovery Education: Habitats Ser.). 32p. (J). (gr. 3-6). 25.25 (978-1-4777-1322-8(0)); pap. 10.00 (978-1-4777-1479-9(0)); pap. 60.00 (978-1-4777-1480-5(4)) Rosen Publishing Group, Inc., The. (PowerKids Pr.).

McKissack, Fredrick L. & McKissack, Lisa Beringer. Counting in the Oceans. 2009. (Counting in the Biomes Ser.). (Illus.). 32p. (J). (gr. 1-3). lib. bdg. 23.94 (978-0-7660-2994-1(8), Enslow Elementary) Enslow Pubs., Inc.

Meltzer Kleinhenz, Sydnie. Coral Reefs. 2004. (ENG., Illus.). 32p. (J). (gr. 4-4). pap. 12.29 (978-0-7652-5223-4(6), Celebration Pr.) Pearson Schl.

Milbourne, Anna. Under the Sea. Shimmen, Cathy, illus. 2007. (Picture Bks). 32p. (J). 9.99 (978-0-7945-1801-1(X), Usborne) EDC Publishing.

Miller-Schroeder, Patricia. Underwater Life. 2007. (Life Science (Weigl Hardcover) Ser.). (Illus.). 32p. (J). (gr. 4-7). lib. bdg. 26.00 (978-1-59036-713-1(8)); per. 9.95 (978-1-59036-714-8(6)) Weigl Pubs., Inc.

Moore, Heidi. Ocean Food Chains, 1 vol. 2010. (Protecting Food Chains Ser.). (ENG., Illus.). 48p. (gr. 3-6). 33.32 (978-1-4329-3859-8(2)); pap. 9.95 (978-1-4329-3866-6(5)) Heinemann-Raintree. (Heinemann InfoSearch).

Morey, Allan. Ocean Food Chains. 2003. (What Eats What? Ser.). (J). pap. (978-1-58417-219-2(3)); lib. bdg. (978-1-58417-218-5(5)) Lake Street Pubs.

Murray, Aaron R. Counting in the Oceans 1-2-3. 2012. (All about Counting in the Biomes Ser.). (Illus.). 24p. (J). (gr. -1-1). 22.60 (978-0-7660-4052-6(6)) Enslow Pubs., Inc.

Newland, Sonya. Sailing the Caribbean Islands. 2016. (Travelling Wild Ser.). (ENG., Illus.). 32p. (J). (gr. 4-6). 17.99 (978-0-7502-9865-0(0), Wayland) Hachette Children's Group GBR. Dist: Hachette Bk. Group.

Newman, Patricia. Sea Otter Heroes: The Predators That Saved an Ecosystem. 2017. (Nonfiction — Grades 4-8 Ser.). (ENG.). 56p. (J). (gr. 4-8). 16.99 **(978-1-5124-3884-0(7))**; 47.99 **(978-1-5124-3885-7(5))**; 47.99 **(978-1-5124-2844-5(2))**; (Illus.). 31.99 (978-1-5124-2631-1(8)) Lerner Publishing Group. (Millbrook Pr.).

O'Neill, Michael Patrick, photos by. Ocean Magic. O'Neill, Michael Patrick, . 2008. (Illus.). 48p. (J). (gr. 1-4). 19.95 (978-0-9728653-5-7(7)) Batfish Bks.

Pettiford, Rebecca. Ocean Food Chains. 2016. (Who Eats What?). 24p. (J). (gr. 2-5). lib. bdg. 25.65 (978-1-62031-302-2(2), Pogo) Jump! Inc.

Pratt Serafini, Kristin Joy, illus. A Swim Through the Sea, 1 vol. 2006. (Simply Nature Bks.). (ENG.). 26p. (J). (gr. -1). bds. 7.95 (978-1-58469-080-1(1)) Dawn Pubns.

Pyers, Greg. Biodiversity of Oceans & Seas. 2011. (Biodiversity 2 Ser.). 32p. (gr. 4). 28.50 (978-1-60870-530-6(7)) Marshall Cavendish GBR. Dist: Marshall Cavendish Corp.

—Biodiversity of Rivers. 2011. (Biodiversity 2 Ser.). 32p. (gr. 4). 28.50 (978-1-60870-531-3(5)) Marshall Cavendish Corp.

Rigby Education Staff. Gardens of the Sea. (Sails Literacy Ser.). (Illus.). 16p. (gr. 1-2). 27.00 (978-0-7635-9923-2(9), 699239C99) Rigby Education.

Riggs, Kate. Food for Life: Oceans. 2015. (Food for Life Ser.). (ENG.). 24p. (J). (gr. 1-3). pap. 9.99 (978-1-62832-102-9(4), Creative Paperbacks) Creative Co., The.

—Oceans. 24p. 2016. (Illus.). (978-1-60818-743-0(8)) 2010. (J). (gr. 1-4). 16.95 (978-1-58341-828-4(8)) Creative Co., The. (Creative Education).

Rissman, Rebecca. Living & Nonliving in the Ocean, 1 vol. 2013. (Is It Living or Nonliving? Ser.). (ENG., Illus.). 24p. (gr. k-2). 23.32 (978-1-4109-5381-0(5)); pap. 6.95 (978-1-4109-5388-9(2)) Heinemann-Raintree.

Rivera, Sheila. Ocean. 2005. (Illus.). 24p. (J). pap. 5.95 (978-0-8225-5372-4(4)) Lerner Publishing Group.

Royston, Angela. Ocean - It's My Home! 2011. (ENG., Illus.). 24p. (J). pap. (978-0-7787-7873-8(8)) Crabtree Publishing Co.

—Ocean Food Chains, 1 vol. 2014. (Food Chains & Webs Ser.). (ENG., Illus.). 32p. (gr. 1-3). 27.32 (978-1-4846-0517-2(9), Heinemann First Library) Heinemann-Raintree.

—Ocean It's My Home! 2011. (Crabtree Connections Ser.). (ENG., Illus.). 24p. (J). (gr. 3-6). (978-0-7787-7851-6(7)) Crabtree Publishing Co.

Rustad, Martha E. H. Clown Fish & Sea Anemones Work Together, 1 vol. 2010. (Animals Working Together Ser.). (ENG.). 24p. (gr. k-1). lib. bdg. 26.65 (978-1-4296-5297-1(7), Pebble Plus) Capstone Press of Coughlan Cos.

Sexton, Colleen. Ponds. 2008. (Learning about the Earth Ser.). (ENG., Illus.). 24p. (J). (gr. k-3). lib. bdg. 25.95 (978-1-60014-230-7(3)) Bellwether Media.

Shocking Sea Creatures. 2016. (Illus.). 32p. (J). (978-1-4222-3528-7(9)) Mason Crest.

Sill, Cathryn. About Habitats-Oceans, 1 vol. Sill, John, illus. 2012. (ENG.). 48p. (J). 16.95 (978-1-56145-618-5(7)) Peachtree Pubs.

Simon, Seymour. Coral Reefs. 2013. (ENG.). 32p. (J). (gr. 1-5). pap. 6.99 (978-0-06-191496-6(7)) HarperCollins Pubs.

Slade, Suzanne. What Eats What in an Ocean Food Chain, 1 vol. McLaughlin, Zack, illus. 2012. (Food Chains Ser.). (ENG.). 24p. (gr. 2-3). pap. 8.95 (978-1-4048-7696-5(0)) Picture Window Bks.

—What If There Were No Sea Otters? A Book about the Ocean Ecosystem, 1 vol. Schwartz, Carol, illus. 2010. (Food Chain Reactions Ser.). (ENG.). 24p. (gr. 2-4). pap. 9.95 (978-1-4048-6397-2(4)) Picture Window Bks.

Smith, Alastair & Tachell, Judy. Under the Sea. Scott, Peter David, illus. 2007. (J). (978-0-545-03305-3(5)) Scholastic, Inc.

Smithyman, Kathryn & Kalman, Bobbie. El Bioma Marino. 2006. (Libro de Bobbie Kalman Ser.). (SPA., Illus.). 32p. (J). (gr. 3-7). pap. (978-0-7787-8414-2(2)); lib. bdg. (978-0-7787-8400-5(2)) Crabtree Publishing Co.

Spilsbury, Louise. Tide Pool. Hanna, Gary, illus. 2013. (Look Inside Ser.). (ENG.). 32p. (gr. 1-3). 27.32 (978-1-4329-7197-7(2)); pap. 8.29 (978-1-4329-7204-2(9)) Heinemann-Raintree. (Heinemann First Library).

Spilsbury, Richard & Spilsbury, Louise. At Home in the Ocean, 01 vols., 1. 2016. (Home in the Biome Ser.). (ENG.). 32p. (J). 26.25 (978-1-5081-4567-7(9), PowerKids Pr.) Rosen Publishing Group, Inc., The.

Stewart, Melissa. Extreme Coral Reef! 2008. (Smithsonian Q & A Ser.). (Illus.). 48p. (J). (gr. k-4). 16.99 (978-0-06-111577-6(0)) Smithsonian Institution Pr.

—A Place for Fish, 1 vol. Bond, Higgins, illus. 2011. (ENG.). 32p. (J). (gr. 1-5). 16.95 (978-1-56145-562-1(8)) Peachtree Pubs.

Stone, Lynn M. Oceans. 2003. (Illus.). 24p. (J). 20.64 (978-1-58952-686-0(4)) Rourke Educational Media.

Storey Publishing Editors. Under the Sea Poster Book. 2005. (ENG., Illus.). 64p. (J). (gr. 2-8). pap. 9.95 (978-1-58017-623-1(2), 67623) Storey Publishing, LLC.

Sullivan, Laura L. 24 Hours in the Ocean. 2017. (J). **(978-1-5026-2478-9(8))** Cavendish Square Publishing.

Summers, Portia & Grady, Colin. The Ocean Biome. 2016. (Zoom in on Biomes Ser.). 24p. (J). (gr. 2-2). pap. 9.35 (978-0-7660-7785-0(3)) Enslow Pubs., Inc.

Sundance/Newbridge LLC Staff. Life in the Sea. 2007. (Early Science Ser.). (gr. k-3). 18.95 (978-1-4007-6386-3(X)); pap. 6.10 (978-1-4007-6382-5(7)) Sundance/Newbridge Educational Publishing.

Tarbox, A. D. An Ocean Food Chain: Nature's Bounty. 2015. (Illus.). 80p. (J). (978-1-60818-541-2(9), Creative Education) Creative Co., The.

Tarbox, A. D. & National Geographic Learning Staff. Ocean. 2010. (ENG.). 48p. (C). (gr. 4-7). pap. 18.95 (978-0-89812-740-9(8)) National Geographic School Publishing, Inc.

Tocci, Salvatore. Marine Habitats: Life in Saltwater. 2004. (Watts Library). (ENG.). (J). 25.50 (978-0-531-12306-5(5), Watts, Franklin) Scholastic Library Publishing.

Ventura, Marne. Exploring the Depths of the Ocean. 2016. (Science Frontiers Ser.). (ENG., Illus.). 32p. (J). pap. 9.95 (978-1-63235-394-8(6), 12-Story Library) Pr. Room Editions LLC.

Wade, Laura. Sea & Sealife. 2003. (Knowledge Masters Ser.). (Illus.). 32p. (YA). pap. incl. cd-rom (978-1-903954-10-2(X), Pavilion Children's Books) Pavilion Bks.

Walker, Pam & Wood, Elaine. The Open Ocean. 2005. (Life in the Sea Ser.). (Illus.). 144p. (YA). (gr. 7-12). 35.00 (978-0-8160-5705-4(2)) Facts On File, Inc.

Walker, Rachel. Help Our Oceans. 2015. (ENG., Illus.). 16p. (-2). pap. (978-1-77654-138-6(3), Red Rocket Readers) Flying Start Bks.

West, David. Tide Pool Animals. 2014. (Nora the Naturalist's Animals Ser.). 24p. (gr. k-3). pap. 8.95 (978-1-62588-054-3(5)) Black Rabbit Bks.

West, Krista, ed. Critical Perspectives on the Oceans. (Scientific American Critical Anthologies on Environment & Climate Ser.). 2009. 208p. (gr. 9-9). 63.90 (978-1-60853-070-0(1)) 2006. (Illus.). 200p. (J). (gr. 3-7). 37.95 (978-1-4042-0692-2(2)) Rosen Publishing Group, Inc., The.

Westerskov, Kim, photos by. Forests in the Sea. 2004. (Illus.). 32p. (J). (978-0-7685-2387-4(7)); pap. (978-0-7685-2116-0(5)) Dominie Pr., Inc.

Woolf, Alex. Sailing the Great Barrier Reef. 2014. (Traveling Wild Ser.). 32p. (J). (gr. 3-6). pap. 63.00 (978-1-4824-1252-9(7)) Stevens, Gareth Publishing LLLP.

Working on Water: Individual Title Six-Packs. (gr. k-1). 23.00 (978-0-7635-8853-3(9)) Rigby Education.

World Book, Inc Staff, contrib. by. Oceans. 2012. (J). (978-0-7166-0447-1(7)) World Bk., Inc.

—Oceans, Islands, & Polar Regions. 2008. (J). (978-0-7166-1402-9(2)) World Bk., Inc.

MARINE FAUNA

see Marine Animals

MARINE FLORA

see Marine Plants

MARINE GEOLOGY

see Submarine Geology

MARINE PAINTING

Baumbusch, Brigitte. Oceans in Art. 2005. (What Makes a Masterpiece? Ser.). (Illus.). 32p. (gr. 1-4). lib. bdg. 23.00 (978-0-8368-4782-6(2), Gareth Stevens Learning Library) Stevens, Gareth Publishing LLLP.

MARINE PLANTS

see also Algae; Freshwater Plants

Diamond, Claudia. What's under the Sea? 2009. (Reading Room Collection 2 Ser.). 24p. (gr. 3-4). 42.50 (978-1-60852-002-2(1), PowerKids Pr.) Rosen Publishing Group, Inc., The.

Fleisher, Paul. Ocean Food Webs in Action. 2013. (Searchlight Books What Is a Food Web Ser.). (ENG., Illus.). 40p. (gr. 3-5). pap. 8.95 (978-1-4677-1556-0(5)); lib. bdg. 27.93 (978-1-4677-1255-2(8), Lerner Pubns.) Lerner Publishing Group.

Hardy, A. S. Sea Stories for Wonder Eyes. 2005. reprint ed. pap. 21.95 (978-1-4191-0670-5(8)) Kessinger Publishing, LLC.

Horsman, Paul. Out of the Blue: A Journey Through the World's Oceans. Seapics.com Staff, photos by. 2005. (ENG., Illus.). 160p. (gr. 17). 32.95 (978-0-262-08341-6(8), 0262083418) MIT Pr.

Kavanagh, James. My First Seashores Nature. Leung, Raymond, illus. 2011. (Nature Activity Book Ser.). (ENG.). 32p. (J). (gr. 2-4). act. bk. ed. 6.95 (978-1-58355-590-3(0)) Western National Parks Assn.

Littlefield, Cindy A. Awesome Ocean Science: Investigating the Secrets of the Underwater World. 2004. (Kids Can Bks.). (Illus.). 120p. (J). (gr. 3-5). pap. 12.95 (978-1-885593-71-9(6), Ideal Pubns.) Worthy Publishing.

Llewellyn, Claire. In the Sea Red Band. Belcher, Andy, photos by. 2016. (Cambridge Reading Adventures Ser.). (ENG., Illus.). 16p. pap. 6.56 (978-1-107-57578-3(8)) Cambridge Univ. Pr.

Merlino, Kim. Ocean Life: Grades 2 Through 4. (Illus.). (J). pap., wbk. ed. 4.99 (978-0-88743-966-7(7)) School Zone Publishing Co.

Munson, Victoria. British Seashore. 2016. (Nature Detective Ser.). (ENG., Illus.). 64p. (J). (gr. 2-4). pap. 9.99 (978-0-7502-9323-5(3), Wayland) Hachette Children's Group GBR. Dist: Hachette Bk. Group.

Richmond, Benjamin. Why Is the Sea Salty? And Other Questions about the Ocean. Azhderian, Cecelia, illus. 2014. (Good Question! Ser.). (ENG.). 32p. (J). (gr. 1). pap. 5.95 (978-1-4549-0677-3(4)) Sterling Publishing Co., Inc.

—Why Is the Sea Salty? And Other Questions about the Oceans. Azhderian, Cecelia, illus. 2014. (Good Question! Ser.). (ENG.). 40p. (J). (gr. 1). 12.95 *(978-1-4549-0676-6(6))* Sterling Publishing Co., Inc.

Rissman, Rebecca. Living & Nonliving in the Ocean, 1 vol. 2013. (Is It Living or Nonliving? Ser.). (ENG., Illus.). 24p. (gr. k-2). 23.32 *(978-1-4109-5381-0(5))*; pap. 6.95 *(978-1-4109-5388-9(2))* Heinemann-Raintree.

Rivera, Sheila. Ocean. 2005. (Illus.). 24p. (J). pap. 5.95 *(978-0-8225-5372-4(4))*; (ENG., lib. bdg. 23.93 *(978-0-8225-2795-4(2)*, Lerner Pubns.) Lerner Publishing Group.

Rushworth, Gary. The Life Cycle of Water Plants: Text Pairs. 2008. (Bridges/Navigators Ser.). (J). (gr. 3). 89.00 *(978-1-4108-8365-0(5))* Benchmark Education Co.

Swanson, Diane. Safari Beneath the Sea: The Wonder World of the North Pacific Coast, 1 vol. Royal British Columbia Museum Staff, photos by. (ENG., Illus.). 64p. (J). pap. 12.95 *(978-1-55110-441-6(5))* Whitecap Bks., Ltd. CAN. Dist: Graphic Arts Ctr. Publishing Co.

Twist, Clint. 1000 Things You Should Know about Oceans. 2008. (1000 Things You Should Know about (Miles Kelley) Ser.). (Illus.). 61p. (J). pap. *(978-1-84236-852-7(4))* Miles Kelly Publishing, Ltd.

Wilkins, John-Paul. What Can Live at the Beach?, 1 vol. 2014. (What Can Live There? Ser.). (ENG., Illus.). 24p. (gr. -1-1). 22.65 *(978-1-4846-0578-3(0)*, Heinemann Read & Learn) Heinemann-Raintree.

World Book, Inc Staff, contrib. by. The Sea & Its Marvels. 2011. (J). *(978-0-7166-1791-4(9))* World Bk., Inc.

MARINE RESOURCES

see also Fisheries

Harper, Joel. All the Way to the Ocean. Spusta, Marq, illus. 2006. (J). 14.95 *(978-0-9714254-1-5(8))* Harper, Joel D.

Mallory, Kenneth. A Home by the Sea: Protecting Coastal Wildlife. 2003. (Illus.). 64p. (YA). (gr. 4-8). reprint ed. 20.00 *(978-0-7567-6562-0(5))* DIANE Publishing Co.

Marine Debris Program (U.S.), Office of Response and Restoration, ed. Understanding Marine Debris: Games & Activities for Kids of All Ages: Marine Debris 101: Games & Activities for Kids of All Ages: Marine Debris 101. 2012. (ENG.). 23p. 7.00 *(978-0-16-091362-4(4)*, National Marine Fisheries Service) United States Government Printing Office.

Perritano, John. Marine Resources, Vol. 12. 2015. (North American Natural Resources Ser.). (Illus.). 64p. (J). (gr. 7). lib. bdg. 23.95 *(978-1-4222-3384-9(7))* Mason Crest.

MARINE ZOOLOGY

see Marine Animals

MARINERS

see Sailors

MARION, FRANCIS, 1732-1795

Kauffman, Scott. Francis Marion: Swamp Fox of South Carolina. 2006. (Forgotten Heroes of the American Revolution Ser.). (Illus.). 88p. (YA). (gr. 5-11). lib. bdg. 23.95 *(978-1-59556-014-8(9))* OTTN Publishing.

MARION, FRANCIS, 1732-1795—FICTION

Gunderson, Jessica. A Rebel among Redcoats: A Revolutionary War Novel. 2015. (Revolutionary War Ser.). (ENG., Illus.). 96p. (gr. 4-4). lib. bdg. 26.65 *(978-1-4342-9701-3(2))* Stone Arch Bks.

MARIONETTES

Anderson, Lynne. Make a Marionette. 2011. (Early Connections Ser.). (J). *(978-1-61672-556-3(7))* Benchmark Education Co.

MARITIME DISCOVERIES

see Discoveries in Geography

MARK, SAINT

Woodman, Ros. Bible Detectives Puzzle Book. 2005. (Activity Ser.). (ENG.). 58p. (J). pap., act. bk. ed. 7.99 *(978-1-85792-674-3(9)*, 8f59622b-b911-4107-a066-1185e34164af) Christian Focus Pubns. GBR. Dist: Bookmasters Distribution.

MARKET GARDENING

see Vegetable Gardening

MARKETING

Adler, David A. Prices! Prices! Prices! Why They Go up & Down. Miller, Edward, illus. 2015. (ENG.). 32p. (J). (gr. 1-5). 17.95 *(978-0-8234-3293-6(9))* Holiday Hse., Inc.

Caraccilo, Dominic. E-Tailing: Careers Selling over the Web. 2009. (Library of E-Commerce & Internet Careers Ser.). 64p. (gr. 5-5). 58.50 *(978-1-60853-587-3(8))* Rosen Publishing Group, Inc., The.

Cohn, Jessica. Fashion Buyer. 2009. (Cool Careers: on the Go Ser.). 32p. (gr. 5-8). pap. 10.50 *(978-1-4339-0166-9(8))*; (YA). lib. bdg. 26.00 *(978-1-4339-0002-0(5))* Stevens, Gareth Publishing LLLP.

Earl, C. F. Marketing Your Business. Madrian, Brigitte, ed. 2013. (Young Adult Library of Small Business & Finance Ser.: 10). 64p. (J). (gr. 7-18). 22.95 *(978-1-4222-2919-4(X))* Mason Crest.

Etzel. Marketing: Student Study Guide. 13th rev. ed. 2004. 368p. (gr. 6-12). pap. *(978-0-07-283785-8(3))* Glencoe/McGraw-Hill.

Gogerly, Liz. Cool Brands. 2012. (On the Radar: Street Style Ser.). (ENG.). 32p. (gr. 4-8). lib. bdg. 26.60 *(978-0-7613-7770-2(0)*, Lerner Pubns.) Lerner Publishing Group.

Jovin, Michelle. Your World: Shopping Secrets: Multiplication (Grade 3) 2017. (Mathematics Readers Ser.). (Illus.). 32p. (J). (gr. 3-3). pap. 8.99 ***(978-1-4807-5796-7(9))*** Teacher Created Materials, Inc.

Loftus, Jennifer. Buying & Selling at the Yard Sale. 2009. (Real Life Readers Ser.). 12p. (gr. 1-2). pap. 5.90 *(978-1-4042-7913-1(X)*, Rosen Classroom) Rosen Publishing Group, Inc., The.

MacDonald, Margaret. Bargaining at the Market. 2011. (Learn-Abouts Ser.). (Illus.). 16p. (J). pap. 7.95 *(978-1-59920-647-9(1))* Black Rabbit Bks.

Malaspina, Ann. False Images, Deadly Promises: Smoking & the Media. 2007. (Tobacco: the Deadly Drug Ser.). (Illus.). 112p. (YA). pap. 12.95 *(978-1-4222-0812-0(5))* Mason Crest.

Meyer, Susan. Branding: Creating an Identity on the Web. 2014. (Digital & Information Literacy Ser.). (Illus.). 48p. (J). (gr. 5-8). 30.25 *(978-1-4777-7647-6(8))*; pap. 70.50 *(978-1-4777-7650-6(8))*; pap. 11.75 *(978-1-4777-7649-0(4))* Rosen Publishing Group, Inc., The.

Mortensen, Lori. Buyers & Sellers. 2016. (Spring Forward Ser.). (J). (gr. 1). *(978-1-4900-9376-5(1))* Benchmark Education Co.

Murley, Leon & Wilson, Antoine. The Distribution of Goods & Services. 2011. 77.70 *(978-1-4488-4750-1(8)*, Rosen Reference); (ENG.). 64p. (YA). (gr. 5-8). pap. 12.95 *(978-1-4488-4718-1(4)*, Rosen Reference); (YA). (gr. 5-9). lib. bdg. 31.95 *(978-1-4488-4710-5(9))* Rosen Publishing Group, Inc., The.

Reeves, Diane Lindsey & Gunzenhauser, Kelly. Career Ideas for Teens in Marketing. 2nd rev. ed. 2012. (Career Ideas for Teens Ser.). (Illus.). 192p. (gr. 6-12). 45.00 *(978-0-8160-8268-1(5)*, Ferguson Publishing Co.) Facts On File, Inc.

Sheen, Barbara. Careers in Sales & Marketing. 2015. (ENG., Illus.). 80p. (YA). lib. bdg. *(978-1-60152-812-4(4))* ReferencePoint Pr., Inc.

Spilsbury, Richard. Hi-Tech Clothes, 1 vol. 2013. (Design & Engineering for STEM Ser.). (ENG., Illus.). 56p. (gr. 6-8). pap. 9.99 *(978-1-4329-7037-6(2)*, NA-h); lib. bdg. 34.65 *(978-1-4329-7032-1(1))* Heinemann-Raintree.

Wittekind, Erika. The Big Push: How Popular Culture Is Always Selling, 1 vol. 2012. (Exploring Media Literacy Ser.). (ENG.). 80p. (gr. 6-7). pap. 9.10 *(978-0-7565-4535-2(8))*; lib. bdg. 34.65 *(978-0-7565-4518-5(8))* Compass Point Bks. (CPB Grades 4-8).

MARKETING—VOCATIONAL GUIDANCE

Ferguson. Advertising & Marketing. 2nd rev. ed. 2009. (Careers in Focus Ser.). 202p. (gr. 6-12). 32.95 *(978-0-8160-7295-8(7)*, Ferguson Publishing Co.) Facts On File, Inc.

Haegele, Katie. E-Advertising & E-Marketing Online Opportunities. 2009. (Library of E-Commerce & Internet Careers Ser.). 64p. (gr. 5-5). 58.50 *(978-1-60853-585-9(1))* Rosen Publishing Group, Inc., The.

Harmon, Daniel E. Careers As a Marketing & Public Relations Specialist. 2013. (Essential Careers Ser.). 80p. (YA). (gr. 7-12). 33.25 *(978-1-4777-1793-6(5))* Rosen Publishing Group, Inc., The.

Nagle, Jeanne. Careers in Internet Advertising & Marketing. 2013. 80p. (YA). (gr. 9-12). 33.25 *(978-1-4488-9596-0(0))* Rosen Publishing Group, Inc., The.

Stinson, Paul. Sales, Marketing, Business & Finance. 2008. (Great Careers with a High School Diploma Ser.). 110p. (C). (gr. 9). 32.95 *(978-0-8160-7051-0(2)*, Ferguson Publishing Co.) Facts On File, Inc.

MARKETING (HOME ECONOMICS)

see Shopping

MARKETING OF FARM PRODUCE

see Farm Produce—Marketing

MARKETS

see also Fairs

Bailey, Diane. How Markets Work. 2011. (Real World Economics Ser.). (ENG.). 80p. (YA). (gr. 7-12). lib. bdg. 33.25 *(978-1-4488-5564-3(0))* Rosen Publishing Group, Inc., The.

Chambers, Catherine. A Day at an Indian Market. 2011. (Big Picture: Food Ser.). (ENG.). 24p. (gr. 1-2). pap. 41.70 *(978-1-4296-6725-8(7)*, First Facts) Capstone Press of Coughlan Cos.

Francis, Amy. The Local Food Movement. 2010. (At Issue Ser.). (ENG.). 128p. (gr. 10-12). 39.40 *(978-0-7377-4888-8(5))*; pap. 27.80 *(978-0-7377-4889-5(3)*, Greenhaven Pr., Inc.) Cengage Gale.

Gorman, Jacqueline Laks. The Shopping Mall (El Centro Comercial) 2005. (I Like to Visit/Me Gusta Visitar Ser.). (ENG & SPA., Illus.). 24p. (gr. k-3). lib. bdg. 22.00 *(978-0-8368-4599-0(4)*, Weekly Reader Leveled Readers) Stevens, Gareth Publishing LLLP.

Gorman, Jacqueline Laks & Laks Gorman, Jacqueline. The Shopping Mall/El Centro Comercial. 2005. (I Like to Visit/ Me gusta visitar Ser.). (ENG & SPA., Illus.). 24p. (gr. k-3). pap. 8.15 *(978-0-8368-4606-5(0)*, Weekly Reader Leveled Readers) Stevens, Gareth Publishing LLLP.

Hawes, Alison. At the Market Pink B Band. Robert, LeyHonor, illus. 2016. (Cambridge Reading Adventures Ser.). (ENG.). 16p. pap. 6.56 *(978-1-107-54993-7(0))* Cambridge Univ. Pr.

Munro, Roxie. Market Maze. 2015. *(978-0-8234-3358-2(7))* Holiday Hse., Inc.

Null Petersen, Casey. Markets Around the World, 1 vol. 2nd rev. ed. 2014. (TIME for KIDS(r) Nonfiction Readers Ser.). (ENG., Illus.). 28p. (J). (gr. 3-3). pap. 25.96 *(978-1-4807-1067-2(9))* Shell Educational Publishing.

—Markets Around the World, 1 vol. 2nd rev. ed. 2011. (TIME for KIDS(r) Nonfiction Readers Ser.). (ENG.). 28p. (J). (gr. 3-3). pap. 8.99 *(978-1-4333-3652-2(9))* Teacher Created Materials, Inc.

Null Petersen, Christine. Mercados Alrededor Del Mundo. 2017. (TIME for Kids en Español - Level 3 Ser.). (SPA.). 32p. (gr. 3-3). lib. bdg. 31.99 ***(978-1-5157-5164-9(3))*** Time for Kids Inc AUS. Dist: Capstone Pub.

Rauen, Amy. Counting at the Market. Pickering, Russell, photos by. 2008. (Getting Started with Math Ser.). (Illus.). 16p. (gr. -1-2). lib. bdg. 19.00 *(978-0-8368-8981-9(9)*, Weekly Reader Leveled Readers) Stevens, Gareth Publishing LLLP.

—Vamos a Contar en el Mercado. 2008. (Matemáticas para empezar (Getting Started with Math) Ser.).Tr. of Counting at the Market. (SPA., Illus.). 16p. (gr. -1-2). pap. 5.30 *(978-0-8368-8996-3(7)*, Weekly Reader Leveled Readers) Stevens, Gareth Publishing LLLP.

—Vamos a Contar en el Mercado. Pickering, Russell, photos by. 2008. (Matemáticas para Empezar (Getting Started with Math) Ser.).Tr. of Counting at the Market. (SPA., Illus.). 16p. (gr. -1-2). lib. bdg. 19.00 *(978-0-8368-8991-8(6)*, Weekly Reader Leveled Readers) Stevens, Gareth Publishing LLLP.

Wolfe, Mike & Sprengelmeyer, Lily. Kid Pickers: How to Turn Junk into Treasure. Right, Mike, illus. 2013. (ENG.). 128p. (J). (gr. 2-7). 19.99 *(978-1-250-00848-0(4)*, 9781250008480); pap. 14.99 *(978-1-250-01930-1(3)*, 9781250019301) Feiwel & Friends.

MARKETS—FICTION

Alakija, Polly. Catch That Goat! A Market Day in Nigeria. Alakija, Polly, illus. 2007. (ENG., Illus.). 40p. (J). (gr. -1-3). 8.99 *(978-1-84686-057-7(1))* Barefoot Bks., Inc.

Alakija, Polly, et al. Catch That Goat! 2004. (Avenues Ser.). (ENG., Illus.). 32p. (C). pap. 11.95 *(978-1-84148-161-6(0))* National Geographic School Publishing, Inc.

Alfaro, Manuel. Griego el Magnífico y la Gotita Verde Golosa Pegajos. Harrington, David, illus. 2007. (SPA.). 36p. per. 15.50 *(978-1-59858-337-3(9))* Dog Ear Publishing, LLC.

Amollo, Regina. When Mother Leaves Home. 2004. (Illus.). 35p. pap. *(978-9970-02-435-3(3))* Fountain Pubs. Ltd. UGA. Dist: Michigan State Univ. Pr.

Averbeck, Jim. The Market Bowl. Averbeck, Jim, illus. 2013. (ENG., Illus.). 32p. (J). (gr. -1-3). lib. bdg. 16.95 *(978-1-58089-368-8(6))* Charlesbridge Publishing, Inc.

Baker, Jeannie. Mirror. Baker, Jeannie, illus. 2010. (ENG., Illus.). 48p. (J). (gr. k-4). 18.99 *(978-0-7636-4848-0(5))* Candlewick Pr.

Capucilli, Alyssa Satin. Monkey Play. 2012. (Step into Reading Ser.). (ENG., Illus.). 32p. (J). (gr. -1-1). pap. 3.99 *(978-0-375-86993-8(X)*, Random Hse. Bks. for Young Readers) Random Hse. Children's Bks.

Charles, Bob. A Trip to the Market: Set Of 6. 2010. (Early Connections Ser.). (J). 37.00 net. *(978-1-4108-1359-6(2))* Benchmark Education Co.

—A Trip to the Market & una visita al Mercado: 6 English, 6 Spanish Adaptations. 2011. (ENG & SPA.). (J). 75.00 net. *(978-1-4108-5642-5(9))* Benchmark Education Co.

Clarke, Lorin. Our Last Trip to the Market. Vane, Mitch, illus. 2017. (ENG.). 32p. (J). (-k). 17.99 ***(978-1-925266-96-2(6))*** Allen & Unwin AUS. Dist: Independent Pubs. Group.

Davies, Lewis. Tai, Troll & the Black & White Cow. 2009. (ENG., Illus.). 30p. (J). pap. 7.95 *(978-1-905762-64-4(X))* Parthian Bks. GBR. Dist: Independent Pubs. Group.

Get Together Girls - Going to the Mall. 2005. (J). bds. *(978-1-4194-0087-2(8))* Paradise Pr., Inc.

Janice Turner & Colleen Connelly. Colleen Goes to the Farmer's Market. Ron Frazier, photos by. 2009. (Illus.). 20p. pap. 12.49 *(978-1-4389-6085-2(9))* AuthorHouse.

Klein, Adria F. Max Goes to the Farmers' Market, 1 vol. Gallagher-Cole, Mernie, illus. 2009. (Read-It! Readers: the Life of Max Ser.). (ENG.). 24p. (gr. -1-2). 21.32 *(978-1-4048-5263-1(8)*, Easy Readers) Picture Window Bks.

Leto, Frank & Scelsa, Greg. Let's Go to the Market. Faulkner, Stacey, ed. 2006. (J). pap. 2.99 *(978-1-59198-317-0(7))* Creative Teaching Pr., Inc.

Lindman, Maj. Flicka, Ricka, Dicka Go to Market. Lindman, Maj, illus. 2012. (ENG., Illus.). 32p. (J). (gr. -1-3). 9.99 *(978-0-8075-2478-7(6))*; (gr. k-3). 9.99 *(978-0-8075-2479-4(4))* Whitman, Albert & Co.

Page, Stefan. We're Going to the Farmers' Market. 2014. (ENG., Illus.). 16p. (J). (gr. -1 — 1). bds. 7.99 *(978-1-4521-1834-5(5))* Chronicle Bks. LLC.

Randolph, Robert. Ben Goes to the Farmer's Market, 1 vol. 2009. 37p. pap. 24.95 *(978-1-4489-1934-5(7))* PublishAmerica, Inc.

Rocky Porch Moore. It's Farm Market Day! 2009. 24p. pap. 12.99 *(978-1-4490-2854-1(3))* AuthorHouse.

Roy, James. Chaz at the Fish Market. Gorissen, Dean, illus. 2015. (J). pap. *(978-1-4966-0251-0(X))* Capstone Classroom.

Taylor, W. Y. Baby Goes to Market. 2009. (ENG.). 12p. bds. 3.95 *(978-1-58117-897-5(2)*, Intervisual/Piggy Toes) Bendon, Inc.

Thong, Roseanne Greenfield. Gai See: What You Can See in Chinatown. Choi, Yangsook, illus. 2007. (ENG.). 40p. (J). (gr. 1-4). 16.95 *(978-0-8109-9337-2(6)*, Abrams Bks. for Young Readers) Abrams, Inc.

Turnbull, Elizabeth. Janjak & Freda Go to the Iron Market. Turnbull, Wally, tr. Jones, Mark, illus. 2013. 36p. 18.95 *(978-1-61153-072-8(5))* Light Messages Publishing.

Turnbull, Elizabeth J. Janjak & Freda Go to the Iron Market. Turnbull, Wally R., tr. Jones, Mark, illus. 2013. 36p. pap. 12.95 *(978-1-61153-062-9(8))* Light Messages Publishing.

Vonthron, Satanta C. Caillov Visits the Farmer's Market. Meier, Kerry L., illus. l.t. ed. 2005. (HRL Board Book Ser.). (J). (gr. -1-k). pap. 10.95 *(978-1-57332-310-9(1)*, HighReach Learning, Incorporated) Carson-Dellosa Publishing, LLC.

Wellington, Monica. Ana Cultiva Manzanas/Apple Farmer Annie. Del Risco, Eida & del Risco, Eida, trs. from ENG. Wellington, Monica, illus. 2004. (ENG & SPA., Illus.). 32p. (J). (gr. -1-2). 16.99 *(978-0-525-47252-0(5)*, Dutton Books for Young Readers) Penguin Young Readers Group.

—Apple Farmer Annie Board Book. Wellington, Monica, illus. 2012. (ENG., Illus.). 24p. (J). (gr. -1 — 1). bds. 5.99 *(978-0-8037-3888-1(9)*, Dial Bks) Penguin Young Readers Group.

MARKSMANSHIP

see Shooting

MARLEY, BOB, 1945-1981

Ellison, Katie. Who Was Bob Marley? Copeland, Gregory, illus. 2017. (Who Was? Ser.). (ENG.). 112p. (J). (gr. 3-7). 5.99 *(978-0-448-48919-3(8)*, Grosset & Dunlap) Penguin Young Readers Group.

—Who Was Bob Marley? 2017. (Who Was...? Ser.). lib. bdg. 16.00 ***(978-0-606-40115-9(6))*** Turtleback Bks.

Jeffrey, Gary. Bob Marley: The Life of a Musical Legend. Riley, Terry, illus. 2007. (Graphic Nonfiction Biographies Ser.). (ENG.). 48p. (YA). (gr. 4-7). lib. bdg. 31.95 *(978-1-4042-0854-4(2))* Rosen Publishing Group, Inc., The.

Medina, Tony. I & I: Bob Marley. Watson, Jesse Joshua, illus. 2009. (ENG.). 48p. (J). (gr. 3-6). 19.95 *(978-1-60060-257-3(6))* Lee & Low Bks., Inc.

Medina, Tony & Watson, Jesse Joshua. I & I Bob Marley, 1 vol. 2009. (ENG., Illus.). 48p. (J). pap. 10.95 *(978-1-62014-030-7(6))* Lee & Low Bks., Inc.

Miller, Calvin Craig. Reggae Poet: The Story of Bob Marley. 2007. (Modern Music Masters Ser.). (Illus.). 128p. (YA). (gr. 9-18). lib. bdg. 27.95 *(978-1-59935-071-4(8))* Reynolds, Morgan Inc.

Waters, Rosa. Bob Marley & the Wailers. (Pop Rock Ser.). (Illus.). 64p. (YA). 2008. (gr. 7-18). lib. bdg. 22.95 *(978-1-4222-0192-3(9))* 2007. pap. 7.95 *(978-1-4222-0317-0(4))* Mason Crest.

MARMOTS

see also Woodchuck

Beer, Amy-Jane. Woodchucks. 2008. (Nature's Children Ser.). (Illus.). 52p. (J). *(978-0-7172-6267-0(7))* Grolier, Ltd.

Royer, Anne. Little Marmots. Castle, Muriel, tr. from FRE. 2005. (Born to Be Wild Ser.). (Illus.). 24p. (gr. k-3). lib. bdg. 23.00 *(978-0-8368-4439-9(4)*, Gareth Stevens Learning Library) Stevens, Gareth Publishing LLLP.

MARMOTS—FICTION

Burchfield, Cindy. Gimme, Gimme Moocher Marmots. Burchfield, Cindy, illus. 2007. (Illus.). 48p. per. 18.95 *(978-1-59858-457-8(X))* Dog Ear Publishing, LLC.

Horvath, Polly. Mr. & Mrs. Bunny: Detectives Extraordinaire! Blackall, Sophie, illus. 2012. (ENG.). 256p. (J). (gr. 3-7). 16.99 *(978-0-375-86755-2(4)*, Schwartz & Wade Bks.) Random Hse. Children's Bks.

Mitchell, George. The Marmots of Lenk & the Long Sleep. 2012. 110p. 25.50 *(978-1-105-61600-6(2))* 2011. 66p. pap. 20.95 *(978-1-4476-2895-8(0))* Lulu Pr., Inc.

MARQUETTE, JACQUES, 1637-1675

Donaldson-Forbes, Jeff. Jacques Marquette & Louis Jolliet. 2009. (Primary Source Library of Famous Explorers Ser.). 24p. (gr. 4-4). 42.50 *(978-1-60854-127-0(4)*, PowerKids Pr.) Rosen Publishing Group, Inc., The.

Harkins, Susan Sales & Harkins, William H. The Life & Times of Father Jacques Marquette. 2008. (Profiles in American History Ser.). (Illus.). 48p. (J). (gr. 4-8). lib. bdg. 29.95 *(978-1-58415-528-7(0))* Mitchell Lane Pubs., Inc.

Larkin, Tanya. Jacques Marquette & Louis Jolliet: Explorers of the Mississippi. 2009. (Library of Explorers & Exploration Ser.). 112p. (gr. 5-8). 66.50 *(978-1-60853-608-5(4)*, Rosen Reference) Rosen Publishing Group, Inc., The.

O'Brien, Cynthia. Explore with Marquette & Jolliet. 2016. (Travel with the Great Explorers Ser.). (ENG., Illus.). 32p. (J). (gr. 3-6). *(978-0-7787-2850-4(1))* Crabtree Publishing Co.

Petrie, Kristin. Marquette & Jolliet, 1 vol. 2007. (Explorers Set 2 Ser.). (ENG., Illus.). 32p. (gr. 4-7). 27.07 *(978-1-59679-745-1(2)*, Checkerboard Library) ABDO Publishing Co.

Zelenyj, Alexander & Zelenyj, Alexander. Marquette & Jolliet: Quest for the Mississippi. 2006. (In the Footsteps of Explorers Ser.). (ENG., Illus.). 32p. (J). (gr. 4-7). pap. *(978-0-7787-2467-4(0))*; lib. bdg. *(978-0-7787-2431-5(X))* Crabtree Publishing Co.

MARRIAGE

see also Dating (Social Customs); Domestic Relations; Family; Family Life; Family Life Education; Intermarriage; Sex; Sexual Ethics

Ascension Press, creator. Theology of the Body for Teens Student Workbook: Discovering God's Plan for Love & Life. 2006. (Illus.). 210p. per. 14.95 *(978-1-932927-86-3(7))* Ascension Pr.

Ayer, Eleanor H. Todo lo que necesitas saber sobre el matrimonio adolescente (Everything You Need to Know about Teen Marriage) 2009. (Todo lo que necesitas (the Need to Know Library) Ser.). (SPA.). 64p. (gr. 6-6). 58.50 *(978-1-60854-408-0(7)*, Editorial Buenas Letras) Rosen Publishing Group, Inc., The.

Bily, Cynthia A. Gay Marriage. Gale, ed. 2014. (Introducing Issues with Opposing Viewpoints Ser.). (ENG., Illus.). 144p. (J). (gr. 10-12). lib. bdg. 42.00 *(978-0-7377-6923-4(8)*, Greenhaven Pr., Inc.) Cengage Gale.

Brown, Kyle. My Wedding Activity Book. 2009. 48p. pap. 9.95 *(978-0-557-06217-1(9))* Lulu Pr., Inc.

Brown, Tracy. Frequently Asked Questions about Same-Sex Marriage & When a Parent Is Gay. 2012. (FAQ: Teen Life Ser.). (ENG., Illus.). 64p. (J). (gr. 7-12). lib. bdg. 31.95 *(978-1-4488-8330-1(X))* Rosen Publishing Group, Inc., The.

Bryan, Dale-Marie. William & Kate. 2012. (Stars of Today Ser.). (ENG.). 32p. (J). (gr. 2-5). 28.50 *(978-1-61473-287-7(6)*, 205049) Child's World, Inc., The.

Center for Learning Network Staff. Charming Billy/at Weddings & Wakes: Curriculum Unit. 2005. (Novel Ser.). 64p. (YA). tchr. ed., spiral bd. 19.95 *(978-1-56077-788-5(5))* Center for Learning, The.

Chastain, Zachary. From the Parlor to the Altar: Romance & Marriage in The 1800s. 2009. (Daily Life in America in the 1800s Ser.). 64p. (YA). (gr. 7-18). pap. 9.95 *(978-1-4222-1852-5(X))*; lib. bdg. 22.95 *(978-1-4222-1779-5(5))* Mason Crest.

Don, Katherine. Nujood Ali & the Fight Against Child Marriage. 2014. (J). *(978-1-59935-466-8(7))* Reynolds, Morgan Inc.

Hillstrom, Kevin. Gay Marriage. Greenhaven Press Editors, ed. 2014. (Hot Topics Ser.). (ENG., Illus.). 128p. (gr. 7-10). lib. bdg. 39.40 *(978-1-4205-0870-3(9))*, Lucent Bks.) Cengage Gale.

Hollander, Barbara Gottfried. Marriage Rights & Gay Rights: Interpreting the Constitution. 2014. (Understanding the United States Constitution Ser.). (Illus.). 112p. (J). (gr. 7-12). 35.60 *(978-1-4777-7514-1(5))* Rosen Publishing Group, Inc., The.

Hossler, Margaret. Spenser Rose Is Born. 2003. 32p. 12.99 *(978-0-9650491-4-6(0))* Send The Light Distribution LLC.

Hunnicutt, M. E. The Wedding Wonderful. 2013. 24p. pap. 24.95 *(978-1-62709-035-3(5))* America Star Bks.

Kiesbye, Stefan. Polygamy. 2012. (At Issue Ser.). (ENG.). 128p. (gr. 10-12). pap. 27.80 *(978-0-7377-6194-8(6)*, Greenhaven Pr., Inc.) Cengage Gale.

Kiesbye, Stefan, ed. Polygamy. 2012. (At Issue Ser.). (ENG.). 128p. (gr. 10-12). lib. bdg. 34.45 *(978-0-7377-6193-1(8)*, Greenhaven Pr., Inc.) Cengage Gale.

Lankford, Ronnie D. Polygamy. 2008. (At Issue Ser.). (ENG., Illus.). 80-128p. (gr. 10-12). pap. 34.45 *(978-0-7377-4106-3(6)*, Greenhaven Pr., Inc.) Cengage Gale.

Meredith, Samantha & Wyk, Hanri van, illus. Weddings Sticker Color Book. 2011. (First Sticker Coloring Bks). 20p. (J). pap. 5.99 *(978-0-7945-3108-9(3)*, Usborne) EDC Publishing.

Open for Debate - Group 5, 4 bks., Set. Incl. National Health Care. Kowalski, Kathiann M. lib. bdg. 42.79 *(978-0-7614-2943-2(3))*; Political Campaigns. Naden, Corinne J. lib. bdg. 42.79 *(978-0-7614-2944-9(1))*; Religious Fundamentalism. Fridell, Ron. lib. bdg. 42.79 *(978-0-7614-2945-6(X))*; Right to Die. Stefoff, Rebecca. lib. bdg. 42.79 *(978-0-7614-2948-7(4))*; 128p. (gr. 7-18). (Open for Debate 5 Ser.). 2008. Set lib. bdg. 171.16

(978-0-7614-2940-1(9), Benchmark Bks.) Marshall Cavendish Corp.

Robert, Na'ima B. Mabrook! a World of Muslim Weddings. Adl, Shirin, illus. 2016. (ENG.). 32p. (J). (gr. -1-2). 17.99 (978-1-84780-588-1(4), Frances Lincoln Children's Bks.) Quarto Publishing Group UK GBR. Dist: Hachette Bk. Group.

Snyder, Gail. Marriage & Family Issues. 2008. (Gallup Major Trends & Events Ser.). (Illus.). 118p. (YA). (gr. 7-18). lib. bdg. 22.95 (978-1-59084-966-8(3), 1260831) Mason Crest.

Spilsbury, Louise. Same-Sex Marriage. 2011. (Ethical Debates Ser.). (ENG., Illus.). 48p. (YA). (gr. 5-8). pap. 11.75 (978-1-4488-7013-4(5)); lib. bdg. 29.25 (978-1-4488-6020-3(2)) Rosen Publishing Group, Inc., The. (Rosen Reference).

Stern, Zoe & Stern, Evan. Divorce Is Not the End of the World: Zoe's & Evan's Coping Guide for Kids. 2nd rev. ed. 2008. (ENG., Illus.). 112p. (J). (gr. 3-7). pap. 9.99 (978-1-58246-241-7(0), Tricycle Pr.) Random Hse. Children's Bks.

Sterngass, Jon. Same Sex Marriage. 2011. (Controversy! 3 Ser.). 112p. (gr. 7). 37.07 (978-1-60870-490-3(4)) Marshall Cavendish Corp.

Stewart, Sheila & Simons, Rae. I Live in Two Homes: Adjusting to Divorce & Remarriage. 2010. (Kids Have Troubles Too Ser.). 48p. (YA). (gr. 5-18). lib. bdg. 19.95 (978-1-4222-1694-1(2)) Mason Crest.

MARRIAGE—FICTION

Alcott, Louisa May. Kitty's Class Day, & Other Stories. 2013. 178p. (J). pap. 8.75 (978-1-61720-920-8(1)) Wilder Pubns., Corp.

Andersen, Hans Christian. The Little Mermaid Retold. Charlotte, J. M., illus. 2013. 48p. 18.00 (978-0-9895422-0-3(3)) MHC Ministries.

Andrews, Julie & Hamilton, Emma Walton. The Very Fairy Princess: Here Comes the Flower Girl! Davenier, Christine, illus. 2012. (Very Fairy Princess Ser.). (ENG.). 32p. (J). (gr. -1-3). 16.99 (978-0-316-18561-5(2)) Little Brown & Co.

Andrews, V. C. Garden of Shadows. 2010. (ENG.). 368p. (YA). (gr. 9). pap. 9.99 (978-1-4424-0643-8(7), Simon Pulse) Simon Pulse.

App, Linda Hoogeveen. Emma Pearl, Flower Girl. 2012. 34p. pap. 16.95 (978-1-4497-6619-1(6), WestBow Pr.) Author Solutions, Inc.

Ariel Make Believe Bride. 2008. (Disney 8*8 Ser.). 24p. pap. (978-1-4075-1620-2(5)) Parragon, Inc.

Armstrong, Rachel. Fair Folk in Knob's End. 2013. 274p. pap. 14.99 (978-1-60820-851-7(6)) MLR Pr., LLC.

Artigas de Sierra, Ione M. Las Bodas del Gallo Perico. (Superbks./Superlibros). (SPA.). (J). (gr. k-1). 21.95 (978-0-88272-488-1(6)); pap. 6.95 (978-0-88272-489-8(4)) Santillana USA Publishing Co., Inc.

—On the Way to the Wedding. (Superbks./Superlibros). (Illus.). 16p. (J). (gr. k-3). pap. 6.95 (978-0-88272-491-1(6)) Santillana USA Publishing Co., Inc.

Austrian, J. J. Worm Loves Worm. Curato, Mike, illus. 2016. 32p. (J). (gr. -1-3). 17.99 (978-0-06-238633-5(6)) HarperCollins Pubs.

Baker, E. D. Princess in Disguise. 2015. (Wide-Awake Princess Ser.: 4). (ENG.). 224p. (YA). (gr. 3-6). 16.99 (978-1-61963-573-9(9), 9781619635739, Bloomsbury USA Childrens) Bloomsbury Publishing USA.

Barkley, Callie. Amy Meets Her Stepsister. Riti, Marsha, illus. 2013. (Critter Club Ser.: 5). (ENG.). 128p. (J). (gr. k-2). 15.99 (978-1-4424-8216-6(8)); pap. 5.99 (978-1-4424-8215-9(X)) Little Simon. (Little Simon).

—Ellie the Flower Girl. Bishop, Tracy, illus. 2016. (Critter Club Ser.: 14). (ENG.). 128p. (J). (gr. k-4). pap. 5.99 (978-1-4814-6718-6(2), Little Simon) Little Simon.

Barnholdt, Lauren. Fake Me a Match. 2012. (Mix Ser.). (ENG.). 304p. (J). (gr. 4-8). pap. 6.99 (978-1-4424-2259-9(9), Aladdin) Simon & Schuster Children's Publishing.

Beach, Kathleen H. & Weeber, Stephanie B. Madison's Mixed-up Flower Girl Magic & Aiden's Amazing Ring Bearer Act Aiden's Amazing Ring Bearer Act. Baisley, Maryann Leake, illus. 2009. 32p. pap. 19.95 (978-1-4251-7059-2(5)) Trafford Publishing.

Beaty, Erin. The Traitor's Kiss. 2017. (Traitor's Trilogy Ser.: 1). (ENG.). 352p. (YA). 18.99 (978-1-250-11794-6(1), 9781250117946) Imprint IND. Dist: Macmillan.

Beauvais, Clémentine. The Royal Wedding Crashers. Moor, Becka, illus. 2015. (ENG.). 240p. (J). (gr. 1-3). pap. 10.99 (978-1-4088-5544-7(5), 9781408855447, Bloomsbury USA Childrens) Bloomsbury Publishing USA.

Berk, Sheryl & Berk, Carrie. Icing on the Cake. 2013. (Cupcake Club Ser.: 4). (ENG.). 160p. (J). (gr. 3-6). pap. 6.99 (978-1-4022-8327-7(X), Sourcebooks Jabberwocky) Sourcebooks, Inc.

Bester, Maryanne. The Long Trousers. Bester, Shayle, illus. 2009. (Cool Nguni Ser.). (ENG.). 32p. (J). (gr. 2-4). pap. 12.00 (978-1-77009-499-4(7)) Jacana Media ZAF. Dist: Independent Pubs. Group.

Birchall, Katy. The It Girl. 2016. (It Girl Ser.: 1). (ENG., Illus.). 352p. (J). (gr. 4-8). 16.99 (978-1-4814-6362-1(4), Aladdin) Simon & Schuster Children's Publishing.

Boat, Patty. A Disappointing Homecoming: (A Soldier's Story), 1 vol. 2009. 158p. pap. 24.95 (978-1-61546-997-0(4)) PublishAmerica, Inc.

Bottner, Barbara. Flower Girl, 0 vols. Grier, Laura, illus. Grier, Laura, photos by. 2012. (ENG.). 32p. (J). (gr. k-3). 16.99 (978-0-7614-6119-7(1), 9780761461197, Amazon Children's Publishing) Amazon Publishing.

Bower, Gary. The Person I Marry. Bower, Jan, illus. 2008. 32p. (J). pap. 11.99 (978-0-9704621-7-6(4)) Storybook Meadow Publishing.

Bradbury, Bianca. Flight into Spring. 2005. (Sally (Bethlehem Books) Ser.). 184p. (YA). (gr. 7). per. 11.95 (978-1-932350-01-2(2)) Bethlehem Bks.

Bradley, Debby. Sophie Wonders about Marriage. Guzman, Lula, illus. 2013. (Sophie Wonders about the Sacraments Ser.). (ENG.). 31p. (J). pap. 4.99 (978-0-7648-2351-0(5)) Liguori Pubns.

Brandon, Demi. Princess Shakina's Locks. 2007. 48p. per. 16.95 (978-1-4241-7195-8(4)) America Star Bks.

Bronte, Jules. The Royal Wedding Adventure. 2012. (Illus.). 188p. pap. (978-1-908804-01-3(7)) Bingham Mayne & Smith, Ltd.

Buehner, Caralyn & Buehner, Mark. Fanny's Dream. Buehner, Caralyn & Buehner, Mark, illus. 2003. (ENG., Illus.). 32p. (J). (gr. k-3). 7.99 (978-0-14-250060-6(7), Puffin Books) Penguin Young Readers Group.

Bunting, Eve. My Mom's Wedding. Papp, Lisa, illus. 2006. (ENG.). 32p. (J). (gr. k-6). 16.95 (978-1-58536-288-2(3)) Sleeping Bear Pr.

Burgis, Stephanie. Renegade Magic. 2012. (Kat, Incorrigible Ser.: 2). (ENG., Illus.). 336p. (J). (gr. 5-9). 16.99 (978-1-4169-9449-7(1), Atheneum Bks. for Young Readers) Simon & Schuster Children's Publishing.

—Stolen Magic. (Kat, Incorrigible Ser.: 3). (ENG., Illus.). 400p. (YA). (gr. 5-8). 2014. pap. 7.99 (978-1-4169-9452-7(1)) 2013. 17.99 (978-1-4169-9451-0(3), Atheneum Bks. for Young Readers) Simon & Schuster Children's Publishing.

Bursting at the Seams. 2014. (Sew Zoey Ser.: 10). (ENG., Illus.). 176p. (J). (gr. 3-7). pap. 6.99 (978-1-4814-1964-2(1), Simon Spotlight) Simon Spotlight.

Cabot, Meg. Royal Wedding Disaster: From the Notebooks of a Middle School Princess. 2016. (From the Notebooks of a Middle School Princess Ser.). (ENG., Illus.). 288p. (J). 16.99 (978-1-250-06604-6(2), 9781250066046) Feiwel & Friends.

Cadell, Ava. NeuroLoveology: The Power to Mindful Love & Sex. 2014. (ENG.). 310p. pap. 14.99 (978-1-4976-6112-7(9)) Open Road Integrated Media, Inc.

Caletti, Deb. The Story of Us. (ENG.). 400p. (YA). (gr. 7). 2013. pap. 9.99 (978-1-4424-2347-3(1)) 2012. 16.99 (978-1-4424-2346-6(3)) Simon Pulse. (Simon Pulse).

Capucilli, Alyssa Satin. Katy Duck, Flower Girl. Cole, Henry, illus. 2013. (Katy Duck Ser.). (ENG.). 24p. (J). (gr. -1-1). 16.99 (978-1-4424-7279-2(0)); pap. 3.99 (978-1-4424-7278-5(2)) Simon Spotlight. (Simon Spotlight).

Carter, Caela. My Best Friend, Maybe. 2014. (ENG.). 352p. (YA). (gr. 9). 17.99 (978-1-59990-970-7(7), 9781599909707, Bloomsbury USA Childrens) Bloomsbury Publishing USA.

Cass, Kiera. The Elite. (Selection Ser.: 2). (ENG.). (YA). (gr. 8). 2014. 352p. pap. 9.99 (978-0-06-205997-0(1)) 2013. 336p. 17.99 (978-0-06-205996-3(3)) HarperCollins Pubs. (HarperTeen).

—LA ÉLITE. 2013. (SPA.). 224p. pap. 20.95 (978-84-9918-613-9(0)) Roca Editorial ESP. Dist: Spanish Pubs., LLC.

—La Elite. 2017. (SPA.). 224p. (YA). (gr. 7-12). pap. 12.95 **(978-84-16240-61-6(2))** Roca Bolsillo ESP. Dist: Spanish Pubs., LLC.

—The Elite. 2014. (Selection Ser.: 2). (YA). lib. bdg. 20.85 (978-0-606-35489-9(1)) Turtleback Bks.

—Happily Ever After. 2015. (Selection Novella Ser.). (ENG., Illus.). (YA). 416p. (gr. 8). 18.99 (978-0-06-241408-3(9), HarperTeen); 320p. (978-0-00-814366-4(8)) HarperCollins Pubs.

—Happily Ever After: Companion to the Selection Series. 2016. (Selection Ser.). (YA). lib. bdg. 20.85 (978-0-606-38919-8(9)) Turtleback Bks.

—The Heir. 2015. (ENG.). 368p. (YA). (Selection Ser.: 4). (gr. 8). 18.99 (978-0-06-234985-9(6), HarperTeen); pap. (978-0-06-239130-8(5)) HarperCollins Pubs.

—The One. (Selection Ser.: 3). (ENG.). (gr. 8). 2015. 368p. (YA). pap. 9.99 (978-0-06-206000-6(7)) 2014. 352p. (J). 17.99 (978-0-06-205999-4(8)) HarperCollins Pubs. (HarperTeen).

—The Selection. (Selection Ser.: 1). (ENG.). (YA). (gr. 8). 2013. 352p. pap. 9.99 (978-0-06-205994-9(7)) 2012. 336p. 17.99 (978-0-06-205993-2(9)) HarperCollins Pubs. (HarperTeen).

—The Selection, 1. (ENG.). 272p. pap. (978-0-00-746669-6(2), HarperCollins Children's Bks.) HarperCollins Pubs. Ltd.

—The Selection. 2013. (Selection Ser.: 1). (YA). lib. bdg. 20.85 (978-0-606-35488-2(3)) Turtleback Bks.

—The Selection Stories: The Prince & the Guard. 2014. (Selection Ser.). (ENG.). 240p. (J). (gr. 8). pap. 9.99 (978-0-06-231832-9(2)) HarperCollins Pubs.

Chambers, Pamela G. My Mommy's Getting Married. Stewart, Muriel, illus. 2009. 32p. (gr. -1-3). 17.95 (978-0-9799487-0-1(3)) Infinity Publishing Co.

Childs, Karin Alfelt. The Balm of Gilead. 2007. 356p. (YA). 15.95 (978-0-9748423-7-0(0)) Fountain Publishing.

Chokshi, Roshani. The Star-Touched Queen. Rothschild, Eileen, ed. 2017. (Star-Touched Ser.). (ENG.). 368p. (YA). pap. 10.99 (978-1-250-10020-7(8), 9781250100207, St. Martin's Griffin) St. Martin's Pr.

—The Star-Touched Queen. 2016. (ENG.). 352p. (YA). (gr. 9). 18.99 (978-1-250-08547-4(0), 9781250085474, St. Martin's Griffin) St. Martin's Pr.

Chopin, Kate. The Awakening: An Icelandic Classic. Davis, Stephen, illus. 2014. (American Classics Ser.). (ENG.). 64p. pap. 6.95 (978-1-906230-78-4(1)) Real Reads Ltd. GBR. Dist: Casemate Pubs. & Bk. Distributors, LLC.

Cleary, Beverly. Sister of the Bride. 2007. (ENG., Illus.). 272p. (J). (gr. 5-18). pap. 9.99 (978-0-380-72807-7(9)) HarperCollins Pubs.

Coe, Mary E. The Prince of Betherland. 2008. 117p. 24.95 (978-0-557-03112-2(5)) Lulu Pr., Inc.

—The Prince of Betherland A Wonderful World of Fantasy. 2009. 66p. pap. 9.95 (978-0-557-08499-9(7)) Lulu Pr., Inc.

—The Prince of Betherland a Wonderful World of Fantasy. 2009. 112p. pap. 9.95 (978-0-557-09297-0(3)) Lulu Pr., Inc.

Cohn, Rachel. Two Steps Forward. 2013. (ENG., Illus.). 240p. (YA). (gr. 7). pap. 11.99 (978-1-4424-9615-6(0), Simon & Schuster Bks. For Young Readers) Simon & Schuster Bks. For Young Readers.

Condie, Ally. Crossed. 2013. (Matched Ser.: 2). (ENG.). 400p. (YA). (gr. 7). pap. 9.99 (978-0-14-242171-0(5), Speak) Penguin Publishing Group.

—Crossed, 2 vols. 2011. (Matched Ser.: 2). (ENG.). 384p. (YA). (gr. 7-18). 17.99 (978-0-525-42365-2(6), Dutton Books for Young Readers) Penguin Young Readers Group.

—Crossed. l.t. ed. 2011. (Matched Trilogy: Bk. 2). (ENG.). 448p. (J). 23.99 (978-1-4104-4325-0(6)) Thorndike Pr.

—Crossed. 2013. (Matched Trilogy Ser.: 2). lib. bdg. 20.85 (978-0-606-26634-5(8), Turtleback) Turtleback Bks.

—Juntos. 2011. (Vintage Espanol Ser.).Tr. of Matched. (SPA.). 352p. (YA). (gr. 7). pap. 10.95 (978-0-307-94778-9(5), Vintage Espanol) Knopf Doubleday Publishing Group.

—Juntos. 2011.Tr. of Matched. (SPA.). lib. bdg. 22.05 (978-0-606-26417-4(5), Turtleback) Turtleback Bks.

—Matched. 2009. (Matched Trilogy: Bk. 1). 11.04 (978-0-7848-3716-0(3), Everbind) Marco Bk. Co.

—Matched. (Matched Ser.: 1). (ENG.). (YA). (gr. 7-18). 2011. 416p. 9.99 (978-0-14-241977-9(X), Speak) 2010. 384p. 17.99 (978-0-525-42364-5(8), Dutton Books for Young Readers) Penguin Young Readers Group.

—Matched. 2011. pap. (978-0-545-39990-6(4)) Scholastic, Inc.

—Matched. l.t. ed. 2011. (Matched Trilogy: Bk. 1). (ENG.). 450p. 23.99 (978-1-4104-3954-3(2)) Thorndike Pr.

—Matched. 2011. (Matched Trilogy Ser.: 1). lib. bdg. 20.85 (978-0-606-23140-4(4), Turtleback) Turtleback Bks.

—Reached. 2012. (Matched Ser.: 3). (ENG.). 528p. (YA). (gr. 7-18). 17.99 (978-0-525-42366-9(4), Dutton Books for Young Readers) Penguin Young Readers Group.

—Reached. l.t. ed. 2012. (Matched Trilogy: Bk. 3). (ENG.). 614p. 23.99 (978-1-4104-5366-2(9)) Thorndike Pr.

Cook, Eileen. Unraveling Isobel. 2012. (ENG.). 320p. (YA). (gr. 9). pap. 9.99 (978-1-4424-1328-3(X), Simon Pulse) Simon Pulse.

—Wishes for Beginners. 2011. (Fourth Grade Fairy Ser.: 2). (ENG.). 160p. (J). (gr. 3-7). pap. 6.99 (978-1-4169-9812-9(8), Aladdin) Simon & Schuster Children's Publishing.

Cooper, Floyd. The Ring Bearer. Cooper, Floyd, illus. 2017. (ENG., Illus.). 32p. (J). (gr. -1-2). 16.99 (978-0-399-16740-9(4), Philomel Bks.) Penguin Young Readers Group.

Couloumbis, Audrey. Lexie. Denos, Julia, illus. 2012. (ENG.). 208p. (J). (gr. 3-7). pap. 6.99 (978-0-375-85633-4(1), Yearling) Random Hse. Children's Bks.

Coven, Wanda. Heidi Heckelbeck Is a Flower Girl. Burris, Priscilla, illus. 2014. (Heidi Heckelbeck Ser.: 11). (ENG.). 128p. (J). (gr. k-2). pap. 4.99 (978-1-4814-0498-3(9), Little Simon) Little Simon.

Cushman, Karen. El Libro de Catherine. 2003.Tr. of Catherine, Called Birdy. (SPA.). 237p. (978-84-236-4600-5(9), ED8017) Edebé ESP. Dist: Lectorum Pubns., Inc.

Daly, Catherine R. Too Many Blooms. 2011. (Petal Pushers Ser.: 1). (ENG.). 192p. (J). (gr. 3-7). pap. 5.99 (978-0-545-21450-6(5), Scholastic Paperbacks) Scholastic, Inc.

Danziger, Paula. Forever Amber Brown. 2008. (Amber Brown Ser.: 5). (ENG.). 128p. (J). (gr. 2-5). 5.99 (978-0-14-241201-5(5), Puffin Books) Penguin Young Readers Group.

Danziger, Paula, et al. Amber Brown Is Tickled Pink. Ross, Tony, illus. 2013. (Amber Brown Ser.: 10). (ENG.). 176p. (J). (gr. 2-5). pap. 5.99 (978-0-14-242757-6(8), Puffin Books) Penguin Young Readers Group.

Danzinger, Paula, et al. Amber Brown Is Tickled Pink. Ross, Tony, illus. 2012. (Amber Brown Ser.). (ENG.). 176p. (J). (gr. 3-7). E-Book (978-1-101-58155-1(7), Puffin Books) Penguin Young Readers Group.

Daswani, Kavita. Lovetorn. 2012. (ENG.). 256p. (YA). (gr. 8). 17.99 (978-0-06-167311-5(0), HarperTeen) HarperCollins Pubs.

Day, Susie. Serafina67 - "Urgently Requires Life" 2010. (ENG.). 256p. (J). (gr. 7-12). 8.99 (978-0-545-07352-3(9), Scholastic Paperbacks) Scholastic, Inc.

de Brunhoff, Laurent & Rose, Phyllis. Babar's Celesteville Games. 2011. (ENG., Illus.). 48p. (J). (gr. k-2). 18.95 (978-1-4197-0006-4(5), Abrams Bks. for Young Readers) Abrams, Inc.

Demas, Corinne. Returning to Shore. 2014. 208p. (YA). (gr. 6-12). 17.95 (978-1-4677-1328-3(7), Carolrhoda Lab™) Lerner Publishing Group.

DeStefano, Lauren. Wither, 9 vols. (Chemical Garden Ser.: 1). (YA). 90.75 (978-1-4561-2060-3(3)); 1.25 (978-1-4561-2064-1(6)); 256.75 (978-1-4561-2059-7(X)); 2011. 120.75 (978-1-4561-2063-4(8)); 2011. 122.75 (978-1-4561-2061-0(1)) Recorded Bks., Inc.

—Wither. 2011. (Chemical Garden Trilogy Ser.: 1). (ENG.). (YA). (gr. 9). 384p. pap. 10.99 (978-1-4424-0906-4(1)); 368p. 19.99 (978-1-4424-0905-7(3)) Simon & Schuster Bks. For Young Readers. (Simon & Schuster Bks. For Young Readers).

Dickerson, Melanie. The Silent Songbird, 1 vol. 2016. (ENG.). 304p. (YA). 14.99 (978-0-7180-2631-8(4)) Nelson, Thomas Inc.

Dijkstra, Lida. Little Mouse. Grobler, Piet, illus. 2004. (ENG.). 32p. (J). 15.95 (978-1-932425-06-2(3), Lemniscaat) Boyds Mills Pr.

Dillon-Hreha, Denise. The Wedding of Q & U. 2007. (Illus.). 48p. per. 16.99 (978-1-4259-8040-5(6)) AuthorHouse.

Disney Book Group. Tangled & Tangled Ever after Read-Along Storybook & CD Bindup. Disney Storybook Art Team, illus. 2017. (Read-Along Storybook & CD Ser.). (ENG.). 64p. (J). (gr. 1-3). pap. 8.99 **(978-1-4847-8780-9(3))** Disney Pr.

Disney Book Group Staff & Bergen, Lara. Tangled Ever After. Disney Storybook Artists Staff, illus. 2012. (Read-Along Storybook & CD Ser.). (ENG.). 32p. (J). (gr. -1 — 1). pap. 6.99 (978-1-4231-6582-8(9)) Disney Pr.

Dolamore, Jaclyn. Dark Metropolis. 2014. (ENG., Illus.). 304p. (YA). (gr. 7-12). 17.99 (978-1-4231-6332-9(X)) Hyperion Bks. for Children.

Donaldson, Julia. The Scarecrows' Wedding. Scheffler, Axel, illus. 2014. (ENG.). 32p. (J). (gr. -1-3). 17.99 (978-0-545-72606-1(9), Levine, Arthur A. Bks.) Scholastic, Inc.

Doty, Linda. Hydrangea Hill: A New Home for Amy Manchester. 2008. 182p. pap. 24.95 (978-1-60610-840-6(9)) America Star Bks.

Doudna, Kelly. Crab Cakes, 1 vol. Haberstroh, Anne, illus. 2007. (Critter Chronicles Ser.). (ENG.). 24p. (J). (gr. k-3). lib. bdg. 24.21 (978-1-59928-434-7(0), SandCastle) ABDO Publishing Co.

DuJardin, Rosamond. Wedding in the Family. 2003. (YA). pap. 12.95 (978-1-930009-72-1(0), 800-691-7779) Image Cascade Publishing.

Dunkle, Clare B. Close Kin. 2nd rev. ed. 2006. (Hollow Kingdom Trilogy Ser.: 2). (ENG.). 224p. (J). (gr. 6-9). pap. 11.99 (978-0-8050-8109-1(7), 9780805081091, Holt, Henry & Co. Bks. For Young Readers) Holt, Henry & Co.

—In the Coils of the Snake. 3rd rev. ed. 2006. (Hollow Kingdom Trilogy Ser.: 3). (ENG.). 240p. (J). (gr. 6-9). pap. 14.99 (978-0-8050-8110-7(0), 9780805081107, Holt, Henry & Co. Bks. For Young Readers) Holt, Henry & Co.

Dyan, Penelope. Someone's Getting Married! 2011. 34p. pap. 11.95 (978-1-935630-64-7(4)) Bellissima Publishing, LLC.

Edwards, Meinir Wyn. Rhys & Meinir. Wade, Gini, illus. 2007. (ENG.). 24p. (J). pap. 4.95 (978-1-84771-020-8(4)) Y Lolfa GBR. Dist: Dufour Editions, Inc.

Elias, Megan J. Stir It Up: Home Economics in American Culture. 2010. (ENG., Illus.). 240p. (C). pap. 22.50 (978-0-8122-2121-3(4)) Univ. of Pennsylvania Pr.

Elliott, Rebecca. A Woodland Wedding. Elliott, Rebecca, illus. 2016. (Owl Diaries: 3). (ENG., Illus.). 80p. (J). (gr. k-2). 15.99 (978-0-545-82558-0(X)) Scholastic, Inc.

English, Karen. Nadia's Hands. Weiner, Jonathan, illus. 2009. (ENG.). 32p. (J). pap. 9.95 (978-1-59078-784-7(6)) Boyds Mills Pr.

—Wedding Drama. Freeman, Laura, illus. 2013. (ENG.). 112p. (J). (gr. 1-4). pap. 5.99 (978-0-544-00324-8(1)) Houghton Mifflin Harcourt Publishing Co.

Essama, Molly Jane. The Prince & the Three Ugly Hags. 2010. 28p. pap. 16.95 (978-1-4490-5587-5(7)) AuthorHouse.

Fantaskey, Beth. Jessica's Guide to Dating on the Dark Side. 2010. (ENG., Illus.). 384p. (YA). (gr. 9-18). pap. 8.99 (978-0-547-25940-6(9)) Houghton Mifflin Harcourt Publishing Co.

Fastje, Shanaya B. Mystery School: Monday Sleepover Disaster. 2009. 24p. pap. 12.99 (978-1-4490-0679-2(5)) AuthorHouse.

Finley, Martha. Elsie at Home. 2006. 27.95 (978-1-4218-2989-0(4)); pap. 12.95 (978-1-4218-3089-6(2)) 1st World Publishing, Inc.

—Elsie at Home. 2007. (ENG.). 152p. pap. 19.99 (978-1-4346-2866-4(3)); 168p. pap. 21.99 (978-1-4346-2901-2(5)) Creative Media Partners, LLC.

—Elsie's Young Folks. 2008. 296p. 34.99 (978-1-58960-287-8(0)) Sovereign Grace Pubs., Inc.

Fisch, Sholly, et al. The Bride & the Bold. 2015. (All-New Batman: the Brave & the Bold Ser.). (ENG., Illus.). 32p. (gr. 2-3). lib. bdg. 22.60 (978-1-4342-9661-0(X)) Stone Arch Bks.

Francoise. Fanchette & Jeannot: A Little Story with Pictures. 2011. 26p. 35.95 (978-1-258-07322-0(6)) Literary Licensing, LLC.

Frederick, Heather Vogel. Wish You Were Eyre. 2013. (Mother-Daughter Book Club Ser.). (ENG.). 480p. (J). (gr. 4-9). pap. 7.99 (978-1-4424-3065-5(6), Simon & Schuster Bks. For Young Readers) Simon & Schuster Bks. For Young Readers.

Friedman, Laurie. Heart to Heart with Mallory. Pollak, Barbara, illus. (Mallory Ser.: 6). (ENG.). 160p. (J). (gr. 2-5). 2007. per. 5.95 (978-0-8225-7133-9(1), First Avenue Editions) 2006. lib. bdg. 15.95 (978-1-57505-932-7(0), Twenty-First Century Bks.) Lerner Publishing Group.

—Mallory on Board. 2008. pap. 34.95 (978-0-8225-9440-6(4)) Lerner Publishing Group.

—Mallory on Board. Pollak, Barbara, illus. 2007. (Mallory Ser.: 7). (ENG.). 176p. (J). (gr. 2-5). 15.95 (978-0-8225-6194-1(8), Carolrhoda Bks.) Lerner Publishing Group.

—A Style All Her Own. Watts, Sharon, illus. 2005. 32p. (J). (gr. -1-3). lib. bdg. 15.95 (978-1-57505-599-2(6)) Lerner Publishing Group.

Friesen, Gayle. For Now. 2007. (ENG.). 248p. (J). (gr. 5-9). 7.95 (978-1-55453-133-2(0)) Kids Can Pr., Ltd. CAN. Dist: Hachette Bk. Group.

Gail, Becky. How the Little White Monkey Became a Woman. 2008. 19p. pap. 24.95 (978-1-60563-471-5(9)) America Star Bks.

Gallagher, Diana G. Bad Luck Bridesmaid: The Complicated Life of Claudia Cristina Cortez, 1 vol. Garvey, Brann, illus. 2009. (Claudia Cristina Cortez Ser.). (ENG.). 88p. (gr. 2-3). 26.65 (978-1-4342-1573-4(3), Claudia Cristina Cortez) Stone Arch Bks.

Garber, Stephanie. Caraval. 2017. (SPA.). 432p. pap. 16.95 **(978-607-07-4044-2(0))** Editorial Planeta, S. A. ESP. Dist: Two Rivers Distribution.

—Caraval. 2017. (Caraval Ser.). (ENG.). (YA). 416p. 18.99 (978-1-250-09525-1(5), 9781250095251); (gr. 8-12). pap. 11.99 **(978-1-250-14149-1(4))** Flatiron Bks.

Godwin, Laura. The Flower Girl. Wallace, John, illus. 2017. (ENG.). 32p. (J). (gr. -1-k). 12.99 (978-1-368-00828-0(3)) Hyperion Bks. for Children.

Graff, Lisa. Lost in the Sun. 2015. (ENG.). 304p. (J). (gr. 5). 16.99 (978-0-399-16406-4(5), Philomel Bks.) Penguin Young Readers Group.

—Lost in the Sun. 2016. lib. bdg. 19.65 (978-0-606-38835-1(4)) Turtleback Bks.

Griffith, Linda Hill, illus. Best Ever Ring Bearer. 2010. (ENG.). 24p. 10.99 (978-1-4022-3818-5(5)) Sourcebooks, Inc.

—Most Special Flower Girl. 2010. (ENG.). 24p. 10.99 (978-1-4022-3817-8(7)) Sourcebooks, Inc.

Grogan, John. Thanks, Mom & Dad! Cowdrey, Richard, illus. 2011. (Marley Ser.). (ENG.). 24p. (J). (gr. -1-2). pap. 3.99 (978-0-06-185381-4(X), HarperFestival) HarperCollins Pubs.

Haines, Lise. Girl in the Arena. (ENG.). 336p. (YA). (gr. 9-13). 2010. pap. 9.99 (978-1-59990-521-1(3), 9781599905211) 2009. 16.99 (978-1-59990-372-9(5), 9781599903729) Bloomsbury Publishing USA. (Bloomsbury USA Childrens).

Hamilton, Elizabeth L. Date with Responsibility. 2004. (Character-in-Action Ser.: No. 2). (Illus.). 384p. (YA). per. 19.95 (978-0-9713749-0-4(2), Character-in-Action) Quiet Impact, Inc.

Hannigan, Kate. Winter Wonders. Hughes, Brooke Boynton, illus. 2016. (Cupcake Cousins Ser.: Bk. 3). (ENG.). 240p. (J). (gr. 3-7). 16.99 (978-1-4847-1663-2(9)) Hyperion Bks. for Children.

Hargreaves, Roger. Little Miss Princess & the Very Special Wedding. 2011. (Mr. Men & Little Miss Ser.). (ENG., Illus.). 24p. (J). (gr. -1-3). (978-1-4052-5996-5(5)) Egmont Bks., Ltd.

Harper, Charise Mericle & Malk, Steven. Just Grace & the Flower Girl Power. (Just Grace Ser.). (ENG., Illus.). 208p. (J). (gr. 1-4). 2013. pap. 5.99 (978-0-544-02283-6(1)) 2012. 15.99 (978-0-547-57720-3(6)) Houghton Mifflin Harcourt Publishing Co.

Hartt-Sussman, Heather. Nana's Getting Married. Graham, Georgia, illus. 2010. (ENG.). 32p. (J). (gr. -1-1). 17.95 (978-0-88776-911-5(X), Tundra Bks.) Tundra Bks. CAN. Dist: Penguin Random Hse. LLC.

Hayes, Rosemary. Payback. 2009. (ENG.). 208p. (J). (gr. 7-10). pap. 8.95 (978-1-84507-935-2(3), Frances Lincoln)

Quarto Publishing Group UK GBR. Dist: Hachette Bk. Group.
Henkes, Kevin. El Gran Dia de Lily, 1 vol. Posada, Maria Candelaria, tr. from ENG. Henkes, Kevin, illus. 2008. (SPA., Illus.). 40p. (J). (gr. -1-3). 17.99 *(978-0-06-136316-0(2))* HarperCollins Pubs.
—Lilly's Big Day. Henkes, Kevin, illus. (Illus.). 40p. (J). (gr. -1-3). 2014. (ENG.). pap. 6.99 *(978-0-06-231358-4(4))* 2006. (ENG., 17.99 *(978-0-06-074236-2(4))* 2006. lib. bdg. 18.89 *(978-0-06-074237-9(2))* HarperCollins Pubs. (Greenwillow Bks.).
—Lilly's Big Day. 2014. (J). lib. bdg. 17.20 *(978-0-606-35472-1(7))* Turtleback Bks.
Hermes, Patricia. Emma Dilemma, the Nanny, & the Wedding, 0 vols. 2012. (Emma Dilemma Ser.: 7). (ENG.). 144p. (J). (gr. 3-6). 16.99 *(978-0-7614-6210-1(4)*, 9780761462101, Amazon Children's Publishing) Amazon Publishing.
Hicks, Betty. Out of Order. 2007. (ENG.). 176p. (J). (gr. 3-7). pap. 14.99 *(978-0-312-37355-9(4)*, 9780312373559) Square Fish.
Hidaka, Banri. V. B. Rose Volume 10. 2010. (Illus.). 208p. pap. 10.99 *(978-1-4278-1160-8(1))* TOKYOPOP, Inc.
—V. B. Rose Volume 9. 2010. (Illus.). 192p. pap. 10.99 *(978-1-4278-0927-8(5))* TOKYOPOP, Inc.
Hidier, Tanuja Desai. Bombay Blues. 2014. (ENG.). 560p. (J). (gr. 9). 18.99 *(978-0-545-38478-0(8)*, PUSH) Scholastic, Inc.
Hingoro, Samira, creator. A Marriage Proposal. 2003. (YA). per. 12.95 *(978-0-9743167-0-3(9))* Faith Pubns.
Hirahara, Naomi. 1001 Cranes. 2009. (ENG.). 240p. (J). (gr. 3-7). 7.99 *(978-0-440-42234-1(5)*, Yearling) Random Hse. Children's Bks.
Hodge, Rosamund. Cruel Beauty. (ENG.). (YA). (gr. 8). 2015. 368p. pap. 9.99 *(978-0-06-222474-3(3))* 2014. 352p. 17.99 *(978-0-06-222473-6(5))* HarperCollins Pubs.
Hoffman, Amalia. Klezmer Bunch. 2009. 36p. 15.95 *(978-965-229-447-0(0))* Gefen Publishing Hse., Ltd ISR. Dist: Strauss Consultants.
Hoffman, Mary. Bravo, Grace! 2011. (ENG.). 112p. (J). (gr. 3-7). 5.99 *(978-0-14-241850-5(1)*, Puffin Books) Penguin Young Readers Group.
Holm, Jennifer L. Middle School Is Worse Than Meatloaf: A Year Told Through Stuff. Castaldi, Elicia, illus. 2011. (ENG.). 128p. (J). (gr. 3-7). pap. 8.99 *(978-1-4424-3663-3(8)*, Atheneum Bks. for Young Readers) Simon & Schuster Children's Publishing.
Hook, Jacqueline A. You're Going to Be a Flower Girl. 2005. (J). per. *(978-0-9664783-3-4(9))* Jacqueline Beverly Hills.
Hooper, Mary. Katie: The Revolting Bridesmaid. Vayssiere, Frederique, illus. 2007. (Katie Ser.). (ENG.). 80p. (J). (gr. 2-4). per. 8.95 *(978-0-7475-8611-1(X))* Bloomsbury Publishing Plc GBR. Dist: Independent Pubs. Group.
—The Revolting Wedding. Vayssiere, Frederique, illus. 2007. (Katie Ser.). (ENG.). 96p. (J). (gr. 2-4). per. 8.95 *(978-0-7475-8612-8(8))* Bloomsbury Publishing Plc GBR. Dist: Independent Pubs. Group.
Howard, Annabelle. As the Mayan Calendars Turn. 2005. (J). pap. *(978-1-4108-4223-7(1))* Benchmark Education Co.
Howard, Elizabeth Fitzgerald. Flower Girl Butterflies. Kromer, Christiane, illus. 2004. 32p. (J). 16.89 *(978-0-688-17810-9(3))* HarperCollins Pubs.
Howitt, Mary Botham. Strive & Thrive a Tale by Mary Howitt. 2006. 180p. per. 18.99 *(978-1-4255-1426-6(X))* Michigan Publishing.
Ignatow, Amy. Love & Other Fiascos with Lydia Goldblatt & Julie Graham-Chang, Bk. 6. 2013. (Popularity Papers). (ENG., Illus.). 208p. (J). (gr. 3-7). 16.95 *(978-1-4197-0859-6(7)*, Amulet Bks.) Abrams, Inc.
Ingalls, Laura. Los Cuatro Primeros Años. 2006. (Little House Bks.). (SPA., Illus.). 126p. (gr. 5-8). pap. 12.99 *(978-84-279-3259-3(6))* Lectorum Pubns., Inc.
Johnson, Annabel & Johnson, Edgar. Wilderness Bride. 2003. 232p. 12.95 *(978-0-9714612-7-7(9))* Green Mansion Pr. LLC.
Jones, Faith. Sprouting Wings, 1 vol. 2010. 96p. pap. 16.95 *(978-1-4489-6366-9(4))* PublishAmerica, Inc.
Jones, Jen. Maren's New Family. Franco, Paula, illus. 2015. (Sleepover Girls Ser.). (ENG.). 128p. (gr. 3-5). lib. bdg. 22.65 *(978-1-4965-0540-8(9))* Stone Arch Bks.
Joyce, Melaine. Cinderella. 2009. (Fairydust Fairytales Ser.). (ENG.). 5p. (J). (gr. -1-k). bds. 6.95 *(978-1-84696-964-5(6)*, TickTock Books) Octopus Publishing Group GBR. Dist: Independent Pubs. Group.
Katherine's Story 1848. 2014. (Secrets of the Manor Ser.: 4). (ENG., Illus.). 160p. (J). (gr. 3-7). pap. 6.99 *(978-1-4814-1843-0(2)*, Simon Spotlight) Simon Spotlight.
Katies Choice. 2005. (YA). per. *(978-1-59872-217-8(4))* Instant Pub.
Kaupp, Rosemarie. The Amberella Tales: Amberella & Double Double Trouble. 2013. 144p. (gr. 2-4). 20.77 *(978-1-4669-9233-7(6))*; pap. 10.77 *(978-1-4669-9234-4(4))* Trafford Publishing.
Keene, Carolyn. Wedding Day Disaster. Pamintuan, Macky, illus. 2008. (Nancy Drew & the Clue Crew Ser.: 17). (ENG.). 96p. (J). (gr. 1-4). pap. 5.99 *(978-1-4169-6778-1(8)*, Aladdin) Simon & Schuster Children's Publishing.
Kelly, Jamie & Benton, Jim. Never Underestimate Your Dumbness. 2008. (Dear Dumb Diary Ser.). (Illus.). 150p. (gr. 4-7). 16.00 *(978-0-7569-8814-2(4))* Perfection Learning Corp.
Kindl, Patrice & Wells, Rosemary. A School for Brides. 2015. (ENG.). 272p. (J). (gr. 7). bds. 17.99 *(978-0-670-78608-4(X)*, Viking Books for Young Readers) Penguin Young Readers Group.
Kiser, Dolores White. The Marriage of White Rabbit. 2005. (J). 10.00 net. *(978-0-9766648-3-3(6))* White Kiser, Dolores.
Kline, Suzy. Horrible Harry & the Wedding Spies. Wummer, Amy, illus. 2016. (Horrible Harry Ser.: 32). (ENG.). 80p. (J). (gr. 2-5). 4.99 *(978-0-14-750968-0(8)*, Puffin Books) Penguin Young Readers Group.
—Horrible Harry & the Wedding Spies. 2016. (Horrible Harry Ser.: 32). lib. bdg. 14.75 *(978-0-606-38389-9(1))* Turtleback Bks.
Konigsburg, E. L. Journey to an 800 Number. 2008. (ENG.). 160p. (J). (gr. 4-8). pap. 6.99 *(978-1-4169-5875-8(4)*, Atheneum Bks. for Young Readers) Simon & Schuster Children's Publishing.
Korba, Joanna. Rough-Face Girl: A Native American Cinderella Tale. 2006. (J). pap. *(978-1-4108-6163-4(5))* Benchmark Education Co.
Kraus, Joanna H. A Night of Tamales & Roses. Caravela, Elena, illus. 2007. (ENG.). 32p. (J). (gr. -1-3). 15.95 *(978-0-9726614-4-7(1))* Shenanigan Bks.
Krider, Dave. Do Animals Go to Heaven?, 1 vol. 2009. 49p. pap. 16.95 *(978-1-61546-049-6(7))* America Star Bks.
Leavitt, Lindsey. The Chapel Wars. 2014. (ENG.). 304p. (YA). (gr. 7). 17.99 *(978-1-59990-788-8(7)*, 9781599907888, Bloomsbury USA Childrens) Bloomsbury Publishing USA.
Lee, Kyanna Shanae. Stepdad? No Thanks...! 2008. 60p. pap. 19.95 *(978-1-60563-422-7(0))* America Star Bks.
Lee, Y. S. Rivals in the City. 2015. (Agency Ser.). (ENG.). 304p. (YA). (gr. 7). 16.99 *(978-0-7636-5914-1(2))* Candlewick Pr.
Levins, Sandra. Do You Sing Twinkle? A Story about Remarriage & New Family. Langdo, Bryan, illus. 2009. 32p. (J). (gr. -1-3). 14.95 *(978-1-4338-0539-4(1))*; pap. 9.95 *(978-1-4338-0551-6(0))* American Psychological Assn. (Magination Pr.).
Lollino, Jessica. Lily & the Big Italian Wedding. Lollino, Jessica, ed. 2008. (Little Lily Mays Ser.: vol. 2). (ENG., Illus.). 32p. (J). pap. 12.95 *(978-0-9712383-2-9(4))* Culturatti Ink.
Looper, Grace W. Great-Grandpa's Hidden Treasure. 2006. (YA). pap. *(978-1-933523-18-7(2))* Bella Rosa Bks.
Lynne, Kimberlee, illus. The Frog & the Mouse. 2011. (First Steps in Music Ser.). (ENG.). 32p. (J). (gr. k-2). 16.95 *(978-1-57999-802-8(X))* G I A Pubns., Inc.
Lyons, Kelly Starling. Ellen's Broom. Minter, Daniel, illus. 2012. (ENG.). 32p. (J). (gr. k-3). 16.99 *(978-0-399-25003-3(4)*, G.P. Putnam's Sons Books for Young Readers) Penguin Young Readers Group.
MacKenzie, Lachlan. The Duke's Daughter: A Story of Faith & Love. Anderson, Jeff, illus. 2008. (Story Time Ser.). (ENG.). 24p. (J). (gr. -1-3). 7.99 *(978-1-84550-326-0(0)*, de5339b0-1f9f-400d-8814-ce3da22de27c) Christian Focus Pubns. GBR. Dist: Bookmasters Distribution.
Malone, Jen & Nall, Gail. You're Invited Too. 2016. (Mix Ser.). (ENG., Illus.). 304p. (J). (gr. 4-8). pap. 7.99 *(978-1-4814-3199-6(4)*, Aladdin) Simon & Schuster Children's Publishing.
Man-Kong, Mary. Wedding Party! (Barbie) Riley, Kellee, illus. 2013. (Pictureback(R) Ser.). (ENG.). 16p. (J). (gr. -1-2). pap. 3.99 *(978-0-307-93116-0(1)*, Random Hse. Bks. for Young Readers) Random Hse. Children's Bks.
Margolis, Leslie. Girls Acting Catty. (Annabelle Unleashed Ser.). (ENG.). (YA). (gr. 3-6). 2010. 208p. pap. 6.99 *(978-1-59990-520-4(5)*, 9781599905204) 2009. 192p. 15.99 *(978-1-59990-237-1(0)*, 9781599902371) Bloomsbury Publishing USA. (Bloomsbury USA Childrens).
Martin, C. K. Kelly. The Lighter Side of Life & Death. 2010. (YA). pap. *(978-0-375-84590-1(9))* Random Hse. Children's Bks.
Mayer, Pamela. Don't Sneeze at the Wedding. Avilés, Martha, illus. 2013. 32p. 17.95 *(978-1-4677-1641-3(3))*; (ENG.). (J). 7.95 *(978-1-4677-0429-8(6)*, Kar-Ben Publishing) Lerner Publishing Group.
—Don't Sneeze at the Wedding. Aviles, Martha, illus. 2013. (Life Cycle Ser.). (ENG.). 32p. (J). (gr. k-3). lib. bdg. 17.95 *(978-1-4677-0428-1(8)*, Kar-Ben Publishing) Lerner Publishing Group.
McDavid-Jones, Elizabeth. Mystery on Skull Island. 2009. (Mysteries Through Time Ser.). 192p. (YA). (gr. 4-8). 31.95 *(978-1-60754-286-5(2))*; pap. 15.25 *(978-1-60754-302-2(8))* Windmill Bks.
McDougal-Littell Publishing Staff, creator. Picture Bride & Related Readings. 2006. (Literature Connections Ser.). 314p. (gr. 6-12). *(978-0-395-77540-0(X)*, 2-80109) Holt McDougal.
McKay, Hilary. Caddy Ever After. (ENG.). 224p. (J). 2007. (gr. 4-8). per. 6.99 *(978-1-4169-0931-6(1))* 2006. (gr. 5-9). 16.99 *(978-1-4169-0930-9(3))* McElderry, Margaret K. Bks. (McElderry, Margaret K. Bks.).
Mead, Richelle. The Glittering Court. 2016. 416p. (YA). pap. *(978-0-448-49385-5(3)*, Razorbill) Penguin Publishing Group.
—The Glittering Court. (Glittering Court Ser.: 1). (ENG.). (YA). (gr. 7). 2017. 432p. pap. 10.99 *(978-1-59514-842-1(6))* 2016. 416p. 19.99 *(978-1-59514-841-4(8))* Penguin Young Readers Group. (Razorbill).
Meadows, Daisy. Blossom the Flower Girl Fairy. 2016. (Rainbow Magic: Special Edition Ser.). (ENG.). 176p. (J). (gr. 2-5). pap. 6.99 *(978-0-545-85202-9(1)*, Scholastic Paperbacks) Scholastic, Inc.
—Mia the Bridesmaid Fairy. 2010. (Rainbow Magic Ser.). (ENG.). 176p. (J). (gr. 2-5). 6.99 *(978-0-545-20251-0(5)*, Scholastic Paperbacks) Scholastic, Inc.
Mejuto, Eva. Run Pumpkin, Run. 2007. (ENG., Illus.). 36p. (J). 17.95 *(978-84-96788-88-6(1))* OQO, Editora ESP. Dist: Baker & Taylor Bks.
Menon, Sandhya. When Dimple Met Rishi. 2017. (ENG., Illus.). 384p. (YA). (gr. 7). 17.99 ***(978-1-4814-7868-7(0)***, Simon Pulse) Simon Pulse.
Meyer, Stephenie. Breaking Dawn. (Twilight Saga Ser.: 4). (ENG.). 768p. (YA). (gr. 7-17). 2012. mass mkt. 7.99 *(978-0-316-22613-4(0))* 2010. pap. 16.99 *(978-0-316-06793-5(8))* 2008. 22.99 *(978-0-316-06792-8(X)*, Tingley, Megan Bks.)Pt. II. 2012. pap. 14.99 *(978-0-316-22642-4(4))* Little, Brown Bks. for Young Readers.
—Breaking Dawn. 2010. (Twilight Saga Ser.: 4). (YA). lib. bdg. 29.40 *(978-0-606-23108-4(0)*, Turtleback) Turtleback Bks.
Michaelis, Antonia. Tiger Moon. 2009. (ENG.). 480p. (YA). (gr. 7-11). pap. 9.95 *(978-0-8109-4499-2(5)*, Amulet Bks.) Abrams, Inc.
Milan, D. S. A Year of Starless Nights. 2013. 154p. pap. 14.95 *(978-1-62432-012-5(0))* Loose Leaves Publishing.
Milde, Jeanette. Once upon a Wedding. Sandin, Joan, tr. from SWE. 2004. (Illus.). 32p. (J). 15.00 *(978-91-29-66048-7(3))* R & S Bks. SWE. Dist: Macmillan.
Mioche, Hilda. The Paper Doll Wedding. 2017. (Little Golden Book Ser.). (ENG., Illus.). 22p. (J). (gr. -1-2). 5.99 ***(978-0-399-55368-4(1)***, Golden Bks.) Random Hse. Children's Bks.
Minke, Shari. The Airplane Story: A Blended Family's Journey. 2010. pap. 12.99 *(978-1-61579-944-2(3))* Salem Author Services.
Monnar, Ana. Heart of Stone. Michaud, Nancy, illus. 2007. 24p. (J). per. 11.99 *(978-0-9768035-5-3(0))* Readers Are Leaders U.S.A., Inc.
Monstrata, Nessi. Monster High Diaries: Draculaura & the New Stepmomster. 2015. (Monster High Diaries: 1). (ENG.). 160p. (J). (gr. 3-7). 9.99 *(978-0-316-30084-1(5))* Little, Brown Bks. for Young Readers.
Mullarkey, Lisa. A Feast of Fun, 1 vol. Franco, Paula, illus. 2016. (ENG.). 112p. (J). lib. bdg. *(978-1-62402-163-3(8))* Magic Wagon.
Mun-Ensor, Michelle. The Ten Bridesmaids. 2011. 28p. pap. 24.95 *(978-1-4560-9003-6(8))* America Star Bks.
Munsch, Robert. Ribbon Rescue. 2004. (Illus.). (J). (gr. k-3). spiral bd. *(978-0-616-01742-5(1))*; spiral bd. *(978-0-616-01743-2(X))* Canadian National Institute for the Blind/Institut National Canadien pour les Aveugles.
—Ribbon Rescue. 2007. (J). 12.65 *(978-0-7569-7466-4(6))* Perfection Learning Corp.
Naylor, Phyllis Reynolds. I Like Him, He Likes Her: Alice Alone; Simply Alice; Patiently Alice. 2010. (Alice Ser.). (ENG.). 640p. (YA). (gr. 7). pap. 12.99 *(978-1-4424-0978-1(9)*, Atheneum Bks. for Young Readers) Simon & Schuster Children's Publishing.
—Including Alice. 2005. (Alice McKinley Ser.: No. 16). 277p. (J). (gr. 4-7). 13.65 *(978-0-7569-5460-4(6))* Perfection Learning Corp.
Nelson, Mary. Catla & the Vikings, 1 vol. 2012. (ENG.). 192p. (J). (gr. 4-7). pap. 9.95 *(978-1-4598-0057-1(5))* Orca Bk. Pubs. USA.
Newhall, Mary & Campbell, Joanna. Bridal Dreams. 2005. (Thoroughbred Ser.). (Illus.). 163p. (gr. 3-7). 15.00 *(978-0-7569-5359-1(6))* Perfection Learning Corp.
Newman, Lesléa. Donovan's Big Day. Dutton, Mike, illus. 2011. (ENG.). 32p. (J). (gr. -1-2). 15.99 *(978-1-58246-332-2(8)*, Tricycle Pr.) Random Hse. Children's Bks.
Newman, Tracy. Uncle Eli's Wedding. Isik, Semur, illus. 2015. (ENG.). 32p. (J). (gr. -1-3). 16.99 *(978-0-8075-8293-0(X))* Whitman, Albert & Co.
Nickerson, Sara. The Secrets of Blueberries, Brothers, Moose & Me. 2015. (ENG.). 336p. (J). (gr. 5). 16.99 *(978-0-525-42654-7(X)*, Dutton Books for Young Readers) Penguin Young Readers Group.
Nolan, Han. Pregnant Pause. 2012. (ENG.). 352p. (YA). (gr. 9). pap. 8.99 *(978-0-547-85414-4(5))* Houghton Mifflin Harcourt Publishing Co.
North, Laura. The Princess & the Frozen Peas. 2014. (ENG., Illus.). 32p. (J). *(978-0-7787-0446-1(7))*; pap. *(978-0-7787-0481-2(5))* Crabtree Publishing Co.
Ohtaka, Shinobu. The Strongest Bride on Earth, 12 vols. 2012. (Sumomomo, Momomo Ser.: 12). (ENG., Illus.). 240p. (gr. 11-17). pap. 13.00 *(978-0-316-20470-5(6)*, Yen Pr.) Orbit.
Olin, Sean. Reckless Hearts. 2015. (Wicked Games Ser.: 2). (ENG.). 336p. (YA). (gr. 9). 17.99 *(978-0-06-219241-7(8)*, Tegen, Katherine Bks) HarperCollins Pubs.
Oliver, Lauren. Requiem. 2013. (Delirium Trilogy: Bk. 3). (ENG.). 400p. (J). (gr. 9). 18.99 *(978-0-06-201453-5(6))* HarperCollins Pubs.
Onyefulu, Ifeoma. New Shoes for Helen. Onyefulu, Ifeoma, photos by. 2011. (First Experiences Ser.). (ENG., Illus.). 32p. (J). (gr. -1-2). 17.95 *(978-1-84780-128-9(5)*, Frances Lincoln) Quarto Publishing Group UK GBR. Dist: Hachette Bk. Group.
Palmer, Robin. Love You Like a Sister. 2017. (Mix Ser.). (ENG., Illus.). 256p. (J). (gr. 4-8). pap. 7.99 ***(978-1-4814-6642-4(9)***, Aladdin) Simon & Schuster Children's Publishing.
—Sealed with a Kiss, 2 vols., No. 2. 2010. (Yours Truly, Lucy B. Parker Ser.: 2). (ENG.). 224p. (J). (gr. 5-18). 6.99 *(978-0-14-241501-6(4)*, Puffin Books) Penguin Young Readers Group.
—Vote for Me!, 3 vols. 2011. (Yours Truly, Lucy B. Parker Ser.: 3). (ENG.). 224p. (J). (gr. 5-18). 6.99 *(978-0-14-241502-3(2)*, Puffin Books) Penguin Young Readers Group.
Paratore, Coleen Murtagh. The Wedding Planner's Daughter. 2005. (Wedding Planner's Daughter Ser.). (ENG.). 208p. (J). (gr. 3-7). 15.95 *(978-0-689-87340-9(9)*, Simon & Schuster Bks. For Young Readers) Simon & Schuster Bks. For Young Readers.
—Willa by Heart. 2008. (Wedding Planner's Daughter Ser.). (ENG.). 240p. (J). (gr. 3-7). 15.99 *(978-1-4169-4076-0(6)*, Simon & Schuster Bks. For Young Readers) Simon & Schuster Bks. For Young Readers.
—Willa by Heart. 2009. (Wedding Planner's Daughter Ser.). (ENG.). 240p. (J). (gr. 4-8). pap. 6.99 *(978-1-4169-7470-3(9)*, Aladdin) Simon & Schuster Children's Publishing.
Parish, Herman. Amelia Bedelia Chapter Book #10: Amelia Bedelia Ties the Knot. Avril, Lynne, illus. 2016. (Amelia Bedelia Ser.). 160p. (J). (gr. 1-5). pap. 4.99 *(978-0-06-233416-9(6)*, Greenwillow Bks.) HarperCollins Pubs.
—Amelia Bedelia Ties the Knot. 2016. (Amelia Bedelia Chapter Book Ser.: 10). (J). lib. bdg. 14.75 *(978-0-606-38762-0(5))* Turtleback Bks.
Parker, Emma. The Wedding Day. 2010. (Illus.). 16p. pap. *(978-1-877561-51-1(7))* First Edition Ltd.
Pate, Ginger. Would You Invite a Skunk to Your Wedding? Blanski, Maribeth, illus. 2009. 32p. (J). 16.95 *(978-1-880851-73-9(3))* Greene Bark Pr., Inc.
Paulsen, Gary. Family Ties. 2014. (ENG.). 144p. (J). (gr. 4-7). 12.99 *(978-0-385-37380-7(5)*, Lamb, Wendy Bks.) Random Hse. Children's Bks.
Peck, Richard. The Best Man, 5 vols. (ENG.). (J). 2017. 44.95 ***(978-0-525-48687-9(9)***, Puffin Books) 2017. 256p. (gr. 4-7). 8.99 ***(978-0-14-751579-7(3)***, Puffin Books) 2016. 240p. (gr. 4-7). 16.99 *(978-0-8037-3839-3(0)*, Dial Bks) Penguin Young Readers Group.
Peterson, John & Slater, Teddy. The Littles Have a Happy Valentine's Day. Rogers, Jacqueline, illus. 2003. (Littles First Readers Ser.: No. 11). (ENG.). 32p. (J). (gr. k-2). pap. 3.99 *(978-0-439-42499-8(2)*, Scholastic Paperbacks) Scholastic, Inc.
Porter, Eleanor H. Miss Billy - Married. 2006. pap. *(978-1-4068-3238-9(3))* Echo Library.
—Miss Billy's Decision. 2006. pap. *(978-1-4068-3240-2(5))* Echo Library.
Posner-Sanchez, Andrea. A Royal Wedding Album (Disney Princess) RH Disney Staff, illus. 2016. (Picture Book Ser.). (ENG.). 48p. (J). (gr. -1-2). 9.99 *(978-0-7364-3477-5(1)*, RH/Disney) Random Hse. Children's Bks.
Powell, Joyce. The Greatest Marriage Ever. Schacher, Tracey, illus. 2011. 26p. pap. 11.95 *(978-1-4575-0215-6(1))* Dog Ear Publishing, LLC.
Prosek, James. The Day My Mother Left. Prosek, James, illus. 2009. (ENG., Illus.). 304p. (J). (gr. 4-7). pap. 7.99 *(978-1-4169-0771-8(8)*, Simon & Schuster Bks. For Young Readers) Simon & Schuster Bks. For Young Readers.
Rajadel, Fernando López. False Love, True Love/Amor Falso, Amor Verdadero: The Alfambra Woman Buried Alive & the Lovers of Teruel. 2010.Tr. of Amor Falso, Amor Verdadero: La enterrada viva de Alfambra & Los amantes de Teruel. (SPA.). 164p. pap. 44.48 *(978-1-4251-8920-4(2))* Trafford Publishing.
Random House Disney Staff. Make-Believe Bride. 2004. (Pictureback(R) Ser.). (ENG., Illus.). 24p. (J). (gr. -1-2). pap. 3.99 *(978-0-7364-2220-8(X)*, RH/Disney) Random Hse. Children's Bks.
—Rapunzel's Royal Wedding/Belle's Royal Wedding (Disney Princess) Random House Disney Staff, illus. 2013. (Pictureback(R) Ser.). (ENG., Illus.). 32p. (J). (gr. -1-2). 4.99 *(978-0-7364-2993-1(X)*, RH/Disney) Random Hse. Children's Bks.
Ray, Christie Jones & Ray, Christie Jones. Eliza Celebrates a Royal Wedding. 2012. (Illus.). 48p. pap. 15.00 *(978-0-9853223-6-6(5))* Rose Water Cottage Pr.
Reiter, David P. Bringing down the Wall. Babajanyan, Sona, illus. 2012. 32p. (J). 18.00 *(978-1-922120-19-9(7)*, IP Kidz) Interactive Pubns. Pty, Ltd. AUS. Dist: Lightning Source, Inc.
RH Disney Staff. Ariel's Royal Wedding/Aurora's Royal Wedding (Disney Princess) RH Disney Staff, illus. 2014. (Pictureback(R) Ser.). (ENG., Illus.). 32p. (J). (gr. -1-2). 4.99 *(978-0-7364-3167-5(5)*, RH/Disney) Random Hse. Children's Bks.
Rinaldi, Ann. Brooklyn Rose. 2006. (ENG., Illus.). 240p. (J). (gr. 5-7). reprint ed. pap. 15.95 *(978-0-15-205538-7(X))* Houghton Mifflin Harcourt Publishing Co.
Rowley, Deborah Pace. My Wedding Day. Harmon, Glenn, illus. 2007. 24p. (J). (gr. -1-3). 15.99 *(978-1-59955-016-9(4))* Cedar Fort, Inc./CFI Distribution.
Roy, Jennifer. Cordially Uninvited. 2012. (ENG., Illus.). 256p. (J). (gr. 3-7). 15.99 *(978-1-4424-3920-7(3)*, Simon & Schuster Bks. For Young Readers) Simon & Schuster Bks. For Young Readers.
Roy, Jennifer Rozines. Cordially Uninvited. 2013. (ENG.). 272p. (J). (gr. 3-7). pap. 6.99 *(978-1-4424-3921-4(1)*, Simon & Schuster Bks. For Young Readers) Simon & Schuster Bks. For Young Readers.
Roy, Ron. A Spy in the White House. Bush, Timothy, tr. Bush, Timothy, illus. 2004. (Capital Mysteries Ser.: No. 4). (ENG.). 96p. (J). (gr. 1-4). 4.99 *(978-0-375-82557-6(6)*, Random Hse. Bks. for Young Readers) Random Hse. Children's Bks.
Rupp, Rebecca. Sarah Simpson's Rules for Living. 2008. (ENG., Illus.). 96p. (J). (gr. 3-7). 14.99 *(978-0-7636-3220-5(1))* Candlewick Pr.
Rylant, Cynthia. Wedding Flowers. Halperin, Wendy Anderson, illus. 2003. (Cobble Street Cousins Ser.). 72p. (gr. 2-5). 15.00 *(978-0-7569-1476-9(0))* Perfection Learning Corp.
Rylant, Cynthia & Halperin, Wendy Anderson. Wedding Flowers. 2003. (Cobble Street Cousins Ser.: 6). (ENG., Illus.). 80p. (J). (gr. 2-5). pap. 5.99 *(978-0-689-83418-9(7)*, Aladdin) Simon & Schuster Children's Publishing.
Saeed, Aisha & Airgood, Ellen. Written in the Stars. 2015. (ENG.). 304p. (YA). (gr. 9). 17.99 *(978-0-399-17170-3(3)*, Nancy Paulsen Books) Penguin Young Readers Group.
Saint, Mimi. The Bride's Price. Wendt, Yohanna, illus. 2013. 16p. pap. 24.95 *(978-1-4241-4249-1(0))* America Star Bks.
Salemi, Dianne K. The Caged Graves. 2014. (ENG.). 336p. (YA). (gr. 7). pap. 8.99 *(978-0-544-33622-3(4)*, HMH Books For Young Readers) Houghton Mifflin Harcourt Publishing Co.
Samuels, Vyanne. Carry Go Bring Come. 2007. (ENG.). 28p. (J). (gr. -1-3). 8.99 *(978-1-4169-6725-5(7)*, Simon & Schuster/Paula Wiseman Bks.) Simon & Schuster/Paula Wiseman Bks.
Saseen, Sharon, illus. Patience & the Flower Girl. 2004. *(978-0-9748425-0-9(8))* Saseen, Sharon.
Sateren, Shelley Swanson. Mudball Molly. Melmon, Deborah, illus. 2015. (Adventures at Hound Hotel Ser.). (ENG.). 72p. (gr. 2-3). lib. bdg. 25.32 *(978-1-4795-5900-8(8)*, Adventures at Hound Hotel) Picture Window Bks.
Scott, Elizabeth. Perfect You. 2008. (ENG.). 304p. (YA). (gr. 9-12). pap. 9.99 *(978-1-4169-5355-5(8)*, Simon Pulse) Simon Pulse.
Shacter, Sara F. Heading to the Wedding: You're Invited to Join Patrick & Evie on the Great Adventure of Becoming (Almost) Perfect Guests. Thornton, Christine, illus. 2006. (ENG.). 32p. (J). (gr. -1-3). 18.95 *(978-1-933176-05-5(9))* Red Rock Pr., Inc.
Shan, Darren, pseud. Zom-B, Bk. 10. 2015. (Zom-B Ser.: 10). (ENG., Illus.). 208p. (YA). (gr. 7-17). 15.99 *(978-0-316-21422-3(1))* Little, Brown Bks. for Young Readers.
Sheth, Kashmira. Keeping Corner. 2009. (ENG.). 304p. (J). (gr. 7-17). pap. 7.99 *(978-0-7868-3860-8(4))* Hyperion Pr.
—Sona & the Wedding Game, 1 vol. Jaeggi, Yoshiko, illus. 2015. (ENG.). 32p. (J). (gr. 1-3). 16.95 *(978-1-56145-735-9(3))* Peachtree Pubs.
Shoup, Barbara. Wish You Were Here. 2008. (ENG.). 336p. (YA). (gr. 7). pap. 9.95 *(978-0-7387-1355-7(4)*, Flux) North Star Editions.
Simmonds, Posy. Lulu & the Chocolate Wedding. 2016. (ENG., Illus.). 32p. (J). (-k). pap. 12.99 *(978-1-78344-407-6(X))* Andersen Pr. GBR. Dist: Independent Pubs. Group.
Simon, Coco. Emma: Lights! Camera! Cupcakes! 2014. (Cupcake Diaries: 19). lib. bdg. 17.20 *(978-0-606-35437-0(9))* Turtleback Bks.
—Emma: Lights! Camera! Cupcakes! Halpin, Abigail, illus. 2014. (Cupcake Diaries: 19). (ENG.). 160p. (J). (gr. 3-7). pap. 6.99 *(978-1-4424-9930-0(3)*, Simon Spotlight) Simon Spotlight.

—Emma on Thin Icing. 2013. (Cupcake Diaries: 3). (ENG., Illus.). 160p. (J). (gr. 3-7). 15.99 (978-1-4424-7492-5(0), Simon Spotlight) Simon Spotlight.

—Emma on Thin Icing. 2011. (Cupcake Diaries: 3). lib. bdg. 17.20 (978-0-606-23734-5(8), Turtleback) Turtleback Bks.

Slater, David Michael. Westley the Wicked & the Rascally Ring Bear. Brooks, S. G., illus. 2012. 36p. pap. 10.95 (978-1-61413-028-4(0)) Puddletown Publishing Group, Inc.

Smith, Jennifer E. The Statistical Probability of Love at First Sight. 2012. (ENG.). 256p. (YA). (gr. 7-17). 17.99 (978-0-316-12238-2(6)) Little Brown & Co.

—The Statistical Probability of Love at First Sight. 2013. (ENG.). 272p. (YA). (gr. 7-17). pap. 10.00 (978-0-316-12239-9(4), Poppy) Little, Brown Bks. for Young Readers.

Smith, Roland. Independence Hall. 2009. (I, Q Ser.: Bk. 1). (ENG., Illus.). 312p. (J). (gr. 5-9). 15.95 (978-1-58536-468-8(1)) Sleeping Bear Pr.

Soentpiet, Chris K., et al. Molly Bannaky. 2009. (ENG., Illus.). 32p. (J). (gr. -1-3). pap. 6.99 (978-0-547-07676-8(2)) Houghton Mifflin Harcourt Publishing Co.

Springer, Nancy. The Case of the Peculiar Pink Fan: An Enola Holmes Mystery. 2010. (Enola Holmes Mystery Ser.: 4). (ENG.). 192p. (J). (gr. 5-7). 6.99 (978-0-14-241517-7(0), Puffin Books) Penguin Young Readers Group.

St. Romain, Rose Anne. Monsieur Durand's Grosse Affaire, 1 vol. Waites, Joan, illus. 2011. (ENG.). 32p. (J). (gr. k-3). 16.99 (978-1-58980-808-9(8)) Pelican Publishing Co., Inc.

Standish, Burt L. Frank Merriwell's Marriage. Rudman, Jack, ed. 2003. (Frank Merriwell Ser.). pap. 9.95 (978-0-8373-9125-0(3)) Merriwell, Frank Inc.

Stapleton, Rhonda. Stupid Cupid. 2009. (ENG.). 272p. (YA). (gr. 7-18). pap. 9.99 (978-1-4169-7464-2(4), Simon Pulse) Simon Pulse.

Stern, A. J. Here Comes the... Trouble! Marts, Doreen Mulryan, illus. 2012. (Frankly, Frannie Ser.: 9). (ENG.). 128p. (J). (gr. 1-3). pap. 5.99 (978-0-448-45752-9(0), Grosset & Dunlap) Penguin Young Readers Group.

Sticker Dolly Dressing Weddings (Revised) 2017. (Sticker Dolly Dressing Ser.). (ENG.). (J). pap. 9.99 **(978-0-7945-3785-2(5)**, Usborne) EDC Publishing.

Stier, Catherine. Welcome to America, Champ. Ettlinger, Doris, illus. 2013. (Tales of the World Ser.). (ENG.). 32p. (J). (gr. 1-4). 17.95 (978-1-58536-606-4(4), 202360) Sleeping Bear Pr.

Strom, Yale. The Wedding That Saved a Town. Prosmitsky, Jenya, illus. 2008. (J). (gr. -1). 17.95 (978-0-8225-7376-0(8), Kar-Ben Publishing) Lerner Publishing Group.

Studio Mouse Staff. Wedding Countdown. 2008. 36p. (J). (gr. -1). 12.99 (978-1-59069-740-5(5)) Studio Mouse LLC.

Suma, Nova Ren. Fade Out. 2012. (ENG.). 288p. (YA). (gr. 7). pap. 9.99 (978-1-4169-7565-6(9), Simon Pulse) Simon Pulse.

Surace, Joan. The Story of Lucia. Rockford, Nancy, illus. 2006. (YA). pap. 8.00 (978-0-8059-7062-3(2)) Dorrance Publishing Co., Inc.

Sutton, Margaret. The Discovery at Dragon's Mouth, No. 31. Doane, Pelagie, illus. 2008. (Judy Bolton Mysteries Ser.). (ENG.). 196p. (J). (gr. 4-7). pap. 14.95 (978-1-4290-9051-3(0)) Applewood Bks.

Sypolt, Carl W. Adventures of David the Honeybee. 2003. 51p. pap. 9.95 (978-0-7414-1526-4(7)) Infinity Publishing.

Thiel, Annie. Cosmos' Blended Family. Edwards, William M., illus. 2007. (Playdate Kids: Let's Be Friends! Ser.). 27p. (J). (gr. -1-3). per. 6.95 (978-1-933721-23-1(5)) Playdate Kids Publishing.

Thiel Annie. Playdate Kids Cosmos' Blended Family. 2007. 32p. 12.95 (978-1-933721-10-1(3)) Playdate Kids Publishing.

Thompson, Kay. Eloise at the Wedding, Pack. 2012. (Eloise Ser.). (ENG.). 192p. (J). (gr. -1-1). pap. 15.96 (978-1-4424-4949-7(7), Simon Spotlight) Simon Spotlight.

The Three Sillies, 6, Pack. (Literatura 2000 Ser.). (gr. 2-3). 33.00 (978-0-7635-0242-3(1)) Rigby Education.

Tougas, Shelley. A Patron Saint for Junior Bridesmaids. 2016. (ENG.). 272p. (J). 16.99 (978-1-62672-403-7(2), 9781626724037) Roaring Brook Pr.

Tucker, Patricia Wright. The Princess Who Couldn't Laugh. 2012. 24p. pap. 24.95 (978-1-4626-8133-4(6)) America Star Bks.

Upham, Linda. Divided Loyalties. Littlejohn, Anna, illus. 2007. 188p. per. (978-0-7552-0302-4(X)) Authors OnLine, Ltd.

Van Draanen, Wendelin. Sammy Keyes & the Wedding Crasher. 2011. (Sammy Keyes Ser.: Bk. 13). (ENG.). 320p. (J). (gr. 5). 7.99 (978-0-375-85456-9(8), Yearling) Random Hse. Children's Bks.

Venkatraman, Padma. Climbing the Stairs. 2010. (ENG., Illus.). 272p. (YA). (gr. 7-18). 9.99 (978-0-14-241490-3(5), Speak) Penguin Young Readers Group.

Vorster, Nicola. A Monkeys' Wedding. 2012. (Illus.). 24p. pap. 21.35 (978-1-4772-3126-5(9)) AuthorHouse.

Wakeman, Lars. Prince Harry the Hairy Prince: A hairy fairy Tale. 2011. 24p. (gr. -1). pap. 12.56 (978-1-4269-6304-9(1)) Trafford Publishing.

Webb, Sarah. Ask Amy Green: Love & Other Drama-Ramas! 2013. (Ask Amy Green Ser.: 4). (ENG.). 256p. (YA). (gr. 5). pap. 6.99 (978-0-7636-5689-8(5)) Candlewick Pr.

—Ask Amy Green: Wedding Belles. 2014. (Ask Amy Green Ser.: 6). (ENG.). 240p. (YA). (gr. 7). 16.99 (978-0-7636-5584-6(8)) Candlewick Pr.

The Wedding of the Mouse: An Asian Folktale. 2006. (J). 17.95 (978-0-9790033-0-1(X)) Playground Pr.

Wells, Rosemary. Max & Ruby at the Warthogs' Wedding. Wells, Rosemary, illus. 2014. (Max & Ruby Ser.). (ENG., Illus.). 40p. (J). (gr. -1-k). 17.99 (978-0-670-78461-5(3), Viking Books for Young Readers) Penguin Young Readers Group.

West, Kathryn E. Garden of Roses. 2007. 328p. per. 19.95 (978-0-595-45295-8(7)) iUniverse, Inc.

Wojciechowski, Susan. Beany & the Dreaded Wedding. Natti, Susanna, illus. 2005. (Beany Adventures Ser.). 121p. (J). 13.65 (978-0-7569-6498-6(9)) Perfection Learning Corp.

MARRIAGE, INTERRACIAL

see Interracial Marriage

MARRIAGE, MIXED

see Intermarriage

MARRIAGE CUSTOMS AND RITES

Dawson, Emily C. Weddings Around the World. 2010. (Special Days Ser.). 24p. (J). 25.65 (978-1-60753-031-2(7)) Amicus Publishing.

Ganeri, Anita. Celebrating Weddings Around the World. 2015. (Cultures & Customs Ser.). (ENG., Illus.). 32p. (gr. 3-3). 30.65 (978-1-4109-8017-5(0)) Heinemann-Raintree.

Hook, Jacqueline A. You're Going to Be a Ring Bearer. 2005. (J). per. (978-0-9664783-4-1(7)) Jacqueline Beverly Hills.

Keyser, Amber. Tying the Knot: A World History of Marriage. 2017. (J). (978-1-4677-9242-4(X)) Twenty First Century Bks.

Mattox, Brenda Sneathen. Wedding Traditions from Around the World Coloring Book. 2007. (Dover Fashion Coloring Book Ser.). (ENG., Illus.). 32p. (gr. 3-5). 3.99 (978-0-486-46232-5(3)) Dover Pubns., Inc.

Onyefulu, Ifeoma & Quarto Generic Staff. Here Comes Our Bride! An African Wedding Story. 2007. (ENG., Illus.). 32p. (J). (gr. 1-4). pap. 8.99 (978-1-84507-113-4(1), Frances Lincoln) Quarto Publishing Group UK GBR. Dist: Hachette Bk. Group.

Randall, Ronne. Marriage. 2017. (Journey of Life Ser.). (ENG., Illus.). 48p. (J). (gr. 4-6). pap. 11.99 (978-0-7502-9654-0(2), Wayland) Hachette Children's Group GBR. Dist: Hachette Bk. Group.

World Book, Inc. Staff, contrib. by. Marriage Celebrations. 2003. (World Book's Celebrations & Rituals Around the World Ser.). (Illus.). 46p. (J). (978-0-7166-5012-6(6)) World Bk., Inc.

MARRIAGE CUSTOMS AND RITES—FICTION

O'Connor, Jane. Fancy Nancy & the Wedding of the Century. Glasser, Robin Preiss, illus. 2014. (Fancy Nancy Ser.). 32p. (J). (gr. -1-3). (ENG.). 17.99 (978-0-06-208319-7(8)); lib. bdg. 18.89 (978-0-06-208320-3(1)) HarperCollins Pubs.

Staples, Suzanne Fisher. Shabanu: Daughter of the Wind. 3rd ed. (J). pap. 3.99 (978-0-13-800053-0(0)) Prentice Hall (Schl. Div.).

Thorpe, Kiki. Wedding Wings. Christy, Jana, illus. 2014. (Stepping Stone Book Series: No. 5). (ENG.). 128p. (J). (gr. 1-4). 5.99 (978-0-7364-3077-7(6), RH/Disney) Random Hse. Children's Bks.

—Wedding Wings. 2014. (Never Girls Ser.: 5). lib. bdg. 16.00 (978-0-606-35544-5(8)) Turtleback Bks.

MARS (PLANET)

Adamson, Thomas K. Do You Really Want to Visit Mars? Fabbri, Daniele, illus. 2013. (Do You Really Want to Visit... ? Ser.). (ENG.). 24p. (gr. 1-4). 27.10 (978-1-60753-198-2(4)) Amicus Publishing.

—Mars [Scholastic]: Revised Edition. 2010. (Exploring the Galaxy Ser.). (ENG.). 24p. pap. 0.49 (978-1-4296-5811-9(8), Pebble Plus) Capstone Press of Coughlan Cos.

Aldrin, Buzz & Dyson, Marianne J. Welcome to Mars: Making a Home on the Red Planet. 2015. (ENG., Illus.). 96p. (J). (gr. 3-7). lib. bdg. 28.90 (978-1-4263-2207-5(0), National Geographic Children's Bks.) National Geographic Society.

Allien Cave Explorers: Meet NASA Inventor William "Red" Whittaker & His Team's. 2017. (J). **(978-0-7166-6163-4(2))** World Bk., Inc.

Anderson, Rane. Stem: Mission to Mars: Problem Solving (Grade 3) 2017. (Mathematics Readers Ser.). (Illus.). 32p. (gr. 3-3). 8.99 **(978-1-4807-5801-8(9))** Teacher Created Materials, Inc.

Baker, David. Inside the Mars Rover. 2017. (Geek's Guide to Space Ser.). 192p. (J). (gr. 12-14). 44.60 **(978-1-4994-6700-0(1)**, Rosen Young Adult) Rosen Publishing Group, Inc., The.

Baker, David & Kissock, Heather. Journey to Mars. (J). 2016. **(978-1-4896-5827-2(0)**, AV2 by Weigl) 2009. (Illus.). 32p. (gr. 2-4). pap. 9.95 (978-1-60596-030-2(6)) 2009. (Illus.). 32p. (gr. 2-4). lib. bdg. 26.00 (978-1-60596-029-6(2)) Weigl Pubs., Inc.

Bellisario, Gina. To Mars! Moran, Mike, illus. 2017. (Cloverleaf Books (tm) — Space Adventures Ser.). (ENG.). 24p. (J). (gr. k-2). 25.32 (978-1-5124-2539-0(7)); pap. 6.99 (978-1-5124-3083-7(8)); 6.99 **(978-1-5124-3888-8(X))**; 38.65 **(978-1-5124-2832-2(9))**; 38.65 **(978-1-5124-3887-1(1))** Lerner Publishing Group. (Millbrook Pr.).

Berger, Melvin & Carson, Mary Kay. Discovering Mars: The Amazing Story of the Red Planet. 2015. lib. bdg. 16.00 (978-0-606-37755-3(7)) Turtleback Bks.

—Discovering Mars: the Amazing Story of the Red Planet: The Amazing Story of the Red Planet. 2015. (ENG.). 64p. (J). (gr. 2-5). pap. 5.99 (978-0-545-83960-0(2), Scholastic Paperbacks) Scholastic, Inc.

Bloom, J. P. Mars, 1 vol. 2014. (Planets Ser.). (ENG., Illus.). 24p. (J). (gr. 2-4). lib. bdg. 28.50 (978-1-62970-717-4(1)) ABDO Publishing Co.

Borgenich, David. Mars: You Decide How to Survive! 2015. (WorstCase Scenario Ultimate Adventure Ser.). (Illus.). 204p. (gr. 3-8). 47.10 (978-1-59920-979-1(9)) Black Rabbit Bks.

Bridges, Andrew. The Inside Story of Mars. 2006. (J). 7.80 (978-0-9753920-8-9(5)) Sally Ride Science.

Capaccio, George. Mars. 2009. (Space!). 64p. (gr. 5-18). lib. bdg. 32.79 (978-0-7614-4247-9(2)) Marshall Cavendish Corp.

Carney, Elizabeth. Mars: the Red Planet. 2016. (ENG., Illus.). 32p. (J). (gr. 1-4). pap. 7.99 (978-1-4263-2754-4(4), National Geographic Children's Bks.) National Geographic Society.

—National Geographic Readers: Mars. 2014. (Readers Ser.). (ENG., Illus.). 48p. (J). (gr. 1-4). pap. 3.99 (978-1-4263-1747-7(6), National Geographic Children's Bks.) National Geographic Society.

Carson, Mary Kay. Far-Out Guide to Mars. 2010. (Far-Out Guide to the Solar System Ser.). (Illus.). 48p. (J). pap. 8.95 (978-1-59845-185-6(5), Enslow Elementary) Enslow Pubs., Inc.

Carson, Mary Kay & Library Association Staff. Far-Out Guide to Mars. 2010. (Far-Out Guide to the Solar System Ser.). 48p. (J). (gr. 2-5). 25.27 (978-0-7660-3183-8(7)) Enslow Pubs., Inc.

Chrismer, Melanie. Mars. 2007. (Scholastic News Nonfiction Readers Ser.). (ENG., Illus.). 24p. (J). (gr. 1-2). 22.00 (978-0-531-14697-2(9)) Scholastic Library Publishing.

Christopher, Nick. Exploring Mars. 2017. (J). **(978-1-5345-2255-8(7)**, KidHaven Publishing) Greenhaven Publishing LLC.

Cobb, Allan B. Mars. (Library of Planets Ser.). 48p. 2009. (gr. 5-8). 55.90 (978-1-60853-817-1(6), Rosen Reference) 2004. (Illus.). (J). lib. bdg. 29.25 (978-1-4042-0169-9(6)) Rosen Publishing Group, Inc., The.

Cornell, Kari. Mars Science Lab Engineer Diana Trujillo. 2016. (STEM Trailblazer Bios Ser.). (ENG., Illus.). 32p. (J). (gr. 2-5). pap. 8.99 (978-1-4677-9721-4(9), Lerner Pubns.) Lerner Publishing Group.

Cosson, M. J. Your Mission to Mars, 1 vol. 2011. (Planets Ser.). (ENG., Illus.). 32p. (J). (gr. k-3). 28.50 (978-1-61641-679-9(3)) Magic Wagon.

Cutting, Robert. Mars Colony. Jeevan, Dhamindra, illus. 2007. 48p. (J). lib. bdg. 23.08 (978-1-4242-1630-7(3)) Fitzgerald Bks.

Dickmann, Nancy. Exploring the Inner Planets. 2015. (Spectacular Space Science Ser.). (ENG., Illus.). 48p. (J). (gr. 5-6). 30.25 (978-1-4994-3629-7(7), Rosen Central) Rosen Publishing Group, Inc., The.

Doyle, Bill. The Space Explorer's Guide to Mars — in 3-D! 2004. (Space University Ser.). (Illus.). 47p. (J). (978-0-439-55748-1(8)) Scholastic, Inc.

Dunn, Mary R. A Look at Mars. (Astronomy Now! Ser.). 24p. (gr. 2-3). 2009. 42.50 (978-1-61511-469-6(6), PowerKids Pr.) 2007. (Illus.). (YA). lib. bdg. 21.25 (978-1-4042-3828-2(X)) Rosen Publishing Group, Inc., The.

Feinstein, Stephen. Mars: A Myreportlinks. com Book. 2005. (Solar System Ser.). (Illus.). 48p. (J). (gr. 4-10). lib. bdg. 26.60 (978-0-7660-5302-1(4), MyReportLinks.com Bks.) Enslow Pubs., Inc.

Goldstein, Margaret J. Mars. 2005. (Pull Ahead Bks.). (Illus.). 32p. (gr. 2-4). lib. bdg. 22.60 (978-0-8225-4651-1(5)) Lerner Publishing Group.

Gruber, Lorin. Journey to Mars. 32p. (J). 2015. (Illus.). (978-1-4898-5169-7(0)) 2014. (ENG.). (gr. 5-5). pap. 11.75 (978-1-4994-0371-8(2), PowerKids Pr.) Rosen Publishing Group, Inc., The.

Hartman, Eve & Meshbesher, Wendy. Mission to Mars, 1 vol. 2011. (Science Missions Ser.). (ENG.). 56p. (gr. 3-3). 34.65 (978-1-4109-3989-0(8), Raintree Freestyle Express) Heinemann-Raintree.

Hollar, Sherman. The Inner Planets: Mercury, Venus, & Mars. 2011. (Illus.). 96p. (J). 31.70 (978-1-61530-512-4(2)) Rosen Publishing Group, Inc., The.

Howard, Fran. Mars, 1 vol. 2007. (Planets Ser.). (ENG.). 32p. (J). (gr. 3-7). lib. bdg. 27.07 (978-1-59928-826-0(5), Buddy Bks.) ABDO Publishing Co.

James, Lincoln. Mars: The Red Planet. 2010. (Our Solar System Ser.). 24p. (J). (gr. k-3). (ENG.). pap. 8.15 (978-1-4339-3825-2(1)); (Illus.). lib. bdg. 22.60 (978-1-4339-3824-5(3)) Stevens, Gareth Publishing LLLP.

Jefferis, David. Mars: Distant Red Planet. 2008. (Exploring Our Solar System Ser.). (ENG., Illus.). 32p. (J). (gr. 3-7). pap. (978-0-7787-3748-3(9)) Crabtree Publishing Co.

Jefferis, David & Irvine, Mat. Exploring Planet Mars. 2007. (Humans in Space Ser.). (ENG., Illus.). 32p. (J). (gr. 4-7). lib. bdg. (978-0-7787-3100-9(6)); pap. (978-0-7787-3114-6(6)) Crabtree Publishing Co.

Kortenkamp, Steve. Mars Exploration Rovers: An Interactive Space Exploration Adventure. 2016. (You Choose: Space Ser.). (ENG., Illus.). 112p. (gr. 3-4). lib. bdg. 31.99 (978-1-4914-8106-6(4), You Choose Bks.) Capstone Press of Coughlan Cos.

Lawrence, Ellen. Mars: The Dusty Planet. 2013. (Zoom into Space Ser.). 24p. (J). (gr. -1-3). lib. bdg. 23.93 (978-1-909673-10-6(2)) Ruby Tuesday Books Limited GBR. Dist: Bearport Publishing Co., Inc.

Lee, Pascal. Mission: Mars. 2013. (ENG.). 48p. (J). (gr. 3-7). pap. 6.99 (978-0-545-56532-5(4)) Scholastic, Inc.

Leedy, Loreen & Schuerger, Andrew. Messages from Mars. Leedy, Loreen, illus. 2006. (ENG., Illus.). 40p. (J). (gr. 3-7). 16.95 (978-0-8234-1954-8(1)) Holiday Hse., Inc.

Loewen, Nancy. Seeing Red: The Planet Mars, 1 vol. Yesh, Jeff, illus. 2008. (Amazing Science: Planets Ser.). (ENG.). 24p. (gr. k-4). lib. bdg. 26.65 (978-1-4048-3953-3(4), 1278905) Picture Window Bks.

Lomberg, Michelle. Mars. (J). 2013. 27.13 (978-1-62127-265-6(6)) 2013. pap. 12.95 (978-1-62127-274-8(5)) 2004. (Illus.). pap. 8.95 (978-1-59036-226-6(8)) 2004. (Illus.). 24p. (gr. 4-7). lib. bdg. 24.45 (978-1-59036-099-6(0)) Weigl Pubs., Inc.

Lomberg, Michelle & Willis, John. Mars. 2016. (Illus.). 24p. (J). (978-1-5105-0977-1(1)) SmartBook Media, Inc.

Markovics, Joyce. Marte: Rocas y Polvo Rojos. 2015. (Fuera de Este Mundo Ser.). (SPA., Illus.). 24p. (J). (gr. -1-3). lib. bdg. 23.93 (978-1-62724-591-3(X)) Bearport Publishing Co., Inc.

Markovics, Joyce L. Mars: Red Rocks & Dust. 2015. (Out of This World Ser.). (ENG.). 24p. (J). (gr. -1-3). lib. bdg. 23.93 (978-1-62724-564-7(2)) Bearport Publishing Co., Inc.

Mars. 2nd rev. ed. 2008. (New Solar System Ser.). 32p. (YA). (gr. 3-6). 23.00 (978-1-60413-211-3(6)) Facts On File, Inc.

Maxwell, Scott & Chambers, Catherine. Mars Rover Driver. 2013. (Coolest Jobs on the Planet Ser.). (ENG., Illus.). 48p. (gr. 5-8). 32.65 (978-1-4109-5483-1(8)); pap. 8.99 (978-1-4109-5488-6(9)) Heinemann-Raintree.

Miller, Ron. Curiosity's Mission on Mars: Exploring the Red Planet. 2014. (ENG., Illus.). 64p. (gr. 6-12). lib. bdg. 33.26 (978-1-4677-1087-9(3), Twenty-First Century Bks.) Lerner Publishing Group.

—Mars. 2006. (Worlds Beyond Ser.). (Illus.). 96p. (YA). (gr. 5-9). 27.93 (978-0-7613-2362-4(7)) Lerner Publishing Group.

Morey, Allan. Mars Rovers. 2017. (Space Tech Ser.). (ENG., Illus.). 24p. (J). (gr. 3-7). lib. bdg. 25.95 **(978-1-62617-703-1(1)**, Epic Bks.) Bellwether Media.

O'Brien, Patrick. You Are the First Kid on Mars. O'Brien, Patrick, illus. 2009. (ENG., Illus.). 32p. (J). (gr. k-3). 16.99 (978-0-399-24634-0(7), G.P. Putnam's Sons Books for Young Readers) Penguin Young Readers Group.

Orme, Helen & Orme, David. Let's Explore Mars. 2007. (Space Launch! Ser.). 24p. (gr. 1-4). pap. 8.15 (978-0-8368-8126-4(5)); (Illus.). lib. bdg. 23.00 (978-0-8368-7941-4(4)) Stevens, Gareth Publishing LLLP. (Gareth Stevens Learning Library).

Owen, Ruth. Mars. 2013. (Explore Outer Space Ser.). 32p. (J). (gr. 3-6). pap. 60.00 (978-1-61533-768-2(7)); pap. 10.00 (978-1-61533-767-5(9)); lib. bdg. 25.25 (978-1-61533-725-5(3)) Windmill Bks.

Owens, L. L. Mars. McGeehan, Dan, illus. 2011. (Space Neighbors Ser.). (ENG.). 32p. (J). (gr. 1-4). lib. bdg. 27.07 (978-1-60954-383-9(1), 200886) Child's World, Inc., The.

Oxlade, Chris. Mars, 1 vol. 2012. (Astronaut Travel Guides). (ENG.). 48p. (gr. 3-6). lib. bdg. 32.65 (978-1-4109-4570-9(7), NA-r) Heinemann-Raintree.

—Mercury, Mars, & Other Inner Planets. 2007. (Earth & Space Ser.). (Illus.). 48p. (YA). (gr. 5-9). lib. bdg. 29.25 (978-1-4042-3735-3(6)) Rosen Publishing Group, Inc., The.

Patenaude, Jeremy & Lock, Peter. Space Quest: Mission to Mars. 2014. (DK Readers Ser.). (ENG.). 32p. (J). (gr. 1-3). 14.99 (978-1-4654-2002-2(9), DK Children) Dorling Kindersley Publishing, Inc.

Portman, Michael. Is There Life on Mars? 2013. (Space Mysteries Ser.). (Illus.). 32p. (J). (gr. 2-5). 25.25 (978-1-4339-8272-9(2)); pap. 10.50 (978-1-4339-8273-6(0)) Stevens, Gareth Publishing LLLP. (Gareth Stevens Learning Library).

Radomski, Kassandra. The Secrets of Mars. 2015. (Planets Ser.). (ENG., Illus.). 32p. (gr. 2-4). lib. bdg. 31.99 (978-1-4914-5865-5(8)) Capstone Press of Coughlan Cos.

Romero, Libby. Discover Mars & Venus. 2006. (J). pap. (978-1-4108-6507-6(X)) Benchmark Education Co.

—Mars & Venus. 2006. (J). pap. (978-1-4108-6504-5(5)) Benchmark Education Co.

Roumanis, Alexis. Mars. 2016. (J). **(978-1-5105-2049-3(X))** SmartBook Media, Inc.

—Mars. 2015. (J). (978-1-4896-3288-3(3)) Weigl Pubs., Inc.

Rusch, Elizabeth. The Mighty Mars Rovers: The Incredible Adventures of Spirit & Opportunity. (Scientists in the Field Ser.). (ENG., Illus.). 80p. (J). (gr. 5-7). 2017. pap. 9.99 (978-0-544-93246-3(3), HMH Books For Young Readers) 2012. 18.99 (978-0-547-47881-4(X)) Houghton Mifflin Harcourt Publishing Co.

—The Mighty Mars Rovers: The Incredible Adventures of Spirit & Opportunity. 2017. (Scientists in the Field Ser.). (ENG.). (J). (gr. 5-7). lib. bdg. 20.85 **(978-0-606-39812-1(0))** Turtleback Bks.

Silverman, Buffy. Mars Missions: A Space Discovery Guide. 2017. (Space Discovery Guides). (ENG.). 48p. (J). (gr. 4-6). 16.99 **(978-1-5124-3809-3(X)**, Lerner Pubns.); 47.99 **(978-1-5124-2795-0(0)**, Lerner Pubns.); 47.99 **(978-1-5124-3810-9(3)**, Lerner Pubns.); (Illus.). 31.99 (978-1-5124-2585-7(0)) Lerner Publishing Group.

Simon, Charnan. Mars. 2011. (21st Century Junior Library: Solar System Ser.). (ENG.). 24p. (gr. 2-5). lib. bdg. 25.64 (978-1-61080-082-2(6), 201074) Cherry Lake Publishing.

Simon, Seymour. Destination: Mars. 2016. (ENG.). 32p. (J). (gr. 1-5). 17.20 (978-0-606-39251-8(3)) Turtleback Bks.

—Destination - Mars. 2016. (Illus.). 32p. (J). (gr. 1-5). 17.99 (978-0-06-234497-7(8)) HarperCollins Pubs.

—Mars. 2004. (ENG.). 32p. (J). (gr. 1-5). pap. 7.99 (978-0-06-054638-0(7)) HarperCollins Pubs.

Siy, Alexandra. Cars on Mars: Roving the Red Planet. 2011. (ENG., Illus.). 64p. (J). (gr. 3-7). pap. 9.95 (978-1-57091-463-8(X)) Charlesbridge Publishing, Inc.

Smith-Llera, Danielle. Mars Rover: How a Self-Portrait Captured the Power of Curiosity. 2017. (Captured Science History Ser.). (ENG.). 64p. (gr. 5-7). lib. bdg. 34.65 **(978-0-7565-5641-9(4)**, CPB Grades 4-8) Compass Point Bks.

Sparrow, Giles. Destination Mars. (Illus.). 32p. (J). 2010. pap. 10.00 (978-1-4358-3459-0(3)) 2009. (ENG., lib. bdg. 25.25 (978-1-4358-3443-9(7)) Rosen Publishing Group, Inc., The. (PowerKids Pr.).

Squire, Ann O. Planet Mars. 2014. (True Book — Space (Revised Edition) Ser.). (ENG.). 48p. (J). lib. bdg. 29.00 (978-0-531-21152-6(5)) Scholastic Library Publishing.

Steinkraus, Kyla. Rocky Planets: Mercury, Venus, Earth, & Mars. 2014. (ENG.). 24p. (gr. k-3). 28.50 (978-1-62717-727-6(2)) Rourke Educational Media.

Storad, Conrad J. Mars. 2009. (Early Bird Astronomy Ser.). (ENG.). 48p. (gr. 2-5). lib. bdg. 26.60 (978-0-7613-4152-9(8)); (Illus.). pap. 8.95 (978-0-7613-4980-8(4), Lerner Pubns.) Lerner Publishing Group.

Sumners, Carolyn T. & Handron, Kerry. An Earthling's Guide to Mars: Travel to Mars with Pathfinder. 2003. (Illus.). 138p. (YA). (gr. 4-7). pap. 12.95 (978-0-07-069635-8(7)) McGraw-Hill Trade.

Teitelbaum, Michael. Mars & Venus Space Exploration: Set Of 6. 2011. (Navigators Ser.). (J). pap. 50.00 net. (978-1-4108-6243-3(7)) Benchmark Education Co.

Ward, D. J. Exploring Mars. 2006. (Cool Science Ser.). (ENG., Illus.). 48p. (gr. 4-8). lib. bdg. 27.93 (978-0-8225-5936-8(6), Lerner Pubns.) Lerner Publishing Group.

Wimmer, Teresa. Mars. 2007. (My First Look at: Planets Ser.). (Illus.). 24p. (J). (gr. -1-3). lib. bdg. 24.25 (978-1-58341-518-4(1), Creative Education) Creative Co., The.

Wittenberg, John C. The Amazing Adventures of Spirit & Opportunity. 2004. (Illus.). 20p. (978-0-9705150-1-8(4)) Aerospace 1 Pubns.

World Book, contrib. by. Mars. 2nd ed. 2006. (World Book's Solar System & Space Exploration Library). (Illus.). 64p. (J). (978-0-7166-9516-5(2)) World Bk., Inc.

World Book, Inc Staff, contrib. by. Mars. 2010. (J). (978-0-7166-9536-3(7)) World Bk., Inc.

Zobel, Derek. Mars. 2010. (Exploring Space Ser.). (ENG., Illus.). 24p. (J). (gr. k-3). lib. bdg. 25.95 (978-1-60014-405-9(5), Blastoff! Readers) Bellwether Media.

MARS (PLANET)—FICTION

Adams, John Joseph, ed. Under the Moons of Mars: New Adventures on Barsoom. 2013. (ENG., Illus.). 368p. (YA). (gr. 7). pap. 9.99 (978-1-4424-2030-4(8), Simon & Schuster Bks. For Young Readers) Simon & Schuster Bks. For Young Readers.

—Under the Moons of Mars: New Adventures on Barsoom. Various Artists, illus. 2012. (ENG.). 368p. (YA). (gr. 7). 16.99 (978-1-4424-2029-8(4), Simon & Schuster Bks. For Young Readers) Simon & Schuster Bks. For Young Readers.

Agee, Jon. Life on Mars. 2017. (ENG., Illus.). 32p. (J). (gr. -1-3). 17.99 (978-0-399-53852-0(6), Dial Bks) Penguin Young Readers Group.

Bach, Tamara. Girl from Mars. Tanaka, Shelley, tr. from GER. 2008. (ENG.). 160p. (J). (gr. 8). 16.95

(978-0-88899-724-1(8)) Groundwood Bks. CAN. Dist: Publishers Group West (PGW).
Barrett, Judi. Cloudy with a Chance of Meatballs 3: Planet of the Pies. Mones, Isidre, illus. 2013. (ENG.). 32p. (J). (gr. -1-3). 17.99 *(978-1-4424-9027-7(6))*, Atheneum Bks. for Young Readers) Simon & Schuster Children's Publishing.
Bean, Raymond. The Curse of Mars. 2016. (Out of This World Ser.). (ENG., Illus.). 112p. (gr. 2-5). lib. bdg. 32.65 *(978-1-4965-3615-0(0))* Out of this World GBR. Dist: Capstone Pub.
Bennett, Jeffrey. Max Goes to Mars: A Science Adventure with Max the Dog. Okamoto, Alan, illus. 2015. (Science Adventures with Max the Dog Ser.). (ENG.). 32p. (J). (gr. 2-4). 15.00 *(978-1-937548-44-5(9))* Big Kid Science.
Bily, Ro. My Red Island in the Sky. 2012. 530p. 34.95 *(978-1-4626-6645-4(0))*; pap. 34.95 *(978-1-4626-6971-4(9))* America Star Bks.
Borgenicht, David & Khan, Hena. Mars: You Decide How to Survive! Labat, Yancey, illus. 2011. (Worst Case Scenario Ser.: WORS). (ENG.). 208p. (J). (gr. 4-7). 12.99 *(978-0-8118-7124-2(X))* Chronicle Bks. LLC.
Brockington, Drew. CatStronauts: Race to Mars. 2017. (CatStronauts Ser.: 2). (J). lib. bdg. 18.40 ***(978-0-606-39901-2(1))*** Turtleback Bks.
Brouwer, Sigmund. Death Trap. 2009. (Robot Wars Ser.: 1). (ENG.). 288p. (YA). pap. 7.99 *(978-1-4143-2309-1(3)*, Tyndale Kids) Tyndale Hse. Pubs.
Burroughs, Edgar Rice. Mars Trilogy: A Princess of Mars - The Gods of Mars - The Warlord of Mars. Fischer, Scott M. et al, illus. 2012. (ENG.). 704p. (YA). (gr. 7). pap. 14.99 *(978-1-4424-2387-9(0)*, Simon & Schuster Bks. For Young Readers) Simon & Schuster Bks. For Young Readers.
Cahill, Byron. Space Pox. 2005. (J). pap. *(978-1-4108-4220-6(7))* Benchmark Education Co.
Catlow, Nikalas & Wesson, Tim. Robots vs. Gorillas in the Desert. Catlow, Nikalas & Wesson, Tim, illus. 2011. (Mega Mash-Up Ser.). (ENG., Illus.). 96p. (J). (gr. 2-5). pap. 6.99 *(978-0-7636-5873-1(1)*, Nosy Crow) Candlewick Pr.
—Romans vs. Dinosaurs on Mars. Catlow, Nikalas & Wesson, Tim, illus. 2011. (Mega Mash-Up Ser.). (ENG., Illus.). 96p. (J). (gr. 2-5). pap. 6.99 *(978-0-7636-5872-4(3)*, Nosy Crow) Candlewick Pr.
Davis, Pat. Estelle & the Escape from Mars: A Children's Novel By. 2009. 136p. pap. 10.99 *(978-1-4389-5432-5(8))* AuthorHouse.
Dingman, Matthew. The Very Different Animal from Mars. 2013. 24p. pap. 24.95 *(978-1-63000-730-0(7))* America Star Bks.
Duane, Diane. A Wizard of Mars Bk. 9. 2011. (Young Wizards Ser.: 9). (ENG.). 560p. (YA). (gr. 7-9). pap. 8.99 *(978-0-15-205449-6(9))* Houghton Mifflin Harcourt Publishing Co.
Duffett-Smith, James. A Curious Robot on Mars! Straker, Bethany, illus. 2013. (ENG.). 32p. (J). (gr. -1-k). 14.95 *(978-1-62087-994-8(8)*, 620994, Sky Pony Pr.) Skyhorse Publishing Co., Inc.
Elam Jr., Richard M. Young Visitor to Mars. Geer, Charles, illus. 2011. 256p. 47.95 *(978-1-258-09909-1(8))* Literary Licensing, LLC.
Gill, David Macinnis. Black Hole Sun. (Black Hole Sun Ser.: 1). (ENG.). (YA). (gr. 9). 2012. 368p. pap. 8.99 *(978-0-06-167306-1(4))* 2010. 352p. 16.99 *(978-0-06-167304-7(8))* HarperCollins Pubs. (Greenwillow Bks.).
—Invisible Sun. (Black Hole Sun Ser.: 2). (ENG.). (YA). (gr. 9). 2013. 400p. pap. 9.99 *(978-0-06-207333-4(8))* 2012. 384p. 16.99 *(978-0-06-207332-7(X))* HarperCollins Pubs. (Greenwillow Bks.).
—Shadow on the Sun. 2013. (Black Hole Sun Ser.: 3). (ENG.). 432p. (YA). (gr. 9). 17.99 *(978-0-06-207335-8(4)*, Greenwillow Bks.) HarperCollins Pubs.
Grahame, Howard. The Wishing Book. 2009. 110p. (J). pap. *(978-1-905809-64-6(6))* Pneuma Springs Publishing.
—The Wishing Book 2 - Return to Mars. 2009. 102p. (J). pap. *(978-1-905809-80-6(8))* Pneuma Springs Publishing.
Guettier, Nancy. Mermaids on Mars. 2013. (ENG.). 36p. (-3). pap. 9.95 *(978-1-61448-670-1(0))*; (Illus.). (gr. 1-3). 19.95 *(978-1-61448-640-4(9))* Morgan James Publishing.
Hays, Barrett K. Mars, Jimmy & Me. 2011. 24p. (gr. 4-6). pap. 11.32 *(978-1-4567-4164-8(0))* AuthorHouse.
Hirschfeld, Robert. Martians Are People, Too. 2011. (Navigators Ser.). (J). pap. *(978-1-61672-969-1(4))* Benchmark Education Co.
Howard, Grahame. The Wishing Book 3 - Extermination. 2010. 170p. (J). pap. *(978-1-905809-90-5(5))* Pneuma Springs Publishing.
Hunt, Elizabeth Singer. The Deadly Race to Space: Russia. 2009. (Secret Agent Jack Stalwart Ser.: 9). (ENG.). 144p. (J). (gr. 1-4). pap. 5.99 *(978-1-60286-078-0(5)*, Weinstein Bks.) Perseus Bks. Group.
The Imaginer: Individual Title Six-Packs. (Bookweb Ser.). 32p. (gr. 6-18). 34.00 *(978-0-7578-0900-2(6))* Rigby Education.
Kelly, Mark. Mousetronaut Goes to Mars. Payne, C. F., illus. 2013. (ENG.). 40p. (J). (gr. -1-3). 16.99 *(978-1-4424-8426-9(8)*, Simon & Schuster/Paula Wiseman Bks.) Simon & Schuster/Paula Wiseman Bks.
Lathrop, Brandy. Jalen Goes to Mars. 2008. 22p. pap. 24.95 *(978-1-4241-9010-2(X))* America Star Bks.
Marsh, Carole. Adventure to the Planet Mars! 2007. (Field Trips (Gallopade International) Ser.). (Illus.). 114p. (J). (gr. 2-9). 14.95 *(978-0-635-06392-2(1))* Gallopade International.
McDougall, Sophia. Mars Evacuees. (J). (gr. 3-7). 2016. 432p. pap. 7.99 *(978-0-06-229400-5(8))* 2015. 416p. 16.99 *(978-0-06-229399-2(0))* HarperCollins Pubs.
McGee, Warner, illus. Mission to Mars. 2006. (Backyardigans Ser.: 4). (ENG.). 24p. (J). (gr. -1-2). pap. 3.99 *(978-1-4169-1486-0(2)*, Simon Spotlight/Nickelodeon) Simon Spotlight/Nickelodeon.
Metz, Melinda. S. M. A. R. T. S. & the Mars Mission Mayhem. McKenzie, Heath, illus. 2016. (S. M. A. R. T. S. Ser.). (ENG.). 128p. (gr. 3-6). lib. bdg. 22.65 *(978-1-4965-3016-5(0))* S.M.A.R.T.S. Learning System.
Oakes, Cory Putman. Dinosaur Boy Saves Mars. 2016. (Dinosaur Boy Ser.: 2). (ENG., Illus.). 224p. (J). (gr. 3-7). 12.99 *(978-1-4926-0540-9(9)*, 9781492605409, Sourcebooks Jabberwocky) Sourcebooks, Inc.
—Dinosaur Boy Saves Mars. 2016. (Dinosaur Boy Ser.: 2). (ENG.). 224p. (J). (gr. 3-7). 18.40 *(978-0-606-39306-5(4))* Turtleback Bks.
Pilkey, Dav. Mighty Robot vs. the Mecha-Monkeys from Mars. Santat, Dan, illus. 2014. (Ricky Ricotta Ser.: 4). (ENG.). 144p. (J). (gr. -1-3). pap. 5.99 *(978-0-545-63012-2(6))* Scholastic, Inc.
Preston, L. M. The Pack. 2010. (ENG.). 316p. (J). pap. 14.99 *(978-0-9841989-7-9(0))* Phenomenal One Pr.
—The Pack - Retribution: Retribution. 2012. (ENG.). 250p. (YA). (gr. 8-12). pap. 11.99 *(978-0-9850251-0-6(7))* Phenomenal One Pr.
Rivers, Karen. Love, Ish. 2017. (ENG.). 288p. (J). (gr. 4-8). 16.95 *(978-1-61620-570-6(9))* Algonquin Bks. of Chapel Hill.
Rockwood, Roy. Lost on the Moon. 2008. 132p. pap. 10.95 *(978-1-60664-236-8(7))* Rodgers, Alan Bks.
Samphire, Patrick. Secrets of the Dragon Tomb. Holmes, Jeremy, illus. 2016. (ENG.). 336p. (J). (gr. 5-8). 16.99 *(978-0-8050-9906-5(9)*, 9780805099065, Holt, Henry & Co. Bks. For Young Readers) Holt, Henry & Co.
Schachner, Judy. Skippyjon Jones, Lost in Spice. Schachner, Judy, illus. 2009. (Skippyjon Jones Ser.). (ENG., Illus.). 32p. (J). (gr. -1-k). 17.99 *(978-0-525-47965-9(1)*, Dutton Books for Young Readers) Penguin Young Readers Group.
—Skippyjon Jones, Lost in Spice. 2009. (Skippyjon Jones Ser.). (J). 1.25 *(978-1-4407-6563-6(4))*; 192.75 *(978-1-4407-6557-5(X))*; 37.75 *(978-1-4407-6558-2(8))* Recorded Bks., Inc.
Slivensky, Katie. The Countdown Conspiracy. 2017. 336p. (J). (gr. 3-7). 16.99 ***(978-0-06-246255-8(5))*** HarperCollins Pubs.
Summers, Kim. Senor Mundo & Me: A Happy Birthday Story. Mariscal, Javier, illus. 2004. 31p. (J). (gr. k-4). 20.00 *(978-0-7567-7759-3(3))* DIANE Publishing Co.
Terrell, Brandon. Mars for Humanity. Foti, Anthony J., illus. 2015. (Exploring Space & Beyond Ser.). (ENG.). 96p. (gr. 3-4). lib. bdg. 26.65 *(978-1-4965-0502-6(6))* Stone Arch Bks.
Trimble, Marcia J. Marsby & the Martian Detectives. Hayden, Jennifer H., illus. 2004. 56p. (J). per. 9.95 *(978-1-891577-52-9(2)*, SAN299-4844) Images Pr.
Wolff, Tracy. Book 4: Arrival. 2016. (Mars Bound Ser.). (ENG.). (J). (gr. 2-8). lib. bdg. 28.50 ***(978-1-62402-200-5(6))*** ABDO Publishing Co.

MARSH, OTHNIEL CHARLES, 1831-1899

Goldish, Meish. The Fossil Feud: Marsh & Cope's Bone Wars. 2006. (Fossil Hunters Ser.). (Illus.). 32p. (YA). (gr. 2-5). lib. bdg. 25.27 *(978-1-59716-256-2(6))* Bearport Publishing Co., Inc.

MARSHALL, GEORGE C. (GEORGE CATLETT), 1880-1959

Gimpel, Lee. Fighting Wars, Planning for Peace: The Story of George C. Marshall. 2005. (World Leaders Ser.). (Illus.). 176p. (J). (gr. 6-12). lib. bdg. 26.95 *(978-1-931798-66-2(4))* Reynolds, Morgan Inc.
Welch, Catherine A. George C. Marshall. (History Maker Bios Ser.). 48p. (J). 2006. (Illus.). (gr. 3-7). lib. bdg. 26.60 *(978-0-8225-2435-9(X)*, Lerner Pubns.) 2005. pap. 8.95 *(978-0-8225-5460-8(7))* Lerner Publishing Group.

MARSHALL, JOHN, 1755-1835

Corrigan, Jim. John Marshall: The Story of John Marshall. 2011. (Supreme Court Justices Ser.). (Illus.). 112p. (J). 28.95 *(978-1-59935-159-9(5))* Reynolds, Morgan Inc.
Wetterer, Charles M. & Wetterer, Margaret K. Chief Justice. Walters, Kurt K. C., illus. 2005. 32p. (J). *(978-1-59336-306-2(0))*; pap. *(978-1-59336-307-9(9))* Mondo Publishing.

MARSHALL, THURGOOD, 1908-1993

Boerst, William J. Galileo Galilei & the Science of Motion. 2004. (Profiles in Science Ser.). (Illus.). 144p. (YA). (gr. 6-12). lib. bdg. 26.95 *(978-1-931798-00-6(1))* Reynolds, Morgan Inc.
Chavez, Emilio. Thurgood Marshall: Supreme Court Justice. 2013. (InfoMax Readers Ser.). (ENG.). 24p. (J). (gr. 3-4). pap. 49.50 *(978-1-4777-2600-6(4))*; pap. 8.25 *(978-1-4777-2599-3(7))* Rosen Publishing Group, Inc., The. (Rosen Classroom).
Collins, Luke. Thurgood Marshall, 1 vol. 2014. (Great African-Americans Ser.). (ENG.). 24p. (gr. k-1). lib. bdg. 21.99 *(978-1-4765-3956-0(1)*, Pebble Bks.) Capstone Press of Coughlan Cos.
Horn, Geoffrey M. Thurgood Marshall. 2004. (Trailblazers of the Modern World Ser.). (Illus.). 48p. (gr. 5-12). pap. 14.05 *(978-0-8368-5258-5(3))*; lib. bdg. 31.00 *(978-0-8368-5098-7(X))* Stevens, Gareth Publishing LLLP. (Gareth Stevens Secondary Library).
Keiser, Cody. Thurgood Marshall: Civil Rights Leader. 2013. (Rosen Readers Ser.). (ENG.). 24p. (J). (gr. 3-4). pap. 49.50 *(978-1-4777-2546-7(6))*; pap. 8.25 *(978-1-4777-2545-0(8))* Rosen Publishing Group, Inc., The. (Rosen Classroom).
Kemp, Kristin. Amazing Americans: Thurgood Marshall, 1 vol. rev. ed. 2014. (Primary Source Readers Content & Literacy Ser.). (ENG., Illus.). 32p. (gr. 3-3). pap. 8.99 *(978-1-4333-7374-9(2))* Teacher Created Materials, Inc.
Mara, Wil. Thurgood Marshall: Champion for Civil Rights. 2004. (Great Life Stories Ser.). (ENG., Illus.). 125p. (J). 30.50 *(978-0-531-12058-3(9)*, Watts, Franklin) Scholastic Library Publishing.
Marshall, Thurgood. Thurgood Marshall. 2004. (Black Americans of Achievement Ser.). (Illus.). 112p. (gr. 6-12). 35.00 *(978-0-7910-8163-1(X)*, Chelsea Hse.) Facts On File, Inc.
Rohan, Rebecca Carey. Thurgood Marshall: The First African-American Supreme Court Justice. 2016. (Great American Thinkers Ser.). 128p. (J). (gr. 9-9). 45.64 *(978-1-5026-1932-7(6))* Cavendish Square Publishing.
Taylor-Butler, Christine. Thurgood Marshall. 2006. (Rookie Biographies Ser.). (ENG., Illus.). 32p. (J). (gr. 1-2). pap. 4.95 *(978-0-516-27099-9(0)*, Children's Pr.) Scholastic Library Publishing.
Wheeler, Jill C. Thurgood Marshall. 2003. (Breaking Barriers Ser.). 64p. (gr. 3-8). 27.07 *(978-1-57765-907-5(4)*, Abdo & Daughters) ABDO Publishing Co.
Whitelaw, Nancy. Mr. Civil Rights: The Story of Thurgood Marshall. 2nd rev. exp. ed. 2004. (Notable Americans Ser.). (Illus.). 144p. (YA). (gr. 6-12). 23.95 *(978-1-931798-02-0(8))* Reynolds, Morgan Inc.
—Thurgood Marshall. 2011. (Supreme Court Justices Ser.). (Illus.). 128p. 28.95 *(978-1-59935-157-5(9))* Reynolds, Morgan Inc.

MARSHES

Bennett, Doraine. Marsh & Swamp. 2009. (J). *(978-1-935077-36-7(8))*; pap. *(978-1-935077-41-1(4))* State Standards Publishing, LLC.
Carlone, Sydney. Life in a Marsh. 2013. (Rosen Readers Ser.). (ENG.). 24p. (J). (gr. 3-4). pap. 49.50 *(978-1-4777-2534-4(2))*; pap. 8.25 *(978-1-4777-2533-7(4))* Rosen Publishing Group, Inc., The. (Rosen Classroom).
Cheshire, Gerard. Day & Night in Swamp. Camm, Martin, illus. 2009. 38p. (J). (gr. 2-5). 14.99 *(978-0-8437-0974-2(X))* Hammond World Atlas Corp.
Declus, Jennifer. What Might I Find in a Swamp. Kalasea, illus. 2004. (J). *(978-0-9743690-3-7(9))* Britt Allcroft Productions.
Johansson, Philip. Marshes & Swamps: A Wetland Web of Life. 2007. (Wonderful Water Biomes Ser.). (Illus.). 48p. (J). (gr. 3-7). lib. bdg. 25.27 *(978-0-7660-2814-2(3)*, Enslow Elementary) Enslow Pubs., Inc.
Lion, David C. A Home in the Swamp. 2006. (Scholastic News Nonfiction Readers Ser.). (ENG., Illus.). 24p. (J). (gr. 1-2). lib. bdg. 22.00 *(978-0-516-25349-7(2))* Scholastic Library Publishing.
—La Vida en el Pantano. 2008. (Scholastic News Nonfiction Readers en Espanol Ser.). 24p. (J). pap. 6.95 *(978-0-531-20648-5(3))*; (SPA., Illus.). 22.00 *(978-0-531-20714-7(5))* Scholastic Library Publishing. (Children's Pr.).
Marais, Vivian. Life in a Swamp: A Wetlands Habitat. 2009. (Real Life Readers Ser.). 24p. (gr. 3-4). pap. 8.25 *(978-1-4358-0141-7(5)*, Rosen Classroom); 42.50 *(978-1-61511-215-9(4)*, PowerKids Pr.) Rosen Publishing Group, Inc., The.
Marais, Vivien. Life in a Swamp: A Wetlands Habitat. 2009. (Look at Life Science Ser.). (J). lib. bdg. 22.60 *(978-1-4358-2972-5(7)*, PowerKids Pr.) Rosen Publishing Group, Inc., The.
Meister, Cari. Do You Really Want to Meet a Swan? Fabbri, Daniele, illus. 2014. (Do You Really Want to Meet... ? Ser.). (ENG.). 24p. (J). (gr. 1-4). 27.10 *(978-1-60753-458-7(4))* Amicus Publishing.
Miller, Mirella S. Life in Freshwater Marshes. 2014. (Life in Water Biomes Ser.). (ENG.). 24p. (J). (gr. 2-5). 28.50 *(978-1-62687-296-7(1)*, 207137) Child's World, Inc., The.
Peterson, Christy. 24 Hours in a Salt Marsh. 2017. (J). ***(978-1-5026-2479-6(6))*** Cavendish Square Publishing.
Root, Phyllis. Big Belching Bog. Bowen, Betsy, illus. 2010. (ENG.). 40p. (gr. 2-3). 15.95 *(978-0-8166-3359-3(2))* Univ. of Minnesota Pr.
Wechsler, Doug. Marvels in the Muck: Life in the Salt Marshes. 2008. (ENG.). 48p. (J). (gr. 5-18). 17.95 *(978-1-59078-588-1(6))* Boyds Mills Pr.

MARSHES—FICTION

Appelt, Kathi. The True Blue Scouts of Sugar Man Swamp. 2014. (ENG., Illus.). 352p. (J). (gr. 3-7). pap. 8.99 *(978-1-4424-2108-0(8)*, Atheneum Bks. for Young Readers) Simon & Schuster Children's Publishing.
—The True Blue Scouts of Sugar Man Swamp. Bricking, Jennifer, illus. 2013. (ENG.). 336p. (J). (gr. 3-7). 16.99 *(978-1-4424-2105-9(3))* Simon & Schuster Children's Publishing.
—The True Blue Scouts of Sugar Man Swamp. 2014. lib. bdg. 19.65 *(978-0-606-35793-7(9))* Turtleback Bks.
Arnosky, Jim. The Pirates of Crocodile Swamp. 2009. (ENG.). 240p. (J). (gr. 4-7). 15.99 *(978-0-399-25068-2(9)*, G.P. Putnam's Sons Books for Young Readers) Penguin Young Readers Group.
Bracegirdle, P. J. Fiendish Deeds. 2009. (Joy of Spooking Ser.: 1). (ENG.). 224p. (J). (gr. 3-7). pap. 5.99 *(978-1-4169-3417-2(0)*, McElderry, Margaret K. Bks.) McElderry, Margaret K. Bks.
Humphreys, Neil. Secrets of the Swamp. Koon, Cheng Puay, illus. 2014. (ENG.). 72p. pap. 11.90 *(978-981-4484-16-9(4))* Marshall Cavendish International (Asia) Private Ltd. SGP. Dist: National Bk. Network.
Hurd, Thacher & Hurd. Mama Don't Allow. Hurd, Thacher, illus. 25th anniv. ed. 2008. (Trophy Picture Bks.). (ENG., Illus.). 40p. (J). (gr. -1-3). pap. 6.99 *(978-0-06-443078-4(2))* HarperCollins Pubs.
Hurd, Thacher & Hurd, T. Mama Don't Allow. 2008. (Illus.). (J). (gr. -1-2). 17.20 *(978-0-8085-3698-7(2)*, Turtleback) Turtleback Bks.
Jaz. Lost Lake: An Adventure for Kids of All Ages. 2008. 172p. pap. 24.95 *(978-1-60703-398-1(4))* America Star Bks.
Jones, C. B. The Cats' Meow. Green, Chris, illus. 2017. (Bog Hollow Boys Ser.). (ENG.). 72p. (gr. 4-5). lib. bdg. 25.32 *(978-1-4965-4057-7(3))* Stone Arch Bks.
—Gone to the Buzzards. Green, Chris, illus. 2017. (Bog Hollow Boys Ser.). (ENG.). 72p. (gr. 4-5). lib. bdg. 25.32 *(978-1-4965-4058-4(1))* Stone Arch Bks.
—Sleeping with the Fishes. Green, Chris, illus. 2017. (Bog Hollow Boys Ser.). (ENG.). 72p. (gr. 4-5). lib. bdg. 25.32 *(978-1-4965-4055-3(7))* Stone Arch Bks.
Key, Watt. Terror at Bottle Creek. 2016. (ENG.). 224p. (J). 16.99 *(978-0-374-37430-3(9)*, 9780374374303, Farrar, Straus & Giroux (BYR)) Farrar, Straus & Giroux.
King, Trey & Kiernan, Kenny. Cops, Crocs, & Crooks! 2015. (Lego City Ser.). (ENG., Illus.). 24p. (J). (gr. -1-3). pap. 3.99 *(978-0-545-78525-9(1))* Scholastic, Inc.
Kurtz, Kevin. A Day in the Salt Marsh, 1 vol. Powell, Consie, illus. 2007. (Day in the Habitat Ser.). (ENG.). 32p. (J). (gr. -1-3). 15.95 *(978-0-9768823-5-0(3))* Arbordale Publishing.
London, Lewis. Wesley Owl. 2010. (Illus.). 36p. (J). pap. 16.99 *(978-1-4490-6122-7(2))* AuthorHouse.
Ouchley, Amy Griffin. Swamper: Letters from a Louisiana Swamp Rabbit. 2013. (ENG., Illus.). 72p. (gr. 4-7). 22.50 *(978-0-8071-5074-0(6)*, 9780807150740) Louisiana State Univ. Pr.
Parker, Natalie C. Beware the Wild. 2014. (Beware the Wild Ser.: 1). (ENG.). 336p. (YA). (gr. 8). 17.99 *(978-0-06-224152-8(4)*, HarperTeen) HarperCollins Pubs.
Preller, James. Swamp Monster. Bruno, Iacopo, illus. 2015. (Scary Tales Ser.: 6). (ENG.). 96p. (J). (gr. 2-5). 15.99 *(978-1-250-04097-8(3)*, 9781250040978) Feiwel & Friends.
Prins, Piet. The Flying Phantom. 2006. (Illus.). 142p. (J). pap. *(978-1-894666-45-9(3))* Inheritance Pubns.
Roberts, Daniel. The Ghost of Froggy's Swamp. 2012. 36p. pap. 18.99 *(978-1-4772-0316-3(8))* AuthorHouse.
Sazaklis, John. Swamp Thing vs the Zombie Pets, 1 vol. Baltazar, Art, illus. 2012. (DC Super-Pets Ser.). (ENG.). 56p. (gr. 2-2). pap. 4.95 *(978-1-4048-7667-5(7))*; lib. bdg. 23.99 *(978-1-4048-6491-7(1))* Picture Window Bks. (DC Super-Pets).
Schaefer, Lola M. Swamp Chomp. Meisel, Paul, illus. 2014. (ENG.). 32p. (J). (gr. -1-3). 16.95 *(978-0-8234-2407-8(3))* Holiday Hse., Inc.
Stine, R. L. Here Comes the Shaggedy. 2016. (Goosebumps Most Wanted Ser.: 9). (Illus.). 140p. (J). lib. bdg. 17.20 *(978-0-606-38587-9(8))* Turtleback Bks.
Stratton-Porter, Gene. Freckles. l.t. ed. 2007. (ENG.). 248p. pap. 22.99 *(978-1-4264-5654-1(9))* Creative Media Partners, LLC.
—Freckles. 2006. 236p. (YA). 19.95 *(978-1-934169-32-2(3))*; pap. 8.95 *(978-1-934169-33-9(1))* Norilana Bks.
—A Girl of the Limberlost. 2006. 336p. (YA). 21.95 *(978-1-934169-30-8(7))*; pap. 10.95 *(978-1-934169-31-5(5))* Norilana Bks.
Turley/Alber. And the Tide Comes In. 2012. (Long Term Ecological Research Ser.). (ENG., Illus.). 32p. (J). (gr. 3-7). 15.95 *(978-0-9817700-5-5(3))* Taylor Trade Publishing.
Vanholme, Virginie. The Vampire from the Marshes. Mauricet, illus. 2008. (Scared to Death Ser.: 1). (ENG.). 46p. pap. 11.95 *(978-1-905460-47-2(3))* CineBook GBR. Dist: National Bk. Network.
Weeks, Sarah. Catfish Kate & the Sweet Swamp Band. Smith, Elwood H., illus. 2009. (ENG.). 32p. (J). (gr. -1-3). 17.99 *(978-1-4169-4026-5(X)*, Atheneum Bks. for Young Readers) Simon & Schuster Children's Publishing.

MARSUPIALS

Bishop, Nic. Marsupials. Bishop, Nic, photos by. 2009. (Nic Bishop Ser.). (ENG., Illus.). 48p. (J). (gr. -1-3). 17.99 *(978-0-439-87758-9(X))* Scholastic, Inc.
Bjorklund, Ruth. Tasmanian Devils. 2013. (Nature's Children Ser.). (ENG.). 48p. (J). 28.00 *(978-0-531-20982-0(2))*; pap. 6.95 *(978-0-531-24308-4(7))* Scholastic Library Publishing. (Children's Pr.).
Clarke, Ginjer L. Pouch Babies. Washburn, Lucia, illus. 2011. (Penguin Young Readers, Level 3 Ser.). (ENG.). 48p. (J). (gr. 1-3). pap. 3.99 *(978-0-448-45107-7(7)*, Penguin Young Readers) Penguin Young Readers Group.
Collard, Sneed B., III. Pocket Babies: And Other Amazing Marsupials. 2007. (Junior Library Guild Selection Ser.). (ENG., Illus.). 72p. (gr. 5-12). 25.26 *(978-1-58196-046-4(8)*, Darby Creek) Lerner Publishing Group.
Fishman, Jon. Meet a Baby Tasmanian Devil. 2017. (Lightning Bolt Books (tm) — Baby Australian Animals Ser.). (ENG.). (J). (gr. 1-3). pap. 6.99 ***(978-1-5124-5590-8(3))*** Lerner Publishing Group.
Fishman, Jon M. Meet a Baby Tasmanian Devil. 2017. (Lightning Bolt Books (tm) — Baby Australian Animals Ser.). (ENG.). 24p. (J). (gr. 1-3). 25.32 ***(978-1-5124-3385-2(3))*** Lerner Publishing Group.
Heos, Bridget. What to Expect When You're Expecting Joeys: A Guide for Marsupial Parents (And Curious Kids) Jorisch, Stéphane, illus. 2011. (Expecting Animal Babies Ser.: 2). (ENG.). 32p. (gr. 2-5). lib. bdg. 25.26 *(978-0-7613-5859-6(5))* Lerner Publishing Group.
Kalman, Bobbie. Baby Marsupials. 2012. (ENG., Illus.). 24p. (J). *(978-0-7787-4074-2(9))*; pap. *(978-0-7787-4079-7(X))* Crabtree Publishing Co.
Kalman, Bobbie & Johnson, Robin. Les Koalas et Autres Marsupiaux. 2010. (Petit Monde Vivant Ser.). (FRE., Illus.). 32p. (J). pap. 9.95 *(978-2-89579-320-5(4))* Bayard Canada Livres CAN. Dist: Crabtree Publishing Co.
Lüsted, Marcia Amidon. Tasmanian Devil: Savage Island Scavenger. 2017. (Illus.). 32p. (J). ***(978-1-68079-776-3(X))*** ABDO Publishing Co.
Markovics, Joyce L. Tasmanian Devil: Nighttime Scavenger. 2008. (Uncommon Animals Ser.). (Illus.). 32p. (YA). (gr. 2-5). lib. bdg. 25.27 *(978-1-59716-733-8(9)*, 1284366) Bearport Publishing Co., Inc.
Morgan, Sally. Marsupials. 2004. (J). lib. bdg. 27.10 *(978-1-59389-175-6(X))* Chrysalis Education.
Racanelli, Marie. Animals with Pockets. 2010. (Crazy Nature Ser.). 24p. (J). (gr. 1-5). lib. bdg., E-Book 42.50 *(978-1-4488-0155-8(9))*; (Illus.). pap. 8.25 *(978-1-4358-9862-2(1)*, PowerKids Pr.); (Illus.). (gr. 1-4). lib. bdg. 22.60 *(978-1-4358-9385-6(9))* Rosen Publishing Group, Inc., The.
Roza, Greg. Tasmanian Devil vs. Hyena. 2015. (Bizarre Beast Battles Ser.). (ENG.). 24p. (J). (gr. 2-3). 22.60 *(978-1-4824-2798-1(2))* Stevens, Gareth Publishing LLLP.
Rustad, Martha E. H. Baby Animals in Pouches. 2017. (Baby Animals & Their Homes Ser.). (ENG., Illus.). 24p. (gr. k-1). lib. bdg. 21.99 *(978-1-5157-3829-9(9))* Capstone Press of Coughlan Cos.
Sill, Cathryn. About Marsupials: A Guide for Children, 1 vol. Sill, John, illus. (ENG.). 48p. (J). 2009. pap. 7.95 *(978-1-56145-407-5(9))* 2006. 15.95 *(978-1-56145-358-0(7))* Peachtree Pubs.
Stefoff, Rebecca. The Marsupial Order. 2007. (Family Trees Ser.). (Illus.). 96p. (gr. 6-7). lib. bdg. 34.21 *(978-0-7614-2697-4(3)*, Benchmark Bks.) Marshall Cavendish Corp.
Tatlock, Ann. Backyard Jungle Safari Opossums: Opossums. 2015. (ENG., Illus.). 32p. (J). 26.50 *(978-1-62469-100-3(5))* Purple Toad Publishing, Inc.
Wignell, Edel. Bilby: Secrets of an Australian Marsupial. Jackson, Mark, illus. 2015. (ENG.). 32p. (J). (gr. k-4). 16.99 *(978-0-7636-6759-7(5))* Candlewick Pr.

MARTHA'S VINEYARD (MASS.)

The Greatest Place on Earth: A Children's Story, A History Lesson, A Scrapbook, A Lifetime Keepsake. 2006. (J). 18.95 *(978-0-9777882-0-0(2)*, Light Works Publishing) I.M. Enterprises.

MARTHA'S VINEYARD (MASS.)—FICTION

Bullen, Alexandra. Wishful Thinking. 2011. (ENG.). 256p. (J). (gr. 9-9). 17.99 *(978-0-545-13907-6(4))* Scholastic, Inc.
Chalfoun, Michelle. The Treasure of Maria Mamoun. 2016. (ENG.). 352p. (J). 16.99 *(978-0-374-30340-2(1)*, 9780374303402, Farrar, Straus & Giroux (BYR)) Farrar, Straus & Giroux.

M N O

Leahy, Sandy & Tarentino, Kathy. The Hibernating House. 2013. 26p. 19.95 *(978-1-4575-1753-2(1))*; pap. 12.95 *(978-1-4575-1670-2(5))* Dog Ear Publishing, LLC.

O'Connell, Jenny. Local Girls: An Island Summer Novel. 2008. (ENG.). 320p. pap. 19.99 *(978-1-4165-6335-8(0))* Pocket Books.

—Rich Boys: An Island Summer Novel. 2008. (ENG.). 288p. pap. 18.99 *(978-1-4165-6336-5(9)*, MTV Bks.) MTV Books.

Schaal, Patty. Nighttide on a Vineyard Farm. Datz, Margot, illus. 2010. (J). *(978-0-9827146-1-4(0))* Vineyard Stories.

Stewart, Jane. The Island Escapade. 2003. 102p. (YA). pap. 9.95 *(978-0-595-27734-6(9))* iUniverse, Inc.

MARTIAL ARTS

see also Archery; Self-Defense

The ABCs of Tae Kwon Do. 2004. (J). 5.95 *(978-0-9754345-0-5(0))* Cannady, John.

ABDO. Inside Martial Arts, 1 vol. 2014. (Inside Martial Arts Ser.: 6). (ENG.). 48p. (gr. 3-6). lib. bdg. 196.74 *(978-1-62403-600-2(7)*, SportsZone) ABDO Publishing Co.

Adams, Colleen. Kelly Clarkson. 2006. (Stars in the Spotlight Ser.: Vol. 3). (Illus.). 32p. (YA). (gr. 4-7). lib. bdg. 25.25 *(978-1-4042-3515-1(9))* Rosen Publishing Group, Inc., The.

Bagnulo, Giancarlo. A Complete Guide to Ju Jitsu. 2017. (Mastering Martial Arts Ser.). 128p. (J). (gr. 6-6). lib. bdg. 37.27 ***(978-0-7660-8545-9(7))*** Enslow Pubs., Inc.

Binder, C. F. Black Belt Attitude. 2003. (Illus.). 16p. (J). 7.70 *(978-1-4120-0351-3(2))* Trafford Publishing.

Bjorklund, Ruth. Aikido. 2011. (Martial Arts in Action 2 Ser.). (Illus.). 48p. (J). (gr. 6). lib. bdg. 29.93 *(978-0-7614-4931-7(0))* Marshall Cavendish Corp.

Castellano, Peter. MMA. 2015. (Daredevil Sports Ser.). (ENG., Illus.). 32p. (J). (gr. 1-1). pap. 10.50 *(978-1-4824-2981-7(0))* Stevens, Gareth Publishing LLLP.

—Mma. 2015. (Daredevil Sports Ser.). (ENG., Illus.). 32p. (J). (gr. 1-1). lib. bdg. 25.25 *(978-1-4824-2982-4(9))* Stevens, Gareth Publishing LLLP.

Chaline, Eric. Martial Arts for Athletic Conditioning. 2003. (Martial & Fighting Arts Ser.). (Illus.). 96p. (J). (gr. 7-18). lib. bdg. *(978-1-59084-397-0(5))* Mason Crest.

—Martial Arts for Athletic Conditioning: Winning Ways. James, Adam, ed. 2015. (Mastering Martial Arts Ser.). (Illus.). 96p. (J). (gr. 5). lib. bdg. 24.95 *(978-1-4222-3241-5(7))* Mason Crest.

—Martial Arts for Women: Winning Ways. James, Adam, ed. 2015. (Mastering Martial Arts Ser.). (Illus.). 96p. (J). (gr. 5). lib. bdg. 24.95 *(978-1-4222-3243-9(3))* Mason Crest.

—Ninjutsu. 2004. (Martial & Fighting Arts Ser.). (Illus.). 96p. (YA). (gr. 7-18). lib. bdg. 22.95 *(978-1-59084-398-7(3))* Mason Crest.

—Ninjutsu: Winning Ways. James, Adam, ed. 2015. (Mastering Martial Arts Ser.). 96p. (J). (gr. 5). lib. bdg. 24.95 *(978-1-4222-3244-6(1))* Mason Crest.

Corporate Contributor. Taylor Lautner. 2012. (ENG.). 32p. (J). *(978-0-7787-7619-2(0))*; pap. *(978-0-7787-7632-1(8))* Crabtree Publishing Co.

Crabtree, Marc. Meet My Neighbor, the Taekwondo Master. 2009. (Meet my Neighbor Ser.). (ENG., Illus.). 24p. (J). (gr. k-2). pap. *(978-0-7787-4582-2(1))* Crabtree Publishing Co.

Crossingham, John & Kalman, Bobbie. High Flying Martial Arts. 2008. (Sports Starters Ser.). (ENG., Illus.). 32p. (J). (gr. 3-7). pap. *(978-0-7787-3172-6(3))*; lib. bdg. *(978-0-7787-3140-5(5))* Crabtree Publishing Co.

Dawson, Patricia. Ninjas: Masters of Stealth & Secrecy. 2015. (J). lib. bdg. *(978-1-62713-413-2(1))*; (ENG., Illus.). 48p. (gr. 4-4). 31.36 *(978-1-5026-0122-3(2))* Cavendish Square Publishing.

Doeden, Matt. Combat Sports. 2015. (Summer Olympic Sports Ser.). (ENG., Illus.). 32p. (J). (gr. 2-4). 19.95 *(978-1-60753-807-3(5))* Amicus Publishing.

—Life as a Ninja: An Interactive History Adventure. 2010. (You Choose: Warriors Ser.). (ENG.). 112p. (gr. 3-4). pap. 41.70 *(978-1-4296-5099-1(0)*, You Choose Bks.) Capstone Press of Coughlan Cos.

Dougherty, Martin. Secrets of Martial Arts Masters. 2010. (Extreme! Ser.). (ENG.). 32p. (gr. 3-4). pap. 47.70 *(978-1-4296-5116-5(4)*, Fact Finders) Capstone Press of Coughlan Cos.

Dougherty, Martin J. Secrets of Martial Arts Masters, 1 vol. 2010. (Extreme Adventures! Ser.). (ENG.). 32p. (gr. 3-4). lib. bdg. 27.32 *(978-1-4296-4561-4(X)*, Fact Finders) Capstone Press of Coughlan Cos.

Durrie, Karen. Artes Marciales. 2012. (J). 27.13 *(978-1-61913-202-3(8))* Weigl Pubs., Inc.

—Martial Arts. 2011. (J). 27.13 *(978-1-61690-941-3(2))* Weigl Pubs., Inc.

Ellis, Carol. Kendo. 2010. (Martial Arts in Action Ser.). 48p. (gr. 6-7). lib. bdg. 29.93 *(978-0-7614-4935-5(3))* Marshall Cavendish Corp.

Etingoff, Kim. All Around Good Habits. 2013. (Junior Martial Arts Ser.: 9). 32p. (J). (gr. 4-18). 19.95 *(978-1-4222-2732-9(4))* Mason Crest.

—Concentration. 2013. (Junior Martial Arts Ser.: 9). 32p. (J). (gr. 4-18). 19.95 *(978-1-4222-2733-6(2))* Mason Crest.

—Confidence. 2013. (Junior Martial Arts Ser.: 9). 32p. (J). (gr. 4-18). 19.95 *(978-1-4222-2734-3(0))* Mason Crest.

—Hand-Eye Coordination. 2013. (Junior Martial Arts Ser.: 9). 32p. (J). (gr. 4-18). 19.95 *(978-1-4222-2735-0(9))* Mason Crest.

—Handling Peer Pressure. 2013. (Junior Martial Arts Ser.: 9). 32p. (J). (gr. 4-18). 19.95 *(978-1-4222-2736-7(7))* Mason Crest.

—Junior Martial Arts, 9 vols. 2014. (Illus.). 9p. (J). *(978-1-4222-2731-2(6))* Mason Crest.

Fishman, Jon M. Ronda Rousey. 2016. (Amazing Athletes Ser.). (ENG., Illus.). 32p. (J). (gr. 2-5). 26.65 *(978-1-5124-1333-5(X))* Lerner Publishing Group.

FitzPatrick, Bill. The Shaolin Action Principles. 2004. Orig. Title: 100 Action Principles of the Shaolin. 128p. pap. 20.00 *(978-1-884864-22-3(8))* American Success Institute, Inc.

Gagne, Tammy. Trends in Martial Arts. 2014. 48p. (gr. 4-8). 29.95 *(978-1-61228-553-5(8))* Mitchell Lane Pubs., Inc.

Gifford, Clive. Combat Sports. 2011. (ENG., Illus.). 32p. (J). pap. 10.95 *(978-1-77092-036-1(6))* Saunders Bk. Co. CAN. Dist: RiverStream Publishing.

—Martial Arts. 2009. (Tell Me about Sports Ser.). 32p. (gr. 3-18). 28.50 *(978-0-7614-4457-2(2))* Marshall Cavendish Corp.

—Martial Arts Legends. 2009. (ENG., Illus.). 32p. (J). (gr. 4-7). lib. bdg. *(978-0-7787-3776-6(4))* Crabtree Publishing Co.

Gitlin, Martin. Martial Arts & Its Greatest Fighters, 1 vol. 2015. (ENG.). 80p. (J). 31.70 *(978-1-62275-588-2(X)*, Britannica Educational Publishing) Rosen Publishing Group, Inc., The.

Group/McGraw-Hill, Wright. Formas de Moverse, 6 vols. (First Explorers. Primeros Exploradores Nonfiction Sets Ser.). (SPA.). (gr. 1-2). 29.95 *(978-0-7699-1473-2(X))* Shortland Pubns. (U. S. A.) Inc.

Gunderson, Jessica. Ninjas: A Guide to the Ancient Assassins, 1 vol. 2011. (History's Greatest Warriors Ser.). (ENG.). 48p. (gr. 3-4). lib. bdg. 31.99 *(978-1-4296-6600-8(5))* Capstone Press of Coughlan Cos.

Hamilton, John. Anderson Silva. 2010. (Xtreme UFC Ser.). 32p. (gr. 3-9). 27.07 *(978-1-61613-478-5(X)*, A&D Xtreme) ABDO Publishing Co.

—B. J. Penn. 2010. (Xtreme UFC Ser.). 32p. (gr. 3-9). 27.07 *(978-1-61613-477-8(1)*, A&D Xtreme) ABDO Publishing Co.

—Forrest Griffin. 2010. (Xtreme UFC Ser.). 32p. (gr. 3-9). 27.07 *(978-1-61613-475-4(5)*, A&D Xtreme) ABDO Publishing Co.

—Georges St-Pierre. 2010. (Xtreme UFC Ser.). 32p. (gr. 3-9). 27.07 *(978-1-61613-479-2(8)*, A&D Xtreme) ABDO Publishing Co.

—Greatest Hits. 2010. (Xtreme UFC Ser.). 32p. (gr. 3-9). 27.07 *(978-1-61613-474-7(7)*, A&D Xtreme) ABDO Publishing Co.

—Inside the Octagon. 2010. (Xtreme UFC Ser.). 32p. (gr. 3-9). 27.07 *(978-1-61613-476-1(3)*, A&D Xtreme) ABDO Publishing Co.

Haney-Withrow, Anna. Tae Kwon Do. 2011. (Martial Arts in Action 2 Ser.). 48p. (gr. 6). lib. bdg. 29.93 *(978-0-7614-4940-9(X))* Marshall Cavendish Corp.

Harbo, Christopher L., et al. The Secrets of Martial Arts: An Isabel Soto History Adventure. 2010. (Graphic Expeditions Ser.). (ENG.). 32p. (gr. 3-4). pap. 47.70 *(978-1-4296-5146-2(6))*; lib. bdg. 30.65 *(978-1-4296-3973-6(3))* Capstone Press of Coughlan Cos. (Graphic Library).

Hillson, Ted. Tae Kwon Do Classic Forms: 21 Hyung — Novice White Belt Through Advanced Black Belt. Kligge, Elizabeth, illus. 2003. 232p. (YA). spiral bd. 22.50 *(978-0-9729293-0-1(4))* Double Dagger Pr.

Hyde, Natalie. Ninjas. 2014. (ENG., Illus.). 48p. (J). *(978-0-7787-1365-4(2))* Crabtree Publishing Co.

James, Sara. Safety. 2013. (Junior Martial Arts Ser.: 9). 32p. (J). (gr. 4-18). 19.95 *(978-1-4222-2737-4(5))* Mason Crest.

—Self-Defense. 2013. (Junior Martial Arts Ser.: 9). 32p. (J). (gr. 4-18). 19.95 *(978-1-4222-2738-1(3))* Mason Crest.

—Self-Discipline. 2013. (Junior Martial Arts Ser.: 9). 32p. (J). (gr. 4-18). 19.95 *(978-1-4222-2739-8(1))* Mason Crest.

—Self-Esteem. 2013. (Junior Martial Arts Ser.: 9). 32p. (J). (gr. 4-18). 19.95 *(978-1-4222-2740-4(5))* Mason Crest.

Johnson, Nathan. Jujutsu: Winning Ways. James, Adam, ed. 2015. (Mastering Martial Arts Ser.). (Illus.). 96p. (J). (gr. 5). lib. bdg. 24.95 *(978-1-4222-3237-8(9))* Mason Crest.

—Kickboxing & MMA: Winning Ways. James, Adam, ed. 2015. (Mastering Martial Arts Ser.). 96p. (J). (gr. 5). lib. bdg. 24.95 *(978-1-4222-3239-2(5))* Mason Crest.

—Martial Arts for Children: Winning Ways. James, Adam, ed. 2015. (Mastering Martial Arts Ser.). (Illus.). 96p. (J). (gr. 5). lib. bdg. 24.95 *(978-1-4222-3242-2(5))* Mason Crest.

Jones, Patrick. Ultimate Fighting: The Brains & Brawn of Mixed Martial Arts. 2013. (Spectacular Sports Ser.). (ENG., Illus.). 64p. (gr. 5-12). lib. bdg. 33.27 *(978-1-4677-0934-7(4)*, Millbrook Pr.) Lerner Publishing Group.

Jones, Richard & Santillan, Jorge. Manga Martial Arts Figures. 2012. (Learn to Draw Manga Ser.). (ENG., Illus.). 32p. (J). (gr. 4-6). pap. 11.75 *(978-1-4488-7946-5(9))*; lib. bdg. 26.50 *(978-1-4488-7875-8(6))* Rosen Publishing Group, Inc., The. (PowerKids Pr.).

Kennedy, Robert C. Would You Dare Be an MMA Fighter? 2016. (Would You Dare? Ser.). 00032p. (J). pap. 10.50 *(978-1-4824-5814-5(4))* Stevens, Gareth Publishing LLLP.

Kortemeier, Todd. Superstars of the UFC. 2016. (Pro Sports Superstars Ser.). (ENG.). 24p. (gr. 1-4). 20.95 *(978-1-60753-939-1(X))* Amicus Publishing.

Lawrence, Katherine Drobot. Jean-Claude Van Damme. 2005. (Martial Arts Masters Ser.). (Illus.). 112p. (YA). (gr. 7-12). lib. bdg. 34.60 *(978-0-8239-3517-8(5))* Rosen Publishing Group, Inc., The.

Levigne, Heather. Les Arts Martiaux. Briere, Marie-Josee, tr. from ENG. Rouse, Bonna, illus. 2007. (Sans Limites Ser.). (FRE.). 32p. (J). pap. 9.95 *(978-2-89579-168-3(6))* Bayard Canada Livres CAN. Dist: Crabtree Publishing Co.

Litmanovich, Ellina. Ronda Rousey: Champion Mixed Martial Arts Star. 2017. (Sports Star Champions Ser.). 48p. (J). (gr. 5-6). lib. bdg. 27.93 ***(978-0-7660-8696-8(8))*** Enslow Pubs., Inc.

Lorini, Walter. A Complete Guide to Tai Chi. 2017. (Mastering Martial Arts Ser.). 128p. (gr. 6-6). lib. bdg. 37.27 ***(978-0-7660-8537-4(6))*** Enslow Pubs., Inc.

MacAulay, Kelley & Kalman, Bobbie. Taekwondo in Action. Crabtree, Marc, photos by. 2004. (Sports in Action Ser.). (ENG., Illus.). 32p. (J). pap. *(978-0-7787-0358-7(4))* Crabtree Publishing Co.

Malam, John. You Wouldn't Want to Be a Ninja Warrior! Antram, David, illus. 2012. (You Wouldn't Want to... Ser.). (ENG.). 32p. (J). pap. 9.95 *(978-0-531-20948-6(2)*, Watts, Franklin) Scholastic Library Publishing.

Martial Arts. 2005. (Martial Arts Ser.). 32p. (gr. 4-6). 112.00 *(978-0-7910-6880-9(3)*, Chelsea Hse.) Facts On File, Inc.

Martial Arts Masters. 2005. (Illus.). (gr. 7-12). lib. bdg. 151.50 *(978-0-8239-9691-9(3))* Rosen Publishing Group, Inc., The.

Martial Arts Sports Zone: Spring 2012 New Releases. 2012. (Martial Arts Sports Zone Ser.). 32p. (gr. 4-8). lib. bdg. 159.60 *(978-0-7613-8901-9(6)*, Lerner Pubns.) Lerner Publishing Group.

Mason, Paul. Tae Kwon Do. 2010. (Combat Sports Ser.). 32p. (J). (gr. 2-5). lib. bdg. 28.50 *(978-1-59771-277-4(9))* Sea-To-Sea Pubns.

Mastering Martial Arts. 2017. (Mastering Martial Arts Ser.). 128p. (gr. 6-6). lib. bdg. 223.62 ***(978-0-7660-8595-4(3))*** Enslow Pubs., Inc.

Mattern, Joanne. Kickboxing. 2008. (Illus.). 24p. (J). lib. bdg. *(978-1-60472-395-3(5))* Rourke Educational Media.

Matthews, Rupert. Ninjas. 2015. (History's Fearless Fighters Ser.). (ENG., Illus.). 48p. (J). (gr. 5-6). pap. 14.05 *(978-1-4824-3173-5(4))* Stevens, Gareth Publishing LLLP.

McDaniel, Sean. Ninja. 2011. (History's Greatest Warriors Ser.). (ENG., Illus.). 24p. (J). (gr. 3-7). lib. bdg. 25.95 *(978-1-60014-630-5(9)*, Torque Bks.) Bellwether Media.

McFee, Shane. Let's Learn Martial Arts. (Let's Get Active Ser.). 24p. 2009. (gr. 2-3). 42.50 *(978-1-61514-250-7(9))* 2008. (Illus.). (J). (gr. 3-7). lib. bdg. 22.60 *(978-1-4042-4196-1(5))* Rosen Publishing Group, Inc., The. (PowerKids Pr.).

McIntosh, J. S. Martial Arts. 2010. (Getting the Edge Ser.). 96p. (YA). lib. bdg. 24.95 *(978-1-4222-1738-2(8))* Mason Crest.

McNab, Chris. Martial Arts for People with Disabilities. 2004. (Martial & Fighting Arts Ser.). (Illus.). 96p. (YA). (gr. 7). lib. bdg. 22.95 *(978-1-59084-399-4(1))* Mason Crest.

Mochizuki, Ken & Lee, Dom. Be Water, My Friend: The Early Years of Bruce Lee, 1 vol. 2006. (ENG., Illus.). 32p. (J). 16.95 *(978-1-58430-265-0(8))* Lee & Low Bks., Inc.

Monnig, Alex. Aikido, 1 vol. 2014. (Inside Martial Arts Ser.). (ENG., Illus.). 48p. (J). (gr. 3-6). lib. bdg. 32.79 *(978-1-62403-601-9(5)*, SportsZone) ABDO Publishing Co.

Montanha. The Brazilian Jiu-Jitsu Mind Set: To Submit Your Opponent from Any Position ! 2004. (Illus.). 108p. per. 12.95 *(978-0-9743380-0-2(1))* Montanha Pr.

Mooney, Carla. Ninjas, 1 vol. 2013. (Great Warriors Ser.). (ENG.). 48p. (J). (gr. 3-6). lib. bdg. 32.79 *(978-1-61783-726-5(1))*; (Illus.). pap. 15.64 *(978-1-61783-776-0(8)*, Core Library) ABDO Publishing Co.

Mostofizadeh, Hoomaz. MMA Coloring Book: Mixed Martial Arts Coloring Book. 2012. (ENG.). 52p. pap. 5.99 *(978-1-937981-60-0(6))* Mikazuki Publishing Hse.

Nishida, Masaki. Drawing Manga Martial Arts Figures. (How to Draw Manga Ser.). 24p. (gr. 3-3). 2009. 47.90 *(978-1-61513-440-3(9)*, PowerKids Pr.) 2007. (Illus.). (J). lib. bdg. 25.25 *(978-1-4042-3850-3(6))* Rosen Publishing Group, Inc., The.

Nixon, James. Martial Arts. 2017. (First Sport Ser.). (ENG., Illus.). 24p. (J). (gr. k-2). pap. 9.99 *(978-1-4451-4905-9(2)*, Franklin Watts) Hachette Children's Group GBR. Dist: Hachette Bk. Group.

Noll, Elizabeth. Mixed Martial Artists. 2017. (Rank It! Ser.). (ENG.). 32p. (gr. 3-7). 31.35 ***(978-1-68072-061-7(9)***, Bolt) Black Rabbit Bks.

Ollhoff, Jim. Grappling, 1 vol. 2008. (World of Martial Arts Ser.). (ENG., Illus.). 32p. (gr. 4-8). 27.07 *(978-1-59928-976-2(8)*, Abdo & Daughters) ABDO Publishing Co.

—Martial Arts Around the Globe, 1 vol. 2008. (World of Martial Arts Ser.). (ENG., Illus.). 32p. (gr. 4-8). 27.07 *(978-1-59928-979-3(2)*, Abdo & Daughters) ABDO Publishing Co.

—Ninja, 1 vol. 2008. (World of Martial Arts Ser.). (ENG.). 32p. (gr. 4-8). 27.07 *(978-1-59928-982-3(2)*, Abdo & Daughters) ABDO Publishing Co.

—Weapons, 1 vol. 2008. (World of Martial Arts Ser.). (ENG.). 32p. (gr. 4-8). 27.07 *(978-1-59928-985-4(7)*, Abdo & Daughters) ABDO Publishing Co.

O'Shei, Tim. Kendo [Scholastic]. 2011. (Martial Arts Ser.). 32p. pap. 1.00 *(978-1-4296-6484-4(3)*, Blazers) Capstone Press of Coughlan Cos.

Page, Jason. Martial Arts, Boxing, & Other Combat Sports: Fencing, Judo, Wrestling, Taekwondo, & a Whole Lot More. 2008. (Olympic Sports Ser.). (ENG., Illus.). 32p. (J). (gr. 3-7). pap. *(978-0-7787-4033-9(1))*; lib. bdg. *(978-0-7787-4016-2(1))* Crabtree Publishing Co.

Park, Y. H. & Tok, Stephanie. Taekwondo for Kids. 2005. (Martial Arts for Kids Ser.). (ENG., Illus.). 48p. (J). (gr. k-3). 13.95 *(978-0-8048-3631-9(0))* Tuttle Publishing.

Pawlett, Mark & Pawlett, Ray. The Tae Kwon Do Handbook. 2008. (Martial Arts Ser.). (Illus.). 256p. (YA). (gr. 7-12). lib. bdg. 42.60 *(978-1-4042-1396-8(1))* Rosen Publishing Group, Inc., The.

Polydoros, Lori. MMA Greats, 1 vol. 2012. (Best of the Best Ser.). (ENG., Illus.). 32p. (gr. 1-2). lib. bdg. 26.65 *(978-1-4296-8433-0(X))* Capstone Press of Coughlan Cos.

Rielly, Robin L. & Tok, Stephanie. Karate for Kids. 2004. (Martial Arts for Kids Ser.). (ENG., Illus.). 48p. (J). (gr. k-3). 13.95 *(978-0-8048-3534-3(9))* Tuttle Publishing.

Roensch, Greg. Bruce Lee. 2005. (Martial Arts Masters Ser.). (Illus.). 112p. (YA). (gr. 7-12). lib. bdg. 34.60 *(978-0-8239-3515-4(9))* Rosen Publishing Group, Inc., The.

Roytman, Arkady. Martial Arts Coloring Book. 2013. (Dover Coloring Bks.). (ENG., Illus.). 32p. (J). (gr. 3-5). pap. 3.99 *(978-0-486-49023-6(8))* Dover Pubns., Inc.

Rumpf, Wolfgang. Taekwondo Kids: From White Belt to Yellow/Green Belt. Dornemann, Volker, illus. 2007. 136p. (J). pap. 14.95 *(978-1-84126-214-7(5))* Meyer & Meyer Sport, Ltd. GBR. Dist: Cardinal Pubs. Group.

Rumpf, Wolfgang & Dornemann, Volker. Taekwondo Kids Volume 2: From Green Belt to Blue Belt. 2008. (Illus.). 144p. (J). (gr. 4-7). pap. 14.95 *(978-1-84126-240-6(4))* Meyer & Meyer Sport, Ltd. GBR. Dist: Cardinal Pubs. Group.

Safe Kids USA Staff. Self-Defense for Kids: Learn Practical & Effective Techniques to Help You Defend Yourself. 2004. (Illus.). 47p. (J). (gr. -1-12). pap. 6.95 *(978-0-9718609-5-7(5))* High Mountain Publishing.

Shaffer, Jody Jensen. Ninja Warriors. 2015. (Ancient Warriors Ser.). (ENG.). 32p. (J). (gr. 2-5). 28.50 *(978-1-63143-757-1(7)*, 208589) Child's World, Inc., The.

Snow, Kevin. Ronda Rousey: Conquering New Ground. 2017. (J). ***(978-1-5026-2832-9(5))*** Cavendish Square Publishing.

Streissguth, Thomas. Kickboxing. 2008. (Action Sports Ser.). (ENG., Illus.). 24p. (J). (gr. 3-7). lib. bdg. 25.95 *(978-1-60014-140-9(4))* Bellwether Media.

Tometich, Annabelle. Mixed Martial Arts, 1 vol. 2014. (Inside Martial Arts Ser.). (ENG., Illus.). 48p. (J). (gr. 3-6). lib. bdg. 32.79 *(978-1-62403-605-7(8)*, SportsZone) ABDO Publishing Co.

Trimble, Aidan, contrib. by. Martial & Fighting Arts, 13 vols., Set. (Illus.). 96p. (YA). (gr. 7-18). lib. bdg. *(978-1-59084-387-1(8))* Mason Crest.

Turnbull, Stephen & Tulloch, Coral. Real Ninja: Over 20 Stories of Japan's Secret Assassins. Field, James, illus. 2008. (ENG.). 48p. (J). (gr. 3-18). 15.95 *(978-1-59270-081-3(0))* Enchanted Lion Bks., LLC.

Uschan, Michael V. Jet Li. 2011. (People in the News Ser.). (ENG., Illus.). 128p. (gr. 7-10). lib. bdg. 39.40 *(978-1-4205-0731-7(1))* Cengage Gale.

Warr, Peter. The Kung Fu Handbook. 2009. (Martial Arts Ser.). 256p. (gr. 8-8). 79.90 *(978-1-61514-369-6(6))* Rosen Publishing Group, Inc., The.

Weiss, Bobbi Jg & Weiss, David Cody. Phonic Comics - Hiro Dragon Warrior: Fight or Flight Level 2, Issue 3. 2011. (ENG., Illus.). 24p. (J). (gr. 1-17). pap. 3.99 *(978-1-60169-111-8(4))* Innovative Kids.

Wells, Garrison. Mixed Martial Arts: Ultimate Fighting Combinations. 2012. (Martial Arts Sports Zone Ser.). (ENG., Illus.). 32p. (gr. 4-8). lib. bdg. 26.60 *(978-0-7613-8455-7(3)*, Lerner Pubns.) Lerner Publishing Group.

—Muay Thai: Kickboxing Combat. 2012. (Martial Arts Sports Zone Ser.). (ENG., Illus.). 32p. (gr. 4-8). lib. bdg. 26.60 *(978-0-7613-8457-1(X)*, Lerner Pubns.) Lerner Publishing Group.

Wiseman, Blaine. UFC Championship. 2010. (Sporting Championships Ser.). 32p. (J). (gr. 4-6). lib. bdg. 27.13 *(978-1-61690-130-1(6))* Weigl Pubs., Inc.

—UFC Championship: Sporting Championships. 2010. (J). pap. 10.95 *(978-1-61690-131-8(4))* Weigl Pubs., Inc.

Wood, Alix. Dueling. Wood, Alix, illus. 2013. (Why'd They Do That? Strange Customs of the Past Ser.). (Illus.). 32p. (J). (gr. 4-6). pap. 10.50 *(978-1-4339-9577-4(8))*; pap. 63.00 *(978-1-4339-9578-1(6))* Stevens, Gareth Publishing LLLP.

—Dueling. 2013. (Why'd They Do That? Strange Customs of the Past Ser.). (ENG., Illus.). 32p. (J). (gr. 4-6). lib. bdg. 26.60 *(978-1-4339-9576-7(X))* Stevens, Gareth Publishing LLLP.

—You Can Be a Martial Artist, Vol. 1. 2014. (Let's Get Moving! Ser.). (ENG.). 32p. (J). (gr. 3-4). 26.60 *(978-1-4824-0279-7(3))* Stevens, Gareth Publishing LLLP.

MARTIAL ARTS—FICTION

Adam D. Levine. Knights: Reign of Hellfire. 2010. (ENG.). 184p. 23.95 *(978-1-4401-7614-2(0))*; pap. 13.95 *(978-1-4401-7618-0(3))* iUniverse, Inc.

Asai, Carrie. The Book of the Pearl. Verhoye, Annabelle & Alarcao, Renato, illus. 2003. (Samurai Girl Ser.: 3). (ENG.). 240p. (YA). (gr. 11). pap. 6.99 *(978-0-689-86432-2(9)*, Simon Pulse) Simon Pulse.

Asai, Carrie & Gray, Mitchel. The Book of the Wind. Verhoye, Annabelle & Alarcão, Renato, illus. 2003. (Samurai Girl Ser.: 4). (ENG.). 224p. (YA). (gr. 11). pap. 6.99 *(978-0-689-86433-9(7)*, Simon Pulse) Simon Pulse.

Binfet, Eric. The Ninja with Bunny Rabbit Slippers. 2012. 34p. pap. 19.99 *(978-1-105-44896-6(7))* Lulu.com GBR. Dist: Lulu Pr., Inc.

Boltonwood-Castle, Tony. Ben,Jay & Ricardo Karate Adventure: The Night the Thieves Came Calling. 2010. 80p. pap. 10.49 *(978-1-4520-8114-4(X))* AuthorHouse.

Bradford, Chris. Hostage, Bk. 2. 2017. (Bodyguard Ser.). (ENG.). 224p. (J). (gr. 5). pap. 8.99 *(978-1-5247-3699-6(6)*, Philomel Bks.) Penguin Young Readers Group.

—Ninja: First Mission. 2012. (Stoke Books Titles Ser.). 64p. (J). (gr. 5-8). pap. 45.32 *(978-0-7613-9221-7(1))*; pap. 7.95 *(978-1-78112-022-4(6))*; lib. bdg. 22.60 *(978-1-78112-021-7(8))* Stoke Bks.

—Recruit, Bk. 1. 2017. (Bodyguard Ser.). (ENG.). 272p. (J). (gr. 5). pap. 8.99 *(978-1-5247-3697-2(X)*, Philomel Bks.) Penguin Young Readers Group.

—The Way of the Warrior, Bk. 1. 2008. (Young Samurai Ser.: 1). (ENG., Illus.). 352p. (J). (gr. 6-10). pap. 12.99 ***(978-0-14-132430-2(9))*** Penguin Bks., Ltd. GBR. Dist: Independent Pubs. Group.

—Young Samurai the Way of the Dragon. l.t. ed. 2012. (Young Samurai Ser.). (ENG.). 644p. (J). (gr. 9-12). 23.99 *(978-1-4104-4466-0(X))* Thorndike Pr.

—Young Samurai: the Way of the Sword. 2011. 448p. pap. 7.99 *(978-1-4231-2937-0(7))* Hyperion Pr.

—Young Samurai the Way of the Sword. l.t. ed. 2012. (Young Samurai Ser.). (ENG.). 547p. (J). (gr. 6-9). 23.99 *(978-1-4104-4404-2(X))* Thorndike Pr.

Brown, K. T. The Adventures of Peter Tucker: Introduction of the Tiger. 2011. 82p. pap. 15.99 *(978-1-4628-7856-7(3))* Xlibris Corp.

Bruchac, Joseph. The Way. 2013. (ENG.). 160p. (YA). (gr. 6-12). pap. 9.95 *(978-1-4677-0862-3(3))* 2007. 156p. (J). (gr. 4-7). 16.95 *(978-1-58196-062-4(X))* Lerner Publishing Group. (Darby Creek).

Cannella, Marco & Marron, Jose Luis, illus. Tattoo of Death. 2007. (Choose Your Own Adventure Ser.: No. 22). 113p. (J). (gr. 4-7). pap. 6.99 *(978-1-933390-22-2(0))* Chooseco LLC.

Caputo, Kenneth. The Adventures of Jay & Tay: Our First Karate Class. 2011. 32p. pap. 14.99 *(978-1-4567-1999-9(8))* AuthorHouse.

Cha, Louis. The Legendary Couple, Vol. 4. Wong, Tony, illus. 2003. 120p. (YA). (gr. 8-18). pap. 13.95 *(978-1-58899-233-8(0))* ComicsOne Corp./Dr. Masters.

Chanda, J-P. Turtle Rescue! Redondo, Jesus, illus. 2004. (Teenage Mutant Ninja Turtles Ser.). 32p. (J). (gr. 4-7). 11.65 *(978-0-7569-5371-3(5))* Perfection Learning Corp.

Chin, Oliver. The Belt of Fire. Chua, Charlene, illus. 2013. (Julie Black Belt Ser.). (ENG.). 36p. (J). (gr. -1-3). 15.95 *(978-1-59702-079-4(6))* Immedium.

Colossal, Eric. Feasts of Fury. 2016. (Rutabaga the Adventure Chef Ser.: 2). (J). lib. bdg. 20.80 *(978-0-606-38205-2(4))* Turtleback Bks.

DaCosta, Barbara. Nighttime Ninja. 2012. (ENG., Illus.). 32p. (J). (gr. -1-3). 16.99 *(978-0-316-20384-5(X))* Little, Brown Bks. for Young Readers.

Davis, Jacky. Black Belt Bunny. Fleck, Jay, illus. 2017. (ENG.). 40p. (J). (-k). 16.99 ***(978-0-525-42902-9(6)***, Dial Bks) Penguin Young Readers Group.

Devine, Eric. Tap Out. 2012. (ENG.). 320p. (YA). (gr. 3-17). pap. 11.95 *(978-0-7624-4569-1(6)*, Running Pr. Kids) Running Pr. Bk. Pubs.

DreamWorks. Kung Fu Panda: Po's Tasty Training. 2008. (J). 13.99 *(978-1-59319-981-4(3))* LeapFrog Enterprises, Inc.

DreamWorks & DreamWorks / LeapFrog. Kung Fu Panda: L'Entrainement Gourmand. 2008. (J). 20.79 *(978-1-59319-946-3(5))* LeapFrog Enterprises, Inc.

Farshtey, Greg. Jay - Ninja of Lightning, Bk. 4. 2012. (Lego Ninjago Ser.). (ENG.). 80p. (J). (gr. 2-5). pap. 4.99 *(978-0-545-36994-7(0))* Scholastic, Inc.

Fusco, John. Little Monk & the Mantis: A Bug, a Boy, & the Birth of a Kung Fu Legend. Lugo, Patrick, illus. 2012. (ENG.). 32p. (J). (gr. -1-3). 16.95 *(978-0-8048-4221-1(3))* Tuttle Publishing.

Gallo, Tina. Like Father, Like Po. 2015. (Kung Fu Panda 8x8 Ser.). lib. bdg. 13.55 *(978-0-606-38257-1(7))* Turtleback Bks.
Gallo, Tina, adapted by. The Po Who Cried Ghost. 2014. (Kung Fu Panda TV Ser.). (ENG., Illus.). 24p. (J). (gr. -1-2). pap. 3.99 *(978-1-4814-0491-4(1),* Simon Spotlight) Simon Spotlight.
Gerver, Jane E. The Santa Snatcher. Spaziante, Patrick, illus. 2004. 32p. (J). lib. bdg. 15.00 *(978-1-4242-0959-0(5))* Fitzgerald Bks.
Gibsen, Cole. Katana. 2012. (Katana Novel Ser.: 1). (ENG.). 384p. (YA). pap. 9.95 *(978-0-7387-3040-0(8),* Flux) North Star Editions.
—Senshi. 2013. (Katana Novel Ser.: 2). (ENG.). 384p. (YA). pap. 9.99 *(978-0-7387-3261-9(3),* Flux) North Star Editions.
—Shinobi. 2014. (Katana Novel Ser.: 3). (ENG.). 288p. (YA). pap. 9.99 *(978-0-7387-3911-3(1),* Flux) North Star Editions.
Goh, Colin & Woo, Yen Yen. Enter the Dumpling, Vol. 1. Lee, Soo, illus. 2013. (ENG.). 144p. (J). pap. 12.99 *(978-0-9881899-0-4(9),* 9780988189904) Yumcha Studios LLC.
Golden Books. Really Spaced Out! (Teenage Mutant Ninja Turtles) Golden Books, illus. 2016. (Little Golden Book Ser.). (ENG., Illus.). 24p. (J). (-k). 4.99 *(978-1-101-93694-8(0),* Golden Bks.) Random Hse. Children's Bks.
Higgins, Simon. Moonshadow #2: the Nightmare Ninja. 2012. (Moonshadow Ser.: 2). (ENG.). 384p. (J). (gr. 3-7). pap. 6.99 *(978-0-316-05534-5(4))* Little, Brown Bks. for Young Readers.
—Moonshadow: Rise of the Ninja. 2011. (Moonshadow Ser.: 1). (ENG.). 352p. (J). (gr. 3-7). pap. 6.99 *(978-0-316-05532-1(8))* Little, Brown Bks. for Young Readers.
Himmelman, John. Bunjitsu Bunny Jumps to the Moon. Himmelman, John, illus. 2016. (Bunjitsu Bunny Ser.). (ENG., Illus.). 128p. (J). 13.99 *(978-1-62779-732-0(7),* 9781627797320, Holt, Henry & Co. Bks. For Young Readers) Holt, Henry & Co.
—Bunjitsu Bunny's Best Move. Himmelman, John, illus. 2015. (Bunjitsu Bunny Ser.: 2). (ENG., Illus.). 128p. (J). (gr. 1-3). 13.99 *(978-0-8050-9971-3(9),* 9780805099713, Holt, Henry & Co. Bks. For Young Readers) Holt, Henry & Co.
—Tales of Bunjitsu Bunny. Himmelman, John, illus. 2014. (Bunjitsu Bunny Ser.: 1). (ENG., Illus.). 128p. (J). (gr. 1-3). 13.99 *(978-0-8050-9970-6(0),* 9780805099706, Holt, Henry & Co. Bks. For Young Readers) Holt, Henry & Co.
Holt, Alex. Kung-Fu Frogs: From the Planet Intellectica. 2012. 40p. pap. 19.57 *(978-1-4669-1973-0(6))* Trafford Publishing.
Hong, Chen Jiang. Little Eagle. 2007. (ENG., Illus.). 32p. (J). (gr. -1-3). 16.95 *(978-1-59270-071-4(3))* Enchanted Lion Bks., LLC.
Ishida, Sanae. Chibi Samurai Wants a Pet: An Adventure with Little Kunoichi the Ninja Girl. 2017. (Little Kunoichi, the Ninja Girl Ser.). (ENG.). 32p. (J). (gr. -1-2). 16.99 ***(978-1-63217-117-7(1),*** Little Bigfoot) Sasquatch Bks.
Ishida, Sanae. Little Kunoichi, the Ninja Girl. 2015. (Little Kunoichi, the Ninja Girl Ser.). (ENG., Illus.). 32p. (J). (gr. -1-2). 16.99 *(978-1-57061-954-0(9),* Little Bigfoot) Sasquatch Bks.
James, Hollis. Space Shark! (Teenage Mutant Ninja Turtles) Spaziante, Patrick, illus. 2016. (Step into Reading Ser.). (ENG.). 24p. (J). (gr. -1-1). 4.99 *(978-1-101-93708-2(4),* Random Hse. Bks. for Young Readers) Random Hse. Children's Bks.
Johnson, Lauren. Beastly Basketball, 1 vol. Garcia, Eduardo, illus. 2014. (Sports Illustrated Kids Graphic Novels Ser.). (ENG.). 72p. (gr. 2-5). lib. bdg. 26.65 *(978-1-4342-6490-9(4))* Stone Arch Bks.
Jones, Patrick. Body Shot. 2013. (Dojo Ser.). (ENG.). 112p. (YA). (gr. 6-12). pap. 7.95 *(978-1-4677-1490-7(9));* lib. bdg. 27.93 *(978-1-4677-0633-9(7))* Lerner Publishing Group. (Darby Creek).
—Head Kick. 2013. (Dojo Ser.). (ENG.). 120p. (YA). (gr. 6-12). pap. 7.95 *(978-1-4677-1489-1(5));* lib. bdg. 27.93 *(978-1-4677-0632-2(9))* Lerner Publishing Group. (Darby Creek).
—Side Control. 2013. (Dojo Ser.). (ENG.). 136p. (YA). (gr. 6-12). pap. 7.95 *(978-1-4677-1488-4(7));* lib. bdg. 27.93 *(978-1-4677-0631-5(0))* Lerner Publishing Group. (Darby Creek).
—Triangle Choke. 2013. (Dojo Ser.). (ENG.). 136p. (YA). (gr. 6-12). pap. 7.95 *(978-1-4677-1487-7(9));* lib. bdg. 27.93 *(978-1-4677-0630-8(2))* Lerner Publishing Group. (Darby Creek).
Kakakios, Melissa. I Love Taekwondo: My First Taekwondo Books. 2013. 28p. pap. 16.95 *(978-1-4525-7668-8(8),* Balboa Pr.) Author Solutions, Inc.
—The Spirit of Courage: My First Tae Kwon Do Books. 2013. 28p. pap. 16.95 *(978-1-4525-8284-9(X),* Balboa Pr.) Author Solutions, Inc.
Kishimoto, Masashi. Naruto: Chapter Book, Vol. 11. Kishimoto, Masashi, illus. 2010. (ENG., Illus.). 80p. (J). pap. 4.99 *(978-1-4215-3041-3(4))* Viz Media.
—Naruto: Chapter Book, Vol. 13. Kishimoto, Masashi, illus. 2010. (ENG., Illus.). 80p. (J). pap. 4.99 *(978-1-4215-3043-7(0))* Viz Media.
Laflamme, Mark. Guys Named Jack. 2013. 308p. pap. 17.95 *(978-1-62646-391-2(3))* Booklocker.com, Inc.
Leibold, Jay. Secret of the Ninja. Nugent, Suzanne & Marron, Jose, illus. 2007. (Choose Your Own Adventure Ser.: Vol. 16). 124p. (J). (gr. 4-7). per. 6.99 *(978-1-933390-16-1(6))* Chooseco LLC.
Leigh, C. J. The Ninjabread Man. Gall, Chris, illus. 2016. (ENG.). 40p. (J). (gr. -1-k). 16.99 *(978-0-545-81430-0(8))* Scholastic, Inc.
Ling, L. M. ZOEY LEE Schoolyard Scuffle. 2011. (ENG., Illus.). 160p. pap. 9.99 *(978-1-937861-00-1(7))* Fear2love Pr.
Lloyd, Alison. Year of the Tiger. 2010. (ENG.). 228p. (YA). (gr. 5-18). pap. 16.95 *(978-0-8234-2277-7(1))* Holiday Hse., Inc.
Ma, Wing Shing. Storm Riders Vol. 1: Invading Sun. 2003. (Illus.). 128p. 9.95 *(978-1-58899-359-5(0))* ComicsOne Corp./Dr. Masters.
Ma, Wing Shing & Lau, Ding Kin. Chinese Hero Vol. 3: Tales of the Blood Sword. Yang, Sue & Stone, Benjamin, eds. Zhao, Yun, tr. from CHI. 2007. (ENG., Illus.). 280p. (YA). pap. 19.95 *(978-1-59796-117-2(5))* DrMaster Pubns. Inc.
Mah, Adeline Yen. Chinese Cinderella & the Secret Dragon Society. 2006. (ENG., Illus.). 256p. (J). (gr. 5-9). pap. 7.99 *(978-0-06-056736-1(8))* HarperCollins Pubs.
Makura, Sho. Panda Man & the Treasure Hunt. Kato, Haruhi, illus. 2011. (ENG.). 96p. (J). (gr. 1-4). pap. 7.99 *(978-1-4215-3521-0(1))* Viz Media.
—Panda Man to the Rescue! Kato, Haruhi, illus. 2010. (ENG.). 96p. (J). pap. 7.99 *(978-1-4215-3520-3(3))* Viz Media.
—Panda Man vs. Chiwanda. Kato, Haruhi, illus. 2011. (ENG.). 96p. (J). (gr. 1-4). pap. 7.99 *(978-1-4215-3522-7(X))* Viz Media.
Mauser McCord, Pat. A Bundle of Sticks. 2nd ed. 2004. (Illus.). 170p. (J). pap. 6.99 *(978-1-880336-86-1(3),* BOS) Turtle Pr.
McCann, James. Flying Feet, 1 vol. 2010. (Orca Sports Ser.). (ENG., Illus.). 152p. (YA). (gr. 6-10). pap. 9.95 *(978-1-55469-290-3(3))* Orca Bk. Pubs. USA.
Ohtaka, Shinobu. The Strongest Bride on Earth, 12 vols. 2012. (Sumomomo, Momomo Ser.: 12). (ENG., Illus.). 240p. (gr. 11-17). pap. 13.00 *(978-0-316-20470-5(6),* Yen Pr.) Orbit.
Orlean, Susan & Bradford, Chris. Young Samurai the Way of the Warrior. l.t. ed. 2011. (Young Samurai Ser.). (ENG.). 628p. (J). 23.99 *(978-1-4104-4329-8(9))* Thorndike Pr.
O'Ryan, Ellie, adapted by. Panda School. 2015. (Kung Fu Panda TV Ser.). (ENG., Illus.). 32p. (J). (gr. k-2). pap. 3.99 *(978-1-4814-3707-3(0),* Simon Spotlight) Simon Spotlight.
Pierce, Terry. Tae Kwon Do! Bonita, Todd, illus. 2006. (Step into Reading Ser.). (ENG.). 32p. (J). (gr. -1-1). per. 3.99 *(978-0-375-83448-6(6),* Random Hse. Bks. for Young Readers) Random Hse. Children's Bks.
Pilkey, Dav. The Adventures of Ook & Gluk, Kung-Fu Cavemen from the Future. Pilkey, Dav, illus. (Captain Underpants Ser.). (ENG., Illus.). 176p. (J). (gr. 2-5). 2011. 5.99 *(978-0-545-38577-0(6))* 2010. 9.99 *(978-0-545-17530-2(5))* Scholastic, Inc.
—The Adventures of Ook & Gluk, Kung-Fu Cavemen from the Future. 2011. lib. bdg. 16.00 *(978-0-606-16381-1(6),* Turtleback) Turtleback Bks.
Pilkey, Dav & Beard, George. The Adventures of Ook & Gluk, Kung-Fu Cavemen from the Future. 2010. lib. bdg. 20.85 *(978-0-606-15003-3(X),* Turtleback) Turtleback Bks.
Random House Disney Staff. Go for the Gold! Random House Disney Staff & Petrossi, Fabrizio, illus. 2016. (Pictureback(R) Ser.). (ENG.). 16p. (J). (gr. -1-2). pap. 4.99 *(978-0-399-55595-4(1),* Random Hse. Bks. for Young Readers) Random Hse. Children's Bks.
Ray, Joanna Z. 'elaran! Isithan! 2007. (ENG.). 92p. (YA). per. 15.95 *(978-1-4116-9393-7(0))* Lulu Pr., Inc.
Richard, Laurent. The Championship! Gauvin, Edward, tr. Ryser, Nicolas, illus. 2014. (ENG.). 64p. (J). (gr. 2-5). pap. 6.95 *(978-1-4677-4459-1(X));* (Tao, the Little Samurai Ser.: 4). lib. bdg. 29.27 *(978-1-4677-2097-7(6))* Lerner Publishing Group. (Graphic Universe™).
—Clowns & Dragons! Gauvin, Edward, tr. from FRE. Ryser, Nicolas, illus. 2014. (Tao, the Little Samurai Ser.: 3). (ENG.). 56p. (J). (gr. 2-5). lib. bdg. 29.27 *(978-1-4677-2096-0(8),* Graphic Universe™) Lerner Publishing Group.
—Ninjas & Knock Outs! Gauvin, Edward, tr. from FRE. Ryser, Nicolas, illus. 2014. (Tao, the Little Samurai Ser.: 2). (ENG.). 64p. (J). (gr. 2-5). lib. bdg. 29.27 *(978-1-4677-3272-7(9),* Graphic Universe™) Lerner Publishing Group.
—Pranks & Attacks! Gauvin, Edward, tr. from FRE. Ryser, Nicolas, illus. 2014. (Tao, the Little Samurai Ser.: 1). (ENG.). 64p. (J). (gr. 2-5). lib. bdg. 29.27 *(978-1-4677-2095-3(X),* Graphic Universe™) Lerner Publishing Group.
—Wild Animals! Gauvin, Edward, tr. from FRE. Ryser, Nicolas, illus. 2014. (Tao, the Little Samurai Ser.: 5). (ENG.). 64p. (J). (gr. 2-5). lib. bdg. 29.27 *(978-1-4677-2098-4(4),* Graphic Universe™) Lerner Publishing Group.
Rocco, John. Fu Finds the Way. Rocco, John, illus. 2009. (ENG., Illus.). 40p. (J). (gr. -1-2). 16.99 *(978-1-4231-0965-5(1))* Hyperion Pr.
Roman, Annette. Passage 2: HIV/AIDS — First Love. Ng, Leandro, illus. 2005. (1 World Manga Ser.: Vol. 2). (ENG.). 40p. (J). pap. 3.99 *(978-0-8213-6406-2(5))* World Bank Pubns.
Schwartz, Corey Rosen. Ninja Red Riding Hood. Santat, Dan, illus. 2014. (ENG.). 40p. (J). (gr. k-3). 16.99 *(978-0-399-16354-8(9),* G.P. Putnam's Sons Books for Young Readers) Penguin Young Readers Group.
—The Three Ninja Pigs. Santat, Dan, illus. 2012. (ENG.). 40p. (J). (gr. k-3). 16.99 *(978-0-399-25514-4(1),* G.P. Putnam's Sons Books for Young Readers) Penguin Young Readers Group.
Schwartz, Corey Rosen & Gomez, Rebecca J. Hensel & Gretel, Ninja Chicks. Santat, Dan, illus. 2016. (ENG.). 40p. (J). (gr. k-3). 17.99 *(978-0-399-17626-5(8),* G.P. Putnam's Sons Books for Young Readers) Penguin Young Readers Group.
Sealed with a Kick. 2015. (Kung Fu Panda TV Ser.). (ENG., Illus.). 32p. (J). (gr. k-2). pap. 3.99 *(978-1-4814-1748-8(7),* Simon Spotlight) Simon Spotlight.
Sensei Teaches Focus. 2004. (J). 10.00 *(978-0-9767483-0-4(4))* Wright's Way Inc.
Shadowboxer. 2014. (ENG.). 288p. (J). (gr. 8). pap. 9.99 *(978-1-78108-282-9(0),* Ravenstone) Rebellion GBR. Dist: Simon & Schuster, Inc.
Sitomer, Alan Lawrence. Noble Warrior. 2015. (Caged Warrior Ser.). (ENG., Illus.). 400p. (YA). (gr. 7-12). 17.99 *(978-1-4847-0528-5(9))* Hyperion Bks. for Children.
Skilton, Sarah. Bruised. 2013. (ENG.). 288p. (YA). (gr. 7-17). 18.95 *(978-1-4197-0387-4(0),* Amulet Bks.) Abrams, Inc.
Smith, James J. & James, Hollis. Mikey's Monster (Teenage Mutant Ninja Turtles) Spaziante, Patrick, illus. 2013. (Step into Reading Ser.). (ENG.). 48p. (J). (gr. k-3). 3.99 *(978-0-449-81826-8(8),* Random Hse. Bks. for Young Readers) Random Hse. Children's Bks.
Stevens, Bonnie. Fighting Chance. 2015. (ENG.). 326p. (YA). pap. 10.95 *(978-1-929345-14-4(3))* Poisoned Pen Pr.
Stone, Jeff. Monkey. 2006. (Five Ancestors Ser.: Bk. 2). (ENG.). 208p. (J). (gr. 3-7). per. 6.99 *(978-0-375-83074-7(X),* Yearling) Random Hse. Children's Bks.
—Tiger. 2006. (Five Ancestors Ser.: Bk. 1). (ENG., Illus.). 208p. (J). (gr. 3-7). reprint ed. 6.99 *(978-0-375-83072-3(3),* Yearling) Random Hse. Children's Bks.
Style Guide Staff, illus. Good Po, Bad Po. 2014. (Kung Fu Panda TV Ser.). (ENG.). 24p. (J). (gr. -1-2). pap. 3.99 *(978-1-4814-0001-5(0),* Simon Spotlight) Simon Spotlight.
—Kung Fu to the Rescue! 2014. (Kung Fu Panda TV Ser.). (ENG.). 96p. (J). (gr. 2-5). pap. 5.99 *(978-1-4814-0511-9(X),* Simon Spotlight) Simon Spotlight.
—Po's Secret Move. 2014. (Kung Fu Panda TV Ser.). (ENG.). 32p. (J). (gr. k-2). pap. 3.99 *(978-1-4424-9995-9(8),* Simon Spotlight) Simon Spotlight.
—Two to Kung Fu. 2014. (Kung Fu Panda TV Ser.). (ENG.). 96p. (J). (gr. 2-5). pap. 4.99 *(978-1-4424-9992-8(3),* Simon Spotlight) Simon Spotlight.
Style Guide, Style, illus. The Furry & the Furious. 2014. (Kung Fu Panda TV Ser.). (ENG.). 96p. (J). (gr. 2-5). pap. 4.99 *(978-1-4814-1703-7(7),* Simon Spotlight) Simon Spotlight.
Styles, Walker. Ghosts & Goblins & Ninja, Oh My! Whitehouse, Ben, illus. 2016. (Rider Woofson Ser.: 4). (ENG.). 128p. (J). (gr. k-4). pap. 5.99 *(978-1-4814-6306-5(3),* Little Simon) Little Simon.
Testa, Maggie. Legendary Legends. Style Guide Staff, illus. 2014. (Kung Fu Panda TV Ser.). (ENG.). 16p. (J). (gr. -1-2). 5.99 *(978-1-4424-9998-0(2),* Simon Spotlight) Simon Spotlight.
Thielbar, Melinda. The Ancient Formula: A Mystery with Fractions. Pantoja, Tintin, illus. 2011. (Manga Math Mysteries Ser.: 5). (ENG.). 46p. (gr. 3-5). pap. 6.95 *(978-0-7613-8134-1(1),* Graphic Universe™) Lerner Publishing Group.
—#5 the Ancient Formula: A Mystery with Fractions. Pantoja, Tintin, illus. 2011. (Manga Math Mysteries Set II Ser.). pap. 39.62 *(978-0-7613-8362-8(X),* Graphic Universe™) Lerner Publishing Group.
Thomas, Jim. Super Slam Turtles! Spaziante, Patrick, illus. 2005. 22p. (J). lib. bdg. 15.00 *(978-1-4242-0971-2(4))* Fitzgerald Bks.
Toriyama, Akira. Dragon Ball Full Color Freeza Arc, Volume 1. 2016. (Dragon Ball Freeza Ser.: 1). lib. bdg. 33.05 *(978-0-606-38706-4(4))* Turtleback Bks.
—Dragon Ball Full Color Freeza Arc, Volume 2. 2016. (Dragon Ball Freeza Ser.: 2). lib. bdg. 33.05 *(978-0-606-38934-1(2))* Turtleback Bks.
—Dragon Ball Z, Vol. 8 (VIZBIG Edition) Toriyama, Akira, illus. 2010. (ENG., Illus.). 560p. pap. 19.99 *(978-1-4215-2071-1(0))* Viz Media.
—Fight to the Finish! Toriyama, Akira, illus. 2010. (Dragon Ball Ser.: 8). (ENG., Illus.). 80p. (J). pap. 4.99 *(978-1-4215-3124-3(0))* Viz Media.
—Let the Tournament Begin! Toriyama, Akira, illus. 2010. (Dragon Ball Ser.: 7). (ENG., Illus.). 80p. (J). pap. 4.99 *(978-1-4215-3123-6(2))* Viz Media.
Tsang, Evonne. Kung Fu Masters, No. 12. Martinez, Alitha E., illus. 2009. (Twisted Journeys (r) Ser.: 12). (ENG.). 112p. (J). (gr. 4-7). 27.93 *(978-0-8225-8878-8(1),* Graphic Universe™) Lerner Publishing Group.
Van Vleet, Carmella. Eliza Bing Is (Not) a Big, Fat Quitter. Donnelly, Karen, illus. 2014. (ENG.). 176p. (J). (gr. 2-6). 16.95 *(978-0-8234-2944-8(X))* Holiday Hse., Inc.
Vernon, Ursula. Attack of the Ninja Frogs. 2nd ed. 2010. (Dragonbreath Ser.: 2). (ENG.). 208p. (J). (gr. 3-7). 12.99 *(978-0-8037-3365-7(8),* Dial Bks) Penguin Young Readers Group.
—Attack of the Ninja Frogs. 2012. (Dragonbreath Ser.: 2). lib. bdg. 17.20 *(978-0-606-26666-6(6),* Turtleback) Turtleback Bks.
Vivès, Bastien, et al. The Royal Cup. 2015. (Last Man Ser.: 2). (ENG., Illus.). 208p. (gr. 9). pap. 9.99 *(978-1-62672-047-3(9),* 9781626720473, First Second Bks.) Roaring Brook Pr.
Wax, Wendy. Meet Leatherhead. Spaziante, Patrick, illus. 2005. 22p. (J). lib. bdg. 15.00 *(978-1-4242-0972-9(2))* Fitzgerald Bks.
Webster, Christy. Green Team! (Teenage Mutant Ninja Turtles) Spaziante, Patrick, illus. 2012. (Step into Reading Ser.). (ENG.). 48p. (J). (gr. k-3). pap. 3.99 *(978-0-307-98070-0(7),* Random Hse. Bks. for Young Readers) Random Hse. Children's Bks.
West, Tracey. Enemy Rising. Phillips, Craig, illus. 2010. (Hiro's Quest Ser.: 1). (ENG.). 96p. (J). (gr. 2-5). 4.99 *(978-0-545-16288-3(2),* Scholastic Paperbacks) Scholastic, Inc.
—The Golden Weapons. 2012. (Lego Ninjago Ser.). (ENG.). 32p. (J). (gr. 2-5). pap. 3.99 *(978-0-545-40115-9(1))* Scholastic, Inc.
—Kung Fu Panda 3 Movie Novelization. 2015. lib. bdg. 17.20 *(978-0-606-38260-1(7))* Turtleback Bks.
—Masters of Spinjitzu. 2012. (Lego Ninjago Ser.). (ENG.). 32p. (J). (gr. -1-3). pap. 3.99 *(978-0-545-40114-2(3))* Scholastic, Inc.
—A Ninja's Path. 2012. (Ninjago Readers Ser.: 5). lib. bdg. 13.55 *(978-0-606-26771-7(9),* Turtleback) Turtleback Bks.

MARTIN DE PORRES, SAINT, 1579-1639

Schmidt, Gary D. Martin de Porres: The Rose in the Desert. Diaz, David, illus. 2012. (ENG.). 32p. (J). (gr. 1-4). lib. bdg. 16.99 *(978-0-547-61218-8(4))* Houghton Mifflin Harcourt Publishing Co.

MARTINIQUE—FICTION

Cendrillon.Tr. of Cinderella. (FRE.). 48p. pap. 12.95 incl. audio compact disk *(978-2-89558-065-2(0))* Coffragants CAN. Dist: Penton Overseas, Inc.

MARX, KARL, 1818-1883

Cates, David. Karl Marx: Philosopher & Revolutionary, 1 vol. 2011. (Essential Lives Set 7 Ser.). (ENG., Illus.). 112p. (J). (gr. 6-12). lib. bdg. 35.64 *(978-1-61783-005-1(4))* ABDO Publishing Co.
Rössig, Wolfgang. Karl Marx. 2009. (Profiles in Economics Ser.). 112p. (YA). lib. bdg. 28.95 *(978-1-59935-132-2(3))* Reynolds, Morgan Inc.

MARXISM

see Communism; Socialism

MARY, BLESSED VIRGIN, SAINT

Aston, Al. A Message for Mary. Hutchinson, Joy, illus. 2005. 16p. 2.00 *(978-1-84427-176-4(5))* Scripture Union GBR. Dist: Send The Light Distribution LLC.
Biffi, Inos, ed. The Life of Mary. Vignazia, Franco, illus. 2007. 28p. (J). (gr. -1-3). 12.95 *(978-1-56854-653-7(X))* Liturgy Training Pubns.
La Casa de Maria.Tr. of Mary's House. (SPA.). (J). *(978-0-7899-0875-9(1),* 496234) Editorial Unilit.
Ficocelli, Elizabeth. Child's Guide to the Rosary. Blake, Anne Catharine, illus. 2009. (J). 10.95 *(978-0-8091-6736-4(0))* Paulist Pr.
Lumsden, Colin, illus. Story of Mary. 2003. (Bible Colour & Learn Ser.). 32p. pap. 2.50 *(978-1-903087-43-5(0))* DayOne Pubns. GBR. Dist: Send The Light Distribution LLC.
Mackenzie, Carine. Martha & Mary: Friends of Jesus. McLaren, Duncan, illus. 2014. (Bible Time Ser.). (ENG.). 32p. (J). (gr. -1-2). pap. 3.99 *(978-1-84550-167-9(5),* 71bfc45e-76c2-452a-846a-4937c26352a8) Christian Focus Pubns. GBR. Dist: Bookmasters Distribution.
MacKenzie, Carine. Mary: Mother of Jesus. McLaren, Duncan, illus. 2012. (Bible Time Ser.). (ENG.). 32p. (J). (gr. -1-2). pap. 3.99 *(978-1-84550-168-6(3),* 9781845501686) Christian Focus Pubns. GBR. Dist: Bookmasters Distribution.
Moore, Alan & Tavner, Gill. Mary of Galilee. Donnelly, Karen, illus. 2014. (New Testament Ser.). (ENG.). 64p. pap. 6.95 *(978-1-906230-25-8(0))* Real Reads Ltd. GBR. Dist: Casemate Pubs. & Bk. Distributors, LLC.
Orfeo, Christine Virginia. My First Book about Mary. Darrenkamp, Julia Mary, illus. 2007. 63p. (Orig.). (J). (gr. 3-7). per. 7.95 *(978-0-8198-4861-1(1))* Pauline Bks. & Media.
Pingry, Patricia A. The Story of Mary. Venturi-Pickett, Stacy, illus. 2006. (ENG.). 32p. (J). (gr. -1-3). pap. 3.95 *(978-0-8249-5546-5(3),* Ideal Pubns.) Worthy Publishing.
Sanders, Nancy I. Mary, 1 vol. 2014. (Get to Know Ser.). (ENG.). 112p. (J). pap. 7.99 *(978-0-310-74480-1(6))* Zonderkidz.
Serrano, Francisco. La Virgen de Guadalupe. Dávalos, Felipe, illus.Tr. of Virgin of Guadalupe. (SPA.). (J). (gr. 2-4). 18.00 *(978-968-494-070-3(X))* Centro de Informacion y Desarrollo de la Comunicacion y la Literatura MEX. Dist: Lectorum Pubns., Inc.

MARY, QUEEN OF SCOTS, 1542-1587

Carruth, J. A., text. Mary Queen of Scots. (Scotland in Words & Pictures Ser.). (Illus.). 32p. pap. 3.95 *(978-0-7117-0147-2(4))* Jarrold Publishing GBR. Dist: 7 Hills Bk. Distributors.
MacDonald, Fiona. You Wouldn't Want to Be Mary Queen of Scots. Antram, David, illus. 2008. (You Wouldn't Want to...: History of the World Ser.). (ENG.). 32p. (J). (gr. 2-5). pap. 9.95 *(978-0-531-14853-2(X),* Watts, Franklin) Scholastic Library Publishing.
—You Wouldn't Want to Be Mary Queen of Scots: A Ruler Who Really Lost Her Head. Antram, David, illus. 2008. (You Wouldn't Want to Ser.). (ENG.). 32p. (J). (gr. 4-7). 29.00 *(978-0-531-13912-7(3))* Scholastic Library Publishing.
Roxburgh, Ellis. Elizabeth I of England vs. Mary, Queen of Scots: Battle for the Throne. 2016. (History's Greatest Rivals Ser.). (ENG., Illus.). 48p. (J). (gr. 6-8). pap. 14.05 *(978-1-4824-4227-4(2))* Stevens, Gareth Publishing LLLP.

MARY, QUEEN OF SCOTS, 1542-1587—FICTION

Blake, Lily. Reign: The Prophecy. 2014. (ENG.). 240p. (YA). (gr. 7-17). pap. 14.00 *(978-0-316-33459-4(6),* Poppy) Little, Brown Bks. for Young Readers.
Hendry, Frances. Quest for a Queen: The Falcon. 2006. pap. *(978-1-905665-06-8(7))* Pollinger In Print.
—Quest for a Queen: The Jackdaw. 2006. pap. *(978-1-905665-05-1(9))* Pollinger In Print.
—Quest for a Queen: The Lark. 2006. (Illus.). 251p. pap. *(978-1-905665-04-4(0))* Pollinger In Print.
Meyer, Carolyn. The Wild Queen: The Days & Nights of Mary, Queen of Scots. 2013. (Young Royals Ser.). (ENG.). 432p. (YA). (gr. 7). pap. 8.99 *(978-0-544-02219-5(X))* Houghton Mifflin Harcourt Publishing Co.
Uttley, Alison & Singh, Mahendra. A Traveller in Time. Bray, Phyllis, illus. 2011. (ENG.). 336p. (J). (gr. 4-7). 17.95 *(978-1-59017-388-6(0),* NYR Children's Collection) New York Review of Bks., Inc., The.

MARYLAND

Blashfield, Jean F. Maryland. 2014. (America the Beautiful Ser.: 3). (ENG., Illus.). 144p. (J). lib. bdg. 40.00 *(978-0-531-24888-1(7))* Scholastic Library Publishing.
Brown, Jonatha A. Maryland. 2006. (Portraits of the States Ser.). (Illus.). 32p. (gr. 2-6). pap. 10.50 *(978-0-8368-4687-4(7));* lib. bdg. 26.00 *(978-0-8368-4668-3(0))* Stevens, Gareth Publishing LLLP. (Gareth Stevens Learning Library).
Brown, Vanessa. Maryland. 2005. (Bilingual Library of the United States of America Ser.: Set 1). (ENG & SPA., Illus.). 32p. (J). (gr. 3-6). lib. bdg. 25.25 *(978-1-4042-3085-9(8))* Rosen Publishing Group, Inc., The.
Bunting, Elaine & D'Amario, Patricia. Counties of Central Maryland, 1 vol. Ramsey, Marcy Dunn, illus. 2009. (ENG.). 160p. (J). 19.95 *(978-0-87033-503-7(0),* 9780870335037, Cornell Maritime Pr./Tidewater Pubs.) Schiffer Publishing, Ltd.
—Counties of Maryland's Lower Eastern Shore, 1 vol. Ramsey, Marcy Dunn, illus. 2009. (ENG.). 168p. (J). 19.95 *(978-0-87033-555-6(3),* 9780870335556, Cornell Maritime Pr./Tidewater Pubs.) Schiffer Publishing, Ltd.
—Counties of Southern Maryland, 1 vol. Ramsey, Marcy Dunn, illus. 2009. (ENG.). 144p. (J). 19.95 *(978-0-87033-535-8(9),* 9780870335358, Cornell Maritime Pr./Tidewater Pubs.) Schiffer Publishing, Ltd.
Connors, Kathleen. People of the Chesapeake Bay. 2013. 32p. (J). (gr. 3-6). 26.60 *(978-1-4339-9776-1(2));* pap. 63.00 *(978-1-4339-9778-5(9));* pap. 10.50 *(978-1-4339-9777-8(0))* Stevens, Gareth Publishing LLLP.
—Plants & Animals of the Chesapeake Bay. 2013. 32p. (J). (gr. 3-6). 26.60 *(978-1-4339-9780-8(0));* pap. 63.00 *(978-1-4339-9782-2(7));* pap. 10.50 *(978-1-4339-9781-5(9))* Stevens, Gareth Publishing LLLP.
Craats, Rennay. Maryland. 2011. (Guide to American States Ser.). (J). (Illus.). 48p. (gr. 3-6). 29.99 *(978-1-61690-792-1(4));* *(978-1-61690-468-5(2))* Weigl Pubs., Inc.
Deinard, Jenny. How to Draw Maryland's Sights & Symbols. 2009. (Kid's Guide to Drawing America Ser.). 32p. (gr. k-k). 50.50 *(978-1-61511-069-8(0),* PowerKids Pr.) Rosen Publishing Group, Inc., The.
Doherty, Craig A. & Doherty, Katherine M. Maryland. 2005. (Thirteen Colonies Ser.). (Illus.). 128p. (gr. 5-8). 35.00 *(978-0-8160-5418-3(5))* Facts On File, Inc.
Franchino, Vicky. Maryland. 2017. (True Book — My United States Ser.). (ENG.). 48p. (J). pap. 7.95

M
N
O

(978-0-531-23288-0(3), Children's Pr.) Scholastic Library Publishing.

Gelletly, LeeAnne. The Mid-Atlantic States: Delaware, Maryland, & Washington, D. C. 2015. (Let's Explore the States Ser.). (Illus.). 64p. (J). (gr. 5). 23.95 *(978-1-4222-3327-6(8))* Mason Crest.

Jensen, Niels R. Maryland, 1 vol. 2009. (United States Ser.). (ENG., Illus.). 48p. (YA). (gr. 2-5). 27.07 *(978-1-60453-655-3(1))* ABDO Publishing Co.

Johnston, Joyce. Maryland. 2012. (J). lib. bdg. 25.26 *(978-0-7613-4537-4(X)*, Lerner Pubns.) Lerner Publishing Group.

Labella, Susan. Maryland. 2005. (Rookie Read-About Geography Ser.). (ENG., Illus.). 32p. (J). (gr. 1-2). lib. bdg. 20.50 *(978-0-516-25256-8(9)*, Children's Pr.) Scholastic Library Publishing.

Latta, Sara L. Who Fixed Babies' Hearts? Vivien Thomas. 2012. (I Like Inventors! Ser.). (Illus.). 24p. (J). (gr. k-3). lib. bdg. 22.60 *(978-0-7660-3963-6(3)*, Enslow Elementary) Enslow Pubs., Inc.

Levy, Debbie & Panza, Rosana. Dozer's Run: A True Story of a Dog & His Race. Opie, David, illus. 2014. (ENG.). 32p. (J). (gr. 1-4). 16.99 *(978-1-58536-896-9(2)*, 203665) Sleeping Bear Pr.

Marsh, Carole. The Marvelous Maryland Coloring Book! 2004. (Maryland Experience! Ser.). (Illus.). 32p. (J). (gr. k-2). pap. 3.95 *(978-0-7933-9615-3(8))* Gallopade International.

—Maryland Current Events Projects: 30 Cool, Activities, Crafts, Experiments & More for Kids to Do to Learn about Your State! 2003. (Maryland Experience Ser.). 32p. (gr. k-8). pap. 5.95 *(978-0-635-02039-0(4)*, Marsh, Carole Bks.) Gallopade International.

—Maryland Geography Projects: 30 Cool, Activities, Crafts, Experiments & More for Kids to Do to Learn about Your State! 2003. (Maryland Experience Ser.). 32p. (gr. k-5). pap. 5.95 *(978-0-635-01839-7(X)*, Marsh, Carole Bks.) Gallopade International.

—Maryland Government Projects: 30 Cool, Activities, Crafts, Experiments & More for Kids to Do to Learn about Your State! 2003. (Maryland Experience Ser.). 32p. (gr. k-5). pap. 5.95 *(978-0-635-01939-4(6)*, Marsh, Carole Bks.) Gallopade International.

—Maryland Jeopardy! Answers & Questions about Our State! 2004. (Maryland Experience! Ser.). (Illus.). 32p. (J). (gr. 3-8). pap. 7.95 *(978-0-7933-9612-2(3))* Gallopade International.

—Maryland "Jography" A Fun Run Thru Our State! 2004. (Maryland Experience! Ser.). (Illus.). 32p. (J). (gr. 3-8). pap. 7.95 *(978-0-7933-9613-9(1))* Gallopade International.

—Maryland People Projects: 30 Cool, Activities, Crafts, Experiments & More for Kids to Do to Learn about Your State! 2003. (Maryland Experience Ser.). 32p. (gr. k-5). pap. 5.95 *(978-0-635-01989-9(2)*, Marsh, Carole Bks.) Gallopade International.

—Maryland Symbols & Facts Projects: 30 Cool, Activities, Crafts, Experiments & More for Kids to Do to Learn about Your State! 2003. (Maryland Experience Ser.). 32p. (gr. k-5). pap. 5.95 *(978-0-635-01889-2(6)*, Marsh, Carole Bks.) Gallopade International.

—My First Book about Maryland. 2004. (Maryland Experience! Ser.). (Illus.). 32p. (J). (gr. k-4). pap. 7.95 *(978-0-7933-9611-5(5))* Gallopade International.

—My First Pocket Guide: Maryland. 2004. (Maryland Experience! Ser.). (Illus.). 96p. (J). (gr. 3-8). per. 6.95 *(978-0-7933-9610-8(7))* Gallopade International.

Menendez, Shirley. B Is for Blue Crab: A Maryland Alphabet. Stutzman, Laura, illus. 2004. (Discover America State by State Ser.). (ENG.). 40p. (J). (gr. 1-3). 17.95 *(978-1-58536-160-1(7)*, 202020) Sleeping Bear Pr.

Murray, Julie. Maryland, 1 vol. 2006. (Buddy Book Ser.). (ENG., Illus.). 32p. (gr. 2-4). 27.07 *(978-1-59197-679-0(0)*, Buddy Bks.) ABDO Publishing Co.

Savage, Jeff. Maryland: A MyReportLinks.com Book. 2003. (States Ser.). (Illus.). 48p. (J). lib. bdg. 25.26 *(978-0-7660-5115-7(3)*, MyReportLinks.com Bks.) Enslow Pubs., Inc.

Saving the Chesapeake Bay. 2013. (Exploring the Chesapeake Bay Ser.). 32p. (J). (gr. 3-6). pap. 63.00 *(978-1-4339-9786-0(X))* Stevens, Gareth Publishing LLLP.

Somervill, Barbara A. Maryland. 2003. (From Sea to Shining Sea Ser.: 2). (ENG., Illus.). 80p. (J). 30.50 *(978-0-516-22384-1(4)*, Children's Pr.) Scholastic Library Publishing.

Swanson, Angie. Maryland. 2016. (States Ser.). (ENG., Illus.). 32p. (gr. 3-4). lib. bdg. 27.32 *(978-1-5157-0407-2(6))* Next Page Pr., The.

Wimmer, Teresa. Maryland. 2008. (This Land Called America Ser.). 32p. (YA). (gr. 3-6). 22.95 *(978-1-58341-645-7(5))* Creative Co., The.

MARYLAND—FICTION

Albritton, Stacy Demoran. The Diary of Marie Landry, Acadian Exile, 1 vol. Haynes, Joyce, illus. 2012. (ENG.). 160p. (J). (gr. 3-7). pap. 14.95 *(978-1-58980-865-2(7))* Pelican Publishing Co., Inc.

Allen, Elaine Ann. Olly's Treasure, 1 vol. Nash, Kelli, illus. 2011. (ENG.). 40p. (J). 16.99 *(978-0-7643-3772-7(6)*, 9780764337727, Schiffer Publishing Ltd) Schiffer Publishing, Ltd.

Altsheler, Joseph A. The Sword of Antietam: A Story of the Nation's Crisis. 2006. (Civil War Ser.: Vol. 4). 296p. (J). reprint ed. 28.95 *(978-1-4218-1776-7(4))*; pap. 13.95 *(978-1-4218-1876-4(0))* 1st World Publishing, Inc. (1st World Library - Literary Society).

—The Sword of Antietam: A Story of the Nation's Crisis. l.t. ed. (Civil War Ser.: Vol. 4). (J). reprint ed. 2006. 262p. pap. 23.99 *(978-1-4264-2714-5(X))* 2011. 358p. (gr. 4-7). pap. 32.75 *(978-1-245-13385-2(3))* 2008. 264p. 28.99 *(978-0-554-22582-1(4))* 2008. 264p. 25.99 *(978-0-554-31885-1(7))* 2007. (ENG.). 242p. pap. 20.99 *(978-1-4264-2657-5(7))* Creative Media Partners, LLC.

—The Sword of Antietam: A Story of the Nation's Crisis. 2006. (Civil War Ser.: Vol. 4). (J). reprint ed. pap. *(978-1-4065-0825-3(X))* Dodo Pr.

—The Sword of Antietam: A Story of the Nation's Crisis. 2007. (Civil War Ser.: Vol. 4). 176p. (J). reprint ed. per. *(978-1-4068-1690-7(6))* Echo Library.

—The Sword of Antietam: A Story of the Nation's Crisis. 2010. (Civil War Ser.: Vol. 4). (Illus.). 160p. (J). (gr. 4-7). reprint ed. pap. 19.99 *(978-1-153-72276-6(3))* General Bks. LLC.

—The Sword of Antietam: A Story of the Nation's Crisis. 2010. (Civil War Ser.: Vol. 4). 224p. (J). reprint ed. pap. *(978-1-4076-4642-8(7))* HardPr.

—The Sword of Antietam: A Story of the Nation's Crisis. (Civil War Ser.: Vol. 4). (J). reprint ed. 2011. 352p. (gr. 4-7). 46.95 *(978-1-169-87969-0(1))* 2010. 352p. (gr. 4-7). 37.56 *(978-1-163-20537-2(0))* 2010. 352p. (gr. 4-7). pap. 25.56 *(978-1-162-77564-7(5))* 2005. 352p. 46.95 *(978-1-4326-1485-0(1))* 2005. pap. 31.95 *(978-0-7661-9405-2(1))* 2004. pap. 1.99 *(978-1-4192-8469-4(X))* Kessinger Publishing, LLC.

—The Sword of Antietam: A Story of the Nation's Crisis. 2011. (Civil War Ser.: Vol. 4). 264p. (J). (gr. 4-7). reprint ed. pap. *(978-3-8424-3211-6(9))* Tredition GmbH.

—The Sword of Antietam: A Story of the Nation's Crisis. 2009. (Civil War Ser.: Vol. 4). (J). reprint ed. pap. 16.95 *(978-1-933573-85-4(6))* Zeezok Publishing, LLC.

Avery, Ben G. Turtle Trouble, 1 vol. Gaudiamo, Adi Darda, illus. 2007. (Z Graphic Novels / TimeFlyz Ser.). (ENG.). 160p. (J). (gr. 3-7). pap. 6.99 *(978-0-310-71362-3(5))* Zondervan.

Baker, Monica S. Freestyle, 1 vol. 2010. (ENG., Illus.). 160p. (J). 14.99 *(978-0-7643-3538-9(3)*, 9780764335389) Schiffer Publishing, Ltd.

Basham, Tom. Sailing Home. Calvert, Lissa, illus. 2012. 168p. *(978-1-77097-370-1(2))* FriesenPress.

Basham, Tom & Calvert, Lissa. Sailing Home. 2012. 168p. pap. *(978-1-77097-371-8(0))* FriesenPress.

Broach, Elise. Shakespeare's Secret. 2007. (Illus.). 258p. (gr. 4-9). 17.00 *(978-0-7569-8204-1(9))* Perfection Learning Corp.

—Shakespeare's Secret. l.t. ed. 2006. (Thorndike Literacy Bridge Ser.). (Illus.). 263p. (J). (gr. 5-10). 22.95 *(978-0-7862-8735-2(7))* Thorndike Pr.

Buffington, Cecil. High School Super-Star: The Junior Year. 2008. 244p. pap. 16.95 *(978-0-595-51914-9(8))* iUniverse, Inc.

Cummings, Priscilla. Blindsided. (ENG.). (J). (gr. 5-18). 2011. 256p. 7.99 *(978-0-14-241902-1(8)*, Puffin Books) 2010. 240p. 16.99 *(978-0-525-42161-0(0)*, Dutton Books for Young Readers) Penguin Young Readers Group.

—A Face First. 2003. (ENG.). 208p. (J). (gr. 4-7). 6.99 *(978-0-14-230247-7(3)*, Puffin Books) Penguin Young Readers Group.

—A Face First. 2003. 197p. (gr. 7-12). 17.00 *(978-0-7569-1547-6(3))* Perfection Learning Corp.

—The Journey Back. 2013. (ENG.). 272p. (J). (gr. 5). pap. 7.99 *(978-0-14-242290-8(8)*, Puffin Books) Penguin Young Readers Group.

Delacre, Lulu. Alicia Afterimage. 2008. (ENG.). 144p. (YA). (gr. 7-18). 19.95 *(978-1-60060-242-9(8))* Lee & Low Bks., Inc.

Eisner, Fern. Saba's Room. 2009. 28p. pap. 15.99 *(978-1-4415-1843-9(6))* Xlibris Corp.

Furtney, Charles S. Tryconnel: An Antebellum Adventure along the C & O Canal. 2004. (Illus.). iii, 156p. (J). pap. *(978-0-9711835-3-7(8))* Local History Co., The.

Gamble, Adam & Jasper, Mark. Good Night Maryland. Veno, Joe et al, illus. 2011. (Good Night Our World Ser.). (ENG.). 20p. (J). (gr. k — 1). bds. 9.95 *(978-1-60219-046-7(1))* Good Night Bks.

Garretson, Dee. Wildfire Run. 2011. (ENG.). 288p. (J). (gr. 3-7). pap. 6.99 *(978-0-06-195350-7(4))* HarperCollins Pubs.

Geithner, Carole. If Only. 2012. (ENG.). 336p. (J). (gr. 5-9). 16.99 *(978-0-545-23499-3(9)*, Scholastic Pr.) Scholastic, Inc.

Hahn, Mary Downing. Promises to the Dead. 2009. (ENG.). 208p. (J). (gr. 5-7). pap. 7.99 *(978-0-547-25838-6(0))* Houghton Mifflin Harcourt Publishing Co.

Hancock, H. Irving. Dave Darrin's First Year at Annapolis. 2007. 180p. per. *(978-1-4065-1974-7(X))* Dodo Pr.

—Dave Darrin's Second Year at Annapolis. 2007. 152p. per. *(978-1-4065-1976-1(6))* Dodo Pr.

Hollenbeck, Kathleen M. Dancing on the Sand: A Story of an Atlantic Blue Crab. 2005. (ENG., Illus.). 32p. (J). (gr. -1-2). 8.95 *(978-1-59249-234-3(7)*, SC4017) Soundprints.

Jackson, Gabrielle E. Peggy Stewart. 2007. 176p. per. *(978-1-4065-1803-0(4))* Dodo Pr.

Jacobs, Lily. The Littlest Bunny in Maryland: An Easter Adventure. Dunn, Robert, illus. 2015. (ENG.). 32p. (J). (-3). 9.99 *(978-1-4926-1111-0(5)*, Sourcebooks Jabberwocky) Sourcebooks, Inc.

James, Eric. A Halloween Scare in Maryland. Le Ray, Marina, illus. 2014. (ENG.). 32p. (J). (-5). 9.99 *(978-1-4926-0603-1(0)*, 9781492606031, Sourcebooks Jabberwocky) Sourcebooks, Inc.

—Santa's Sleigh Is on Its Way to Maryland: A Christmas Adventure. Dunn, Robert, illus. 2016. (ENG.). 32p. (J). (-2). 12.99 *(978-1-4926-4335-7(1)*, 9781492643357, Sourcebooks Jabberwocky) Sourcebooks, Inc.

Johnson-Simon. Anaya Visits the James E Lewis Museum of Art at Morgan State University. 2009. 40p. pap. 16.99 *(978-1-4490-1884-9(X))* AuthorHouse.

Kehne, Carroll Harrison, Jr. Buried Treasure, a Pirate's Tale, 1 vol. 2009. (ENG., Illus.). 34p. (J). (gr. 3-7). 12.95 *(978-0-87033-601-0(0)*, 9780870336010, Cornell Maritime Pr./Tidewater Pubs.) Schiffer Publishing, Ltd.

LeFlore, Lyah B. The World Is Mine. Warfield, D. L., illus. 2009. (Come Up Ser.). (ENG.). 304p. (YA). (gr. 9-18). pap. 8.99 *(978-1-4169-7963-0(8)*, Simon Pulse) Simon Pulse.

Litzenberg, Corinne M. The Sand Lady: An Ocean City, Maryland, Tale, 1 vol. 2007. (ENG., Illus.). 32p. (J). 14.95 *(978-0-7643-2684-4(8)*, 9780764326844) Schiffer Publishing, Ltd.

Lockhart, Lynne N. & Lockhart, Barbara M. Rambling Raft, 1 vol. Lockhart, Lynne N., illus. 2009. (ENG., Illus.). 30p. (J). (gr. 2-18). 7.95 *(978-0-87033-392-7(5)*, 9780870333927, Cornell Maritime Pr./Tidewater Pubs.) Schiffer Publishing, Ltd.

Lorton, Barbara. Sidney Seagull Marks Lighthouses & Buoys of the Chesapeake. 2013. (Illus.). 28p. pap. 16.99 *(978-1-4582-1055-5(3)*, Abbott Pr.) Author Solutions, Inc.

Lyga, Barry. Hero Type. 2009. (ENG.). 312p. (YA). (gr. 7). pap. 8.99 *(978-0-547-24877-6(6))* Houghton Mifflin Harcourt Publishing Co.

Mair, J. Samia. The Great Race to Sycamore Street. 2013. (ENG., Illus.). 196p. (J). (gr. 3-6). pap. 12.99 *(978-1-84774-057-1(X))* Kube Publishing Ltd. GBR. Dist: Consortium Bk. Sales & Distribution.

Maxson, H. A. & Young, Claudia H. Tea Party at Chestertown. Kosits, Andrew, illus. 2003. (Magical History Tours Ser.). 55p. (J). per. 8.95 *(978-0-9741713-0-2(1))* Bay Oak Pubs., Ltd.

Messner, Kate. Long Road to Freedom. McMorris, Kelley, illus. 2015. (Ranger in Time Ser.: 3). (ENG.). 160p. (J). (gr. 2-5). pap. 5.99 *(978-0-545-63920-0(4))* Scholastic, Inc.

Mills, Charles. Storm on Shadow Mountain. 2003. 127p. (J). 7.99 *(978-0-8163-1993-0(6))* Pacific Pr. Publishing Assn.

Molinari, Laurice E. Pillars of Fire, 1 vol. 2016. (Ether Novel Ser.). (ENG.). 368p. (J). pap. 8.99 *(978-0-310-73562-5(9))* Zonderkidz.

Molinari, Laurice Elehwany. The Ether: Vero Rising, 1 vol. 2014. (Ether Novel Ser.). (ENG.). 368p. (J). pap. 8.99 *(978-0-310-73561-8(0))* Zonderkidz.

—Pillars of Fire, 1 vol. 2015. (Ether Novel Ser.). (ENG.). 368p. (J). 16.99 *(978-0-310-73556-4(4))* Zonderkidz.

Moore, Kelly, et al. Amber House. (Amber House Ser.: 1). (ENG.). (J). 2013. 384p. (gr. 7). pap. 9.99 *(978-0-545-43417-1(3))* 2012. 368p. (gr. 9). 17.99 *(978-0-545-43416-4(5))* Scholastic, Inc. (Levine, Arthur A. Bks.).

—Neverwas. 2014. (YA). pap. *(978-0-545-43419-5(X))*; (Amber House Ser.: 2). (ENG.). 320p. (J). (gr. 9). 17.99 *(978-0-545-43418-8(1)*, Levine, Arthur A. Bks.) Scholastic, Inc.

Naylor, Phyllis Reynolds. Alice in Charge. (Alice Ser.: 22). (ENG., (YA). (gr. 9). 2011. Illus.). 304p. pap. 8.99 *(978-1-4169-7555-7(1))* 2010. 336p. 16.99 *(978-1-4169-7552-6(7))* Simon & Schuster Children's Publishing. (Atheneum Bks. for Young Readers).

—Alice on Board. 2012. (Alice Ser.: 24). (ENG., Illus.). 288p. (YA). (gr. 9). 16.99 *(978-1-4424-4588-8(2)*, Atheneum Bks. for Young Readers) Simon & Schuster Children's Publishing.

—Dangerously Alice. 2007. (Alice Ser.: 19). (ENG.). 304p. (YA). (gr. 9-12). 15.99 *(978-0-689-87094-1(9)*, Atheneum Bks. for Young Readers) Simon & Schuster Children's Publishing.

—Dangerously Alice. 2008. (Alice Ser.: No. 19). (ENG.). 320p. (YA). mass mkt. 6.99 *(978-0-689-87095-8(7)*, Simon Pulse) Simon Pulse.

—Incredibly Alice. (Alice Ser.: 23). (ENG., (YA). (gr. 9). 2012. Illus.). 304p. pap. 8.99 *(978-1-4169-7556-4(X))* 2011. 288p. 16.99 *(978-1-4169-7553-3(5))* Simon & Schuster Children's Publishing. (Atheneum Bks. for Young Readers).

—Intensely Alice. 2009. (Alice Ser.: 21). (ENG.). 288p. (YA). (gr. 9-18). 16.99 *(978-1-4169-7551-9(9)*, Atheneum Bks. for Young Readers) Simon & Schuster Children's Publishing.

—Intensely Alice. 2010. (Alice Ser.: 21). (ENG.). 288p. (YA). (gr. 9). mass mkt. 6.99 *(978-1-4169-7554-0(3)*, Simon Pulse) Simon Pulse.

—Lovingly Alice. 2004. (Alice Bks.). 166p. (J). (gr. 4-6). 13.65 *(978-0-7569-6604-1(3))* Perfection Learning Corp.

—Lovingly Alice. 2006. (Alice Ser.). (ENG., Illus.). 176p. (J). (gr. 4-7). pap. 5.99 *(978-0-689-84400-3(X)*, Atheneum Bks. for Young Readers) Simon & Schuster Children's Publishing.

—Now I'll Tell You Everything. 2013. (Alice Ser.: 25). (ENG., Illus.). 528p. (YA). (gr. 9). 17.99 *(978-1-4424-4590-1(4))* Simon & Schuster Children's Publishing.

—Please Don't Be True: Dangerously Alice; Almost Alice; Intensely Alice. 2011. (Alice Ser.). (ENG., Illus.). 768p. (YA). (gr. 9). pap. 12.99 *(978-1-4424-1721-2(8)*, Atheneum Bks. for Young Readers) Simon & Schuster Children's Publishing.

—You & Me & the Space in Between: Alice in Charge; Incredibly Alice; Alice on Board. 2013. (Alice Ser.). (ENG., Illus.). 880p. (YA). (gr. 9). pap. 10.99 *(978-1-4424-8664-5(3)*, Atheneum Bks. for Young Readers) Simon & Schuster Children's Publishing.

Now I'll Tell You Everything. 2014. (Alice Ser.: 25). (ENG., Illus.). 544p. (YA). (gr. 9). pap. 12.99 *(978-1-4424-4591-8(2)*, Atheneum Bks. for Young Readers) Simon & Schuster Children's Publishing.

Oneill, Elizabeth. Alfred Visits Maryland. 2008. 24p. (J). pap. 12.00 *(978-0-9799121-7-7(2))* Global Business Information Strategies, Inc.

Otis, James. Calvert of Maryland A Story of Lord Baltimore's Colony. 2005. reprint ed. pap. 21.95 *(978-1-4179-3369-3(0))* Kessinger Publishing, LLC.

Papp, Lisa & Papp, Robert. The Town That Fooled the British: A War of 1812 Story. Papp, Lisa & Papp, Robert, illus. 2011. (Tales of Young Americans Ser.). (ENG., Illus.). 32p. (J). (gr. 1-5). 16.95 *(978-1-58536-484-8(3))* Sleeping Bear Pr.

Rosenthal, Betsy R. Looking for Me: In This Great Big Family. 2013. (ENG., Illus.). 176p. (J). (gr. 5-7). pap. 6.99 *(978-0-544-02271-3(8))* Houghton Mifflin Harcourt Publishing Co.

Roy, Ron. The Ghost at Camp David. Bush, Timothy, illus. 2010. (Capital Mysteries Ser.: 12). (ENG.). 96p. (J). (gr. 1-4). pap. 4.99 *(978-0-375-85925-0(X)*, Random Hse. Bks. for Young Readers) Random Hse. Children's Bks.

—The Ghost at Camp David. 2010. (Capital Mysteries Ser.: 12). lib. bdg. 14.75 *(978-0-606-14010-2(7)*, Turtleback) Turtleback Bks.

Sharpe, Susan. Waterman's Boy. 2007. (ENG.). 176p. (J). (gr. 3-7). pap. 11.95 *(978-1-4169-6453-7(3)*, Simon & Schuster/Paula Wiseman Bks.) Simon & Schuster/Paula Wiseman Bks.

Silvano, Wendi. Love Is All Around Maryland. Czernichowska, Joanna, illus. 2016. (ENG.). 32p. (J). (-6). 12.99 *(978-1-4926-2932-0(4)*, Sourcebooks Jabberwocky) Sourcebooks, Inc.

Siwak, Brenda S. Counting on the Bay. Dodge, Barbara A., illus. 2006. (J). per. 14.95 *(978-0-9790906-0-8(1))* Pleasant Plains Pr.

Smallman, Steve. Santa Is Coming to Maryland. Dunn, Robert, illus. 2013. (ENG.). 32p. (J). (-3). 9.99 *(978-1-4022-8812-8(3)*, Sourcebooks Jabberwocky) Sourcebooks, Inc.

Soentpiet, Chris K., et al. Molly Bannaky. 2009. (ENG., Illus.). 32p. (J). (gr. -1-3). pap. 6.99 *(978-0-547-07676-8(2))* Houghton Mifflin Harcourt Publishing Co.

Standiford, Natalie. The Secret Tree. 2012. 245p. (J). pap. *(978-0-545-48976-8(8)*, Scholastic Pr.) Scholastic, Inc.

Step up 2: the Streets. 2008. 160p. pap. 4.99 *(978-1-4231-1319-5(5))* Disney Pr.

Stout, Shawn K. Ballerina Weather Girl. Martini, Angela, illus. 2013. (Not-So-Ordinary Girl Ser.: 1). (ENG.). 192p. (J). (gr. 1-5). pap. 5.99 *(978-1-4424-7401-7(7)*, Aladdin) Simon & Schuster Children's Publishing.

—Ballerina Weather Girl. Martini, Angela, illus. 2013. (Not-So-Ordinary Girl Ser.: 1). (ENG.). 192p. (J). (gr. 1-5). 15.99 *(978-1-4424-7402-4(5)*, Simon & Schuster/Paula Wiseman Bks.) Simon & Schuster/Paula Wiseman Bks.

—Don't Chicken Out. Ying, Victoria, illus. 2013. (Not-So-Ordinary Girl Ser.: 3). (ENG.). 176p. (J). (gr. 1-5). pap. 5.99 *(978-1-4169-7111-5(4)*, Aladdin) Simon & Schuster Children's Publishing.

—Don't Chicken Out. Ying, Victoria, illus. 2013. (Not-So-Ordinary Girl Ser.: 3). (ENG.). 176p. (J). (gr. 1-5). 15.99 *(978-1-4169-7929-6(8)*, Simon & Schuster/Paula Wiseman Bks.) Simon & Schuster/Paula Wiseman Bks.

—Fiona Finkelstein, Big-Time Ballerina!! Martini, Angela, illus. 2010. (ENG.). 192p. (J). pap. 4.99 *(978-1-4169-7109-2(2)*, Simon & Schuster/Paula Wiseman Bks.) Simon & Schuster/Paula Wiseman Bks.

—Miss Matched. Martini, Angela, illus. 2013. (Not-So-Ordinary Girl Ser.: 2). (ENG.). 176p. (J). (gr. 1-5). pap. 5.99 *(978-1-4424-7404-8(1)*, Aladdin) Simon & Schuster Children's Publishing.

—Miss Matched. Martini, Angela, illus. 2013. (Not-So-Ordinary Girl Ser.: 2). (ENG.). 160p. (J). (gr. 1-5). 15.99 *(978-1-4424-7405-5(X)*, Simon & Schuster/Paula Wiseman Bks.) Simon & Schuster/Paula Wiseman Bks.

Sully, Katherine. Night-Night Maryland. Poole, Helen, illus. 2017. (ENG.). 20p. (J). (-1). bds. 9.99 *(978-1-4926-4768-3(3)*, 9781492647683, Sourcebooks Jabberwocky) Sourcebooks, Inc.

Szymanski, Lois K. Grandfather's Secret, 1 vol. 2010. (ENG., Illus.). 64p. (J). pap. 12.99 *(978-0-7643-3535-8(9)*, 9780764335358) Schiffer Publishing, Ltd.

Thompson, Kimberly. Toulouse Tangled up in Lights. Easey, Chris, illus. 2011. 64p. (J). 19.95 *(978-0-9818976-1-5(4))* Little Pigeon Bks.

Trimper, Marty. Hermione: Shipwrecked! in Ocean City, Maryland. Amy, Holloway, illus. 2004. (J). *(978-1-886068-28-5(3))* Fruitbearer Publishing, LLC.

Troeger, Virginia B. Secret along the St. Mary's. Swisher, Michael-Che, tr. Swisher, Michael-Che, illus. 2003. (Mysteries in Time Ser.). 92p. (gr. 4). 14.95 *(978-1-893110-35-9(4))* Silver Moon Pr.

Winstead, Amy. The Star-Spangled Banner. Dacey, Bob & Bandelin, Debra, illus. 2003. (ENG.). 32p. (J). 18.65 *(978-0-8249-5462-8(9)*, Ideal Pubns.) Worthy Publishing.

MARYLAND—HISTORY

Bachmann, Elaine Rice. While a Tree Grew: The Story of Maryland's Wye Oak, 1 vol. Harrell, Kim, illus. 2009. (ENG.). 30p. (gr. -1-3). 10.50 *(978-0-87033-577-8(4)*, 9780870335778, Cornell Maritime Pr./Tidewater Pubs.) Schiffer Publishing, Ltd.

Brown, Vanessa. Maryland. 2009. (Bilingual Library of the United States of America Ser.). (ENG & SPA.). 32p. (gr. 2-2). 47.90 *(978-1-60853-365-7(4)*, Editorial Buenas Letras) Rosen Publishing Group, Inc., The.

Bunting, Elaine & D'Amario, Patricia. Counties of Northern Maryland, 1 vol. Ramsey, Marcy Dunn, illus. 2010. (ENG.). 176p. (J). (gr. 4-7). 19.95 *(978-0-87033-520-4(0)*, 9780870335204, Cornell Maritime Pr./Tidewater Pubs.) Schiffer Publishing, Ltd.

Connors, Kathleen. Visiting the Chesapeake Bay. 2013. 32p. (J). (gr. 3-6). 26.60 *(978-1-4339-9788-4(6))*; pap. 10.50 *(978-1-4339-9789-1(4))* Stevens, Gareth Publishing LLLP.

Craats, Rennay. Maryland: The Old Line State. 2016. (J). *(978-1-4896-4875-4(5))* Weigl Pubs., Inc.

Cunningham, Kevin. The Maryland Colony. 2011. (True Bk Ser.). (ENG., Illus.). 48p. (J). pap. 6.95 *(978-0-531-26603-8(6))*; lib. bdg. 29.00 *(978-0-531-25390-8(2))* Scholastic Library Publishing. (Children's Pr.).

Damanda, Lori. The Story of the "Star-Spangled Banner" 2009. (Real Life Readers Ser.). 32p. (J). (ENG., Illus.). (gr. 5-6). pap. 10.00 *(978-1-4358-0205-6(5))*; (gr. 4-6). lib. bdg. 25.25 *(978-1-4358-3015-8(6))* Rosen Publishing Group, Inc., The. (PowerKids Pr.).

Dans, Peter E. Sergeant Bill & His Horse Bob. Corpus, Mary Grace, illus. 2015.Tr. of 28. (ENG.). (J). 17.95 *(978-1-933822-97-6(X))* Camino Bks., Inc.

Doak, Robin. Maryland, 1634-1776. 2007. (National Geographic Voices from ColonialAmerica Ser.). (ENG., Illus.). 112p. (J). (gr. 5-9). 21.95 *(978-1-4263-0143-8(X))*; lib. bdg. 32.90 *(978-1-4263-0144-5(8))* National Geographic Society. (National Geographic Children's Bks.).

Doherty, Craig A. & Doherty, Katherine M. Maryland. 2005. (Thirteen Colonies Ser.). (Illus.). 128p. (gr. 5-8). 35.00 *(978-0-8160-5418-3(5))* Facts On File, Inc.

Exploring the Chesapeake Bay. 2013. (Exploring the Chesapeake Bay Ser.). 32p. (J). (gr. 3-6). 159.60 *(978-1-4339-9843-0(2))*; pap. 378.00 *(978-1-4339-9845-4(9))*; pap. 63.00 *(978-1-4339-9844-7(0))* Stevens, Gareth Publishing LLLP.

Friddell, Claudia. Goliath: Hero of the Great Baltimore Fire. Howell, Troy, illus. 2010. (True Stories Ser.). (ENG.). 32p. (J). (gr. 1-4). 17.95 *(978-1-58536-455-8(X)*, 202179) Sleeping Bear Pr.

Grau, Maritta, ed. The ABCs of Frederick Maryland: A Historic Coloring Book. Grau, Ryon, illus. 2007. 32p. 8.95 *(978-0-9772559-0-0(5))* Grau, Ryon.

Hama, Larry. The Battle of Antietam: The Bloodiest Day of Battle. (Graphic Civil War Battles Ser.). (ENG.). 48p. 2009. (YA). (gr. 4-5). 58.50 *(978-1-61512-897-6(2)*, Rosen Reference) 2007. (Illus.). (gr. 5-8). pap. 14.05 *(978-1-4042-6475-5(2)*, Rosen Classroom) Rosen Publishing Group, Inc., The.

—The Battle of Antietam: The Bloodiest Day of Battle. Moore, Scott, illus. 2007. (Graphic Battles of the Civil War Ser.). (ENG.). 48p. (YA). (gr. 4-7). lib. bdg. 31.95 *(978-1-4042-0775-2(9))* Rosen Publishing Group, Inc., The.

History of the Chesapeake Bay. 2013. (Exploring the Chesapeake Bay Ser.). 32p. (J). (gr. 3-6). pap. 63.00 *(978-1-4339-9774-7(6))* Stevens, Gareth Publishing LLLP.

Jensen, Ann. The World Turned Upside Down: Children of 1776, 1 vol. Ramsey, Marcy Dunn, illus. 2009. (ENG.). 80p. (J). pap. 9.95 *(978-0-87033-534-1(0)*, 9780870335341,

Cornell Maritime Pr./Tidewater Pubs.) Schiffer Publishing, Ltd.

Jerome, Kate B. Lucky to Live in Maryland. 2017. (Arcadia Kids Ser.). (ENG., Illus.). 32p. (J). 16.99 **(978-0-7385-2785-7(8))** Arcadia Publishing.

—The Wise Animal Handbook Maryland. 2017. (Arcadia Kids Ser.). (ENG., Illus.). 32p. (J). 16.99 **(978-0-7385-2824-3(2))** Arcadia Publishing.

Landau, Elaine. The National Anthem. 2007. (True Book(tm), a — American History Ser.). (ENG., Illus.). 48p. (J). (gr. 3-5). lib. bdg. 31.00 *(978-0-531-12633-2(1)*, Children's Pr.) Scholastic Library Publishing.

Loker, Aleck. The Murder of Joseph Henry Ching: A Legend Examined. 2003. (Illus.). 28p. 6.00 *(978-1-928874-04-1(5))* Solitude Pr.

Lusted, Marcia Amidon. Maryland: The Old Line State. 2010. (Our Amazing States Ser.). (Illus.). 24p. (J). pap. 8.25 *(978-1-4358-9794-6(3))*; lib. bdg. 22.60 *(978-1-4358-9350-4(6))* Rosen Publishing Group, Inc., The. (PowerKids Pr.).

Marsh, Carole. Exploring Maryland Through Project-Based Learning. 2016. (Maryland Experience Ser.). (ENG.). (J). pap. 9.99 *(978-0-635-12344-2(4))* Gallopade International.

—I'm Reading about Maryland. 2014. (Maryland Experience Ser.). (ENG., Illus.). (J). pap., pap. 8.99 *(978-0-635-11295-8(7))* Gallopade International.

—Let's Discover Maryland! 2004. (J). (gr. 2-8). cd-rom 14.95 *(978-0-7933-9617-7(4))* Gallopade International.

—Lords of Baltimore, Founders of Maryland. 2004. 12p. (gr. k-4). 2.95 *(978-0-635-02368-1(7))* Gallopade International.

—Maryland History Projects: 30 Cool, Activities, Crafts, Experiments & More for Kids to Do to Learn about Your State! 2003. (Maryland Experience Ser.). 32p. (gr. k-5). pap. 5.95 *(978-0-635-01789-5(X)*, Marsh, Carole Bks.) Gallopade International.

Marsico, Katie. The Chesapeake Bay. 2013. (Explorer Library: Social Studies Explorer Ser.). (ENG.). 32p. (gr. 4-8). pap. 14.21 *(978-1-62431-037-9(0)*, 202505); lib. bdg. 28.50 *(978-1-62431-013-3(3)*, 202503) Cherry Lake Publishing.

The Maryland Adventure: New Maryland 4th Grade, 1 vol. l.t. ed. 2009. 360p. (gr. 4-4). 47.95 *(978-1-4236-0583-6(7))* Gibbs Smith, Publisher.

The Maryland Adventure Program Kit: All program components for the Maryland Adventure, 1 vol. 2009. pap. 169.95 *(978-1-4236-0719-9(8))* Gibbs Smith, Publisher.

Mattern, Joanne. Maryland: Past & Present. 2010. (United States: Past & Present Ser.). (ENG., Illus.). 48p. (J). pap. 11.75 *(978-1-4358-8488-5(4))*; lib. bdg. 29.25 *(978-1-4358-3519-1(0))* Rosen Publishing Group, Inc., The. (Rosen Reference).

McDowell, Pamela. Maryland: The Old Line State. 2012. (J). *(978-1-61913-359-4(8))*; pap. *(978-1-61913-360-0(1))* Weigl Pubs., Inc.

Mills, Clifford W. Lord Baltimore. 2010. (Leaders of the Colonial Era Ser.). 128p. (gr. 5-8). 35.00 *(978-1-60413-738-5(X)*, Chelsea Hse.) Facts On File, Inc.

Mis, Melody S. The Colony of Maryland: A Primary Source History. (Primary Source Library of the Thirteen Colonies & the Lost Colony Ser.). 24p. (gr. 3-4). 2009. 42.50 *(978-1-60854-139-3(8))* 2006. (Illus.). (J). lib. bdg. 22.60 *(978-1-4042-3434-5(9))* Rosen Publishing Group, Inc., The. (PowerKids Pr.).

Murphy, Jim. A Savage Thunder: Antietam & the Bloody Road to Freedom. 2009. (ENG.). 112p. (J). (gr. 3-7). 19.99 *(978-0-689-87633-2(5)*, McElderry, Margaret K. Bks.) McElderry, Margaret K. Bks.

Murray, Julie. Maryland, 1 vol. 2012. (Explore the United States Ser.). (ENG.). 32p. (J). (gr. 2-5). lib. bdg. 28.50 *(978-1-61783-358-8(4)*, Big Buddy Bks.) ABDO Publishing Co.

Nagelhout, Ryan. Saving the Chesapeake Bay. 2013. (Exploring the Chesapeake Bay Ser.). (Illus.). 32p. (J). (gr. 3-6). pap. 10.50 *(978-1-4339-9785-3(1))*; (ENG., lib. bdg. 26.60 *(978-1-4339-9784-6(3))* Stevens, Gareth Publishing LLLP.

Niver, Heather Moore. Tributaries of the Chesapeake Bay. 2013. (Exploring the Chesapeake Bay Ser.). (Illus.). 32p. (J). (gr. 3-6). pap. 10.50 *(978-1-4339-9793-8(2))*; lib. bdg. 26.60 *(978-1-4339-9792-1(4))* Stevens, Gareth Publishing LLLP.

Otfinoski, Steven & Steinitz, Andy. Maryland. 2014. (It's My State! (r) Ser.). (Illus.). 80p. (J). (gr. 4-8). lib. bdg. 34.21 *(978-1-62712-743-1(7))* Cavendish Square Publishing.

—Maryland. 2nd rev. ed. 2010. (It's My State! Ser.). 80p. (gr. 3-18). lib. bdg. 31.36 *(978-1-60870-052-3(6))* Marshall Cavendish Corp.

Pietrzyk, Leslie & Kneib, Martha. Maryland. 2nd rev. ed. 2008. (Celebrate the States Ser.). 144p. (gr. 6-18). lib. bdg. 42.79 *(978-0-7614-3004-9(0)*, Benchmark Bks.) Marshall Cavendish Corp.

Raum, Elizabeth & Doak, Robin S. Exploring the Maryland Colony. 2016. (Exploring the 13 Colonies Ser.). (ENG., Illus.). 48p. (gr. 3-4). lib. bdg. 31.99 *(978-1-5157-2238-0(4))* Capstone Press of Coughlan Cos.

Shea, Therese. History of the Chesapeake Bay. 2013. 32p. (J). (gr. 3-6). 26.60 *(978-1-4339-9772-3(X))*; pap. 10.50 *(978-1-4339-9773-0(8))* Stevens, Gareth Publishing LLLP.

Somervill, Barbara A. Maryland. 2008. (ENG.). 80p. (J). pap. 7.95 *(978-0-531-20807-6(9)*, Children's Pr.) Scholastic Library Publishing.

Sonneborn, Liz. The Colony of Maryland. 2006. (Primary Sources of the Thirteen Colonies & the Lost Colony Ser.). (ENG., Illus.). 64p. (gr. 4-8). per. 12.95 *(978-1-4042-0672-4(8))* Rosen Publishing Group, Inc., The.

—A Primary Source History of the Colony of Maryland. (Primary Sources of the Thirteen Colonies & the Lost Colony Ser.). 64p. 2009. (gr. 5-8). 58.50 *(978-1-60851-879-1(5))* 2006. (Illus.). (YA). (gr. 4-7). lib. bdg. 31.95 *(978-1-4042-0427-0(X))* Rosen Publishing Group, Inc., The.

Tributaries of the Chesapeake Bay. 2013. (Exploring the Chesapeake Bay Ser.). 32p. (J). (gr. 3-6). pap. 63.00 *(978-1-4339-9794-5(0))* Stevens, Gareth Publishing LLLP.

Visiting the Chesapeake Bay. 2013. (Exploring the Chesapeake Bay Ser.). 32p. (J). (gr. 3-6). pap. 63.00 *(978-1-4339-9790-7(8))* Stevens, Gareth Publishing LLLP.

Walker, Sally. Ghost Walls: The Story of a 17th-Century Colonial Homestead. 2014. (Illus.). 136p. (J). (gr. 6-12). lib. bdg. 20.95 *(978-0-7613-5408-6(5)*, Carolrhoda Bks.) Lerner Publishing Group.

Whiting, Jim. The Maryland Colony: Lord Baltimore. 2007. (Building America Ser.). (Illus.). 48p. (J). (gr. 4-8). lib. bdg. 29.95 *(978-1-58415-547-8(7))* Mitchell Lane Pubs., Inc.

Wyckoff, Edwin Brit. The African-American Heart Surgery Pioneer: The Genius of Vivien Thomas. 2013. (Genius Inventors & Their Great Ideas Ser.). 48p. (J). (gr. 3-4). pap. 8.95 *(978-1-4644-0210-4(8)*, Enslow Elementary) Enslow Pubs., Inc.

Yasuda, Anita. What's Great about Maryland? 2015. (ENG., Illus.). 32p. (J). (gr. 2-5). 26.65 *(978-1-4677-3875-0(1))* Lerner Publishing Group.

MASAI (AFRICAN PEOPLE)

Alexander, Florence & Alexander, Stanley. Come with Me & See — African People: Venga Conmigo y Vea — la Gente de Africa. 2003. (SPA & ENG., Illus.). 34p. (J). *(978-964-8313-41-3(5))* Ebon Research Systems Publishing, LLC.

—Come with Me & See... African People. l.t. ed. 2003. (ENG & SPA., Illus.). 13p. (J). 3.99 *(978-0-9648313-8-4(4))* Ebon Research Systems Publishing, LLC.

Craats, Rennay. Maasai. (Indigenous Peoples Ser.). 32p. 2005. pap. 9.95 *(978-1-59036-255-6(1))* 2004. (Illus.). (J). lib. bdg. 26.00 *(978-1-59036-219-8(5))* Weigl Pubs., Inc.

Deedy, Carmen Agra. 14 Cows for America, 1 vol. González, Thomas, illus. 2009. (ENG.). 36p. (J). (gr. 1-5). 17.95 *(978-1-56145-490-7(7))* Peachtree Pubs.

—14 Cows for America. Gonzalez, Thomas, illus. 2016. (ENG.). 36p. (J). (gr. -1-3). lib. bdg. 19.60 *(978-0-606-39065-1(0))* Turtleback Bks.

Deedy, Carmen Agra & Naiyomah, Wilson Kimeli. 14 Cows for America, 1 vol. González, Thomas, illus. 2016. (ENG.). 36p. (J). (gr. 1-5). pap. 8.95 *(978-1-56145-961-2(5))* Peachtree Pubs.

Lekuton, Joseph & Viola, Herman J. Facing the Lion: Growing up Maasai on the African Savanna. 2006. (Reader's Workshop Ser.). (ENG., Illus.). 112p. (C). pap. 21.95 *(978-0-7362-3133-6(1))* CENGAGE Learning.

Lekuton, Joseph Lemasolai. Facing the Lion: Growing up Maasai on the African Savanna. (ENG., Illus.). 144p. (YA). (gr. 7-18). 2005. 23.90 *(978-0-7922-8328-7(7))* 2003. 15.95 *(978-0-7922-5125-5(3))* National Geographic Society. (National Geographic Children's Bks.).

Scott, Jonathan & Scott, Angela. The Masai: Tribe of Warriors. Scott, Jonathan & Scott, Angela, illus. 2007. (Collins Big Cat Ser.). (ENG., Illus.). 48p. (J). (gr. 3-4). pap. 8.99 *(978-0-00-723097-6(4))* HarperCollins Pubs. Ltd. GBR. Dist: Independent Pubs. Group.

MASAI (AFRICAN PEOPLE)—FICTION

Barasch, Lynne. First Come the Zebra. Barasch, Lynne, illus. (ENG., Illus.). 40p. (J). 2009. (gr. 1-6). 18.95 *(978-1-60060-365-5(3))* 2005. pap. 10.95 *(978-1-62014-029-1(2))* Lee & Low Bks., Inc.

Joosse, Barbara M. & Lavallee, Barbara. Papa, Do You Love Me? Lavallee, Barbara, illus. 2005. (Mama Ser.: MAMA). (ENG., Illus.). 36p. (J). (gr. -1-7). 15.99 *(978-0-8118-4265-5(7))* Chronicle Bks. LLC.

MASERS, OPTICAL

see Lasers

MASKS

Anastasio, Dina. Mask Making Around the World. 2011. (Early Connections Ser.). (J). *(978-1-61672-588-4(5))* Benchmark Education Co.

—Mask Making Around the World: Set Of 6. 2011. (Early Connections Ser.). (J). pap. 37.00 net. *(978-1-4108-1069-4(0))* Benchmark Education Co.

Cryan, Mary Beth. Make Your Own Masks: Tear Them, Share Them, Color & Wear Them! 2015. (ENG.). 64p. (J). (gr. 1-4). pap. 7.99 *(978-0-486-79406-8(7))* Dover Pubns., Inc.

D'Cruz, Anna-Marie. Make Your Own Masks. 2009. (Do It Yourself Projects! Ser.). 24p. (J). (gr. 3-5). (ENG.). pap. 9.40 *(978-1-4358-2923-7(9))*; lib. bdg. 25.25 *(978-1-4358-2853-7(4))* Rosen Publishing Group, Inc., The. (PowerKids Pr.).

Doney, Meryl. Masks. 2004. (Crafts from Many Cultures Ser.). (Illus.). 32p. (gr. 2-5). lib. bdg. 26.00 *(978-0-8368-4044-5(5)*, Gareth Stevens Learning Library) Stevens, Gareth Publishing LLLP.

Hodge, Susie. Masks. 2006. (Design & Make Ser.). (Illus.). 32p. (J). (gr. 4-7). lib. bdg. 28.50 *(978-1-58340-952-7(1))* Black Rabbit Bks.

Holden, Pam. Masks, 6 pack. 2009. (Red Rocket Readers Ser.). (ENG., Illus.). 16p. (gr. 1-1). pap. *(978-1-877490-19-4(9))* Flying Start Bks.

Humphrey, Paul. How to Make a Mask. Fairclough, Chris, photos by. 2007. (Crafty Kids Ser.). (Illus.). 24p. (J). (gr. -1-3). lib. bdg. 24.25 *(978-1-59771-101-2(2))* Sea-To-Sea Pubns.

Issa, Joanna. I Can Make a Mask, 1 vol. 2014. (What Can I Make Today? Ser.). (ENG., Illus.). 24p. (gr. k-2). 22.65 *(978-1-4846-0461-8(X)*, Heinemann Read & Learn) Heinemann-Raintree.

Kenney, Karen Latchana. Super Simple Masks: Fun & Easy-to-Make Crafts for Kids, 1 vol. 2009. (Super Simple Crafts Ser.). (ENG., Illus.). 32p. (gr. k-4). 27.07 *(978-1-60453-627-0(6)*, Super SandCastle) ABDO Publishing Co.

LaFosse, Michael G. Making Origami Masks Step by Step. 2009. (Kid's Guide to Origami Ser.). 24p. (gr. 3-4). 47.90 *(978-1-61511-188-6(3)*, PowerKids Pr.) Rosen Publishing Group, Inc., The.

Morris, Ting & Morris, Neil. Masks. 2006. (Sticky Fingers Ser.). (Illus.). 32p. (J). lib. bdg. 28.50 *(978-1-59771-030-5(X))* Sea-To-Sea Pubns.

Rudolph, Nancy Lyn. Paper Animal Masks from Northwest Tribal Tales. 2004. (Illus.). 80p. (J). (gr. 4-8). reprint ed. 20.00 *(978-0-7567-7073-0(4))* DIANE Publishing Co.

Smith, A. G. Masks of the World Coloring Book. 2003. (Dover History Coloring Book Ser.). (ENG., Illus.). 32p. (J). (gr. 3-8). pap. 3.99 *(978-0-486-43039-3(1))* Dover Pubns., Inc.

Smith, Thomasina. Amazing Masks to Make Yourself: 25 Projects for Funny & Frightening Faces to Wear! 2014. (ENG., Illus.). 64p. (J). (gr. 3-8). 9.99 *(978-1-84322-913-1(7)*, Armadillo) Anness Publishing GBR. Dist: National Bk. Network.

Storey, Rita. Masks. Rhodes, Harry, illus. Rhodes, Harry, photos by. 2014. (J). lib. bdg. 26.60 *(978-1-4677-4195-8(7)*, Lerner Pubns.) Lerner Publishing Group.

Thomas, Isabel. Masks & Face Painting, 1 vol. 2011. (Start with Art Ser.). (ENG.). 24p. (gr. k-2). 23.32 *(978-1-4329-5190-0(4)*, Heinemann Read & Learn) Heinemann-Raintree.

Valat, Pierre-Marie. Animal Faces: 15 Punch-Out Masks. 3rd ed. 2007. (ENG., Illus.). 32p. (J). (gr. -1-7). per. 16.95 *(978-1-59354-196-5(1)*, Handprint Bks.) Chronicle Bks. LLC.

Yates, Jane. Paper-Mache Masks. 2016. (Cool Crafts for Kids Ser.). 00032p. (J). (gr. 3-3). pap. 11.75 *(978-1-4994-8234-8(5)*, Windmill Bks.) Rosen Publishing Group, Inc., The.

MASONRY

Willett, Edward. A Career As a Mason, 01 vols., 1. 2016. (Essential Careers Ser.). (ENG.). 80p. (J). 34.25 *(978-1-4994-6217-3(4)*, Rosen Young Adult) Rosen Publishing Group, Inc., The.

MASS COMMUNICATION

see Communication

MASS MEDIA

Adams, Simon. Politics. 2010. (Media Power Ser.). 48p. (YA). (gr. 5-9). 35.65 *(978-1-60753-114-2(3))* Amicus Publishing.

Ali, Dominic. Media Madness: An Insider's Guide to Media. Cho, Michael, illus. 2005. (ENG.). 64p. (J). (gr. 5-9). 9.95 *(978-1-55337-175-5(5))* Kids Can Pr., Ltd. CAN. Dist: Hachette Bk. Group.

Anderson, Judith. Celebrity & Fame. 2010. (Media Power Ser.). 48p. (YA). (gr. 5-9). 35.65 *(978-1-60753-112-8(7))* Amicus Publishing.

—Celebrity & Fame. 2011. (Inside Crime Ser.). 48p. (YA). (gr. 5-9). lib. bdg. 34.25 *(978-1-59920-398-0(7))* Black Rabbit Bks.

—Crime. 2010. (Media Power Ser.). 48p. (YA). (gr. 5-9). 35.65 *(978-1-60753-113-5(5))* Amicus Publishing.

—War & Conflict. 2010. (Media Power Ser.). 48p. (J). 35.65 *(978-1-60753-116-6(X))* Amicus Publishing.

Anderson, Judith & Flinthart, Dirk. War & Conflict. 2011. (Inside Crime Ser.). 48p. (YA). (gr. 5-9). lib. bdg. 34.25 *(978-1-59920-399-7(5))* Black Rabbit Bks.

Anderson, Judith & Vaughan, Jenny. Crime. 2011. (Inside Crime Ser.). 48p. (YA). (gr. 5-9). lib. bdg. 34.25 *(978-1-59920-400-0(2))* Black Rabbit Bks.

Anniss, Matthew. Media Genius. 2016. (Media Genius Ser.). (ENG.). 48p. (gr. 5-8). 133.28 *(978-1-4109-8117-2(7))* Heinemann-Raintree.

Bailey, Gerry & Way, Steve. Communication. 2008. (Simply Science Ser.). (Illus.). 32p. (YA). (gr. 3-6). lib. bdg. 26.00 *(978-0-8368-9226-0(7))* Stevens, Gareth Publishing LLLP.

Ball, Jacqueline A., et al. Communication Inventions: From Hieroglyphics to DVDs. 2006. (Which Came First? Ser.). (Illus.). 32p. (YA). (gr. 3-6). lib. bdg. 25.27 *(978-1-59716-129-9(2))* Bearport Publishing Co., Inc.

Barber, Phil. Football & Player Safety. 2017. (Illus.). 64p. (J). *(978-1-4222-3576-8(9))* Mason Crest.

Bauder, Julia. Media Ethics. 2008. (Current Controversies Ser.). (ENG., Illus.). 176-240p. (gr. 10-12). 28.45 *(978-0-7377-4145-2(7))*; 40.95 *(978-0-7377-4144-5(9))* Cengage Gale. (Greenhaven Pr., Inc.).

Berlatsky, Noah, ed. Media Violence. 2012. (Opposing Viewpoints Ser.). (ENG., Illus.). 240p. (gr. 10-12). 42.95 *(978-0-7377-6328-7(0))*; pap. 29.45 *(978-0-7377-6329-4(9))* Cengage Gale. (Greenhaven Pr., Inc.).

Bozzo, Linda & Library. Staying in Touch in the Past, Present, & Future. 2010. (Imagining the Future Ser.). (Illus.). 24p. (J). lib. bdg. 22.60 *(978-0-7660-3438-9(0)*, Enslow Elementary) Enslow Pubs., Inc.

Cefrey, Holly. Coping with Media Violence. 2005. (Coping Ser.). (Illus.). 192p. (YA). (gr. 7-12). lib. bdg. 34.60 *(978-0-8239-2893-4(4))* Rosen Publishing Group, Inc., The.

Cooper, Alison. Media Power? 2005. (Viewpoints (Sea to Sea) Ser.). (Illus.). 32p. (J). (gr. 5-9). lib. bdg. 27.10 *(978-1-932889-61-1(2))* Sea-To-Sea Pubns.

DeGaetano, Gloria. Parenting Well in a Media Age: Keeping Our Kids Human. 2004. (ENG.). 272p. pap. 18.95 *(978-1-932181-12-8(1))* Personhood Pr.

Donovan, Sandy. Media: From News Coverage to Political Advertising. 2015. (ENG.). 64p. (J). (gr. 6-8). 26.65 *(978-1-4677-7909-8(1))* Lerner Publishing Group.

Dugan, Christine. Tech World: The Language of Social Media (Level 5) 2017. (Exploring Reading Ser.). (Illus.). 48p. (J). (gr. 5-5). pap. 10.99 **(978-1-4258-4989-4(X))** Teacher Created Materials, Inc.

Endich, Roberta. Media Literacy: Activities for Understanding the Scripted World, 1 vol. 2003. (Linworth Learning Ser.). (Illus.). 150p. (C). pap. 29.95 *(978-1-58683-094-6(5)*, A2374P, Linworth Publishing, Inc.) ABC-CLIO, LLC.

Gifford, Clive. Violence on the Screen. 2010. (Voices Ser.). (Illus.). 48p. pap. *(978-0-237-54218-4(8))* Evans Brothers, Ltd.

Haerens, Margaret. Mass Media. Greenhaven Press Editors, ed. 2014. (Opposing Viewpoints Ser.). (ENG.). 224p. (gr. 10-12). lib. bdg. 48.80 *(978-0-7377-6660-8(3)*, Greenhaven Pr., Inc.) Cengage Gale.

—Mass Media. Greenhaven Press Editors & Gale Editors, eds. 2014. (Opposing Viewpoints Ser.). (ENG., Illus.). 224p. (gr. 7-12). pap. 33.80 *(978-0-7377-6661-5(1)*, Greenhaven Pr., Inc.) Cengage Gale.

Hand, Carol. Getting Paid to Produce Videos. 2016. (Turning Your Tech Hobbies into a Career Ser.). 00080p. (J). (gr. 7-7). 35.75 *(978-1-5081-7292-5(7))* Rosen Publishing Group, Inc., The.

Harmon, Daniel E. Dream Jobs in Sports Media. 2014. (Great Careers in the Sports Industry Ser.). (Illus.). 160p. (YA). (gr. 7-12). 40.95 *(978-1-4777-7523-3(4))* Rosen Publishing Group, Inc., The.

Harper, Leslie. Cómo Mantenerse Informado. 2014. (Sé un líder de la Comunidad (Be a Community Leader) Ser.). (SPA.). 32p. (J). (gr. 4-6). pap. 60.00 *(978-1-4777-6923-2(4)*, PowerKids Pr.) Rosen Publishing Group, Inc., The.

—Cómo Mantenerse Informados. 2014. (Sé un líder de la Comunidad (Be a Community Leader) Ser.). (SPA.). 32p. (J). (gr. 4-6). lib. bdg. 26.25 *(978-1-4777-6921-8(8)*, PowerKids Pr.) Rosen Publishing Group, Inc., The.

—How to Stay Informed. 2014. (Be a Community Leader Ser.). 32p. (J). (gr. 4-6). lib. bdg. 26.25 *(978-1-4777-6701-6(0)*, PowerKids Pr.) Rosen Publishing Group, Inc., The.

Haugen, David M. Media Violence. 2008. (Opposing Viewpoints Ser.). (ENG., Illus.). 232p. (YA). (gr. 10-12). 29.45 *(978-0-7377-4219-0(4)*, LML02109-243141); pap. 42.95 *(978-0-7377-4218-3(6)*, LML02109-243108) Cengage Gale. (Greenhaven Pr., Inc.).

Hermansson, Casie. Parental Guidance Ratings. 2013. (Hot Topics in Media EBook Ser.). (ENG.). 48p. (J). pap. 15.64 *(978-1-61783-784-5(9))* ABDO Publishing Co.

Hernández, Roger E. Teens & the Media. 2008. (Gallup Youth Survey, Major Issues & Trends Ser.). (Illus.). 112,128p. (YA). lib. bdg. 22.95 *(978-1-59084-874-6(8))* Mason Crest.

Hernandez, Roger E. Teens & the Media. Developed in Association with the Gallup Organization Staff, ed. 2013. (Gallup Youth Survey: Major Issues & Trends Ser.: 14). 112p. (J). (gr. 7-18). 24.95 *(978-1-4222-2954-5(8))* Mason Crest.

Hollingsworth, Tamara. Unforgettable News Reports, 1 vol. 2nd rev. ed. 2013. (Nonfiction Readers Ser.). (ENG., Illus.). 64p. (J). (gr. 5-5). pap. 31.96 *(978-1-4333-7444-9(7))* Teacher Created Materials, Inc.

Horn, Geoffrey M. Political Parties, Interest Groups & the Media. 2003. (World Almanac Library of American Government). (Illus.). 48p. (gr. 5-12). pap. 14.05 *(978-0-8368-5483-1(7))*; lib. bdg. 31.00 *(978-0-8368-5478-7(0))* Stevens, Gareth Publishing LLLP. (Gareth Stevens Secondary Library).

Kerr, Jim. Sports. 2010. (Media Power Ser.). 48p. (YA). (gr. 5-9). 35.65 *(978-1-60753-115-9(1))* Amicus Publishing.

Lane, Yvet-Renee. Cambridge Checkpoints VCE Media 2005. 2004. (Cambridge Checkpoints Ser.). (ENG.). pap., stu. ed. 12.00 *(978-0-521-61223-4(3))* Cambridge Univ. Pr.

Ledbetter, Ebonie. Media Bias. 2015. (Introducing Issues with Opposing Viewpoints Ser.). (ENG., Illus.). 144p. (J). (gr. 7-10). 42.00 *(978-0-7377-7236-4(0)*, Greenhaven Pr., Inc.) Cengage Gale.

Lewis, Clare. Entertainment Through the Years: How Having Fun Has Changed in Living Memory. 2015. (History in Living Memory Ser.). (ENG.). 24p. (gr. k-2). 23.32 *(978-1-4846-0923-1(9)*, Heinemann Read & Learn) Heinemann-Raintree.

Malaspina, Ann. False Images, Deadly Promises: Smoking & the Media. 2007. (Tobacco: the Deadly Drug Ser.). (Illus.). 112p. (YA). pap. 12.95 *(978-1-4222-0812-0(5))* Mason Crest.

Miller, Adam. Mastering Media, 1 vol., Set. Incl. Entertainment & Gaming. Botzakis, Stergios. 34.65 *(978-1-4109-3844-2(1))*; News Never Stops. Price, Sean Stewart & DiConsiglio, John. 34.65 *(978-1-4109-3843-5(3))*; (Illus.). (gr. 7-8). (Mastering Media Ser.). (ENG.). 56p. 2010. 69.30 *(978-1-4109-3846-6(8)*, Raintree Freestyle) Heinemann-Raintree.

Open for Debate - Group 5, 4 bks., Set. Incl. National Health Care. Kowalski, Kathiann M. lib. bdg. 42.79 *(978-0-7614-2943-2(3))*; Political Campaigns. Naden, Corinne J. lib. bdg. 42.79 *(978-0-7614-2944-9(1))*; Religious Fundamentalism. Fridell, Ron. lib. bdg. 42.79 *(978-0-7614-2945-6(X))*; Right to Die. Stefoff, Rebecca. lib. bdg. 42.79 *(978-0-7614-2948-7(4))*; 128p. (gr. 7-18). (Open for Debate 5 Ser.). 2008. Set lib. bdg. 171.16 *(978-0-7614-2940-1(9)*, Benchmark Bks.) Marshall Cavendish Corp.

Pelusey, Michael & Pelusey, Jane. The Media. 2005. (Media Ser.). (Illus.). 32p. (gr. 5-8). 131.70 *(978-0-7910-9093-0(0)*, Chelsea Hse.) Facts On File, Inc.

Peters, Jennifer. Critical Perspectives on Media Bias. 2017. (J). **(978-0-7660-9169-6(4))** Enslow Pubs., Inc.

Reeves, Diane Lindsey. Career Ideas for Kids Who Like Talking. Bond, Nancy, illus. 2nd rev. ed. 2007. (Career Ideas for Kids Ser.). 208p. (gr. 4-9). 32.95 *(978-0-8160-6553-0(5)*, Checkmark Bks.) Facts On File, Inc.

Regulating Violence in Entertainment. 2010. (Point/Counterpoint Ser.). (Illus.). 152p. (C). (gr. 9-18). 35.00 *(978-1-60413-510-7(7)*, Chelsea Hse.) Facts On File, Inc.

Robinson, Tom. Media Ownership, 1 vol. 2009. (Essential Viewpoints Set 4 Ser.). (ENG., Illus.). 112p. (J). (gr. 6-12). lib. bdg. 35.64 *(978-1-60453-534-1(2))* ABDO Publishing Co.

Rooney, Anne. Creative & Media Careers. 2010. (In the Workplace Ser.). 48p. (J). lib. bdg. 34.25 *(978-1-60753-090-9(2))* Amicus Publishing.

Rooney, Anne & Savery, Annabel. Creative & Media Careers. 2011. (Been There! Ser.). 32p. (J). (gr. 3-6). lib. bdg. 28.50 *(978-1-59920-470-3(3))* Black Rabbit Bks.

Rustad, Martha E. H. Learning about Fact & Opinion. 2015. (Media Literacy for Kids Ser.). (ENG.). 24p. (gr. k-1). lib. bdg. 26.65 *(978-1-4914-1831-4(1)*, Pebble Plus) Capstone Press of Coughlan Cos.

Summers, Sue L. Media Alert! 200 Activities to Create Media-Savvy Kids. (J). pap. 15.00 *(978-0-9676616-0-5(9))* Media Alert!

Tuyl, Christine Van & Merino, Noël. Media Violence. 2010. (OPPOSING VIEWPOINTS VISUALS Ser.). (Illus.). 128p. (YA). (gr. 7-12). 36.95 *(978-0-7377-4480-4(4))* Cengage Gale.

Vander Hook, Sue. Rupert Murdoch: News Corporation Magnate, 1 vol. 2011. (Essential Lives Set 6 Ser.). (ENG., Illus.). 112p. (J). (gr. 6-12). lib. bdg. 35.64 *(978-1-61714-782-1(6)*, Essential Library) ABDO Publishing Co.

Vaughan, Jenny. Causes & Campaigns. 2010. (Media Power Ser.). 48p. (YA). (gr. 5-9). 35.65 *(978-1-60753-111-1(9))* Amicus Publishing.

Williams, Mary E. Media Bias. 2011. (Introducing Issues with Opposing Viewpoints Ser.). 144p. lib. bdg. 36.95 *(978-0-7377-5199-4(1)*, Greenhaven Pr., Inc.) Cengage Gale.

Wilson, Rosie. Media & Communications Industry. 2010. (Closer Look: Global Industries Ser.). (ENG.). 48p. (YA). lib. bdg. 29.25 *(978-1-4358-9632-1(7)*, Rosen Reference) Rosen Publishing Group, Inc., The.

Wittekind, Erika. Violence as Entertainment: Why Aggression Sells. 2012. (Exploring Media Literacy Ser.). (ENG.). 80p. (gr. 6-7). pap. 9.10 *(978-0-7565-4536-9(6))*; lib. bdg. 34.65 *(978-0-7565-4520-8(X))* Compass Point Bks. (CPB Grades 4-8).

M
N
O

MASSACHUSETTS

Baker, Helen. Shopping the Cape, 1 book. 2003. 160p. per. 12.95 *(978-0-9743511-0-0(5))* Baker, Helen Interiors, Inc.

Bruun, Erik. Massachusetts. 2006. (ENG., Illus.). 48p. (J). (gr. -1-17). 9.95 *(978-1-57912-230-0(2),* 81230, Black Dog & Leventhal Pubs. Inc.) Hachette Bks.

Crane, Cody. Massachusetts. 2017. (True Book — My United States Ser.). (ENG.). 48p. (J). pap. 7.95 ***(978-0-531-23289-7(1),*** Children's Pr.) Scholastic Library Publishing.

Deinard, Jenny. How to Draw Massachusetts's Sights & Symbols. 2009. (Kid's Guide to Drawing America Ser.). 32p. (gr. k-k). 50.50 *(978-1-61511-070-4(4),* PowerKids Pr.) Rosen Publishing Group, Inc., The.

Ewing, Juliana Horatia. Story of A Short Life. 2006. pap. 24.95 *(978-1-4286-3593-7(9))* Kessinger Publishing, LLC.

Fairley, Melissa & Brown, Jonatha A. Massachusetts. 2005. (Portraits of the States Ser.). (Illus.). 32p. (gr. 2-6). pap. 10.50 *(978-0-8368-4645-4(1));* lib. bdg. 26.00 *(978-0-8368-4626-3(5))* Stevens, Gareth Publishing LLLP. (Gareth Stevens Learning Library).

Freedman, Jeri. Massachusetts: Past & Present. 2009. (J). 70.50 *(978-1-4358-5587-8(6));* (J). pap. 11.75 *(978-1-4358-5586-1(8));* (ENG., Illus.). 48p. (YA). lib. bdg. 29.25 *(978-1-4358-5294-5(X))* Rosen Publishing Group, Inc., The. (Rosen Reference).

Gaarder-Juntti, Oona. Buster's Trip to Cape Cod: A Story about Massachusetts, 1 vol. Doucet, Bob, illus. 2010. (Fact & Fable: State Stories Set 2 Ser.). (ENG.). 24p. (J). (gr. -1-2). 25.65 *(978-1-60453-921-9(6))* ABDO Publishing Co.

Hale, Kate. Little Massachusetts. Brett, Jeannie, illus. 2016. (Little State Ser.). (ENG.). 20p. (J). (gr. -1-k). 9.95 *(978-1-58536-949-2(7),* 204035) Sleeping Bear Pr.

Jerome, Kate Boehm. Massachusetts: What's So Great about This State? 2011. (Arcadia Kids Ser.). (ENG., Illus.). 32p. (J). pap. 7.99 *(978-1-58973-019-9(4))* Arcadia Publishing.

Knudsen, Shannon. Alice Ray & the Salem Witch Trials. Palmer, Ruth, illus. 2011. (History Speaks: Picture Books Plus Reader's Theater Ser.). 48p. pap. 56.72 *(978-0-7613-7629-3(1));* (ENG.). (gr. 2-4). pap. 9.95 *(978-0-7613-7114-4(1))* Lerner Publishing Group.

Marsh, Carole. Massachusetts Current Events Projects: 30 Cool, Activities, Crafts, Experiments & More for Kids to Do to Learn about Your State! 2003. (Massachusetts Experience Ser.). 32p. (gr. k-8). pap. 5.95 *(978-0-635-02040-6(8),* Marsh, Carole Bks.) Gallopade International.

—Massachusetts Geography Projects: 30 Cool, Activities, Crafts, Experiments & More for Kids to Do to Learn about Your State! 2003. (Massachusetts Experience Ser.). 32p. (gr. k-5). pap. 5.95 *(978-0-635-01840-3(3),* Marsh, Carole Bks.) Gallopade International.

—Massachusetts Government Projects: 30 Cool, Activities, Crafts, Experiments & More for Kids to Do to Learn about Your State! 2003. (Massachusetts Experience Ser.). 32p. (gr. k-5). pap. 5.95 *(978-0-635-01940-0(X),* Marsh, Carole Bks.) Gallopade International.

—Massachusetts People Projects: 30 Cool, Activities, Crafts, Experiments & More for Kids to Do to Learn about Your State! 2003. (Massachusetts Experience Ser.). 32p. (gr. k-5). pap. 5.95 *(978-0-635-01990-5(6),* Marsh, Carole Bks.) Gallopade International.

—Massachusetts Symbols & Facts Projects: 30 Cool, Activities, Crafts, Experiments & More for Kids to Do to Learn about Your State! 2003. (Massachusetts Experience Ser.). 32p. (gr. k-5). pap. 5.95 *(978-0-635-01890-8(X),* Marsh, Carole Bks.) Gallopade International.

Massachusetts. 2003. (Switched on Schoolhouse Ser.). cd-rom 24.95 *(978-0-7403-0645-7(6))* Alpha Omega Pubns., Inc.

McDowell, Pamela. Massachusetts: The Bay Btate. 2012. (J). *(978-1-61913-361-7(X));* pap. *(978-1-61913-362-4(8))* Weigl Pubs., Inc.

Murray, Julie. Massachusetts, 1 vol. 2006. (Buddy Book Ser.). (ENG., Illus.). 32p. (gr. 2-4). 27.07 *(978-1-59197-680-6(4),* Buddy Bks.) ABDO Publishing Co.

Naden, Corinne J. & Blue, Rose. Massachusetts: A MyReportLinks.com Book. 2003. (States Ser.). (Illus.). 48p. (J). (gr. 4-10). lib. bdg. 25.26 *(978-0-7660-5107-2(2),* MyReportLinks.com Bks.) Enslow Pubs., Inc.

Obregon, Jose Maria. Massachusetts. Brusca, Maria Cristina, tr. 2005. (Bilingual Library of the United States of America Ser.: Set 1). (ENG & SPA., Illus.). 32p. (J). (gr. 3-6). lib. bdg. 25.25 *(978-1-4042-3086-6(6))* Rosen Publishing Group, Inc., The.

Pezzi, Bryan. Massachusetts. 2011. (Guide to American States Ser.). (Illus.). 48p. (YA). (gr. 3-6). 29.99 *(978-1-61690-793-8(2));* (J). *(978-1-61690-469-2(0))* Weigl Pubs., Inc.

Smith, Rich. Massachusetts, 1 vol. 2009. (United States Ser.). (ENG., Illus.). 48p. (YA). (gr. 2-5). 27.07 *(978-1-60453-656-0(X))* ABDO Publishing Co.

Stemple, Heidi E. Y. One If by Land: A Massachusetts Number Book. Brett, Jeannie, illus. 2006. (Count Your Way Across the U. S. A. Ser.). (ENG.). 40p. (J). 17.95 *(978-1-58536-186-1(0))* Sleeping Bear Pr.

Strain Trueit, Trudi. Massachusetts. 2014. (America the Beautiful Ser.: 3). (ENG.). 144p. (J). lib. bdg. 40.00 *(978-0-531-24889-8(5))* Scholastic Library Publishing.

Troupe, Thomas Kingsley. Paul Revere's Ride: a Fly on the Wall History. Tejido, Jomike, illus. 2017. (Fly on the Wall History Ser.). (ENG.). 32p. (gr. 1-3). lib. bdg. 27.32 *(978-1-4795-9785-7(6))* Picture Window Bks.

—The Pilgrims' Voyage to America: a Fly on the Wall History. Tejido, Jomike, illus. 2017. (Fly on the Wall History Ser.). (ENG.). 32p. (gr. 1-3). lib. bdg. 27.32 *(978-1-4795-9786-4(4))* Picture Window Bks.

Trueit, Trudi Strain. Massachusetts. 2011. (America the Beautiful, Third Ser.). (Illus.). 144p. (J). pap. 12.95 *(978-0-531-22920-0(3),* Children's Pr.) Scholastic Library Publishing.

Warner, J. F. Massachusetts. 2012. (J). lib. bdg. 25.26 *(978-0-7613-4538-1(8),* Lerner Pubns.) Lerner Publishing Group.

Wimmer, Teresa. Massachusetts. 2008. (This Land Called America Ser.). 32p. (YA). (gr. 3-6). 22.95 *(978-1-58341-646-4(3))* Creative Co., The.

Winter, Jonah. Paul Revere & the Bell Ringers. Dodson, Bert, illus. 2003. (Ready-To-read COFA Ser.). (ENG.). 32p. (J). (gr. k-2). pap. 3.99 *(978-0-689-85635-8(0),* Simon Spotlight) Simon Spotlight.

MASSACHUSETTS—FICTION

Alderson, Sarah. The Sound. 2014. (ENG., Illus.). 320p. (YA). (gr. 9). 17.99 *(978-1-4424-9933-1(8),* Simon Pulse) Simon Pulse.

Angelini, Josephine. Starcrossed. 2011. (Starcrossed Trilogy Ser.: 1). (ENG.). 496p. (YA). (gr. 8-18). 17.99 *(978-0-06-201199-2(5),* HarperTeen) HarperCollins Pubs.

Armistead, Cal. Being Henry David. (ENG.). 312p. (YA). (gr. 8-12). 2014. pap. 9.99 *(978-0-8075-0616-5(8))* 2013. 16.99 *(978-0-8075-0615-8(X))* Whitman, Albert & Co.

Atkinson, Elizabeth. From Alice to Zen & Everyone in Between. (gr. 4-7). 2013. (ENG.). 248p. (J). pap. 9.95 *(978-1-4677-0861-6(5),* Carolrhoda Bks.) 2008. 247p. (YA). 16.95 *(978-0-8225-7271-8(0))* Lerner Publishing Group.

—I, Emma Freke. (Exceptional Reading & Language Arts Titles for Intermediate Grades Ser.). (ENG.). 240p. (J). (gr. 4-7). 2012. 9.95 *(978-0-7613-8500-4(2))* 2010. 16.95 *(978-0-7613-5604-2(5))* Lerner Publishing Group. (Carolrhoda Bks.).

Barnhart, Judy. Sand Angels in the Snow. 2007. 68p. per. 8.95 *(978-0-595-45154-8(3))* iUniverse, Inc.

Barnholdt, Lauren. Hailey Twitch & the Great Teacher Switch. Beaky, Suzanne, illus. 2010. (Hailey Twitch Ser.: 2). (ENG.). 176p. (J). (gr. 2-4). pap. 6.99 *(978-1-4022-2445-4(1),* Sourcebooks Jabberwocky) Sourcebooks, Inc.

—Hailey Twitch Is Not a Snitch. Beaky, Suzanne, illus. 2010. (Hailey Twitch Ser.: 1). (ENG.). 160p. (J). (gr. 2-4). pap. 6.99 *(978-1-4022-2444-7(3),* Sourcebooks Jabberwocky) Sourcebooks, Inc.

Bestul, Nancy M. The Final Clue: An Historical Novel. 2014. (Illus.). 150p. (J). pap. *(978-1-4951-1481-6(3))* Independent Pub.

Birdsall, Jeanne. The Penderwicks: A Summer Tale of Four Sisters, Two Rabbits, & a Very Interesting Boy. (Penderwicks Ser.). (ENG.). (J). (gr. 3-7). 2007. 288p. 7.99 *(978-0-440-42047-7(4),* Yearling) 2005. 272p. 16.99 *(978-0-375-83143-0(6),* Knopf Bks. for Young Readers) Random Hse. Children's Bks.

—The Penderwicks: A Summer Tale of Four Sisters, Two Rabbits & a Very Interesting Boy. 2007. (Penderwicks (Hardback) Ser.). 262p. (gr. 3-7). 18.00 *(978-0-7569-7798-6(3))* Perfection Learning Corp.

—The Penderwicks: A Summer Tale of Four Sisters, Two Rabbits, & a Very Interesting Boy. 2007. (Penderwicks Ser.: 1). (Illus.). 262p. (gr. 4-7). lib. bdg. 18.40 *(978-1-4177-7275-9(1))* Turtleback Bks.

—The Penderwicks: A Summer Tale of Four Sisters, Two Rabbits & a Very Interesting Boy. 2009. 8.80 *(978-0-7848-2826-7(1),* Everbind) Marco Bk. Co.

—The Penderwicks: A Summer Tale of Four Sisters, Two Rabbits & a Very Interesting Boy. l.t. ed. 2006. (Penderwick Ser.). 304p. (J). (gr. 3-7). 23.95 *(978-0-7862-8897-7(3))* Thorndike Pr.

—The Penderwicks in Spring. 2015. (Penderwicks Ser.). (ENG.). 352p. (J). (gr. 3-7). 16.99 *(978-0-375-87077-4(6),* Knopf Bks. for Young Readers) Random Hse. Children's Bks.

—The Penderwicks on Gardam Street. 2011. (Playaway Children Ser.). (J). (gr. 3-6). 44.99 *(978-1-61707-435-6(7))* Findaway World, LLC.

—The Penderwicks on Gardam Street. (Penderwicks Ser.). (ENG.). (J). (gr. 3-7). 2010. 336p. 7.99 *(978-0-440-42203-7(5),* Yearling) 2008. 320p. 16.99 *(978-0-375-84090-6(7),* Knopf Bks. for Young Readers) Random Hse. Children's Bks.

—The Penderwicks on Gardam Street. 2010. (Penderwicks Ser.: 2). lib. bdg. 18.40 *(978-0-606-14418-6(8),* Turtleback) Turtleback Bks.

Bolte, Marissa. Arrested for Witchcraft! Nickolas Flux & the Salem Witch Trials, 1 vol. Ginevra, Dante, illus. 2014. (Nickolas Flux History Chronicles Ser.). (ENG.). (gr. 3-4). 40p. pap. 7.95 *(978-1-4765-5151-7(0));* 32p. lib. bdg. 30.65 *(978-1-4765-3947-8(2))* Capstone Press of Coughlan Cos. (Graphic Library).

Bruchac, Joseph. Squanto's Journey: The Story of the First Thanksgiving. Shed, Greg, illus. 2007. (ENG.). 32p. (J). (gr. -1-3). pap. 7.99 *(978-0-15-206044-2(8),* HMH Books For Young Readers) Houghton Mifflin Harcourt Publishing Co.

Bryant, Annie. Ghost Town. 2007. (Beacon Street Girls Ser.: No. 11). (Illus.). 217p. (J). (gr. 4-7). per. 7.10 *(978-1-933566-09-2(4))* B*tween Productions, Inc.

—Just Kidding. 2007. (Beacon Street Girls Ser.: No. 10). (Illus.). 247p. (J). (gr. 3-8). per. 7.99 *(978-1-933566-07-8(8))* B*tween Productions, Inc.

—Letters from the Heart. 2008. (Beacon Street Girls Ser.: 3). (ENG., Illus.). 256p. (J). (gr. 4-8). pap. 6.99 *(978-1-4169-6426-1(6),* Aladdin) Simon & Schuster Children's Publishing.

Burak, Kathryn. Emily's Dress & Other Missing Things. 2012. (ENG.). 240p. (YA). (gr. 8-12). 17.99 *(978-1-59643-736-4(7))* Roaring Brook Pr.

Burnham, Niki. Sticky Fingers. 2005. (ENG.). 288p. (YA). (gr. 9-18). pap. 7.99 *(978-0-689-87649-3(1),* Simon Pulse) Simon Pulse.

Chetkowski, Emily. Amasa Walker's Spendid Garment. Peterson, Dawn, illus. 2003. 48p. (gr. 5-8). reprint ed. pap. 9.95 *(978-0-911469-21-9(4))* Hood, Alan C. & Co., Inc.

Clark, Eleanor Linton, et al. Dodo's Dream Boat or the Voyage of the Seven Seas. 2008. (Illus.). 45p. (J). *(978-0-9816873-2-2(6))* West Barnstable Pr.

Clements, Andrew. In Harm's Way. Stower, Adam, illus. (Benjamin Pratt & the Keepers of the School Ser.: 4). (ENG.). (J). (gr. 2-5). 2014. 240p. pap. 7.99 *(978-1-4169-3910-8(5))* 2013. 224p. 14.99 *(978-1-4169-3889-7(3))* Simon & Schuster Children's Publishing. (Atheneum Bks. for Young Readers).

Cochran, Molly. Legacy. (Legacy Ser.). (ENG.). (YA). (gr. 9). 2012. 448p. pap. 9.99 *(978-1-4424-1740-3(4))* 2011. 432p. 17.99 *(978-1-4424-1739-7(0))* Simon & Schuster/Paula Wiseman Bks. (Simon & Schuster/Paula Wiseman Bks.).

—Poison. (Legacy Ser.). (ENG., 368p. (YA). (gr. 9). 2014. Illus.). pap. 9.99 *(978-1-4424-5051-6(7))* 2012. 17.99 *(978-1-4424-5050-9(9))* Simon & Schuster/Paula Wiseman Bks. (Simon & Schuster/Paula Wiseman Bks.).

Collins, Pat Lowery. Daughter of Winter. 2010. (ENG., Illus.). 352p. (YA). (gr. 5-18). 16.99 *(978-0-7636-4500-7(1))* Candlewick Pr.

Collins, Renee. Until We Meet Again. 2015. (ENG.). 336p. (YA). (gr. 8-12). 16.99 *(978-1-4926-2116-4(1),* 9781492621164) Sourcebooks, Inc.

Cooper, Susan. Ghost Hawk. 2014. (ENG., Illus.). 352p. (J). (gr. 5-9). pap. 7.99 *(978-1-4424-8142-8(0),* McElderry, Margaret K. Bks.) McElderry, Margaret K. Bks.

Cotler, Steve. Cheesie Mack Is Not a Genius or Anything. McCauley, Adam, illus. (Cheesie Mack Ser.). (ENG.). 240p. (J). (gr. 3-7). 2012. 6.99 *(978-0-375-86394-3(X),* Yearling) 2011. 15.99 *(978-0-375-86437-7(7),* Random Hse. Bks. for Young Readers) Random Hse. Children's Bks.

—Cheesie Mack Is Not Exactly Famous. Holgate, Douglas, illus. 2014. (Cheesie Mack Ser.). (ENG.). 256p. (J). (gr. 3-7). 15.99 *(978-0-385-36984-8(0),* Random Hse. Bks. for Young Readers) Random Hse. Children's Bks.

—Cheesie Mack Is Sort of Freaked Out. Holgate, Douglas, illus. 2014. (Cheesie Mack Ser.). (ENG.). 256p. (J). (gr. 3-7). 15.99 *(978-0-385-36988-6(3),* Random Hse. Bks. for Young Readers) Random Hse. Children's Bks.

Cusick, John M. Girl Parts. 2010. (ENG., Illus.). 240p. (YA). (gr. 9-18). 16.99 *(978-0-7636-4930-2(9))* Candlewick Pr.

Daneshvari, Gitty. Class Is Not Dismissed! 2011. (School of Fear Ser.: 2). (ENG.). 336p. (J). (gr. 3-7). pap. 8.99 *(978-0-316-03329-9(4))* Little, Brown Bks. for Young Readers.

—The Final Exam. (School of Fear Ser.: 3). (ENG.). (J). (gr. 3-7). 2012. 352p. pap. 8.99 *(978-0-316-18285-0(0))* 2011. 336p. 16.99 *(978-0-316-18287-4(7))* Little, Brown Bks. for Young Readers.

Darrows, Eva. The Awesome. 2015. (ENG.). 352p. (YA). (gr. 10). pap. 9.99 *(978-1-78108-324-6(X),* Ravenstone) Rebellion GBR. Dist: Simon & Schuster, Inc.

Davis, Rachel. My Life at Mapleleaf Cabin. 2nd ed. 2004. (YA). per. 10.00 *(978-0-9741176-8-3(4))* Wu Li Turtle Corp.

Dionne, Erin. Notes from an Accidental Band Geek. 2012. (ENG.). 304p. (J). (gr. 5). pap. 6.99 *(978-0-14-242247-2(9),* Puffin Books) Penguin Young Readers Group.

Dixon, Franklin W. Thrill Ride. 2005. 154p. (J). lib. bdg. 16.92 *(978-1-4242-0386-4(4))* Fitzgerald Bks.

Dorato, A. P. Arthur, Donna, & the Magic Crown of Tiabora. 2006. pap. 24.95 *(978-1-4137-8898-3(X))* PublishAmerica, Inc.

Easer, Katherine. Vicious Little Darlings. 2012. (ENG.). 320p. (YA). (gr. 9-12). pap. 9.99 *(978-1-59990-854-0(9),* 9781599908540, Bloomsbury USA Childrens) Bloomsbury Publishing USA.

Ehrlich, Esther. Nest. 2016. (ENG.). 336p. (J). (gr. 5). pap. 7.99 *(978-0-385-38610-4(9),* Yearling) Random Hse. Children's Bks.

Fleming, Candace. A Big Cheese for the White House: The True Tale of a Tremendous Cheddar. Schindler, S. D., illus. 2004. (ENG.). 32p. (J). (gr. -1-3). reprint ed. pap. 8.99 *(978-0-374-40627-1(8),* 9780374406271) Square Fish.

Foard, Judith P. Senior Year. 2013. 416p. pap. 16.95 *(978-1-4759-6552-0(4));* (gr. 10-12). 26.95 *(978-1-4759-6554-4(0))* iUniverse, Inc.

Frederick, Heather Vogel. The Mother-Daughter Book Club. (Mother-Daughter Book Club Ser.). (ENG.). (J). 2008. 288p. (gr. 4-7). pap. 7.99 *(978-1-4169-7079-8(7))* 2007. (Illus.). 256p. (gr. 5-7). 17.99 *(978-0-689-86412-4(4))* Simon & Schuster Bks. For Young Readers. (Simon & Schuster Bks. For Young Readers).

—Pies & Prejudice. 2010. (Mother-Daughter Book Club Ser.). (ENG.). 384p. (J). (gr. 4-7). 15.99 *(978-1-4169-7431-4(8),* Simon & Schuster Bks. For Young Readers) Simon & Schuster Bks. For Young Readers.

Friend, Natasha. For Keeps. 2011. (ENG.). 272p. (YA). (gr. 7-18). 7.99 *(978-0-14-241846-8(3),* Speak) Penguin Young Readers Group.

Gagnon, Mary. Are Those Your Shoes? 2008. 120p. pap. 11.95 *(978-1-4357-2942-1(0))* Lulu Pr., Inc.

Gaylord, Glance. Culm Rock, the Story of a Year: What it Brought & What it Taught. 2007. (Illus.). 188p. per. *(978-1-4065-2819-0(6))* Dodo Pr.

Gerber, Alyson. Braced. 2017. (ENG.). 304p. (J). (gr. 3-7). 16.99 *(978-0-545-90214-4(2))* Scholastic, Inc.

Gleason, Barbara. My Hometown: Barnstable. 2010. 28p. pap. 15.99 *(978-1-4490-6928-5(2))* AuthorHouse.

Gold, Maya. Spellbinding. 2013. (ENG.). 272p. (J). (gr. 7). pap. 8.99 *(978-0-545-43380-8(0))* Scholastic, Inc.

Grab, Daphne. Halftime. 2010. (J). *(978-0-385-73783-8(1));* *(978-0-385-90693-7(5))* Random House Publishing Group. (Delacorte Pr).

Green, Jacqueline. Kiss & Tell. 2015. (Truth or Dare Ser.: 3). (ENG.). 288p. (YA). (gr. 10-17). 18.00 *(978-0-316-22033-0(7),* Poppy) Little, Brown Bks. for Young Readers.

—Secrets & Lies. 2014. (Truth or Dare Ser.: 2). (ENG.). 336p. (YA). (gr. 10-17). pap. 21.99 *(978-0-316-22030-9(2),* Poppy) Little, Brown Bks. for Young Readers.

—Truth or Dare. (Truth or Dare Ser.: 1). (ENG.). (YA). (gr. 10-17). 2014. 416p. pap. 10.99 *(978-0-316-22035-4(3))* 2013. 400p. 18.00 *(978-0-316-22036-1(1))* Little, Brown Bks. for Young Readers. (Poppy).

Greenburg, Dan. It's Itchcraft! Davis, Jack E., illus. 2004. (Zack Files Ser.). 118p. lib. bdg. 15.00 *(978-0-7569-2238-2(0))* Perfection Learning Corp.

Greenspan, Paul. Crystal of Dreams. 2007. 192p. pap. 12.96 *(978-0-615-13477-2(7))* Flying Cloud Bks.

Griffin, Adele. Amandine. 2003. (ENG.). 208p. (gr. 5-9). pap. 6.99 *(978-0-7868-1441-1(1))* Disney Pr.

Haines, Lise. Girl in the Arena. (ENG.). 336p. (YA). (gr. 9-13). 2010. pap. 9.99 *(978-1-59990-521-1(3),* 9781599905211) 2009. 16.99 *(978-1-59990-372-9(5),* 9781599903729) Bloomsbury Publishing USA. (Bloomsbury USA Childrens).

Harley, Bill. Night of the Spadefoot Toads, 1 vol. 2008. (ENG.). 192p. (J). (gr. 3-7). 15.95 *(978-1-56145-459-4(1))* Peachtree Pubs.

Harrington, K. A. Forget Me. 2014. (ENG.). 288p. (YA). (gr. 7). 17.99 *(978-0-399-16529-0(0),* G.P. Putnam's Sons Books for Young Readers) Penguin Young Readers Group.

Hoffman, Alice. Nightbird. (ENG., Illus.). 208p. (J). (gr. 5). 2016. pap. 7.99 *(978-0-385-38961-7(2),* Yearling) 2015. 16.99 *(978-0-385-38958-7(2),* Lamb, Wendy Bks.) Random Hse. Children's Bks.

—Nightbird. 2016. lib. bdg. 18.40 *(978-0-606-38451-3(0))* Turtleback Bks.

Horvath, Polly. Northward to the Moon. 2012. (ENG.). 256p. (J). (gr. 5-8). 7.99 *(978-0-307-92980-8(9),* Yearling) Random Hse. Children's Bks.

Howe, Katherine. Conversion. (ENG.). 432p. (YA). (gr. 7). 2015. pap. 10.99 *(978-0-14-751155-3(0),* Speak) 2014. 18.99 *(978-0-399-16777-5(3),* G.P. Putnam's Sons Books for Young Readers) Penguin Young Readers Group.

Hubbard, Jenny. And We Stay. 2014. (ENG.). 240p. (YA). (gr. 9). lib. bdg. 19.99 *(978-0-375-98955-1(2),* Delacorte Pr.) Random Hse. Children's Bks.

Hughes, Lynn Gordon. To Live a Truer Life: A Story of the Hopedale Community. Lindro, illus. 2003. 32p. (J). 10.00 *(978-0-9725017-2-9(X))* Blackstone Editions.

Jacobs, Lily. The Littlest Bunny in Massachusetts: An Easter Adventure. 2015. (ENG.). 32p. (J). (-3). 9.99 *(978-1-4926-1114-1(X),* Sourcebooks Jabberwocky) Sourcebooks, Inc.

James, Eric. A Halloween Scare in Massachusetts. Le Ray, Marina, illus. 2015. (ENG.). 32p. (J). (-5). 9.99 *(978-1-4926-2381-6(4),* 9781492623816, Sourcebooks Jabberwocky) Sourcebooks, Inc.

—Santa's Sleigh Is on Its Way to Massachusetts: A Christmas Adventure. Dunn, Robert, illus. 2016. (ENG.). 32p. (J). (-2). 12.99 *(978-1-4926-4336-4(X),* 9781492643364, Sourcebooks Jabberwocky) Sourcebooks, Inc.

Katherine, Paterson. Lyddie. 2014. (Puffin Modern Classics Ser.). (ENG.). 192p. (J). (gr. 1-4). 11.24 *(978-1-63245-222-1(7))* Lectorum Pubns., Inc.

Klausner, Julie. Art Girls Are Easy. 2013. (ENG.). 240p. (YA). (gr. 10-17). pap. 18.99 *(978-0-316-24362-9(0),* Poppy) Little, Brown Bks. for Young Readers.

Koller, Jackie French. Someday. 2010. 228p. pap. 14.95 *(978-1-4401-8675-2(8))* iUniverse, Inc.

Konigsberg, Bill. Honestly Ben. 2017. (ENG.). 336p. (J). (gr. 9). 17.99 *(978-0-545-85826-7(7))* Scholastic, Inc.

—Openly Straight. 2013. (ENG.). 336p. (J). (gr. 9). 17.99 *(978-0-545-50989-3(0),* Levine, Arthur A. Bks.) Scholastic, Inc.

Kurtz, Jane. Lanie's Real Adventures. Papp, Robert, illus. 2010. (American Girl Today Ser.). (ENG.). 112p. (YA). (gr. 3-18). 12.95 *(978-1-59369-685-6(X))* American Girl Publishing, Inc.

Lenzi, Danielle E. My Search for Prince Charming's Normal Brother. 2011. 136p. pap. 25.70 *(978-1-4634-0446-8(8));* (gr. 10-12). 33.70 *(978-1-4634-0445-1(X))* AuthorHouse.

Lockhart, E. We Were Liars. 2014. (Illus.). 227p. (YA). *(978-0-385-39009-5(2),* Delacorte Pr) Random House Publishing Group.

—We Were Liars. (ENG., (YA). (gr. 7). 2014. Illus.). 240p. 17.99 *(978-0-385-74126-2(X))* 2017. 272p. 18.99 ***(978-1-5247-6458-6(2))*** Random Hse. Children's Bks. (Delacorte Pr.).

Look, Lenore. Alvin Ho: Allergic to Babies, Burglars, & Other Bumps in the Night. Pham, LeUyen, illus. 2013. (Alvin Ho Ser.). (ENG.). 192p. (J). (gr. 1-4). 15.99 *(978-0-375-87033-0(4),* Schwartz & Wade Bks.) Random Hse. Children's Bks.

—Alvin Ho: Allergic to Birthday Parties, Science Projects, & Other Man-Made Catastrophes. Pham, LeUyen, illus. 2011. (Alvin Ho Ser.). (ENG.). 192p. (J). (gr. 1-4). 6.99 *(978-0-375-87369-0(4),* Yearling) Random Hse. Children's Bks.

—Alvin Ho: Allergic to Camping, Hiking, & Other Natural Disasters. Pham, LeUyen, illus. 2010. (Alvin Ho Ser.). (ENG.). 192p. (J). (gr. 1-4). 6.99 *(978-0-375-85750-8(8),* Yearling) Random Hse. Children's Bks.

—Alvin Ho: Allergic to Babies, Burglars, & Other Bumps in the Night. Pham, LeUyen, illus. 2014. (Alvin Ho Ser.). (ENG.). 192p. (J). (gr. 1-4). 6.99 *(978-0-385-38600-5(1),* Yearling) Random Hse. Children's Bks.

—Alvin Ho: Allergic to Dead Bodies, Funerals, & Other Fatal Circumstances. Pham, LeUyen, illus. 2012. (Alvin Ho Ser.). (ENG.). 208p. (J). (gr. 1-4). 6.99 *(978-0-307-97695-6(5),* Yearling) Random Hse. Children's Bks.

Lupica, Mike. Million-Dollar Throw. 2010. (ENG.). 272p. (J). (gr. 5-18). 7.99 *(978-0-14-241558-0(8),* Puffin Books) Penguin Young Readers Group.

—Million-Dollar Throw. 2010. (Million Dollar Sports Ser.). lib. bdg. 18.40 *(978-0-606-25316-1(5),* Turtleback) Turtleback Bks.

MacColl, Michaela. Nobody's Secret. (ENG.). (gr. 7-17). 2014. 256p. (YA). pap. 9.99 *(978-1-4521-2854-2(5))* 2013. 241p. (J). 16.99 *(978-1-4521-0860-5(9))* Chronicle Bks. LLC.

—The Revelation of Louisa May. 2015. (ENG.). 272p. (J). (gr. 7-12). 16.99 *(978-1-4521-3357-7(3))* Chronicle Bks. LLC.

Malone, Lee Gjertsen. The Last Boy at St. Edith's. 2017. lib. bdg. 18.40 ***(978-0-606-40157-9(1))*** Turtleback Bks.

Mancusi, Mari. Gamer Girl. 2010. (ENG.). 256p. (YA). (gr. 7-18). 7.99 *(978-0-14-241509-2(X),* Speak) Penguin Young Readers Group.

Manning, Matthew K. The Salem Witch Showdown. Neely, Scott, illus. 2017. (You Choose Stories: Scooby-Doo Ser.). (ENG.). 112p. (gr. 2-3). lib. bdg. 32.65 *(978-1-4965-4334-9(3),* You Choose Bks.) Capstone Press of Coughlan Cos.

Marshall, Peter, et al. Mercy Clifton: Pilgrim Girl. 2007. 208p. (J). pap. 9.99 *(978-0-8054-4395-0(9),* B&H Bks.) B&H Publishing Group.

Martin, Ann M. Needle & Thread. Andreasen, Dan, illus. 2007. 205p. (J). pap. *(978-0-545-03660-3(7))* Scholastic, Inc.

—'Tis the Season. 2007. (Main Street Ser.). (Illus.). 195p. (J). (gr. 4-7). 14.65 *(978-0-7569-8327-7(4))* Perfection Learning Corp.

Mather, Adriana. How to Hang a Witch. 2016. (ENG.). 368p. (YA). (gr. 7). 17.99 *(978-0-553-53947-9(7),* Knopf Bks. for Young Readers) Random Hse. Children's Bks.

McGuire, Roberta Libby. The Adventures of the Cape Cod Bear. 2012. 24p. pap. 15.99 *(978-1-4771-5266-9(0))* Xlibris Corp.

Metaxas, Eric. Princess Scargo & the Birthday Pumpkin, 1 vol. Barbour, Karen, illus. 2004. (Rabbit Ears-A Classic Tale

Ser.). (ENG.). 40p. (gr. k-5). 25.65 *(978-1-59197-769-8(X))* Spotlight.

Miceli, Mary Anne. Boston North Shore's ... Salem's Golden Broomstick. 2013. 44p. pap. 20.00 *(978-0-9888654-0-2(8))* Miceli, Mary Anne.

Montague, Gay & Wise, Erin. Peace Is a Bright Delight. 2008. 28p. pap. 13.99 *(978-1-4389-2153-2(5))* AuthorHouse.

Nardone, Frank. Something's Brewing in Salem. 2013. 164p. pap. 9.99 *(978-0-9884024-1-6(6))* Dragon Tree Bks.

O'Neill, Elizabeth. Alfred Visits Massachusetts. 2006. (Illus.). 24p. (J). (gr. -1-3). pap. 12.00 *(978-0-9771836-7-8(X))* Global Business Information Strategies, Inc.

Osborne, Mary Pope, et al. Jueves de Acción de Gracias. Murdocca, Sal, illus. 2014. 27. (SPA.). 88p. (J). (gr. 2-4). pap. 5.99 *(978-1-933032-94-8(4))* Lectorum Pubns., Inc.

Otis, James. Ruth of Boston: A story of the Massachusetts Bay Colony. 2007. 140p. per. 9.95 *(978-0-9790876-3-9(5))* Living Bks. Pr.

Palmer, Robin. Sealed with a Kiss, 2 vols., No. 2. 2010. (Yours Truly, Lucy B. Parker Ser.: 2). (ENG.). 224p. (J). (gr. 5-18). 6.99 *(978-0-14-241501-6(4),* Puffin Books) Penguin Young Readers Group.

Paratore, Coleen Murtagh. The Funeral Director's Son. 2008. (Funeral Director's Son Ser.). (ENG.). 144p. (J). (gr. 3-7). 15.99 *(978-1-4169-3594-0(0),* Simon & Schuster Bks. For Young Readers) Simon & Schuster Bks. For Young Readers.

—Kip Campbell's Gift. 2009. (ENG.). 160p. (J). (gr. 3-7). 15.99 *(978-1-4169-3596-4(7),* Simon & Schuster Bks. For Young Readers) Simon & Schuster Bks. For Young Readers.

—The Wedding Planner's Daughter. McGregor, Barbara, illus. 2006. (Wedding Planner's Daughter Ser.). (ENG.). 208p. (J). (gr. 3-8). reprint ed. pap. 6.99 *(978-1-4169-1854-7(X),* Simon & Schuster Bks. For Young Readers) Simon & Schuster Bks. For Young Readers.

Phillips, Merrill. Tell Me Again Grampa. 2013. 172p. pap. 13.96 *(978-1-4669-9676-2(5))* Trafford Publishing.

Ramsey, Jo. Shoulder Pads & Flannel. 2016. (ENG., Illus.). (J). 24.99 ***(978-1-63533-072-4(6),*** Harmony Ink Pr.) Dreamspinner Pr.

Rees, Douglas. Vampire High. 2010. (ENG.). 240p. (YA). (gr. 7-18). pap. 9.99 *(978-0-385-73920-7(6),* Delacorte Bks. for Young Readers) Random Hse. Children's Bks.

Reinhardt, Dana. A Brief Chapter in My Impossible Life. 2007. (ENG.). 256p. (YA). (gr. 9-12). pap. 8.99 *(978-0-375-84691-5(3),* Ember) Random Hse. Children's Bks.

Rohr, Rebecca. Flocks: A Buster Bird Adventure. 2011. pap. 8.95 *(978-0-7414-6735-5(6))* Infinity Publishing.

Sales, Leila. Mostly Good Girls. (ENG.). 368p. (YA). (gr. 9). 2011. pap. 9.99 *(978-1-4424-0680-3(1))* 2010. 17.99 *(978-1-4424-0679-7(8))* Simon Pulse. (Simon Pulse).

Sanchez, Anita. The Invasion of Sandy Bay. 2008. (ENG.). 148p. (J). (gr. 5-7). 16.95 *(978-1-59078-560-7(6),* Calkins Creek) Boyds Mills Pr.

Schmidt, Gary D. What Came from the Stars. 2014. (ENG.). 304p. (J). (gr. 5-7). pap. 6.99 *(978-0-544-33636-0(4),* HMH Books For Young Readers) Houghton Mifflin Harcourt Publishing Co.

Shults, Sylvia. Double Double Love & Trouble. 2013. 150p. pap. 12.99 *(978-0-9848931-3-3(X))* Dark Continents Publishing.

Silvano, Wendi. Love Is All Around Massachusetts. Czernichowska, Joanna, illus. 2016. (ENG.). 32p. (J). (-6). 12.99 *(978-1-4926-2933-7(2),* Sourcebooks Jabberwocky) Sourcebooks, Inc.

Smallman, Steve. Santa Is Coming to Massachusetts. Dunn, Robert, illus. 2014. (ENG.). 32p. (J). (-3). 9.99 *(978-1-4926-0673-4(1),* Sourcebooks Jabberwocky) Sourcebooks, Inc.

Speare, Elizabeth George. The Witch of Blackbird Pond. 2004. 223p. (J). (gr. 4-7). pap., tchr.'s planning gde. ed. 38.00 incl. audio *(978-0-8072-0862-5(0),* Listening Library) Random Hse. Audio Publishing Group.

Specter, Baron. Drama at Dungeon Rock: #6, 1 vol. Evans, Dustin, illus. 2010. (Ghostly Graphic Adventures Ser.). (ENG.). 32p. (J). (gr. 3-6). 28.50 *(978-1-60270-775-7(8))* ABDO Publishing Co.

—The Lighthouse of Terror, 1 vol., Bk. 3. Evans, Dustin, illus. 2010. (Ghostly Graphic Adventures Ser.). (ENG.). 32p. (J). (gr. 3-6). 28.50 *(978-1-60270-772-6(3))* ABDO Publishing Co.

Stanley, Diane. Thanksgiving on Plymouth Plantation. Berry, Holly, illus. 2004. (Time-Traveling Twins Ser.). (ENG.). 48p. (J). (gr. k-5). 16.99 *(978-0-06-027069-8(1))* HarperCollins Pubs.

Stewart, Whitney. Marshall, the Sea Dog. 2010. (ENG.). 56p. (J). (gr. 4-7). 17.95 *(978-1-60727-183-3(4))* Soundprints.

Stone, Phoebe. The Boy on Cinnamon Street. 2012. 234p. (J). *(978-0-545-43368-6(1),* Levine, Arthur A. Bks.) Scholastic, Inc.

Tashjian, Janet. Larry & the Meaning of Life. 2014. (Larry Ser.: 3). (ENG., Illus.). 240p. (YA). (gr. 7-12). pap. 9.99 *(978-1-250-05035-9(9),* 9781250050359) Square Fish.

Tea, Michelle. Girl at the Bottom of the Sea. Verwey, Amanda, illus. 2015. (ENG.). 240p. (gr. 6). 19.95 *(978-1-940450-00-1(4))* McSweeney's Publishing.

—Mermaid in Chelsea Creek. Polan, Jason, illus. 2013. (ENG.). 240p. (gr. 5-11). 19.95 *(978-1-938073-36-6(3))* McSweeney's Publishing.

Tiernan, Cate. Immortal Beloved. (Immortal Beloved Ser.: 1). (ENG.). (YA). (gr. 7-17). 2012. 432p. pap. 9.99 *(978-0-316-03591-0(2))* 2010. 416p. 16.99 *(978-0-316-03592-7(0))* Little, Brown Bks. for Young Readers.

Vrettos, Adrienne Maria. Best Friends for Never. 2016. (ENG.). 240p. (J). (gr. 3-7). 16.99 *(978-0-545-56149-5(3),* Scholastic Pr.) Scholastic, Inc.

Wittlinger, Ellen. Blind Faith. 2007. (ENG.). 304p. (YA). (gr. 7-12). pap. 9.99 *(978-1-4169-4906-0(2),* Simon & Schuster Bks. For Young Readers) Simon & Schuster Bks. For Young Readers.

—Love & Lies: Marisol's Story. (ENG.). (YA). 2009. 272p. (gr. 7). pap. 8.99 *(978-1-4169-7914-2(X))* 2008. 256p. (gr. 9-18). 16.99 *(978-1-4169-1623-9(7))* Simon & Schuster Bks. For Young Readers. (Simon & Schuster Bks. For Young Readers).

Young, Janet Ruth. The Babysitter Murders. 2011. (ENG., Illus.). 336p. (YA). (gr. 9-18). 16.99 *(978-1-4169-5944-1(0),* Atheneum Bks. for Young Readers) Simon & Schuster Children's Publishing.

—My Beautiful Failure. (ENG., Illus.). 320p. (YA). (gr. 7). 2013. pap. 9.99 *(978-1-4424-8269-2(9))* 2012. 16.99 *(978-1-4169-5489-7(9))* Simon & Schuster Children's Publishing. (Atheneum Bks. for Young Readers).

MASSACHUSETTS—HISTORY

Allen, David. Early Maps of Greenfield, Massachusetts, 1717-1918. 2003. (Illus.). 64p. cd-rom 27.95 *(978-0-911653-10-6(4))* Old Maps.

Arenstam, Peter. The Mighty Mastiff of the Mayflower. 2012. Orig. Title: The Mighty Mastiff of the Mayflower. (ENG., Illus.). 112p. 14.99 *(978-1-60949-609-8(4),* History Pr., The) Arcadia Publishing.

Aretha, David. Mitt Romney. 2012. (Illus.). 112p. (J). *(978-1-59935-344-9(X))* Reynolds, Morgan Inc.

Barber, Nicola. Who Journeyed on the Mayflower?, 1 vol. HL Studios Staff, illus. 2014. (Primary Source Detectives Ser.). (ENG.). 64p. (gr. 7-8). lib. bdg. 35.99 *(978-1-4329-9602-4(9))* Heinemann-Raintree.

Bauer, Marion Dane. Celebrating Massachusetts: 50 States to Celebrate. Canga, C. B., illus. 2014. (Green Light Readers Level 3 Ser.). (ENG.). 40p. (J). (gr. 1-4). 12.99 *(978-0-544-11944-4(4),* HMH Books For Young Readers) Houghton Mifflin Harcourt Publishing Co.

Baxter, Roberta. The Battle of Gettysburg: A History Perspectives Book. 2013. (Perspectives Library). (ENG., Illus.). 32p. (J). (gr. 4-8). 28.50 *(978-1-62431-415-5(5),* 202780); pap. 14.21 *(978-1-62431-491-9(0),* 202782) Cherry Lake Publishing.

Benge, Janet & Benge, Geoff. William Bradford: Plymouth's Rock. 2016. (ENG., Illus.). 200p. (J). pap. 9.99 *(978-1-62486-092-8(3))* Emerald Bks.

Bjorklund, Ruth & Fitzgerald, Stephanie. Massachusetts. 2014. (It's My State! (r) Ser.). 80p. (J). (gr. 4-8). lib. bdg. 34.21 *(978-1-62712-500-0(0))* Cavendish Square Publishing.

—Massachusetts. 2nd rev. ed. 2010. (It's My State! Ser.). 80p. (gr. 3-18). lib. bdg. 31.36 *(978-1-60870-053-0(4))* Marshall Cavendish Corp.

Brandt, Keith & Macken, JoAnn Early. Paul Revere, Son of Liberty. Livingston, Francis, illus. 2007. 50p. (J). *(978-0-439-02017-6(4))* Scholastic, Inc.

Caswell, Max. My Life in the Plymouth Colony. 2017. (My Place in History Ser.). 24p. (J). (gr. 2-3). pap. 8.15 ***(978-1-5382-0305-7(7))***; pap. 48.90 ***(978-1-5382-0306-4(5))*** Stevens, Gareth Publishing LLLP.

Cherry, Lynne. A River Ran Wild. 2005. 17.00 *(978-0-7569-5231-0(X))* Perfection Learning Corp.

Clark, Mary. Biographical Sketches of the Fathers of New England. 2003. 180p. 89.00 *(978-0-7950-4738-1(X))* New Library Press LLC.

Colonel Edward Howland Robinson Green & the World He Created at Round Hill. 2003. 39.95 *(978-0-9743731-0-2(9),* 2500) Bedell, Barbara F.

Connors, Kathleen. The First Thanksgiving, Vol. 1. 2014. (What You Didn't Know about History Ser.). (Illus.). 24p. (J). (gr. 2-3). (ENG.). 22.60 *(978-1-4824-0581-1(4))*; pap. 8.15 *(978-1-4824-0582-8(2))* Stevens, Gareth Publishing LLLP.

Cook, Peter. You Wouldn't Want to Sail on the Mayflower! A Trip That Took Entirely Too Long. Whelan, Kevin, illus. rev. ed. 2013. (ENG.). 40p. (J). (gr. 3-12). pap. 9.95 *(978-0-531-23858-5(X))* Scholastic Library Publishing.

Cook, Peter & Whelan, Kevin. You Wouldn't Want to Sail on the Mayflower! A Trip That Took Entirely Too Long. rev. ed. 2013. (ENG.). 32p. (J). 29.00 *(978-0-531-27107-0(2),* Watts, Franklin) Scholastic Library Publishing.

Cox, Clinton. Undying Glory: The Story of the Massachusetts 54th Regiment. 2007. 196p. (YA). (gr. 4-7). per. 15.95 *(978-0-595-45116-6(0),* Backinprint.com) iUniverse, Inc.

Davidson, Tish. Southern New England: Connecticut, Massachusetts, Rhode Island, Vol. 19. 2015. (Let's Explore the States Ser.). (Illus.). 64p. (J). (gr. 5). 23.95 *(978-1-4222-3333-7(2))* Mason Crest.

Davis, Daniel K. Miles Standish. 2010. (Leaders of the Colonial Era Ser.). 120p. (gr. 5-8). 35.00 *(978-1-60413-739-2(8),* Chelsea Hse.) Facts On File, Inc.

Doherty, Craig A. & Doherty, Katherine M. Massachusetts, 13 vols. 2005. (Thirteen Colonies Ser.). (Illus.). 160p. (gr. 5-8). 35.00 *(978-0-8160-5407-7(X))* Facts On File, Inc.

Downey, Tika. Massachusetts: The Bay State. (Illus.). 24p. (J). 2010. pap. 8.25 *(978-1-4358-3342-5(2),* 1300528) 2009. lib. bdg. 22.60 *(978-1-4042-8111-0(8),* 1300528) Rosen Publishing Group, Inc., The. (PowerKids Pr.).

Dreyer, Ellen. A Band of Brave Men: The Story of the 54th Massachusetts Regiment. 2004. (ENG., Illus.). 31p. (J). (gr. 5-5). pap. 11.47 net. *(978-0-7652-5247-0(3),* Celebration Pr.) Pearson Schl.

Duris, Joan & Jones, Gillian. B Is for Berkshires. 2015. (ENG.). 32p. 17.95 *(978-1-939017-51-2(3),* e79df012-d55f-4ec1-9a59-318cc001d57e) Islandport Pr., Inc.

Edwards, Roberta. Who Was Paul Revere? Harrison, Nancy & O'brien, John, illus. 2011. (Who Was? Ser.). (ENG.). 112p. (J). (gr. 3-7). pap. 5.99 *(978-0-448-45715-4(6),* Grosset & Dunlap) Penguin Young Readers Group.

Englar, Mary. The Pilgrims & the First Thanksgiving, 1 vol. McDonnell, Peter, illus. 2006. (Graphic History Ser.). (ENG.). 32p. (gr. 3-4). 8.10 *(978-0-7368-9656-6(2),* Graphic Library) Capstone Press of Coughlan Cos.

Ford, Barbara. Paul Revere: American Patriot. 2015. (Legendary American Biographies Ser.). 96p. (J). (gr. 6-12). pap. 10.95 *(978-0-7660-6486-7(7))* Enslow Pubs., Inc.

Fradin, Dennis Brindell. The Mayflower Compact. 2006. (Turning Points in U. S. History Ser.). (Illus.). 47p. (J). (gr. 3-7). lib. bdg. 31.36 *(978-0-7614-2125-2(4),* Benchmark Bks.) Marshall Cavendish Corp.

Gamble, Adam & Jasper, Mark. Good Night Massachusetts. 2013. (Good Night Our World Ser.). (ENG., Illus.). 20p. (J). (— 1). bds. 9.95 *(978-1-60219-084-9(4))* Good Night Bks.

Gleason, Barbara. My Hometown: Mashpee. 2009. 28p. pap. 14.99 *(978-1-4389-9984-5(4))* AuthorHouse.

Goddu, Krystyna Poray. What's Your Story, Paul Revere? 2016. (Cub Reporter Meets Famous Americans Ser.). (ENG., Illus.). 32p. (J). (gr. k-3). pap. 8.99 *(978-1-4677-9641-5(7),* Lerner Pubns.) Lerner Publishing Group.

Golden, Nancy. The British Are Coming! The Midnight Ride of Paul Revere. 2009. (Great Moments in American History Ser.). 32p. (gr. 3-3). 47.90 *(978-1-61513-136-5(1))* Rosen Publishing Group, Inc., The.

The Greatest Place on Earth: A Children's Story, A History Lesson, A Scrapbook, A Lifetime Keepsake. 2006. (J). 18.95 *(978-0-9777882-0-0(2),* Light Works Publishing) I.M. Enterprises.

Griffis, William Elliot. Young People's History of the Pilgrims. 353p. reprint ed. 98.00 *(978-0-7222-6679-3(0))* Library Reprints, Inc.

Gunderson, Jessica. Life on the Mayflower, 1 vol. Dumm, Brian Caleb, illus. 2011. (Thanksgiving Ser.). (ENG.). 24p. (gr. 1-2). pap. 7.95 *(978-1-4048-6719-2(8))* Picture Window Bks.

—The Pilgrims' First Thanksgiving, 1 vol. Lucke, Deb, illus. (Thanksgiving Ser.). (ENG.). 24p. (gr. 1-2). 2011. pap. 8.95 *(978-1-4048-6720-8(1))* 2010. lib. bdg. 27.32 *(978-1-4048-6285-2(4))* Picture Window Bks.

Harness, Cheryl. The Adventurous Life of Myles Standish & the Amazing-but-True Survival Story of Plymouth Colony. Harness, Cheryl, illus. 2006. (Cheryl Harness Histories Ser.). (ENG., Illus.). 144p. (J). (gr. 5-9). 16.95 *(978-0-7922-5918-3(1))*; lib. bdg. 25.90 *(978-0-7922-5919-0(X))* National Geographic Society. (National Geographic Children's Bks.).

Hicks, Dwayne. Paul Revere: American Patriot. 2012. (Beginning Biographies Ser.). (ENG., Illus.). 24p. (J). (gr. 1-3). 22.60 *(978-1-4488-8599-2(X),* PowerKids Pr.) Rosen Publishing Group, Inc., The.

Hinman, Bonnie. The Massachusetts Bay Colony: The Puritans Arrive from England. 2006. (Building America Ser.). (Illus.). 48p. (J). (gr. 3-7). lib. bdg. 29.95 *(978-1-58415-460-0(8))* Mitchell Lane Pubs., Inc.

Holub, Joan. What Was the First Thanksgiving? 2013. (What Was? Ser.). (ENG., Illus.). 112p. (J). (gr. 3-7). pap. 5.99 *(978-0-448-46463-3(2),* Penguin Workshop) Penguin Young Readers Group.

—What Was the First Thanksgiving? 2013. (What Was... ? Ser.). lib. bdg. 16.00 *(978-0-606-31687-3(6),* Turtleback) Turtleback Bks.

Honders, Christine. Mayflower Compact. 2016. (Documents of American Democracy Ser.). (Illus.). 32p. (J). (gr. 5-5). pap. 10.00 *(978-1-4994-2085-2(4),* PowerKids Pr.) Rosen Publishing Group, Inc., The.

Jeffrey, Gary. Paul Revere & His Midnight Ride. 2011. (Graphic Heroes of the American Revolution Ser.). 24p. (J). (gr. 3-6). lib. bdg. 23.95 *(978-1-4339-6019-2(2))*; pap. 8.15 *(978-1-4339-6020-8(6),* Gareth Stevens Learning Library) Stevens, Gareth Publishing LLLP.

Jerome, Kate B. Lucky to Live in Massachusetts. 2017. (Arcadia Kids Ser.). (ENG., Illus.). 32p. (J). 16.99 ***(978-0-7385-2795-6(5))*** Arcadia Publishing.

Kallio, Jamie. Mayflower Compact, 1 vol. 2013. (Foundations of Our Nation Ser.). (ENG.). 48p. (J). (gr. 3-6). lib. bdg. 32.79 *(978-1-61783-711-1(3))*; (Illus.). pap. 15.64 *(978-1-61783-761-6(X),* Core Library) ABDO Publishing Co.

Kamma, Anne. If You Lived at the Time of Squanto. Johnson, Pamela Ford, illus. 2006. 63p. (J). pap. *(978-0-439-87628-5(1))* Scholastic, Inc.

Kauffman, Dorothy. Two Villages: Two Hundred Years Apart. 2005. (Oxford Picture Dictionary for the Content Areas Ser.). (ENG., Illus.). 22p. pap. 7.56 *(978-0-19-430952-3(5))* Oxford Univ. Pr., Inc.

Keller, Susanna. The True Story of Paul Revere's Ride. 2013. (What Really Happened? Ser.). (ENG., Illus.). 24p. (J). (gr. 3-6). pap. 8.25 *(978-1-4488-9838-1(2))*; lib. bdg. 22.60 *(978-1-4488-9690-5(8))* Rosen Publishing Group, Inc., The. (PowerKids Pr.).

Landau, Elaine. Celebrate the First Thanksgiving with Elaine Landau. 2006. (Explore Colonial America with Elaine Landau Ser.). (Illus.). 48p. (J). (gr. 3-7). lib. bdg. 25.27 *(978-0-7660-2556-1(X),* Enslow Elementary) Enslow Pubs., Inc.

—Sacco & Vanzetti. 2004. (Cornerstones of Freedom Ser.). (ENG., Illus.). 48p. (YA). (gr. 4-7). 26.00 *(978-0-516-24237-8(7))* Scholastic Library Publishing.

—Witness the Salem Witchcraft Trials. 2006. (Explore Colonial America with Elaine Landau Ser.). (Illus.). 48p. (J). (gr. 3-4). lib. bdg. 25.27 *(978-0-7660-2558-5(6),* Enslow Elementary) Enslow Pubs., Inc.

Lanser, Amanda. What's Great about Massachusetts? 2014. (Our Great States Ser.). (Illus.). 32p. (gr. 2-5). (J). lib. bdg. 26.60 *(978-1-4677-3331-1(8),* Lerner Pubns.); (ENG., pap. 7.95 *(978-1-4677-4525-3(1))* Lerner Publishing Group.

LeVert, Suzanne & Orr, Tamra. Massachusetts. 2nd rev. ed. 2008. (Celebrate the States Ser.). 144p. (gr. 6-18). lib. bdg. 42.79 *(978-0-7614-3005-6(9),* Benchmark Bks.) Marshall Cavendish Corp.

Lusted, Marcia Amidon. The Battle of Bunker Hill: A History Perspectives Book. 2013. (Perspectives Library). (ENG., Illus.). 32p. (J). (gr. 4-8). 28.50 *(978-1-62431-414-8(7),* 202776); pap. 14.21 *(978-1-62431-490-2(2),* 202778) Cherry Lake Publishing.

Mara, Wil. Paul Revere. (Rookie Biographies(r) Ser.). (ENG., Illus.). 32p. (J). 2015. pap. 5.95 *(978-0-531-20597-6(5))* 2005. (gr. 1-2). pap. 4.95 *(978-0-516-25820-1(6))* Scholastic Library Publishing. (Children's Pr.).

Marie, June. Harry the Plum Island Fisherman. 2012. 24p. pap. 15.99 *(978-1-4797-0009-7(6))* Xlibris Corp.

Marsh, Carole. Exploring Massachusetts Through Project-Based Learning: Geography, History, Government, Economics & More. 2016. (Massachusetts Experience Ser.). (ENG.). (J). pap. 9.99 *(978-0-635-12345-9(2))* Gallopade International.

—I'm Reading about Massachusetts. 2014. (Massachusetts Experience Ser.). (ENG., Illus.). (J). pap., pap. 8.99 *(978-0-635-11296-5(5))* Gallopade International.

—Massachusetts History Projects: 30 Cool, Activities, Crafts, Experiments & More for Kids to Do to Learn about Your State! 2003. (Massachusetts Experience Ser.). 32p. (gr. k-5). pap. 5.95 *(978-0-635-01790-1(3),* Marsh, Carole Bks.) Gallopade International.

Mase, Tina. Spencer: A Sense of Heritage. 2009. 108p. pap. 19.95 *(978-1-4290-9110-7(X))* Applewood Bks.

McCarthy, Rose. Paul Revere: Freedom Rider. 2009. (Primary Sources of Famous People in American History Ser.). 32p. (gr. 2-3). 47.90 *(978-1-60851-714-5(4))* Rosen Publishing Group, Inc., The.

—Paul Revere: Freedom Rider / Jinete de la causa Revolucionaria. 2009. (Famous People in American History/Grandes personajes en la historia de los Estados Unidos Ser.). (ENG & SPA.). 32p. (gr. 2-3). 47.90 *(978-1-61512-553-1(1),* Editorial Buenas Letras) Rosen Publishing Group, Inc., The.

—Paul Revere: Jinete de la causa revolucionaria (Paul Revere: Freedom Rider) 2009. (Grandes personajes en la historia de los Estados Unidos (Famous People in American History) Ser.). (SPA.). 32p. (gr. 2-3). 47.90 *(978-1-61512-806-8(9),* Editorial Buenas Letras) Rosen Publishing Group, Inc., The.

McNeil, Tom & Benchmark Education Co. Staff. Take-Off: A Pilot's Memoir. 2014. (Text Connections Ser.). (J). (gr. 6). *(978-1-4900-1536-1(1))* Benchmark Education Co.

Mills, Jordan. Massachusetts. 2016. (States Ser.). (ENG., Illus.). 32p. (gr. 3-4). lib. bdg. 27.32 *(978-1-5157-0408-9(4))* Next Page Pr., The.

Mills, Nathan & Hicks, Dwayne. Paul Revere: American Patriot. 2012. (Rosen Readers Ser.). (ENG., Illus.). 24p. (J). (gr. 1-2). pap. 8.25 *(978-1-4488-8836-8(0),* Rosen Classroom) Rosen Publishing Group, Inc., The.

Min, Ellen. The Midnight Ride of Paul Revere: One If by Land, Two If by Sea. 2015. (Spotlight on American History Ser.). (ENG., Illus.). 24p. (J). (gr. 4-6). pap. 10.00 *(978-1-4994-1734-0(9),* PowerKids Pr.) Rosen Publishing Group, Inc., The.

Murray, Julie. Massachusetts, 1 vol. 2012. (Explore the United States Ser.). (ENG.). 32p. (J). (gr. 2-5). lib. bdg. 28.50 *(978-1-61783-359-5(2),* Big Buddy Bks.) ABDO Publishing Co.

Nelson, Maria. The Life of Paul Revere. 2012. (Famous Lives Ser.). (ENG.). 24p. (J). (gr. k-3). lib. bdg. 22.60 *(978-1-4339-6353-7(1))*; (gr. 1-4). pap. 8.15 *(978-1-4339-6355-1(8))* Stevens, Gareth Publishing LLLP.

—The Life of Paul Revere / la Vida de Paul Revere. 2012. (Famous Lives / Vidas extraordinarias Ser.). (ENG & SPA., Illus.). 24p. (J). (gr. k-3). 22.60 *(978-1-4339-6657-6(3))* Stevens, Gareth Publishing LLLP.

Niz, Xavier & Niz, Xavier W. Paul Revere's Ride. Bascle, Brian, illus. 2005. (Graphic History Ser.). (ENG.). 32p. (gr. 3-4). 30.65 *(978-0-7368-4965-4(3),* Graphic Library) Capstone Press of Coughlan Cos.

Obregón, José María. Massachusetts. 2009. (Bilingual Library of the United States of America Ser.). (ENG & SPA.). 32p. (gr. 2-2). 47.90 *(978-1-60853-366-4(2),* Editorial Buenas Letras) Rosen Publishing Group, Inc., The.

Oney, Yannick. First American Colonies. 2004. (World Discovery History Readers Ser.). (Illus.). 32p. (J). pap. *(978-0-439-66555-1(8))* Scholastic, Inc.

Osborne, Mary Pope & Boyce, Natalie Pope. Pilgrims: A Nonfiction Companion to Thanksgiving on Thursday. Murdocca, Sal, illus. 2005. (Magic Tree House - Fact Tracker Ser.: 13). (ENG.). 128p. (J). (gr. 2-5). 6.99 *(978-0-375-83219-2(X),* Random Hse. Bks. for Young Readers) Random Hse. Children's Bks.

Owens, L. L. Pilgrims in America. 2006. (Events in American History Ser.). (Illus.). 48p. (J). (gr. -1-1). lib. bdg. 31.36 *(978-1-60044-122-6(X))* Rourke Educational Media.

Pezzi, Bryan. Massachusetts: The Bay State. 2016. (J). *(978-1-4896-4878-5(X))* Weigl Pubs., Inc.

Philbrick, Nathaniel. In the Heart of the Sea (Young Readers Edition) 2015. (ENG., Illus.). 208p. (J). (gr. 3-7). 8.99 *(978-1-101-99776-5(1),* Puffin Books) Penguin Young Readers Group.

—The Mayflower & the Pilgrims' New World. 2009. (ENG.). 368p. (J). (gr. 5-18). 8.99 *(978-0-14-241458-3(1),* Puffin Books) Penguin Young Readers Group.

Plimoth Plantation Staff, et al. Mayflower 1620: A New Look at a Pilgrim Voyage. 2013. (ENG.). 48p. (J). (gr. 3-7). lib. bdg. 27.00 *(978-1-4263-1631-9(3),* National Geographic Children's Bks.) National Geographic Society.

—Mayflower 1620: A New Look at a Pilgrim Voyage. Coulson, Cotton, photos by. 2007. (ENG., Illus.). 48p. (J). (gr. 3-7). per. 6.95 *(978-0-7922-6276-3(X),* National Geographic Children's Bks.) National Geographic Society.

Poolos, J. The Mayflower: A Primary Source History of the Pilgrims' Journey to the New World. 2009. (Primary Sources in American History Ser.). 64p. (gr. 5-8). 58.50 *(978-1-60851-499-1(4))* Rosen Publishing Group, Inc., The.

Rajczak, Michael. Life on the Mayflower, Vol. 1. 2014. (What You Didn't Know about History Ser.). (ENG.). 24p. (J). (gr. 2-3). 22.60 *(978-1-4824-0591-0(1))* Stevens, Gareth Publishing LLLP.

Raum, Elizabeth. The Mayflower Compact, 1 vol. 2012. (Documenting U. S. History Ser.). (ENG.). 48p. (gr. 3-6). pap. 9.95 *(978-1-4329-6759-8(2))*; lib. bdg. 32.65 *(978-1-4329-6750-5(9))* Heinemann-Raintree. (NA-h).

Rechner, Amy. Massachusetts. 2013. (Exploring the States Ser.). (ENG., Illus.). 32p. (gr. 3-7). lib. bdg. 26.95 *(978-1-62617-020-9(7),* Blastoff! Readers) Bellwether Media.

Rooney, Thomas L. Tobey Boland & the Blackstone Canal. Donovan, Patte, illus. 2005. 30p. (J). *(978-1-929039-30-2(1))* Ambassador Bks., Inc.

Santella, Andrew. The First Thanksgiving. 2003. (Cornerstones of Freedom Ser.). (ENG., Illus.). 48p. (YA). (gr. 4-7). 26.00 *(978-0-516-24204-0(0))* Scholastic Library Publishing.

Schulte, Mary. Dover Demon. 2009. (Mysterious Encounters Ser.). (ENG., Illus.). 48p. (J). 29.00 *(978-0-7377-4570-2(3),* Greenhaven Pr., Inc.) Cengage Gale.

Shea, Therese. The Boston Massacre, Vol. 1. 2014. (What You Didn't Know about History Ser.). (ENG.). 24p. (J). (gr. 2-3). 22.60 *(978-1-4824-0580-4(6))* Stevens, Gareth Publishing LLLP.

Slavicek, Louise Chipley. The Salem Witch Trial: Hysteria in Colonial America. 2011. (Milestones in American History Ser.). (Illus.). 124p. (gr. 6-12). 35.00 *(978-1-60413-763-7(0),* Chelsea Hse.) Facts On File, Inc.

Smith, Andrea P. A Day in the Life of Colonial Silversmith Paul Revere. 2012. (Illus.). 24p. (J). 63.60 *(978-1-4488-5217-8(X))*; pap. 10.60 *(978-1-4488-5216-1(1))*; lib. bdg. 25.25 *(978-1-4488-5189-8(0))* Rosen Publishing Group, Inc., The. (PowerKids Pr.).

—The First Thanksgiving. 2012. (Illus.). 24p. (J). 63.60 *(978-1-4488-5213-0(7))*; pap. 10.60 *(978-1-4488-5212-3(9))*; lib. bdg. 25.25 *(978-1-4488-5187-4(4))* Rosen Publishing Group, Inc., The. (PowerKids Pr.).

—The Journey of the Mayflower. 2012. (Illus.). 24p. (J). 63.60 *(978-1-4488-5211-6(0))*; pap. 10.60 *(978-1-4488-5210-9(2))*; lib. bdg. 25.25 *(978-1-4488-5186-7(6))* Rosen Publishing Group, Inc., The. (PowerKids Pr.).

—The Salem Witch Trials. 2012. (Illus.). 24p. 63.60 *(978-1-4488-5215-4(3))*; pap. 10.60 *(978-1-4488-5214-7(5))*; lib. bdg. 25.25 *(978-1-4488-5188-1(2))* Rosen Publishing Group, Inc., The. (PowerKids Pr.).

Smolik, Jane Petrlik. The Great Massachusetts Puzzle Book: Over 75 Puzzles about Life in the Bay State. rev. ed. 2005. (Illus.). 96p. (J). (gr. 2-7). per. 11.95 *(978-0-9664095-5-0(8))* MidRun Pr.

Spooner, J. B. & Seeley, Terre Lamb. The Little Black Dog Has Puppies. Seeley, Terre Lamb, illus. 2011. (Little Black Dog Ser.). (ENG., Illus.). 32p. (J). (gr. -1-k). 16.95 *(978-1-61145-006-4(3)*, 611006, Arcade Publishing) Skyhorse Publishing Co., Inc.

Sullivan, Laura L. The Colonial Minuteman. 2015. (Colonial People Ser.). (ENG., Illus.). 48p. (J). (gr. 4-4). lib. bdg. 31.36 *(978-1-5026-0478-1(7))* Cavendish Square Publishing.

—Life As a Passenger on the Mayflower. 2016. (Life As... Ser.). (Illus.). 32p. (J). (gr. 3-3). 28.50 *(978-1-5026-1789-7(7))* Cavendish Square Publishing.

Tieck, Sarah. Paul Revere, 1 vol. 2006. (First Biographies Ser.). (ENG., Illus.). 32p. (gr. -1-3). 27.07 *(978-1-59679-787-1(8)*, Buddy Bks.) ABDO Publishing Co.

Tougias, Michael J. & Sherman, Casey. The Finest Hours: The True Story of a Heroic Sea Rescue. 2014. (True Storm Rescues Ser.). (ENG., Illus.). 176p. (YA). (gr. 4-8). 17.99 *(978-0-8050-9764-1(3)*, 9780805097641, Holt, Henry & Co. Bks. For Young Readers) Holt, Henry & Co.

—The Finest Hours: The True Story of a Heroic Sea Rescue. 2015. (ENG., Illus.). 208p. (YA). (gr. 4-8). pap. 7.99 *(978-1-250-04423-5(5)*, 9781250044235) Square Fish.

Tracy, Kathleen. The Plymouth Colony: The Pilgrims Settle in New England. 2006. (Building America Ser.). (Illus.). 48p. (J). (gr. 3-7). lib. bdg. 29.95 *(978-1-58415-459-4(4))* Mitchell Lane Pubs., Inc.

Vierow, Wendy. The Assault on Fort Wagner: Black Union Soldiers Make a Stand in South Carolina Battle. 2004. (Headlines from History Ser.). (Illus.). 24p. (YA). (gr. 2-5). lib. bdg. 22.60 *(978-0-8239-6223-5(7))* Rosen Publishing Group, Inc., The.

Wagner, Heather Lehr. Paul Revere: Messenger for Freedom. 2005. (Leaders of the American Revolution Ser.). (Illus.). 128p. (gr. 5-8). lib. bdg. 30.00 *(978-0-7910-8624-7(0))* Facts On File, Inc.

—William Bradford. 2010. (Leaders of the Colonial Era Ser.). 120p. (gr. 5-8). 35.00 *(978-1-60413-743-9(6)*, Chelsea Hse.) Facts On File, Inc.

Waters, Kate. A Day in the Life of a Pilgrim Girl. Kendall, Russell, illus. 2008. (Sarah Morton's Day Ser.). (ENG.). 32p. (J). (gr. -1-3). pap. 7.99 *(978-0-439-81220-7(8)*, Scholastic Paperbacks) Scholastic, Inc.

Waxman, Laura Hamilton. Why Did the Pilgrims Come to the New World? And Other Questions about the Plymouth Colony. 2010. (Six Questions of American History Ser.). (ENG., Illus.). 48p. (gr. 4-6). lib. bdg. 30.60 *(978-1-58013-665-5(6))* Lerner Publishing Group.

—Why Did the Pilgrims Come to the New World? & Other Questions about the Plymouth Colony. 2010. pap. 56.72 *(978-0-7613-6951-6(1))* Lerner Publishing Group.

Weintraub, Aileen. Boston Light: The First Lighthouse in North America. 2009. (Great Lighthouses of North America Ser.). 24p. (gr. 3-3). 42.50 *(978-1-61513-128-0(0)*, PowerKids Pr.) Rosen Publishing Group, Inc., The.

Whitcraft, Melissa. The Mayflower Compact. 2003. (Cornerstones of Freedom Ser.). (ENG., Illus.). 48p. (YA). (gr. 4-7). 26.00 *(978-0-516-24203-3(2))* Scholastic Library Publishing.

Whitehurst, Susan. The Mayflower. 2009. (Library of the Pilgrims Ser.). 24p. (gr. 3-4). 42.50 *(978-1-60853-914-7(8)*, PowerKids Pr.) Rosen Publishing Group, Inc., The.

—The Pilgrims Before the Mayflower. 2009. (Library of the Pilgrims Ser.). 24p. (gr. 3-4). 42.50 *(978-1-60853-915-4(6)*, PowerKids Pr.) Rosen Publishing Group, Inc., The.

—Plymouth Partnership: Pilgrims & Native Americans. 2009. (Library of the Pilgrims Ser.). 24p. (gr. 3-4). 42.50 *(978-1-60853-912-3(1)*, PowerKids Pr.) Rosen Publishing Group, Inc., The.

—William Bradford & Plymouth: A Colony Grows. 2009. (Library of the Pilgrims Ser.). 24p. (gr. 3-4). 42.50 *(978-1-60853-916-1(4)*, PowerKids Pr.) Rosen Publishing Group, Inc., The.

Williams, Gianna & Riehecky, Janet. La Colonia de Plymouth. 2006. (Hitos de la historia de Estados Unidos (Landmark Events in American History) Ser.). (SPA.). 48p. (gr. 5-12). pap. 11.70 *(978-0-8368-7471-6(4)*, Gareth Stevens Learning Library); (Illus.). lib. bdg. 27.00 *(978-0-8368-7464-8(1)*, Gareth Stevens Secondary Library) Stevens, Gareth Publishing LLLP.

Woelfle, Gretchen. Mumbet's Declaration of Independence. Delinois, Alix, illus. 2014. (ENG.). 32p. (J). (gr. 1-4). 17.95 *(978-0-7613-6589-1(3)*, Carolrhoda Bks.) Lerner Publishing Group.

Yero, Judith Lloyd & National Geographic Learning Staff. The Mayflower Compact. 2007. (Reading Expeditions Ser.). (ENG., Illus.). 32p. (J). pap. 17.95 *(978-0-7922-4553-7(9))* CENGAGE Learning.

MASSACHUSETTS—HISTORY—COLONIAL PERIOD, CA. 1600-1775

Abrams, Dennis. Cotton Mather. 2010. (Leaders of the Colonial Era Ser.). 128p. (gr. 5-8). 35.00 *(978-1-60413-736-1(3)*, Chelsea Hse.) Facts On File, Inc.

Aller, Susan Bivin. Anne Hutchinson. 2010. (History Maker Biographies Ser.). (ENG.). 48p. (gr. 3-6). lib. bdg. 27.93 *(978-0-7613-5208-2(2)*, Lerner Pubns.) Lerner Publishing Group.

Avett, Harper. The Colony of Massachusetts. 2015. (Spotlight on the 13 Colonies Ser.). (ENG., Illus.). 24p. (J). (gr. 4-5). pap. 8.25 *(978-1-4994-0511-8(1)*, PowerKids Pr.) Rosen Publishing Group, Inc., The.

Burgan, Michael. Massachusetts, 1620-1776. 2005. (National Geographic Voices from ColonialAmerica Ser.). (ENG., Illus.). 112p. (J). (gr. 5-9). 21.95 *(978-0-7922-6383-8(9))*; lib. bdg. 32.90 *(978-0-7922-6599-3(8))* National Geographic Society. (National Geographic Children's Bks.).

Cunningham, Kevin. The Massachusetts Colony. 2011. (True Book-the Thirteen Colonies Ser.). (ENG., Illus.). 48p. (J). lib. bdg. 29.00 *(978-0-531-25391-5(0))*; (gr. 3-5). pap. 6.95 *(978-0-531-26604-5(4))* Scholastic Library Publishing. (Children's Pr.).

Doherty, Craig A. & Doherty, Katherine M. Massachusetts, 13 vols. 2005. (Thirteen Colonies Ser.). (Illus.). 160p. (gr. 5-8). 35.00 *(978-0-8160-5407-7(X))* Facts On File, Inc.

Edwards, Judith. The Plymouth Colony & the Pilgrim Adventure in American History. 2003. (In American History Ser.). (Illus.). 128p. (J). (gr. 5-12). lib. bdg. 26.60 *(978-0-7660-1989-8(6))* Enslow Pubs., Inc.

Englar, Mary. The Pilgrims & the First Thanksgiving, 1 vol. McDonnell, Peter, illus. 2006. (Graphic History Ser.). (ENG.). 32p. (gr. 3-4). 30.65 *(978-0-7368-5492-4(4)*, Graphic Library) Capstone Press of Coughlan Cos.

Freedman, Jeri. A Primary Source History of the Colony of Massachusetts. (Primary Sources of the Thirteen Colonies & the Lost Colony Ser.). 64p. 2009. (gr. 5-8). 58.50 *(978-1-60851-880-7(9))* 2006. (Illus.). (YA). (gr. 4-7). lib. bdg. 31.95 *(978-1-4042-0428-7(8))* 2006. (ENG., Illus.). (gr. 4-8). per. 12.95 *(978-1-4042-0671-7(X))* Rosen Publishing Group, Inc., The.

Harness, Cheryl. The Adventurous Life of Myles Standish & the Amazing-but-True Survival Story of Plymouth Colony: Barbary Pirates, the Mayflower, the First Thanksgiving, & Much, Much More. 2008. (Cheryl Harness Histories Ser.). (ENG., Illus.). 144p. (J). (gr. 5-9). 9.95 *(978-1-4263-0284-8(3)*, National Geographic Children's Bks.) National Geographic Society.

Hawthorne, Nathaniel. Grandfather's Chair: A History for Youth. 2010. 292p. pap. 17.95 *(978-1-4290-4522-3(1))* Applewood Bks.

Koestler-Grack, Rachel A. Pilgrims, 1 vol. 2005. (American Moments Ser.). (ENG., Illus.). 48p. (gr. 4-8). 27.07 *(978-1-59197-937-1(4)*, Abdo & Daughters) ABDO Publishing Co.

Lynch, P. J. The Boy Who Fell off the Mayflower, or John Howland's Good Fortune. Lynch, P. J., illus. 2015. (ENG., Illus.). 64p. (J). (gr. 2-5). 17.99 *(978-0-7636-6584-5(3))* Candlewick Pr.

Marsh, Carole. Anne Hutchinson. 2004. 12p. (gr. k-4). 2.95 *(978-0-635-02370-4(9))* Gallopade International.

Miller, Barbara Kiely. Anne Hutchinson. 2007. (Great Americans Ser.). 24p. (gr. 1-4). pap. 8.15 *(978-0-8368-8324-4(1))*; (SPA.). pap. 8.15 *(978-0-8368-8337-4(3))*; (Illus.). lib. bdg. 22.00 *(978-0-8368-8317-6(9))*; (SPA., Illus.). lib. bdg. 22.00 *(978-0-8368-8330-5(6))* Stevens, Gareth Publishing LLLP. (Weekly Reader Leveled Readers).

Miller, Jake. The Colony of Massachusetts: A Primary Source History. (Primary Source Library of the Thirteen Colonies & the Lost Colony Ser.). 24p. 2009. (gr. 3-4). 42.50 *(978-1-60854-142-3(8)*, PowerKids Pr.) 2006. (Illus.). (YA). (gr. 4-7). lib. bdg. 22.60 *(978-1-4042-3028-6(9))* Rosen Publishing Group, Inc., The.

Moe, Barbara A. The Charter of the Massachusetts Bay Colony: A Primary Source Investigation of the 1629 Charter. 2005. (Great American Political Documents Ser.). (Illus.). 112p. (YA). (gr. 7-12). lib. bdg. 34.60 *(978-0-8239-3801-8(8))* Rosen Publishing Group, Inc., The.

Shea, Therese. The Boston Massacre, Vol. 1. 2014. (What You Didn't Know about History Ser.). 24p. (J). (gr. 2-5). pap. 8.15 *(978-1-4824-3328-9(1))* Stevens, Gareth Publishing LLLP.

Slavicek, Louise Chipley. Anne Hutchinson. 2010. (Leaders of the Colonial Era Ser.). 120p. (gr. 5-8). 35.00 *(978-1-60413-741-5(X)*, Chelsea Hse.) Facts On File, Inc.

Smith-Llera, Danielle. Exploring the Massachusetts Bay Colony. 2016. (Exploring the 13 Colonies Ser.). (ENG., Illus.). 48p. (gr. 3-4). lib. bdg. 31.99 *(978-1-5157-2237-3(6))* Capstone Press of Coughlan Cos.

Wolfe, James & Moe, Barbara A. Understanding the Charter of the Massachusetts Bay Colony. 2015. (Primary Sources of American Political Documents Ser.). (ENG., Illus.). 112p. (J). (gr. 7-7). 37.27 *(978-0-7660-6870-4(6))* Enslow Pubs., Inc.

MASSACHUSETTS—HISTORY—FICTION

Alger, Horatio. Do & Dare: Or, A Brave Boy's Fight for Fortune. 2006. 182p. pap. 19.99 *(978-1-4264-0880-9(3))*; 170p. pap. 21.99 *(978-1-4264-0861-8(7))* Creative Media Partners, LLC.

—Do & Dare: Or, A Brave Boy's Fight for Fortune. 2006. pap. *(978-1-4065-0701-0(6))* Dodo Pr.

Anderson, M. T. The Kingdom on the Waves. 2009. (Astonishing Life of Octavian Nothing, Traitor to the Nation Ser.: Vol. 2). (ENG., Illus.). 592p. (YA). (gr. 9). pap. 12.99 *(978-0-7636-4626-4(1))* Candlewick Pr.

—The Pox Party. 2006. (Astonishing Life of Octavian Nothing, Traitor to the Nation Ser.: Vol. 1). (ENG., Illus.). 368p. (YA). (gr. 9-12). 17.99 *(978-0-7636-2402-6(0))* Candlewick Pr.

Axelrod, Amy. Your Friend in Fashion, Abby Shapiro. 2011. (ENG.). 288p. (J). (gr. 3-7). 17.95 *(978-0-8234-2340-8(9))* Holiday Hse., Inc.

Barker, M. P. A Difficult Boy. 2009. (ENG.). 272p. (YA). (gr. 5-18). pap. 7.95 *(978-0-8234-2244-9(5))* Holiday Hse., Inc.

Brodeur, Tom. Regina Silsby's Phantom Militia. 2005. (Illus.). 267p. (J). (gr. 3-7). 7.49 *(978-1-59166-385-0(7))* BJU Pr.

Cooney, Caroline B. The Ransom of Mercy Carter. 2011. (ENG.). 256p. (YA). (gr. 7). pap. 8.99 *(978-0-385-74046-3(8)*, Ember) Random Hse. Children's Bks.

Cooper, Susan. Ghost Hawk. 2013. (ENG.). 336p. (J). (gr. 5-9). 16.99 *(978-1-4424-8141-1(2)*, McElderry, Margaret K. Bks.) McElderry, Margaret K. Bks.

Fama, Elizabeth. Monstrous Beauty. 2013. (ENG.). 352p. (YA). (gr. 7-12). pap. 9.99 *(978-1-250-03425-0(6))* Square Fish.

Figley, Marty Rhodes. Emily & Carlo. Stock, Catherine, illus. 2012. (ENG.). 32p. (J). (gr. k-3). 15.95 *(978-1-58089-274-2(4))* Charlesbridge Publishing, Inc.

Gibbs, Gretchen. The Book of Maggie Bradstreet. 2012. (Bradstreet Chronicles). (ENG.). 183p. (YA). pap. 9.99 *(978-0-9852948-0-9(9))* Glenmere Pr.

Gomes, Linda Nunes. Special Words: A Story about Multicultural Families & Their Pets. Levine, Lenora D., illus. 2007. (YA). per. 12.99 *(978-1-934400-02-9(5))* Rock Village Publishing.

Harlow, Joan Hiatt. Midnight Rider. 2006. (ENG.). 384p. (J). (gr. 4-9). pap. 8.99 *(978-0-689-87010-1(8)*, McElderry, Margaret K. Bks.) McElderry, Margaret K. Bks.

Hearn, Julie. The Minister's Daughter. 2006. (ENG.). 272p. (YA). (gr. 7-12). pap. 7.99 *(978-0-689-87691-2(2)*, Atheneum Bks. for Young Readers) Simon & Schuster Children's Publishing.

Hurst, Carol Otis. Terrible Storm. 2007. (Illus.). 32p. (J). (gr. k-3). lib. bdg. 17.89 *(978-0-06-009002-9(2))* HarperCollins Pubs.

Klimo, Kate. Dog Diaries #5: Dash. Jessell, Tim, illus. 2014. (Dog Diaries). (ENG.). 160p. (J). (gr. 2-5). pap. 7.99 *(978-0-385-37338-8(4)*, Random Hse. Bks. for Young Readers) Random Hse. Children's Bks.

Lasky, Kathryn. A Journey to the New World: The Diary of Remember Patience Whipple, Mayflower 1620. 2010. (Dear America Ser.). (ENG.). 192p. (J). (gr. 3-7). 12.99 *(978-0-545-23801-4(3)*, Scholastic Pr.) Scholastic, Inc.

Latham, Jean Lee. Carry on, Mr. Bowditch. 2003. (ENG., Illus.). 256p. (YA). (gr. 7). pap. 7.99 *(978-0-618-25074-5(3))* Houghton Mifflin Harcourt Publishing Co.

Limbaugh, Rush H., III. Rush Revere & the Brave Pilgrims: Time-Travel Adventures with Exceptional Americans. 2013. (ENG., Illus.). 224p. 19.99 *(978-1-4767-5586-1(8)*, Threshold Editions) Threshold Editions.

Moody Publishing Staff & Lawton, Wendy G. Freedom's Pen: A Story Based on the Life of Freed Slave & Author Phillis Wheatley 2009. (Daughters of the Faith Ser.). (ENG.). 144p. (gr. 3-7). pap. 7.99 *(978-0-8024-7639-5(2))* Moody Pubs.

Parker, Robert. Edenville Owls. 2008. 194p. (gr. 4-6). 18.00 *(978-0-7569-8920-0(5))* Perfection Learning Corp.

Paterson, Katherine. Bread & Roses, Too. 2008. (ENG.). 288p. (J). (gr. 5-7). pap. 7.99 *(978-0-547-07651-5(7))* Houghton Mifflin Harcourt Publishing Co.

Rees, Celia. Witch Child. unabr. ed. 2004. (Young Adult Cassette Librariestm Ser.). 304p. (J). (gr. 5-9). pap. 40.00 incl. audio *(978-0-8072-1198-4(2)*, S YA 343 SP, Listening Library) Random Hse. Audio Publishing Group.

Rinaldi, Ann. Hang a Thousand Trees with Ribbons: The Story of Phillis Wheatley. 2005. (Great Episodes Ser.). (ENG.). 352p. (YA). (gr. 7-8). pap. 8.99 *(978-0-15-205393-2(X))* Houghton Mifflin Harcourt Publishing Co.

—Hang a Thousand Trees with Ribbons: The Story of Phillis Wheatley. 2005. (Great Episodes Ser.). 336p. (gr. 5-9). 18.00 *(978-0-7569-5018-7(X))* Perfection Learning Corp.

Roy, Ron. Mayflower Treasure Hunt. Gurney, John Steven, illus. 2nd ed. 2007. (to Z Mysteries Ser.: 2). (ENG.). 128p. (J). (gr. 1-4). per. 5.99 *(978-0-375-83937-5(2)*, Random Hse. Bks. for Young Readers) Random Hse. Children's Bks.

—Mayflower Treasure Hunt. Gurney, John Steven, illus. 2007. (to Z Mysteries Ser.: 28). 114p. (gr. 4-7). lib. bdg. 16.00 *(978-1-4177-9141-5(1)*, Turtleback) Turtleback Bks.

Sheely, Robert. In the Hands of the Enemy. Killcoyne, Hope L., ed. Martin, John F., illus. 2003. (Adventures in America Ser.: Vol. 8). 75p. (gr. 4). 14.95 *(978-1-893110-31-1(1))* Silver Moon Pr.

Smith, Mary P. Boy Captive of Old Deerfield. (Illus.). (J). (gr. 5-6). reprint ed. lib. bdg. 22.95 *(978-0-89190-961-3(3)*, Rivercity Pr.) Amereon Ltd.

Spykman, E. C. Terrible, Horrible Edie. 2010. (ENG.). 232p. (J). (gr. 4-7). 16.95 *(978-1-59017-353-4(8)*, NYR Children's Collection) New York Review of Bks., Inc., The.

Strohmeier, Lenice & Strohmeier. Mingo, 1 vol. Farnsworth, Bill, illus. 2003. (ENG.). 32p. (J). 16.95 *(978-0-7614-5111-2(0))* Marshall Cavendish Corp.

Thomas, Carroll, creator. Under the Open Sky: A Matty Trescott Novel. 2005. (Illus.). 184p. (J). per. 12.95 *(978-0-9762091-2-6(8))* Antrim Hse.

Thompson, Paul B. The Devil's Door: A Salem Witchcraft Story. 2010. (Historical Fiction Adventures (HFA) Ser.). (Illus.). 160p. (J). pap. 10.95 *(978-1-59845-214-3(2))*; (gr. 3-6). 29.27 *(978-0-7660-3367-0(2))* Enslow Pubs., Inc.

—Liberty's Son: A Spy Story of the American Revolution. 2009. (Historical Fiction Adventures (HFA) Ser.). (Illus.). 160p. (J). (gr. 3-6). lib. bdg. 29.27 *(978-0-7660-3309-2(0))* Enslow Pubs., Inc.

Warburton, Carol. Edge of Night: A Novel. 2004. (Illus.). 278p. pap. 14.95 *(978-1-59156-013-5(6))* Covenant Communications, Inc.

Wiley, Melissa. Little House by Boston Bay. 2007. (Little House Prequel Ser.). (ENG.). 160p. (J). (gr. 3-7). pap. 5.99 *(978-0-06-114828-6(8))* HarperCollins Pubs.

Wolk, Lauren. Beyond the Bright Sea. 2017. (ENG.). 304p. (J). (gr. 5). 16.99 ***(978-1-101-99485-6(1)**,* Dutton Books for Young Readers) Penguin Young Readers Group.

MASSACHUSETTS—POLITICS AND GOVERNMENT

Marsh, Carole. Exploring Massachusetts Through Project-Based Learning: Geography, History, Government, Economics & More. 2016. (Massachusetts Experience Ser.). (ENG.). (J). pap. 9.99 *(978-0-635-12345-9(2))* Gallopade International.

MASTODON

Goecke, Michael P. American Mastodon, 1 vol. 2003. (Prehistoric Animals Set II Ser.). (ENG., Illus.). 24p. (gr. k-4). 25.65 *(978-1-57765-973-0(2)*, Buddy Bks.) ABDO Publishing Co.

MATERIA MEDICA

see also Poisons

Claybourne, Anna. Sick at Sea? Cure It or Cut It Off! 2010. (ENG.). 32p. (J). *(978-0-7787-9901-6(8))* Crabtree Publishing Co.

Lawrence, Ellen. Healing Plants. 2015. (Plant-Ology Ser.). (ENG., Illus.). 24p. (J). (gr. -1-3). lib. bdg. 23.93 *(978-1-62724-866-2(8))* Bearport Publishing Co., Inc.

Woods, Michael & Woods, Mary B. Ancient Medical Technology: From Herbs to Scalpels. 2011. (Technology in Ancient Cultures Ser.). (ENG.). 96p. (gr. 6-12). lib. bdg. 31.93 *(978-0-7613-6522-8(2))* Lerner Publishing Group.

MATERIALS

Addison, D. R. Cement Mixers at Work. 2009. (Big Trucks Ser.). (Illus.). 24p. (J). (gr. k-2). pap. 8.25 *(978-1-4358-3087-5(3)*, PowerKids Pr.) Rosen Publishing Group, Inc., The.

Angliss, Sarah, et al. Hands-On Science: Matter & Materials. 2013. (Hands-On Science Ser.). (ENG., Illus.). 32p. (J). (gr. 2-5). pap. 7.99 *(978-0-7534-6973-6(1)*, 9780753469736, Kingfisher) Roaring Brook Pr.

Ballard, Carol. Exploring Natural & Man-Made Materials. 2008. (How Does Science Work? Ser.). (Illus.). 32p. (J). (gr. 3-7). lib. bdg. 26.50 *(978-1-4042-4278-4(3)*, PowerKids Pr.) Rosen Publishing Group, Inc., The.

Barton, Chris. The Day-Glo Brothers: The True Story of Bob & Joe Switzer's Bright Ideas & Brand-New Colors. Persiani, Tony, illus. 2009. (ENG.). 44p. (J). (gr. 2-5). 19.95 *(978-1-57091-673-1(X))* Charlesbridge Publishing, Inc.

Bentley, Joyce. Rough. 2006. (Things Around Us Ser.). (J). *(978-1-59389-276-0(4))* Chrysalis Education.

—Smooth. 2006. (Things Around Us Ser.). (J). *(978-1-59389-277-7(2))* Chrysalis Education.

Brill, Marlene Targ. Concrete Mixers. 2006. (Pull Ahead Books-Mighty Movers Ser.). (ENG., Illus.). 32p. (gr. k-3). lib. bdg. 22.60 *(978-0-8225-6011-1(9)*, Lerner Pubns.) Lerner Publishing Group.

Canavan, Thomas. Magnificent Experiments with Materials. Linley, Adam, illus. 2017. (Mind-Blowing Science Experiments Ser.). 32p. (gr. 4-5). pap. 63.00 ***(978-1-5382-0732-1(X))*** Stevens, Gareth Publishing LLLP.

Carr, Aaron. Natural o Hecho Por el Hombre. 2013. (SPA., Illus.). 24p. (J). *(978-1-62127-607-4(4))* Weigl Pubs., Inc.

Claybourne, Anna. Materials. 2016. (Mind Webs Ser.). (ENG., Illus.). 32p. (J). (gr. 4-6). pap. 11.99 *(978-0-7502-8984-9(8)*, Wayland) Hachette Children's Group GBR. Dist: Hachette Bk. Group.

—Materials. 2012. (Illus.). 24p. (gr. k-4). pap. 7.95 *(978-1-926853-58-1(X))* Saunders Bk. Co. CAN. Dist: RiverStream Publishing.

Colich, Abby. Exploring Materials. 2013. (Exploring Materials Ser.). (ENG.). 24p. (gr. -1-1). pap. 41.93 *(978-1-4329-8029-0(7))*; lib. bdg. 158.55 *(978-1-4329-8021-4(1))* Heinemann-Raintree. (Acorn).

Enz, Tammy. Bend It! 2017. (Shaping Materials Ser.). (ENG.). 24p. (gr. k-2). lib. bdg. 23.32 ***(978-1-4846-4097-5(7)**,* Heinemann Read & Learn) Heinemann-Raintree.

—Shaping Materials. 2017. (Shaping Materials Ser.). (ENG.). 24p. (gr. k-2). 93.28 ***(978-1-4846-4116-3(7)**,* Heinemann Read & Learn) Heinemann-Raintree.

—Squash It! 2017. (Shaping Materials Ser.). (ENG.). 24p. (gr. k-2). lib. bdg. 23.32 ***(978-1-4846-4095-1(0)**,* Heinemann Read & Learn) Heinemann-Raintree.

—Stretch It! 2017. (Shaping Materials Ser.). (ENG.). 24p. (gr. k-2). lib. bdg. 23.32 ***(978-1-4846-4094-4(2)**,* Heinemann Read & Learn) Heinemann-Raintree.

—Twist It! 2017. (Shaping Materials Ser.). (ENG.). 24p. (gr. k-2). lib. bdg. 23.32 ***(978-1-4846-4096-8(9)**,* Heinemann Read & Learn) Heinemann-Raintree.

Goldsmith, Mike. Discover Science: Materials. 2012. (Discover Science Ser.). (ENG., Illus.). 56p. (J). (gr. -1-3). 9.99 *(978-0-7534-6781-7(X)*, 9780753467817, Kingfisher) Roaring Brook Pr.

Guillain, Charlotte. Brillante U Opaco, 1 vol. 2010. (Las Propiedades de Los Materiales Ser.). (SPA.). 24p. (gr. -1-1). pap. 6.29 *(978-1-4329-4249-6(2)*, Bellota) Heinemann-Raintree.

—Caliente o Frío, 1 vol. 2010. (Las Propiedades de Los Materiales Ser.). (SPA.). 24p. (gr. -1-1). 22.65 *(978-1-4329-4239-7(5))*; pap. 6.29 *(978-1-4329-4247-2(6))* Heinemann-Raintree. (Bellota).

—Liso O Áspero. 2010. (Las Propiedades de Los Materiales Ser.).Tr. of Smooth or Rough. (SPA.). 24p. (gr. -1-1). 22.65 *(978-1-4329-4242-7(5))*; pap. 6.29 *(978-1-4329-4250-2(6))* Heinemann-Raintree. (Bellota).

Hawkins, Jay. Material World: The Science of Matter. 2013. (Big Bang Science Experiments Ser.). (ENG., Illus.). 32p. (gr. 3-6). 26.50 *(978-1-4777-0323-6(3))*; pap. 11.75 *(978-1-4777-0367-0(5))* Windmill Bks.

Hughes, Susan. Is It Transparent or Opaque? 2012. (ENG., Illus.). 24p. (J). *(978-0-7787-2052-2(7))*; pap. *(978-0-7787-2059-1(4))* Crabtree Publishing Co.

Is It Natural or Human-Made? 2014. (ENG., Illus.). 24p. (J). *(978-0-7787-0535-2(8))* Crabtree Publishing Co.

Issues, Evidence & You - Water Mega Module Complete Materials Package. 2003. (Illus.). tchr. ed., ring bd. *(978-1-887725-42-2(3))*; (YA). tchr. ed., stu. ed., per. *(978-1-887725-60-6(1))* Lab-Aids, Inc.

Issues, Evidence & You Complete Materials Package. 2003. (Illus.). (YA). tchr. ed., ring bd. *(978-1-887725-71-2(7))* Lab-Aids, Inc.

Issues, Evidence & You Complete Materials Package: Includes Teacher's Guide & Student Books. 2003. (Illus.). (YA). *(978-1-887725-72-9(5))* Lab-Aids, Inc.

Jennings, Terry. Materials. 2009. (Science Alive Ser.). (Illus.). 32p. (J). (gr. 4-7). pap. *(978-1-897563-58-8(2))* Saunders Bk. Co.

Kalman, Bobbie. What Is It Made From? 2011. (ENG.). 16p. (J). lib. bdg. *(978-0-7787-9562-9(4))*; (My World Ser.: No. 60). pap. *(978-0-7787-9587-2(X))* Crabtree Publishing Co.

Kerrod, Robin. New Materials. 2003. (21st Century Science Ser.). 48p. (J). lib. bdg. 27.10 *(978-1-58340-353-2(1))* Black Rabbit Bks.

Langley, Andrew. Everyday Materials. 2008. (ENG., Illus.). 24p. (J). (gr. 4-7). *(978-0-7787-4125-1(7))* Crabtree Publishing Co.

Law, Felicia. Materials. 2015. (Stone Age Science Ser.). (ENG., Illus.). 32p. (J). *(978-0-7787-1889-5(1))* Crabtree Publishing Co.

Lunis, Natalie. Squishy Sponges. 2007. (No Backbone! Ser.). (Illus.). 24p. (J). (gr. k-3). lib. bdg. 21.28 *(978-1-59716-512-9(3))* Bearport Publishing Co., Inc.

Lüsted, Marcia Amidon. Bit Rot: Preserving the Documents Most Important to You. 2016. (Digital & Information Literacy Ser.). 00048p. (J). (gr. 6-6). pap. 11.75 *(978-1-4994-6515-0(7))* Rosen Publishing Group, Inc., The.

Mason, Adrienne. Touch It! Materials, Matter & You. Dávila, Claudia, illus. 2005. (Primary Physical Science Ser.). (ENG.). 32p. (J). (gr. -1-2). 7.95 *(978-1-55337-761-0(3))* Kids Can Pr., Ltd. CAN. Dist: Hachette Bk. Group.

Materials. 2004. (Illus.). lib. bdg. 7.95 *(978-0-8225-4789-1(9))* Lerner Publishing Group.

Materials & Their Uses, 6 vols., Pack. (Discovery World Ser.). 24p. (gr. 1-2). 33.00 *(978-0-7635-8479-5(7))* Rigby Education.

Mooney, Carla. Becoming Invisible: From Camouflage to Cloaks. 2010. (Great Idea Ser.). 48p. (J). (gr. 4-6). lib. bdg. 26.60 *(978-1-59953-378-0(2))* Norwood Hse. Pr.

Newson, Lesley & Wadsworth, Pamela. Defnyddiau. 2005. (WEL., Illus.). 24p. pap. *(978-1-85596-235-4(7))* Dref Wen.

—Rhagor Am Ddefnyddiau. 2005. (WEL., Illus.). 24p. pap. *(978-1-85596-236-1(5))* Dref Wen.

Newton, David E. Chemistry of New Materials. 2007. (New Chemistry Ser.). (Illus.). 192p. (gr. 6-12). 35.00 *(978-0-8160-5278-3(6))* Facts On File, Inc.

Nunn, Daniel. Buttons & Beads, 1 vol. 2011. (From Trash to Treasures Ser.). (ENG.). 24p. (gr. k-2). 23.32 *(978-1-4329-5152-8(1)*, Heinemann Read & Learn) Heinemann-Raintree.

O'Hara, Nicholas. Sort It by Texture. 2015. (Sort It Out! Ser.). (ENG.). 24p. (J). (gr. k-1). pap. 8.15 *(978-1-4824-2581-9(5))* Stevens, Gareth Publishing LLLP.

Orme, Helen. What Things Are Made Of. 2010. (Science Everywhere! Ser.). 24p. 24.25 *(978-1-84898-298-7(4))* Black Rabbit Bks.

Oxlade, Chris. Calentar, 1 vol. 2010. (Materiales Cambiantes Ser.). (SPA.). 32p. (gr. 1-3). 27.32 *(978-1-4329-4429-2(0))*; pap. 8.95 *(978-1-4329-4434-6(7))* Heinemann-Raintree.

—Cambiar la Forma, 1 vol. 2010. (Materiales Cambiantes Ser.).Tr. of Changing Shape. (SPA & ENG.). 32p. (gr. 1-3). 27.32 *(978-1-4329-4428-5(2))*; pap. 8.95 *(978-1-4329-4433-9(9))* Heinemann-Raintree.

—Changing Materials. 2007. (Working with Materials Ser.). (ENG., Illus.). 32p. (J). (gr. -1-3). pap. *(978-0-7787-3648-6(2))* Crabtree Publishing Co.

—Conductors & Insulators, 1 vol. 2012. (It's Electric! Ser.). (ENG., Illus.). 32p. (gr. 2-4). pap. 8.95 *(978-1-4329-5678-3(7))*; lib. bdg. 26.65 *(978-1-4329-5673-8(6))* Heinemann-Raintree. (NA-h).

—Enfriar, 1 vol. 2010. (Materiales Cambiantes Ser.).Tr. of Cooling. (SPA.). 32p. (gr. 1-3). 27.32 *(978-1-4329-4430-8(4))*; pap. 8.95 *(978-1-4329-4435-3(5))* Heinemann-Raintree.

—Experiments with Matter & Materials, 1 vol. 2015. (ENG.). 32p. (J). lib. bdg. 27.50 *(978-1-4777-5969-1(7)*, PowerKids Pr.) Rosen Publishing Group, Inc., The.

—Heating, 1 vol. 2012. (How Does My Home Work? Ser.). (ENG.). 24p. (gr. k-1). lib. bdg. 23.32 *(978-1-4329-6564-8(6)*, Heinemann Read & Learn) Heinemann-Raintree.

—Joining Materials. 2007. (Working with Materials Ser.). (ENG.). 32p. (J). pap. *(978-0-7787-3649-3(0))*; (Illus.). (gr. -1-3). lib. bdg. *(978-0-7787-3639-4(3))* Crabtree Publishing Co.

—Shaping Materials. 2007. (Working with Materials Ser.). (ENG., Illus.). 32p. (J). (gr. -1-3). pap. *(978-0-7787-3651-6(2))* Crabtree Publishing Co.

Rau, Dana Meachen. Builders. 2007. (J). pap. 6.99 *(978-0-7614-3289-0(2))* Marshall Cavendish Corp.

Rigby Education Staff. Discovery World Red Materials. (Discovery World Ser.). 12p. (gr. 1-2). 31.00 *(978-0-7635-2706-8(8))* Rigby Education.

Riley, Peter. Everyday Materials. 2016. (Ways into Science Ser.). (ENG., Illus.). 32p. (J). (gr. k-2). pap. 11.99 *(978-1-4451-3480-2(2)*, Franklin Watts) Hachette Children's Group GBR. Dist: Hachette Bk. Group.

Riley, Peter D. Materials. 2011. (Real Scientist Investigates Ser.). (Illus.). 32p. (J). (gr. 3-5). lib. bdg. 28.50 *(978-1-59771-282-8(5))* Sea-To-Sea Pubns.

Rising, Heather. Is It Smooth or Rough? 2012. (ENG., Illus.). 24p. (J). *(978-0-7787-2051-5(9))*; pap. *(978-0-7787-2058-4(6))* Crabtree Publishing Co.

Rissman, Rebecca. Materials: Real Size Science, 1 vol. 2013. (Real Size Science Ser.). (ENG.). 24p. (gr. -1-1). 22.65 *(978-1-4329-7878-5(0))*; pap. 6.95 *(978-1-4329-7885-3(3))* Heinemann-Raintree. (Acorn).

Rivera, Sheila. How Does It Feel? (First Step Nonfiction - Properties of Matter Ser.). 2005. (ENG.). 8p. (gr. -1-1). pap. 4.95 *(978-0-8225-5405-9(4))* 2004. (J). lib. bdg. 23.99 *(978-0-8225-2863-0(0))* Lerner Publishing Group. (Lerner Pubns.).

Rustad, Martha E. H. What Is It Made Of? Noticing Types of Materials. Schneider, Christine M., illus. 2015. (ENG.). 24p. (J). (gr. k-2). 25.32 *(978-1-4677-8561-7(X)*, Millbrook Pr.) Lerner Publishing Group.

Smith, A. Materials. 2004. (Internet-Linked Library of Science). 64p. (J). pap. 9.95 *(978-0-7945-0085-6(4)*, Usborne) EDC Publishing.

Snedden, Robert. Materials Engineering & Exploring Properties. 2015. (ENG., Illus.). 32p. (J). *(978-0-7787-7514-0(3))* Crabtree Publishing Co.

Spilsbury, Louise & Spilsbury, Richard. Materials, 1 vol. (Essential Physical Science Ser.). (ENG., 48p. (gr. 4-6). 2014. Illus.). lib. bdg. 33.32 *(978-1-4329-8149-5(8))* 2013. pap. 9.95 *(978-1-4329-8158-7(7))* Heinemann-Raintree. (Heinemann InfoSearch).

Sundance/Newbridge LLC Staff. Properties of Materials. 2007. (Early Science Ser.). (gr. k-3). 18.95 *(978-1-4007-6576-8(5))*; pap. 6.10 *(978-1-4007-6572-0(2))* Sundance/Newbridge Educational Publishing.

Thomas, Isabel. Experiments with Materials. 2015. (Read & Experiment Ser.). (ENG., Illus.). 32p. (gr. 2-4). 30.65 *(978-1-4109-7923-0(7))* Heinemann-Raintree.

Wadsworth, Pamela. Golwg Gyntaf Ar Ddefnyddiau. 2005. (WEL., Illus.). 24p. pap. *(978-1-85596-251-4(9))* Dref Wen.

Ward, D. J. Materials Science. 2009. pap. 52.95 *(978-0-7613-4784-2(4))* 2008. (ENG.). 48p. (gr. 4-8). 27.93 *(978-0-8225-7588-7(4))* Lerner Publishing Group.

Way, Steve. Materials. 2009. (Simply Science Ser.). (Illus.). 32p. (YA). (gr. 3-6). lib. bdg. 26.00 *(978-1-4339-0033-4(5))* Stevens, Gareth Publishing LLLP.

Wood & Other Materials: Individual Title Six-Packs. (Discovery World Ser.). 16p. (gr. 1-2). 28.00 *(978-0-7635-8460-3(6))* Rigby Education.

York, M. J. Henry Ford: Manufacturing Mogul, 1 vol. 2010. (Essential Lives Set 5 Ser.). (ENG.). 112p. (J). (gr. 6-12). lib. bdg. 35.64 *(978-1-61613-514-0(X))* ABDO Publishing Co.

MATERNITY

see Mothers

MATHEMATICAL DRAWING

see Geometrical Drawing; Mechanical Drawing

MATHEMATICAL RECREATIONS

Activity Guide Feast of Fracts. 2004. 40p. (J). *(978-1-59242-147-3(4))* Delta Education, LLC.

Activity Guide Fraction Burger. 2004. 92p. (J). *(978-1-59242-146-6(6))* Delta Education, LLC.

Allen, Robert, et al. Train Your Brain: Brain-Scrambling Challenges. 2015. (Train Your Brain Puzzle Bks.). (ENG.). 96p. (J). (gr. 2-6). pap. 7.99 *(978-1-4380-0766-3(3))* Barron's Educational Series, Inc.

Author, Oxford. Number Challenge Games Interactive: Champion. 2014. (ENG.). 1p. audio compact disk 191.00 *(978-1-874099-91-8(X))* Oxford Univ. Pr., Inc.

—Number Challenge Interactive: Brainbox. 2014. (ENG.). 1p. audio compact disk 191.00 *(978-1-874099-90-1(1))* Oxford Univ. Pr., Inc.

Babb, Joanna. Playing with Numbers: A Playbook to Build Numeracy for 3-7 Year Olds, Including Counting, Measuring, Sizes, Shapes, Patterns, Groups & Telling the Time. 2008. (ENG., Illus.). 64p. (J). (gr. -1-3). pap. 7.99 *(978-1-84476-534-8(2))* Anness Publishing GBR. Dist: National Bk. Network.

Big Book of English & Math. 2003. (Bumper Gold Stars Ser.). (Illus.). 240p. (J). 9.98 *(978-1-4054-1719-8(6))*; 9.98 *(978-1-4054-1720-4(X))* Parragon, Inc.

Blakely, April. Math Brainteasers. 2nd ed. 2005. (Illus.). 90p. (YA). (gr. 8-12). per. 12.95 *(978-1-59647-036-1(4))* Good Year Bks.

Blum, Raymond. Mathamusements. Date not set. (J). 5.95 *(978-0-8069-3190-6(6))* Sterling Publishing Co., Inc.

Blum, Raymond, et al. Giant Book of Science Fun/Giant Book of Math Fun: Flip Book. Sterling Publishing Company Staff, ed. (Illus.). 512p. pap. 9.98 *(978-1-4027-0469-7(0))* Sterling Publishing Co., Inc.

Bortz, Trudy & Rappaport, Josh. Math Games That Roam the Concept Range. Blakemore, Sally, illus. 2010. (Card Game Roundup Ser.: 0). (ENG.). 96p. (gr. -1-3). per. 12.95 *(978-0-9659113-9-9(X))* Singing Turtle Pr.

Cameron, Antonia & Fosnot, Catherine Twomey. Games for Early Number Sense. 2008. (ENG.). 96p. (gr. k-1). pap. 31.25 *(978-0-325-01009-0(9)*, E01009, Firsthand) Heinemann.

Canavan, Thomas. Computation Skills: 50 Math Super Puzzles. 2011. (Math Standards Workout Ser.). (ENG., Illus.). 48p. (YA). (gr. 5-8). pap. 11.75 *(978-1-4488-6680-9(4)*, Rosen Reference); lib. bdg. 29.25 *(978-1-4488-6673-1(1))* Rosen Publishing Group, Inc., The.

—Making Connections: 50 Math Super Puzzles. 2011. (Math Standards Workout Ser.). (ENG., Illus.). 48p. (YA). (gr. 5-8). pap. 11.75 *(978-1-4488-6681-6(2)*, Rosen Reference); lib. bdg. 29.25 *(978-1-4488-6674-8(X))* Rosen Publishing Group, Inc., The.

—Mental Math: 50 Math Super Puzzles. 2011. (Math Standards Workout Ser.). (ENG., Illus.). 48p. (YA). (gr. 5-8). pap. 11.75 *(978-1-4488-6684-7(7)*, Rosen Reference); lib. bdg. 29.25 *(978-1-4488-6677-9(4))* Rosen Publishing Group, Inc., The.

—Number Magic, 1. Mostyn, David, illus. 2014. (Miraculous Magic Tricks Ser.). (ENG.). 32p. (J). (gr. 3-6). 27.50 *(978-1-4777-9069-4(1)*, Windmill Bks.) Rosen Publishing Group, Inc., The.

—Problem Solving: 50 Math Super Puzzles. 2011. (Math Standards Workout Ser.). (ENG., Illus.). 48p. (YA). (gr. 5-8). pap. 11.75 *(978-1-4488-6682-3(0)*, Rosen Reference); lib. bdg. 29.25 *(978-1-4488-6675-5(8))* Rosen Publishing Group, Inc., The.

—Shapes & Symmetry: 50 Math Super Puzzles. 2011. (Math Standards Workout Ser.). (ENG., Illus.). 48p. (YA). (gr. 5-8). pap. 11.75 *(978-1-4488-6683-0(9)*, Rosen Reference); lib. bdg. 29.25 *(978-1-4488-6676-2(6))* Rosen Publishing Group, Inc., The.

—Symbols & Algebra: 50 Math Super Puzzles. 2011. (Math Standards Workout Ser.). (ENG., Illus.). 48p. (YA). (gr. 5-8). pap. 11.75 *(978-1-4488-6685-4(5)*, Rosen Reference); lib. bdg. 29.25 *(978-1-4488-6678-6(2))* Rosen Publishing Group, Inc., The.

Chwast, Seymour & Moskof, Martin. Still Another Number Book. 2014. (ENG., Illus.). 64p. (J). (gr. -1). pap. 9.99 *(978-0-486-49201-8(X))* Dover Pubns., Inc.

Colgan, Lynda. Mathemagic! Number Tricks. Kurisu, Jane, illus. 2011. (ENG.). 40p. (J). (gr. 5-9). 16.95 *(978-1-55453-425-8(9))* Kids Can Pr., Ltd. CAN. Dist: Hachette Bk. Group.

Disney Mickey, Disney. Disney Imagicademy: Math Adventures. 2016. (ENG.). 14p. (J). (gr. -1-2). 12.99 *(978-0-7944-3595-0(5))* Studio Fun International.

Dot-to-Dot 1-100+ Spanish Version. 2007. (J). per. *(978-1-58232-163-9(9))* ECS Learning Systems, Inc.

Eastaway, Rob & Wyndham. Why Do Buses Come in Threes? 2004. (Illus.). 156p. pap. *(978-1-86105-247-6(2)*, Robson Bks. Ltd.) Pavilion Bks.

English/Math 3-4. 2003. (Illus.). 48p. (J). wbk. ed. 7.98 *(978-1-4054-1264-3(X))* Parragon, Inc.

English/Math 4-5. 2003. (Illus.). 48p. (J). wbk. ed. 7.98 *(978-1-4054-1265-0(8))* Parragon, Inc.

English/Math 5-6. 2003. (Illus.). 48p. (J). wbk. ed. 7.98 *(978-1-4054-1266-7(6))* Parragon, Inc.

English/Math 6-7. 2003. (Illus.). 48p. (YA). wbk. ed. 7.98 *(978-1-4054-1267-4(4))* Parragon, Inc.

Faulkner, Keith & Holmes, Stephen. Animal ? Math. Faulkner, Keith & Holmes, Stephen, illus. 2003. (Illus.). (J). *(978-0-439-62755-9(9))* Scholastic, Inc.

Fleisher, Paul. Brain Food: 100+ Games That Make Kids Think. 2008. (ENG.). 208p. (gr. 4-12). pap. 24.95 *(978-1-59363-331-8(9))* Prufrock Pr.

Free Spirit Publishing Staff & Stein, Deborah Jiang. Math. 2009. (In a Jar(r) Ser.). (ENG.). (J). 9.99 *(978-1-57542-937-3(3))* Free Spirit Publishing, Inc.

Freudenthal. Reflections on Numbers. 3rd ed. 2003. (Math in Context Ser.). (Illus.). 7.86 *(978-0-03-071704-8(3))* Holt McDougal.

Ganesan, C. T. Fun with Maths. 2005. (Illus.). 188p. (gr. 4-7). per. *(978-1-84549-027-0(4))* arima publishing.

Gardner, Martin. Mental Magic: Surefire Tricks to Amaze Your Friends. Sinclair, Jeff, illus. 2010. (Dover Children's Activity Bks.). (ENG.). 96p. (J). (gr. 3-5). pap. 4.99 *(978-0-486-47495-3(X))* Dover Pubns., Inc.

Gave, Marc. Number Games Around the World & Juegos de números alrededor del Mundo: 6 English, 6 Spanish Adaptations 2011. (Navigators Ser.). (ENG & SPA.). (J). instr.'s gde. ed. 97.00 net. *(978-1-4108-1765-5(2))* Benchmark Education Co.

George, Rebecca. Super Smart Math: 180 Warm-Ups & Challenging Activities. 2006. (ENG., Illus.). 220p. per. 19.95 *(978-1-59363-200-7(2))* Prufrock Pr.

Hanson, Anders & Mann, Elissa. Cool Flexagon Art: Creative Activities That Make Math & Science Fun for Kids!, 1 vol. 2013. (Cool Art with Math & Science Ser.). (ENG.). 32p. (J). (gr. 3-6). lib. bdg. 28.50 *(978-1-61783-821-7(7)*, Checkerboard Library) ABDO Publishing Co.

—Cool String Art: Creative Activities That Make Math & Science Fun for Kids!, 1 vol. 2013. (Cool Art with Math & Science Ser.). (ENG.). 32p. (J). (gr. 3-6). lib. bdg. 28.50 *(978-1-61783-824-8(1)*, Checkerboard Library) ABDO Publishing Co.

—Cool Structures: Creative Activities That Make Math & Science Fun for Kids!, 1 vol. 2013. (Cool Art with Math & Science Ser.). (ENG.). 32p. (J). (gr. 3-6). lib. bdg. 28.50 *(978-1-61783-825-5(X)*, Checkerboard Library) ABDO Publishing Co.

—Cool Tessellations: Creative Activities That Make Math & Science Fun for Kids!, 1 vol. 2013. (Cool Art with Math & Science Ser.). (ENG.). 32p. (J). (gr. 3-6). lib. bdg. 28.50 *(978-1-61783-826-2(8)*, Checkerboard Library) ABDO Publishing Co.

Highlights for Children Editorial Staff, creator. Numbers, Please! 2015. (Highlights(tm) Puzzlemania(r) Activity Bks.). (ENG.). 144p. (J). (gr. k). pap. 9.95 *(978-1-62979-420-4(1)*, Highlights) Boyds Mills Pr.

Kiernan, Denise. Fractions & Decimals: Familiar & Flexible Games with Dozens of Variations That Help Struggling Learners Practice & Really Master Basic Fraction & Decimal Facts. 2007. (Math Games to Master Basic Skills Ser.). (ENG., Illus.). 48p. pap. 10.99 *(978-0-439-51772-0(9)*, Teaching Resources) Scholastic, Inc.

—Multiplication & Division: Familiar & Flexible Games with Dozens of Variations That Help Struggling Learners Practice & Really Master Multiplication & Division Facts. 2007. (Math Games to Master Basic Skills Ser.). (ENG., Illus.). 48p. pap. 10.99 *(978-0-439-51773-7(7)*, Teaching Resources) Scholastic, Inc.

Leech, Bonnie Coulter. Mesopotamia: Creating & Solving Word Puzzles. 2006. (Math Big Bookstm Ser.). (ENG.). 32p. (gr. 6-7). 47.50 *(978-1-4042-6364-2(0))* Rosen Publishing Group, Inc., The.

Levy, Janey. At Sea on a Viking Ship: Solving Problems of Length & Weight Using the Four Math Operations. 2009. (PowerMath Ser.). (ENG., Illus.). 24p. (gr. 3-4). pap. 8.25 *(978-0-8239-8922-5(4)*, PowerKids Pr.) Rosen Publishing Group, Inc., The.

Lewis, J. Patrick. Arithme-Tickle: An Even Number of Odd Riddle-Rhymes. Remkiewicz, Frank, illus. 2007. (ENG.). 32p. (J). (gr. 1-4). pap. 7.99 *(978-0-15-205848-7(6))* Houghton Mifflin Harcourt Publishing Co.

Linde, Barbara M. Working at the Farmer's Market: Solving Money Problems Involving the Four Math Operations. 2009. (PowerMath Ser.). (Illus.). 24p. (gr. 3-4). pap. 8.25 *(978-0-8239-8920-1(8)*, PowerKids Pr.) Rosen Publishing Group, Inc., The.

Lund, Charles. Math Games & Activies with Cards. 2008. (ENG.). 64p. tchr. ed. 14.95 *(978-1-934218-01-3(4)*, EM 500) IPMG Publishing.

—Math games & activities with Dice. 2008. (ENG.). 84p. pap. 14.95 *(978-1-934218-03-7(0)*, EM 590) IPMG Publishing.

—Place Mat Math, 1. 2009. (ENG.). 14.95 *(978-1-934218-04-4(9)*, EM 595) IPMG Publishing.

Mental Math. 2004. (Help with Homework Ser.). 32p. (J). (gr. 1-4). wbk. ed. 3.99 *(978-1-904586-26-5(0))* Byeway Bks.

Morgan, Rowland. Brain Bafflers. 2003. (Illus.). 96p. (J). pap. 3.99 *(978-0-330-36783-7(8)*, Macmillan Children's Bks.) Pan Macmillan GBR. Dist: Trafalgar Square Publishing.

Neuschwander, Cindy. Sir Cumference & the Sword in the Cone. Geehan, Wayne, illus. 2003. (Make the Math-Literature Connection Ser.). (ENG.). 32p. (J). (gr. 3-7). pap. 7.95 *(978-1-57091-601-4(2))* Charlesbridge Publishing, Inc.

Newman-D'Amico, Fran. My First Book of Number Fun. 2006. (Dover Children's Activity Bks.). (ENG., Illus.). 64p. (J). (gr. -1-2). per. 4.95 *(978-0-486-45226-5(3))* Dover Pubns., Inc.

Niederman, Derrick. Mind-Stretching Math Puzzles. 2005. (Illus.). 112p. (J). *(978-1-4156-0492-2(4))* Sterling Publishing Co., Inc.

Nobleman, Marc Tyler. Math Puzzles: Grades 3 & 4. (Illus.). (J). pap., wbk. ed. 4.99 *(978-0-88743-846-2(6))* School Zone Publishing Co.

Overdeck, Laura. Fun Excuse to Stay up Late. Paillot, Jim, illus. 2013. (Bedtime Math Ser.). (ENG.). 96p. (J). (gr. -1-2). 15.99 *(978-1-250-03585-1(6)*, 9781250035851) Feiwel & Friends.

—This Time It's Personal. Paillot, Jim, illus. 2014. (Bedtime Math Ser.). (ENG.). 96p. (J). (gr. -1-2). 15.99 *(978-1-250-04096-1(5)*, 9781250040961) Feiwel & Friends.

Paré, Roger. Les Chiffres. 2004. (Livres-jeux Ser.). (FRE.). 12p. (J). (gr. -1). pap. *(978-2-89021-654-9(3))* Diffusion du livre Mirabel (DLM).

Pressnall, Debra Olson. Colorful File Folder Games: Skill-Building Center Activities for Language Arts & Math. 2006. (ENG., Illus.). 160p. (gr. -1 — 1). per. 22.99 *(978-0-88724-268-7(5)*, CD-104047) Carson-Dellosa Publishing, LLC.

Prior, Jennifer Overend & Prior, Jennifer. Time & Money: 14 Reproducible Games That Help Struggling Learners Practice & Really Master Basic Time & Money Skills. 2007. (Math Games to Master Basic Skills Ser.). (ENG., Illus.). 48p. pap. 10.99 *(978-0-439-55414-5(4)*, Teaching Resources) Scholastic, Inc.

Rooney, Anne. 50 Amazing Things Kids Need to Know about Math. 2012. (ENG., Illus.). 192p. (J). (gr. 2-7). pap. 12.95 *(978-1-61608-507-0(X)*, 608507, Sky Pony Pr.) Skyhorse Publishing Co., Inc.

Ruffin, Frances E. Creating a City Park: Dividing Three-Digit Numbers by One-Digit Numbers Without Remainders. (PowerMath Ser.). (Illus.). 24p. 2009. (ENG.). (gr. 3-4). pap. 8.25 *(978-0-8239-8926-3(7)*, PowerKids Pr.) 2004. (J). (gr. 5-9). lib. bdg. 22.50 *(978-0-8239-8978-2(X))* Rosen Publishing Group, Inc., The.

—Creating a City Park: Dividing Three-digit Numbers by One-digit Numbers Without Remainders. 2009. (PowerMath: Intermediate Ser.). 24p. (gr. 3-4). 45.00 *(978-1-60851-380-2(7)*, PowerKids Pr.) Rosen Publishing Group, Inc., The.

Sargent, Brian. Grandfather's Shape Story. 2006. (Rookie Read-About Math Ser.). (ENG., Illus.). 32p. (J). (gr. -1-3). 20.50 *(978-0-516-29919-8(0)*, Children's Pr.) Scholastic Library Publishing.

Schwartz, Linda. Math Critical Thinking, Grades 2-4: Creative Puzzles to Challenge the Brain. VanBlaricum, Pam, ed. Armstrong, Bev & Grayson, Rick, illus. 2005. 64p. (J). pap. 11.99 *(978-0-88160-383-5(X)*, LW-422) Creative Teaching Pr., Inc.

Steck-Vaughn Staff. Math Level H-J: How Big Is a Cat? 2003. (Illus.). pap. *(978-0-7398-7657-2(0))* Steck-Vaughn.

Super Sticker Math. Date not set. 64p. (J). 3.98 *(978-0-7525-9774-4(4))* Parragon, Inc.

Tang, Greg. The Grapes of Math. Briggs, Harry, illus. 2004. (Scholastic Bookshelf Ser.). (ENG.). 40p. (J). (gr. 2-5). pap. 6.99 *(978-0-439-59840-8(0)*, Scholastic Paperbacks) Scholastic, Inc.

—The Grapes of Math: Mind-Stretching Math Riddles. Briggs, Harry, illus. 2004. (Scholastic Bookshelf Ser.). (gr. 2-5). 17.00 *(978-0-7569-3195-7(9))* Perfection Learning Corp.

—Math Appeal. Briggs, Harry, illus. 2003. (Mind-Stretching Math Riddles Ser.). (ENG.). 40p. (J). (gr. -1-3). 18.99 *(978-0-439-21046-1(1)*, Scholastic Pr.) Scholastic, Inc.

Thompson, Helen. Travel Math. 2013. (Math 24/7 Ser.: 10). 48p. (J). (gr. 5-18). 19.95 *(978-1-4222-2911-8(4))* Mason Crest.

Tremaine, Jon. Magic with Numbers. 2012. (Illus.). 32p. (gr. 3-5). pap. 8.95 *(978-1-926853-82-6(2))* Saunders Bk. Co. CAN. Dist: RiverStream Publishing.

Weiss, Ellen. Math on the Playground. 2007. (Scholastic News Nonfiction Readers Ser.). (ENG., Illus.). 24p. (J). (gr. 1-2). 22.00 *(978-0-531-18533-9(8))* Scholastic Library Publishing.

Yoder, Eric & Yoder, Natalie. One Minute Mysteries: 65 Short Mysteries You Solve with Math! 2010. (One Minute Mysteries Ser.). (ENG., Illus.). 192p. (J). (gr. 5-9). pap. 12.95 *(978-0-9678020-0-8(8))* Platypus Media, L.L.C.

Zaslavsky, Claudia. More Math Games & Activities from Around the World. 2003. (ENG.). 176p. (J). (gr. 4). pap. 16.95 *(978-1-55652-501-8(X))* Chicago Review Pr., Inc.

MATHEMATICAL SETS

see Set Theory

MATHEMATICIANS

Alan Turing: Computing Genius & Wartime Code Breaker. 2011. (Makers of Modern Science Ser.). (Illus.). 160p. (J). (gr. 6-12). 35.00 *(978-0-8160-6175-4(0)*, Chelsea Hse.) Facts On File, Inc.

Bailey, Gerry & Foster, Karen. Galileo's Telescope. Noyes, Leighton & Radford, Karen, illus. 2008. (Stories of Great People Ser.). (ENG.). 40p. (J). (gr. 3-6). lib. bdg. *(978-0-7787-3694-3(6))*; pap. *(978-0-7787-3716-2(0))* Crabtree Publishing Co.

Bodden, Valerie. Programming Pioneer ADA Lovelace. 2016. (STEM Trailblazer Bios Ser.). (ENG.). 32p. (J). (gr. 2-5). 26.65 *(978-1-5124-0784-6(4))* Lerner Publishing Group.

Bradley, Michael J. The Birth of Mathematics: Ancient Times To 1300. 2006. (Pioneers in Math Ser.). (Illus.). 160p. (YA). (gr. 7-12). 35.00 *(978-0-8160-5423-7(1))* Facts On File, Inc.

—The Foundations of Mathematics: 1800 To 1900. 2006. (Pioneers in Math Ser.). (Illus.). 176p. (YA). (gr. 7-12). 35.00 *(978-0-8160-5425-1(8))* Facts On File, Inc.

—Mathematics Frontiers: 1950 to Present. 2006. (Pioneers in Math Ser.). (Illus.). 160p. (YA). (gr. 7-12). 35.00 *(978-0-8160-5427-5(4))* Facts On File, Inc.

—Modern Mathematics: 1900-1950. 2006. (Pioneers in Math Ser.). (Illus.). 176p. (YA). (gr. 7-12). 35.00 *(978-0-8160-5426-8(6))* Facts On File, Inc.

Campbell, Josette & Hayhurst, Chris. Euclid: The Father of Geometry. 2015. (Greatest Greek Philosophers Ser.). (ENG., Illus.). 112p. (J). (gr. 7-8). 35.60 *(978-1-4994-6128-2(3)*, Rosen Young Adult) Rosen Publishing Group, Inc., The.

Coakley, Louis C., ed. Top 101 Mathematicians. 2016. (People You Should Know Ser.). 184p. (J). (gr. 8-8). lib. bdg. 36.25 *(978-1-68048-508-0(3))* Rosen Publishing Group, Inc., The.

Coakley, Louis C. & Karamanides, Dimitra. Pythagoras: Mathematician & Mystic. 2015. (Greatest Greek Philosophers Ser.). (ENG., Illus.). 112p. (J). (gr. 7-8). 35.60 *(978-1-4994-6132-9(1)*, Rosen Young Adult) Rosen Publishing Group, Inc., The.

Collier, Bruce & Maclachlan, James. Charles Babbage & the Engines of Perfection. 2006. (Illus.). 123p. reprint ed. pap. 12.00 *(978-1-4223-5040-9(1))* DIANE Publishing Co.

Corrigan, Jim. Alan Turing. 2007. (Profiles in Mathematics Ser.). 112p. (J). (gr. 4-7). lib. bdg. 28.95 *(978-1-59935-064-6(5))* Reynolds, Morgan Inc.

Faulkner, Nicholas & Hosch, William L. Algebra & Trigonometry. 2017. (J). lib. bdg. ***(978-1-68048-774-9(4))*** Rosen Publishing Group, Inc., The.

Flood, Raymond & Wilson, Robin. Great Mathematicians. 2012. (Great People in History Ser.). (ENG., Illus.). 128p. (YA). (gr. 8-12). 34.60 *(978-1-4777-0402-8(7))* Rosen Publishing Group, Inc., The.

Gow, Mary. Archimedes: Genius Mathematician. 2015. (Genius Scientists & Their Genius Ideas Ser.). 96p. (J). (gr. 5-12). 27.94 *(978-0-7660-6530-7(8))*; pap. 10.95 *(978-0-7660-6531-4(6))* Enslow Pubs., Inc.

—Archimedes: Mathematical Genius of the Ancient World. 2005. (Great Minds of Science Ser.). (Illus.). 128p. (J). (gr. 4-10). lib. bdg. 27.94 *(978-0-7660-2502-8(0))* Enslow Pubs., Inc.

—Measuring the Earth: Eratosthenes & His Celestial Geometry. 2009. (Great Minds of Ancient Science & Math Ser.). (Illus.). 128p. (J). (gr. 4-7). lib. bdg. 33.27 *(978-0-7660-3120-3(9))* Enslow Pubs., Inc.

Graham, Amy. Astonishing Ancient World Scientists: Eight Great Brains. 2009. (Great Scientists & Famous Inventors Ser.). (Illus.). 128p. (J). (gr. 5-9). lib. bdg. 34.60 *(978-1-59845-079-8(4))* Enslow Pubs., Inc.

Gunzehauser, Kelly. Find Your Future in Mathematics. 2016. (Bright Futures Press: Find Your Future in STEAM Ser.). (ENG., Illus.). 32p. (J). (gr. 4-6). 29.93 *(978-1-63471-902-5(6)*, 208929) Cherry Lake Publishing.

Hagler, Gina. ADA Lovelace, 01 vols., 1. 2016. (Tech Pioneers Ser.). (ENG.). 112p. (J). 35.60 *(978-1-4994-6282-1(4)*, Rosen Young Adult) Rosen Publishing Group, Inc., The.

—Careers for Tech Girls in Math. 2015. (Tech Girls Ser.). (ENG., Illus.). 80p. (J). (gr. 7-8). 34.25 *(978-1-4994-6101-5(1)*, Rosen Young Adult) Rosen Publishing Group, Inc., The.

Hasan, Heather. Archimedes: The Father of Mathematics. (Library of Greek Philosophers Ser.). 112p. 2009. (gr. 6-6). 66.50 *(978-1-60853-657-3(2)*, Rosen Reference) 2005. (Illus.). (YA). (gr. 5-9). lib. bdg. 34.60 *(978-1-4042-0774-5(0))* Rosen Publishing Group, Inc., The.

Heiligman, Deborah. The Boy Who Loved Math: The Improbable Life of Paul Erdös. Pham, LeUyen, illus. 2013. (ENG.). 48p. (J). (gr. -1-2). 18.99 *(978-1-59643-307-6(8)*, 9781596433076) Roaring Brook Pr.

Hightower, Paul. The Father of Geometry: Euclid & His 3-D World. 2010. (Great Minds of Ancient Science & Math Ser.). 112p. (J). 33.27 *(978-0-7660-3409-9(7))* Enslow Pubs., Inc.

—The Greatest Mathematician: Archimedes & His Eureka! Moment. 2009. (Great Minds of Ancient Science & Math Ser.). (Illus.). 128p. (J). (gr. 4-7). lib. bdg. 33.27 *(978-0-7660-3408-2(9))* Enslow Pubs., Inc.

Jones, Viola & Hasan, Heather. Archimedes: Innovative Mathematician, Engineer, & Inventor. 2015. (Greatest Greek Philosophers Ser.). (ENG., Illus.). 112p. (J). (gr. 7-8). 35.60 *(978-1-4994-6124-4(0)*, Rosen Young Adult) Rosen Publishing Group, Inc., The.

Keating, Susan. Archimedes: Ancient Greek Mathematician. 2013. (People of Importance Ser.: 21). (Illus.). 32p. (J). (gr. 4-18). 19.95 *(978-1-4222-2841-8(X))* Mason Crest.

Kraft Rector, Rebecca. Alan Turing, 01 vols., 1. 2016. (Tech Pioneers Ser.). (ENG.). 112p. (J). 35.60 *(978-1-4994-6280-7(8)*, Rosen Young Adult) Rosen Publishing Group, Inc., The.

Labrecque, Ellen. Ada Lovelace & Computer Algorithms. 2017. (21st Century Junior Library: Women Innovators Ser.). (ENG., Illus.). 24p. (J). (gr. 2-5). lib. bdg. 27.07 *(978-1-63472-177-6(2)*, 209280) Cherry Lake Publishing.

Leech, Bonnie. Geometry's Great Thinkers: The History of Geometry. 2009. (PowerMath: Advanced Proficiency Plus Ser.). 32p. (gr. 5-5). 47.90 *(978-1-60851-355-0(6)*, PowerKids Pr.) Rosen Publishing Group, Inc., The.

Leech, Bonnie Coulter. Geometry's Great Thinkers: The History of Geometry. (Math for the Real World Ser.). (Illus.). 32p. 2009. (ENG.). (gr. 6-7). pap. 10.00 *(978-1-4042-6073-3(0))* 2006. (YA). (gr. 5-9). lib. bdg. 25.25 *(978-1-4042-3360-7(1))* Rosen Publishing Group, Inc., The.

Lew, Kristi. ADA Lovelace: Mathematician & First Programmer. 2017. (J). ***(978-1-5383-0022-0(2))*** Rosen Publishing Group, Inc., The.

Lim, Bridget & Brezina, Corona. Al-Khwarizmi. 2016. (Physicians, Scientists, & Mathematicians of the Islamic World Ser.). 112p. (J). (gr. 6-6). 37.10 *(978-1-5081-7144-7(0))* Rosen Publishing Group, Inc., The.

Love, D. Anne. Of Numbers & Stars: The Story of Hypatia. Paparone, Pamela & Paparone, Pam, illus. 2006. (ENG.). 32p. (J). (gr. 4-8). 16.95 *(978-0-8234-1621-9(6))* Holiday Hse., Inc.

Nichols, Susan. Al-Karaji: Tenth Century Mathematician & Engineer. 2016. (Physicians, Scientists, & Mathematicians of the Islamic World Ser.). 112p. (J). (gr. 6-6). 37.10 *(978-1-5081-7143-0(2))* Rosen Publishing Group, Inc., The.

Pioneers in Math, 5 vols., Set. 2006. (Pioneers in Math Ser.). 128p. (gr. 6-12). 175.00 *(978-0-8160-5422-0(3))* Facts On File, Inc.

Profiles in Mathematics, vols. 7, vol. 7. Incl. Alan Turing. Corrigan, Jim. 112p. 2007. lib. bdg. 28.95 *(978-1-59935-064-6(5))*; Carl Friedrich Gauss. West, Krista. (Illus.). 112p. 2008. lib. bdg. 28.95 *(978-1-59935-063-9(7))*; René Descartes. Gimbel, Steven. (Illus.). 128p. 2008. lib. bdg. 28.95 *(978-1-59935-060-8(2))*; Sophie Germain. Ornes, Stephen. (Illus.). 112p. 2008. lib. bdg. 28.95 *(978-1-59935-062-2(9))*; Women Mathematicians. Venkatraman, Padma. (Illus.). 160p. 2008. lib. bdg. 28.95 *(978-1-59935-091-2(2))*; (J). (gr. 4-7). 2008. Set lib. bdg. 202.65 *(978-1-59935-093-6(9))* Reynolds, Morgan Inc.

Reed, Jennifer. Computer Scientist Jean Bartik. 2016. (STEM Trailblazer Bios Ser.). (ENG., Illus.). 32p. (J). (gr. 2-5). 26.65 *(978-1-5124-0789-1(5))* Lerner Publishing Group.

Robinson, Fiona. Ada's Ideas: The Story of Ada Lovelace, the World's First Computer Programmer. 2016. (ENG., Illus.). 40p. (J). (gr. 1-4). 17.95 *(978-1-4197-1872-4(X)*, Abrams Bks. for Young Readers) Abrams, Inc.

Rooney, Anne. Alan Turing & His Binary Computer Code. 2012. (Miracle Makers Ser.). (ENG., Illus.). 48p. (YA). (gr. 5-8). 27.95 *(978-1-4488-6037-1(7)*, Rosen Reference) Rosen Publishing Group, Inc., The.

Schwartz, Heather E. Code-Breaker & Mathematician Alan Turing. 2017. (J). ***(978-1-5124-9980-3(3))*** Lerner Publishing Group.

—NASA Mathematician Katherine Johnson. 2017. (STEM Trailblazer Bios Ser.). (ENG.). 32p. (J). (gr. 2-5). 26.65 ***(978-1-5124-5703-2(5))*** Lerner Publishing Group.

Shaffer, Jody Jensen. Benjamin Banneker: Self-Made Man. 2016. (Primary Source Readers Ser.). (Illus.). 32p. (J). (gr. 4-5). pap. 8.99 *(978-1-4938-3082-4(1))* Teacher Created Materials, Inc.

Sheen, Barbara. Careers If You Like Math. 2016. (ENG.). 80p. (YA). (gr. 5-12). *(978-1-68282-004-9(1))* ReferencePoint Pr., Inc.

Sherman, Josepha. Charles Babbage & the Story of the First Computer. 2005. (Uncharted, Unexplored, & Unexplained Ser.). (Illus.). 48p. (J). (gr. 4-8). lib. bdg. 29.95 *(978-1-58415-372-6(5))* Mitchell Lane Pubs., Inc.

Shetterly, Margot Lee. Hidden Figures. Freeman, Laura, illus. 2018. (ENG.). 40p. (J). (gr. -1-3). 17.99 ***(978-0-06-274246-9(9))*** HarperCollins Pubs.

—Hidden Figures. 2016. 240p. (J). (gr. 3-7). 16.99 *(978-0-06-266238-5(4))*; (Illus.). pap. 7.99 *(978-0-06-266237-8(6))* HarperCollins Pubs.

—Hidden Figures. 2016. (Illus.). 231p. (J). lib. bdg. 18.40 ***(978-0-606-39623-3(3))*** Turtleback Bks.

Stanley, Diane. Ada Lovelace. Hartland, Jessie, illus. 2016. (ENG.). 40p. (J). (gr. -1-3). 17.99 *(978-1-4814-5249-6(5)*, Simon & Schuster Bks. For Young Readers) Simon & Schuster Bks. For Young Readers.

Steffens, Bradley. Big Data Analyst. 2017. (ENG.). 64p. (YA). (gr. 5-12). ***(978-1-68282-176-3(5))*** ReferencePoint Pr., Inc.

Sullivan, Anne Marie. Sir Isaac Newton: Famous English Scientist. 2013. (People of Importance Ser.: 21). (Illus.). 32p. (J). (gr. 4-18). 19.95 *(978-1-4222-2856-2(8))* Mason Crest.

Sullivan, Erin. Mathematical Thinkers & Los Matemáticos: 6 English, 6 Spanish Adaptations, 122 vols., Vol. 2. 2011. (Navigators Ser.). (ENG & SPA.). (J). instr.'s gde. ed. 97.00 net. *(978-1-4108-1773-0(3)*, 17733) Benchmark Education Co.

Tent, M. B. W. Emmy Noether: The Mother of Modern Algebra. 2008. (ENG., Illus.). 184p. (C). 35.95 *(978-1-56881-430-8(5)*, K00391) AK Peters, Ltd.

Wallmark, Laurie. Ada Byron Lovelace & the Thinking Machine. Chu, April, illus. 2015. (ENG.). 40p. (J). (gr. k). 17.99 *(978-1-939547-20-0(2))* Creston Bks.

Zannos, Susan. The Life & Times of Archimedes. 2004. (Biography from Ancient Civilizations Ser.). (Illus.). 48p. (J). (gr. 4-8). lib. bdg. 29.95 *(978-1-58415-242-2(7))* Mitchell Lane Pubs., Inc.

MATHEMATICS

see also Algebra; Arithmetic; Binary System (Mathematics); Calculus; Geometry; Measurement; Mechanics; Number Theory; Set Theory; Trigonometry

ABDO Publishing Company Staff & Kompelien, Tracy. Math Made Fun. 2007. (Math Made Fun Ser.: 24). (ENG.). 24p. (J). (gr. k-3). lib. bdg. 581.04 *(978-1-59928-503-0(7)*, SandCastle) ABDO Publishing Co.

Aboff, Marcie. If You Were a Set [LTD Commodities]. Dillard, Sarah, illus. 2010. (Math Fun Ser.). 24p. pap. 3.50 *(978-1-4048-6258-6(7)*, Nonfiction Picture Bks.) Picture Window Bks.

Abramson, Marcie F. Painless Math Word Problems. 2nd rev. ed. 2010. (Painless Ser.). (ENG.). 288p. pap. 11.99 *(978-0-7641-4335-9(2))* Barron's Educational Series, Inc.

Accelerated Curriculum for Mathematics Grade 11 Exit TAKS Teacher Edition. 2005. (Region IV ESC Resources for Mathematics Ser.). spiral bd. *(978-1-932797-25-1(4))* Region IV Education Service Ctr.

Accelerated Curriculum for Mathematics Grade 5 Student Edition Spanish. 2005. (Region IV ESC Resources for Mathematics Ser.). (SPA.). (J). (gr. 5). stu. ed., spiral bd. *(978-1-932797-83-1(1))* Region IV Education Service Ctr.

Accelerated Math Learning Cards - Basic Math. 2004. 199.00 *(978-1-59455-122-2(7))* Renaissance Learning, Inc.

Accelerated Math West Virginia State Tagged Grade 3 Library. 2004. cd-rom 1199.00 *(978-1-59455-107-9(3))* Renaissance Learning, Inc.

Accelerated Math West Virginia State Tagged Grade 5 Library. 2004. cd-rom 1199.00 *(978-1-59455-109-3(X))* Renaissance Learning, Inc.

Accelerated Math West Virginia State Tagged Grade 6 Library. 2004. cd-rom 1199.00 *(978-1-59455-110-9(3))* Renaissance Learning, Inc.

Accelerated Math West Virginia State Tagged Grade 7 Library. 2004. cd-rom 1199.00 *(978-1-59455-111-6(1))* Renaissance Learning, Inc.

Accelerated Math West Virginia State Tagged Pre-Algebra Library. 2004. cd-rom 1199.00 *(978-1-59455-112-3(X))* Renaissance Learning, Inc.

ACT Mathematics Victory Student Textbook. 2nd ed. 2005. per. *(978-1-58894-031-5(4))* Cambridge Educational Services, Inc.

Activities for Base Ten Blocks. rev. ed. 2004. (J). per. 9.95 *(978-1-56911-547-3(8))* Learning Resources, Inc.

Activity Cards for Equivalency Cubes. 2004. (J). 12.95 *(978-1-56911-925-9(2))* Learning Resources, Inc.

Adams, Jim, Sr., creator. Math Made Easy As 1+2+3= 2003. (Illus.). 24p. spiral bd. 16.99 *(978-0-9729189-4-7(9))* Adams Publishing.

Adams, Presley. Let's Go to Acadia National Park: Solve Problems Involving the Four Operations, 1 vol. 2015. (InfoMax Common Core Math Readers Ser.). (ENG.). 24p. (J). pap. 8.25 *(978-1-4777-4687-5(0)*, Rosen Classroom) Rosen Publishing Group, Inc., The.

Adams, Scott. Ben's Bug Collection: Understanding Addition. 2013. (Rosen Math Readers Ser.). (ENG.). 16p. (J). (gr. k-1). pap. 42.00 *(978-1-4777-1621-2(1))*; (Illus.). pap. 7.00 *(978-1-4777-1620-5(3))* Rosen Publishing Group, Inc., The. (Rosen Classroom).

Adamson, Thomas K. & Adamson, Heather. 2, 4, Skip Count Some More, 1 vol. 2012. (Fun with Numbers Ser.). (ENG.). 32p. (gr. 1-2). pap. 8.10 *(978-1-4296-7856-8(9))*; lib. bdg. 27.32 *(978-1-4296-7707-3(4))* Capstone Press of Coughlan Cos. (Aplus Bks.).

Adbåge, Emma. Outdoor Math: Fun Activities for Every Season. Adbåge, Emma, illus. 2016. (ENG., Illus.). 26p. (J). (gr. k-3). 15.95 *(978-1-77138-612-8(6))* Kids Can Pr., Ltd. CAN. Dist: Hachette Bk. Group.

Add-On Package. 2003. 187.95 *(978-0-673-76009-8(X))*; 129.95 *(978-0-673-76011-1(1))*; 187.95 *(978-0-673-76007-4(3))* Celebration Pr.

Adding. 2003. (Gold Star Workbooks Ser.). (Illus.). 32p. (J). 2.98 *(978-1-4054-1191-2(0))*; 2.98 *(978-1-4054-1190-5(2))* Parragon, Inc.

Adler, David A. Fractions, Decimals, & Percents. Miller, Edward, illus. 2010. (ENG.). 32p. (J). (gr. 1-5). 17.95 *(978-0-8234-2199-2(6))* Holiday Hse., Inc.

—Fun with Roman Numerals. Miller, Edward, III, illus. (ENG.). 32p. (J). (gr. 1-5). 2009. pap. 6.95 *(978-0-8234-2255-5(0))* 2008. 16.95 *(978-0-8234-2060-5(4))* Holiday Hse., Inc.

—Let's Estimate: A Book about Estimating & Rounding Numbers. Miller, Edward, illus. 2017. (ENG.). 32p. (J). (gr. 1-5). 17.95 *(978-0-8234-3668-2(3))* Holiday Hse., Inc.

—Place Value. Miller, Edward, illus. 2016. (ENG.). 32p. (J). (gr. k-3). 17.95 *(978-0-8234-3550-0(4))* Holiday Hse., Inc.

—You Can, Toucan, Math: Word Problem-Solving Fun. Miller, Edward, illus. 2006. (ENG.). 32p. (J). (gr. -1-3). 17.95 *(978-0-8234-1919-7(3))* Holiday Hse., Inc.

Advanced Mathematics: Precalculus with Discrete Mathematics & Data Analysis. 2003. (gr. 11-12). tchr. ed. *(978-0-618-25039-4(5)*, 2-06020) Holt McDougal.

Aihara, Masaaki & Sarris, Eno, eds. Grade 1 Addition: Kumon Math Workbooks. 2008. (J). per. 7.95 *(978-1-933241-49-4(7))* Kumon Publishing North America, Inc.

—Grade 1 Subtraction: Kumon Math Workbooks. 2008. (J). per. 7.95 *(978-1-933241-50-0(0))* Kumon Publishing North America, Inc.

—Grade 3 Addition & Subtraction: Kumon Math Workbooks. 2008. (J). per. 7.95 *(978-1-933241-53-1(5))* Kumon Publishing North America, Inc.

—Grade 3 Division: Kumon Math Workbooks. 2008. (J). per. 7.95 *(978-1-933241-55-5(1))* Kumon Publishing North America, Inc.

—Grade 3 Multiplication: Kumon Math Workbooks. 2008. (J). per. 7.95 *(978-1-933241-54-8(3))* Kumon Publishing North America, Inc.

—Grade 4 Division: Kumon Math Workbooks. 2008. (J). per. 7.95 *(978-1-933241-57-9(8))* Kumon Publishing North America, Inc.

—Grade 4 Multiplication: Kumon Math Workbooks. 2008. (J). per. 7.95 *(978-1-933241-56-2(X))* Kumon Publishing North America, Inc.

Alaina, Maria. Adding Animals, 1 vol. 2013. (Wonder Readers Next Steps: Math Ser.). (ENG.). 20p. (gr. -1-1). lib. bdg. 22.65 *(978-1-4765-0032-4(0)*, Wonder Readers) Capstone Press of Coughlan Cos.

—Both Sides Are the Same, 1 vol. 2011. (Wonder Readers Early Level Ser.). (ENG.). 32p. (gr. -1-1). pap. 5.99 *(978-1-4296-7797-4(X)*, Wonder Readers) Capstone Press of Coughlan Cos.

—Estimating, 1 vol. 2011. (Wonder Readers Early Level Ser.). (ENG.). 32p. (gr. -1-1). pap. 5.99 *(978-1-4296-7802-5(X)*, Wonder Readers) Capstone Press of Coughlan Cos.

—Patterns in Nature, 1 vol. (Wonder Readers Next Steps: Math Ser.). (ENG.). (gr. -1-1). 2013. 20p. lib. bdg. 22.65 *(978-1-4765-0034-8(7))* 2011. 16p. pap. 35.94 *(978-1-4296-8138-4(1))* 2011. 32p. pap. 5.99 *(978-1-4296-7815-5(1))* Capstone Press of Coughlan Cos. (Wonder Readers).

—Wonder Readers Next Steps: Math. 2013. (Wonder Readers Next Steps: Math Ser.). (ENG.). 20p. (gr. -1-1). lib. bdg. 181.20 *(978-1-4765-3751-1(8))*; lib. bdg. 90.60 *(978-1-4765-3752-8(6))*; lib. bdg. 90.60 *(978-1-4765-0044-7(4))* Capstone Press of Coughlan Cos. (Wonder Readers).

Alexander, Emmett. Tamaños / Sort It by Size. de la Vega, Eida, tr. from SPA. 2015. (Vamos a Agrupar Por... / Sort It Out! Ser.). (ENG & SPA., Illus.). 24p. (J). (gr. k-1). lib. bdg. 22.60 *(978-1-4824-3219-0(6))* Stevens, Gareth Publishing LLLP.

Alpha Omega Publishing Staff. Mathematics, 2 bks., Set. 2004. (Illus.). pap. 59.95 *(978-0-7403-0313-5(9)*, JKC120, Horizons) Alpha Omega Pubns., Inc.

Amazing World of Science & Math. 2016. (Amazing World of Science & Math Ser.). 48p. (gr. 5-5). pap. 56.20 *(978-1-4824-5335-5(5))*; lib. bdg. 127.80 *(978-1-4824-4970-9(6))* Stevens, Gareth Publishing LLLP.

America's Math Teacher. Mastering Essential Math Skills Book Two: Middle Grades/High School: 20 Minutes a Day to Success. 2007. (Mastering Essential Math Skills Ser.). (Illus.). 127p. (J). (gr. 6-13). pap. 39.95 *(978-0-9821901-1-1(5))* Math Essentials.

Analysis II: Differenzierbarkeit von Funktionen und Kurvendiskussion. (Duden Abiturhilfen Ser.). (GER.). 112p. (YA). (gr. 11-12). *(978-3-411-70172-8(2))* Bibliographisches Institut & F. A. Brockhaus AG DEU. Dist: International Bk. Import Service, Inc.

Anderson, Lynne. The Aquarium Adds Up: Set Of 6. 2011. (Early Connections Ser.). (J). pap. 37.00 net. *(978-1-4108-1070-0(4))* Benchmark Education Co.

Andres, Ken & Johnson, Diane. Math Go Figure Student Book. 2004. 160p. per. *(978-1-59318-179-6(5))* Cambium Education, Inc.

Andrews, Ken & Johnson, Diane. You Can Be Algebra Ready. 2003. Pt. 1. 244p. spiral bd. *(978-1-57035-848-7(6)*, 185STU1)Pt. 2. 256p. spiral bd. *(978-1-57035-849-4(4)*, 185STU2) Cambium Education, Inc.

Apple, Michael W. Rosie the Counting Rabbit. (J). (gr. k-2). 75.00 *(978-0-669-13447-6(3))* Houghton Mifflin Harcourt School Pubs.

Applied Mathematics. 2016. (Applied Mathematics Ser.). 128p. (gr. 9-9). lib. bdg. 273.84 *(978-1-5026-2003-3(0))* Cavendish Square Publishing.

Arcturus Publishing. Math Is Awesome! 101 Incredible Things Every Kid Should Know. 2017. (ENG.). 128p. (J). pap. 9.95 *(978-1-78599-873-7(0)*, 9781785998737) Arcturus Publishing GBR. Dist: Bookmasters Distribution.

Arcturus Publishing Staff. Magic Adding & Subtracting. 2013. (ENG.). 24p. (J). 9.95 *(978-1-78212-219-7(2))* Arcturus Publishing GBR. Dist: Bookmasters Distribution.

Arias, Lisa. Edgy Equations: One-Variable Equations. 2014. (ENG.). 32p. (gr. 3-6). 32.79 *(978-1-62717-721-4(3))* Rourke Educational Media.

—Multiplication Meltdown: Factors & Multiples. 2014. (ENG.). 32p. (gr. 3-6). 32.79 *(978-1-62717-711-5(6))* Rourke Educational Media.

—Powerful Place Value: Patterns & Power. 2014. (ENG.). 32p. (gr. 3-6). 32.79 *(978-1-62717-707-8(8))* Rourke Educational Media.

Arlene, Sonday. The Sonday System - Let's Play Learn: Shapes & Numbers Book. Cindy, Breckman, ed. l.t. ed. 2004. (Illus.). 29p. (J). per. *(978-1-891602-12-2(8))* Winsor Learning, Inc.

Arroyo, Sheri, et al. How Crime Fighters Use Math. 2009. (Math in the Real World Ser.). 32p. (gr. 4-6). 28.00 *(978-1-60413-602-9(2)*, Chelsea Clubhouse) Facts On File, Inc.

—How Race Car Drivers Use Math. 2009. (Math in the Real World Ser.). 32p. (gr. 4-6). 28.00 *(978-1-60413-609-8(X)*, Chelsea Clubhouse) Facts On File, Inc.

Arthur's Christmas Cookies. 2003. 22.95 *(978-0-673-75906-1(7))* Celebration Pr.

Aseervatham, Aloysius & Aseervatham, Leslie. Graduated Numerical Skills: For the Young Scholar. 2011. (Illus.). 268p. pap. 74.94 *(978-1-4567-7355-7(0))* AuthorHouse.

Asker, Nick & Morrison, Karen. GCSE Mathematics for OCR Foundation Homework Book. 2015. (GCSE Mathematics OCR Ser.). (ENG.). 118p. pap. 10.30 *(978-1-107-49700-9(0))* Cambridge Univ. Pr.

Atkinson, Sue. New Cambridge Mathematics. 2005. (WEL., Illus.). 32p. pap. *(978-1-86085-267-1(X))* ICA Video.

Austin, Judi. Making My Breakfast: Learning the Sequential Steps of a Process. 2009. (Math for the REAL World Ser.). 12p. (gr. 1-2). pap. 5.90 *(978-0-8239-8889-1(9)*, Rosen Classroom) Rosen Publishing Group, Inc., The.

Avenues PreK Level: Plastic Magnetic Numbers. (gr. -1-12). 11.04 *(978-0-7362-2467-3(X))* CENGAGE Learning.

Awal, Pia. Travel Math. 2008. (Math Alive! Ser.). 32p. (gr. 4-18). lib. bdg. 28.50 *(978-0-7614-3217-3(5)*, Benchmark Bks.) Marshall Cavendish Corp.

Babb, Joanna. Playing with Numbers: A Playbook to Build Numeracy for 3-7 Year Olds, Including Counting, Measuring, Sizes, Shapes, Patterns, Groups & Telling the Time. 2008. (ENG., Illus.). 64p. (J). (gr. -1-3). pap. 7.99 *(978-1-84476-534-8(2))* Anness Publishing GBR. Dist: National Bk. Network.

Bailey, Rhonda, et al. Mathematics: Applications & Concepts. 2004. (MATH APPLIC & CONN CRSE Ser.). (ENG., Illus.). 736p. (gr. 5-6). stu. ed. 101.60 *(978-0-07-865253-0(7)*, 0078652537) McGraw-Hill Higher Education.

Baker, David & Kervegant, Ffion. Allwedd Mathemateg 71. 2005. (WEL., Illus.). 416p. pap. *(978-1-85644-427-9(9))* CAA.

—Allwedd Mathemateg 83. 2005. (WEL., Illus.). 382p. pap. *(978-1-85644-576-4(3))* CAA.

—Allwedd Mathemateg TGAU. 2005. (WEL., Illus.). 508p. pap. *(978-1-85644-862-8(2))* CAA.

Baker, David, et al. Allwedd Mathemateg TGAU. Jones, Eirian, ed. Kervegant, Ffion, tr. 2005. (WEL., Illus.). 468p. pap. *(978-1-85644-863-5(0))* CAA.

Baker, Linda R. Learning Division with Puppies & Kittens. 2017. (J). pap. ***(978-0-7660-9073-6(6))*** Enslow Pubs., Inc.

—Learning Multiplication with Puppies & Kittens. 2017. (J). pap. ***(978-0-7660-9072-9(8))*** Enslow Pubs., Inc.

—Using Math in Cooking. 2017. (Math You Will Actually Use Ser.). 48p. (J). (gr. 10-10). pap. 11.75 ***(978-1-4994-3856-7(7)***, Rosen Central) Rosen Publishing Group, Inc., The.

Ball, Barbara & Ball, Derek. Task Maths Interactive 1: Sequence Machines. 2005. (ENG.). cd-rom 190.00 *(978-1-84565-124-4(3))* Cambridge Univ. Pr.

—Task Maths Interactive 3: Is it Possible? 2006. (ENG.). cd-rom 190.00 *(978-1-84565-946-2(5))* Cambridge Univ. Pr.

—Task Maths Interactive 4: Number Pyramids. 2006. (ENG.). cd-rom 177.00 *(978-1-84565-947-9(3))* Cambridge Univ. Pr.

Ball, Johnny. Go Figure! A Totally Cool Book about Numb. 2016. (Big Questions Ser.). (ENG., Illus.). 96p. (J). (gr. 3-7). pap. 9.99 *(978-1-4654-4385-4(1)*, DK Children) Dorling Kindersley Publishing, Inc.

—Why Pi? 2016. (Big Questions Ser.). (ENG., Illus.). 96p. (J). (gr. 2-5). pap. 9.99 *(978-1-4654-4387-8(8)*, DK Children) Dorling Kindersley Publishing, Inc.

Ball, Susan, et al. Formula One Mathematics Gold. 2003. (Illus.). 216p. pap., pupil's gde. ed. 39.50 *(978-0-340-86932-1(1)*, Hodder Education) Hodder Education Group GBR. Dist: Trans-Atlantic Pubns., Inc.

—Formula One Maths Gold B. 2004. (Illus.). 240p. pap., pupil's gde. ed. 39.50 *(978-0-340-86933-8(X)*, Hodder Education) Hodder Education Group GBR. Dist: Trans-Atlantic Pubns., Inc.

Bando Irvin, Barbara. Math Readiness K-1. deluxe ed. 2004. (ENG.). 64p. (J). pap. 3.99 *(978-1-58947-322-5(1)*, 02208) School Zone Publishing Co.

Bardos, Laszlo C. Amazing Math: Projects You Can Build Yourself. Carbaugh, Samuel, illus. 2010. (Build It Yourself Ser.). (ENG.). 128p. (J). (gr. 3-7). 21.95 *(978-1-934670-58-3(8))* Octavio Publishing.

Bardos, Laszlo C. & Carbaugh, Samuel. Amazing Math Projects. 2010. (Build It Yourself Ser.). (ENG., Illus.). 128p. (J). (gr. 3-7). pap. 15.95 *(978-1-934670-57-6(X))* Octavio Publishing.

Barker, Lori. On the Road: Ratios & Proportions. rev. ed. 2012. (Mathematics Readers Ser.). (ENG.). 32p. (J). (gr. 6-6). pap. 8.99 *(978-1-4333-3450-4(X))* Teacher Created Materials, Inc.

—Our New Car. rev. ed. 2012. (Mathematics Readers Ser.). (ENG.). 32p. (J). (gr. 6-6). pap. 8.99 *(978-1-4333-3451-1(8))* Teacher Created Materials, Inc.

Barnes, John, et al. Science, Maths & Technology. 2003. (ENG., Illus.). 184p. pap. *(978-0-7487-7121-9(2))* Nelson Thornes Ltd.

Barnett, Carne S., et al. General Math. 128p. (YA). (gr. 7-12). pap. 33.95 *(978-0-201-25188-3(4))* Globe Fearon Educational Publishing.

—Pre-Algebra. 152p. (YA). (gr. 7-12). pap. 33.95 *(978-0-201-25976-6(1))* Globe Fearon Educational Publishing.

Baron, Jessica. What's in the Garden? Learning to Compare Two Sets of Objects. 2009. (Math for the Real World: Early Emergent Ser.). (ENG., Illus.). 8p. (gr. k-1). pap. 5.15 *(978-0-8239-8860-0(0))* Rosen Publishing Group, Inc., The.

Barth, April. Mira nuestros Patrones. 2010. (Rising Readers Ser.). (SPA.). (J). 3.49 *(978-1-60719-661-7(1))* Newmark Learning LLC.

Baseball Math Kindergarten Workbook. 2006. (J). *(978-0-9787458-0-6(9))* Sport Workbooks.

Basher, Simon & Green, Dan. Math: A Book You Can Count On! Basher, Simon, illus. 2010. (Basher Basics Ser.). (ENG., Illus.). 64p. (J). (gr. 3-7). pap. 8.99 *(978-0-7534-6419-9(5)*, 9780753464199, Kingfisher) Roaring Brook Pr.

Basic Facts To 18 (Gr. 2-3) 2003. (J). *(978-1-58232-084-7(5))* ECS Learning Systems, Inc.

Basic Facts to 18 Spanish Version. 2007. (J). per. *(978-1-58232-153-0(1))* ECS Learning Systems, Inc.

Basic Math Skills, Chapter 2, Activities. 2005. (Illus.). 52p. (YA). pap. 5.00 *(978-1-59476-036-5(5))* Paradigm Accelerated Curriculum.

Basic Math Skills, Chapter 2, Text. 2005. (Illus.). 72p. (YA). pap. 7.00 *(978-1-59476-024-2(1))* Paradigm Accelerated Curriculum.

Basic Math Skills, Chapter 3, Activities. 2005. (Illus.). 42p. (YA). pap. 5.00 *(978-1-59476-037-2(3))* Paradigm Accelerated Curriculum.

Basic Math Skills, Chapter 3, Text. 2005. (Illus.). 68p. (YA). pap. 7.00 *(978-1-59476-025-9(X))* Paradigm Accelerated Curriculum.

Basic Math Skills, Chapter 4, Activities. 2005. (Illus.). 48p. (YA). pap. 5.00 *(978-1-59476-038-9(1))* Paradigm Accelerated Curriculum.

Basic Math Skills, Chapter 4, Text. 2005. (Illus.). 70p. (YA). pap. 7.00 *(978-1-59476-026-6(8))* Paradigm Accelerated Curriculum.

Basic Math Skills, Chapter 5, Activities. 2005. (Illus.). 40p. (YA). pap. 5.00 *(978-1-59476-039-6(X))* Paradigm Accelerated Curriculum.

Basic Math Skills, Chapter 5, Text. 2005. (Illus.). 62p. (YA). pap. 7.00 *(978-1-59476-027-3(6))* Paradigm Accelerated Curriculum.

Basic Math Skills, Chapter 6, Activities. 2005. (Illus.). 52p. (YA). pap. 5.00 *(978-1-59476-040-2(3))* Paradigm Accelerated Curriculum.

Basic Math Skills, Chapter 6, Text. 2005. (Illus.). 70p. (YA). pap. 7.00 *(978-1-59476-028-0(4))* Paradigm Accelerated Curriculum.

Basiswissen Mathematik zur Physik. (Duden Abiturhilfen Ser.). (GER.). 96p. (YA). (gr. 11-13). *(978-3-411-04841-0(7))* Bibliographisches Institut & F. A. Brockhaus AG DEU. Dist: International Bk. Import Service, Inc.

Bear's Book of Numbers. 2004. 12p. (J). bds. 2.99 *(978-1-85997-429-2(5))* Byeway Bks.

Beck, Esther & Doudna, Kelly. Please Don't Laugh, I Can Use a Graph!, 1 vol. 2007. (Science Made Simple Ser.). (ENG., Illus.). 24p. (J). (gr. k-3). lib. bdg. 24.21 *(978-1-59928-614-3(9)*, SandCastle) ABDO Publishing Co.

Beck, Ray, et al. Practicing Basic Skills in Math: Grades 2-3. 2004. (One-Minute Fluency Builders Ser.). 560p. (gr. 2-3). per. 62.95 *(978-1-59318-001-0(2)*, 237MATH2-3) Cambium Education, Inc.

—Practicing Basic Skills in Math: Grades 4-5. 2004. (One-Minute Fluency Builders Ser.). 592p. (gr. 4-5). per. 62.95 *(978-1-59318-002-7(0)*, 237MATH4-5) Cambium Education, Inc.

—Practicing Basic Skills in Math: Grades 6-8. 2004. (One-Minute Fluency Builders Ser.). 558p. (gr. 6-8). per. 62.95 *(978-1-59318-003-4(9)*, 237MATH6-8) Cambium Education, Inc.

—Practicing Basic Skills in Math: Grades K-1. 2004. (One-Minute Fluency Builders Ser.). 352p. (gr. k-1). per. 49.95 *(978-1-59318-000-3(4)*, 237MATHK-1) Cambium Education, Inc.

—Practicing Basic Skills in Math: Secondary Remedial. 2004. (One-Minute Fluency Builders Ser.). 766p. per. 69.49 *(978-1-59318-004-1(7)*, 237MATHREM) Cambium Education, Inc.

Becker, Helaine. Lines, Bars & Circles: How William Playfair Invented Graphs. Tremblay, Marie-Ève, illus. 2017. (ENG.). 36p. (J). (gr. 1-4). 17.95 *(978-1-77138-570-1(7))* Kids Can Pr., Ltd. CAN. Dist: Hachette Bk. Group.

Beers, Jack. Anchors Grade 1. 2003. (Voyages Ser.). (J). (gr. 1). stu. ed., per. 11.95 *(978-1-58830-345-5(4))* Metropolitan Teaching & Learning Co.

—Anchors Grade 1 SP. 2004. (Voyages Ser.). (J). (gr. 1). stu. ed., per. 16.53 *(978-1-58830-990-7(8))* Metropolitan Teaching & Learning Co.

—Anchors Grade 2. 2003. (Voyages Ser.). (J). (gr. 2). stu. ed., per. 13.95 *(978-1-58830-346-2(2))* Metropolitan Teaching & Learning Co.

—Anchors Grade 2 SP. 2004. (Voyages Ser.). (J). (gr. 2). stu. ed., per. 16.53 *(978-1-58830-991-4(6))* Metropolitan Teaching & Learning Co.

—Anchors Grade 3. 2003. (Voyages Ser.). (J). (gr. 3). stu. ed., per. 13.95 *(978-1-58830-347-9(0))* Metropolitan Teaching & Learning Co.

—Anchors Grade 3 SP. 2004. (Voyages Ser.). (J). (gr. 3). stu. ed., per. 16.53 *(978-1-58830-992-1(4))* Metropolitan Teaching & Learning Co.

—Anchors Grade 4. 2003. (Voyages Ser.). (J). (gr. 4). stu. ed., per. 13.95 *(978-1-58830-348-6(9))* Metropolitan Teaching & Learning Co.

—Anchors Grade 5 Student Edition. 2003. (Voyages Ser.). (J). (gr. 5). per. 13.95 *(978-1-58830-470-4(1))* Metropolitan Teaching & Learning Co.

—Bridges-Blue. 2003. (Metro Math Bridges Ser.). (J). (gr. 8). stu. ed., per. 13.95 *(978-1-58830-191-8(5))* Metropolitan Teaching & Learning Co.

—Bridges-Gold. 2003. (Metro Math Bridges Ser.). (gr. 7). tchr. ed., per. 19.95 *(978-1-58830-613-5(5))* Metropolitan Teaching & Learning Co.

—Bridges-Red. 2003. (Metro Math Bridges Ser.). (J). (gr. 6). stu. ed., per. 13.95 *(978-1-58830-190-1(7))* Metropolitan Teaching & Learning Co.

Beissinger, Janet & Pless, Vera. The Cryptoclub: Using Mathematics to Make & Break Secret Codes. 2006. (ENG., Illus.). 200p. (C). pap. 43.95 *(978-1-56881-223-6(X)*, K00700) AK Peters, Ltd.

Bellos, Alex & Harriss, Edmund. Visions of the Universe: A Coloring Journey Through Math's Great Mysteries. 2016. (ENG., Illus.). 144p. pap. 14.95 *(978-1-61519-367-7(7))* Experiment LLC, The.

Benchmark Education Company, LLC Staff, compiled by. Early Math Theme Set. 2006. (J). 1295.00 *(978-1-4108-7078-0(2))* Benchmark Education Co.

—Early/Fluent Math Theme Set. 2006. (J). 258.00 *(978-1-4108-7095-7(2))* Benchmark Education Co.

—Math Standards Set. 2005. spiral bd. 3950.00 *(978-1-4108-5456-8(6))* Benchmark Education Co.

—Math Strands Set. 2005. spiral bd. 2580.00 *(978-1-4108-5458-2(2))*; spiral bd. 695.00 *(978-1-4108-5561-9(9))* Benchmark Education Co.

—Math Texts Set. 2005. spiral bd. 750.00 *(978-1-4108-3827-8(7))*; spiral bd. 95.00 *(978-1-4108-3837-7(4))*; spiral bd. 100.00 *(978-1-4108-3836-0(6))*; spiral bd. 335.00 *(978-1-4108-3834-6(X))*; spiral bd. 835.00 *(978-1-4108-3832-2(3))*; spiral bd. 3685.00 *(978-1-4108-3821-6(8))*; (J). spiral bd. 575.00 *(978-1-4108-5332-5(2))* Benchmark Education Co.

—Math Themes. 2006. spiral bd. 1295.00 *(978-1-4108-7055-1(3))* Benchmark Education Co.

—My First Reader's Theater Lap Books. 2009. (My First Reader's Theater Ser.). (J). (gr. k-1). 575.00 *(978-1-4108-8455-8(4))* Benchmark Education Co.

—Numbers & Operations. 2005. spiral bd. 120.00 *(978-1-4108-5859-7(6))*; spiral bd. 905.00 *(978-1-4108-5858-0(8))*; spiral bd. 120.00 *(978-1-4108-5448-3(5))*; spiral bd. 1095.00 *(978-1-4108-5447-6(7))*; spiral bd. 1020.00 *(978-1-4108-4509-2(5))*; spiral bd. 75.00 *(978-1-4108-3912-1(5))*; spiral bd. 95.00 *(978-1-4108-3911-4(7))*; spiral bd. 50.00 *(978-1-4108-3907-7(9))*; spiral bd. 75.00 *(978-1-4108-3906-0(0))*; spiral bd. 75.00 *(978-1-4108-3905-3(2))*; spiral bd. 75.00 *(978-1-4108-3904-6(4))*; spiral bd. 370.00 *(978-1-4108-3890-2(0))*; spiral bd. 695.00 *(978-1-4108-3889-6(7))*; spiral bd. 420.00 *(978-1-4108-3882-7(X))*; spiral bd. 615.00 *(978-1-4108-3881-0(1))* Benchmark Education Co.

—Numbers & Operations: Theme Set. 2006. (J). spiral bd. 258.00 *(978-1-4108-7094-0(4))* Benchmark Education Co.

—Spanish Math Standard Sets. 2005. spiral bd. 2775.00 *(978-1-4108-5867-2(7))* Benchmark Education Co.

—Using Maps, Graphs & Charts: Theme Set. 2006. (J). 109.00 *(978-1-4108-7091-9(X))* Benchmark Education Co.

Bennett, Clinton. Math: Chapter Resource: Indiana Middle School Edition. 4th ed. 2004. (J). 60.40 *(978-0-03-070979-1(2))* Harcourt Schl. Pubs.

—Math: Chapter Resources: Illinois Middle School Edition. 4th ed. 2004. (J). 58.60 *(978-0-03-070978-4(4))* Harcourt Schl. Pubs.

—Math: Chapter Resources: New York Middle School Edition. 4th ed. 2004. (J). 58.60 *(978-0-03-070981-4(4))* Harcourt Schl. Pubs.

—Math: Chapter Resourses: Florida Middle School Edition. 4th ed. 2004. (J). 60.40 *(978-0-03-070977-7(6))* Harcourt Schl. Pubs.

Bernardo, Kat. Stem: The Science of Travel: Multiplication (Grade 3) 2017. (Mathematics Readers Ser.). (Illus.). 32p. (J). (gr. 3-3). pap. 8.99 ***(978-1-4807-5797-4(7))*** Teacher Created Materials, Inc.

Berry, Minta. Building Sets of Ten. Crabtree Publishing Staff, ed. 2011. (My Path to Math Ser.: No. 36). (ENG.). 24p. (J). pap. *(978-0-7787-5266-0(6))* Crabtree Publishing Co.

Bertoletti, John C., et al. How Baseball Managers Use Math. 2009. (Math in the Real World Ser.). 32p. (gr. 4-6). 28.00 *(978-1-60413-604-3(9)*, Chelsea Clubhouse) Facts On File, Inc.

—How Fashion Designers Use Math. 2009. (Math in the Real World Ser.). 32p. (gr. 4-6). 28.00 *(978-1-60413-606-7(5)*, Chelsea Clubhouse) Facts On File, Inc.

Besel, Jennifer M. Lions & Tigers & Graphs! Oh My! (Data Mania Ser.). (ENG.). 24p. (gr. 1-2). 2011. pap. 41.70 *(978-1-4296-6466-0(5))* 2010. lib. bdg. 25.32 *(978-1-4296-4527-0(X))* Capstone Press of Coughlan Cos. (First Facts).

Big Book Tote Bag, 2, Pack. 2003. (Metro Reading Ser.). (J). (gr. 12). 26.45 *(978-1-58120-613-5(5))* Metropolitan Teaching & Learning Co.

Blackwood, Melissa, et al. Letts Monster Practice e Maths Age 5-6. 2014. (Letts Monster Practice Ser.). (ENG.). 32p. (J). (gr. k-1). pap. 6.95 *(978-1-84419-774-3(3))* HarperCollins Pubs. Ltd. GBR. Dist: Independent Pubs. Group.

—Maths Age 6-7. 2014. (Letts Monster Practice Ser.). (ENG.). 32p. (J). (gr. 1-2). pap. 6.95 *(978-1-84419-775-0(1))* HarperCollins Pubs. Ltd. GBR. Dist: Independent Pubs. Group.

Blanchard, Emma. Seeds I See: Work with 11-19 to Gain Foundations for Place Value. 2013. (Rosen Math Readers Ser.). (ENG.). 16p. (J). (gr. k-1). pap. 42.00 *(978-1-4777-1606-9(8))*; (Illus.). pap. 7.00 *(978-1-4777-1605-2(X))* Rosen Publishing Group, Inc., The. (Rosen Classroom).

Blane, Francisco. Stripes at the Beach: Lap Book. 2009. (My First Reader's Theater Set B Ser.). (J). 28.00 *(978-1-60634-988-5(0))* Benchmark Education Co.

Blask, Tina. I Can Help My Teacher: Use Place Value & Properties of Operation to Add. 2013. (InfoMax Math Readers Ser.). (ENG.). 24p. (J). (gr. 1-2). pap. 8.25 *(978-1-4777-2198-8(3)*, Rosen Classroom) Rosen Publishing Group, Inc., The.

—I Can Help My Teacher: Use Place Value & Properties of Operations to Add. 2013. (InfoMax Math Readers Ser.). (ENG.). 24p. (J). (gr. 1-2). pap. 49.50 *(978-1-4777-2199-5(1)*, Rosen Classroom) Rosen Publishing Group, Inc., The.

Blundell, Gillian & Graham, Noel. Problem Solving Activities with Mottik. (Illus.). 64p. (J). (gr. k-4). pap. 12.50 *(978-1-871098-21-1(1))* Claire Pubns. GBR. Dist: Parkwest Pubns., Inc.

Blythe, Peter, et al. Mathematical Studies: Oxford IB Diploma Program. 2015. (IB Diploma Program Ser.). (ENG.). 624p. 59.00 *(978-0-19-835506-9(8))* Oxford Univ. Pr., Inc.

Bodach, Vijaya Khisty. Gráficas Circulares. 2012. (Hacer Gráficas/Making Graphs Ser.).Tr. of Pie Graphs. (MUL & SPA.). 32p. (gr. 1-2). pap. 8.10 *(978-1-4296-8539-9(5))*; pap. 47.70 *(978-1-4296-8540-5(9))* Capstone Press of Coughlan Cos. (A+ Bilingue/Bilingual).

—Gráficas de Barras. (Hacer Gráficas/Making Graphs Ser.).Tr. of Bar Graphs. 32p. (gr. 1-2). 2012. (MUL.). pap. 47.70 *(978-1-4296-8543-6(3))* 2012. (MUL & SPA.). pap. 8.10 *(978-1-4296-8542-9(5))* 2010. (SPA, ENG & MUL.). lib. bdg. 27.32 *(978-1-4296-6100-3(3))* Capstone Press of Coughlan Cos. (A+ Bilingue/Bilingual).

—Hacer Gráficas. 2012. (Hacer Gráficas/Making Graphs Ser.).Tr. of Making Graphs. (MUL.). 32p. (gr. 1-2). pap. 190.80 *(978-1-4296-8549-8(2))*; pap. 24.30 *(978-1-4296-8548-1(4))* Capstone Press of Coughlan Cos. (A+ Bilingue/Bilingual).

—Pictografías. 2010. (Hacer Gráficas/Making Graphs Ser.). (MUL, SPA & ENG.). 32p. (gr. 1-2). lib. bdg. 27.32 *(978-1-4296-6101-0(1)*, A+ Bilingue/Bilingual) Capstone Press of Coughlan Cos.

—Pictografías/Pictographs. 2012. (Hacer Gráficas/Making Graphs Ser.). (MUL.). 32p. (gr. 1-2). pap. 47.70 *(978-1-4296-8545-0(X)*, A+ Bilingue/Bilingual) Capstone Press of Coughlan Cos.

—Tableros de Conteo. 2012. (Hacer Gráficas/Making Graphs Ser.).Tr. of Tally Charts. (MUL.). 32p. (gr. 1-2). pap. 47.70 *(978-1-4296-8547-4(6))*; pap. 8.10 *(978-1-4296-8546-7(8))* Capstone Press of Coughlan Cos. (A+ Bilingue/Bilingual).

—Tableros de Conteo/Tally Charts, 1 vol. 2010. (Hacer Gráficas/Making Graphs Ser.). (SPA, ENG & MUL.). 32p. (gr. 1-2). lib. bdg. 27.32 *(978-1-4296-6103-4(8)*, A+ Bilingue/Bilingual) Capstone Press of Coughlan Cos.

Bolster. Mathematics Grade 3. (Illus.). (J). pap., stu. ed. 6.59 *(978-0-673-11812-7(6))* Addison-Wesley Educational Pubs., Inc.

Book Company, Popular. Complete Math Workout, Volume 7. 2008. 271p. (J). pap. *(978-1-897164-49-5(1))* Popular Bk. Co. (Canada) Ltd.

—Complete Math Workout, Volume 8. 2008. 271p. (J). pap. *(978-1-897164-50-1(5))* Popular Bk. Co. (Canada) Ltd.

Books are Fun Exclusive Start Math, 4, Bk. 2, Set. 2005. (J). lib. bdg. *(978-1-59566-163-0(8))* QEB Publishing Inc.

Boothroyd, Jennifer. Grouping. 2007. (First Step Nonfiction - Early Math Ser.). (ENG.). 8p. (gr. -1-1). pap. 4.95 *(978-0-8225-6826-1(8))* Lerner Publishing Group.

Borovsky, Ivan. Our Trip to the Ocean: Understand Place Value. 2013. (InfoMax Math Readers Ser.). (ENG.). 24p. (J). (gr. 1-2). pap. 49.50 *(978-1-4777-2131-5(2))*; (Illus.). pap. 8.25 *(978-1-4777-2130-8(4))* Rosen Publishing Group, Inc., The. (Rosen Classroom).

Boston, Paul, illus. In Space. 2017. (Find Your Way Ser.). (ENG.). 32p. (J). (gr. k-3). 14.95 *(978-1-68297-047-8(7)*, QED Publishing) Quarto Publishing Group UK GBR. Dist: Hachette Bk. Group.

Boswell, Shannon. Savannah's Snorkeling Adventure! Use Place Value Understanding, 1 vol. 2015. (InfoMax Common Core Math Readers Ser.). (ENG.). 24p. (J). pap. 8.25 *(978-1-4777-4681-3(1)*, Rosen Classroom) Rosen Publishing Group, Inc., The.

Boyd, Amanda. Near & Far at the Beach: Learning Spatial Awareness Concepts. 2009. (Math for the Real World: Early Emergent Ser.). (ENG., Illus.). 8p. (gr. k-1). pap. 5.15 *(978-0-8239-8911-9(9))* Rosen Publishing Group, Inc., The.

—A Trip Around Town: Learning to Add 3 One-Digit Numbers. 2009. (Math for the REAL World Ser.). 12p. (gr. 1-2). pap. 5.90 *(978-0-8239-8915-7(1)*, Rosen Classroom) Rosen Publishing Group, Inc., The.

Braidich, Victoria. Shapes at Home: Learning to Recognize Basic Geometric Shapes. 2009. (Math for the REAL World Ser.). 12p. (gr. 1-2). pap. 5.90 *(978-0-8239-8863-1(5)*, Rosen Classroom) Rosen Publishing Group, Inc., The.

Brezina, Corona. Top STEM Careers in Math. 2014. (Cutting-Edge STEM Careers Ser.). (Illus.). 128p. (J). (gr. 9-12). pap. 113.10 *(978-1-4777-7679-7(6))* Rosen Publishing Group, Inc., The.

Bridger, Maggie. What Time Is It? A Content Area Reader-math. 2005. (Emergent/Early (Prek-2) Math Package Ser.). 16p. (gr. k-2). 25.20 *(978-0-8215-7824-7(3))* Sadlier, William H. Inc.

Briggs, D. Sharon. Mysteries in Knowledge Challenge Your Children: Complete Multiplication Tables. 2006. (J). per. 75.00 *(978-0-615-13051-4(8))* Briggs, Sharon.

Bright & Beyond - Math. 2004. (J). *(978-0-9763648-0-1(8))* Pal Toys, LLC.

Broadbent, Paul. Being A Cartoonist. 2007. (Trackers-Math Ser.). (gr. 2-5). pap. 5.00 *(978-1-59055-937-6(1))* Pacific Learning, Inc.

—Beneath Our Feet. 2007. (Trackers-Math Ser.). (gr. 2-5). pap. 5.00 *(978-1-59055-929-1(0))* Pacific Learning, Inc.

—Dance Fever. 2007. (Trackers-Math Ser.). (gr. 2-5). pap. 5.00 *(978-1-59055-930-7(4))* Pacific Learning, Inc.

—Detective Work. 2007. (Trackers-Math Ser.). (gr. 2-5). pap. 5.00 *(978-1-59055-931-4(2))* Pacific Learning, Inc.

—Down under Vacation. 2007. (Trackers-Math Ser.). (gr. 2-5). pap. 5.00 *(978-1-59055-940-6(1))* Pacific Learning, Inc.

—Rock Stars. 2007. (Trackers-Math Ser.). (gr. 2-5). pap. 5.00 *(978-1-59055-939-0(8))* Pacific Learning, Inc.

—Scuba Diving. 2007. (Trackers-Math Ser.). (gr. 2-5). pap. 5.00 *(978-1-59055-938-3(X))* Pacific Learning, Inc.

—What Are You Scared Of? 2007. (Trackers-Math Ser.). (gr. 2-5). pap. 5.00 *(978-1-59055-928-4(2))* Pacific Learning, Inc.

Broadbent, Paul & Letts Staff. Challenging Maths Age 10-11. 2015. (Letts KS2 Success Ser.). (ENG.). 64p. (J). (gr. 5-6). pap. 8.95 *(978-1-84419-846-7(4))* HarperCollins Pubs. Ltd. GBR. Dist: Independent Pubs. Group.

Broadbent, Paul, et al. Make It Easy. 2015. (Letts Make It Easy Ser.). (ENG.). 64p. (J). (gr. 3-4). pap. 8.95 *(978-1-84419-850-4(2))* HarperCollins Pubs. Ltd. GBR. Dist: Independent Pubs. Group.

—Maths Age 5-6. 2015. (Letts Make It Easy Ser.). (ENG.). 64p. (J). (gr. k-1). pap. 8.95 *(978-1-84419-847-4(2))* HarperCollins Pubs. Ltd. GBR. Dist: Independent Pubs. Group.

—Maths Age 6-7. 2015. (Letts Make It Easy Ser.). (ENG.). 64p. (J). (gr. 1-2). pap. 8.95 *(978-1-84419-848-1(0))* HarperCollins Pubs. Ltd. GBR. Dist: Independent Pubs. Group.

—Maths, Age 9-10. 2015. (Letts KS2 Success Ser.). (ENG., Illus.). 64p. (J). (gr. 4-5). pap. 8.95 *(978-1-84419-855-9(3))* HarperCollins Pubs. Ltd. GBR. Dist: Independent Pubs. Group.

—Maths & English, Age 9-10. 2015. (Letts KS2 Success Ser.). (ENG., Illus.). 128p. (J). (gr. 4-5). pap. 12.95 *(978-1-84419-857-3(X))* HarperCollins Pubs. Ltd. GBR. Dist: Independent Pubs. Group.

Brookie, Anna, et al. Mathematics & Statistics for the New Zealand Curriculum Year 9. 2nd ed. 2013. (ENG.). pap., stu. ed. *(978-1-107-62840-3(7))* Cambridge Univ. Pr.

Brown, Melony A. Solving Word Problems for Life, Grades 6-8, 1 vol. 2009. (Illus.). 146p. (C). pap. 27.00 *(978-1-59158-947-1(9)*, A2643P, Libraries Unlimited) ABC-CLIO, LLC.

Brown, Robin. Practice Papers: Advanced Maths. 2nd ed. (Illus.). 32p. (YA). pap. *(978-0-340-72690-7(3))* Hodder & Stoughton.

—Practice Papers: Maths. 2nd ed. (Illus.). 32p. (YA). pap. *(978-0-340-72689-1(X))* Hodder & Stoughton.

Brownlee, Joan, et al. Geofinity. 2003. (J). spiral bd. 15.95 *(978-1-931334-26-6(9))* Pieces of Learning.

Bruchgleichungen und Bruchungleichungen. (Duden-Schuelerhilfen Ser.). (GER.). 96p. (YA). (gr. 8). *(978-3-411-02614-2(6))* Bibliographisches Institut & F. A. Brockhaus AG DEU. Dist: International Bk. Import Service, Inc.

Brueche. (Duden-Schuelerhilfen Ser.). (GER.). 112gerp. (YA). (gr. 6-7). *(978-3-411-70692-1(9))* Bibliographisches Institut & F. A. Brockhaus AG DEU. Dist: International Bk. Import Service, Inc.

Bumcrot, Curt & Bumcrot, Jenny. Achieving Peak Performance New Edition. Krischke, Nikki, ed. 2nd rev. ed. 2003. 19p. (gr. 2-18). pap. 5.00 *(978-1-888786-39-2(6))* Basic Skills Assessment & Educational Services.

Burganti, Darien. Fun at the Dojo: Use Place Value Understanding & Properties of Operations to Add. 2014. (Math Masters: Number & Operations in Base Ten Ser.). 24p. (J). (gr. 2-3). 23.60 *(978-1-4777-6433-6(X))*; (ENG.). pap. 8.25 *(978-1-4777-4717-9(6))* Rosen Publishing Group, Inc., The. (Rosen Classroom).

Burgess, Lynne. Shapes: Individual Title Six-Packs. (Discovery World Ser.). 12p. (gr. k-1). 28.00 *(978-0-7635-8446-7(0))* Rigby Education.

Burnett, Betty. Cool Careers Without College for Math & Science Wizards. 2009. (Cool Careers Without College Ser.). 144p. (gr. 6-6). 66.50 *(978-1-61511-959-2(0))* Rosen Publishing Group, Inc., The.

Burnett, James & Irons, Calvin. A Dozen Dizzy Dinosaurs: A Book about Division (Equal Groups) 2012. (J). *(978-1-921959-30-1(4))* Origo Education.

—How Many Legs? A Book about Number Combinations. 2012. (J). *(978-1-921358-97-5(1))* Origo Education.

Burns, Kylie. Roman Numerals & Ordinals. 2010. (ENG., Illus.). 24p. (J). *(978-0-7787-5250-9(X))*; pap. *(978-0-7787-5297-4(6))* Crabtree Publishing Co.

Burrill, Gail F., et al. Advanced Modeling & Matrices. (Data-Driven Mathematics Ser.). 136p. (YA). (gr. 7-12). pap., stu. ed. 18.95 *(978-1-57232-255-4(1))* Seymour, Dale Pubns.

—Exploring Symbols. (Data-Driven Mathematics Ser.). 120p. (YA). (gr. 7-12). pap., stu. ed. 18.95 *(978-1-57232-230-1(6))* Seymour, Dale Pubns.

Burton, Margie, et al. Looking for Numbers. 2011. (Early Connections Ser.). (J). *(978-1-61672-300-2(9))* Benchmark Education Co.

—What Comes in Twos? 2011. (Early Connections Ser.). (J). *(978-1-61672-276-0(2))* Benchmark Education Co.

Bussell, Linda. Vamos a Usar Datos de División en el Jardín. 2008. (Las matemáticas en nuestro mundo - Nivel 3 (Math in Our World - Level 3) Ser.). (SPA.). 24p. (gr. 2-5). pap. 8.15 *(978-0-8368-9393-9(X)*, Weekly Reader Leveled Readers) Stevens, Gareth Publishing LLLP.

—Vamos a Usar la División en el Campamento de Deportes. 2008. (Matemáticas en Nuestro Mundo - Nivel 3 (Math in Our World - Level 3) Ser.). (SPA.). 24p. (gr. 2-5). (J). lib. bdg. 22.00 *(978-0-8368-9296-3(8))*; pap. 8.15 *(978-0-8368-9395-3(6))* Stevens, Gareth Publishing LLLP. (Weekly Reader Leveled Readers).

Bussiere, Desireé. Bowling by the Numbers, 1 vol. 2013. (Sports by the Numbers Ser.). (ENG.). 24p. (J). (gr. k-3). lib. bdg. 24.21 *(978-1-61783-842-2(X)*, SandCastle) ABDO Publishing Co.

—Gymnastics by the Numbers, 1 vol. 2013. (Sports by the Numbers Ser.). (ENG.). 24p. (J). (gr. k-3). lib. bdg. 24.21 *(978-1-61783-844-6(6)*, SandCastle) ABDO Publishing Co.

Cain, Michael. Mathability: Math in the Real World. 2005. (ENG.). 80p. (gr. 5-8). pap. 16.95 *(978-1-59363-106-2(5)*, 9781593631062) Prufrock Pr.

Callella, Trisha. I Have, Who Has? Math, Grades 3-4: 38 Interactive Card Games. Hamaguchi, Carla, ed. Hillam, Corbin, illus. 2006. (I Have, Who Has? Ser.). 204p. (J). (gr. 3-4). per. 19.99 *(978-1-59198-230-2(8)*, 2208) Creative Teaching Pr., Inc.

Campbell, Sarah C. Mysterious Patterns: Finding Fractals in Nature. Campbell, Sarah C. & Campbell, Richard P., photos by. 2014. (ENG., Illus.). 32p. (J). (gr. 2-5). 16.95 *(978-1-62091-627-8(4))* Boyds Mills Pr.

Canavan, Thomas. Making Connections: 50 Math Super Puzzles. 2011. (Math Standards Workout Ser.). (ENG., Illus.). 48p. (YA). (gr. 5-9). lib. bdg. 29.25 *(978-1-4488-6674-8(X))* Rosen Publishing Group, Inc., The.

—Math Adds Up. 2016. (Amazing World of Science & Math Ser.). 48p. (gr. 5-5). pap. 14.05 *(978-1-4824-4986-0(2))* Stevens, Gareth Publishing LLLP.

—Mental Math: 50 Math Super Puzzles. 2011. (Math Standards Workout Ser.). (ENG., Illus.). 48p. (YA). (gr. 5-8). pap. 11.75 *(978-1-4488-6684-7(7)*, Rosen Reference) Rosen Publishing Group, Inc., The.

Canetti, Yanitzia. Rhyming Tongue-Twisters Math. 2010. 32p. (J). pap. 6.99 *(978-1-59835-263-4(6)*, BrickHouse Education) Cambridge BrickHouse, Inc.

Capote, Lori. Monster Knows Math. Wass, Chip, illus. 2013. (Monster Knows Math Ser.). (ENG.). 24p. (gr. 3-4). lib. bdg. 98.60 *(978-1-4048-7950-8(1))* Picture Window Bks.

Capstone Press. Data Mania. 2010. (Data Mania Ser.). (ENG.). 32p. lib. bdg. 95.96 *(978-1-4296-5929-1(7)*, First Facts) Capstone Press of Coughlan Cos.

—Real World Math, 1 vol. 2010. (Real World Math - Level 4 Ser.). (ENG.). 32p. lib. bdg. 405.12 *(978-1-4296-5915-4(7))* Capstone Press of Coughlan Cos.

Captain B's Boat, 6 vols. (Sunshinetm Ser.). 16p. (gr. k-18). 29.50 *(978-0-7802-5441-1(4))* Wright Group/McGraw-Hill.

Caron, Lucille & Jacques, Philip M. Addition & Subtraction Smarts! 2011. (Math Smarts! Ser.). (Illus.). 64p. (J). (gr. 5-18). lib. bdg. 29.27 *(978-0-7660-3939-1(0))* Enslow Pubs., Inc.

Caron, Lucille & St. Jacques, Philip M. Addition & Subtraction Smarts! 2011. (Math Smarts! Ser.). (Illus.). 64p. (J). (gr. 5-18). pap. 8.95 *(978-1-59845-318-8(1))* Enslow Pubs., Inc.

—Math Success, 7 bks., Set. Incl. Addition & Subtraction. 2001. lib. bdg. 23.94 *(978-0-7660-1432-9(0))*; Fractions & Decimals. 2000. lib. bdg. 23.94 *(978-0-7660-1430-5(4))*; Multiplication & Division. 2001. lib. bdg. 23.94 *(978-0-7660-1431-2(2))*; Percents & Ratios. 2000. lib. bdg. 23.94 *(978-0-7660-1435-0(5))*; Pre-Algebra & Algebra. 2000. lib. bdg. 23.94 *(978-0-7660-1434-3(7))*; 64p. (J). (gr. 4-10). (Illus.). Set lib. bdg. 107.70 *(978-0-7660-1601-9(3))* Enslow Pubs., Inc.

—Pre-Algebra & Algebra Smarts! 2011. (Math Smarts! Ser.). (Illus.). 64p. (J). (gr. 5-18). pap. 8.95 *(978-1-59845-319-5(X))* Enslow Pubs., Inc.

Caron, Lucille, et al. Pre-Algebra & Algebra Smarts! 2011. (Math Smarts! Ser.). (Illus.). 64p. (J). (gr. 5-18). lib. bdg. 29.27 *(978-0-7660-3938-4(2))* Enslow Pubs., Inc.

Carr, Barbara, et al. Revise for Cambridge Primary Checkpoint Maths. 2013. (Cambridge International Examinations Ser.). 96p. (gr. 7-9). pupil's gde. ed. 27.50 *(978-1-4441-7829-6(6))* Hodder Education Group GBR. Dist: Trans-Atlantic Pubns., Inc.

Carroll, Danielle. Tiling with Shapes. 2005. (Yellow Umbrella Fluent Level Ser.). (ENG., Illus.). 16p. (gr. k-1). pap. 35.70 *(978-0-7368-5323-1(5)*, Yellow Umbrella Bks.) Capstone Press of Coughlan Cos.

Carson-Dellosa Publishing Staff. Beginning Math, Grade 1. 2010. (Home Workbooks Ser.). (ENG.). 64p. (gr. 1-1). pap. 4.49 *(978-1-60418-790-8(5))* Carson-Dellosa Publishing, LLC.

—Beginning Math, Grade K. 2010. (Home Workbooks Ser.). (ENG.). 64p. (gr. k-k). pap. 4.49 *(978-1-60418-776-2(X))* Carson-Dellosa Publishing, LLC.

Carson-Dellosa Publishing Staff, compiled by. Early Skills, Grade 1. 2013. (Complete Ser.). (ENG.). 352p. (gr. 1-1). pap. 14.95 *(978-1-62399-096-1(3))* Carson-Dellosa Publishing, LLC.

—Early Skills, Grade K. 2013. (Complete Ser.). (ENG.). 352p. (gr. k-k). pap. 14.95 *(978-1-62399-095-4(5))* Carson-Dellosa Publishing, LLC.

—Early Skills, Grade PK. 2013. (Complete Ser.). (ENG.). 352p. (gr. -1 — 1). pap. 14.95 *(978-1-62399-094-7(7))* Carson-Dellosa Publishing, LLC.

Carson, Janet. In the Forest: Learning Directional Concepts. (Math for the REAL World Ser.). 12p. (gr. 1-2). 2009. pap. 5.90 *(978-0-8239-8916-4(X)*, Rosen Classroom) 2004. (ENG.). 33.50 *(978-0-8239-7634-8(3))* Rosen Publishing Group, Inc., The.

Carter, Denine, ed. Gotta Have Graphs. 2003. 144p. (gr. 1-6). 16.95 *(978-1-56234-573-0(7)*, Mailbox Bks., The) Education Ctr., Inc.

Cartogna, Eileen. Jobs Around Town: Learning to Sort & Classify. (Math for the Real World: Early Emergent Ser.). (ENG., Illus.). 8p. (gr. k-1). 2009. pap. 5.15 *(978-0-8239-8910-2(0))* 2004. 29.95 *(978-0-8239-7629-4(7))* Rosen Publishing Group, Inc., The.

Cernak, Kim & Williams, Rozanne Lanczak. Build-a-Skill Instant Books Math Facts To 20. Faulkner, Stacey, ed. Campbell, Jenny, illus. 2007. (J). 4.99 *(978-1-59198-418-4(1))* Creative Teaching Pr., Inc.

Challen, Paul & Peppas, Lynn. Math Words & Symbols. 2009. (ENG.). 24p. (J). lib. bdg. *(978-0-7787-4347-7(0))*; pap. *(978-0-7787-4365-1(9))* Crabtree Publishing Co.

Chambers, Jo. All about Cars. 2007. (Trackers-Math Ser.). (gr. 2-5). pap. 5.00 *(978-1-59055-923-9(1))* Pacific Learning, Inc.

—Art Gallery. 2007. (Trackers-Math Ser.). (gr. 2-5). pap. 5.00 *(978-1-59055-927-7(4))* Pacific Learning, Inc.

—Caring for Wild Animals. 2007. (Trackers-Math Ser.). (gr. 2-5). pap. 5.00 *(978-1-59055-933-8(9))* Pacific Learning, Inc.

—Discovering India. 2007. (Trackers-Math Ser.). (gr. 2-5). pap. 5.00 *(978-1-59055-926-0(6))* Pacific Learning, Inc.

—Extreme Earth. 2007. (Trackers-Math Ser.). (gr. 2-5). pap. 5.00 *(978-1-59055-913-0(4))* Pacific Learning, Inc.

—High Tech. 2007. (Trackers-Math Ser.). (gr. 2-5). pap. 5.00 *(978-1-59055-934-5(7))* Pacific Learning, Inc.

—Making Movies. 2007. (Trackers-Math Ser.). (gr. 2-5). pap. 5.00 *(978-1-59055-932-1(0))* Pacific Learning, Inc.

—That's Extreme. 2007. (Trackers-Math Ser.). (gr. 2-5). pap. 5.00 *(978-1-59055-936-9(3))* Pacific Learning, Inc.

—Tropical Rainforest. 2007. (Trackers-Math Ser.). (gr. 2-5). pap. 5.00 *(978-1-59055-924-6(X))* Pacific Learning, Inc.

Chapman, Joan. Heavy & Light: Learning to Compare Weights of Objects. 2009. (Math for the Real World: Early Emergent Ser.). (ENG., Illus.). 8p. (gr. k-1). pap. 5.15 *(978-0-8239-8844-0(9))* Rosen Publishing Group, Inc., The.

Chapmann, Helen. The Art of Maths. 2007. (Action Numeracy Middle Primary Ser.). 32p. pap. 9.95 *(978-0-86431-654-7(2))* ACER Pr. AUS. Dist: ISBS Publisher Services.

Charles, et al. Problem-Solving Experiences in Mathematics. 2003. (gr. 7-8). suppl. ed. 30.95 *(978-0-201-20688-3(9))* Seymour, Dale Pubns.

Charles, R., et al. Problem-Solving Experience in Mathematics. 2003. 30.95 *(978-0-201-20689-0(7))*; (gr. 3). 30.95 *(978-0-201-20684-5(6))*; (gr. 4). 30.95 *(978-0-201-20685-2(4))*; (gr. 5). 30.95 *(978-0-201-20686-9(2))*; (gr. 6). 30.95 *(978-0-201-20687-6(0))* Seymour, Dale Pubns.

—Problem-Solving Experiences in Mathematics. 2nd ed. 2003. 16.50 *(978-0-201-49361-0(6))* Seymour, Dale Pubns.

—Problem-Solving Experiences in Mathematics, Grade 2, BLM. Anderson, Cathy & Apple, Mali, eds. 2nd ed. 2003. (Illus.). 17.50 *(978-0-201-49363-4(2))* Seymour, Dale Pubns.

Charles, Randall I. & Prentice Hall Directories Staff. Pre-Algebra, 3 vols. 5th ed. 2003. (ENG.). 954p. (YA). (gr. 7-9). 477.00 *(978-0-13-068608-4(5)*, Prentice Hall) Pearson Schl.

Charles, Randall I. & Prentice Hall Staff. Prentice Hall Mathematics, 3 vols. 2003. (ENG.). 828p. (YA). (gr. 6-8). 414.00 *(978-0-13-063136-7(1)*, Prentice Hall) Pearson Schl.

Charles, Randall I., et al. Problem-Solving Experiences in Mathematics: Prob Solv Exper. 2005. (Problem Solving Experiences Ser.). (J). (gr. k-8). stu. ed. 56.95 *(978-0-7690-3250-4(8))*; (gr. 4-18). stu. ed. 56.95 *(978-0-7690-3251-1(6))* Seymour, Dale Pubns.

Charlesworth, Eric. Solve & Match Math Practice Pages: 50+ Motivating, Self-Checking Activities That Help Kids Review & Master Essential Math Skills. 2011. (ENG.). 64p. (gr. 2-3). pap. 11.99 *(978-0-545-28815-6(0))*; (gr. 4-6). pap. 11.99 *(978-0-545-28816-3(9))* Scholastic, Inc. (Teaching Resources).

Chen, John. Helping at the Book Sale: Represent & Solve Subtraction Problems. 2013. (Rosen Math Readers Ser.). 24p. (J). (gr. 1-2). (ENG.). pap. 8.25 *(978-1-4777-2052-3(9)*, Rosen Classroom); (ENG.). pap. 49.50 *(978-1-4777-2053-0(7)*, Rosen Classroom); lib. bdg. 22.60 *(978-1-4777-2208-4(4)*, PowerKids Pr.) Rosen Publishing Group, Inc., The.

Chilson, Martin. Carmen Cooks Healthy! Represent & Solve Problems Involving Division. 2014. (Math Masters: Operations & Algebraic Thinking Ser.). 24p. (J). (gr. 3-4). 23.60 *(978-1-4777-6410-7(0))*; (ENG.). pap. 8.25 *(978-1-4777-4965-4(9))* Rosen Publishing Group, Inc., The. (Rosen Classroom).

Chrismer, Melanie. Odd & Even Socks. 2005. (Rookie Read-About Math Ser.). (ENG., Illus.). 32p. (J). (gr. 1-2). lib. bdg. 20.50 *(978-0-516-25265-0(8)*, Children's Pr.) Scholastic Library Publishing.

Cipriano, Jeri S. It's Time!, 6 vols., Set. 2003. (Yellow Umbrella Early Level Ser.). (ENG.). 16p. (gr. k-1). pap. 35.70 *(978-0-7368-2993-9(8)*, Yellow Umbrella Bks.) Capstone Press of Coughlan Cos.

—Making a Difference. 2003. (Shutterbug Books: Social Studies). (Illus.). 16p. (J). (gr. -1-3). pap. 4.10 *(978-0-7398-7647-3(3))* Steck-Vaughn.

Clarke, Peter, ed. Software 1. 2nd ed. 2008. (Collins New Primary Maths Ser.). (ENG.). 48p. (J). (gr. 1-1). cd-rom 264.00 *(978-0-00-721997-1(0))* HarperCollins Pubs. Ltd. GBR. Dist: Independent Pubs. Group.

Cleary, Brian P. A-B-a-B-A: A Book of Pattern Play. Gable, Brian, illus. 2010. (Math Is CATegorical (r) Ser.). (ENG.). 32p. (J). (gr. k-3). lib. bdg. 16.95 *(978-0-8225-7880-2(8))* Lerner Publishing Group.

— A-B-A-B-A: A Book of Pattern Play. Gable, Brian, illus. 2012. (Math Is CATegorical (r) Ser.). (ENG.). 32p. (gr. k-3). pap. 6.95 *(978-0-7613-8502-8(9))*, Millbrook Pr.) Lerner Publishing Group.

—The Action of Subtraction. Gable, Brian, illus. 2008. (Math Is CATegorical (r) Ser.). (ENG.). 32p. (gr. k-3). pap. 6.95 *(978-1-58013-843-7(8)*, First Avenue Editions) Lerner Publishing Group.

Clements, Andrew. A Million Dots. Reed, Mike, illus. 2006. (ENG.). 48p. (J). (gr. -1-3). 17.99 *(978-0-689-85824-6(8)*, Atheneum Bks. for Young Readers) Simon & Schuster Children's Publishing.

Clemson, Wendy & Clemson, David. Digging for Dinosaurs. 2007. (Math Adventures Ser.). (Illus.). 32p. (gr. 1-4). pap. 10.50 *(978-0-8368-8137-0(0))*; lib. bdg. 26.00 *(978-0-8368-7838-7(8))* Stevens, Gareth Publishing LLLP. (Gareth Stevens Learning Library).

—Firefighters to the Rescue. 2007. (Math Adventures Ser.). (Illus.). 32p. (gr. 1-4). pap. 10.50 *(978-0-8368-8138-7(9))*; lib. bdg. 26.00 *(978-0-8368-7839-4(6))* Stevens, Gareth Publishing LLLP. (Gareth Stevens Learning Library).

—Ocean Giants. 2007. (Math Adventures Ser.). (Illus.). 32p. (gr. 1-4). pap. 10.50 *(978-0-8368-8139-4(7))*; lib. bdg. 26.00 *(978-0-8368-7840-0(X))* Stevens, Gareth Publishing LLLP. (Gareth Stevens Learning Library).

—Rocket to the Moon. 2007. (Math Adventures Ser.). (Illus.). 32p. (gr. 1-4). (SPA.). pap. 10.50 *(978-0-8368-8140-0(0))*; lib. bdg. 26.00 *(978-0-8368-7841-7(8))* Stevens, Gareth Publishing LLLP. (Gareth Stevens Learning Library).

—Times Tables! (Illus.). 32p. (J). pap. 11.99 *(978-0-590-24755-9(7))* Scholastic, Inc.

—Treasure Hunt in the Jungle. 2007. (Math Adventures Ser.). (Illus.). 32p. (gr. 1-4). pap. 10.50 *(978-0-8368-8141-7(9))*; lib. bdg. 26.00 *(978-0-8368-7842-4(6))* Stevens, Gareth Publishing LLLP. (Gareth Stevens Learning Library).

Clissold, Caroline. All about Pirates. 2007. (Trackers-Math Ser.). (gr. 2-5). pap. 5.00 *(978-1-59055-918-5(5))* Pacific Learning, Inc.

—Dinosaur. 2007. (Trackers-Math Ser.). (gr. 2-5). pap. 5.00 *(978-1-59055-914-7(2))* Pacific Learning, Inc.

—Extreme Earth. 2007. (Trackers-Math Ser.). (gr. 2-5). pap. 5.00 *(978-1-59055-912-3(6))* Pacific Learning, Inc.

—Food Around the World. 2007. (Trackers-Math Ser.). (gr. 2-5). pap. 5.00 *(978-1-59055-910-9(X))* Pacific Learning, Inc.

—Out of This World. 2007. (Trackers-Math Ser.). (gr. 2-5). pap. 5.00 *(978-1-59055-917-8(7))* Pacific Learning, Inc.

CMSP Projects Staff. Applied Math Concepts: Lines & Perimeters Area & Volume. rev. ed. (Illus.). 91p. (YA). reprint ed. pap. *(978-0-942851-01-4(3))* CMSP Projects.

Cocca, Lisa Colozza. Bar Graphs. 2013. (Explorer Junior Library: Math Explorer Junior Ser.). (ENG.). 24p. (gr. 1-4). 28.50 *(978-1-61080-911-5(4)*, 202623); pap. 12.79 *(978-1-61080-936-8(X)*, 202625) Cherry Lake Publishing.

—Graphing Story Problems. 2013. (J). *(978-1-61080-989-4(0))*; (ENG.). 24p. (gr. 1-4). 28.50 *(978-1-61080-914-6(9)*, 202635); (ENG.). 24p. (gr. 1-4). pap. 12.79 *(978-1-61080-939-9(4)*, 202637) Cherry Lake Publishing.

—Line Graphs. 2013. (J). *(978-1-61080-987-0(4))*; (ENG.). 24p. (gr. 1-4). 28.50 *(978-1-61080-912-2(2)*, 202627); (ENG.). 24p. (gr. 1-4). pap. 12.79 *(978-1-61080-937-5(8)*, 202629) Cherry Lake Publishing.

—Pie Graphs. 2013. (J). *(978-1-61080-990-0(4))*; (ENG.). 24p. (gr. 1-4). 28.50 *(978-1-61080-915-3(7)*, 202639); (ENG.). 24p. (gr. 1-4). pap. 12.79 *(978-1-61080-940-5(8)*, 202641) Cherry Lake Publishing.

Cognitive Tutor (R) Integrated Math II Software Manual. 2003. spiral bd. *(978-1-930804-43-2(1))* Caregie Learning Inc.

Cognitive Tutor (R) Integrated Math II Student. 2003. per. *(978-1-930804-54-8(7))* Caregie Learning Inc.

Cohen, Marina. Money Problems. 2010. (ENG.). 24p. (J). *(978-0-7787-6782-4(5))*; pap. *(978-0-7787-6791-6(4))* Crabtree Publishing Co.

Collins Easy Learning Staff. Maths Ages 9-11. 2014. (Collins Easy Learning Ser.). (ENG.). 48p. (J). (gr. 4-6). pap. 7.99 *(978-0-00-755983-1(6))* HarperCollins Pubs. Ltd. GBR. Dist: Independent Pubs. Group.

Collins Easy Learning Staff & Collins UK. Maths Ages 6-8. 2014. (Collins Easy Learning Ser.). (ENG.). 32p. (J). (gr. 1-3). pap. 6.99 *(978-0-00-755980-0(1))* HarperCollins Pubs. Ltd. GBR. Dist: Independent Pubs. Group.

Collins Easy Learning Staff, et al. Numbers. 2015. (Collins Easy Learning Ser.). (ENG.). 32p. (J). (gr. 1-2). pap. 6.95 *(978-0-00-813431-0(6))* HarperCollins Pubs. Ltd. GBR. Dist: Independent Pubs. Group.

Collins, Kathleen. On the Trail with Lewis & Clark: Learning to Use Line Graphs. 2004. (Math Big Bookstm Ser.). (ENG.). 16p. (gr. 2-3). 37.95 *(978-0-8239-7639-3(4))* Rosen Publishing Group, Inc., The.

Collins Publishers Staff. KS3 Maths. 2014. (ENG., Illus.). 216p. (YA). (gr. 6-9). pap. 16.95 *(978-0-00-756279-4(9))* HarperCollins Pubs. Ltd. GBR. Dist: Independent Pubs. Group.

—KS3 Maths Advanced. 2014. (ENG., Illus.). 144p. (YA). (gr. 6-9). pap. 12.95 *(978-0-00-756278-7(0))* HarperCollins Pubs. Ltd. GBR. Dist: Independent Pubs. Group.

Collins Publishers Staff & Collins KS3 Staff. KS3 Maths. 2014. (ENG., Illus.). 144p. (YA). (gr. 6-9). pap. 12.95 *(978-0-00-756276-3(4))* HarperCollins Pubs. Ltd. GBR. Dist: Independent Pubs. Group.

—KS3 Maths Standard. 2014. (ENG., Illus.). 216p. (YA). (gr. 6-9). pap. 16.95 *(978-0-00-756277-0(2))* HarperCollins Pubs. Ltd. GBR. Dist: Independent Pubs. Group.

—KS3 Maths, Year 7. 2014. (ENG., Illus.). 80p. (J). (gr. 6-7). pap., wbk. ed. 8.95 *(978-0-00-756266-4(7))* HarperCollins Pubs. Ltd. GBR. Dist: Independent Pubs. Group.

—KS3 Maths Year 8. 2014. (ENG., Illus.). 80p. (J). (gr. 7-8). pap., wbk. ed. 8.95 *(978-0-00-756267-1(5))* HarperCollins Pubs. Ltd. GBR. Dist: Independent Pubs. Group.

—KS3 Maths, Year 9. 2014. (ENG., Illus.). 80p. (YA). (gr. 8-9). pap., wbk. ed. 8.95 *(978-0-00-756268-8(3))* HarperCollins Pubs. Ltd. GBR. Dist: Independent Pubs. Group.

Collins UK Publishing Staff. Maths Ages 5-7. 2014. (Collins Easy Learning Ser.). (ENG.). 32p. (J). (gr. k-2). pap. 6.99 *(978-0-00-755979-4(8))* HarperCollins Pubs. Ltd. GBR. Dist: Independent Pubs. Group.

—Maths Ages 7-9. 2014. (Collins Easy Learning Ser.). (ENG.). 32p. (J). (gr. 2-4). pap. 6.99 *(978-0-00-755981-7(X))* HarperCollins Pubs. Ltd. GBR. Dist: Independent Pubs. Group.

—Maths Ages 8-10. 2014. (Collins Easy Learning Ser.). (ENG.). 48p. (J). (gr. 3-5). pap. 7.99 *(978-0-00-755982-4(8))* HarperCollins Pubs. Ltd. GBR. Dist: Independent Pubs. Group.

—Shanghai Maths - Shanghai Maths Workbook Year 5. Fan, Lianghuo, ed. 2016. (Shanghai Maths Ser.). (ENG., Illus.). 252p. (J). pap. 13.95 *(978-0-00-814466-1(4))* HarperCollins Pubs. Ltd. GBR. Dist: Independent Pubs. Group.

Collins UK Publishing Staff & Greenway, Karen. English for Mathematics, Bk. A. 2016. (ENG., Illus.). 80p. (J). pap. 9.95 *(978-0-00-813570-6(3))* HarperCollins Pubs. Ltd. GBR. Dist: Independent Pubs. Group.

Collins UK Publishing Staff & Letts KS1 Staff. Maths, Age 5-7. 2016. (ENG.). 96p. (gr. k-2). pap. 9.95 *(978-1-84419-818-4(9))* HarperCollins Pubs. Ltd. GBR. Dist: Independent Pubs. Group.

—Maths & English Practice Test Papers. 2016. (ENG.). 192p. (J). (gr. 1-2). pap. 15.95 *(978-1-84419-819-1(7))* HarperCollins Pubs. Ltd. GBR. Dist: Independent Pubs. Group.

Collins UK Publishing Staff & Letts KS2 Staff. Maths & English Practice Test Papers. 2016. (Letts KS2 Success Ser.). (ENG.). 216p. (J). (gr. 3-6). pap. 15.95 *(978-1-84419-835-1(9))* HarperCollins Pubs. Ltd. GBR. Dist: Independent Pubs. Group.

—Maths, English & Science Test Practice Papers. 2016. (Letts KS2 Success Ser.). (ENG.). 280p. (gr. 3-6). pap. 20.95 *(978-1-84419-836-8(7))* HarperCollins Pubs. Ltd. GBR. Dist: Independent Pubs. Group.

—Maths Practice Test Papers, Age 7-11. 2016. (Letts KS2 Success Ser.). (ENG.). 112p. (J). (gr. 3-6). pap. 9.95 *(978-1-84419-832-0(4))* HarperCollins Pubs. Ltd. GBR. Dist: Independent Pubs. Group.

Collins UK Staff & Collins KS1 Staff. Maths, Age 6-7. 2016. (ENG.). 128p. (J). (gr. 1-2). pap., wbk. ed. 9.95 *(978-0-00-817900-7(X))* HarperCollins Pubs. Ltd. GBR. Dist: Independent Pubs. Group.

Collins UK Staff & Collins KS2 Staff. Maths, Age 10-11. 2016. (Collins KS2 SATs Revision & Practice Ser.). (ENG.). 128p. (J). (gr. 5-6). pap. 9.95 *(978-0-00-817549-8(7))* HarperCollins Pubs. Ltd. GBR. Dist: Independent Pubs. Group.

Colson, Rob. Super Sums: Addition, Subtraction, Multiplication, & Division. 2017. (Math Everywhere Ser.). (ENG.). 32p. (J). pap. 8.95 ***(978-0-531-23320-7(0))***; lib. bdg. 27.00 ***(978-0-531-22884-5(3))*** Scholastic Library Publishing. (Children's Pr.).

Cominskey, Michael J. The Number System & Common & Decimal Fractions, 1 vol. 2015. (ENG.). 64p. (J). 31.70 *(978-1-62275-524-0(3)*, Britannica Educational Publishing) Rosen Publishing Group, Inc., The.

Concentrate on! — Grades 7, 8. 2003. (J). spiral bd. 15.95 *(978-1-58123-333-9(7))* Larson Learning, Inc.

Concentrate on! Grades 6/7. 2003. (J). spiral bd. 15.95 *(978-1-58123-335-3(3))* Larson Learning, Inc.

Concentrate on! Prealgebra. 2003. spiral bd. 15.95 *(978-1-58123-334-6(5))* Larson Learning, Inc.

Connecting People Pattern Cards. 2003. (J). 7.95 *(978-1-56911-144-4(8))* Learning Resources, Inc.

Connolly, Techla & Meyers-Herron, Carrie. Test Practice for Common Core. 2015. (Barron's Core Focus Ser.). (ENG.). 216p. pap. 14.99 *(978-1-4380-0706-9(X))* Barron's Educational Series, Inc.

Cooper, Terry, ed. Reading & Math. 2005. (ENG.). 320p. pap., wbk. ed. 14.99 *(978-0-439-78603-4(7)*, Teaching Resources) Scholastic, Inc.

—Reading & Math, Grade 3. 2005. (ENG.). 320p. pap., wbk. ed. 14.99 *(978-0-439-78602-7(9)*, Teaching Resources) Scholastic, Inc.

Cooper, Terry, ed. Reading & Math. Cooper, Terry, . 2005. (ENG.). 320p. pap., wbk. ed. 14.99 *(978-0-439-78599-0(5)*, Teaching Resources) Scholastic, Inc.

Core Math Skills: Numbers & Operations in Base 10. 2013. (Core Math Skills: Numbers & Operations in Base 10 Ser.). 24p. (J). (gr. 1-2). 135.60 *(978-1-4777-2235-0(1)*, Rosen Classroom) Rosen Publishing Group, Inc., The.

Core Math Skills (Grades 1 - 2) 2013. (Core Math Skills Ser.). 24p. (J). (gr. 1-2). 406.80 *(978-1-4777-2374-6(9)*, Rosen Classroom) Rosen Publishing Group, Inc., The.

Cortina, Janice. The Lonely Sixteenth. 2010. 40p. 16.99 *(978-1-4520-2406-6(5))* AuthorHouse.

Costa, David. What's the Difference? Frink, Phil, photos by. 2004. (Illus.). 24p. (J). per. 26.99 *(978-1-4134-4855-9(0))* Xlibris Corp.

Cotton, Anthony, et al. Maths. 2014. (ENG., Illus.). 184p. pap., wbk. ed. 20.00 *(978-0-19-839459-4(4))* Oxford Univ. Pr., Inc.

—Oxford International Primary Maths 5. 2014. (ENG., Illus.). 184p. pap. 28.00 *(978-0-19-839463-1(2))* Oxford Univ. Pr., Inc.

—Oxford International Primary Maths, Stage 3. 2014. (ENG., Illus.). 176p. pap. 25.00 *(978-0-19-839461-7(6))* Oxford Univ. Pr., Inc.

The Cotton Tale. abr. ed. 2004. (Thrilling Tales in Time Ser.: Vol. 41). (J). 19.95 *(978-1-58123-372-8(8))* Larson Learning, Inc.

Count down to Math Grade 5. 2005. (ENG.). *(978-0-9766802-9-1(7))* Educational Tools, Inc.

Counting Cards Staff. LP-Counting: Level 1 Math. 2004. (ENG.). (J). 9.99 *(978-1-59204-013-1(6))* Learning Wrap-Ups, Inc.

Cozens, Gaynor & Thomas, Cheryl Ann. Numeracy Matters Grade 1 IsiXhosa. 2003. (AFR.). 48p. pap., wbk. ed. 2.05 *(978-0-521-53868-8(8))* Cambridge Univ. Pr.

—Numeracy Matters Grade 1 Sesotho Translation. 2003. (AFR.). 48p. pap., wbk. ed. 2.05 *(978-0-521-53866-4(1))* Cambridge Univ. Pr.

—Numeracy Matters Grade 1 Xitsonga Tranlation. 2003. (AFR.). 48p. pap., wbk. ed. 2.05 *(978-0-521-53867-1(X))* Cambridge Univ. Pr.

—Numeracy Matters Grade 2 isiXhosa Translation. 2003. (AFR.). 48p. pap., wbk. ed. 2.05 *(978-0-521-53874-9(2))* Cambridge Univ. Pr.

—Numeracy Matters Grade 2 Sesotho Translation. 2003. (AFR.). 48p. pap., wbk. ed. 2.05 *(978-0-521-53872-5(6))* Cambridge Univ. Pr.

—Numeracy Matters Grade 2 Xitsonga Translation. 2003. (AFR.). 48p. pap., wbk. ed. 2.05 *(978-0-521-53873-2(4))* Cambridge Univ. Pr.

—Numeracy Matters, Grade 3. 2003. (AFR.). 48p. pap., wbk. ed. 2.05 *(978-0-521-53879-4(3))* Cambridge Univ. Pr.

—Numeracy Matters Grade 3 Sesotho Translation. 2003. (AFR.). 48p. pap., wbk. ed. 2.05 *(978-0-521-53878-7(5))* Cambridge Univ. Pr.

Crabtree Publishing, creator. My Path to Math: Math Concepts Made Simple. 2008. (J). pap. *(978-0-7787-4354-5(3))* Crabtree Publishing Co.

Critical Thinking Publishing Staff & Husted, Terri. Math Detective A1: Higher-Order Thinking Reading Writing in Mathematics. 2010. (Math Detective Ser.). 128p. (gr. 5-6). pap. 19.99 *(978-0-89455-803-0(X))* Critical Thinking Co., The.

—Math Detective Beginning: Higher-Order Thinking Reading Writing in Mathematics. 2013. (Math Detective Ser.). 112p. (gr. 3-4). pap. 19.99 *(978-0-89455-802-3(1))* Critical Thinking Co., The.

Crum, Anna-Maria. Math to Build On: Set Of 6. 2011. (Navigators Ser.). (J). pap. 48.00 net. *(978-1-4108-0421-1(6))* Benchmark Education Co.

—Math to Build on & Matemáticas para Construir: 6 English, 6 Spanish Adaptations. 2011. (ENG & SPA.). (J). 97.00 net. *(978-1-4108-5696-8(8))* Benchmark Education Co.

Cuenta Conmigo. (Mathematics Ser.). (SPA.). (J). *(978-958-04-7725-9(6))*; *(978-958-04-7726-6(4))*; *(978-958-04-7727-3(2))* Norma S.A. COL. Dist: Distribuidora Norma, Inc.

Cuisenaire Rods Addition & Subtraction Activity Cards. 2003. (J). 19.95 *(978-1-56911-140-6(5))* Learning Resources, Inc.

Cuisenaire Rods Fractions & Decimals Activity Cards. 2003. (J). 19.95 *(978-1-56911-142-0(1))* Learning Resources, Inc.

Cuisenaire Rods Multiplication & Division Activity Cards. 2003. (J). 19.95 *(978-1-56911-141-3(3))* Learning Resources, Inc.

Curriculum Associates Staff. Ready New York CCLS Common Core Math Instruction 2014: Grade 4. 2014. pap. *(978-0-7609-8433-8(6))* Curriculum Assocs., LLC.

Dacey, Linda. Strategies to Integrate the Arts in Mathematics, 1 vol. rev. ed. 2013. (Strategies to Integrate the Arts Ser.). (ENG.). 280p. (gr. k-12). pap. 45.99 *(978-1-4258-1088-7(8))* Shell Educational Publishing.

Dahl, Michael. Huevos y Patas: Cuenta de Dos en Dos. Ouren, Todd, illus. 2010. (Apréndete Tus Números/Know Your Numbers Ser.).Tr. of Eggs & Legs/Counting by Twos. (MUL & SPA.). 24p. (gr. -1-2). lib. bdg. 26.65 *(978-1-4048-6296-8(X))* Picture Window Bks.

—Lots of Ladybugs! Counting by Fives, 1 vol. Ouren, Todd, illus. 2005. (Know Your Numbers Ser.). (ENG.). 24p. (gr. -1-2). 26.65 *(978-1-4048-0944-4(9))* Picture Window Bks.

—¡Montones de Mariquitas! Cuenta de Cinco en Cinco. Ouren, Todd, illus. 2010. (Apréndete Tus Números/Know Your Numbers Ser.).Tr. of Lots of Ladybugs! - Counting by Fives. (SPA & MUL.). 24p. (gr. -1-2). lib. bdg. 26.65 *(978-1-4048-6297-5(8))* Picture Window Bks.

Dale Seymour Staff. Mathematics: Problem Solving Activities. (J). 69p. 12.95 net. *(978-0-86651-256-5(X)*, DSO1529); 77p. (gr. 3). 12.95 net. *(978-0-86651-254-1(3)*, DSO1527); 71p. (gr. 6). 13.95 net. *(978-0-86651-257-2(8)*, DSO1530) Seymour, Dale Pubns.

Dalton, Julie. Patterns Everywhere. 2006. (Rookie Read-About Math Ser.). (ENG., Illus.). 32p. (J). (gr. 1-2). per. 5.95 *(978-0-516-25367-1(0)*, Children's Pr.) Scholastic Library Publishing.

Danellis, Charles W., ed. Group Theory: Classes, Representation & Connections, & Applications. 2010. (Mathematics Research Developments Ser.). (Illus.). 331p. (J). 145.00 *(978-1-60876-175-3(4))* Nova Science Pubs., Inc.

Daronco, Mickey. Circus in the City: Set Of 6. 2011. (BuildUp Ser.). (J). pap. 27.00 net. *(978-1-4108-0774-8(6))* Benchmark Education Co.

Daronco, Mickey & Ohanesian, Diane. The Big Clock: Set Of 6. 2nd rev. ed. 2004. (BuildUp Ser.). (J). pap. 27.00 net. *(978-1-4108-1526-2(9))* Benchmark Education Co.

—Can We Pick It? Set Of 6. 2nd rev. ed. 2004. (BuildUp Ser.). (J). pap. 27.00 net. *(978-1-4108-1534-7(X))* Benchmark Education Co.

—Is It Big? Set Of 6. 2nd rev. ed. 2004. (BuildUp Ser.). (J). pap. 27.00 net. *(978-1-4108-1530-9(7))* Benchmark Education Co.

—More Corn: Set of 6. 2nd rev. ed. 2003. (BuildUp Ser.). (J). pap. 22.00 *(978-1-4108-0766-3(5))* Benchmark Education Co.

—My Turn to Fit: Set Of 6. 2nd rev. ed. 2011. (BuildUp Ser.). Orig. Title: Will It or Will It Not? (J). pap. 27.00 net. *(978-1-4108-0765-6(7))* Benchmark Education Co.

—One to Ten: Set Of 6. 2nd rev. ed. 2004. (BuildUp Ser.). (J). pap. 27.00 net. *(978-1-4108-1527-9(7))* Benchmark Education Co.

—Two by Two: Set Of 6. 2nd rev. ed. 2004. (BuildUp Ser.). (J). pap. 27.00 net. *(978-1-4108-1535-4(8))* Benchmark Education Co.

Daronco, Mickey & Presti, Lori. Instrumentos para Medir: Set Of 6. 2011. (Primeras Conexiones Ser.).Tr. of Measuring Tools. (SPA.). (J). 40.00 net. *(978-1-4108-0330-6(9))* Benchmark Education Co.

Data Mania, 1 vol. 2010. (Data Mania Ser.). (ENG.). 24p. (gr. 1-2). lib. bdg. 75.96 *(978-1-4296-4530-0(X),* First Facts) Capstone Press of Coughlan Cos.

Davies, Ann & Ne, Harriet. Sum Fun. (Illus.). 40p. (J). 19.95 *(978-1-85479-226-6(1))* O'Mara, Michael Bks., Ltd. GBR. Dist: Trans-Atlantic Pubns., Inc.

Davis, Graeme. Earthquakes. 2012. (21st Century Skills Library: Real World Math Ser.). (ENG., Illus.). 32p. (J). (gr. 4-8). pap. 14.21 *(978-1-61080-411-0(2),* 201343); lib. bdg. 28.50 *(978-1-61080-323-6(X),* 201308) Cherry Lake Publishing.

—Floods. 2012. (21st Century Skills Library: Real World Math Ser.). (ENG., Illus.). 32p. (J). (gr. 4-8). pap. 14.21 *(978-1-61080-409-7(0),* 201341); lib. bdg. 28.50 *(978-1-61080-324-3(8),* 201304) Cherry Lake Publishing.

Day Two PSAE Student Textbook. 3rd ed. 2005. per. *(978-1-58894-035-3(7))* Cambridge Educational Services, Inc.

De Long, Ron, et al. Dream-Makers Mathematics: Art & Mathematics. De Long, Ron et al, eds. 2007. (Illus.). 104p. spiral bd. 9.99 *(978-0-86696-327-5(8))* Binney & Smith, Inc.

Dean, Arlan. Mathematical Thinking Ideas Procedures. 2004. (BrainBuilders Ser.). (ENG.). 48p. (gr. k-4). pap. 5.25 *(978-1-4042-8528-6(8))* Rosen Publishing Group, Inc., The.

Decoding Math Word Problems - Grade 3. 2004. (J). pap. 14.95 *(978-1-56911-156-7(1))* Learning Resources, Inc.

Decoding Math Word Problems - Grade 4. 2004. (J). pap. 14.95 *(978-1-56911-157-4(X))* Learning Resources, Inc.

Decoding Math Word Problems - Grade 5. 2004. (J). pap. 14.95 *(978-1-56911-158-1(8))* Learning Resources, Inc.

Dee, Nora. Making Circle Graphs. 2014. (Graph It! Ser.). 24p. (J). (gr. 1-3). 22.60 *(978-1-4824-0829-4(5))* Stevens, Gareth Publishing LLLP.

Deen, Marilyn. Tiling Shapes. 2011. (Wonder Readers Fluent Level Ser.). (ENG.). 16p. (gr. -1-2). pap. 35.94 *(978-1-4296-8188-9(8),* Wonder Readers) Capstone Press of Coughlan Cos.

—Wonder Readers: Mathematics. (Wonder Readers: Mathematics Ser.). (ENG.). 20p. (gr. k-1). 2012. lib. bdg. 181.20 *(978-1-4296-9619-7(2))* 2012. lib. bdg. 90.60 *(978-1-4296-9618-0(4))* 2011. lib. bdg. 90.60 *(978-1-4296-8633-4(2))* Capstone Press of Coughlan Cos. (Wonder Readers).

Delrose, Julian. Feeding Time at the Farm. 2013. (Core Math Skills: Numbers & Operations in Base 10 Ser.). 24p. (J). (gr. 1-2). 22.60 *(978-1-4777-2226-8(2),* Rosen Classroom) Rosen Publishing Group, Inc., The.

—Feeding Time at the Farm: Use Place Value & Properties of Operation to Subtract. 2013. (Rosen Math Readers Ser.). (ENG.). 24p. (J). (gr. 1-2). pap. 8.25 *(978-1-4777-2043-1(X),* Rosen Classroom) Rosen Publishing Group, Inc., The.

—Feeding Time at the Farm: Use Place Value & Properties of Operations to Subtract. 2013. (Rosen Math Readers Ser.). (ENG.). 24p. (J). (gr. 1-2). pap. 49.50 *(978-1-4777-2044-8(8),* Rosen Classroom) Rosen Publishing Group, Inc., The.

Denman, Gregory. Mathematics: Strategies for Explaining Thinking. rev. ed. 2013. (Think It Show It Ser.). (ENG.). 192p. (gr. 3-8). pap. 39.99 *(978-1-4258-1051-1(9))* Shell Educational Publishing.

Dessen, Maci. Let's Go Snorkeling! Use Place Value Understanding. 2014. (Rosen Common Core Math Readers Ser.). (ENG.). 24p. (J). (gr. 3-4). pap. 8.25 *(978-1-4777-4938-8(1),* Rosen Classroom) Rosen Publishing Group, Inc., The.

Developmental Studies Center Staff. AfterSchool KidzMath 3-6 Games. ldr.'s ed. 2005. spiral bd. 70.00 *(978-1-57621-452-7(4))* Center for the Collaborative Classroom.

Dezimalbrueche. (Duden-Schuelerhilfen Ser.). (GER.). 112p. (J). (gr. 6). *(978-3-411-70112-4(9))* Bibliographisches Institut & F. A. Brockhaus AG DEU. Dist: International Bk. Import Service, Inc.

Disbrow, Sheri. Math Warm-Ups: Developing Fluency in Math. 2005. (Math Warm-Ups Ser.). (ENG.). 82p. (gr. 2-2). pap. 14.95 *(978-1-59363-103-1(0));* 82p. (gr. 3-3). pap. 14.95 *(978-1-59363-104-8(9));* 80p. (gr. 4-4). pap. 14.95 *(978-1-59363-105-5(7))* Prufrock Pr.

—Math Warm-Ups, Grade 2. 2004. per. 12.95 *(978-1-883055-64-6(4))* Dandy Lion Pubns.

—Math Warm-Ups, Grade 3. 2004. per. 12.95 *(978-1-883055-65-3(2))* Dandy Lion Pubns.

—Math Warm-Ups, Grade 4. 2004. per. 12.95 *(978-1-883055-66-0(0))* Dandy Lion Pubns.

Dise, Molly. A Math Hike. 2011. (Math Ser.). (ENG.). 16p. (gr. -1-1). 25.95 *(978-1-4296-8541-2(7),* Wonder Readers) Capstone Press of Coughlan Cos.

Disney Mickey, Disney. Disney Imagicademy: Math Adventures. 2016. (ENG.). 14p. (J). (gr. -1-2). 12.99 *(978-0-7944-3595-0(5))* Studio Fun International.

Dix, Colton. The Popcorn Sale: Understand Place Value. 2013. (Rosen Math Readers Ser.). (ENG.). 24p. (J). (gr. 1-2). pap. 49.50 *(978-1-4777-2095-0(2));* (Illus.). pap. 8.25 *(978-1-4777-2094-3(4))* Rosen Publishing Group, Inc., The. (Rosen Classroom).

Dockery, L. D. The Multiplication Song Book. 2012. 24p. pap. 17.99 *(978-1-4772-6900-8(2))* AuthorHouse.

Dolphin, Colleen. Angles to Zeros: Mathematics from A to Z, 1 vol. 2008. (Let's Look A to Z Ser.). (ENG., Illus.). 32p. (gr. k-4). 27.07 *(978-1-60453-011-7(1),* Super SandCastle) ABDO Publishing Co.

Donovan, Barabara. Numbers Everywhere: A Content Area Reader-math. 2005. (Sadlier Phonics Reading Program). 12p. (gr. k-2). 25.20 *(978-0-8215-7823-0(5))* Sadlier, William H. Inc.

Dooley, Virginia. Reading & Math. Cooper, Terry, ed. 2005. (ENG.). 320p. pap., wbk. ed. 14.99 *(978-0-439-78600-3(2),* Teaching Resources) Scholastic, Inc.

Dooley, Virginia & Teaching Resources Staff. Reading & Math Jumbo. Cooper, Terry, ed. 2005. (ENG.). 320p. pap., wbk. ed. 14.99 *(978-0-439-78598-3(7),* Teaching Resources) Scholastic, Inc.

Dorling Kindersley Publishing Staff. Amazing Visual Math. 2014. (ENG.). 18p. (J). (gr. 3-7). 14.99 *(978-1-4654-2017-6(7),* DK Children) Dorling Kindersley Publishing, Inc.

—How to Do Math. 2016. (ENG., Illus.). 320p. (J). (gr. 2-5). pap. 19.99 *(978-1-4654-3575-0(1),* DK Children) Dorling Kindersley Publishing, Inc.

—The Incredible Math Games Book. 2015. (ENG.). 16p. (J). (gr. 1-4). 16.99 *(978-1-4654-3628-3(6),* DK Children) Dorling Kindersley Publishing, Inc.

—10 Minutes a Day: Math Grade 5. 2013. (ENG.). 80p. (J). (gr. 4-7). pap. 9.99 *(978-1-4654-0230-1(6),* DK Children) Dorling Kindersley Publishing, Inc.

—10 Minutes a Day - Math, Grade 4. 2013. (ENG.). 80p. (J). (gr. 2-4). pap. 9.99 *(978-1-4654-0229-5(2),* DK Children) Dorling Kindersley Publishing, Inc.

—10 Minutes a Day - Math, Grade K. 2013. (ENG.). 80p. (J). (gr. -1-k). pap. 9.99 *(978-1-4654-0232-5(2),* DK Children) Dorling Kindersley Publishing, Inc.

—10 Minutes a Day: Decimals, Fourth Grade: Decimals, Fourth Grade. 2014. (ENG.). 80p. (J). (gr. 3-7). pap. 9.99 *(978-1-4654-2823-3(2),* DK Children) Dorling Kindersley Publishing, Inc.

—10 Minutes a Day Math, Grade 2. 2013. (ENG.). 80p. (J). (gr. k-4). pap. 9.99 *(978-1-4654-0231-8(4),* DK Children) Dorling Kindersley Publishing, Inc.

Dorling Kindersley Publishing Staff & Goldsmith, Mike. How to Be a Math Genius. 2012. (ENG., Illus.). 128p. (J). (gr. 5-12). 15.99 *(978-0-7566-9796-9(4),* DK Children) Dorling Kindersley Publishing, Inc.

Dorling Kindersley Publishing Staff & Vorderman, Carol. Math Dictionary. 2009. (ENG., Illus.). 128p. (J). (gr. 3-7). 14.99 *(978-0-7566-5194-7(8),* DK Children) Dorling Kindersley Publishing, Inc.

Dot-to-Dot 1-100+ (Gr. 2-4) 2003. (J). *(978-1-58232-104-2(3))* ECS Learning Systems, Inc.

Dowdy, Penny. Body Math. 2008. (Math Alive! Ser.). 32p. (gr. 4-18). lib. bdg. 28.50 *(978-0-7614-3215-9(9),* Benchmark Bks.) Marshall Cavendish Corp.

—Estimation. 2008. (My Path to Math Ser.). (ENG., Illus.). 24p. (J). (gr. k-3). pap. *(978-0-7787-4355-2(1))* Crabtree Publishing Co.

—Nature Math. 2008. (Math Alive! Ser.). 32p. (gr. 4-18). lib. bdg. 28.50 *(978-0-7614-3214-2(0),* Benchmark Bks.) Marshall Cavendish Corp.

Dowdy, Penny & Becker, Ann. Subtraction. 2009. (My Path to Math Ser.). (ENG.). 24p. (J). (gr. k-1). pap. *(978-0-7787-4368-2(3))* Crabtree Publishing Co.

Draze, Dianne. The Loose Caboose & Other Math Mysteries. 2005. 64p. 11.95 *(978-1-59363-136-9(7))* Prufrock Pr.

—Math-a-Logic. 2005. (ENG.). 81p. (gr. 5-8). pap. 14.95 *(978-1-59363-107-9(3))* Prufrock Pr.

Dreieckskonstruktionen. (Duden-Schuelerhilfen Ser.). (GER.). 112p. (YA). (gr. 7-8). *(978-3-411-05671-2(1))* Bibliographisches Institut & F. A. Brockhaus AG DEU. Dist: International Bk. Import Service, Inc.

Dreisatz, Prozente, Zinsen. (Duden-Schuelerhilfen Ser.). (GER.). 112p. (YA). (gr. 6-8). *(978-3-411-70762-1(3))* Bibliographisches Institut & F. A. Brockhaus AG DEU. Dist: International Bk. Import Service, Inc.

Drill, Practice, & Apply (Gr. 1-2) 2003. (J). *(978-1-58232-100-4(0))* ECS Learning Systems, Inc.

Drill, Practice, & Apply Gr. 1-2 Spanish Version. 2007. (J). per. *(978-1-58232-159-2(0))* ECS Learning Systems, Inc.

Drill, Practice, & Apply (Gr. 2-3) 2003. (J). *(978-1-58232-101-1(9))* ECS Learning Systems, Inc.

Drill, Practice, & Apply Gr. 2-3 Spanish Version. 2007. (J). per. *(978-1-58232-160-8(4))* ECS Learning Systems, Inc.

Drill, Practice, & Apply (Gr. 3-4) 2003. (J). *(978-1-58232-102-8(7))* ECS Learning Systems, Inc.

Drill, Practice, & Apply Gr. 3-4 Spanish Version. 2007. (J). per. *(978-1-58232-161-5(2))* ECS Learning Systems, Inc.

Drill, Practice, & Apply (Gr. 4-5) 2003. (J). *(978-1-58232-103-5(5))* ECS Learning Systems, Inc.

Drill, Practice, & Apply Gr. 4-5 Spanish Version. 2007. (J). per. *(978-1-58232-162-2(0))* ECS Learning Systems, Inc.

Dugan, Christine & Lane, Chloe. Pack It Up: Surface Area & Volume. rev. ed. 2012. (Mathematics Readers Ser.). (ENG.). 32p. (J). (gr. 6-6). pap. 8.99 *(978-1-4333-3461-0(5))* Teacher Created Materials, Inc.

Duke, Shirley. What's the Place Value? 2012. (ENG.). 24p. (gr. -1-1). pap. 8.95 *(978-1-61810-208-9(7))* Rourke Educational Media.

Duncan, Neil, et al. Cambridge Checkpoints HSC General Mathematics 2014. 2013. (Cambridge Checkpoints Ser.). (ENG.). pap. *(978-1-107-64370-3(8))* Cambridge Univ. Pr.

—Cambridge Checkpoints HSC Mathematics Extension 1 2014. 2013. (Cambridge Checkpoints Ser.). (ENG.). pap. *(978-1-107-64350-5(3))* Cambridge Univ. Pr.

—HSC Mathematics 2014. 2013. (Cambridge Checkpoints Ser.). (ENG.). pap. *(978-1-107-69277-0(6))* Cambridge Univ. Pr.

DynaNotes Grade 9 Math Review Guide Transparency Set. 2006. (YA). trans. *(978-1-933854-34-2(0))* DynaStudy, Inc.

DynaNotes Grade 9 Math TAKS Review Guide. 2006. (YA). pap. *(978-1-933854-30-4(8))* DynaStudy, Inc.

Eastaway, Rob & Askew, Mike. Maths on the Go: 101 Fun Ways to Play with Maths. 2016. (ENG., Illus.). 208p. 16.99 ***(978-0-224-10162-2(5))*** Random Hse. GBR. Dist: Independent Pubs. Group.

Ebbutt, Sheila. Playing with Maths Interactive, Vol. 2. 2014. (ENG.). audio compact disk 141.00 *(978-1-906224-37-0(4))* Oxford Univ. Pr., Inc.

Edson, Ann & Schwartz, Allan A. Read & Solve Math Problems, Vol. 2. (J). (gr. 4-6). pap., act. bk. ed., pupil's gde. ed. 79.00 incl. audio *(978-0-89525-196-1(5),* AKC 319) Educational Activities, Inc.

Education.com. All That Math: A Workbook of Basic Operations & Small Numbers. 2015. (ENG.). 128p. (J). (gr. 3-3). pap. 7.99 *(978-0-486-80268-8(X))* Dover Pubns., Inc.

—Count It: A Workbook of Patterning, Counting, & Addition. 2015. (ENG.). 128p. (J). (gr. 1-1). pap. 7.99 *(978-0-486-80260-2(4))* Dover Pubns., Inc.

—Creatures & Counting: A Workbook of Counting, Sorting, & Discovery. 2015. (ENG.). 128p. (J). (gr. -1-k). pap. 7.99 *(978-0-486-80274-9(4))* Dover Pubns., Inc.

—Earth & Sky: A Workbook of Science Facts & Math Practice. 2015. (ENG.). 112p. (J). (gr. 3-3). pap. 7.99 *(978-0-486-80269-5(8))* Dover Pubns., Inc.

—Math Mania: A Workbook of Whole Numbers, Fractions, & Decimals. 2015. (ENG.). 112p. (J). (gr. 4-4). pap. 7.99 *(978-0-486-80271-8(X))* Dover Pubns., Inc.

Edwards, Roy. School Mathematics Project 11-16, Llyfr 1. 2005. (WEL., Illus.). 64p. *(978-1-86085-065-3(0))* ICA Video.

Edwards, Roy, et al. Mathemateg Cynradd Caergrawnt. 2005. (WEL., Illus.). 128p. pap. *(978-1-86085-070-7(7))* ICA Video.

Egan, Jill & Stewart, Rhea A. How Video Game Designers Use Math. 2009. (Math in the Real World Ser.). 32p. (gr. 4-6). 28.00 *(978-1-60413-603-6(0),* Chelsea Clubhouse) Facts On File, Inc.

Eikum, John. The 4th Dimension & Beyond: Imagining Worlds with 0, 1, 2, 3, 4 Dimensions & More. 2007. 120p. (J). per. 16.95 *(978-1-59298-172-4(0))* Beaver's Pond Pr., Inc.

Einhorn, Karna. Number of the Week Flip Chart: Lively, Interactive Acvtive Pages That Teaches Each Number from 0 to 30. 2013. (ENG.). 28p. (gr. -1-2). pap. 25.99 *(978-0-545-45709-5(2),* Teaching Resources) Scholastic, Inc.

Elementary Mathematics for Diverse Learners - Training Kit. 2004. (Region IV ESC Resources for Special Education Ser.). cd-rom *(978-1-932797-04-6(1))* Region IV Education Service Ctr.

Ellis, Rob & Collins UK. Edexcel GCSE Maths - Higher Practice Book: Use & Apply Standard Techniques. 4th ed. 2015. (Collins GCSE Maths Ser.). (ENG.). 184p. (YA). (gr. 9-11). pap. 12.95 *(978-0-00-811387-2(4))* HarperCollins Pubs. Ltd. GBR. Dist: Independent Pubs. Group.

Ellis, Rob & Collins UK Publishing Staff. Maths Higher Practice Book: Use & Apply Standard Techniques. 4th rev. ed. 2015. (Collins GCSE Maths Ser.). (ENG.). 184p. (J). (gr. 9-11). pap. 12.95 *(978-0-00-811383-4(1))* HarperCollins Pubs. Ltd. GBR. Dist: Independent Pubs. Group.

Encyclopaedia Britannica, Inc. Staff, compiled by. Britannica Math in Context Test & Practice Generator with Examview Assessment Suite. 2010. cd-rom 175.00 *(978-1-61535-441-2(7))* Encyclopaedia Britannica, Inc.

Encyclopaedia Britannica Publishers, Inc. Staff. Math in Context. 6th ed. 2005. (Math in Context Ser.). Level 1. 79.73 *(978-0-03-040374-3(X))*Level 2. 79.73 *(978-0-03-040377-4(4))*Level 3. 79.73 *(978-0-03-040378-1(2))* Harcourt Schl. Pubs.

—Math in Context: Building Formulas. 6th ed. 2005. (Math in Context Ser.). pap. 10.60 *(978-0-03-038559-9(8))* Harcourt Schl. Pubs.

—Math in Context: Dealing with Data. 6th ed. 2005. (Math in Context Ser.). pap. 10.60 *(978-0-03-038566-7(0))* Harcourt Schl. Pubs.

—Math in Context: Facts & Factors. 6th ed. 2005. (Math in Context Ser.). pap. 10.60 *(978-0-03-038564-3(4))* Harcourt Schl. Pubs.

—Math in Context: Great Predictions. 6th ed. 2005. (Math in Context Ser.). pap. 10.60 *(978-0-03-038572-8(5))* Harcourt Schl. Pubs.

—Math in Context: It's All the Same. 6th ed. 2005. (Math in Context Ser.). (gr. 8). pap. 10.60 *(978-0-03-038567-4(9))* Harcourt Schl. Pubs.

—Math in Context: Made to Measure. 6th ed. 2005. (Math in Context Ser.). (gr. 7). pap. 10.60 *(978-0-03-042404-5(6))* Harcourt Schl. Pubs.

—Math in Context: More or Less. 6th ed. 2006. (Math in Context Ser.). pap. 10.60 *(978-0-03-039618-2(2))* Harcourt Schl. Pubs.

—Math in Context: Number Tools. 6th ed. 2006. (Math in Context Ser.). pap., wbk. ed. 12.70 *(978-0-03-040384-2(7))* Harcourt Schl. Pubs.

—Math in Context: Operations. 6th ed. 2005. (Math in Context Ser.). pap. 10.60 *(978-0-03-038561-2(X))* Harcourt Schl. Pubs.

—Math in Context: Ratios & Rates. 6th ed. 2005. (Math in Context Ser.). (gr. 7). pap. 10.60 *(978-0-03-039629-8(8))* Harcourt Schl. Pubs.

—Math in Context: Reallotment. 6th ed. 2005. (Math in Context Ser.). pap. 10.60 *(978-0-03-039614-4(X))* Harcourt Schl. Pubs.

—Math in Context: Second Chance. 6th ed. 2005. (Math in Context Ser.). (gr. 7). pap. 10.60 *(978-0-03-038558-2(X))* Harcourt Schl. Pubs.

—Math in Context: Take a Chance. 6th ed. 2006. (Math in Context Ser.). (gr. 6). pap. 10.60 *(978-0-03-039613-7(1))* Harcourt Schl. Pubs.

—Math in Context: Ups & Downs. 6th ed. 2005. (Math in Context Ser.). pap. 10.60 *(978-0-03-038576-6(8))* Harcourt Schl. Pubs.

Enderle, Dotti. Storytime Discoveries: Math. Ginger Illustrations Staff, illus. 2004. 64p. (J). pap. 9.95 *(978-1-57310-440-1(X))* Teaching & Learning Co.

Essential Words Math Activity Book (Elementary) Elementary. 2006. (J). 8.95 *(978-1-933655-04-8(6))* New Leaf Educ., Inc.

Essential Words Math Activity Book (Intermediate) Intermediate/Middle School. 2005. (Illus.). 42p. (J). 8.95 *(978-0-9722452-9-6(4))* New Leaf Educ., Inc.

Evan-Moor. Basic Math Skills Grade 1. 2003. (Basic Math Skills Ser.). (ENG.). 304p. (J). (gr. 1). pap. 29.99 *(978-1-55799-896-5(5),* EMC 3014) Evan-Moor Educational Pubs.

—Basic Math Skills Grade 2. 2003. (Basic Math Skills Ser.). (ENG.). 304p. (J). (gr. 2). pap. 29.99 *(978-1-55799-897-2(3),* EMC 3015) Evan-Moor Educational Pubs.

—Basic Math Skills Grade 3. 2003. (Basic Math Skills Ser.). (ENG.). 304p. (J). (gr. 3). pap. 29.99 *(978-1-55799-898-9(1),* EMC 3016) Evan-Moor Educational Pubs.

—Basic Math Skills, Grade 4. 2005. (ENG.). 304p. (J). (gr. 4-18). pap. 29.99 *(978-1-55799-937-5(6),* EMC 3017) Evan-Moor Educational Pubs.

—Math Centers, Grades 2-3. 2004. (ENG., Illus.). 192p. (J). (gr. 2-3). pap. 21.99 *(978-1-55799-978-8(3),* EMC 3021) Evan-Moor Educational Pubs.

—Math Centers, Grades 3-4. 2004. (ENG., Illus.). 192p. (J). (gr. 3-4). pap. 21.99 *(978-1-55799-979-5(1),* EMC 3022) Evan-Moor Educational Pubs.

—Skill Sharpeners, Math, Grade 1. 2005. (ENG.). 144p. (J). pap. 9.99 *(978-1-59673-053-3(6),* emc 4545) Evan-Moor Educational Pubs.

—Skill Sharpeners Math, Grade 2. 2005. (ENG.). 144p. (J). pap. 9.99 *(978-1-59673-054-0(4),* emc 4546) Evan-Moor Educational Pubs.

—Skill Sharpeners Math, Grade 3. 2005. (ENG.). 144p. (J). pap. 9.99 *(978-1-59673-055-7(2),* emc 4547) Evan-Moor Educational Pubs.

—Skill Sharpeners Math, Grade 4. 2005. (ENG.). 144p. (J). pap. 9.99 *(978-1-59673-056-4(0),* emc 4548) Evan-Moor Educational Pubs.

—Skill Sharpeners Math, Grade 5. 2005. (ENG.). 144p. (J). pap. 9.99 *(978-1-59673-057-1(9),* emc 4549) Evan-Moor Educational Pubs.

—Skill Sharpeners, Math, Grade 6+ 2005. (ENG.). 144p. (J). pap. 9.99 *(978-1-59673-058-8(7),* emc 4550) Evan-Moor Educational Pubs.

—Skill Sharpeners Math, Grade K. 2005. (ENG., Illus.). 144p. (J). pap. 9.99 *(978-1-59673-052-6(8),* emc 4544) Evan-Moor Educational Pubs.

—Skill Sharpeners Math, Grade PreK. 2005. (ENG.). 144p. (J). pap. 9.99 *(978-1-59673-051-9(X),* emc 4543) Evan-Moor Educational Pubs.

Evans, Kevin, et al. Edexcel GCSE Maths Foundation. 4th rev. ed. 2015. (Collins GCSE Maths Ser.). (ENG.). 700p. (YA). (gr. 9-11). pap., stu. ed. 31.95 *(978-0-00-811382-7(3))* HarperCollins Pubs. Ltd. GBR. Dist: Independent Pubs. Group.

—Homework, Bk. 3. 3rd ed. 2014. (Maths Frameworking Ser.). (ENG., Illus.). 120p. (YA). (gr. 9-9). pap. 12.99 *(978-0-00-753765-5(4))* HarperCollins Pubs. Ltd. GBR. Dist: Independent Pubs. Group.

—Maths Frameworking. 3rd ed. 2014. (Maths Frameworking Ser.). (ENG., Illus.). 360p. (YA). (gr. 9-9). pap. 25.99 *(978-0-00-753779-2(4))* HarperCollins Pubs. Ltd. GBR. Dist: Independent Pubs. Group.

—Pupil Book. 3rd ed. 2014. (Maths Frameworking Ser.). (ENG., Illus.). 360p. (YA). (gr. 9-9). pap. 25.99 *(978-0-00-753777-8(8))* HarperCollins Pubs. Ltd. GBR. Dist: Independent Pubs. Group.

Evans, Lesli. Transport Math. 2008. (Math Alive! Ser.). 32p. (gr. 4-18). lib. bdg. 28.50 *(978-0-7614-3211-1(6),* Benchmark Bks.) Marshall Cavendish Corp.

Evans, Lory. One-Page Math Games: 30 Super-Easy, Super-Fun, Reproducible Games for Seatwork, Centers, Homework, & More! 2011. (ENG.). 48p. pap. 10.99 *(978-0-545-31475-6(5),* Teaching Resources) Scholastic, Inc.

Exploring Acadia National Park: Solve Problems Involving the Four Operations. 2014. (Rosen Common Core Math Readers Ser.). (ENG., Illus.). 24p. (J). (gr. 3-4). pap. 8.25 *(978-1-4777-4944-9(6),* PowerKids Pr.) Rosen Publishing Group, Inc., The.

Exploring Geometric Solids. 2004. (J). per. 4.95 *(978-1-56911-538-1(9))* Learning Resources, Inc.

Extend the Day! a Guide to Using Larson's Intermediate Math in Before-School & after-School Programs. 2003. spiral bd. 0.00 *(978-1-58123-339-1(6))* Larson Learning, Inc.

Extend the Day! a Guide to Using Larson's Prealgebra & Larson's Algebra 1 in Before-School & after-School Programs. 2003. spiral bd. 0.00 *(978-1-58123-340-7(X))* Larson Learning, Inc.

Fact Families Staff. LP-Fact Families: Level 1 Math. 2004. (ENG.). (J). 9.99 *(978-1-59204-016-2(0))* Learning Wrap-Ups, Inc.

Falvo, David C. Passport to Mathematics Practice Workbook: Book 1. 2006. (Illus.). 87p. (gr. 6-12). stu. ed., per., wbk. ed. *(978-0-395-89626-6(6),* 2-77680) Holt McDougal.

Fannon, Paul, et al. Mathematics Higher Level for the IB Diploma Option Topic 8 Sets, Relations & Groups. 2013. (IB Diploma Ser.). (ENG., Illus.). 148p. pap. 18.44 *(978-1-107-64628-5(6))* Cambridge Univ. Pr.

—Mathematics Higher Level Statistics & Probability for the IB Diploma. 2013. (IB Diploma Ser.). (ENG., Illus.). 172p. pap. 18.44 *(978-1-107-68226-9(6))* Cambridge Univ. Pr.

Faulkner, Nicholas & Gregersen, Erik. Analysis & Calculus. 2017. (J). ***(978-1-68048-775-6(2))*** Rosen Publishing Group, Inc., The.

Feldman, Jean & Karapetkova, Holly. Math Songs. unabr. ed. 2010. (ENG.). 16p. (gr. -1-k). 12.99 *(978-1-61741-588-3(X))* Rourke Educational Media.

Feldman, Jean R. & Karapetkova, Holly. Addition Pokey (Tune, Hokey Pokey) Lap Book. 2010. (ENG., Illus.). 12p. (gr. -1-k). 9.95 *(978-1-61590-198-2(1))* Rourke Educational Media.

Feldman, Sarah. Symmetry in Our World: Set Of 6. 2011. (Early Connections Ser.). (J). pap. 39.00 net. *(978-1-4108-1545-3(5))* Benchmark Education Co.

Femiano, Robert. Dr. Funster's Quick Thinks Math C1: Fun Math Brain Teasers. 2003. (Dr. Funster's Ser.). 44p. (gr. 8-10). pap. 3.99 *(978-0-89455-831-3(5))* Critical Thinking Co., The.

Ferguson. Careers in Focus: Mathematics & Physics. 2nd rev. ed. 2008. (Careers in Focus Ser.). 202p. (gr. 6-12). 32.95 *(978-0-8160-7274-3(4),* Ferguson Publishing Co.) Facts On File, Inc.

Ferrie, Chris. ABC's of Mathematics. 2017. (Baby University Ser.: 0). (ENG.). 26p. (J). bds. 9.99 ***(978-1-4926-5628-9(3),*** Sourcebooks Jabberwocky) Sourcebooks, Inc.

First-Glance Finance. 2015. (First-Glance Finance Ser.). (ENG.). 48p. (J). (gr. 4-4). 188.16 *(978-1-5026-0292-3(X))* Cavendish Square Publishing.

First Number Skills Spanish Version. 2007. (J). per. *(978-1-58232-150-9(7))* ECS Learning Systems, Inc.

First Picture Math. 2007. (First Picture Board Bks.). (Illus.). 16p. (J). (gr. -1-k). bds. 11.99 *(978-0-7945-1642-0(4),* Usborne) EDC Publishing.

First, Rachel. Math Beginnings. 2016. (Math Beginnings Ser.: 6). (ENG.). 24p. (J). (gr. k-3). lib. bdg. 145.26 *(978-1-62403-931-7(6),* SandCastle) ABDO Publishing Co.

—Weigh It! Fun with Weight, 1 vol. 2016. (Math Beginnings Ser.). (ENG., Illus.). 24p. (J). (gr. k-3). 24.21 *(978-1-62403-936-2(7))* ABDO Publishing Co.

Fisher, Richard W. Mastering Essential Math Skills, Book One: Grades 4 And 5: 20 Minutes a Day to Success. 2007. (Mastering Essential Math Skills Ser.). (Illus.). 142p. (J). (gr. 6-13). pap. 19.95 *(978-0-9821901-0-4(7))* Math Essentials.

Fishman, Seth. A Hundred Billion Trillion Stars. Greenberg, Isabel, illus. 2017. 40p. (J). (gr. -1-3). 17.99 *(978-0-06-245578-9(8),* Collins Design) HarperCollins Pubs.

Fitzsimmons, Jim & Whiteford, Rhona. Maths Tests. (Illus.). 32p. (J). pap. 6.99 (978-0-340-68070-4(9)) Hodder & Stoughton GBR. Dist: Trafalgar Square Publishing.

Fix, Natalie. Graphing Death Valley: Represent & Interpret Data, 1 vol. 2015. (InfoMax Common Core Math Readers Ser.). (ENG.). 24p. (J). pap. 8.25 (978-1-4777-4600-4(5), Rosen Classroom) Rosen Publishing Group, Inc., The.

Flaherty, Liz. Cooking up a Storm. 2007. (Action Numeracy Middle Primary Ser.). 32p. pap. 9.95 (978-0-86431-670-7(4)) ACER Pr. AUS. Dist: ISBS Publisher Services.

Flash Kids Editors, ed. Division Activities: Grade 3 (Flash Skills) 2010. (Flash Skills Ser.). (ENG.). 64p. (J). pap. 3.95 (978-1-4114-3443-1(9), Spark Publishing Group) Sterling Publishing Co., Inc.

—Main Idea: Grade 3 (Flash Skills) 2010. (Flash Skills Ser.). (ENG.). 64p. (J). pap. 3.95 (978-1-4114-3442-4(0), Spark Publishing Group) Sterling Publishing Co., Inc.

—Math Drills: Grade 1 (Flash Skills) 2010. (Flash Skills Ser.). (ENG.). 64p. (J). pap. 3.95 (978-1-4114-3460-8(9), Spark Publishing Group) Sterling Publishing Co., Inc.

—Math Drills: Grade 2 (Flash Skills) 2010. (Flash Skills Ser.). (ENG.). 64p. (J). pap. 3.95 (978-1-4114-3451-6(X), Spark Publishing Group) Sterling Publishing Co., Inc.

—Math Drills: Grade 3 (Flash Skills) 2010. (Flash Skills Ser.). (ENG.). 64p. (J). pap. 3.95 (978-1-4114-3454-7(4), Spark Publishing Group) Sterling Publishing Co., Inc.

—Multiplication Activities: Grade 3 (Flash Skills) 2010. (Flash Skills Ser.). (ENG.). 64p. (J). pap. 3.95 (978-1-4114-3452-3(8), Spark Publishing Group) Sterling Publishing Co., Inc.

—Number Puzzles & Games: Grade Pre-K-K (Flash Skills) 2010. (Flash Skills Ser.). (ENG.). 64p. (J). pap. 3.95 (978-1-4114-3464-6(1), Spark Publishing Group) Sterling Publishing Co., Inc.

—Place Value: Grade 1 (Flash Skills) 2010. (Flash Skills Ser.). (ENG.). 64p. (J). pap. 3.95 (978-1-4114-3455-4(2), Spark Publishing Group) Sterling Publishing Co., Inc.

—Subtraction Activities: Grade 1 (Flash Skills) 2010. (Flash Skills Ser.). (ENG.). 64p. (J). pap. 3.95 (978-1-4114-3457-8(9), Spark Publishing Group) Sterling Publishing Co., Inc.

—Subtraction Activities: Grade 2 (Flash Skills) 2010. (Flash Skills Ser.). (ENG.). 64p. (J). pap. 3.95 (978-1-4114-3456-1(0), Spark Publishing Group) Sterling Publishing Co., Inc.

Flash Kids Editors, Flash Kids, ed. Summer Study, Grade 1. 2016. (Summer Study Ser.). (ENG., Illus.). 160p. (J). (gr. 1-1). pap. 9.95 (978-1-4114-7857-2(6), Spark Publishing Group) Sterling Publishing Co., Inc.

—Summer Study, Grade 2. 2016. (Summer Study Ser.). (ENG., Illus.). 160p. (J). (gr. 2-2). pap. 9.95 (978-1-4114-7858-9(4), Spark Publishing Group) Sterling Publishing Co., Inc.

—Summer Study, Grade 3. 2016. (Summer Study Ser.). (ENG., Illus.). 160p. (J). (gr. 3-3). pap. 9.95 (978-1-4114-7859-6(2), Spark Publishing Group) Sterling Publishing Co., Inc.

—Summer Study, Grade 4. 2016. (Summer Study Ser.). (ENG., Illus.). 160p. (J). (gr. 4-4). pap. 9.95 (978-1-4114-7860-2(6), Spark Publishing Group) Sterling Publishing Co., Inc.

—Summer Study, Grade 5. 2016. (Summer Study Ser.). (ENG., Illus.). 160p. (J). (gr. 5-5). pap. 9.95 (978-1-4114-7861-9(4), Spark Publishing Group) Sterling Publishing Co., Inc.

—Summer Study, Kindergarten. 2016. (Summer Study Ser.). (ENG., Illus.). 160p. (J). (gr. k-k). pap. 9.95 (978-1-4114-7862-6(2), Spark Publishing Group) Sterling Publishing Co., Inc.

Flatt, Lizann. Counting on Fall. Barron, Ashley & Owlkids Books Inc. Staff, illus. 2012. (Math in Nature Ser.: 1). (ENG.). 32p. (J). (gr. k-2). 15.95 (978-1-926973-36-4(4), Owlkids) Owlkids Bks. Inc. CAN. Dist: Publishers Group West (PGW).

—Line Graphs. 2016. (Get Graphing! Building Data Literacy Skills Ser.). (ENG., Illus.). 24p. (J). (gr. k-3). (978-0-7787-2625-8(8)) Crabtree Publishing Co.

—Sorting Through Spring. Barron, Ashley, illus. 2013. (Math in Nature Ser.: 2). (ENG.). 32p. (J). (gr. 1-4). 15.95 (978-1-926973-59-3(3), Owlkids) Owlkids Bks. Inc. CAN. Dist: Publishers Group West (PGW).

Flip over Math: Addition & Subtraction. 2004. (J). spiral bd. 14.95 (978-1-56911-540-4(0)) Learning Resources, Inc.

Flip over Math: Multiplication & Division. 2004. (J). spiral bd. 14.95 (978-1-56911-541-1(9)) Learning Resources, Inc.

Flip over Math: Story Problems. 2004. (J). spiral bd. 14.95 (978-1-56911-542-8(7)) Learning Resources, Inc.

Flockhart, Dan. Fantasy Basketball & Mathematics: Student Workbook. 2007. (Fantasy Sports & Mathematics Ser.: 5). (ENG., Illus.). 216p. (gr. 4-7). per. 9.95 (978-0-7879-9449-5(9), Jossey-Bass) Wiley, John & Sons, Inc.

—Fantasy Football & Mathematics: Student Workbook. 2007. (Fantasy Sports & Mathematics Ser.: 3). (ENG., Illus.). 144p. (gr. 4-7). stu. ed., per., wbk. ed. 9.95 (978-0-7879-9448-8(0), Jossey-Bass) Wiley, John & Sons, Inc.

Foresman, Scott. Scott Foresman - Addison Wesley Mathematics: Additional Resources. 2003. (ENG.). (gr. k-2). 42.47 net. (978-0-328-08111-0(6)); (gr. 5-6). 42.47 net. (978-0-328-08113-4(2)) Pearson Schl. (Scott Foresman).

—Scott Foresman-Addison Wesley Mathematics. 2003. (ENG.). (gr. k-k). pap., stu. ed. 28.47 net. (978-0-328-07586-7(8)); (gr. k-k). pap., wbk. ed. 5.47 net. (978-0-328-04952-3(2)); (gr. k-k). pap., wbk. ed. 8.97 net. (978-0-328-04931-8(X)); (gr. 1-1). pap., stu. ed. 41.97 net. (978-0-328-03016-3(3)) Pearson Schl. (Scott Foresman).

—Scott Foresman-Addison Wesley Mathematics: Pre-K Mathematics. 2003. (ENG.). (gr. k-6). cd-rom 46.47 net. (978-0-328-08590-3(1), Scott Foresman) Pearson Schl.

—Scott Foresman-Addison Wesley Mathematics: Pupil Edition. 2003. (ENG.). (gr. 2-2). pap. 41.97 net. (978-0-328-03017-0(1), Scott Foresman) Pearson Schl.

—Scott Foresman-Addison Wesley Mathematics: Workbooks. 2003. (ENG.). (gr. 1-1). pap., wbk. ed. 8.97 net. (978-0-328-07556-0(6)); (gr. 2-2). pap., wbk. ed. 8.97 net. (978-0-328-07557-7(4)); (gr. 3-3). pap., wbk. ed. 8.97 net. (978-0-328-07558-4(2)); (gr. 4-4). pap., wbk. ed. 8.97 net. (978-0-328-07559-1(0)); (gr. 5-5). pap., wbk. ed. 8.97 net. (978-0-328-07560-7(4)); (gr. 6-6). pap., wbk. ed. 8.97 net. (978-0-328-07561-4(2)); (gr. 1-1). pap., wbk. ed. 8.97 net. (978-0-328-04932-5(8)); (gr. 1-1). pap., wbk. ed. 5.47 net. (978-0-328-04953-0(0)); (gr. 1-1). pap., wbk. ed. 5.47 net. (978-0-328-04959-2(X)); (gr. 2-2). pap., wbk. ed. 8.97 net. (978-0-328-04933-2(6)); (gr. 2-2). pap., wbk. ed. 5.47 net. (978-0-328-04954-7(9)); (gr. 2-2). pap., wbk. ed. 5.47 net. (978-0-328-04960-8(3)); (gr. 2-2). pap., wbk. ed. 8.97 net. (978-0-328-04966-0(2)); (gr. 3-3). pap., wbk. ed. 8.97 net. (978-0-328-04934-9(4)); (gr. 3-3). pap., wbk. ed. 5.47 net. (978-0-328-04961-5(1)); (gr. 3-3). pap., wbk. ed. 5.47 net. (978-0-328-04955-4(7)); (gr. 3-3). pap., wbk. ed. 8.97 net. (978-0-328-04967-7(0)); (gr. 4-4). pap., wbk. ed. 8.97 net. (978-0-328-04968-4(9)); (gr. 4-4). pap., wbk. ed. 5.47 net. (978-0-328-04956-1(5)); (gr. 4-4). pap., wbk. ed. 5.47 net. (978-0-328-04962-2(X)); (gr. 4-4). pap., wbk. ed. 8.97 net. (978-0-328-04935-6(2)); (gr. 5-5). pap., wbk. ed. 8.97 net. (978-0-328-04936-3(0)); (gr. 5-5). pap., wbk. ed. 8.97 net. (978-0-328-04969-1(7)); (gr. 5-5). pap., wbk. ed. 5.47 net. (978-0-328-04957-8(3)); (gr. 5-5). pap., wbk. ed. 5.47 net. (978-0-328-04963-9(8)); (gr. 6-6). pap., wbk. ed. 8.97 net. (978-0-328-04970-7(0)); (gr. 6-6). pap., wbk. ed. 5.47 net. (978-0-328-04958-5(1)); (gr. 6-6). pap., wbk. ed. 8.97 net. (978-0-328-04937-0(9)); (gr. 6-6). pap., wbk. ed. 5.47 net. (978-0-328-04964-6(6)) Pearson Schl. (Scott Foresman).

—Scott Foresman-Addison Wesley Mathematics 2. 2003. (ENG.). (gr. k-k). stu. ed. 175.97 net. (978-0-328-06321-5(5), Scott Foresman) Pearson Schl.

—Scott Foresman-Addison Wesley Mathematics 3. 2003. (ENG.). (gr. k-k). stu. ed. 175.97 net. (978-0-328-06322-2(3), Scott Foresman) Pearson Schl.

—Scott Foresman-Addison Wesley Mathematics 4. 2003. (ENG.). (gr. k-k). stu. ed. 175.97 net. (978-0-328-06323-9(1), Scott Foresman) Pearson Schl.

—Scott Foresman-Addison Wesley Mathematics 1. 2003. (ENG.). (gr. k-k). stu. ed. 175.97 net. (978-0-328-06320-8(7), Scott Foresman) Pearson Schl.

—Scott Foresman Math Around the Clock. 2003. (ENG.). (gr. 1-1). pap., wbk. ed. 46.47 net. (978-0-328-06427-4(0)); (gr. 1-1). pap., wbk. ed. 46.47 net. (978-0-328-06428-1(9)); (gr. 1-1). pap., wbk. ed. 46.47 net. (978-0-328-06426-7(2)); (gr. 1-1). pap., wbk. ed. 46.47 net. (978-0-328-06429-8(7)); (gr. 1-1). pap., wbk. ed. 46.47 net. (978-0-328-06430-4(0)); (gr. 1-1). pap., wbk. ed. 46.47 net. (978-0-328-06431-1(9)); (gr. 1-1). pap., wbk. ed. 46.47 net. (978-0-328-06432-8(7)); (gr. 1-1). pap., wbk. ed. 46.47 net. (978-0-328-06433-5(5)); (gr. 2-2). pap., wbk. ed. 46.47 net. (978-0-328-06434-2(3)); (gr. 2-2). pap., wbk. ed. 46.47 net. (978-0-328-06439-7(4)); (gr. 2-2). pap., wbk. ed. 46.47 net. (978-0-328-06435-9(1)); (gr. 2-2). pap., wbk. ed. 46.47 net. (978-0-328-06436-6(X)); (gr. 2-2). pap., wbk. ed. 46.47 net. (978-0-328-06437-3(8)); (gr. 2-2). pap., wbk. ed. 46.47 net. (978-0-328-06438-0(6)); (gr. 2-2). pap., wbk. ed. 46.47 net. (978-0-328-06440-3(8)); (gr. 3-3). pap., wbk. ed. 46.47 net. (978-0-328-06442-7(4)); (gr. 3-3). pap., wbk. ed. 46.47 net. (978-0-328-06443-4(2)); (gr. 3-3). pap., wbk. ed. 46.47 net. (978-0-328-06444-1(0)); (gr. 3-3). pap., wbk. ed. 46.47 net. (978-0-328-06441-0(6)); (gr. 3-3). pap., wbk. ed. 46.47 net. (978-0-328-06445-8(9)); (gr. 3-3). pap., wbk. ed. 46.47 net. (978-0-328-06446-5(7)); (gr. 3-3). pap., wbk. ed. 46.47 net. (978-0-328-06447-2(5)); (gr. 3-3). pap., wbk. ed. 46.47 net. (978-0-328-06448-9(3)); (gr. 4-4). pap., wbk. ed. 46.47 net. (978-0-328-06449-6(1)); (gr. 4-4). pap., wbk. ed. 46.47 net. (978-0-328-06450-2(5)); (gr. 4-4). pap., wbk. ed. 46.47 net. (978-0-328-06451-9(3)); (gr. 4-4). pap., wbk. ed. 46.47 net. (978-0-328-06453-3(X)); (gr. 4-4). pap., wbk. ed. 46.47 net. (978-0-328-06454-0(8)); (gr. 4-4). pap., wbk. ed. 46.47 net. (978-0-328-06455-7(6)); (gr. 5-5). pap., wbk. ed. 46.47 net. (978-0-328-06456-4(4)); (gr. 5-5). pap., wbk. ed. 46.47 net. (978-0-328-06457-1(2)); (gr. 5-5). pap., wbk. ed. 46.47 net. (978-0-328-06458-8(0)); (gr. 5-5). pap., wbk. ed. 46.47 net. (978-0-328-06459-5(9)); (gr. 5-5). pap., wbk. ed. 46.47 net. (978-0-328-06460-1(2)); (gr. 5-5). pap., wbk. ed. 46.47 net. (978-0-328-06461-8(0)); (gr. 5-5). pap., wbk. ed. 46.47 net. (978-0-328-06462-5(9)); (gr. 5-5). pap., wbk. ed. 46.47 net. (978-0-328-06463-2(7)); (gr. 6-6). pap., wbk. ed. 46.47 net. (978-0-328-06464-9(5)); (gr. 6-6). pap., wbk. ed. 46.47 net. (978-0-328-06465-6(3)); (gr. 6-6). pap., wbk. ed. 46.47 net. (978-0-328-06466-3(1)); (gr. 6-6). pap., wbk. ed. 46.47 net. (978-0-328-06467-0(X)); (gr. 6-6). pap., wbk. ed. 46.47 net. (978-0-328-06468-7(8)); (gr. 6-6). pap., wbk. ed. 46.47 net. (978-0-328-06469-4(6)); (gr. 6-6). pap., wbk. ed. 46.47 net. (978-0-328-06470-0(X)) Pearson Schl. (Scott Foresman).

Forest, Anne. My Lemonade Stand: Represent & Interpret Data. 2013. (InfoMax Math Readers Ser.). (ENG.). 24p. (J). (gr. 1-2). pap. 49.50 (978-1-4777-2173-5(8)); (Illus.). pap. 8.25 (978-1-4777-2172-8(X)) Rosen Publishing Group, Inc., The. (Rosen Classroom).

Forte, Imogene. Ready to Learn Beginning Math. 2003. (Illus.). 64p. per. 7.95 (978-0-86530-594-6(3)) Incentive Pubns., Inc.

Fortunado, Hector. Jose's Hardware Store: Understand Place Value. 2013. (InfoMax Math Readers Ser.). (ENG., Illus.). 24p. (J). (gr. 1-2). pap. 8.25 (978-1-4777-2192-6(4), Rosen Classroom) Rosen Publishing Group, Inc., The.

—Jos's Hardware Store: Understand Place Value. 2013. (InfoMax Math Readers Ser.). (ENG.). 24p. (J). (gr. 1-2). pap. 49.50 (978-1-4777-2193-3(2), Rosen Classroom) Rosen Publishing Group, Inc., The.

Franchino, Vicky. Droughts. 2012. (21st Century Skills Library: Real World Math Ser.). (ENG., Illus.). 32p. (J). (gr. 4-8). pap. 14.21 (978-1-61080-407-3(4), 201339); lib. bdg. 28.50 (978-1-61080-322-9(1), 201300) Cherry Lake Publishing.

Franco, Betsy. Counting Poems Flip Chart: 20 Playful Poems That Teach Numbers, Counting, & More. 2004. (ENG.). 10p. pap. 19.99 (978-0-439-51761-4(3), Teaching Resources) Scholastic, Inc.

Frary, Mark. Mathematics Explained, 1 vol., 1. 2014. (Guide for Curious Minds Ser.). (ENG.). 136p. (YA). (gr. 7-12). 38.25 (978-1-4777-2971-7(2)) Rosen Publishing Group, Inc., The.

Freese, Joan. Tablas y Graficas de Cosas Saludables. 2007. (Matimáticas en Nuestro Mundo (Math in Our World) Ser.). (SPA., Illus.). 24p. (gr. 1-2). lib. bdg. 22.00 (978-0-8368-8489-0(2), Weekly Reader Leveled Readers) Stevens, Gareth Publishing LLLP.

—TABLAS y GRÁFICAS de Cosas Saludables. 2007. (Las matimaticas en nuestro mundo (Spanish- Math in Our World) Ser.).Tr. of Tables & Graphs of Healthy Things. (SPA.). 24p. (gr. 1-2). pap. 8.15 (978-0-8368-8498-2(1), Weekly Reader Leveled Readers) Stevens, Gareth Publishing LLLP.

—Tables & Graphs of Healthy Things. 2007. (Math in Our World Ser.). 24p. (gr. 1-2). pap. 8.15 (978-0-8368-8480-7(9)); (Illus.). lib. bdg. 22.00 (978-0-8368-8471-5(X)) Stevens, Gareth Publishing LLLP. (Weekly Reader Leveled Readers).

French. Consumer Mathematics. (J). (gr. 7-12). 32.97 (978-0-13-166729-7(7)) Prentice Hall (Schl. Div.).

Freudentha, H. Powers of Ten: Math Context. 3rd ed. 2003. (Math in Context Ser.). 8.33 (978-0-03-071529-7(6)) Holt McDougal.

—Re-Allotment Math/Context. 3rd ed. 2003. (Math in Context Ser.). 8.33 (978-0-03-071511-2(3)) Holt McDougal.

Freudenthal. Expressions & Formulas. 3rd ed. 2003. (Math in Context Ser.). (Illus.). 8.33 (978-0-03-071444-3(3)) Holt McDougal.

—Growth. 3rd ed. 2003. (Math in Context Ser.). (Illus.). 8.33 (978-0-03-071667-6(5)) Holt McDougal.

—Patterns & Symbols. 3rd ed. 2003. (Math in Context Ser.). (Illus.). 8.33 (978-0-03-071283-8(1)) Holt McDougal.

—Percentage Sense. 3rd ed. 2003. (Math in Context Ser.). (Illus.). 8.33 (978-0-03-071286-9(6)) Holt McDougal.

Fried, Ellen. What's the Chance? 2007. (Reading Expeditions Ser.). (ENG., Illus.). 24p. (J). pap. 14.95 (978-0-7922-4590-2(3)) CENGAGE Learning.

Friedman, Matthew. Tic-Tac-Math: 50 Reproducible, Leveled Game Sheets That Kids Can Use Independently or in Small Groups to Practice Important Math Skills. 2005. (Tic-Tac-Math Ser.). (ENG.). 64p. (gr. 3-4). pap. 11.99 (978-0-439-62920-1(9), Teaching Resources) Scholastic, Inc.

Frith, Alex. What's Math All About? 2012. (What's Math All about? Ser.). 96p. (J). pap. 10.99 (978-0-7945-3126-3(1), Usborne) EDC Publishing.

Frith, Alex & Lacey, Minna. See Inside Math - Internet Referenced. 2008. (See Inside Board Bks). 16p. (J). bds. 12.99 (978-0-7945-2093-9(6), Usborne) EDC Publishing.

Fronczak, Blaine. Haley Helps at School. 2013. (Core Math Skills: Numbers & Operations in Base 10 Ser.). 24p. (J). (gr. 1-2). 22.60 (978-1-4777-2225-1(4)); (ENG.). pap. 8.25 (978-1-4777-2097-4(9)) Rosen Publishing Group, Inc., The. (Rosen Classroom).

—Haley Helps at School: Use Place Value & Properties of Operations to Add. 2013. (Rosen Math Readers Ser.). (ENG.). 24p. (J). (gr. 1-2). pap. 49.50 (978-1-4777-2098-1(7), Rosen Classroom) Rosen Publishing Group, Inc., The.

Fuerst, Jeffrey B. Sorting at My Desk: Lap Book. 2009. (My First Reader's Theater Set B Ser.). (J). 28.00 (978-1-60634-987-8(2)) Benchmark Education Co.

Fuller, Jill. Springtime Addition. 2005. (Rookie Read-About Math Ser.). (ENG., Illus.). 32p. (J). (gr. 1-2). pap. 5.95 (978-0-516-24668-0(2), Children's Pr.) Scholastic Library Publishing.

—Toy Box Subtraction. 2004. (Rookie Read-About Math Ser.). (J). 20.50 (978-0-516-24423-5(X), Children's Pr.) Scholastic Library Publishing.

Furgang, Kathy. Math Fun at the Fair. 2011. (Early Connections Ser.). (J). (978-1-61672-589-1(3)) Benchmark Education Co.

—Math Fun at the Fair: Set Of 6. 2011. (Early Connections Ser.). (J). pap. 37.00 net. (978-1-4108-1076-2(3)) Benchmark Education Co.

—Pizza Parts: Set Of 6. 2011. (Early Connections Ser.). (J). pap. 39.00 net. (978-1-4108-1548-4(X)) Benchmark Education Co.

Furstinger, Nancy. Discovering Cylinders. 2016. (J). (978-1-4896-4980-5(8)) Weigl Pubs., Inc.

Ganesan, C. T. Fun with Maths. 2005. (Illus.). 188p. (gr. 4-7). per. (978-1-84549-027-0(4)) arima publishing.

Gannett, Barbara. Count Your Money: A Content Area Reader-math. 2005. (Emergent/Early (Prek-2) Math Package Ser.). 20p. (gr. k-2). 25.20 (978-0-8215-7821-6(9)) Sadlier, William H. Inc.

Gardner, Colin. Pythagorean Triangle Properties & Attributes Samples (Enlarged), As Independently Discovered by Colin Gardner, Physicist: Pythagorean triples are everwhere, & have an application in nearly every math lesson(6th grade thru College. 2nd ed. 2004. Orig. Title: Pythagorean Triangle Properties & Attriibutes Samples. (Illus.). 6p. (YA). (gr. 6-18). 7.95 (978-0-9720348-5-2(4)) Gardner, Colin.

Gardner, Harvey. Fun in Fall: Work with Addition & Subtraction Equations. 2013. (Rosen Math Readers Ser.). (ENG.). 24p. (J). (gr. 1-2). pap. 49.50 (978-1-4777-2035-6(9)); (Illus.). pap. 8.25 (978-1-4777-2034-9(0)) Rosen Publishing Group, Inc., The. (Rosen Classroom).

Gassman, Nathan, des. Math Fun, 6 vols., Set. Incl. If You Were a Plus Sign. Shaskan, Trisha Speed. Carabelli, Francesca, illus. 27.99 (978-1-4048-4784-2(7)); If You Were a Set. Aboff, Marcie. Dillard, Sarah, illus. 27.99 (978-1-4048-4799-6(5)); If You Were an Even Number. Aboff, Marcie. Dillard, Sarah, illus. 27.99 (978-1-4048-4796-5(0)); (gr. 2-4). 2008. (Math Fun Ser.). (ENG.). 24p. 2008. 83.97 (978-1-4048-4803-0(7)) Picture Window Bks.

Gave, Marc. Number Games Around the World & Juegos de números alrededor del Mundo: 6 English, 6 Spanish Adaptations 2011. (Navigators Ser.). (ENG & SPA.). (J). instr.'s gde. ed. 97.00 net. (978-1-4108-1765-5(2)) Benchmark Education Co.

Gaydos, Nora. Math Madness, Independent. 2003. (Now I'm Reading!). (Illus.). 128p. (J). 14.99 (978-1-58476-248-5(9)) Innovative Kids.

Gensmer, Laura. Score One for Math! 2011. (Math Ser.). (ENG.). 16p. (gr. -1-1). 25.95 (978-1-4296-8671-6(5), Wonder Readers) Capstone Press of Coughlan Cos.

GER Math Tool Kit A. 2006. (J). 19.95 (978-1-934046-10-4(8)) Global Education Resources, LLC.

Ghim, John Y. Ghim's Critical Exercises of HIgh School Math. 2004. (Illus.). 340p. (YA). (gr. 9-12). pap. 35.99 (978-0-9656864-1-9(8)) Ghim, John Yun.

—Ghim's Critical Exercises of High School Math Answers & Explanations. 2004. (YA). per. 12.95 (978-0-9656864-2-6(6)) Ghim, John Yun.

Giganti, Paul. Numeros Importantes. Grbich, Aaron, illus. (SPA.). (J). (gr. 1-3). pap. 3.16 net. (978-0-590-48700-9(0), Scholastic Pr.) Scholastic, Inc.

Ginsburg, Herbert P., et al. Acorn Hunt. 2003. (Illus.). 9.95 (978-0-7690-3046-3(7)) Seymour, Dale Pubns.

—Big Math for Little Kids: Classroom Manipulative Kit. 2003. (Illus.). 382.50 (978-0-7690-3063-0(7)); 251.50 (978-0-7690-3064-7(5)) Seymour, Dale Pubns.

—Dobee Doubler. 2003. (Illus.). 9.95 (978-0-7690-3042-5(4)) Seymour, Dale Pubns.

—Jenny Saves the Day. 2003. (Illus.). 9.95 (978-0-7690-3047-0(5)) Seymour, Dale Pubns.

—Leftover Muffins. 2003. (Illus.). 9.95 (978-0-7690-3040-1(8)) Seymour, Dale Pubns.

—Rafael's Messy Room. 2003. (Illus.). 9.95 (978-0-7690-3045-6(9)) Seymour, Dale Pubns.

—So Many Fives! 2003. (Illus.). 9.95 (978-0-7690-3044-9(0)) Seymour, Dale Pubns.

—The Table of Phinneas Fable. 2003. (Illus.). 9.95 (978-0-7690-3048-7(3)) Seymour, Dale Pubns.

—Tick-Tock! 2003. (Illus.). 9.95 (978-0-7690-3041-8(6)) Seymour, Dale Pubns.

—The Trees of Mrs. Mcgee. 2003. (Illus.). 9.95 (978-0-7690-3049-4(1)) Seymour, Dale Pubns.

Girard, Robert. The American Flag: Learning to Identify Two-Digit Numbers up To 50. 2004. (Math Big Bookstm Ser.). (ENG.). 12p. (gr. 1-2). 33.50 (978-0-8239-7632-4(7)) Rosen Publishing Group, Inc., The.

Glasscock, Sarah, et al. How Nurses Use Math. 2009. (Math in the Real World Ser.). 32p. (gr. 4-6). 28.00 (978-1-60413-607-4(3), Chelsea Clubhouse) Facts On File, Inc.

Gleichungen mit zwei Unbekannten. (Duden-Schuelerhilfen Ser.). (GER.). 96p. (YA). (gr. 8-9). (978-3-411-02622-7(7)) Bibliographisches Institut & F. A. Brockhaus AG DEU. Dist: International Bk. Import Service, Inc.

Gleichungen und Ungleichungen 1. 2nd ed. (Duden-Schuelerhilfen Ser.). (GER.). 112p. (J). (gr. 5-6). (978-3-411-70872-7(7)) Bibliographisches Institut & F. A. Brockhaus AG DEU. Dist: International Bk. Import Service, Inc.

Gleichungen und Ungleichungen 2. (Duden-Schuelerhilfen Ser.). (GER.). 112p. (YA). (gr. 7-8). (978-3-411-70682-2(1)) Bibliographisches Institut & F. A. Brockhaus AG DEU. Dist: International Bk. Import Service, Inc.

Glencoe McGraw-Hill Staff, creator. Mathematics: Applications & Concepts. 2003. (MATH APPLIC & CONN CRSE Ser.). (ENG., Illus.). 90p. (gr. 6-8). pap., wbk. ed. 7.20 (978-0-07-860085-2(5), 0078600855); pap., wbk. ed. 7.20 (978-0-07-860086-9(3), 0078600863) McGraw-Hill Education.

—Mathematics: Applications & Concepts, Course 3, Practice Skills Worbook. 2003. (MATH APPLIC & CONN CRSE Ser.). (ENG., Illus.). 95p. (gr. 6-8). per. 7.20 (978-0-07-860163-7(0), 0078601630) McGraw-Hill Education.

—Mathematics - Applications & Concepts. 2003. (MATH APPLIC & CONN CRSE Ser.). (ENG., Illus.). 720p. (gr. 6-8). lib. bdg., stu. ed. 101.60 (978-0-07-829631-4(5), 0078296315) McGraw-Hill Education.

—Quick Review Math Handbook - Hot Words, Hot Topics, Bk. 3. 2003. (MATH APPLIC & CONN CRSE Ser.). (ENG., Illus.). 512p. (gr. 6-8). stu. ed. 41.12 (978-0-07-860160-6(6), 0078601606) McGraw-Hill Higher Education.

Goba, Busisiwe, et al. Mathematics for Zambia Basic Education Grade 7 Pupil's Book. 2007. pap., stu. ed. (978-0-521-70345-1(X)) Cambridge Univ. Pr.

Goldie, Sophie, et al. Formula One Maths Gold. 2004. (Illus.). 228p. pap., pupil's gde. ed. 39.50 (978-0-340-86934-5(8), Hodder Education) Hodder Education Group GBR. Dist: Trans-Atlantic Pubns., Inc.

Goldsmith, Mike. I Wish I Knew That. 2012. (J). (978-1-60652-474-9(7)) Reader's Digest Assn., Inc., The.

Goldstone, Bruce. Great Estimations. Goldstone, Bruce, illus. 2010. (ENG., Illus.). 32p. (J). (gr. 2-5). pap. 7.99 (978-0-312-60887-3(X), 9780312608873) Square Fish.

Gottwald, Siegfried, et al. Meyers Kleine Enzyklopädie Mathematik. 14th ed. (GER., Illus.). 810p. (978-3-411-07771-7(9)) Bibliographisches Institut & F. A. Brockhaus AG DEU. Dist: i. b. d., Ltd.

Gow, Mary. Archimedes: Mathematical Genius of the Ancient World. 2005. (Great Minds of Science Ser.). (Illus.). 128p. (J). (gr. 4-10). lib. bdg. 27.94 (978-0-7660-2502-8(0)) Enslow Pubs., Inc.

Graham, Amy. Astonishing Ancient World Scientists: Eight Great Brains. 2009. (Great Scientists & Famous Inventors Ser.). (Illus.). 128p. (J). (gr. 5-9). lib. bdg. 34.60 (978-1-59845-079-8(4)) Enslow Pubs., Inc.

Graham, Noel & Blundell, Graham. Graph Pack. (Illus.). 22p. (J). (gr. k-3). 10.00 (978-1-871098-29-7(7)) Claire Pubns. GBR. Dist: Parkwest Pubns., Inc.

Graham, Oakley. 123 Dreams. Orkrania, Alexia, illus. 2014. (ENG.). 12p. (J). (gr. -1-k). 7.99 (978-1-78244-534-0(X)) Top That! Publishing PLC GBR. Dist: Independent Pubs. Group.

Graham, Roland. Let's Vote! Learning to Use Simple Bar Graphs. 2004. (Math Big Bookstm Ser.). (ENG.). 12p. (gr. 1-2). 33.50 (978-0-8239-7635-5(1)) Rosen Publishing Group, Inc., The.

Graham, Roland & National Geographic Learning Staff. Let's Vote! Learning to Use Simple Bar Graphs. 2010. (Rise & Shine Ser.). (ENG.). 12p. (C). (gr. 1-2). pap. 9.95 (978-0-8239-8864-8(3)) National Geographic School Publishing, Inc.

Grant, Mackensey. Roman's Road Trip: Understand Place Value. 2014. (Rosen Common Core Math Readers Ser.). 24p. (J). (gr. 2-3). (ENG., Illus.). pap. 8.25 (978-1-4777-4657-8(9)); 23.60 (978-1-4777-6429-9(1)) Rosen Publishing Group, Inc., The. (Rosen Classroom).

The Great Big Book of Math Kindergarten Costco Edition. 2008. (J). pap. (978-1-59566-624-6(9)) QEB Publishing Inc.

The Great Big Book of Math Preschool Costco Edition. 2008. (J). pap. (978-1-59566-625-3(7)) QEB Publishing Inc.

Great Source Education Group Staff. Math on Call. 2nd ed. 2003. (Math on Call Ser.). (ENG.). 480p. (gr. 6-8). 30.45 (978-0-669-50818-5(7)) Great Source Education Group, Inc.

—Math on Call: A Mathematics Handbook. 2003. (gr. 5-8). lib. bdg. 41.10 *(978-0-613-73010-5(0),* Turtleback) Turtleback Bks.

Great Source Education Group Staff, creator. Math to Know Book A: Problem Solving. 2007. (Illus.). 123p. per. 22.50 *(978-0-669-50047-9(X))* Great Source Education Group, Inc.

Greaves, Helen & Greaves, Simon. Doodle Yourself Smart ... Math. 2012. (Doodle Bks.). (ENG., Illus.). 128p. pap. 12.95 *(978-1-60710-441-4(5),* Thunder Bay Pr.) Readerlink Distribution Services, LLC.

Greene, Lila. Henry Ford's Fantastic Factory: Identify & Explain Patterns in Arithmetic. 2014. (Rosen Common Core Math Readers Ser.). (ENG., Illus.). 24p. (J). (gr. 3-4). pap. 8.25 *(978-1-4777-4941-8(1),* Rosen Classroom) Rosen Publishing Group, Inc., The.

Greenes, Carole E., et al. Navigating through Problem Solving & Reasoning in Grade 2. House, Peggy A. & Greenes, Carole E., eds. 2004. (Navigations Ser.). (Illus.). 50p. pap. 24.95 *(978-0-87353-551-9(0),* 12584) National Council of Teachers of Mathematics.

Greenway, Linda, et al. English for Mathematics, Bk. B. 2016. (ENG., Illus.). 80p. (J). pap. 9.95 *(978-0-00-813571-3(1))* HarperCollins Pubs. Ltd. GBR. Dist: Independent Pubs. Group.

Gregorich, Barbara. Brain Quest, Grade 4: A Whole Year of Curriculum-Based Exercises & Activities in One Fun Book! McGee, Patty, ed. 2008. (ENG., Illus.). 320p. (J). (gr. 4-4). pap., wbk. ed. 12.95 *(978-0-7611-5018-3(8),* 15018) Workman Publishing Co., Inc.

Gregorich, Barbara & Jennison, Christopher. Racing Math: Checkered Flag Activities & Projects for Grades 4-8. 2nd ed. 2005. (Good Year Bks.). (Illus.). 160p. (YA). (gr. 9-14). per. 12.95 *(978-1-59647-060-6(7))* Good Year Bks.

Group/McGraw-Hill, Wright. Wonder World Complete Sets: Math Set - 1 Each of 30 Titles. (Wonder Worldtm Ser.). (gr. k-6). 153.95 *(978-0-322-06715-8(4))* Wright Group/McGraw-Hill.

—Wonder World Early & Upper Emergent Sets: Math Set - 1 Each of 20 Titles. (Wonder Worldtm Ser.). (gr. k-6). 92.50 *(978-0-322-06722-6(7))* Wright Group/McGraw-Hill.

—Wonder World Early Fluency & Fluency: Math Set - 1 Each of 10 Titles. (Wonder Worldtm Ser.). (gr. k-6). 61.95 *(978-0-322-06718-9(9))* Wright Group/McGraw-Hill.

Guillain, Charlotte. Math, 1 vol. 2012. (Jobs If You Like... Ser.). (ENG.). 32p. (gr. 1-3). pap. 8.29 *(978-1-4329-6819-9(X),* Heinemann First Library) Heinemann-Raintree.

Gunzehauser, Kelly. Find Your Future in Mathematics. 2016. (Bright Futures Press: Find Your Future in STEAM Ser.). (ENG., Illus.). 32p. (J). (gr. 4-6). 29.93 *(978-1-63471-902-5(6),* 208929) Cherry Lake Publishing.

Gunzi, Christiane, contrib. by. Los Colores. 2004. (My Very First Look At Ser.).Tr. of Colors. (SPA & ENG., Illus.). 24p. (J). (gr. -1-k). 9.95 *(978-1-58728-270-6(4))* Cooper Square Publishing Llc.

Guscott, Maggie. On the Job, Book 3. 2005. (Practical Math in Context Ser.). (Illus.). 104p. per. 9.95 *(978-1-56254-764-6(X),* SP764X) Saddleback Educational Publishing, Inc.

Guzman, Sienna. Visiting Death Valley: Represent & Interpret Data. 2014. (Rosen Common Core Math Readers Ser.). (ENG.). 24p. (J). (gr. 3-4). pap. 8.25 *(978-1-4777-4909-8(8),* Rosen Classroom) Rosen Publishing Group, Inc., The.

Hagler, Gina. Careers for Tech Girls in Math. 2015. (Tech Girls Ser.). (ENG., Illus.). 80p. (J). (gr. 7-8). 34.25 *(978-1-4994-6101-5(1),* Rosen Young Adult) Rosen Publishing Group, Inc., The.

Hake, Stephen & Saxon, John. Saxon Math 5/4: An Incremental Development. 3rd ed. 2003. (Saxon Math 5/4 Ser.). (ENG., Illus.). 640p. (gr. 4-4). stu. ed. 75.40 *(978-1-56577-503-9(1),* 503) Houghton Mifflin Harcourt Publishing Co.

—Saxon Math 7/6. 4th ed. 2003. (Saxon Math 7/6 Ser.). (ENG., Illus.). 756p. (gr. 6-6). stu. ed. 78.35 *(978-1-56577-507-7(4),* 5074) Houghton Mifflin Harcourt Publishing Co.

—Saxon Math 8/7. 3rd ed. 2003. (Saxon Math 8/7 Ser.). (ENG., Illus.). 944p. (gr. 7-7). stu. ed. 81.40 *(978-1-56577-509-1(0),* 509-0) Houghton Mifflin Harcourt Publishing Co.

Hakizimana, Laurence. Quadrature: Pi, at Last, a Rational Number Equal to 3.125. 2004. 63p. pap. 19.95 *(978-1-4137-4558-0(X))* America Star Bks.

Hammelef, Danielle S. The Case of the Ad That Subtracts & Other True Math Mysteries for You to Solve, 1 vol. 2012. (Seriously True Mysteries Ser.). (ENG.). 32p. (gr. 3-4). lib. bdg. 27.32 *(978-1-4296-7624-3(8),* Fact Finders) Capstone Press of Coughlan Cos.

—Fun with Fives. 2006. (Early Explorers Ser.). (J). pap. *(978-1-4108-6116-0(3))* Benchmark Education Co.

Hammelef, Danielle S., et al. Seriously True Mysteries. 2012. (Seriously True Mysteries Ser.). (ENG.). 32p. (gr. 3-4). lib. bdg. 109.28 *(978-1-4296-8162-9(4),* Fact Finders) Capstone Press of Coughlan Cos.

Hands: Level B, 6 vols. 8p. 24.95 *(978-0-7802-8915-4(3))* Wright Group/McGraw-Hill.

Hankes, Judith E. & Fast, Gerald R. Lost & Found & Found Again: A Math Adventure. 2005. (Illus.). 167p. per. 15.00 *(978-0-9758592-1-6(8))* Mindsong Math.

Hanrahan, Val. Additional Mathematics for Ocr. Porkess, R., ed. 2004. (Illus.). 272p. pap. 42.00 *(978-0-340-86960-4(7),* Hodder Education) Hodder Education Group GBR. Dist: Trans-Atlantic Pubns., Inc.

Hansen, Sue. 50 Reproducible, Leveled Game Sheets That Kids Can Use Independently or in Small Groups to Practice Important Math Skills. 2005. (Tic-Tac-Math Ser.). (ENG.). 64p. (gr. k-2). pap. 11.99 *(978-0-439-62919-5(5),* Teaching Resources) Scholastic, Inc.

Hanson, Anders & Mann, Elissa. Cool Tessellations: Creative Activities That Make Math & Science Fun for Kids!, 1 vol. 2013. (Cool Art with Math & Science Ser.). (ENG.). 32p. (J). (gr. 3-6). lib. bdg. 28.50 *(978-1-61783-826-2(8),* Checkerboard Library) ABDO Publishing Co.

Harasymiw, R. Mann. Problem Solving with Pigs. 2013. (Animal Math Ser.). (ENG., Illus.). 24p. (J). (gr. 1-3). lib. bdg. 22.60 *(978-1-4339-9323-7(6))* Stevens, Gareth Publishing LLLP.

Harasymiw, Raymond. Problem Solving with Pigs. 2013. (Animal Math Ser.). 24p. (J). (gr. 1-3). pap. 48.90 *(978-1-4339-9325-1(2))* Stevens, Gareth Publishing LLLP.

Harasymiw, Raymond & Harasymiw, R. P. Problem Solving with Pigs. 2013. 24p. (J). (gr. 1-3). pap. 8.15 *(978-1-4339-9324-4(4))* Stevens, Gareth Publishing LLLP.

Harasymiw, Therese. Making Venn Diagrams. 2014. (Graph It! Ser.). 24p. (J). (gr. 1-3). 22.60 *(978-1-4824-0934-5(8))* Stevens, Gareth Publishing LLLP.

Harcourt, creator. Achieve Arizona Mathematics 5. 2007. (Illus.). 61p. (J). (gr. 4-7). per. *(978-1-4190-0486-5(7))* Harcourt.

—I Know Big & Small: Math Concept Reader. 2007. (Illus.). (J). pap. 31.53 *(978-0-15-379897-9(1))* Houghton Mifflin Harcourt School Pubs.

—Summertime Math: Math Concept Reader. 2007. (Illus.). (J). pap. 31.53 *(978-0-15-379898-6(X))* Houghton Mifflin Harcourt School Pubs.

Harcourt Achieve, creator. Top Line Math: Data, Tables & Graphs. 2005. (Top Line Math Ser.). (Illus.). 53p. pap. 5.49 *(978-1-4190-0371-4(2))* Steck-Vaughn.

Harcourt School Publishers, creator. Professional Development for Math: Fraction Operations, Grades 3-6. 2004. (ENG.). 219.27 *(978-0-15-341946-1(6))* Harcourt Schl. Pubs.

Harcourt School Publishers Staff. Harcourt Matematicas: CA & National Family Involvement Activities. 2nd ed. 2003. (Harcourt Matematicas Ser.). (SPA., Illus.). (gr. k-6). 25.30 *(978-0-15-321566-7(6))*; (gr. 1-18). 31.10 *(978-0-15-321567-4(4))*; (gr. 2-18). 31.10 *(978-0-15-321568-1(2))*; (gr. 3-18). 35.80 *(978-0-15-321569-8(0))*; (gr. 4-18). 35.80 *(978-0-15-321570-4(4))*; (gr. 5-18). 35.80 *(978-0-15-321571-1(2))*; (gr. 6-18). 36.20 *(978-0-15-321572-8(0))* Harcourt Schl. Pubs.

—Harcourt Matematicas: Challenge Workbook. 2nd ed. 2003. (Harcourt Matematicas Ser.). (SPA., Illus.). (gr. k-6). wbk. ed., pupil's gde. ed. 11.80 *(978-0-15-321642-8(5))*; (gr. 1-18). wbk. ed. 12.50 *(978-0-15-321643-5(3))*; (gr. 2-18). wbk. ed. 12.50 *(978-0-15-321644-2(1))*; (gr. 3-18). wbk. ed. 13.50 *(978-0-15-321645-9(X))*; (gr. 4-18). wbk. ed. 13.50 *(978-0-15-321646-6(8))*; (gr. 5-18). wbk. ed. 13.50 *(978-0-15-321647-3(6))*; (gr. 6-18). wbk. ed. 14.50 *(978-0-15-321648-0(4))* Harcourt Schl. Pubs.

—Harcourt Matematicas: Checklist for Knowledge Enrichment. 2nd ed. 2003. (Harcourt Matematicas Ser.). (SPA., Illus.). (gr. 5-18). 13.10 *(978-0-15-326116-9(1))* Harcourt Schl. Pubs.

—Harcourt Matematicas: Practice Workbook. 2nd ed. 2003. (Harcourt Matematicas Ser.). (SPA., Illus.). (gr. 3-18). wbk. ed. 11.60 *(978-0-15-321631-2(X))*; (gr. 4-18). wbk. ed. 11.60 *(978-0-15-321632-9(8))*; (gr. 5-18). wbk. ed. 11.60 *(978-0-15-321633-6(6))*; (gr. 6-18). wbk. ed. 12.00 *(978-0-15-321634-3(4))* Harcourt Schl. Pubs.

—Harcourt Matematicas: Problem Solving & Reading Strategies Workbook. 2nd ed. 2003. (Harcourt Matematicas Ser.). (SPA., Illus.). (gr. 1-18). wbk. ed. 11.00 *(978-0-15-321668-8(9))*; (gr. 2-18). wbk. ed. 11.00 *(978-0-15-321669-5(7))*; (gr. 3-18). wbk. ed. 12.00 *(978-0-15-321670-1(0))*; (gr. 4-18). wbk. ed. 12.00 *(978-0-15-321671-8(9))*; (gr. 5-18). wbk. ed. 12.00 *(978-0-15-321672-5(7))*; (gr. 6-18). wbk. ed. 12.50 *(978-0-15-321673-2(5))* Harcourt Schl. Pubs.

—Harcourt Matematicas: Resource Package. 2nd ed. 2003. (Harcourt Matematicas Ser.). (SPA., Illus.). (gr. k-6). 992.20 *(978-0-15-321844-6(4))* Harcourt Schl. Pubs.

—Harcourt Matemáticas Práctica. 4th ed. 2004. (Harcourt Matematicas Ser.). (SPA.). 168p. (gr. 3-3). pap., wbk. ed. 14.10 *(978-0-15-341132-8(5))* Harcourt Schl. Pubs.

—Harcourt Math. 4th ed. 2004. (Harcourt Matematicas Ser.). (SPA.). Vol. 1. 544p. (gr. k-k). tchr. ed., spiral bd. 197.25 *(978-0-15-341109-0(0))* Vol. 1. 588p. (gr. 5-5). tchr. ed., spiral bd. 131.55 *(978-0-15-341123-6(6))* Vol. 2. 400p. (gr. k-k). tchr. ed., spiral bd. 197.25 *(978-0-15-341110-6(4))* Vol. 2. 540p. (gr. 5-5). tchr. ed., spiral bd. 131.55 *(978-0-15-341124-3(4))* Vol. 3. 432p. (gr. 2-2). tchr. ed. 121.55 *(978-0-15-341116-8(3))* Vol. 3. 564p. (gr. 5-5). tchr. ed., spiral bd. 131.55 *(978-0-15-341125-0(2))* Harcourt Schl. Pubs.

—Harcourt Math: MEAP Resource Book. 3rd ed. 2003. (gr. 1). pap. 7.50 *(978-0-15-340989-9(4))*; (gr. 2). pap. 7.50 *(978-0-15-340990-5(8))*; (gr. 3). pap. 9.60 *(978-0-15-340991-2(6))*; (gr. 4). pap. 9.60 *(978-0-15-340992-9(4))*; (gr. 5). pap. 9.60 *(978-0-15-340993-6(2))*; (gr. 6). pap. 9.60 *(978-0-15-340994-3(0))* Harcourt Schl. Pubs.

—Harcourt Math Collection, Grade 1, Vols. 1-3. 3rd ed. 2003. tchr. ed. 276.00 *(978-0-15-338863-7(3))* Harcourt Schl. Pubs.

—Harcourt Math Collection, Grade 2, Vols. 1-3. 3rd ed. 2003. tchr. ed. 276.00 *(978-0-15-338864-4(1))* Harcourt Schl. Pubs.

—Harcourt Math Collection, Grade 3, Vols. 1-3. 3rd ed. 2003. tchr. ed. 276.00 *(978-0-15-338865-1(X))* Harcourt Schl. Pubs.

—Harcourt Math Collection, Grade 4, Vols. 1-3. 3rd ed. 2003. tchr. ed. 276.00 *(978-0-15-338866-8(8))* Harcourt Schl. Pubs.

—Harcourt Math Collection, Grade 5, Vols. 1-3. 3rd ed. 2003. tchr. ed. 276.00 *(978-0-15-338867-5(6))* Harcourt Schl. Pubs.

—Harcourt Math Collection, Grade 6, Vols. 1-3. 3rd ed. 2003. tchr. ed. 276.00 *(978-0-15-338868-2(4))* Harcourt Schl. Pubs.

—Harcourt Math, Grade 1. 4th ed. 2004. (Harcourt Matematicas Ser.). (SPA.). (gr. 1-1). Vol. 1. 504p. tchr. ed., spiral bd. 131.55 *(978-0-15-341111-3(2))* Vol. 2. 528p. tchr. ed., spiral bd. 131.55 *(978-0-15-341112-0(0))* Vol. 3. 456p. tchr. ed., spiral bd. 131.55 *(978-0-15-341113-7(9))* Harcourt Schl. Pubs.

—Harcourt Math, Grade 3. 4th ed. 2004. (Harcourt Matematicas Ser.). (SPA.). (gr. 3-3). Vol. 1. 672p. tchr. ed., spiral bd. 131.55 *(978-0-15-341117-5(1))* Vol. 2. 528p. tchr. ed., spiral bd. 131.55 *(978-0-15-341118-2(X))* Vol. 3. 420p. tchr. ed., spiral bd. 131.55 *(978-0-15-341119-9(8))* Harcourt Schl. Pubs.

—Harcourt Math, Grade 6. 4th ed. 2004. (Harcourt Matematicas Ser.). (SPA.). (gr. 6-6). Vol. 1. 688p. tchr. ed., spiral bd. 131.55 *(978-0-15-341126-7(0))* Vol. 2. 504p. tchr. ed., spiral bd. 131.55 *(978-0-15-341127-4(9))* Vol. 3. 480p. tchr. ed., spiral bd. 131.55 *(978-0-15-341128-1(7))* Harcourt Schl. Pubs.

—Harcourt Math, Grade K Vol. 2. 3rd ed. 2003. tchr. ed. 138.00 *(978-0-15-338908-5(7))* Harcourt Schl. Pubs.

—Harcourt School Publishers Matematicas. 4th ed. 2004. (Harcourt Matematicas Ser.). (SPA.). 396p. (gr. k-k). pap., stu. ed. 39.45 *(978-0-15-341102-1(3))*; 600p. (gr. 1-1). pap., stu. ed. 53.95 *(978-0-15-341103-8(1))*; 160p. (gr. 1-1). pap., wbk. ed. 14.10 *(978-0-15-341130-4(9))*; 624p. (gr. 2-2). pap., stu. ed. 53.95 *(978-0-15-341104-5(X))*; 176p. (gr. 2-2). pap., wbk. ed. 14.10 *(978-0-15-341131-1(7))*; 736p. (gr. 3-3). stu. ed. 98.65 *(978-0-15-341105-2(8))*; 168p. (gr. 4-4). pap., wbk. ed. 14.10 *(978-0-15-341133-5(3))*; 176p. (gr. 5-5). pap., wbk. ed. 14.10 *(978-0-15-341134-2(1))*; 144p. (gr. 6-6). pap., wbk. ed. 14.10 *(978-0-15-341135-9(X))* Harcourt Schl. Pubs.

—Matemáticas. 4th ed. 2004. (Harcourt Matematicas Ser.). (SPA.). 104p. (gr. k-k). pap., stu. ed., wbk. ed. 13.90 *(978-0-15-341129-8(5))* Harcourt Schl. Pubs.

—Matematicas 2005, Vol. 2. 4th ed. 2004. (Harcourt School Publishers Matematicas Ser.). (SPA.). 444p. (gr. 2-2). tchr. ed. 121.55 *(978-0-15-341115-1(5))* Harcourt Schl. Pubs.

—Mathemáticas. 4th ed. 2004. (Harcourt School Publishers Matematicas Ser.). (SPA.). 768p. (gr. 4-4). stu. ed. 98.65 *(978-0-15-341106-9(6))* Harcourt Schl. Pubs.

—Problem Solving. 4th ed. 2004. pap., tchr.'s training gde. ed. 54.90 *(978-0-15-341942-3(3))*; (ENG.). 120p. (gr. 6-6). pap., pupil's gde. ed. 15.45 *(978-0-15-341943-0(1))* Harcourt Schl. Pubs.

Hardyman, Robyn. Exploring Amazing Adaptations with Math. 2016. (Math Attack: Exploring Life Science with Math Ser.). 00032p. (J). (gr. 3-4). pap. 10.00 *(978-1-4994-3113-1(9),* PowerKids Pr.) Rosen Publishing Group, Inc., The.

—Exploring Awesome Animal Bodies with Math. 2016. (Math Attack: Exploring Life Science with Math Ser.). 00032p. (J). (gr. 3-4). pap. 10.00 *(978-1-4994-3117-9(1),* PowerKids Pr.) Rosen Publishing Group, Inc., The.

—Exploring Deadly Habitats with Math. 2016. (Math Attack: Exploring Life Science with Math Ser.). 00032p. (J). (gr. 3-4). pap. 10.00 *(978-1-4994-3121-6(X),* PowerKids Pr.) Rosen Publishing Group, Inc., The.

—Exploring Food Chains with Math. 2016. (Math Attack: Exploring Life Science with Math Ser.). 00032p. (J). (gr. 3-4). pap. 10.00 *(978-1-4994-3125-4(2),* PowerKids Pr.) Rosen Publishing Group, Inc., The.

—Exploring Killer Plants with Math. 2016. (Math Attack: Exploring Life Science with Math Ser.). 00032p. (J). (gr. 3-4). pap. 10.00 *(978-1-4994-3129-2(5),* PowerKids Pr.) Rosen Publishing Group, Inc., The.

—Exploring Lethal Life Cycles with Math. 2016. (Math Attack: Exploring Life Science with Math Ser.). 00032p. (J). (gr. 3-4). pap. 10.00 *(978-1-4994-3133-9(3),* PowerKids Pr.) Rosen Publishing Group, Inc., The.

Harnadek, Anita. Math Word Problems Level C: Mixed Concepts: Whole Numbers to Percents. 2006. (Math Word Problems Ser.). 96p. (gr. 5-10). pap. 14.99 *(978-0-89455-822-1(6))* Critical Thinking Co., The.

Harris, Brooke. Playing at My House: Lap Book. 2009. (My First Reader's Theater Set B Ser.). (J). 28.00 *(978-1-60634-986-1(4))* Benchmark Education Co.

Harris, Janelle. Bree's Building Blocks: Work with 11-19 to Gain Foundations for Place Value. 2013. (Rosen Math Readers Ser.). (ENG.). 16p. (J). (gr. k-1). pap. 42.00 *(978-1-4777-1672-4(6))*; (Illus.). pap. 7.00 *(978-1-4777-1671-7(8))* Rosen Publishing Group, Inc., The. (Rosen Classroom).

Harris, Nancy & Rissman, Rebecca. Be the Best at Math, 1 vol. 2012. (Top Tips Ser.). (ENG.). 32p. (gr. 1-3). 29.99 *(978-1-4109-4765-9(3),* Read Me!) Heinemann-Raintree.

Harrison, Paul & Montague-Smith, Ann. Extension for All Through Problem Solving. 2003. (Apex Maths Ser.: Vol. 5). (ENG., Illus.). 48p. pap., stu. ed. 14.94 *(978-0-521-75494-1(1))*; pap., stu. ed. 14.20 *(978-0-521-75496-5(8))* Cambridge Univ. Pr.

Harrison, Paul & Mumford, Jeannette. Math Extension Activities for Year 6. 2004. (6 Plus Ser.). (ENG., Illus.). 144p. pap., stu. ed. 18.65 *(978-0-521-54290-6(1))* Cambridge Univ. Pr.

Harrison, Sharon, et al. Mathemateg Newydd Caergrawnt. 2005. (WEL., Illus.). 32p. pap. *(978-1-86085-272-5(6))* ICA Video.

Hausmann, Gisela. Hands on Mathemagical Dice. 2005. (Illus.). 30p. (J). cd-rom 13.00 *(978-0-9664217-4-3(4))* Educ-Easy Bks.

Hayhurst, Chris. Euclid: The Great Geometer. 2009. (Library of Greek Philosophers Ser.). 112p. (gr. 6-6). 66.50 *(978-1-60853-659-7(9),* Rosen Reference) Rosen Publishing Group, Inc., The.

Head, Debby & Pollett, Libby. Bby Practice Pages: 04-Addition Facts 0-10. 2004. (ENG., Illus.). 93p. spiral bd. 37.00 *(978-1-885775-20-7(2))* bby Publications at The University of West Alabama.

—Bby Practice Pages: 05-Subtraction Facts 0-10. 2004. (ENG., Illus.). spiral bd. 37.00 *(978-1-885775-21-4(0))* bby Publications at The University of West Alabama.

—Bby Practice Pages: 08-Beginning Addition 0-10. 2004. (ENG.). spiral bd. 37.00 *(978-1-885775-24-5(5))* bby Publications at The University of West Alabama.

—Bby Practice Pages: 10-Addition Facts 11-20. 2004. (ENG., Illus.). spiral bd. 37.00 *(978-1-885775-26-9(1))* bby Publications at The University of West Alabama.

—Bby Practice Pages: 11-Subtraction Facts 11-20. 2004. (ENG., Illus.). spiral bd. 37.00 *(978-1-885775-27-6(X))* bby Publications at The University of West Alabama.

—Bby Practice Pages: 12-Making Change Through $1.00. 2004. (ENG., Illus.). spiral bd. 37.00 *(978-1-885775-28-3(8))* bby Publications at The University of West Alabama.

Heaney, Shane. Food from Around the World: Represent & Solve Problems Involving Division. 2014. (Rosen Common Core Math Readers Ser.). 24p. (J). (gr. 3-4). (ENG.). pap. 49.50 *(978-1-4777-4978-4(0),* Rosen Classroom); (ENG., Illus.). pap. 8.25 *(978-1-4777-4977-7(2),* PowerKids Pr.); (Illus.). lib. bdg. 23.60 *(978-1-4777-6446-6(1),* PowerKids Pr.) Rosen Publishing Group, Inc., The.

Heath Mathematics. (J). (gr. 1). wbk. ed. 10.44 *(978-0-669-10473-8(6))*; wbk. ed. *(978-0-669-10502-5(3))* Houghton Mifflin Harcourt School Pubs.

Hein, Marilyn B. Math Phonics Pre-Algebra. Wheeler, Ron, illus. 2004. 96p. (J). pap. 10.65 *(978-1-57310-438-8(8))* Teaching & Learning Co.

Hennings, Mark. Cambridge Pre-U Mathematics Coursebook. 2017. (Pre-U Ser.). (ENG.). 788p. pap. 64.94 *(978-1-316-63575-9(9))* Cambridge Univ. Pr.

Hense, Mary, et al. How Astronauts Use Math. 2009. (Math in the Real World Ser.). 32p. (gr. 4-6). 28.00 *(978-1-60413-610-4(3),* Chelsea Clubhouse) Facts On File, Inc.

—How Fighter Pilots Use Math. 2009. (Math in the Real World Ser.). 32p. (gr. 4-6). 28.00 *(978-1-60413-605-0(7),* Chelsea Clubhouse) Facts On File, Inc.

Heos, Bridget. Making Graphs. Longhi, Katya, illus. 2015. (Math World Ser.). 24p. (J). lib. bdg. 27.10 *(978-1-60753-463-1(0))* Amicus Publishing.

Herbst, Kailee. Lots of Clocks: Learning about Tools That Measure Time. 2009. (Math for the Real World: Early Emergent Ser.). (ENG., Illus.). 8p. (gr. k-1). pap. 5.15 *(978-0-8239-8858-7(9))* Rosen Publishing Group, Inc., The.

Hicer, Nancy. Pennies, Nickles, & Dimes. 2015. (Rosen REAL Readers: STEM & STEAM Collection). (ENG.). 8p. pap. 5.46 *(978-1-4994-9723-6(7),* Rosen Classroom) Rosen Publishing Group, Inc., The.

Hinkler Books Staff, ed. Early Math. 2009. (ENG.). 24p. (J). 9.99 *(978-0-8249-1401-1(5),* Ideal Pubns.) Worthy Publishing.

Hinkler Studios Staff., ed. Cars: Numbers & Early Math. 2011. 12p. 9.99 *(978-1-74183-870-1(3))* Hinkler Bks. Pty, Ltd. AUS. Dist: Ideals Pubns.

Hinton, John. Hot or Cold? Describe & Compare Measurable Attributes. 2013. (Rosen Math Readers Ser.). (ENG.). 16p. (J). (gr. k-1). pap. 42.00 *(978-1-4777-1627-4(0))*; (Illus.). pap. 7.00 *(978-1-4777-1626-7(2))* Rosen Publishing Group, Inc., The. (Rosen Classroom).

Hironaka, Heisuke & Sugiyama, Yoshishige, eds. Tokyo Shoseki's Mathematics 4 for Elementary School (Grade 4A & 4B, 2 vol. Set) 2006. Orig. Title: Atarashii Sansuu 4 (Jo/Ge). pap. 24.99 *(978-1-934046-04-3(3))* Global Education Resources, LLC.

—Tokyo Shoseki's Mathematics 5 for Elementary School (Grades 5A & 5B, 2 vol. Set) 2006. Orig. Title: Atarashii Sansuu 5 (Jo/Ge). pap. 24.99 *(978-1-934046-05-0(1))* Global Education Resources, LLC.

—Tokyo Shoseki's Mathematics 6 for Elementary School (Grade 6A & 6B, 2 vol. Set) 2006. Orig. Title: Atarashii Sansuu 6 (Jo/Ge). pap. 24.99 *(978-1-934046-06-7(X))* Global Education Resources, LLC.

Hobbs, Chris & Perryman, Richard. The Largest Number Smaller Than Five. 2007. (ENG.). 128p. per. 19.99 *(978-1-4303-0630-6(0))* Lulu Pr., Inc.

Hoena, Blake. Circles & Crescents: A Song about Drawing with Shapes. Palin, Tim, illus. 2017. (Sing & Draw! Ser.). (ENG.). 24p. (gr. 1-3). 33.99 ***(978-1-68410-015-6(1))*** Cantata Learning.

—Rectangles & Triangles: A Song about Drawing with Shapes. Palin, Tim, illus. 2017. (Sing & Draw! Ser.). (ENG.). 24p. (gr. 1-3). 33.99 ***(978-1-68410-047-7(X))*** Cantata Learning.

Hollis, Matthew. Jada Makes Jewelry: Use Place Value Understanding & Properties of Operations to Add & Subtract. 2014. (Math Masters: Number & Operations in Base Ten Ser.). 24p. (J). (gr. 2-3). 23.60 *(978-1-4777-6402-2(X))*; (ENG.). pap. 8.25 *(978-1-4777-4742-1(7))* Rosen Publishing Group, Inc., The. (Rosen Classroom).

Holmes, Rebecca. Allie's Art Class: Analyze, Compare, Create, & Compose Shapes. 2013. (Rosen Math Readers Ser.). (ENG.). 16p. (J). (gr. k-1). pap. 42.00 *(978-1-4777-1645-8(9))*; (Illus.). pap. 7.00 *(978-1-4777-1644-1(0))* Rosen Publishing Group, Inc., The. (Rosen Classroom).

HOLT MCDOUGAL. Go Math! Student Interactive Worktext Accelerated 7 2014. 2013. (Go Math! Ser.). (ENG.). 840p. (gr. 7-7). pap. 20.80 *(978-0-544-14716-4(2))* Big Ideas Learning, LLC.

Holt, Rinehart and Winston Staff. Decision Making: Math Context. 3rd ed. 2003. tchr. ed. 33.53 *(978-0-03-071523-5(7))* Holt McDougal.

—Math: CIM Test Preparation Book: Oregon High School Edition: 3rd ed. 2003. (YA). pap. 12.16 *(978-0-03-070452-9(9))* Holt, Rinehart & Winston of Canada, Ltd. CAN. Dist: Harcourt Canada, Ltd.

—Math: Middle School: Interactive Posters & Worksheets. 4th ed. 2004. (Illus.). pap. 55.66 *(978-0-03-068634-4(2))* Holt McDougal.

—Math Course 1: Middle School: Chapter Resources. 4th ed. Date not set. pap. 367.00 *(978-0-03-070832-9(X))* Holt McDougal.

—Math Course 1: Middle School: Interactive Posters & Worksheets. 4th ed. 2004. (Illus.). pap. 55.66 *(978-0-03-068623-8(7))* Holt McDougal.

—Math Course 2: Middle School: Chapter Resources. 4th ed. Date not set. pap. 367.00 *(978-0-03-070833-6(8))* Holt McDougal.

—Math Course 2: Middle School: Standard Test Practice. 4th ed. Date not set. (YA). pap., wbk. ed. 8.40 *(978-0-03-070821-3(4))* Holt McDougal.

—Math Course 2: Middle School: Standard Test Practice with Answer Key. 4th ed. Date not set. pap., wbk. ed. 12.60 *(978-0-03-070822-0(2))* Holt McDougal.

—Math Course 3: Middle School: Chapter Resources. 4th ed. Date not set. pap. 367.00 *(978-0-03-070834-3(6))* Holt McDougal.

—Math Course 3: Middle School: Interactive Posters & Worksheets. 4th ed. 2004. (Illus.). pap. 55.66 *(978-0-03-068646-7(6))* Holt McDougal.

—Math Course 3: Middle School: Standard Test Practice. 4th ed. Date not set. pap., wbk. ed. 8.40 *(978-0-03-070823-7(0))* Holt McDougal.

—Math Chapter Resources: Arizona Edition. 4th ed. 2004. (YA). tchr. ed. 110.60 *(978-0-03-073509-7(2))* Holt McDougal.

—Math Chapter Resources: Maine Edition. 4th ed. 2004. (YA). tchr. ed. 110.60 *(978-0-03-073291-1(3))*; tchr. ed. 110.60 *(978-0-03-073292-8(1))* Holt McDougal.
—Math Chapter Resources: New Jersey Edition. 4th ed. 2004. (YA). 110.60 *(978-0-03-073289-8(1))*; tchr. ed. 110.60 *(978-0-03-073288-1(3))* Holt McDougal.
—Math Chapter Resources: Pennsylvania Edition. 4th ed. 2004. (YA). tchr. ed. 110.60 *(978-0-03-073492-2(4))*; tchr. ed. 110.60 *(978-0-03-073493-9(2))*; tchr. ed. 110.60 *(978-0-03-073491-5(6))* Holt McDougal.
—Math Know-It Notebook: Middle School. 4th ed. 2004. (Holt Mathematics Ser.). (ENG., Illus.). 272p. (gr. 6-6). pap. 15.50 *(978-0-03-038016-7(2))*; 272p. (gr. 7-7). pap. 15.50 *(978-0-03-038017-4(0))*; 256p. (gr. 8-8). pap. 15.50 *(978-0-03-038018-1(9))* Houghton Mifflin Harcourt Publishing Co.
—Middle School Math: New York Review & Test Preparation Workbook. 4th ed. (Holt Middle School Math Ser.). 2004. pap. 8.40 *(978-0-03-070812-1(5))* 2003. pap. 8.40 *(978-0-03-070811-4(7))* 2003. pap. 8.40 *(978-0-03-070809-1(5))* Holt McDougal.
—Middle School Math Chapter 4: Resource Book. 4th ed. 2004. pap. 38.33 *(978-0-03-067962-9(1))* Holt McDougal.
—Middle School Math Chapter 5: Resource Book. 4th ed. 2004. pap. 38.33 *(978-0-03-067963-6(X))* Holt McDougal.
—Middle School Math Chapter 6: Resource Book. 4th ed. 2004. pap. 38.33 *(978-0-03-067964-3(8))* Holt McDougal.
—Middle School Math Chapter 7: Resource Book. 4th ed. 2004. pap. 38.33 *(978-0-03-067966-7(4))* Holt McDougal.
—Middle School Math Chapter 8: Resource Book. 4th ed. 2004. pap. 38.33 *(978-0-03-067967-4(2))* Holt McDougal.
—Middle School Math Chapter 9: Resource Book. 4th ed. 2004. pap. 38.33 *(978-0-03-067968-1(0))* Holt McDougal.
—Middle School Math Chapter 10: Resource Book. 4th ed. 2004. pap. 38.33 *(978-0-03-067969-8(9))* Holt McDougal.
—Middle School Math Chapter 11: Resource Book. 4th ed. 2004. pap. 38.33 *(978-0-03-067971-1(0))* Holt McDougal.
—Middle School Math Chapter 12: Resource Book. 4th ed. 2004. pap. 38.33 *(978-0-03-067972-8(9))* Holt McDougal.
—Middle School Math Course 1: Chapter Resources: Oregon Edition. 4th ed. 2004. (YA). tchr. ed. 110.60 *(978-0-03-073513-4(0))* Holt McDougal.
—Middle School Math Course 2: Chapter Resources: Oregon Edition. 4th ed. 2004. (YA). tchr. ed. 110.60 *(978-0-03-073514-1(9))* Holt McDougal.
—Middle School Math Course 2: Maryland Edition. 4th ed. 2004. (J). tchr. ed. 110.60 *(978-0-03-072832-7(0))* Holt McDougal.
—Middle School Math Course 3: Chapter Resources: Oregon Edition. 4th ed. 2004. (YA). tchr. ed. 110.60 *(978-0-03-073516-5(5))* Holt McDougal.
—Middle School Math Course 3: Consumer/Career Mathematics. 4th ed. 2004. (Illus.). pap. 22.26 *(978-0-03-066231-7(1))* Holt McDougal.
—Middle School Math Course 3: Homework/Practice Workbook with Answer Key - Spanish Edition. 4th ed. Date not set. pap. 11.00 *(978-0-03-068296-4(7))* Holt McDougal.
—Middle School Math Course 3: Maryland Edition. 4th annot. ed. 2004. (J). tchr. ed. 110.60 *(978-0-03-072833-4(9))* Holt McDougal.
—Middle School Math Course 3: Success for English Language Students. 4th ed. Date not set. pap. 79.53 *(978-0-03-066257-7(5))* Holt McDougal.
—Middle School Math 2: Spanish Homework & Practice Workbook. 4th ed. Date not set. (Holt Mathematics Ser.). pap. 8.40 *(978-0-03-067973-5(7))* Holt McDougal.
—New in Numbers. 3rd ed. 2003. (Math in Context Ser.). (Illus.). pap. 15.05 *(978-0-03-072432-9(5))* Holt McDougal.
—Pre-Algebra: Hands-on Lab Activities with Answer Key. 4th ed. 2004. pap. 21.53 *(978-0-03-069698-5(4))* Holt McDougal.
—Pre-Algebra: Tech Lab Activities with Answer Key. 4th ed. 2003. pap. 21.53 *(978-0-03-069861-3(8))* Holt McDougal.
—Pre-Algebra: Test Preparation Tool Kit. 4th ed. 2004. pap. 264.66 *(978-0-03-069616-9(X))* Holt McDougal.
—Pre-Algebra Chptr. 4: Resource Book with Answer Key. 4th ed. 2004. pap. 38.86 *(978-0-03-069683-1(6))* Holt McDougal.
—Pre-Algebra Chptr. 5: Resource Book with Answer Key. 4th ed. 2004. pap. 38.86 *(978-0-03-069684-8(4))* Holt McDougal.
—Science Spectrum: Physics Math Skills. 4th ed. 2004. pap., wbk. ed. 11.13 *(978-0-03-067084-8(5))* Holt McDougal.
HOP LLC Staff. Hooked on Math - Addition & Subtraction. 2005. (J). (gr. 6-7). 64.99 *(978-1-931020-50-3(7))* HOP, LLC.
Houghton Mifflin Company Staff, creator. Math Practice Workbook, Grade 3. 2003. (Houghton Mifflin Math Ser.). (ENG., Illus.). 160p. (gr. 3-3). pap. 12.30 *(978-0-618-38959-9(8))* Houghton Mifflin Harcourt Publishing Co.
—Math-Trips, Grades 4-6. 2011. (Steck-Vaughn School Supply Ser.). (ENG., Illus.). 79p. (J). pap. 14.99 *(978-0-547-62559-1(6))* Houghton Mifflin Harcourt Trade & Reference Pubs.
Hughes, Haley. What's near & Far? Describe & Compare Measurable Attributes. 2013. (InfoMax Math Readers Ser.). (ENG.). 16p. (J). (gr. k-1). pap. 7.00 *(978-1-4777-1925-1(3)*, Rosen Classroom) Rosen Publishing Group, Inc., The.
Hughes, Holly. What's near & Far? Describe & Compare Measurable Attributes. 2013. (InfoMax Math Readers Ser.). (ENG.). 16p. (J). (gr. k-1). pap. 42.00 *(978-1-4777-1926-8(1)*, Rosen Classroom) Rosen Publishing Group, Inc., The.
Hulme, Joy N. Wild Fibonacci: Nature's Secret Code Revealed. Schwartz, Carol, illus. 2010. (ENG.). 32p. (J). (gr. -1-2). pap. 7.99 *(978-1-58246-324-7(7)*, Tricycle Pr.) Random Hse. Children's Bks.
Hunt, Darleen L. Dad's Pancakes: Number Reduction. Komarck, Michael, illus. 2003. (Sherman's Math Corner Ser.). (J). (gr. -1-3). *(978-1-929591-04-6(7))* Reading Rock, Inc.
—Dog & Cat Compare: Comparing Amounts. Komarck, Michael, illus. 2003. (Sherman's Math Corner Ser.). (J). (gr. -1-3). *(978-1-929591-09-1(8))* Reading Rock, Inc.
—Dog's Dollars: Patterns. Komarck, Michael, illus. 2003. (Sherman's Math Corner Ser.). (J). (gr. -1-3). *(978-1-929591-08-4(X))* Reading Rock, Inc.
—Harvey T. Crow Puts It All Together: Addition. Komarck, Michael, illus. 2003. (Sherman's Math Corner Ser.). (J). (gr. -1-3). *(978-1-929591-02-2(0))* Reading Rock, Inc.
—Samanta Uses Patterns: Patterns. Komarck, Michael, illus. 2003. (Sherman's Math Corner Ser.). (J). (gr. -1-3). *(978-1-929591-10-7(1))* Reading Rock, Inc.
—Spider Inventories: Count & Record. Komarck, Michael, illus. 2003. (Sherman's Math Corner Ser.). (J). (gr. -1-3). *(978-1-929591-05-3(5))* Reading Rock, Inc.
Husted, Terri. Math Detective B1: Higher-Order Thinking Reading Writing in Mathematics. 2013. (Math Detective Ser.). 136p. (gr. 7-8). pap. 19.99 *(978-0-89455-864-1(1))* Critical Thinking Co., The.
Hutton, Kallie, et al. Mathematics for Zambia Basic Education Grade 5 Pupil's Book. 2008. pap. 3.99 *(978-0-521-69868-9(5))* Cambridge Univ. Pr.
Hynson, Colin. Dream Jobs in Math. 2017. (Illus.). 32p. (J). ***(978-0-7787-2963-1(X))*** Crabtree Publishing Co.
I Love Math Series, 12 bks. Incl. Alice in Numberland: Fantasy Math. Time-Life Books Editors. Mark, Sara et al, eds. 1993. 16.95 *(978-0-8094-9978-6(9))*; Case of the Missing Zebra Stripes: Zoo Math. Time-Life Books Editors. Daniels, Patricia et al, eds. 1992. 16.95 *(978-0-8094-9954-0(1))*; From Head to Toe: Body Math. Time-Life Books Editors. Daniels, Patricia & Crawford, Jean B., eds. 1992. 16.95 *(978-0-8094-9966-3(5))*; How Do Octopi Eat Pizza Pie? Pizza Math. Time-Life Books Editors. Daniels, Patricia et al, eds. 1992. 16.95 *(978-0-8094-9950-2(9))*; Mystery Mansion: House Math. Mark, Sara, ed. 1993. 16.95 *(978-0-8094-9986-1(X))*; Pterodactyl Tunnel: Amusement Park Math. Crawford, Jean B., ed. 1993. 16.95 *(978-0-8094-9990-8(8))*; Search for the Mystery Planet: Space Math. Time-Life Books Editors. Crawford, Jean B., ed. 1993. 16.95 *(978-0-8094-9982-3(7))*; (Illus.). 64p. (J). (gr. 1-4). 172.89 *(978-0-8094-9991-5(6))* Time-Life, Inc.
Ikids Staff. Fast Facts - Division. 2005. (ENG.). 14p. (J). (gr. 2-17). 7.99 *(978-1-58476-315-4(9))* Innovative Kids.
—Fast Facts - Multiplication. 2005. (ENG.). 14p. (J). (gr. 2-17). 7.99 *(978-1-58476-314-7(0))* Innovative Kids.
—Math Gear: Fast Facts - Addition. 2005. (ENG.). 14p. (J). (gr. 2-17). 9.99 *(978-1-58476-326-0(4))* Innovative Kids.
—Math Gear: Fast Facts - Subtraction. 2005. (ENG.). 14p. (J). (gr. 2-17). 9.99 *(978-1-58476-327-7(2))* Innovative Kids.
In Step with the Standards - Computation & Estimation. 2005. (J). spiral bd. 15.95 *(978-1-58123-376-6(0))* Larson Learning, Inc.
In Step with the Standards - Data, Statistics, & Probability. 2005. (J). spiral bd. 15.95 *(978-1-58123-378-0(7))* Larson Learning, Inc.
Inchworms Activity Cards. 2003. (J). 17.95 *(978-1-56911-143-7(X))* Learning Resources, Inc.
Infomax Common Core Math Readers: Levels a - D. 2013. (InfoMax Common Core Math Readers Ser.). 16p. (J). (gr. k-1). pap. 1683.00 *(978-1-4777-2215-2(7))*; pap. 280.50 *(978-1-4777-2216-9(5))* Rosen Publishing Group, Inc., The. (Rosen Classroom).
Infomax Common Core Math Readers: Levels d - I. 2013. (InfoMax Common Core Math Readers Ser.). 24p. (J). (gr. 1-2). pap. 1534.50 *(978-1-4777-2218-3(1))*; pap. 255.75 *(978-1-4777-2217-6(3))* Rosen Publishing Group, Inc., The. (Rosen Classroom).
Integrating Grade 11 TAKS Geometry into Algebra II Student Edition. 2004. (Region IV ESC Resources for Mathematics Ser.). pap. *(978-1-932797-71-8(8))* Region IV Education Service Ctr.
Intermediate Math Skills, Chapter 1, Activities. 2005. (Illus.). 50p. (YA). per. 7.00 *(978-1-59476-041-9(1))* Paradigm Accelerated Curriculum.
Intermediate Math Skills, Chapter 1, Text. 2005. (Illus.). 50p. (YA). pap. 7.00 *(978-1-59476-029-7(2))* Paradigm Accelerated Curriculum.
Intermediate Math Skills, Chapter 2, Activities. 2005. (Illus.). 58p. (YA). pap. 5.00 *(978-1-59476-042-6(X))* Paradigm Accelerated Curriculum.
Intermediate Math Skills, Chapter 2, Text. 2005. (Illus.). 64p. (YA). pap. 7.00 *(978-1-59476-030-3(6))* Paradigm Accelerated Curriculum.
Intermediate Math Skills, Chapter 3, Activities. 2005. (Illus.). 52p. (YA). pap. 5.00 *(978-1-59476-043-3(8))* Paradigm Accelerated Curriculum.
Intermediate Math Skills, Chapter 3, Text. 2005. (Illus.). 62p. (YA). pap. 7.00 *(978-1-59476-031-0(4))* Paradigm Accelerated Curriculum.
Intermediate Math Skills, Chapter 4, Activities. 2005. (Illus.). 60p. (YA). pap. 5.00 *(978-1-59476-044-0(6))* Paradigm Accelerated Curriculum.
Intermediate Math Skills, Chapter 4, Text. 2005. (Illus.). 70p. (YA). pap. 7.00 *(978-1-59476-032-7(2))* Paradigm Accelerated Curriculum.
Intermediate Math Skills, Chapter 5, Activities. 2005. (Illus.). 68p. (YA). pap. 5.00 *(978-1-59476-045-7(4))* Paradigm Accelerated Curriculum.
Intermediate Math Skills, Chapter 5, Text. 2005. (Illus.). 56p. (YA). pap. 7.00 *(978-1-59476-033-4(0))* Paradigm Accelerated Curriculum.
Intermediate Math Skills, Chapter 6, Activities. 2005. 68p. (YA). pap. 5.00 *(978-1-59476-046-4(2))* Paradigm Accelerated Curriculum.
Intermediate Math Skills, Chapter 6, Text. 2005. (Illus.). 68p. (YA). pap. 7.00 *(978-1-59476-034-1(9))* Paradigm Accelerated Curriculum.
Intermediate Math Skills Full Course Kit with TRK & CD-ROM. 2005. (Illus.). 1042p. (YA). 87.00 *(978-1-59476-203-1(1))* Paradigm Accelerated Curriculum.
Investigations in Number, Data, & Space. 2004. (gr. k-5). *(978-0-328-01881-9(3*, Scott Foresman) Addison-Wesley Educational Pubs., Inc.
Investigations in Number, Data, & Space: Complete Program. 2004. (gr. k-18). *(978-0-201-37792-7(6))*; (gr. 1-18). *(978-0-201-37793-4(4))*; (gr. 2-18). *(978-0-201-37794-1(2))*; (gr. 3-18). *(978-0-201-37795-8(0))*; (gr. 4-18). *(978-0-201-37796-5(9))*; (gr. 5-18). *(978-0-201-37797-2(7))* Addison-Wesley Educational Pubs., Inc. (Scott Foresman).
Investigations in Number, Data, & Space: Individual Components (Additional Resources) 2004. (gr. k-18). *(978-0-328-01883-3(X))*; (gr. k-18). *(978-0-328-01882-6(1))*; (gr. k-2). *(978-0-201-43436-1(9))*; (gr. 2-18). *(978-0-201-37586-2(9))*; (gr. 3-5). *(978-0-201-43438-5(5))* Addison-Wesley Educational Pubs., Inc. (Scott Foresman).
Irvin, Barbara Bando. Multiplication Facts Made Easy 3-4. Boyer, Robin, illus. 2005. (ENG.). 64p. (J). (gr. 3-4). pap. 3.99 *(978-1-58947-328-7(0)*, 02214) School Zone Publishing Co.
Jackson, Dona. Let's Get Moving! Tell & Write Time. 2013. (InfoMax Math Readers Ser.). (ENG.). 24p. (J). (gr. 1-2). pap. 49.50 *(978-1-4777-2176-6(2))*; (Illus.). pap. 8.25 *(978-1-4777-2175-9(4))* Rosen Publishing Group, Inc., The. (Rosen Classroom).
Jackson, Richelle. Running for Class President: Represent & Solve Problems Involving Division. 2014. (Rosen Common Core Math Readers Ser.). 24p. (J). (gr. 3-4). (ENG.). pap. 49.50 *(978-1-4777-4960-9(8)*, Rosen Classroom); (ENG., Illus.). pap. 8.25 *(978-1-4777-4959-3(4)*, PowerKids Pr.); (Illus.). lib. bdg. 23.60 *(978-1-4777-6448-0(8)*, PowerKids Pr.) Rosen Publishing Group, Inc., The.
Jacobs, Daniel. City Shapes, 6 vols., Set. 2003. (Yellow Umbrella Early Level Ser.). (ENG.). 16p. (gr. k-1). pap. 35.70 *(978-0-7368-2992-2(X)*, Yellow Umbrella Bks.) Capstone Press of Coughlan Cos.
—Count Your Chickens, 6 vols., Set. 2003. (Yellow Umbrella Early Level Ser.). (ENG.). 16p. (gr. k-1). pap. 35.70 *(978-0-7368-2995-3(4)*, Yellow Umbrella Bks.) Capstone Press of Coughlan Cos.
Jason Math Adventure: Proportional Reasoning & the Disappearing Wetlands. 2004. (J). *(978-0-9763809-3-1(5))* JASON Project, The.
Jennison, Christopher. Baseball Math: Grandslam Activities & Projects. 3rd ed. 2005. (Illus.). 104p. (J). (gr. 4-8). per. 12.95 *(978-1-59647-007-1(0))* Good Year Bks.
Jeopardy Math Grade 3. 2006. (J). 28.00 *(978-1-933178-56-1(6))* Pflaum Publishing Group.
Jeopardy Math Grade 4. 2006. (J). 28.00 *(978-1-933178-57-8(4))* Pflaum Publishing Group.
Jeopardy Math Grade 5. 2006. (J). 28.00 *(978-1-933178-58-5(2))* Pflaum Publishing Group.
Jerome, Kate Boehm. How Many Ants in an Anthill? 2007. (Reading Expeditions Ser.). (ENG., Illus.). 24p. (J). pap. 14.95 *(978-0-7922-4587-2(3))* CENGAGE Learning.
—Number Know-How. 2007. (Reading Expeditions Ser.). (ENG., Illus.). 24p. (J). pap. 14.95 *(978-0-7922-4591-9(1))* CENGAGE Learning.
Johns, Bobbie. Secure Maths - Secure Year 6: A Primary Maths Intervention Programme. 2017. (ENG.). 144p. (J). pap. 71.99 ***(978-0-00-822152-2(9))*** HarperCollins Pubs. Ltd. GBR. Dist: Independent Pubs. Group.
Johnson, Rebecca L. Crunching Numbers. 2007. (Reading Expeditions Ser.). (ENG., Illus.). 24p. (J). pap. 14.95 *(978-0-7922-4592-6(X))* CENGAGE Learning.
—Decoding Data. 2007. (Reading Expeditions Ser.). (ENG., Illus.). 24p. (J). pap. 14.95 *(978-0-7922-4588-9(1))* CENGAGE Learning.
—Puzzling Out Patterns. 2007. (Nonfiction Reading & Writing Workshops Ser.). (ENG., Illus.). 24p. (J). pap. 14.95 *(978-0-7922-4594-0(6))* CENGAGE Learning.
Johnson, Virginia. Hands-on Math, Grades K-1: Manipulative Activities for the Classroom. Hamaguchi, Carla, ed. Weller, Linda, illus. 2nd ed. 2006. 144p. (J). (gr. k-1). per. 19.99 *(978-1-59198-232-6(4)*, 2568) Creative Teaching Pr., Inc.
Johnstone, Drummond & Wakefield, Chris. Numbers Game, Theparent Booklet: It's a Real Cure for Maths Fright. 2013. (ENG.). 26p. pap. 3.25 *(978-1-85741-181-2(1))* Southgate Pubs. GBR. Dist: Parkwest Pubns., Inc.
Jones, Dee. Winston Wonders about Capacity: A mathematical Story. Klaus, Machelle, illus. 2010. 36p. pap. 14.95 *(978-1-60844-181-5(4))* Dog Ear Publishing, LLC.
Jones, Otis. Geonopolis, the Shapely City of Geometry. 2003. (ENG., Illus.). 21p. (J). *(978-0-9744123-0-6(9))* Jeb Cool Kids Entertainment, Inc.
Jones, Rob Lee. Mathematics 1 for Young Catholics. 2013. pap. 15.00 *(978-1-60704-113-9(8))* Seton Pr.
Jordan, Christopher. Hockey 123. 2011. (My First NHL Book Ser.). (ENG.). 30p. (J). (gr. k-k). bds. 6.95 *(978-1-77049-347-6(6)*, Fenn-Tundra) Tundra Bks. CAN. Dist: Penguin Random Hse. LLC.
Jovin, Michelle. Your World: Shopping Secrets: Multiplication (Grade 3) 2017. (Mathematics Readers Ser.). (Illus.). 32p. (J). (gr. 3-3). pap. 8.99 ***(978-1-4807-5796-7(9))*** Teacher Created Materials, Inc.
Kaplan, Andrew & DeBold, Carol. Math on Call: A Mathematics Handbook. 2nd ed. 2003. (Math on Call Ser.). (ENG., Illus.). 480p. (gr. 6-8). pap. 25.55 *(978-0-669-50819-2(5))* Great Source Education Group, Inc.
Karapetian, Marjam. Bilingual Content Dictionary: English to Spanish. 2004. (SPA & ENG., Illus.). 4.95 *(978-0-9764829-0-1(8))* WizdomInc.
Karapetkova, Holly & Robertson, J. Jean. ?un Cuadrado? ! un Rectangulo! A Square? a Rectangle! 2008. (ENG & SPA., Illus.). 24p. (J). 19.44 *(978-1-60472-506-3(0))* Rourke Educational Media.
Kauffman, Dorothy. Math Every Day. 2005. (Oxford Picture Dictionary for the Content Areas Ser.). (ENG., Illus.). 24p. 7.56 *(978-0-19-430958-5(4))* Oxford Univ. Pr., Inc.
Kay, Stephanie. Let's Go to the Parade! Understand Place Value. 2013. (InfoMax Math Readers Ser.). (ENG.). 24p. (J). (gr. 1-2). pap. 49.50 *(978-1-4777-2164-3(9))*; (Illus.). pap. 8.25 *(978-1-4777-2163-6(0))* Rosen Publishing Group, Inc., The. (Rosen Classroom).
Keen Kite Books. KS2 Maths SATs. 2017. (ENG.). 128p. (J). (gr. 5-6). pap. 113.99 ***(978-0-00-824195-7(3))*** HarperCollins Pubs. Ltd. GBR. Dist: Independent Pubs. Group.
Kelly, Lynne. Maths Wizard. (Illus.). (J). (gr. 2-6). pap. *(978-1-876367-35-0(0))* Wizard Bks.
Keman, Elizabeth. How Long Is It? Learning to Measure with Nonstandard Units. 2009. (Math for the Real World: Early Emergent Ser.). (ENG., Illus.). 8p. (gr. k-1). pap. 5.15 *(978-0-8239-8843-3(0))* Rosen Publishing Group, Inc., The.
Kessler, Colleen. Math Problem Solvers: Using Word Problems to Enhance Mathematical Problem Solving. 2005. 44p. 14.95 *(978-1-59363-026-3(3))* Prufrock Pr.
Kids Can Press Staff. Math Stories: Subtraction. 2003. (Kids Can Learn with Franklin Ser.). (ENG., Illus.). 32p. (J). (gr. 1-3). 3.95 *(978-1-55337-597-5(1))* Kids Can Pr., Ltd. CAN. Dist: Hachette Bk. Group.
—Measurement. 2003. (Kids Can Learn with Franklin Ser.). (ENG., Illus.). 32p. (J). (gr. k-1). 3.95 *(978-1-55337-595-1(5))* Kids Can Pr., Ltd. CAN. Dist: Hachette Bk. Group.
Kidzup Productions Staff. Addition & Subtraction. 2003. (Interactive Learning Kits Ser.). (Illus.). 24p. (J). (gr. k-2). audio, audio compact disk 13.99 *(978-1-894281-01-0(2))* Kidzup Productions.
Kim, Hy. The Complete Book of Multiplication & Division: Basic Facts & Advanced Number Theories. Applebaum, Teri L. & Rous, Sheri, eds. 2004. (Illus.). 144p. (J). pap. 16.99 *(978-1-59198-035-3(6)*, CTP 2572) Creative Teaching Pr., Inc.
—The Complete Book of Multiplication & Division: Grades 2-3. Applebaum, Teri L. & Rous, Sheri, eds. Hillam, Corbin, illus. 2004. 144p. per. 16.99 *(978-1-59198-034-6(8)*, CTP 2571) Creative Teaching Pr., Inc.
—Math Cycles: Problems & Quizzes that Strengthen Math Skills. 2008. pap. 24.95 *(978-1-59647-141-2(7))* Good Year Bks.
King, Julie, et al. Adding & Subtracting Rational Expressions, Bk. 7. 2012. (Key To... workbooks Ser.: Bk. 7). (ENG., Illus.). 40p. (gr. 6-8). spiral bd. 5.64 *(978-1-55953-007-1(3)*, 1559530073) McGraw-Hill Education.
Kirk, Karly. All My Cousins: Understand & Apply Properties of Operations. 2013. (InfoMax Math Readers Ser.). (ENG.). 24p. (J). (gr. 1-2). pap. 49.50 *(978-1-4777-2184-1(3))*; (Illus.). pap. 8.25 *(978-1-4777-2183-4(5))* Rosen Publishing Group, Inc., The. (Rosen Classroom).
Kirkman, Steve & McAlister, Kerrie. Maths in Practice Workbook 2. 2013. (ENG.). pap., stu. ed. *(978-1-107-62846-5(6))* Cambridge Univ. Pr.
—Maths in Practice Workbook 2 & Hotmaths Bundle. 2013. (ENG.). pap., stu. ed. *(978-1-107-63382-7(6))* Cambridge Univ. Pr.
Kleist, Nick. Super Sports Numbers: Understand Place Value. 2014. (Math Masters: Number & Operations in Base Ten Ser.). 24p. (J). (gr. 2-3). 23.60 *(978-1-4777-6401-5(1))*; (ENG.). pap. 8.25 *(978-1-4777-4666-0(8))* Rosen Publishing Group, Inc., The. (Rosen Classroom).
Koenig, Jenaya. Jumping Animals! Relate Addition & Subtraction to Length. 2014. (Math Masters: Measurement & Data Ser.). 24p. (J). (gr. 2-3). (Illus.). 23.60 *(978-1-4777-6439-8(9))*; (ENG.). pap. 8.25 *(978-1-4777-4816-9(4))* Rosen Publishing Group, Inc., The. (Rosen Classroom).
Kofman, Victoria. Guni-Pi Academy, Math & Logic: Hands-On Textbook for 4 - 7 Year Olds. 2006. spiral bd. *(978-0-9777171-0-1(0))* VK Publishing, Inc.
—Guni-Pi Academy, Math & Logic: Hands-on Textbook for 4 - 7 Year Olds - Non-Laminated. 2006. spiral bd. *(978-0-9777171-2-5(7))* VK Publishing, Inc.
Koizim, Jessica. Mathematical Thinking Expressing Ideas Strategies. 2004. (BrainBuilders Ser.). (ENG.). 48p. (gr. k-4). pap. 5.25 *(978-1-4042-8523-1(7))* Rosen Publishing Group, Inc., The.
—Mathematical Thinking Linking Math. 2004. (BrainBuilders Ser.). (ENG.). 48p. (gr. k-4). pap. 5.25 *(978-1-4042-8524-8(5))* Rosen Publishing Group, Inc., The.
Koll, Hilary & Mills, Steve. A Math Journey Around the Wonders of the World. 2016. (ENG., Illus.). 32p. (J). *(978-0-7787-2321-9(6))* Crabtree Publishing Co.
—A Math Journey Through Computer Games. 2016. (ENG.). 32p. (J). *(978-0-7787-2311-0(9))* Crabtree Publishing Co.
—A Math Journey Through Extreme Sports. 2016. (ENG., Illus.). 32p. (J). *(978-0-7787-2313-4(5))* Crabtree Publishing Co.
—A Math Journey under the Ocean. 2016. (ENG., Illus.). 32p. (J). *(978-0-7787-2315-8(1))* Crabtree Publishing Co.
Koll, Hilary, et al. Using Math in the ER. 2006. (Mathworks!). (Illus.). 32p. (gr. 2-6). pap. 10.50 *(978-0-8368-6769-5(6))*; lib. bdg. 26.00 *(978-0-8368-6762-6(9))* Stevens, Gareth Publishing LLLP. (Gareth Stevens Learning Library).
—Using Math to Build a Skyscraper. 2006. (Mathworks!). (Illus.). 32p. (gr. 2-6). pap. 10.50 *(978-0-8368-6771-8(8))*; lib. bdg. 26.00 *(978-0-8368-6764-0(5))* Stevens, Gareth Publishing LLLP. (Gareth Stevens Learning Library).
—Using Math to Design a Roller Coaster. 2006. (Mathworks!). (Illus.). 32p. (gr. 2-6). pap. 10.50 *(978-0-8368-6773-2(4))*; lib. bdg. 26.00 *(978-0-8368-6766-4(1))* Stevens, Gareth Publishing LLLP. (Gareth Stevens Learning Library).
—Using Math to Survive in the Wild. 2006. (Mathworks!). 32p. (gr. 2-6). pap. 10.50 *(978-0-8368-6774-9(2))*; (Illus.). lib. bdg. 26.00 *(978-0-8368-6767-1(X))* Stevens, Gareth Publishing LLLP. (Gareth Stevens Learning Library).
Kompelien, Tracy. Lets Sort, Its a Real Sport!, 1 vol. 2007. (Math Made Fun Ser.). (ENG., Illus.). 24p. (J). (gr. k-3). lib. bdg. 24.21 *(978-1-59928-539-9(8)*, SandCastle) ABDO Publishing Co.
Kramer, Alan. In Search of Numbers. 2004. (Reader's Theater Ser.). (J). pap. *(978-1-4108-1137-0(9))* Benchmark Education Co.
—No Math Day at School. 2004. (Reader's Theater Ser.). (J). pap. *(978-1-4108-0792-2(4))* Benchmark Education Co.
Krech, Bob. Math Word Problems Made Easy: Surefire Strategies-With 100+ Guided & Independent Practice Problems-That Give Kids the Tools to Tackle All Kinds of Word Problems. 2005. (Math Word Problems Made Easy Ser.). (ENG.). 80p. pap. 12.99 *(978-0-439-52972-3(7))*; pap. 12.99 *(978-0-439-52971-6(9))* Scholastic, Inc. (Teaching Resources).
Krech, Bob & Kennan, Audrey. Multiplication & Division: Mini-Lessons, Games, & Activities to Review & Reinforce Essential Math Concepts & Skills. 2008. (Reteaching Math Ser.). (ENG.). 96p. (gr. 4-6). pap. 14.99 *(978-0-439-52967-9(0)*, Teaching Resources) Scholastic, Inc.
Krech, Bob, et al. Geometry & Measurement: Mini-Lessons, Games, & Activities to Review & Reinforce Essential Math Concepts & Skills. 2008. (Reteaching Math Ser.). (ENG.). 96p. (gr. 2-4). pap. 14.99 *(978-0-439-52968-6(9)*, Teaching Resources) Scholastic, Inc.
Kreloff, Elliot, illus. Matching Puzzle Cards - Numbers. 2012. (ENG.). 36p. (J). (gr. k-12). 9.99 *(978-1-60905-221-8(8))* Blue Apple Bks.
Kumon Publishing, creator. Addition Grade 2: Kumon Math Workbooks. 2008. (Kumon Workbooks Ser.). 96p. (J). (gr.

-1-3). pap. 7.95 *(978-1-933241-51-7(9))* Kumon Publishing North America, Inc.

—My Book of Simple Multiplication. 2007. (Kumon Workbooks Ser.). (Illus.). 80p. (J). (gr. 1-3). per. 7.95 *(978-1-933241-41-8(1))* Kumon Publishing North America, Inc.

Kumon Publishing, ed. Focus on Multiplication & Division with Decimals. 2012. (Illus.). 64p. (J). pap. 5.95 *(978-4-7743-0025-2(X))* Kumon Publishing North America, Inc.

—Focus on Multiplication Numbers 1-10. 2012. (ENG., Illus.). 64p. (J). pap. 5.95 *(978-4-7743-0023-8(3))* Kumon Publishing North America, Inc.

—Multiplication & Division with Decimals. 2012. (ENG., Illus.). 64p. (J). pap. 5.95 *(978-1-935800-42-2(6))* Kumon Publishing North America, Inc.

—My Book of Number Games 1-70. 2004. (ENG., Illus.). 82p. (J). per. 7.95 *(978-4-7743-0759-6(9))* Kumon Publishing North America, Inc.

—Subtraction, Grade 2. 2008. (Illus.). 96p. (J). (gr. 2). pap. 7.95 *(978-1-933241-52-4(7))* Kumon Publishing North America, Inc.

—Velocity, Proportion & Ratio. 2012. (Illus.). 64p. (J). pap. 5.95 *(978-4-7743-0024-5(1))* Kumon Publishing North America, Inc.

LaCompte, Angie. Math for Fun. 2011. (Math Ser.). (ENG.). 16p. (gr. -1-1). 25.95 *(978-1-4296-8669-3(3))*, Wonder Readers) Capstone Press of Coughlan Cos.

Lalley, Kristine. How Many Legs? Learning to Multiply Using Repeated Addition. 2009. (PowerMath: Beginning Ser.). 16p. (gr. 2-2). 37.50 *(978-1-60851-373-4(4)*, PowerKids Pr.) Rosen Publishing Group, Inc., The.

Lane, Chloe. Package Design. rev. ed. 2012. (Mathematics Readers Ser.). (ENG.). 32p. (J). (gr. 6-6). pap. 8.99 *(978-1-4333-3460-3(7))* Teacher Created Materials, Inc.

Lane County Mathematics Project Staff. Problem Solving in Mathematics. 432p. (J). (gr. 4). pap. 27.95 *(978-0-86651-181-0(4)*, DSO1407); (YA). (gr. 8). pap. 27.95 *(978-0-86651-185-8(7)*, DSO1411) Globe Fearon Educational Publishing.

Lappan, Glenda. Connected Mathematics, 3 vols. 2004. 760p. (YA). (gr. 6-18). 380.00 *(978-0-13-180833-1(8))* Prentice Hall Pr.

Lappan, Glenda & Prentice Hall Staff. Connected Mathematics, 2 vols. 2003. (ENG.). 676p. (YA). (gr. 8-8). 338.00 *(978-0-13-180835-5(4)*, Prentice Hall) Pearson Schl.

Large, Tori. Illustrated Dictionary of Math: Internet-Linked. 2004. (Illustrated Dictionaries Ser.). 128p. (J). lib. bdg. 20.99 *(978-1-58086-645-3(X)*, Usborne) EDC Publishing.

—The Usborne Illustrated Dictionary of Math. 2004. (Illustrated Dictionaries Ser.). (ENG., Illus.). 128p. (J). pap. 12.99 *(978-0-7945-0662-9(3)*, Usborne) EDC Publishing.

Larson, Nancy. Lesson Planner Instruction. Saxon Publishers Staff, tr. 2nd rev. ed. 2003. (gr. k-4). incl. cd-rom *(978-1-59141-299-1(4)*, 2994) Saxon Pubs., Inc.

—Teacher Resource Instruction. Saxon Publishers Staff, tr. 2nd rev. ed. 2003. (gr. k-4). tchr. ed. incl. audio compact disk *(978-1-59141-298-4(6)*, 2986) Saxon Pubs., Inc.

Larson, Ron. Middle School Math, Course 2. l.t. ed. 2004. (McDougal Littell Math Ser.). (YA). (gr. 6-9). stu. ed. 63.96 *(978-0-618-24974-9(5)*, 2-06002) Holt McDougal.

—Precalculus Advanced Placement. 6th ed. 2003. (YA). (gr. 11-12). 161.56 *(978-0-618-31435-5(0)*, 332741) CENGAGE Learning.

Larson, Ron, et al. McDougall Littell Middle School Math Course 3. l.t. ed. 2006. (Illus.). 797p. (gr. 6-9). lib. bdg., stu. ed. 66.12 *(978-0-618-25000-4(X)*, 2-06003) Holt McDougal.

—Passport to Mathematics, Vol. 2. 2006. (Illus.). 706p. (gr. 6-12). lib. bdg., stu. ed. *(978-0-618-18599-3(2)*, 2-05511) Holt McDougal.

Law, Karina & Collins Easy Learning Staff. Handwriting, Bk. 2. 2011. (Collins Easy Learning Age 7-11 Ser.). (ENG.). 16p. (J). pap., wbk. ed. 6.99 *(978-0-00-727759-9(8))* HarperCollins Pubs. Ltd. GBR. Dist: Independent Pubs. Group.

Lawrence, Paul. Communicator Mathematics#8482; Content Series — Fraction Addition & Subtraction Teacher Guide: W/DVD Book G. 2005. 368p. spiral bd. 45.95 *(978-1-59699-177-4(1))* Lawrence Educational Services, Inc.

—Communicator Mathematics#8482; Content Series - Concepts of Fractions & Decimals Teacher Guide: W/DVD Book F. 2005. 268p. spiral bd. 45.95 *(978-1-59699-170-5(4))* Lawrence Educational Services, Inc.

—Communicator Mathematics#8482; Content Series - Whole Number Addition & Subtraction Teacher Guide: W/DVD Book C. 2005. 436p. spiral bd. 51.95 *(978-1-59699-167-5(4))* Lawrence Educational Services, Inc.

—Communicator Mathematics#8482; Content Series - Whole Numbers: Multiplication & Division Beyond Facts Teacher Guide: W/DVD Book E. 2005. 408p. spiral bd. 51.95 *(978-1-59699-169-9(0))* Lawrence Educational Services, Inc.

—Communicator Mathematics#8482; Content Series - Whole Numbers: Understanding & Mastering Multiplication & Division Facts Teacher Guide: W/DVD Book D. 2005. 464p. spiral bd. 49.95 *(978-1-59699-168-2(2))* Lawrence Educational Services, Inc.

—Communicator Mathematics#8482; Content Series- Decimal Addition & Subtraction Teacher Guide I: W/DVD Book I. 2005. 210p. spiral bd. 42.95 *(978-1-59699-171-2(2))* Lawrence Educational Services, Inc.

—Communicator Mathematics#8482; Content Series Fractions & Decimals - Decimals Multiplication & Division Teacher Guide: W/DVD Book J. 2005. 148p. spiral bd. 40.95 *(978-1-59699-176-7(3))* Lawrence Educational Services, Inc.

—Communicator Mathematics#8482; Fractions Multiplacation & Division Teacher Guide: W/DVD Book H. 2005. 262p. spiral bd. 45.95 *(978-1-59699-178-1(X))* Lawrence Educational Services, Inc.

—Communicator#8482; Mathematics Content Series- — Decimal Multiplication & Division: Book J Student Pak. 2005. 88p. ring bd. 3.95 *(978-1-59699-352-5(9))* Lawrence Educational Services, Inc.

—Communicator#8482; Mathematics Content Series- Concepts of Fractions & Decimals: Book F Student Pak. 2005. 144p. spiral bd. 4.95 *(978-1-59699-353-2(7))* Lawrence Educational Services, Inc.

—Communicator#8482; Mathematics Content Series- Fraction Multiplication & Division: Book H Student Pak. 2005. 120p. spiral bd. 3.95 *(978-1-59699-355-6(3))* Lawrence Educational Services, Inc.

—Communicator#8482; Mathematics Content Series- Perspective on Numbers Assessment: Book B Student Pak. 2005. 232p. spiral bd. 6.95 *(978-1-59699-347-1(2))* Lawrence Educational Services, Inc.

—Communicator#8482; Mathematics Content Series- Whole Number Addition & Subtraction: Book C Student Pak. 2005. 208p. spiral bd. 7.95 *(978-1-59699-348-8(0))* Lawrence Educational Services, Inc.

—Communicator#8482; Mathematics Content Series- Whole Numbers: Multiplication & Division Beyond Facts: Book E Student Pak. 2005. 232p. spiral bd. 7.95 *(978-1-59699-350-1(2))* Lawrence Educational Services, Inc.

—Communicator#8482; Mathematics Content Series- Whole Numbers: Understanding & Mastering Multiplication & Division Facts: Book D Student Pak. 2005. 312p. spiral bd. 7.95 *(978-1-59699-349-5(9))* Lawrence Educational Services, Inc.

—Communicator#8482; Mathematics Content Series-Decimal Addition & Subtraction: Book I Student Pak. 2005. 152p. spiral bd. 4.95 *(978-1-59699-351-8(0))* Lawrence Educational Services, Inc.

Lawrence, Paul R. Question Quest HSPA Math - Level A, 1 volume. 2003. (Illus.). (YA). pap. 10.95 *(978-1-931104-20-3(4))* L L Teach.

—Question Quest HSPA Math - Level B, 1 volume. 2003. (Illus.). (YA). pap. 10.95 *(978-1-931104-22-7(0))* L L Teach.

—Question Quest HSPA Math Algebra Companion, 1 volume. 2003. (Illus.). (YA). pap. 8.95 *(978-1-931104-18-0(2))* L L Teach.

—Question Quest HSPA Math Geometry Companion. 2003. (Illus.). (YA). pap. 8.95 *(978-1-931104-16-6(6))* L L Teach.

Learning Company Books Staff, ed. Mighty Math: Money & Decimals. 2003. (Illus.). (J). 32p. pap., wbk. ed. *(978-0-7630-7631-3(7))*; 32p. pap., wbk. ed. *(978-0-7630-7632-0(5))*; 320p. (gr. 2-3). pap., wbk. ed. *(978-0-7630-7636-8(8))* Magma.

—Reader Rabbit Math: Addition & Subtraction. 2003. (Illus.). (J). 32p. pap., wbk. ed. *(978-0-7630-7638-2(4))*; 32p. pap., wbk. ed. *(978-0-7630-7639-9(2))*; 320p. pap., wbk. ed. *(978-0-7630-7637-5(6))* Magma.

Learning Company, Inc. Staff. Pre-K Math. 2012. (Learning with Curious George Ser.). (ENG., Illus.). 64p. (J). (gr. -1-3). pap. 4.99 *(978-0-547-79055-8(4))* Houghton Mifflin Harcourt Publishing Co.

Learning Wrap Ups Palette Base. 2004. (ENG.). (J). 14.99 *(978-1-59204-000-1(4))* Learning Wrap-Ups, Inc.

Lechner, Judith. Our New Fish Tank: Learning to Estimate & Round Numbers to the Nearest Ones, Tens, & Hundreds Places. (Math for the REAL World Ser.). 16p. (gr. 2-3). 2009. pap. 7.05 *(978-0-8239-8881-5(3)*, Rosen Classroom) 2004. (ENG.). 37.95 *(978-0-8239-7640-9(8))* Rosen Publishing Group, Inc., The.

Leckie and Leckie, Leckie and, et al. CfE Advanced Higher Maths Student Book. 2017. (ENG.). 392p. (YA). (gr. 8). pap. 45.00 ***(978-0-00-820903-2(0))*** HarperCollins Pubs. Ltd. GBR. Dist: Independent Pubs. Group.

Lee, Cora. The Great Number Rumble: A Story of Math in Surprising Places. Gray, Virginia & Gray, Virginia, illus. 2007. (ENG.). 108p. (J). (gr. 4-6). 24.95 *(978-1-55451-032-0(5)*, 9781554510320) Annick Pr., Ltd. CAN. Dist: Publishers Group West (PGW).

Lee, Cora & O'Reilly, Gillian. The Great Number Rumble: A Story of Math in Surprising Places. Crump, Lil, illus. 2nd ed. 2016. (ENG.). 104p. (J). (gr. 3-7). pap. 12.95 *(978-1-55451-849-4(0))* Annick Pr., Ltd. CAN. Dist: Publishers Group West (PGW).

Leech, Bonnie. Mesopotamia: Creating & Solving World Problems. 2009. (PowerMath: Advanced Proficiency Plus Ser.). 32p. (gr. 5-5). 47.90 *(978-1-60851-362-8(9)*, PowerKids Pr.) Rosen Publishing Group, Inc., The.

Leech, Bonnie Coulter. Mesopotamia: Creating & Solving Word Problems. (Math for the Real World Ser.). (Illus.). 32p. 2009. (ENG.). (gr. 6-7). pap. 10.00 *(978-1-4042-6067-2(6))* 2006. (YA). (gr. 5-9). lib. bdg. 25.25 *(978-1-4042-3357-7(1))* Rosen Publishing Group, Inc., The.

Lehoczky, Sandor & Rusczyk, Richard. The Art of Problem Solving Vol. 1: The Basics. Date not set. 361p. (YA). (gr. 7-12). pap. 29.00 *(978-1-885875-01-3(0))* Mu Alpha Theta, National High Schl. Mathematics Club.

Leigh, Autumn. On the Ball: Learning to Identify the Place Values of Ones & Tens. 2009. (Math for the Real World: Early Emergent Ser.). (ENG., Illus.). 8p. (gr. k-1). pap. 5.15 *(978-0-8239-8859-4(7))* Rosen Publishing Group, Inc., The.

—Signs on the Road: Learning to Identify the Four Basic Geometric Shapes. 2009. (Math for the Real World: Early Emergent Ser.). (ENG., Illus.). 8p. (gr. k-1). pap. 5.15 *(978-0-8239-8857-0(0))* Rosen Publishing Group, Inc., The.

Leimbach, Judy & Eckert, Sharon. Math Extension Units, Bk. 1. 2005. (Math Extension Units Ser.: 1). (ENG.). 64p. (gr. 2-3). pap. 16.95 *(978-1-59363-099-7(9)*, 9781593630997) Prufrock Pr.

Leimbach, Judy & Leimbach, Kathy. Math Extension Units, Bk. 2. 2005. (Math Extension Units Ser.: 2). (ENG.). 64p. (gr. 4-5). pap. 16.95 *(978-1-59363-100-0(6))* Prufrock Pr.

Lent, Patricia & Fosnot, Catherine Twomey. Trades, Jumps, & Stops: Early Algebra. 2008. (ENG.). 96p. (gr. 1-2). pap. 31.25 *(978-0-325-01015-1(3)*, E01015, Firsthand) Heinemann.

LernerClassroom Editors. First Step Nonfiction-Early Math Teaching Guide. 2009. pap. 7.95 *(978-0-8225-6881-0(0))* Lerner Publishing Group.

Levy, Janey. A Journey along the Erie Canal: Dividing Multidigit Numbers by a One-Digit Number Without Remainders. 2009. (PowerMath Ser.). (ENG., Illus.). 32p. (gr. 4-5). pap. 10.00 *(978-0-8239-8904-1(6))* Rosen Publishing Group, Inc., The.

Lift-The-Flap Fractions & Decimals IR. 2017. (Advanced Lift-The-Flap BDs* Ser.). (ENG.). (J). bds. 14.99 ***(978-0-7945-3727-2(8)***, Usborne) EDC Publishing.

Linde, Barbara. Math in Our Solar System: Applying Problem-Solving Strategies. 2009. (PowerMath: Proficiency Plus Ser.). 32p. (gr. 4-5). 47.90 *(978-1-60851-413-7(7)*, PowerKids Pr.) Rosen Publishing Group, Inc., The.

Linde, Barbara M. Math in Our Solar System: Applying Problem-Solving Strategies. (PowerMath Ser.). 32p. 2009. (ENG.). (gr. 5-6). pap. 10.00 *(978-1-4042-5135-9(9))* 2005. (Illus.). (J). (gr. 3-6). lib. bdg. 25.25 *(978-1-4042-2936-5(1)*, PowerKids Pr.) Rosen Publishing Group, Inc., The.

—A Shopping Trip: Learning to Add Dollars & Cents up to $10.00 Without Regrouping. 2009. (Math for the REAL World Ser.). 16p. (gr. 2-3). pap. 7.05 *(978-0-8239-8900-3(3)*, Rosen Classroom) Rosen Publishing Group, Inc., The.

—Working at the Post Office: Learning to Subtract 2 Three-Digit Numbers Without Renaming. 2009. (Math for the REAL World Ser.). 16p. (gr. 2-3). pap. 7.05 *(978-0-8239-8855-6(4)*, Rosen Classroom) Rosen Publishing Group, Inc., The.

Lindsay, Kristine. Basic Math Practice 5 - Rounding, Reasonableness & Estimating. 2005. (YA). ring bd. 49.95 *(978-1-58804-405-1(X))* P C I Education.

—Coupon Math. 2004. (YA). ring bd. 59.95 *(978-1-58804-355-9(X))* P C I Education.

Literacy & Math Centers. 2005. (J). pap. *(978-1-60015-019-7(5))* Steps To Literacy, LLC.

Litton, Jonathan. Mesmerizing Math. Flintham, Thomas, illus. 2013. (ENG.). 16p. (J). (gr. 2-5). 18.99 *(978-0-7636-6881-5(8)*, Templar) Candlewick Pr.

Llewellyn, Claire & Holden, Arianne. It's Great to Play & Fun to Learn: A Stimulating Play-And-Learn Book with over 130 Amazing Facts, Exercises & Projects, & More Than 5000 Bright Action-Packed Photographs. 2014. (ENG., Illus.). 256p. (J). (gr. k-4). 16.99 *(978-1-84322-981-0(1)*, Armadillo) Anness Publishing GBR. Dist: National Bk. Network.

Loader, Mair. Meistrgopiau. 2005. (WEL., Illus.). 123p. pap. *(978-0-86174-782-5(8))* Drake Educational Assocs. Ltd.

—Yr Haen Fathemateg. 2005. (WEL., Illus.). 112p. pap. *(978-0-86174-781-8(X))* Drake Educational Assocs. Ltd.

Lock, Deborah & Dorling Kindersley Publishing Staff. Math, Grade 3. 2013. (ENG., Illus.). 80p. (J). (gr. 2-4). pap. 9.99 *(978-1-4654-1717-6(6)*, DK Children) Dorling Kindersley Publishing, Inc.

—10 Minutes a Day: Math, Grade 1. 2013. (ENG., Illus.). 80p. (J). (gr. k-4). pap. 9.99 *(978-1-4654-1716-9(8)*, DK Children) Dorling Kindersley Publishing, Inc.

Lockerd, Jodi. Nocturnal Animals: Represent & Solve Problems Involving Multiplication. 2014. (Rosen Common Core Math Readers Ser.). (Illus.). 24p. (J). (gr. 3-4). (ENG.). pap. 8.25 *(978-1-4777-4968-5(3))*; lib. bdg. 23.60 *(978-1-4777-6447-3(X))* Rosen Publishing Group, Inc., The. (PowerKids Pr.).

Loesen von Sachaufgaben. (Duden-Schuelerhilfen Ser.). (GER.). 112p. (J). (gr. 5-6). *(978-3-411-04872-4(7))* Bibliographisches Institut & F. A. Brockhaus AG DEU. Dist: International Bk. Import Service, Inc.

Logarithmen und Exponentialgleichungen. (Duden-Schuelerhilfen Ser.). (GER.). 112p. (YA). (gr. 10). *(978-3-411-05661-3(4))* Bibliographisches Institut & F. A. Brockhaus AG DEU. Dist: International Bk. Import Service, Inc.

Logue, Damien. Favorite Foods: Classify & Count Objects in Each Category. 2013. (Rosen Math Readers Ser.). (ENG.). 16p. (J). (gr. k-1). pap. 42.00 *(978-1-4777-1654-0(8))*; (Illus.). pap. 7.00 *(978-1-4777-1653-3(X))* Rosen Publishing Group, Inc., The. (Rosen Classroom).

Long, Lynette. Math Smarts: Tips, Tricks, & Secrets for Making Math More Fun! McGuinness, Tracy, illus. 2004. (AmericanGirl Library). (ENG.). 64p. (J). pap. 8.95 *(978-1-58485-875-1(3))* American Girl Publishing, Inc.

Loop, Katherine. Principles of Mathematics Book 1 Set. 2016. (ENG.). (J). pap. 79.98 ***(978-0-89051-914-1(5))*** Master Bks.

Loughran, Donna. Herding a Hundred: Counting the Sheep. 2013. (IMath Ser.). (Illus.). 24p. (J). (gr. k-2). lib. bdg. 21.27 *(978-1-59953-547-0(5))* Norwood Hse. Pr.

—On the Playground: How Do You Build Place Value? 2013. (IMath Ser.). (Illus.). 24p. (J). (gr. k-2). pap. 11.94 *(978-1-60357-488-4(3))* Norwood Hse. Pr.

—Toy Tally: How Many Toys Are There? 2013. (IMath Ser.). (Illus.). 24p. (J). (gr. k-2). pap. 11.94 *(978-1-60357-492-1(1))*; lib. bdg. 21.27 *(978-1-59953-553-1(X))* Norwood Hse. Pr.

Loughran, Donna & Brunner-Jass, Renata. Finding the Treasure: Coordinate Grids. 2013. (IMath Ser.). (Illus.). 48p. (J). (gr. 5-6). pap. 11.94 *(978-1-60357-512-6(X))*; lib. bdg. 23.94 *(978-1-59953-573-9(4))* Norwood Hse. Pr.

—Winning the Game: Putting Miles in Their Place. 2013. (IMath Ser.). (Illus.). 48p. (J). (gr. 5-6). pap. 11.94 *(978-1-60357-506-5(5))*; lib. bdg. 23.94 *(978-1-59953-567-8(X))* Norwood Hse. Pr.

Low, Emma & Wood, Mary. Cambridge Primary Mathematics Stage 5 Learner's Book. 2014. (Cambridge Primary Maths Ser.). (ENG.). 129p. pap. 19.94 *(978-1-107-63822-8(4))* Cambridge Univ. Pr.

—Cambridge Primary Mathematics Stage 6 Learner's Book. 2014. (Cambridge Primary Maths Ser.). (ENG.). 131p. pap. 19.94 *(978-1-107-61859-6(2))* Cambridge Univ. Pr.

LP-Addition: Level 2 Math. 2004. (ENG.). (J). 9.99 *(978-1-59204-018-6(7))* Learning Wrap-Ups, Inc.

LP-Blends & Digraphs: Level 1 Reading. 2004. (ENG.). (J). 9.99 *(978-1-59204-005-6(5))* Learning Wrap-Ups, Inc.

LP-Capitalization & Punctuation: Level 2 Reading. 2004. (ENG.). (J). 9.99 *(978-1-59204-009-4(8))* Learning Wrap-Ups, Inc.

LP-Place Value: Level 2 Math. 2004. (ENG.). (J). 9.99 *(978-1-59204-017-9(9))* Learning Wrap-Ups, Inc.

LP-Reading Comprehension: Level 2 Reading. 2004. (ENG.). (J). 9.99 *(978-1-59204-011-7(X))* Learning Wrap-Ups, Inc.

LP-Subtraction: Level 2 Math. 2004. (ENG.). (J). 9.99 *(978-1-59204-019-3(5))* Learning Wrap-Ups, Inc.

Lucas, Vivien. A Puzzle a Day: A Collection of Mathematical Problems for Every Day of the Year. 2004. (Illus.). 96p. 14.00 *(978-1-899618-52-1(X))* Tarquin Pubns. GBR. Dist: Parkwest Pubns., Inc.

Macfarlane, Katherine. The Father of the Atom: Democritus & the Nature of Matter. 2009. (Great Minds of Ancient Science & Math Ser.). (Illus.). 112p. (J). (gr. 4-7). lib. bdg. 33.27 *(978-0-7660-3410-5(0))* Enslow Pubs., Inc.

MacGillivray, Helen & Petocz, Peter. Statistics & Probability in the Australian Curriculum Years 7 And 8. 2013. (ENG.). pap. *(978-1-107-61421-5(X))* Cambridge Univ. Pr.

MacGregor, Helen. Tom Thumb's Musical Maths: Developing Maths Skills with Simple Songs. 2005. (Songbooks Ser.). (ENG., Illus.). 64p. (J). pap. 22.95 ***(978-0-7136-7295-4(1))*** HarperCollins Pubs. Ltd. GBR. Dist: Independent Pubs. Group.

Mack, Steve. Numbers. Flash Kids Editors, ed. 2012. (Flash Kids Preschool Activity Bks.). (ENG., Illus.). 80p. (J). pap. 5.95 *(978-1-4114-5810-9(9)*, Spark Publishing Group) Sterling Publishing Co., Inc.

MacPhee, K. M. Maths & English: Basics Manual for Young People. 2010. 254p. pap. *(978-0-7552-0482-3(4))* Authors OnLine, Ltd.

Mahaney, Ian F. The Math of Basketball. 2011. (J). 49.50 *(978-1-4488-2695-7(0)*, PowerKids Pr.); (J). pap. 8.25 *(978-1-4488-2694-0(2)*, PowerKids Pr.); (YA). (gr. 2-5). lib. bdg. 22.60 *(978-1-4488-2593-6(8))* Rosen Publishing Group, Inc., The.

Make Believe Ideas. I Love to Learn Math Games. 2013. (ENG.). 40p. (J). pap. 4.99 *(978-1-78235-201-3(5))* Make Believe Ideas GBR. Dist: Nelson, Thomas Inc.

—I Love to Learn Math Puzzles. 2013. (ENG.). 40p. (J). pap. 4.99 *(978-1-78235-209-9(0))* Make Believe Ideas GBR. Dist: Nelson, Thomas Inc.

Making Connection with Measurement, Grade 11 TAKS - Student. 2004. (Region IV ESC Resources for Mathematics Ser.). pap., wbk. ed. *(978-1-932797-53-4(X))* Region IV Education Service Ctr.

Making Connections with Measurement, Grade 1 - Student Workbook - Spanish. 2004. (Region IV ESC Resources for Mathematics Ser.). pap. *(978-1-932797-62-6(9))* Region IV Education Service Ctr.

Making Connections with Measurement, Grade 1 TEKS - Student Workbook. 2004. (Region IV ESC Resources for Mathematics Ser.). pap. *(978-1-932797-43-5(2))* Region IV Education Service Ctr.

Making Connections with Measurement, Grade 10 TAKS - Student Workbook. 2004. (Region IV ESC Resources for Mathematics Ser.). pap. *(978-1-932797-52-7(1))* Region IV Education Service Ctr.

Making Connections with Measurement, Grade 2 TEKS - Student Workbook. 2004. (Region IV ESC Resources for Mathematics Ser.). pap. *(978-1-932797-44-2(0))* Region IV Education Service Ctr.

Making Connections with Measurement, Grade 3 TAKS - Student Workbook. 2004. (Region IV ESC Resources for Mathematics Ser.). pap. *(978-1-932797-45-9(9))* Region IV Education Service Ctr.

Making Connections with Measurement, Grade 4 TEKS - Student Workbook. 2004. (Region IV ESC Resources for Mathematics Ser.). pap. *(978-1-932797-46-6(7))* Region IV Education Service Ctr.

Making Connections with Measurement, Grade 5 TAKS - Student Workbook. 2004. (Region IV ESC Resources for Mathematics Ser.). pap. *(978-1-932797-47-3(5))* Region IV Education Service Ctr.

Making Connections with Measurement, Grade 5 TAKS - Teacher Edition. 2004. (Region IV ESC Resources for Mathematics Ser.). spiral bd. *(978-1-932797-35-0(1))* Region IV Education Service Ctr.

Making Connections with Measurement, Grade 6 TAKS - Student Workbook. 2004. (Region IV ESC Resources for Mathematics Ser.). pap. *(978-1-932797-48-0(3))* Region IV Education Service Ctr.

Making Connections with Measurement, Grade 7 TAKS - Student Workbook. 2004. (Region IV ESC Resources for Mathematics Ser.). pap. *(978-1-932797-49-7(1))* Region IV Education Service Ctr.

Making Connections with Measurement, Grade 8 TAKS - Student Workbook. 2004. (Region IV ESC Resources for Mathematics Ser.). pap. *(978-1-932797-50-3(5))* Region IV Education Service Ctr.

Making Connections with Measurement, Grade 9 TAKS - Student Workbook. 2004. (Region IV ESC Resources for Mathematics Ser.). pap. *(978-1-932797-51-0(3))* Region IV Education Service Ctr.

Making Connections with Measurement, Grade K TEKS - Student Workbook. 2004. (Region IV ESC Resources for Mathematics Ser.). pap. *(978-1-932797-42-8(4))* Region IV Education Service Ctr.

Making Connections with Measurement, Grade K TEKS - Student Workbook Spanish. 2004. (Region IV ESC Resources for Mathematics Ser.). pap. *(978-1-932797-61-9(0))* Region IV Education Service Ctr.

Making Connections with Measurement, TAKS Preparation Grade 2 - Student Workbook. 2004. (Region IV ESC Resources for Mathematics Ser.). pap. *(978-1-932797-63-3(7))* Region IV Education Service Ctr.

Malchik, E. The Great Depression by the Numbers & Los números de la Gran Depresión: 6 English, 6 Spanish Adaptations. 2011. (ENG & SPA.). (J). 101.00 net. *(978-1-4108-5730-9(1))* Benchmark Education Co.

Malue, Jenna. Recycling Plastic: Understand Place Value. 2014. (Math Masters: Number & Operations in Base Ten Ser.). (Illus.). 24p. (J). (gr. 2-3). 23.60 *(978-1-4777-6427-5(5))*; (ENG., pap. 8.25 *(978-1-4777-4651-6(X))* Rosen Publishing Group, Inc., The. (Rosen Classroom).

Mansk, Anne. You Can Measure: A Content Area Reader-math. 2005. (Emergent/Early (Prek-2) Math Package Ser.). 16p. (YA). (gr. -1-2). 25.20 *(978-0-8215-7825-4(1))* Sadlier, William H. Inc.

Mapua, Jeff. Using Math in Science. 2017. (Math You Will Actually Use Ser.). 48p. (J). (gr. 10-10). pap. 11.75 ***(978-1-4994-3868-0(0)***, Rosen Central) Rosen Publishing Group, Inc., The.

Marrewa, Jennifer. Graphing Favorite Things. 2008. (Math in Our World - Level 2 Ser.). 24p. (gr. 1-4). pap. 8.15 *(978-0-8368-9017-4(5)*, Weekly Reader Leveled Readers) Stevens, Gareth Publishing LLLP.

—Graphing Favorite Things. Espinosa, Patrick, photos by. 2008. (Math in Our World: Level 2 Ser.). (Illus.). 24p. (gr. 1-4). lib. bdg. 22.00 *(978-0-8368-9008-2(6)*, Weekly Reader Leveled Readers) Stevens, Gareth Publishing LLLP.

—Vamos a Hacer Graficas de Nuestras Cosas Favoritas. Espinosa, Patrick, photos by. 2008. (Matemáticas en Nuestro Mundo - Nivel 2 (Math in Our World - Level 2) Ser.). (SPA., Illus.). 24p. (gr. 1-4). lib. bdg. 22.00 *(978-0-8368-9026-6(4)*, Weekly Reader Leveled Readers) Stevens, Gareth Publishing LLLP.

—Vamos a Hacer Graficás de Nuestras Cosas Favoritas. 2008. (Las Matemáticas en Nuestro Mundo Ser.). (SPA.). 24p. (gr. 1-4). pap. 8.15 *(978-0-8368-9035-8(3)*, Weekly Reader Leveled Readers) Stevens, Gareth Publishing LLLP.

Marsh, Carole. Math for Girls Grades 3-6: The Book with the Number to Help Girls Love & Excel in Math! Beard, Chad, ed. 2004. (Math Ser.). (Illus.). 32p. (J). (gr. 2-6). pap. 7.95 *(978-0-635-02445-9(4))* Gallopade International.

Marsico, Katie. Ball Game Math. 2014. (Math Everywhere! Ser.). (Illus.). 32p. (gr. 3-4). (J). lib. bdg. 26.60 *(978-1-4677-1885-1(8)*, Lerner Pubns.); pap. 7.95 *(978-1-4677-4512-3(X))* Lerner Publishing Group.

—Fitness Math. 2015. (ENG., Illus.). 32p. (J). (gr. 3-4). 26.65 *(978-1-4677-8578-5(4))* Lerner Publishing Group.

—Investing: Making Your Money Work for You. 2015. (21st Century Skills Library: Real World Math Ser.). (ENG., Illus.). 32p. (J). (gr. 4-7). 29.93 *(978-1-63362-571-6(0)*, 206468) Cherry Lake Publishing.

—Kitchen Math. 2014. (Math Everywhere! Ser.). (Illus.). 32p. (gr. 3-4). (J). lib. bdg. 26.60 *(978-1-4677-1883-7(1)*, Lerner Pubns.); pap. 7.95 *(978-1-4677-4513-0(8))* Lerner Publishing Group.

—Math on the Move. 2014. (Math Everywhere! Ser.). (Illus.). 32p. (J). (gr. 3-4). lib. bdg. 26.60 *(978-1-4677-1882-0(3)*, Lerner Pubns.) Lerner Publishing Group.

—Money Math. 2015. (ENG., Illus.). 32p. (J). (gr. 3-4). 26.65 *(978-1-4677-8579-2(2)*, Lerner Pubns.) Lerner Publishing Group.

—Shopping Trip Math. 2014. (Math Everywhere! Ser.). (Illus.). 32p. (gr. 3-4). (J). lib. bdg. 26.60 *(978-1-4677-1884-4(X)*, Lerner Pubns.); pap. 7.95 *(978-1-4677-4515-4(4))* Lerner Publishing Group.

—Understanding Taxes. 2015. (21st Century Skills Library: Real World Math Ser.). (ENG., Illus.). 32p. (J). (gr. 4-7). 29.93 *(978-1-63362-577-8(X)*, 206492) Cherry Lake Publishing.

—Using Credit Wisely. 2015. (21st Century Skills Library: Real World Math Ser.). (ENG., Illus.). 32p. (J). (gr. 4-7). 29.93 *(978-1-63362-578-5(8)*, 206496) Cherry Lake Publishing.

—Weather Math. 2015. (ENG., Illus.). 32p. (J). (gr. 3-4). 26.65 *(978-1-4677-1886-8(6))* Lerner Publishing Group.

Martin, Elena. Look at Both Sides, 6 vols., Set. 2003. (Yellow Umbrella Early Level Ser.). (ENG.). 16p. (gr. k-1). pap. 35.70 *(978-0-7368-3013-3(8)*, Yellow Umbrella Bks.) Capstone Press of Coughlan Cos.

Martin, Hope. Career Math. 2007. 100p. per. 9.95 *(978-1-59647-253-2(7))* Good Year Bks.

Martin, Jannelle. ABC Math Riddles. Levin, Freddie, illus. 2003. (ABC Riddles Ser.). 32p. (J). 13.95 *(978-0-939217-57-1(0))* Peel Productions, Inc.

Martin, Sandra. Mathopedia Level 1. 2003. (Illus.). 118p. spiral bd. 49.99 *(978-0-9718488-1-8(5))* Specialty Educational Pubs.

Martinelli, Marjorie. Brain Quest Grade 2 Math. 2nd rev. ed. 2006. (ENG.). 150p. (J). (gr. 2-2). 11.95 *(978-0-7611-4136-5(7)*, 14136) Workman Publishing Co., Inc.

Martinelli, Marjorie & Brain Quest Editors. Brain Quest Grade 1 Math. 2nd rev. ed. 2006. (ENG.). 150p. (J). (gr. 1-1). 11.95 *(978-0-7611-4135-8(9)*, 14135) Workman Publishing Co., Inc.

Marzollo, Jean. Help Me Learn Addition. Phillips, Chad, photos by. 2012. (ENG., Illus.). 32p. (J). 15.95 *(978-0-8234-2398-9(0))* Holiday Hse., Inc.

Mastering Math Word Problems. 2016. (Mastering Math Word Problems Ser.). 48p. (J). pap. 70.20 *(978-0-7660-8401-8(9))* Enslow Pubs., Inc.

Masters, Nancy Robinson. Volcanic Eruptions. 2012. (21st Century Skills Library: Real World Math Ser.). (ENG., Illus.). 32p. (J). (gr. 4-8). pap. 14.21 *(978-1-61080-414-1(7)*, 201346); lib. bdg. 28.50 *(978-1-61080-328-1(0)*, 201314) Cherry Lake Publishing.

Matematicas 2000. (SPA.). (YA). (gr. 10). pap. 19.95 *(978-958-02-0533-3(7)*, 0333); (SPA.). (YA). (gr. 11). pap. 19.95 *(978-958-02-0534-0(5)*, 0334); (J). (gr. 6). pap. 19.95 *(978-958-02-0529-6(9)*, 0329); (SPA.). (J). (gr. 7). pap. 19.95 *(978-958-02-0530-2(2)*, 0330); (SPA.). (YA). (gr. 8). pap. 19.95 *(978-958-02-0531-9(0)*, 0331); (SPA.). (YA). (gr. 9). pap. 19.95 *(978-958-02-0532-6(9)*, 0332) Norma S.A. COL. Dist: Continental Bk. Co., Inc.

El Matematico de Primaria 1. (Matematicos Ser.). (SPA.). (J). 15.50 *(978-968-416-840-4(3)*, 5101) Fernandez USA Publishing.

El Matematico de Primaria 2. (Matematicos Ser.). (SPA.). (J). 15.50 *(978-968-416-841-1(1)*, FN8411) Fernandez USA Publishing.

El Matematico de Primaria 3. (Matematicos Ser.). (SPA.). (J). 15.50 *(978-968-416-842-8(X)*, 5103) Fernandez USA Publishing.

El Matematico de Primaria 4, Level 4. (Matematicos Ser.). (SPA.). (J). 15.50 *(978-968-416-843-5(8)*, 5104) Fernandez USA Publishing.

El Matematico de Primaria 5, Level 5. (SPA.). (J). 15.50 *(978-968-416-844-2(6)*, 5105) Fernandez USA Publishing.

El Matematico Preescolar Avanzado. (Matematicos Ser.). (SPA.). (J). 11.95 *(978-970-03-1141-8(4)*, FN4736) Fernandez USA Publishing.

El Matematico Preescolar Basic. (Matematicos Ser.). (SPA.). (J). 11.95 *(978-970-03-1140-1(6)*, FN4728) Fernandez USA Publishing.

El Matematico Preescolar Inicial. (Matematicos Ser.). (SPA.). (J). 11.95 *(978-970-03-1139-5(2)*, FN471X) Fernandez USA Publishing.

Math. 2011. (New Discovering Careers for Your Future Ser.). (Illus.). 128p. (gr. 4-9). 24.95 *(978-0-8160-8052-6(6)*, Ferguson Publishing Co.) Facts On File, Inc.

Math: Grades 5 & 6. (Illus.). (J). pap., wbk. ed. 4.99 *(978-0-88743-847-9(4))* School Zone Publishing Co.

Math: Student Testing Kit. 2004. (gr. 1-8). pap., stu. ed. 5.00 *(978-1-58095-815-8(X)*, MD001); (gr. 7-12). pap., stu. ed. 5.00 *(978-1-58095-817-2(6)*, MD002) Alpha Omega Pubns., Inc. (Lifepac).

Math 1 Reviews. 3rd ed. 2006. pap., act. bk. ed. 14.00 *(978-1-59166-322-5(9))* BJU Pr.

Math 1 Student Manipulatives. 3rd ed. 2006. (J). 12.00 *(978-1-59166-325-6(3))* BJU Pr.

Math 1 Testpack. 3rd ed. 2006. 10.00 *(978-1-59166-326-3(1))* BJU Pr.

Math 4: Version 3. 1, 2 vols. 2003. (gr. 6-12). stu. ed. 40.00 *(978-1-885145-48-2(9)*, M4-489) CPM Educational Program.

Math 5: Version 3. 0, 2 vols. 2003. (gr. 6-12). stu. ed. 50.00 *(978-1-931287-28-9(7)*, M5-287) CPM Educational Program.

Math Activities (Gr. 1) 2003. (J). *(978-1-58232-046-5(2))* ECS Learning Systems, Inc.

Math Activities (K) 2003. (J). *(978-1-58232-044-1(6))* ECS Learning Systems, Inc.

Math Ad Libs: Addition & Subtraction. 2004. (J). per. 9.95 *(978-1-56911-543-5(5))* Learning Resources, Inc.

Math Ad Libs: Fractions & Decimals. 2004. (J). per. 9.95 *(978-1-56911-545-9(1))* Learning Resources, Inc.

Math Ad Libs: Multiplication & Division. 2004. (J). per. 9.95 *(978-1-56911-544-2(3))* Learning Resources, Inc.

Math Alive!, 6 bks., Set. Incl. Body Math. Dowdy, Penny. lib. bdg. 28.50 *(978-0-7614-3215-9(9))*; Building Math. Perritano, John. lib. bdg. 28.50 *(978-0-7614-3210-4(8))*; Nature Math. Dowdy, Penny. lib. bdg. 28.50 *(978-0-7614-3214-2(0))*; Science Math. Stosch, Dawn. lib. bdg. 28.50 *(978-0-7614-3213-5(2))*; Transport Math. Evans, Lesli. lib. bdg. 28.50 *(978-0-7614-3211-1(6))*; Travel Math. Awal, Pia. lib. bdg. 28.50 *(978-0-7614-3217-3(5))*; 32p. (gr. 4-18). (Math Alive! Ser.). 2008. Set lib. bdg. 171.00 *(978-0-7614-3208-1(6)*, Benchmark Bks.) Marshall Cavendish Corp.

Math Around Us. 2015. (Math Around Us Ser.). (ENG.). 24p. (J). (gr. 1-1). 145.26 *(978-1-5026-0301-2(2))*; 49.32 *(978-1-5026-0329-6(2))* Cavendish Square Publishing.

Math Art (Gr. 1-2) 2003. (J). *(978-1-58232-105-9(1))* ECS Learning Systems, Inc.

Math Art (Gr. 2-3) 2003. (J). *(978-1-58232-106-6(X))* ECS Learning Systems, Inc.

Math Exploration: Using Math to Learn about the Continents. 2015. (Math Exploration: Using Math to Learn about the Continents Ser.). (ENG.). 32p. (J). (gr. 3-4). pap., pap., pap. 360.00 *(978-1-4994-1304-5(1)*, PowerKids Pr.) Rosen Publishing Group, Inc., The.

Math Grade Eight. 2004. (ACSI Elementary Mathmatics). tchr. ed., ring bd. *(978-1-58331-198-1(X)*, 7225) Assn. of Christian Schls. International.

Math Is Everywhere, 6 vols. (Sunshinetm Ser.). 16p. (gr. k-18). 29.50 *(978-0-7802-5442-8(2))* Wright Group/McGraw-Hill.

Math Is Everywhere! Set 1. 2016. (Math Is Everywhere! Ser.). 24p. (gr. k-k). pap. 48.90 *(978-1-4824-5290-7(1))*; lib. bdg. 135.60 *(978-1-4824-4520-6(4))* Stevens, Gareth Publishing LLLP.

Math Is Everywhere! Set 2. 2016. (Math Is Everywhere! Ser.). 00024p. (J). lib. bdg. 135.60 ***(978-1-4824-5543-4(9))*** Stevens, Gareth Publishing LLLP.

Math Is Fun. 2004. (Play & Learn Pads Ser.). 48p. (J). 3.99 *(978-1-85997-720-0(0))* Byeway Bks.

Math Journal. 2004. (J). pap. 19.95 *(978-1-56911-182-6(0))* Learning Resources, Inc.

Math on Target for Grade 3. 2005. (J). stu. ed., per. 10.95 *(978-1-59230-064-8(2))* Englefield & Assocs., Inc.

Math on Target for Grade 4: Student Workbook. 2006. (J). per. 10.95 *(978-1-59230-161-4(4))* Englefield & Assocs., Inc.

Math on Target for Grade 5: Student Workbook. 2005. (J). stu. ed., per. 10.95 *(978-1-59230-111-9(8))* Englefield & Assocs., Inc.

Math Plus Literature, Set. (J). (gr. 2). pap. *(978-0-8136-8824-4(8))* Modern Curriculum Pr.

Math Program, Early Level. 2003. (Yellow Umbrella Early Level Ser.). (ENG.). 16p. (gr. k-1). pap. 453.35 *(978-0-7368-3064-5(2)*, Yellow Umbrella Bks.) Capstone Press of Coughlan Cos.

Math Puzzle Pad (was Math Games Pad) 2017. (Tear-Off Pads Ser.). (ENG.). (J). pap. 5.99 ***(978-0-7945-3805-7(3)***, Usborne) EDC Publishing.

Math Rod Activity Cards - Addition & Subtraction. 2004. (J). 9.95 *(978-1-56911-164-2(2))* Learning Resources, Inc.

Math Rod Activity Cards - Kindergarten. 2004. (J). 9.95 *(978-1-56911-163-5(4))* Learning Resources, Inc.

Math Rod Activity Cards - Multiplication & Division. 2004. (J). 9.95 *(978-1-56911-165-9(0))* Learning Resources, Inc.

Math Shark. 2005. (J). *(978-1-60015-034-0(9))* Steps To Literacy, LLC.

Math Spanish Content Area Standard Set. 2005. spiral bd. 2095.00 *(978-1-4108-4532-0(X))* Benchmark Education Co.

Math Student Text: Grade 7. 2004. 32.00 *(978-0-89084-842-5(4))* BJU Pr.

Math You Will Actually Use. 2017. (Math You Will Actually Use Ser.). 48p. (gr. 10-10). 190.50 ***(978-1-4777-8987-2(1))***; pap. 70.50 ***(978-1-4777-8989-6(8))*** Rosen Publishing Group, Inc., The. (Rosen Central).

Mathematics. 2004. (Illus.). (gr. 5). tchr. ed., stu. ed. 47.95 *(978-1-58095-725-0(0)*, MAT0515);Set. (gr. 2). tchr. ed., stu. ed. 47.95 *(978-1-58095-716-8(1)*, MAT0215) Alpha Omega Pubns., Inc. (Lifepac).

Mathematics: Algebra II, 11 vols., Set. 2004. (Illus.). (gr. 11-12). tchr. ed., stu. ed. 52.95 *(978-1-58095-743-4(9)*, MAT1115, Lifepac) Alpha Omega Pubns., Inc.

Mathematics: Trigonometry, 11 vols., Set. 2004. (Illus.). (gr. 12). tchr. ed., stu. ed. 52.95 *(978-1-58095-746-5(3)*, MAT1215, Lifepac) Alpha Omega Pubns., Inc.

Mathematik I. (Duden-Schuelerduden Ser.). (GER., Illus.). 544p. (YA). *(978-3-411-04206-7(0))* Bibliographisches Institut & F. A. Brockhaus AG DEU. Dist: International Bk. Import Service, Inc.

Mathematik II. 4th ed. (Duden-Schuelerduden Ser.). (GER.). 480p. (YA). *(978-3-411-04274-6(5))* Bibliographisches Institut & F. A. Brockhaus AG DEU. Dist: International Bk. Import Service, Inc.

Maths 3-4. Date not set. (Illus.). 32p. (J). 2.98 *(978-0-7525-9560-3(1))* Parragon, Inc.

Maths 4-5. Date not set. (Gold Stars Workbook Ser.). (Illus.). 32p. (J). 2.98 *(978-0-7525-9561-0(X))* Parragon, Inc.

Maths 5-6. Date not set. (Gold Stars Workbook Ser.). (Illus.). 32p. (J). 2.98 *(978-0-7525-9562-7(8))* Parragon, Inc.

Maths 6-7. Date not set. (Gold Stars Workbook Ser.). (Illus.). 32p. (J). 2.98 *(978-0-7525-9563-4(6))* Parragon, Inc.

Matrix Math: Innovative Educational Software for Grades 1 Thru 8+ 2004. (J). cd-rom *(978-0-9763833-0-7(6))* Stellar Learning.

Mattern, Joanne. At the Football Game: Learning the Symbols , And = 2009. (Math for the REAL World Ser.). 16p. (gr. 2-3). pap. 7.05 *(978-0-8239-8875-4(9)*, Rosen Classroom) Rosen Publishing Group, Inc., The.

Matthews, Jean, et al. Formula One Maths. 2003. (Illus.). Vol. 1. 96p. pap. 18.50 *(978-0-340-85928-5(8))* Vol. 1. 96p. pap. 18.50 *(978-0-340-85926-1(1))* Vol. 2. 96p. (J). pap. 18.50 *(978-0-340-85929-2(6))* Vol. 2. 88p. pap. 18.50 *(978-0-340-85927-8(X))* Vol. 2. 96p. pap. 18.50 *(978-0-340-85925-4(3))* Vol. 3. 96p. pap. 18.50 *(978-0-340-85930-8(X))* Hodder Education Group GBR. (Hodder Education). Dist: Trans-Atlantic Pubns., Inc.

Mayfield-Ingram, Karen. The Journey Through Middle School Math. Humphrey Williams, Ann, illus. Crews, Elizabeth, photos by. 2005. (Equals Ser.). 140p. pap. 18.95 *(978-0-912511-31-3(1)*, EQUALS) Univ. of California, Berkeley, Lawrence Hall of Science.

McAneney, Caitlin. North American Birds: Represent & Solve Problems Involving Multiplication. 2014. (Rosen Common Core Math Readers Ser.). (Illus.). 24p. (J). (gr. 3-4). (ENG.). pap. 8.25 *(978-1-4777-4971-5(3))*; lib. bdg. 23.60 *(978-1-4777-6445-9(3))* Rosen Publishing Group, Inc., The. (PowerKids Pr.).

McCallum, Ann. The Secret Life of Math: Discover How (and Why) Numbers Have Survived from the Cave Dwellers to Us! Norton, Carolyn McIntyre, illus. 2005. (Kids Can Ser.). (ENG.). 128p. (J). (gr. 3-7). per. 14.25 *(978-0-8249-6755-0(0))*; (gr. 4-7). 14.95 *(978-0-8249-6779-6(8))* Worthy Publishing. (Ideal Pubns.).

McDonnell, Rory. Matemáticas con el Tiempo / Math with Weather. de la Vega, Eida, tr. 2016. (¡Matemáticas en Todas Partes! / Math Is Everywhere! Ser.). (ENG & SPA.). 24p. (gr. k-k). lib. bdg. 22.60 *(978-1-4824-5212-9(X))* Stevens, Gareth Publishing LLLP.

—Matemáticas con Juguetes / Math with Toys. de la Vega, Eida, tr. 2016. (¡Matemáticas en Todas Partes! / Math Is Everywhere! Ser.). (ENG & SPA.). 24p. (gr. k-k). lib. bdg. 22.60 *(978-1-4824-5214-3(6))* Stevens, Gareth Publishing LLLP.

—Matemáticas con Ruedas / Math with Wheels. de la Vega, Eida, tr. 2016. (¡Matemáticas en Todas Partes! / Math Is Everywhere! Ser.). (ENG & SPA.). 24p. (gr. k-k). lib. bdg. 22.60 *(978-1-4824-5218-1(9))* Stevens, Gareth Publishing LLLP.

McDougal-Littell Publishing Staff. McDougal Littell Middle School Math: Notetaking Guide. 2003. (McDougal Littell Middle School Math Ser.). (ENG.). 304p. (gr. 7-7). pap. 12.20 *(978-0-618-25618-1(0)*, 2-06021) Great Source Education Group, Inc.

—Middle School Math. 2003. (McDougal Littell Middle School Math Ser.). (ENG.). 304p. (gr. 8-8). pap. 12.20 *(978-0-618-25656-3(3)*, 2-06022) Great Source Education Group, Inc.

—Middle School Math: Practice Workbook. 2003. (McDougal Littell Middle School Math Ser.). (ENG.). 192p. (gr. 8-8). pap. 4.90 *(978-0-618-25757-7(8)*, 2-06027); (gr. 7-7). pap. 4.90 *(978-0-618-25755-3(1)*, 2-06026) Great Source Education Group, Inc.

—Middle School Math, Course 1: Notetaking Guide. 2003. (McDougal Littell Middle School Math Ser.). (ENG.). 320p. (gr. 6-6). pap. 12.20 *(978-0-618-25035-6(2)*, 2-06018) Great Source Education Group, Inc.

—Middle School Math, Course 1: Practice Workbook, PE. 2003. (McDougal Littell Middle School Math, Course 1 Ser.). (ENG.). 192p. (gr. 6-6). pap. 4.90 *(978-0-618-25754-6(3)*, 2-06025) Great Source Education Group, Inc.

—Notetaking Guide: Pre-Algebra. 2004. (McDougal Littell Middle School Math Ser.). (ENG.). 312p. (gr. 7-8). per. 12.20 *(978-0-618-25657-0(1)*, 2-06023) Great Source Education Group, Inc.

—Pre-Algebra. 2004. (McDougal Littell Middle School Math Ser.). (ENG.). 208p. (gr. 7-8). pap., wbk. ed. 4.90 *(978-0-618-25752-2(7)*, 2-06024) Great Source Education Group, Inc.

—Pre-Algebra: Exercises in Spanish. 2004. (McDougal Littell Middle School Math Ser.). (SPA.). 304p. (gr. 7-8). pap. 25.70 *(978-0-618-43362-9(7)*, 2-05834) Great Source Education Group, Inc.

McFadden, Jesse. Franklin's Farm Stand: Understand Place Value. 2014. (Math Masters: Number & Operations in Base Ten Ser.). (Illus.). 24p. (J). (gr. 2-3). 23.60 *(978-1-4777-6428-2(3))*; (ENG., pap. 8.25 *(978-1-4777-4654-7(4))* Rosen Publishing Group, Inc., The. (Rosen Classroom).

McGrath, Barbara Barbieri. Teddy Bear Math. Nihoff, Tim, illus. 2011. (McGrath Math Ser.). (ENG.). 32p. (J). (gr. k-3). 16.95 *(978-1-58089-283-4(3))*; pap. 7.95 *(978-1-58089-284-1(1))* Charlesbridge Publishing, Inc.

McGraw-Hill - Jamestown Education Staff. Timed Readings Plus in Mathematics: Book 1, Bk. 1. 2005. (Jamestown Education Ser.). 78p. (J). per. 17.32 *(978-0-07-872659-0(X)*, 9780078726590) Glencoe/McGraw-Hill.

—Timed Readings Plus in Mathematics: Book 2, Bk. 2. 2005. (Jamestown Education Ser.). 78p. (J). per. 17.32 *(978-0-07-872660-6(3)*, 9780078726606) Glencoe/McGraw-Hill.

—Timed Readings Plus in Mathematics: Book 3, Bk. 3. 2005. (Jamestown Education Ser.). 78p. (J). per. 17.32 *(978-0-07-872661-3(1)*, 9780078726613) Glencoe/McGraw-Hill.

—Timed Readings Plus in Mathematics: Book 4, Bk. 4. 2005. (Jamestown Education Ser.). 78p. (J). per. 17.32 *(978-0-07-872662-0(X)*, 9780078726620) Glencoe/McGraw-Hill.

—Timed Readings Plus in Mathematics: Book 5, Bk. 5. 2005. (Jamestown Education Ser.). 78p. (J). per. 17.32 *(978-0-07-872663-7(8)*, 9780078726637) Glencoe/McGraw-Hill.

McGraw-Hill Editors. Math, Grade 5. 2012. (ENG., Illus.). 160p. pap. 13.00 *(978-0-07-177558-8(7)*, 0071775587) McGraw-Hill Cos., The.

—McGraw-Hill Math Grade 2. 2012. (ENG., Illus.). 128p. pap. 11.99 *(978-0-07-177598-4(6)*, 0071775986) McGraw-Hill Education.

McGraw-Hill Editors & McGraw-Hill Education Staff. McGraw-Hill Math Grade 1. 2012. (ENG., Illus.). 128p. pap. 11.99 *(978-0-07-177556-4(0)*, 0071775560) McGraw-Hill Education.

McGraw-Hill Education Editors. Buyer Beware: Rates, Ratios, Percents, & Proportions. 2004. (Creative Pub: Mathscape Ser.). (ENG., Illus.). 45p. (gr. 7-7). per. 15.88 *(978-0-07-866806-7(9)*, 0078668069) McGraw-Hill Higher Education.

—ESL Math Overhead Manipulatives. 2003. (Mmgh Mathematics Ser.). (ENG.). (gr. 4-4). 213.56 *(978-0-02-104468-9(6)*, 0021044686) Macmillan/McGraw-Hill Schl. Div.

—Getting down to Business: Functions & Spreasheets. 2004. (Creative Pub: Mathscape Ser.). (ENG., Illus.). 42p. (gr. 7-7). stu. ed., per. 15.88 *(978-0-07-866816-6(6)*, 0078668166) McGraw-Hill Education.

—Macmillan/McGraw-Hill Math: Pupil Edition. 2004. (Mmgh Mathematics Ser.). (ENG.). (gr. 1-1). pap., stu. ed. 57.12 *(978-0-02-105012-3(0)*, 0021050120); (gr. 2-2). pap. 57.12 *(978-0-02-105015-4(5)*, 0021050155) Macmillan/McGraw-Hill Schl. Div.

—Math Skills Maintenance Workbook: Course 3. 2005. (Elc: Impact Math Ser.). (ENG., Illus.). 80p. (gr. 6-8). pap., wbk. ed. 7.08 *(978-0-07-860733-2(7)*, 0078607337) McGraw-Hill Education.

—McGraw-Hill Math Grade 3. 2012. (ENG., Illus.). 160p. pap. 13.00 *(978-0-07-177562-5(5)*, 0071775625) McGraw-Hill Education.

—McGraw-Hill Math Grade 4. 2012. (ENG., Illus.). 160p. pap. 13.00 *(978-0-07-177560-1(9)*, 0071775609) McGraw-Hill Education.

—Roads & Ramps: Slopes, Angles, & Ratios. 2004. (Creative Pub: Mathscape Ser.). (ENG., Illus.). 42p. (gr. 8-8). per. 15.88 *(978-0-07-866830-2(1)*, 0078668301) McGraw-Hill Education.

—What Does the Data Say? Graphs & Averages. 2004. (Creative Pub: Mathscape Ser.). (ENG., Illus.). 47p. (gr. 6-6). stu. ed., per. 15.88 *(978-0-07-866792-3(5)*, 0078667925) McGraw-Hill Education.

McGraw-Hill Education Staff. Beside the Point: Operating with Decimals, Percents, & Integers. 2004. (Creative Pub: Mathscape Ser.). (ENG., Illus.). 66p. (gr. 6-6). stu. ed., per. 15.88 *(978-0-07-866800-5(X)*, 007866800X) McGraw-Hill Education.

—Designing Spaces: Visualizing, Planning, & Building. 2004. (Creative Pub: Mathscape Ser.). (ENG., Illus.). 40p. (gr. 6-6). stu. ed., per. 15.88 *(978-0-07-866798-5(4)*, 0078667984) McGraw-Hill Education.

—Exploring the Unknown: Writing & Solving Equations. 2004. (Creative Pub: Mathscape Ser.). (ENG., Illus.). 40p. (gr. 8-8). per. 15.88 *(978-0-07-866828-9(X)*, 007866828X) McGraw-Hill Education.

—Family Portraits: Comparing Function Families. 2004. (Creative Pub: Mathscape Ser.). (ENG., Illus.). 42p. (gr. 8-8). stu. ed., per. 15.88 *(978-0-07-866832-6(8)*, 0078668328) McGraw-Hill Education.

—Gulliver's Worlds: Measuring & Scaling. 2004. (Creative Pub: Mathscape Ser.). (ENG., Illus.). 40p. (gr. 6-6). per. 15.88 *(978-0-07-866802-9(6)*, 0078668026) McGraw-Hill Education.

—Looking Behind the Numbers: Correlations, Rankings, & Permutations. 2004. (Creative Pub: Mathscape Ser.). (ENG., Illus.). 45p. (gr. 8-8). per. 15.88 *(978-0-07-866820-3(4)*, 0078668204) McGraw-Hill Higher Education.

—Math Grd. 7: Power up Your Math Skills. 2011. (ENG.). 160p. pap. 13.00 *(978-0-07-174863-6(6)*, 0071748636) McGraw-Hill Education.

—Math Skills Maintenance Workbook, Course 1. 2003. (Elc: Impact Math Ser.). (ENG.). 95p. (gr. 6-8). pap., wbk. ed. 7.20 *(978-0-07-860721-9(3)*, 0078607213) McGraw-Hill Education.

—McGraw-Hill's Math, Grade 6. 2011. (ENG., Illus.). 160p. pap. 13.00 *(978-0-07-174730-1(3)*, 0071747303) McGraw-Hill Cos., The.

—Shapes & Space: Thinking Three-Dimensionally. 2004. (Creative Pub: Mathscape Ser.). (ENG., Illus.). 40p. (gr. 8-8). per. 15.88 *(978-0-07-866824-1(7)*, 0078668247) McGraw-Hill Education.

McGraw-Hill Staff. Contemporary Mathematics in Context Pt. A: A Unified Approach. 2nd ed. 2003. (Elc: Core Plus Ser.). (ENG., Illus.). 369p. (gr. 11-12). 52.24 *(978-0-07-827549-4(0)*, 0078275490) McGraw-Hill Higher Education.

—Mathematics: Applications & Concepts. (MATH APPLIC & CONN CRSE Ser.). (ENG., Illus.). (gr. 6-8). 2004. 784p. lib. bdg., stu. ed. 103.28 *(978-0-07-865265-3(0)*, 0078652650) 2nd ed. 2003. 92p. per., wbk. ed. 7.20 *(978-0-07-860129-3(0)*, 0078601290) McGraw-Hill Education.

—Mathematics: Applications & Concepts, Course 2. 2006. (MATH APPLIC & CONN CRSE Ser.). (ENG., Illus.). 704p. (gr. 6-8). lib. bdg., stu. ed. 103.28 *(978-0-07-865263-9(4)*, 0078652634) McGraw-Hill Education.

—Mathematics: Applications & Concepts, Course 2, StudentWorks. 2003. (MATH APPLIC & CONN CRSE Ser.). (ENG.). (gr. 6-7). 119.16 *(978-0-07-860279-5(3)*, 0078602793) Glencoe/McGraw-Hill.

—MathScape Bk. 3: Seeing & Thinking Mathematically. 2nd ed. 2004. (Creative Pub: Mathscape Ser.). (ENG., Illus.). 329p. (gr. 8-8). lib. bdg., stu. ed. 110.40 *(978-0-07-860468-3(0)*, 0078604680) McGraw-Hill Education.

—Skills Intervention for Pre-Algebra: Diagnosis & Remediation. 2004. (Merrill Pre-Algebra Ser.). (ENG.). 176p. (gr. 8-10). pap., wbk. ed. 7.08 *(978-0-07-867808-0(0)*, 0078678080) McGraw-Hill Education.

McGraw-Hill Staff, creator. Chance Encounters: Probability in Games & Simulations. 2004. (Creative Pub: Mathscape Ser.). (ENG., Illus.). 42p. (gr. 7-7). per., instr.'s gde. ed. 15.88 *(978-0-07-866808-1(5)*, 0078668085) McGraw-Hill Education.

—From the Ground Up: Modeling, Measuring, & Constructing Homes. 2004. (Creative Pub: Mathscape Ser.). (ENG., Illus.). 40p. (gr. 7-7). per. 15.88 *(978-0-07-866812-8(3)*, 0078668123) McGraw-Hill Education.

—From Wholes to Parts: Operating with Factors, Multiples, & Fractions. 2004. (Creative Pub: Mathscape Ser.). (ENG., Illus.). 66p. (gr. 6-6). per. 15.88 *(978-0-07-866796-1(8)*, 0078667968) McGraw-Hill Education.

—Intervención para Mejorar Destrezas para Pre-Álgebra: Diagnóstico y Remediación - Libro de Ejercicios para el Alumno. 2004. (Merrill Pre-Algebra Ser.). (SPA., Illus.). 176p. (gr. 6-9). per. 7.08 *(978-0-07-867809-7(9)*, 0078678099) McGraw-Hill Higher Education.
—The Language of Algebra: Equations, Tables, & Graphs. 2004. (Creative Pub: Mathscape Ser.). (ENG., Illus.). 40p. (gr. 7-7). stu. ed., per. 15.88 *(978-0-07-866814-2(X)*, 007866814X) McGraw-Hill Education.
—The Language of Numbers: Inventing & Comparing Number Systems. 2004. (Creative Pub: Mathscape Ser.). (ENG., Illus.). 38p. (gr. 6-6). per. 15.88 *(978-0-07-866794-7(1)*, 0078667941) McGraw-Hill Education.
—Making Mathematical Arguments: Generalizing about Numbers. 2004. (Creative Pub: Mathscape Ser.). (ENG., Illus.). 40p. (gr. 7-7). per. 15.88 *(978-0-07-866810-4(7)*, 0078668107) McGraw-Hill Education.
—Math Skills Maintenance. 2003. (Elc: Impact Math Ser.). (ENG.). 77p. (gr. 6-8). pap., wbk. ed. 7.08 *(978-0-07-860727-1(2)*, 0078607272) McGraw-Hill Education.
—Mathematics: Applications & Concepts. 2003. (MATH APPLIC & CONN CRSE Ser.). (ENG., Illus.). 92p. (gr. 6-8). pap. 7.20 *(978-0-07-860130-9(4)*, 0078601304) McGraw-Hill Education.
—Mathematics: Applications & Concepts. 2003. (MATH APPLIC & CONN CRSE Ser.). (SPA., Illus.). 90p. (gr. 5-6). pap., wbk. ed. 7.20 *(978-0-07-860092-0(8)*, 0078600928) McGraw-Hill Higher Education.
—Mathematics Practice: Word Problems Workbook: Applications & Concepts, Course 1. 2003. (MATH APPLIC & CONN CRSE Ser.). (ENG., Illus.). 90p. (gr. 6-8). pap. 7.20 *(978-0-07-860087-6(1)*, 0078600871) McGraw-Hill Education.
—Mathematics Practice: Word Problems Workbook: Applications & Concepts, Course 3. 2003. (MATH APPLIC & CONN CRSE Ser.). (ENG., Illus.). 95p. (gr. 7-8). pap. 7.20 *(978-0-07-860164-4(9)*, 0078601649) McGraw-Hill Higher Education.
—Patterns in Numbers & Shapes: Using Algebraic Thinking. 2004. (Creative Pub: Mathscape Ser.). (ENG., Illus.). 42p. (gr. 6-6). per. 15.88 *(978-0-07-866804-3(2)*, 0078668042) McGraw-Hill Education.
McGuinness, Daniel. Cool Careers Without College for People Who Are Really Good at Science & Math. 2013. (New Cool Careers Without College Ser.). (Illus.). 144p. (J). (gr. 7-12). 35.95 *(978-1-4777-1823-0(0))* Rosen Publishing Group, Inc., The.
McKay, Lucia & Guscott, Maggie. Budgeting & Banking Math. 2005. (Practical Math in Context Ser.). (Illus.). 104p. per. 9.95 *(978-1-56254-758-5(5)*, SP7585) Saddleback Educational Publishing, Inc.
—Everyday Life, Book 1. 2005. (Practical Math in Context Ser.). (Illus.). 104p. per. 9.95 *(978-1-56254-760-8(7)*, SP7607) Saddleback Educational Publishing, Inc.
—Home & School, Book 2. 2005. (Practical Math in Context Ser.). (Illus.). 104p. per. 9.95 *(978-1-56254-762-2(3)*, SP7623) Saddleback Educational Publishing, Inc.
—Smart Shopping Math. 2005. (Practical Math in Context Ser.). (Illus.). 104p. per. 9.95 *(978-1-56254-756-1(9)*, SP7569) Saddleback Educational Publishing, Inc.
McKell, Theresa Kane. Pre-Algebra. 2003. (Skills for Success Ser.). (ENG.). 128p. (gr. 6-8). pap. 16.99 *(978-0-88724-952-5(3)*, CD-4323) Carson-Dellosa Publishing, LLC.
McKinney, Devon. Monuments of Washington, D. C. Use Place Value Understanding & Properties of Operations to Add & Subtract. 2014. (Math Masters: Number & Operations in Base Ten Ser.). (Illus.). 24p. (J). (gr. 2-3). 23.60 *(978-1-4777-6435-0(6))*; (ENG., pap. 8.25 *(978-1-4777-4771-1(0))* Rosen Publishing Group, Inc., The. (Rosen Classroom).
McMahon, Philip & Letts 11+ Staff. Maths. 2016. (Letts 11+ Success Ser.). (ENG.). 80p. (J). (gr. 4-5). pap. 9.95 ***(978-1-84419-890-0(1))*** HarperCollins Pubs. Ltd. GBR. Dist: Independent Pubs. Group.
McManaman, Yelena & Droujkova, Maria. Moebius Noodles: Adventurous Math for the Playground Crowd. 2015. (Natural Math Ser.: 3). (Illus.). 88p. pap. 15.00 *(978-0-9776939-5-5(3))* Delta Stream Media.
McNeil, Niki, et al. HOCPP 1115 Multiplication Party. 2006. spiral bd. 21.00 *(978-1-60308-115-3(1))* In the Hands of a Child.
MCP Mathematics: Level K. 2005. (J). (gr. k-6). stu. ed. 28.50 *(978-0-7652-6054-3(9))* Seymour, Dale Pubns.
The MEAP Solution: Middle School Edition. 2003. 70p. (YA). (gr. 5-9). 19.95 *(978-0-9718019-1-2(6))* Twianie Roberts Consulting.
Measuring Worms Activity Cards. 2004. (J). 7.95 *(978-1-56911-529-9(X))* Learning Resources, Inc.
Menotti, Andrea. How Many Jelly Beans? A Giant Book of Giant Numbers! Labat, Yancey, illus. 2012. (ENG.). 28p. (J). (gr. -1-1). 18.99 *(978-1-4521-0206-1(6))* Chronicle Bks. LLC.
Mental Math. 2004. (Help with Homework Ser.). 32p. (J). (gr. 1-4). wbk. ed. 3.99 *(978-1-904586-26-5(0))* Byeway Bks.
Meyer, Jan. Brain Quest, Grade 3: A Whole Year of Curriculum-Based Exercises & Activities in One Fun Book! Shults, Anna, ed. 2008. (ENG., Illus.). 320p. (J). (gr. 3-3). wbk. ed. 12.95 *(978-0-7611-4916-3(3)*, 14916) Workman Publishing Co., Inc.
Meyer, Jan & Brain Quest Editors. Brain Quest Grade 3 Math. 2nd rev. ed. 2006. (ENG.). 150p. (J). (gr. 3-3). 11.95 *(978-0-7611-4137-2(5)*, 14137) Workman Publishing Co., Inc.
Meyrick, Caroline & Dwamena, Kwame. Mathematical Studies Standard Level for the IB Diploma Coursebook. 2013. (IB Diploma Ser.). (ENG., Illus.). 772p. pap. 53.13 *(978-1-107-69140-7(0))* Cambridge Univ. Pr.
Michaels, Chris. Animal Babies. 2010. (Sight Word Readers Ser.). (J). 3.49 *(978-1-60719-628-0(X))* Newmark Learning LLC.
—On My Desk. 2010. (Sight Word Readers Ser.). (J). 3.49 *(978-1-60719-625-9(5))* Newmark Learning LLC.
Middle School Math, Course 1: EEdition. 2004. (gr. 6-9). cd-rom *(978-0-618-36400-8(5)*, 2-06524) Holt McDougal.
Middle School Math, Course 1: EEdition Plus Online with print purchase - 1 Year. 2004. (gr. 6-9). *(978-0-618-39416-6(8)*, 2-05569) Holt McDougal.
Middle School Math, Course 1: EEdition Plus Online without print purchase - 6 Years. 2004. (gr. 6-9). *(978-0-618-36956-0(2)*, 2-06527) Holt McDougal.
Middle School Math, Course 1: ETutorial. 2004. (gr. 6-9). cd-rom *(978-0-618-39811-9(2)*, 2-05641); cd-rom *(978-0-618-39810-2(4)*, 2-05640); cd-rom *(978-0-618-36393-3(9)*, 2-06517) Holt McDougal.
Middle School Math, Course 1: ETutorial Plus Online. 2004. (gr. 6-9). *(978-0-618-39410-4(9)*, 2-05563) Holt McDougal.
Middle School Math, Course 1: EWorkbook Plus Online. 2004. (gr. 6-9). *(978-0-618-39413-5(3)*, 2-05566) Holt McDougal.
Middle School Math, Course 1: Exercises in Spanish. 2004. (gr. 6-9). *(978-0-618-37054-2(4)*, 2-06338) Holt McDougal.
Middle School Math, Course 1: Notetaking Guide, TE. 2004. (gr. 6-9). *(978-0-618-33453-7(X)*, 2-06212) Holt McDougal.
Middle School Math, Course 1: Practice Workbook, TE. 2004. (gr. 6-9). *(978-0-618-34360-7(1)*, 2-06229) Holt McDougal.
Middle School Math, Course 1: Pupil's Edition. 2004. (gr. 6-12). *(978-0-618-06730-5(2)*, 2-78042); *(978-0-618-08759-4(1)*, 2-06000) Holt McDougal.
Middle School Math, Course 1: Spanish Study Guide. 2004. (gr. 6-9). *(978-0-618-26962-4(2)*, 2-05798) Holt McDougal.
Middle School Math, Course 1: Test & Practice Generator. 2004. (gr. 6-9). cd-rom *(978-0-618-15838-6(3)*, 2-99755) Holt McDougal.
Middle School Math, Course 1: Worked-Out Solution Key. 2004. (gr. 6-9). *(978-0-618-28026-1(X)*, 2-06102) Holt McDougal.
Middle School Math, Course 2: EEdition. 2004. (gr. 6-12). cd-rom *(978-0-618-36401-5(3)*, 2-06525) Holt McDougal.
Middle School Math, Course 2: EEdition Plus Online with print purchase - 1 Year. 2004. (gr. 6-12). *(978-0-618-39422-7(2)*, 2-05575) Holt McDougal.
Middle School Math, Course 2: EEdition Plus Online without print purchase - 6 Years. 2004. (gr. 6-12). *(978-0-618-36957-7(0)*, 2-06528) Holt McDougal.
Middle School Math, Course 2: ETutorial. 2004. (gr. 6-12). cd-rom *(978-0-618-39813-3(9)*, 2-05643); cd-rom *(978-0-618-39812-6(0)*, 2-05642); cd-rom *(978-0-618-36396-4(3)*, 2-06520) Holt McDougal.
Middle School Math, Course 2: ETutorial Plus Online. 2004. (gr. 6-12). *(978-0-618-39411-1(7)*, 2-05564) Holt McDougal.
Middle School Math, Course 2: EWorkbook Plus Online. 2004. (gr. 6-12). *(978-0-618-39414-2(1)*, 2-05567) Holt McDougal.
Middle School Math, Course 2: Spanish Study Guide. 2004. (gr. 6-12). *(978-0-618-26882-5(0)*, 2-06083) Holt McDougal.
Middle School Math, Course 2: Worked-Out Solution Key. 2004. (gr. 6-12). *(978-0-618-28036-0(7)*, 2-06106) Holt McDougal.
Middle School Math, Course 3: EEdition. 2004. (gr. 6-12). cd-rom *(978-0-618-36402-2(1)*, 2-06526) Holt McDougal.
Middle School Math, Course 3: EEdition Plus Online with print purchase - 1 Year. 2004. (gr. 6-12). *(978-0-618-39428-9(1)*, 2-05581) Holt McDougal.
Middle School Math, Course 3: EEdition Plus Online with print purchase - 6 Years. 2004. (gr. 6-12). *(978-0-618-39433-3(8)*, 2-05586) Holt McDougal.
Middle School Math, Course 3: EEdition Plus Online without print purchase - 6 Years. 2004. (gr. 6-12). *(978-0-618-36958-4(9)*, 2-06529) Holt McDougal.
Middle School Math, Course 3: ETutorial. 2004. (gr. 6-12). cd-rom *(978-0-618-36383-4(1)*, 2-06507); cd-rom *(978-0-618-39815-7(5)*, 2-05645); cd-rom *(978-0-618-39814-0(7)*, 2-05644) Holt McDougal.
Middle School Math, Course 3: ETutorial Plus Online. 2004. (gr. 6-12). *(978-0-618-39412-8(5)*, 2-05565) Holt McDougal.
Middle School Math, Course 3: EWorkbook Plus Online. 2004. (gr. 6-12). *(978-0-618-39415-9(X)*, 2-05568) Holt McDougal.
Middle School Math, Course 3: Worked-Out Solution Key. 2004. (gr. 6-12). *(978-0-618-28040-7(5)*, 2-06110) Holt McDougal.
Mighton, John. Jump at Home: Math Worksheets for the Elementary Curriculum. 2007. (Illus.). pap. *(978-0-88784-721-9(8))*; pap. *(978-0-88784-722-6(6))*; pap. *(978-0-88784-719-6(6))* House of Anansi Pr.
—JUMP at Home — Grade 4: Math Worksheets for the Elementary Curriculum. 2007. (Illus.). pap. *(978-0-88784-720-2(X))* House of Anansi Pr.
Mihaly, Christy. Using Math in Fashion. 2017. (Math You Will Actually Use Ser.). 48p. (J). (gr. 10-10). pap. 11.75 ***(978-1-4994-3860-4(5)***, Rosen Central) Rosen Publishing Group, Inc., The.
Milanese, Celestine Marie & Peck, Carolyn. Math 8 X-treme Review: Concise Training for NYS Math Intermediate Assessment. Stich, Paul, ed. Garnsey, Wayne, illus. 2007. 160p. per. 13.95 *(978-0-935487-85-5(9)*, X-treme Reviews) N&N Publishing Co., Inc.
Miller, Elizabeth D. Read It! Draw It! Solve It! 2003. (Illus.). 192p. (YA). (gr. 3-18). 20.50 *(978-1-57232-436-7(8)*, 33802) Seymour, Dale Pubns.
—Read It! Draw It! Solve It! Animal Book. 2003. (Illus.). 192p. (J). 34.95 *(978-1-57232-437-4(6))* Seymour, Dale Pubns.
Miller, Nate. Sam's Soccer Game: Work with Addition & Subtraction Equations. 2013. (InfoMax Math Readers Ser.). (ENG.). 24p. (J). (gr. 1-2). pap. 8.25 *(978-1-4777-2189-6(4))*; pap. 49.50 *(978-1-4777-2190-2(8))* Rosen Publishing Group, Inc., The. (Rosen Classroom).
Miller, Reagan & Berry, Minta. Beginner Word Problems. 2011. (ENG., Illus.). 24p. (J). lib. bdg. *(978-0-7787-5274-5(7))* Crabtree Publishing Co.
—Beginner Word Problems. Crabtree Publishing Co. Staff, ed. 2011. (My Path to Math Ser.: No. 33). (ENG., Illus.). 24p. (J). (gr. k-3). pap. *(978-0-7787-5263-9(1))* Crabtree Publishing Co.
—Building Sets of Ten. 2011. (ENG.). 24p. (J). lib. bdg. *(978-0-7787-5277-6(1))* Crabtree Publishing Co.
—Patterning. Crabtree Publishing Staff, ed. 2011. (My Path to Math Ser.: No. 37). (ENG.). 24p. (J). (gr. k-3). pap. *(978-0-7787-5267-7(4))* Crabtree Publishing Co.
—Patterning. 2011. (ENG.). 24p. (J). lib. bdg. *(978-0-7787-5278-3(X))* Crabtree Publishing Co.
Millington, Jon. Mathematical Snacks: A Collection of Interesting Ideas to Fill Those Spare Moments. 2004. (Illus.). 96p. 14.00 *(978-1-899618-51-4(1))* Tarquin Pubns. GBR. Dist: Parkwest Pubns., Inc.
—Tables Cubes: Make These Two Sets of Special Cubes & Use Them for Tables Practice. 2004. (Illus.). 24p. (J). 10.00 *(978-1-899618-17-0(1))* Tarquin Pubns. GBR. Dist: Parkwest Pubns., Inc.
Mills, Nathan & Jefferson, Dave. Let's Do Math at the Store. 2012. (Rosen Readers Ser.). (ENG., Illus.). 24p. (J). (gr. 1-2). pap. 8.25 *(978-1-4488-8809-2(3)*, Rosen Classroom) Rosen Publishing Group, Inc., The.
Mills, Steve & Koll, Hilary. Fast Forward Maths. 2003. (Illus.). pap., tchr. ed. 78.50 *(978-0-340-78201-9(3)*, Hodder Education) Hodder Education Group GBR. Dist: Trans-Atlantic Pubns., Inc.
—Quick Revision KS3 Maths. 2007. (Illus.). 46p. pap. 9.95 *(978-0-340-94306-9(8)*, Hodder Education) Hodder Education Group GBR. Dist: Trans-Atlantic Pubns., Inc.
Minden, Cecilia. Basketball. 2008. (21st Century Skills Library: Real World Math Ser.). (ENG., Illus.). 32p. (gr. 4-8). lib. bdg. 28.50 *(978-1-60279-245-6(3)*, 200196) Cherry Lake Publishing.
—Exercise by the Numbers. 2007. (21st Century Skills Library: Real World Math Ser.). (ENG., Illus.). 32p. (gr. 4-8). lib. bdg. 28.50 *(978-1-60279-010-0(8)*, 200063) Cherry Lake Publishing.
—Real World Math: Health & Wellness, 8 vols., Set. Incl. Breakfast by the Numbers. (Illus.). lib. bdg. 28.50 *(978-1-60279-011-7(6)*, 200060); Cooking by the Numbers. (Illus.). lib. bdg. 28.50 *(978-1-60279-007-0(8)*, 200061); Dinner by the Numbers. (Illus.). lib. bdg. 28.50 *(978-1-60279-013-1(2)*, 200062); Exercise by the Numbers. (Illus.). lib. bdg. 28.50 *(978-1-60279-010-0(8)*, 200063); Gardening by the Numbers. (Illus.). lib. bdg. 28.50 *(978-1-60279-008-7(6)*, 200064); Grocery Shopping by the Numbers. (Illus.). lib. bdg. 28.50 *(978-1-60279-006-3(X)*, 200065); Lunch by the Numbers. (Illus.). lib. bdg. 28.50 *(978-1-60279-012-4(4)*, 200066); Restaurants by the Numbers. lib. bdg. 28.50 *(978-1-60279-009-4(4)*, 200067); (gr. 4-8). 32p. 2007. Set lib. bdg. 159.60 *(978-1-60279-103-9(1)*, 200059) Cherry Lake Publishing.
—Saving for the Future. 2015. (21st Century Skills Library: Real World Math Ser.). (ENG., Illus.). 32p. (J). (gr. 4-7). 29.93 *(978-1-63362-574-7(5)*, 206480) Cherry Lake Publishing.
—Smart Shopping. 2015. (21st Century Skills Library: Real World Math Ser.). (ENG., Illus.). 32p. (J). (gr. 4-7). 29.93 *(978-1-63362-575-4(3)*, 206484) Cherry Lake Publishing.
—Starting Your Own Business. (21st Century Skills Library: Real World Math Ser.). (ENG., 32p. (gr. 4-7). 2015. Illus.). (J). 29.93 *(978-1-63362-576-1(1)*, 206488) 2009. lib. bdg. 28.50 *(978-1-60279-313-2(1)*, 200209) Cherry Lake Publishing.
Misztal, Maggie. Be Creative with Beads! Use Place Value Understanding & Properties of Operations to Add & Subtract, 1 vol. 2015. (InfoMax Common Core Math Readers Ser.). (ENG.). 24p. (J). pap. 8.25 *(978-1-4777-4797-1(4)*, Rosen Classroom) Rosen Publishing Group, Inc., The.
Mitchell, Cindi. Dazzling Math Line Designs: Dozens of Reproducible Activities That Help Build Addition, Subtraction. 2003. (ENG., Illus.). 64p. pap. 9.95 *(978-0-590-00086-4(1))* Scholastic, Inc.
—Math Line Designs from Around the World: Dozens of Engaging Practice Pages That Build Skills in Addition, Subtraction, Multiplication Facts, & More. 2008. (ENG., Illus.). 64p. pap. 11.99 *(978-0-439-37660-0(2)*, Teaching Resources) Scholastic, Inc.
—Math Line Designs from Around the World: Dozens of Engaging Practice Pages That Build Skills in Multiplication, Division, Fractions, Decimals, & More. 2008. (ENG., Illus.). 64p. pap. 11.99 *(978-0-439-37661-7(0)*, Teaching Resources) Scholastic, Inc.
—Quilt Math: 100 Reproducible Activities That Motivate Kids to Practice Multi-Digit Addition & Subtraction, Multiplication & Division, Fractions, Decimals, & More. 2005. (ENG., Illus.). 112p. (gr. 4-6). per. 15.99 *(978-0-439-38533-6(4)*, Teaching Resources) Scholastic, Inc.
Modern Curriculum Press Mathematics. 2003. Level C. (J). 28.50 *(978-0-8136-3111-0(4))*Level C. pap., tchr. ed. 32.50 net. *(978-0-8136-3118-9(1))*Level D. (J). pap., wbk. ed. 28.50 *(978-0-8136-3112-7(2))*Level D. tchr. ed. 29.50 *(978-0-8136-3119-6(X))*Level A. (J). 28.50 *(978-0-8136-3109-7(2))*Level A. pap., tchr. ed. 32.50 net. *(978-0-8136-3116-5(5))*Level B. (J). 28.50 *(978-0-8136-3110-3(6))*Level B. pap., tchr. ed. 32.50 net. *(978-0-8136-3117-2(3))*Level E. pap., tchr. ed. 32.50 net. *(978-0-8136-3120-2(3))*Level F. tchr. ed. 32.50 net. *(978-0-8136-3121-9(1))*Level K. (J). 28.50 *(978-0-8136-3108-0(4))*Level K. pap., tchr. ed. 32.50 net. *(978-0-8136-3115-8(7))* Modern Curriculum Pr.
Molding Mental Mathemagicians Student Worksheets. 2005. (J). pap., wbk. ed. *(978-0-9766926-1-4(9))* JCTT, LLC.
Moldovo, Eustacia & Murphy, Patricia J. Learning Addition with Puppies & Kittens. 2017. (J). ***(978-0-7660-9069-9(8))*** Enslow Pubs., Inc.
—Learning How to Measure with Puppies & Kittens. 2017. (J). pap. ***(978-0-7660-9074-3(4))*** Enslow Pubs., Inc.
—Learning Subtraction with Puppies & Kittens. 2017. (J). pap. ***(978-0-7660-9071-2(X))*** Enslow Pubs., Inc.
Money Matters Series. 2005. (J). pap. *(978-1-60015-017-3(9))* Steps To Literacy, LLC.
Montague-Smith, Ann. Dividing, 8 vols. 2005. (QEB Math Club Ser.). (Illus.). 24p. (J). (gr. k-1). lib. bdg. 15.95 *(978-1-59566-115-9(8))* QEB Publishing Inc.
—Numbers. 2004. (QEB Start Math Ser.). (Illus.). 24p. (J). Vol. 1. lib. bdg. 15.95 *(978-1-59566-025-1(9))* Vol. 2. lib. bdg. 15.95 *(978-1-59566-029-9(1))* QEB Publishing Inc.
—Subtracting, 8 vols. 2005. (QEB Math Club Ser.). (Illus.). 24p. (J). (gr. k-1). lib. bdg. 15.95 *(978-1-59566-097-8(6))* QEB Publishing Inc.
—Using Numbers. 2005. (QEB Math Club Ser.). (Illus.). 24p. (J). (gr. k-1). lib. bdg. 15.95 *(978-1-59566-113-5(1))* QEB Publishing Inc.
—Using Numbers Book One, 8 vols. 2005. (QEB Math Club Ser.). (Illus.). 24p. (J). (gr. k-1). lib. bdg. 15.95 *(978-1-59566-095-4(X))* QEB Publishing Inc.
Montague-Smith, Ann & Harrison, Paul. Extension for All Through Problem Solving, Bk. 2. 2003. (Apex Maths Ser.: Vol. 2). (ENG., Illus.). 48p. pap., stu. ed. 14.94 *(978-0-521-75488-0(7))* Cambridge Univ. Pr.
Mooney, Carla. Using Math in Sports. 2017. (Math You Will Actually Use Ser.). 48p. (J). (gr. 10-10). pap. 11.75 ***(978-1-4994-3872-7(9)***, Rosen Central) Rosen Publishing Group, Inc., The.
Moreau, Nancy & Moreau, Wayne. Math A STAReview: Math Grade 9-10 Test Preparation. Stich, Paul, ed. 2003. (ENG., Illus.). 352p. (YA). per. 12.67 *(978-0-935487-78-7(6)*, STAReviews) N&N Publishing Co., Inc.
Morrison, Chloe. Laura's Lemonade Stand: Represent & Interpret Data. 2013. (Rosen Math Readers Ser.). (ENG.). 24p. (J). (gr. 1-2). pap. 8.25 *(978-1-4777-2079-0(0))*; pap. 49.50 *(978-1-4777-2080-6(4))* Rosen Publishing Group, Inc., The. (Rosen Classroom).
Morrison, Karen. Nelson International Mathematics, Bk. 4. 2nd ed. 2014. (ENG.). 128p. pap., stu. ed. 13.00 *(978-1-4085-1903-5(8))* Oxford Univ. Pr., Inc.
Moseley, Cherri & Rees, Janet. Cambridge Primary Mathematics Stage 1 Learner's Book. 2014. (Cambridge Primary Maths Ser.). (ENG.). 90p. pap. 19.94 *(978-1-107-63131-1(9))* Cambridge Univ. Pr.
—Cambridge Primary Mathematics Stage 2 Learner's Book. 2014. (Cambridge Primary Maths Ser.). (ENG.). 78p. pap. 19.94 *(978-1-107-61582-3(8))* Cambridge Univ. Pr.
—Cambridge Primary Mathematics Stage 3 Learner's Book. 2014. (Cambridge Primary Maths Ser.). (ENG.). 138p. pap. 19.94 *(978-1-107-66767-9(4))* Cambridge Univ. Pr.
Mother Goose Cares about Math & Science: Professional Development Manual. 2004. *(978-0-9753985-2-4(0))* Mother Goose Programs.
Mother Goose Programs, prod. What's the BIG Idea? Shapes & Spaces Librarian Manual. 2008. 70p. pap. *(978-0-9753985-9-3(8))* Mother Goose Programs.
Mottershead, Lorraine. Metamorphosis. 196p. (J). (gr. 7-10). 15.95 *(978-0-86651-466-8(X)*, DS01716) Seymour, Dale Pubns.
Multiplication & Division. 2004. (Help with Homework Ser.). 32p. (J). (gr. 1-4). wbk. ed. 3.99 *(978-1-904586-21-0(X))* Byeway Bks.
Multiplication & Division. 2003. Level C. tchr. ed. 19.50 *(978-0-7652-1316-7(8))*Level C. stu. ed. 14.50 *(978-0-7652-1304-4(4))*Level D. tchr. ed. 19.50 *(978-0-7652-1320-4(6))*Level D. stu. ed. 14.50 *(978-0-7652-1308-2(7))*Level E. tchr. ed. 19.50 *(978-0-7652-1324-2(9))*Level E. stu. ed. 14.50 *(978-0-7652-1312-9(5))* Modern Curriculum Pr.
Multiplication & Division Game Board Book. 2004. (J). bds. 16.95 *(978-1-56911-161-1(8))* Learning Resources, Inc.
Mumford, Jeanette, et al. Busy Ant Maths. Evans, Steve et al, illus. 2014. (Busy Ant Maths Ser.). (ENG.). 128p. (gr. 4). Bk. 5A. pap. 12.95 *(978-0-00-756833-8(9))*Bk. 5B. pap. 12.95 *(978-0-00-756834-5(7))*Bk. 5C. pap. 12.95 *(978-0-00-756835-2(5))*Bk. 6B. pap. 12.95 *(978-0-00-756837-6(1))*Bk. 6C. pap. 12.95 *(978-0-00-756838-3(X))* HarperCollins Pubs. Ltd. GBR. Dist: Independent Pubs. Group.
—Busy Ant Maths - Pupil Book, Bk. 3B. Evans, Steve et al, illus. 2014. (Busy Ant Maths Ser.). (ENG.). 16p. (gr. 2). pap., stu. ed. 11.99 *(978-0-00-756238-1(1))* HarperCollins Pubs. Ltd. GBR. Dist: Independent Pubs. Group.
—Busy Ant Maths - Year 6 Pupil, Bk. 6A. Evans, Steve et al, illus. 2014. (Busy Ant Maths Ser.). (ENG.). 128p. (gr. 4). pap. 12.95 *(978-0-00-756836-9(3))* HarperCollins Pubs. Ltd. GBR. Dist: Independent Pubs. Group.
Murphy, Patricia J. Counting with an Abacus: Learning the Place Values of Ones, Tens, & Hundreds. 2009. (Math for the REAL World Ser.). 16p. (gr. 2-3). pap. 7.05 *(978-0-8239-8880-8(5)*, Rosen Classroom) Rosen Publishing Group, Inc., The.
Murphy, Stuart J. Double the Ducks. Petrone, Valeria, illus. 2003. (MathStart Ser.). 40p. (J). 15.99 *(978-0-06-028922-5(8))* HarperCollins Pubs.
—Earth Day - Hooray!, Vol. 50. Andriani, Renee, illus. 2004. (MathStart 3 Ser.). (ENG.). 40p. (J). (gr. 2-18). pap. 5.99 *(978-0-06-000129-2(1))* HarperCollins Pubs.
—Earth Day — Hooray! Andriani, Renee, illus. 2004. (MathStart 3 Ser.). (ENG.). 40p. (J). (gr. 2-18). 17.99 *(978-0-06-000127-8(5))* HarperCollins Pubs.
—Mall Mania. Andriani, Renee W., illus. 2006. (MathStart Ser.). (ENG.). 40p. (J). (gr. 1-4). 15.99 *(978-0-06-055776-8(1))*; pap. 5.99 *(978-0-06-055777-5(X))* HarperCollins Pubs.
—Same Old Horse. Björkman, Steve, illus. 2005. (MathStart Ser.). 40p. (J). 15.99 *(978-0-06-055770-6(2))*; (ENG.). (gr. 1). pap. 5.99 *(978-0-06-055771-3(0))* HarperCollins Pubs.
Murray, Stuart A. P. Score with Baseball Math. 2013. (Score with Sports Math Ser.). 48p. (J). lib. bdg. 25.27 *(978-0-7660-4174-5(3)*, Enslow Elementary) Enslow Pubs., Inc.
—Score with Race Car Math. 2013. (Score with Sports Math Ser.). 48p. (J). lib. bdg. 25.27 *(978-0-7660-4177-6(8)*, Enslow Elementary) Enslow Pubs., Inc.
—Score with Soccer Math. 2013. (Score with Sports Math Ser.). 48p. (J). lib. bdg. 25.27 *(978-0-7660-4175-2(1)*, Enslow Elementary) Enslow Pubs., Inc.
—Score with Track & Field Math. 2013. (Score with Sports Math Ser.). 48p. (J). lib. bdg. 25.27 *(978-0-7660-4176-9(X)*, Enslow Elementary) Enslow Pubs., Inc.
Muschla, Gary Robert. Practice Makes Perfect Multiplication & Division. 2012. (Practice Makes Perfect Ser.). (ENG.). 192p. pap. 18.00 *(978-0-07-177285-3(5)*, 0071772855) McGraw-Hill Education.
NCPTA Staff, et al. Better Maths. (Illus.). 32p. pap. 6.99 *(978-0-340-64668-7(3)*, Coronet) Hodder & Stoughton GBR. Dist: Trafalgar Square Publishing.
—Maths for the Brighter Child. (Illus.). 24p. pap. 6.99 *(978-0-340-71680-9(0)*, Coronet) Hodder & Stoughton GBR. Dist: Trafalgar Square Publishing.
Nelson, Robin. Let's Make a Bar Graph. 2012. (First Step Nonfiction - Graph It! Ser.). (ENG., Illus.). 24p. (gr. k-2). (J). lib. bdg. 23.93 *(978-0-7613-8972-9(5)*, Lerner Pubns.); pap. 6.95 *(978-1-57505-947-1(9))* Lerner Publishing Group.
—Let's Make a Circle Graph. 2012. (First Step Nonfiction - Graph It! Ser.). (ENG., Illus.). 24p. (gr. k-2). pap. 6.95 *(978-1-58013-675-4(3))*; lib. bdg. 23.93 *(978-0-7613-8974-3(1)*, Lerner Pubns.) Lerner Publishing Group.

M
N
O

—Let's Make a Picture Graph. 2012. (First Step Nonfiction - Graph It! Ser.). (ENG., Illus.). 24p. (gr. k-2). pap. 6.95 *(978-1-57505-965-5(7))*; lib. bdg. 23.93 *(978-0-7613-8973-6(3)*, Lerner Pubns.) Lerner Publishing Group.

—Let's Make a Tally Chart. 2012. (First Step Nonfiction - Graph It! Ser.). (ENG., Illus.). 24p. (gr. k-2). pap. 6.95 *(978-1-58013-946-5(9))* Lerner Publishing Group.

—Tally Charts. 2012. (First Step Nonfiction - Graph It! Ser.). (ENG., Illus.). 24p. (gr. k-2). lib. bdg. 23.93 *(978-0-7613-8975-0(X)*, Lerner Pubns.) Lerner Publishing Group.

Neuschwander, Cindy. Sir Cumference & the Fracton Faire. Geehan, Wayne, illus. 2017. (ENG.). 32p. (J). (gr. 2-5). lib. bdg. 16.99 *(978-1-57091-771-4(X))* Charlesbridge Publishing, Inc.

—Sir Cumference & the Viking's Map. Geehan, Wayne, illus. 2012. (Sir Cumference Ser.). lib. bdg. 18.40 *(978-0-606-26445-7(0)*, Turtleback) Turtleback Bks.

New BaseTen Fries. 2004. (J). *(978-1-59242-143-5(1))* Delta Education, LLC.

New Maths Frameworking: Matches the Revised KS3 Framework. 2nd ed. 2008. (New Maths Frameworking Ser.). (ENG., Illus.). 32p. (YA). (gr. 8-9). pap. 10.99 *(978-0-00-726804-7(1))* HarperCollins Pubs. Ltd. GBR. Dist: Independent Pubs. Group.

New York Middle School Mathematics. 2005. (J). (gr. 7-8). pap., stu. ed. 13.95 *(978-0-13-024192-4(X))* Globe Fearon Educational Publishing.

New York Middle School Mathematics: Answer Key. 2005. (J). (gr. 7-8). pap. 1.50 *(978-0-13-023913-6(5))* Globe Fearon Educational Publishing.

Nickson, Marilyn. Teaching & Learning Mathematics: A Teacher's Guide to Recent Research & Its Application. (J). pap. *(978-0-8264-7026-3(2))* Bloomsbury Publishing Plc.

Niederman, Derrick. Mind-Stretching Math Puzzles. 2005. (Illus.). 112p. (J). *(978-1-4156-0492-2(4))* Sterling Publishing Co., Inc.

Noah, Ian & Logan, Stephanie. Mike's Math Club Presents the Monstrously Fun Fraction Book. Noah, Ian et al, eds. Milken-Noah, Joni et al, eds. 2003. (Illus.). 382p. pap. 24.95 *(978-0-9646425-1-5(4))* Milken Family Foundation.

Noble, Jonathan & Owen, Ruth. Pole Position! 2010. (Top Score Maths Ser.). (Illus.). 32p. pap. *(978-0-237-54283-2(8))* Evans Brothers, Ltd.

Nolan, Henry. Sophia Sows Seeds: Work with 11-19 to Gain Foundations for Place Value. 2013. (InfoMax Math Readers Ser.). (ENG.). 16p. (J). (gr. k-1). pap. 7.00 *(978-1-4777-1991-6(1))*; pap. 42.00 *(978-1-4777-1992-3(X))* Rosen Publishing Group, Inc., The. (Rosen Classroom).

Nowark, Jennifer. At the Flower Shop: Learning Simple Division by Forming Equal Groups. 2009. (Math for the REAL World Ser.). 16p. (gr. 2-3). pap. 7.05 *(978-0-8239-8930-0(5)*, Rosen Classroom) Rosen Publishing Group, Inc., The.

Numbers for 3-5 Years. Date not set. (Play & Learn Ser.). (Illus.). 192p. (J). 3.98 *(978-0-7525-6912-3(0))* Parragon, Inc.

Numbers for 5-7 Years. Date not set. (Play & Learn Ser.). 192p. (J). 3.98 *(978-0-7525-6913-0(9))* Parragon, Inc.

Numbers on the Farm. (Padded Large Learners Ser.). (Illus.). (J). bds. *(978-0-7525-9889-5(9))* Parragon, Inc.

Nunn, Daniel. Patterns Outside, 1 vol. 2012. (Math Every Day Ser.). (ENG.). 24p. (gr. -1-k). pap. 9.95 *(978-1-4329-5736-0(8))*; lib. bdg. 25.99 *(978-1-4329-5731-5(7))* Heinemann-Raintree.

Objects in the Sky, 6 bks., Set. Incl. Exploring Comets. Way, Jennifer. lib. bdg. 22.60 *(978-1-4042-3469-7(1)*, PowerKids Pr.); Exploring Earth. Olien, Rebecca. lib. bdg. 22.60 *(978-1-4042-3465-9(9))*; Exploring Meteors. Olien, Rebecca. lib. bdg. 22.60 *(978-1-4042-3468-0(3)*, PowerKids Pr.); Exploring the Moon. Olien, Rebecca. lib. bdg. 22.60 *(978-1-4042-3466-6(7)*, PowerKids Pr.); Exploring the Planets in Our Solar System. Olien, Rebecca. lib. bdg. 22.60 *(978-1-4042-3467-3(5)*, PowerKids Pr.); Exploring the Sun. Olien, Rebecca. lib. bdg. 22.60 *(978-1-4042-3464-2(0)*, PowerKids Pr.); (Illus.). 24p. (J). (gr. 3-7). 2007. 2007. Set lib. bdg. 127.50 *(978-1-4042-3502-1(7)*, PowerKids Pr.) Rosen Publishing Group, Inc., The.

O'Brien, Thomas C. Off the Path Math with Tobbs, Vol. 1. Reynolds, Peter H., illus. 2003. 59p. (J). 14.50 *(978-1-891405-09-9(8))* FableVision Pr.

O'Dell, Angela & Carlson, Kyrsten. Math Lessons for a Living Education Level 2. 2016. (ENG.). 352p. pap. 36.99 *(978-0-89051-924-0(2))* Master Bks.

—Math Lessons for a Living Education Level 3. 2016. (ENG.). 360p. pap. 36.99 *(978-0-89051-925-7(0))* Master Bks.

—Math Lessons for a Living Education Level 4. 2016. (ENG.). 388p. pap. 36.99 *(978-0-89051-926-4(9))* Master Bks.

—Math Lessons for a Living Education Level 5. 2016. (ENG.). 341p. (J). pap. 36.99 *(978-0-89051-927-1(7))* Master Bks.

O'Donnell, Kerri. The Ancient Civilizations of Greece & Rome: Solving Algebraic Equations. (PowerMath Ser.). 32p. (gr. 5-6). 2009. (ENG.). pap. 10.00 *(978-1-4042-5123-6(5)*, PowerKids Pr.) 2005. (Illus.). (YA). lib. bdg. 25.25 *(978-1-4042-2930-3(2))* Rosen Publishing Group, Inc., The.

—The Ancient Civilizations of Greece & Rome: Solving Algebraic Equations Big Book. 2005. (Math for the REAL World Ser.). (J). pap. 39.95 *(978-1-4042-5292-9(4)*, Rosen Classroom) Rosen Publishing Group, Inc., The.

—The Ancient Civilizations of Greece & Rome: Solving Algebraic Equations (Big Book) 2005. (Math for the REAL World Ser.). 32p. 47.50 *(978-1-4042-5222-6(3)*, Rosen Classroom) Rosen Publishing Group, Inc., The.

—The California Gold Rush: Multiplying & Dividing Using Three- & Four-Digit Numbers. (PowerMath: Proficiency Plus Ser.). 32p. 2009. (gr. 4-5). 47.90 *(978-1-60851-419-9(6)*, PowerKids Pr.) 2005. 47.50 *(978-1-4042-5221-9(5)*, Rosen Classroom) Rosen Publishing Group, Inc., The.

Olliges, Rob. Que Viene Primero/What Comes First. Mallick, David, tr. 2006. (My First Math Discovery Ser.). (SPA., Illus.). 24p. (J). (gr. -1-3). lib. bdg. 22.79 *(978-1-60044-288-9(9))* Rourke Educational Media.

Olsen, Alana. What Do You Know about Bugs? Understand Place Value. 2014. (Math Masters: Number & Operations in Base Ten Ser.). (Illus.). 24p. (J). (gr. 2-3). 23.60 *(978-1-4777-6431-2(3))*; (ENG., pap. 8.25 *(978-1-4777-4663-9(3))* Rosen Publishing Group, Inc., The. (Rosen Classroom).

Onish, Liane. Brain Quest, Grade 2: A Whole Year of Curriculum-Based Exercises & Activities in One Fun Book! Swann, Jill, ed. 2008. (ENG., Illus.). 320p. (J). (gr. 2-2). wbk. ed. 12.95 *(978-0-7611-4915-6(5)*, 14915) Workman Publishing Co., Inc.

—Brain Quest, Pre-K: A Whole Year of Curriculum-Based Exercises & Activities in One Fun Book! Fung, Jane, ed. 2008. (ENG., Illus.). 320p. (J). (gr. -1 — 1). wbk. ed. 12.95 *(978-0-7611-4961-3(9)*, 14961) Workman Publishing Co., Inc.

Open Court Staff. Real Math: Level 8. (J). stu. ed. *(978-0-8126-0638-6(8)*, 60638) Open Court Publishing Co.

Opie, Brenda & McAvinn, Douglas. Masterminds Riddlemath for Elementary: Measurement, Fractions, Probability, & Logical Thinking. 2004. (Illus.). 96p. (J). per. 11.95 *(978-0-86530-611-0(7))* Incentive Pubns., Inc.

Orr, Tamra B. Tornadoes. 2012. (21st Century Skills Library: Real World Math Ser.). (ENG., Illus.). 32p. (J). (gr. 4-8). pap. 14.21 *(978-1-61080-413-4(9)*, 201345); lib. bdg. 28.50 *(978-1-61080-326-7(4)*, 201312) Cherry Lake Publishing.

—Tsunamis. 2012. (21st Century Skills Library: Real World Math Ser.). (ENG.). 32p. (J). (gr. 4-8). pap. 14.21 *(978-1-61080-410-3(4)*, 201342); lib. bdg. 28.50 *(978-1-61080-327-4(2)*, 201306) Cherry Lake Publishing.

—Wildfires. 2012. (21st Century Skills Library: Real World Math Ser.). (ENG., Illus.). 32p. (J). (gr. 4-8). pap. 14.21 *(978-1-61080-412-7(0)*, 201344); lib. bdg. 28.50 *(978-1-61080-329-8(9)*, 201310) Cherry Lake Publishing.

Oswald, Nina. Saving Endangered Animals: Develop Understanding of Fractions & Numbers, 1 vol. 2015. (InfoMax Common Core Math Readers Ser.). (ENG.). 24p. (J). pap. 8.25 *(978-1-4777-4612-7(9)*, Rosen Classroom) Rosen Publishing Group, Inc., The.

Overdeck, Laura. How Many Guinea Pigs Can Fit on a Plane? Answers to Your Most Clever Math Questions. 2017. (ENG., Illus.). 144p. (J). pap. 9.99 *(978-1-250-12368-8(2)*, 9781250123688) Feiwel & Friends.

—This Time It's Personal. Paillot, Jim, illus. 2014. (Bedtime Math Ser.). (ENG.). 96p. (J). (gr. -1-2). 15.99 *(978-1-250-04096-1(5)*, 9781250040961) Feiwel & Friends.

Pallotta, Jerry. Multiplication. Bolster, Rob, illus. 2008. 32p. (J). *(978-0-545-00686-6(4))* Scholastic, Inc.

Palmer, Stuart, et al. Cambridge Mathematics NSW Syllabus for the Australian Curriculum Year 10 5. 1, 5. 2 & 5. 3 & Hotmaths Bundle. 2014. (ENG.). pap. *(978-1-107-66567-5(1))* Cambridge Univ. Pr.

—Cambridge Mathematics NSW Syllabus for the Australian Curriculum Year 8. 2014. (ENG.). pap. *(978-1-107-67181-2(7))* Cambridge Univ. Pr.

Pappas, Theoni. Do the Math! Math Challenges to Exercise Your Mind. 2015. (ENG., Illus.). 224p. (gr. 5). pap. 12.95 *(978-1-884550-74-4(6))* Wide World Publishing/Tetra.

—Further Adventures of Penrose the Mathematical Cat. 2004. (ENG., Illus.). 128p. (J). pap. 10.95 *(978-1-884550-32-4(0))* Wide World Publishing/Tetra.

—More Math Adventures with Penrose the Mathematical Cat. 2017. (ENG., Illus.). 128p. (gr. 1). pap. 12.95 *(978-1-884550-76-8(2))* Wide World Publishing/Tetra.

Pardoe, Mary. Formula One Interactive Oral & Mental Starters. unabr. ed. 2005. (Illus.). cd-rom *(978-0-340-91333-8(9))* Hodder & Stoughton.

Parham, Donna. Splash of Math K-3: K-3. 2003. (Illus.). 28p. (J). (gr. k-3). tchr. ed. 5.99 *(978-1-893698-35-2(1)*, T13, SeaWorld Education Dept.) SeaWorld, Inc.

Partil, Sravan. Measuring Quilts: Understand Concepts of Area, 1 vol. 2015. (InfoMax Common Core Math Readers Ser.). (ENG.). 24p. (J). pap. 8.25 *(978-1-4777-4591-5(2)*, Rosen Classroom) Rosen Publishing Group, Inc., The.

Payne, Ruby K. Mental Models for Math: Grades 6-12. 2006. (YA). per. 13.00 *(978-1-929229-53-6(4))* aha! Process, Inc.

Pearce, Chris. Maths Skills Builder. 3rd ed. 2014. (Maths Frameworking Ser.). (ENG., Illus.). 80p. (YA). (gr. 7-9). pap. 9.99 *(978-0-00-753780-8(8))* HarperCollins Pubs. Ltd. GBR. Dist: Independent Pubs. Group.

Penn, M. W. Pebble Math. (Pebble Math Ser.). (ENG.). 24p. (gr. k-1). 2012. pap. 12.58 *(978-1-4296-8309-8(0))* 2012. pap. 214.20 *(978-1-4296-8311-1(2))* 2012. pap. 25.16 *(978-1-4296-8310-4(4))* 2012. lib. bdg. 131.94 *(978-1-4296-8107-0(1))* 2012. lib. bdg. 43.98 *(978-1-4296-8106-3(3))* 2011. pap. 142.80 *(978-1-4296-7076-0(2))* 2011. pap. 12.58 *(978-1-4296-7075-3(4))* 2011. lib. bdg. 87.96 *(978-1-4296-6041-9(4))* Capstone Press of Coughlan Cos. (Pebble Bks.).

People Together: E-Journals. (Technology: Social Studies). (SPA.). (gr. 2-18). *(978-0-02-147229-1(7))* Macmillan/McGraw-Hill Schl. Div.

Peppas, Lynn & Challen, Paul. Addition. 2009. (ENG.). 24p. (J). lib. bdg. *(978-0-7787-4345-3(4))* Crabtree Publishing Co.

Perritano, John. Building Math. 2008. (Math Alive! Ser.). 32p. (gr. 4-18). lib. bdg. 28.50 *(978-0-7614-3210-4(8)*, Benchmark Bks.) Marshall Cavendish Corp.

Petersen, Jamee. Math & Nonfiction, Grades K-2. 2004. (ENG., Illus.). 144p. (gr. k-2). pap. 29.95 *(978-0-941355-61-2(6))* Math Solutions.

Pezzimenti, Grace. The Pizza Party: Learning Basic Problem-Solving Skills. 2004. (Math Big Bookstm Ser.). (ENG.). 12p. (gr. 1-2). 33.50 *(978-0-8239-7636-2(X))* Rosen Publishing Group, Inc., The.

Pfister, Marcus. Rainbow Fish Counting. 2013. (Rainbow Fish Ser.). (ENG., Illus.). 12p. (J). (gr. 1-1). bds. 7.95 *(978-0-7358-4148-2(9))* North-South Bks., Inc.

Phillips, Vivian A. Intrique Math. Date not set. (Illus.). 16p. (Orig.). (YA). pap. *(978-1-888413-04-5(2))* Seasoning Quilting (Arts & Crafts).

Piddock, Claire. Line, Bar, & Circle Graphs. 2010. (ENG., Illus.). 24p. (J). *(978-0-7787-5247-9(X))*; pap. *(978-0-7787-5294-3(1))* Crabtree Publishing Co.

—Slides, Flips, & Turns. 2010. (ENG., Illus.). 24p. (J). *(978-0-7787-5251-6(8))*; pap. *(978-0-7787-5298-1(4))* Crabtree Publishing Co.

Pistoia, Sara. Graphs. 2016. (J). *(978-1-4896-5107-5(1))* Weigl Pubs., Inc.

—Measurements. 2016. (J). *(978-1-4896-5110-5(1))* Weigl Pubs., Inc.

—Patterns. 2016. (J). *(978-1-4896-5116-7(0))* Weigl Pubs., Inc.

Place Value Skills (Gr. 1-2) 2003. (J). *(978-1-58232-088-5(8))* ECS Learning Systems, Inc.

Place Value Skills Spanish Version. 2007. (J). per. *(978-1-58232-157-8(4))* ECS Learning Systems, Inc.

Polette, Nancy & Ebbesmeyer, Joan. Math in Fables & Myths: Solving Word Problems with Readers' Theatre. 2004. (J). pap. 14.95 *(978-1-931334-58-7(7))* Pieces of Learning.

Pomerleau, Annie. At the Arcade: Understand Place Value. 2014. (Rosen Common Core Math Readers Ser.). 24p. (J). (gr. 2-3). (ENG.). pap. 49.50 *(978-1-4777-4661-5(7))*; (Illus.). 23.60 *(978-1-4777-6430-5(5))* Rosen Publishing Group, Inc., The. (Rosen Classroom).

Ponka, Katherine. Math on the Sun. 2016. (Solve It! Math in Space Ser.). (Illus.). 24p. (J). (gr. 3-2). 22.60 *(978-1-4824-4936-5(6))* Stevens, Gareth Publishing LLLP.

Portable Press Staff. See Ya Later Calculator. 2017. (ENG., Illus.). 224p. 14.99 *(978-1-62686-758-1(5)*, Portable Pr.) Readerlink Distribution Services, LLC.

Poskitt, Kjartan & Watson, Richard. Maths Adventure. 2016. (ENG., Illus.). 14p. (J). (gr. k-2). 14.99 *(978-1-4052-7661-0(4))* Egmont Bks., Ltd. GBR. Dist: Independent Pubs. Group.

Power Math: Sets 7,8, And 9. (Illus.). (J). (gr. 3-6). 405.00 *(978-1-4042-2967-9(1))* Rosen Publishing Group, Inc., The.

Power Math Set 10. (J). (gr. k-5). 79.50 *(978-1-4042-3383-6(0))* Rosen Publishing Group, Inc., The.

Power Math Set 7. (Illus.). (J). (gr. 3-6). 135.00 *(978-1-4042-2974-7(4))* Rosen Publishing Group, Inc., The.

Power Math Set 8. (Illus.). (J). (gr. 3-6). 135.00 *(978-1-4042-2975-4(2))* Rosen Publishing Group, Inc., The.

Power Math Set 9. (Illus.). (J). (gr. 3-6). 135.00 *(978-1-4042-2976-1(0))* Rosen Publishing Group, Inc., The.

Practice Power School Bus Book: First Grade Mathematics. 2003. (Illus.). 24p. (J). (gr. k-1). spiral bd. *(978-1-930355-44-6(0))* Bright of America.

Pre-Algebra: EEdition. 2005. (gr. 6-12). cd-rom *(978-0-618-43339-1(2)*, 2-05812) Holt McDougal.

Pre-Algebra: ETutorial. 2005. (gr. 6-12). cd-rom *(978-0-618-43355-1(4)*, 2-05828); cd-rom *(978-0-618-43356-8(2)*, 2-05829); cd-rom *(978-0-618-43351-3(1)*, 2-05824) Holt McDougal.

Pre-Algebra: ETutorial Plus Online. 2005. (gr. 6-12). *(978-0-618-43357-5(0)*, 2-05830) Holt McDougal.

Pre-Algebra: EWorkbook Plus Online. 2005. (gr. 6-12). *(978-0-618-43358-2(9)*, 2-05831) Holt McDougal.

Pre-Algebra: Pupil's Edition. 2005. (McDougal Littell Math Ser.). (gr. 6-12). *(978-0-618-25003-5(4)*, 2-06006) Holt McDougal.

Pre-Algebra: Worked-Out Solution Key. 2005. (gr. 6-12). *(978-0-618-28044-5(8)*, 2-06114) Holt McDougal.

PRESS, Celebration. Fractals: The Art of Math. 2003. (ENG.). (J). (gr. 6-8). pap. 37.95 *(978-0-7652-3250-2(2)*, Celebration Pr.) Pearson Schl.

Priddy, Roger. Play & Learn with Wallace: Everyday Math. 2015. (Play & Learn with Wallace Ser.). (ENG.). 56p. (J). (gr. -1-1). spiral bd. 12.99 *(978-0-312-51872-1(2)*, 9780312518721, Priddy Bks.) St. Martin's Pr.

Primary Mathematics Intensive Practice U. S. Edition 1A. 2004. per. 8.50 *(978-1-932906-00-4(2))* SingaporeMath.com, Inc.

Primary Mathematics Intensive Practice U. S. Edition 1B. 2004. per. 8.50 *(978-1-932906-01-1(0))* SingaporeMath.com, Inc.

Primary Mathematics Intensive Practice U. S. Edition 2A. 2004. per. 8.50 *(978-1-932906-02-8(9))* SingaporeMath.com, Inc.

Primary Mathematics Intensive Practice U. S. Edition 2B. 2004. per. 8.50 *(978-1-932906-03-5(7))* SingaporeMath.com, Inc.

Primary Mathematics Intensive Practice U. S. Edition 3A. 2004. per. 8.50 *(978-1-932906-04-2(5))* SingaporeMath.com, Inc.

Primary Mathematics Intensive Practice U. S. Edition 3B. 2004. per. 8.50 *(978-1-932906-05-9(3))* SingaporeMath.com, Inc.

Primary Mathematics Intensive Practice U. S. Edition 4A. 2004. per. 8.50 *(978-1-932906-06-6(1))* SingaporeMath.com, Inc.

Primary Mathematics Intensive Practice U. S. Edition 4B. 2004. per. 8.50 *(978-1-932906-07-3(X))* SingaporeMath.com, Inc.

Primary Mathematics Intensive Practice U. S. Edition 5A. 2004. per. 8.50 *(978-1-932906-08-0(8))* SingaporeMath.com, Inc.

Primary Mathematics Intensive Practice U. S. Edition 5B. 2004. per. 8.50 *(978-1-932906-09-7(6))* SingaporeMath.com, Inc.

Primary Mathematics Intensive Practice U. S. Edition 6A. 2004. per. 8.50 *(978-1-932906-10-3(X))* SingaporeMath.com, Inc.

Primary Mathematics Intensive Practice U. S. Edition 6B. 2004. per. 8.50 *(978-1-932906-11-0(8))* SingaporeMath.com, Inc.

Primary Mathematics Teacher's Guide 3B. 2004. spiral bd. 21.00 *(978-0-9741573-5-1(X))* SingaporeMath.com, Inc.

Primmer, Rachel. Pentomino Piazza, Vol. 1. 2006. (J). 24.99 *(978-0-9787021-0-6(7)*, P001) Knowtivate, LLC.

Problem Solving. 2003. Level C. tchr. ed. 19.50 *(978-0-7652-1314-3(1))*Level C. stu. ed. 14.50 *(978-0-7652-1112-5(2))*Level D. tchr. ed. 19.50 *(978-0-7652-1318-1(4))*Level D. stu. ed. 14.50 *(978-0-7652-1306-8(0))*Level E. tchr. ed. 19.50 *(978-0-7652-1322-8(2))* Modern Curriculum Pr.

PUBLICATIONS, Dale Seymour. MCP Mathematics: Level A. 2004. (ENG.). (J). (gr. 1-1). pap., stu. ed. 28.50 *(978-0-7652-6056-7(5)*, Dale Seymour Publications) Pearson Schl.

—MCP Mathematics: Level B. 2004. (ENG.). (J). (gr. 2-3). pap., stu. ed. 28.50 *(978-0-7652-6058-1(1)*, Dale Seymour Publications) Pearson Schl.

—MCP Mathematics: Level C. 2004. (ENG.). (J). (gr. 3-3). pap., stu. ed. 28.50 *(978-0-7652-6060-4(3)*, Dale Seymour Publications) Pearson Schl.

—MCP Mathematics: Level F. 2004. (ENG.). (J). (gr. 6-6). pap., stu. ed. 28.50 *(978-0-7652-6066-6(2)*, Dale Seymour Publications) Pearson Schl.

Publications International Ltd. Staff, ed. Preschool Reading & Math Activities. 2010. 128p. 11.98 *(978-1-60553-180-9(4))* Publications International, Ltd.

QEB Maths Club National Book Stores Edition: Using Numbers Book 1. 2006. (J). per. *(978-1-59566-286-6(3))* QEB Publishing Inc.

QEB Maths Club National Book Stores Edition: Using Numbers Book 2. 2006. (J). per. *(978-1-59566-290-3(1))* QEB Publishing Inc.

Quadratische Gleichungen und Ungleichungen. (Duden-Schuelerhilfen Ser.). (GER.). 112p. (YA). (gr. 9). *(978-3-411-70102-5(1))* Bibliographisches Institut & F. A. Brockhaus AG DEU. Dist: International Bk. Import Service, Inc.

A Question of Math. 2004. (Illus.). lib. bdg. 5.95 *(978-0-8225-4440-1(7))* Lerner Publishing Group.

Rainbow Bridge Publishing Staff & Bosse, Nancy Rogers. Math Connection¿, Grade 3. 2004. (Connections(tm) Ser.). (ENG., Illus.). 160p. (gr. 3-3). pap. 9.95 *(978-1-887923-79-8(9))* Rainbow Bridge Publishing.

Randolph, Joanne. Math Exploration: Using Math to Learn about the Continents Set. 2015. (Math Exploration: Using Math to Learn about the Continents Ser.). (ENG.). 32p. (J). (gr. 3-4). 157.50 *(978-1-4994-0706-8(8)*, PowerKids Pr.) Rosen Publishing Group, Inc., The.

Rapoport, Rebecca & Yoder, J. Math Lab for Kids: Fun Projects for Learning about Shapes & Numbers. 2017. (Lab Ser.). (ENG., Illus.). 144p. (J). (gr. 2-5). pap. 24.99 *(978-1-63159-252-2(1)*, Quarry Bks.) Quarto Publishing Group USA.

Rasmussen, Steven & Key Curriculum Press Staff. Adding & Subtracting, BK. 3. 2012. (Key To... workbooks Ser.: Bk. 3). (ENG.). 40p. (gr. 6-8). spiral bd., wbk. ed. 5.64 *(978-0-913684-93-1(7)*, 0913684937) McGraw-Hill Education.

Rasmussen, Steven, et al. Percent Concepts, Bk. 1. 2012. (Key To... workbooks Ser.: Bk. 1). (ENG.). 48p. (gr. 6-8). spiral bd. 5.64 *(978-0-913684-57-3(0)*, 0913684570) McGraw-Hill Education.

—Percents & Decimals, Bk. 3. 2012. (Key To... workbooks Ser.: Bk. 3). (ENG.). 48p. (gr. 6-8). spiral bd. 5.64 *(978-0-913684-59-7(7)*, 0913684597) McGraw-Hill Education.

—Percents & Fractions, Bk. 2. 2012. (Key To... workbooks Ser.: Bk. 2). (ENG.). 48p. (gr. 6-8). spiral bd., wbk. ed. 5.64 *(978-0-913684-58-0(9)*, 0913684589) McGraw-Hill Education.

Rawlins, Jeanne & Rainbow Bridge Publishing Staff. Math Comprehension Grade 6. 2004. (Skill Builders Ser.). 80p. (gr. 6-18). pap. 3.99 *(978-1-932210-05-7(9))* Rainbow Bridge Publishing.

Reagan, Naomi. Butterflies & Moths: Represent & Interpret Data. 2014. (Rosen Common Core Math Readers Ser.). (ENG., Illus.). 24p. (J). (gr. 3-4). pap. 8.25 *(978-1-4777-4901-2(2)*, Rosen Classroom) Rosen Publishing Group, Inc., The.

Real World Math: Sports, 8 vols. Incl. Baseball. Minden, Cecilia. (Illus.). lib. bdg. 28.50 *(978-1-60279-243-2(7)*, 200194); Basketball. Minden, Cecilia. (Illus.). lib. bdg. 28.50 *(978-1-60279-245-6(3)*, 200196); Football. Marsico, Katie. (Illus.). lib. bdg. 28.50 *(978-1-60279-247-0(X)*, 200198); Running. Marsico, Katie. (Illus.). lib. bdg. 28.50 *(978-1-60279-249-4(6)*, 200032); Soccer. Minden, Cecilia. (Illus.). lib. bdg. 28.50 *(978-1-60279-244-9(5)*, 200195); Speed Skating. Marsico, Katie. lib. bdg. 28.50 *(978-1-60279-250-0(X)*, 200128); Swimming. Minden, Cecilia. (Illus.). lib. bdg. 28.50 *(978-1-60279-246-3(1)*, 200197); Tennis. Marsico, Katie. (Illus.). lib. bdg. 28.50 *(978-1-60279-248-7(8)*, 200127); (gr. 4-8). 32p. 2008. Set lib. bdg. 159.60 *(978-1-60279-289-0(5)*, 200185) Cherry Lake Publishing.

Recreational Mathematics, 3 vols. 2004. (Illus.). 497p. spiral bd. 45.75 *(978-1-931084-23-9(8))* Balloon Magic.

Reed, Janet. Parts of a Whole, 6 vols., Set. 2003. (Yellow Umbrella Early Level Ser.). (ENG.). 16p. (gr. k-1). pap. 35.70 *(978-0-7368-3012-6(X)*, Yellow Umbrella Bks.) Capstone Press of Coughlan Cos.

Reeves, Diane Lindsey. Career Ideas for Kids Who Like Math & Money. Bond, Nancy, illus. 2nd rev. ed. 2007. (Career Ideas for Kids Ser.). 208p. (gr. 4-9). 32.95 *(978-0-8160-6545-5(4)*, Ferguson Publishing Co.); per. 16.95 *(978-0-8160-6546-2(2)*, Checkmark Bks.) Facts On File, Inc.

Region 4 Education Service Center. Integrating Grade 11 TAKS Geometry Objectives into Algebra II Teacher Edition. 2004. (Region IV ESC Resources for Mathematics Ser.). pap. *(978-1-932797-70-1(X))* Region IV Education Service Ctr.

—Making Connection with Measurement, TAKS Preparation Grade 6 - Student Workbook - Spanish. 2004. (Region IV ESC Resources for Mathematics Ser.). pap. *(978-1-932797-67-1(X))* Region IV Education Service Ctr.

—Making Connections with Measurement, TAKS Preparation Grade 3 TAKS - Student Workbook - Spanish. 2004. (Region IV ESC Resources for Mathematics Ser.). pap. *(978-1-932797-64-0(5))* Region IV Education Service Ctr.

—Making Connections with Measurement, TAKS Preparation Grade 4 TAKS - Student Workbook - Spanish. 2004. (Region IV ESC Resources for Mathematics Ser.). pap. *(978-1-932797-65-7(3))* Region IV Education Service Ctr.

—Making Connections with Measurement, TAKS Preparation Grade 5 - Student Workbook - Spanish. 2004. (Region IV ESC Resources for Mathematics Ser.). pap. *(978-1-932797-66-4(1))* Region IV Education Service Ctr.

—TAKS Mathematics Preparation Grade 6 - Spanish. 2004. stu. ed., per., wbk. ed. *(978-1-932524-86-4(X))* Region IV Education Service Ctr.

Regrouping Skills (Gr. 2-3) 2003. (J). *(978-1-58232-085-4(3))* ECS Learning Systems, Inc.

Regrouping Skills Spanish Version. 2007. (J). per. *(978-1-58232-154-7(X))* ECS Learning Systems, Inc.

Renaissance Learning, Inc. Staff. Getting Started with Accelerated Math & Math Renaissance (Foundation & RP) Guide may be used by Foundation or RP Customers. 2004. 48p. per. 12.95 *(978-1-931819-55-8(6))* Renaissance Learning, Inc.

—Math Power Lessons for Grade 4: Instruction for Accelerated Math Objectives. 2004. 164p. spiral bd. 39.95 *(978-1-931819-53-4(X))* Renaissance Learning, Inc.

—Math Power Lessons for Grade 5: Instruction for Accelerated Math Objectives. 2004. 207p. spiral bd. 39.95 *(978-1-931819-54-1(8))* Renaissance Learning, Inc.

—STAR Math Made EZ (v 3. 1) RP: Quick Guide to the Software. 2004. 27p. spiral bd. 21.95 *(978-1-931819-40-4(8))* Renaissance Learning, Inc.

Research Masters Staff & Barron's Educational Staff. Barron's Common Core Success Grade 1 Math Workbook: Preparing Students for a Brilliant Future. 2015. (Barron's Common Core Success Ser.). (ENG., Illus.). 144p. (gr. 1-1). pap. 12.99 *(978-1-4380-0670-3(5))* Barron's Educational Series, Inc.

—Barron's Common Core Success Grade 2 Math Workbook: Preparing Students for a Brilliant Future. 2015. (Barron's Common Core Success Ser.). (ENG., Illus.). 144p. (gr. 2-2). pap. 12.99 *(978-1-4380-0672-7(1))* Barron's Educational Series, Inc.

Rice, Dona. Use Your Math Mind: Group It. 2015. (TIME for KIDS(r) Nonfiction Readers Ser.). (ENG., Illus.). 12p. (gr. k-k). 4.99 *(978-1-4938-2144-0(X))* Teacher Created Materials, Inc.

Richardson, Erik. Applying Functions to Everyday Life. 2016. (Applied Mathematics Ser.). (Illus.). 128p. (J). (gr. 9-9). 45.64 *(978-1-5026-1967-9(9))* Cavendish Square Publishing.

Ring, Susan. I See Shapes. 2005. (Emergent/Early (Prek-2) Math Package Ser.). 12p. (gr. -1-1). 25.20 *(978-0-8215-7843-8(X))* Sadlier, William H. Inc.

—Money Math, 6 vols., Set. 2003. (Yellow Umbrella Early Level Ser.). (ENG.). 16p. (gr. k-1). pap. 35.70 *(978-0-7368-3011-9(1)*, Yellow Umbrella Bks.) Capstone Press of Coughlan Cos.

—One Green Frog, 6 vols., Set. 2003. (Yellow Umbrella Early Level Ser.). (ENG.). 16p. (gr. k-1). pap. 35.70 *(978-0-7368-2994-6(6)*, Yellow Umbrella Bks.) Capstone Press of Coughlan Cos.

Ripley, Catherine. Great Math Ideas. 2007. (ENG., Illus.). 16p. (J). (gr. 2-2). pap. 9.47 net. *(978-0-7652-8598-0(3)*, Celebration Pr.) Pearson Schl.

Robinson, C. L. MATH1on1 Units of Measure. 2006. (YA). per. 9.99 *(978-0-9786767-4-2(2))* Robinson, Consuelo.

Robles, D. & Minquini, Lourdes. Los 100 Mejores Acertijos Matematicos (The One Hundred Best Word Problems) (SPA., Illus.). 151p. (J). (gr. k-6). pap. 7.95 *(978-968-416-820-6(9)*, FN8209) Fernandez USA Publishing.

Rock, Nathaniel. Math for Everyone Combo Book: 7th Grade Math, Algebra I, Geometry I, Algebra II, Math Analysis, Calculus. 2007. 480p. per. 49.99 *(978-1-59980-009-7(8))* Nathaniel Max Rock.

Rock, Nathaniel Max. Math Is Easy So Easy, Combo Book. 2008. 540p. pap. 59.99 *(978-1-59980-050-9(0))* Nathaniel Max Rock.

Rodgers, Linda. King Joe's Garden: Unit 2: Data Analysis, Statistics & Probability, 6 vols. l.t. ed. 2003. (Illus.). 88p. per. *(978-0-9728596-1-5(6))* King Joe Educational Enterprises, Inc.

Romaine, Claire. Matemáticas con Mascotas / Math with Pets. de la Vega, Eida, tr. 2016. (¡Matemáticas en Todas Partes! / Math Is Everywhere! Ser.). (ENG & SPA.). 24p. (gr. k-k). lib. bdg. 22.60 *(978-1-4824-5216-7(2))* Stevens, Gareth Publishing LLLP.

—Matemáticas en el Parque / Math at the Park. de la Vega, Eida, tr. 2016. (¡Matemáticas en Todas Partes! / Math Is Everywhere! Ser.). (ENG & SPA.). 24p. (gr. k-k). lib. bdg. 22.60 *(978-1-4824-5220-4(0))* Stevens, Gareth Publishing LLLP.

Romanek, Trudee. Science, Medicine, & Math in the Early Islamic World. 2012. (ENG.). 48p. (J). lib. bdg. *(978-0-7787-2170-3(1))* Crabtree Publishing Co.

Rookie Read-About Math, 8 bks., Set. Incl. Grouping at the Dog Show. Ribke, Simone T. lib. bdg. 20.50 *(978-0-516-24959-9(2))*; Guess the Order. Sargent, Brian. lib. bdg. 20.50 *(978-0-516-24963-6(0))*; How Much Does It Hold? Sargent, Brian. lib. bdg. 20.50 *(978-0-516-24957-5(6))*; Look & Count. Dalton, Julie. lib. bdg. 20.50 *(978-0-516-24958-2(4))*; Making Change at the Fair. Dalton, Julie. lib. bdg. 20.50 *(978-0-516-24960-5(6))*; Math Tools. Chrismer, Melanie. lib. bdg. 20.50 *(978-0-516-24961-2(4))*; Slumber Party Problem Solving. Sargent, Brian. lib. bdg. 20.50 *(978-0-516-24962-9(2))*; (Illus.). 32p. (J). (gr. 1-2). 2006. 2006. 156.00 o.p. *(978-0-516-25416-6(2)*, Children's Pr.) Scholastic Library Publishing.

Rooney, Anne. A Math Journey Through Planet Earth. 2014. (ENG.). 32p. (J). *(978-0-7787-0728-8(8))* Crabtree Publishing Co.

—A Math Journey Through Space. 2014. (ENG.). 32p. (J). *(978-0-7787-0730-1(X))* Crabtree Publishing Co.

—A Math Journey Through the Animal Kingdom. 2014. (ENG.). 32p. (J). *(978-0-7787-0732-5(6))* Crabtree Publishing Co.

—A Math Journey Through the Human Body. 2014. (ENG.). 32p. (J). *(978-0-7787-0734-9(2))* Crabtree Publishing Co.

—50 Amazing Things Kids Need to Know about Math. 2012. (ENG., Illus.). 192p. (J). (gr. 2-7). pap. 12.95 *(978-1-61608-507-0(X)*, 608507, Sky Pony Pr.) Skyhorse Publishing Co., Inc.

Roper, Dawn. 30 Fun Ways to Learn about Time & Money. 2011. (30 Fun Ways to Learn Ser.). (ENG.). 80p. (gr. -1-k). pap. 12.95 *(978-0-87659-370-7(8)*, Gryphon House Inc) Gryphon Hse., Inc.

Rosario, Miguel. Kitchen Math. 2015. (J). pap. *(978-1-62713-452-1(2))* Cavendish Square Publishing.

Rose, Mary. Week-by-Week Homework for Building Math Skills. 2006. (Week by Week Homework Ser.). (ENG., Illus.). 96p. pap. 13.99 *(978-0-439-53134-4(9)*, Teaching Resources) Scholastic, Inc.

Rosen Common Core Math Readers: Levels a - D. 2013. (Rosen Common Core Math Readers Ser.). 16p. (J). (gr. k-1). pap. 1683.00 *(978-1-4777-2214-5(9))*; pap. 280.50 *(978-1-4777-2213-8(0))* Rosen Publishing Group, Inc., The. (Rosen Classroom).

Rosen Common Core Math Readers: Levels d - I. 2013. (Rosen Common Core Math Readers Ser.). 24p. (J). (gr. 1-2). pap. 255.75 *(978-1-4777-2220-6(3))*; pap. 1534.50 *(978-1-4777-2219-0(X))* Rosen Publishing Group, Inc., The. (Rosen Classroom).

Rosen Common Core Math Readers: Levels I - L. 2014. (Rosen Common Core Math Readers Ser.). 24p. (J). (gr. 2-3). pap. 1683.00 *(978-1-4777-5170-1(X))*; pap. 280.50 *(978-1-4777-5171-8(8))* Rosen Publishing Group, Inc., The. (Rosen Classroom).

Rosen Common Core Math Readers: Levels I - O. 2014. (Rosen Common Core Math Readers Ser.). 24p. (J). (gr. 3-4). pap. 1534.50 *(978-1-4777-5172-5(6))*; pap. 255.75 *(978-1-4777-5173-2(4))* Rosen Publishing Group, Inc., The. (Rosen Classroom).

Rosen, Michael J. Mind-Boggling Numbers. Patton, Julia, illus. 2016. (ENG.). 32p. (gr. 2-5). 38.65 *(978-1-5124-1108-9(6)*, Millbrook Pr.) Lerner Publishing Group.

—Mind-Boggling Numbers: Math for the Curious. Patton, Julia, illus. 2016. (ENG.). 32p. (J). (gr. 2-5). 19.99 *(978-1-4677-3489-9(6)*, Millbrook Pr.) Lerner Publishing Group.

Rosen Publishing Staff. Infomax Common Core Math Readers: Levels I - L, 1 vol. 2015. (InfoMax Common Core Math Readers Ser.). (ENG.). 24p. (J). 280.50 *(978-1-4777-5175-6(0)*, Rosen Classroom) Rosen Publishing Group, Inc., The.

—Infomax Common Core Math Readers: Levels I - O, 1 vol. 2015. (InfoMax Common Core Math Readers Ser.). (ENG.). 24p. (J). 255.75 *(978-1-4777-5177-0(7)*, Rosen Classroom) Rosen Publishing Group, Inc., The.

—The Story of Math: Core Principles of Mathematics, 1 vol. 2015. (Story of Math Ser.). (ENG.). (YA). 190.20 *(978-1-62275-536-3(7)*, Britannica Educational Publishing) Rosen Publishing Group, Inc., The.

Rosenberg, Mary. Math Review, Grade 3. 2003. (Practice Makes Perfect Ser.). (ENG.). 48p. (gr. 3). pap. 5.99 *(978-0-7439-3743-6(0))* Teacher Created Resources, Inc.

—Math Review, Grade 4. 2003. (Practice Makes Perfect Ser.). (ENG.). 48p. (gr. 4). pap. 5.99 *(978-0-7439-3744-3(9))* Teacher Created Resources, Inc.

—Math Review, Grade 6. 2003. (Practice Makes Perfect Ser.). (ENG.). 48p. (gr. 6). pap. 5.99 *(978-0-7439-3746-7(5))* Teacher Created Resources, Inc.

—Place Value, Grade 2. 2004. (Practice Makes Perfect Ser.). (ENG.). 48p. pap. 5.99 *(978-0-7439-8602-1(4))* Teacher Created Resources, Inc.

Rosenberg, Mary & ROSENBERG, Mary. Math Review, Grade 5. 2003. (Practice Makes Perfect Ser.). (ENG., Illus.). 48p. (gr. 5). pap. 5.99 *(978-0-7439-3745-0(7))* Teacher Created Resources, Inc.

Rosenthal, Cynthia. Matt Does Math at the Ball Game. 2012. (InfoMax Readers Ser.). (ENG., Illus.). 24p. (J). (gr. 1-2). pap. 8.25 *(978-1-4488-9028-6(4)*, Rosen Classroom) Rosen Publishing Group, Inc., The.

Roy, Jennifer Rozines & Roy, Gregory. Holiday Fractions. 2005. (Math All Around Ser.). (Illus.). 32p. (gr. 2-7). lib. bdg. 29.93 *(978-0-7614-2001-9(0)*, Benchmark Bks.) Marshall Cavendish Corp.

—Math All Around, 6 bks., Set. Incl. Addition in the Forest. lib. bdg. 29.93 *(978-0-7614-2000-2(2))*; Holiday Fractions. lib. bdg. 29.93 *(978-0-7614-2001-9(0))*; Numbers on the Street. lib. bdg. 29.93 *(978-0-7614-2002-6(9))*; Patterns in Nature. lib. bdg. 29.93 *(978-0-7614-1999-0(3))*; Sorting at the Ocean. lib. bdg. 29.93 *(978-0-7614-1998-3(5))*; Subtraction at School. lib. bdg. 29.93 *(978-0-7614-2003-3(7))*; (Illus.). 32p. (gr. 2-7). (Math All Around Ser.). 2005. 179.57 *(978-0-7614-1997-6(7)*, Benchmark Bks.) Marshall Cavendish Corp.

—Math All Around Group 2, 6 bks., Set. Incl. Division with Toys. 32p. (gr. 2-7). lib. bdg. 29.93 *(978-0-7614-2269-3(2))*; Graphing in the Desert. 32p. (gr. 2-7). lib. bdg. 29.93 *(978-0-7614-2262-4(5))*; Measuring at Home. 32p. (gr. 2-7). lib. bdg. 29.93 *(978-0-7614-2263-1(3))*; Money at the Store. 32p. (gr. 2-7). lib. bdg. 29.93 *(978-0-7614-2264-8(1))*; Multiplication on the Farm. 32p. (gr. 2-7). lib. bdg. 29.93 *(978-0-7614-2268-6(4))*; Shapes in Transportation. 31p. (J). (gr. 3-7). lib. bdg. 29.93 *(978-0-7614-2265-5(X))*; (Illus.). 2006. 2007. Set lib. bdg. 179.57 *(978-0-7614-2261-7(7)*, Benchmark Bks.) Marshall Cavendish Corp.

—Patterns in Nature. 2005. (Math All Around Ser.). (Illus.). 32p. (gr. 2-7). lib. bdg. 29.93 *(978-0-7614-1999-0(3)*, Benchmark Bks.) Marshall Cavendish Corp.

Royce, Ron. At the Butterfly Conservatory: Represent & Interpret Data, 1 vol. 2015. (InfoMax Common Core Math Readers Ser.). (ENG.). 24p. (J). pap. 8.25 *(978-1-4777-4597-7(1)*, Rosen Classroom) Rosen Publishing Group, Inc., The.

Roza, Greg. An Optical Artist: Exploring Patterns & Symmetry. 2009. (PowerMath Ser.). (Illus.). 32p. (gr. 5-6). pap. 10.00 *(978-1-4042-5117-5(0))* Rosen Publishing Group, Inc., The.

—Space Math. (Reading Room Collection 2 Ser.). 24p. 2009. (gr. 3-4). 42.50 *(978-1-60851-989-7(9)*, PowerKids Pr.) 2003. (Illus.). (J). lib. bdg. 22.60 *(978-0-8239-3705-9(4))* Rosen Publishing Group, Inc., The.

Ruffin, Frances E. Let's Have a Bake Sale: Calculating Profit & Unit Cost. (PowerMath Ser.). (gr. 3-4). 2009. (ENG., Illus.). 224p. pap. 8.25 *(978-0-8239-8893-8(7)*, PowerKids Pr.) 2004. 24p. 43.95 *(978-0-8239-7645-4(9))* Rosen Publishing Group, Inc., The.

Safro, Jill. Math Word Problems Made Easy: Surefire Strategies-With 100+ Guided & Independent Practice Problems-That Give Kids the Tools to Tackle All Kinds of Word Problems. 2005. (Math Word Problems Made Easy Ser.). (ENG.). 80p. pap. 12.99 *(978-0-439-52974-7(3))*; pap. 12.99 *(978-0-439-52973-0(5))* Scholastic, Inc. (Teaching Resources).

Sain, Judy L. Daily Math SKills Review Grade 4: Practice for Mastery of Math Standards. 2004. (J). spiral bd. 22.00 *(978-1-929229-23-9(2))* aha! Process, Inc.

Salzmann, Mary Elizabeth. Money for Clothes, 1 vol. 2010. (Your Piggy Bank: A Guide to Spending & Saving for Kids! Ser.). (ENG.). 24p. (J). (gr. k-3). 27.07 *(978-1-61641-027-8(2))* Magic Wagon.

—Money for Entertainment, 1 vol. 2010. (Your Piggy Bank: A Guide to Spending & Saving for Kids! Ser.). (ENG., Illus.). 24p. (J). (gr. k-3). 27.07 *(978-1-61641-028-5(0))* Magic Wagon.

—Money for Food, 1 vol. 2010. (Your Piggy Bank: A Guide to Spending & Saving for Kids! Ser.). (ENG.). 24p. (J). (gr. k-3). 27.07 *(978-1-61641-029-2(9))* Magic Wagon.

—Money for Hobbies, 1 vol. 2010. (Your Piggy Bank: A Guide to Spending & Saving for Kids! Ser.). (ENG.). 24p. (J). (gr. k-3). 27.07 *(978-1-61641-030-8(2))* Magic Wagon.

—Money for School, 1 vol. 2010. (Your Piggy Bank: A Guide to Spending & Saving for Kids! Ser.). (ENG.). 24p. (J). (gr. k-3). 27.07 *(978-1-61641-031-5(0))* Magic Wagon.

—Money for Toys, 1 vol. 2010. (Your Piggy Bank: A Guide to Spending & Saving for Kids! Ser.). (ENG.). 24p. (J). (gr. k-3). 27.07 *(978-1-61641-032-2(9))* Magic Wagon.

Sanders, Nancy I. Cut & Paste Mini-Books: Math: 15 Fun, Interactive Mini-Books That Reinforce Key Math Concepts & Boost Reading Skills. 2010. (ENG.). 128p. (gr. k-1). pap. 16.99 *(978-0-439-60630-1(6)*, Teaching Resources) Scholastic, Inc.

Sandviks HOP, Inc. Staff. Hooked on First Grade. 2007. 39.99 *(978-1-60143-750-1(1))* HOP, LLC.

—Hooked on Kindergarten. 2007. 39.99 *(978-1-60143-788-4(9))* HOP, LLC.

Sargent, Brian. Places along the Way. 2006. (Rookie Read-About Math Ser.). (ENG., Illus.). 32p. (J). (gr. 1-2). 20.50 *(978-0-516-29917-4(4))* Scholastic Library Publishing.

Saunders, Hal. When Are We Ever Gonna Have to Use This? (Illus.). 14p. (J). (gr. k-6). 14.95 *(978-1-57232-364-3(7))* Seymour, Dale Pubns.

Saxon Manipulatives Kit. 2004. (gr. k-3). 64.50 *(978-0-01-210520-7(1))* Saxon Pubs., Inc.

Saxon Math 54 Answer Key & Test. 2004. 18.00 *(978-0-01-205170-2(5))* Saxon Pubs., Inc.

Saxon Math 54 Home Study Kit. 2004. 68.50 *(978-1-59141-331-8(1))* Saxon Pubs., Inc.

Saxon Math 65 Answer Key & Test. 2004. 18.00 *(978-0-01-205173-3(X))* Saxon Pubs., Inc.

Saxon Math 76 Answer Key & Test. 2004. 18.00 *(978-0-01-205176-4(4))* Saxon Pubs., Inc.

Saxon Math 87 Answer Key & Test. 2004. pap. 18.00 *(978-0-01-210332-6(2))* Saxon Pubs., Inc.

Saxon Math 87 Home Study Kit. 2004. 57.75 *(978-0-01-204723-1(6))* Saxon Pubs., Inc.

Saxon Publishers Staff & Hake, Stephen. Saxon Math 6/5 Homeschool Kit, 3 vols. rev. ed. 2004. 69.50 *(978-1-59141-348-6(6)*, 3486) Saxon Pubs., Inc.

Schieber, Jennifer. A contar en las Olimpiadas: Fiction-to-Fact Big Book. enl. ed. 2004. (SPA.). (J). pap. 26.00 *(978-1-4108-2360-1(1)*, 23601) Benchmark Education Co.

—Insects Measure Up! 2004. (Shared Connections Ser.). (J). instr.'s gde. ed. 34.00 net. *(978-1-4108-1610-8(9))* Benchmark Education Co.

Scholastic, Inc. Staff. Brain Play 1st-3rd. 2008. (J). 29.99 *(978-0-545-05207-8(6))* Scholastic, Inc.

—Brain Play Preschool-1st. 2008. (J). 29.99 *(978-0-439-81350-1(6))* Scholastic, Inc.

Scholastic, Inc. Staff, contrib. by. Early Math: 25 Ready-to-Go Manipulative Wheels That Help Children Practice & Master Key Early Math Skills. 2010. (ENG.). 112p. (gr. -1-1). 20.99 *(978-0-545-22376-8(8)*, Teaching Resources) Scholastic, Inc.

—Math Picture Puzzles for Little Learners: Dozens of Age-Perfect Practice Pages That Help Children Build Key Early Math Skills, Grades PreK-K. 2011. (ENG.). 48p. pap. 10.99 *(978-0-545-30068-1(1)*, Teaching Resources) Scholastic, Inc.

—Which Is Different? 2015. (Rookie Toddler(r) Ser.). (ENG.). 12p. (J). bds. 6.95 *(978-0-531-20572-3(X))* Scholastic Library Publishing.

—100 Day Count up Calendar with100 Open & Peek Door. 2003. (ENG.). 4p. (J). pap. 12.95 *(978-0-439-08248-8(X))* Scholastic, Inc.

School Mathematics Project. SMP Interact for Key Stage 3 Mathematics: Projectable PDFs for the T (Support) tier. 2009. (ENG.). cd-rom 189.00 *(978-0-521-15861-9(3))* Cambridge Univ. Pr.

School Zone, ed. Transition Math K-1. deluxe ed. 2004. (ENG.). 64p. (J). pap., wbk. ed. 3.99 *(978-1-58947-321-8(3)*, 02207) School Zone Publishing Co.

School Zone Interactive Staff. Math Basics. rev. ed. 2004. (ENG.). 64p. (J). (gr. k-2). wbk. ed. 15.99 *(978-1-58947-802-2(9))*; 15.99 *(978-1-58947-803-9(7))* School Zone Publishing Co.

School Zone Publishing. Math 1. 2003. (ENG.). cd-rom 19.99 *(978-1-58947-908-1(4))* School Zone Publishing Co.

—Math 2. 2003. (ENG.). cd-rom 19.99 *(978-1-58947-909-8(2))* School Zone Publishing Co.

—Math 3. 2003. (ENG.). cd-rom 19.99 *(978-1-58947-910-4(6))* School Zone Publishing Co.

—Multiplication & Division. 2003. (ENG.). (J). (gr. 3-4). cd-rom 19.99 *(978-1-58947-927-2(0))* School Zone Publishing Co.

School Zone Publishing Company Staff. Bilingual Math Basics 1. 2007. (ENG.). 64p. (J). pap. 3.99 *(978-1-58947-966-1(1))* School Zone Publishing Co.

—Bilingual Math Basics 2. 2007. (ENG.). 64p. (J). pap. 3.99 *(978-1-58947-967-8(X))* School Zone Publishing Co.

—Matematicas Basicas Math Basics. 2007. (ENG.). 64p. (J). (gr. k-3). pap. 2.69 *(978-1-58947-968-5(8))* School Zone Publishing Co.

—Math: Grades 5 & 6. (Illus.). (J). 19.99 incl. audio compact disk *(978-0-88743-953-7(5))* School Zone Publishing Co.

—Math 1-2 Software. 2004. (ENG.). 64p. (J). wbk. ed. 15.99 *(978-1-58947-369-0(8))* School Zone Publishing Co.

—Math 4. (Illus.). (J). 19.99 incl. audio compact disk *(978-0-88743-952-0(7))* School Zone Publishing Co.

—Math Readiness. 2007. (ENG.). 64p. (J). pap. 2.69 *(978-1-58947-964-7(5))* School Zone Publishing Co.

—Numbers Fun! Hours of Reusable Fun! rev. ed. 2005. (ENG.). 26p. (J). (gr. k-1). pap. 3.99 *(978-1-58947-786-5(3))* School Zone Publishing Co.

Schuette, Sarah L. Eating Pairs (Comer Pares) Counting Fruits & Vegetables by Two (Contar Frutas y Vegetales de DOS en DOS) 2012. (Vamos a Contar / Counting Bks.). (ENG, SPA & MUL.). 32p. (gr. 1-2). lib. bdg. 27.32 *(978-1-4296-8251-0(5)*, A+ Bilingue/Bilingual) Capstone Press of Coughlan Cos.

Schultz-Ferrell, Karren, et al. Introduction to Reasoning & Proof, Grades 3-5. 2007. (ENG., Illus.). 160p. (C). (gr. 3-5). pap. 36.25 *(978-0-325-01033-5(1)*, E01033) Heinemann.

Schwartz, David M. How Much Is a Million? Kellogg, Steven, illus. 20th anniv. ed. 2004. (Reading Rainbow Bks.). (ENG.). 40p. (J). (gr. -1-3). pap. 7.99 *(978-0-688-09933-6(5))* HarperCollins Pubs.

—How Much Is a Million? 2004. (J). (gr. k-3). 18.40 *(978-0-8085-7914-4(2)*, Turtleback) Turtleback Bks.

Schwartz, Linda. Math Quiz Whiz 3-5, Vol. 431. VanBlaricum, Pam, ed. Armstrong, Beverly, illus. 2004. 128p. (J). (gr. 3-5). pap. 10.99 *(978-0-88160-374-3(0)*, LW-431) Creative Teaching Pr., Inc.

—Primary Math Quiz Whiz, Vol. 428. VanBlaricum, Pam, ed. Mason, Mark, illus. 2004. 128p. (J). (gr. 1-3). pap. 14.99 *(978-0-88160-371-2(6)*, LW-428) Creative Teaching Pr., Inc.

Schweppe, Deirdre. Migrating Animals: Use Place Value Understanding & Properties of Operations to Add & Subtract. 2014. (Math Masters: Number & Operations in Base Ten Ser.). 24p. (J). (gr. 2-3). 23.60 *(978-1-4777-6434-3(8))*; (ENG.). pap. 8.25 *(978-1-4777-4751-3(6))* Rosen Publishing Group, Inc., The. (Rosen Classroom).

Sciarrino, Stephanie. Multiplication at the Marina: Multiply Within 100. 2014. (Rosen Common Core Math Readers Ser.). (Illus.). 24p. (J). (gr. 3-4). (ENG.). pap. 8.25 *(978-1-4777-4950-0(0))*; lib. bdg. 23.60 *(978-1-4777-6451-0(8))* Rosen Publishing Group, Inc., The. (PowerKids Pr.).

Scillian, Devin & Scillian, Corey. One Kansas Farmer: A Kansas Number Book. Bowles, Doug, illus. 2009. (Discover America State by State Ser.). (ENG.). 40p. (J). (gr. k-6). 16.95 *(978-1-58536-182-3(8))* Sleeping Bear Pr.

Scott Foresman - Addison Wesley Mathematics: Additional Resources. 2004. (gr. 1-18). *(978-0-328-07382-5(2))*; (gr. 2-18). *(978-0-328-07383-2(0))*; (gr. 3-18). *(978-0-328-07384-9(9))*; (gr. 3-4). *(978-0-328-08112-7(4))*; (gr. 4-18). *(978-0-328-07385-6(7))*; (gr. 5-18). *(978-0-328-07386-3(5))*; (gr. 6-18). *(978-0-328-07387-0(3))* Addison-Wesley Educational Pubs., Inc. (Scott Foresman).

Scott Foresman-Addison Wesley Mathematics. 2004. (gr. k-18). stu. ed. *(978-0-328-03015-6(5)*, Scott Foresman) Addison-Wesley Educational Pubs., Inc.

Scott Foresman-Addison Wesley Mathematics: Additional Resources. 2004. (gr. k-18). *(978-0-328-07549-2(3))*; (gr. k-18). *(978-0-328-08559-0(6))*; (gr. k-18). *(978-0-328-04989-9(1))*; (gr. k-18). *(978-0-328-04945-5(X))*; (gr. k-18). *(978-0-328-03816-9(4))*; (gr. k-5). *(978-0-328-08797-6(1))*; (gr. k-6). *(978-0-328-07636-9(8))*; (gr. k-6). *(978-0-328-06313-0(4))*; (gr. 1-18). *(978-0-328-03817-6(2))*; (gr. 1-18). *(978-0-328-07550-8(7))*; (gr. 1-18). *(978-0-328-08560-6(X))*; (gr. 1-18). *(978-0-328-04990-5(5))*; (gr. 1-18). *(978-0-328-04946-2(8))*; (gr. 2-18). *(978-0-328-08561-3(8))*; (gr. 2-18). *(978-0-328-04991-2(3))*; (gr. 2-18). *(978-0-328-03818-3(0))*; (gr. 2-18). *(978-0-328-07551-5(5))*; (gr. 2-18). *(978-0-328-04947-9(6))*; (gr. 3-18). *(978-0-328-08562-0(6))*; (gr. 3-18). *(978-0-328-09245-1(2))*; (gr. 3-18). *(978-0-328-04948-6(4))*; (gr. 3-18). *(978-0-328-07552-2(3))*; (gr. 3-18). *(978-0-328-03819-0(9))*; (gr. 3-18). *(978-0-328-04992-9(1))*; (gr. 3-4). *(978-0-328-07619-2(8))*; (gr. 4-18). *(978-0-328-04949-3(2))*; (gr. 4-18). *(978-0-328-07553-9(1))*; (gr. 4-18). *(978-0-328-03820-6(2))*; (gr. 4-18). *(978-0-328-09246-8(0))*; (gr. 4-18). *(978-0-328-08563-7(4))*; (gr. 4-18). *(978-0-328-05007-9(5))*; (gr. 5-18). *(978-0-328-08564-4(2))*; (gr. 5-18). *(978-0-328-03821-3(0))*; (gr. 5-18). *(978-0-328-09247-5(9))*; (gr. 5-18). *(978-0-328-04950-9(6))*; (gr. 5-18). *(978-0-328-04993-6(X))*; (gr. 5-18). *(978-0-328-07554-6(X))*; (gr. 5-6). *(978-0-328-07620-8(1))*; (gr. 6-18). *(978-0-328-03822-0(9))*; (gr. 6-18). *(978-0-328-09248-2(7))*; (gr. 6-18). *(978-0-328-08565-1(0))*; (gr. 6-18). *(978-0-328-04951-6(4))*; (gr. 6-18). *(978-0-328-07555-3(8))*; (gr. 6-18). *(978-0-328-04994-3(8))* Addison-Wesley Educational Pubs., Inc. (Scott Foresman).

Scott Foresman-Addison Wesley Mathematics: Assessment, Diagnosis, & Intervention. 2004. (gr. k-18). *(978-0-328-05519-7(0))*; (gr. 1-18). *(978-0-328-06131-0(X))*; (gr. 1-18). *(978-0-328-05520-3(4))*; (gr. 1-18). *(978-0-328-06125-9(5))*; (gr. 1-18). *(978-0-328-09313-7(0))*; (gr. 2-18). *(978-0-328-05521-0(2))*; (gr. 2-18). *(978-0-328-06132-7(8))*; (gr. 2-18). *(978-0-328-06126-6(3))*; (gr. 2-18). *(978-0-328-09314-4(9))*; (gr. 3-18). *(978-0-328-06137-2(9))*; (gr. 3-18). *(978-0-328-06133-4(6))*; (gr. 3-18). *(978-0-328-09315-1(7))*; (gr. 3-18). *(978-0-328-06127-3(1))*; (gr. 3-18). *(978-0-328-05522-7(0))*; (gr. 4-18). *(978-0-328-09316-8(5))*; (gr. 4-18). *(978-0-328-06138-9(7))*; (gr. 4-18). *(978-0-328-05523-4(9))*; (gr. 4-18). *(978-0-328-06134-1(4))*; (gr. 4-18). *(978-0-328-06128-0(X))*; (gr. 5-18). *(978-0-328-06139-6(5))*; (gr. 5-18). *(978-0-328-06129-7(8))*; (gr. 5-18). *(978-0-328-06135-8(2))*; (gr. 5-18). *(978-0-328-09317-5(3))*; (gr. 5-18). *(978-0-328-05524-1(7))*; (gr. 6-18). *(978-0-328-06136-5(0))*; (gr. 6-18). *(978-0-328-09318-2(1))*; (gr. 6-18). *(978-0-328-06140-2(9))*; (gr. 6-18). *(978-0-328-05525-8(5))*; (gr. 6-18). *(978-0-328-06130-3(1))* Addison-Wesley Educational Pubs., Inc. (Scott Foresman).

Scott Foresman-Addison Wesley Mathematics: Pre-K Mathematics. 2004. (Scott Foresman Addison Wesley Math Ser.). (gr. -1-18). *(978-0-328-09243-7(6))*; *(978-0-328-08088-5(8))*; *(978-0-328-09227-7(4))*; *(978-0-328-08086-1(1))*; *(978-0-328-09366-3(1))*; *(978-0-328-09168-3(5))*; *(978-0-328-09244-4(4))*; *(978-0-328-09229-1(0))*; *(978-0-328-09365-6(3))*; *(978-0-328-09228-4(2))*; tchr. ed. *(978-0-328-08087-8(X))* Addison-Wesley Educational Pubs., Inc. (Scott Foresman).

Scott Foresman-Addison Wesley Mathematics: Pupil Edition, 4 vols. 2004. (gr. k-18). *(978-0-328-07587-4(6)*, Scott Foresman) Addison-Wesley Educational Pubs., Inc.

Scott Foresman-Addison Wesley Mathematics: Technology. 2004. (gr. k-18). *(978-0-328-08602-3(9))*; (gr. k-18). E-Book incl. cd-rom *(978-0-328-08566-8(9))*; (gr. 1-18). *(978-0-328-08603-0(7))*; (gr. 1-18). *(978-0-328-09350-2(5))*; (gr. 1-18). E-Book incl. cd-rom *(978-0-328-08567-5(7))*; (gr. 1-18). cd-rom *(978-0-328-08579-8(0))*; (gr. 1-18). cd-rom *(978-0-328-08591-0(X))*; (gr. 1-18). cd-rom *(978-0-328-07764-9(X))*; (gr. 2-18). *(978-0-328-08604-7(5))*; (gr. 2-18). *(978-0-328-09351-9(3))*; (gr. 2-18). E-Book incl. cd-rom *(978-0-328-08568-2(5))*; (gr. 2-18). cd-rom *(978-0-328-08592-7(8))*; (gr. 2-18). cd-rom

MNO

(978-0-328-07765-6(8)); (gr. 2-18). cd-rom (978-0-328-08580-4(4)); (gr. 3-18). (978-0-328-08605-4(3)); (gr. 3-18). (978-0-328-09352-6(1)); (gr. 3-18). E-Book incl. cd-rom (978-0-328-08569-9(3)); (gr. 3-18). cd-rom (978-0-328-08581-1(2)); (gr. 3-18). cd-rom (978-0-328-07766-3(6)); (gr. 3-18). cd-rom (978-0-328-08593-4(6)); (gr. 4-18). (978-0-328-08606-1(1)); (gr. 4-18). (978-0-328-09353-3(X)); (gr. 4-18). E-Book incl. cd-rom (978-0-328-08570-5(7)); (gr. 4-18). cd-rom (978-0-328-08582-8(0)); (gr. 4-18). cd-rom (978-0-328-07767-0(4)); (gr. 4-18). cd-rom (978-0-328-08594-1(4)); (gr. 4-6). (978-0-328-09311-3(4)); (gr. 4-6). (978-0-328-09312-0(2)); (gr. 5-18). (978-0-328-09354-0(8)); (gr. 5-18). (978-0-328-08607-8(X)); (gr. 5-18). E-Book incl. cd-rom (978-0-328-08571-2(5)); (gr. 5-18). cd-rom (978-0-328-07768-7(2)); (gr. 5-18). cd-rom (978-0-328-08583-5(9)); (gr. 5-18). cd-rom (978-0-328-08595-8(2)); (gr. 6-18). (978-0-328-09355-7(6)); (gr. 6-18). (978-0-328-08608-5(8)); (gr. 6-18). E-Book incl. cd-rom (978-0-328-08572-9(3)); (gr. 6-18). cd-rom (978-0-328-07769-4(0)); (gr. 6-18). cd-rom (978-0-328-08584-2(7)); (gr. 6-18). cd-rom (978-0-328-08596-5(0)) Addison-Wesley Educational Pubs., Inc. (Scott Foresman).

Scott Foresman-Addison Wesley Mathematics: Workbooks. 2004. (gr. 1-18). wbk. ed. (978-0-328-04965-3(4), Scott Foresman) Addison-Wesley Educational Pubs., Inc.

Scott Foresman Math Around the Clock. 2003. (Scott Foreman Math Around the Clock Ser.). (gr. 1-18). (978-0-328-07264-4(8)); (gr. 1-18). tchr. ed. (978-0-328-06304-8(5)); (gr. 1-2). (978-0-328-01697-6(7)); (gr. 2-18). (978-0-328-07265-1(6)); (gr. 2-18). tchr. ed. (978-0-328-06305-5(3)); (gr. 3-18). (978-0-328-07266-8(4)); (gr. 3-18). tchr. ed. (978-0-328-06306-2(1)); (gr. 3-4). (978-0-328-01698-3(5)); (gr. 4-18). (978-0-328-07267-5(2)); (gr. 4-18). tchr. ed. (978-0-328-06307-9(X)); (gr. 4-18). wbk. ed. (978-0-328-06452-6(1)); (gr. 5-18). (978-0-328-07268-2(0)); (gr. 5-18). tchr. ed. (978-0-328-06308-6(8)); (gr. 5-6). (978-0-328-01880-2(5)); (gr. 6-18). (978-0-328-07269-9(9)); (gr. 6-18). tchr. ed. (978-0-328-06309-3(6)) Addison-Wesley Educational Pubs., Inc. (Scott Foresman).

Scott, Kimberley, illus. Wipe-Clean First Math. 2014. (ENG.). (J). (gr. k-4). pap. 7.99 (978-0-7945-3354-0(X), Usborne) EDC Publishing.

Segal, Kevin & Levy, Nathan. 101 Things Everyone Should Know about Math — TEST BOOKLET. 2009. (101 Things Everyone Should Know Ser.). (ENG., Illus.). 16p. (YA). 2.95 (978-0-9678020-2-2(4)) Science, Naturally!

Seymour, Dale. Balanced Assessment for the Mathematics Curriculum. 2003. (Illus.). 184p. (J). (gr. 3-5). 42.95 (978-0-7690-0063-3(0));Package 2. 42.95 (978-0-7690-0064-0(9)) Seymour, Dale Pubns.

—Developing Skills in Estimation, Bk. A. 55p. (J). (gr. 7-8). 14.95 net. (978-0-86651-010-3(9), DSO1161) Seymour, Dale Pubns.

Sganga, Francis. Introducing Gifted Students to the Wonders of Mathematics: Preparation for High School & Higher Mathematics, Grades 4-8. 2004. (Illus.). 75p. (978-0-910609-47-0(0)) Gifted Education Pr.

Shae, Jordan. Handy Measuring: Measure Lengths. 2013. (InfoMax Math Readers Ser.). (ENG.). 24p. (J). (gr. 1-2). pap. 49.50 (978-1-4777-2202-2(5)); pap. 8.25 (978-1-4777-2201-5(7)) Rosen Publishing Group, Inc., The. (Rosen Classroom).

Shah, Keiran. Making Pictographs. 2014. (Graph It! Ser.). 24p. (J). (gr. 1-3). 22.60 (978-1-4824-0839-3(2)) Stevens, Gareth Publishing LLLP.

Shakes, Suzanna, et al. Maths in Practice Year 8, Bk. 1. 2009. (Illus.). 204p. stu. ed. 39.59 (978-0-340-94858-3(2)) Hodder Education Group GBR. Dist: Trans-Atlantic Pubns., Inc.

Shakes, Suzanne, et al. Maths in Practice. 2009. (Dynamic Learning Ser.). (Illus.). Bk. 2. 244p. stu. ed. 36.50 (978-0-340-94859-0(0))Bk. 3. 284p. stu. ed. 39.50 (978-0-340-94860-6(4)) Hodder Education Group GBR. Dist: Trans-Atlantic Pubns., Inc.

—Maths in Practice Year 7, 4 vols. 2009. Bk. 1. (Illus.). stu. ed. 37.50 (978-0-340-94848-4(5))Bk. 2. stu. ed. 37.50 (978-0-340-94849-1(3))Bk. 3. (Illus.). 37.50 (978-0-340-94850-7(7)) Hodder Education Group GBR. Dist: Trans-Atlantic Pubns., Inc.

Shaskan, Trisha Speed. If You Were a Divided-By Sign, 1 vol. Dillard, Sarah, illus. 2009. (Math Fun Ser.). (ENG.). 24p. (gr. 2-4). pap. 7.95 (978-1-4048-5196-2(8)); lib. bdg. 27.99 (978-1-4048-5195-5(X)) Picture Window Bks.

—If You Were a Minus Sign [LTD Commodities]. Carabelli, Francesca, illus. 2010. (Math Fun Ser.). 24p. pap. 3.50 (978-1-4048-6256-2(0), Nonfiction Picture Bks.) Picture Window Bks.

—If You Were a Minus Sign [Scholastic]. Carabelli, Francesca, illus. 2010. (Math Fun Ser.). 24p. pap. 0.52 (978-1-4048-6173-2(4), Nonfiction Picture Bks.) Picture Window Bks.

—If You Were a Plus Sign, 1 vol. Carabelli, Francesca, illus. 2008. (Math Fun Ser.). (ENG.). 24p. (gr. 2-4). 27.99 (978-1-4048-4784-2(7)) Picture Window Bks.

—If You Were a Plus Sign [LTD Commodities]. Carabelli, Francesca, illus. 2010. (Math Fun Ser.). 24p. pap. 3.50 (978-1-4048-6257-9(9), Nonfiction Picture Bks.) Picture Window Bks.

—If You Were a Plus Sign [Scholastic]. Carabelli, Francesca, illus. 2010. (Math Fun Ser.). 24p. pap. 0.52 (978-1-4048-6172-5(6), Nonfiction Picture Bks.) Picture Window Bks.

—If You Were a Times Sign, 1 vol. Dillard, Sarah, illus. 2009. (Math Fun Ser.). (ENG.). 24p. (gr. 2-4). pap. 7.95 (978-1-4048-5211-2(5)); lib. bdg. 27.99 (978-1-4048-5210-5(7)) Picture Window Bks.

Shea, Bobby Kennedy. Patterns with Pandas. 2013. (Animal Math Ser.). 24p. (J). (gr. 1-3). pap. 48.90 (978-1-4339-9320-6(1)); (ENG., Illus.). lib. bdg. 22.60 (978-1-4339-9318-3(X)) Stevens, Gareth Publishing LLLP.

Shea, Bobby Kennedy & Kennedy Shea, Bobby. Patterns with Pandas. 2013. 24p. (J). (gr. 1-3). pap. 8.15 (978-1-4339-9319-0(8)) Stevens, Gareth Publishing LLLP.

Shea, Mary Molly. Making Line Graphs. 2014. (Graph It! Ser.). 24p. (J). (gr. 1-3). 22.60 (978-1-4824-0834-8(1)) Stevens, Gareth Publishing LLLP.

Shea, Therese. Biosphere 2: Solving Word Problems. (PowerMath Ser.). 32p. 2009. (ENG., Illus.). (gr. 5-6). pap. 10.00 (978-1-4042-5150-2(2), PowerKids Pr.) 2009. (gr. 4-5). 47.90 (978-1-60851-406-9(4), PowerKids Pr.) 2005. (Illus.). (YA). (gr. 5-9). lib. bdg. 25.25 (978-1-4042-2943-3(4)) Rosen Publishing Group, Inc., The.

—Climbing Mount Everest: Understanding Commutative, Associative, & Distributive Properties. (PowerMath Ser.). (Illus.). 32p. (gr. 5-6). 2009. (ENG.). pap. 10.00 (978-1-4042-5142-7(1), PowerKids Pr.) 2005. (YA). lib. bdg. 25.25 (978-1-4042-2939-6(6)) Rosen Publishing Group, Inc., The.

—Climbing Mount Everest: Understanding Commutative, Associative & Distributive Properties. 2009. (PowerMath: Proficiency Plus Ser.). 32p. (gr. 4-5). 47.90 (978-1-60851-408-3(0), PowerKids Pr.) Rosen Publishing Group, Inc., The.

—The Great Barrier Reef: Using Graphs & Charts to Solve Word Problems. 2009. (PowerMath: Advanced Proficiency Plus Ser.). 32p. (gr. 5-5). 47.90 (978-1-60851-367-3(X), PowerKids Pr.) Rosen Publishing Group, Inc., The.

Sheen, Barbara. Careers If You Like Math. 2016. (ENG.). 80p. (YA). (gr. 5-12). (978-1-68282-004-9(1)) ReferencePoint Pr., Inc.

Sherratt, Andrew. International Mathematics, Bk. 2. 2009. (Illus.). 264p. pap. 39.50 (978-0-340-96743-0(9)); 48p. pap., wbk. ed. 19.50 (978-0-340-96749-2(8)) Hodder Education Group GBR. Dist: Trans-Atlantic Pubns., Inc.

Shieber, Jennifer. Insects Measure Up! Small Book. 2004. (Shared Connections Ser.). (J). pap. (978-1-4108-1634-4(6)) Benchmark Education Co.

Shiotsu, Vicky. Preschool Math: Learning Basic Concepts Through Experimenting & Play. 2006. (Early Learning Ser.). (Illus.). 128p. (J). (gr. -1-1). per. 13.99 (978-1-59198-224-1(3), 2567) Creative Teaching Pr., Inc.

Show What You Know Publishing, ed. Show What You Know on the CSAP for Grade 6, Mathematics Student Workbook. 2007. (J). per. 14.95 (978-1-59230-238-3(6)) Englefield & Assocs., Inc.

Sikkens, Crystal. Bar Graphs. 2016. (Get Graphing! Building Data Literacy Skills Ser.). (ENG., Illus.). 24p. (J). (gr. k-3). (978-0-7787-2624-1(X)) Crabtree Publishing Co.

—Picture Graphs. 2016. (Get Graphing! Building Data Literacy Skills Ser.). (ENG., Illus.). 24p. (J). (gr. k-3). (978-0-7787-2632-6(0)) Crabtree Publishing Co.

Silbey, Robyn. Math Hooks. 2004. (Illus.). 80p. (gr. 1). pap. 10.95 (978-0-673-58916-3(1)); (gr. 2). pap. 10.95 (978-0-673-58917-0(X)) Good Year Bks.

Simonds, Lucy. Celebrations. 2007. (Trackers-Math Ser.). (gr. 2-5). pap. 5.00 (978-1-59055-919-2(3)) Pacific Learning, Inc.

—Indoor Sports. 2007. (Trackers-Math Ser.). (gr. 2-5). pap. 5.00 (978-1-59055-921-5(5)) Pacific Learning, Inc.

—The Olympics. 2007. (Trackers-Math Ser.). (gr. 2-5). pap. 5.00 (978-1-59055-911-6(8)) Pacific Learning, Inc.

—People & Pets. 2007. (Trackers-Math Ser.). (gr. 2-5). pap. 5.00 (978-1-59055-920-8(7)) Pacific Learning, Inc.

—The Sky Is the Limit. 2007. (Trackers-Math Ser.). (gr. 2-5). pap. 5.00 (978-1-59055-922-2(3)) Pacific Learning, Inc.

—Wonders of the World. 2007. (Trackers-Math Ser.). (gr. 2-5). pap. 5.00 (978-1-59055-925-3(8)) Pacific Learning, Inc.

Simons, Lisa M. Bolt. Unusual & Awesome Jobs Using Math: Stunt Coordinator, Cryptologist, & More. 2015. (You Get Paid for THAT? Ser.). (ENG., Illus.). 32p. (gr. 3-4). 27.99 (978-1-4914-2030-0(8)) Capstone Press of Coughlan Cos.

Simons, Rae. Business Math. 2013. (Math 24/7 Ser.: 10). 48p. (J). (gr. 5-18). 19.95 (978-1-4222-2903-3(3)) Mason Crest.

Simpson, Audrey. Cambridge O Level Mathematics: Volume 2. 2012. (ENG.). 495p. pap. 26.20 (978-0-521-18605-6(6)) Cambridge Univ. Pr.

Simpson, Jeff. Sharing Big Numbers, 2nd Edition, Student Edition: Count, Notice & Remember Math Intervention Volume I, MD-2. Simpson, Marilyn, ed. 2nd ed. 2007. (Count, Notice & Remember Ser.: Volume I, MD-2). ring bd. 50.00 (978-1-888976-44-1(6)) Mastery Learning Systems.

Simpson, Marilyn Bohlen, ed. Percents, Ratios, & Rates, Student Edition: Count, Notice & Remember Math Intervention, Volume 3. 2007. ring bd. 59.95 (978-1-888976-50-2(0)) Mastery Learning Systems.

Skinner, Anna. Maths Outside & in for the Early Years Foundation Stage, Vol. 7. 2014. (ENG.). 104p. pap. 55.00 (978-1-906224-92-9(7)) Oxford Univ. Pr., Inc.

Smith, Jodene. Cut & Paste - Math, Grades 1-3. 2003. (ENG.). 96p. pap. 12.99 (978-0-7439-3708-5(2)) Teacher Created Resources, Inc.

Smith, Paula & Colozza Cocca, Lisa. Calendar Math. 2013. (ENG.). 24p. (J). (978-0-7787-1075-2(0)); pap. (978-0-7787-1091-2(2)) Crabtree Publishing Co.

—Time Word Problems. 2013. (ENG.). 24p. (J). (978-0-7787-1077-6(7)); pap. (978-0-7787-1093-6(9)) Crabtree Publishing Co.

Smith, Paula & Mason, Helen. Length Word Problems. 2013. (ENG.). 24p. (J). (978-0-7787-1079-0(3)); pap. (978-0-7787-1095-0(5)) Crabtree Publishing Co.

—Word Problems: Mass & Volume. 2013. (ENG., Illus.). 24p. (J). (978-0-7787-1081-3(5)); pap. (978-0-7787-1097-4(1)) Crabtree Publishing Co.

Solodar, Marisol. Bailey's Band: Develop Understanding of Fractions & Numbers, 1 vol. 2015. (InfoMax Common Core Math Readers Ser.). (ENG.). 24p. (J). pap. 8.25 (978-1-4777-4618-9(8), Rosen Classroom) Rosen Publishing Group, Inc., The.

Solve It! Math in Space. 2016. (Solve It! Math in Space Ser.). 24p. (gr. 3-2). pap. 48.90 (978-1-4824-5325-6(8)); lib. bdg. 135.60 (978-1-4824-4602-9(2)) Stevens, Gareth Publishing LLLP.

Somervill, Barbara A. Hurricanes. 2012. (21st Century Skills Library: Real World Math Ser.). (ENG., Illus.). 32p. (J). (gr. 4-8). pap. 14.21 (978-1-61080-408-0(2), 201340); lib. bdg. 28.50 (978-1-61080-325-0(6), 201302) Cherry Lake Publishing.

Soriano, Al. Excursions Gr 1 Sp. 2004. (Voyages Ser.). (J). (gr. 1). stu. ed., per. 10.55 (978-1-58830-875-7(8)) Metropolitan Teaching & Learning Co.

—Excursions Gr 2 Sp. 2004. (Voyages Ser.). (J). (gr. 2). stu. ed., per. 10.55 (978-1-58830-876-4(6)) Metropolitan Teaching & Learning Co.

—Excursions Gr 3 Sp. 2004. (Voyages Ser.). (J). (gr. 3). stu. ed., per. 10.55 (978-1-58830-877-1(4)) Metropolitan Teaching & Learning Co.

—Excursions Grade 1. 2003. (Voyages Ser.). (J). (gr. 1). stu. ed., per. 8.95 (978-1-58830-612-8(7)) Metropolitan Teaching & Learning Co.

—Excursions Grade 2. 2003. (Voyages Ser.). (J). (gr. 2). stu. ed., per. 8.95 (978-1-58830-627-2(5)) Metropolitan Teaching & Learning Co.

—Excursions Grade 3. 2003. (Voyages Ser.). (J). (gr. 3). stu. ed., per. 8.95 (978-1-58830-628-9(3)) Metropolitan Teaching & Learning Co.

—Excursions Grade 4. 2003. (Voyages Ser.). (J). (gr. 4). stu. ed., per. 8.95 (978-1-58830-629-6(1)) Metropolitan Teaching & Learning Co.

—Excursions Grade 5. 2003. (Voyages Ser.). (J). (gr. 5). stu. ed., per. 8.95 (978-1-58830-630-2(5)) Metropolitan Teaching & Learning Co.

—Metro Math Voyages Kindergarten Kit Sp. 2004. (Voyages Ser.). (J). (gr. k). 474.75 (978-1-58830-977-8(0)) Metropolitan Teaching & Learning Co.

—Voyages Gr 1 Student Kit Sp. 2004. (Voyages Ser.). (J). (gr. 1). 31.37 (978-1-58830-980-8(0)) Metropolitan Teaching & Learning Co.

—Voyages Gr 2 Student Kit Sp. 2004. (Voyages Ser.). (J). (gr. 2). 31.37 (978-1-58830-981-5(9)) Metropolitan Teaching & Learning Co.

—Voyages Gr 3 Student Kit Sp. 2004. (Voyages Ser.). (J). (gr. 3). 31.37 (978-1-58830-982-2(7)) Metropolitan Teaching & Learning Co.

—Voyages Grade 2 Complete Program Sp. 2005. (Voyages Ser.). (J). (gr. 2). 758.67 (978-1-58830-868-9(5)) Metropolitan Teaching & Learning Co.

—Voyages Grade 3 Complete Program Sp. 2005. (Voyages Ser.). (J). (gr. 3). 758.67 (978-1-58830-869-6(3)) Metropolitan Teaching & Learning Co.

—Voyages Kinder Sp Activity Cards Deck a Sp. 2004. (Voyages Ser.). (J). (gr. k). 62.85 (978-1-58830-974-7(6)) Metropolitan Teaching & Learning Co.

—Voyages Kinder Sp Activity Cards Deck B Sp. 2004. (Voyages Ser.). (J). (gr. k). 26.45 (978-1-58830-973-0(8)) Metropolitan Teaching & Learning Co.

—Voyages Kinder Sp Student. 2004. (Voyages Ser.). (J). (gr. k). per., act. bk. ed. 13.73 (978-1-58830-975-4(4)) Metropolitan Teaching & Learning Co.

Somson, Bob. Essential Math Skills: Over 250 Activities to Develop Deep Learning, 1 vol. rev. ed. 2014. (Classroom Resources Ser.). (ENG., Illus.). 168p. (gr. -1-3). pap. 24.99 (978-1-4258-1211-9(2)) Shell Educational Publishing.

—Math Moms & Dads Home Program: Developing Symbolic Math Skills for Ages 5 to 8. 2004. 10.00 (978-0-9755415-1-7(X)) Early Learning Foundation, LLC.

Somson, Robert. The Math Moms & Dads Home Program: Preschool & Kindergarten Level, for ages 3 to 6. 2004. (978-0-9755415-0-0(1)) Early Learning Foundation, LLC.

Sort It Out! 2015. (Sort It Out! Ser.). (ENG.). 24p. (J). (gr. k-1). 135.60 (978-1-4824-2538-3(6)); pap., pap., pap. 48.90 (978-1-4824-3494-1(6)); pap., pap., pap. 293.40 (978-1-4824-3493-4(8)) Stevens, Gareth Publishing LLLP.

Souviney, Randall. Solving Math Problems Kids Care About. 2nd ed. 2005. (Illus.). 140p. (YA). (gr. 9-14). per. 14.95 (978-1-59647-061-3(5)) Good Year Bks.

Souviney, Randall J., et al. Mathematical Investigations, Bk. 3. 208p. (J). 24.95 net. (978-0-86651-585-6(2), DS21145) Seymour, Dale Pubns.

Spangler, David. Mathematics Explorations. 2007. 112p. (gr. 6-10). per. 9.95 (978-1-59647-254-9(5)) Good Year Bks.

Spanish TAKS MASTER Math, Gr. 5. 2004. (J). (978-1-57022-473-7(0)) ECS Learning Systems, Inc.

Spanish TAKS MASTER Math, Gr. 6. 2004. (J). (978-1-57022-501-7(X)) ECS Learning Systems, Inc.

Spanish TAKS MASTER Math Grade 3. 2004. (978-1-57022-466-9(8)) ECS Learning Systems, Inc.

Spanish TAKS MASTER Math Grade 4. 2004. (978-1-57022-467-6(6)) ECS Learning Systems, Inc.

Spectrum, compiled by. Spectrum Math & Language Arts Kit, Grade 3. 2013. (Spectrum Ser.). (ENG.). 12p. (gr. 3-3). 18.99 (978-1-4838-0199-5(3), Spectrum) Carson-Dellosa Publishing, LLC.

—Spectrum Math & Language Arts Kit, Grade 4. 2013. (Spectrum Ser.). (ENG.). 12p. (gr. 4-4). 18.99 (978-1-4838-0200-8(0), Spectrum) Carson-Dellosa Publishing, LLC.

—Spectrum Math & Language Arts Kit, Grade 5. 2013. (Spectrum Ser.). (ENG.). 12p. (gr. 5-5). 18.99 (978-1-4838-0201-5(9), Spectrum) Carson-Dellosa Publishing, LLC.

—Spectrum Math & Language Arts Kit, Grade 6. 2013. (Spectrum Ser.). (ENG.). 12p. (gr. 6-6). 18.99 (978-1-4838-0202-2(7), Spectrum) Carson-Dellosa Publishing, LLC.

Spooky Math. 2015. (Spooky Math Ser.: 6). (ENG.). 32p. (J). (gr. -1-3). lib. bdg. 159.60 (978-1-62724-329-2(1)) Bearport Publishing Co., Inc.

Stanley, Anne, illus. Listen in Addition. 2007. (ENG.). 16p. (J). 16.99 (978-0-9796150-0-9(3)) Jandie Jams Music LLC.

Stanley, Mandy. Arty Numbers: Early Learning Through Art. 2017. (Arty Mouse Wipe Clean with Pen Ser.). (ENG., Illus.). 24p. (J). (gr. -1-2). pap. 7.99 (978-1-78445-865-2(1)) Top That! Publishing PLC GBR. Dist: Independent Pubs. Group.

STAR Math RP Norms Upgrade. 2004. cd-rom (978-1-59455-183-3(9)) Renaissance Learning, Inc.

STAR Math RP Student Subscription. 2004. cd-rom 0.99 (978-1-59455-180-2(4)) Renaissance Learning, Inc.

STAR Math RP Student Subscription Renewal. 2004. cd-rom (978-1-59455-181-9(2)) Renaissance Learning, Inc.

STAR Math RP Subscription Package. 2004. cd-rom (978-1-59455-178-9(2)) Renaissance Learning, Inc.

Starr, Will. Circus Math. 2008. 132p. pap. 38.95 (978-1-4389-0836-6(9)) AuthorHouse.

Stckvagn. AC Ems Decimals & Percents. 2004. pap. (978-0-7398-9858-1(2)) Harcourt Schl. Pubs.

—AC Ems Whole Numbers. 2004. pap. (978-0-7398-9857-4(4)) Harcourt Schl. Pubs.

Steck-Vaughn Company, creator. Taste Like Math!, Grades K-6. 2011. (Fun Math Ser.). (ENG., Illus.). 128p. (J). (gr. k-6). pap. 16.99 (978-0-547-62555-3(3)) Heinemann-Raintree.

Steck-Vaughn Staff. Applied Math Intermediate, 8 pack. 2004. pap. 68.00 (978-0-7398-9930-4(9)); pap. 8.50 (978-0-7398-9849-9(3)) Harcourt Schl. Pubs.

—Applied Math Introductory. 2004. pap. 8.50 (978-0-7398-9853-6(1)) Harcourt Schl. Pubs.

—Applied Math Introductory 8-Pack. 2004. pap. 68.00 (978-0-7398-9934-2(1)) Harcourt Schl. Pubs.

—At-Home Workbooks: Division. 2004. (Illus.). pap., wbk. ed. (978-0-7398-8532-1(4)) Steck-Vaughn.

—At-Home Workbooks: Multiplication. 2004. (Illus.). (J). pap., wbk. ed. 5.99 (978-0-7398-8531-4(6)) Steck-Vaughn.

—At-Home Workbooks: Subtraction. 2004. (Illus.). pap., wbk. ed. (978-0-7398-8534-5(0)) Steck-Vaughn.

—Computational & Applied Mathematics. 2004. pap. 8.50 (978-0-7398-9846-8(9));8 Pack. pap. 68.00 (978-0-7398-9927-4(9)) Harcourt Schl. Pubs.

—Early Math: 2 Digit Addition & Subtraction. 2005. pap. 2.99 (978-1-4190-0332-5(1)) Steck-Vaughn.

—Early Math: 2 Digit Addition with Regrouping. 2005. pap. 2.99 (978-1-4190-0333-2(X)) Steck-Vaughn.

—Early Math: Mixed Operations. 2005. pap. 2.99 (978-1-4190-0326-4(7)) Steck-Vaughn.

—Early Math: Money I, 10 Pack. 2005. pap. 29.95 (978-1-4190-0352-3(6)); pap. 2.99 (978-1-4190-0328-8(3)) Steck-Vaughn.

—Early Math: Money II. 2005. pap. 2.99 (978-1-4190-0338-7(0)); pap. 29.95 (978-1-4190-0362-2(3)) Steck-Vaughn.

—Early Math: Problem Solving I, 10 Pack. 2005. pap. 29.95 (978-1-4190-0355-4(0)); pap. 2.99 (978-1-4190-0331-8(3)) Steck-Vaughn.

—Early Math: Problem Solving II, 10 Pack. 2005. pap. 29.95 (978-1-4190-0365-3(8)); pap. 2.99 (978-1-4190-0341-7(0)) Steck-Vaughn.

—Early Math: Readiness. 2005. pap. 2.99 (978-1-4190-0318-9(6)); pap. 29.95 (978-1-4190-0342-4(9)) Steck-Vaughn.

—Early Math: Readiness for Problem Solving, 10 Pack. 2005. pap. 29.95 (978-1-4190-0345-5(3)); pap. 2.99 (978-1-4190-0321-9(6)) Steck-Vaughn.

—Early Math: Time I, 10 Pack. 2005. pap. 29.95 (978-1-4190-0351-6(8)) Steck-Vaughn.

—Early Math: Time II, 10 Pack. 2005. pap. 29.95 (978-1-4190-0361-5(5)) Steck-Vaughn.

—Focus on Math Level C: Decimals. 2005. pap. 2.99 (978-1-4190-0268-7(6)) Harcourt Schl. Pubs.

—Focus on Math Level C: Problem Solving. 2005. pap. 2.99 (978-1-4190-0271-7(6)) Harcourt Schl. Pubs.

—Focus on Math Level C 10-pack: Decimals. 2005. pap. 29.95 (978-1-4190-0292-2(9)) Harcourt Schl. Pubs.

—Focus on Math Level C 10-pack: Problem Solving. 2005. pap. 29.95 (978-1-4190-0295-3(3)) Harcourt Schl. Pubs.

—Focus on Math Level D: Decimals. 2005. pap. 2.99 (978-1-4190-0274-8(0)) Harcourt Schl. Pubs.

—Focus on Math Level D: Measurement. 2005. pap. 2.99 (978-1-4190-0275-5(9)) Harcourt Schl. Pubs.

—Focus on Math Level D: Mixed Operations. 2005. pap. 2.99 (978-1-4190-0272-4(4)) Harcourt Schl. Pubs.

—Focus on Math Level D: Problem Solving. 2005. pap. 2.99 (978-1-4190-0277-9(5)) Harcourt Schl. Pubs.

—Focus on Math Level D 10-pack: Decimals. 2005. pap. 29.95 (978-1-4190-0298-4(8)) Harcourt Schl. Pubs.

—Focus on Math Level D 10-pack: Measurement. 2005. pap. 29.95 (978-1-4190-0299-1(6)) Harcourt Schl. Pubs.

—Focus on Math Level D 10-pack: Problem Solving. 2005. pap. 29.95 (978-1-4190-0301-1(1)) Harcourt Schl. Pubs.

—Focus on Math Level E: Decimals. 2005. pap. 2.99 (978-1-4190-0279-3(1)) Harcourt Schl. Pubs.

—Focus on Math Level E: Mixed Operations. 2005. pap. 2.99 (978-1-4190-0278-6(3)) Harcourt Schl. Pubs.

—Focus on Math Level E: Problem Solving. 2005. pap. 2.99 (978-1-4190-0283-0(X)) Harcourt Schl. Pubs.

—Focus on Math Level E: Ratio Percent. 2005. pap. 2.99 (978-1-4190-0282-3(1)) Harcourt Schl. Pubs.

—Focus on Math Level E 10-pack: Decimals. 2005. pap. 29.95 (978-1-4190-0303-5(8)) Harcourt Schl. Pubs.

—Focus on Math Level E 10-pack: Problem Solving. 2005. pap. 29.95 (978-1-4190-0307-3(0)) Harcourt Schl. Pubs.

—Focus on Math Level F: Problem Solving. 2005. pap. 2.99 (978-1-4190-0288-5(0)) Harcourt Schl. Pubs.

—Focus on Math Level F 10-pack: Problem Solving. 2005. pap. 29.95 (978-1-4190-0312-7(7)) Harcourt Schl. Pubs.

—Grade Level Math. 2005. (gr. 5). pap. 14.99 (978-0-7398-9941-0(4)); (gr. 6). pap. 14.99 (978-0-7398-9942-7(2)) Steck-Vaughn.

—Hey Theres Math in My Literature. 2004. (Illus.). (J). pap. 12.99 (978-0-7398-8474-4(3)) Steck-Vaughn.

—Just-a-Minute Math: Build Math Strength Through Timed Drills. 2003. (Just-A-Minute Math Ser.). (ENG.). 224p. (gr. 1-8). pap. 23.99 (978-0-7398-7940-5(5)) Houghton Mifflin Harcourt Publishing Co.

—Looking for Patterns. 2003. pap. 4.10 (978-0-7398-7659-6(7)) Steck-Vaughn.

—Mastering Math. 2004. (Steck-Vaughn Mastering Math Ser.). (ENG.). 160p. (gr. 4-4). pap. 25.70 (978-0-7398-9203-9(7)); 176p. (gr. 6-6). pap. 25.70 (978-0-7398-9205-3(3)); (Illus.). 48p. (gr. 1-1). pap. 11.90 (978-0-7398-9206-0(1)); (Illus.). 48p. (gr. 2-2). pap. 11.90 (978-0-7398-9207-7(X)); (Illus.). 48p. (gr. 3-3). pap. 11.90 (978-0-7398-9208-4(8)); (Illus.). 48p. (gr. 4-4). pap. 11.90 (978-0-7398-9209-1(6)); (Illus.). 48p. (gr. 5-5). pap. 11.90 (978-0-7398-9210-7(X));Level C. 160p. (gr. 3-3). pap. 25.70 (978-0-7398-9202-2(9));Level A. 160p. (gr. 1-1). pap., stu. ed. 25.70 (978-0-7398-9200-8(2));Level B. 160p. (gr. 2-2). pap. 25.70 (978-0-7398-9201-5(0));Level E. 176p. (gr. 5-5). pap. 25.70 (978-0-7398-9204-6(5)) Houghton Mifflin Harcourt Publishing Co.

—Mastering Math, Level F. 2004. (Steck-Vaughn Mastering Math Ser.). (ENG., Illus.). 48p. (gr. 6-6). pap. 11.90 (978-0-7398-9211-4(8)) Houghton Mifflin Harcourt Publishing Co.

—Math: Data Analysis & Statistics. 2004. pap. 5.00 (978-0-7398-9844-4(2)) Harcourt Schl. Pubs.

—Math 10-Pack: Data, Analysis & Statistics. 2004. pap. 44.95 (978-0-7398-9925-0(2)) Harcourt Schl. Pubs.

—Math Computation Intermediate. 2004. pap. 8.50 (978-0-7398-9850-5(7)) Harcourt Schl. Pubs.

—Math Computation Intermediate 8-Pack. 2004. pap. 68.00 (978-0-7398-9931-1(7)) Harcourt Schl. Pubs.

—Math Computation Introductory. 2004. pap. 8.50 (978-0-7398-9854-3(X)) Harcourt Schl. Pubs.

—That Makes Ten! 2003. pap. 4.10 (978-0-7398-7656-5(2)) Steck-Vaughn.

—Top Line Math: Probability. 2005. pap. 5.49 (978-1-4190-0374-5(7)) Steck-Vaughn.

—Top Line Math: Proportions. 2005. pap. 5.49 (978-1-4190-0369-1(0)) Harcourt Schl. Pubs.

—Top Line Math: Special Topics in Math. 2005. pap., tchr. ed. 5.95 (978-1-4190-0385-1(2)) Harcourt Schl. Pubs.

—Top Line Math: Special Topics in Math. 2005. pap. 5.49 (978-1-4190-0375-2(5)) Steck-Vaughn.

—Top Line Math: Tables & Maps. 2005. pap., tchr. ed. 5.95 (978-1-4190-0381-3(X)) Harcourt Schl. Pubs.

Steck-Vaughn Staff, creator. Test Fundamentals Math Computation: Basic. 2004. (Illus.). pap. 68.00 (978-0-7398-9935-9(X)) Harcourt Schl. Pubs.

Steffora, Tracey. Animal Math. 2013. (Animal Math Ser.). (ENG.). 24p. (gr. -1-1). pap. 29.95 (978-1-4329-7571-5(4)); lib. bdg. 113.25 (978-1-4329-7564-7(1)) Heinemann-Raintree. (NA-h).

—Animal Math: Adding, Taking Away, & Skip Counting, 1 vol. 2014. (Animal Math Ser.). (ENG.). 32p. (gr. -1-1). 29.99 (978-1-4846-0061-0(4), NA-h) Heinemann-Raintree.

—Math Around Us, 7 vols., Set. Incl. Counting in the City. pap. 6.29 (978-1-4329-4929-7(2)); Measuring in the Garden. pap. 6.29 (978-1-4329-4934-1(9)); Patterns at the Museum. pap. 6.29 (978-1-4329-4931-0(4)); Shapes in the Kitchen. pap. 6.29 (978-1-4329-4930-3(6)); Sorting at the Market. pap. 6.29 (978-1-4329-4935-8(7)); Using Addition at Home. pap. 6.29 (978-1-4329-4932-7(2)); Using Subtraction at the Park. pap. 6.29 (978-1-4329-4933-4(0)); (gr. -1-1). (Math Around Us Ser.). (ENG.). 24p. 2011. Set pap. 44.03 (978-1-4329-4936-5(5)); Set lib. bdg. 135.90 (978-1-4329-4928-0(4)) Heinemann-Raintree. (Acorn).

—Math at the Airport, 1 vol. 2013. (Math on the Job Ser.). (ENG., Illus.). 24p. (gr. k-2). pap. 6.29 (978-1-4329-7158-8(1)); lib. bdg. 22.65 (978-1-4329-7151-9(4)) Heinemann-Raintree. (Acorn).

—Math at the Hospital, 1 vol. 2013. (Math on the Job Ser.). (ENG., Illus.). 24p. (gr. k-2). pap. 6.29 (978-1-4329-7159-5(X)); lib. bdg. 22.65 (978-1-4329-7152-6(2)) Heinemann-Raintree. (Acorn).

—Math at the Store, 1 vol. 2013. (Math on the Job Ser.). (ENG., Illus.). 24p. (gr. k-2). pap. 6.29 (978-1-4329-7160-1(3)); lib. bdg. 22.65 (978-1-4329-7153-3(0)) Heinemann-Raintree. (Acorn).

—Math at the Train Station, 1 vol. 2013. (Math on the Job Ser.). (ENG., Illus.). 24p. (gr. k-2). pap. 6.29 (978-1-4329-7161-8(1)); lib. bdg. 22.65 (978-1-4329-7154-0(9)) Heinemann-Raintree. (Acorn).

—Math at the Vet, 1 vol. 2013. (Math on the Job Ser.). (ENG., Illus.). 24p. (gr. k-2). lib. bdg. 22.65 (978-1-4329-7155-7(7), Acorn) Heinemann-Raintree.

—Math on the Farm, 1 vol. 2013. (Math on the Job Ser.). (ENG., Illus.). 24p. (gr. k-2). pap. 6.29 (978-1-4329-7163-2(8)); lib. bdg. 22.65 (978-1-4329-7156-4(5)) Heinemann-Raintree. (Acorn).

—Math on the Job. 2013. (Math on the Job Ser.). (ENG.). 24p. (gr. k-2). pap. 35.94 (978-1-4329-7164-9(6)); lib. bdg. 135.90 (978-1-4329-7157-1(3)) Heinemann-Raintree. (Acorn).

—What Is Math?, 1 vol. 2011. (ENG.). 24p. (gr. -1-1). 25.99 (978-1-4329-5356-0(7), Acorn Read-Aloud) Heinemann-Raintree.

Stetson, Raymond. Math Mage: A Position in Addition, 1 vol. 2010. 40p. pap. 24.95 (978-1-4489-7976-9(5)) PublishAmerica, Inc.

Stevens, Judith. Maths in Stories, 2. 2014. (ENG.). 80p. pap. 58.00 (978-1-874099-65-9(0)) Oxford Univ. Pr., Inc.

Stewart, Rhea A. & Technology Education Design Forum Staff. Math in the Real World Set, 10-Volumes. 2009. (Math in the Real World Ser.). 277p. (gr. 4-6). 280.00 (978-1-60413-828-3(9), Chelsea Clubhouse) Facts On File, Inc.

Stites, Ranae & Buethe, Amanda. Cooperative Mathematics. 2008. (J). per. 29.00 (978-1-879097-36-0(2)) Kagan Publishing.

Stosch, Dawn. Science Math. 2008. (Math Alive! Ser.). 32p. (gr. 4-18). lib. bdg. 28.50 (978-0-7614-3213-5(2), Benchmark Bks.) Marshall Cavendish Corp.

Stowasser, Peter & Burnett, James. Cupcake Capers: A Book about Take-Away Subtraction. 2012. (J). (978-1-921959-27-1(4)) Origo Education.

Strazzabosco, John. Mathematical Thinking Reasoning Proof. 2004. (BrainBuilders Ser.). (ENG.). 48p. (gr. k-4). pap. 5.25 (978-1-4042-8522-4(9)) Rosen Publishing Group, Inc., The.

Stuart, Carrie. Kinds of Coins: Learning the Values of Pennies, Nickels, Dimes & Quarters. 2009. (Math for the REAL World Ser.). 12p. (gr. 1-2). pap. 5.90 (978-0-8239-8862-4(7), Rosen Classroom) Rosen Publishing Group, Inc., The.

Stuart, Liam. The Parade: Understand Place Value. 2013. (Rosen Math Readers Ser.). (ENG., Illus.). 24p. (J). (gr. 1-2). pap. 8.25 (978-1-4777-2070-7(7), Rosen Classroom) Rosen Publishing Group, Inc., The.

Suen, Anastasia. Top STEM Careers in Science. 2014. (Cutting-Edge STEM Careers Ser.). (Illus.). 128p. (J). (gr. 9-12). 35.60 (978-1-4777-7664-3(8)) Rosen Publishing Group, Inc., The.

Sugiyama, Yoshishige, ed. Tokyo Shoseki's Mathematics for Elementary School (Grades 1 - 6 set, 11 vol. Set), 11 vols. 2006. Orig. Title: Atarashii Sansuu 1. (Illus.). pap. 129.55 (978-1-934046-00-5(0)) Global Education Resources, LLC.

Sulley, Robert. First Aid in Mathematics. 2010. 208p. pap. 17.95 (978-1-4441-1658-8(4)) Hodder Education Group GBR. Dist: Trans-Atlantic Pubns., Inc.

Sullivan. Computerized Test Bank to Accompany Finite Mathema Tics: An Applied Approach. 9th ed. 2004. (YA). (978-0-471-44818-1(4)) Wiley, John & Sons, Inc.

—Test Bank to Accompany Finite Mathematics: An Appl led Approach, Ninth Edition. 9th ed. 2004. (YA). (978-0-471-44821-1(4)) Wiley, John & Sons, Inc.

Sullivan, Erin. Mathematical Thinkers & Los Matemáticos: 6 English, 6 Spanish Adaptations, 122 vols., Vol. 2. 2011. (Navigators Ser.). (ENG & SPA.). (J). instr.'s gde. ed. 97.00 net. (978-1-4108-1773-0(3), 17733) Benchmark Education Co.

—Sports Math & Matemáticas en los Deportes: 6 English, 6 Spanish Adaptations, 122 vols., Vol. 2. 2011. (Navigators Ser.). (J). instr.'s gde. ed. 97.00 net. (978-1-4108-1774-7(1), 17741) Benchmark Education Co.

Sullivan, Erin Ash. The Class Election: Set Of 6. 2010. (Early Connections Ser.). (J). pap. 37.00 net. (978-1-4108-1085-4(2)) Benchmark Education Co.

—Human Body Math: Set Of 6. 2010. (Navigators Ser.). (J). 44.00 net. (978-1-4108-0408-2(9)) Benchmark Education Co.

—Human Body Math & Matemáticas del cuerpo Humano: 6 English, 6 Spanish Adaptations. 2011. (ENG & SPA.). (J). 89.00 net. (978-1-4108-5682-1(8)) Benchmark Education Co.

—Math Around the Globe: Set Of 6. 2011. (Navigators Ser.). (J). pap. 48.00 net. (978-1-4108-0417-4(8)) Benchmark Education Co.

—Math Around the Globe & Matemáticas alrededor del Mundo: 6 English, 6 Spanish Adaptations. 2011. (ENG & SPA.). (J). 97.00 net. (978-1-4108-5689-0(5)) Benchmark Education Co.

—Math at the Olympics: Set Of 6. 2011. (Navigators Ser.). (J). 48.00 net. (978-1-4108-0433-4(X)) Benchmark Education Co.

—Math at the Olympics & Matemáticas en las Olimpiadas: 6 English, 6 Spanish Adaptations. 2011. (ENG & SPA.). (J). 97.00 net. (978-1-4108-5707-1(7)) Benchmark Education Co.

—Math in a Democracy: Set Of 6. 2011. (Navigators Ser.). (J). pap. 48.00 net. (978-1-4108-0437-2(2)) Benchmark Education Co.

—Math in a Democracy & Matemáticas en una Democracia: 6 English, 6 Spanish Adaptations. 2011. (ENG & SPA.). (J). 97.00 net. (978-1-4108-5715-6(8)) Benchmark Education Co.

—Metric Math: Set Of 6. 2011. (Navigators Ser.). (J). pap. 44.00 net. (978-1-4108-0414-3(3)) Benchmark Education Co.

—Metric Math & Matemáticas Métricas: 6 English, 6 Spanish Adaptations. 2011. (ENG & SPA.). (J). 89.00 net. (978-1-4108-5681-4(X)) Benchmark Education Co.

—Music Counts: Set Of 6. 2011. (Navigators Ser.). (J). 44.00 net. (978-1-4108-0405-1(4)) Benchmark Education Co.

—Patterns in Nature: Set Of 6. 2010. (Early Connections Ser.). (J). pap. 37.00 net. (978-1-4108-1079-3(8)) Benchmark Education Co.

Sundance/Newbridge LLC Staff. From Circles to Cubes. 2004. (Reading PowerWorks Ser.). (gr. 1-3). 37.50 (978-0-7608-7839-2(0)); pap. 6.10 (978-0-7608-7840-8(4)) Sundance/Newbridge Educational Publishing.

—Make a Good Guess. 2004. (Reading PowerWorks Ser.). (gr. 1-3). 37.50 (978-0-7608-9317-3(9)); pap. 6.10 (978-0-7608-9318-0(7)) Sundance/Newbridge Educational Publishing.

—Parts of a Whole. 2004. (Reading PowerWorks Ser.). (gr. 1-3). 37.50 (978-0-7608-9293-0(8)); pap. 6.10 (978-0-7608-9294-7(6)) Sundance/Newbridge Educational Publishing.

Super Achievement. Math Magic Workbook. 2007. (Illus.). 88p. per. 16.99 (978-0-9799545-1-1(7)) Magic Works Publishing & Production.

Super Achievement, creator. Multimagic Table. 2007. (Illus.). 2p. 9.97 (978-0-9799545-0-4(9)) Magic Works Publishing & Production.

Swain, Cynthia. Sorting at the Park. 2006. (Early Explorers Ser.). (J). pap. (978-1-4108-6036-1(1)) Benchmark Education Co.

Swann, Kristina. Meaningful Math. 2005. (YA). ring bd. 49.95 (978-1-58804-402-0(5)) P C I Education.

Swenson, Julie. High-Speed Trains: Use Place Value Understanding & Properties of Operations to Add & Subtract. 2014. (Rosen Common Core Math Readers Ser.). (ENG.). 24p. (J). (gr. 2-3). pap. 8.25 (978-1-4777-4759-9(1), Rosen Classroom) Rosen Publishing Group, Inc., The.

Sylvan Learning. Sylvan Kick Start for First Grade. 2013. (Sylvan Language Arts Bundles Ser.). (ENG.). 96p. (J). (gr. 1-4). 19.99 (978-0-307-94614-0(2), Sylvan Learning Publishing) Random Hse. Children's Bks.

Sylvan Learning Staff. Kindergarten Page per Day: Math Skills. 2012. (Sylvan Page per Day Series, Math Ser.). (ENG.). 64p. (J). (gr. -1-2). pap. 6.99 (978-0-307-94458-0(1), Sylvan Learning Publishing) Random Hse. Children's Bks.

—Pre-K Page per Day: Numbers. 2012. (Sylvan Page per Day Series, Math Ser.). (ENG.). 64p. (J). (gr. -1-2). pap. 6.99 (978-0-307-94456-6(5), Sylvan Learning Publishing) Random Hse. Children's Bks.

Tabletop Pocket Chart Addition & Subtraction Card Set. 2004. (J). 8.95 (978-1-56911-170-3(7)) Learning Resources, Inc.

TAKS MASTER Power Practice, Math Gr. 3. 2004. (J). (978-1-57022-535-2(4)) ECS Learning Systems, Inc.

TAKS MASTER Power Practice, Math Gr. 4. 2004. (J). (978-1-57022-536-9(2)) ECS Learning Systems, Inc.

TAKS MASTER Power Practice, Math Gr. 5. 2004. (J). (978-1-57022-537-6(0)) ECS Learning Systems, Inc.

TAKS MASTER Power Practice, Math Gr. 6. 2004. (J). (978-1-57022-538-3(9)) ECS Learning Systems, Inc.

TAKS MASTER Power Practice, Math Gr. 7. 2004. (J). (978-1-57022-539-0(7)) ECS Learning Systems, Inc.

TAKS MASTER Power Practice, Math Gr. 8. 2004. (YA). (978-1-57022-540-6(0)) ECS Learning Systems, Inc.

TAKS MASTER Practice Test Math, Gr. 3. 2004. (J). (978-1-57022-474-4(9)) ECS Learning Systems, Inc.

TAKS MASTER Practice Test Math, Gr. 4. 2004. (J). (978-1-57022-516-1(8)) ECS Learning Systems, Inc.

TAKS MASTER Practice Test Math, Gr. 5. 2004. (J). (978-1-57022-517-8(6)) ECS Learning Systems, Inc.

TAKS MASTER Practice Test Math, Gr. 6. 2004. (J). (978-1-57022-518-5(4)) ECS Learning Systems, Inc.

TAKS MASTER Practice Test Math, Gr. 7. 2004. (J). (978-1-57022-519-2(2)) ECS Learning Systems, Inc.

TAKS MASTER Practice Test Math, Gr. 8. 2004. (YA). (978-1-57022-520-8(6)) ECS Learning Systems, Inc.

TAKS Mathematics Preparation Grade 1. 2004. (Region IV ESC Resources for Mathematics Ser.). (J). (gr. 1). stu. ed., per., wbk. ed. (978-1-932524-51-2(7)) Region IV Education Service Ctr.

TAKS Mathematics Preparation Grade 1- Spanish. 2004. (SPA.). stu. ed., per., wbk. ed. (978-1-932524-81-9(9)) Region IV Education Service Ctr.

TAKS Mathematics Preparation Grade 10. 2004. (Region IV ESC Resources for Mathematics Ser.). stu. ed., per., wbk. ed. (978-1-932524-60-4(6)) Region IV Education Service Ctr.

TAKS Mathematics Preparation Grade 11 Exit. 2003. (Region IV ESC Resources for Mathematics Ser.). stu. ed., per., wbk. ed. (978-1-932524-61-1(4)) Region IV Education Service Ctr.

TAKS Mathematics Preparation Grade 2. 2004. (Region IV ESC Resources for Mathematics Ser.). (gr. 2). stu. ed., per., wbk. ed. (978-1-932524-52-9(5)) Region IV Education Service Ctr.

TAKS Mathematics Preparation Grade 2 - Spanish. 2004. (SPA.). stu. ed., per. (978-1-932524-82-6(7)) Region IV Education Service Ctr.

TAKS Mathematics Preparation Grade 3. 2004. (Region IV ESC Resources for Mathematics Ser.). (J). (gr. 3). stu. ed., per., wbk. ed. (978-1-932524-53-6(3)) Region IV Education Service Ctr.

TAKS Mathematics Preparation Grade 3 - Spanish. 2004. (SPA.). stu. ed., per., wbk. ed. (978-1-932524-83-3(5)) Region IV Education Service Ctr.

TAKS Mathematics Preparation Grade 4. 2004. (Region IV ESC Resources for Mathematics Ser.). (J). (gr. 4). stu. ed., per., wbk. ed. (978-1-932524-54-3(1)) Region IV Education Service Ctr.

TAKS Mathematics Preparation Grade 4 - Spanish. 2004. (SPA.). stu. ed., per., wbk. ed. (978-1-932524-84-0(3)) Region IV Education Service Ctr.

TAKS Mathematics Preparation Grade 5. 2003. (Region IV ESC Resources for Mathematics Ser.). (J). (gr. 5). stu. ed., per., wbk. ed. (978-1-932524-55-0(X)) Region IV Education Service Ctr.

TAKS Mathematics Preparation Grade 5 - Spanish. 2004. (SPA.). per., wbk. ed. (978-1-932524-85-7(1)) Region IV Education Service Ctr.

TAKS Mathematics Preparation Grade 6. 2004. (Region IV ESC Resources for Mathematics Ser.). (J). (gr. 6). stu. ed., per., wbk. ed. (978-1-932524-56-7(8)) Region IV Education Service Ctr.

TAKS Mathematics Preparation Grade 7. 2004. (Region IV ESC Resources for Mathematics Ser.). (YA). (gr. 7). stu. ed., per., wbk. ed. (978-1-932524-57-4(6)) Region IV Education Service Ctr.

TAKS Mathematics Preparation Grade 8. 2003. (Region IV ESC Resources for Mathematics Ser.). stu. ed., per., wbk. ed. (978-1-932524-58-1(4)) Region IV Education Service Ctr.

TAKS Mathematics Preparation Grade 9. 2004. (Region IV ESC Resources for Mathematics Ser.). stu. ed., per., wbk. ed. (978-1-932524-59-8(2)) Region IV Education Service Ctr.

TAKS Mathematics Preparation Grade K. 2004. (Region IV ESC Resources for Mathematics Ser.). stu. ed., per., wbk. ed. (978-1-932524-50-5(9)) Region IV Education Service Ctr.

TAKS Mathematics Preparation Grade K - Spanish. 2004. (SPA.). stu. ed., per., wbk. ed. (978-1-932524-80-2(0)) Region IV Education Service Ctr.

Tallinda, Theodore. Math at Henry Ford's Factory: Identify & Explain Patterns in Arithmetic, 1 vol. 2015. (InfoMax Common Core Math Readers Ser.). (ENG.). 24p. (J). pap. 8.25 (978-1-4777-4684-4(6), Rosen Classroom) Rosen Publishing Group, Inc., The.

Tamambang, Andrew Tangang, et al. Mastering Mathematics Form 3 Student's Book: Volume 0, Part 0. 2007. pap. 6.00 (978-0-521-70145-7(7)) Cambridge Univ. Pr.

Tang, Greg. Math Appeal. Briggs, Harry, illus. 2003. (Mind-Stretching Math Riddles Ser.). (ENG.). 40p. (J). (gr. -1-3). 18.99 (978-0-439-21046-1(1), Scholastic Pr.) Scholastic, Inc.

—Math for All Seasons. Briggs, Harry, illus. 2005. (Scholastic Bookshelf Ser.). (ENG.). 40p. (J). (gr. -1-3). pap. 6.99 (978-0-439-75537-5(9), Scholastic Paperbacks) Scholastic, Inc.

Tang, Greg & Greg, Tang. Un, Dos, Tres, el Ano Se Fue. Briggs, Harry, illus. 2003.Tr. of Math for All Seasons. (SPA.). 40p. (J). (gr. 2-3). 14.99 (978-84-241-8074-4(7)) Everest Editora ESP. Dist: Lectorum Pubns., Inc.

Tangang Tamambang, Andrew, et al. Mastering Mathematics Form 1 Student's Book. 2008. pap., stu. ed. 4.00 (978-0-521-69301-1(2)) Cambridge Univ. Pr.

—Mastering Mathematics Form 2 Student's Book. 2008. pap., stu. ed. 6.00 (978-0-521-69300-4(4)) Cambridge Univ. Pr.

Tastes Like Math. 2003. (J). pap., stu. ed. 10.95 (978-1-58123-341-4(8)) Larson Learning, Inc.

Tate, Kelly. Selling Popcorn: Understand Place Value. 2013. (InfoMax Math Readers Ser.). (ENG.). 24p. (J). (gr. 1-2). pap. 49.50 (978-1-4777-2196-4(7)); (Illus.). pap. 8.25 (978-1-4777-2195-7(9)) Rosen Publishing Group, Inc., The. (Rosen Classroom).

Taylor-Butler, Christine. Understanding Charts & Graphs. 2012. (True Book(tm), a — Information Literacy Ser.). (ENG.). 48p. (J). lib. bdg. 31.00 (978-0-531-26009-8(7)); pap. 6.95 (978-0-531-26240-5(5)) Scholastic Library Publishing.

Teaching Resources Staff. Reading & Math. Cooper, Terry, ed. 2005. (ENG., Illus.). 320p. (gr. 2-2). pap., wbk. ed. 14.99 (978-0-439-78601-0(0), Teaching Resources) Scholastic, Inc.

TestSMART Plus Math Processes, Level B-1. 2004. (J). (978-1-57022-507-9(9)) ECS Learning Systems, Inc.

TestSMART Plus Math Processes, Level B-2. 2004. (J). (978-1-57022-508-6(7)) ECS Learning Systems, Inc.

TestSMART Plus Math Processes, Level C. 2004. (J). (978-1-57022-509-3(5)) ECS Learning Systems, Inc.

TestSMART Plus Math Processes, Level D. 2004. (J). (978-1-57022-510-9(9)) ECS Learning Systems, Inc.

TestSMART Plus Math Processes, Level E. 2004. (J). (978-1-57022-511-6(7)) ECS Learning Systems, Inc.

TestSMART Plus Math Processes, Level F. 2004. (J). (978-1-57022-512-3(5)) ECS Learning Systems, Inc.

TestSMART Plus Math Processes, Level G. 2004. (J). (978-1-57022-513-0(3)) ECS Learning Systems, Inc.

TestSMART Plus Math Processes, Level H. 2004. (J). (978-1-57022-514-7(1)) ECS Learning Systems, Inc.

TestSMART Plus Math Processes, Level I. 2004. (YA). (978-1-57022-515-4(X)) ECS Learning Systems, Inc.

TestSMART Plus Numeration, Level A-1. 2004. (J). (978-1-57022-522-2(2)) ECS Learning Systems, Inc.

TestSMART Plus Numeration, Level A-2. 2004. (J). (978-1-57022-523-9(0)) ECS Learning Systems, Inc.

TestSMART Plus Numeration, Level B. 2004. (J). (978-1-57022-524-6(9)) ECS Learning Systems, Inc.

TestSmart Plus Numeration Level C/D. 2004. (J). (978-1-57022-525-3(7)) ECS Learning Systems, Inc.

TestSmart Plus Numeration Level E/F. 2004. (J). (978-1-57022-526-0(5)) ECS Learning Systems, Inc.

TestSmart Plus Numeration Level G/H. 2004. (J). (978-1-57022-527-7(3)) ECS Learning Systems, Inc.

TestSMART Plus Whole Numbers, Level A. 2004. (J). (978-1-57022-488-1(9)) ECS Learning Systems, Inc.

The Research Masters Staff & Barron's Educational Staff. Barron's Common Core Success Grade 6 Math Workbook: Preparing Students for a Brilliant Future. 2015. (Barron's Common Core Success Ser.). (ENG., Illus.). 208p. (gr. 6-6). pap. 12.99 (978-1-4380-0680-2(2)) Barron's Educational Series, Inc.

Thomas, Mary Ann. Our Train Trip: Learning to Add Times by the Half Hour. 2009. (Math for the REAL World Ser.). 12p. (gr. 1-2). pap. 5.90 (978-0-8239-8849-5(X), Rosen Classroom) Rosen Publishing Group, Inc., The.

Thomas, Penny. Powwow Counting in Cree. Josie, Melinda, illus. 2013. (CRE & ENG.). 24p. (978-1-55379-392-2(7), 9781553793922, HighWater Pr.) Portage & Main Pr.

Thompson, Becki & Reinke, Missy. Building Math Vocabulary: 70 Engaging Reproducible Activities That Go Beyond the Textbook to Help Students Practice & Really Learn the Math Terms They Need to Know. 2009. (ENG.). 80p. pap. 14.99 (978-0-545-04875-0(3), Teaching Resources) Scholastic, Inc.

Thompson, Helen. Shopping Math. 2013. (Math 24/7 Ser.: 10). 48p. (J). (gr. 5-18). 19.95 (978-1-4222-2908-8(4)) Mason Crest.

—Understanding Business Math & Budgets. Madrian, Brigitte, ed. 2013. (Young Adult Library of Small Business & Finance Ser.: 10). 64p. (J). (gr. 7-18). 22.95 (978-1-4222-2921-7(1)) Mason Crest.

Three Bear Family: Addition & Subtraction Activity Book. 2003. (J). pap. 4.95 (978-1-56911-103-1(0)) Learning Resources, Inc.

Three Bear Family: Matching & Sorting Activity Book. 2003. (J). pap. 4.95 (978-1-56911-101-7(4)) Learning Resources, Inc.

The TI-108 Calculator, 30. 2004. (gr. k-6). suppl. ed. 202.50 (978-0-201-23151-9(4)); suppl. ed. 74.25 (978-0-201-23150-2(6)) Addison-Wesley Educational Pubs., Inc. (Scott Foresman).

Time & Money Skills (Gr. 1-2) 2003. (J). (978-1-58232-082-3(9)) ECS Learning Systems, Inc.

Tiner, John Hudson. Exploring the World of Mathematics: From Ancient Record Keeping to the Latest Advances in Computers. 2004. (Sense of Wonder Ser.). 157p. pap. 14.99 (978-0-89051-412-2(7), 303-050) Master Bks.

Tipler, Maryanne. Mathematics, Vol. 9. 2014. (ENG., Illus.). 448p. pap., stu. ed. 30.00 (978-0-7487-8614-5(7)) Oxford Univ. Pr., Inc.

To Market, to Market. 2004. cd-rom 119.00 (978-1-889775-52-4(5)) Learning in Motion.

Top That Publishing. Writing My First Sums. 2007. (Early Days Ser.). (Illus.). 10p. bds. (978-1-84666-338-3(5)) Top That! Publishing PLC.

Torres Moliner, Isabel & Puche, Lola Soriano. Espacio Espacial. 2005. (In-genio Ser.). (Illus.). 47p. (J). (gr. 4-7). per. 14.95 (978-84-95895-09-7(9)) Editorial Brief ESP. Dist: Independent Pubs. Group.

Torres Moliner, Isabel & Soriano Puche, Lola. Domino Domino. 2005. (In-genio Ser.). (Illus.). 48p. (J). (gr. 4-7). pap. 14.95 (978-84-95895-01-1(3)) Editorial Brief ESP. Dist: Independent Pubs. Group.

Trapolsi, Audrey. Teaching Struggling Readers to Tackle Math Word Problems: Effective Strategies & Practice Pages That Help Kids Develop the Skills They Need to Read & Solve Math Word Problems. 2012. (ENG.). 64p. (gr. 3-3). pap. 11.99 (978-0-545-20717-1(7), Teaching Resources) Scholastic, Inc.

Trumbauer, Lisa. Let's Graph, 6 vols., Set. 2003. (Yellow Umbrella Early Level Ser.). (ENG.). 16p. (gr. k-1). pap. 35.70 (978-0-7368-3009-6(X), Yellow Umbrella Bks.) Capstone Press of Coughlan Cos.

Twin Sisters(r) Staff & Thompson, Kim Mitzo. Subtraction. 2011. (J). (gr. k-1). audio compact disk 4.99 (978-1-59922-567-8(0)) Twin Sisters IP, LLC.

Unswood, Cassie. Exploring Plane Figures: Understand Concepts of Area, 1 vol. 2015. (InfoMax Common Core Math Readers Ser.). (ENG.). 24p. (J). pap. 8.25 (978-1-4777-4594-6(7), Rosen Classroom) Rosen Publishing Group, Inc., The.

Vamos a Agrupar Por... / Sort It Out! 2015. (Vamos a Agrupar Por... / Sort It Out! Ser.). (ENG & SPA.). 24p. (J). (gr. k-1). 135.60 (978-1-4824-2976-3(4)) Stevens, Gareth Publishing LLLP.

Van Horn, Stephanie. Math Rapmatics: Mathematical Rhymes Right on Time. Daniel, Rick, illus. 2011. 24p. (J). 18.00 (978-0-9814945-9-3(5)) AK Classics, LLC.

Vanderbilt, Amy & Vanderbilt, Sabrina. Negative Nine: Book 1 of the Early Math Series. Vanderbilt, Amy, illus. 2008. (Illus.). 28p. (J). 14.99 (978-0-7639-0719-8(7)) Trend Factor Pr.

VanVoorst, Jennifer. Can You Guess?, 6 vols., Set. 2003. (Yellow Umbrella Early Level Ser.). (ENG.). 16p. (gr. k-1). pap. 35.70 (978-0-7368-3008-9(1), Yellow Umbrella Bks.) Capstone Press of Coughlan Cos.

—Making Shapes, 6 vols., Set. 2003. (Yellow Umbrella Early Level Ser.). (ENG.). 16p. (gr. k-1). pap. 35.70 (978-0-7368-3010-2(3), Yellow Umbrella Bks.) Capstone Press of Coughlan Cos.

Vaughan, Susan. Let's Eat Lunch: Learning about Picture Graphs. 2009. (Math for the Real World: Early Emergent Ser.). (ENG., Illus.). 8p. (gr. k-1). pap. 5.15 *(978-0-8239-8885-3(6))* Rosen Publishing Group, Inc., The.

Vaughn, Sydney. At the Track Meet: Understand Place Value. 2013. (InfoMax Math Readers Ser.). (ENG.). 24p. (J). (gr. 1-2). pap. 49.50 *(978-1-4777-2134-6(7))*; pap. 8.25 *(978-1-4777-2133-9(9))* Rosen Publishing Group, Inc., The. (Rosen Classroom).

Vedic Mathematics. 2003. per. *(978-0-9727877-0-3(4))* Consciousness-Based Education Association.

Velasquez, Maria. Pet Parade. Mooney, Alyssa, illus. 2007. (J). pap. 21.00 *(978-0-15-379895-5(5))* Houghton Mifflin Harcourt School Pubs.

Viajando a traves de los Numeros - America Aponte. 2005. 32.95 *(978-1-881744-70-2(1))* Editorial Panamericana, Inc.

Vicario, Evelyn. Mathematics for Life Practice Workbook - Kindergarten. 2013. (ENG.). 118p. (J). pap. 12.99 *(978-0-9826276-2-4(9),* Bibia Publishing) Bibia, LLC.

Visaint, Henock. Math Pack Bilingual English, Haitian Creole: PakMat. Date not set. (Illus.). 64p. (J). (gr. 1-3). wbk. ed. 5.50 *(978-1-881839-64-4(8))* Educa Vision Inc.

Virtual Math Tutor V2. 0: CD Installable. 2005. (YA). cd-rom 60.00 *(978-1-59807-032-3(0))* American Bk. Co.

Virtual Math Tutor V2. 0: CD Playable. 2005. (YA). cd-rom 60.00 *(978-1-59807-031-6(2))* American Bk. Co.

Visto, Joy. Where Does a Graph Go? 2015. (Illus.). 48p. (J). *(978-1-60818-575-7(3),* Creative Education) Creative Co., The.

—Where Does a Graph Go? Making Math Work. 2016. (Making Math Work Ser.). (ENG.). 48p. (J). (gr. 5-9). pap. 12.00 *(978-1-62832-176-0(8),* Creative Paperbacks) Creative Co., The.

Wagner, Sy. Brownie Math. 2003. (Rosen Real Readers: Upper Emergent Ser.). (ENG., Illus.). 12p. (gr. 1-2). pap. 5.90 *(978-0-8239-6366-9(7))* Rosen Publishing Group, Inc., The.

Walch Publishing Staff. Assessment Strategies for Math. 2003. 86p. 24.99 *(978-0-8251-4492-9(2))* Walch Education.

Walch Publishing Staff, creator. Math & Science. 2007. (Daily Warm-Ups Ser.). 204p. (gr. 5-6). tchr. ed., spiral bd. 24.99 *(978-0-8251-6447-7(8))* Walch Education.

Wall, Terry & Pimental, Ric. Checkpoint Mathematics, Vol. 3. 2005. (Illus.). 192p. pap. 36.50 *(978-0-340-81293-8(1),* Hodder Education) Hodder Education Group GBR. Dist: Trans-Atlantic Pubns., Inc.

Wall, Terry & Pimentel, Ric. Checkpoint Maths, Vol. 1. 2004. (Illus.). 180p. (YA). pap. 36.50 *(978-0-340-81295-2(8),* Hodder Education) Hodder Education Group GBR. Dist: Trans-Atlantic Pubns., Inc.

Warren, Sandra J. Times to Remember, the Fun & Easy Way to Memorize the Multiplication Tables: Home & Classroom Resources. Vasquez, Juan Jose, illus. 2012. 246p. pap. 19.95 *(978-0-9836580-1-6(3))* Joyful Learning Publications, LLC.

Warren, Sandra Jane. Times to Remember, the Fun & Easy Way to Memorize the Multiplication Tables. Vásquez, Juan José, illus. 2012. 86p. pap. 24.95 *(978-0-9836580-0-9(5))* Joyful Learning Publications, LLC.

Waters, Jennifer. Todo Tipo de Movimiento. 2011. (Ciencia Fisica/Physical Science Ser.).Tr. of All Kinds of Motion. (SPA, ENG & MUL.). 24p. (gr. k-1). 26.65 *(978-1-4296-6905-4(5))* Capstone Press of Coughlan Cos.

Watt, Fiona. Big Book of Sticker Math. Wells, Rachel, illus. 2008. (Usborne Sticker Math Ser.). 151p. (J). (gr. -1-3). pap. 12.99 *(978-0-7945-1825-7(7),* Usborne) EDC Publishing.

Watt, Fiona & Wells, Rachel. Numbers. 2004. (Usborne Sticker Math Ser.). (ENG., Illus.). 1p. (J). (gr. k-1). pap., act. bk. ed. 6.95 *(978-0-7460-3731-7(7))* EDC Publishing.

—Sticker Maths: Adding. 2004. (Usborne Sticker Math Ser.). (ENG., Illus.). 1p. (J). (gr. k-1). pap., act. bk. ed. 6.95 *(978-0-7460-3728-7(7))* EDC Publishing.

—Sticker Maths: Taking Away. 2004. (Usborne Sticker Math Ser.). (ENG., Illus.). 1p. (J). (gr. k-1). pap., act. bk. ed. 6.95 *(978-0-7460-3734-8(1))* EDC Publishing.

Weakland, Mark. Solve It with Scooby-Doo!: Math: Math, 1 vol. Gross, Scott, illus. 2014. (Solve It with Scooby-Doo!: Math Ser.). (ENG.). 24p. (gr. k-2). 111.96 *(978-1-4914-1543-6(6))* Capstone Press of Coughlan Cos.

Weill, Cynthia. Count Me In: A Parade of Mexican Folk Art Numbers in English & Spanish. Aguilar Sisters Staff, illus. 2012. (First Concepts in Mexican Folk Art Ser.). (ENG & SPA.). 32p. (J). (gr. k-k). 14.95 *(978-1-935955-39-9(X))* Cinco Puntos Pr.

Weiss, Ellen. Math in the Backyard. 2007. (Scholastic News Nonfiction Readers Ser.). (ENG., Illus.). 24p. (J). (gr. 1-2). 22.00 *(978-0-531-18529-2(X))* Scholastic Library Publishing.

—Math in the Car. 2007. (Scholastic News Nonfiction Readers Ser.). (ENG., Illus.). 24p. (J). (gr. 1-2). 22.00 *(978-0-531-18530-8(3))* Scholastic Library Publishing.

—Math in the Kitchen. 2007. (Scholastic News Nonfiction Readers Ser.). (ENG., Illus.). 24p. (J). (gr. 1-2). 22.00 *(978-0-531-18531-5(1))* Scholastic Library Publishing.

—Math in the Neighborhood. 2007. (Scholastic News Nonfiction Readers Ser.). (ENG., Illus.). 24p. (J). (gr. 1-2). 22.00 *(978-0-531-18532-2(X))*; pap. 6.95 *(978-0-531-18785-2(3))* Scholastic Library Publishing.

Wells, Robert E. Can You Count to a Googol? 2012. (J). *(978-1-61913-144-6(7))* Weigl Pubs., Inc.

White, Billy. Kids & Money. 2009. pap. *(978-1-61623-010-4(X))* Independent Pub.

White, Jason & Letts KS2 Staff. Maths Age 10-11. 2015. (Letts KS2 Success Ser.). (ENG., Illus.). 64p. (J). (gr. 5-6). pap. 8.95 *(978-1-84419-856-6(1))* HarperCollins Pubs. Ltd. GBR. Dist: Independent Pubs. Group.

White, Jason, et al. Maths & English Ages, 10-11. 2015. (Letts KS2 Success Ser.). (ENG., Illus.). 128p. (J). (gr. 5-6). pap. 12.95 *(978-1-84419-858-0(8))* HarperCollins Pubs. Ltd. GBR. Dist: Independent Pubs. Group.

White, Nancy. Make a Pattern: A Content Area Reader-math. 2005. (Emergent/Early (Prek-2) Math Package Ser.). 12p. (gr. k-2). 25.20 *(978-0-8215-7822-3(7))* Sadlier, William H. Inc.

Whiteford, Rhona, et al. Complete Maths, 4 bks. in 1. (Illus.). 96p. (YA). pap. 15.99 *(978-0-340-71581-9(2))* Hodder & Stoughton GBR. Dist: Trafalgar Square Publishing.

Whitmore, Andre. Math Lingo Homework Helper. 2007. 162p. pap. 22.50 *(978-0-615-16443-4(9))* American World Publishing.

Whyte, Elizabeth. Making Tally Charts. 2014. (Graph It! Ser.). 24p. (J). (gr. 1-3). 22.60 *(978-1-4824-0844-7(9))* Stevens, Gareth Publishing LLLP.

Wilkinson, Colin. Using Math in Construction. 2017. (Math You Will Actually Use Ser.). 48p. (J). (gr. 10-10). pap. 11.75 ***(978-1-4994-3852-9(4),*** Rosen Central) Rosen Publishing Group, Inc., The.

William H. Sadlier Staff. Count with Me. 2005. (Mathematics Ser.). (gr. -1-1). 24.00 net. *(978-0-8215-8928-1(8))* Sadlier, William H. Inc.

—Counting Sheep. 2005. (Emergent/Early (Prek-2) Math Package Ser.). 12p. (gr. -1-1). 25.20 *(978-0-8215-7842-1(1))* Sadlier, William H. Inc.

—New Progress in Mathematics. 2003. (New Progress in Mathematics Ser.). (gr. 7-18). stu. ed. 48.00 net. *(978-0-8215-1677-5(9))*; (gr. 8-18). stu. ed. 48.00 net. *(978-0-8215-1678-2(7))* Sadlier, William H. Inc.

—Over, under, Left, Right. 2005. (Emergent/Early (Prek-2) Math Package Ser.). 12p. (gr. -1-1). 25.20 *(978-0-8215-7844-5(8))* Sadlier, William H. Inc.

—Progress in Mathematics. 2006. (Progress in Mathematics 2006 Ser.). stu. ed., wbk. ed. 8.00 net. *(978-0-8215-8222-0(4))*; pap., stu. ed. 31.00 net. *(978-0-8215-8202-2(X))*; (gr. k-2). stu. ed. 8.00 net. *(978-0-8215-8220-6(8))*; (gr. k-2). pap., stu. ed. 23.00 net. *(978-0-8215-8200-8(3))*; (gr. 1-2). stu. ed. 8.00 net. *(978-0-8215-8221-3(6))*; (gr. 1-2). pap., stu. ed. 31.00 net. *(978-0-8215-8201-5(1))* Sadlier, William H. Inc.

—Yes, You Can. 2005. (Mathematics Ser.). (gr. -1-1). 24.00 net. *(978-0-8215-8918-2(0))* Sadlier, William H. Inc.

—You Can Sort. 2005. (Emergent/Early (Prek-2) Math Package Ser.). 12p. (gr. -1-1). 25.20 *(978-0-8215-7841-4(3))* Sadlier, William H. Inc.

Williams, Rozanne Lanczak. Adding. Jarrett, Michael, illus. Jarrett, Michael, photos by. 2004. (I Can Do Math Ser.). 24p. (gr. k-3). lib. bdg. 22.00 *(978-0-8368-4108-4(5),* Gareth Stevens Learning Library) Stevens, Gareth Publishing LLLP.

—Subtracting. Jarrett, Michael, photos by. 2004. (I Can Do Math Ser.). (Illus.). 24p. (gr. k-3). lib. bdg. 22.00 *(978-0-8368-4113-8(1),* Gareth Stevens Learning Library) Stevens, Gareth Publishing LLLP.

Williams, Zachary. Cleaning up the Park: Learning to Count by Fives. 2009. (Math for the REAL World Ser.). 12p. (gr. 1-2). pap. 5.90 *(978-0-8239-8892-1(9),* Rosen Classroom) Rosen Publishing Group, Inc., The.

Williams, Zella & Wingard-Nelson, Rebecca. Word Problems Using Addition & Subtraction. 2016. (Mastering Math Word Problems Ser.). (Illus.). 48p. (J). pap. 11.70 *(978-0-7660-8252-6(0))* Enslow Pubs., Inc.

Williamson, Brian. Comic Maths: Sue. 2012. 116p. pap. *(978-0-9561602-1-8(2))* Captain PapadopoulosPublishing Company, The.

Willoughby, Alana. Real Math Fourth Grade. (J). (gr. 4). stu. ed. *(978-0-8126-0504-4(7),* 60504) SRA/McGraw-Hill.

Willoughby, Stephen S., et al. Real Math. 2006. (Illus.). pap., stu. ed. 107.00 *(978-0-07-603002-6(4))* Open Court Publishing Co.

Wilson, Robert B. Learn it Fast! NJ ASK4 Math. 2005. per. 34.95 *(978-0-9772020-0-3(3))* Global Institute for Maximizing Potential, Incorporated.

Wingard-Nelson, Rebecca. Algebra & Pre-Algebra. 2008. (Math Busters Ser.). (Illus.). 64p. (J). (gr. 3-7). lib. bdg. 29.27 *(978-0-7660-2879-1(8))* Enslow Pubs., Inc.

—Algebra & Pre-Algebra: It's Easy. 2014. (Easy Genius Math Ser.). 64p. (J). (gr. 4-18). lib. bdg. 29.27 *(978-0-7660-4251-3(0))* Enslow Pubs., Inc.

—Data, Graphing, & Statistics Smarts! 2011. (Math Smarts! Ser.). (Illus.). 64p. (J). (gr. 5-18). pap. 8.95 *(978-1-59845-323-2(8))*; lib. bdg. 29.27 *(978-0-7660-3942-1(0))* Enslow Pubs., Inc.

—Division & Multiplication. 2008. (Math Busters Ser.). (Illus.). 64p. (J). (gr. 3-7). lib. bdg. 29.27 *(978-0-7660-2876-0(3))* Enslow Pubs., Inc.

—Fractions & Decimals Made Easy. Tom, LaBaff, illus. 2005. (Making Math Easy Ser.). 48p. (J). (gr. 2-4). lib. bdg. 25.27 *(978-0-7660-2513-4(6),* Enslow Elementary) Enslow Pubs., Inc.

—I Can Do Money Word Problems. 2009. (I Like Money Math! Ser.). (Illus.). 24p. (J). pap. 7.95 *(978-0-7660-3659-8(6),* Enslow Elementary); (gr. 1-3). lib. bdg. 22.60 *(978-0-7660-3145-6(4))* Enslow Pubs., Inc.

—Pre-Algebra & Algebra. 2012. (Ace Your Math Test Ser.). (Illus.). 104p. (J). (gr. 5-18). 33.27 *(978-0-7660-3782-3(7))* Enslow Pubs., Inc.

—Problem Solving & Word Problem Smarts! 2011. (Math Smarts! Ser.). (Illus.). 64p. (J). (gr. 5-18). pap. 8.95 *(978-1-59845-325-6(4))*; lib. bdg. 29.27 *(978-0-7660-3943-8(9))* Enslow Pubs., Inc.

—Ratios & Percents. 2008. (Math Busters Ser.). (Illus.). 64p. (J). (gr. 3-7). lib. bdg. 29.27 *(978-0-7660-2878-4(X))* Enslow Pubs., Inc.

—Ready for Addition. 2014. (Ready for Math Ser.). (Illus.). 48p. (J). (gr. 3-18). 25.27 *(978-0-7660-4245-2(6))* Enslow Pubs., Inc.

—Ready for Addition. LaBaff, Tom, illus. 2014. (Ready for Math Ser.). 48p. (J). pap. 8.95 *(978-1-4644-0433-7(X),* Enslow Elementary) Enslow Pubs., Inc.

—Ready for Word Problems & Problem Solving. LaBaff, Tom, illus. 2014. (Ready for Math Ser.). 48p. (J). pap. 8.95 *(978-1-4644-0443-6(7),* Enslow Elementary); (gr. 3-18). 25.27 *(978-0-7660-4250-6(2))* Enslow Pubs., Inc.

—Space Word Problems Starring Ratios & Proportions: Math Word Problems Solved. 2009. (Math Word Problems Solved Ser.). (Illus.). 48p. (J). (gr. 2-5). lib. bdg. 25.27 *(978-0-7660-2921-7(2))* Enslow Pubs., Inc.

—Sports Word Problems Starring Decimals & Percents. 2009. (Math Word Problems Solved Ser.). (Illus.). 48p. (J). (gr. 2-5). lib. bdg. 25.27 *(978-0-7660-2920-0(4))* Enslow Pubs., Inc.

—Word Problems Made Easy. LaBaff, Tom, illus. 2005. (Making Math Easy Ser.). 48p. (J). (gr. 2-4). lib. bdg. 25.27 *(978-0-7660-2512-7(8),* Enslow Elementary) Enslow Pubs., Inc.

Wingard-Nelson, Rebecca & Library. Geometry Word Problems: No Problem! 2010. (Math Busters Word Problems Ser.). (Illus.). 64p. (J). lib. bdg. 29.27 *(978-0-7660-3368-9(6))* Enslow Pubs., Inc.

—Graphing & Probability Word Problems: No Problem! 2010. (Math Busters Word Problems Ser.). (Illus.). 64p. (J). lib. bdg. 29.27 *(978-0-7660-3372-6(4))* Enslow Pubs., Inc.

—Math Measurement Word Problems: No Problem! 2010. (Math Busters Word Problems Ser.). (Illus.). 64p. (J). lib. bdg. 29.27 *(978-0-7660-3369-6(4))* Enslow Pubs., Inc.

Wise & Paco Dog's Multiplication Books. 2003. 3.99 *(978-0-915960-35-4(4))* Ebon Research Systems Publishing, LLC.

Witt, Joe & Gallaway, Kate. Managing Your Mathematics Classroom. 2005. 88p. 19.49 *(978-1-59318-484-1(0))* Cambium Education, Inc.

Woodford, Chris. Height. 2012. (Measure up Math Ser.). (Illus.). 32p. (J). (gr. 4-6). pap. 10.50 *(978-1-4339-7442-7(8))*; lib. bdg. 26.60 *(978-1-4339-7441-0(X))* Stevens, Gareth Publishing LLLP.

Woods, Mark. Xtreme! Owen, Ruth, illus. 2010. (Top Score Maths Ser.). 32p. pap. *(978-0-237-54282-5(X))* Evans Brothers, Ltd.

Woods, Mark & Owen, Ruth. Ace! 2010. (Top Score Maths Ser.). (Illus.). 32p. pap. *(978-0-237-54280-1(3))* Evans Brothers, Ltd.

—Goal! 2010. (Top Score Maths Ser.). (Illus.). 32p. pap. *(978-0-237-54279-5(X))* Evans Brothers, Ltd.

—Scrum! 2010. (Top Score Maths Ser.). (Illus.). 32p. pap. *(978-0-237-54281-8(1))* Evans Brothers, Ltd.

—Slam Dunk! 2010. (Top Score Maths Ser.). (Illus.). 32p. pap. *(978-0-237-54278-8(1))* Evans Brothers, Ltd.

Woods, Michael & Woods, Mary B. Ancient Computing Technology: From Abacuses to Water Clocks. 2011. (Technology in Ancient Cultures Ser.). (ENG.). 96p. (gr. 6-12). lib. bdg. 31.93 *(978-0-7613-6528-0(1))* Lerner Publishing Group.

World Almanac Puzzler Deck for Kids: Math (BoMC) World Almanac Deck: Math, 11-13. 2007. 9.95 *(978-0-8118-6243-1(7))* Chronicle Bks. LLC.

Wren, Coretta. Counting on God. 2006. 82p. (YA). per., act. bk. ed. *(978-0-9790934-0-1(6))* Know Me Pubn. LLC.

Wright, Joe. Math's Mate Orange: Student Pad. Tutos, Joanna, ed. McKenna, Lou, illus. 2013. 72p. pap. *(978-1-921535-55-0(5))* Educational Advantage Pty, Ltd.

Wright, Joseph B. Math's Mate Rose: Student Pad. Tutos, Joanna, ed. McKenna, Lou, illus. 2013. 72p. pap. *(978-1-921535-56-7(3))* Educational Advantage Pty, Ltd.

WRITE IT! Problem Solving with Numbers & Words, Grades 1-2. 2004. (J). per. 10.95 *(978-1-58123-363-6(9))* Larson Learning, Inc.

WRITE IT! Problem Solving with Numbers & Words Grades 3-4 SE. 2004. (J). per. 10.95 *(978-1-58123-361-2(2))* Larson Learning, Inc.

WRITE IT! Problem Solving with Numbers & Words, Grades 5-6. 2004. (J). per. 10.95 *(978-1-58123-365-0(5))* Larson Learning, Inc.

WRITE IT! Problem Solving with Numbers & Words, Grades 7-8. 2004. (J). per. 10.95 *(978-1-58123-367-4(1))* Larson Learning, Inc.

Wunderlich, Richard. Math on the Job. 2016. (ENG., Illus.). 32p. (J). lib. bdg. *(978-0-7787-2360-8(7))* Crabtree Publishing Co.

Wunderlich, Rick. Math on the Job: Building a Business. 2016. (ENG., Illus.). 32p. (J). *(978-0-7787-2357-8(7))* Crabtree Publishing Co.

—Math on the Job: Caring for Marine Animals. 2016. (ENG., Illus.). 32p. (J). *(978-0-7787-2358-5(5))* Crabtree Publishing Co.

—Math on the Job: Keeping People Healthy. 2016. (ENG., Illus.). 32p. (J). *(978-0-7787-2359-2(3))* Crabtree Publishing Co.

—Math on the Job: Working in Construction. 2016. (ENG., Illus.). 32p. (J). *(978-0-7787-2361-5(5))* Crabtree Publishing Co.

—Math on the Job: Working in Sports. 2016. (ENG., Illus.). 32p. (J). *(978-0-7787-2362-2(3))* Crabtree Publishing Co.

Wyborney, Steve. Week-By-Week Math Review for the Digital Classroom: Grade 1: Ready-To-Use, Animated PowerPoint(r) Slideshows with Practice Pages That Help Students Master Key Math Skills & Concepts. 2015. (Week-By-Week Math Review for the Digital Classroom Ser.). (ENG., Illus.). 80p. (gr. 1-1). pap. 12.99 *(978-0-545-77337-9(7),* Teaching Resources) Scholastic, Inc.

—Week-By-Week Math Review for the Digital Classroom: Grade 2: Ready-To-Use, Animated PowerPoint(r) Slideshows with Practice Pages That Help Students Master Key Math Skills & Concepts. 2015. (ENG., Illus.). 80p. (gr. 2-2). pap. 12.99 *(978-0-545-77339-3(3),* Teaching Resources) Scholastic, Inc.

—Week-By-Week Math Review for the Digital Classroom: Grade 3: Ready-To-Use, Animated PowerPoint(r) Slideshows with Practice Pages That Help Students Master Key Math Skills & Concepts. 2015. (ENG., Illus.). 80p. (gr. 3-3). pap. 12.99 *(978-0-545-77340-9(7),* Teaching Resources) Scholastic, Inc.

—Week-By-Week Math Review for the Digital Classroom: Grade 4: Ready-To-Use, Animated PowerPoint(r) Slideshows with Practice Pages That Help Students Master Key Math Skills & Concepts. 2015. (ENG., Illus.). 80p. (gr. 4-4). pap. 12.99 *(978-0-545-77342-3(3),* Teaching Resources) Scholastic, Inc.

—Week-By-Week Math Review for the Digital Classroom: Grade 5: Ready-To-Use, Animated PowerPoint(r) Slideshows with Practice Pages That Help Students Master Key Math Skills & Concepts. 2015. (ENG., Illus.). 80p. (gr. 5-5). pap. 12.99 *(978-0-545-77343-0(1),* Teaching Resources) Scholastic, Inc.

—Week-By-Week Math Review for the Digital Classroom: Grade 6: Ready-To-Use, Animated PowerPoint(r) Slideshows with Practice Pages That Help Students Master Key Math Skills & Concepts. 2015. (ENG., Illus.). 80p. (gr. 6-6). pap. 12.99 *(978-0-545-77344-7(X),* Teaching Resources) Scholastic, Inc.

Yates, Irene. Christmas Activities for ks1 Maths. 2005. pap. *(978-1-903853-68-9(0))* Brilliant Pubns.

—Christmas Activities for Ks2 Maths. 2005. (Illus.). 64p. pap. *(978-1-903853-69-6(9))* Brilliant Pubns.

Yeatts, Karol, et al. Navigating through problem Solving & Reasoning in Grade 3. House, Peggy A. & Litwiller, Bonnie H., eds. 2004. (Principles & Standards for School Mathematics Navigations Ser.). (Illus.). 65p. pap. 28.95 *(978-0-87353-557-1(X),* 12719) National Council of Teachers of Mathematics.

Yemm, Caterhine. Maths Problem Solving: Year 1, 6 vols. Endersby, Frank, illus. 2005. 106p. pap. *(978-1-903853-74-0(5))* Brilliant Pubns.

—Maths Problem Solving: Year 2, 6 vols. Endersby, Frank, illus. 2005. 106p. pap. *(978-1-903853-75-7(3))* Brilliant Pubns.

—Maths Problem Solving: Year 3, 6 vols. Endersby, Frank, illus. 2005. 80p. pap. *(978-1-903853-76-4(1))* Brilliant Pubns.

—Maths Problem Solving: Year 4, 6 vols. Endersby, Frank, illus. 2005. 80p. pap. *(978-1-903853-77-1(X))* Brilliant Pubns.

—Maths Problem Solving: Year 5, 6 vols. Endersby, Frank, illus. 2005. 80p. pap. *(978-1-903853-78-8(8))* Brilliant Pubns.

—Maths Problem Solving: Year 6, 6 vols. Endersby, Frank, illus. 2006. 80p. pap. *(978-1-903853-79-5(6))* Brilliant Pubns.

Yoder, Eric & Yoder, Natalie. Short Mysteries You Solve with Math! ¡Misterios Cortos Que Resuelves con Matemáticas! Geating, Karen & Villalobos, Yana Alfaro, trs. 2017. (One Minute Mysteries Ser.). (ENG & SPA., Illus.). 224p. (J). (gr. 6-9). pap. 12.95 *(978-1-938492-22-8(6))* Science, Naturally!

Yoon, Ae-hae. Who Eats First? Cruise, ed. Yang, Hae-won, illus. 2015. (ENG.). 38p. (J). (gr. -1-k). 16.95 *(978-1-939248-00-8(0))* Tantan Publishing.

York, Jamie. Making Math Meaningful: A 6th Grade. 2003. stu. ed. 8.95 *(978-1-892857-05-7(7))* Whole Spirit Pr.

—Making Math Meaningful: A 7th Grade. 2004. (YA). tchr. ed., spiral bd. 18.95 *(978-1-892857-11-8(1))* Whole Spirit Pr.

—Making Math Meaningful: A 7th Grade Student's Workbook. 2004. (YA). wbk. ed. 15.95 *(978-1-892857-12-5(X))* Whole Spirit Pr.

—Making Math Meaningful: A Middle School Math Curriculum for Teachers & Parents. 2nd ed. 2003. (J). spiral bd. 17.95 *(978-1-892857-04-0(9))* 3rd ed. 2004. per. 22.95 *(978-1-892857-08-8(1))* Whole Spirit Pr.

—Making Math Meaningful: An 8th Grade. 2004. (YA). tchr. ed., spiral bd. 18.95 *(978-1-892857-09-5(X))* Whole Spirit Pr.

—Making Math Meaningful: An 8th Grade Student's Workbook. 2004. (YA). wbk. ed. 15.95 *(978-1-892857-10-1(3))* Whole Spirit Pr.

Youssef, Jagger. Making Bar Graphs. 2014. (Graph It! Ser.). 24p. (J). (gr. 1-3). 22.60 *(978-1-4824-0779-2(5))* Stevens, Gareth Publishing LLLP.

Yoyo Books, creator. Numbers. 2011. (Baby's First Library). (ENG., Illus.). 40p. (gr. -1-k). bds. *(978-94-6033-702-4(3))* YoYo Bks.

Zable, Stacy. City by the Lake: Set Of 6. 2011. (Early Connections Ser.). (J). pap. 39.00 net. *(978-1-4108-1542-2(0))* Benchmark Education Co.

—Four Faces in Rock: Set Of 6. 2010. (Early Connections Ser.). (J). pap. 39.00 net. *(978-1-4108-1539-2(0))* Benchmark Education Co.

Zahn, Peter. Let's Recycle. 2013. (Rosen Math Readers Ser.). (ENG.). 24p. (J). (gr. 1-2). pap. 8.25 *(978-1-4777-2109-4(6),* Rosen Classroom) Rosen Publishing Group, Inc., The.

—Let's Recycle: Represent & Solve Addition Problems. 2013. (Rosen Math Readers Ser.). 24p. (J). (gr. 1-2). (ENG.). pap. 49.50 *(978-1-4777-2110-0(X),* Rosen Classroom); lib. bdg. 22.60 *(978-1-4777-2207-7(6),* PowerKids Pr.) Rosen Publishing Group, Inc., The.

Zander, Alex. The School Track Meet. 2013. (Core Math Skills: Numbers & Operations in Base 10 Ser.). 24p. (J). (gr. 1-2). 22.60 *(978-1-4777-2223-7(8),* Rosen Classroom) Rosen Publishing Group, Inc., The.

—The School Track Meet: Understand Place Value. 2013. (Rosen Math Readers Ser.). (ENG.). 24p. (J). (gr. 1-2). pap. 49.50 *(978-1-4777-2041-7(3))*; pap. 8.25 *(978-1-4777-2040-0(5))* Rosen Publishing Group, Inc., The. (Rosen Classroom).

Zike, Dinah & McGraw-Hill-Glencoe Staff. Mathematics - Applications & Concepts. 2004. (MATH APPLIC & CONN CRSE Ser.). (ENG., Illus.). 304p. (gr. 6-7). per. 34.32 *(978-0-07-868215-5(0),* 0078682150) McGraw-Hill Higher Education.

Zolty, Howard. What Is Math? Answer: Math Is Everything. 2005. 28p. 14.21 *(978-1-4116-6717-4(4))* Lulu Pr., Inc.

Zuchora-Walske, Christine. Working in Math. 2018. (ENG.). 32p. (gr. 3-6). ***(978-1-63235-446-4(2),*** 12-Story Library) Pr. Room Editions LLC.

MATHEMATICS—DATA PROCESSING

Allen-Conn, B. J. & Rose, Kim. Powerful Ideas in the Classroom Using Squeak to Enhance Math & Science Learning. 2003. (Illus.). 86p. per. *(978-0-9743131-0-8(6))* Viewpoints Research Institute, Inc.

Drew, Jon. Matt's Field Day: Represent & Interpret Data. 2013. (InfoMax Math Readers Ser.). (ENG.). 24p. (J). (gr. 1-2). pap. 49.50 *(978-1-4777-2140-7(1))*; (Illus.). pap. 8.25 *(978-1-4777-2139-1(8))* Rosen Publishing Group, Inc., The. (Rosen Classroom).

Harris, Patricia. Understanding Coding by Building Algorithms. 2016. (Spotlight on Kids Can Code Ser.). 00024p. (J). (gr. 4-5). pap. 11.75 *(978-1-4994-2793-6(X),* PowerKids Pr.) Rosen Publishing Group, Inc., The.

Saddleback Publishing, creator. Math Computation Skills & Strategies: Level 3. 2006. (Math Computation Skills & Strategies Ser.). (Illus.). 143p. (YA). per. *(978-1-56254-966-4(9))* Saddleback Educational Publishing, Inc.

—Math Computation Skills & Strategies: Level 4. 2006. (Math Computation Skills & Strategies Ser.). (Illus.). 144p. per. *(978-1-56254-967-1(7))* Saddleback Educational Publishing, Inc.

—Math Computation Skills & Strategies: Level 5. 2006. (Math Computation Skills & Strategies Ser.). (Illus.). 144p. per. *(978-1-56254-968-8(5))* Saddleback Educational Publishing, Inc.

—Math Computation Skills & Strategies: Level 6. 2006. (Math Computation Skills & Strategies Ser.). (Illus.). 144p. (YA). per. *(978-1-56254-969-5(3))* Saddleback Educational Publishing, Inc.

—Math Computation Skills & Strategies: Level 7. 2006. (Math Computation Skills & Strategies Ser.). (Illus.). 144p. (YA). per.

19.95 *(978-1-56254-970-1(7))* Saddleback Educational Publishing, Inc.

—Math Computation Skills & Strategies: Level 8. 2006. (Math Computation Skills & Strategies Ser.). (Illus.). 144p. (YA). per. *(978-1-56254-971-8(5))* Saddleback Educational Publishing, Inc.

Stuart, Liam. The Parade: Understand Place Value. 2013. (Rosen Math Readers Ser.). (ENG.). 24p. (J). (gr. 1-2). pap. 49.50 *(978-1-4777-2071-4(5),* Rosen Classroom) Rosen Publishing Group, Inc., The.

MATHEMATICS—DICTIONARIES

Abdelnoor, R. E. Jason. A Mathematical Dictionary for IGCSE. 2014. (ENG., Illus.). 136p. pap. 13.00 *(978-0-7487-8196-6(X))* Oxford Univ. Pr., Inc.

Collins Dictionaries, Collins & Broadbent, Paul. Collins Maths Dictionary: Trusted Support for Learning. 2017. (ENG., Illus.). 144p. (J). (gr. k-6). pap. 15.99 ***(978-0-00-821237-7(6))*** HarperCollins Pubs. Ltd. GBR. Dist: Independent Pubs. Group.

De Klerk, Judith. Illustrated Maths Dictionary for Australian Schools. 2nd ed. Date not set. (Illus.). 123p. pap. 59.50 *(978-0-582-87045-1(3))* Addison-Wesley Longman, Ltd. GBR. Dist: Trans-Atlantic Pubns., Inc.

Fitzgerald, Theresa R. Math Dictionary for Kids: The #1 Guide for Helping Kids with Math. 5th rev. ed. 2016. (ENG., Illus.). 175p. (J). (gr. 4-9). pap. 13.95 *(978-1-61821-617-5(1))* Prufrock Pr.

—Math Dictionary for Kids: The Essential Guide to Math Terms, Strategies, & Tables. 2005. (ENG., Illus.). 110p. (gr. 4-7). pap. 12.95 *(978-1-59363-160-4(X))* Prufrock Pr.

Gardner, Kay. Maths Dictionary. 2005. (Collins Primary Dictionaries Ser.). (ENG., Illus.). 16p. (J). pap. 15.99 *(978-0-00-720783-1(2))* HarperCollins Pubs. Ltd. GBR. Dist: Independent Pubs. Group.

Large, Tori. The Usborne Illustrated Dictionary of Math. Constantine, Adam, illus. 2007. 128p. (J). (gr. 4-7). pap. 12.99 *(978-0-7945-1629-1(7),* Usborne) EDC Publishing.

—The Usborne Illustrated Dictionary of Math. Rogers, Kirsteen, ed. Constantine, Adam, illus. 2007. (Usborne Illustrated Dictionaries Ser.). 128p. (YA). (gr. 7). lib. bdg. 20.99 *(978-1-60130-013-3(1),* Usborne) EDC Publishing.

Middle School Math, Course 1: Multi-Language Visual Glossary. 2004. (gr. 6-9). *(978-0-618-26963-1(0),* 2-05799) Holt McDougal.

PRAESA & Press, Karen. The Cambridge Mathematics Dictionary for Schools Afrikaans Translation. 2008. pap. *(978-0-521-70883-8(4))* Cambridge Univ. Pr.

Rogers, Kirsteen. First Illustrated Math Dictionary IR. 2013. (Illustrated Dictionaries Ser.). 136p. (J). pap. 12.99 *(978-0-7945-3197-3(0),* Usborne) EDC Publishing.

Rogers, Kirsteen & Large, Tori. Illustrated Elementary Math Dictionary. 2010. (Illustrated Dictionaries Ser.). 135p. (YA). (gr. 3-18). pap. 12.99 *(978-0-7945-2143-1(6),* Usborne) EDC Publishing.

University of Cape Town Staff & Press, Karen. The Cambridge Mathematics Dictionary for Schools. 2008. pap. *(978-0-521-70882-1(6))* Cambridge Univ. Pr.

MATHEMATICS—HISTORY

Baptiste, Tracey. Mathematics: The Study of Numbers, Quantity, & Space, 1 vol. 2015. (ENG.). 64p. (YA). 31.70 *(978-1-62275-530-1(8),* Britannica Educational Publishing) Rosen Publishing Group, Inc., The.

Downey, Tika. How the Arabs Invented Algebra: The History of the Concept of Variables. 2009. (Powermath Ser.). (ENG., Illus.). 32p. (gr. 4-5). pap. 10.00 *(978-0-8239-8879-2(1),* PowerKids Pr.) Rosen Publishing Group, Inc., The.

Flood, Raymond & Wilson, Robin. Great Mathematicians. 2012. (Great People in History Ser.). (ENG., Illus.). 128p. (YA). (gr. 8-12). 34.60 *(978-1-4777-0402-8(7))* Rosen Publishing Group, Inc., The.

Flynn, Mike. Infinity Explained, 1 vol. 2015. (ENG.). 136p. (J). 38.25 *(978-1-4777-8127-2(7),* Rosen Young Adult) Rosen Publishing Group, Inc., The.

Levy, Joel. Exploring the Mysteries of Mathematics. 2016. (STEM Guide to the Universe Ser.). (ENG.). 192p. (gr. 9-9). lib. bdg. 46.10 *(978-1-4994-6406-1(1))* Rosen Publishing Group, Inc., The.

World Book, Inc. Staff, contrib. by. Counting Pebbles to Writing Code: A Timeline of Mathematics & Computers. 2016. (J). *(978-0-7166-3541-3(0))* World Bk., Inc.

MATHEMATICS—POETRY

Franco, Betsy & Salerno, Steven. Mathematickles! 2006. (Illus.). (gr. k-5). 18.00 *(978-0-7569-6709-3(0))* Perfection Learning Corp.

Souders, Taryn. Whole-Y Cow! Fractions Are Fun. Mai-Wyss, Tatjana, illus. 2010. (ENG & ACE.). 40p. (J). (gr. 1-4). 15.95 *(978-1-58536-460-2(6),* 202182) Sleeping Bear Pr.

Vergo, Franny. Mathapalooza: A Collection of Math Poetry for Primary & Intermediate Students. 2012. 56p. pap. 11.95 *(978-1-4685-4269-1(9))* AuthorHouse.

MATHEMATICS—STUDY AND TEACHING

Ali, Fayad W. Practice Tests for NCSE Mathematics. 2014. (ENG.). 96p. spiral bd. 13.00 *(978-1-4085-0553-3(3))* Oxford Univ. Pr., Inc.

Anderson, Jill. Money Math with Sebastian Pig & Friends at the Farmer's Market. Huntington, Amy, illus. 2009. (Math Fun with Sebastian Pig & Friends! Ser.). 32p. (J). (gr. k-3). lib. bdg. 23.94 *(978-0-7660-3364-1(3))* Enslow Pubs., Inc.

Anderson, Wendy. Expeditions. 2007. (Action Numeracy Middle Primary Ser.). 32p. pap. 9.95 *(978-0-86431-646-2(1))* ACER Pr. AUS. Dist: ISBS Publisher Services.

Arroyo, Sheri, et al. How Chefs Use Math. 2009. (Math in the Real World Ser.). 32p. (gr. 4-6). 28.00 *(978-1-60413-608-1(1),* Chelsea Clubhouse) Facts On File, Inc.

—How Deep Sea Divers Use Math. 2009. (Math in the Real World Ser.). 32p. (gr. 4-6). 28.00 *(978-1-60413-611-1(1),* Chelsea Clubhouse) Facts On File, Inc.

Atkinson, Sue. Supermaths: Age 4-5. 2003. (Illus.). 32p. pap. *(978-0-340-80559-6(5),* Hodder Children's Books) Hachette Children's Group.

—Supermaths 3: Age 3-6. 2003. (Illus.). 32p. pap. *(978-0-340-80561-9(7),* Hodder Children's Books) Hachette Children's Group.

Atkinson, Sue & Baxter, Cathy. Modwl 1 - Llyfr Gweithgareddau 5. 2005. (WEL., Illus.). 15p. *(978-1-86085-035-6(9))* ICA Video.

Atkinson, Sue & Canals, Sonia. A Modwl 1 - Llyfr Cyswllt Cartref. 2005. (WEL., Illus.). 15p. *(978-1-86085-045-5(6))* ICA Video.

Bartch, Marian. Math & Stories, Grades K-3. Street Level Studio, illus. 2007. 173p. per. 17.95 *(978-1-59647-222-8(7))* Good Year Bks.

Bennett, Clinton. Middle School Math Course 1. 4th ed. 2004. (Holt Middle School Math Ser.). (SPA., Illus.). 60.40 *(978-0-03-070976-0(8))* Holt McDougal.

—Middle School Math Course 2. 4th ed. 2004. (Hold Middle School Math Ser.). (SPA., Illus.). 62.46 *(978-0-03-071098-8(7))* Holt McDougal.

Bingham, Chauna. A Guide to Middle School Math. 2009. 96p. pap. 15.99 *(978-1-4415-3390-6(7))* Xlibris Corp.

Bolster. Exploring Mathematics. (J). pap., wbk. ed. 9.10 *(978-0-673-33130-4(X));* (gr. 1). pap., wbk. ed. 9.95 *(978-0-673-33131-1(8));* (gr. 5). pap., wbk. ed. 11.85 *(978-0-673-33135-9(0))* Addison-Wesley Educational Pubs., Inc.

Braidich, Victoria. Animals on the Farm: Learning to Compare Size. 2009. (Math for the REAL World Ser.). 12p. (gr. 1-2). pap. 5.90 *(978-0-8239-8847-1(3),* Rosen Classroom) Rosen Publishing Group, Inc., The.

Collins, Kathleen. A Day with the Baker: Learning to Tell Time by Quarter Hours. 2009. (Math for the REAL World Ser.). 16p. (gr. 2-3). pap. 7.05 *(978-0-8239-8854-9(6),* Rosen Classroom) Rosen Publishing Group, Inc., The.

Cortland, D J. A Look at Books: Learning to Count by Tens to 50. 2009. (Math for the REAL World Ser.). 12p. (gr. 1-2). pap. 5.90 *(978-0-8239-8890-7(2),* Rosen Classroom) Rosen Publishing Group, Inc., The.

Cotugno, Megan. Measure It!, 1 vol., Set. Incl. Distance, Area, & Volume. Somervill, Barbara A. pap. 8.29 *(978-1-4329-3769-0(3));* Mass & Weight. Somervill, Barbara A. pap. 8.29 *(978-1-4329-3771-3(5));* Speed & Acceleration. Somervill, Barbara A. pap. 8.29 *(978-1-4329-3770-6(7));* Temperature. Rand, Casey. pap. 8.29 *(978-1-4329-3773-7(1));* Time. Rand, Casey. pap. 8.29 *(978-1-4329-3772-0(3));* (Illus.). (gr. 3-6). (Measure It! Ser.). (ENG.). 32p. 2010. Set pap. 39.95 *(978-1-4329-3774-4(X),* Heinemann InfoSearch) Heinemann-Raintree.

Dorling Kindersley Publishing Staff. Math Grade 1. 2014. (ENG.). 60p. (J). (gr. k-4). pap., wbk. ed. 6.99 *(978-1-4654-1733-6(8),* DK Children) Dorling Kindersley Publishing, Inc.

—Math Grade 2. 2014. (ENG.). 60p. (J). (gr. 1-4). pap. 6.99 *(978-1-4654-1734-3(6),* DK Children) Dorling Kindersley Publishing, Inc.

—Math Grade 3. 2014. (ENG.). 60p. (J). (gr. 2-4). pap. 6.99 *(978-1-4654-1735-0(4),* DK Children) Dorling Kindersley Publishing, Inc.

—Math Grade K. 2014. (ENG.). 60p. (J). (gr. -1-1). pap. 6.99 *(978-1-4654-1732-9(X),* DK Children) Dorling Kindersley Publishing, Inc.

—Math Grade Pre-K. 2014. (ENG.). 60p. (J). (gr. -1-k). pap. 6.99 *(978-1-4654-1731-2(1),* DK Children) Dorling Kindersley Publishing, Inc.

Dukes, Dorothy. Kg - 2nd Grade Basic Math Elements. 2009. 121p. pap. 10.34 *(978-0-557-16210-9(6))* Lulu Pr., Inc.

Epps, S. Emmanuel & Robateau, Lisa. Bubble Brain: Story Time Rhymes That Build the Mind. 2013. 34p. pap. 12.95 *(978-0-9911410-0-5(8))* Addi-Boo Bks.

ETA Cuisenaire Staff. Hands-On-Standards, Common Core Edition, Teacher's Resource Guide, Grade 1: Book. 2012. (ENG.). (gr. k-8). pap. 67.95 *(978-0-7406-9430-1(8))* ETA hand2mind.

—Hands-On-Standards, Common Core Edition, Teacher's Resource Guide, Grade 2: Book. 2012. (ENG.). (gr. k-8). pap. 67.95 *(978-0-7406-9431-8(6))* ETA hand2mind.

—Hands-On-Standards, Common Core Edition, Teacher's Resource Guide, Grade 3: Book. 2012. (ENG.). (gr. k-8). pap. 67.95 *(978-0-7406-9432-5(4))* ETA hand2mind.

—Hands-On-Standards, Common Core Edition, Teacher's Resource Guide, Grade 4: Book. 2012. (ENG.). (gr. k-8). pap. 67.95 *(978-0-7406-9433-2(2))* ETA hand2mind.

—Hands-On-Standards, Common Core Edition, Teacher's Resource Guide, Grade 5: Book. 2012. (ENG.). (gr. k-8). pap. 67.95 *(978-0-7406-9434-9(0))* ETA hand2mind.

—Hands-On-Standards, Common Core Edition, Teacher's Resource Guide, Grade 6: Book. 2012. (ENG.). (gr. k-8). pap. 67.95 *(978-0-7406-9444-8(8))* ETA hand2mind.

—Hands-On-Standards, Common Core Edition, Teacher's Resource Guide, Grade 7: Book. 2012. (ENG.). (gr. k-8). pap. 67.95 *(978-0-7406-9445-5(6))* ETA hand2mind.

—Hands-On-Standards, Common Core Edition, Teacher's Resource Guide, Grade 8: Book. 2012. (ENG.). (gr. k-8). pap. 67.95 *(978-0-7406-9446-2(4))* ETA hand2mind.

—Hands-On-Standards, Common Core Edition, Teacher's Resource Guide, Grade K: Book. 2012. (ENG.). (gr. k-8). pap. 67.95 *(978-0-7406-9429-5(4))* ETA hand2mind.

Evan-Moor Educational Publishers, creator. At-Home Tutor Math, Grade 2. 2014. (ENG., Illus.). 89p. (J). (gr. 2). pap. 9.99 *(978-1-61368-982-0(9))* Evan-Moor Educational Pubs.

Everhart, Loretta Jean. Math Vitamins: Daily Dose for Students Learning How to Solve Word Problems. 2011. 164p. pap. 12.95 *(978-1-4620-3251-8(6))* iUniverse, Inc.

Exploring Mathematics. (J). (gr. 2). pap., wbk. ed. 9.95 *(978-0-673-33132-8(6));* (gr. 3). pap., wbk. ed. 11.85 *(978-0-673-33133-5(4))* Addison-Wesley Educational Pubs., Inc.

Flash Kids Editors, ed. Addition Activities: Grade 1 (Flash Skills) 2010. (Flash Skills Ser.). (ENG.). 64p. (J). pap. 3.95 *(978-1-4114-3458-5(7),* Spark Publishing Group) Sterling Publishing Co., Inc.

—Addition Activities: Grade 2 (Flash Skills) 2010. (Flash Skills Ser.). (ENG.). 64p. (J). pap. 3.95 *(978-1-4114-3453-0(6),* Spark Publishing Group) Sterling Publishing Co., Inc.

Franco, Betsy. Funny Fairy Tale Math, Grades 3-4: 15 Rib-Tickling Reproducible Stories with Companion Word Problems That Build Key Math Skills & Concepts. 2011. (ENG.). 64p. (gr. 3-4). pap. 11.99 *(978-0-545-28510-0(0),* Teaching Resources) Scholastic, Inc.

Freudentha, H. Digging Numbers: Math/Context. 3rd ed. 2003. (J). 7.86 *(978-0-03-071716-1(7))* Holt, Rinehart & Winston of Canada, Ltd. CAN. Dist: Harcourt Canada, Ltd.

—Pattern & Figures: Math/Context. 3rd ed. 2003. (Math in Context Ser.). (J). 7.86 *(978-0-03-071702-4(7))* Holt, Rinehart & Winston of Canada, Ltd. CAN. Dist: Harcourt Canada, Ltd.

—Re-Allotment: Math/Context. 3rd ed. 2003. (SPA.). (J). 7.86 *(978-0-03-072354-4(X))* Holt, Rinehart & Winston of Canada, Ltd. CAN. Dist: Harcourt Canada, Ltd.

George, Abigail. Freaky Bug Facts! Understand Place Value, 1 vol. 2015. (InfoMax Common Core Math Readers Ser.). (ENG.). 24p. (J). pap. 8.25 *(978-1-4777-4837-4(7),* Rosen Classroom) Rosen Publishing Group, Inc., The.

Goodman, Jenny. Cambridge Mathematics NSW Syllabus for the Australian Curriculum Year 8 Teacher Edition. 2014. (ENG.). pap., tchr. ed. *(978-1-107-65058-9(5))* Cambridge Univ. Pr.

Goren, Ada. Math Story Mats: 16 Ready-to-Use Story Mats That Boost Essential Listening & Math Skills. 2012. (Follow-The-Directions Ser.). (ENG.). 80p. (gr. k-2). pap. 12.99 *(978-0-545-28072-3(9),* Teaching Resources) Scholastic, Inc.

Gow, Mary. Archimedes: Genius Mathematician. 2015. (Genius Scientists & Their Genius Ideas Ser.). 96p. (J). (gr. 5-12). 27.94 *(978-0-7660-6530-7(8));* pap. 10.95 *(978-0-7660-6531-4(6))* Enslow Pubs., Inc.

Hall, Kevin. 10 Great Makerspace Projects Using Math. 2017. (Using Makerspaces for School Projects Ser.). 64p. (gr. 11-11). 34.45 ***(978-1-4994-3846-8(X),*** Rosen Central) Rosen Publishing Group, Inc., The.

Hammelef, Danielle S. That Figures! A Crash Course in Math, 1 vol. 2014. (Crash Course Ser.). (ENG.). 64p. (gr. 4-5). lib. bdg. 34.65 *(978-1-4914-0774-5(3))* Capstone Press of Coughlan Cos.

Harcourt School Publishers Staff. Harcourt Matematicas, Grade 1. 2nd ed. 2003. (Harcourt Matematicas Ser.). (SPA.). (gr. 1-18). Vol. 1. tchr. ed. 140.60 *(978-0-15-321616-9(6))* Vol. 2. tchr. ed. 140.60 *(978-0-15-321617-6(4))* Harcourt Schl. Pubs.

—Harcourt Matematicas, Grade 2. 2nd ed. 2003. (Harcourt Matematicas Ser.). (SPA.). (gr. 2-18). Vol. 1. tchr. ed. 140.60 *(978-0-15-321618-3(2))* Vol. 2. tchr. ed. 140.60 *(978-0-15-321619-0(0))* Harcourt Schl. Pubs.

—Harcourt Matematicas, Grade 3. 2nd ed. 2003. (Harcourt Matematicas Ser.). (SPA.). (gr. 3-18). Vol. 1. tchr. ed. 157.50 *(978-0-15-321620-6(4))* Vol. 2. tchr. ed. 157.50 *(978-0-15-321621-3(2))* Harcourt Schl. Pubs.

—Harcourt Matematicas, Grade 4. 2nd ed. 2003. (Harcourt Matematicas Ser.). (SPA.). (gr. 4-18). Vol. 1. tchr. ed. 158.90 *(978-0-15-321622-0(0))* Vol. 2. tchr. ed. 158.90 *(978-0-15-321623-7(9))* Harcourt Schl. Pubs.

—Harcourt Matematicas, Grade 4: Practice Workbook. 2nd ed. 2003. (Harcourt Matematicas Ser.). (SPA.). (gr. 4-18). tchr. ed., wbk. ed. 23.30 *(978-0-15-321639-8(5))* Harcourt Schl. Pubs.

—Harcourt Matematicas, Grade 5. 2nd ed. 2003. (Harcourt Matematicas Ser.). (SPA.). (gr. 5-18). Vol. 1. tchr. ed. 158.90 *(978-0-15-321624-4(7))* Vol. 2. tchr. ed. 158.90 *(978-0-15-321625-1(5))* Harcourt Schl. Pubs.

—Harcourt Matematicas, Grade 6. 2nd ed. 2003. (Harcourt Matematicas Ser.). (SPA.). (gr. 6-18). Vol. 1. tchr. ed. 158.90 *(978-0-15-321626-8(3))* Vol. 2. tchr. ed. 158.90 *(978-0-15-321627-5(1))* Harcourt Schl. Pubs.

—Harcourt Matematicas, Grade K: Teacher's Resource Book. 2nd ed. 2003. (Harcourt Matematicas Ser.). (SPA.). (gr. k-6). tchr. ed. 63.90 *(978-0-15-321680-0(8))* Harcourt Schl. Pubs.

—Harcourt Math: Practice Workbook. 2nd ed. 2003. (Harcourt School Publishers Math Ser.). (Illus.). (ENG.). 176p. (gr. 4-4). pap., wbk. ed. 13.25 *(978-0-15-320769-3(8));* (gr. 6-18). wbk. ed. 9.80 *(978-0-15-320786-0(8))* Harcourt Schl. Pubs.

—Zoo Zillions: User's Guide. 98th ed. 2003. (Mighty Mathtm Ser.). (Illus.). (gr. k-3). pap., pupil's gde. ed. 11.00 *(978-0-15-307970-2(3))* Harcourt Schl. Pubs.

Hirakawa, Diane M. Math 101 for Busy Families: K-6 Monthly Activities. 2007. (Illus.). 48p. pap. 12.95 *(978-1-890035-63-1(7))* New Century Pr.

Holt, Rinehart and Winston Staff. Digging Numbers: Math/Context. 3rd ed. 2003. (J). tchr. ed. 31.60 *(978-0-03-071717-8(5))* Holt, Rinehart & Winston of Canada, Ltd. CAN. Dist: Harcourt Canada, Ltd.

—Holt Science & Technology: Math Skills Worksheets. 5th ed. 2004. (Illus.). pap., wbk. ed. 11.60 *(978-0-03-035198-3(7))* Holt McDougal.

—Insights & Data: Math/Context. 3rd ed. 2003. (J). tchr. ed. 31.60 *(978-0-03-071701-7(9))* Holt, Rinehart & Winston of Canada, Ltd. CAN. Dist: Harcourt Canada, Ltd.

—Number Tools: Math Context. 3rd ed. 2003. (SPA.). (J). pap. 42.66 *(978-0-03-072433-6(3))* Holt, Rinehart & Winston of Canada, Ltd. CAN. Dist: Harcourt Canada, Ltd.

—Number Tools Vol. 2: Math/Context. 3rd ed. 2003. (SPA.). (J). 42.66 *(978-0-03-072428-2(7))* Holt, Rinehart & Winston of Canada, Ltd. CAN. Dist: Harcourt Canada, Ltd.

—Number Tools Workbook Math/Contt. 3rd ed. 2003. (Math in Context Ser.). (J). pap., wbk. ed. 24.66 *(978-0-03-072582-1(8))* Holt, Rinehart & Winston of Canada, Ltd. CAN. Dist: Harcourt Canada, Ltd.

—Reflections & Numbers: Math/Context. 3rd ed. 2003. (J). tchr. ed. 31.60 *(978-0-03-071709-3(4))* Holt, Rinehart & Winston of Canada, Ltd. CAN. Dist: Harcourt Canada, Ltd.

—Teaching Math to All Students Package. 4th ed. 2004. 1200.00 *(978-0-03-037951-2(2));* 5333.36 *(978-0-03-037953-6(9));* 2266.67 *(978-0-03-037952-9(0))* Holt McDougal.

James, Rosemary. What Do Scientists Do? Solve Problems Involving Measurement & Estimation, 1 vol. 2015. (InfoMax Common Core Math Readers Ser.). (ENG.). 24p. (J). pap. 8.25 *(978-1-4777-4603-5(X),* Rosen Classroom) Rosen Publishing Group, Inc., The.

Kaufman, Elliott, photos by. Numbers Everywhere. 2013. (ENG., Illus.). 32p. (J). (gr. -1). 12.95 *(978-0-7892-1157-6(2),* Abbeville Kids) Abbeville Pr., Inc.

Kiernan, Denise & Mitchell, Cindi. Motivating Math Homework: 80 Reproducible Practice Pages That Reinforce Key Math Skills. 2009. (ENG.). 96p. (gr. 2-3). pap. 14.99 *(978-0-545-16832-8(5),* Teaching Resources) Scholastic, Inc.

Kovacs, Nicola. Digging Deep. 2007. (Action Numeracy Middle Primary Ser.). 32p. pap. 9.95 *(978-0-86431-694-3(1))* ACER Pr. AUS. Dist: ISBS Publisher Services.

Layne, Steven L. Number 1 Teacher: A School Counting Book. Ettlinger, Doris & Layne, Deborah, illus. 2008. (ENG.). 40p. (J). (gr. k-6). 17.95 *(978-1-58536-307-0(3))* Sleeping Bear Pr.

LernerClassroom Editors, ed. Teaching Guide for Manga Math Mysteries. 2010. pap. 5.95 *(978-0-7613-6679-9(2))* Lerner Publishing Group.

Levy, Joel. Exploring the Mysteries of Mathematics. 2016. (STEM Guide to the Universe Ser.). (ENG.). 192p. (gr. 9-9). lib. bdg. 46.10 *(978-1-4994-6406-1(1))* Rosen Publishing Group, Inc., The.

Lindeen, Mary. Forest Doubles, 1 vol. 2011. (Wonder Readers Fluent Level Ser.). (ENG.). (gr. -1-2). 32p. pap. 5.99 *(978-1-4296-7922-0(0));* 16p. pap. 35.94 *(978-1-4296-8089-9(X))* Capstone Press of Coughlan Cos. (Wonder Readers).

Loughran, Donna & Brunner-Jass, Renata. Field of Play: Measuring Distance, Rate, & Time. 2013. (IMath Ser.). (Illus.). 48p. (J). (gr. 5-6). pap. 11.94 *(978-1-60357-510-2(3));* lib. bdg. 23.94 *(978-1-59953-571-5(8))* Norwood Hse. Pr.

Maletsky, Evan A., et al. Check What You Know: Intervention Practice Books. 2003. (Harcourt Math Ser.). (gr. 3-18). 10.70 *(978-0-15-324442-1(9));* (gr. 4-18). 10.70 *(978-0-15-324443-8(7));* (gr. 5-18). 11.50 *(978-0-15-324444-5(5));* (gr. 6-18). 12.10 *(978-0-15-324445-2(3))* Harcourt Schl. Pubs.

Marie-France, Marcie & Lebuis, Peter. Additions Chansons et Activités, 2 vols. 2013. (ENG & FRE.). 64p. 19.95 *(978-1-55386-226-0(0),* 9781553862260) Jordan, Sara Publishing.

—Divisions Chansons et Activités, 1 vol. 2013. (ENG & FRE.). 64p. 19.95 *(978-1-55386-235-2(X),* 9781553862352) Jordan, Sara Publishing.

—Multiplications Chansons et Activités, 2 vols. 2013. (ENG & FRE.). 64p. 19.95 *(978-1-55386-229-1(5),* 9781553862291) Jordan, Sara Publishing.

—Soustractions Chansons et Activités, 2 vols. 2013. (ENG & FRE.). 64p. 19.95 *(978-1-55386-232-1(5),* 9781553862321) Jordan, Sara Publishing.

McCallum, Ann. A Kid's Multicultural Math Adventure: Amazing Activities to Explore Math's Global Roots! Norton, Carolyn, illus. 2004. (Williamson Multicultural Kids Can! Book Ser.). 128p. (J). pap. 14.95 *(978-1-885593-92-4(9),* Ideal Pubns.) Worthy Publishing.

MCP Mathematics, Level E. 2003. (J). 28.50 *(978-0-8136-3113-4(0))* Modern Curriculum Pr.

MCP Mathematics. 2005. (J). (gr. k-6). tchr. ed. 29.95 *(978-0-7652-6065-9(4));* tchr. ed. 29.95 *(978-0-7652-6063-5(8))* Seymour, Dale Pubns.

Mercer, Susan. Pathway to Pre-Algebra Proficiency. 2008. 76p. per. 14.95 *(978-1-4327-1719-3(7))* Outskirts Pr., Inc.

Miles Kelly Staff. Science & Maths. 2003. (Flip Quiz Ser.). (Illus.). 38p. (J). (gr. 10-11). spiral bd. 5.95 *(978-1-84236-032-3(9));* (gr. 11-12). spiral bd. 5.95 *(978-1-84236-033-0(7));* (gr. 7-9). spiral bd. 5.95 *(978-1-84236-030-9(2));* (gr. 9-10). spiral bd. 5.95 *(978-1-84236-031-6(0))* Miles Kelly Publishing, Ltd. GBR. Dist: Independent Pubs. Group.

Murphy, Patricia J. A Frog's Life: Learning Sequential Order Using a Timeline. 2009. (Math for the REAL World Ser.). 16p. (gr. 2-3). pap. 7.05 *(978-0-8239-8905-8(4),* Rosen Classroom) Rosen Publishing Group, Inc., The.

Muschla, Gary Robert & Muschla, Judith A. Math Games: 180 Reproducible Activities to Motivate, Excite, & Challenge Students, Grades 6-12. 2004. (Educational Trade Ser.: 1). (ENG.). 240p. (gr. 6-12). pap. 29.95 *(978-0-7879-7081-9(6),* Wiley) Wiley, John & Sons, Inc.

Nurk, Enn & Telgmaa, Aksel. Mathematics 6. Harte, Will, tr. from RUS. 2003. Orig. Title: Matematika 6. Uchebnik Dlya Obshcheobrazovatel'Nykh Uchebnikh Zavedenij. (Illus.). ix, 310p. per. 38.50 *(978-0-9740234-0-3(X))* Perpendicular Pr.

Palmer, Stuart, et al. Cambridge Mathematics NSW Syllabus for the Australian Curriculum Year 10 5. 1 & 5. 2 & Hotmaths Bundle. 2014. (ENG.). pap. *(978-1-107-69185-8(0))* Cambridge Univ. Pr.

Perritano, John. Football Numbers: Graphing Data. 2013. (IMath Ser.). 32p. (J). (gr. 3-4). lib. bdg. 22.60 *(978-1-59953-566-1(1))* Norwood Hse. Pr.

PUBLICATIONS, Dale Seymour. MCP Mathematics. 2004. (ENG.). (J). (gr. 4-4). pap., stu. ed. 28.50 *(978-0-7652-6062-8(X));* (gr. 5-5). pap., stu. ed. 28.50 *(978-0-7652-6064-2(6))* Pearson Schl. (Dale Seymour Publications).

Publications International Ltd. Staff, ed. Kindergarten Boot Camp. 2010. (J). 20.98 *(978-1-4508-0069-3(6))* Publications International, Ltd.

Rankie, Barbara. Addition Unplugged, 2 vols. 2nd ed. 2013. (ENG.). 64p. 19.95 *(978-1-55386-216-1(3),* 1553862163) Jordan, Sara Publishing.

—Subtraction Unplugged, 2 vols. 2nd ed. 2013. (ENG.). 64p. 19.95 *(978-1-55386-217-8(1),* 1553862171) Jordan, Sara Publishing.

Research Masters Staff & Barron's Educational Staff. Barron's Common Core Success Grade 5 Math Workbook: Preparing Students for a Brilliant Future. 2015. (Barron's Common Core Success Ser.). (ENG.). 184p. (gr. 5-5). pap. 12.99 *(978-1-4380-0678-9(0))* Barron's Educational Series, Inc.

Roy, Jennifer Rozines & Roy, Gregory. Money at the Store. 2007. (J). pap. 6.99 *(978-0-7614-3385-9(6))* Marshall Cavendish Corp.

Saddleback Educational Publishing Staff, ed. Everyday Life Math 2011, 1 vol. 2011. (21st Century Lifeskills Math Ser.). (ENG.). 109p. (gr. 6-12). pap., tchr. ed. 24.95 *(978-1-61651-408-2(6))* Saddleback Educational Publishing, Inc.

—On the Job Math, 1 vol. 2011. (21st Century Lifeskills Math Ser.). (ENG.). 110p. (gr. 6-12). pap., tchr. ed. 24.95 *(978-1-61651-410-5(8))* Saddleback Educational Publishing, Inc.

—Smart Shopping Math, 1 vol. 2011. (21st Century Lifeskills Math Ser.). (ENG.). 110p. (gr. 6-12). pap., tchr. ed. 24.95 *(978-1-61651-406-8(X))* Saddleback Educational Publishing, Inc.

Scholastic, Inc. Staff, contrib. by. Addition & Subtraction. 2010. (Scholastic Success with Ser.). (ENG.). 48p. (gr. 1-1). pap.

5.99 (978-0-545-20098-1(9)); (gr. 2-2). pap. 5.99 (978-0-545-20097-4(0)) Scholastic, Inc. (Teaching Resources).

—Addition, Subtraction, Multiplication & Division. 2010. (Scholastic Success with Ser.). (ENG.). 48p. (gr. 4-4). pap. 5.99 (978-0-545-20072-1(5)); (gr. 5-5). pap. 5.99 (978-0-545-20101-8(2)) Scholastic, Inc. (Teaching Resources).

—Scholastic Success with Addition & Subtraction. 2010. (Scholastic Success with Ser.). (ENG.). 48p. (gr. 3-3). pap. 5.99 (978-0-545-20096-7(2), Teaching Resources) Scholastic, Inc.

School Specialty Publishing Staff & Carson-Dellosa Publishing Staff. 70 Must-Know Word Problems. 2009. (Singapore Math Ser.). (ENG.). 160p. (gr. 1-2). pap. 12.99 (978-0-7682-4011-5(5), Frank Schaffer Pubns.) Carson-Dellosa Publishing, LLC.

School Zone Publishing. Transition Math. 2003. (ENG.). (J). (gr. k-1). cd-rom 19.99 (978-1-58947-911-1(4)) School Zone Publishing Co.

Spilsbury, Richard. I'M Good at Math... What Job Can I Get? 2012. (What's a Good Job for Me? Ser.). (ENG., Illus.). 32p. (J). (gr. 5-6). (978-1-4488-6629-8(4), PowerKids Pr.) Rosen Publishing Group, Inc., The.

Steffens, Bradley. Big Data Analyst. 2017. (ENG.). 64p. (YA). (gr. 5-12). **(978-1-68282-176-3(5))** ReferencePoint Pr., Inc.

Sundance/Newbridge LLC Staff. Charts & Graphs. 2004. (Reading PowerWorks Ser.). (gr. 1-3). 37.50 (978-0-7608-8987-9(2)); pap. 6.10 (978-0-7608-8988-6(0)) Sundance/Newbridge Educational Publishing.

—Dollars & Cents. 2004. (Reading PowerWorks Ser.). (gr. 1-3). 37.50 (978-0-7608-8964-0(3)); pap. 6.10 (978-0-7608-8965-7(1)) Sundance/Newbridge Educational Publishing.

Taylor, Helen & Harris, Andrew J. R., eds. Learning & Teaching Mathematics 0-8. 2013. (ENG., Illus.). 280p. (C). 110.00 (978-1-4462-5331-1(7), B53311C); pap. 47.00 (978-1-4462-5332-8(5), B53311P) SAGE Pubns., Ltd. GBR. Dist: SAGE Pubns., Inc.

Taylor, Roger & Taylor, Robert J. Move on Maths Ages 9-11: 50+ Flexible Maths Activities, Volume 2. 2009. (ENG., Illus.). 128p. 46.95 (978-0-415-47154-1(0), RX10799) Fulton, David Pubs. GBR. Dist: Taylor & Francis Group.

Van Doren, Elizabeth. Get Ready for Kindergarten: Math & Science. 2010. (ENG., Illus.). 240p. (J). (gr. -1-2). 17.95 (978-1-57912-830-2(0), 81830, Black Dog & Leventhal Pubs. Inc.) Hachette Bks.

Webb, Barbara L. Graph It! 2012. (ENG., Illus.). 24p. (gr. -1-1). pap. 8.95 (978-1-61810-203-4(6)) Rourke Educational Media.

Workman Publishing Company Staff. Everything You Need to Ace Math in One Big Fat Notebook: A Middle School Study Guide. 2016. (Big Fat Notebooks Ser.). (ENG., Illus.). 512p. (J). (gr. 6-8). pap. 14.95 (978-0-7611-6096-0(5)) Workman Publishing Co., Inc.

Year 1 Impact Intervention. 2017. (ENG.). 96p. (J). (gr. k-1). pap. 43.99 **(978-0-00-822838-5(8))** HarperCollins Pubs. Ltd. GBR. Dist: Independent Pubs. Group.

Zaccaro, Edward D. Primary Grade Challenge Math. 2003. (ENG., Illus.). 311p. (J). pap. 24.95 (978-0-9679915-3-5(6)) Hickory Grove Pr.

MATINICUS ROCK LIGHTHOUSE (ME.)

Keep the Lights Burning. 9.95 (978-1-59112-293-7(7)) Live Oak Media.

Roop, Connie & Roop, Peter. Keep the Lights Burning, Abbie. Hanson, Peter E., illus. 2016. (On My Own History Ser.). (ENG.). 40p. (J). (gr. 2-4). 38.65 (978-1-5124-1862-0(5), Millbrook Pr.) Lerner Publishing Group.

Roop, Peter & Roop, Connie. Manten Las Luces Encendidas, Abbie. Hanson, Peter E., illus. 2005. (Yo Solo - Historia (on My Own - History) Ser.). (SPA.). 48p. (gr. 2-4). lib. bdg. 25.26 (978-0-8225-3098-5(8)) Lerner Publishing Group.

—The Stormy Adventure of Abbie Burgess, Lighthouse Keeper. 2010. pap. 51.02 (978-0-7613-6922-6(8)) Lerner Publishing Group.

—The Stormy Adventure of Abbie Burgess, Lighthouse Keeper. Trover, Zachary, illus. 2010. (History's Kid Heroes Ser.). (ENG.). 32p. (gr. 3-5). 26.60 (978-0-7613-6172-5(3)); pap. 8.95 (978-0-7613-6191-6(X), Graphic Universe™) Lerner Publishing Group.

MATISSE, HENRI, 1869-1954

Fillion, Susan. Miss Etta & Dr. Claribel: Bringing Matisse to America. 2011. (Illus.). 92p. (YA). (gr. 5-18). 18.95 (978-1-56792-434-3(4)) Godine, David R. Pub.

Geis, Patricia. Henri Matisse: Meet the Artist! 2014. (Meet the Artist Ser.). (ENG., Illus.). 16p. (J). (gr. 2-7). 24.95 (978-1-61689-282-1(X)) Princeton Architectural Pr.

Hollein, Nina & Hollein, Max. Cut-Out Fun with Matisse. 2014. (ENG., Illus.). 40p. (J). (gr. 3-7). pap. 9.95 (978-3-7913-7192-4(4)) Prestel Verlag GmbH & Co KG. DEU. Dist: Penguin Random Hse. LLC.

Hyde, Margaret E., ed. Matisse for Kids, 1 vol. 2003. (Great Art for Kids Ser.). (ENG., Illus.). 10p. (J). (gr. -1 — 1). bds. 8.95 (978-1-58980-204-9(7)) Pelican Publishing Co., Inc.

Le Tord, Bijou. A Bird or Two: A Story about Henri Matisse. Le Tord, Bijou, illus. 2004. (Illus.). 32p. (gr. 2-7). 18.00 (978-0-8028-5184-0(3)) Eerdmans, William B. Publishing Co.

MacLachlan, Patricia. The Iridescence of Birds: A Book about Henri Matisse. Hooper, Hadley, illus. 2014. (ENG.). 40p. (J). (gr. -1-3). 17.99 (978-1-59643-948-1(3), 9781596439481) Roaring Brook Pr.

Parker, Marjorie Blain & Matisse, Henri. Colorful Dreamer: The Story of Artist Henri Matisse. Berry, Holly, illus. 2012. (ENG.). 32p. (J). (gr. -1-k). 16.99 (978-0-8037-3758-7(0), Dial Bks) Penguin Young Readers Group.

Rubin, Susan Goldman. Matisse Dance for Joy. 2008. (ENG., Illus.). 26p. (J). (gr. -1 — 1). bds. 6.99 (978-0-8118-6288-2(7)) Chronicle Bks. LLC.

Stephens, Pamela Geiger. Dropping in on Matisse. McNeill, Jim, illus. 2004. 32p. (J). 15.95 (978-1-56290-322-0(5)) Crystal Productions.

Winter, Jeanette. Henri's Scissors. Winter, Jeanette, illus. 2013. (ENG., Illus.). 40p. (J). (gr. k-3). 17.99 (978-1-4424-6484-1(4), Beach Lane Bks.) Beach Lane Bks.

MATRIMONY

see Marriage

MATTER

Aloian, Molly. Atoms & Molecules. 2008. (Why Chemistry Matters Ser.). (ENG., Illus.). 32p. (J). (gr. 3-7). pap. (978-0-7787-4247-0(4)) Crabtree Publishing Co.

Anderson, Michael. The Nature of Planets, Dwarf Planets, & Space Objects. 2011. (Illus.). 96p. (J). lib. bdg. 31.70 (978-1-61530-517-9(3)) Rosen Publishing Group, Inc., The.

Barkan, Joanne. What Is Density? 2006. (Rookie Read-About Science Ser.). (ENG., Illus.). 32p. (J). (gr. 1-2). pap. 4.95 (978-0-516-24660-4(7), Children's Pr.) Scholastic Library Publishing.

Benchmark Education Company. Matter Is Everywhere (Teacher Guide) Solids, Liquids, & Gases. 2005. (978-1-4108-4658-7(X)) Benchmark Education Co.

—Measuring Matter (Teacher Guide) Solids, Liquids, & Gases. 2005. (978-1-4108-4651-8(2)) Benchmark Education Co.

—This Is Matter (Teacher Guide) Solids, Liquids, & Gases. 2005. (978-1-4108-4644-0(X)) Benchmark Education Co.

Benchmark Education Company, LLC Staff, compiled by. Matter. 2006. spiral bd. 330.00 (978-1-4108-7013-1(8)) 2006. (J). 148.00 (978-1-4108-7032-2(4)) 2005. (J). spiral bd. 265.00 (978-1-4108-5757-6(3)) Benchmark Education Co.

—Matter: Theme Set. 2006. (J). 105.00 (978-1-4108-7060-5(X)) Benchmark Education Co.

—Science Theme: Matter. 2005. spiral bd. 115.00 (978-1-4108-5311-0(X)) Benchmark Education Co.

Biskup, Agnieszka. The Solid Truth about States of Matter with Max Axiom, Super Scientist, 1 vol. Martin, Cynthia & Schulz, Barbara, illus. 2009. (Graphic Science Ser.). (ENG.). 32p. (gr. 3-4). pap. 8.10 (978-1-4296-3451-9(0), Graphic Library) Capstone Press of Coughlan Cos.

—The Solid Truth about States of Matter with Max Axiom, Super Scientist. Martin, Cynthia & Schulz, Barbara, illus. 2008. (Life Cycles Ser.). 24p. 289.10 (978-1-4296-2451-0(5)) Capstone Press of Coughlan Cos.

Bloom, Chrissa. In the Kitchen with Solids, Liquids, & Gases. 2009. (Real Life Readers Ser.). 12p. (gr. 1-2). pap. 5.90 (978-1-4042-7897-4(4), Rosen Classroom) Rosen Publishing Group, Inc., The.

Boothroyd, Jennifer. How Big? How Heavy? How Dense? A Look at Matter. 2011. (Lightning Bolt Books Exploring Physical Science Ser.). 32p. pap. 45.32 (978-0-7613-7649-1(6)); (ENG.). pap. 7.95 (978-0-7613-7105-2(2)); (ENG.). lib. bdg. 26.60 (978-0-7613-6095-7(6)) Lerner Publishing Group.

—Many Kinds of Matter: A Look at Solids, Liquids, & Gases. 2011. (Lightning Bolt Books Exploring Physical Science Ser.). 32p. pap. 45.32 (978-0-7613-7651-4(8)); (ENG.). pap. 7.95 (978-0-7613-7106-9(0)) Lerner Publishing Group.

Campbell, Margaret Christine & Goldstein, Natalie. Discovering Atoms. 2011. (Scientist's Guide to Physics Ser.). (YA). (gr. 7-12). lib. bdg. 34.60 (978-1-4488-4700-6(1)) Rosen Publishing Group, Inc., The.

Canavan, Thomas. Why Do Ice Cubes Float? Questions & Answers about the Science of Everyday Materials. 2013. (Science F. A. Q. Ser.). (Illus.). 32p. (gr. 3-6). 31.35 (978-1-78212-396-5(2)) Arcturus Publishing GBR. Dist: Black Rabbit Bks.

Cardenas, Ernesto A. What Is Matter? 2009. pap. 4.95 (978-1-60698-076-7(9)) Milo Educational Bks. & Resources.

Clark, John O. E. The Basics of Matter. 2014. (Core Concepts Ser.). (Illus.). 96p. (YA). (gr. 7-12). 35.60 (978-1-4777-7752-7(0)) Rosen Publishing Group, Inc., The.

Claybourne, Anna. Make It Change!, 1 vol. Scott, Kimberly & Dean, Venetia, illus. 2014. (Whiz Kid Science Ser.). (ENG.). 32p. (gr. 2-4). 29.99 (978-1-4109-6746-6(8), Read Me!) Heinemann-Raintree.

Curry, Don L. What Is Matter? 2005. (Rookie Read-About Science Ser.). (ENG., Illus.). 32p. (J). (gr. 1-2). pap. 4.95 (978-0-516-24667-3(4), Children's Pr.) Scholastic Library Publishing.

Dicker, Katie. Properties of Matter. 2010. (Sherlock Bones Looks at Physical Science Ser.). (ENG.). 32p. (YA). (gr. 3-6). lib. bdg. 25.25 (978-1-61533-214-4(6)) Windmill Bks.

Field, Andrea R. Matter. 2012. (Introduction to Physics Ser.). (ENG., Illus.). 80p. (YA). (gr. 7-12). 31.70 (978-1-61530-839-2(3)) Rosen Publishing Group, Inc., The.

Field, Andrea R., ed. Matter. 2012. (Introduction to Physics Ser.). (ENG., Illus.). 80p. (YA). (gr. 7-12). 63.40 (978-1-61530-848-4(2)) Rosen Publishing Group, Inc., The.

Gardner, Robert. Atoms & Molecules Experiments Using Ice, Salt, Marbles, & More: One Hour or Less Science Experiments. 2012. (Last-Minute Science Projects Ser.). 48p. (J). (gr. 5-18). 25.27 (978-0-7660-3961-2(7)) Enslow Pubs., Inc.

Goldsmith, Mike. Discover Science: Materials. 2012. (Discover Science Ser.). (ENG., Illus.). 56p. (J). (gr. -1-3). 9.99 (978-0-7534-6781-7(X), 9780753467817, Kingfisher) Roaring Brook Pr.

Hansen, Amy S. Matter Comes in All Shapes. 2011. (ENG., Illus.). 24p. (gr. 1-2). pap. 8.95 (978-1-61741-941-6(9)) Rourke Educational Media.

Hanson-Harding, Alexandra. What Is Matter? 2014. (Let's Find Out! Ser.). 32p. (J). (gr. 3-6). 23.45 (978-1-62275-487-8(5)) Windmill Bks.

Hirsch, Rebecca. Science Lab: Properties of Matter. 2011. (Explorer Library: Language Arts Explorer Ser.). (ENG.). 32p. (gr. 4-8). pap. 14.21 (978-1-61080-295-6(0), 201217); lib. bdg. 28.50 (978-1-61080-206-2(3), 201188) Cherry Lake Publishing.

Holt, Rinehart and Winston Staff. Holt Science Spectrum Chptr. 3: States of Matter. 4th ed. Date not set. pap. 11.20 (978-0-03-068586-6(9)) Holt McDougal.

Jennings, Terry J. Hot & Cold. 2009. (J). 28.50 (978-1-59920-274-7(3)) Black Rabbit Bks.

Karam, P. Andrew & Stein, Ben P. Matter & Energy. 2011. (Science Foundations Ser.). (Illus.). 128p. (gr. 6-12). 35.00 (978-1-60413-345-5(7), Chelsea Hse.) Facts On File, Inc.

Kjelle, Marylou Morano. The Properties of Metals. 2007. (Library of Physical Sciences). (ENG., Illus.). 24p. (gr. 4-8). pap. 7.05 (978-1-4042-2164-2(6), PowerKids Pr.) Rosen Publishing Group, Inc., The.

—The Properties of Salts. 2006. (Library of Physical Science Ser.). (Illus.). 24p. (YA). (gr. 4-7). lib. bdg. 22.60 (978-1-4042-3425-3(X)) Rosen Publishing Group, Inc., The.

—The Properties of Solids. 2006. (Library of Physical Science Ser.). (Illus.). 24p. (YA). (gr. 4-7). lib. bdg. 22.60 (978-1-4042-3421-5(7)) Rosen Publishing Group, Inc., The.

Larson, Daniel T. The Nature of Matter. 2007. (Physics in Action Ser.). (Illus.). 107p. (YA). (gr. 9-12). lib. bdg. 35.00 (978-0-7910-8929-3(0)) Facts On File, Inc.

LernerClassroom Editors. First Step Nonfiction-States of Matter Teaching Guide. 2009. pap. 7.95 (978-0-8225-6883-4(7)) Lerner Publishing Group.

Lilly, Melinda. Solid, Liquid, & Gas. Thompson, Scott M., illus. 2003. 24p. (J). 20.64 (978-1-58952-648-8(1)) Rourke Educational Media.

Macfarlane, Katherine. The Father of the Atom: Democritus & the Nature of Matter. 2009. (Great Minds of Ancient Science & Math Ser.). (Illus.). 112p. (J). (gr. 4-7). lib. bdg. 33.27 (978-0-7660-3410-5(0)) Enslow Pubs., Inc.

Manolis, Kay. Matter. 2007. (First Science Ser.). (ENG., Illus.). 24p. (J). (gr. 2-5). lib. bdg. 25.95 (978-1-60014-130-0(7), Blastoff! Readers) Bellwether Media.

Marsico, Katie. Key Discoveries in Physical Science. 2015. (Science Discovery Timelines Ser.). (ENG., Illus.). 48p. (J). (gr. 6-8). pap. 8.99 (978-1-4677-6160-4(5)); lib. bdg. 30.65 (978-1-4677-5785-0(3)) Lerner Publishing Group. (Lerner Pubns.).

Matos, Rebecca. Matter Is Everywhere: Solids, Liquids, & Gases. 2005. (J). pap. (978-1-4108-4610-5(5)) Benchmark Education Co.

—Measuring Matter: Solids, Liquids, & Gases. 2005. (J). pap. (978-1-4108-4603-7(2)) Benchmark Education Co.

—This Is Matter: Solids, Liquids, & Gases. 2005. (J). pap. (978-1-4108-4596-2(6)) Benchmark Education Co.

Matter & Energy Lesson Plans & Blackline Masters (National Version) 2009. (Journeys Ser.). 20.00 (978-1-4042-9489-9(9), Rosen Classroom) Rosen Publishing Group, Inc., The.

Matter & Energy Word-picture match cards, Memory game cards, Labeled picture Cards. 2008. (Journeys Ser.). 46.60 (978-1-4042-9490-5(2), Rosen Classroom) Rosen Publishing Group, Inc., The.

Meredith, Susan Markowitz. The States of Matter: Set Of 6. 2010. (Early Connections Ser.). (J). pap. 37.00 net. (978-1-4108-1083-0(6)) Benchmark Education Co.

Merrill, Amy French. Everyday Physical Science Experiments with Solids. 2009. (Science Surprises Ser.). 24p. (gr. 3-3). 42.50 (978-1-60853-064-9(7), PowerKids Pr.) Rosen Publishing Group, Inc., The.

Michele, Tracey. Having Fun with Matter. 2011. (Learn-Abouts Ser.). (Illus.). 16p. (J). pap. 7.95 (978-1-59920-628-8(5)) Black Rabbit Bks.

Moore, Elizabeth. Matter Is Everything! 2011. (Wonder Readers Early Level Ser.). (ENG.). 16p. (gr. -1-1). pap. 35.94 (978-1-4296-8126-1(8), Wonder Readers) Capstone Press of Coughlan Cos.

Morano-Kjelle, Marylou. Gases, 1 vol., 1. 2014. (Ultimate Science: Physical Science Ser.). (ENG.). 24p. (gr. 3-6). 23.60 (978-1-4777-6081-9(4), PowerKids Pr.) Rosen Publishing Group, Inc., The.

—Liquids, 1 vol., 1. 2014. (Ultimate Science: Physical Science Ser.). (ENG.). 24p. (gr. 3-6). pap. 7.05 (978-1-4777-6078-9(4), PowerKids Pr.) Rosen Publishing Group, Inc., The.

—Solids, 1 vol., 1. 2014. (Ultimate Science: Physical Science Ser.). (ENG.). 24p. (gr. 3-6). pap. 7.05 (978-1-4777-6004-8(0), PowerKids Pr.) Rosen Publishing Group, Inc., The.

Mullins, Matt & Plummer, Todd. Super Cool Science Experiments: States of Matter. 2009. (Explorer Library: Science Explorer Ser.). (ENG., Illus.). 32p. (gr. 4-8). lib. bdg. 28.50 (978-1-60279-535-8(5), 200299) Cherry Lake Publishing.

Murray, Julie. Matter, 1 vol. 2006. (First Science - 12 Titles Ser.). (ENG., Illus.). 24p. (gr. k-4). 25.65 (978-1-59679-828-1(9), Buddy Bks.) ABDO Publishing Co.

National Geographic Learning Staff. Solids,Liquids, & Gases, Level 3. 2011. (World Windows Ser.). (ENG., Illus.). 16p. (J). stu. ed. 9.95 (978-1-133-49276-4(2)) Cengage Heinle.

Oxlade, Chris. Solids: An Investigation. 2008. (Science Investigations Ser.). (Illus.). 32p. (YA). (gr. 4-7). lib. bdg. 26.50 (978-1-4042-4284-5(8)) Rosen Publishing Group, Inc., The.

Paris, Morgaine. Composition of Matter. 2015. (Science Readers: Content & Literacy Ser.). (Illus.). 32p. (J). (gr. 5-5). pap. 8.99 (978-1-4807-4720-3(3)) Teacher Created Materials, Inc.

Parker, Janice. The Science of Liquids & Solids. 2003. (Living Science Ser.). (Illus.). 32p. (J). (gr. 1-3). pap. 9.95 (978-1-930954-11-3(5)) Weigl Pubs., Inc.

Peppas, Lynn. What Is a Solid? 2012. (ENG.). 24p. (J). (978-0-7787-0771-4(7)); (Illus.). pap. (978-0-7787-0778-3(4)) Crabtree Publishing Co.

Petersen, Kristen. Understanding Kinetic Energy. 2015. (J). lib. bdg. (978-1-62713-435-4(2)); (ENG.). 48p. (gr. 7-7). 31.36 (978-1-5026-0144-5(3)) Cavendish Square Publishing.

Phelan, Glen. What Is Matter? 2007. (Language, Literacy, & Vocabulary - Reading Expeditions Ser.). (ENG., Illus.). 36p. (J). pap. 18.95 (978-0-7922-5442-3(2)) CENGAGE Learning.

Reilly, Kathleen M. Explore Solids & Liquids! With 25 Great Projects. Stone, Bryan, illus. 2014. (Explore Your World Ser.). (ENG.). 96p. (J). (gr. 1-5). 19.95 (978-1-61930-171-9(7)) Open City Bks.

Riley, Peter. Matter. 2016. (Moving up with Science Ser.). 00032p. (J). (gr. 3-4). pap. 10.00 (978-1-4994-3149-0(X), PowerKids Pr.) Rosen Publishing Group, Inc., The.

Rivera, Sheila. Cutting. 2007. (First Step Nonfiction - Changing Matter Ser.). (ENG.). 8p. (gr. -1-1). pap. 4.95 (978-0-8225-6413-3(0)) Lerner Publishing Group.

—Dissolving. 2007. (First Step Nonfiction - Changing Matter Ser.). (ENG.). 8p. (gr. -1-1). pap. 4.95 (978-0-8225-6414-0(9)) Lerner Publishing Group.

—Heating. 2007. (First Step Nonfiction - Changing Matter Ser.). (ENG., Illus.). 8p. (gr. -1-1). pap. 4.95 (978-0-8225-6415-7(7)) Lerner Publishing Group.

Rodriguez, Cindy & Siemens, Jared. Gas. 2016. (J). **(978-1-4896-5752-7(5))** Weigl Pubs., Inc.

—Liquid. 2016. (J). **(978-1-4896-5746-6(0))** Weigl Pubs., Inc.

Schaefer, Lola M. What Is Matter? 2011. (Early Connections Ser.). (J). (978-1-61672-656-0(3)) Benchmark Education Co.

Schuh, Mari. All about Matter, 1 vol. 2011. (Science Builders Ser.). (ENG.). 24p. (gr. k-1). pap. 7.29 (978-1-4296-7105-7(X), Pebble Plus) Capstone Press of Coughlan Cos.

Schuh, Mari C. All about Matter. 2011. (Science Builders Ser.). (ENG.). 24p. (gr. k-1). pap. 41.70 (978-1-4296-7111-8(4), Pebble Plus) Capstone Press of Coughlan Cos.

Silverman, Buffy. State of Confusion: Solids, Liquids, & Gases. 2016. (Raintree Fusion: Physical Science Ser.). (ENG.). 32p. (gr. 2-2). pap. 8.29 (978-1-4109-8520-0(2), Raintree Fusion) Heinemann-Raintree.

Slade, Suzanne. Splat! Wile E. Coyote Experiments with States of Matter, 1 vol. Cornia, Christian, illus. 2014. (Wile E. Coyote, Physical Science Genius Ser.). (ENG.). 32p. (gr. 3-4). 30.65 (978-1-4765-4224-9(4)) Capstone Press of Coughlan Cos.

—The Structure of Atoms. (Library of Physical Science Ser.). 24p. (gr. 4-4). 2009. 42.50 (978-1-60853-795-2(1)) 2007. (ENG., Illus.). pap. 7.05 (978-1-4042-2161-1(1)) Rosen Publishing Group, Inc., The. (PowerKids Pr.).

Slingerland, Janet. Werewolves & States of Matter, 1 vol. Mosquito, Angel, illus. 2011. (Monster Science Ser.). (ENG.). 32p. (gr. 3-4). pap. 8.10 (978-1-4296-7333-4(8)); pap. 47.70 (978-1-4296-7334-1(6)); lib. bdg. 30.65 (978-1-4296-6578-0(5)) Capstone Press of Coughlan Cos. (Graphic Library).

Sohn, Emily & Tsang, Nina. Matter & Energy: Finding the Power. 2011. (IScience Readers Ser.). 32p. (J). (gr. 3-4). lib. bdg. 22.60 (978-1-59953-416-9(9)) Norwood Hse. Pr.

Solway, Andrew. Energy & Matter. 2010. (CC: 21st Century Science Ser.). 112p. (gr. 6-12). 42.80 (978-1-933834-72-6(2)) Brown Bear Bks.

Spilsbury, Louise & Spilsbury, Richard. Solids, Liquids, & Gases, 1 vol. (Essential Physical Science Ser.). (ENG., Illus.). 48p. (gr. 4-6). 2014. lib. bdg. 33.32 (978-1-4329-8151-8(X)) 2013. pap. 9.95 (978-1-4329-8160-0(9)) Heinemann-Raintree. (Heinemann InfoSearch).

Stille, Darlene R. Matter: See It, Touch It, Taste It, Smell It, 1 vol. Boyd, Sheree, illus. 2004. (Amazing Science Ser.). (ENG.). 24p. (gr. k-4). per. 8.95 (978-1-4048-0344-2(0)) Picture Window Bks.

Stille, Darlene R. & Picture Window Books Staff. La Materia: Mira, Toca, Prueba, Huele, 1 vol. Robledo, Sol, tr. from ENG. Boyd, Sheree, illus. 2007. (Ciencia Asombrosa Ser.). (SPA.). 24p. (gr. k-4). 26.65 (978-1-4048-3221-3(1)) Picture Window Bks.

Strauss, Michael J. Investigating the Natural World of Chemistry with Kids: Experiments, Writing, & Drawing Activities for Learning Science. 2012. 226p. pap. 25.95 (978-1-61233-155-3(6)) Universal Pubs.

Sullivan, Erin Ash. Measuring Matter: Set Of 6. 2010. (Navigators Ser.). (J). pap. 44.00 net. (978-1-4108-5070-6(6)) Benchmark Education Co.

—Measuring Matter: Text Pairs. 2008. (Bridges/Navigators Ser.). (J). (gr. 3). 94.00 (978-1-4108-8367-4(1)) Benchmark Education Co.

Sundance/Newbridge LLC Staff. Matter Is Everything. 2004. (Reading PowerWorks Ser.). (gr. 1-3). 37.50 (978-0-7608-8900-8(7)); pap. 6.10 (978-0-7608-8901-5(5)) Sundance/Newbridge Educational Publishing.

—What Is Matter? 2007. (Early Science Ser.). (gr. k-3). 18.95 (978-1-4007-6477-8(7)); pap. 6.10 (978-1-4007-6473-0(4)) Sundance/Newbridge Educational Publishing.

Trumbauer, Lisa. What Are Atoms. 2005. (Rookie Read-About Science Ser.). (ENG., Illus.). 32p. (J). (gr. 1-2). pap. 4.95 (978-0-516-24665-9(8), Children's Pr.) Scholastic Library Publishing.

Walker, Denise. Materials. 2006. (Core Chemistry/Evans Brothers Ser.). (Illus.). 48p. (YA). (gr. 5-9). 34.25 (978-1-58340-817-9(7)) Black Rabbit Bks.

Walker, Sally M. Investigating Matter. 2011. (Searchlight Books How Does Energy Work Ser.). (ENG., Illus.). (gr. 3-6). pap. 51.01 (978-0-7613-8409-0(X)); 40p. 27.93 (978-0-7613-5776-6(9)); 40p. pap. 8.95 (978-0-7613-7875-4(8)) Lerner Publishing Group.

—La Materia. Translations.com Staff, tr. from ENG. King, Andy, photos by. 2007. (Libros de Energía para madrugadores (Early Bird Energy) Ser.). (SPA., Illus.). 48p. (gr. 2-5). lib. bdg. 26.60 (978-0-8225-7721-8(6)) Lerner Publishing Group.

—La Materia; Matter. 2008. pap. 52.95 (978-0-8225-9870-1(1)) Lerner Publishing Group.

—Matter. 2006. (Illus.). 48p. (J). pap. 8.95 (978-0-8225-2844-9(4)) Lerner Publishing Group.

Weakland, Mark. The Solid Truth about Matter. Lum, Bernice, illus. 2012. (LOL Physical Science Ser.). (ENG.). 32p. (gr. 3-4). pap. 47.70 (978-1-4296-9303-5(7), Fact Finders) Capstone Press of Coughlan Cos.

Weakland, Mark Andrew. The Solid Truth about Matter, 1 vol. Lum, Bernice, illus. 2012. (LOL Physical Science Ser.). (ENG.). 32p. (gr. 3-4). pap. 8.10 (978-1-4296-9302-8(9), Fact Finders) Capstone Press of Coughlan Cos.

Weir, Jane. Inside the World of Matter, 1 vol. 2007. (Science Readers Ser.). (ENG.). 32p. (J). (gr. 4-4). pap. 8.99 (978-0-7439-0567-1(9)) Shell Educational Publishing.

—Max Planck: Uncovering the World of Matter, 1 vol. 2007. (Science Readers Ser.). (ENG.). 32p. (J). (gr. 3-3). pap. 8.99 (978-0-7439-0568-8(7)) Shell Educational Publishing.

Woodford, Chris & Clowes, Martin. Atoms & Molecules: Investigating the Building Blocks of Matter. 2012. (Scientific Pathways Ser.). (ENG., Illus.). 48p. (J). (gr. 5-8). lib. bdg. 27.95 (978-1-4488-7196-4(4), Rosen Reference) Rosen Publishing Group, Inc., The.

World Book, Inc Staff, contrib. by. Encyclopedia of Matter & Energy. 2013. (Illus.). 245p. (J). (978-0-7166-7521-1(8)) World Bk., Inc.

—Matter & How It Changes. 2011. (J). (978-0-7166-1428-9(6)) World Bk., Inc.

Young, June. Energy Is Everywhere. 2006. (Rookie Read-About Science Ser.). (ENG., Illus.). 32p. (J). (gr. 1-2). pap. 4.95 (978-0-516-28003-5(1), Children's Pr.) Scholastic Library Publishing.

MATTER—PROPERTIES

Adams, Tom. Super Science: Matter Matters! Flintman, Thomas, illus. 2012. (ENG.). 18p. (J). (gr. 2-5). 18.99 (978-0-7636-6096-3(5), Templar) Candlewick Pr.

Aloian, Molly. Mixtures & Solutions. 2008. (Why Chemistry Matters Ser.). (ENG., Illus.). 32p. (J). (gr. 3-7). pap. (978-0-7787-4250-0(4)) Crabtree Publishing Co.

Angliss, Sarah, et al. Hands-On Science: Matter & Materials. 2013. (Hands-On Science Ser.). (ENG., Illus.). 32p. (J). (gr. 2-5). pap. 7.99 (978-0-7534-6973-6(1), 9780753469736, Kingfisher) Roaring Brook Pr.

Barkan, Joanne. What Is Density? 2006. (Rookie Read-About Science Ser.). (ENG., Illus.). 32p. (J). (gr. 1-2). lib. bdg. 20.50 (978-0-516-23618-6(0)) Scholastic Library Publishing.

Bateman, Graham, ed. Atoms, Molecules, & States of Matter. 2011. (Facts at Your Fingertips: Introducing Chemistry Ser.). 64p. (YA). (gr. 7-12). lib. bdg. 35.65 (978-1-936333-10-3(4)) Brown Bear Bks.

—Electricity & Electronics. 2011. (FAYFT: Introducing Physics Ser.). 64p. (gr. 4-10). lib. bdg. 39.95 (978-1-936333-09-7(0)) Brown Bear Bks.

Baxter, Roberta. States of Matter in the Real World. 2013. (Science in the Real World EBook Ser.). (ENG.). 48p. (J). pap. 15.64 (978-1-61783-795-1(4), Core Library); (gr. 3-6). lib. bdg. 32.79 (978-1-61783-745-6(8)) ABDO Publishing Co.

Boothroyd, Jennifer. Many Kinds of Matter: A Look at Solids, Liquids, & Gases. 2011. (Lightning Bolt Books (tm) — Exploring Physical Science Ser.). (ENG.). 32p. (gr. k-2). 26.60 (978-0-7613-6096-4(4)) Lerner Publishing Group.

Brannon, Barbara. Discover Solids. 2005. (J). pap. (978-1-4108-5117-8(6)) Benchmark Education Co.

Braun, Eric. Curious Pearl Explains States of Matter: 4D an Augmented Reality Science Experience. Dehennin, Stephanie, illus. 2017. (Curious Pearl, Science Girl 4D Ser.). (ENG.). 24p. (gr. k-2). lib. bdg. 20.65 **(978-1-5158-1342-2(8))** Picture Window Bks.

Braun, Eric. Joe-Joe the Wizard Brews up Solids, Liquids, & Gases, 1 vol. Boyden, Robin, illus. 2012. (In the Science Lab Ser.). (ENG.). 24p. (gr. 2-3). pap. 9.95 (978-1-4048-7238-7(8)) Picture Window Bks.

Cardenas, Ernesto & Saavedra, Patricia. Qué es la Materia? l.t. ed. 2006. (SPA., Illus.). 16p. pap. 4.95 (978-1-933668-16-1(4)) Milo Educational Bks. & Resources.

Carr, Aaron. Solids. 2012. (What Is Matter? Ser.). (ENG., Illus.). 24p. (J). (gr. -1-3). lib. bdg. 27.13 (978-1-61913-601-4(5), AV2 by Weigl) Weigl Pubs., Inc.

Carr, Aaron & Evans Ogden, Lesley J. Studying Properties of Matter. 2016. (Illus.). 24p. (J). (978-1-5105-1128-6(8)) SmartBook Media, Inc.

Carr, Aaron & Siemens, Jared. Solid. 2016. (J). **(978-1-4896-5749-7(5))** Weigl Pubs., Inc.

Clark, John. Matter & Materials. 2006. (Real World Science Ser.). (Illus.). 32p. (gr. 2-6). lib. bdg. 26.00 (978-0-8368-6307-9(0), Gareth Stevens Learning Library) Stevens, Gareth Publishing LLLP.

Claybourne, Anna. The Science of a Glass of Water: The Science of States of Matter. 2009. (Science of... Ser.). (Illus.). 32p. (YA). (gr. 3-6). lib. bdg. 26.00 (978-1-4339-0041-9(6)) Stevens, Gareth Publishing LLLP.

Cook, Trevor M. Experiments with States of Matter. 2009. (Science Lab Ser.). (J). (ENG., Illus.). 32p. (gr. 4-6). pap. 10.00 (978-1-4358-3218-3(3)); lib. bdg. 26.50 (978-1-4358-2805-6(4)) Rosen Publishing Group, Inc., The. (PowerKids Pr.).

Cooper, Chris. The Basics of Energy & Reactions. 2013. (Core Concepts Ser.). 96p. (YA). (gr. 7-12). 34.60 (978-1-4777-2710-2(8)) Rosen Publishing Group, Inc., The.

Curry, Don L. What Is Mass? 2005. (Rookie Read-About Science Ser.). (ENG., Illus.). 32p. (J). (gr. 1-2). pap. 4.95 (978-0-516-24666-6(6), Children's Pr.) Scholastic Library Publishing.

Dingrando, Laurel, et al. Chemistry: Matter & Change. 2nd ed. 2004. (Glencoe Chemistry Ser.). (ENG., Illus.). 1024p. (gr. 10-12). stu. ed. 123.44 (978-0-07-866418-2(7), 0078664187) Glencoe/McGraw-Hill.

Does It Absorb or Repel Liquid? 2014. (ENG., Illus.). 24p. (J). (978-0-7787-0537-6(4)) Crabtree Publishing Co.

Duke, Shirley. What's the Matter? 2016. (Let's Explore Science Ser.). (ENG., Illus.). 48p. (gr. 5-8). 35.64 (978-1-68191-393-3(3)) Rourke Educational Media.

Dunne, Abbie. Matter. 2016. (Physical Science Ser.). (ENG., Illus.). 24p. (gr. k-1). lib. bdg. 26.65 (978-1-5157-0939-8(6), Pebble Plus) Capstone Press of Coughlan Cos.

Enz, Tammy. Squash It! 2017. (Shaping Materials Ser.). (ENG.). 24p. (gr. k-2). lib. bdg. 23.32 **(978-1-4846-4095-1(0)**, Heinemann Read & Learn) Heinemann-Raintree.

Evans Ogden, Lesley J. Properties of Matter. 2011. (J). (gr. 4-6). pap. 12.95 (978-1-61690-734-1(7), AV2 by Weigl); (Illus.). 24p. (gr. 3-6). 27.13 (978-1-61690-730-3(4)) Weigl Pubs., Inc.

Fletcher, Sheila. Is It Flexible or Rigid? 2012. (ENG., Illus.). 24p. (J). (978-0-7787-2047-8(0)); pap. (978-0-7787-2054-6(3)) Crabtree Publishing Co.

Flynn, James J. Air. 2003. (Matter & Materials Ser.). (J). pap. (978-1-58417-169-0(3)); lib. bdg. (978-1-58417-163-8(4)) Lake Street Pubs.

Gaff, Jackie. Looking at Solids, Liquids, & Gases: How Does Matter Change? 2008. (Looking at Science: How Things Change Ser.). (Illus.). 32p. (J). (gr. 3-7). lib. bdg. 23.94 (978-0-7660-3092-3(X), Enslow Elementary) Enslow Pubs., Inc.

Gardner, Robert. Melting, Freezing, & Boiling Science Projects with Matter. 2006. (Fantastic Physical Science Experiments Ser.). (Illus.). 48p. (J). (gr. 4-7). lib. bdg. 25.27 (978-0-7660-2589-9(6), Enslow Elementary) Enslow Pubs., Inc.

—Science Fair Projects about the Properties of Matter, Revised & Expanded Using the Scientific Method. LaBaff, Stephanie, illus. 2010. (Physics Science Projects Using the Scientific Method Ser.). 160p. (J). (gr. 5-18). 35.94 (978-0-7660-3417-4(8)) Enslow Pubs., Inc.

—Science Fair Projects about the Properties of Matter Using Marbles, Water, Balloons, & More. Tom, LaBaff, illus. 2004. (Physics! Best Science Projects Ser.). 128p. (J). lib. bdg. 27.94 (978-0-7660-2128-0(9)) Enslow Pubs., Inc.

—Solids, Liquids, & Gases Science Projects. 2013. (Exploring Hands-On Science Projects Ser.). 128p. (J). (gr. 5-18). lib. bdg. 27.94 (978-0-7660-4145-5(X)) Enslow Pubs., Inc.

Garrett, Ginger. Solids, Liquids, & Gases. 2005. (Rookie Read-About Science Ser.). (ENG., Illus.). 32p. (J). (gr. 1-2). pap. 4.95 (978-0-516-24663-5(1), Children's Pr.) Scholastic Library Publishing.

Gordon, Sharon. Duro Blando. 2006. (Bookworms Ser.). (SPA & ENG., Illus.). 24p. (gr. k-1). lib. bdg. 15.95 (978-0-7614-2368-3(0)) Marshall Cavendish Corp.

—Hard/Soft. 2007. (J). pap. 6.99 (978-0-7614-3282-1(5)) Marshall Cavendish Corp.

—Hard/Soft/Duro/Blando. 2006. (Bookworms Ser.). (ENG & SPA., Illus.). 24p. (gr. k-1). lib. bdg. 15.95 (978-0-7614-2448-2(2)) Marshall Cavendish Corp.

Gregory, Josh. Experiment with Solids. 2010. (Explorer Junior Library: Science Explorer Junior Ser.). (ENG.). 32p. (gr. 3-6). lib. bdg. 28.50 (978-1-60279-845-8(1), 200556) Cherry Lake Publishing.

Guillain, Charlotte. Duro o Blando, 1 vol. 2010. (Las Propiedades de Los Materiales Ser.).Tr. of Hard or Soft. (SPA.). 24p. (gr. -1-1). 22.65 (978-1-4329-4238-0(7)); pap. 6.29 (978-1-4329-4246-5(8)) Heinemann-Raintree. (Bellota).

—Es Rigido o Se Dobla, 1 vol. 2010. (Las Propiedades de Los Materiales Ser.). (SPA., Illus.). 24p. (gr. -1-1). pap. 6.29 (978-1-4329-4252-6(2), Bellota) Heinemann-Raintree.

—Pesado o Liviano, 1 vol. 2010. (Las Propiedades de Los Materiales Ser.).Tr. of Heavy or Light. (SPA.). 24p. (gr. -1-1). 22.65 (978-1-4329-4240-3(9)); pap. 6.29 (978-1-4329-4248-9(4)) Heinemann-Raintree. (Bellota).

—Es Rigido O Se Dobla. 2010. (Las Propiedades de Los Materiales Ser.).Tr. of Stiff or Bendable. (SPA., Illus.). 24p. (gr. -1-1). 22.65 (978-1-4329-4244-1(1), Bellota) Heinemann-Raintree.

Hewitt, Sally. Amazing Materials. 2007. (Amazing Science Ser.). (ENG.). 32p. (J). pap. (978-0-7787-3627-1(X)) Crabtree Publishing Co.

Holland, Gini. Soft & Hard/Blando Y Duro. 2007. (I Know Opposites/Conceptos Contrarios Ser.). (SPA & ENG., Illus.). 16p. (gr. -1-3). lib. bdg. 19.00 (978-0-8368-8306-0(3), Weekly Reader Leveled Readers) Stevens, Gareth Publishing LLLP.

Holt, Rinehart and Winston Staff. Holt Science & Technology Chapter 2: Physical Science: Properties of Matter. 5th ed. 2004. (Illus.). pap. 12.86 (978-0-03-030361-6(3)) Holt McDougal.

Housel, Debra J. The Nature of Matter, 1 vol. rev. ed. 2014. (Science Readers: Content & Literacy Ser.). (ENG.). 32p. (gr. 2-2). pap. 8.99 (978-1-4807-4603-9(7)) Teacher Created Materials, Inc.

Hughes, Susan. Does It Sink or Float? 2014. (ENG., Illus.). 24p. (J). lib. bdg. (978-0-7787-0536-9(6)) Crabtree Publishing Co.

—Is It Heavy or Light? 2012. (ENG., Illus.). 24p. (J). (978-0-7787-2048-5(9)); pap. (978-0-7787-2055-3(1)) Crabtree Publishing Co.

—Is It Hot or Cold? 2012. (ENG., Illus.). 24p. (J). (978-0-7787-2049-2(7)); pap. (978-0-7787-2056-0(X)) Crabtree Publishing Co.

—Is It Transparent or Opaque? 2012. (ENG., Illus.). 24p. (J). (978-0-7787-2052-2(7)); pap. (978-0-7787-2059-1(4)) Crabtree Publishing Co.

Hurd, Will. Changing States: Solids, Liquids, & Gases. 2016. (Do It Yourself Ser.). (ENG.). 48p. (gr. 3-6). pap. 8.99 (978-1-4846-3818-7(2), NA-h) Heinemann-Raintree.

Is It Hard or Soft? 2014. (ENG., Illus.). 24p. (J). (978-0-7787-0538-3(2)) Crabtree Publishing Co.

Is It Natural or Human-Made? 2014. (ENG., Illus.). 24p. (J). (978-0-7787-0535-2(8)) Crabtree Publishing Co.

Ives, Rob. Fun Experiments with Matter: Invisible Ink, Giant Bubbles, & More. Sassin, Eva, illus. 2017. (Amazing Science Experiments Ser.). (ENG.). (J). (gr. 3-6). lib. bdg. 26.65 **(978-1-5124-3216-9(4))** Lerner Publishing Group.

Jackson, Tom. The Basics of Atoms & Molecules. 2013. (Core Concepts Ser.). 96p. (YA). (gr. 7-12). 34.60 (978-1-4777-2715-7(9)) Rosen Publishing Group, Inc., The.

James, Emily. The Simple Science of Matter. 2017. (Simply Science Ser.). (ENG.). 32p. (gr. 1-2). lib. bdg. 27.32 **(978-1-5157-7081-7(8)**, Aplus Bks.) Capstone Press of Coughlan Cos.

Kenney, Karen Latchana. The Science of Stars: Exploring Matter, 1 vol. 2016. (Science in Action Ser.). (ENG., Illus.). 32p. (J). (gr. 3-6). 27.07 (978-1-62403-965-2(0)) ABDO Publishing Co.

Kenney, Karen Latchana. States of Matter Investigations. 2017. (Key Questions in Physical Science Ser.). (ENG.). 32p. (J). (gr. 3-6). 27.99 **(978-1-5124-4006-5(X))** Lerner Publishing Group.

Kjelle, Marylou Morano. The Properties of Liquids. (Library of Physical Science Ser.). 24p. (gr. 4-4). 2009. 42.50 (978-1-60853-791-4(9)) 2007. (ENG., Illus.). pap. 7.05 (978-1-4042-2169-7(7)) Rosen Publishing Group, Inc., The. (PowerKids Pr.).

—The Properties of Metals. (Library of Physical Science Ser.). 24p. 2009. (gr. 4-4). 42.50 (978-1-60853-792-1(7), PowerKids Pr.) 2006. (Illus.). (J). (gr. 3-7). lib. bdg. 22.60 (978-1-4042-3417-8(9)) Rosen Publishing Group, Inc., The.

—The Properties of Salts. (Library of Physical Science Ser.). 24p. (gr. 4-4). 2009. 42.50 (978-1-60853-793-8(5)) 2007. (ENG., Illus.). pap. 7.05 (978-1-4042-2172-7(7)) Rosen Publishing Group, Inc., The. (PowerKids Pr.).

—The Properties of Solids. (Library of Physical Science Ser.). 24p. (gr. 4-4). 2009. 42.50 (978-1-60853-794-5(3)) 2007. (ENG., Illus.). pap. 7.05 (978-1-4042-2168-0(9)) Rosen Publishing Group, Inc., The. (PowerKids Pr.).

Larson, Karen. Changing Matter, 1 vol. 2015. (Science Readers: Content & Literacy Ser.). (ENG., Illus.). 32p. (J). (gr. 3-3). pap. 8.99 (978-1-4807-4642-8(8)) Teacher Created Materials, Inc.

Leber, Nancy. Solids: Text Pairs. 2008. (Bridges/Navigators Ser.). (J). (gr. 3). 89.00 (978-1-4108-8372-8(8)) Benchmark Education Co.

Lindeen, Mary. Color & Shape. 2017. (BeginningtoRead Ser.). (ENG.). 32p. (J). (-2). 22.60 **(978-1-59953-882-2(2))**; pap. 11.94 **(978-1-68404-101-5(5))** Norwood Hse. Pr.

Marshall Cavendish Benchmark, prod. Heavy/Light. 2nd rev. ed. 2011. (Bookworms 2nd Edition: Opposites Ser.). 16p. (gr. k-1). 21.36 (978-1-60870-408-8(4)) Marshall Cavendish Corp.

Mason, Adrienne. Change It! Solids, Liquids, Gases & You. Dávila, Claudia, illus. 2006. (Primary Physical Science Ser.). (ENG.). 32p. (J). (gr. -1-2). 7.95 (978-1-55337-838-9(5)) Kids Can Pr., Ltd. CAN. Dist: Hachette Bk. Group.

—Touch It! Materials, Matter & You. Dávila, Claudia, illus. 2005. (Primary Physical Science Ser.). (ENG.). 32p. (J). (gr. -1-2). 7.95 (978-1-55337-761-0(3)) Kids Can Pr., Ltd. CAN. Dist: Hachette Bk. Group.

Maurer, Daniel D. Do You Really Want to Skate on Thin Ice? A Book about States of Matter. Alberini, Teresa, illus. 2016. (Adventures in Science Ser.). (ENG.). 24p. (J). (gr. k-3). 20.95 (978-1-60753-958-2(6)) Amicus Publishing.

Maurer, Tracy Nelson. Changing Matter: Understanding Physical & Chemical Changes. 2012. (ENG.). 24p. (gr. 4-5). pap. 8.95 (978-1-61810-240-9(0)) Rourke Educational Media.

—Mix It up! Solution or Mixture? 2012. (ENG.). 24p. (gr. 3-4). pap. 8.95 (978-1-61810-227-0(3)) Rourke Educational Media.

—The Scoop about Measuring Matter. 2012. (ENG.). 24p. (gr. 3-4). pap. 8.95 (978-1-61810-226-3(5)) Rourke Educational Media.

Mezzanotte, Jim. Gases. 2006. (States of Matter Ser.). (Illus.). 24p. (gr. 1-4). pap. 8.15 (978-0-8368-6802-9(1)); lib. bdg. 22.00 (978-0-8368-6797-8(1)) Stevens, Gareth Publishing LLLP. (Weekly Reader Leveled Readers).

—Sólidos. 2006. (Estados de la materia (States of Matter) Ser.). (ENG & SPA.). 24p. (gr. 1-4). pap. 8.15 (978-0-8368-7410-5(2)); (Illus.). lib. bdg. 22.00 (978-0-8368-7405-1(6)) Stevens, Gareth Publishing LLLP. (Weekly Reader Leveled Readers).

—Solids. 2006. (States of Matter Ser.). (Illus.). 24p. (gr. 1-4). lib. bdg. 22.00 (978-0-8368-6800-5(5), Weekly Reader Leveled Readers) Stevens, Gareth Publishing LLLP.

Miller, Heather. Matter. 2009. (21st Century Skills Library: Real World Science Ser.). (ENG., Illus.). 32p. (J). (gr. 4-8). lib. bdg. 28.50 (978-1-60279-460-3(X), 200235) Cherry Lake Publishing.

Monroe, Tilda. What Do You Know about States of Matter? 2010. (20 Questions: Physical Science Ser.). (ENG.). 24p. (J). pap. 8.25 (978-1-4488-1246-2(1), PowerKids Pr.); (gr. 2-5). lib. bdg. 22.60 (978-1-4488-0670-6(4)) Rosen Publishing Group, Inc., The.

Montgomery, Anne. Solid or Liquid?, 1 vol. rev. ed. 2014. (Science Readers: Content & Literacy Ser.). (ENG., Illus.). 24p. (gr. k-k). pap. 8.99 (978-1-4807-4527-8(8)) Teacher Created Materials, Inc.

Moore, David. Expl on Your Own Cookie Time. 2009. (Explore on Your Own Ser.). (ENG.). (C). pap. 7.95 (978-0-7362-5543-1(5)) National Geographic School Publishing, Inc.

—Expl on Your Own Decorating AVase. 2009. (Explore on Your Own Ser.). (ENG.). (C). pap. 7.95 (978-0-7362-5541-7(9)) National Geographic School Publishing, Inc.

—Expl on Your Own Postcards from My Trip. 2009. (Explore on Your Own Ser.). (ENG., Illus.). 12p. (C). pap. 7.95 (978-0-7362-5601-8(6)) National Geographic School Publishing, Inc.

Moore, Elizabeth. Matter Is Everything! 2011. (Wonder Readers Early Level Ser.). (ENG.). 32p. (gr. -1-1). pap. 5.99 (978-1-4296-8059-2(8), Wonder Readers) Capstone Press of Coughlan Cos.

Murphy, John, ed. Physics: Understanding the Properties of Matter & Energy. 2014. (Study of Science Ser.). (Illus.). 160p. (J). (gr. 7-12). 35.25 (978-1-62275-418-2(2)) Rosen Publishing Group, Inc., The.

Murray, Julie. Solids, Liquids, & Gasses, 1 vol. 2006. (First Science Ser.). (ENG., Illus.). 24p. (gr. k-4). 25.65 (978-1-59679-830-4(0), Buddy Bks.) ABDO Publishing Co.

National Geographic Learning Staff. Solids,Liquids, & Gases, Level 3. 2011. (World Windows Ser.). (ENG., Illus.). 16p. (J). stu. ed. 9.95 (978-1-133-49276-4(2)) Cengage Heinle.

O'Neal, Claire. A Project Guide to Matter. 2011. (Physical Science Projects for Kids Ser.). (Illus.). 48p. (J). (gr. 3-6). lib. bdg. 29.95 (978-1-58415-967-4(7)) Mitchell Lane Pubs., Inc.

Oxlade, Chris. Experiments with Matter & Materials, 1 vol. 2015. (ENG.). 32p. (J). lib. bdg. 27.50 (978-1-4777-5969-1(7), PowerKids Pr.) Rosen Publishing Group, Inc., The.

—Mixing & Separating. 2007. (ENG., Illus.). 32p. (J). (gr. -1-3). pap. (978-0-7787-3650-9(4)) Crabtree Publishing Co.

Peterson, Megan Cooley. Scooby-Doo! a States of Matter Mystery: Revenge from a Watery Grave. Cornia, Christian, illus. 2016. (Scooby-Doo Solves It with S. T. E. M. Ser.). (ENG.). 32p. (gr. 3-4). 27.99 (978-1-5157-2592-3(8)) Capstone Press of Coughlan Cos.

Randolph, Joanne. Solids in My World. 2009. (My World of Science Ser.). 24p. (gr. 2-2). 37.50 (978-1-61514-728-1(4), PowerKids Pr.) Rosen Publishing Group, Inc., The.

—Solids in My World/Los sólidos en mi Mundo. 2009. (My World of Science/la ciencia en mi mundo Ser.). (ENG & SPA.). 48p. (gr. 2-2). 37.50 (978-1-61514-740-3(3), Editorial Buenas Letras) Rosen Publishing Group, Inc., The.

Rees, Peter. Why Does Water Freeze? Level 3 Factbook. 2010. (Cambridge Young Readers Ser.). (ENG., Illus.). 16p. pap. 6.00 (978-0-521-13712-6(8)) Cambridge Univ. Pr.

Rising, Heather. Is It Smooth or Rough? 2012. (ENG., Illus.). 24p. (J). (978-0-7787-2051-5(9)); pap. (978-0-7787-2058-4(6)) Crabtree Publishing Co.

Rising, Trudy L. Is It Magnetic or Nonmagnetic? 2012. (ENG., Illus.). 24p. (J). (978-0-7787-2050-8(0)); pap. (978-0-7787-2057-7(8)) Crabtree Publishing Co.

Rivera, Sheila. Mixing. 2007. (First Step Nonfiction - Changing Matter Ser.). (ENG., Illus.). 8p. (gr. -1-1). pap. 4.95 (978-0-8225-6411-9(4)) Lerner Publishing Group.

Rodriguez, Cindy. Gases. 2013. (SPA.). (J). (978-1-62127-601-2(5)) Weigl Pubs., Inc.

—Gases, with Code. 2012. (What Is Matter? Ser.). (ENG., Illus.). 24p. (J). (gr. -1-3). pap. 12.95 (978-1-61913-604-5(X), AV2 by Weigl) Weigl Pubs., Inc.

—Gases with Code. 2012. (What Is Matter? Ser.). (ENG., Illus.). 24p. (J). (gr. -1-3). lib. bdg. 27.13 (978-1-61913-602-1(3), AV2 by Weigl) Weigl Pubs., Inc.

—Líquidos. 2013. (SPA.). (J). (978-1-62127-603-6(1)) Weigl Pubs., Inc.

—Liquids, with Code. 2012. (What Is Matter? Ser.). (ENG., Illus.). 24p. (J). (gr. -1-3). pap. 12.95 (978-1-61913-605-2(8), AV2 by Weigl) Weigl Pubs., Inc.

—Liquids with Code. 2012. (What Is Matter? Ser.). (ENG., Illus.). 24p. (J). (gr. -1-3). lib. bdg. 27.13 (978-1-61913-603-8(1), AV2 by Weigl) Weigl Pubs., Inc.

—Sólidos. 2013. (SPA.). (J). (978-1-62127-605-0(8)) Weigl Pubs., Inc.

Rompella, Natalie. Experiments in Material & Matter with Toys & Everyday Stuff. 2015. (Fun Science Ser.). (ENG., Illus.). 24p. (gr. 1-2). lib. bdg. 25.32 (978-1-4914-5034-5(7)) Capstone Press of Coughlan Cos.

Rustad, Martha E. H. What Is It Made Of? Noticing Types of Materials. Schneider, Christine M., illus. 2015. (ENG.). 24p. (J). (gr. k-2). 25.32 (978-1-4677-8561-7(X), Millbrook Pr.) Lerner Publishing Group.

Ryback, Carol & Mezzanotte, Jim. Solids. 2006. (States of Matter Ser.). (Illus.). 24p. (gr. 1-4). pap. 8.15 (978-0-8368-6805-0(6), Weekly Reader Leveled Readers) Stevens, Gareth Publishing LLLP.

Schuh, Mari C. All about Matter, 1 vol. 2011. (Science Builders Ser.). (ENG.). 24p. (gr. k-1). 26.65 (978-1-4296-6068-6(6), Pebble Plus) Capstone Press of Coughlan Cos.

Selwyn, Josephine. When Does Water Turn into Ice? 2014. (Little Books of Answers: Level F Ser.). (Illus.). 16p. (gr. k-2). pap. 7.95 (978-1-927136-59-1(8)) Three Crows Media NZL. Dist: RiverStream Publishing.

Silverstein, Alvin, et al. Matter. 2008. (Science Concepts, Second Ser.). (Illus.). 112p. (YA). (gr. 5-9). lib. bdg. 31.93 (978-0-8225-7515-3(9)) Lerner Publishing Group.

Slade, Suzanne. Atoms, 1 vol., 1. 2014. (Ultimate Science: Physical Science Ser.). (ENG.). 24p. (gr. 3-6). 23.60 (978-1-4777-6089-5(X), PowerKids Pr.) Rosen Publishing Group, Inc., The.

—Atoms & Chemical Reactions. (Library of Physical Science Ser.). 24p. (gr. 4-4). 2009. 42.50 (978-1-60853-780-8(3), PowerKids Pr.) 2007. (ENG., Illus.). pap. 7.05 (978-1-4042-2162-8(X), PowerKids Pr.) 2006. (Illus.). (YA). lib. bdg. 22.60 (978-1-4042-3415-4(2)) Rosen Publishing Group, Inc., The.

—Different States of Matter, 1 vol., 1. 2014. (Ultimate Science: Physical Science Ser.). (ENG.). 24p. (gr. 3-6). 23.60 (978-1-4777-6093-2(8), PowerKids Pr.) Rosen Publishing Group, Inc., The.

—Scientific Instruments: Looking at Atoms & Molecules. 2009. (Library of Physical Science Ser.). 24p. (gr. 4-4). 42.50 (978-1-60853-786-0(2), PowerKids Pr.) Rosen Publishing Group, Inc., The.

—States of Matter. 24p. (gr. 4-4). 2009. (Library of Physical Science Ser.). 42.50 (978-1-60853-789-1(7), PowerKids Pr.) 2007. (Library of Physical Sciences). (ENG., Illus.). pap. 7.05 (978-1-4042-2163-5(8), PowerKids Pr.) 2006. (Library of Physical Science Ser.: Vol. 3). (Illus.). (YA). lib. bdg. 22.60 (978-1-4042-3416-1(0)) Rosen Publishing Group, Inc., The.

Smith, Ben. Where Can You Find Hard & Soft Things? 2014. (Little Books of Answers: Level e Ser.). (Illus.). 16p. (gr. k-2). pap. 7.95 (978-1-927136-49-2(0)) Three Crows Media NZL. Dist: RiverStream Publishing.

Smith, Erica. Solid, Liquid, Gas: What Is Matter? 2009. (Reading Room Collection 2 Ser.). 24p. (gr. 3-4). 42.50 (978-1-60851-988-0(0), PowerKids Pr.) Rosen Publishing Group, Inc., The.

Smith, Sian. Hard & Soft, 1 vol. 2014. (Opposites Ser.). (ENG.). 24p. (gr. -1-1). pap. 5.99 (978-1-4846-0333-8(8), Acorn) Heinemann-Raintree.

Solway, Andrew. The Science of a Loaf of Bread: The Science of Changing Properties. 2009. (Science of... Ser.). (Illus.). 32p. (YA). (gr. 3-6). lib. bdg. 26.00 (978-1-4339-0043-3(2)) Stevens, Gareth Publishing LLLP.

Spilsbury, Richard & Spilsbury, Louise. What Are Solids, Liquids, & Gases? Exploring Science with Hands-on Activities. 2008. (In Touch with Basic Science Ser.). (Illus.). 32p. (J). (gr. 3-4). lib. bdg. 23.94 (978-0-7660-3094-7(6), Enslow Elementary) Enslow Pubs., Inc.

Stephens, David. A Material World: What Is Matter?, 1 vol., 1. 2014. (Discovery Education: How It Works). (ENG.). 32p. (gr. 3-6). 26.25 (978-1-4777-6325-4(2), PowerKids Pr.) Rosen Publishing Group, Inc., The.

Taylor-Butler, Christine. Experiments with Solids, Liquids, & Gases. 2011. (True Bk Ser.). (ENG., Illus.). 48p. (J). pap. 6.95 (978-0-531-26649-6(4)); lib. bdg. 29.00 (978-0-531-26349-5(5)) Scholastic Library Publishing. (Children's Pr.).

Troupe, Thomas Kingsley. Why Do Dead Fish Float? Learning about Matter with the Garbage Gang, 1 vol. Toye, Derek, illus. 2014. (Garbage Gang's Super Science Questions Ser.). (ENG.). 24p. (gr. k-2). 26.65 (978-1-4795-5479-9(0)) Picture Window Bks.

Walker, Sally M. Matter. King, Andy, illus. 2005. (Early Bird Energy Ser.). 48p. (J). (gr. 3-7). lib. bdg. 25.26 (978-0-8225-5131-7(4), Lerner Pubns.) Lerner Publishing Group.

Weir, Kirsten & Brent, Lynnette. States of Matter. 2008. (Why Chemistry Matters Ser.). (ENG., Illus.). 32p. (J). (gr. 3-7). pap. (978-0-7787-4251-7(2)) Crabtree Publishing Co.

West, Krista. States of Matter: Gases, Liquids, & Solids. 2008. (Essential Chemistry Ser.). 128p. (YA). (gr. 7-12). 35.00 (978-0-7910-9521-8(5)) Facts On File, Inc.

Williams, Zella. Experiments with Solids, Liquids, & Gases. (Do-It-Yourself Science Ser.). 24p. 2009. (gr. 2-3). 47.90 (978-1-61512-190-8(0), PowerKids Pr.) 2007. (Illus.). (J). 42.30 (978-1-4042-4013-1(6), PowerKids Pr.) 2007. (Illus.). (J). (gr. 2-5). lib. bdg. 25.25 (978-1-4042-3658-5(9)) Rosen Publishing Group, Inc., The.

World Book, Inc Staff, contrib. by. Learning about Matter. 2011. (J). (978-0-7166-0234-7(2)) World Bk., Inc.

—Matter & Its Properties. 2011. 32p. (J). (978-0-7166-1429-6(4)) World Bk., Inc.

Young, June. Look How It Changes! 2006. (Rookie Read-About Science Ser.). (ENG., Illus.). 32p. (J). (gr. 1-2). pap. 4.95 (978-0-516-28178-0(X), Children's Pr.) Scholastic Library Publishing.

MATTHEW, SAINT, APOSTLE

Mackenzie, Carine & Gair, Cyhoeddiadau'r. Actau. Taylor, Jane, illus. 2005. (WEL.). 16p. pap. (978-1-85994-271-0(7)) Cyhoeddiadau'r Gair.

Woodman, Ros. Matthew - Bible Detectives. 2005. (Activity Ser.). (ENG.). 64p. (J). pap., act. bk. ed. 7.99 (978-1-85792-673-6(0), 81c9df0c-5d0a-4c8e-bf79-57c337cb3e6d) Christian Focus Pubns. GBR. Dist: Bookmasters Distribution.

MAURITANIA

Blauer, Ettagale & Lauré, Jason. Mauritania. 2008. (Cultures of the World Ser.). (Illus.). 144p. (gr. 6-18). lib. bdg. 42.79 (978-0-7614-3116-9(0), Benchmark Bks.) Marshall Cavendish Corp.

MAXI (FICTITIOUS CHARACTER)—FICTION

Bennett, Jeffrey. Max Goes to Mars: A Science Adventure with Max the Dog. Okamoto, Alan, illus. 2015. (Science Adventures with Max the Dog Ser.). (ENG.). 32p. (J). (gr. 2-4). 15.00 (978-1-937548-44-5(9)) Big Kid Science.

Sykes, Julie. Beware the Werepup & Other Stories. Reed, Nathan, illus. unabr. ed. 2014. (ENG.). 384p. (J). (gr. 2-4). pap. 8.99 (978-1-4472-1961-3(9)) Pan Macmillan GBR. Dist: Independent Pubs. Group.

MAXIMS

see Proverbs

MAY DAY—FICTION

Mora, Pat. The Rainbow Tulip. Sayles, Elizabeth, illus. 2003. (ENG.). 32p. (J). (gr. k-3). 6.99 (978-0-14-250009-5(7), Puffin Books) Penguin Young Readers Group.

—Rainbow Tulip. 2014. 17.00 (978-1-63419-680-2(5)) Perfection Learning Corp.

Silverman, Erica. On the Morn of Mayfest. Frazee, Marla, illus. 2011. (ENG.). 32p. (J). (gr. -1-2). pap. 13.99 (978-1-4424-4341-9(3), Simon & Schuster Bks. For Young Readers) Simon & Schuster Bks. For Young Readers.

MAYAS

see Indians of Mexico—Mayas

MAYFLOWER (SHIP)

Arenstam, Peter. The Mighty Mastiff of the Mayflower. 2012. Orig. Title: The Mighty Mastiff of the Mayflower. (ENG., Illus.). 112p. 14.99 (978-1-60949-609-8(4), History Pr., The) Arcadia Publishing.

Arenstam, Peter, et al. MayFlower 1620: A New Look at a Pilgrim Voyage. 2004. (Illus.). 47p. (J). (gr. k-4). 18.00 (978-0-7567-7967-2(7)) DIANE Publishing Co.

Barber, Nicola. Who Journeyed on the Mayflower?, 1 vol. HL Studios Staff, illus. 2014. (Primary Source Detectives Ser.). (ENG.). 64p. (gr. 7-8). lib. bdg. 35.99 (978-1-4329-9602-4(9)) Heinemann-Raintree.

Cook, Peter. You Wouldn't Want to Sail on the Mayflower! A Trip That Took Entirely Too Long. Whelan, Kevin, illus. rev. ed. 2013. (ENG.). 40p. (J). (gr. 3-12). pap. 9.95 (978-0-531-23858-5(X)) Scholastic Library Publishing.

Cook, Peter & Whelan, Kevin. You Wouldn't Want to Sail on the Mayflower! A Trip That Took Entirely Too Long. rev. ed. 2013. (ENG.). 32p. (J). 29.00 (978-0-531-27107-0(2), Watts, Franklin) Scholastic Library Publishing.

Fradin, Dennis Brindell. The Mayflower Compact. 2006. (Turning Points in U. S. History Ser.). (Illus.). 47p. (J). (gr. 3-7). lib. bdg. 31.36 (978-0-7614-2125-2(4), Benchmark Bks.) Marshall Cavendish Corp.

Greenwood, Mark. The Mayflower. Lessac, Frané, illus. 2014. (ENG.). 32p. (J). (gr. -1-3). 16.95 (978-0-8234-2943-1(1)) Holiday Hse., Inc.

Gunderson, Jessica. Life on the Mayflower, 1 vol. Dumm, Brian Caleb, illus. 2011. (Thanksgiving Ser.). (ENG.). 24p. (gr. 1-2). pap. 7.95 (978-1-4048-6719-2(8)) Picture Window Bks.

Honders, Christine. Mayflower Compact. 2016. (Documents of American Democracy Ser.). (Illus.). 32p. (J). (gr. 5-5). pap. 10.00 (978-1-4994-2085-2(4), PowerKids Pr.) Rosen Publishing Group, Inc., The.

Kallio, Jamie. Mayflower Compact, 1 vol. 2013. (Foundations of Our Nation Ser.). (ENG.). 48p. (J). (gr. 3-6). lib. bdg. 32.79 (978-1-61783-711-1(3)); (Illus.). pap. 15.64 (978-1-61783-761-6(X), Core Library) ABDO Publishing Co.

Lassieur, Allison. El Viaje del Mayflower. McDonnell, Peter, illus. 2006. (Historia Gráficas Ser.). (SPA.). 32p. (gr. 3-4). 30.65 (978-0-7368-6613-2(2)) Capstone Press of Coughlan Cos.

Lynch, P. J. The Boy Who Fell off the Mayflower, or John Howland's Good Fortune. Lynch, P. J., illus. 2015. (ENG., Illus.). 64p. (J). (gr. 2-5). 17.99 (978-0-7636-6584-5(3)) Candlewick Pr.

Plimoth Plantation Staff, et al. Mayflower 1620: A New Look at a Pilgrim Voyage. 2013. (ENG.). 48p. (J). (gr. 3-7). lib. bdg. 27.00 (978-1-4263-1631-9(3), National Geographic Children's Bks.) National Geographic Society.

—Mayflower 1620: A New Look at a Pilgrim Voyage. Coulson, Cotton, photos by. 2007. (ENG., Illus.). 48p. (J). (gr. 3-7). per. 6.95 (978-0-7922-6276-3(X), National Geographic Children's Bks.) National Geographic Society.

Poolos, J. The Mayflower. 2004. (Primary Sources in American History Ser.). (Illus.). 64p. (J). (gr. 5-8). lib. bdg. 31.95 (978-0-8239-4514-6(6), Rosen Reference) Rosen Publishing Group, Inc., The.

—The Mayflower: A Primary Source History of the Pilgrims' Journey to the New World. 2009. (Primary Sources in American History Ser.). 64p. (gr. 5-8). 58.50 (978-1-60851-499-1(4)) Rosen Publishing Group, Inc., The.

Rajczak, Kristen. The Mayflower Compact. 2013. (Documents That Shaped America Ser.). (Illus.). 32p. (J). (gr. 4-6). pap. 10.50 (978-1-4339-9006-9(7)); (ENG., lib. bdg. 26.60 (978-1-4339-9005-2(9)) Stevens, Gareth Publishing LLLP.

Rajczak, Michael. Life on the Mayflower, Vol. 1. 2014. (What You Didn't Know about History Ser.). (ENG.). 24p. (J). (gr. 2-3). 22.60 (978-1-4824-0591-0(1)) Stevens, Gareth Publishing LLLP.

Rajczak Nelson, Kristen. The Mayflower Compact. 2013. (Documents That Shaped America Ser.). (Illus.). 32p. (J). (gr. 4-6). pap. 63.00 (978-1-4339-9007-6(5)) Stevens, Gareth Publishing LLLP.

Raum, Elizabeth. The Mayflower Compact, 1 vol. 2012. (Documenting U. S. History Ser.). (ENG.). 48p. (gr. 3-6). pap. 9.95 (978-1-4329-6759-8(2)); lib. bdg. 32.65 (978-1-4329-6750-5(9)) Heinemann-Raintree. (NA-h).

Smith, Andrea P. The Journey of the Mayflower. 2012. (Illus.). 24p. (J). 63.60 (978-1-4488-5211-6(0)); pap. 10.60 (978-1-4488-5210-9(2)); lib. bdg. 25.25 (978-1-4488-5186-7(6)) Rosen Publishing Group, Inc., The. (PowerKids Pr.).

Waxman, Laura Hamilton. Why Did the Pilgrims Come to the New World? And Other Questions about the Plymouth Colony. 2010. (Six Questions of American History Ser.). (ENG., Illus.). 48p. (gr. 4-6). lib. bdg. 30.60 (978-1-58013-665-5(6)) Lerner Publishing Group.

—Why Did the Pilgrims Come to the New World? & Other Questions about the Plymouth Colony. 2010. pap. 56.72 (978-0-7613-6951-6(1)) Lerner Publishing Group.

Whitcraft, Melissa. The Mayflower Compact. 2003. (Cornerstones of Freedom Ser.). (ENG., Illus.). 48p. (YA). (gr. 4-7). 26.00 (978-0-516-24203-3(2)) Scholastic Library Publishing.

Whitehurst, Susan. The Mayflower. 2009. (Library of the Pilgrims Ser.). 24p. (gr. 3-4). 42.50 (978-1-60853-914-7(8), PowerKids Pr.) Rosen Publishing Group, Inc., The.

Yero, Judith Lloyd & National Geographic Learning Staff. The Mayflower Compact. 2007. (Reading Expeditions Ser.). (ENG., Illus.). 32p. (J). pap. 17.95 (978-0-7922-4553-7(9)) CENGAGE Learning.

MAYFLOWER (SHIP)—FICTION

Klimo, Kate. Dog Diaries #5: Dash. Jessell, Tim, illus. 2014. (Dog Diaries). (ENG.). 160p. (J). (gr. 2-5). pap. 7.99 (978-0-385-37338-8(4), Random Hse. Bks. for Young Readers) Random Hse. Children's Bks.

Lasky, Kathryn. A Journey to the New World: The Diary of Remember Patience Whipple, Mayflower 1620. 2010. (Dear America Ser.). (ENG.). 192p. (J). (gr. 3-7). 12.99 (978-0-545-23801-4(3), Scholastic Pr.) Scholastic, Inc.

Lawton, Wendy G. Almost Home: A Story Based on the Life of the Mayflower's Mary Chilton. 2003. (Daughters of the Faith Ser.). (ENG.). 160p. (YA). (gr. 3). pap. 7.99 (978-0-8024-3637-5(4)) Moody Pubs.

Limbaugh, Rush H., III. Rush Revere & the Brave Pilgrims: Time-Travel Adventures with Exceptional Americans. 2013. (ENG., Illus.). 224p. 19.99 (978-1-4767-5586-1(8), Threshold Editions) Threshold Editions.

Roy, Ron. Mayflower Treasure Hunt. Gurney, John Steven, illus. 2nd ed. 2007. (to Z Mysteries Ser.: 2). (ENG.). 128p. (J). (gr. 1-4). per. 5.99 (978-0-375-83937-5(2), Random Hse. Bks. for Young Readers) Random Hse. Children's Bks.

MAYORS

Bankston, John. Rudy Giuliani. l.t. ed. 2003. (Blue Banner Biography Ser.). (Illus.). 32p. (J). (gr. 3-8). lib. bdg. 25.70 (978-1-58415-194-4(3)) Mitchell Lane Pubs., Inc.

Dawson, Emily C. Town Leaders. 2010. (My Community Ser.). 24p. (J). 25.65 (978-1-60753-025-1(2)) Amicus Publishing.

Gorman, Jacqueline Laks. Alcalde (Mayor) 2009. (Conoce tu gobierno (Know Your Government) Ser.). (SPA.). 24p. (J). (gr. 2-4). lib. bdg. 22.00 (978-1-4339-0100-3(5), Weekly Reader Leveled Readers) Stevens, Gareth Publishing LLLP.

—Mayor. 2009. (Know Your Government Ser.). 24p. (J). (gr. 2-4). pap. 8.15 (978-1-4339-0121-8(8)); lib. bdg. 22.00 (978-1-4339-0093-8(9)) Stevens, Gareth Publishing LLLP. (Weekly Reader Leveled Readers).

Jakubiak, David J. What Does a Mayor Do? 2010. (How Our Government Works Ser.). 24p. (J). (gr. 3-6). lib. bdg., E-Book 42.50 (978-1-4488-0026-1(9)); (Illus.). pap. 8.25 (978-1-4358-9814-1(1), PowerKids Pr.); (Illus.). (gr. 3-6). lib. bdg. 22.60 (978-1-4358-9359-7(X), PowerKids Pr.) Rosen Publishing Group, Inc., The.

Jeffries, Joyce. Meet the Mayor. 2013. (People Around Town Ser.). 24p. (J). (gr. k-2). pap. 8.15 (978-1-4339-9378-7(3)); pap. 48.90 (978-1-4339-9379-4(1)); (ENG., Illus.). lib. bdg. 22.60 (978-1-4339-9377-0(5)) Stevens, Gareth Publishing LLLP.

—Meet the Mayor / Conoce a Los Alcaldes. 2013. (People Around Town / Gente de Mi Ciudad Ser.). (SPA & ENG., Illus.). 24p. (J). (gr. k-2). 22.60 (978-1-4339-9470-8(4)) Stevens, Gareth Publishing LLLP.

Knudsen, Shannon. Mayors. 2005. (Pull Ahead Bks.). (Illus.). 32p. (J). (gr. 3-7). lib. bdg. 22.60 (978-0-8225-2829-6(0), Lerner Pubns.) Lerner Publishing Group.

Laks Gorman, Jacqueline. Alcalde (Mayor) 2009. (Conoce tu gobierno (Know Your Government) Ser.). (SPA.). 24p. (J). (gr. 2-4). pap. 8.15 (978-1-4339-0128-7(5), Weekly Reader Leveled Readers) Stevens, Gareth Publishing LLLP.

Manning, Jack. The City Mayor, 1 vol. 2014. (Our Government Ser.). (ENG.). 24p. (gr. 1-2). 25.32 (978-1-4914-0336-5(5), First Facts) Capstone Press of Coughlan Cos.

Marsh, Carole. Meet Shirley Franklin, Mayor of Atlanta! 2003. 32p. (gr. 3-8). 21.95 (978-0-635-01141-7(7)) Gallopade International.

Shichtman, Sandra H. Michael Bloomberg. 2010. (Political Profiles Ser.). 112p. (J). 28.95 (978-1-59935-135-3(8)) Reynolds, Morgan Inc.

Silate, Jennifer. Your Mayor: Local Government in Action. 2009. (Primary Source Library of American Citizenship Ser.). 24p. (gr. 5-5). 47.90 (978-1-61511-237-1(5), Rosen Reference) Rosen Publishing Group, Inc., The.

MAYS, WILLIE, 1931-

Doeden, Matt. Willie Mays. 2010. (Sports Heroes & Legends Ser.). (ENG.). 120p. (gr. 5-12). lib. bdg. 30.60 (978-0-7613-5370-6(4)) Lerner Publishing Group.

Mandel, Peter. Say Hey! A Song of Willie Mays. Tate, Don, illus. 2004. 30p. (J). (gr. k-2). reprint ed. 16.00 (978-0-7567-8162-0(0)) DIANE Publishing Co.

Smith, Linda J. Willie Mays: The Say Hey Kid. 2005. (Illus.). 112p. (J). pap. (978-1-59421-015-0(2)) Seacoast Publishing, Inc.

Winter, Jonah. You Never Heard of Willie Mays?! Widener, Terry, illus. 2016. (ENG.). 40p. (J). (gr. -1-3). 7.99 (978-1-101-93421-0(2), Dragonfly Bks.) Random Hse. Children's Bks.

MAZE PUZZLES

Adam, Winky. Native American Mazes. 2003. (Dover Little Activity Bks.). (ENG., Illus.). 64p. (J). (gr. k-3). pap. 1.99 (978-0-486-42616-7(5)) Dover Pubns., Inc.

Altmann, Scott. Vampire Mazes. 2011. (Dover Children's Activity Bks.). (ENG., Illus.). 48p. (J). (gr. 3-4). pap. 4.99 (978-0-486-47922-4(6)) Dover Pubns., Inc.

Andrews McMeel Publishing Staff. Go Fun! Big Book of Mazes. 2014. (Go Fun! Ser.: 3). (ENG.). 144p. (J). pap. 8.99 (978-1-4494-6485-1(8)) Andrews McMeel Publishing.

—Go Fun! Big Book of Mazes 2. 2015. (Go Fun! Ser.: 9). (ENG.). 128p. (J). pap. 8.99 (978-1-4494-7227-6(3)) Andrews McMeel Publishing.

Artymowska, Aleksandra, illus. Amazed. 2017. (ENG.). 32p. (J). (gr. 1-4). 16.99 **(978-1-78627-051-1(X))** King, Laurence Publishing GBR. Dist: Hachette Bk. Group.

Blundell, Kim & Tyler, Jenny. Treasure Mazes. rev. ed. 2003. (Illus.). 23p. (J). pap. 5.99 (978-0-7945-0537-0(6), Usborne) EDC Publishing.

Brightfield, Rick. Amazing Mazes: Groovy, Graphic Games. 2012. (Dover Children's Activity Bks.). (ENG.). 80p. (gr. 4). pap. 6.99 (978-0-486-48939-1(6)) Dover Pubns., Inc.

Bulleman, Curtis David. Car Crazy: Tricked Out Activity Book. 2012. (Dover Children's Activity Bks.). (ENG.). 48p. (J). (gr. 2-5). pap. 4.99 (978-0-486-48375-7(4)) Dover Pubns., Inc.

Carpenter, Elizabeth. DinoMazes: The Colossal Fossil Book - 31 Poster-Size Prehistoric Fossil Nazes. 2011. (ENG., Illus.). 41p. (J). (gr. 3-12). pap. 11.95 (978-0-7611-6575-0(4), 16575) Workman Publishing Co., Inc.

—MummyMaze: The Tomb Treasures Maze Book. 2nd rev. ed. 2007. (J). pap. 19.99 (978-0-9793043-0-9(X)) Mazeology.

Donahue, Peter. Robot Mazes. 2008. (Dover Children's Activity Bks.). (ENG., Illus.). 48p. (J). (gr. k-5). pap. 4.99 (978-0-486-46825-9(9)) Dover Pubns., Inc.

Dover Staff & Radtke, Becky. Girls on the Go Mazes. 2011. (Dover Little Activity Bks.). (ENG.). 64p. (J). (gr. k-3). pap. 1.50 (978-0-486-47526-4(3)) Dover Pubns., Inc.

Elder, Jeremy. Monsters Destroyed My City! Mazes. 2012. (Dover Children's Activity Bks.). (ENG.). 48p. (J). (gr. 3-5). pap. 4.99 (978-0-486-48157-9(3)) Dover Pubns., Inc.

—Pinball Mazes Activity Book: Can You Top the High Score? 2012. (Dover Children's Activity Bks.). (ENG.). 48p. (J). (gr. 3-8). 4.99 (978-0-486-49003-8(3)) Dover Pubns., Inc.

Griffiths, Andy & Griffiths, Jill. The Treehouse Fun Book. Denton, Terry, illus. 2016. (Treehouse Bks.). (ENG.). 192p. (J). 12.99 (978-1-250-11775-5(5), 9781250117755) Feiwel & Friends.

Highlights for Children Editorial Staff, compiled by. Amazing Mazes - Off We Go! 2011. (Highlights(tm) Amazing Mazes Ser.). (ENG., Illus.). 72p. (J). (gr. 1-4). pap. 6.95 (978-1-59078-902-5(4), Highlights) Boyds Mills Pr.

Highlights for Children Editorial Staff, creator. Amazing Mazes: Lost & Found. 2011. (Highlights(tm) Amazing Mazes Ser.). (ENG., Illus.). 72p. (J). (gr. 1-4). pap. 6.95 (978-1-59078-903-2(2), Highlights) Boyds Mills Pr.

HOP, LLC. Hooked on Learning Puzzles & Mazes. 2006. 64p. 3.79 (978-1-933863-90-0(0)) HOP, LLC.

Kalz, Jill. School Adventure. Cerato, Mattia, illus. 2010. (A-MAZE-Ing Adventures Ser.). (ENG.). 32p. (gr. 1-2). lib. bdg. 26.65 (978-1-4048-6039-1(8)) Picture Window Bks.

—Zoo Adventure. Cerato, Mattia, illus. 2010. (A-MAZE-Ing Adventures Ser.). (ENG.). 32p. (gr. 1-2). lib. bdg. 26.65 (978-1-4048-6024-7(X)) Picture Window Bks.

Kumon Publishing, ed. Amazing Mazes. 2004. (Illus.). 80p. (J). per. 7.95 (978-4-7743-0710-7(6)) Kumon Publishing North America, Inc.

Lamb, Stacey, illus. Wipe-Clean Mazes. 2012. (Wipe-Clean Bks). 20p. (J). pap. 7.99 (978-0-7945-3257-4(8), Usborne) EDC Publishing.

Lonely Planet Publications Staff. Lonely Planet Amelia's Maze Adventure, 1 vol. 2017. (Lonely Planet Kids Ser.). (ENG., Illus.). 96p. (J). pap. 9.99 **(978-1-78657-436-7(5)**, 5374) Lonely Planet Pubns.

—Lonely Planet Marco's Maze Mission, 1 vol. 2017. (Lonely Planet Kids Ser.). (ENG., Illus.). 96p. (J). pap. 9.99 **(978-1-78657-687-3(2)**, 5510) Lonely Planet Pubns.

Matthies, Don-Oliver. Detective Mazes. 2004. (ENG., Illus.). 40p. (J). pap. 3.95 (978-1-4027-1293-7(6)) Sterling Publishing Co., Inc.

—Magician's Castle. 2005. (ENG., Illus.). 40p. (J). (gr. 2-4). per. 3.95 (978-1-4027-2652-1(X)) Sterling Publishing Co., Inc.

Matthies, Don-Oliver & Arena Verlag Staff. Castle Mazes. 2003. (ENG., Illus.). 40p. (J). pap. 3.95 (978-1-4027-0605-9(7)) Sterling Publishing Co., Inc.

—Mummy Mazes. 2003. (ENG., Illus.). 40p. (J). pap. 3.95 (978-1-4027-0548-9(4)) Sterling Publishing Co., Inc.

—Pirate Mazes. 2003. (ENG., Illus.). 40p. (J). pap. 3.95 (978-1-4027-0603-5(0)) Sterling Publishing Co., Inc.

Mazes for 1st Grade. 2003. (J). (978-1-58232-059-5(4)) ECS Learning Systems, Inc.

Mazes for 2nd Grade. 2003. (J). (978-1-58232-060-1(8)) ECS Learning Systems, Inc.

Mazurkiewicz, Jessica. Eco-Mania Mazes. 2010. (Dover Little Activity Bks.). (ENG., Illus.). 64p. (J). (gr. -1-5). pap. 1.50 (978-0-486-47561-5(1)) Dover Pubns., Inc.

Munro, Roxie. Market Maze. 2015. (978-0-8234-3358-2(7)) Holiday Hse., Inc.

—Market Maze. Munro, Roxie, illus. 2015. (ENG., Illus.). 32p. (J). (gr. -1-3). 16.95 (978-0-8234-3092-5(8)) Holiday Hse., Inc.

My First Mazes (Gr. K-1) 2003. (J). (978-1-58232-058-8(6)) ECS Learning Systems, Inc.

Newman-D'Amico, Fran. Alphabet Mazes. 2006. (Dover Children's Activity Bks.). (ENG., Illus.). 32p. (J). (gr. -1-2). 3.99 (978-0-486-44894-7(0)) Dover Pubns., Inc.

—Zoo Animal Mazes. 2004. (Dover Coloring Bks.). (ENG., Illus.). 32p. (J). (gr. -1-2). pap. 3.99 (978-0-486-43769-9(8)) Dover Pubns., Inc.

Peters, Andy. Around the Universe in 80 Mazes. 2012. (ENG.). 96p. (J). pap. 9.95 (978-1-84858-449-5(0)) Arcturus Publishing GBR. Dist: Bookmasters Distribution.

—Maze Quest: Navigate the Mazes, Complete the Search & Find, Solve the Puzzle Fun. 2012. (ENG.). 64p. (J). pap. 10.95 (978-1-84858-369-6(9)) Arcturus Publishing GBR. Dist: Bookmasters Distribution.

Phillips, Dave. Big Book of Adventure Mazes. 2003. (Dover Children's Activity Bks.). (ENG.). 128p. (J). (gr. 2-8). pap. 8.95 (978-0-486-42900-7(8)) Dover Pubns., Inc.

—Set Puzzles: Find Sets, Group Them, Fill the Grid. 2012. (ENG.). 48p. pap. 12.95 (978-0-486-49055-7(6)) Dover Pubns., Inc.

Radtke, Becky. On the Go Mazes. 2005. (Dover Little Activity Bks.). (ENG., Illus.). 64p. (J). (gr. 3-5). per. 1.99 (978-0-486-44103-0(2)) Dover Pubns., Inc.

Robson, Kirsten. Big Maze Book. 2013. (Doodle Bks). 64p. (J). pap. 9.99 (978-0-7945-3345-8(0), Usborne) EDC Publishing.

Sallows, Lee C. F. Geometric Magic Squares: A Challenging New Twist Using Colored Shapes Instead of Numbers. 2013. (Dover Recreational Math Ser.). (ENG., Illus.). 160p. (C). pap. 19.95 (978-0-486-48909-4(4)) Dover Pubns., Inc.

School Zone Interactive Staff. Mazes. Simard, Remy, illus. rev. ed. 2006. (ENG.). 64p. (J). (gr. 1-2). wbk. ed. 7.99 (978-1-58947-300-3(0)) School Zone Publishing Co.

School Zone Publishing. Mazes Animals. 2004. (ENG.). 32p. (J). pap. 2.99 (978-1-58947-386-7(8), 02191) School Zone Publishing Co.

School Zone Staff, ed. Mazes Preschool. 2006. (ENG.). 32p. (J). pap. 2.99 (978-1-58947-394-2(9), 02196) School Zone Publishing Co.

Sheehan, Peter. Maze of Twisted Tales. 2008. (ENG., Illus.). 32p. (J). (gr. 2-7). pap. 7.95 (978-1-921272-03-5(1)) Little Hare Bks. AUS. Dist: Independent Pubs. Group.

Tallarico, Tony. Nature Trivia Mazes. 2007. (Dover Children's Activity Bks.). (ENG., Illus.). 48p. (J). (gr. 3-3). per. 4.99 (978-0-486-45364-4(2)) Dover Pubns., Inc.

Tallarico, Tony J., Jr. Bugs! Bugs! Bugs! 2012. (Dover Children's Activity Bks.). (ENG.). 48p. (J). (gr. 3-8). pap. 4.99 (978-0-486-48399-3(1)) Dover Pubns., Inc.

The Ultimate Maze Craze. 2003. (Illus.). 40p. (J). 3.95 (978-0-9729026-0-1(0)) Midwest Cylinder Management, Inc.

University Games Staff, compiled by. i-Ballers: University Games. 2005. (I-Ballers Ser.). (ENG.). 60p. pap. 4.95 (978-1-57528-952-6(0)) Univ. Games.

White, Graham. A Maze Adventure: Search for Pirate Treasure. 2009. (ENG., Illus.). 32p. (J). (gr. 4-7). pap. 8.95 (978-1-4263-0459-0(5), National Geographic Children's Bks.) National Geographic Society.

Woodworth, Viki. A-B-C Mazes. 2006. (Dover Little Activity Bks.). (ENG., Illus.). 64p. (J). (gr. k-3). per. 1.50 (978-0-486-44726-1(X)) Dover Pubns., Inc.

—Little Monster Mazes. 2006. (Dover Little Activity Bks.). (ENG., Illus.). 64p. (J). (gr. 3-5). per. 1.50 (978-0-486-45189-3(5)) Dover Pubns., Inc.

—Maze Mania. 2005. (Dover Children's Activity Bks.). (ENG., Illus.). 32p. (J). (gr. 3-5). per. 4.99 (978-0-486-44604-2(2)) Dover Pubns., Inc.

—Princess Mazes. 2012. (Dover Children's Activity Bks.). (ENG.). 48p. (J). (gr. 1-4). pap. 4.99 (978-0-486-49058-8(0)) Dover Pubns., Inc.

—United States Maze Craze. 2009. (Dover Children's Activity Bks.). (ENG., Illus.). 64p. (J). (gr. 3-4). pap. 4.99 (978-0-486-46831-0(3)) Dover Pubns., Inc.

—World of Mazes. 2007. (Dover Children's Activity Bks.). (ENG., Illus.). 48p. (J). (gr. 3-5). per. 4.99 (978-0-486-45640-9(4)) Dover Pubns., Inc.

MEAD, MARGARET, 1901-1978

Bankston, John. Margaret Mead: Pioneer of Social Anthropology. 2006. (Great Minds of Science Ser.). (Illus.). 128p. (J). (gr. 4-10). lib. bdg. 33.27 (978-0-7660-2507-3(1)) Enslow Pubs., Inc.

Horn, Geoffrey M. Margaret Mead. 2004. (Trailblazers of the Modern World Ser.). (Illus.). 48p. (gr. 5-12). pap. 14.05 (978-0-8368-5259-2(1)); lib. bdg. 31.00 (978-0-8368-5099-4(8)) Stevens, Gareth Publishing LLLP. (Gareth Stevens Secondary Library).

MEAL PLANNING

see Menus; Nutrition

MEASLES

Colligan, L. H. Measles & Mumps. 2010. (Health Alert 7 Ser.). (Illus.). 64p. (J). (gr. 4-7). 32.79 (978-0-7614-4819-8(5)) Marshall Cavendish Corp.

Hawkins, Trisha. Everything You Need to Know about Measles & Rubella. (Need to Know Library). 64p. 2009. (gr. 5-5). 58.50 (978-1-60854-075-4(8)) 2005. (Illus.). (YA). (gr. 7-12). 31.95 (978-0-8239-3322-8(9)) Rosen Publishing Group, Inc., The.

Rosaler, Maxine. Measles. (Epidemics Ser.). 64p. 2009. (gr. 5-5). 58.50 (978-1-61512-296-7(6)) 2004. (Illus.). (YA). (gr. 7-12). lib. bdg. 31.95 (978-1-4042-0256-6(0)) Rosen Publishing Group, Inc., The.

Shmaefsky, Brian R. Rubella & Rubeola. 2009. (Deadly Diseases & Epidemics Ser.). (Illus.). 120p. (C). (gr. 9-18). 34.95 (978-1-60413-230-4(2), Chelsea Hse.) Facts On File, Inc.

MEASUREMENT

Here are entered works on the general process of measuring. Works on the science of measurement or of weights and measures are entered under Metrology.

see also Geodesy; Measuring Instruments; Metrology; Surveying; Weights and Measures

Adamson, Heather. Measure It!, 1 vol., Set. Incl. How Do You Measure Liquids? Adamson, Thomas K. lib. bdg. 27.32 (978-1-4296-4457-0(5)); How Do You Measure Time? Adamson, Tom. lib. bdg. 27.32 (978-1-4296-4459-4(1)); How Do You Measure Weight? Adamson, Tom. lib. bdg. 27.32 (978-1-4296-4458-7(3)); (gr. 1-2). (Measure It! Ser.). (ENG.). 32p. 2010. Set lib. bdg. 81.96 (978-1-4296-4487-7(7), Aplus Bks.) Capstone Press of Coughlan Cos.

Adamson, Thomas K. & Adamson, Heather. How Do You Measure Length & Distance?, 1 vol. 2011. (Measure It! Ser.). (ENG.). 32p. (gr. 1-2). pap. 8.10 (978-1-4296-6330-4(8), Aplus Bks.) Capstone Press of Coughlan Cos.

—How Do You Measure Liquids?, 1 vol. (Measure It! Ser.). (ENG.). 32p. (gr. 1-2). 2011. pap. 8.10 (978-1-4296-6331-1(6)) 2010. lib. bdg. 27.32 (978-1-4296-4457-0(5)) Capstone Press of Coughlan Cos. (Aplus Bks.).

—How Do You Measure Time?, 1 vol. 2011. (Measure It! Ser.). (ENG.). 32p. (gr. 1-2). pap. 8.10 (978-1-4296-6332-8(4), Aplus Bks.) Capstone Press of Coughlan Cos.

Adamson, Thomas K. and Heather. How Do You Measure Length & Distance? 2011. (Measure It! Ser.). (ENG.). 32p. (gr. 1-2). pap. 47.70 (978-1-4296-6457-8(6), Aplus Bks.) Capstone Press of Coughlan Cos.

—How Do You Measure Liquids? 2011. (Measure It! Ser.). (ENG.). 32p. (gr. 1-2). pap. 47.70 *(978-1-4296-6458-5(4),* Aplus Bks.) Capstone Press of Coughlan Cos.

—How Do You Measure Time? 2011. (Measure It! Ser.). (ENG.). 32p. (gr. 1-2). pap. 47.70 *(978-1-4296-6459-2(2),* Aplus Bks.) Capstone Press of Coughlan Cos.

—Mídelo. 2011. (Mídelo/Measure It Ser.).Tr. of Measure It. (MUL.). 32p. (gr. 1-2). lib. bdg. 54.64 *(978-1-4296-6893-4(8),* A+ Bilingue/Bilingual) Capstone Press of Coughlan Cos.

Adamson, Tom & Adamson, Heather. How Do You Measure Time?, 1 vol. 2010. (Measure It! Ser.). (ENG.). 32p. (gr. 1-2). lib. bdg. 27.32 *(978-1-4296-4459-4(1),* Aplus Bks.) Capstone Press of Coughlan Cos.

—How Do You Measure Weight?, 1 vol. 2010. (Measure It! Ser.). (ENG.). 32p. (gr. 1-2). lib. bdg. 27.32 *(978-1-4296-4458-7(3),* Aplus Bks.) Capstone Press of Coughlan Cos.

Alaina, Maria. Measuring Time, 1 vol. 2011. (Wonder Readers Early Level Ser.). (ENG.). 32p. (gr. -1-1). pap. 5.99 *(978-1-4296-7834-6(8),* Wonder Readers) Capstone Press of Coughlan Cos.

Anderson, Jill. Measuring with Sebastian Pig & Friends on a Road Trip. Amy Huntington, illus. 2013. (Math Fun with Sebastian Pig & Friends! Ser.). 32p. (J). (gr. k-3). pap. 7.95 *(978-0-7660-5982-5(0),* Enslow Elementary) Enslow Pubs., Inc.

Baer, T. H. Measuring Distance. 2016. (Measure It! Ser.). (ENG., Illus.). 24p. (J). (gr. 1-2). pap. 8.15 *(978-1-4824-3856-7(9))* Stevens, Gareth Publishing LLLP.

—Measuring Height. 2016. (Measure It! Ser.). (ENG.). 24p. (J). (gr. 1-2). pap. 8.15 *(978-1-4824-3860-4(7))* Stevens, Gareth Publishing LLLP.

—Measuring Temperature. 2016. (Measure It! Ser.). (ENG., Illus.). 24p. (J). (gr. 1-2). pap. 8.15 *(978-1-4824-3868-0(2))* Stevens, Gareth Publishing LLLP.

—Measuring Volume. 2016. (Measure It! Ser.). (ENG., Illus.). 24p. (J). (gr. 1-2). pap. 8.15 *(978-1-4824-3872-7(0))* Stevens, Gareth Publishing LLLP.

Bailer, Darice. Measuring Length. Petelinsek, Kathleen, illus. 2014. (Explorer Junior Library: Math Explorer Junior Ser.). (ENG.). 24p. (J). (gr. 1-4). 28.50 *(978-1-62431-647-0(6),* 203100) Cherry Lake Publishing.

Baker, Maryann. My Mom Is a Carpenter: Relate Addition & Subtraction to Length. 2014. (Rosen Common Core Math Readers Ser.). (ENG.). 24p. (J). (gr. 2-3). pap. 8.25 *(978-1-4777-4813-8(X),* Rosen Classroom) Rosen Publishing Group, Inc., The.

Barner, Bob. Ants Rule: The Long & Short of It. 2017. (ENG.). 32p. (J). (gr. -1-3). 16.95 *(978-0-8234-3660-6(8));* ***(978-0-8234-3790-0(6))*** Holiday Hse., Inc.

Beck, Esther & Doudna, Kelly. Im on the Trail to Learn about Scale!, 1 vol. 2007. (Science Made Simple Ser.). (ENG., Illus.). 24p. (J). (gr. k-3). lib. bdg. 24.21 *(978-1-59928-592-4(4),* SandCastle) ABDO Publishing Co.

Bellavia, Rebecca. Planting Sunflowers: Represent & Interpret Data. 2014. (Math Masters: Measurement & Data Ser.). 24p. (J). (gr. 2-3). 23.60 *(978-1-4777-6408-4(9));* (ENG.). pap. 8.25 *(978-1-4777-4825-1(3))* Rosen Publishing Group, Inc., The. (Rosen Classroom).

Benchmark Education Company, LLC Staff, compiled by. Measurement. 2005. spiral bd. 330.00 *(978-1-4108-5865-8(0));* spiral bd. 295.00 *(978-1-4108-5866-5(9));* spiral bd. 315.00 *(978-1-4108-5455-1(8));* spiral bd. 635.00 *(978-1-4108-5454-4(X));* spiral bd. 420.00 *(978-1-4108-4513-9(3));* spiral bd. 35.00 *(978-1-4108-3914-5(1));* spiral bd. 50.00 *(978-1-4108-3910-7(9));* spiral bd. 110.00 *(978-1-4108-3903-9(6));* spiral bd. 295.00 *(978-1-4108-3902-2(8));* spiral bd. 120.00 *(978-1-4108-3896-4(X));* spiral bd. 270.00 *(978-1-4108-3895-7(1));* spiral bd. 165.00 *(978-1-4108-3888-9(9));* spiral bd. 305.00 *(978-1-4108-3887-2(0))* Benchmark Education Co.

—Measuring: Theme Set. 2006. (J). 109.00 *(978-1-4108-7090-2(1))* Benchmark Education Co.

Bishop, Celeste. Core Math Skills: Measurement & Geometry. 2013. (Core Math Skills: Measurement & Geometry Ser.). 24p. (J). (gr. 1-2). 135.60 *(978-1-4777-2236-7(X),* Rosen Classroom) Rosen Publishing Group, Inc., The.

—Gone Fishing! 2013. (Core Math Skills: Measurement & Geometry Ser.). 24p. (J). (gr. 1-2). 22.60 *(978-1-4777-2227-5(0),* Rosen Classroom) Rosen Publishing Group, Inc., The.

—Gone Fishing! Measure Lengths. 2013. (Rosen Math Readers Ser.). (ENG.). 24p. (J). (gr. 1-2). pap. 49.50 *(978-1-4777-2077-6(4));* pap. 8.25 *(978-1-4777-2076-9(6))* Rosen Publishing Group, Inc., The. (Rosen Classroom).

—Tall & Short: Describe & Compare Measurable Attributes. 2013. (InfoMax Math Readers Ser.). (ENG.). 16p. (J). (gr. k-1). pap. 42.00 *(978-1-4777-1923-7(7));* (Illus.). pap. 7.00 *(978-1-4777-1922-0(9))* Rosen Publishing Group, Inc., The. (Rosen Classroom).

Bodach, Vijaya Khisty. Measuring. 2008. (Discovering & Exploring Science Ser.). (Illus.). 16p. (J). (gr. -1-3). lib. bdg. 12.95 *(978-0-7569-8256-0(1))* Perfection Learning Corp.

Borden, Louise. Sea Clocks: The Story of Longitude. Blegvad, Erik, illus. 2004. (ENG.). 48p. (J). (gr. 2-5). 19.99 *(978-0-689-84216-0(3),* McElderry, Margaret K. Bks.) McElderry, Margaret K. Bks.

Bryant-Mole, Karen. Starting to Measure. 2004. (First Learning Ser.). (ENG., Illus.). 1p. (J). (gr. -1-18). pap., act. bk. ed. 4.95 *(978-0-7460-3801-7(1))* EDC Publishing.

Burstein, John. Measuring: The Perfect Playhouse. 2003. (Weekly Reader Early Learning Library). (Illus.). 24p. (J). (gr. k-4). pap. 8.15 *(978-0-8368-3828-2(9),* Weekly Reader Leveled Readers) Stevens, Gareth Publishing LLLP.

—Measuring: The Perfect Playhouse. Destiny Images Staff, illus. 2003. (Math Monsters Ser.). 24p. (J). (gr. k-4). lib. bdg. 21.00 *(978-0-8368-3813-8(0),* Weekly Reader Leveled Readers) Stevens, Gareth Publishing LLLP.

Burton, Margie, et al. Bigger Than? Smaller Than? 2011. (Early Connections Ser.). (J). *(978-1-61672-249-4(5))* Benchmark Education Co.

—Measure Up! 2011. (Early Connections Ser.). (J). *(978-1-61672-500-6(1))* Benchmark Education Co.

—What Can You Measure with a Lollipop? & ¿Qué puedes medir con una Paleta? 6 English, 6 Spanish Adaptations. 2011. (J). spiral bd. 75.00 net. *(978-1-4108-5627-2(5))* Benchmark Education Co.

Bussiere, Desirée. Let's Measure More, 1 vol. 2013. (Let's Measure More Ser.: 6). (ENG.). 24p. (J). (gr. -1-3). lib. bdg. 145.26 *(978-1-61783-594-0(3),* SandCastle) ABDO Publishing Co.

—What in the World Is a Baker's Dozen? & Other Interesting Measurements, 1 vol. 2013. (Let's Measure More Ser.). (ENG.). 24p. (J). (gr. -1-3). lib. bdg. 24.21 *(978-1-61783-595-7(1),* SandCastle) ABDO Publishing Co.

—What in the World Is a Centimeter? & Other Metric Measurements, 1 vol. 2013. (Let's Measure More Ser.). (ENG.). 24p. (J). (gr. -1-3). lib. bdg. 24.21 *(978-1-61783-596-4(X),* SandCastle) ABDO Publishing Co.

—What in the World Is a Mile? & Other Distance Measurements, 1 vol. 2013. (Let's Measure More Ser.). (ENG.). 24p. (J). (gr. -1-3). lib. bdg. 24.21 *(978-1-61783-598-8(6),* SandCastle) ABDO Publishing Co.

—What in the World Is a Ton? & Other Weight & Volume Measurements, 1 vol. 2013. (Let's Measure More Ser.). (ENG.). 24p. (J). (gr. -1-3). lib. bdg. 24.21 *(978-1-61783-599-5(4),* SandCastle) ABDO Publishing Co.

—What in the World Is an Acre? & Other Land & Sea Measurements, 1 vol. 2013. (Let's Measure More Ser.). (ENG.). 24p. (J). (gr. -1-3). lib. bdg. 24.21 *(978-1-61783-600-8(1),* SandCastle) ABDO Publishing Co.

Caes, Charles J. Discovering the Speed of Light. 2011. (Scientist's Guide to Physics Ser.). (Illus.). 112p. (YA). (gr. 7-12). lib. bdg. 34.60 *(978-1-4488-4699-3(4))* Rosen Publishing Group, Inc., The.

Cardenas, Ernesto A. Measurement. 2009. pap. 4.95 *(978-1-60698-070-5(X))* Milo Educational Bks. & Resources.

—What Do You Use to Measure? 2009. 23.95 *(978-1-60698-050-7(5));* pap. 4.95 *(978-1-60698-048-4(3))* Milo Educational Bks. & Resources.

Chanko, Pamela. Shoe Box Learning Centers: Time & Measurement: 30 Instant Centers with Reproducible Templates & Activities That Help Kids Practice Important Math Skills-Independently! 2012. (ENG.). 80p. (gr. k-2). pap. 12.99 *(978-0-545-46873-2(6),* Teaching Resources) Scholastic, Inc.

Chigeza, Philemon. Measurement Ideas & Possibilities. 2012. 28p. pap. 32.70 *(978-1-4691-8015-1(4))* Xlibris Corp.

Cleary, Brian. How Long or How Wide? A Measuring Guide. Gable, Brian, illus. 2009. (Math Is CATegorical (r) Ser.). (ENG.). 32p. (gr. k-3). pap. 6.95 *(978-1-58013-844-4(6),* First Avenue Editions) Lerner Publishing Group.

Colson, Rob. Get the Measure: Units & Measurements. 2017. (Math Everywhere Ser.). (ENG.). 32p. (J). pap. 8.95 ***(978-0-531-23319-1(7));*** lib. bdg. 27.00 ***(978-0-531-22883-8(5))*** Scholastic Library Publishing. (Children's Pr.).

Corcorane, Ann. Measuring. 2011. (Wonder Readers Emergent Level Ser.). (ENG.). (gr. -1-1). 16p. pap. 35.94 *(978-1-4296-8128-5(4));* 32p. pap. 5.99 *(978-1-4296-7867-4(4))* Capstone Press of Coughlan Cos. (Wonder Readers).

Cotugno, Megan. Measure It!, 1 vol., Set. Incl. Distance, Area, & Volume. Somervill, Barbara A. pap. 8.29 *(978-1-4329-3769-0(3));* Mass & Weight. Somervill, Barbara A. pap. 8.29 *(978-1-4329-3771-3(5));* Speed & Acceleration. Somervill, Barbara A. pap. 8.29 *(978-1-4329-3770-6(7));* Temperature. Rand, Casey. pap. 8.29 *(978-1-4329-3773-7(1));* Time. Rand, Casey. pap. 8.29 *(978-1-4329-3772-0(3));* (Illus.). (gr. 3-6). (Measure It! Ser.). (ENG.). 32p. 2010. Set pap. 39.95 *(978-1-4329-3774-4(X),* Heinemann InfoSearch) Heinemann-Raintree.

Dase, Pam. Hurricane Hunters. rev. ed. 2012. (Mathematics Readers Ser.). (ENG.). 32p. (J). (gr. 6-6). pap. 8.99 *(978-1-4333-3462-7(3))* Teacher Created Materials, Inc.

—Tornado Chasers. rev. ed. 2012. (Mathematics Readers Ser.). (ENG.). 32p. (J). (gr. 6-6). pap. 8.99 *(978-1-4333-3463-4(1))* Teacher Created Materials, Inc.

Davenport, Jefferson. Our Fishing Trip: Measure Lengths. 2013. (InfoMax Math Readers Ser.). (ENG.). 24p. (J). (gr. 1-2). pap. 49.50 *(978-1-4777-2170-4(3));* (Illus.). pap. 8.25 *(978-1-4777-2169-8(X))* Rosen Publishing Group, Inc., The. (Rosen Classroom).

Davies, Ann. Fun Size. (Illus.). 40p. (J). 19.95 *(978-1-85479-230-3(X))* O'Mara, Michael Bks., Ltd. GBR. Dist: Trans-Atlantic Pubns., Inc.

Deen, Marilyn. Measure by Measure, 1 vol. (Wonder Readers: Mathematics Ser.). (ENG.). (gr. -1-2). 2012. 20p. lib. bdg. 22.65 *(978-1-4296-9607-4(9))* 2011. 16p. pap. 35.94 *(978-1-4296-8127-8(6))* 2011. 32p. pap. 5.99 *(978-1-4296-7930-5(1))* Capstone Press of Coughlan Cos. (Wonder Readers).

Dell, Pamela. Feet & Meters. 2016. (Spring Forward Ser.). (J). (gr. 2). *(978-1-4900-9416-8(4))* Benchmark Education Co.

Dreyer, Kira. My New Bedroom: Estimate Lengths in Standard Units. 2014. (Math Masters: Measurement & Data Ser.). 24p. (J). (gr. 2-3). 23.60 *(978-1-4777-6438-1(0));* (ENG.). pap. 8.25 *(978-1-4777-4801-5(6))* Rosen Publishing Group, Inc., The. (Rosen Classroom).

Erickson, Amelia. My First Airplane Trip: Solve Problems Involving Measurement, 1 vol. 2015. (InfoMax Common Core Math Readers Ser.). (ENG.). 24p. (J). pap. 8.25 *(978-1-4777-4606-6(4),* Rosen Classroom) Rosen Publishing Group, Inc., The.

Faulkner, Nicholas & Hosch, William L. Numbers & Measurements. 2017. (J). lib. bdg. ***(978-1-68048-778-7(7),*** Britannica Educational Publishing) Rosen Publishing Group, Inc., The.

Fiedler, Heidi. The Know-Nonsense Guide to Measurements: The Awesomely Fun Guide to How Things Are Measured! Kearney, Brendan, illus. 2017. (Know Nonsense Ser.). (ENG.). 64p. (J). (gr. 3-7). 14.95 *(978-1-63322-297-7(7),* Walter Foster Jr) Quarto Publishing Group USA.

First, Rachel. Measure It! Fun with Length & Distance, 1 vol. 2016. (Math Beginnings Ser.). (ENG., Illus.). 24p. (J). (gr. k-3). 24.21 *(978-1-62403-934-8(0))* ABDO Publishing Co.

Flatt, Lizann. Sizing up Winter. Barron, Ashley & Owlkids Books Inc. Staff, illus. 2013. (Math in Nature Ser.: 3). (ENG.). 32p. (J). (gr. k-3). 15.95 *(978-1-926973-82-1(8),* Owlkids) Owlkids Bks. Inc. CAN. Dist: Publishers Group West (PGW).

Formichelli, Linda & Martin, W. Eric. Timekeeping: Explore the History & Science of Telling Time with 15 Projects. Carbaugh, Sam, illus. 2012. (Build It Yourself Ser.). (ENG.). 128p. (J). (gr. 3-7). 21.95 *(978-1-61930-136-8(9))* Open City Bks.

Formichelli, Linda, et al. Timekeeping: Explore the History & Science of Telling Time with 15 Projects. Carbaugh, Samuel, illus. 2012. (Build It Yourself Ser.). (ENG.). 128p. (J). (gr. 3-7). pap. 15.95 *(978-1-61930-033-0(8))* Open City Bks.

Franco, Betsy. Finding Area & Volume Using English Units, 3. 2012. (Key To... workbooks Ser.: Bk. 3). (ENG.). 56p. (gr. 6-8). spiral bd. 5.64 *(978-1-55953-023-1(5),* 1559530235) McGraw-Hill Education.

Franco, Betsy & Key Curriculum Press Staff. English Units of Length, Bk. 1. 2012. (Key To... workbooks Ser.: Bk. 1). (ENG.). 48p. (gr. 6-8). spiral bd. 5.64 *(978-1-55953-021-7(9),* 1559530219) McGraw-Hill Education.

—Measuring Length & Perimeter Using English Units, 2. 2012. (Key To... workbooks Ser.: Bk. 2). (ENG.). 48p. (gr. 6-8). spiral bd. 5.64 *(978-1-55953-022-4(7),* 1559530227) McGraw-Hill Education.

—Measuring Length & Perimeter Using Metric Units, Bk. 2. 2012. (Key To... workbooks Ser.: Bk. 2). (ENG., Illus.). 48p. (gr. 6-8). spiral bd., wbk. ed. 5.64 *(978-1-55953-326-3(9),* 1559533269) McGraw-Hill Education.

Freeman, Marcia S. Measuring Our World. 2003. (ENG.). 16p. (gr. 2-3). pap. 6.33 *(978-1-59515-272-5(5))* Rourke Educational Media.

Furgang, Kathy. Measuring Length. 2011. (Early Connections Ser.). (J). *(978-1-61672-590-7(7))* Benchmark Education Co.

Garcia, Joy. My Paper Ruler: A Garcia Hands-on Learn-about Book. 2009. (Skinny Minis Ser.). (ENG., Illus.). 44p. (J). (gr. -1-3). per. 4.99 *(978-1-59092-144-9(5))* Blue Forge Pr.

Gardner, Robert. Far-Out Science Projects with Height & Depth: How High Is up? How Low Is Down? 2003. (Sensational Science Experiments Ser.). (Illus.). 48p. (J). (gr. 1-4). lib. bdg. 25.27 *(978-0-7660-2016-0(9))* Enslow Pubs., Inc.

—How Heavy Is Heavy? Science Projects with Weight. 2015. (Hot Science Experiments Ser.). 48p. (J). (gr. 3-4). 25.27 *(978-0-7660-6600-7(2))* Enslow Pubs., Inc.

—How High Is High? Science Projects with Height & Depth. 2015. (Hot Science Experiments Ser.). 48p. (J). (gr. 3-4). 25.27 *(978-0-7660-6595-6(2));* pap. 8.95 *(978-0-7660-6596-3(0),* Enslow Elementary) Enslow Pubs., Inc.

Gunderson, Jessica. How Long? Wacky Ways to Compare Length, 1 vol. Sinkovec, Igor, illus. 2013. (Wacky Comparisons Ser.). (ENG.). 24p. (J). (gr. -1-2). 27.99 *(978-1-4048-8324-6(X));* pap. 8.95 *(978-1-4795-1914-9(6))* Picture Window Bks.

Gunderson, Jessica & Weakland, Mark. Wacky Comparisons. Bolton, Bill & Sinkovec, Igor, illus. 2013. (Wacky Comparisons Ser.). (ENG.). 32p. (gr. -1-2). 14.95 *(978-1-62370-037-9(X))* Capstone Young Readers of Coughlan Cos.

—Wacky Comparisons. 2013. (Wacky Comparisons Ser.). (ENG.). 24p. (gr. -1-2). pap. 31.80 *(978-1-4795-1970-5(7));* lib. bdg. 111.96 *(978-1-4048-8145-7(X))* Picture Window Bks.

Heos, Bridget. Measure It. Longhi, Katya, illus. 2015. (Math World Ser.). 24p. (J). lib. bdg. 27.10 *(978-1-60753-464-8(9))* Amicus Publishing.

—What Are Measurements? 2014. (Let's Find Out! Ser.). 32p. (J). (gr. 3-6). 23.45 *(978-1-62275-507-3(3))* Rosen Publishing Group, Inc., The.

Hunt, Darleen L. Mr. Reed's Class Estimates: Estimating. Komarck, Michael, illus. 2003. (Sherman's Math Corner Ser.). (J). (gr. -1-3). *(978-1-929591-06-0(3))* Reading Rock, Inc.

In Step with the Standards - Measurement. 2005. (J). spiral bd. 15.95 *(978-1-58123-377-3(9))* Larson Learning, Inc.

Jerome, Kate Boehm. How Many Ants in an Anthill? 2007. (Reading Expeditions Ser.). (ENG., Illus.). 24p. (J). pap. 14.95 *(978-0-7922-4587-2(3))* CENGAGE Learning.

Jones, Tammy. What Is the Time? 2009. (Sight Word Readers Set A Ser.). (J). 3.49 net. *(978-1-60719-150-6(4))* Newmark Learning LLC.

Kompelein, Tracy. I Can Measure Weight at Any Rate, 1 vol. 2007. (Math Made Fun Ser.). (ENG., Illus.). 24p. (J). (gr. k-3). lib. bdg. 24.21 *(978-1-59928-519-1(3),* SandCastle) ABDO Publishing Co.

Kompelien, Tracy. I Can Measure Length, It Has No Strength!, 1 vol. 2007. (Math Made Fun Ser.). (ENG., Illus.). 24p. (J). (gr. k-3). lib. bdg. 24.21 *(978-1-59928-517-7(7),* SandCastle) ABDO Publishing Co.

—Lets All Assume, We Can Measure Volume!, 1 vol. 2007. (Math Made Fun Ser.). (ENG., Illus.). 24p. (J). (gr. k-3). lib. bdg. 24.21 *(978-1-59928-535-1(5),* SandCastle) ABDO Publishing Co.

Kralick, Evelyn. Famous Fossils: Measure Lengths in Standard Units. 2014. (Math Masters: Measurement & Data Ser.). 24p. (J). (gr. 2-3). 23.60 *(978-1-4777-6437-4(2));* (ENG.). pap. 8.25 *(978-1-4777-4792-6(3))* Rosen Publishing Group, Inc., The. (Rosen Classroom).

Krishnaswami, Uma. Learn to Estimate. 2006. (Early Explorers Ser.). (J). pap. *(978-1-4108-6132-0(5))* Benchmark Education Co.

Levy, Janey. At Sea on a Viking Ship: Solving Problems of Length & Weight Using the Four Math Operations. 2004. (Math Big Bookstm Ser.). (ENG.). 24p. (gr. 3-4). 43.95 *(978-0-8239-7642-3(4))* Rosen Publishing Group, Inc., The.

—The Great Pyramid of Giza: Measuring Length, Area, Volume, & Angles. (Math for the Real World Ser.). 32p. 2009. (ENG., Illus.). (gr. 6-7). pap. 10.00 *(978-1-4042-6059-7(5))* 2009. (gr. 5-5). 47.90 *(978-1-60851-368-0(8),* PowerKids Pr.) 2006. (Illus.). (YA). (gr. 5-9). lib. bdg. 25.25 *(978-1-4042-3353-9(9))* Rosen Publishing Group, Inc., The.

Linde, Barbara M. Building Washington, D. C. Measuring the Area of Rectangular Spaces. 2009. (PowerMath Ser.). (Illus.). 32p. (gr. 4-5). pap. 10.00 *(978-0-8239-8867-9(8),* PowerKids Pr.) Rosen Publishing Group, Inc., The.

—Building Washington, DC: Measuring the Area of Rectangular Shapes. 2004. (PowerMath: Proficiency Ser.). (Illus.). 32p. (YA). (gr. 5-9). lib. bdg. 25.25 *(978-0-8239-8980-5(1))* Rosen Publishing Group, Inc., The.

Loughran, Donna. A Day at Mini-Golf: What's the Length? 2013. (IMath Ser.). (Illus.). 24p. (J). (gr. k-2). pap. 11.94 *(978-1-60357-495-2(6));* lib. bdg. 21.27 *(978-1-59953-556-2(4))* Norwood Hse. Pr.

—How Long Is It? 2005. (Rookie Read-About Math Ser.). (ENG., Illus.). 32p. (J). (gr. 1-2). pap. 5.95 *(978-0-516-24671-0(2),* Children's Pr.) Scholastic Library Publishing.

Loughran, Donna & Brunner-Jass, Renata. Field of Play: Measuring Distance, Rate, & Time. 2013. (IMath Ser.). (Illus.). 48p. (J). (gr. 5-6). pap. 11.94 *(978-1-60357-510-2(3))* Norwood Hse. Pr.

—A Year at the Fairgrounds: Finding Volume. 2013. (IMath Ser.). (Illus.). 48p. (J). (gr. 5-6). pap. 11.94 *(978-1-60357-514-0(6));* lib. bdg. 23.94 *(978-1-59953-575-3(0))* Norwood Hse. Pr.

Lowery, Lawrence F. How Tall Was Milton? Smith, Phil, illus. 2012. (I Wonder Why Ser.). (ENG.). 32p. (J). (gr. k-3). pap. 11.95 *(978-1-936959-43-3(7))* National Science Teachers Assn.

Maloof, Torrey. Your World: Investigating Measurement: Volume & Mass (Grade 3) 2017. (Mathematics Readers Ser.). (Illus.). 32p. (gr. 3-3). 8.99 ***(978-1-4807-5807-0(8))*** Teacher Created Materials, Inc.

Markovics, Joyce. Measure It! 2012. (ENG.). 24p. (gr. -1-1). pap. 8.95 *(978-1-61810-210-2(9))* Rourke Educational Media.

Marrewa, Jennifer. ¿A qué distancia? Vamos a Comparar Viajes. 2008. (Las matemáticas en nuestro mundo - Nivel 2 (Math in Our World - Level 2) Ser.). (SPA.). 24p. (gr. 1-4). pap. 8.15 *(978-0-8368-9033-4(7),* Weekly Reader Leveled Readers) Stevens, Gareth Publishing LLLP.

—¿A qué distancia? Vamos a Comparar Viajes. 2008. (Matemáticas en Nuestro Mundo - Nivel 2 (Math in Our World - Level 2) Ser.). (SPA., Illus.). 24p. (gr. 1-4). lib. bdg. 22.00 *(978-0-8368-9024-2(8),* Weekly Reader Leveled Readers) Stevens, Gareth Publishing LLLP.

—How Far Away? Comparing Trips. 2008. (Math in Our World - Level 2 Ser.). 24p. (gr. 1-4). pap. 8.15 *(978-0-8368-9015-0(9),* Weekly Reader Leveled Readers) Stevens, Gareth Publishing LLLP.

—How Far Away? Comparing Trips. 2008. (Math in Our World: Level 2 Ser.). (Illus.). 24p. (gr. 1-4). lib. bdg. 22.00 *(978-0-8368-9006-8(X),* Weekly Reader Leveled Readers) Stevens, Gareth Publishing LLLP.

—Measuring on a Treasure Hunt. 2008. (Math in Our World - Level 2 Ser.). 24p. (gr. 1-4). pap. 8.15 *(978-0-8368-9016-7(7));* (Illus.). lib. bdg. 22.00 *(978-0-8368-9007-5(8))* Stevens, Gareth Publishing LLLP. (Weekly Reader Leveled Readers).

—Midiendo para una Búsqueda Del Tesoro. 2008. (Las matemáticas en nuestro mundo - Nivel 2 (Math in Our World - Level 2) Ser.). (SPA.). 24p. (gr. 1-4). pap. 8.15 *(978-0-8368-9034-1(5),* Weekly Reader Leveled Readers) Stevens, Gareth Publishing LLLP.

—Midiendo para una Búsqueda del Tesoro. McKinley, Kay, photos by. 2008. (Matemáticas en Nuestro Mundo - Nivel 2 (Math in Our World - Level 2) Ser.). (SPA., Illus.). 24p. (gr. 1-4). lib. bdg. 22.00 *(978-0-8368-9025-9(6),* Weekly Reader Leveled Readers) Stevens, Gareth Publishing LLLP.

Maurer, Tracy Nelson. The Scoop about Measuring Matter. 2012. (ENG.). 24p. (gr. 3-4). pap. 8.95 *(978-1-61810-226-3(5))* Rourke Educational Media.

Maxwell, Yolonda. Famous Bridges of the World: Measuring Length, Weight, & Volume. (PowerMath Ser.). (Illus.). 32p. 2009. (ENG.). (gr. 5-6). pap. 10.00 *(978-1-4042-5137-3(5))* 2005. (J). (gr. 3-6). lib. bdg. 25.25 *(978-1-4042-2937-2(X))* Rosen Publishing Group, Inc., The. (PowerKids Pr.).

Measure It! (Measure It! Ser.). (ENG.). 32p. (gr. 1-2). 2011. pap. 190.80 *(978-1-4296-6461-5(4))* 2010. pap. 31.80 *(978-1-4296-6334-2(0))* Capstone Press of Coughlan Cos. (Aplus Bks.).

Measurement & Geometry. 2003. Level C. tchr. ed. 19.50 *(978-0-7652-1317-4(6))*Level C. stu. ed. 14.50 *(978-0-7652-1305-1(2))*Level D. tchr. ed. 19.50 *(978-0-7652-1321-1(4))*Level D. stu. ed. 14.50 *(978-0-7652-1309-9(5))*Level E. tchr. ed. 19.50 *(978-0-7652-1325-9(7))*Level E. stu. ed. 14.50 *(978-0-7652-1313-6(3))* Modern Curriculum Pr.

Measuring. 2005. (J). Bk. 1. per. 8.95 *(978-1-59566-156-2(5))*Bk. 2. per. 8.95 *(978-1-59566-160-9(3))* QEB Publishing Inc.

Metz, Lorijo. Using Rulers & Tape Measures. 2013. (Science Tools Ser.). (ENG., Illus.). 24p. (J). (gr. 3-6). 22.60 *(978-1-4488-9688-2(6));* pap. 8.25 *(978-1-4488-9834-3(X))* Rosen Publishing Group, Inc., The. (PowerKids Pr.).

Mian measurement Gr4-5. 2004. (Math in A Nutshell Ser.). (gr. 4-5). *(978-1-59242-185-5(7))* Delta Education, LLC.

Minden, Cecilia. How Tall? How Wide? 2010. (21st Century Basic Skills Library: Measurements Ser.). (ENG.). 24p. (gr. k-3). lib. bdg. 22.79 *(978-1-60279-848-9(6),* 200562) Cherry Lake Publishing.

Moldovo, Eustacia & Murphy, Patricia J. Learning How to Measure with Puppies & Kittens. 2017. (J). pap. ***(978-0-7660-9074-3(4))*** Enslow Pubs., Inc.

Montague-Smith, Ann. Measuring. 2004. (QEB Start Math Ser.). (Illus.). 24p. (J). Vol. 1. lib. bdg. 15.95 *(978-1-59566-027-5(5))* Vol. 2. lib. bdg. 15.95 *(978-1-59566-031-2(3))* QEB Publishing Inc.

Morgan, Elizabeth. Around My Town: Describe & Compare Measurable Attributes. 2013. (InfoMax Math Readers Ser.). (ENG.). 16p. (J). (gr. k-1). pap. 42.00 *(978-1-4777-1983-1(0));* (Illus.). pap. 7.00 *(978-1-4777-1982-4(2))* Rosen Publishing Group, Inc., The. (Rosen Classroom).

Mortensen, Lori. Made to Measure. 2016. (Spring Forward Ser.). (J). (gr. 2). *(978-1-4900-9442-7(3))* Benchmark Education Co.

Multiplication Dot-to-Dot Spanish Version. 2007. (J). *(978-1-58232-166-0(3))* ECS Learning Systems, Inc.

Multiplication Facts Spanish Version. 2007. (J). per. *(978-1-58232-155-4(8))* ECS Learning Systems, Inc.

Multiplication Skills Spanish Version. 2007. (J). per. *(978-1-58232-156-1(6))* ECS Learning Systems, Inc.

Murphy, Patricia J. Measuring Puppies & Kittens. 2007. (Puppy & Kitten Math Ser.). (Illus.). 32p. (J). (gr. 1-2). lib. bdg. 23.94

(978-0-7660-2727-5(9), Enslow Elementary) Enslow Pubs., Inc.

Murphy, Stuart J. Polly's Pen Pal. Simard, Remy, illus. 2005. (MathStart 3 Ser.). (ENG.). 40p. (J). (gr. 2-18). pap. 5.99 (978-0-06-053170-6(3)) HarperCollins Pubs.

Nielsen, Aubrie. After School. rev. ed. 2011. (Mathematics Readers Ser.). (ENG.). 32p. (J). (gr. k-k). pap. 8.99 (978-1-4333-3440-5(2)) Teacher Created Materials, Inc.

—At School. rev. ed. 2011. (Mathematics Readers Ser.). (ENG.). 32p. (J). (gr. k-k). pap. 8.99 (978-1-4333-3441-2(0)) Teacher Created Materials, Inc.

Nussbaum, Ben. PEEP Measuring. 2004. 32p. (J). (gr. -1-2). 14.95 (978-1-59249-377-7(7), 1C004) Soundprints.

Parker, Vic. How Far Is Far? Comparing Geographical Distances, 1 vol. 2010. (Measuring & Comparing Ser.). (ENG., Illus.). 32p. (gr. 1-3). 27.32 (978-1-4329-3956-4(4), Heinemann First Library) Heinemann-Raintree.

—How Full Is Full? Comparing Bodies of Water, 1 vol. 2010. (Measuring & Comparing Ser.). (ENG.). 32p. (gr. 1-3). 27.32 (978-1-4329-3957-1(2), Heinemann First Library) Heinemann-Raintree.

—How Heavy Is Heavy? Comparing Vehicles, 1 vol. 2010. (Measuring & Comparing Ser.). (ENG.). 32p. (gr. 1-3). 27.32 (978-1-4329-3954-0(8), Heinemann First Library) Heinemann-Raintree.

—How Long Is Long? Comparing Animals, 1 vol. 2010. (Measuring & Comparing Ser.). (ENG.). 32p. (gr. 1-3). 27.32 (978-1-4329-3958-8(0), Heinemann First Library) Heinemann-Raintree.

Patterson, Haley. Fossils Around the World: Measure Lengths in Standard Units, 1 vol. 2015. (InfoMax Common Core Math Readers Ser.). (ENG.). 24p. (J). pap. 8.25 (978-1-4777-4777-3(X), Rosen Classroom) Rosen Publishing Group, Inc., The.

Pecorella, Jane. How a Quilt Is Built: Learning to Measure an Object Using Inches. 2009. (Math for the REAL World Ser.). 16p. (gr. 2-3). pap. 7.05 (978-0-8239-8924-9(0), Rosen Classroom) Rosen Publishing Group, Inc., The.

Peppas, Lynn. How Do We Measure Matter? 2012. (ENG.). 24p. (J). (978-0-7787-0768-4(7)); (Illus.). pap. (978-0-7787-0775-2(X)) Crabtree Publishing Co.

Perritano, John. A Toy Store Summer: Finding Area. 2013. (iMath Ser.). (Illus.). 32p. (J). (gr. 3-4). pap. 11.94 (978-1-60357-504-1(9)) Norwood Hse. Pr.

Pisano, Sal. Measurement. 2004. (BrainBuilders Ser.). (ENG.). 48p. (gr. k-4). pap. 5.25 (978-1-4042-8543-9(1)) Rosen Publishing Group, Inc., The.

Pistoia, Sara. Measurement. 2013. (Simply Math Ser.). (ENG.). 24p. (J). (gr. -1-2). 27.07 (978-1-62323-531-4(6), 206337) Child's World, Inc., The.

—Measurements. 2016. (J). (978-1-4896-5110-5(1)) Weigl Pubs., Inc.

Pluckrose, Henry. What Size Is It? 2006. (Let's Explore, Maths Set Ser.). (Illus.). 32p. (J). (gr. -1-3). lib. bdg. 27.10 (978-1-59771-040-4(7)) Sea-To-Sea Pubns.

QEB Start Math Book Stores Edition: Measuring - Book 1. 2006. (J). per. (978-1-59566-274-3(X)) QEB Publishing Inc.

QEB Start Math Book Stores Edition: Measuring Book 2. 2006. (J). per. (978-1-59566-278-1(2)) QEB Publishing Inc.

Rauen, Amy. Finding Shortest & Longest. 2008. (Getting Started with Math Ser.). 16p. (gr. -1-2). pap. 5.30 (978-0-8368-8987-1(8)); (Illus.). lib. bdg. 19.00 (978-0-8368-8982-6(7)) Stevens, Gareth Publishing LLLP. (Weekly Reader Leveled Readers).

Rauen, Amy & Ayers, Amy. Measuring at the Dog Show. 2007. (Math in Our World Ser.). 24p. (gr. 1-2). pap. 8.15 (978-0-8368-8483-8(3), Weekly Reader Leveled Readers) Stevens, Gareth Publishing LLLP.

—Measuring at the Dog Show. Walter, Lorin, photos by. 2007. (Math in Our World Ser.). (Illus.). 24p. (gr. 1-2). lib. bdg. 22.00 (978-0-8368-8474-6(4), Weekly Reader Leveled Readers) Stevens, Gareth Publishing LLLP.

—Midiendo en la Exposicion de Perros. 2007. (Las matimaticas en nuestro mundo (Spanish- Math in Our World) Ser.). (SPA.). 24p. (gr. 1-2). pap. 8.15 (978-0-8368-8501-9(5), Weekly Reader Leveled Readers) Stevens, Gareth Publishing LLLP.

Reagan, Naomi. Butterflies & Moths: Represent & Interpret Data. 2014. (Rosen Common Core Math Readers Ser.). (ENG., Illus.). 24p. (J). (gr. 3-4). pap. 8.25 (978-1-4777-4901-2(2), Rosen Classroom) Rosen Publishing Group, Inc., The.

Reinhart, Robin. Fierce Freshwater Fish: Measure Lengths in Standard Units. 2014. (Math Masters: Measurement & Data Ser.). (Illus.). 24p. (J). (gr. 2-3). 23.60 (978-1-4777-6404-6(6), Rosen Classroom) Rosen Publishing Group, Inc., The.

Rey, Molly. Measuring with Footsteps. 2013. (Rosen Math Readers Ser.). (ENG.). 24p. (J). (gr. 1-2). pap. 8.25 (978-1-4777-2100-1(2), Rosen Classroom) Rosen Publishing Group, Inc., The.

—Measuring with Footsteps: Measure Lengths. 2013. (Rosen Math Readers Ser.). (ENG.). 24p. (J). (gr. 1-2). pap. 49.50 (978-1-4777-2101-8(0), Rosen Classroom) Rosen Publishing Group, Inc., The.

Rice, Dona. Use Your Math Mind: Describe It. 2015. (TIME for KIDS(r) Nonfiction Readers Ser.). (ENG., Illus.). 12p. (gr. k-k). 4.99 (978-1-4938-2142-6(3)) Teacher Created Materials, Inc.

Rice, Dona Herweck. USA Las Matemáticas (Use Math - Describe It) 2016. (TIME for KIDS(r) Nonfiction Readers Ser.). (SPA.). 12p. (gr. k-k). 4.99 (978-1-4938-3023-7(6)) Teacher Created Materials, Inc.

Robbins, Eliza. Which Holds More? Learning to Compare Volume. (Math for the Real World: Early Emergent Ser.). (ENG., Illus.). 8p. (gr. k-1). 2009. pap. 5.15 (978-0-8239-8845-7(1)) 2004. 29.95 (978-0-8239-7631-7(9)) Rosen Publishing Group, Inc., The.

Roberts, Abigail B. Using Measuring Cups. 2017. (Super Science Tools Ser.). 24p. (gr. 1-2). pap. 8.15 **(978-1-4824-6397-2(0))** Stevens, Gareth Publishing LLLP.

Roman, Nora. Using a Scale. 2017. (Super Science Tools Ser.). 24p. (gr. 1-2). 22.60 **(978-1-4824-6407-8(1))** Stevens, Gareth Publishing LLLP.

Roy, Jennifer Rozines & Roy, Gregory. Measuring at Home. 2006. (Math All Around Ser.). (Illus.). 32p. (gr. 2-7). lib. bdg. 29.93 (978-0-7614-2263-1(3), Benchmark Bks.) Marshall Cavendish Corp.

Roza, Greg. Measurement. 2004. (BrainBuilders Ser.). (ENG.). 48p. (gr. k-4). pap. 5.25 (978-1-4042-8537-8(7)) Rosen Publishing Group, Inc., The.

—Where We Play Sports: Measuring the Perimeters of Polygons. 2009. (PowerMath Ser.). (ENG., Illus.). 24p. (gr. 3-4). pap. 8.25 (978-0-8239-8895-2(3), PowerKids Pr.) Rosen Publishing Group, Inc., The.

Salzmann, Mary Elizabeth. What in the World Is a Cup? CD & Book. 2010. (Let's Measure CD+Book Ser.). 24p. (gr. k-3). audio compact disk 42.70 (978-1-61613-313-9(9), SandCastle) ABDO Publishing Co.

—What in the World Is a Cup? Site CD & Book. 2010. (Let's Measure Site CD+Book Ser.). 24p. (gr. k-3). cd-rom 78.42 (978-1-61613-285-9(X), SandCastle) ABDO Publishing Co.

—What in the World Is a Foot? CD & Book. 2010. (Let's Measure CD+Book Ser.). 24p. (gr. k-3). audio compact disk 42.70 (978-1-61613-314-6(7), SandCastle) ABDO Publishing Co.

—What in the World Is a Foot? Site CD & Book. 2010. (Let's Measure Site CD+Book Ser.). 24p. (gr. k-3). cd-rom 78.42 (978-1-61613-286-6(8), SandCastle) ABDO Publishing Co.

—What in the World Is a Gallon? CD & Book. 2010. (Let's Measure CD+Book Ser.). 24p. (gr. k-3). audio compact disk 42.70 (978-1-61613-315-3(5), SandCastle) ABDO Publishing Co.

—What in the World Is a Gallon? Site CD & Book. 2010. (Let's Measure Site CD+Book Ser.). 24p. (gr. k-3). cd-rom 78.42 (978-1-61613-287-3(6), SandCastle) ABDO Publishing Co.

—What in the World Is a Pound? CD & Book. 2010. (Let's Measure CD+Book Ser.). 24p. (gr. k-3). audio compact disk 42.70 (978-1-61613-316-0(3), SandCastle) ABDO Publishing Co.

—What in the World Is a Pound? Site CD & Book. 2010. (Let's Measure Site CD+Book Ser.). 24p. (gr. k-3). cd-rom 78.42 (978-1-61613-288-0(4), SandCastle) ABDO Publishing Co.

—What in the World Is an Inch? CD & Book. 2010. (Let's Measure CD+Book Ser.). 24p. (gr. k-3). audio compact disk 42.70 (978-1-61613-317-7(1), SandCastle) ABDO Publishing Co.

—What in the World Is an Inch? Site CD & Book. 2010. (Let's Measure Site CD+Book Ser.). 24p. (gr. k-3). cd-rom 78.42 (978-1-61613-289-7(2), SandCastle) ABDO Publishing Co.

—What in the World Is an Ounce? CD & Book. 2010. (Let's Measure CD+Book Ser.). 24p. (gr. k-3). audio compact disk 42.70 (978-1-61613-318-4(X), SandCastle) ABDO Publishing Co.

—What in the World Is an Ounce? Site CD & Book. 2010. (Let's Measure Site CD+Book Ser.). 24p. (gr. k-3). cd-rom 78.42 (978-1-61613-290-3(6), SandCastle) ABDO Publishing Co.

Sargent, Brian. How Much Does It Hold? 2006. (Rookie Read-About Math Ser.). (ENG., Illus.). 32p. (J). (gr. 1-2). pap. 5.95 (978-0-516-29812-2(7)); lib. bdg. 20.50 (978-0-516-24957-5(6)) Scholastic Library Publishing. (Children's Pr.).

Schwartz, David M. Millions to Measure. Kellogg, Steven, illus. 2006. (ENG.). 40p. (J). (gr. k-7). reprint ed. pap. 6.99 (978-0-06-084806-4(5)) HarperCollins Pubs.

Schwartz, David M. & Schwartz, David. Millions to Measure. Kellogg, Steven, illus. 2003. (ENG.). 40p. (J). (gr. k-7). 17.99 (978-0-688-12916-3(1)) HarperCollins Pubs.

Science Stories Foss Spanish Measurement EA CR05. 2005. (J). (978-1-59242-586-0(0)) Delta Education, LLC.

Shae, Jordan. Handy Measuring: Measure Lengths. 2013. (InfoMax Math Readers Ser.). (ENG.). 24p. (J). (gr. 1-2). pap. 49.50 (978-1-4777-2202-2(5)); pap. 8.25 (978-1-4777-2201-5(7)) Rosen Publishing Group, Inc., The. (Rosen Classroom).

Simpson, Jeffrey L. Measurement & Geometry, Student Edition: Count, Notice & Remember Math Intervention, Volume 6. Simpson, Marilyn Bohlen, ed. 2007. ring bd. 59.95 (978-1-888976-59-5(4)) Mastery Learning Systems.

Smith, Paula. Measure It! 2015. (ENG., Illus.). 24p. (J). pap. (978-0-7787-1544-3(2)) Crabtree Publishing Co.

Sohn, Emily & Sharp, Katie. Measurement: The Measured Mystery. 2011. (iScience Readers Ser.). 32p. (J). (gr. 3-4). lib. bdg. 22.60 (978-1-59953-417-6(7)) Norwood Hse. Pr.

Somervill, Barbara A. & Capstone Press Staff. Measure It! 2010. (Measure It! Ser.). (ENG.). 32p. lib. bdg. 103.96 (978-1-4296-5944-4(0), Aplus Bks.) Capstone Press of Coughlan Cos.

Steck-Vaughn Company, creator. Measure Mints, Grades K-6. 2011. (ENG., Illus.). 200p. (J). (gr. k-6). pap. 19.99 (978-0-547-62558-4(8)) Heinemann-Raintree.

Steck-Vaughn Staff. Early Math: Measurement I. 2005. pap. 2.99 (978-1-4190-0329-5(1)) Steck-Vaughn.

—Early Math: Measurement II. 2005. pap. 2.99 (978-1-4190-0339-4(9)); pap. 29.95 (978-1-4190-0363-9(1)) Steck-Vaughn.

—Early Measurement 10-pack: Measurement I. 2005. pap. 29.95 (978-1-4190-0353-0(4)) Steck-Vaughn.

—Focus on Math Level C: Measurement. 2005. pap. 2.99 (978-1-4190-0269-4(4)) Harcourt Schl. Pubs.

—Focus on Math Level C 10-pack: Measurement. 2005. pap. 29.95 (978-1-4190-0293-9(7)) Harcourt Schl. Pubs.

—Measure That Tongue! 2003. pap. 4.10 (978-0-7398-7653-4(8)) Steck-Vaughn.

—Measurement & Geometry. 2004. pap. 14.95 (978-0-7398-9855-0(8)) Harcourt Schl. Pubs.

—Top Line Math: Measurement. 2005. pap. 5.49 (978-1-4190-0370-7(4)) Harcourt Schl. Pubs.

Steffora, Tracey. Animal Math: Comparing & Measuring, 1 vol. 2014. (Animal Math Ser.). (ENG.). 32p. (gr. -1-1). 29.99 (978-1-4846-0062-7(2), NA-h) Heinemann-Raintree.

—Measuring in the Garden, 1 vol. 2011. (Math Around Us Ser.). (ENG.). 24p. (gr. -1-1). 22.65 (978-1-4329-4926-6(8)); pap. 6.29 (978-1-4329-4934-1(9)) Heinemann-Raintree. (Acorn).

—Measuring with Monkeys, 1 vol. 2013. (Animal Math Ser.). (ENG.). 24p. (gr. -1-1). 22.65 (978-1-4329-7560-9(9)); pap. 6.95 (978-1-4329-7567-8(6)) Heinemann-Raintree. (NA-h).

Strazzabosco, John. Measurement. 2004. (BrainBuilders Ser.). (ENG.). 48p. (gr. k-4). pap. 5.25 (978-1-4042-8530-9(X)) Rosen Publishing Group, Inc., The.

Sullivan, Martha. Around My City: Describe & Compare Measurable Attributes. 2013. (Rosen Math Readers Ser.). (ENG.). 16p. (J). (gr. k-1). pap. 42.00 (978-1-4777-1597-0(5)); (Illus.). pap. 7.00 (978-1-4777-1596-3(7)) Rosen Publishing Group, Inc., The. (Rosen Classroom).

Sullivan, Navin. Area, Distance, & Volume. 2006. (Measure Up! Ser.). (Illus.). 48p. (gr. 4-7). lib. bdg. 31.36 (978-0-7614-2323-2(0), Benchmark Bks.) Marshall Cavendish Corp.

—Measure Up!, 5 bks., Set. Incl. Area, Distance, & Volume. lib. bdg. 31.36 (978-0-7614-2323-2(0)); Speed. lib. bdg. 31.36 (978-0-7614-2325-6(7)); Temperature. lib. bdg. 31.36 (978-0-7614-2322-5(2)); Time. lib. bdg. 31.36 (978-0-7614-2321-8(4)); Weight. lib. bdg. 31.36 (978-0-7614-2324-9(9)); (Illus.). 48p. (gr. 4-7). (Measure up! Ser.). 2006. Set lib. bdg. 156.80 (978-0-7614-2320-1(6), Benchmark Bks.) Marshall Cavendish Corp.

—Speed. 2006. (Measure Up! Ser.). (Illus.). 48p. (gr. 4-7). lib. bdg. 31.36 (978-0-7614-2325-6(7), Benchmark Bks.) Marshall Cavendish Corp.

Thanner, Eric. Leaping Lengths! Relate Addition & Subtraction to Length, 1 vol. 2015. (InfoMax Common Core Math Readers Ser.). (ENG.). 24p. (J). pap. 8.25 (978-1-4777-4760-5(5), Rosen Classroom) Rosen Publishing Group, Inc., The.

Truran, Stacy. Troy's Tree Fort: Measure Lengths in Standard Units. 2014. (Rosen Common Core Math Readers Ser.). (ENG.). 24p. (J). (gr. 2-3). pap. 8.25 (978-1-4777-4784-1(2), Rosen Classroom) Rosen Publishing Group, Inc., The.

Tuxworth, Nicola. Sizes. 2016. (ENG., Illus.). 20p. bds. 6.99 (978-1-84322-751-9(7), Armadillo) Anness Publishing GBR. Dist: National Bk. Network.

Unswood, Cassie. Exploring Plane Figures: Understand Concepts of Area, 1 vol. 2015. (InfoMax Common Core Math Readers Ser.). (ENG.). 24p. (J). pap. 8.25 (978-1-4777-4594-6(7), Rosen Classroom) Rosen Publishing Group, Inc., The.

Visto, Joy. Whose Foot Is a Foot? 2015. (Illus.). 48p. (J). (978-1-60818-576-4(1), Creative Education) Creative Co., The.

—Whose Foot Is a Foot? Making Math Work. 2016. (Making Math Work Ser.). (ENG.). 48p. (J). (gr. 5-9). pap. 12.00 (978-1-62832-177-7(6), Creative Paperbacks) Creative Co., The.

Vogel, Julia. Measuring Length. Marten, Luanne, illus. 2012. (Simple Measurement Ser.). (ENG.). 24p. (J). (gr. -1-2). 27.07 (978-1-61473-279-2(5), 204984) Child's World, Inc., The.

—Measuring Time: The Calendar. Marten, Luanne, illus. 2012. (Simple Measurement Ser.). (ENG.). 24p. (J). (gr. -1-2). 27.07 (978-1-61473-281-5(7), 204986) Child's World, Inc., The.

—Measuring Time: The Clock. Marten, Luanne, illus. 2012. (Simple Measurement Ser.). (ENG.). 24p. (J). (gr. -1-2). 27.07 (978-1-61473-282-2(5), 204987) Child's World, Inc., The.

—Measuring Volume. Marten, Luanne, illus. 2012. (Simple Measurement Ser.). (ENG.). 24p. (J). (gr. -1-2). 27.07 (978-1-61473-283-9(3), 204988) Child's World, Inc., The.

Weakland, Mark. How Tall? Wacky Ways to Compare Height, 1 vol. Sinkovec, Igor, illus. 2013. (Wacky Comparisons Ser.). (ENG.). 24p. (gr. -1-2). 27.99 (978-1-4048-8323-9(1)); pap. 8.95 (978-1-4795-1913-2(8)) Picture Window Bks.

Weaver, Madeline. Near & Far at the Park: Describe & Compare Measurable Attributes. 2013. (Rosen Math Readers Ser.). (ENG.). 16p. (J). (gr. k-1). pap. 42.00 (978-1-4777-1636-6(X)); (Illus.). pap. 7.00 (978-1-4777-1635-9(1)) Rosen Publishing Group, Inc., The. (Rosen Classroom).

Wingard-Nelson, Rebecca & Library. Math Measurement Word Problems: No Problem! 2010. (Math Busters Word Problems Ser.). (Illus.). 64p. (J). lib. bdg. 29.27 (978-0-7660-3369-6(4)) Enslow Pubs., Inc.

Woodford, Chris. Area. 2012. (Measure up Math Ser.). (Illus.). 32p. (J). (gr. 4-6). pap. 10.50 (978-1-4339-7434-2(7)); lib. bdg. 26.60 (978-1-4339-7433-5(9)) Stevens, Gareth Publishing LLLP.

—Distance. 2012. (Measure up Math Ser.). (Illus.). 32p. (J). (gr. 4-6). pap. 10.50 (978-1-4339-7438-0(X)); lib. bdg. 26.60 (978-1-4339-7437-3(1)) Stevens, Gareth Publishing LLLP.

—Height. 2012. (Measure up Math Ser.). (Illus.). 32p. (J). (gr. 4-6). pap. 10.50 (978-1-4339-7442-7(8)); lib. bdg. 26.60 (978-1-4339-7441-0(X)) Stevens, Gareth Publishing LLLP.

MEASUREMENT—FICTION

Berkes, Marianne. The Tortoise & Hare's Amazing Race, 1 vol. Morrison, Cathy, illus. 2015. (ENG & SPA.). 32p. (J). (gr. k-3). 17.95 (978-1-62855-635-3(8)) Arbordale Publishing.

deRubertis, Barbara & National Geographic Learning Staff. Lulu's Lemonade. Billin-Frye, Paige, illus. 2010. (Rise & Shine Ser.). (ENG.). 32p. (C). (gr. -1-3). pap. 10.95 (978-1-57565-093-7(2)) National Geographic School Publishing, Inc.

Dussling, Jennifer. If the Shoe Fits: Nonstandard Units of Measurement. Dussling, Deborah, illus. 2015. (ENG.). 32p. (J). (gr. -1-1). lib. bdg. 22.60 (978-1-57565-800-1(3)) Kane Press, Inc.

Fletcher, Corina. Small Smaller Smallest. Marshall, Natalie, illus. 2015. (ENG.). 12p. (J). (— 1). bds. 8.95 (978-1-4549-1559-1(5)) Sterling Publishing Co., Inc.

Gabriel, Nat. Sam Y Sus Cuadrados de Zapatos (Sam's Sneaker Squares) 2009. (SPA.). pap. 34.95 (978-0-7613-4790-3(9)) Lerner Publishing Group.

Gabriel, Nat & Ramirez, Alma. Sam y Sus Cuadrados de Zapatos. Fritz, Ronald, illus. 2009. (Math Matters en Espanol Ser.). (SPA.). 32p. (J). (gr. 1-3). pap. 5.95 (978-1-57565-276-4(5)) Kane Press, Inc.

Greve, Meg. Mud Pie Queen. Poole, Helen, illus. 2012. (ENG.). 24p. (gr. k-1). pap. 8.95 (978-1-61810-303-1(2)) Rourke Educational Media.

Hosford, Kate. Infinity & Me. Swiatkowska, Gabi, illus. 2012. (Carolrhoda Picture Bks.). (ENG.). 32p. (J). (gr. k-4). lib. bdg. 16.95 (978-0-7613-6726-0(8)) Lerner Publishing Group.

Kayaalp, Suzan. Inch Worm Inch Worm. Merrifield, Monarca, illus. 2013. 20p. pap. 12.95 (978-1-62838-072-9(1)) Page Publishing Inc.

Klein, Adria F. Tia Tape Measure, 1 vol. Rowland, Andrew, illus. 2011. (Tool School Ser.). (ENG.). 32p. (gr. 1-2). pap. 6.25 (978-1-4342-3388-2(X)); lib. bdg. 22.65 (978-1-4342-3046-1(5)) Stone Arch Bks.

—Tia Tape Measure & the Move, 1 vol. Rowland, Andrew, illus. 2012. (Tool School Ser.). (ENG.). 32p. (gr. 1-3). pap. 6.25 (978-1-4342-4236-5(6)); lib. bdg. 22.65 (978-1-4342-4023-1(1)) Stone Arch Bks.

Law, Felicia & Way, Steve. Mirage in the Mist: Measurement in Action. Spoor, Mike & Mostyn, David, illus. 2010. (Mandrill Mountain Math Mysteries Ser.). 32p. (J). (gr. 2-6). pap. 10.55 (978-1-60754-823-2(2)) Windmill Bks.

—Mirage in the Mist: Measurements in Action. Spoor, Mike & Mostyn, David, illus. 2010. (Mandrill Mountain Math Mysteries Ser.). 32p. (J). (gr. 2-6). 22.60 (978-1-60754-818-8(6)) Windmill Bks.

May, Eleanor. Let's Go, Snow! Pillo, Cary, illus. 2017. (Math Matters (r) Ser.). (ENG.). 32p. (J). (gr. k-3). pap. 5.95 (978-1-57565-807-0(0)) Kane Press, Inc.

May, Eleanor. Let's Go, Snow! Temperature Measurement. Pillo, Cary, illus. 2017. (Math Matters (r) Ser.). (ENG.). 32p. (gr. k-3). 23.99 **(978-1-57565-808-7(9))** Kane Press, Inc.

Meredith, Susan Markowitz. The Royal Zookeeper. 2011. (Early Connections Ser.). (J). (978-1-61672-678-2(4)) Benchmark Education Co.

Naylor, Phyllis Reynolds. Lovingly Alice. 2006. (Alice Ser.). (ENG., Illus.). 176p. (J). (gr. 4-7). pap. 5.99 (978-0-689-84400-3(X), Atheneum Bks. for Young Readers) Simon & Schuster Children's Publishing.

Spoor, Mike, illus. Desperate Measures: Units of Measurement in Action. 2010. (Mandrill Mountain Math Mysteries Ser.). (ENG.). 32p. (J). (gr. 2-6). pap. 10.55 (978-1-60754-925-3(5)) Windmill Bks.

—Desperate Measures: Units of Measurement in Action. 2010. (Mandrill Mountain Math Mysteries Ser.). (ENG.). 32p. (J). (gr. 2-6). lib. bdg. 22.60 (978-1-60754-920-8(4)) Windmill Bks.

Thielbar, Melinda. The Secret Ghost. 3rd rev. ed. 2010. pap. 39.62 (978-0-7613-6944-8(9)) Lerner Publishing Group.

—The Secret Ghost: A Mystery with Distance & Measurement. Ota, Yuko, illus. 2010. (Manga Math Mysteries Ser.: 3). (ENG.). 46p. (gr. 3-5). pap. 6.95 (978-0-7613-5245-7(7), Graphic Universe™) Lerner Publishing Group.

Weston Woods Staff, creator. Inch by Inch. 2011. 38.75 (978-0-439-90543-5(5)) Weston Woods Studios, Inc.

MEASURES

see Weights and Measures

MEASURING

see Measurement

MEASURING INSTRUMENTS

Allen, Nancy. My Math Toolbox. 2011. (ENG., Illus.). 24p. (gr. -1-1). pap. 8.95 (978-1-61741-960-7(5)) Rourke Educational Media.

Benchmark Education Company. Measuring Matter (Teacher Guide) Solids, Liquids, & Gases. 2005. (978-1-4108-4651-8(2)) Benchmark Education Co.

Benchmark Education Company, LLC Staff. Science Measuring Tools Teacher's Guide. 2004. (978-1-4108-2588-9(4)) Benchmark Education Co.

Cardenas, Ernesto A. What Do You Use to Measure? 2009. 23.95 (978-1-60698-050-7(5)); pap. 4.95 (978-1-60698-048-4(3)) Milo Educational Bks. & Resources.

Chrismer, Melanie & National Geographic Learning Staff. Math Tools. 2010. (Rise & Shine Ser.). (ENG., Illus.). 32p. (C). (gr. 1-2). pap. 19.95 (978-0-516-25550-7(9)) National Geographic School Publishing, Inc.

Doudna, Kelly. She'll Use a Ruler So You Won't Fool Her!, 1 vol. 2007. (Science Made Simple Ser.). (ENG., Illus.). 24p. (J). (gr. k-3). lib. bdg. 24.21 (978-1-59928-618-1(1), SandCastle) ABDO Publishing Co.

Eboch, Chris. Science Measurements: How Heavy? How Long? How Hot? Davis, Jon, illus. 2006. (Amazing Science Ser.). (ENG.). 24p. (gr. k-4). 26.65 (978-1-4048-2197-2(X)) Picture Window Bks.

Furgang, Kathy. Science Measuring Tools: Set Of 6. 2011. (Navigators Ser.). (J). pap. 50.00 net. (978-1-4108-2573-5(6)) Benchmark Education Co.

—Science Measuring Tools & Instrumentos para medir en Ciencias: 6 English, 6 Spanish Adaptations. 2011. (ENG & SPA.). (J). 101.00 net. (978-1-4108-5727-9(1)) Benchmark Education Co.

Mangieri, Catherine. Using Measuring Tools. 2009. (Real Life Readers Ser.). 12p. (gr. 1-2). pap. 5.90 (978-1-4042-7921-6(0), Rosen Classroom) Rosen Publishing Group, Inc., The.

Markovics, Joyce. Measure It! 2012. (ENG.). 24p. (gr. -1-1). pap. 8.95 (978-1-61810-210-2(9)) Rourke Educational Media.

Marsico, Katie. Tape Measures. 2013. (21st Century Junior Library: Basic Tools Ser.). (ENG.). 24p. (J). (gr. 2-5). 25.64 (978-1-62431-173-4(3), 203012); pap. 12.79 (978-1-62431-305-9(1), 203014) Cherry Lake Publishing.

Matos, Rebecca. Measuring Matter: Solids, Liquids, & Gases. 2005. (J). pap. (978-1-4108-4603-7(2)) Benchmark Education Co.

Pearson Learning Staff, creator. A Visit to the Doctor. 2007. (ENG.). (J). (gr. 2-2). pap. 10.92 (978-0-7652-8602-4(5), Celebration Pr.) Pearson Schl.

Peppas, Lynn. How Do We Measure Matter? 2012. (ENG.). 24p. (J). (978-0-7787-0768-4(7)); (Illus.). pap. (978-0-7787-0775-2(X)) Crabtree Publishing Co.

Rivera, Sheila. Measuring Cup. 2006. (First Step Nonfiction - Simple Tools Ser.). (ENG., Illus.). 8p. (gr. -1-1). pap. 4.95 (978-0-8225-5714-2(2), Lerner Pubns.) Lerner Publishing Group.

—Ruler. 2006. (First Step Nonfiction - Simple Tools Ser.). (ENG., Illus.). 8p. (gr. -1-1). pap. 4.95 (978-0-8225-5715-9(0), Lerner Pubns.) Lerner Publishing Group.

Roy, Jennifer Rozines & Roy, Gregory. Measuring at Home. 2007. (J). pap. 6.99 (978-0-7614-3384-2(8)) 2006. (Illus.). 32p. (gr. 2-7). lib. bdg. 29.93 (978-0-7614-2263-1(3), Benchmark Bks.) Marshall Cavendish Corp.

Salzmann, Mary Elizabeth. What in the World Is a Cup?, 1 vol. 2009. (Let's Measure Ser.). (ENG., Illus.). 24p. (J). (gr. k-3). lib. bdg. 24.21 (978-1-60453-162-6(2)) ABDO Publishing Co.

—What in the World Is a Cup? CD & Book. 2010. (Let's Measure CD+Book Ser.). 24p. (gr. k-3). audio compact disk 42.70 (978-1-61613-313-9(9), SandCastle) ABDO Publishing Co.

—What in the World Is a Cup? Site CD & Book. 2010. (Let's Measure Site CD+Book Ser.). 24p. (gr. k-3). cd-rom 78.42 *(978-1-61613-285-9(X)*, SandCastle) ABDO Publishing Co.
Sullivan, Erin Ash. Measuring Matter: Set Of 6. 2010. (Navigators Ser.). (J). pap. 44.00 net. *(978-1-4108-5070-6(6))* Benchmark Education Co.
Sundance/Newbridge LLC Staff. Let's Measure It! 2004. (Reading PowerWorks Ser.). (gr. 1-3). 37.50 *(978-0-7608-7831-6(5))*; pap. 6.10 *(978-0-7608-7832-3(3))* Sundance/Newbridge Educational Publishing.

MEAT INDUSTRY AND TRADE

Francis, Amy. Vegetarianism. 2015. (Current Controversies Ser.). (ENG.). 224p. (J). (gr. 10-12). 46.40 *(978-0-7377-7227-2(1)*, Greenhaven Pr., Inc.) Cengage Gale.
Hasan, Heather. Meat: From the Farm to Your Table. 2012. (Truth about the Food Supply Ser.). (ENG., Illus.). 48p. (J). (gr. 5-8). lib. bdg. 27.95 *(978-1-4488-6797-4(5)*, Rosen Reference) Rosen Publishing Group, Inc., The.
Lee, Sally. The Powerful Protein Group, 1 vol. Swift, Gary, illus. 2011. (First Graphics: Myplate & Healthy Eating Ser.). (ENG.). 24p. (gr. 1-2). lib. bdg. 23.99 *(978-1-4296-6091-4(0))* Capstone Press of Coughlan Cos.
Lynette, Rachel. Producing Meat, 1 vol. 2012. (Technology of Farming Ser.). (ENG.). 48p. (gr. 4-6). lib. bdg. 33.32 *(978-1-4329-6410-8(0)*, Heinemann InfoSearch) Heinemann-Raintree.
Nelson, Robin. Meats & Proteins. 2003. (First Step Nonfiction - Food Groups Ser.). (ENG., Illus.). 24p. (gr. k-2). 23.93 *(978-0-8225-4630-6(2))* Lerner Publishing Group.
Singer, Jane E. Meat. 2013. (Feeding the World Ser.: 8). (Illus.). 48p. (J). (gr. 4-18). 19.95 *(978-1-4222-2746-6(4))* Mason Crest.

MECHANICAL BRAINS

see Computers

MECHANICAL DRAWING

see also Architectural Drawing; Geometrical Drawing; Graphic Methods; Lettering

Welsbacher, Anne. Earth-Friendly Design. 2008. (Saving Our Living Earth Ser.). 72p. (YA). (gr. 4-7). lib. bdg. 30.60 *(978-0-8225-7564-1(7))* Lerner Publishing Group.

MECHANICAL DRAWING—VOCATIONAL GUIDANCE

AIMS Education Foundation, et al. Machine Shop. 2007. (ENG.). 248p. (gr. 5-9). pap. 24.95 *(978-1-881431-39-8(8)*, 1311) AIMS Education Foundation.

MECHANICAL ENGINEERING

see also Electric Engineering; Engines; Machinery; Power (Mechanics)

Corporate Contributor & Snedden, Robert. Mechanical Engineering & Simple Machines. 2012. (ENG.). 32p. (J). *(978-0-7787-7498-3(8))* Crabtree Publishing Co.
Crabtree Staff & Snedden, Robert. Mechanical Engineering & Simple Machines. 2012. (ENG., Illus.). 32p. (J). pap. *(978-0-7787-7503-4(8))* Crabtree Publishing Co.
Domaine, Helena. Robotics. 2005. (Cool Science Ser.). (ENG., Illus.). 48p. (gr. 4-8). lib. bdg. 27.93 *(978-0-8225-2112-9(1)*, Lerner Pubns.) Lerner Publishing Group.
Eboch, Chris. Amazing Feats of Mechanical Engineering, 1 vol. 2014. (Great Achievements in Engineering Ser.). (ENG.). 112p. (J). (gr. 6-12). lib. bdg. 35.64 *(978-1-62403-430-5(6)*, Essential Library) ABDO Publishing Co.
Enz, Tammy. Zoom It: Invent New Machines That Move, 1 vol. 2012. (Invent It Ser.). (ENG.). 32p. (gr. 3-4). pap. 8.10 *(978-1-4296-7984-8(0))*; pap. 47.70 *(978-1-4296-8458-3(5))*; lib. bdg. 27.32 *(978-1-4296-7634-2(5))* Capstone Press of Coughlan Cos. (Fact Finders).
Herweck, Don. All about Mechanical Engineering, 1 vol. 2007. (Science Readers Ser.). (ENG.). 32p. (J). (gr. 4-4). pap. 8.99 *(978-0-7439-0577-0(6))* Shell Educational Publishing.
Hinton, Kerry. A Career As an Operating & Stationary Engineer, 01 vols., 1. 2016. (Essential Careers Ser.). (ENG.). 80p. (J). 34.25 *(978-1-4994-6223-4(9)*, Rosen Young Adult) Rosen Publishing Group, Inc., The.
Holland, Gini. Soft & Hard. 2007. (I Know Opposites Ser.). 16p. (gr. -1-2). pap. 5.30 *(978-0-8368-8301-5(2))*; lib. bdg. 19.00 *(978-0-8368-8296-4(2))* Stevens, Gareth Publishing LLLP. (Weekly Reader Leveled Readers).
Juarez, Christine. John Danny Olivas. 2016. (Great Hispanic & Latino Americans Ser.). (ENG.). 24p. (gr. k-1). lib. bdg. 21.99 *(978-1-5157-1890-1(5)*, Pebble Bks.) Capstone Press of Coughlan Cos.
LaMachia, Dawn. Pulleys at Work. 2015. (Zoom in on Simple Machines Ser.). (ENG.). 24p. (J). (gr. 2-2). 22.60 *(978-0-7660-6736-3(X))* Enslow Pubs., Inc.
McBride, Carol & Gonzales, Francisco L. Engineer This! 15 Amazing Projects for Young Mechanical Engineers. 2017. (Other Ser.). (ENG.). 150p. (J). (gr. 4-7). pap. 14.95 ***(978-1-61821-629-8(5))*** Prufrock Pr.
Miller, Tim. Inclined Planes in My Makerspace. 2017. (Simple Machines in My Makerspace Ser.). (ENG., Illus.). 32p. (J). ***(978-0-7787-3370-6(X))*** Crabtree Publishing Co.
—Pulleys in My Makerspace. 2017. (Simple Machines in My Makerspace Ser.). (ENG., Illus.). 32p. (J). ***(978-0-7787-3372-0(6))*** Crabtree Publishing Co.
—Screws in My Makerspace. 2017. (Simple Machines in My Makerspace Ser.). (ENG., Illus.). 32p. (J). ***(978-0-7787-3373-7(4))*** Crabtree Publishing Co.
—Wedges in My Makerspace. 2017. (Simple Machines in My Makerspace Ser.). (ENG., Illus.). 32p. (J). ***(978-0-7787-3374-4(2))*** Crabtree Publishing Co.
Mooney, Carla. Becoming Invisible: From Camouflage to Cloaks. 2010. (Great Idea Ser.). 48p. (J). (gr. 4-6). lib. bdg. 26.60 *(978-1-59953-378-0(2))* Norwood Hse. Pr.
Moore Niver, Heather. Getting to Know Arduino. 2014. (Code Power: a Teen Programmer's Guide Ser.). (Illus.). 64p. (J). (gr. 5-8). pap. 12.95 *(978-1-4777-7501-1(3)*, Rosen Reference) Rosen Publishing Group, Inc., The.
Randolph, Joanne. Gears in My World. 2006. (My World of Science Ser.). (Illus.). 24p. (J). (gr. 3-7). lib. bdg. 18.75 *(978-1-4042-3311-9(3)*, PowerKids Pr.) Rosen Publishing Group, Inc., The.
—Gears in My World: Engranajes en Mi Mundo. 2006. (My World of Science/ Mi mundo y la Ciencia Ser.). (ENG & SPA.). (J). (gr. k-3). 16.00 *(978-1-4042-3323-2(7))* Rosen Publishing Group, Inc., The.
—Inclined Planes in My World. 2006. (My World of Science Ser.). (Illus.). 24p. (J). (gr. 3-7). lib. bdg. 18.75 *(978-1-4042-3312-6(1)*, PowerKids Pr.) Rosen Publishing Group, Inc., The.
—Inclined Planes in My World: Planos Inclinados en Mi Mundo. 2006. (My World of Science/ Mi mundo y la Ciencia Ser.). (ENG & SPA.). (J). (gr. k-3). 16.00 *(978-1-4042-3324-9(5))* Rosen Publishing Group, Inc., The.
—Levers in My World. 2006. (My World of Science Ser.). (Illus.). 24p. (J). (gr. 3-7). lib. bdg. 18.75 *(978-1-4042-3309-6(1)*, PowerKids Pr.) Rosen Publishing Group, Inc., The.
—Levers in My World: Palancas en Mi Mundo. 2006. (My World of Science/ Mi mundo y la Ciencia Ser.). (ENG & SPA.). (J). (gr. k-3). 16.00 *(978-1-4042-3321-8(0))* Rosen Publishing Group, Inc., The.
—Pulleys in My World. 2006. (My World of Science Ser.). (Illus.). 24p. (J). (gr. 3-7). lib. bdg. 18.75 *(978-1-4042-3308-9(3)*, PowerKids Pr.) Rosen Publishing Group, Inc., The.
—Pulleys in My World: Poleas en Mi Mundo. 2006. (My World of Science/ Mi mundo y la Ciencia Ser.). (ENG & SPA., Illus.). 24p. (J). (gr. k-3). 16.00 *(978-1-4042-3320-1(2))* Rosen Publishing Group, Inc., The.
—Wedges in My World. 2006. (My World of Science Ser.). (Illus.). 24p. (J). (gr. 3-7). lib. bdg. 18.75 *(978-1-4042-3310-2(5)*, PowerKids Pr.) Rosen Publishing Group, Inc., The.
—Wedges in My World: Cuñas en Mi Mundo. 2006. (My World of Science/ Mi mundo y la Ciencia Ser.). (ENG & SPA.). (J). (gr. k-3). 16.00 *(978-1-4042-3322-5(9))* Rosen Publishing Group, Inc., The.
Rivera, Sheila. Bending. 2007. (First Step Nonfiction - Changing Matter Ser.). (ENG.). 8p. (gr. -1-1). pap. 4.95 *(978-0-8225-6416-4(5))* Lerner Publishing Group.
Rooney, Anne. Optical Engineering & the Science of Light. 2013. (ENG.). 32p. (J). *(978-0-7787-1228-2(1))*; (Illus.). pap. *(978-0-7787-1232-9(X))* Crabtree Publishing Co.
Royston, Angela. Pulleys & Gears, 1 vol. 2003. (Machines in Action Ser.). (ENG., Ilus.). 32p. (gr. 3-5). pap. 7.99 *(978-1-4034-4085-3(9)*, NA-h) Heinemann-Raintree.
Shea, Therese. Solving Real World Problems with Mechanical Engineering, 01 vols., 1. 2016. (Let's Find Out! Ser.). (ENG., Illus.). 32p. (J). pap. 12.90 *(978-1-5081-0079-9(9)*, Britannica Educational Publishing) Rosen Publishing Group, Inc., The.
Weakland, Mark. Gears Go, Wheels Roll, 1 vol. 2011. (Science Starts Ser.). (ENG., Illus.). 32p. (gr. 1-2). pap. 8.10 *(978-1-4296-6143-0(7)*, Aplus Bks.) Capstone Press of Coughlan Cos.

MECHANICAL MODELS

see Machinery—Models

MECHANICS

see also Dynamics; Force and Energy; Hydrostatics; Liquids; Machinery; Motion; Power (Mechanics); Steam-Engines; Vibration

Bateman, Graham, ed. Electricity & Electronics. 2011. (FAYFT: Introducing Physics Ser.). 64p. (gr. 4-10). lib. bdg. 39.95 *(978-1-936333-09-7(0))* Brown Bear Bks.
Cavell-Clarke, Steffi. Pushes & Pulls. 2017. (First Science Ser.). 24p. (J). (gr. 1-1). pap. 8.25 ***(978-1-5345-2080-6(5))***; lib. bdg. 24.60 ***(978-1-5345-2082-0(1))*** Greenhaven Publishing LLC. (KidHaven Publishing).
Clark, John O. E. The Basics of Mechanics. 2014. (Core Concepts Ser.). (Illus.). 96p. (YA). (gr. 7-12). 35.60 *(978-1-4777-7754-1(7))* Rosen Publishing Group, Inc., The.
Eason, Sarah. How Does a Car Work? 2010. (How Does It Work? Ser.). (Illus.). 32p. (J). (gr. 3-6). pap. 10.50 *(978-1-4339-3463-6(9))*; lib. bdg. 26.00 *(978-1-4339-3462-9(0))* Stevens, Gareth Publishing LLLP. (Gareth Stevens Learning Library).
Gardner, Robert. How Fast Is Fast? Science Projects with Speed. 2015. (Hot Science Experiments Ser.). 48p. (J). (gr. 3-4). 25.27 *(978-0-7660-6615-1(0))* Enslow Pubs., Inc.
—The Physics of Toys & Games Science Projects. 2013. (Exploring Hands-On Science Projects Ser.). 128p. (J). (gr. 5-12). pap. 10.95 *(978-1-4644-0219-7(1))*; lib. bdg. 27.94 *(978-0-7660-4143-1(3))* Enslow Pubs., Inc.
Hoffmann, Sara. Rolling. 2012. (First Step Nonfiction - Balance & Motion Ser.). (ENG., Illus.). 8p. (gr. -1-1). pap. 4.95 *(978-1-4677-0514-1(4)*, Lerner Pubns.) Lerner Publishing Group.
Hoyt, Linda & Therriault, Teresa. Mastering the Mechanics: Ready-to-Use Lessons for Modeled, Guided, & Independent Editing. 2008. (Mastering the Mechanics Ser.). (ENG., Illus.). 192p. (gr. 2-3). pap. 22.99 *(978-0-545-04878-1(8))*; (gr. 4-5). pap. 22.99 *(978-0-545-04879-8(6))* Scholastic, Inc. (Teaching Resources).
Ivancic, Linda. What Is a Wave? 2016. (Unseen Science Ser.). (ENG., Illus.). 32p. (J). (gr. 3-3). pap. 10.58 *(978-1-5026-0917-5(7))* Cavendish Square Publishing.
Kawa, Katie. Loaders. 2011. (Big Machines Ser.). (Illus.). 24p. (gr. k-2). 69.20 *(978-1-4339-6890-7(8))* Stevens, Gareth Publishing LLLP.
Kraul, Walter. Earth, Water, Fire & Air: Playful Explorations in the Four Elements, 1 vol. Maclean, Donald, tr. from GER. 3rd rev. ed. 2010. Orig. Title: Spielen mit Wasser und Luft & Spielen mit Feuer und Erde. (ENG., Illus.). 104p. (J). (gr. 1-7). pap. 25.00 *(978-0-86315-768-4(8))* Floris Bks. GBR. Dist: SteinerBooks, Inc.
Mara, Wil. How Do Waves Form? 2010. (Tell Me Why, Tell Me How 4 Ser.). 32p. (gr. 3-5). 29.93 *(978-0-7614-4829-7(2))* Marshall Cavendish Corp.
Mechanik I: Bewegungslehre. (Duden Abiturhilfen Ser.). (GER.). 96p. (YA). (gr. 11). *(978-3-411-04451-1(9))* Bibliographisches Institut & F. A. Brockhaus AG DEU. Dist: International Bk. Import Service, Inc.
Mechanik II: Erhaltungssaetze. (Duden Abiturhilfen Ser.). (GER.). 96p. (YA). (gr. 11). *(978-3-411-05181-6(7))* Bibliographisches Institut & F. A. Brockhaus AG DEU. Dist: International Bk. Import Service, Inc.
Miller, Malinda. Modern Mechanics: Maintaining Tomorrow's Green Vehicles. 2010. (New Careers for the 21st Century Ser.). (Illus.). 64p. (YA). (gr. 7-18). lib. bdg. 22.95 *(978-1-4222-1818-1(X))* Mason Crest.
Paris, Stephanie. ¡Brumm! Velocidad y Aceleración. 2016. (TIME for Kids en Español - Level 5 Ser.). (SPA.). 64p. (gr. 5-5). lib. bdg. 31.99 *(978-1-5157-2932-7(X))* Time for Kids Inc AUS. Dist: Capstone Pub.
Randolph, Joanne. Gears in My World. 2007. (Journeys Ser.). (ENG.). 24p. (gr. k-8). pap. 7.05 *(978-1-4042-8423-4(0)*, Rosen Classroom) Rosen Publishing Group, Inc., The.
Somervill, Barbara A. Speed & Acceleration, 1 vol. 2010. (Measure It! Ser.). (ENG., Illus.). 32p. (gr. 3-6). 33.32 *(978-1-4329-3764-5(2))*; pap. 8.29 *(978-1-4329-3770-6(7))* Heinemann-Raintree. (Heinemann InfoSearch).
Sootin, Harry. Experiments with MacHines & Matter. Aloise, Frank, illus. 2012. 96p. 38.95 *(978-1-258-23744-8(X))*; pap. 23.95 *(978-1-258-24341-8(5))* Literary Licensing, LLC.
Walker, Sally M. & Feldmann, Roseann. Tornillos. King, Andy, photos by. 2005. (Libros de Física para Madrugadores (Early Bird Physics) Ser.). (SPA & ENG., Illus.). 48p. (gr. 3-6). lib. bdg. 26.60 *(978-0-8225-2974-3(2)*, Ediciones Lerner) Lerner Publishing Group.
Walker, Sally M., et al. Work. 2005. (Early Bird Physics Ser.). (Illus.). 48p. (gr. 3-6). lib. bdg. 25.26 *(978-0-8225-2217-1(9))* Lerner Publishing Group.
Wells, Robert E. How Do You Lift a Lion? 2012. (J). 34.28 *(978-1-61913-159-0(5))* Weigl Pubs., Inc.

MECHANICS (PERSONS)

Ferguson. Careers in Focus: Mechanics. 3rd rev. ed. 2008. (Careers in Focus Ser.). 202p. (gr. 6-12). 32.95 *(978-0-8160-7275-0(2)*, Ferguson Publishing Co.) Facts On File, Inc.
Liebman, Dan. I Want to Be a Mechanic. 2003. (I Want to Be Ser.). (ENG., Illus.). 24p. (J). (gr. -1-2). pap. 3.99 *(978-1-55297-693-7(9)*, 9781552976937) Firefly Bks., Ltd.
Liebman, Daniel & Liebman, Dan. I Want to Be a Mechanic. 2003. (I Want to Be Ser.). (ENG., Illus.). 24p. (J). (gr. -1-2). 14.95 *(978-1-55297-695-1(5)*, 9781552976951) Firefly Bks., Ltd.
—Quiero Ser Mecanico. 2003. (Quiero Ser.). (SPA., Illus.). 24p. (J). (gr. -1-2). pap. 5.99 *(978-1-55297-728-6(5)*, 9781552977286) Firefly Bks., Ltd.
Marsico, Katie. Auto Technician. 2010. (21st Century Skills Library: Cool Careers Ser.). (ENG.). 32p. (gr. 4-8). lib. bdg. 28.50 *(978-1-60279-937-0(7)*, 200619) Cherry Lake Publishing.
Rogers, Kate. Mechanics, 01 vols., 1. 2016. (Hands-On Jobs Ser.). (ENG., Illus.). 24p. (J). pap. 8.25 *(978-1-5081-4367-3(6)*, PowerKids Pr.) Rosen Publishing Group, Inc., The.

MEDAL OF HONOR

Collier, Peter. Choosing Courage: Inspiring Stories of What It Means to Be a Hero. (ENG., Illus.). (J). 2016. 272p. (gr. 4-6). pap. 8.95 *(978-1-57965-705-5(2))* 2015. 240p. 18.95 *(978-1-57965-596-9(3))* Artisan.
Mikaelian, Allen & Wallace, Mike. Medal of Honor: Profiles of America's Military Heroes from the Civil War to the Present. 2003. (ENG.). 336p. (gr. 8-17). pap. 20.99 *(978-0-7868-8576-3(9))* Hyperion Pr.
Stevens, Paul D., ed. The Congressional Medal of Honor: The Names, the Deeds. 2003. (Illus.). 1105p. 27.50 *(978-0-918495-01-3(6))* Sharp & Dunnigan.

MEDICAL BOTANY

see Botany, Medical

MEDICAL CENTERS

see also Hospitals

Smith, Ian. First Experiences: Going to the Doctor. 2004. (QEB Start Talking Ser.). (Illus.). 24p. (J). lib. bdg. 15.95 *(978-1-59566-003-9(8))* QEB Publishing Inc.

MEDICAL ELECTRONICS

Moe, Barbara. The Revolution in Medical Imaging. 2009. (Library of Future Medicine Ser.). 64p. (gr. 5-5). 58.50 *(978-1-60853-634-4(3))* Rosen Publishing Group, Inc., The.

MEDICAL PROFESSION

see Medicine; Physicians

MEDICAL RESEARCH

see Medicine—Research

MEDICAL TECHNOLOGY

Allen, John. How Gene Therapy Is Changing Society. 2015. (ENG., Illus.). 80p. (J). mass mkt. *(978-1-60152-898-8(1))* ReferencePoint Pr., Inc.
Allman, Toney. Cutting Edge Medical Technology. 2016. (ENG.). 80p. (YA). (gr. 5-12). lib. bdg. *(978-1-68282-042-1(4))* ReferencePoint Pr., Inc.
Bailey, Diane. Biomedical Engineers!, Vol. 10. 2015. (Scientists in Action Ser.). (Illus.). 48p. (J). (gr. 5). 20.95 *(978-1-4222-3420-4(7))* Mason Crest.
Balien, Karen Gunnison. Seven Wonders of Medicine. 2010. (Seven Wonders Ser.). (YA). (gr. 5-9). lib. bdg. 33.26 *(978-0-7613-4239-7(7))* Twenty First Century Bks.
Bickerstaff, Linda. Technology & Infertility: Assisted Reproduction & Modern Society. 2009. (Science & Society Ser.). 64p. (gr. 5-6). 58.50 *(978-1-60853-011-3(6))*; (Illus.). (YA). (gr. 7-12). lib. bdg. 31.95 *(978-1-4358-5024-8(6))* Rosen Publishing Group, Inc., The.
Boudreau, Hélène. Miraculous Medicines. 2008. (ENG., Illus.). 32p. (J). (gr. 3-7). lib. bdg. *(978-0-7787-4168-8(0))* Crabtree Publishing Co.
Bryant, Jill. Medical Inventions: The Best of Health. 2013. (ENG., Illus.). 48p. (J). *(978-0-7787-0212-2(X))*; (gr. 4-8). pap. *(978-0-7787-0232-0(4))* Crabtree Publishing Co.
Carr, Denis. The 10 Most Significant Medical Breakthroughs. 2008. 14.99 *(978-1-55448-491-1(X))* Scholastic Library Publishing.
Faust, Daniel R. Medical Robots. 2016. (Robots & Robotics Ser.). 32p. (J). (gr. 5-5). pap. 11.75 *(978-1-4994-2175-0(3)*, PowerKids Pr.) Rosen Publishing Group, Inc., The.
Gardner, Jane P. Health Science, Vol. 11. Lewin, Russ, ed. 2015. (Science 24/7 Ser.). (Illus.). 48p. (J). (gr. 5). 20.95 *(978-1-4222-3411-2(8))* Mason Crest.
Hagler, Gina. Careers As a First Responder. 2012. (Essential Careers Ser.). (ENG., Illus.). 80p. (YA). (gr. 7-12). lib. bdg. 33.25 *(978-1-4488-8234-2(6))* Rosen Publishing Group, Inc., The.
Higgins, Nadia. Medical Robots. 2017. (Robotics in Our World Ser.). (ENG.). 32p. (gr. 1-4). 20.95 *(978-1-68151-143-6(6))* Amicus Publishing.
Jacobson, Ryan. Marvelous Medical Inventions. 2013. (Awesome Inventions You Use Every Day Ser.). (ENG., Illus.). 32p. (gr. 3-6). lib. bdg. 26.60 *(978-1-4677-1095-4(4)*, Lerner Pubns.) Lerner Publishing Group.
Kenney, Karen Latchana. What Makes Medical Technology Safer? 2015. (ENG., Illus.). 32p. (gr. 4-6). (J). 26.65 *(978-1-4677-7916-6(4))*; 26.65 *(978-1-4677-8651-5(9))* Lerner Publishing Group. (Lerner Pubns.).
Kopp, Megan. Bionic Bodies. 2017. (Illus.). 32p. (J). ***(978-0-7787-3584-7(2))*** Crabtree Publishing Co.
Kroll, Jennifer. A la Vanguardia: Adelantos en Tecnología. 2016. (TIME for Kids en Español - Level 5 Ser.). (SPA.). 64p. (gr. 5-5). lib. bdg. 31.99 *(978-1-5157-2927-3(3))* Time for Kids Inc AUS. Dist: Capstone Pub.
Latta, Sara L. Zoom in on Medical Robots. 2017. (J). ***(978-0-7660-9228-0(3))*** Enslow Pubs., Inc.
McFadzean, Lesley. Technology & Treatments. 2012. (Discovery Education: Technology Ser.). (ENG., Illus.). 32p. (J). (gr. 3-6). 25.25 *(978-1-4488-7886-4(1))*; pap. 10.00 *(978-1-4488-7968-7(X))* Rosen Publishing Group, Inc., The. (PowerKids Pr.).
Merino, Noel. Genetic Engineering. 2013. (Opposing Viewpoints Ser.). (ENG., Illus.). 224p. (gr. 10-12). pap. 33.80 *(978-0-7377-6425-3(2)*, Greenhaven Pr., Inc.) Cengage Gale.
Merino, No'l, ed. Genetic Engineering. 2013. (Opposing Viewpoints Ser.). (ENG., Illus.). 224p. (gr. 10-12). lib. bdg. 48.80 *(978-0-7377-6424-6(4)*, Greenhaven Pr., Inc.) Cengage Gale.
Moe, Barbara. The Revolution in Medical Imaging. (Library of Future Medicine Ser.). 64p. 2009. (gr. 5-5). 58.50 *(978-1-60853-634-4(3))* 2005. (Illus.). (YA). (gr. 7-12). lib. bdg. 31.95 *(978-0-8239-3672-4(4))* Rosen Publishing Group, Inc., The.
Mooney, Carla. Medical Technology & Engineering. 2012. (ENG.). 48p. (gr. 4-6). pap. 10.95 *(978-1-61810-256-0(7))* Rourke Educational Media.
—Wearable Robots. 2016. (Tech Bytes Ser.). (ENG.). 48p. (J). (gr. 4-6). pap. 13.26 *(978-1-60357-868-4(4))*; (Illus.). lib. bdg. 26.60 *(978-1-59953-760-3(5))* Norwood Hse. Pr.
Morrison, Heather S. Inventors of Health & Medical Technology. 2015. (Designing Engineering Solutions Ser.). (ENG., Illus.). 144p. (J). (gr. 8-8). 42.79 *(978-1-5026-0658-7(5))* Cavendish Square Publishing.
Newquist, H. P. & Wells, Rosemary. The Human Body. 2015. (Smithsonian: Invention & Impact Ser.: 1). (ENG., Illus.). 112p. (J). (gr. 3-7). bds. 18.99 *(978-0-451-47643-2(3)*, Viking Books for Young Readers) Penguin Young Readers Group.
Noll, Elizabeth. Medical Robots. 2017. (World of Robots Ser.). (ENG., Illus.). 32p. (J). (gr. 3-8). lib. bdg. 26.95 ***(978-1-62617-689-8(2)***, Blastoff! Discovery) Bellwether Media.
Rooney, Anne. Machines in Medicine. 2007. (Cutting Edge Medicine Ser.). (Illus.). 64p. (gr. 6-12). lib. bdg. 34.00 *(978-0-8368-7867-7(1)*, Gareth Stevens Secondary Library) Stevens, Gareth Publishing LLLP.
Sheen, Barbara. Artificial Eyes. 2016. (Tech Bytes Ser.). (ENG., Illus.). 48p. (J). (gr. 4-6). lib. bdg. 26.60 *(978-1-59953-761-0(3))* Norwood Hse. Pr.
Sjonger, Rebecca. Biomedical Engineering & Human Body Systems. 2015. (ENG., Illus.). 32p. (J). *(978-0-7787-7505-8(4))* Crabtree Publishing Co.
Snedden, Robert. Medical Technology. 2009. (New Technology Ser.). (YA). (gr. 7-12). 34.25 *(978-1-59920-164-1(X))* Black Rabbit Bks.
—Medical Technology. 2010. (New Technology Ser.). (ENG., Illus.). 48p. (J). 23.99 *(978-0-237-53427-1(4))* Evans Brothers, Ltd. GBR. Dist: Independent Pubs. Group.
Solway, Andrew. Seeing Inside the Body. 2007. (Cutting Edge Medicine Ser.). (Illus.). 64p. (gr. 6-12). lib. bdg. 34.00 *(978-0-8368-7869-1(8)*, Gareth Stevens Secondary Library) Stevens, Gareth Publishing LLLP.
Steffens, Bradley. Biomedical Engineer. 2017. (ENG.). 64p. (YA). (gr. 5-12). ***(978-1-68282-178-7(1))*** ReferencePoint Pr., Inc.
Strange, Cordelia. Medical Technicians: Health-Care Support for the 21st Century. 2010. (New Careers for the 21st Century Ser.). 64p. (YA). (gr. 7-18). pap. 9.95 *(978-1-4222-2038-2(9))* Mason Crest.
Thompson, Tamara. Expanding the Human Lifespan. Greenhaven Press Editors, ed. 2013. (At Issue Ser.). (ENG.). 128p. (gr. 10-12). 39.40 *(978-0-7377-6836-7(3)*, Greenhaven Pr., Inc.) Cengage Gale.
Vaughan, Jenny. Making New Life. 2010. (J). 34.25 *(978-1-59920-318-8(9))* Black Rabbit Bks.
Williams, Kara. Fertility Technology: The Baby Debate. 2003. (Focus on Science & Society Ser.). (Illus.). 64p. (YA). (gr. 4-6). lib. bdg. 26.50 *(978-0-8239-3210-8(9)*, FSFETE) Rosen Publishing Group, Inc., The.
World Book, Inc. Staff, contrib. by. Leeches to Lasers: A Timeline of Medicine. 2016. (J). *(978-0-7166-3542-0(9))* World Bk.-Childcraft International.
World Book, Inc Staff, contrib. by. Medicine. 2009. *(978-0-7166-0384-9(5))* World Bk., Inc.

MEDICAL TECHNOLOGY—VOCATIONAL GUIDANCE

Bryan, Nichol. Paramedics, 1 vol. 2003. (Everyday Heroes Ser.). (ENG., Illus.). 32p. (gr. k-6). 27.07 *(978-1-57765-856-6(6)*, Checkerboard Library) ABDO Publishing Co.

MEDICI, LORENZO DE', 1449-1492

Hancock, Lee. Lorenzo de' Medici: Florence's Great Leader & Patron of the Arts. (Rulers, Scholars, & Artists of the Renaissance Ser.). 112p. 2009. (gr. 5-8). 66.50 *(978-1-60852-942-1(8)*, Rosen Reference) 2004. (Illus.). (J). lib. bdg. 34.60 *(978-1-4042-0315-0(X))* Rosen Publishing Group, Inc., The.

MEDICINAL PLANTS

see Botany, Medical

MEDICINE

see also Anatomy; Bacteriology; Botany, Medical; Health; Hospitals; Hypnotism; Materia Medica; Mind and Body; Nursing; Pathology; Pharmacy; Physiology also headings beginning with the word Medical

ABDO Publishing Company Staff. Medical Marvels. 2013. (Medical Marvels Ser.: 6). (ENG.). 112p. (J). (gr. 6-12). lib. bdg. 213.84 *(978-1-61783-899-6(3)*, Essential Library) ABDO Publishing Co.

MNO

Abramavitz. Online Privacy & Healthcare. 2014. (Privacy in the Online World). (ENG., Illus.). 80p. (YA). lib. bdg. *(978-1-60152-652-6(0))* ReferencePoint Pr., Inc.

Anderson, Catherine Corley. John F. Kennedy. 2005. (Just the Facts Biographies Ser.). (ENG., Illus.). 112p. (gr. 5-12). lib. bdg. 27.93 *(978-0-8225-2643-8(3)*, Lerner Pubns.) Lerner Publishing Group.

Anderson, Sheila. Clinic. 2008. pap. 22.95 *(978-0-8225-9370-6(X))*; (ENG.). 8p. (gr. -1-1). pap. 4.95 *(978-0-8225-8840-5(4))* Lerner Publishing Group.

Bayden, Maya. Medical Science, 1 vol., 1. 2016. (Study of Science Ser.). (ENG.). 96p. (J). (gr. 8-8). lib. bdg. 36.25 *(978-1-68048-229-4(7)*, Britannica Educational Publishing) Rosen Publishing Group, Inc., The.

Bayden, Maya, ed. Medical Science. 2016. (Study of Science Ser.). 96p. (gr. 8-8). 72.50 *(978-1-68048-228-7(9)*, Britannica Educational Publishing) Rosen Publishing Group, Inc., The.

Benchmark Education Company. Fighting Disease (Teacher Guide) 2005. *(978-1-4108-4657-0(1))* Benchmark Education Co.

Billitteri, Thomas J. & Davis, Catherine. Alternative Medicine. 2012. (USA TODAY Health Reports: Diseases & Disorders Ser.). (ENG.). 112p. (gr. 6-12). lib. bdg. 34.60 *(978-0-7613-8145-7(7))* Lerner Publishing Group.

Blount, Rachel. Paramedic. 2017. (Here to Help Ser.). (ENG., Illus.). 24p. (J). (gr. k-2). 16.99 *(978-1-4451-4014-8(4)*, Franklin Watts) Hachette Children's Group GBR. Dist: Hachette Bk. Group.

Boring, Mel & Dendy, Leslie. Guinea Pig Scientists. Mordan, C. B., illus. 2014. (ENG.). 224p. (J). (gr. 5-12). pap. 12.99 *(978-1-250-05065-6(0)*, 9781250050656) Square Fish.

Boudreau, Hélène. Miraculous Medicines. 2008. (ENG., Illus.). 32p. (J). (gr. 3-7). pap. *(978-0-7787-4175-6(3))* Crabtree Publishing Co.

Bredeson, Carmen. Don't Let the Barber Pull Your Teeth: Could You Survive Medieval Medicine? Kelley, Gerald, illus. 2011. (Ye Yucky Middle Ages Ser.). 48p. (J). (gr. 5-18). pap. 8.95 *(978-1-59845-373-7(4))*; (gr. 7-12). lib. bdg. 25.27 *(978-0-7660-3693-2(6))* Enslow Pubs., Inc.

Brill, Marlene Targ. Doctors. (Pull Ahead Bks.). (Illus.). 32p. (J). 2005. lib. bdg. 22.60 *(978-0-8225-1689-7(6))* 2004. pap. 5.95 *(978-0-8225-2531-8(3)*, Lerner Pubns.) Lerner Publishing Group.

Bryan, Dale-Marie. Living with Celiac Disease, 1 vol. 2012. (Living with Health Challenges Set 1 Ser.). (ENG.). 112p. (J). (gr. 6-12). lib. bdg. 35.64 *(978-1-61783-125-6(5)*, Essential Library) ABDO Publishing Co.

Burgan, Michael. Medicine & Health Care, Vol. 10. 2016. (Stem in Current Events Ser.). (Illus.). 64p. (J). (gr. 7). 23.95 *(978-1-4222-3594-2(7))* Mason Crest.

Burstein, John. The Exciting Endocrine System: How Do My Glands Work? 2009. (Slim Goodbody's Body Buddies Ser.). (ENG., Illus.). 32p. (J). (gr. 3-5). pap. *(978-0-7787-4432-0(9))* Crabtree Publishing Co.

Carlson, Dale. ¿Adonde Vamos? Dentro y Fuera de tu mente. Guix, Joan Carles, tr. from ENG. Nicklaus, Carol, illus. 2004.Tr. of In & Out of your Mind. Where are we Going? (SPA.). 64p. *(978-84-9754-117-6(0)*, 88303) Ediciones Oniro S.A.

Chancellor, Deborah. Ambulance Rescue. 2013. (Emergency Vehicles Ser.). 24p. (gr. k-3). 28.50 *(978-1-59920-888-6(1))* Black Rabbit Bks.

Chandler, Alton. A Salute to African American in Medicine: Learning. Chapman, L., ed. Still, Wayne A., illus. 24p. (Orig.). (J). (gr. 3-8). pap. 1.75 *(978-1-877804-17-5(7))* Chandler/White Publishing Co.

Chilman-Blair, Kim. Superheroes on a Medical Mission, 6 vols., Set. Incl. "What's up with Bill?" Medikidz Explain Epilepsy. Taddeo, John. lib. bdg. 29.25 *(978-1-4358-3533-7(6))*; "What's up with David?" Medikidz Explain Food Allergies. Taddeo, John. lib. bdg. 29.25 *(978-1-4358-3537-5(9)*, Rosen Reference); "What's up with Ella?" Medikidz Explain Diabetes. Taddeo, John. lib. bdg. 29.25 *(978-1-4358-3538-2(7)*, Rosen Reference); "What's up with Max?" Medikidz Explain Asthma. Taddeo, John. lib. bdg. 29.25 *(978-1-4358-3534-4(4)*, Rosen Reference); What's up with Pam? Medikidz Explain Childhood Obesity. Taddeo, John. lib. bdg. 29.25 *(978-1-4358-3535-1(2)*, Rosen Reference); "What's up with Sean?" Medikidz Explain Scoliosis. Taddeo, Sean & Noordeen, Hilali. lib. bdg. 29.25 *(978-1-4358-3536-8(0)*, Rosen Reference); (YA). (gr. 5-8). (Illus.). 40p. 2010. Set lib. bdg. 175.50 *(978-1-4358-9423-5(5)*, Rosen Reference) Rosen Publishing Group, Inc., The.

Chmielewski, Gary. The Medical Zone: Jokes, Riddles, Tongue Twisters & Daffynitions. Caputo, Jim, illus. rev. ed. 2009. (Funny Zone Ser.). (ENG.). 24p. (J). (gr. 2-4). lib. bdg. 22.60 *(978-1-59953-299-8(9))* Norwood Hse. Pr.

Cobb, Allan B. First Responders. (Extreme Careers Ser.). 64p. 2009. (gr. 5-5). 58.50 *(978-1-61512-393-3(8)*, Rosen Reference) 2007. (Illus.). (J). (gr. 3-7). lib. bdg. 26.50 *(978-1-4042-0944-2(1))* Rosen Publishing Group, Inc., The.

Cox, Judith. The Wellness Tree. Rogers, Denny, illus. 2003. (ENG.). 32p. (J). (gr. k-4). 19.95 *(978-1-878044-29-7(X))* Mayhaven Publishing, Inc.

Crabtree, Marc. Meet My Neighbor, the Doctor. 2013. (ENG., Illus.). 24p. (J). *(978-0-7787-0871-1(3))*; pap. *(978-0-7787-0875-9(6))* Crabtree Publishing Co.

Davies, Gill. The Illustrated Timeline of Medicine. 2011. (History Timelines Ser.). (Illus.). 226p. (YA). (gr. 7-12). lib. bdg. 50.60 *(978-1-4488-4796-9(6))* Rosen Publishing Group, Inc., The.

Dawson, Ian. Prehistoric & Egyptian Medicine. 2005. (ENG., Illus.). 64p. (J). (gr. 4). 19.95 *(978-1-59270-035-6(7))* Enchanted Lion Bks., LLC.

Dawson, Patricia. A Doctor's Job. 2014. (Community Workers Ser.). 24p. (J). (gr. k-2). pap. 8.22 *(978-1-62712-991-6(X))*; lib. bdg. 24.21 *(978-1-62712-990-9(1))* Cavendish Square Publishing.

Dittmer, Lori. The Future of Medicine. 2012. (What's Next? Ser.). (Illus.). 48p. (J). (gr. 5-12). 23.95 *(978-1-60818-222-0(3)*, Creative Education) Creative Co., The.

Donovan, Sandy. Does It Really Take Seven Years to Digest Swallowed Gum? And Other Questions You've Always Wanted to Ask. 2010. (Is That a Fact? Ser.). (ENG., Illus.). 40p. (J). (gr. 4-6). lib. bdg. 26.60 *(978-0-8225-9085-9(9)*, 1306473) Lerner Publishing Group.

Ebner, Aviva. Health Science Experiments. 2011. (Experiments for Future Scientists Ser.). (Illus.). 160p. (gr. 5-8). 35.00 *(978-1-60413-853-5(X))* Facts On File, Inc.

Edwards, Hazel & Alexander, Goldie. Talking about Illnesses. 2010. (Healthy Living Ser.). (Illus.). 32p. (YA). (gr. 3-6). lib. bdg. 26.00 *(978-1-4339-3657-9(7))* Stevens, Gareth Publishing LLLP.

Elliott, Lynne. Medieval Medicine & the Plague. 2005. (Medieval World Ser.). (ENG., Illus.). 32p. (J). (gr. 5-9). lib. bdg. *(978-0-7787-1358-6(X))* Crabtree Publishing Co.

Ellis, Catherine. Cars & Trucks. 2007. (Mega Military Machines Ser.). (Illus.). 24p. (J). (gr. 3-7). lib. bdg. 22.60 *(978-1-4042-3669-1(4))* Rosen Publishing Group, Inc., The.

Engdahl, Sylvia, ed. Alternative Therapies. 2011. (Current Controversies Ser.). 240p. pap. 28.45 *(978-0-7377-5611-1(X)*, Greenhaven Pr., Inc.) Cengage Gale.

Espejo, Roman. Should Vaccinations Be Mandatory? Gale, G., ed. 2014. (At Issue Ser.). (ENG.). 128p. (gr. 10-12). lib. bdg. 39.40 *(978-0-7377-6862-6(2)*, Greenhaven Pr., Inc.) Cengage Gale.

Etingoff, Kim. Women in Medicine. Karlon, Ann Lee, ed. 2013. (Major Women in Science Ser.: 10). 64p. (J). (gr. 7-18). 22.95 *(978-1-4222-2929-3(7))* Mason Crest.

Evans, Michael. The Adventures of Medical Man: Kids' Illnesses & Injuries Explained. Williams, Gareth, illus. 2010. (ENG.). 72p. (J). (gr. 3-5). 21.95 *(978-1-55451-263-8(8)*, 9781554512638); pap. 12.95 *(978-1-55451-262-1(X)*, 9781554512621) Annick Pr., Ltd. CAN. Dist: Publishers Group West (PGW).

Faison, Ashley Starr & Ackerman, Bettie Bennett. The Garden of Hope: A Story about the Hospice Experience. 2005. (Illus.). (J). *(978-0-9774691-0-9(7))* Hospice & Community Care Pubns.

Freedman, Jeri. Careers in Women's Health. 2017. (J). ***(978-1-5383-8158-8(3)***, Rosen Young Adult) Rosen Publishing Group, Inc., The.

Freedman, Jeri. Professional Wrestling: Steroids in & Out of the Ring. 2009. (Disgraced! the Dirty History of Performance-Enhancing Drugs in Sports Ser.). (Illus.). 48p. (YA). (gr. 5-9). 29.25 *(978-1-4358-5305-8(9))* Rosen Publishing Group, Inc., The.

Gardner, Jane P. Health Science, Vol. 11. Lewin, Russ, ed. 2015. (Science 24/7 Ser.). (Illus.). 48p. (J). (gr. 5). 20.95 *(978-1-4222-3411-2(8))* Mason Crest.

Gardner, Robert & Conklin, Joshua. Experiments for Future Doctors. 2016. (Experiments for Future STEM Professionals Ser.). 128p. (J). (gr. 6-6). 37.27 *(978-0-7660-7854-3(X))* Enslow Pubs., Inc.

Geis, Patricia. Let's Get Well! Folch, Sergio, illus. 2009. (Good Habits with Coco & Tula Ser.). 16p. (J). (gr. -1-k). bds. 11.40 *(978-1-60754-407-4(5))* Windmill Bks.

Giddens, Sandra. Everything You Need to Know about Crohn's Disease & Ulcerative Colitis. 2009. (Need to Know Library). 64p. (gr. 5-5). 58.50 *(978-1-60854-061-7(8))* Rosen Publishing Group, Inc., The.

Goldish, Meish. Doctors to the Rescue. 2011. (Work of Heroes: First Responders in Action Ser.). 32p. (YA). (gr. 1-4). lib. bdg. 25.27 *(978-1-61772-285-1(5))* Bearport Publishing Co., Inc.

Gordon, Sharon. What's Inside an Ambulance? 2007. (J). pap. 6.99 *(978-0-7614-3343-9(0))* Marshall Cavendish Corp.

Gorman, Jacqueline Laks. Doctors. 2010. (People in My Community Ser.). (ENG.). 24p. (J). (gr. k-3). pap. 8.15 *(978-1-4339-3804-7(9))*; lib. bdg. 22.60 *(978-1-4339-3803-0(0))* Stevens, Gareth Publishing LLLP.

Gow, Mary. The Greatest Doctor of Ancient Times: Hippocrates & His Oath. 2009. (Great Minds of Ancient Science & Math Ser.). (Illus.). 128p. (J). (gr. 4-7). lib. bdg. 33.27 *(978-0-7660-3118-0(7))* Enslow Pubs., Inc.

Gray, Leon. Dirty Bombs & Shell Shock: Biology Goes to War. 2017. (STEM on the Battlefield Ser.). (ENG., Illus.). 48p. (J). (gr. 4-6). 31.99 ***(978-1-5124-3928-1(2))*** Lerner Publishing Group.

Gray, Susan H. Artificial Limbs. 2008. (21st Century Skills Innovation Library: Innovation in Medicine Ser.). (ENG., Illus.). 32p. (gr. 4-8). lib. bdg. 28.50 *(978-1-60279-229-6(1)*, 200160) Cherry Lake Publishing.

Greenhaven Press Editors & Haugen, David M. Alternative Medicine. Zott, Lynn, ed. 2012. (Opposing Viewpoints Ser.). (ENG., Illus.). 224p. (gr. 10-12). pap. 33.80 *(978-0-7377-5439-1(7))*; lib. bdg. 48.80 *(978-0-7377-5438-4(9))* Cengage Gale. (Greenhaven Pr., Inc.).

Gregory, Josh. Sports Medicine: Science, Technology, & Engineering. 2016. (Calling All Innovators: a Career for You Ser.). (ENG., Illus.). 64p. (J). lib. bdg. 32.00 *(978-0-531-23004-6(X)*, Children's Pr.) Scholastic Library Publishing.

—What Do They Do? Doctors. 2010. (Community Connections: What Do They Do? Ser.). (ENG.). 24p. (gr. 2-5). lib. bdg. 25.64 *(978-1-60279-805-2(2)*, 200500) Cherry Lake Publishing.

Greve, Tom. Emt: Crisis Care for Injuries & Illness. 2014. (ENG.). 32p. (gr. 4-8). 32.79 *(978-1-62717-651-4(9))* Rourke Educational Media.

Hapka, Cathy, pseud. My Little Doctor Bag Book. Sharp, Paul, illus. 2005. (J). *(978-1-57151-754-8(5))* Playhouse Publishing.

HarrisNic. MEDICINE: OLD AND NEW LOW INTERMEDIATE BOOK WITH ONLINE ACCESS. 2014. (ENG., Illus.). 24p. (J). pap. 9.50 *(978-1-107-65866-0(7))* Cambridge Univ. Pr.

Harrison, Lorraine. Doctors on the Job. 2017. (Jobs in Our Community Ser.). 24p. (J). (gr. k-k). pap. 49.50 *(978-1-5345-2138-4(0))*; (gr. 1-1). 24.60 *(978-1-5345-2139-1(9))*; (gr. 1-1). pap. 8.25 *(978-1-5345-2137-7(2))* Cengage Gale.

Hersh, Iffy. Mommy Is an Histologist. (What Does Mommy Do? Ser.). (Illus.). (Orig.). (J). (gr. k-2). pap. 10.00 *(978-0-936735-04-7(X))* Grove Educational Technologies.

Horn, Geoffrey M. Sports Therapist. 2008. (Cool Careers Ser.). 32p. (gr. 5-8). pap. 10.50 *(978-0-8368-9329-8(8))*; lib. bdg. 26.00 *(978-0-8368-9196-6(1))* Stevens, Gareth Publishing LLLP.

Huffman, Julie. 101 Ways to Gross Out Your Friends. Paillot, Jim, illus. 2017. (101 Ser.). (ENG.). 144p. (J). (gr. 3-5). 33.32 *(978-1-942875-16-1(9))* Quarto Publishing Group USA.

Human Relations Media, prod. Clued in! on Medicines. 2005. (ENG.). (J). pap. 4.95 *(978-1-55548-149-0(3))* Human Relations Media.

Hunsaker, Jennifer. Respiratory Therapists. 2017. (Careers in Healthcare Ser.: Vol. 13). (ENG.). (YA). (gr. 7-12). 23.95 ***(978-1-4222-3805-9(9))*** Mason Crest.

—Ultrasound Technicians. 2017. (Careers in Healthcare Ser.: Vol. 13). (ENG.). (YA). (gr. 7-12). 23.95 ***(978-1-4222-3807-3(5))*** Mason Crest.

Iserson, Kenneth V. Get into Medical School! A Guide for the Perplexed. 2nd ed. 2004. (Illus.). 512p. (Orig.). pap. 36.95 *(978-1-883620-31-8(7))* Galen Pr., Ltd.

Jankowski, Connie. Hippocrates: Making the Way for Medicine, 1 vol. 2007. (Science Readers Ser.). (ENG.). 32p. (J). (gr. 3-3). pap. 8.99 *(978-0-7439-0596-1(2))* Shell Educational Publishing.

Jerome, Kate Boehm & National Geographic Learning Staff. Fighting Disease. 2007. (Rise & Shine Ser.). (ENG., Illus.). 32p. (J). pap. 17.95 *(978-0-7922-8865-7(3))* CENGAGE Learning.

Kavanaugh, Beatrice. Medical Discoveries. 2017. (Illus.). 80p. (J). ***(978-1-4222-3710-6(9))*** Mason Crest.

Kawa, Katie. My First Trip to the Doctor / Mi Primera Visita Al MéDico. 2012. (My First Adventures / Mis primeras aventuras Ser.). (ENG & SPA., Illus.). 24p. (J). (gr. k-2). 22.60 *(978-1-4339-6629-3(8))* Stevens, Gareth Publishing LLLP.

Kelley, K. C. & Buckley, James. Paramedic, Vol. 12. 2015. (On a Mission Ser.). (Illus.). 48p. (J). (gr. 5). 20.95 *(978-1-4222-3398-6(7))* Mason Crest.

Kidd, Renee A. Potent Natural Medicines: Mother Nature's Pharmacy. 2005. (Science & Society Ser.). (Illus.). 176p. (gr. 6-12). 35.00 *(978-0-8160-5607-1(2))* Facts On File, Inc.

Kopp, Megan. Bionic Bodies. 2017. (Illus.). 32p. (J). ***(978-0-7787-3584-7(2))*** Crabtree Publishing Co.

Kummer, Patricia K. Sports Medicine Doctor. 2008. (21st Century Skills Library: Cool Careers Ser.). (ENG.). 32p. (gr. 4-8). lib. bdg. 28.50 *(978-1-60279-302-6(6)*, 200141) Cherry Lake Publishing.

Labrecque, Ellen. Gertrude B. Elion & Pharmacology. 2017. (21st Century Junior Library: Women Innovators Ser.). (ENG., Illus.). 24p. (J). (gr. 2-5). pap. 12.79 *(978-1-63472-314-5(7)*, 209301) Cherry Lake Publishing.

Langwith, Jacqueline. Alternative Medicine. 2009. (Introducing Issues with Opposing Viewpoints Ser.). (ENG.). 144p. (gr. 10-12). 42.00 *(978-0-7377-4333-3(6)*, Greenhaven Pr., Inc.) Cengage Gale.

Lawrence, Ellen. Poop Cures. 2017. (Scoop on Poop Ser.). (ENG.). (J). (gr. -1-3). lib. bdg. 17.95 ***(978-1-68402-249-6(5))*** Bearport Publishing Co., Inc.

Lew, Kristi. Bat Spit, Maggots, & Other Amazing Medical Wonders, 1 vol. (Nasty (but Useful!) Science Ser.). (ENG.). 32p. (gr. 3-4). 2011. pap. 8.10 *(978-1-4296-6344-1(8))* 2011. pap. 47.70 *(978-1-4296-6470-7(3))* 2010. lib. bdg. 27.32 *(978-1-4296-4537-9(7))* Capstone Press of Coughlan Cos. (Fact Finders).

Libal, Autumn. Drug Therapy & Psychosomatic Disorders. 2003. (Psychiatric Disorders: Drugs & Psychology for the Mind & Bod Ser.). (Illus.). 124p. (YA). (gr. 4-7). pap. 14.95 *(978-1-4222-0397-2(2))* Mason Crest.

Libal, Joyce. Drug Therapy & Mental Disorders Due to a Medical Condition. 2003. (Psychiatric Disorders: Drugs & Psychology for the Mind & Bod Ser.). (Illus.). 126p. (YA). (gr. 8-12). pap. 14.95 *(978-1-4222-0391-0(3))* Mason Crest.

—Mental Disorders Due to a Medical Condition. McDonnell, Mary Ann & Esherick, Donald, eds. 2013. (State of Mental Illness & Its Therapy Ser.: 19). 128p. (J). (gr. 7-18). 24.95 *(978-1-4222-2828-9(2))* Mason Crest.

The Library of Future Medicine. 2005. (Illus.). (gr. 7-12). lib. bdg. 159.00 *(978-0-8239-3902-2(2))* Rosen Publishing Group, Inc., The.

Loh-Hagan, Virginia. Acupuncturist. 2015. (Illus.). 32p. (J). pap. *(978-1-63470-057-3(0))* Cherry Lake Publishing.

Loria, Laura. Poop Medicine. 2017. (J). pap. ***(978-0-7660-9111-5(2))*** Enslow Pubs., Inc.

Lusted, Marcia. Hippocrates. 2017. (Junior Biography From Ancient Civilization Ser.). (gr. 4-6). 29.95 *(978-1-68020-030-0(5))* Mitchell Lane Pubs., Inc.

MacDonald, Fiona. The Plague & Medicine in the Middle Ages. 2005. (World Almanac Library of the Middle Ages). (Illus.). 48p. (gr. 5-12). pap. 14.05 *(978-0-8368-5907-2(3)*, Gareth Stevens Secondary Library) Stevens, Gareth Publishing LLLP.

Marquardt, Meg. Discover Cutting-Edge Medicine. 2016. (Searchlight Books (tm) — What's Cool about Science? Ser.). (ENG., Illus.). 40p. (J). (gr. 3-5). 30.65 *(978-1-5124-0808-9(5))* Lerner Publishing Group.

Mayo Clinic Staff, contrib. by. Alternative Medicine & Your Health. 2004. (Mayo Clinic on Health Ser.). (Illus.). 36,52p. (YA). (gr. 8-18). lib. bdg. 15.95 *(978-1-59084-248-5(0))* Mason Crest.

Meachen Rau, Dana. EMTs. 2007. (Tools We Use Ser.). (Illus.). 32p. (gr. k-2). lib. bdg. 15.95 *(978-0-7614-2660-8(4)*, Benchmark Bks.) Marshall Cavendish Corp.

—EMTs/Los Paramedicos. 2007. (Tools We Use/Instrumentos de Trabajo Ser.). (SPA & ENG., Illus.). 32p. (gr. k-2). lib. bdg. 15.95 *(978-0-7614-2825-1(9)*, Benchmark Bks.) Marshall Cavendish Corp.

—Los Paramedicos. 2007. (Instrumentos de Trabajo Ser.). (SPA & ENG., Illus.). 32p. (gr. k-2). lib. bdg. 15.95 *(978-0-7614-2801-5(1)*, Benchmark Bks.) Marshall Cavendish Corp.

Medical Care. (YA). (gr. 6-12). pap. 10.95 *(978-0-8224-4365-0(1))* Globe Fearon Educational Publishing.

Miller, Debra A. Alternative Therapies. 2008. (Current Controversies Ser.). (ENG., Illus.). 176-240p. (gr. 10-12). 27.50 *(978-0-7377-4129-2(5))*; pap. 39.70 *(978-0-7377-4128-5(7))* Cengage Gale. (Greenhaven Pr., Inc.).

Miracles of Medicine. 2016. (Miracles of Medicine Ser.). 00048p. (J). lib. bdg. 191.70 ***(978-1-4824-6122-0(6))*** Stevens, Gareth Publishing LLLP.

Montgomery, Sharon, text. Your Invisible Bodies: A Reference Book for Children & Adults about Human Energy Fields. 2011. (Illus.). *(978-0-9811089-2-6(X))* Words By Montgomery.

Murphy, Patricia. Everything You Need to Know about Staying in the Hospital. 2009. (Need to Know Library). 64p. (gr. 5-5). 58.50 *(978-1-60854-088-4(X))* Rosen Publishing Group, Inc., The.

Murray, Aaron R. EMTs Help Us. 2012. (All about Community Helpers Ser.). (Illus.). 24p. (J). (gr. -1-1). 22.60 *(978-0-7660-4050-2(X)*, Enslow Elementary) Enslow Pubs., Inc.

Nelson, Kristin L. EMTs. 2005. (Pull Ahead Books: Community Helpers Ser.). (gr. k-3). (ENG.). 32p. pap. 7.95 *(978-0-8225-5475-2(5))*; (Illus.). (J). 22.60 *(978-0-8225-1690-3(X))* Lerner Publishing Group.

Newquist, H. P. & Wells, Rosemary. The Human Body. 2015. (Smithsonian: Invention & Impact Ser.: 1). (ENG., Illus.). 112p. (J). (gr. 3-7). bds. 18.99 *(978-0-451-47643-2(3)*, Viking Books for Young Readers) Penguin Young Readers Group.

Parks, Peggy J. The Dangers of Painkillers. 2016. (ENG.). 80p. (YA). (gr. 5-12). *(978-1-68282-024-7(6))* ReferencePoint Pr., Inc.

Parry, Ann. Doctors Without Borders: Medecins Sans Frontieres. 2005. (Humanitarian Organizations Ser.). (Illus.). 32p. (gr. 5-8). lib. bdg. 25.00 *(978-0-7910-8817-3(0)*, Chelsea Hse.) Facts On File, Inc.

Parsons, Michelle Hyde. Fighting Disease. 2005. (J). pap. *(978-1-4108-4609-9(1))* Benchmark Education Co.

Pearson Learning Staff, creator. A Visit to the Doctor. 2007. (ENG.). (J). (gr. 2-2). pap. 10.92 *(978-0-7652-8602-4(5)*, Celebration Pr.) Pearson Schl.

Peppas, Lynn. Plague! 2013. (ENG.). 48p. (J). *(978-0-7787-1102-5(1))*; pap. *(978-0-7787-1122-3(6))* Crabtree Publishing Co.

Phillips, Hannah. Doctor. 2016. (Here to Help Ser.). (ENG., Illus.). 24p. (J). (gr. k-2). 16.99 *(978-1-4451-3991-3(X)*, Franklin Watts) Hachette Children's Group GBR. Dist: Hachette Bk. Group.

Rajczak, Kristen. Freaky Stories about Our Bodies. 2015. (Freaky True Science Ser.). (ENG.). 32p. (J). (gr. 4-5). 26.60 *(978-1-4824-2962-6(4))* Stevens, Gareth Publishing LLLP.

Ramen, Fred. Albucasis (Abu al-Qasim Al-Zahrawi) Renowned Muslim Surgeon of the Tenth Century. 2009. (Great Muslim Philosophers & Scientists of the Middle Ages Ser.). 112p. (gr. 6-6). 66.50 *(978-1-61513-178-5(7)*, Rosen Reference) Rosen Publishing Group, Inc., The.

—Sleeping Sickness & Other Parasitic Tropical Diseases. 2009. (Epidemics Ser.). 64p. (gr. 5-5). 58.50 *(978-1-61512-301-8(6))* Rosen Publishing Group, Inc., The.

Randolph, Joanne. Ambulances. 2008. (To the Rescue! Ser.). (Illus.). 24p. (J). (gr. 3-7). lib. bdg. 22.60 *(978-1-4042-4150-3(7)*, PowerKids Pr.) Rosen Publishing Group, Inc., The.

—Emergency Helicopters. 2009. (To the Rescue! Ser.). 24p. (gr. 1-1). 42.50 *(978-1-60854-396-0(X)*, PowerKids Pr.) Rosen Publishing Group, Inc., The.

—Emergency Helicopters/Helicopteros de Emergencia. 2009. (To the Rescue! / ¡Al rescate! Ser.). (ENG & SPA.). 24p. (gr. 1-1). 42.50 *(978-1-60854-402-8(8)*, Editorial Buenas Letras) Rosen Publishing Group, Inc., The.

Rau, Dana Meachen. EMTs. 2007. (J). pap. 6.99 *(978-0-7614-3292-0(2))* Marshall Cavendish Corp.

Reeves, Diane Lindsey. Health Sciences. 2017. (Bright Futures Press: World of Work Ser.). (ENG., Illus.). 32p. (J). (gr. 4-7). lib. bdg. 29.93 *(978-1-63472-624-5(3)*, 209530) Cherry Lake Publishing.

Riggs, Kate. Ambulances. 2015. (Illus.). 24p. (J). *(978-1-60818-578-8(8)*, Creative Education) Creative Co., The.

Ringstad, Arnold. Medical Myths, Busted! 2017. (Science Myths, Busted! Ser.). (ENG., Illus.). 32p. (J). (gr. 3-6). 21.95 *(978-1-63235-303-0(2))* Pr. Room Editions LLC.

Rissman, Rebecca. Going to the Doctor: Comparing Past & Present, 1 vol. 2014. (Comparing Past & Present Ser.). (ENG., Illus.). 24p. (gr. -1-1). lib. bdg. 22.65 *(978-1-4329-8992-7(8)*, Acorn) Heinemann-Raintree.

Rivera, Sheila. Doctor. 2005. (First Step Nonfiction - Work People Do Ser.). (ENG.). 8p. (gr. -1-1). pap. 4.95 *(978-0-8225-5357-1(0)*, Lerner Pubns.) Lerner Publishing Group.

Roberts, Russell. Medicine: A Matter of Life & Death, 1 vol. 2014. (History of Science Ser.). (ENG., Illus.). 112p. (YA). (gr. 6-12). lib. bdg. 35.64 *(978-1-62403-563-0(9)*, Essential Library) ABDO Publishing Co.

Romanek, Trudee. Science, Medicine, & Math in the Early Islamic World. 2012. (ENG.). 48p. (J). lib. bdg. *(978-0-7787-2170-3(1))* Crabtree Publishing Co.

Romero, Libby. Discover Medical Chemistry. 2006. (J). pap. *(978-1-4108-6502-1(9))* Benchmark Education Co.

Rooney, Anne. Health & Medicine: The Impact of Science & Technology. 2009. (Pros & Cons Ser.). (ENG.). 64p. (YA). (gr. 5-9). lib. bdg. 35.00 *(978-1-4339-1988-6(5))* Stevens, Gareth Publishing LLLP.

—World after Super-Plague. 2013. (World After Ser.). (ENG.). 56p. (gr. 7-8). pap. 9.95 *(978-1-4329-7626-2(5))* Heinemann-Raintree.

Rosario, Miguel. A Paramedic's Job. 2014. (Community Workers Ser.). 24p. (J). (gr. k-2). lib. bdg. 24.21 *(978-1-62712-996-1(0))* Cavendish Square Publishing.

Rosario, Miguel & Rosario, Miguel T. A Paramedic's Job. 2014. (Community Workers Ser.). 24p. (J). (gr. k-2). pap. 8.22 *(978-1-62712-997-8(9))* Cavendish Square Publishing.

Rosen, Michael J. & Kassoy, Ben. Odd Medical Cures. Sandy, Pat, illus. 2013. (No Way! Ser.). (ENG.). 32p. (gr. 3-5). lib. bdg. 26.60 *(978-0-7613-8987-3(3)*, Millbrook Pr.) Lerner Publishing Group.

Royston, Angela. Heroes of Medicine & Their Discoveries. 2010. (ENG., Illus.). 32p. (J). *(978-0-7787-9897-2(6))*; pap. *(978-0-7787-9918-4(2))* Crabtree Publishing Co.

Ruffin, David C. The Duties & Responsibilities of the Secretary of Health & Human Services. (Your Government in Action Ser.). 32p. 2009. (gr. 3-3). 43.90 *(978-1-60854-917-7(8))* 2005. (Illus.). (J). lib. bdg. 23.95 *(978-1-4042-2691-3(5))* Rosen Publishing Group, Inc., The. (PowerKids Pr.).

Sally Ride Science Editors, Sally Ride Science. What Do You Want to Be? Explore Health Sciences. 2004. (J). 6.00 *(978-0-9753920-3-4(4))* Sally Ride Science.

Sargent, Brian. The Placebo Effect: The Power of Positive Thinking. 2014. (ENG., Illus.). 28p. pap. 9.50 *(978-1-107-62263-0(8))* Cambridge Univ. Pr.

Sharafeddine, Fatima. The Amazing Discoveries of Ibn Sina, 1 vol. Ali, Intelaq Mohammed, illus. 2015. (ENG.). 32p. (J). (gr. 1-6). 17.95 *(978-1-55498-710-8(5))* Groundwood Bks. CAN. Dist: Publishers Group West (PGW).

Shepherd, Jodie. A Day with Doctors. 2012. (Rookie Read-About Community Ser.). (ENG., Illus.). 32p. (J). pap. 5.95 *(978-0-531-29250-1(9))* Scholastic Library Publishing.

—A Day with Paramedics. 2012. (Rookie Read-About Community Ser.). (ENG., Illus.). 32p. (J). pap. 5.95 *(978-0-531-29254-9(1))*; lib. bdg. 23.00 *(978-0-531-28954-9(0))* Scholastic Library Publishing.

Sherrow, Victoria. Medical Imaging. 2006. (Great Inventions Ser.). (Illus.). 128p. (gr. 8-10). lib. bdg. 29.95 *(978-0-7614-2231-0(5)*, Benchmark Bks.) Marshall Cavendish Corp.

Sieling, Peter. Folk Medicine. 2004. (North American Folklore Ser.). (Illus.). 112p. (YA). (gr. 7-18). lib. bdg. 22.95 *(978-1-59084-341-3(X))* Mason Crest.

Silverstein, Alvin, et al. Tapeworms, Foot Fungus, Lice, & More: The Yucky Disease Book. Kelley, Gerald, illus. 2010. (Yucky Science Ser.). 48p. (J). (gr. 5-9). 25.27 *(978-0-7660-3314-6(7))* Enslow Pubs., Inc.

Simon, Samantha. Emts & Paramedics. 2017. (Careers in Healthcare Ser.: Vol. 13). (ENG.). (YA). (gr. 7-12). 23.95 ***(978-1-4222-3799-1(0))*** Mason Crest.

—Orthotists & Prosthetists. 2017. (Careers in Healthcare Ser.: Vol. 13). (ENG.). (YA). (gr. 7-12). 23.95 ***(978-1-4222-3802-8(4))*** Mason Crest.

Sohn, Emily, frwd. Health & Medicine. 2006. (Science News for Kids Ser.). (Illus.). 160p. (gr. 4-6). lib. bdg. 30.00 *(978-0-7910-9122-7(8)*, Chelsea Clubhouse) Facts On File, Inc.

Soloway, Cindy. Mommy, What's an MRI? Steve, Sumner, ed. Susan, Lisbin, illus. 2006. (J). mass mkt. *(978-0-9765060-2-7(5))* TouchSmart Publishing, LLC.

Solway, Andrew. Genetics in Medicine. 2007. (Cutting Edge Medicine Ser.). (Illus.). 64p. (gr. 6-12). lib. bdg. 34.00 *(978-0-8368-7865-3(5)*, Gareth Stevens Secondary Library) Stevens, Gareth Publishing LLLP.

Staniford, Linda. Ambulances to the Rescue Around the World. 2016. (To the Rescue! Ser.). (ENG., Illus.). 24p. (gr. k-2). lib. bdg. 23.32 *(978-1-4846-2752-5(0)*, Heinemann Read & Learn) Heinemann-Raintree.

Steffens, Bradley. Careers in Medical Technology. 2017. (ENG.). 80p. (YA). (gr. 5-12). ***(978-1-68282-116-9(1))*** ReferencePoint Pr., Inc.

Stefoff, Rebecca. Magic & Medicine. 2014. 48p. pap. 29.93 *(978-1-62712-515-4(9))* Cavendish Square Publishing.

Stephens, Ronald, ed. Sports. 2014. (Safety First Ser.: 11). 48p. (J). (gr. 5-18). 20.95 *(978-1-4222-3053-4(8))* Mason Crest.

Stoyles, Pennie. The A-Z of Health. 2010. (a to Z of Health Ser.). 32p. (gr. 4-7). Vol. 1. lib. bdg. 31.35 *(978-1-59920-541-0(6))* Vol. 2. lib. bdg. 31.35 *(978-1-59920-542-7(4))* Vol. 3. lib. bdg. 31.35 *(978-1-59920-543-4(2))* Vol. 4. lib. bdg. 31.35 *(978-1-59920-544-1(0))* Vol. 6. lib. bdg. 31.35 *(978-1-59920-546-5(7))* Black Rabbit Bks.

Stoyles, Pennie & Pentland, Peter. Medicine & Health. 2011. (Energy in Action Ser.). (Illus.). 32p. (J). (gr. 4). 28.50 *(978-1-60870-568-9(4))* Marshall Cavendish Corp.

Strange, Cordelia. Medical Technicians: Health-Care Support for the 21st Century. 2010. (New Careers for the 21st Century Ser.). 64p. (YA). (gr. 7-18). lib. bdg. 22.95 *(978-1-4222-1817-4(1))* Mason Crest.

Syrewicz, Connor. Masseur & Massage Therapist. 2013. (Earning $50,000 - $100,000 with a High School Diploma or Less Ser.: 14). 64p. (J). (gr. 7-18). 22.95 *(978-1-4222-2896-8(7))* Mason Crest.

Tartakoff, Katy. Burned & Beautiful. Shields, Laurie, illus. 54p. (Orig.). (J). stu. ed. 14.95 *(978-0-9629365-1-7(0))* Children's Legacy.

—Let Me Show You My World. Shields, Laurie, illus. 54p. (Orig.). (J). stu. ed. 14.95 *(978-0-9629365-2-4(9))* Children's Legacy.

Thornton, Denise. Living with Cancer: The Ultimate Teen Guide. 2011. (It Happened to Me Ser.: 30). (ENG.). 190p. 45.00 *(978-0-8108-7277-6(3))* Scarecrow Pr., Inc.

Toriello, James. The Human Genome Project. (Library of Future Medicine Ser.). 64p. 2009. (gr. 5-5). 58.50 *(978-1-60853-632-0(7))* 2005. (Illus.). (YA). (gr. 7-12). lib. bdg. 31.95 *(978-0-8239-3671-7(6))* Rosen Publishing Group, Inc., The.

Vickers, Rebecca. Medicine, 1 vol. 2010. (From Fail to Win! Learning from Bad Ideas Ser.). (ENG., Illus.). 56p. (gr. 5-8). 34.65 *(978-1-4109-3908-1(1)*, Raintree Freestyle) Heinemann-Raintree.

Waters, Rosa. Over-The-Counter Medications. Borus, Joshua, ed. 2014. (Downside of Drugs Ser.: 11). (Illus.). 48p. (J). (gr. 5-18). lib. bdg. 20.95 *(978-1-4222-3025-1(2))* Mason Crest.

Waters, Sophie. Seeing the Gynecologist. 2009. (Girls' Health Ser.). 48p. (gr. 5-6). 53.00 *(978-1-61512-731-3(3)*, Rosen Reference) Rosen Publishing Group, Inc., The.

Watson, Stephanie. Brain Injuries in Football, 1 vol. 2014. (Essential Issues Set 4 Ser.). (ENG., Illus.). 112p. (J). (gr. 6-12). lib. bdg. 35.64 *(978-1-62403-417-6(9)*, Essential Library) ABDO Publishing Co.

—Endometriosis. 2009. (Library of Sexual Health Ser.). 64p. (gr. 6-6). 58.50 *(978-1-60853-842-3(7))* Rosen Publishing Group, Inc., The.

Waxman, Laura Hamilton. Ambulances on the Move. 2011. (Lightning Bolt Books Vroom-Vroom Ser.). 32p. pap. 45.32 *(978-0-7613-7615-6(1))*; (ENG.). pap. 7.95 *(978-0-7613-7110-6(9))* Lerner Publishing Group.

Way, Steve. Fighting Disease. 2011. (Planet SOS Ser.). (Illus.). 48p. (J). (gr. 3-6). pap. 14.05 *(978-1-4339-4971-5(7))*; lib. bdg. 31.95 *(978-1-4339-4970-8(9))* Stevens, Gareth Publishing LLLP. (Gareth Stevens Learning Library).

Weber, Rebecca. Science & Your Health, 1 vol. (Health & Your Body Ser.). (ENG.). 24p. (gr. k-1). 2011. pap. 7.29 *(978-1-4296-7130-9(0))* 2011. pap. 41.70 *(978-1-4296-7136-1(X))* 2010. lib. bdg. 26.65 *(978-1-4296-6612-1(9))* Capstone Press of Coughlan Cos. (Pebble Plus).

Whiting, Jim. The Life & Times of Hippocrates. 2006. (Biography from Ancient Civilizations Ser.). (Illus.). 48p. (J). (gr. 3-7). lib. bdg. 29.95 *(978-1-58415-512-6(4)*, 1259600) Mitchell Lane Pubs., Inc.

Woods, Michael & Woods, Mary B. Ancient Medical Technology: From Herbs to Scalpels. 2011. (Technology in Ancient Cultures Ser.). (ENG.). 96p. (gr. 6-12). lib. bdg. 31.93 *(978-0-7613-6522-8(2))* Lerner Publishing Group.

World Book, Inc Staff, contrib. by. Medicine. 2009. *(978-0-7166-0384-9(5))* World Bk., Inc.

Wunderlich, Rick. Math on the Job: Keeping People Healthy. 2016. (ENG., Illus.). 32p. (J). *(978-0-7787-2359-2(3))* Crabtree Publishing Co.

Yomtov, Nelson. Medical Illustrator. 2015. (21st Century Skills Library: Cool STEAM Careers Ser.). (ENG.). 32p. (gr. 4-7). pap. 14.21 *(978-1-63362-042-1(5)*, 205925) Cherry Lake Publishing.

Zuchora-Walske, Christine. Your Head Shape Reveals Your Personality! Science's Biggest Mistakes about the Human Body. 2014. (Science Gets It Wrong Ser.). (ENG., Illus.). 32p. (J). (gr. 4-6). lib. bdg. 26.60 *(978-1-4677-3661-9(9)*, Lerner Pubns.) Lerner Publishing Group.

MEDICINE—BIOGRAPHY

Harvey, Joanna & Crabtree, Marc. Meet My Neighbor, the Paramedic. 2010. (ENG., Illus.). 24p. (J). pap. *(978-0-7787-4585-3(6))*; lib. bdg. *(978-0-7787-4575-4(9))* Crabtree Publishing Co.

Hitchcock, Susan Tyler. Karen Horney: Pioneer of Feminine Psychology. 2004. (Women in Medicine Ser.). (Illus.). 112p. (gr. 6-12). 30.00 *(978-0-7910-8025-2(0)*, Chelsea Hse.) Facts On File, Inc.

Lim, Bridget & Ramen, Fred. Albucasis: The Father of Modern Surgery. 2016. (Physicians, Scientists, & Mathematicians of the Islamic World Ser.). 112p. (gr. 6-6). 37.10 *(978-1-5081-7140-9(8))* Rosen Publishing Group, Inc., The.

Morrison, John. Mathilde Krim. 2004. (Women in Medicine Ser.). (Illus.). 112p. (YA). (gr. 6-12). 30.00 *(978-0-7910-8026-9(9)*, Chelsea Hse.) Facts On File, Inc.

MEDICINE—DATA PROCESSING

Benedict, Aaron & Gallaher, David. Using Computer Science in High-Tech Health & Wellness Careers. 2017. (Coding Your Passion Ser.). 80p. (J). (gr. 12-12). 35.75 ***(978-1-5081-7515-5(2)***, Rosen Young Adult) Rosen Publishing Group, Inc., The.

MEDICINE, DENTAL

see Dentistry; Teeth

MEDICINE—FICTION

Accardo, Reba, told to. Surgery for Me? 2005. (J). pap. 8.00 *(978-0-8059-6697-8(8))* Dorrance Publishing Co., Inc.

Bailey, Leslie J. Jacub's Journey. DeBroeck, Sarah, illus. 2011. 28p. pap. 24.95 *(978-1-4560-9951-0(5))* America Star Bks.

Birney, Roxanne. Johannah's Lazy Eye. 2009. 28p. pap. 12.49 *(978-1-4389-3673-4(7))* AuthorHouse.

Brix-Maffei, Angela & Brix-Maffei, John. The Christmas Dinosaur. 2008. 48p. pap. 22.49 *(978-1-4389-0499-3(1))* AuthorHouse.

Bryers, Paul. Kobal. 2009. 1.00 *(978-1-4074-4320-1(8))* Recorded Bks., Inc.

Burgess, Melvin. Sara's Face. 2008. (ENG.). 288p. (YA). (gr. 9-12). pap. 7.99 *(978-1-4169-5815-4(0)*, Simon Pulse) Simon Pulse.

Cowan, Charlotte. Sadie's Sore Throat. Bratun, Katy, illus. 2007. (Dr. Hippo Ser.). (ENG.). 32p. (J). (gr. 3-7). 17.95 *(978-0-9753516-4-2(8))* Hippocratic Pr., The.

Cummings, K. M. I Hate Medicine! 2007. 24p. per. 10.95 *(978-1-4327-1382-9(5))* Outskirts Pr., Inc.

Cushman, Karen. Matilda Bone. 2014. (ENG.). 176p. (J). (gr. 5-7). pap. 6.99 *(978-0-547-72242-9(7)*, HMH Books For Young Readers) Houghton Mifflin Harcourt Publishing Co.

—Matilda Bone. unabr. ed. 2004. (Middle Grade Cassette Librariestm Ser.). 176p. (J). (gr. 5-9). pap. 36.00 incl. audio *(978-0-8072-1725-2(5)*, S YA 252 SP, Listening Library) Random Hse. Audio Publishing Group.

Dahl, Roald. La Maravillosa Medicina de Jorge. Blake, Quentin, illus. 2005. (Alfaguara Ser.).Tr. of George's Marvellous Medicine Spanish. (SPA.). 118p. (gr. 3-5). per. 11.95 *(978-968-19-0547-7(4))* Santillana USA Publishing Co., Inc.

Danziger, Paula. The Pistachio Prescription. (J). (gr. 4-6). 154p. pap. 3.99 *(978-0-8072-1525-8(2))*; 160p. pap. 3.99 *(978-0-8072-1374-2(8))* Random Hse. Audio Publishing Group. (Listening Library).

DeFelice, Cynthia C. The Apprenticeship of Lucas Whitaker. 2007. (ENG.). 160p. (J). (gr. 5-9). per. 9.99 *(978-0-374-40014-9(8)*, 9780374400149) Square Fish.

Dempsey, Tami. We Are a Champion! 2010. 36p. pap. 15.49 *(978-1-4490-8102-7(9))* AuthorHouse.

Dixon, Heather. Illusionarium. 2015. (ENG.). 368p. (YA). (gr. 8). 17.99 *(978-0-06-200105-4(1)*, Greenwillow Bks.) HarperCollins Pubs.

Dusablon, David. Dee Dee's First Shot, 1 vol. Spoerl, Amber, illus. 2009. 17p. pap. 24.95 *(978-1-60749-113-2(3))* America Star Bks.

Ecton, Emily. The Curse of Cuddles McGee. 2008. (ENG.). 272p. (J). (gr. 3-7). pap. 12.99 *(978-1-4169-6450-6(9)*, Simon & Schuster/Paula Wiseman Bks.) Simon & Schuster/Paula Wiseman Bks.

Gaydos, Nora. Now I'm Growing! - A Visit to the Doctor. Gutierrez, Akemi, illus. 2011. (ENG.). 30p. (J). (gr. -1-17). 8.99 *(978-1-60169-153-8(X))* Innovative Kids.

Guerra, Juan J. The Little Doctor / el Doctorcito. Castillo, Victoria, illus. 2017. (ENG & SPA.). 32p. (J). (gr. k-3). 17.95 *(978-1-55885-846-6(6)*, Piñata Books) Arte Publico Pr.

Hansell, Donna. The Adventures of Kirbey the Kidney. 2012. 20p. pap. 11.59 *(978-1-4669-4527-2(3))* Trafford Publishing.

Hare, Eric B. Dr. Rabbit. Bohlmann, Siegfried, illus. fac. ed. 2010. 127p. per. 11.95 *(978-1-57258-278-1(2)*, 945-6131) TEACH Services, Inc.

James, M. R. The Five Jars. 2008. 96p. pap. *(978-1-84830-112-2(X)*, Wildhern Pr.) Echo Library.

K/H (Pathways). Kindergarten Stepping Stones: Kindergarten the Bravest Dog Ever - The True Story of Balto Trade Book. rev. ed. 2010. (ENG.). 48p. pap. 9.00 *(978-0-7575-8646-0(5))* Kendall Hunt Publishing Co.

Kellerman, Faye & Kellerman, Aliza. Prism. (YA). 2010. (ENG.). 288p. (gr. 8). pap. 8.99 *(978-0-06-168724-2(3))* 2009. 272p. (gr. 7-18). lib. bdg. 17.89 *(978-0-06-168722-8(7)*, HarperTeen) HarperCollins Pubs.

Klein, Adria F. Max Goes to the Doctor, 1 vol. Gallagher-Cole, Mernie, illus. 2007. (Read-It! Readers: the Life of Max Ser.). (ENG.). 24p. (gr. -1-2). lib. bdg. 21.32 *(978-1-4048-3680-8(2)*, Easy Readers) Picture Window Bks.

Krossing, Karen. Pure, 1 vol. 2006. (ENG.). 245p. (YA). (gr. 7-9). per. 10.95 *(978-1-896764-96-2(7))* Second Story Pr. CAN. Dist: Orca Bk. Pubs. USA.

Krovatin, Christopher. Venomous. Yates, Kelly, illus. 2008. (ENG.). 336p. (YA). (gr. 8-18). 16.99 *(978-1-4169-2487-6(6)*, Atheneum Bks. for Young Readers) Simon & Schuster Children's Publishing.

Ladd, Debbie. Nurse Robin's Hats. Nakasone, Shaun, illus. 2006. 52p. (J). 16.95 *(978-0-9727615-3-6(5))* Deb on Air Bks.

Lansdowne, Marcella. The Adventures of Patty & Annabel: Apache Lake & the Chakras. 2009. 28p. pap. 15.95 *(978-1-4389-1643-9(4))* AuthorHouse.

Milford, Kate. The Boneshaker. Offermann, Andrea, illus. 2011. (ENG.). 384p. (J). (gr. 5-7). pap. 7.99 *(978-0-547-55004-6(9))* Houghton Mifflin Harcourt Publishing Co.

Morgan, Nicola. Fleshmarket. 2003. (ENG.). 272p. (J). (gr. 7-17). pap. 9.99 *(978-0-340-85557-7(6))* Hodder & Stoughton GBR. Dist: Hachette Bk. Group.

Parish, Herman. Calling Doctor Amelia Bedelia. Sweat, Lynn, illus. 2004. (I Can Read Level 2 Ser.). (ENG.). 64p. (J). (gr. k-3). pap. 3.99 *(978-0-06-008780-7(3)*, Greenwillow Bks.) HarperCollins Pubs.

Patton, Katherine. Bam Bam the Bandage. 2010. 16p. pap. 10.99 *(978-1-4343-4967-5(5))* AuthorHouse.

Pelow, Lawrence. Little Larry of Lewiston Meets Bobby the Backyard Bully. 2006. 2p. 6.71 *(978-1-4116-9172-8(5))* Lulu Pr., Inc.

Penson, Mary E. Martha Mary Overstreet, M. D. 2007. (Chaparral Bks.). (ENG.). 142p. (J). per. 11.95 *(978-0-87565-345-7(6))* Texas Christian Univ. Pr.

Powers, J. L. This Thing Called the Future. 2011. (FRS & ENG.). 208p. (J). (gr. 7-11). 16.95 *(978-1-933693-95-8(9))* Cinco Puntos Pr.

Riner, Kendall F. The Rescue Adventures of Fireman Frank. 2006. (Illus.). 52p. (J). pap. 12.00 *(978-0-9786369-1-3(0))* Warwick Hse. Publishing.

Rivera-Ashford, Roni Capin. My Tata's Remedies - Los Remedios de Mi Tata. Castro L., Antonio, illus. 2015. (ENG & SPA.). 40p. (J). (gr. 1-6). pap. 8.95 *(978-1-935955-89-4(6))* Cinco Puntos Pr.

Royster, Ka-Sandra. Cough Syrup in Mommy's Hair. 2013. 24p. pap. *(978-1-4602-2600-1(3))* FriesenPress.

Ryden, David. Andy the Ambulance: My Two Partners. 2012. 34p. 24.95 *(978-1-4626-5372-0(3))* PublishAmerica, Inc.

Samples, Suzanne. Pivot. 2011. 208p. pap. 13.00 *(978-1-257-03969-2(5))* Lulu Pr., Inc.

Sateren, Shelley Swanson. Max & Zoe at the Doctor, 1 vol. Sullivan, Mary, illus. 2011. (Max & Zoe Ser.). (ENG.). 32p. (gr. k-2). lib. bdg. 21.32 *(978-1-4048-6212-8(9)*, Max & Zoe) Picture Window Bks.

Stewart, Jennifer J. Close Encounters of a Third World Kind. 2004. (ENG.). 128p. (J). (gr. 4-6). tchr. ed. 16.95 *(978-0-8234-1850-3(2))* Holiday Hse., Inc.

Walsh, Ann. The Doctor's Apprentice. 2005. 160p. (YA). (gr. 3-8). pap., tchr. ed. 8.95 *(978-0-88878-389-9(2))* Beach Holme Pubs., Ltd. CAN. Dist: Literary Pr. Group of Canada.

—The Doctor's Apprentice: A Barkerville Mystery. 2007. (Barkerville Mystery Ser.: 2). (ENG.). 160p. (J). pap. 9.99 *(978-1-55002-633-7(X)*, Sandcastle Bks.) Dundurn CAN. Dist: Ingram Publisher Services.

Wells, Dan. Partials. (ENG.). (YA). 2013. (Partials Sequence Ser.: 1). 528p. (gr. 9). pap. 9.99 *(978-0-06-207105-7(X))* 2012. (Partials Sequence Ser.: 1). 480p. (gr. 9). 17.99 *(978-0-06-207104-0(1))* 2012. 496p. pap. 9.99 *(978-0-06-213569-8(4))* HarperCollins Pubs.

White, Paul. Jungle Doctor Looks for Trouble. 2009. (Flamingo Fiction 9-13s Ser.). (ENG., Illus.). 160p. (J). pap. 8.99 *(978-1-84550-499-1(2)*, 9302ad19-8b28-4030-be88-ef9afc9f3a6c) Christian Focus Pubns. GBR. Dist: Bookmasters Distribution.

—Jungle Doctor on Safari. 2011. (Flamingo Fiction 9-13s Ser.). (ENG., Illus.). 144p. (J). 8.99 *(978-1-84550-391-8(0)*, 9781845503918) Christian Focus Pubns. GBR. Dist: Bookmasters Distribution.

—Jungle Doctor Operates. 2009. (Flamingo Fiction 9-13s Ser.). (ENG., Illus.). 160p. (J). pap. 8.99 *(978-1-84550-500-4(X)*, 5b5acc8e-b6fe-4477-b9ac-b1a8ea9426ea) Christian Focus Pubns. GBR. Dist: Bookmasters Distribution.

—Jungle Doctor Stings a Scorpion. 2008. (Flamingo Fiction 9-13s Ser.). (ENG., Illus.). 160p. (J). 8.99 *(978-1-84550-390-1(2)*, 21dc615c-019a-4cfe-b2da-d2c676461510) Christian Focus Pubns. GBR. Dist: Bookmasters Distribution.

—Jungle Doctor to the Rescue. 2009. (Flamingo Fiction 9-13s Ser.). (ENG., Illus.). 176p. (J). pap. 8.99 *(978-1-84550-516-5(6)*, 052662e3-f01a-4a40-9e4d-88634018ee06) Christian Focus Pubns. GBR. Dist: Bookmasters Distribution.

—Jungle Doctor's Africa. 2011. (Flamingo Fiction 9-13s Ser.). (ENG., Illus.). 144p. (J). 8.99 *(978-1-84550-388-8(0)*, 97eef3f6-1cd9-4ca5-866c-66b47f498800) Christian Focus Pubns. GBR. Dist: Bookmasters Distribution.

Yager, Jeff. Atom & Eve. 2013. (ENG.). (YA). 255p. 29.95 *(978-1-938998-36-2(7))*; 262p. (gr. 8-12). pap. 16.95 *(978-1-938998-34-8(0))* Hannacroix Creek Bks., Inc.

Young, Lena. One World Healing. Tsai, Dora, illus. 2005. 26p. (J). pap. *(978-1-933554-01-3(0))* Primordia.

MEDICINE—HISTORY

Allman, Toney. Medieval Medicine & Disease. 2014. (The Library of Medieval Times Ser). (ENG., Illus.). 80p. (J). lib. bdg. *(978-1-60152-656-4(3))* ReferencePoint Pr., Inc.

Anniss, Matt. Science vs. Disease. 2013. (Science Fights Back Ser.). (Illus.). 48p. (gr. 4-6). 31.95 *(978-1-4339-8687-1(6))*; pap. 14.05 *(978-1-4339-8688-8(4))* Stevens, Gareth Publishing LLLP. (Gareth Stevens Learning Library).

Atkinson, Mary. Pills & Potions: A History of Remedies. 2007. (Shockwave: Life Science & Medicine Ser.). (ENG., Illus.). 36p. (J). (gr. 4-6). lib. bdg. 25.00 *(978-0-531-17767-9(X)*, Children's Pr.) Scholastic Library Publishing.

Auden, Scott. Medical Mysteries: Science Researches Conditions from Bizarre to Deadly. 2008. (National Geographic Investigates Ser.). (ENG., Illus.). 64p. (J). (gr. 5). lib. bdg. 27.90 *(978-1-4263-0261-9(4)*, National Geographic Children's Bks.) National Geographic Society.

Auden, Scott & National Geographic Kids Staff. Medical Mysteries: Science Researches Conditions from Bizarre to Deadly. 2008. (National Geographic Investigates Science Ser.). (ENG., Illus.). 64p. (J). (gr. 5). 17.95 *(978-1-4263-0356-2(4)*, National Geographic Children's Bks.) National Geographic Society.

Bankston, John. Joseph Lister & the Story of Antiseptics. 2004. (Uncharted, Unexplored, & Unexplained Ser.). (Illus.). 48p. (J). (gr. 4-8). lib. bdg. 29.95 *(978-1-58415-262-0(1))* Mitchell Lane Pubs., Inc.

Bearce, Stephanie. Medical Mayhem. 2017. (Twisted True Tales from Science Ser.: 0). (ENG., Illus.). 125p. (J). (gr. 4-7). pap. 8.95 *(978-1-61821-572-7(8))* Prufrock Pr.

Beccia, Carlyn. I Feel Better with a Frog in My Throat: History's Strangest Cures. 2010. (ENG., Illus.). 48p. (J). (gr. 1-4). 17.99 *(978-0-547-22570-8(9))* Houghton Mifflin Harcourt Publishing Co.

Biskup, Agnieszka. Medical Marvels: The Next 100 Years of Medicine. Pota, Giovanni & Brown, Alan, illus. 2016. (Our World: the Next 100 Years Ser.). (ENG.). 32p. (gr. 3-4). lib. bdg. 30.65 *(978-1-4914-8264-3(8)*, Graphic Library) Capstone Press of Coughlan Cos.

Carmichael, Lindsey. Innovations in Health. 2016. (Problem Solved! Your Turn to Think Big Ser.). (ENG., Illus.). 32p. (J). (gr. 3-6). *(978-0-7787-2681-4(9))* Crabtree Publishing Co.

Clayboume, Anna. Sick at Sea? Cure It or Cut It Off! 2010. (ENG.). 32p. (J). *(978-0-7787-9901-6(8))* Crabtree Publishing Co.

Coan, Sharon. STEM Careers. 2017. (TIME for KIDS(r) Nonfiction Readers Ser.). (Illus.). 48p. (J). (gr. 7-7). pap. 9.99 *(978-1-4938-3621-5(8))* Teacher Created Materials, Inc.

Farndon, John. Quacks & con Artists: The Dubious History of Doctors. Dean, Venitia, illus. 2017. (Sickening History of Medicine Ser.). (ENG.). 32p. (J). (gr. 3-6). 26.65 *(978-1-5124-1560-5(X))*; 19.99 ***(978-1-5124-3636-5(4))***; 30.65 ***(978-1-5124-3635-8(6))***; 30.65 ***(978-1-5124-2712-7(8))*** Lerner Publishing Group.

—Strange Medicine. Dean, Venitia, illus. 2017. (Sickening History of Medicine Ser.). (ENG.). 32p. (J). (gr. 3-6). 26.65 *(978-1-5124-1559-9(6))* Lerner Publishing Group.

—Strange Medicine: A History of Medical Remedies. Dean, Venitia, illus. 2017. (Sickening History of Medicine Ser.). (ENG.). 32p. (J). (gr. 3-6). 19.99 ***(978-1-5124-3640-2(2))***; 30.65 ***(978-1-5124-3638-9(0))***; 30.65 ***(978-1-5124-2711-0(X))*** Lerner Publishing Group.

—Tiny Killers: When Bacteria & Viruses Attack. Dean, Venitia, illus. 2017. (Sickening History of Medicine Ser.). (ENG.). 32p. (J). (gr. 3-6). 26.65 *(978-1-5124-1558-2(8))*; 19.99 ***(978-1-5124-3642-6(9))***; 30.65 ***(978-1-5124-2710-3(1))***; 30.65 ***(978-1-5124-3641-9(0))*** Lerner Publishing Group.

Goldsmith, Connie. Cutting-Edge Medicine. 2008. pap. 52.95 *(978-0-8225-9327-0(0))* 2007. (ENG., Illus.). 48p. (gr. 4-8). lib. bdg. 27.93 *(978-0-8225-6770-7(9)*, Lerner Pubns.) Lerner Publishing Group.

Green, Jen. Medicine. 2004. (Routes of Science Ser.). (Illus.). 40p. (J). (gr. 4-7). 23.70 *(978-1-4103-0168-0(0)*, Blackbirch Pr., Inc.) Cengage Gale.

Hardman, Lizabeth. The History of Medicine. 2012. (World History Ser.). (ENG., Illus.). 128p. (gr. 7-10). 39.90 *(978-1-4205-0671-6(4))* Cengage Gale.

Hollar, Sherman. Pioneers in Medicine: From the Classical World to Today. 2012. (Inventors & Innovators Ser.). (ENG., Illus.). 112p. (YA). (gr. 7-12). 65.80 *(978-1-61530-785-2(0))* Rosen Publishing Group, Inc., The.

—Pioneers in Medicine: From the Classical World to Today. 2012. (Inventors & Innovators Ser.). (ENG., Illus.). 112p. (J). (gr. 7-12). lib. bdg. 32.90 *(978-1-61530-669-5(2))* Rosen Publishing Group, Inc., The.

Jeffrey, Gary. Medical Breakthroughs. (Graphic Discoveries Ser.). (ENG.). 48p. 2009. (YA). (gr. 5-5). 58.50 *(978-1-61512-932-4(4)*, Rosen Reference) 2008. (gr. 3-8). pap. 14.05 *(978-1-4042-9587-2(9))* Rosen Publishing Group, Inc., The.

—Medical Breakthroughs. Riley, Terry, illus. 2008. (Graphic Discoveries Ser.). (ENG.). 48p. (YA). (gr. 5-9). lib. bdg. 31.95 *(978-1-4042-1086-8(5))* Rosen Publishing Group, Inc., The.

Johnson, Rose. Discoveries in Medicine That Changed the World, 1 vol. 2015. (ENG.). 48p. (YA). 30.25 *(978-1-4777-8611-6(2)*, Rosen Reference) Rosen Publishing Group, Inc., The.

Klepeis, Alicia. Bizarre Things We've Called Medicine. 2015. (History of the Bizarre Ser.). (ENG., Illus.). 32p. (gr. 3-4). lib. bdg. 27.99 *(978-1-4914-4266-1(2))* Capstone Press of Coughlan Cos.

Kudlinski, Kathleen V. Boy, Were We Wrong about the Human Body! Tilley, Debbie, illus. 2015. (ENG.). 32p. (J). (gr. -1-3). 16.99 *(978-0-8037-3792-1(0)*, Dial Bks) Penguin Young Readers Group.

Langley, Andrew. Ancient Medicine, 1 vol. 2012. (Medicine Through the Ages Ser.). (ENG.). 48p. (gr. 6-7). lib. bdg. 34.65 *(978-1-4109-4642-3(8)*, Raintree Freestyle) Heinemann-Raintree.

Life in the American Colonies. 2011. (Life in the American Colonies Ser.). (ENG.). 32p. (gr. 3-4). pap. 31.80 *(978-1-4296-7221-4(8)*, Fact Finders) Capstone Press of Coughlan Cos.

Marsico, Katie. The Doctor. 2011. (Colonial People 2 Ser.). 48p. (gr. 3). 29.93 *(978-1-60870-412-5(2))* Marshall Cavendish Corp.

Morrison, Heather S. Inventors of Health & Medical Technology. 2015. (Designing Engineering Solutions Ser.). (ENG., Illus.). 144p. (J). (gr. 8-8). 42.79 *(978-1-5026-0658-7(5))* Cavendish Square Publishing.

Orr, Tamra B. Antibiotics. 2016. (True Book(tm), a — Greatest Discoveries & Discoverers Ser.). (ENG., Illus.). 48p. (J). lib. bdg. 31.00 *(978-0-531-21860-0(0)*, Children's Pr.) Scholastic Library Publishing.

Raum, Elizabeth, et al. Life in the American Colonies. 2011. (Life in the American Colonies Ser.). (ENG.). 32p. (gr. 3-4). pap. 190.80 *(978-1-4296-7222-1(6))*; lib. bdg. 54.64 *(978-1-4296-6493-6(2))* Capstone Press of Coughlan Cos. (Fact Finders).

Rooney, Anne. The History of Medicine. 2012. (History of Science Ser.). (ENG., Illus.). 208p. (YA). (gr. 7-12). 42.60 *(978-1-4488-7228-2(6))* Rosen Publishing Group, Inc., The.
Sandvold, Lynnette Brent. Revolution in Medicine. 2009. (It Works! Ser.). 32p. (gr. 3). 28.50 *(978-0-7614-4376-6(2))* Marshall Cavendish Corp.
Senior, Kathryn. You Wouldn't Want to Be Sick in the 16th Century! (Revised Edition) 2014. (You Wouldn't Want to... Ser.). (ENG.). 32p. (J). lib. bdg. 29.00 *(978-0-531-21176-2(2)*, Watts, Franklin) Scholastic Library Publishing.
Strange, Matthew. Bleeding, Blistering, & Purging: Health & Medicine in The 1800s. 2009. (Daily Life in America in the 1800s Ser.). 64p. (YA). (gr. 7-18). pap. 9.95 *(978-1-4222-1848-8(1))*; lib. bdg. 22.95 *(978-1-4222-1775-7(2))* Mason Crest.
Strom, Laura Layton. Dr. Medieval: Medicine in the Middle Ages. 2007. (Shockwave: Life Science & Medicine Ser.). (ENG., Illus.). 36p. (J). (gr. 3-5). 25.00 *(978-0-531-17765-5(3)*, Children's Pr.) Scholastic Library Publishing.
Vickers, Rebecca. Industrial Age Medicine, 1 vol. 2012. (Medicine Through the Ages Ser.). (ENG.). 48p. (gr. 6-7). pap. 9.49 *(978-1-4109-4651-5(7))*; lib. bdg. 34.65 *(978-1-4109-4645-4(2))* Heinemann-Raintree. (Raintree Freestyle).
Ward, Brian. The History of Medicine: Healthcare Around the World & Through the Ages. 2016. (ENG., Illus.). 64p. 12.99 *(978-1-86147-724-8(4)*, Armadillo) Anness Publishing GBR. Dist: National Bk. Network.
Ward, Brian R. The Story of Medicine. 2011. (Journey Through History Ser.). (J). lib. bdg. 31.95 *(978-1-4488-4792-1(3)*, Rosen Reference) Rosen Publishing Group, Inc., The.
World Book, Inc. Staff, contrib. by. Leeches to Lasers: A Timeline of Medicine. 2016. (J). *(978-0-7166-3542-0(9))* World Bk.-Childcraft International.
Zuchora-Walske, Christine. Your Head Shape Reveals Your Personality! Science's Biggest Mistakes about the Human Body. 2014. (Science Gets It Wrong Ser.). (Illus.). 32p. (gr. 4-6). pap. 7.95 *(978-1-4677-4551-2(0))* Lerner Publishing Group.

MEDICINE, PEDIATRIC

see Children—Diseases

MEDICINE—PRACTICE

Beccia, Carlyn. I Feel Better with a Frog in My Throat: History's Strangest Cures. 2010. (ENG., Illus.). 48p. (J). (gr. 1-4). 17.99 *(978-0-547-22570-8(9))* Houghton Mifflin Harcourt Publishing Co.

MEDICINE, PREVENTIVE

see Bacteriology; Health; Immunity; Public Health

MEDICINE—RESEARCH

Brocker, Susan & Furgang, Kathy. Pioneers in Medicine & Médicos Pioneros: 6 English, 6 Spanish Adaptations. 2011. (ENG & SPA.). (J). 97.00 net. *(978-1-4108-5701-9(8))* Benchmark Education Co.
Eboch, M. M. The 12 Biggest Breakthroughs in Medicine. 2014. (ENG., Illus.). 32p. (J). *(978-1-63235-015-2(7))* Pr. Room Editions LLC.
Foy, Debbie. Medical Pioneers. 2011. (20th Century Lives Ser.). (ENG.). 32p. (YA). (gr. 3-6). lib. bdg. 26.50 *(978-1-4488-3293-4(4))* Rosen Publishing Group, Inc., The.
Jacobson, Ryan. Marvelous Medical Inventions. 2013. (Awesome Inventions You Use Every Day Ser.). (ENG., Illus.). 32p. (gr. 3-6). lib. bdg. 26.60 *(978-1-4677-1095-4(4)*, Lerner Pubns.) Lerner Publishing Group.
Kjelle, Marylou Morano. Conquering Disease. 2014. 48p. (J). (gr. 4-8). 29.95 *(978-1-61228-576-4(7))* Mitchell Lane Pubs., Inc.
Oransky Wittenstein, Vicki. For the Good of Mankind? The Shameful History of Human Medical Experimentation. 2013. (ENG., Illus.). 96p. (gr. 6-12). 35.93 *(978-1-4677-0659-9(0)*, Twenty-First Century Bks.) Lerner Publishing Group.

MEDICINE—UNITED STATES

Engdahl, Sylvia. Medical Rights. 2008. (Issues on Trial Ser.). (ENG., Illus.). 240p. (gr. 10-12). 48.30 *(978-0-7377-4179-7(1)*, Greenhaven Pr., Inc.) Cengage Gale.
Hantula, Richard. Jonas Salk. 2004. (Trailblazers of the Modern World Ser.). (Illus.). 48p. (gr. 5-12). lib. bdg. 31.00 *(978-0-8368-5100-7(5)*, Gareth Stevens Secondary Library) Stevens, Gareth Publishing LLLP.
Naden, Corinne J. Health Care: A Right or a Privilege? 2009. (Controversy! Ser.). 112p. (gr. 7-9). lib. bdg. 37.07 *(978-0-7614-4231-8(6))* Marshall Cavendish Corp.
Porterfield, Jason. The Law & Personal Health: Your Legal Rights. 2015. (Know Your Rights Ser.). (ENG., Illus.). 64p. (J). (gr. 6-6). 33.25 *(978-1-4777-8052-7(1)*, Rosen Young Adult) Rosen Publishing Group, Inc., The.
Raum, Elizabeth. The Cold, Hard Facts about Science & Medicine in Colonial America, 1 vol. 2011. (Life in the American Colonies Ser.). (ENG.). 32p. (gr. 3-4). pap. 8.10 *(978-1-4296-7215-3(3))*; pap. 47.70 *(978-1-4296-7216-0(1))* Capstone Press of Coughlan Cos. (Fact Finders).
Schroeder-Lein, Glenna R. The Encyclopedia of Civil War Medicine. 2008. (ENG., Illus.). 457p. (C). 158.00 *(978-0-7656-1171-0(6)*, Y184328) Routledge.

MEDICINE, VETERINARY

see Veterinary Medicine

MEDICINE—VOCATIONAL GUIDANCE

Asher, Dana. Epidemiologists: Life Tracking Deadly Diseases. 2005. (Extreme Careers Ser.). (Illus.). 64p. (YA). (gr. 5-8). 31.95 *(978-0-8239-3633-5(3))* Rosen Publishing Group, Inc., The.
Bell, Samantha. Sports Medicine Doctor. 2015. (21st Century Skills Library: Cool STEAM Careers Ser.). (ENG., Illus.). 32p. (J). (gr. 4-7). pap. 14.21 *(978-1-63362-654-6(7)*, 206441) Cherry Lake Publishing.
Benedict, Aaron & Gallaher, David. Using Computer Science in High-Tech Health & Wellness Careers. 2017. (Coding Your Passion Ser.). 80p. (J). (gr. 12-12). 35.75 ***(978-1-5081-7515-5(2)**,* Rosen Young Adult) Rosen Publishing Group, Inc., The.
Boyd, Nicole. A Doctor's Busy Day. 2009. (Reading Room Collection 2 Ser.). 24p. (gr. 3-4). 42.50 *(978-1-60851-952-1(X)*, PowerKids Pr.) Rosen Publishing Group, Inc., The.
Christy, Lee Louis. I Go to Work as a Doctor. 2003. (I Go to Work As Ser.). (Illus.). (J). *(978-1-58417-042-6(5))*; pap. *(978-1-58417-107-2(3))* Lake Street Pubs.
Coan, Sharon. STEM Careers: Metamorphosis of Medicine. 2017. (Time for Kids Nonfiction Readers Ser.). lib. bdg. 20.85 ***(978-0-606-40281-1(0))*** Turtleback Bks.
Colby, Jennifer. Hospital. 2016. (21st Century Junior Library: Explore a Workplace Ser.). (ENG.). 24p. (J). (gr. 2-5). 27.07 *(978-1-63471-074-9(6)*, 208375) Cherry Lake Publishing.
Currie-McGhee, L. K. Careers in Medicine. 2017. (ENG.). 80p. (YA). (gr. 5-12). ***(978-1-68282-200-5(1))*** ReferencePoint Pr., Inc.
Extraordinary Jobs in Health & Science. 2006. (Extraordinary Jobs Ser.). 176p. (gr. 6-12). 40.00 *(978-0-8160-5858-7(X)*, Ferguson Publishing Co.) Facts On File, Inc.
Ferguson. Therapists. 2nd rev. ed. 2008. (Careers in Focus Ser.). 202p. (gr. 6-12). 32.95 *(978-0-8160-7286-6(8)*, Ferguson Publishing Co.) Facts On File, Inc.
Ferguson Publishing Staff, contrib. by. Physicians. 3rd rev. ed. 2010. (Careers in Focus Ser.). (Illus.). 229p. (gr. 6-12). 32.95 *(978-0-8160-8027-4(5)*, Ferguson Publishing Co.) Facts On File, Inc.
Geriatric Care. 3rd rev. ed. 2010. (Careers in Focus Ser.). 208p. (gr. 6-12). 32.95 *(978-0-8160-8025-0(9)*, Ferguson Publishing Co.) Facts On File, Inc.
Henneberg, Susan. The Vo-Tech Track to Success in Health Care. 2014. (Learning a Trade, Preparing for a Career Ser.). (Illus.). 80p. (J). (gr. 7-12). 34.25 *(978-1-4777-7730-5(X))* Rosen Publishing Group, Inc., The.
Hubbard, Rita L. What Degree Do I Need to Pursue a Career in Health Care?, 1 vol. 2015. (ENG., Illus.). 80p. (J). 34.60 *(978-1-4777-7869-2(1)*, Rosen Young Adult) Rosen Publishing Group, Inc., The.
J. G. Ferguson Publishing Company Staff. Exploring Health Care Careers. 3rd rev. ed. 2006. (Illus.). 960p. (C). (gr. 9-18). 125.00 *(978-0-8160-6448-9(2)*, Ferguson Publishing Co.) Facts On File, Inc.
J. G. Ferguson Publishing Company Staff, contrib. by. Discovering Careers for Your Future: English. 2nd rev. ed. 2005. (Discovering Careers for Your Future Ser.). (Illus.). 96p. (gr. 4-9). 21.95 *(978-0-8160-5872-3(5)*, Ferguson Publishing Co.) Facts On File, Inc.
Mattern, Joanne. Tecnicos en Emergencias Medicas. 2004. (Trabajo en Grupo (Working Together) Ser.). (SPA & ENG., Illus.). 24p. (J). (gr. 3-6). lib. bdg. 22.60 *(978-0-8239-6839-8(1)*, Editorial Buenas Letras) Rosen Publishing Group, Inc., The.
McAlpine, Margaret. Working in Health Care. 2004. (My Future Career Ser.). (Illus.). 64p. (gr. 3-7). lib. bdg. 27.00 *(978-0-8368-4238-8(3)*, Gareth Stevens Learning Library) Stevens, Gareth Publishing LLLP.
Porterfield, Deborah. Great Careers with a High School Diploma: Health Care, Medicine, & Science. 2008. (Great Careers with a High School Diploma Ser.). 115p. (C). (gr. 9). 32.95 *(978-0-8160-7047-3(4)*, Ferguson Publishing Co.) Facts On File, Inc.
Reeves, Diane Lindsey. Career Ideas for Teens in Health Science. 2006. (Career Ideas for Teens Ser.). (Illus.). 192p. (gr. 8-12). per. 16.95 *(978-0-8160-6920-0(4)*, Checkmark Bks.) Facts On File, Inc.
Shepherd, Jodie. A Day with Doctors. 2012. (ENG., Illus.). 32p. (J). lib. bdg. 23.00 *(978-0-531-28950-1(8))* Scholastic Library Publishing.
Silverstone, Michael. Paramedics to the Rescue: When Every Second Counts. 2004. (High Five Reading - Purple Ser.). (ENG., Illus.). 64p. (gr. 3-4). per. 9.00 *(978-0-7368-3849-8(X)*, High Five Reading (RBL)) Capstone Press of Coughlan Cos.

MEDIEVAL ART

see Art, Medieval

MEDIEVAL CIVILIZATION

see Civilization, Medieval

MEDIEVAL LITERATURE

see Literature, Medieval

MEDITATIONS

Abato, Andrew. Alphabet Mandalas - Beautiful Letter-Based Mandalas for Colouring in, Learning & Meditation. 2010. 56p. pap. 14.90 *(978-3-8391-4871-6(5))* Bks. on Demand.
—Christmas Mandalas - Beautiful Christmas Mandalas for Colouring In. 2010. 52p. pap. 15.50 *(978-3-8391-4000-0(5))* Bks. on Demand.
Ayer, Jane E. Guided Meditations for Junior High: Good Judgment, Gifts, Obedience, Inner Blindness. 2003. (Quiet Place Apart Ser.). 48p. pap., tchr. ed. 9.95 *(978-0-88489-500-8(9))* St. Mary's Pr. of MN.
Babour Staff & Frazier, April. 3-Minute Devotions for Teen Girls: 180 Encouraging Readings. 2015. (3-Minute Devotions Ser.). (ENG.). 192p. pap. 4.99 *(978-1-63058-856-4(3)*, Barbour Bks.) Barbour Publishing, Inc.
Berg, Yehuda. The 72 Names of God for Kids: A Treasury of Timeless Wisdom. 2006. (ENG., Illus.). 192p. (gr. 1-7). *(978-1-57189-543-1(4))* Klein, Richard A. scaneg Verlag.
Brost, Corey. Gospel Connections for Teens: Reflections for Sunday Mass, Cycle C. 2006. 129p. (YA). (gr. 8-12). per. 6.25 *(978-0-88489-641-8(2))* St. Mary's Pr. of MN.
Brown, Monica & Musgrave, Hilary. Be Still & know... God Is Here: Be Still. 2011. (J). pap. *(978-0-9750732-8-5(1))* Emmaus Productions.
Freeman, Laurence. A Simple Way: The Path of Christian Meditation. 2004. 43p. (YA). pap. 9.95 *(978-0-9725627-6-8(1))* Medio Media Publishing.
Gates, Mariam. Meditate with Me: A Step-By-Step Mindfulness Journey. Sumaite, Margarita, illus. 2017. (ENG.). 40p. (J). (gr. -1-3). 17.99 ***(978-0-399-18661-5(1)**,* Dial Bks) Penguin Young Readers Group.
Gyatso, Geshe Kelsang. What Is Meditation? Buddhism for Children Level 4. 2013. (Buddhism for Children Ser.). (ENG., Illus.). 32p. (J). (gr. 4-7). 8.95 *(978-1-61606-024-4(7))* Tharpa Pubns. GBR. Dist: Ingram Publisher Services.
Hamilton, Amy. Indigo Dreaming: Meditations for Children. 2006. (Illus.). 141p. per. *(978-0-9757953-7-8(6))* Joshua Bks.
Hascall, Glenn & Barbour Publishing Staff. 3-Minute Devotions for Guys: 180 Encouraging Readings for Teens. 2015. (3-Minute Devotions Ser.). (ENG.). 192p. pap. 4.99 *(978-1-63058-857-1(1)*, Barbour Bks.) Barbour Publishing, Inc.
Henry, Deborah, ed. My Devotions: Fifty Years. 50th anniv. ed. 2008. 368p. (J). 12.99 *(978-0-7586-1593-0(0))* Concordia Publishing Hse.
Hodgson, Joan. Our Father. Ripper, Peter, illus. 2003. 24p. (gr. k-7). 5.95 *(978-0-85487-040-0(7))* White Eagle Publishing Trust GBR. Dist: DeVorss & Co.
Nghiem, Thuc, et al. Each Breath a Smile. Dong, Nguyen & Hop, Nguyen Thi, illus. 2005. (ENG.). 32p. (J). (gr. -1-2). pap. 10.95 *(978-1-888375-22-0(1)*, Plum Blossom Bks.) Parallax Pr.
Parrish, MariLee. God Hearts Me: 3-Minute Devotions for Girls on the Go! 2015. (3-Minute Devotions Ser.). (ENG.). 160p. (J). pap. 4.99 *(978-1-63058-609-6(9)*, Barbour Bks.) Barbour Publishing, Inc.
Paynter, Roxanne. Small Souls: Meditations for Children. 2004. 86p. (Orig.). (J). pap. *(978-0-9581891-0-1(2)*, 305-004) Joshua Bks.
Simhananda, B. Jyoti for Kids: A Meditative Technique of Purification by the Light. 2011. (ENG., Illus.). 34p. (J). pap. *(978-0-9809694-6-7(8)*, 9780980969467) Orange Palm & Magnificent Magus Pubns., Inc.
Singh, Rajinder. Jyoti Meditation for Children. Schulbaum, Michael, illus. 2011. 24p. (J). (gr. -1-3). 10.00 *(978-0-918224-81-1(0))* Radiance Pubs.
Swanson, Gary B. Click Here: Interactive Devotionals for Teens. 2003. 144p. (YA). pap. 10.99 *(978-0-8280-1726-8(3))* Review & Herald Publishing Assn.
Thiruvalluvar. Tirukkural Manthiram Coloring Book with Meditation. 2006. (ENG, FRE & ZUL., Illus.). (J). 5.00 incl. audio *(978-0-9676212-3-4(2))* International Tamil Language Foundation.
Viegas, Marneta. Relax Kids: Little Book of Stars. 2015. (ENG., Illus.). 126p. pap. 14.95 *(978-1-78279-460-8(3)*, Our Street Bks.) Hunt, John Publishing Ltd. GBR. Dist: National Bk. Network.
—Relax Kids: The Wishing Star. 2015. (ENG.). 128p. pap. 14.95 *(978-1-78279-870-5(6)*, Our Street Bks.) Hunt, John Publishing Ltd. GBR. Dist: National Bk. Network.
—Relax Kids - Aladdin's Magic Carpet: Let Snow White, the Wizard of Oz & Other Fairytale Characters Show You & Your Child How to Meditate & Relax. 2015. (ENG.). 120p. pap. 14.95 *(978-1-78279-869-9(2)*, Our Street Bks.) Hunt, John Publishing Ltd. GBR. Dist: National Bk. Network.
Wan, Jian Q. Meditating into Wellness with San He Qigong. 2003. per. 13.00 *(978-1-892686-10-7(4))* Manning, Laurie.
Yaconelli, Mike. Devotion: A Raw-Truth Journal on Following Jesus, 1 vol. 2004. (Invert Ser.). (ENG., Illus.). 80p. (YA). pap. 10.99 *(978-0-310-25559-8(7))* Zondervan.
Ytreeide, Arnold. Tabitha's Travels: A Family Story for Advent, 1 vol. 2010. (Illus.). 160p. (J). (gr. 7-18). pap. 15.99 *(978-0-8254-4172-1(2))* Kregel Pubns.

MEDITERRANEAN REGION

Behnke, Alison, et al. Cooking the Mediterranean Way. 2nd rev. ed. 2005. (Easy Menu Ethnic Cookbooks 2nd Edition Ser.). (ENG., Illus.). 72p. (gr. 5-12). 25.26 *(978-0-8225-1237-0(8)*, Lerner Pubns.) Lerner Publishing Group.
Collier, Paul H. & O'Neill, Robert John. World War II: The Mediterranean 1940-1945. 2010. (World War II: Essential Histories Ser.). (Illus.). 96p. (YA). (gr. 9-12). lib. bdg. 33.25 *(978-1-4358-9132-6(5))* Rosen Publishing Group, Inc., The.
Greeley, August. Writing in Ancient Phoenicia. 2009. (Writing in the Ancient World Ser.). 24p. (gr. 3-3). 42.50 *(978-1-60854-908-5(9)*, PowerKids Pr.) Rosen Publishing Group, Inc., The.
Green, Jen. Mediterranean Sea. 2006. (Oceans & Seas Ser.). (Illus.). 48p. (gr. 5-12). pap. 14.05 *(978-0-8368-6282-9(1))*; lib. bdg. 31.00 *(978-0-8368-6274-4(0))* Stevens, Gareth Publishing LLLP. (Gareth Stevens Secondary Library).
Heing, Bridey. Phoenician Trade Routes. 2017. (J). ***(978-1-5026-2861-9(9))*** Cavendish Square Publishing.
Jeffrey, Gary. North Africa & the Mediterranean. 2012. (ENG., Illus.). 48p. (J). *(978-0-7787-4193-0(1))*; pap. *(978-0-7787-4200-5(8))* Crabtree Publishing Co.
Kuskowski, Alex. Super Simple Mediterranean Art: Fun & Easy Art from Around the World, 1 vol. 2014. (Super Simple Cultural Art Set 2 Ser.). (ENG.). 32p. (gr. 5-10). lib. bdg. 27.07 *(978-1-62403-282-0(6)*, Super SandCastle) ABDO Publishing Co.
Micklos, John. Mediterranean Trade Routes. 2017. (J). ***(978-1-5026-2693-6(4))*** Cavendish Square Publishing.
Stefoff, Rebecca. The Ancient Mediterranean World. 2004. (World Historical Atlases Ser.). (Illus.). 48p. (gr. 5). 26.95 *(978-0-7614-1641-8(2)*, Benchmark Bks.) Marshall Cavendish Corp.
—Redbeard. 2015. (J). lib. bdg. *(978-1-62713-533-7(2))*; (ENG.). 48p. (gr. 3-3). 31.36 *(978-1-5026-0199-5(0))* Cavendish Square Publishing.
Tubb, Jonathan. Bible Lands. 2016. (DK Eyewitness Bks.). (ENG., Illus.). 64p. (J). (gr. 3-7). lib. bdg. 19.99 *(978-1-4654-4011-2(9)*, 1405880, DK Children) Dorling Kindersley Publishing, Inc.
Weintraub, Aileen. The Barbarossa Brothers: 16th-Century Pirates of the Barbary Coast. 2009. (Library of Pirates Ser.). 24p. (gr. 3-3). 42.50 *(978-1-60853-814-0(1)*, PowerKids Pr.) Rosen Publishing Group, Inc., The.

MEDITERRANEAN REGION—FICTION

Fox, Robin C. & Fox, Carol White. The Traveling Adventures of the Robin & the Fox Around the World We Go! A Cruise Through the Mediterranean. 2013. 44p. pap. 20.45 *(978-1-4908-1763-7(8)*, WestBow Pr.) Author Solutions, Inc.
Friesner, Esther & Friesner, Esther M. Nobody's Princess. 2008. (Princesses of Myth Ser.). (ENG., Illus.). 336p. (YA). (gr. 7-11). pap. 8.99 *(978-0-375-87529-8(8)*, Ember) Random Hse. Children's Bks.
Harrison, Francesca. Obus the Eucalyptus Tree Fairy. 2012. 26p. pap. *(978-1-909381-03-2(9))* Foote, Douglas.
Le Clézio, J. M. G. Lullaby. Lemoine, Georges, illus. 2007. (FRE.). 72p. (J). (gr. 5-10). pap. *(978-2-07-061258-1(9))* Gallimard, Editions.
Paver, Michelle. The Burning Shadow. 2015. (Gods & Warriors Ser.: 2). (ENG.). 320p. (J). (gr. 5). 7.99 *(978-0-14-242285-4(1)*, Puffin Books) Penguin Young Readers Group.
—Gods & Warriors. 2013. (Gods & Warriors Ser.: 1). (ENG.). 336p. (J). (gr. 5). pap. 8.99 *(978-0-14-242284-7(3)*, Puffin Books) Penguin Young Readers Group.
—Warrior Bronze. 2017. (Gods & Warriors Ser.). (ENG.). 272p. (J). (gr. 3-7). 16.99 *(978-0-8037-3884-3(6)*, Dial Bks) Penguin Young Readers Group.
Saunders, Harry M. Teenagers on an Adventure: Journey of Two Boys & a Girl. 2013. 168p. pap. 19.95 *(978-1-62709-466-5(0))* America Star Bks.

MEDUSAE

Nagle, Frances. Medusa. 2016. (Monsters! Ser.). (Illus.). 32p. (J). (gr. 2-1). pap. 10.50 *(978-1-4824-4867-2(X))* Stevens, Gareth Publishing LLLP.

MEIR, GOLDA, 1898-1978

Aboff, Marcie. Golda Meir Iron Lady of Israel. 2016. (Spring Forward Ser.). (J). (gr. 2). *(978-1-4900-9454-0(7))* Benchmark Education Co.
Blashfield, Jean F. Golda Meir. 2010. (Leading Women Ser.). 96p. (YA). (gr. 7-12). 39.93 *(978-0-7614-4960-7(4))* Marshall Cavendish GBR. Dist: Marshall Cavendish Corp.
Krasner, Barbara. Goldie Takes a Stand! Golda Meir's First Crusade. Garrity-Riley, Kelsey, illus. 2014. (ENG.). 32p. (J). (gr. k-4). 17.95 *(978-1-4677-1200-2(0))* Lerner Publishing Group.
—Goldie Takes a Stand: Golda Meir's First Crusade. Garrity-Riley, Kelsey, illus. 2014. (ENG.). 32p. (J). (gr. k-4). 7.95 *(978-1-4677-1201-9(9)*, Kar-Ben Publishing) Lerner Publishing Group.
World Book, Inc Staff, contrib. by. Golda Meir: With Profiles of David Ben-Gurion & Yitzhak Rabin. 2006. (Biographical Connections Ser.). (Illus.). 112p. (J). *(978-0-7166-1829-4(X))* World Bk., Inc.

MEITNER, LISE, 1878-1968

Barron, Rachel Stiffler. Lise Meitner: Discoverer of Nuclear Fission. 2004. (Profiles in Science Ser.). (Illus.). 112p. (YA). (gr. 6-12). lib. bdg. 23.95 *(978-1-883846-52-7(8)*, First Biographies) Reynolds, Morgan Inc.
Conkling, Winifred. Radioactive! How Irene Curie & Lise Meitner Revolutionized Science & Changed the World. 2016. (ENG., Illus.). 240p. (J). (gr. 5-9). 17.95 *(978-1-61620-415-0(X))* Algonquin Bks. of Chapel Hill.
Venezia, Mike. Lise Meitner: Had the Right Vision about Nuclear Fission. Venezia, Mike, illus. 2010. (Getting to Know the World's Greatest Inventors & Scientists Ser.). (ENG., Illus.). 32p. (J). (gr. 3-4). pap. 6.95 *(978-0-531-20776-5(5)*, Children's Pr.) Scholastic Library Publishing.

MELVILLE, HERMAN, 1819-1891

Bloom, Harold, ed. Herman Melville's Moby-Dick. 2nd rev. ed. 2007. (Bloom's Modern Critical Interpretations Ser.). 256p. (C). (gr. 9-12). 45.00 *(978-0-7910-9363-4(8)*, Chelsea Hse.) Facts On File, Inc.
Faiella, Graham. Moby Dick & the Whaling Industry of the 19th Century. 2009. (Looking at Literature Through Primary Sources Ser.). 64p. (gr. 5-8). 58.50 *(978-1-61514-305-4(X))* Rosen Publishing Group, Inc., The.
Gibson, Karen Bush. Herman Melville. 2006. (J). lib. bdg. *(978-1-58415-453-2(5))* Mitchell Lane Pubs., Inc.
Meltzer, Milton. Herman Melville: A Biography. 2005. (Literary Greats Ser.). (ENG., Illus.). 128p. (gr. 7-12). 33.26 *(978-0-7613-2749-3(5)*, Twenty-First Century Bks.) Lerner Publishing Group.
Saddleback Educational Publishing Staff, ed. Moby Dick. 2011. (Timeless Classics Ser.). (ENG.). 48p. (YA). (gr. 9-12). cd-rom 19.95 *(978-1-61651-144-9(3))* Saddleback Educational Publishing, Inc.

MEMOIRS

see Autobiographies; Biography

MEMORY

Beck, Esther. Cool Eyewitness Encounters: How's Your Memory?, 1 vol. 2009. (Cool CSI Ser.). (ENG., Illus.). 32p. (YA). (gr. 3-6). 28.50 *(978-1-60453-485-6(0))* ABDO Publishing Co.
Berry, Joy. Help Me Be Good about Being Forgetful. 2009. (Help Me Be Good Ser.). 32p. pap. 7.95 *(978-1-60577-102-1(3))* Berry, Joy Enterprises.
Berry, Joy Wilt. A Book about Being Forgetful. 2005. (Illus.). (J). *(978-0-7172-8589-1(8))* Scholastic, Inc.
Coirault, Christine, illus. My First Book of Learning. 2009. (J). *(978-1-74089-930-7(X))* Fog City Pr.
Cusimano/Achieve Publications Staff. Achieve Levels I-IV: A Visual Memory Program Levels I-IV, 4 vols., Set. 2003. (ENG.). 412p. tchr. ed., ring bd. 79.95 *(978-0-9727762-0-2(6)*, 206) Achieve Pubns.
—Achieve Levels V & VI: A Visual Memory Program Levels V & VI, 2 vols., Set. 2003. 242p. tchr. ed., ring bd. 43.95 *(978-0-9727762-1-9(4))* Achieve Pubns.
Dwyer, Helen, ed. Intellectual Development. 2011. (CC: Psychology Ser.). (Illus.). 112p. (gr. 6-12). lib. bdg. 42.80 *(978-1-936333-18-9(X))* Brown Bear Bks.
Eastaway, Rob. How to Remember (Almost) Everything, Ever! Tips, Tricks & Fun to Turbo-Charge Your Memory. 2016. (ENG., Illus.). 176p. (YA). (gr. 7). 15.95 *(978-1-910232-24-8(6)*, Pavilion) Pavilion Bks. GBR. Dist: Independent Pubs. Group.
Fry, Ron. Surefire Tips to Improve Your Memory Skills, 01 vols., 1. 2016. (Surefire Study Success Ser.). (ENG.). 128p. (YA). 35.60 *(978-1-5081-7089-1(4)*, Rosen Young Adult) Rosen Publishing Group, Inc., The.
Martin, Steve. Miss Pell Never Misspells: More Cool Ways to Remember Stuff. Remphry, Martin, illus. 2013. (ENG.). 128p. (J). (gr. 5-9). 9.99 *(978-0-545-49477-9(X)*, Scholastic Reference) Scholastic, Inc.
Murphy, Patricia J. Never Eat Soggy Waffles: Fun Mnemonic Memory Tricks. LaBaff, Tom, illus. 2009. (Prime (Elementary) Ser.). 48p. (J). (gr. 2-5). lib. bdg. 25.27 *(978-0-7660-2710-7(4))* Enslow Pubs., Inc.
O'Brien, Cynthia. Amazing Brain Mysteries. 2015. (ENG., Illus.). 32p. (J). *(978-0-7787-8070-0(8))* Crabtree Publishing Co.
Olson, Elsie. Memory Fun: Facts, Trivia, & Quizzes. 2017. (Mind Games Ser.). (ENG., Illus.). (J). (gr. 2-5). lib. bdg. 27.99 ***(978-1-5124-3418-7(3))*** Lerner Publishing Group.
Randol, Susan. I Before e (Except after C) Easy, Cool Ways to Remember Facts. 2011. (ENG.). 144p. (YA). (gr. 4-6). 9.99 *(978-1-60652-348-3(1))* Reader's Digest Assn., Inc., The.

Wells, Marcia. Mystery on Museum Mile. Calo, Marcos, illus. 2015. (Eddie Red Undercover Ser.). (ENG.). 256p. (J). (gr. 5-7). pap. 7.99 *(978-0-544-43940-5(6)*, HMH Books For Young Readers) Houghton Mifflin Harcourt Publishing Co.

MEN

see also Human Beings

Carlinsky, Dan. Do You Know Your Boyfriend? 2013. (Do You Know? Ser.). (ENG.). 48p. (YA). (gr. 9-12). pap. 5.99 *(978-1-4022-8539-4(6))* Sourcebooks, Inc.

Chin-Lee, Cynthia. Akira to Zoltan: Twenty-Six Men Who Changed the World. Addy, Sean & Halsey, Megan, illus. 2008. (ENG.). 32p. (J). (gr. 3-7). pap. 7.95 *(978-1-57091-580-2(6))* Charlesbridge Publishing, Inc.

—Akira to Zoltan: Twenty-Six Men Who Changed the World. Halsey, Megan & Addy, Sean, illus. 2006. (ENG.). 32p. (J). (gr. 3-7). lib. bdg. 15.95 *(978-1-57091-579-6(2))* Charlesbridge Publishing, Inc.

Guys' Guides. 2005. (Illus.). 48p. (gr. 5-8). lib. bdg. 95.80 *(978-0-8239-4094-3(2))* Rosen Publishing Group, Inc., The.

Guys' Guides, 6 bks. Incl. Real Deal: A Guy's Guide to Being a Guy. Roberts, Jeremy. (YA). lib. bdg. 29.25 *(978-0-8239-3104-0(8)*, GUREDE); Stay Cool: A Guy's Guide to Handling Conflict. Hayhurst, Chris. (YA). lib. bdg. 29.25 *(978-0-8239-3159-0(5)*, GUSTCO); You Ought to Know: A Guy's Guide to Sex. Kelly, Bill. (J). lib. bdg. 29.25 *(978-0-8239-3084-5(X)*, GUYOSH); 48p. (gr. 5-8). 2005. (Illus.). Set lib. bdg. 107.70 o.p. *(978-0-8239-9088-7(5)*, GUGUID, Rosen Reference) Rosen Publishing Group, Inc., The.

McCann, Michelle Roehm. Boys Who Rocked the World: Heroes from King Tut to Bruce Lee. Hahn, David, illus. 2012. (ENG.). 256p. (J). (gr. 3-7). 18.99 *(978-1-58270-362-6(0))*; pap. 10.99 *(978-1-58270-331-2(0))* Aladdin/Beyond Words.

Mccann, Michelle Roehm. Boys Who Rocked the World: Heroes from King Tut to Shaun White. 2012. lib. bdg. 22.10 *(978-0-606-26897-4(9)*, Turtleback) Turtleback Bks.

McCarthy, Meghan. Strong Man: The Story of Charles Atlas. 2015. (ENG., Illus.). 40p. (J). (gr. k-3). 7.99 *(978-0-553-11354-9(2)*, Dragonfly Bks.) Random Hse. Children's Bks.

Morkes, Andrew & McKenna, Amy. Nontraditional Careers for Women & Men: More Than 30 Great Jobs for Women & Men with Apprenticeships Through Phds. 2011. (ENG.). (J). pap. 19.95 *(978-0-9745251-9-8(7))* College & Career Pr., LLC.

Roberts, Jeremy. The Real Deal: A Guy's Guide to Being a Guy. 2005. (Guys' Guides). (Illus.). 48p. (YA). (gr. 5-8). lib. bdg. 29.25 *(978-0-8239-3104-0(8)*, GUREDE) Rosen Publishing Group, Inc., The.

Shone, Rob. Bigfoot & Other Strange Beasts. 2009. (Graphic Mysteries Ser.). (ENG.). 48p. (YA). (gr. 5-5). 58.50 *(978-1-61512-961-4(8)*, Rosen Reference) Rosen Publishing Group, Inc., The.

MENDEL, GREGOR, 1822-1884

Bankston, John. Gregor Mendel & the Discovery of the Gene. 2004. (Uncharted, Unexplored, & Unexplained Ser.). (Illus.). 48p. (J). (gr. 4-8). lib. bdg. 29.95 *(978-1-58415-266-8(4))* Mitchell Lane Pubs., Inc.

Bardoe, Cheryl. Gregor Mendel: The Friar Who Grew Peas. Smith, Jos. A., illus. (ENG.). (J). (gr. k-4). 2015. 32p. pap. 9.95 *(978-1-4197-1840-3(1))* 2006. 40p. 21.95 *(978-0-8109-5475-5(3))* Abrams, Inc. (Abrams Bks. for Young Readers).

Bortz, Fred. The Laws of Genetics & Gregor Mendel. 2013. (Revolutionary Discoveries of Scientific Pioneers Ser.). (Illus.). 80p. (J). (gr. 7-12). 33.25 *(978-1-4777-1806-3(0))* Rosen Publishing Group, Inc., The.

Klare, Roger. Gregor Mendel: Genius of Genetics. 2015. (J). *(978-0-7660-6565-9(0))* Enslow Pubs., Inc.

Leech, Bonnie. Gregor Mendel's Genetic Theory: Understanding & Applying Concepts of Probability. (PowerMath: Advanced Proficiency Plus Ser.). 2009. 32p. (gr. 5-5). 47.90 *(978-1-60851-356-7(4))* 2007. 36p. pap. 23.95 *(978-1-4358-3820-8(3))* Rosen Publishing Group, Inc., The. (PowerKids Pr.).

Leech, Bonnie Coulter. Gregor Mendel's Genetic Theory: Understanding & Applying Concepts of Probability. (Math for the Real World Ser.). (Illus.). 32p. 2009. (ENG.). (gr. 6-7). pap. 10.00 *(978-1-4042-6063-4(3))* 2006. (YA). (gr. 5-9). lib. bdg. 25.25 *(978-1-4042-3355-3(5))* Rosen Publishing Group, Inc., The.

Van Gorp, Lynn. Gregor Mendel: Genetics Pioneer, 1 vol. 2007. (Science Readers Ser.). (ENG.). 32p. (J). (gr. 3-3). pap. 8.99 *(978-0-7439-0598-5(9))* Shell Educational Publishing.

MENDELEYEV, DMITRY IVANOVICH, 1834-1907

Zannos, Susan. Dmitri Mendeleyev & the Periodic Table. 2004. (Uncharted, Unexplored, & Unexplained Ser.). (Illus.). 48p. (J). (gr. 4-8). lib. bdg. 29.95 *(978-1-58415-267-5(2))* Mitchell Lane Pubs., Inc.

MENDEL'S LAW

Leech, Bonnie. Gregor Mendel's Genetic Theory: Understanding & Applying Concepts of Probability. 2009. (PowerMath: Advanced Proficiency Plus Ser.). 32p. (gr. 5-5). 47.90 *(978-1-60851-356-7(4)*, PowerKids Pr.) Rosen Publishing Group, Inc., The.

MENNONITES

see also Amish

Fleming, Alice. The King of Prussia & a Peanut Butter Sandwich. 2009. (ENG.). 48p. (J). (gr. 2-4). pap. 6.99 *(978-1-4424-1215-6(1)*, Atheneum Bks. for Young Readers) Simon & Schuster Children's Publishing.

Null, David. Introduction to Mennonite Doctrine & Practice. 2004. 90p. 3.25 *(978-0-7399-2316-0(1)*, 2356) Rod & Staff Pubs., Inc.

Therrien, Patricia. Amish & Mennonite Cooking. (American Regional Cooking Library). (Illus.). 72p. 2006. (YA). lib. bdg. 19.95 *(978-1-59084-612-4(5))* 2005. (J). lib. bdg. 299.25 *(978-1-59084-609-4(5))* Mason Crest.

MENNONITES—FICTION

Barry, Rick. Gunner's Run: A World War II Novel. 2007. 215p. (YA). (gr. 8-12). per. 8.99 *(978-1-59166-761-2(5))* BJU Pr.

Brenneman, Lynette Leaman, photos by. Susanna's Surprise: A Day at the Hans Herr House. 2012. (Illus.). 32p. (J). *(978-0-9859737-0-4(6))* Brenneman, Lynette.

Byers, Arlene. Rainbows for Rosa. Halverson, Randal, illus. 2016. 172p. ***(978-0-7399-2521-8(0))*** Rod & Staff Pubs., Inc.

Dueck, Adele. Nettie's Journey, 1 vol. 2005. (From Many Peoples Ser.). (ENG., Illus.). 216p. (J). (gr. 4-7). per. 7.95 *(978-1-55050-322-7(7))* Coteau Bks. CAN. Dist: Orca Bk. Pubs. USA.

Gerber, Mary Lichty. Mary's Family Stories. Whitehead, Victoria E. & Shirk, Linda, illus. 2015. 124p. (J). ***(978-0-7399-2512-6(1))*** Rod & Staff Pubs., Inc.

Gugler, Laurel Dee. Catching Forever, 1 vol. 2007. (Lorimer Streetlights Ser.). (ENG.). 104p. (J). (gr. 2-5). 7.95 *(978-1-55028-954-1(3)*, 9781550289541) Lorimer, James & Co., Ltd., Pubs. CAN. Dist: Casemate Pubs. & Bk. Distributors, LLC.

—A Piece of Forever, 1 vol. 2008. (Lorimer Streetlights Ser.). (ENG.). 168p. (J). (gr. 2-4). 8.95 *(978-1-55277-026-9(5)*, 9781552770269) Lorimer, James & Co., Ltd., Pubs. CAN. Dist: Casemate Pubs. & Bk. Distributors, LLC.

Hege, Lynnita. The Little Black Hen. Keyes, Tina Misrasi, illus. 2013. 208p. (J). *(978-0-7399-2465-5(6))* Rod & Staff Pubs., Inc.

Horrocks, Anita. Almost Eden. 2006. (ENG.). 288p. (J). (gr. 5-9). pap. 9.95 *(978-0-88776-742-5(7)*, Tundra Bks.) Tundra Bks. CAN. Dist: Penguin Random Hse. LLC.

Hurst, Elva. Autumn Days: Based on a True Story. 2015. (Farm Life Ser.). (ENG., Illus.). 80p. (J). pap. 6.99 *(978-0-7369-6094-6(5))* Harvest Hse. Pubs.

—The Pony Cart Adventure. 2014. (Farm Life Ser.). 64p. pap. 6.99 *(978-0-7369-6089-2(9))* Harvest Hse. Pubs.

—The Pony Cart Adventure: A True Story. 2014. (Farm Life Ser.). (ENG., Illus.). 64p. (J). pap. 6.99 *(978-0-7369-6088-5(0))* Harvest Hse. Pubs.

—Summer on the Farm. 2014. (Farm Life Ser.). 80p. pap. 6.99 *(978-0-7369-6091-5(0))* Harvest Hse. Pubs.

—Summer on the Farm: A True Story. 2014. (Farm Life Ser.). (ENG., Illus.). 80p. (J). pap. 6.99 *(978-0-7369-6090-8(2))* Harvest Hse. Pubs.

—When School Bells Call: Based on a True Story. 2015. (Farm Life Ser.). (ENG.). 80p. (J). pap. 6.99 *(978-0-7369-6092-2(9))* Harvest Hse. Pubs.

Klassen, Kirsten L. Katelyn's Affection. 2004. (ENG.). 280p. pap. 11.99 *(978-0-8361-9281-0(8))* Herald Pr.

Krahn, Maria. Charity Prays for Rain. Eshbach, Ariel, illus. 2014. 32p. (J). *(978-0-7399-2475-4(3))* Rod & Staff Pubs., Inc.

Kuepfer, Sharon (Durksen) Schnupp. Little Prairie Girl: Are We Rich ... or Poor? 2009. (ENG., Illus.). 115p. pap. 7.95 *(978-0-60126-187-8(X))* Masthof Pr.

Martin, Elaine S. Bowman. The Rooster's Fate: And Other Stories. Hackman, Evelyn, illus. 2014. 184p. (J). *(978-0-7399-2481-5(8))* Rod & Staff Pubs., Inc.

Martin, Joanna F. Betsey's Wishes. 2010. (Illus.). 255p. (J). (gr. 3-6). 9.80 *(978-0-7399-2424-2(9))* Rod & Staff Pubs., Inc.

Martin, Mabel. Days with Mary. Hoover, Charity, illus. 2015. 159p. (J). *(978-0-7399-2515-7(6))* Rod & Staff Pubs., Inc.

Martin, Mary. God Made Nuts. Derstine, Charlene, illus. 2012. 53p. (J). *(978-0-7399-2501-0(6))* Rod & Staff Pubs., Inc.

—Grandma's Goose. Hoover, Charity, illus. 2012. 188p. *(978-0-7399-2452-5(4))* Rod & Staff Pubs., Inc.

Martin, Mildred A. Growing with the Millers. Burkholder, Edith, illus. 2012. 144p. (J). *(978-1-884377-23-5(8))* Green Pastures Pr.

Martin, Rebecca. Blossoms on the Roof. 2015. (Amish Frontier Ser.). (ENG.). 160p. (J). (gr. 2-7). pap. 8.99 *(978-0-7369-6367-1(7))* Harvest Hse. Pubs.

—Joanna's Journey. Yoder, Laura & Weaver, Lisa, illus. 2006. 168p. (YA). pap. 9.99 *(978-1-933753-01-0(3))* Carlisle Pr.-Walnut Creek.

Sawyer, Kim Vogel. Katy's New World, 1 vol. 2010. (Katy Lambright Ser.: No. 1). (ENG.). 208p. (YA). (gr. 8-11). pap. 9.99 *(978-0-310-71924-3(0))* Zondervan.

Seyfert, Ella Maie. Amish Moving Day. Jones, Henrietta, illus. 2011. 132p. 40.95 *(978-1-258-01315-8(0))* Literary Licensing, LLC.

Smith, Eunice Geil. Treasure Hunt. 2006. 119p. (J). (gr. 3-7). per. 9.99 *(978-0-8361-9332-9(6))* Herald Pr.

Snider, Cindy Gay. Finding Anna Bee. Chambers, Mary, illus. 2007. 163p. (J). (gr. 3-7). per. 9.99 *(978-0-8361-9392-3(X))* Herald Pr.

Trottier, Maxine. Migrant, 1 vol. Arsenault, Isabelle, illus. 2011. (ENG.). 40p. (J). (gr. -1-2). 18.95 *(978-0-88899-975-7(5))* Groundwood Bks. CAN. Dist: Publishers Group West (PGW).

Weaver, Anna E. Stories From Grandma's Day. 2011. (Illus.). 285p. (YA). (gr. 4-9). pap. 8.90 *(978-0-7399-2426-6(5))* Rod & Staff Pubs., Inc.

MENSTRUATION

Bonnice, Sherry. Premenstrual Disorders. McDonnell, Mary Ann & Esherick, Donald, eds. 2013. (State of Mental Illness & Its Therapy Ser.: 19). 128p. (J). (gr. 7-18). 24.95 *(978-1-4222-2833-3(9))* Mason Crest.

Byers, Ann. Menstruation. 2009. (Girls' Health Ser.). 48p. (gr. 5-6). 53.00 *(978-1-61512-730-6(5)*, Rosen Reference) Rosen Publishing Group, Inc., The.

Feinmann, Jane. Everything a Girl Needs to Know about Her PeriodS. 2003. (Illus.). 144p. pap. 14.95 *(978-1-56906-555-6(1)*, BTM-555) Sellers Publishing, Inc.

Growing Up, 9 vols., Set. Incl. Going to the Hospital. Parker, Steve & Parker, Vic. 23.32 *(978-1-4329-4797-2(4))*; Having a Hearing Test. Parker, Steve & Parker, Vic. 23.32 *(978-1-4329-4799-6(0))*; Having an Eye Test. Parker, Steve & Parker, Vic. 23.32 *(978-1-4329-4798-9(2))*; Moving. Parker, Steve & Parker, Vic. 23.32 *(978-1-4329-4800-9(8))*; My First Day at a New School. Guillain, Charlotte. 23.32 *(978-1-4329-4796-5(6))*; My First Sleepover. Guillain, Charlotte. 23.32 *(978-1-4329-4802-3(4))*; My First Trip on an Airplane. Parker, Steve & Parker, Vic. 23.32 *(978-1-4329-4801-6(6))*; New Brother or Sister. Guillain, Charlotte. 23.32 *(978-1-4329-4803-0(2))*; Visiting the Dentist. Guillain, Charlotte. 23.32 *(978-1-4329-4804-7(0))*; (gr. k-2). (Growing Up Ser.). (ENG., Illus.). 24p. 2011. Set lib. bdg. 209.88 *(978-1-4329-4805-4(9)*, Heinemann Read & Learn) Heinemann-Raintree.

Morais, Joan. A Time to Celebrate: A Celebration of a Girl's First Menstrual Period. 2004. (Illus.). 112p. (YA). per. 16.95 *(978-0-9746304-5-8(4)*, 1196060) Lua Publishing.

Movsessian, Shushann. Puberty Girl. 2005. (ENG., Illus.). 128p. (J). (gr. 4-7). pap. 19.95 *(978-1-74114-104-7(4))* Allen & Unwin AUS. Dist: Independent Pubs. Group.

Orr, Tamra. Amenorrhea: Why Your Period Stops. 2009. (Library of Sexual Health Ser.). 64p. (gr. 6-6). 58.50 *(978-1-60853-838-6(9))* Rosen Publishing Group, Inc., The.

Parker, Steve & Parker, Vic. Growing Up, 9 vols., Set. Incl. My First Trip on an Airplane. (ENG.). 24p. (gr. k-2). 2011. pap. 6.79 *(978-1-4329-4811-5(3)*, Heinemann Read & Learn); (Growing Up Ser.). (ENG.). 24p. 2011. Set pap. 13.58 o.p. *(978-1-4329-4815-3(6)*, Heinemann Read & Learn) Heinemann-Raintree.

Parker, Vic. The Little Book of Growing Up. 2007. (ENG., Illus.). 128p. (J). (gr. 7-17). pap. 6.99 *(978-0-340-93099-1(3))* Headline Publishing Group GBR. Dist: Hachette Bk. Group.

Parker, Victoria. Girls Only! All about Periods & Growing-Up Stuff. 2014. (ENG., Illus.). 112p. (J). (gr. k-7). pap. 9.99 *(978-0-340-87828-6(2))* Hodder & Stoughton GBR. Dist: Hachette Bk. Group.

Thomson, Ruth & Thomson, Chloë. Have You Started Yet? You & Your Period - Getting the Facts Straight. Eccles, Jane, illus. unabr. ed. 2013. (ENG.). 128p. (J). (gr. 4-7). pap. 9.99 *(978-1-4472-2611-6(9))* Pan Macmillan GBR. Dist: Independent Pubs. Group.

Waters, Sophie. Dealing with PMS. (Girls' Health Ser.). 48p. 2009. (gr. 5-6). 53.00 *(978-1-61512-729-0(1)*, Rosen Reference) 2007. (Illus.). (YA). (gr. 7-12). lib. bdg. 29.25 *(978-1-4042-1949-6(8))* Rosen Publishing Group, Inc., The.

MENSTRUATION—FICTION

Fraustino, Lisa Rowe, ed. Don't Cramp My Style: Stories about That Time of the Month. 2012. (ENG.). 304p. (YA). (gr. 7). pap. 14.99 *(978-1-4424-8109-1(9)*, Simon & Schuster Bks. For Young Readers) Simon & Schuster Bks. For Young Readers.

Gordon, Lorell Cynthia. Tilly's Birthday: A Young Girl's Introduction to Menstruation. 2005. (Illus.). 64p. (J). per. 6.99 *(978-0-9763961-0-9(6))* Learning All About Me, LLC.

Naylor, Phyllis Reynolds. Lovingly Alice. 2004. (Alice Bks.). 166p. (J). (gr. 4-6). 13.65 *(978-0-7569-6604-1(3))* Perfection Learning Corp.

MENSURATION

see Measurement

MENTAL DEFICIENCY

see People with Mental Disabilities

MENTAL DEPRESSION

see Depression, Mental

MENTAL DISEASES

see Mental Illness; Psychology, Pathological

MENTAL HEALTH

see also Mental Illness; Mind and Body; Psychology, Pathological

Belfield, Annie. Stressed-Out Girl? Girls Dealing with Feelings. 2014. (ENG.). 64p. (J). (gr. 5-12). 15.95 *(978-1-62293-040-1(1))* Enslow Pubs., Inc.

Bonnice, Sherry. Drug Therapy & Adjustment Disorders. 2003. (Psychiatric Disorders: Drugs & Psychology for the Mind & Bod Ser.). (Illus.). 126p. (YA). (gr. 4-7). pap. 14.95 *(978-1-4222-0384-2(0))* Mason Crest.

—Drug Therapy for Adjustment Disorders. 2004. (Encyclopedia of Psychiatric Drugs & Their Disorders Ser.). (Illus.). 128p. (YA). lib. bdg. 24.95 *(978-1-59084-560-8(9))* Mason Crest.

Brinkerhoff, Shirley. Drug Therapy & Anxiety Disorders. (Encyclopedia of Psychiatric Drugs & Their Disorders Ser.). (Illus.). (YA). 2004. 128p. lib. bdg. 24.95 *(978-1-59084-561-5(7))* 2003. 124p. (gr. 7). pap. 14.95 *(978-1-4222-0385-9(9))* Mason Crest.

—Drug Therapy & Childhood & Adolescent Disorders. 2003. (Psychiatric Disorders: Drugs & Psychology for the Mind & Bod Ser.). (Illus.). 125p. (YA). (gr. 4-7). pap. 14.95 *(978-1-4222-0386-6(7))* Mason Crest.

Clark, Travis. A Stressed-Out Guy's Guide: How to Deal. 2014. (ENG.). 64p. (J). (gr. 5-12). 15.95 *(978-1-62293-010-4(X))* Enslow Pubs., Inc.

Conte, Paola, et al. Someone to Talk To: Getting Good at Feeling Better. 2017. (Illus.). 64p. (J). pap. ***(978-1-4338-2672-6(0)***, Magination Pr.) American Psychological Assn.

Engdahl, Sylvia. Mental Health. 2010. (Issues on Trial Ser.). (J). 42.15 *(978-0-7377-4738-6(2)*, Greenhaven Pr., Inc.) Cengage Gale.

Fisher, Beverly. Mental Toughness for Personal Fitness: Workbook for Life 2004. (Illus.). 64p. pap. 10.99 *(978-0-9745066-0-9(5))* Sports In Mind.

—Mental Toughness for Weight Management: Workbook for Life. 2004. (Illus.). 60p. pap. 10.99 *(978-0-9745066-1-6(3))* Sports In Mind.

Harmon, Daniel E. Careers in Mental Health. 2017. (J). ***(978-1-5383-8154-0(0)***, Rosen Young Adult) Rosen Publishing Group, Inc., The.

Kuskowski, Alex. Cool Thinking: Healthy & Fun Ways to Train Your Brain, 1 vol. 2012. (Cool Health & Fitness Ser.). (ENG.). 32p. (J). (gr. 3-6). lib. bdg. 27.07 *(978-1-61783-430-1(0)*, Checkerboard Library) ABDO Publishing Co.

Lambillion, Paul. Staying Cool. 2004. (Illus.). 196p. pap. 13.95 *(978-0-7171-3598-1(5))* M.H. Gill & Co. U. C. IRL. Dist: Hushion Hse. Publishing, Ltd.

Libal, Autumn. Drug Therapy & Postpartum Disorders. 2003. (Psychiatric Disorders: Drugs & Psychology for the Mind & Bod Ser.). (Illus.). 124p. (YA). (gr. 4-7). pap. 14.95 *(978-1-4222-0395-8(6))* Mason Crest.

McPherson, Stephanie Sammartino. Stressed Out in School? Learning to Deal with Academic Pressure. 2009. (Issues in Focus Today Ser.). (Illus.). 112p. (J). (gr. 6-18). lib. bdg. 33.27 *(978-0-7660-3069-5(5))* Enslow Pubs., Inc.

Miller, Susan B. When Parents Have Problems: A Book for Teens & Older Children Who Have a Disturbed or Difficult Parent. 2nd ed. 2012. xiv, 105p. (J). pap. 19.95 *(978-0-398-08713-5(X))* Thomas, Charles C. Pub., Ltd.

Morse, Philip C. Kick Out Stress - Teen Stress Reduction Program: Improving Self-Esteem, Optimizing Performance in School & Sports & Improving Physical & Emotional Health. 2004. (YA). (gr. 8-12). pap. *(978-0-9748548-0-9(8))* Mind/Body Workshops.

Parks, Peggy J. Teens & Stress. 2015. (ENG., Illus.). 96p. (J). lib. bdg. *(978-1-60152-768-4(3))* ReferencePoint Pr., Inc.

Reber, Deborah. Chill: Stress-Reducing Techniques for a More Balanced, Peaceful You. 2008. 208p. (YA). (gr. 7-12). pap. 9.99 *(978-1-4169-6555-8(6)*, Simon Pulse) Simon Pulse.

Simpson, Carolyn & Simpson, Dwain. Coping with Post-Traumatic Stress Disorder (PTSD) Dealing with Tragedy. 2005. (Coping Ser.). (Illus.). 192p. (YA). (gr. 7-12). lib. bdg. 34.60 *(978-0-8239-3456-0(X))* Rosen Publishing Group, Inc., The.

Spalding, Maddie. 12 Tips to Maintain Brain Health. 2017. (Healthy Living Ser.). (ENG., Illus.). 32p. (J). (gr. 3-6). 21.95 *(978-1-63235-368-9(7))* Pr. Room Editions LLC.

Spalding, Maddie & Ventura, Marne. 12 Tips to Maintain Brain Health. 2016. (Healthy Living Ser.). (ENG., Illus.). 32p. (J). pap. 9.95 *(978-1-63235-386-3(5))* Pr. Room Editions LLC.

Teen Mental Health, 6 vols., Set. Incl. Addictive Personality. Juzwiak, Richard. lib. bdg. 29.25 *(978-1-4042-1802-4(5))*; Anxiety & Panic Attacks. Levin, Judith. lib. bdg. 29.25 *(978-1-4042-1797-3(5))*; Depression & Mood Disorders. Levin, Judith. lib. bdg. 29.25 *(978-1-4042-1798-0(3))*; Meditation. Moore, Andrew. lib. bdg. 29.25 *(978-1-4042-1799-7(1))*; (Illus.). 48p. (YA). (gr. 7-12). 2008. 2009. Set lib. bdg. 159.00 *(978-1-4042-1888-8(2))* Rosen Publishing Group, Inc., The.

Teen Mental Health: Set 4. 2013. (Teen Mental Health Ser.). 48p. (YA). (gr. 7-12). 179.70 *(978-1-4777-1761-5(7))* Rosen Publishing Group, Inc., The.

Tousey, Ben. Acting Your Dreams: Using Acting Techniques to Interpret Your Dreams, 1. 2003. (C). per. 14.95 *(978-0-9724292-0-7(4))* Yhabbut Publishing.

Ward, James. Asylum Light: Stories from the George A. Zeller Era & Beyond, Peoria State Hospital, Galesburg Mental Health Center, & George A. Zeller Mental Health Center. 2005. (Illus.). 298p. pap. 19.95 *(978-0-9748742-0-3(5)*, 1210408) Mental Health Historic Preservation Society Of Central Illinois.

Williams, Dinah. Abandoned Insane Asylums. 2008. (Scary Places Ser.). (Illus.). 32p. (YA). (gr. 4-7). lib. bdg. 25.27 *(978-1-59716-575-4(1))* Bearport Publishing Co., Inc.

Wroble, Lisa A. Dealing with Stress. 2011. (Life—a How-To Guide Ser.). (Illus.). 128p. (J). (gr. 6-18). pap. 10.95 *(978-1-59845-309-6(2))* Enslow Pubs., Inc.

MENTAL HYGIENE

see Mental Health

MENTAL ILLNESS

see also Mental Health

Abramovitz, Melissa. Mental Retardation. 2007. (Diseases & Disorders Ser.). (ENG., Illus.). 104p. (YA). (gr. 7-12). lib. bdg. 34.95 *(978-1-59018-412-7(2)*, LML02109-192008) Cengage Gale.

Bjorklund, Ruth. Tourette Syndrome. 2009. (Health Alert 6 Ser.). 64p. (gr. 4). 32.79 *(978-0-7614-3985-1(4))* Marshall Cavendish Corp.

Bleuel, Amy & Chapman, Wesley. Project Semicolon: Your Story Isn't Over. 2017. 352p. (YA). (gr. 9). pap. 9.99 ***(978-0-06-246652-5(6))*** HarperCollins Pubs.

Bonnice, Sherry. Drug Therapy & Adjustment Disorders. 2003. (Psychiatric Disorders: Drugs & Psychology for the Mind & Bod Ser.). (Illus.). 126p. (YA). (gr. 4-7). pap. 14.95 *(978-1-4222-0384-2(0))* Mason Crest.

—Drug Therapy & Premenstrual Disorders. 2003. (Psychiatric Disorders: Drugs & Psychology for the Mind & Bod Ser.). (Illus.). 124p. (YA). (gr. 4-7). pap. 14.95 *(978-1-4222-0396-5(4))* Mason Crest.

Bonnice, Sherry & Hoard, Carolyn. Drug Therapy & Cognitive Disorders. (Encyclopedia of Psychiatric Drugs & Their Disorders Ser.). (Illus.). (YA). 2004. 128p. lib. bdg. 24.95 *(978-1-59084-562-2(5))* 2003. 126p. (gr. 7). pap. 14.95 *(978-1-4222-0387-3(5))* Mason Crest.

Brinkerhoff, Shirley. Drug Therapy & Obsessive-Compulsive Disorders. 2003. (Psychiatric Disorders: Drugs & Psychology for the Mind & Bod Ser.). (Illus.). 124p. (YA). (gr. 7). pap. 14.95 *(978-1-4222-0393-4(X))* Mason Crest.

—Drug Therapy & Personality Disorders. (Encyclopedia of Psychiatric Drugs & Their Disorders Ser.). (Illus.). (YA). 2004. 128p. lib. bdg. 24.95 *(978-1-59084-571-4(4))* 2003. 126p. (gr. 4-7). pap. 14.95 *(978-1-4222-0394-1(8))* Mason Crest.

—Drug Therapy & Schizophrenia. 2003. (Psychiatric Disorders: Drugs & Psychology for the Mind & Bod Ser.). (Illus.). 124p. (YA). (gr. 4-7). pap. 14.95 *(978-1-4222-0398-9(0))* Mason Crest.

—Schizophrenia. McDonnell, Mary Ann & Esherick, Donald, eds. 2013. (State of Mental Illness & Its Therapy Ser.: 19). 128p. (J). (gr. 7-18). 24.95 *(978-1-4222-2835-7(5))* Mason Crest.

Bryfonski, Dedria. Depression in J. D. Salinger's The Catcher in the Rye. 2008. (Social Issues in Literature Ser.). (ENG., Illus.). 218p. (YA). (gr. 10-12). pap. 40.95 *(978-0-7377-4256-5(9)*, LML02109-243169, Greenhaven Pr., Inc.) Cengage Gale.

Burnett, Betty. Coping with Multiple Sclerosis. 2009. (Coping Ser.). 192p. (gr. 7-12). 63.90 *(978-1-61512-005-5(X))* Rosen Publishing Group, Inc., The.

Cefrey, Holly. Antidepressants. 2005. (Drug Abuse Prevention Library). (Illus.). 64p. (J). (gr. 7-12). lib. bdg. 31.95 *(978-0-8239-3283-2(4)*, DRANDE) Rosen Publishing Group, Inc., The.

Centore, Michael. Drug Use & Mental Health, Vol. 13. Becker, Sara, ed. 2016. (Drug Addiction & Recovery Ser.). (Illus.). 64p. (J). (gr. 7). 23.95 *(978-1-4222-3601-7(3))* Mason Crest.

Chastain, Zachary. Sick All the Time: Kids with Chronic Illness. 2009. (Kids with Special Needs Ser.). 48p. (YA). (gr. 5-18). pap. 7.95 *(978-1-4222-1922-5(4))* Mason Crest.

Chou, Joey. Crazy by the Letters. Chou, Joey, illus. 2006. (Illus.). 15.99 *(978-0-9788670-0-3(9))* Choo Choo Clan.

Clarke, Lisa Anne. Wishing Wellness: A Workbook for Children of Parents with Mental Illness. Candace, Bonnie & Ellen, illus. 2006. 127p. (J). (gr. 1-7). per. 14.95 *(978-1-59147-313-8(6)*, Magination Pr.) American Psychological Assn.

de Sosa, Linda. I'm Not Crazy: A Workbook for Teens with Depression & Bipolar Disorder. 2010. 128p. pap. 13.95 *(978-0-595-52118-0(5))* iUniverse, Inc.

Encyc of Psychol Disorders. 2005. (Encyclopedia of Psychological Disorders Ser.). (gr. 6-12). 490.00 *(978-0-7910-9164-7(3)*, Chelsea Hse.) Facts On File, Inc.

M
N
O

Engdahl, Sylvia. Mental Health. 2010. (Issues on Trial Ser.). (J). 42.15 (978-0-7377-4738-6(2), Greenhaven Pr., Inc.) Cengage Gale.

Esherick, Joan. The FDA & Psychiatric Drugs: How a Drug Is Approved. McDonnell, Mary Ann & Esherick, Donald, eds. 2013. (State of Mental Illness & Its Therapy Ser.: 19). 128p. (J). (gr. 7-18). 24.95 (978-1-4222-2826-5(6)) Mason Crest.

Farrell, Courtney. Mental Disorders, 1 vol. 2010. (Essential Issues Set 1 Ser.). (ENG.). 112p. (J). (gr. 6-12). lib. bdg. 35.64 (978-1-60453-956-1(9), Essential Library) ABDO Publishing Co.

Freedman, Jeri. Tay-Sachs Disease. 2009. (Genes & Disease Ser.). (Illus.). 128p. (YA). (gr. 7-12). 35.00 (978-0-7910-9634-5(3)) Facts On File, Inc.

Goldstein, Natalie. Parkinson's Disease. 2008. (Genes & Disease Ser.). (Illus.). 128p. (YA). (gr. 7-12). 35.00 (978-0-7910-9584-3(3)) Facts On File, Inc.

Hall, Kirk. Carina & Her Care Partner Gramma. Paolini, Alison, illus. 2013. 26p. 19.95 (978-1-61314-158-8(0)); pap. 15.95 (978-1-61314-171-7(8)) Innovo Publishing, LLC.

Hyman, Bruce M. & Pedrick, Cherry. Obsessive-Compulsive Disorder. 2008. (Twenty-First Century Medical Library). (YA). (gr. 7-12). lib. bdg. 33.26 (978-0-8225-8579-4(0)) Twenty First Century Bks.

Iorizzo, Carrie. Schizophrenia & Other Psychotic Disorders. 2013. (ENG., Illus.). 48p. (J). (978-0-7787-0085-2(2)) Crabtree Publishing Co.

—Schizophrenia & Psychotic Disorders. 2013. (ENG., Illus.). 48p. (J). pap. (978-0-7787-0091-3(7)) Crabtree Publishing Co.

Jovinelly, Joann. Coping with Bipolar Disorder & Manic-Depressive Illness. (Coping Ser.). 192p. (gr. 7-12). 2009. 63.90 (978-1-61511-992-9(2)) 2005. (Illus.). (YA). lib. bdg. 34.60 (978-0-8239-3193-4(5)) Rosen Publishing Group, Inc., The.

Juettner, Bonnie, et al. Dementia. 2009. (Diseases & Disorders Ser.). (ENG., Illus.). 128p. (YA). (gr. 7-10). lib. bdg. 34.95 (978-1-4205-0042-4(2), LML02109-240029, Lucent Bks.) Cengage Gale.

Kelly, Evelyn. Coping with Schizophrenia. 2009. (Coping Ser.). 192p. (gr. 7-12). 63.90 (978-1-61512-011-6(4)) Rosen Publishing Group, Inc., The.

Kelly, Pat. Coping with Schizophrenia. 2005. (Coping Ser.). (Illus.). 192p. (YA). (gr. 7-12). lib. bdg. 34.60 (978-0-8239-2853-8(5)) Rosen Publishing Group, Inc., The.

Kent, Deborah. Snake Pits, Talking Cures, & Magic Bullets: A History of Mental Illness. 2003. (Single Titles Ser.). (ENG., Illus.). 160p. (gr. 7-12). lib. bdg. 26.60 (978-0-7613-2704-2(5), Twenty-First Century Bks.) Lerner Publishing Group.

Larson, Elaine Marie. The Kaleidoscope Kid: Focusing on the Strengths of Children with Asperger Syndrome & High-Functioning Autism. Strand, Vivian, illus. 2007. 35p. 17.95 (978-1-931282-41-3(2)) Autism Asperger Publishing Co.

Leicester, Mal. Can I Tell You about Tourette Syndrome? A Guide for Friends, Family & Professionals. Apsley House, London Staff, illus. 2013. (Can I Tell You About... ? Ser.). (ENG.). 56p. pap. 13.95 (978-1-84905-407-2(X), 5896) Kingsley, Jessica Pubs. GBR. Dist: Macmillan Distribution Ltd.

Libal, Autumn. Drug Therapy & Dissociative Disorders. 2003. (Psychiatric Disorders: Drugs & Psychology for the Mind & Bod Ser.). (Illus.). 124p. (YA). (gr. 7). pap. 14.95 (978-1-4222-0388-0(3)) Mason Crest.

—Drug Therapy & Impulse Control Disorders. 2003. (Psychiatric Disorders: Drugs & Psychology for the Mind & Bod Ser.). (Illus.). 124p. (YA). (gr. 4-7). pap. 14.95 (978-1-4222-0390-3(5)) Mason Crest.

—Drug Therapy & Psychosomatic Disorders. (Encyclopedia of Psychiatric Drugs & Their Disorders Ser.). (Illus.). (YA). 2004. 128p. lib. bdg. 24.95 (978-1-59084-573-8(0)) 2003. 124p. (gr. 4-7). pap. 14.95 (978-1-4222-0397-2(2)) Mason Crest.

—The FDA & Psychiatric Drugs: Drugs & Psychology for the Mind & Body, 19 vols., Set. 2004. (Psychiatric Disorders Ser.). (Illus.). 128p. (J). lib. bdg. (978-1-59084-559-2(5)) Mason Crest.

Libal, Joyce. Drug Therapy & Mental Disorders Due to a Medical Condition. 2003. (Psychiatric Disorders: Drugs & Psychology for the Mind & Bod Ser.). (Illus.). 126p. (YA). (gr. 8-12). pap. 14.95 (978-1-4222-0391-0(3)) Mason Crest.

Marcovitz, Hal. Bipolar Disorder. 2009. (Compact Research Ser.). 112p. (YA). (gr. 7-12). 25.95 (978-1-60152-066-1(2)) ReferencePoint Pr., Inc.

Marcus, Mary Brophy. Sleep Disorders. 2009. (Psychological Disorders Ser.). (Illus.). 128p. (YA). (gr. 7-12). 37.50 (978-1-60413-085-0(7)) Facts On File, Inc.

McIntosh, Kenneth & Livingston, Phyllis. Youth with Juvenile Schizophrenia: The Search for Reality. 2009. (Helping Youth with Mental, Physical, & Social Challenges Ser.). (Illus.). 128p. (YA). (gr. 7-18). lib. bdg. 24.95 (978-1-4222-0148-0(1)) Mason Crest.

Meisel, Abigail. Depression & Bipolar Disorder: Examining Chemical Imbalances & Mood Disorders. 2014. (Diseases, Disorders, Symptoms Ser.). (Illus.). 96p. (J). (gr. 9-12). 27.94 (978-1-62293-060-9(6)) Enslow Pubs., Inc.

Moe, Barbara. Coping with Mental Illness. (Coping Ser.). 192p. (gr. 7-12). 2009. 63.90 (978-1-61512-004-8(1)) 2005. (Illus.). (YA). lib. bdg. 34.60 (978-0-8239-3205-4(2)) Rosen Publishing Group, Inc., The.

mooney, carla. Mental Illness Research. 2011. (Inside Science Ser.). 96p. (YA). (gr. 7-12). lib. bdg. 37.27 (978-1-60152-234-4(7)) ReferencePoint Pr., Inc.

Palmer, Libbi. The PTSD Workbook for Teens: Simple, Effective Skills for Healing Trauma. 2012. (ENG.). 160p. (YA). (gr. 6-12). pap. 17.95 (978-1-60882-321-5(0), Instant Help Books) New Harbinger Pubns.

parks, peggy j. Schizophrenia. 2011. (YA). lib. bdg. (978-1-60152-140-8(5)) ReferencePoint Pr., Inc.

Phillips, Jane E. & Ketelsen, David P. Schizophrenia. 2003. (Diseases & People Ser.). (Illus.). 112p. (J). (gr. 6-12). lib. bdg. 26.60 (978-0-7660-1896-9(2)) Enslow Pubs., Inc.

Rice, Donna. The Magic Is Me. Rice, Doug, illus. 2012. 34p. (J). mass mkt. 15.99 (978-1-936497-16-4(6)) Searchlight Pr.

Rose, Deborah. Joshua Wears A Red Cape. 2007. 44p. 25.45 (978-1-4357-0006-2(6)) Lulu Pr., Inc.

Ross, Allison J. Coping When a Parent Is Mentally Ill. 2005. (Coping Ser.). (Illus.). 192p. (YA). (gr. 7-12). lib. bdg. 34.60 (978-0-8239-3359-4(8)) Rosen Publishing Group, Inc., The.

Rykken, Cheryl. My Shaky Grandma. 2008. 32p. pap. 11.50 (978-1-4357-3496-8(3)) Lulu Pr., Inc.

Sabin, Ellen & Driscoll, Patricia. The Healing Heroes Book: Braving the Changes When Someone You Love Is Wounded in Service. 2012. (ENG., Illus.). 64p. (J). spiral bd. 19.95 (978-0-9826416-0-6(5)) Watering Can.

Shea, Therese. Dementia. 2011. (Understanding Brain Diseases & Disorders Ser.). (ENG.). 64p. (YA). (gr. 7-12). lib. bdg. 31.95 (978-1-4488-5545-2(4)) Rosen Publishing Group, Inc., The.

Simpson, Carolyn. Coping with Post-Traumatic Stress Disorder (PTSD) Dealing with Tragedy. 2009. (Coping Ser.). 192p. (gr. 7-12). 63.90 (978-1-61512-008-6(4)) Rosen Publishing Group, Inc., The.

Smith, Paula. Schizophrenia & Other Psychotic Disorders. 2013. 48p. (J). (978-0-7787-0834-6(9)); (Illus.). pap. (978-0-7787-0861-2(6)) Crabtree Publishing Co.

Sommers, Michael A. Everything You Need to Know about Bipolar Disorder & Manic Depressive Illness. (Need to Know Library). 64p. 2009. (gr. 5-5). 58.50 (978-1-60854-055-6(3)) 2005. (Illus.). (YA). (gr. 4-6). lib. bdg. 31.95 (978-0-8239-3768-4(2)) Rosen Publishing Group, Inc., The.

Veague, Heather Barnett. Schizophrenia. 2007. (Psychological Disorders Ser.). (Illus.). 114p. (YA). (gr. 7-12). lib. bdg. 37.50 (978-0-7910-8544-8(9)) Facts On File, Inc.

Veague, Heather Barnett & Collins, Christine. Cutting & Self-Harm. 2008. (Psychological Disorders Ser.). (Illus.). 120p. (YA). (gr. 7-12). 37.50 (978-0-7910-9003-9(5)) Facts On File, Inc.

MENTAL ILLNESS—FICTION

Adams, Mark. Bucky's Best Friend, Vol. 1. Dolan, Amy, illus. 2006. 15p. (J). pap. 5.00 (978-0-9670245-4-7(4)) Enthusi Adams, Inc.

Anderson, Jessica Lee. Border Crossing. 2009. (ENG.). 160p. (J). (gr. 5-10). pap. 8.00 (978-1-57131-691-2(4)) Milkweed Editions.

Anderson, Laurie Halse. The Impossible Knife of Memory. 2015. (ENG.). 416p. (YA). (gr. 7). pap. 9.99 (978-0-14-751072-3(4), Speak) Penguin Publishing Group.

—The Impossible Knife of Memory. 2014. (ENG.). 384p. (YA). (gr. 7). 18.99 (978-0-670-01209-1(2), Viking Books for Young Readers) Penguin Young Readers Group.

—The Impossible Knife of Memory. 2015. (ENG.). (YA). (gr. 7). lib. bdg. 20.60 **(978-1-68065-510-0(8))** Perfection Learning Corp.

—The Impossible Knife of Memory. 2015. lib. bdg. 20.85 (978-0-606-36798-1(5)) Turtleback Bks.

Andrews, Emily. The Finer Points of Becoming Machine. 2008. (Cutting Edge Ser.). (ENG.). 200p. pap. (978-1-84167-714-9(0)) Ransom Publishing Ltd.

Armstrong, Kelley. The Summoning. (Darkest Powers Ser.: 1). (YA). (gr. 8). 2009. 416p. pap. 9.99 (978-0-06-145054-9(5)) 2008. 400p. 17.99 (978-0-06-166269-0(0)) HarperCollins Pubs.

—The Summoning, 7 vols. 2009. (Darkest Powers Ser.: 1). (J). 81.75 (978-1-4361-9717-5(1)); 243.75 (978-1-4361-9718-2(X)) Recorded Bks., Inc.

Arnold, David. Mosquitoland. 2015. (ENG.). 352p. (YA). (gr. 7). 17.99 (978-0-451-47077-5(X), Viking Books for Young Readers) Penguin Young Readers Group.

Atwater-Rhodes, Amelia. Persistence of Memory. 2010. (Den of Shadows Ser.: Bk. 4). (ENG.). 224p. (YA). (gr. 7). pap. 8.99 (978-0-440-24004-4(2), Delacorte Pr.) Random Hse. Children's Bks.

Averett, Edward. Cameron & the Girls. 2014. (ENG.). 224p. (YA). (gr. 9). pap. 8.99 (978-0-544-30162-7(5), HMH Books For Young Readers) Houghton Mifflin Harcourt Publishing Co.

Bailey, Em. Shift. 2016. (ENG.). 288p. (YA). (gr. 9). pap. 17.99 **(978-1-76012-698-8(5))** Hardie Grant Egmont Pty, Ltd. AUS. Dist: Independent Pubs. Group.

Boyne, John. Stay Where You Are & Then Leave. Jeffers, Oliver, illus. 2014. (ENG.). 256p. (J). (gr. 4-7). 16.99 (978-1-62779-031-4(4), 9781627790314, Holt, Henry & Co. Bks. For Young Readers) Holt, Henry & Co.

Brewer, Zac. Madness. 2017. 304p. (YA). (gr. 9). 17.99 **(978-0-06-245785-1(3))** HarperCollins Pubs.

Caletti, Deb. Love Is All You Need: Wild Roses - The Nature of Jade. 2013. (ENG.). 608p. (YA). (gr. 7-7). pap. 11.99 (978-1-4424-6636-4(7), Simon Pulse) Simon Pulse.

—Wild Roses. (ENG.). (YA). (gr. 7-12). 2008. 320p. pap. 8.99 (978-1-4169-5782-9(0)) 2005. (Illus.). 304p. 15.95 (978-0-689-86766-8(2)) Simon Pulse. (Simon Pulse).

Carey, Becky. 47 Strings: Tessa's Special Code. Stidwell O'Boyle, Carrie, ed. Leick, Bonnie, illus. 2012. (ENG.). 36p. 16.95 (978-0-9849245-6-1(6)) Little Creek Press.

Carter, Alden R. Walkaway. 2008. (ENG.). 192p. (YA). (gr. 7-18). 16.95 (978-0-8234-2106-0(6)) Holiday Hse., Inc.

Chand, Emlyn. Farsighted. 2012. 260p. 19.95 (978-0-9839308-2-2(1)) Blue Crown Pr.

Clark, Clara Gillow. Hattie on Her Way. Thompson, John, illus. 2005. (ENG.). 208p. (J). (gr. 5-18). 15.99 (978-0-7636-2286-2(9)) Candlewick Pr.

Cleaver, Vera & Cleaver, Bill. Donde Florecen los Lirios. (SPA.). 168p. (YA). (gr. 5-8). (978-84-204-3648-7(8), AF0285) Ediciones Alfaguara ESP. Dist: Lectorum Pubns., Inc.

Cody, Paul. Love Is Both Wave & Particle. 2017. (ENG.). 320p. (YA). 17.99 (978-1-62672-688-8(4), 9781626726888) Roaring Brook Pr.

Colbert, Brandy. Little & Lion. 2017. (ENG.). 336p. (YA). (gr. 9-17). 17.99 **(978-0-316-34900-0(3))** Little, Brown Bks. for Young Readers.

Colfer, Eoin. Artemis Fowl & the Atlantis Complex. 2012. (ENG.). 384p. (J). (gr. 5-9). pap. 8.99 (978-1-4231-2972-1(5)) Hyperion Pr.

—The Atlantis Complex. 2010. (Artemis Fowl Ser.: 7). (ENG.). 368p. (J). (gr. 5-9). 17.99 (978-1-4231-2819-9(2)) Hyperion Pr.

—The Atlantis Complex. 2012. (Artemis Fowl Ser.: 7). (J). lib. bdg. 19.65 (978-0-606-23614-0(7), Turtleback) Turtleback Bks.

Curtis, Christopher Paul. The Madman of Piney Woods. (Illus.). (J). 2016. (ENG.). 384p. (gr. 3-7). pap. 7.99 (978-0-545-15665-3(3)) 2014. 363p. (978-0-545-63376-5(1)) 2014. (ENG., 384p. (gr. 3-7). 16.99 (978-0-545-15664-6(5)) Scholastic, Inc. (Scholastic Pr.).

De la Peña, Matt. I Will Save You. 2011. (ENG.). 320p. (YA). (gr. 9). pap. 9.99 (978-0-385-73828-6(5), Ember) Random Hse. Children's Bks.

Dolamore, Jaclyn. Dark Metropolis. 2014. (ENG., Illus.). 304p. (YA). (gr. 7-12). 17.99 (978-1-4231-6332-9(X)) Hyperion Bks. for Children.

Downes, Patrick. Ten Miles One Way. 2017. (ENG.). 208p. (YA). (gr. 9). 17.99 (978-0-399-54499-6(2), Philomel Bks.) Penguin Young Readers Group.

Durmush, F. Ayshe, an Anatolian Tale. 2007. (ENG.). 84p. per. (978-1-84747-171-0(4)) Chipmunkapublishing.

Easton, Kelly. To Be Mona. (ENG.). 224p. (YA). (gr. 7). 2009. pap. 7.99 (978-1-4169-0055-9(1)) 2008. 16.99 (978-1-4169-0054-2(3)) McElderry, Margaret K. Bks. (McElderry, Margaret K. Bks.).

Eden, Alexandra. Holy Smoke: A Bones & the Duchess Mystery. 2004. (ENG., Illus.). 117p. (J). 16.00 (978-1-888310-46-7(4)) Knoll, Allen A. Pubs.

Evangelista, Kate. No Love Allowed. 2016. (Dodge Cove Trilogy Ser.). (ENG.). 256p. (YA). pap. 9.99 (978-1-250-07390-7(1), 9781250073907) Feiwel & Friends.

Firmston, Kim. Schizo, 1 vol. 2011. (Lorimer SideStreets Ser.). (ENG.). 152p. (YA). (gr. 9-12). pap. 9.95 (978-1-55277-871-5(1), 9781552778715) Lorimer, James & Co., Ltd., Pubs. CAN. Dist: Casemate Pubs. & Bk. Distributors, LLC.

Fortunati, Karen. The Weight of Zero. 2016. (ENG.). 400p. (YA). (gr. 9). 17.99 (978-1-101-93889-8(7), Delacorte Pr.) Random Hse. Children's Bks.

Franklin, Emily. Last Night at the Circle Cinema. 2015. (ENG.). 200p. (YA). (gr. 8-12). 18.99 (978-1-4677-7489-5(8)) Lerner Publishing Group.

Franklin, Kristine L. Dove Song. 2006. (ENG.). 192p. (J). (gr. 5-9). per. 5.99 (978-0-7636-3219-9(8)) Candlewick Pr.

Friedman, Robin. Nothing. 2008. (ENG.). 240p. (YA). (gr. 8-18). pap. 9.95 (978-0-7387-1304-5(X), Flux) North Star Editions.

Friend, Natasha. Where You'll Find Me. 2016. (ENG.). 272p. (YA). 16.99 (978-0-374-30230-6(8), 9780374302306, Farrar, Straus & Giroux (BYR)) Farrar, Straus & Giroux.

—Where You'll Find Me. 2017. (YA). lib. bdg. 20.85 **(978-0-606-39591-5(1))** Turtleback Bks.

Gale, Emily. Girl Out Loud. 2012. (YA). (978-0-545-30439-9(3)); (ENG.). 288p. (J). (gr. 7-7). 17.99 (978-0-545-30438-2(5)) Scholastic, Inc. (Chicken Hse., The).

Gephart, Donna. Lily & Dunkin. 2016. (ENG.). 352p. (J). (gr. 5). 16.99 (978-0-553-53674-4(5), Delacorte Bks. for Young Readers) Random Hse. Children's Bks.

Ghislain, Gary. How I Stole Johnny Depp's Alien Girlfriend. 2011. (ENG., Illus.). 208p. (YA). (gr. 7-17). 16.99 (978-0-8118-7460-1(5)) Chronicle Bks. LLC.

Gornall, Louise. Under Rose-Tainted Skies. 2017. (ENG.). 336p. (YA). (gr. 7). 17.99 (978-0-544-73651-1(6), Clarion Bks.) Houghton Mifflin Harcourt Trade & Reference Pubs.

Green, John. Turtles All the Way Down. 2017. lib. bdg. 33.05 **(978-0-606-40748-9(0))** Turtleback Bks.

Greenberg, Joanne. I Never Promised You a Rose Garden. 256p. (YA). (gr. 7-18). pap. 5.99 (978-0-8072-1362-9(4), Listening Library) Random Hse. Audio Publishing Group.

Griffin, Adele. Tighter. (ENG.). (YA). (gr. 7). 2012. 240p. pap. 8.99 (978-0-375-85933-5(0), Ember) 2011. 224p. 16.99 (978-0-375-86645-6(0), Knopf Bks. for Young Readers) Random Hse. Children's Bks.

—Where I Want to Be. 2007. (ENG.). 176p. (YA). (gr. 7-18). 7.99 (978-0-14-240948-0(0), Speak) Penguin Young Readers Group.

Griffin, Paul. The Orange Houses. 2011. (ENG.). 176p. (YA). (gr. 9-18). 8.99 (978-0-14-241982-3(6), Speak) Penguin Young Readers Group.

Guest, Jacqueline. Racing Fear, 1 vol. 2004. (Lorimer SideStreets Ser.). (ENG.). 160p. (YA). (gr. 9-12). 9.95 (978-1-55028-838-4(5), 9781550288384); 16.95 (978-1-55028-839-1(3), 9781550288391) Lorimer, James & Co., Ltd., Pubs. CAN. Dist: Casemate Pubs. & Bk. Distributors, LLC.

Halliday, John. Shooting Monarchs. 2007. (ENG.). 144p. (YA). (gr. 8). pap. 8.95 (978-1-4169-5559-7(3), McElderry, Margaret K. Bks.) McElderry, Margaret K. Bks.

Halpern, Julie. Get Well Soon. 2009. (ENG.). 224p. (YA). (gr. 7-12). pap. 9.99 (978-0-312-58148-0(3), 9780312581480) Square Fish.

—Have a Nice Day. 2013. (ENG.). 352p. (YA). (gr. 7-12). pap. 10.99 (978-1-250-03420-5(5), 9781250034205) Square Fish.

Harrington, Karen. Sure Signs of Crazy. (ENG.). (J). 2014. 304p. (gr. 5-17). pap. 7.99 (978-0-316-21049-2(8)) 2013. 288p. (gr. 4-17). 17.00 (978-0-316-21058-4(7)) Little, Brown Bks. for Young Readers.

Hautman, Pete. Invisible. Hautman, Pete, illus. 2006. (ENG., Illus.). 160p. (YA). (gr. 7-12). reprint ed. pap. 9.99 (978-0-689-86903-7(7), Simon & Schuster Bks. For Young Readers) Simon & Schuster Bks. For Young Readers.

Hopkins, Ellen. Impulse. (ENG.). (YA). (gr. 9-12). 2008. 688p. pap. 12.99 (978-1-4169-0357-4(7)) 2007. 672p. 22.99 (978-1-4169-0356-7(9)) McElderry, Margaret K. Bks. (McElderry, Margaret K. Bks.).

Howard, A. G. Splintered. 2013. (Splintered Ser.). (ENG., Illus.). 384p. (YA). (gr. 9-17). 17.95 (978-1-4197-0428-4(1), Amulet Bks.) Abrams, Inc.

—Splintered. 2014. (Splintered Ser.: 1). (J). lib. bdg. 19.60 (978-0-606-35235-2(X)) Turtleback Bks.

—Unhinged. (Splintered Ser.). (ENG.). (YA). (gr. 9-17). 2015. 416p. pap. 9.99 (978-1-4197-1373-6(6)) 2014. 400p. 17.95 (978-1-4197-0971-5(2)) Abrams, Inc. (Amulet Bks.).

—Unhinged. 2015. (Splintered Ser.: 2). (J). lib. bdg. 19.60 (978-0-606-36565-9(6)) Turtleback Bks.

Hoyle, Alice. Pretend Friends: A Story about Schizophrenia & Other Illnesses That Can Cause Hallucinations. Reis, Lauren, illus. 2015. (ENG.). 36p. 14.95 (978-1-84905-624-3(2), 7689) Kingsley, Jessica Pubs. GBR. Dist: Macmillan Distribution Ltd.

Huston, Donna. Inch by Inch. 2006. (J). spiral bd. 19.95 (978-0-9771192-3-3(8)) Shayne Publishing.

Ireland, Justina. Vengeance Bound. 2013. (ENG.). 320p. (YA). (gr. 9). 17.99 (978-1-4424-4462-1(2), Simon & Schuster Bks. For Young Readers) Simon & Schuster Bks. For Young Readers.

James, Caleb. Haffling. 2nd ed. 2016. (ENG., Illus.). 250p. pap. 14.99 (978-1-63476-795-8(0), DSP Pubns.) Dreamspinner Pr.

Jean, Emiko. We'll Never Be Apart. 2015. (ENG.). 288p. (YA). (gr. 9). 17.99 (978-0-544-48200-5(X), HMH Books For Young Readers) Houghton Mifflin Harcourt Publishing Co.

Johansson, J. R. Insomnia. 2013. (Night Walkers Ser.: 1). (ENG.). 360p. (YA). pap. 9.99 (978-0-7387-3593-1(0), Flux) North Star Editions.

Kehret, Peg. Deadly Stranger. 2012. (ENG.). 176p. (J). (gr. 3-7). pap. 9.99 (978-1-4424-6044-7(X), Simon & Schuster/Paula Wiseman Bks.) Simon & Schuster/Paula Wiseman Bks.

King, Wesley. OCDaniel. (ENG., Illus.). 304p. (J). (gr. 3-7). 2017. pap. 8.99 (978-1-4814-5532-9(X)) 2016. 17.99 (978-1-4814-5531-2(1)) Simon & Schuster/Paula Wiseman Bks. (Simon & Schuster/Paula Wiseman Bks.).

—OCDaniel. 2017. lib. bdg. 18.40 **(978-0-606-39743-8(4))** Turtleback Bks.

Kraus, Daniel. Scowler. 2014. (ENG.). 304p. (YA). (gr. 9). pap. 9.99 (978-0-385-74310-5(6), Ember) Random Hse. Children's Bks.

Kuehn, Stephanie. Complicit. (ENG.). 256p. (YA). 2016. pap. 10.99 (978-1-250-04460-0(X), 9781250044600) 2014. (gr. 8-12). 19.99 (978-1-250-04459-4(6), 9781250044594) St. Martin's Pr. (St. Martin's Griffin).

—Delicate Monsters. 2015. (ENG.). 240p. (YA). (gr. 9-12). 19.99 (978-1-250-06384-7(1), 9781250063847, St. Martin's Griffin) St. Martin's Pr.

Lahey, Sandra. Let's Talk. 2016. (ENG., Illus.). 26p. (J). pap. 28.22 **(978-1-5245-1995-7(2))** Xlibris Corp.

Leavitt, Martine. Calvin: Just because You See Something Doesn't Mean It's Really There. 2015. (ENG.). 192p. (YA). (gr. 7). 17.99 (978-0-374-38073-1(2), 9780374380731, Farrar, Straus & Giroux (BYR)) Farrar, Straus & Giroux.

Levithan, David. Every You, Every Me. Levithan, David & Farmer, Jonathan, photos by. 2012. (ENG., Illus.). 256p. (YA). (gr. 7). pap. 9.99 (978-0-375-85451-4(7), Ember) Random Hse. Children's Bks.

—Every You, Every Me. Farmer, Jonathan, photos by. 2012. (Illus.). lib. bdg. 20.85 (978-0-606-26816-5(2), Turtleback) Turtleback Bks.

Levoy, Myron. Alan & Naomi. 2011. 14.12 (978-0-7848-3566-1(7), Everbind) Marco Bk. Co.

The Lonely. 2014. (ENG.). 288p. (YA). pap. 9.99 (978-0-7387-4133-8(7), Flux) North Star Editions.

Lord, Emery. When We Collided. 2016. (ENG.). 352p. (YA). 17.99 (978-1-61963-845-7(2), 9781619638457, Bloomsbury USA Childrens) Bloomsbury Publishing USA.

Lowenstein, Sallie Claire. Waiting for Eugene. 2006. (Illus.). 201p. (J). (978-1-4156-6166-6(9)) Book Wholesalers, Inc.

Masciola, Carol. The Yearbook. 2015. (ENG.). 224p. (YA). 17.99 (978-1-4405-8897-6(X), Simon Pulse) Simon Pulse.

McCombs, A. Lisa. Abby. 2011. 184p. (978-1-77067-327-4(X)) FriesenPress.

McCombs, Lisa A. Abby. 2011. 184p. pap. (978-1-77067-328-1(8)) FriesenPress.

McGinnis, Mindy. This Darkness Mine. 2017. 384p. (YA). (gr. 9). 17.99 **(978-0-06-256159-6(6)**, Tegen, Katherine Bks) HarperCollins Pubs.

McNish, Cliff. Angel. 2008. (Exceptional Reading & Language Arts Titles for Intermediate Grades Ser.). 311p. (YA). (gr. 8-12). 16.95 (978-0-8225-8900-6(1)) Lerner Publishing Group.

Meadows, Jodi. Before She Ignites. 2017. (Fallen Isles Ser.: 1). 496p. (YA). (gr. 8). 17.99 **(978-0-06-246940-3(1)**, Tegen, Katherine Bks) HarperCollins Pubs.

Michaels, Rune. Nobel Genes. (ENG., (YA). (gr. 7). 2011. Illus.). 208p. pap. 8.99 (978-1-4424-2401-2(X)) 2010. 192p. 16.99 (978-1-4169-1259-0(2)) Simon & Schuster Children's Publishing. (Atheneum Bks. for Young Readers).

Miller, Barnabas. The Girl with the Wrong Name. 2016. (ENG., Illus.). 272p. (YA). (gr. 9). pap. 10.99 (978-1-61695-704-9(2), Soho Teen) Soho Pr., Inc.

Moore, Meredith. Fiona. 2016. (ENG.). 384p. (YA). (gr. 7). 17.99 (978-1-59514-784-4(5), Razorbill) Penguin Young Readers Group.

Moulton, Erin E. Chasing the Milky Way. 2014. (ENG.). 288p. (J). (gr. 3-7). 16.99 (978-0-399-16449-1(9), Philomel Bks.) Penguin Young Readers Group.

Myers, Kate Kae. The Vanishing Game. (ENG.). (YA). (gr. 7). 2014. 384p. pap. 9.99 (978-1-61963-127-4(X), 9781619631274) 2012. 368p. 17.99 (978-1-59990-694-2(5), 9781599906942) Bloomsbury Publishing USA. (Bloomsbury USA Childrens).

Napoli, Donna Jo. Dark Shimmer. 2015. (ENG., Illus.). 368p. (YA). (gr. 9). 16.99 (978-0-385-74655-7(5), Lamb, Wendy Bks.) Random Hse. Children's Bks.

Neale, Jonathan. Lost at Sea. 2004. (ENG.). 112p. (J). (gr. 5-7). reprint ed. pap. 8.95 (978-0-618-43236-3(1)) Houghton Mifflin Harcourt Publishing Co.

Nelson, R. A. Breathe My Name. 2008. (ENG.). 320p. (YA). (gr. 7-18). 9.99 (978-1-59514-186-6(3), Razorbill) Penguin Young Readers Group.

Neufeld, John. Lisa, Bright & Dark: A Novel. 2007. 152p. per. 12.95 (978-0-595-45048-0(2), Backinprint.com) iUniverse, Inc.

Nolan, Han. Crazy. 2010. (ENG.). 352p. (YA). (gr. 7-18). 17.00 (978-0-15-205109-9(0)) Houghton Mifflin Harcourt Publishing Co.

Olson, Norah. Twisted Fate. (YA). (gr. 8). 2016. 288p. pap. 9.99 (978-0-06-227206-5(3), Tegen, Katherine Bks) 2015. (ENG.). 272p. 17.99 (978-0-06-227204-1(7)) HarperCollins Pubs.

Phillips, Linda Vigen. Crazy. 2014. (ENG.). 320p. (YA). pap. 9.00 (978-0-8028-5437-7(0), Eerdmans Bks For Young Readers) Eerdmans, William B. Publishing Co.

Pickering, Amanda. Alfred the Alien: Number Adventure. 2011. 18p. pap. 15.95 (978-1-4327-7522-3(7)) Outskirts Pr., Inc.

Pixley, Marcella. Without Tess. 2014. (ENG.). 304p. (YA). (gr. 7-12). pap. 9.99 (978-1-250-04435-8(9), 9781250044358) Square Fish.

Plitt, Kay. Why Isn't Bobby Like Me, Mom? 2010. 32p. 14.75 (978-1-4269-4038-5(6)) Trafford Publishing.

Polsky, Sara. This Is How I Find Her. (ENG.). 272p. (YA). (gr. 8-12). 2015. pap. 9.99 (978-0-8075-7880-3(0)) 2013. 16.99 (978-0-8075-7877-3(0)) Whitman, Albert & Co.

Prinz, Yvonne. If You're Lucky. (ENG.). 288p. (YA). (gr. 9-12). 2016. pap. 9.95 (978-1-61620-639-0(X)) 2015. 17.95 (978-1-61620-463-1(X)) Algonquin Bks. of Chapel Hill.

Ransom, Marty. Our Father, Our Soldier, Our Hero. 2011. 36p. pap. 24.95 (978-1-4626-1377-9(2)) America Star Bks.

Redford, Ali & Stickleberry, Plum. The Boy Who Built a Wall Around Himself. Simpson, Kara, illus. 2015. (ENG.). 32p. (J). 15.95 (978-1-84905-683-0(8), 8121) Kingsley, Jessica Pubs. GBR. Dist: Macmillan Distribution Ltd.

Reed, Amy. Crazy. (ENG., (YA). (gr. 9). 2013. Illus.). 416p. pap. 9.99 (978-1-4424-1348-1(4)) 2012. 384p. 16.99 (978-1-4424-1347-4(6)) Simon Pulse. (Simon Pulse).

Reeves, Dia. Bleeding Violet. 2010. (ENG.). 480p. (YA). (gr. 9). pap. 20.99 (978-1-4169-8619-5(7), Simon Pulse) Simon Pulse.

Rilla, Donald. The Three Italian Foster Kids. 2012. 68p. pap. 15.99 (978-1-4797-1582-4(4)) Xlibris Corp.

Rinaldi, Ann. Or Give Me Death. 2004. (Great Episodes Ser.). 226p. (gr. 5-9). 17.00 (978-0-7569-3462-0(1)) Perfection Learning Corp.

Roux, Madeleine. Asylum. (ENG.). (gr. 9). 2014. 336p. (J). pap. 9.99 (978-0-06-222097-4(7)) 2013. (Illus.). 320p. (YA). 17.99 (978-0-06-222096-7(9)) HarperCollins Pubs.

—Asylum. 2015. (SPA.). 320p. (YA). (gr. 9-12). pap. 20.99 (978-987-612-778-3(0)) V&R Editoras.

Scelsa, Kate. Fans of the Impossible Life. 2015. (ENG.). 368p. (YA). (gr. 9). 17.99 (978-0-06-233175-5(2)) HarperCollins Pubs.

Schantz, Sarah Elizabeth. Fig. 2016. (ENG.). 352p. (YA). (gr. 9). pap. 10.99 (978-1-4814-2359-5(2), McElderry, Margaret K. Bks.) McElderry, Margaret K. Bks.

Schindler, Holly. A Blue So Dark. 2010. (ENG.). 288p. (YA). (gr. 9-18). pap. 11.99 (978-0-7387-1926-9(9), Flux) North Star Editions.

Schraff, Anne. The Vandal. 2008. 132p. (J). (gr. 4-7). 13.95 (978-0-7569-8388-8(6)) Perfection Learning Corp.

Scott, Kieran. What Waits in the Woods. 2017. (ENG.). 288p. (J). (gr. 7). pap. 9.99 **(978-0-545-83763-7(4))** Scholastic, Inc.

Shaw, Susan. Black-Eyed Suzie. 2007. (ENG.). 176p. (J). (gr. 6-9). pap. 9.95 (978-1-59078-533-1(9), Front Street) Boyds Mills Pr.

Sheff, Nic. Schizo: A Novel. 2015. (ENG.). 272p. (YA). (gr. 9). pap. 9.99 (978-0-14-750885-0(1), Speak) Penguin Young Readers Group.

Shusterman, Neal. Challenger Deep. Shusterman, Brendan, illus. 320p. (YA). (gr. 9). 2016. pap. 9.99 (978-0-06-113414-2(7), HarperTeen) 2015. (ENG.). 17.99 (978-0-06-113411-1(2)) HarperCollins Pubs.

Singleton, Paul. Sometimes Mama's Just Like That. 2013. 30p. pap. 17.99 (978-0-578-13425-3(X)) Drinking Gourd Pr.

Sirowy, Alexandra. The Creeping: If You Hunt for Monsters, You'll Find Them. 2015. (ENG., Illus.). 400p. (YA). (gr. 7). 17.99 (978-1-4814-1886-7(6)) Simon & Schuster Children's Publishing.

Sloan, Holly Goldberg. I'll Be There. (ENG.). (YA). (gr. 7-17). 2012. 416p. pap. 11.99 (978-0-316-12276-4(9)) 2011. (Illus.). 400p. 18.00 (978-0-316-12279-5(3)) Little, Brown Bks. for Young Readers.

Stahler, David, Jr. Spinning Out. 2011. (ENG.). 288p. (YA). (gr. 7-17). 16.99 (978-0-8118-7780-0(9)) Chronicle Bks. LLC.

Strasser, Todd. The Wave. 2013. lib. bdg. 20.85 (978-0-606-27009-0(4), Turtleback) Turtleback Bks.

Taree, Aerle. Molly's Mental Health: Love Me Too. 2008. 36p. pap. 24.95 (978-1-60441-064-8(7)) PublishAmerica, Inc.

Toten, Teresa. Beware That Girl. 2016. (ENG.). 336p. (YA). (gr. 9). 17.99 (978-0-553-50790-4(7), Delacorte Pr.) Random Hse. Children's Bks.

Trueman, Terry. Inside Out. 128p. 2003. (J). lib. bdg. 16.89 (978-0-06-623963-7(X)) 2004. (ENG.). (YA). (gr. 9). reprint ed. pap. 8.99 (978-0-06-447376-7(7), HarperTeen) HarperCollins Pubs.

Truly Blessed Ink. I Know You Won't Forget. Jordan, Carol, illus. 2007. (ENG.). 40p. (J). 16.95 (978-0-9789066-1-0(6)) Square Circle Pr. LLC.

Vaught, Susan. Footer Davis Probably Is Crazy. Reinhardt, Jennifer Black, illus. 2015. (ENG.). 240p. (J). (gr. 5-9). 16.99 (978-1-4814-2276-5(6), Simon & Schuster Bks. For Young Readers) Simon & Schuster Bks. For Young Readers.

—Freaks Like Us. 2014. (ENG.). 256p. (YA). (gr. 7). pap. 9.99 (978-1-61963-163-2(6), 9781619631632, Bloomsbury USA Childrens) Bloomsbury Publishing USA.

Ventresca, Yvonne. Black Flowers, White Lies. 2016. (ENG.). 272p. (YA). (gr. 6). 16.99 (978-1-5107-0988-1(6), Sky Pony Pr.) Skyhorse Publishing Co., Inc.

Vizzini, Ned. It's Kind of a Funny Story. 2007. (ENG.). 464p. (YA). (gr. 7-12). per. 9.99 (978-0-7868-5197-3(X)) Disney Publishing Worldwide.

—It's Kind of a Funny Story. 2011. 11.04 (978-0-7848-3383-4(4), Everbind) Marco Bk. Co.

—It's Kind of a Funny Story. 2007. (YA). lib. bdg. 20.85 (978-1-4178-1818-1(2), Turtleback) Turtleback Bks.

Walton, Julia. Words on Bathroom Walls. 2017. (ENG.). 304p. (YA). (gr. 7). 17.99 **(978-0-399-55088-1(7))**; lib. bdg. 20.99 **(978-0-399-55089-8(5))** Random Hse. Children's Bks. (Random Hse. Bks. for Young Readers).

Weeks, Sarah. So B. It. 2009. 9.00 (978-0-7848-3326-1(5), Everbind) Marco Bk. Co.

—So B. It. 2005. 17.00 (978-0-7569-5112-2(7)) Perfection Learning Corp.

—So B. It. 2007. (J). 1.25 (978-1-4193-7988-8(7)) Recorded Bks., Inc.

Weeks, Sarah & Weeks. So B. It. (ENG.). (J). (gr. 5). 2005. 288p. pap. 7.99 (978-0-06-441047-2(1)) 2004. 256p. 16.99 (978-0-06-623622-3(3)) HarperCollins Pubs.

Wexler, Django. The Mad Apprentice. Jansson, Alexander, illus. 2015. (Forbidden Library). (ENG.). 352p. (J). (gr. 5). 16.99 (978-0-8037-3976-5(1), Kathy Dawson Books) Penguin Young Readers Group.

Winfrey, Kerry. Love & Other Alien Experiences. 2017. (ENG.). 272p. (YA). pap. 10.99 (978-1-250-11952-0(9), 9781250119520) Feiwel & Friends.

Woods, Elizabeth. Choker. (ENG.). 240p. (YA). (gr. 9). 2012. pap. 9.99 (978-1-4424-1234-7(8)) 2011. (Illus.). 16.99 (978-1-4424-1233-0(X)) Simon & Schuster Bks. For Young Readers. (Simon & Schuster Bks. For Young Readers).

Woolston, Blythe. The Freak Observer. 2012. (Carolrhoda YA Ser.). (ENG.). 208p. (YA). (gr. 9-12). pap. 9.95 (978-0-7613-8132-7(5), Carolrhoda Lab™) Lerner Publishing Group.

Wunder, Wendy. The Museum of Intangible Things. 2015. (ENG.). 256p. (YA). (gr. 7). pap. 9.99 (978-1-59514-576-5(1), Razorbill) Penguin Young Readers Group.

Young, Janet Ruth. My Beautiful Failure. (ENG., Illus.). 320p. (YA). (gr. 7). 2013. pap. 9.99 (978-1-4424-8269-2(9)) 2012. 16.99 (978-1-4169-5489-7(9)) Simon & Schuster Children's Publishing. (Atheneum Bks. for Young Readers).

—Things I Shouldn't Think. 2012. (ENG., Illus.). 352p. (YA). (gr. 9). pap. 8.99 (978-1-4424-5107-0(6), Atheneum Bks. for Young Readers) Simon & Schuster Children's Publishing.

Zappia, Francesca. Made You Up. (YA). (gr. 9). 2017. 464p. pap. 9.99 (978-0-06-229011-3(8)) 2015. (ENG.). 448p. 17.99 (978-0-06-229010-6(X)) HarperCollins Pubs. (Greenwillow Bks.).

MENTAL PHILOSOPHY

see Philosophy; Psychology

MENTAL TELEPATHY

see Thought Transference

MENTALLY DISABLED PERSONS

see People with Mental Disabilities

MENTALLY HANDICAPPED

see People with Mental Disabilities

MENTALLY ILL

see also People with Mental Disabilities

Abramovitz, Melissa. What Is Schizophrenia? 2015. (ENG., Illus.). 80p. (J). lib. bdg. (978-1-60152-926-8(0)) ReferencePoint Pr., Inc.

Brinkerhoff, Shirley. Childhood & Adolescent Disorders. McDonnell, Mary Ann & Esherick, Donald, eds. 2013. (State of Mental Illness & Its Therapy Ser.: 19). 128p. (J). (gr. 7-18). 24.95 (978-1-4222-2822-7(3)) Mason Crest.

Champion, Gina. Anna & Her Mommy. Mitchell, Nanci, illus. 2005. 36p. (J). (gr. k-6). pap. 10.00 (978-1-884363-20-7(2)) Odenwald Pr.

Clarke, Lisa Anne. Wishing Wellness: A Workbook for Children of Parents with Mental Illness. Candace, Bonnie & Ellen, illus. 2006. 127p. (J). (gr. 1-7). per. 14.95 (978-1-59147-313-8(6), Magination Pr.) American Psychological Assn.

Evans, Jan. Repetitive Rhonda: A Coloring Book. 2007. (Illus.). 16p. (J). (978-0-9720176-8-8(2)) Breath & Shadows Productions.

Goldman, Stan. CPCS Mental Health Proceedings in Massachusetts. 2014. (ENG.). pap. 125.00 (978-1-57589-853-7(5)) Massachusetts Continuing Legal Education, Inc.

Knight, S. Black Magic. 2007. (ENG.). 156p. per. (978-1-84747-007-2(6)) Chipmunkapublishing.

Landau, Elaine. Schizophrenia. 2004. (Life Balance Ser.). (ENG.). 80p. (J). 20.50 (978-0-531-12215-0(8), Watts, Franklin) Scholastic Library Publishing.

Marzilli, Alan. Mental Health Reform. 2003. (Point/Counterpoint Ser.). (Illus.). 112p. (C). (gr. 9-13). 35.00 (978-0-7910-7372-8(6), Chelsea Hse.) Facts On File, Inc.

Miller, Maia. Drugs & Mental Illness. 2005. (Drug Abuse Prevention Library). (Illus.). 64p. (YA). (gr. 7-12). lib. bdg. 31.95 (978-0-8239-3155-2(2), DRMEIL) Rosen Publishing Group, Inc., The.

Nakaya, Andrea C. What Is Bipolar Disorder? 2015. (ENG., Illus.). 80p. (J). lib. bdg. (978-1-60152-922-0(8)) ReferencePoint Pr., Inc.

Netzley, Patricia D. What Impact Does Mental Illness Have on Crime? 2014. (In Controversy Ser.). (ENG., Illus.). 96p. (J). lib. bdg. (978-1-60152-660-1(1)) ReferencePoint Pr., Inc.

Ross, Allison J. Coping When a Parent Is Mentally Ill. (Coping Ser.). 192p. (gr. 7-12). 2009. 63.90 (978-1-61511-987-5(6)) 2005. (Illus.). (YA). lib. bdg. 34.60 (978-0-8239-3359-4(8)) Rosen Publishing Group, Inc., The.

Rustad, Martha E. H. Some Kids Have Autism, 1 vol. Saunders-Smith, Gail, ed. 2008. (Understanding Differences Ser.). (ENG., Illus.). 24p. (gr. k-1). pap. 6.29 (978-1-4296-1772-7(1), Pebble Bks.) Capstone Press of Coughlan Cos.

Stewart, Sheila. Something's Wrong! Kids with Emotional Disturbance. 2009. (Kids with Special Needs Ser.). 48p. (YA). (gr. 5-18). pap. 7.95 (978-1-4222-1923-2(2)) Mason Crest.

MENTALLY ILL—FICTION

Anderson, R. J. Ultraviolet. 2013. (ENG.). 312p. (YA). (gr. 7-12). pap. 9.95 (978-1-4677-0914-9(X), Carolrhoda Lab™) Lerner Publishing Group.

Barnes, John. Losers in Space. 2012. (ENG.). 448p. (YA). (gr. 9-18). 18.99 (978-0-670-06156-3(5), Viking Books for Young Readers) Penguin Young Readers Group.

Bateson, Catherine. Being Bee. (ENG.). 136p. (J). 2008. (gr. 3-7). pap. 7.95 (978-0-8234-2208-1(9)) 2007. (Illus.). (gr. 4-7). 16.95 (978-0-8234-2104-6(X)) Holiday Hse., Inc.

Bodeen, S. A. The Compound. 2008. (Compound Ser.: 1). (ENG.). 256p. (YA). (gr. 7-12). 18.99 (978-0-312-37015-2(6), 9780312370152) Feiwel & Friends.

—The Compound. 2009. (Compound Ser.: 1). (ENG.). 272p. (YA). (gr. 7-12). pap. 9.99 (978-0-312-57860-2(1), 9780312578602) Square Fish.

Brown, Jahla. Nathan Is Nathan. 2009. (ENG., Illus.). 20p. (J). pap. 19.95 (978-0-9778083-8-0(6)) Everlasting Publishing.

Buckell, Tobias S. & Monti, Joe, eds. Diverse Energies. 2012. (ENG., Illus.). 368p. (YA). pap. 10.95 (978-1-62014-011-6(X)) Lee & Low Bks., Inc.

Dorfman, Joaquin. The Long Wait for Tomorrow. 2009. (YA). (978-0-375-84696-0(4)) Random Hse., Inc.

Elizabeth Arkward Newton. The Little Boy Who Wished God Had Not Given Him a Brain: Big Momma Books. 2009. 36p. pap. 18.99 (978-1-4389-0133-6(X)) AuthorHouse.

Firmston, Kim. Schizo, 1 vol. 2011. (Lorimer SideStreets Ser.). (ENG.). 152p. (YA). (gr. 9-12). 16.95 (978-1-55277-872-2(X), 9781552778722) Lorimer, James & Co., Ltd., Pubs. CAN. Dist: Casemate Pubs. & Bk. Distributors, LLC.

Ford, J. One in Four. 2007. pap. (978-1-84747-173-4(0)) Chipmunkapublishing.

Friesen, Jonathan. Jerk, California. 2008. (ENG.). 352p. (YA). (gr. 7-18). 9.99 (978-0-14-241203-9(1), Speak) Penguin Young Readers Group.

Greenberg, Joanne. I Never Promised You a Rose Garden. 256p. (YA). (gr. 7-18). pap. 5.99 (978-0-8072-1362-9(4), Listening Library) Random Hse. Audio Publishing Group.

Heiman, Herb. Running on Dreams. 2007. 293p. (YA). (gr. 8-14). per. 22.95 (978-1-931282-28-4(5)) Autism Asperger Publishing Co.

Hills, Curt. Hannah's Legalized Kidnapping: A Rush to React Took Her Away for 207 Days. 2007. 68p. per. 12.95 (978-1-4327-0668-5(3)) Outskirts Pr., Inc.

Jayne, Hannah. The Escape. 2015. (ENG., Illus.). 256p. (YA). (gr. 8-12). pap. 9.99 (978-1-4926-1654-2(0), 9781492616542) Sourcebooks, Inc.

Ketchen, Susan. Made That Way. 2010. (ENG.). 160p. (J). pap. 12.95 (978-0-88982-270-2(0)) Oolichan Bks. CAN. Dist: Univ. of Toronto Pr.

Kuderick, Madeleine. Kiss of Broken Glass. 2014. (ENG.). 224p. (YA). (gr. 9). 17.99 (978-0-06-230656-2(1), HarperTeen) HarperCollins Pubs.

Leno, Katrina. The Half Life of Molly Pierce. 2014. (ENG.). 240p. (YA). (gr. 8). 17.99 (978-0-06-223117-8(0), HarperTeen) HarperCollins Pubs.

Lorenz, Nancy. The Strength of Ballerinas. 2014. 249p. (YA). pap. 15.99 (978-1-4621-1452-8(0)) Cedar Fort, Inc./CFI Distribution.

Mayfield, Jamie. A Broken Kind of Life. 2016. (ENG., Illus.). (YA). (gr. 9-12). 24.99 **(978-1-63477-926-5(6)**, Harmony Ink Pr.) Dreamspinner Pr.

Moskowitz, Hannah. Break. 2009. (ENG.). 272p. (YA). (gr. 9-18). pap. 10.99 (978-1-4169-8275-3(2), Simon Pulse) Simon Pulse.

Oliver, Lauren. Vanishing Girls. (gr. 9). 2016. 384p. (YA). pap. 9.99 (978-0-06-222411-8(5)) 2015. (ENG.). 368p. (J). 18.99 (978-0-06-222410-1(7)) HarperCollins Pubs.

—Vanishing Girls. 2016. (YA). lib. bdg. 20.85 (978-0-606-38171-0(6)) Turtleback Bks.

Peters, Andrew Fusek & Peters, Polly. The Color Thief. Littlewood, Karin, illus. 2015. (ENG.). 24p. (J). (gr. -1-3). 16.99 (978-0-8075-1273-9(7)) Whitman, Albert & Co.

Peterson, Lois J. Three Good Things, 1 vol. 2015. (Orca Currents Ser.). (ENG.). 144p. (J). (gr. 5-9). pap. 9.95 (978-1-4598-0985-7(8)) Orca Bk. Pubs. USA.

Porter, Pamela. The Crazy Man. 2013. 164p. pap. (978-1-4596-6446-3(9)) ReadHowYouWant.com, Ltd.

Roorda, Julie. Wings of a Bee, 1 vol. 2008. (ENG., Illus.). 224p. (YA). (gr. 7-11). pap. (978-1-894549-68-4(6), Sumach Pr.) Canadian Scholars.

Stauffacher, Sue. Donuthead. 2005. (ENG.). 176p. (J). (gr. 3-7). reprint ed. per. 6.99 (978-0-440-41934-1(4), Yearling) Random Hse. Children's Bks.

Stone, Tamara Ireland. Every Last Word. 2017. (ENG.). 384p. (YA). (gr. 7-12). pap. 9.99 (978-1-4847-2364-7(3)) Hyperion Bks. for Children.

Winegar, Tracy. Keeping Keller. 2008. 207p. pap. 14.99 (978-1-59955-115-9(2)) Cedar Fort, Inc./CFI Distribution.

MENTALLY RETARDED PERSONS

see People with Mental Disabilities

MENUS

Silate, Jennifer. Planning & Preparing Healthy Meals & Snacks: A Day-to-Day Guide to a Healthier Diet. (Library of Nutrition Ser.). 48p. 2009. (gr. 5-8). 53.00 (978-1-60853-776-1(5), Rosen Reference) 2008. (ENG., Illus.). (gr. 5-8). per. 11.75 (978-1-4042-1634-1(0)) 2004. (Illus.). (J). lib. bdg. 26.50 (978-1-4042-0302-0(8)) Rosen Publishing Group, Inc., The.

Tuminelly, Nancy. Super Simple Dinners: Easy No-Bake Recipes for Kids, 1 vol. 2010. (Super Simple Cooking Ser.). (ENG.). 32p. (gr. k-4). 27.07 (978-1-61613-385-6(6), Super SandCastle) ABDO Publishing Co.

MERCHANDISE

see Commercial Products

MERCHANDISING

see Marketing; Retail Trade

MERCHANTS

Behnke, Alison. Grocers. 2005. (Pull Ahead Bks.). (Illus.). 32p. (J). (gr. 3-7). lib. bdg. 22.60 (978-0-8225-2801-2(0), Lerner Pubns.) Lerner Publishing Group.

Bennett, Eric G. Pull up the Ladder Jack: Seamen Behaving Badly. 2012. 182p. 29.99 (978-1-4797-3476-4(4)); pap. 19.99 (978-1-4797-3475-7(6)) Xlibris Corp.

Bow, James. Your Guide to Trade in the Middle Ages. 2017. (Destination: Middle Ages Ser.). (ENG., Illus.). 32p. (J). **(978-0-7787-2996-9(6))**; pap. **(978-0-7787-3052-1(2))** Crabtree Publishing Co.

Dyan, Penelope. The Place of Tales — - a Kid's Guide to Canterbury, Kent, England. Weigand, John, photos by. 2011. (Illus.). 40p. pap. 12.95 (978-1-935630-66-1(0)) Bellissima Publishing, LLC.

Gogerly, Liz. Shopkeeper. 2017. (Play the Part Ser.). (ENG., Illus.). 24p. (J). (gr. k-2). pap. 10.99 (978-0-7502-9706-6(9), Wayland) Hachette Children's Group GBR. Dist: Hachette Bk. Group.

Hull, Robert. Merchant. 2009. (Medieval Lives Ser.). (J). 32.80 (978-1-59920-170-2(4)) Black Rabbit Bks.

Mead, Wendy. The Merchant. 2013. 48p. (J). (gr. 4-8). 29.93 (978-1-60870-415-6(7)); pap. 12.93 (978-1-62712-047-0(5)) Cavendish Square Publishing.

O'Brien, Cynthia. Go West with Merchants & Traders. 2016. (ENG.). 32p. (J). (978-0-7787-2326-4(7)) Crabtree Publishing Co.

Twist, Clint. Marco Polo: History's Great Adventurer. 2011. (Historical Notebooks Ser.). (ENG., Illus.). 30p. (J). (gr. 3-7). 19.99 (978-0-7636-5286-9(5), Templar) Candlewick Pr.

MERCURY (PLANET)

Adamson, Thomas K. Do You Really Want to Visit Mercury? Fabbri, Daniele, illus. 2013. (Do You Really Want to Visit... ? Ser.). (ENG.). 24p. (gr. 1-4). 27.10 (978-1-60753-195-1(X)) Amicus Publishing.

—Mercury [Scholastic]: Revised Edition. 2010. (Exploring the Galaxy Ser.). (ENG.). 24p. pap. 0.49 (978-1-4296-5812-6(6), Pebble Plus) Capstone Press of Coughlan Cos.

Asimov, Isaac & Hantula, Richard. Mercurio. Porras, Carlos & D'Andrea, Patricia, trs. from ENG. 2003. (Isaac Asimov's Biblioteca del Universo del Siglo XXI).Tr. of Mercury: The Quick Planet. (SPA., Illus.). 32p. (gr. 2-6). lib. bdg. 26.00 (978-0-8368-3857-2(2), Gareth Stevens Learning Library) Stevens, Gareth Publishing LLLP.

Berne, Emma Carlson. The Secrets of Mercury. 2015. (Planets Ser.). (ENG., Illus.). 32p. (gr. 2-4). lib. bdg. 31.99 (978-1-4914-5866-2(6)) Capstone Press of Coughlan Cos.

Bloom, J. P. Mercury, 1 vol. 2014. (Planets Ser.). (ENG.). 24p. (J). (gr. 2-4). lib. bdg. 28.50 (978-1-62970-718-1(X)) ABDO Publishing Co.

Carson, Mary Kay. Far-Out Guide to Mercury. 2010. (Far-Out Guide to the Solar System Ser.). (Illus.). 48p. (J). pap. 8.95 (978-1-59845-181-8(2), Enslow Elementary) Enslow Pubs., Inc.

Carson, Mary Kay & Library Association Staff. Far-Out Guide to Mercury. 2010. (Far-Out Guide to the Solar System Ser.). 48p. (J). (gr. 2-5). 25.27 (978-0-7660-3180-7(2)) Enslow Pubs., Inc.

Colligan, L. H. Mercury. 2009. (Space!). 64p. (gr. 5-18). lib. bdg. 32.79 (978-0-7614-4239-4(1)) Marshall Cavendish Corp.

Croce, Carlo P. Mercury. (Library of Planets Ser.). 48p. (gr. 5-8). 2009. 55.90 (978-1-60853-818-8(4), Rosen Reference) 2008. (Illus.). (YA). lib. bdg. 29.25 (978-1-4042-1427-9(5)) Rosen Publishing Group, Inc., The.

Dickmann, Nancy. Exploring the Inner Planets. 2015. (Spectacular Space Science Ser.). (ENG., Illus.). 48p. (J). (gr. 5-6). 30.25 (978-1-4994-3629-7(7), Rosen Central) Rosen Publishing Group, Inc., The.

Dunn, Mary R. A Look at Mercury. (Astronomy Now! Ser.). 24p. (gr. 2-3). 2009. 42.50 (978-1-61511-470-2(X), PowerKids Pr.) 2007. (Illus.). (YA). lib. bdg. 22.60 (978-1-4042-3825-1(5)) Rosen Publishing Group, Inc., The.

Glaser, Chaya. Mercurio: El MÁS PequeÑo de Todos. 2015. (Fuera de Este Mundo Ser.). (SPA., Illus.). 24p. (J). (gr. -1-3). lib. bdg. 23.93 (978-1-62724-592-0(8)) Bearport Publishing Co., Inc.

—Mercury: The Smallest of All. 2015. (Out of This World Ser.). (ENG.). 24p. (J). (gr. -1-3). lib. bdg. 23.93 (978-1-62724-561-6(8)) Bearport Publishing Co., Inc.

Goldstein, Margaret J. Mercury. 2005. (Pull Ahead Bks.). (Illus.). 32p. (gr. 2-4). lib. bdg. 22.60 (978-0-8225-4648-1(5)) Lerner Publishing Group.

Hamilton, Robert M. Exploring Mercury. 2017. (J). **(978-1-5345-2256-5(5)**, KidHaven Publishing) Greenhaven Publishing LLC.

Hollar, Sherman. The Inner Planets: Mercury, Venus, & Mars. 2011. (Illus.). 96p. (J). 31.70 (978-1-61530-512-4(2)) Rosen Publishing Group, Inc., The.

Howard, Fran. Mercury, 1 vol. 2007. (Planets Ser.). (ENG.). 32p. (gr. 3-7). 27.07 (978-1-59928-823-9(0), Buddy Bks.) ABDO Publishing Co.

James, Lincoln. Mercury: The Iron Planet. 2010. (Our Solar System Ser.). 24p. (J). (gr. k-3). (ENG.). pap. 8.15 (978-1-4339-3828-3(6)); (Illus.). lib. bdg. 22.60 (978-1-4339-3827-6(8)) Stevens, Gareth Publishing LLLP.

Jefferis, David. Hot Planets: Mercury & Venus. 2008. (ENG., Illus.). 32p. (J). (gr. 3-7). pap. (978-0-7787-3751-3(9)) Crabtree Publishing Co.

Kazunas, Ariel. Mercury. 2011. (21st Century Junior Library: Solar System Ser.). (ENG.). 24p. (gr. 2-5). lib. bdg. 25.64 (978-1-61080-088-4(5), 201086) Cherry Lake Publishing.

Lawrence, Ellen. Mercury: The High-Speed Planet. 2013. (Zoom into Space Ser.). 24p. (J). (gr. -1-3). lib. bdg. 23.93 (978-1-909673-02-1(1)) Ruby Tuesday Books Limited GBR. Dist: Bearport Publishing Co., Inc.

Lew, Kristi. Mercury. 2009. (Understanding the Elements of the Periodic Table Ser.). 48p. (gr. 6-6). 53.00 (978-1-60854-666-4(7), Rosen Reference) Rosen Publishing Group, Inc., The.

Loewen, Nancy. Nearest to the Sun: The Planet Mercury, 1 vol. Yesh, Jeff, illus. 2008. (Amazing Science: Planets Ser.). (ENG.). 24p. (gr. k-4). lib. bdg. 26.65 (978-1-4048-3954-0(2), 1278902) Picture Window Bks.

Mercury. 2nd rev. ed. 2008. (New Solar System Ser.). 32p. (YA). (gr. 3-6). 23.00 (978-1-60413-208-3(6)) Facts On File, Inc.

Miller, Ron. Mercury & Pluto. 2003. (Worlds Beyond Ser.). (Illus.). 80p. (J). (gr. 7-18). lib. bdg. 27.93 (978-0-7613-2361-7(9), Twenty-First Century Bks.) Lerner Publishing Group.

O'Connell, Kim A. Mercury: A Myreportlinks. com Book. 2005. (Solar System Ser.). (Illus.). 48p. (J). (gr. 4-10). lib. bdg. 26.60 (978-0-7660-5209-3(5), MyReportLinks.com Bks.) Enslow Pubs., Inc.

Orme, Helen & Orme, David. Let's Explore Mercury. 2007. (Space Launch! Ser.). 24p. (gr. 1-4). pap. 8.15 (978-0-8368-8127-1(3)); (Illus.). lib. bdg. 23.00 (978-0-8368-7942-1(2)) Stevens, Gareth Publishing LLLP. (Gareth Stevens Learning Library).

Owen, Ruth. Mercury. 2013. (Explore Outer Space Ser.). 32p. (J). (gr. 3-6). pap. 60.00 (978-1-61533-762-0(8)); pap. 10.00 (978-1-61533-761-3(X)); lib. bdg. 25.25 (978-1-61533-722-4(9)) Windmill Bks.

Oxlade, Chris. Mercury, Mars, & Other Inner Planets. 2007. (Earth & Space Ser.). (Illus.). 48p. (YA). (gr. 5-9). lib. bdg. 29.25 (978-1-4042-3735-3(6)) Rosen Publishing Group, Inc., The.

Rhodes, Mary Wilson. Journey to Mercury, 1 vol. 2014. (Spotlight on Space Science Ser.). (ENG.). 32p. (J). (gr. 5-5). pap. 11.75 (978-1-4994-0372-5(0), PowerKids Pr.) Rosen Publishing Group, Inc., The.

Ring, Susan. Mercury. (J). 2013. 27.13 (978-1-62127-266-3(4)) 2013. pap. 12.95 (978-1-62127-275-5(3)) 2004. (Illus.). pap. 8.95 (978-1-59036-225-9(X)) 2004. (Illus.). 24p. (gr. 4-7). lib. bdg. 24.45 (978-1-59036-098-9(2)) Weigl Pubs., Inc.

Ring, Susan & Roumanis, Alexis. Mercury. 2016. (Illus.). 24p. (J). (978-1-5105-0980-1(1)) SmartBook Media, Inc.

Roumanis, Alexis. Mercury. 2016. (J). **(978-1-5105-2051-6(1))** SmartBook Media, Inc.

—Mercury. 2015. (Illus.). 24p. (J). (978-1-4896-3292-0(1)) Weigl Pubs., Inc.

Sparrow, Giles. Destination Mercury. 32p. (J). 2010. (Illus.). pap. 10.00 (978-1-4358-3455-2(0)) 2009. (ENG.). lib. bdg. 25.25 (978-1-4358-3441-5(0)) Rosen Publishing Group, Inc., The. (PowerKids Pr.).

M
N
O

Squire, Ann O. Planet Mercury. 2014. (True Book — Space (Revised Edition) Ser.). (ENG.). 48p. (J). lib. bdg. 29.00 (978-0-531-21153-3(3)) Scholastic Library Publishing.

Steinkraus, Kyla. Rocky Planets: Mercury, Venus, Earth, & Mars. 2014. (ENG.). 24p. (gr. k-3). 28.50 (978-1-62717-727-6(2)) Rourke Educational Media.

Taylor-Butler, Christine. Mercury. 2007. (Scholastic News Nonfiction Readers Ser.). (ENG., Illus.). 24p. (J). (gr. 1-2). 22.00 (978-0-531-14698-9(7)) Scholastic Library Publishing.

Thomas, Isabel. Mercury & Venus, 1 vol. 2012. (Astronaut Travel Guides). (ENG.). 48p. (gr. 3-6). lib. bdg. 32.65 (978-1-4109-4571-6(5), NA-r) Heinemann-Raintree.

Tocci, Salvatore. Mercury. 2005. (True Bks.). (ENG., Illus.). 48p. (J). (gr. 3-7). lib. bdg. 25.00 (978-0-516-23700-8(4), Children's Pr.) Scholastic Library Publishing.

Vogt, Gregory. Mercury. 2009. (Early Bird Astronomy Ser.). (ENG.). 48p. (gr. 2-5). lib. bdg. 26.60 (978-0-7613-4150-5(1)) Lerner Publishing Group.

Wimmer, Teresa. Mercury. 2007. (My First Look at: Planets Ser.). (Illus.). 24p. (J). (gr. -1-3). lib. bdg. 24.25 (978-1-58341-519-1(X), Creative Education) Creative Co., The.

World Book, contrib. by. Mercury & Venus. 2nd ed. 2006. (World Book's Solar System & Space Exploration Library). (Illus.). 64p. (J). (978-0-7166-9517-2(0)) World Bk., Inc.

World Book, Inc. Staff, contrib. by. Mercury & Venus. 2006. (World Book's Solar System & Space Exploration Library). (Illus.). 63p. (J). (978-0-7166-9502-8(2)) World Bk., Inc.

World Book, Inc Staff, contrib. by. Mercury & Venus. 2010. (J). (978-0-7166-9534-9(0)) World Bk., Inc.

Zobel, Derek. Mercury. 2010. (Exploring Space Ser.). (ENG., Illus.). 24p. (J). (gr. k-3). lib. bdg. 25.95 (978-1-60014-402-8(0), Blastoff! Readers) Bellwether Media.

Zuchora-Walske, Christine. Your Mission to Mercury, 1 vol. 2011. (Planets Ser.). (ENG., Illus.). 32p. (J). (gr. k-3). 28.50 (978-1-61641-680-5(7)) Magic Wagon.

MERCURY PROJECT

see Project Mercury (U.S.)

MERCY DEATH

see Euthanasia

MERCY KILLING

see Euthanasia

MEREDITH, JAMES, 1933-

Bausum, Ann & National Geographic Kids Staff. The March Against Fear: The Last Great Walk of the Civil Rights Movement & the Emergence of Black Power. 2017. (ENG., Illus.). 144p. (J). (gr. 7-9). 18.99 (978-1-4263-2665-3(3), National Geographic Children's Bks.) National Geographic Society.

MERLIN (LEGENDARY CHARACTER)—FICTION

Barron, T. A. The Book of Magic, 12 vols., Bk. 12. Hall, August, illus. 2011. (Merlin Saga Ser.: 12). (ENG.). 160p. (J). (gr. 5-18). 17.99 (978-0-399-24741-5(6), Philomel Bks.) Penguin Young Readers Group.

—Doomraga's Revenge, 7 vols., Bk. 7. 2011. (Merlin Saga Ser.: 7). (ENG.). 272p. (J). (gr. 5-18). 8.99 (978-0-14-241925-0(7), Puffin Books) Penguin Young Readers Group.

—The Dragon of Avalon, Bk. 6. 2011. (Merlin Saga Ser.: 6). (ENG.). 336p. (J). (gr. 5-18). 8.99 (978-0-14-241924-3(9), Puffin Books) Penguin Young Readers Group.

—The Lost Years, Bk. 1. 2011. (Merlin Saga Ser.: 1). (ENG.). 352p. (J). (gr. 5-18). 8.99 (978-0-14-241889-5(7), Puffin Books) Penguin Young Readers Group.

—The Raging Fires, Bk. 3. 2011. (Merlin Saga Ser.: 2). (ENG.). 288p. (J). (gr. 5-18). 8.99 (978-0-14-241921-2(4), Puffin Books) Penguin Young Readers Group.

—The Seven Songs, Bk. 2. 2011. (Merlin Saga Ser.: 2). (ENG.). 336p. (J). (gr. 5-18). 8.99 (978-0-14-241920-5(6), Puffin Books) Penguin Young Readers Group.

—The Wisdom of Merlin: 7 Magical Words for a Meaningful Life. 2015. (ENG.). 80p. (J). (gr. 5). 12.99 (978-0-399-17325-7(0), Philomel Bks.) Penguin Young Readers Group.

—The Wizard's Wings, Bk. 5. 2011. (Merlin Saga Ser.: 5). (ENG.). 384p. (J). (gr. 5-18). 8.99 (978-0-14-241923-6(0), Puffin Books) Penguin Young Readers Group.

Côté, Denis. La Forêt aux Mille et un Périls, Tome 2. Poulin, Stephane, illus. 2004. (Roman Jeunesse Ser.). (FRE.). 96p. (J). (gr. 4-7). pap. (978-2-89021-696-9(9)) Diffusion du livre Mirabel (DLM).

Epstein, Alex. The Circle Cast, 1 vol. 2011. (ENG., Illus.). 304p. (YA). (gr. 2-4). pap. 12.95 (978-1-896580-63-0(7)) Tradewind Bks. CAN. Dist: Orca Bk. Pubs. USA.

Gale, Eric Kahn. The Wizard's Dog. 2017. (ENG., Illus.). 288p. (J). (gr. 3-7). 16.99 (978-0-553-53736-9(9), Crown Books For Young Readers) Random Hse. Children's Bks.

Guerra, Elisa Puricelli. Merlin's Island, 1 vol. Pernigotti, Chiara, tr. from ITA. Bernstein, Gabo León, illus. 2014. (Minerva Mint Ser.). (ENG.). 160p. (gr. 2-4). pap. 7.99 (978-1-4342-6514-2(5)) Capstone Young Readers of Coughlan Cos.

—Merlin's Island, 1 vol. Pernigotti, Chiara, tr. from ITA. Bernstein, Gabo León, illus. 2014. (Minerva Mint Ser.). (ENG.). 160p. (gr. 2-4). 25.32 (978-1-4342-6511-1(0)) Stone Arch Bks.

Hodges, Margaret & Malory, Sir Thomas. Merlin & the Making of the King. Hyman, Trina Schart, tr. Hyman, Trina Schart, illus. 2004. (ENG.). 40p. (J). (gr. 4-6). tchr. ed. 16.95 (978-0-8234-1647-9(X)) Holiday Hse., Inc.

Liess, Claudia Schmidt. Henry the Magical, Mythical Dragon. 2008. 74p. pap. 19.95 (978-1-60672-956-4(X)) America Star Bks.

Memling, Carl. The Sword in the Stone (Disney) Random House Disney Staff, illus. 2015. (Little Golden Book Ser.). (ENG.). 24p. (J). (-k). 4.99 (978-0-7364-3374-7(0), Golden/Disney) Random Hse. Children's Bks.

Pilkington, Linda Rash. Arthur Collins & the Three Wishes: Arthur the Brave! 322p. (YA). (gr. 4-18). 2009. pap. 13.95 (978-0-615-26743-2(2)) 2008. 20.95 (978-0-615-22213-4(7)) City Castles Publishing.

Salemi, Dianne K. The Inquisitor's Mark. 2015. (Eighth Day Ser.: 2). (ENG.). 352p. (J). (gr. 3-7). 16.99 (978-0-06-227218-8(7)) HarperCollins Pubs.

Spinner, Stephanie. The Magic of Merlin. Sokolova, Valerie, illus. 2004. (Stepping Stones: A Chapter Book: Fantasy Ser.). 42p. (J). 11.65 (978-0-7569-0905-5(8)) Perfection Learning Corp.

Treskillard, Robert. Merlin's Nightmare, 1 vol. 2014. (Merlin Spiral Ser.). (ENG.). 432p. (YA). pap. 12.99 (978-0-310-73509-0(2)) Blink.

Yolen, Jane. The Young Merlin Trilogy: Passager, Hobby, & Merlin. 2004. (ENG., Illus.). 276p. (J). (gr. 2-5). pap. 16.95 (978-0-15-205211-9(9)) Houghton Mifflin Harcourt Publishing Co.

MERMAIDS

Altmann, Scott. Mermaids — Sirens of the Sea. 2009. (Dover Coloring Bks.). (ENG., Illus.). 32p. (J). (gr. 1-5). pap. 3.99 (978-0-486-46990-4(5)) Dover Pubns., Inc.

Hile, Lori. Mermaids, 1 vol. 2013. (Solving Mysteries with Science Ser.). (ENG., Illus.). 48p. (gr. 5-5). pap. 9.95 (978-1-4109-4994-3(X)); lib. bdg. 29.99 (978-1-4109-4989-9(3)) Heinemann-Raintree.

Hinds, Kathryn. Mermaids. 2013. (Creatures of Fantasy Ser.). 64p. (J). (gr. 4-8). pap. 15.28 (978-1-62712-053-1(X)) Cavendish Square Publishing.

I Want to Be a Mermaid. 2008. (Magnetic Board Books Ser.). 7p. bds. (978-1-4075-1417-8(2)) Parragon, Inc.

Jeffrey, Gary. Mermaids. Boccanfuso, Emanuele, illus. 2012. (Graphic Mythical Creatures Ser.). (ENG.). 24p. (J). (gr. 3-5). pap. 8.15 (978-1-4339-6765-8(0)); lib. bdg. 23.95 (978-1-4339-6763-4(4)) Stevens, Gareth Publishing LLLP. (Gareth Stevens Learning Library).

Johnson, Sheri A. The Girl's Guide to Mermaids: Everything Alluring about These Mythical Beauties. 2011. (Girls' Guides to Everything Unexplained Ser.). (ENG.). 32p. (gr. 3-4). lib. bdg. 27.99 (978-1-4296-6557-5(2), Snap Bks.) Capstone Press of Coughlan Cos.

Knudsen, Shannon. Mermaids & Mermen. 2009. (Fantasy Chronicles Ser.). (ENG.). 48p. (gr. 4-7). lib. bdg. 27.93 (978-0-8225-9981-4(3)) Lerner Publishing Group.

Loh-Hagan, Virginia. Mermaids. 2017. (Magic, Myth, & Mystery Ser.). (ENG., Illus.). 32p. (J). (gr. 4-8). lib. bdg. 29.93 (978-1-63472-149-3(7), 209168, 45th Parallel Press) Cherry Lake Publishing.

Pratt, Leonie. Mermaid things to make & Do. 2005. 32p. (J). pap. 6.95 (978-0-7945-1062-6(0), Usborne) EDC Publishing.

Publications International Ltd. Staff, creator. Look & Find: Disney Princess: the Little Mermaid. 2013. 24p. (J). (gr. 1-3). 7.98 (978-1-4508-6996-6(3), 23104826-4b2a-459d-8edc-2f0362eaf16d) Phoenix International Publications, Inc.

Rau, Dana Meachen. Mermaids. 2010. (Bookworms Chapter Books: for Real? Ser.). 24p. (gr. 2-3). 22.79 (978-0-7614-4862-4(4)) Marshall Cavendish Corp.

Redmond, Shirley Raye. Mermaids. 2007. (Monsters Ser.). (ENG., Illus.). 48p. (gr. 4-7). lib. bdg. 35.20 (978-0-7377-3634-2(8)) Cengage Gale.

Schomp, Virginia & Hinds, Kathryn. Mermaids. 2013. (Illus.). 64p. (J). (gr. 4-8). 34.21 (978-0-7614-4924-9(8)) Cavendish Square Publishing.

The Summer Mermaid: R-Controlled e, i, u: Level B, 6 vols. (Wright Skills Ser.). 16p. (gr. k-3). 26.50 (978-0-322-01488-6(3)) Wright Group/McGraw-Hill.

Summers, Portia & Rau, Dana Meachen. Are Mermaids Real? 2016. (I Want to Know Ser.). (Illus.). 32p. (J). pap. 10.52 (978-0-7660-8240-3(7)) Enslow Pubs., Inc.

Watt, Fiona. Mermaids. Cartwright, Stephen, illus. 2004. 10p. (J). 15.95 (978-0-7945-0727-5(1), Usborne) EDC Publishing.

MERMAIDS—FICTION

Aaron, Chester. Home to the Sea 2004. (Illus.). 125p. (YA). (gr. 8-12). per. 10.95 (978-0-9746481-2-5(4)) Brown Barn Bks.

Andersen, Hans Christian. Ariel & the Secret Grotto. (Read-Along Ser.). (J). 7.99 incl. audio (978-0-7634-0287-7(7)) Walt Disney Records.

—The Little Mermaid. Santore, Charles, illus. 2013. Orig. Title: Lille havfrue. (ENG.). 48p. (J). 16.95 (978-1-60433-377-0(4), Applesauce Pr.) Cider Mill Pr. Bk. Pubs., LLC.

—The Little Mermaid. Capdevila, Francesc, illus. 2003. (Bilingual Fairy Tales Ser.: BILI).Tr. of Sirenita. (ENG & SPA.). 32p. (J). (gr. -1-7). pap. 6.99 (978-0-8118-3911-2(7)) Chronicle Bks. LLC.

—The Little Mermaid & the Princess & the Pea: Two Tales & Their Histories. Brown, Carron, ed. 2009. (World of Fairy Tales Ser.). (Illus.). 32p. (J). (gr. -1-2). pap. 10.55 (978-1-60754-638-2(8)); lib. bdg. 22.60 (978-1-60754-637-5(X)) Windmill Bks.

—The Little Mermaid Retold. Charlotte, J. M., illus. 2013. 48p. 18.00 (978-0-9895422-0-3(3)) MHC Ministries.

Appelt, Kathi. Keeper. Hall, August, illus. (ENG.). (J). (gr. 3-7). 2012. 432p. pap. 8.99 (978-1-4169-5061-5(3)) 2010. 416p. 17.99 (978-1-4169-5060-8(5)) Simon & Schuster Children's Publishing. (Atheneum Bks. for Young Readers).

Ariel Make Believe Bride. 2008. (Disney 8*8 Ser.). 24p. pap. (978-1-4075-1620-2(5)) Parragon, Inc.

Artful Doodlers Limited Staff. Dora Salva a las Sirenas. 2007. (Dora la Exploradora Ser.). (SPA., Illus.). 24p. (J). (gr. -1-2). pap. 3.99 (978-1-4169-4725-7(6), Libros Para Ninos) Libros Para Ninos.

Artful Doodlers Ltd Staff. Dora Saves Mermaid Kingdom! 2007. (Dora the Explorer Ser.: 24). (ENG., Illus.). 24p. (J). (gr. -1-2). pap. 3.99 (978-1-4169-3841-5(9), Simon Spotlight/Nickelodeon) Simon Spotlight/Nickelodeon.

Balletta, Janet. The Legend of the Colombian Mermaid. Mejía, Estella, illus. 2013. 36p. (J). pap. 14.95 (978-0-9856762-9-2(9)) WRB Pub.

Banks, Rosie. Mermaid Reef. 2014. (Secret Kingdom Ser.: 4). lib. bdg. 14.75 (978-0-606-35842-2(0)) Turtleback Bks.

—Secret Kingdom #4: Mermaid Reef. 2014. (Secret Kingdom Ser.: 4). (ENG.). 128p. (J). (gr. 2-5). pap. 4.99 (978-0-545-53556-4(5), Scholastic Paperbacks) Scholastic, Inc.

Bar-el, Dan. That One Spooky Night. Huyck, David, illus. 2012. (ENG.). 80p. (J). (gr. 2-5). 8.95 (978-1-55453-752-5(5)); 16.95 (978-1-55453-751-8(7)) Kids Can Pr., Ltd. CAN. Dist: Hachette Bk. Group.

Bardhan-Quallen, Sudipta. Purrmaids #1: the Scaredy Cat. 2017. (Purrmaids Ser.: 1). (ENG.). 96p. (J). (gr. 1-4). lib. bdg. 12.99 **(978-1-5247-0162-8(9))**; (Illus.). 4.99 **(978-1-5247-0161-1(0))** Random Hse. Children's Bks. (Random Hse. Bks. for Young Readers).

—Purrmaids #2: the Catfish Club. 2017. (Purrmaids Ser.: 2). (ENG.). 96p. (J). (gr. 1-4). lib. bdg. 12.99 **(978-1-5247-0165-9(3))**; (Illus.). 4.99 **(978-1-5247-0164-2(5))** Random Hse. Children's Bks. (Random Hse. Bks. for Young Readers).

Barella, Laura, illus. The Little Mermaid. 2010. (Flip-Up Fairy Tales Ser.). (ENG.). 24p. (J). (gr. -1-2). audio compact disk (978-1-84643-331-3(2)) Child's Play International Ltd.

Baxter, Nicola. The Mermaid & the Star. Rigby, Deborah, illus. 2025. 14p. (J). bds. (978-1-84322-907-0(2), Armadillo) Anness Publishing.

Beinstein, Phoebe. ¡A nadar, Boots! (Swim, Boots, Swim!) Roper, Robert, illus. 2009. (Dora la Exploradora Ser.). (SPA.). 24p. (J). pap. 3.99 (978-1-4169-7939-5(5), Libros Para Ninos) Libros Para Ninos.

—Swim, Boots, Swim! Roper, Robert, illus. 2009. (Dora the Explorer Ser.: 29). (ENG.). 24p. (J). (gr. -1-2). pap. 3.99 (978-1-4169-7195-5(5), Simon Spotlight/Nickelodeon) Simon Spotlight/Nickelodeon.

Belle, Trixie & Caruso-Scott, Melissa. The Little Mermaid: Les Petits Fairytales. Lake, Oliver, illus. 2013. (Petits Fairytales Ser.). (ENG.). 26p. (J). (gr. -1 — 1). bds. 7.99 (978-0-8050-9789-4(9), 9780805097894, Holt, Henry & Co. Bks. For Young Readers) Holt, Henry & Co.

Berg, Deva Jean. A Tail of Two Sisters. Berg, Deva Jean, illus. 2013. (Illus.). 26p. pap. 9.95 (978-1-939790-07-1(7)) Lorian Assn., The.

Berk, Ari. The Secret History of Mermaids & Creatures of the Deep. Anderson, Wayne, illus. 2009. (ENG.). 48p. (J). (gr. 3-7). 17.99 (978-0-7636-4515-1(X)) Candlewick Pr.

Bernstein, Danielle V. The Magic in a Mermaid's Tear. 2013. 28p. pap. 24.95 (978-1-62709-604-1(3)) America Star Bks.

Booker, Dwayne. Mia the Mermaid: Looking at Data. 2017. (Computer Science for the Real World Ser.). 12p. (gr. 6-7). pap. 7.05 **(978-1-5383-5122-2(6)**, Rosen Classroom) Rosen Publishing Group, Inc., The.

Borgia, Mary. Tales of the Texas Mermaid: The Charro. 2007. (J). 17.95 (978-0-9778451-1-8(7)) Goretti Publishing.

Boudreau, Helene. Real Mermaids Don't Hold Their Breath. 2012. (ENG.). 240p. (J). (gr. 4-8). pap. 9.99 (978-1-4022-6446-7(1), Sourcebooks Jabberwocky) Sourcebooks, Inc.

—Real Mermaids Don't Need High Heels. 2013. (ENG.). 240p. (J). (gr. 4-8). pap. 6.99 (978-1-4022-6458-0(5), Sourcebooks Jabberwocky) Sourcebooks, Inc.

Brennan-Nelson, Denise & Hartung, Susan Kathleen. Tallulah: Mermaid of the Great Lakes. 2015. (ENG., Illus.). 40p. (J). (gr. 1-4). 16.99 (978-1-58536-909-6(8), 203812) Sleeping Bear Pr.

Brett, Jan. The Mermaid. Brett, Jan, illus. 2017. (ENG., Illus.). 32p. (J). (gr. -1-3). 18.99 **(978-0-399-17072-0(3)**, G.P. Putnam's Sons Books for Young Readers) Penguin Young Readers Group.

Brown, Anne Greenwood. Deep Betrayal. 2013. (ENG.). 352p. (YA). (gr. 7). pap. 9.99 (978-0-385-74204-7(5), Ember) Random Hse. Children's Bks.

—Lies Beneath. 2013. (ENG.). 320p. (YA). (gr. 7). pap. 8.99 (978-0-385-74202-3(9), Ember) Random Hse. Children's Bks.

Bryan, Barbara. Starfish, Seashells, Coral & Gems. 2010. 47p. (J). pap. 27.95 (978-1-4327-6265-0(6)); pap. 21.95 (978-1-4327-6009-0(2)) Outskirts Pr., Inc.

Bubble Guppies, Bubble. Bubble Guppies: Let's Play, Bubble Puppy! A PeekABoo Book. 2015. (ENG.). 10p. (J). (gr. -1-k). bds. 10.99 (978-0-7944-3470-0(3), Reader's Digest Children's Bks.) Studio Fun International.

Burns, Laura J. Magic Below. 2016. (Bewitched in Oz Ser.). (ENG.). 240p. (gr. 4-8). lib. bdg. 30.65 (978-1-4965-2603-8(1)) Stone Arch Bks.

Cabell, Robert W. The Mermaid Adventures of Princess Miranda: Volume One. Cabell, Robert W., illus. 2013. (Illus.). 128p. pap. 7.95 (978-0-9890974-3-7(9), Oceanus Bks.) Warrington Pubns.

Childs, Tera Lynn. Fins Are Forever. 2012. (Forgive My Fins Ser.: 2). (ENG.). 288p. (YA). (gr. 8). pap. 8.99 (978-0-06-191470-6(3), Tegen, Katherine Bks) HarperCollins Pubs.

—Forgive My Fins. (Forgive My Fins Ser.: 1). (ENG.). (YA). (gr. 8). 2011. 336p. pap. 8.99 (978-0-06-191467-6(3)) 2010. 304p. 16.99 (978-0-06-191465-2(7)) HarperCollins Pubs. (Tegen, Katherine Bks).

—Just for Fins. 2013. (Forgive My Fins Ser.: 3). (ENG.). 256p. (YA). (gr. 8). pap. 9.99 (978-0-06-219208-0(6), Tegen, Katherine Bks) HarperCollins Pubs.

Clibbon, Meg. Shimmering Mermaids. Clibbon, Lucy, illus. 2011. (My World Of Ser.). (ENG.). 32p. (J). (gr. k-2). pap. 9.99 (978-1-84089-594-0(2)) Meg and Lucy Bks. GBR. Dist: Independent Pubs. Group.

Collins, Michael. Anu & the Blue. 2009. 166p. pap. 16.68 (978-0-557-20316-1(3)) Lulu Pr., Inc.

Córdova, Zoraida. The Vicious Deep. 2012. (Vicious Deep Ser.: 1). (ENG.). 384p. (YA). (gr. 7-12). pap. 9.99 (978-1-4022-7441-1(6)) Sourcebooks, Inc.

Crump, Fred, Jr., illus. & retold by. The Little Mermaid. Crump, Fred, Jr., retold by. 2007. 32p. (J). 12.95 (978-1-934056-72-1(3)); pap. 9.95 (978-1-60352-063-8(5)) UMI (Urban Ministries, Inc.).

Dadey, Debbie. Battle of the Best Friends. Avakyan, Tatevik, illus. 2012. (Mermaid Tales Ser.: 2). (ENG.). 112p. (J). (gr. 1-4). 15.99 (978-1-4424-4979-4(9)); pap. 5.99 (978-1-4424-2982-6(8)) Simon & Schuster Children's Publishing. (Aladdin).

—Books vs. Looks. Avakyan, Tatevik, illus. 2016. (Mermaid Tales Ser.: 15). (ENG.). 128p. (J). (gr. 1-4). pap. 5.99 (978-1-4814-4081-3(0), Aladdin) Simon & Schuster Children's Publishing.

—The Crook & the Crown. Avakyan, Tatevik, illus. 2015. (Mermaid Tales Ser.: 13). (ENG.). 128p. (J). (gr. 1-4). pap. 5.99 (978-1-4814-4075-2(6), Aladdin) Simon & Schuster Children's Publishing.

—Danger in the Deep Blue Sea. Avakyan, Tatevik, illus. 2013. (Mermaid Tales Ser.: 4). (ENG.). 112p. (J). (gr. 1-4). 15.99 (978-1-4424-5319-7(2)); pap. 5.99 (978-1-4424-2986-4(0)) Simon & Schuster Children's Publishing. (Aladdin).

—Dream of the Blue Turtle. Avakyan, Tatevik, illus. 2014. (Mermaid Tales Ser.: 7). (ENG.). 128p. (J). (gr. 1-4). 16.99 (978-1-4424-8264-7(8)); pap. 5.99 (978-1-4424-8263-0(X)) Simon & Schuster Children's Publishing. (Aladdin).

—The Lost Princess. Avakyan, Tatevik, illus. 2013. (Mermaid Tales Ser.: 5). (ENG.). 128p. (J). (gr. 1-4). 15.99 (978-1-4424-8258-6(3)); pap. 5.99 (978-1-4424-8257-9(5)) Simon & Schuster Children's Publishing. (Aladdin).

—Mermaid Tales 3-Books-In-1! Trouble at Trident Academy; Battle of the Best; a Whale of a Tale. Avakyan, Tatevik, illus. 2016. (Mermaid Tales Ser.). (ENG.). 320p. (J). (gr. 1-4). pap. 8.99 (978-1-4814-8555-5(5), Aladdin) Simon & Schuster Children's Publishing.

—Mermaid Tales 4-Books-In-1! Trouble at Trident Academy; Battles of the Best Friends; a Whale of a Tale; Danger in the Deep Blue Sea. Avakyan, Tatevik, illus. 2016. (Mermaid Tales Ser.). (ENG.). 416p. (J). (gr. 1-4). 14.99 (978-1-4814-7592-1(4), Aladdin) Simon & Schuster Children's Publishing.

—A Mermaid Tales Sparkling Collection: Trouble at Trident Academy - Battle of the Best Friends - A Whale of a Tale - Danger in the Deep Blue Sea - The Lost Princess. Avakyan, Tatevik, illus. 2013. (Mermaid Tales Ser.). (ENG.). 592p. (J). (gr. 1-4). pap. 29.99 (978-1-4814-0055-8(X), Aladdin) Simon & Schuster Children's Publishing.

—The Polar Bear Express. Avakyan, Tatevik, illus. 2015. (Mermaid Tales Ser.: 11). (ENG.). 128p. (J). (gr. 1-4). pap. 5.99 (978-1-4814-0260-6(9), Aladdin) Simon & Schuster Children's Publishing.

—A Tail of Two Sisters. Avakyan, Tatevik, illus. 2015. (Mermaid Tales Ser.: 10). (ENG.). 128p. (J). (gr. 1-4). 17.99 (978-1-4814-0258-3(7), Aladdin) Simon & Schuster Children's Publishing.

—A Tale of Two Sisters. Avakyan, Tatevik, illus. 2015. (Mermaid Tales Ser.: 10). (ENG.). 128p. (J). (gr. 1-4). pap. 5.99 (978-1-4814-0257-6(9), Aladdin) Simon & Schuster Children's Publishing.

—Treasure in Trident City. Avakyan, Tatevik, illus. 2014. (Mermaid Tales Ser.: 8). (ENG.). 128p. (J). (gr. 1-4). pap. 5.99 (978-1-4424-8266-1(4), Aladdin) Simon & Schuster Children's Publishing.

—Trouble at Trident Academy. Avakyan, Tatevik, illus. 2012. (Mermaid Tales Ser.: 1). (ENG.). 112p. (J). (gr. 1-4). 15.99 (978-1-4424-4978-7(0)); pap. 5.99 (978-1-4424-2980-2(1)) Simon & Schuster Children's Publishing. (Aladdin).

—Twist & Shout. Avakyan, Tatevik, illus. 2016. (Mermaid Tales Ser.: 14). (ENG.). 112p. (J). (gr. 1-4). pap. 5.99 (978-1-4814-4078-3(0), Aladdin) Simon & Schuster Children's Publishing.

—A Whale of a Tale. Avakyan, Tatevik, illus. 2012. (Mermaid Tales Ser.: 3). (ENG.). 128p. (J). (gr. 1-4). 14.99 (978-1-4424-5318-0(4)); pap. 5.99 (978-1-4424-2984-0(4)) Simon & Schuster Children's Publishing. (Aladdin).

Dadey, Debby. Mermaid Tales. 2015. (Mermaid Tales Ser.: Vol. 8). (ENG.). (J). 193.68 (978-1-61479-321-2(2), Spotlight) ABDO Publishing Co.

Dadey, Debby & Dadey, Debbie. Battle of the Best Friends, 1 vol., Bk. 2. 2015. (Mermaid Tales Ser.). (ENG.). 104p. (J). (gr. 2-4). 24.21 (978-1-61479-323-6(9), Spotlight) ABDO Publishing Co.

—Danger in the Deep Blue Sea, 1 vol., Bk. 4. 2015. (Mermaid Tales Ser.). (ENG.). 104p. (J). (gr. 2-4). 24.21 (978-1-61479-325-0(5), Spotlight) ABDO Publishing Co.

—Dream of the Blue Turtle, 1 vol., Bk. 7. 2015. (Mermaid Tales Ser.). (ENG.). 112p. (J). (gr. 2-4). 24.21 (978-1-61479-328-1(X), Spotlight) ABDO Publishing Co.

—Secret Sea Horse, 1 vol., Bk. 6. 2015. (Mermaid Tales Ser.). (ENG.). 96p. (J). (gr. 2-4). 24.21 (978-1-61479-327-4(1), Spotlight) ABDO Publishing Co.

—Treasure in Trident City, 1 vol., Bk. 8. 2015. (Mermaid Tales Ser.). (ENG.). 120p. (J). (gr. 2-4). 24.21 (978-1-61479-329-8(8), Spotlight) ABDO Publishing Co.

—Trouble at Trident Academy, 1 vol., Bk. 1. 2015. (Mermaid Tales Ser.). (ENG.). 104p. (J). (gr. 2-4). 24.21 (978-1-61479-322-9(0), Spotlight) ABDO Publishing Co.

—Whale of a Tale, 1 vol., Bk. 3. 2015. (Mermaid Tales Ser.). (ENG.). 120p. (J). (gr. 2-4). 24.21 (978-1-61479-324-3(7), Spotlight) ABDO Publishing Co.

Dahl, Michael. The Marshmallow Mermaid. Crowther, Jeff, illus. 2010. (Graphic Sparks Ser.). (ENG.). 40p. (gr. 1-3). pap. 5.95 (978-1-4342-2802-4(9), Graphic Sparks) Stone Arch Bks.

Davidson, Susanna. Stories of Mermaids. 2009. (Young Reading 1 Ser.). 48p. (J). (gr. 2). 6.99 (978-0-7945-2589-7(X), Usborne) EDC Publishing.

de Brunhoff, Jean. Babar & Zephir. de Brunhoff, Jean, illus. 2005. (Illus.). 38p. (J). (gr. k-4). reprint ed. 16.00 (978-0-7567-8935-0(4)) DIANE Publishing Co.

Deep Trouble (Book 5) 2017. (Secret Mermaid Ser.). (ENG.). (J). pap. 4.99 **(978-0-7945-3685-5(9)**, Usborne) EDC Publishing.

Dipinto, Michael J. The Princess Mermaid & the Missing Sea Shells. Marsh, Bobbie, illus. 2013. 36p. pap. 15.95 (978-1-61493-151-5(8)) Peppertree Pr., The.

Disney & Disney / LeapFrog. Disney Princess: Les aventures D'Ariel. 2008. (J). 20.79 (978-1-59319-944-9(9)) LeapFrog Enterprises, Inc.

Disney Book Group. The Little Mermaid: The Story of Ariel. Disney Storybook Art Team, illus. 2016. (ENG.). 112p. (J). (gr. -1-k). 12.99 (978-1-4847-6728-3(4)) Disney Pr.

Disney Book Group Staff. The Little Mermaid Read-Along Storybook & CD. Disney Storybook Artists Staff, illus. 2013. (Read-Along Storybook & CD Ser.). (ENG.). 32p. (J). (gr. -1-k). pap. 6.99 (978-1-4231-6889-8(5)) Disney Pr.

—Part of Their World. Disney Storybook Artists Staff, illus. 2013. (ENG.). 40p. (J). (gr. -1-17). 15.99 (978-1-4231-6757-0(0)) Disney Pr.

Disney Princess Staff & Disney Book Group Staff. Ariel: The Birthday Surprise. Cagol, Andrea & Studio Iboix Staff, illus. 2010. (Disney Princess Chapter Book: Series #1 Ser.). (ENG.). 96p. (J). (gr. 1-3). pap. 4.99 (978-1-4231-2971-4(7)) Disney Pr.

Disney Storybook Artists Staff & Thammavongsa, Christine, illus. The Little Mermaid. 2007. (Play-A-Sound Bks.). 18p. (J). (gr. -1-3). bds. 16.98 (978-1-4127-8775-8(0)) Publications International, Ltd.

Donaldson, Julia & Axworthy, Anni. The Mermaid & the Octopus. 2006. (Collins Big Cat Ser.). (ENG., Illus.). 16p. (J). (gr. 1-1). pap. 5.99 (978-0-00-718684-6(3)) HarperCollins Pubs. Ltd. GBR. Dist: Independent Pubs. Group.

Donnelly, Jennifer. Dark Tide. 2015. (Waterfire Saga Ser.: Bk. 3). (ENG.). 400p. (YA). (gr. 7-12). 17.99 *(978-1-4231-8201-6(4))* Hyperion Bks. for Children.
—Deep Blue. 2014. (Waterfire Saga Novel Ser.: Bk. 1). (ENG., Illus.). 352p. (YA). (gr. 7-12). 17.99 *(978-1-4231-3316-2(1))* Disney Pr.
—Deep Blue. 2015. (Waterfire Saga Ser.: Bk. 1). (ENG.). 368p. (YA). (gr. 7-12). pap. 9.99 *(978-1-4847-1310-5(9))* Hyperion Bks. for Children.
—Rogue Wave. 2015. (Waterfire Saga Novel Ser.: Bk. 2). (ENG.). 320p. (YA). (gr. 7-12). 17.99 *(978-1-4231-8200-9(6))* Disney Pr.
—Rogue Wave. 2016. (Waterfire Saga Ser.: Bk. 2). (ENG.). 336p. (YA). (gr. 7-12). pap. 9.99 *(978-1-4847-1301-3(X))* Hyperion Bks. for Children.
—Waterfire Saga, Book Four: Sea Spell. 2016. (Waterfire Saga Novel Ser.). (ENG.). 368p. (YA). (gr. 7-12). 17.99 *(978-1-4847-1290-0(0))* Hyperion Bks. for Children.
—Waterfire Saga, Book Four Sea Spell. 2017. (Waterfire Saga Ser.). (ENG.). 368p. (YA). (gr. 7-12). pap. 9.99 ***(978-1-4847-1303-7(6))*** Hyperion Bks. for Children.
Donnelly, Jennifer. Waterfire Saga, Book Three Dark Tide. 2016. (Waterfire Saga Ser.). (ENG.). 416p. (YA). (gr. 7-12). pap. 9.99 *(978-1-4847-1302-0(8))* Hyperion Bks. for Children.
Dunmore, Helen. The Crossing of Ingo. 2009. (ENG.). 368p. (J). 15.99 *(978-1-55468-247-8(9))* HarperCollins Pubs.
—Ingo. 2008. (Ingo Ser.: 1). 336p. (YA). (gr. 5). per. 7.99 *(978-0-06-081854-8(9))* HarperCollins Pubs.
—The Tide Knot. 2008. 330p. (J). 5.99 *(978-0-06-081857-9(3))*; (Ingo Ser.: 2). (ENG.). 336p. (YA). (gr. 5-8). 16.99 *(978-0-06-081855-5(7))* HarperCollins Pubs.
Ealy, Gerald & Ealy, Gerald. I Made a Wish to Be a Fish. 2012. 32p. pap. 9.95 *(978-0-9843837-5-7(1))* G340 Publishing.
Eberly, Chelsea. Surf Princess. 2012. (Barbie Step into Reading Level 2 Ser.). lib. bdg. 13.55 *(978-0-606-23718-5(6),* Turtleback) Turtleback Bks.
Epperson, Kathy. Mermaids. 2013. 28p. pap. 24.95 *(978-1-4626-9631-4(7))* America Star Bks.
Fama, Elizabeth. Monstrous Beauty. 2013. (ENG.). 352p. (YA). (gr. 7-12). pap. 9.99 *(978-1-250-03425-0(6))* Square Fish.
Farmer, Nancy. The Islands of the Blessed. 2012. (ENG., Illus.). 496p. (YA). (gr. 7). pap. 11.99 *(978-1-4169-0738-1(6),* Atheneum Bks. for Young Readers) Simon & Schuster Children's Publishing.
—The Islands of the Blessed. Foster, Jon, illus. 2009. (ENG.). 496p. (YA). (gr. 7-9). 18.99 *(978-1-4169-0737-4(8),* Atheneum/Richard Jackson Bks.) Simon & Schuster Children's Publishing.
—The Islands of the Blessed. l.t. ed. 2010. (Sequel to the Land of the Silver Apples Ser.). (ENG.). 520p. (J). 23.95 *(978-1-4104-2253-8(4))* Thorndike Pr.
Felix, Rebecca. The Little Mermaid. Petelinsek, Kathleen, illus. 2013. (Fairy Tale Collection). (ENG.). 24p. (J). (gr. k-3). 28.50 *(978-1-62323-612-0(6),* 206379) Child's World, Inc., The.
Filakosky, Sandra. Star the Mermaid. Anderson, Susan, illus. 2010. 20p. pap. 10.49 *(978-1-4389-8626-5(2))* AuthorHouse.
Froeb, Lori C. Disney Princess: Part of Your World. 2015. (Spin Arounds Ser.: 2). (ENG.). 12p. (J). (gr. -1-k). bds. 10.99 *(978-0-7944-3291-1(3),* Reader's Digest Children's Bks.) Studio Fun International.
Funke, Cornelia. Lilly & Fin: A Mermaid's Tale. LatschLit, Inc., tr. from GER. 2017. (ENG., Illus.). 96p. (J). (gr. 2-5). 9.99 ***(978-1-5247-0101-7(7))***; lib. bdg. 12.99 ***(978-1-5247-0102-4(5))*** Random Hse. Children's Bks. (Random Hse. Bks. for Young Readers).
Gallemore, M. H. Annie & the Mermaid. 2005. 9.00 *(978-0-8059-9787-3(3))* Dorrance Publishing Co., Inc.
Gamble, Adam & Jasper, Mark. Good Night Mermaids. Chan, Suwin, illus. 2015. (Good Night Our World Ser.). (ENG.). 20p. (J). (— 1). bds. 9.95 *(978-1-60219-226-3(X))* Good Night Bks.
George, Kallie. The Melancholic Mermaid. Halpin, Abigail, illus. 2011. (ENG.). 64p. (J). (gr. k-4). 16.95 *(978-1-897476-53-6(1))* Simply Read Bks. CAN. Dist: Ingram Publisher Services.
Gilbert, Julie. Fire & Ice: A Mermaid's Journey. Fagan, Kirbi, illus. 2017. (Dark Waters Ser.). (ENG.). 160p. (gr. 2-4). lib. bdg. 26.65 *(978-1-4965-4168-0(5))* Stone Arch Bks.
—Into the Storm: A Mermaid's Journey. Fagan, Kirbi, illus. 2017. (Dark Waters Ser.). (ENG.). 160p. (gr. 2-4). pap. 6.95 *(978-1-4965-4175-8(8))*; lib. bdg. 26.65 *(978-1-4965-4171-0(5))* Stone Arch Bks.
—Neptune's Trident: A Mermaid's Journey. Fagan, Kirbi, illus. 2017. (Dark Waters Ser.). (ENG.). 160p. (gr. 2-4). lib. bdg. 26.65 *(978-1-4965-4169-7(3))* Stone Arch Bks.
—The Sighting: A Mermaid's Journey. Fagan, Kirbi, illus. 2017. (Dark Waters Ser.). (ENG.). 160p. (gr. 2-4). lib. bdg. 26.65 *(978-1-4965-4170-3(7))* Stone Arch Bks.
Golden Books. Bubble Guppies Little Golden Book Favorites (Bubble Guppies) Golden Books, illus. 2015. (Little Golden Book Favorites Ser.). (ENG., Illus.). 80p. (J). (gr. -1-2). 7.99 *(978-0-553-52115-3(2),* Golden Bks.) Random Hse. Children's Bks.
Guettier, Nancy. Mermaids on Mars. 2013. (ENG.). 36p. (-3). pap. 9.95 *(978-1-61448-670-1(0))*; (Illus.). (gr. 1-3). 19.95 *(978-1-61448-640-4(9))* Morgan James Publishing.
Gurtler, Janet. Cora's Decision. Wood, Katie, illus. 2015. (Mermaid Kingdom Ser.). (ENG.). 96p. (gr. 3-5). 23.99 *(978-1-4342-9695-5(4))* Stone Arch Bks.
—Deep-Water Drama. Wood, Katie, illus. 2016. (Mermaid Kingdom Ser.). (ENG.). 288p. (gr. 3-5). 12.95 *(978-1-62370-632-6(7))* Capstone Young Readers of Coughlan Cos.
—Rachel's Secret. Wood, Katie, illus. 2015. (Mermaid Kingdom Ser.). (ENG.). 96p. (gr. 3-5). 23.99 *(978-1-4342-9694-8(6))* Stone Arch Bks.
—Rachel's Worry. Wood, Katie, illus. 2016. (Mermaid Kingdom Ser.). (ENG.). 96p. (gr. 3-5). 23.99 *(978-1-4965-2607-6(4))* Stone Arch Bks.
—Secrets Beneath the Sea. Wood, Katie, illus. 2015. (Mermaid Kingdom Ser.). (ENG.). 288p. (gr. 3-5). 12.95 *(978-1-62370-187-1(2))* Capstone Young Readers of Coughlan Cos.
—Shyanna's Song. Wood, Katie, illus. 2015. (Mermaid Kingdom Ser.). (ENG.). 96p. (gr. 3-5). lib. bdg. 23.99 *(978-1-4342-9693-1(8))* Stone Arch Bks.
—Shyanna's Wish. Wood, Katie, illus. 2015. (Mermaid Kingdom Ser.). (ENG.). 96p. (gr. 3-5). 23.99 *(978-1-4342-9696-2(2))* Stone Arch Bks.
Hanes, Tracey. The Adventures of Kung Foo Poo. 2009. 84p. pap. 15.99 *(978-1-4415-4045-4(8))* Xlibris Corp.
Hargreaves, Roger & Hargreaves, Adam. Little Miss Trouble & the Mermaid. Hargreaves, Adam, illus. 2008. (Mr. Men & Little Miss Ser.). (ENG., Illus.). 32p. (J). (gr. -1-2). mass mkt. 3.99 *(978-0-8431-3277-9(9),* Grosset & Dunlap) Penguin Young Readers Group.
Harper, Suzanne. A Mischief of Mermaids. 2013. (Unseen World of Poppy Malone Ser.: 3). (ENG.). 288p. (J). (gr. 3-7). 16.99 *(978-0-06-199613-9(0),* Greenwillow Bks.) HarperCollins Pubs.
Haydon, Elizabeth. The Tree of Water. Dorman, Brandon, illus. 2014. (Lost Journals of Ven Polypheme Ser.: 4). (ENG.). 400p. (J). (gr. 5-9). 17.99 *(978-0-7653-2059-9(2),* 9780765320599, Starscape) Doherty, Tom Assocs., LLC.
Hecker, Vera, illus. A Home for Rainbow. 2007. 32p. (J). *(978-0-9799729-0-4(6))* Banta, Sandra.
Heinrichs, Cynthia. Mermaids. Lee, Jumin, illus. 2011. (ENG.). 32p. (J). (gr. -1-3). 16.95 *(978-1-897476-37-6(X))* Simply Read Bks. CAN. Dist: Ingram Publisher Services.
Herman, Gail & Studio Iboix Staff. Ariel: The Birthday Surprise, 1 vol. 2012. (Disney Princess Ser.). (ENG., Illus.). 96p. (J). (gr. 2-5). 24.21 *(978-1-59961-877-7(X))* Spotlight.
Hicks, Angie, illus. Moonlight & the Mermaid. 2012. (ENG.). 24p. (J). 9.95 *(978-1-84135-833-8(9))* Award Pubns. Ltd. GBR. Dist: Parkwest Pubns., Inc.
Hinkler Books Staff. CD Storybook: Beauty & the Beast; The Little Mermaid; Cinderella; Snow White. rev. ed. 2004. (Illus.). 128p. (J). (gr. 4-12). 14.95 incl. cd-rom *(978-1-86515-754-2(6))* Hinkler Bks. Pty, Ltd. AUS. Dist: Penton Overseas, Inc.
Homberg, Ruth. The Little Mermaid. 2013. (Disney Princess Step into Reading Ser.). lib. bdg. 13.55 *(978-0-606-32202-7(7),* Turtleback) Turtleback Bks.
—The Little Mermaid Step into Reading (Disney Princess) RH Disney Staff, illus. 2013. (Step into Reading Ser.). (ENG.). 32p. (J). (gr. -1-1). 3.99 *(978-0-7364-8128-1(1),* RH/Disney) Random Hse. Children's Bks.
Hoppey, Tim. Pedro, the Pirate. Bonder, Dianna, illus. 2012. (ENG & SPA.). 32p. (J). lib. bdg. 16.95 *(978-1-936299-18-8(6),* Raven Tree Pr.,Csi) Continental Sales, Inc.
Hunter, Mollie. The Mermaid Summer. 2003. 118p. (J). *(978-1-4131-4688-2(0),* Harper Trophy) HarperCollins Pubs.
Hutchinson, Kerrian. The Fish People. 2011. 18p. pap. 16.95 *(978-1-4626-2692-2(0))* PublishAmerica, Inc.
Jackson, Susan. The Secret of Mermaid Island. 2004. (J). per. 9.95 *(978-0-9748087-1-0(7))* Journey Pubns., LLC.
Jarek, Janice. Mya & the Mermaid. 2012. 28p. 24.95 *(978-1-4626-3277-0(7))* America Star Bks.
Johnson, Gillian. Thora. Johnson, Gillian, illus. 2003. (Illus.). 128p. *(978-0-207-19815-1(2))* HarperCollins Pubs. Australia.
—Thora & the Green Sea-Unicorn. Johnson, Gillian, illus. 2005. (Illus.). 272p. *(978-0-207-20016-8(5))* HarperCollins Pubs. Australia.
—Thora & the Incredible Crystals. 2007. (Illus.). 272p. *(978-0-207-20017-5(3))* HarperCollins Pubs. Australia.
Jones, Cheri. The Adventures of a Mermaid Princess. 2013. 76p. (gr. -1). pap. 10.84 *(978-1-4907-0598-9(8))* Trafford Publishing.
Kann, Victoria. Aqualicious. Kann, Victoria, illus. 2015. (ENG., Illus.). 40p. (J). (gr. -1-3). 17.99 *(978-0-06-233016-1(0))* HarperCollins Pubs.
—Pinkalicious & Aqua, the Mini-Mermaid. Kann, Victoria, illus. 2016. (Pinkalicious Ser.). (Illus.). 24p. (J). (gr. -1-3). pap. 4.99 *(978-0-06-241075-7(X),* HarperFestival) HarperCollins Pubs.
—Pinkalicious & Aqua, the Mini-Mermaid. 2016. (Pinkalicious Ser.). (J). lib. bdg. 14.75 *(978-0-606-38773-6(0))* Turtleback Bks.
Kessler, Liz. The Castle in the Mist. Ledwidge, Natacha & Gibb, Sarah, illus. 2007. (Emily Windsnap Ser.: 3). (ENG.). 208p. (J). (gr. 3-7). 15.99 *(978-0-7636-3330-1(5))* Candlewick Pr.
—The Castle in the Mist. 2012. (Emily Windsnap Ser.: 3). lib. bdg. 16.00 *(978-0-606-25596-7(6),* Turtleback) Turtleback Bks.
—Emily Windsnap & the Castle in the Mist. Ledwidge, Natacha, illus. 2012. (Emily Windsnap Ser.: 3). (ENG.). 208p. (J). (gr. 3-7). pap. 5.99 *(978-0-7636-6017-8(5))* Candlewick Pr.
—Emily Windsnap & the Land of the Midnight Sun. Gibb, Sarah & Ledwidge, Natacha, illus. 2013. (Emily Windsnap Ser.: 5). (ENG.). 288p. (J). (gr. 3-7). 15.99 *(978-0-7636-5824-3(3))* Candlewick Pr.
—Emily Windsnap & the Land of the Midnight Sun. 2014. (Emily Windsnap Ser.: 5). lib. bdg. 16.00 *(978-0-606-35165-2(5))* Turtleback Bks.
—Emily Windsnap & the Monster from the Deep. Gibb, Sarah, illus. 2012. (Emily Windsnap Ser.: 2). (ENG.). 240p. (J). (gr. 3-7). pap. 5.99 *(978-0-7636-6018-5(3))* Candlewick Pr.
—Emily Windsnap & the Monster from the Deep. 2012. (Emily Windsnap Ser.: 2). lib. bdg. 16.00 *(978-0-606-25573-8(7),* Turtleback) Turtleback Bks.
—Emily Windsnap & the Siren's Secret. (Emily Windsnap Ser.: 4). (ENG., Illus.). 304p. (J). (gr. 3-7). 2012. pap. 5.99 *(978-0-7636-6019-2(1))* 2010. 15.99 *(978-0-7636-4374-4(2))* Candlewick Pr.
—Emily Windsnap & the Siren's Secret. 2012. (Emily Windsnap Ser.: 4). lib. bdg. 16.00 *(978-0-606-25601-8(6),* Turtleback) Turtleback Bks.
—Emily Windsnap: Two Magical Mermaid Tales. Gibb, Sarah, illus. 2014. (Emily Windsnap Ser.). (ENG.). 464p. (J). (gr. 3-7). pap. 9.99 *(978-0-7636-7452-6(4))* Candlewick Pr.
—The Tail of Emily Windsnap. Gibb, Sarah, illus. 2012. (Emily Windsnap Ser.: 1). (ENG.). 224p. (J). (gr. 3-7). pap. 5.99 *(978-0-7636-6020-8(5))* Candlewick Pr.
—The Tail of Emily Windsnap. 2012. (Emily Windsnap Ser.: 1). lib. bdg. 16.00 *(978-0-606-25544-8(3),* Turtleback) Turtleback Bks.
King-smith, Dick. The Merman. unabr. ed. 2004. 102p. (J). (gr. 3-7). pap. 29.00 incl. audio *(978-0-8072-8132-1(8),* Listening Library) Random Hse. Audio Publishing Group.
Klimo, Kate. The Dragon in the Sea. Shroades, John, illus. 2013. (Dragon Keepers Ser.: 5). (ENG.). 224p. (J). (gr. 3-7). 6.99 *(978-0-375-87116-0(0),* Yearling) Random Hse. Children's Bks.
—Dragon Keepers #4: the Dragon in the Volcano. Shroades, John, illus. 2012. (Dragon Keepers Ser.). (ENG.). 256p. (J). (gr. 3-7). 6.99 *(978-0-375-86688-3(4),* Yearling) Random Hse. Children's Bks.
Kusama, Yayoi & Andersen, Hans Christian. The Little Mermaid. 2016. (ENG., Illus.). 96p. 45.00 *(978-87-92877-59-8(1))* Louisana DNK. Dist: D.A.P./Distributed Art Pubs.
La Rose, Melinda & Ward, Kelly. Treasure of the Tides. 2014. (Illus.). (J). *(978-1-4844-3449-9(8))* Disney Publishing Worldwide.
Lagonegro, Melissa. The Little Mermaid Junior Novelization (Disney Princess) Random House Disney Staff, illus. 2013. (Junior Novel Ser.). (ENG.). 128p. (J). (gr. 3-7). 4.99 *(978-0-7364-2983-2(2),* RH/Disney) Random Hse. Children's Bks.
—Sealed with a Kiss. Marrucchi, Elisa, illus. 2005. (Step into Reading Ser.). (ENG.). 32p. (J). (gr. k-3). per. 3.99 *(978-0-7364-2363-2(X),* RH/Disney) Random Hse. Children's Bks.
Larkin, Rochelle, ed. The Little Mermaid & Other Stories. (Illus.). 239p. (J). 9.95 *(978-0-86611-676-3(1))* Waldman Publishing Corp.
Larose, Melinda. Treasure of the Tides. 2014. (Jake & the Never Land Pirates Ser.). (J). lib. bdg. 13.55 *(978-0-606-35269-7(4))* Turtleback Bks.
LaRose, Melinda & Disney Book Group Staff. Jake & the Never Land Pirates Treasure of the Tides. Disney Storybook Artists Staff, illus. 2014. (ENG.). 32p. (J). (gr. -1-k). pap. 3.99 *(978-1-4231-9422-4(5))* Disney Pr.
Lasaracina, Barbara. Mermaid Tears: A Magical Sea Tale. Peer, Nancy, illus. 2010. 28p. pap. 11.99 *(978-1-60844-451-9(1))* Dog Ear Publishing, LLC.
Lasky, Kathryn. Hannah. 2011. (Daughters of the Sea Ser.: 1). (ENG.). 320p. (J). (gr. 7-7). pap. 9.99 *(978-0-545-23803-8(X))* Scholastic, Inc.
—Lucy. 2012. (Daughters of the Sea Ser.: 3). (ENG.). 320p. (J). (gr. 7). 17.99 *(978-0-439-78312-5(7),* Scholastic Pr.) Scholastic, Inc.
—May. (Daughters of the Sea Ser.). (ENG.). 336p. (J). (gr. 7-7). 2012. pap. 9.99 *(978-0-545-24331-5(9))* 2011. 17.99 *(978-0-439-78311-8(9))* Scholastic, Inc. (Scholastic Pr.).
Levine, Gail Carson. Fairy Haven & the Quest for the Wand. Christiana, David, illus. 2007. 191p. (J). *(978-1-4287-6391-3(0))* Disney Pr.
Little Mermaid. 2009. (Disney Glitter Board Book Ser.). 5p. *(978-1-4054-9825-8(0))* Parragon, Inc.
Little Reader Digital Storybook: The Little Mermaid. 2005. (J). cd-rom 11.99 *(978-0-9767657-0-7(5))* Mullings Media.
Little Sticker Dolly Dressing Mermaids. 2017. (Little Sticker Dolly Dressing Ser.). (ENG.). (J). pap. 8.99 ***(978-0-7945-3809-5(6),*** Usborne) EDC Publishing.
Lovric, Michelle. The Undrowned Child. 2012. (ENG.). 464p. (J). (gr. 5). 7.99 *(978-0-375-86597-8(7),* Yearling) Random Hse. Children's Bks.
Madigan, L. K. The Mermaid's Mirror. 2011. (ENG.). 320p. (YA). (gr. 7). pap. 8.99 *(978-0-547-57735-7(4))* Houghton Mifflin Harcourt Publishing Co.
Man-Kong, Mary. Barbie in a Mermaid Tale. Golden Books Staff, illus. 2010. (Little Golden Book Ser.). (ENG.). (J). (gr. -1-2). 24p. 4.99 *(978-0-375-85733-1(8),* Golden Bks.); 16p. pap. 3.99 *(978-0-375-85735-5(4),* Random Hse. Bks. for Young Readers) Random Hse. Children's Bks.
—A Fairy-Tail Adventure. 2012. (Barbie 8X8 Ser.). lib. bdg. 13.55 *(978-0-606-23850-2(6),* Turtleback) Turtleback Bks.
—A Fin-Tastic Journey! Golden Books Staff, illus. 2012. (Color Plus Chunky Crayons Ser.). (ENG.). 48p. (J). (gr. k-k). pap. 3.99 *(978-0-307-92978-5(7),* Golden Bks.) Random Hse. Children's Bks.
—Magical Mermaid Adventure. 2014. (Pictureback(R) Ser.). (ENG., Illus.). 16p. (J). (gr. -1-2). 3.99 *(978-0-385-37308-1(2),* Random Hse. Bks. for Young Readers) Random Hse. Children's Bks.
Manson, Beverlie, illus. The Mermaid's Secret Diaries. 2013. (ENG.). 96p. (J). (gr. -1-2). 9.95 *(978-1-907967-59-7(1))* Boxer Bks., Ltd. GBR. Dist: Sterling Publishing Co., Inc.
Marks, Alan, illus. The Little Mermaid. 2005. 48p. (J). (gr. 4-7). 8.95 *(978-0-7945-1122-7(8),* Usborne) EDC Publishing.
Marroquin, Melissa. Tide Day, 1000 vols. 2016. (ENG., Illus.). (J). (gr. -1-3). 16.95 *(978-1-59298-684-2(6))* Beaver's Pond Pr., Inc.
Massenot, Véronique. The Mermaid & the Parakeet: A Children's Book Inspired by Henri Matisse. Hié, Vanessa, illus. 2016. (ENG.). 32p. (J). (gr. -1-3). 14.95 *(978-3-7913-7265-5(3))* Prestel Verlag GmbH & Co KG. DEU. Dist: Penguin Random Hse. LLC.
McDermott, Noel. Kiviuq & the Mermaids, 1 vol. Feizo Gas, Toma, illus. 2016. (ENG.). 40p. (J). (gr. 4-7). 16.95 *(978-1-77227-082-2(2))* Inhabit Media Inc. CAN. Dist: Independent Pubs. Group.
McFadden, Deanna & Andersen, Hans Christian. The Little Mermaid. Mims, Ashley, illus. 2013. (Silver Penny Stories Ser.). (ENG.). 48p. (J). (gr. -1-1). 4.95 *(978-1-4027-8336-4(1))* Sterling Publishing Co., Inc.
McGann, Oisín. Mad Grandad & the Mutant River. 2005. (Flyers Ser.: 14). (ENG., Illus.). 64p. (J). pap. 9.95 *(978-0-86278-939-8(7))* O'Brien Pr., Ltd., The IRL. Dist: Dufour Editions, Inc.
McGuire Woods, Molly. The Pearl Princess. 2014. (Junior Novel Ser.). (ENG.). 128p. (J). (gr. 3-7). 5.99 *(978-0-385-37517-7(4),* Random Hse. Bks. for Young Readers) Random Hse. Children's Bks.
McKenzie, J. Lee. Vampires Don't Believe in Mermaids. 2011. 54p. pap. 16.95 *(978-1-4560-1157-4(X))* America Star Bks.
McLaren, Heather. Mythos. 2013. (ENG.). 260p. pap. 17.95 *(978-1-60619-093-7(8))* Twilight Times Bks.
McLeod, Kris Aro. Hush-a-Bye Counting: A Bedtime Book. Allyn, Virginia, illus. 2008. (ENG.). 20p. (J). (gr. -1). 14.95 *(978-1-58117-785-5(2),* Intervisual/Piggy Toes) Bendon, Inc.
Mlynowski, Sarah. Sink or Swim. (Whatever After Ser.: 3). (J). 2014. (ENG.). 176p. (gr. 3-7). pap. 5.99 *(978-0-545-41570-5(5))* 2013. 165p. *(978-0-545-53316-4(3))*Bk. 3. 2013. (ENG.). 176p. (gr. 3-7). 14.99 *(978-0-545-41569-9(1))* Scholastic, Inc. (Scholastic Pr.).
Moffitt, Sara. Merlin & the Frog Meet Chatly & Noble. 2011. 25p. (J). pap. 18.95 *(978-1-4327-5921-6(3))* Outskirts Pr., Inc.
Morpurgo, Michael. Mairi's Mermaid. 2006. (Blue Bananas Ser.). (ENG., Illus.). 48p. (J). (gr. -1-3). lib. bdg. *(978-0-7787-0851-3(9))* Crabtree Publishing Co.
Munro, Moira. The Mermaid Who Came to School. 2012. 64p. pap. *(978-0-9571099-0-2(3))* Paperchard Bks.
Nagaraj, Josephine. Giddy-Up, Guppies! (Bubble Guppies) Huxtable, John, illus. 2014. (Step into Reading Ser.). (ENG.). 32p. (J). (gr. -1-1). 3.99 *(978-0-385-36974-9(3),* Random Hse. Bks. for Young Readers) Random Hse. Children's Bks.
Nail, Eric. The Wave Wranglers & the New Order of the Pyramid. 2007. 268p. (YA). pap. 18.95 *(978-1-4303-2254-2(3))* Lulu Pr., Inc.
Napoli, Donna Jo. Fish Girl. 2017. (ENG.). (J). (gr. 5-7). lib. bdg. 30.60 ***(978-0-606-39824-4(4))*** Turtleback Bks.
Napoli, Donna Jo & Wiesner, David. Fish Girl. Wiesner, David, illus. 2017. (ENG., Illus.). 192p. (J). (gr. 5-7). 25.00 *(978-0-544-81512-4(2))*; pap. 17.99 *(978-0-547-48393-1(7))* Houghton Mifflin Harcourt Trade & Reference Pubs. (Clarion Bks.).
Nesbit, E. Wet Magic. 2006. 188p. (gr. -1-7). 26.95 *(978-1-59818-174-6(2))* Aegypan.
—Wet Magic. 2006. 200p. (gr. -1-7). per. *(978-1-84350-095-7(7))* Soft Editions Ltd.
Nickelodeon. Swim, Boots, Swim! 2013. (Dora the Explorer 8X8 Ser.). lib. bdg. 13.55 *(978-0-606-31933-1(6),* Turtleback) Turtleback Bks.
Noble, Trinka Hakes. The Legend of Sea Glass. Ettlinger, Doris, illus. 2016. (Myths, Legends, Fairy & Folktales Ser.). (ENG.). 32p. (J). (gr. 1-4). pap. 17.99 *(978-1-58536-611-8(0),* 204027) Sleeping Bear Pr.
Owen, Sarah. The Enchanted Tales. 2009. 39p. pap. 26.50 *(978-1-4452-5948-2(6))* Lulu Pr., Inc.
Paquette, Ammi-Joan. The Tiptoe Guide to Tracking Mermaids. LeTourneau, Marie, illus. 2012. (ENG.). 32p. (J). (gr. -1-3). 16.95 *(978-1-933718-59-0(5))* Tanglewood Pr.
Parker, Emma. The Lucky Pearl. 2010. (Illus.). 20p. pap. *(978-1-877561-18-4(5))* First Edition Ltd.
Parker, Vic, ed. The Little Mermaid & Other Stories. 2015. (Scary Fairy Tales Ser.). (ENG.). 40p. (J). (gr. 3-4). pap. 14.05 *(978-1-4824-3085-1(1))* Stevens, Gareth Publishing LLLP.
PC Treasures Staff, prod. The Little Mermaid. 2007. (J). *(978-1-60072-020-8(X))* PC Treasures, Inc.
Pearl, Paige. ARTLANTICA: the Secret Kingdom Beneath Galveston Island. 2008. 38p. 18.95 *(978-1-4357-0389-6(8))* Lulu Pr., Inc.
Peck, Dale. Drift House: The First Voyage. 2006. (ENG.). 464p. (YA). (gr. 5). per. 7.95 *(978-1-59990-005-6(X),* 9781599900056, Bloomsbury USA Childrens) Bloomsbury Publishing USA.
Peetoom, Laura. Mermaid in the Bathtub, 1 vol. Fernandes, Eugenie, illus. 2006. (First Flight: Level 4 Ser.). (ENG.). 104p. (J). (gr. 4-7). pap. 4.95 *(978-1-55041-362-5(7))* Fitzhenry & Whiteside, Ltd. CAN. Dist: F&W Media, Inc.
Perrault, Charles, contrib. by. The Little Mermaid. 2012. (Musical Fairy Tales Ser.). (ENG., Illus.). 12p. (J). (gr. -1-3). bds. 15.95 *(978-1-61889-066-5(2))* AZ Bks. LLC.
La Petite Sirene.Tr. of Little Mermaid. (FRE.). 48p. (J). pap. 12.95 incl. audio compact disk *(978-2-89558-071-3(5))* Coffragants CAN. Dist: Penton Overseas, Inc.
Philips, A. If You Believe in Mermaids Don't Tell. 2007. 160p. per. 12.95 *(978-1-59858-359-5(X))* Dog Ear Publishing, LLC.
Phillips, Beth Ann. Crystal Kingdom, 1 vol. 2009. 63p. pap. 19.95 *(978-1-60813-003-0(7))* America Star Bks.
Playmore Publishers Staff. Sirenita. 2011. pap. 4.95 *(978-0-86611-653-4(2))* Waldman Publishing Corp.
Porter, Sarah. Lost Voices. 2011. (Lost Voices Trilogy Ser.: 1). (ENG.). 304p. (YA). (gr. 7-18). 16.99 *(978-0-547-48250-7(7))* Houghton Mifflin Harcourt Publishing Co.
—The Twice Lost. (Lost Voices Trilogy Ser.: 3). (ENG.). 480p. (YA). (gr. 7). 2014. pap. 8.99 *(978-0-547-48255-2(8),* HMH Books For Young Readers) 2013. 16.99 *(978-0-547-48252-1(3))* Houghton Mifflin Harcourt Publishing Co.
—Waking Storms. (Lost Voices Trilogy Ser.: 2). (ENG.). (YA). (gr. 7). 2013. 416p. pap. 8.99 *(978-0-547-48254-5(X))* 2012. 400p. 16.99 *(978-0-547-48251-4(5))* Houghton Mifflin Harcourt Publishing Co.
Posner-Sanchez, Andrea. Ariel Is My Babysitter (Disney Princess) Cortes, Mario et al, illus. 2016. (Little Golden Book Ser.). (ENG.). 24p. (J). (gr. -1-k). 4.99 *(978-0-7364-3446-1(1),* Golden/Disney) Random Hse. Children's Bks.
—Ariel's Dolphin Adventure - Snow White's New Friend, 2 bks. in 1. Random House Disney Staff, illus. 2010. (Pictureback(R) Ser.). (ENG.). 32p. (J). (gr. -1-2). pap. 4.99 *(978-0-7364-2654-1(X),* RH/Disney) Random Hse. Children's Bks.
—Bath Time with Ariel (Disney Princess) DiCicco, Sue, illus. 2015. (Board Book Ser.). (ENG.). 24p. (J). (— 1). bds. 6.99 *(978-0-7364-3310-5(4),* RH/Disney) Random Hse. Children's Bks.
Publications International Ltd. Staff, ed. Disney Princess Ariel. 2011. 14p. (J). bds. 16.98 *(978-1-4127-9206-6(1))* Publications International, Ltd.
Quinn, Jordan. The Secret World of Mermaids. McPhillips, Robert, illus. 2015. (Kingdom of Wrenly Ser.: 8). (ENG.). 128p. (J). (gr. k-4). pap. 5.99 *(978-1-4814-3122-4(6),* Little Simon) Little Simon.
Rakos, Lynnda, et al. Princesses, Mermaids & Fairies Coloring Book. 2012. (Dover Coloring Bks.). (ENG.). 32p. (J). (gr. -1-2). pap. 3.99 *(978-0-486-48664-2(8))* Dover Pubns., Inc.
Random House. Magical Mermaids! Random House, illus. 2017. (Step into Reading Ser.). (ENG., Illus.). 24p. (J). (gr. -1-1). pap. 4.99 *(978-0-399-55886-3(1),* Random Hse. Bks. for Young Readers) Random Hse. Children's Bks.
Random House Disney Staff. The Little Mermaid Big Golden Book (Disney Princess) Random House Disney Staff, illus.

MNO

2013. (Big Golden Book Ser.). (ENG., Illus.). 64p. (J). (gr. -1-2). 9.99 *(978-0-7364-2988-7(3)*, Golden/Disney) Random Hse. Children's Bks.

Random House Staff. Legend of the Blue Mermaid (Team Umizoomi) Fruchter, Jason, illus. 2013. (Pictureback(R) Ser.). (ENG.). 24p. (J). (gr. -1-2). 3.99 *(978-0-449-81758-2(X)*, Random Hse. Bks. for Young Readers) Random Hse. Children's Bks.

—Swim, Boots, Swim! (Dora the Explorer) Random House Staff, illus. 2013. (Pictureback(R) Ser.). (ENG., Illus.). 24p. (J). (gr. -1-2). 3.99 *(978-0-449-81850-3(0)*, Random Hse. Bks. for Young Readers) Random Hse. Children's Bks.

Ray, Jane. Can You Catch a Mermaid? Ray, Jane, illus. 2003. (ENG., Illus.). 32p. (J). (gr. -1-12). pap. 9.99 *(978-1-84121-296-8(2))* Hodder & Stoughton GBR. Dist: Hachette Bk. Group.

Raymundo, Peter. Third Grade Mermaid. 2017. (ENG.). 208p. (J). (gr. 1-3). 12.99 *(978-0-545-91816-9(2)*, Scholastic Pr.) Scholastic, Inc.

Reef Rescue (Book 4) 2017. (Secret Mermaid Ser.). (ENG.). (J). pap. 4.99 ***(978-0-7945-3686-2(7)**, Usborne)* EDC Publishing.

Rees, Gwyneth. Mermaid Magic. Hudson, Annabel, illus. 2016. (ENG.). 96p. (J). (gr. k-2). pap. 9.99 *(978-1-5098-1869-3(3))* Pan Macmillan GBR. Dist: Independent Pubs. Group.

—Rani's Sea Spell. 2016. (ENG., Illus.). 96p. (J). (gr. k-2). pap. 9.99 *(978-1-5098-1870-9(7))* Pan Macmillan GBR. Dist: Independent Pubs. Group.

—The Shell Princess. 2016. (ENG., Illus.). 96p. (J). (gr. k-2). pap. 9.99 *(978-1-5098-1871-6(5))* Pan Macmillan GBR. Dist: Independent Pubs. Group.

Reese, Jenn. Horizon. 2015. (Above World Ser.). (ENG.). 400p. (J). (gr. 5). pap. 7.99 *(978-0-7636-7667-4(5))* Candlewick Pr.

—Mirage. 2014. (Above World Ser.). (ENG.). 368p. (J). (gr. 5). pap. 7.99 *(978-0-7636-6929-4(6))* Candlewick Pr.

Reeve, Philip. Oliver & the Sea Monkeys. McIntyre, Sarah, illus. 2016. (Not-So-Impossible Tale Ser.). (ENG.). 224p. (J). (gr. 2-5). pap. 6.99 *(978-0-385-38789-7(X)*, Yearling) Random Hse. Children's Bks.

—Oliver & the Seawigs. McIntyre, Sarah, illus. 2014. (Not-So-Impossible Tale Ser.). (ENG.). 208p. (J). (gr. 2-5). 12.99 *(978-0-385-38788-0(1)*, Random Hse. Bks. for Young Readers) Random Hse. Children's Bks.

Reilly, Antoinette. Mr. Lobster & the Mermaid. 2011. 24p. pap. 14.93 *(978-1-4269-5683-6(5))* Trafford Publishing.

Return of the Dark Queen (Book 6) 2017. (Secret Mermaid Ser.). (ENG.). (J). pap. 4.99 ***(978-0-7945-3684-8(0)**,* Usborne) EDC Publishing.

RH Disney Staff & Calmenson, Stephanie. The Little Mermaid. Mateu, Francesca, illus. 2003. (Pictureback(R) Ser.). (ENG.). 24p. (J). (gr. -1-2). pap. 3.99 *(978-0-7364-2128-7(9)*, RH/Disney) Random Hse. Children's Bks.

Roberts, Roxanne. Angel Wings, Faery Dust & Other Magical Things: A Story about Merpeople. 2011. 24p. pap. 11.50 *(978-1-61204-588-7(X)*, Strategic Bk. Publishing) Strategic Book Publishing & Rights Agency (SBPRA).

Robleda, Margarita. Suenos. Suarez, Maribel, illus. (Rana, Rema, Rimas Ser.). (SPA.). 16p. (J). (gr. k-3). 7.95 *(978-1-59437-821-8(5))* Santillana USA Publishing Co., Inc.

Rodriguez, Ashley. A Mermaid Tale. 2010. 60p. pap. 10.50 *(978-0-557-65601-1(X))* Lulu Pr., Inc.

Rossi, Francesca, illus. The Little Mermaid. 2015. (Fairy Tale Adventures Ser.). (ENG.). 64p. (J). (gr. 2-6). 7.95 *(978-1-4549-1509-6(9))* Sterling Publishing Co., Inc.

A Royal Tea. 2014. (Mermaid Tales Ser.: 9). (ENG., Illus.). 112p. (J). (gr. 1-4). pap. 5.99 *(978-1-4814-0254-5(4)*, Aladdin) Simon & Schuster Children's Publishing.

Sabuda, Robert. The Little Mermaid. Sabuda, Robert, illus. 2013. (ENG., Illus.). 12p. (J). (gr. 1). 34.99 *(978-1-4169-6080-5(5)*, Little Simon) Little Simon.

Saxton, Patricia. The Book of Mermaids. Saxton, Patricia, illus. 2006. (ENG., Illus.). 32p. (J). (gr. 1-5). 14.95 *(978-0-9726614-6-1(8))* Shenanigan Bks.

Schlegl, Stacey Lynn & Schlegl, Abigail. MerMountain. 2012. 84p. (J). pap. 11.95 *(978-0-9850272-2-3(3))* Jan-Carol Publishing, INC.

Schreiber, Ellen. Teenage Mermaid. 2003. 160p. (J). (gr. 4-18). lib. bdg. 16.89 *(978-0-06-008205-5(4))* HarperCollins Pubs.

Selfors, Suzanne. To Catch a Mermaid. 2009. (ENG.). 272p. (J). (gr. 3-7). pap. 8.00 *(978-0-316-01817-3(1))* Little, Brown Bks. for Young Readers.

Shields, Gillian. Holly Takes a Risk. Turner, Helen, illus. 2008. (Mermaid S. O. S. Ser.: 4). (ENG.). 96p. (J). (gr. 1-4). pap. 4.50 *(978-1-59990-214-2(1)*, 9781599902142, Bloomsbury USA Childrens) Bloomsbury Publishing USA.

—Sophie Makes a Splash. Turner, Helen, illus. 2008. (Mermaid S. O. S. Ser.: 3). (ENG.). 96p. (J). (gr. 1-4). pap. 4.50 *(978-1-59990-212-8(5)*, 9781599902128, Bloomsbury USA Childrens) Bloomsbury Publishing USA.

Silver Dolphin & Andersen, Hans Christian. Little Mermaid: a Coloring Book. Dulac, Edmund, illus. 2017. (Classic Coloring Book Ser.). (ENG.). 96p. (J). (gr. k). pap. 15.99 *(978-1-62686-886-1(7)*, Silver Dolphin Bks.) Readerlink Distribution Services, LLC.

Sky Koster, Amy & Patrick, Ella. Ariel & the Big Baby/Rapunzel Finds a Friend (Disney Princess) Thomas, Jeffrey, illus. 2017. (Pictureback(R) Ser.). (ENG.). 48p. (J). (gr. -1-2). pap. 5.99 ***(978-0-7364-3747-9(9)**,* RH/Disney) Random Hse. Children's Bks.

Steele-Saccio, Eva. The Marvelous Book of Magical Mermaids. 2014. (ENG.). 50p. (J). (gr. 1). 19.99 *(978-0-545-69214-4(8))* Klutz.

Stine, R. L. Deep Trouble. 2008. (Classic Goosebumps Ser.: 2). (ENG.). 144p. (J). (gr. 3-7). 6.99 *(978-0-545-03519-4(8)*, Scholastic Paperbacks) Scholastic, Inc.

Studio Mouse Editorial. Ariel: The Brave Little Mermaid. 2008. (ENG., Illus.). 36p. (gr. -1-k). 7.99 *(978-1-59069-434-3(1))* Studio Mouse LLC.

Taylor, C. J. Spirits, Fairies, & Merpeople: Native Stories of Other Worlds. 2009. (ENG., Illus.). 40p. (J). (gr. 2-4). 19.95 *(978-0-88776-872-9(5)*, Tundra Bks.) Tundra Bks. CAN. Dist: Penguin Random Hse. LLC.

Taylor, Dereen. The Mermaid's Treasure Hunt. East, Jacqueline, illus. 2012. (ENG.). 12p. (J). (gr. -1-12). 16.99 *(978-1-84322-762-5(2))* Anness Publishing GBR. Dist: National Bk. Network.

Tea, Michelle. Girl at the Bottom of the Sea. Verwey, Amanda, illus. 2015. (ENG.). 240p. (gr. 6). 19.95 *(978-1-940450-00-1(4))* McSweeney's Publishing.

—Mermaid in Chelsea Creek. Polan, Jason, illus. 2013. (ENG.). 240p. (gr. 5-11). 19.95 *(978-1-938073-36-6(3))* McSweeney's Publishing.

Teitelbaum, Michael. The Little Mermaid. DiCicco, Sue, illus. 2003. (Little Golden Book Ser.). (ENG.). 24p. (J). (gr. -1-2). 4.99 *(978-0-7364-2177-5(7)*, Golden/Disney) Random Hse. Children's Bks.

Thomas Nelson. Little Mermaid. 2015. (ENG., Illus.). 12p. (J). (gr. -1-k). bds. *(978-1-78393-499-7(9))* Make Believe Ideas.

Thorpe, Kiki. Under the Lagoon. Christy, Jana, illus. 2016. (Never Girls Ser.). (ENG.). 128p. (J). (gr. 1-4). 5.99 *(978-0-7364-3529-1(8)*, RH/Disney) Random Hse. Children's Bks.

Tillworth, Mary. Bubble Ball Game! (Bubble Guppies) MJ Illustrations, illus. 2015. (Pictureback Ser.). (ENG.). 16p. (J). (gr. -1-2). 4.99 *(978-0-385-37439-2(9)*, Random Hse. Bks. for Young Readers) Random Hse. Children's Bks.

—Mermaid Treasure Hunt. 2015. (Dora the Explorer 8X8 Ser.). lib. bdg. 13.55 *(978-0-606-36395-2(5))* Turtleback Bks.

ToyBox Innovations, creator. Disney's the Little Mermaid. abr. ed. 2006. (Disney's Read along Collection). (ENG.). (J). (gr. -1-3). pap. *(978-0-7634-2184-7(7))* Walt Disney Records.

—Disney's the Little Mermaid: Read-along. 2006. (Disney's Read Along Ser.). (ENG., Illus.). 24p. (J). pap. *(978-0-7634-2174-8(X))* Walt Disney Records.

Toybox Innovations Staff & Toybox Innovations, creators. Disney Read along Little Mermaid Collection, 3 vols. 2009. (ENG., Illus.). (J). (gr. -1-1). *(978-0-7634-1202-9(3))* Walt Disney Records.

Trowell, Michelle. Magical Mermaids. Top That Publishing Staff, ed. Richards, Kirsten, illus. 2008. (Magnetic Story & Play Scene Ser.). 9p. (J). (gr. -1). *(978-1-84666-442-7(X)*, Tide Mill Pr.) Top That! Publishing PLC.

Ungaro, Marley. Darling Dozen of the Deep. 2012. (ENG.). (J). pap. 24.99 *(978-1-4675-4418-4(3))* Independent Pub.

Valencia, O. R. Savior in the Blue Mermaid. 2008. 180p. pap. 14.35 *(978-1-4251-2824-1(6))* Trafford Publishing.

Valentino, Serena. Poor Unfortunate Soul: A Tale of the Sea Witch. Disney Storybook Art Team, illus. 2016. (Villains Ser.: 3). (ENG.). 208p. (J). (gr. 5-9). 17.99 *(978-1-4847-2405-7(4))* Disney Pr.

Van Fleet, Mara. Three Little Mermaids. Van Fleet, Mara, illus. 2011. (ENG., Illus.). 16p. (J). (gr. -1-k). 15.99 *(978-1-4424-1286-6(0)*, Simon & Schuster/Paula Wiseman Bks.) Simon & Schuster/Paula Wiseman Bks.

Wade, Judith. Mermaid Dreams. 2005. (J). per. 5.99 *(978-0-9728958-3-5(3))* Riley Pr.

—The Mermaid's Gift. 2004. 140p. (J). per. 5.99 *(978-0-9728958-1-1(7)*, 750) Riley Pr.

—The Secret of Mermaid Island. 2003. 136p. (J). mass mkt. 5.99 *(978-0-9728958-0-4(9))* Riley Pr.

Watt, Fiona. That's Not My Mermaid. rev. ed. 2012. (Touchy-Feely Board Bks). 10p. (J). bds. 9.99 *(978-0-7945-3307-6(8)*, Usborne) EDC Publishing.

Webster, Christy. Barbie in a Mermaid Tale. Random House Editors, illus. 2010. (Step into Reading Ser.). (ENG.). 32p. (J). (gr. -1-1). pap. 3.99 *(978-0-375-86450-6(4)*, Random Hse. Bks. for Young Readers) Random Hse. Children's Bks.

—Barbie in a Mermaid Tale. 2010. (Barbie Step into Reading Level 2 Ser.). lib. bdg. 13.55 *(978-0-606-07031-7(1)*, Turtleback) Turtleback Bks.

Weinberg, Jennifer Liberts. Pretty Pearl Mermaid. 2014. (Step into Reading Ser.). (ENG., Illus.). 32p. (J). (gr. -1-1). 3.99 *(978-0-385-37307-4(4)*, Random Hse. Bks. for Young Readers) Random Hse. Children's Bks.

Wiese, Fritz H. & Wiese, Erika J. Erika & the Mermaids. 2011. 180p. 29.99 *(978-1-4568-6364-7(9))*; pap. 19.99 *(978-1-4568-6363-0(0))* Xlibris Corp.

Williams, Becky. Ten Little Mermaids. East, Jacqueline, illus. 2007. (Story Book Ser.). 22p. (J). (gr. -1). bds. *(978-1-84666-375-8(X)*, Tide Mill Pr.) Top That! Publishing PLC.

Witcher, Lillie. Ican & the Little Mermaid. 2006. (Illus.). (J). 8.95 *(978-1-56167-945-4(3)*, Shooting Star Edition) American Literary Pr.

Young, Sarah. Gasparilla's Key & the Revenge of the Purple Mermaid. 2013. 254p. pap. 15.99 *(978-1-935986-58-4(9))* Liberty University Press.

MERRIMACK (FRIGATE)

Abnett, Dan. The Monitor Versus the Merrimac: Ironclads at War. Verma, Dheeraj, illus. 2007. (Graphic Battles of the Civil War Ser.). (ENG.). 48p. (YA). (gr. 4-7). lib. bdg. 31.95 *(978-1-4042-0778-3(3))* Rosen Publishing Group, Inc., The.

Brager, Bruce L. The Monitor vs. the Merrimack. 2003. (Great Battles Through the Ages Ser.). (Illus.). 112p. (gr. 6-12). 30.00 *(978-0-7910-7439-8(0)*, Chelsea Hse.) Facts On File, Inc.

O'Brien, Patrick. Duel of the Ironclads: The Monitor vs. the Virginia. 2003. (Illus.). 40p. (J). (gr. 1-5). 18.85 *(978-0-8027-8843-6(2))* Walker & Co.

MERRIMACK (FRIGATE)—FICTION

Aviation Staff. Iron Thunder: The Battle Between the Monitor & the Merrimac. 2009. (ENG.). 208p. (J). (gr. 3-7). pap. 7.99 *(978-1-4231-0518-3(4))* Hyperion Pr.

MERRY-GO-ROUND

Bodden, Valerie. Carousels. 2012. (Illus.). 24p. (J). 25.65 *(978-1-60818-112-4(X)*, Creative Education) Creative Co., The.

MERRY-GO-ROUND—FICTION

Branson, Terri & Wilks, Jackie. Mirror of the Carousel. l.t. ed. 2006. (Illus.). 24p. (J). per. 14.99 *(978-0-9765786-8-0(9))* Dragonfly Publishing, Inc.

Carousel Writers' Group Staff, contrib. by. Every Pony Has a Tale. 2003. (Illus.). 88p. (J). pap. *(978-0-89802-787-7(X))* Beautiful America Publishing Co.

Demeritt, Mary Anne. The Twilight Ride of the Pink Fairy. Daniel, Ellen, illus. 2006. 36p. (J). pap. 17.95 *(978-1-58597-410-8(2))* Leathers Publishing.

Fiddick, Calay. The Fortieth Horse. Levy, Shaun & Jamieson, Eden, illus. 2006. 32p. (J). *(978-1-55306-876-1(9)*, Epic Pr.) Essence Publishing.

Graves, Sue. Harry & the Horse. 2011. (Tadpoles Ser.). (ENG., Illus.). 24p. (J). (gr. k-2). *(978-0-7787-0579-6(X))*; pap. *(978-0-7787-0590-1(0))* Crabtree Publishing Co.

Hyde, Heidi Smith. Feivel's Flying Horses. van der Sterre, Johanna, illus. 2010. (ENG.). 32p. (J). (gr. k-4). lib. bdg. 17.95 *(978-0-7613-3957-1(4))*; pap. 7.95 *(978-0-7613-3959-5(0))* Lerner Publishing Group. (Kar-Ben Publishing).

Parker, Emma. The Carousel. 2010. (Illus.). 16p. pap. *(978-1-877561-73-3(8))* First Edition Ltd.

Shire, Poppy. Flame the Desert Pony. Berg, Ron, illus. 2008. (Magic Pony Carousel Ser.: 5). (ENG.). 96p. (J). (gr. 2-5). pap. 3.99 *(978-0-06-083794-5(2))* HarperCollins Pubs.

—Jewel the Midnight Pony. Berg, Ron, illus. 2008. (Magic Pony Carousel Ser.: 4). (ENG.). 96p. (J). (gr. 2-5). pap. 3.99 *(978-0-06-083788-4(8))* HarperCollins Pubs.

Towell, Katy. Skary Childrin & the Carousel of Sorrow. 2013. (ENG.). 272p. (J). (gr. 3-7). pap. 8.99 *(978-0-375-87240-2(X)*, Knopf Bks. for Young Readers) Random Hse. Children's Bks.

Ward, Lindsay. Please Bring Balloons. 2013. (ENG., Illus.). 32p. (J). (gr. -1-k). 16.99 *(978-0-8037-3878-2(1)*, Dial Bks) Penguin Young Readers Group.

Wing, Carol. Lio the Carousel Horse. Moen, Ruth, illus. 2010. (ENG.). 32p. (J). (gr. -1-2). 14.95 *(978-1-933067-37-7(3))* Beachhouse Publishing, LLC.

MERTON, THOMAS, 1915-1968

Ryan, Gregory & Ryan, Elizabeth. The ABC's of Thomas Merton: A Monk at the Heart of the World. 2017. (ENG.). 32p. (J). (gr. k-4). 16.99 ***(978-1-61261-847-0(2))*** Paraclete Pr., Inc.

MESA VERDE NATIONAL PARK (COLO.)

Blake, Kevin & Yates, Martha. Cliff Dwellings: Empty Windows. 2015. (Abandoned: Towns Without People Ser.). (ENG.). 32p. (J). (gr. 2-7). lib. bdg. 26.60 *(978-1-62724-522-7(7))* Bearport Publishing Co., Inc.

Brannon, Barbara. Discover Mesa Verde. 2005. (J). pap. *(978-1-4108-5143-7(5))* Benchmark Education Co.

Collins, Terry, et al. The Mesa Verde Cliff Dwellers: An Isabel Soto Archaeology Adventure, 1 vol. 2010. (Graphic Expeditions Ser.). (ENG.). 32p. (gr. 3-4). pap. 8.10 *(978-1-4296-4861-5(9))*; pap. 47.70 *(978-1-4296-5144-8(X))* Capstone Press of Coughlan Cos. (Graphic Library).

—The Mesa Verde Cliff Dwellers: An Isabel Soto Archaeology Adventure, 1 vol. Anderson, Bill, illus. 2010. (Graphic Expeditions Ser.). (ENG.). 32p. (gr. 3-4). lib. bdg. 30.65 *(978-1-4296-3971-2(7)*, Graphic Library) Capstone Press of Coughlan Cos.

Fay, Gail. Secrets of Mesa Verde: Cliff Dwellings of the Pueblo, 1 vol. 2014. (Archaeological Mysteries Ser.). (ENG.). 32p. (gr. 3-4). lib. bdg. 27.99 *(978-1-4765-9918-2(1))* Capstone Press of Coughlan Cos.

MESA VERDE NATIONAL PARK (COLO.)—FICTION

Skurzynski, Gloria & Ferguson, Alane. Cliff-Hanger: A Mystery in Mesa Verde National Park. 2007. (Mysteries in Our National Park Ser.). (ENG., Illus.). 160p. (J). (gr. 3-7). per. 4.99 *(978-1-4263-0092-9(1)*, National Geographic Children's Bks.) National Geographic Society.

MESMERISM

see Hypnotism

MESOPOTAMIA

see Iraq—History—To 634

METABOLISM

see also Nutrition

Barchers, Suzanne I. Energy in Action, 1 vol. 2015. (Science Readers: Content & Literacy Ser.). (ENG., Illus.). 32p. (gr. 3-3). pap. 8.99 *(978-1-4807-4643-5(6))* Teacher Created Materials, Inc.

Cole, Joanna. Inside the Human Body. Degen, Bruce, illus. 2011. (Magic School Bus Ser.). (ENG.). (J). (gr. 2-5). 9.99 *(978-0-545-24083-3(2))* Scholastic, Inc.

Curran, Christine Perdan, ed. Metabolic Processes & Energy Transfers: An Anthology of Current Thought. (Contemporary Discourse in the Field of Biology Ser.). 2009. 224p. (gr. 10-12). 63.90 *(978-1-61511-911-0(6))* 2005. (Illus.). 192p. (YA). (gr. 7-12). lib. bdg. 35.95 *(978-1-4042-0399-0(0))* Rosen Publishing Group, Inc., The.

Eaton, Louise & Rogers, Kara. Examining Biochemical Reactions. 2017. (J). lib. bdg. ***(978-1-5383-0006-0(0))*** Rosen Publishing Group, Inc., The.

McLaughlin, Marc, et al. How Cells Send, Receive, & Process Information, 1 vol. 2015. (ENG.). 64p. (YA). 31.70 *(978-1-62275-800-5(5)*, Britannica Educational Publishing) Rosen Publishing Group, Inc., The.

Morgan, Philip & Turnbull, Stephanie. Generating Energy. 2011. (Secrets of Magic Ser.). 32p. (gr. 4-7). lib. bdg. 31.35 *(978-1-59920-495-6(9))* Black Rabbit Bks.

Shryer, Donna. Body Fuel: A Guide to Good Nutrition. 2007. (Food & Fitness Ser.). (Illus.). 128p. (YA). (gr. 7-12). lib. bdg. 38.50 *(978-0-7614-2552-6(7))* Marshall Cavendish Corp.

Stewart, Melissa. Summertime Sleep. Chen, Jordan, illus. 2017. (J). lib. bdg. *(978-1-58089-716-7(9))* Charlesbridge Publishing, Inc.

Stoffwechsel und Energieumsatz: Fachliche Inhalte und Uebungsaufgaben. 2nd ed. (Duden Abiturhilfen Ser.). (GER.). 112p. (YA). (gr. 12-13). *(978-3-411-04282-1(6))* Bibliographisches Institut & F. A. Brockhaus AG DEU. Dist: International Bk. Import Service, Inc.

Williams, Mary E. Growth Disorders. 2011. (Perspectives on Diseases & Disorders Ser.). (ENG., Illus.). 144p. (gr. 10-12). 44.30 *(978-0-7377-5774-3(4))* Cengage Gale.

METAL-WORK

see also Jewelry; Silversmithing; Steel

Felix, Rebecca. Cool Metalworking Projects: Fun & Creative Workshop Activities. 2016. (ENG., Illus.). 32p. (J). *(978-1-68078-129-8(4))* ABDO Publishing Co.

Nelson, David Erik. Soldering. 2014. (21st Century Skills Innovation Library: Makers As Innovators Ser.). (ENG., Illus.). 32p. (J). (gr. 4-8). 28.50 *(978-1-63137-774-7(4)*, 205339) Cherry Lake Publishing.

Orr, Tamra. Careers in Sheet Metal & Ironwork, 01 vols., 1. 2016. (Essential Careers Ser.). (ENG.). 80p. (J). 34.25 *(978-1-4994-6221-0(2)*, Rosen Young Adult) Rosen Publishing Group, Inc., The.

Parramon's Editorial Team Staff & Parramon's Editorial Team. Metal. Parramon's Editorial Team Staff, photos by. 2004. (Let's Create! Ser.). (Illus.). 32p. (gr. 1-4). lib. bdg. 26.00 *(978-0-8368-4016-2(X)*, Gareth Stevens Learning Library) Stevens, Gareth Publishing LLLP.

Petersen, Christine. The Blacksmith. 2010. (Colonial People Ser.). 48p. (gr. 3-18). 29.93 *(978-0-7614-4799-3(7))* Marshall Cavendish Corp.

Scheunemann, Pam. Cool Metal Projects: Creative Ways to Upcycle Your Trash into Treasure, 1 vol. 2012. (Cool Trash to Treasure Ser.). (ENG., Illus.). 32p. (J). (gr. 3-6). lib. bdg. 27.07 *(978-1-61783-434-9(3)*, Checkerboard Library) ABDO Publishing Co.

METALS

Adair, Rick. Beryllium. 2009. (Understanding the Elements of the Periodic Table Ser.). 48p. (gr. 6-6). 53.00 *(978-1-60854-634-3(9)*, Rosen Reference) Rosen Publishing Group, Inc., The.

Beatty, Richard. The Lanthanides. 2007. (Elements Ser.). (Illus.). 32p. (J). (gr. 4-7). lib. bdg. 28.50 *(978-0-7614-2687-5(6)*, Benchmark Bks.) Marshall Cavendish Corp.

—Manganese. 2004. (J). 25.64 *(978-0-7614-1813-9(X)*, Benchmark Bks.) Marshall Cavendish Corp.

Colich, Abby. Metal, 1 vol. 2013. (Exploring Materials Ser.). (ENG.). 24p. (gr. -1-1). 22.65 *(978-1-4329-8015-3(7))*; pap. 6.95 *(978-1-4329-8023-8(8))* Heinemann-Raintree. (Acorn).

Crabtree Publishing Company Staff & Montgomerie, Adrienne. Metals. 2012. (ENG., Illus.). 32p. (J). *(978-0-7787-4231-9(8))*; pap. *(978-0-7787-4235-7(0))* Crabtree Publishing Co.

Jennings, Terry. Metal. 2006. (Illus.). 32p. (YA). (gr. 1-18). lib. bdg. 27.10 *(978-1-932333-01-5(0))* Chrysalis Education.

Johanson, Paula. Cobalt. 2009. (Understanding the Elements of the Periodic Table Ser.). 48p. (gr. 6-6). 53.00 *(978-1-60854-645-9(4)*, Rosen Reference) Rosen Publishing Group, Inc., The.

—Lithium. 2009. (Understanding the Elements of the Periodic Table Ser.). 48p. (gr. 6-6). 53.00 *(978-1-60854-661-9(6)*, Rosen Reference) Rosen Publishing Group, Inc., The.

Kjelle, Marylou Morano. The Properties of Metals. 24p. 2009. (Library of Physical Science Ser.). (gr. 4-4). 42.50 *(978-1-60853-792-1(7)*, PowerKids Pr.) 2007. (Library of Physical Sciences). (ENG., Illus.). (gr. 4-8). pap. 7.05 *(978-1-4042-2164-2(6)*, PowerKids Pr.) 2006. (Library of Physical Science Ser.: Vol. 3). (Illus.). (J). (gr. 3-7). lib. bdg. 22.60 *(978-1-4042-3417-8(9))* Rosen Publishing Group, Inc., The.

Langley, Andrew. Metal. 2008. (ENG., Illus.). 24p. (J). (gr. k-3). pap. *(978-0-7787-4134-3(6))* Crabtree Publishing Co.

Llewellyn, Claire. Metal. 2005. (I Know That! Ser.). (Illus.). 24p. (J). (gr. 1-4). lib. bdg. 22.80 *(978-1-932889-52-9(3))* Sea-To-Sea Pubns.

McDowell, Julie. Metals. 2008. (Essential Chemistry Ser.). (Illus.). 105p. (YA). (gr. 7-12). 35.00 *(978-0-7910-9535-5(5))* Facts On File, Inc.

Mitchell, Melanie S. Metal. 2003. (First Step Nonfiction - Materials Ser.). (ENG., Illus.). 24p. (gr. k-2). lib. bdg. 23.93 *(978-0-8225-4622-1(1))* Lerner Publishing Group.

Morris, Neil. Metals. 2010. (Materials That Matter Ser.). 32p. (YA). (gr. 4-7). 28.50 *(978-1-60753-066-4(X))* Amicus Publishing.

Morris, Neil & Johnson, Jinny. Metals. 2011. (Watery Worlds Ser.). 32p. (gr. 3-6). lib. bdg. 31.35 *(978-1-59920-506-9(8))* Black Rabbit Bks.

National Geographic Learning Staff. Magnets, Level 3 - World Windows. 2011. (World Windows Ser.). (ENG., Illus.). 16p. (J). stu. ed. 9.95 *(978-1-133-49266-5(5))* Cengage Heinle.

Parramon's Editorial Team Staff & Parramon's Editorial Team. Metal. Parramon's Editorial Team Staff, photos by. 2004. (Let's Create! Ser.). (Illus.). 32p. (gr. 1-4). lib. bdg. 26.00 *(978-0-8368-4016-2(X)*, Gareth Stevens Learning Library) Stevens, Gareth Publishing LLLP.

Rau, Dana Meachen. Metal. 2011. (Bookworms Chapter Books: Use It! Reuse It! Ser.). 24p. (gr. 2-3). 22.79 *(978-1-60870-516-0(1))* Marshall Cavendish GBR. Dist: Marshall Cavendish Corp.

Royston, Angela. Metal: Let's Look at a Knife & Fork. 2005. (J). *(978-1-4109-1822-2(X))*; (ENG.). 24p. pap. *(978-1-4109-1831-4(9))* Steck-Vaughn.

Roza, Greg. Chromium. 2009. (Understanding the Elements of the Periodic Table Ser.). 48p. (gr. 6-6). 53.00 *(978-1-60854-644-2(6)*, Rosen Reference) Rosen Publishing Group, Inc., The.

—Titanium, Vol. 1. 2014. (Rare & Precious Metals Ser.). (ENG.). 24p. (J). (gr. 2-3). 22.60 *(978-1-4824-0518-7(0))* Stevens, Gareth Publishing LLLP.

—Zirconium. 2009. (Understanding the Elements of the Periodic Table Ser.). 48p. (gr. 6-6). 53.00 *(978-1-60854-690-9(X)*, Rosen Reference) Rosen Publishing Group, Inc., The.

Scheunemann, Pam. Cool Metal Projects: Creative Ways to Upcycle Your Trash into Treasure, 1 vol. 2012. (Cool Trash to Treasure Ser.). (ENG., Illus.). 32p. (J). (gr. 3-6). lib. bdg. 27.07 *(978-1-61783-434-9(3)*, Checkerboard Library) ABDO Publishing Co.

Sherman, Jill. Minerals & Heavy Metals. 2017. (J). pap. ***(978-0-7660-9147-4(3))*** Enslow Pubs., Inc.

Sparrow, Giles. Nickel. 2004. (J). 25.64 *(978-0-7614-1811-5(3)*, Benchmark Bks.) Marshall Cavendish Corp.

Storey, Rita. Metal. 2007. (How We Use Materials/Watts Ser.). (Illus.). 30p. (J). (gr. 4-7). lib. bdg. 28.50 *(978-1-59920-003-3(1))* Black Rabbit Bks.

Taylor-Butler, Christine. Experiments with Magnets & Metals, 1 vol. 2011. (My Science Investigations Ser.). (ENG.). 32p. (gr. 1-3). pap. 8.29 *(978-1-4329-5365-2(6)*, Heinemann First Library) Heinemann-Raintree.

Thomas, Michele. Sodium. 2009. (Understanding the Elements of the Periodic Table Ser.). 48p. (gr. 6-6). 53.00 *(978-1-60854-685-5(3)*, Rosen Reference) Rosen Publishing Group, Inc., The.

Tocci, Salvatore. Lead. 2005. (True Bks.). (ENG., Illus.). 48p. (J). (gr. 3-7). lib. bdg. 25.00 *(978-0-516-23699-5(7)*, Children's Pr.) Scholastic Library Publishing.

—Zinc. 2005. (True Bks.). (ENG., Illus.). 48p. (J). (gr. 3-7). lib. bdg. 25.00 *(978-0-516-23703-9(9)*, Children's Pr.) Scholastic Library Publishing.

West, Krista. The Basics of Metals & Metalloids. 2013. (Core Concepts Ser.). 96p. (YA). (gr. 7-12). 34.60 *(978-1-4777-2713-3(2))* Rosen Publishing Group, Inc., The.
Zronik, John Paul & Zronik, John. Metals. 2004. (Rocks, Minerals, & Resources Ser.). (ENG., Illus.). 32p. (J). lib. bdg. *(978-0-7787-1418-7(7))* Crabtree Publishing Co.
—Metals - Shaping Our World. 2004. (Rocks, Minerals, & Resources Ser.). (ENG., Illus.). 32p. (J). pap. *(978-0-7787-1450-7(0))* Crabtree Publishing Co.

METALWORK

see Metal-Work

METAMORPHIC ROCKS

see Rocks

METEORITES

Alter, Judy. Souvenirs from Space: The Oscar E. Monnig Meteorite Gallery. Normand, Hal, illus. 2007. (ENG.). 24p. (J). (gr. 4-7). pap. 4.95 *(978-0-87565-346-4(4))* Texas Christian Univ. Pr.
Howard, Fran. Asteroids, Comets, & Meteoroids, 1 vol. 2008. (Universe Ser.). (ENG.). 32p. (gr. k-4). 27.07 *(978-1-59928-925-0(3),* Buddy Bks.) ABDO Publishing Co.
Nicolson, Cynthia. Discover Space Rocks. Slavin, Bill, illus. 2006. 32p. (J). lib. bdg. 15.38 *(978-1-4242-1195-1(6))* Fitzgerald Bks.
Nicolson, Cynthia Pratt & Nicolson, Cynthia. Discover Space Rocks. Slavin, Bill, illus. 2006. (Kids Can Read Ser.). (ENG.). 32p. (J). (gr. 1-3). 3.95 *(978-1-55337-901-0(2))* Kids Can Pr., Ltd. CAN. Dist: Hachette Bk. Group.
Orme, David. Comets. 2009. (Fact to Fiction Ser.). (Illus.). 36p. (J). pap. 6.95 *(978-0-7891-7899-2(0))* Perfection Learning Corp.
Orr, Tamra B. I See Falling Stars. 2015. (Tell Me Why Library). (ENG., Illus.). 24p. (J). (gr. 2-5). pap. 12.79 *(978-1-63362-035-3(2),* 205897) Cherry Lake Publishing.
—Searching the Sky. 2014. (Explorer Library: Follow the Clues Ser.). (ENG., Illus.). 32p. (J). (gr. 4-8). 28.50 *(978-1-62431-782-8(0),* 203324) Cherry Lake Publishing.
Parker, Steve. Space Objects: Comets, Asteroids & Meteors. 2007. (Earth & Space Ser.). (Illus.). 48p. (YA). (gr. 5-9). lib. bdg. 29.25 *(978-1-4042-3738-4(0))* Rosen Publishing Group, Inc., The.
Rose, Simon. Meteors. 2016. (J). ***(978-1-4896-5818-0(1),*** AV2 by Weigl) Weigl Pubs., Inc.

METEOROLOGICAL INSTRUMENTS

see also Barometer; Thermometers

Hanson, Anders. Meteorologist's Tools, 1 vol. 2011. (Professional Tools Ser.). (ENG., Illus.). 24p. (J). (gr. 3-5). lib. bdg. 25.65 *(978-1-61613-580-5(8),* Super SandCastle) ABDO Publishing Co.
Kampff, Joseph. What Are Weather Instruments?, 1 vol. 2015. (ENG.). 32p. (J). 23.45 *(978-1-62275-791-6(2),* Britannica Educational Publishing) Rosen Publishing Group, Inc., The.
Wills, Susan & Wills, Steven R. Meteorology: Predicting the Weather. 2003. (Innovators Ser.: Vol. 12). (Illus.). 144p. (gr. 5-18). lib. bdg. 21.95 *(978-1-881508-61-8(7))* Oliver Pr., Inc.

METEOROLOGICAL SATELLITES

Baker, David & Kissock, Heather. Satellites. 2016. (J). ***(978-1-4896-5830-2(0),*** AV2 by Weigl) Weigl Pubs., Inc.
Cobb, Allan. Weather Observation Satellites. 2003. 68p. pap. 29.25 *(978-1-4358-3643-3(X))* Rosen Publishing Group, Inc., The.
Hansen, Jim & Burns, John. How to Draw Dragons. 2007. (Drawing Fantasy Art Ser.: Vol. 4). (Illus.). 32p. (J). (gr. 4-7). lib. bdg. 26.50 *(978-1-4042-3856-5(5))* Rosen Publishing Group, Inc., The.

METEOROLOGISTS

Brezina, Corona. Careers in Meteorology. 2012. (Essential Careers Ser.). (ENG., Illus.). 80p. (YA). (gr. 7-12). lib. bdg. 33.25 *(978-1-4488-8241-0(9))* Rosen Publishing Group, Inc., The.
Careers in Focus: Meteorology. 2nd rev. ed. 2011. (Careers in Focus Ser.). (Illus.). 192p. (gr. 6-12). 32.95 *(978-0-8160-8033-5(X),* Ferguson Publishing Co.) Facts On File, Inc.
Demarest, Chris L. Hurricane Hunters! Riders on the Storm. Demarest, Chris L., illus. 2006. (ENG., Illus.). 40p. (J). (gr. -1-5). 19.99 *(978-0-689-86168-0(0),* McElderry, Margaret K. Bks.) McElderry, Margaret K. Bks.
Dreier, David. Be a Storm Chaser. 2008. (Scienceworks! Ser.). (Illus.). 32p. (gr. 3-5). lib. bdg. 26.00 *(978-0-8368-8929-1(0))* Stevens, Gareth Publishing LLLP.
Dreier, David Louis. Be a Storm Chaser. 2008. (Scienceworks! Ser.). 32p. pap. 8.95 *(978-0-8368-8936-9(3))* Stevens, Gareth Publishing LLLP.
Gaffney, Timothy R. Storm Scientist: Careers Chasing Severe Weather. 2009. (Wild Science Careers Ser.). (Illus.). 112p. (J). (gr. 5-18). lib. bdg. 33.27 *(978-0-7660-3050-3(4))* Enslow Pubs., Inc.
Hanson, Anders. Meteorologist's Tools, 1 vol. 2011. (Professional Tools Ser.). (ENG., Illus.). 24p. (J). (gr. 3-5). lib. bdg. 25.65 *(978-1-61613-580-5(8),* Super SandCastle) ABDO Publishing Co.
Hollar, Sherman. Pioneers in the World of Weather & Climatology. 2012. (Inventors & Innovators Ser.). (ENG., Illus.). 112p. (YA). (gr. 7-12). 65.80 *(978-1-61530-787-6(7));* 32.90 *(978-1-61530-702-9(8))* Rosen Publishing Group, Inc., The.
Horn, Geoffrey M. Meteorologist. 2008. (Cool Careers Ser.). 32p. (gr. 5-8). pap. 10.50 *(978-0-8368-9327-4(1));* (YA). lib. bdg. 26.00 *(978-0-8368-9194-2(5))* Stevens, Gareth Publishing LLLP.
Jeffrey, Gary. Hurricane Hunters & Tornado Chasers. 2009. (Graphic Careers Ser.). (ENG.). 48p. (YA). (gr. 5-5). 58.50 *(978-1-61512-885-3(9),* Rosen Reference) Rosen Publishing Group, Inc., The.
Lindop, Laurie. Chasing Tornadoes. 2003. (Science on the Edge Ser.). (Illus.). 80p. (gr. 5-18). lib. bdg. 26.90 *(978-0-7613-2703-5(7),* Twenty-First Century Bks.) Lerner Publishing Group.
Martin, Jacqueline Briggs. Snowflake Bentley. Azarian, Mary, illus. 2009. (ENG.). 32p. (J). (gr. -1-3). pap. 7.99 *(978-0-547-24829-5(6))* Houghton Mifflin Harcourt Publishing Co.
—Snowflake Bentley. 2004. (Illus.). (J). (gr. -1-3). spiral bd. *(978-0-616-01714-2(6))* Canadian National Institute for the Blind/Institut National Canadien pour les Aveugles.
Owen, Ruth. Climatologists & Meteorologists. 2013. (Out of the Lab: Extreme Jobs in Science Ser.). 32p. (J). (gr. 3-6). 25.25 *(978-1-4777-1288-7(7));* pap. 10.00 *(978-1-4777-1376-1(X));* pap. 60.00 *(978-1-4777-1377-8(8))* Rosen Publishing Group, Inc., The. (PowerKids Pr.).
Peterson, Judy Monroe. Weather Watchers: Climate Scientists. 2009. (Extreme Scientists Ser.). 24p. (gr. 2-3). 42.50 *(978-1-61512-454-1(3),* PowerKids Pr.); (Illus.). (YA). lib. bdg. 22.60 *(978-1-4042-4527-3(8))* Rosen Publishing Group, Inc., The.
Rajczak, Kristen. Be a Meteorologist. 2014. (Be a Scientist! Ser.). (Illus.). 32p. (J). (gr. 3-6). pap. 10.50 *(978-1-4824-1210-9(1));* pap. 63.00 *(978-1-4824-1197-3(0))* Stevens, Gareth Publishing LLLP.
Spangenburg, Ray, et al. Alfred Wegener: Puzzle of the Continents. 2009. (Makers of Modern Science Ser.). (Illus.). 176p. (gr. 6-12). 35.00 *(978-0-8160-6174-7(2),* Chelsea Hse.) Facts On File, Inc.
Tieck, Sarah. Storm Chasers, 1 vol. 2011. (Extreme Jobs Ser.). (ENG., Illus.). 32p. (J). (gr. 2-5). 28.50 *(978-1-61783-028-0(3))* ABDO Publishing Co.
Weston Woods Staff, creator. Snowflake Bentley. 2011. 18.95 *(978-0-545-31414-5(3));* 38.75 *(978-0-545-31415-2(1))* Weston Woods Studios, Inc.
Wheeler, Jill C. Joanne Simpson: Magnificent Meteorologist, 1 vol. 2012. (Women in Science Ser.). (ENG., Illus.). 32p. (J). (gr. 3-6). lib. bdg. 27.07 *(978-1-61783-449-3(1),* Checkerboard Library) ABDO Publishing Co.
Wills, Susan & Wills, Steven R. Meteorology: Predicting the Weather. 2003. (Innovators Ser.: Vol. 12). (Illus.). 144p. (gr. 5-18). lib. bdg. 21.95 *(978-1-881508-61-8(7))* Oliver Pr., Inc.

METEOROLOGY

see also Air; Atmosphere; Climate; Clouds; Floods; Fog; Hurricanes; Lightning; Rain and Rainfall; Seasons; Snow; Solar Radiation; Storms; Thunderstorms; Tornadoes; Weather; Weather Forecasting; Winds

Allaby, Michael. The World's Weather. 2012. (ENG., Illus.). 48p. (J). 15.00 *(978-1-899762-81-1(7))* Award Pubns. Ltd. GBR. Dist: Parkwest Pubns., Inc.
Anaxos Inc. Staff, contrib. by. UXL Encyclopedia of Weather & Natural Disasters. 2007. (J). *(978-1-4144-1884-1(1)); (978-1-4144-1882-7(5)); (978-1-4144-1883-4(3)); (978-1-4144-1880-3(9)); (978-1-4144-1881-0(7))* Cengage Gale.
Bang, Molly & Chisholm, Penny. Buried Sunlight: How Fossil Fuels Have Changed the Earth. Bang, Molly, illus. 2014. (ENG., Illus.). 48p. (J). (gr. -1-3). 18.99 *(978-0-545-57785-4(3))* Scholastic, Inc.
—Ocean Sunlight: How Tiny Plants Feed the Seas. Bang, Molly, illus. 2012. (ENG., Illus.). 48p. (J). (gr. -1-3). 18.99 *(978-0-545-27322-0(6),* Blue Sky Pr., The) Scholastic, Inc.
Berger, Melvin & Berger, Gilda. Hurricanes Have Eyes but Can't See: And Other Amazing Facts about Wild Weather. 2003. (Illus.). 48p. (J). *(978-0-439-54980-6(9))* Scholastic, Inc.
Birch, Robin. How Weather Works. 2009. (Weather & Climate Ser.). 32p. (gr. 3). 28.50 *(978-0-7614-4466-4(1))* Marshall Cavendish Corp.
Blackwell, Amy Hackney, ed. U-X-L Encyclopedia of Weather & Natural Disasters, 5 vols. 2nd ed. 2016. (U-X-L Encyclopedia of Weather & Natural Disasters Ser.). (ENG., Illus.). 1200p. (J). (gr. 6-8). 458.00 *(978-1-4103-3290-5(X),* UXL) Cengage Gale.
Boothroyd, Jennifer. Playing with Light & Shadows. 2014. (First Step Nonfiction - Light & Sound Ser.). (ENG., Illus.). 24p. (gr. k-2). lib. bdg. 23.93 *(978-1-4677-3912-2(X),* Lerner Pubns.) Lerner Publishing Group.
Brezina, Corona. Careers in Meteorology. 2012. (Essential Careers Ser.). (ENG., Illus.). 80p. (YA). (gr. 7-12). lib. bdg. 33.25 *(978-1-4488-8241-0(9))* Rosen Publishing Group, Inc., The.
Bright, Michael. Weather Explained, 1 vol. 2015. (ENG.). 136p. (YA). 38.25 *(978-1-4777-8129-6(3),* Rosen Young Adult) Rosen Publishing Group, Inc., The.
Brodfuehrer, Marc. Measuring the Weather. 2009. (Real Life Readers Ser.). 16p. (gr. 2-3). pap. 7.05 *(978-1-4358-0105-9(9),* Rosen Classroom) Rosen Publishing Group, Inc., The.
Challen, Paul C. & Challen, Paul. Drought & Heat Wave Alert! 2004. (Disaster Alert! Ser.). (ENG., Illus.). 32p. (J). pap. *(978-0-7787-1610-5(4));* lib. bdg. *(978-0-7787-1578-8(7))* Crabtree Publishing Co.
Chambers, Catherine. Stickmen's Guide to Earth's Atmosphere in Layers. Dean, Venitia & De Quay, John Paul, illus. 2016. (Stickmen's Guides to This Incredible Earth Ser.). (ENG.). 32p. (J). (gr. 3-6). 26.65 *(978-1-5124-0617-7(1))* Lerner Publishing Group.
Children's Weather Encyclopedia. (Children's Reference Ser.). 224p. *(978-1-4054-9554-7(5))* Parragon, Inc.
Clarke, Catriona. Weather: Level 7. Chen, Kuo Kang, illus. 2006. (Usborne Beginners Ser.). 32p. (J). (gr. 4-7). lib. bdg. 12.99 *(978-1-58086-892-1(4),* Usborne) EDC Publishing.
Cobb, Allan. Weather Observation Satellites. 2003. 68p. pap. 29.25 *(978-1-4358-3643-3(X))* Rosen Publishing Group, Inc., The.
Como Ser un Experto en Clima. (Coleccion Ciencia y Proyectos). (SPA., Illus.). (YA). (gr. 5-8). pap. *(978-950-724-283-0(X),* LMA8238) Lumen ARG. Dist: Lectorum Pubns., Inc.
Corbett, Sean. Heat Waves. 2015. (Illus.). 32p. (J). *(978-1-5105-0078-5(2))* SmartBook Media, Inc.
—Heat Waves. 2014. (J). *(978-1-4896-3272-2(7))* Weigl Pubs., Inc.
El Cuerpo Humano, 6 vols. (Explorers. Exploradores Nonfiction Sets Ser.). (SPA.). 32p. (gr. 3-6). 44.95 *(978-0-7699-0635-5(4))* Shortland Pubns. (U. S. A.) Inc.
El Cuerpo Humano. (Coleccion Estrella del Saber). (SPA., Illus.). (J). 14.95 *(978-950-11-0035-8(9),* SGM035) Sigmar ARG. Dist: Continental Bk. Co., Inc.
D'Aubuisson, Elisabeth. Rainy Days. 2007. (What's the Weather? Ser.). (Illus.). 24p. (J). (gr. 3-7). lib. bdg. 22.60 *(978-1-4042-3682-0(1),* PowerKids Pr.) Rosen Publishing Group, Inc., The.
d'Aubuisson, Elisabeth. Rainy Days. 2009. (What's the Weather? Ser.). 24p. (gr. 2-3). 42.50 *(978-1-60854-775-3(2),* PowerKids Pr.) Rosen Publishing Group, Inc., The.
DeLallo, Laura. Hammered by a Heat Wave! 2010. (Disaster Survivors Ser.). (Illus.). 32p. (YA). (gr. 4-7). lib. bdg. 25.27 *(978-1-936087-51-8(0))* Bearport Publishing Co., Inc.
DiSiena, Laura Lyn & Eliot, Hannah. Rainbows Never End: And Other Fun Facts. Oswald, Pete, illus. 2014. (Did You Know? Ser.). (ENG.). 32p. (J). (gr. -1-3). 17.99 *(978-1-4814-0277-4(3));* pap. 5.99 *(978-1-4814-0275-0(7))* Little Simon. (Little Simon).
Dolphin, Colleen. Advisories to Zero Degrees: Weather from A to Z, 1 vol. 2007. (Let's See A to Z Ser.). (ENG., Illus.). 32p. (gr. -1-3). 27.07 *(978-1-59928-879-6(6),* Super SandCastle) ABDO Publishing Co.
Extreme Threats, 4 vols., Set. Incl. Asteroids & Comets. Nardo, Don. (YA). lib. bdg. 28.95 *(978-1-59935-121-6(8));* Climate Change. Nardo, Don. (J). lib. bdg. 28.95 *(978-1-59935-119-3(6));* Wildfires. Cunningham, Kevin. (YA). lib. bdg. 28.95 *(978-1-59935-120-9(X));* 112p. 2009. 2009. Set lib. bdg. 115.80 *(978-1-59935-128-5(5))* Reynolds, Morgan Inc.
Fleisher, Paul. Gases, Pressure, & Wind: The Science of the Atmosphere. 2010. (Weatherwise Ser.). (ENG., Illus.). 48p. (gr. 4-8). lib. bdg. 29.27 *(978-0-8225-7537-5(X))* Lerner Publishing Group.
—Vapor, Rain, & Snow: The Science of Clouds & Precipitation. 2010. (Weatherwise Ser.). (ENG.). 48p. (gr. 4-8). lib. bdg. 29.27 *(978-0-8225-7534-4(5))* Lerner Publishing Group.
Gaffney, Timothy R. Storm Scientist: Careers Chasing Severe Weather. 2009. (Wild Science Careers Ser.). (Illus.). 112p. (J). (gr. 5-18). lib. bdg. 33.27 *(978-0-7660-3050-3(4))* Enslow Pubs., Inc.
Ganeri, Anita. El Sol. 2004. (tiempo de aqui (Weather Around You- Spanish) Ser.). (SPA.). 24p. (gr. 1-4). lib. bdg. 22.00 *(978-0-8368-4365-1(7),* Weekly Reader Leveled Readers) Stevens, Gareth Publishing LLLP.
Gardner, Robert. Meteorology Experiments in Your Own Weather Station. 2015. (Design, Build, Experiment Ser.). (ENG.). 128p. (J). (gr. 7-7). lib. bdg. 37.27 *(978-0-7660-6957-2(5))* Enslow Pubs., Inc.
—Meteorology Projects with a Weather Station You Can Build. 2008. (Build-A-Lab! Science Experiments Ser.). (Illus.). 128p. (J). (gr. 5-18). lib. bdg. 33.27 *(978-0-7660-2807-4(0))* Enslow Pubs., Inc.
Gardner, Robert & Conklin, Joshua. Experiments for Future Meteorologists. 2016. (Experiments for Future STEM Professionals Ser.). (Illus.). 128p. (J). 37.27 *(978-0-7660-8196-3(6))* Enslow Pubs., Inc.
Gibbons, Gail. It's Raining! Gibbons, Gail, illus. 2014. (ENG., Illus.). 32p. (J). (gr. -1-3). 17.95 *(978-0-8234-2924-0(5))* Holiday Hse., Inc.
Goldstein, Natalie. Drought & Heat Waves: A Practical Survival Guide. 2009. (Library of Emergency Preparedness Ser.). 64p. (gr. 6-6). 29.25 *(978-1-60853-592-7(4),* Rosen Reference) Rosen Publishing Group, Inc., The.
Gregory, Josh. Climate Scientist. 2013. (21st Century Skills Library: Cool STEM Careers Ser.). (ENG.). 32p. (J). (gr. 4-8). 28.50 *(978-1-62431-002-7(8),* 202459); pap. 14.21 *(978-1-62431-026-3(5),* 202461) Cherry Lake Publishing.
Hackney Blackwell, Amy & Manar, Elizabeth P. U-X-L Encyclopedia of Weather & Natural Disasters. 2016. (Illus.). (J). *(978-1-4103-3291-2(8)); (978-1-4103-3292-9(6))* Cengage Gale. (Blackbirch Pr., Inc.).
Hand, Carol. Science Lab: Weather Patterns. 2011. (Explorer Library: Language Arts Explorer Ser.). (ENG.). 32p. (gr. 4-8). pap. 14.21 *(978-1-61080-299-4(3),* 201221); lib. bdg. 28.50 *(978-1-61080-210-9(1),* 201196) Cherry Lake Publishing.
—Weather Myths, Busted! 2017. (Science Myths, Busted! Ser.). (ENG.). 32p. (J). (gr. 3-6). 21.95 *(978-1-63235-307-8(5),* 12-Story Library) Pr. Room Editions LLC.
—Weather Myths, Busted! 12 Groundbreaking Discoveries. 2016. (Science Myths, Busted! Ser.). (ENG., Illus.). 32p. (J). pap. 9.95 *(978-1-63235-357-3(1),* 12-Story Library) Pr. Room Editions LLC.
Hansen, Jim & Burns, John. How to Draw Dragons. 2007. (Drawing Fantasy Art Ser.: Vol. 4). (Illus.). 32p. (J). (gr. 4-7). lib. bdg. 26.50 *(978-1-4042-3856-5(5))* Rosen Publishing Group, Inc., The.
Higgins, Nadia. Types of Precipitation. Infante, Sara, illus. 2017. (Water All Around Us Ser.). (ENG.). 24p. (gr. 1-3). 33.99 ***(978-1-68410-057-6(7))*** Cantata Learning.
Hirschmann, Kris. It's Wet Out!, 1 vol. 2008. (What's It Like Out? Ser.). (ENG.). 32p. (gr. k-6). 27.07 *(978-1-59928-944-1(X),* Checkerboard Library) ABDO Publishing Co.
Hollar, Sherman. Pioneers in the World of Weather & Climatology. 2012. (Inventors & Innovators Ser.). (ENG., Illus.). 112p. (YA). (gr. 7-12). 65.80 *(978-1-61530-787-6(7));* 32.90 *(978-1-61530-702-9(8))* Rosen Publishing Group, Inc., The.
Hunter, Nick. Science vs. Climate Change. 2013. (Science Fights Back Ser.). (Illus.). 48p. (gr. 4-6). 31.95 *(978-1-4339-8678-9(7));* pap. 14.05 *(978-1-4339-8679-6(5))* Stevens, Gareth Publishing LLLP. (Gareth Stevens Learning Library).
Johnson, Robin. What Is a Heat Wave? 2016. (ENG., Illus.). 24p. (J). *(978-0-7787-2397-4(6))* Crabtree Publishing Co.
—What Is Precipitation? 2012. (ENG.). 24p. (J). *(978-0-7787-0754-7(7));* (Illus.). pap. *(978-0-7787-0761-5(X))* Crabtree Publishing Co.
Kerrod, Robin. Exploring Science: Weather an Amazing Fact File & Hands-On Project Book. 2014. (ENG., Illus.). 64p. (J). (gr. 3-7). 12.99 *(978-1-86147-307-3(9),* Armadillo) Anness Publishing GBR. Dist: National Bk. Network.
Kjelle, Marylou Morano. A Project Guide to Wind, Weather, & the Atmosphere. 2010. (Earth Science Projects for Kids Ser.). (Illus.). 48p. (J). (gr. 4-7). lib. bdg. 29.95 *(978-1-58415-869-1(7))* Mitchell Lane Pubs., Inc.
Lawrence, Ellen. How are Rain, Snow, & Hail Alike? 2012. (Weather Wise Ser.). 24p. (J). (gr. -1-3). lib. bdg. 23.93 *(978-1-61772-403-9(3))* Bearport Publishing Co., Inc.
Lunis, Natalie. Making a Weather Station. 2011. (Early Connections Ser.). (J). *(978-1-61672-613-3(X))* Benchmark Education Co.
Mara, Wil. Why Does It Rain? 2009. (Tell Me Why, Tell Me How Ser.). 32p. (gr. 3-18). 29.93 *(978-0-7614-3991-2(9))* Marshall Cavendish Corp.
Marsico, Katie. Wild Weather Days. 2006. (Scholastic News Nonfiction Readers Ser.). (ENG., Illus.). 24p. (J). (gr. 1-2). lib. bdg. 22.00 *(978-0-531-16771-7(2))* Scholastic Library Publishing.
Martin, Bobi. What Are Air Masses & Weather Fronts?, 1 vol. 2015. (ENG.). 32p. (J). 23.45 *(978-1-62275-787-9(4),* Britannica Educational Publishing) Rosen Publishing Group, Inc., The.
Mattern, Joanne. What Are Weather & Climate?, 1 vol. 2015. (ENG.). 32p. (J). 23.45 *(978-1-62275-779-4(3),* Britannica Educational Publishing) Rosen Publishing Group, Inc., The.
McAneney, Caitie. Precipitation. 2016. (Where's the Water? Ser.). (Illus.). 24p. (J). (gr. 3-2). pap. 8.15 *(978-1-4824-4684-5(7));* lib. bdg. 22.60 *(978-1-4824-4686-9(3))* Stevens, Gareth Publishing LLLP.
Morgan, Emily. Next Time You See a Cloud. 2017. (Next Time You See Ser.). (ENG., Illus.). 32p. (J). (gr. 2-4). pap. 12.95 *(978-1-938946-36-3(7))* National Science Teachers Assn.
Mullins, Matt. Think Like a Scientist in the Backyard. 2011. (Explorer Junior Library: Science Explorer Junior Ser.). (ENG.). 32p. (gr. 4-8). lib. bdg. 28.50 *(978-1-61080-167-6(9),* 201104) Cherry Lake Publishing.
El Mundo de la Meteorologia, 6 vols., Vol. 3. (Explorers. Exploradores Nonfiction Sets Ser.). (SPA.). (gr. 3-6). *(978-0-7699-0654-6(0))* Shortland Pubns. (U. S. A.) Inc.
Oard, Michael. The New Weather Book. 2015. (Illus.). 96p. (J). 16.99 *(978-0-89051-861-8(0))* Master Bks.
Orr, Tamra. Experiment with Weather. 2010. (Explorer Junior Library: Science Explorer Junior Ser.). (ENG.). 32p. (gr. 3-6). lib. bdg. 28.50 *(978-1-60279-841-0(9),* 200548) Cherry Lake Publishing.
Oxlade, Chris. Weather Infographics, 1 vol. 2014. (Infographics Ser.). (ENG.). 32p. (gr. 1-3). lib. bdg. 29.99 *(978-1-4109-6219-5(9),* Read Me!) Heinemann-Raintree.
Parker, Janice. Weather. 2016. (J). ***(978-1-5105-2243-5(3))*** SmartBook Media, Inc.
Peterson, Judy Monroe. Weather Watchers: Climate Scientists. 2009. (Extreme Scientists Ser.). 24p. (gr. 2-3). 42.50 *(978-1-61512-454-1(3),* PowerKids Pr.); (Illus.). (YA). lib. bdg. 22.60 *(978-1-4042-4527-3(8))* Rosen Publishing Group, Inc., The.
Poolos, Christine. What Is an Object in the Sky? 2014. (Let's Find Out! Ser.). 32p. (J). (gr. 3-6). 23.45 *(978-1-62275-471-7(9))* Rosen Publishing Group, Inc., The.
Purdie, Kate. Sunshine & Drought. 2010. (Weatherwise Ser.). 32p. (ENG.). (J). pap. 10.60 *(978-1-61532-278-7(7),* PowerKids Pr.); (Illus.). (YA). (gr. 3-6). lib. bdg. 26.50 *(978-1-61532-266-4(3))* Rosen Publishing Group, Inc., The.
Purslow, Frances. Precipitation. 2015. (Illus.). 24p. (J). *(978-1-5105-0054-9(5))* SmartBook Media, Inc.
—Precipitation. 2016. (J). ***(978-1-4896-5797-8(5))*** 2010. (Illus.). 24p. (J). (gr. 3-5). pap. 11.95 *(978-1-61690-008-3(3))* 2010. (Illus.). 24p. (YA). (gr. 3-6). lib. bdg. 25.70 *(978-1-61690-002-1(4))* 2005. (Illus.). 24p. (J). (gr. 3-7). pap. 8.95 *(978-1-59036-311-9(6))* 2005. (Illus.). 24p. (J). (gr. 3-7). lib. bdg. 24.45 *(978-1-59036-305-8(1))* Weigl Pubs., Inc.
Richards, Jon. Light & Sight. 2009. (Science Factory Ser.). 32p. (gr. 4-5). 50.50 *(978-1-60853-022-9(1),* PowerKids Pr.) Rosen Publishing Group, Inc., The.
Roker, Al. Al Roker's Extreme Weather. 2017. 48p. (J). (gr. 3-7). 16.99 ***(978-0-06-248499-4(0))*** HarperCollins Pubs.
Rowe, Brooke. Creating Rain. Bane, Jeff, illus. 2016. (My Early Library: My Science Fun Ser.). (ENG.). 24p. (J). (gr. k-1). 28.50 *(978-1-63471-027-5(4),* 208188) Cherry Lake Publishing.
Schuetz, Kristin. Precipitation. 2015. (Understanding Weather Ser.). (ENG., Illus.). 24p. (J). (gr. k-3). lib. bdg. 25.95 *(978-1-62617-253-1(6),* Blastoff! Readers) Bellwether Media.
Sherman, Josepha. Amazing Science - Weather, 6 bks. Incl. Flakes & Flurries: A Book about Snow. Yesh, Jeff, illus. 26.65 *(978-1-4048-0098-4(0));* Gusts & Gales: A Book about Wind. Wesley, Omarr, illus. 26.65 *(978-1-4048-0094-6(8));* Shapes in the Sky: A Book about Clouds. Wesley, Omarr, illus. 26.65 *(978-1-4048-0097-7(2));* (gr. -1-3). (Amazing Science: Weather Ser.). (ENG.). 24p. 2003. Set lib. bdg. 159.90 o.p. *(978-1-4048-0092-2(1))* Picture Window Bks.
Silverstein, Alvin, et al. Weather & Climate. 2007. (Science Concepts, Second Ser.). (Illus.). 96p. (J). (gr. 6-8). lib. bdg. 31.93 *(978-0-8225-6796-7(2),* Twenty-First Century Bks.) Lerner Publishing Group.
Smith, Alastair & Clarke, Phillip. Weather: With Internet Links. 2006. (Usborne Spotter's Guides). (Illus.). 64p. (J). (gr. 2). lib. bdg. 13.99 *(978-1-58086-915-7(7),* Usborne) EDC Publishing.
Sneideman, Joshua & Twamley, Erin. Climate Change: Discover How It Impacts Spaceship Earth. Crosier, Mike, illus. 2015. (Build It Yourself Ser.). (ENG.). 128p. (gr. 3-7). 22.95 *(978-1-61930-269-3(1))* Open City Bks.
Taylor-Butler, Christine. Meteorology: The Study of Weather. 2012. (True Book Ser.). (ENG., Illus.). 48p. (J). pap. 6.95 *(978-0-531-28272-4(4));* lib. bdg. 29.00 *(978-0-531-24678-8(7))* Scholastic Library Publishing. (Children's Pr.).
Thompson, Jean M. Water Wonders Every Child Should Know: L. 2005. reprint ed. pap. 26.95 *(978-1-4179-3339-6(9))* Kessinger Publishing, LLC.
USA Today Staff, contrib. by. USA Today Weather Wonders: Discover What's up & What's Coming Down. 2009. (Illus.). 80p. (J). *(978-1-4027-6534-6(7),* Sterling Innovation) Sterling Publishing Co., Inc.
Way, Jennifer L. & Gaffney, Timothy R. Severe-Storm Scientists: Chasing Tornadoes & Hurricanes. 2015. (Extreme Science Careers Ser.). (ENG., Illus.). 128p. (J). (gr. 7-7). 37.27 *(978-0-7660-6968-8(0))* Enslow Pubs., Inc.
Whitt, Kelly Kizer. Solar System Forecast, 1 vol. Klein, Laurie Allen, illus. 2012. (SPA.). 32p. (J). (gr. -1-4). pap. 9.95 *(978-1-62855-425-0(8))* Arbordale Publishing.
Whitt, Kelly Kizer. El Pronóstico Del Sistema Solar, 1 vol. Klein, Laurie Allen, illus. 2012. (SPA & ENG.). 32p. (J). (gr. -1-4). 17.95 *(978-1-60718-678-6(0))* Arbordale Publishing.
—Solar System Forecast, 1 vol. Klein, Laurie Allen, illus. 2012. 32p. (J). (gr. -1-4). (ENG & SPA.). 17.95 *(978-1-60718-523-9(7));* (SPA & ENG.). pap. 9.95 *(978-1-60718-532-1(6))* Arbordale Publishing.
Williams, Judith. En Busca de Tormentas con un Cientifico/Searching for Storms with a Scientist. 2008. (I Like Science! Bilingual Ser.).Tr. of Searching for Storms with a

MNO

Scientist. (SPA & ENG., Illus.). 24p. (J). (gr. 1-3). lib. bdg. 22.60 *(978-0-7660-2980-4(8),* Enslow Elementary) Enslow Pubs., Inc.

—Searching for Stormy Weather with a Scientist. 2004. (I Like Science! Ser.). (Illus.). 24p. (J). lib. bdg. 22.60 *(978-0-7660-2271-3(4))* Enslow Pubs., Inc.

World Book, Inc Staff, contrib. by. Heat Waves. (J). 2007. *(978-0-7166-9807-4(2))* 2nd ed. 2009. (Illus.). 47p. *(978-0-7166-9823-4(4))* World Bk., Inc.

—Learning about Weather. 2011. (J). *(978-0-7166-0235-4(0))* World Bk., Inc.

Zoehfeld, Kathleen Weidner. School of Dragons #3: Storm Approaching! (DreamWorks Dragons) Random House, illus. 2017. (ENG.). 80p. (J). (gr. 2-5). pap. 7.99 *(978-1-101-93343-5(7),* Random Hse. Bks. for Young Readers) Random Hse. Children's Bks.

METEOROLOGY—VOCATIONAL GUIDANCE

Cortinas, John. On the Job with a Meteorologist. 2003. (Adventures in Science Professions Ser.). (J). *(978-1-58417-061-7(1));* pap. *(978-1-58417-124-9(3))* Lake Street Pubs.

Horn, Geoffrey M. Meteorologist. 2008. (Cool Careers Ser.). 32p. (gr. 5-8). pap. 10.50 *(978-0-8368-9327-4(1));* (YA). lib. bdg. 26.00 *(978-0-8368-9194-2(5))* Stevens, Gareth Publishing LLLP.

Mullins, Matt. Meteorologist. 2011. (21st Century Skills Library: Cool Science Careers Ser.). (ENG.). 32p. (gr. 4-8). lib. bdg. 28.50 *(978-1-61080-034-1(6),* 200994) Cherry Lake Publishing.

Rajczak, Kristen. Be a Meteorologist. 2014. (Be a Scientist! Ser.). (Illus.). 32p. (J). (gr. 3-6). pap. 10.50 *(978-1-4824-1210-9(1))* Stevens, Gareth Publishing LLLP.

METEORS

see also Meteorites

Asimov, Isaac & Hantula, Richard. Comets & Meteors. 2005. (Isaac Asimov's 21st Century Library of the Universe). (Illus.). 32p. (gr. 2-6). lib. bdg. 26.00 *(978-0-8368-3966-1(8),* Gareth Stevens Learning Library) Stevens, Gareth Publishing LLLP.

Atkinson, Stuart. Comets, Asteroids, & Meteors, 1 vol. 2012. (Astronaut Travel Guides). (ENG.). 48p. (gr. 3-6). pap. 9.95 *(978-1-4109-4576-1(6));* lib. bdg. 32.65 *(978-1-4109-4567-9(7))* Heinemann-Raintree. (NA-r).

Cutting, Robert. Falling Star. Ng, Drew, illus. 2007. 48p. (J). lib. bdg. 23.08 *(978-1-4242-1625-3(7))* Fitzgerald Bks.

Dickmann, Nancy. Exploring Comets, Asteroids, & Other Objects in Space. 2015. (Spectacular Space Science Ser.). (ENG., Illus.). 48p. (J). (gr. 5-6). 30.25 *(978-1-4994-3637-2(8),* Rosen Central) Rosen Publishing Group, Inc., The.

Dybvik, Tina. Space Cowboy Caleb & the Night Sky Round-Up: Learning about the Night Sky, 1 vol. Record, Adam, illus. 2013. (Take It Outside Ser.). (ENG.). 24p. (gr. k-2). pap. 8.95 *(978-1-4795-1938-5(3));* lib. bdg. 27.32 *(978-1-4048-8317-8(7))* Picture Window Bks.

Gifford, Clive. The Solar System, Meteors, & Comets. 2015. (Watch This Space! Ser.). (ENG., Illus.). 32p. (J). (gr. 3-7). lib. bdg. *(978-0-7787-2023-2(3))* Crabtree Publishing Co.

Kelley, J. A. Meteor Showers. (True Book(tm), A — Space Ser.). (ENG.). 48p. (J). 2009. (gr. 2-5). 31.00 *(978-0-531-16897-4(2))* 2010. (Illus.). pap. 6.95 *(978-0-531-22804-3(5),* Children's Pr.) Scholastic Library Publishing.

Lawrence, Ellen. Comets, Meteors, & Asteroids: Voyagers of the Solar System. 2013. (Zoom into Space Ser.). 24p. (J). (gr. -1-3). lib. bdg. 23.93 *(978-1-909673-22-9(6))* Ruby Tuesday Books Limited GBR. Dist: Bearport Publishing Co., Inc.

Mason Crest. Comets & Meteors, Vol. 7. 2016. (Solar System Ser.: Vol. 7). (ENG., Illus.). 48p. (J). (gr. 5-8). 20.95 *(978-1-4222-3548-5(3))* Mason Crest.

Miller, Ron. Asteroids, Comets, & Meteors. 2006. (Worlds Beyond Ser.). (Illus.). 80p. (J). (gr. 5-9). 27.93 *(978-0-7613-2363-1(5),* Twenty-First Century Bks.) Lerner Publishing Group.

—Seven Wonders of Asteroids, Comets, & Meteors. 2011. (Seven Wonders Ser.). (ENG.). 80p. (gr. 5-8). lib. bdg. 33.26 *(978-0-7613-5451-2(4))* Lerner Publishing Group.

Olien, Rebecca. Exploring Meteors. (Objects in the Sky Ser.). 24p. (gr. 3-3). 2009. 42.50 *(978-1-60851-139-6(1))* 2007. (Illus.). (J). lib. bdg. 22.60 *(978-1-4042-3468-0(3))* Rosen Publishing Group, Inc., The. (PowerKids Pr.).

Orr, Tamra B. I See Falling Stars. 2015. (Tell Me Why Library). (ENG., Illus.). 24p. (J). (gr. 2-5). pap. 12.79 *(978-1-63362-035-3(2),* 205897) Cherry Lake Publishing.

—Searching the Sky. 2014. (Explorer Library: Follow the Clues Ser.). (ENG., Illus.). 32p. (J). (gr. 4-8). 28.50 *(978-1-62431-782-8(0),* 203324) Cherry Lake Publishing.

Rajczak, Kristen. Shooting Stars. 2012. (Nature's Light Show Ser.). (Illus.). 24p. (J). (gr. 2-5). pap. 8.15 *(978-1-4339-7036-8(8));* lib. bdg. 22.60 *(978-1-4339-7035-1(X))* Stevens, Gareth Publishing LLLP.

Rose, Simon. Meteors. 2016. (J). ***(978-1-4896-5818-0(1),*** AV2 by Weigl) 2011. (J). (gr. 4-6). pap. 13.95 *(978-1-61690-638-2(3),* AV2 by Weigl) 2011. (Illus.). 32p. (YA). (gr. 2-5). 28.55 *(978-1-61690-634-4(0))* Weigl Pubs., Inc.

Sherman, Josepha. Asteroids, Meteors, & Comets. 2009. (Space!). 64p. (gr. 5-18). lib. bdg. 32.79 *(978-0-7614-4252-3(9))* Marshall Cavendish Corp.

Sparrow, Giles. Destination Asteroids, Comets, & Meteors. 2009. (Destination Solar System Ser.). (Illus.). 32p. (J). 25.25 *(978-1-4358-3449-1(6));* pap. 10.00 *(978-1-4358-3469-9(0))* Rosen Publishing Group, Inc., The. (PowerKids Pr.).

Stewart, Melissa. Meteors. 2015. (Readers Ser.). (ENG.). 32p. (J). (gr. 1-4). pap. 3.99 *(978-1-4263-1943-3(6),* National Geographic Children's Bks.) National Geographic Society.

Stiefel, Chana. Comets & Meteors: Shooting Through Space. 2014. (ENG.). 24p. (gr. k-3). 28.50 *(978-1-62717-732-0(9))* Rourke Educational Media.

The Sun. 2017. (Illus.). 40p. (J). ***(978-1-4222-3547-8(5))*** Mason Crest.

Vogt, Gregory. Meteors & Comets. 2010. (Early Bird Astronomy Ser.). (ENG.). 48p. (gr. 2-5). lib. bdg. 26.60 *(978-0-7613-3876-5(4))* Lerner Publishing Group.

Wilkins, Mary-Jane. Asteroids, Comets, & Meteors. 2017. (Fast Track: Our Solar System Ser.). 24p. (gr. k-3). 28.50 ***(978-1-78121-368-1(2))*** Brown Bear Bks.

Woolf, Alex. Meteor: Perspectives on Asteroid Strikes, 1 vol. 2014. (Disaster Dossiers Ser.). (ENG., Illus.). 56p. (gr. 7-8). 34.65 *(978-1-4846-0182-2(3))* Heinemann-Raintree.

METER

see Versification

METER (UNIT)

see Metric System

METHOD OF STUDY

see Study Skills

METHODIST CHURCH

Benge, Janet & Benge, Geoff. Christian Heroes - Then & Now - John Wesley: The World, His Parish. 2007. (Christian Heroes Ser.). (ENG.). 192p. (YA). (gr. 3-7). pap. 9.99 *(978-1-57658-382-1(1))* YWAM Publishing.

METRIC SYSTEM

Arias, Lisa. Marvelous Measurement: Conversions. 2014. (ENG.). 32p. (gr. 3-6). 32.79 *(978-1-62717-712-2(4))* Rourke Educational Media.

Benjamin, Lindsay. Measurement Action! 2005. (Yellow Umbrella Fluent Level Ser.). (ENG., Illus.). 16p. (gr. k-1). pap. 35.70 *(978-0-7368-5322-4(7),* Yellow Umbrella Bks.) Capstone Press of Coughlan Cos.

Bussell, Linda. Measuring at the Pond. 2008. (Math in Our World - Level 3 Ser.). 24p. (gr. 2-5). (J). lib. bdg. 22.00 *(978-0-8368-9291-8(7));* pap. 8.15 *(978-0-8368-9390-8(5))* Stevens, Gareth Publishing LLLP. (Weekly Reader Leveled Readers).

—Vamos a Medir en el Estanque. 2008. (Matemáticas en Nuestro Mundo - Nivel 3 (Math in Our World - Level 3) Ser.). (SPA.). 24p. (gr. 2-5). (J). lib. bdg. 22.00 *(978-0-8368-9299-4(2));* pap. 8.15 *(978-0-8368-9398-4(0))* Stevens, Gareth Publishing LLLP. (Weekly Reader Leveled Readers).

Bussiere, Desirée. What in the World Is a Centimeter? & Other Metric Measurements, 1 vol. 2013. (Let's Measure More Ser.). (ENG.). 24p. (J). (gr. -1-3). lib. bdg. 24.21 *(978-1-61783-596-4(X),* SandCastle) ABDO Publishing Co.

Challen, Paul. The Metric System. 2009. (ENG.). 24p. (J). lib. bdg. *(978-0-7787-4352-1(7));* pap. *(978-0-7787-4313-2(6))* Crabtree Publishing Co.

Fandel, Jennifer. The Metric System. 2006. (What in the World? Ser.). (Illus.). 48p. (J). (gr. 4-7). lib. bdg. 21.95 *(978-1-58341-430-9(4),* Creative Education) Creative Co., The.

Mattern, Joanne. Let's Visit Canada: The Metric System. 2009. (PowerMath Ser.). (Illus.). 24p. (gr. 3-4). pap. 8.25 *(978-0-8239-8872-3(4),* PowerKids Pr.) Rosen Publishing Group, Inc., The.

Murphy, Stuart J. Polly's Pen Pal. Simard, Remy, illus. 2005. (MathStart 3 Ser.). (ENG.). 40p. (J). (gr. 2-18). pap. 5.99 *(978-0-06-053170-6(3))* HarperCollins Pubs.

O'Donnell, Kerri. Natural Wonders of the World: Converting Distance Measurements to Metric Units. 2009. (PowerMath: Proficiency Plus Ser.). 32p. (gr. 4-5). 47.90 *(978-1-60851-414-4(5),* PowerKids Pr.) Rosen Publishing Group, Inc., The.

—Natural Wonders of the World: Converting Measurements to Metric Units. 2005. (PowerMath: Proficiency Plus Ser.). (Illus.). 32p. (J). (gr. 3-6). lib. bdg. 25.25 *(978-1-4042-2928-0(0),* PowerKids Pr.) Rosen Publishing Group, Inc., The.

—Natural Wonders of the World: Understanding & Representing Numbers in the Billions. 2009. (Math for the REAL World Ser.). (Illus.). 32p. (gr. 5-6). pap. 10.00 *(978-1-4042-5119-9(7))* Rosen Publishing Group, Inc., The.

Schwartz, David M. Millions to Measure. Kellogg, Steven, illus. 2006. (ENG.). 40p. (J). (gr. k-7). reprint ed. pap. 6.99 *(978-0-06-084806-4(5))* HarperCollins Pubs.

Schwartz, David M. & Schwartz, David. Millions to Measure. Kellogg, Steven, illus. 2003. (ENG.). 40p. (J). (gr. k-7). 17.99 *(978-0-688-12916-3(1))* HarperCollins Pubs.

Sullivan, Erin Ash. Metric Math & Matemáticas Métricas: 6 English, 6 Spanish Adaptations. 2011. (ENG & SPA.). (J). 89.00 net. *(978-1-4108-5681-4(X))* Benchmark Education Co.

Sullivan, Navin. Area, Distance, & Volume. 2006. (Measure Up! Ser.). (Illus.). 48p. (gr. 4-7). lib. bdg. 31.36 *(978-0-7614-2323-2(0),* Benchmark Bks.) Marshall Cavendish Corp.

METROLOGY

Here are entered works on the science of measurement or of weights and measures. Works on the general process of measuring are entered under Measurement. Works on a system of standard units of measure are entered under Weights and Measures.

see also Measurement; Weights and Measures

Branson, Sam. Let's Measure the Weather. 2012. (InfoMax Readers Ser.). (ENG., Illus.). 24p. (J). (gr. 1-2). pap. 8.25 *(978-1-4488-9019-4(5),* Rosen Classroom) Rosen Publishing Group, Inc., The.

Gardner, Robert. Ace Your Math & Measuring Science Project: Great Science Fair Ideas. 2009. (Ace Your Physics Science Project Ser.). (Illus.). 128p. (J). (gr. 5-18). lib. bdg. 33.27 *(978-0-7660-3224-8(8))* Enslow Pubs., Inc.

Sohn, Emily & Sharp, Katie. Measurement: The Measured Mystery. 2011. (iScience Readers Ser.). 32p. (J). (gr. 3-4). lib. bdg. 22.60 *(978-1-59953-417-6(7))* Norwood Hse. Pr.

METROPOLITAN MUSEUM OF ART (NEW YORK, N.Y.)

Gregory, Joy. The Metropolitan Museum of Art. 2014. (Illus.). 24p. (J). *(978-1-4896-1194-9(0))* Weigl Pubs., Inc.

Metropolitan Museum of Art Staff, contrib. by. Museum Colors: The Metropolitan Museum of Art. 2006. (J). 16.99 *(978-1-58839-183-4(3))* Metropolitan Museum of Art, The.

MEXICAN AMERICANS

see also Mexicans—United States

Abrams, Dennis. Gary Soto. 2008. (Who Wrote That? Ser.). (Illus.). 120p. (gr. 6-12). 35.00 *(978-0-7910-9529-4(0),* Chelsea Hse.) Facts On File, Inc.

Adler, David A. & Adler, Michael S. A Picture Book of Cesar Chavez. Olofsdotter, Marie, illus. 2010. (ENG.). 32p. (J). (gr. -1-3). 17.95 *(978-0-8234-2202-9(X))* Holiday Hse., Inc.

Alaniz, Valeria & Garcia, Sarah Rafael. Barrio Writers: Empowering Teens Through Creative Writing —: A Collection of Works by Teens for Teens, Teachers & Our Communities. 2012. (SPA & ENG.). 147p. (YA). pap. *(978-1-890701-32-1(7))* La Mancha Publishing Group.

Alter, Judy. Martin de León: Tejano Empresario. Messersmith, Patrick, illus. 2007. (Stars of Texas Ser.: 4). (ENG.). 72p. (gr. 4-7). 14.95 *(978-1-933337-08-1(7))* State Hse. Pr.

Ancona, George. Mi Casa: My House. 2005. (Somos Latinos (We Are Latinos) Ser.). (SPA & ENG., Illus.). 32p. (J). (gr. 1-3). pap. 8.95 *(978-0-516-25065-6(5),* Children's Pr.) Scholastic Library Publishing.

—Mis Juegos/My Games. 2005. (Somos Latinos (We Are Latinos) Ser.). (ENG & SPA., Illus.). 32p. (J). (gr. 1-3). lib. bdg. 21.00 *(978-0-516-25293-3(3),* Children's Pr.) Scholastic Library Publishing.

Angel, Ann. A Reader's Guide to Sandra Cisneros's the House on Mango Street. 2010. (Multicultural Literature Ser.). (Illus.). 128p. (YA). 33.27 *(978-0-7660-3167-8(5))* Enslow Pubs., Inc.

Anza, Ana Luisa. Amigos del Otro Lado. Gomez, Eddie Martinez, illus. rev. ed. 2004. (Castillo de la Lectura Naranja Ser.). (SPA & ENG.). 136p. (J). pap. 7.95 *(978-970-20-0130-0(7))* Castillo, Ediciones, S. A. de C. V. MEX. Dist: Macmillan.

Apte, Sunita. Cesar Chavez: We Can Do It! 2005. (Defining Moments Ser.). (Illus.). 32p. (J). (gr. 2-5). lib. bdg. 25.27 *(978-1-59716-073-5(3))* Bearport Publishing Co., Inc.

Baughan, Brian. Cesar Chavez. 2009. (Sharing the American Dream Ser.). (Illus.). 64p. (YA). (gr. 7-12). 22.95 *(978-1-4222-0582-2(7))* Mason Crest.

Behnke, Alison. Mexicans in America. 2004. (In America Ser.). (ENG., Illus.). 80p. (gr. 5-8). lib. bdg. 27.93 *(978-0-8225-3955-1(1))* Lerner Publishing Group.

Berne, Emma Carlson. What's Your Story, Cesar Chavez? 2015. (ENG.). 32p. (J). (gr. k-3). 26.65 *(978-1-4677-7967-8(9))* Lerner Publishing Group.

Bloom, Barbara Lee. The Mexican Americans. 2005. (Immigrants in America Ser.). (ENG., Illus.). 112p. (J). 30.85 *(978-1-56006-753-5(5),* Lucent Bks.) Cengage Gale.

Boyer Binns, Tristan. Mexican Americans. 2003. (We Are America Ser.). (Illus.). 32p. (J). (gr. 2-4). lib. bdg. 24.22 *(978-1-4034-0163-2(2))* Heinemann-Raintree.

Braun, Eric. Cesar Chavez: Fighting for Farmworkers, 1 vol. Roland, Harry et al, illus. 2005. (Graphic Biographies Ser.). (ENG.). 32p. (gr. 3-4). 30.65 *(978-0-7368-4631-8(X),* Graphic Library) Capstone Press of Coughlan Cos.

Brimner, Larry Dane. Strike! The Farm Workers' Fight for Their Rights. 2014. (ENG., Illus.). 172p. (J). (gr. 5). 16.95 *(978-1-59078-997-1(0),* Calkins Creek) Boyds Mills Pr.

Brown, Jonatha A. César Chávez. (People We Should Know Ser.). 2005. (SPA.). 24p. (gr. 1-4). pap. 8.15 *(978-0-8368-4766-6(0),* Weekly Reader Leveled Readers) 2005. (Illus.). 24p. (gr. 1-4). lib. bdg. 22.00 *(978-0-8368-4745-1(8),* Weekly Reader Leveled Readers) 2005. (SPA., Illus.). 24p. (gr. 1-4). lib. bdg. 22.00 *(978-0-8368-4759-8(8),* Weekly Reader Leveled Readers) 2004. (Illus.). 48p. (gr. 5-12). pap. 14.05 *(978-0-8368-5257-8(5),* Gareth Stevens Secondary Library) 2004. (Illus.). 48p. (gr. 5-12). lib. bdg. 31.00 *(978-0-8368-5097-0(1),* Gareth Stevens Secondary Library) Stevens, Gareth Publishing LLLP.

Brown, Jonatha A., et al. César Chávez. McHargue, D., illus. 2007. (Biografías Gráficas (Graphic Biographies) Ser.). (SPA.). 32p. (gr. 5-8). lib. bdg. 27.00 *(978-0-8368-7879-0(5))* Stevens, Gareth Publishing LLLP.

Brown, Monica. Lado a Lado: La Historia de Dolores Huerta y Cesar Chavez. Cepeda, Joe, illus. 2010.Tr. of Side by Side - The Story of Dolores Huerta & Cesar Chavez. (SPA & ENG.). 32p. (J). (gr. -1-3). 16.99 *(978-0-06-122781-3(1),* Rayo) HarperCollins Pubs.

Bryan, Nichol. Mexican Americans, 1 vol. 2004. (One Nation Set 1 Ser.). (ENG.). 32p. (gr. k-6). 27.07 *(978-1-57765-987-7(2),* Checkerboard Library) ABDO Publishing Co.

Cesar Chavez, Lider Laboral. 2003. pap. 48.95 *(978-0-8136-9205-0(9))* Modern Curriculum Pr.

Charlesworth, Eric. Easy Reader Biographies: Cesar Chavez: A Leader for Change. 2007. (ENG.). 16p. pap. 2.99 *(978-0-439-77416-1(0),* Teaching Resources) Scholastic, Inc.

Collard, Sneed B., III. Cesar Chavez: The Farm Workers' Best Friend. 2009. (American Heroes Ser.). 48p. (gr. 3-18). 29.93 *(978-0-7614-4055-0(0))* Marshall Cavendish Corp.

Collins, David R. Cesar Chavez. 2005. (Just the Facts Biographies Ser.). (Illus.). 112p. (J). (gr. 6-12). 27.93 *(978-0-8225-2248-5(9))* Lerner Publishing Group.

Cruz, Bárbara C. Cesar Chavez: A Voice for Farmworkers. 2005. (Latino Biography Library). (Illus.). 128p. (J). (gr. 6-13). lib. bdg. 33.27 *(978-0-7660-2489-2(X))* Enslow Pubs., Inc.

Cruz, Bárbara C. César Chávez: Civil Rights Activist. 2016. (Influential Latinos Ser.). (ENG.). 128p. (J). (gr. 7-8). lib. bdg. 37.27 *(978-0-7660-7179-7(0))* Enslow Pubs., Inc.

Cuesta, Vivian. It Can Be Done: The Life & Legacy of César Chávez. 2003. (ENG., Illus.). 32p. (J). (gr. 6-8). pap. 8.47 net. *(978-0-7652-3271-7(5),* Celebration Pr.) Pearson Schl.

Deiters, Erika & Deiters, Jim. The Mexican Community in America. 2003. (J). *(978-1-58417-030-3(1));* pap. *(978-1-58417-092-1(1))* Lake Street Pubs.

DePietro, Frank. Mexican Americans. 2013. (Illus.). 64p. (J). pap. *(978-1-4222-2345-1(0))* Mason Crest.

—Mexican Americans. Limón, José E., ed. 2012. (Hispanic Americans: Major Minority Ser.). (Illus.). 64p. (J). (gr. 4). 22.95 *(978-1-4222-2328-4(0))* Mason Crest.

Dunn, Joeming W. Cesar Chavez, 1 vol. Espinosa, Rod, illus. 2008. (Bio-Graphics Ser.). (ENG.). 32p. (gr. 3-5). 28.50 *(978-1-60270-172-4(5),* Graphic Planet- Nonfiction) ABDO Publishing Co.

Ebon Research Systems Staff. Dare to Be... A Hero Vol. 3: Cesar Chavez. I.t. ed. 2003.Tr. of Atrevete Ser... Un Heroe Cesar Chavez. (ENG & SPA., Illus.). 16p. (J). 3.99 *(978-0-9648313-6-0(8))* Ebon Research Systems Publishing, LLC.

Eddy, Susan & National Geographic Learning Staff. Cesar Chavez. 2010. (Rise & Shine Ser.). (ENG., Illus.). 32p. (C). (gr. 1-2). pap. 7.95 *(978-0-516-27923-7(8))* National Geographic School Publishing, Inc.

Feinstein, Stephen. Lee Sobre Cesar Chavez. 2006. (I Like Biographies! Bilingual Ser.).Tr. of Read about Cesar Chavez. (ENG & SPA., Illus.). 24p. (J). (gr. -1-3). lib. bdg. 22.60 *(978-0-7660-2744-2(9),* Enslow Elementary) Enslow Pubs., Inc.

—Read about Cesar Chavez. 2004. (I Like Biographies! Ser.). (Illus.). 24p. (J). lib. bdg. 22.60 *(978-0-7660-2296-6(X))* Enslow Pubs., Inc.

Finley, Toiya Kristen. Russell Simmons. 2007. (Sharing the American Dream Ser.). 64p. (YA). (gr. 7-18). pap. 9.95 *(978-1-4222-0762-8(5))* Mason Crest.

Flynn, Jean. Henry B. Gonzalez: Rebel with a Cause. 2003. (Illus.). v, 140p. (J). 16.95 *(978-1-57168-780-7(7),* Eakin Pr.) Eakin Pr.

Frey, Wendy. Citizen Heroes. 2007. (Illus.). 68p. (J). *(978-1-4105-0888-1(9)); (978-1-4105-0887-4(0))* Johnston, Don Inc.

Gallegos, Yuliana. Mi Sueno de America/My American Dream. Baeza, Georgina, tr. 2009. (ENG & SPA., Illus.). 55p. (J). (gr. 4-7). pap. 9.95 *(978-1-55885-534-2(3),* Piñata Books) Arte Publico Pr.

Gelletly, LeeAnne. Mexican Immigration. 2005. (Changing Face of North America Ser.). (Illus.). 112p. (YA). lib. bdg. 24.95 *(978-1-59084-680-3(X))* Mason Crest.

Gnojewski, Carol. Celebrating Cinco de Mayo. 2012. (Celebrating Holidays Ser.). (Illus.). 48p. (J). (gr. 3-4). pap. 8.95 *(978-1-59845-399-7(8),* Enslow Elementary) Enslow Pubs., Inc.

Gotsch, Patrice. Cesar Chavez: Changing Lives. Arreola, Gil, illus. 2006. 19p. pap. 6.30 *(978-1-55501-780-4(0))* Ballard & Tighe Pubs.

Grande, Reyna. The Distance Between Us: A Memoir. 2017. (ENG., Illus.). 336p. (J). (gr. 5-9). pap. 7.99 ***(978-1-4814-6370-6(5),*** Aladdin) Simon & Schuster Children's Publishing.

—The Distance Between Us: A Memoir. 2016. (ENG., Illus.). 336p. (J). (gr. 5-9). 17.99 *(978-1-4814-6371-3(3),* Simon & Schuster/Paula Wiseman Bks.) Simon & Schuster/Paula Wiseman Bks.

Guzman, Lila & Guzman, Rick. Cesar Chavez: Fighting for Fairness. 2006. (Famous Latinos Ser.). (Illus.). 32p. (J). (gr. 3-7). lib. bdg. 22.60 *(978-0-7660-2370-3(2),* Enslow Elementary) Enslow Pubs., Inc.

Hernández, Roger E. 1898 to World War II. 2009. (Hispanic America 2 Ser.). 80p. (gr. 5). 34.21 *(978-0-7614-4176-2(X))* Marshall Cavendish Corp.

Herrera, Juan Felipe. El Canto de las Palomas/Calling the Doves. 2004. (Illus.). (J). (gr. 3-6). spiral bd. *(978-0-616-14607-1(8))* Canadian National Institute for the Blind/Institut National Canadien pour les Aveugles.

—The Upside down Boy. Gómez, Elizabeth, illus. 2011. (Rise & Shine Ser.).Tr. of Nino de Cabeza. (SPA & ENG.). 32p. (C). (gr. k-3). per. 14.95 *(978-0-89239-217-9(7))* National Geographic School Publishing, Inc.

Honders, Christine. Mexican American Rights Movement. 2016. (Civic Participation: Working for Civil Rights Ser.). 00032p. (J). (gr. 5-5). pap. 10.00 *(978-1-4994-2684-7(4),* PowerKids Pr.) Rosen Publishing Group, Inc., The.

Ingram, Scott. Mexican Americans. 2006. (World Almanac Library of American Immigration). (Illus.). 48p. (gr. 5-12). lib. bdg. 31.00 *(978-0-8368-7316-0(5),* Gareth Stevens Secondary Library) Stevens, Gareth Publishing LLLP.

Juarez, Christine. Cesar Chavez. 2016. (Great Hispanic & Latino Americans Ser.). (ENG.). 24p. (gr. k-1). lib. bdg. 21.99 *(978-1-5157-1892-5(1),* Pebble Bks.) Capstone Press of Coughlan Cos.

—Hector P. Garcia. 2016. (Great Hispanic & Latino Americans Ser.). (ENG.). 24p. (gr. k-1). lib. bdg. 21.99 *(978-1-5157-1891-8(3),* Pebble Bks.) Capstone Press of Coughlan Cos.

—José Antonio Navarro. 2016. (Great Hispanic & Latino Americans Ser.). (ENG.). 24p. (gr. k-1). lib. bdg. 21.99 *(978-1-5157-1889-5(1),* Pebble Bks.) Capstone Press of Coughlan Cos.

Keedle, Jayne. Mexican Americans. 2009. (New Americans Ser.). 80p. (gr. 5). 35.64 *(978-0-7614-4307-0(X))* Marshall Cavendish Corp.

Kent, Deborah. Mario Molina: Chemist & Nobel Prize Winner. 2004. (Proud Heritage: the Hispanic Library). (ENG., Illus.). 40p. (J). (gr. 3-6). 29.93 *(978-1-59296-170-2(3),* 200011) Child's World, Inc., The.

Kirkpatrick, Rob. Oscar de la Hoya: Boxeador de Medalla de Oro (Gold-Medal Boxer) 2009. (Grandes Idolos (Hot Shots) Ser.). (SPA.). 24p. (gr. 1-1). 42.50 *(978-1-61512-738-2(0),* Editorial Buenas Letras) Rosen Publishing Group, Inc., The.

—Oscar de la Hoya: Gold-Medal Boxer / Boxeador de Medalla de Oro. 2009. (Hot Shots/Grandes ídolos Ser.). (ENG & SPA.). 24p. (gr. 1-1). 42.50 *(978-1-61513-416-8(6),* Editorial Buenas Letras) Rosen Publishing Group, Inc., The.

—Oscar de la Hoya, Gold Medal Boxer/Boxeador de Medalla de Oro. De Leon, Mauricio Velzaquez, tr. 2008. (Reading Power Ser.). (ENG., Illus.). 24p. (gr. 1-6). per. 8.85 *(978-0-8239-6211-2(3))* Rosen Publishing Group, Inc., The.

Krull, Kathleen. Cosechando Esperanza: La Historia de César Chávez. Campoy, F. Isabel & Flor Ada, Alma, trs. Morales, Yuyi, illus. 2004. (SPA & ENG.). 48p. (J). (gr. -1-3). pap. 7.99 *(978-0-15-205169-3(4))* Houghton Mifflin Harcourt Publishing Co.

—Harvesting Hope: The Story of Cesar Chavez. Morales, Yuyi, illus. 2003. (ENG.). 48p. (J). (gr. -1-3). 17.99 *(978-0-15-201437-7(3))* Houghton Mifflin Harcourt Publishing Co.

Lieurance, Suzanne. Mexico: A MyReportLinks. com Book. 2004. (Top Ten Countries of Recent Immigrants Ser.). (Illus.). 48p. (J). lib. bdg. 26.60 *(978-0-7660-5177-5(3),* MyReportLinks.com Bks.) Enslow Pubs., Inc.

Magoon, Kekla. Cesar Chavez: Crusader for Labor Rights, 1 vol. 2010. (Essential Lives Set 5 Ser.). (ENG., Illus.). 112p. (J). (gr. 6-12). lib. bdg. 35.64 *(978-1-61613-512-6(3))* ABDO Publishing Co.

Marcovitz, Hal. Mexican Americans. (Successful Americans Ser.). 64p. (YA). 2009. (gr. 9-12). 22.95 *(978-1-4222-0515-0(0))* 2007. (gr. 7-18). pap. 9.95 *(978-1-4222-0865-6(6))* Mason Crest.

—Pat Mora. 2007. (Who Wrote That? Ser.). (Illus.). 135p. (gr. 6-12). lib. bdg. 35.00 *(978-0-7910-9528-7(2),* Chelsea Hse.) Facts On File, Inc.

Martinez, Diana Davila. A School Named for Someone Like Me (Una Escuela Con un Nombre Como ell Mio) (Illus.).

48p. (YA). (gr. 3-8). pap. 7.95 *(978-1-55885-334-8(0)*, Piñata Books) Arte Publico Pr.
Marvis, Barbara J. Selena. 2003. (Blue Banner Biography Ser.). (Illus.). 32p. (J). (gr. 3-8). lib. bdg. 25.70 *(978-1-58415-226-2(5))* Mitchell Lane Pubs., Inc.
Mattern, Joanne. Celebrate Cinco de Mayo. 2006. (Celebrate Holidays Ser.). (Illus.). 104p. (J). (gr. 5-6). lib. bdg. 33.27 *(978-0-7660-2579-0(9))* Enslow Pubs., Inc.
Medina, Jane & National Geographic Learning Staff. Tomás Rivera. Martinez, Edward, illus. 2004. (Green Light Readers Level 2 Ser.). (ENG.). 24p. (J). (gr. -1-3). pap. 3.95 *(978-0-15-205145-7(7)*, HMH Books For Young Readers) Houghton Mifflin Harcourt Publishing Co.
Miklowitz, Gloria. Cesar Chavez. 2009. pap. 13.25 *(978-1-60559-056-1(8))* Hameray Publishing Group, Inc.
Miklowitz, Gloria D. César Chávez. 2004. (ENG., Illus.). 29p. (J). (gr. 2-5). pap. 5.97 net. *(978-0-7685-1215-1(8)*, Dominie Elementary) Pearson Schl.
Moreno, Barry. The Mexican Americans. (Major American Immigration Ser.). (YA). 2010. (Illus.). 64p. (gr. 9-12). 22.95 *(978-1-4222-0614-0(9))* 2007. pap. 9.95 *(978-1-4222-0681-2(5))* Mason Crest.
Parker, Lewis K. Why Mexican Immigrants Came to America. (Coming to America Ser.). 24p. 2009. (gr. 2-3). 42.50 *(978-1-61511-887-8(X))* 2003. (Illus.). (J). lib. bdg. 22.60 *(978-0-8239-6459-8(0))* Rosen Publishing Group, Inc., The. (PowerKids Pr.).
Peppas, Lynn. Why Martín de Léon Matters to Texas. 2014. (Illus.). 32p. (J). lib. bdg. 26.25 *(978-1-4777-0916-0(9))* Rosen Publishing Group, Inc., The.
Randolph, Joanne. The Angel of Goliad: Francisca Alvarez & the Texas War for Independence. 2009. (Great Moments in American History Ser.). 32p. (gr. 3-3). 47.90 *(978-1-61513-151-8(5))* Rosen Publishing Group, Inc., The.
Rice, Liz. Bill Richardson. (Sharing the American Dream Ser.). 64p. (YA). (gr. 7-12). 2009. 22.95 *(978-1-4222-0589-1(4))* 2007. pap. 9.95 *(978-1-4222-0761-1(7))* Mason Crest.
Rinaldo, Denise. Cesar Chavez: With a Discussion of Compassion. 2003. (Values in Action Ser.). (J). *(978-1-59203-064-4(5))* Learning Challenge, Inc.
Ruiz, José. Mexican Immigrants. 2017. (Illus.). 112p. (J). ***(978-1-4222-3679-6(X))*** Mason Crest.
Sanna, Ellyn. Mexican Americans' Role in the United States: A History of Pride, a Future of Hope. 2007. (Hispanic Heritage Ser.). (Illus.). 112p. (YA). (gr. 4-7). lib. bdg. 22.95 *(978-1-59084-926-2(4))* Mason Crest.
Seidman, David. Cesar Chavez: Labor Leader. 2004. (Great Life Stories Ser.). (ENG., Illus.). 127p. (J). 30.50 *(978-0-531-12319-5(7)*, Watts, Franklin) Scholastic Library Publishing.
Seymour, Isobel. I am Mexican American. (Our American Family Ser.). 24p. 2009. (gr. 2-3). 42.50 *(978-1-60851-149-5(9))* 2004. (J). 22.60 *(978-1-4042-2907-5(8))* Rosen Publishing Group, Inc., The. (PowerKids Pr.).
Shane, C. J. The Mexicans. 2005. pap. 22.45 *(978-0-7377-2157-7(X)*, Greenhaven Pr., Inc.) Cengage Gale.
Soto, Gary. Cesar Chavez: A Hero for Everyone. Lohstoeter, Lori, illus. 2003. (Milestone Ser.). (ENG.). 80p. (J). (gr. 2-5). pap. 6.99 *(978-0-689-85922-9(8)*, Simon & Schuster/Paula Wiseman Bks.) Simon & Schuster/Paula Wiseman Bks.
Tait, Leia. Cinco de Mayo. (American Celebrations Ser.). (Illus.). 24p. (J). (gr. 3-5). 2010. pap. 11.95 *(978-1-60596-934-3(6))* 2010. lib. bdg. 25.70 *(978-1-60596-776-9(9))* 2006. lib. bdg. 24.45 *(978-1-59036-460-4(0))* 2006. per. 8.95 *(978-1-59036-463-5(5))* Weigl Pubs., Inc.
Thompson, E. L. Cesar Chavez, with Profiles of Terence V. Powderly & Dolores Huerta. 2006. (Biographical Connections Ser.). (Illus.). 112p. (J). *(978-0-7166-1827-0(3))* World Bk., Inc.
Tol, Alex Van & National Geographic Learning Staff. Dolores Huerta: Voice for the Working Poor. 2010. (ENG., Illus.). 112p. (J). pap. *(978-0-7787-2545-9(6))* Crabtree Publishing Co.
Van Tol, Alex. Dolores Huerta: Voice for the Working Poor. 2010. (Crabtree Groundbreaker Biographies Ser.). (ENG., Illus.). 112p. (J). (gr. 5-8). lib. bdg. *(978-0-7787-2536-7(7))* Crabtree Publishing Co.
Wadsworth, Ginger. Cesar Chavez. Schroeder, Mark, illus. 2005. (Yo Solo - Biografías (on My Own - Biographies) Ser.). (SPA.). 48p. (J). (gr. 2-4). per. 6.95 *(978-0-8225-3125-8(9))* Lerner Publishing Group.
—Cesar Chavez. 2005. (On My Own Biography Ser.). (Illus.). 48p. (J). 25.26 *(978-1-57505-652-4(6)*, Carolrhoda Bks.) Lerner Publishing Group.
—Cesar Chavez. Schroder, Mark, illus. 2005. (On My Own Biography Ser.). (ENG.). 48p. (gr. 2-4). pap. 6.95 *(978-1-57505-826-9(X))* Lerner Publishing Group.
—César Chávez. Fitzpatrick, Julia, tr. from ENG. Schroder, Mark, illus. 2005. (Yo Solo: Biografías (on My Own Biographies) Ser.). (SPA.). 48p. (gr. 2-4). lib. bdg. 25.26 *(978-0-8225-3124-1(0)*, Ediciones Lerner) Lerner Publishing Group.
Warren, Sarah E. Dolores Huerta: A Hero to Migrant Workers, 0 vols. Casilla, Robert, illus. 2012. (ENG.). 32p. (J). (gr. 2-5). 17.99 *(978-0-7614-6107-4(8)*, 9780761461074, Amazon Children's Publishing) Amazon Publishing.
Warrick, Karen Clemens. Sandra Cisneros: Inspiring Latina Author. 2009. (Latino Biography Library). (Illus.). 128p. (J). (gr. 6-18). lib. bdg. 33.27 *(978-0-7660-3162-3(4))* Enslow Pubs., Inc.
Webster, Christine. Sandra Cisneros: My Favorite Writer. 2008. (J). 29.05 *(978-1-59036-933-3(5))* Weigl Pubs., Inc.
Wheeler, Jill C. Cesar Chavez. 2003. (Breaking Barriers Ser.). 64p. (gr. 3-8). 27.07 *(978-1-57765-905-1(8)*, Abdo & Daughters) ABDO Publishing Co.
World Book, Inc Staff, contrib. by. !Feliz Navidad¡: Celebrating a Mexican Christmas. 2015. 80p. (J). *(978-0-7166-0830-1(8))* World Bk., Inc.
Worth, Richard. Mexican Immigrants. 2004. (Immigration to the United States Ser.). (Illus.). 96p. (gr. 4-9). 35.00 *(978-0-8160-5690-3(0))* Facts On File, Inc.
—The Texas War of Independence. 2008. (Hispanic America Ser.). 80p. (gr. 5-18). lib. bdg. 34.21 *(978-0-7614-2934-0(4)*, Benchmark Bks.) Marshall Cavendish Corp.
Young, Jeff C. Cesar Chavez. 2007. (American Workers Ser.). (Illus.). 160p. (J). (gr. 3-7). lib. bdg. 27.95 *(978-1-59935-036-3(X))* Reynolds, Morgan Inc.

MEXICAN AMERICANS—FICTION

Abraham, Susan Gonzales & Abraham, Denise Gonzales. Surprising Cecilia. 2005. (Latino Fiction for Young Adults Ser.). (ENG., Illus.). 216p. (J). (gr. -1-7). 16.95 *(978-0-938317-96-8(2))* Cinco Puntos Pr.
Alegria, Malin. Cruzar el Límite (Crossing the Boundary) 2012. (Border Town (Spanish) Ser.: 1). (SPA.). lib. bdg. 16.00 *(978-0-606-26239-2(3)*, Turtleback) Turtleback Bks.
—Estrella's Quinceañera. (ENG.). (YA). (gr. 7-18). 2007. 288p. pap. 10.99 *(978-0-689-87810-7(9))* 2006. (Illus.). 272p. 15.99 *(978-0-689-87809-1(5))* Simon & Schuster Bks. For Young Readers. (Simon & Schuster Bks. For Young Readers).
—Guerra de Quinceaneras (Quince Clash) 2013. (Border Town (Spanish) Ser.: 2). (SPA.). lib. bdg. 16.00 *(978-0-606-32401-4(1)*, Turtleback) Turtleback Bks.
—Sofi Mendoza's Guide to Getting Lost in Mexico. 2008. (ENG.). 304p. (YA). (gr. 7). pap. 10.99 *(978-0-689-87812-1(5)*, Simon & Schuster Bks. For Young Readers) Simon & Schuster Bks. For Young Readers.
Alexander, William. Ambassador. 2015. (ENG.). 256p. (J). (gr. 3-7). pap. 7.99 *(978-1-4424-9765-8(3)*, McElderry, Margaret K. Bks.) McElderry, Margaret K. Bks.
—Nomad. 2015. (ENG., Illus.). 272p. (J). (gr. 3-7). 16.99 *(978-1-4424-9767-2(X)*, McElderry, Margaret K. Bks.) McElderry, Margaret K. Bks.
Alvarez, Julia. Devolver Al Remitente. 2010.Tr. of Return to Sender. (SPA & ENG.). 368p. (J). (gr. 3-7). 7.99 *(978-0-375-85124-7(0)*, Yearling) Random Hse. Children's Bks.
—How Tía Lola Ended up Starting Over. 2012. (Tía Lola Stories Ser.). (ENG.). 160p. (J). (gr. 3-7). pap. 6.99 *(978-0-375-87320-1(1)*, Yearling) Random Hse. Children's Bks.
Anaya, Rudolfo A. The Santero's Miracle: A Bilingual Story. Lamadrid, Enrique R., tr. Córdova, Amy, illus. 2004. (ENG & SPA.). 32p. (J). 19.95 *(978-0-8263-2847-2(4))* Univ. of New Mexico Pr.
Aragón, Carla, et al. Dance of the Eggshells: Baile de los Cascarones. Saville, Kathy Dee, illus. 2010. (SPA & ENG.). 32p. (J). (gr. 1). 18.95 *(978-0-8263-4770-1(3))* Univ. of New Mexico Pr.
Armas, Teresa. Remembering Grandma / Recordando a Abuela. Ventura, Gabriela Baeza, tr. from ENG. Rodriguez Howard, Pauline, illus. 2003. (ENG & SPA.). 32p. (J). 16.95 *(978-1-55885-344-7(8)*, Piñata Books) Arte Publico Pr.
Baca, Ana. Benito's Sopaipillas/Las Sopaipillas de Benito. Villarroel, Carolina, tr. Accardo, Anthony, illus. 2007. (ENG & SPA.). 32p. (J). (gr. -1-2). 16.95 *(978-1-55885-370-6(7)*, Piñata Books) Arte Publico Pr.
—Chiles for Benito (Chiles para Benito) Colin, Jose Juan, tr. Accardo, Anthony, illus. (ENG & SPA.). 32p. (J). 16.95 *(978-1-55885-389-8(8)*, Piñata Books) Arte Publico Pr.
—Tía's Tamales. Chilton, Noel, illus. (ENG & SPA.). 32p. 2012. (J). pap. 16.95 *(978-0-8263-5027-5(5))* 2011. (YA). (gr. 4-18). 16.95 *(978-0-8263-5026-8(7))* Univ. of New Mexico Pr.
Banks, Anna. Joyride. 2015. (ENG.). 288p. (YA). (gr. 7). 17.99 *(978-1-250-03961-3(4)*, 9781250039613) Feiwel & Friends.
Belford, Bibi. Canned & Crushed. 2015. (ENG.). 192p. (J). (gr. 2-7). 14.99 *(978-1-63220-435-6(5)*, Sky Pony Pr.) Skyhorse Publishing Co., Inc.
Bertrand, Diane Gonzales. Cecilia & Miguel Are Best Friends. Ventura, Gabriela Baeza, tr. Muraida, Thelma, illus. 2014.Tr. of Cecilia y Miguel Son Mejores Amigos. (SPA & ENG.). 32p. (J). 17.95 *(978-1-55885-794-0(X))* Arte Publico Pr.
—The Empanadas That Abuela Made/Las Empandas Que Hacia la Abuela. Ventura, Gabriela Baeza, tr. DeLange, Alex Pardo, illus. (ENG & SPA.). 32p. (J). 16.95 *(978-1-55885-388-1(X)*, Piñata Books) Arte Publico Pr.
—El Momento de Trino. Sanmiguel, Rosario, tr. from ENG. 2006. (SPA.). 181p. (J). (gr. 3-7). per. 9.95 *(978-1-55885-473-4(8)*, Piñata Books) Arte Publico Pr.
—Sip, Slurp, Soup, Soup/Caldo, Caldo, Caldo. Castilla, Julia Mercedes, tr. Delange, Alex Pardo, illus. 2008. (SPA & ENG.). 32p. (J). (gr. -1-2). pap. 7.95 *(978-1-55885-241-9(7)*, Piñata Books) Arte Publico Pr.
—Sip, Slurp, Soup Soup/Caldo Caldo Caldo: CD & Book Set. DeLange, Alex Pardo, illus. 2008. 32p. (J). pap. 19.95 *(978-0-9815686-1-4(0))* Lorito Bks., Inc.
Billingsley, ReShonda Tate. Friends 'Til the End. 2009. (Good Girlz Ser.: 6). (ENG., Illus.). 208p. pap. 11.00 *(978-1-4165-5877-4(2)*, Gallery Bks.) Gallery Bks.
Brammer, Ethriam Cash. My Tata's Guitar / la guitarra de mi Tata. Lechon, Daniel, illus. (ENG & SPA.). 32p. (J). 16.95 *(978-1-55885-369-0(3)*, Piñata Books) Arte Publico Pr.
—The Rowdy, Rowdy Ranch / Alla en el Rancho Grande. Cruz, D. Nina, illus. 2003. (ENG & SPA.). 32p. (J). 16.95 *(978-1-55885-409-3(6)*, Piñata Books) Arte Publico Pr.
Brightwood, Laura, illus. Growing up in East L. A. Brightwood, Laura, . 2006. (J). *(978-0-9779290-8-5(6))* 3-C Institute for Social Development.
Brooks, Melanie & Spenser and Mom Staff. Spenser Goes to el Paso. Jacobsen, Amie, illus. 2010. (SpenserNation Ser.). 32p. (J). 14.95 *(978-0-9817598-3-8(1))* Simple Fish Bk. Co., LLC.
Brown, Monica. Butterflies on Carmen Street/Mariposas en la Calle Carmen. Ward, April, illus. 2007. (SPA & ENG.). 32p. (J). (gr. -1-2). 16.95 *(978-1-55885-484-0(3)*, Piñata Books) Arte Publico Pr.
Camper, Cathy. Low Riders in Space. Raúl, III, illus. 2014. (ENG & SPA.). 112p. (J). (gr. 3-7). pap. 9.99 *(978-1-4521-2869-6(3))*;Bk. 1. 22.99 *(978-1-4521-2155-0(9))* Chronicle Bks. LLC.
—Lowriders to the Center of the Earth. 2016. (ENG., Illus.). 128p. (J). (gr. 3-7). 22.99 *(978-1-4521-2343-1(8))* Chronicle Bks. LLC.
Campos, Tito. Muffler Man el Hombre Mofle. Alvarez, Lamberto, illus. 2009. 32p. (J). pap. 7.95 *(978-1-55885-557-1(2)*, Piñata Books) Arte Publico Pr.
Canales, Viola. The Tequila Worm. 2007. (ENG., Illus.). 208p. (YA). (gr. 7-11). pap. 7.99 *(978-0-375-84089-0(3)*, Lamb, Wendy Bks.) Random Hse. Children's Bks.
Castan, Mike. Fighting for Dontae. 2012. (ENG.). 144p. (YA). 16.95 *(978-0-8234-2348-4(4))* Holiday Hse., Inc.
—The Price of Loyalty. 2011. (ENG., Illus.). 256p. (YA). (gr. 7-18). 17.95 *(978-0-8234-2268-5(2))* Holiday Hse., Inc.
Castilla, Julia Mercedes. Strange Parents. 2009. 144p. (J). (gr. 6-18). pap. 9.95 *(978-1-55885-590-8(4)*, Piñata Books) Arte Publico Pr.
Center for Learning Network Staff. The House on Mango Street: Curriculum Unit. 2005. (Novel Ser.). (YA). tchr. ed., spiral bd. 19.95 *(978-1-56077-783-0(4))* Center for Learning, The.
Cervantes, Jennifer. Tortilla Sun. 2014. (ENG.). 224p. (J). (gr. 3-7). pap. 6.99 *(978-1-4521-3150-4(3))* Chronicle Bks. LLC.
Chambers, Veronica. The Go-Between. 2017. (ENG.). 208p. (YA). (gr. 7). 16.99 ***(978-1-101-93095-3(0)**, Delacorte Pr.)* Random Hse. Children's Bks.
Conkling, Winifred. Sylvia & Aki. (ENG.). 160p. (J). 2013. (gr. 4-7). 6.99 *(978-1-58246-345-2(X)*, Yearling) 2011. (Illus.). (gr. 3-7). 16.99 *(978-1-58246-337-7(9)*, Tricycle Pr.) Random Hse. Children's Bks.
Contreras, Kathleen & Lindmark, Margaret. Sweet Memories/Dulces Recuerdos. Lindmark, Margaret, illus. 2014. (SPA & ENG., Illus.). 32p. (J). (gr. 2-4). pap. 14.99 *(978-1-933032-91-7(X))* Lectorum Pubns., Inc.
Costales, Amy. Sundays on Fourth Street/Los Domingos en la Calle Cuatro. Jerome, Elaine, illus. 2009. (SPA & ENG.). 32p. (J). (gr. -1-3). 16.95 *(978-1-55885-520-5(3))* Arte Publico Pr.
Cox, Judy. Carmen Learns English. Dominguez, Angela N., illus. 2010. (ENG.). 32p. (J). (gr. -1-3). 16.95 *(978-0-8234-2174-9(0))* Holiday Hse., Inc.
Cruz, Maria Colleen. Border Crossing. 2003. 128p. (J). pap. 9.95 *(978-1-55885-405-5(3)*, Piñata Books) Arte Publico Pr.
—Border Crossing. 2006. 122p. (gr. 8-12). 19.95 *(978-0-7569-6587-7(X))* Perfection Learning Corp.
De Anda, Diane. Kikiriki / Quiquiriquí. Hernández, Karina, tr. from ENG. Lechón, Daniel, illus. 2004. (ENG & SPA.). 32p. 16.95 *(978-1-55885-382-9(0)*, Piñata Books) Arte Publico Pr.
De la Peña, Matt. The Hunted. 2015. (ENG.). 384p. (YA). (gr. 9). lib. bdg. 20.99 *(978-0-375-98992-6(7)*, Delacorte Pr.) Random Hse. Children's Bks.
—The Living. (ENG.). (YA). (gr. 9). 2015. 336p. pap. 9.99 *(978-0-385-74121-7(9)*, Ember) 2013. 320p. lib. bdg. 20.99 *(978-0-375-98991-9(9)*, Delacorte Pr.) Random Hse. Children's Bks.
de la Vega, Eida, tr. from ENG. Estela en el Mercado de Pulgas. Sanchez, Enrique O., illus. 2005. (SPA.). 32p. (J). (gr. -1-k). 16.95 *(978-1-58430-245-2(3))* Lee & Low Bks., Inc.
Diamond, Jill. Lou Lou & Pea & the Mural Mystery. Vamos, Lesley, illus. 2016. (ENG.). 272p. (J). 16.99 *(978-0-374-30295-5(2)*, 9780374302955, Farrar, Straus & Giroux (BYR)) Farrar, Straus & Giroux.
Dix, Catherine R. Rosetta Stones. 2009. (ENG.). 213p. pap. 14.95 *(978-0-9798452-2-2(X))* Central Ave. Pr.
Dumas Lachtman, Ofelia. Looking for la Unica. 2004. (ENG & SPA., Illus.). 190p. (J). pap. 9.95 *(978-1-55885-412-3(6)*, Piñata Books) Arte Publico Pr.
Edwards, Michelle. A Hat for Mrs. Goldman: A Story about Knitting & Love. Karas, G. Brian, illus. 2016. (ENG.). 40p. (J). (gr. -1-3). 17.99 *(978-0-553-49710-6(3)*, Schwartz & Wade Bks.) Random Hse. Children's Bks.
Elkeles, Simone. Chain Reaction. 2015. (Perfect Chemistry Novel Ser.). (ENG.). 336p. (YA). (gr. 9). pap. 9.99 *(978-1-61963-703-0(0)*, 9781619637030, Bloomsbury USA Childrens) Bloomsbury Publishing USA.
—Rules of Attraction. 2015. (Perfect Chemistry Novel Ser.). (ENG.). 352p. (YA). (gr. 9). pap. 9.99 *(978-1-61963-702-3(2)*, 9781619637023, Bloomsbury USA Childrens) Bloomsbury Publishing USA.
Elya, Susan Middleton. Al fin en Casa. Davalos, Felipe, illus. 2011.Tr. of Home at Last. (SPA.). 32p. (J). pap. 8.95 *(978-1-60060-654-0(7))* Lee & Low Bks., Inc.
—Home at Last. Dávalos, Felipe, illus. 2013. (ENG.). 32p. (J). 16.95 *(978-1-58430-020-5(5))* Lee & Low Bks., Inc.
Estevis, Anne. Chicken Foot Farm. 2008. 154p. (J). (gr. 6-18). pap. 10.95 *(978-1-55885-505-2(X)*, Piñata Books) Arte Publico Pr.
—Down Garrapata Road. 2003. 128p. (J). pap. 12.95 *(978-1-55885-397-3(9))* Arte Publico Pr.
Flor Ada, Alma. Celebrate Thanksgiving Day with Beto & Gaby. Hayes, Joe & Franco, Sharon, trs. Rueda, Claudia, illus. 2006. (Cuentos para Celebrar / Stories to Celebrate Ser.). 30p. (gr. k-6). per. 11.95 *(978-1-59820-133-8(6))* Santillana USA Publishing Co., Inc.
—I Love Saturdays y Domingos. Savadier, Elivia, illus. 2004. (ENG.). 32p. (J). (gr. -1-3). reprint ed. 7.99 *(978-0-689-87409-3(X)*, Atheneum Bks. for Young Readers) Simon & Schuster Children's Publishing.
—El Vuelo de los Colibries. Jacobson, Judith, illus. 32p. (J). (gr. 3-6). pap. 9.95 *(978-1-56492-211-3(1))* Laredo Publishing Co., Inc.
Flor Ada, Alma & Zubizarreta, Gabriel M. Con Cariño, Amalia. (SPA., Illus.). (J). (gr. 3-7). 2013. 160p. pap. 6.99 *(978-1-4424-2406-7(0))* 2012. 144p. 15.99 *(978-1-4424-2405-0(2)*, Atheneum Bks. for Young Readers) Simon & Schuster Children's Publishing.
—Dancing Home. (ENG., (J). (gr. 3-7). 2013. Illus.). 176p. pap. 7.99 *(978-1-4424-8175-6(7))* 2011. 160p. 15.99 *(978-1-4169-0088-7(8))* Simon & Schuster Children's Publishing. (Atheneum Bks. for Young Readers).
—Love, Amalia. 2012. (ENG., Illus.). 144p. (J). (gr. 3-7). 15.99 *(978-1-4424-2402-9(8)*, Atheneum Bks. for Young Readers) Simon & Schuster Children's Publishing.
—Nacer Bailando (Dancing Home) 2011. (SPA.). 160p. (J). (gr. 3-7). lib. bdg. 16.99 *(978-1-4424-2061-8(8)*, Atheneum Bks. for Young Readers) Simon & Schuster Children's Publishing.
Flores-Scott, Patrick. Jumped In. 2013. (ENG.). 304p. (YA). (gr. 7). 16.99 *(978-0-8050-9514-2(4)*, 9780805095142, Holt, Henry & Co. Bks. For Young Readers) Holt, Henry & Co.
—Jumped In. 2014. (ENG., Illus.). 304p. (YA). (gr. 7). pap. 10.99 *(978-1-250-05398-5(6)*, 9781250053985) Square Fish.
Fontes, Justine. Deadly Drive. 2013. (Surviving Southside Ser.). (ENG.). 104p. (YA). (gr. 6-12). pap. 7.95 *(978-1-4677-0704-6(X))*; lib. bdg. 27.93 *(978-1-4677-0310-9(9))* Lerner Publishing Group.
Freschet, Gina. Beto & the Bone Dance. Freschet, Gina, illus. 2005. (Illus.). 30p. (J). (gr. 4-8). reprint ed. 16.00 *(978-0-7567-8933-6(8))* DIANE Publishing Co.
Galindo, Mary Sue. Icy Watermelon/Sandia Fria. Rodriguez Howard, Pauline & Howard, Pauline Rodriguez, illus. 2008. (J). (gr. -1-2). pap. 7.95 *(978-1-55885-307-2(3)*, Piñata Books) Arte Publico Pr.
Garcia, Nasario. Grandpa Lolo & Trampa: A Story of Surprise & Mystery = Abuelito Lolo y Trampa: Un Cuento de Sorpresa y Misterio. Montoya, Jeremy, illus. 2014. (SPA & ENG.). (J). 9.99 *(978-1-936744-30-5(9))* LPD Pr.
—Grandpa Lolo's Navajo Saddle Blanket: La Tilma de Abuelito Lolo. Moeller, Richard, illus. Moeller, Richard, photos by. 2012. (J). *(978-0-8263-5078-7(X))*; (SPA.). 72p. pap. *(978-0-8263-5079-4(8))*; 61p. pap. *(978-0-8263-5080-0(1))* Univ. of New Mexico Pr.
Garcia, Nasario & Aragon, Dolores, illus. Grandpa Lolo's Matanza: A New Mexican Tradition = la Matanza de Abuelito Lolo: Una Tradición Nuevo Mexicana. 2015. (SPA & ENG.). 70p. (J). *(978-1-936744-47-3(3)*, Rio Grande Bks.) LPD Pr.
Garza, Xavier. Charro Claus & the Tejas Kid. 2008. (SPA & ENG., Illus.). 40p. (J). (gr. k-6). 17.95 *(978-1-933693-24-8(X))* Cinco Puntos Pr.
—Maximilian & the Bingo Rematch: A Lucha Libre Sequel. 2013. (Max's Lucha Libre Adventures Ser.). (ENG., Illus.). 208p. (J). (gr. 2-7). pap. 12.95 *(978-1-935955-46-7(2))* Cinco Puntos Pr.
Garza, Xavier, illus. Maximilian & the Bingo Rematch: A Lucha Libre Sequel. 2013. (Max's Lucha Libre Adventures Ser.). (ENG.). 208p. (J). 19.95 *(978-1-935955-59-7(4))* Cinco Puntos Pr.
—Maximilian & the Mystery of the Guardian Angel. 2011. (Max's Lucha Libre Adventures Ser.). (SPA & ENG.). 160p. (J). (gr. 5-8). pap. 12.95 *(978-1-933693-98-9(3))* Cinco Puntos Pr.
Garza, Xavier & Villarroel, Carolina. Zulema & the Witch Owl/Zulema y la Bruja Lechuza. Garza, Xavier, illus. 2009. (SPA & ENG., Illus.). 32p. (J). (gr. -1-4). 16.95 *(978-1-55885-515-1(7)*, Piñata Books) Arte Publico Pr.
Gates, J. Gabriel & Keel, Charlene. Ghost Crown. 2012. (Tracks Ser.). (ENG.). 456p. (YA). (gr. 6-12). pap. 9.95 *(978-0-7573-1594-7(1)*, HCI Teens) Health Communications, Inc.
Gonzalez, Genaro. A So-Called Vacation. 2009. 192p. (YA). (gr. 9-18). pap. 10.95 *(978-1-55885-545-8(9)*, Piñata Books) Arte Publico Pr.
Gonzalez, Maya Christina & Perez, Amada Irma. My Very Own Room: Mi Propio Cuartito. 2013. (ENG & SPA., Illus.). 32p. (J). (gr. k-4). pap. 9.95 *(978-0-89239-223-0(1))* Lee & Low Bks., Inc.
Griffith, Gretchen. When Christmas Feels Like Home. Farias, Carolina, illus. 2013. (ENG.). 32p. (J). (gr. -1-3). 16.99 *(978-0-8075-8872-7(5))* Whitman, Albert & Co.
Harvey, Gwen. Esperanza Means Hope. Porfirio, Guy, illus. 2010. (J). *(978-0-910037-51-8(5))*; pap. *(978-0-910037-52-5(3))* Arizona Historical Society.
Hayes, Joe. Ghost Fever (Mal de Fantasma) 2006. (ENG & SPA., Illus.). 90p. (J). (gr. 4-6). pap. 8.95 *(978-1-933693-03-3(7))* Cinco Puntos Pr.
—Ghost Fever (Mal de Fantasma) Pennypacker, Mona, illus. 2004. (ENG & SPA.). 80p. (J). (gr. 4-6). 14.95 *(978-0-938317-83-8(0))* Cinco Puntos Pr.
Herrera, Juan Felipe. Grandma & Me at the Flea: Los Meros Meros Remateros. De Lucio-Brock, Anita, illus. 2013. (ENG & SPA.). 32p. (J). pap. 9.95 *(978-0-89239-279-7(7)*, Children's Book Press) Lee & Low Bks., Inc.
Herrera, Juan Felipe & Cuevas, Ernesto, illus. Featherless. 2013.Tr. of Desplumado. (SPA & ENG.). 32p. (J). pap. 8.95 *(978-0-89239-303-9(3))* Lee & Low Bks., Inc.
Herrera, Juan Felipe & Herrera, Juan. La Superrnina del Cilantro. Robledo Tapia, Honorio, illus. 2003.Tr. of Super Cilantro Girl. (ENG & SPA.). 32p. (J). 16.95 *(978-0-89239-187-5(1))* Lee & Low Bks., Inc.
Hobbs, Will. Crossing the Wire. 2007. (ENG.). 224p. (J). (gr. 5-9). pap. 7.99 *(978-0-06-074140-2(6))* HarperCollins Pubs.
Iyengar, Malathi Michelle. Romina's Rangoli. Wanardi, Jennifer, illus. 2007. (Romina's Rangoli Ser.). 32p. (J). (gr. -1-3). 16.95 *(978-1-885008-32-9(5)*, Shen's Bks.) Lee & Low Bks., Inc.
Jiménez, Francisco. La Mariposa. Silva, Simon, illus. 2004. 38p. (J). (gr. k-4). reprint ed. pap. 14.00 *(978-0-7567-8433-1(6))* DIANE Publishing Co.
Jiménez, Francisco. Taking Hold: From Migrant Childhood to Columbia University. 2017. (ENG.). 208p. (YA). (gr. 9). pap. 8.99 ***(978-1-328-74209-4(1)**, HMH Books For Young Readers)* Houghton Mifflin Harcourt Publishing Co.
Johnson, LouAnne. Muchacho. 2011. (ENG.). 208p. (YA). (gr. 7). pap. 9.99 *(978-0-375-85903-8(9)*, Ember) Random Hse. Children's Bks.
Johnston, Tony. Any Small Goodness. Colón, Raúl, illus. 2003. (Any Small Goodness Ser.). (ENG.). 128p. (J). (gr. 2-5). per. 6.99 *(978-0-439-23384-2(4)*, Scholastic Paperbacks) Scholastic, Inc.
—Any Small Goodness: A Novel of the Barrio. Colón, Raúl, illus. 2005. (Reader's Workshop Ser.). (ENG.). 120p. (C). pap. 19.95 *(978-0-7362-2797-1(0))* CENGAGE Learning.
—My Abuelita. Morales, Yuyi, illus. 2009. (ENG.). 32p. (J). (gr. -1-3). 17.99 *(978-0-15-216330-3(1))* Houghton Mifflin Harcourt Publishing Co.
Jones, Patrick. Always Faithful. 2015. (ENG.). 112p. (YA). (gr. 6-12). lib. bdg. 27.99 *(978-1-4677-8052-0(9))*; 7.99 *(978-1-4677-9014-7(1))* Lerner Publishing Group. (Darby Creek).
Juan, Felipe Herrera. Coralito's Bay: Bahia de Coralito. 2004. (SPA & ENG.). 41p. 14.95 *(978-0-9742810-0-1(X))* Monterey Bay Sanctuary Foundation.
Korman, Susan. Overexposed. 2013. (Surviving Southside Ser.). (ENG.). 104p. (YA). (gr. 6-12). lib. bdg. 27.93 *(978-1-4677-0312-3(5))* Lerner Publishing Group.
Korman, Susan J. Overexposed. 2013. (Surviving Southside Ser.). (ENG.). 104p. (YA). (gr. 6-12). pap. 7.95 *(978-1-4677-0706-0(6)*, Darby Creek) Lerner Publishing Group.
Laínez, René Colato. From North to South/Del Norte Al Sur. Cepeda, Joe, illus. 2010.Tr. of Del norte al Sur. (ENG & SPA.). 32p. (J). (gr. k-3). 17.95 *(978-0-89239-231-5(2))* Lee & Low Bks., Inc.
Lamadrid, Enrique R. Amadito & the Hero Children: Amadito y los Ninos Heroes. Cordova, Amy, illus. 2011. (SPA & ENG.). 60p. (J). 19.95 *(978-0-8263-4979-8(X))* Univ. of New Mexico Pr.

MNO

—Amadito & the Hero Children: Amadito y Los Niños Héroes. Córdova, Amy, illus. 2011. (SPA & ENG.). (J). (978-0-8263-4980-4(3)); (978-0-8263-4978-1(1)) Univ. of New Mexico Pr.
Lozano, José. Once Around the Block (Una Vuelta a la Manzana) Crosthwaite, Luis Humberto, tr. 2009. (SPA & ENG., Illus.). 32p. (J). (gr. -1-4). 16.95 (978-1-933693-57-6(6)) Cinco Puntos Pr.
Luenn, Nancy. A Gift for Abuelita/Un Regalo para Abuelita: Celebrating the Day of the Dead/En Celebration del Dia de los Muertos. Chapman, Robert, illus. 2004.Tr. of Un Regalo para Abuelita: En Celebration del Dia de los Muertos. (ENG, SPA & MUL.). 32p. (J). (gr. k-3). 15.95 (978-0-87358-688-7(3)) Cooper Square Publishing Llc.
Lupica, Mike. Long Shot. 1 vol. 2012. (Comeback Kids Ser.). (ENG.). 192p. (J). (gr. 4-8). lib. bdg. 27.07 (978-1-59961-176-1(7)) Spotlight.
Lupita Manana. 3rd ed. (J). pap., stu. ed. (978-0-13-772500-7(0)) Prentice Hall (Schl. Div.).
Lynch, Janet Nichols. Addicted to Her. 2010. (ENG.). 256p. (YA). (gr. 7-18). pap. 17.95 (978-0-8234-2186-4(2)) Holiday Hse., Inc.
The Magic Paper (Mexicans) 76p. (YA). (gr. 6-12). pap. 9.95 (978-0-8224-3686-7(8)) Globe Fearon Educational Publishing.
Martinez, Victor. Parrot in the Oven. Scott, Steve, illus. rev. ed. 2004. (ENG.). 240p. (YA). (gr. 8-18). pap. 8.99 (978-0-06-447186-2(1), Rayo) HarperCollins Pubs.
May, Eleanor. The Best Mother's Day Ever. Pilz, M. H., illus. 2010. (Social Studies Connects Ser.). 32p. (J). (gr. 1-3). pap. 5.95 (978-1-57565-299-3(4)) Kane Press, Inc.
McCall, Guadalupe Garcia. Summer of the Mariposas. 2012. (ENG.). 352p. (YA). 19.95 (978-1-60060-900-8(7), Tu Bks.) Lee & Low Bks., Inc.
—Under the Mesquite. 2013. (ENG., Illus.). 224p. (J). (gr. 7-18). 17.95 (978-1-60060-429-4(3)) Lee & Low Bks., Inc.
Meister, Cari. Airplane Adventure. Janovitz, Marilyn, illus. 2010. (My First Graphic Novel Ser.). 32p. pap. 4.95 (978-1-4342-3602-9(1), My First Graphic Novel) Stone Arch Bks.
Mikaelsen, Ben. Sparrow Hawk Red. 2010. (ENG.). 192p. (J). (gr. 3-7). pap. 5.99 (978-1-4231-3361-2(7)) Hyperion Pr.
Mora, Pat. Una Cesta de Cumpleanos para Tia Abuela. Lang, Cecily, illus. (SPA.). (J). (gr. k-2). pap. 3.16 net. (978-0-395-78817-2(X), HMS088) Houghton Mifflin Harcourt Publishing Co.
—The Rainbow Tulip. Sayles, Elizabeth, illus. 2003. (ENG.). 32p. (J). (gr. k-3). 6.99 (978-0-14-250009-5(7), Puffin Books) Penguin Young Readers Group.
—Rainbow Tulip. 2014. 17.00 (978-1-63419-680-2(5)) Perfection Learning Corp.
—Tomas & the Library Lady. Colón, Raúl, illus. 2007. (gr. k-3). 18.00 (978-0-7569-7935-5(8)) Perfection Learning Corp.
—Tomas y la Senora de la Biblioteca. 2004. (SPA., Illus.). (J). (gr. k-3). spiral bd. (978-0-616-03092-9(4)) Canadian National Institute for the Blind/Institut National Canadien pour les Aveugles.
Mora, Pat & Martinez, Libby. I Pledge Allegiance. Barton, Patrice, illus. 2014. (ENG.). 40p. (J). (gr. -1-2). 16.99 (978-0-307-93181-8(1), Knopf Bks. for Young Readers) Random Hse. Children's Bks.
Naylor, Phyllis Reynolds. Eating Enchiladas. 0 vols. Ramsey, Marcy, illus. 2011. (Simply Sarah Ser.: 0). (ENG.). 80p. (J). (gr. 1-4). pap. 9.99 (978-0-7614-5885-2(9), 9780761458852, Amazon Children's Publishing) Amazon Publishing.
Neil Wallace, Sandra. Muckers. 2013. (ENG.). 288p. (YA). (gr. 7). 16.99 (978-0-375-86754-5(6), Knopf Bks. for Young Readers) Random Hse. Children's Bks.
Ofelia, Dumas Lachtman. Big Enough Bastante Grande. Enrique, Sanchez, illus. 2008. 32p. (J). pap. 7.95 (978-1-55885-239-6(5)) Arte Publico Pr.
O'Neill, Alexis. Estela en el Mercado de Pulgas. de la Vega, Eida, tr. from ENG. Sanchez, Enrique O., illus. 2005. (SPA.). 32p. (J). (gr. -1-k). pap. 9.95 (978-1-58430-246-9(1)) Lee & Low Bks., Inc.
O'Neill, Alexis & Sanchez, Enrique O. Estela's Swap. 1 vol. 2005. (ENG., Illus.). 32p. (J). (gr. -1-3). pap. 9.95 (978-1-60060-253-5(3)) Lee & Low Bks., Inc.
Ortega, Cristina. The Eyes of the Weaver: Los Ojos Del Tejedor. Garcia, Patricio E., illus. 2006. (ENG.). 64p. (J). 19.95 (978-0-8263-3990-4(5)) Univ. of New Mexico Pr.
Parker, Amy Christine. Smash & Grab. 2016. (ENG.). 384p. (YA). (gr. 7). 17.99 (978-0-553-53382-8(7), Random Hse. Bks. for Young Readers) Random Hse. Children's Bks.
Parra, Kelly. Graffiti Girl. 2007. (ENG.). 256p. (gr. 8-12). pap. 16.99 (978-1-4165-3461-7(X), MTV Bks.) MTV Books.
Perales, Alonso M. Brujas, Lechuzas y Espantos/Witches, Owls & Spooks. Pluecker, John, tr. from SPA. 2008. (ENG & SPA., Illus.). 96p. (J). (gr. 3-7). pap. 9.95 (978-1-55885-512-0(2), Piñata Books) Arte Publico Pr.
Pérez, Amada Irma. Mi Diario de Aquí Hasta Allá. Gonzalez, Maya Christina, illus. 2013.Tr. of My Diary from Here to There. (ENG & SPA.). 32p. (J). (gr. k). pap. 9.95 (978-0-89239-230-8(4)) Lee & Low Bks., Inc.
Perez, Amada Irma. Mi Propio Cuartito. 2004. (SPA & ENG., Illus.). (J). (gr. k-3). spiral bd. (978-0-616-14609-5(4)) Canadian National Institute for the Blind/Institut National Canadien pour les Aveugles.
Pérez, Amada Irma. Nana's Big Surprise. Gonzalez, Maya Christina, illus. 2013.Tr. of Nana, ¡Qué Sorpresa! (ENG & SPA.). 32p. (J). pap. 9.95 (978-0-89239-307-7(6), Children's Book Press) Lee & Low Bks., Inc.
Perez, Amada Irma & Children's Book Press Staff. Nana, Que Sorpresa! Gonzalez, Maya Christina, illus. 2007.Tr. of Nana's Big Surprise. (ENG & SPA.). 32p. (J). (gr. k-2). lib. bdg. 16.95 (978-0-89239-190-5(1)) Lee & Low Bks., Inc.
Pérez, Ashley Hope. Out of Darkness. 2015. (ENG., Illus.). 408p. (YA). (gr. 8-12). 18.99 (978-1-4677-4202-3(3), Carolrhoda Lab™) Lerner Publishing Group.
—What Can't Wait. 2011. (Carolrhoda YA Ser.). (ENG.). 240p. (YA). (gr. 9-12). 17.95 (978-0-7613-6155-8(3), Carolrhoda Bks.) Lerner Publishing Group.
Pérez, Celia C. The First Rule of Punk. 2017. (ENG., Illus.). 336p. (J). (gr. 4-7). 16.99 **(978-0-425-29040-8(9)**, Viking Books for Young Readers) Penguin Young Readers Group.
Peschke, Marci. Daisy & the Spring Dance. 1 vol., Bk. 6. Pilz, M. H., illus. 2011. (Growing up Daisy Ser.). (ENG.). 80p. (gr. 3-8). 27.07 (978-1-61641-119-0(8), Calico Chapter Bks) Magic Wagon.
—Daisy for President. 1 vol., Bk. 2. Pilz, M. H., illus. 2011. (Growing up Daisy Ser.). (ENG.). 80p. (gr. 3-8). 27.07 (978-1-61641-115-2(5), Calico Chapter Bks) Magic Wagon.
—Daisy Has the Holiday Blues. 1 vol., Bk. 5. Pilz, MH, illus. 2011. (Growing up Daisy Ser.). (ENG.). 80p. (gr. 3-8). 27.07 (978-1-61641-118-3(X), Calico Chapter Bks) Magic Wagon.
—Daisy's Fall Festival. 1 vol., Bk. 4. Pilz, M. H., illus. 2011. (Growing up Daisy Ser.). (ENG.). 80p. (gr. 3-8). 27.07 (978-1-61641-117-6(1), Calico Chapter Bks) Magic Wagon.
—Daisy's Field Trip Adventure. 1 vol., Bk. 3. Pilz, M. H., illus. 2011. (Growing up Daisy Ser.). (ENG.). 80p. (gr. 3-8). 27.07 (978-1-61641-116-9(3), Calico Chapter Bks) Magic Wagon.
—Daisy's Summer Essay. 1 vol., Bk. 1. Pilz, M. H., illus. 2011. (Growing up Daisy Ser.). (ENG.). 80p. (gr. 3-8). 27.07 (978-1-61641-114-5(7), Calico Chapter Bks) Magic Wagon.
Price, Mara & Ventura, Gabriela Baeza. Grandma's Chocolate/El Chocolate de Abuelita. Fields, Lisa, illus. 2010. (SPA.). 32p. (J). (gr. -1-3). 16.95 (978-1-55885-587-8(4), Piñata Books) Arte Publico Pr.
Quintero, Isabel. Gabi, a Girl in Pieces. 2014. (ENG.). 208p. (J). pap. 11.95 (978-1-935955-95-5(0)); (YA). 17.95 (978-1-935955-94-8(2)) Cinco Puntos Pr.
Resau, Laura. Estrella en el Bosque (Star in the Forest) 2016. (ENG & SPA.). 160p. (J). (gr. 2-5). 18.40 (978-0-606-39132-0(0)) Turtleback Bks.
—Star in the Forest. 2012. (ENG.). 160p. (J). (gr. 2-5). 6.99 (978-0-375-85410-1(X), Yearling) Random Hse. Children's Bks.
Rice, David. Crazy Loco. 2008. 135p. 16.00 (978-0-7569-8951-4(5)) Perfection Learning Corp.
Rice, David & Garcia, Mike D. Heart-Shaped Cookies. 2011. (YA). pap. (978-1-931010-79-5(X)) Bilingual Pr./Editorial Bilingue.
Rivera-Ashford, Roni Capin & Johnson, Richard. Hip Hip Hooray, It's Monsoon Day! 2007. (ENG & SPA.). (YA). pap. 15.95 (978-1-886679-36-8(3)) Arizona Sonora Desert Museum Pr.
Rodriguez, Emma Vera & Scogin, Connie. Blanca Rosa's Quinceaner. 2011. 34p. pap. 13.50 (978-1-60911-444-2(2), Eloquent Bks.) Strategic Book Publishing & Rights Agency (SBPRA).
Romeyn, Debra. Passage to Monterey. May, Dan, tr. May, Dan, illus. 2003. (Adventures of Juan & Mariano Ser.: No. 1). 39p. (J). pap. 9.95 (978-0-9729016-0-4(4)) Gossamer Bks.
Ruiz, Joseph J. Angel on Daniel's Shoulder. 2004. (SPA & ENG., Illus.). 108p. (J). pap. 12.95 (978-0-86534-402-0(7)) Sunstone Pr.
—Manuel & the Magic Ring. 2003. (SPA & ENG., Illus.). 108p. (J). pap. 12.95 (978-0-86534-399-3(3)) Sunstone Pr.
Ryan, Pam Muñoz. Becoming Naomi Leon. 2005. (ENG.). 272p. (J). (gr. 3-7). reprint ed. per. 7.99 (978-0-439-26997-1(0), Scholastic Paperbacks) Scholastic, Inc.
—Esperanza Rising. 2005. (Reader's Workshop Ser.). (ENG.). 264p. (C). pap. 19.95 (978-0-7362-2817-6(9)) CENGAGE Learning.
Sáenz, Benjamin Alire. Aristotle & Dante Discover the Secrets of the Universe. (ENG., Illus.). 368p. (YA). (gr. 7). 2014. pap. 12.99 (978-1-4424-0893-7(6)) 2012. 21.99 (978-1-4424-0892-0(8)) Simon & Schuster Bks. For Young Readers. (Simon & Schuster Bks. For Young Readers).
—A Gift from Papa Diego: Un Regalo de Papa Diego. Garcia, Geronimo, illus. 2008. (Little Diego Book Ser.). (ENG & SPA.). 40p. (J). pap. 10.95 (978-0-938317-33-3(4)) Cinco Puntos Pr.
—He Forgot to Say Goodbye. 2008. (ENG.). 336p. (YA). (gr. 7-12). 18.99 (978-1-4169-4963-3(1), Simon & Schuster Bks. For Young Readers) Simon & Schuster Bks. For Young Readers.
—The Inexplicable Logic of My Life. 2017. (ENG.). 464p. (gr. 7). 17.99 (978-0-544-58650-5(6)) Houghton Mifflin Harcourt Publishing Co.
—La Perrita Que le Encantaban las Tortillas. Garcia, Geronimo, illus. 2009. (Little Diego Book Ser.).Tr. of Dog Who Loved Tortillas. (SPA & ENG.). 40p. (J). (gr. 1-4). 17.95 (978-1-933693-54-5(1)) Cinco Puntos Pr.
Saldaña, Jr. A Good Long Way. 2010. 128p. (J). (gr. 6-18). pap. 10.95 (978-1-55885-607-3(2), Piñata Books) Arte Publico Pr.
Saldaña, René. Dancing with the Devil & Other Tales from Beyond / Bailando con el Diablo y Otros Cuentos del Más Allá. Baeza Ventura, Gabriela, tr. from ENG. 2012. (SPA & ENG.). (YA). pap. 9.95 (978-1-55885-744-5(3), Piñata Books) Arte Publico Pr.
Saldana, Rene, Jr. The Jumping Tree. 2008. 181p. (gr. 5-7). 16.50 (978-0-7569-8950-7(7)) Perfection Learning Corp.
—A Mystery Bigger Than Big / un Misterio Mas Grande Que Grandisimo: A Mickey Rangel Mystery / Colección Mickey Rangel, Detective Privado. 2016. (Mickey Rangel Mystery / Coleccion Mickey Rangel, Detective P Ser.). (MUL, ENG & SPA., Illus.). 64p. (J). (gr. 3-6). pap. 9.95 (978-1-55885-824-4(5), Piñata Books) Arte Publico Pr.
Saldana, Rene. The Whole Sky Full of Stars. 2008. (ENG.). 144p. (YA). (gr. 7-11). mass mkt. 5.99 (978-0-440-23791-4(2), Laurel Leaf) Random Hse. Children's Bks.
Sanchez, Alex. Bait. (ENG.). 256p. (YA). (gr. 7). 2010. pap. 12.99 (978-1-4169-3774-6(9)) 2009. 17.99 (978-1-4169-3772-2(2)) Simon & Schuster Bks. For Young Readers. (Simon & Schuster Bks. For Young Readers).
—Getting It. Mehta, Sangeeta, ed. 2007. (ENG., Illus.). 240p. (YA). (gr. 7-12). pap. 8.99 (978-1-4169-0898-2(6), Simon & Schuster Bks. For Young Readers) Simon & Schuster Bks. For Young Readers.
—So Hard to Say. Weiss, Jennifer, ed. 2006. (ENG., Illus.). 232p. (YA). (gr. 7-12). reprint ed. pap. 11.99 (978-1-4169-1189-0(8), Simon & Schuster Bks. For Young Readers) Simon & Schuster Bks. For Young Readers.
Sandoval, Victor. Roll over, Big Toben. 2003. 128p. (J). pap. 9.95 (978-1-55885-401-7(0), Piñata Books) Arte Publico Pr.
Schraff, Anne. The Lost. 1 vol. unabr. ed. 2011. (Urban Underground Ser.). (ENG.). 198p. (YA). (gr. 9-12). pap. 9.95 (978-1-61651-585-0(6)) Saddleback Educational Publishing, Inc.
Serros, Michele. ¡Scandalosa! A Honey Blonde Chica Novel. 2008. (ENG.). 320p. (YA). (gr. 9). pap. 14.99 (978-1-4169-1594-2(X), Simon Pulse) Simon Pulse.
Sitomer, Alan Lawrence. The Secret Story of Sonia Rodriguez. 2010. (ENG.). 320p. (J). (gr. 6-8). pap. 9.99 (978-1-4231-3027-7(8), Jump at the Sun) Hyperion Bks. for Children.
Soto, Gary. Buried Onions. 2006. (ENG., Illus.). 176p. (YA). (gr. 7-12). pap. 6.95 (978-0-15-206265-1(3)) Houghton Mifflin Harcourt Publishing Co.
—Buried Onions. 2006. 149p. 16.95 (978-0-7569-7218-9(3)) Perfection Learning Corp.
—Chato & the Party Animals. Guevara, Susan, illus. (Chato Ser.). 28.95 incl. audio compact disk (978-1-59112-920-2(6)); 25.95 incl. audio (978-1-59112-460-3(3)); 28.95 incl. audio compact disk (978-1-59112-920-2(6)); pap. 37.95 incl. audio (978-1-59112-461-0(1)); pap. 39.95 incl. audio compact disk (978-1-59112-921-9(4)) Live Oak Media.
—Chato & the Party Animals. Guevara, Susan, illus. 2004. (Chato Ser.). (ENG.). 32p. (J). (gr. -1-3). reprint ed. pap. 7.99 (978-0-14-240032-6(7), Puffin Books) Penguin Young Readers Group.
—Chato & the Party Animals. Guevara, Susan, illus. 2004. (Chato Ser.). (gr. -1-3). 17.00 (978-0-7569-2921-3(0)) Perfection Learning Corp.
—Chato Goes Cruisin' Guevara, Susan, illus. 2008. (Chato Ser.). (J). 25.95 incl. audio (978-1-59519-906-5(3)) Live Oak Media.
—Chato Goes Cruisin' Guevara, Susan, illus. 2007. (Chato Ser.). (J). (gr. -1-3). 14.65 (978-0-7569-8147-1(6)) Perfection Learning Corp.
—Chato's Kitchen. Guevara, Susan, illus. 2003. (Chato Ser.). (J). (gr. -1-2). pap. 39.95 (978-1-59112-527-3(8)) Live Oak Media.
—Facts of Life. 2012. (ENG.). 192p. (YA). (gr. 7-7). pap. 7.99 (978-0-547-57734-0(6)) Houghton Mifflin Harcourt Publishing Co.
—Help Wanted: Stories. 2007. (ENG., Illus.). 240p. (YA). (gr. 7-12). pap. 6.95 (978-0-15-205663-6(7)) Houghton Mifflin Harcourt Publishing Co.
—Jesse. 2006. (ENG., Illus.). 192p. (YA). (gr. 7-12). pap. 7.99 (978-0-15-205425-0(1)) Houghton Mifflin Harcourt Publishing Co.
—Jesse. 2006. 166p. (gr. 7-12). 16.95 (978-0-7569-6688-1(4)) Perfection Learning Corp.
—Petty Crimes. 2006. (ENG., Illus.). 176p. (J). (gr. 5-7). pap. 6.99 (978-0-15-205437-3(5)) Houghton Mifflin Harcourt Publishing Co.
Spenser & Brooks, Melanie. Spenser Via a el Paso. Jacobsen, Amie, illus. 2010. (SpenserNation Ser.). (SPA.). 32p. (J). 14.95 (978-0-9817598-5-2(8)) Simple Fish Bk. Co., LLC.
Stewart, Sarah. The Quiet Place. 1 vol. Small, David, illus. 2012. (ENG.). 44p. (J). (gr. k-4). 17.99 (978-0-374-32565-7(0), 9780374325657, Farrar, Straus & Giroux (BYR)) Farrar, Straus & Giroux.
Stites, Clara. Rosalba of Santa Juanita: A California Story. 2015. (ENG., Illus.). 100p. (J). pap. 8.95 (978-1-56474-394-7(2), Fithian Pr) Daniel & Daniel, Pubs., Inc.
Stork, Francisco X. The Last Summer of the Death Warriors. 2010. (ENG.). 352p. (J). (gr. 9-7). 18.99 (978-0-545-15133-7(3), Levine, Arthur A. Bks.) Scholastic, Inc.
—The Memory of Light. 2016. (Arthur a Levine Novel Bks.). (ENG.). 336p. (YA). (gr. 7). 17.99 (978-0-545-47432-0(9)) Scholastic, Inc.
Tafolla, Carmen. Fiesta Babies. Córdova, Amy, illus. 2010. (ENG & SPA.). 24p. (J). (gr. k — 1). 12.99 (978-1-58246-319-3(0), Tricycle Pr.) Random Hse. Children's Bks.
—What Can You Do with a Paleta? Morales, Magaly, illus. (ENG.). 32p. (J). (gr. -1-2). 2014. 7.99 (978-0-385-77537-5(6), Dragonfly Bks.) 2009. 14.99 (978-1-58246-221-9(6), Tricycle Pr.) Random Hse. Children's Bks.
—What Can You Do with a Paleta? (¿Que Puede Hacer con una Paleta?) Morales, Magaly, illus. 2009. (SPA & ENG.). 32p. (J). (gr. -1-2). 14.99 (978-1-58246-289-9(5), Tricycle Pr.) Random Hse. Children's Bks.
—What Can You Do with a Rebozo? ?Qué Puedes Hacer con un Rebozo? Córdova, Amy & Cordova, Amy, illus. 2009. (SPA & ENG.). 32p. (J). (gr. -1-2). pap. 7.99 (978-1-58246-271-4(2), Tricycle Pr.) Random Hse. Children's Bks.
—What Can You Do with a Rebozo? (¿Qué Puedes Hacer Con un Rebozo?) Córdova, Amy & Cordova, Amy, illus. 2009. (SPA & ENG.). 30p. (J). (gr. -1-2). 14.99 (978-1-58246-270-7(4), Tricycle Pr.) Random Hse. Children's Bks.
Tonatiuh, Duncan. Dear Primo: A Letter to My Cousin. 2010. (ENG., Illus.). 32p. (J). (gr. k-2). 16.95 (978-0-8109-3872-4(3), Abrams Bks. for Young Readers) Abrams, Inc.
Torres, Jennifer. Stef Soto, Taco Queen. 2017. (ENG.). 176p. (J). (gr. 3-7). 16.99 (978-0-316-30686-7(X)) Little Brown & Co.
Tripp, Valerie. Josefina Story Collection. Tibbles, Jean-Paul, illus. 2008. 420p. pap. 29.95 (978-1-59369-453-1(9)) American Girl Publishing, Inc.
Velasquez, Gloria. Teen Angel. 2003. (Roosevelt High School Ser.). 160p. (J). pap. 9.95 (978-1-55885-391-1(X), Piñata Books) Arte Publico Pr.
Villareal, Ray. Alamo Wars. 2008. 187p. (J). (gr. 6-18). pap. 10.95 (978-1-55885-513-7(0), Piñata Books) Arte Publico Pr.
—Body Slammed! 2012. (YA). pap. 11.95 (978-1-55885-749-0(4), Piñata Books) Arte Publico Pr.
—Who's Buried in the Garden? 2009. 160p. (YA). (gr. 6-18). pap. 10.95 (978-1-55885-546-5(7), Piñata Books) Arte Publico Pr.
Villasenor, Victor. The Stranger & the Red Rooster: El Forastero y el Gallo Rojo. Ventura, Gabriela Baeza, tr. Jara, Jose, illus. 2005. (ENG & SPA.). 26p. (J). (gr. -1-2). 16.95 (978-1-55885-420-8(7), Piñata Books) Arte Publico Pr.
Volponi, Paul. Homestretch. 2009. (ENG.). 160p. (YA). (gr. 7-18). 16.99 (978-1-4169-3987-0(3), Atheneum Bks. for Young Readers) Simon & Schuster Children's Publishing.
Weston Woods Staff, creator. Chato & the Party Animals. 2011. 38.75 (978-0-439-84581-6(5)) 2011. 18.95 (978-0-439-73984-9(5)) 2004. 29.95 (978-1-55592-703-5(3)) Weston Woods Studios, Inc.
—Chato's Kitchen. 2004. (J). 38.75 (978-1-55592-388-4(7)); 18.95 (978-1-55592-386-0(0)) Weston Woods Studios, Inc.
—Too Many Tamales. 2011. 18.95 (978-0-439-87361-1(4)); 38.75 (978-0-439-84580-9(7)) Weston Woods Studios, Inc.
Worsham, Adria F. Max Celebrates Cinco de Mayo. 1 vol. Gallagher-Cole, Memie, illus. 2008. (Read-It! Readers: the Life of Max Ser.). (ENG.). 24p. (gr. -1-2). lib. bdg. 21.32 (978-1-4048-4759-0(6), Easy Readers) Picture Window Bks.
Yardi, Robin. The Midnight War of Mateo Martinez. 2016. (ENG.). 184p. (J). (gr. 3-6). 17.99 (978-1-4677-8306-4(4), Carolrhoda Bks.) Lerner Publishing Group.

MEXICAN WAR, 1846-1848

Behnke, Alison. A Timeline History of the Mexican-American War. 2015. (ENG., Illus.). 48p. (J). (gr. 5-8). 30.65 (978-1-4677-8583-9(0)) Lerner Publishing Group.
Cantor, Carrie & Cantor, Carrie Nichols. The Mexican War: How the United States Gained Its Western Lands. 2003. (Proud Heritage: the Hispanic Library). (ENG., Illus.). 40p. (J). (gr. 3-6). 29.93 (978-1-56766-176-7(9), 200017) Child's World, Inc., The.
Deem, James M. Primary Source Accounts of the Mexican-American War. 2006. (America's Wars Through Primary Sources Ser.). (Illus.). 128p. (J). (gr. 4-7). lib. bdg. 34.60 (978-1-59845-005-7(0), MyReportLinks.com Bks.) Enslow Pubs., Inc.
DiConsiglio, John. The Mexican-American War. 1 vol. 2012. (Living Through... Ser.). (ENG.). 80p. (gr. 7-8). pap. 11.95 (978-1-4329-6007-0(5)); lib. bdg. 37.32 (978-1-4329-5998-2(0)) Heinemann-Raintree.
Feldman, Ruth Tenzer. The Mexican-American War. 2004. (Chronicle of America's Wars Ser.). (Illus.). 96p. (J). (gr. 5-12). 27.93 (978-0-8225-0831-1(1)) Lerner Publishing Group.
Gaddi, Rosalie. The U.S.-Mexican War & Its Impact on the United States. 2016. (Spotlight on American History Ser.). (Illus.). 24p. (J). (gr. 6-4). 26.25 (978-1-5081-4946-0(1), PowerKids Pr.) Rosen Publishing Group, Inc., The.
Kachur, Matthew & Sterngass, Jon. The Mexican-American War. 2006. (Wars That Changed American History Ser.). (Illus.). 48p. (gr. 5-12). pap. 14.05 (978-0-8368-7299-6(1), Gareth Stevens Secondary Library) Stevens, Gareth Publishing LLLP.
Loria, Laura. The Mexican-American War. 2017. (J). **(978-1-5383-0014-5(1)**, Britannica Educational Publishing) Rosen Publishing Group, Inc., The.
Mexican-American War. 2003. (ENG., Illus.). 288p. (J). lib. bdg. 106.00 (978-0-7876-6537-1(1), GML00502-182439, UXL) Cengage Gale.
Mills, Bronwyn. U. S. -Mexican War. 3rd rev. ed. 2010. (America at War Ser.). 192p. (gr. 6-12). 45.00 (978-0-8160-8195-0(6), Chelsea Hse.) Facts On File, Inc.
O'Connell, Kim A. The Mexican-American War: A MyReportLinks.com Book. 2003. (U.S. Wars Ser.). (Illus.). 48p. (J). lib. bdg. 26.60 (978-0-7660-5131-7(5)) Enslow Pubs., Inc.
Porterfield, Jason. The Treaty of Guadalupe Hidalgo 1848: A Primary Source Examination of the Treaty That Ended the Mexican-American War. (Primary Sources of American Treaties Ser.). 64p. 2009. (gr. 5-8). 58.50 (978-1-60851-516-5(8)) 2006. (Illus.). (J). (gr. k-3). lib. bdg. 31.95 (978-1-4042-0440-9(7)) Rosen Publishing Group, Inc., The.
Poulakidas, Georgene. The Mexican-American War. (Primary Sources of American Wars Ser.). 24p. 2009. (gr. 3-4). 42.50 (978-1-60851-527-1(3), PowerKids Pr.) 2006. (Illus.). (YA). (gr. 4-7). lib. bdg. 22.60 (978-1-4042-2683-8(4)) Rosen Publishing Group, Inc., The.
Raabe, Emily. The Mexican-American War. (Westward Ho! Ser.). 24p. 2009. (gr. 2-3). 42.50 (978-1-60854-760-9(4)) 2003. (Illus.). (J). lib. bdg. 22.60 (978-0-8239-6497-0(3)) Rosen Publishing Group, Inc., The. (PowerKids Pr.).
Rice, Earle. Causes of the Mexican-American War. 2010. (J). lib. bdg. (978-1-59556-033-9(5)) OTTN Publishing.
Rose, Simon. Mexican-American War. 2014. (J). pap. (978-1-4896-0509-2(6)) Weigl Pubs., Inc.
Shoup, Kate. Texas & the Mexican War. 2016. (Expanding America Ser.). (ENG., Illus.). 96p. (J). (gr. 8-8). 42.79 (978-1-5026-0964-9(9)) Cavendish Square Publishing.
Sonneborn, Liz. The Mexican-American War. 2005. (Primary Sources in American History Ser.). (Illus.). 64p. (J). (gr. 5-8). lib. bdg. 31.95 (978-1-4042-0180-4(7)) Rosen Publishing Group, Inc., The.
—The Mexican-American War: A Primary Source History of the Expansion of the Western Lands of the United States. 2009. (Primary Sources in American History Ser.). 64p. (gr. 5-8). 58.50 (978-1-60851-500-4(1)) Rosen Publishing Group, Inc., The.
Stein, R. Conrad. Mexican-American War. 2011. (Story of Mexico Ser.). 144p. (gr. 7-12). 28.95 (978-1-59935-160-5(9)) Reynolds, Morgan Inc.
Worth, Richard. The Texas War of Independence. 2008. (Hispanic America Ser.). 80p. (gr. 5-18). lib. bdg. 34.21 (978-0-7614-2934-0(4), Benchmark Bks.) Marshall Cavendish Corp.

MEXICAN WAR, 1846-1848—FICTION

Dell, Pamela. Blood in the Water: A Story of Friendship During the Mexican War. 2003. (Scrapbooks of America Ser.). (ENG., Illus.). 48p. (J). (gr. 3-6). 32.79 (978-1-59187-042-5(9), 200805) Child's World, Inc., The.
Fleischman, Sid. The Giant Rat of Sumatra. Hendrix, John, illus. 208p. (J). (gr. 5-18). 2005. 15.99 (978-0-06-074238-6(0)) 2006. (ENG.). reprint ed. pap. 6.99 (978-0-06-074240-9(2), Greenwillow Bks.) HarperCollins Pubs.

MEXICANS—UNITED STATES

Egan, Tracie. Francisca Alvarez: El ángel de Goliad (Francisca Alvarez: the Angel of Goliad) 2009. (Grandes personajes en la historia de los Estados Unidos (Famous People in American History) Ser.). (SPA.). 32p. (gr. 2-3). 47.90 (978-1-61512-798-6(4), Editorial Buenas Letras) Rosen Publishing Group, Inc., The.

—Francisca Alvarez: The Angel of Goliad. 2009. (Primary Sources of Famous People in American History Ser.). 32p. (gr. 2-3). 47.90 (978-1-60851-675-9(X)) Rosen Publishing Group, Inc., The.

—Francisca Alvarez: The Angel of Goliad / el ángel de Goliad. 2009. (Famous People in American History/Grandes personajes en la historia de los Estados Unidos Ser.). (ENG & SPA.). 32p. (gr. 2-3). 47.90 (978-1-61512-544-9(2), Editorial Buenas Letras) Rosen Publishing Group, Inc., The.

Taylor, Theodore. The Maldonado Miracle. 2003. (ENG.). 176p. (J). (gr. 2-5). pap. 6.95 (978-0-15-205036-8(1)) Houghton Mifflin Harcourt Publishing Co.

MEXICO

Alaníz, Eduardo Martínez. Hugo Sanchez. 2012. (Superstars of Soccer SPANISH Ser.). (SPA.). 32p. (J). (gr. 4). 19.95 (978-1-4222-2615-5(8)) Mason Crest.

—Hugo Sanchez. 2012. (Superstars of Soccer ENGLISH Ser.). (Illus.). 32p. (J). (gr. 4). 19.95 (978-1-4222-2668-1(9)) Mason Crest.

Alvarez, Mateo. Diego Rivera: Famous Mexican Painter. 2015. (Exceptional Latinos Ser.). (ENG.). 24p. (J). (gr. 3-4). pap. 9.35 (978-0-7660-6702-8(5)) Enslow Pubs., Inc.

Arturo Miranda Bravo, Jorge. Andres Guardado. 2012. (Superstars of Soccer ENGLISH Ser.). 32p. (J). (gr. 4). 19.95 (978-1-4222-2666-7(2)); (SPA., Illus.). 19.95 (978-1-4222-2613-1(1)) Mason Crest.

Aykroyd, Clarissa. The Government of Mexico. (Mexico: Beautiful Land, Diverse People Ser.). 64p. (YA). (gr. 7-12). 2009. (Illus.). 21.95 (978-1-4222-0662-1(9)) 2007. pap. 9.95 (978-1-4222-0729-1(3)) Mason Crest.

Blaxland, Wendy. Mexican Food. 2011. (I Can Cook ! Ser.). 32p. (YA). (gr. 2-5). 28.50 (978-1-59920-668-4(4)) Black Rabbit Bks.

Blevins, Wiley. Mexico. 2017. (Follow Me Around Ser.). (ENG.). 32p. (J). pap. 7.95 (**978-0-531-23972-8(1)**); lib. bdg. 27.00 (**978-0-531-23706-9(0)**) Scholastic Library Publishing. (Children's Pr.).

Burt, Janet. The Pacific North States of Mexico. (Mexico: Beautiful Land, Diverse People Ser.). 64p. (YA). (gr. 7-12). 2009. (Illus.). 21.95 (978-1-4222-0667-6(X)) 2007. pap. 9.95 (978-1-4222-0734-5(X)) Mason Crest.

Day-MacLeod, Deirdre. The States of Central Mexico. (Mexico: Beautiful Land, Diverse People Ser.). 64p. (YA). (gr. 7-12). 2009. (Illus.). 21.95 (978-1-4222-0664-5(5)) 2007. pap. 9.95 (978-1-4222-0731-4(5)) Mason Crest.

—The States of Northern Mexico. (Mexico: Beautiful Land, Diverse People Ser.). 64p. (YA). (gr. 7-12). 2009. (Illus.). 21.95 (978-1-4222-0665-2(3)) 2007. pap. 9.95 (978-1-4222-0732-1(3)) Mason Crest.

Elzaurdia, Paco. Cuauhtemoc Blanco. 2012. (Superstars of Soccer SPANISH Ser.). (Illus.). 32p. (J). (gr. 4). (SPA.). 19.95 (978-1-4222-2614-8(X)); 19.95 (978-1-4222-2667-4(0)) Mason Crest.

—Rafael Marquez. 32p. (J). 2013. (Illus.). (978-1-4222-2594-3(1)) 2012. (SPA.). (gr. 4). 19.95 (978-1-4222-2598-1(4)) Mason Crest.

Farrell, Courtney. The Mexican Drug War, 1 vol. 2011. (Essential Issues Set 3 Ser.). (ENG., Illus.). 112p. (J). (gr. 6-12). lib. bdg. 35.64 (978-1-61783-136-2(0)) ABDO Publishing Co.

George, Lynn. Teotihuacan: Designing an Ancient Mexican City: Calculating Perimeters & Areas of Squares & Rectangles. (PowerMath Ser.). (Illus.). 32p. 2009. (ENG.). (gr. 4-5). pap. 10.00 (978-0-8239-8876-1(7)) 2004. (J). lib. bdg. 25.25 (978-0-8239-8983-6(6)) Rosen Publishing Group, Inc., The. (PowerKids Pr.).

Gitlin, Marty. Mexico. 2017. (Country Profiles Ser.). (ENG., Illus.). 32p. (J). (gr. 3-8). lib. bdg. 26.95 (**978-1-62617-685-0(X)**, Blastoff! Discovery) Bellwether Media.

Golden, Nancy. Exploring Mexico with the Five Themes of Geography. (Library of the Western Hemisphere Ser.). 24p. 2009. (gr. 4-4). 42.50 (978-1-60853-928-4(8), PowerKids Pr.) 2005. (Illus.). (J). (gr. 5-7). lib. bdg. 22.60 (978-1-4042-2668-5(0), PowerKids Pr.) 2005. (ENG., Illus.). (gr. 3-8). pap. 8.25 (978-0-8239-4628-0(2)) Rosen Publishing Group, Inc., The.

Green, Jen. Caribbean Sea & Gulf of Mexico. 2006. (Oceans & Seas Ser.). (Illus.). 48p. (gr. 5-12). lib. bdg. 31.00 (978-0-8368-6272-0(4), Gareth Stevens Secondary Library) Stevens, Gareth Publishing LLLP.

Green, Yuko. Let's Learn about MEXICO: Activity & Coloring Book. 2013. (Dover Children's Activity Bks.). (ENG.). 48p. (J). (gr. 1-5). pap. 4.99 (978-0-486-48994-0(9)) Dover Pubns., Inc.

Gritzner, Charles F. Mexico. 2nd rev. ed. 2011. (Modern World Nations Ser.). 136p. (gr. 6-12). 35.00 (978-1-60413-938-9(2), Chelsea Hse.) Facts On File, Inc.

Group/McGraw-Hill, Wright. Mexico: Land of Old & New, 6 vols. (Book2WebTM Ser.). (gr. 4-8). 36.50 (978-0-322-04445-6(6)) Wright Group/McGraw-Hill.

Gruber, Beth. Mexico. 2009. (Countries of the World Ser.). (ENG., Illus.). 64p. (J). (gr. 5). pap. 12.95 (978-1-4263-0566-5(4), National Geographic Children's Bks.) National Geographic Society.

Hardwick, Susan, ed. Mexico. 2004. (World-Wise Kids Project Guides). (Illus.). 96p. (978-1-59258-079-8(3)) Hylas Publishing.

Johnston, Tony. P Is for Pinata. Parra, John, illus. 2008. (Discover the World Ser.). (ENG.). 40p. (J). (gr. 1-5). 17.95 (978-1-58536-144-1(5)) Sleeping Bear Pr.

Juarez, Christine. Mexico, 1 vol. 2013. (Countries Ser.). (ENG.). 24p. (gr. k-1). 26.65 (978-1-4765-3076-5(9), Pebble Plus) Capstone Press of Coughlan Cos.

Junior Worldmark Encyclopedia of the Mexican States. 2nd rev. ed. 2007. (ENG., Illus.). 456p. (J). 106.00 (978-1-4144-1112-5(X), UXL) Cengage Gale.

Kalman, Bobbie. Mexico: The Culture. 3rd rev. ed. 2008. (Lands, Peoples, & Cultures Ser.). (ENG., Illus.). 32p. (J). (gr. 3-9). lib. bdg. (978-0-7787-9295-6(1)) Crabtree Publishing Co.

—Mexico - The Land. 3rd rev. ed. 2008. (Lands, Peoples, & Cultures Ser.). (ENG., Illus.). 32p. (J). (gr. 3-9). pap. (978-0-7787-9661-9(2)) Crabtree Publishing Co.

Kuskowski, Alex. Super Simple Mexican Art: Fun & Easy Art from Around the World, 1 vol. 2012. (ENG.). 32p. 27.07 (978-1-61783-213-0(8), Super SandCastle) ABDO Publishing Co.

Landau, Elaine. Mexico. 2008. (True Bks.). (ENG.). 48p. (J). pap. 6.95 (978-0-531-20727-7(7), Children's Pr.) Scholastic Library Publishing.

Lieurance, Suzanne. Mexico: A MyReportLinks. com Book. 2004. (Top Ten Countries of Recent Immigrants Ser.). (Illus.). 48p. (J). lib. bdg. 26.60 (978-0-7660-5177-5(3), MyReportLinks.com Bks.) Enslow Pubs., Inc.

Lindeen, Mary. Welcome to Mexico!, 1 vol. 2011. (Wonder Readers Fluent Level Ser.). (ENG.). 32p. (gr. -1-2). pap. 5.99 (978-1-4296-7973-2(5), Wonder Readers) Capstone Press of Coughlan Cos.

—Welcome to Mexico, 1 vol. 2011. (Wonder Readers: Social Studies). (ENG.). 20p. (gr. -1-2). lib. bdg. 22.65 (978-1-4296-8642-6(1), Wonder Readers) Capstone Press of Coughlan Cos.

—Welcome to North America, 1 vol. 2011. (Wonder Readers Fluent Level Ser.). (ENG.). 32p. (gr. -1-2). pap. 5.99 (978-1-4296-7974-9(3), Wonder Readers) Capstone Press of Coughlan Cos.

El maravilloso maiz de Mexico: 6 Small Books. (Saludos Ser.: Vol. 2). (SPA.). (gr. 3-5). 31.00 (978-0-7635-1815-8(8)) Rigby Education.

Marsh, Carole. Mexico: A Colorful Land of Exotic Culture! 2009. (It's Your World Ser.). 48p. (J). (gr. 2-9). pap. 7.99 (978-0-635-06821-7(4)) Gallopade International.

Martínez Alaníz, Eduardo. Hugo Sanchez. 2013. (Illus.). 32p. (J). (978-1-4222-2647-6(6)) Mason Crest.

McCartney Lewis, Pat. The Colors of the Coloni: Los Colores de la Colonia. 2009. 36p. pap. 16.99 (978-1-4389-2306-2(6)) AuthorHouse.

McDonnell, Ginger. Next Stop - Mexico, 1 vol. 2nd rev. ed. 2011. (Nonfiction Readers Ser.). (ENG.). 24p. (J). (gr. 2-2). pap. 6.99 (978-1-4333-3610-2(3)) Teacher Created Materials, Inc.

McNamara, Margaret. Mexico. 2006. (J). pap. (978-1-4108-6456-7(1)) Benchmark Education Co.

Moon, Walt K. Exploremos Cuba. 2017. (Bumba Books (tm) en Español — Exploremos Países (Let's Explore Countries) Ser.). (SPA.). 24p. (J). (gr. -1-1). lib. bdg. 25.32 (**978-1-5124-4123-9(6)**) Lerner Publishing Group.

—Exploremos México. 2017. (Bumba Books (tm) en Español — Exploremos Países (Let's Explore Countries) Ser.). (SPA.). 24p. (J). (gr. -1-1). lib. bdg. 25.32 (**978-1-5124-4121-5(X)**) Lerner Publishing Group.

—Let's Explore Mexico. 2017. (Bumba Books (tm) — Let's Explore Countries Ser.). (ENG.). 24p. (J). (gr. -1-1). 12.99 (**978-1-5124-3741-6(7)**, Lerner Pubns.); 38.65 (**978-1-5124-3023-3(4)**, Lerner Pubns.); 38.65 (**978-1-5124-3740-9(9)**, Lerner Pubns.); (Illus.). 25.32 (978-1-5124-3005-9(6)) Lerner Publishing Group.

Nantus, Sheryl. The Pacific South States of Mexico. (Mexico: Beautiful Land, Diverse People Ser.). 64p. (YA). (gr. 7-12). 2009. (Illus.). 21.95 (978-1-4222-0666-9(1)) 2007. pap. 9.95 (978-1-4222-0733-8(1)) Mason Crest.

Obregón, José María. Mexico/México. Benson, Megan, tr. 2009. (Great National Soccer Teams / Grandes Selecciones Del Fútbol Mundial Ser.). (SPA & ENG., Illus.). 24p. (J). (gr. 2-5). lib. bdg. 22.60 (978-1-4358-2497-3(0), PowerKids Pr.) Rosen Publishing Group, Inc., The.

—Mexico/México. 2009. (SPA & ENG.). (J). 49.50 (978-1-4358-3234-3(5)); pap. 8.25 (978-1-4358-2498-0(9)) Rosen Publishing Group, Inc., The. (PowerKids Pr.).

O'Donnell, Kerri. A Primary Source Guide to Mexico. (Countries of the World). (Illus.). 24p. 2004. (J). (gr. k-5). lib. bdg. 22.60 (978-0-8239-6592-2(9)) 2003. (ENG., (gr. 3-6). pap. 8.25 (978-0-8239-8076-5(6)) Rosen Publishing Group, Inc., The. (PowerKids Pr.).

Orr, Tamra. Meet Our New Student from Mexico. 2008. (Meet Our New Student Ser.). (Illus.). 48p. (YA). (gr. 2-5). lib. bdg. 29.95 (978-1-58415-646-8(5)) Mitchell Lane Pubs., Inc.

Otto, Carolyn. Celebrate Cinco de Mayo: With Fiestas, Music, & Dance. 2008. (Holidays Around the World Ser.). (ENG., Illus.). 32p. (J). (gr. 1-4). 23.90 (978-1-4263-0216-9(9), National Geographic Children's Bks.) National Geographic Society.

Pohl, Kathleen. Looking at Mexico. 2007. (Looking at Countries Ser.). 32p. (gr. 1-5). pap. 10.50 (978-0-8368-8179-0(6)); (Illus.). lib. bdg. 26.00 (978-0-8368-8172-1(9)) Stevens, Gareth Publishing LLLP. (Gareth Stevens Learning Library).

Richardson, Adele. Mexico. 2006. (My First Look at Countries Ser.). (Illus.). 24p. (J). (gr. -1-3). lib. bdg. 15.95 (978-1-58341-448-4(7), Creative Education) Creative Co., The.

Ring, Susan. Come to Mexico. 2005. (Yellow Umbrella Fluent Level Ser.). (ENG.). 16p. (gr. k-1). pap. 35.70 (978-0-7368-5310-1(3), Yellow Umbrella Bks.) Capstone Press of Coughlan Cos.

Rose, Elizabeth. A Primary Source Guide to Mexico. 2009. (Countries of the World). 24p. (gr. 2-3). 42.50 (978-1-61512-039-0(4), PowerKids Pr.) Rosen Publishing Group, Inc., The.

Sabeca International Investment Staff. Enciclopedia de Mexico. 2004. (SPA., Illus.). (YA). cd-rom (978-1-56409-069-0(8)) EBP Latin America Group, Inc.

Sanna, Ellyn. Mexico: Facts & Figures. 2009. (Mexico: Beautiful Land, Diverse People Ser.). (Illus.). 64p. (YA). (gr. 7-12). 21.95 (978-1-4222-0660-7(2)) Mason Crest.

Simpson, Kathleen. Geography of Mexico: Set Of 6. 2011. (Navigators Ser.). (J). pap. 50.00 net. (978-1-4108-6263-1(1)) Benchmark Education Co.

Somervill, Barbara. Mexico. 2010. (Explorer Library: Social Studies Explorer Ser.). (ENG.). 48p. (gr. 4-8). lib. bdg. 31.36 (978-1-60279-833-5(8), 200532) Cherry Lake Publishing.

Sonneborn, Liz. Mexico. 2017. (Enchantment of the World Ser.). (ENG.). 144p. (J). lib. bdg. 40.00 (**978-0-531-23570-6(X)**, Children's Pr.) Scholastic Library Publishing.

Stein, R. Conrad. Mexico. rev. ed. 2006. (Enchantment of the World Ser.). (ENG., Illus.). 144p. (J). (gr. 5-9). 39.00 (978-0-516-24868-4(5), Children's Pr.) Scholastic Library Publishing.

Stokes, Erica M. The Economy of Mexico. (Mexico: Beautiful Land, Diverse People Ser.). 64p. (YA). (gr. 7-12). 2009. (Illus.). 21.95 (978-1-4222-0658-4(0)) 2007. pap. 9.95 (978-1-4222-0725-3(0)) Mason Crest.

Streissguth, Thomas. Mexico. 2007. (Country Explorers Ser.). (Illus.). 48p. (J). (gr. k-2). lib. bdg. 27.93 (978-0-8225-7130-8(7), Lerner Pubns.) Lerner Publishing Group.

Streissguth, Tom. Mexico. 2008. pap. 40.95 (978-0-8225-9305-8(X)) Lerner Publishing Group.

Tidmarsh, Celia. Focus on Mexico. 2006. (World in Focus Ser.). (Illus.). 64p. (gr. 5-12). lib. bdg. 34.00 (978-0-8368-6219-5(8), Gareth Stevens Secondary Library) Stevens, Gareth Publishing LLLP.

Urrutia, Maria Cristina, et al. Cinco de Mayo. 2nd ed. 2008. (ENG., Illus.). 32p. (J). (gr. 4). pap. 7.95 (978-0-88899-877-4(5)) Groundwood Bks. CAN. Dist: Publishers Group West (PGW).

Williams, Colleen Madonna Flood. The Geography of Mexico. (Mexico: Beautiful Land, Diverse People Ser.). 64p. (YA). (gr. 7-12). 2009. (Illus.). 21.95 (978-1-4222-0661-4(0)) 2007. pap. 9.95 (978-1-4222-0728-4(5)) Mason Crest.

World Book, Inc Staff, contrib. by. !Feliz Navidad¡: Celebrating a Mexican Christmas. 2015. 80p. (J). (978-0-7166-0830-1(8)) World Bk., Inc.

Zocchi, Judy. In Mexico. Brodie, Neale, illus. 2005. (Global Adventures II Ser.). 32p. (J). per. 10.95 (978-1-59646-136-9(5)) Dingles & Co.

—In Mexico/en México. Brodie, Neale, illus. 2005. (Global Adventures II Ser.).Tr. of En México. (ENG & SPA.). 32p. (J). per. 10.95 (978-1-59646-138-3(1)) Dingles & Co.

MEXICO—ANTIQUITIES

Hofer, Charles. Ancient Maya Technology. 2016. (Spotlight on the Maya, Aztec, & Inca Civilizations Ser.). (Illus.). 32p. (J). (gr. 6-4). 26.25 (978-1-4994-1983-2(X), PowerKids Pr.) Rosen Publishing Group, Inc., The.

Mahoney, Emily Jankowski. Ancient Aztec Technology. 2016. (Spotlight on the Maya, Aztec, & Inca Civilizations Ser.). (Illus.). 32p. (J). (gr. 6-4). pap. 11.75 (978-1-4994-1923-8(6), PowerKids Pr.) Rosen Publishing Group, Inc., The.

Woods, Mary B. & Woods, Michael. Seven Wonders of Ancient North America. 2008. (Seven Wonders Ser.). (ENG., Illus.). 80p. (gr. 5-8). lib. bdg. 33.26 (978-0-8225-7572-6(8)) Lerner Publishing Group.

MEXICO—BIOGRAPHY

Antonio Lopez de Santa Anna. 2010. (Great Hispanic Heritage Ser.). (Illus.). 104p. (gr. 6-12). 35.00 (978-1-60413-734-7(7), Chelsea Hse.) Facts On File, Inc.

Brown, Monica. Frida Kahlo & Her Animalitos. Parra, John, illus. 2017. (ENG.). 40p. (J). (gr. -1-3). 17.95 (**978-0-7358-4269-4(8)**) North-South Bks., Inc.

Carew-Miller, Anna. Famous People of Mexico. (Mexico: Beautiful Land, Diverse People Ser.). 64p. (YA). (gr. 7-12). 2009. (Illus.). 21.95 (978-1-4222-0659-1(9)) 2007. pap. 9.95 (978-1-4222-0726-0(9)) Mason Crest.

Contro, Arturo. Rafael Marquez. Benson, Megan, tr. from SPA. 2008. (World Soccer Stars / Estrellas Del Fútbol Mundial Ser.). (SPA., Illus.). 24p. (J). (gr. 2-5). lib. bdg. 22.60 (978-1-4042-7667-3(X)) Rosen Publishing Group, Inc., The.

Dickens, Lydia. The Little Donkey Nico / el Burrito Nico. 2012. 32p. pap. 19.99 (978-1-4772-7026-4(4)) AuthorHouse.

Dougherty, Terri. Salma Hayek. 2008. (People in the News Ser.). (ENG., Illus.). 128p. (gr. 7-10). lib. bdg. 39.40 (978-1-4205-0096-7(1), LML02109-242100, Lucent Bks.) Cengage Gale.

Elzaurdia, Paco. Rafael Marquez. 2012. (Superstars of Soccer ENGLISH Ser.). (Illus.). 32p. (J). (gr. 4). 19.95 (978-1-4222-2651-3(4)) Mason Crest.

Fabiny, Sarah. Who Was Frida Kahlo? Hoare, Jerry, illus. 2013. (Who Was? Ser.). (ENG.). 112p. (J). (gr. 3-7). 5.99 (978-0-448-47938-5(9), Grosset & Dunlap) Penguin Young Readers Group.

Foard, Sheila Wood. Diego Rivera. 2nd rev. ed. 2010. (Great Hispanic Heritage Ser.). (Illus.). 120p. (gr. 6-12). 35.00 (978-1-60413-845-0(9), Chelsea Hse.) Facts On File, Inc.

Gaines, Ann Graham & Gaines, Ann. Vicente Fox: The Road to the Mexican Presidency. 2003. (Proud Heritage: the Hispanic Library). (ENG., Illus.). 40p. (J). (gr. 3-6). 29.93 (978-1-56766-177-4(7), 200018) Child's World, Inc., The.

Gordon, Nick. Alberto Del Rio. 2012. (Pro Wrestling Champions Ser.). (ENG., Illus.). 24p. (J). (gr. 3-7). lib. bdg. 25.95 (978-1-60014-782-1(8), Torque Bks.) Bellwether Media.

Guzmán, Lila & Guzmán, Rick. Diego Rivera: Artist of Mexico. 2006. (Famous Latinos Ser.). (Illus.). 32p. (J). (gr. 3-4). lib. bdg. 23.94 (978-0-7660-2641-4(8), Enslow Elementary) Enslow Pubs., Inc.

Hart, Paul. Emiliano Zapata: Mexico's Social Revolutionary. 2017. (World in a Life Ser.). (ENG.). 320p. (C). pap. 19.95 (**978-0-19-068808-0(4)**) Oxford Univ. Pr., Inc.

Hillstrom, Laurie & Hillstrom, Kevin. Diego Rivera, Muralist. 2008. (Twentieth Century's Most Influential Hispanics Ser.). (ENG., Illus.). 110p. (gr. 7-12). 39.40 (978-1-4205-0018-9(X)) Cengage Gale.

Jauregui, Diego. Libros de Arte para Ninos: Diego Rivera.Tr. of Art Books for Children: Diego Rivera. (SPA., Illus.). 73p. (YA). (gr. 5-8). pap. (978-968-494-026-0(2)) Centro de Informacion y Desarrollo de la Comunicacion y la Literatura.

Lazaro, Georgina. Juana Ines. Preza, Bruno Gonzalez, illus. 2007. (SPA.). 32p. (J). (gr. 3-5). 14.99 (978-1-930332-57-7(2)) Lectorum Pubns., Inc.

Loria, Laura. Malinche: Indigenous Translator for Hernán Cortés in Mexico. 2017. (Women Who Changed History Ser.). 48p. (gr. 10-12). pap. 14.05 (**978-1-68048-649-0(7)**, Britannica Educational Publishing) Rosen Publishing Group, Inc., The.

Marín, Guadalupe Rivera. My Papá Diego & Me (Mi Papa Diego y Yo) Memories of My Father & His Art (Recuerdos de Mi Padre y Su Arte) Rivera, Diego, illus. 2013. (SPA & ENG.). 32p. (J). (gr. k-5). 18.95 (978-0-89239-228-5(2)) Lee & Low Bks., Inc.

Marsh, Carole. Diego Rivera: Acclaimed Mural Painter: Acclaimed Mural Painter. 2003. 12p. (gr. k-4). 2.95 (978-0-635-02137-3(4)) Gallopade International.

Morales, Yuyi. Viva Frida. O'Meara, Tim, photos by. 2014. (ENG., Illus.). 40p. (J). (gr. -1-3). 17.99 (978-1-59643-603-9(4), 9781596436039) Roaring Brook Pr.

Morrison, John. Frida Kahlo. 2nd rev. ed. 2010. (Great Hispanic Heritage Ser.). (Illus.). 128p. (J). (gr. 6-12). 35.00 (978-1-60413-846-7(7), Chelsea Hse.) Facts On File, Inc.

Nardo, Don, ed. Frida Kahlo. 2012. (Eye on Art Ser.). (ENG., Illus.). 128p. (J). (gr. 7-10). lib. bdg. 34.80 (978-1-4205-0850-5(4), Lucent Bks.) Cengage Gale.

Obregón, José María. Cuauhtémoc Blanco. 2009. (World Soccer Stars / Estrellas Del Fútbol Mundial Ser.). (SPA, ENG & MUL., Illus.). 24p. (J). lib. bdg. 22.60 (978-1-4358-2731-8(7), Editorial Buenas Letras) Rosen Publishing Group, Inc., The.

Owens, L. L. A Journey with Hernán Cortés. 2017. (Primary Source Explorers Ser.). (ENG.). 40p. (J). (gr. 3-5). 30.65 (978-1-5124-0777-8(1)) Lerner Publishing Group.

Ramen, Fred. Hernán Cortés: The Conquest of Mexico & the Aztec Empire. 2009. (Library of Explorers & Exploration Ser.). 112p. (gr. 5-8). 66.50 (978-1-60853-606-1(8), Rosen Reference) Rosen Publishing Group, Inc., The.

Reef, Catherine. Frida & Diego: Art, Love, Life. 2014. (ENG., Illus.). 176p. (J). (gr. 7-12). 18.99 (978-0-547-82184-9(0), Clarion Bks.) Houghton Mifflin Harcourt Publishing Co.

Richards, Virginia Helen & Halpin, D. Thomas, illus. Blessed Miguel Pro. 2011. (J). pap. 2.95 (978-0-8198-1192-9(0)) Pauline Bks. & Media.

Rubin, Susan Goldman. Diego Rivera: An Artist for the People. 2013. (ENG., Illus.). 56p. (J). (gr. 3-7). 22.95 (978-0-8109-8411-0(3), Abrams Bks. for Young Readers) Abrams, Inc.

Sapet, Kerrily. Salma Hayek. (Transcending Race in America Ser.). 64p. (YA). (gr. 5-18). 2010. (Illus.). lib. bdg. 22.95 (978-1-4222-1616-3(0)) 2009. pap. 9.95 (978-1-4222-1630-9(6)) Mason Crest.

Stein, R. Conrad. Emiliano Zapata & the Mexican Revolution. 2011. (Story of Mexico Ser.). (Illus.). 144p. (gr. 7-12). 28.95 (978-1-59935-163-6(3)) Reynolds, Morgan Inc.

—Hernando Cortés: Conquistador & Empire Builder. 2004. (Proud Heritage: the Hispanic Library). (ENG., Illus.). 40p. (J). (gr. 3-6). 29.93 (978-1-59296-169-6(X), 200009) Child's World, Inc., The.

Tieck, Sarah. Diego Rivera, 1 vol. 2006. (First Biographies Ser.). (ENG., Illus.). 32p. (gr. -1-3). 27.07 (978-1-59679-785-7(1), Buddy Bks.) ABDO Publishing Co.

Tonatiuh, Duncan. Danza! Amalia Hernández & Mexico's Folkloric Ballet. 2017. (ENG., Illus.). 32p. (J). (gr. 1-5). 18.95 (**978-1-4197-2532-6(7)**, Abrams Bks. for Young Readers) Abrams, Inc.

—Diego Rivera: His World & Ours. 2011. (ENG., Illus.). 40p. (J). (gr. 1-4). 17.95 (978-0-8109-9731-8(2), Abrams Bks. for Young Readers) Abrams, Inc.

—Funny Bones: Posada & His Day of the Dead Calaveras. 2015. (ENG., Illus.). 40p. (J). (gr. 1-5). 18.95 (978-1-4197-1647-8(6), Abrams Bks. for Young Readers) Abrams, Inc.

Valay, Ana Patricia. Giovani Dos Santos. 2012. (Superstars of Soccer SPANISH Ser.). (SPA.). 32p. (J). (gr. 4). 19.95 (978-1-4222-2597-4(6)) Mason Crest.

Wagner, Heather Lehr. Hernan Cortes. 2009. (Great Explorers Ser.). (Illus.). 120p. (gr. 6-12). 30.00 (978-1-60413-424-7(0), Chelsea Hse.) Facts On File, Inc.

Walker, Paul Robert. Remember the Alamo: Texians, Tejanos, & Mexicans Tell Their Stories. 2007. (Remember Ser.). (ENG., Illus.). 64p. (gr. 5-8). lib. bdg. 27.90 (978-1-4263-0011-0(5), National Geographic Children's Bks.) National Geographic Society.

West, David. Hernán Cortés: The Life of a Spanish Conquistador. 2009. (Graphic Nonfiction Biographies Ser.). (ENG.). 48p. (YA). (gr. 4-5). 58.50 (978-1-61513-019-1(5), Rosen Reference) Rosen Publishing Group, Inc., The.

Wine, Bill. Salma Hayek. (Sharing the American Dream Ser.). 64p. (YA). (gr. 7-12). 2009. (Illus.). 22.95 (978-1-4222-0585-3(1)) 2007. pap. 9.95 (978-1-4222-0748-2(X)) Mason Crest.

MEXICO CITY (MEXICO)

Bingham, Jane. Aztec Empire (Freestyle Express) 2014. 22.50 (978-1-63419-686-4(4)) Perfection Learning Corp.

Croy, Anita. Solving the Mysteries of Aztec Cities. 2008. (Digging into History Ser.). 32p. (gr. 4-18). lib. bdg. 29.93 (978-0-7614-3102-2(0), Benchmark Bks.) Marshall Cavendish Corp.

Morrison, Marion. Mexico City. 2003. (Great Cities of the World Ser.). (Illus.). 48p. (gr. 5-12). lib. bdg. 31.00 (978-0-8368-5023-9(8), Gareth Stevens Secondary Library) Stevens, Gareth Publishing LLLP.

Parker, Edward. Mexico City. Parker, Edward, photos by. 2006. (Global Cities Ser.). (Illus.). 61p. (gr. 5-8). 30.00 (978-0-7910-8854-8(5), Chelsea Hse.) Facts On File, Inc.

Pugliano-Martin, Carol. Discover Mexico City. 2006. (J). pap. (978-1-4108-6423-9(5)) Benchmark Education Co.

—Mexico City, Mexico. 2006. (J). pap. (978-1-4108-6420-8(0)) Benchmark Education Co.

MEXICO—FICTION

Abraham, Susan Gonzales & Abraham, Denise Gonzales. Cecilia's Year. 2004. (Latino Fiction for Young Adults Ser.). (ENG., Illus.). 160p. (J). (gr. 7-9). 16.95 (978-0-938317-87-6(3)) Cinco Puntos Pr.

Agustin, Jose. La Panza del Tepozteco. Tino, illus. 2003. (SPA.). 118p. (J). (gr. 8-12). pap. 12.95 (978-968-19-0187-5(8)) Santillana USA Publishing Co., Inc.

Ahern, Carolyn L. Tino Turtle Travels to Mexico City, Mexico. Burt Sullivan, Neallia, illus. 2008. (ENG & SPA.). 32p. (J). (gr. -1-4). 19.95 incl. audio compact disk (978-0-9793158-2-4(4)) Tino Turtle Travels, LLC.

Alegria, Malin. Sofi Mendoza's Guide to Getting Lost in Mexico. 2008. (ENG.). 304p. (YA). (gr. 7). pap. 10.99 (978-0-689-87812-1(5), Simon & Schuster Bks. For Young Readers) Simon & Schuster Bks. For Young Readers.

Alsaid, Adi. North of Happy. 2017. (ENG.). 304p. 18.99 (978-0-373-21228-6(3), Harlequin Teen) Harlequin Enterprises, Ltd. CAN. Dist: HarperCollins Pubs.

Anaya, Rudolfo. Curse of the ChupaCabra. 2013. (ENG.). 176p. (YA). pap. 19.95 (978-0-8263-4115-0(2)) Univ. of New Mexico Pr.

—The First Tortilla: A Bilingual Story. Lamadrid, Enrique R., tr. Córdova, Amy, illus. 2012. (ENG & SPA.). 32p. (J). pap. 16.95 (978-0-8263-4215-7(9)) Univ. of New Mexico Pr.

Anaya, Rudolfo A. & Anaya, Rudolfo. The First Tortilla: A Bilingual Story. Lamadrid, Enrique R., tr. from ENG.

Córdova, Amy, illus. 2007. (SPA & ENG.). 32p. (J). (gr. 4-7). 16.95 *(978-0-8263-4214-0(0))* Univ. of New Mexico Pr.
And Then it was Sugar, 6 vols. (Multicultural Programs Ser.). 16p. (gr. 1-6). 31.95 *(978-0-7802-8324-4(4))* Wright Group/McGraw-Hill.
Angel, Ido. Vipo in Mexico: The Maya Treasure Mystery. 2015. (AV2 Animated Storytime Ser.). (ENG.). (J). lib. bdg. 29.99 *(978-1-4896-3908-0(X),* AV2 by Weigl) Weigl Pubs., Inc.
Anza, Ana Luisa. El Misterio de la Casa Chueca (y el Bulto Color Mugre) The Mystery of the Crooked House. Escobar, Antonio Rocha, illus. rev. ed. 2006. (Castillo de la Lectura Naranja Ser.). (SPA & ENG.). 120p. (J). (gr. 4-7). pap. 7.95 *(978-970-20-0200-0(1))* Castillo, Ediciones, S. A. de C. V. MEX. Dist: Macmillan.
Appleton, Victor. Tom Swift in the City of Gold. 2005. 27.95 *(978-1-4218-1510-7(9));* 204p. pap. 12.95 *(978-1-4218-1610-4(5))* 1st World Publishing, Inc. (1st World Library - Literary Society).
—Tom Swift in the City of Gold or Marvelo. 2006. pap. *(978-1-4065-0916-8(7))* Dodo Pr.
Archbold, David M. The Amazing Adventures of Chumley, Robin, Snickers & Mac. 2011. 48p. (gr. 4-6). pap. 19.26 *(978-1-4634-1518-1(4))* AuthorHouse.
Avalon-Pai, Phyllis. Children's Stories from Around the World. Arrott, Nancy, illus. 2008. 70p. pap. 9.95 *(978-0-9788283-8-7(0))* Acacia Publishing, Inc.
Bennett, Marilyn J. The Poinsettia Adventure. 2010. 60p. pap. 21.99 *(978-1-4490-7108-0(2))* AuthorHouse.
Blair, Kathryn S. Diario de Lucia (1939) 2003. (Mexican Diaries). (SPA., Illus.). 132p. (J). pap. *(978-970-690-039-5(X),* SOM7943) Planeta Mexicana Editorial S. A. de C. V. MEX. Dist: Lectorum Pubns., Inc.
Brammer, Ethriam Cash. The Rowdy, Rowdy Ranch / Alla en el Rancho Grande. Cruz, D. Nina, illus. 2003. (ENG & SPA.). 32p. (J). 16.95 *(978-1-55885-409-3(6),* Piñata Books) Arte Publico Pr.
Brandeis, Madeline. The Little Mexican Donkey Boy. 2011. 226p. 44.95 *(978-1-258-09794-3(X))* Literary Licensing, LLC.
Bray, Diane E. B. First Generation: The Story of Annie. 2008. 53p. pap. 16.95 *(978-1-60563-516-3(2))* America Star Bks.
Brooks, Melanie & Spenser and Mom Staff. Spenser Goes to el Paso. Jacobsen, Amie, illus. 2010. (SpenserNation Ser.). 32p. (J). 14.95 *(978-0-9817598-3-8(1))* Simple Fish Bk. Co., LLC.
Brown, Jeff. The Amazing Mexican Secret. Pamintuan, Macky, illus. 2010. (Flat Stanley's Worldwide Adventures Ser.: 5). (ENG.). 112p. (J). (gr. 2-5). pap. 4.99 *(978-0-06-142998-9(8));*No. 5. 15.99 *(978-0-06-142999-6(6))* HarperCollins Pubs.
Bruner, Roger & Bruner, Kristi Rae. Found in Translation: An Unforgettable Mission Trip Where Faith, Obedience, & Forgiveness Intersect. 2011. (Altered Hearts Ser.: 1). (ENG.). 368p. (YA). (gr. 9-12). pap. 9.99 *(978-1-60260-961-7(6),* Barbour Bks.) Barbour Publishing, Inc.
Cantwell, Michael. The Rising of the Fifth Sun. 2012. 120p. (gr. 4-6). 20.95 *(978-1-4620-7203-3(8));* pap. 10.95 *(978-1-4620-7201-9(1))* iUniverse, Inc.
Carlson, Melody. Notes from a Spinning Planet - Mexico. 2007. (Notes from a Spinning Planet Ser.). (ENG.). 256p. (YA). (gr. 7). pap. 12.99 *(978-1-4000-7146-3(1),* WaterBrook Pr.) Crown Publishing Group.
Carr, Pat. Border Ransom. 2006. (Chaparral Bks.). (ENG., Illus.). 178p. (J). (gr. 3-7). per. 11.95 *(978-0-87565-332-7(4))* Texas Christian Univ. Pr.
Carter, Aubrey Smith. The Enchanted Lizard: La Lagartijita Mágica. Nelson, Esther Whitt, ed. Branton, Molly, illus. 2006. (ENG & SPA.). 96p. (J). 18.95 *(978-1-893271-38-8(2),* Maverick Bks.) Trinity Univ. Pr.
Cohn. Dream Carver Pb. 2009. (Illus.). 40p. pap. 6.99 *(978-0-8118-7050-4(2))* Chronicle Bks. LLC.
Cruz, Maria Colleen. Border Crossing. 2003. 128p. (J). pap. 9.95 *(978-1-55885-405-5(3),* Piñata Books) Arte Publico Pr.
—Border Crossing. 2006. 122p. (gr. 8-12). 19.95 *(978-0-7569-6587-7(X))* Perfection Learning Corp.
Cuesy, Silvia. Diario de Mercedes (1844-48) 2003. (Mexican Diaries). (SPA., Illus.). 161p. (J). pap. *(978-970-690-037-1(3),* SOM7983) Planeta Mexicana Editorial S. A. de C. V. MEX. Dist: Lectorum Pubns., Inc.
DaColl, Ivar. El Dia de Muertos. 2004.Tr. of Day of the Dead. (SPA., Illus.). (J). 14.95 *(978-1-930332-44-7(0))* Lectorum Pubns., Inc.
Darnitz, Charlie. Diving for el Corazon. Diefendorf, Cathy, illus. 2007. (ENG.). 101p. (J). pap. 7.95 *(978-0-9744446-3-5(4))* All About Kids Publishing.
Dear Abuelita, 6, Pack. (Greetings Ser.: Vol. 2). (gr. 3-5). 31.00 *(978-0-7635-1765-6(8))* Rigby Education.
Death at the Border. 64p. (YA). (gr. 6-12). pap. *(978-0-8224-2361-4(8))* Globe Fearon Educational Publishing.
Desisti, Sam F. The Paco & Angelina Stories, 1 vol. 2009. 48p. pap. 16.95 *(978-1-61582-604-9(1))* America Star Bks.
Diederich, Phillippe. Playing for the Devil's Fire. 2016. (ENG.). 232p. (J). (gr. 6-10). 16.95 *(978-1-941026-29-8(X))* Cinco Puntos Pr.
Duncklee, John. Manchado & His Friends Manchado Y Sus Amigos. 2009. 52p. pap. 9.95 *(978-1-4401-2496-9(5))* iUniverse, Inc.
Emerson, Kevin. The Dark Shore. 2013. (Atlanteans Ser.: 2). (ENG.). 480p. (YA). (gr. 8). 17.99 *(978-0-06-206282-6(4))* HarperCollins Pubs.
Estrada Michel, Rafael, tr. Diario de Lupita. 2003. (Mexican Diaries). (SPA., Illus.). 179p. (J). pap. *(978-970-690-114-9(0))* Planeta Mexicana Editorial S. A. de C. V.
Estrada, Pau. Pedro's Burro. Estrada, Pau, illus. 2007. (My First I Can Read Bks.). (Illus.). 32p. (J). (gr. -1-k). lib. bdg. 16.89 *(978-0-06-056032-4(0))* HarperCollins Pubs.
Estrada, Pau & Capucilli, Alyssa Satin. Pedro's Burro. Estrada, Pau, illus. 2008. (My First I Can Read Ser.). (ENG., Illus.). 32p. (J). (gr. -1 — 1). pap. 3.99 *(978-0-06-056033-1(9))* HarperCollins Pubs.
Evans, Cordelia. Bet on It. Reel FX Inc. Staff, illus. 2014. (Book of Life Ser.). (ENG.). 16p. (J). (gr. -1-3). pap. 5.99 *(978-1-4814-2564-3(1),* Simon Spotlight) Simon Spotlight.
Ezirim, E. C. Jet Black & the Ebony Knights. 2010. 40p. 16.99 *(978-1-4520-7567-9(0))* AuthorHouse.
Feliciano, Maria Inez. Meximan. 2012. 28p. pap. 24.95 *(978-1-4626-9248-4(6))* America Star Bks.
Fine, Edith Hope. Bajo la Luna de Limon. 2004. (SPA., Illus.). (J). (gr. k-3). spiral bd. *(978-0-616-03089-9(4))* Canadian National Institute for the Blind/Institut National Canadien pour les Aveugles.
—Under the Lemon Moon. Moreno, Rene King, illus. 2010.Tr. of Bajo la Luna de Limon. (ENG.). 32p. (C). pap. 14.95 *(978-1-58430-051-9(5))* National Geographic School Publishing, Inc.
Fine, Edith Hope & Josephson, Judith Pinkerton. Armando & the Blue Tarp School, 1 vol. Sosa, Hernan, illus. 2007. (ENG.). 32p. (J). (gr. -1-3). lib. bdg. 16.95 *(978-1-58430-278-0(X))* Lee & Low Bks., Inc.
—Armando y la Escuela de Lona Azul. Sosa, Hernan, illus. 2015.Tr. of Armando & the Blue Tarp School. (SPA & ENG.). 32p. (J). (gr. k-4). pap. 10.95 *(978-1-60060-449-2(8))* Lee & Low Bks., Inc.
Fleischman, Sid. The Dream Stealer. Sis, Peter, illus. (ENG.). (J). 2011. 128p. pap. 6.99 *(978-0-06-178729-4(9))* 2009. 96p. (gr. 4-18). 16.99 *(978-0-06-175563-7(X))* HarperCollins Pubs. (Greenwillow Bks.).
Flitcroft, Jean. The Chupacabra. 2014. (Cryptid Files Ser.: No. 2). 232p. (gr. 4-8). (J). lib. bdg. 27.93 *(978-1-4677-3265-9(6));* (ENG.). (YA). pap. 7.95 *(978-1-4677-3483-7(7))* Lerner Publishing Group. (Darby Creek).
Flor Ada, Alma. Celebra el Cinco de Mayo con un Jarabe Tapatio. Gomez, Marcela & Silva, David, illus. 2006. (Cuentos para Celebrar / Stories to Celebrate Ser.). 30p. (gr. k-6). per. 11.95 *(978-1-59820-118-5(2))* Ediciones Alfaguara ESP. Dist: Santillana USA Publishing Co., Inc.
Flowers, J. J. Juan Pablo & the Butterflies. 2017. (ENG., Illus.). 224p. (YA). (gr. 9-12). 17.99 *(978-1-5072-0214-2(8),* Simon Pulse) Simon Pulse.
Fowler, Frank. The Broncho Rider Boys with Funston at Vera Cruz: Or: Upholding the Honor of the Stars & Stripes. 2007. (ENG.). 190p. pap. 19.99 *(978-1-4346-3206-7(7));* 202p. pap. 22.99 *(978-1-4346-3207-4(5))* Creative Media Partners, LLC.
Garza, Xavier. Lucha Libre: The Man in the Silver Mask - A Bilingual Cuento. Garza, Xavier, illus. 2007. (SPA & ENG., Illus.). 40p. (J). (gr. 4-6). pap. 8.95 *(978-1-933693-10-1(X))* Cinco Puntos Pr.
—Lucha Libre: The Man in the Silver Mask - A Bilingual Cuento. Crosthwaite, Luis Humberto, tr. Garza, Xavier, illus. 2005. (ENG & SPA., Illus.). 40p. (J). (gr. 4-6). 17.95 *(978-0-938317-92-0(X))* Cinco Puntos Pr.
Geeslin, Campbell. Elena's Serenade. Juan, Ana, illus. 2004. (ENG.). 40p. (J). (gr. -1-2). 19.99 *(978-0-689-84908-4(7),* Atheneum Bks. for Young Readers) Simon & Schuster Children's Publishing.
Gill, Heidi & Carter, Kris. 2 Kurious Kids: Mexico. 2012. (Illus.). 38p. (J). 14.95 *(978-1-936319-91-6(8))* Mascot Bks., Inc.
Goldman, Judy. Uncle Monarch & the Day of the Dead. Moreno, Rene King, illus. 2008. (ENG.). 32p. (J). (gr. 2-4). 16.95 *(978-1-59078-425-9(1))* Boyds Mills Pr.
Gollub, Matthew. The Twenty-Five Mixtec Cats. Martinez, Leovigildo, illus. 2004. (J). *(978-1-889910-30-7(9))* Tortuga Pr.
Guillain, Adam. Bella Balistica & the Izta Warriors. 2012. (Bella Balistica Ser.). (ENG., Illus.). 170p. (J). (gr. 4-7). pap. 9.95 *(978-1-84059-771-4(2))* Milet Publishing.
Hancock, H. Irving. Dave Darrin at Vera Cruz. rev. ed. 2006. 216p. 27.95 *(978-1-4218-1745-3(4));* pap. 12.95 *(978-1-4218-1845-0(0))* 1st World Publishing, Inc. (1st World Library - Literary Society).
—Dave Darrin at Vera Cruz. 2007. 180p. per. *(978-1-4065-1973-0(1))* Dodo Pr.
—The Young Engineers in Mexico. rev. ed. 2006. 208p. 27.95 *(978-1-4218-1738-5(1));* pap. 12.95 *(978-1-4218-1838-2(8))* 1st World Publishing, Inc. (1st World Library - Literary Society).
—The Young Engineers in Mexico. 2007. 176p. per. *(978-1-4065-1994-5(4))* Dodo Pr.
Herman-O'Neal, Jackie. Moctezuma's Zoo: A Tale from an Enchanted City. 2013. 28p. pap. 24.95 *(978-1-62709-271-5(4))* America Star Bks.
Hoena, Blake A. & Terrell, Brandon. Tony Hawk's 900 Revolution. 2013. (Tony Hawk's 900 Revolution Ser.). (ENG.). 128p. (gr. 3-4). 106.60 *(978-1-4342-4109-2(2),* Tony Hawk's 900 Revolution) Stone Arch Bks.
Hunt, Elizabeth Singer. The Quest for Aztec Gold - Mexico, Bk. 10. 2009. (Secret Agent Jack Stalwart Ser.: 10). (ENG.). 128p. (J). (gr. 1-4). pap. 5.99 *(978-1-60286-079-7(3),* Weinstein Bks.) Perseus Bks. Group.
Irwin, Bindi, et al. Surfing with Turtles: Bindi Wildlife Adventures. 2013. (Bindi's Wildlife Adventures Ser.: 8). (ENG.). 112p. (J). (gr. 3-6). pap. 4.99 *(978-1-4022-8094-8(7),* Sourcebooks Jabberwocky) Sourcebooks, Inc.
Isabel, Delgado Maria. Chave's Memories / Los Recuerdos de Chave. Yvonne, Symank, illus. 2008. 32p. (J). pap. 7.95 *(978-1-55885-244-0(1),* Piñata Books) Arte Publico Pr.
Jaramillo, Ann. La Linea. 2008. (ENG.). 144p. (J). (gr. 5-9). pap. 8.99 *(978-0-312-37354-2(6),* 9780312373542) Square Fish.
Johnston, Tony. Isabel's House of Butterflies. Guevara, Susan, illus. 2005. 32p. pap. 6.95 *(978-1-58685-844-5(0))* Gibbs Smith, Publisher.
Jungle Crossing. 2011. (ENG.). 228p. (J). (gr. 5-7). pap. 13.99 *(978-0-547-55009-1(X))* Houghton Mifflin Harcourt Publishing Co.
Kasischke, Laura. Feathered. 2008. (ENG.). 272p. (YA). (gr. 9-18). 16.99 *(978-0-06-081317-8(2),* HarperTeen) HarperCollins Pubs.
Keep, Richard. Clatter Bash! A Day of the Dead Celebration, 1 vol. Keep, Richard, illus. 2004. (ENG., Illus.). 32p. (J). (gr. k-3). 15.95 *(978-1-56145-322-1(6))* Peachtree Pubs.
Kephart, Beth. The Heart Is Not a Size. 2010. (ENG.). 256p. (YA). (gr. 8-18). 16.99 *(978-0-06-147048-6(1),* HarperTeen) HarperCollins Pubs.
Kerr, Cora. Love Lessons on Bird Beach. 2010. 88p. pap. 26.50 *(978-1-60860-713-6(5),* Strategic Bk. Publishing) Strategic Book Publishing & Rights Agency (SBPRA).
King, Dedie. I See the Sun in Mexico, 1 vol. Inglese, Judith, illus. 2012. (I See the Sun Ser.: 5). (ENG.). 40p. (J). (gr. 1-2). pap. 12.95 *(978-1-935874-14-0(4))* Satya Hse. Pubns.
Krensky, Stephen. The Tale of la Llorona: A Mexican Folktale. 2009. pap. 40.95 *(978-0-7613-4819-1(0))* Lerner Publishing Group.
Laínez, René Colato. From North to South. Cepeda, Joe, illus. 2013.Tr. of Del Norte Al Sur. (ENG & SPA.). 32p. (J). pap. 9.95 *(978-0-89239-304-6(1),* Children's Book Press) Lee & Low Bks., Inc.
—From North to South/Del Norte Al Sur. Cepeda, Joe, illus. 2010.Tr. of Del norte al Sur. (ENG & SPA.). 32p. (J). (gr. k-3). 17.95 *(978-0-89239-231-5(2))* Lee & Low Bks., Inc.
—Playing Loteria Mexicana: El Juego de la Loteria Mexicana. Arena, Jillayne, illus. 2005. (ENG, SPA & MUL.). 32p. (J). (gr. -1-3). 15.95 *(978-0-87358-881-2(9))* Cooper Square Publishing Llc.
Landman, Tanya. I Am Apache. 2008. (ENG., Illus.). 320p. (YA). (gr. 7-18). 17.99 *(978-0-7636-3664-7(9))* Candlewick Pr.
Leal, Luis, compiled by. Cuentos Mexicanos - de los origenes a la Revolucion. 2007. (SPA.). 184p. (J). per. 23.90 *(978-1-934768-04-4(9))* Stockcero, Inc.
LeBlanc, Margaret Ann. The Mexico Adventure: Book Three of Ms. Maddy Series, 1 vol. 2010. 72p. pap. 19.95 *(978-1-4489-8090-1(9))* America Star Bks.
Levy, Janice & Arisa, Miguel. I Remember Abuelito: A Day of the Dead Story. Lopez, Loretta, illus. 2012.Tr. of Yo Recuerdo a Abuelito - Un Cuento del Dia de los Muertos. (SPA & ENG.). (J). *(978-1-61913-114-9(5))* Weigl Pubs., Inc.
Long, Eula. Pirate's Doll: The Story of the China Poblana. 2011. 82p. 37.95 *(978-1-258-08444-8(9))* Literary Licensing, LLC.
Lorraine, Nancy. Tatty, the Lonely Monarch. Herron, Dorothy, illus. 2013. 48p. pap. 17.50 *(978-0-9893063-8-6(0))* ProsePress.
Lowery, Linda. The Tale of la Llorona: A Mexican Folktale. 2008. 48p. (J). pap. 6.95 *(978-0-8225-6743-1(1),* First Avenue Editions) Lerner Publishing Group.
—Truth & Salsa, 1 vol. (ENG.). 176p. (J). 2009. pap. 7.95 *(978-1-56145-498-3(2))* 2006. (gr. 3-7). 15.95 *(978-1-56145-366-5(8))* Peachtree Pubs.
Luedtke, Courtney. Baby Boo: The Happy Beginning. 2009. (Illus.). 72p. pap. 27.49 *(978-1-4389-2696-4(0))* AuthorHouse.
MacLachlan, Patricia. More Perfect Than the Moon. 2005. 16.00 *(978-0-7569-5437-6(1))* Perfection Learning Corp.
Madrigal, Antonio Hernandez. Erandi's Braids. dePaola, Tomie, illus. 2015. 32p. pap. 7.00 *(978-1-61003-530-9(5))* Center for the Collaborative Classroom.
Marquez, Sofia. Pepe Perez Mexican Mouse: Pepe Perez Comes to the United States: Book 1, 1 vol. Marquez, Sofia, illus. 2009. (Illus.). 20p. pap. 24.95 *(978-1-61546-496-8(4))* America Star Bks.
—Pepe Perez Mexican Mouse: Pepe Perez Comes to the United States: Book 1, 1 vol. 2010. 20p. 24.95 *(978-1-4489-6600-4(0))* PublishAmerica, Inc.
Marsden, Carolyn. Starfields. 2011. (ENG., Illus.). 224p. (J). (gr. 5). 15.99 *(978-0-7636-4820-6(5))* Candlewick Pr.
Matthews. Death in the Desert. (Thumbprint Mysteries Ser.). 32.86 *(978-0-8092-0416-8(9))* McGraw-Hill/Contemporary.
May, Eleanor. The Best Mother's Day Ever. Pilz, M. H., illus. 2010. (Social Studies Connects Ser.). 32p. (J). (gr. 1-3). pap. 5.95 *(978-1-57565-299-3(4))* Kane Press, Inc.
McAlister, Caroline. Holy Mole! A Folktale from Mexico. Czernecki, Stefan, illus. 2006. (ENG.). 32p. (J). (gr. k-3). 16.95 *(978-0-87483-775-9(8))* August Hse. Pubs., Inc.
McDougal-Littell Publishing Staff. Literature Connections English: A Place Where the Sea Remembers. 2004. (McDougal Littell Literature Connections Ser.). (ENG.). 208p. (gr. 10-10). 16.25 *(978-0-395-83361-2(2),* 2-70784) Great Source Education Group, Inc.
McKenzie, Precious. A Vacation in Ruins. 2015. (ENG.). 96p. (gr. 3-6). 31.36 *(978-1-63430-393-4(8))* Rourke Educational Media.
McLennan, Connie, illus. Domitila: A Cinderella Tale from the Mexican Tradition. 2014. (ENG.). 32p. (J). pap. 9.95 *(978-1-885008-43-5(0),* Shen's Bks.) Lee & Low Bks., Inc.
Medina, Meg. The Girl Who Could Silence the Wind. (ENG.). 256p. (YA). (gr. 9). 2013. pap. 8.99 *(978-0-7636-6419-0(7))* 2012. (Illus.). 17.99 *(978-0-7636-4602-8(4))* Candlewick Pr.
Meek, S. P. Pagan: A Border Patrol Horse. 2011. 254p. 46.95 *(978-1-258-08439-4(2))* Literary Licensing, LLC.
Meister, Cari. Airplane Adventure, 1 vol. Janovitz, Marilyn, illus. 2010. (My First Graphic Novel Ser.). (ENG.). 32p. (gr. k-2). pap. 6.25 *(978-1-4342-2286-2(1),* My First Graphic Novel) Stone Arch Bks.
Mervis (Pantoja), Judith. Yuyi & la Ram: Yuyi y la Rama. 2012. 24p. pap. 17.99 *(978-1-4685-7600-9(3))* AuthorHouse.
Mikaelsen, Ben. Sparrow Hawk Red. 2010. (ENG.). 192p. (J). (gr. 3-7). pap. 5.99 *(978-1-4231-3361-2(7))* Hyperion Pr.
Molina, Silvia & Silvia, Molina. Le Comieron la Lengua los Ratones. Rodriguez, Mari, illus. 2005. (Montana Encantada Ser.). (SPA.). 96p. (YA). (gr. 3-5). pap. 9.50 *(978-84-241-8557-2(9))* Everest Editora ESP. Dist: Lectorum Pubns., Inc.
Mora, Pat & Ventura, Gabriela Baeza. The Remembering Day / el Día de Los Muertos. Casilla, Robert, illus. 2015. (SPA & ENG.). 32p. (J). (gr. k-3). 17.95 *(978-1-55885-805-3(9),* Piñata Books) Arte Publico Pr.
Mora, Pat, et al. La Hermosa Señora: Nuestra Señora de Guadalupe. Johnson, Steve & Fancher, Lou, illus. 2012. (SPA & ENG.). 40p. (J). (gr. k-3). pap. 8.99 *(978-0-375-86840-5(2),* Dragonfly Bks.) Random Hse. Children's Bks.
Nail, Eric. The Wave Wranglers & the New Order of the Pyramid. 2007. 268p. (YA). pap. 18.95 *(978-1-4303-2254-2(3))* Lulu Pr., Inc.
Naylor, Phyllis Reynolds. Eating Enchiladas, 0 vols. Ramsey, Marcy, illus. 2011. (Simply Sarah Ser.: 0). (ENG.). 80p. (J). (gr. 1-4). pap. 9.99 *(978-0-7614-5885-2(9),* 9780761458852, Amazon Children's Publishing) Amazon Publishing.
Nelson, Suzanne. Heart & Salsa. 2006. (S. A. S. S. Ser.). (ENG., Illus.). 224p. (YA). (gr. 7-18). 6.99 *(978-0-14-240647-2(3),* Speak) Penguin Young Readers Group.
O'Dell, Scott. The Black Pearl. 2010. (ENG.). 144p. (gr. 5-7). pap. 7.99 *(978-0-547-33400-4(1),* HMH Books For Young Readers) Houghton Mifflin Harcourt Publishing Co.
—The King's Fifth. 2006. (ENG., Illus.). 272p. (YA). (gr. 7). pap. 7.99 *(978-0-618-74783-2(4))* Houghton Mifflin Harcourt Publishing Co.
Olberg, Henry, illus. The Magical Tooth Fairies: A Surprise in Mexico. 2012. (J). *(978-0-86715-568-6(X))* Edition Q, Inc.
Oliver, Juanbjuan, illus. The Prince & the Three Oranges a Fairy Tale from Mexico. 2017. (Text Connections Guided Close Reading Ser.). (J). (gr. 1). *(978-1-4900-1822-5(0))* Benchmark Education Co.
Oppenheim, Joanne F. El Milagro de la Primera Flora de Nochebuena: Un Cuento Mexicano Sobre la Navidad. Negrin, Fabian, illus. 2003. (SPA & ENG.). 32p. (J). 16.99 *(978-1-84148-308-5(7))* Barefoot Bks., Inc.
—The Miracle of the First Poinsettia. Negrin, Fabian, illus. 2003. (ENG.). 32p. (J). 16.99 *(978-1-84148-245-3(5))* Barefoot Bks., Inc.
Orozco, Rebeca & Muro, Claudia Burr. Dona Josefa y sus Conspiraciones. 2005. (Ya Veras Ser.). (SPA., Illus.). (J). (gr. 3-5). pap. 9.95 *(978-968-7381-29-9(9))* Tecolote, Ediciones, S.A. de C.V. MEX. Dist: Iaconi, Mariuccia Bk. Imports.
Osborne, Mary Pope. Shadow of the Shark. 2017. (Magic Tree House Merlin Mission Ser.: 25). (ENG., Illus.). 144p. (J). (gr. 2-5). 5.99 ***(978-0-553-51084-3(3),*** Random Hse. Bks. for Young Readers) Random Hse. Children's Bks.
—Shadow of the Shark. Murdocca, Sal, illus. 2015. (Magic Tree House Merlin Mission Ser.: No. 25). (ENG.). 144p. (J). (gr. 2-5). lib. bdg. 15.99 *(978-0-553-51082-9(7),* Random Hse. Bks. for Young Readers) Random Hse. Children's Bks.
—Soccer on Sunday. Murdocca, Sal, illus. (Magic Tree House Merlin Missions Ser.: No. 24). (ENG.). (J). (gr. 2-5). 2016. 144p. 5.99 *(978-0-307-98056-4(1))* 2014. 128p. 12.99 *(978-0-307-98053-3(7))* Random Hse. Children's Bks. (Random Hse. Bks. for Young Readers).
Paulsen, Gary. The Crossing. 2006. (Point Ser.). (ENG.). 128p. (J). (gr. 2-5). per. 6.99 *(978-0-439-78661-4(4),* Scholastic Paperbacks) Scholastic, Inc.
Pedraza, M. Eugenia Rueda. Nico's Voyage. 2013. 32p. pap. *(978-1-4602-2360-4(8))* FriesenPress.
Pequeña the Burro: Evaluation Guide. 2006. (J). *(978-1-55942-420-2(6))* Witcher Productions.
Petretti, Silvia I. Rachel's Easter Vacation in Mexico. James, Elizabeth, ed. 2011. (Illus.). 50p. (J). pap. 14.99 *(978-1-931671-37-8(0))* FM Publishing Co.
Pidutti, Nancy L. José the Donkey. 2013. 36p. pap. 16.99 *(978-1-4497-9213-8(8),* WestBow Pr.) Author Solutions, Inc.
Pugliano-Martin, Carol. Quetzacoatl Brings Corn to His People: A Legend from Mexico. 2006. (J). pap. *(978-1-4108-7168-8(1))* Benchmark Education Co.
Ralphson, G. Harvey. Boy Scouts in Mexico. 2007. 112p. (gr. 4-7). per. *(978-1-4068-3728-5(8))* Echo Library.
—Boy Scouts in Mexico or on Guard with un. 2005. pap. 27.95 *(978-1-885529-52-7(X))* Stevens Publishing.
—Boy Scouts in Mexico,Or on Guard with Uncle Sam. 2003. 136p. pap. 14.99 *(978-1-59224-085-2(2))* Wildside Pr., LLC.
Resau, Laura. The Lightning Queen. 2015. (ENG.). 336p. (J). (gr. 3-7). 16.99 *(978-0-545-80084-6(6),* Scholastic Pr.) Scholastic, Inc.
—Red Glass. 2009. (ENG.). 304p. (YA). (gr. 7). pap. 8.99 *(978-0-440-24025-9(5),* Delacorte Bks. for Young Readers) Random Hse. Children's Bks.
Rice, Dona Herwick & Isecke, Harriet. Remember the Alamo, 1 vol. 2009. (Building Fluency Through Reader's Theater Ser.). (ENG., Illus.). 32p. (J). (gr. 3-5). pap. 7.99 *(978-1-4333-0541-2(0))* Teacher Created Materials, Inc.
Richardson, Arleta. Across the Border. 2016. (Beyond the Orphan Train Ser.: 4). (ENG.). 192p. (J). (gr. 3-6). pap. 7.99 *(978-0-7814-1358-9(3))* Cook, David C.
Romeu, Emma. Gregorio Vuelve a Mexico. 2003. (SPA., Illus.). 148p. (J). (gr. 5-8). pap. 9.95 *(978-968-19-0367-1(6))* Santillana USA Publishing Co., Inc.
Rosas, Alejandro. Diario de Aurora. 2003. (Mexican Diaries). (SPA.). 164p. (J). pap. *(978-968-406-990-9(1),* SOM7961) Planeta Mexicana Editorial S. A. de C. V. MEX. Dist: Lectorum Pubns., Inc.
Rosenthal, S. L. Mama, Where Do Our Butterflies Go in the Winter? 2011. 40p. pap. 24.95 *(978-1-4560-7498-2(9))* America Star Bks.
Rothshank, Brooke, illus. Cups Held Out. 2006. 40p. (J). (gr. -1-3). per. 12.99 *(978-0-8361-9316-9(4))* Herald Pr.
Ryan, Pam Muñoz. Becoming Naomi Leon. 2005. (ENG.). 272p. (J). (gr. 3-7). reprint ed. per. 7.99 *(978-0-439-26997-1(0),* Scholastic Paperbacks) Scholastic, Inc.
—Esperanza Rising. 2016. (gr. 5-8). lib. bdg. 17.20 *(978-0-613-53807-7(2),* Turtleback) Turtleback Bks.
—Mice & Beans. Cepeda, Joe, illus. 2005. (gr. -1-3). lib. bdg. 17.00 *(978-0-7569-5089-7(9))* Perfection Learning Corp.
Sanchez, Juanita L. Pancho the Green Parrot Lays an Egg, 1 vol. Ramirez, Samuel, illus. 2009. 24p. pap. 24.95 *(978-1-61546-150-9(7))* America Star Bks.
Sanderson, Nancy. Horse of the Four Winds. 2011. 152p. (gr. 10-12). pap. 14.50 *(978-1-4634-4802-8(3))* AuthorHouse.
Scieszka, Jon. Me Oh Maya. McCauley, Adam, illus. 2005. (Time Warp Trio Ser.: 13). (ENG.). 96p. (J). (gr. 2-4). 5.99 *(978-0-14-240300-6(8),* Puffin Books) Penguin Young Readers Group.
—Me Oh Maya. McCauley, Adam, illus. 2005. (Time Warp Trio Ser.: No. 13). 69p. (gr. 2-6). 15.00 *(978-0-7569-5060-6(0))* Perfection Learning Corp.
Sclafani, Terry. The Thompson Twins Western Adventure. 2009. 114p. pap. 11.95 *(978-1-4327-3783-2(X))* Outskirts Pr., Inc.
Silva, Carlos. Diario de Fernando. 2003. (Mexican Diaries). (SPA., Illus.). 172p. (J). pap. *(978-970-690-244-3(9))* Planeta Mexicana Editorial S. A. de C. V.
Smallman, Steve. Santa Is Coming to Durango. Dunn, Robert, illus. 2013. (ENG.). 32p. (J). (-3). 9.99 *(978-1-4022-9133-3(7),* Sourcebooks Jabberwocky) Sourcebooks, Inc.
Smith, Emilie & Tejada, Marguerita. Viva Zapata!, 1 vol. Czernecki, Stefan, illus. 2009. (ENG.). 32p. (J). (gr. -1-3). 14.95 *(978-1-896580-55-5(6))* Tradewind Bks. CAN. Dist: Orca Bk. Pubs. USA.
Smith, Roland. Eruption. 2012. (Storm Runners Ser.: 3). (ENG.). 160p. (J). (gr. 3-7). 16.99 *(978-0-545-08174-0(2),* Scholastic Pr.) Scholastic, Inc.

Spenser & Brooks, Melanie. Spenser Via a el Paso. Jacobsen, Amie, illus. 2010. (SpenserNation Ser.). (SPA.). 32p. (J). 14.95 *(978-0-9817598-5-2(8))* Simple Fish Bk. Co., LLC.

Stalcup. La Loncheria. Arroyo, illus. 2008. (SPA & ENG.). 28p. (J). pap. 8.95 *(978-1-60448-006-1(8))* Lectura Bks.

—La Loncheria. Arroyo, illus. 2008. (SPA & ENG.). 28p. (J). 15.95 *(978-1-60448-005-4(X))* Lectura Bks.

Stanton, Karen. Papi's Gift. Moreno, Rene King, illus. 2007. (ENG.). 32p. (J). (gr. 2-4). 16.95 *(978-1-59078-422-8(7))* Boyds Mills Pr.

Stavans, Ilan. Golemito. Villegas, Teresa, illus. 2013. (ENG.). 32p. (J). 16.95 *(978-1-58838-292-4(3),* NewSouth Bks.) NewSouth, Inc.

StJohn, Amanda. Medio Pollito (Half-Chick) A Mexican Folktale. Todd, Sue, illus. 2011. (Folktales from Around the World Ser.). (ENG.). 24p. (J). (gr. k-3). 28.50 *(978-1-60973-141-0(7),* 201144) Child's World, Inc., The.

Stokes, Erica M. Sports of Mexico. 2009. (Mexico: Beautiful Land, Diverse People Ser.). (Illus.). 64p. (YA). (gr. 7-12). 21.95 *(978-1-4222-0654-6(8))* Mason Crest.

Sutton, Laurie S. The Mystery of the Aztec Tomb, 1 vol. Neely, Scott, illus. 2014. (You Choose Stories: Scooby-Doo Ser.). (ENG.). 112p. (gr. 2-3). 32.65 *(978-1-4342-9127-1(8),* You Choose Bks.) Capstone Press of Coughlan Cos.

Terrell, Brandon & Tortosa, Wilson. Exiled, Vol. 7. Ito, Leonardo, illus. 2012. (Tony Hawk's 900 Revolution Ser.). (ENG.). 128p. (gr. 3-4). pap. 7.19 *(978-1-4342-3889-4(X));* lib. bdg. 26.65 *(978-1-4342-3313-4(8))* Stone Arch Bks. (Tony Hawk's 900 Revolution).

Titus, Eve. Basil in Mexico. Galdone, Paul, illus. 2016. (Great Mouse Detective Ser.: 3). (ENG.). 112p. (J). (gr. 1-4). pap. 5.99 *(978-1-4814-6407-9(8),* Aladdin) Simon & Schuster Children's Publishing.

Tonatiuh, Duncan. Dear Primo: A Letter to My Cousin. 2010. (ENG., Illus.). 32p. (J). (gr. k-2). 16.95 *(978-0-8109-3872-4(3),* Abrams Bks. for Young Readers) Abrams, Inc.

Tony Hawk's 900 Revolution. 2013. (Tony Hawk's 900 Revolution Ser.). (ENG.). 128p. (gr. 3-4). 319.80 *(978-1-4342-4110-8(6),* Tony Hawk's 900 Revolution) Stone Arch Bks.

Toretto, Jordana. The Runaway Children. 2013. 30p. pap. 16.95 *(978-1-63004-706-1(6))* America Star Bks.

Torres, Eliseo & Sawyer, Timothy L. Stories of Mexico's Independence Days & Other Bilingual Children's Fables. Ramirez, Herman, illus. 2005. (ENG & SPA.). 70p. (J). (gr. 3-7). pap. 15.95 *(978-0-8263-3886-0(0))* Univ. of New Mexico Pr.

Trottier, Maxine. Migrant, 1 vol. Arsenault, Isabelle, illus. 2011. (ENG.). 40p. (J). (gr. -1-2). 18.95 *(978-0-88899-975-7(5))* Groundwood Bks. CAN. Dist: Publishers Group West (PGW).

Unrau, Adela. A Big Change, 1 vol. Friesen, Anni, illus. 2010. 16p. pap. 24.95 *(978-1-4489-7672-0(3))* PublishAmerica, Inc.

Vernon, Ursula. Dani Bocafuego. la Cueva Del Murcielago Gigante. 2012. (SPA.). 204p. (J). (gr. 4-6). pap. 20.99 *(978-84-246-3599-2(X))* La Galera, S.A. Editorial ESP. Dist: Lectorum Pubns., Inc.

—Lair of the Bat Monster. 4th ed. (Dragonbreath Ser.: 4). (ENG.). 208p. (J). (gr. 3-7). 2014. pap. 6.99 *(978-0-14-751320-5(0),* Puffin Books) 2011. 12.99 *(978-0-8037-3525-5(1),* Dial Bks) Penguin Young Readers Group.

—Lair of the Bat Monster. 2014. (Dragonbreath Ser.: 4). lib. bdg. 17.20 *(978-0-606-35711-1(4))* Turtleback Bks.

Villalpando, Jose Manuel. Diario de Clara Eugenia (1864-67) 2003. (Diarios Mexicanos Coleccion). (SPA., Illus.). 174p. (J). (gr. 5-8). pap. *(978-968-406-900-8(6),* SOM7940) Planeta Mexicana Editorial S. A. de C. V.

Villanueva, Pedro. Chronicle of a New Kid. 2017. (Text Connections Guided Close Reading Ser.). (J). (gr. 1). *(978-1-4900-1825-6(5))* Benchmark Education Co.

Voorhees, Coert. In Too Deep. 2014. (ENG.). 336p. (YA). (gr. 7-12). pap. 8.99 *(978-1-4231-4473-1(2))* Hyperion Bks. for Children.

Walker, Kathryn. Unsolved! 2008. (J). (gr. 4-7). *(978-0-7787-4140-4(0))* Crabtree Publishing Co.

Wells, Marcia. Mystery in Mayan Mexico. Calo, Marcos, illus. 2016. (Eddie Red Undercover Ser.: 2). (ENG.). 224p. (J). (gr. 5-7). pap. 7.99 *(978-0-544-66850-8(2),* HMH Books For Young Readers) Houghton Mifflin Harcourt Publishing Co.

—Mystery in Mayan Mexico. 2016. (Eddie Red Undercover Ser.: 2). lib. bdg. 18.40 *(978-0-606-39664-6(0))* Turtleback Bks.

Williams, Geoffrey T. The Devil Fish. Artful Doodlers, illus. Campbell, Tom, photos by. 2008. (Save Our Seas Adventure Bks.). (ENG.). 64p. (J). (gr. 4-7). 8.95 *(978-0-9800444-1-6(3))* Save Our Seas, Ltd.

Zepeda, Monique. Las Pinatas. Graullera, Fabiola, illus.Tr. of Pinatas. (SPA.). 26p. (J). (gr. 3-5). pap. 6.95 *(978-968-19-0612-2(8))* Santillana USA Publishing Co., Inc.

Zevin, Gabrielle. Because It Is My Blood, 1 vol. 2012. (Birthright Ser.: 2). (ENG.). 368p. (YA). (gr. 7). 17.99 *(978-0-374-38074-8(0),* 9780374380748, Farrar, Straus & Giroux (BYR)) Farrar, Straus & Giroux.

—Because It Is My Blood. 2013. (Birthright Ser.: 2). (ENG.). 384p. (YA). (gr. 7). pap. 9.99 *(978-1-250-03422-9(1),* 9781250034229) Square Fish.

MEXICO—FOREIGN RELATIONS

Porterfield, Jason. The Treaty of Guadalupe Hidalgo 1848: A Primary Source Examination of the Treaty That Ended the Mexican-American War. 2009. (Primary Sources of American Treaties Ser.). 64p. (gr. 5-8). 58.50 *(978-1-60851-516-5(8))* Rosen Publishing Group, Inc., The.

Yomtov, Nelson. The United States & Mexico. 2013. (Cornerstones of Freedom™, Third Ser.). (ENG., Illus.). 64p. (J). pap. 8.95 *(978-0-531-21963-8(1));* lib. bdg. 30.00 *(978-0-531-23605-5(6))* Scholastic Library Publishing.

MEXICO—HISTORY

Abnett, Dan. Hernán Cortés y la Caída Del Imperio Azteca. 2009. (Historietas Juveniles: Biografías (Jr. Graphic Biographies) Ser.). (SPA., Illus.). 24p. (gr. 3-8). pap. 10.60 *(978-1-4358-3314-2(7))* Rosen Publishing Group, Inc., The.

—Hernán Cortés y la Caída Del Imperio Azteca. Abregón, José María, tr. 2009. (Historietas Juveniles: Biografías (Jr. Graphic Biographies) Ser.). (SPA., Illus.). 24p. (J). (gr. 2-5). 25.25 *(978-1-4358-8560-8(0))* Rosen Publishing Group, Inc., The.

Aykroyd, Clarissa. Meeting Future Challenges: The Government of Mexico. 2014. (Mexico: Leading the Southern Hemisphere Ser.: 16). 64p. (J). (gr. 7-18). lib. bdg. 22.95 *(978-1-4222-3223-1(9))* Mason Crest.

Brooks, Susie. Mexico. 2016. (Unpacked Ser.). (ENG., Illus.). 32p. (J). (gr. 4-6). pap. 11.99 *(978-0-7502-9171-2(0),* Wayland) Hachette Children's Group GBR. Dist: Hachette Bk. Group.

Brownlie Bojang, Ali. Mexico, 1 vol. 2011. (Countries Around the World Ser.). (ENG.). 48p. (gr. 3-6). pap. 9.95 *(978-1-4329-5238-9(2),* NA-h) Heinemann-Raintree.

Buckley, A. M. Mexico, 1 vol. 2011. (Countries of the World Set 1 Ser.). (ENG., Illus.). 144p. (J). (gr. 6-12). lib. bdg. 37.07 *(978-1-61783-116-4(6))* ABDO Publishing Co.

Burt, Janet. Mexico's Pacific North States. 2014. (Mexico: Leading the Southern Hemisphere Ser.: 16). 64p. (J). (gr. 7-18). lib. bdg. 22.95 *(978-1-4222-3225-5(5))* Mason Crest.

Cain, Marie Mowery. George Takes a Road Trip, Mexico. 2013. (Big Books, Red Ser.). (ENG & SPA., Illus.). 16p. pap. 33.00 *(978-1-59246-206-3(5))* Big Books, by George!

Carew-Miller, Anna. Famous People of Mexican History. 2014. (Mexico: Leading the Southern Hemisphere Ser.: 16). 64p. (J). (gr. 7-18). lib. bdg. 22.95 *(978-1-4222-3215-6(8))* Mason Crest.

—Vital & Creative: The Art & Architecture of Mexico. 2014. (Mexico: Leading the Southern Hemisphere Ser.: 16). 64p. (J). (gr. 7-18). lib. bdg. 22.95 *(978-1-4222-3219-4(0))* Mason Crest.

Celebrate: Mexico. 2009. (Celebrate Country Ser.). 32p. (gr. 4-6). 28.00 *(978-1-60413-267-0(1),* Chelsea Clubhouse) Facts On File, Inc.

Cobb, Allan B. Mexico: A Primary Source Cultural Guide. 2009. (Primary Sources of World Cultures Ser.). 128p. (gr. 4-5). 79.90 *(978-1-60851-927-9(9))* Rosen Publishing Group, Inc., The.

Conklin, Wendy. Moctezuma: Aztec Ruler, 1 vol. 2007. (Primary Source Readers Ser.). (ENG.). 32p. (J). (gr. 4-4). pap. 8.99 *(978-0-7439-0457-5(5))* Shell Educational Publishing.

Dawson, Imogen. Food & Feasts with the Aztecs. 2004. (Illus.). 32p. (J). (gr. 4-8). reprint ed. 14.00 *(978-0-7567-7143-0(9))* DIANE Publishing Co.

Field, Randi. Mexico's Gulf States. 2014. (Mexico: Leading the Southern Hemisphere Ser.: 16). 64p. (J). (gr. 7-18). lib. bdg. 22.95 *(978-1-4222-3224-8(7))* Mason Crest.

Gagne, Tammy. We Visit Mexico. 2010. (Your Land & My Land Ser.). (Illus.). 64p. (J). (gr. 3-6). lib. bdg. 33.95 *(978-1-58415-889-9(1))* Mitchell Lane Pubs., Inc.

Ganeri, Anita. Mexico: A Benjamin Blog & His Inquisitive Dog Guide, 1 vol. Isik, Sernur, illus. 2014. (Country Guides, with Benjamin Blog & His Inquisitive Dog Ser.). (ENG.). 32p. (gr. 1-3). 29.99 *(978-1-4109-6664-3(X),* Read Me!) Heinemann-Raintree.

Garbus, Julie. Mexico. Greenhaven Press Staff, ed. 2015. (Introducing Issues with Opposing Viewpoints Ser.). (ENG., Illus.). 144p. (J). (gr. 7-10). lib. bdg. 42.00 *(978-0-7377-7237-1(9),* Greenhaven Pr., Inc.) Cengage Gale.

García Dávila, Sandra. Los Antepasados Para Ninos. 2006. (SPA.). 142p. (YA). pap. *(978-970-643-359-6(7))* Selector, S.A. de C.V.

George, Lynn. Teotihuacan: Designing an Ancient Mexican City: Calculating Perimeters & Areas of Squares & Rectangles. 2009. (PowerMath: Proficiency Ser.). 32p. (gr. 4-5). 47.90 *(978-1-60851-400-7(5),* PowerKids Pr.) Rosen Publishing Group, Inc., The.

Goddard, Phyllis M. Spratling Silver: Recognizing a Spratling Silver Treasure: a Field Guide. 2003. (Illus.). 152p. per. 39.95 *(978-0-9740907-3-3(5))* Keenan Tyler Paine.

Hart, Paul. Emiliano Zapata: Mexico's Social Revolutionary. 2017. (World in a Life Ser.). (ENG.). 320p. (C). pap. 19.95 ***(978-0-19-068808-0(4))*** Oxford Univ. Pr., Inc.

Higgins, Nadia. Spanish Missions of the Old West. 2006. (Events in American History Ser.). (Illus.). 48p. (YA). (gr. 3-6). lib. bdg. 31.36 *(978-1-60044-128-8(9))* Rourke Educational Media.

Hoyt-Goldsmith, Diane. Cinco de Mayo: Celebrating the Traditions of Mexico. Migdale, Lawrence, illus. 2008. (ENG.). 32p. (J). (gr. 3-7). 16.95 *(978-0-8234-2107-7(4))* Holiday Hse., Inc.

Hudak, Heather C. A Refugee's Journey from Guatemala. 2017. 32p. (J). ***(978-0-7787-3673-8(3))*** Crabtree Publishing Co.

Hunter, Amy N. Ancient Land with a Fascinating Past: The History of Mexico. 2014. (Mexico: Leading the Southern Hemisphere Ser.: 16). 64p. (J). (gr. 7-18). lib. bdg. 22.95 *(978-1-4222-3218-7(2))* Mason Crest.

—The History of Mexico. 2009. (Mexico: Beautiful Land, Diverse People Ser.). (Illus.). 64p. (YA). (gr. 7-12). 21.95 *(978-1-4222-0653-9(X))* Mason Crest.

Ingram, Scott. Mexican Americans. 2006. (World Almanac Library of American Immigration). (Illus.). 48p. (gr. 5-12). pap. 14.05 *(978-0-8368-7329-0(7));* lib. bdg. 31.00 *(978-0-8368-7316-0(5))* Stevens, Gareth Publishing LLLP. (Gareth Stevens Secondary Library).

Jermyn, Leslie & Conboy, Fiona. Mexico. 2010. (Welcome to My Country Ser.). 48p. (gr. 3). 28.50 *(978-1-60870-157-5(3))* Marshall Cavendish Corp.

Jovinelly, Joann. The Crafts & Culture of the Aztecs. 2009. (Crafts of the Ancient World Ser.). 48p. (gr. 5-8). 58.50 *(978-1-61512-064-2(5),* Rosen Reference) Rosen Publishing Group, Inc., The.

Juarez, Christine. Mexico, 1 vol. 2013. (Countries Ser.). (ENG.). 24p. (gr. k-1). pap. 6.95 *(978-1-4765-3516-6(7),* Pebble Bks.) Capstone Press of Coughlan Cos.

Kalman, Bobbie & Walker, Niki. Conoce México. 2009. (Conoce Mi País Ser.). (SPA.). 32p. (J). (gr. 2-5). pap. *(978-0-7787-8215-5(8))* Crabtree Publishing Co.

—Spotlight on Mexico. 2007. (Spotlight on My Country Ser.). (ENG., Illus.). 32p. (J). (gr. 4-7). pap. *(978-0-7787-3477-2(3))* Crabtree Publishing Co.

Kauffman, Dorothy. Letters from Canada & Mexico. 2005. (Oxford Picture Dictionary for the Content Areas Ser.). (ENG., Illus.). 22p. pap. 7.56 *(978-0-19-430951-6(7))* Oxford Univ. Pr., Inc.

Kent, Deborah. Mexico. 2011. (Enchantment of the World Ser.). (ENG.). 144p. (J). (gr. 5-9). lib. bdg. 40.00 *(978-0-531-25355-7(4))* Scholastic Library Publishing.

King, David C. Projects about the Ancient Aztecs. 2006. (Hands-On History Ser.). (Illus.). 48p. (gr. 3-7). lib. bdg. 21.95 *(978-0-7614-2256-3(0),* Benchmark Bks.) Marshall Cavendish Corp.

Kopp, Megan. Mexico. 2014. (J). *(978-1-4896-1022-5(7))* Weigl Pubs., Inc.

Levy, Janey. Mexico. 2006. (Tony Stead Independent Reading Collection). (ENG.). 24p. (gr. 3-6). pap. 8.85 *(978-1-4042-5669-9(5))* Rosen Publishing Group, Inc., The.

Lindeen, Mary. Welcome to Mexico! 2011. (Wonder Readers Fluent Level Ser.). (ENG.). 16p. (gr. -1-2). pap. 35.94 *(978-1-4296-8202-2(7),* Wonder Readers) Capstone Press of Coughlan Cos.

—Welcome to North America, 1 vol. (Wonder Readers: Social Studies). (ENG.). (gr. -1-2). 2012. 20p. lib. bdg. 22.65 *(978-1-4296-9617-3(6))* 2011. 16p. pap. 35.94 *(978-1-4296-8204-6(3))* Capstone Press of Coughlan Cos. (Wonder Readers).

MacLeod, Deirdre Day. Mexico's Central States. 2014. (Mexico: Leading the Southern Hemisphere Ser.: 16). 64p. (J). (gr. 7-18). lib. bdg. 22.95 *(978-1-4222-3228-6(X))* Mason Crest.

—Mexico's Northern States. 2014. (Mexico: Leading the Southern Hemisphere Ser.: 16). 64p. (J). (gr. 7-18). lib. bdg. 22.95 *(978-1-4222-3227-9(1))* Mason Crest.

Madonna, Colleen & Williams, Flood. Beautiful Diversity: The Geography of Mexico. 2014. (Mexico: Leading the Southern Hemisphere Ser.: 16). 64p. (J). (gr. 7-18). lib. bdg. 22.95 *(978-1-4222-3214-9(X))* Mason Crest.

—Fiesta! the Festivals of Mexico. 2014. (Mexico: Leading the Southern Hemisphere Ser.: 16). 64p. (J). (gr. 7-18). lib. bdg. 22.95 *(978-1-4222-3217-0(4))* Mason Crest.

—Spirit of a Nation: The People of Mexico. 2014. (Mexico: Leading the Southern Hemisphere Ser.: 16). 64p. (J). (gr. 7-18). lib. bdg. 22.95 *(978-1-4222-3216-3(6))* Mason Crest.

Maloy, Jackie. The Ancient Maya. (True Book(tm), a — Ancient Civilizations Ser.). (ENG.). 48p. (J). 2009. (gr. 2-5). 31.00 *(978-0-531-25229-1(9))* 2010. (Illus.). (gr. 3-5). pap. 6.95 *(978-0-531-24110-3(6))* Scholastic Library Publishing.

Marsico, Katie. The Colorado River. 2013. (Explorer Library: Social Studies Explorer Ser.). (ENG.). 32p. (J). (gr. 4-8). 28.50 *(978-1-62431-014-0(1),* 202507); pap. 14.21 *(978-1-62431-038-6(9),* 202509) Cherry Lake Publishing.

—The Rio Grande. 2013. (Explorer Library: Social Studies Explorer Ser.). (ENG.). 32p. (J). (gr. 4-8). 28.50 *(978-1-62431-012-6(5),* 202499); pap. 14.21 *(978-1-62431-036-2(2),* 202501) Cherry Lake Publishing.

McCullough, Naomi V. The Technology of the Aztecs. 2016. (Ancient Innovations Ser.). 64p. (J). 34.21 *(978-1-5026-2239-6(4))* Cavendish Square Publishing.

McDaniel, Jan. Zesty & Colorful Cuisine: The Food of Mexico. 2014. (Mexico: Leading the Southern Hemisphere Ser.: 16). 64p. (J). (gr. 7-18). lib. bdg. 22.95 *(978-1-4222-3222-4(0))* Mason Crest.

McDonnell, Ginger. Next Stop: Mexico, 1 vol. 2nd rev. ed. 2013. (Nonfiction Readers Ser.). (ENG., Illus.). 24p. (J). (gr. 2-2). pap. 23.96 *(978-1-4807-1037-5(7))* Shell Educational Publishing.

McNamara, Margaret. Discover Mexico. 2006. (J). pap. *(978-1-4108-6459-8(6))* Benchmark Education Co.

The Mexican Revolution. 2011. (Milestones in Modern World History Ser.). (Illus.). 128p. (J). (gr. 9). 35.00 *(978-1-60413-459-9(3),* Chelsea Hse.) Facts On File, Inc.

Mexican Revolution 2003. (Illus.). (YA). spiral bd. *(978-0-9759194-6-0(6))* Publicaciones Papelandia.

Mexico: Leading the Southern Hemisphere. 2015. (Illus.). (J). *(978-1-4222-3213-2(1))* Mason Crest.

Mexico's Desert Country 2003. (Illus.). (YA). spiral bd. *(978-0-9759194-7-7(4))* Publicaciones Papelandia.

Morris, Ting. Arts & Crafts of the Aztecs & Maya. Young, Emma, illus. 2006. (Arts & Crafts of the Ancient World Ser.). 32p. (J). lib. bdg. 28.50 *(978-1-58340-915-2(7),* 1262694) Black Rabbit Bks.

Nantus, Sheryl. Mexico's Pacific South States. 2014. (Mexico: Leading the Southern Hemisphere Ser.: 16). 64p. (J). (gr. 7-18). lib. bdg. 22.95 *(978-1-4222-3226-2(3))* Mason Crest.

Nicholson, Dorinda Makanaōnalani. The School the Aztec Eagles Built, 1 vol. Nicholson, Dorinda Makanaōnalani, photos by. 2016. (ENG., Illus.). 48p. (J). 18.95 *(978-1-60060-440-9(4))* Lee & Low Bks., Inc.

Noticias de Fin de Siglo. 2005. (SPA.). (J). pap. *(978-968-7381-10-7(8))* Tecolote, Ediciones, S.A. de C.V.

Palos, Lilia. Acercate a la Historia 3 de las Raices Indigenas al Mexico Contemprineo Actores Sociales, Vida Cotidiana, Mentalidades y Cultura. 2003. (SPA.). 350p. (YA). *(978-968-7903-42-2(2))* Edere, S. A. de C. V.

Parker, Lewis K. Why Mexican Immigrants Came to America. (Coming to America Ser.). 24p. 2009. (gr. 2-3). 42.50 *(978-1-61511-887-8(X))* 2003. (Illus.). (J). lib. bdg. 22.60 *(978-0-8239-6459-8(0))* Rosen Publishing Group, Inc., The. (PowerKids Pr.).

Perkins, Chloe. Living in ... Mexico. Woolley, Tom, illus. 2016. (Living In... Ser.). (ENG.). 32p. (J). (gr. k-2). pap. 3.99 *(978-1-4814-6050-7(1),* Simon Spotlight) Simon Spotlight.

Pliego, Jane. La Reforma para Ninos. (SPA.). (J). 8.98 *(978-970-643-394-7(5))* Selector, S.A. de C.V. MEX. Dist: AIMS International Bks., Inc.

Pohl, Kathleen. Descubramos México. 2007. (Descubramos paises del mundo (Spanish- Looking at Countries) Ser.). (SPA.). 32p. (gr. 1-5). pap. 10.50 *(978-0-8368-8193-6(1),* Gareth Stevens Learning Library) Stevens, Gareth Publishing LLLP.

Ponto, Joanna & Gnojewski, Carol. Day of the Dead. 2016. (Story of Our Holidays Ser.). (Illus.). 32p. (J). (gr. 3-3). pap. 10.52 *(978-0-7660-7642-6(3))* Enslow Pubs., Inc.

Powell, Jillian. Descubramos Mexico. 2007. (Descubramos Paises Del Mundo (Looking at Countries) Ser.). (SPA., Illus.). 32p. (gr. 1-5). lib. bdg. 26.00 *(978-0-8368-8186-8(9),* Gareth Stevens Learning Library) Stevens, Gareth Publishing LLLP.

Revolucion a Todo Vapor (Rev. Full Stream Ahead) 2005. (SPA.). (J). pap. *(978-968-7381-08-4(6))* Tecolote, Ediciones, S.A. de C.V.

Richardson, Adele. Mexico. 2011. (My First Look At Ser.). (ENG.). 24p. (J). (gr. 1-17). pap. 7.99 *(978-1-926722-38-2(8),* Creative Paperbacks) Creative Co., The.

Robinson, Joanna J. Mexico. 2015. (One World, Many Countries Ser.). (ENG.). 32p. (J). (gr. 1-4). 28.50 *(978-1-63407-053-9(4),* 208877) Child's World, Inc., The.

Rosenthal, Cynthia. A Day in Mexico. 2013. (InfoMax Readers Ser.). (ENG.). 24p. (J). (gr. 2-3). pap. 49.50 *(978-1-4777-2316-6(1));* (Illus.). pap. 8.25 *(978-1-4777-2315-9(3))* Rosen Publishing Group, Inc., The. (Rosen Classroom).

Rudolph, Jessica. Mexico. 2015. (Countries We Come From Ser.). (ENG., Illus.). 32p. (J). (gr. k-3). lib. bdg. 26.60 *(978-1-62724-853-2(6))* Bearport Publishing Co., Inc.

Sanna, Ellyn. Mexican Americans' Role in the United States: A History of Pride, a Future of Hope. 2007. (Hispanic Heritage Ser.). (Illus.). 112p. (YA). (gr. 4-7). lib. bdg. 22.95 *(978-1-59084-926-2(4))* Mason Crest.

—Mexican Facts & Figures. 2014. (Mexico: Leading the Southern Hemisphere Ser.: 16). 64p. (J). (gr. 7-18). lib. bdg. 22.95 *(978-1-4222-3229-3(8))* Mason Crest.

Savery, Annabel. Mexico. 2011. (ENG., Illus.). 32p. (J). pap. 10.95 *(978-1-77092-026-2(9))* Saunders Bk. Co. CAN. Dist: RiverStream Publishing.

Scholl, Elizabeth J. The Mayan Civilization. 2009. (How'd They Do That? Ser.). (Illus.). 64p. (J). (gr. 4-8). lib. bdg. 33.95 *(978-1-58415-822-6(0))* Mitchell Lane Pubs., Inc.

Senker, Cath. Mexico. 2016. (Land & the People Ser.). 48p. (gr. 5-5). pap. 14.05 *(978-1-4824-5099-6(2))* Stevens, Gareth Publishing LLLP.

Serrano, Francisco. The Poet King of Tezcoco: A Great Leader of Ancient Mexico, 1 vol. Balch, Trudy & Engelbert, Jo Anne, trs. from SPA. Serrano, Pablo, illus. 2007. (ENG.). 48p. (J). (gr. 3-6). 18.95 *(978-0-88899-787-6(6))* Groundwood Bks. CAN. Dist: Publishers Group West (PGW).

Sexton, Colleen. Mexico. 2010. (Exploring Countries Ser.). (ENG., Illus.). 32p. (J). (gr. 3-7). lib. bdg. 26.95 *(978-1-60014-487-5(X),* Blastoff! Readers) Bellwether Media.

Simpson, Kathleen. Geography of Mexico: Text Pairs. 2008. (Bridges/Navigators Ser.). (J). (gr. 6). 94.00 *(978-1-4108-8439-8(2))* Benchmark Education Co.

Snedden, Robert. Aztec, Inca & Maya. 2009. (Technology in Times Past Ser.). (J). 32.80 *(978-1-59920-299-0(9))* Black Rabbit Bks.

Stein, R. Conrad. Ancient Mexico. 2011. (Story of Mexico Ser.). (Illus.). 144p. (gr. 7-12). 28.95 *(978-1-59935-161-2(7))* Reynolds, Morgan Inc.

—Emiliano Zapata & the Mexican Revolution. 2011. (Story of Mexico Ser.). (Illus.). 144p. (gr. 7-12). 28.95 *(978-1-59935-163-6(3))* Reynolds, Morgan Inc.

—Hernando Cortés: Conquistador & Empire Builder. 2004. (Proud Heritage: the Hispanic Library). (ENG., Illus.). 40p. (J). (gr. 3-6). 29.93 *(978-1-59296-169-6(X),* 200009) Child's World, Inc., The.

—Modern Mexico. 2011. (Story of Mexico Ser.). (Illus.). 144p. (gr. 7-12). 28.95 *(978-1-59935-162-9(5))* Reynolds, Morgan Inc.

—The Story of Mexico Set, vols. 8, vol. 8. Incl. Ancient Mexico. (Illus.). 144p. (gr. 7-12). 2011. 28.95 *(978-1-59935-161-2(7));* Benito Juarez & the French Intervention. (Illus.). 160p. (YA). (gr. 8-12). 2007. lib. bdg. 27.95 *(978-1-59935-052-3(1));* Cortes & the Spanish Conquest. (Illus.). 160p. (J). (gr. 3-7). 2007. lib. bdg. 27.95 *(978-1-59935-053-0(X));* Emiliano Zapata & the Mexican Revolution. (Illus.). 144p. (gr. 7-12). 2011. 28.95 *(978-1-59935-163-6(3));* Mexican-American War. 144p. (gr. 7-12). 2011. 28.95 *(978-1-59935-160-5(9));* Mexican Revolution. (Illus.). 160p. (YA). (gr. 7-18). 2007. lib. bdg. 27.95 *(978-1-59935-051-6(3));* Mexican War of Independence. (Illus.). 144p. (J). (gr. 3-7). 2007. lib. bdg. 27.95 *(978-1-59935-054-7(8));* Modern Mexico. (Illus.). 144p. (gr. 7-12). 2011. 28.95 *(978-1-59935-162-9(5));* 2007. Set lib. bdg. 231.60 *(978-1-59935-074-5(2))* Reynolds, Morgan Inc.

Stokes, Erica M. Finding a Financial Balance: The Economy of Mexico. 2014. (Mexico: Leading the Southern Hemisphere Ser.: 16). 64p. (J). (gr. 7-18). lib. bdg. 22.95 *(978-1-4222-3221-7(2))* Mason Crest.

—Sports of Mexico. 2007. (Mexico: Beautiful Land, Diverse People Ser.). 64p. (YA). (gr. 7-18). pap. 9.95 *(978-1-4222-0721-5(8))* Mason Crest.

—Victoria! the Sports of Mexico. 2014. (Mexico: Leading the Southern Hemisphere Ser.: 16). 64p. (J). (gr. 7-18). lib. bdg. 22.95 *(978-1-4222-3220-0(4))* Mason Crest.

Taylor, Trace. Mexico. 2010. pap. 39.62 *(978-1-61541-127-6(5))* American Reading Co.

Taylor, Trace & SáNchez, LucíA M. Mexico. 2010. pap. 39.62 *(978-1-61541-150-4(X))* American Reading Co.

Taylor, Trace & Sánchez, Lucía M. Mexico. 2010. (1Y Nuestro Mundo Ser.). (SPA.). 16p. (J). (gr. k-1). pap. 6.99 *(978-1-61541-149-8(6))* American Reading Co.

Tieck, Sarah. Mexico, 1 vol. 2013. (Explore the Countries Ser.). (ENG.). 40p. (J). (gr. 2-5). lib. bdg. 29.93 *(978-1-61783-816-3(0),* Big Buddy Bks.) ABDO Publishing Co.

Trueba, Jose Luis. Descubre... Las Raices de Mexico. Cortes, Osvaldo, illus. 2004. (Ser. Descubre). (SPA.). 96p. (J). (gr. 3-5). pap. 18.95 *(978-970-29-0508-0(7))* Santillana USA Publishing Co., Inc.

Trujillo, Francisco. Conquista para Ninos. (SPA.). (J). 7.98 *(978-970-643-360-2(0))* Selector, S.A. de C.V. MEX. Dist: AIMS International Bks., Inc.

Wagner, Heather Lehr. Hernan Cortes. 2009. (Great Explorers Ser.). (Illus.). 120p. (gr. 6-12). 30.00 *(978-1-60413-424-7(0),* Chelsea Hse.) Facts On File, Inc.

Worth, Richard. Independence for Latino America. 2006. (Latino-American History Ser.). 112p. (YA). (gr. 5-9). 35.00 *(978-0-8160-6441-0(5))* Facts On File, Inc.

Zocchi, Judy. In Mexico. Brodie, Neale, illus. 2005. (Global Adventures I Ser.). 32p. (J). pap. 10.95 *(978-1-59646-135-2(7));* lib. bdg. 21.65 *(978-1-59646-002-7(4))* Dingles & Co.

—In Mexico/en México. Brodie, Neale, illus. 2005. (Global Adventures I Ser.).Tr. of En México. (ENG & SPA.). 32p. (J). pap. 10.95 *(978-1-59646-137-6(3));* lib. bdg. 21.65 *(978-1-59646-003-4(2))* Dingles & Co.

MEXICO—HISTORY—CONQUEST, 1519-1540

Abnett, Dan. Hernan Cortes & the Fall of the Aztec Empire. (Jr. Graphic Biographies Ser.). (ENG.). 24p. 2009. (J). (gr. 2-3).

47.90 *(978-1-61513-819-7(6)*, PowerKids Pr.) 2007. (Illus.). (J). (gr. 2-5). lib. bdg. 25.25 *(978-1-4042-3391-1(1))* 2007. (Illus.). (gr. 3-8). pap. 10.60 *(978-1-4042-2144-4(1)*, PowerKids Pr.) Rosen Publishing Group, Inc., The.

Gaff, Jackie. Hernan Cortes: The Life of a Spanish Conquistador. 2005. (Graphic Nonfiction Biographies Ser.). (ENG., Illus.). 48p. (YA). (gr. 4-7). lib. bdg. 31.95 *(978-1-4042-0244-3(7))* Rosen Publishing Group, Inc., The.

Green, Carl R. Cortés: Conquering the Powerful Aztec Empire. 2010. (Great Explorers of the World Ser.). (Illus.). 112p. (J). (gr. 7-12). 33.27 *(978-1-59845-099-6(9))* Enslow Pubs., Inc.

Johnson, Sylvia A. The Spanish Conquest of Mexico. 2009. (Pivotal Moments in History Ser.). (ENG.). 160p. (gr. 9-12). 38.60 *(978-0-8225-9079-8(4))* Lerner Publishing Group.

Koestler-Grack, Rachel A. Hernando Cortes & the Fall of the Aztecs. Goetzmann, William H., ed. 2005. (Explorers of New Lands Ser.). (Illus.). 176p. (gr. 5-8). lib. bdg. 30.00 *(978-0-7910-8609-4(7))* Facts On File, Inc.

Petrie, Kristin. Hernan Cortes, 1 vol. 2004. (Explorers Set 1 Ser.). (ENG., Illus.). 32p. (gr. k-6). 27.07 *(978-1-59197-598-4(0)*, Checkerboard Library) ABDO Publishing Co.

Ramen, Fred. Hernán Cortés: The Conquest of Mexico & the Aztec Empire. 2015. (Incredible Explorers Ser.). (ENG., Illus.). 64p. (J). (gr. 7-7). 34.21 *(978-1-5026-0129-2(X))* Cavendish Square Publishing.

—Hernán Cortés: The Conquest of Mexico & the Aztec Empire. 2009. (Library of Explorers & Exploration Ser.). 112p. (gr. 5-8). 66.50 *(978-1-60853-606-1(8)*, Rosen Reference) Rosen Publishing Group, Inc., The.

Schulz, Elizabeth. Montezuma II. 2017. (J). ***(978-1-5026-2789-6(2))*** Cavendish Square Publishing.

Serrano, Francisco. La Malinche: The Princess Who Helped Cortés Conquer the Aztec Empire, 1 vol. Ouriou, Susan, tr. from SPA. Serrano, Pablo, illus. 2012. (ENG.). 36p. (J). (gr. 3-7). 18.95 *(978-1-55498-111-3(5))* Groundwood Bks. CAN. Dist: Publishers Group West (PGW).

Stein, R. Conrad. Cortes & the Spanish Conquest. 2007. (Story of Mexico Ser.). (Illus.). 160p. (J). (gr. 3-7). lib. bdg. 27.95 *(978-1-59935-053-0(X))* Reynolds, Morgan Inc.

West, David. Hernán Cortés: The Life of a Spanish Conquistador. 2009. (Graphic Nonfiction Biographies Ser.). (ENG.). 48p. (YA). (gr. 4-5). 58.50 *(978-1-61513-019-1(5)*, Rosen Reference) Rosen Publishing Group, Inc., The.

Whiting, Jim. The Life & Times of Hernando Cortes. 2006. (Profiles in American History Ser.). (Illus.). 48p. (J). (gr. 3-7). lib. bdg. 29.95 *(978-1-58415-449-5(7))* Mitchell Lane Pubs., Inc.

MEXICO—HISTORY—CONQUEST, 1519-1540—FICTION

Bronson, Wilfrid S., illus. Stooping Hawk & Stranded Whale, Sons of Liberty. 2009. 236p. (J). pap. 22.95 *(978-0-86534-715-1(8))* Sunstone Pr.

O'Dell, Scott. The Seven Serpents Trilogy. 2009. (ENG.). 560p. (J). (gr. 4-6). pap. 19.99 *(978-1-4022-1836-1(2)*, Sourcebooks Jabberwocky) Sourcebooks, Inc.

MEXICO—HISTORY—SPANISH COLONY, 1540-1810

Burr, Claudia, et al. When the Viceroy Came. 2006. (Illus.). 29p. (J). (gr. 4-8). reprint ed. 16.00 *(978-1-4223-5465-0(2))* DIANE Publishing Co.

MEXICO—HISTORY—SPANISH COLONY, 1540-1810—FICTION

Barrera, Norma. Diario de Tlauhquechol (1518) 2003. (Mexican Diaries). (SPA., Illus.). 146p. (J). pap. *(978-970-690-042-5(X)*, SOM7948) Planeta Mexicana Editorial S. A. de C. V. MEX. Dist: Lectorum Pubns., Inc.

Zarco, Carmen Saucedo. Diario de Mariana (1695-95) 2003. (Mexican Diaries). (SPA., Illus.). 164p. (J). pap. *(978-970-690-113-2(2)*, SOM7943) Planeta Mexicana Editorial S. A. de C. V. MEX. Dist: Lectorum Pubns., Inc.

MEXICO—SOCIAL LIFE AND CUSTOMS

Aloian, Molly & Peppas, Lynn. Cultural Traditions in Mexico. 2012. (ENG.). 32p. (J). lib. bdg. *(978-0-7787-7587-4(9))* Crabtree Publishing Co.

Aloian, Molly & Peppas, Lynne. Cultural Traditions in Mexico. 2012. (ENG.). 32p. (J). pap. *(978-0-7787-7594-2(1))* Crabtree Publishing Co.

Andrade, Mary J., photos by. Day of the Dead A Passion for Life: Día de los Muertos Pasión por la Vida. Andrade, Mary J., . 2nd ed. 2007. (SPA & ENG., Illus.). 200p. lib. bdg., stu. ed., tchr.'s training gde. ed. 29.95 *(978-0-9791624-0-4(8))* La Oferta Publishing Co.

Augustin, Byron. The Food of Mexico. 2011. (Flavors of the World Ser.). 64p. (gr. 4). 31.36 *(978-1-60870-237-4(5))* Marshall Cavendish Corp.

Barker, Geoff. The World of Food - Mexico. 2010. (World of Food Ser.). 32p. (YA). (gr. 4-7). lib. bdg. 24.95 *(978-1-934545-13-3(9))* Oliver Pr., Inc.

Berg, Elizabeth. Mexico. 2010. (Festivals of the World Ser.). 32p. (gr. 3). 28.50 *(978-1-60870-104-9(2))* Marshall Cavendish GBR. Dist: Marshall Cavendish Corp.

Bingham, Jane. Mexico. 2008. (Costume Around the World Ser.). (Illus.). 32p. (gr. 4-6). 28.00 *(978-0-7910-9771-7(4)*, Chelsea Clubhouse) Facts On File, Inc.

Brooks, Susie. Mexico. 2016. (Unpacked Ser.). (ENG., Illus.). 32p. (J). (gr. 4-6). 17.99 *(978-0-7502-9169-9(9))*; pap. 11.99 *(978-0-7502-9171-2(0))* Hachette Children's Group GBR. (Wayland). Dist: Hachette Bk. Group.

Bullard, Lisa. Daniela's Day of the Dead. Conger, Holli, illus. 2012. (Cloverleaf Books (tm) — Fall & Winter Holidays Ser.). (ENG.). 24p. (gr. k-2). 6.95 *(978-0-7613-8585-1(1))*; lib. bdg. 23.93 *(978-0-7613-5084-2(5))* Lerner Publishing Group. (Millbrook Pr.).

—Marco's Cinco de Mayo. Conger, Holli, illus. 2012. (Holidays & Special Days Ser.). 24p. (J). (gr. k-2). pap. 39.62 *(978-0-7613-9249-1(1)*, Millbrook Pr.) Lerner Publishing Group.

—Marco's Cinco de Mayo. Conger, Holli, illus. 2012. (Cloverleaf Books — Holidays & Special Days Ser.). (ENG.). 24p. (J). (gr. k-2). lib. bdg. 23.93 *(978-0-7613-5082-8(9))* Lerner Publishing Group.

—Marco's Cinco de Mayo. Conger, Holli, illus. 2012. (Cloverleaf Books — Holidays & Special Days Ser.). (ENG.). 24p. (gr. k-2). pap. 6.95 *(978-0-7613-8580-6(0)*, Millbrook Pr.) Lerner Publishing Group.

Cassriel, Betsy. My Teenage Life in Mexico. 2017. (Custom & Cultures of the World Ser.). (ENG.). (YA). (gr. 7-12). 23.95 ***(978-1-4222-3907-0(1))*** Mason Crest.

Celebrate: Mexico. 2009. (Celebrate Country Ser.). 32p. (gr. 4-6). 28.00 *(978-1-60413-267-0(1)*, Chelsea Clubhouse) Facts On File, Inc.

Centore, Michael. Mexico, Vol. 12. 2015. (Major Nations in a Global World: Tradition, Culture, & Daily Life Ser.). (Illus.). 64p. (J). (gr. 7). 23.95 *(978-1-4222-3348-1(0))* Mason Crest.

Coleman, Miriam. The Culture & Crafts of Mexico. 2015. (Cultural Crafts Ser.). (ENG., Illus.). 32p. (J). (gr. 4-6). pap. 11.75 *(978-1-4994-1126-3(X)*, PowerKids Pr.) Rosen Publishing Group, Inc., The.

Cordero, Flor de Maria. M Is for Mexico. 2014. (World Alphabets Ser.). (ENG., Illus.). 32p. (J). (gr. -1-2). pap. 8.95 *(978-1-84780-257-6(5)*, Frances Lincoln) Quarto Publishing Group UK GBR. Dist: Hachette Bk. Group.

Cordero, Flor de Maria, photos by. M Is for Mexico. 2008. (World Alphabets Ser.). (ENG., Illus.). 32p. (J). (gr. -1-2). 16.95 *(978-1-84507-593-4(5)*, Frances Lincoln) Quarto Publishing Group UK GBR. Dist: Hachette Bk. Group.

Cunningham, Patrick. Mexico. 2010. (Letters from Around the World Ser.). (Illus.). 32p. pap. *(978-1-84234-614-3(8))* Cherrytree Bks.

Enderlein, Cheryl L. Christmas in Mexico, 1 vol. 2013. (Christmas Around the World Ser.). (ENG.). 24p. (gr. 1-2). lib. bdg. 25.32 *(978-1-62065-138-4(6))* Capstone Press of Coughlan Cos.

Flood Williams, Colleen Madonna, et al. The Festivals of Mexico. 2009. (Mexico: Beautiful Land, Diverse People Ser.). (Illus.). 64p. (YA). (gr. 7-12). 21.95 *(978-1-4222-0657-7(2))* Mason Crest.

Garcia, James. Cinco de Mayo: A Mexican Holiday about Unity & Pride. 2003. (Proud Heritage: the Hispanic Library). (ENG., Illus.). 40p. (J). (gr. 3-6). 29.93 *(978-1-56766-174-3(2)*, 200003) Child's World, Inc., The.

Gnojewski, Carol. Celebrating Cinco de Mayo. 2012. (Celebrating Holidays Ser.). 48p. (J). (gr. 3-4). (Illus.). pap. 8.95 *(978-1-59845-399-7(8))*; 25.27 *(978-0-7660-4032-8(1))* Enslow Pubs., Inc. (Enslow Elementary).

—Day of the Dead: A Latino Celebration of Family & Life. 2005. (Finding Out about Holidays Ser.). (Illus.). 48p. (J). lib. bdg. 23.93 *(978-0-7660-1780-1(X)*, Enslow Elementary) Enslow Pubs., Inc.

Gnojewski, Carol & Ponto, Joanna. Cinco de Mayo. 2016. (Story of Our Holidays Ser.). (Illus.). 32p. (J). pap. 10.52 *(978-0-7660-8328-8(4))* Enslow Pubs., Inc.

Grack, Rachel. Cinco de Mayo. 2017. (Celebrating Holidays! Ser.). (ENG.). 24p. (J). (gr. k-3). lib. bdg. 25.95 ***(978-1-62617-617-1(5)***, Blastoff! Readers) Bellwether Media.

—Day of the Dead. 2017. (Celebrating Holidays! Ser.). (ENG.). 24p. (J). (gr. k-3). lib. bdg. 25.95 ***(978-1-62617-618-8(3)***, Blastoff! Readers) Bellwether Media.

Hawker, Frances & Paz, Noemi. Christianity in Mexico. Campbell, Bruce, photos by. 2009. (ENG., Illus.). 32p. (J). (gr. 3-6). *(978-0-7787-5007-9(8))*; pap. *(978-0-7787-5024-6(8))* Crabtree Publishing Co.

Heinrichs, Ann. Cinco de Mayo. Petelinsek, Kathleen, illus. 2013. (Holidays & Celebrations Ser.). (ENG.). 32p. (J). (gr. k-3). 27.07 *(978-1-62323-505-5(7)*, 206277) Child's World, Inc., The.

Holm, Kirsten C. Everyday Life in the Maya Civilization. 2012. (Jr. Graphic Ancient Civilizations Ser.). (ENG.). 24p. (J). (gr. 3-6). pap. 10.60 *(978-1-4488-6393-8(7))*; lib. bdg. 25.25 *(978-1-4488-6217-7(5))* Rosen Publishing Group, Inc., The.

Howell, Izzi. Aztecs. 2017. (Explore! Ser.). (ENG., Illus.). 32p. (J). (gr. 4-6). 16.99 *(978-1-5263-0059-1(1)*, Wayland) Hachette Children's Group GBR. Dist: Hachette Bk. Group.

Hoyt-Goldsmith, Diane. Cinco de Mayo: Celebrating the Traditions of Mexico. Migdale, Lawrence, illus. 2008. (ENG.). 32p. (J). (gr. 3-7). 16.95 *(978-0-8234-2107-7(4))* Holiday Hse., Inc.

—Cinco de Mayo: Celebrating the traditions of Mexico. Migdale, Lawrence, illus. 2010. (ENG.). 32p. (J). (gr. 1-5). pap. 7.95 *(978-0-8234-2279-1(8))* Holiday Hse., Inc.

Jones, Theodore. Celebrating Day of the Dead. 2016. (History of Our Holidays Ser.). (ENG., Illus.). 24p. (J). (gr. 1-2). pap. 8.15 *(978-1-4824-3886-4(0))* Stevens, Gareth Publishing LLLP.

Kalman, Bobbie. Mexico: The Culture. 3rd rev. ed. 2008. (Lands, Peoples, & Cultures Ser.). (ENG., Illus.). 32p. (J). (gr. 3-9). pap. *(978-0-7787-9663-3(9))* Crabtree Publishing Co.

—Mexico: The People. 3rd rev. ed. 2008. (Lands, Peoples, & Cultures Ser.). (ENG., Illus.). 32p. (J). (gr. 3-9). lib. bdg. *(978-0-7787-9294-9(3))* Crabtree Publishing Co.

—Mexico - The People. 3rd rev. ed. 2008. (Lands, Peoples, & Cultures Ser.). (ENG., Illus.). 32p. (J). (gr. 3-9). pap. *(978-0-7787-9662-6(0))* Crabtree Publishing Co.

Kaplan, Leslie. Cinco de Mayo. 2003. (Library of Holidays Ser.). (Illus.). 24p. (J). (gr. 4-7). lib. bdg. 22.60 *(978-0-8239-6662-2(3)*, PowerKids Pr.) Rosen Publishing Group, Inc., The.

Kaplan, Leslie C. Cinco de Mayo. 2009. (Library of Holidays Ser.). 24p. (gr. 2-3). 42.50 *(978-1-60853-708-2(0)*, PowerKids Pr.) Rosen Publishing Group, Inc., The.

King, Aven. My Mexican Heritage. 2013. (Rosen Readers Ser.). (ENG.). 24p. (J). (gr. 2-3). pap. 8.25 *(978-1-4777-2331-9(5))*; pap. 49.50 *(978-1-4777-2332-6(3))* Rosen Publishing Group, Inc., The. (Rosen Classroom).

Krebs, Laurie. Off We Go to Mexico. Corr, Christopher, illus. 2006. (ENG.). 32p. (J). 16.99 *(978-1-905236-40-4(9))* Barefoot Bks., Inc.

Krebs, Laurie & Blackstone, Stella. Nos Vamos a Mexico! Una Aventura Bajo el Sol. Canetti, Yanitzia James, tr. from ENG. Corr, Christopher, illus. 2006. (ENG & SPA.). 32p. (J). (gr. k-5). pap. 8.99 *(978-1-84686-014-0(8))* Barefoot Bks., Inc.

Krebs, Laurie & Corr, Christopher. Off We Go to Mexico! An Adventure in the Sun. 2008. (ENG., Illus.). 32p. (J). (gr. k-5). 8.99 *(978-1-84686-159-8(4))* Barefoot Bks., Inc.

Laufer, Peter. Hecho en México. Reyes, Victor, tr. Roth, Susan L., illus. 2008. (SPA.). 32p. (J). (gr. 3-7). 16.95 *(978-1-4263-0364-7(5)*, National Geographic Children's Bks.) National Geographic Society.

Lowery, Linda. Cinco de Mayo. Knutson, Barbara, illus. 2005. (On My Own Holidays Ser.). 48p. (J). (gr. k-3). per. 6.95 *(978-1-57505-764-4(6))*; (gr. 2-4). 25.26 *(978-1-57505-654-8(2))* Lerner Publishing Group.

—Day of the Dead. Knutson, Barbara, illus. 2003. (On My Own Holidays Ser.). (ENG.). 48p. (gr. 2-4). lib. bdg. 25.26 *(978-0-87614-914-0(X))* Lerner Publishing Group.

MacMillan, Dianne M. Mexican Independence Day & Cinco de Mayo. rev. ed. 2008. (Best Holiday Bks.). (Illus.). 48p. (J). (gr. 4-7). lib. bdg. 25.27 *(978-0-7660-3044-2(X))* Enslow Pubs., Inc.

Mattern, Joanne. Celebrate Cinco de Mayo. 2006. (Celebrate Holidays Ser.). (Illus.). 104p. (J). (gr. 5-6). lib. bdg. 33.27 *(978-0-7660-2579-0(9))* Enslow Pubs., Inc.

McGill, Jordan, ed. Cinco de Mayo. 2011. (J). (gr. 3-5). pap. 12.95 *(978-1-61690-688-7(X)*, AV2 by Weigl); (Illus.). 24p. (gr. 2-5). 27.13 *(978-1-61690-682-5(0))* Weigl Pubs., Inc.

McManus, Lori. Mexican Culture, 1 vol. 2012. (Global Cultures Ser.). (ENG.). 48p. (gr. 4-6). pap. 9.95 *(978-1-4329-6792-5(4))*; 32.65 *(978-1-4329-6783-3(5))* Heinemann-Raintree. (NA-h).

Murray, Julie. Cinco de Mayo, 1 vol. 2005. (Buddy Book Ser.). (ENG., Illus.). 24p. (gr. k-4). 25.65 *(978-1-59197-586-1(7)*, Buddy Bks.) ABDO Publishing Co.

Murray, Laura K. Exploring the Aztec Empire. 2018. (ENG.). 32p. (gr. 3-6). ***(978-1-63235-467-9(5)***, 12-Story Library) Pr. Room Editions LLC.

Otto, Carolyn. Celebremos el Cinco de Mayo: Con Fiestas, Musica y Baile. 2008. (Holidays Around the World Ser.). (SPA., Illus.). 32p. (J). (gr. 1-4). 15.95 *(978-1-4263-0363-0(7)*, National Geographic Children's Bks.) National Geographic Society.

Owens, L. L. Cinco de Mayo, 1 vol. Conger, Holli, illus. 2009. (Cultural Holidays Ser.). (ENG.). 32p. (gr. -1-4). 28.50 *(978-1-60270-602-6(6)*, Looking Glass Library- Nonfiction) Magic Wagon.

Pearce, Kevin. Foods of Mexico. 2011. (Culture in the Kitchen Ser.). 24p. (J). (gr. 2-5). pap. 8.15 *(978-1-4339-5716-1(7))*; lib. bdg. 22.60 *(978-1-4339-5714-7(0))* Stevens, Gareth Publishing LLLP. (Gareth Stevens Learning Library).

Roholt, Christine VeLure. Foods of Mexico. 2014. (Cook with Me Ser.). (ENG.). 24p. (J). (gr. 3-7). 25.95 *(978-1-62617-121-3(1)*, Express Bks.) Bellwether Media.

San Vicente, Luis, illus. The Festival of Bones / el Festival de Las Calaveras. 2014. (ENG.). 32p. (J). 7.95 *(978-1-941026-03-8(6))* Cinco Puntos Pr.

Sheen, Barbara. Growing up in Mexico. 2017. (Growing up Around the World Ser.). (ENG.). 80p. (YA). (gr. 5-12). ***(978-1-68282-221-0(4))*** ReferencePoint Pr., Inc.

Somervill, Barbara A. Ancient Maya. 2012. (Ancient World Ser.). (ENG.). 112p. (J). pap. 9.95 *(978-0-531-25981-8(1))*; (gr. 6-9). lib. bdg. 34.00 *(978-0-531-25181-2(0))* Scholastic Library Publishing.

Stevenson, Mónica. Tradiciones Mexicanas Para Ninos. 2006. (SPA.). 136p. (YA). (gr. 4-7). pap. *(978-968-403-934-6(4))* Selector, S.A. de C.V.

Stuckey, Rachel. Ancient Maya Inside Out. 2017. (Ancient Worlds Inside Out Ser.). (ENG.). 32p. (J). ***(978-0-7787-2878-8(1))***; (Illus.). pap. ***(978-0-7787-2892-4(7))*** Crabtree Publishing Co.

Tabor, Nancy Maria Grande. Celebraciones: Días Feriados de los Estados Unidos y Mexico. Tabor, Nancy Maria Grande, illus. 2004.Tr. of Celebrations - Holidays of the United States of America & Mexico. (SPA & ENG., Illus.). 32p. (J). (gr. -1-2). pap. 7.95 *(978-1-57091-550-5(4))* Charlesbridge Publishing, Inc.

Tait, Leia. Cinco de Mayo. (American Celebrations Ser.). (Illus.). 24p. (J). (gr. 3-5). 2010. pap. 11.95 *(978-1-60596-934-3(6))* 2010. lib. bdg. 25.70 *(978-1-60596-776-9(9))* 2006. lib. bdg. 24.45 *(978-1-59036-460-4(0))* 2006. per. 8.95 *(978-1-59036-463-5(5))* Weigl Pubs., Inc.

Taylor, Trace & Sánchez, Lucía M. Mexico. 2010. (1Y Nuestro Mundo Ser.). (SPA.). 16p. (J). (gr. k-1). pap. 6.99 *(978-1-61541-149-8(6))* American Reading Co.

Torpie, Kate. Cinco de Mayo. 2008. (Celebrations In My World Ser.). (ENG., Illus.). 32p. (J). (gr. k-3). pap. *(978-0-7787-4299-9(7))* Crabtree Publishing Co.

Turck, Mary C. Mexico & Central America: A Fiesta of Cultures, Crafts, & Activities for Ages 8-12. 2004. (ENG., Illus.). 160p. (J). (gr. 4-7). pap. 16.95 *(978-1-55652-525-4(7))* Chicago Review Pr., Inc.

Urrutia, Maria Cristina & Orozco, Rebeca. Cinco de Mayo: Yesterday & Today. 2006. (SPA., Illus.). 29p. (J). (gr. 4-8). reprint ed. 16.00 *(978-1-4223-5464-3(4))* DIANE Publishing Co.

VanVoorst, Jennifer Fretland. The Ancient Maya, 1 vol. 2012. (Exploring the Ancient World Ser.). (ENG., Illus.). 48p. (gr. 5-6). 29.32 *(978-0-7565-4564-2(1))* Compass Point Bks.

—The Ancient Maya, 1 vol. 2012. (Exploring the Ancient World Ser.). (ENG., Illus.). 48p. (gr. 5-6). pap. 9.10 *(978-0-7565-4584-0(6))* Compass Point Bks.

Wade, Mary Dodson. Cinco de Mayo. 2003. (Rookie Read-About Holidays Ser.). (ENG., Illus.). 32p. (J). (gr. 1-2). pap. 5.95 *(978-0-516-27489-8(9)*, Children's Pr.) Scholastic Library Publishing.

Weston Woods Staff, creator. The Day of the Dead / el Día de Los Muertos. 2011. (ENG & SPA.). 18.95 *(978-0-545-42606-0(5))*; 38.75 *(978-0-545-42607-7(3))*; 29.95 *(978-0-545-37417-0(0))* Weston Woods Studios, Inc.

Wiseman, Blaine & Kissock, Heather. Aztecs. 2016. (Illus.). 32p. (J). *(978-1-5105-1094-4(X))* SmartBook Media, Inc.

Wood, Ira. A Mexican Feast: The Foods & Recipes of Mexico. 2009. (Reading Room Collection 2 Ser.). 24p. (gr. 3-4). 42.50 *(978-1-60851-953-8(8)*, PowerKids Pr.) Rosen Publishing Group, Inc., The.

Zocchi, Judy. In Mexico. Brodie, Neale, illus. 2005. (Global Adventures I Ser.). 32p. (J). lib. bdg. 21.65 *(978-1-59646-002-7(4))* Dingles & Co.

—In Mexico/en México. Brodie, Neale, illus. 2005. (Global Adventures I Ser.).Tr. of En México. (ENG & SPA.). 32p. (J). pap. 10.95 *(978-1-59646-137-6(3))*; lib. bdg. 21.65 *(978-1-59646-003-4(2))* Dingles & Co.

MEXICO, GULF OF

Benoit, Peter. The BP Oil Spill. 2011. (J). pap. *(978-0-531-29029-3(8))* Children's Pr., Ltd.

—The BP Oil Spill. 2011. (True Bks.). 48p. (J). (gr. 3-5). lib. bdg. 29.00 *(978-0-531-20630-0(0))*; (ENG., Illus.). pap. 6.95 *(978-0-531-28999-0(0))* Scholastic Library Publishing. (Children's Pr.).

Brennan, Linda Crotta. Gulf Oil Spill, 1 vol. 2013. (History's Greatest Disasters Ser.). (ENG.). 48p. (J). (gr. 3-6). lib. bdg. 32.79 *(978-1-61783-957-3(4))* ABDO Publishing Co.

—Gulf Oil Spill Paperback. 2013. (J). 15.65 *(978-1-62403-022-2(X)*, Core Library) ABDO Publishing Co.

Farrell, Courtney. The Gulf of Mexico Oil Spill, 1 vol. 2011. (Essential Events Set 6 Ser.). (ENG., Illus.). 112p. (J). (gr. 6-12). lib. bdg. 35.64 *(978-1-61714-765-4(6))* ABDO Publishing Co.

Field, Randi. The Gulf States of Mexico. (Mexico: Beautiful Land, Diverse People Ser.). 64p. (YA). (gr. 7-12). 2009. (Illus.). 21.95 *(978-1-4222-0668-3(8))* 2007. pap. 9.95 *(978-1-4222-0735-2(8))* Mason Crest.

Friedman, Lauri S. The BP Oil Spill. Greenhaven Press Editors, ed. 2011. (Writing the Critical Essay Ser.). (ENG., Illus.). 128p. (gr. 6-10). 38.30 *(978-0-7377-5833-7(3))* Cengage Gale.

Goldish, Meish. Oil Spill: Deepwater Horizon. 2017. (Eco-Disasters Ser.). (ENG.). 32p. (J). (gr. 2-7). 19.95 ***(978-1-68402-226-7(6))*** Bearport Publishing Co., Inc.

Green, Jen. Caribbean Sea & Gulf of Mexico. 2006. (Oceans & Seas Ser.). (Illus.). 48p. (gr. 5-12). pap. 14.05 *(978-0-8368-6280-5(5)*, Gareth Stevens Secondary Library) Stevens, Gareth Publishing LLLP.

Haugen, David M. The BP Oil Spill. 2011. (At Issue Ser.). (ENG.). 128p. (gr. 10-12). pap. 27.80 *(978-0-7377-5569-5(5)*, Greenhaven Pr., Inc.) Cengage Gale.

—Drilling in the Gulf of Mexico. 2011. (At Issue Ser.). (ENG.). 128p. (gr. 10-12). 39.40 *(978-0-7377-5568-8(7))* Cengage Gale.

Marsico, Katie. The Gulf of Mexico. 2013. (Explorer Library: Social Studies Explorer Ser.). (ENG.). 32p. (gr. 4-8). pap. 14.21 *(978-1-62431-040-9(0)*, 202517); lib. bdg. 28.50 *(978-1-62431-016-4(8)*, 202515) Cherry Lake Publishing.

Mitchell, Mark. Raising la Belle. Mitchell, Mark, illus. (Professor Wigglestix & the Weather Ser.). (Illus.). 112p. 10.95 *(978-1-57168-703-6(3))* Eakin Pr.

Peppas, Lynn. Gulf Oil Spill. 2011. (ENG., Illus.). 32p. (J). *(978-0-7787-1592-4(2))*; (Disaster Alert! Ser.: No. 20). (gr. 3-6). pap. *(978-0-7787-1625-9(2))* Crabtree Publishing Co.

Stone, Adam. The Deepwater Horizon Oil Spill. 2014. (Disaster Stories Ser.). (ENG., Illus.). 24p. (J). (gr. 3-8). 29.95 *(978-1-62617-152-7(1)*, Black Sheep) Bellwether Media.

MIAMI DOLPHINS (FOOTBALL TEAM)

Adamson, Thomas K. The Miami Dolphins Story. 2016. (NFL Teams Ser.). (ENG., Illus.). 32p. (J). (gr. 3-7). lib. bdg. 26.95 *(978-1-62617-371-2(0)*, Torque Bks.) Bellwether Media.

Burgess, Zack. Meet the Miami Dolphins. 2016. (Big Picture Sports Ser.). (ENG., Illus.). 24p. (J). (gr. k-3). lib. bdg. 22.60 *(978-1-59953-733-7(8))* Norwood Hse. Pr.

Caffrey, Scott. The Story of the Miami Dolphins. 2009. (NFL Today Ser.). 48p. (YA). (gr. 5-9). 22.95 *(978-1-58341-761-4(3))* Creative Co., The.

Frisch, Aaron. Miami Dolphins. 2011. (Super Bowl Champions Ser.). (J). (gr. 1-3). 24.25 *(978-1-60818-021-9(2))* Creative Co., The.

—Miami Dolphins. 2014. (Illus.). 24p. (J). *(978-1-60818-379-1(3)*, Creative Education) Creative Co., The.

Leboutillier, Nate. Miami Dolphins. 2005. (Super Bowl Champions Ser.). (Illus.). 24p. (J). (gr. 1-4). lib. bdg. 16.95 *(978-1-58341-385-2(5)*, Creative Education) Creative Co., The.

MacRae, Sloan. The Miami Dolphins. 2011. (America's Greatest Teams Ser.). (Illus.). 24p. (J). pap. 8.25 *(978-1-4488-3172-2(5))*; lib. bdg. 22.60 *(978-1-4488-3167-8(9))* Rosen Publishing Group, Inc., The. (PowerKids Pr.).

McMahon, Dave. Miami Dolphins, 1 vol. 2010. (Inside the NFL Ser.). (ENG.). 48p. (YA). (gr. 3-6). lib. bdg. 32.79 *(978-1-61714-017-4(1))* ABDO Publishing Co.

Miami Dolphins, 1 vol. 2014. (NFL's Greatest Teams Ser.). (ENG.). 32p. (gr. 7-11). 28.50 *(978-1-62403-362-9(8))* ABDO Publishing Co.

Schmalzbauer, Adam. The History of the Miami Dolphins. 2004. (NFL Today Ser.). (Illus.). 32p. (YA). (gr. 5-9). 18.95 *(978-1-58341-302-9(2))* Creative Co., The.

Whiting, Jim. NFL Today: Miami Dolphins. 2013. (NFL Today Ser.). (ENG., Illus.). 48p. (J). (gr. 4-7). pap. 12.00 *(978-0-89812-861-1(7)*, Creative Paperbacks) Creative Co., The.

—The Story of the Miami Dolphins. 2013. (Illus.). 48p. (J). 35.65 *(978-1-60818-308-1(4)*, Creative Education) Creative Co., The.

Wilner, Barry. Miami Dolphins. 2015. (Insider's Guide to Pro Football Ser.). (ENG.). 32p. (J). (gr. k-3). 28.50 *(978-1-63143-988-9(X)*, 208823) Child's World, Inc., The.

Wyner, Zach. Miami Dolphins. (Illus.). 32p. 2015. pap. *(978-1-4896-0847-5(8))* 2014. (ENG.). (J). (gr. 4-7). lib. bdg. 28.55 *(978-1-4896-0846-8(X)*, AV2 by Weigl) Weigl Pubs., Inc.

MICE

Coppendale, Jean. Mice. 2004. (QEB You & Your Pet Ser.). (Illus.). 32p. (J). lib. bdg. 18.95 *(978-1-59566-056-5(9))* QEB Publishing Inc.

Jackson, Tom. Mice. 2008. (Nature's Children Ser.). (Illus.). 52p. (J). *(978-0-7172-6239-7(1))* Grolier, Ltd.

Johnson, Jinny. Rats & Mice. 2009. (Get to Know Your Pet Ser.). (J). 28.50 *(978-1-59920-091-0(0))* Black Rabbit Bks.

—Rats & Mice. 2009. (Get to Know Your Pet Ser.). (Illus.). 32p. (J). (gr. 4-7). pap. *(978-1-897563-33-5(7))* Saunders Bk. Co.

Leavitt, Amie Jane. Care for a Pet Mouse. 2007. (How to Convince Your Parents You Can ... Ser.). (Illus.). 32p. (J). (gr. 1-4). lib. bdg. 25.70 *(978-1-58415-606-2(6))* Mitchell Lane Pubs., Inc.

Lupo, Tamar. Caring for Your Mouse. 2006. (Caring for Your Pet Ser.). (Illus.). 32p. (J). (gr. 3-7). lib. bdg. 26.00 *(978-1-59036-472-7(4))* Weigl Pubs., Inc.

Markle, Sandra. Outside & Inside Rats & Mice. 2008. (ENG.). 44p. (J). (gr. k-4). 10.99 *(978-1-4169-7571-7(3)*, Simon & Schuster/Paula Wiseman Bks.) Simon & Schuster/Paula Wiseman Bks.

Meinking, Mary. Owl vs. Mouse, 1 vol. 2011. (Predator vs. Prey Ser.). (ENG., Illus.). 32p. (gr. 1-2). 29.99 *(978-1-4109-3936-4(7))*; pap. 8.29 *(978-1-4109-3945-6(6))* Heinemann-Raintree. (Read Me!).

Mice at School: Individual Title Six-Packs. (Story Steps Ser.). (gr. k-2). 32.00 (978-0-7635-9825-9(9)) Rigby Education.

Moose, Jay. Ratoncitos Pequeitos / Itty Bitty Mice, Vol. 1. 2014. (Animales Pequeñitos / Itty Bitty Animals Ser.). (SPA & BYN.). 24p. (J). (gr. k-2). 22.60 (978-1-4339-9912-3(9)) Stevens, Gareth Publishing LLLP.

Morgan, Sally. Rats & Mice. 2012. (Pets Plus Ser.). (Illus.). 32p. (gr. 3-6). lib. bdg. 31.35 (978-1-59920-703-2(6)) Black Rabbit Bks.

Morris Mouse: Individual Title Six-Pack. (Story Steps Ser.). (gr. k-2). 23.00 (978-0-7635-9827-3(5)) Rigby Education.

Nardi, James. In Mouse's Backyard, 1 vol. 2011. (ENG., Illus.). 40p. (J). 16.99 (978-0-7643-3833-5(1), 9780764338335, Schiffer Publishing Ltd) Schiffer Publishing, Ltd.

Nice Mice! Long Vowel i, CVCe Pattern: Level B, 6 vols. (Wright Skills Ser.). 16p. (gr. k-3). 17.95 (978-0-322-03102-9(8)) Wright Group/McGraw-Hill.

Riggs, Kate. Mice. (In My Backyard Ser.). (Illus.). 24p. (J). 2017. (ENG.). (gr. 1-3). pap. 8.99 (978-1-62832-295-8(0), Creative Paperbacks) 2016. (978-1-60818-699-0(7), Creative Education) Creative Co., The.

Rissman, Rebecca. Mice: Nocturnal Explorers, 1 vol. 2014. (Night Safari Ser.). (ENG., Illus.). 24p. (gr. k-2). 23.32 (978-1-4846-0311-6(7), Heinemann Read & Learn) Heinemann-Raintree.

Roza, Greg. Your Neighbor the Mouse. 2011. (City Critters Ser.). (ENG., Illus.). 24p. (J). (gr. k-5). pap. 8.25 (978-1-4488-5125-6(4)); lib. bdg. 22.60 (978-1-4488-4998-7(5)) Windmill Bks.

Rustad, Martha E. H. Mice. 2013. (ENG., Illus.). 24p. (J). lib. bdg. 25.65 (978-1-62031-070-0(8)) Jump! Inc.

Savage, Stephen. Mouse. 2009. (Animal Neighbors Ser.). 32p. (gr. k-5). pap. 10.60 (978-1-4042-4567-9(7), Rosen Classroom); (Illus.). (J). (gr. 3-6). lib. bdg. 23.95 (978-1-4358-4990-7(6), PowerKids Pr.) Rosen Publishing Group, Inc., The.

Scheunemann, Pam. Mice Squeak!, 1 vol. 2011. (Animal Sounds Set 2 Ser.). (ENG., Illus.). 24p. (J). (gr. k-3). lib. bdg. 24.21 (978-1-61613-573-7(5), SandCastle) ABDO Publishing Co.

Schuetz, Kari. Mice. 2014. (Backyard Wildlife Ser.). (ENG., Illus.). 24p. (J). (gr. k-3). lib. bdg. 25.95 (978-1-62617-060-5(6), Blastoff! Readers) Bellwether Media.

Shusterman, Danielle. Here I Come, Mouse! 2016. (1G Predator Animals Ser.). (ENG., Illus.). 28p. (J). pap. 5.99 **(978-1-63437-570-2(X))** American Reading Co.

—A Mouse Is a Mouse. 2016. (1-3Y Animals Ser.). (ENG., Illus.). 16p. (J). pap. 5.99 **(978-1-63437-573-3(4))** American Reading Co.

Sjonger, Rebecca & Kalman, Bobbie. Mice. Crabtree, Marc, illus. Crabtree, Marc, photos by. 2003. (Pet Care Ser.). (ENG.). 32p. (J). pap. (978-0-7787-1786-7(0)); lib. bdg. (978-0-7787-1754-6(2)) Crabtree Publishing Co.

Sjonger, Rebecca, et al. Les Souris. 2011. (Petit Monde Vivant (Small Living World) Ser.: No. 77). (FRE., Illus.). 32p. (J). pap. 9.95 (978-2-89579-371-7(9)) Bayard Canada Livres CAN. Dist: Crabtree Publishing Co.

Stills, Caroline. Mice Mischief: Math Facts in Action. Rossell, Judith, illus. 2014. (ENG.). 24p. (J). (gr. -1-1). 16.95 (978-0-8234-2947-9(4)) Holiday Hse., Inc.

Storm, Marysa. Mice. 2017. (Spot Backyard Animals Ser.). (ENG.). 16p. (J). (gr. k-3). 17.95 **(978-1-68151-093-4(6))** Amicus Publishing.

—El Ratón (Mice) 2017. (Spot Backyard Animals Ser.). (ENG & SPA.). 16p. (J). (gr. k-3). 17.95 **(978-1-68151-273-0(4)**, Amicus Readers) Amicus Publishing.

Tait, Leia. Mice. 2009. (Backyard Animals Ser.). (Illus.). 24p. (J). (gr. 3-5). pap. 8.95 (978-1-60596-081-4(0)); lib. bdg. 24.45 (978-1-60596-080-7(2)) Weigl Pubs., Inc.

Watts, Barrie. Mouse. 2004. (Illus.). 32p. (J). (gr. -1-17). lib. bdg. 24.25 (978-1-58340-231-3(4)) Black Rabbit Bks.

MICE—FICTION

Abbott, Simon. Little Mouse Visits Grandma: Mouse on Ribbon, Flaps, Acetates. Abbott, Simon, illus. 2006. (ENG., Illus.). 16p. (J). (gr. -1-k). 15.99 (978-1-85707-668-4(0)) Tango Bks. GBR. Dist: Independent Pubs. Group.

Adam, Sally. The Cats of Ellis Island. 2009. 28p. pap. 12.50 (978-1-4389-6012-8(3)) AuthorHouse.

Adams, Tina. Chris Mouse & the Promise. 2012. 24p. (-18). pap. 9.99 (978-1-939217-01-1(6)) 5 Prince Publishing.

Aesop. The Country Mouse & the City Mouse. 2012. (J). 29.99 (978-1-61913-100-2(5)) Weigl Pubs., Inc.

—The Lion & the Mouse. 2016. (ENG.). 79.82 **(978-1-367-86708-6(8))** Blurb, Inc.

—The Lion & the Mouse. 2017. (Let's Learn Aesop's Fables Ser.). 24p. (gr. 6-7). 24.60 **(978-1-4994-8369-7(4))**; pap. 8.25 **(978-1-4994-8374-1(0))** Rosen Publishing Group, Inc., The. (Windmill Bks.).

Aesop. The Lion & the Mouse Tuff Book. 2011. (ENG., Illus.). 28p. (J). 6.95 (978-0-7358-4028-7(8)) North-South Bks., Inc.

Aesop Enterprise Inc. Staff. The Lion & the Mouse. Watts, Bernadette, illus. 2007. (ENG.). 32p. (J). (gr. -1-3). pap. 8.95 (978-0-7358-2129-3(1)) North-South Bks., Inc.

Alborozo, Gabriel. The Mouse & the Moon. Alborozo, Gabriel, illus. 2016. (ENG., Illus.). 32p. (J). 16.99 (978-1-62779-224-0(4), 9781627792240, Holt, Henry & Co. Bks. For Young Readers) Holt, Henry & Co.

Alfred Oscar Valentine: Tales from Spoon Creek: New Beginnings. 2006. (J). 12.00 (978-0-9766894-5-4(6)) Stanley, Donna Lacy.

Allen, Eleanor. Mouse Monk in a Christmas Adventure. 2009. 36p. pap. 15.49 (978-1-4490-2197-9(2)) AuthorHouse.

Alrawi, Karim. The Mouse Who Saved Egypt. Willey, Bee, illus. 2011. 32p. (J). (gr. -1-3). 16.95 (978-1-56656-856-2(0), Crocodile Bks.) Interlink Publishing Group, Inc.

Ammirato, Lidia. Why Does the Dog Chase the Cat & the Cat Chase the Mouse? 2012. 24p. pap. 15.99 (978-1-4771-0651-8(0)) Xlibris Corp.

Anderson, Sorrel. The Clumsies Make a Mess, 1. 2010. (Clumsies Ser.: 1). (ENG., Illus.). 112p. (J). pap. 5.99 (978-0-00-733090-4(1), HarperCollins Children's Bks.) HarperCollins Pubs. Ltd. GBR. Dist: HarperCollins Pubs.

—Clumsies Make a Mess of the Big Show, 3. Slater, Nicola, illus. 2011. (ENG.). 112p. (J). (gr. 2-4). 6.99 (978-0-00-733936-5(4)) HarperCollins Pubs. Ltd. GBR. Dist: Independent Pubs. Group.

—Make a Mess of the Seaside, 2. 2010. (Clumsies Ser.: 2). (ENG., Illus.). 112p. (J). pap. 5.99 (978-0-00-733935-8(6), HarperCollins Children's Bks.) HarperCollins Pubs. Ltd. GBR. Dist: HarperCollins Pubs.

Andrews, Julie & Hamilton, Emma Walton. The Great American Mousical. Walton, Tony, illus. 2006. (Julie Andrews Collection). (J). (gr. k-4). 160p. 15.99 (978-0-06-057918-0(8), Julie Andrews Collection); 147p. lib. bdg. 16.89 (978-0-06-057919-7(6)) HarperCollins Pubs.

Anfousse, Ginette. Polo et L'anniversaire. Sarrazin, Marisol, tr. 2003. (Polo Baby Board Bks.). (FRE., Illus.). 16p. (J). (— 1). bds. (978-2-89021-656-3(X)) Diffusion du livre Mirabel (DLM).

Archambault, John. Boom Chicka Rock. Chitwood, Suzanne Tanner & Chitwood, Suzanne, illus. 2004. (ENG.). 32p. (J). (gr. -1-k). 16.99 (978-0-399-23587-0(6), Philomel Bks.) Penguin Young Readers Group.

Archambault, Marc. Mommy Is Too Tired to Play. 2010. 32p. 18.97 (978-0-557-23350-2(X)) Lulu Pr., Inc.

Aremds, Donald L. Norm the Ninja River Mouse. 2006. (J). (978-0-9768880-1-7(7)) Mission Manuscripts, Inc.

Arenstam, Peter. Nicholas: A New Hampshire Tale. Holman, Karen Busch, illus. 2009. (Nicholas Northeastern Ser.: 3). (ENG.). 144p. (J). (gr. k-7). 14.95 (978-1-58726-521-1(4), Mitten Pr.) Ann Arbor Editions LLC.

—Nicholas: A Vermont Tale. Holman, Karen Busch, illus. 2010. (Nicholas Northeastern Ser.: 4). (ENG.). 144p. (J). (gr. k-7). 14.95 (978-1-58726-522-8(2), Mitten Pr.) Ann Arbor Editions LLC.

—Nicholas, a New Hampshire Tale. Holman, Karen Busch, illus. 2015. (Nicholas Northeastern Ser.: 3). (ENG.). 158p. (J). (gr. k-7). pap. 8.95 (978-1-938170-68-3(7), Mitten Pr.) Ann Arbor Editions LLC.

Asch, Frank. Battle in a Bottle. Kanzler, John, illus. 2014. (Class Pets Ser.). (ENG.). 96p. (J). (gr. 2-6). pap. 13.99 (978-1-4814-3625-0(2), Simon & Schuster/Paula Wiseman Bks.) Simon & Schuster/Paula Wiseman Bks.

—The Ghost of P. S. 42. Kanzler, John, illus. 2014. (Class Pets Ser.). (ENG.). 96p. (J). (gr. 2-5). pap. 13.99 (978-1-4814-3624-3(4), Simon & Schuster/Paula Wiseman Bks.) Simon & Schuster/Paula Wiseman Bks.

—Here Comes the Cat! Vagin, Vladimir, illus. 25th ed. 2011. (ENG & RUS.). 32p. (J). (gr. -1-3). 12.95 (978-1-936365-41-8(3)) McSweeney's Publishing.

—Mr. Maxwell's Mouse, 0 vols. Asch, Devin, illus. 2014. (ENG.). 32p. (J). (gr. k-4). pap. 8.95 (978-1-77138-117-8(5)) Kids Can Pr., Ltd. CAN. Dist: Hachette Bk. Group.

—Mrs. Marlowe's Mice. Asch, Devin, illus. 2007. (ENG.). 32p. (J). (gr. k-4). 17.95 (978-1-55453-022-9(9)) Kids Can Pr., Ltd. CAN. Dist: Hachette Bk. Group.

—Survival School. Kanzler, John, illus. 2014. (Class Pets Ser.). (ENG.). 96p. (J). (gr. 2-6). pap. 13.99 (978-1-4814-3627-4(9), Simon & Schuster/Paula Wiseman Bks.) Simon & Schuster/Paula Wiseman Bks.

Asch, Frank & Asch, Devin. Mr. Maxwell's Mouse. Asch, Frank & Asch, Devin, illus. 2004. (ENG., Illus.). 32p. (J). (gr. k-4). 18.95 (978-1-55337-486-2(X)) Kids Can Pr., Ltd. CAN. Dist: Hachette Bk. Group.

Avi. Poppy. Floca, Brian, illus. 2006. (Poppy Stories Ser.). (ENG.). 192p. (J). (gr. 3-7). pap. 6.99 (978-0-380-72769-8(2)) HarperCollins Pubs.

—Poppy. 2006. (Poppy Stories Ser.: 2). (J). (gr. 3-6). lib. bdg. 17.20 (978-0-613-03338-1(8), Turtleback) Turtleback Bks.

—Poppy & Ereth. Floca, Brian, illus. 2011. (Poppy Stories Ser.). (ENG.). 224p. (J). (gr. 3-7). pap. 6.99 (978-0-06-111971-2(7)) HarperCollins Pubs.

—Poppy & Rye. Floca, Brian, illus. 2006. (Poppy Stories Ser.). (ENG.). 240p. (J). (gr. 3-7). pap. 6.99 (978-0-380-79717-2(8)) HarperCollins Pubs.

—Poppy & Rye. Floca, Brian, illus. 2006. (Poppy Stories Ser.: 3). 182p. (J). (gr. 3-7). lib. bdg. 17.20 (978-0-613-17447-3(X), Turtleback) Turtleback Bks.

—Ragweed. Howard, E., ed. Floca, Brian, illus. 2006. (Poppy Stories Ser.). (ENG.). 224p. (J). (gr. 3-7). pap. 6.99 (978-0-380-80167-1(1)) HarperCollins Pubs.

Aviation Book Company Staff. Ragweed. 2006. (Poppy Stories Ser.: 1). (J). (gr. 3-6). lib. bdg. 17.20 (978-0-613-26699-4(4), Turtleback) Turtleback Bks.

Award, Anna & Aesop. The Lion & the Mouse with the Donkey & the Lapdog. Biro, Val, illus. 2014. (ENG.). 24p. (J). pap. 6.95 (978-1-84135-953-3(X)) Award Pubns. Ltd. GBR. Dist: Parkwest Pubns., Inc.

Award, Anna, et al. The Eagle & the Man with the Town Mouse & the Country Mouse. 2014. (ENG.). 24p. (J). pap. 6.95 (978-1-84135-958-8(0)) Award Pubns. Ltd. GBR. Dist: Parkwest Pubns., Inc.

Baglio, Ben M. The Midnight Mouse. Ellis, Andy, illus. 2003. 59p. (J). (978-0-439-41916-1(6)) Scholastic, Inc.

Bailey, Mark & Oatman, Michael. Tiny Pie. Hemingway, Edward, illus. 2013. (ENG.). 32p. (J). (gr. -1-17). 15.95 (978-0-7624-4482-3(7), Running Pr. Kids) Running Pr. Bk. Pubs.

Baker, Alan, illus. Two Tiny Mice: A Mouse-Eye Exploration of Nature. rev. ed. 2014. (ENG.). 40p. (J). (gr. -1-3). 16.95 (978-1-62914-627-0(7), Sky Pony Pr.) Skyhorse Publishing Co., Inc.

Baker, Keith. Hickory Dickory Dock. 2007. (ENG., Illus.). 32p. (J). (gr. -1-3). 17.99 (978-0-15-205818-0(4)) Houghton Mifflin Harcourt Publishing Co.

Balian, Lorna. Mother's Mother's Day, 1 vol. 2004. (ENG., Illus.). 32p. (J). 8.95 (978-1-932065-39-8(3)) Star Bright Bks., Inc.

Bardhan-Quallen, Sudipta. Snoring Beauty. Manning, Jane, illus. 2014. (J). (978-0-06-087405-6(8)) Harper & Row Ltd.

—Snoring Beauty. Manning, Jane, illus. 2014. (ENG.). 32p. (J). (gr. -1-3). 17.99 (978-0-06-087403-2(1)) HarperCollins Pubs.

Barklem, Jill. Autumn Story. Barklem, Jill, illus. 2011. (Brambly Hedge Ser.). (ENG., Illus.). 32p. (J). 9.99 (978-0-00-183739-3(7), HarperCollins Children's Bks.) HarperCollins Pubs. Ltd. GBR. Dist: HarperCollins Pubs.

—Spring Story. Barklem, Jill, illus. 2011. (Brambly Hedge Ser.). (ENG., Illus.). 32p. (J). 9.99 (978-0-00-183922-9(5), HarperCollins Children's Bks.) HarperCollins Pubs. Ltd. GBR. Dist: HarperCollins Pubs.

—Summer Story. Barklem, Jill, illus. 2011. (Brambly Hedge Ser.). (ENG., Illus.). 32p. (J). 9.99 (978-0-00-183923-6(3), HarperCollins Children's Bks.) HarperCollins Pubs. Ltd. GBR. Dist: HarperCollins Pubs.

Barlone, M. J. A Mouse & Rabbits Tale. 2010. (Illus.). 40p. pap. 16.99 (978-1-4490-7771-6(4)) AuthorHouse.

Barnes, Cheryl Shaw & Barnes, Peter W., illus. Liberty Lee's Tail of Independence. 2012. (ENG.). 36p. (J). (gr. k-3). 16.95 (978-1-59698-792-0(8), Little Patriot Pr.) Regnery Publishing, Inc., An Eagle Publishing Co.

Barnes, Peter W. House Mouse, Senate Mouse. Barnes, Cheryl S., illus. 2012. (ENG.). 40p. (J). (gr. k-3). 16.99 (978-1-59698-790-6(1), Little Patriot Pr.) Regnery Publishing, Inc., An Eagle Publishing Co.

—Maestro Mouse: And the Mystery of the Missing Baton. Barnes, Cheryl Shaw, illus. 2005. 32p. (J). 16.95 (978-1-893622-17-3(7), VSP Bks.) Vacation Spot Publishing.

—Marshall, the Courthouse Mouse: A Tail of the U. S. Supreme Court. Barnes, Cheryl S., illus. 2012. (ENG.). 40p. (J). (gr. k). 16.95 (978-1-59698-789-0(8), Little Patriot Pr.) Regnery Publishing, Inc., An Eagle Publishing Co.

—Woodrow, the White House Mouse. Barnes, Cheryl Shaw, illus. 2012. (ENG.). 40p. (J). (gr. k-3). 16.95 (978-1-59698-788-3(X), Little Patriot Pr.) Regnery Publishing, Inc., An Eagle Publishing Co.

Barnes, Peter W. & Barnes, Cheryl S., illus. Maestro Mouse: And the Mystery of the Missing Baton. 2013. (ENG.). 40p. (J). (gr. k-5). 16.95 (978-1-62157-036-3(3), Little Patriot Pr.) Regnery Publishing, Inc., An Eagle Publishing Co.

Bassett, Madge A. At Bumblebee Farm. Bassett, Madge A., illus. 2009. (Illus.). 20p. pap. 13.46 (978-1-4251-9230-3(0)) Trafford Publishing.

Bauer, Marion Dane. Christmas in the Forest. Hearn, Diane Dawson, illus. (Holiday House Reader Ser.). (ENG.). 48p. (J). (gr. k-3). tchr. ed. 15.95 (978-0-8234-1371-3(3)) Holiday Hse., Inc.

Beander, Lillian. Mylah's Bedtime Stories, 1 vol. 2009. 48p. pap. 16.95 (978-1-61546-981-9(8)) America Star Bks.

Beam, Emily. The Rose Cottage Tales. 2010. (Tumtum & Nutmeg Ser.: 2). (ENG., Illus.). 416p. (J). (gr. 3-7). 16.99 (978-0-316-08599-1(5)) Little, Brown Bks. for Young Readers.

—Tumtum & Nutmeg: Adventures Beyond Nutmouse Hall. 2011. (Tumtum & Nutmeg Ser.: 1). (ENG., Illus.). 512p. (J). (gr. 3-7). pap. 10.00 (978-0-316-07574-9(4)) Little, Brown Bks. for Young Readers.

Becker, Bonny. A Bedtime for Bear. Denton, Kady MacDonald, illus. 2010. (J). (Bear & Mouse Ser.: 3). (ENG.). 48p. (gr. -1-2). 16.99 (978-0-7636-4101-6(4)); (978-0-7636-5364-4(0)) Candlewick Pr.

—A Birthday for Bear. Denton, Kady MacDonald, illus. (Candlewick Sparks Ser.). (ENG.). (J). 2013. 56p. (gr. k-4). pap. 3.99 (978-0-7636-6861-7(3)) 2012. 48p. (gr. -1-2). 16.99 (978-0-7636-5823-6(5)) Candlewick Pr.

—The Sniffles for Bear. Denton, Kady MacDonald, illus. 2011. (Bear & Mouse Ser.). (ENG.). 32p. (J). (gr. -1-2). 16.99 (978-0-7636-4756-8(X)) Candlewick Pr.

—A Visitor for Bear. Denton, Kady MacDonald, illus. (Bear & Mouse Ser.). (ENG.). 56p. (J). 2012. (gr. k-k). pap. 6.99 (978-0-7636-4611-0(3)) 2008. (gr. -1-2). 16.99 (978-0-7636-2807-9(7)) Candlewick Pr.

—A Visitor for Bear. Denton, Kady MacDonald, illus. 2012. lib. bdg. 17.20 (978-0-606-26930-8(4), Turtleback) Turtleback Bks.

Beckler, Bruce. The Secrets of the Green Mansion. l.t. ed. 2004. (Illus.). 240p. (J). per. 13.99 (978-0-9745210-1-5(9)) Myers Publishing Co.

Beiser, Tim. Miss Mousie's Blind Date. Berman, Rachel, illus. 2012. (ENG.). 24p. (J). (gr. -1-2). 17.95 (978-1-77049-251-6(8), Tundra Bks.) Tundra Bks. CAN. Dist: Penguin Random Hse. LLC.

Bennett, Diane. Put a Smile on Your Face. 2008. 24p. per. 24.95 (978-1-4241-9895-5(X)) America Star Bks.

Benson, Jeffrey. The Adventures of Avortit & Rooney. 2005. pap. (978-1-84401-490-3(8)) Athena Pr.

Bently, Peter. The Cat, the Mouse, & the Runaway Train. Cox, Steve, illus. 2013. (J). (978-1-4351-4968-7(8)) Barnes & Noble, Inc.

Beraducci, Deborah. Tyler's Halloween Horror, 1 vol. Eyre, Jane, illus. 2009. 22p. pap. 24.95 (978-1-4489-2133-1(3)) America Star Bks.

Berkowitz, Barbara. A Mouse in the House. 2009. 32p. pap. 14.49 (978-1-4490-4258-5(9)) AuthorHouse.

Bernheimer, Kate. The Girl Who Wouldn't Brush Her Hair. Parker, Jake, illus. 2013. (ENG.). 40p. (J). (gr. -1-3). 17.99 (978-0-375-86878-8(X), Schwartz & Wade Bks.) Random Hse. Children's Bks.

Berry, Wendell. Whitefoot: A Story from the Center of the World. Te Selle, Davis, illus. 2010. (ENG.). 64p. pap. (978-1-58243-640-1(1)) Ebury Publishing.

Berry, Wendell & Rorer, Abigail. Whitefoot: A Story from the Center of the World. Te Selle, Davis, illus. 2008. (Port William Ser.). (ENG.). 64p. (gr. 2-7). 22.00 (978-1-58243-432-2(8)) Eastern National.

Bertagnolli, Daniel. Now You Seed It, Now You Don't. 2012. 40p. pap. 16.46 (978-1-4669-2622-6(8)) Trafford Publishing.

Best, Jessica Gabrielle. The Wish Giver's Promise. 2011. 16p. 16.95 (978-1-4567-1385-0(X)) AuthorHouse.

Beverly-Barrier, Essie. Ouse the Mouse. Allen, Joshua, illus. 2009. 20p. pap. 12.99 (978-1-4389-4518-7(3)) AuthorHouse.

Beverly, Cleary. The Mouse & the Motorcycle. 2014. (Mouse & the Motorcycle Ser.). (ENG.). 208p. (J). (gr. 2-5). 11.24 (978-1-63245-245-0(6)) Lectorum Pubns., Inc.

Billingsley, Franny. Big Bad Bunny. Karas, G. Brian, illus. 2008. (ENG.). 40p. (J). (gr. k-3). 17.99 (978-1-4169-0601-8(0), Atheneum/Richard Jackson Bks.) Simon & Schuster Children's Publishing.

Bird, Benjamin. A Cat Is Chasing Me Through This Book!, 1 vol. Pérez, Carmen, illus. 2014. (Tom & Jerry Ser.). (ENG.). 32p. (gr. -1-2). 22.65 (978-1-4795-5229-0(1)) Picture Window Bks.

—Don't Give This Book a Bowl of Milk!, 1 vol. Pérez, Carmen, illus. 2014. (Tom & Jerry Ser.). (ENG.). 32p. (gr. -1-2). 22.65 (978-1-4795-5230-6(5)) Picture Window Bks.

—This Book Is Not a Piece of Cheese!, 1 vol. Pérez, Carmen, illus. 2014. (Tom & Jerry Ser.). (ENG.). 32p. (gr. -1-2). 22.65 (978-1-4795-5231-3(3)) Picture Window Bks.

Bishop, Anne. Anne Bishop's Christmas Dram: The Gift of Three. 2013. 28p. pap. 24.95 (978-1-4626-8276-8(6)) America Star Bks.

Bishop, Brandy. The Christmas Mice, 1 vol. 2010. 30p. 24.95 (978-1-4489-4438-5(4)) PublishAmerica, Inc.

Björkman, Steve. Look Out, Mouse! Björkman, Steve, illus. 2015. (I Like to Read(r) Ser.). (ENG., Illus.). 24p. (J). (gr. -1-3). 6.99 (978-0-8234-3397-1(8)) Holiday Hse., Inc.

Björkman, Steve, illus. Look Out, Mouse! 2015. (I Like to Read(r) Ser.). (ENG.). 24p. (J). (gr. -1-3). 14.95 (978-0-8234-2953-0(9)) Holiday Hse., Inc.

Blair, Eric. Belling the Cat: A Retelling of Aesop's Fable, 1 vol. Silverman, Dianne, illus. 2013. (My First Classic Story Ser.). (ENG.). 24p. (gr. k-3). pap. 7.10 (978-1-4795-1854-8(9), My First Classic Story) Picture Window Bks.

—The Country Mouse & the City Mouse: A Retelling of Aesop's Fable, 1 vol. Silverman, Dianne, illus. 2013. (My First Classic Story Ser.). (ENG.). 24p. (gr. k-3). pap. 7.10 (978-1-4795-1858-6(1), My First Classic Story) Picture Window Bks.

—El Raton de Campo y el Raton de Ciudad: Versión de la Fábula de Esopo. Abello, Patricia, tr. from ENG. Silverman, Dianne, illus. 2006. (Read-It! Readers en Español: Fábulas Ser.).Tr. of Country Mouse & the City Mouse - A Retelling of Aesop's Fable. (SPA.). 24p. (gr. k-3). 21.32 (978-1-4048-1617-6(8), Easy Readers) Picture Window Bks.

Blair, Eric & Aesop Enterprise Inc. Staff. The Country Mouse & the City Mouse: A Retelling of Aesop's Fable, 1 vol. Silverman, Dianne, illus. 2011. (My First Classic Story Ser.). (ENG.). 24p. (gr. k-3). lib. bdg. 22.65 (978-1-4048-6510-5(1), My First Classic Story) Picture Window Bks.

Blanchard, Patricia & Suhr, Joanne. There Was a Mouse. Gorbachev, Valeri, illus. 2003. (ENG.). 16p. (J). pap. 15.00 (978-1-57274-702-9(1), BB2210, Bks. for Young Learners) Owen, Richard C. Pubs., Inc.

Bloser, Cheryl. Little Mouse & the Muddy Feet. 2012. 28p. pap. 9.99 (978-0-9836771-1-6(5)) Mindstir Media.

Bloumis, Joy. An Adventure in Fairyland. 2013. 84p. pap. 10.50 (978-1-62212-835-8(4), Strategic Bk. Publishing) Strategic Book Publishing & Rights Agency (SBPRA).

Bogart, Jo Ellen & Bogart, Jill. Out & about with the Big Tree Gang, 1 vol. Griffiths, Dean, illus. 2006. (Orca Echoes Ser.). (ENG.). 64p. (J). (gr. 2-3). per. 4.99 (978-1-55143-603-6(5)) Orca Bk. Pubs. USA.

Bolander, Sharon Miller. At the Stroke of Midnight. 2012. 40p. pap. 24.95 (978-1-4626-8905-7(1)) America Star Bks.

Bond, Felicia. The Halloween Play. Bond, Felicia, illus. 2008. Orig. Title: The Halloween Performance. (ENG., Illus.). 32p. (J). (gr. -1-1). pap. 7.99 (978-0-06-135796-1(0)) HarperCollins Pubs.

Bonnell, Kris. Mmm, Apples. 2006. (J). pap. 3.95 (978-1-933727-22-6(5)) Reading Reading Bks., LLC.

Botha, Ingrid. Chikin & Scrub. 2011. 108p. pap. 10.50 (978-1-60976-295-7(9), Strategic Bk. Publishing) Strategic Book Publishing & Rights Agency (SBPRA).

Bottner, Barbara & Kruglik, Gerald. Wallace's Lists. Landstrom, Olof, tr. Landstrom, Olof, illus. 2004. (ENG.). 40p. (J). (gr. -1-2). 16.99 (978-0-06-000224-4(7), Tegen, Katherine Bks) HarperCollins Pubs.

—Wallace's Lists. Landstrom, Olof, illus. 2011. (J). (gr. 1-3). 29.95 (978-0-545-04275-8(5)) Weston Woods Studios, Inc.

Bowen, Marvin. Adventures of the Fluffytail Mouse. 2011. 52p. (gr. -1). pap. 12.99 (978-1-4670-3879-9(2)) AuthorHouse.

Bowman, Crystal. Little David & His Best Friend. Hartung, Susan Kathleen & Endersly, Frank, illus. 2010. (I Can Read! / Little David Ser.). (ENG.). 32p. (J). pap. 3.99 (978-0-310-71710-2(8)) Zonderkidz.

—Little David's Brave Day, 1 vol. Hartung, Susan Kathleen & Endersly, Frank, illus. 2010. (I Can Read! / Little David Ser.). (ENG.). 32p. (J). pap. 3.99 (978-0-310-71709-6(4)) Zonderkidz.

Boyd, Ken. Tinsel Tail Mouse. 2009. 48p. pap. 16.25 (978-1-60860-403-6(9), Eloquent Bks.) Strategic Book Publishing & Rights Agency (SBPRA).

Bradford James Nolan. The Mouse Who Lived in Fenway Park. Jim Connelly, illus. 2009. 36p. pap. 19.99 (978-1-4389-4491-3(8)) AuthorHouse.

Bratun, Katy. Gingerbread Mouse. Bratun, Katy, illus. (Illus.). 32p. (J). (gr. -1-3). 2007. (ENG.). per. 6.99 (978-0-06-009082-1(0)) 2003. lib. bdg. 13.89 (978-0-06-009081-4(2)) HarperCollins Pubs.

Braun, Sebastien. Back to Bed, Ed!, 1 vol. Braun, Sebastien, illus. (Illus.). 32p. (J). (gr. -1-3). 2014. (ENG.). pap. 7.95 (978-1-56145-775-5(2)) 2010. 15.95 (978-1-56145-518-8(0)) Peachtree Pubs.

—Mayday Mouse. Braun, Sebastien, illus. (Child's Play Library). (ENG., Illus.). 32p. (J). (gr. k-3). 2017. (978-1-84643-759-5(8)) 2016. pap. (978-1-84643-758-8(X)) Child's Play International Ltd.

Brave Little Mouse: Individual Title Six-Packs. (Story Steps Ser.). (gr. k-2). 32.00 (978-0-7635-9831-0(3)) Rigby Education.

Breitrose, Prudence & Yue, Stephanie. Mousemobile: When Mice Hit the Road. 2014. (Mousenet Book Ser.). (ENG., Illus.). 288p. (J). (gr. 3-7). pap. 7.99 (978-1-4231-7438-7(0)) Hyperion Bks. for Children.

Bright, Rachel. The Lion Inside. Field, Jim, illus. 2016. (ENG.). 32p. (J). (gr. -1-k). 16.99 (978-0-545-87350-5(9), Scholastic Pr.) Scholastic, Inc.

—Side by Side. Gliori, Debi, illus. 2015. (ENG.). 32p. (J). (gr. -1-k). 17.99 (978-0-545-81326-6(3), Scholastic Pr.) Scholastic, Inc.

Brightwood, Laura, illus. Lion & Mousie. Brightwood, Laura, . 2007. (J). DVD (978-1-934409-00-8(6)) 3-C Institute for Social Development.

Broom, Jenny. The Lion & the Mouse: Turn-And-Tell Tales. Noj, Nahta, illus. 2014. (ENG.). 32p. (J). (gr. -1-2). 14.99 (978-0-7636-6619-4(X), Templar) Candlewick Pr.

Brown, Palmer. Cheerful. 2012. (ENG., Illus.). 72p. (J). (gr. -1-2). 12.95 (978-1-59017-501-9(8), NYR Children's Collection) New York Review of Bks., Inc., The.

—Hickory. Brown, Palmer, illus. 2013. (ENG., Illus.). 56p. (J). (gr. -1-2). 16.95 (978-1-59017-627-6(8), NYR Children's Collection) New York Review of Bks., Inc., The.

—Something for Christmas. Brown, Palmer, illus. 2011. (ENG., Illus.). 40p. (J). (gr. -1-2). 12.95 (978-1-59017-462-3(3), NYR Children's Collection) New York Review of Bks., Inc., The.

Brown, Ruth. The Tale of Two Mice. Brown, Ruth, illus. 2008. (ENG., Illus.). 32p. (J). (gr. -1-3). 17.99 (978-0-7636-4015-6(8)) Candlewick Pr.

Brown, Ruth, illus. The Christmas Mouse. 2013. (J). (978-1-4351-5021-8(X)) Barnes & Noble, Inc.

Bucklaschuk, Angela. My Doggy the Big Helper. 2012. 30p. pap. 11.95 (978-1-61286-124-1(5)) Avid Readers Publishing Group.

Buehner, Caralyn. Merry Christmas, Mr. Mouse. Buehner, Mark, illus. 2015. (ENG.). 40p. (J). (gr. -1-k). 17.99 (978-0-8037-4010-5(7), Dial Bks) Penguin Young Readers Group.

Bunting, Eve. The Mother's Day Mice. Brett, Jan, illus. 2017. (ENG.). 40p. (J). (gr. -1-3). 8.99 (978-0-544-88033-7(1), HMH Books For Young Readers) Houghton Mifflin Harcourt Publishing Co.

—Whose Shoe? Ruzzier, Sergio, illus. 2015. (ENG.). 32p. (J). (gr. -1-3). 16.99 (978-0-544-30210-5(9)) Houghton Mifflin Harcourt Publishing Co.

Burgess, Thornton W. The Adventures of Danny Meadow Mouse. (J). 18.95 (978-0-8488-0377-3(9)) Amereon Ltd.

—Tommy & the Wishing-Stone. Cady, Harrison, illus. 2012. (Dover Children's Thrift Classics Ser.). (ENG.). 240p. (J). (gr. k-3). pap. 4.00 (978-0-486-48105-0(0)) Dover Pubns., Inc.

—Whitefoot the Wood Mouse. (J). 18.95 (978-0-8488-0395-7(7)) Amereon Ltd.

—Whitefoot the Wood Mouse. Cady, Harrison, illus. 2006. (Dover Children's Thrift Classics Ser.). (ENG.). 112p. (J). (gr. 3-8). per. 4.00 (978-0-486-44944-9(0)) Dover Pubns., Inc.

—Whitefoot the Woodmouse. 2007. 120p. per. 10.95 (978-1-60312-258-0(3)); 22.95 (978-1-60312-756-1(9)) Aegypan.

—Whitefoot the Woodmouse. 2011. 118p. 23.95 (978-1-4638-9567-9(4)) Rodgers, Alan Bks.

Burke, Christina. Melvin et le Grand Match de Hockey. Minguet, Anne, tr. Franfou, illus. 2013. 52p. (978-0-9918561-3-8(9)); pap. (978-0-9918561-2-1(0)) Stars Aligned Publishing.

Burkert, Rand. Mouse & Lion. Burkert, Nancy Ekholm, illus. 2011. (ENG.). 32p. (J). (gr. -1-3). 18.99 (978-0-545-10147-9(6), Di Capua, Michael) Scholastic, Inc.

Burton, Jeffrey. The Itsy Bitsy Pilgrim. Rescek, Sanja, illus. 2016. (Itsy Bitsy Ser.). (ENG.). 16p. (J). (gr. -1 — 1). bds. 5.99 (978-1-4814-6852-7(9), Little Simon) Little Simon.

Burton, Katherine. One Gray Mouse. Fernandes, Kim, illus. 2006. (ENG.). 24p. (J). (gr. -1 — 1). bds. 7.95 (978-1-55453-026-7(1)) Kids Can Pr., Ltd. CAN. Dist: Hachette Bk. Group.

—Une Souris Grise. Fernandes, Kim, illus.Tr. of Souris Grise. (FRE.). 24p. (J). pap. 6.99 (978-0-590-16023-0(0)) Scholastic, Inc.

Bush, Robert Quacken. The Return of Pete Pack Rat. Bush, Robert Quacken, ed. rev. deluxe ed. 2005. (Illus.). 64p. (J). (gr. 2-4). reprint ed. 12.95 (978-0-9712757-1-3(8)); pap. 6.95 (978-0-9712757-2-0(6)) Quackenbush, Robert Studios.

Bushnell, Steven G. The Neighbors of Little Church Mouse: The Parables of Jesus. 2009. 96p. pap. 31.99 (978-1-4490-0620-4(5)) AuthorHouse.

Butterworth, Nick. Jingle Bells. 2014. (ENG.). 32p. (J). 9.99 (978-0-00-758399-7(0), HarperCollins Children's Bks.) HarperCollins Pubs. Ltd. GBR. Dist: HarperCollins Pubs.

Byers, Marcella. Mitsy & Marty Mouse Visit Grandpa. Grant, Cheryl, illus. 2014. (ENG.). 32p. (gr. -1-2). pap. 8.95 (978-1-61448-740-1(5), 9781614487401) Morgan James Publishing.

Cabral, Noel. Rachel's Four-Legged Friend. 2012. 24p. 24.95 (978-1-4626-6089-6(4)) America Star Bks.

Calmenson, Stephanie. Birthday at the Panda Palace. Cushman, Doug, illus. 2007. 32p. (J). (gr. -1-3). 15.99 (978-0-06-052663-4(7)) HarperCollins Pubs.

Camp, V. Ray. The Little Mouse on the Prairie. Baker, David, illus. 2011. 28p. pap. 24.95 (978-1-4560-1028-7(X)) America Star Bks.

Can I Come Too?, 1 vol. 2014. (ENG., Illus.). 32p. (J). (gr. -1-3). pap. 16.95 (978-1-56145-796-0(5)) Peachtree Pubs.

Carlson, Nancy. First Grade, Here I Come! 2006. (Illus.). (J). (978-1-4156-8114-5(7), Viking Adult) Penguin Publishing Group.

—Henry & the Bully. 2012. (ENG.). 32p. (J). (gr. -1-1). pap. 6.99 (978-0-14-242120-8(0), Puffin Books) Penguin Young Readers Group.

—Henry's Show & Tell. Carlson, Nancy, illus. 2012. (Nancy Carlson Picture Bks). (Illus.). 32p. (J). (gr. k-2). (ENG.). 9.95 (978-0-7613-8953-8(9)); 56.72 (978-0-7613-9308-5(0)) Lerner Publishing Group. (Carolrhoda Bks.).

Carman, Debby. I'm Maximum Cat, That's a Fact! 2007. (Illus.). 28p. (J). 14.99 (978-0-9777340-2-3(1)) Faux Paw Media Group.

Carpenter, Joyce M. An Unexpected Friend. 2010. 24p. 11.49 (978-1-4520-0758-8(6)) AuthorHouse.

Carr, Jan. Toe Shoe Mouse. Bell, Jennifer, illus. 2014. (ENG.). 32p. (J). (gr. -1-3). 16.95 (978-0-8234-2406-1(5)) Holiday Hse., Inc.

Carroll, Claudia. Missy Mouse & the Rocket Ship. 2008. 65p. pap. 9.95 (978-0-557-01769-0(6)) Lulu Pr., Inc.

Carroll, Harlsha. Miracle Mouse & Jesus - Book: (Short Stories 1) 2012. 36p. pap. 24.95 (978-1-4626-6615-7(9)) America Star Bks.

—Miracle Mouse & Jesus Book #3: Short Stories 2. 2013. 32p. pap. 24.95 (978-1-4626-6647-8(7)) America Star Bks.

Carter, David A. & Carter, Noelle. Little Mouse & Daddy. Carter, David A. & Carter, Noelle, illus. 2005. (Little Mouse Ser.). (Illus.). 12p. (J). 7.95 (978-1-58117-223-2(0), Intervisual/Piggy Toes) Bendon, Inc.

—Little Mouse & Mommy. Carter, David A. & Carter, Noelle, illus. 2005. (Little Mouse Ser.). (Illus.). 12p. (J). 7.95 (978-1-58117-224-9(9), Intervisual/Piggy Toes) Bendon, Inc.

—Little Mouse Plays Peek-a-Boo. Carter, David A. & Carter, Noelle, illus. 2005. (Little Mouse Ser.). (Illus.). 12p. (J). 7.95 (978-1-58117-225-6(7), Intervisual/Piggy Toes) Bendon, Inc.

—Little Mouse's Christmas. Carter, David A. & Carter, Noelle, illus. 2005. (Illus.). 12p. (J). 7.95 (978-1-58117-226-3(5), Intervisual/Piggy Toes) Bendon, Inc.

Cartlidge, Michelle. The Mouse Christmas House: A Press-Out Model Book. (Illus.). 32p. (J). (978-1-904613-67-1(5), Buster Bks.) O'Mara, Michael Bks., Ltd.

Casey, Grandpa. Meet the Müsh-Mice. 2008. 32p. per. 24.95 (978-1-60441-061-7(2)) America Star Bks.

—The Trilogy: Three adventures of the Müsh-Mice. Brennan, Lisa, illus. 2011. 48p. pap. 24.95 (978-1-4626-2095-1(7)) America Star Bks.

Chandler, Paul. Mouse of Commons - Mouse of Lords. 2006. 186p. pap. 14.99 (978-1-4116-8447-8(8)) Lulu Pr., Inc.

Charles, Faustin. The Selfish Crocodile. Terry, Michael, illus. 2010. (Selfish Crocodile Ser.). (ENG.). 32p. (J). (gr. -1-k). pap. 9.99 (978-0-7475-4193-6(0), 9780747541936, Bloomsbury USA Childrens) Bloomsbury Publishing USA.

Charles, Faustin & Terry, Michael. The Selfish Crocodile Book of Nursery Rhymes. Terry, Michael, illus. 2008. (ENG., Illus.). 1p. (J). (gr. -1-k). 25.95 (978-0-7475-9523-6(2)) Bloomsbury Publishing Plc GBR. Dist: Independent Pubs. Group.

Charlie Church Mouse Bible Adventures! Early Elementary. 2003. (J). cd-rom 19.98 (978-0-9714753-1-1(8)) LifeLine Studios, Inc.

The Cheshire Cheese Cat, 1 vol. 2014. (ENG., Illus.). 234p. (J). (gr. 3-6). pap. 8.95 (978-1-56145-810-3(4)) Peachtree Pubs.

Child, Jeremy. Mouse. Davies, Caroline, illus. 2013. (Rock & Rattle Bks.). (ENG.). 8p. (J). (gr. -1 — 1). bds. 3.99 (978-0-7641-6591-7(7)) Barron's Educational Series, Inc.

Chinnery, Karen. Secret Agent Squirrel. 2006. (ENG.). 48p. per. 16.95 (978-1-4241-5459-3(6)) America Star Bks.

Choi, SeoYun. Let's Be Friends. Furukawa, Masumi, illus. rev. ed. 2014. (MySELF Bookshelf Ser.). (ENG.). 32p. (J). (gr. k-2). pap. 11.94 (978-1-60357-658-1(4)) Norwood Hse. Pr.

Christian, Norma. A Christmas Mouse. 2012. 32p. pap. 13.99 (978-1-4624-0328-8(X), Inspiring Voices) Author Solutions, Inc.

Christie, R. Gregory. Mousetropolis. (ENG., Illus.). 32p. (J). (gr. -1-3). 2016. 6.99 (978-0-8234-3692-7(6)) 2015. 16.95 (978-0-8234-2319-4(0)) Holiday Hse., Inc.

Church, Caroline Jayne. Ruff! And the Wonderfully Amazing Busy Day. Church, Caroline Jayne, illus. 2013. (ENG., Illus.). 32p. (J). (gr. k-3). 17.99 (978-0-06-201498-6(6)) HarperCollins Pubs.

Clairmont, Patsy. 5 Cheesy Stories: About Friendship, Bravery, Bullying, & More, 1 vol. Oeltjenbruns, Joni, illus. 2007. (Tails from the Pantry Ser.). (ENG.). 144p. (gr. -1-2). 15.99 (978-1-4003-1042-5(3)) Nelson, Thomas Inc.

Clark, Ruth. Airport Mouse Explores on Opening Day. 2008. (ENG.). 32p. (J). 15.95 (978-0-9792963-4-5(X)) Huntington Ludlow Media Group.

—Airport Mouse Works the Nightshift. 2008. (ENG.). 32p. (J). 15.95 (978-0-9792963-3-8(1)) Hollywood Operating System.

Clark, Ruth E. Airport Mouse. Jones, Phil, illus. 2008. (ENG.). 32p. (J). (gr. -1-3). 15.95 (978-0-9792963-2-1(3)) Hibiscus Publishing.

—Airport Mouse Activity Fun Book 1. Jones, Phil, illus. 2010. 16p. (J). pap. 5.99 (978-0-9792963-6-9(6)) Huntington Ludlow Media Group.

—Airport Mouse Becomes a VIP/VIM World Traveler. Jones, Phil, illus. 2009. 32p. (J). 15.95 (978-0-9792963-5-2(8)) Kimball, Jane A.

—Airport Mouse Becomes a VIP/VIM World Traveler Activity Fun Book 4. Jones, Phil, illus. 2010. 16p. (J). pap. 5.99 (978-0-9792963-9-0(0)) Huntington Ludlow Media Group.

—Airport Mouse Explores on Opening Day Activity Fun Book 3. Jones, Phil, illus. 2010. 16p. (J). pap. 5.99 (978-0-9792963-8-3(2)) Kimball, Jane A.

—Airport Mouse Works the Night Shift Activity Fun Book 2. Jones, Phil, illus. 2010. 16p. (J). pap. 5.99 (978-0-9792963-7-6(4)) Huntington Ludlow Media Group.

Clark, Seneca & Girardi, Sandy. Frankie Goes to Fenway: The Tale of the Faithful, Red Sox-Loving Mouse. Decedue, Julie, illus. 2008. 56p. (J). 18.95 (978-0-9767276-3-7(3)) Three Bean Pr.

Clarke, Jane. Clover the Bunny. 2016. (Dr. KittyCat Ser.: 2). (ENG.). 96p. (J). (gr. 2-5). pap. 4.99 (978-0-545-87336-9(3), Scholastic Paperbacks) Scholastic, Inc.

Clarke, Roger & Wight, Al. Do Mice Eat Rice? 2005. (ENG., Illus.). 32p. (J). (gr. -1-3). 12.95 (978-0-8048-3643-2(4)) Tuttle Publishing.

Cleary, Beverly. The Mouse & the Motorcycle. Darling, Louis et al, illus. (Ralph Mouse Ser.: 1). (ENG.). 208p. (J). (gr. 3-7). 2014. 16.99 (978-0-688-21698-6(6)) 2016. reprint ed. pap. 6.99 (978-0-380-70924-3(4)) HarperCollins Pubs.

—The Mouse & the Motorcycle: a Harper Classic. Rogers, Jacqueline, illus. 2017. (Harper Classic Ser.). 224p. (J). (gr. 3-7). 16.99 (978-0-06-265798-5(4)) HarperCollins Pubs.

—The Ralph Mouse Collection. 2006. (Ralph Mouse Ser.). 592p. (J). (gr. 3-7). pap. 14.99 (978-0-06-441004-5(8)) HarperCollins Pubs.

—Ralph S. Mouse. Zelinsky, Paul O. & Rogers, Jacqueline, illus. 2014. (Ralph Mouse Ser.: 3). (ENG.). 192p. (J). (gr. 3-7). pap. 7.99 (978-0-380-70957-1(0)) HarperCollins Pubs.

—Ralph S. Mouse. Zelinsky, Paul O. et al, illus. 2014. (Ralph Mouse Ser.: 3). (ENG.). 192p. (J). (gr. 3-7). 16.99 (978-0-688-01452-0(6)) HarperCollins Pubs.

—Ralph S. Mouse. (Mouse & the Motorcycle Ser.). 160p. (J). (gr. 3-5). pap. 4.95 (978-0-8072-1476-3(0), Listening Library) Random Hse. Audio Publishing Group.

—El Ratoncito de la Moto, 1 vol. Netto, Lydia, tr. Darling, Louis, illus. 2006. (Ralph Mouse Ser.: 1).Tr. of Mouse & the Motorcycle. (SPA.). 160p. (J). (gr. 3-7). pap. 5.99 (978-0-06-000057-8(0)) HarperCollins Pubs.

—El Ratoncito de la Moto. 2006.Tr. of Mouse & the Motorcycle. (SPA.). (J). (gr. 3-6). 16.00 (978-0-613-67220-7(8), Turtleback) Turtleback Bks.

—Runaway Ralph. Darling, Louis et al, illus. 2014. (Ralph Mouse Ser.: 2). (ENG.). 224p. (J). (gr. 3-7). pap. 7.99 (978-0-380-70953-3(8)) HarperCollins Pubs.

Cochran, Kate & Benchmark Education Co., LLC Staff. Why Mice Hide. 2015. (BuildUp Ser.). (J). (gr. 1). (978-1-4900-0728-1(8)) Benchmark Education Co.

Cohen, Lee. The Surprise Party. Neuville, Loyal de, illus. 2010. (ENG.). 32p. (J). (gr. -1-12). lib. bdg. 16.95 (978-1-934960-85-1(3), Raven Tree Pr.,Csi) Continental Sales, Inc.

Cole, Henry. A Nest for Celeste: A Story about Art, Inspiration, & the Meaning of Home. Cole, Henry, illus. (Nest for Celeste Ser.: 1). (ENG., Illus.). 352p. (J). (gr. 3-7). 2012. pap. 6.99 (978-0-06-170412-3(1)) 2010. 16.99 (978-0-06-170410-9(5)) HarperCollins Pubs. (Tegen, Katherine Bks).

—The Somewhat True Adventures of Sammy Shine, 1 vol. Cole, Henry, illus. 2016. (ENG., Illus.). 272p. (J). (gr. 3-6). 16.95 (978-1-56145-866-0(X)) Peachtree Pubs.

Collicott, Sharleen. Mildred & Sam. Collicott, Sharleen, illus. (I Can Read Bks.). (Illus.). (J). 2008. 64p. (gr. -1-2). lib. bdg. 17.89 (978-0-06-058115-2(8), Geringer, Laura Book) 2004. (ENG., 48p. (gr. k-3). pap. 3.99 (978-0-06-000200-8(X)) 2003. 48p. (gr. -1-18). 15.99 (978-0-06-026681-3(3)) HarperCollins Pubs.

—Mildred & Sam & Their Babies. Collicott, Sharleen, illus. 2005. (I Can Read Bks.). (Illus.). 48p. (J). (gr. -1-2). 15.99 (978-0-06-058111-4(5), Geringer, Laura Book) HarperCollins Pubs.

Condenzio, Mary. The Mouse & the Star. Long, Paulette Rich, illus. 2008. 13p. pap. 24.95 (978-1-60441-449-3(9)) America Star Bks.

Cook, Sherry & Johnson, Terri. Mary Motion, 26 vols. Kuhn, Jesse, illus. l.t. ed. 2006. (Quirkles — Exploring Phonics through Science Ser.: 13). 32p. (J). 7.99 (978-1-933815-12-1(4), Quirkles, The) Creative 3, LLC.

Coons, Susan. The Lighthouse Mouse. 2006. 19.99 (978-0-9721410-1-7(4)) Vinland Pr.

Coons, Susan Anderson. Lighthouse Mouse Meets Simon the Cat. Sanne, Don, illus. 2012. 52p. pap. 10.03 (978-1-4669-1223-6(5)) Trafford Publishing.

Corderoy, Tracey. I Want My Mommy! Edgson, Alison, illus. 2014. (ENG.). 32p. (J). (gr. -1-3). mass mkt. 3.99 (978-1-58925-453-4(8)) Tiger Tales.

—Squish Squash Squeeze! Chapman, Jane, illus. 2016. (ENG.). 32p. (J). (gr. -1-2). 16.99 (978-1-68010-011-2(4)) Tiger Tales.

Cosson, Kip. Ned Visits New York. 2006. (ENG., Illus.). 40p. (J). 16.95 (978-0-9789384-0-6(2)) Kip Kids of New York.

Cote, Nancy. Watch the Cookie! Cote, Nancy, illus. 2014. (ENG., Illus.). 32p. (J). (gr. -1-k). 16.95 (978-1-62914-630-0(7), Sky Pony Pr.) Skyhorse Publishing Co., Inc.

Cote, Nancy, illus. Watch the Birdie! 2016. (ENG.). 32p. (J). (gr. -1-k). 16.99 (978-1-63450-202-3(7), Sky Pony Pr.) Skyhorse Publishing Co., Inc.

Cousins, Lucy. Los Alimentos de Maisy. Cousins, Lucy, illus. 2009. (Maisy Ser.). (SPA & ENG., Illus.). 16p. (J). (gr. -1-2). bds. 5.99 (978-0-7636-4519-9(2)) Candlewick Pr.

—Count with Maisy, Cheep, Cheep, Cheep! Cousins, Lucy, illus. 2015. (Maisy Ser.). (ENG., Illus.). 32p. (J). (-k). 15.99 (978-0-7636-7643-8(8)) Candlewick Pr.

—Los Juguetes de Maisy. Cousins, Lucy, illus. 2009. (Maisy Ser.). (SPA & ENG., Illus.). 16p. (J). (gr. -1-2). bds. 5.99 (978-0-7636-4520-5(6)) Candlewick Pr.

—Maisy Goes Camping. Cousins, Lucy, illus. 2009. (Maisy Ser.). (ENG., Illus.). 32p. (J). (gr. k-k). pap. 6.99 (978-0-7636-4368-3(8)) Candlewick Pr.

—Maisy Goes Camping. 2009. (Maisy First Experiences Ser.). lib. bdg. 17.20 (978-0-606-06667-9(5), Turtleback) Turtleback Bks.

—Maisy Goes on a Sleepover. Cousins, Lucy, illus. 2016. (Maisy Ser.). (ENG., Illus.). 32p. (J). (gr. -1-2). 6.99 (978-0-7636-8947-6(5)) Candlewick Pr.

—Maisy Goes on Vacation. Cousins, Lucy, illus. 2012. (Maisy Ser.). (ENG., Illus.). 32p. (J). (gr. -1-2). pap. 6.99 (978-0-7636-6039-0(6)) Candlewick Pr.

—Maisy Goes Swimming. Cousins, Lucy, illus. 2017. (Maisy Ser.). (ENG., Illus.). 16p. (J). (-k). 14.99 (978-0-7636-9461-6(4)) Candlewick Pr.

—Maisy Goes to Bed. Cousins, Lucy, illus. 2016. (Maisy Ser.). (ENG., Illus.). 16p. (J). (gr. -1-2). 14.99 (978-0-7636-9249-0(2)) Candlewick Pr.

—Maisy Goes to London. Cousins, Lucy, illus. 2016. (Maisy Ser.). (ENG., Illus.). 32p. (J). (-k). 15.99 (978-0-7636-8399-3(X)) Candlewick Pr.

—Maisy Goes to Preschool: A Maisy First Experiences Book. Cousins, Lucy, illus. (Maisy Ser.). (ENG., Illus.). 32p. (J). 2010. (gr. k-k). pap. 6.99 (978-0-7636-5086-5(2)) 2009. (gr. -1-k). 12.99 (978-0-7636-4254-9(1)) Candlewick Pr.

—Maisy Goes to the City. Cousins, Lucy, illus. 2014. (Maisy Ser.). (ENG., Illus.). 32p. (J). (gr. -1-2). 6.99 (978-0-7636-6834-1(6)) Candlewick Pr.

—Maisy Goes to the City. 2014. (Maisy First Experiences Ser.). lib. bdg. 17.20 (978-0-606-35157-7(4)) Turtleback Bks.

—Maisy Goes to the Hospital. Cousins, Lucy, illus. 2009. (Maisy Ser.). (ENG., Illus.). 32p. (J). (gr. k-k). pap. 6.99 (978-0-7636-4372-0(6)) Candlewick Pr.

—Maisy Goes to the Library. Cousins, Lucy, illus. 2009. (Maisy Ser.). (ENG., Illus.). 32p. (J). (gr. k-k). pap. 6.99 (978-0-7636-4371-3(8)) Candlewick Pr.

—Maisy Goes to the Library. 2009. (Maisy First Experiences Ser.). lib. bdg. 17.20 (978-0-606-06687-7(X), Turtleback) Turtleback Bks.

—Maisy Goes to the Local Bookstore: A Maisy First Experiences Book. Cousins, Lucy, illus. 2017. (Maisy Ser.). (ENG., Illus.). 32p. (J). (-k). 12.99 (978-0-7636-9255-1(7)) Candlewick Pr.

—Maisy Goes to the Museum. Cousins, Lucy, illus. 2009. (Maisy Ser.). (ENG., Illus.). 32p. (J). (gr. k-k). pap. 6.99 (978-0-7636-4370-6(X)) Candlewick Pr.

—Maisy Grows a Garden. 2013. (Maisy Ser.). (ENG., Illus.). 16p. (J). (-k). 14.99 (978-0-7636-6242-4(9)) Candlewick Pr.

—Maisy Learns to Swim. Cousins, Lucy, illus. (Maisy Ser.). (ENG., Illus.). 32p. (J). 2015. (-k). 6.99 (978-0-7636-7749-7(3)) 2013. (gr. -1-k). 12.99 (978-0-7636-6480-0(4)) Candlewick Pr.

—Maisy's Amazing Big Book of Learning. 2011. (Maisy Ser.). (ENG., Illus.). 48p. (J). (gr. k-k). 14.99 (978-0-7636-5481-8(7)) Candlewick Pr.

—Maisy's Amazing Big Book of Words. Cousins, Lucy, illus. 2007. (Maisy Ser.). (ENG., Illus.). 64p. (J). (gr. k-k). 14.99 (978-0-7636-0794-4(0)) Candlewick Pr.

—Maisy's Animals (Los Animales de Maisy) Cousins, Lucy, illus. 2009. (Maisy Ser.). (SPA & ENG., Illus.). 16p. (J). (gr. -1-2). bds. 5.99 (978-0-7636-4517-5(6)) Candlewick Pr.

—Maisy's Band. Cousins, Lucy, illus. 2012. (Maisy Ser.). (ENG., Illus.). 16p. (J). (gr. -1-2). 17.99 (978-0-7636-6044-4(2)) Candlewick Pr.

—Maisy's Clothes/La Ropa de Maisy. Cousins, Lucy, illus. 2009. (Maisy Ser.). (SPA & ENG., Illus.). 16p. (J). (gr. -1-2). bds. 5.99 (978-0-7636-4518-2(4)) Candlewick Pr.

—Maisy's Field Day. Cousins, Lucy, illus. 2016. (Maisy Ser.). (ENG., Illus.). 32p. (J). (-k). 12.99 (978-0-7636-8441-9(4)) Candlewick Pr.

—Maisy's Fire Engine. Cousins, Lucy, illus. 2009. (Maisy Ser.). (ENG., Illus.). 16p. (J). (gr. k-k). bds. 5.99 (978-0-7636-4252-5(5)) Candlewick Pr.

—Maisy's First Clock. Cousins, Lucy, illus. 2011. (Maisy Ser.). (ENG., Illus.). 16p. (J). (gr. k-k). bds. 14.99 (978-0-7636-5095-7(1)) Candlewick Pr.

—Maisy's Moon Landing: A Maisy First Science Book. Cousins, Lucy, illus. 2017. (Maisy Ser.). (ENG., Illus.). 16p. (J). (-k). 15.99 (978-0-7636-9040-3(6)) Candlewick Pr.

—Maisy's Pool. 2015. 24p. pap. 4.00 (978-1-61003-408-1(2)) Center for the Collaborative Classroom.

—Maisy's Train. Cousins, Lucy, illus. 2009. (Maisy Ser.). (ENG., Illus.). 16p. (J). (gr. k-k). bds. 5.99 (978-0-7636-4251-8(7)) Candlewick Pr.

—La Nochebuena de Maisy. 2004.Tr. of Maisy's Christmas Eve. (SPA., Illus.). 32p. (J). 16.99 (978-84-8488-106-3(7)) Serres, Ediciones, S. L. ESP. Dist: Lectorum Pubns., Inc.

—Suenos de Colores. 2004.Tr. of Maisy's Rainbow Dream. (SPA., Illus.). 32p. (J). 18.99 (978-84-8488-108-7(3)) Serres, Ediciones, S. L. ESP. Dist: Lectorum Pubns., Inc.

—Sweet Dreams, Maisy. Cousins, Lucy, illus. 2009. (Maisy Ser.). (ENG., Illus.). 32p. (J). (gr. -1-2). bds. 6.99 (978-0-7636-4532-8(X)) Candlewick Pr.

—El Tren de Maisy. 2006.Tr. of Maisy's Train. (CAT & SPA., Illus.). 28p. (J). (gr. -1-k). 18.50 (978-84-8488-043-1(5)) Serres, Ediciones, S. L. ESP. Dist: Lectorum Pubns., Inc.

—Where Are Maisy's Friends? Cousins, Lucy, illus. 2010. (Maisy Ser.). (ENG., Illus.). 12p. (J). (-k). bds. 5.99 (978-0-7636-4669-1(5)) Candlewick Pr.

—Where Does Maisy Live? 2010. 12p. bds. 4.99 (978-976-3-64668-7(5)) Candlewick Pr.

—Where Does Maisy Live? Cousins, Lucy, illus. 2010. (Maisy Ser.). (ENG., Illus.). 12p. (J). (-k). bds. 5.99 (978-0-7636-4668-4(7)) Candlewick Pr.

—Where Is Maisy? Cousins, Lucy, illus. 2010. (Maisy Ser.). (ENG., Illus.). 14p. (J). (gr. k-k). bds. 5.99 (978-0-7636-4673-8(3)) Candlewick Pr.

Cowhard, Patricia Ann. B J 's Underground Adventure. 2011. 28p. pap. 15.99 (978-1-4628-5577-3(6)) Xlibris Corp.

Cox, Judy. Cinco de Mouse-O! Ebbeler, Jeffrey, illus. (SPA & ENG.). 32p. (J). 2011. pap. 6.95 (978-0-8234-2328-6(X)) 2010. (gr. -1-3). 16.95 (978-0-8234-2194-7(5)) Holiday Hse., Inc.

—Haunted House, Haunted Mouse. Ebbeler, Jeffrey, illus. (ENG.). 32p. (J). (gr. -1-2). 2012. pap. 7.99 (978-0-8234-2544-0(4)) 2011. 16.95 (978-0-8234-2315-6(8)) Holiday Hse., Inc.

—One Is a Feast for Mouse: A Thanksgiving Tale. Ebbeler, Jeffrey, illus. 2009. (ENG.). 32p. (J). (gr. -1-3). pap. 7.99 (978-0-8234-2231-9(3)) Holiday Hse., Inc.

—Snow Day for Mouse. Ebbeler, Jeffrey, illus. (ENG.). 32p. (J). (gr. -1). 2013. pap. 7.99 (978-0-8234-2913-4(X)) 2012. 16.95 (978-0-8234-2408-5(1)) Holiday Hse., Inc.

Cox, Phil Roxbee. Mouse Moves House. Tyler, Jenny, ed. Cartwright, Stephen, illus. rev. ed. 2006. (Phonic Readers Ser.). 16p. (J). (gr. -1-3). pap. 6.99 (978-0-7945-1507-2(X), Usborne) EDC Publishing.

Cox, Phil Roxbee & Cartwright, Stephen. Mouse Moves House. 2004. (Easy Words to Read Ser.). (Illus.). 16p. (J). (gr. 1-18). pap. 6.95 (978-0-7945-0367-3(5), Usborne) EDC Publishing.

Crane, Walter, illus. Mr Michael Mouse Unfolds His Tale. 2011. 36p. pap. 35.95 (978-1-258-07891-1(0)) Literary Licensing, LLC.

Creed, Elizabeth. Millie's Merry Christmas. 2011. 26p. (J). pap. 12.95 (978-1-4327-0580-0(6)) Outskirts Pr., Inc.

Creighton, B. L. Max's Seaworthy Adventure. 2009. 28p. pap. 13.99 (978-1-4389-7329-6(2)) AuthorHouse.

Crespeno, John. Toby: The Mouse Who Lived in a Pumpkin. 2011. 84p. pap. 28.68 (978-1-4634-1632-4(6)) AuthorHouse.

Crippa, Luca, et al. The Discovery of America. Cooper-McGuinness, Nanette, tr. de Pretto, Lorenzo, illus. 2009. (Geronimo Stilton Graphic Novels Ser.). (ENG.). 56p. (J). (gr. 2-6). 9.99 (978-1-59707-158-1(7), 9781597071581) Papercutz.

Crofoot, Nancy. Christmas in the Barn, 1 vol. Rawat, Tania, illus. 2009. 37p. pap. 24.95 (978-1-61582-585-1(1)) America Star Bks.

—Sandy & Mitzi: Their First Adventure, 1 vol. Rawat, Tania, illus. 2009. 31p. pap. 24.95 (978-1-60836-707-8(X)) America Star Bks.

Crouch, Kathryn L. Nibbly Noshers. 2010. (Illus.). 44p. pap. 16.99 (978-1-4490-9448-5(1)) AuthorHouse.

Crow, Nosy. Pip & Posy: the Bedtime Frog. Scheffler, Axel, illus. 2014. (Pip & Posy Ser.). (ENG.). 32p. (J). (-k). 12.99 (978-0-7636-7068-9(5), Nosy Crow) Candlewick Pr.

—Pip & Posy: the Scary Monster. Scheffler, Axel, illus. 2014. (Pip & Posy Ser.). (ENG.). 24p. (J). (-k). bds. 6.99 (978-0-7636-7231-7(9), Nosy Crow) Candlewick Pr.

—Teeny Weeny Looks for His Mommy: A Tiny Tab Book. Ho, Jannie, illus. 2014. (Tiny Tab Ser.). (ENG.). 8p. (J). (— 1). bds. 7.99 (978-0-7636-7273-7(4), Nosy Crow) Candlewick Pr.

Curato, Mike. Little Elliot, Big City. Curato, Mike, illus. 2014. (Little Elliot Ser.). (ENG., Illus.). 40p. (J). (gr. -1-3). 16.99 (978-0-8050-9825-9(9), 9780805098259, Holt, Henry & Co. Bks. For Young Readers) Holt, Henry & Co.

—Little Elliot, Big Family. Curato, Mike, illus. 2015. (Little Elliot Ser.). (ENG., Illus.). 40p. (J). (gr. -1-3). 17.99 (978-0-8050-9826-6(7), 9780805098266, Holt, Henry & Co. Bks. For Young Readers) Holt, Henry & Co.

—Little Elliot, Big Fun. Curato, Mike, illus. 2016. (Little Elliot Ser.). (ENG., Illus.). 40p. (J). 17.99 (978-0-8050-9827-3(5), 9780805098273, Holt, Henry & Co. Bks. For Young Readers) Holt, Henry & Co.

Currey, Anna. Truffle Goes to Town. Currey, Anna, illus. 2003. (Illus.). 32p. (YA). (978-1-85602-429-7(6), Pavilion Children's Books) Pavilion Bks.

Curtis, Shelly. Shellbear's Adventures. 2012. 56p. pap. (978-1-4602-0601-0(0)) FriesenPress.

D. Carlo the Mouse/ Book 1: Too Many Rules for One Little Mouse. 2013. 40p. pap. 19.99 (978-1-4575-1917-8(8)) Dog Ear Publishing, LLC.

Dachman, Adam. The Player Piano Mouse. Julich, Jenniffer, illus. 2008. 32p. (J). 14.99 (978-0-9797794-0-4(5)) Player Piano Mouse Productions (PPMP).

Dahl, Michael. Mouse Says Sorry, 1 vol. Vidal, Oriol, illus. 2011. (Hello Genius Ser.). (ENG.). 20p. (gr. 1-2). bds. 7.99 (978-1-4048-6789-5(9)) Picture Window Bks.

Dahl, Roald. The Witches. Blake, Quentin, illus. 2007. (ENG.). 224p. (J). (gr. 3-7). 7.99 (978-0-14-241011-0(X), Puffin Books) Penguin Young Readers Group.

Danby, Aaron. Jazzmin's Jamboree. Martin, M. J., illus. 2005. 40p. 13.95 (978-0-9730583-3-8(1)) Lion & Mouse Tales, Inc. CAN. Dist: Hushion Hse. Publishing, Ltd.

Daniel, Martha Ann. Mimi Mouse Meets Roger Rat: A Tail of Bullying. 2012. 32p. (-18). pap. 19.99 (978-1-4772-8295-3(5)) AuthorHouse.

Danielson, Diane K. There Is a Mouse That Is Haunting Our House. 2012. (ENG.). 28p. (J). pap. 14.99 (978-0-9885157-0-3(9)) SDP Publishing.

Das, Christina. Munchy Mouse. l.t. ed. 2005. (Illus.). 32p. (J). 15.95 (978-0-9763082-0-1(7), A JuneOne Production) JuneOne Publishing Hub.

Dashney, John. The Adventures of Walter the Weremouse; the Adventures of Mishka the Mousewere. Somerville, Sheila, illus. 2005. 202p. (J). pap. (978-0-9633236-7-5(9)) Storm Peak Pr.

Davey, Keith Peter. Squeaks Narrow Squeaks. Frost, Justine, illus. 2009. 32p. pap. 14.62 (978-1-4120-4402-8(2)) Trafford Publishing.

Davies, Kate, illus. Little Squeak School. 2014. (J). (978-1-4351-5582-4(3)) Barnes & Noble, Inc.

—Welcome to the Mouse House. 2014. (J). (978-1-4351-5583-1(1)) Barnes & Noble, Inc.

De Boer, Joan. THE SULTAN AND THE MICE. 2007. (ENG., Illus.). 36p. (J). 18.95 (978-84-96788-84-8(9)) OQO, Editora ESP. Dist: Baker & Taylor Bks.

de Las Casas, Dianne. The House That Santa Built, 1 vol. Stone-Barker, Holly, illus. 2013. (ENG.). 32p. (J). (gr. -1-k). 16.99 (978-1-4556-1750-0(4)) Pelican Publishing Co., Inc.

De Long, Robert & De Long, Janice. Redwall Study Guide. 2003. ring bd. 14.99 (978-1-58609-196-5(4)) Progeny Pr.

De Sena, Joseph. Mrs. Mouse & the Golden Flower. 2007. 56p. per. 19.95 (978-1-4327-1525-0(9)) Outskirts Pr., Inc.

Dean, Barbara. Rattalia's Birthday Stories. 2nd ed. 2013. 132p. (978-0-9572470-4-8(4)); pap. (978-0-9572470-5-5(2)) Newpole Bks.

Deedy, Carmen Agra & Wright, Randall. The Cheshire Cheese Cat: A Dickens of a Tale, 1 vol. Moser, Barry, illus. 2011. (ENG.). 256p. (J). 16.95 (978-1-56145-595-9(4)) Peachtree Pubs.

Deem, Saitofi Anne. Myrtle Teachable Moments Series, 16 vols. Incl. Myrtle Learns about Asthma. 8p. (gr. -1-3). pap. 7.95 (978-1-930694-00-2(8)); Myrtle Learns about Dangerous Situations. 8p. (gr. -1-3). pap. 7.95 (978-1-930694-03-3(2)); Myrtle Learns about Diabetes. 12p. (gr. -1-3). pap. 7.95 (978-1-930694-04-0(0)); Myrtle Learns about Hygiene. 8p. (gr. -1-3). pap. 7.95 (978-1-930694-09-5(1)); Myrtle Learns about Lice. 12p. (gr. -1-3). pap. 7.95 (978-1-930694-11-8(3)); Myrtle Learns about Medicine. 8p. (gr. -1-3). pap. 7.95 (978-1-930694-12-5(1)); Myrtle Learns about Safety. 8p. (gr. -1-3). pap. 7.95 (978-1-930694-13-2(X)); Myrtle Learns about Seizures. 8p. (gr. -1-3). pap. 7.95 (978-1-930694-14-9(8)); Myrtle Learns How You Catch an Illness. 8p. (gr. -1-3). pap. 7.95 (978-1-930694-10-1(5)); Myrtle Learns to Eat Well. 12p. (gr. -1-3). pap. 7.95 (978-1-930694-05-7(9)); Myrtle Learns to Get Along. 8p. (gr. -1-3). pap. 7.95 (978-1-930694-08-8(3)); Myrtle Learns to Make Friends. 8p. (gr. -1-3). pap. 7.95 (978-1-930694-07-1(5)); Myrtle Learns to Take Care of Boo Boos. 12p. (gr. -1-3). pap. 7.95 (978-1-930694-01-9(6)); Myrtle Learns Why Exercise Is Important. 8p. pap. 7.95 (978-1-930694-06-4(7)); Myrtle Makes a Choice. 8p. (gr. -1-3). pap. 7.95 (978-1-930694-02-6(4)); Myrtle's Friend Is Very Sick. 8p. (gr. -1-3). pap. 7.95 (978-1-930694-15-6(6)); (J). 1998. (Illus.). Set pap. 114.48 (978-1-930694-16-3(4)) Myrtle Learns.

Del Moral, Susana. La Casa de Violet. Zaidi, Nadeem, illus. 2005. (Baby Einstein: Libros de Carton Ser.). (SPA.). 10p. (J). (gr. -1). bds. (978-970-718-305-6(5), Silver Dolphin en Español) Advanced Marketing, S. de R. L. de C. V.

Delaney, Ned. Two Strikes, Four Eyes. Date not set. (J). pap. (978-0-679-84172-2(5)); lib. bdg. (978-0-679-94172-9(X)) Random Hse. Children's Bks. (Random Hse. Bks. for Young Readers).

DeLuise, Dom & Brown, Tim. No Place Like Home. 2007. 240p. pap. 9.95 (978-0-9769369-1-6(7)) Bacchus Bks.

Demas, Corinne. Two Christmas Mice. Roth, Stephanie, illus. 2005. (ENG.). 32p. (J). (gr. -1-3). 16.95 (978-0-8234-1785-8(9)) Holiday Hse., Inc.

Dennis, Chantal. Sammy the Mouse. 2011. 36p. pap. 32.70 (978-1-4568-2773-1(1)) Xlibris Corp.

DePrisco, Dorothea. Country Mouse & City Mouse. 2006. (ENG.). 12p. 10.95 (978-1-58117-479-3(9), Intervisual/Piggy Toes) Bendon, Inc.

Detwiler, Susan. Fine Life for a Country Mouse. Detwiler, Susan, illus. 2014. (Penguin Core Concepts Ser.). (ENG., Illus.). 32p. (J). (gr. -1-k). 3.99 (978-0-448-48061-9(1), Grosset & Dunlap) Penguin Young Readers Group.

Diaz, S. Jemmy & the Little Spider of Hope. 2012. 40p. pap. 20.99 (978-1-4772-7032-5(9)) AuthorHouse.

DiCamillo, Kate. The Tale of Despereaux: Being the Story of a Mouse, a Princess, Some Soup & a Spool of Thread. Ering, Timothy Basil, illus. (J). 2015. (ENG.). 272p. (gr. 2-5). pap. 8.99 (978-0-7636-8089-3(3)) 2013. 296p. (978-0-7636-7205-8(X)) 2003. (ENG.). 272p. (gr. 2-5). 17.99 (978-0-7636-1722-6(9)) 2008. (ENG.). 272p. (gr. 2-5). 29.99 (978-0-7636-2928-1(6)) Candlewick Pr.

—The Tale of Despereaux: Being the Story of a Mouse, a Princess, Some Soup & a Spool of Thread. 2008. (J). 34.99 (978-0-7393-7105-3(3)) Findaway World, LLC.

—The Tale of Despereaux: Being the Story of a Mouse, a Princess, Some Soup & a Spool of Thread. 2009. 9.84 (978-0-7848-3043-7(6), Everbind) Marco Bk. Co.

—The Tale of Despereaux: Being the Story of a Mouse, a Princess, Some Soup & a Spool of Thread. 2006. 272p. (gr. 4-6). 18.00 (978-0-7569-6580-8(2)) Perfection Learning Corp.

—The Tale of Despereaux: Being the Story of a Mouse, a Princess, Some Soup & a Spool of Thread, 3 vols. 2006. 42.75 (978-1-4193-7734-1(5)) Recorded Bks., Inc.

—The Tale of Despereaux: Being the Story of a Mouse, a Princess, Some Soup & a Spool of Thread. Ering, Timothy Basil, illus. 2003. pap. (978-0-439-70167-9(8), Scholastic) Scholastic, Inc.

—The Tale of Despereaux: Being the Story of a Mouse, a Princess, Some Soup & a Spool of Thread. Ering, Timothy Basil, illus. l.t. ed. 2004. (Thorndike Literacy Bridge Ser.). (ENG.). 247p. (J). pap. 11.95 (978-1-4104-1527-1(9)) Thorndike Pr.

—The Tale of Despereaux: Being the Story of a Mouse, a Princess, Some Soup & a Spool of Thread. 2015. lib. bdg. 18.40 (978-0-606-37888-8(X)) Turtleback Bks.

—The Tale of Despereaux Student Packet. 2004. (J). (gr. 3-4). stu. ed. 12.99 (978-1-58130-524-1(9)) Novel Units, Inc.

DiCamillo, Kate & Candlewick Press Staff. The Tale of Despereaux: Glow-in-the-Dark Sticker Book. movie tie-in ed. 2008. (Tale of Despereaux Ser.). (ENG., Illus.). 8p. (J). (gr. -1-3). pap. 6.99 (978-0-7636-4079-8(4)) Candlewick Pr.

DiCamillo, Kate & Ering, Timothy Basil. The Tale of Despereaux: Being the Story of a Mouse, a Princess, Some Soup & a Spool of Thread. 2005. (CHI.). (J). pap. 12.95 (978-7-5307-3545-9(4)) New Buds Publishing Hse. CHN. Dist: Chinasprout, Inc.

Dickson, Robert. Sam Ferret Mysteries. 2010. 88p. pap. 14.95 (978-1-4259-2741-7(6)) AuthorHouse.

Dijkstra, Lida. Little Mouse. Grobler, Piet, illus. 2004. (ENG.). 32p. (J). 15.95 (978-1-932425-06-2(3), Lemniscaat) Boyds Mills Pr.

Dillard, Sarah. Mouse Scouts. 2016. (Mouse Scouts Ser.). (ENG., Illus.). 128p. (J). (gr. 2-5). 12.99 (978-0-385-75599-3(6), Knopf Bks. for Young Readers) Random Hse. Children's Bks.

—Mouse Scouts: Make a Difference. 2016. (Mouse Scouts Ser.). (ENG., Illus.). 144p. (J). (gr. 2-5). 12.99 (978-0-385-75603-7(8), Knopf Bks. for Young Readers) Random Hse. Children's Bks.

Dinardo, Jeff. Mr. Mouse's Motel: Helping Others. Lubach, Peter, illus. 2014. (Funny Bone Readers: Being a Friend Ser.). 24p. (gr. -1-1). pap. 4.99 (978-1-939656-05-6(2)) Red Chair Pr.

Disney Storybook Art Team, illus. Cinderella: The Great Mouse Mistake. 2010. (Disney Princess Chapter Book Ser.). (ENG.). 80p. (J). (gr. 1-3). pap. 4.99 (978-1-4231-2978-3(4)) Disney Pr.

Dixon, Amy. Marathon Mouse. Denlinger, Sam, illus. 2012. (ENG.). 32p. (J). (gr. -1-k). 16.95 (978-1-61608-966-5(0), 608966, Sky Pony Pr.) Skyhorse Publishing Co., Inc.

Doerrfeld, Cori. Little Bunny Foo Foo: The Real Story. (ENG., Illus.). 32p. (J). 2016. (-k). pap. 8.99 (978-1-101-99774-1(5), Puffin Books) 2012. (gr. -1-k). 16.99 (978-0-8037-3470-8(0), Dial Bks) Penguin Young Readers Group.

Donaldson, Julia. El Grufalo. Scheffler, Axel, illus. 2003. (SPA.). 32p. (J). (gr. k-2). 7.96 (978-84-233-3145-1(8), DS4478) Ediciones Destino ESP. Dist: Lectorum Pubns., Inc.

—The Gruffalo. Harris, Ben, tr. from ENG. Scheffler, Axel, illus. 2012. (LAT, SPA & ENG.). 32p. (J). (gr. -1-2). 19.99 (978-0-230-75932-9(7)) Pan Macmillan GBR. Dist: Independent Pubs. Group.

—The Gruffalo. Scheffler, Axel, illus. (ENG.). (J). (gr. -1-2). 2006. 32p. pap. 7.99 (978-0-14-240387-7(3), Puffin Books) 2005. 26p. bds. 8.99 (978-0-8037-3047-2(0), Dial Bks) Penguin Young Readers Group.

—The Gruffalo. Scheffler, Axel, illus. 2005. (ENG.). 32p. (J). (gr. -1-2). 17.99 (978-0-8037-3109-7(4), Dial Bks) Penguin Young Readers Group.

—The Gruffalo. 2006. lib. bdg. 18.40 (978-0-606-23141-1(2), Turtleback) Turtleback Bks.

—The Gruffalo in Scots. Robertson, James, tr. from ENG. Scheffler, Axel, illus. 2012. (ENG.). 32p. (J). (-k). pap. 10.99 (978-1-84502-503-8(2)) Black and White Publishing Ltd. GBR. Dist: Independent Pubs. Group.

—The Gruffalo Theatre, 1. Scheffler, Axel, illus. 2008. (ENG.). 18p. (gr. 2-5). 34.95 (978-0-230-53179-6(2), Macmillan) Pan Macmillan GBR. Dist: Trans-Atlantic Pubns., Inc.

—The Gruffalo's Child. Scheffler, Axel, illus. 2007. (ENG.). 32p. (J). (gr. -1-2). pap. 7.99 (978-0-14-240754-7(2), Puffin Books) Penguin Young Readers Group.

Donofrio, Beverly. Where's Mommy? McClintock, Barbara, illus. 2014. (Mary & the Mouse Ser.). (ENG.). 32p. (J). (gr. -1-2). 17.99 (978-0-375-84423-2(6), Schwartz & Wade Bks.) Random Hse. Children's Bks.

Donovan, Michelle O. Joshua, Helmut, & Bethlehem. 2011. 56p. pap. 8.95 (978-1-4620-5867-9(1)) iUniverse, Inc.

Douglas, Babette. Miss Evonne: And the Mice of Nice! Johnson, John, illus. 2006. (Kiss a Me Teacher Creature Stories Ser.). (J). (gr. -1-3). 9.99 (978-1-890343-19-4(6)) Kiss A Me Productions, Inc.

Doyen, Denise. Once upon a Twice. Moser, Barry, illus. 2013. (Picture Book Ser.). (ENG.). 32p. (J). (gr. -1-2). pap. 7.99 (978-0-449-81794-0(6), Dragonfly Bks.) Random Hse. Children's Bks.

Driscoll, Laura. Count off, Squeak Scouts! Melmon, Deborah, illus. 2013. (Mouse Math Ser.). 32p. (J). (gr. -1-1). 22.60 (978-1-57565-524-6(1)); (ENG.). pap. 7.95 (978-1-57565-525-3(X)) Kane Press, Inc.

—A Mousy Mess. Melmon, Deborah, illus. 2014. (Mouse Math (r) Ser.). 32p. (J). (gr. -1-1). 22.60 (978-1-57565-646-5(9)) Kane Press, Inc.

Dubuc, Marianne & Ghione, Yvette. Mr. Postmouse's Rounds. Dubuc, Marianne, illus. 2015. (ENG., Illus.). 24p. (J). (gr. -1-2). 17.95 (978-1-77138-572-5(3)) Kids Can Pr., Ltd. CAN. Dist: Hachette Bk. Group.

Duncan, Sharyn. The Mouse House & other Stories: You Are the Artist. 2004. 40p. (J). 9.95 (978-1-933002-04-0(2)) PublishingWorks.

Dussling, Jennifer. If the Shoe Fits: Nonstandard Units of Measurement. Dussling, Deborah, illus. 2015. (ENG.). 32p. (J). (gr. -1-1). lib. bdg. 22.60 (978-1-57565-800-1(3)) Kane Press, Inc.

Dyan, Penelope. The Day an Elephant Flies! Dyan, Penelope, illus. 2013. (Illus.). 34p. pap. 11.95 (978-1-61477-113-5(8)) Bellissima Publishing, LLC.

—The Warrior Mouse of Forest Hollow. Quinn, Courtney, illus. 2008. 108p. 17.95 (978-1-935118-00-8(5)) Bellissima Publishing, LLC.

—The Warrior Mouse of Forest Hollow. 2005. (J). per. 5.95 (978-0-9771916-5-9(6)) Bellissima Publishing, LLC.

Earhart, Kristin. Roscoe & the Pony Parade. Gurney, John Steven, illus. 2008. (Little Apple Ser.). 88p. (J). (978-0-545-08094-1(0)) Scholastic, Inc.

East, Jacqueline, illus. The Town Mouse & the Country Mouse. 2007. (Picture Book Classics Ser.). (J). (gr. -1-3). 24p. 9.99 (978-0-7945-1877-6(X)); 48p. 8.99 (978-0-7945-1613-0(0)) EDC Publishing. (Usborne).

Eaton, Gordon J. Piebald & the Parade of Small Animals. 2009. 184p. pap. 14.99 (978-1-60791-991-9(5)) Salem Author Services.

Eberle, Dina P. The Mice Next Door, 1 vol. 2010. 18p. 24.95 (978-1-4512-1206-8(2)) PublishAmerica, Inc.

Ebie, Mora. Little Mouse's Hawaiian Christmas Present. Braffet, Holly, illus. 2011. 28p. (J). (978-1-56647-956-1(8)) Mutual Publishing LLC.

Edwards, Pamela Duncan. Livingstone Mouse II. 2005. 32p. (J). pap. (978-0-7868-1171-7(4)) Hyperion Bks. for Children.

Egan, Tim. Dodsworth in Paris. Egan, Tim, illus. 2010. (Dodsworth Book Ser.). (ENG., Illus.). 48p. (J). (gr. 1-4). pap. 3.99 (978-0-547-33192-8(4)) Houghton Mifflin Harcourt Publishing Co.

Eggleton, Jill. Brave Mouse, 3 vols., Pack. Taylor, Clive, illus. (Sails Literacy Ser.). 24p. (gr. 1-18). 57.00 (978-0-7578-3205-5(9)) Rigby Education.

Egielski, Richard. Slim & Jim. Egielski, Richard, illus. 2005. (Illus.). 37p. (J). (gr. k-4). reprint ed. 16.00 (978-0-7567-8936-7(2)) DIANE Publishing Co.

Ehlert, Lois. Boo to You! Ehlert, Lois, illus. 2009. (ENG., Illus.). 42p. (J). (gr. -1-2). 17.99 (978-1-4169-8625-6(1), Beach Lane Bks.) Beach Lane Bks.

—The Scraps Book: Notes from a Colorful Life. Ehlert, Lois, illus. 2014. (ENG., Illus.). 72p. (J). (gr. k-5). 17.99 (978-1-4424-3571-1(2)) Simon & Schuster Children's Publishing.

Eldarova, Sofia. Builder Mouse. 2016. (ENG., Illus.). 32p. (J). (gr. -1-3). 16.99 (978-0-544-35766-2(3), Clarion Bks.) Houghton Mifflin Harcourt Trade & Reference Pubs.

Emberley, Rebecca & Emberley, Ed. The Lion & the Mice. 2011. (I Like to Read(r) Ser.). (ENG., Illus.). 24p. (J). (gr. -1-2). 14.95 (978-0-8234-2357-6(3)) Holiday Hse., Inc.

—Mice on Ice. 2013. (I Like to Read(r) Ser.). (ENG.). 24p. (J). (gr. -1-3). pap. 6.99 (978-0-8234-2908-0(3)) Holiday Hse., Inc.

Emberley, Rebecca & Emberley, Edward R. The Lion & the Mice. Emberley, Rebecca & Emberley, Edward R., illus. 2012. (I Like to Read(r) Ser.). (ENG., Illus.). 24p. (J). (gr. -1-2). pap. 6.99 (978-0-8234-2641-6(6)) Holiday Hse., Inc.

—Mice on Ice. Emberley, Rebecca & Emberley, Edward R., illus. 2012. (I Like to Read(r) Ser.). (ENG., Illus.). 24p. (J). (gr. -1-3). 14.95 (978-0-8234-2576-1(2)) Holiday Hse., Inc.

Engelbreit, Mary. Mary Engelbreit's A Merry Little Christmas: Celebrate from A to Z. Engelbreit, Mary, illus. 2006. (Illus.). 40p. (J). (gr. -1-3). lib. bdg. 17.89 (978-0-06-074159-4(7)) HarperCollins Pubs.

—Mary Engelbreit's a Merry Little Christmas: Celebrate from A to Z. Engelbreit, Mary, illus. 2010. (ENG., Illus.). 40p. (J). (gr. -1-3). pap. 6.99 (978-0-06-074160-0(0)) HarperCollins Pubs.

Epstein, Diane & Sullivan, Abigail. Three Nearsighted Mice. 2009. 32p. pap. 14.49 (978-1-4343-8822-3(0)) AuthorHouse.

Evelyn. Lucy the Elephant & Sami the Mouse: A Bedtime Story. Conforti, John W., tr. Conforti, John W., illus. 2003. (J). (978-0-9740115-0-9(9)) WeBeANS Corp.

—Lucy the Elephant & Sami the Mouse: The Birthday Party. Conforti, John W., illus. 2004. (J). (978-0-9740115-1-6(7)) WeBeANS Corp.

Fagan, Cary. Ten Old Men & a Mouse. Clement, Gary, illus. 2007. (ENG.). 32p. (J). (gr. -1-1). 18.95 (978-0-88776-716-6(8), Tundra Bks.) Tundra Bks. CAN. Dist: Penguin Random Hse. LLC.

Falla, Lynne. World of the Weeples: Sophie & the Weeples. 2012. 24p. pap. 15.99 (978-1-4771-2078-1(5)) Xlibris Corp.

Farley, Jan. Fleur, a Lonely Pocket Mouse. 2011. 32p. pap. 16.95 (978-1-4560-4073-4(1)) America Star Bks.

Feierabend, John M. The Tailor & the Mouse. McGann, James, illus. 2012. (First Steps in Music Ser.). (ENG.). 32p. (J). (gr. -1-k). 16.95 (978-1-57999-903-2(4)) G I A Pubns., Inc.

Felix, Monique. The Alphabet. Felix, Monique, illus. 2012. (Mouse Book Ser.). (ENG., Illus.). 32p. (J). (gr. -1-k). 12.99 (978-1-56846-226-4(3), Creative Editions) Creative Co., The.

Félix, Monique. The Alphabet. 2015. (J). pap. (978-1-62832-262-0(4), Creative Paperbacks) Creative Co., The.

Felix, Monique. The Colors. Felix, Monique, illus. 2013. (ENG., Illus.). 32p. (J). (gr. -1-k). 12.99 (978-1-56846-234-9(4), Creative Editions) Creative Co., The.

—Mouse Book: the Valentine. Felix, Monique, illus. 2013. (Mouse Book Ser.). (ENG., Illus.). 32p. (J). (gr. -1-k). 12.99 (978-1-56846-247-9(6), Creative Editions) Creative Co., The.

—The Numbers. Felix, Monique, illus. 2013. (ENG., Illus.). 32p. (J). (gr. -1-k). 12.99 (978-1-56846-235-6(2), Creative Editions) Creative Co., The.

—The Wind. 2012. (Mouse Book Ser.). (ENG.). 32p. (J). (gr. -1-k). 12.99 (978-1-56846-227-1(1), Creative Editions) Creative Co., The.

Felix, Monique, creator. Mouse Books: the Boat. 2014. (ENG.). 32p. (J). (gr. -1-k). 12.99 (978-1-56846-252-3(2), Creative Editions) Creative Co., The.

—Mouse Books: the Opposites. 2014. (ENG.). 32p. (J). (gr. -1-k). 12.99 (978-1-56846-251-6(4), Creative Editions) Creative Co., The.

Fiedler, Lisa. Hopper's Destiny. To, Vivienne, illus. 2016. (Mouseheart Ser.: 2). (ENG.). 368p. (J). (gr. 3-7). pap. 7.99 (978-1-4814-2090-7(9), McElderry, Margaret K. Bks.) McElderry, Margaret K. Bks.

—Mouseheart. To, Vivienne, illus. (Mouseheart Ser.: 1). (ENG.). (J). (gr. 3-7). 2015. 336p. pap. 7.99 (978-1-4424-8783-3(6)) 2014. 320p. 16.99 (978-1-4424-8781-9(X)) McElderry, Margaret K. Bks. (McElderry, Margaret K. Bks.).

—Return of the Forgotten. To, Vivienne, illus. 2015. (Mouseheart Ser.: 3). (ENG.). 320p. (J). (gr. 3-7). 16.99 (978-1-4814-2092-1(5), McElderry, Margaret K. Bks.) McElderry, Margaret K. Bks.

Filoche, Eric. Hey ! We're Talking about Ourselves ! 2013. 68p. pap. (978-2-9538737-4-0(0)) Koshkindom.

Finch, Mary & Messing, Debra. The Little Red Hen. Slater, Kate, illus. 2013. (ENG.). 32p. (J). pap. 7.99 (978-1-78285-041-0(4)); (gr. -1-2). 16.99 (978-1-84686-575-6(1)); (gr. -1-2). 9.99 (978-1-84686-751-4(7)) Barefoot Bks., Inc.

Finkelstein, Ruth. Mendel the Mouse, Bk. 1. (Illus.). (J). 10.00 (978-0-914131-43-4(5), D350) Torah Umesorah Pubns.

Fisher, Meaghan. Mousekabitz. Dunnier, Tina, illus. 2013. (ENG.). 32p. (J). pap. 8.99 (978-1-938768-31-6(0)) Gypsy Pubns.

Fitch, Sheree. There's a Mouse in My House! braille ed. 2004. (Illus.). (J). (gr. k-3). spiral bd. (978-0-616-07234-9(1)); spiral bd. (978-0-616-07235-6(X)) Canadian National Institute for the Blind/Institut National Canadien pour les Aveugles.

Fitzgerald, June. Squeaky: The Little Mouse Who Didn't Listen. 2013. (ENG.). 20p. (J). pap. 14.95 (978-1-4787-1559-7(6)) Outskirts Pr., Inc.

Fitzpatrick-Hale-Herself, Donna Marie. Snake & Mouse: Ryan's birthday Tea. 2011. (Illus.). 44p. pap. 17.04 (978-1-4567-8590-1(7)) AuthorHouse.

Fleming, Denise. Alphabet under Construction. Fleming, Denise, illus. 2006. (ENG., Illus.). 32p. (J). (gr. -1-k). reprint ed. pap. 7.99 (978-0-8050-8112-1(7), 9780805081121) Square Fish.

—Go, Shapes, Go! Fleming, Denise, illus. 2014. (ENG., Illus.). 40p. (J). (gr. -1-3). 17.99 (978-1-4424-8240-1(0), Beach Lane Bks.) Beach Lane Bks.

—Lunch. 2014. 32p. pap. 8.00 (978-1-61003-225-4(X)) Center for the Collaborative Classroom.

—Shout! Shout It Out! Fleming, Denise, illus. 2011. (ENG., Illus.). 40p. (J). (gr. -1-1). 16.99 (978-0-8050-9237-0(4), 9780805092370, Holt, Henry & Co. Bks. For Young Readers) Holt, Henry & Co.

Fleming, Maria & Scholastic Canada Ltd. Staff. 30 Mice Are Very Nice. Borlasca, Hector, illus. 2005. (Number Tales Ser.). (ENG.). 16p. (J). (gr. -1-1). pap. 2.99 (978-0-439-69026-3(9)) Scholastic, Inc.

Floen, Douglas. Knowing Noah: The Adventures of a Mouse Who Could Read. 2012. 88p. pap. 13.95 (978-1-4772-4506-4(5)) AuthorHouse.

Fontes, Justine. Showdown in Crittertown. 2014. (Cheddar's Tales Ser.). (ENG.). 176p. (J). (gr. 2-4). pap. 5.99 (978-1-4380-0360-3(9)) Barron's Educational Series, Inc.

Fox, Mem. This & That. Horacek, Judy, illus. 2017. (ENG.). 32p. (J). (gr. -1-k). 17.99 (978-1-338-03780-7(3), Scholastic Pr.) Scholastic, Inc.

Fraggalosch, Audrey. Let's Explore, Moose! Forest, Crista, illus. 2003. (Soundprints' Read-and-Discover Ser.). (ENG.). 32p. (J). (gr. -1-1). 12.95 (978-1-59249-152-0(9), PS2017) Soundprints.

Frederick, Heather Vogel. The Black Paw. 2013. (Spy Mice Ser.: 1). (ENG., Illus.). 224p. (J). (gr. 3-6). pap. 7.99 (978-1-4424-6701-9(0), Simon & Schuster Bks. For Young Readers) Simon & Schuster Bks. For Young Readers.

—For Your Paws Only. 2013. (Spy Mice Ser.: 2). (ENG., Illus.). 240p. (J). (gr. 3-6). pap. 6.99 (978-1-4424-6703-3(7), Simon & Schuster Bks. For Young Readers) Simon & Schuster Bks. For Young Readers.

—For Your Paws Only. Comport, Sally Wern, illus. 2006. (Spy Mice Ser.: 2). (ENG.). 272p. (J). (gr. 3-6). pap. 5.99 (978-1-4169-4025-8(1), Simon & Schuster Bks. For Young Readers) Simon & Schuster Bks. For Young Readers.

—For Your Paws Only. Comport, Sally Wern, illus. 2005. (Spy Mice Ser.). (ENG.). 272p. (J). (gr. 4-6). 9.95 (978-1-4169-0573-8(1)) Simon & Schuster Children's Publishing.

—Goldwhiskers. 2013. (Spy Mice Ser.: 3). (ENG., Illus.). 272p. (J). (gr. -1-6). pap. 6.99 (978-1-4424-6705-7(3), Simon & Schuster Bks. For Young Readers) Simon & Schuster Bks. For Young Readers.

—Hide-and-Squeak. Payne, C. F., illus. 2011. (ENG.). 32p. (J). (gr. -1-1). 16.99 (978-0-689-85570-2(2), Simon & Schuster Bks. For Young Readers) Simon & Schuster Bks. For Young Readers.

Freedman, Claire. A Magical Christmas. Yerrill, Gail, illus. 2008. 24p. (J). (gr. 4-7). 12.95 (978-1-58925-828-0(2)) Tiger Tales.

—The Monster of the Woods! Julian, Russell, illus. 2013. (ENG.). 32p. (J). pap. (978-0-545-51571-9(8), Cartwheel Bks.) Scholastic, Inc.

Freedman, Deborah. By Mouse & Frog. Freedman, Deborah, illus. 2015. (ENG., Illus.). 32p. (J). (gr. -1-k). 16.99 (978-0-670-78490-5(7), Viking Books for Young Readers) Penguin Young Readers Group.

Freeman, Martha. The Orphan & the Mouse. McPhail, David, illus. 2014. (ENG.). 176p. (J). (gr. 3-7). 16.95 (978-0-8234-3167-0(3)) Holiday Hse., Inc.

Friedman, J. S. Casablanca. Beatrice, Chris, illus. 2013. (Maurice's Valises: Moral Tails in an Immoral World Ser.: Vol. 3). (ENG.). 45p. (J). (gr. k-4). pap. (978-94-91613-09-8(X)) Mouse Prints Pr.

—In the Beginning. Beatrice, Chris, illus. 2013. (Maurice's Valises: Moral Tails in an Immoral World Ser.: Vol. 1). (ENG.). 45p. (J). (gr. k-4). (978-94-91613-03-6(0)) Mouse Prints Pr.

—The Micetro of Moscow. Beatrice, Chris, illus. 2013. (Maurice's Valises: Moral Tails in an Immoral World Ser.: Vol. 2). (ENG.). 37p. (J). (gr. k-4). pap. (978-94-91613-06-7(5)) Mouse Prints Pr.

Fuerst, Jeffrey B. Three Blind Mice. Walker, Sholto, illus. 2010. (Rising Readers Ser.). (J). 3.49 (978-1-60719-707-2(3)) Newmark Learning LLC.

Fujikawa, Brian. The Adventures of Bibole, Rivol & Michelle: The French Fry Caper. 2013. 72p. pap. 24.27 (978-1-4907-0954-3(1)) Trafford Publishing.

Furie, Matt. The Night Riders. 2012. (ENG., Illus.). 48p. 17.95 (978-1-936365-56-2(1)) McSweeney's Publishing.

Fyleman, Rose. Mice. Ehlert, Lois, illus. 2012. (ENG.). 40p. (J). (gr. -1-k). 16.99 (978-1-4424-5684-6(1), Beach Lane Bks.) Beach Lane Bks.

Gall, Allan R. Of Mouse & Magic. 2011. (ENG., Illus.). 269p. (J). (gr. 3-7). pap. 12.95 (978-1-936401-78-9(9)) Salem Author Services.

Gallagher, Diana G. Mice Capades, 1 vol. Juarez, Adriana & Puglisi, Adriana, illus. 2013. (Pet Friends Forever Ser.). (ENG.). 88p. (gr. 1-3). pap. 5.95 (978-1-4795-1863-0(8)); lib. bdg. 25.32 (978-1-4048-7500-5(X)) Picture Window Bks.

Galvin, Laura Gates. Deer Mouse at Old Farm Road. 2005. (Smithsonian's Backyard Ser.). (ENG., Illus.). 32p. (J). (gr. -1-2). 8.95 (978-1-59249-223-7(1), SC5015); pap. 6.95 (978-1-59249-195-7(2), S5015) Soundprints.

Gandy, Deborah A. A Squeaky Little Mouse Named Rainbow. 2011. 44p. pap. 21.99 (978-1-4568-7546-6(9)) Xlibris Corp.

Gannon, Patty. Desdemona & the Eggs. 2011. 52p. pap. 23.00 (978-1-4567-1581-6(X)) AuthorHouse.

Garfein, Stanley Joe. Tales of the Temple Mice. 2006. (Illus.). 92p. (J). 14.95 (978-0-9787422-0-1(6)) Garfein, Stanley.

Garland, Michael. Big & Little: A Story of Two Friends. 2017. (ENG., Illus.). 32p. (J). (gr. -1-k). 14.99 (978-0-545-87097-9(6)) Scholastic, Inc.

—Hooray José!, 1 vol. Garland, Michael, illus. 2007. (ENG., Illus.). 32p. (J). (gr. -1-3). 16.99 (978-0-7614-5345-1(8)) Marshall Cavendish Corp.

Gauthier, Lance C., text. The One-Eared Mouse of Pasture Hill. 2003. 55p. (J). per. 6.95 (978-1-884540-70-7(8)) Haley's.

George, Joshua. Fame-Mouse. Bakos, Barbara, illus. 2017. (ENG.). 32p. (J). (gr. -1-k). pap. 9.99 ***(978-1-78445-704-4(3))*** Top That! Publishing PLC GBR. Dist: Independent Pubs. Group.

George, Kallie. Fall. Graegin, Stephanie, illus. 2017. (Heartwood Hotel Ser.). (ENG.). 176p. (J). (gr. 2-5). 14.99 ***(978-1-4847-3161-1(1))*** Disney Pr.

—The Greatest Gift. 2017. (Heartwood Hotel Ser.: 2). (J). lib. bdg. 16.00 ***(978-0-606-39967-8(4))*** Turtleback Bks.

—Heartwood Hotel, Book 2 the Greatest Gift. Graegin, Stephanie, illus. 2017. (Heartwood Hotel Ser.). (ENG.). 176p. (J). (gr. 2-5). 14.99 ***(978-1-4847-3234-2(0))***; pap. 5.99 ***(978-1-4847-4639-4(2))*** Hyperion Bks. for Children.

—A True Home. 2017. (Heartwood Hotel Ser.: 1). (J). lib. bdg. 16.00 ***(978-0-606-39968-5(2))*** Turtleback Bks.

George, Lindsay Barrett. Inside Mouse, Outside Mouse. George, Lindsay Barrett, illus. 2004. (ENG., Illus.). 40p. (J). (gr. -1-3). 17.99 (978-0-06-000466-8(5), Greenwillow Bks.) HarperCollins Pubs.

George, Lindsay Barrett & George, Lindsay B. Inside Mouse, Outside Mouse. George, Lindsay Barrett, illus. 2006. (ENG., Illus.). 40p. (J). (gr. -1-3). reprint ed. pap. 6.99 (978-0-06-000468-2(1), Greenwillow Bks.) HarperCollins Pubs.

Geronimo Stilton Staff. The Cheese Experiment. 2016. (Geronimo Stilton Ser.: 63). (ENG.). 128p. (J). (gr. 2-5). pap. 7.99 (978-0-545-87252-2(9), Scholastic Paperbacks) Scholastic, Inc.

—The Christmas Toy Factory. 2006. (Geronimo Stilton Ser.: 27). (ENG., Illus.). 128p. (J). (gr. 2-5). pap. 7.99 (978-0-439-84118-4(6), Scholastic Paperbacks) Scholastic, Inc.

—Mouse House Hunter. 2015. (Geronimo Stilton Ser.: 61). (ENG.). 128p. (J). (gr. 2-5). pap. 7.99 (978-0-545-83554-1(2), Scholastic Paperbacks) Scholastic, Inc.

—The Wizard's Wand. 2016. (ENG.). 320p. (J). (gr. 2-5). 14.99 (978-1-338-03291-8(7), Scholastic Paperbacks) Scholastic, Inc.

Getsinger, Mary. A Dream Come True. 2009. 20p. pap. 9.50 (978-1-4251-8885-6(0)) Trafford Publishing.

Gibbs, Lynne. Molly Mouse Is Shy: A Story of Shyness. Mitchell, Melanie, illus. 2009. (Let's Grow Together Ser.). 32p. (J). (gr. -1-2). pap. 10.55 (978-1-60754-761-7(9)); lib. bdg. 22.60 (978-1-60754-756-3(2)) Windmill Bks.

Gibson, Josephine. Is There a Mouse in the House? 2014. (ENG., Illus.). 32p. (J). (gr. -1-2). 13.99 (978-1-4814-2523-0(4), Simon & Schuster Bks. For Young Readers) Simon & Schuster Bks. For Young Readers.

Gifford, Dorinda. Harriet the Ferret, 1 vol. Luevano, Raul, illus. 2009. 20p. pap. 24.95 (978-1-59129-405-4(3)) America Star Bks.

Gill, Bob. The Green-Eyed Mouse & the Blue-Eyed Mouse. 2010. (ENG., Illus.). 28p. (gr. -1-k). 14.95 (978-0-7148-4887-7(5)) Phaidon Pr., Inc.

Gillis, Jennifer Blizin. Two Nice Mice. Krejca, Gary, illus. 2006. (Reader's Clubhouse Level 2 Reader Ser.). (ENG.). 24p. (J). (gr. 1-4). pap. 3.99 (978-0-7641-3295-7(4)) Barron's Educational Series, Inc.

Glass, Bryan J. L. Mice Templar, Vol. 3. 2012. (ENG., Illus.). 250p. (YA). 29.99 (978-1-60706-457-2(X), 9781607064572) Image Comics.

Godden, Rumer. Mouse House. Adams, Adrienne, illus. 2016. (ENG.). 72p. (J). (gr. -1-2). 15.95 (978-1-59017-998-7(6), NYR Children's Collection) New York Review of Bks., Inc., The.

—The Mousewife. du Bois, William Pène, illus. 2009. (ENG.). 56p. (J). (gr. -1-2). 16.95 (978-1-59017-310-7(4), NYR Children's Collection) New York Review of Bks., Inc., The.

Goodhart, Pippa. Big Cat. 2011. (Tadpoles Ser.: No. 28). (ENG., Illus.). 24p. (J). (gr. k-3). pap. (978-0-7787-0585-7(4)) Crabtree Publishing Co.

—Little Nelly's Big Book. Rowland, Andy, illus. 2012. (ENG.). 32p. (J). (gr. -1-3). 16.99 (978-1-59990-779-6(8), 9781599907796, Bloomsbury USA Childrens) Bloomsbury Publishing USA.

Goodrich, Carter & Moore, Clement C. A Creature Was Stirring: One Boy's Night Before Christmas. Goodrich, Carter, illus. 2006. (ENG., Illus.). 40p. (J). (gr. -1-3). 17.99 (978-0-689-86399-8(3), Simon & Schuster Bks. For Young Readers) Simon & Schuster Bks. For Young Readers.

Gore, Emily. And Nick. Gore, Leonid, illus. 2015. (ENG.). 40p. (J). (gr. -1-3). 17.99 (978-1-4169-5506-1(2)) Simon & Schuster Children's Publishing.

Gore, Leonid. Mommy, Where Are You? Gore, Leonid, illus. 2009. (ENG., Illus.). 32p. (J). (gr. -1-2). 16.99 (978-1-4169-5505-4(4), Atheneum Bks. for Young Readers) Simon & Schuster Children's Publishing.

Grammy Sunshine. The Adventures of Mouse: The Mouse Who Wanted to Be A Pig. 2009. 20p. pap. 12.49 (978-1-4389-9268-6(8)) AuthorHouse.

Grandpa Casey. Another Müsh-Mice Adventure. Brennan, Lisa, illus. 2012. 48p. 24.95 (978-1-4626-9379-5(2)) America Star Bks.

—Another Müsh-Mice Adventure: Florida Vacation, 1 vol. Brennan, Lisa, illus. 2009. 45p. pap. 24.95 (978-1-60813-329-1(X)) America Star Bks.

—Going Green: Another Müsh-Mice Adventure, 1 vol. Brennan, Lisa, illus. 2010. 34p. pap. 24.95 (978-1-4489-7375-0(9)) America Star Bks.

—Meet the Müsh-Mice. Brennan, Lisa, illus. 2012. 28p. 24.95 (978-1-4626-9380-1(6)) America Star Bks.

—The Trilogy: Three Adventures of the Müsh-Mice. Brenn, Lisa, illus. 2012. 46p. 24.95 (978-1-4626-9378-8(4)) America Star Bks.

Grandpa Dennis, as told by. George Washington's Smallest Army: The Miracle Before Trenton. 2009. 216p. (J). pap. 17.49 (978-1-4389-3147-0(6)) AuthorHouse.

Grant, Rose. Right Where You Need Me. Bryant, Julie, illus. 2012. 16p. pap. 15.99 (978-1-4685-6856-1(6)) AuthorHouse.

Grant, V. F. Stories from Grimley Forest. 2011. 48p. (gr. 1-2). pap. 19.50 (978-1-4567-4709-1(6)) AuthorHouse.

Gravett, Emily. Little Mouse's Big Book of Fears. Gravett, Emily, illus. 2008. (ENG., Illus.). 32p. (J). (gr. -1-3). 19.99 (978-1-4169-5930-4(0), Simon & Schuster Bks. For Young Readers) Simon & Schuster Bks. For Young Readers.

Gravett, Emily, illus. Little Mouse's Big Book of Beasts. 2016. (ENG.). 32p. (J). (gr. -1-3). 17.99 (978-1-4814-3929-9(4), Simon & Schuster Bks. For Young Readers) Simon & Schuster Bks. For Young Readers.

Greathouse, Cindy. Wilbur Learns to Forgive, 1 vol. 2010. 18p. 24.95 (978-1-4489-7374-3(0)) PublishAmerica, Inc.

Greaves, Margaret. The Mice of Nibbling Village. Pinkney, Jane, illus. 2011. (ENG.). 32p. (J). (gr. -1-k). 14.99 (978-1-84365-189-5(0)) National Trust, Aylesbury GBR. Dist: Independent Pubs. Group.

Green, Poppy. The Clover Curse. Bell, Jennifer A., illus. 2016. (Adventures of Sophie Mouse Ser.: 7). (ENG.). 128p. (J). (gr. k-4). 16.99 (978-1-4814-5184-0(7), Little Simon) Little Simon.

—The Emerald Berries. Bell, Jennifer A., illus. 2015. (Adventures of Sophie Mouse Ser.: 2). (ENG.). 128p. (J). (gr. k-4). pap. 5.99 (978-1-4814-2835-4(7), Little Simon) Little Simon.

—Forget-Me-Not Lake. Bell, Jennifer A., illus. 2015. (Adventures of Sophie Mouse Ser.: 3). (ENG.). 128p. (J). (gr. k-4). 16.99 (978-1-4814-3000-5(9), Little Simon) Little Simon.

—The Great Big Paw Print. Bell, Jennifer A., illus. 2016. (Adventures of Sophie Mouse Ser.: 9). (ENG.). 128p. (J). (gr. k-4). 16.99 (978-1-4814-7149-7(X), Little Simon) Little Simon.

—The Maple Festival. Bell, Jennifer A., illus. 2015. (Adventures of Sophie Mouse Ser.: 5). (ENG.). 128p. (J). (gr. k-4). pap. 5.99 (978-1-4814-4196-4(5), Little Simon) Little Simon.

—A New Friend. Bell, Jennifer A., illus. 2015. (Adventures of Sophie Mouse Ser.: 1). (ENG.). 128p. (J). (gr. k-4). pap. 5.99 (978-1-4814-2832-3(2), Little Simon) Little Simon.

—A Surprise Visitor. Bell, Jennifer A., illus. 2016. (Adventures of Sophie Mouse Ser.: 8). (ENG.). 128p. (J). (gr. k-4). pap. 5.99 (978-1-4814-6698-1(4), Little Simon) Little Simon.

—Winter's No Time to Sleep! Bell, Jennifer A., illus. 2015. (Adventures of Sophie Mouse Ser.: 6). (ENG.). 128p. (J). (gr. k-4). pap. 5.99 (978-1-4814-4199-5(X), Little Simon) Little Simon.

Greene, Stephanie. Christmas at Stony Creek. Sheban, Chris, illus. 2007. 96p. (gr. -1-3). lib. bdg. 15.89 (978-0-06-121487-5(6)) HarperCollins Pubs.

—The Show-Off, 0 vols. Mathieu, Joe, illus. 2013. (Moose & Hildy Ser.). (ENG.). 64p. (J). (gr. 1-4). pap. 9.99 (978-1-4778-1686-8(0), 9781477816868, Amazon Children's Publishing) Amazon Publishing.

Grey, Mini. Hermelin the Detective Mouse. 2014. (ENG.). 32p. (J). (gr. k-3). 17.99 (978-0-385-75433-0(7), Knopf Bks. for Young Readers) Random Hse. Children's Bks.

Griffin, Daniel. The Adventures of Merlin the Mouse 2005. (Illus.). 44p. (J). (978-0-9768348-0-9(4)) DiGuiseppi, Joseph.

Grubman, Bonnie. How Do You Get a Mouse to Smile?, 1 vol. Van Wright, Cornelius, illus. 2009. (ENG.). 32p. (J). (gr. -1-3). pap. 6.50 (978-1-59572-167-9(3)) Star Bright Bks., Inc.

Guibert, Emmanuel. The Little Rats of the Opera. 2017. (Ariol Ser.: 10). (J). lib. bdg. 24.50 ***(978-0-606-39879-4(1))*** Turtleback Bks.

Gump, Granny. The Giraffe Who Went to School. 2011. 48p. pap. 21.99 (978-1-4568-5805-6(X)) Xlibris Corp.

Gutman, Anne. Gaspard et Lisa au Musee. (FRE.). pap. 19.95 (978-2-01-224132-9(8)) Hachette Groupe Livre FRA. Dist: Distribooks, Inc.

Hall, Shirley. The Adventure of Molly the Mouse. 2012. (ENG.). (J). pap. 14.95 (978-1-4675-1717-1(8)) Independent Pub.

Haller, Reese. The Adventures Begin. Lynn, Galsterer, illus. 2005. (Fred the Mouse Ser.). 108p. (J). (gr. -1-3). per. 4.97 (978-0-9616046-8-4(9)) Personal Power Pr.

—Making Friends, 2. Galsterer, Lynne, illus. 2nd ed. 2006. (Fred the Mouse Ser.). 112p. (J). per. 4.97 (978-0-9772321-0-9(7)) Personal Power Pr.

—Rescuing Freedom. Haller, Thomas, illus. 3rd ed. 2006. (Fred the Mouse Ser.). 112p. (J). (gr. k-4). per. 4.97 (978-0-9772321-3-0(1)) Personal Power Pr.

Halliday-King, Michaela. The Pennine Mouse. 2012. (Illus.). 40p. pap. 27.99 (978-1-4678-8709-0(9)) AuthorHouse.

Hamilton, Laura, reader. Sheila Rae, the Brave. 2003. (Illus.). (J). (gr. -1-2). 28.95 incl. audio compact disk (978-1-59112-550-1(2)) Live Oak Media.

Harff, David. Mouse Mayhem, 1 vol. 2009. 24p. pap. 24.95 (978-1-60749-610-6(0)) America Star Bks.

Harms, Jeanine, illus. Boss Mouse Coloring Book & Theme Song. 2006. (J). 4.00 (978-1-4276-0118-6(6)) Aardvark Global Publishing.

Harris, Christine. Four Tails: An Anthology of Four Tales for Children. 2011. (Illus.). 92p. (gr. -1). pap. 12.10 (978-1-4520-7643-0(X)) AuthorHouse.

Harris, Robie H. Adios, Ratoncito. Rioja, Alberto Jimenez, tr. Ormerod, Jan, illus. (SPA.). (J). (gr. k-2). 16.00 (978-1-930332-34-8(3), LC8567) Lectorum Pubns., Inc.

—Goodbye Mousie. Ormerod, Jan, illus. 2004. (ENG.). 32p. (J). (gr. -1-3). reprint ed. 16.99 (978-0-689-87134-4(1), Aladdin) Simon & Schuster Children's Publishing.

Harrison, Paul. Three Blind Mice Team up with the Three Little Pigs. Epelbaum, Mariano, illus. 2016. (Fairy Tale Mix-Ups Ser.). (ENG.). 24p. (J). (gr. k-2). lib. bdg. 23.32 (978-1-4109-8301-5(3)) Heinemann-Raintree.

Hart, Melissa. A Guide for Using the Tale of Despereaux in the Classroom. 2005. (ENG.). 48p. pap. 9.99 (978-1-4206-3164-7(0)) Teacher Created Resources, Inc.

Harvey, Keith. Tiberius & the Chocolate Cake. Kirk, Heather, illus. 2010. (Tiberius Tales Ser.). 24p. (J). (gr. -1-2). pap. 8.15 (978-1-60754-836-2(4)); lib. bdg. 22.60 (978-1-60754-832-4(1)) Windmill Bks.

—Tiberius & the Friendly Dragon. Kirk, Heather, illus. 2010. (Tiberius Tales Ser.). 24p. (J). (gr. -1-2). pap. 8.15 (978-1-60754-834-8(8)); lib. bdg. 22.60 (978-1-60754-830-0(5)) Windmill Bks.

—Tiberius Goes to School. Brown, Kate & Hickman, Paula, illus. 2014. (ENG.). 24p. pap. 8.95 (978-1-84135-919-9(X)) Award Pubns. Ltd. GBR. Dist: Parkwest Pubns., Inc.

—Tiberius Goes to School. Brown, Kait, illus. 2010. (Tiberius Tales Ser.). 24p. (J). (gr. -1-2). pap. 8.15 (978-1-60754-837-9(2)); lib. bdg. 22.60 (978-1-60754-833-1(X)) Windmill Bks.

—Tiberius Meets Sneaky Cat. Hickman, Paula, illus. 2010. (Tiberius Tales Ser.). 24p. (J). (gr. -1-2). pap. 8.15 (978-1-60754-835-5(6)); lib. bdg. 22.60 (978-1-60754-831-7(3)) Windmill Bks.

Harvey, Keith & Kirk, Heather. Tiberius & the Friendly Dragon. 2014. (ENG., Illus.). 24p. pap. 8.95 (978-1-84135-917-5(3)) Award Pubns. Ltd. GBR. Dist: Parkwest Pubns., Inc.

Harvey, Tom. Rat in the Red Truck. 2011. 44p. 17.99 (978-1-4269-6236-3(3)) Trafford Publishing.

Hash, Stella. The Christmas Caravan. 2011. 32p. pap. 24.95 (978-1-4626-0533-0(8)) America Star Bks.

Hayes, Geoffrey. Benny & Penny in Just Pretend, 1 vol. 2013. (Toon Bks). (ENG.). 36p. (J). (gr. 1-2). lib. bdg. 27.07 (978-1-61479-148-5(1)) Spotlight.

—Benny & Penny in Just Pretend. 2013. (Toon Books Level 2 Ser.). lib. bdg. 14.75 (978-0-606-31597-5(7), Turtleback) Turtleback Bks.

—Benny & Penny in Lights Out! Hayes, Geoffrey, illus. 2012. (Benny & Penny Ser.). (ENG., Illus.). 32p. (J). (gr. -1-3). 12.95 (978-1-935179-20-7(9)) TOON Books / RAW Junior, LLC.

—Benny & Penny in Lost & Found. Hayes, Geoffrey, illus. 2013. (Benny & Penny Ser.). (ENG., Illus.). 40p. (J). (gr. -1-3). 12.95 (978-1-935179-64-1(0)) TOON Books / RAW Junior, LLC.

—Benny & Penny in the Big No-No! Mouly, Francoise, ed. Hayes, Geoffrey, illus. 2009. (Benny & Penny Ser.). (ENG., Illus.). 32p. (J). (gr. -1-3). 12.95 (978-0-9799238-9-0(1)) TOON Books / RAW Junior, LLC.

—Benny & Penny in the Big No-No! 2014. (Toon Books Level 1 Ser.). lib. bdg. 14.75 (978-0-606-32102-0(0), Turtleback) Turtleback Bks.

—Benny & Penny in the Toy Breaker. Mouly, Francoise, ed. Hayes, Geoffrey, illus. 2010. (Benny & Penny Ser.). (ENG., Illus.). 32p. (J). (gr. -1-3). 12.95 (978-1-935179-07-8(1)) TOON Books / RAW Junior, LLC.

—Benny & Penny in the Toy Breaker. 2013. (Toon Books Level 2 Ser.). lib. bdg. 14.75 (978-0-606-31598-2(5), Turtleback) Turtleback Bks.

—How to Say Goodbye. Hayes, Geoffrey, illus. 2016. (Benny & Penny Ser.). (ENG., Illus.). 32p. (J). (gr. -1-3). 12.95 (978-1-935179-99-3(3)) TOON Books / RAW Junior, LLC.

Hayes, Geoffrey & Rosenstiehl, Agnes. Toon Books. 2013. (Toon Bks: 10). 36p. (J). (gr. k-3). lib. bdg. 270.70 (978-1-61479-147-8(3)) Spotlight.

Hays, Ethel, illus. The Town Mouse & the Country Mouse. 2007. (Shape Bks.). (ENG.). 14p. (J). (gr. -1-3). pap. 9.95 (978-1-59583-192-7(4), 9781595831927, Green Tiger Pr.) Laughing Elephant.

Hazel, Jan. Marshall Meets the Little Dragons. 2013. 38p. pap. 9.99 (978-1-62509-396-7(9)) Salem Author Services.

Hazlewood, Leyland. Chester Goes to Afric. 2011. 32p. pap. 21.99 (978-1-4568-6466-8(1)) Xlibris Corp.

Hegarty, Patricia. Who's There? Beware! 2015. (Amazing Changing Pictures! Ser.). (ENG.). 14p. (J). (gr. -1-3). 12.99 (978-1-68010-000-6(9)) Tiger Tales.

Heim, Julia & Dami, Elisabetta. The Little Book of Happiness. Bluecheese, Wally, illus. 2013. 42p. (J). pap. (978-0-545-48255-4(0)) Scholastic, Inc.

Hellberg, Joanne S. Thomas S Tucker & the Silver Buckle. 2009. 32p. pap. 12.99 (978-1-4389-8723-1(4)) AuthorHouse.

Henderson, Virginia. Zippy the Dreamer. 2010. 20p. 13.77 (978-1-4269-3448-3(3)) Trafford Publishing.

Hendry, Diana. Que Noche Mas Ruidosa! Chapman, Jane, illus. 2003. (SPA.). 28p. (J). (gr. k-2). 16.95 (978-84-488-0865-5(7), BS3550) Beascoa, Ediciones S.A. ESP. Dist: Lectorum Pubns., Inc.

—The Very Snowy Christmas. Chapman, Jane, illus. (J). 2013. (ENG.). 16p. (gr. -1). bds. 8.95 (978-1-58925-617-0(4)) 2007. 32p. pap. 6.95 (978-1-58925-406-0(6)) 2005. 32p. (gr. -1-2). 15.95 (978-1-58925-051-2(6)) Tiger Tales.

Henkes, Kevin. Chester's Way. (Illus.). 25.95 incl. audio (978-1-59112-968-4(0)); 28.95 incl. audio compact disk (978-1-59112-972-1(9)); pap. 33.95 incl. audio (978-1-59112-969-1(9)); pap. 35.95 incl. audio compact disk (978-1-59112-973-8(7)) Live Oak Media.

—El Gran Dia de Lily, 1 vol. Posada, Maria Candelaria, tr. from ENG. Henkes, Kevin, illus. 2008. (SPA., Illus.). 40p. (J). (gr. -1-3). 17.99 (978-0-06-136316-0(2)) HarperCollins Pubs.

—Julius, el Rey de la Casa. 2017.Tr. of Julius, the Baby of the World. (SPA.). (J). pap. ***(978-1-63245-668-7(0))*** Lectorum Pubns., Inc.

—Lilly's Big Day. Henkes, Kevin, illus. 2006. (Illus.). 40p. (J). (gr. -1-3). (ENG.). 17.99 (978-0-06-074236-2(4)); lib. bdg. 18.89 (978-0-06-074237-9(2)) HarperCollins Pubs. (Greenwillow Bks.).

—Lilly's Big Day. 2014. (J). lib. bdg. 17.20 (978-0-606-35472-1(7)) Turtleback Bks.

—Lilly's Purple Plastic Purse. Henkes, Kevin, illus. 10th anniv. ed. 2006. (ENG., Illus.). 40p. (J). (gr. -1-4). 17.99 (978-0-688-12897-5(1), Greenwillow Bks.) HarperCollins Pubs.

—Lilly's Purple Plastic Purse. Henkes, Kevin, illus. (Illus.). pap. 18.95 incl. audio compact disk (978-1-59112-347-7(X)); pap. incl. audio (978-0-87499-688-3(0)); pap. 16.95 incl. audio (978-0-87499-686-9(4)); pap. incl. audio compact disk (978-1-59112-557-0(X)) Live Oak Media.

—Lilly's Purple Plastic Purse 20th Anniversary Edition. Henkes, Kevin, illus. 20th ed. 2016. (Illus.). 40p. (J). (gr. -1-3). 17.99 (978-0-06-242419-8(X), Greenwillow Bks.) HarperCollins Pubs.

—Lily y Su Bolso de Plastico Morado. 2017.Tr. of Lilly's Purple Plastic Purse. (SPA.). (J). pap. ***(978-1-63245-667-0(2))*** Lectorum Pubns., Inc.

—Owen. 2017. (SPA.). (J). pap. ***(978-1-63245-665-6(6))*** Lectorum Pubns., Inc.

—Penny & Her Doll. Henkes, Kevin, illus. 2012. (Illus.). 32p. (J). (gr. -1-3). (ENG.). 12.99 (978-0-06-208199-5(3)); lib. bdg. 14.89 (978-0-06-208200-8(0)) HarperCollins Pubs. (Greenwillow Bks.).

—Penny & Her Doll. 2013. (I Can Read! Level 1 Ser.). (J). lib. bdg. 13.55 (978-0-606-27147-9(3), Turtleback) Turtleback Bks.

—Penny & Her Marble. Henkes, Kevin, illus. 2013. (I Can Read Level 1 Ser.). (Illus.). 48p. (J). (gr. -1-3). (ENG.). pap. 3.99 (978-0-06-208205-3(1)); (ENG., 12.99 (978-0-06-208203-9(5)); 14.89 (978-0-06-208204-6(3)) HarperCollins Pubs. (Greenwillow Bks.).

—Penny & Her Marble. 2013. (J). lib. bdg. 13.55 (978-0-606-32151-8(9), Turtleback) Turtleback Bks.

—Penny & Her Song. Henkes, Kevin, illus. 2012. (I Can Read Level 1 Ser.). (Illus.). 32p. (J). (gr. -1-3). (ENG.). pap. 3.99 (978-0-06-208197-1(7)); (ENG., 12.99 (978-0-06-208195-7(0)); lib. bdg. 14.89 (978-0-06-208196-4(9)) HarperCollins Pubs. (Greenwillow Bks.).

—Penny & Her Song. 2012. (J). lib. bdg. 13.55 (978-0-606-26847-9(2), Turtleback) Turtleback Bks.

—Prudencia Se Preocupa. 2017.Tr. of Wemberly Worried. (SPA.). (J). pap. ***(978-1-63245-666-3(4))*** Lectorum Pubns., Inc.

—Sheila Rae, the Brave. Henkes, Kevin, illus. (Illus.). 9.95 (978-1-59112-865-6(X)) Live Oak Media.

—Wemberly Worried. Henkes, Kevin, illus. 2010. (ENG., Illus.). 32p. (J). (gr. -1-4). pap. 6.99 (978-0-06-185776-8(9), Greenwillow Bks.) HarperCollins Pubs.

—Wemberly Worried. Henkes, Kevin, illus. (Illus.). pap. 16.95 incl. audio (978-0-87499-806-1(9)); pap. incl. audio (978-0-87499-808-5(5)); pap. 18.95 incl. audio compact disk (978-1-59112-359-0(3)); pap. 39.95 incl. audio compact disk (978-1-59112-561-7(8)) Live Oak Media.

—Wemberly Worried. 2010. (J). lib. bdg. 17.20 (978-0-606-14757-6(8), Turtleback) Turtleback Bks.

Henkes, Kevin & Kevin, Henkes. Owen. 2006. (Coleccion Rascacielos Ser.). (SPA., Illus.). 32p. (gr. k-1). pap. 9.99 (978-84-241-1519-7(8)) Everest Editora ESP. Dist: Lectorum Pubns., Inc.

Henry, Jed. Cheer up, Mouse! Henry, Jed, illus. 2013. (ENG., Illus.). 32p. (J). (gr. -1-3). 12.99 (978-0-547-68107-8(0)) Houghton Mifflin Harcourt Publishing Co.

—Good Night, Mouse! Henry, Jed, illus. 2013. (ENG., Illus.). 32p. (J). (gr. -1-3). 16.99 (978-0-547-98156-7(2)) Houghton Mifflin Harcourt Publishing Co.

Herman, R. A. Littlest Pumpkin. Ogden, Betina, illus. 2006. (ENG.). (J). (gr. -1-3). 18.95 (978-0-439-89837-9(4)) Scholastic, Inc.

Hickman, B. Jo. Old Cat, Fat Rat, & Boo. 2011. 28p. pap. 15.99 (978-1-4653-3615-6(X)) Xlibris Corp.

Higginson, Sheila Sweeny & Disney Book Group Staff. Minnie's Rainbow. Loter Inc. Staff & Disney Storybook Art Team, illus. rev. ed. 2008. (ENG.). 24p. (J). (gr. -1-k). pap. 3.99 (978-1-4231-0743-9(8)) Disney Pr.

—Minnie's Valentine. Loter Inc. Staff & Disney Storybook Art Team, illus. rev. ed. 2007. (ENG.). 24p. (J). (gr. -1-k). pap. 4.99 (978-1-4231-0746-0(2)) Disney Pr.

Hines, D. H. L. College Mouse. 2009. 24p. pap. 16.49 (978-1-4490-2976-0(0)) AuthorHouse.

Hinkelman, Carole & Rebik, Nan. The Herman Chronicles: *Herman the Horrible Trailer Mouse *Herman & the Donkeys * Herman's Midnight Trek * Herman's Vacation. 2012. 84p. (gr. 2-4). pap. 11.50 (978-1-4669-5202-7(4)) Trafford Publishing.

Hobbs, Brice Edward. Beth's Woodpecker. 2004. 108p. 26.45 (978-1-4208-0135-4(X)) AuthorHouse.

Hockerman, Dennis, illus. The Country Mouse & the City Mouse: A Tale of Tolerance. 2006. (J). 6.99 (978-1-59939-003-1(5)) Cornerstone Pr.

—The Lion & the Mouse: A Tale about Being Helpful. 2006. (J). 6.99 (978-1-59939-007-9(8)) Cornerstone Pr.

Hockinson, Liz. Marcello: The Movie Mouse. Otoshi, Kathryn, illus. 2005. (ENG.). 40p. (J). (gr. k). 16.95 (978-0-9723946-2-8(1)) KO Kids Bks.

Hodgkinson, Jo. A Big Day for Migs. Hodgkinson, Jo, illus. 2014. (ENG., Illus.). 32p. (J). (gr. -1-3). 16.95 (978-1-4677-5014-1(X)) Lerner Publishing Group.

Hodgkinson, Leigh. Boris & the Wrong Shadow. 2012. (ENG.). 32p. (J). pap. (978-1-58925-434-3(1)) Tiger Tales.

Hoenecke, Karen. Little Mouse. Gedeon, Gloria, illus. l.t. ed. 2005. (ENG.). 12p. (gr. k-2). pap. 7.95 (978-1-57874-023-9(1), Kaeden Bks.) Kaeden Corp.

Hoeye, Michael. Una Cuestion de Tiempo. (SPA.). 304p. (J). (gr. 6-8). 17.56 (978-84-8441-167-3(2), MO1007) Grijalbo Mondadori, S.A.-Montena ESP. Dist: Lectorum Pubns., Inc.

—The Sands of Time. 2007. (ENG.). 288p. (J). (gr. 3-7). pap. 8.99 (978-0-14-240983-1(9), Puffin Books) Penguin Young Readers Group.

—The Sands of Time: A Hermux Tantamoq AdventureTM. 2004. 288p. (J). (gr. 5-9). pap. 40.00 incl. audio (978-1-4000-9016-7(4), Listening Library) Random Hse. Audio Publishing Group.

—Time Stops for No Mouse. 2007. (ENG.). 272p. (J). (gr. 3-7). 7.99 (978-0-14-240984-8(7), Puffin Books) Penguin Young Readers Group.

—Time Stops for No Mouse. 2003. (Hermux Tantamoq Adventure Ser.). (Illus.). 250p. (J). (gr. 4-7). 18.40 (978-0-613-62122-9(0), Turtleback) Turtleback Bks.

—Time Stops for No Mouse: A Hermux Tantamoq AdventureTM. 2004. 272p. (J). (gr. 5-9). pap. 40.00 incl. audio (978-0-8072-2280-5(1), Listening Library) Random Hse. Audio Publishing Group.

Hoffman, Karen Burkinshaw. The Story about Tee Low: A Mouse with a Knot in His Tail. 2013. 36p. pap. 18.41 *(978-1-4669-9715-8(X))* Trafford Publishing.
Holm, Jennifer L. Little Babymouse & the Christmas Cupcakes. Holm, Matthew, illus. 2016. (ENG.). 40p. (J). (gr. -1-2). 17.99 *(978-1-101-93743-3(2),* Random Hse. Bks. for Young Readers) Random Hse. Children's Bks.
Holm, Jennifer L. & Holm, Matthew. Babymouse for President. Holm, Jennifer L. & Holm, Matthew, illus. 2012. (Babymouse Ser.: 16). (ENG., Illus.). 96p. (J). (gr. 2-5). 12.99 *(978-0-375-96780-1(X));* pap. 6.99 *(978-0-375-86780-4(5))* Random Hse. Children's Bks. (Random Hse. Bks. for Young Readers).
—Babymouse for President. 2012. (Babymouse Ser.: 16). lib. bdg. 17.20 *(978-0-606-26404-4(3),* Turtleback) Turtleback Bks.
—Babymouse Goes for the Gold. Holm, Jennifer L. & Holm, Matthew, illus. 2016. (Babymouse Ser.: 20). (ENG., Illus.). 96p. (J). (gr. 2-5). pap. 6.99 *(978-0-307-93163-4(3),* Random Hse. Bks. for Young Readers) Random Hse. Children's Bks.
—Bad Babysitter. Holm, Jennifer L. & Holm, Matthew, illus. 2015. (Babymouse Ser.: 19). (ENG., Illus.). 96p. (J). (gr. 2-5). pap. 6.99 *(978-0-307-93162-7(5),* Random Hse. Bks. for Young Readers) Random Hse. Children's Bks.
—Beach Babe. 2006. (Babymouse Ser.: 3). (ENG., Illus.). 96p. (J). (gr. 2-5). pap. 6.99 *(978-0-375-83231-4(9));* No. 3. lib. bdg. 12.99 *(978-0-375-93231-1(3))* Random Hse. Children's Bks. (Random Hse. Bks. for Young Readers).
—Burns Rubber. 2010. (Babymouse Ser.: 12). lib. bdg. 17.20 *(978-0-606-07025-6(7),* Turtleback) Turtleback Bks.
—Camp Babymouse. 2007. (Babymouse Ser.: No. 6). (Illus.). 91p. (J). (gr. 2-5). 13.65 *(978-0-7569-8344-4(4))* Perfection Learning Corp.
—Camp Babymouse. 2007. (Babymouse Ser.: 6). (ENG., Illus.). 96p. (J). (gr. 2-5). pap. 6.99 *(978-0-375-83988-7(7));* lib. bdg. 12.99 *(978-0-375-93988-4(1))* Random Hse. Children's Bks. (Random Hse. Bks. for Young Readers).
—Camp Babymouse. 2007. (Babymouse Ser.: 6). lib. bdg. 17.20 *(978-1-4177-8070-9(3),* Turtleback) Turtleback Bks.
—Dragonslayer. Holm, Jennifer L. & Holm, Matthew, illus. 2009. (Babymouse Ser.: 11). (ENG., Illus.). 96p. (J). (gr. 2-5). pap. 6.99 *(978-0-375-85712-6(5));* lib. bdg. 12.99 *(978-0-375-95712-3(X))* Random Hse. Children's Bks. (Random Hse. Bks. for Young Readers).
—Extreme Babymouse. Holm, Jennifer L. & Holm, Matthew, illus. 2013. (Babymouse Ser.: 17). (ENG., Illus.). 96p. (J). (gr. 2-5). pap. 6.99 *(978-0-307-93160-3(9));* lib. bdg. 12.99 *(978-0-375-97096-2(7))* Random Hse. Children's Bks. (Random Hse. Bks. for Young Readers).
—Extreme Babymouse. 2013. (Babymouse Ser.: 17). lib. bdg. 17.20 *(978-0-606-26999-5(1),* Turtleback) Turtleback Bks.
—Happy Birthday, Babymouse! Holm, Jennifer L. & Holm, Matthew, illus. 2014. (Babymouse Ser.: 18). (ENG., Illus.). 96p. (J). (gr. 2-5). 12.99 *(978-0-375-97097-9(5),* Random Hse. Bks. for Young Readers) Random Hse. Children's Bks.
—Happy Birthday, Babymouse. Holm, Jennifer L. & Holm, Matthew, illus. 2014. (Babymouse Ser.: 18). (ENG., Illus.). 96p. (J). (gr. 2-5). pap. 6.99 *(978-0-307-93161-0(7),* Random Hse. Bks. for Young Readers) Random Hse. Children's Bks.
—Happy Birthday, Babymouse. 2014. (Babymouse Ser.: 18). lib. bdg. 17.20 *(978-0-606-35567-4(7))* Turtleback Bks.
—Heartbreaker. 2006. (Babymouse Ser.: 5). (ENG., Illus.). 96p. (J). (gr. 2-5). lib. bdg. 12.99 *(978-0-375-93798-9(6),* Random Hse. Bks. for Young Readers) Random Hse. Children's Bks.
—Mad Scientist. Holm, Jennifer L. & Holm, Matthew, illus. 2011. (Babymouse Ser.: No. 14). (ENG., Illus.). 96p. (J). (gr. 2-5). pap. 6.99 *(978-0-375-86574-9(8));* lib. bdg. 12.99 *(978-0-375-96574-6(2))* Random Hse. Children's Bks. (Random Hse. Bks. for Young Readers).
—Monster Mash. Holm, Jennifer L. & Holm, Matthew, illus. 2008. (Babymouse Ser.: 9). (ENG., Illus.). 96p. (J). (gr. 2-5). pap. 6.99 *(978-0-375-84387-7(6));* lib. bdg. 12.99 *(978-0-375-93789-7(7))* Random Hse. Children's Bks. (Random Hse. Bks. for Young Readers).
—The Musical. Holm, Jennifer L. & Holm, Matthew, illus. 2009. (Babymouse Ser.: 10). (ENG., Illus.). 96p. (J). (gr. 2-5). pap. 6.99 *(978-0-375-84388-4(4));* lib. bdg. 12.99 *(978-0-375-93791-0(9))* Random Hse. Children's Bks. (Random Hse. Bks. for Young Readers).
—Our Hero. 2005. (Babymouse Ser.: 2). (ENG., Illus.). 96p. (J). (gr. 2-5). pap. 6.99 *(978-0-375-83230-7(0));* lib. bdg. 12.99 *(978-0-375-93230-4(5))* Random Hse. Children's Bks. (Random Hse. Bks. for Young Readers).
—Queen of the World! 2005. (Babymouse Ser.: 1). (ENG., Illus.). 96p. (J). (gr. 2-5). pap. 6.99 *(978-0-375-83229-1(7));* lib. bdg. 12.99 *(978-0-375-93229-8(1))* Random Hse. Children's Bks. (Random Hse. Bks. for Young Readers).
—Rock Star. 2006. (Babymouse Ser.: 4). (ENG., Illus.). 96p. (J). (gr. 2-5). pap. 6.99 *(978-0-375-83232-1(7));* lib. bdg. 12.99 *(978-0-375-93232-8(1))* Random Hse. Children's Bks. (Random Hse. Bks. for Young Readers).
—A Very Babymouse Christmas. Holm, Jennifer L. & Holm, Matthew, illus. 2011. (Babymouse Ser.: 15). (ENG., Illus.). 96p. (J). (gr. 2-5). 12.99 *(978-0-375-96779-5(6));* pap. 6.99 *(978-0-375-86779-8(1))* Random Hse. Children's Bks. (Random Hse. Bks. for Young Readers).
Hood, Susan. The Tooth Mouse. Nadeau, Janice, illus. 2012. (ENG.). 32p. (J). (gr. -1-2). 16.95 *(978-1-55453-565-1(4))* Kids Can Pr., Ltd. CAN. Dist: Hachette Bk. Group.
Horácek, Petr. The Mouse Who Ate the Moon. Horácek, Petr, illus. 2014. (ENG., Illus.). 32p. (J). (gr. -1-2). 15.99 *(978-0-7636-7059-7(6))* Candlewick Pr.
—The Mouse Who Reached the Sky. Horácek, Petr, illus. 2016. (ENG., Illus.). 32p. (J). (-k). 16.99 *(978-0-7636-7916-3(X))* Candlewick Pr.
—A Surprise for Tiny Mouse. Horácek, Petr, illus. 2015. (ENG., Illus.). 16p. (J). (— 1). bds. 8.99 *(978-0-7636-7967-5(4))* Candlewick Pr.
Horender, Philip M. A Brave New Mouse: Ellis Island Approved Immigrant, 1 vol. Wolek, Guy, illus. 2013. (Maximilian P. Mouse, Time Traveler Ser.). (ENG.). 112p. (J). (gr. 3-6). lib. bdg. 27.07 *(978-1-61641-961-5(X),* Calico Chapter Bks) Magic Wagon.
—Head West, Young Mouse: Transcontinental Railroad Traveler, 1 vol. Wolek, Guy, illus. 2013. (Maximilian P. Mouse, Time Traveler Ser.). (ENG.). 112p. (J). (gr. 3-6). lib. bdg. 27.07 *(978-1-61641-959-2(8),* Calico Chapter Bks) Magic Wagon.
—Homeward Bound: Civil Rights Mouse Leader, 1 vol. Wolek, Guy, illus. 2013. (Maximilian P. Mouse, Time Traveler Ser.). (ENG.). 112p. (J). (gr. 3-6). lib. bdg. 27.07 *(978-1-61641-962-2(8),* Calico Chapter Bks) Magic Wagon.
—The Mighty Maximilian: Samuel Clemens's Traveling Companion, 1 vol. Wolek, Guy, illus. 2013. (Maximilian P. Mouse, Time Traveler Ser.). (ENG.). 112p. (J). (gr. 3-6). lib. bdg. 27.07 *(978-1-61641-960-8(1),* Calico Chapter Bks) Magic Wagon.
—Patriotic Mouse: Boston Tea Party Participant, 1 vol. Wolek, Guy, illus. 2013. (Maximilian P. Mouse, Time Traveler Ser.). (ENG.). 112p. (J). (gr. 3-6). lib. bdg. 27.07 *(978-1-61641-957-8(1),* Calico Chapter Bks) Magic Wagon.
—Yankee Mouse: Gettysburg Address Observer, 1 vol. Wolek, Guy, illus. 2013. (Maximilian P. Mouse, Time Traveler Ser.). (ENG.). 112p. (J). (gr. 3-6). lib. bdg. 27.07 *(978-1-61641-958-5(X),* Calico Chapter Bks) Magic Wagon.
Houdek, Andi. Mice in My Tummy. 2006. (J). per. 16.95 *(978-0-9771939-9-8(3),* 012) New World Publishing.
Houdek, Andrea. Mice in My Tummy. Collier, Kevin Scott, illus. 2012. 16p. pap. 9.95 *(978-1-61633-219-8(0))* Guardian Angel Publishing, Inc.
Houran, Lori Haskins. Bravo, Albert! Melmon, Deborah, illus. 2017. (Mouse Math (r) Ser.). (ENG.). 32p. (J). (gr. -1-1). lib. bdg. 22.65 *(978-1-57565-856-8(9))* Kane Press, Inc.
—Bravo, Albert! Melmon, Deborah, illus. 2017. (Mouse Math (r) Ser.). (ENG.). 32p. (gr. -1-1). 7.95 *(978-1-57565-859-9(3))* Kane Press, Inc.
—Bravo, Albert! Patterns. Melmon, Deborah, illus. 2017. (Mouse Math (r) Ser.). (ENG.). 32p. (gr. -1-1). 34.65 ***(978-1-57565-862-9(3))*** Kane Press, Inc.
Houran, Lori Haskins. Make a Wish, Albert: 3-D Shapes. Melmon, Deborah, illus. 2015. (ENG.). 32p. (J). (gr. -1-1). lib. bdg. 22.60 *(978-1-57565-797-4(X))* Kane Press, Inc.
Howe, James. Horace & Morris, but Mostly Dolores. Waldrod, Amy, illus. 2003. pap. 39.95 incl. audio compact disk *(978-1-59112-538-9(3));* pap. 37.95 incl. audio *(978-1-59112-243-2(0))* Live Oak Media.
—Horace & Morris but Mostly Dolores. Walrod, Amy, illus. 2003. 30p. (J). (gr. -1-3). 15.65 *(978-0-7569-2936-7(9))* Perfection Learning Corp.
—Horace & Morris Join the Chorus (but What about Dolores?) Walrod, Amy, illus. 2006. (J). pap. 44.95 incl. audio compact disk *(978-1-59112-909-7(5));* pap. incl. audio *(978-1-59112-449-8(2))* Live Oak Media.
—Horace & Morris Join the Chorus (but What about Dolores?) Walrod, Amy, illus. 2005. (ENG.). 32p. (J). (gr. -1-3). 7.99 *(978-1-4169-0616-2(9),* Atheneum Bks. for Young Readers) Simon & Schuster Children's Publishing.
—Horace & Morris Say Cheese (Which Makes Dolores Sneeze!) Walrod, Amy, illus. (ENG.). 32p. (J). (gr. -1-3). 2010. 7.99 *(978-0-689-87177-1(5))* 2009. 16.99 *(978-0-689-83940-5(5))* Simon & Schuster Children's Publishing. (Atheneum Bks. for Young Readers).
Howie, Vicki. Silent Night. Kallai, Kriszta Nagy, illus. 2009. 32p. (J). (gr. -1). pap. 13.49 *(978-0-7586-1779-8(8))* Concordia Publishing Hse.
Hubery, Julia. When Grandma Saved Christmas. Pedler, Caroline, illus. 2014. (ENG.). 32p. (J). (gr. -1-3). 16.99 *(978-1-58925-164-9(4))* Tiger Tales.
Huck, Jeremy. Charlie, the Christmas Caterpillar, & Marvin Mouse. 2013. 16p. pap. 24.95 *(978-1-62709-632-4(9))* America Star Bks.
Hughes, Mónica. Little Mouse Deer & the Crocodile. Moricuchi, Mique, illus. 2004. 24p. (J). lib. bdg. 23.65 *(978-1-59646-684-5(7))* Dingles & Co.
Hurrell, Dianne. Tom Burrows & Friends: Short Stories, Rhymes & Poems. 2010. (ENG., Illus.). 50p. pap. *(978-1-84748-782-7(3))* Athena Pr.
Husar, Stephane. Cat & Mouse Come to My House! Mehee, Loic, illus. 2015. (Av2 Fiction Readalong 2016 Ser.). (ENG.). (J). lib. bdg. 34.28 *(978-1-4896-3804-5(0),* AV2 by Weigl) Weigl Pubs., Inc.
—Cat & Mouse Eat Good Food! Mehee, Loic, illus. 2015. (Av2 Fiction Readalong 2016 Ser.). (ENG.). (J). lib. bdg. 34.28 *(978-1-4896-3807-6(5),* AV2 by Weigl) Weigl Pubs., Inc.
—Cat & Mouse Feelings. Mehee, Loic, illus. 2015. (Av2 Fiction Readalong 2016 Ser.). (ENG.). (J). lib. bdg. 34.28 *(978-1-4896-3810-6(5),* AV2 by Weigl) Weigl Pubs., Inc.
—Cat & Mouse Let's Go Shopping! Mehee, Loic, illus. 2015. (Av2 Fiction Readalong 2016 Ser.). (ENG.). (J). lib. bdg. 34.28 *(978-1-4896-3816-8(4),* AV2 by Weigl) Weigl Pubs., Inc.
—Cat & Mouse Meet the Animals! Mehee, Loic, illus. 2015. (Av2 Fiction Readalong 2016 Ser.). (ENG.). (J). lib. bdg. 34.28 *(978-1-4896-3819-9(9),* AV2 by Weigl) Weigl Pubs., Inc.
Hutton, John. Flowers for Mr. President. 2012. (Illus.). (J). *(978-0-9789608-3-4(1))* Salem Academy & College.
—Sister Maus: A Small Tale of Sisters House in Salem. 2006. (Illus.). 32p. (J). 20.00 *(978-0-9789608-0-3(7))* Salem Academy & College.
Huusmann, Thomas-Bo & Fables, Aesops. The Lion & the Mouse. 2013. 26p. pap. *(978-87-995724-4-1(3))* Huusmann, Thomas-Bo.
I Am a Painter: Individual Title, 6 Packs. (Sails Literacy Ser.). 16p. (gr. k-18). 27.00 *(978-0-7635-4410-2(8))* Rigby Education.
I Can: Individual Title Six-Packs. (Sails Literacy Ser.). 16p. (gr. k-18). 27.00 *(978-0-7635-4396-9(9))* Rigby Education.
I Like Boxes: Individual Title, 6 Packs. (Sails Literacy Ser.). 16p. (gr. k-18). 27.00 *(978-0-7635-4442-3(6))* Rigby Education.
I Like Riding: Individual Title, 6 Packs. (Sails Literacy Ser.). 16p. (gr. k-18). 27.00 *(978-0-7635-4400-3(0))* Rigby Education.
ImageBooks Staff. Little Mouse. 2007. (Little Finger Puppet Board Bks.: FING). (ENG., Illus.). 12p. (J). (gr. -1 — 1). bds. 6.99 *(978-0-8118-6110-6(4))* Chronicle Bks. LLC.
Isbell, Shaun. The Mouse & the Witch, 1 vol. 2009. 56p. pap. 16.95 *(978-1-61546-892-8(7))* PublishAmerica, Inc.
Iwamura, Kazuo. Seven Little Mice Have Fun on the Ice. 2011. (ENG., Illus.). 32p. (J). (gr. -1-2). 16.95 *(978-0-7358-4048-5(2))* North-South Bks., Inc.
Iwamura, Kazuo & Yamashita, Haruo. Seven Little Mice Go to School. 2011. (ENG., Illus.). 32p. (J). (gr. -1-k). 17.95 *(978-0-7358-4012-6(1))* North-South Bks., Inc.
Jacques, Brian. Doomwyte. 2008. (Redwall Ser.). (ENG., Illus.). 384p. (J). (gr. 5-18). 23.99 *(978-0-399-24544-2(8),* Philomel Bks.) Penguin Young Readers Group.
—The Legend of Luke. 2005. (Redwall Ser.). (ENG., Illus.). 384p. (J). (gr. 5-7). pap. 8.99 *(978-0-14-250109-2(3),* Firebird) Penguin Young Readers Group.
—Mariel of Redwall. Chalk, Gary, illus. 2003. (Redwall Ser.). (ENG.). 400p. (J). (gr. 5-5). pap. 9.99 *(978-0-14-230239-2(2),* Firebird) Penguin Young Readers Group.
—Mariel of Redwall. 2004. (Redwall Ser.). 1.00 *(978-1-4175-6449-1(0))* Recorded Bks., Inc.
—Martin the Warrior. Chalk, Gary, illus. 2004. (Redwall Ser.). (ENG.). 384p. (J). (gr. 5-18). pap. 9.99 *(978-0-14-240055-5(6),* Firebird) Penguin Young Readers Group.
—Mattimeo. Chalk, Gary, illus. 2003. (Redwall Ser.). (ENG.). 448p. (J). (gr. 5-7). pap. 9.99 *(978-0-14-230240-8(6),* Firebird) Penguin Young Readers Group.
—Mattimeo. 2003. (Redwall Ser.). 1.00 *(978-1-4175-5316-7(2))* Recorded Bks., Inc.
—Die Mauer. pap. 19.95 *(978-3-570-26021-0(6))* Bertelsman, Verlagsgruppe C. GmbH DEU. Dist: Distribooks, Inc.
—Redwall. Chalk, Gary, illus. 20th anniv. ed. 2007. (Redwall Ser.). (ENG.). 352p. (J). (gr. 5-18). 23.99 *(978-0-399-24794-1(7),* Philomel Bks.) Penguin Young Readers Group.
James, Rosalind. Bertie Rides Again. 2012. (Illus.). 126p. 29.99 *(978-1-4771-2272-3(9))* Xlibris Corp.
Jaskiewicz, A. E. Hickory & the Big Clock. 2006. (ENG.). 56p. per. 16.95 *(978-1-4241-6024-2(3))* America Star Bks.
Jasnoch, Dorothy. Adventure of Little Mouse Maggie. Kern, Kimberly, ed. Jasnoch, Dorothy, illus. 2012. (ENG., Illus.). 36p. pap. 14.99 *(978-1-937752-06-4(2))* Owl About Bks. Pub., Inc.
Jeffs, Stephanie. Llygoden y Nadolig. Wyn, Delyth, tr. from ENG. Thorne, Jenny, illus. 2005. (WEL.). 28p. *(978-1-85994-497-4(3))* Cyhoeddiadau'r Gair.
Jenkins, Amanda. The Lion & the Mouse Shoot Hoops. 2006. (J). pap. *(978-1-4108-7173-2(8))* Benchmark Education Co.
Jeong, SoYun. Lulu the Shy Piglet. Orsolini, Laura, illus. rev. ed. 2014. (MySELF Bookshelf Ser.). (ENG.). 32p. (J). (gr. k-2). pap. 11.94 *(978-1-60357-654-3(1));* lib. bdg. 25.27 *(978-1-59953-645-3(5))* Norwood Hse. Pr.
Jepsen, D. R. Fabulous Fred Gets the Cheese. 2007. 16p. per. 24.95 *(978-1-4241-8456-9(8))* America Star Bks.
Jeram, Anita. Bunny My Honey. Jeram, Anita, illus. 2009. (ENG., Illus.). 22p. (J). (gr. k-k). bds. 7.99 *(978-0-7636-4645-5(8))* Candlewick Pr.
Jerome, Kate Boehm. Miniature Golf Madness. 2005. (Illus.). 32p. (J). 15.95 *(978-0-9769087-3-9(5))* Vertical Connect Pr.
Jeswald, Mary J. The Crazy Adventure of Nicholas Mouse. Trimble, Anne M., illus. 2004. 32p. (J). 14.99 *(978-0-9760651-0-4(X))* OrangeFoot Publishing Co.
Jewell, Teresa. How Charlie Mouse Learned about Cystic Fibrosis. 2011. 48p. pap. 21.66 *(978-1-4567-2557-0(2))* AuthorHouse.
Jitchotvisut, Donna M. Mittens for Christmas. 2009. 376p. 31.95 *(978-1-4401-0372-8(0));* pap. 21.95 *(978-1-4401-0370-4(4))* iUniverse, Inc.
Johnson, Gerald J. J. Bessie's Little Mouse Day Care. Miltenberger, Dave & Miltenberger, Jeri, illus. 2012. 32p. pap. 24.95 *(978-1-62709-430-6(X))* America Star Bks.
—The Mouse Family Christmas, 1 vol. Bousum, Julie, illus. 2009. 26p. pap. 24.95 *(978-1-61546-536-1(7))* America Star Bks.
Johnson, Joanna. Phoebe's Sweater. Johnson, Eric, illus. 2010. (ENG.). 38p. (J). 18.95 *(978-0-578-04697-6(0))* Slate Falls Pr., LLC.
Johnson, Spencer. Who Moved My Cheese? - For Kids: An A-Mazing Way to Change & Win! Pileggi, Steve, illus. 2003. (ENG.). 64p. (J). (gr. -1-3). 20.99 *(978-0-399-24016-4(0),* G.P. Putnam's Sons Books for Young Readers) Penguin Young Readers Group.
Johnston-Brown, A. M. The Chronicles of Pleasant Grove. 2006. (J). pap. 12.95 *(978-0-9760718-5-3(1))* Retriever Pr.
—The Chronicles of Pleasant Grove (Glossary of Terms) 2006. (J). pap. 1.95 *(978-0-9760718-6-0(X))* Retriever Pr.
Jones, Anna, illus. Goodnight, Mouse: A Peek-A-Boo Adventure. 2012. (J). *(978-1-4351-4387-6(6))* Barnes & Noble, Inc.
Jones, Brenda. The Adventures of Murphy the Mouse. Moore, Dwain, illus. 2007. (J). per. 12.99 *(978-1-59712-069-2(3))* Catawba Publishing Co.
Jones, Carroll. Grandma Battles the Mouse. Giovannini, Jody, illus. 2007. 52p. pap. 16.95 *(978-0-9774260-1-0(7))* Orndee Omnimedia, Inc.
Jones, Janey Louise. Martha the Little Mouse. Poh, Jennie, illus. 2016. (Superfairies Ser.). (ENG.). 56p. (gr. k-3). lib. bdg. 23.99 *(978-1-4795-8643-1(9))* Picture Window Bks.
Jones, Rosemary. The Mouse House. 2010. (ENG., Illus.). 52p. pap. *(978-1-84748-818-3(8))* Athena Pr.
Jules, Jacqueline. The Missing Mouse. Smith, Kim, illus. 2015. (Sofia Martinez Ser.). (ENG.). 32p. (gr. k-2). lib. bdg. 21.32 *(978-1-4795-5774-5(9),* Sofia Martinez) Picture Window Bks.
Kabir, Shohag. Mice & Squirrel. 2009. 24p. pap. 13.99 *(978-1-4389-9164-1(9))* AuthorHouse.
Kakugawa, Frances. Wordsworth Dances the Waltz. DeSica, Melissa, illus. 2007. 32p. (J). 10.95 *(978-0-9790647-3-9(2))* Watermark Publishing, LLC.
Kakugawa, Francis. Wordsworth the Poet. Goto, Scott, illus. 2003. 32p. (J). (gr. -1-3). 10.95 *(978-0-9742672-0-3(1))* Watermark Publishing, LLC.
Kawai, Ritsuko. Hamtaro Gets Lost & Other Stories. Kawai, Ritsuko, illus. 2003. (Adventures of Hamtaro Ser.: Vol. 2). (ENG., Illus.). 92p. (J). (gr. 1-3). 9.95 *(978-1-56931-817-1(4))* Viz Media.
—Hamtaro, Vol. 3. Kawai, Ritsuko, illus. 2003. (ENG., Illus.). 16p. (J). pap. 7.95 *(978-1-56931-816-4(6))* Viz Media.
—Let's Play! Vol. 4: A Playground for Ham-Ham. Kawai, Ritsuko, illus. 2003. (Hamtaro Ser.). (ENG., Illus.). 16p. (J). (gr. 1-3). pap. 7.95 *(978-1-56931-821-8(2))* Viz Media.
Keane, Sarah. The Town Mouse & the Country Mouse: An Aesop Fable Retold by Sarah Keane, 1 vol. 2013. (Fiction Readers Ser.). (ENG., Illus.). 24p. (J). (gr. 2-2). pap. 6.99 *(978-1-4333-5525-7(6))* Shell Educational Publishing.
Kellingley, Krystina. Mistflower - the Loneliest Mouse. 2013. (ENG., Illus.). 112p. (J). (gr. -1-12). pap. 9.95 *(978-1-78099-468-0(0),* Our Street Bks.) Hunt, John Publishing Ltd. GBR. Dist: National Bk. Network.
Kelly, Mark. Mousetronaut: Based on a (Partially) True Story. Payne, C. F., illus. 2012. (ENG.). 40p. (J). (gr. -1-3). 17.99 *(978-1-4424-5824-6(0),* Simon & Schuster/Paula Wiseman Bks.) Simon & Schuster/Paula Wiseman Bks.
—Mousetronaut Goes to Mars. Payne, C. F., illus. 2013. (ENG.). 40p. (J). (gr. -1-3). 16.99 *(978-1-4424-8426-9(8),* Simon & Schuster/Paula Wiseman Bks.) Simon & Schuster/Paula Wiseman Bks.
Kelso, Mary Jean & Snider, K. C. Rv Mouse. 2013. 24p. 19.95 *(978-1-61633-399-7(5))* Guardian Angel Publishing, Inc.
Kennedy, Kim & Kennedy, Doug. Hee-Haw-Dini & the Great Zambini. 2009. (ENG., Illus.). 32p. (J). (gr. k-2). 15.95 *(978-0-8109-7025-0(2),* Abrams Bks. for Young Readers) Abrams, Inc.
Kernahan, J. C. & Kernahan, C. Tom, Dot & Talking Mouse & Other Bedtime Stories. 2007. (Illus.). 48p. per. *(978-1-4065-1897-9(2))* Dodo Pr.
Kilgore, Lee. The Mr. Munch Adventures: Six Short Stories, 1 vol. 2010. 73p. pap. 19.95 *(978-1-4489-2876-7(1))* America Star Bks.
Kilner, Dorothy. The Life & Perambulations of a Mouse. 2005. 26.95 *(978-1-4218-0923-6(0),* 1st World Library - Literary Society) 1st World Publishing, Inc.
—Life & Perambulations of a Mouse. 2005. 96p. pap. 10.95 *(978-1-59540-623-1(9),* 1st World Library - Literary Society) 1st World Publishing, Inc.
—The Life & Perambulations of a Mouse. 2004. reprint ed. pap. 15.95 *(978-1-4191-6941-0(6))* Kessinger Publishing, LLC.
—The Life & Perambulations of A Mouse. 2004. reprint ed. pap. 1.99 *(978-1-4192-6941-7(0))* Kessinger Publishing, LLC.
Kim, YeShil. The Very Best Teacher. Moriuchi, Mique, illus. 2015. (ENG.). 24p. (J). (-3). 12.99 *(978-1-4926-0998-8(6))* Sourcebooks, Inc.
King-smith, Dick. Three Terrible Trins. 105p. (J). pap. 4.99 *(978-0-8072-1482-4(5),* Listening Library) Random Hse. Audio Publishing Group.
Kirk, Daniel. Library Mouse, No. 1. 2007. (ENG., Illus.). 32p. (J). (gr. 1-4). 17.95 *(978-0-8109-9346-4(5),* Abrams Bks. for Young Readers) Abrams, Inc.
—Library Mouse. 2010. (ENG., Illus.). 32p. (J). (gr. 1-4). pap. 7.95 *(978-0-8109-8929-0(8))* UK Abrams Bks. for Young Readers.
—Library Mouse: A World to Explore. 2010. (ENG., Illus.). 32p. (J). (gr. 1-4). 17.95 *(978-0-8109-8968-9(9),* Abrams Bks. for Young Readers) Abrams, Inc.
—Library Mouse: Home Sweet Home. 2013. (ENG., Illus.). 40p. (J). (gr. 1-4). 17.95 *(978-1-4197-0544-1(X),* Abrams Bks. for Young Readers) Abrams, Inc.
—Library Mouse Bk. 2: A Friend's Tale. 2009. (ENG., Illus.). 32p. (J). (gr. 1-4). 17.95 *(978-0-8109-8927-6(1),* Abrams Bks. for Young Readers) Abrams, Inc.
—Library Mouse No. 2: A Friend's Tale. 2010. (ENG., Illus.). 32p. (J). (gr. 1-4). pap. 7.95 *(978-0-8109-8930-6(1))* UK Abrams Bks. for Young Readers.
Kirkwood, Jeff. The Adventures of Little Mouse. 2008. (ENG.). 24p. pap. 12.99 *(978-1-4389-2874-6(2))* AuthorHouse.
Kleven, Elisa. Welcome Home, Mouse. Kleven, Elisa, illus. 2010. (ENG., Illus.). 32p. (J). (gr. -1-2). 15.99 *(978-1-58246-277-6(1),* Tricycle Pr.) Random Hse. Children's Bks.
Kimpton, Diana. Amy Wild, Animal Talker - the Musical Mouse. 2013. pap. 4.99 *(978-0-7945-3145-4(8),* Usborne) EDC Publishing.
Kline, Trish & Donev, Mary. Don't Frown, Clown! KA Reader 9. 2007. (Illus.). 32p. (J). per. 20.00 *(978-1-934307-02-1(5))* Ghost Hunter Productions.
Klise, Kate. Pop Goes the Circus! Klise, M. Sarah, illus. 2015. (Three-Ring Rascals Ser.: 4). (ENG.). 144p. (J). (gr. 2-5). 15.95 *(978-1-61620-464-8(8))* Algonquin Bks. of Chapel Hill.
Klise, Kate & Klise, M. Sarah. The Greatest Star on Earth. Klise, M. Sarah, illus. 2014. (Three-Ring Rascals Ser.: 2). (ENG., Illus.). 144p. (J). (gr. 2-5). 15.95 *(978-1-61620-245-3(9),* 73245) Algonquin Bks. of Chapel Hill.
Knight, Hilary. A Firefly in a Fir Tree: A Carol for Mice. Knight, Hilary, illus. 2004. (Illus.). 32p. (J). (gr. -1-3). lib. bdg. 15.89 *(978-0-06-000992-2(6),* Tegen, Katherine Bks) HarperCollins Pubs.
Knowles, Daniel S. Mouse. 2011. 710p. pap. 23.99 *(978-1-4535-9629-6(1))* Xlibris Corp.
Koch, Theresa F. The Gift of Laughter. 2007. 16p. per. 24.95 *(978-1-4241-8343-2(X))* America Star Bks.
Kousky, Vern. Otto the Owl Who Loved Poetry. Kousky, Vern, illus. 2015. (ENG., Illus.). 32p. (J). (gr. k-3). 16.99 *(978-0-399-16440-8(5),* Nancy Paulsen Books) Penguin Young Readers Group.
Kraus, Robert. Whose Mouse Are You? Aruego, Jose, illus. 2005. (ENG.). 40p. (J). (gr. -1-3). 4.99 *(978-1-4169-0311-6(9),* Simon & Schuster/Paula Wiseman Bks.) Simon & Schuster/Paula Wiseman Bks.
Krause, John & Chua, Maria. Poco Loco, 0 vols. 2013. (ENG.). 32p. (J). (gr. -1-3). 15.99 *(978-1-4778-1649-3(6),* 9781477816493, Amazon Children's Publishing) Amazon Publishing.
Krensky, Stephen. Case of the Missing Mice: A Simon Mystery. 2003. (Illus.). 14.95 *(978-1-59319-022-4(0))* LeapFrog Enterprises, Inc.
—Malarkey & the Big Trap. Shortley, Michele, illus. 2011. 29p. (J). pap. *(978-0-7680-3487-5(6))* SAE Intl.
Kroll, Steven. The Biggest Christmas Tree Ever. Bassett, Jeni, illus. 2009. (ENG.). 32p. (J). (gr. -1-3). pap. 4.99 *(978-0-545-12119-4(1),* Cartwheel Bks.) Scholastic, Inc.
—The Biggest Easter Basket Ever. Bassett, Jeni, illus. 2008. (ENG.). 32p. (J). (gr. -1-3). pap. 4.99 *(978-0-545-01702-2(5),* Cartwheel Bks.) Scholastic, Inc.
—The Biggest Pumpkin Ever. Bassett, Jeni, illus. 2007. (ENG.). 32p. (J). (gr. -1-k). pap. 4.99 *(978-0-439-92946-2(6))* Scholastic, Inc.

—The Biggest Snowman Ever. Bassett, Jeni, illus. 2005. (ENG.). 32p. (J). (gr. -1-3). 4.99 (978-0-439-62768-9(0), Cartwheel Bks.) Scholastic, Inc.

—The Biggest Valentine Ever. Bassett, Jeni, illus. 2006. (ENG.). 32p. (J). (gr. -1-1). pap. 3.99 (978-0-439-76419-3(X)) Scholastic, Inc.

—The Hanukkah Mice, 0 vols. Shapiro, Michelle, illus. 2012. (ENG.). 42p. (J). (gr. -1-3). pap. 7.99 (978-0-7614-5988-0(X), 9780761459880, Amazon Children's Publishing) Amazon Publishing.

Kroupa, Robert J. Just Like You. 2011. (J). (978-0-9825503-4-2(0)) IGI Pr.

Kuhlmann, Torben. Armstrong: The Adventurous Journey of a Mouse to the Moon. 2016. (ENG., Illus.). 128p. (J). 19.95 (978-0-7358-4262-5(0)) North-South Bks., Inc.

—Lindbergh: The Tale of a Flying Mouse. 2014. (ENG., Illus.). 96p. (J). (gr. k-k). 19.95 (978-0-7358-4167-3(5)) North-South Bks., Inc.

Labadie, Sally Zolkosky. The Schoolhouse Mouse. 2013. 32p. pap. (978-1-4602-3128-9(7)) FriesenPress.

Lamb, Lenny. Facing Your Fears: Greener Grass Volume 4. 2012. 48p. pap. 24.95 (978-1-4626-5398-0(7)) America Star Bks.

Lambert, Jonny. The Great AAA-OOO! Lambert, Jonny, illus. 2016. (ENG., Illus.). 32p. (J). (gr. -1-2). 16.99 (978-1-68010-032-7(7)) Tiger Tales.

Landa, Norbert. The Secret House of Papa Mouse. Turk, Hanne, illus. 2004. (Picture Books/Quality Time Ser.). 32p. (gr. k-3). lib. bdg. 26.00 (978-0-8368-4106-0(9), Gareth Stevens Learning Library) Stevens, Gareth Publishing LLLP.

Lang, Andrew. The Queen & the Mouse: A Story about Friendship. Lohmann, Renate, illus. 2006. (J). (978-1-59939-081-9(7), Reader's Digest Young Families, Inc.) Studio Fun International.

Lange, Willem. The White-Footed Mouse. Dodson, Bert, illus. 2012. (ENG.). 32p. (J). (gr. 1-3). 17.95 (978-1-59373-109-0(4)) Bunker Hill Publishing, Inc.

Langford, Virginia. Monty Says Mice Are Nice. 2009. 20p. pap. 12.95 (978-1-4389-3429-7(7)) AuthorHouse.

Langley, Noel. Desbarolida, the Waltzing Mouse. Ardizzone, Edward, illus. 2008. 80p. pap. (978-1-905946-01-3(5)) Durrant Publishing.

LaRochelle, David. This Is Not a Cat. Wohnoutka, Mike, illus. 2016. (ENG.). 40p. (J). (gr. -1). 14.95 (978-1-4549-1574-4(9)) Sterling Publishing Co., Inc.

Larson, Angela. Anthony Smoochiano: First Loves. 2012. pap. (978-1-4507-7998-2(0)) Independent Pub.

Le Gall, Frank. Freedom! Balthazar, Flore, illus. 2012. (Miss Annie Ser.). 48p. (J). (gr. 2-4). pap. 39.62 (978-0-7613-9281-1(5)); (ENG.). lib. bdg. 29.27 (978-0-7613-7884-6(7)) Lerner Publishing Group. (Graphic Universe™).

—Miss Annie. Balthazar, Flore, illus. 2012. (Miss Annie Ser.). 48p. (J). (gr. 2-4). lib. bdg. 58.54 (978-0-7613-8902-6(4), Graphic Universe™) Lerner Publishing Group.

—Miss Annie: 6Pack Set. Balthazar, Flore, illus. 2012. (Miss Annie Ser.). 48p. (J). (gr. 2-4). pap. 79.23 (978-0-7613-9284-2(X), Graphic Universe™) Lerner Publishing Group.

—Miss Annie: Single Copy Set. Balthazar, Flore, illus. 2012. (Miss Annie Ser.). 48p. (J). (gr. 2-4). pap. 13.21 (978-0-7613-9283-5(1), Graphic Universe™) Lerner Publishing Group.

—Rooftop Cat. Balthazar, Flore, illus. 2012. (Miss Annie Ser.). 48p. (J). (gr. 2-4). pap. 39.62 (978-0-7613-9282-8(3)); (ENG.). lib. bdg. 29.27 (978-0-7613-7885-3(5)) Lerner Publishing Group. (Graphic Universe™).

Le Guin, Ursula K. Tom Mouse. 2004. (Illus.). (J). (gr. k-3). spiral bd. (978-0-616-14584-5(5)) Canadian National Institute for the Blind/Institut National Canadien pour les Aveugles.

Leathers, Philippa. How to Catch a Mouse. Leathers, Philippa, illus. 2015. (ENG., Illus.). 40p. (J). (gr. -1-2). 15.99 (978-0-7636-6912-6(1)) Candlewick Pr.

Leavitt, Lindsey. The Big Move. Ford, A. G., illus. 2016. (Commander in Cheese Ser.: 1). (ENG.). 112p. (J). (gr. 2-5). 4.99 (978-1-101-93112-7(4), Random Hse. Bks. for Young Readers) Random Hse. Children's Bks.

—Have a Mice Flight! Ford, A. G., illus. 2016. (Commander in Cheese Ser.: 3). (ENG.). 112p. (J). (gr. 2-5). 4.99 (978-1-101-93118-9(3), Random Hse. Bks. for Young Readers) Random Hse. Children's Bks.

—Oval Office Escape. Ford, A. G., illus. 2016. (Commander in Cheese Ser.: 2). (ENG.). 112p. (J). (gr. 2-5). 4.99 (978-1-101-93115-8(9), Random Hse. Bks. for Young Readers) Random Hse. Children's Bks.

LeBaron, Cecilia. Nat & Tab. 2007. (Illus.). 16p. (J). 5.95 (978-0-9798869-0-4(2)) Crush Publishing.

Lecaye, Olga. El Ratoncito Perez. (SPA.). 40p. 18.95 (978-84-95150-03-5(4)); 2005. 24p. (J). 9.95 (978-84-8470-051-7(8)) Corimbo, Editorial S.L. ESP. Dist: Distribooks, Inc., Iaconi, Mariuccia Bk. Imports.

Lee, P. Janet. Ella Elephant: And Her Fear of Mice. 2007. (ENG., Illus.). 36p. (J). per. 15.95 (978-1-59800-713-8(0)) Outskirts Pr., Inc.

Leeson, Christine. Just for You! Ellis, Andy, illus. (Tiger Tales Ser.). (J). 2008. 24p. (gr. -1-2). pap. 6.95 (978-1-58925-408-4(2)) 2004. 32p. tchr. ed. 15.95 (978-1-58925-042-0(7)) Tiger Tales.

—Molly & the Storm. Hansen, Gaby, illus. 2003. 32p. (J). (gr. k-2). tchr. ed. 15.95 (978-1-58925-027-7(3)) Tiger Tales.

—The Snow Angel. Chapman, Jane, illus. 2016. (ENG.). 32p. (J). (gr. -1-2). mass mkt. 3.99 (978-1-58925-494-7(5)) Tiger Tales.

Leonard, Nellie M. Grand Daddy Whiskers, M. D. 2004. reprint ed. pap. 1.99 (978-1-4192-2227-6(9)); pap. 15.95 (978-1-4191-2227-9(4)) Kessinger Publishing, LLC.

Lestelle, Wende. Science Mouse. 2004. pap. (978-1-930493-65-0(7)) Athena Pr.

LeTourneau, Marie & Baty, Danielle Reed. The Mice of Bistrot des Sept Frères. 2008. (ENG & FRE.). 32p. (J). (gr. -1-3). pap. 7.95 (978-1-933718-18-7(8)) Tanglewood Pr.

Leung, Julie. Mice of the Round Table #2: Voyage to Avalon. Carr, Lindsey, illus. 2017. (Mice of the Round Table Ser.: 2). 336p. (J). (gr. 3-7). 16.99 **(978-0-06-240402-2(4))** HarperCollins Pubs.

Leung, Julie. A Tail of Camelot. Carr, Lindsey, illus. 2016. (Mice of the Round Table Ser.: 1). 304p. (J). (gr. 3-7). 16.99 (978-0-06-240399-5(0)) HarperCollins Pubs.

Lias, Joe. The Wood Rats Dragging Their Long Tales. 2005. 183p. pap. 24.95 (978-1-4137-5900-6(9)) America Star Bks.

Lieberman, Sylvia. Archibald's Swiss Cheese Mountain. Wendell, Jeremy, illus. 2007. 44p. (J). (gr. k-2). 17.95 (978-0-9795852-5-8(2)) Seven Locks Pr.

Linehan, Jess Golden. Martin Mixed-Up at the Beach. 2011. (ENG., Illus.). 32p. (J). 15.95 (978-0-615-45705-5(3)) Salty Pond Pubs.

Lionni, Leo. Alexander & the Wind-Up Mouse. 2014. (Step into Reading Ser.). (ENG., Illus.). 40p. (J). (gr. 1-4). 3.99 (978-0-385-75551-1(1), Random Hse. Bks. for Young Readers) Random Hse. Children's Bks.

—Frederic. (FRE.). (J). pap. 14.95 (978-2-211-06589-4(9)) Archimede Editions FRA. Dist: Distribooks, Inc.

—Frederick. 2017. (ENG.). 32p. (J). (gr. -1-2). 7.99 (978-0-399-55552-7(8), Dragonfly Bks.) Random Hse. Children's Bks.

—Geraldine, the Music Mouse. Lionni, Leo, illus. 2016. (ENG., Illus.). 32p. (J). (gr. -1-2). 17.99 (978-0-394-84238-7(3)); 20.99 (978-0-394-94238-4(8)) Random Hse. Children's Bks. (Knopf Bks. for Young Readers).

—Geraldine, the Music Mouse. 2009. (ENG., Illus.). 32p. (J). (gr. -1-2). pap. 7.99 (978-0-375-85514-6(9), Dragonfly Bks.) Random Hse. Children's Bks.

—The Greentail Mouse. 2003. (ENG., Illus.). 32p. (J). (gr. -1-2). 15.95 (978-0-375-82399-2(9), Knopf Bks. for Young Readers) Random Hse. Children's Bks.

—Let's Play. 2003. (ENG., Illus.). 28p. (J). (— 1). bds. 6.99 (978-0-375-82528-6(2), Knopf Bks. for Young Readers) Random Hse. Children's Bks.

—Nicolas, Where Have You Been? 2010. (ENG., Illus.). 32p. (J). (gr. -1-2). pap. 6.99 (978-0-375-85549-8(1), Dragonfly Bks.) Random Hse. Children's Bks.

—El Sueno de Matias. (SPA.). 32p. (J). (gr. 1-3). 13.56 (978-84-264-3675-7(7), LM4689) Editorial Lumen ESP. Dist: Lectorum Pubns., Inc.

—Tillie & the Wall. Lionni, Leo, illus. 2014. (ENG., Illus.). 32p. (J). (gr. -1-2). 17.99 (978-0-394-82155-9(6), Knopf Bks. for Young Readers) Random Hse. Children's Bks.

Listening with Zachary. (J). pap. 13.75 (978-0-8136-4655-8(3)) Modern Curriculum Pr.

Litchmore, Michael. The MB Force: Heroes at the Best! 2007. 56p. pap. 9.00 (978-0-8059-7399-0(0)) Dorrance Publishing Co., Inc.

Lithgow, John. Mahalia Mouse Goes to College. Oleynikov, Igor, illus. 2007. (ENG.). 40p. (J). (gr. -1-3). 17.99 (978-1-4169-2715-0(8), Simon & Schuster Bks. For Young Readers) Simon & Schuster Bks. For Young Readers.

Litton, Jonathan. Mouse in the Haunted House. Anderson, Nicola, illus. 2015. (Planet Pop-Up Ser.). (ENG.). 12p. (J). (gr. -1). 12.95 (978-1-62686-485-6(3), Silver Dolphin Bks.) Readerlink Distribution Services, LLC.

Lobel, Arnold. Historias de Ratones. 2003. (SPA.). 64p. (978-84-95123-95-4(9), KA7695) Kalandraka Editora, S.L. ESP. Dist: Lectorum Pubns., Inc.

—Sopa de Ratón. 2003. (SPA., Illus.). 62p. (gr. 1-3). pap. 10.99 (978-980-257-286-1(1)) Ekare, Ediciones VEN. Dist: Lectorum Pubns., Inc.

Lois, Lowry & Rohmann, Eric. Bless This Mouse. Lois, Lowry & Rohmann, Eric, illus. 2011. (ENG., Illus.). 160p. (J). (gr. 2-5). 16.99 (978-0-547-39009-3(2)) Houghton Mifflin Harcourt Publishing Co.

Long, Ethan. Me & My Big Mouse, 0 vols. 2014. (ENG.). 32p. (J). (gr. -1-k). 16.99 (978-1-4778-4728-2(6), 9781477847282, Amazon Children's Publishing) Amazon Publishing.

Long, Julie Anne. A Notorious Countess Confesses: Pennyroyal Green Series. 2012. (Pennyroyal Green Ser.: 7). (ENG.). 384p. mass mkt. 5.99 (978-0-06-211802-8(1), Avon Bks.) HarperCollins Pubs.

Lord, Cynthia. Hot Rod Hamster. Anderson, Derek, illus. 2010. (ENG.). 40p. (J). (gr. -1-k). 18.99 (978-0-545-03530-9(9), Scholastic Pr.) Scholastic, Inc.

—Hot Rod Hamster & the Awesome ATV Adventure! Anderson, Derek, illus. 2015. (ENG.). 32p. (J). 16.99 (978-0-545-76734-7(2)); pap. 3.99 (978-0-545-62680-4(3)) Scholastic, Inc. (Scholastic Pr.).

—Hot Rod Hamster Meets His Match! Anderson, Derek, illus. 2016. (Scholastic Reader, Level 2 Ser.). (ENG.). 32p. (J). (gr. -1-2). pap. 3.99 (978-0-545-82591-7(1), Scholastic Pr.) Scholastic, Inc.

Lord, Pia. The Adventures of M M , Music Mouse. 2011. 50p. pap. 16.95 (978-1-4626-3755-3(8)) America Star Bks.

Louthain, J. A. Ame the Elephant: Terrorized by Evil Mice. Eberbach, Andrea, illus. 2nd l.t. ed. 2003. 48p. (J). 12.97 (978-0-9679416-2-2(8), 0-9679416-2-8) Alexie Bks.

Low, Alice. Blueberry Mouse. Friend, David Michael, tr. Friend, David Michael, illus. 2004. (J). 15.95 (978-1-59336-111-2(4)); pap. (978-1-59336-112-9(2)) Mondo Publishing.

Lowe, Nakesha. It's All about Me. 2010. 12p. 17.50 (978-1-4490-8464-6(8)) AuthorHouse.

Loyd, Mark. Big Ben: A Little Known Story. Loyd, Mark, illus. 2005. (Illus.). (J). (978-0-9773317-1-0(7)) Too Fun Publshing.

Lucado, Max. Itsy Bitsy Christmas: You're Never Too Little for His Love, 1 vol. 2013. (ENG., Illus.). 32p. (J). 14.99 (978-1-4003-2262-6(6)); pap. 9.99 (978-1-4003-2404-0(1)) Nelson, Thomas Inc.

Lurie, Susan. Will You Be My Friend? Head, Murray, illus. 2016. (ENG.). 32p. (J). 16.99 (978-1-250-04643-7(2), 9781250046437) Feiwel & Friends.

Lynne, Kimberlee, illus. The Frog & the Mouse. 2011. (First Steps in Music Ser.). (ENG.). 32p. (J). (gr. k-2). 16.95 (978-1-57999-802-8(X)) G I A Pubns., Inc.

Lyon, Tammie Speer, illus. Hickory Dickory Dock! gif. ed. 2006. 10p. (J). (gr. -1-k). bds. 10.95 (978-1-57791-213-2(6)) Brighter Minds Children's Publishing.

MacDonald, Alan. Scaredy Mouse. Warnes, Tim, illus. 2007. (Storytime Board Bks.). 16p. (J). (gr. -1-k). bds. 6.95 (978-1-58925-827-3(4)) Tiger Tales.

Macho, Geri. A Beautiful Mouse, 1 vol. 2009. 44p. pap. 24.95 (978-1-60703-004-1(7)) America Star Bks.

Mack, Jeff. Mine. 2017. (ENG., Illus.). 40p. (J). 16.99 (978-1-4521-5234-9(9)) Chronicle Bks. LLC.

Mack, Jeff, illus. Good News, Bad News. 2012. (ENG.). 40p. (J). (gr. -1-1). 16.99 (978-1-4521-0110-1(8)) Chronicle Bks. LLC.

Madonna, Lenae. Lost & Found. Conde, Manuel, illus. 2012. 38p. (J). 16.95 (978-1-60131-115-3(X), Castlebridge Bks.) Big Tent Bks.

Make Believe Ideas, creator. Twinkle Book & Mouse Plush. 2007. (Illus.). (J). (gr. -1-3). (978-1-84610-694-1(X)) Make Believe Ideas.

Malaspina, Ann. The Mouse & the Wizard: A Hindu Folktale. Sylvaine, Jenny, illus. 2013. (Folktales from Around the World Ser.). (ENG.). 24p. (J). (gr. k-3). 28.50 (978-1-62323-633-5(9), 206384) Child's World, Inc., The.

Mangum, Ariana. Carlos, the Mouse Who Discovered Americ. 2008. 272p. pap. 17.99 (978-1-4343-6344-2(9)) AuthorHouse.

Mariconda, Barbara. ¡Clasifícalo! Rogers, Sherry, illus. 2008.Tr. of Sort it Out! (SPA.). 32p. (J). (gr. k-4). 17.95 (978-1-60718-695-3(0)) Arbordale Publishing.

Marinaro, Stacy. The Cat who rules the Star Mice. 2009. 32p. pap. 15.95 (978-0-557-08180-6(7)) Lulu Pr., Inc.

Marquez, Sofia. Pepe Perez Mexican Mouse: Pepe Perez Comes to the United States: Book 1, 1 vol. Marquez, Sofia, illus. 2009. (Illus.). 20p. pap. 24.95 (978-1-61546-496-8(4)) America Star Bks.

Martin, David Lozell. All for Pie, Pie for All. Gorbachev, Valeri, illus. 2008. (ENG.). 32p. (J). (gr. -1-2). pap. 6.99 (978-0-7636-3891-7(9)) Candlewick Pr.

Martin, Lisa & Martin, Valerie. Anton & Cecil, Book 2: Cats on Track. Murphy, Kelly, illus. 2015. (Anton & Cecil Ser.: 2). (ENG.). 272p. (J). (gr. 3-7). 16.95 (978-1-61620-419-8(2)) Algonquin Bks. of Chapel Hill.

Martin, Rosemary. Rosie's Story. 2011. (ENG., Illus.). 32p. pap. (978-1-84876-699-0(8)) Troubador Publishing Ltd.

Martin, Yvonne. A Mouse in the House. 2012. 28p. pap. 18.65 (978-1-4691-3819-0(0)) Xlibris Corp.

Marwood, Diane. The Lion & the Mouse. 2012. (ENG., Illus.). 24p. (J). (978-0-7787-7893-6(2)); pap. (978-0-7787-7905-6(X)) Crabtree Publishing Co.

Matsutani, Miyoko. Peek-A-Boo. Segawa, Yasuo, illus. 2006. 20p. (J). (gr. -1). 10.95 (978-1-74126-047-2(7)) R.I.C. Pubns. AUS. Dist: SCB Distributors.

May, Eleanor. Albert Adds Up! Melmon, Deborah, illus. 2014. (Mouse Math (r) Ser.). 32p. (J). (gr. -1-1). 22.60 (978-1-57565-744-8(9)) Kane Press, Inc.

—Albert Doubles the Fun. Melmon, Deborah, illus. 2017. (Mouse Math (r) Ser.). (ENG.). 32p. (gr. -1-1). 22.65 (978-1-57565-834-6(8)) Kane Press, Inc.

—Albert Doubles the Fun: Adding Doubles. Melmon, Deborah, illus. 2017. (Mouse Math (r) Ser.). (ENG.). 32p. (gr. -1-1). 34.65 **(978-1-57565-836-0(4))** Kane Press, Inc.

—Albert Helps Out: Counting Money. Melmon, Deborah, illus. 2017. (Mouse Math (r) Ser.). (ENG.). 32p. (gr. -1-1). 7.95 (978-1-57565-860-5(7)) Kane Press, Inc.

—Albert Helps Out: Counting Money. Melmon, Deborah, illus. 2017. (Mouse Math (r) Ser.). (ENG.). 32p. (gr. -1-1). lib. bdg. 22.65 (978-1-57565-857-5(7)) Kane Press, Inc.

—Albert Is Not Scared. Melmon, Deborah, illus. 2013. (Mouse Math Ser.). (ENG.). 32p. (J). (gr. -1-1). pap. 7.95 (978-1-57565-629-8(9)); lib. bdg. 22.60 (978-1-57565-628-1(0)) Kane Press, Inc.

—Albert Is Not Scared. 2013. 32p. 22.60 (978-1-57565-630-4(2)) Kane Press, Inc.

—Albert Starts School. Melmon, Deborah, illus. 2015. (Mouse Math (r) Ser.). (ENG.). 32p. (J). (gr. -1-1). 22.60 (978-1-57565-741-7(4)) Kane Press, Inc.

—Albert the Muffin-Maker. Melmon, Deborah, illus. 2014. (Mouse Math Ser.). 32p. (gr. -1-1). lib. bdg. 22.60 (978-1-57565-631-1(0)) Kane Press, Inc.

—Albert's Amazing Snail. Melmon, Deborah, illus. 2012. (Mouse Math Ser.). (ENG.). 32p. (J). (gr. -1-1). 22.60 (978-1-57565-448-5(2)); pap. 7.95 (978-1-57565-442-3(3)) Kane Press, Inc.

—Albert's Bigger Than Big Idea. Melmon, Deborah, illus. 2013. (Mouse Math Ser.). (ENG.). 32p. (gr. -1-1). pap. 7.95 (978-1-57565-522-2(5)) Kane Press, Inc.

—A Beach for Albert. Melmon, Deborah, illus. 2013. (Mouse Math Ser.). 32p. (gr. -1-1). (ENG.). pap. 7.95 (978-1-57565-531-4(4)); lib. bdg. 22.60 (978-1-57565-530-7(6)) Kane Press, Inc.

—Lost in the Mouseum. Melmon, Deborah, illus. 2015. (Mouse Math (r) Ser.). (ENG.). 32p. (J). (gr. -1-1). 22.60 (978-1-57565-643-4(4)) Kane Press, Inc.

—Mice on Ice. Melmon, Deborah, illus. 2013. (Mouse Math Ser.). 32p. (J). (gr. -1-1). 22.60 (978-1-57565-527-7(6)); (ENG.). pap. 7.95 (978-1-57565-528-4(4)) Kane Press, Inc.

—The Mousier the Merrier. Melmon, Deborah, illus. 2012. (Mouse Math Ser.). (ENG.). 32p. (J). (gr. -1-1). 22.60 (978-1-57565-447-8(4)); pap. 7.95 (978-1-57565-440-9(7)) Kane Press, Inc.

—Where's Albert? Counting & Skip Counting. Melmon, Deborah, illus. 2017. (Mouse Math (r) Ser.). (ENG.). 32p. (gr. -1-1). lib. bdg. 22.65 (978-1-57565-855-1(0)) Kane Press, Inc.

—Where's Albert? Counting & Skip Counting. Melmon, Deborah, illus. 2017. (Mouse Math (r) Ser.). (ENG.). 32p. (gr. -1-1). 7.95 (978-1-57565-858-2(5)) Kane Press, Inc.

Maya Z And Nadajia R. Hall. The New-Fangled Adventures of Alexia & Z: The Case of Grams' Missing Teeth. 2009. 36p. pap. 15.95 (978-1-4389-4508-8(6)) AuthorHouse.

Mayerhofer, Felix. Horace the Great Harmonica King. MacFarlane, John, illus. 2006. 31p. (J). (gr. -1-7). per. 16.95 (978-1-60002-255-5(3), 4313) Mountain Valley Publishing, LLC.

Mayhew, James. Bubble & Squeak. Vulliamy, Clara, illus. 2013. (J). (978-1-4351-4770-6(7)) Barnes & Noble, Inc.

Mazula, Derek. A Drifen's Tale. 2009. 48p. pap. 24.99 (978-1-4490-2782-7(2)) AuthorHouse.

Mcadams, Kate. Flynn the Post Office Mouse. 2010. 28p. pap. 12.49 (978-1-4520-0816-5(7)) AuthorHouse.

Mcaleney, Kimberly. The Mouse & the Music Box: A Bedtime Story. 2008. 16p. pap. 8.49 (978-1-4389-3134-0(4)) AuthorHouse.

McAllister, Angela. A Mouse So Small. Pedler, Caroline, illus. 2015. (ENG.). 32p. (J). (gr. -1-3). 16.99 (978-1-58925-194-6(6)) Tiger Tales.

McCully, Emily Arnold. First Snow. McCully, Emily Arnold, illus. 2003. (ENG., Illus.). 32p. (J). (gr. -1-3). 17.99 (978-0-06-623852-4(8)) HarperCollins Pubs.

—Late Nate in a Race. McCully, Emily Arnold, illus. 2013. (I Like to Read(r) Ser.). (ENG., Illus.). 24p. (J). (gr. -1-3). pap. 6.99 (978-0-8234-2755-0(2)) Holiday Hse., Inc.

—Picnic. McCully, Emily Arnold, illus. 2003. (Illus.). 32p. (J). (gr. -1-k). 16.89 (978-0-06-623855-5(2)); (ENG., 17.99 (978-0-06-623854-8(4)) HarperCollins Pubs.

—School. McCully, Emily Arnold, illus. 2005. (Illus.). 32p. (J). lib. bdg. 16.89 (978-0-06-623857-9(9)) HarperCollins Pubs.

McElreath, Kim. Mikey the Schoolhouse Mouse. 2006. (J). 13.95 (978-0-9769271-1-2(X)) McElreath, K.M.

McGowan, Steve. The Adventures of Keke & the Golden Coconut. 2012. 48p. pap. 21.92 (978-1-4251-4407-4(1)) Trafford Publishing.

McGregor, Suzy. The Garden Fairy & Mrs. Mouse. 2013. 58p. pap. 14.95 (978-0-9824926-6-6(9)) Lollipop Media Productions, LP.

McHeffey, Adam. Rudy & Claude Splash into Art, 0 vols. 2014. (ENG., Illus.). 32p. (J). (gr. -1-2). 16.99 (978-1-4778-4777-0(4), 9781477847770, Amazon Children's Publishing) Amazon Publishing.

McIntyre, Mel & Mcintyre, Mel. Flutter Bunnies Fossil of Fortune. Grady, Kit, illus. 2011. 20p. pap. 9.95 (978-1-61633-170-2(4)) Guardian Angel Publishing, Inc.

McMillan, Bruce. Mouse Views. 2014. 32p. pap. 7.00 (978-1-61003-308-4(6)) Center for the Collaborative Classroom.

McMullan, Kate. One Funny Day. Alley, R. W., illus. 2012. (Pearl & Wagner Ser.: 1). (ENG.). 48p. (J). (gr. 1-3). pap. 3.99 (978-0-448-45866-3(7), Penguin Young Readers) Penguin Young Readers Group.

—Pearl & Wagner: Three Secrets. 2013. (Penguin Young Readers Level 3 Ser.). lib. bdg. 13.55 (978-0-606-31708-5(2), Turtleback) Turtleback Bks.

—Three Secrets. Alley, R. W., illus. 2013. (Pearl & Wagner Ser.: 3). (ENG.). 48p. (J). (gr. 1-3). pap. 3.99 (978-0-448-46472-5(1), Penguin Young Readers) Penguin Young Readers Group.

—Two Good Friends. Alley, R. W., illus. 2011. (Pearl & Wagner Ser.: 2). (ENG.). 48p. (J). (gr. 1-3). pap. 3.99 (978-0-448-45690-4(7), Penguin Young Readers) Penguin Young Readers Group.

Meachen Rau, Dana. Sweet Pea: Escape in the Garden. Hannon, Holly, illus. 2006. (J). (978-1-58987-200-4(2)) Kindermusik International.

The Meadow Mouse Treasury: Stories, Poems, Pictures from Canada's Finest Authors & Illustrators. (Illus.). (J). 9.99 (978-0-88899-249-9(1)) Groundwood Bks. CAN. Dist: Publishers Group West (PGW).

Meadows, Daisy. Molly Twinkletail Runs Away. 2015. (Magic Animal Friends Ser.: 2). (ENG.). 112p. (J). (gr. 2-5). pap. 4.99 (978-0-545-68644-0(X), Scholastic Paperbacks) Scholastic, Inc.

Meadows, Michelle. Itsy-Bitsy Baby Mouse. Cordell, Matthew, illus. 2012. (ENG.). 40p. (J). (gr. -1-2). 15.99 (978-1-4169-3786-9(2), Simon & Schuster Bks. For Young Readers) Simon & Schuster Bks. For Young Readers.

Meek, Jeffrey/K. Nimble the Thimble Mouse, 1. Dungey, Thomas, illus. 2007. 21p. (J). 9.95 (978-0-9794522-0-8(1)) Thimble Mouse Publishing, Inc.

Messimer, Wanda Fay. Tiny Teacup & Pot Belly Pig Go to Africa to Meet the 'Great Lion' 2013. 24p. pap. 24.95 (978-1-4626-8736-7(9)) America Star Bks.

Messner, Kate. Fergus & Zeke. Ross, Heather, illus. 2017. (ENG.). 56p. (J). (gr. k-3). 14.99 (978-0-7636-7846-3(5)) Candlewick Pr.

Mice & Other Stories: Individual Title Six-Pack. (Story Steps Ser.). (gr. k-2). 48.00 (978-0-7635-9823-5(2)) Rigby Education.

Mice on Ice: KinderReaders Individual Title Six-Packs. (Kinderstarters Ser.). 8p. (gr. -1-1). 21.00 (978-0-7635-8664-5(1)) Rigby Education.

Miceli, Mary Anne. Boston North Shore's... Mouse Tales of Early Salem. 2013. 44p. pap. 20.00 (978-0-9888654-1-9(6)) Miceli, Mary Anne.

Milbourne, A. & Wells, R. Mouse on the Moon. 2004. (Touchy-Feely Board Bks.). (Illus.). 10p. (J). (gr. -1-18). 4.95 (978-0-7945-0163-1(X), Usborne) EDC Publishing.

Milgrim, David. See Pip Point. Milgrim, David, illus. 2016. (Adventures of Otto Ser.). (ENG., Illus.). 32p. (J). (gr. -1-k). pap. 3.99 (978-1-4814-6784-1(0), Simon Spotlight) Simon Spotlight.

Miller, Dorothy North. How Mr Foxy Fox Was Outfoxed. 2009. 32p. pap. 14.95 (978-0-9825086-1-9(1)) Fiction Publishing, Inc.

Miller, Linda K. Ronald the Church Mouse. 2008. 96p. pap. 12.00 (978-1-60693-063-2(X), Eloquent Bks.) Strategic Book Publishing & Rights Agency (SBPRA).

Milway, Alex. The Curse of Mousebeard. 2011. (ENG.). 368p. (J). (gr. 3-7). pap. 6.99 (978-0-316-07745-3(3)) Little, Brown Bks. for Young Readers.

Miracle Mouse Cranky's Miracle. 2006. (J). lib. bdg. 19.95 (978-1-934017-00-5(0)) Hignites, Tom Miracle Studio.

Mitchard, Jacquelyn. Starring Prima! The Mouse of the Ballet Jolie. Tusa, Tricia, illus. 2004. 160p. (J). (gr. 3-18). 16.89 (978-0-06-057357-7(0)); (ENG.). 15.99 (978-0-06-057356-0(2)) HarperCollins Pubs.

Mitchell, Carolyn. The Tale of the Pumpkin Seed Squad. 2006. (ENG.). 40p. per. 16.99 (978-1-4259-7004-8(4)) AuthorHouse.

Mitchell, Gloria. The Mouse That Went to Find Christmas. Johnson, Jerome A., illus. (J). pap. (978-0-9706186-0-3(3)) Fourth Generation Pubs.

Mitchell, Sheena. Out of the Ark. 2012. 48p. pap. 18.41 (978-1-4669-1489-6(0)) Trafford Publishing.

Mitton, Tony & Parker, Ant. Super Submarines. 2014. (Amazing Machines Ser.). (ENG., Illus.). 24p. (J). (gr. -1-k). 4.99 (978-0-7534-7208-8(2), 9780753472088, Kingfisher) Roaring Brook Pr.

—Super Submarines. 2014. (Amazing Machines Ser.). (J). lib. bdg. 14.75 (978-0-606-36133-0(2)) Turtleback Bks.

Moerder, Lynne. Things That Go Burp! in the Night. Moerder, Lynne, illus. 2015. (ENG., Illus.). 32p. (J). (gr. -1-k). 16.99 (978-1-4847-1669-4(8)) Hyperion Bks. for Children.

Molk, Laurel. Eeny, Meeny, Miney, Mo, & Flo. Molk, Laurel, illus. 2015. (ENG., Illus.). 32p. (J). (gr. -1-k). 16.99 *(978-0-670-01538-2(5),* Viking Books for Young Readers) Penguin Young Readers Group.

Molloy, Tom. Everything but the Beach: A Slice of Manchester Life. 2012. (Illus.). 192p. (J). pap. 9.60 *(978-1-291-15817-5(0))* Lulu Pr., Inc.

Moncure, Jane Belk. Mousekin's Special Day: A Book about Special Days. Gallagher-Cole, Mernie, illus. 2013. (Magic Castle Readers Ser.). (ENG.). 32p. (J). (gr. -1-2). 25.64 *(978-1-62323-586-4(3),* 206321) Child's World, Inc., The.

Monks, Lydia. Eeeek, Mouse! 2015. (ENG., Illus.). 32p. (J). (gr. -1-k). pap. 10.99 *(978-1-4052-7692-4(4))* Egmont Bks., Ltd. GBR. Dist: Independent Pubs. Group.

Moore, Suzi. Whoops! Ayto, Russell, illus. 2016. (ENG.). 32p. (J). (gr. -1-2). 16.99 *(978-0-7636-8180-7(6),* Templar) Candlewick Pr.

Moore, Thomas. Zoe & the Back Yard Boys: The Magic Garden Haunted House Adventure. 2012. 24p. pap. 17.99 *(978-1-4772-9086-6(9))* AuthorHouse.

Mora, Pat & Martinez, Libby. Bravo, Chico Canta! Bravo!, 1 vol. Carling, Amelia Lau, illus. 2014. (ENG.). 32p. (J). (gr. -1-2). 17.95 *(978-1-55498-343-8(6))* Groundwood Bks. CAN. Dist: Publishers Group West (PGW).

—Bravo, Chico Canta! Bravo!, 1 vol. Iribarren, Elena, tr. from ENG. Carling, Amelia Lau, illus. 2014. (SPA.). 32p. (J). (gr. -1-2). 8.95 *(978-1-55498-344-5(4))* Groundwood Bks. CAN. Dist: Publishers Group West (PGW).

Morgan, Mary. Hear Me Squeak! 2009. 24p. pap. 11.84 *(978-1-4389-4632-0(5))* AuthorHouse.

—Sleep Tight, Little Mouse. Morgan, Mary, illus. 2015. (ENG., Illus.). 32p. (J). (gr. -1-2). bds. 6.99 *(978-0-553-49829-5(0),* Knopf Bks. for Young Readers) Random Hse. Children's Bks.

Morgan, Michaela. Mouse with No Name. Mikhail, Jess, illus. 2004. (ENG.). 24p. (J). lib. bdg. 23.65 *(978-1-59646-682-1(0))* Dingles & Co.

Morrissey, Dean & Krensky, Stephen. The Wizard Mouse. Morrissey, Dean, illus. 2011. (ENG., Illus.). 32p. (J). (gr. k-4). 16.99 *(978-0-06-008066-2(3))* HarperCollins Pubs.

Morse, William A. Bip & the Bulb. 2009. 64p. pap. 23.49 *(978-1-4490-2498-7(X))* AuthorHouse.

Mortensen, Lori. Mousequerade Ball: A Counting Tale. Lewin, Betsy, illus. 2016. (ENG.). 32p. (J). 16.99 *(978-1-61963-422-0(8),* 9781619634220, Bloomsbury USA Childrens) Bloomsbury Publishing USA.

Mortimer, Anne. Christmas Mouse. Mortimer, Anne, illus. 2013. (ENG., Illus.). 40p. (J). (gr. -1-3). 12.99 *(978-0-06-208928-1(5),* Tegen, Katherine Bks) HarperCollins Pubs.

—Pumpkin Cat. Mortimer, Anne, illus. 2011. (ENG., Illus.). 24p. (J). (gr. -1-2). 14.99 *(978-0-06-187485-7(X),* Tegen, Katherine Bks) HarperCollins Pubs.

Moser, Erwin, et al. Manuel y Didi y el Coche de Maiz. (Manuel & Didi Ser.).Tr. of Manuel & Didi & the Corn Car. (SPA., Illus.). 48p. (J). *(978-84-392-8721-6(6))* Gaviota Ediciones ESP. Dist: Lectorum Pubns., Inc.

Moulton, Bob. Rosey & Josey Meet Big Feet. 2010. 20p. 10.49 *(978-1-4490-9151-4(2))* AuthorHouse.

Moulton, Mark K. A Royal Wedding. Good, Karen H., illus. 2007. (ENG.). 32p. (J). (gr. k-3). 14.99 *(978-0-8249-8677-3(6),* Ideal Pubns.) Worthy Publishing.

Moulton, Mark Kimball. One Enchanted Evening. Crouch, Karen Hillard, illus. 2003. 32p. (J). 14.95 *(978-0-8249-5480-2(7),* Ideal Pubns.) Worthy Publishing.

The Mouse & the Grouse. 2006. (J). lib. bdg. *(978-0-9787826-0-3(7))* Happy Bks. Pr.

The Mouse in the House. (J). (gr. 1). *(978-0-669-17653-7(2))* Houghton Mifflin Harcourt School Pubs.

A Mouse on the Moon. Date not set. 5.95 *(978-0-89868-347-9(5))* ARO Publishing Co.

Mr. Cheesehead Goes for a Ride... 2nd rev. ed. 2005. (Illus.). 32p. (J). 12.99 *(978-0-9764463-1-6(6))* Vertigo Publishing.

Murphy, Mary. A Kiss Like This. Murphy, Mary, illus. 2012. (ENG., Illus.). 32p. (J). (gr. k-k). 12.99 *(978-0-7636-6182-3(1))* Candlewick Pr.

Nakagawa, Masafumi. Dr. Mouse's Mission. Perry, Mia Lynn, tr. Yamawaki, Yuriko, illus. 2007. (R. I. C. Story Chest Ser.). 27p. (J). (gr. -1-1). 14.95 incl. audio compact disk *(978-1-74126-051-9(5))* R.I.C. Pubns. AUS. Dist: SCB Distributors.

Nastanlieva, Vanya. Mo & Beau. 2015. (ENG., Illus.). 36p. (J). (gr. -1-3). 15.95 *(978-1-927018-63-7(3))* Simply Read Bks. CAN. Dist: Ingram Publisher Services.

Needham, T. L. Kitty Claus. 2012. (ENG.). 27p. (J). (-18). pap. 19.95 *(978-1-4787-1788-1(2))* Outskirts Pr., Inc.

Newell, Jeff. Skimper-Scamper. Hranilovich, Barbara, illus. 2005. (Green Light Readers Level 2 Ser.). (J). (gr. k-2). 11.60 *(978-0-7569-5244-0(1))* Perfection Learning Corp.

Newman, Robin. The Case of the Poached Egg. Zemke, Deborah, illus. 2017. (Wilcox & Griswold Mystery Ser.). (ENG.). 48p. (J). (gr. -1-3). 15.95 *(978-1-939547-30-9(X))* Creston Bks.

Newman, Vivian. Moti the Mitzvah Mouse. Knopp-Kilpert, Inga, illus. 2017. (ENG.). 24p. (J). (gr. -1-k). 17.99 ***(978-1-5124-2647-2(4))***; pap. 7.99 ***(978-1-5124-2649-6(0))*** Lerner Publishing Group. (Kar-Ben Publishing).

Newton, Lesley. Ralphie's Christmas Story, 1 vol. 2010. 16p. pap. 24.95 *(978-1-4489-2674-9(2))* PublishAmerica, Inc.

Nibble, Nibble, Nibble: KinderConcepts Individual Title Six-Packs. (Kinderstarters Ser.). 8p. (gr. -1-1). 21.00 *(978-0-7635-8716-1(8))* Rigby Education.

Nimmo, Jenny. Matty Mouse. 2006. (Blue Bananas Ser.). (ENG., Illus.). 48p. (J). (gr. -1-3). *(978-0-7787-0898-6(5))*; lib. bdg. *(978-0-7787-0852-0(7))* Crabtree Publishing Co.

—Matty Mouse. Rivers, Ruth, illus. 2003. (Blue Bananas Ser.). (ENG.). 48p. (J). (gr. k-2). pap. 5.99 *(978-1-4052-0591-7(1))* Egmont Bks., Ltd. GBR. Dist: Independent Pubs. Group.

Norton, Miriam. The Kitten Who Thought He Was a Mouse. Williams, Garth, illus. 2008. (Little Golden Book Ser.). (ENG.). 24p. (J). (gr. -1-2). 4.99 *(978-0-375-84822-3(3),* Golden Bks.) Random Hse. Children's Bks.

Nosy Crow Staff. Pip & Posy: the Little Puddle. Scheffler, Axel, illus. 2011. (Pip & Posy Ser.). (ENG.). 32p. (J). (gr. k-k). 12.99 *(978-0-7636-5878-6(2),* Nosy Crow) Candlewick Pr.

—Pip & Posy: the New Friend. Scheffler, Axel, illus. 2017. (Pip & Posy Ser.). (ENG.). 32p. (J). (-k). 12.99 *(978-0-7636-9339-8(1),* Nosy Crow) Candlewick Pr.

—Pip & Posy: the Super Scooter. Scheffler, Axel, illus. 2011. (Pip & Posy Ser.). (ENG.). 32p. (J). (gr. k-k). 12.99 *(978-0-7636-5877-9(4),* Nosy Crow) Candlewick Pr.

Numeroff, Laura Joffe. The Best Mouse Cookie. Bond, Felicia, illus. 2006. (If You Give... Ser.). (ENG.). 32p. (J). (gr. -1-2). 9.99 *(978-0-06-113760-0(X))* HarperCollins Pubs.

—Happy Birthday, Mouse! Bond, Felicia, illus. 2012. (If You Give... Ser.). (ENG.). 24p. (J). (gr. -1 — 1). bds. 6.99 *(978-0-694-01425-5(7))* HarperCollins Pubs.

—Happy Valentine's Day, Mouse! Bond, Felicia, illus. 2009. (If You Give... Ser.). (ENG.). 24p. (J). (gr. -1-3). bds. 6.99 *(978-0-06-180432-8(0))* HarperCollins Pubs.

—Happy Valentine's Day, Mouse! Lap Edition. Bond, Felicia, illus. 2015. (If You Give... Ser.). (ENG.). 24p. (J). (gr. -1-3). bds. 12.99 *(978-0-06-242740-3(7))* HarperCollins Pubs.

—If You Give a Mouse a Brownie. Bond, Felicia, illus. 2016. (If You Give... Ser.). (ENG.). 32p. (J). (gr. -1-3). 17.99 *(978-0-06-027571-6(5))* HarperCollins Pubs.

—If You Give a Mouse a Cookie. 2004. (Illus.). (J). (gr. k-3). spiral bd. *(978-0-616-01752-4(9))*; spiral bd. *(978-0-616-01751-7(0))* Canadian National Institute for the Blind/Institut National Canadien pour les Aveugles.

—If You Give a Mouse a Cookie. Bond, Felicia, illus. (J). (gr. -1-2). Date not set. 32p. 4.95 *(978-0-06-443166-8(5))* 2013. (ENG.). 40p. 16.99 *(978-0-06-230594-7(8),* Balzer & Bray) 25th anniv. ed. 2015. (ENG.). 40p. 16.99 *(978-0-06-024586-3(7))* HarperCollins Pubs.

—If You Take a Mouse to School. 2004. (Illus.). (J). (gr. k-3). spiral bd. *(978-0-616-14594-4(2))*; spiral bd. *(978-0-616-14593-7(4))* Canadian National Institute for the Blind/Institut National Canadien pour les Aveugles.

—If You Take a Mouse to the Movies. 2004. (Illus.). (J). (gr. k-3). spiral bd. *(978-0-616-11128-4(2))*; spiral bd. *(978-0-616-11129-1(0))* Canadian National Institute for the Blind/Institut National Canadien pour les Aveugles.

—If You Take a Mouse to the Movies. Bond, Felicia, illus. 2009. (If You Give... Ser.). (ENG.). 72p. (J). (gr. -1-3). 18.99 *(978-0-06-176280-2(6))* HarperCollins Pubs.

—It's Pumpkin Day, Mouse! Bond, Felicia, illus. 2012. (If You Give... Ser.). (ENG.). 24p. (J). (gr. -1 — 1). bds. 6.99 *(978-0-694-01429-3(X))* HarperCollins Pubs.

—Merry Christmas, Mouse! Bond, Felicia, illus. 2007. (If You Give... Ser.). (ENG.). 24p. (J). (gr. -1 — 1). bds. 6.99 *(978-0-06-134499-2(0))* HarperCollins Pubs.

—A Mouse Cookie First Library: If You Give a Mouse a Cookie; If You Take a Mouse to School. Bond, Felicia, illus. 2007. (If You Give... Ser.). (ENG.). 100p. (J). (gr. -1-2). bds. 15.99 *(978-0-06-117479-7(3),* HarperFestival) HarperCollins Pubs.

—Mouse Cookies & More: A Treasury. Bond, Felicia, illus. 2015. (If You Give... Ser.). (ENG.). 224p. (J). (gr. -1-3). 24.99 *(978-0-06-113763-1(4))* HarperCollins Pubs.

—Mouse's Family Album. Date not set. 32p. (J). 10.99 *(978-0-06-028561-6(3),* Geringer, Laura Book) HarperCollins Pubs.

—Si Llevas un Ratón a la Escuela, 1 vol. Bond, Felicia, illus. 2003. (If You Give... Ser.).Tr. of If You Take a Mouse to School. (SPA.). 32p. (J). (gr. -1-3). 16.99 *(978-0-06-052340-4(9))* HarperCollins Pubs.

—Time for School, Mouse! Bond, Felicia, illus. 2008. (If You Give... Ser.). (ENG.). 24p. (J). (gr. -1 — 1). bds. 6.99 *(978-0-06-143307-8(1),* HarperFestival) HarperCollins Pubs.

Oakley, Graham. Church Mice Take a Break. (Illus.). 25p. (J). 17.99 *(978-0-340-73254-0(7))* Hodder & Stoughton GBR. Dist: Trafalgar Square Publishing.

O'Brien, Robert C. Mrs. Frisby & the Rats of NIMH. 2006. (KOR.). 280p. (J). (gr. 4-7). ***(978-89-90794-37-6(4))*** Green Bks. Co., Ltd.

—Mrs. Frisby & the Rats of NIMH. (J). 2009. 73.75 *(978-1-4618-3748-0(0))* 2003. 81.75 *(978-1-4025-6007-1(9))* Recorded Bks., Inc.

Ocker, Christ Holder. A Mouse Without a House. 2006. (J). per. *(978-1-59872-711-1(7))* Instant Pub.

Oe, Patricia Daly. Blue Mouse, Yellow Mouse. Oe, Patricia Daly, illus. 2007. (R. I. C. Story Chest Ser.). (Illus.). 20p. (J). (gr. -1-k). 11.95 incl. audio compact disk *(978-1-74126-439-5(1))* R.I.C. Pubns. AUS. Dist: SCB Distributors.

Oelschlager, Vanita. Elefante. Blackwood, Kristin, illus. 2011. 20p. (J). (gr. k-k). (ENG.). bds. 6.95 *(978-0-9826366-4-0(4))*; (SPA.). bds. 6.95 *(978-0-9826366-5-7(2))* VanitaBooks.

Oeming, Michael Avon & Glass, Bryan J. L. Mice Templar Volume 4. 1 HC. 2013. (ENG., Illus.). 248p. (YA). 29.99 *(978-1-60706-822-8(2),* 9781607068228) Image Comics.

Ofoche, Uzo. Monte & Me. 2012. 20p. pap. 10.95 *(978-1-60911-511-1(2),* Eloquent Bks.) Strategic Book Publishing & Rights Agency (SBPRA).

Oh, Jiwon. Mr. Monkey's Classroom. Oh, Jiwon, illus. 2005. (Illus.). 32p. (J). (gr. -1-2). lib. bdg. 15.89 *(978-0-06-055722-5(2))* HarperCollins Pubs.

O'Malley, Kevin. Herbert Fieldmouse, Secret Agent. 2003. (Illus.). 32p. (J). pap. *(978-1-59336-043-6(6))*; (gr. 1-6). 15.95 *(978-1-59336-042-9(8))* Mondo Publishing.

Oram, Hiawyn. The Giant Surprise: A Narnia Story. Humphries, Tudor, illus. 2005. (Step into Narnia Ser.). 40p. (J). (gr. -1-2). lib. bdg. 16.89 *(978-0-06-001360-8(5))* HarperCollins Pubs.

—Mr Strongmouse & the Baby. Chapman, Lynne, illus. 2006. 32p. (J). pap. *(978-1-84362-588-9(1),* Orchard Bks.) Scholastic, Inc.

Orliczky P. T., Kristina. Mona's Mitten: A Story to Move To. 2011. 32p. (gr. -1). pap. 14.49 *(978-1-4567-3306-3(0))* AuthorHouse.

Orshoski, Paul. We Both Read Bilingual Edition-The Mouse in My House/un Raton en Mi Casa. Canetti, Yanitzia, tr. from ENG. Ebbeler, Jeffrey, illus. 2014. (We Both Read - Level 1 (Quality) Ser.). (ENG & SPA.). 44p. (J). (gr. 1). pap. 4.99 *(978-1-60115-056-1(3))* Treasure Bay, Inc.

—We Both Read-The Mouse in My House. Ebbeler, Jeffrey, illus. 2012. 44p. (J). 9.95 *(978-1-60115-257-2(4))*; pap. 4.99 *(978-1-60115-258-9(2))* Treasure Bay, Inc.

Orshoski, Paul & Max, Dave. We Both Read-The Ant & the Pancake. 2015. (ENG., Illus.). 44p. (J). (gr. k-1). pap. 4.99 *(978-1-60115-272-5(8))* Treasure Bay, Inc.

O'Ryan, Ellie & Studio IBOIX. Cinderella: The Great Mouse Mistake, 1 vol. 2012. (Disney Princess Ser.). (ENG., Illus.). 96p. (J). (gr. 2-5). 24.21 *(978-1-59961-879-1(6))* Spotlight.

Otten, Charlotte. The Flying Mouse. Crawford, Greg, illus. 2014. (ENG.). 32p. (J). 17.95 *(978-1-59373-152-6(3))* Bunker Hill Publishing, Inc.

Oud, Pauline. Christmas with Lily & Milo. 2012. (Clavis Toddler: Language Development Ser.). (ENG.). 30p. (J). (gr. k — 1). 12.95 *(978-1-60537-128-3(9))* Cobblestone Publishing Co.

—Eating with Lily & Milo. Oud, Pauline, illus. 2010. (Lily & Milo Ser.). (ENG., Illus.). 30p. (J). (gr. k — 1). 12.95 *(978-1-60537-055-2(X))* Cobblestone Publishing Co.

—Getting Dressed with Lily & Milo. Oud, Pauline, illus. 2010. (Lily & Milo Ser.). (ENG., Illus.). 30p. (J). (gr. k — 1). 12.95 *(978-1-60537-060-6(6))* Cobblestone Publishing Co.

—Going to the Beach with Lily & Milo. Oud, Pauline, illus. 2011. (Lily & Milo Ser.). (ENG., Illus.). 28p. (J). (gr. k — 1). 12.95 *(978-1-60537-094-1(0))* Cobblestone Publishing Co.

—Going to the Zoo with Lily & Milo. Oud, Pauline, illus. 2011. (Lily & Milo Ser.). (ENG., Illus.). 28p. (J). (gr. k — 1). 12.95 *(978-1-60537-093-4(2))* Cobblestone Publishing Co.

—Having a Party with Lily & Milo. Oud, Pauline, illus. 2012. (Clavis Toddler: Skills Ser.). (ENG., Illus.). 24p. (J). (— 1). 12.95 *(978-1-60537-129-0(7))* Cobblestone Publishing Co.

Packard, Albert. Cavern of Babel. Boyles, Shawn, illus. 2006. (J). per. 14.95 *(978-0-9790652-0-0(8))* Diamond Triple C Ranch.

Page, J. & Rainier, S. T. Curiosity Strikes: Ben & Elvis Adventures. Rainier, S. T., illus. 2011. (Illus.). 28p. (J). pap. 8.99 *(978-0-9829669-3-8(8))* Elv Enterprises.

Pankiw, Dr Mary & Pankiw, Mary. Misilla Mouse. 2011. 32p. pap. *(978-1-4269-5476-4(X))* Trafford Publishing (UK) Ltd.

Parker, Emma & Aesop. The Lion & the Mouse. 2010. (Illus.). pap. *(978-1-877547-45-4(X))* First Edition Ltd.

Parker, Jake. Rescue on Tankium, No. 3. 2011. (Missile Mouse Ser.: 2). (ENG.). 160p. (J). (gr. 3-7). pap. 10.99 *(978-0-545-11717-3(8),* Graphix) Scholastic, Inc.

—Rescue on Tankium3. 2011. (Missile Mouse Ser.: 2). (ENG.). 160p. (J). (gr. 3-7). 21.99 *(978-0-545-11716-6(X),* Graphix) Scholastic, Inc.

Parker, Vic, ed. The Mice & the Weasels & Other Fables. 2014. (Aesop's Fables Ser.). 40p. (J). (gr. 2-5). pap. 84.95 *(978-1-4824-1259-8(4))* Stevens, Gareth Publishing LLLP.

—The Town Mouse & the Country Mouse & Other Fables. 2014. (Aesop's Fables Ser.). 40p. (J). (gr. 2-5). pap. 84.95 *(978-1-4824-1260-4(8))* Stevens, Gareth Publishing LLLP.

Parr, Garnet A. Mosey. 2012. 60p. pap. 31.99 *(978-1-4691-7928-5(8))* Xlibris Corp.

Patrick, Jim. The Adventures of Artemous Bk. 1: Mouse in the Museum. 2015. (ENG., Illus.). 52p. (J). pap. 12.95 *(978-1-62287-915-1(5))* First Edition Design eBook Publishing.

Patterson, James & Grabenstein, Chris. Word of Mouse. Sutphin, Joe, illus. 2016. (ENG.). 304p. (J). (gr. 3-7). 13.99 *(978-0-316-34956-7(9),* Jimmy Patterson) Little Brown & Co.

Pearson, Judith Frank. Chester the Christmas Church Mouse. 2013. 18p. pap. 9.95 *(978-1-61493-176-8(3))* Peppertree Pr., The.

Peck, Richard. The Mouse with the Question Mark Tail. 2014. (ENG.). 256p. (J). (gr. 3-7). pap. 7.99 *(978-0-14-242530-5(3),* Puffin Books) Penguin Young Readers Group.

—The Mouse with the Question Mark Tail. Murphy, Kelly, illus. 2013. (ENG.). 240p. (J). (gr. 3-7). 16.99 *(978-0-8037-3838-6(2),* Dial Bks) Penguin Young Readers Group.

—Secrets at Sea. 2012. (ENG.). 272p. (J). (gr. 3-7). pap. 7.99 *(978-0-14-242183-3(9),* Puffin Books) Penguin Young Readers Group.

—Secrets at Sea. Murphy, Kelly, illus. 2011. (ENG.). 256p. (J). (gr. 3-7). 16.99 *(978-0-8037-3455-5(7),* Dial Bks) Penguin Young Readers Group.

Pellegata, Donna, illus. The Harp Mouse Chooses Her Home: The Adventure Begins. 2008. 24p. (J). pap. 6.95 *(978-0-9742174-1-3(7))* Heart & Harp LLC.

Perry, Phyllis J. The Secrets of the Rock. Lipking, Ron, illus. 2004. (Fribble Mouse Library Mystery Ser.). 96p. (J). 16.95 *(978-1-932146-22-6(9),* 1237661) Highsmith Inc.

Peters, Andrew Fusek. Dragon & Mousie. Wade, Gini, illus. 2006. (ENG.). 32p. (J). pap. 7.95 *(978-0-86243-650-6(8))* Y Lolfa GBR. Dist: Dufour Editions, Inc.

—Dragon & Mousie & the Snow Factory. Wade, Gini, illus. 2007. (ENG.). 32p. (J). pap. 7.95 *(978-0-86243-945-3(0))* Y Lolfa GBR. Dist: Dufour Editions, Inc.

Peters, Suzanne. Misee Mouse. 2011. 36p. pap. 15.49 *(978-1-4269-5738-3(6))* Trafford Publishing.

Pfanner, Louise. Little Lucies Diary. 2006. (Illus.). 24p. pap. *(978-1-877003-98-1(0))* Little Hare Bks. AUS. Dist: HarperCollins Pubs. Australia.

Pfister, Marcus. Milo & the Magical Stones. Pfister, Marcus, illus. 2010. (Milo Ser.). (ENG., Illus.). 32p. (J). (gr. k-3). 17.95 *(978-0-7358-2253-5(0))* North-South Bks., Inc.

Pham, LeUyen. A Piece of Cake. Pham, LeUyen, illus. 2014. (ENG., Illus.). 40p. (J). (gr. -1-3). 16.99 *(978-0-06-199264-3(X))* HarperCollins Pubs.

Pierre, Dana. Mousey, Mousey Finds Cheese? Illustrated by Wellon Pierre. 2006. 17.00 *(978-0-8059-9867-2(5))* Dorrance Publishing Co., Inc.

Pilkey, Dav. Dogzilla. Pilkey, Dav, illus. 2014. (Illus.). 32p. pap. 7.00 *(978-1-61003-187-5(3))* Center for the Collaborative Classroom.

—Dogzilla. 2003. (ENG., Illus.). 32p. (J). (gr. -1-3). pap. 5.95 *(978-0-15-204949-2(5))* Houghton Mifflin Harcourt Publishing Co.

—Kat Kong. 2003. (ENG., Illus.). 32p. (J). pap. 5.95 *(978-0-15-204950-8(9))* Houghton Mifflin Harcourt Publishing Co.

—Kat Kong. 2003. (gr. k-3). lib. bdg. 15.95 *(978-0-613-71635-2(3),* Turtleback) Turtleback Bks.

—Mighty Robot vs. the Mecha-Monkeys from Mars. Santat, Dan, illus. 2014. (Ricky Ricotta Ser.: 4). (ENG.). 144p. (J). (gr. -1-3). pap. 5.99 *(978-0-545-63012-2(6))* Scholastic, Inc.

—Mighty Robot vs. the Mutant Mosquitoes from Mercury. Santat, Dan, illus. 2014. (Ricky Ricotta Ser.: 2). (ENG.). 128p. (J). (gr. -1-3). pap. 5.99 *(978-0-545-63010-8(X))* Scholastic, Inc.

—Mighty Robot vs. the Naughty Nightcrawlers from Neptune. Santat, Dan, illus. 2016. (Ricky Ricotta Ser.: 8). (ENG.). 128p. (J). (gr. -1-3). 15.99 *(978-0-439-37708-9(0))* Scholastic, Inc.

—Ricky Ricotta's Mighty Robot. Santat, Dan, illus. 2014. (Ricky Ricotta Ser.: 1). (ENG.). 112p. (J). (gr. -1-3). pap. 5.99 *(978-0-545-63009-2(6))*; lib. bdg. 15.99 *(978-0-545-63106-8(8))* Scholastic, Inc.

—Ricky Ricotta's Mighty Robot. 2014. (Ricky Ricotta's Mighty Robot Ser.: 1). lib. bdg. 16.00 *(978-0-606-35799-9(8))* Turtleback Bks.

—Ricky Ricotta's Mighty Robot vs. the Jurassic Jackrabbits from Jupiter. Santat, Dan, illus. 2014. (Ricky Ricotta Ser.: 5). (ENG.). 128p. (J). (gr. -1-3). pap. 5.99 *(978-0-545-63013-9(4))* Scholastic, Inc.

—Ricky Ricotta's Mighty Robot vs. the Naughty Nightcrawlers from Neptune. Santat, Dan, illus. 2016. (Ricky Ricotta Ser.: 8). (ENG.). 128p. (J). (gr. -1-3). pap. 5.99 *(978-0-439-37709-6(9))* Scholastic, Inc.

—Ricky Ricotta's Mighty Robot vs. the Unpleasant Penguins from Pluto. Santat, Dan, illus. 2016. (Ricky Ricotta's Mighty Robot Ser.: 9). (ENG.). 128p. (J). (gr. -1-3). 15.99 *(978-0-545-63016-0(9))* Scholastic, Inc.

—Uranium Unicorns from Uranus., Bk. 7. 2015. (Ricky Ricotta Ser.: 7). (ENG., Illus.). 128p. (J). (gr. -1-3). pap. 5.99 *(978-0-545-63015-3(0))* Scholastic, Inc.

—The Voodoo Vultures from Venus. Santat, Dan, illus. 2014. (Ricky Ricotta Ser.: 3). (ENG.). 128p. (J). (gr. -1-3). pap. 5.99 *(978-0-545-63011-5(8))* Scholastic, Inc.

Pinkwater, Daniel M. Mrs. Noodlekugel & Four Blind Mice. Stower, Adam, illus. (Mrs. Noodlekugel Ser.). (ENG.). 96p. (J). (gr. k-4). 2015. pap. 5.99 *(978-0-7636-7658-2(6))* 2013. 14.99 *(978-0-7636-5054-4(4))* Candlewick Pr.

Pistinier, Caroline. La Noche Del Ratoncito Perez. 2004. (SPA.). 40p. (J). 19.99 *(978-84-8470-055-5(0))* Corimbo, Editorial S.L. ESP. Dist: Lectorum Pubns., Inc.

Platt, Cynthia. Little Bit of Love. Whitty, Hannah, illus. 2011. (ENG.). 32p. (J). (gr. -1-2). pap. 7.95 *(978-1-58925-426-8(0))* Tiger Tales.

—A Little Bit of Love. Whitty, Hannah, illus. 2011. (ENG.). 32p. (J). (gr. -1-2). 15.95 *(978-1-58925-095-6(8))* Tiger Tales.

Plourde, Lynn. You're Doing That in the Talent Show?! Cornelison, Sue, illus. 2016. (ENG.). 32p. (J). (gr. -1-k). 16.99 *(978-1-4847-1491-1(1))* Disney Pr.

—You're Wearing That to School?! Cornelison, Sue, illus. 2013. (ENG.). 32p. (J). (gr. -1-3). 16.99 *(978-1-4231-5510-2(6))* Disney Pr.

Pogo the Clown. A Little Gray Mouse: Harley's Great Adventures. Miller, Richard D., illus. 2005. (J). 12.95 *(978-0-9755253-7-1(9))* Chilinc Pubns.

Posner-Sanchez, Andrea. Shop with Minnie. Random House Disney Staff, illus. 2012. (Little Golden Book Ser.). (ENG.). 24p. (J). (gr. k-k). 4.99 *(978-0-7364-3031-9(8),* Golden/Disney) Random Hse. Children's Bks.

Posner-Sanchez, Andrea & Weinberg, Jennifer Liberts. Bow-Bot Robot (Disney Junior: Minnie's Bow Toons) RH Disney Staff, illus. 2014. (Little Golden Book Ser.). (ENG.). 24p. (J). (-k). 4.99 *(978-0-7364-3078-4(4),* Golden/Disney) Random Hse. Children's Bks.

Postgate, Oliver. Noggin & the Moon Mouse. Firmin, Peter, illus. 2017. (Noggin the Nog Ser.: 5). (ENG.). 48p. (J). (gr. 1-4). 8.99 ***(978-1-4052-8141-6(3))*** Egmont Bks., Ltd. GBR. Dist: Independent Pubs. Group.

Potter, Beatrix. The Tailor of Gloucester, 1 vol. Jorgensen, David, illus. 2007. (Rabbit Ears: A Classic Tale Ser.). (ENG.). 40p. (gr. -1-3). 25.65 *(978-1-59961-312-3(3))* Spotlight.

—The Tale of Mrs. Tittlemouse. Rasmussen, Wendy, illus. 2009. (Classic Tales by Beatrix Potter Ser.). (ENG.). 24p. (J). (gr. k-3). 28.50 *(978-1-60253-294-6(X),* 200120) Child's World, Inc., The.

—A Tale of Two Bad Mice, 1 vol. McClintock, Barbara, illus. 2007. (Rabbit Ears: A Classic Tale Ser.). (ENG.). 40p. (gr. -1-3). 25.65 *(978-1-59961-314-7(X))* Spotlight.

Powell, Richard. Quiet as a Mouse: A Moving Picture Storybook. Hendra, Sue, illus. 2003. 16p. (J). 7.95 *(978-1-58925-678-1(6))* Tiger Tales.

Powell, Richard & Davis, Caroline. Mouse's Tail. 2003. (Animal Tails Ser.). (Illus.). 10p. (J). 3.95 *(978-1-58925-675-0(1))* Tiger Tales.

Prentice-Hall Staff. Of Mice & Men. 2nd ed. (J). stu. ed. *(978-0-13-717018-0(1))* Prentice Hall (Schl. Div.).

Previn, Stacey. Aberdeen. 2016. (ENG., Illus.). 40p. (J). (-k). 16.99 *(978-0-451-47148-2(2),* Viking Books for Young Readers) Penguin Young Readers Group.

Price, Kathryn. The Mouse & the Buddha. Price, Traer, illus. 2006. (ENG.). 36p. (J). (gr. -1-k). 14.95 *(978-0-9773812-0-3(X))* Little Hse. Pr.

Prince, April Jones. Dig In! Berg, Michelle, illus. 2013. (ENG.). 14p. (J). (gr. -1 — 1). bds. 7.95 *(978-1-4197-0522-9(9))* Abrams, Inc.

—Dive In! Berg, Michelle, illus. 2013. (ENG.). 14p. (J). (gr. -1 — 1). bds. 7.95 *(978-1-4197-0523-6(7))* Abrams, Inc.

The Pumpkin House, 6 Packs. (Literatura 2000 Ser.). (gr. 2-3). 33.00 *(978-0-7635-0182-2(4))* Rigby Education.

Pursglove, Sheila. Mouse Ate the House. 2008. pap. 16.95 *(978-1-932399-19-6(4))* Huron River Pr.

Puttock, Simon. Mouse's First Night at Moonlight School. Pye, Ali, illus. 2015. (ENG.). 32p. (J). (gr. -1-2). 16.99 *(978-0-7636-7607-0(1),* Nosy Crow) Candlewick Pr.

Quayle, Susan. Mouse & the Storm. Muldoon, Melissa, illus. 2017. (ENG.). 56p. 15.95 *(978-1-84819-344-4(0),* 9047, Singing Dragon) Kingsley, Jessica Pubs. GBR. Dist: Macmillan Distribution Ltd.

Quintanilla, Billie. The Greatest Mousemas Ever! Barnum, Tabatha, illus. 2012. 36p. 24.95 *(978-1-4626-9725-0(9))*; pap. 24.95 *(978-1-4626-5236-5(0))* America Star Bks.

Quinton, Sasha. Eek-A-Squeak: A Phonics Reader. 2009. (Illus.). pap. *(978-1-936199-05-1(X))* Book Shop, Ltd., The.

Rabei, Carolina. Crunch! Rabei, Carolina, illus. 2016. (Child's Play Library). (ENG., Illus.). 36p. (J). *(978-1-84643-733-5(4))* Child's Play International Ltd.

Rabley, Stephen. Marcel & the Mona Lisa. 2nd ed. 2009. (ENG., Illus.). 20p. pap. 11.99 *(978-1-4058-6955-3(0))* Pearson Education.

Ramsay, Kim Heaton. Will You Be My Friend? 2012. 16p. pap. 15.99 *(978-1-4772-9503-8(8))* AuthorHouse.

Ramsay, Mark. The Good Neighbors' Cheese Feast: A Cheesy Mouse Tale of Subtraction with Regrouping. Robinson, Susan G., illus. 2010. (ENG.). 32p. (J). pap. 9.95 *(978-0-9842863-1-7(4))* Strategic Educational Tools.

—The Good Neighbors Store an Award: A Cheesy Mouse Tale of Addition with Regrouping. Robinson, Susan G., illus. 2010. (ENG.). 32p. (J). pap. 9.95 *(978-0-9842863-0-0(6))* Strategic Educational Tools.

Randall, Ronne. The Hanukkah Mice. Kneep, Maggie, illus. 2010. (ENG.). 18p. (J). (gr. -1-1). 9.99 *(978-0-8118-7663-6(2))* Chronicle Bks. LLC.

Rath, Tom H. Donkey Oatie's Field Trip. Gaudet, Christine, illus. 2013. 26p. pap. *(978-0-9918033-4-7(5))* Wood Islands Prints.

Ratnayake, Kumari/Keiko. Monsieur Bagel's War. Ratnayake, Kumari/Keiko, illus. 2007. (Illus.). 25p. (J). spiral bd. 15.00 net. *(978-0-9797015-1-1(1))* Augustana College Geology Dept. Pr.

Ray, Christie Jones & Ray, Christie Jones. Eliz. 2012. (Illus.). 28p. pap. 15.00 *(978-0-9853223-1-1(4))* Rose Water Cottage Pr.

—Eliza & a Cottage Door. 2012. (Illus.). 40p. pap. 15.00 *(978-0-9853223-0-4(6))* Rose Water Cottage Pr.

—Eliza Celebrates a Royal Wedding. 2012. (Illus.). 48p. pap. 15.00 *(978-0-9853223-6-6(5))* Rose Water Cottage Pr.

—Eliza Has a Cousin. 2012. (Illus.). 32p. pap. 15.00 *(978-0-9853223-5-9(7))* Rose Water Cottage Pr.

—Eliza Will Not Be Afraid. 2012. (Illus.). 24p. pap. 12.00 *(978-0-9853223-7-3(3))* Rose Water Cottage Pr.

—Pick-A-Pick-a-Pumpkin. 2012. (Illus.). 36p. pap. 12.00 *(978-0-9853223-4-2(9))* Rose Water Cottage Pr.

Rayner, Catherine. The Bear Who Shared. 2011. (ENG.). 32p. (J). (gr. -1-k). 16.99 *(978-0-8037-3576-7(6)*, Dial Bks) Penguin Young Readers Group.

Read, Miss. The Christmas Mouse. Goodall, John S., illus. (J). lib. bdg. 14.95 *(978-0-8488-1452-6(5))* Amereon Ltd.

Reasoner, Charles. Inside Jolly Rodger's Pirate Ship. 2014. (Illus.). (J). *(978-1-4351-5466-7(5))* Barnes & Noble, Inc.

—The 3 Blind Mice Inside the Spooky Scary & Creepy Haunted House. Reasoner, Charles, illus. 2007. (Story Book Ser.). (Illus.). 10p. (J). (gr. -1-3). bds. *(978-1-84666-381-9(4)*, Tide Mill Pr.) Top That! Publishing PLC.

Reed, Patricia. Mousetrap. 2005. pap. 15.99 *(978-1-4196-0540-6(2))* CreateSpace Independent Publishing Platform.

Reeve, Rosie. Lullaby Moon. Reeve, Rosie, illus. 2010. (ENG., Illus.). 20p. (J). (gr. k — 1). bds. 8.99 *(978-0-545-21146-8(8)*, Cartwheel Bks.) Scholastic, Inc.

Reid, Barbara. The Subway Mouse. Reid, Barbara, illus. 2005. (Illus.). (J). *(978-0-439-77430-7(6))* Scholastic, Inc.

Remsburg, Rebecca. The Camping Trip, 1 vol. 2010. 22p. pap. 24.95 *(978-1-4489-2508-7(8))* PublishAmerica, Inc.

Reyes, Analisse. It Wasn't Me! 2011. (Illus.). 25p. (J). pap. 14.95 *(978-1-4327-6851-5(4))* Outskirts Pr., Inc.

Reynolds, Paul A. Sydney & Simon: Going Green! Reynolds, Paul A. & Reynolds, Peter H., illus. 2015. (Sydney & Simon Ser.). (ENG.). 48p. (J). (gr. 1-4). lib. bdg. 12.95 *(978-1-58089-677-1(4))* Charlesbridge Publishing, Inc.

—Sydney & Simon: To the Moon & Beyond! Reynolds, Peter H., illus. 2017. (ENG.). 48p. (J). (gr. 1-4). lib. bdg. 12.99 *(978-1-58089-679-5(0))* Charlesbridge Publishing, Inc.

RH Disney. Gus Loves Cinderella (Disney Princess) RH Disney, illus. 2016. (Padded Board Book Ser.). (ENG., Illus.). 26p. (J). (gr. -1-1). bds. 9.99 *(978-0-7364-3706-6(1)*, RH/Disney) Random Hse. Children's Bks.

Rice, Dona Herwick. The Lion & the Mouse, 1 vol. 2008. (Building Fluency Through Reader's Theater Ser.). (ENG.). 24p. (J). (gr. 1-3). pap. 6.99 *(978-1-4333-0293-0(4))* Teacher Created Materials, Inc.

Rice, Dona Herwick & Housel, Debra. The Town Mouse & the Country Mouse, 1 vol. 2008. (Building Fluency Through Reader's Theater Ser.). (ENG., Illus.). 24p. (J). (gr. 1-3). pap. 6.99 *(978-1-4333-0294-7(2))* Teacher Created Materials, Inc.

Rigby, Ed & Dooley, Angela. Mouse of the Match. 2009. 41p. pap. 10.50 *(978-1-4452-2692-7(8))* Lulu Pr., Inc.

Rigby Education Staff. A Mouse Manual. (Sails Literacy Ser.). (Illus.). 16p. (gr. 2-3). 27.00 *(978-0-7635-9942-3(5)*, 699425C99) Rigby Education.

Robaard, Jedda. The Little Mouse Who Lost Her Squeak. 2015. (ENG., Illus.). 12p. (J). (gr. -1-k). 7.99 *(978-1-4998-0002-9(9))* Little Bee Books Inc.

Roberts, Bethany. Fourth of July Mice! 2004. (ENG., Illus.). 32p. (J). (gr. -1-1). tchr. ed. 13.00 *(978-0-618-31367-9(2)*, Clarion Bks.) Houghton Mifflin Harcourt Trade & Reference Pubs.

—Halloween Mice! Cushman, Doug, illus. 2011. (ENG.). 28p. (J). (gr. k — 1). bds. 5.99 *(978-0-547-57573-5(4))* Houghton Mifflin Harcourt Publishing Co.

—Thanksgiving Mice! Cushman, Doug, illus. 2005. (ENG.). 32p. (J). (gr. -1 — 1). 5.95 *(978-0-618-60486-9(3))* Houghton Mifflin Harcourt Publishing Co.

—Valentine Mice! Cushman, Doug, illus. 2016. (Green Light Readers Level 1 Ser.). (ENG.). 32p. (J). (gr. -1-3). 12.99 *(978-0-544-80897-3(5)*, HMH Books For Young Readers) Houghton Mifflin Harcourt Publishing Co.

—Valentine Mice! Board Book. Cushman, Doug, illus. 2011. (ENG.). 28p. (J). (gr. k — 1). bds. 5.99 *(978-0-547-37144-3(6))* Houghton Mifflin Harcourt Publishing Co.

Roberts, Daniel. Mouse & His Balloon. 2011. 32p. pap. 14.95 *(978-1-4634-2090-1(0))* AuthorHouse.

Roberts, Smith. A House for a Mouse. Roberts, Smith, illus. 2003. (Illus.). 56p. (J). per. 16.00 *(978-0-9727315-3-9(9))* Prospero's Pr.

Robinson Ed. D., Shannon R. The Adventures of Katie Koala: Oops! My Momma Is Lost!, 1 vol. Swope, Brenda, illus. 2009. 23p. pap. 24.95 *(978-1-60749-733-2(6))* America Star Bks.

Robleda, Margarita. Ramon y Su Raton. Suarez, Maribel, illus. (Rana, Rema, Rimas Ser.). (SPA.). 16p. (J). (gr. k-3). 7.95 *(978-1-59437-818-8(5))* Santillana USA Publishing Co., Inc.

Rockas, Leo. Mice Make War. 2007. 53p. 16.95 *(978-1-4241-5708-2(0))* America Star Bks.

Roddie, Shen. You're Too Small! Lavis, Steve, illus. 2004. 32p. (J). 6.95 *(978-1-58925-385-8(X))*; tchr. ed. 15.95 *(978-1-58925-038-3(9))* Tiger Tales.

Rodrigues, Naomi. Molly Mouse & the Christmas Mystery. 2013. 24p. pap. 15.99 *(978-1-4797-6511-9(2))* Xlibris Corp.

Rogers, Anne. Sooty Wooty Is a Cat. 2008. 32p. pap. 23.95 *(978-1-4092-2565-2(8))* Lulu Pr., Inc.

Rohmann, Eric. My Friend Rabbit. Rohmann, Eric, illus. 2011. (ENG., Illus.). 36p. (J). (gr. -1-3). bds. 7.99 *(978-1-59643-641-1(7)*, 9781596436411) Roaring Brook Pr.

—My Friend Rabbit. Rohmann, Eric, illus. 2007. (ENG., Illus.). 32p. (J). (gr. -1-3). per. 7.99 *(978-0-312-36752-7(X)*, 9780312367527) Square Fish.

Rohmann, Eric, creator. My Friend Rabbit & the Snow Geese. 2013. (My Readers Ser.). (ENG., Illus.). 32p. (J). (gr. -1-1). pap. 3.99 *(978-1-250-01661-4(4)*, 9781250016614) Square Fish.

Rose, Chloe Gayle & Rose, Tammy Marie. The Snake That Eats Cake. 2012. 28p. pap. 24.95 *(978-1-4626-9882-0(4))* America Star Bks.

Ross, Dev. We Both Read-Frank & the Tiger. Reinhart, Larry, illus. 2012. 44p. (J). pap. 4.99 *(978-1-60115-260-2(4))* Treasure Bay, Inc.

Roth, Susan L. Mi Amor Por Ti/My Love for You. 2003. (ENG & SPA., Illus.). 26p. (J). (gr. -1 — 1). bds. 6.99 *(978-0-8037-2944-5(8)*, Dial Bks) Penguin Young Readers Group.

Rourke, Janet W. The New Baby: Featuring Marta the Mouse. 2004. (Illus.). 20p. (J). 7.99 *(978-0-9729563-1-8(2))* Hale Publishing.

Rowland, Patty. Marvelous Max, the Mansion Mouse. Rasmussen, Wendy, tr. Rasmussen, Wendy, illus. 2003. 32p. (J). 17.95 *(978-0-9649934-4-0(9))* Norfleet Pr., Inc.

Roy, Philip. Mouse Tales. Torrey Balsara, Andrea, illus. 2014. (ENG.). 32p. pap. 9.95 *(978-1-55380-262-4(4))* Ronsdale Pr. CAN. Dist: SPD-Small Pr. Distribution.

Rubin, Bruce Joel & Michaels, Julie. Stuart Little 2 Vol. 2: El Libro de la Pelicula. 2003. (SPA., Illus.). 60p. (J). (gr. 3-5). 14.95 *(978-84-204-6503-6(8))* Santillana USA Publishing Co., Inc.

Rudy, Maggie & Abrams, Pam. The House That Mouse Built. Wolf, Bruce, photos by. 2011. (ENG., Illus.). 32p. (J). (gr. -1). 14.99 *(978-1-935703-25-9(0))* Downtown Bookworks.

Russell, Allyson. The Lizard Who Wanted to Be a Mouse. Bubp, Jennifer, illus. 2009. 28p. pap. 12.95 *(978-1-59858-938-2(5))* Dog Ear Publishing, LLC.

Russell, John. Sam & Socrates. 2012. 60p. (gr. 4-6). pap. 8.95 *(978-1-4620-6830-2(8))* iUniverse, Inc.

Ruzzier, Sergio. Two Mice. 2015. (ENG., Illus.). 32p. (J). (gr. -1-3). 12.99 *(978-0-544-30209-9(5))* Houghton Mifflin Harcourt Publishing Co.

Ryan, Mary C., illus. & text. Twitcher Mcgee & the Wonderful Tree. Ryan, Mary C., text. 2008. 12p. (J). 4.95 *(978-0-9678115-3-6(8))* Dragonseed Pr.

Ryan, Pam Muñoz. Mice & Beans. Cepeda, Joe, illus. 2005. (gr. -1-3). lib. bdg. 17.00 *(978-0-7569-5089-7(9))* Perfection Learning Corp.

Rylant, Cynthia. The Eagle. McDaniels, Preston, illus. 2004. (Lighthouse Family Ser.: 3). (ENG.). 64p. (J). (gr. 1-5). 15.99 *(978-0-689-86243-4(1)*, Simon & Schuster Bks. For Young Readers) Simon & Schuster Bks. For Young Readers.

—The Eagle. McDaniels, Preston, illus. 2005. (Lighthouse Family Ser.: 3). (ENG.). 64p. (J). (gr. 1-5). pap. 5.99 *(978-0-689-86311-0(X)*, Simon & Schuster Bks. For Young Readers) Simon & Schuster Bks. For Young Readers.

—The Octopus. McDaniels, Preston, illus. 2005. (Lighthouse Family Ser.: 5). (ENG.). 64p. (J). (gr. 1-5). 15.99 *(978-0-689-86246-5(6)*, Simon & Schuster Bks. For Young Readers) Simon & Schuster Bks. For Young Readers.

Sabuda, Robert. Uh-Oh, Leonardo! The Adventures of Providence Traveler. Sabuda, Robert, illus. 2007. (ENG., Illus.). 48p. (J). (gr. k-3). 12.99 *(978-1-4169-6164-2(X)*, Aladdin) Simon & Schuster Children's Publishing.

Said Mouse to Mole. 2005. (J). per. 8.95 *(978-1-59566-139-5(5))* QEB Publishing Inc.

Sales, Kyle M. On Our Way to Fontinasi. 2011. 60p. pap. 23.88 *(978-1-4634-2739-9(5))* AuthorHouse.

Sally, Zak. Sammy the Mouse #1 (Ignatz) 2007. (ENG.). 32p. pap. 7.95 *(978-1-56097-865-7(1))* Fantagraphics Bks.

Salmassian, Jennifer. Sally Saves the Mice. 2007. (J). per. 0.01 net. *(978-1-60402-115-8(2))* Independent Pub.

Sammel, Rochelle. Tales of Two Mouse Brothers. 2008. 45p. pap. 24.95 *(978-1-4241-9798-9(8))* America Star Bks.

San Souci, Robert D. Zigzag. Czernecki, Stefan, illus. 2005. (ENG.). 32p. (J). (gr. -1-2). 16.95 *(978-0-87483-764-3(2))* August Hse. Pubs., Inc.

Sanders, Jeane F. Ramón. 2008. 100p. pap. 19.95 *(978-1-60610-768-3(2))* America Star Bks.

Sandifer, Audie Cavett. The Exciting Adventures of Eekie & Squeeky. 2011. 52p. (gr. -1). pap. 12.95 *(978-1-4567-4289-8(2))* AuthorHouse.

Sanna, Charles A. Daddy. Daddy There's a Mouse in the House. Hill, Dave, illus. 2006. (J). 10.00 *(978-0-9762839-1-1(3))* Elizabooks.

Santat, Dan, illus. Mighty Robot vs. the Stupid Stinkbugs from Saturn. 2015. (Ricky Ricotta Ser.: 6). (ENG.). 128p. (J). (gr. -1-3). 15.99 *(978-0-545-63121-1(1))* Scholastic, Inc.

—Stupid Stinkbugs from Saturn. 2015. (Ricky Ricotta Ser.: 6). (ENG.). 128p. (J). (gr. -1-3). pap. 5.99 *(978-0-545-63014-6(2))* Scholastic, Inc.

Sargent, Dave & Sargent, Pat. Big Jake: I'm Very Curious, 56 vols., Vol. 12. Huff, Jeane, illus. 2nd rev. ed. 2003. (Animal Pride Ser.: 12). 42p. (J). lib. bdg. 20.95 *(978-1-56763-781-6(7))* Ozark Publishing.

Scam, Busta. The Kingdom of Nome. 2006. (Illus.). 44p. pap. 12.95 *(978-1-59663-516-6(9)*, Castle Keep Pr.) Rock, James A. & Co. Pubs.

Scarry, Patsy, et al. Richard Scarry's Best Little Golden Books Ever! Scarry, Richard, illus. 2014. (Little Golden Book Treasury Ser.). (ENG.). 224p. (J). (-k). 12.99 *(978-0-385-37912-0(9)*, Golden Bks.) Random Hse. Children's Bks.

Scarry, Richard. Christmas Mice. Scarry, Richard, illus. 2014. (Little Golden Book Ser.). (ENG., Illus.). 24p. (J). (-k). 4.99 *(978-0-385-38421-6(1)*, Golden Bks.) Random Hse. Children's Bks.

Schade, Susan. Riff Raff Sails the High Cheese. Kennedy, Anne, illus. 2014. (I Can Read Level 2 Ser.). (ENG.). 24p. (J). (gr. -1-3). pap. 3.99 *(978-0-06-230509-1(3))* HarperCollins Pubs.

—Riff Raff the Mouse Pirate. Kennedy, Anne, illus. 2014. (I Can Read Level 2 Ser.). (ENG.). 24p. (J). (gr. -1-3). pap. 3.99 *(978-0-06-230507-7(7))* HarperCollins Pubs.

Scharer, Niko. Emily's House, 1 vol. Fitzgerald, Joanne, illus. 2010. (ENG.). 22p. (J). (gr. k — 1). bds. 7.95 *(978-0-88899-831-6(7))* Groundwood Bks. CAN. Dist: Publishers Group West (PGW).

Scheer, Ruth D. The Mouse & the Angel. 2003. (J). lib. bdg. 15.95 *(978-0-9671761-3-0(1))* Scheer Delight Publishing.

Schertle, Alice. Such a Little Mouse. Yue, Stephanie, illus. 2015. (ENG.). 32p. (J). (gr. -1-k). 16.99 *(978-0-545-64929-2(3))* Scholastic, Inc.

Schmidt, Hans-Christian & Bieber, Hartmut. The Wondrous Day. 2004. (Illus.). 18p. (J). 10.99 *(978-1-59384-047-1(0))* Parklane Publishing.

Schoenherr, Ian. Cat & Mouse. Schoenherr, Ian, illus. 2008. (Illus.). 40p. (J). (gr. -1). lib. bdg. 17.89 *(978-0-06-136314-6(6)*, Greenwillow Bks.) HarperCollins Pubs.

—Pip & Squeak. Schoenherr, Ian, illus. 2007. (Illus.). 32p. (J). (gr. -1-k). 18.89 *(978-0-06-087254-0(3))* HarperCollins Pubs.

Schomberger, Mary. The Adventures of Goldy the Mouse. 2013. 36p. pap. 16.95 *(978-1-4908-0375-3(0)*, WestBow Pr.) Author Solutions, Inc.

Schreck, Tabatha M. Welcome to God's Big Backyard: Little Mouse's Adventure. 2012. 28p. pap. 14.95 *(978-1-4520-5524-4(6))* AuthorHouse.

Schubert, Ingrid & Schubert, Dieter. Elephant Soup. 2010. (ENG., Illus.). 32p. (J). (gr. -1-3). 17.95 *(978-1-59078-807-3(9)*, 9781590788073) Lemniscaat USA.

—My Hero. 2005. (ENG., Illus.). 32p. (J). (gr. -1-3). 16.95 *(978-1-932425-10-9(1)*, 9781932425109) Lemniscaat USA.

Schwabauer, Daniel. Runt the Hunted. 2007. (ENG., Illus.). 304p. (J). (gr. 4-7). 17.99 *(978-0-9742972-3-1(2))* Clear Water Pr.

Schwartz, Roslyn. The Vole Brothers. Schwartz, Roslyn & Owlkids Books Inc. Staff, illus. 2011. (ENG.). 32p. (J). (gr. -1-2). 15.95 *(978-1-926818-83-2(0)*, Owlkids) Owlkids Bks. Inc. CAN. Dist: Publishers Group West (PGW).

Scott, Cathy. Lily Mouse. 2011. (Illus.). 32p. pap. 12.95 *(978-1-4575-0305-4(0))* Dog Ear Publishing, LLC.

Scott, Janine. Mars Mouse. Wood, Hannah, illus. 2009. (Treasure Chest Readers Ser.). 24p. (J). (gr. -1-2). pap. 8.15 *(978-1-60754-677-1(9))*; lib. bdg. 22.60 *(978-1-60754-676-4(0))* Windmill Bks.

Scott, Nathan Kumar. Mangoes & Bananas. Balaji, T., illus. 2nd ed. 2006. (ENG.). 32p. (J). *(978-81-86211-06-9(3))* Temmen, Edition, Horst Temmen.

Scotton, Rob. The Name of the Game. Scotton, Rob, illus. 2012. (I Can Read Level 1 Ser.). (ENG., Illus.). 32p. (J). (gr. -1-3). 16.99 *(978-0-06-209015-7(1))* HarperCollins Pubs.

—On with the Snow. 2013. (Splat the Cat 8X8 Ser.). (J). lib. bdg. 13.55 *(978-0-606-27152-3(X)*, Turtleback) Turtleback Bks.

—Splat the Cat. 2011. (J). (gr. -1-2). 29.95 *(978-0-545-23794-9(7))* Weston Woods Studios, Inc.

—Splat the Cat: Big Reading Collection. Scotton, Rob, illus. 2012. (I Can Read Level 1 Ser.). (ENG., Illus.). 100p. (J). (gr. k-3). pap. 16.99 *(978-0-06-209029-4(1))* HarperCollins Pubs.

—Twice the Mice. 2015. (Splat the Cat: I Can Read Ser.). (J). lib. bdg. 13.55 *(978-0-606-37633-4(X))* Turtleback Bks.

—Up in the Air at the Fair. 2014. (Splat the Cat: I Can Read Ser.). (J). lib. bdg. 13.55 *(978-0-606-35059-4(4)*, Turtleback) Turtleback Bks.

Scriber, Christian. The Adventures of Almighty Mouse: And Tales of His Friends. 2009. 112p. pap. 10.99 *(978-1-4389-4313-8(X))* AuthorHouse.

Seaman, Lucy. Mr Mouse Morgan. Swope, Brenda, illus. 2011. 28p. pap. 24.95 *(978-1-4560-0916-8(8))* America Star Bks.

Seddon, Jane. Tales of Bermy Wood, 1 vol. 2010. 64p. pap. 19.95 *(978-1-4489-2195-9(3))* America Star Bks.

Segal, Andrew. Clarissa the Clown. Scott, Peter & JessT, Grant, illus. 2007. 32p. per. *(978-1-905823-20-8(7))* Panoma Pr. Ltd.

Seigel, Jonathan & Rother, Beverly S. Myrtle the Turtle & Popeye the Mouse: Learning about Our Solar System. 2012. 40p. pap. 24.95 *(978-1-4626-6587-7(X))* America Star Bks.

Selden, George. The Cricket in Times Square. Williams, Garth, illus. 2008. (Chester Cricket & His Friends Ser.: 1). (ENG.). 144p. (J). (gr. 1-4). pap. 6.99 *(978-0-312-38003-8(8)*, 9780312380038) Square Fish.

—Harry Kitten & Tucker Mouse. Williams, Garth, illus. 2009. (Chester Cricket & His Friends Ser.). (ENG.). 144p. (J). (gr. 1-4). pap. 8.99 *(978-0-312-58248-7(X)*, 9780312582487) Square Fish.

—Tucker's Countryside. Williams, Garth, illus. 2012. (ENG.). 192p. (J). (gr. 3-7). pap. 7.99 *(978-1-250-00256-3(7)*, 9781250002563) Square Fish.

Seltzer, Eric. Bake, Mice, Bake! Rosenberg, Natascha, illus. 2012. (Penguin Young Readers, Level 1 Ser.). (ENG.). 32p. (J). (gr. k-1). mass mkt. 3.99 *(978-0-448-45763-5(6)*, Penguin Young Readers) Penguin Young Readers Group.

—Bake, Mice, Bake! 2012. (Penguin Young Readers Level 1 Ser.). lib. bdg. 13.55 *(978-0-606-23625-6(2)*, Turtleback) Turtleback Bks.

Shea, Therese. A House for Mouse. 2006. (Neighborhood Readers Ser.). (ENG.). 8p. (gr. -1-3). pap. 5.15 *(978-1-4042-5672-9(5)*, Rosen Classroom) Rosen Publishing Group, Inc., The.

Shelton, Crystal G. Theodore's Rings. 2013. 24p. pap. 24.95 *(978-1-62709-378-1(8))* America Star Bks.

Shepard, Aaron. The Adventures of Mouse Deer. Gamble, Kim, illus. 2005. 48p. (J). (gr. -1-4). pap. 10.00 *(978-0-938497-32-5(4)*, Skyhook Pr.) Shepard Pubns.

Shields, Christine. The Tiny Little Scary Mouse. 2012. 20p. pap. 12.68 *(978-1-4669-2147-4(1))* Trafford Publishing.

Shimberg, Elaine Fantle. Helga, the Hippopotamouse. Walling, Sandy Seeley, illus. 2008. (ENG.). 36p. (J). 7.95 *(978-0-9741940-4-2(2))* Abernathy Hse. Publishing.

Shock, Tanya & Thomson, Roger. Walking in Courage: Stories of Virtue's Forest. 2012. 24p. pap. 12.95 *(978-1-4497-3443-5(X)*, WestBow Pr.) Author Solutions, Inc.

Shope, Ray & Shope, Lois. Sandy Claws & Chris Mouse. White, Michael, illus. 2003. 32p. (J). 13.95 *(978-0-9714734-0-9(4))* Flutter-By Productions.

Sif, Birgitta. Swish & Squeak's Noisy Day. 2017. (ENG.). 32p. (J). (-k). 16.99 ***(978-0-399-55622-7(2))***; lib. bdg. 19.99 ***(978-0-399-55623-4(0))*** Random Hse. Children's Bks. (Knopf Bks. for Young Readers).

Sivola, Liz. Little Mouse Finds a New Home. DuPont, Brittany, illus. 2013. 24p. pap. 9.99 *(978-1-937165-42-0(6))* Orange Hat Publishing.

Simi, Gillingham & Gillingham, Sara. In My Patch. Siminovich, Lorena, illus. 2010. (ENG.). 12p. (J). (gr. -1 — 1). bds. 8.99 *(978-0-8118-7567-7(9))* Chronicle Bks. LLC.

Singh, Jay. Once upon a Time in a Forest Far Away. 2009. 394p. pap. 33.12 *(978-1-4251-9122-1(3))* Trafford Publishing.

Skinner, Daphne. Albert Keeps Score. Melmon, Deborah, illus. 2012. (Mouse Math Ser.). (ENG.). 32p. (J). (gr. -1-1). lib. bdg. 22.60 *(978-1-57565-449-2(0))* Kane Press, Inc.

—The Right Place for Albert. Melmon, Deborah, illus. 2012. (Mouse Math Ser.). (ENG.). 32p. (J). (gr. -1-1). 7.95 *(978-1-57565-438-6(5))*; lib. bdg. 22.60 *(978-1-57565-446-1(6))* Kane Press, Inc.

Skinner, Daphne & May, Eleanor. Albert Keeps Score. Melmon, Deborah, illus. 2012. (Mouse Math Ser.). (ENG.). 32p. (J). (gr. -1-1). 7.95 *(978-1-57565-444-7(X))* Kane Press, Inc.

Skrbina, Daniel William. A Knight to Remember: Gulliver's Journey Continues, 1 vol. 2009. 74p. pap. 19.95 *(978-1-60836-737-5(1))* America Star Bks.

Slanina, Anne M. Baby Brother Goes to the Hospital. Agnew, Alicia, illus. 2007. (Adventures of Annie Mouse Ser.: Bk. 2). 28p. (J). 18.99 *(978-0-9793379-1-8(7))*; per. 9.99 *(978-0-9793379-0-1(9))* Annie Mouse Bks.

Slanina, Anne Marc. Annie Mouse's Route 66 Adventure: A Photo Journal, vols. 6, vol. 5. Collins, Kelsey, illus. 2011. (ENG.). 48p. (J). pap. 14.99 *(978-0-9793379-6-3(8))* Annie Mouse Bks.

Small, Lily. Chloe the Kitten. 2015. (Fairy Animals of Misty Wood Ser.: 1). (ENG., Illus.). 144p. (J). (gr. k-3). pap. 5.99 *(978-1-62779-141-0(8)*, 9781627791410, Holt, Henry & Co. Bks. For Young Readers) Holt, Henry & Co.

—Mia the Mouse. 2015. (Fairy Animals of Misty Wood Ser.: 4). (ENG., Illus.). 144p. (J). (gr. k-3). pap. 5.99 *(978-1-62779-144-1(2)*, 9781627791441, Holt, Henry & Co. Bks. For Young Readers) Holt, Henry & Co.

—Mia the Mouse, Poppy the Pony, & Hailey the Hedgehog Bindup. Small, Lily, illus. 2016. (Fairy Animals of Misty Wood Ser.). (ENG., Illus.). 416p. (J). pap. 10.99 *(978-1-250-11399-3(7)*, 9781250113993, Holt, Henry & Co. Bks. For Young Readers) Holt, Henry & Co.

Smiley, Jeremy. Mice City. 2007. 48p. per. 24.95 *(978-1-4241-8835-2(0))* America Star Bks.

Smith, Gloria. Annie Elf Meets Mitty Mouse. Smith, Claire, illus. 2012. 24p. 29.95 *(978-1-62709-398-9(2))*; pap. 24.95 *(978-1-4626-8151-8(4))* America Star Bks.

Smith, Holly C. Tyler the Monkey & Andy the Mouse. 2012. 28p. (-18). pap. 24.95 *(978-1-4626-9501-0(9))* America Star Bks.

Smith, Jeff. Little Mouse Gets Ready. 2009. (ENG., Illus.). 32p. (J). (gr. -1-3). 12.95 *(978-1-935179-01-6(2))* TOON Books / RAW Junior, LLC.

—Little Mouse Gets Ready. 2013. (Toon Books Level 1 Ser.). lib. bdg. 14.75 *(978-0-606-31593-7(4)*, Turtleback) Turtleback Bks.

—Little Mouse Gets Ready, Level 1. 2013. (ENG., Illus.). 32p. (J). (gr. -1-3). pap. 6.99 *(978-1-935179-24-5(1))* TOON Books / RAW Junior, LLC.

Smith, Sindy. Ervin & Alma's Little Mouse House. 2013. 38p. 24.95 *(978-1-63004-209-7(9))*; 40p. pap. 24.95 *(978-1-62709-189-3(0))* America Star Bks.

Snively, Carolyn. Zippo's First Christmas. 2012. 19.95 *(978-0-7414-7383-7(6))*; pap. 11.95 *(978-0-7414-7382-0(8))* Infinity Publishing.

Solomon, Martha. Christmas in Da Hood. 2012. 28p. pap. 12.50 *(978-0-9883126-3-0(8))* iScribe Pubns. LLC.

Sommer, Carl. If Only I Were. . . 2003. (Another Sommer-Time Story Ser.). (Illus.). 48p. (J). (gr. 1-4). 16.95 incl. audio *(978-1-57537-551-9(6))* Advance Publishing, Inc.

—If Only I Were. . . James, Kennon, illus. 2003. (Another Sommer-Time Story Ser.). (ENG.). 48p. (J). 16.95 incl. audio compact disk *(978-1-57537-502-1(8))* Advance Publishing, Inc.

—If Only I Were- James, Kennon, illus. 2014. (J). pap. *(978-1-57537-954-8(6))* Advance Publishing, Inc.

—If Only I Were...(Si Yo Fuese...) James, Kennon, illus. 2009. (Another Sommer-Time Story Bilingual Ser.). (SPA & ENG.). 48p. (J). lib. bdg. 16.95 *(978-1-57537-154-2(5))* Advance Publishing, Inc.

—The Lion & the Mouse. Mercado, Jorge, illus. 2014. (Sommer-Time Story Classics Ser.). (ENG.). 32p. (J). (gr. k-4). 16.95 *(978-1-57537-082-8(4))* Advance Publishing, Inc.

—Noise! Noise! Noise! James, Kennon, illus. (J). 2014. pap. *(978-1-57537-963-0(5))* 2003. (ENG.). 48p. 9.95 *(978-1-57537-020-0(4))* 2003. (ENG.). 48p. lib. bdg. 16.95 *(978-1-57537-069-9(7))* 2003. (ENG.). 48p. (gr. 1-4). 16.95 incl. audio compact disk *(978-1-57537-519-9(2))* Advance Publishing, Inc.

—Noise! Noise! Noise! 2003. (Another Sommer-Time Story Ser.). (Illus.). 48p. (J). (gr. 1-4). 16.95 incl. audio *(978-1-57537-568-7(0))* Advance Publishing, Inc.

—Noise! Noise! Noise! Read-along 2003. (Another Sommer-Time Story Ser.). (Illus.). 48p. (J). lib. bdg. 23.95 incl. audio *(978-1-57537-769-8(1))* Advance Publishing, Inc.

—Noise! Noise! Noise!(Ruido! Ruido! Ruido!) James, Kennon, illus. 2009. (Another Sommer-Time Story Bilingual Ser.). (SPA & ENG.). 48p. (J). lib. bdg. 16.95 *(978-1-57537-161-0(8))* Advance Publishing, Inc.

Sorenson, Margo. Ambrose & the Cathedral Dream. Szegedi, Katalin, illus. 2006. (ENG.). 32p. (J). (gr. -1-3). 4.24 *(978-0-8146-3004-4(9))* Liturgical Pr.

—Ambrose & the Princess. Szegedi, Katalin, illus. 2005. (ENG.). 32p. (J). (gr. -1-3). 16.95 *(978-0-8146-3043-3(X))* Liturgical Pr.

Soto, Gary. Chato's Kitchen. Guevara, Susan, illus. 2003. (Chato Ser.). (J). (gr. -1-2). pap. 39.95 *(978-1-59112-527-3(8))* Live Oak Media.

Spangenberg, Greg. A Christmas Eve Victory. Lodwick, Sarah, illus. l.t. ed. 2006. 32p. (J). 16.99 *(978-1-59879-140-2(0))* Lifevest Publishing, Inc.

—Churchy & the Light on Christmas Eve. Lodwick, Sarah, illus. l.t. ed. 2006. 40p. (J). (gr. -1-7). 14.99 *(978-1-59879-017-7(X))* Lifevest Publishing, Inc.

Spellmeyer, William. Ick-N-Pog: The Encounter Book 2. 2012. 104p. (gr. 2-4). pap. 12.81 *(978-1-4251-9237-2(8))* Trafford Publishing.

Spin & Match - Tell Me a Story: The Grasshopper & the Ants, the Fox & the Grapes, the Turtle & the Rabbit. 2006. (ENG.). 66p. (J). 9.99 *(978-1-59204-202-9(3))* Learning Wrap-Ups, Inc.

Spinelli, Eileen. Now It Is Summer. DePalma, Mary Newell, illus. 2011. (ENG.). 36p. (YA). (gr. -1-3). 16.00 *(978-0-8028-5340-0(4)*, Eerdmans Bks For Young Readers) Eerdmans, William B. Publishing Co.

—Now It Is Winter. DePalma, Mary Newell, illus. 2004. 32p. (J). 16.00 *(978-0-8028-5244-1(0))* Eerdmans, William B. Publishing Co.

—Together at Christmas. Lee, Bin, illus. 2012. (ENG.). 24p. (J). (gr. -1-3). 15.99 *(978-0-8075-8010-3(4))* Whitman, Albert & Co.

Springman, I. C. More. Lies, Brian, illus. 2012. (ENG.). 40p. (J). (gr. -1-3). 16.99 *(978-0-547-61083-2(1))* Houghton Mifflin Harcourt Publishing Co.

Square Cat ABC. 2014. (ENG., Illus.). 32p. (J). (gr. -1-3). 15.99 *(978-1-4424-9895-2(1)*, Aladdin) Simon & Schuster Children's Publishing.

St. Pierre, Todd-Michael. Chicory & Roux: The Creole Mouse & the Cajun Mouse, 1 vol. Randall, Lee Brandt, illus. 2017. (ENG.). 32p. (J). (gr. k-3). 16.99 ***(978-1-4556-2237-5(0))*** Pelican Publishing Co., Inc.

Staehli, Melissa. Charlie's Gingerbread House. Rottinger, Amy, illus. 2012. 24p. pap. 11.95 *(978-1-61244-063-7(0))* Halo Publishing International.

Stahl, Stephanie. The Best Snowman Ever! Vasylenko, Veronica, illus. 2013. (ENG.). 16p. (J). (gr. -1-k). bds. 8.95 *(978-1-58925-605-7(0))* Tiger Tales.

Stave, Mel. How Harry Found the Meaning of Friendship. 2010. (Illus.). 40p. pap. 14.95 *(978-1-60911-147-2(8)*, Eloquent Bks.) Strategic Book Publishing & Rights Agency (SBPRA).

Steig, William. Abel's Island. 2007. (Newbery Award & Honor Bks.). (Illus.). 117p. (gr. 3-7). 17.00 *(978-0-7569-8290-4(1))* Perfection Learning Corp.

—Abel's Island. Steig, William, illus. 2007. (ENG., Illus.). 128p. (J). (gr. 3-7). per. 6.99 *(978-0-312-37143-2(8)*, 9780312371432) Square Fish.

—Amos & Boris. 2011. 8.30 *(978-0-7848-3427-5(X)*, Everbind) Marco Bk. Co.

—Amos & Boris. Steig, William, illus. 2009. (ENG., Illus.). 32p. (J). (gr. k-3). pap. 7.99 *(978-0-312-53566-7(X)*, 9780312535667) Square Fish.

—Amos & Boris. 2009. (J). (gr. -1-2). lib. bdg. 18.40 *(978-0-8085-2709-1(6)*, Turtleback) Turtleback Bks.

—Doctor de Soto. 2003. (Picture Books Collection). (SPA.). 32p. (J). (gr. k-3). 16.95 *(978-84-372-6616-9(5))* Altea, Ediciones, S.A. - Grupo Santillana ESP. Dist: Santillana USA Publishing Co., Inc.

—Doctor de Soto. 2004. (J). (gr. k-3). spiral bd. *(978-0-616-01785-2(5))*; spiral bd. *(978-0-616-01784-5(7))* Canadian National Institute for the Blind/Institut National Canadien pour les Aveugles.

—Doctor de Soto. Steig, William, illus. 2010. (ENG., Illus.). 32p. (J). (gr. -1-3). pap. 7.99 *(978-0-312-61189-7(7)*, 9780312611897) Square Fish.

—Doctor de Soto. 2010. (J). lib. bdg. 18.40 *(978-0-606-14606-7(7)*, Turtleback) Turtleback Bks.

Stein, David Ezra. Love, Mouserella. Stein, David Ezra, illus. 2011. (ENG., Illus.). 32p. (J). (gr. -1-k). 15.99 *(978-0-399-25410-9(2)*, Nancy Paulsen Books) Penguin Young Readers Group.

Stengel, Joyce A. St. Patrick & the Three Brave Mice, 1 vol. Leonhard, Herb, illus. 2009. (ENG.). 32p. (J). (gr. k-3). 16.99 *(978-1-58980-663-4(8))* Pelican Publishing Co., Inc.

Stewart, Shawna. Amazing Tails of Zomber Doodles & Buttons, 1 vol. 2010. 30p. pap. 24.95 *(978-1-4489-7913-4(7))* PublishAmerica, Inc.

Stewig, John Warren. Nobody Asked the Pea. Van Wright, Cornelius, illus. 2013. (ENG.). 32p. (J). (gr. 1-5). 16.95 *(978-0-8234-2224-1(0))* Holiday Hse., Inc.

Stilton, Geronimo. All Because of a Cup of Coffee. Wolf, Matt, illus. 2004. (Geronimo Stilton Ser.: 10). (ENG.). 128p. (J). (gr. 2-5). pap. 7.99 *(978-0-439-55972-0(3)*, Scholastic Paperbacks) Scholastic, Inc.

—The Amazing Voyage. Barozzi, Danilo, illus. 2011. (Geronimo Stilton & the Kingdom of Fantasy Ser.: 3). (ENG.). 320p. (J). (gr. 2-5). 14.99 *(978-0-545-30771-0(6))* Scholastic, Inc.

—Back in Time. 2015. (Geronimo Stilton Special Edition: the Journey Through Time Ser.: 2). (ENG.). 320p. (J). (gr. 2-5). 14.99 *(978-0-545-74618-2(3)*, Scholastic Paperbacks) Scholastic, Inc.

—Beware! Space Junk! 2016. (Geronimo Stilton Spacemice Ser.: 7). (ENG.). 128p. (J). (gr. 2-5). pap. 7.99 *(978-0-545-87245-4(6)*, Scholastic Paperbacks) Scholastic, Inc.

—Cat & Mouse in a Haunted House. Wolf, Matt & Keys, Larry, illus. 2004. (Geronimo Stilton Ser.: 3). (ENG.). 128p. (J). (gr. -1-3). pap. 7.99 *(978-0-439-55965-2(0)*, Scholastic Paperbacks) Scholastic, Inc.

—Cat & Mouse in a Haunted House. 2004. (Geronimo Stilton Ser.: 3). (gr. 3-6). lib. bdg. 18.40 *(978-0-613-72224-7(8)*, Turtleback) Turtleback Bks.

—Christmas Catastrophe. 2007. (Geronimo Stilton Ser.). (Illus.). 93p. (J). (gr. 2-5). 14.65 *(978-0-7569-8804-3(7))* Perfection Learning Corp.

—Christmas Catastrophe. 2007. (Geronimo Stilton Special Edition Ser.). (ENG., Illus.). 128p. (J). (gr. 2-5). pap. 8.99 *(978-0-545-00902-7(2)*, Scholastic Paperbacks) Scholastic, Inc.

—The Curse of the Cheese Pyramid. Wolf, Matt & Keys, Larry, illus. 2004. (Geronimo Stilton Ser.: 2). (ENG.). 128p. (J). (gr. 2-5). pap. 7.99 *(978-0-439-55964-5(2))* Scholastic, Inc.

—The Curse of the Cheese Pyramid. 2004. (Geronimo Stilton Ser.: 2). (gr. 3-6). lib. bdg. 18.40 *(978-0-613-72223-0(X)*, Turtleback) Turtleback Bks.

—Don't Wake the Dinosaur! 2014. (Geronimo Stilton Cavemice Ser.: 6). (ENG.). 128p. (J). (gr. 2-5). pap. 7.99 *(978-0-545-65603-0(6)*, Scholastic Paperbacks) Scholastic, Inc.

—Don't Wake the Dinosaur! 2014. (Geronimo Stilton Cavemice Ser.: 6). lib. bdg. 18.40 *(978-0-606-36057-9(3))* Turtleback Bks.

—Down & Out down Under. 2007. (Geronimo Stilton Ser.: 29). lib. bdg. 18.40 *(978-1-4177-7837-9(7)*, Turtleback) Turtleback Bks.

—The Dragon of Fortune: An Epic Kingdom of Fantasy Adventure. 2017. (Geronimo Stilton & the Kingdom of Fantasy Ser.: 2). (ENG.). 592p. (J). (gr. 2-5). 19.99 ***(978-1-338-15939-4(9)***, Scholastic Paperbacks) Scholastic, Inc.

—The Dragon Prophecy. 2012. (Geronimo Stilton & the Kingdom of Fantasy Ser.: Bk. 4). (ENG.). 320p. (J). (gr. 2-5). 14.99 *(978-0-545-39351-5(5)*, Scholastic Paperbacks) Scholastic, Inc.

—The Enormouse Pearl Heist. 2012. (Geronimo Stilton Ser.: 51). lib. bdg. 18.40 *(978-0-606-26756-4(5)*, Turtleback) Turtleback Bks.

—A Fabumouse School Adventure. 2009. (Geronimo Stilton Ser.: 38). (ENG.). 128p. (J). (gr. 2-5). pap. 7.99 *(978-0-545-02138-8(3)*, Scholastic Paperbacks) Scholastic, Inc.

—A Fabumouse School Adventure. 2009. (Geronimo Stilton Ser.: 38). lib. bdg. 18.40 *(978-0-606-00229-5(4)*, Turtleback) Turtleback Bks.

—A Fabumouse Vacation for Geronimo. Keys, Larry, illus. 2004. (Geronimo Stilton Ser.: 9). (ENG.). 128p. (J). (gr. 2-5). pap. 7.99 *(978-0-439-55971-3(5)*, Scholastic Paperbacks) Scholastic, Inc.

—The Fast & the Frozen. 2014. (Geronimo Stilton Cavemice Ser.: 4). (ENG., Illus.). 128p. (J). (gr. 2-5). pap. 7.99 *(978-0-545-64291-0(4)*, Scholastic Paperbacks) Scholastic, Inc.

—Field Trip to Niagara Falls. 2006. (Geronimo Stilton Ser.: 24). (ENG., Illus.). 128p. (J). (gr. 2-5). pap. 7.99 *(978-0-439-69146-8(X)*, Scholastic Paperbacks) Scholastic, Inc.

—Flight of the Red Bandit. 2014. (ENG., Illus.). 128p. (J). (gr. 2-5). pap. 7.99 *(978-0-545-55630-9(9)*, Scholastic Paperbacks) Scholastic, Inc.

—Flood Mission. 2015. (Illus.). 117p. (J). *(978-0-545-92010-0(8))* Scholastic, Inc.

—Following the Trail of Marco Polo, No. 4. Cooper-McGuinness, Nanette, tr. 2010. (Geronimo Stilton Graphic Novels Ser.). (ENG., Illus.). 56p. (J). (gr. 2-6). 9.99 *(978-1-59707-188-8(9)*, 9781597071888) Papercutz.

—Four Mice Deep in the Jungle. Wolf, Matt & Keys, Larry, illus. 2004. (Geronimo Stilton Ser.: 5). (ENG.). 128p. (J). (gr. 2-5). pap. 7.99 *(978-0-439-55967-6(7)*, Scholastic Paperbacks) Scholastic, Inc.

—Fright Night. 2013. (Geronimo Stilton — Creepella Von Cacklefur Ser.: 5). lib. bdg. 18.40 *(978-0-606-26181-4(8)*, Turtleback) Turtleback Bks.

—The Galactic Goal. 2015. (Geronimo Stilton Spacemice Ser.: 4). (ENG., Illus.). 128p. (J). (gr. 2-5). pap. 7.99 *(978-0-545-74620-5(5)*, Scholastic Paperbacks) Scholastic, Inc.

—Geronimo & the Gold Medal Mystery. 2008. (Geronimo Stilton Ser.). (Illus.). 87p. (J). (gr. 2-5). lib. bdg. 14.65 *(978-0-7569-8803-6(9))* Perfection Learning Corp.

—Geronimo & the Gold Medal Mystery. 2008. (Geronimo Stilton Ser.: 33). (ENG., Illus.). 128p. (J). (gr. 2-5). pap. 7.99 *(978-0-545-02133-3(2)*, Scholastic Paperbacks) Scholastic, Inc.

—Geronimo Stilton Bk. 59: Welcome to Moldy Manor. 2014. (ENG., Illus.). 128p. (J). (gr. 2-5). pap. 7.99 *(978-0-545-74613-7(2)*, Scholastic Paperbacks) Scholastic, Inc.

—Geronimo Stilton Bks. 7-9: Red Pizzas for a Blue Count, Attack of the Bandit Cats, a Fabumouse Vacation for Gernimo. 2005. (J). *(978-0-439-79161-8(8))* Scholastic, Inc.

—Geronimo Stilton Boxed Set: Vol. #4 - 6. 2011. (Geronimo Stilton Graphic Novels Ser.). (ENG., Illus.). 168p. (J). (gr. 2-6). 29.99 *(978-1-59707-271-7(0)*, 9781597072717) Papercutz.

—Geronimo Stilton Boxed Set Vol. #7-9. 2012. (Geronimo Stilton Graphic Novels Ser.). (ENG., Illus.). 168p. (J). (gr. 2-6). 29.99 *(978-1-59707-344-8(X)*, 9781597073448) Papercutz.

—Geronimo Stilton Cavemice Bk. 7: I¿m a Scaredy-Mouse! 2015. (Geronimo Stilton Cavemice Ser.: 7). (ENG., Illus.). 128p. (J). (gr. 2-5). pap. 6.99 *(978-0-545-74616-8(7)*, Scholastic Paperbacks) Scholastic, Inc.

—Geronimo Stilton Heromice Bk. 3: Flood Mission. 2015. (Illus.). 128p. (J). pap. *(978-0-545-66814-9(X))* Scholastic, Inc.

—Geronimo's Valentine, No. 36. 2009. (Geronimo Stilton Ser.: 36). (ENG.). 128p. (J). (gr. 2-5). pap. 7.99 *(978-0-545-02136-4(7)*, Scholastic Paperbacks) Scholastic, Inc.

—Geronimo's Valentine. 2009. (Geronimo Stilton Ser.: 36). (Illus.). 103p. (J). 18.40 *(978-1-4364-5051-5(9)*, Turtleback) Turtleback Bks.

—Get the Scoop, Geronimo! 2015. (Geronimo Stilton Cavemice Ser.: 9). 128p. (J). lib. bdg. 17.20 *(978-0-606-37779-9(4))* Turtleback Bks.

—Ghost Pirate Treasure. 2012. (Creepella Von Cacklefur Ser.: 3). (ENG.). 128p. (J). (gr. 2-5). pap. 7.99 *(978-0-545-30744-4(9)*, Scholastic Paperbacks) Scholastic, Inc.

—Ghost Pirate Treasure. 2012. (Geronimo Stilton — Creepella Von Cacklefur Ser.: 3). lib. bdg. 18.40 *(978-0-606-23931-8(6)*, Turtleback) Turtleback Bks.

—The Golden Statue Plot. 2013. (Geronimo Stilton Ser.: 55). lib. bdg. 18.40 *(978-0-606-32380-2(5)*, Turtleback) Turtleback Bks.

—The Great Ice Age. Cooper-McGuinness, Nanette, tr. 2010. (Geronimo Stilton Graphic Novels Ser.). (ENG., Illus.). 56p. (J). (gr. 2-6). 9.99 *(978-1-59707-202-1(8)*, 9781597072021) Papercutz.

—The Great Mouse Race. 2014. (Geronimo Stilton Cavemice Ser.: 5). (ENG., Illus.). 128p. (J). (gr. 2-5). pap. 7.99 *(978-0-545-64654-3(5)*, Scholastic Paperbacks) Scholastic, Inc.

—The Haunted Castle. 2011. (ENG.). 128p. (J). (gr. 2-5). pap. 7.99 *(978-0-545-10374-9(6)*, Scholastic Paperbacks) Scholastic, Inc.

—Help, I'm in Hot Lava! 2013. (Geronimo Stilton Cavemice Ser.: 3). (ENG., Illus.). 128p. (J). (gr. 2-5). pap. 7.99 *(978-0-545-64290-3(6)*, Scholastic Paperbacks) Scholastic, Inc.

—Help, I'm in Hot Lava! 2013. (Geronimo Stilton Cavemice Ser.: 3). lib. bdg. 17.20 *(978-0-606-32407-6(0)*, Turtleback) Turtleback Bks.

—The Hour of Magic. 2016. (ENG.). 320p. (J). (gr. 2-5). 14.99 *(978-0-545-82336-4(6))* Scholastic, Inc.

—The Hunt for the Curious Cheese. 2015. (Geronimo Stilton Special Edition Ser.). (ENG., Illus.). 224p. (J). (gr. 2-5). 14.99 *(978-0-545-79151-9(0)*, Scholastic Paperbacks) Scholastic, Inc.

—The Hunt for the Secret Papyrus. 2016. (Geronimo Stilton Special Edition Ser.). (ENG.). 224p. (J). (gr. 2-5). 14.99 *(978-0-545-87250-8(2)*, Scholastic Paperbacks) Scholastic, Inc.

—Ice Planet Adventure. 2015. (Geronimo Stilton Spacemice Ser.: 3). (ENG., Illus.). 128p. (J). (gr. 2-5). pap. 7.99 *(978-0-545-74619-9(1)*, Scholastic Paperbacks) Scholastic, Inc.

—I'm Not a Supermouse! 2010. (ENG.). 128p. (J). (gr. 2-5). pap. 7.99 *(978-0-545-10375-6(4)*, Scholastic Paperbacks) Scholastic, Inc.

—I'm Too Fond of My Fur! Wolf, Matt, illus. 2004. (Geronimo Stilton Ser.: No. 4). 116p. (J). lib. bdg. 10.00 *(978-1-4242-0698-8(7))* Fitzgerald Bks.

—I'm Too Fond of My Fur! Wolf, Matt & Keys, Larry, illus. 2004. (Geronimo Stilton Ser.: 4). (ENG.). 128p. (J). (gr. 2-5). pap. 7.99 *(978-0-439-55966-9(9)*, Scholastic Paperbacks) Scholastic, Inc.

—I'm Too Fond of My Fur! 2004. (Geronimo Stilton Ser.: 4). (gr. 3-6). lib. bdg. 18.40 *(978-0-613-72225-4(6)*, Turtleback) Turtleback Bks.

—It's Halloween, You 'Fraidy Mouse! Wolf, Matt, illus. 2004. 113p. (J). lib. bdg. 10.00 *(978-1-4242-0280-5(9))* Fitzgerald Bks.

—It's Halloween, You 'Fraidy Mouse! Wolf, Matt, illus. 2004. (Geronimo Stilton Ser.: 11). (ENG.). 128p. (J). (gr. 2-5). pap. 7.99 *(978-0-439-55973-7(1)*, Scholastic Paperbacks) Scholastic, Inc.

—Journey Through Time. 2014. (Geronimo Stilton Special Edition Ser.). (ENG.). 320p. (J). (gr. 2-5). 14.99 *(978-0-545-55623-1(6)*, Scholastic Paperbacks) Scholastic, Inc.

—The Karate Mouse. 2010. (Geronimo Stilton Ser.: 40). (ENG., Illus.). 128p. (J). (gr. 2-5). 7.99 *(978-0-545-10369-5(X)*, Scholastic Paperbacks) Scholastic, Inc.

—The Karate Mouse. 2010. (Geronimo Stilton Ser.: 40). lib. bdg. 18.40 *(978-0-606-06847-5(3)*, Turtleback) Turtleback Bks.

—Lost Treasure of the Emerald Eye. Wolf, Matt, illus. 2004. (Geronimo Stilton Ser.: No. 1). 116p. (J). lib. bdg. 10.00 *(978-1-4242-0695-7(2))* Fitzgerald Bks.

—Lost Treasure of the Emerald Eye. Wolf, Matt & Keys, Larry, illus. 2004. (Geronimo Stilton Ser.: 1). (ENG.). 128p. (J). (gr. 2-5). pap. 7.99 *(978-0-439-55963-8(4)*, Scholastic Paperbacks) Scholastic, Inc.

—Meet Me in Horrorwood. 2011. (Geronimo Stilton — Creepella Von Cacklefur Ser.: 2). (Illus.). 112p. (J). lib. bdg. 18.40 *(978-0-606-22947-0(7)*, Turtleback) Turtleback Bks.

—Merry Christmas, Geronimo! Wolf, Matt, illus. 2004. (Geronimo Stilton Ser.: 12). (ENG.). 128p. (J). (gr. 2-5). pap. 7.99 *(978-0-439-55974-4(X)*, Scholastic Paperbacks) Scholastic, Inc.

—The Mona Mousa Code. Wolf, Matt, illus. 2005. (Geronimo Stilton Ser.: No. 15). 113p. (J). lib. bdg. 10.00 *(978-1-4242-0284-3(1))* Fitzgerald Bks.

—Mouse House Hunter. 2015. (Geronimo Stilton Ser.: 61). lib. bdg. 18.40 *(978-0-606-37780-5(8))* Turtleback Bks.

—The Mouse Island Marathon. 2007. (Geronimo Stilton Ser.: 30). (ENG., Illus.). 128p. (J). (gr. 2-5). pap. 7.99 *(978-0-439-84121-4(6)*, Scholastic Paperbacks) Scholastic, Inc.

—The Mouse Island Marathon. 2007. (Geronimo Stilton Ser.: 30). lib. bdg. 18.40 *(978-1-4177-7839-3(3)*, Turtleback) Turtleback Bks.

—The Mummy with No Name. 2006. (Geronimo Stilton Ser.: 26). (ENG., Illus.). 128p. (J). (gr. 2-5). pap. 7.99 *(978-0-439-84117-7(8)*, Scholastic Paperbacks) Scholastic, Inc.

—My Name Is Stilton, Geronimo Stilton. 2005. (Geronimo Stilton Ser.: 19). (ENG., Illus.). 128p. (J). (gr. 2-5). pap. 7.99 *(978-0-439-69142-0(7)*, Scholastic Paperbacks) Scholastic, Inc.

—The Mysterious Cheese Thief. 2007. (Geronimo Stilton Ser.). (Illus.). 111p. (J). (gr. 2-5). 14.65 *(978-0-7569-8303-1(7))* Perfection Learning Corp.

—The Mysterious Cheese Thief. 2007. (Geronimo Stilton Ser.: 31). (Illus.). 111p. (gr. 4-7). 18.40 *(978-1-4177-9646-5(4)*, Turtleback) Turtleback Bks.

—The Mystery in Venice. 2012. (Geronimo Stilton Ser.: Bk. 48). (ENG.). 128p. (J). (gr. 2-5). pap. 7.99 *(978-0-545-34097-7(7)*, Scholastic Paperbacks) Scholastic, Inc.

—The Mystery in Venice. 2012. (Geronimo Stilton Ser.: 48). lib. bdg. 18.40 *(978-0-606-23729-1(1)*, Turtleback) Turtleback Bks.

—Paws Off, Cheddarface! Wolf, Matt & Keys, Larry, illus. 2004. (Geronimo Stilton Ser.: 6). (ENG.). 128p. (J). (gr. 2-5). pap. 7.99 *(978-0-439-55968-3(5))* Scholastic, Inc.

—The Peculiar Pumpkin Thief. 2010. (Geronimo Stilton Ser.: 42). (ENG.). 128p. (J). (gr. 2-5). 7.99 *(978-0-545-10372-5(X)*, Scholastic Paperbacks) Scholastic, Inc.

—The Phantom of the Subway. Wolf, Matt, illus. 2004. (Geronimo Stilton Ser.: No. 13). 112p. (J). lib. bdg. 10.00 *(978-1-4242-0282-9(5))* Fitzgerald Bks.

—The Phantom of the Subway. 2004. (Geronimo Stilton Ser.: No. 13). (ENG., Illus.). 128p. (J). (gr. 2-5). pap. 7.99 *(978-0-439-66162-1(5)*, Scholastic Paperbacks) Scholastic, Inc.

—The Race Across America. 2009. (Geronimo Stilton Ser.: 37). lib. bdg. 18.40 *(978-0-606-00228-8(6)*, Turtleback) Turtleback Bks.

—The Race Against Time: The Third Journey Through Time. 2016. (Geronimo Stilton Journey Through Time Ser.: 3). (ENG.). 320p. (J). (gr. 2-5). 14.99 *(978-0-545-87241-6(3)*, Scholastic Paperbacks) Scholastic, Inc.

—Red Pizzas for a Blue Count. Wolf, Matt & Keys, Larry, illus. 2004. (Geronimo Stilton Ser.: 7). (ENG.). 128p. (J). (gr. 2-5). pap. 7.99 *(978-0-439-55969-0(3))* Scholastic, Inc.

—Rescue Rebellion. 2015. (Geronimo Stilton Spacemice Ser.: 5). lib. bdg. 17.20 *(978-0-606-37775-1(1))* Turtleback Bks.

—Return of the Vampire. 2012. (Geronimo Stilton — Creepella Von Cacklefur Ser.: 4). lib. bdg. 18.40 *(978-0-606-26180-7(X)*, Turtleback) Turtleback Bks.

—Ride for Your Life! 2014. (Geronimo Stilton — Creepella Von Cacklefur Ser.: 6). lib. bdg. 18.40 *(978-0-606-35847-7(1))* Turtleback Bks.

—Rumble in the Jungle. 2013. (Geronimo Stilton Ser.: 53). lib. bdg. 18.40 *(978-0-606-31527-2(6)*, Turtleback) Turtleback Bks.

—Save the White Whale! 2011. (ENG.). 128p. (J). (gr. 2-5). pap. 7.99 *(978-0-545-10377-0(0)*, Scholastic Paperbacks) Scholastic, Inc.

—The Search for Sunken Treasure. Wolf, Matt, illus. 2006. (Geronimo Stilton Ser.: No. 25). 111p. (J). lib. bdg. 10.00 *(978-1-4242-1519-5(6))* Fitzgerald Bks.

—The Search for Treasure. 2014. (ENG.). 320p. (J). (gr. 2-5). 14.99 *(978-0-545-65604-7(4)*, Scholastic Paperbacks) Scholastic, Inc.

—The Secret of Cacklefur Castle. 2005. (Geronimo Stilton Ser.: 22). (ENG., Illus.). 128p. (J). (gr. 2-5). pap. 7.99 *(978-0-439-69145-1(1)*, Scholastic Paperbacks) Scholastic, Inc.

—Singing Sensation. 2009. (Geronimo Stilton Ser.: 39). lib. bdg. 18.40 *(978-0-606-00230-1(8)*, Turtleback) Turtleback Bks.

—The Stinky Cheese Vacation. 2014. (Geronimo Stilton Ser.). (ENG., Illus.). 128p. (J). (gr. 2-5). pap. 7.99 *(978-0-545-55631-6(7)*, Scholastic Paperbacks) Scholastic, Inc.

—The Stinky Cheese Vacation. 2014. (Geronimo Stilton Ser.: 57). lib. bdg. 18.40 *(978-0-606-35843-9(9))* Turtleback Bks.

—The Stone of Fire. 2013. (Geronimo Stilton Cavemice Ser.: 1). lib. bdg. 18.40 *(978-0-606-31526-5(8)*, Turtleback) Turtleback Bks.

—A Suitcase Full of Ghosts. 2015. (Creepella Von Cacklefur Ser.: 7). (ENG.). 128p. (J). (gr. 2-5). pap. 7.99 *(978-0-545-74611-3(6)*, Scholastic Paperbacks) Scholastic, Inc.

—Super Chef Contest. 2014. (ENG., Illus.). 128p. (J). (gr. 2-5). pap. 7.99 *(978-0-545-65600-9(1)*, Scholastic Paperbacks) Scholastic, Inc.

—The Super Chef Contest. 2014. (Geronimo Stilton Ser.: 58). lib. bdg. 18.40 *(978-0-606-36056-2(5))* Turtleback Bks.

—The Temple of the Ruby of Fire. Wolf, Matt, illus. 2004. (Geronimo Stilton Ser.: No. 14). 109p. (J). lib. bdg. 10.00 *(978-1-4242-0283-6(3))* Fitzgerald Bks.

—The Temple of the Ruby of Fire. 2004. (Geronimo Stilton Ser.: 14). (ENG., Illus.). 128p. (J). (gr. 2-5). pap. 7.99 *(978-0-439-66163-8(3)*, Scholastic Paperbacks) Scholastic, Inc.

—The Golden Statue Plot. 2013. (ENG.). 128p. (J). (gr. 2-5). pap. 7.99 *(978-0-545-55629-3(5)*, Scholastic Paperbacks) Scholastic, Inc.

—Thea Stilton & the Dragon's Code. 2009. (Geronimo Stilton Special Edition Ser.: No. 1). (Illus.). 158p. 18.00 *(978-1-60686-420-3(3))* Perfection Learning Corp.

—Thea Stilton & the Dragon's Code. 2009. (Thea Stilton Ser.: 1). lib. bdg. 19.65 *(978-0-606-00231-8(6)*, Turtleback) Turtleback Bks.

—This Hotel Is Haunted! 2012. (Geronimo Stilton Ser.: 50). lib. bdg. 18.40 *(978-0-606-26182-1(6)*, Turtleback) Turtleback Bks.

—The Underwater Planet. 2016. (Geronimo Stilton Spacemice Ser.: 6). (ENG., Illus.). 128p. (J). (gr. 2-5). pap. 7.99 *(978-0-545-87243-0(X)*, Scholastic Paperbacks) Scholastic, Inc.

—Valentine's Day Disaster. Keys, Larry et al, illus. 2006. (Geronimo Stilton Ser.: No. 23). 122p. (J). lib. bdg. 18.46 *(978-1-4242-0292-8(2))* Fitzgerald Bks.

—Valentine's Day Disaster. 2006. (Geronimo Stilton Ser.: No. 23). (ENG., Illus.). 128p. (J). (gr. 2-5). pap. 7.99 *(978-0-439-69147-5(8)*, Scholastic Paperbacks) Scholastic, Inc.

—Valley of the Giant Skeletons. 2008. (Illus.). 111p. (J). lib. bdg. 15.38 *(978-1-4242-4303-7(3))* Fitzgerald Bks.

—Valley of the Giant Skeletons. 2008. (Geronimo Stilton Ser.). (Illus.). 110p. (gr. 2-5). 17.00 *(978-0-7569-8805-0(5))* Perfection Learning Corp.

—Valley of the Giant Skeletons. 2008. (Geronimo Stilton Ser.: 32). (ENG., Illus.). 128p. (J). (gr. 2-5). pap. 7.99 *(978-0-545-02132-6(4)*, Scholastic Paperbacks) Scholastic, Inc.

—Valley of the Giant Skeletons. 2008. (Geronimo Stilton Ser.: 32). lib. bdg. 18.40 *(978-1-4364-2713-5(4))* Turtleback Bks.

—A Very Merry Christmas. 2008. (Geronimo Stilton Ser.: 35). (ENG.). 128p. (J). (gr. 2-5). pap. 7.99 *(978-0-545-02135-7(9)*, Scholastic Paperbacks) Scholastic, Inc.

—The Volcano of Fire. 2013. (Geronimo Stilton & the Kingdom of Fantasy Ser.: Bk. 5). (ENG., Illus.). 320p. (J). (gr. 2-5). 14.99 *(978-0-545-55625-5(2)*, Scholastic Paperbacks) Scholastic, Inc.

—Watch Your Tail! 2013. (Geronimo Stilton Cavemice Ser.: 2). lib. bdg. 18.40 *(978-0-606-31998-0(0)*, Turtleback) Turtleback Bks.

—The Way of the Samurai. 2012. (Geronimo Stilton Ser.: No. 49). (ENG.). 128p. (J). (gr. 2-5). pap. 7.99 *(978-0-545-34101-1(9)*, Scholastic Paperbacks) Scholastic, Inc.

—The Way of the Samurai. 2012. (Geronimo Stilton Ser.: 49). lib. bdg. 18.40 *(978-0-606-26094-7(3)*, Turtleback) Turtleback Bks.

—Wedding Crasher. 2007. (Geronimo Stilton Ser.: 28). (ENG., Illus.). 128p. (J). (gr. 2-5). pap. 7.99 *(978-0-439-84119-1(4)*, Scholastic Paperbacks) Scholastic, Inc.

—Welcome to Moldy Manor. 2014. (Geronimo Stilton Ser.: 59). lib. bdg. 18.40 *(978-0-606-36351-8(3))* Turtleback Bks.

—We'll Always Have Paris. Cooper-McGuinness, Nanette, tr. from ITA. 2012. (Geronimo Stilton Graphic Novels Ser.). (ENG., Illus.). 56p. (J). (gr. 2-6). 9.99 *(978-1-59707-347-9(4),* 9781597073479) Papercutz.

—You're Mine, Captain! 2014. (Geronimo Stilton Spacemice Ser.: 2). (ENG., Illus.). 128p. (J). (gr. 2-5). pap. 7.99 *(978-0-545-64652-9(9),* Scholastic Paperbacks) Scholastic, Inc.

—You're Mine, Captain! 2014. (Geronimo Stilton Spacemice Ser.: 2). lib. bdg. 18.40 *(978-0-606-35845-3(5))* Turtleback Bks.

Stilton, Geronimo & Dami, Elisabetta. The Enchanted Charms: The Seventh Adventure in the Kingdom of Fantasy. Barozzi, Danilo, illus. 2015. (ENG.). 320p. (J). (gr. 2-5). 14.99 *(978-0-545-74615-1(9))* Scholastic, Inc.

—The Phoenix of Destiny. 2015. (Geronimo Stilton & the Kingdom of Fantasy: Special Edition Ser.). (ENG.). 592p. (J). (gr. 2-5). 19.99 *(978-0-545-82907-6(0))* Scholastic, Inc.

Stilton, Geronimo & Geronimo Stilton Staff. Attack of the Dragons. 2016. (Geronimo Stilton Micekings Ser.: 1). (ENG.). 128p. (J). (gr. 2-5). pap. 6.99 *(978-0-545-87238-6(3),* Scholastic Paperbacks) Scholastic, Inc.

—My Autosaurus Will Win! 2016. (Geronimo Stilton Cavemice Ser.: 10). (ENG.). 128p. (J). (gr. 2-5). pap. 7.99 *(978-0-545-87246-1(4),* Scholastic Paperbacks) Scholastic, Inc.

Stilton, Geronimo & Heim, Julia. The Perilous Plants. Usai, Luca et al, illus. 2016. 117p. (J). ***(978-0-545-93092-5(8))*** Scholastic, Inc.

Stilton, Geronimo & Pizzelli, Anna. The Underwater Planet. Facciotto, Giuseppe & Verzini, Daniele, illus. 2016. 113p. (J). ***(978-1-5182-0303-9(5))*** Scholastic, Inc.

Stilton, Geronimo & Stilton, Thea. Thea Stilton & the Ghost of the Shipwreck. 2010. (Thea Stilton Ser.: 3). lib. bdg. 19.65 *(978-0-606-06843-7(0),* Turtleback) Turtleback Bks.

—Thea Stilton & the Mountain of Fire. 2009. (Thea Stilton Ser.: 2). lib. bdg. 19.65 *(978-0-606-00232-5(4),* Turtleback) Turtleback Bks.

—Thea Stilton & the Mystery in Paris. 2010. (Thea Stilton Ser.: 5). (ENG.). 176p. (J). (gr. 2-5). pap. 8.99 *(978-0-545-22773-5(9),* Scholastic Paperbacks) Scholastic, Inc.

—Thea Stilton & the Secret of the Old Castle. 2012. (Thea Stilton Ser.: 10). (ENG., Illus.). 176p. (J). (gr. 2-5). pap. 8.99 *(978-0-545-34107-3(8),* Scholastic Paperbacks) Scholastic, Inc.

—Thea Stilton & the Star Castaways. 2011. (Thea Stilton Ser.: 7). (ENG.). 176p. (J). (gr. 2-5). pap. 8.99 *(978-0-545-22774-2(7),* Scholastic Paperbacks) Scholastic, Inc.

Stilton, Geronimo & Tramontozzi, Lidia Morson. The Treasure of Easter Island. Ferrario, Giuseppe & Fausone, Flavio, illus. 2015. 106p. (J). *(978-1-4844-5770-2(6))* Scholastic, Inc.

Stilton, Geronimo & Wolf, Matt. All Because of a Cup of Coffee. 2004. (Geronimo Stilton Ser.: No. 10). (Illus.). 112p. (J). lib. bdg. 10.00 *(978-1-4242-0279-9(5))* Fitzgerald Bks.

Stilton, Geronimo, et al. Get the Scoop, Geronimo! Facciotto, Giuseppe & Costa, Alessandro, illus. 2015. 113p. (J). ***(978-1-5182-0417-3(1))*** Scholastic, Inc.

—The Journey Through Time. 2014. (Illus.). 94p. (J). *(978-0-545-61129-9(6))* Scholastic, Inc.

—Robot Attack. Usai, Luca & Verzini, Daniele, illus. 2015. 117p. (J). *(978-0-545-86796-2(7))* Scholastic, Inc.

Stilton, Thea. The Journey to Atlantis. 2012. (Thea Stilton Special Edition Ser.). (ENG.). 320p. (J). (gr. 2-5). 14.99 *(978-0-545-44020-2(3),* Scholastic Paperbacks) Scholastic, Inc.

—The Secret of the Fairies. 2013. (Thea Stilton Ser.). (ENG., Illus.). 320p. (J). (gr. 2-5). 14.99 *(978-0-545-55624-8(4),* Scholastic Paperbacks) Scholastic, Inc.

—Thea Stilton & the Blue Scarab Hunt. 2012. (Thea Stilton Ser.: 11). lib. bdg. 19.65 *(978-0-606-26183-8(4),* Turtleback) Turtleback Bks.

—Thea Stilton & the Chocolate Sabotage. 2014. (Thea Stilton Ser.: 19). (ENG., Illus.). 176p. (J). (gr. 2-5). pap. 8.99 *(978-0-545-64656-7(1),* Scholastic Paperbacks) Scholastic, Inc.

—Thea Stilton & the Dancing Shadows. 2013. (Thea Stilton Ser.: 14). lib. bdg. 19.65 *(978-0-606-31528-9(4),* Turtleback) Turtleback Bks.

—Thea Stilton & the Frozen Fiasco. 2017. (Thea Stilton Ser.: 25). lib. bdg. 19.65 ***(978-0-606-40181-4(4))*** Turtleback Bks.

—Thea Stilton & the Frozen Fiasco: a Geronimo Stilton Adventure (Thea Stilton #25) 2017. (Thea Stilton Ser.: 25). (ENG.). 176p. (J). (gr. 2-5). pap. 8.99 ***(978-1-338-08786-4(X),*** Scholastic Paperbacks) Scholastic, Inc.

—Thea Stilton & the Great Tulip Heist. 2014. (Thea Stilton Ser.: 18). (ENG.). 176p. (J). (gr. 2-5). pap. 8.99 *(978-0-545-55628-6(7),* Scholastic Paperbacks) Scholastic, Inc.

—Thea Stilton & the Great Tulip Heist. 2014. (Thea Stilton Ser.: 18). lib. bdg. 19.65 *(978-0-606-35386-1(0))* Turtleback Bks.

—Thea Stilton & the Hollywood Hoax. 2016. (Thea Stilton Ser.: 23). lib. bdg. 18.40 *(978-0-606-38799-6(4))* Turtleback Bks.

—Thea Stilton & the Legend of the Fire Flowers. 2013. (Thea Stilton Ser.: 15). (ENG., Illus.). 176p. (J). (gr. 2-5). pap. 8.99 *(978-0-545-48188-5(0),* Scholastic Paperbacks) Scholastic, Inc.

—Thea Stilton & the Lost Letters. 2015. (Thea Stilton Ser.: 21). (Illus.). 159p. (J). lib. bdg. 18.40 *(978-0-606-37061-5(7))* Turtleback Bks.

—Thea Stilton & the Missing Myth. 2014. (Thea Stilton Ser.: 20). (ENG.). 176p. (J). (gr. 2-5). pap. 8.99 *(978-0-545-65601-6(X),* Scholastic Paperbacks) Scholastic, Inc.

—Thea Stilton & the Missing Myth. 2014. (Thea Stilton Ser.: 20). lib. bdg. 19.65 *(978-0-606-36058-6(1))* Turtleback Bks.

—Thea Stilton & the Prince's Emerald. 2012. (Thea Stilton Ser.: 12). lib. bdg. 19.65 *(978-0-606-26534-8(1),* Turtleback) Turtleback Bks.

—Thea Stilton & the Secret of the Old Castle. 2012. (Thea Stilton Ser.: 10). lib. bdg. 19.65 *(978-0-606-23930-1(8),* Turtleback) Turtleback Bks.

—Thea Stilton & the Tropical Treasure. 2015. (Thea Stilton Ser.: 22). (ENG.). 176p. (J). (gr. 2-5). pap. 8.99 *(978-0-545-83552-7(6),* Scholastic Paperbacks) Scholastic, Inc.

—The Treasure of the Sea. 5th ed. 2016. (Thea Stilton Special Edition Ser.: 5). (ENG.). 320p. (J). (gr. 2-5). 14.99 *(978-1-338-03290-1(9),* Scholastic Paperbacks) Scholastic, Inc.

Stilton, Thea & Stilton, Geronimo. Secret of the Snow: A Geronimo Stilton Adventure. 2014. (Thea Stilton Special Edition Ser.). (ENG.). 320p. (J). (gr. 2-5). 14.99 *(978-0-545-65605-4(2),* Scholastic Paperbacks) Scholastic, Inc.

Stompin' Boots. 2013. (Illus.). 24p. pap. *(978-1-4602-2767-1(0))* FriesenPress.

Stone, Kate. Happy Birthday, Mouse! (ENG.). 16p. (J). 2014. bds. 5.99 *(978-1-4494-4387-0(7))* 2012. (Illus.). bds. 10.99 *(978-1-4494-0838-1(9))* Andrews McMeel Publishing.

—Mouse Goes to School. 2012. (ENG.). 16p. (J). bds. 10.99 *(978-1-4494-1788-8(4))* Andrews McMeel Publishing.

Suarez, Maribel, illus. Ramon & His Mouse. (Rowing Frog's Rhymes Ser.). 16p. (J). (gr. k-3). 7.95 *(978-1-59437-839-3(8))* Santillana USA Publishing Co., Inc.

Susan, Paradis. Edna. Susan, Paradis, illus. 2013. (Illus.). 32p. pap. 11.95 *(978-1-60898-153-3(3))* namelos llc.

Swanson, Maggie, illus. The Tale of Two Bad Mice. 2006. (J). 6.99 *(978-1-59939-030-7(2))* Cornerstone Pr.

Swarbrick, David E. Peggy's Play House. 2011. 24p. pap. 24.95 *(978-1-4626-1989-4(4))* America Star Bks.

Sweeney, Kimberly A. Tippy Meets the Easter Bunny! 2012. 24p. pap. 17.99 *(978-1-4685-8460-8(X))* AuthorHouse.

Talbot, Amy. Deer & His Dear Friends: A Tale from India. 2006. (J). pap. *(978-1-4108-6173-3(2))* Benchmark Education Co.

Tara, Stephanie Lisa. Little Library Mouse. Walton, Alex, illus. 2006. 32p. (J). (gr. k). lib. bdg. 16.95 *(978-1-933285-39-9(7))* Brown Books Publishing Group.

Tashiro, Chisato. Five Nice Mice & the Great Car Race. Tashiro, Chisato, illus. 2014. (Five Nice Mice Ser.). (ENG., Illus.). 40p. (J). (gr. k-2). 17.99 *(978-988-8240-73-9(0))* Neugebauer, Michael (Publishing) Limited HKG. Dist: Independent Pubs. Group.

Taylor, Sean. The World-Famous Cheese Shop Break-In. Shaw, Hannah, illus. 2015. (ENG.). 32p. (J). (gr. -1-2). 17.99 *(978-1-84780-430-3(6),* Frances Lincoln) Quarto Publishing Group UK GBR. Dist: Hachette Bk. Group.

Teague, Patricia. Gilda the Gluten Free Mouse: A Story about Living Gloriously with Celiac Sprue Disease. 2013. 24p. pap. 10.95 *(978-1-4908-1276-2(8),* WestBow Pr.) Author Solutions, Inc.

Terada, Junzo. A Good Home for Max. 2014. (ENG., Illus.). 40p. (J). (gr. -1-k). 16.99 *(978-1-4521-2702-6(6))* Chronicle Bks. LLC.

Terrian, Michael W. Chalie's Brand New Coat. 2011. 24p. pap. 12.50 *(978-1-4670-3858-4(X))* AuthorHouse.

Tetrick, Jack E. Joey the Motor Home Mouse. 2012. 110p. 20.95 *(978-1-4759-3702-2(4));* pap. 10.95 *(978-1-4759-3703-9(2))* iUniverse, Inc.

Thea Stilton Staff. The Cloud Castle. 2015. (Thea Stilton Special Edition Ser.: 4). (ENG.). 320p. (J). (gr. 2-5). 14.99 *(978-0-545-83536-7(4),* Scholastic Paperbacks) Scholastic, Inc.

Thomas, Jan. Pumpkin Trouble. Thomas, Jan, illus. 2011. (ENG., Illus.). 40p. (J). (gr. -1-3). 9.99 *(978-0-06-169284-0(0))* HarperCollins Pubs.

Thomas, Mikey. The Mouse & the House. 2012. 24p. pap. 24.95 *(978-1-4626-7854-9(8))* America Star Bks.

Thomas Nelson. Hickory Dickory Dock. 2015. (ENG., Illus.). 12p. (gr. -1). bds. *(978-1-78393-534-5(0))* Make Believe Ideas.

Thomas, Patricia. Mouse's Christmas Cookie, 0 vols. Nez, Jon, illus. 2013. (ENG.). 24p. (J). (gr. -1-2). 14.99 *(978-1-4778-4704-6(9),* 9781477847046, Amazon Children's Publishing) Amazon Publishing.

Thomas, Shelley Moore. This Book Is Not about Dragons. Koehler, Fred, illus. 2016. (ENG.). 32p. (J). (gr. -1-2). 16.95 *(978-1-62979-168-5(7))* Boyds Mills Pr.

Thompson, Lauren. Little Lamb. Butler, John, illus. 2014. (J). *(978-1-4351-5352-3(9),* Simon & Schuster Bks. For Young Readers) Simon & Schuster Bks. For Young Readers.

—Mouse Loves School. Erdogan, Buket, illus. 2011. (Mouse Ser.). (ENG.). 24p. (J). (gr. -1-k). pap. 3.99 *(978-1-4424-2898-0(8));* lib. bdg. 16.99 *(978-1-4424-2899-7(6))* Simon Spotlight. (Simon Spotlight).

—Mouse's First Christmas. Erdogan, Buket, illus. 2003. (ENG.). 32p. (J). (gr. -1-3). 7.99 *(978-0-689-86348-6(9),* Simon & Schuster Bks. For Young Readers) Simon & Schuster Bks. For Young Readers.

—Mouse's First Christmas. Erdogan, Buket, illus. 2003. (gr. -1-1). lib. bdg. 18.40 *(978-0-613-91039-2(7),* Turtleback) Turtleback Bks.

—Mouse's First Day of School. Erdogan, Buket, illus. 2010. (Mouse Ser.). (ENG.). 34p. (J). (gr. -1 — 1). bds. 7.99 *(978-1-4169-9476-3(9),* Little Simon) Little Simon.

—Mouse's First Fall. Erdogan, Buket, illus. 2010. (Classic Board Bks.). (ENG.). 34p. (J). (gr. -1 — 1). bds. 7.99 *(978-1-4169-9477-0(7),* Little Simon) Little Simon.

—Mouse's First Fall. Erdogan, Buket, illus. 2006. (ENG.). 32p. (J). (gr. -1-1). 15.99 *(978-0-689-85837-6(X),* Simon & Schuster Bks. For Young Readers) Simon & Schuster Bks. For Young Readers.

—Mouse's First Halloween. Erdogan, Buket, illus. 2003. (Classic Board Bks.). (ENG.). 34p. (J). (gr. -1 — 1). bds., bds. 7.99 *(978-0-689-85584-9(2),* Little Simon) Little Simon.

—Mouse's First Snow. Erdogan, Buket, illus. 2011. (Classic Board Bks.). (ENG.). 34p. (J). (gr. -1 — 1). bds. 7.99 *(978-1-4424-2651-1(9),* Little Simon) Little Simon.

—Mouse's First Snow. Erdogan, Buket, illus. 2005. (ENG.). 32p. (J). (gr. -1-3). 15.99 *(978-0-689-85836-9(1),* Simon & Schuster Bks. For Young Readers) Simon & Schuster Bks. For Young Readers.

—Mouse's First Spring. Erdogan, Buket, illus. 2012. (Classic Board Bks.). (ENG.). 34p. (J). (gr. -1-3). bds. 7.99 *(978-1-4424-3431-8(7),* Little Simon) Little Simon.

—Mouse's First Spring. Erdogan, Buket, illus. 2005. (ENG.). 32p. (J). (gr. -1-3). 17.99 *(978-0-689-85838-3(8),* Simon & Schuster Bks. For Young Readers) Simon & Schuster Bks. For Young Readers.

—Mouse's First Summer. Erdogan, Buket, illus. 2013. (Classic Board Bks.). (ENG.). 34p. (J). (gr. -1 — 1). bds. 7.99 *(978-1-4424-5842-0(9),* Little Simon) Little Simon.

—Mouse's First Summer. Erdogan, Buket, illus. 2014. (J). *(978-1-4351-5506-0(8))* Simon & Schuster.

—Mouse's First Summer. Erdogan, Buket, illus. 2004. (ENG.). 32p. (J). (gr. -1-3). 17.99 *(978-0-689-85835-2(3),* Simon & Schuster Bks. For Young Readers) Simon & Schuster Bks. For Young Readers.

—Mouse's First Valentine. Erdogan, Buket, illus. 2004. (Classic Board Bks.). (ENG.). 34p. (J). (gr. -1 — 1). bds. 7.99 *(978-0-689-85585-6(0),* Little Simon) Little Simon.

—Wee Little Lamb. Butler, John, illus. 2009. (Wee Little Ser.). (ENG.). 32p. (J). (gr. -1-3). 16.99 *(978-1-4169-3469-1(3),* Simon & Schuster Bks. For Young Readers) Simon & Schuster Bks. For Young Readers.

Thompson, Lauren & Jackson, Livia. Mouse's First Day of School. Erdogan, Buket, illus. 2003. (Mouse Ser.). (ENG.). 32p. (J). (gr. -1-3). 15.99 *(978-0-689-84727-1(0),* Simon & Schuster Bks. For Young Readers) Simon & Schuster Bks. For Young Readers.

Tibbs, Ely. The Mouse under My House - Ingle & the Cats Meow. 2010. 73p. pap. 27.81 *(978-0-557-39421-0(X))* Lulu Pr., Inc.

Tirado, Raquel. That Sticky Cat. 2012. 20p. pap. 17.99 *(978-1-4685-8857-6(5))* AuthorHouse.

Titus, Eve. Anatole. 2010. (ENG., Illus.). 32p. (J). (gr. k-3). pap. 7.99 *(978-0-375-85546-7(7),* Dragonfly Bks.) Random Hse. Children's Bks.

—Anatole. Galdone, Paul, illus. 50th ed. 2006. (ENG.). 40p. (J). (gr. k-3). 14.95 *(978-0-375-83901-6(1),* Knopf Bks. for Young Readers) Random Hse. Children's Bks.

—Anatole & the Cat. 2010. (ENG., Illus.). 32p. (J). (gr. k-3). pap. 7.99 *(978-0-375-85547-4(5),* Dragonfly Bks.) Random Hse. Children's Bks.

—Basil & the Cave of Cats. Galdone, Paul, illus. 2016. (Great Mouse Detective Ser.: 2). (ENG.). 112p. (J). (gr. 1-4). pap. 5.99 *(978-1-4814-6404-8(3),* Aladdin) Simon & Schuster Children's Publishing.

—Basil & the Lost Colony. Galdone, Paul, illus. 2017. (Great Mouse Detective Ser.: 5). (ENG.). 96p. (J). (gr. 1-4). pap. 5.99 ***(978-1-4814-6413-0(2),*** Aladdin) Simon & Schuster Children's Publishing.

—Basil in Mexico. Galdone, Paul, illus. 2016. (Great Mouse Detective Ser.: 3). (ENG.). 112p. (J). (gr. 1-4). pap. 5.99 *(978-1-4814-6407-9(8),* Aladdin) Simon & Schuster Children's Publishing.

—Basil of Baker Street. Galdone, Paul, illus. 2016. (Great Mouse Detective Ser.: 1). (ENG.). 112p. (J). (gr. 1-4). 16.99 *(978-1-4814-6402-4(7));* pap. 5.99 *(978-1-4814-6401-7(9))* Simon & Schuster Children's Publishing. (Aladdin).

Tolan, Stephanie S. Bartholomew's Blessing. Moore, Margie, illus. 2004. 32p. (J). (gr. -1-3). lib. bdg. 16.89 *(978-0-06-001198-7(X))* HarperCollins Pubs.

Tolstoy, Aleksei, et al. The Gigantic Turnip. 2009. (ENG., Illus.). (J). 16.99 *(978-1-84686-298-4(1))* Barefoot Bks., Inc.

Tomos, Angharad. Cosyn. 2005. (WEL., Illus.). 24p. pap. *(978-0-86243-566-0(8))* Y Lolfa.

Toms, Kate. Twinkle Twinkle Box Set. 2007. (Illus.). 26p. (gr. -1). per. *(978-1-84610-672-9(9))* Make Believe Ideas.

—Twinkle, Twinkle, Little Star. 2007. (Kate Toms Ser.). (Illus.). 26p. (gr. -1). bds. 7.99 *(978-1-84610-485-5(8))* Make Believe Ideas GBR. Dist: Nelson, Thomas Inc.

Top That Publishing Staff, ed. Mr. Mouse Needs House. 2005. (Illus.). 8p. *(978-1-84510-128-2(6))* Top That! Publishing PLC.

Toporoff, Debi. Roscoe Goes to the Gym. Butler, Gregory J., illus. 2007.Tr. of Rosco Va Al Gimnasio. (ENG.). 32p. (gr. -1-3). 9.99 *(978-1-59979-215-6(X),* Creation Hse.) Charisma Media.

Touma, Patricia. Happy Times, Book: Ish & Mish Go to the Carnival. 2007. 56p. per. 9.95 *(978-1-59899-093-5(4))* Long Dash Publishing.

Town Mouse & Country Mouse. 2005. (Folk Tales Set 2 Ser.). (J). 5.33 *(978-1-58453-303-0(X))* Pioneer Valley Bks.

Town Mouse & Country Mouse: Individual Title Six-Packs. (Story Steps Ser.). (gr. k-2). 32.00 *(978-0-7635-9826-6(7))* Rigby Education.

Townsend, Stephanie Z. Not Too Small at All: A Mouse Tale. Looney, Bill, illus. 2008. 30p. (J). (gr. -1). 13.99 *(978-0-89051-524-2(7))* Master Bks.

Toybox Innovations, creator. Pixar's Ratatouille. 2007. (Ratatouille Ser.). (ENG.). (J). (gr. -1-3). pap. *(978-0-7634-2185-4(5))* Walt Disney Records.

Travis, Lucille. The Far Journey. 2009. 160p. (J). (gr. 4-7). 8.99 *(978-1-60682-023-0(0))* BJU Pr.

Trimble, Gina. The Little Tiny Mouse, 1 vol. 2009. 17p. pap. 24.95 *(978-1-61546-540-8(5))* America Star Bks.

Tupera, Tupera. Polar Bear's Underwear. 2015. (ENG., Illus.). 32p. (J). (gr. -1-k). 16.99 *(978-1-4521-4199-2(1))* Chronicle Bks. LLC.

Turley, Sandy. The Clock & the Mouse: A Teaching Rhyme about Time. Peterson, Sara & Lindstrom, Brita, illus. 2006. 32p. (J). lib. bdg. 26.95 *(978-0-9778548-0-6(9))* Helps4Teachers.

Tuttle, Lucia. There's a Mouse in the House. 2008. 36p. pap. 19.99 *(978-1-4363-4000-7(4))* Xlibris Corp.

Twigger, J. Nicci & Her Amazing Adventure. 2008. (Illus.). 40p. pap. 18.49 *(978-1-4389-1295-0(1))* AuthorHouse.

Twohy, Mike. Mouse & Hippo. Twohy, Mike, illus. 2017. (ENG., Illus.). 32p. (J). (gr. -1-3). 17.99 *(978-1-4814-5124-6(3),* Simon & Schuster/Paula Wiseman Bks.) Simon & Schuster/Paula Wiseman Bks.

Ugarte, Ane Miren De Rotaeche. A Very Special Tea Party. 2010. 24p. (J). 25.99 *(978-1-4500-5378-5(5))* Xlibris Corp.

Underwood, Deborah. Here Comes the Tooth Fairy Cat. Rueda, Claudia, illus. 2015. (ENG.). 96p. (J). (gr. -1-k). 16.99 *(978-0-525-42774-2(0),* Dial Bks) Penguin Young Readers Group.

Unger-Pengilly, Elaine. Rat. Trockstad, Marcy, illus. 2013. 120p. *(978-1-4602-2262-1(8))* FriesenPress.

Urban, Linda. Mouse Was Mad. Cole, Henry, illus. (ENG.). 40p. (J). (gr. -1-3). 2012. pap. 7.99 *(978-0-547-72750-9(X))* 2009. 16.99 *(978-0-15-205337-6(9))* Houghton Mifflin Harcourt Publishing Co.

—Mouse Was Mad Big Book. Cole, Henry, illus. 2015. (ENG.). 40p. (J). (gr. -1-3). 26.99 *(978-0-544-45607-5(6),* HMH Books For Young Readers) Houghton Mifflin Harcourt Publishing Co.

Urbanek Reese, Dorothy. When Mice Sing — the Story of Mei & Yu. 2008. 138p. pap. 13.95 *(978-1-4357-6104-9(9))* Lulu Pr., Inc.

Van Durme, Leen. Mo & Mac: Socks On! Van Durme, Leen, illus. 2013. (ENG., Illus.). 16p. (J). (— 1). 9.95 *(978-1-60537-176-4(9))* Cobblestone Publishing Co.

Van Leeuwen, Jean. The Great Cheese Conspiracy, 0 vols. 2011. (ENG.). 96p. (J). (gr. 1-4). 15.99 *(978-0-7614-5972-9(3),* 9780761459729, Amazon Children's Publishing) Amazon Publishing.

Vaniko, K. L. Why the Dog Chases the Cat & the Cat Chases the Mouse. 2006. 189p. 30.99 *(978-1-59926-863-7(9))* Xlibris Corp.

Vasquez, Paula. I Spy with My Little Eye, 1 vol. 2017. (ENG., Illus.). 40p. (J). bds. 8.99 *(978-1-4236-4687-7(8))* Gibbs Smith, Publisher.

Vaswani, Navina. A Wonderful Christmas. 2004. (YA). per. *(978-0-9754818-5-1(1))* Creative Bk. Pubs.

Vasylenko, Veronica. Deck the Halls. Tiger Tales Staff, ed. 2011. (ENG., Illus.). 20p. bds. 8.95 *(978-1-58925-868-6(1))* Tiger Tales.

—Jingle Bells. Tiger Tales Staff, ed. 2011. (ENG., Illus.). 20p. bds. 8.95 *(978-1-58925-869-3(X))* Tiger Tales.

Vere, Ed. Max el Valiente. 2014. (SPA.). 36p. (gr. k-2). 20.99 *(978-84-261-4071-5(8))* Juventud, Editorial ESP. Dist: Lectorum Pubns., Inc.

—Max the Brave. (ENG.). (J). 2017. 30p. bds. 7.99 ***(978-1-4926-5706-4(9))*** 2015. (Max Ser.: 1). 32p. 16.99 *(978-1-4926-1651-1(6),* 9781492616511) Sourcebooks, Inc. (Sourcebooks Jabberwocky).

Verrett, Michael. Galid's Christmas Wish. 2010. 44p. pap. 22.90 *(978-0-557-29109-0(7))* Lulu Pr., Inc.

Vidal, Séverine. Mega Mouse. Barroux, Stephane, illus. 2015. (Mega Hero Bks.). (ENG.). 28p. (J). (gr. k-2). 12.95 *(978-1-77085-639-4(0),* 9781770856394) Firefly Bks., Ltd.

Villarreal, Tanya E. Izzie's First Christmas, 1 vol. Villarreal, Tanya E., illus. 2009. (Illus.). 28p. pap. 24.95 *(978-1-61546-093-9(4))* America Star Bks.

Villeneuve, Marie-Paule & Audet, Patrice. Qui a Enleve Polka? 2004. (FRE., Illus.). 122p. (J). 8.95 *(978-2-922565-81-2(5))* Editions de la Paix CAN. Dist: World of Reading, Ltd.

Vincent, Karen. Robbie Learns a Lesson on Truth. 2010. 20p. pap. 12.49 *(978-1-4490-5772-5(1))* AuthorHouse.

Viva, Frank. A Trip to the Bottom of the World with Mouse. Viva, Frank, illus. 2012. (ENG., Illus.). 32p. (J). (gr. -1-k). 12.95 *(978-1-935179-19-1(5))* TOON Books / RAW Junior, LLC.

Vize, Bonnie. The Mystery of the Park Pavilion. 2009. pap. 14.22 *(978-1-61584-491-3(0))* Independent Pub.

Vizzi, Maria. Morely: The Mouse in the Bakery. 2011. 24p. (gr. 1-2). pap. 13.33 *(978-1-4567-4621-6(9))* AuthorHouse.

Voigt, Cynthia. Young Fredle. Yates, Louise, illus. 2011. (ENG.). 240p. (J). (gr. 3-7). 16.99 *(978-0-375-86457-5(1),* Knopf Bks. for Young Readers) Random Hse. Children's Bks.

Von Buhler, Cynthia. But Who Will Bell the Cats? Von Buhler, Cynthia, illus. 2009. (ENG., Illus.). 32p. (J). (gr. -1-3). 17.00 *(978-0-618-99718-3(0))* Houghton Mifflin Harcourt Publishing Co.

Wahl, Jan. Pleasant Fieldmouse. Sendak, Maurice, illus. 2007. (Sendak Reissues Ser.). (ENG.). 72p. (J). 15.95 *(978-0-06-029725-1(5))* HarperCollins Pubs.

Wall, Pauline & Smith, Shelley. What the Mouse Saw: An Easter Story. 2013. 20p. pap. 16.82 *(978-1-4669-3503-7(0))* Trafford Publishing.

Wallace, Chad. The Mouse & the Meadow, 1 vol. Wallace, Chad, illus. 2014. (ENG., Illus.). 32p. (J). (gr. k-4). 16.95 *(978-1-58469-481-6(5))* Dawn Pubns.

Wallace, Karen. Ghost Mouse. Blake, Beccy, illus. 2009. (Go! Readers Ser.). 48p. (J). (gr. 2-5). pap. 12.85 *(978-1-60754-273-5(0));* lib. bdg. 29.25 *(978-1-60754-272-8(2))* Windmill Bks.

Wallace, Nancy Elizabeth & Friedlaender, Linda. Look! Look! Look! at Sculpture, 0 vols. 2012. (ENG.). 40p. (J). (gr. k-3). 17.99 *(978-0-7614-6132-6(9),* 9780761461326, Amazon Children's Publishing) Amazon Publishing.

Walsh, Ellen Stoll. Dot & Jabber & the Big Bug Mystery. 2017. (Green Light Readers — Level 2 Ser.: Vol. 3). (ENG.). (J). (gr. -1-3). lib. bdg. 13.55 ***(978-0-606-39827-5(9))*** Turtleback Bks.

—Dot & Jabber & the Great Acorn Mystery. 2016. (Green Light Readers Level 2 Ser.). (ENG., Illus.). 32p. (J). (gr. -1-3). 12.99 *(978-0-544-79164-0(9),* HMH Books For Young Readers) Houghton Mifflin Harcourt Publishing Co.

—Dot & Jabber & the Mystery of the Missing Stream. 2016. (Green Light Readers Level 2 Ser.). (ENG., Illus.). 32p. (J). (gr. -1-3). 12.99 *(978-0-544-79166-4(5),* HMH Books For Young Readers) Houghton Mifflin Harcourt Publishing Co.

—Mouse Paint: Lap-Sized Board Book. 2006. (ENG., Illus.). 15p. (J). (gr. k — 1). bds. 11.99 *(978-0-15-205533-2(9))* Houghton Mifflin Harcourt Publishing Co.

—Mouse Paint - Pintura de Ratón. 2010. (ENG & SPA., Illus.). 30p. (J). (gr. k — 1). bds. 4.99 *(978-0-547-33332-8(3))* Houghton Mifflin Harcourt Publishing Co.

—Mouse Shapes. 2017. (ENG., Illus.). 40p. (J). (gr. -1-3). pap. 7.99 ***(978-1-328-74053-3(6),*** HMH Books For Young Readers) Houghton Mifflin Harcourt Publishing Co.

Walsh, Ellen Stoll. Where Is Jumper? Walsh, Ellen Stoll, illus. 2015. (ENG., Illus.). 32p. (J). (gr. -1-3). 17.99 *(978-1-4814-4508-5(1),* Beach Lane Bks.) Beach Lane Bks.

Walsh, Ellen Stoll & Amosky, Jim. Mouse Shapes. 2007. (ENG., Illus.). 40p. (J). (gr. -1-3). 16.99 *(978-0-15-206091-6(X))* Houghton Mifflin Harcourt Publishing Co.

Ward, Helen. The Town Mouse & the Country Mouse. Ward, Helen, illus. 2012. (ENG., Illus.). 48p. (J). (gr. -1-3). 16.99 *(978-0-7636-6098-7(1),* Templar) Candlewick Pr.

Wargin, Kathy-jo. Minn from Minnesota. Holman, Karen Busch, illus. 2006. (Mitt Midwest Ser.: 2). (ENG.). 144p. (J). (gr. k-7). 14.95 *(978-1-58726-304-0(1),* Mitten Pr.) Ann Arbor Editions LLC.

—Mitt & Minn at the Wisconsin Cheese Jamboree. Holman, Karen Busch, illus. 2007. (Mitt Midwest Ser.: 3). (ENG.). 144p. (J). (gr. k-7). 14.95 (978-1-58726-305-7(X), Mitten Pr.) Ann Arbor Editions LLC.

—Mitt & Minn's Illinois Adventure. Holman, Karen Busch, illus. 2007. (Mitt Midwest Ser.: 4). (ENG.). 144p. (J). (gr. k-7). 14.95 (978-1-58726-306-4(8), Mitten Pr.) Ann Arbor Editions LLC.

Warner, Jeremy. Hidden Mickeys: A Mouse in the Land. Warner, Danielle, illus. 2012. 68p. pap. 5.95 (978-0-9853555-2-4(2)) Portrait Health Publishing.

Warnes, Tim. Chalk & Cheese. Warnes, Tim, illus. 2008. (ENG., Illus.). 32p. (J). (gr. -1-3). 18.99 (978-1-4169-1378-8(5), Simon & Schuster Bks. For Young Readers) Simon & Schuster Bks. For Young Readers.

Waters, Tony. Cinnamon's Busy Year. Waters, Tony, illus. 2003. (Illus.). 32p. (J). (gr. -1-3). pap. 5.95 (978-0-9710278-2-4(X)) All About Kids Publishing.

Watkins, Greg. Brendon Mouse's Big Idea to Save the Bad Bird Bunch. 2006. (Illus.). 29p. (J). 14.95 (978-0-9761318-0-9(3)) Cute & Cuddly Productions, Inc.

—Brendon Mouse's Big Idea to Save the Bad Bird Bunch, 1 vol. Watkins, Greg, illus. 2007. (Big Bill & Buddies Ser.). (ENG., Illus.). 32p. (J). (gr. k-3). 16.99 (978-1-58980-449-4(X)) Pelican Publishing Co., Inc.

Watson, Louise. The Mouse in Our House. 2005. (J). pap. 8.00 (978-0-8059-6719-7(2)) Dorrance Publishing Co., Inc.

Watt, Fiona. Christmas Eve. Wells, Rachel, illus. 2007. (Luxury Touchy-Feely Board Bks). 10p. (J). (gr. -1-k). bds. 11.99 (978-0-7945-1478-5(2), Usborne) EDC Publishing.

—Christmas Mice. 2004. (Big Touchy Feely Board Bks.). (Illus.). 10p. (J). 11.95 (978-0-7945-0482-3(5), Usborne) EDC Publishing.

—That's Not My Kitten. Wells, Rachel, illus. rev. ed. 2006. (Touchy-Feely Board Bks.). 10p. (J). (gr. -1-k). bds. 7.99 (978-0-7945-1266-8(6), Usborne) EDC Publishing.

Watts, Frances. Goodnight, Mice! Watson, Judy, illus. 2017. 24p. bds. 6.99 (978-0-7333-3530-3(6)) ABC Bks. AUS. Dist: HarperCollins Pubs.

—The Song of the Winns: the Spies of Gerander. 2013. (ENG., Illus.). 320p. (J). (gr. -1-2). 12.95 (978-0-7624-4658-2(7), Running Pr. Kids) Running Pr. Bk. Pubs.

Waugh, Peter. Cannon Beach Mouse Caper. 2007. 128p. per. 13.95 (978-0-944638-68-2(6)) Educare Pr.

The Wedding of the Mouse: An Asian Folktale. 2006. (J). 17.95 (978-0-9790033-0-1(X)) Playground Pr.

Weeks, Sarah. Pip Squeak. Manning, Jane K., illus. (I Can Read Level 1 Ser.). 32p. (J). 2008. (ENG.). (gr. k-3). pap. 3.99 (978-0-06-075638-3(1)) 2007. (gr. -1-3). lib. bdg. 16.89 (978-0-06-075637-6(3), Geringer, Laura Book) HarperCollins Pubs.

Weigl Publishers, creator. The Lion & the Mouse: Can Little Friends Be Great Friends? 2013. (AV2 Animated Storytime Ser.: Vol. 15). (ENG., Illus.). 32p. (J). (gr. -1-3). lib. bdg. 29.99 (978-1-62127-919-8(7), AV2 by Weigl) Weigl Pubs., Inc.

Welling, Peter J. Darlene Halloween & the Great Chicago Fire, 1 vol. Welling, Peter J., illus. 2007. (ENG., Illus.). 32p. (J). (gr. k-3). 16.99 (978-1-58980-479-1(1)) Pelican Publishing Co., Inc.

Wellington-Johnson, Sharon. A Mouse in My House. 2008. 28p. pap. 15.99 (978-1-4363-3113-5(7)) Xlibris Corp.

Wells, Rosemary. Julieta, Estate Quieta! (SPA.). 43p. (J). 5.50 (978-84-372-1523-5(4)) Santillana USA Publishing Co., Inc.

—Sophie's Terrible Twos. Wells, Rosemary, illus. 2014. (ENG., Illus.). 32p. (J). (gr. -1-k). 16.99 (978-0-670-78512-4(1), Viking Books for Young Readers) Penguin Young Readers Group.

—Ten Kisses for Sophie! Wells, Rosemary, illus. 2016. (ENG., Illus.). 32p. (J). (— 1). 16.99 (978-0-670-01665-5(9), Viking Books for Young Readers) Penguin Young Readers Group.

Werntz, Terry. Grace the Church Mouse. 2010. (ENG.). 28p. pap. 9.95 (978-1-4564-4191-3(4)) CreateSpace Independent Publishing Platform.

Westling, Vicki Diane. Hannibal Goes to the Hospital: A Sam & Friends Book. 2011. 32p. pap. 15.99 (978-1-4634-0997-5(4)) AuthorHouse.

Weston Woods Staff, creator. Chato's Kitchen. 2004. (J). 38.75 (978-1-55592-388-4(7)); 18.95 (978-1-55592-386-0(0)) Weston Woods Studios, Inc.

—Chrysanthemum. 2004. (SPA.). (J). 18.95 (978-1-55592-395-2(X)); 38.75 (978-1-55592-397-6(6)) Weston Woods Studios, Inc.

—A Dark, Dark Tale. 2004. (J). 18.95 (978-1-55592-804-9(8)); 38.75 (978-1-55592-821-6(8)) Weston Woods Studios, Inc.

—Doctor de Soto. 2011. (SPA.). 29.95 (978-0-439-73624-4(2)); 38.75 (978-0-439-78365-1(8)) Weston Woods Studios, Inc.

—Doctor Desoto. 2004. (SPA.). (J). 18.95 (978-0-7882-0950-5(7)) Weston Woods Studios, Inc.

—The Island of the Skog. 2011. 38.75 (978-0-545-23367-5(4)); 18.95 (978-0-545-23366-8(6)); 29.95 (978-0-545-23365-1(8)) Weston Woods Studios, Inc.

—Norman the Doorman. 2011. 29.95 (978-0-439-78648-5(7)) Weston Woods Studios, Inc.

—Owen. 2011. (SPA.). 18.95 (978-0-439-02177-7(4)); 38.75 (978-0-439-02178-4(2)); 29.95 (978-0-439-02310-8(6)) Weston Woods Studios, Inc.

—Seven Blind Mice. 2011. 38.75 (978-0-439-02777-9(2)) Weston Woods Studios, Inc.

—A Weeekend with Wendell. 2004. 29.95 (978-1-55592-129-3(9)); (J). 18.95 (978-1-55592-116-3(7)) Weston Woods Studios, Inc.

—A Weekend with Wendell. 2004. (J). 38.75 (978-1-55592-647-2(9)) Weston Woods Studios, Inc.

Westover, Gail. Mrs Mouse's Garden Party in Giggleswick Village. Daly, Karen Anne, illus. 2012. 26p. pap. 9.95 (978-0-9821507-9-5(2)) Thistlewood Publishing.

Wheatley, Sandra. Marmaduke the Mighty. 2010. (Illus.). 28p. (gr. -1). 13.99 (978-1-4490-4290-5(2)) AuthorHouse.

Wheeler, Lisa. One Dark Night. Bates, Ivan, illus. 2006. (ENG.). 32p. (J). (gr. -1-3). reprint ed. pap. 6.99 (978-0-15-205888-3(5)) Houghton Mifflin Harcourt Publishing Co.

Wherry, Alwyn. The Hungry Little Mouse. 2006. 17p. (J). 12.08 (978-1-4116-8056-2(1)) Lulu Pr., Inc.

White, E. B. Le Avventure di Stuart Little.Tr. of Stuart Little. (ITA.). pap. 17.95 (978-88-451-2736-6(2)) Fabbri Editori - RCS Libri ITA. Dist: Distribooks, Inc.

—Stuart Little. Date not set. 141p. 18.95 (978-0-8488-2602-4(7)) Amereon Ltd.

—Stuart Little. 2008. (J). 34.99 (978-0-7393-7101-5(0)) Findaway World, LLC.

—Stuart Little. Williams, Garth, illus. 60th anniv. ed. 2005. (Trophy Bk.). (ENG.). 144p. (J). (gr. 3-7). pap. 6.99 (978-0-06-440056-5(5)) HarperCollins Pubs.

—Stuart Little. Williams, Garth & Wells, Rosemary, illus. 60th anniv. ed. 2005. (Stuart-Little Ser.). (ENG.). 144p. (J). (gr. 3-7). pap. 8.99 (978-0-06-441092-2(7)) HarperCollins Pubs.

—Stuart Little. Williams, Garth, illus. 60th anniv. ed. 2005. (Stuart-Little Ser.). (ENG.). 144p. (J). (gr. 3-7). 16.99 (978-0-06-026395-9(4)) HarperCollins Pubs.

—Stuart Little. 131p. (J). pap. 5.95 (978-0-8072-8333-2(9)); 2004. (gr. 3-7). pap. 29.00 incl. audio (978-0-8072-8332-5(0), YA165SP) Random Hse. Audio Publishing Group. (Listening Library).

—Stuart Little. Williams, Garth, illus. 2004. (SPA.). 144p. (gr. 3-5). pap. 10.95 (978-1-59437-554-5(2)) Santillana USA Publishing Co., Inc.

—Stuart Little Book & Charm. Williams, Garth, illus. 2006. (Charming Classics). 144p. (J). (gr. 3-7). 6.99 (978-0-06-082334-4(8), HarperFestival) HarperCollins Pubs.

White, E. B. & White, E. Stuart Little. 2005. (J). (gr. 3-6). lib. bdg. 17.20 (978-0-8085-3806-6(3), Turtleback) Turtleback Bks.

White, Loricia. Little Tail's Rhyming Roots. 2012. 74p. pap. 19.95 (978-1-4626-6885-4(2)) America Star Bks.

White, Mark. The Lion & the Mouse: A Retelling of Aesop's Fable, 1 vol. Pérez, Sara Rojo, illus. 2010. (My First Classic Story Ser.). (ENG.). 24p. (gr. k-3). pap. 7.10 (978-1-4048-7365-0(1), My First Classic Story) Picture Window Bks.

White, Mark & Aesop Enterprise Inc. Staff. The Lion & the Mouse: A Retelling of Aesop's Fable, 1 vol. Pérez, Sara Rojo, illus. 2010. (My First Classic Story Ser.). (ENG.). 24p. (gr. k-3). lib. bdg. 22.65 (978-1-4048-6525-9(X), My First Classic Story) Picture Window Bks.

Whybrow, Ian. Miss Wire's Christmas Surprise. Chichester Clark, Emma, illus. 2007. 45p. (J). (gr. -1-3). pap. 3.95 (978-0-7534-6136-5(6), Kingfisher) Roaring Brook Pr.

Wilbur, Richard. Loudmouse. 2015. (ENG., Illus.). 64p. (J). pap. 9.99 (978-0-486-79807-3(0)) Dover Pubns., Inc.

William H. Sadlier Staff. The Lion & the Mouse, Vol. 2. 2005. (Fluent Library). (gr. 1-3). 29.34 (978-0-8215-8968-7(7)) Sadlier, William H. Inc.

Williams, Brenda May. The Shop of Magical Things. 2013. (Illus.). 44p. pap. 13.50 (978-1-78035-526-9(2), Fastprint Publishing) Upfront Publishing Ltd. GBR. Dist: Printondemand-worldwide.com.

—The Unusual Pet Shop. Williams, Raymond, illus. 2012. 24p. pap. 11.50 (978-1-61897-798-4(9), Strategic Bk. Publishing) Strategic Book Publishing & Rights Agency (SBPRA).

Williams, Sherri. The Adventures of Little Mouse: (Life Outside the Mouse Hole) 2012. 48p. pap. 21.99 (978-1-4772-2937-8(X)) AuthorHouse.

Willis, Jeanne. Cottonball Colin. Ross, Tony, illus. 2008. 26p. (J). (gr. -1-4). 16.00 (978-0-8028-5331-8(5), Eerdmans Bks For Young Readers) Eerdmans, William B. Publishing Co.

—Never Too Little to Love. Fearnley, Jan, illus. 2013. (ENG.). 32p. (J). (gr. -1-2). 8.99 (978-0-7636-6656-9(4)) Candlewick Pr.

Wilsdon, Christina. An Alligator Adventure in Florida. Mayo, Frank, illus. 2006. 26p. (J). 7.99 (978-1-59939-010-9(8)) Cornerstone Pr.

—An Amusement Park Mystery in Ohio. Ebert, Len, illus. 2006. 26p. (J). 7.99 (978-1-59939-013-0(2)) Cornerstone Pr.

—Lights! Action! California! Hockerman, Dennis, illus. 2006. 26p. (J). 7.99 (978-1-59939-009-3(4)) Cornerstone Pr.

—A New York Sailing Adventure. Hockerman, Dennis, illus. 2006. 26p. (J). 7.99 (978-1-59939-014-7(0)) Cornerstone Pr.

—On the Trail of Bigfoot in Washington. McCreary, Jane, illus. 2006. 26p. (J). 7.99 (978-1-59939-012-3(4)) Cornerstone Pr.

—A Wild Ride in Texas. Jaekel, Susan, illus. 2006. 26p. (J). 7.99 (978-1-59939-011-6(6)) Cornerstone Pr.

Wilson, Karma. Bear Counts. Chapman, Jane, illus. 2015. (Bear Bks.). (ENG.). 32p. (J). (gr. -1-2). 16.99 (978-1-4424-8092-6(0), McElderry, Margaret K. Bks.) McElderry, Margaret K. Bks.

—Big Bear, Small Mouse. Chapman, Jane, illus. 2016. (Bear Bks.). (ENG.). 32p. (J). (gr. -1-2). 16.99 (978-1-4814-5971-6(6), McElderry, Margaret K. Bks.) McElderry, Margaret K. Bks.

—Mortimer's First Garden. Andreasen, Dan, illus. 2009. (ENG.). 32p. (J). (gr. -1-3). 17.99 (978-1-4169-4203-0(3), McElderry, Margaret K. Bks.) McElderry, Margaret K. Bks.

—Who Goes There? Currey, Anna, illus. 2013. (ENG.). 40p. (J). (gr. -1-3). 16.99 (978-1-4169-8002-5(4), McElderry, Margaret K. Bks.) McElderry, Margaret K. Bks.

Wilson, Rosalee. A Mushy Mouse Tale. 2009. 69p. pap. 24.58 (978-0-557-10084-2(4)) Lulu Pr., Inc.

Wilton, Briar. The Strongest Mouse (Big Book Edition) A Tale from East Africa. Corke, Estelle, illus. 2016. 24p. (J). pap. (978-1-927244-69-2(2)) Flying Start Bks.

Winter, Rosalind. The Mice of St Goran. 2010. 70p. pap. (978-1-84923-461-0(2)) YouWriteOn.

Wise, William. Christopher Mouse. 2004. (J). (978-1-58234-961-9(4)) Bloomsbury Publishing USA.

—Christopher Mouse: The Tale of a Small Traveler. Benson, Patrick, illus. 2006. (ENG.). 160p. (YA). (gr. 2-5). per. 7.99 (978-1-58234-708-0(5), 9781582347080, Bloomsbury USA Childrens) Bloomsbury Publishing USA.

—Christopher Mouse: The Tale of a Small Traveler. Benson, Patrick, tr. Benson, Patrick, illus. 2004. (ENG.). 160p. (YA). (gr. 3-6). 15.95 (978-1-58234-878-0(2), 9781582348780, Bloomsbury USA Childrens) Bloomsbury Publishing USA.

Wood, Amanda & Kneen, Maggie. Christmas in the Mouse House. Kneen, Maggie, illus. 2011. (ENG., Illus.). 16p. (J). (gr. -1-2). 14.99 (978-0-7636-5287-6(3), Templar) Candlewick Pr.

Wood, Audrey & Wood, Don. The Little Mouse, the Red Ripe Strawberry, & the Big Hungry Bear. Wood, Don, illus. 2007. (Child's Play Library). (ENG., Illus.). 32p. (J). audio compact disk (978-1-84643-050-3(X)) Child's Play International Ltd.

Wood, David & Wood, Aimee. The Beautiful Swan. 2008. 24p. pap. 14.95 (978-1-59858-624-4(6)) Dog Ear Publishing, LLC.

Wood, Kathryn J. Morty Mouse: I Wish I Could Fly. 2012. 24p. pap. 15.99 (978-1-4771-1116-1(6)) Xlibris Corp.

Wright, Mary H. & Frontiera, Deborah K. Simon & Company: Flea Market Mice. Scott, Korey, illus. l.t. ed. 2016. (ENG.). 110p. (J). (gr. 2). pap. 11.99 (978-1-940591-04-9(X)) By Grace Enterprises.

Wright, Sky'asia. The Big, Blue Raspberry. 2012. 30p. pap. 5.99 (978-0-9857095-1-8(0)) RRJ Publishing, Inc.

Wright, Unasue Sellers. Dr. Chubby. 2013. 32p. pap. 13.95 (978-1-4497-8931-2(5), WestBow Pr.) Author Solutions, Inc.

Wyman, Susan. Pipsqueak's Puny Peepholes. 2013. 40p. pap. 15.99 (978-1-4908-0412-5(9), WestBow Pr.) Author Solutions, Inc.

Wyneken, Cherise. Spaceship Lands in Africa, 1 vol. 2010. 50p. pap. 16.95 (978-1-4489-5417-9(7)) America Star Bks.

Wynne-Jones, Tim. Ned Mouse Breaks Away, 1 vol. Petricic, Dusan, illus. 2003. (ENG.). 68p. (J). (gr. 3-18). 14.95 (978-0-88899-474-5(5)) Groundwood Bks. CAN. Dist: Publishers Group West (PGW).

Yang, Stella, illus. My Family: Individual Title Six-Packs. (Sails Literacy Ser.). 16p. (gr. k-18). 27.00 (978-0-7635-4393-8(4)) Rigby Education.

Yee, Wong Herbert. Abracadabra! Magic with Mouse & Mole. 2010. (Mouse & Mole Story Ser.). (ENG., Illus.). 48p. (J). (gr. -1-3). pap. 3.99 (978-0-547-40621-3(5)) Houghton Mifflin Harcourt Publishing Co.

—A Brand-New Day with Mouse & Mole. (Mouse & Mole Story Ser.). (ENG., Illus.). 48p. (J). (gr. 1-4). 2012. pap. 3.99 (978-0-547-72209-2(5)) 2008. 15.00 (978-0-618-96676-9(5)) Houghton Mifflin Harcourt Publishing Co.

—A Brand-New Day with Mouse & Mole. 2012. (Green Light Readers — Level 3 Ser.). lib. bdg. 13.55 (978-0-606-24437-4(9), Turtleback) Turtleback Bks.

—Fine Feathered Friends. Yee, Wong Herbert, illus. 2011. (Mouse & Mole Story Ser.). (ENG., Illus.). 48p. (J). (gr. 1-4). pap. 3.99 (978-0-547-51977-7(X)) Houghton Mifflin Harcourt Publishing Co.

—Mouse & Mole, a Winter Wonderland. Yee, Wong Herbert, illus. 2011. (Mouse & Mole Story Ser.). (ENG., Illus.). 48p. (J). (gr. 1-4). pap. 3.99 (978-0-547-57697-8(8)) Houghton Mifflin Harcourt Publishing Co.

—A Perfect Halloween. 2011. (Mouse & Mole Story Ser.). (ENG., Illus.). 48p. (J). (gr. 1-4). 14.99 (978-0-547-55152-4(5)) Houghton Mifflin Harcourt Publishing Co.

—Secret Valentine. Yee, Wong Herbert, illus. 2013. (Mouse & Mole Story Ser.). (ENG., Illus.). 48p. (J). (gr. 1-4). 15.99 (978-0-547-88719-7(1)) Houghton Mifflin Harcourt Publishing Co.

—Upstairs Mouse, Downstairs Mole. 12th ed. 2007. (Mouse & Mole Story Ser.). (ENG., Illus.). 48p. (J). (gr. -1-3). 3.99 (978-0-618-91586-6(9)) Houghton Mifflin Harcourt Publishing Co.

Yeoman, John. Mouse Trouble. Blake, Quentin, illus. 2011. (ENG.). 32p. (J). (gr. -1-k). pap. 12.99 (978-1-84939-201-3(3)) Andersen Pr. GBR. Dist: Independent Pubs. Group.

Yost-Filgate, Susan. A Good Day for Abbey. Filgate, Leonard, illus. 2009. (ENG.). 12p. (J). (gr. -1-12). 6.99 (978-1-934960-45-5(4), Raven Tree Pr.,Csi) Continental Sales, Inc.

—Rip Squeak & His Friends. Filgate, Leonard, illus. 2009. (ENG.). 32p. (J). (gr. -1-3). 16.95 (978-1-934960-40-0(3), Raven Tree Pr.,Csi) Continental Sales, Inc.

—Rip Squeak's A to Z Book. Filgate, Leonard, illus. 2009. (ENG.). 22p. (J). (gr. -1-12). 7.95 (978-1-934960-44-8(6), Raven Tree Pr.,Csi) Continental Sales, Inc.

—The Treasure. 2009. (ENG.). 32p. (J). (gr. -1-3). 16.95 (978-1-934960-41-7(1), Raven Tree Pr.,Csi) Continental Sales, Inc.

Young, Ed. Seven Blind Mice. Young, Ed, illus. 2007. (Illus.). pap. 14.95 incl. audio (978-0-439-02784-7(5)); (J). 24.95 incl. audio (978-0-439-02782-3(9)) Scholastic, Inc.

—Seven Blind Mice. Young, Ed, illus. 2011. (Illus.). 18.95 (978-0-439-02785-4(3)); (J). 29.95 (978-0-439-02783-0(7)) Weston Woods Studios, Inc.

Young, Ed, ed. Siete Ratones Ciegos. Uribe, Verónica, tr. 2009. (SPA., Illus.). 40p. (gr. k-2). pap. 9.99 (978-980-257-255-7(1)) Ekare, Ediciones VEN. Dist: Lectorum Pubns., Inc.

Younger, David. Spanky, the Brave Space Mouse, 1 vol. 2010. 18p. 24.95 (978-1-4489-4661-7(1)) PublishAmerica, Inc.

Zalben, Jane Breskin. Mousterpiece. Zalben, Jane Breskin, illus. 2012. (ENG., Illus.). 36p. (J). (gr. -1-2). 16.99 (978-1-59643-549-0(6), 9781596435490) Roaring Brook Pr.

Ziefert, Harriet. The Best Smelling Christmas Book Ever: 9 Scents to Scratch & Sniff! Rader, Laura, illus. 2004. 18p. (J). (gr. k-4). reprint ed. 13.00 (978-0-7567-7600-8(7)) DIANE Publishing Co.

Zimmerman, Michael. The Mouse & the Acorn. 2007. 32p. per. 11.95 (978-1-4327-0462-9(1)) Outskirts Pr., Inc.

Zinner, Gennieve. The UFB's of Bugsville, Florida USA, 1 vol. Ballinger, Carolyn, illus. 2010. 48p. pap. 24.95 (978-1-4489-7977-6(3)) PublishAmerica, Inc.

Zoboli, Giovanna. A Most Remarkable Mouse. D'Andrea, Lisa, illus. 2016. (ENG.). 40p. (J). (gr. -1-4). 17.95 (978-1-59270-213-8(9)) Enchanted Lion Bks., LLC.

MICE—POETRY

Akister, Finola, et al, selected by. Sports Poems & Mouse Poems. 2008. (Illus.). 32p. (J). pap. 10.95 (978-1-59646-619-7(7)) Dingles & Co.

Akister, Finola, et al. Sports Poems & Mouse Poems. 2008. (Illus.). 32p. (J). lib. bdg. 23.65 (978-1-59646-618-0(9)) Dingles & Co.

MICHELANGELO BUONARROTI, 1475-1564

Bailer, Darice. Michelangelo. Morrow, J. T., illus. 2014. (World's Greatest Artists Ser.). (ENG.). 24p. (J). (gr. 2-5). 28.50 (978-1-62687-352-0(6), 207192) Child's World, Inc., The.

Carr, Simonetta. Michelangelo for Kids: His Life & Ideas, with 21 Activities. 2016. (For Kids Ser.). (ENG., Illus.). 144p. (J). (gr. 4). pap. 18.99 (978-1-61373-193-2(0)) Chicago Review Pr., Inc.

Carvalho de Magalhaes, Roberto. Michelangelo. 2005. (Great Artists Ser.). (Illus.). 40p. (J). (gr. 4-7). per. 7.95 (978-1-59270-049-3(7)) Enchanted Lion Bks., LLC.

Connolly, Sean & Michelangelo Buonarroti. Michelangelo. 2004. (Lives of the Artists Ser.). (Illus.). 48p. (gr. 5-12). pap. 14.05 (978-0-8368-5605-7(8)); lib. bdg. 31.00 (978-0-8368-5600-2(7)) Stevens, Gareth Publishing LLLP. (Gareth Stevens Secondary Library).

Cook, Diane. Michelangelo: Renaissance Artist. (Illus.). 32p. (J). 2013. (People of Importance Ser.: 21). (gr. 4-18). 19.95 (978-1-4222-2851-7(7)) 2004. (Great Names Ser.). (gr. 3-18). lib. bdg. 19.95 (978-1-59084-156-3(5)) Mason Crest.

De Salvia, Maria Siponta. Michelangelo. 2003. (Great Artists Ser.). (Illus.). 40p. (J). 15.95 (978-1-59270-008-0(X)) Enchanted Lion Bks., LLC.

Di Cagno, Gabriella. Michelangelo. 2008. (Art Masters Ser.). 64p. (YA). (gr. 6-18). lib. bdg. 24.95 net. (978-1-934545-01-0(5)) Oliver Pr., Inc.

Emert, Phyllis, ed. Michelangelo. 2012. (Eye on Art Ser.). (ENG., Illus.). 128p. (gr. 7-10). lib. bdg. 39.40 (978-1-4205-0696-9(X), Lucent Bks.) Cengage Gale.

Fandel, Jennifer & Richardson, Adele. Michelangelo. 2017. (Odysseys in Artistry Ser.). (ENG., Illus.). 80p. (J). (gr. 7-11). pap. 14.99 (978-1-62832-315-3(9), Creative Paperbacks) Creative Co., The.

Howse, Jennifer. Michelangelo. 2016. (Illus.). 32p. (J). (978-1-4896-4623-1(X)) Weigl Pubs., Inc.

Mattern, Joanne. Michelangelo, 1 vol. 2005. (Great Artists Set 1 Ser.). (ENG., Illus.). 32p. (gr. k-6). 27.07 (978-1-59197-845-9(9), Checkerboard Library) ABDO Publishing Co.

McNeese, Tim. Michelangelo: Painter, Sculptor & Architect. 2005. (Makers of the Middle Ages & Renaissance Ser.). (Illus.). 160p. (gr. 5-8). lib. bdg. 32.95 (978-0-7910-8627-8(5), Chelsea Hse.) Facts On File, Inc.

Nichols, Catherine. Michelangelo Buonarroti. (Primary Source Library of Famous Artists Ser.). 32p. (gr. 3-4). 2009. 42.50 (978-1-60854-102-7(9)) 2006. (Illus.). (J). lib. bdg. 23.95 (978-1-4042-2763-7(6)) Rosen Publishing Group, Inc., The. (PowerKids Pr.).

Quill, Charlie. Michelangelo: His Life & Art. 2009. (Reading Room Collection 2 Ser.). 24p. (gr. 3-4). 42.50 (978-1-60851-980-4(5), PowerKids Pr.) Rosen Publishing Group, Inc., The.

Richardson, Adele. Michelangelo. 2016. (Illus.). 80p. (J). (978-1-60818-719-5(5), Creative Education) Creative Co., The.

Stanley, Diane. Michelangelo. Stanley, Diane, illus. 2003. (ENG., Illus.). 48p. (J). (gr. 2-18). pap. 6.99 (978-0-06-052113-4(9)) HarperCollins Pubs.

Sutcliffe, Jane. Stone Giant: Michelangelo's David & How He Came to Be. Shelley, John, illus. 2014. (J). 32p. pap. 16.95 (978-1-60734-614-2(1)); (ENG.). 32p. (gr. 1-4). lib. bdg. 16.95 (978-1-58089-295-7(7)); pap. (978-1-58089-296-4(5)) Charlesbridge Publishing, Inc.

Venezia, Mike. Michelangelo. Venezia, Mike, illus. rev. ed. 2014. (Getting to Know the World's Greatest Artists Ser.). (ENG., Illus.). 40p. (J). lib. bdg. 29.00 (978-0-531-21977-5(1)) Scholastic Library Publishing.

—Michelangelo (Revised Edition) 2014. (Getting to Know the World's Greatest Artists Ser.). (ENG.). 40p. (J). pap. 7.95 (978-0-531-22538-7(0)) Scholastic Library Publishing.

Whiting, Jim. Michelangelo. 2007. (Art Profiles for Kids Ser.). (Illus.). 48p. (YA). (gr. 4-7). lib. bdg. 29.95 (978-1-58415-562-1(0)) Mitchell Lane Pubs., Inc.

Wilkinson, Philip. Michelangelo: The Young Artist Who Dreamed of Perfection. 2006. (National Geographic World History Biographies Ser.). (ENG., Illus.). 64p. (J). (gr. 3-7). 17.95 (978-0-7922-5533-8(X)); lib. bdg. 27.90 (978-0-7922-5534-5(8)) National Geographic Society. (National Geographic Children's Bks.).

MICHELANGELO BUONARROTI, 1475-1564—FICTION

Brezina. Who Can Open Michelangelo's Seven Seals? (Illus.). 112p. (978-3-7913-3555-1(3)) Prestel Verlag GmbH & Co KG.

Hi-stories presents Michelangelo Bunnyrroti. 2006. (J). bds. 14.99 (978-0-9763233-2-7(X)) Little Germ That Could...Creations, Inc., The.

MICHIGAN

Abramowski, Christina. Something Special. (Illus.). 32p. (J). (gr. 2-4). 9.95 (978-0-9634927-0-8(5)) Junior League of Grand Rapids Michigan, Inc.

Aretha, David. Michigan: A MyReportLinks.com Book. 2003. (States Ser.). (Illus.). 48p. (J). lib. bdg. 25.26 (978-0-7660-5154-6(4), MyReportLinks.com Bks.) Enslow Pubs., Inc.

Arrathoon, Leigh A. & Davio, John. Jody's Travelbooks for Kids Vol. I: Frankenmuth, Michigan. Morris, Jeanne L., illus. 48p. (J). (gr. 2-6). pap. 4.95 (978-0-9648564-7-9(6)) Archus Pr., LLC.

—Jody's Travelbooks for Kids Vol. II: Holland, Michigan. Morris, Jeanne L., illus. 48p. (J). (gr. 2-6). pap. 4.95 (978-0-9648564-8-6(4)) Archus Pr., LLC.

—Jody's Travelbooks for Kids Vol. III: Mackinaw, Michigan. Morris, Jeanne L., illus. 48p. (J). (gr. 2-6). pap. 4.95 (978-0-9648564-9-3(2)) Archus Pr., LLC.

Bower, Gary. I'm a Michigan Kid! Bower, Jan, illus. 2005. 48p. (J). 17.99 (978-0-9704621-6-9(6)) Storybook Meadow Publishing.

Brill, Marlene Targ. Michigan. 2nd rev. ed. 2006. (Celebrate the States Ser.). (Illus.). 144p. (gr. 6-7). lib. bdg. 42.79 (978-0-7614-2351-5(6), Benchmark Bks.) Marshall Cavendish Corp.

Brown, Jonatha A. & Dubois, Muriel L. Michigan. 2005. (Portraits of the States Ser.). (Illus.). 32p. (gr. 2-6). lib. bdg. 26.00 (978-0-8368-4627-0(3), Gareth Stevens Learning Library) Stevens, Gareth Publishing LLLP.

Craats, Rennay. Michigan. 2011. (Guide to American States Ser.). (Illus.). 48p. (YA). (gr. 3-6). 29.99 (978-1-61690-794-5(0)); (J). (978-1-61690-470-8(4)) Weigl Pubs., Inc.

Deinard, Jenny. How to Draw Michigan's Sights & Symbols. 2009. (Kid's Guide to Drawing America Ser.). 32p. (gr. k-k). 50.50 (978-1-61511-071-1(2), PowerKids Pr.) Rosen Publishing Group, Inc., The.

Dubois, Muriel L. & Brown, Jonatha A. Michigan. 2005. (Portraits of the States Ser.). (Illus.). 32p. (gr. 2-6). pap. 10.50

M
N
O

(978-0-8368-4646-1(X), Gareth Stevens Learning Library) Stevens, Gareth Publishing LLLP.

Eisbruch, Emily. Curious Kids Activity Guide to Michigan. 2007. pap. 9.95 (978-0-9789140-0-4(7)) Curious Kids Guides.

Gregory, Josh. Michigan. 2017. (True Book — My United States Ser.). (J). pap. 7.95 **(978-0-531-23290-3(5),** Children's Pr.) Scholastic Library Publishing.

Haney, Johannah. Michigan. 2005. (It's My State! Ser.). (Illus.). 79p. (J). (gr. 4-7). lib. bdg. 27.07 (978-0-7614-1861-0(X), Benchmark Bks.) Marshall Cavendish Corp.

Heidtke, John. Family Golf Adventures on Michigan Links. 2010. 242p. (J). pap. 12.95 (978-1-60920-000-8(4)) Ajoyin Publishing, Inc.

Jensen, Niels R. Michigan, 1 vol. 2009. (United States Ser.). (ENG., Illus.). 48p. (YA). (gr. 2-5). 27.07 (978-1-60453-657-7(8)) ABDO Publishing Co.

Jerome, Kate B. The Wise Animal Handbook Michigan. 2017. (Arcadia Kids Ser.). (ENG., Illus.). 32p. (J). 16.99 **(978-0-7385-2826-7(9))** Arcadia Publishing.

Kammeraad, Kevin & Kammeraad, Stephanie. A Curious Glimpse of Michigan. Kammeraad, Kevin & Hipp, Ryan, illus. 32p. (J). 2006. (gr. 4-7). pap. 9.95 (978-0-9749412-9-5(8)) 2004. (gr. 3-7). 19.95 (978-0-9712692-9-3(7)) EDCO Publishing, Inc.

L Is for Ludington: An alphabet book about Ludington, MI created by Children. 2006. (J). pap. 10.00 (978-0-9786128-0-1(9)) Bosse, Andre Ctr.

Lewis, Anne Margaret & Campbell, Janis. Hidden Michigan. Popko, Wendy, illus. 2006. (ENG.). 40p. (J). (gr. 1-4). 12.95 (978-1-934133-01-9(9), Mackinac Island Press, Inc.) Charlesbridge Publishing, Inc.

Mader, Jan. Michigan. 2003. (Rookie Read-About Geography Ser.). (ENG., Illus.). 32p. (J). (gr. 1-2). 20.50 (978-0-516-22736-8(X), Children's Pr.) Scholastic Library Publishing.

Marsh, Carole. The Magnificant Michigan Coloring Book. 2004. (Michigan Experience! Ser.). (Illus.). 32p. (J). (gr. k-2). pap. 3.95 (978-0-7933-9567-5(4)) Gallopade International.

—Michigan Current Events Projects: 30 Cool, Activities, Crafts, Experiments & More for Kids to Do to Learn about Your State! 2003. (Michigan Experience Ser.). 32p. (gr. k-8). pap. 5.95 (978-0-635-02041-3(6), Marsh, Carole Bks.) Gallopade International.

—The Michigan Experience Pocket Guide. 2004. (Michigan Experience! Ser.). (Illus.). 96p. (J). (gr. 3-8). pap. 6.95 (978-0-7933-9562-0(3)) Gallopade International.

—Michigan Geography Projects: 30 Cool, Activities, Crafts, Experiments & More for Kids to Do to Learn about Your State! 2003. (Michigan Experience Ser.). 32p. (gr. k-5). pap. 5.95 (978-0-635-01841-0(1), Marsh, Carole Bks.) Gallopade International.

—Michigan Government Projects: 30 Cool, Activities, Crafts, Experiments & More for Kids to Do to Learn about Your State! 2003. (Michigan Experience Ser.). 32p. (gr. k-5). pap. 5.95 (978-0-635-01941-7(8), Marsh, Carole Bks.) Gallopade International.

—Michigan Jeopardy! Answers & Questions about Our State! 2004. (Michigan Experience! Ser.). (Illus.). 32p. (J). (gr. 3-8). pap. 7.95 (978-0-7933-9564-4(X)) Gallopade International.

—Michigan "Jography" A Fun Run Thru Our State! 2004. (Michigan Experience! Ser.). (Illus.). 32p. (J). (gr. 3-8). pap. 7.95 (978-0-7933-9565-1(8)) Gallopade International.

—Michigan People Projects: 30 Cool, Activities, Crafts, Experiments & More for Kids to Do to Learn about Your State! 2003. (Michigan Experience Ser.). 32p. (gr. k-5). pap. 5.95 (978-0-635-01991-2(4), Marsh, Carole Bks.) Gallopade International.

—Michigan Symbols & Facts Projects: 30 Cool, Activities, Crafts, Experiments & More for Kids to Do to Learn about Your State! 2003. (Michigan Experience Ser.). 32p. (gr. k-5). pap. 5.95 (978-0-635-01891-5(8), Marsh, Carole Bks.) Gallopade International.

—My First Book about Michigan. 2004. (Michigan Experience! Ser.). (Illus.). 32p. (J). (gr. k-4). pap. 7.95 (978-0-7933-9563-7(1)) Gallopade International.

—Texas's Big Activity Book. 2004. (Texas Experience! Ser.). (Illus.). 96p. (J). (gr. 2-6). pap. 9.95 (978-0-7933-9465-4(1)) Gallopade International.

McNamara, Connie. My First Michigan Words. 2004. (J). bds. 11.95 (978-0-9743244-6-3(9)) Shamrock Publishing, Inc.

Mills, Jordan. Michigan. 2016. (States Ser.). (ENG., Illus.). 32p. (gr. 3-4). lib. bdg. 27.32 (978-1-5157-0409-6(2)) Next Page Pr., The.

Murray, Julie. Michigan, 1 vol. 2006. (Buddy Book Ser.). (ENG., Illus.). 32p. (gr. 2-4). 27.07 (978-1-59197-681-3(2), Buddy Bks.) ABDO Publishing Co.

Obregon, Jose Maria. Michigan. Brusca, Maria Cristina, tr. 2005. (Bilingual Library of the United States of America Ser.: Set 1). (ENG & SPA., Illus.). 32p. (J). (gr. 3-6). lib. bdg. 25.25 (978-1-4042-3087-3(4)) Rosen Publishing Group, Inc., The.

Raatma, Lucia. Michigan. 2014. (America the Beautiful Ser.: 3). (ENG.). 144p. (J). lib. bdg. 40.00 (978-0-531-24890-4(9)) Scholastic Library Publishing.

Riggs, Kate. Michigan. 2008. (This Land Called America Ser.). (Illus.). 32p. (YA). (gr. 3-6). 22.95 (978-1-58341-647-1(1)) Creative Co., The.

Sirvaitis, Karen. Michigan. 2012. (J). lib. bdg. 25.26 (978-0-7613-4539-8(6), Lerner Pubns.) Lerner Publishing Group.

MICHIGAN—FICTION

Andrews, Randall. The Last Guardian of Magic. 2008. 448p. (YA). per. 23.95 (978-0-595-47345-8(8)) iUniverse, Inc.

Anthony, David & David, Charles. Heroes A2Z #1: (Heroes a to Z): Alien Ice Cream. Blakeslee, Lys, illus. 2007. 128p. (J). pap. 4.99 (978-0-9728461-8-9(2)) Sigil Publishing.

—Heroes A2Z #2: (Heroes a to Z): Bowling over Halloween: Bowling over Halloween. Blakeslee, Lys, illus. 2007. (Heroes A2Z Ser.). 128p. (J). pap. 4.99 (978-0-9728461-9-6(0)) Sigil Publishing.

Arrathoon, Leigh A. Summer of the Bear: An Historical Novel about the Anishinabeg & the Fur Traders in Michigan. 2005. (Journals of Kevin Murphy Ser.: Bk. 1). (J). (978-1-893047-07-5(5)) Archus Pr., LLC.

Arrathroon, Leigh A. Magical Adventures in Michigan. 2003. (Illus.). viii, 349p. (978-1-893047-10-5(5)) Archus Pr., LLC.

Balash, Sue Beth. Mimi the Inchworm. 2009. (ENG.). 32p. pap. 10.95 (978-1-933916-44-6(3), Ferne Pr.) Nelson Publishing & Marketing.

Balliett, Blue. The Danger Box. 2012. (ENG.). 320p. (J). (gr. 3-7). pap. 7.99 (978-0-439-85210-4(2), Scholastic Paperbacks) Scholastic, Inc.

Baumer, Dawn McVay, creator. Dune Daze: Silver Lake. 2004. (Illus.). (J). (978-0-9754960-0-8(X)) Butters Pr.

Bellairs, John. The House with a Clock in Its Walls. Gorey, Edward, illus. 2004. (Lewis Barnavelt Ser.: Bk. 1). (ENG.). 192p. (J). (gr. 3-7). pap. 6.99 (978-0-14-240257-3(5), Puffin Books) Penguin Young Readers Group.

—The House with a Clock in Its Walls. (Lewis Barnavelt Ser.: Bk. 1). 179p. (J). (gr. 4-6). pap. 4.50 (978-0-8072-1423-7(X), Listening Library) Random Hse. Audio Publishing Group.

Birkholz, Gay Lyn. Veneti: Lake Michigan's Treasure. Williamson, Linda K., illus. 2010. 52p. pap. 17.00 (978-1-60860-129-5(3), Strategic Bk. Publishing) Strategic Book Publishing & Rights Agency (SBPRA).

Blos, Joan W. Brothers of the Heart: A Story of the Old Northwest, 1837-1838. 2008. (ENG.). 176p. (J). (gr. 3-7). pap. 5.99 (978-1-4169-7561-8(6), Simon & Schuster/Paula Wiseman Bks.) Simon & Schuster/Paula Wiseman Bks.

Bower, Gary. I'm a Michigan Kid Coloring & Activity Book. Bower, Jan & Bower, Brittany, illus. 2006. 48p. (J). pap. 7.95 (978-0-9704621-5-2(8), Bower Bks.) Storybook Meadow Publishing.

Brewer, Heather. The Cemetery Boys. 2016. 304p. (YA). (gr. 8). pap. 9.99 (978-0-06-230789-7(4), HarperTeen) HarperCollins Pubs.

—The Cemetery Boys. 2016. (YA). lib. bdg. 20.85 (978-0-606-38741-5(2)) Turtleback Bks.

Carr, Annie Roe. Nan Sherwoods Winter Holidays or Rescuin. 2007. pap. (978-1-4065-1296-0(6)) Dodo Pr.

Carter, Aimée. The Goddess Test. 2011. (Goddess Test Ser.: 1). lib. bdg. 20.85 (978-0-606-26943-8(6), Turtleback) Turtleback Bks.

Cory, Kim Delmar. Home to Mackinac: The Tale of Young Jack Murphy's Discovery of Loyalty, Family, & Forgiveness. Evans, Laura, illus. 2007. (ENG.). 175p. (J). (gr. 3-7). per. 9.95 (978-0-911872-87-3(6)) Mackinac State Historic Parks.

—Tending Ben's Garden. 2009. (J). pap. (978-0-88092-778-9(X)) Royal Fireworks Publishing Co.

Curtis, Christopher Paul. Bucking the Sarge. 2006. (Readers Circle Ser.). (ENG.). 288p. (YA). (gr. 7-7). reprint ed. mass mkt. 6.99 (978-0-440-41331-8(1), Laurel Leaf) Random Hse. Children's Bks.

—Bud, Not Buddy. unabr. ed. 2004. 256p. (J). (gr. 4-7). pap. 36.00 incl. audio (978-0-8072-8210-6(3), LYA 140 S{, Listening Library) Random Hse. Audio Publishing Group.

—Bud, Not Buddy. 2004. (ENG., Illus.). 288p. (J). (gr. 3-7). mass mkt. 7.99 (978-0-553-49410-5(4), Laurel Leaf) Random Hse. Children's Bks.

—The Mighty Miss Malone. (ENG.). 320p. (J). (gr. 4-7). 2013. pap. 7.99 (978-0-440-42214-3(0), Yearling) 2012. 15.99 (978-0-385-73491-2(3), Lamb, Wendy Bks.) Random Hse. Children's Bks.

—The Mighty Miss Malone. 2013. lib. bdg. 18.40 (978-0-606-27007-6(8), Turtleback) Turtleback Bks.

—Mr. Chickee's Funny Money. 2007. (ENG.). 160p. (J). (gr. 3-7). 6.99 (978-0-440-22919-3(7), Yearling) Random Hse. Children's Bks.

—Mr. Chickee's Messy Mission. 2008. (ENG., Illus.). 240p. (J). (gr. 3-7). 6.99 (978-0-440-22922-3(7), Yearling) Random Hse. Children's Bks.

—The Watsons Go to Birmingham — 1963. 2013. (ENG.). 224p. (J). (gr. 3-7). 7.99 (978-0-385-38294-6(4), Yearling) Random Hse. Children's Bks.

—The Watsons Go to Birmingham 1963. 210p. (YA). (gr. 5-18). pap. 5.50 (978-0-8072-8336-3(3)); 2004. (J). (gr. 4-18). pap. 38.00 incl. audio (978-0-8072-8335-6(5), YA166SP) Random Hse. Audio Publishing Group. (Listening Library).

Curtis, Christopher Paul & Vega, Eida de la. Los Watson Van a Birmingham - 1963. 2016. (SPA.). 200p. (J). (gr. 5-12). pap. 12.99 **(978-1-63245-640-3(0))** Lectorum Pubns., Inc.

Dalton, Michelle. Fifteenth Summer. 2013. (ENG.). 272p. (YA). (gr. 7). 17.99 (978-1-4424-7267-9(7)); (Illus.). pap. 10.99 (978-1-4424-7266-2(9)) Simon Pulse. (Simon Pulse).

Damerau, Diane Deci. The Petoskey Stones, 1 vol. 2009. 135p. pap. 24.95 (978-1-60749-903-9(7)) America Star Bks.

Day, Karen. No Cream Puffs. 2010. (ENG.). 224p. (J). (gr. 3-7). 6.99 (978-0-375-83776-0(0), Yearling) Random Hse. Children's Bks.

DeCamp, Alison. My Near-Death Adventures: I Almost Died. Again. 2016. (ENG., Illus.). 288p. (J). (gr. 3-7). 16.99 (978-0-385-39048-4(3), Crown Books For Young Readers) Random Hse. Children's Bks.

Delco, Bobby. Lil Mack Jr. 2009. 108p. pap. 11.99 (978-1-4389-0473-3(8)) AuthorHouse.

Derby, Sally. Kyle's Island. (ENG.). 192p. (J). (gr. 5). 2014. pap. 7.95 (978-1-58089-317-6(1)) 2010. 16.95 (978-1-58089-316-9(3)) Charlesbridge Publishing, Inc.

Deshone, Jerry Michael. Bear in Mind. 2011. 24p. pap. 24.95 (978-1-4626-2973-2(3)) America Star Bks.

Dunn, Robert, illus. The Littlest Bunny in Michigan: An Easter Adventure. 2015. (ENG.). 32p. (J). (-3). 9.99 (978-1-4926-1117-2(4), Sourcebooks Jabberwocky) Sourcebooks, Inc.

Elster, Jean Alicia. Who's Jim Hines? 2008. (Great Lakes Books Ser.). (ENG., Illus.). 146p. (J). pap. 14.99 (978-0-8143-3402-7(4), 2162) Wayne State Univ. Pr.

Frost, Helen. Crossing Stones. 2009. (ENG., Illus.). 192p. (YA). (gr. 7-18). 18.99 (978-0-374-31653-2(8), 9780374316532, Farrar, Straus & Giroux (BYR)) Farrar, Straus & Giroux.

Gaertner, Connie. Wake-Up Calls. 2013. 154p. (gr. 10-12). pap. 12.95 (978-1-4759-6646-6(6)) iUniverse, Inc.

Gamble, Adam. Good Night Michigan. Rosen, Anne, illus. 2011. (Good Night Our World Ser.). (ENG.). 20p. (J). (gr. k — 1). bds. 9.95 (978-1-60219-054-2(2)) Good Night Bks.

Giff, Patricia Reilly. Willow Run. 2007. 149p. (J). 13.65 (978-0-7569-7769-6(X)) Perfection Learning Corp.

—Willow Run. 2007. (ENG.). 160p. (J). (gr. 3-7). per. 5.99 (978-0-440-23801-0(3), Yearling) Random Hse. Children's Bks.

Grund, Carol A. Anna Mei, Blessing in Disguise. 2011. 181p. (J). pap. (978-0-8198-0796-0(6)) Pauline Bks. & Media.

—Anna Mei, Escape Artist. 2011. 168p. (J). (gr. 4-7). pap. 8.95 (978-0-8198-0794-6(X)) Pauline Bks. & Media.

Guarneri, Cristina. The Invincible, 1 vol. 2010. 48p. pap. 16.95 (978-1-4489-4086-8(9)) America Star Bks.

Hahn, Cathe. Step Up!, 1 vol. Artley, Bob, illus. 2005. (ENG.). 32p. (J). (gr. k-3). 16.99 (978-1-58980-214-8(4)) Pelican Publishing Co., Inc.

Hannigan, Kate. Summer Showers. Hughes, Brooke Boynton, illus. (Cupcake Cousins Ser.: Bk. 2). (ENG.). (J). (gr. 3-7). 2016. 256p. pap. 6.99 (978-1-4847-2362-3(7))Bk. 2. 2015. 240p. 16.99 (978-1-4847-1662-5(0)) Hyperion Bks. for Children.

—Winter Wonders. Hughes, Brooke Boynton, illus. 2016. (Cupcake Cousins Ser.: Bk. 3). (ENG.). 240p. (J). (gr. 3-7). 16.99 (978-1-4847-1663-2(9)) Hyperion Bks. for Children.

Haynes, Marilee. Pictures of Me. 2016. 149p. (J). pap. (978-0-8198-6019-4(0)) Pauline Bks. & Media.

Holbrook, Sara. The Enemy: Detroit 1954. 2017. (ENG.). 224p. (J). (gr. 4-9). 17.95 (978-1-62979-498-3(8), Calkins Creek) Boyds Mills Pr.

Howard, Ellen. The Log Cabin Wedding. Himler, Ronald, illus. 2006. (ENG.). 64p. (J). (gr. -1-3). 15.95 (978-0-8234-1989-0(4)) Holiday Hse., Inc.

James, Eric. A Halloween Scare in Michigan. Le Ray, Marina, illus. 2014. (ENG.). 32p. (J). (-5). 9.99 (978-1-4926-0606-2(5), 9781492606062, Sourcebooks Jabberwocky) Sourcebooks, Inc.

—Santa's Sleigh Is on Its Way to Michigan. Dunn, Robert, illus. 2015. (ENG.). 32p. (J). (-2). 12.99 (978-1-4926-2741-8(0), Sourcebooks Jabberwocky) Sourcebooks, Inc.

Johnson, Lois Walfrid. Mystery of the Missing Map. 2009. (J). 8.99 (978-0-88062-283-7(0)) Mott Media.

Langley, Jan. Captain & Harry Haunting Tail. 2004. pap. (978-0-9724777-0-3(5)) Captain & Harry LLC, The.

Lewis, Anne Margaret. The Runaway Mitten. Zenz, Aaron, illus. 2015. (ENG.). 40p. (J). (gr. -1-k). 15.99 (978-1-63450-213-9(2), Sky Pony Pr.) Skyhorse Publishing Co., Inc.

MacPherson, M. j. The Magic Thread: Overcoming challenges during World War II, a young girl discovers secrets that change adversity into Adventure. 2009. 208p. pap. 17.95 (978-0-595-52812-7(0)) iUniverse, Inc.

Magsamen, Sandra. I Love Michigan (an ABC Adventure) 2015. (ENG.). 40p. (J). (-5). 12.99 (978-1-4926-2844-6(1), Sourcebooks Jabberwocky) Sourcebooks, Inc.

Marsh, Barry. Good Harbor Bay. 2009. (J). 14.95 (978-0-9767268-1-4(5)) Crofton Creek Pr.

McCahan, Erin. I Now Pronounce You Someone Else. 2010. (ENG.). 272p. (J). (gr. 7-18). 16.99 (978-0-545-08818-3(6), Levine, Arthur A. Bks.) Scholastic, Inc.

Merkel, Ruth Vitrano. Hannah's Girls: Elaine. 2008. (Hannah's Girls Ser.: 5). (Illus.). 176p. (J). pap. 9.99 (978-0-8280-1955-2(X)) Review & Herald Publishing Assn.

Noble, Trinka Hakes. The Legend of Michigan. Van Frankenhuyzen, Gijsbert, illus. 2006. (Legend (Sleeping Bear) Ser.). (ENG.). 40p. (J). (gr. -1-3). 17.95 (978-1-58536-278-3(6)) Sleeping Bear Pr.

Nye, Naomi Shihab. The Turtle of Oman. 2014. (ENG.). 304p. (J). (gr. 3-7). 16.99 (978-0-06-201972-1(4)) HarperCollins Pubs.

O'Neill, Elizabeth. Alfred Visits Michigan. 2006. (Illus.). 24p. pap. 12.00 (978-0-9771836-6-1(1)) Global Business Information Strategies, Inc.

Otten, Charlotte F. Home in a Wilderness Fort: Copper Harbor 1844. 2006. (Illus.). 232p. (J). (gr. 2-7). per. 14.95 (978-0-9766104-5-8(0)) Arbutus Pr.

Panagopoulos, Janie Lynn. A Castle at the Straits. Evans, Laura, illus. 2003. 48p. (J). (gr. 1-6). (978-0-911872-83-5(3)) Mackinac State Historic Parks.

—Mark of the Bear Claw. 2007. 224p. (J). pap. 8.95 (978-0-938682-83-7(0)) River Road Pubns., Inc.

Paul, Curtis Christopher. Bud, Not Buddy. 2014. (ENG.). 256p. (J). (gr. 12-12). 11.24 (978-1-63245-063-0(1)) Lectorum Pubns., Inc.

—The Watsons Go to Birmingham 1963. 2014. (ENG.). 224p. (J). (gr. 12-12). 11.24 (978-1-63245-108-8(5)) Lectorum Pubns., Inc.

Phelan, Matt. Bluffton: My Summers with Buster. Phelan, Matt, illus. 2017. (ENG., Illus.). 232p. (J). (gr. 4-7). pap. 12.99 (978-0-7636-8706-9(5)) Candlewick Pr.

—Bluffton: My Summers with Buster. Phelan, Matt, illus. 2017. (ENG., Illus.). (J). (gr. 4-7). lib. bdg. 24.50 **(978-0-606-39837-4(6))** Turtleback Bks.

Pirzada, Nefes & Simeone, Angelique. Young Equestrian: Something in Common. 2012. 386p. (gr. 4-18). pap. 21.14 (978-1-4669-5242-3(3)) Trafford Publishing.

Polacco, Patricia. The Mermaid's Purse. Polacco, Patricia, illus. 2016. (ENG., Illus.). 48p. (J). (gr. k-3). 17.99 (978-0-399-16692-1(0), G.P. Putnam's Sons Books for Young Readers) Penguin Young Readers Group.

Pyke, Helen Godfrey. Pinch River: Growing up Hard & Fast on the Michigan Frontier. 2008. (J). pap. 7.97 (978-0-8163-2250-3(3)) Pacific Pr. Publishing Assn.

Quackenbush-Douglas, Diane. That's Just the Way it Was! (Not a Fairy Tale) 2010. 28p. 15.49 (978-1-4520-2941-2(5)) AuthorHouse.

Rand, Jonathan. Michigan Chillers #14 Bionic Bats Bay City. 2007. 208p. (J). pap. 5.99 (978-1-893699-65-6(X)) AudioCraft Publishing, Inc.

Richards, Sonja. Comet Kid. 2007. 31p. pap. 8.95 (978-0-9794935-0-8(1)) Olde Towne Publishing.

—My Maize & Blue Day. Viall, Pauline, illus. 2008. 32p. (J). 19.95 (978-0-9794935-1-5(X)) Olde Towne Publishing.

Robinson, A. M. Vampire Crush. 2010. (ENG.). 416p. (YA). (gr. 8-18). pap. 8.99 (978-0-06-198971-1(1), HarperTeen) HarperCollins Pubs.

Rought, A. E. Broken. 2013. (ENG.). 320p. (J). (gr. 9). pap. 9.99 (978-1-908844-31-6(0), Strange Chemistry) Watkins Media Limited GBR. Dist: Penguin Random Hse. LLC.

Schröder, Monika. Be Light Like a Bird. 2016. (ENG.). 240p. (gr. 3-7). lib. bdg. 14.95 (978-1-62370-749-1(8)) Capstone Young Readers of Coughlan Cos.

—Be Light Like a Bird. 2016. (Middle-Grade Novels Ser.). (ENG.). 240p. (gr. 4-7). 26.65 (978-1-4965-3301-2(1)) Stone Arch Bks.

Shabazz, Ilyasah & Magoon, Kekla. X. 2016. (ENG.). 384p. (J). (gr. 9). pap. 8.99 (978-0-7636-9092-2(9)) Candlewick Pr.

Shaw, J. D. Leave No Footprints. 2011. (ENG.). 276p. (J). (gr. 7). pap. 14.95 (978-0-9845318-6-8(6)) Tiny Stachel Pr.

Silvano, Wendi. Love Is All Around Michigan. Czernichowska, Joanna, illus. 2016. (ENG.). 32p. (J). (-6). 12.99 (978-1-4926-2934-4(0), 9781492629344, Sourcebooks Jabberwocky) Sourcebooks, Inc.

Smallman, Steve. Santa Is Coming to Grand Rapids. Dunn, Robert, illus. 2015. (ENG.). 32p. (J). (-3). 9.99 (978-1-4926-2657-2(0), Sourcebooks Jabberwocky) Sourcebooks, Inc.

—Santa Is Coming to Michigan. Dunn, Robert, illus. 2012. (ENG.). 32p. (J). (-3). 9.99 (978-1-4022-7539-5(0), Sourcebooks Jabberwocky) Sourcebooks, Inc.

Smallman, Steve, et al. My First Santa's Coming to Michigan. Dunn, Robert, illus. 2015. (ENG.). 18p. (J). bds. 9.99 (978-1-4926-2873-6(5), Sourcebooks Jabberwocky) Sourcebooks, Inc.

Smith, Ruth. Buddy Bear: Visits Michigan Lighthouses. 2010. 28p. pap. 13.99 (978-1-4490-8363-2(3)) AuthorHouse.

Smucker, Anna Egan. To Keep the South Manitou Light. (Great Lakes Books Ser.). (ENG., Illus.). 144p. (J). 2006. (gr. 3-7). per. 15.99 (978-0-8143-3236-8(6), 1147) 2004. 23.95 (978-0-8143-3235-1(8), 1148, Painted Turtle) Wayne State Univ. Pr.

Stinson, Aimee & Somson, Kathy. The Bearless City, 1 vol. 2009. 22p. pap. 24.95 (978-1-60749-406-5(X)) America Star Bks.

Stupp, Robert Dock. The Fable of Freddy & the Frockett. 2011. 194p. pap. 16.95 (978-1-4327-4327-7(9)) Outskirts Pr., Inc.

Sully, Katherine. Night-Night Michigan. Kolanovic, Dubravka & Poole, Helen, illus. 2016. (ENG.). 20p. (J). (-1). bds. 9.99 (978-1-4926-3934-3(6), 9781492639343, Sourcebooks Jabberwocky) Sourcebooks, Inc.

Thoms, Susan Collins. The Twelve Days of Christmas in Michigan. Pilutti, Deb, illus. (Twelve Days of Christmas in America Ser.). (ENG.). (J). (— 1). 2017. 22p. bds. 7.95 **(978-1-4549-2284-1(2))** 2010. 40p. 12.95 (978-1-4027-6351-9(4)) Sterling Publishing Co., Inc.

Thorne, K. C. The Troll of MacKinac. Johnson, Vickie, illus. 2010. 32p. pap. 13.00 (978-1-60911-178-6(8), Eloquent Bks.) Strategic Book Publishing & Rights Agency (SBPRA).

Tillson, M. C. Secret of Bete Grise Bay: A Michigan Lighthouse Adventure. Bailey, Lisa, illus. 2008. (ENG.). (J). (gr. 1-5). pap. 9.95 (978-0-9764824-2-0(8)) A & M Writing and Publishing.

Tracy, Kristen. Crimes of the Sarahs. 2014. (ENG., Illus.). 384p. (YA). (gr. 9). pap. 9.99 (978-1-4424-8100-8(5), Simon Pulse) Simon Pulse.

Van Frankenhuyzen, Robbyn Smith. Kelly of Hazel Ridge. van Frankenhuyzen, Gijsbert, illus. 3rd rev. ed. 2006. (Hazel Ridge Farm Stories Ser.). (ENG.). 32p. (J). (gr. k-5). 17.95 (978-1-58536-268-4(9)) Sleeping Bear Pr.

Walter, Debbie. Introducing Russell. Walter, Debbie, illus. 2007. (Illus.). 68p. (J). per. 6.95 (978-0-9766315-2-1(0)) Moose Run Productions.

Wargin, Kathy-jo. Mitt, the Michigan Mouse. Holman, Karen Busch, illus. 2015. (Mitt Midwest Ser.: 1). (ENG.). 160p. (J). (gr. k-7). pap. 8.95 (978-1-938170-65-2(2), Mitten Pr.) Ann Arbor Editions LLC.

Whelan, Gloria. Forgive the River, Forgive the Sky. 2004. 96p. (J). pap. 8.00 (978-0-8028-5256-4(4)) Eerdmans, William B. Publishing Co.

—Mackinac Bridge: The Story of the Five-Mile Poem. van Frankenhuyzen, Gijsbert, illus. 2006. (Tales of Young Americans Ser.). (ENG.). 32p. (J). 17.95 (978-1-58536-283-7(2)) Sleeping Bear Pr.

Winfield, Arthur M. The Rover Boys on the Great Lakes. 2004. reprint ed. pap. 22.95 (978-1-4191-8119-1(X)) Kessinger Publishing, LLC.

Winfield, Arthur M. The Rover Boys on the Great Lakes. 2004. reprint ed. pap. 1.99 (978-1-4192-8119-8(4)) Kessinger Publishing, LLC.

Wood, David. The Little House on Buchanan Street. 2007. 24p. per. 12.95 (978-1-934246-64-1(6)) Peppertree Pr., The.

MICHIGAN—HISTORY

Bernard-Nollins, Sonya M. Here I Stand: A Musical History of African Americans in Battle Creek, Michigan. 2003. (Illus.). (YA). pap. 15.00 (978-0-9741611-0-5(1)) Fortitude Graphic Design & Printing.

Brennan-Nelson, Denise. Little Michigan. Monroe, Michael Glenn, illus. 2010. (My Little State Ser.). (ENG.). 22p. (J). 9.95 (978-1-58536-479-4(7)) Sleeping Bear Pr.

Connery-Boyd, Peg. Totally Michigan! 2016. (Hawk's Nest Activity Bks.: 0). (ENG.). 64p. (J). (-3). pap. 8.99 (978-1-4926-4191-9(X), 9781492641919, Sourcebooks Jabberwocky) Sourcebooks, Inc.

Craats, Rennay. Michigan: The Wolverine State. 2016. (J). (978-1-4896-4881-5(X)) Weigl Pubs., Inc.

Foster, Tracy, et al. Benson's Adventures in Michigan. 2016. (Illus.). 32p. (J). 17.95 (978-0-9980066-0-4(2)) Britton & Case Prs.

Frank, David. The Kids & Sites of Kalamazoo. 2004. 80p. (978-0-9756971-0-2(1)) Artstreet LLC.

Gamble, Adam & Jasper, Mark. Count to Sleep Michigan. Veno, Joe, illus. 2014. (Count to Sleep Ser.). (ENG.). 20p. (J). (— 1). bds. 7.95 (978-1-60219-327-7(4)) Good Night Bks.

Glupker, Dianne. Great Tastes of Michigan. Delsi, Dawna, illus. 2006. (J). per. 9.95 (978-0-9769846-1-0(X)) Harambee Pr.

Haney, Johannah & Hantula, Richard. Michigan. 2nd rev. ed. 2011. (It's My State! 2 Ser.). 80p. (gr. 3). 31.36 (978-1-60870-523-8(4)) Marshall Cavendish Corp.

Haney, Johannah, et al. Michigan. 2016. (It's My State! (r) Ser.). (Illus.). 80p. (J). (gr. 4-4). 34.21 (978-1-62713-163-6(9)) Cavendish Square Publishing.

Harmon, Daniel E. Minnesota: Past & Present. 2010. (United States: Past & Present Ser.). (ENG., Illus.). 48p. (J). lib. bdg. 29.25 (978-1-4358-3524-5(7), Rosen Reference) Rosen Publishing Group, Inc., The.

Helweg, Laura. Eastern Great Lakes: Indiana, Michigan, Ohio, Vol. 19. 2015. (Let's Explore the States Ser.). 64p. (J). (gr. 5). 23.95 (978-1-4222-3323-8(5)) Mason Crest.

Hoffman, Mary Hramiec. Elizabeth Whitney Williams & the Little Traverse Light. 2004. (Illus.). 38p. (J). 17.95 (978-0-9746901-0-0(4)) Hramiec Hoffman Publishing.

Jerome, Kate B. Lucky to Live in Michigan. 2017. (Arcadia Kids Ser.). (ENG., Illus.). 32p. (J). 16.99 ***(978-0-7385-2777-2(7))*** Arcadia Publishing.

Killingbeck, Dale. Michigan Triumphs & Tragedies 2005. (Illus.). 160p. per. 9.95 *(978-0-9762758-0-0(5))* Killingbeck, Dale.

Levy, Janey. Michigan: Past & Present. 2010. (United States: Past & Present Ser.). (ENG., Illus.). 48p. (J). pap. 11.75 *(978-1-4358-8496-0(5))*; lib. bdg. 29.25 *(978-1-4358-3523-8(9))* Rosen Publishing Group, Inc., The. (Rosen Reference).

Mac, Janie. The Moon over Michigan. 2013. 20p. pap. 13.77 *(978-1-4669-5238-6(5))* Trafford Publishing.

Marsh, Carole. Exploring Michigan Through Project-Based Learning: Geography, History, Government, Economics & More. 2016. (Michigan Experience Ser.). (ENG.). (J). pap. 9.99 *(978-0-635-12346-6(0))* Gallopade International.

—I'm Reading about Michigan. 2014. (Michigan Experience Ser.). (ENG., Illus.). (J). pap., pap. 8.99 *(978-0-635-11297-2(3))* Gallopade International.

—Michigan History Projects: 30 Cool, Activities, Crafts, Experiments & More for Kids to Do to Learn about Your State! 2003. (Michigan Experience Ser.). 32p. (gr. k-5). pap. 5.95 *(978-0-635-01791-8(1),* Marsh, Carole Bks.) Gallopade International.

McDowell, Pamela. Michigan: The Wolverine State. 2012. (J). *(978-1-61913-363-1(6))*; pap. *(978-1-61913-364-8(4))* Weigl Pubs., Inc.

McGraw-Hill Education Editors. Michigan 2009 Gr 3 Practice & Activity Workbook. 2009. (ENG.). (gr. 3). pap. 5.48 *(978-0-02-153646-7(5),* 0021536465) Macmillan/McGraw-Hill Schl. Div.

Murray, Julie. Michigan, 1 vol. 2012. (Explore the United States Ser.). (ENG., Illus.). 32p. (J). (gr. 2-5). lib. bdg. 28.50 *(978-1-61783-360-1(6),* Big Buddy Bks.) ABDO Publishing Co.

Newman, Mark. Sooper Yooper: Environmental Defender. Heckman, Mark, illus. 2010. 48p. (J). 17.95 *(978-1-933272-26-9(0))* Thunder Bay Pr.

Obregón, José María. Michigan. 2009. (Bilingual Library of the United States of America Ser.). (ENG & SPA.). 32p. (gr. 2-2). 47.90 *(978-1-60853-367-1(0),* Editorial Buenas Letras) Rosen Publishing Group, Inc., The.

Powell, Jennifer. The Colors of Mackinac Island. Powell, Jennifer, photos by. 2015. (ENG., Illus.). 30p. (J). (gr. 1-2). 10.95 *(978-1-933272-49-8(X))* Thunder Bay Pr.

Smucker, Anna Egan. To Keep the South Manitou Light. 2006. (Great Lakes Books Ser.). (ENG., Illus.). 144p. (J). (gr. 3-7). per. 15.99 *(978-0-8143-3236-8(6),* 1147) Wayne State Univ. Pr.

Wargin, Kathy-jo. S Is for Sleeping Bear Dunes: A National Lakeshore Alphabet. Frankenhuyzen, Gijsbert van, illus. 2015. (ENG.). 32p. (J). (gr. 2-4). 16.99 *(978-1-58536-917-1(9),* 203818) Sleeping Bear Pr.

Wells, Sherry A. Father, Ford, $5 a Day: The Mullers from Missouri. Bulla, Randy, illus. 2003. 128p. lib. bdg. 14.00 *(978-0-934981-11-8(6))* Lawells Publishing.

Yasuda, Anita. What's Great about Michigan? 2015. (ENG., Illus.). 32p. (J). (gr. 2-5). 26.65 *(978-1-4677-3886-6(7))* Lerner Publishing Group.

MICHIGAN, LAKE

Crane, Carol. The Christmas Tree Ship. Ellison, Chris, illus. 2011. (ENG.). 32p. (J). (gr. k-6). 15.95 *(978-1-58536-285-1(9))* Sleeping Bear Pr.

MICHIGAN, LAKE—FICTION

Chellis, Marie. The Hayburner, 1 vol. 2010. 60p. pap. 19.95 *(978-1-4512-9053-0(5))* America Star Bks.

Hannigan, Kate. Summer Showers. Hughes, Brooke Boynton, illus. 2016. (Cupcake Cousins Ser.: Bk. 2). (ENG.). 256p. (J). (gr. 3-7). pap. 6.99 *(978-1-4847-2362-3(7))* Hyperion Bks. for Children.

Jean. Jean's Story. 2009. 40p. pap. 18.49 *(978-1-4389-4531-6(0))* AuthorHouse.

McCahan, Erin. The Lake Effect. 2017. (ENG.). 400p. (YA). (gr. 7). 17.99 ***(978-0-8037-4052-5(2),*** Dial Bks) Penguin Young Readers Group.

Prestwood, Donna. Center World. 2006. 120p. per. 10.95 *(978-1-59824-206-5(7))* E-BookTime LLC.

MICKEY MOUSE (FICTITIOUS CHARACTER)—FICTION

Ambrosio, Stefano. Mouse Magic. Pastrovicchio, Lorenzo, illus. 2010. (ENG.). 112p. (J). 24.99 *(978-1-60886-550-5(9))*; Vol. 1. pap. 9.99 *(978-1-60886-541-3(X))* Boom! Studios.

—Wizards of Mickey - Grand Tournament, Vol. 2. Pastrovicchio, Lorenzo & Magic Eye Studios, illus. 2010. (Wizards of Mickey Ser.). (ENG.). 128p. (J). (gr. 3-6). pap. 9.99 *(978-1-60886-564-2(9))* Boom! Studios.

Amerikaner, Susan. Goofy at Bat. 2013. (Mickey & Friends World of Reading Ser.). (J). lib. bdg. 13.55 *(978-0-606-27117-2(1),* Turtleback) Turtleback Bks.

Barks, Carl, et al. Walt Disney's Christmas Parade #5. 2008. (Illus.). 80p. pap. 9.50 *(978-1-60360-005-7(1))* Gemstone Publishing, Inc.

—Walt Disney's Comics & Stories #702. 2009. 64p. pap. 7.99 *(978-1-60360-092-7(2))* Gemstone Publishing, Inc.

—Walt Disney's Comics & Stories #704. 2009. 64p. pap. 7.99 *(978-1-60360-094-1(9))* Gemstone Publishing, Inc.

Castellan, Andrea. Mickey Mouse & the Orbiting Nightmare. 2011. (ENG., Illus.). 128p. (J). pap. *(978-1-60886-630-4(0))* Boom! Studios.

Castellan, Andrea "Casty". Mickey Mouse & the World to Come. Castellan, Andrea "Casty" & Mazzon, Michelle, illus. 2010. (ENG.). 112p. (J). (gr. 3-6). pap. 9.99 *(978-1-60886-562-8(2))* Boom! Studios.

Clark, John, ed. Mickey Mouse Adventures, Vol. 5. 2005. (ENG., Illus.). 128p. (YA). pap. 7.95 *(978-0-911903-70-6(4),* 9780911903706) Gemstone Publishing, Inc.

—Mystery of the Old Mansion, Vol. 6. 2005. (ENG., Illus.). 128p. (YA). pap. 7.95 *(978-0-911903-71-3(2),* 9780911903713) Gemstone Publishing, Inc.

Disney Book Group. M Is for Mickey. Disney Storybook Art Team, illus. 2017. (ENG.). 26p. (J). (gr. -1-k). bds. 12.99 *(978-1-4847-8221-7(6))* Disney Pr.

—Mickey & Minnie's Storybook Collection. Disney Storybook Art Team, illus. 2015. (Storybook Collection). (ENG.). 304p. (J). (gr. -1-1). 16.99 *(978-1-4231-3508-1(3))* Disney Pr.

—Mickey Mouse Clubhouse Everyone Loves Mickey. Disney Storybook Art Team, illus. 2015. (ENG.). 12p. (J). (gr. -1-k). bds. 6.99 *(978-1-4847-2720-1(7))* Disney Pr.

—Mickey Mouse Clubhouse Mickey's Halloween. Disney Storybook Art Team, illus. 2015. (ENG.). 10p. (J). (gr. -1-k). bds. 8.99 *(978-1-4847-2096-7(2))* Disney Pr.

Disney Book Group Staff. Haunted Clubhouse. 2010. (ENG., Illus.). 12p. (J). (gr. -1-k). bds. 6.99 *(978-1-4231-2832-8(X))* Disney Pr.

—Mickey & Friends Mickey's Spooky Night: Purchase Includes Digital App! Disney Storybook Artists Staff & Disney Storybook Art Team, illus. 2014. (ENG.). 24p. (J). (gr. 1-3). bds. 10.99 *(978-1-4847-0841-5(5))* Disney Pr.

—Mickey Mouse Clubhouse Choo Choo Express. 2009. (ENG.). 16p. (J). (gr. -1-k). pap. 4.99 *(978-1-4231-2230-2(5))* Disney Pr.

—Mickey Saves Santa. Disney Storybook Artists Staff, illus. 2009. (ENG.). 24p. (J). (gr. -1-k). pap. 5.99 *(978-1-4231-1846-6(4))* Disney Pr.

—5-Minute Minnie Tales. Disney Storybook Artists Staff, illus. 2014. (5-Minute Stories Ser.). (ENG.). 192p. (J). (gr. 1-3). 12.99 *(978-1-4847-0452-3(5))* Disney Pr.

Disney Book Group Staff & Higginson, Sheila Sweeny. Minnie: Minnie's Valentine. Disney Storybook Artists Staff, illus. 2013. 10p. 5.99 *(978-1-4231-8811-7(X))* Disney Pr.

Disney Book Group Staff & Kelman, Marcy. Animal ABCs. Disney Storybook Art Team, illus. 2014. (ENG.). 10p. (J). (gr. -1-k). bds. 10.99 *(978-1-4231-8488-1(2))* Disney Pr.

Disney Book Group Staff & Scollon, William. Mickey Mouse Clubhouse a Goofy Fairy Tale. Disney Storybook Art Team, illus. 2014. (ENG.). 24p. (J). (gr. -1-k). pap. 4.99 *(978-1-4231-8900-8(0))* Disney Pr.

Disney Mickey Mouse Clubhouse, ed. Clubhouse ABCs: Mickey Mouse Clubhouse. 2009. (ENG.). 24p. 7.99 *(978-1-59069-771-9(5))* Studio Mouse LLC.

Disney Press Staff, ed. Mickey's New Friend. 2011. (Illus.). 32p. (J). *(978-1-4231-4585-1(2))* Disney Pr.

Disney Press Staff & Disney Book Group Staff. Road Trip. Disney Storybook Art Team, illus. 2011. (ENG.). 10p. (J). (gr. -1-k). bds. 8.99 *(978-1-4231-4416-8(3))* Disney Pr.

Disney Storybook Artists Staff, illus. Disney Mickey Mouse Clubhouse Movie Theater: Storybook & Movie Projector. 2012. (Movie Theater Ser.). (ENG.). 32p. (J). (gr. k-3). 19.99 *(978-0-7944-2587-6(9))* Reader's Digest Assn., Inc., The.

Feldman, Thea & Disney Book Group Staff. Mickey's Halloween Treat. Disney Storybook Artists Staff, illus. 2008. (ENG.). 16p. (J). (gr. -1-k). pap. 4.99 *(978-1-4231-0983-9(X))* Disney Pr.

Flood, Heather. Mousey Mousey & the Witches' Revenge. 2012. 220p. pap. *(978-1-909359-03-1(3))* My Voice Publishing.

Galvin, Laura Gates. Mickey Mouse Clubhouse Fun with Numbers & Shapes. 2008. (ENG.). 20p. (J). (gr. -1-3). 9.99 *(978-1-59069-655-2(7))* Studio Mouse LLC.

—Mickey Mouse Clubhouse Teamwork: Let's Do It Together. 2008. (ENG.). 40p. (J). (gr. -1). 12.99 *(978-1-59069-738-2(3))* Studio Mouse LLC.

—Musical Fun: Colors & Patterns. Williams, Tracee, ed. 2011. (Carry a Tune Ser.). (ENG., Illus.). 22p. (J). (gr. -1-1). pap. 4.99 incl. audio compact disk *(978-1-60727-305-9(5))* Studio Mouse LLC.

Gilbert, Michael T., et al. Mickey Mouse Adventures, Vol. 8. Clark, John, ed. 2006. (ENG., Illus.). 128p. (YA). pap. 7.95 *(978-1-888472-09-7(X),* 9781888472097) Gemstone Publishing, Inc.

—Walt Disney's Comics & Stories #693. Clark, John, ed. 2008. (ENG., Illus.). 64p. pap. 7.99 *(978-1-60360-038-5(8),* 9781603600385) Gemstone Publishing, Inc.

Gold, Gina. Disney Mickey Mouse Clubhouse - Hugs from Mickey: A Hugs Book. Guell, Fernanado, illus. 2014. (Hugs Book Ser.). (ENG.). 10p. (J). (gr. -1-k). bds. 10.99 *(978-0-7944-3288-1(3))* Reader's Digest Assn., Inc., The.

Gottfredson, Floyd. Race to Death Valley, Vol. 1. Gerstein, David & Groth, Gary, eds. 2011. (Walt Disney's Mickey Mouse Ser.: 0). (ENG., Illus.). 320p. 29.99 *(978-1-60699-441-2(7),* 699441) Fantagraphics Bks.

Gottfredson, Floyd, et al. Walt Disney's Comics & Stories #700. 2008. 80p. pap. 9.99 *(978-1-60360-057-6(4))* Gemstone Publishing, Inc.

Hamilton, Tisha. Mickey Mouse Clubhouse. Disney Storybook Artists Staff, illus. 2008. (Carry along Treasury Ser.). (ENG.). 14p. (J). (gr. -1-1). bds. 14.99 *(978-0-7944-1481-8(8))* Reader's Digest Assn., Inc., The.

Hinkler Studios Staff., ed. Mickey Mouse Clubhouse: Preschool Skills. 2011. 12p. 9.99 *(978-1-74183-869-5(X))* Hinkler Bks. Pty, Ltd. AUS. Dist: Ideals Pubns.

Jippes, Daan, et al. Walt Disney's Comics & Stories #703. 2009. 64p. pap. 7.99 *(978-1-60360-093-4(0))* Gemstone Publishing, Inc.

Keast, Jennifer H. Mickey Mouse Clubhouse (Giant First Play-a-Sound) 2010. 10p. (J). bds. 17.98 *(978-1-60553-545-6(1))* Phoenix International Publications, Inc.

Kelman, Marcy & Disney Book Group Staff. Hoppy Clubhouse Easter. Disney Storybook Art Team, illus. 2011. (ENG.). 12p. (J). (gr. -1-k). bds. 6.99 *(978-1-4231-3910-2(0))* Disney Pr.

Korhonen, Kari, et al. Walt Disney's Comics & Stories #705. 2009. 64p. pap. 7.99 *(978-1-60360-095-8(7))* Gemstone Publishing, Inc.

Kruse, Jan, et al. Walt Disney's Spring Fever Volume 3. 2009. 80p. pap. 9.99 *(978-1-60360-097-2(3))* Gemstone Publishing, Inc.

Kurchinski, Alessandra. Disney Story. 2010. 36p. pap. 17.30 *(978-0-557-25447-7(7))* Lulu Pr., Inc.

Marsoli, Lisa Ann. Minnierella. 2013. (Mickey & Friends World of Reading Ser.). (J). lib. bdg. 13.55 *(978-0-606-34103-5(X),* Turtleback) Turtleback Bks.

McGreal, Pat, et al. Walt Disney's Comics & Stories #701. 2009. 64p. pap. 7.99 *(978-1-60360-091-0(4))* Gemstone Publishing, Inc.

Parragon Staff. Mickey Mouse: Adventure Tales & Stories. 2010. (Disney Diecut Classics). 72p. (J). (gr. -1-1). *(978-1-4075-8937-4(7))* Parragon, Inc.

Posner-Sanchez, Andrea. Shop with Minnie. Random House Disney Staff, illus. 2012. (Little Golden Book Ser.). (ENG.). 24p. (J). (gr. k). 4.99 *(978-0-7364-3031-9(8),* Golden/Disney) Random Hse. Children's Bks.

Publications International Ltd. Staff. BK & Plush Mickey Mouse Club House. 2010. (J). 12.98 *(978-1-4127-8864-9(1))* Phoenix International Publications, Inc.

—Little Sound Mickey Mouse Club. 2007. 10p. (J). 10.98 *(978-1-4127-6711-8(3))* Phoenix International Publications, Inc.

—Mickey Mouse Club First Look & Find. 2008. 18p. (J). bds. 9.98 *(978-1-4127-7455-0(1))* Phoenix International Publications, Inc.

—Mickey Mouse Club House Little Pop up Sd. 2008. 8p. (J). 10.50 *(978-1-4127-8869-4(2))* Phoenix International Publications, Inc.

Publications International Ltd. Staff, ed. Disney(r) Mickey Mouse ClubhouseCalling All Pals. 2015. 14p. (J). bds. *(978-1-4508-9352-7(X),* 145089352X) Publications International, Ltd.

—Disney(r) Mickey Mouse Clubhouself You're Happy & You Know It. 2015. 12p. (J). bds. *(978-1-4508-7437-3(1),* 1450874371) Publications International, Ltd.

—Goof's Adventure. 2010. 24p. (J). 19.98 *(978-1-4127-5367-8(8),* PIL Kids) Publications International, Ltd.

—Little Lift & Listen Sound Mickey Mouse Clubhouse. 2007. (J). 10.98 *(978-1-4127-8457-3(3))* Phoenix International Publications, Inc.

—Look & Find Activity Pad Mickey Mouse. 2011. 64p. (J). 10.98 *(978-1-4508-0733-3(X))* Publications International, Ltd.

—Mickey Mouse Clubhouse. 2010. 128p. (J). pap. 12.98 *(978-1-60553-129-8(4),* PIL Kids) Publications International, Ltd.

—Mickey Mouse Clubhouse: Ask a Silly Question. 2010. (J). bds. 5.98 *(978-1-60553-037-6(9))* Phoenix International Publications, Inc.

—Mickey Mouse Clubhouse: Hot Dog! Sing Along! 2010. 10p. (J). bds. 14.98 *(978-1-60553-047-5(6))* Publications International, Ltd.

—Mickey Mouse Clubhouse: Las canciones de piano de Mickey. 2011. 24p. (J). 17.98 *(978-1-4508-1616-8(9))* Publications International, Ltd.

—Mickey Mouse Clubhouse: Lights on, Lights Off! 2011. 12p. (J). (gr. k-3). bds. 10.99 *(978-1-4508-0763-0(1),* 1450807631) Phoenix International Publications, Inc.

—Mickey Mouse Clubhouse: Mickey & Friends (Look & Find) 2010. 24p. (J). 7.98 *(978-1-60553-747-4(0))* Publications International, Ltd.

—Mickey Mouse Clubhouse: Mickey's Silly Shadow Book. 2011. 14p. (J). bds. 8.45 net. *(978-1-4508-0564-3(7))* Phoenix International Publications, Inc.

—Mickey Mouse Clubhouse: Telling Time with Mickey. 2011. 12p. (J). bds. 13.98 *(978-1-4508-0914-6(6))* Publications International, Ltd.

—Mickey Mouse Clubhouse - Who's Not Sleepy? 2011. 12p. (J). bds. *(978-1-4508-0398-4(9))* Publications International, Ltd.

—Mickey Mouse Clubhouse (book Block) 2010. (J). 10.98 *(978-1-4508-0673-2(2))* Publications International, Ltd.

—Mickey Mouse Clubhouse: Colors: Sing & Learn. 2010. 12p. (J). bds. 10.98 *(978-1-4127-1729-8(9))* Publications International, Ltd.

—Mickey Mouse Clubhouse: Mickey's Surprise! 2013. 14p. (J). (gr. k-3). bds. 16.99 *(978-1-4508-2188-9(X),* 87b7723a-b11c-4ce1-8b21-522e3e8ff7e2) Phoenix International Publications, Inc.

—Mickey Mouse Clubhouse: Sing-along Christmas Songs: Holiday Play-a-Song Book. 2010. 10p. (J). bds. 12.98 *(978-1-4127-7862-6(X))* Publications International, Ltd.

—Mickey Mouse Clubhouse Super Look & Find Activity Pad with Stickers. 2010. 64p. (J). *(978-1-4508-0732-6(1),* 1450807321) Phoenix International Publications, Inc.

—Mickey Mouse Clubhouse Super Look & Find Activity Pad with Stickers. 2011. 64p. (J). 10.98 *(978-1-4508-1887-2(0))* Publications International, Ltd.

—Mickey's Adventure. 2010. 24p. (J). bds. 16.98 *(978-1-4127-4599-4(3))* Phoenix International Publications, Inc.

—Mickey's Piano Songs Play & Learn. 2010. 24p. (J). 12.98 *(978-1-4508-0114-0(5))* Phoenix International Publications, Inc.

—Who's Not Sleepy? 2010. 18p. (J). bds. 10.98 *(978-1-60553-463-3(3),* PIL Kids) Publications International, Ltd.

Reader's Digest Staff. Mickey Mouse Clubhouse Gift Set. 2012. (ENG.). 64p. (J). 39.98 *(978-0-7944-2669-9(7))* Reader's Digest Assn., Inc., The.

Reader's Digest Staff & Rhodes, Lilly. Guess Who, Minnie! Loter Inc. Staff, illus. 2013. (Guess Who Ser.: 1). (ENG.). 10p. (J). (gr. -1-k). 10.99 *(978-0-7944-2555-5(0))* Reader's Digest Assn., Inc., The.

Ring, Susan. Pete's Surprise. 2009. (ENG.). 24p. (J). pap. 3.99 *(978-1-4231-1827-5(8))* Disney Pr.

Ritchey, Kate. A Perfect Picnic. 2013. (Mickey & Friends World of Reading Ser.). (J). lib. bdg. 13.55 *(978-0-606-31753-5(8),* Turtleback) Turtleback Bks.

Sarda, Bruno. Mickey & Donald: the Search for the Zodiac Stone. Vita, Massimo de & Valussi, Franco, illus. 2016. (Mickey Mouse Ser.). (ENG.). 368p. 39.99 *(978-1-63140-706-2(6),* 9781631407062) Idea & Design Works, LLC.

Scollon, Bill. A Goofy Fairy Tale. 2014. (Mickey Mouse 8x8 Ser.). (J). lib. bdg. 14.75 *(978-0-606-35900-9(1))* Turtleback Bks.

—Super Adventure. Disney Book Group Staff & Disney Storybook Artists Staff, illus. 2013. (ENG.). 24p. (J). (gr. -1-k). pap. 4.99 *(978-1-4231-8657-1(5))* Disney Pr.

Scollon, William & Disney Book Group Staff. Mickey & Donald Have a Farm. Disney Storybook Art Team, illus. 2012. (ENG.). 32p. (J). (gr. -1-k). pap. 5.99 *(978-1-4231-4946-0(7))* Disney Pr.

Silver Dolphin en Español Staff, creator. Mickey Mouse: Tesoros para Llevar: Una Coleccion de Cuentos Adaptada de los Dibujos Animados Clasicos de Mickey. 2006. (Tesoros para Llevar Ser.). (Illus.). 24p. (J). (gr. -1-k). bds. *(978-970-718-357-5(8),* Silver Dolphin en Español) Advanced Marketing, S. de R. L. de C. V.

Werner, Jane. Mickey Mouse & His Spaceship (Disney: Mickey Mouse) RH Disney, illus. 2016. (Little Golden Book Ser.). (ENG.). 24p. (J). (-k). 4.99 *(978-0-7364-3633-5(2),* Golden/Disney) Random Hse. Children's Bks.

Wright, Bill, et al. Mickey Mouse: Timeless Tales Volume 1: Timeless Tales Volume 1. Murry, Paul, illus. 2016. (Mickey Mouse Ser.). (ENG.). 260p. 29.99 *(978-1-63140-580-8(2),* 9781631405808) Idea & Design Works, LLC.

MICROBES

see Bacteriology; Microorganisms; Viruses

MICROBIOLOGY

see also Bacteriology; Microorganisms; Microscopes

Alphin, Elaine Marie. Germ Hunter: A Story about Louis Pasteur. Verstraete, Elaine, illus. 2003. (Creative Minds Biographies Ser.). (ENG.). 64p. (gr. 4-8). per. 8.95 *(978-0-87614-929-4(8),* Carolrhoda Bks.) Lerner Publishing Group.

Bacteria up Close. 2013. (Under the Microscope Ser.). 32p. (J). (gr. 4-6). pap. 70.20 *(978-1-4339-8336-8(2))* Stevens, Gareth Publishing LLLP.

Basher, Simon & Green, Dan. Basher Science: Microbiology. Basher, Simon, illus. 2015. (Basher Science Ser.). (ENG., Illus.). 128p. (J). (gr. 5-9). pap. 8.99 *(978-0-7534-7194-4(9),* 9780753471944, Kingfisher) Roaring Brook Pr.

Crewe, Sabrina. In Rivers, Lakes, & Ponds. 2010. (Under the Microscope Ser.). 32p. (gr. 2-4). 30.00 *(978-1-60413-826-9(2),* Chelsea Clubhouse) Facts On File, Inc.

Davies, Nicola. Tiny Creatures: The World of Microbes. Sutton, Emily, illus. 2016. (Read & Wonder Ser.). (ENG.). 40p. (J). (gr. k-3). pap. 7.99 *(978-0-7636-8904-9(1))* Candlewick Pr.

Eamer, Claire. Inside Your Insides: A Guide to the Microbes That Call You Home. Tremblay, Marie-Eve, illus. 2016. (ENG.). 36p. (J). (gr. 3-7). 17.95 *(978-1-77138-332-5(1))* Kids Can Pr., Ltd. CAN. Dist: Hachette Bk. Group.

Ebola & Marburg Virus. 2nd rev. ed. 2010. (Deadly Diseases & Epidemics Ser.). (Illus.). 104p. (C). (gr. 9). 34.95 *(978-1-60413-252-6(3),* Chelsea Hse.) Facts On File, Inc.

Feinstein, Stephen. Louis Pasteur: The Father of Microbiology. 2008. (Inventors Who Changed the World Ser.). (Illus.). 128p. (J). (gr. 6-18). lib. bdg. 34.60 *(978-1-59845-078-1(6),* MyReportLinks.com Bks.) Enslow Pubs., Inc.

Hirsch, Rebecca E. The Human Microbiome: The Germs That Keep You Healthy. 2016. (ENG., Illus.). 112p. (gr. 7-12). (J). 34.65 *(978-1-4677-8568-6(7))*; (YA). 51.99 *(978-1-5124-1140-9(X),* Twenty-First Century Bks.) Lerner Publishing Group.

Hollar, Sherman. A Closer Look at Biology, Microbiology, & the Cell. 2011. (J). lib. bdg. 31.70 *(978-1-61530-514-8(9))* Rosen Publishing Group, Inc., The.

Kornberg, Arthur. Germ Stories. Alaniz, Adam, illus. Kolter, Roberto, photos by. 2007. 70p. (J). (gr. 3-7). 34.00 *(978-1-891389-51-1(3))* Univ. Science Bks.

Kroll, Jennifer. Pequeños Poderosos: Cosas Diminutas - Grandes Resultados. 2016. (TIME for Kids en Español - Level 5 Ser.). (SPA.). 64p. (gr. 5-5). lib. bdg. 31.99 *(978-1-5157-2926-6(5))* Time for Kids Inc AUS. Dist: Capstone Pub.

Latta, Sara L. The Good, the Bad, the Slimy: The Secret Life of Microbes. Kunkel, Dennis, photos by. 2006. (Prime (Middle/Senior) Ser.). (Illus.). 128p. (J). (gr. 4-9). lib. bdg. 33.27 *(978-0-7660-1294-3(8))* Enslow Pubs., Inc.

Levy, Janey. Tiny Bugs up Close. 2013. (Under the Microscope Ser.). 32p. (J). (gr. 4-6). pap. 11.70 *(978-1-4339-8351-1(6))*; lib. bdg. 26.60 *(978-1-4339-8350-4(8))* Stevens, Gareth Publishing LLLP.

Lew, Kristi. The Exterminator: Wiping Out the World's Most Infectious Diseases. 2009. (Current Science Ser.). 48p. (YA). (gr. 4-7). lib. bdg. 31.00 *(978-1-4339-2061-5(1))* Stevens, Gareth Publishing LLLP.

Mitchell, Melanie. Killing Germs. 2005. (Pull Ahead Bks.). (Illus.). 32p. (J). (gr. -1-3). lib. bdg. 22.60 *(978-0-8225-2450-2(3),* Lerner Pubns.) Lerner Publishing Group.

—Matar los Gérmenes. Aguirre, Barbara & Fitzpatrick, Julia, trs. 2005. (Libros para Avanzar-La Salud (Pull Ahead Books-Health) Ser.). (SPA., Illus.). 32p. (gr. k-3). lib. bdg. 22.60 *(978-0-8225-3144-9(5),* Ediciones Lerner) Lerner Publishing Group.

Murray, Julie. Home, 1 vol. 2009. (That's Gross!:A Look at Science Ser.). (ENG., Illus.). 32p. (J). (gr. 2-5). 28.50 *(978-1-60453-555-6(5))* ABDO Publishing Co.

Ollhoff, Jim. The Germ Detectives, 1 vol. 2009. (History of Germs Ser.). (ENG., Illus.). 32p. (YA). (gr. 5-9). 27.07 *(978-1-60453-499-3(0))* ABDO Publishing Co.

Orr, Tamra. Public Health Microbiologist. 2007. (21st Century Skills Library: Cool Science Careers Ser.). (ENG.). 32p. (gr. 4-8). pap. 14.21 *(978-1-60279-082-7(5),* 200643); (Illus.). lib. bdg. 29.93 *(978-1-60279-053-7(1),* 200015) Cherry Lake Publishing.

Owen, Ruth. Creepy Backyard Invaders. 2011. (Up Close & Gross Ser.). 24p. (YA). (gr. 2-5). lib. bdg. 22.61 *(978-1-61772-125-0(5))* Bearport Publishing Co., Inc.

—Icky House Invaders. 2011. (Up Close & Gross Ser.). 24p. (YA). (gr. 2-5). lib. bdg. 22.61 *(978-1-61772-124-3(7))* Bearport Publishing Co., Inc.

Rainis, Kenneth G. Cell & Microbe Science Fair Projects. rev. exp. ed. 2010. (Biology Science Projects Using the Scientific Method Ser.). (Illus.). 160p. (J). (gr. 5-18). 35.94 *(978-0-7660-3420-4(8))* Enslow Pubs., Inc.

—Cell & Microbe Science Fair Projects: Using Microscopes, Mold, & More. 2005. (Biology! Best Science Projects Ser.). (Illus.). 128p. (J). (gr. 6-12). lib. bdg. 27.94 *(978-0-7660-2369-7(9))* Enslow Pubs., Inc.

Roza, Greg. Bacteria up Close. 2013. 32p. (J). (gr. 4-6). 26.60 *(978-1-4339-8334-4(6))*; pap. 11.70 *(978-1-4339-8335-1(4))* Stevens, Gareth Publishing LLLP.

—Deadly Bacteria. 2011. (Small but Deadly Ser.). (Illus.). 24p. (J). (gr. 2-5). pap. 8.15 *(978-1-4339-5728-4(0))*; lib. bdg. 22.60 *(978-1-4339-5726-0(4))* Stevens, Gareth Publishing LLLP. (Gareth Stevens Learning Library).

Sherman, Josepha. The War Against Germs. 2009. (Germs: the Library of Disease-Causing Organisms Ser.). 48p. (gr. 5-5). 53.00 *(978-1-61512-718-4(6))* Rosen Publishing Group, Inc., The.

Spilsbury, Louise & Spilsbury, Richard. Microorganisms, 1 vol. (Essential Life Science Ser.). (ENG., 48p. (gr. 4-6). 2014. Illus.). 33.32 *(978-1-4329-7811-2(X))* 2013. pap. 9.95

M N O

(978-1-4329-7842-6(X)) Heinemann-Raintree. (Heinemann InfoSearch).

Stefoff, Rebecca. The Moneran Kingdom. 2008. (Family Trees Ser.). 96p. (gr. 6-18). lib. bdg. 34.21 *(978-0-7614-3076-6(8),* Benchmark Bks.) Marshall Cavendish Corp.

Swanson, Jennifer. Uninvited Guests: Invisible Creatures Lurking in Your Home. 2011. (Tiny Creepy Creatures Ser.). (ENG.). 32p. (gr. 3-4). pap. 47.70 *(978-1-4296-7276-4(5),* Edge Bks.) Capstone Press of Coughlan Cos.

Taylor-Butler, Christine. Tiny Life in the Air. 2005. (Rookie Read-About Science Ser.). (ENG., Illus.). 32p. (J). (gr. 1-2). lib. bdg. 20.50 *(978-0-516-25273-5(9),* Children's Pr.) Scholastic Library Publishing.

Tiny Bugs up Close. 2013. (Under the Microscope Ser.). 32p. (J). (gr. 4-6). pap. 70.20 *(978-1-4339-8352-8(4))* Stevens, Gareth Publishing LLLP.

Trumbauer, Lisa. Tiny Life in Your Home. 2005. (Rookie Read-About Science Ser.). (ENG., Illus.). 32p. (J). (gr. 1-2). lib. bdg. 20.50 *(978-0-516-25274-2(7),* Children's Pr.) Scholastic Library Publishing.

Wanjie, Anne, ed. The Basics of Microbes. 2013. (Core Concepts Ser.). (ENG., Illus.). 96p. (YA). (gr. 7-12). lib. bdg. 34.60 *(978-1-4777-0550-6(3))* Rosen Publishing Group, Inc., The.

MICROCOMPUTERS

Graham, Ian. Great Electronic Gadget Designs 1900-Today. 2015. (Iconic Designs Ser.). (ENG., Illus.). 48p. (gr. 4-6). pap. 8.99 *(978-1-4846-2623-8(0),* Heinemann InfoSearch) Heinemann-Raintree.

Rooney, Anne. Communicate Online. 2004. (QEB Learn Computing Ser.). (Illus.). 32p. (J). lib. bdg. 18.95 *(978-1-59566-043-5(7))* QEB Publishing Inc.

—Fact Factory. 2004. (QEB Learn Computing Ser.). (Illus.). 32p. (J). lib. bdg. 18.95 *(978-1-59566-042-8(9))* QEB Publishing Inc.

Severance, Charles R. & Fontichiaro, Kristin. Raspberry Pi. 2013. (21st Century Skills Innovation Library: Makers As Innovators Ser.). (ENG., Illus.). 32p. (J). (gr. 4-8). 28.50 *(978-1-62431-139-0(3),* 202876); pap. 14.21 *(978-1-62431-271-7(3),* 202878) Cherry Lake Publishing.

Weber, Sandra. Personal Computer. 2003. (Transforming Power of Technology Ser.). (Illus.). 112p. (C). (gr. 9-13). 30.00 *(978-0-7910-7450-3(1),* Chelsea Hse.) Facts On File, Inc.

MICROCOMPUTERS—PROGRAMMING

Dorling Kindersley Publishing Staff, et al. DK Workbooks: Coding in Scratch: Projects Workbook. 2016. (ENG.). 40p. (J). (gr. 1-4). pap. 5.99 *(978-1-4654-4402-8(5),* DK Children) Dorling Kindersley Publishing, Inc.

Harris, Patricia. Understanding Coding with Hopscotch, 01 vols., 1. 2016. (Kids Can Code Ser.). (ENG., Illus.). 24p. (J). pap. 11.75 *(978-1-5081-4459-5(1),* PowerKids Pr.) Rosen Publishing Group, Inc., The.

—Understanding Coding with Raspberry Pi(tm), 01 vols., 1. 2016. (Kids Can Code Ser.). (ENG., Illus.). 24p. (J). pap. 11.75 *(978-1-5081-4478-6(8),* 1399024, PowerKids Pr.) Rosen Publishing Group, Inc., The.

—Understanding Coding with Scratch, 01 vols., 1. 2016. (Kids Can Code Ser.). (ENG., Illus.). 24p. (J). pap. 11.75 *(978-1-5081-4482-3(6),* PowerKids Pr.) Rosen Publishing Group, Inc., The.

Sweigart, Al. Scratch Programming Playground: Learn to Program by Making Cool Games. 2016. (ENG., Illus.). 288p. (J). (gr. 2). pap. 24.95 *(978-1-59327-762-8(8))* No Starch Pr., Inc.

MICROGRAPHIC ANALYSIS

see Microscopes

MICRONESIA

Department of Chamorro Affairs, Division of Research, Publication and Training Staff. I Manfayi Vol. I: Who's Who in Chamorro History. (Hale'-ta Ser.). (Illus.). 250p. (J). (gr. 6-7). pap. 30.00 *(978-1-883488-04-8(4))* Dept. of Chamorro Affairs.

—I Manfayi Vol. II: Who's Who in Chamorro History. Date not set. (Illus.). 250p. (J). (gr. 6-7). pap. 25.00 *(978-1-883488-06-2(0))* Dept. of Chamorro Affairs.

Millhoff, Brian L. The Micronesian Coloring Book. 2nd l.t. ed. 2006. (Illus.). 68p. (J). per. 6.50 net. *(978-0-9790111-0-8(8))* M-m-mauleg Publishing.

MICROORGANISMS

see also Bacteriology; Microbiology; Microscopes; Protozoa; Viruses

Anderson, Rodney P. The Invisible ABC's: Exploring the World of Microbes..., 1 vol. 2006. (ENG., Illus.). 64p. (gr. 3-7). 19.95 *(978-1-55581-386-4(0),* 9781555813864) ASM Pr.

Benchmark Education Company, LLC Staff, compiled by. Organisms: Past & Present. 2005. (English Explorers Ser.). (J). spiral bd. 265.00 *(978-1-4108-5758-3(1))* Benchmark Education Co.

—Organisms: Theme Set. 2006. (J). 303.00 *(978-1-4108-7122-0(3))* Benchmark Education Co.

—Organisms Past & Present. 2006. spiral bd. 330.00 *(978-1-4108-7016-2(2))* Benchmark Education Co.

Burillo-Kirch, Christine. Microbes: Discover an Unseen World. Casteel, Tom, illus. 2015. (Build It Yourself Ser.). (ENG.). 128p. (gr. 3-7). 22.95 *(978-1-61930-306-5(X))* Open City Bks.

Crewe, Sabrina. In the Backyard. 2010. (Under the Microscope Ser.). 32p. (gr. 2-4). 30.00 *(978-1-60413-822-1(X),* Chelsea Clubhouse) Facts On File, Inc.

—In the Home. 2010. (Under the Microscope Ser.). 32p. (gr. 2-4). 30.00 *(978-1-60413-823-8(8),* Chelsea Clubhouse) Facts On File, Inc.

—In Your Body. 2010. (Under the Microscope Ser.). 32p. (gr. 2-4). 30.00 *(978-1-60413-825-2(4),* Chelsea Clubhouse) Facts On File, Inc.

Davies, Nicola. Tiny Creatures: The World of Microbes. Sutton, Emily, illus. 2016. (Read & Wonder Ser.). (ENG.). 40p. (J). (gr. k-3). pap. 7.99 *(978-0-7636-8904-9(1))* Candlewick Pr.

Day, Trevor. Body Bugs! [Scholastic]: Uninvited Guests on Your Body. 2010. (Extreme! Ser.). 32p. pap. 0.65 *(978-1-4296-4993-3(3),* Fact Finders) Capstone Press of Coughlan Cos.

DiConsiglio, John. Superbugs, 1 vol. 2012. (Hot Topics Ser.). (ENG.). 64p. (gr. 7-8). 34.65 *(978-1-4329-6037-7(7));* pap. 10.95 *(978-1-4329-6045-2(8))* Heinemann-Raintree. (NA-h).

Eamer, Claire. Inside Your Insides: A Guide to the Microbes That Call You Home. Tremblay, Marie-Ève, illus. 2016. (ENG.). 36p. (J). (gr. 3-7). 17.95 *(978-1-77138-332-5(1))* Kids Can Pr., Ltd. CAN. Dist: Hachette Bk. Group.

Eason, Sarah, ed. Plants & Microorganisms. 2011. (FAYFT: Introducing Biology Ser.). 64p. (gr. 4-10). lib. bdg. 39.95 *(978-1-936333-02-8(3))* Brown Bear Bks.

Favor, Lesli J. Eukaryotic & Prokaryotic Cell Structures: Understanding Cells with & Without a Nucleus. 2009. (Library of Cells Ser.). 48p. (gr. 5-5). 53.00 *(978-1-60853-571-2(1))* Rosen Publishing Group, Inc., The.

Gardy, Jennifer. It's Catching: The Infectious World of Germs & Microbes. Holinaty, Josh, illus. 2014. (ENG.). 64p. (J). (gr. 3-7). pap. 13.95 *(978-1-77147-053-7(4),* Owlkids) Owlkids Bks. Inc. CAN. Dist: Publishers Group West (PGW).

Germ Warfare: Individual Title Six-Packs. (Bookweb Ser.). 32p. (gr. 5-18). 34.00 *(978-0-7635-3798-2(5))* Rigby Education.

Germs: Disease Causing Organisms. 2016. (Germs: Disease Causing Organisms Ser.). 48p. (gr. 5-5). 190.50 *(978-1-4994-3839-0(7));* pap. 70.50 *(978-1-4777-8982-7(0))* Rosen Publishing Group, Inc., The. (Rosen Central).

Gibson, Brylee. Unseen by the Eye. 2007. (Connectors Ser.). (gr. 2-5). pap. *(978-1-877453-00-7(5))* Global Education Systems Ltd.

Graham, Ian. Microscopic Scary Creatures. 2009. (Scary Creatures Ser.). (ENG.). 32p. (J). (gr. 3-5). pap. 8.95 *(978-0-531-21044-4(8),* Watts, Franklin); (Illus.). 27.00 *(978-0-531-21673-6(X),* Children's Pr.) Scholastic Library Publishing.

Green, Jen. Inside Animals. 2010. (Invisible Worlds Ser.). 48p. (gr. 4). 28.50 *(978-0-7614-4195-3(6))* Marshall Cavendish Corp.

Harrison, Paul. Micro Bugs. (Up Close Ser.). 24p. (gr. 3-3). 2009. 47.90 *(978-1-60854-696-1(9))* 2007. (Illus.). (J). lib. bdg. 25.25 *(978-1-4042-3760-5(7))* Rosen Publishing Group, Inc., The. (PowerKids Pr.).

Holt, Rinehart and Winston Staff. Holt Science & Technology Chapter 11: Life Science: Protists & Fungi. 5th ed. 2004. (Illus.). pap. 12.86 *(978-0-03-030211-4(0))* Holt McDougal.

—Microorganisms, Fungi, & Plants. 5th ed. 2003. (Holt Science & Technology [Short Course] Ser.: Vol. A). (ENG.). 192p. (gr. 6-8). stu. ed. 28.60 *(978-0-03-025533-5(3))* Houghton Mifflin Harcourt Publishing Co.

Hyde, Natalie. Micro Life in Soil. 2010. (Everybody Digs Soil Ser.). (ENG., Illus.). 32p. (J). (gr. 3-6). pap. *(978-0-7787-5415-2(4));* lib. bdg. *(978-0-7787-5402-2(2))* Crabtree Publishing Co.

Kelly, Evelyn B., et al. Investigating Tuberculosis & Superbugs: Real Facts for Real Lives. 2010. (Investigating Diseases Ser.). 160p. (YA). (gr. 9-12). 35.94 *(978-0-7660-3343-6(0))* Enslow Pubs., Inc.

Kroll, Jennifer. Mighty Macros: Little Things, Big Results, 1 vol. 2nd rev. ed. 2013. (TIME for KIDS(r) Nonfiction Readers Ser.). (ENG.). 64p. (J). (gr. 5-5). pap. 10.99 *(978-1-4333-4948-5(5))* Teacher Created Materials, Inc.

Latta, Sara L. The Good, the Bad, the Slimy: The Secret Life of Microbes. Kunkel, Dennis, photos by. 2006. (Prime (Middle/Senior) Ser.). (Illus.). 128p. (J). (gr. 4-9). lib. bdg. 33.27 *(978-0-7660-1294-3(8))* Enslow Pubs., Inc.

Leet, Karen M. Yard Monsters: Invisible Creatures Lurking in Your Backyard. 2011. (Tiny Creepy Creatures Ser.). (ENG.). 32p. (gr. 3-4). pap. 47.70 *(978-1-4296-7278-8(1));* lib. bdg. 27.99 *(978-1-4296-6533-9(5))* Capstone Press of Coughlan Cos. (Edge Bks.).

Levy, Janey. The World of Microbes: Bacteria, Viruses, & Other Microorganisms. 2010. (Understanding Genetics Ser.). (ENG.). 80p. (YA). lib. bdg. 33.25 *(978-1-4358-9536-2(3))* Rosen Publishing Group, Inc., The.

Lew, Kristi. The Exterminator: Wiping Out the World's Most Infectious Diseases. 2009. (Current Science Ser.). 48p. (gr. 4-7). (YA). lib. bdg. 31.00 *(978-1-4339-2061-5(1));* (ENG.). (J). pap. 8.95 *(978-1-4339-2132-2(4),* Gareth Stevens Learning Library) Stevens, Gareth Publishing LLLP.

Lindstrom, Karin. Tiny Life on Plants. (Rookie Read-About Science Ser.). (ENG., Illus.). 32p. (J). (gr. 1-2). 2006. per. 4.95 *(978-0-516-25478-4(2))* 2005. lib. bdg. 20.50 *(978-0-516-25297-1(6))* Scholastic Library Publishing. (Children's Pr.).

Markovics, Joyce L. Tiny Invaders! Deadly Microorganisms, 1 vol. 2013. (Nature's Invaders Ser.). (ENG.). 32p. (gr. 3-4). lib. bdg. 27.99 *(978-1-4765-0142-0(4))* Capstone Press of Coughlan Cos.

May, Suellen. Invasive Microbes. 2007. (Invasive Species Ser.). (Illus.). 100p. (gr. 6-12). lib. bdg. 30.00 *(978-0-7910-9131-9(7),* Chelsea Hse.) Facts On File, Inc.

Merchant, Raina G. & Favor, Lesli J. How Eukaryotic & Prokaryotic Cells Differ, 1 vol. 2015. (ENG.). 64p. (YA). 31.70 *(978-1-62275-806-7(4),* Britannica Educational Publishing) Rosen Publishing Group, Inc., The.

Micromonsters: Microscopic Life up Close. 2016. (Micromonsters: Microscopic Life up Close Ser.). 32p. (gr. 4-4). 105.00 *(978-1-4994-2251-1(2));* pap. 40.00 *(978-1-4994-2450-8(7))* Rosen Publishing Group, Inc., The. (PowerKids Pr.).

Minden, Cecilia. Germ Free. 2010. (21st Century Basic Skills Library: Keep It Clean Ser.). (ENG.). 24p. (gr. k-3). lib. bdg. 22.79 *(978-1-60279-857-1(5),* 200580) Cherry Lake Publishing.

Murphy, Jim & Blank, Alison. Invincible Microbe: Tuberculosis & the Never-Ending Search for a Cure. 2012. (ENG., Illus.). 160p. (J). (gr. 5-7). 18.99 *(978-0-618-53574-3(8))* Houghton Mifflin Harcourt Publishing Co.

Oetting, Judy. Germs. Herr, Tad, illus. 2006. (Rookie Reader Skill Set Ser.). (ENG.). 32p. (J). (gr. k-2). pap. 4.95 *(978-0-516-24995-7(9))* Scholastic Library Publishing.

Owen, Ruth. Creepy Backyard Invaders. 2011. (Up Close & Gross Ser.). 24p. (YA). (gr. 2-5). lib. bdg. 22.61 *(978-1-61772-125-0(5))* Bearport Publishing Co., Inc.

—Up Close & Gross: Microscopic Creatures, 4 vols., Set. Incl. Creepy Backyard Invaders. lib. bdg. 22.61 *(978-1-61772-125-0(5));* Disgusting Food Invaders. lib. bdg. 22.61 *(978-1-61772-127-4(1));* Gross Body Invaders. lib. bdg. 22.61 *(978-1-61772-126-7(3));* Icky House Invaders. lib. bdg. 22.61 *(978-1-61772-124-3(7));* (YA). (gr. 2-5). 24p. 2011. Set lib. bdg. 90.44 *(978-1-61772-123-6(9))* Bearport Publishing Co., Inc.

Porter, Esther. What's Sprouting in My Trash? A Book about Composting. 2013. (Earth Matters Ser.). (ENG.). 32p. (gr. 1-2). pap. 47.70 *(978-1-62065-746-1(5));* lib. bdg. 27.32 *(978-1-62065-047-9(9))* Capstone Press of Coughlan Cos. (Aplus Bks.).

Rake, Jody Sullivan. Why Feet Smell & Other Gross Facts about Your Body, 1 vol. 2012. (Gross Me Out Ser.). (ENG.). 24p. (gr. 1-2). pap. 7.29 *(978-1-4296-7955-8(7));* pap. 41.70 *(978-1-4296-8377-7(5));* lib. bdg. 25.32 *(978-1-4296-7610-6(8))* Capstone Press of Coughlan Cos. (First Facts).

Romano, Amy. Germ Warfare. 2004. (Germs: the Library of Disease-Causing Organisms Ser.). (Illus.). 48p. (gr. 7-12). lib. bdg. 29.25 *(978-0-8239-4493-4(X))* Rosen Publishing Group, Inc., The.

Schitt, Christine. Journey into the Invisible: The World from under the Microscope. Brandt, Chris, tr. from GER. 2013. (ENG., Illus.). 80p. (J). (gr. -1-k). 16.95 *(978-1-62087-116-4(5),* 620116, Sky Pony Pr.) Skyhorse Publishing Co., Inc.

Sherman, Josepha. The War Against Germs. 2009. (Germs: the Library of Disease-Causing Organisms Ser.). 48p. (gr. 5-5). 53.00 *(978-1-61512-718-4(6))* Rosen Publishing Group, Inc., The.

Sian revision Microworlds. 2004. (J). *(978-1-59242-045-2(1))* Delta Education, LLC.

Sian revision sm Wonders. 2004. (J). *(978-1-59242-067-4(2))* Delta Education, LLC.

Spilsbury, Louise. Garbage Can. Hanna, Gary, illus. 2013. (Look Inside Ser.). (ENG.). 32p. (gr. 1-3). 27.32 *(978-1-4329-7195-3(6));* pap. 8.29 *(978-1-4329-7202-8(2))* Heinemann-Raintree. (Heinemann First Library).

—Pond. Hanna, Gary, illus. 2013. (Look Inside Ser.). (ENG.). 32p. (gr. 1-3). 27.32 *(978-1-4329-7196-0(4));* pap. 8.29 *(978-1-4329-7203-5(0))* Heinemann-Raintree. (Heinemann First Library).

—Tide Pool. Hanna, Gary, illus. 2013. (Look Inside Ser.). (ENG.). 32p. (gr. 1-3). 27.32 *(978-1-4329-7197-7(2));* pap. 8.29 *(978-1-4329-7204-2(9))* Heinemann-Raintree. (Heinemann First Library).

Spilsbury, Louise & Spilsbury, Richard. Microorganisms, 1 vol. (Essential Life Science Ser.). (ENG., 48p. (gr. 4-6). 2014. Illus.). 33.32 *(978-1-4329-7811-2(X))* 2013. pap. 9.95 *(978-1-4329-7842-6(X))* Heinemann-Raintree. (Heinemann InfoSearch).

Spilsbury, Richard. Cave. Hanna, Gary, illus. 2013. (Look Inside Ser.). (ENG.). 32p. (gr. 1-3). 27.32 *(978-1-4329-7194-6(8));* pap. 8.29 *(978-1-4329-7201-1(4))* Heinemann-Raintree. (Heinemann First Library).

—Tree. Hanna, Gary, illus. 2013. (Look Inside Ser.). (ENG.). 32p. (gr. 1-3). 27.32 *(978-1-4329-7198-4(0));* pap. 8.29 *(978-1-4329-7205-9(7))* Heinemann-Raintree. (Heinemann First Library).

Stewart, Melissa. Do People Really Have Tiny Insects Living in Their Eyelashes? And Other Questions about the Microscopic World. 2010. (Is That a Fact? Ser.). (ENG.). 40p. (gr. 4-6). lib. bdg. 26.60 *(978-0-7613-4916-7(2))* Lerner Publishing Group.

Swanson, Jennifer. Body Bugs: Invisible Creatures Lurking Inside You, 1 vol. 2011. (Tiny Creepy Creatures Ser.). (ENG.). 32p. (gr. 3-4). pap. 8.29 *(978-1-4296-7271-9(4));* pap. 47.70 *(978-1-4296-7272-6(2));* lib. bdg. 27.99 *(978-1-4296-6530-8(0))* Capstone Press of Coughlan Cos. (Edge Bks.).

—Uninvited Guests: Invisible Creatures Lurking in Your Home. 2011. (Tiny Creepy Creatures Ser.). (ENG.). 32p. (gr. 3-4). pap. 47.70 *(978-1-4296-7276-4(5));* lib. bdg. 27.99 *(978-1-4296-6531-5(9))* Capstone Press of Coughlan Cos. (Edge Bks.).

Thomas, Isabel. Micro-Organisms. 2015. (Collins Big Cat Ser.). (ENG., Illus.). 80p. (J). (gr. 5). pap. 9.95 *(978-0-00-812798-5(0))* HarperCollins Pubs. Ltd. GBR. Dist: Independent Pubs. Group.

Townsend, John. Rotters: Decomposition. 2016. (Raintree Fusion: Life Science Ser.). (ENG.). 32p. (gr. 2-2). pap. 8.29 *(978-1-4109-8650-4(0),* Raintree Fusion) Heinemann-Raintree.

Wanjie, Anne, ed. The Basics of Microbes. 2013. (Core Concepts Ser.). (ENG., Illus.). 96p. (YA). (gr. 7-12). lib. bdg. 34.60 *(978-1-4777-0550-6(3))* Rosen Publishing Group, Inc., The.

Watson, Stephanie. Superbugs: The Rise of Drug-Resistant Germs. 2010. (In the News Ser.). 64p. (YA). (ENG.). pap. 12.95 *(978-1-4358-8553-0(8));* (Illus.). (gr. 7-12). lib. bdg. 31.95 *(978-1-4358-3585-6(9))* Rosen Publishing Group, Inc., The.

Weakland, Mark. Gut Bugs, Dust Mites, & Other Microorganisms You Can't Live Without. (Nasty (but Usefull) Science Ser.). (ENG.). 32p. (gr. 3-4). 2011. pap. 8.10 *(978-1-4296-6346-5(4))* 2011. pap. 47.70 *(978-1-4296-6472-1(X))* 2010. lib. bdg. 27.32 *(978-1-4296-4538-6(5))* Capstone Press of Coughlan Cos. (Fact Finders).

Yount, Lisa. Antoni Van Leeuwenhoek: Genius Discoverer of Microscopic Life. 2015. (Genius Scientists & Their Genius Ideas Ser.). 96p. (J). (gr. 5-12). pap. 10.95 *(978-0-7660-6526-0(X))* Enslow Pubs., Inc.

Zamosky, Lisa. Investigating Simple Organisms, 1 vol. 2007. (Science Readers Ser.). (ENG., Illus.). 32p. (J). (gr. 4-4). pap. 8.99 *(978-0-7439-0587-9(3))* Shell Educational Publishing.

MICROPROCESSORS

High-Tech DIY Projects with Microcontrollers. 2014. (Maker Kids Ser.). (Illus.). 32p. (J). (gr. 3-6). pap. 70.50 *(978-1-4777-6658-3(8),* PowerKids Pr.) Rosen Publishing Group, Inc., The.

MICROSCOPE AND MICROSCOPY

see Microscopes; Microscopy

MICROSCOPES

Here are entered works on microscopes in general as well as works specifically on light or optical microscopes.

Beckett, Leslie. Miguel Uses a Microscope. 2013. (Rosen Readers Ser.). (ENG.). 24p. (J). (gr. 3-4). pap. 49.50 *(978-1-4777-2499-6(0));* pap. 8.25 *(978-1-4777-2498-9(2))* Rosen Publishing Group, Inc., The. (Rosen Classroom).

Bullock, Linda. Looking Through a Microscope. 2004. (Rookie Read-About Science Ser.). (ENG., Illus.). 32p. (J). (gr. 1-2). pap. 4.95 *(978-0-516-27912-1(2),* Children's Pr.) Scholastic Library Publishing.

Crewe, Sabrina. In Your Body. 2010. (Under the Microscope Ser.). 32p. (gr. 2-4). 30.00 *(978-1-60413-825-2(4),* Chelsea Clubhouse) Facts On File, Inc.

Crewe, Sabrina & Camper, Anne K. Under the Microscope, 6 vols., Set. 2010. (Under the Microscope Ser.). (gr. 2-4). 180.00 *(978-1-60413-965-5(X),* Chelsea Clubhouse) Facts On File, Inc.

Gikow, Louise. Science. 2004. (True Tales Ser.). (ENG., Illus.). 48p. (J). 22.50 *(978-0-516-23729-9(2),* Children's Pr.) Scholastic Library Publishing.

Greg's Microscope. 2003. 22.95 *(978-0-673-75918-4(0))* Celebration Pr.

Hall, Kirsten. Up Close & Gross. Jankowski, Dan, illus. 2009. 64p. (J). *(978-0-545-13583-2(4))* Scholastic, Inc.

Kramer, Stephen. Hidden Worlds: Looking Through a Scientist's Microscope. Kunkel, Dennis, photos by. 2003. (Scientists in the Field Ser.). (ENG., Illus.). 64p. (J). (gr. 5-7). pap. 9.99 *(978-0-618-35405-4(0))* Houghton Mifflin Harcourt Publishing Co.

—Hidden Worlds: Looking Through a Scientist's Microscope. Kunkel, Dennis, photos by. 2005. (Illus.). 57p. (gr. 4-7). 20.00 *(978-0-7569-5188-7(7))* Perfection Learning Corp.

—Hidden Worlds: Looking Through a Scientist's Microscope. 2003. (gr. k-3). lib. bdg. 20.85 *(978-0-613-88665-9(8),* Turtleback) Turtleback Bks.

Levine, Shar & Johnstone, Leslie. The Ultimate Guide to Your Microscope. 2008. (ENG., Illus.). 144p. (J). (gr. 5). pap. 9.95 *(978-1-4027-4329-0(7))* Sterling Publishing Co., Inc.

Lopez, Max. How Do Microscopes Work? 2013. (InfoMax Readers Ser.). (ENG.). 24p. (J). (gr. 3-4). pap. 49.50 *(978-1-4777-2505-4(9));* pap. 8.25 *(978-1-4777-2504-7(0))* Rosen Publishing Group, Inc., The. (Rosen Classroom).

Melendez, Alicia & Benchmark Education Co. Staff. Behind the Microscope: Solving Scientific Mysteries. 2014. (Text Connections Ser.). (J). (gr. 6). *(978-1-4900-1532-3(9))* Benchmark Education Co.

Oxlade, C. & Stockley, C. Micro Kit (Box) rev. ed. 2008. (Kid Kits Ser.). 48p. (J). pap. 29.99 *(978-1-60130-108-6(1),* Usborne) EDC Publishing.

Oxlade, Chris & Stockley, Corinne. The World of the Microscope. Chen, Kuo Kang et al, illus. 2008. (Usborne Science & Experiments Ser.). 48p. (J). (gr. 5-11). pap. 8.99 *(978-0-7945-1524-9(X),* Usborne) EDC Publishing.

Rainis, Kenneth G. Microscope Science Projects & Experiments: Magnifying the Hidden World. 2003. (Science Fair Success Ser.). (Illus.). 128p. (J). lib. bdg. 26.60 *(978-0-7660-2090-0(8))* Enslow Pubs., Inc.

Rivera, Sheila. Microscope. 2007. (First Step Nonfiction - Simple Tools Ser.). (ENG., Illus.). 8p. (gr. -1-1). pap. 4.95 *(978-0-8225-6853-7(5))* Lerner Publishing Group.

Rodgers, Kirsteen. El Gran Libro del Microscopio. 2004. (Complete Bks.).Tr. of Complete Book of the Microscope. (SPA., Illus.). 96p. (J). (gr. 3-18). lib. bdg. 22.95 *(978-1-58086-317-9(5),* EU31324) EDC Publishing.

Rogers, K. Complete Book of the Microscope. 2004. (Complete Bks.). (SPA., Illus.). 96p. (J). lib. bdg. 22.95 *(978-1-58086-384-1(1))* EDC Publishing.

Rogers, Kirsteen. The Complete Book of the Microscope. Dowswell, Paul, ed. Lane, Kim, illus. rev. ed. 2005. (Complete Bks.). 96p. (J). pap. 14.99 *(978-0-7945-1558-4(4),* Usborne) EDC Publishing.

Schitt, Christine. Journey into the Invisible: The World from under the Microscope. Brandt, Chris, tr. from GER. 2013. (ENG., Illus.). 80p. (J). (gr. -1-k). 16.95 *(978-1-62087-116-4(5),* 620116, Sky Pony Pr.) Skyhorse Publishing Co., Inc.

See & Learn Science: A Curriculum Guide for Using Your Digital Microscope. 2007. (J). *(978-1-933229-69-0(1))* APTE, Inc.

Slade, Suzanne. Looking at Atoms & Molecules. 2006. (Library of Physical Sciences). (Illus.). 24p. (J). (gr. 3-7). lib. bdg. 21.25 *(978-1-4042-3419-2(5),* PowerKids Pr.) Rosen Publishing Group, Inc., The.

—Scientific Instruments for Studying Atoms & Molecules. 2007. (Library of Physical Sciences). (ENG., Illus.). 24p. (gr. 4-8). pap. 7.05 *(978-1-4042-2166-6(2),* PowerKids Pr.) Rosen Publishing Group, Inc., The.

Stefoff, Rebecca. Microscopes & Telescopes. 2006. (Great Inventions Ser.). (Illus.). 128p. (J). (gr. 3-7). lib. bdg. 39.93 *(978-0-7614-2230-3(7),* Benchmark Bks.) Marshall Cavendish Corp.

Under the Microscope. 2013. (Under the Microscope Ser.). 32p. (J). (gr. 4-6). 159.60 *(978-1-4339-8358-0(3));* pap. 70.20 *(978-1-4339-9735-8(5));* pap. 421.20 *(978-1-4339-9736-5(3))* Stevens, Gareth Publishing LLLP.

Yount, Lisa. Antoni Van Leeuwenhoek: First to See Microscopic Life. rev. ed. 2008. (Great Minds of Science Ser.). (Illus.). 128p. (J). (gr. k-5). lib. bdg. 33.27 *(978-0-7660-3012-1(1))* Enslow Pubs., Inc.

—Antoni Van Leeuwenhoek: Genius Discoverer of Microscopic Life. 2015. (Genius Scientists & Their Genius Ideas Ser.). 96p. (J). (gr. 5-12). 27.94 *(978-0-7660-6525-3(1));* pap. 10.95 *(978-0-7660-6526-0(X))* Enslow Pubs., Inc.

MICROSCOPIC ANALYSIS

see Microscopy

MICROSCOPIC ORGANISMS

see Microorganisms

MICROSCOPY

Here are entered works on microscopy in general as well as works specifically on light or optical microscopy.

Bacteria up Close. 2013. (Under the Microscope Ser.). 32p. (J). (gr. 4-6). pap. 70.20 *(978-1-4339-8336-8(2))* Stevens, Gareth Publishing LLLP.

Crewe, Sabrina. In Rivers, Lakes, & Ponds. 2010. (Under the Microscope Ser.). 32p. (gr. 2-4). 30.00 *(978-1-60413-826-9(2),* Chelsea Clubhouse) Facts On File, Inc.

—In the Backyard. 2010. (Under the Microscope Ser.). 32p. (gr. 2-4). 30.00 *(978-1-60413-822-1(X),* Chelsea Clubhouse) Facts On File, Inc.

—In the Home. 2010. (Under the Microscope Ser.). 32p. (gr. 2-4). 30.00 *(978-1-60413-823-8(8)*, Chelsea Clubhouse) Facts On File, Inc.
—In Your Body. 2010. (Under the Microscope Ser.). 32p. (gr. 2-4). 30.00 *(978-1-60413-825-2(4)*, Chelsea Clubhouse) Facts On File, Inc.
Early, Bobbi. Tiny Life in a Puddle. 2005. (Rookie Read-About Science Ser.). (ENG., Illus.). 32p. (J). (gr. 1-2). lib. bdg. 20.50 *(978-0-516-25272-8(0)*, Children's Pr.) Scholastic Library Publishing.
Kramer, Stephen. Hidden Worlds: Looking Through a Scientist's Microscope. Kunkel, Dennis, photos by. 2003. (Scientists in the Field Ser.). (ENG., Illus.). 64p. (J). (gr. 5-7). pap. 9.99 *(978-0-618-35405-4(0))* Houghton Mifflin Harcourt Publishing Co.
—Hidden Worlds: Looking Through a Scientist's Microscope. Kunkel, Dennis, photos by. 2005. (Illus.). 57p. (gr. 4-7). 20.00 *(978-0-7569-5188-7(7))* Perfection Learning Corp.
—Hidden Worlds: Looking Through a Scientist's Microscope. 2003. (gr. k-3). lib. bdg. 20.85 *(978-0-613-88665-9(8)*, Turtleback) Turtleback Bks.
Levine, Shar & Johnstone, Leslie. The Ultimate Guide to Your Microscope. 2008. (ENG., Illus.). 144p. (J). (gr. 5). pap. 9.95 *(978-1-4027-4329-0(7))* Sterling Publishing Co., Inc.
Levy, Janey. Tiny Bugs up Close. 2013. (Under the Microscope Ser.). 32p. (J). (gr. 4-6). pap. 11.70 *(978-1-4339-8351-1(6))*; lib. bdg. 26.60 *(978-1-4339-8350-4(8))* Stevens, Gareth Publishing LLLP.
Metz, Lorijo. Using Hand Lenses & Microscopes. 2013. (Science Tools Ser.). (ENG., Illus.). 24p. (J). (gr. 3-6). 22.60 *(978-1-4488-9687-5(8))*; pap. 8.25 *(978-1-4488-9832-9(3))* Rosen Publishing Group, Inc., The. (PowerKids Pr.).
Nelson, Maria. Cells up Close. 2013. (Under the Microscope Ser.). 32p. (J). (gr. 4-6). pap. 70.20 *(978-1-4339-8340-5(0))*; (Illus.). 26.60 *(978-1-4339-8338-2(9))*; (Illus.). pap. 11.70 *(978-1-4339-8339-9(7))* Stevens, Gareth Publishing LLLP.
Rogers, Kirsteen. The Complete Book of the Microscope. Dowswell, Paul, ed. Lane, Kim, illus. rev. ed. 2005. (Complete Bks.). 96p. (J). pap. 14.99 *(978-0-7945-1558-4(4)*, Usborne) EDC Publishing.
Roza, Greg. Bacteria up Close. 2013. 32p. (J). (gr. 4-6). 26.60 *(978-1-4339-8334-4(6))*; pap. 11.70 *(978-1-4339-8335-1(4))* Stevens, Gareth Publishing LLLP.
Schlitt, Christine. Journey into the Invisible: The World from under the Microscope. Brandt, Chris, tr. from GER. 2013. (ENG., Illus.). 80p. (J). (gr. -1-k). 16.95 *(978-1-62087-116-4(5)*, 620116, Sky Pony Pr.) Skyhorse Publishing Co., Inc.
Stewart, Melissa. Do People Really Have Tiny Insects Living in Their Eyelashes? And Other Questions about the Microscopic World. 2010. (Is That a Fact? Ser.). (ENG.). 40p. (gr. 4-6). lib. bdg. 26.60 *(978-0-7613-4916-7(2))* Lerner Publishing Group.
Tiny Bugs up Close. 2013. (Under the Microscope Ser.). 32p. (J). (gr. 4-6). pap. 70.20 *(978-1-4339-8352-8(4))* Stevens, Gareth Publishing LLLP.

MICROSOFT SOFTWARE

Glencoe McGraw-Hill Staff & Glencoe Staff. Microsoft PowerPoint 2007: Real World Applications. 2008. (Achieve Microsoft Office 2003 Ser.). (ENG., Illus.). 288p. (gr. 9-12). stu. ed. 93.72 *(978-0-07-880267-6(9)*, 0078802679) McGraw-Hill Education.
Goff, Terry. 44 Fast & Fun Microsoft Word Activities. 2008. 130p. (J). per. 34.95 *(978-0-9774748-5-1(2))* Brewer Technologies.
Gregory, Josh. Bill & Melinda Gates. 2013. (True Book(tm), A — Biographies Ser.). (ENG., Illus.). 48p. (J). lib. bdg. 31.00 *(978-0-531-21905-8(4))*; pap. 6.95 *(978-0-531-23876-9(8))* Scholastic Library Publishing.
Lesinski, Jeanne M. Bill Gates. rev. ed. 2007. (Biography Ser.). (Illus.). 112p. (J). (gr. 6-9). lib. bdg. 29.27 *(978-0-8225-7363-0(6)*, Twenty-First Century Bks.) Lerner Publishing Group.
Napier, H. Albert, et al. Learning with Computers I. 2nd ed. 2011. (Middle School Solutions Ser.). (ENG & ABK., Illus.). 464p. (C). 70.95 *(978-0-538-45070-6(3))* Cengage South-Western.
—Learning with Computers II. 2nd ed. 2011. (Middle School Solutions Ser.). (ENG & ABK., Illus.). 512p. (C). pap. 87.95 *(978-0-538-45071-3(1))* Cengage South-Western.
Wanniarachchi, Ruwan. Early Childhood Computer Learning Workbook - Level 1. 2007. 79p. pap. 18.50 *(978-0-615-17026-8(9))* Wanniarachchige, Somiruwan.

MIDDLE AGES

see also Art, Medieval; Chivalry; Civilization, Medieval; Knights and Knighthood; Literature, Medieval; Renaissance

Allen, Kathy. The Horrible, Miserable Middle Ages: The Disgusting Details About Life During Medieval. 2011. (Disgusting History Ser.). (ENG.). 32p. (gr. 3-4). pap. 47.70 *(978-1-4296-6479-0(7)*, Fact Finders) Capstone Press of Coughlan Cos.
—The Horrible, Miserable Middle Ages: The Disgusting Details about Life During Medieval Times. (Disgusting History Ser.). (ENG.). 32p. (gr. 3-4). 2011. pap. 8.10 *(978-1-4296-6350-2(2))* 2010. lib. bdg. 27.32 *(978-1-4296-3958-3(X))* Capstone Press of Coughlan Cos. (Fact Finders).
Bauer, Susan Wise. The Middle Ages. 2003. (Story of the World: Vol. 2). (ENG., Illus.). 200p. (J). act. bk. ed. 29.95 *(978-0-9714129-4-1(4)*, AB2) Well-Trained Mind Pr.
—The Middle Ages Vol. 2: From the Fall of Rome to the Rise of the Renaissance. 2003. (Story of the World: Vol. 2). (ENG., Illus.). 1p. 21.95 *(978-0-9714129-8-9(7))*; 336p. (J). pap. 16.95 *(978-0-9714129-3-4(6)*, SOTW2) Well-Trained Mind Pr.
Baum, Margaux & Bhote, Tehmina. Foods, Feasts, & Celebrations. 2016. (Life in the Middle Ages Ser.). 00064p. (J). (gr. 5-5). 34.45 *(978-1-4994-6470-2(3)*, Rosen Central) Rosen Publishing Group, Inc., The.
Baum, Margaux & Hopkins, Andrea. The Lives of Women in the Middle Ages. 2016. (J). *(978-1-4994-6467-2(3))* Rosen Publishing Group, Inc., The.
Benduhn, Tea. La Edad Media. 2007. (vida en el pasado (Life Long Ago) Ser.). (SPA., Illus.). 24p. (gr. 1-4). pap. 8.15 *(978-0-8368-8040-3(4))*; lib. bdg. 22.00 *(978-0-8368-8035-9(8))* Stevens, Gareth Publishing LLLP. (Weekly Reader Leveled Readers).
—The Middle Ages. 2007. (Life Long Ago Ser.). (Illus.). 24p. (gr. 1-4). pap. 8.15 *(978-0-8368-7789-2(6))*; lib. bdg. 22.00 *(978-0-8368-7784-7(5))* Stevens, Gareth Publishing LLLP. (Weekly Reader Leveled Readers).
Bingham, Jane. Medieval world - internet Linked. Firenze, Inklink, illus. rev. ed. 2004. 96p. (J). pap. 14.95 *(978-0-7945-0815-9(4)*, Usborne) EDC Publishing.
Bingham, Marjorie. An Age of Empires, 1200-1750. 2006. 32.95 *(978-0-19-522268-5(7))* Oxford Univ. Pr., Inc.
Bingham, Marjorie Wall. An Age of Empires, 1200-1750. 2005. (Medieval & Early Modern World Ser.: 4). (ENG., Illus.). 160p. (YA). 32.95 *(978-0-19-517839-5(4))* Oxford Univ. Pr., Inc.
Bodden, Valerie. Barbarians. 2017. (J). *(978-1-60818-811-6(6)*, Creative Education) 2013. 24p. pap. *(978-1-60818-466-8(8))* Creative Co., The.
—Great Warriors: Barbarians. 2014. (Great Warriors Ser.). (ENG.). 24p. (J). (gr. 1-3). pap. 9.99 *(978-1-62832-066-4(4)*, Creative Paperbacks) Creative Co., The.
Bow, James. Your Guide to Trade in the Middle Ages. 2017. (Destination: Middle Ages Ser.). (ENG., Illus.). 32p. (J). ***(978-0-7787-2996-9(6))***; pap. ***(978-0-7787-3052-1(2))*** Crabtree Publishing Co.
Bower & Bower, Bert. History Alive! The Medieval World & Beyond. 2011. (Illus.). xiv, 505p. (J). *(978-1-58371-916-9(4))* Teachers' Curriculum Institute.
Chambers, Catherine. A King's Guide. Pentney, Ryan, illus. 2017. (How-To Guides for Fiendish Rulers Ser.). (ENG.). 32p. (J). (gr. 3-6). lib. bdg. 26.65 *(978-1-5124-1550-6(2))*; 7.99 ***(978-1-5124-3624-2(0))***; 39.99 ***(978-1-5124-3623-5(2))***; 39.99 ***(978-1-5124-2706-6(3))*** Lerner Publishing Group.
—Why Why Why... Did Knights Wear Heavy Armor? 2010. (Why Why Why Ser.). (Illus.). 32p. (J). (gr. 1-3). lib. bdg. 18.95 *(978-1-4222-1575-3(X))* Mason Crest.
Corbishley, Mike. The Middle Ages. 3rd rev. ed. 2007. (Cultural Atlas for Young People Ser.). (Illus.). 96p. (YA). (gr. 5-9). 35.00 *(978-0-8160-6825-8(9))* Facts On File, Inc.
Corrick, James A. The Early Middle Ages. 2005. (World History Ser.). (ENG., Illus.). 112p. (J). (gr. 5-8). lib. bdg. 34.95 *(978-1-59018-652-7(4)*, Lucent Bks.) Cengage Gale.
Delaware, Steven S. Art & Culture of the Medieval World. 2010. (Ancient Art & Cultures Ser.). 40p. (YA). (gr. 5-8). lib. bdg., E-Book 53.00 *(978-1-61532-966-3(8))* Rosen Publishing Group, Inc., The.
Delaware, Steven S., et al. Art & Culture of the Medieval World. 2010. (Ancient Art & Cultures Ser.). (Illus.). 40p. (J). pap. 11.75 *(978-1-61532-887-1(4))*; (YA). (gr. 5-8). lib. bdg. 26.50 *(978-1-4358-3592-4(1))* Rosen Publishing Group, Inc., The. (Rosen Reference).
Dorling Kindersley Publishing Staff & Langley, Andrew. Medieval Life. 2011. (DK Eyewitness Bks.). (ENG.). 72p. (J). (gr. 3-7). 16.99 *(978-0-7566-7316-1(X)*, DK Children) Dorling Kindersley Publishing, Inc.
Dwyer, Helen. The Middle Ages, 600 to 1492. 2010. (CC: Atlas of World History Ser.). 112p. (gr. 6-12). 42.80 *(978-1-933834-67-2(6))* Brown Bear Bks.
Eastwood, Kay. Medieval Society. 2003. (Medieval World Ser.). (ENG., Illus.). 32p. (J). (gr. 5). pap. *(978-0-7787-1377-7(6))* Crabtree Publishing Co.
—Women & Girls in the Middle Ages. 2003. (Medieval World Ser.). (ENG., Illus.). 32p. (J). (gr. 5). pap. *(978-0-7787-1378-4(4))* Crabtree Publishing Co.
English Heritage Staff. My Life as a Knight. 2005. (Illus.). 32p. pap. 19.95 *(978-1-85074-985-1(X))* Historic England Publishing GBR. Dist: Casemate Academic.
—My Life as a Princess. 2005. (Illus.). 32p. pap. 19.95 *(978-1-85074-984-4(1))* Historic England Publishing GBR. Dist: Casemate Academic.
Exploring the Ancient & Medieval Worlds. 2015. (Exploring the Ancient & Medieval Worlds Ser.). (ENG.). 160p. (YA). (gr. 8-8). 456.40 *(978-1-5026-0374-6(8))* Cavendish Square Publishing.
Ganeri, Anita. How to Live Like a Medieval Knight. Epelbaum, Mariano, illus. 2015. (How to Live Like... Ser.). (ENG.). 32p. (J). (gr. 3-6). lib. bdg. 26.65 *(978-1-4677-6353-0(5))* Lerner Publishing Group.
George, Enzo. The Middle Ages. 2016. (Primary Sources in World History Ser.). (ENG.). 48p. (YA). (gr. 6-6). 31.36 *(978-1-5026-1800-9(1))* Cavendish Square Publishing.
Gitlin, Marty. The Totally Gross History of Medieval Europe, 01 vols., 1. 2016. (Totally Gross History Ser.). (ENG.). 48p. (J). pap. 11.75 *(978-1-4994-3764-5(1)*, Rosen Central) Rosen Publishing Group, Inc., The.
Grant, Neil. Medieval Europe. 2003. (Uncovering History Ser.). 46p. (J). lib. bdg. 28.50 *(978-1-58340-254-2(3))* Black Rabbit Bks.
Hanawalt, Barbara. The European World, 400-1450. 2006. (Illus.). 189p. 32.95 *(978-0-19-522267-8(9))* Oxford Univ. Pr., Inc.
Hanawalt, Barbara A. The European World, 400-1450. 2005. (Medieval & Early Modern World Ser.). (ENG., Illus.). 192p. (YA). 36.95 *(978-0-19-517844-9(0))* Oxford Univ. Pr., Inc.
Harding, Samuel. The Story of the Middle Ages. 2008. 116p. pap. 9.45 *(978-1-60459-530-7(2))* Wilder Pubns., Corp.
Harding, Samuel Bannister. The Story of the Middle Ages (Yesterday's Classics) 2006. (Illus.). 228p. (YA). per. 10.95 *(978-1-59915-157-1(X))* Yesterday's Classics.
Hattstein, Markus & Udelhoven, Hermann-Josef. The Middle Ages & the Early Modern Period: From the 5th Century to the 18th Century. 2012. (Witness to History: A Visual Chronicle of the World Ser.). (ENG., Illus.). 200p. (J). (gr. 7-12). 46.50 *(978-1-4488-7223-7(5))* Rosen Publishing Group, Inc., The.
Hazen, Walter. Middle Ages. 2005. (Everyday Life (Good Year Books) Ser.). (Illus.). 92p. (J). (gr. 6-9). per. 12.95 *(978-1-59647-059-0(3))* Good Year Bks.
Helget, Nicole Lea. Barbarians. 2012. (Fearsome Fighters Ser.). 48p. (gr. 5-12). 23.95 *(978-1-60818-182-7(0)*, Creative Education) Creative Co., The.
Heos, Bridget. Who Wants to Be a Princess? What It Was Really Like to Be a Medieval Princess. Migy, illus. 2017. (ENG.). 32p. (J). 16.99 *(978-0-8050-9769-6(4)*, 9780805097696, Holt, Henry & Co. Bks. For Young Readers) Holt, Henry & Co.
Hindley, Judy, et al. Time Traveler: Visit Medieval Times, the Viking Age, the Roman World & Ancient Egypt. rev. ed. 2004. (Time Travelers Bks.). (Illus.). 130p. (J). (gr. 3-6). 22.95 *(978-0-7460-3365-4(6))* EDC Publishing.
Hinds, Kathryn. Everyday Life in Medieval Europe. 2008. (Everyday Life in... Ser.). 288p. (gr. 6-18). lib. bdg. 42.79 *(978-0-7614-3927-1(7)*, Benchmark Bks.) Marshall Cavendish Corp.
Hopkins, Andrea. Damsels Not in Distress: The True Story of Women in Medieval Times. 2009. (Library of the Middle Ages Ser.). 64p. (gr. 5-8). 58.50 *(978-1-60853-898-0(2)*, Rosen Reference) Rosen Publishing Group, Inc., The.
Hunt, Norman Bancroft. Living in the Middle Ages. 2008. (Living in the Ancient World Ser.). (Illus.). 96p. (YA). (gr. 7-12). 35.00 *(978-0-8160-6341-3(9))* Facts On File, Inc.
Jovinelly, Joann. The Crafts & Culture of a Medieval Cathedral. 2009. (Crafts & Cultures of the Middle Ages Ser.). 48p. (gr. 5-5). 58.50 *(978-1-61512-054-3(8)*, Rosen Reference) Rosen Publishing Group, Inc., The.
—The Crafts & Culture of a Medieval Guild. 2009. (Crafts & Cultures of the Middle Ages Ser.). 48p. (gr. 5-5). 58.50 *(978-1-61512-055-0(6)*, Rosen Reference) Rosen Publishing Group, Inc., The.
—The Crafts & Culture of a Medieval Manor. 2009. (Crafts & Cultures of the Middle Ages Ser.). 48p. (gr. 5-5). 58.50 *(978-1-61512-053-6(X)*, Rosen Reference) Rosen Publishing Group, Inc., The.
Jovinelly, Joann & Netelkos, Jason. The Crafts & Culture of a Medieval Cathedral. 2006. (Crafts & Cultures of the Middle Ages Ser.). (Illus.). 48p. (J). (gr. 3-7). lib. bdg. 29.25 *(978-1-4042-0758-5(9))* Rosen Publishing Group, Inc., The.
—The Crafts & Culture of a Medieval Guild. 2006. (Crafts & Cultures of the Middle Ages Ser.). (Illus.). 48p. (J). (gr. 3-7). lib. bdg. 29.25 *(978-1-4042-0757-8(0))* Rosen Publishing Group, Inc., The.
—The Crafts & Culture of a Medieval Manor. 2006. (Crafts & Cultures of the Middle Ages Ser.). (Illus.). 48p. (J). (gr. 3-7). lib. bdg. 29.25 *(978-1-4042-0756-1(2))* Rosen Publishing Group, Inc., The.
Kenney, Karen Latchana. Harsh or Heroic? The Middle Ages. 2007. (Shockwave: History & Politics Ser.). (ENG., Illus.). 36p. (J). (gr. 3-5). 25.00 *(978-0-531-17754-9(8)*, Children's Pr.) Scholastic Library Publishing.
Kerns, Ann. Did Castles Have Bathrooms? And Other Questions about the Middle Ages. 2010. (Is That a Fact? Ser.). (ENG.). 40p. (gr. 4-6). lib. bdg. 26.60 *(978-0-7613-4915-0(4))* Lerner Publishing Group.
Koestler-Grack, Rachel A. Eleanor of Aquitaine: Heroine of the Middle Ages. 2005. (Makers of the Middle Ages & Renaissance Ser.). (Illus.). 168p. (gr. 5-8). lib. bdg. 32.95 *(978-0-7910-8633-9(X)*, Chelsea Hse.) Facts On File, Inc.
Kroll, Steven. Barbarians! Byrd, Robert, illus. 2009. (ENG.). 48p. (J). (gr. 3-7). 20.99 *(978-0-525-47958-1(9)*, Dutton Books for Young Readers) Penguin Young Readers Group.
Lassieur, Allison. The Middle Ages: An Interactive History Adventure. 2016. (You Choose: Historical Eras Ser.). (ENG.). 112p. (gr. 3-4). pap. 6.95 *(978-1-5157-4250-0(4)*, You Choose Bks.) Capstone Press of Coughlan Cos.
Levy, Janey. 20 Fun Facts about Women of the Middle Ages. 2015. (Fun Fact File: Women in History Ser.). (ENG., Illus.). 32p. (J). (gr. 2-3). pap. 10.50 *(978-1-4824-2824-7(5))* Stevens, Gareth Publishing LLLP.
Life in the Middle Ages. 2016. (Life in the Middle Ages Ser.). 00064p. (J). (gr. 5-5). 206.70 *(978-1-5081-7364-9(8)*, Rosen Central) Rosen Publishing Group, Inc., The.
Macdonald, Fiona. The Medieval Chronicles: Vikings, Knights, & Castles. Antram, David, illus. 2013. 92p. (J). *(978-1-4351-5067-6(8))* Barnes & Noble, Inc.
MacDonald, Fiona. Monarchs in the Middle Ages. 2005. (World Almanac Library of the Middle Ages). (Illus.). 48p. (gr. 5-12). pap. 14.05 *(978-0-8368-5905-8(7)*, Gareth Stevens Secondary Library) Stevens, Gareth Publishing LLLP.
—Monarchs in the Middle Ages. 2005. (World Almanac Library of the Middle Ages). (Illus.). 48p. (gr. 5-12). lib. bdg. 31.00 *(978-0-8368-5896-9(4)*, Gareth Stevens Secondary Library) Stevens, Gareth Publishing LLLP.
Macdonald, Fiona. You Wouldn't Want to Be in a Medieval Dungeon! Prisoners You'd Rather Not Meet. Antram, David, illus. 2013. (You Wouldn't Want to... Ser.). (ENG.). (J). 40p. pap. 9.95 *(978-0-531-24504-0(7))*; 32p. 29.00 *(978-0-531-25948-1(X))* Scholastic Library Publishing. (Watts, Franklin).
—You Wouldn't Want to Be in a Medieval Dungeon! Prisoners You'd Rather Not Meet. 2013. (You Wouldn't Want To... Ser.). lib. bdg. 20.80 *(978-0-606-31629-3(9)*, Turtleback) Turtleback Bks.
—You Wouldn't Want to Work on a Medieval Cathedral! A Difficult Job That Never Ends. 2010. (You Wouldn't Want to... Ser.). 32p. (J). 29.00 *(978-0-531-20504-4(5)*, Watts, Franklin) Scholastic Library Publishing.
MacDonald, Fiona. You Wouldn't Want to Work on a Medieval Cathedral! A Difficult Job That Never Ends. 2010. (You Wouldn't Want to... Ser.). (ENG., Illus.). 32p. (J). (gr. 3-18). pap. 9.95 *(978-0-531-13784-0(8)*, Watts, Franklin) Scholastic Library Publishing.
Mayer, Cassie. Knights & Castles. 2012. (Illus.). 64p. (J). pap. 12.99 *(978-1-62267-007-9(8))* Bright Connections Media.
McNeil, Niki, et al. HOCPP 1054 Middle Ages. 2006. spiral bd. 21.00 *(978-1-60308-054-5(6))* In the Hands of a Child.
Medieval Africa DBA. 2003. spiral bd. 16.95 *(978-1-56004-170-2(6))* Social Studies Schl. Service.
Middle Ages: Fun Projects for World History. 2006. cd-rom 29.95 net. *(978-1-56004-252-5(4))* Social Studies Schl. Service.
Miles, Liz. Meet the Medievals. 2014. (Encounters with the Past Ser.). 32p. (J). (gr. 3-6). 26.60 *(978-1-4824-0889-8(9))* Stevens, Gareth Publishing LLLP.
Nikola-lisa, W. Till Year's Good End. Manson, Christopher, illus. 2009. (ENG.). 36p. (J). (gr. 1-4). 12.99 *(978-1-4424-0225-6(3)*, Atheneum Bks. for Young Readers) Simon & Schuster Children's Publishing.
O'Brian, Pliny. Empires, Crusaders, & Invasions Through the Middle Ages. 2015. (Exploring the Ancient & Medieval Worlds Ser.). (ENG., Illus.). 160p. (J). (gr. 8-8). lib. bdg. 45.64 *(978-1-5026-0679-2(8))* Cavendish Square Publishing.
O'Brien, Cynthia. Your Guide to Knights & the Age of Chivalry. 2017. (Destination: Middle Ages Ser.). (ENG., Illus.). 32p. (J). ***(978-0-7787-2992-1(3))***; pap. ***(978-0-7787-2998-3(2))*** Crabtree Publishing Co.
—Your Guide to the Arts in the Middle Ages. 2017. (Destination: Middle Ages Ser.). (ENG., Illus.). 32p. (J). ***(978-0-7787-2995-2(8))***; pap. ***(978-0-7787-3002-6(6))*** Crabtree Publishing Co.
Paprocki, Greg, illus. C Is for Castle: A Medieval Primer. 1 vol. 2016. (ENG.). 32p. (J). bds. 9.99 *(978-1-4236-4281-7(3))* Gibbs Smith, Publisher.
Park, Louise. Life in the Middle Ages. 2013. (Discovery Education: Ancient Civilizations Ser.). (ENG., Illus.). 32p. (J). (gr. 3-6). pap. 10.00 *(978-1-4777-0095-2(1))*; lib. bdg. 25.25 *(978-1-4777-0055-6(2))* Rosen Publishing Group, Inc., The. (PowerKids Pr.).
Plain, Nancy. Eleanor of Aquitaine & the High Middle Ages. 2005. (Rulers & Their Times Ser.). (Illus.). 80p. (gr. 6-7). lib. bdg. 23.95 *(978-0-7614-1834-4(2)*, Benchmark Bks.) Marshall Cavendish Corp.
Powell, Jillian & Buckingham, Matt. The Middle Ages. 2010. (Gruesome Truth about Ser.). (ENG.). 32p. (J). (gr. 4-6). lib. bdg. 22.60 *(978-1-61533-219-9(7))* Windmill Bks.
Roscoe, Kelly, ed. The End of the Middle Ages. 2017. (Power & Religion in Medieval & Renaissance Times Ser.). 112p. (gr. 14-15). 36.25 ***(978-1-68048-623-0(3)***, Britannica Educational Publishing) Rosen Publishing Group, Inc., The.
Samuels, Charlie. Timeline of the Middle Ages. 2010. (History Highlights: A Gareth Stevens Timeline Ser.). (Illus.). 48p. (gr. 6-8). (J). pap. 14.05 *(978-1-4339-3484-1(1))*; (YA). lib. bdg. 31.95 *(978-1-4339-3483-4(3))* Stevens, Gareth Publishing LLLP. (Gareth Stevens Secondary Library).
Shapiro, Stephen. It's a Feudal, Feudal World: A Different Medieval History. Kinnaird, Ross, illus. 2013. (ENG.). 48p. (J). (gr. 4-8). lib. bdg. 24.95 *(978-1-55451-553-0(X)*, 9781554515530); 2nd ed. pap. 14.95 *(978-1-55451-552-3(1)*, 9781554515523) Annick Pr., Ltd. CAN. Dist: Publishers Group West (PGW).
Smith, Bonnie G. & Kelley, Donald R. The Medieval & Early Modern World: Primary Sources & Reference Volume. 2006. 32.95 *(978-0-19-522300-2(4))* Oxford Univ. Pr., Inc.
—The Medieval & Early Modern World: Primary Sources & Reference Volume. 2005. (Medieval & Early Modern World Ser.). (ENG., Illus.). 176p. (YA). 32.95 *(978-0-19-517848-7(3))* Oxford Univ. Pr., Inc.
Stefoff, Rebecca. The Medieval World. 2004. (World Historical Atlases Ser.). (Illus.). 48p. (gr. 5). 26.95 *(978-0-7614-1642-5(0)*, Benchmark Bks.) Marshall Cavendish Corp.
Stevens, Catrin, et al. Yr Oesoedd Canol Cythryblus. 2005. (WEL., Illus.). 144p. pap. 4.99 *(978-1-84323-423-4(8))* Gomer Pr. GBR. Dist: Gomer Pr.
Stewart, David. You Wouldn't Want to Be in a Medieval Dungeon! Antram, David, illus. rev. ed. 2013. (You Wouldn't Want to... Ser.). (ENG.). 32p. (J). 29.00 *(978-0-531-25949-8(8)*, Watts, Franklin) Scholastic Library Publishing.
Stiefel, Chana. Ye Castle Stinketh: Could You Survive Living in a Castle? Kelley, Gerald, illus. 2011. (Ye Yucky Middle Ages Ser.). 48p. (J). (gr. 5-18). pap. 8.95 *(978-1-59845-374-4(2))*; (gr. 7-12). lib. bdg. 25.27 *(978-0-7660-3786-1(X))* Enslow Pubs., Inc.
Stuckey, Rachel. Your Guide to Medieval Society. 2017. (Destination: Middle Ages Ser.). (ENG., Illus.). 32p. (J). ***(978-0-7787-2991-4(5))***; pap. ***(978-0-7787-2997-6(4))*** Crabtree Publishing Co.
Taylor, Barbara. The Amazing History of Castles & Knights. 2016. (ENG., Illus.). 64p. (J). (gr. -1-12). 12.99 *(978-1-86147-717-0(1)*, Armadillo) Anness Publishing GBR. Dist: National Bk. Network.
Templeman, Henry. Knights: The Secrets of Medieval Warriors. 2015. (ENG., Illus.). 80p. (J). (gr. 3). pap. 16.95 *(978-1-78312-146-5(7))* Carlton Kids GBR. Dist: Sterling Publishing Co., Inc.
Trembinski, Donna. Famous People of the Middle Ages. 2005. (Medieval World Ser.). (ENG., Illus.). 32p. (J). (gr. 5-9). lib. bdg. *(978-0-7787-1356-2(3))* Crabtree Publishing Co.
Walker, Jane. Knights & Castles. 2013. (Illus.). 48p. (J). *(978-1-4351-5093-5(7))* Barnes & Noble, Inc.
—100 Things You Should Know about Knights & Castles. 2008. (Illus.). 64p. *(978-1-84236-002-6(7))* Miles Kelly Publishing, Ltd.
Whitfield, Cathy. History Odyssey, Middle Ages - Level One. 2006. (J). ring bd. 31.00 *(978-0-9766057-7-5(5))* Pandia Pr.
Wiesner-Hanks, Merry E. An Age of Voyages, 1350-1600. 2005. (Medieval & Early Modern World Ser.: 5). (ENG., Illus.). 192p. (YA). (gr. 7-18). lib. bdg. 32.95 *(978-0-19-517672-8(3))* Oxford Univ. Pr., Inc.
Wiesner, Merry E. An Age of Voyages, 1450-1600. 2006. (Illus.). 189p. 32.95 *(978-0-19-522264-7(4))* Oxford Univ. Pr., Inc.
Wilkinson, Carole. How to Live in the Dark Ages. 2007. 96p. (J). pap. *(978-1-4207-0725-0(6))* Sundance/Newbridge Educational Publishing.
Woog, Adam. The Early Middle Ages. 2011. (Understanding World History Ser.). (ENG., Illus.). 96p. (YA). (gr. 7-12). lib. bdg. 27.95 *(978-1-60152-151-4(0))* ReferencePoint Pr., Inc.
—A Medieval Knight. 2003. (Daily Life Ser.). (ENG., Illus.). 48p. (J). (gr. 4-6). pap. 27.00 *(978-0-7377-0992-6(8)*, Kidhaven) Cengage Gale.

MIDDLE AGES—BIOGRAPHY

Dixon, Darla, illus. What Really Happened During the Middle Ages: A Collection of Historical Biographies, 4. 2007. (What Really Happened Ser.). 222p. per. 15.95 *(978-1-932786-22-4(8))* Knowledge Quest.
Trembinski, Donna. Famous People of the Middle Ages. 2005. (Medieval World Ser.). (ENG., Illus.). 32p. (J). (gr. 5-9). pap. *(978-0-7787-1388-3(1))* Crabtree Publishing Co.

MIDDLE AGES—FICTION

Avi. Crispin: La Cruz de Plomo. 2004.Tr. of Crispin: The Cross of Lead. (SPA., Illus.). (YA). pap. 7.99 *(978-84-348-9601-7(X))* SM Ediciones ESP. Dist: Lectorum Pubns., Inc.
—Crispin: The Cross of Lead. 2004. (Crispin Ser.). (ENG.). 320p. (J). (gr. 3-7). reprint ed. pap. 7.99 *(978-0-7868-1658-3(9))* Hyperion Pr.
—The End of Time. (ENG.). 240p. (J). (gr. 5). 2011. pap. 6.99 *(978-0-06-174083-1(7))*No. 3. 2010. 16.99 *(978-0-06-174080-0(2))* HarperCollins Pubs.

MNO

Aviation Book Company Staff. Crispin: The Cross of Lead. 2004. (J). (gr. 3-6). 18.40 (978-0-613-74965-7(0), Turtleback) Turtleback Bks.

Banks, Steven. Lost in Time. The Artifact Group, illus. 2006. 22p. (J). lib. bdg. 15.00 (978-1-4242-0977-4(3)) Fitzgerald Bks.

Barnhouse, Rebecca. The Book of the Maidservant. 2011. (ENG., Illus.). 240p. (J). (gr. 3-7). pap. 7.99 (978-0-375-85857-4(1), Yearling) Random Hse. Children's Bks.

Biggs, Stephen. The Time Barrel. 2009. 152p. pap. (978-1-84923-434-4(5)) YouWriteOn.

Bilgrey, Marc. And Don't Forget to Rescue the Other Princess. 2009. 252p. 25.95 (978-1-59414-744-9(2), Five Star) Cengage Gale.

Black, Kat. A Templar's Apprentice. 2009. (Book of Tormod Ser.: 1). (ENG.). 288p. (J). (gr. 7-18). 17.99 (978-0-545-05654-0(3)) Scholastic, Inc.

—A Templar's Destiny. 2012. (Book of Tormod Ser.). (ENG.). 256p. (J). (gr. 7-7). 17.99 (978-0-545-05677-9(2), Scholastic Pr.) Scholastic, Inc.

—A Templar's Gifts. 2011. (Book of Tormod Ser.: 2). (ENG.). 272p. (J). (gr. 7-7). 17.99 (978-0-545-05675-5(6), Scholastic Pr.) Scholastic, Inc.

Bonneval, Gwen de & Smith, Owen. William & the Lost Spirit. Smith, Anne Collins, tr. from FRE. Bonhomme, Matthieu, illus. 2013. (ENG.). 160p. (J). (gr. 8-12). lib. bdg. 30.60 (978-0-7613-8567-7(3), Graphic Universe™) Lerner Publishing Group.

Clayton, Colleen. What Happens Next. 2013. (ENG.). 320p. (YA). (gr. 10-17). pap. 10.00 (978-0-316-19869-1(2), Poppy) Little, Brown Bks. for Young Readers.

Coats, J. Anderson. The Wicked & the Just. (ENG.). 352p. (YA). (gr. 7). 2012. 16.99 (978-0-547-68837-4(7)) 2013. pap. 9.99 (978-0-544-02221-8(1)) Houghton Mifflin Harcourt Publishing Co.

Cody, Matthew. Will in Scarlet. 2014. (ENG., Illus.). 272p. (J). (gr. 5). pap. 6.99 (978-0-375-87292-1(2), Yearling) Random Hse. Children's Bks.

Comrie, Margaret S. The Heroes of Castle Bretten. 2003. (Illus.). 229p. (J). (978-1-894666-65-7(8)) Inheritance Pubns.

Connolly, Kara. No Good Deed. 2017. (ENG.). 352p. (YA). (gr. 9). 17.99 **(978-0-385-74393-8(9))**; lib. bdg. 20.99 **(978-0-375-99140-0(9))** Random Hse. Children's Bks. (Delacorte Pr.).

Costanza, Stephen, illus. Smudge & the Book of Mistakes: A Christmas Story. 2012. (ENG.). 48p. (J). (gr. 1-5). 17.95 (978-1-58536-483-1(5)) Sleeping Bear Pr.

Cremer, Andrea. Rift. 2013. (Nightshade Ser.). (ENG.). 480p. (YA). (gr. 9). pap. 9.99 (978-0-14-242493-3(5), Speak) Penguin Young Readers Group.

Crossley-Holland, Kevin. At the Crossing-Places. 2004. (Arthur Trilogy). (Illus.). 394p. (YA). (gr. 7-12). 15.65 (978-0-7569-3182-7(7)) Perfection Learning Corp.

—Crossing to Paradise. 2008. (J). pap. (978-0-545-05868-1(6), Levine, Arthur A. Bks.) Scholastic, Inc.

Cushman, Karen. Catherine, Called Birdy. 2012. lib. bdg. 18.40 (978-0-606-24712-2(2), Turtleback) Turtleback Bks.

—Grayling's Song. 2016. (ENG.). 224p. (J). (gr. 5-7). 16.99 (978-0-544-30180-1(3), Clarion Bks.) Houghton Mifflin Harcourt Trade & Reference Pubs.

—Matilda Bone. 2014. (ENG.). 176p. (J). (gr. 5-7). pap. 6.99 (978-0-547-72242-9(7), HMH Books For Young Readers) Houghton Mifflin Harcourt Publishing Co.

—Matilda Bone. unabr. ed. 2004. (Middle Grade Cassette Librariestm Ser.). 176p. (J). (gr. 5-9). pap. 36.00 incl. audio (978-0-8072-1725-2(5), S YA 252 SP, Listening Library) Random Hse. Audio Publishing Group.

—The Midwife's Apprentice. 2012. lib. bdg. 18.40 (978-0-606-24696-5(7), Turtleback) Turtleback Bks.

—Will Sparrow's Road. 2012. (ENG.). 224p. (J). (gr. 5-7). 16.99 (978-0-547-73962-5(1)) Houghton Mifflin Harcourt Publishing Co.

Davis, Tony. Roland Wright: at the Joust. Rogers, Gregory, illus. 2011. (ENG.). 144p. (J). (gr. 1-4). 6.99 (978-0-375-87328-7(7), Yearling) Random Hse. Children's Bks.

—Roland Wright: Brand-New Page. Rogers, Gregory, illus. 2011. (Roland Wright Ser.). (ENG.). 144p. (J). (gr. 1-4). 6.99 (978-0-385-73803-3(X), Yearling) Random Hse. Children's Bks.

De Bonneval, Gwen. William & the Lost Spirit. Smith, Anne, tr. Bonhomme, Matthieu, illus. 2013. (ENG.). 160p. (YA). (gr. 8-12). pap. 9.95 (978-1-4677-0807-4(0), Graphic Universe™) Lerner Publishing Group.

Dickerson, Melanie. The Huntress of Thornbeck Forest, 1 vol. 2015. (Medieval Fairy Tale Ser.: 1). (ENG.). 320p. pap. 15.99 (978-0-7180-2624-0(1)) Nelson, Thomas Inc.

—The Noble Servant, 1 vol. 2017. (ENG.). 336p. (J). 14.99 (978-0-7180-2660-8(8)) Nelson, Thomas Inc.

Flusfeder, David. John the Pupil. 2015. 240p. 24.99 (978-0-06-233918-8(4)) HarperCollins Pubs.

French, Allen. The Story of Rolf & the Viking Bow. 2008. 148p. (gr. 7-12). pap. 8.15 (978-1-60459-522-2(1)) Wilder Pubns., Corp.

French, Jackie. My Dad the Dragon. King, Stephen Michael, illus. 2004. 128p. (978-0-207-19950-9(7)) HarperCollins Pubs. Australia.

Gashler, Stephen. The Bent Sword. 2010. (YA). pap. 15.99 (978-1-59955-401-3(1)) Cedar Fort, Inc./CFI Distribution.

Gaughen, A. C. Lion Heart. 2015. (Scarlet Trilogy: No. 3). (ENG.). 352p. (YA). 17.99 (978-0-8027-3616-1(5), 9780802736161, Bloomsbury USA Childrens) Bloomsbury Publishing USA.

Gidwitz, Adam. The Inquisitor's Tale: Or, the Three Magical Children & Their Holy Dog. Aly, Hatem, illus. 2016. (ENG.). 384p. (J). (gr. 5). 17.99 (978-0-525-42616-5(7), Dutton Books for Young Readers) Penguin Young Readers Group.

Gilman, Laura Anne. The Camelot Spell. 2006. (Grail Quest Ser.: No. 1). 291p. (J). (gr. 5-9). 10.99 (978-0-06-077279-6(4)) HarperCollins Pubs.

Golding, Julia. The Silver Sea, 0 vols. 2013. (ENG.). 352p. (YA). (gr. 7-11). pap. 9.99 (978-1-4778-1598-4(8), 9781477815984, Amazon Children's Publishing) Amazon Publishing.

Grant, K. M. Blood Red Horse. 2006. (DeGranville Trilogy Ser.). (ENG.). 320p. (YA). (gr. 5-9). per. 10.99 (978-0-8027-7734-8(1), 9780802777348, Bloomsbury USA Childrens) Bloomsbury Publishing USA.

Gray, Elizabeth Janet. Adam of the Road. Lawson, Robert, illus. 2006. (Puffin Modern Classics Ser.). (ENG.). 320p. (J). (gr. 3-7). 7.99 (978-0-14-240659-5(7), Puffin Books) Penguin Young Readers Group.

Hardinge, Frances. Fly by Night. 2006. 487p. (J). (gr. 5-9). 16.99 (978-0-06-087627-2(1)) HarperCollins Pubs.

Hedlund, Jody. A Daring Sacrifice, 1 vol. 2016. (ENG.). 224p. (YA). pap. 12.99 (978-0-310-74937-0(9)) Zondervan.

Herz, Henry, et al. When You Give an Imp a Penny, 1 vol. Larson, Abigail, illus. 2016. (ENG.). 32p. (J). (gr. k-3). 16.99 (978-1-4556-2144-6(7)) Pelican Publishing Co., Inc.

Hidden. 2014. (ENG., Illus.). 384p. (YA). (gr. 7). 17.99 (978-1-4424-8300-2(8), Simon & Schuster/Paula Wiseman Bks.) Simon & Schuster/Paula Wiseman Bks.

Hulme-Cross, Benjamin. The Knight's Enemies. Rinaldi, Angelo, illus. 2015. (ENG.). 160p. (J). (978-0-7787-1765-2(8)) Crabtree Publishing Co.

Jackson, Marilee. Midnight Runner. 2015. 261p. (YA). pap. 17.99 (978-1-4621-1615-7(9)) Cedar Fort, Inc./CFI Distribution.

Jinks, Catherine. Babylonne. 2008. (ENG., Illus.). 400p. (YA). (gr. 7). 18.99 (978-0-7636-3650-0(9)) Candlewick Pr.

—Pagan in Exile. 2004. (Pagan Chronicles Ser.: 2). (ENG., Illus.). 336p. (YA). (gr. 9-18). 15.99 (978-0-7636-2020-2(3)) Candlewick Pr.

Jones, Rob Lloyd. The Story of Robin Hood. Marks, Alan, illus. 2010. (Picture Book Classics Ser.). 24p. (J). 9.99 (978-0-7945-2859-1(7), Usborne) EDC Publishing.

Keller, John E. The Emperor's Elephant. 2006. 127p. (YA). per. 12.95 (978-0-942566-45-1(9)) LinguaText, LLC.

Laird, Elizabeth. Crusade. 2016. (ENG.). 400p. (J). (gr. 4-7). pap. 8.99 (978-1-5098-0296-8(7)) Pan Macmillan GBR. Dist: Independent Pubs. Group.

Lamprey, L. Masters of the Guild. l.t. ed. 2006. 168p. pap. 21.99 (978-1-4264-2076-4(5)) Creative Media Partners, LLC.

Lawrence, Michael. Jiggy's Magic Balls: A Medieval Mess! 2010. (ENG.). 176p. (J). (gr. k-2). pap. 7.99 (978-1-4083-0803-5(7)) Hodder & Stoughton GBR. Dist: Hachette Bk. Group.

Love, D. Anne. The Puppeteer's Apprentice. 2004. (ENG., Illus.). 192p. (J). (gr. 3-7). reprint ed. pap. 9.99 (978-0-689-84425-6(5), McElderry, Margaret K. Bks.) McElderry, Margaret K. Bks.

—The Puppeteer's Apprentice. 2004. (Aladdin Historical Fiction Ser.). 185p. (gr. 3-7). 17.00 (978-0-7569-4323-3(X)) Perfection Learning Corp.

Massey, Eithne. Where the Stones Sing: Who Are the Mysterious Voices in Christ Church? 2012. (ENG., Illus.). 208p. (J). pap. 12.95 (978-1-84717-277-8(6)) O'Brien Pr., Ltd., The IRL. Dist: Dufour Editions, Inc.

McMullan, Kate. Countdown to the Year 1000. Basso, Bill, illus. 2003. (Dragon Slayers' Academy Ser.: 8). (ENG.). 112p. (J). (gr. 2-5). pap. 5.99 (978-0-448-43508-4(X), Grosset & Dunlap) Penguin Young Readers Group.

Millen, C. M. The Ink Garden of Brother Theophane. Wisnewski, Andrea, illus. 2010. (ENG.). 32p. (J). (gr. k-3). 17.95 (978-1-58089-179-0(9)) Charlesbridge Publishing, Inc.

Morris, Gerald. The Adventures of Sir Balin the Ill-Fated. Renier, Aaron, illus. 2013. (Knights' Tales Ser.: 4). (ENG.). 112p. (J). (gr. 1-4). pap. 5.99 (978-0-544-10488-4(9)) Houghton Mifflin Harcourt Publishing Co.

—The Lioness & Her Knight. 2008. (Squire's Tales Ser.: 7). (ENG.). 352p. (J). (gr. 5-7). pap. 7.99 (978-0-547-01485-2(6)) Houghton Mifflin Harcourt Publishing Co.

—Parsifal's Page. 2008. (Squire's Tales Ser.: 4). (ENG.). 240p. (J). (gr. 5-7). pap. 7.99 (978-0-547-01434-0(1)) Houghton Mifflin Harcourt Publishing Co.

Moss, Barbara E. The Adventures of Sir Goblin, the Feline Knight. Houx, Emily Marie Cornell du, illus. 2009. 336p. pap. 15.95 (978-1-882190-03-4(3)) Porcupine Communications.

Muir, Suzanne. The Magic Tile. 2007. (Illus.). 48p. (J). lib. bdg. 15.00 (978-1-4242-1619-2(2)) Dingles & Co.

Murphy, Shirley Rousseau. Silver Woven in My Hair. 2015. (ENG., Illus.). 128p. (J). (gr. 3-7). pap. 13.99 (978-1-4814-5865-8(5), Atheneum Bks. for Young Readers) Simon & Schuster Children's Publishing.

Nunes, Rachel Ann. The Secret of the King. Ward, Jay Bryant, illus. 2005. 32p. (J). (gr. -1-3). 17.95 (978-1-59038-241-7(2), Shadow Mountain) Shadow Mountain Publishing.

Osborne, Mary Pope. The Knight at Dawn. unabr. ed. 2004. (Magic Tree House Ser.: No. 2). 66p. (J). (gr. k-3). pap. 17.00 incl. audio (978-0-8072-0331-6(9), Listening Library) Random Hse. Audio Publishing Group.

—The Knight at Dawn. Murdocca, Sal, illus. 20th anniv. ed. 2013. (Magic Tree House Ser.). (ENG.). 96p. (J). (gr. 1-4). 14.99 (978-0-449-81822-0(5), Random Hse. Bks. for Young Readers) Random Hse. Children's Bks.

Picard, Barbara Leonie. Ransom for a Knight. 2008. (Nautilus Ser.). (ENG.). 314p. (J). (gr. 6). pap. 14.95 (978-1-58988-043-6(9)) Dry, Paul Bks., Inc.

Platt, Richard. Castle Diary: The Journal of Tobias Burgess. Riddell, Chris, illus. 2003. (ENG.). 128p. (J). (gr. 4-7). 6.99 (978-0-7636-2164-3(1)) Candlewick Pr.

Pringle, Eric. Big George & the Winter King. Paine, Colin, illus. 2004. (ENG.). 208p. (J). pap. 12.99 (978-0-7475-6341-9(1)) Bloomsbury Publishing Plc GBR. Dist: Independent Pubs. Group.

Pyle, Howard. Otto of the Silver Hand. 2008. 72p. pap. 8.15 (978-1-60459-556-7(6)) Wilder Pubns., Corp.

Rautenberg, Karen Rita. Lady Lucy's Gallant Knight. 2007. (ENG.). 156p. (J). (gr. 4-7). per. (978-1-933255-22-4(6)) DNA Pr.

Santillo, LuAnn. Medieval Magic, 6 vols. Santillo, LuAnn, ed. 2003. (Half-Pint Kids Readers Ser.). (Illus.). 42p. (J). (gr. -1-1). pap. 6.95 (978-1-59256-049-3(0)) Half-Pint Kids, Inc.

Service, Pamela F. The Wizards of Wyrd World. Gorman, Mike, illus. (Way-Too-Real Aliens Ser.: 3). (ENG.). 112p. (J). (gr. 4-6). 2015. 34.65 (978-1-4677-5962-5(7), Lerner Digital) 2013. pap. 6.95 (978-0-7613-7922-5(3), Darby Creek) 2012. 15.95 (978-0-7613-7920-1(7)) Lerner Publishing Group.

Sleiman, Dina L. Chivalrous. 2015. (Valiant Hearts Ser.: 2). (ENG.). 368p. (YA). pap. 16.00 (978-0-7642-1313-7(X)) Bethany Hse. Pubs.

—Courageous. 2016. (Valiant Hearts Ser.: 3). (ENG.). 368p. (YA). pap. 13.99 (978-0-7642-1314-4(8)) Bethany Hse. Pubs.

—Dauntless. 2015. (Valiant Hearts Ser.: 1). (ENG.). 368p. (YA). pap. 13.99 (978-0-7642-1312-0(1)) Bethany Hse. Pubs.

Smith, Danna. The Hawk of the Castle: A Story of Medieval Falconry. Ibatouilline, Bagram, illus. 2017. (ENG.). 40p. (J). (gr. -1-3). 16.99 (978-0-7636-7992-7(5)) Candlewick Pr.

Spradlin, Michael. Orphan of Destiny: Book 3, 3 vols. 2011. (Youngest Templar Ser.: 3). (ENG.). 272p. (J). (gr. 5-18). 7.99 (978-0-14-241959-5(1), Puffin Books) Penguin Young Readers Group.

Spradlin, Michael P. Keeper of the Grail, Bk. 1. 2009. (Youngest Templar Ser.: 1). (ENG.). 272p. (J). (gr. 5-6). 7.99 (978-0-14-241461-3(1), Puffin Books) Penguin Young Readers Group.

—Trail of Fate, 2 vols., Bk. 2. 2010. (Youngest Templar Ser.: 2). (ENG.). 256p. (J). (gr. 5-7). 7.99 (978-0-14-241707-2(6), Puffin Books) Penguin Young Readers Group.

Springer, Nancy. Wild Boy. 2005. (Tales of Rowan Hood Ser.). 115p. (J). (gr. 3). 13.65 (978-0-7569-5490-1(8)) Perfection Learning Corp.

Stine, Faye. The Golden Goblet: 200 Years in a Medieval Castle. 2013. (ENG.). 169p. (YA). pap. 12.95 (978-1-4787-1063-9(2)) Outskirts Pr., Inc.

Williams, Laura E. The Executioner's Daughter. 2007. (ENG.). 144p. (YA). (gr. 5-9). pap. 9.99 (978-0-8050-8186-2(0), 9780805081862, Holt, Henry & Co. Bks. For Young Readers) Holt, Henry & Co.

MIDDLE ATLANTIC STATES

see Atlantic States

MIDDLE EARTH (IMAGINARY PLACE)—FICTION

Tolkien, J. R. R. El Hobbit. 2003. (Lord of the Rings Ser.). (SPA.). 320p. (YA). 17.95 (978-84-450-7141-0(6), MQ9001) Minotauro Ediciones ESP. Dist: Distribooks, Inc.

—The Hobbit. Tolkien, J. R. R., illus. 70th anniv. ed. 2011. (ENG., Illus.). 400p. mass mkt. (978-0-261-10221-7(4)) HarperCollins Pubs. Ltd.

—The Hobbit. movie tie-in ed. 2012. lib. bdg. 19.65 (978-0-606-26240-8(7), Turtleback) Turtleback Bks.

—Senhor dos Aneis. pap. 36.95 (978-85-336-1337-9(7)) Livraria Martins Editora BRA. Dist: Distribooks, Inc.

MIDDLE EAST

Here are entered works on the region consisting of Asia west of Pakistan, northeastern Africa, and occasionally Greece and Pakistan. Works treating collectively the Arabic-speaking countries of Asia and Africa, or of Asia only, are entered under Arab Countries.

Alcraft, Rob. Dubai from the Sky. 2015. (Collins Big Cat Ser.). (ENG., Illus.). 24p. (J). (gr. 2-2). pap. 7.95 (978-0-00-759115-2(2)) HarperCollins Pubs. Ltd. GBR. Dist: Independent Pubs. Group.

Alcraft, Rob & Collins UK Publishing Staff. Dubai from the Sky. 2016. (Collins Big Cat Arabic Ser.). (ARA & ENG.). 24p. (J). pap. 6.95 (978-0-00-815653-4(0)) HarperCollins Pubs. Ltd. GBR. Dist: Independent Pubs. Group.

Brimson, Samuel. Sierra Leone-United Arab Emirates, 8 vols. 2003. (Nations of the World Ser.: Vol. 7). (Illus.). 64p. (gr. 5-12). lib. bdg. 31.00 (978-0-8368-5491-6(8), Gareth Stevens Secondary Library) Stevens, Gareth Publishing LLLP.

Conklin, Blane. Modern Middle East, 1 vol. 2007. (Primary Source Readers Ser.). (ENG.). 32p. (J). (gr. 5-5). pap. 8.99 (978-0-7439-0674-6(8)) Shell Educational Publishing.

Downing, David. Geography & Resources of the Middle East. 2006. (World Almanac Library of the Middle East). (Illus.). 48p. (gr. 5-12). pap. 14.05 (978-0-8368-7341-2(6)); lib. bdg. 31.00 (978-0-8368-7334-4(3)) Stevens, Gareth Publishing LLLP. (Gareth Stevens Secondary Library).

—Governments & Leaders of the Middle East. 2006. (World Almanac Library of the Middle East). (Illus.). 48p. (gr. 5-12). pap. 14.05 (978-0-8368-7342-9(4)); lib. bdg. 31.00 (978-0-8368-7335-1(1)) Stevens, Gareth Publishing LLLP. (Gareth Stevens Secondary Library).

Gelletly, LeeAnne. The Kurds. 2010. (Major Muslim Nations Ser.). (Illus.). 120p. (J). (gr. 5-18). lib. bdg. 25.95 (978-1-4222-1407-7(9)) Mason Crest.

Gunderson, Cory Gideon. Religions of the Middle East. 2003. (World in Conflict-the Middle East Ser.). 32p. (gr. 4-8). 27.07 (978-1-59197-412-3(7), Abdo & Daughters) ABDO Publishing Co.

Heing, Bridey. The Children Soldiers of ISIS. 2017. (J). **(978-0-7660-9211-2(9))** Enslow Pubs., Inc.

King, David C. The United Arab Emirates. 2007. (Cultures of the World Ser.). 144p. (gr. 6). lib. bdg. 42.79 (978-0-7614-2565-6(9), Benchmark Bks.) Marshall Cavendish Corp.

Kort, Michael G. The Handbook of the Middle East. 2007. (Handbook Of... Ser.). (Illus.). 320p. (YA). (gr. 7-12). lib. bdg. 39.93 (978-0-8225-7143-8(9)) Twenty First Century Bks.

The Making of the Middle East, 10 vols., Set. Incl. Arab-Israeli Relations, 1950-1979. Baughan, Brian. 80p. (YA). (gr. 3-7). 2009. lib. bdg. 22.95 (978-1-4222-0171-8(6)); Arabian Peninsula in the Age of Oil. Calvert, John. 88p. (YA). (gr. 3-7). 2009. lib. bdg. 22.95 (978-1-4222-0172-5(4)); Cold War in the Middle East, 1950-1991. Sasley, Brent. 80p. (YA). (gr. 7-18). 2009. lib. bdg. 22.95 (978-1-4222-0173-2(2)); First World War & the End of the Ottoman Order. Brennan, Kristine. 80p. (YA). (gr. 7-18). 2009. lib. bdg. 22.95 (978-1-4222-0168-8(6)); Iranian Revolution & the Resurgence of Islam. Rubin, Barry A. 88p. (YA). (gr. 7-18). 2009. lib. bdg. 22.95 (978-1-4222-0174-9(0)); Middle East in the Age of Uncertainty, 1991-Present. Rubin, Barry A. 78p. (YA). (gr. 3-7). 2009. lib. bdg. 22.95 (978-1-4222-0176-3(7)); Ottoman & Qajar Empires in the Age of Reform. Robbins, Gerald. 80p. (YA). (gr. 7-18). 2009. lib. bdg. 22.95 (978-1-4222-0167-1(8)); Palestine Mandate & the Creation of Israel, 1920-1949. Luxenberg, Alan. 80p. (J). (gr. 3-7). 2007. lib. bdg. 22.95 (978-1-4222-0170-1(8)); Rise of Nationalism: The Arab World, Turkey, & Iran. Spyer, Jonathan & Brown, Cameron. 80p. (YA). (gr. 7-18). 2007. lib. bdg. 22.95 (978-1-4222-0169-5(4)); Tensions in the Gulf, 1978-1991. Peterson, J. E. 88p. (J). (gr. 3-7). 2007. lib. bdg. 22.95 (978-1-4222-0175-6(9)); (Illus.). (Making of the Middle East Ser.). 2009. Set lib. bdg. 229.95 (978-1-4222-0166-4(X)) Mason Crest.

Marsh, Carole. Middle East: Ancient Countries of Current Events Headlines! 2009. (It's Your World Ser.). 48p. (J). (gr. 2-9). pap. 7.99 (978-0-635-06808-8(7)) Gallopade International.

McCoy, Lisa. Middle East: Facts & Figures. 2010. (Major Muslim Nations Ser.). 112p. (YA). (gr. 5-18). lib. bdg. 25.95 (978-1-4222-1400-8(1)) Mason Crest.

—United Arab Emirates. 2010. (Major Muslim Nations Ser.). (Illus.). 112p. (YA). (gr. 5-18). lib. bdg. 25.95 (978-1-4222-1390-2(0), 1306268) Mason Crest.

Miller, Debra A. The Middle East. 2007. (Current Controversies Ser.). (ENG., Illus.). 224p. (gr. 10-12). 46.40 (978-0-7377-3960-2(6)); pap. 32.00 (978-0-7377-3961-9(4), Greenhaven Pr., Inc.) Cengage Gale.

Somervill, Barbara A. United Arab Emirates. 2016. (Enchantment of the World Ser.). (ENG., Illus.). 144p. (J). lib. bdg. 40.00 (978-0-531-23298-9(0), Children's Pr.) Scholastic Library Publishing.

Stacey, Gill. Religions of the Middle East. 2006. (World Almanac Library of the Middle East). (Illus.). 48p. (gr. 5-12). pap. 14.05 (978-0-8368-7345-0(9)); lib. bdg. 31.00 (978-0-8368-7338-2(6)) Stevens, Gareth Publishing LLLP. (Gareth Stevens Secondary Library).

Townsend, Chris. The Violent Rise of ISIS. 2017. (J). **(978-0-7660-9210-5(0))** Enslow Pubs., Inc.

Wimmer, Teresa. Causes. 2011. (War on Terror Ser.). (Illus.). 48p. (J). (gr. 5-9). 34.25 (978-1-60818-097-4(2)) Creative Co., The.

Woods, Michael & Woods, Mary B. Seven Natural Wonders of Asia & the Middle East. 2009. (Seven Wonders Ser.). (ENG., Illus.). 80p. (gr. 5-8). 33.26 (978-0-8225-9073-6(5)) Lerner Publishing Group.

MIDDLE EAST—ANTIQUITIES

Down, David. Archaeology Book. 2009. 96p. (YA). 16.99 (978-0-89051-573-0(5)) Master Bks.

Heing, Bridey. The Cultural Destruction of ISIS. 2017. (J). **(978-0-7660-9215-0(1))** Enslow Pubs., Inc.

Robinson Jr., Charles Alexander. The First Book of Ancient Mesopotamia & Persi. 2011. 70p. 36.95 (978-1-258-10112-1(2)) Literary Licensing, LLC.

Tubb, Jonathan. DK Eyewitness Books: Bible Lands. 2016. (DK Eyewitness Bks.). (ENG., Illus.). 64p. (J). (gr. 3-7). pap. 9.99 (978-1-4654-4010-5(0), 1405880, DK Children) Dorling Kindersley Publishing, Inc.

MIDDLE EAST—DESCRIPTION AND TRAVEL

Collins Maps Staff. Atlas for the Middle East. 2014. (Collins Primary Geography Ser.). (ENG.). 72p. (J). pap. 14.99 (978-0-00-756370-8(1)) HarperCollins Pubs. Ltd. GBR. Dist: Independent Pubs. Group.

Feiler, Bruce. Walking the Bible: An Illustrated Journey for Kids Through the Greatest Stories Ever Told. Meret, Sasha, tr. Meret, Sasha, illus. 2004. 112p. (J). (gr. 2-7). 16.99 (978-0-06-051117-3(6)) HarperCollins Pubs.

Goldsworthy, Kaite. Burj Khalifa. 2012. (J). 27.13 (978-1-61913-252-8(4)); pap. 12.95 (978-1-61913-258-0(3)) Weigl Pubs., Inc.

Groner, Judye & Wikler, Madeline. Let's Visit Israel. Nathan, Cheryl, illus. 2004. (ENG.). 12p. (J). (gr. -1 — 1). 5.95 (978-1-58013-087-5(9), Kar-Ben Publishing) Lerner Publishing Group.

Kallen, Stuart. Burj Khalifa: The Tallest Tower in the World. 2014. (Great Idea Ser.). (ENG.). 48p. (J). (gr. 4-6). pap. 13.26 (978-1-60357-578-2(2)) Norwood Hse. Pr.

Kallen, Stuart A. Burj Khalifa: The Tallest Tower in the World. 2014. (Great Idea Ser.). (ENG.). 48p. (J). (gr. 4-6). lib. bdg. 26.60 (978-1-59953-598-2(X)) Norwood Hse. Pr.

MIDDLE EAST—FICTION

Addison, George R. Iii. When Mom Came Home. 2012. 32p. pap. 21.99 (978-1-4691-6406-9(X)) Xlibris Corp.

Al Mansour, Haifaa. The Green Bicycle. 2015. (ENG.). 352p. (J). (gr. 5). 16.99 (978-0-525-42806-0(2), Dial Bks) Penguin Young Readers Group.

Appelt, Kathi. Keeper. Hall, August, illus. 2010. (ENG.). 416p. (J). (gr. 3-7). 17.99 (978-1-4169-5060-8(5), Atheneum Bks. for Young Readers) Simon & Schuster Children's Publishing.

Bhoola, Prisha. Hashay Says Goodbye & Hello. 2013. 24p. pap. 22.68 (978-1-4669-9209-2(3)) Trafford Publishing.

Bowen, Carl & Fuentes, Benny. Dark Agent, 1 vol. Tortosa, Wilson, illus. 2014. (Shadow Squadron Ser.). (ENG.). 112p. (gr. 4-8). 26.65 (978-1-4342-9170-7(7)) Stone Arch Bks.

—Rogue Agent. Tortosa, Wilson, illus. 2015. (Shadow Squadron Ser.). (ENG.). 224p. (gr. 4-8). pap. 8.95 (978-1-62370-296-0(8)) Capstone Young Readers of Coughlan Cos.

—Steel Hammer. Tortosa, Wilson, illus. 2015. (Shadow Squadron Ser.). (ENG.). 112p. (gr. 4-8). lib. bdg. 26.65 (978-1-4965-0385-5(6)) Stone Arch Bks.

Carleson, J. C. The Tyrant's Daughter. 2015. (ENG.). 304p. (YA). (gr. 7). pap. 9.99 (978-0-449-80999-0(4), Ember) Random Hse. Children's Bks.

Center for Learning Staff. Habibi/Seven Daughters & Seven Sons: Novel Curriculum Unit. 2004. (Novel Ser.). 73p. (YA). tchr. ed., spiral bd. 19.95 (978-1-56077-770-0(2)) Center for Learning, The.

Clinton, Cathryn. A Stone in My Hand. 2010. (ENG., Illus.). 208p. (J). (gr. 5). pap. 6.99 (978-0-7636-4772-8(1)) Candlewick Pr.

Collingwood, Harry. The Cruise of The 'Esmeralda' 2009. 220p. pap. 15.95 (978-1-60664-391-4(6)) Rodgers, Alan Bks.

Cowley, Marjorie. The Golden Bull. 2012. (ENG.). 216p. (J). (gr. 4-7). pap. 8.95 (978-1-58089-182-0(9)) Charlesbridge Publishing, Inc.

Dahl, Michael. The Girl Who Breathed Fire. Piatti, Federico, illus. 2010. (Dragonblood Ser.). (ENG.). 40p. (gr. 1-3). lib. bdg. 23.99 (978-1-4342-1925-1(9), Zone Bks.) Stone Arch Bks.

E. O., Monalisa. Dan & Derrick's Prayer to the Troops. 2007. 36p. per. 16.95 (978-1-4327-0753-8(1)) Outskirts Pr., Inc.

Edwards, Wayne. Ali & the Magic Ball. Golden, Rayna, illus. 2009. 24p. pap. 12.50 *(978-1-60860-367-1(9),* Eloquent Bks.) Strategic Book Publishing & Rights Agency (SBPRA).
Ellis, Deborah. The Breadwinner Trilogy, 1 vol. 2009. (ENG.). 520p. (J). (gr. 4-9). pap. 18.95 *(978-0-88899-959-7(3))* Groundwood Bks. CAN. Dist: Publishers Group West (PGW).
Etheridge, Judy. Olivia's Wish. 2009. 32p. pap. 21.99 *(978-1-4415-3915-1(8))* Xlibris Corp.
Fletcher, Susan. Alphabet of Dreams. 2006. (ENG., Illus.). 304p. (YA). (gr. 7-12). 16.95 *(978-0-689-85042-4(5),* Atheneum Bks. for Young Readers) Simon & Schuster Children's Publishing.
Forbidden. 2014. (Forbidden Ser.: 1). (ENG.). 400p. (YA). (gr. 9). 17.99 *(978-0-06-219497-8(6))* HarperCollins Pubs.
Formento, Alison Ashley. Twigs. 2013. (ENG.). 272p. (YA). 17.99 *(978-1-4405-6565-6(1),* Simon Pulse) Simon Pulse.
Gormally, Eleanor. St Paul: The Man with the Letters. 2010. (ENG., Illus.). 32p. (J). pap. 16.95 *(978-1-84730-177-2(0))* Veritas Pubns. IRL. Dist: Dufour Editions, Inc.
Goscinny, René. The Caliph's Vacation. 2009. (Iznogoud Ser.: 2). (ENG., Illus.). 48p. (J). (gr. 4-7). pap. 11.95 *(978-1-905460-61-8(9))* CineBook GBR. Dist: National Bk. Network.
—The Grand Vizier Iznogoud, Vol. 9. Tabary, illus. 2012. (Iznogoud Ser.: 9). (ENG.). 52p. (J). (gr. 3-12). pap. 13.95 *(978-1-84918-131-0(4))* CineBook GBR. Dist: National Bk. Network.
—Iznogoud - The Infamous, Vol. 7. Tabary, illus. 2011. (Iznogoud Ser.: 7). (ENG.). 48p. (gr. 3-17). pap. 11.95 *(978-1-84918-074-0(1))* CineBook GBR. Dist: National Bk. Network.
—Iznogoud Vol. 10: Iznogoud the Relentless. Tabary, Jean, illus. 2013. (Iznogoud Ser.: 10). (ENG.). 48p. (J). (gr. 3-12). pap. 11.95 *(978-1-84918-181-5(0))* CineBook GBR. Dist: National Bk. Network.
—Rockets to Stardom - Iznogoud, Vol. 8. Tabary, illus. 2011. (Iznogoud Ser.: 8). (ENG.). 48p. pap. 11.95 *(978-1-84918-092-4(X))* CineBook GBR. Dist: National Bk. Network.
—The Wicked Wiles of Iznogoud, Vol. 1. Tabary, Armelle, illus. 2008. (Iznogoud Ser.: 1). (ENG.). 48p. (J). (gr. -1-12). pap. 13.95 *(978-1-905460-46-5(5))* CineBook GBR. Dist: National Bk. Network.
Goscinny, René & Tabary, Jean. A Carrot for Iznogoud, Vol. 5. 2010. (Iznogoud Ser.: 5). (ENG., Illus.). 48p. (J). (gr. 4-7). pap. 11.95 *(978-1-84918-021-4(0))* CineBook GBR. Dist: National Bk. Network.
Hancock, H. Irving. The Young Engineers on the Gulf. rev. ed. 2006. 216p. 27.95 *(978-1-4218-1752-1(7));* pap. 12.95 *(978-1-4218-1852-8(3))* 1st World Publishing, Inc. (1st World Library - Literary Society).
Hapka, Catherine, pseud. Yatimah. Sanderson, Ruth, illus. 2011. (Horse Diaries). (ENG.). 176p. (J). (gr. 3-7). pap. 7.99 *(978-0-375-86719-4(8),* Random Hse. Bks. for Young Readers) Random Hse. Children's Bks.
Hathorn, Sarah Alexandra. Teenagents: World Challenge. 2012. 240p. pap. 12.99 *(978-2-9700738-2-6(X))* Simon & Schuster, Inc.
Higgins, Jack & Richards, Justin. Sharp Shot. 2010. (Rich & Jade Ser.: Bk. 3). (ENG.). 240p. (YA). (gr. 7-18). 8.99 *(978-0-14-241730-0(0),* Speak) Penguin Young Readers Group.
Hillman, John E. Ancient Stories of the Hodj. 2012. (Illus.). 52p. pap. 27.45 *(978-1-4685-8215-4(1))* AuthorHouse.
Horowitz, Anthony. Scorpia Rising. (Alex Rider Ser.). (ENG.). (J). (gr. 5-18). 2012. 432p. 8.99 *(978-0-14-241985-4(0),* Puffin Books) 2011. 416p. 17.99 *(978-0-399-25057-6(3),* Philomel Bks.) Penguin Young Readers Group.
—Scorpia Rising, 9 vols. (J). 2012. 256.75 *(978-1-4561-3362-7(4))* 2012. 1.25 *(978-1-4640-0577-0(X))* 2012. 90.75 *(978-1-4561-3363-4(2))* 2011. 122.75 *(978-1-4561-3365-8(9))* 2011. 120.75 *(978-1-4561-3367-2(5))* Recorded Bks., Inc.
—Scorpia Rising. 2012. (Alex Rider Ser.: 9). lib. bdg. 19.65 *(978-0-606-23638-6(4),* Turtleback) Turtleback Bks.
Islam, M. N. Hamza's Journey of a Lifetime. 2012. 124p. pap. *(978-1-909395-70-1(6))* Legend Pr.
Jolin, Paula. In the Name of God. 2008. (ENG.). 224p. (YA). (gr. 9-12). pap. 18.99 *(978-0-312-38455-5(6),* 9780312384555) Square Fish.
Kimmel, Eric A. The Three Princes. Fisher, Leonard Everett, illus. 2005. (Ala Notable Book Ser.). (ENG.). 32p. (J). (gr. k-3). pap. 6.95 *(978-0-8234-1553-3(8))* Holiday Hse., Inc.
Kirby, Matthew J. Cave of Wonders. 2013. (Infinity Ring Ser.: 5). (ENG.). 192p. (J). (gr. 3-7). 16.99 *(978-0-545-48460-2(X))* Scholastic, Inc.
LaFevers, R. L. Flight of the Phoenix Bk. 1. Murphy, Kelly, illus. 2010. (Nathaniel Fludd, Beastologist Ser.: 1). (ENG.). 144p. (J). (gr. 1-4). pap. 5.99 *(978-0-547-40845-3(5))* Houghton Mifflin Harcourt Publishing Co.
Lieberman, Leanne. The Book of Trees, 1 vol. 2010. (ENG.). 256p. (YA). (gr. 8-12). pap. 12.95 *(978-1-55469-265-1(2))* Orca Bk. Pubs. USA.
Litrel, Suzanne. Jackie Tempo & the House of Wisdom. 2012. 150p. (gr. 10-12). 21.95 *(978-1-4620-5887-7(6));* pap. 11.95 *(978-1-4620-5886-0(8))* iUniverse, Inc.
Lough, Amber. The Blind Wish. 2015. (Jinni Wars Ser.: 2). (ENG.). 320p. (YA). (gr. 7). 17.99 *(978-0-385-36980-0(8),* Random Hse. Bks. for Young Readers) Random Hse. Children's Bks.
Luedke, Robert James. Eye Witness: A Fictional Tale of Absolute Truth. 2005. (Eye Witness Ser.). (ENG., Illus.). 96p. pap. 13.99 *(978-0-9758924-0-4(1));* lib. bdg. 24.99 *(978-0-9758924-1-1(X))* Head Pr. Publishing.
Marsden, Carolyn. The White Zone. (ENG.). 192p. (J). (gr. 4-8). 2014. pap. 9.95 *(978-1-4677-5177-3(4))* 2012. 17.95 *(978-0-7613-7383-4(7))* Lerner Publishing Group. (Carolrhoda Bks.).
Marston, Elsa. Figs & Fate: Stories about Growing up in the Arab World Today. 2005. (ENG.). 146p. (J). 22.50 *(978-0-8076-1551-5(X));* pap. 15.95 *(978-0-8076-1554-6(4))* Braziller, George Inc.
—Santa Claus in Baghdad & Other Stories about Teens in the Arab World. 2008. (ENG.). 216p. (gr. 3-7). pap. 15.95 *(978-0-253-22004-2(1),* 0253220041) Indiana Univ. Pr.
Mason, Prue. Camel Rider. 2011. 9.49 *(978-0-7848-3618-7(3),* Everbind) Marco Bk. Co.
Mazer, Harry & Lerangis, Peter. Somebody, Please Tell Me Who I Am. 2013. (ENG.). 160p. (YA). (gr. 7). pap. 9.99 *(978-1-4169-3896-5(6),* Simon & Schuster Bks. For Young Readers) Simon & Schuster Bks. For Young Readers.
McCormick, Patricia. Purple Heart. 2009. (ENG.). 208p. (YA). (gr. 8-18). 16.99 *(978-0-06-173090-0(4))* HarperCollins Pubs.
McKay, Sharon E. Enemy Territory. 2012. (ENG., Illus.). 200p. (YA). (gr. 6-10). 21.95 *(978-1-55451-431-1(2),* 9781554514311); pap. 12.95 *(978-1-55451-430-4(4),* 9781554514304) Annick Pr., Ltd. CAN. Dist: Publishers Group West (PGW).
Montgomery, R. A. Trouble on Planet Earth. 2007. 144p. (J). pap. *(978-1-86504-933-5(6))* Chooseco LLC.
—Trouble on Planet Earth. Trod, Mariano et al, illus. 2006. (Choose Your Own Adventure Ser.: No. 11). 144p. (J). (gr. 4-8). per. 6.99 *(978-1-933390-11-6(5),* CHCL11) Chooseco LLC.
—Trouble on Planet Earth. 2005. (Illus.). 113p. (J). pap. *(978-0-7608-9699-0(2))* Sundance/Newbridge Educational Publishing.
Myers, Walter Dean. Sunrise over Fallujah. 2009. (ENG.). 320p. (J). (gr. 7). 8.99 *(978-0-439-91625-7(9),* Scholastic Pr.) Scholastic, Inc.
—Sunrise over Fallujah. l.t. ed. 2008. 468p. (YA). 23.95 *(978-1-4104-1019-1(6))* Thorndike Pr.
Nye, Naomi Shihab. The Turtle of Oman. 2014. (ENG.). 304p. (J). (gr. 3-7). 16.99 *(978-0-06-201972-1(4))* HarperCollins Pubs.
Osborne, Mary Pope. Season of the Sandstorms. 2014. (Magic Tree House Merlin Missions Ser.: No. 6). 15.00 *(978-1-63419-681-9(3))* Perfection Learning Corp.
—Season of the Sandstorms. Murdocca, Sal, illus. 2006. (Magic Tree House Merlin Mission Ser.: No. 6). (ENG.). 144p. (J). (gr. 2-5). 5.99 *(978-0-375-83032-7(4),* Random Hse. Bks. for Young Readers) Random Hse. Children's Bks.
Osborne, Mary Pope, et al. La Estación de Las Tormentas de Arena. Murdocca, Sal, illus. 2016. (SPA.). (J). (gr. 2-4). pap. 5.99 ***(978-1-63245-644-1(3))*** Lectorum Pubns., Inc.
Parry, Rosanne. Heart of a Shepherd. 2010. (ENG.). 176p. (J). (gr. 3-7). pap. 7.99 *(978-0-375-84803-2(7),* Yearling) Random Hse. Children's Bks.
Powell, Martin. The Seven Voyages of Sinbad, 1 vol. Pérez, Daniel et al, illus. 2010. (Classic Fiction Ser.). (ENG.). 72p. (gr. 2-3). 27.99 *(978-1-4342-1987-9(9),* Graphic Revolve) Stone Arch Bks.
—The Seven Voyages of Sinbad. Pérez, Daniel et al, illus. 2010. (Classic Fiction Ser.). (ENG.). 72p. (gr. 2-3). pap. 7.15 *(978-1-4342-2775-1(8),* Graphic Revolve) Stone Arch Bks.
Raether, Erin F. When Auntie Angie Left for Iraq & Remi Came to Stay. 2008. 15p. pap. 24.95 *(978-1-4241-8735-5(4))* America Star Bks.
Romagnoli, L. M. The Worn-Out Backpack. Campbell, Lisa, illus. 2008. 15p. pap. 24.95 *(978-1-60563-934-5(6))* America Star Bks.
Rumford, James. Silent Music: A Story of Baghdad. Rumford, James, illus. 2008. (ENG., Illus.). 32p. (J). (gr. -1-3). 18.99 *(978-1-59643-276-5(4),* 9781596432765) Roaring Brook Pr.
Serafin, Mike. 7 Stories from Baghdad. 2005. 50p. pap. 16.95 *(978-1-4137-8808-2(4))* PublishAmerica, Inc.
Shah, Idries. The Silly Chicken. Jackson, Jeff, illus. 2005. 32p. (J). pap., pap. 6.99 *(978-1-883536-50-3(2),* Hoopoe Bks.) I S H K.
—The Silly Chicken/el Pollo Bobo. Wirkala, Rita, tr. Jackson, Jeff, illus. 2005. 32p. (J). (gr. -1-3). 18.00 *(978-1-883536-37-4(5),* Hoopoe Bks.) I S H K.
Smith, Chris. One City, Two Brothers. Fronty, Aurélia, illus. 2007. (ENG.). 32p. (J). (gr. -1-3). 16.99 *(978-1-84686-042-3(3))* Barefoot Bks., Inc.
Sovago-Royal, Sandra. Magimus. 2009. 33p. (J). pap. 19.95 *(978-1-4327-4375-8(9))* Outskirts Pr., Inc.
Summers, Susan. The Greatest Gift: The Story of the Other Wise Man. Morris, Jackie, illus. 2011. (ENG.). 30p. (J). 16.99 *(978-1-84686-578-7(6))* Barefoot Bks., Inc.
Townsend, S. P. The Star of Persia. 2008. 120p. pap. 12.50 *(978-1-84799-532-2(2))* Lulu Pr., Inc.
Weulersse, Odile & Merz, Kathleen. Nasreddine. Dautremer, Rebecca, illus. 2013. (ENG.). 34p. (J). 17.00 *(978-0-8028-5416-2(8),* Eerdmans Bks For Young Readers) Eerdmans, William B. Publishing Co.
Whelan, Gloria. Parade of Shadows. 2007. 304p. (J). (gr. 5-18). lib. bdg. 16.89 *(978-0-06-089029-2(0))* HarperCollins Pubs.
Williams, David Morgan. Ebony & Ivory. 2007. (ENG.). 136p. (J). pap. 11.95 *(978-0-86243-972-9(8))* Y Lolfa GBR. Dist: Dufour Editions, Inc.
Williams, Emma. The Story of Hurry. Quraishi, Ibrahim, illus. 2014. (ENG.). 38p. (J). (gr. -1-2). 16.95 *(978-1-60980-589-0(5),* Triangle Square) Seven Stories Pr.

MIDDLE EAST—HISTORY

ABDO Publishing Company Staff. World in Conflict-the Middle East. 2003. (World in Conflict-the Middle East Ser.). (gr. 4-8). 324.84 *(978-1-59197-409-3(7),* Abdo & Daughters) ABDO Publishing Co.
Adamson, Heather. United Arab Emirates. 2016. (Exploring Countries Ser.). (ENG., Illus.). 32p. (J). (gr. 3-7). lib. bdg. 26.95 *(978-1-62617-346-0(X),* Blastoff! Readers) Bellwether Media.
Bowden, Rob. The Middle East & North Africa. 2016. (Regions of the World Ser.). (ENG.). 64p. pap. 9.99 *(978-1-4846-4021-0(7),* NA-h) Heinemann-Raintree.
Bryan, Antonia D. United Arab Emirates. 2009. (True Book Ser.). (ENG.). 48p. (J). pap. 6.95 *(978-0-531-21361-2(7),* Children's Pr.) Scholastic Library Publishing.
Coletti, Sharon. Everything You Need to Teach the Middle East. 2005. (YA). ring bd. 149.95 *(978-1-933558-04-2(0))* InspirEd Educators.
Crisp, Peter. Mesopotamia: Iraq in Ancient Times. 2004. (Picturing the Past Ser.). (Illus.). 32p. (J). 15.95 *(978-1-59270-024-0(1))* Enchanted Lion Bks., LLC.
Darraj, Susan Muaddi & Puller, Meredyth. United Arab Emirates. 2008. (Creation of the Modern Middle East Ser.). (Illus.). 120p. (gr. 6-12). 35.00 *(978-1-60413-071-3(7),* Chelsea Hse.) Facts On File, Inc.
Davenport, John. A Brief Political & Geographic History of the Middle East: Where Are... Persia, Babylon, & the Ottoman Empire. 2007. (Places in Time Ser.). (Illus.). 112p. (YA). (gr. 5-9). lib. bdg. 37.10 *(978-1-58415-622-2(8))* Mitchell Lane Pubs., Inc.
DeCarlo, Carolyn. The Islamic Caliphate. 2017. (J). ***(978-1-68048-783-1(3),*** Britannica Educational Publishing) Rosen Publishing Group, Inc., The.
Dell, Pamela. Queen Noor. 2013. 128p. (YA). (gr. 7-12). 39.93 *(978-0-7614-4958-4(2));* pap. 19.99 *(978-1-62712-116-3(1))* Cavendish Square Publishing.
Doak, Robin. Empire of the Islamic World, Revised Edition. 2nd rev. ed. 2009. (Great Empires of the Past Ser.). (Illus.). 144p. (gr. 6-12). 35.00 *(978-1-60413-161-1(6),* Chelsea Hse.) Facts On File, Inc.
Don, Katherine. Nujood Ali & the Fight Against Child Marriage. 2014. (J). *(978-1-59935-466-8(7))* Reynolds, Morgan Inc.
Downing, David. Conflicts of the Middle East. 2006. (World Almanac Library of the Middle East). (Illus.). 48p. (gr. 5-12). pap. 14.05 *(978-0-8368-7340-5(8));* lib. bdg. 31.00 *(978-0-8368-7333-7(5))* Stevens, Gareth Publishing LLLP. (Gareth Stevens Secondary Library).
—History of the Middle East. 2006. (World Almanac Library of the Middle East). (Illus.). 48p. (gr. 5-12). pap. 14.05 *(978-0-8368-7343-6(2));* lib. bdg. 31.00 *(978-0-8368-7336-8(X))* Stevens, Gareth Publishing LLLP. (Gareth Stevens Secondary Library).
Doyle, Bill H. Behind Enemy Lines: Under Fire in the Middle East. 2011. 136p. (J). pap. *(978-0-545-33463-1(2))* Scholastic, Inc.
Eugster, Rachel & Whiting, Jim. The Role of Religion in the Early Islamic World. 2012. (ENG., Illus.). 48p. (J). lib. bdg. *(978-0-7787-2169-7(8))* Crabtree Publishing Co.
Flatt, Lizann. Early Islamic Empires. 2013. (ENG.). 48p. (J). lib. bdg. *(978-0-7787-2171-0(X))* Crabtree Publishing Co.
Gale. Middle East Conflict: Almanac. 2nd ed. 2012. (Middle East Conflict Reference Library). (ENG.). 400p. 106.00 *(978-1-4144-8608-6(1),* UXL) Cengage Gale.
—Middle East Conflict: Biographies. 2nd ed. 2012. (Middle East Conflict Reference Library). (ENG.). 400p. 106.00 *(978-1-4144-8609-3(X),* UXL) Cengage Gale.
—Middle East Conflict: Primary Sources. 2nd ed. 2012. (Middle East Conflict Reference Library). (ENG.). 400p. 106.00 *(978-1-4144-8610-9(3),* UXL) Cengage Gale.
—Middle East Conflict Reference Library, 3 vols. 2nd ed. 2012. (Middle East Conflict Reference Library). (ENG.). 1200p. 286.00 *(978-1-4144-8607-9(3));* (Illus.). 400p. 5.00 *(978-1-4144-8612-3(X))* Cengage Gale. (UXL).
Gelletly, LeeAnne. The Kurds, Vol. 13. 2015. (Major Nations of the Modern Middle East Ser.). (Illus.). 120p. (J). (gr. 7). lib. bdg. 25.95 *(978-1-4222-3454-9(1))* Mason Crest.
Gillespie, Frances & Al-Naimi, Faisal. Hidden in the Sands: Uncovering Qatar's Past. 2013. (ENG., Illus.). 48p. pap. 12.99 *(978-1-909339-06-4(7))* Medina Publishing, Ltd. GBR. Dist: Casemate Pubs. & Bk. Distributors, LLC.
—Hidden in the Sands - Arabic: Uncovering Qatar's Past. 2013. (ARA., Illus.). 48p. pap. 12.99 *(978-1-909339-03-3(2))* Medina Publishing, Ltd. GBR. Dist: Casemate Pubs. & Bk. Distributors, LLC.
Hampton, Wilborn. War in the Middle East: A Reporter's Story: Black September & the Yom Kippur War. (ENG., Illus.). 128p. (J). (gr. 5). 2009. pap. 9.99 *(978-0-7636-4376-8(9))* 2007. 19.99 *(978-0-7636-2493-4(4))* Candlewick Pr.
Hudak, Heather C. A Refugee's Journey from Yemen. 2017. 32p. (J). ***(978-0-7787-3677-6(6))*** Crabtree Publishing Co.
January, Brendan. Isis: The Global Face of Terrorism. 2017. (ENG.). (J). (gr. 8-12). 37.32 ***(978-1-5124-2998-5(8),*** Twenty-First Century Bks.) Lerner Publishing Group.
Kent, Deborah. Middle Eastern Migration, 1 vol. 2011. (Children's True Stories: Migration Ser.). (ENG.). 32p. (gr. 3-3). 30.65 *(978-1-4109-4073-5(X),* Raintree Perspectives) Heinemann-Raintree.
Kerrigan, Michael, et al. Exploring the Life, Myth, & Art of the Ancient near East. 2016. (Civilizations of the World Ser.). (ENG.). 144p. (J). (gr. 8-8). lib. bdg. 45.10 *(978-1-4994-6397-2(9))* Rosen Publishing Group, Inc., The.
Krasner, Barbara. Ancient Mesopotamian Daily Life. 2016. (Spotlight on the Rise & Fall of Ancient Civilizations Ser.). 48p. (J). (gr. 6-6). pap. 11.75 *(978-1-4777-8905-6(7))* Rosen Publishing Group, Inc., The.
Liberman, Sherri. A Historical Atlas of Azerbaijan. 2009. (Historical Atlases of South Asia, Central Asia, & the Middle East Ser.). 64p. (gr. 6-6). 61.20 *(978-1-61513-316-1(X))* Rosen Publishing Group, Inc., The.
LoBaido, Anthony C., et al. The Kurds of Asia. 2005. (First Peoples Ser.). (Illus.). 48p. (gr. 4-8). lib. bdg. 23.95 *(978-0-8225-0664-5(5))* Lerner Publishing Group.
Lowery, Zoe & Levy, Janey. The Darfur Genocide. 2016. (Bearing Witness: Genocide & Ethnic Cleansing in the Modern World Ser.). 64p. (J). (gr. 6-6). 34.45 *(978-1-4994-6306-4(5))* Rosen Publishing Group, Inc., The.
Lucks, Naomi. Makeda (Queen of Sheba) 2008. (Ancient World Leaders Ser.). 112p. (gr. 6-12). 30.00 *(978-0-7910-9579-9(7),* Chelsea Hse.) Facts On File, Inc.
Macaulay, David. Mosque. 2008. (ENG., Illus.). 96p. (YA). (gr. 4-7). pap. 9.95 *(978-0-547-01547-7(X))* Houghton Mifflin Harcourt Publishing Co.
Malaspina, Ann & Woog, Adam. Nubia. 2012. (Lost Worlds & Mysterious Civilizations Ser.). (Illus.). 104p. (gr. 6-12). 35.00 *(978-1-60413-973-0(0),* Chelsea Hse.) Facts On File, Inc.
Matters, Print & Blackwell, Amy Hackney. Lent, Yom Kippur, & Other Atonement Days. 2009. (Holidays & Celebration Ser.). (Illus.). 112p. (gr. 5-8). 40.00 *(978-1-60413-100-0(4),* Chelsea Hse.) Facts On File, Inc.
Maury, Rob. Immigration from the Middle East. 2005. (Changing Face of North America Ser.). (Illus.). 112p. (YA). lib. bdg. 24.95 *(978-1-59084-695-7(8))* Mason Crest.
Maxim, Bailey, ed. The Colonial & Postcolonial Middle East. 2016. (Colonial & Postcolonial Experience Ser.). 00128p. (J). (gr. 10-10). 54.00 *(978-1-5081-0437-7(9),* Britannica Educational Publishing) Rosen Publishing Group, Inc., The.
O'Neal, Claire. We Visit Yemen. 2011. (Your Land & My Land Ser.). (Illus.). 64p. (J). (gr. 4-7). lib. bdg. 33.95 *(978-1-58415-961-2(8))* Mitchell Lane Pubs., Inc.
Perliger, Arie. Middle Eastern Terrorism. Eubank, Bill, ed. 2006. (Roots of Terrorism Ser.). (Illus.). 111p. (gr. 6-12). 35.00 *(978-0-7910-8309-3(8),* Chelsea Hse.) Facts On File, Inc.
Podany, Amanda H. & McGee, Marni. The Ancient near Eastern World. 2005. (World in Ancient Times Ser.). (ENG., Illus.). 176p. (YA). (gr. 7-12). 36.95 *(978-0-19-516159-5(9))* Oxford Univ. Pr., Inc.
Rauf, Don. Near East, Vol. 10. 2016. (Social Progress & Sustainability Ser.). (Illus.). 80p. (J). (gr. 7). 24.95 *(978-1-4222-3497-6(5))* Mason Crest.
Rice Jr., Earle. Islamic State. 2017. lib. bdg. 29.95 ***(978-1-68020-055-3(0))*** Mitchell Lane Pubs., Inc.
Rodger, Ellen. A Refugee's Journey from South Sudan. 2017. 32p. (J). ***(978-0-7787-3676-9(8))*** Crabtree Publishing Co.
Romanek, Trudee. Science, Medicine, & Math in the Early Islamic World. 2012. (ENG.). 48p. (J). lib. bdg. *(978-0-7787-2170-3(1))* Crabtree Publishing Co.
Romano, Amy. A Historical Atlas of United Arab Emirates. 2004. (Historical Atlases of South Asia, Central Asia, & the Middle East Ser.). (Illus.). 64p. (gr. 7-12). lib. bdg. 31.95 *(978-0-8239-4501-6(4))* Rosen Publishing Group, Inc., The.
—A Historical Atlas of Yemen. 2004. (Historical Atlases of South Asia, Central Asia, & the Middle East Ser.). (Illus.). 64p. (gr. 7-12). lib. bdg. 31.95 *(978-0-8239-4502-3(2))* Rosen Publishing Group, Inc., The.
Rubin, Barry A. The Middle East in the Age of Uncertainty, 1991-Present. 2009. (Making of the Middle East Ser.). (Illus.). 78p. (YA). (gr. 3-7). lib. bdg. 22.95 *(978-1-4222-0176-3(7))* Mason Crest.
Scheppler, Bill. Al-Biruni: Master Astronomer & Muslim Scholar of the Eleventh Century. 2009. (Great Muslim Philosophers & Scientists of the Middle Ages Ser.). 112p. (gr. 6-6). 66.50 *(978-1-61513-177-8(9),* Rosen Reference) Rosen Publishing Group, Inc., The.
Senker, Cath. Israel & the Middle East. 2011. (Our World Divided Ser.). (ENG.). 48p. (YA). (gr. 5-8). 27.95 *(978-1-4488-6032-6(6),* Rosen Reference) Rosen Publishing Group, Inc., The.
Stefoff, Rebecca. The Ancient Near East. 2004. (World Historical Atlases Ser.). (J). 31.36 *(978-0-7614-1639-5(0),* Benchmark Bks.) Marshall Cavendish Corp.
Stokes, Jamie. The Muslim World. 2010. (Global Issues Ser.). 400p. (C). (gr. 9). 45.00 *(978-0-8160-8086-1(0))* Facts On File, Inc.
Understanding the Cultures of the Middle East. 2016. (Understanding the Cultures of the Middle East Ser.). 112p. (YA). lib. bdg. 171.16 *(978-1-5026-2372-0(2))* Cavendish Square Publishing.
Wagner, Heather Lehr. The Division of the Middle East: The Treaty of Sevres. 2004. (Arbitrary Borders Ser.). (Illus.). 120p. (C). (gr. 9-13). 35.00 *(978-0-7910-7831-0(0),* Chelsea Hse.) Facts On File, Inc.
Warms, Ed. Immigration to North America: Middle Eastern Immigrants, Vol. 11. Anderson, Stuart, ed. 2016. (Immigration to North America Ser.: Vol. 11). (ENG., Illus.). 112p. (J). (gr. 7-12). 25.95 *(978-1-4222-3689-5(7))* Mason Crest.
Young Voices from the Arab World: The Lives & Times of Five Teenagers. 2004. 139p. (YA). (gr. 5-18). tchr. ed. 35.00 incl. VHS *(978-0-913957-15-8(1))* AMIDEAST.

MIDDLE EAST—POLITICS AND GOVERNMENT

Burns, Jann. Can Democracy Succeed in the Middle East? Einfeld, Jann, ed. 2006. (At Issue Ser.). (ENG., Illus.). 128p. (gr. 10-12). 39.40 *(978-0-7377-3393-8(4))* Cengage Gale.
Conklin, Blane. Leaders of the Middle East, 1 vol. 2007. (Primary Source Readers Ser.). (ENG.). 32p. (J). (gr. 4-4). pap. 8.99 *(978-0-7439-0675-3(6))* Shell Educational Publishing.
Foreign Policy Research Institute Staff, ed. Modern Middle East Nations & Their Strategic Places in the World, 25 vols., Set. 2003. (Illus.). 112,128p. (YA). (gr. 7-18). lib. bdg. *(978-1-59084-504-2(8))* Mason Crest.
Gunderson, Cory Gideon. The Need for Oil. 2003. (World in Conflict-the Middle East Ser.). 32p. (gr. 4-8). 27.07 *(978-1-59197-417-8(8),* Abdo & Daughters) ABDO Publishing Co.
Haugen, David M., et al. Iraq. 2009. (Opposing Viewpoints Ser.). (ENG., Illus.). 240p. (YA). (gr. 10-12). 29.45 *(978-0-7377-4525-2(8),* LML02109-246006);No. 9. pap. 42.95 *(978-0-7377-4524-5(X),* LML02109-245978) Cengage Gale. (Greenhaven Pr., Inc.).
Heing, Bridget. Geography, Government, & Conflict Across the Middle East. 2016. (Understanding the Cultures of the Middle East Ser.). 112p. (YA). lib. bdg. 42.79 *(978-1-5026-2367-6(6))* Cavendish Square Publishing.
Hunnicutt, Susan C. The Middle East Peace Process. 2010. (Opposing Viewpoints Ser.). (ENG.). 224p. (gr. 10-12). 48.80 *(978-0-7377-4976-2(8));* pap. 33.80 *(978-0-7377-4977-9(6))* Cengage Gale. (Greenhaven Pr., Inc.).
Romanek, Trudee. Government & Law in the Early Islamic World. 2013. (ENG.). 48p. (J). lib. bdg. *(978-0-7787-2168-0(X))* Crabtree Publishing Co.
Sasley, Brent. The Cold War in the Middle East, 1950-1991. 2009. (Making of the Middle East Ser.). (Illus.). 80p. (YA). (gr. 7-18). lib. bdg. 22.95 *(978-1-4222-0173-2(2))* Mason Crest.
Steele, Philip. Uprisings in the Middle East & North Africa. 2016. (Illus.). 48p. (J). *(978-0-7787-2589-3(8))* Crabtree Publishing Co.
Wagner, Heather Lehr. Anwar Sadat & Menachem Begin: Negotiating Peace in the Middle East. 2007. (Modern Peacemakers Ser.). (Illus.). 122p. (YA). (gr. 9-12). lib. bdg. 30.00 *(978-0-7910-9000-8(0))* Facts On File, Inc.
Witte, Sam. Gamal Abdel Nasser. 2009. (Middle East Leaders Ser.). 112p. (gr. 5-8). 66.50 *(978-1-61514-646-8(6),* Rosen Reference) Rosen Publishing Group, Inc., The.
Woog, Adam. The Palestinian National Authority. 2nd rev. ed. 2008. (Creation of the Modern Middle East Ser.). (Illus.). 136p. (gr. 6-12). 35.00 *(978-1-60413-020-1(2),* Chelsea Hse.) Facts On File, Inc.

MIDDLE STATES

see Atlantic States

MIDDLE WEST

Here are entered works on the region of the United States between the Rocky Mountains and the Allegheny Mountains and north of the Ohio River and the southern border of Missouri and Kansas, generally including the states of Ohio, Indiana, Michigan, Illinois, Wisconsin, Minnesota, Iowa, Missouri, Kansas, Nebraska, South Dakota and North Dakota.

Benchmark Education Company. The Midwest Region (Teacher Guide) 2005. *(978-1-4108-4653-2(9))* Benchmark Education Co.
Codell, Esmé Raji. Seed by Seed: The Legend & Legacy of John Appleseed Anniversary. Perkins, Lynne Rae, illus. 2012. 32p. (J). (gr. -1-3). 17.89 *(978-0-06-145516-2(4),* Greenwillow Bks.) HarperCollins Pubs.
—Seed by Seed: The Legend & Legacy of John Appleseed Chapman. Perkins, Lynne Rae, illus. 2012. (ENG.). 32p. (J). (gr. -1-3). 16.99 *(978-0-06-145515-5(6),* Greenwillow Bks.) HarperCollins Pubs.
Leonardo, Victoria. The Midwest Region. 2005. (J). pap. *(978-1-4108-4605-1(9))* Benchmark Education Co.
Miller, Reagan & Johnson, Robin. What's in the Midwest? Crabtree Publishing Staff, ed. 2011. (All Around the U.S. Ser.). (ENG.). 32p. (J). (gr. 3-6). pap. *(978-0-7787-1829-1(8))* Crabtree Publishing Co.
—What's in the Midwest? 2011. (ENG.). 32p. (J). lib. bdg. *(978-0-7787-1823-9(9))* Crabtree Publishing Co.
Orr, Tamra B. It's Cool to Learn about the United States Midwest. 2011. (Explorer Library: Social Studies Explorer Ser.). (ENG.). 48p. (gr. 4-8). pap. 15.64 *(978-1-61080-302-1(7),* 201198) Cherry Lake Publishing.
Radomski, Kassandra. People & Places of the Midwest. 2016. (United States by Region Ser.). (ENG., Illus.). 32p. (gr. 3-4). lib. bdg. 27.32 *(978-1-5157-2440-7(9),* Fact Finders) Capstone Press of Coughlan Cos.
Roop, Peter & Roop, Connie. Explore the Midwest. 2007. (Language, Literacy, & Vocabulary - Reading Expeditions Ser.). (ENG., Illus.). 36p. (J). pap. 18.95 *(978-0-7922-5458-4(9))* CENGAGE Learning.
Schaeffer, Julia. The Midwest States: Set Of 6. 2011. (Navigators Ser.). (J). pap. 48.00 net. *(978-1-4108-6253-2(4))* Benchmark Education Co.
Schaffer, Julia. The Midwest States: Text Pairs. 2008. (Bridges/Navigators Ser.). (J). (gr. 4). 89.00 *(978-1-4108-8390-2(6))* Benchmark Education Co.
U. S. National Geographic Society Staff, contrib. by. The Midwest Today. 2007. (Reading Expeditions Ser.). (ENG., Illus.). 32p. (J). pap. 17.95 *(978-0-7922-4534-6(2))* CENGAGE Learning.
Wiseman, Blaine. The Midwest. 2016. (Illus.). 48p. (J). *(978-1-5105-1136-1(9))* SmartBook Media, Inc.
Yomtov, Nel. The Children's Blizzard Of 1888: A Cause-And-Effect Investigation. 2016. (Cause-And-Effect Disasters Ser.). (ENG., Illus.). 40p. (J). (gr. 4-6). lib. bdg. 30.65 *(978-1-5124-1118-8(3))* Lerner Publishing Group.

MIDDLE WEST—FICTION

Bean, Margo Cronbaugh. Brutus the Bull. Perry, Aumi Kauffman, illus. 2013. 24p. 19.95 *(978-1-61633-373-7(1));* pap. 11.95 *(978-1-61633-374-4(X))* Guardian Angel Publishing, Inc.
Chand, Emlyn. Farsighted. 2012. 260p. pap. 12.95 *(978-0-9839308-3-9(X))* Blue Crown Pr.
Damron, Dugan. Further Adventures of Old Shorty: Tales of a Midwest Country Boy, 1 vol. 2010. 112p. pap. 19.95 *(978-1-4489-5838-2(5))* America Star Bks.
Geisert, Arthur, creator. Thunderstorm. 2015. (ENG., Illus.). 34p. (J). (gr. k). 60.00 *(978-1-59270-170-4(1))* Enchanted Lion Bks., LLC.
Hammond, John, as told by. Lucky in Life. 2003. 150p. (YA). per. 13.95 *(978-1-885631-76-3(6))* Hutchison, G.F. Pr.
Kegerreis, Carl. Tibby & His Friend's Big Secret. 2010. 96p. pap. 13.95 *(978-1-4327-4449-6(6))* Outskirts Pr., Inc.
Kraus, Daniel. Rotters. 2012. (ENG.). 464p. (YA). (gr. 9). pap. 10.99 *(978-0-385-73858-3(7),* Ember) Random Hse. Children's Bks.
L'Allier, Peter Wesley Thomas. Rotten Robbie & the Legend of Wanabinoo. 2006. (Illus.). 215p. 18.95 *(978-0-9724022-8-6(4))* TangleTown Media Inc.
Lewis, Richard. The Demon Queen. 2012. (ENG.). 240p. (YA). (gr. 7). pap. 11.99 *(978-1-4169-3590-2(8),* Simon & Schuster Bks. For Young Readers) Simon & Schuster Bks. For Young Readers.
Lillehaug-Collins, Yvonne. Little Dragon. 2009. 70p. pap. 21.00 *(978-1-60693-344-2(2),* Eloquent Bks.) Strategic Book Publishing & Rights Agency (SBPRA).
Macaraeg, Diane. Last Meal. 2008. 132p. pap. *(978-3-639-03548-3(8))* AV Akademikerverlag GmbH & Co. KG.
Peck, Richard. The Ghost Belonged to Me. 2005. 176p. (YA). 21.00 *(978-0-8446-7275-5(0),* 3590) Smith, Peter Pub., Inc.
Rapp, Adam. 33 Snowfish. Ering, Timothy Basil, illus. 2006. (ENG.). 192p. (YA). (gr. 9-12). per. 7.99 *(978-0-7636-2917-5(0))* Candlewick Pr.
Tilson, Gina L. Patches: Adventures of a Country Cavalier. 2011. 48p. pap. 9.99 *(978-1-4567-6386-2(5))* AuthorHouse.
Wargin, Kathy-jo. Mitt & Minn at the Wisconsin Cheese Jamboree. Holman, Karen Busch, illus. 2007. (Mitt Midwest Ser.: 3). (ENG.). 144p. (J). (gr. k-7). 14.95 *(978-1-58726-305-7(X),* Mitten Pr.) Ann Arbor Editions LLC.
—Mitt & Minn's Illinois Adventure. Holman, Karen Busch, illus. 2007. (Mitt Midwest Ser.: 4). (ENG.). 144p. (J). (gr. k-7). 14.95 *(978-1-58726-306-4(8),* Mitten Pr.) Ann Arbor Editions LLC.
Weaver, Will. Checkered Flag Cheater. 2010. (Motor Novels Ser.: 3). (ENG.). 208p. (YA). (gr. 7-12). 19.99 *(978-0-374-35062-8(0),* 9780374350628, Farrar, Straus & Giroux (BYR)) Farrar, Straus & Giroux.
Weber, Richard D. Elvis & Me. 2004. 511p. (YA). per. 17.41 *(978-1-4116-0549-7(7))* Lulu Pr., Inc.
Wilder, Laura Ingalls. Pioneer Sisters. Kim, Ji-Hyuk, illus. 2017. (Little House Chapter Book Ser.: 2). 112p. (J). (gr. 1-5). pap. 4.99 *(978-0-06-237710-4(8))* HarperCollins Pubs.

MIDDLE WEST—HISTORY

Allen, Nancy. Midwest & Great Lakes Regions. 2014. (ENG.). 32p. (gr. 3-5). 32.79 *(978-1-62717-671-2(3))* Rourke Educational Media.
Benjamin, Margaret. Johnny Appleseed. 2014. (Illus.). 31p. (J). pap. *(978-1-62712-278-8(8))* Cavendish Square Publishing.
Blair, Eric. Johnny Appleseed, 1 vol. Muehlenhardt, Amy Bailey, illus. 2011. (My First Classic Story Ser.).Tr. of Johnny Appleseed. (ENG.). 32p. (gr. k-3). pap. 7.10 *(978-1-4048-7367-4(8),* My First Classic Story) Picture Window Bks.
Brannon, Barbara. Discover the Midwest Region. 2005. (J). pap. *(978-1-4108-5151-2(6))* Benchmark Education Co.
Burkes-Larrañaga, Dustin, illus. Johnny Appleseed Plants Trees Across the Land, 1 vol. 2014. (American Folk Legends Ser.). (ENG.). 32p. (gr. k-2). lib. bdg. 27.32 *(978-1-4795-5428-7(6))* Picture Window Bks.
Chandler, Matt. Bachelor's Grove Cemetery & Other Haunted Places of the Midwest, 1 vol. 2014. (Haunted America Ser.). (ENG.). 32p. (gr. 3-4). lib. bdg. 27.99 *(978-1-4765-3913-3(8),* Edge Bks.) Capstone Press of Coughlan Cos.
Connors, Kathleen. Let's Explore the Midwest. 2013. (Road Trip: Exploring America's Regions Ser.). 24p. (J). (gr. 2-5). pap. 8.15 *(978-1-4339-9130-1(6));* (ENG., Illus.). lib. bdg. 22.60 *(978-1-4339-9129-5(2))* Stevens, Gareth Publishing LLLP.
Doherty, Kieran. Voyageurs, Lumberjacks & Farmers: Pioneers of the Midwest. 2003. (Shaping America Ser.: Vol. 5). (Illus.). 176p. (gr. 7-18). lib. bdg. 22.95 *(978-1-881508-54-0(4))* Oliver Pr., Inc.
Garland, Sherry. Voices of the Dust Bowl, 1 vol. Hierstein, Judith, illus. 2012. (Voices of History Ser.). (ENG.). 40p. (J). (gr. 3-3). 17.99 *(978-1-58980-964-2(5))* Pelican Publishing Co., Inc.
Herschbach, Elisabeth. Lower Plains: Kansas, Nebraska, Vol. 19. 2015. (Let's Explore the States Ser.). (Illus.). 64p. (J). (gr. 5). 23.95 *(978-1-4222-3326-9(X))* Mason Crest.
Let's Explore the Midwest. 2013. (Road Trip: Exploring America's Regions Ser.). 24p. (J). (gr. 2-5). pap. 48.90 *(978-1-4339-9131-8(4))* Stevens, Gareth Publishing LLLP.
Meachen-Rau, Dana. The Midwest. 2012. (True Book Ser.). (ENG., Illus.). 48p. (J). pap. 6.95 *(978-0-531-28325-7(9),* Children's Pr.) Scholastic Library Publishing.
The Midwest. 2014. (Land That I Love: Regions of the United States Ser.). (Illus.). 32p. (J). (gr. 3-6). pap. 60.00 *(978-1-4777-6637-8(5),* PowerKids Pr.) Rosen Publishing Group, Inc., The.
Miller, Dean & Talbot, Jeffrey. Johnny Appleseed. 2014. (Illus.). 32p. (J). 28.50 *(978-1-62712-277-1(X))* Cavendish Square Publishing.
Orr, Tamra B. Midwest. 2011. (Explorer Library: Social Studies Explorer Ser.). (ENG.). 48p. (gr. 4-8). lib. bdg. 31.36 *(978-1-61080-179-9(2),* 201152) Cherry Lake Publishing.
Rau, Dana Meachen. The Midwest. 2012. (True Book Ser.). (ENG., Illus.). 48p. (J). (gr. 3-5). 29.00 *(978-0-531-24850-8(X),* Children's Pr.) Scholastic Library Publishing.
Vander Hook, Sue. Southern Atlantic Coast Region. 2014. (ENG.). 32p. (gr. 3-5). 32.79 *(978-1-62717-676-7(4))* Rourke Educational Media.
Westcott, Jim. Upper Plains: Montana, North Dakota, South Dakota, Vol. 19. 2015. (Let's Explore the States Ser.). (Illus.). 64p. (J). (gr. 5). 23.95 *(978-1-4222-3336-8(7))* Mason Crest.
Wiseman, Blaine. The Midwest. 2014. (Illus.). 32p. (J). *(978-1-4896-1226-7(2))* Weigl Pubs., Inc.
Yomtov, Nel. The Children's Blizzard Of 1888: A Cause-And-Effect Investigation. 2016. (Cause-And-Effect Disasters Ser.). (ENG., Illus.). 40p. (J). (gr. 4-6). 46.65 *(978-1-5124-1129-4(9),* Lerner Pubns.) Lerner Publishing Group.

MIDGETS

see Dwarfs

MIDWAY, BATTLE OF, 1942

Abnett, Dan. The Battle of Midway: The Destruction of the Japanese Fleet. Elson, Richard, illus. 2007. (Graphic Battles of World War II Ser.). (ENG.). 48p. (YA). (gr. 4-7). lib. bdg. 31.95 *(978-1-4042-0783-7(X))* Rosen Publishing Group, Inc., The.
Mara, Wil. The Battle of Midway: Turning the Tide of World War II. 2017. (Major Battles in US History (paperback) Ser.). (ENG., Illus.). 32p. (J). (gr. 4-7). pap. 9.95 ***(978-1-63517-077-1(X),*** Focus Readers) North Star Editions.
White, Steve. The Battle of Midway: The Destruction of the Japanese Fleet. 2008. (Graphic Battles of World War II Ser.). (ENG., Illus.). 48p. (gr. 3-8). pap. 14.05 *(978-1-4042-7424-2(3))* Rosen Publishing Group, Inc., The.

MIDWEST

see Middle West

MIDWIFERY

see Childbirth

MIGRANT LABOR

Here are entered works dealing with casual or seasonal workers who move from place to place in search of employment. Works on the movement of population within a country for permanent settlement are entered under Migration, Internal.

Cruz, Bárbara C. César Chávez: Civil Rights Activist. 2016. (Influential Latinos Ser.). (ENG.). 128p. (J). (gr. 7-8). lib. bdg. 37.27 *(978-0-7660-7179-7(0))* Enslow Pubs., Inc.
Dunn, Joeming W. Cesar Chavez, 1 vol. Espinosa, Rod, illus. 2008. (Bio-Graphics Ser.). (ENG.). 32p. (gr. 3-5). 28.50 *(978-1-60270-172-4(5),* Graphic Planet- Nonfiction) ABDO Publishing Co.
Herrera, Juan Felipe. El Canto de las Palomas/Calling the Doves. 2004. (Illus.). (J). (gr. 3-6). spiral bd. *(978-0-616-14607-1(8))* Canadian National Institute for the Blind/Institut National Canadien pour les Aveugles.
Kent, Deborah. Migrant Farmworkers: Hoping for a Better Life. 2005. (Proud Heritage: the Hispanic Library). (ENG., Illus.). 40p. (J). (gr. 3-6). 29.93 *(978-1-59296-386-7(2),* 200012) Child's World, Inc., The.
Zuchora-Walske, Christine. The Dust Bowl: A History Perspectives Book. 2013. (Perspectives Library). (ENG., Illus.). 32p. (J). (gr. 4-8). 28.50 *(978-1-62431-417-9(1),* 202788); pap. 14.21 *(978-1-62431-493-3(7),* 202790) Cherry Lake Publishing.

MIGRANT LABOR—FICTION

Altman, Linda Jacobs. El Camino de Amelia. 2004. (SPA., Illus.). (J). (gr. k-3). spiral bd. *(978-0-616-14603-3(5))* Canadian National Institute for the Blind/Institut National Canadien pour les Aveugles.
Alvarez, Julia. Devolver Al Remitente. 2010.Tr. of Return to Sender. (SPA & ENG.). 368p. (J). (gr. 3-7). 7.99 *(978-0-375-85124-7(0),* Yearling) Random Hse. Children's Bks.
—Return to Sender. 2010. (ENG.). 352p. (J). (gr. 3-7). 6.99 *(978-0-375-85123-0(2),* Yearling) Random Hse. Children's Bks.
Castillo, Gary D. Quesadilla Moon. 2007. 100p. (J). (gr. 3-7). per. 9.95 *(978-1-55885-433-8(9),* Piñata Books) Arte Publico Pr.
Gonzalez, Genaro. A So-Called Vacation. 2009. 192p. (YA). (gr. 9-18). pap. 10.95 *(978-1-55885-545-8(9),* Piñata Books) Arte Publico Pr.
Literature Connections English: ... & the Earth Did Not Devour Him. 2004. (gr. 6-12). *(978-0-395-77139-6(0),* 2-70217) Holt McDougal.
Lord, Cynthia. A Handful of Stars. 2015. (ENG.). 192p. (J). (gr. 3-7). 16.99 *(978-0-545-70027-6(2),* Scholastic Pr.) Scholastic, Inc.
Lowery, Linda. Truth & Salsa, 1 vol. (ENG.). 176p. (J). 2009. pap. 7.95 *(978-1-56145-498-3(2))* 2006. (gr. 3-7). 15.95 *(978-1-56145-366-5(8))* Peachtree Pubs.
Mora, Pat. Tomas & the Library Lady. Colón, Raúl, illus. 2007. (gr. k-3). 18.00 *(978-0-7569-7935-5(8))* Perfection Learning Corp.
—Tomas y la Senora de la Biblioteca. 2004. (SPA., Illus.). (J). (gr. k-3). spiral bd. *(978-0-616-03092-9(4))* Canadian National Institute for the Blind/Institut National Canadien pour les Aveugles.
Paulsen, Gary. The Beet Fields. 2011. (ENG.). 174p. (YA). (gr. 9). pap. 7.99 *(978-0-375-87305-8(8),* Delacorte Bks. for Young Readers) Random Hse. Children's Bks.
Prinz, Yvonne. All You Get Is Me. 2010. (ENG.). 288p. (YA). (gr. 9-18). 16.99 *(978-0-06-171580-8(8))* HarperCollins Pubs.
Rio, Adam del & Arroyo, David. Vines of the Earth. Rio, Adam del & Arroyo, David, illus. 2006. (SPA & ENG., Illus.). 27p. *(978-0-9772852-7-3(8));* pap. *(978-0-9772852-6-6(X))* Lectura Bks.
Smothers, Ethel Footman & Smothers, Ethel F. Hard-Times Jar. Holyfield, John, illus. 2003. (ENG.). 32p. (J). (gr. k-3). 18.99 *(978-0-374-32852-8(8),* 9780374328528, Farrar, Straus & Giroux (BYR)) Farrar, Straus & Giroux.
Tonatiuh, Duncan. Pancho Rabbit & the Coyote: A Migrant's Tale. 2013. (ENG., Illus.). 32p. (J). (gr. 1-4). 17.95 *(978-1-4197-0583-0(0),* Abrams Bks. for Young Readers) Abrams, Inc.

MIGRANT LABOR—UNITED STATES

Brown, Jonatha A. César Chávez. (People We Should Know Ser.). 2005. (SPA.). 24p. (gr. 1-4). pap. 8.15 *(978-0-8368-4766-6(0),* Weekly Reader Leveled Readers) 2005. (Illus.). 24p. (gr. 1-4). lib. bdg. 22.00 *(978-0-8368-4745-1(8),* Weekly Reader Leveled Readers) 2005. (SPA., Illus.). 24p. (gr. 1-4). lib. bdg. 22.00 *(978-0-8368-4759-8(8),* Weekly Reader Leveled Readers) 2004. (Illus.). 48p. (gr. 5-12). pap. 14.05 *(978-0-8368-5257-8(5),* Gareth Stevens Secondary Library) 2004. (Illus.). 48p. (gr. 5-12). lib. bdg. 31.00 *(978-0-8368-5097-0(1),* Gareth Stevens Secondary Library) Stevens, Gareth Publishing LLLP.
Cruz, Bàrbara C. Cesar Chavez: A Voice for Farmworkers. 2005. (Latino Biography Library). (Illus.). 128p. (J). (gr. 6-13). lib. bdg. 33.27 *(978-0-7660-2489-2(X))* Enslow Pubs., Inc.
DePietro, Frank. Latino Migrant Workers. 2013. (Illus.). 64p. (J). pap. *(978-1-4222-2343-7(4))* Mason Crest.
—Latino Migrant Workers. Limón, José E., ed. 2012. (Hispanic Americans: Major Minority Ser.). (Illus.). 64p. (J). (gr. 4). 22.95 *(978-1-4222-2326-0(4))* Mason Crest.
Feinstein, Stephen. Lee Sobre Cesar Chavez. 2006. (I Like Biographies! Bilingual Ser.).Tr. of Read about Cesar Chavez. (ENG & SPA., Illus.). 24p. (J). (gr. -1-3). lib. bdg. 22.60 *(978-0-7660-2744-2(9),* Enslow Elementary) Enslow Pubs., Inc.
Guzman, Lila & Guzman, Rick. Cesar Chavez: Fighting for Fairness. 2006. (Famous Latinos Ser.). (Illus.). 32p. (J). (gr. 3-7). lib. bdg. 22.60 *(978-0-7660-2370-3(2),* Enslow Elementary) Enslow Pubs., Inc.
Krull, Kathleen. Cosechando Esperanza: La Historia de César Chávez. Campoy, F. Isabel & Flor Ada, Alma, trs. Morales, Yuyi, illus. 2004. (SPA & ENG.). 48p. (J). (gr. -1-3). pap. 7.99 *(978-0-15-205169-3(4))* Houghton Mifflin Harcourt Publishing Co.
—Harvesting Hope: The Story of Cesar Chavez. Morales, Yuyi, illus. 2003. (ENG.). 48p. (J). (gr. -1-3). 17.99 *(978-0-15-201437-7(3))* Houghton Mifflin Harcourt Publishing Co.
Rinaldo, Denise. Cesar Chavez: With a Discussion of Compassion. 2003. (Values in Action Ser.). (J). *(978-1-59203-064-4(5))* Learning Challenge, Inc.
Seidman, David. Cesar Chavez: Labor Leader. 2004. (Great Life Stories Ser.). (ENG., Illus.). 127p. (J). 30.50 *(978-0-531-12319-5(7),* Watts, Franklin) Scholastic Library Publishing.
Soto, Gary. Cesar Chavez: A Hero for Everyone. Lohstoeter, Lori, illus. 2003. (Milestone Ser.). (ENG.). 80p. (J). (gr. 2-5). pap. 6.99 *(978-0-689-85922-9(8),* Simon & Schuster/Paula Wiseman Bks.) Simon & Schuster/Paula Wiseman Bks.
Thompson, E. L. Cesar Chavez, with Profiles of Terence V. Powderly & Dolores Huerta. 2006. (Biographical Connections Ser.). (Illus.). 112p. (J). *(978-0-7166-1827-0(3))* World Bk., Inc.
Wheeler, Jill C. Cesar Chavez. 2003. (Breaking Barriers Ser.). 64p. (gr. 3-8). 27.07 *(978-1-57765-905-1(8),* Abdo & Daughters) ABDO Publishing Co.

MIGRANTS

see Immigrants; Migrant Labor

MIGRATION

see Emigration and Immigration

MIGRATION, INTERNAL

Cunningham, Kevin. Migration from Africa, 1 vol. 2011. (Children's True Stories: Migration Ser.). (ENG.). 32p. (gr. 3-3). pap. 8.29 *(978-1-4109-4078-0(0));* 30.65 *(978-1-4109-4072-8(1))* Heinemann-Raintree. (Raintree Perspectives).
De Medeiros, James. The Migration North. 2013. (J). 29.99 *(978-1-62127-193-2(5))* 2013. (J). pap. 14.95 *(978-1-62127-199-4(4))* 2008. (Illus.). 48p. (YA). (gr. 5-8). pap. 10.95 *(978-1-59036-881-7(9))* 2008. (Illus.). 48p. (YA). (gr. 5-8). lib. bdg. 29.05 *(978-1-59036-880-0(0))* Weigl Pubs., Inc.
Harris, Irene. African American Migrations in North America, 01 vols., 1. 2016. (Spotlight on Immigration & Migration Ser.). (ENG., Illus.). 24p. (J). pap. 10.00 *(978-1-5081-4046-7(4),* PowerKids Pr.) Rosen Publishing Group, Inc., The.
Naidoo, Beverley. Making It Home: Real-Life Stories from Children Forced to Flee. 2005. (Illus.). 117p. (gr. 3-7). 17.00 *(978-0-7569-5823-7(7))* Perfection Learning Corp.
Obadina, Tunde. Population & Overcrowding. Ojakorotu, Victor & Rotberg, Robert I., eds. 2013. (Africa: Progress & Problems Ser.: 13). (Illus.). 112p. (J). (gr. 7-18). 24.95 *(978-1-4222-2945-3(9))* Mason Crest.
Rosen Classroom, creator. Map Activities for Primary Sources of Immigration & Migration in America: Reproducible Blackline Masters. 2011. (Illus.). 15p. (J). pap. 15.99 *(978-0-8239-4597-9(9),* Rosen Classroom) Rosen Publishing Group, Inc., The.
Sioux, Tracee. Immigrants, Migration, & the Growth of the American City. 2004. (Primary Sources of Immigration & Migration in America Ser.). (Illus.). 24p. (J). lib. bdg. 22.60 *(978-0-8239-6828-2(6),* PowerKids Pr.) Rosen Publishing Group, Inc., The.
—Immigrants, Migration, & the Industrial Revolution. 2004. (Primary Sources of Immigration & Migration in America Ser.). (Illus.). 24p. (J). lib. bdg. 22.60 *(978-0-8239-6826-8(X),* PowerKids Pr.) Rosen Publishing Group, Inc., The.
—Immigration, Migration, & the Growth of the American City. 2004. (Primary Sources of Immigration & Migration in America Ser.). (ENG., Illus.). 24p. (gr. 4-8). pap. 9.40 *(978-0-8239-8954-6(2),* PowerKids Pr.) Rosen Publishing Group, Inc., The.
—Immigration, Migration, & the Industrial Revolution. 2004. (Primary Sources of Immigration & Migration in America Ser.). (ENG., Illus.). 24p. (gr. 4-8). pap. 9.40 *(978-0-8239-8998-0(4),* PowerKids Pr.) Rosen Publishing Group, Inc., The.
Walker, Robert. Pushes & Pulls: Why Do People Migrate? 2010. (Investigating Human Migration & Settlement Ser.). (ENG., Illus.). 48p. (J). (gr. 5-8). *(978-0-7787-5183-0(X));* pap. *(978-0-7787-5198-4(8))* Crabtree Publishing Co.

MIGRATION OF ANIMALS

see Animals—Migration

MIGRATION OF BIRDS

see Birds—Migration

MIGRATORY WORKERS

see Migrant Labor

MILITARY AERONAUTICS

see Aeronautics, Military

MILITARY AIR BASES

see Air Bases

MILITARY AIRPLANES

see Airplanes, Military

MILITARY ART AND SCIENCE

see also Aeronautics, Military; Armies; Battles; Disarmament; Fortification; Guerrilla Warfare; Ordnance; Signals and Signaling; Soldiers; Spies; War; Weapons

also headings beginning with the word Military

ABDO. Ready for Military Action, 1 vol. 2014. (Ready for Military Action Ser.: 8). (ENG.). 48p. (gr. 3-6). lib. bdg. 262.32 *(978-1-62403-648-4(1))* ABDO Publishing Co.
AZ Books Staff. Great Warriors. Aksinovich, Natalia & Yaroshevich, Angelica, eds. 2012. (Sounds Around Us Ser.). (ENG.). 16p. (J). (gr. 1-3). bds. 17.95 *(978-1-61889-033-7(6))* AZ Bks. LLC.
Barnham, Kay. The Fact or Fiction Behind Battles & Wars. 2016. (Fact or Phony? Ser.). (ENG.). 96p. (J). (gr. 5-6). lib. bdg. 33.25 *(978-1-4824-4268-7(X))* Stevens, Gareth Publishing LLLP.
Baum, Margaux & Hilliam, Paul. Weapons & Warcraft. 2016. (Life in the Middle Ages Ser.). 00064p. (J). (gr. 5-5). 34.45 *(978-1-4994-6472-6(X))* Rosen Publishing Group, Inc., The.
Bodden, Valerie. Barbarians. 2017. (J). *(978-1-60818-811-6(6),* Creative Education) Creative Co., The.
—Great Warriors: Barbarians. 2014. (Great Warriors Ser.). (ENG.). 24p. (J). (gr. 1-3). pap. 9.99 *(978-1-62832-066-4(4),* Creative Paperbacks) Creative Co., The.
Bow, James. Your Guide to Castles & Medieval Warfare. 2017. (Destination: Middle Ages Ser.). (ENG., Illus.). 32p. (J). ***(978-0-7787-2994-5(X))***; pap. ***(978-0-7787-3000-2(X))*** Crabtree Publishing Co.
Bozzo, Linda. Marine Expeditionary Units. 2015. (Serving in the Military Ser.). (Illus.). 32p. (J). 28.50 *(978-1-60753-493-8(2))* Amicus Publishing.
Browne, G. Waldo. With Rogers' Rangers: Woodranger Tales. 2011. 296p. 48.95 *(978-1-258-06137-1(6))* Literary Licensing, LLC.
Burgan, Michael. Chronology of U.S. Special Ops. 2016. (U. S. Special Ops Ser.). (ENG., Illus.). 48p. (gr. 3-4). lib. bdg. 29.32 *(978-1-5157-1850-5(6))* Capstone Press of Coughlan Cos.
—Weapons Technology: Science, Technology, & Engineering. 2016. (Calling All Innovators: a Career for You Ser.). (ENG., Illus.). 64p. (J). lib. bdg. 32.00 *(978-0-531-21891-4(0),* Children's Pr.) Scholastic Library Publishing.
Burrows, Terry. Robots, Drones, & Radar: Electronics Go to War. 2017. (STEM on the Battlefield Ser.). (ENG., Illus.). (J). (gr. 4-6). lib. bdg. 31.99 ***(978-1-5124-3930-4(4))*** Lerner Publishing Group.
Calkhoven, Laurie. Flash, Boom, Blast! Amazing Inventions from the War Front. 2004. (Illus.). 72p. (J). pap. *(978-0-439-68357-9(2))* Scholastic, Inc.
Caraccilo, Dominic J. Military Intelligence Technology of the Future. 2005. (Library of Future Weaponry Ser.). (Illus.). 64p. (YA). (gr. 7-12). lib. bdg. 31.95 *(978-1-4042-0528-4(4))* Rosen Publishing Group, Inc., The.
Cassell, John. The Marching Book / Marchar. 2009. (Let's Get Moving / Diviértete en movimiento Ser.). (SPA.). 24p. (gr. k-1). 42.50 *(978-1-61514-235-4(5),* Editorial Buenas Letras) Rosen Publishing Group, Inc., The.
Chambers, Catherine. Silent Soldiers. Bustamante, Maryin & Juta, Jason, illus. 2016. (Warriors! Ser.). (ENG.). 32p. (J). (gr. 3-6). lib. bdg. 26.65 *(978-1-4677-9356-8(6))* Lerner Publishing Group.
Chapman, Caroline. Battles & Weapons: Exploring History Through Art. 2007. (Picture That Ser.). (ENG., Illus.). 64p. (J). (gr. 3-17). 19.95 *(978-1-58728-588-2(6))* Cooper Square Publishing Llc.

Christian, Mary Blount. Special Ops: Tactical Training, 1 vol. 2015. (ENG.). 64p. (YA). 32.95 *(978-1-4777-7547-9(1)*, Rosen Reference) Rosen Publishing Group, Inc., The.

Coleman, Miriam. Mujeres en Las Fuerzas Armadas (Women in the Military) 2015. (Ellas Abrieron Camino (Women Groundbreakers) Ser.). (ENG & SPA.). 32p. (J). (gr. 4-5). 26.25 *(978-1-4994-0522-4(7)*, PowerKids Pr.) Rosen Publishing Group, Inc., The.

Dell, Pamela & Raatma, Lucia. The Science of Soldiers, 1 vol. 2012. (Science of War Ser.). (ENG.). 48p. (gr. 5-6). pap. 9.10 *(978-0-7565-4526-0(9))*; lib. bdg. 33.99 *(978-0-7565-4460-7(2))* Compass Point Bks. (CPB Grades 4-8).

Derkins, Susie. The Irish Republican Army. 2005. (Inside the World's Most Infamous Terrorist Organizations Ser.). (Illus.). 64p. (YA). (gr. 7-12). lib. bdg. 31.95 *(978-0-8239-3822-3(0))* Rosen Publishing Group, Inc., The.

Doeden, Matt. Can You Survive in the Special Forces? An Interactive Survival Adventure, 1 vol. 2012. (You Choose: Survival Ser.). (ENG., Illus.). 112p. (gr. 3-4). pap. 6.95 *(978-1-4296-9480-3(7))*; lib. bdg. 31.99 *(978-1-4296-8582-5(4))* Capstone Press of Coughlan Cos. (You Choose Bks.).

Doeden, Matt & Hoena, Blake. War in Afghanistan: An Interactive Modern History Adventure, 1 vol. 2014. (You Choose: Modern History Ser.). (ENG.). 112p. (gr. 3-4). pap. 6.95 *(978-1-4765-5221-7(5))*; 31.99 *(978-1-4765-4190-7(6))* Capstone Press of Coughlan Cos. (You Choose Bks.).

Donovan, Sandy. U. S. Naval Special Warfare Forces. 2004. (U. S. Armed Forces Ser.). (ENG., Illus.). 64p. (gr. 4-8). lib. bdg. 26.60 *(978-0-8225-1650-7(0))* Lerner Publishing Group.

Dorling Kindersley Publishing Staff & Adams, Simon. Soldier. 2009. (DK Eyewitness Bks.). (ENG.). 72p. (J). (gr. 3-7). 16.99 *(978-0-7566-4539-7(5)*, DK Children) Dorling Kindersley Publishing, Inc.

Dougherty, Martin. The Most Amazing Weapons of War. 2010. (Extreme! Ser.). (ENG.). 32p. (gr. 3-4). pap. 47.70 *(978-1-4296-5133-2(4)*, Fact Finders) Capstone Press of Coughlan Cos.

Dougherty, Martin J. Land Warfare. 2010. (Modern Warfare Ser.). (Illus.). 32p. (YA). (gr. 2-5). lib. bdg. 26.00 *(978-1-4339-2727-0(6))* Stevens, Gareth Publishing LLLP.

Earl, C. F. World's Best Soldiers. 2010. (Special Forces Ser.). 64p. (YA). (gr. 7-18). lib. bdg. 22.95 *(978-1-4222-1846-4(5))* Mason Crest.

Earl, C. F. & Vanderhoof, Gabrielle. Army Rangers. 2010. (Special Forces Ser.). (Illus.). 64p. (YA). (gr. 7-18). lib. bdg. 22.95 *(978-1-4222-1838-9(4))* Mason Crest.

Ellis, Catherine. Helicopters/Helicopteros. Brusca, Maria Cristina, tr. 2007. (Mega Military Machines / Megamaquinas Militares Ser.). (ENG & SPA., Illus.). 24p. (J). lib. bdg. 22.60 *(978-1-4042-7621-5(1)*, PowerKids Pr.) Rosen Publishing Group, Inc., The.

Farndon, John. Special Forces. 2010. (Remarkable Man & Beast Ser.). (Illus.). 48p. (J). (gr. 3-18). lib. bdg. 19.95 *(978-1-4222-1976-8(3))* Mason Crest.

Felber, Bill. The Horse in War. 2005. (Horse Library). (Illus.). 64p. (gr. 5-8). 125.00 *(978-0-7910-6650-8(9)*, Chelsea Hse.) Facts On File, Inc.

Ferguson, Amanda. SAS: British Special Air Service. 2003. (Inside Special Operations Ser.). (Illus.). 64p. (YA). (gr. 5-8). lib. bdg. 31.95 *(978-0-8239-3810-0(7)*, Rosen Reference) Rosen Publishing Group, Inc., The.

Fowler, Will. The Story of Modern Weapons & Warfare. 2011. (Journey Through History Ser.). (J). lib. bdg. 31.95 *(978-1-4488-4793-8(1))* Rosen Publishing Group, Inc., The.

Freedman, Jeri. Special Ops: Air Commandos, 1 vol. 2015. (ENG.). 64p. (YA). 32.95 *(978-1-4777-7993-4(0)*, Rosen Reference) Rosen Publishing Group, Inc., The.

Fremont-Barnes, Gregory. Rescue at the Iranian Embassy: The Most Daring SAS Raid. 2011. (Most Daring Raids in History Ser.). (Illus.). 64p. (YA). (gr. 7-12). lib. bdg. 31.95 *(978-1-4488-1869-3(9))* Rosen Publishing Group, Inc., The.

Fridell, Ron. Military Technology. 2007. (Cool Science Ser.). (ENG., Illus.). 48p. (gr. 4-8). lib. bdg. 27.93 *(978-0-8225-6769-1(5)*, Lerner Pubns.) Lerner Publishing Group.

Frontline Families. 2015. (Frontline Families Ser.). (ENG.). 48p. (J). (gr. 5-6). 191.70 *(978-1-4824-2558-1(0))* Stevens, Gareth Publishing LLLP.

Gitlin, Martin. Green Berets. 2013. (Great Warriors EBook Ser.). (Illus.). 48p. pap. 32.79 *(978-1-61783-773-9(3))* ABDO Publishing Co.

Glass, Maya. The Marching Book. 2009. (Let's Get Moving Ser.). 24p. (gr. k-k). 42.50 *(978-1-61514-229-3(0)*, PowerKids Pr.) Rosen Publishing Group, Inc., The.

Gonzalez, Lissette. Bomb Squads in Action. 2007. (Dangerous Jobs Ser.). (Illus.). 24p. (J). (gr. 1-3). lib. bdg. 22.60 *(978-1-4042-3781-0(X)*, PowerKids Pr.) Rosen Publishing Group, Inc., The.

Gordon, Nick. Marine Expeditionary Units. 2013. (U. S. Military Ser.). (ENG., Illus.). 24p. (J). (gr. 3-7). lib. bdg. 25.95 *(978-1-60014-876-7(X)*, Epic Bks.) Bellwether Media.

Graham, Ian. Military Technology. 2010. (New Technology Ser.). (ENG., Illus.). 48p. (J). 23.99 *(978-0-237-53428-8(2))* Evans Brothers, Ltd. GBR. Dist: Independent Pubs. Group.

Gregory, Josh. Special Ops. 2012. (21st Century Skills Library: Cool Military Careers Ser.). (ENG.). 32p. (gr. 4-8). 28.50 *(978-1-61080-446-2(5)*, 202056); pap. 14.21 *(978-1-61080-620-6(4)*, 202230) Cherry Lake Publishing.

Guinta, Peter & Cribbs, Randy. Illumination Rounds. 2004. (Illus.). 192p. (YA). per. *(978-0-9725796-4-3(8)*, 9051945) River Pr.

Hamilton, John. Special Forces, 1 vol. 2007. (Defending the Nation Ser.). (ENG., Illus.). 32p. (gr. 4-7). 27.07 *(978-1-59679-759-8(2)*, Checkerboard Library) ABDO Publishing Co.

—Weapons of World War I, 1 vol. 2004. (World War I Ser.). (ENG.). 32p. (gr. 4-8). 27.07 *(978-1-57765-917-4(1)*, Abdo & Daughters) ABDO Publishing Co.

Hand, Carol. Special Ops: Search & Rescue Operations, 1 vol. 2015. (ENG.). 64p. (J). 32.95 *(978-1-4777-7997-2(3)*, Rosen Reference) Rosen Publishing Group, Inc., The.

Harasymiw, M. Alexander. Pararescuemen. 2012. (US Special Forces Ser.). (ENG., Illus.). 32p. (J). (gr. 3-6). pap. 10.50 *(978-1-4339-6571-5(2))*; lib. bdg. 26.60 *(978-1-4339-6569-2(0))* Stevens, Gareth Publishing LLLP. (Gareth Stevens Learning Library).

Heppermann, Christine. Samurai. 2013. (Great Warriors EBook Ser.). (ENG., Illus.). 48p. (J). pap. 15.64 *(978-1-61783-777-7(6)*, Core Library) ABDO Publishing Co.

History's Greatest Warriors. 2015. (History's Greatest Warriors Ser.). (ENG.). 48p. (J). (gr. 4-4). 156.80 *(978-1-5026-0296-1(2))* Cavendish Square Publishing.

Holmes, Richard. Battle. 2009. (DK Eyewitness Bks.). (ENG.). 72p. (J). (gr. 3-7). 16.99 *(978-0-7566-5027-8(5)*, DK Children) Dorling Kindersley Publishing, Inc.

Hubbard, Ben. Samurai Warriors. 2016. (Conquerors & Combatants Ser.). 224p. (YA). lib. bdg. 55.00 *(978-1-5026-2459-8(1))* Cavendish Square Publishing.

Ives, Rob. Ready, Aim, Launch! Make Your Own Small Launchers. Paul de Quay, John, illus. 2016. (Tabletop Wars Ser.). (ENG.). 32p. (J). (gr. 3-6). lib. bdg. 26.65 *(978-1-5124-0636-8(8))* Lerner Publishing Group.

—Surprise the Enemy: Make Your Own Traps & Triggers. Paul de Quay, John, illus. 2016. (Tabletop Wars Ser.). (ENG.). 32p. (J). (gr. 3-6). lib. bdg. 26.65 *(978-1-5124-0637-5(6))* Lerner Publishing Group.

Janeczko, Paul B. Double Cross: Deception Techniques in War. 2017. (ENG.). 256p. (J). (gr. 5-9). 16.99 *(978-0-7636-6042-0(6))* Candlewick Pr.

Kamberg, Mary-Lane. Special Ops: Snipers, 1 vol. 2015. (ENG., Illus.). 64p. (J). 32.95 *(978-1-4777-7989-7(2)*, Rosen Reference) Rosen Publishing Group, Inc., The.

Kassnoff, David. Special Ops: Weapons & Gear, 1 vol. 2015. (ENG.). 64p. (J). 32.95 *(978-1-4777-7567-7(6)*, Rosen Reference) Rosen Publishing Group, Inc., The.

Labrecque, Ellen. Fighting Crime, 1 vol. 2012. (Heroic Jobs Ser.). (ENG.). 32p. (gr. 1-2). pap. 8.29 *(978-1-4109-4362-0(3))*; lib. bdg. 29.99 *(978-1-4109-4355-2(0))* Heinemann-Raintree. (Read Me!).

—Special Forces, 1 vol. 2012. (Heroic Jobs Ser.). (ENG., Illus.). 32p. (gr. 1-2). pap. 8.29 *(978-1-4109-4366-8(6))*; lib. bdg. 29.99 *(978-1-4109-4359-0(3))* Heinemann-Raintree. (Read Me!).

Leavitt, Amie Jane. Stories from Those Who Fought in America's Special Ops. 2016. (U. S. Special Ops Ser.). (ENG., Illus.). 48p. (gr. 3-4). lib. bdg. 29.32 *(978-1-5157-1851-2(4)*, Connect) Stone Arch Bks.

Levete, Sarah. The Army. 2016. (Defend & Protect Ser.). (ENG.). 48p. (J). (gr. 4-5). pap. 14.05 *(978-1-4824-4119-2(5))* Stevens, Gareth Publishing LLLP.

—Special Forces. 2016. (Defend & Protect Ser.). (ENG.). 48p. (J). (gr. 4-5). pap. 14.05 *(978-1-4824-4115-4(2))* Stevens, Gareth Publishing LLLP.

—Undercover Operations. 2016. (Defend & Protect Ser.). (ENG.). 48p. (J). (gr. 4-5). pap. 14.05 *(978-1-4824-4127-7(6))* Stevens, Gareth Publishing LLLP.

Lusted, Marcia Amidon. Ninja Science: Camouflage, Weapons, & Stealthy Attacks. 2016. (Warrior Science Ser.). (ENG., Illus.). 32p. (gr. 3-4). lib. bdg. 27.99 *(978-1-4914-8115-8(3)*, Edge Bks.) Capstone Press of Coughlan Cos.

Marciniak, Kristin. Navy Seals, 1 vol. 2013. (Great Warriors Ser.). (ENG.). 48p. (J). (gr. 3-6). lib. bdg. 32.79 *(978-1-61783-725-8(3))* ABDO Publishing Co.

—Navy SEALs. 2013. (Great Warriors EBook Ser.). (ENG., Illus.). 48p. (J). pap. 15.64 *(978-1-61783-775-3(X)*, Core Library) ABDO Publishing Co.

Marcovitz, Dan. Critical World Issues: The Arms Trade, Vol. 16. 2016. (Critical World Issues Ser.: Vol. 16). (ENG., Illus.). 112p. (J). (gr. 7-12). 25.95 *(978-1-4222-3648-2(X))* Mason Crest.

Margulies, Philip. Strategic Defense Systems of the Future. 2005. (Library of Future Weaponry Ser.). (Illus.). 64p. (J). (gr. 2-7). lib. bdg. 31.95 *(978-1-4042-0527-7(6))* Rosen Publishing Group, Inc., The.

Margulies, Phillip. Strategic Defense Systems of the Future. 2009. (Library of Future Weaponry Ser.). 64p. (gr. 6-6). 58.50 *(978-1-60853-641-2(6))* Rosen Publishing Group, Inc., The.

Martin, Martha. D-Day. 2012. (ENG.). 48p. (J). *(978-0-7787-7924-7(6))*; pap. *(978-0-7787-7933-9(5))* Crabtree Publishing Co.

Marx, Christy. Battlefield Command Systems of the Future. (Library of Future Weaponry Ser.). 64p. 2009. (gr. 6-6). 58.50 *(978-1-60853-636-8(X))* 2005. (Illus.). (J). (gr. 2-7). lib. bdg. 31.95 *(978-1-4042-0521-5(7))* Rosen Publishing Group, Inc., The.

Marx, Mandy R. Amazing Military Facts. 2016. (Amazing Military Facts Ser.). (ENG.). 24p. (gr. k-1). 106.60 *(978-1-5157-1362-3(8)*, Pebble Plus) Capstone Press of Coughlan Cos.

Maybury, Richard J. World War II: The Rest of the Story & How It Affects You Today, 1930 to September 11 2001. Williams, Jane A., ed. rev. ed. 2003. ("Uncle Eric" Bk.: 11). (ENG., Illus.). 349p. pap. 19.95 *(978-0-942617-43-6(6))* Bluestocking Pr.

McIntosh, J. S. Elite Forces Selection. 2010. (Special Forces Ser.). 64p. (YA). (gr. 7-18). lib. bdg. 22.95 *(978-1-4222-1839-6(2))* Mason Crest.

Mercer, Abbie. Happy 4th of July. 2007. (Holiday Fun Ser.). (Illus.). 24p. (J). (gr. -1-3). lib. bdg. 22.60 *(978-1-4042-3810-7(7))* Rosen Publishing Group, Inc., The.

Minay, Rachel. A Heroic History of Gladiators & Ancient Warriors. 2017. (Blast Through the Past Ser.). (ENG., Illus.). 32p. (J). (gr. 2-4). 16.99 ***(978-1-4451-4929-5(X)***, Franklin Watts) Hachette Children's Group GBR. Dist: Hachette Bk. Group.

Montana, Jack. Urban Warfare. 2010. (Special Forces Ser.). 64p. (YA). (gr. 7-18). lib. bdg. 22.95 *(978-1-4222-1844-0(9))* Mason Crest.

Mooney, Carla. Becoming Invisible: From Camouflage to Cloaks. 2010. (Great Idea Ser.). 48p. (J). (gr. 4-6). lib. bdg. 26.60 *(978-1-59953-378-0(2))* Norwood Hse. Pr.

Murrell, Deborah Jane & Dennis, Peter. Samurai. 2012. (Illus.). 32p. (gr. 3-5). pap. 8.95 *(978-1-926853-55-0(5))* Saunders Bk. Co. CAN. Dist: RiverStream Publishing.

O'Brian, Pliny. Knights: Warriors of the Middle Ages. 2015. (History's Greatest Warriors Ser.). (ENG., Illus.). 48p. (J). (gr. 4-4). 31.36 *(978-1-5026-0120-9(6))* Cavendish Square Publishing.

Orr, Tamra B. USMC Special Reaction Teams. 2009. (Inside Special Operations Ser.). (Illus.). 64p. (gr. 5-8). pap. 12.95 *(978-1-4358-5130-6(7)*, Rosen Classroom) Rosen Publishing Group, Inc., The.

Oxlade, Chris. Inside Tanks & Heavy Artillery. Viana, Tatio, illus. 2017. (Inside Military Machines Ser.). (ENG.). (J). (gr. 3-6). lib. bdg. 26.65 ***(978-1-5124-3226-8(1))*** Lerner Publishing Group.

Park, Louise & Love, Timothy. The Japanese Samurai. 2009. (Ancient & Medieval People Ser.). 32p. (gr. 5). 28.50 *(978-0-7614-4448-0(3))* Marshall Cavendish Corp.

Parker, Steve. A Brief Illustrated History of Warfare. 2017. (J). pap. *(978-1-4747-2708-2(5))* Capstone Press of Coughlan Cos.

Perritano, John. War & the Military, Vol. 10. 2016. (Stem in Current Events Ser.). (Illus.). 64p. (J). (gr. 7). 23.95 *(978-1-4222-3597-3(1))* Mason Crest.

Peters, Andrew Fusek. Free Running. 2014. (Collins Big Cat Progress Ser.). (ENG., Illus.). 32p. (J). (gr. 3-4). pap. 7.99 *(978-0-00-751934-7(6))* HarperCollins Pubs. Ltd. GBR. Dist: Independent Pubs. Group.

Poolos, J. Army Rangers: Surveillance & Reconnaissance for the U. S. Army. (Inside Special Operations Ser.). 64p. 2009. (gr. 6-6). 58.50 *(978-1-61513-549-3(9))* 2003. (Illus.). (YA). (gr. 5-8). lib. bdg. 31.95 *(978-0-8239-3805-6(0))* Rosen Publishing Group, Inc., The. (Rosen Reference).

Porterfield, Jason. USAF Special Tactics Teams. (Inside Special Operations Ser.). (Illus.). 64p. 2009. (gr. 5-8). pap. 12.95 *(978-1-4358-5131-3(5)*, Rosen Classroom) 2008. (J). lib. bdg. 31.95 *(978-1-4042-1753-9(3))* Rosen Publishing Group, Inc., The.

Protecting Our Country. 2013. (Protecting Our Country Ser.). 32p. (J). (gr. 3-6). 126.25 *(978-1-4777-1543-7(6))*; pap. 300.00 *(978-1-4777-2686-0(1))*; pap. 50.00 *(978-1-4777-2685-3(3))* Rosen Publishing Group, Inc., The. (PowerKids Pr.).

Rice, Rob S. Ancient Greek Warfare. 2009. (Ancient Warfare Ser.). (Illus.). 32p. (J). (gr. 5-8). lib. bdg. 26.00 *(978-1-4339-1972-5(9)*, Gareth Stevens Learning Library) Stevens, Gareth Publishing LLLP.

Ripley, Tim. Torpedoes, Missiles, & Cannons: Physics Goes to War. 2017. (STEM on the Battlefield Ser.). (ENG., Illus.). 48p. (J). (gr. 4-6). 31.99 ***(978-1-5124-3926-7(6)***, Lerner Pubns.) Lerner Publishing Group.

Roberts, Jeremy. U. S. Air Force Special Operations. 2004. (U. S. Armed Forces Ser.). (ENG., Illus.). 64p. (gr. 4-8). lib. bdg. 26.60 *(978-0-8225-1644-6(6))* Lerner Publishing Group.

Rose, Simon. Air Force Special Operations. 2014. (Illus.). 24p. (J). *(978-1-62127-448-3(9))* Weigl Pubs., Inc.

—Marine Corps Special Operations. 2013. (J). 27.13 *(978-1-62127-452-0(7))*; pap. *(978-1-62127-458-2(6))* Weigl Pubs., Inc.

Rosen Publishing Staff. Inside Special Forces: Set 2, 1 vol. 2015. (Inside Special Forces Ser.). (ENG.). 64p. (YA). 197.70 *(978-1-4777-8001-5(7)*, Rosen Central) Rosen Publishing Group, Inc., The.

Rudolph, Jessica. CIA Paramilitary Operatives in Action. 2013. (Special Ops II Ser.). 32p. (J). (gr. 2-7). lib. bdg. 26.60 *(978-1-61772-892-1(6))* Bearport Publishing Co., Inc.

Russell, Marcia. A Visit to a Marine Base, 1 vol. 2nd rev. ed. 2014. (TIME for KIDS(r) Nonfiction Readers Ser.). (ENG., Illus.). 24p. (J). (gr. 2-2). pap. 23.96 *(978-1-4807-1036-8(9))* Shell Educational Publishing.

Sandler, Michael. Marine Force Recon in Action. 2008. (Special Ops Ser.). (Illus.). 32p. (J). (gr. 3-6). lib. bdg. 25.27 *(978-1-59716-634-8(0))* Bearport Publishing Co., Inc.

—Pararescuemen in Action. 2008. (Special Ops Ser.). (Illus.). 32p. (J). (gr. 3-6). lib. bdg. 25.27 *(978-1-59716-633-1(2))* Bearport Publishing Co., Inc.

Scheppler, Bill. British Royal Marines: Amphibious Division of the United Kingdom's Royal Navy. 2003. (Inside Special Operations Ser.). (Illus.). 64p. (YA). (gr. 5-8). lib. bdg. 31.95 *(978-0-8239-3806-3(9)*, Rosen Reference) Rosen Publishing Group, Inc., The.

Schmidt, Roderic D. Infantry of the Future. (Library of Future Weaponry Ser.). 64p. 2009. (gr. 6-6). 58.50 *(978-1-60853-637-5(8))* 2005. (Illus.). (J). (gr. 2-7). lib. bdg. 31.95 *(978-1-4042-0525-3(X))* Rosen Publishing Group, Inc., The.

—Land Warfare of the Future. (Library of Future Weaponry Ser.). 64p. 2009. (gr. 6-6). 58.50 *(978-1-60853-638-2(6))* 2005. (Illus.). (J). (gr. 2-7). lib. bdg. 31.95 *(978-1-4042-0524-6(1))* Rosen Publishing Group, Inc., The.

Shea, Therese. Black Ops & Other Special Missions of the U. S. Army Green Berets. 2012. (Inside Special Forces Ser.). (ENG., Illus.). 64p. (YA). (gr. 5-8). pap. 12.95 *(978-1-4488-8387-5(3))*; lib. bdg. 31.95 *(978-1-4488-8381-3(4))* Rosen Publishing Group, Inc., The.

Silverstein Gray, Judy & Baldwin Kiland, Taylor. Cyber Technology: Using Computers to Fight Terrorism. 2016. (Military Engineering in Action Ser.). 48p. (J). (gr. 6-5). pap. 11.70 *(978-0-7660-7535-1(4))* Enslow Pubs., Inc.

Slater, Lee. Special Ops. 2016. (Special Ops Ser.: 6). (ENG.). 32p. (J). (gr. 3-6). lib. bdg. 162.42 *(978-1-62403-966-9(9)*, Checkerboard Library) ABDO Publishing Co.

Sodaro, Craig. The U. S. Marines Special Operations Regiment: The Missions. 2012. (American Special Ops Ser.). (ENG., Illus.). 48p. (gr. 3-4). 31.99 *(978-1-4296-8658-7(8))* Capstone Press of Coughlan Cos.

Special Forces: Protecting, Building, Teaching & Fighting, 10 vols., Set. Incl. Air Force. Vanderhoof, Gabrielle. lib. bdg. 22.95 *(978-1-4222-1837-2(6))*; Army Rangers. Earl, C. F. & Vanderhoof, Gabrielle. (Illus.). lib. bdg. 22.95 *(978-1-4222-1838-9(4))*; Elite Forces Selection. McIntosh, J. S. lib. bdg. 22.95 *(978-1-4222-1839-6(2))*; Green Berets. Earl, C. F. lib. bdg. 22.95 *(978-1-4222-1841-9(4))*; Marines. Montana, Jack. lib. bdg. 22.95 *(978-1-4222-1842-6(2))*; Navy SEALs. Montana, Jack. lib. bdg. 22.95 *(978-1-4222-1843-3(0))*; Parachute Regiment. Montana, Jack. lib. bdg. 22.95 *(978-1-4222-1845-7(7))*; Urban Warfare. Montana, Jack. lib. bdg. 22.95 *(978-1-4222-1844-0(9))*; World's Best Soldiers. Earl, C. F. lib. bdg. 22.95 *(978-1-4222-1846-4(5))*; 64p. (YA). (gr. 7-18). 2010. 2011. Set lib. bdg. 229.50 *(978-1-4222-1836-5(8))* Mason Crest.

Steele, Tara. Medieval Warfare. 2003. (Medieval World Ser.). (ENG., Illus.). 32p. (J). (gr. 5). pap. *(978-0-7787-1376-0(8))* Crabtree Publishing Co.

Stewart, Alex. Greek Soldiers. 2013. (Greatest Warriors Ser.). 32p. (gr. 3-7). 28.50 *(978-1-78212-399-6(7))* Arcturus Publishing GBR. Dist: Black Rabbit Bks.

Sutherland, Adam. Armed Services. 2012. (On the Radar: Defend & Protect Ser.). (ENG., Illus.). 32p. (gr. 4-8). lib. bdg. 26.60 *(978-0-7613-7771-9(9)*, Lerner Pubns.) Lerner Publishing Group.

—Special Forces. 2012. (On the Radar: Defend & Protect Ser.). (ENG., Illus.). 32p. (gr. 4-8). lib. bdg. 26.60 *(978-0-7613-7772-6(7)*, Lerner Pubns.) Lerner Publishing Group.

Terrell, Brandon. Guarding Area 51. 2016. (Highly Guarded Places Ser.). (ENG.). 24p. (J). (gr. 2-5). 28.50 *(978-1-5038-0809-6(2)*, 210644) Child's World, Inc., The.

Tools of War. (Illus.). 192p. (J). *(978-0-7835-0154-3(4))* Time-Life Education, Inc.

Tougas, Shelley. The Science of Weapons, 1 vol. 2012. (Science of War Ser.). (ENG.). 48p. (gr. 5-6). lib. bdg. 33.99 *(978-0-7565-4461-4(0)*, CPB Grades 4-8) Compass Point Bks.

Weapons & Warfare. 2003. (Illus.). 32p. (YA). pap. *(978-1-904516-31-6(9)*, Pavilion Children's Books) Pavilion Bks.

Whiting, Jim. Air Force Special Operations Command. 2014. (J). *(978-1-60818-460-6(9)*, Creative Education) Creative Co., The.

Williams, Brian. Special Forces, 1 vol. 2011. (War Stories Ser.). (ENG.). 32p. (gr. 3-6). 30.65 *(978-1-4329-4831-3(8)*, NA-h) Heinemann-Raintree.

Wilson, Patrick. Survival Equipment. Carney, John, ed. 2014. (Extreme Survival in the Military Ser.: 12). 64p. (J). (gr. 7-18). lib. bdg. 23.95 *(978-1-4222-3085-5(6))* Mason Crest.

Wolny, Philip. Weapons Satellites. 2009. (Library of Satellites Ser.). 64p. (gr. 5-8). 58.50 *(978-1-60853-834-8(6)*, Rosen Reference) Rosen Publishing Group, Inc., The.

Woog, Adam. Careers in Homeland Security. 2013. (J). 34.21 *(978-1-60870-959-5(0))* Marshall Cavendish Corp.

World Book, Inc. Staff, contrib. by. Wooden Spears to Military Drones: A Timeline of Warfare. 2016. (J). *(978-0-7166-3544-4(5))* World Bk.-Childcraft International.

Yomtov, Nel. Special Ops. 2016. (Military Missions Ser.). (ENG., Illus.). 24p. (J). (gr. 3-7). 25.95 *(978-1-62617-439-9(3)*, Epic Bks.) Bellwether Media.

Zaloga, Steven J. The Most Daring Raid of World War II: D-Day — Pointe-Du-Hoc. 2011. (Most Daring Raids in History Ser.). (Illus.). 64p. (YA). (gr. 7-12). lib. bdg. 31.95 *(978-1-4488-1867-9(2))* Rosen Publishing Group, Inc., The.

MILITARY ART AND SCIENCE—HISTORY

Abdo Publishing. Great Warriors, 1 vol. 2013. (Great Warriors Ser.: 8). (ENG.). 48p. (J). (gr. 3-6). lib. bdg. 262.32 *(978-1-61783-721-0(0))* ABDO Publishing Co.

Baum, Margaux & Hopkins, Andrea. Jousts, Tournaments, & War Training. 2016. (Life in the Middle Ages Ser.). 00064p. (J). (gr. 5-5). 34.45 *(978-1-4994-6474-0(6))* Rosen Publishing Group, Inc., The.

Bergin, Mark. Warfare in the 16th to 19th Centuries. 2015. (Warriors Ser.). (Illus.). 48p. (gr. 4-7). 37.10 *(978-1-62588-357-5(9))* Black Rabbit Bks.

—Warfare in the Ancient World. 2015. (Warriors Ser.). (Illus.). 48p. (gr. 4-7). 37.10 *(978-1-62588-355-1(2))* Black Rabbit Bks.

Bodden, Valerie. Barbarians. 2013. 24p. pap. *(978-1-60818-466-8(8))* Creative Co., The.

Bougie, Matt. Strategic Inventions of the Cold War. 2016. (Tech in the Trenches Ser.). (ENG., Illus.). 112p. (J). (gr. 9-9). 42.79 *(978-1-5026-1022-5(1))* Cavendish Square Publishing.

Brian, Dittmar. Mongol Warriors. 2012. (History's Greatest Warriors Ser.). (ENG., Illus.). 24p. (J). (gr. 3-7). lib. bdg. 25.95 *(978-1-60014-746-3(1)*, Torque Bks.) Bellwether Media.

Burrows, Terry. Hovercraft & Humvees: Engineering Goes to War. 2017. (STEM on the Battlefield Ser.). (ENG.). 48p. (J). (gr. 4-6). 31.99 ***(978-1-5124-3929-8(0))*** Lerner Publishing Group.

Cooke, Tim, ed. Weapons, Tactics, & Strategy. 2011. (CC: Civil War Ser.). 112p. (gr. 6-12). 42.80 *(978-1-936333-46-2(5))* Brown Bear Bks.

Cooper, Meghan. Sun Tzu. 2017. (J). ***(978-1-5026-2867-1(8))*** Cavendish Square Publishing.

Fowler, Will. The Children's History of Weapons: Ancient & Modern. 2014. (ENG., Illus.). 128p. (J). (gr. -1-12). 14.99 *(978-1-86147-359-2(1)*, Armadillo) Anness Publishing GBR. Dist: National Bk. Network.

—The Story of Ancient Weapons. 2010. (Journey Through History Ser.). (ENG.). 64p. (YA). lib. bdg. 31.95 *(978-1-4488-0623-2(2)*, Rosen Reference) Rosen Publishing Group, Inc., The.

Graham, Ian. Military & Government Technology, 1 vol. 2010. (From Fail to Win! Learning from Bad Ideas Ser.). (ENG., Illus.). 56p. (gr. 5-8). 34.65 *(978-1-4109-3910-4(3)*, Raintree Freestyle) Heinemann-Raintree.

Gunderson, Jessica. Conquistadors. 2012. (Fearsome Fighters Ser.). 48p. (gr. 5-12). 23.95 *(978-1-60818-183-4(9)*, Creative Education) Creative Co., The.

Helget, Nicole Lea. Mongols. 2012. (Fearsome Fighters Ser.). (Illus.). 48p. (J). (gr. 5-12). 23.95 *(978-1-60818-184-1(7)*, Creative Education) Creative Co., The.

Jackson, Tom. Military & Security. 2012. (FAYFT: Invention & Technology Ser.). 64p. (gr. 4-10). lib. bdg. 39.95 *(978-1-936333-40-0(6))* Brown Bear Bks.

Jestice, Phyllis G. Ancient Egyptian Warfare. 2009. (Ancient Warfare Ser.). (Illus.). 32p. (J). (gr. 5-8). lib. bdg. 26.00 *(978-1-4339-1971-8(0)*, Gareth Stevens Learning Library) Stevens, Gareth Publishing LLLP.

—Ancient Persian Warfare. 2009. (Ancient Warfare Ser.). (Illus.). 32p. (J). (gr. 5-8). lib. bdg. 26.00 *(978-1-4339-1973-2(7)*, Gareth Stevens Learning Library) Stevens, Gareth Publishing LLLP.

Larson, Kirsten W. Statistics about U. S. Special Ops - Past & Present. 2016. (U. S. Special Ops Ser.). (ENG., Illus.). 48p. (gr. 3-4). lib. bdg. 29.32 *(978-1-5157-1852-9(2))* Capstone Press of Coughlan Cos.

MacDonald, Fiona. Knights & Castles. 2009. (History Explorers Ser.). (ENG.). 24p. (J). (gr. k-2). pap. 5.95 *(978-1-84696-215-8(3)*, TickTock Books) Octopus Publishing Group GBR. Dist: Independent Pubs. Group.

—Knights, Castles, & Warfare in the Middle Ages. 2005. (World Almanac Library of the Middle Ages). (Illus.). 48p. (gr.

5-12). lib. bdg. 31.00 *(978-0-8368-5895-2(6)*, Gareth Stevens Secondary Library) Stevens, Gareth Publishing LLLP.

Macdonald, Fiona. Top 10 Worst Ruthless Warriors. Antram, David, illus. 2012. (Top 10 Worst Ser.). (ENG.). 32p. (J). (gr. 3-6). pap. 10.50 *(978-1-4339-6686-6(7))*; lib. bdg. 26.60 *(978-1-4339-6685-9(9))* Stevens, Gareth Publishing LLLP. (Gareth Stevens Learning Library).

—Warfare in the Middle Ages. 2015. (Warriors Ser.). (Illus.). 48p. (gr. 4-7). 37.10 *(978-1-62588-356-8(0))* Black Rabbit Bks.

Malam, John. Warriors. 2010. (Remarkable Man & Beast Ser.). (Illus.). 48p. (J). (gr. 3-18). lib. bdg. 19.95 *(978-1-4222-1979-9(8))* Mason Crest.

Matthews, Rupert. Weapons & Armor. 2015. (100 Facts You Should Know Ser.). (ENG., Illus.). 48p. (J). (gr. 4-5). lib. bdg. 31.95 *(978-1-4824-2193-4(3))* Stevens, Gareth Publishing LLLP.

Murrell, Deborah Jane. Fighting a Battle. 2008. (Medieval Warfare Ser.). 32p. (gr. 5-8). (J). lib. bdg. 26.00 *(978-0-8368-9209-3(7)*, Gareth Stevens Secondary Library); pap. 10.50 *(978-0-8368-9336-6(0))* Stevens, Gareth Publishing LLLP.

—Weapons. 2008. (Medieval Warfare Ser.). 32p. (gr. 5-8). (J). lib. bdg. 26.00 *(978-0-8368-9211-6(9)*, Gareth Stevens Secondary Library); pap. 10.50 *(978-0-8368-9338-0(7))* Stevens, Gareth Publishing LLLP.

Murrell, Deborah Jane & Dennis, Peter. Greek Warrior. 2012. (Illus.). 32p. (gr. 3-5). pap. 8.95 *(978-1-926853-53-6(9))* Saunders Bk. Co. CAN. Dist: RiverStream Publishing.

Nardo, Don. In the Water: Strategies & Tactics. 2014. (J). *(978-1-59935-464-4(0))* Reynolds, Morgan Inc.

O'Brian, Pliny. Knights: Warriors of the Middle Ages. 2015. (J). lib. bdg. *(978-1-62713-407-1(7))* Cavendish Square Publishing.

Park, Louise. The Pharaohs' Armies. 2009. (Ancient & Medieval People Ser.). 32p. (gr. 5). 28.50 *(978-0-7614-4451-0(3))* Marshall Cavendish Corp.

Rice, Rob S. Ancient Roman Warfare. 2009. (Ancient Warfare Ser.). (Illus.). 32p. (J). (gr. 5-8). lib. bdg. 26.00 *(978-1-4339-1974-9(5)*, Gareth Stevens Learning Library) Stevens, Gareth Publishing LLLP.

Ripley, Tim. Smoke Screens & Gas Masks: Chemistry Goes to War. 2017. (STEM on the Battlefield Ser.). (ENG.). 48p. (J). (gr. 4-6). 31.99 ***(978-1-5124-3925-0(8))*** Lerner Publishing Group.

Robertshaw, Andrew. Warfare in the 20th Century. 2015. (Warriors Ser.). (Illus.). 48p. (gr. 4-7). 37.10 *(978-1-62588-358-2(7))* Black Rabbit Bks.

Scheppler, Bill. British Royal Marines: Amphibious Division of the United Kingdom's Royal Navy. 2009. (Inside Special Operations Ser.). 64p. (gr. 6-6). 58.50 *(978-1-61513-550-9(2)*, Rosen Reference) Rosen Publishing Group, Inc., The.

Sodaro, Craig. The Dangerous, Disastrous, Unusual History of War, 1 vol. 2012. (Unusual Histories Ser.). (ENG., Illus.). 48p. (gr. 3-4). lib. bdg. 31.99 *(978-1-4296-7536-9(5))* Capstone Press of Coughlan Cos.

Soriano, Joan & Malizia, Diana, eds. A Visual History of Soldiers & Armies Around the World. 2016. (Visual History of the World Ser.). 00096p. (YA). (gr. 8-8). 37.10 *(978-1-4994-6592-1(0)*, Rosen Young Adult) Rosen Publishing Group, Inc., The.

Steele, Tara. Medieval Warfare. 2003. (Medieval World Ser.). (ENG., Illus.). 32p. (J). (gr. 5). lib. bdg. *(978-0-7787-1344-9(X))* Crabtree Publishing Co.

Woods, Mary B. & Woods, Michael. Ancient Warfare: From Clubs to Catapults. 2005. (Ancient Technology Ser.). (Illus.). 96p. (gr. 6-12). 25.26 *(978-0-8225-2999-6(8))* Lerner Publishing Group.

—Ancient Warfare Technology: From Javelins to Chariots. 2011. (Technology in Ancient Cultures Ser.). (ENG.). 96p. (gr. 6-12). lib. bdg. 31.93 *(978-0-7613-6525-9(7))* Lerner Publishing Group.

World Book, Inc Staff, contrib. by. Warfare. 2009. (J). *(978-0-7166-0388-7(8))* World Bk., Inc.

Worth, Richard. Gunpowder. 2003. (Transforming Power of Technology Ser.). (Illus.). 112p. (C). (gr. 9-13). 30.00 *(978-0-7910-7448-0(X)*, Chelsea Hse.) Facts On File, Inc.

MILITARY ART AND SCIENCE—STUDY AND TEACHING

see Military Education

MILITARY ART AND SCIENCE—VOCATIONAL GUIDANCE

see Armed Forces—Vocational Guidance

MILITARY BIOGRAPHY

see Generals

MILITARY EDUCATION

see also names of military schools, e.g. United States Military Academy, West Point; etc.

Goldish, Meish. Army: Civilian to Soldier. 2010. (Becoming a Soldier Ser.). 24p. (YA). (gr. 3-6). lib. bdg. 22.61 *(978-1-936088-11-9(8))* Bearport Publishing Co., Inc.

—Navy: Civilian to Sailor. 2010. (Becoming a Soldier Ser.). 24p. (YA). (gr. 3-6). lib. bdg. 22.61 *(978-1-936088-14-0(2))* Bearport Publishing Co., Inc.

Wehrertuchtigungslager der Hitler-Jugend, 1942-1945. (GER.). *(978-3-928379-00-7(3))* Verein zur Forderung der Umweltforschung.

MILITARY ENGINEERING

see also Fortification

Military Engineering in Action. 2015. (Military Engineering in Action Ser.). (ENG.). 48p. (J). (gr. 6-6). 167.58 *(978-0-7660-6692-2(4))*; pap., pap., pap. 70.20 *(978-0-7660-7071-4(9))*; pap., pap., pap. 421.20 *(978-0-7660-7072-1(7))* Enslow Pubs., Inc.

Military Engineering in Action: Set 2. 2016. (Military Engineering in Action Ser.). 48p. (gr. 6-5). pap. 70.20 *(978-0-7660-7970-0(8))*; lib. bdg. 167.58 *(978-0-7660-7499-6(4))* Enslow Pubs., Inc.

MILITARY FORCES

see Armies

MILITARY HISTORY

see also Battles; Naval History

also names of countries with the subdivision Army or History, Military

Baum, Margaux & Hilliam, Paul. Weapons & Warcraft. 2016. (Life in the Middle Ages Ser.). 00064p. (J). (gr. 5-5). 34.45 *(978-1-4994-6472-6(X))* Rosen Publishing Group, Inc., The.

Bow, James. Your Guide to Castles & Medieval Warfare. 2017. (Destination: Middle Ages Ser.). (ENG., Illus.). 32p. (J). ***(978-0-7787-2994-5(X))***; pap. ***(978-0-7787-3000-2(X))*** Crabtree Publishing Co.

Cawthorne, Nigel. Military Commanders: The 100 Greatest Throughout History. 2004. (Illus.). 208p. 18.95 *(978-1-59270-029-5(2))* Enchanted Lion Bks., LLC.

—Victory: 100 Great Military Commanders. 2012. (Illus.). 208p. (J). *(978-1-4351-4242-8(X))* Metro Bks.

Dargie, Richard. Castles under Siege. 2008. (Age of Castles Ser.). (Illus.). 48p. (J). (gr. 3-7). lib. bdg. 29.25 *(978-1-4042-4294-4(5)*, PowerKids Pr.) Rosen Publishing Group, Inc., The.

Donaldson, Madeline. Deadly Bloody Battles. 2013. (ShockZone — Deadly & Dangerous Ser.). (ENG., Illus.). 32p. (gr. 5-8). pap. 8.95 *(978-1-4677-0889-0(5))*; lib. bdg. 26.60 *(978-1-4677-0601-8(9)*, Lerner Pubns.) Lerner Publishing Group.

Dougherty, Martin J. Land Warfare. 2010. (Modern Warfare Ser.). (Illus.). 32p. (YA). (gr. 2-5). lib. bdg. 26.00 *(978-1-4339-2727-0(6))* Stevens, Gareth Publishing LLLP.

Frontline Families. 2015. (Frontline Families Ser.). (ENG.). 48p. (J). (gr. 5-6). pap., pap., pap. 84.30 *(978-1-4824-3472-9(5))* Stevens, Gareth Publishing LLLP.

Gale Editors, ed. Worldmark Conflict & Diplomacy: 2 Volume Set, 2 vols. 2014. (Worldmark Conflict & Diplomacy Ser.). (ENG.). 1000p. 329.00 *(978-1-57302-726-7(X))* Cengage Gale.

Guillain, Charlotte. Great Escapes, 1 vol. 2011. (War Stories Ser.). (ENG.). 32p. (gr. 3-6). 30.65 *(978-1-4329-4835-1(0)*, NA-h) Heinemann-Raintree.

Hanson, Anders & Mann, Elissa. Biggest, Baddest Book of Warriors, 1 vol. 2012. (Biggest, Baddest Books for Boys Ser.). (ENG.). 24p. (J). (gr. k-4). 25.65 *(978-1-61783-409-7(2))* ABDO Publishing Co.

Hargrove, Julia. Tomb of the Unknowns. 2003. (Historic Monuments Ser.). (Illus.). 48p. (J). pap. 6.95 *(978-1-57310-405-0(1))* Teaching & Learning Co.

Henry, Claire. The World's Deadliest Wars, 1 vol., 1. 2014. (World's Deadliest Ser.). (ENG.). 32p. (J). (gr. 3-6). 26.25 *(978-1-4777-6153-3(5)*, PowerKids Pr.) Rosen Publishing Group, Inc., The.

Hull, Robert. Trade & Warfare. 2007. (World of Ancient Greece Ser.). (Illus.). 32p. (YA). (gr. 3-6). lib. bdg. 27.10 *(978-1-59771-062-6(8))* Sea-To-Sea Pubns.

Jestice, Phyllis G. Ancient Egyptian Warfare. 2009. (Ancient Warfare Ser.). (Illus.). 32p. (J). (gr. 5-8). lib. bdg. 26.00 *(978-1-4339-1971-8(0)*, Gareth Stevens Learning Library) Stevens, Gareth Publishing LLLP.

—Ancient Persian Warfare. 2009. (Ancient Warfare Ser.). (Illus.). 32p. (J). (gr. 5-8). lib. bdg. 26.00 *(978-1-4339-1973-2(7)*, Gareth Stevens Learning Library) Stevens, Gareth Publishing LLLP.

Johnson, Cynthia. Worldmark Conflict & Diplomacy. 2014. (J). *(978-1-57302-727-4(8))* Cengage Gale.

Macdonald, Fiona. Top 10 Worst Ruthless Warriors. Antram, David, illus. 2012. (Top 10 Worst Ser.). (ENG.). 32p. (J). (gr. 3-6). pap. 10.50 *(978-1-4339-6686-6(7))*; lib. bdg. 26.60 *(978-1-4339-6685-9(9))* Stevens, Gareth Publishing LLLP. (Gareth Stevens Learning Library).

Malam, John. Warriors. 2013. (Illus.). 48p. (J). *(978-1-4351-5100-0(3))* Barnes & Noble, Inc.

—Warriors. 2010. (Remarkable Man & Beast Ser.). (Illus.). 48p. (J). (gr. 3-18). lib. bdg. 19.95 *(978-1-4222-1979-9(8))* Mason Crest.

—You Wouldn't Want to Be a Ninja Warrior! A Secret Job That's Your Destiny. Antram, David, illus. 2012. (ENG.). 32p. (J). (gr. 3-12). lib. bdg. 29.00 *(978-0-531-20873-1(7))* Scholastic Library Publishing.

The Most Daring Raids in History, 6 vols., Set. Incl. Counterterrorism in West Africa: The Most Dangerous SAS Assault. Fowler, Will. lib. bdg. 31.95 *(978-1-4488-1871-6(0))*; Entebbe: The Most Daring Raid of Israel's Special Forces. Dunstan, Simon. 31.95 *(978-1-4488-1868-6(0))*; Most Daring Raid of the Civil War: The Great Locomotive Chase. Rottman, Gordon L. 31.95 *(978-1-4488-1870-9(2))*; Most Daring Raid of the Samurai. Turnbull, Stephen R. lib. bdg. 31.95 *(978-1-4488-1872-3(9))*; Most Daring Raid of World War II: D-Day — Pointe-Du-Hoc. Zaloga, Steven J. lib. bdg. 31.95 *(978-1-4488-1867-9(2))*; Rescue at the Iranian Embassy: The Most Daring SAS Raid. Fremont-Barnes, Gregory. lib. bdg. 31.95 *(978-1-4488-1869-3(9))*; (YA). (gr. 7-12). (Most Daring Raids in History Ser.). (Illus.). 64p. 2011. Set lib. bdg. 175.50 *(978-1-4488-1956-0(3))* Rosen Publishing Group, Inc., The.

Nardo, Don. Bad Days in Battle. 2017. (Whoops! a History of Bad Days Ser.). (ENG., Illus.). 48p. (gr. 5-8). lib. bdg. 33.32 *(978-1-4109-8562-0(8))* Heinemann-Raintree.

Nelson, Sheila & Zoldak, Joyce. In Defense of Our Country: Survivors of Military Conflict. 2009. (J). pap. 24.95 *(978-1-4222-1465-7(6))* Mason Crest.

Nelson, Sheila, et al. In Defense of Our Country: Survivors of Military Conflict. 2010. (Survivors Ser.). 128p. (YA). (gr. 7-12). 24.95 *(978-1-4222-0452-8(9))* Mason Crest.

Oxlade, Chris. The Top Ten Battles That Changed the World. 2009. (J). 60.00 *(978-1-4358-9178-4(3)*, PowerKids Pr.); (J). pap. 10.00 *(978-1-4358-9177-7(5)*, PowerKids Pr.); (Illus.). 32p. (YA). (gr. 3-6). 26.50 *(978-1-4358-9176-0(7))* Rosen Publishing Group, Inc., The.

Rice, Rob S. Ancient Greek Warfare. 2009. (Ancient Warfare Ser.). (Illus.). 32p. (J). (gr. 5-8). lib. bdg. 26.00 *(978-1-4339-1972-5(9)*, Gareth Stevens Learning Library) Stevens, Gareth Publishing LLLP.

—Ancient Roman Warfare. 2009. (Ancient Warfare Ser.). (Illus.). 32p. (J). (gr. 5-8). lib. bdg. 26.00 *(978-1-4339-1974-9(5)*, Gareth Stevens Learning Library) Stevens, Gareth Publishing LLLP.

Simons, Lisa M. Bolt, et al. Military by the Numbers, 1 vol. 2014. (Military by the Numbers Ser.). (ENG.). 32p. (gr. 3-4). lib. bdg. 111.96 *(978-1-4765-7837-8(0)*, Edge Bks.) Capstone Press of Coughlan Cos.

Sodaro, Craig. The Dangerous, Disastrous, Unusual History of War, 1 vol. 2012. (Unusual Histories Ser.). (ENG., Illus.). 48p. (gr. 3-4). lib. bdg. 31.99 *(978-1-4296-7536-9(5))* Capstone Press of Coughlan Cos.

Steele, Tara. Medieval Warfare. 2003. (Medieval World Ser.). (ENG., Illus.). 32p. (J). (gr. 5). pap. *(978-0-7787-1376-0(8))* Crabtree Publishing Co.

Turner, Tracey. Hard As Nails in Wars & Battles. Lenman, Jamie, illus. 2015. (ENG.). 64p. (J). pap. *(978-0-7787-1526-9(4))* Crabtree Publishing Co.

—Hard as Nails Warriors. Lenman, Jamie, illus. 2015. (ENG.). 64p. (J). pap. *(978-0-7787-1517-7(5))* Crabtree Publishing Co.

Voices of War. 2010. (Voices of War Ser.). (ENG.). 32p. (gr. 3-4). pap. 190.80 *(978-1-4296-5705-1(7)*, Edge Bks.) Capstone Press of Coughlan Cos.

Woods, Mary B. & Woods, Michael. Ancient Warfare Technology: From Javelins to Chariots. 2011. (Technology in Ancient Cultures Ser.). (ENG.). 96p. (gr. 6-12). lib. bdg. 31.93 *(978-0-7613-6525-9(7))* Lerner Publishing Group.

MILITARY LIFE

see Soldiers; United States—Army—Military Life

MILITARY POWER

see Armies; Disarmament; Military Art and Science; Sea Power

MILITARY SCHOOLS

see Military Education

MILITARY SCIENCE

see Military Art and Science

MILITARY SERVICE, COMPULSORY

see Draft

MILITARY SIGNALING

see Signals and Signaling

MILITARY TRAINING

see Military Education

MILITARY UNIFORMS

Bell, Samantha S. Cool Military Gear, 1 vol. 2014. (Ready for Military Action Ser.). (ENG.). 48p. (gr. 3-6). lib. bdg. 32.79 *(978-1-62403-650-7(3))* ABDO Publishing Co.

Carman, William Y. The Ackermann Military Prints: Uniforms of the British & Indian Armies, 1840-1855, 1 vol. 2003. (ENG., Illus.). 176p. (gr. 10-13). 59.95 *(978-0-7643-1671-5(0)*, 9780764316715) Schiffer Publishing, Ltd.

Equipped for Battle: Weapons, Gear, & Uniforms of America's Wars. 2014. (Equipped for Battle Ser.). (ENG.). 176p. pap. 12.95 *(978-1-4765-7653-4(X)*, Edge Bks.) Capstone Press of Coughlan Cos.

Harris, Carol & Brown, Mike. Ceremonial Costumes. 2004. (Twentieth-Century Developments in Fashion & Costume Ser.). (Illus.). 64p. (YA). (gr. 7-18). lib. bdg. 19.95 *(978-1-59084-424-3(6))* Mason Crest.

—Military Uniforms. 2004. (Twentieth-Century Developments in Fashion & Costume Ser.). (Illus.). 64p. (YA). (gr. 7-18). lib. bdg. 19.95 *(978-1-59084-418-2(1))* Mason Crest.

Mingo, Norman. Navy Scouts Paper Dolls. Taliadoros, Jenny, ed. Mingo, Norman & Ernst, Clara, illus. 2007. (ENG.). 16p. pap. 12.00 *(978-0-9790668-3-2(2))* Paper Studio Pr.

Stowell, Louie. Sticker Dressing Second World War. 2012. (Sticker Dressing Ser.). 24p. (J). pap. 8.99 *(978-0-7945-3314-4(0)*, Usborne) EDC Publishing.

Tucker, Louise, ed. The Visual Dictionary of Military Uniforms. Eyewitness Visual Dictionaries. 2004. (Illus.). 64p. (J). (gr. 4-8). reprint ed. 18.00 *(978-0-7567-7820-0(4))* DIANE Publishing Co.

MILITARY VEHICLES

see Vehicles, Military

MILITARY WEAPONS

see also Disarmament; Ordnance

Bergin, Mark. Warfare in the Ancient World. 2015. (Warriors Ser.). (Illus.). 48p. (gr. 4-7). 37.10 *(978-1-62588-355-1(2))* Black Rabbit Bks.

Blackford, Cheryl. This Book Is Top Secret: A Collection of Awesome Military Trivia, 1 vol. 2012. (Super Trivia Collection). (ENG., Illus.). 32p. (gr. 3-4). lib. bdg. 27.99 *(978-1-4296-8591-7(3))* Capstone Press of Coughlan Cos.

Bow, James. Tech to Protect. 2017. (Illus.). 32p. (J). ***(978-0-7787-3606-6(7))*** Crabtree Publishing Co.

Brezina, Corona. Weapons of Mass Destruction: Proliferation & Control. 2004. (Library of Weapons of Mass Destruction Ser.). (Illus.). 64p. (J). lib. bdg. 31.95 *(978-1-4042-0298-6(6))* Rosen Publishing Group, Inc., The.

Burgan, Michael. Weapons, Gear, & Uniforms of the American Revolution, 1 vol. 2012. (Equipped for Battle Ser.). (ENG.). 32p. (gr. 3-4). lib. bdg. 27.99 *(978-1-4296-7647-2(7)*, Edge Bks.) Capstone Press of Coughlan Cos.

—Weapons, Gear, & Uniforms of World War II, 1 vol. 2012. (Equipped for Battle Ser.). (ENG.). 32p. (gr. 3-4). lib. bdg. 27.99 *(978-1-4296-7650-2(7)*, Edge Bks.) Capstone Press of Coughlan Cos.

Burgan, Michael, et al. Equipped for Battle. 2012. (Equipped for Battle Ser.). (ENG.). 32p. (gr. 3-4). lib. bdg. 167.94 *(978-1-4296-8191-9(8)*, Edge Bks.) Capstone Press of Coughlan Cos.

Burrows, Terry. Hovercraft & Humvees: Engineering Goes to War. 2017. (STEM on the Battlefield Ser.). (ENG.). 48p. (J). (gr. 4-6). 31.99 ***(978-1-5124-3929-8(0))*** Lerner Publishing Group.

—Robots, Drones, & Radar: Electronics Go to War. 2017. (STEM on the Battlefield Ser.). (ENG., Illus.). (J). (gr. 4-6). lib. bdg. 31.99 ***(978-1-5124-3930-4(4))*** Lerner Publishing Group.

Campbell, Geoffrey A. Weapons of War. 2004. (American War Library). (Illus.). 112p. (J). (gr. 7-10). 30.85 *(978-1-59018-544-5(7)*, Lucent Bks.) Cengage Gale.

Chambers, Catherine. Mighty Fighting Machines. Bustamante, Martin, illus. 2016. (Warriors! Ser.). (ENG.). 32p. (J). (gr. 3-6). lib. bdg. 26.65 *(978-1-4677-9358-2(2))* Lerner Publishing Group.

Cohn, Jessica. Military Machines. 2013. (Machines in Motion Ser.). 48p. (J). (gr. 3-5). pap. 84.30 *(978-1-4339-9606-1(5))*; pap. 14.05 *(978-1-4339-9605-4(7))*; (ENG., Illus.). lib. bdg. 31.95 *(978-1-4339-9604-7(9))* Stevens, Gareth Publishing LLLP.

Davis, Graeme. The Weapons & Gear of the Revolutionary War. 2012. (Story of the American Revolution Ser.). (ENG.). 32p. (gr. 3-4). pap. 47.70 *(978-1-4296-9289-2(8)*, Fact Finders); (Illus.). lib. bdg. 27.32 *(978-1-4296-8588-7(3))* Capstone Press of Coughlan Cos.

Doeden, Matt. Weapons of the Civil War. 2017. (Weapons of War Ser.). (ENG.). 32p. (gr. 2-3). lib. bdg. 26.65 ***(978-1-5157-7909-4(2))*** Capstone Press of Coughlan Cos.

—Weapons of the Revolutionary War. 2017. (Weapons of War Ser.). (ENG.). 32p. (gr. 2-3). lib. bdg. 26.65 ***(978-1-5157-7908-7(4))*** Capstone Press of Coughlan Cos.

—Weapons of World War I. 2017. (Weapons of War Ser.). (ENG.). 32p. (gr. 2-3). lib. bdg. 26.65 ***(978-1-5157-7907-0(6))*** Capstone Press of Coughlan Cos.

—Weapons of World War II. 2017. (Weapons of War Ser.). (ENG.). 32p. (gr. 2-3). lib. bdg. 26.65 ***(978-1-5157-7906-3(8))*** Capstone Press of Coughlan Cos.

Dougherty, Martin J. Weapons & Technology. 2010. (Modern Warfare Ser.). 32p. (YA). (gr. 2-5). lib. bdg. 26.00 *(978-1-4339-2741-6(1))* Stevens, Gareth Publishing LLLP.

Equipped for Battle: Weapons, Gear, & Uniforms of America's Wars. 2014. (Equipped for Battle Ser.). (ENG.). 176p. pap. 12.95 *(978-1-4765-7653-4(X)*, Edge Bks.) Capstone Press of Coughlan Cos.

Fein, Eric. Weapons, Gear, & Uniforms of the Civil War, 1 vol. 2012. (Equipped for Battle Ser.). (ENG.). 32p. (gr. 3-4). lib. bdg. 27.99 *(978-1-4296-7648-9(5)*, Edge Bks.) Capstone Press of Coughlan Cos.

—Weapons, Gear, & Uniforms of World War I, 1 vol. 2012. (Equipped for Battle Ser.). (ENG.). 32p. (gr. 3-4). lib. bdg. 27.99 *(978-1-4296-7649-6(3)*, Edge Bks.) Capstone Press of Coughlan Cos.

Gagne, Tammy. Incredible Military Weapons, 1 vol. 2014. (Ready for Military Action Ser.). (ENG.). 48p. (gr. 3-6). lib. bdg. 32.79 *(978-1-62403-652-1(X))* ABDO Publishing Co.

Hamilton, John. Weapons of the American Revolution. 2013. (American Revolution Ser.). 32p. (J). (gr. 5-9). lib. bdg. 27.07 *(978-1-61783-683-1(4)*, Abdo & Daughters) ABDO Publishing Co.

—World War II: Weapons, 1 vol. 2011. (World War II Ser.). (ENG., Illus.). 32p. (YA). (gr. 5-9). 27.07 *(978-1-61783-064-8(X))* ABDO Publishing Co.

Kassnoff, David. Special Ops: Weapons & Gear, 1 vol. 2015. (ENG.). 64p. (J). 32.95 *(978-1-4777-7567-7(6)*, Rosen Reference) Rosen Publishing Group, Inc., The.

Macdonald, Fiona. Warfare in the Middle Ages. 2015. (Warriors Ser.). (Illus.). 48p. (gr. 4-7). 37.10 *(978-1-62588-356-8(0))* Black Rabbit Bks.

Mapua, Jeff. Weaponizing Poop. 2017. (J). pap. ***(978-0-7660-9093-4(0))*** Enslow Pubs., Inc.

Matthews, Rupert. Weapons & Armor. 2015. (100 Facts You Should Know Ser.). (ENG., Illus.). 48p. (J). (gr. 4-5). lib. bdg. 31.95 *(978-1-4824-2193-4(3))* Stevens, Gareth Publishing LLLP.

Mighty Military Machines. 2015. (Mighty Military Machines Ser.). (ENG.). 32p. (J). (gr. 1-1). 159.60 *(978-1-4824-1649-7(2))* Stevens, Gareth Publishing LLLP.

Murrell, Deborah Jane. Weapons. 2008. (Medieval Warfare Ser.). 32p. (gr. 5-8). (J). lib. bdg. 26.00 *(978-0-8368-9211-6(9)*, Gareth Stevens Secondary Library); pap. 10.50 *(978-0-8368-9338-0(7))* Stevens, Gareth Publishing LLLP.

Nardo, Don. The Civil War. 2009. (American History Ser.). pap. 24.10 *(978-1-4205-0302-9(2)*, Lucent Bks.) Cengage Gale.

Ollhoff, Jim. The Civil War: Weapons, 1 vol. 2012. (Civil War Ser.). (ENG.). 32p. (J). (gr. 5-9). 27.07 *(978-1-61783-278-9(2))* ABDO Publishing Co.

Parker, Steve. Military Machines. 2010. (How It Works Ser.). 40p. (J). (gr. 3-18). lib. bdg. 19.95 *(978-1-4222-1797-9(3))* Mason Crest.

Perritano, John. War & the Military, Vol. 10. 2016. (Stem in Current Events Ser.). (Illus.). 64p. (J). (gr. 7). 23.95 *(978-1-4222-3597-3(1))* Mason Crest.

Ripley, Tim. Smoke Screens & Gas Masks: Chemistry Goes to War. 2017. (STEM on the Battlefield Ser.). (ENG.). 48p. (J). (gr. 4-6). 31.99 ***(978-1-5124-3925-0(8))*** Lerner Publishing Group.

Robertshaw, Andrew. Warfare in the 20th Century. 2015. (Warriors Ser.). (Illus.). 48p. (gr. 4-7). 37.10 *(978-1-62588-358-2(7))* Black Rabbit Bks.

Samuels, Charlie. Machines & Weaponry of the Vietnam War. 2013. (Machines That Won the War Ser.). (Illus.). 48p. (J). (gr. 5-8). pap. 14.05 *(978-1-4339-8600-0(0))*; lib. bdg. 31.95 *(978-1-4339-8599-7(3))* Stevens, Gareth Publishing LLLP.

—Machines & Weaponry of World War I. 2013. (Machines That Won the War Ser.). (Illus.). 48p. (J). (gr. 5-8). pap. 14.05 *(978-1-4339-8604-8(3))*; lib. bdg. 31.95 *(978-1-4339-8603-1(5))* Stevens, Gareth Publishing LLLP.

—Machines & Weaponry of World War II. 2013. (Machines That Won the War Ser.). (Illus.). 48p. (J). (gr. 5-8). pap. 14.05 *(978-1-4339-8608-6(6))*; lib. bdg. 31.95 *(978-1-4339-8607-9(8))* Stevens, Gareth Publishing LLLP.

Schmidt, Roderic D. Infantry of the Future. 2005. (Library of Future Weaponry Ser.). (Illus.). 64p. (J). (gr. 2-7). lib. bdg. 31.95 *(978-1-4042-0525-3(X))* Rosen Publishing Group, Inc., The.

Sheen, Barbara. Cutting Edge Military Technology. 2016. (ENG.). 80p. (J). (gr. 5-12). *(978-1-68282-044-5(0))* ReferencePoint Pr., Inc.

Sherman, Jill. Guarding Nuclear Weapons Facilities. 2016. (Highly Guarded Places Ser.). (ENG.). 24p. (J). (gr. 2-5). 28.50 *(978-1-5038-0813-3(0)*, 210647) Child's World, Inc., The.

Small, Cathleen. Strategic Inventions of the Korean War. 2016. (Tech in the Trenches Ser.). 112p. (J). 42.79 *(978-1-5026-2345-4(5))* Cavendish Square Publishing.

Swanson, Jennifer. Top Secret Science: Projects You Aren't Supposed to Know About, 1 vol. 2014. (Scary Science Ser.). (ENG.). 32p. (gr. 3-4). lib. bdg. 27.32 *(978-1-4765-3926-3(X)*, Fact Finders) Capstone Press of Coughlan Cos.

Tougas, Shelley. The Science of Weapons, 1 vol. 2012. (Science of War Ser.). (ENG.). 48p. (gr. 5-6). lib. bdg. 33.99 *(978-0-7565-4461-4(0)*, CPB Grades 4-8) Compass Point Bks.

—Weapons, Gear, & Uniforms of the Iraq War, 1 vol. 2012. (Equipped for Battle Ser.). (ENG.). 32p. (gr. 3-4). lib. bdg. 27.99 *(978-1-4296-7652-6(3)*, Edge Bks.) Capstone Press of Coughlan Cos.

—Weapons, Gear, & Uniforms of the Vietnam War, 1 vol. 2012. (Equipped for Battle Ser.). (ENG.). 32p. (gr. 3-4). lib. bdg. 27.99 *(978-1-4296-7651-9(5)*, Edge Bks.) Capstone Press of Coughlan Cos.

Woods, Mary B. & Woods, Michael. Ancient Warfare Technology: From Javelins to Chariots. 2011. (Technology in Ancient Cultures Ser.). (ENG.). 96p. (gr. 6-12). lib. bdg. 31.93 *(978-0-7613-6525-9(7))* Lerner Publishing Group.
Wright, Susan. Weapons of Mass Destruction: Illicit Trade & Trafficking. 2004. (Library of Weapons of Mass Destruction Ser.). (Illus.). 64p. (J). lib. bdg. 31.95 *(978-1-4042-0297-9(8))* Rosen Publishing Group, Inc., The.

MILK

Benduhn, Tea. Milk & Cheese. 2007. (Find Out about Food Ser.). 24p. (gr. k-3). pap. 8.15 *(978-0-8368-8260-5(1))*; (Illus.). lib. bdg. 22.00 *(978-0-8368-8253-7(9))* Stevens, Gareth Publishing LLLP. (Weekly Reader Leveled Readers).
—Milk & Cheese/Leche y Queso. 2007. (Find Out about Food/Conoce la Comida Ser.). (SPA & ENG., Illus.). 24p. (gr. k-3). lib. bdg. 22.00 *(978-0-8368-8457-9(4)*, Weekly Reader Leveled Readers) Stevens, Gareth Publishing LLLP.
The Book Carton, 6 vols. (Let's Read about... Ser.). (Illus.). 10p. (J). *(978-2-7643-0028-2(X))* Phidal Publishing, Inc./Editions Phidal, Inc.
Dilkes, D. H. Milk & Dairy. 2011. (All about Good Foods We Eat Ser.). (Illus.). 24p. (J). (gr. -1-18). pap. 7.95 *(978-1-59845-253-2(3)*, Enslow Elementary); (gr. k-3). lib. bdg. 22.60 *(978-0-7660-3924-7(2))* Enslow Pubs., Inc.
Donlon, Bridget. Got Milk? How? Chelsey, Emily, illus. 2012. 26p. (-18). 29.95 *(978-1-62709-613-3(2))* America Star Bks.
Hewitt, Sally. Milk & Cheese. 2008. (Good for Me Ser.). (Illus.). 24p. (J). (gr. -1-3). lib. bdg. 22.60 *(978-1-4042-4268-5(6)*, PowerKids Pr.) Rosen Publishing Group, Inc., The.
Kalz, Jill. Dairy Products. 2003. 24p. (J). lib. bdg. 21.35 *(978-1-58340-297-9(7))* Black Rabbit Bks.
Lee, Sally. The Delicious Dairy Group, 1 vol. Poling, Kyle, illus. 2011. (First Graphics: Myplate & Healthy Eating Ser.). (ENG.). 24p. (gr. 1-2). lib. bdg. 23.99 *(978-1-4296-6092-1(9))*; pap. 35.70 *(978-1-4296-7165-1(3))* Capstone Press of Coughlan Cos.
Malam, John. Journey of a Glass of Milk, 1 vol. 2012. (Journey of A... Ser.). (ENG.). 32p. (gr. 1-3). pap. 8.29 *(978-1-4329-6610-2(3))*; lib. bdg. 27.32 *(978-1-4329-6603-4(0))* Heinemann-Raintree. (Heinemann First Library).
Martineau, Susan & James, Hel. Milk, Butter, & Cheese. 2012. (Healthy Eating Ser.). (Illus.). 32p. (gr. 2-6). pap. 8.95 *(978-1-59920-245-7(X))* Black Rabbit Bks.
Mayo, Gretchen Will. Milk. 2004. (Weekly Reader Early Learning Library). (Illus.). 24p. (gr. 1-4). pap. 8.15 *(978-0-8368-4074-2(7)*, Weekly Reader Leveled Readers) Stevens, Gareth Publishing LLLP.
Murray, Julie. Grass to Milk, 1 vol. 2006. (Beginning to End Ser.). (ENG., Illus.). 24p. (gr. k-4). 25.65 *(978-1-59679-837-3(8)*, Buddy Bks.) ABDO Publishing Co.
—Milk to Ice Cream, 1 vol. 2006. (Beginning to End Ser.). (ENG., Illus.). 24p. (gr. k-4). 25.65 *(978-1-59679-838-0(6)*, Buddy Bks.) ABDO Publishing Co.
Nelson, Maria. I'm Allergic to Milk. 2014. (I'm Allergic Ser.). 24p. (J). (gr. 1-3). 22.60 *(978-1-4824-0968-0(2))* Stevens, Gareth Publishing LLLP.
Owen, Ruth. Milk! Life on a Dairy Farm. 2012. (Food from Farmers Ser.). (ENG.). 32p. (J). (gr. k-3). pap. 11.75 *(978-1-61533-534-3(X))*; lib. bdg. 26.50 *(978-1-61533-528-2(5))* Windmill Bks.
Shores, Erika L. How Food Gets from Farms to Store Shelves. 2016. (Here to There Ser.). (ENG.). 24p. (gr. k-1). lib. bdg. 26.65 *(978-1-4914-8428-9(4)*, Pebble Plus) Capstone Press of Coughlan Cos.
Smith, Linda Wasmer. Louis Pasteur: Genius Disease Fighter. 2015. (Genius Scientists & Their Genius Ideas Ser.). 96p. (J). (gr. 5-12). 27.94 *(978-0-7660-6575-8(8))*; pap. 10.95 *(978-0-7660-6576-5(6))* Enslow Pubs., Inc.
Squire, Ann O. Milk. 2017. (True Book(tm), a — Farm to Table Ser.). (ENG., Illus.). 48p. (J). lib. bdg. 31.00 *(978-0-531-22933-0(5)*, Children's Pr.) Scholastic Library Publishing.
Taus-Bolstad, Stacy. From Grass to Milk. (ENG., Illus.). 24p. (gr. k-3). 2012. (Start to Finish, Second Series: Food Ser.: No. 2). pap. 6.95 *(978-1-58013-966-3(3))* 2012. (Start to Finish, Second Series: Food Ser.: No. 2). lib. bdg. 23.93 *(978-0-7613-9179-1(7)*, Lerner Pubns.) 2003. (Start to Finish Ser.). 19.93 *(978-0-8225-4664-1(7)*, Lerner Pubns.) Lerner Publishing Group.

MILKWEED

Holland, Mary. Milkweed Visitors. Holland, Mary, photos by. 2006. (Illus.). 32p. (J). per. 10.95 *(978-0-9657472-4-0(7))* Bas Relief, LLC.

MILL AND FACTORY BUILDINGS

see Factories

MILLIPEDES

Clapper, Nikki Bruno. Millipedes. 2015. (Creepy Crawlers Ser.). (ENG., Illus.). 24p. (gr. k-1). lib. bdg. 26.65 *(978-1-4914-6214-0(0))* Capstone Press of Coughlan Cos.
Clark, Willow & Rockwood, Leigh. Centipedes & Millipedes Are Gross! 2010. (Creepy Crawlies Ser.). 24p. (J). (ENG.). pap. 8.25 *(978-1-4488-1363-6(8)*, PowerKids Pr.); (Illus.). lib. bdg. 22.60 *(978-1-4488-0701-7(8))* Rosen Publishing Group, Inc., The.
Rhodes, Wendell. Millipedes. 2016. (Dig Deep! Bugs That Live Underground Ser.). 24p. (J). (gr. 3-3). pap. 8.25 *(978-1-4994-2058-6(7)*, PowerKids Pr.) Rosen Publishing Group, Inc., The.
Ross, Michael Elsohn. Millipedeology. Erickson, Darren, illus. Grogan, Brian, photos by. 2005. (Backyard Buddies Ser.). 48p. (gr. 3-6). lib. bdg. 19.93 *(978-1-57505-398-1(5))* Lerner Publishing Group.
Schuetz, Kari. Millipedes. 2015. (Creepy Crawlies Ser.). (ENG., Illus.). 24p. (J). (gr. k-3). lib. bdg. 25.95 *(978-1-62617-225-8(0)*, Blastoff! Readers) Bellwether Media.

MILLIPEDES—FICTION

Ross, Bakthi. Millipede Curl. 2007. 17.00 *(978-0-8059-8820-8(3))* Dorrance Publishing Co., Inc.

MILNE, A. A. (ALAN ALEXANDER), 1882-1956

Ellison, Virginia H. The Winnie-the-Pooh Cookbook. Shepard, Ernest H., illus. 2010. (Winnie-the-Pooh Ser.). (ENG.). 112p. (J). (gr. 3-7). 19.99 *(978-0-525-42359-1(1)*, Dutton Books for Young Readers) Penguin Young Readers Group.
Guillain, Charlotte. A. A. Milne, 1 vol. 2012. (Author Biographies Ser.). (ENG.). 24p. (gr. 1-2). 23.32 *(978-1-4329-5958-6(1))*; pap. 6.79 *(978-1-4329-5964-7(6))* Heinemann-Raintree. (Heinemann Read & Learn).
Ward, S. Meet A. A. Milne. 2009. (About the Author Ser.). 24p. (gr. 4-4). 42.50 *(978-1-61511-243-2(X)*, PowerKids Pr.) Rosen Publishing Group, Inc., The.

MILWAUKEE (WIS.)

Ruebartsch, John, photos by. All about Wisconsin: Todo Acerca de Wisconsin. 2007.Tr. of Todo Acerca de Wisconsin. (ENG & SPA., Illus.). 84p. (J). pap. 16.00 *(978-0-9770816-3-9(X))* SHARP Literacy, Inc.

MILWAUKEE (WIS.)—FICTION

Calford, Farley. The Complete Disaster, Rhonda's Birthday Party. 2009. 86p. pap. 9.95 *(978-1-60860-210-0(9)*, Eloquent Bks.) Strategic Book Publishing & Rights Agency (SBPRA).

MILWAUKEE (WIS.)—HISTORY

Stotts, Stuart. Father Groppi: Marching for Civil Rights. 2013. (Badger Biographies Ser.). (ENG., Illus.). 160p. (J). pap. 12.95 *(978-0-87020-575-0(7))* Wisconsin Historical Society.

MILWAUKEE BREWERS (BASEBALL TEAM)

Derong, Gary. Milwaukee Brewers, 1 vol. (Inside MLB Ser.). (ENG., 48p. (gr. 3-6). 2011. Illus.). (YA). lib. bdg. 32.79 *(978-1-61714-049-5(X))* 2014. lib. bdg. 32.79 *(978-1-62403-475-6(6)*, SportsZone) ABDO Publishing Co.
Epstein, Brad M. Milwaukee Brewers 101: My First Team-Board-Book. I.t. ed. 2007. (101 — My First Text-Board Books). (Illus.). 22p. (J). *(978-1-932530-75-9(4)*, 101 Bk.) Michaelson Entertainment.
Gilbert, Sara. The Story of the Milwaukee Brewers. (Illus.). 48p. 2011. (J). 35.65 *(978-1-60818-046-2(8)*, Creative Education) 2007. (YA). (gr. 4-7). lib. bdg. 32.80 *(978-1-58341-492-7(4))* Creative Co., The.
Stewart, Mark. The Milwaukee Brewers. 2012. (Team Spirit Ser.). 48p. (J). (gr. 3-6). lib. bdg. 29.27 *(978-1-59953-487-9(8))* Norwood Hse. Pr.

MIND

see Intellect; Psychology

MIND AND BODY

see also Dreams; Hypnotism; Nervous System; Psychoanalysis; Psychology, Pathological; Sleep

Be Your Best Self. 2017. (Be Your Best Self Ser.). 158p. (gr. 12-14). 223.00 ***(978-1-4994-6658-4(7)**, Rosen Young Adult)* Rosen Publishing Group, Inc., The.
Chopra, Deepak. Teens Ask Deepak: All the Right Questions. Barchowsky, Damien, illus. 2006. (ENG.). 208p. (YA). (gr. 7). pap. 15.99 *(978-0-689-86218-2(0)*, Simon Pulse) Simon Pulse.
Cook, David Fuller, compiled by. A Balanced Approach to Long Life & Vitality, Signature Edition: As Used in Fitness, Wellness, Clinical Weight Loss, & Cardiac Rehabilitation Programs. 2003. (Illus.). 80p. spiral bd. 31.95 *(978-0-9741629-0-4(6))* Cook, David.
Dahn Healer School. Home Massage Therapy Book 1: Heal Yourself & Your Loved Ones, 2 vols. 2004. (Dahnhak, the Way to Perfect Health Ser.: Vol. 2). (Illus.). 142p. per. 17.95 *(978-0-9720282-9-5(3))* Healing Society, Inc.
Esherick, Joan. Diet & Your Emotions: The Comfort Food Falsehood. 2004. (Obesity Ser.). (Illus.). 104p. (J). (gr. 4-7). lib. bdg. 23.95 *(978-1-59084-950-7(7))* Mason Crest.
Fisher, Beverly. Level One Workbook: Getting Started 2004. (Illus.). pap. 9.99 *(978-0-9745066-2-3(1))* Sports In Mind.
Hanson, Paul & Nagourney, Eric. My Silly Body: A User's Manual for Boys & Girls. 2009. (ENG., Illus.). 64p. (J). (gr. -1-3). bds. 13.95 *(978-0-7611-5409-9(4)*, 15409) Workman Publishing Co., Inc.
Leavitt, Amy. Yoga Fitness. 2014. (ENG.). 48p. (gr. 4-8). 29.95 *(978-1-61228-551-1(1))* Mitchell Lane Pubs., Inc.
Lite, Lori. Affirmation Weaver: A Believe in Yourself Story Designed to Help Children Increase Self-Esteem While Decreasing Stress & Anxiety. 2nd ed. 2011. 24p. pap. 14.95 *(978-0-9836256-9-8(7))* Stress Free Pubs.
—Angry Octopus: An Anger Management Story Introducing Active Progressive Muscular Relaxation & Deep Breathing. 2011. (Illus.). 30p. (gr. -1-3). pap. 14.95 *(978-0-9836256-8-1(9))* Stress Free Pubs.
—A Boy & a Turtle: A Relaxation Story Teaching Young Children Visualization Techniques to Increase Creativity While Lowering Stress & Anxiety Lev. 3rd ed. 2012.Tr. of niño y una Tortuga. (ENG.). 16p. (J). pap. 12.95 *(978-1-937985-13-4(X))* Stress Free Pubs.
—Bubble Riding: A Relaxation Story Designed to Teach Children Visualization Techniques to Increase Creativity While Lowering Stress & Anxiety. 2012.Tr. of Montando Burbujas. (ENG.). (J). pap. 14.95 *(978-1-937985-03-5(2))* Stress Free Pubs.
—Buenas Noches Oruga: Una Historia para la Relajación Que Ayuda a Los Niños a Controlar la Ira y el Estrés para Que Se Queden Dormidos Sosegadamente. 2012.Tr. of Goodnight Caterpillar. (SPA., Illus.). 16p. (J). pap. 12.95 *(978-1-937985-16-5(4))* Stress Free Pubs.
—Caleta de la Nutria Marina: Un Cuento para la Ansiedad Infantil, Enseña la Relajación, la Respiración Profunda para Reducir la Ansiedad, el Estrés y la Ira, a la Vez Que Fomenta el Sueño Sosegado. 2011.Tr. of Sea Otter Cove. (SPA., Illus.). 28p. (J). pap. 14.95 *(978-1-937985-11-0(3))* Stress Free Pubs.
—The Goodnight Caterpillar: A Children's Relaxation Story to Improve Sleep, Manage Stress, Anxiety, Anger. 3rd abr. ed. 2011.Tr. of Buenas Noches, Oruga. (ENG.). 18p. (J). pap. 12.95 *(978-1-937985-00-4(8))* Stress Free Pubs.
—Montando Burbujas: Un Cuento con Ejercicios de Relajación para Niños, Diseñada para Enseñar a Los Niños Técnicas de Visualización para Aumentar la Creatividad Mientras Disminuyen Sus Niveles de Ansiedad y de Estrés. 2012.Tr. of Bubble Riding. (SPA., Illus.). 32p. (J). pap. 14.95 *(978-1-937985-12-7(1))* Stress Free Pubs.
—El Niño y la Tortuga: Un Cuento para Promover la Relajación. 2012.Tr. of Boy & a Turtle. (SPA., Illus.). 16p. (J). pap. 12.95 *(978-1-937985-17-2(2))* Stress Free Pubs.
—El Pulpo Enojado: Un Cuento Sobre Cómo Controlar la Ira Que Enseña la Relajación Muscular Activa y Progresiva, y la Respiración: un Cuento Sobre Cómo Controlar la Ira Que Enseña la Relajación Muscular Activa y Progresiva, y la Respiración. 2012.Tr. of Angry Octopus. (SPA., Illus.). 30p. (J). pap. 14.95 *(978-1-937985-01-1(6))* Stress Free Pubs.
—Sea Otter Cove: A Relaxation Story, Introducing Deep Breathing to Decrease Anxiety, Stress & Anger While Promoting Peaceful Sleep. 2nd ed. 2012.Tr. of Caleta de la Nutria Marina. (SPA & ENG., Illus.). 24p. (J). 14.95 *(978-1-937985-08-0(3))* Stress Free Pubs.
—Tejedor de Afirmaciones: Un Cuento Que Aumenta la Autoestima en Los Niños, Creer en Ellos Mismos, Mientras Que Reducen Su Estrés y Su Ansiedad. 2012.Tr. of Affirmation Weaver. (SPA., Illus.). 24p. (J). pap. 14.95 *(978-1-937985-02-8(4))* Stress Free Pubs.
Mather, Kelly. The Five Keys to Wellness. Schneller, Lisa, illus. 2006. 46p. *(978-0-9787179-8-8(8))* Harmony Healing Hse.
Mattern, Joanne. Famous Mystics & Psychics. 2004. (gr. 7-10). 27.45 *(978-1-59018-558-2(7))* Cengage Gale.
Ripley Entertainment Staff, contrib. by. Body & Mind. 2010. (Ripley's Believe It or Not Ser.). 36p. (YA). (gr. 3-18). lib. bdg. 19.95 *(978-1-4222-1532-6(6))* Mason Crest.
Sargent, Brian. The Placebo Effect: The Power of Positive Thinking. 2014. (ENG., Illus.). 28p. pap. 9.50 *(978-1-107-62263-0(8))* Cambridge Univ. Pr.
Steps to Healthy Touching: Activities to Help Kids Understand & Control Their Problems with Touching. 2nd ed. 2003. (Illus.). 128p. (J). per., wbk. ed. 14.95 *(978-1-55864-138-9(6))* JIST Publishing.
Wells, Rosemary & Rosemary, Wells. El Mundo Que Nos Rodea. Fernandez, Leire Amigo, tr. Koelsch, Michael, illus. 2004. (SPA.). (J). (gr. -1-1). 14.99 *(978-84-241-8711-8(3))* Everest Editora ESP. Dist: Lectorum Pubns., Inc.
Willard, Christopher. The Mindfulness for Teen Anxiety: A Workbook for Overcoming Anxiety at Home, at School, & Everywhere Else. 2014. (ENG.). 168p. (YA). (gr. 5-12). pap. 16.95 *(978-1-60882-910-1(3))* New Harbinger Pubns.

MIND CURE

see Christian Science; Mind and Body

MINERAL INDUSTRIES

see Mines and Mineral Resources

MINERAL LANDS

see Mines and Mineral Resources

MINERAL OIL

see Petroleum

MINERAL RESOURCES

see Mines and Mineral Resources

MINERALOGY

see also Gems; Precious Stones

ABDO Publishing Company Staff. Rocks & Minerals. 2014. (Rocks & Minerals Ser.: 8). (ENG.). 48p. (gr. 8-12). lib. bdg. 262.32 *(978-1-62403-383-4(0))* ABDO Publishing Co.
Allen, Nancy Kelly. Minerals & Rocks. 2009. (Rock It! Ser.). 24p. (ENG.). (J). (gr. 3-6). pap. 8.25 *(978-1-4358-3184-1(5))*; (gr. 3-4). 42.50 *(978-1-60852-492-1(2)*, PowerKids Pr.); (YA). (gr. 2-5). lib. bdg. 22.60 *(978-1-4358-2761-5(9))* Rosen Publishing Group, Inc., The.
Anderson, Michael. Investigating Minerals, Rocks, & Fossils. 2011. (Illus.). 88p. (J). lib. bdg. 31.70 *(978-1-61530-500-1(9))* Rosen Publishing Group, Inc., The.
Aston, Dianna Hutts. A Rock Is Lively. Long, Sylvia, illus. 2012. (ENG.). 40p. (J). (gr. k-5). 16.99 *(978-1-4521-0645-8(2))* Chronicle Bks. LLC.
—A Rock Is Lively. 2015. (J). lib. bdg. 18.40 *(978-0-606-37444-6(2))* Turtleback Bks.
Atwood, Frederick D. Rocks & Minerals - Pb: A Portrait of the Natural World. 2013. (Portrait of the Natural World Ser.). (Illus.). 72p. pap. 9.95 *(978-1-59764-332-0(7))* New Line Bks.
Basher, Simon & Green, Dan. Rocks & Minerals: A Gem of a Book! Basher, Simon, illus. 2009. (Basher Science Ser.). (ENG., Illus.). 128p. (J). (gr. 5-9). pap. 8.99 *(978-0-7534-6314-7(8)*, 9780753463147, Kingfisher) Roaring Brook Pr.
Baxter, Roberta. Minerals. 2016. (Geology Rocks! Ser.). (ENG.). 24p. (J). (gr. 3-6). 28.50 *(978-1-5038-0803-4(3)*, 210639) Child's World, Inc., The.
Benchmark Education Company, LLC Staff, compiled by. Rocks & Minerals: Theme Set. 2006. (J). 215.00 *(978-1-4108-7135-0(5))* Benchmark Education Co.
—Rocky Tales & Earth Systems. 2005. spiral bd. 225.00 *(978-1-4108-5819-1(7))* Benchmark Education Co.
Bowman, Chris. Minerals. (Illus.). 24p. (J). 2015. lib. bdg. *(978-0-531-20588-4(6))* 2014. (ENG., lib. bdg. 25.95 *(978-1-60014-960-1(4)*, Blastoff! Readers) Bellwether Media.
Brannon, Cecelia H. A Look at Minerals. 2016. (Rock Cycle Ser.). (ENG.). 32p. (J). (gr. 3-4). pap. 10.52 *(978-0-7660-7307-4(6))*; (Illus.). 25.27 *(978-0-7660-7309-8(2))* Enslow Pubs., Inc.
Brinkman, Patricia. Discover Minerals. 2006. (J). pap. *(978-1-4108-6495-6(2))* Benchmark Education Co.
—Minerals. 2006. (J). pap. *(978-1-4108-6492-5(8))* Benchmark Education Co.
Brown, Cynthia Light & Brown, Nick. Explore Rocks & Minerals! 20 Great Projects, Activities, Experiments. Stone, Bryan, illus. 2010. (Explore Your World Ser.). (ENG.). 96p. (J). (gr. k-4). pap. 12.95 *(978-1-934670-61-3(8))* Octavio Publishing.
Burns, T. D. BOOST Rocks & Minerals Coloring Book. 2013. (BOOST Educational Ser.). (ENG.). 48p. (J). (gr. 3-5). pap. 5.99 *(978-0-486-49437-1(3))* Dover Pubns., Inc.
Centore, Michael. Vitamins & Minerals. 2017. (J). ***(978-1-4222-3745-8(1))*** Mason Crest.
Challoner, Jack. Find Out about Rocks & Minerals: With 23 Projects & More Than 350 Pictures. 2013. (ENG., Illus.). 64p. (J). (gr. k-8). 9.99 *(978-1-84322-747-2(9)*, Armadillo) Anness Publishing GBR. Dist: National Bk. Network.
Challoner, Jack & Walshaw, Rodney. Rocks & Minerals: Crystals; Erosion; Geology; Fossils. 2015. (ENG., Illus.). 64p. 12.99 *(978-1-86147-465-0(2)*, Armadillo) Anness Publishing GBR. Dist: National Bk. Network.
Clarke, Phillip & Tudhope, Simon, eds. 100 Rocks & Minerals to Spot. 2009. (Spotter's Cards Ser.). 52p. (J). 9.99 *(978-0-7945-2255-1(6)*, Usborne) EDC Publishing.
Close, Edward. Earth's Treasures: Rocks & Minerals: Rocks & Minerals, 1 vol., 1. 2014. (Discovery Education: Earth & Space Science Ser.). (ENG.). 32p. (gr. 3-6). 26.25 *(978-1-4777-6170-0(5)*, PowerKids Pr.) Rosen Publishing Group, Inc., The.
Corriel, Michele. Weird Rocks, 1 vol. Bilyeu, Dan, illus. 2013. (ENG.). 36p. (J). 12.00 *(978-0-87842-597-6(7))* Mountain Pr. Publishing Co., Inc.
Cull, Selby. Rocks & Minerals. 2009. (Restless Earth Ser.). (Illus.). 112p. (YA). (gr. 5-9). 35.00 *(978-0-7910-9702-1(1))* Facts On File, Inc.
Dayton, Connor. Crystals. (Rocks & Minerals Ser.). 24p. (gr. 2-3). 2009. 42.50 *(978-1-60852-498-3(1)*, PowerKids Pr.) 2007. (Illus.). (YA). lib. bdg. 22.60 *(978-1-4042-3687-5(2))* Rosen Publishing Group, Inc., The.
—Minerals. (Rocks & Minerals Ser.). 24p. (gr. 2-3). 2009. 42.50 *(978-1-60852-501-0(5)*, PowerKids Pr.) 2007. (Illus.). (YA). lib. bdg. 22.60 *(978-1-4042-3691-2(0))* Rosen Publishing Group, Inc., The.
—Rocks & Minerals, 6 bks., Set. Incl. Crystals. lib. bdg. 22.60 *(978-1-4042-3687-5(2))*; Fossils. lib. bdg. 22.60 *(978-1-4042-3689-9(9))*; Gemstones. lib. bdg. 22.60 *(978-1-4042-3686-8(4))*; Minerals. lib. bdg. 22.60 *(978-1-4042-3691-2(0))*; Rock Formations. lib. bdg. 22.60 *(978-1-4042-3690-5(2))*; Volcanic Rocks. lib. bdg. 22.60 *(978-1-4042-3688-2(0))*; (Illus.). 24p. (YA). (gr. 2-5). 2007. 2007. Set lib. bdg. 127.50 *(978-1-4042-3610-3(4)*, PowerKids Pr.) Rosen Publishing Group, Inc., The.
Dee, Willa. Earth's Rock Cycle, 1 vol., 1. 2014. (Rocks: the Hard Facts Ser.). (ENG.). 24p. (J). (gr. 3-6). 23.60 *(978-1-4777-2903-8(8)*, PowerKids Pr.) Rosen Publishing Group, Inc., The.
—Minerals, 1 vol., 1. 2014. (Rocks: the Hard Facts Ser.). (ENG.). 24p. (J). (gr. 3-6). 23.60 *(978-1-4777-2905-2(4)*, PowerKids Pr.) Rosen Publishing Group, Inc., The.
Dorling Kindersley Publishing Staff. Pocket Genius: Rocks & Minerals. 2016. (Pocket Genius Ser.). (ENG., Illus.). 160p. (J). (gr. 3-7). pap. 4.99 *(978-1-4654-4590-2(0)*, DK Children) Dorling Kindersley Publishing, Inc.
—Rocks & Minerals. 2014. (ENG.). (J). 96p. (gr. 2-4). pap. 12.99 *(978-1-4654-1654-4(4))*; 56p. (gr. k-4). 10.99 *(978-1-4654-1559-2(9))* Dorling Kindersley Publishing, Inc. (DK Children).
Dorling Kindersley Publishing Staff & Dennie, Devin P. My Book of Rocks & Minerals. 2017. (ENG., Illus.). 96p. (J). (gr. 1-4). 12.99 ***(978-1-4654-6190-2(6)**,* DK Children) Dorling Kindersley Publishing, Inc.
Dunlop, Jenna & Morganelli, Adrianna. Minerals. 2004. (Rocks, Minerals, & Resources Ser.). (ENG., Illus.). 32p. (J). lib. bdg. *(978-0-7787-1415-6(2))* Crabtree Publishing Co.
Eid, Alain. 1000 Photos of Minerals & Fossils. Viard, Michel, illus. 2003. (One Thousand Photos Ser.). 128p. (YA). (gr. 5-18). pap. 24.95 *(978-0-7641-5218-4(1))* Barron's Educational Series, Inc.
Encyclopaedia Britannica, Inc. Staff, compiled by. Britannica Illustrated Science Library: Rocks & Minerals, 16 vols. 2008. (Illus.). (J). 29.95 *(978-1-59339-396-0(2))* Encyclopaedia Britannica, Inc.
Ethan, Eric. Diamonds. 2011. (Gems: Nature's Jewels Ser.). (Illus.). 24p. (J). (gr. 2-5). 22.60 *(978-1-4339-4715-5(3))*; pap. 8.15 *(978-1-4339-4716-2(1))* Stevens, Gareth Publishing LLLP. (Gareth Stevens Learning Library).
—Emeralds. 2011. (Gems: Nature's Jewels Ser.). (Illus.). 24p. (J). (gr. 2-5). pap. 8.15 *(978-1-4339-4720-9(X))*; lib. bdg. 22.60 *(978-1-4339-4719-3(6))* Stevens, Gareth Publishing LLLP. (Gareth Stevens Learning Library).
—Opals. 2011. (Gems: Nature's Jewels Ser.). (Illus.). 24p. (gr. 2-5). 22.60 *(978-1-4339-4723-0(4))*; pap. 8.15 *(978-1-4339-4724-7(2))* Stevens, Gareth Publishing LLLP. (Gareth Stevens Learning Library).
—Rubies. 2011. (Gems: Nature's Jewels Ser.). (Illus.). 24p. (gr. 2-5). 22.60 *(978-1-4339-4727-8(7))*; pap. 8.15 *(978-1-4339-4728-5(5))* Stevens, Gareth Publishing LLLP. (Gareth Stevens Learning Library).
—Sapphires. 2011. (Gems: Nature's Jewels Ser.). (Illus.). 24p. (gr. 2-5). 22.60 *(978-1-4339-4731-5(5))*; pap. 8.15 *(978-1-4339-4732-2(3))* Stevens, Gareth Publishing LLLP. (Gareth Stevens Learning Library).
—Turquoise. 2011. (Gems: Nature's Jewels Ser.). (Illus.). 24p. (J). (gr. 2-5). pap. 8.15 *(978-1-4339-4712-4(9))*; lib. bdg. 22.60 *(978-1-4339-4711-7(0))* Stevens, Gareth Publishing LLLP. (Gareth Stevens Learning Library).
Farndon, John. Rocks, Gems, Minerals. 2016. (ENG., Illus.). 120p. (J). (gr. 6-10). 24.95 *(978-1-77085-740-7(0)*, 9781770857407) Firefly Bks., Ltd.
—Rocks, Minerals & Gems. 2016. (ENG., Illus.). 120p. (J). (gr. 6-10). pap. 12.95 *(978-1-77085-868-8(7)*, 9781770858688) Firefly Bks., Ltd.
Gardner, Robert. Smashing Science Projects about Earth's Rocks & Minerals. LaBaff, Tom, illus. 2007. (Rockin' Earth Science Experiments Ser.). 48p. (J). (gr. 3-4). lib. bdg. 25.27 *(978-0-7660-2731-2(7)*, Enslow Elementary) Enslow Pubs., Inc.
Glaser, Jason. Minerals up Close. 2013. (Under the Microscope Ser.). 32p. (J). (gr. 4-6). pap. 11.70 *(978-1-4339-8347-4(8))*; pap. 70.20 *(978-1-4339-8348-1(6))*; lib. bdg. 26.60 *(978-1-4339-8346-7(X))* Stevens, Gareth Publishing LLLP.
Goldman, Phyllis B., ed. Monkeyshines on Rocks & Minerals. (Illus.). 148p. (J). (gr. -1-7). reprint ed. pap. 26.95 *(978-1-888325-14-0(3))* Allosaurus Pubs.
Green, Dan. Rocks & Minerals. 2013. (Scholastic Discover More Ser.). (ENG.). 112p. (J). (gr. 5-9). 15.99 *(978-0-545-50511-6(9)*, Scholastic Reference) Scholastic, Inc.
Gregorovna, Anna. Inside Earth: Rocks & Minerals. 2012. (InfoMax Readers Ser.). (ENG., Illus.). 24p. (J). (gr. 1-2). pap. 8.25 *(978-1-4488-9043-9(8)*, Rosen Classroom) Rosen Publishing Group, Inc., The.
Group/McGraw-Hill, Wright. Materials Que Hay en la Tierra, 6 vols. (First Explorers. Primeros Exploradores Nonfiction Sets Ser.). (SPA.). (gr. 1-2). 29.95 *(978-0-7699-1468-8(3))* Shortland Pubns. (U. S. A.) Inc.
Hand, Carol. Experiments with Rocks & Minerals. 2011. (True Bk Ser.). (ENG., Illus.). 48p. (J). pap. 6.95 *(978-0-531-26648-9(6))*; lib. bdg. 29.00 *(978-0-531-26348-8(7))* Scholastic Library Publishing. (Children's Pr.).
Hansen, Grace. Menas. 2016. (¡Súper Geología! Ser.). (SPA.). 24p. (J). (gr. 1-6). pap. 7.95 *(978-1-4966-0681-5(7))* Capstone Classroom.
—Minerales. 2016. (¡Súper Geología! Ser.). (SPA.). 24p. (J). (gr. 1-6). pap. 7.95 *(978-1-4966-0680-8(9))* Capstone Classroom.

—Minerals, 1 vol. 2016. (ENG., Illus.). 24p. (J). *(978-1-62970-907-9(7)*, 1391186) ABDO Publishing Co.
—Ores, 1 vol. 2016. (ENG., Illus.). 24p. *(978-1-62970-908-6(5)*, 1391188) ABDO Publishing Co.
—Rocks, 1 vol. 2016. (ENG., Illus.). 24p. (J). *(978-1-62970-909-3(3)*, 1391189) ABDO Publishing Co.
Hantula, Richard. Rocks & Fossils. 2007. (Gareth Stevens Vital Science: Earth Science Ser.). (Illus.). 48p. (gr. 5-12). pap. 14.05 *(978-0-8368-7876-9(0)*, Gareth Stevens Secondary Library) Stevens, Gareth Publishing LLLP.
Harrison, Lorraine. All Kinds of Rocks. 2013. (InfoMax Readers Ser.). (ENG.). 24p. (J). (gr. 2-3). pap. 49.50 *(978-1-4777-2408-8(7))*; (Illus.). pap. 8.25 *(978-1-4777-2407-1(9))* Rosen Publishing Group, Inc., The. (Rosen Classroom).
Hirschmann, Kris. Rocks & Minerals. 2004. (World Discovery Science Readers Ser.). (Illus.). 31p. (J). pap. 4.95 *(978-0-439-56630-8(4))* Scholastic, Inc.
Hodge, Judith. Riches from Earth & Las riquezas de la Tierra: 6 English, 6 Spanish Adaptations. 2011. (ENG & SPA.). (J). 97.00 net. *(978-1-4108-5716-3(6))* Benchmark Education Co.
Hoffman, Steven M. Rock Study: A Guide to Looking at Rocks. 2011. (Rock It! Ser.). (Illus.). 24p. (J). pap. 8.25 *(978-1-4488-2713-8(2))*; lib. bdg. 22.60 *(978-1-4488-2562-2(8))* Rosen Publishing Group, Inc., The. (PowerKids Pr.).
Hyde, Natalie. How to Be a Rock Collector. 2012. (Let's Rock! Ser.). (ENG., Illus.). 32p. (J). (gr. 3-6). lib. bdg. *(978-0-7787-7212-5(8))* Crabtree Publishing Co.
—What Are Minerals? 2012. (ENG., Illus.). 32p. (J). pap. *(978-0-7787-7220-0(9))*; (gr. 3-6). lib. bdg. *(978-0-7787-7215-6(2))* Crabtree Publishing Co.
Hyler, Nelson W. The How & Why Wonder Book of Rocks & Minerals. Blackwood, Paul E., ed. Shannon, Kenyon, illus. 2011. 52p. 36.95 *(978-1-258-10482-5(2))* Literary Licensing, LLC.
Ivancic, Linda. Soil for Tools & Art. 2016. (Science of Soil Ser.). 48p. (J). 31.36 *(978-1-5026-2166-5(5))* Cavendish Square Publishing.
Lawrence, Ellen. How Do People Use Rocks? 2014. (Science Slam!: Rock-Ology Ser.). (ENG.). 24p. (J). (gr. -1-3). lib. bdg. 23.93 *(978-1-62724-303-2(8))* Bearport Publishing Co., Inc.
—Rocks & Minerals. 2015. (FUN-Damental Experiments Ser.). (ENG.). 24p. (J). (gr. -1-3). lib. bdg. 23.93 *(978-1-62724-540-1(5))* Bearport Publishing Co., Inc.
Lockwood, Sophie. Super Cool Science Experiments: Minerals. 2009. (Explorer Library: Science Explorer Ser.). (ENG., Illus.). 32p. (gr. 4-8). lib. bdg. 28.50 *(978-1-60279-524-2(X)*, 200291) Cherry Lake Publishing.
MacAulay, Kelley. Why Do We Need Rocks & Minerals? 2014. (ENG., Illus.). 24p. (J). *(978-0-7787-0492-8(0))*; pap. *(978-0-7787-0496-6(3))* Crabtree Publishing Co.
Maloof, Torrey. Rocks & Minerals, 1 vol. rev. ed. 2014. (Science Readers: Content & Literacy Ser.). (ENG.). 32p. (gr. 2-2). pap. 8.99 *(978-1-4807-4610-7(X))* Teacher Created Materials, Inc.
Mattern, Joanne. Minerals & the Rock Cycle. (Shaping & Reshaping of Earth's Surface Ser.). 24p. (gr. 4-4). 2009. 42.50 *(978-1-60854-218-5(1)*, PowerKids Pr.) 2006. (Illus.). (YA). lib. bdg. 22.60 *(978-1-4042-3199-3(4))* Rosen Publishing Group, Inc., The.
McQueen, David. The Mineral Book. 2014. 96p. 16.99 *(978-0-89051-802-1(5))* Master Bks.
Meredith, Susan. Las Rocas, los Minerales y el Suelo. 2012. (SPA & ENG.). 48p. (gr. 4-8). pap. 10.95 *(978-1-61810-470-0(5))* Rourke Educational Media.
—Rocks, Minerals, & Soil. 2009. (Let's Explore Science Ser.). (Illus.). 48p. (gr. 4-8). (J). lib. bdg. 32.79 *(978-1-60694-411-0(8))*; (ENG., pap. 10.95 *(978-1-60694-529-2(7))* Rourke Educational Media.
Miles, Lisa. Usborne Rocks & Minerals Sticker Book. Khan, Sarah & Armstrong, Carrie, eds. Freeman, Mike & Julings, Emma, photos by. rev. ed. 2006. (Spotter's Guides Sticker Books - New Format Ser.). (Illus.). 16p. (J). (gr. 2-5). pap. 8.99 *(978-0-7945-1413-6(8)*, Usborne) EDC Publishing.
Miller-Schroeder, Patricia. Minerals. (Focus on Earth Science Ser.). (gr. 3-7). 2015. (ENG.). (J). lib. bdg. 27.13 *(978-1-4896-4085-7(1)*, AV2 by Weigl) 2010. (Illus.). 24p. (J). pap. 11.95 *(978-1-60596-977-0(X))* 2010. (Illus.). 24p. (YA). lib. bdg. 25.70 *(978-1-60596-976-3(1))* 2006. (Illus.). 24p. (J). lib. bdg. 24.45 *(978-1-59036-214-3(4))* Weigl Pubs., Inc.
Mills, Nathan & Roza, Greg. Exploring Rocks & Minerals. 2012. (Rosen Readers Ser.). (ENG., Illus.). 24p. (J). (gr. 1-2). pap. 49.50 *(978-1-4488-8831-3(X)*, 1348003); pap. 8.25 *(978-1-4488-8830-6(1)*, 1348003) Rosen Publishing Group, Inc., The. (Rosen Classroom).
Mooney, Carla. What Are Minerals?, 01 vols., 1. 2016. (Junior Geologist Ser.). (ENG., Illus.). 32p. (J). pap. 12.90 *(978-1-5081-0049-2(7)*, Britannica Educational Publishing) Rosen Publishing Group, Inc., The.
National Geographic Kids Staff & Honovich, Nancy. Rocks & Minerals. 2016. (ENG., Illus.). 160p. (J). (gr. 3-7). lib. bdg. 22.90 *(978-1-4263-2302-7(6)*, National Geographic Children's Bks.) National Geographic Society.
—Rocks & Minerals: Find Adventure! - Go Outside! - Have Fun! - Be a Rock Hound! 2016. (ENG., Illus.). 160p. (J). (gr. 3-7). pap. 12.99 *(978-1-4263-2301-0(8)*, National Geographic Children's Bks.) National Geographic Society.
Natural History Museum Collection Staff. Rocks & Minerals Sticker Book. 2013. (ENG.). 14p. (J). (gr. -1-1). pap. 7.99 *(978-0-565-09300-6(2))* Natural History Museum Pubns. GBR. Dist: Independent Pubs. Group.
Nelson, Maria. Earth's Minerals. 2013. (That Rocks! Ser.). 24p. (J). (gr. 2-5). pap. 48.90 *(978-1-4339-8311-5(7))*; (Illus.). pap. 8.15 *(978-1-4339-8310-8(9))*; (Illus.). lib. bdg. 22.60 *(978-1-4339-8309-2(5))* Stevens, Gareth Publishing LLLP.
Nsrc, prod. Science & Technology for Children BOOKS: Rocks & Minerals. 2007. (J). *(978-1-933008-40-0(7)*, Science and Technology Concepts (STC)) Smithsonian Science Education Ctr. (SSEC).
O'Donoghue, Michael. Rocks & Minerals of the World. 2004. (World Book's Science & Nature Guides Ser.). (Illus.). 80p. (J). *(978-0-7166-4217-6(4))* World Bk., Inc.
Ostopowich, Melanie. Rocks. 2010. (Earth Science Ser.). (Illus.). 24p. (gr. 3-5). (J). pap. 11.95 *(978-1-60596-962-6(1))*; (YA). lib. bdg. 25.70 *(978-1-60596-961-9(3))* Weigl Pubs., Inc.
Oxlade, Chris. Minerals. 2016. (Rock On! Ser.). (ENG., Illus.). 32p. (gr. 2-4). lib. bdg. 30.65 *(978-1-4109-8137-0(1)*, Raintree Perspectives) Heinemann-Raintree.
—Rocks & Minerals, 1 vol. (Essential Physical Science Ser.). (ENG., 48p. (gr. 4-6). 2014. Illus.). 33.32 *(978-1-4329-8150-1(1))* 2013. pap. 9.95 *(978-1-4329-8159-4(5))* Heinemann-Raintree. (Heinemann InfoSearch).
Pellant, Chris & Pellant, Helen. Crystals & Gemstones. 2008. (Rock Stars Ser.). (Illus.). 24p. (J). (gr. 1-4). lib. bdg. 23.00 *(978-0-8368-9222-2(4))* Stevens, Gareth Publishing LLLP.
—Minerals. 2008. (Rock Stars Ser.). (Illus.). 24p. (J). (gr. 1-4). lib. bdg. 23.00 *(978-0-8368-9224-6(0))* Stevens, Gareth Publishing LLLP.
—Quartz & Other Minerals. 2007. (Guide to Rocks & Minerals Ser.). (Illus.). 32p. (gr. 3-6). lib. bdg. 26.00 *(978-0-8368-7908-7(2)*, Gareth Stevens Learning Library) Stevens, Gareth Publishing LLLP.
Petersen, Christine. Jade, 1 vol. 2013. (Earth's Treasures Ser.). (ENG.). 32p. (J). (gr. 3-6). lib. bdg. 27.07 *(978-1-61783-872-9(1)*, Checkerboard Library) ABDO Publishing Co.
—Mighty Minerals, 1 vol. 2010. (Rock on!: a Look at Geology Ser.). (ENG.). 32p. (YA). (gr. 3-6). 27.07 *(978-1-60453-744-4(2))* ABDO Publishing Co.
—Outrageous Ores, 1 vol. 2010. (Rock on!: a Look at Geology Ser.). (ENG.). 32p. (YA). (gr. 3-6). 27.07 *(978-1-60453-745-1(0))* ABDO Publishing Co.
Phelan, Glen. Rocks & Minerals. 2007. (Nonfiction Reading & Writing Workshops Ser.). (ENG., Illus.). 32p. (J). pap. 17.95 *(978-0-7922-4571-1(7))* CENGAGE Learning.
Pinet, Michele. Be Your Own Rock & Mineral Expert. Greenbaum, Fay, tr. from FRE. Korkos, Alain, illus. 2003. 40p. (J). (gr. 5-7). 14.95 *(978-0-8069-9580-9(7))* Sterling Publishing Co., Inc.
Prokos, Anna. Rocks & Minerals. 2004. (Discovery Channel School Science Ser.). (Illus.). 32p. (gr. 4-8). lib. bdg. 26.00 *(978-0-8368-3384-3(8)*, Gareth Stevens Learning Library) Stevens, Gareth Publishing LLLP.
Rajczak Nelson, Kristen. What Are Minerals? 2017. (Look at Earth's Rocks Ser.). 32p. (J). (gr. 2-2). 26.60 ***(978-1-4824-6244-9(3))*** Stevens, Gareth Publishing LLLP.
Rau, Dana Meachen. Rocks & Minerals. 2009. (21st Century Skills Library: Real World Science Ser.). (ENG.). 32p. (gr. 4-8). lib. bdg. 28.50 *(978-1-60279-463-4(4)*, 200233) Cherry Lake Publishing.
Reynolds, Shaye. Volcanoes. 2016. (Spotlight on Earth Science Ser.). 00024p. (J). (gr. 4-6). pap. 10.00 *(978-1-4994-2537-6(6)*, PowerKids Pr.) Rosen Publishing Group, Inc., The.
Rocks & Minerals. 2005. 48p. (J). per. 6.99 *(978-1-59441-202-8(2)*, CD-104110) Carson-Dellosa Publishing, LLC.
Rocks & Minerals. 2009. (Hammond Undercover Ser.). 72p. (J). (gr. 3-7). 15.95 *(978-0-8437-1932-1(X))* Hammond World Atlas Corp.
Roza, Greg. Exploring Rocks & Minerals. 2012. (Exploring Earth & Space Ser.). (ENG., Illus.). 24p. (J). (gr. 1-3). 22.60 *(978-1-4488-8576-3(0)*, 1348003, PowerKids Pr.) Rosen Publishing Group, Inc., The.
Salzano, Tammi J. Rocks, Minerals, & Gemstones. Jankowski, Daniel, illus. 2009. 24p. (J). pap. *(978-0-545-19868-4(2))* Scholastic, Inc.
Scholastic, Inc. Staff, contrib. by. Rocks & Minerals. 2015. (Scholastic Discover More Reader, Level 2 Ser.). (ENG.). 32p. (J). (gr. 1-3). pap. 3.99 *(978-0-545-83947-1(5)*, Scholastic Reference) Scholastic, Inc.
Scholastic, Inc. Staff, et al. Rocks, Minerals & Gems. 2016. (ENG.). 224p. (J). (gr. 3-7). 19.99 *(978-0-545-94719-0(7)*, Scholastic Nonfiction) Scholastic, Inc.
Schuh, Mari C. Learning about Rocks, 1 vol. 2011. (Science Builders Ser.). (ENG.). 24p. (gr. k-1). pap. 7.29 *(978-1-4296-7108-8(4))*; pap. 41.70 *(978-1-4296-7114-9(9))*; lib. bdg. 26.65 *(978-1-4296-6072-3(4))* Capstone Press of Coughlan Cos. (Pebble Plus).
Science stories foss spanish earth materials ea Cr05. 2005. (J). *(978-1-59242-590-7(9))* Delta Education, LLC.
Sherman, Jill. Minerals & Heavy Metals. 2017. (J). pap. ***(978-0-7660-9147-4(3))*** Enslow Pubs., Inc.
Simon, Seymour. Rocks & Minerals. 2017. 48p. (J). (gr. 1-5). pap. 6.99 ***(978-0-06-228917-9(9))*** HarperCollins Pubs.
Spilsbury, Louise. Minerales. 2011. (Las Rocas Ser.). (SPA.). 32p. (gr. 3-5). pap. 8.29 *(978-1-4329-5661-5(2)*, Heinemann InfoSearch) Heinemann-Raintree.
Spilsbury, Louise & Spilsbury, Richard. Minerals, 1 vol. 2011. (Let's Rock Ser.). (ENG.). 32p. (gr. 3-6). 33.32 *(978-1-4329-4683-8(8))*; pap. 8.29 *(978-1-4329-4691-3(9))* Heinemann-Raintree. (Heinemann InfoSearch).
Squire, Ann O. Minerals. 2012. (True Book(tm), a — Earth Science Ser.). (ENG.). 48p. (J). lib. bdg. 31.00 *(978-0-531-26144-6(1))*; pap. 6.95 *(978-0-531-26252-8(9))* Scholastic Library Publishing.
—Rocks. 2012. (True Book(tm), a — Earth Science Ser.). (ENG.). 48p. (J). lib. bdg. 31.00 *(978-0-531-26145-3(X))*; pap. 6.95 *(978-0-531-26253-5(7))* Scholastic Library Publishing.
Stamper, Judith Bauer. Rocks & Minerals. 2010. (Illus.). 32p. (J). pap. *(978-0-545-28544-5(5))* Scholastic, Inc.
Stewart, Melissa. Extreme Rocks & Minerals! 2007. (Smithsonian Q & A Ser.). (ENG., Illus.). 48p. (J). (gr. k-4). pap. 8.99 *(978-0-06-089981-3(6)*, Collins) HarperCollins Pubs.
Symes, R. F. DK Eyewitness Books: Rocks & Minerals: Rocks & Minerals. 2014. (DK Eyewitness Bks.). (ENG.). 72p. (J). (gr. 3-7). pap. 9.99 *(978-1-4654-2056-5(8)*, DK Children) Dorling Kindersley Publishing, Inc.
Tomecek, Steve. Rocks & Minerals. Poling, Kyle, illus. 2010. (Jump into Science Ser.). (ENG.). 32p. (J). (gr. -1-3). 16.95 *(978-1-4263-0538-2(9))*; lib. bdg. 25.90 *(978-1-4263-0539-9(7))* National Geographic Society. (National Geographic Children's Bks.).
Tomecek, Steve & National Geographic Kids Staff. National Geographic Kids Everything Rocks & Minerals: Dazzling Gems of Photos & Info That Will Rock Your World. 2011. (ENG., Illus.). 64p. (J). (gr. 3-7). pap. 12.95 *(978-1-4263-0768-3(3)*, National Geographic Children's Bks.) National Geographic Society.
Tomecek, Steve the Dirtmeister. Rocks & Minerals: Dazzling Gems of Photos & Info That Will Rock Your World. 2011. (National Geographic Kids Everything Ser.). (ENG., Illus.). 64p. (J). (gr. 3-7). 25.90 *(978-1-4263-0801-7(9)*, National Geographic Children's Bks.) National Geographic Society.
Trueit, Trudi Strain. Rocks, Gems, & Minerals. 2003. (Watts Library). (ENG.). 64p. (gr. 5-7). pap. 8.95 *(978-0-531-16241-5(9)*, Watts, Franklin) Scholastic Library Publishing.
Tuchman, Gail. Rocks & Minerals. 2015. (Scholastic Reader Level 2 Ser.). lib. bdg. 13.55 *(978-0-606-37757-7(3))* Turtleback Bks.
Walker, Sally M. Marveling at Minerals. 2013. (Searchlight Books (tm) — Do You Dig Earth Science? Ser.). (ENG.). 40p. (gr. 3-5). lib. bdg. 27.93 *(978-1-4677-0022-1(3)*, Lerner Pubns.); (Illus.). pap. 8.95 *(978-1-4677-0792-3(9))* Lerner Publishing Group.
—Minerals. (Early Bird Earth Science Ser.). (Illus.). 48p. (J). 2007. pap. 8.95 *(978-0-8225-6620-5(6))* 2006. (gr. 3-7). lib. bdg. 25.26 *(978-0-8225-5946-7(3))* Lerner Publishing Group. (Lerner Pubns.).
Watson, Stephanie. Vitamins & Minerals: Getting the Nutrients Your Body Needs. 2010. (Healthy Habits Ser.). (Illus.). 64p. (YA). (gr. 5-8). pap. 12.95 *(978-1-4488-0613-3(5))*; lib. bdg. 31.95 *(978-1-4358-9443-3(X))* Rosen Publishing Group, Inc., The. (Rosen Reference).
Woolley, A. Rocks & Minerals. 2004. (Spotter's Guides). (Illus.). 64p. (J). lib. bdg. 13.95 *(978-1-58086-309-4(4))* EDC Publishing.
Woolley, Alan. Rocks & Minerals Spotter's Guide: With Internet Links. Freeman, Mike, photos by. rev. ed. 2007. (Spotter's Guides). (Illus.). 64p. (J). pap. 5.99 *(978-0-7945-1304-7(2)*, Usborne) EDC Publishing.
Wooster, Patricia. Show Me Rocks & Minerals. 2013. (My First Picture Encyclopedias Ser.). (ENG., Illus.). 32p. (gr. 1-2). 7.95 *(978-1-4765-3346-9(6)*, Aplus Bks.) Capstone Press of Coughlan Cos.
—Show Me Rocks & Minerals: My First Picture Encyclopedia, 1 vol. 2013. (My First Picture Encyclopedias Ser.). (ENG.). 32p. (gr. 1-2). 27.32 *(978-1-4765-0116-1(5))*; pap. 8.10 *(978-1-4765-3350-6(4))* Capstone Press of Coughlan Cos. (Aplus Bks.).
Zoehfeld, Kathleen Weidner. National Geographic Readers: Rocks & Minerals. 2012. (Readers Ser.). (ENG., Illus.). 32p. (J). (gr. k-3). lib. bdg. 13.90 *(978-1-4263-1039-3(0)*, National Geographic Children's Bks.) National Geographic Society.
—Rocks & Minerals. 2012. (Readers Ser.). (ENG., Illus.). 32p. (J). (gr. k-3). pap. 3.99 *(978-1-4263-1038-6(2)*, National Geographic Children's Bks.) National Geographic Society.

MINERALS

see Mineralogy

MINERS

Gordon, Nick. Coal Miner. 2013. (Dangerous Jobs Ser.). (ENG., Illus.). 24p. (J). (gr. 3-7). lib. bdg. 25.95 *(978-1-60014-893-4(X)*, Torque Bks.) Bellwether Media.
Hyde, Natalie. Life in a Mining Community. 2009. (Learn about Rural Life Ser.). (ENG., Illus.). 32p. (J). (gr. 3-6). pap. *(978-0-7787-5087-1(6))*; lib. bdg. *(978-0-7787-5074-1(4))* Crabtree Publishing Co.
Landau, Elaine. The California Gold Rush: Would You Go for the Gold? 2010. (What Would You Do? Ser.). (Illus.). 48p. (J). pap. 8.95 *(978-1-59845-193-1(6)*, Enslow Elementary) Enslow Pubs., Inc.
Lyon, George Ella. Which Side Are You On? The Story of a Song. Cardinale, Christopher, illus. 2011. (ENG.). 40p. (J). (gr. 2-4). 17.95 *(978-1-933693-96-5(7))* Cinco Puntos Pr.
O'Brien, Cynthia. Go West with Miners, Prospectors, & Loggers. 2016. (ENG.). 32p. (J). *(978-0-7787-2328-8(3))* Crabtree Publishing Co.
Savage, Jeff. Rugged Gold Miners: True Tales of the Wild West. 2012. (True Tales of the Wild West Ser.). (Illus.). 48p. (J). (gr. 5-18). 22.60 *(978-0-7660-4020-5(8))* Enslow Pubs., Inc.
Stanbridge, Joanne. Maurice Ruddick: Un Survivant. 2004. (FRE., Illus.). (J). *(978-2-7650-0744-9(6))* Les Editions de la Cheneliere, Inc.
Tieck, Sarah. Miners, 1 vol. 2011. (Extreme Jobs Ser.). (ENG., Illus.). 32p. (J). (gr. 2-5). 28.50 *(978-1-61783-026-6(7))* ABDO Publishing Co.

MINERS—FICTION

Blackwater Mine, 6 Pack. (Bookweb Ser.). 32p. (gr. 6-18). 34.00 *(978-0-7578-0893-7(X))* Rigby Education.
Croker, Verity. May Day Mine. (ENG., Illus.). (J). 2016. 24.99 ***(978-1-63533-048-9(3))*** 2015. 180p. pap. 14.99 *(978-1-63216-717-0(4))* Dreamspinner Pr. (Harmony Ink Pr.).
Gregory, Kristiana. My Darlin' Clementine. 2009. (ENG.). 192p. (J). (gr. 5-18). 16.95 *(978-0-8234-2198-5(8))* Holiday Hse., Inc.
Hancock, H. Irving. The Young Engineers in Mexico. 2007. 176p. per. *(978-1-4065-1994-5(4))* Dodo Pr.
Marsh, Carole. The Gosh Awful! Gold Rush Mystery. (Real Kids, Real Places Ser.). (Illus.). 146p. (J). 2009. lib. bdg. 18.99 *(978-0-635-07026-5(X)*, Marsh, Carole Mysteries) 2007. (gr. 2-8). 14.95 *(978-0-635-06390-8(5))* Gallopade International.
St. John, Patricia. A Home for Virginia. Smith, Helen, illus. 2005. (ENG.). 24p. (J). (gr. 4-7). 9.99 *(978-1-85792-961-4(6)*, 61d6526b-9c8a-4a92-bdf8-4e663de02131) Christian Focus Pubns. GBR. Dist: Bookmasters Distribution.
Steele, Michael Anthony & Scholastic Editors. Look Out Below! Kiernan, Kenny, illus. 2012. (LEGO City Scholastic Readers Level 1 Ser.). lib. bdg. 13.55 *(978-0-606-26236-1(9)*, Turtleback) Turtleback Bks.
Varonka, Steve. Hard Coal Times: Pennsylvania Anthracite Stories, Vol. 1. 2003. (Illus.). 40p. (J). 4.72 *(978-0-9709630-2-4(5))* Coal Hole Productions.
Whale Watch, 6 Packs. (Bookweb Ser.). 32p. (gr. 6-18). 34.00 *(978-0-7578-0895-1(6))* Rigby Education.
Wiseman, David. Jeremy Visick. 2005. 176p. (YA). (gr. 5-18). 21.25 *(978-0-8446-7271-7(8)*, 3594) Smith, Peter Pub., Inc.

MINES AND MINERAL RESOURCES

see also Mineralogy; Mining Engineering; Precious Metals also specific types of mines and mining, e.g. Coal Mines and Mining; etc.

Blake, Kevin. Deadly Mine: Libby, Montana. 2017. (Eco-Disasters Ser.). (ENG.). 32p. (J). (gr. 2-7). 19.95 ***(978-1-68402-222-9(3))*** Bearport Publishing Co., Inc.
Crowther, Robert. Deep down under Ground: A Pop-up Book of Amazing Facts & Feats. Crowther, Robert, illus. 2004. (Illus.). 18p. (J). (gr. 3-8). reprint ed. pap. 22.00 *(978-0-7567-7179-9(X))* DIANE Publishing Co.
Forman, Lillian E. The Diamond Trade, 1 vol. 2010. (Essential Viewpoints Set 5 Ser.). (ENG.). 112p. (J). (gr. 6-12). lib. bdg. 35.64 *(978-1-61613-520-1(4)*, Essential Library) ABDO Publishing Co.
Hayhurst, Chris. John Sutter: California Pioneer. 2009. (Primary Sources of Famous People in American History Ser.). 32p. (gr. 2-3). 47.90 *(978-1-60851-696-4(2))* Rosen Publishing Group, Inc., The.
Holt, Rinehart and Winston Staff. Environmental Science Chptr. 16: Mining & Mineral Resources. 4th ed. 2004. pap. 11.20 *(978-0-03-068077-9(8))* Holt McDougal.
Hyde, Natalie. Life in a Mining Community. 2009. (Learn about Rural Life Ser.). (ENG., Illus.). 32p. (J). (gr. 3-6). pap. *(978-0-7787-5087-1(6))*; lib. bdg. *(978-0-7787-5074-1(4))* Crabtree Publishing Co.
Kovacs, Nicola. Digging Deep. 2007. (Action Numeracy Middle Primary Ser.). 32p. pap. 9.95 *(978-0-86431-694-3(1))* ACER Pr. AUS. Dist: ISBS Publisher Services.
Lendroth, Susan. Calico Dorsey: Mail Dog of the Mining Camps. Gustavson, Adam, illus. 2010. (ENG.). 32p. (J). (gr. -1-2). 16.99 *(978-1-58246-318-6(2)*, Tricycle Pr.) Random Hse. Children's Bks.
MacAulay, Kelley. Why Do We Need Rocks & Minerals? 2014. (ENG., Illus.). 24p. (J). *(978-0-7787-0492-8(0))*; pap. *(978-0-7787-0496-6(3))* Crabtree Publishing Co.
Marsico, Katie. What's It Like to Live Here? Mining Town. 2014. (Community Connections: What's It Like to Live Here? Ser.). (ENG., Illus.). 24p. (J). (gr. 2-5). pap. 12.79 *(978-1-62431-582-4(8)*, 203253) Cherry Lake Publishing.
McDonnell, Julia. How Precious Metals Form. 2016. (From the Earth: How Resources Are Made Ser.). (Illus.). 32p. (J). (gr. 4-3). pap. 10.50 *(978-1-4824-4727-9(4))* Stevens, Gareth Publishing LLLP.
Miles, Lisa. Rocks & Minerals. 2003. (Usborne Hotshots Ser.). (ENG., Illus.). 1p. (YA). (gr. 2-18). pap. 2.95 *(978-0-7460-2790-5(7))* EDC Publishing.
O'Neal, Claire. A Project Guide to Rocks & Minerals. 2010. (Earth Science Projects for Kids Ser.). (Illus.). 48p. (J). (gr. 4-7). lib. bdg. 29.95 *(978-1-58415-866-0(2))* Mitchell Lane Pubs., Inc.
Stanbridge, Joanne. Maurice Ruddick: Un Survivant. 2004. (FRE., Illus.). (J). *(978-2-7650-0744-9(6))* Les Editions de la Cheneliere, Inc.
Zronik, John Paul & Zronik, John. Metals. 2004. (Rocks, Minerals, & Resources Ser.). (ENG., Illus.). 32p. (J). lib. bdg. *(978-0-7787-1418-7(7))* Crabtree Publishing Co.
—Metals - Shaping Our World. 2004. (Rocks, Minerals, & Resources Ser.). (ENG., Illus.). 32p. (J). pap. *(978-0-7787-1450-7(0))* Crabtree Publishing Co.

MINES AND MINERAL RESOURCES—FICTION

Blaine, John. The Blue Ghost Mystery: A Rick Brant Science Adventure Story. 2011. 188p. 42.95 *(978-1-258-09526-0(2))* Literary Licensing, LLC.
Boyce, Frank Cottrell. Framed, 1. Lenton, Steven, illus. 2nd ed. 2008. (ENG.). 336p. 17.95 *(978-0-330-45292-2(4)*, Macmillan) Pan Macmillan GBR. Dist: Trans-Atlantic Pubns., Inc.
Fraustino, Lisa Rowe. The Hole in the Wall. 2011. (ENG.). 232p. (J). (gr. 2-8). pap. 8.00 *(978-1-57131-698-1(1))* Milkweed Editions.
Glaze, Dave. Danger in Dead Man's Mine, 1 vol. 2009. (1912: the Mackenzie Davis Files Ser.). (ENG., Illus.). 176p. (J). (gr. 4-7). pap. 8.95 *(978-1-55050-416-3(9))* Coteau Bks. CAN. Dist: Orca Bk. Pubs. USA.
Kay, Ross. The Go Ahead Boys & Simon's Mine. Owen, R. Emmett, illus. 2007. 184p. per. *(978-1-4065-1857-3(3))* Dodo Pr.
—The Go Ahead Boys & Simon's Mine. 2007. 112p. per. *(978-1-4068-1924-3(7))* Echo Library.
Lewis, R. C. Stitching Snow. 2014. (ENG., Illus.). 332p. (YA). (gr. 9-17). 17.99 *(978-1-4231-8507-9(2))* Hyperion Bks. for Children.
Moyer, Jenny. Flashfall. 2016. (Flashfall Ser.). (ENG.). 352p. (YA). 17.99 *(978-1-62779-481-7(6)*, 9781627794817, Holt, Henry & Co. Bks. For Young Readers) Holt, Henry & Co.
Stamper, Judith Bauer. Rocky Road Trip. Gangloff, Hope, illus. 2004. (Magic School Bus Science Chapter Bks.). 89p. (gr. 2-5). lib. bdg. 15.00 *(978-0-7569-3093-6(6))* Perfection Learning Corp.
Steele, Michael Anthony & Scholastic Editors. Look Out Below! Kiernan, Kenny, illus. 2012. (LEGO City Scholastic Readers Level 1 Ser.). lib. bdg. 13.55 *(978-0-606-26236-1(9)*, Turtleback) Turtleback Bks.
Sylvester, Kevin. Miners. 2016. (MiNRS Ser.: 1). (ENG., Illus.). 352p. (J). (gr. 3-7). pap. 8.99 *(978-1-4814-4040-0(3)*, McElderry, Margaret K. Bks.) McElderry, Margaret K. Bks.
—MiNRS. (MiNRS Ser.: 2). (ENG., Illus.). (J). (gr. 3-7). 2016. 352p. 17.99 *(978-1-4814-4042-4(X))* 2015. 336p. 16.99 *(978-1-4814-4039-4(X))* McElderry, Margaret K. Bks. (McElderry, Margaret K. Bks.).
Wells, Helen. Cherry Ames, Island Nurse. 2007. (Cherry Ames Nurse Stories Ser.). 224p. (J). (gr. 3-7). 14.95 *(978-0-8261-0423-6(1))* Springer Publishing Co., Inc.
Wiechman, Kathy Canon. Empty Places. 2016. (ENG., Illus.). 240p. (J). (gr. 3-7). 17.95 *(978-1-62979-451-8(1)*, Calkins Creek) Boyds Mills Pr.
Williams, Michael. Diamond Boy. 2014. (Illus.). 384p. (YA). *(978-0-316-32067-2(6))* Little Brown & Co.
Winfield, Arthur M. The Rover Boys Out West. 2007. 228p. 26.95 *(978-1-4218-4140-3(1))*; per. 11.95 *(978-1-4218-4238-7(6))* 1st World Publishing, Inc. (1st World Library - Literary Society).

MINIATURE CAMERAS

see Cameras

MINIATURE GARDENS

see Gardens, Miniature

MINIATURE OBJECTS
see Dollhouses; Models and Modelmaking; Toys
see names of objects with the subdivision Models, e.g. Airplanes—Models

MINING
see Mines and Mineral Resources; Mining Engineering

MINING ENGINEERING

Linde, Barbara M. Strip Mining. 2014. (Illus.). 32p. (J). *(978-1-4339-9862-1(9))* Stevens, Gareth Publishing LLLP.

Thomas, Mark. Discoverer Enterprise: La plataforma de perforación más grande del mundo (the Discoverer Enterprise: World's Largest Offshore Drilling Rig) 2009. (Estructuras extraordinarias (Record-Breaking Structures) Ser.). (SPA.). 24p. (gr. 1-2). 42.50 *(978-1-61512-310-0(5),* Editorial Buenas Letras) Rosen Publishing Group, Inc., The.

—The Discoverer Enterprise: World's Largest Offshore Drilling Rig. 2009. (Record-Breaking Structures Ser.). 24p. (gr. 1-2). 42.50 *(978-1-60852-454-9(X),* PowerKids Pr.) Rosen Publishing Group, Inc., The.

Troupe, Thomas Kingsley. Blow It Up!, 1 vol. 2013. (Destruction Ser.). (ENG.). 24p. (gr. k-1). lib. bdg. 26.65 *(978-1-4765-2086-5(0),* Pebble Plus) Capstone Press of Coughlan Cos.

MINISTERS (DIPLOMATIC AGENTS)
see Diplomats

MINISTERS OF THE GOSPEL
see Clergy

MINKS

Gray, Susan H. American Mink. 2008. (21st Century Skills Library: Animal Invaders Ser.). (ENG.). 32p. (gr. 4-8). lib. bdg. 28.50 *(978-1-60279-114-5(7),* 200092) Cherry Lake Publishing.

MINKS—FICTION

Burgess, Thornton W. Billy Mink. (J). 18.95 *(978-0-8488-0397-1(3))* Amereon Ltd.

—Billy Mink. Cady, Harrison, illus. 2012. (Dover Children's Thrift Classics Ser.). (ENG.). 128p. (J). (gr. k-3). pap. 4.00 *(978-0-486-48107-4(7))* Dover Pubns., Inc.

—Tommy & the Wishing-Stone. Cady, Harrison, illus. 2012. (Dover Children's Thrift Classics Ser.). (ENG.). 240p. (J). (gr. k-3). pap. 4.00 *(978-0-486-48105-0(0))* Dover Pubns., Inc.

Kink the Mink: KinderReaders Individual Title Six-Packs. (Kinderstarters Ser.). 8p. (gr. -1-1). 21.00 *(978-0-7635-8652-2(8))* Rigby Education.

Sargent, Dave & Sargent, Pat. Mad Jack: I Throw Fits, 15 vols., Vol. 16. Huff, Jeane, illus. 2nd rev. ed. 2003. (Animal Pride Ser.: 16). 42p. (J). pap. 10.95 *(978-1-56763-790-8(6));* lib. bdg. 20.95 *(978-1-56763-789-2(2))* Ozark Publishing.

MINNESOTA

Brown, Vanessa. Minnesota. 2009. (Bilingual Library of the United States of America Ser.). (ENG & SPA.). 32p. (gr. 2-2). 47.90 *(978-1-60853-368-8(9),* Editorial Buenas Letras) Rosen Publishing Group, Inc., The.

—Minnesota. Brusca, Maria Cristina, tr. 2005. (Bilingual Library of the United States of America Ser.: Set 1). (ENG & SPA., Illus.). 32p. (J). (gr. 3-6). lib. bdg. 25.25 *(978-1-4042-3088-0(2))* Rosen Publishing Group, Inc., The.

Dolan, Sean J. Minnesota. 2005. (Rookie Read-About Geography Ser.). (ENG., Illus.). 32p. (J). (gr. 1-2). lib. bdg. 20.50 *(978-0-516-25257-5(7),* Children's Pr.) Scholastic Library Publishing.

Draper, Penny. Red River Raging, 1 vol. 2014. (Disaster Strikes! Ser.: 8). (ENG.). 168p. (J). (gr. 5-8). pap. 8.95 *(978-1-55050-584-9(X))* Coteau Bks. CAN. Dist: Orca Bk. Pubs. USA.

Feinstein, Stephen. Minnesota: A MyReportLinks.com Book. 2003. (States Ser.). (Illus.). 48p. (J). (gr. 4-10). lib. bdg. 25.26 *(978-0-7660-5096-9(3),* MyReportLinks.com Bks.) Enslow Pubs., Inc.

Gedatus, Gustav Mark. Minnesota. 2006. (Portraits of the States Ser.). (Illus.). 32p. (gr. 2-6). pap. 10.50 *(978-0-8368-4688-1(5));* lib. bdg. 26.00 *(978-0-8368-4669-0(9))* Stevens, Gareth Publishing LLLP. (Gareth Stevens Learning Library).

Greenberg, Keith Elliot. Jesse Ventura. 2003. (Biography Ser.). (Illus.). 112p. (YA). (gr. 6-12). pap. 7.95 *(978-0-8225-9680-6(6),* Carolrhoda Bks.) Lerner Publishing Group.

Kuedee, Jaycee. How to Draw Minnesota's Sights & Symbols. 2009. (Kid's Guide to Drawing America Ser.). 32p. (gr. k-k). 50.50 *(978-1-61511-072-8(0),* PowerKids Pr.) Rosen Publishing Group, Inc., The.

Lowrie, Paul. Hooray for Minnesota Lakes. 2008. 19.95 *(978-0-9755801-8-9(3))* Questmarc Publishing.

—Hooray for Minnesota Winters. 2008. 19.95 *(978-0-9755801-9-6(1))* Questmarc Publishing.

Magsamen, Sandra. I Love Minnesota. 2016. (ENG.). 40p. (J). (-5). 12.99 *(978-1-4926-2838-5(7),* Sourcebooks Jabberwocky) Sourcebooks, Inc.

Marsh, Carole. Minnesota Current Events Projects: 30 Cool, Activities, Crafts, Experiments & More for Kids to Do to Learn about Your State! 2003. (Minnesota Experience Ser.). 32p. (gr. k-8). pap. 5.95 *(978-0-635-02042-0(4),* Marsh, Carole Bks.) Gallopade International.

—Minnesota Geography Projects: 30 Cool, Activities, Crafts, Experiments & More for Kids to Do to Learn about Your State! 2003. (Minnesota Experience Ser.). 32p. (gr. k-5). pap. 5.95 *(978-0-635-01842-7(X),* Marsh, Carole Bks.) Gallopade International.

—Minnesota Government Projects: 30 Cool, Activities, Crafts, Experiments & More for Kids to Do to Learn about Your State! 2003. (Minnesota Experience Ser.). 32p. (gr. k-5). pap. 5.95 *(978-0-635-01942-4(6),* Marsh, Carole Bks.) Gallopade International.

—Minnesota People Projects: 30 Cool, Activities, Crafts, Experiments & More for Kids to Do to Learn about Your State! 2003. (Minnesota Experience Ser.). 32p. (gr. k-5). pap. 5.95 *(978-0-635-01992-9(2),* Marsh, Carole Bks.) Gallopade International.

—Minnesota Symbols & Facts Projects: 30 Cool, Activities, Crafts, Experiments & More for Kids to Do to Learn about Your State! 2003. (Minnesota Experience Ser.). 32p. (gr. k-5). pap. 5.95 *(978-0-635-01892-2(6),* Marsh, Carole Bks.) Gallopade International.

Moore, Cyd. Diary of a Minnesota Kid. 2010. (State Journal Ser.). (ENG.). 128p. (J). (gr. 4-8). pap. 9.95 *(978-1-58536-539-5(4),* 202217) Sleeping Bear Pr.

Moore, Dave, compiled by. A Free People: Tracing Our Hmong Roots. 2nd ed. 2003. (ENG., Illus.). 144p. (J). per. 19.95 *(978-1-888194-42-5(1))* Master Communications, Inc.

Murray, Julie. Minnesota, 1 vol. 2006. (United States Ser.). (ENG., Illus.). 32p. (gr. 2-4). 27.07 *(978-1-59197-682-0(0),* Buddy Bks.) ABDO Publishing Co.

Paplow, Paula. Hands upon the Rock. 2013. 48p. 19.99 *(978-0-9884268-0-1(3))* Little Cottonwood River Bks.

Paulsen, Gary. Woodsong. unabr. ed. 2004. 132p. (J). (gr. 6-18). pap. 29.00 incl. audio *(978-0-8072-0460-3(9),* Listening Library) Random Hse. Audio Publishing Group.

—Woodsong. 2007. (ENG., Illus.). 144p. (J). (gr. 5-9). pap. 7.99 *(978-1-4169-3939-9(3),* Simon & Schuster Bks. For Young Readers) Simon & Schuster Bks. For Young Readers.

Peterson, Sheryl. Minnesota. 2008. (This Land Called America Ser.). 32p. (YA). (gr. 3-6). 22.95 *(978-1-58341-648-8(X))* Creative Co., The.

Porter, A. P. Minnesota. (J). 2012. lib. bdg. 25.26 *(978-0-7613-4188-8(9),* Lerner Pubns.) 2nd rev. exp. ed. 2003. (Illus.). 84p. (gr. 3-6). pap. 6.95 *(978-0-8225-4149-3(1))* Lerner Publishing Group.

Purslow, Neil. Minnesota. 2011. (Guide to American States Ser.). (Illus.). 48p. (YA). (gr. 3-6). 29.99 *(978-1-61690-795-2(9))* Weigl Pubs., Inc.

River Lake Press. An Osprey Summer. 2010. (Illus.). 32p. (J). 17.95 *(978-0-615-36951-8(0))* River Lake Pr.

Schwabacher, Martin & Kummer, Patricia K. Minnesota. 2nd rev. ed. 2007. (Celebrate the States Ser.). 144p. (gr. 6). lib. bdg. 42.79 *(978-0-7614-2716-2(3),* Benchmark Bks.) Marshall Cavendish Corp.

Thompson, Gabrielle. The ABCs of Childhood Cancer. 2008. (Illus.). (J). *(978-1-59298-247-9(6))* Beaver's Pond Pr., Inc.

Van Hoven, Constance. The Twelve Days of Christmas in Minnesota. Wohnoutka, Mike, illus. 2016. (Twelve Days of Christmas in America Ser.). (ENG.). 22p. (J). (— 1). bds. 7.95 *(978-1-4549-2057-1(2))* Sterling Publishing Co., Inc.

Wargin, Kathy-jo. Minnesota. Wargin, Ed, photos by. 2008. (I Spy with My Little Eye Ser.). (ENG., Illus.). 32p. (J). (gr. 1-4). 13.95 *(978-1-58536-359-9(6),* 202144) Sleeping Bear Pr.

—North Star Numbers: A Minnesota Number Book. Caple, Laurie, illus. 2008. (Count Your Way Across the U. S. A. Ser.). (ENG.). 40p. (J). (gr. -1-3). 17.95 *(978-1-58536-187-8(9))* Sleeping Bear Pr.

—V Is for Viking: A Minnesota Alphabet. Latham, Karen & Latham, Rebecca, illus. 2003. (Discover America State by State Ser.). (ENG.). 40p. (J). 17.95 *(978-1-58536-125-0(9))* Sleeping Bear Pr.

What's Great about Minnesota? 2014. (Our Great States Ser.). (ENG.). 32p. (gr. 2-5). lib. bdg. 26.60 *(978-1-4677-3388-5(1),* Lerner Pubns.) Lerner Publishing Group.

MINNESOTA—FICTION

Applegate, Katherine. Home of the Brave. 2008. (ENG.). 272p. (J). (gr. 5-9). pap. 7.99 *(978-0-312-53563-6(5),* 9780312535636) Square Fish.

Baum, Diane Ganzer & Olson, Dan. Dakota's Trail. 2011. 48p. pap. 11.99 *(978-1-61286-029-9(X))* Avid Readers Publishing Group.

Bissonette, Aimee M. North Woods Girl. McGehee, Claudia, illus. 2015. (ENG.). 32p. (J). 16.95 *(978-0-87351-966-3(3))* Minnesota Historical Society Pr.

Blume, Lesley M. M. The Rising Star of Rusty Nail. 2009. (ENG.). 288p. (J). (gr. 3-7). 7.99 *(978-0-440-42111-5(X),* Yearling) Random Hse. Children's Bks.

Bredeson, Michelle. Legends. 2012. 220p. pap. *(978-1-61706-158-5(1))* Roxby Media Ltd.

Brezenoff, Steve. Guy in Real Life. (ENG.). 400p. (YA). (gr. 9). 2015. pap. 9.99 *(978-0-06-226684-2(5))* 2014. 17.99 *(978-0-06-226683-5(7))* HarperCollins Pubs.

Brost, Diane. Courage at Crow Wing River, 1 vol. 2010. 36p. 24.95 *(978-1-4512-1254-9(2))* PublishAmerica, Inc.

Bullard, Lisa. Turn Left at the Cow. 2013. (ENG.). 304p. (J). (gr. 5-7). 16.99 *(978-0-544-02900-2(3))* Houghton Mifflin Harcourt Publishing Co.

Carlson-Voiles, Polly. Summer of the Wolves. 2013. (ENG.). 352p. (J). (gr. 5-7). pap. 7.99 *(978-0-544-02276-8(9))* Houghton Mifflin Harcourt Publishing Co.

Carson, John & Carson, Marlene. Ramblin' Rose: The Chinese Fortune Cookie. 2008. 291p. pap. 8.99 *(978-0-9800034-1-3(5))* BBM Bks.

Casanova, Mary. Frozen. 2013. (Fesler-Lampert Minnesota Heritage Ser.). (ENG.). 256p. pap. 11.95 *(978-0-8166-8057-3(4))* Univ. of Minnesota Pr.

—Ice-Out. 2016. (ENG., Illus.). 264p. (YA). 16.95 *(978-0-8166-9417-4(6))* Univ. of Minnesota Pr.

—When Eagles Fall. 2014. (Fesler-Lampert Minnesota Heritage Ser.). (ENG.). 160p. pap. 9.95 *(978-0-8166-9211-8(4))* Univ. of Minnesota Pr.

Clement-Moore, Rosemary. Spirit & Dust. 2014. (ENG.). 400p. (YA). (gr. 7). pap. 9.99 *(978-0-385-74081-4(6),* Ember) Random Hse. Children's Bks.

Cochrane, Mick. Fitz. (ENG.). 192p. (YA). (gr. 7). 2013. pap. 8.99 *(978-0-375-84611-3(5),* Ember) 2012. 16.99 *(978-0-375-85683-9(8),* Knopf Bks. for Young Readers) Random Hse. Children's Bks.

Cronn-Mills, Kirstin. Beautiful Music for Ugly Children. 2012. (ENG.). 288p. (YA). pap. 11.99 *(978-0-7387-3251-0(6),* Flux) North Star Editions.

—Original Fake. Johnson, E. Eero, illus. 2016. (ENG.). 352p. (YA). (gr. 7). 17.99 *(978-0-399-17326-4(9),* G.P. Putnam's Sons Books for Young Readers) Penguin Young Readers Group.

Debruzzi, Jeremy. A Minnesota Fish Tail. 2012. 48p. 24.99 *(978-1-4628-8580-0(2));* pap. 15.99 *(978-1-4628-8579-4(9))* Xlibris Corp.

Delsol, Wendy. Stork. (ENG., Illus.). (YA). (gr. 7). 2011. 368p. pap. 8.99 *(978-0-7636-5687-4(9))* 2010. 357p. 15.99 *(978-0-7636-4844-2(2))* Candlewick Pr.

Despain, Bree. The Dark Divine. 2010. (ENG.). 384p. (gr. 7). pap. 9.99 *(978-1-60684-154-9(8),* Carolrhoda Lab™) Lerner Publishing Group.

Downing, Erin. Kiss It. 2010. (ENG.). 288p. (YA). (gr. 9-18). pap. 9.99 *(978-1-4169-9700-9(8),* Simon Pulse) Simon Pulse.

Durbin, William. Blackwater Ben. 2014. (Fesler-Lampert Minnesota Heritage Ser.). (ENG., Illus.). 216p. pap. 11.95 *(978-0-8166-9192-0(4))* Univ. of Minnesota Pr.

Durbin, William & Durbin, Barbara. Dead Man's Rapids. 2017. (J). pap. **(978-1-5179-0224-7(X))** Univ. of Minnesota Pr.

Ellsworth, Loretta. The Shrouding Woman. 2007. (ENG., Illus.). 160p. (YA). (gr. 4-9). pap. 17.99 *(978-0-8050-8185-5(2),* 9780805081855, Holt, Henry & Co. Bks. For Young Readers) Holt, Henry & Co.

Gamble, Adam. Good Night Minnesota. Veno, Joe, illus. 2009. (Good Night Our World Ser.). (ENG.). 20p. (J). (gr. k — 1). bds. 9.95 *(978-1-60219-034-4(8))* Good Night Bks.

Ganser, Sara. The Weekend Getaway. 2009. 24p. pap. 15.59 *(978-1-4490-2423-9(8))* AuthorHouse.

Glaser, Linda. Hannah's Way. Gustavson, Adam, illus. 2012. (Shabbat Ser.). (ENG.). 32p. (J). (gr. k-3). pap. 7.95 *(978-0-7613-5138-2(8),* Kar-Ben Publishing) Lerner Publishing Group.

Goode, Laura. Sister Mischief. (ENG.). 384p. (YA). (gr. 9). 2013. pap. 8.99 *(978-0-7636-6456-5(1))* 2011. (Illus.). 16.99 *(978-0-7636-4640-0(7))* Candlewick Pr.

Griffin, Molly Beth. Silhouette of a Sparrow. 2013. (Milkweed Prize for Children's Literature Ser.). (ENG., Illus.). 208p. pap. 8.00 *(978-1-57131-704-9(X))* Milkweed Editions.

Groethe, Kd. The Virtual Adventures of Megan & Timmy. 2012. 230p. (gr. 4-6). 27.99 *(978-1-4685-5050-4(0));* pap. 16.95 *(978-1-4685-5049-8(7))* AuthorHouse.

Harbo, Gary. The Northern Woods Adventure: Advanced Reader, 6 vols. Harbo, Gary, illus. l.t. ed. 2004. (If You Want to Succeed, You Need to Read! Ser.: 6). (Illus.). 33p. (J). per. 10.95 *(978-1-884149-15-3(4))* Kutie Kari Bks., Inc.

Hautman, Pete. The Big Crunch. 2011. (ENG.). 288p. (J). (gr. 7-8). 17.99 *(978-0-545-24075-8(1),* Scholastic Pr.) Scholastic, Inc.

—Mr. Was. 2012. (ENG.). 240p. (YA). (gr. 7). pap. 8.99 *(978-1-4424-3337-3(X),* Simon & Schuster Bks. For Young Readers) Simon & Schuster Bks. For Young Readers.

Havill, Juanita. Grow, 1 vol. Kodman, Stansislawa, illus. 2011. (ENG.). 160p. (J). (gr. 3-7). pap. 7.95 *(978-1-56145-575-1(X))* Peachtree Pubs.

—Grow, 1 vol. Kodman, Stanislawa, illus. 2008. (ENG.). 144p. (J). (gr. 3-7). 14.95 *(978-1-56145-441-9(9))* Peachtree Pubs.

Hayles, Marsha. Breathing Room. 2013. (ENG., Illus.). 272p. (J). (gr. 5-9). pap. 9.99 *(978-1-250-03411-3(6),* 9781250034113) Square Fish.

Herbach, Geoff. Fat Boy vs. the Cheerleaders. 2014. (ENG.). 320p. (YA). (gr. 7-12). 16.99 *(978-1-4022-9141-8(8),* 9781402291418) Sourcebooks, Inc.

—Gabe Johnson Takes Over. 2015. (ENG.). 352p. (YA). (gr. 6-12). pap. 9.99 *(978-1-4926-0865-3(3))* Sourcebooks, Inc.

Hoena, Blake A. & Tortosa, Wilson. Amplified, Vol. 5. Ito, Leonardo, illus. 2012. (Tony Hawk's 900 Revolution Ser.). (ENG.). 128p. (gr. 3-4). pap. 7.19 *(978-1-4342-3887-0(3));* lib. bdg. 26.65 *(978-1-4342-3311-0(1))* Stone Arch Bks. (Tony Hawk's 900 Revolution).

Holmes, Katherine L. The Wide Awake Loons. 2013. 188p. pap. 9.95 *(978-1-938083-18-1(0))* Silver Knight Publishing, LLC.

Jacobs, Lily. The Littlest Bunny in Minnesota: An Easter Adventure. Dunn, Robert, illus. 2015. (ENG.). 32p. (J). (-3). 9.99 *(978-1-4926-1120-2(4),* Sourcebooks Jabberwocky) Sourcebooks, Inc.

James, Eric. A Halloween Scare in Minnesota. Le Ray, Marina, illus. 2014. (ENG.). 32p. (J). (-5). 9.99 *(978-1-4926-0609-3(X),* 9781492606093, Sourcebooks Jabberwocky) Sourcebooks, Inc.

—Santa's Sleigh Is on Its Way to Minnesota. Dunn, Robert, illus. 2015. (ENG.). 32p. (J). (-2). 12.99 *(978-1-4926-2748-7(8),* Sourcebooks Jabberwocky) Sourcebooks, Inc.

Johnson, Kristin F. Deep Freeze. 2017. (Day of Disaster Ser.). (ENG.). 104p. (gr. 6-12). (J). 26.65 *(978-1-5124-2776-9(4));* (YA). 12.99 **(978-1-5124-3510-8(4),** Darby Creek); (YA). 39.99 **(978-1-5124-3509-2(0),** Darby Creek); (YA). 39.99 **(978-1-5124-2783-7(7),** Darby Creek) Lerner Publishing Group.

Jones, Patrick. Doing Right. 2015. (J). 27.99 *(978-1-4677-7691-2(2));* (ENG.). 104p. (gr. 6-12). lib. bdg. 27.99 *(978-1-4677-5803-1(5))* Lerner Publishing Group.

—Taking Sides. 2015. (J). 97p. 9.99 *(978-1-4677-7703-2(X));* (ENG.). 104p. (gr. 6-12). lib. bdg. 27.99 *(978-1-4677-5800-0(0))* Lerner Publishing Group.

Jones, Patrick & Clark, Marshunna. Duty or Desire. 2016. (Unbarred Ser.). (ENG.). 112p. (YA). (gr. 6-12). lib. bdg. 27.99 *(978-1-5124-0002-1(5),* Darby Creek) Lerner Publishing Group.

—Duty or Desire. 2016. (Unbarred Ser.). (ENG.). 112p. (YA). (gr. 6-12). pap. 7.99 *(978-1-5124-0089-2(0),* Darby Creek) Lerner Publishing Group.

—Duty or Desire. 2016. (Unbarred Ser.). (ENG.). 112p. (YA). (gr. 6-12). 42.65 *(978-1-5124-0090-8(4),* Darby Creek) Lerner Publishing Group.

Kadence, Sam. On the Right Track. 2016. (ENG., Illus.). (YA). (gr. 9-12). 24.99 **(978-1-63533-057-1(2))** 2013. 184p. pap. 14.99 *(978-1-62798-069-2(5))* Dreamspinner Pr. (Harmony Ink Pr.).

Kallander, Susan & Boomgaarden, Larry. Up in Smoke. 2010. (Illus.). 24p. pap. 11.50 *(978-1-60860-934-5(0),* Eloquent Bks.) Strategic Book Publishing & Rights Agency (SBPRA).

Kantar, Andrew. Game Face. Keleher, Fran, illus. 2013. 160p. pap. 12.95 *(978-1-61160-566-2(0))* Whiskey Creek Restorations.

Long, Loren & Bildner, Phil. Water, Water Everywhere. Long, Loren, illus. (Sluggers Ser.: 4). (ENG., Illus.). (J). (gr. 3-7). 2010. 288p. pap. 7.99 *(978-1-4169-1890-5(6))* 2009. 272p. 14.99 *(978-1-4169-1866-0(3))* Simon & Schuster Bks. For Young Readers. (Simon & Schuster Bks. For Young Readers).

Lovelace, Maud Hart. The Betsy-Tacy Treasury: The First Four Betsy-Tacy Books. 2011. (P. S. Ser.). (ENG.). 736p. pap. 15.99 *(978-0-06-209587-9(0),* Harper Perennial) HarperCollins Pubs.

Maddox, Jake. Slap-Shot Slump. 2015. (Jake Maddox JV Ser.). (ENG.). 96p. (gr. 3-4). lib. bdg. 25.99 *(978-1-4342-9635-1(0))* Stone Arch Bks.

Malloy, Brian. Twelve Long Months. 2010. (ENG.). 320p. (J). (gr. 7). 9.99 *(978-0-439-87763-3(6),* Scholastic Paperbacks) Scholastic, Inc.

Marsh, Carole. The Mystery in the Twin Cities. Baker, Janice, ed. 2011. (Carole Marsh Mysteries Ser.). (Illus.). (J). pap. 7.99 *(978-0-635-07960-2(7),* Marsh, Carole Mysteries) Gallopade International.

—The Mystery on the Mighty Mississippi. 2009. (Real Kids, Real Places Ser.). (Illus.). 146p. (J). lib. bdg. 18.99 *(978-0-635-07001-2(4),* Marsh, Carole Mysteries) Gallopade International.

Marvin, Isabel R. A Bride for Anna's Papa. 2004. (Historical Fiction for Young Readers Ser.). (ENG., Illus.). 144p. (J). pap. 6.95 *(978-1-57131-650-9(7))* Milkweed Editions.

—The Tenth Rifle. Costner, Howard, illus. Date not set. 128p. (Orig.). (J). (gr. 3-8). pap. 9.95 *(978-0-89896-109-6(2))* Larksdale.

Mcghee, Alison. Julia Gillian - And the Art of Knowing. Kozjan, Drazen, illus. 2009. (Julia Gillian Ser.). (ENG.). 304p. (J). (gr. 3-7). 6.99 *(978-0-545-03349-7(7),* Scholastic Paperbacks) Scholastic, Inc.

McGhee, Allison. Julia Gillian 3. 2010. *(978-0-545-10467-8(X))* Scholastic, Inc.

McMann, Lisa. Dead to You. 2012. (ENG.). (YA). (gr. 9). 272p. pap. 10.99 *(978-1-4424-0389-5(6));* 256p. 16.99 *(978-1-4424-0388-8(8))* Simon Pulse. (Simon Pulse).

Mercier, Deborah. The Captain's Hat. Mills, Faythe, illus. 2007. 32p. (J). 17.99 *(978-0-9799410-0-9(8))* Minnewaska Pr.

Miller-Burke, Jude. Snowball, Come Home! 2005. (Illus.). 32p. (J). bds. 16.95 *(978-1-59298-093-2(7))* Beaver's Pond Pr., Inc.

Mullin, Michael & Skewes, John. Larry Gets Lost in the Twin Cities. Skewes, John, illus. 2012. (Larry Gets Lost Ser.). (ENG., Illus.). 32p. (J). (gr. -1-2). 17.99 *(978-1-57061-754-6(6),* Little Bigfoot) Sasquatch Bks.

Oceanak, Karla. Cahoots. Spanjer, Kendra, illus. 2011. (Aldo Zelnick Comic Novel Ser.: 3). (ENG.). 151p. (J). (gr. 3-7). 12.95 *(978-1-934649-08-4(2))* Bailiwick Pr.

O'Neill, Elizabeth. Alfred Visits Minnesota. 2007. (Illus.). 24p. (J). pap. 12.00 *(978-0-9799121-2-2(1))* Global Business Information Strategies, Inc.

Paulsen, Gary. Dancing Carl. 2007. (ENG.). 112p. (J). (gr. 5-9). pap. 8.99 *(978-1-4169-3938-2(5),* Simon & Schuster Bks. For Young Readers) Simon & Schuster Bks. For Young Readers.

—Foxman. l.t. ed. 2004. (YA). (gr. 6-12). 27.95 *(978-1-58118-112-8(4))* LRS.

Perry, Marie. A Gift for Sadia. Perry, Marie, illus. l.t. ed. 2005. (Illus.). 32p. (J). lib. bdg. 15.95 *(978-0-9755675-1-7(9))* Buttonweed Pr., L.L.C.

Peterson, Jay D. & Morgan, Collette A., eds. Sky Blue Water: Great Stories for Young Readers. 2016. (ENG.). 240p. (J). 19.95 *(978-0-8166-9876-9(7))* Univ. of Minnesota Pr.

Pietron, Barbara. Thunderstone. 2013. (ENG.). 262p. (YA). pap. 12.99 *(978-1-940368-91-7(X))* Scribe Publishing Co.

Polinski, Jo. Minnesota Moon. Webber, Carol, illus. 2007. 20p. per. 12.95 *(978-1-933482-60-6(5))* White Turtle Bks.

Preus, Margi. Enchantment Lake: A Northwoods Mystery. 2015. (ENG.). 200p. (YA). 16.95 *(978-0-8166-8302-4(6))* Univ. of Minnesota Pr.

Puck. 123 Minnesota: A Cool Counting Book. 2012. (Cool Counting Bks.). (ENG.). 22p. (J). (gr. k — 1). bds. 8.95 *(978-0-9838121-2-8(8))* Duo Pr. LLC.

Qualey, Marsha. Come in from the Cold. 2008. (ENG.). 224p. (YA). (gr. 7). pap. 14.95 *(978-0-547-01439-5(2))* Houghton Mifflin Harcourt Publishing Co.

Rempel, Leah. Hey, Hmong Girl, Whassup? The Journal of Choua Vang. 2004. (Illus.). v, 138p. (YA). pap. *(978-0-9723721-5-2(6))* Hamline Univ. Pr.

Rich, Juliann. Caught in the Crossfire. 2014. (ENG.). 264p. (J). (gr. 7). pap. 11.95 *(978-1-62639-070-6(3))* Bold Strokes Bks.

Root, Phyllis. One North Star: A Counting Book. Prange, Beckie & Bowen, Betsy, illus. 2016. (ENG.). 36p. (J). 16.95 *(978-0-8166-5063-7(2))* Univ. of Minnesota Pr.

Rubens, Michael. Sons of The 613. 2012. (ENG.). 320p. (YA). (gr. 7). 16.99 *(978-0-547-61216-4(8))* Houghton Mifflin Harcourt Publishing Co.

Rylant, Cynthia. Old Town in the Green Groves. 2007. (Little House Ser.). (ENG.). 192p. (J). (gr. 3-7). pap. 6.99 *(978-0-06-088546-5(7))* HarperCollins Pubs.

Scaletta, Kurtis. Mudville. 2010. (ENG.). 272p. (J). (gr. 3-7). 8.99 *(978-0-375-84472-0(4),* Yearling) Random Hse. Children's Bks.

Schindler, Holly. Playing Hurt. 2011. (ENG.). 312p. (YA). (gr. 7-18). pap. 9.95 *(978-0-7387-2287-0(1),* Flux) North Star Editions.

Schultz, Jan Neubert. Firestorm. 2003. (Adventures in Time Ser.). 204p. (YA). (gr. 4-7). 15.95 *(978-0-87614-276-9(5),* Carolrhoda Bks.) Lerner Publishing Group.

—Horse Sense: The Story of Will Sasse, His Horse Star & the Outlaw Jesse James. 2005. (Adventures in Time Ser.). (Illus.). 180p. (J). (gr. 4-8). 15.95 *(978-1-57505-998-3(3))* Lerner Publishing Group.

Schultz, Leslie & Braulick, J. J. M. And Sometimes Y. Newman, Heather, illus. 2013. 302p. pap. 12.99 *(978-1-937848-07-1(8))* Do Life Right, Inc.

Scott, Luke. Through a Crystal Doorknob. 2012. 88p. 24.95 *(978-1-4626-9420-4(9));* pap. 19.95 *(978-1-4626-7361-2(9))* America Star Bks.

Shaw, Janet. Kirsten Story Collection. Graef, Renee, illus. 2008. 380p. 29.95 *(978-1-59369-454-8(7))* American Girl Publishing, Inc.

—Kirsten's Short Story Collection. Lewis, Kim & Graef, Renee, illus. 2006. (American Girls Collection). 213p. (J). (gr. 3-8). 12.95 *(978-1-59369-323-7(0))* American Girl Publishing, Inc.

Sheehan, Judy. I Woke up Dead at the Mall. 2016. (ENG.). 288p. (YA). (gr. 7). 17.99 *(978-0-553-51246-5(3),* Delacorte Pr.) Random Hse. Children's Bks.

Siemsen, Nancy. The Girl Who Loved Jupiter. 2005. 151p. pap. 24.95 *(978-1-4137-9004-7(6))* America Star Bks.

Silvano, Wendi. Love Is All Around Minnesota. Czernichowska, Joanna, illus. 2016. (ENG.). 32p. (J). (-6). 12.99 *(978-1-4926-2935-1(9),* Sourcebooks Jabberwocky) Sourcebooks, Inc.

Sims, Lori. Starvin' Marvin & Skinny Minnie Melt Minnesota. 2010. 115p. pap. 11.95 *(978-1-4327-5628-4(1))* Outskirts Pr., Inc.

Smallman, Steve. Santa Is Coming to Duluth. Dunn, Robert, illus. 2013. (ENG.). 32p. (J). (-3). 9.99 *(978-1-4022-9027-5(6),* Sourcebooks Jabberwocky) Sourcebooks, Inc.
—Santa Is Coming to Minnesota. Dunn, Robert, illus. 2012. (ENG.). 32p. (J). (-3). 9.99 *(978-1-4022-7530-2(7),* Sourcebooks Jabberwocky) Sourcebooks, Inc.
Smallman, Steve, et al. My First Santa's Coming to Minnesota. Dunn, Robert, illus. 2015. (ENG.). 18p. (J). bds. 9.99 *(978-1-4926-2879-8(4),* Sourcebooks Jabberwocky) Sourcebooks, Inc.
Sommerdorf, Norma. Red River Girl. 2006. (ENG., Illus.). 192p. (J). (gr. 3-7). 16.95 *(978-0-8234-1903-6(7))* Holiday Hse., Inc.
Sommers, Jackie Lea. Truest. 2015. (ENG.). 384p. (YA). (gr. 8). 17.99 *(978-0-06-234825-8(6),* Tegen, Katherine Bks) HarperCollins Pubs.
Springer, Michael. The Bootlegger's Secret. 2010. (Illus.). 164p. pap. 15.95 *(978-1-4327-5792-2(X))* Outskirts Pr., Inc.
St. Anthony, Jane. Isabelle Day Refuses to Die of a Broken Heart. 2015. (ENG.). 152p. (J). 14.95 *(978-0-8166-9799-1(X))* Univ. of Minnesota Pr.
St. Antoine, Sarah. Three Bird Summer. 2014. (ENG.). 256p. (J). (gr. 5). 16.99 *(978-0-7636-6564-7(9))* Candlewick Pr.
Sully, Katherine. Night-Night Minnesota. Kolanovic, Dubravka & Poole, Helen, illus. 2016. (ENG.). 20p. (J). (-1). bds. 9.99 *(978-1-4926-3940-4(0),* 9781492639404, Sourcebooks Jabberwocky) Sourcebooks, Inc.
Tagged. 2015. (ENG.). 288p. (YA). (gr. 7). lib. bdg. 16.95 *(978-1-58089-583-5(2))* Charlesbridge Publishing, Inc.
Terrell, Brandon. Fearless, 1 vol. Cano, Fernando, illus. 2014. (Tony Hawk: Live2Skate Ser.). (ENG.). 72p. (gr. 4-5). 25.32 *(978-1-4342-9141-7(3),* Tony Hawk's 900 Revolution) Stone Arch Bks.
Tetzlaff, Wendy Jo. Summertime: A Girl Named Frannie, 1 vol. 2010. 38p. pap. 24.95 *(978-1-4489-2598-8(3))* PublishAmerica, Inc.
Treacy, Ann. The Search for the Homestead Treasure: A Mystery. 2016. (ENG., Illus.). 160p. 16.95 *(978-0-8166-9956-8(9))* Univ. of Minnesota Pr.
Wargin, Kathy-jo. The Legend of Minnesota. Geister, David, illus. 2006. (Legend (Sleeping Bear) Ser.). (ENG.). 40p. (J). (gr. 3-7). 17.95 *(978-1-58536-262-2(X))* Sleeping Bear Pr.
—Minn from Minnesota. Holman, Karen Busch, illus. 2006. (Mitt Midwest Ser.: 2). (ENG.). 144p. (J). (gr. k-7). 14.95 *(978-1-58726-304-0(1),* Mitten Pr.) Ann Arbor Editions LLC.
Weaver, Will. Clay. 2004. 232p. (YA). (gr. 8-12). 14.65 *(978-0-7569-4594-7(1))* Perfection Learning Corp.
—Saturday Night Dirt. 2009. (Motor Novels Ser.: 1). (ENG.). 192p. (YA). (gr. 7-12). pap. 14.99 *(978-0-312-56131-4(8),* 9780312561314) Square Fish.
—The Survivors. 2012. (ENG.). 320p. (YA). (gr. 8). 17.99 *(978-0-06-009476-8(1),* HarperTeen) HarperCollins Pubs.
Wedgeworth, Anthony G. Nums of Shoreview: Baka's Curse. 2010. 68p. pap. 9.97 *(978-0-578-04710-2(1))* Wedgeworth, Anthony G.
Westlund, Emmaline. Fatim. 2012. 42p. pap. 16.95 *(978-1-4626-9660-4(0))* America Star Bks.
Wilder, Laura Ingalls. On the Banks of Plum Creek. Williams, Garth, illus. (Little House Ser.: 4). (ENG.). 352p. (J). (gr. 3-7). 2008. pap. 7.99 *(978-0-06-440004-6(2))* 2004. pap. 9.99 *(978-0-06-058183-1(2))* HarperCollins Pubs.
Williams, Heather. Farmer Boy Goes West. 2012. (Little House Sequel Ser.). (ENG.). 320p. (J). (gr. 3-7). 16.99 *(978-0-06-124251-9(9))* HarperCollins Pubs.
Wood, Gail. Lizzie & the Big Lake Mystery. 2015. (Illus.). ix, 93p. (J). pap. *(978-1-57249-416-9(6),* White Mane Kids) White Mane Publishing Co., Inc.
—Lizzie, Light Feather & the Quarry Bluff Storm. 2015. (Illus.). viii, 88p. (J). pap. *(978-1-57249-415-2(8),* White Mane Kids) White Mane Publishing Co., Inc.

MINNESOTA—HISTORY

Anderson, Debby L. Minnesota for Mini-Sotans. 2004. (Illus.). spiral bd. 24.95 *(978-0-9759281-0-3(4))* Busy Bee Bks.
Brill, Marlene Targ & Kaplan, Elizabeth. Minnesota. 2014. (It's My State! (r) Ser.). 80p. (J). (gr. 4-8). lib. bdg. 34.21 *(978-1-62712-748-6(8))* Cavendish Square Publishing.
—Minnesota. 2nd rev. ed. 2010. (It's My State! Ser.). 80p. (gr. 3-18). lib. bdg. 31.36 *(978-1-60870-054-7(2))* Marshall Cavendish Corp.
Carlson, Nancy & McCool, Barry. T Is for Twin Cities: A Minneapolis/St. Paul Alphabet. Geister, David, illus. 2012. (City Alphabet Ser.). (ENG.). 32p. (J). (gr. 1-5). 16.95 *(978-1-58536-583-8(1))* Sleeping Bear Pr.
Coleman, Karlyn. Where Are All the Minnesotans? Hartman, Carrie, illus. 2017. (ENG.). 32p. (J). 16.95 ***(978-1-68134-040-1(2))*** Minnesota Historical Society Pr.
Davis, W. Harry. Changemaker: W. Harry Davis. Sturdevant, Lori, ed. 2004. (Illus.). 136p. (J). pap. 17.95 *(978-1-890434-60-1(4))* Afton Historical Society Pr.
Eggerling, Kristin J. Breath of Wilderness: The Life of Sigurd Olson. 2014. (ENG., Illus.). 112p. (J). (gr. 4-7). pap. 12.95 *(978-1-938486-10-4(2))* Fulcrum Publishing.
Ellis, Paula. Minnesota Activity Book, 1 vol. Nitzsche, Shane, illus. 2013. (Color & Learn Ser.). (ENG.). 64p. (J). (gr. k-2). pap. 5.95 *(978-1-59193-377-9(3))* Adventure Pubns.
Freshman, Wendy & Jansson, Kristin. Making History: Have a Blast with 15 Crafts. 2014. (ENG., Illus.). 216p. (J). (gr. 2-6). pap. 17.95 *(978-0-87351-919-9(1))* Minnesota Historical Society Pr.
Gold, Susan Dudley. Protecting Hate Speech: R.A.V. V. St. Paul. 2014. lib. bdg. *(978-1-62712-393-8(8))* Cavendish Square Publishing.
Gove-Berg, Christie. Minnesota Must-See for Families: An A-Z List. 2015. (ENG.). 64p. pap. 12.95 *(978-1-59193-525-4(3))* Adventure Pubns.
Graham, Joan Claire. Minnesota Memories 3. 2003. (Illus.). 192p. per. 13.95 *(978-0-9711971-2-1(1))* Megyeri, Graham Bks.
Graham, JoanClaire, compiled by. Minnesota Memories 4. 2004. 208p. per. 13.95 *(978-0-9711971-3-8(X))* Megyeri, Graham Bks.
Green, Sara. Target. 2015. (Brands We Know Ser.). (ENG., Illus.). 24p. (J). (gr. 3-8). lib. bdg. 25.95 *(978-1-62617-289-0(7),* Pilot Bks.) Bellwether Media.
Harmon, Daniel E. Minnesota: Past & Present. 2010. (United States: Past & Present Ser.). (ENG., Illus.). 48p. (J). pap. 11.75 *(978-1-4358-8498-4(1),* Rosen Reference) Rosen Publishing Group, Inc., The.
Heinrichs, Ann. Minnesota (Revised Edition) 2014. (America the Beautiful, Third Ser. (Revised Edition) Ser.). (ENG.). 144p. (J). lib. bdg. 40.00 *(978-0-531-28281-6(3))* Scholastic Library Publishing.
Higgins, Nadia. What's Great about Minnesota? 2014. (Our Great States Ser.). (ENG., Illus.). 32p. (gr. 2-5). pap. 7.95 *(978-1-4677-4538-3(3))* Lerner Publishing Group.
Jensen, Niels R. Minnesota, 1 vol. 2009. (United States Ser.). (ENG., Illus.). 48p. (YA). (gr. 2-5). 27.07 *(978-1-60453-658-4(6))* ABDO Publishing Co.
Jerome, Kate B. Lucky to Live in Minnesota. 2017. (Arcadia Kids Ser.). (ENG., Illus.). 32p. (J). 16.99 ***(978-0-7385-2786-4(6))*** Arcadia Publishing.
—The Wise Animal Handbook Minnesota. 2017. (Arcadia Kids Ser.). (ENG., Illus.). 32p. (J). 16.99 ***(978-0-7385-2827-4(7))*** Arcadia Publishing.
Kallas, Randi & Dougherty, Mike, eds. Rochester, Minnesota: A Visual & Historic Journey. 2003. (Illus.). 136p. pap. 24.95 *(978-0-9659875-3-0(1))* Riggott, Dean Photography.
Kenney, Dave. Northern Lights: The Stories of Minnesota's Past. 2nd ed. 2013. (ENG.). (gr. 5-6). 62.50 *(978-0-87351-885-7(3))* Minnesota Historical Society Pr.
Kenney, Dave, et al. Northern Lights: The Stories of Minnesota's Past. 2nd ed. 2003. (Illus.). 352p. 25.00 *(978-0-87351-440-8(8))* Minnesota Historical Society Pr.
Lackner, Michelle Myers. Finding Hope, 1 vol. North American Bear Center Staff, photos by. 2013. (ENG., Illus.). 40p. (J). (gr. -1-3). pap. 14.95 *(978-1-59193-373-1(0))* Adventure Pubns.
Marling, Karal Ann. Minnesota Hail to Thee! A Sesquicentennial History. 2008. (Illus.). 163p. (J). (gr. 3-7). 28.00 *(978-1-890434-78-6(7))* Afton Historical Society Pr.
Marsh, Carole. Exploring Minnesota Through Project-Based Learning: Geography, History, Government, Economics & More. 2016. (Minnesota Experience Ser.). (ENG.). (J). pap. 9.99 *(978-0-635-12347-3(9))* Gallopade International.
—I'm Reading about Minnesota. 2014. (Minnesota Experience Ser.). (ENG., Illus.). (J). pap., pap. 8.99 *(978-0-635-11298-9(1))* Gallopade International.
—Minnesota History Projects: 30 Cool, Activities, Crafts, Experiments & More for Kids to Do to Learn about Your State! 2003. (Minnesota Experience Ser.). 32p. (gr. k-5). pap. 5.95 *(978-0-635-01792-5(X),* Marsh, Carole Bks.) Gallopade International.
McDowell, Pamela. Minnesota: The North Star State. 2012. (J). *(978-1-61913-365-5(2));* pap. *(978-1-61913-366-2(0))* Weigl Pubs., Inc.
Mills, Jordan. Minnesota. 2016. (States Ser.). (ENG., Illus.). 32p. (gr. 3-4). lib. bdg. 27.32 *(978-1-5157-0410-2(6))* Next Page Pr., The.
Minneapolis, Jewish Family and Children's Service of. M Is for Minnesota. 2016. (See My State Ser.). (ENG., Illus.). 32p. (J). 13.99 *(978-1-943328-07-9(2),* West Winds Pr.) Graphic Arts Ctr. Publishing Co.
Murray, Julie. Minnesota, 1 vol. 2012. (Explore the United States Ser.). (ENG.). 32p. (J). (gr. 2-5). lib. bdg. 28.50 *(978-1-61783-361-8(4),* Big Buddy Bks.) ABDO Publishing Co.
Purslow, Neil. Minnesota: The North Star State. 2016. (J). *(978-1-4896-4884-6(4))* Weigl Pubs., Inc.
Rossi, Joe, photos by. Minnesota's Hidden Alphabet. 2010. (ENG., Illus.). 48p. (J). (gr. -1-1). 16.95 *(978-0-87351-808-6(X))* Minnesota Historical Society Pr.
Ruff, Carolyn. Keystones of the Stone Arch Bridge. Washam, Christie, illus. 2014. (ENG.). 80p. (J). (gr. 2-3). pap. 7.95 *(978-0-87351-923-6(X))* Minnesota Historical Society Pr.
Scheunemann, Pam. Lena & the Lady's Slippers: A Story about Minnesota, 1 vol. Doucet, Bob, illus. 2011. (Fact & Fable: State Stories Set 3 Ser.). (ENG.). 24p. (J). (gr. -1-2). 25.65 *(978-1-61714-681-7(1))* ABDO Publishing Co.
Van Hoven, Constance. The Twelve Days of Christmas in Minnesota. Wohnoutka, Mike, illus. 2009. (Twelve Days of Christmas in America Ser.). (ENG.). 40p. (J). (gr. k). 12.95 *(978-1-4027-6395-3(6))* Sterling Publishing Co., Inc.
Wargin, Kathy-jo. Little Minnesota. Urban, Helle, illus. 2011. (My Little State Ser.). (ENG.). 22p. (J). 9.95 *(978-1-58536-174-8(7))* Sleeping Bear Pr.
Ziff, John. Western Great Lakes: Illinois, Minnesota, Wisconsin, Vol. 19. 2015. (Let's Explore the States Ser.). (Illus.). 64p. (J). (gr. 5). 23.95 *(978-1-4222-3338-2(3))* Mason Crest.

MINNESOTA TWINS (BASEBALL TEAM)

Bissen, Joe. Minnesota Twins, 1 vol. 2011. (Inside MLB Ser.). (ENG., Illus.). 48p. (YA). (gr. 3-6). lib. bdg. 32.79 *(978-1-61714-050-1(3))* ABDO Publishing Co.
Connery-Boyd, Peg. Minnesota Twins. 2016. (Hawk's Nest Activity Bks.: 0). (ENG.). 64p. (J). (gr. k-3). pap., act. bk. ed. 8.99 *(978-1-4926-3374-7(7))* Sourcebooks, Inc.
Epstein, Brad. Minnesota Twins 101: My First Team-Board-book. 2008. (Illus.). 22p. (J). pap. *(978-1-932530-97-1(5),* 101 Bk.) Michaelson Entertainment.
Frisch, Aaron. Minnesota Twins. 2009. (World Series Champions Ser.). (Illus.). 23p. (J). (gr. 2-3). 24.25 *(978-1-58341-695-2(1),* Creative Education) Creative Co., The.
Gilbert, Sara. Minnesota Twins. 2013. (Illus.). 24p. (J). 25.65 *(978-1-60818-267-1(3),* Creative Education) Creative Co., The.
—World Series Champs: Minnesota Twins. 2013. (World Series Champions Ser.). (ENG.). 24p. (J). (gr. 1-3). pap. 7.99 *(978-0-89812-818-5(8),* Creative Paperbacks) Creative Co., The.
Howell, Brian. Joe Mauer: All-Star Catcher, 1 vol. 2011. (Playmakers Ser.). (ENG., Illus.). 32p. (YA). (gr. 3-6). 27.07 *(978-1-61714-749-4(4))* ABDO Publishing Co.
LeBoutillier, Nate. The Story of the Minnesota Twins. 2011. (J). 35.65 *(978-1-60818-047-9(6),* Creative Education) Creative Co., The.
Leboutillier, Nate. The Story of the Minnesota Twins. 2007. (Baseball, the Great American Game Ser.). (Illus.). 48p. (YA). (gr. 4-7). lib. bdg. 32.80 *(978-1-58341-493-4(2))* Creative Co., The.
MacRae, Sloan. The Minnesota Twins. 2012. 24p. (J). 49.50 *(978-1-4488-5158-4(0));* pap. 8.25 *(978-1-4488-5157-7(2));* lib. bdg. 22.60 *(978-1-4488-5012-9(6))* Rosen Publishing Group, Inc., The. (PowerKids Pr.).
Stewart, Mark. The Minnesota Twins. 2012. (Team Spirit Ser.). 48p. (J). (gr. 3-6). lib. bdg. 29.27 *(978-1-59953-488-6(6))* Norwood Hse. Pr.
Zuehlke, Jeffrey. Joe Mauer. 2011. 32p. 25.26 *(978-0-7613-7204-2(0))* 2008. pap. 40.95 *(978-0-8225-9490-1(0))* 2011. (ENG.). 32p. (gr. 2-5). 25.26 *(978-0-7613-7066-6(8))* 2011. (ENG.). 32p. (gr. 2-5). pap. 7.95 *(978-0-7613-7068-0(4))* Lerner Publishing Group.
—Joe Mauer (Revised Edition) 2011. (Amazing Athletes Ser.). 32p. (J). pap. 45.32 *(978-0-7613-7653-8(4))* Lerner Publishing Group.

MINNESOTA VIKINGS (FOOTBALL TEAM)

Adamson, Thomas K. The Minnesota Vikings Story. 2016. (NFL Teams Ser.). (ENG., Illus.). 32p. (J). (gr. 3-7). lib. bdg. 26.95 *(978-1-62617-372-9(9),* Torque Bks.) Bellwether Media.
Burgess, Zack. Meet the Minnesota Vikings. 2016. (Big Picture Sports Ser.). (ENG., Illus.). 24p. (J). (gr. k-3). lib. bdg. 22.60 *(978-1-59953-752-8(4))* Norwood Hse. Pr.
Epstein, Brad M. Minnesota Vikings 101. 2010. (ENG., Illus.). 24p. (J). bds. *(978-1-60730-117-2(2),* 101 Bk.) Michaelson Entertainment.
Frisch, Aaron. The History of the Minnesota Vikings. 2004. (NFL Today Ser.). (Illus.). 32p. (YA). (gr. 5-9). 18.95 *(978-1-58341-303-6(0))* Creative Co., The.
Frisch, Aaron & Bodden, Valerie. The Big Time: Adrian Peterson. 2014. (Big Time Ser.). (ENG.). 24p. (J). (gr. 1-3). pap. 9.99 *(978-1-62832-060-2(5),* Creative Paperbacks) Creative Co., The.
Gilbert, Sara. NFL Today: Minnesota Vikings. 2013. (NFL Today Ser.). (ENG., Illus.). 48p. (J). (gr. 4-7). pap. 12.00 *(978-0-89812-862-8(5),* Creative Paperbacks) Creative Co., The.
—The Story of the Minnesota Vikings. 2013. (Illus.). 48p. (J). 35.65 *(978-1-60818-309-8(2),* Creative Education) Creative Co., The.
Gitlin, Martin. Adrian Peterson: Record-Setting Running Back, 1 vol. 2012. (Playmakers Ser.). (ENG.). 32p. (J). (gr. 3-6). 27.07 *(978-1-61783-293-2(6))* ABDO Publishing Co.
Grabowski, John F. The Minnesota Vikings. 2003. (Great Sports Teams in History Ser.). (ENG., Illus.). 112p. (J). 30.85 *(978-1-56006-943-0(0),* Lucent Bks.) Cengage Gale.
Howell, Brian. Minnesota Vikings. 2015. (Insider's Guide to Pro Football Ser.). (ENG.). 32p. (J). (gr. k-3). 28.50 *(978-1-63407-010-2(0),* 208845) Child's World, Inc., The.
LeBoutillier, Nate. The Story of the Minnesota Vikings. 2009. (NFL Today Ser.). (Illus.). 48p. (YA). (gr. 5-9). 22.95 *(978-1-58341-762-1(1))* Creative Co., The.
Lobby, Mackenzie & Gitlin, Martin. Minnesota Vikings, 1 vol. 2010. (Inside the NFL Ser.). (ENG.). 48p. (YA). (gr. 3-6). lib. bdg. 32.79 *(978-1-61714-018-1(X))* ABDO Publishing Co.
MacRae, Sloan. The Minnesota Vikings. 2011. (America's Greatest Teams Ser.). (Illus.). 24p. (J). pap. 8.25 *(978-1-4488-3174-6(1));* lib. bdg. 22.60 *(978-1-4488-3168-5(7))* Rosen Publishing Group, Inc., The. (PowerKids Pr.).
Sandler, Michael. Adrian Peterson. 2010. (Football Heroes Making a Difference Ser.). (Illus.). 24p. (YA). (gr. 2-5). lib. bdg. 22.61 *(978-1-936087-59-4(6))* Bearport Publishing Co., Inc.
Savage, Jeff. Adrian Peterson. 2010. (Amazing Athletes Ser.). (ENG.). 32p. (gr. 2-5). 25.26 *(978-0-7613-5746-9(7));* pap. 7.95 *(978-0-7613-5758-2(0))* Lerner Publishing Group.
Scarpati, Kevin. Minnesota Vikings. 2014. (Inside the NFL Ser.). (ENG., Illus.). 32p. (J). (gr. 4-7). lib. bdg. 28.55 *(978-1-4896-0850-5(8),* AV2 by Weigl) Weigl Pubs., Inc.
Stewart, Mark. The Minnesota Vikings. rev. ed. 2012. (Team Spirit Ser.). (ENG.). 48p. (J). (gr. 3-6). lib. bdg. 29.27 *(978-1-59953-529-6(7))* Norwood Hse. Pr.
Wyner, Zach. Minnesota Vikings. 2015. (Illus.). 32p. pap. *(978-1-4896-0851-2(6))* Weigl Pubs., Inc.
Zappa, Marcia. Minnesota Vikings, 1 vol. 2014. (NFL's Greatest Teams Set 2 Ser.). (ENG.). 32p. (gr. 2-5). 28.50 *(978-1-62403-587-6(6))* ABDO Publishing Co.

MINORITIES

see also Assimilation (Sociology); Discrimination; Race Relations

African American Eras. 2010. *(978-1-4144-3598-5(3)); (978-1-4144-3599-2(1)); (978-1-4144-3600-5(9)); (978-1-4144-3597-8(5))* Cengage Gale. (UXL).
Anderson, Sonya, et al, eds. Facing Racism in Education. 3rd ed. 2005. (Harvard Educational Review Ser.: No. 39). (Illus.). 324p. (YA). pap. 29.95 *(978-0-916690-42-7(3),* Harvard Educational Review Reprint Series) Harvard Education Publishing Group (HEPG).
Bauchner, Elizabeth. Teen Minorities in Rural North America: Growing up Different. 2009. (Youth in Rural North America Ser.). (Illus.). 96p. (YA). (gr. 3-7). lib. bdg. 22.95 *(978-1-4222-0014-8(0))* Mason Crest.
Berlatsky, Noah, ed. Interracial America. 2011. (Opposing Viewpoints Ser.). (Illus.). 240p. pap. 29.45 *(978-0-7377-5728-6(0),* Greenhaven Pr., Inc.) Cengage Gale.
Books, Golson. The African Americans, 7 vols. 2011. (Multicultural America Ser.). (Illus.). 256p. (gr. 6-12). 55.00 *(978-0-8160-7813-4(0))* Facts On File, Inc.
—The Arab Americans, 7 vols. 2011. (Multicultural America Ser.). (Illus.). 208p. (gr. 6-12). 55.00 *(978-0-8160-7812-7(2))* Facts On File, Inc.
—The Asian Americans, 7 vols. 2011. (Multicultural America Ser.). (Illus.). 272p. (gr. 6-12). 55.00 *(978-0-8160-7814-1(9))* Facts On File, Inc.
—The European Americans, 7 vols. 2011. (Multicultural America Ser.). (Illus.). 256p. (gr. 6-12). 55.00 *(978-0-8160-7816-5(5))* Facts On File, Inc.
—The Hispanic Americans, 7 vols. 2011. (Multicultural America Ser.). (Illus.). 256p. (gr. 6-12). 55.00 *(978-0-8160-7811-0(4))* Facts On File, Inc.
—The Jewish Americans, 7 vols. 2011. (Multicultural America Ser.). (Illus.). 256p. (gr. 6-12). 55.00 *(978-0-8160-7815-8(7))* Facts On File, Inc.
—Multicultural America, 7 vols. Set. 2011. (Multicultural America Ser.). (Illus.). (gr. 6-12). 385.00 *(978-0-8160-7810-3(6))* Facts On File, Inc.
—The Native Americans, 7 vols. 2011. (Multicultural America Ser.). (Illus.). 256p. (gr. 6-12). 55.00 *(978-0-8160-7817-2(3))* Facts On File, Inc.
Brezina, Corona. Standing up to Bullying at School. 2017. (LGBTQ+ Guide to Beating Bullying Ser.). 64p. (J). (gr. 12-11). pap. 12.95 ***(978-1-5081-7429-5(6),*** Rosen Young Adult) Rosen Publishing Group, Inc., The.
Buckley, A. M. Racism, 1 vol. 2011. (Essential Issues Set 2 Ser.). (ENG., Illus.). 112p. (J). (gr. 6-12). lib. bdg. 35.64 *(978-1-61714-777-7(X),* Essential Library) ABDO Publishing Co.
Burgan, Michael. The Voting Rights Act of 1965: An Interactive History Adventure. 2015. (You Choose: History Ser.). (ENG.). 112p. (gr. 3-4). pap. 6.95 *(978-1-4914-1805-5(2),* You Choose Bks.) Capstone Press of Coughlan Cos.
Cosson, M. J. Affirmative Action, 1 vol. 2007. (Essential Viewpoints Set 1 Ser.). (ENG., Illus.). 112p. (J). (gr. 6-12). lib. bdg. 35.64 *(978-1-59928-857-4(5))* ABDO Publishing Co.
Cronn-Mills, Kirstin. Transgender Lives: Complex Stories, Complex Voices. 2014. 88p. (J). (gr. 6-12). lib. bdg. 34.60 *(978-0-7613-9022-0(7),* Twenty-First Century Bks.) Lerner Publishing Group.
Descola, Philippe. Diversité des Natures, Diversité des Cultures. 2010. (FRE.). 84p. *(978-2-227-48207-4(9))* Bayard Editions.
Espejo, Roman. Transgender People. 2010. (At Issue Ser.). (ENG.). 128p. pap. 24.45 *(978-0-7377-4897-0(4),* Greenhaven Pr., Inc.); (YA). (gr. 9-12). 34.45 *(978-0-7377-4896-3(6))* Cengage Gale.
Gayle-Evans, Guda. An Annotated Bibliography of Multi-Cultural Literature for Children Three to Ten Years. 2004. (Mellen Studies in Children's Literature: Vol. 6). (Illus.). 204p. 109.95 *(978-0-7734-6474-2(3))* Mellen, Edwin Pr., The.
Grinapol, Corinne. Racial Profiling & Discrimination: Your Legal Rights. 2015. (Know Your Rights Ser.). (ENG., Illus.). 64p. (J). (gr. 6-6). pap. 12.95 *(978-1-4777-8619-2(8),* Rosen Young Adult) Rosen Publishing Group, Inc., The.
Grinapol, Corinne. Racial Profiling & Discrimination: Your Legal Rights. 2015. (Know Your Rights Ser.). (ENG., Illus.). 64p. (J). (gr. 6-6). 33.25 *(978-1-4777-8020-6(3),* Rosen Young Adult) Rosen Publishing Group, Inc., The.
Hansen-Krening, Nancy, et al, eds. Kaleidoscope: A Multicultural Booklist for Grades K-8. 4th ed. 2003. (NCTE Bibliography Ser.). (Illus.). 118p. (J). pap. 30.95 *(978-0-8141-2539-7(5),* 25395) National Council of Teachers of English.
Hearn, Emily & Milne, Marywinn, eds. Our New Home: Immigrant Children Speak, 1 vol. 2008. (ENG., Illus.). 128p. (J). (gr. 4-8). pap. 13.95 *(978-1-897187-32-6(7))* Orca Bk. Pubs. USA.
Hermann, Spring. The Struggle for Equality: Women & Minorities in America. 2006. (American Saga Ser.). (Illus.). 128p. (J). (gr. 5-9). lib. bdg. 33.27 *(978-0-7660-2573-8(X))* Enslow Pubs., Inc.
Hernandez, Daniel. They Call Me a Hero: A Memoir of My Youth. 2013. (ENG., Illus.). 240p. (YA). (gr. 7). 17.99 *(978-1-4424-6228-1(0),* Simon & Schuster Bks. For Young Readers) Simon & Schuster Bks. For Young Readers.
Hiber, Amanda. Is the U. S. Ready for a Minority President? 2007. (At Issue Ser.). (ENG., Illus.). 128p. (gr. 10-12). pap. 27.80 *(978-0-7377-3879-7(0),* Greenhaven Pr., Inc.) Cengage Gale.
—Is the United States Ready for a Minority President? 2007. (At Issue Ser.). (ENG., Illus.). 128p. (gr. 10-12). 39.40 *(978-0-7377-3878-0(2),* Greenhaven Pr., Inc.) Cengage Gale.
Higgins, Melissa. We All Come from Different Cultures, 1 vol. 2012. (Celebrating Differences Ser.). (ENG.). 24p. (gr. k-1). 26.65 *(978-1-4296-7577-2(2));* pap. 41.70 *(978-1-4296-8320-3(1));* pap. 7.29 *(978-1-4296-7887-2(9))* Capstone Press of Coughlan Cos. (Pebble Plus).
Hirschmann, Kris. Understanding Sexual Identity & Orientation. 2017. (Understanding Psychology Ser.). (ENG.). 80p. (YA). (gr. 5-12). ***(978-1-68282-281-4(8))*** ReferencePoint Pr., Inc.
Holt, David H. Religious, Cultural, & Minority Rights, Vol. 8. Lansford, Tom, ed. 2016. (Foundations of Democracy Ser.). (Illus.). 64p. (J). (gr. 7). 23.95 *(978-1-4222-3632-1(3))* Mason Crest.
Howse, Jennifer. Reconstruction. 2013. (J). *(978-1-62127-194-9(3));* pap. *(978-1-62127-200-7(1))* Weigl Pubs., Inc.
Hunter, Miranda. Story of Latino Civil Rights: Fighting for Justice. 2007. (Hispanic Heritage Ser.). (Illus.). 112p. (YA). lib. bdg. 22.95 *(978-1-59084-934-7(5))* Mason Crest.
Hyde, Natalie. LGBTQ Rights. 2017. 48p. (J). ***(978-0-7787-3942-5(2))*** Crabtree Publishing Co.
Jones, Patrick. Teen Incarceration: From Cell Bars to Ankle Bracelets. 2016. (ENG., Illus.). 120p. (YA). (gr. 7-12). lib. bdg. 37.32 *(978-1-4677-7572-4(X));* 55.99 *(978-1-5124-1138-6(8),* Twenty-First Century Bks.) Lerner Publishing Group.
Kootz, Russell & Seidman, David. Understanding Civil Rights. 2011. (Personal Freedom & Civic Duty Ser.). (Illus.). 184p. (J). lib. bdg. 35.95 *(978-1-4488-4666-5(8))* Rosen Publishing Group, Inc., The.
Kortemeier, Todd. Unsung Heroes of Social Justice. 2017. (Unsung Heroes Ser.). (ENG., Illus.). 32p. (J). (gr. 3-6). 21.95 *(978-1-63235-310-8(5))* Pr. Room Editions LLC.
Marcovitz, Hal. Race Relations. 2008. (Gallup Major Trends & Events Ser.). (Illus.). 127p. (YA). (gr. 7-18). lib. bdg. 22.95 *(978-1-59084-968-2(X))* Mason Crest.
Nagle, Jeanne. Are You LGBTQ? 2016. (Got Issues? Ser.). (ENG.). 112p. (YA). (gr. 7-8). lib. bdg. 37.27 *(978-0-7660-7139-1(1))* Enslow Pubs., Inc.
Naidoo, Jamie Campbell. Rainbow Family Collections: Selecting & Using Children's Books with Lesbian, Gay, Bisexual, Transgender, & Queer Content, 1 vol. 2012. (Children's & Young Adult Literature Reference Ser.). (Illus.). 260p. (C). 50.00 *(978-1-59884-960-8(3),* A3634C) Pearson Education GBR. Dist: ABC-CLIO, LLC.
Perrin, Pat. Getting Started-America's Melting Pot. 2004. (Illus.). (J). *(978-1-932663-04-4(5))* History Compass, LLC.
—Getting Started-Our 50 United States. 2004. (Illus.). (J). *(978-1-932663-03-7(7))* History Compass, LLC.
—Getting Started-Our Government. 2004. (Illus.). (J). *(978-1-932663-02-0(9))* History Compass, LLC.
Pobst, Sandy. The Newest Americans, 5 vols. 2003. (Middle School Reference Ser.). (Illus.). 144p. (C). (gr. 6-8). 242.00

(978-0-313-32553-3(7), MS2553, Greenwood) ABC-CLIO, LLC.

Prager, Sarah. Queer, There, & Everywhere: 23 People Who Changed the World. O'Ferrall, Zoë More, illus. 2017. 272p. (YA). (gr. 8). 17.99 *(978-0-06-247431-5(6))* HarperCollins Pubs.

Radzilowski, John. Ukrainian Americans. 2007. (New Immigrants Ser.). (Illus.). 128p. (gr. 6-12). lib. bdg. 30.00 *(978-0-7910-8789-3(1)*, Chelsea Hse.) Facts On File, Inc.

Robins, Maureen Picard. One Land, Many Cultures. 2012. (ENG.). 24p. (gr. k-2). pap. 8.95 *(978-1-61810-276-8(1))* Rourke Educational Media.

Rosen Publishing Staff. Remarkable Lgbtq Lives, 1 vol. 2015. (Remarkable LGBTQ Lives Ser.). (ENG.). 112p. (YA). 213.60 *(978-1-4777-7903-3(5)*, Rosen Young Adult) Rosen Publishing Group, Inc., The.

Seba, Jaime. Gay People of Color: Facing Prejudices, Forging Identities. 2009. (Gallup's Guide to Modern Gay, Lesbian, & Transgender Lifestyle Ser.). 64p. (YA). (gr. 7-18). pap. 9.95 *(978-1-4222-1877-8(5))*; (Illus.). lib. bdg. 22.95 *(978-1-4222-1748-1(5))* Mason Crest.

Stanek, Muriel. We Came from Vietnam. McMahon, Wm. Franklin, photos by. 2004. (Illus.). 46p. (J). (gr. k-4). reprint ed. *(978-0-7567-7795-1(X))* DIANE Publishing Co.

Steele, Philip. Race & Crime. 2016. (Illus.). 48p. (J). *(978-0-7787-2588-6(X))* Crabtree Publishing Co.

Takaki, Ronald. A Different Mirror for Young People: A History of Multicultural America. 2012. (For Young People Ser.). (ENG., Illus.). 378p. (J). (gr. 5). pap. 18.95 *(978-1-60980-416-9(3)*, Triangle Square) Seven Stories Pr.

Thomas, Zachary & Wilson, Natashya. The Melting Pot: The People & Cultures of New York. 2012. (Illus.). 24p. (J). 60.00 *(978-1-4488-5768-5(6))*; pap. 10.00 *(978-1-4488-5767-8(8))*; lib. bdg. 22.60 *(978-1-4488-5747-0(3))* Rosen Publishing Group, Inc., The. (PowerKids Pr.).

Wright, John D. Race & Crime. 2004. (Crime & Detection Ser.). (Illus.). 96p. (YA). (gr. 7-18). lib. bdg. 22.95 *(978-1-59084-378-9(9))* Mason Crest.

—Race & Crime, Vol. 20. Gomez, Manny, ed. 2016. (Crime & Detection Ser.). (Illus.). 96p. (J). (gr. 7). 24.95 *(978-1-4222-3485-3(1))* Mason Crest.

MINTS

Morrison, Taylor. The Buffalo Nickel. Morrison, Taylor, illus. 2006. (Illus.). 32p. (J). (gr. 4-8). reprint ed. 16.00 *(978-1-4223-5858-0(5))* DIANE Publishing Co.

Vox, Everett. The U. S. Mint: The History of U. S. Money. 2017. (Landmarks of Democracy: American Institutions Ser.). 24p. (J). (gr. 7-8). pap. 8.25 ***(978-1-5081-6101-1(1)***, PowerKids Pr.) Rosen Publishing Group, Inc., The.

MIRACLE PLAYS

see Bible Plays

MIRRORS

Edom, H. Science Activities, Vol. 1. 2010. (Science Activities Ser.). 72p. (J). 13.99 *(978-0-7945-2752-5(3)*, Usborne) EDC Publishing.

Holden, Pam. Look in the Mirror. 2015. (ENG., Illus.). 16p. (-1). pap. *(978-1-77654-082-2(4)*, Red Rocket Readers) Flying Start Bks.

Priddy, Roger. Hello Baby. 2012. (Hello Baby Ser.). (ENG., Illus.). 6p. (J). (gr. -1 — 1). 9.99 *(978-0-312-51510-2(3)*, 9780312515102, Priddy Bks.) St. Martin's Pr.

Strom, Laura Layton. Mirror Power. 2007. (Shockwave: Technology & Manufacturing Ser.). (ENG., Illus.). 36p. (J). (gr. 3-5). 25.00 *(978-0-531-17588-0(X)*, Children's Pr.) Scholastic Library Publishing.

Tullet, Hervé. The Game of Mirrors. 2014. (ENG., Illus.). 14p. (gr. -1-17). 12.95 *(978-0-7148-6687-1(3))* Phaidon Pr., Inc.

MISDEMEANORS

see Crime

MISS SPIDER (FICTITIOUS CHARACTER)—FICTION

Kirk, David. Miss Spider's Tea Party. unabr. ed. 2008. (Scholastic Bookshelf Ser.). (ENG., Illus.). (J). (gr. -1-3). 18.95 *(978-0-545-02979-7(1))* Scholastic, Inc.

Kirk, David & Scholastic / LeapFrog. Miss Spider's Tea Party. 2008. (J). 13.99 *(978-1-59319-934-0(1))* LeapFrog Enterprises, Inc.

MISSILES, GUIDED

see Guided Missiles

MISSING PERSONS

Herbst, Judith. Vanished. 2004. (Unexplained Ser.). (Illus.). 48p. (J). pap. 8.95 *(978-0-8225-2404-5(X)*, Lerner Pubns.); (ENG., (gr. 5-12). lib. bdg. 26.60 *(978-0-8225-1631-6(4))* Lerner Publishing Group.

Hutt, Sarah. Missing, 1 vol. unabr. ed. 2012. (Astonishing Headlines Ser.). (ENG.). 92p. (YA). (gr. 9-12). 8.95 *(978-1-61651-923-0(1))* Saddleback Educational Publishing, Inc.

Purney, Dawn. Lost & Found, 1 vol. unabr. ed. 2012. (Astonishing Headlines Ser.). (ENG.). 92p. (YA). (gr. 9-12). 8.95 *(978-1-61651-922-3(3))* Saddleback Educational Publishing, Inc.

Rollason, Jane. Killer Bees Level 2 Elementary/Lower-intermediate American English. 2010. (ENG., Illus.). 64p. pap. 12.00 *(978-0-521-14896-2(0))* Cambridge Univ. Pr.

Stewart, Gail B. Missing Persons. 2011. (Crime Scene Investigations Ser.). (ENG.). 128p. (gr. 10-10). lib. bdg. 40.40 *(978-1-4205-0534-4(3)*, Lucent Bks.) Cengage Gale.

Townsend, John. Gone Missing. 2010. (Amazing Mysteries Ser.). (YA). (gr. 3-6). 28.50 *(978-1-59920-364-5(2))* Black Rabbit Bks.

MISSING PERSONS—FICTION

Abbott, Tony. The Battle Begins. 2012. (Underworlds Ser.: 1). lib. bdg. 14.75 *(978-0-606-23928-8(6)*, Turtleback) Turtleback Bks.

Abrahams, Peter. Reality Check. 2010. (ENG.). 352p. (YA). (gr. 8). pap. 8.99 *(978-0-06-122768-4(4)*, HarperTeen) HarperCollins Pubs.

Adam, Paul. Escape from Shadow Island. (ENG.). 304p. (J). (gr. 5). 2011. (Max Cassidy Ser.: Bk. 1). pap. 5.99 *(978-0-06-186325-7(4))* 2010. 16.99 *(978-0-06-186323-3(8))* HarperCollins Pubs. (Waldon Pond Pr.).

Adler, David A. Bones & the Football Mystery. 2013. (Bones Ser.: 9). (ENG.). 32p. (J). (gr. 1-3). pap. 3.99 *(978-0-448-47942-2(7)*, Penguin Young Readers) Penguin Young Readers Group.

—Cam Jansen & the Spaghetti Max Mystery. Allen, Joy, illus. 2014. (Cam Jansen Ser.: 33). (ENG.). 64p. (J). (gr. 2-5). pap. 4.99 *(978-0-14-751232-1(8)*, Puffin Books) Penguin Young Readers Group.

—Young Cam Jansen & the Circus Mystery. Natti, Susanna, illus. 2013. (Young Cam Jansen Ser.: 17). (ENG.). 32p. (J). (gr. 1-3). pap. 3.99 *(978-0-448-46614-9(7)*, Penguin Young Readers) Penguin Young Readers Group.

—Young Cam Jansen & the Goldfish Mystery. Natti, Susanna, illus. 2013. (Young Cam Jansen Ser.: 19). (ENG.). 32p. (J). (gr. 1-3). 14.99 *(978-0-670-01259-6(9)*, Penguin Young Readers) Penguin Young Readers Group.

—Young Cam Jansen & the Magic Bird Mystery. Natti, Susanna, illus. 2013. (Young Cam Jansen Ser.: 18). (ENG.). 32p. (J). (gr. 1-3). pap. 3.99 *(978-0-448-46613-2(9)*, Penguin Young Readers) Penguin Young Readers Group.

Aiken, Joan. Black Hearts in Battersea, No. 2. 2004. (ENG., Illus.). 256p. (J). pap. 10.95 *(978-0-09-945639-1(7)*, Red Fox) Random House Children's Books GBR. Dist: Random Hse. of Canada.

Alexander, William. Goblin Secrets. (ENG., Illus.). (J). (gr. 3-7). 2013. 256p. pap. 7.99 *(978-1-4424-2727-3(2))* 2012. 240p. 16.99 *(978-1-4424-2726-6(4))* McElderry, Margaret K. Bks. (McElderry, Margaret K. Bks.).

Alphin, Elaine Marie. Picture Perfect. 2003. (ENG., Illus.). 256p. (YA). (gr. 5-12). 15.95 *(978-0-8225-0535-8(5))* Lerner Publishing Group.

Alpine, Rachele. A Void the Size of the World. 2017. (ENG., Illus.). 368p. (YA). (gr. 9). 17.99 ***(978-1-4814-8571-5(7)***, Simon Pulse) Simon Pulse.

Altebrando, Tara. The Leaving. 2016. (ENG.). 432p. (YA). 17.99 *(978-1-61963-803-7(7)*, 9781619638037, Bloomsbury USA Childrens) Bloomsbury Publishing USA.

Anastasiu, Heather & Brown, Anne Greenwood. Girl Last Seen. 2016. (ENG.). 272p. (YA). (gr. 8-12). pap. 9.99 *(978-0-8075-8141-4(0))* Whitman, Albert & Co.

Anderson, E. V. The Many Lives of Lilith Lane, 0 vols. unabr. ed. 2012. (ENG.). 162p. (YA). (gr. 7-9). pap. 9.99 *(978-1-61109-792-4(4)*, 9781611097924, Amazon Children's Publishing) Amazon Publishing.

Armentrout, Jennifer L. Don't Look Back. 2014. (Novel Ser.: 1). (ENG.). 384p. (YA). (gr. 9-17). 16.99 *(978-1-4231-7512-4(3))* Hyperion Bks. for Children.

Arsenault, Emily. The Leaf Reader. 2017. (ENG.). 240p. (YA). (gr. 9). 18.99 *(978-1-61695-782-7(4)*, Soho Teen) Soho Pr., Inc.

Ashley, Bernard. A Present for Paul. Mitchell, David, illus. 2004. 28p. (J). *(978-1-85269-360-2(6))*; *(978-1-85269-359-6(2))* Mantra Lingua.

Atlas, Lilly. Journey to the Deep Woods. 2008. 36p. pap. 16.99 *(978-1-4389-2596-7(4))* AuthorHouse.

Austin, Jamie Lea-Elizabeth. Reverie. 2012. 312p. 29.95 *(978-1-4626-6734-5(1))* PublishAmerica, Inc.

Bachmann, Stefan. The Whatnot. 2014. (Peculiar Ser.: 2). (ENG.). 432p. (J). (gr. 3-7). pap. 8.99 *(978-0-06-219522-7(0)*, Greenwillow Bks.) HarperCollins Pubs.

Bacon, C. G. Mean Mandy. 2009. 103p. pap. 11.00 *(978-0-557-05740-5(X))* Lulu Pr., Inc.

Bailey, Margaret A. Dragonworld & the Room of Strange Hangings. 2009. 172p. pap. 11.99 *(978-1-4389-8252-6(6))* AuthorHouse.

Ballantyne, R. M. Silver Lake. 2004. reprint ed. pap. 1.99 *(978-1-4192-4729-3(8))*; pap. 19.95 *(978-1-4191-4729-6(3))* Kessinger Publishing, LLC.

Ballantyne, Robert Michael. Jarwin & Cuffy. l.t. ed. 2007. (ENG.). 102p. pap. 19.99 *(978-1-4346-3724-6(7))* Creative Media Partners, LLC.

—Silver Lake. 2007. (ENG.). 116p. pap. 18.99 *(978-1-4346-3759-8(X))*; 130p. pap. 19.99 *(978-1-4346-3773-4(5))* Creative Media Partners, LLC.

Balliett, Blue. The Calder Game. Helquist, Brett, illus. (ENG.). (J). (gr. 3-7). 2010. 416p. 7.99 *(978-0-439-85208-1(0)*, Scholastic Paperbacks) 2008. 400p. 17.99 *(978-0-439-85207-4(2)*, Scholastic Pr.) Scholastic, Inc.

—Hold Fast. 2015. (ENG.). 288p. (J). (gr. 3-7). pap. 6.99 *(978-0-545-29989-3(6)*, Scholastic Paperbacks) Scholastic, Inc.

Balmer, Fred. Festus & the Stranger. Miller, Callie, ed. Newcomb, Kristene, illus. 2007. 30p. (J). per. 7.00 *(978-0-9760790-4-0(6))* Folsom Fallies Pr.

Banim, Lisa. Case of the Missing She-Geek. 2004. 125p. (J). lib. bdg. 16.92 *(978-1-4242-0683-4(9))* Fitzgerald Bks.

Baptiste, Tracey. The Rise of the Jumbies. 2017. (Jumbies Ser.). (ENG.). 256p. (J). (gr. 3-7). 16.95 ***(978-1-61620-665-9(9))*** Algonquin Bks. of Chapel Hill.

Barrett, Tracy. The Missing Heir. 2012. (Sherlock Files Ser.: 4). (ENG., Illus.). 192p. (J). (gr. 3-7). pap. 8.99 *(978-1-250-00480-2(2)*, 9781250004802) Square Fish.

—The Missing Heir. 2012. (Sherlock Files Ser.: 4). (J). lib. bdg. 19.65 *(978-0-606-26131-9(1)*, Turtleback) Turtleback Bks.

Barwin, Steven. Hurricane Heat, 1 vol. 2013. (Orca Sports Ser.). (ENG.). 176p. (YA). (gr. 6-10). pap. 9.95 *(978-1-4598-0213-1(6))* Orca Bk. Pubs. USA.

Bashe, Kayla. Kitty Cadawell & the Shadowslayers of Fyrn. 2008. 290p. pap. 16.50 *(978-0-557-01916-8(8))* Lulu Pr., Inc.

Baum, L. Frank. L Frank Baum's Book of Santa Claus. 2007. 84p. per. 7.99 *(978-1-60459-118-7(8))* Wilder Pubns., Corp.

Baumgartner, John Robert. Like Losing Your Left Hand. 2011. 244p. pap. 24.95 *(978-1-4560-4043-7(X))* America Star Bks.

Beaufrand, M. J. The Rise & Fall of the Gallivanters. 2015. (ENG., Illus.). 288p. (YA). (gr. 9-17). 16.95 *(978-1-4197-1495-5(3)*, Amulet Bks.) Abrams, Inc.

Beaumier, Randy P. Snapshot Billy: I Remember. 2012. 36p. pap. 24.95 *(978-1-4626-1787-6(5))* America Star Bks.

Beauvais, Clémentine. Sleuth on Skates. Home, Sarah, illus. 2014. (Sesame Seade Mystery Ser.: 1). (ENG.). 224p. (J). (gr. 2-5). 16.95 *(978-0-8234-3197-7(5))* Holiday Hse., Inc.

Beckham, David. Charlie Barker & the Secret of the Deep Dark Woods. 2006. 570p. pap. 33.20 *(978-1-4120-9264-7(7))* Trafford Publishing.

Behems, Kathryn J. Breakdown. 2016. (Atlas of Cursed Places Ser.). (ENG.). 96p. (YA). (gr. 6-12). lib. bdg. 26.65 *(978-1-5124-1323-6(2)*, Darby Creek) Lerner Publishing Group.

Berenstain, Jan & Berenstain, Mike. The Berenstain Bears & the Little Lost Cub, 1 vol. 2011. (I Can Read! / Berenstain Bears / Good Deed Scouts / Living Lights Ser.). (ENG.). 32p. (J). pap. 3.99 *(978-0-310-72100-0(8))* Zonderkidz.

Bergstrom, Scott. The Cruelty. 2017. (Cruelty Ser.). (ENG.). 384p. (YA). 18.99 *(978-1-250-10818-0(7)*, 9781250108180) Feiwel & Friends.

Bessen, Luc. Arthur & the Minimoys. Sowchek, Ellen, tr. from FRE. 2005. (ENG.). 240p. (J). 15.99 *(978-0-06-059623-1(6))* HarperCollins Pubs.

Besson, Luc. Arthur & the Minimoys. 2005. (Illus.). 240p. (J). lib. bdg. 16.89 *(978-0-06-059624-8(4))* HarperCollins Pubs.

Bilen, Tracy. What She Left Behind. 2012. (ENG.). 256p. (YA). (gr. 9). pap. 9.99 *(978-1-4424-3951-1(3)*, Simon Pulse) Simon Pulse.

Birch, Beverley. Rift. 2008. (ENG., Illus.). 224p. (YA). (gr. 7-18). pap. 9.95 *(978-1-4052-1589-3(5))* Egmont Bks., Ltd. GBR. Dist: Independent Pubs. Group.

Black, Holly. Kin. Naifeh, Ted, illus. (Good Neighbors Ser.: 1). (ENG.). 144p. (J). (gr. 7). 2009. pap. 12.99 *(978-0-439-85565-5(9))* 2008. 16.99 *(978-0-439-85562-4(4))* Scholastic, Inc. (Graphix).

—Kith. Naifeh, Ted, illus. 2010. (Good Neighbors Ser.: 2). (ENG.). 128p. (J). (gr. 3-7). pap. 12.99 *(978-0-439-85566-2(7)*, Graphix) Scholastic, Inc.

Black, Yelena. Dance of Shadows. (Dance of Shadows Ser.). (ENG., Illus.). 384p. (YA). (gr. 7). 2014. pap. 9.99 *(978-1-61963-185-4(7)*, 9781619631854) 2013. 17.99 *(978-1-59990-940-0(5)*, 9781599909400) Bloomsbury Publishing USA. (Bloomsbury USA Childrens).

Blackstock, Terri. Southern Storm, 1 vol. 2014. (Cape Refuge Ser.). (ENG.). 400p. pap. 15.99 *(978-0-310-34280-9(5))* Zondervan.

Bliss, Harry. Luke on the Loose. Bliss, Harry, illus. 2009. (ENG., Illus.). 32p. (J). (gr. -1-3). 12.95 *(978-1-935179-00-9(4))* TOON Books / RAW Junior, LLC.

—Luke on the Loose. 2014. (Toon Books Level 2 Ser.). lib. bdg. 14.75 *(978-0-606-32101-3(2)*, Turtleback) Turtleback Bks.

Bobulski, Chelsea. The Wood. 2017. (ENG.). 320p. (YA). 17.99 *(978-1-250-09426-1(7)*, 9781250094261) Feiwel & Friends.

Bond, Gwenda. Strange Alchemy. 2017. (ENG.). 336p. (gr. 9-12). 17.95 ***(978-1-63079-076-9(1))*** Switch Pr.

Bosch, Pseudonymous. This Book Is Not Good for You. 2009. (Secret Ser.: 3). (ENG.). 400p. (J). (gr. 3-7). 17.99 *(978-0-316-04086-0(X))* Little, Brown Bks. for Young Readers.

Bowler, Tim. Frozen Fire. 2010. (ENG.). 352p. (YA). (gr. 7-18). 8.99 *(978-0-14-241465-1(4)*, Speak) Penguin Young Readers Group.

Bracegirdle, P. J. Sinister Scenes. (Joy of Spooking Ser.). (ENG.). 320p. (J). (gr. 3-7). 2012. pap. 6.99 *(978-1-4169-3421-9(9))* 2011. 15.99 *(978-1-4169-3420-2(0))* McElderry, Margaret K. Bks. (McElderry, Margaret K. Bks.).

Bradbury, Jennifer. Shift. (ENG., Illus.). (YA). (gr. 7). 2012. 272p. pap. 10.99 *(978-1-4424-0852-4(9))* 2008. 256p. 17.99 *(978-1-4169-4732-5(9))* Simon & Schuster Children's Publishing. (Atheneum Bks. for Young Readers).

Bradley, Timothy. Ripple Effect. rev. ed. 2014. (Sci Hi Ser.). (ENG., Illus.). 176p. (J). (gr. 3-6). lib. bdg. 26.96 *(978-1-4807-4216-1(3))* Teacher Created Materials, Inc.

Branning, Debe. The Adventures of Chickolet Pigolet: The Bribe of Frankenbeans. Knold, Nijlon, illus. 2008. 48p. pap. 7.95 *(978-1-935137-40-5(9))* Guardian Angel Publishing, Inc.

Brauning, Kate. How We Fall. 2014. (ENG.). 304p. (YA). 17.99 *(978-1-4405-8179-3(7)*, Simon Pulse) Simon Pulse.

Brezenoff, Steven. The Case of the Missing Mom. Weber, Lisa K., illus. 2016. (Museum Mysteries Ser.). (ENG.). 128p. (gr. 2-3). 26.65 *(978-1-4965-2517-8(5))* Stone Arch Bks.

—The Missing Bully: An Interactive Mystery Adventure. Calo, Marcos, illus. 2017. (You Choose Stories: Field Trip Mysteries Ser.). (ENG.). 112p. (gr. 3-7). lib. bdg. 32.65 *(978-1-4965-2642-7(2))* Stone Arch Bks.

Brian, Kate, pseud. Ominous. 2011. (Private Ser.). (ENG.). 224p. (YA). (gr. 9-18). pap. 9.99 *(978-1-4169-8472-6(0)*, Simon & Schuster Bks. For Young Readers) Simon & Schuster Bks. For Young Readers.

Briggs, Andy. The Savage Lands. 2013. (Tarzan Ser.). (ENG.). 212p. (J). (gr. 3-6). pap. 12.99 *(978-1-4804-0014-6(9)*, Open Road Media E-riginal) Open Road Integrated Media, Inc.

—Tarzan: The Greystoke Legacy. 2011. (ENG.). 304p. pap. *(978-0-571-27238-9(X))* Faber & Faber, Ltd.

Briley, Randy. Mr Underneath. 2013. 134p. pap. 12.99 *(978-0-9896269-0-3(3))* Raven Mad Studios.

Brown, Anne Greenwood & Anastasiu, Heather. Girl Last Seen. 2016. (ENG.). 272p. (YA). (gr. 8-12). 16.99 *(978-0-8075-8140-7(2))* Whitman, Albert & Co.

Brown, Jo. Where's My Mommy? Brown, Jo, illus. 2006. (Storytime Board Bks.). (Illus.). 18p. (J). (gr. -1-3). bds. 6.95 *(978-1-58925-795-5(2))* Tiger Tales.

Brummit, Ariyana. A Soldier's Way Home. 2013. 124p. pap. 11.97 *(978-0-9801060-7-7(9))* Heard Word Publishing, LLC.

Buckingham, Royce. The Dead Boys. 2010. (ENG.). 208p. (J). (gr. 5-18). 16.99 *(978-0-399-25222-8(3)*, G.P. Putnam's Sons Books for Young Readers) Penguin Young Readers Group.

Bullock, Rob. Noah Ramsbottom & the Cave Elves. 2009. 48p. pap. 12.25 *(978-1-60860-335-0(0)*, Strategic Bk. Publishing) Strategic Book Publishing & Rights Agency (SBPRA).

Bumgarner, Sam. Little Sami's Silly Again, 1 vol. 2009. 32p. pap. 24.95 *(978-1-60813-863-0(1))* America Star Bks.

Burak, Kathryn. Emily's Dress & Other Missing Things. 2012. (ENG.). 240p. (YA). (gr. 8-12). 17.99 *(978-1-59643-736-4(7))* Roaring Brook Pr.

Bursztyn, Dina. The Land of Lost Things: El País de las Cosas Perdidas. Bursztyn, Dina, illus. 2011. (SPA & ENG., Illus.). 32p. (J). (gr. -1-3). 16.95 *(978-1-55885-690-5(0)*, Piñata Books) Arte Publico Pr.

Busby, Cylin. The Stranger Game. 2016. 288p. (YA). (gr. 8). 17.99 *(978-0-06-235460-0(4))* HarperCollins Pubs.

Butler, Dori Hillestad. The Buddy Files Bk. 3: The Case of the Missing Family. Tugeau, Jeremy, illus. 2010. (Buddy Files Ser.: 3). (ENG.). 128p. (J). (gr. 1-5). 14.99 *(978-0-8075-0912-8(4))* Whitman, Albert & Co.

—The Case of the Lost Boy. Tugeau, Jeremy, illus. 2010. (Buddy Files Ser.: 1). (ENG.). 128p. (J). (gr. 1-5). 14.99 *(978-0-8075-0910-4(8))*;Bk. 1. pap. 5.99 *(978-0-8075-0932-6(9))* Whitman, Albert & Co.

—The Case of the Missing Family, 1 vol., Bk. 3. Tugeau, Jeremy, illus. 2010. (Buddy Files Ser.: 3). (ENG.). 144p. (J). (gr. 1-5). pap. 5.99 *(978-0-8075-0934-0(5))* Whitman, Albert & Co.

Cabot, Meg. Safe House - Sanctuary. 2011. (Vanished Ser.: Bks. 3 & 4). (ENG.). 512p. (YA). (gr. 7). pap. 12.99 *(978-1-4424-0631-5(3)*, Simon Pulse) Simon Pulse.

—When Lightning Strikes; Code Name Cassandra. 2010. (Vanished Ser.: Bks. 1 & 2). (ENG., Illus.). 560p. (YA). (gr. 7). pap. 12.99 *(978-1-4424-0629-2(1)*, Simon Pulse) Simon Pulse.

Cain, Janan. Roonie B. Moonie: Lost & Alone. 2007. (Illus.). 32p. (J). (gr. -1-3). 15.95 *(978-0-9740190-8-6(9))* Illumination Arts Publishing Co., Inc.

Caine, Rachel, pseud. Kiss of Death, 8 vols. 2010. (Morganville Vampires Ser.: 8). (ENG.). 256p. (YA). (gr. 9-18). 6.99 *(978-0-451-22973-1(8)*, Berkley) Penguin Publishing Group.

—The Morganville Vampires, Vol. 4. 2011. (Morganville Vampires Ser.: Bks. 7-8). (ENG.). 464p. (YA). (gr. 9-18). 9.99 *(978-0-451-23426-1(X)*, Berkley) Penguin Publishing Group.

Cameron, Sam. The Missing Juliet: a Fisher Key Adventure. 2013. (ENG.). 264p. (gr. 7). pap. 11.95 *(978-1-60282-959-6(4))* Bold Strokes Bks.

Cantor, Jillian. The September Sisters. 2009. (ENG.). 368p. (YA). (gr. 8-18). 16.99 *(978-0-06-168648-1(4)*, HarperTeen) HarperCollins Pubs.

Capeci, Anne. Missing!, 1 vol. Casale, Paul, illus. 2005. (Cascade Mountain Railroad Mysteries Ser.). (ENG.). 144p. (J). (gr. 2-5). 12.95 *(978-1-56145-334-4(X))* Peachtree Pubs.

Carey, Benedict. Island of the Unknowns. 2011. (ENG., Illus.). 288p. (YA). (gr. 3-7). pap. 6.95 *(978-0-8109-9663-2(4)*, Amulet Bks.) Abrams, Inc.

—The Unknowns: A Mystery. 2009. (ENG., Illus.). 272p. (YA). (gr. 3-7). 17.95 *(978-0-8109-7991-8(8)*, Amulet Bks.) Abrams, Inc.

Carlson, Caroline. The Terror of the Southlands. Phillips, Dave, illus. 2014. (ENG.). 336p. (J). pap. *(978-0-06-236178-3(3))* Harper & Row Ltd.

Carlson, Melody. Bad Connection. 2006. (Secret Life of Samantha Mcgregor Ser.: No. 1). (ENG.). 256p. (J). (gr. 7-12). per. 12.99 *(978-1-59052-692-7(9)*, Multnomah) Doubleday Religious Publishing Group, The.

Caron, Eleonore. Gizmo & Ellen Mysteries: The Case of the Missing Boy. 2012. 24p. pap. 24.95 *(978-1-4626-6747-5(3))* America Star Bks.

Carr, Debra. Misty Is Missing. Carr, Stephen, illus. 2008. 52p. pap. 8.95 *(978-0-9816172-7-5(1))* Westview Publishing Co., Inc.

Carroll, Jenny, pseud. Safe House. 2011. (1-800-Where-R-You Ser.: 3). (ENG.). 272p. (YA). (gr. 9). pap. 12.99 *(978-1-4424-3084-6(2)*, Simon Pulse) Simon Pulse.

Carroll, Jenny, pseud & Cabot, Meg. Code Name Cassandra. 2007. (1-800-Where-R-You Ser.: No. 2). (ENG., Illus.). 272p. (YA). (gr. 9-12). mass mkt. 6.99 *(978-1-4169-2704-4(2)*, Simon Pulse) Simon Pulse.

Carson, Jack. Swampland Slam. 2013. (ENG., Illus.). 128p. (J). pap. 7.99 *(978-0-85707-563-5(2)*, Simon & Schuster Children's) Simon & Schuster, Ltd. GBR. Dist: Simon & Schuster, Inc.

Carter, Rachel. So Close to You. 2013. (ENG.). 336p. (YA). (gr. 9). pap. 9.99 *(978-0-06-208106-3(3)*, HarperTeen) HarperCollins Pubs.

—This Strange & Familiar Place. 2013. (ENG.). 272p. (YA). (gr. 9). 17.99 *(978-0-06-208108-7(X)*, HarperTeen) HarperCollins Pubs.

Cartwright, Ran. The Adventures of Billy Space Boy, 1 vol. 2010. 208p. pap. 24.95 *(978-1-4489-3901-5(1))* America Star Bks.

Chan, Queenie. The Dreaming Collection. 2010. (ENG., Illus.). 576p. pap. 19.99 *(978-1-4278-1871-3(1))* TOKYOPOP, Inc.

Chapman, Clay McLeod. Camp Cannibal. 2014. (Tribe Novel Ser.). (ENG.). 320p. (J). (gr. 3-7). 16.99 *(978-1-4231-5222-4(0))* Hyperion Bks. for Children.

Chappell, Crissa-Jean. Snow Birds. 2017. (ENG.). 272p. (YA). 17.99 *(978-1-5072-0069-8(2)*, Simon Pulse) Simon Pulse.

Charbonneau, Joelle. The Testing. (Testing Ser.: 1). (ENG.). 352p. (YA). (gr. 7). 2015. pap. 9.99 *(978-0-544-33623-0(2)*, HMH Books For Young Readers) 2013. 17.99 *(978-0-547-95910-8(9))* Houghton Mifflin Harcourt Publishing Co.

The Children of the Lost, Bk. 1. 2010. (Hardy Boys (All New) Undercover Brothers Ser.: 34). (ENG.). 192p. (J). (gr. 3-7). pap. 5.99 *(978-1-4424-0262-1(8)*, Aladdin) Simon & Schuster Children's Publishing.

Childress, Jamie. Galactic Treasure Hunt 5: Lost Fortress of Light. Braun, Chris, illus. 2010. (Galactic Treasure Hunt Ser.). (ENG.). 230p. pap. 6.99 *(978-1-935487-06-7(X))* Adventures Unlimited Pr.

Clarke, Cat. The Lost & the Found. 2016. (ENG.). 368p. (YA). (gr. 9). 17.99 *(978-1-101-93204-9(X)*, Crown Books For Young Readers) Random Hse. Children's Bks.

Clarke, E. J. Oakwing: A Fairy's Tale. 2017. (Oakwing Ser.: 1). (ENG., Illus.). 192p. (J). (gr. 2-6). 16.99 ***(978-1-4814-8191-5(6)***, Aladdin) Simon & Schuster Children's Publishing.

—Oakwing: A Fairy's Tale. 2017. (J). pap. ***(978-1-4814-8190-8(8)***, Simon & Schuster/Paula Wiseman Bks.) Simon & Schuster/Paula Wiseman Bks.

Clement-Moore, Rosemary. Spirit & Dust. 2014. (ENG.). 400p. (YA). (gr. 7). pap. 9.99 *(978-0-385-74081-4(6)*, Ember) Random Hse. Children's Bks.

Clugston-Flores, Chynna. Lumberjanes/Gotham Academy. 2017. lib. bdg. 33.05 ***(978-0-606-39766-7(3))*** Turtleback Bks.

Coben, Harlan. Shelter. (Mickey Bolitar Novel Ser.: 1). (ENG.). (YA). (gr. 7-18). 2011. 288p. 18.99 *(978-0-399-25650-9(4)*, G.P. Putnam's Sons Books for Young Readers)Bk. 1. 2012. 336p. pap. 9.99 *(978-0-14-242203-6(7)*, Speak) Penguin Young Readers Group.

—Shelter. l.t. ed. 2011. (Mickey Bolitar Ser.: Bk. 1). (ENG.). 354p. (J). (gr. 9-12). 23.99 *(978-1-4104-4365-6(5))* Thorndike Pr.

M
N
O

—Shelter. 2012. (Mickey Bolitar Ser.: 1). lib. bdg. 20.85 *(978-0-606-26669-7(0)*, Turtleback) Turtleback Bks.

Coburn, Ann. Glint. 2007. 423p. (J). (gr. 4-7). 17.99 *(978-0-06-084723-4(9))* HarperCollins Pubs.

Coleman, K. R. Truth or Dare. 2017. (Midnight Ser.). (ENG.). 104p. (YA). (gr. 6-12). lib. bdg. 26.65 *(978-1-5124-2768-4(3))*; 12.99 ***(978-1-5124-3495-8(7))***; 39.99 ***(978-1-5124-2788-2(8))***; 39.99 ***(978-1-5124-3494-1(9))*** Lerner Publishing Group. (Darby Creek).

Coley, Liz. Pretty Girl-13. 2013. (ENG.). 352p. (YA). (gr. 9). 17.99 *(978-0-06-212737-2(3)*, Tegen, Katherine Bks) HarperCollins Pubs.

Collins, Suzanne. Gregor, Set. Nos. 1-5. 2009. (Underland Chronicles Ser.). (ENG.). (J). (gr. 3-7). pap., pap., pap. 39.95 *(978-0-545-16681-2(0))* Scholastic, Inc.

Cook, Eileen. The Almost Truth. (ENG., (YA). (gr. 9). 2013. Illus.). 272p. pap. 9.99 *(978-1-4424-4020-3(1))* 2012. 256p. 16.99 *(978-1-4424-4019-7(8))* Simon Pulse. (Simon Pulse).

Cook, Philip. Erden: Flame of the Creator. 2014. xiii, 259p. (YA). *(978-1-4908-2033-0(7)*, WestBow Pr.) Author Solutions, Inc.

Cooney, Caroline B. Janie Face to Face. 2014. (ENG.). 352p. (YA). (gr. 7). pap. 9.99 *(978-0-385-74207-8(X)*, Ember) Random Hse. Children's Bks.

Cooper, E. E. Vanished. 2015. (Vanished Ser.: 1). (ENG.). 320p. (YA). (gr. 9). 17.99 *(978-0-06-229390-9(7)*, Tegen, Katherine Bks) HarperCollins Pubs.

Couloumbis, Audrey. Say Yes. 2003. (ENG.). 208p. (J). (gr. 3-7). pap. 7.99 *(978-0-14-250186-3(7)*, Speak) Penguin Young Readers Group.

Coyle, Katie. Vivian Apple Needs a Miracle. 2015. (ENG.). 304p. (YA). (gr. 7). 17.99 *(978-0-544-39042-3(3)*, HMH Books For Young Readers) Houghton Mifflin Harcourt Publishing Co.

Cray, Jordan. Stalker. 2009. (Danger. com Ser.: 5). (ENG.). 224p. (YA). (gr. 7). pap. 10.99 *(978-1-4169-9850-1(0)*, Simon Pulse) Simon Pulse.

Creech, Sharon. The Boy on the Porch. 2014. (ENG.). 176p. (J). (gr. 3-7). pap. 6.99 *(978-0-06-189238-7(6))* HarperCollins Pubs.

Crockett, S. D. After the Snow. 2012. (After the Snow Ser.: 1). (ENG.). 304p. (YA). (gr. 7-12). 16.99 *(978-0-312-64169-6(9))* Feiwel & Friends.

—After the Snow. 2013. (After the Snow Ser.: 1). (ENG.). 320p. (YA). (gr. 7-12). pap. 9.99 *(978-1-250-01676-8(2))* Square Fish.

Crowl, Janice. Kili & the Singing Snails. Orme, Harinani, illus. 2011. (J). 16.95 *(978-1-58178-104-5(0))* Bishop Museum Pr.

Crowley, James. Monsterland. 2017. (ENG.). 384p. (J). (gr. 5). 16.99 *(978-0-399-17589-3(X)*, G.P. Putnam's Sons Books for Young Readers) Penguin Young Readers Group.

Culwell, Lori. The Dirt. 2011. (ENG.). 208p. (YA). pap. 11.95 *(978-1-935961-36-9(5)*, Booktrope Editions) Booktrope.

Curtis, Vanessa & Quarto Generic Staff. The Taming of Lilah May. 2012. (ENG.). 192p. (J). (gr. 7-9). pap. 8.99 *(978-1-84780-149-4(8)*, Frances Lincoln) Quarto Publishing Group UK GBR. Dist: Hachette Bk. Group.

Dahl, Lisa. Gorm the Viking: The Lost Voyage. 2013. 282p. (gr. 4-6). 26.95 *(978-1-4759-5809-6(9))*; pap. 16.95 *(978-1-4759-5807-2(2))* iUniverse, Inc.

Dahl, Michael. The Wizard & the Wormhole, 1 vol. Weber, Lisa K., illus. 2014. (Hocus Pocus Hotel Ser.). (ENG.). 128p. (gr. 2-3). 25.32 *(978-1-4342-6507-4(2))* Stone Arch Bks.

Daneshvari, Gitty. Who's That Ghoulfriend? 2013. Bk. 3. (ENG., Illus.). 272p. (J). (gr. 3-7). 13.00 *(978-0-316-22254-9(2))* Little, Brown Bks. for Young Readers.

Danziger, Paula. Es Dia de Feria, Ambar Dorado. Ross, Tony, illus. 2007. (de Ámbar / a Is for Amber Easy-To-Read Ser.).Tr. of It's a Fair Day, Amber Brown. (SPA.). 48p. (gr. k-3). pap. 8.95 *(978-1-59820-596-1(X))* Santillana USA Publishing Co., Inc.

—It's a Fair Day, Amber Brown. Ross, Tony, illus. 2003. pap. 31.95 incl. audio compact disk *(978-1-59112-564-8(2))*; (J). (gr. -1-2). audio compact disk 28.95 *(978-1-59112-565-5(0))* Live Oak Media.

David, Jamie. Johann Sebastian Humpbach. David, Jamie, illus. 2009. (Illus.). 167p. pap. 14.95 *(978-0-615-31840-0(1))* Chai Yo Maui Pr.

Davis, Harold. The Starrigans of Little Brook Bottom, 1 vol. Carter, Dana, illus. 2007. (ENG.). 150p. (J). (gr. 3-7). per. 8.95 *(978-1-894294-85-0(8)*, Tuckamore Bks) Creative Bk. Publishing CAN. Dist: Orca Bk. Pubs. USA.

Dawn, Sasha. Splinter. 2017. (ENG.). 304p. (YA). (gr. 8-12). 18.99 *(978-1-5124-1151-5(5))*; 9.99 ***(978-1-5124-3434-7(5)***, Carolrhoda Lab™); 38.65 ***(978-1-5124-3435-4(3)***, Carolrhoda Lab™); 38.65 ***(978-1-5124-2695-3(4)***, Carolrhoda Lab™) Lerner Publishing Group.

de Beer, Hans, pseud. Little Polar Bear. 2016. (ENG., Illus.). 32p. (J). 16.95 *(978-0-7358-4264-9(7))* North-South Bks., Inc.

De la Cruz, Melissa. Angels on Sunset Boulevard. 2008. (Angels on Sunset Boulevard Ser.: Bk. 1). (ENG.). 240p. (YA). (gr. 9-18). pap. 8.99 *(978-1-4169-3991-7(1)*, Simon & Schuster Bks. For Young Readers) Simon & Schuster Bks. For Young Readers.

Decker, Wendy. The Bedazzling Bowl. 2006. pap. 13.99 *(978-1-60034-468-8(2))* Salem Author Services.

Defoe, Daniel. Robinson Crusoe, Level 4. 2009. (ENG.). 96p. pap. 12.75 *(978-84-8323-553-9(6))* Cambridge Univ. Pr.

Despain, Bree. The Dark Divine. 2009. (ENG.). 384p. (J). (gr. 7-18). 17.99 *(978-1-60684-057-3(6)*, Carolrhoda Lab™) Lerner Publishing Group.

di Vries, Maggie. Rabbit Ears. 2014. 288p. (YA). (gr. 8). pap. 8.99 *(978-0-06-233290-5(2))* HarperCollins Pubs.

DiCamillo, Kate. The Magician's Elephant. Tanaka, Yoko, illus. (ENG.). (J). (gr. 3-7). 2015. 224p. pap. 7.99 *(978-0-7636-8088-6(5))* 2009. 208p. 16.99 *(978-0-7636-4410-9(2))* Candlewick Pr.

—The Magician's Elephant. l.t. ed. 2010. (ENG.). 242p. 23.95 *(978-1-4104-2493-8(6))* Thorndike Pr.

—The Magician's Elephant. 2015. lib. bdg. 17.20 *(978-0-606-37891-8(X))* 2011. lib. bdg. 17.20 *(978-0-606-15375-1(6)*, Turtleback) Turtleback Bks.

Diederich, Phillippe. Playing for the Devil's Fire. 2016. (ENG.). 232p. (J). (gr. 6-10). 16.95 *(978-1-941026-29-8(X))* Cinco Puntos Pr.

Dillon, Elena. Crushing. 2013. 368p. (YA). pap. 13.99 *(978-0-9886353-4-0(8))* Dillon, Elena.

Ding, Yuhui Andrew. Warrior Soul. 2009. 28p. pap. 15.99 *(978-1-4415-6734-5(8))* Xlibris Corp.

Disney Book Group Staff. Finding Nemo. 2012. (Read-Along Storybook & CD Ser.). (ENG.). 912p. (J). (gr. -1 — 1). pap. 6.99 *(978-1-4231-6028-1(2))* Disney Pr.

Dixon, Franklin W. Double Down. 26th ed. 2008. (Hardy Boys (All New) Undercover Brothers Ser.: 26). (ENG.). 172p. (J). (gr. 3-7). pap. 5.99 *(978-1-4169-7446-8(6)*, Aladdin) Simon & Schuster Children's Publishing.

—The Madman of Black Bear Mountain. 2016. (Hardy Boys Adventures Ser.: 12). (ENG., Illus.). 144p. (J). (gr. 3-7). pap. 6.99 *(978-1-4814-3880-3(8)*, Aladdin) Simon & Schuster Children's Publishing.

—Pushed. 18th ed. 2007. (Hardy Boys (All New) Undercover Brothers Ser.: 18). (ENG., Illus.). 160p. (J). (gr. 3-7). pap. 5.99 *(978-1-4169-4802-5(3)*, Aladdin) Simon & Schuster Children's Publishing.

d'Lacey, Chris. A Crown of Dragons. 2016. (UFiles Ser.: 3). (ENG.). 320p. (J). (gr. 3-7). 16.99 *(978-0-545-60883-1(X)*, Scholastic Pr.) Scholastic, Inc.

—A Dark Inheritance. 2014. (UFiles Ser.). (ENG.). 304p. (J). (gr. 3-7). 16.99 *(978-0-545-60876-3(7)*, Scholastic Pr.) Scholastic, Inc.

—UFiles #1: a Dark Inheritance. 2014. (UFiles Ser.: 1). (ENG.). 304p. (J). (gr. 3-7). pap. 7.99 *(978-0-545-60878-7(3)*, Scholastic Paperbacks) Scholastic, Inc.

Dormer, Frank W. The Sword in the Stove. Dormer, Frank W., illus. 2016. (ENG., Illus.). 40p. (J). (gr. -1-3). 17.99 *(978-1-4814-3167-5(6))* Simon & Schuster, Inc.

Doro, Ann. The Missing Canary. l.t. ed. 2005. 93p. 12.95 *(978-0-9745052-2-0(6)*, Peeper & Friends) Tree Of Life Publishing.

Dotlich, Rebecca Kai. Peanut & Pearl's Picnic Adventure. Alley, R. W., illus. 2008. (My First I Can Read Ser.). (ENG.). 32p. (J). (gr. -1 — 1). pap. 3.99 *(978-0-06-054922-0(X))* HarperCollins Pubs.

Double Deception, Bk. 3. 2009. (Hardy Boys (All New) Undercover Brothers Ser.: 27). (ENG.). 176p. (J). (gr. 3-7). pap. 5.99 *(978-1-4169-6766-8(4)*, Aladdin) Simon & Schuster Children's Publishing.

Dowd, Siobhan. The London Eye Mystery. 2009. (ENG.). 336p. (J). (gr. 3-7). 7.99 *(978-0-385-75184-1(2)*, Yearling) Random Hse. Children's Bks.

—The London Eye Mystery. 2009. lib. bdg. 18.40 *(978-0-606-14413-1(7)*, Turtleback) Turtleback Bks.

Duey, Kathleen & Bale, Karen A. Swamp: Louisiana 1851. 2016. (Survivors Ser.). (ENG., Illus.). 160p. (J). (gr. 3-7). pap. 6.99 *(978-1-4814-2783-8(0)*, Aladdin) Simon & Schuster Children's Publishing.

Duff, Hilary. Elixir. 2011. (Playaway Young Adult Ser.). (YA). 59.99 *(978-1-4417-7416-3(5))* Findaway World, LLC.

—Elixir. 2011. (Elixir Ser.). (ENG.). 336p. (YA). (gr. 9). pap. 9.99 *(978-1-4424-0854-8(5)*, Simon & Schuster Bks. For Young Readers) Simon & Schuster Bks. For Young Readers.

Duff, Hilary & Allen, Elise. Elixir. 2010. (Elixir Ser.). (ENG.). 336p. (YA). (gr. 9-18). 17.99 *(978-1-4424-0853-1(7)*, Simon & Schuster Bks. For Young Readers) Simon & Schuster Bks. For Young Readers.

Dunham, Wendy. My Name Is River. 2015. (ENG.). 144p. (J). (gr. 2-7). pap. 7.99 *(978-0-7369-6461-6(4))* Harvest Hse. Pubs.

Dunker, Kristina. Summer Storm, 0 vols. Dembo, Margot Battauer, tr. from GER. unabr. ed. 2011. (ENG.). 146p. (YA). (gr. 7-9). pap. 9.95 *(978-1-61109-030-7(X)*, 9781611090307) Amazon Publishing.

Durant, Alan. Little Miss Muffet's Big Scare. Heming, Leah-Ellen, illus. 2012. (ENG.). 32p. (J). *(978-0-7787-8030-4(9))*; pap. *(978-0-7787-8041-0(4))* Crabtree Publishing Co.

Durrant, Geraldine. Twinbane: an Appalling True History. 2010. 142p. pap. 16.95 *(978-1-4457-7998-0(6))* Lulu Pr., Inc.

Dver, Alyssa. When Whizzly Wanders. 2005. 15p. 6.78 *(978-1-4116-4667-4(3))* Lulu Pr., Inc.

Dyer, Hadley. Johnny Kellock Died Today. 2007. (ENG.). 192p. (J). mass mkt. 6.92 ***(978-0-00-639534-8(1)***, Harper Trophy) HarperCollins Pubs.

Eastman, Brock D. & Eastman, Brock. Taken. 2011. (Illus.). 315p. (J). pap. *(978-1-59638-245-9(7))* P & R Publishing.

Eichler, Ken. Swift Eagle's Wagon Train Adventure, 1 vol. 2010. 80p. pap. 19.95 *(978-1-4489-4364-7(7))* America Star Bks.

Eldridge, Courtney. Ghost Time. (ENG.). (YA). 2016. 418p. pap. 9.99 *(978-1-4778-1697-4(6)*, 9781477816974) 2013. 416p. (gr. 9-12). 17.99 *(978-1-4778-1657-8(7)*, 9781477816578, Amazon Children's Publishing) Amazon Publishing.

Elgert, C. J. The Elder Brothers & the Padstow Crystals. 2013. 208p. *(978-1-4602-1788-7(8))*; pap. *(978-1-4602-1789-4(6))* FriesenPress.

Elish, Dan. The School for the Insanely Gifted. 2011. (ENG.). 304p. (J). (gr. 3-7). 15.99 *(978-0-06-113873-7(8))* HarperCollins Pubs.

Elizabeth's Story 1848. 2014. (Secrets of the Manor Ser.: 3). (ENG., Illus.). 160p. (J). (gr. 3-7). pap. 6.99 *(978-1-4814-1840-9(8)*, Simon Spotlight) Simon Spotlight.

Ellis, Deborah. Parvana's Journey, 1 vol. 2015. (Breadwinner Ser.). (ENG., Illus.). 200p. (J). (gr. 4-9). pap. 9.95 *(978-1-55498-770-2(9))* Groundwood Bks. CAN. Dist: Publishers Group West (PGW).

Emerson, Alice B. Ruth Fielding at Snow Camp: Or, Lost in the Backwoods. 2007. (ENG.). 134p. pap. 18.99 *(978-1-4264-5024-2(9))*; 144p. pap. 19.99 *(978-1-4264-5325-0(6))* Creative Media Partners, LLC.

Emerson, Kevin. The Fellowship for Alien Detection. 2013. (ENG.). 432p. (J). (gr. 3-7). 16.99 *(978-0-06-207185-9(8)*, Waldon Pond Pr.) HarperCollins Pubs.

Emerson, Scott. The Case of the Cat with the Missing Ear: From the Notebooks of Edward R. Smithfield, D. V. M. Mullett, Viv, illus. 2011. (Adventures of Samuel Blackthorne Ser.: 1). (ENG.). 240p. (J). (gr. 3-7). pap. 11.99 *(978-0-689-87615-8(7)*, Simon & Schuster Bks. For Young Readers) Simon & Schuster Bks. For Young Readers.

Evans, Ann. Cry Danger. 2006. 184p. per. *(978-1-904529-31-6(3)*, Back to Front) Solidus.

Evans, Richard. Michael Vey 5. 2015. (Michael Vey Ser.: 5). (ENG., Illus.). 288p. (YA). (gr. 7). 18.99 *(978-1-4814-4410-1(7)*, Simon Pulse/Mercury Ink) Simon Pulse/Mercury Ink.

Everheart, Chris. Concrete Gallery. 2014. (ENG.). 96p. (J). *(978-1-63235-053-4(X))* Pr. Room Editions LLC.

Fantich, Susanna. A Cat's Tale. 2012. 210p. 33.99 *(978-1-4582-0527-8(4))*; pap. 15.99 *(978-1-4582-0525-4(8))* Author Solutions, Inc. (Abbott Pr.).

Fearing, Mark & Rummel, Tim. Earthling! 2012. (ENG., Illus.). 248p. (J). (gr. 3-7). 22.99 *(978-0-8118-7106-8(1))* Chronicle Bks. LLC.

—Earthling. 2012. (ENG., Illus.). 248p. (J). (gr. 3-7). pap. 12.99 *(978-1-4521-0906-0(0))* Chronicle Bks. LLC.

Feehan-Vileria, Elaine. The Legend of Old Mr. Clarke. 2004. 58p. per. 17.95 *(978-1-4116-1523-6(9))* Lulu Pr., Inc.

Feiffer, Kate. Signed by Zelda. (ENG.). 240p. (J). (gr. 3-7). 2013. pap. 6.99 *(978-1-4424-3332-8(9))* 2012. (Illus.). 16.99 *(978-1-4424-3331-1(0))* Simon & Schuster/Paula Wiseman Bks. (Simon & Schuster/Paula Wiseman Bks.).

Ferguson, Alane & Skurzynski, Gloria. Running Scared. 2008. (Mysteries in Our National Park Ser.). (ENG., Illus.). 160p. (J). (gr. 3-7). mass mkt. 4.99 *(978-1-4263-0182-7(0)*, National Geographic Children's Bks.) National Geographic Society.

Fiani, M. A Cat Named Monkey. 2008. 24p. pap. 14.99 *(978-1-4389-1966-9(2))* AuthorHouse.

Fickey, Brenda. Whispering Darkness. 2007. (ENG.). 136p. per. 24.95 *(978-1-4241-6932-0(1))* America Star Bks.

Fields, Jan. Ghost Light Burning: An Up2U Mystery Adventure, 1 vol. Fabbretti, Valerio, illus. 2015. (ENG.). 80p. (J). *(978-1-62402-092-6(5))* Magic Wagon.

Fishbone, Greg. The Penguins of Doom. 2007. (From the Desk of Septina Nash Ser.). (ENG., Illus.). 182p. (J). (gr. 2-7). 13.95 *(978-1-933831-03-9(0))* Blooming Tree Pr.

Fisher, Catherine. The Slanted Worlds. 2015. (Obsidian Mirror Ser.: 2). (ENG.). 384p. (YA). (gr. 7). pap. 9.99 *(978-0-14-242678-4(4)*, Speak) Penguin Young Readers Group.

Fitzgerald, Sarah Moore. The Apple Tart of Hope. 2016. (ENG.). 208p. (J). (gr. 5). 16.95 *(978-0-8234-3561-6(X))* Holiday Hse., Inc.

Fletcher, Christopher. The Guardian Angel. 2008. 212p. pap. *(978-1-84923-031-5(5))* YouWriteOn.

Fletcher, J. S. Scarhaven Keep. 2011. (YA). *(978-1-60682-173-2(3))* BJU Pr.

Flinn, Alex. Cloaked. 2011. (YA). 341p. lib. bdg. 17.89 *(978-0-06-087423-0(6))*; (ENG.). 352p. (gr. 8-18). 16.99 *(978-0-06-087422-3(8))* HarperCollins Pubs. (HarperTeen).

—Towering. 2013. (YA). (Kendra Chronicles Ser.: 3). (ENG.). 304p. (gr. 9). 17.99 *(978-0-06-202417-6(5)*, HarperTeen); (Kendra Chronicles Ser.: 3). 304p. (gr. 9). lib. bdg. 18.89 *(978-0-06-202418-3(3)*, HarperTeen); 296p. *(978-0-06-227632-2(8))* HarperCollins Pubs.

Fogg, K. L. Diamondback Cave: A Novel. 2008. 377p. (J). *(978-1-59811-512-3(X))* Covenant Communications.

Foreman, Michael. Tufty. Foreman, Michael, illus. 2016. (ENG., Illus.). 32p. (gr. -1-3). 35.99 *(978-1-5124-0448-7(9))* Lerner Publishing Group.

Forever Lost. 2011. (Hardy Boys (All New) Undercover Brothers Ser.: 36). (ENG.). 160p. (J). (gr. 3-7). pap. 6.99 *(978-1-4424-0264-5(4)*, Aladdin) Simon & Schuster Children's Publishing.

Formento, Alison Ashley. Twigs. 2013. (ENG.). 272p. (YA). 17.99 *(978-1-4405-6565-6(1)*, Simon Pulse) Simon Pulse.

Frazier, Angie. The Midnight Tunnel: A Suzanna Snow Mystery. 2011. (ENG.). 288p. (J). (gr. 3-7). 17.99 *(978-0-545-20862-8(9)*, Scholastic Pr.) Scholastic, Inc.

Freeman, Martha. Who Stole Uncle Sam? 2008. (Chickadee Court Mystery Ser.). (ENG., Illus.). 128p. (J). (gr. 3-7). 16.95 *(978-0-8234-2091-9(4))* Holiday Hse., Inc.

Friedman, Stanley. Quantum Outlaws. 2010. 210p. pap. 11.95 *(978-1-935630-09-8(1))* Bellissima Publishing, LLC.

Friedmann, Patty. Taken Away. 2010. (ENG.). 427p. (J). (gr. 6). pap. 18.95 *(978-0-9845318-2-0(3))* Tiny Stachel Pr.

Fry, Jason. Servants of the Empire: The Secret Academy. 2015. (ENG.). 192p. (J). (gr. 3-7). pap. 6.99 *(978-1-4847-1661-8(2)*, Disney Lucasfilm Press) Disney Publishing Worldwide.

Galvin, Laura Gates. Baby Duck Gets Lost. 2007. (Baby Animals Ser.). (ENG., Illus.). 16p. (gr. -1-k). 6.95 *(978-1-59249-747-8(0))* Soundprints.

Gamble, Paul. The Ministry of S. U. I. T. S. 2016. (Ministry of SUITs Ser.: 1). (ENG.). 384p. (J). 16.99 *(978-1-250-07682-3(X)*, 9781250076823) Feiwel & Friends.

Gardner, Sally. The Vanishing of Billy Buckle. Roberts, David, illus. 2015. (Wings & Co Ser.: 3). (ENG.). 240p. (J). (gr. 2-5). 13.99 *(978-0-8050-9915-7(8)*, 9780805099157, Holt, Henry & Co. Bks. For Young Readers) Holt, Henry & Co.

Garis, Howard Roger. Larry Dexter's Great Search or, the Hunt for the Missing Millionaire. 2007. 196p. per. *(978-1-4065-2768-1(8))* Dodo Pr.

Garrick, Veda. The Place: Jello. 2012. 302p. pap. 19.99 *(978-1-4525-5081-7(6))* Balboa Pr.

Gershator, David. Where Did the Baby Go? Gershator, Phillis, illus. 2016. (J). pap. *(978-1-934370-57-5(6))* Editorial Campana.

Gibbons, Alan. The Dying Photo. 2012. (Stoke Books Titles Ser.). 64p. (J). (gr. 5-8). pap. 45.32 *(978-0-7613-9217-0(3))*; pap. 7.95 *(978-1-78112-020-0(X))*; lib. bdg. 22.60 *(978-1-78112-019-4(6))* Stoke Bks.

Giff, Patricia Reilly. Until I Find Julian. 2015. (ENG.). 160p. (J). (gr. 3-7). 16.99 *(978-0-385-74482-9(X)*, Lamb, Wendy Bks.) Random Hse. Children's Bks.

Gilbert, David D. Feodor Fitz: Journey to Harmony Ville. 2012. 40p. pap. 17.57 *(978-1-4772-1983-6(8))*; pap. 20.99 *(978-1-4685-8122-5(8))* AuthorHouse.

Godwin, Jane. Falling from Grace. 2007. (ENG.). 204p. (J). (gr. 6-12). 16.95 *(978-0-8234-2105-3(8))* Holiday Hse., Inc.

Goeglein, T. M. Cold Fury. 2013. (Cold Fury Novel Ser.: 1). (ENG.). 336p. (YA). (gr. 7). pap. 9.99 *(978-0-14-242631-9(8)*, Speak) Penguin Young Readers Group.

—Flicker & Burn. 2014. (Cold Fury Novel Ser.: 2). (ENG.). 368p. (YA). (gr. 7). pap. 9.99 *(978-0-14-751141-6(0)*, Speak) Penguin Young Readers Group.

Goodman, Nancy. The Camping Kids Adventures. 2010. 74p. pap. 10.99 *(978-1-60957-474-1(5))* Salem Author Services.

Goodrich, Carter. We Forgot Brock! Goodrich, Carter, illus. 2015. (ENG., Illus.). 48p. (J). (gr. -1-3). 17.99 *(978-1-4424-8090-2(4)*, Simon & Schuster Bks. For Young Readers) Simon & Schuster Bks. For Young Readers.

Gordon, Roderick. Deeper, 15 vols. 2009. (J). 128.75 *(978-1-4361-3717-1(9))*; 134.75 *(978-1-4361-3721-8(7))*; 126.75 *(978-1-4361-3719-5(5))*; 301.75 *(978-1-4361-3718-8(7))*; 1.25 *(978-1-4361-3714-0(4))*; 132.75 *(978-1-4361-3723-2(3))* Recorded Bks., Inc.

Graphman, Wm. Matthew. Chel & Riley Adventures: The K9 Kidnapping Adventure. 2011. 80p. (gr. 4-6). pap. 9.99 *(978-1-4567-9574-0(0))* AuthorHouse.

Gratton, Tessa. The Apple Throne. 2015. (YA). *(978-0-307-97756-4(0))* Random Hse., Inc.

Gray, Grandpa. The Land of the Three Elves Vol. 1: Beginnings. 2012. (ENG.). 317p. pap. 14.95 *(978-1-4327-9551-1(1))* Outskirts Pr., Inc.

Green, John. Paper Towns. 2011. 11.04 *(978-0-7848-3497-8(0)*, Everbind) Marco Bk. Co.

—Paper Towns. movie tie-in ed. 2015. (ENG.). 336p. (YA). (gr. 9). pap. 10.99 *(978-0-14-751765-4(6)*, Penguin Books) Penguin Publishing Group.

—Paper Towns. (ENG.). (YA). (gr. 9-18). 2009. 336p. 10.99 *(978-0-14-241493-4(X)*, Speak) 2008. 320p. 18.99 *(978-0-525-47818-8(3)*, Dutton Books for Young Readers) Penguin Young Readers Group.

—Paper Towns. 2010. (ENG., Illus.). 305p. (gr. 9-12). 20.00 *(978-1-60686-913-0(2))* Perfection Learning Corp.

—Paper Towns. 2009. lib. bdg. 20.85 *(978-0-606-10658-0(8)*, Turtleback) Turtleback Bks.

Green, John. Turtles All the Way Down. 2017. lib. bdg. 33.05 ***(978-0-606-40748-9(0))*** Turtleback Bks.

Green, Judith. A Family Secret. Hammah, Aisha, illus. 2013. 32p. pap. *(978-0-9810759-7-6(5))* WTL International.

Green, Poppy. Looking for Winston. Bell, Jennifer A., illus. 2015. (Adventures of Sophie Mouse Ser.: 4). (ENG.). 128p. (J). (gr. k-4). pap. 5.99 *(978-1-4814-3003-6(3)*, Little Simon) Little Simon.

Griffin, M. A. Lifers. 2017. (ENG.). 288p. (J). (gr. 7). 17.99 *(978-1-338-06553-4(X)*, Chicken Hse., The) Scholastic, Inc.

Griffiths, Andy. The 52-Story Treehouse. Denton, Terry, illus. 2016. (Treehouse Bks.: 4). (ENG.). 336p. (J). (gr. 2-5). 13.99 *(978-1-250-02693-4(8)*, 9781250026934) Feiwel & Friends.

—The 52-Story Treehouse. Denton, Terry, illus. 2017. (Treehouse Bks.). (ENG.). 352p. (J). pap. 6.99 *(978-1-250-10379-6(7)*, 9781250103796) Square Fish.

—The 52-Story Treehouse. 2017. (Treehouse Adventures Ser.: 4). (J). lib. bdg. 17.20 ***(978-0-606-40350-4(7))*** Turtleback Bks.

Griggs, Terry. Nieve. L'Hirondelle, Cheryl, illus. 2010. (ENG.). 264p. (J). (gr. 4-10). pap. 14.95 *(978-1-897231-87-6(3))* Biblioasis CAN. Dist: Consortium Bk. Sales & Distribution.

Grinti, Mike & Grinti, Rachel. Claws. 2012. (J). *(978-0-545-43314-3(2))*; (ENG.). 256p. (gr. 5-9). 16.99 *(978-0-545-43313-6(4))* Scholastic, Inc. (Chicken Hse., The).

Grove, S. E. The Golden Specific. 2015. (Mapmakers Trilogy Ser.: 2). (ENG., Illus.). 528p. (J). (gr. 5). 17.99 *(978-0-670-78503-2(2)*, Viking Books for Young Readers) Penguin Young Readers Group.

—The Golden Specific. 2016. (Mapmakers Ser.: 2). lib. bdg. 19.65 *(978-0-606-38836-8(2))* Turtleback Bks.

Guest, Elissa Haden. Iris & Walter & the Field Trip. Davenier, Christine, illus. 2013. (Green Light Readers Level 3 Ser.). (ENG.). 44p. (J). (gr. 1-4). pap. 3.99 *(978-0-544-10665-9(2))* Houghton Mifflin Harcourt Publishing Co.

—Iris & Walter & the Field Trip. Davenier, Christine, illus. 2007. (Iris & Walter Ser.). 44p. (J). (gr. 1-4). 13.60 *(978-0-7569-8041-2(0))* Perfection Learning Corp.

—Iris & Walter & the Field Trip. 2013. (Iris & Walter — Green Light Reader Ser.). lib. bdg. 13.55 *(978-0-606-33987-2(6)*, Turtleback) Turtleback Bks.

Hagen, George. Gabriel Finley & the Raven's Riddle. Bakal, Scott, illus. 2014. (ENG.). 384p. (J). (gr. 4-7). 16.99 *(978-0-385-37103-2(9)*, Schwartz & Wade Bks.) Random Hse. Children's Bks.

Haig, Matt. To Be a Cat. Curtis, Stacy, illus. (ENG.). 304p. (J). (gr. 3-7). 2014. pap. 8.99 *(978-1-4424-5406-4(7))* 2013. 16.99 *(978-1-4424-5405-7(9))* Simon & Schuster Children's Publishing.

Hannibal, James R. The Lost Property Office. 2016. (Section 13 Ser.: 1). (ENG., Illus.). 400p. (J). (gr. 3-7). 16.99 *(978-1-4814-6709-4(3)*, Simon & Schuster Bks. For Young Readers) Simon & Schuster Bks. For Young Readers.

Harper, Ken. Mystery in Mansfield. 2008. 60p. pap. 19.95 *(978-1-60441-055-6(8))* America Star Bks.

Harris, Lewis. A Taste for Red. 2010. (ENG.). 180p. (J). (gr. 5-7). pap. 12.95 *(978-0-547-39851-8(4))* Houghton Mifflin Harcourt Publishing Co.

Harrison, Michelle. The Thirteen Treasures. 2014. (ENG., Illus.). 352p. pap. 8.99 *(978-1-4711-2167-8(4)*, Simon & Schuster Children's) Simon & Schuster, Ltd. GBR. Dist: Simon & Schuster, Inc.

Hartnett, Sonya. What the Birds See. 2007. (ENG., Illus.). 208p. (YA). (gr. 9). pap. 7.99 *(978-0-7636-3680-7(0))* Candlewick Pr.

Harvey, Pam & Panckridge, Michael. Into the Fire. 2008. 192p. (J). *(978-0-207-20061-8(0))* HarperCollins Pubs. Australia.

Hatfield, Ruth. The Book of Storms. Call, Greg, illus. 2015. (Book of Storms Trilogy Ser.: 1). (ENG.). 368p. (J). (gr. 5-9). 16.99 *(978-0-8050-9998-0(0)*, 9780805099980, Holt, Henry & Co. Bks. For Young Readers) Holt, Henry & Co.

Hathorn, Sarah Alexandra. Teenagents: World Challenge. 2012. 240p. pap. 12.99 *(978-2-9700738-2-6(X))* Simon & Schuster, Inc.

Hautman, Pete. The Cydonian Pyramid. (Klaatu Diskos Ser.). (ENG.). 368p. (YA). (gr. 7). 2014. pap. 8.99 *(978-0-7636-6933-1(4))* 2013. 16.99 *(978-0-7636-5404-7(3))* Candlewick Pr.

—The Obsidian Blade. 2012. (Klaatu Diskos Ser.). (ENG., Illus.). 320p. (YA). (gr. 7). 16.99 *(978-0-7636-5403-0(5))* Candlewick Pr.

Hawkes, Kevin. The Wicked Big Toddlah Goes to New York. 2011. (ENG., Illus.). 40p. (J). (gr. -1-2). 16.99 *(978-0-375-86188-8(2)*, Knopf Bks. for Young Readers) Random Hse. Children's Bks.

Hayes, Juliana. Ari Sylph Valley. 2012. 84p. 19.95 (978-1-4626-6912-7(3)) America Star Bks.
Heimbuch, Carol. Shadow Stallion. 2011. 170p. pap. 11.50 (978-1-59330-693-9(8)) Aventine Pr.
Heltzel, Anne. Charlie, Presumed Dead. (ENG.). 272p. (YA). (gr. 9). 2016. pap. 8.99 (978-0-544-66869-0(3)) 2015. 17.99 (978-0-544-38849-9(6)) Houghton Mifflin Harcourt Publishing Co. (HMH Books For Young Readers).
Henry, April. The Night She Disappeared. 2013. (ENG.). 256p. (YA). (gr. 7-12). pap. 10.99 (978-1-250-01674-4(6), 9781250016744) Square Fish.
Hergé. Prisoners of the Sun. 2014. (Adventures of Tintin: Young Readers Edition Ser.). (ENG., Illus.). 96p. (J). (gr. 3-17). pap. 9.00 (978-0-316-40917-9(0)) Little, Brown Bks. for Young Readers.
Hesse, Monica. Girl in the Blue Coat. (ENG.). 320p. (gr. 7-17). 2017. (YA). pap. 9.99 (978-0-316-26063-3(0)) 2016. 17.99 (978-0-316-26060-2(6)) 2016. (YA). E-Book (978-0-316-26064-0(9)) Little, Brown Bks. for Young Readers.
—Girl in the Blue Coat. 2017. (YA). lib. bdg. 20.85 **(978-0-606-39918-0(6))** Turtleback Bks.
Hiaasen, Carl. Chomp. (ENG.). 304p. (J). (gr. 5). 2013. pap. 8.99 (978-0-375-86827-6(5), Ember) 2012. 16.99 (978-0-375-86842-9(9), Knopf Bks. for Young Readers) Random Hse. Children's Bks.
—Chomp. l.t. ed. 2012. (ENG.). 364p. 23.99 (978-1-4104-5101-9(1)) Thorndike Pr.
—Chomp. 2013. lib. bdg. 19.65 (978-0-606-27006-9(X), Turtleback) Turtleback Bks.
—Scat. 2011. 10.54 (978-0-7848-3574-6(8), Everbind) Marco Bk. Co.
—Scat. (ENG.). (J). (gr. 5). 2012. 400p. 7.99 (978-0-440-42104-7(7), Yearling) 2010. 384p. pap. 8.99 (978-0-375-83487-5(7), Ember) 2009. 384p. 16.99 (978-0-375-83486-8(9), Knopf Bks. for Young Readers) Random Hse. Children's Bks.
—Scat. 2012. lib. bdg. 18.40 (978-0-606-26532-4(5), Turtleback) Turtleback Bks.
—Skink - No Surrender. (ENG.). 288p. (gr. 7). 2015. (YA). pap. 9.99 (978-0-307-93059-0(9), Ember) 2014. (J). 18.99 (978-0-375-87051-4(2), Knopf Bks. for Young Readers) Random Hse. Children's Bks.
Hill, Michelle M. Stanley. 2012. 12p. pap. 15.99 (978-1-4772-2923-1(X)) AuthorHouse.
Hobbs, Leigh. Mr Badger & the Missing Ape. l.t. ed. 2012. 120p. (J). pap. (978-1-4596-3344-5(X)) ReadHowYouWant.com, Ltd.
Hof, Marjolijn. Against the Odds. 1 vol. Prins, Johanna, tr. 2011.Tr. of Een Kleine Kans. (ENG.). 128p. (J). (gr. 3-7). pap. 8.95 (978-0-88899-950-4(X)) Groundwood Bks. CAN. Dist: Publishers Group West (PGW).
Hollyer, Belinda. Secrets, Lies & My Sister Kate. 2009. (ENG.). 144p. (J). (gr. 3-7). 16.95 (978-0-8234-2179-4(1)) Holiday Hse., Inc.
Holt, K. A. Gnome-A-geddon. Jack, Colin, illus. 2017. (ENG.). 304p. (J). (gr. 3-7). 16.99 **(978-1-4814-7845-8(1)**, McElderry, Margaret K. Bks.) McElderry, Margaret K. Bks.
—Gnomeageddon. 2017. (Illus.). 285p. (J). pap. **(978-1-4814-7846-5(X)**, McElderry, Margaret K. Bks.) McElderry, Margaret K. Bks.
Horowitz, Nancy Ellis. Nicely Dunn & the Lost Little Sister. 2009. 88p. pap. 30.49 (978-1-4389-3011-4(9)) AuthorHouse.
Howard, Martin. Shaun the Sheep Movie - the Junior Novel. 2015. (Tales from Mossy Bottom Farm Ser.). (ENG.). 152p. (J). (gr. 2-4). pap. 5.99 (978-0-7636-7736-7(1), Candlewick Entertainment) Candlewick Pr.
Hughes, Alison. Lost in the Backyard, 1 vol. 2015. (ENG.). 144p. (J). (gr. 4-7). pap. 9.95 (978-1-4598-0794-5(4)) Orca Bk. Pubs. USA.
Hulst, W. G. van de & Hulst, Willem G. van de, illus. The Rockity Rowboat. 2014. (J). (978-1-928136-18-7(4)) Inheritance Pubns.
Hunt, Elizabeth Singer. The Mystery of the Mona Lisa, Bk. 3. Williamson, Brian, illus. 2007. (Secret Agent Jack Stalwart Ser.: 3). (ENG.). 128p. (J). (gr. 1-4). per. 5.99 (978-1-60286-001-8(7), Weinstein Bks.) Perseus Bks. Group.
—The Search for the Sunken Treasure. Williamson, Brian, illus. 2007. (Secret Agent Jack Stalwart Ser.: 2). (ENG.). 128p. (J). (gr. 1-4). per. 5.99 (978-1-60286-002-5(5), Weinstein Bks.) Perseus Bks. Group.
Impey, Rose. Introducing Scarlett Lee. 2008. (ENG.). 240p. (J). (gr. 4-6). pap. 8.99 (978-1-84616-706-5(X)) Hodder & Stoughton GBR. Dist: Hachette Bk. Group.
Into Thin Air. 2013. (Hardy Boys Adventures Ser.: 4). (ENG., Illus.). 128p. (J). (gr. 3-7). 15.99 (978-1-4424-7345-4(2)); pap. 6.99 (978-1-4424-5983-0(2)) Simon & Schuster Children's Publishing. (Aladdin).
Irwin, Chris. Nightmare of Shadows. 2007. 140p. pap. 18.95 (978-0-615-15008-6(X)) Irwin, Christine.
Jacobson, Jennifer Richard. Andy Shane & the Barn Sale Mystery. Carter, Abby, illus. 2010. (Andy Shane Ser.: 5). (ENG.). 64p. (J). (gr. k-3). 4.99 (978-0-7636-4827-5(2)) Candlewick Pr.
Jacques, Karen. Monsters Have My Brother. Cahanes, Erin, illus. 2015. (ENG.). 16.95 (978-1-59298-863-1(6)) Beaver's Pond Pr., Inc.
Jaimet, Kate. Slam Dunk, 1 vol. 2009. (Orca Sports Ser.). (ENG.). 176p. (YA). (gr. 6-10). pap. 9.95 (978-1-55469-132-6(X)) Orca Bk. Pubs. USA.
James, Caleb. Haffling. 2nd ed. 2016. (ENG., Illus.). 250p. pap. 14.99 (978-1-63476-795-8(0), DSP Pubns.) Dreamspinner Pr.
James, Ellie. Shattered Dreams: A Midnight Dragonfly Novel. 2011. (Midnight Dragonfly Novel Ser.: 1). (ENG.). 352p. (YA). (gr. 7). pap. 22.99 (978-0-312-64702-5(6), 9780312647025, St. Martin's Griffin) St. Martin's Pr.
Jasper, Rick & Reece, Richard. Thaw. 2010. (Night Fall Ser.). (ENG.). 112p. (YA). (gr. 6-12). pap. 7.95 (978-0-7613-6161-9(8)) Lerner Publishing Group.
Jenisch, Betty. Rennie. 2007. 9.00 (978-0-8059-8947-2(1)) Dorrance Publishing Co., Inc.
Jenkins, Carla LaVern. The Disappearance of Mrs. Brown: A Jenkins Girl Mystery. 2010. 72p. 23.55 (978-1-4269-4537-3(X)); pap. 13.55 (978-1-4251-6659-5(8)) Trafford Publishing.
Jenkins, Jerry B. & Fabry, Chris. Phantom Writer. 2005. (Red Rock Mysteries Ser.: 6). (ENG.). 256p. (YA). pap. 5.99 (978-1-4143-0145-7(6), Tyndale Kids) Tyndale Hse. Pubs.
—Windy City Danger. 2006. (Red Rock Mysteries Ser.: 11). (ENG.). 246p. (YA). (gr. 8-12). per. 6.99 (978-1-4143-0150-1(2), Tyndale Kids) Tyndale Hse. Pubs.
Johnson, Elana. Possession. 2012. (ENG.). 432p. (YA). (gr. 9). pap. 9.99 (978-1-4424-2126-4(6), Simon Pulse) Simon Pulse.
Johnson, Terry Lynn. Falcon Wild. 2017. (ENG.). 176p. (J). (gr. 5). lib. bdg. 16.99 **(978-1-58089-788-4(6))** Charlesbridge Publishing, Inc.
Jones, Carrie. Entice. (Need Ser.). (ENG.). (YA). 2011. 288p. pap. 9.99 (978-1-59990-693-5(7), 9781599906935) 2010. 272p. (gr. 7-12). 17.99 (978-1-59990-553-2(1), 9781599905532) Bloomsbury Publishing USA. (Bloomsbury USA Childrens).
Jordan, Cat. The Leaving Season. 2016. 352p. (J). (gr. 8). 17.99 (978-0-06-235137-1(0), HarperTeen) HarperCollins Pubs.
Joyce, William. The Sandman & the War of Dreams. Joyce, William, illus. 2013. (Guardians Ser.: 4). (ENG., Illus.). 240p. (J). (gr. 2-6). 15.99 (978-1-4424-3054-9(0), Atheneum Bks. for Young Readers) Simon & Schuster Children's Publishing.
Jules, Jacqueline. Shopping Trip Trouble Smith, Kim, illus. 2017. (Sofia Martinez Ser.). (ENG.). 32p. (gr. k-2). lib. bdg. 21.32 (978-1-5158-0729-2(0), Sofia Martinez) Picture Window Bks.
Justis, Jon. Pumpkin & the Great Dragon Caper. 2012. 32p. pap. 24.95 (978-1-4626-9733-5(X)) America Star Bks.
Kaaberbøl, Lene. Heartbreak Island. 2005. (W. I. T. C. H. Adventures Ser.: Bk. 3). (Illus.). 105p. (J). lib. bdg. 11.00 (978-1-4242-0786-2(X)) Fitzgerald Bks.
Kantor, Melissa. The Amanda Project. 2011. 287p. (J). 8.99 (978-0-06-202706-1(9), HarperTeen) HarperCollins Pubs.
Kanu, Rosslyn. The Little Girl Called Princess: Princess Where Are You? 2012. 32p. pap. 19.99 (978-1-4685-2375-1(9)) AuthorHouse.
Kasischke, Laura. Feathered. 2008. (ENG.). 272p. (YA). (gr. 9-18). 16.99 (978-0-06-081317-8(2), HarperTeen) HarperCollins Pubs.
Kelly, Erin Entrada. Hello, Universe. Roxas, Isabel, illus. 2017. 320p. (J). (gr. 3-7). 16.99 (978-0-06-241415-1(1), Greenwillow Bks.) HarperCollins Pubs.
Kenah, Katharine. The Best Seat in Second Grade. Carter, Abby, illus. 2006. (I Can Read Bks.). 48p. (J). (gr. -1-3). 11.65 (978-0-7569-6979-0(4)) Perfection Learning Corp.
Kennedy, Emma. The Case of the Putrid Poison, 2 vols. Marc, Sylvain & Dorman, Brandon, illus. 2011. (Wilma Tenderfoot Ser.: 2). (ENG.). 336p. (J). (gr. 3-7). 16.99 (978-0-8037-3541-5(3), Dial Bks) Penguin Young Readers Group.
Kessler, Liz. North of Nowhere. (ENG.). 272p. (J). (gr. 4-7). 2015. pap. 7.99 (978-0-7636-7672-8(1)) 2013. (Illus.). 15.99 (978-0-7636-6727-6(7)) Candlewick Pr.
Kilgras, Heidi. Peanut. Reed, Mike, illus. 2003. (Step into Reading Ser.). (ENG.). 32p. (J). (gr. -1-1). pap. 3.99 (978-0-375-80618-6(0), Random Hse. Bks. for Young Readers) Random Hse. Children's Bks.
King, A. S. Everybody Sees the Ants. 2011. (ENG.). 288p. (YA). (gr. 10-17). 18.00 (978-0-316-12928-2(3)) Little Brown & Co.
—Everybody Sees the Ants. 2012. (ENG.). 320p. (YA). (gr. 10-17). pap. 10.00 (978-0-316-12927-5(5)) Little, Brown Bks. for Young Readers.
King, Caro. Shadow Spell. 2012. (ENG.). 320p. (J). (gr. 3-7). pap. 6.99 (978-1-4423-3908-8(X), Aladdin) Simon & Schuster Children's Publishing.
—Shadow Spell. 2012. (ENG.). 320p. (J). (gr. 3-7). 15.99 (978-1-4424-2045-8(6), Simon & Schuster/Paula Wiseman Bks.) Simon & Schuster/Paula Wiseman Bks.
King, Caro & Bowater, Charlie. Seven Sorcerers. 2012. (ENG.). 352p. (J). (gr. 3-7). pap. 6.99 (978-1-4424-2043-4(X), Aladdin) Simon & Schuster Children's Publishing.
Klim, Christopher. Firecracker Jones Is on the Case. 2006. (Illus.). 116p. (J). lib. bdg. 19.95 (978-1-933435-11-4(9)) Hopewell Pubns., LLC.
Kline, Suzy. Horrible Harry & the Missing Diamond. Wummer, Amy, illus. 2013. (Horrible Harry Ser.: 30). (ENG.). 80p. (J). (gr. 2-4). 14.99 (978-0-670-01426-2(5), Viking Books for Young Readers) Penguin Young Readers Group.
Klise, Kate. Regarding the Sink: Where, Oh Where, Did Waters Go? Klise, M. Sarah, illus. 2006. (Regarding The ... Ser.: Bk. 2). (ENG.). 144p. (J). (gr. 2-5). pap. 6.99 (978-0-15-205544-8(4)) Houghton Mifflin Harcourt Publishing Co.
Knight, Barbara. The Lost Boy. 2008. (Illus.). 32p. (J). 14.95 (978-0-9766270-3-6(5)) Mustang BKS.
Knight, Christopher. World Is Black & White. 2008. 459p. (YA). pap. 14.95 (978-1-893699-97-7(8)) AudioCraft Publishing, Inc.
Krokos, Dan. The Black Stars. 2015. (ENG., Illus.). 304p. (J). (gr. 3-8). pap. 21.99 (978-0-7653-7668-8(7), 9780765376688, Starscape) Doherty, Tom Assocs., LLC.
Kropp, Paul. The Kid Is Lost. Melanson, Matt, illus. 2004. (New Series Canada). 88p. (J). pap. (978-1-897039-04-5(2)) High Interest Publishing (HIP).
Krosoczka, Jarrett J. Lunch Lady & the Author Visit Vendetta. 2009. (Lunch Lady Ser.). (ENG.). 96p. (J). (gr. 3-7). pap. 6.99 (978-0-375-86094-2(0), Knopf Bks. for Young Readers) Random Hse. Children's Bks.
Krulik, Nancy. Get Lost!, 6 vols. John and Wendy Staff, illus. 2006. (Katie Kazoo, Switcheroo Ser.: 6). (ENG.). 80p. (J). (gr. 2-4). pap. 4.99 (978-0-448-43101-7(7), Grosset & Dunlap) Penguin Young Readers Group.
Lackey, Mercedes & Edghill, Rosemary. Dead Reckoning. 2012. (ENG.). 336p. (YA). (gr. 7-12). 16.99 (978-1-59990-684-3(8), 9781599906843, Bloomsbury USA Childrens) Bloomsbury Publishing USA.
LaFevers, R. L. The Basilisk's Lair. Murphy, Kelly, illus. 2nd ed. 2010. (Nathaniel Fludd, Beastologist Ser.: 2). (ENG.). 160p. (J). (gr. 1-4). 15.00 (978-0-547-23867-8(3)) Houghton Mifflin Harcourt Publishing Co.
Laird, Chynna. Dark Water. 2012. 166p. pap. (978-1-926997-76-6(X)) Imajin Bks.
Lane, Andrew. Fire Storm. 2013. (Sherlock Holmes: the Legend Begins Ser.: 4). (ENG.). 352p. (YA). (gr. 7-12). 17.99 (978-0-374-32311-0(9), 9780374323110, Farrar, Straus & Giroux (BYR)) Farrar, Straus & Giroux.
—Fire Storm. 2014. (Sherlock Holmes: the Legend Begins Ser.: 4). (ENG.). 368p. (YA). (gr. 7-12). pap. 12.99 (978-1-250-05072-4(3), 9781250050724) Square Fish.
—Snake Bite. 2014. (Sherlock Holmes: the Legend Begins Ser.: 5). (ENG.). 304p. (YA). (gr. 7-12). 17.99 (978-0-374-37090-9(7), 9780374370909, Farrar, Straus & Giroux (BYR)) Farrar, Straus & Giroux.
LaReau, Kara. Unintentional Adventures of the Bland Sisters. Hill, Jen, illus. 2017. (ENG.). 176p. (J). (gr. 3-7). 14.95 (978-1-4197-2136-6(4), Amulet Bks.) Abrams, Inc.
Larson, Hope. Compass South. 2017. (Four Points Ser.: 1). (J). lib. bdg. 24.50 **(978-0-606-39953-1(4))** Turtleback Bks.
Lawrence, Caroline. The Secrets of Vesuvius. 2004. (Roman Mysteries Ser.). (Illus.). 173p. (J). (gr. 3-7). 13.65 (978-0-7569-5947-0(0)) Perfection Learning Corp.
Legrand, Claire. The Cavendish Home for Boys & Girls. Watts, Sarah, illus. (ENG.). (J). (gr. 5). 2013. 368p. pap. 7.99 (978-1-4424-4292-4(1)) 2012. 352p. 16.99 (978-1-4424-4291-7(3)) Simon & Schuster Bks. For Young Readers. (Simon & Schuster Bks. For Young Readers).
Leighton-Porter, Wendy. The Shadow of Camelot. 2013. 262p. pap. (978-1-909411-06-7(X)) Mauve Square Publishing.
Les Becquets, Diane. Season of Ice. 2008. (ENG.). 288p. (YA). (gr. 9-13). 16.95 (978-1-59990-063-6(7), 9781599900636, Bloomsbury USA Childrens) Bloomsbury Publishing USA.
Leveen, Tom. Hellworld. 2017. (ENG., Illus.). 304p. (YA). (gr. 9). 17.99 (978-1-4814-6633-2(X), Simon Pulse) Simon Pulse.
Littman, Sarah Darer. Want to Go Private? (ENG.). 336p. (J). 2013. (gr. 7). pap. 10.99 (978-0-545-15147-4(3)) 2011. (gr. 9-9). 17.99 (978-0-545-15146-7(5), Scholastic Pr.) Scholastic, Inc.
Lobdell, Scott. Haley Danelle's Top Eight! 2008. (Hardy Boys Graphic Novels Ser.: 14). (ENG., Illus.). 96p. (J). (gr. 3-7). pap. 7.95 (978-1-59707-113-0(7), 9781597071130) Papercutz.
Lord, Gabrielle. Black Ops Missing: Conspiracy 365. 2014. 192p. (J). 10.99 (978-1-61067-168-2(6)) Kane Miller.
The Lost Boy. 2008. (Illus.). 32p. (Orig.). (J). per. 14.95 (978-0-9766720-3-6(0)) Mustang BKS.
Lück, Stefanie. Carla's Worlds. 2010. 222p. pap. 20.90 (978-3-8391-4857-0(X)) Bks. on Demand.
Ludwig, Elisa. Pretty Sly. 2014. (Pretty Crooked Trilogy Ser.: 2). (ENG.). 336p. (YA). (gr. 8). 17.99 (978-0-06-206609-1(9), Tegen, Katherine Bks) HarperCollins Pubs.
MacGregor, Roy. The Secret of the Deep Woods, No. 17. 2003. (ENG.). 128p. (J). (gr. 4-18). mass mkt. 4.95 (978-0-7710-5646-8(X), Screech Owls) McClelland & Stewart CAN. Dist: Penguin Random Hse. LLC.
MacIntyre, R. P. Revved. 2006. (ENG.). 220p. pap. 12.95 (978-1-894345-46-0(0)) Thistledown Pr., Ltd. CAN. Dist: Univ. of Toronto Pr.
Mackey, Heather. Dreamwood. 2014. (ENG.). 352p. (J). (gr. 5). 16.99 (978-0-399-25067-5(0), G.P. Putnam's Sons Books for Young Readers) Penguin Young Readers Group.
MacPhail, Catherine. Hide & Seek. 2012. (Stoke Books Titles Ser.). 72p. (J). (gr. 5-8). pap. 7.95 (978-1-78112-024-8(2)); lib. bdg. 22.60 (978-1-78112-023-1(4)) Stoke Bks.
Madonia, Kristen-Paige. Invisible Fault Lines. 2016. (ENG.). 320p. (YA). (gr. 7). 17.99 (978-1-4814-3071-5(8), Simon & Schuster Bks. For Young Readers) Simon & Schuster Bks. For Young Readers.
Mafi, Tahereh. Furthermore. 2016. (ENG.). 416p. (J). (gr. 4-7). 17.99 (978-1-101-99476-4(2), Dutton Books for Young Readers) Penguin Young Readers Group.
—Furthermore. 2017. lib. bdg. 19.65 **(978-0-606-40493-8(7))** Turtleback Bks.
Magoon, Kekla. Shadows of Sherwood. (Robyn Hoodlum Adventure Ser.). (ENG.). 368p. 2016. (J). pap. 7.99 (978-1-68119-023-5(0), 9781681190235) 2015. (YA). (gr. 3-6). 16.99 (978-1-61963-634-7(4), 9781619636347) Bloomsbury Publishing USA. (Bloomsbury USA Childrens).
—Shadows of Sherwood. 2016. (Robyn Hoodlum Ser.: 1). (ENG.). 355p. (J). (gr. 3-6). 18.40 (978-0-606-39281-5(5)) Turtleback Bks.
Malkin, Nina. Swear. (ENG.). 480p. (YA). (gr. 11). 2012. pap. 9.99 (978-1-4424-2111-0(8)) 2011. 17.99 (978-1-4424-2110-3(X)) Simon Pulse. (Simon Pulse).
Mammina, David. The Circle Stone Group: Book 1: the Beginning. 2009. 112p. pap. 13.35 (978-1-4269-1478-2(4)) Trafford Publishing.
Manushkin, Fran. Katie Woo, Where Are You?, 1 vol. Lyon, Tammie, illus. 2011. (Katie Woo Ser.). (ENG.). 32p. (gr. k-2). pap. 5.95 (978-1-4048-6853-3(4)); lib. bdg. 21.32 (978-1-4048-6517-4(9)) Picture Window Bks.
Margaret I. Pascuzzo. Anton Finds a Treasure. Bicking, Judith, illus. 2008. 16p. pap. 12.00 (978-1-4251-8683-8(1)) Trafford Publishing.
Margolin, Phillip & Rome, Ami Margolin. Vanishing Acts. 2012. (ENG.). 176p. (J). (gr. 3-7). pap. 8.99 (978-0-06-188558-7(4)) HarperCollins Pubs.
Margolis, Leslie. Vanishing Acts. (Maggie Brooklyn Mystery Ser.). (ENG.). (YA). (gr. 3-6). 2013. 256p. pap. 6.99 (978-1-59990-981-3(2), 9781599909813) 2012. 240p. 15.99 (978-1-59990-536-5(1), 9781599905365) Bloomsbury Publishing USA. (Bloomsbury USA Childrens).
Marsh, Carole. The Mystery at Fort Sumter. Friedlander, Randolyn, illus. 2010. (Real Kids, Real Places Ser.). 32p. (J). pap. 7.99 (978-0-635-07432-4(X), Marsh, Carole Mysteries) Gallopade International.
—The Mystery at Fort Sumter: First Shot Fired in the Civil War! 2010. (Real Kids, Real Places Ser.). (Illus.). 158p. (J). 18.99 (978-0-635-07430-0(3), Marsh, Carole Mysteries) Gallopade International.
Marsh, Sarah Glenn. Fear the Drowning Deep. 2016. (ENG.). 312p. (YA). (gr. 6). 16.99 (978-1-5107-0348-3(9), Sky Pony Pr.) Skyhorse Publishing Co., Inc.
Marsham, Liz. Wonder Woman: Maze of Magic. 2017. (I Can Read! Level 2 Ser.). lib. bdg. 13.55 **(978-0-606-40057-2(5))** Turtleback Bks.
Martin, Amy. Symphony City. 2011. (ENG., Illus.). 48p. (J). (gr. -1-4). 17.95 (978-1-936365-39-5(1)) McSweeney's Publishing.
Martin, Laura. The Ark Plan. DesChamps, Eric, illus. 2017. (Edge of Extinction Ser.: 1). (ENG.). (J). (gr. 3-7). lib. bdg. 17.20 **(978-0-606-40046-6(X))** Turtleback Bks.
Martin, R. T. Dark Star. 2017. (Midnight Ser.). (ENG.). 96p. (YA). (gr. 6-12). 26.65 (978-1-5124-2769-1(1)); 12.99 **(978-1-5124-3486-6(8)**, Darby Creek); 39.99 **(978-1-5124-3485-9(X)**, Darby Creek); 39.99 **(978-1-5124-2789-9(6)**, Darby Creek) Lerner Publishing Group.
Maselli, Christopher P. N. The Runaway Mission. 2004. 104p. 5.99 (978-1-57562-805-9(8)) Copeland, Kenneth Pubns.
Mathieu, Jennifer. Afterward. 2016. (ENG.). 320p. (YA). 17.99 (978-1-62672-238-5(2), 9781626722385) Roaring Brook Pr.
—Afterward. 2017. (ENG.). 336p. (YA). pap. 9.99 **(978-1-250-12962-8(1)**, 9781250129628) Square Fish.
—Afterward. 2017. (YA). lib. bdg. 20.85 **(978-0-606-40590-4(9))** Turtleback Bks.
Matuszak, Pat. Simone's Secret, 2, Bk 2. 2009. (Angel Light Ser.: 2). (ENG.). 192p. (gr. 11). pap. 12.99 (978-0-89957-876-7(4)) AMG Pubs.
May, Eleanor. Lost in the Mouseum. Melmon, Deborah, illus. 2015. (Mouse Math (r) Ser.). (ENG.). 32p. (J). (gr. -1-1). 22.60 (978-1-57565-643-4(4)) Kane Press, Inc.
McBride, Anthony & McBride, Autumn. The Lost Cat. 2007. (Illus.). pap. 11.00 (978-1-56411-540-9(2), CB Publishing & Design) UBUS Communications Systems.
McClintock, Norah. About That Night, 1 vol. 2014. (ENG.). 248p. (YA). (gr. 8-12). pap. 12.95 (978-1-4598-0594-1(1)) Orca Bk. Pubs. USA.
McCracken, Connie. Indigo Boy & Crystalline Girl. Craig, Chris, illus. 2009. 24p. pap. 10.95 (978-1-4269-0423-3(1)) Trafford Publishing.
McCreight, Kimberly. The Outliers. (Outliers Ser.: 1). (YA). (gr. 9). 2017. 368p. pap. 9.99 (978-0-06-235910-0(X)) 2016. (ENG.). 352p. 18.99 (978-0-06-235909-4(6)) HarperCollins Pubs.
McCullough, Victoria. Charlotte's Hummock: a Young Adult Woman's Mystery Detective Novel. 2007. 124p. per. 19.95 (978-1-4241-6703-6(5)) America Star Bks.
McDonald, Megan. Girl Detective. Reynolds, Peter H., illus. (Judy Moody Ser.: 9). (ENG.). 192p. (J). (gr. 1-4). 2011. pap. 5.99 (978-0-7636-4349-2(1))Bk. 9. 2010. 15.99 (978-0-7636-3450-6(6)) Candlewick Pr.
—When the Library Lights Go Out. Tillotson, Katherine, illus. 2009. (ENG.). 40p. (J). (gr. -1-1). 8.99 (978-1-4169-8028-5(8), Atheneum Bks. for Young Readers) Simon & Schuster Children's Publishing.
—When the Library Lights Go Out. Tillotson, Katherine, tr. Tillotson, Katherine, illus. 2005. (ENG.). 40p. (J). (gr. -1-3). 19.99 (978-0-689-86170-3(2), Atheneum/Richard Jackson Bks.) Simon & Schuster Children's Publishing.
McDonnell, Margot. Torn to Pieces. 2010. (ENG.). 272p. (YA). (gr. 7). pap. 8.99 (978-0-385-73557-5(X), Delacorte Bks. for Young Readers) Random Hse. Children's Bks.
McDougall, Sophia. Mars Evacuees. (J). (gr. 3-7). 2016. 432p. pap. 7.99 (978-0-06-229400-5(8)) 2015. 416p. 16.99 (978-0-06-229399-2(0)) HarperCollins Pubs.
McMann, Lisa. Cryer's Cross. 2011. (ENG.). (YA). (gr. 9). 256p. pap. 9.99 (978-1-4169-9482-4(3)); (Illus.). 240p. 16.99 (978-1-4169-9481-7(5)) Simon Pulse. (Simon Pulse).
McMillan, Frank. Cezanne Is Missing. 2006. (ENG.). 323p. (YA). (gr. 7). per. 14.95 (978-0-9711359-4-9(0)) Cambridge Hse. Publishing Co., LLC.
McMullan, Kate. I'm Big! McMullan, Jim, illus. 2010. (ENG.). 40p. (J). (gr. -1-3). 16.99 (978-0-06-122974-9(1)) HarperCollins Pubs.
McNeal, Tom. Far Far Away. (ENG.). (YA). (gr. 7). 2014. 400p. pap. 9.99 (978-0-375-84329-7(9), Ember) 2013. 384p. 17.99 (978-0-375-84972-5(6), Knopf Bks. for Young Readers) Random Hse. Children's Bks.
McNeece, Alexander. Sam Iver: Imminent Threat. 2009. 138p. pap. 10.95 (978-1-935278-02-3(9), iUniverse Star) iUniverse, Inc.
McSorley, Paul J. & Bearss, Patricia. The Adventures of Forealdo: Finding Millie. 2012. 34p. 24.95 (978-1-4626-6721-5(X)) America Star Bks.
Meadows, Michelle. Itsy-Bitsy Baby Mouse. Cordell, Matthew, illus. 2012. (ENG.). 40p. (J). (gr. -1-2). 15.99 (978-1-4169-3786-9(2), Simon & Schuster Bks. For Young Readers) Simon & Schuster Bks. For Young Readers.
Meloy, Colin. Wildwood. Ellis, Carson, illus. 2011. (Wildwood Chronicles Ser.: 1). (ENG.). 560p. (J). (gr. 3-7). 17.99 (978-0-06-202468-8(X)) HarperCollins Pubs.
—Wildwood. Ellis, Carson, illus. 2012. (Wildwood Chronicles Ser.: 1). (J). lib. bdg. 20.85 (978-0-606-26864-6(2), Turtleback) Turtleback Bks.
Methods, Bryan. The Shanghai Incident. 2017. (Master Diplexito & Mr. Scant Ser.). (ENG.). 264p. (J). (gr. 5-8). 17.99 **(978-1-5124-0580-4(9)**, Carolrhoda Bks.) Lerner Publishing Group.
Meyer, Deanna. Buffalo on the Ridge. 2010. pap. 12.95 (978-0-7414-6103-2(X)) Infinity Publishing.
Meyer, Marissa. Scarlet. 2013. (Lunar Chronicles: Bk. 2). (ENG.). 464p. (YA). (gr. 7). 19.99 (978-0-312-64296-9(2), 9780312642969) Feiwel & Friends.
—Scarlet. 2014. (Lunar Chronicles Ser.: 2). (ENG.). 512p. (YA). (gr. 7-12). pap. 9.99 (978-1-250-00721-6(6), 9781250007216) Square Fish.
—Scarlet. l.t. ed. 2013. (Lunar Chronicles: Bk. 2). (ENG.). 572p. 23.99 (978-1-4104-5623-6(4)) Thorndike Pr.
—Scarlet. 2014. (Lunar Chronicles Ser.: 2). (YA). lib. bdg. 20.85 (978-0-606-35097-6(7), Turtleback) Turtleback Bks.
—Scarlet. 2016. (SPA.). 430p. (YA). (gr. 9-12). pap. 20.99 (978-987-612-990-9(2)) V&R Editoras.
Meyers, Susan. Bear in the Air. Bates, Amy, illus. 2010. (ENG.). 32p. (J). (gr. k-2). 15.95 (978-0-8109-8398-4(2), Abrams Bks. for Young Readers) Abrams, Inc.
Michael Batdorf. Pair of Jacks: A Novel. 2009. 332p. 29.95 (978-1-4401-4482-0(6)); pap. 19.95 (978-1-4401-4479-0(6)) iUniverse, Inc.
Michaelis, Antonia. The Secret of the Twelfth Continent. Hosmer-Dillard, Mollie, tr. from GER. Nievelstein, Ralf, illus. 2013. (ENG.). 288p. (J). (gr. 2-7). 14.95

(978-1-62087-539-1(X), 620539, Sky Pony Pr.) Skyhorse Publishing Co., Inc.

Miklowitz, Gloria D. The Enemy Has a Face. 2004. 143p. (YA). pap. 8.00 *(978-0-8028-5261-8(0))* Eerdmans, William B. Publishing Co.

Millet, Lydia. The Fires Beneath the Sea. 2012. (Dissenters Ser.). (ENG.). 256p. (J). (gr. 3-7). pap. 12.00 *(978-1-931520-47-8(X)*, Big Mouth Hse.) Small Beer Pr.

—The Shimmers in the Night. 2012. (Dissenters Ser.). (ENG.). 256p. (J). (gr. 3-7). 16.95 *(978-1-931520-78-2(X)*, Big Mouth Hse.) Small Beer Pr.

Milway, Alex. Operation Robot Storm: The Mythical 9th Division. Milway, Alex, illus. 2013. (ENG., Illus.). 224p. (J). pap. 5.99 *(978-1-61067-074-6(4))* Kane Miller.

Mishica, Clare. Samantha Stays Safe. Dubin, Jill, illus. 2012. 32p. (J). pap. 8.00 *(978-1-935014-40-9(4))* Hutchings, John Pubs.

The Missing Man & the Twenty Dragons. 2nd ed. 2005. (ENG., Illus.). 204p. (J). reprint ed. per. 11.99 *(978-0-9760045-1-6(8)*, Reluctant Reader Bks.) Cronus College.

Molk, Laurel. Eeny, Meeny, Miney, Mo, & Flo. Molk, Laurel, illus. 2015. (ENG., Illus.). 32p. (J). (gr. -1-k). 16.99 *(978-0-670-01538-2(5)*, Viking Books for Young Readers) Penguin Young Readers Group.

Monaghan, Annabel. A Girl Named Digit: Undercover, under Pressure, & Underestimated. 2012. (ENG., Illus.). 192p. (YA). (gr. 7). 16.99 *(978-0-547-66852-9(X))* Houghton Mifflin Harcourt Publishing Co.

Moriarty, Jaclyn. A Corner of White. 2013. (Colors of Madeleine Ser.: 1). (ENG.). 384p. (J). (gr. 7). 18.99 *(978-0-545-39736-0(7)*, Levine, Arthur A. Bks.) Scholastic, Inc.

—The Cracks in the Kingdom. 2014. (Colors of Madeleine Ser.: 2). (ENG.). 480p. (J). (gr. 7). 18.99 *(978-0-545-39738-4(3)*, Levine, Arthur A. Bks.) Scholastic, Inc.

—A Tangle of Gold. 2016. (Colors of Madeleine Ser.: 3). (ENG.). 480p. (YA). (gr. 7). 18.99 *(978-0-545-39740-7(5)*, Levine, Arthur A. Bks.) Scholastic, Inc.

Mowry, Jess. Tyger Tales. 2007. 227p. per. 14.99 *(978-1-59092-358-0(8))* Blue Forge Pr.

Mrozek, Elizabeth. The Fifth Chair. Mrozek, Elizabeth, illus. 2013. (Illus.). 38p. 19.95 *(978-1-935766-80-3(5))* Windy City Pubs.

Munday, Dj. The Secret Dummy of Joshua Bean. 2008. 84p. pap. *(978-1-84923-029-2(3))* YouWriteOn.

Murphy, Stuart J. En Busca de Freda. Mlawer, Teresa, tr. from ENG. Jones, Tim, illus. 2012. (I See I Learn Ser.). (SPA & ENG.). 32p. (J). (-k). 14.95 *(978-1-58089-494-4(1))*; pap. 6.95 *(978-1-58089-495-1(X))* Charlesbridge Publishing, Inc.

—Freda Is Found. 2011. (I See I Learn Ser.). (ENG., Illus.). 32p. (J). (-k). 14.95 *(978-1-58089-462-3(3))*; pap. 6.95 *(978-1-58089-463-0(1))* Charlesbridge Publishing, Inc.

Narsimhan, Mahtab. The Third Eye. 2007. (Tara Trilogy Ser.: 1). (ENG.). 240p. (YA). (gr. 5-7). pap. 12.99 *(978-1-55002-750-1(6)*, Boardwalk Bks.) Dundurn CAN. Dist: Ingram Publisher Services.

Neil, Deanna. The Land of Curiosities (Book 2)) Lost in Yellowstone, 1872-1873. 2009. 320p. (J). pap. 12.95 *(978-0-9798800-2-5(5))* EcoSeekers, The.

Nichols, Lee. Deception. 2010. (Haunting Emma Ser.). (ENG.). 336p. (YA). (gr. 9-12). 16.99 *(978-1-59990-308-8(3)*, 9781599903088); pap. 9.99 *(978-1-59990-421-4(7)*, 9781599904214) Bloomsbury Publishing USA. (Bloomsbury USA Childrens).

Nix, Garth. The Fall. 2004. (Seventh Tower Ser.). 195p. (gr. 4-7). 18.00 *(978-0-7569-3516-0(4))* Perfection Learning Corp.

Noël, Alyson. Unrivaled. 2017. (Beautiful Idols Ser.: 1). (YA). lib. bdg. 20.85 *(978-0-606-39609-7(8))* Turtleback Bks.

Nolan, Han. Crazy. 2010. (ENG.). 352p. (YA). (gr. 7-18). 17.00 *(978-0-15-205109-9(0))* Houghton Mifflin Harcourt Publishing Co.

Norris, Elizabeth. Unbreakable. 2013. (Unraveling Ser.: 2). (ENG.). 496p. (YA). (gr. 9). 17.99 *(978-0-06-210376-5(8))* HarperCollins Pubs.

Northrop, Michael. Gentlemen. 2009. (ENG.). 256p. (J). (gr. 9-18). 17.99 *(978-0-545-09749-9(5)*, Scholastic Pr.) Scholastic, Inc.

—Surrounded by Sharks. 2014. (ENG.). 224p. (J). (gr. 4-7). 17.99 *(978-0-545-61545-7(3)*, Scholastic Pr.) Scholastic, Inc.

O'Brien, Joe. Beyond the Cherry Tree. McGann, Oisín, illus. 2012. (ENG.). 224p. (J). pap. 12.95 *(978-1-84717-212-9(1))* O'Brien Pr., Ltd., The IRL. Dist: Dufour Editions, Inc.

Oliver, Lauren. Vanishing Girls. (gr. 9). 2016. 384p. (YA). pap. 9.99 *(978-0-06-222411-8(5))* 2015. (ENG.). 368p. (J). 18.99 *(978-0-06-222410-1(7))* HarperCollins Pubs.

—Vanishing Girls. 2016. (YA). lib. bdg. 20.85 *(978-0-606-38171-0(6))* Turtleback Bks.

Oliver, Lin. Danger! Tiger Crossing. 2016. (Illus.). 115p. (J). pap. *(978-0-448-48086-2(7)*, Grosset & Dunlap) Penguin Young Readers Group.

O'Neil-Andrews, Milly. Bandolines & Bubbles. 2011. 88p. pap. 11.25 *(978-1-4269-3089-8(5))* Trafford Publishing.

Ostlere, Cathy. Karma. 2012. (ENG.). 544p. (YA). (gr. 7-18). 9.99 *(978-1-59514-384-6(X)*, Razorbill) Penguin Young Readers Group.

Painchaud, Michelle. Pretending to Be Erica. 2015. (ENG.). 272p. (YA). (gr. 7). 17.99 *(978-0-670-01497-2(4)*, Viking Books for Young Readers) Penguin Young Readers Group.

Panitch, Amanda. Never Missing, Never Found. 2016. (ENG.). 320p. (YA). (gr. 9). 17.99 *(978-0-553-50764-5(8)*, Random Hse. Bks. for Young Readers) Random Hse. Children's Bks.

Papp, Robert, illus. The Vanishing Passenger. 2006. (Boxcar Children Mysteries Ser.: 106). (ENG.). 128p. (J). (gr. 1-5). 14.99 *(978-0-8075-1066-7(1))* Whitman, Albert & Co.

Paratore, Coleen Murtagh. Wish I Might. 2011. (ENG.). 176p. (J). (gr. 5-9). pap. 6.99 *(978-0-545-09402-3(X)*, Scholastic Paperbacks) Scholastic, Inc.

—Wish I Might: From the Life of Willa Havisham. 2010. (ENG.). 176p. (J). (gr. 5-9). 16.99 *(978-0-545-09406-1(2)*, Scholastic Pr.) Scholastic, Inc.

Parker, Natalie C. Beware the Wild. 2014. (Beware the Wild Ser.: 1). (ENG.). 336p. (YA). (gr. 8). 17.99 *(978-0-06-224152-8(4)*, HarperTeen) HarperCollins Pubs.

Parrish, Harry. Kate & Alice. 2009. 28p. pap. 13.40 *(978-1-4389-3120-3(4))* AuthorHouse.

Patterson, James & Grabenstein, Chris. Danger down the Nile. Neufeld, Juliana, illus. 2014. (Treasure Hunters Ser.). (ENG.). 480p. (J). (gr. 3-7). 14.99 *(978-0-316-37086-8(X)*, Jimmy Patterson) Little Brown & Co.

—Secret of the Forbidden City. Neufeld, Juliana, illus. 2015. (Treasure Hunters Ser.: 3). (ENG.). 448p. (J). (gr. 3-7). 14.99 *(978-0-316-28480-6(7)*, Jimmy Patterson) Little Brown & Co.

—Treasure Hunters. Neufeld, Juliana, illus. (Treasure Hunters Ser.: 1). (ENG.). 480p. (J). (gr. 3-7). 2015. pap. 8.00 *(978-0-316-20757-7(8))* 2013. 14.99 *(978-0-316-20756-0(X))* Little Brown & Co. (Jimmy Patterson).

—Treasure Hunters. 2015. (Treasure Hunters Ser.: 1). (J). lib. bdg. 18.45 *(978-0-606-37305-0(5))* Turtleback Bks.

Patterson, James, et al. Treasure Hunters. Neufeld, Juliana, illus. 2013. 451p. (J). *(978-0-316-24262-2(4))* Little Brown & Co.

Pattison, Darcy. The Journey of Oliver K. Woodman. Cepeda, Joe, illus. 2009. (ENG.). 52p. (J). (gr. -1-3). pap. 7.99 *(978-0-15-206118-0(5))* Houghton Mifflin Harcourt Publishing Co.

Paulsen, Gary. Mudshark. 2010. (ENG.). 96p. (J). (gr. 3-7). 6.99 *(978-0-553-49464-8(3)*, Yearling) Random Hse. Children's Bks.

Peacock, Shane. Vanishing Girl: The Boy Sherlock Holmes, His 3rd Case. 2010. (Boy Sherlock Holmes Ser.). (ENG., Illus.). 326p. (YA). (gr. 5-9). pap. 11.99 *(978-1-77049-234-9(8)*, Tundra Bks.) Tundra Bks. CAN. Dist: Penguin Random Hse. LLC.

Pearce, Jackson. The Doublecross: (And Other Skills I Learned As a Superspy) 2015. (ENG.). 304p. (YA). (gr. 3-6). 16.99 *(978-1-61963-414-5(7)*, 9781619634145, Bloomsbury USA Childrens) Bloomsbury Publishing USA.

Pearce, Margaret. A Belinda Robinson Novel Book 2: Belinda & the Holidays It Rained. 2013. 78p. pap. *(978-1-922233-22-6(6))* Writers Exchange E-Publishing.

Pedraza, M. Eugenia Rueda. Nico's Voyage. 2013. 32p. pap. *(978-1-4602-2360-4(8))* FriesenPress.

Peet, Mal. The Penalty. (ENG.). 272p. 2016. (J). (gr. 7). pap. 8.99 *(978-0-7636-8747-2(2))* 2007. (Illus.). (YA). (gr. 9-12). 16.99 *(978-0-7636-3399-8(2))* Candlewick Pr.

Pennypacker, Sara. Clementine, Friend of the Week. Frazee, Marla, illus. 2010. (ENG.). 176p. (J). (gr. 2-5). 14.99 *(978-1-4231-1355-3(1))* Hyperion Pr.

Perry, Michael. The Scavengers. (ENG.). 336p. (J). (gr. 3-7). 2015. pap. 6.99 *(978-0-06-202617-0(8))* 2014. 16.99 *(978-0-06-202616-3(X))* HarperCollins Pubs.

Perry, Naresha S. Zora's Valentine. 2005. (J). per. 13.00 *(978-0-9767189-0-1(1))* Better Day Publishing LLC.

Peters, Andrew J. The Seventh Pleiade. 2013. (ENG.). 264p. (gr. 7). pap. 11.95 *(978-1-60282-960-2(8))* Bold Strokes Bks.

Petrucha, Stefan & Kinney, Sarah. High School Musical Mystery. 2010. (Nancy Drew Graphic Novels: Girl Detective Ser.). (ENG., Illus.). 96p. (J). (gr. 3-7). pap. 8.99 *(978-1-59707-178-9(1)*, 9781597071789) Papercutz.

Pett, Mark. The Boy & the Airplane. Pett, Mark, illus. 2013. (ENG., Illus.). 40p. (J). 15.99 *(978-1-4424-5123-0(8)*, Simon & Schuster Bks. For Young Readers) Simon & Schuster Bks. For Young Readers.

Pfoutz, Sally. Missing Person. 2009. 192p. (gr. 7-18). pap. 12.95 *(978-1-4401-5108-8(3))* iUniverse, Inc.

Phillips, Helen. Here Where the Sunbeams Are Green. (ENG.). 304p. (J). (gr. 5). 2013. 7.99 *(978-0-307-93145-0(5)*, Yearling) 2012. E-Book *(978-0-307-97487-7(1)*, Delacorte Bks. for Young Readers) Random Hse. Children's Bks.

Plum-Ucci, Carol. The Body of Christopher Creed. 2008. (ENG., Illus.). 272p. (YA). (gr. 7). pap. 7.99 *(978-0-15-206386-3(2))* Houghton Mifflin Harcourt Publishing Co.

Podos, Rebecca. The Mystery of Hollow Places. 2016. 304p. (YA). (gr. 9). 17.99 *(978-0-06-237334-2(X))* HarperCollins Pubs.

Polak, Monique. Flip Turn, 1 vol. 2004. (Lorimer Sports Stories Ser.: 67). (ENG.). 104p. (J). (gr. 4-8). 16.95 *(978-1-55028-819-3(9)*, 9781550288193) Lorimer, James & Co., Ltd., Pubs. CAN. Dist: Casemate Pubs. & Bk. Distributors, LLC.

Porter, Kevin Don. Missing. 2013. 166p. pap. 11.99 *(978-0-9857014-7-5(1))* Artists' Orchard, LLC, The.

Portes, Andrea & Silverman, Joel. Liberty: The Spy Who (Kind of) Liked Me. 2017. 400p. (YA). (gr. 8). 17.99 *(978-0-06-242199-9(9)*, HarperTeen) HarperCollins Pubs.

Poth, Karen. Sheerluck Holmes & the Case of the Missing Friend, 1 vol. 2014. (I Can Read! / Big Idea Books / VeggieTales Ser.). (ENG.). 32p. (J). pap. 3.99 *(978-0-310-74171-8(8))* Zonderkidz.

Potter, Noel Gyro. Lost in the Mall, 1 vol. Cannon, Joseph, illus. 2008. (Adventures of Marshall & Art Ser.). (ENG.). 32p. (gr. -1-4). 28.50 *(978-1-60270-198-4(9)*, Looking Glass Library) ABDO Publishing Co.

Powell, Laura. Witch Fire. 2013. (ENG.). 336p. (YA). (gr. 7). 17.99 *(978-1-61963-006-2(0)*, 9781619630062, Bloomsbury USA Childrens) Bloomsbury Publishing USA.

Pryor, Michael. The Missing Kin. 2009. (Chronicles of Krangor Ser.: 2). (ENG.). 208p. (J). (gr. 4-7). pap. 7.99 *(978-1-74166-175-0(7))* Random Hse. Australia AUS. Dist: Independent Pubs. Group.

Pyron, Bobbie. A Dog's Way Home. Jessell, Tim, illus. 2011. (ENG.). 336p. (J). (gr. 3-7). 16.99 *(978-0-06-198674-1(7)*, Tegen, Katherine Bks) HarperCollins Pubs.

Radice, Teresa, et al. Tinker Bell & the Wings of Rani. Vetro, Daniela et al, illus. 2010. (Disney Fairies Ser.: 2). (ENG.). 80p. (J). (gr. 1-6). pap. 7.99 *(978-1-59707-226-7(5)*, 9781597072267) Papercutz.

Redwine, C. J. Defiance. (Defiance Trilogy Ser.: 1). (ENG.). (YA). (gr. 8). 2013. 432p. pap. 9.99 *(978-0-06-211717-5(3))* 2012. 416p. 17.99 *(978-0-06-211718-2(1))* HarperCollins Pubs.

Reeve, Philip. Oliver & the Sea Monkeys. McIntyre, Sarah, illus. 2016. (Not-So-Impossible Tale Ser.). (ENG.). 224p. (J). (gr. 2-5). pap. 6.99 *(978-0-385-38789-7(X)*, Yearling) Random Hse. Children's Bks.

—Oliver & the Seawigs. McIntyre, Sarah, illus. 2014. (Not-So-Impossible Tale Ser.). (ENG.). 208p. (J). (gr. 2-5). 12.99 *(978-0-385-38788-0(1)*, Random Hse. Bks. for Young Readers) Random Hse. Children's Bks.

Reid, F. J. The Midwinter Child. 2009. 224p. pap. *(978-1-84923-496-2(5))* YouWriteOn.

Renner, Ellen. Castle of Shadows. 2013. (ENG., Illus.). 400p. (J). (gr. 5-7). pap. 7.99 *(978-0-544-02270-6(X))* Houghton Mifflin Harcourt Publishing Co.

Rewalt, Nancy E. Lost & Found: Goldilocks & the Three Bears Revisited. Cranford, Darren, illus. 2012. 64p. (J). pap. 6.95 *(978-0-9821110-2-4(9))* Ronan Enterprises, Inc.

Rex, Adam. The True Meaning of Smekday. Rex, Adam, illus. 2015. (ENG., Illus.). 432p. (J). (gr. 3-7). pap. 7.99 *(978-1-4847-2946-5(3))* Hyperion Bks. for Children.

—The True Meaning of Smekday. Rex, Adam, illus. 2009. (Smek Smeries Ser.). (ENG., Illus.). 432p. (J). (gr. 3-7). pap. 7.99 *(978-0-7868-4901-7(0))* Hyperion Pr.

—The True Meaning of Smekday. 2009. (Illus.). 423p. 18.00 *(978-1-60686-525-5(0))* Perfection Learning Corp.

Richard Richtmyer. A Bit of Magic: A Novel. 2009. 116p. pap. 10.95 *(978-1-4401-5565-9(8))* iUniverse, Inc.

Roach, Joyce Gibson, tr. Cowgirl of the Rocking R. 2003. (J). *(978-0-9726573-0-3(4))* Crosswinds Bks.

Roberts, Kelly Hughes. The Road to Chianti. 2012. 214p. (gr. 4-6). 33.99 *(978-1-4525-5963-6(5))*; pap. 15.99 *(978-1-4525-5961-2(9))* Balboa Pr.

Robins, Eleanor. Where Is Mr. Zane?, 1 vol. unabr. ed. 2011. (Carter High Mysteries Ser.). (ENG.). 48p. (YA). (gr. 9-12). 7.95 *(978-1-61651-569-0(4))* Saddleback Educational Publishing, Inc.

Roehrig, Caleb. Last Seen Leaving. 2016. (ENG.). 336p. (YA). 17.99 *(978-1-250-08563-4(2)*, 9781250085634) Feiwel & Friends.

Rollason, Jane. Killer Bees. 2009. (ENG.). 64p. pap. 12.00 *(978-84-8323-503-4(X))* Cambridge Univ. Pr.

Rollins, James. Jake Ransom & the Howling Sphinx. 2011. (Jake Ransom Ser.: 2). (ENG.). 384p. (J). (gr. 5-18). 16.99 *(978-0-06-147382-1(0))* HarperCollins Pubs.

—Jake Ransom & the Skull King's Shadow. 2010. (Jake Ransom Ser.: 1). (ENG.). 432p. (J). (gr. 5). pap. 7.99 *(978-0-06-147381-4(2))* HarperCollins Pubs.

Rooftoppers. 2014. (ENG., Illus.). 304p. (J). (gr. 3-7). pap. 7.99 *(978-1-4424-9059-8(4)*, Simon & Schuster Bks. For Young Readers) Simon & Schuster Bks. For Young Readers.

Root, Phyllis. Lilly & the Pirates. Shepperson, Rob, illus. (ENG.). (J). 2013. 180p. (gr. 3-7). pap. 8.95 *(978-1-62091-027-6(6))* 2010. 116p. (gr. 4-6). 16.95 *(978-1-59078-583-6(5)*, Front Street) Boyds Mills Pr.

Rosenthal, Eileen. Bobo the Sailor Man! Rosenthal, Marc, illus. 2013. (ENG.). 40p. (J). (gr. -1-1). 15.99 *(978-1-4424-4443-0(6))* Simon & Schuster Children's Publishing.

Rosoff, Meg. Picture Me Gone. 2013. (ENG.). 256p. (J). (gr. 7). 17.99 *(978-0-399-25765-0(9)*, G.P. Putnam's Sons Books for Young Readers) Penguin Young Readers Group.

Ross, Jeff. Dawn Patrol, 1 vol. 2012. (Orca Sports Ser.). (ENG.). 160p. (YA). (gr. 6-10). pap. 9.95 *(978-1-4598-0062-5(1))* Orca Bk. Pubs. USA.

Roy, Ron. A to Z Mysteries Collection, No. 1. Gurney, John Steven, illus. 2010. (to Z Mysteries Ser.: Nos. 1-4). (ENG.). 384p. (J). (gr. 1-4). 9.99 *(978-0-375-85946-5(2)*, Random Hse. Bks. for Young Readers) Random Hse. Children's Bks.

—Operation Orca. Gurney, John Steven, illus. 2015. (to Z Mysteries Ser.). (ENG.). 144p. (J). (gr. 1-4). 12.99 *(978-0-553-52397-3(X)*, Random Hse. Bks. for Young Readers) Random Hse. Children's Bks.

Rubin, Sarah. The Impossible Clue. 2017. (J). pap. ***(978-0-545-94272-0(1)***, Chicken Hse., The) Scholastic, Inc.

Rundell, Katherine. Rooftoppers. Fan, Terry, illus. 2013. (ENG.). 288p. (J). (gr. 3-7). 16.99 *(978-1-4424-9058-1(6)*, Simon & Schuster Bks. For Young Readers) Simon & Schuster Bks. For Young Readers.

Rushford, Patricia H. Secrets of Ghost Island. 2007. (J). *(978-88-02-46255-4(0))* Moody Pubs.

Ruth, Greg. The Lost Boy. 2013. (ENG.). 192p. (J). (gr. 3-7). pap. 12.99 *(978-0-439-82332-6(3)*, Graphix) Scholastic, Inc.

Rykken, John. Bloodwood: The Chronicles of Max Mayhem. 2011. 264p. (gr. 10-12). 26.95 *(978-1-4620-0656-4(6))*; pap. 16.95 *(978-1-4620-0657-1(4))* iUniverse, Inc.

Sage, Angie. Todhunter Moon. Zug, Mark, illus. 2015. (World of Septimus Heap Ser.: 1). (ENG.). 496p. (J). (gr. 3-7). pap. 7.99 *(978-0-06-227246-1(2)*, Tegen, Katherine Bks) HarperCollins Pubs.

Salomon, Peter Adam. All Those Broken Angels. 2014. (ENG.). 240p. (YA). pap. 11.99 *(978-0-7387-4079-9(9)*, Flux) North Star Editions.

Sanderson, Nancy. Horse of the Four Winds. 2011. 152p. (gr. 10-12). pap. 14.50 *(978-1-4634-4802-8(3))* AuthorHouse.

Santiago, Brianna A. Why Is the Moon Following Us? 2008. 16p. pap. 24.95 *(978-1-60474-944-1(X))* America Star Bks.

Santopolo, Jill. The Nina, the Pinta, & the Vanishing Treasure. 2009. (Alec Flint Mystery Ser.: 1). (ENG.). 192p. (J). (gr. 2-5). pap. 6.99 *(978-0-439-90353-0(X)*, Scholastic Paperbacks) Scholastic, Inc.

Sargent, Dave & Sargent, Pat. Young Dike: Teamwork! Woodward, Elaine, illus. 2003. (Young Animal Pride Ser.: 5). 24p. (J). 5. pap. 6.95 *(978-1-56763-872-1(4))* Vol. 5. lib. bdg. 20.95 *(978-1-56763-871-4(6))* Ozark Publishing.

Sazaklis, John. Return of the Dinobot. 2014. (Transformers 8x8 Ser.). (J). lib. bdg. 13.55 *(978-0-606-35296-3(1))* Turtleback Bks.

Schmidt, Werner. The Forests of Adventure. 2005. 137p. pap. 12.50 *(978-1-4116-4721-3(1))* Lulu Pr., Inc.

Schoon, Christian. Under Nameless Stars. 2014. (ENG.). 368p. (J). (gr. 9). pap. 9.99 *(978-1-908844-87-3(6)*, Strange Chemistry) Watkins Media Limited GBR. Dist: Penguin Random Hse. LLC.

Schraff, Anne. Lost & Found. Langan, Paul, ed. 2007. (Bluford High Ser.). 133p. (gr. 8-12). 16.00 *(978-0-7569-8076-4(3))* Perfection Learning Corp.

—Lost & Found. 2007. (Bluford High — Scholastic Ser.: 1). lib. bdg. 16.00 *(978-1-4177-7141-7(0)*, Turtleback) Turtleback Bks.

—Something Dreadful down Below, 1 vol. unabr. ed. 2010. (Q Reads Ser.). (ENG.). 32p. (YA). (gr. 9-12). pap. 6.95 *(978-1-61651-205-7(9))* Saddleback Educational Publishing, Inc.

Seaman, Kathleen. Annycole, 1 vol. 2009. 49p. pap. 16.95 *(978-1-4489-1970-3(3))* America Star Bks.

Sedgwick, Marcus. She Is Not Invisible. 2014. (ENG.). 224p. (YA). (gr. 7). 16.99 *(978-1-59643-801-9(0)*, 9781596438019) Roaring Brook Pr.

—She Is Not Invisible. 2015. (ENG.). 240p. (YA). (gr. 7). pap. 9.99 *(978-1-250-05698-6(5)*, 9781250056986) Square Fish.

Sedoti, Chelsea. The Hundred Lies of Lizzie Lovett. 2017. (ENG.). 400p. (YA). (gr. 8-12). 17.99 *(978-1-4926-3608-3(8)*, 9781492636083) Sourcebooks, Inc.

Sharp, Lydia. Whenever I'm with You. 2017. (ENG.). 304p. (J). (gr. 7). 17.99 *(978-1-338-04749-3(3)*, Scholastic Pr.) Scholastic, Inc.

Shaw, J. D. The Secrets of Loon Lake. 2010. (ENG.). 338p. (J). (gr. 5). pap. 16.95 *(978-0-9845318-0-6(7))* Tiny Stachel Pr.

Sheninger, Rick. Buddy the Duck Gets Lost. 2012. 20p. pap. 15.99 *(978-1-4685-8371-7(9))* AuthorHouse.

Shepard, Sara. Pretty Little Liars Bind-Up #1: Pretty Little Liars & Flawless. 2014. (Pretty Little Liars Ser.). (ENG.). 656p. (YA). (gr. 9). pap. 10.99 *(978-0-06-232292-0(3)*, HarperTeen) HarperCollins Pubs.

Sherrard, Valerie. Chasing Shadows. 2004. (ENG.). 216p. (YA). pap. 9.99 *(978-1-55002-502-6(3))* Dundurn CAN. Dist: Ingram Publisher Services.

—Searching for Yesterday: A Shelby Belgarden Mystery. 2008. (ENG.). 224p. (YA). (gr. 6-10). pap. 12.99 *(978-1-55002-788-4(3)*, Boardwalk Bks.) Dundurn CAN. Dist: Ingram Publisher Services.

Sheth, Kashmira. Boys Without Names. 2010. (ENG.). 320p. (J). (gr. 4-7). 16.99 *(978-0-06-185760-7(2))* HarperCollins Pubs.

Shurtliff, Liesl. Jack: The True Story of Jack & the Beanstalk. 2015. (ENG.). 304p. (J). (gr. 3-7). 16.99 *(978-0-385-75579-5(1)*, Knopf Bks. for Young Readers) Random Hse. Children's Bks.

Silvey, Diane. Time of the Thunderbird. Mantha, John, illus. 2008. (ENG.). 88p. (J). (gr. 6-5). pap. 11.99 *(978-1-55002-792-1(1)*, Sandcastle Bks.) Dundurn CAN. Dist: Ingram Publisher Services.

Siobhan, Dowd. The London Eye Mystery. 2014. (ENG.). 336p. (J). (gr. 3-7). 12.24 *(978-1-63245-320-4(7))* Lectorum Pubns., Inc.

Sirowy, Alexandra. The Creeping: If You Hunt for Monsters, You'll Find Them. 2015. (ENG., Illus.). 400p. (YA). (gr. 7). 17.99 *(978-1-4814-1886-7(6))* Simon & Schuster Children's Publishing.

Skuse, C. J. Pretty Bad Things. 2011. (ENG.). 256p. (J). (gr. 7-7). 17.99 *(978-0-545-28973-3(4)*, Chicken Hse., The) Scholastic, Inc.

Sloane, Roxy. Missing: The Heather Harding Mysteries. 2011. 100p. pap. 15.99 *(978-1-4628-9061-3(X))* Xlibris Corp.

Small, Lily. Chloe the Kitten. 2015. (Fairy Animals of Misty Wood Ser.: 1). (ENG., Illus.). 144p. (J). (gr. k-3). pap. 5.99 *(978-1-62779-141-0(8)*, 9781627791410, Holt, Henry & Co. Bks. For Young Readers) Holt, Henry & Co.

Smith, Holly C. Tyler the Monkey & Andy the Mouse. 2012. 28p. (-18). pap. 24.95 *(978-1-4626-9501-0(9))* America Star Bks.

Smith, R. L. The Journals of Underwich: Book One. 2007. 253p. pap. 27.95 *(978-1-60441-490-5(1))* America Star Bks.

Smith-Ready, Jeri. This Side of Salvation. 2014. (ENG., Illus.). 384p. (YA). (gr. 9). 17.99 *(978-1-4424-3948-1(3)*, Simon Pulse) Simon Pulse.

Smith, Roland. Chupacabra. (J). 2015. (ENG.). 304p. (gr. 3-7). pap. 7.99 *(978-0-545-17818-1(5)*, Scholastic Paperbacks) 2013. (Illus.). xv, 285p. pap. *(978-0-545-62984-3(5)*, Scholastic Pr.) Scholastic, Inc.

—Mutation. (ENG.). 352p. (J). (gr. 3-7). 2016. (Cryptid Hunters Ser.: 4). pap. 6.99 *(978-0-545-08181-8(5))* 2014. 16.99 *(978-0-545-08180-1(7))* Scholastic, Inc. (Scholastic Pr.).

—Tentacles. 2009. (ENG.). 336p. (J). (gr. 3-7). 16.99 *(978-0-545-16688-1(8)*, Scholastic Pr.) Scholastic, Inc.

Snicket, Lemony, pseud. When Did You See Her Last? Seth, illus. (All the Wrong Questions Ser.: 2). (ENG.). (J). (gr. 3-17). 2014. 304p. pap. 7.99 *(978-0-316-33684-0(X))* 2013. 288p. 16.00 *(978-0-316-12305-1(6))* 2013. 304p. 29.99 *(978-0-316-23993-6(3))* Little, Brown Bks. for Young Readers.

Soontornvat, Christina. The Changelings. (Changelings Ser.: 1). (ENG.). (J). (gr. 5-8). 2017. 304p. pap. 7.99 ***(978-1-4926-4795-9(0))*** 2016. 288p. 16.99 *(978-1-4926-3260-3(0)*, 9781492632603) Sourcebooks, Inc. (Sourcebooks Jabberwocky).

Sparkes, Ali. Alligator Action. Collins, Ross, illus. 2014. (S. W. I. T. C. H. Ser.: 14). (ENG.). 112p. (J). (gr. 2-5). lib. bdg. 27.93 *(978-1-4677-2117-2(4)*, Darby Creek) Lerner Publishing Group.

Specter, Baron. To Werewolf or Not to Werewolf, 1 vol. Kneupper, Setch, illus. 2012. (Graveyard Diaries Ser.). (ENG.). 128p. (J). (gr. 3-8). 27.07 *(978-1-61641-901-1(6))* Magic Wagon.

Spoor, Mike, illus. Desperate Measures: Units of Measurement in Action. 2010. (Mandrill Mountain Math Mysteries Ser.). (ENG.). 32p. (J). (gr. 2-6). pap. 10.55 *(978-1-60754-925-3(5))* Windmill Bks.

—Desperate Measures: Units of Measurement in Action. 2010. (Mandrill Mountain Math Mysteries Ser.). (ENG.). 32p. (J). (gr. 2-6). lib. bdg. 22.60 *(978-1-60754-920-8(4))* Windmill Bks.

—The Emperor's Guards: Concepts of Time. 2010. (Mandrill Mountain Math Mysteries Ser.). (ENG.). 32p. (J). (gr. 2-6). pap. 10.55 *(978-1-60754-927-7(1))*; lib. bdg. 22.60 *(978-1-60754-922-2(0))* Windmill Bks.

—The Hidden Valley: Reasoning in Action. 2010. (Mandrill Mountain Math Mysteries Ser.). (ENG.). 32p. (J). (gr. 2-6). pap. 10.55 *(978-1-60754-924-6(7))*; lib. bdg. 22.60 *(978-1-60754-919-2(0))* Windmill Bks.

Springer, Nancy. The Case of the Bizarre Bouquets. 2009. (Enola Holmes Mystery Ser.: 3). (ENG.). 176p. (J). (gr. 3-7). pap. 6.99 *(978-0-14-241390-6(9)*, Puffin Books) Penguin Young Readers Group.

—The Case of the Cryptic Crinoline. 2011. (Enola Holmes Mystery Ser.: 5). (ENG.). 176p. (J). (gr. 5-7). 6.99 *(978-0-14-241690-7(8)*, Puffin Books) Penguin Young Readers Group.

—The Case of the Missing Marquess. 2007. (Enola Holmes Mystery Ser.: 1). (ENG.). 240p. (J). (gr. 3-7). 7.99

(978-0-14-240933-6(2), Puffin Books) Penguin Young Readers Group.

Stanfield, Michael. Bucky & Becky - the Magic of Wigglepoo Mountain. 2009. 144p. pap. 14.96 *(978-0-557-02614-2(8))* Lulu Pr., Inc.

Starmer, Aaron. The Riverman. 2015. (Riverman Trilogy Ser.: 1). (ENG.). 336p. (YA). (gr. 5-9). pap. 8.99 *(978-1-250-05685-6(3),* 9781250056856) Square Fish.

—The Storyteller. 2016. (Riverman Trilogy Ser.: 3). (ENG.). 336p. (J). 16.99 *(978-0-374-36313-0(7),* 9780374363130, Farrar, Straus & Giroux (BYR)) Farrar, Straus & Giroux.

Steig, William. Sylvester & the Magic Pebble. Steig, William, illus. 2012. (ENG., Illus.). 32p. (J). (gr. -1-2). pap. 9.99 *(978-1-4424-3560-5(7),* Little Simon) Little Simon.

—Sylvester & the Magic Pebble. Steig, William, illus. 2006. (Stories to Go! Ser.). (Illus.). 32p. (J). (gr. -1-3). 4.99 *(978-1-4169-1857-8(4),* Simon & Schuster/Paula Wiseman Bks.) Simon & Schuster/Paula Wiseman Bks.

Steinkraus, Kyla. Curious Case of the Ransom Riddler. 2015. (ENG.). 64p. (gr. 3-6). 29.95 *(978-1-63430-382-8(2))* Rourke Educational Media.

Stevenson, S. Roy. The Magic Act: A Mystery by S. Roy Stevenson. 2008. 108p. 20.95 *(978-0-595-51841-8(9));* pap. 10.95 *(978-0-595-53062-5(1))* iUniverse, Inc.

Stewart, Joel. Tree Soup. 2011. (Stanley Wells Mystery Ser.: 2). (ENG., Illus.). 180p. (J). (gr. 2-4). pap. 9.99 *(978-0-440-86717-3(7))* Transworld Publishers Ltd. GBR. Dist: Independent Pubs. Group.

Stewart, Trenton Lee. The Mysterious Benedict Society & the Perilous Journey. Sudyka, Diana, illus. 2009. (Mysterious Benedict Society Ser.: 2). (ENG.). 464p. (J). (gr. 3-7). pap. 8.99 *(978-0-316-03673-3(0))* Little Brown & Co.

—The Mysterious Benedict Society & the Perilous Journey. Sudyka, Diana, illus. 2008. (Mysterious Benedict Society Ser.: 2). (ENG.). 448p. (J). (gr. 3-7). 18.99 *(978-0-316-05780-6(0))* Little, Brown Bks. for Young Readers.

—The Mysterious Benedict Society & the Perilous Journey. 2009. (Mysterious Benedict Society Ser.: 2). (J). lib. bdg. 19.65 *(978-0-606-07462-9(7),* Turtleback) Turtleback Bks.

Stilton, Geronimo. Fright Night. 2013. (Creepella Von Cacklefur Ser.: 5). (ENG.). 128p. (J). (gr. 2-5). pap. 7.99 *(978-0-545-39349-2(3),* Scholastic Paperbacks) Scholastic, Inc.

—Ride for Your Life! 2014. (Geronimo Stilton — Creepella Von Cacklefur Ser.: 6). lib. bdg. 18.40 *(978-0-606-35847-7(1))* Turtleback Bks.

—Thea Stilton & the Dragon's Code. 2009. (Geronimo Stilton Special Edition Ser.: No. 1). (Illus.). 158p. 18.00 *(978-1-60686-420-3(3))* Perfection Learning Corp.

—Thea Stilton & the Dragon's Code. 2009. (Thea Stilton Ser.: 1). lib. bdg. 19.65 *(978-0-606-00231-8(6),* Turtleback) Turtleback Bks.

Stilton, Geronimo & Stilton, Thea. Thea Stilton & the Dragon's Code. 2009. (Thea Stilton Ser.: 1). (ENG.). 176p. (J). (gr. 2-5). pap. 8.99 *(978-0-545-10367-1(3),* Scholastic Paperbacks) Scholastic, Inc.

—Thea Stilton & the Ghost of the Shipwreck. 2010. (Thea Stilton Ser.: 3). (ENG., Illus.). 176p. (J). (gr. 2-5). mass mkt. 8.99 *(978-0-545-15059-0(0),* Scholastic Paperbacks) Scholastic, Inc.

—Thea Stilton & the Ghost of the Shipwreck. 2010. (Thea Stilton Ser.: 3). lib. bdg. 19.65 *(978-0-606-06843-7(0),* Turtleback) Turtleback Bks.

—Thea Stilton & the Secret of the Old Castle. 2012. (Thea Stilton Ser.: 10). (ENG., Illus.). 176p. (J). (gr. 2-5). pap. 8.99 *(978-0-545-34107-3(8),* Scholastic Paperbacks) Scholastic, Inc.

Stilton, Thea. Thea Stilton & the Frozen Fiasco. 2017. (Thea Stilton Ser.: 25). lib. bdg. 19.65 ***(978-0-606-40181-4(4))*** Turtleback Bks.

—Thea Stilton & the Missing Myth. 2014. (Thea Stilton Ser.: 20). lib. bdg. 19.65 *(978-0-606-36058-6(1))* Turtleback Bks.

—Thea Stilton & the Secret of the Old Castle. 2012. (Thea Stilton Ser.: 10). lib. bdg. 19.65 *(978-0-606-23930-1(8),* Turtleback) Turtleback Bks.

Stokes, Paula. Liars, Inc. 2015. (ENG.). 368p. (YA). (gr. 8). 17.99 *(978-0-06-232328-6(8),* HarperTeen) HarperCollins Pubs.

Stolarz, Laurie Faria. Deadly Little Lessons. 2013. (Touch Novel Ser.). (ENG., Illus.). 346p. (YA). (gr. 7-12). pap. 8.99 *(978-1-4231-3498-5(2))* Hyperion Pr.

Stoop, Naoko. Red Knit Cap Girl to the Rescue. 2013. (ENG., Illus.). 40p. (J). (gr. -1-3). 17.00 *(978-0-316-22885-5(0))* Little, Brown Bks. for Young Readers.

Strasnick, Lauren. Then You Were Gone. (ENG., 272p. (YA). (gr. 9). 2014. Illus.). pap. 9.99 *(978-1-4424-2716-7(7))* 2013. 16.99 *(978-1-4424-2715-0(9))* Simon Pulse. (Simon Pulse).

Strasser, Todd. Wish You Were Dead. (ENG.). 240p. (gr. 9). 2010. (J). pap. 8.99 *(978-1-60684-138-9(6))* 2009. 16.99 *(978-1-60684-007-8(X))* Lerner Publishing Group. (Carolrhoda Lab™).

Sturman, Jennifer. And Then Everything Unraveled. 2010. (ENG.). 256p. (J). (gr. 7). 8.99 *(978-0-545-08723-0(6))* Scholastic, Inc.

—And Then I Found Out the Truth. 2010. (ENG.). 272p. (J). (gr. 7-18). 16.99 *(978-0-545-08724-7(4))* Scholastic, Inc.

Summers, Courtney. All the Rage. (ENG.). 336p. (YA). 2016. pap. 10.99 *(978-1-250-06915-3(7),* 9781250069153) 2015. (gr. 9-13). 18.99 *(978-1-250-02191-5(X),* 9781250021915) St. Martin's Pr. (St. Martin's Griffin).

Summy, Barrie. The Disappearance of Emily H. 2015. (ENG.). 256p. (J). (gr. 5). 16.99 *(978-0-385-73943-6(5),* Delacorte Bks. for Young Readers) Random Hse. Children's Bks.

Sutiff, Jamie. The Elves of Owl's Head Mountain. Blumberg, Christine A., ed. Evens, Kevin C., illus. 2007. 276p. pap. 10.95 *(978-0-9712867-8-8(7))* Cold River Pubns.

—The Elves of Owl's Head Mountain. Blumberg, Christine A., ed. Evans, Kevin, illus. 2007. 280p. (gr. 8-12). 26.95 *(978-0-9712867-7-1(9))* Cold River Pubns.

Sutton, Laurie S. Legend of the Gator Man. Neely, Scott, illus. 2016. (Scooby-Doo Comic Chapter Bks.). (ENG.). 88p. (gr. 3-7). pap. 5.95 *(978-1-4965-3588-7(X))* Capstone Press of Coughlan Cos.

Sutton, Margaret. The Clue in the Patchwork Quilt, No. 14. Doane, Pelagie, illus. 2008. (Judy Bolton Mysteries Ser.). (ENG.). 228p. (J). (gr. 4-7). pap. 14.95 *(978-1-4290-9034-6(0))* Applewood Bks.

—The Riddle of the Double Ring, No. 10. Doane, Pelagie, illus. 2008. (Judy Bolton Mysteries Ser.). (ENG.). 236p. (J). (gr. 4-7). pap. 14.95 *(978-1-4290-9030-8(8))* Applewood Bks.

Swindells, Robert. Shrapnel. 2009. (ENG., Illus.). 224p. (YA). (gr. 7-18). pap. 14.99 *(978-0-552-55930-0(X))* Transworld Publishers Ltd. GBR. Dist: Independent Pubs. Group.

Tafuri, Nancy. Have You Seen My Duckling? Tafuri, Nancy, illus. 2007. (Illus.). (gr. -1-k). 17.00 *(978-0-7569-7869-3(6))* Perfection Learning Corp.

Tharp, Tim. Mojo. 2014. (ENG.). 288p. (YA). (gr. 7). pap. 8.99 *(978-0-375-86402-5(4),* Ember) Random Hse. Children's Bks.

Theo. Oscar & Hoo. Dudok de Wit, Michael, illus. 2003. 32p. (J). (gr. -1-2). 17.99 *(978-0-00-710793-3(5),* HarperCollins Children's Bks.) HarperCollins Pubs. Ltd. GBR. Dist: Trafalgar Square Publishing.

Thiel Annie. The Playdate Kids Dakota Gets Lost. 2007. 32p. 12.95 *(978-1-933721-08-8(1))* Playdate Kids Publishing.

Thiel, Annie & Fanning, Tena. Dakota Gets Lost. Edwards, William M., illus. 2007. (Playdate Kids: Let's Be Friends! Ser.). 27p. (J). (gr. -1-3). per. 6.95 *(978-1-933721-20-0(0))* Playdate Kids Publishing.

Thomas, Kara. Little Monsters. 2017. (ENG.). 336p. (YA). (gr. 9). 17.99 ***(978-0-553-52149-8(7),*** Delacorte Pr.) Random Hse. Children's Bks.

Thomas, Shelley Moore. Secrets of Selkie Bay. 2015. (ENG.). 208p. (J). (gr. 3-7). 15.99 *(978-0-374-36749-7(3),* 9780374367497, Farrar, Straus & Giroux (BYR)) Farrar, Straus & Giroux.

Thompson, Lisa. The Goldfish Boy. 2017. (ENG.). 320p. (J). (gr. 3-7). 16.99 *(978-1-338-05392-0(2),* Scholastic Pr.) Scholastic, Inc.

Thorpe, Kiki. A Dandelion Wish. Christy, Jana, illus. 2013. (Stepping Stone Book Series: No. 3). (ENG.). 128p. (J). (gr. 1-4). 5.99 *(978-0-7364-2796-8(1),* RH/Disney) Random Hse. Children's Bks.

—A Dandelion Wish. Christy, Jana, illus. 2013. (Never Girls Ser.: 3). lib. bdg. 16.00 *(978-0-606-32199-0(3),* Turtleback) Turtleback Bks.

Timberlake, Amy. One Came Home. 2013. (ENG., Illus.). 272p. (J). (gr. 4-7). 16.99 *(978-0-375-86925-9(5),* Knopf Bks. for Young Readers) Random Hse. Children's Bks.

Torres, Jennifer. The Disappearing. 2014. (Briny Deep Mysteries Ser.). (Illus.). 96p. (J). (gr. 4-9). 17.95 *(978-1-62285-172-0(2));* pap. 10.95 *(978-1-62285-173-7(0))* Enslow Pubs., Inc.

—The Return. 2014. (Briny Deep Mysteries Ser.: Bk. 2). (Illus.). 96p. (J). (gr. 4-9). 17.95 *(978-1-62285-181-2(1));* pap. 10.95 *(978-1-62285-182-9(X))* Enslow Pubs., Inc.

Townley, Roderick. A Bitter Magic. 2015. (ENG.). 304p. (J). (gr. 4-7). 16.99 *(978-0-449-81649-3(4),* Knopf Bks. for Young Readers) Random Hse. Children's Bks.

Tromly, Stephanie. Trouble Is a Friend of Mine. 2015. (ENG.). 336p. (YA). (gr. 7-12). 17.99 *(978-0-525-42840-4(2),* Kathy Dawson Books) Penguin Young Readers Group.

—Trouble Makes a Comeback. (ENG.). (YA). (gr. 7). 2017. 320p. pap. 10.99 ***(978-0-14-751544-5(0),*** Speak) 2016. 304p. 17.99 *(978-0-525-42841-1(0),* Kathy Dawson Books) Penguin Young Readers Group.

Tucker, Mark. Super Phil & the Missing Mom. Patete, Christine, illus. 2003. 24p. (J). 4.50 *(978-1-882440-01-6(3))* God's World Pubns. Inc.

Umansky, Kaye. Clover Twig & the Perilous Path. Wright, Johanna, illus. 2013. (ENG.). 272p. (J). (gr. 3-7). pap. 7.99 *(978-1-250-02727-6(6),* 9781250027276) Square Fish.

Ure, Jean. Is Anybody There? Seeing Is Believing... Donnelly, Karen, illus. 2004. (ENG.). 192p. (J). (gr. 4-7). pap. 9.95 *(978-0-00-716136-2(0),* HarperCollins Children's Bks.) HarperCollins Pubs. Ltd. GBR. Dist: HarperCollins Pubs.

Valentine, Jenny. Me, the Missing, & the Dead. 2010. 224p. (YA). (gr. 9). pap. 8.99 *(978-0-06-085070-8(1),* HarperTeen) HarperCollins Pubs.

Valverde, Mikel. Paula en Nueva York. 2006. (SPA., Illus.). 32p. (J). (gr. 6-8). 14.99 *(978-1-933032-15-3(4))* Lectorum Pubns., Inc.

Van Draanen, Wendelin. Sammy Keyes & the Killer Cruise. (Sammy Keyes Ser.). (ENG.). (J). (gr. 5). 2014. 352p. 7.99 *(978-0-307-93062-0(9),* Yearling) 2013. 336p. 16.99 *(978-0-375-87054-5(7),* Knopf Bks. for Young Readers) Random Hse. Children's Bks.

—Sammy Keyes & the Night of Skulls. 2012. (Sammy Keyes Ser.: 14). (ENG.). 336p. (J). (gr. 5-7). 8.99 *(978-0-375-85457-6(6),* Yearling) Random Hse. Children's Bks.

—Sammy Keyes & the Power of Justice Jack. 2012. (Sammy Keyes Ser.: Bk. 15). (ENG.). 320p. (J). (gr. 5-7). 7.99 *(978-0-307-93060-6(2),* Yearling) Random Hse. Children's Bks.

Vandepeer, Helen. Gifts. 2008. 76p. pap. 35.80 *(978-0-557-03191-7(5))* Lulu Pr., Inc.

The Vanishing Game. 2013. (Hardy Boys Adventures Ser.: 3). (ENG.). 144p. (J). (gr. 3-7). 15.99 *(978-1-4424-7344-7(4));* (Illus.). pap. 6.99 *(978-1-4424-5981-6(6))* Simon & Schuster Children's Publishing. (Aladdin).

Vaught, Susan. Footer Davis Probably Is Crazy. Reinhardt, Jennifer Black, illus. 2015. (ENG.). 240p. (J). (gr. 5-9). 16.99 *(978-1-4814-2276-5(6),* Simon & Schuster Bks. For Young Readers) Simon & Schuster Bks. For Young Readers.

—Freaks Like Us. 2014. (ENG.). 256p. (YA). (gr. 7). pap. 9.99 *(978-1-61963-163-2(6),* 9781619631632, Bloomsbury USA Childrens) Bloomsbury Publishing USA.

Vegas, Peter. The Iron Tomb. 2016. (Pyramid Hunters Ser.: 1). (ENG., Illus.). 304p. (J). (gr. 5-9). 16.99 *(978-1-4814-4578-8(2),* Aladdin) Simon & Schuster Children's Publishing.

Via, Jennifer Welsh. The Foggy Meadow Discovery. 2007. 216p. per. 14.95 *(978-0-595-44680-3(9))* iUniverse, Inc.

Voake, Steve. Daisy Dawson & the Big Freeze. Meserve, Jessica, illus. 2011. (Daisy Dawson Ser.). (ENG.). 96p. (J). (gr. 1-4). pap. 5.99 *(978-0-7636-5627-0(5))* Candlewick Pr.

Voigt, Cynthia. Mister Max: the Book of Kings: Mister Max 3. Bruno, Iacopo, illus. 2016. (Mister Max Ser.). (ENG.). 352p. (J). (gr. 3-7). 7.99 *(978-0-307-97688-8(2),* Yearling) Random Hse. Children's Bks.

—Mister Max: the Book of Lost Things: Mister Max 1. Bruno, Iacopo, illus. 2014. (Mister Max Ser.). (ENG.). 400p. (J). (gr. 3-7). 7.99 *(978-0-307-97682-6(3),* Yearling) Random Hse. Children's Bks.

—Mister Max: the Book of Secrets. Bruno, Iacopo, illus. 2014. (Mister Max Ser.). (ENG.). 384p. (J). (gr. 3-7). 16.99 *(978-0-307-97684-0(X),* Knopf Bks. for Young Readers) Random Hse. Children's Bks.

—Mister Max: the Book of Secrets: Mister Max 2. Bruno, Iacopo, illus. 2015. (Mister Max Ser.). (ENG.). 384p. (J). (gr. 3-7). 6.99 *(978-0-307-97685-7(8),* Yearling) Random Hse. Children's Bks.

—The Book of Kings. Bruno, Iacopo, illus. 2015. (Mister Max Ser.). (ENG.). 352p. (J). (gr. 3-7). 16.99 *(978-0-307-97687-1(4),* Knopf Bks. for Young Readers) Random Hse. Children's Bks.

Voskuil, Hannah. Horus & the Curse of Everlasting Regret. 2016. (ENG.). 224p. (J). (gr. 3-7). 16.99 *(978-1-101-93333-6(X),* Knopf Bks. for Young Readers) Random Hse. Children's Bks.

Vrettos, Adrienne Maria. Sight. 2008. (ENG.). 272p. (YA). (gr. 7). pap. 8.99 *(978-1-4169-0658-2(4),* McElderry, Margaret K. Bks.) McElderry, Margaret K. Bks.

Wallach, Diana Rodriguez. Proof of Lies. 2017. (Anastasia Phoenix Ser.). (ENG.). 400p. (YA). pap. 9.99 *(978-1-63375-608-3(4),* 9781633756083) Entangled Publishing, LLC.

Walsh, Sara. The Dark Light. (ENG., (YA). (gr. 9). 2013. Illus.). 512p. pap. 9.99 *(978-1-4424-3458-5(9))* 2012. 496p. 16.99 *(978-1-4424-3455-4(4))* Simon Pulse. (Simon Pulse).

Walter, Lee. The Gifts That Are Forgotten. 2006. 60p. pap. 16.95 *(978-1-4137-9070-2(4))* PublishAmerica, Inc.

Warden, John. The Chronicles of Zabaduk. 2009. 116p. pap. 13.53 *(978-1-4251-6488-1(9))* Trafford Publishing.

Warner, Gertrude Chandler, creator. The Mystery of the Missing Pop Idol. 2015. (Boxcar Children Mysteries Ser.: 138). (ENG., Illus.). 128p. (J). (gr. 1-5). 15.99 *(978-0-8075-5605-4(X))* Whitman, Albert & Co.

—The Vanishing Passenger. 2006. (Boxcar Children Mysteries Ser.: 106). (ENG., Illus.). 112p. (J). (gr. 1-5). per. 6.99 *(978-0-8075-1067-4(X))* Whitman, Albert & Co.

Warner, Penny. The Hunt for the Missing Spy. 2016. (Code Busters Club Ser.: 5). (ENG.). 168p. (gr. 3-6). (J). 16.99 *(978-1-5124-0304-6(0));* 33.32 *(978-1-5124-0305-3(9))* Lerner Publishing Group.

Watson, Michael. Search, Secrets, & Spies. 2011. 32p. pap. 13.00 *(978-1-61204-357-9(7),* Strategic Bk. Publishing) Strategic Book Publishing & Rights Agency (SBPRA).

Webb, Philip. Where the Rock Splits the Sky. 2014. (ENG.). 272p. (J). (gr. 9). 17.99 *(978-0-545-55701-6(1),* Chicken Hse., The) Scholastic, Inc.

Weber, Elka. One Little Chicken. Kleven, Elisa, illus. 2011. (ENG.). 32p. (J). (gr. -1-2). 16.99 *(978-1-58246-374-2(3),* Tricycle Pr.) Random Hse. Children's Bks.

Weeks, Sarah. Angel Face. Diaz, David, illus. 2014. (ENG.). 32p. (J). (gr. -1-2). 13.99 *(978-1-4814-5045-4(X),* Atheneum Bks. for Young Readers) Simon & Schuster Children's Publishing.

Weingarten, Lynn. Wherever Nina Lies. 2010. (ENG.). 320p. (J). (gr. 7-12). 8.99 *(978-0-545-06633-4(6))* Scholastic, Inc.

Welch, J. D. The Einstein Code. 2016. (ENG.). 304p. (J). pap. 13.95 *(978-1-78612-987-1(6),* 1524d2d4-f042-4c83-8186-8bc8e3b6d93d) Austin, Stan AUS. Dist: Bookmasters Distribution.

Welvaert, Scott R. The Alabaster Ring. 2014. (ENG.). 96p. (J). *(978-1-63235-052-7(1))* Pr. Room Editions LLC.

West, Carly Anne. The Bargaining. 2015. (ENG., Illus.). 416p. (YA). (gr. 9). 17.99 *(978-1-4424-4182-8(8),* Simon Pulse) Simon Pulse.

West, Jacqueline. The Strangers. Bernatene, Poly, illus. 2013. (Books of Elsewhere Ser.: 4). (ENG.). 320p. (J). (gr. 5). 16.99 *(978-0-8037-3690-0(8),* Dial Bks) Penguin Young Readers Group.

Westerfeld, Scott. Horizon. 2017. (Horizon Ser.: 1). (ENG.). 256p. (J). (gr. 4-7). 16.99 ***(978-1-338-19658-0(8))*** Scholastic, Inc.

Westerfeld, Scott. So Yesterday. (ENG.). (YA). (gr. 7-12). 2004. 240p. 16.99 *(978-1-59514-000-5(X))* 2005. 256p. reprint ed. 8.99 *(978-1-59514-032-6(8))* Penguin Young Readers Group. (Razorbill).

Weston, Carrie. If a Chicken Stayed for Supper. Fatus, Sophie, illus. 2007. (ENG.). 32p. (J). (gr. -1-3). 16.95 *(978-0-8234-2067-4(1))* Holiday Hse., Inc.

Weston Woods Staff, creator. Children Make Terrible Pets. 2011. 29.95 *(978-0-545-40221-7(2))* Weston Woods Studios, Inc.

—Sylvester & the Magic Pebble. 2011. 38.75 *(978-0-439-72898-0(3));* 29.95 *(978-0-439-73522-3(X))* Weston Woods Studios, Inc.

Whaley, John Corey. Where Things Come Back. (ENG., Illus.). (YA). (gr. 9). 2012. 256p. pap. 11.99 *(978-1-4424-1334-4(4))* 2011. 240p. 16.99 *(978-1-4424-1333-7(6))* Simon & Schuster Children's Publishing. (Atheneum Bks. for Young Readers).

Whelan, Gloria. The Disappeared. 2010. (ENG.). 144p. (YA). (gr. 7-18). 6.99 *(978-0-14-241540-5(5),* Speak) Penguin Young Readers Group.

Wiggin, Kate Douglas. A Summer in a Canyon. 2007. 140p. 24.95 *(978-1-60312-626-7(0))* Aegypan.

Wilhelm, Hans. Little Whale in Deep Trouble: A Story Inspired by a True Event. 2017. (ENG., Illus.). 32p. (J). (gr. -1-2). 9.99 *(978-0-7641-6851-2(7))* Barron's Educational Series, Inc.

Willey, Margaret. Four Secrets. Hauser, Bill, illus. 2014. (ENG.). 288p. (YA). (gr. 7-12). pap. 9.95 *(978-1-4677-1626-0(X),* Carolrhoda Lab™) Lerner Publishing Group.

Williams, Geoffrey T. The Hammerheads of Treasure Island. 2010. (ENG., Illus.). 64p. (J). (gr. 3-7). 8.95 *(978-0-9800444-2-3(1))* Save Our Seas, Ltd.

Willis, Jeanne. Shamanka. 2009. (J). pap. *(978-0-7636-3767-5(X))* Candlewick Pr.

Wilson, Karma. Bear Feels Scared. Chapman, Jane, illus. 2011. (Bear Bks.). (ENG.). 34p. (J). (gr. -1 — 1). bds. 7.99 *(978-1-4424-2755-6(8),* Little Simon) Little Simon.

—Bear Feels Scared. Chapman, Jane, illus. 2008. (Bear Bks.). (ENG.). 40p. (J). (gr. -1-3). 17.99 *(978-0-689-85986-1(4),* McElderry, Margaret K. Bks.) McElderry, Margaret K. Bks.

Wilson, N. D. Leepike Ridge. 2008. (ENG., Illus.). 256p. (J). (gr. 3-7). 6.99 *(978-0-375-83874-3(0),* Yearling) Random Hse. Children's Bks.

Winget, Dianna Dorisi. A Million Ways Home. 2014. (ENG.). 272p. (J). (gr. 3-7). 16.99 *(978-0-545-66706-7(2),* Scholastic Pr.) Scholastic, Inc.

Wirt, Mildred A. Whispering Walls. 2011. 174p. pap. 9.99 *(978-1-935774-83-9(2),* Resurrected Pr.) Intrepid Ink, LLC.

Wright, Peter M. The Stone Prince, 1 vol. 2009. 48p. pap. 16.95 *(978-1-4489-2591-9(6))* America Star Bks.

Wunder, Wendy. The Museum of Intangible Things. 2015. (ENG.). 256p. (YA). (gr. 7). pap. 9.99 *(978-1-59514-576-5(1),* Razorbill) Penguin Young Readers Group.

Wundram, Bill. Finnius: The Tale of a Lost Little Elephant. Tucker, Eric, illus. 2003. (J). *(978-1-59152-011-5(8),* Sweetgrass Bks.) Farcountry Pr.

Yovanoff, Brenna. The Replacement. 2011. (ENG.). 368p. (YA). (gr. 7-18). 8.99 *(978-1-59514-381-5(5),* Razorbill) Penguin Young Readers Group.

—The Space Between. 2012. (ENG., Illus.). 384p. (YA). (gr. 9). pap. 8.99 *(978-1-59514-483-6(8),* Razorbill) Penguin Young Readers Group.

Yusuf. Butterfly & Bumble Bee: Adventure in Yellow Stone National Park. 2010. 16p. 8.49 *(978-1-4520-4022-6(2))* AuthorHouse.

Zadoff, Allen. I Am the Weapon. 2014. (Unknown Assassin Ser.: 1). (ENG.). 368p. (YA). (gr. 10-17). pap. 10.99 *(978-0-316-19967-4(2))* Little, Brown Bks. for Young Readers.

Zahler, Diane. A True Princess. (ENG.). (J). (gr. 3-7). 2012. 208p. pap. 6.99 *(978-0-06-182503-3(4))* 2011. 192p. 15.99 *(978-0-06-182501-9(8))* HarperCollins Pubs.

Zhang, Kat. The Emperor's Riddle. 2017. (ENG., Illus.). 256p. (J). (gr. 3-7). 16.99 ***(978-1-4814-7862-5(1),*** Aladdin) Simon & Schuster Children's Publishing.

Zucker, Jonny. Mission 6: Short Circuit. Woodman, Ned, illus. 2013. (Max Flash Ser.: 6). (ENG.). 144p. (gr. 2-5). pap. 7.95 *(978-1-4677-1480-8(1));* lib. bdg. 27.93 *(978-1-4677-1211-8(6))* Lerner Publishing Group. (Darby Creek).

4RV Publishing LLC Staff. Case of the Missing Coach. 2007. (Illus.). 144p. (J). per. 18.99 *(978-0-9797513-1-8(4))* 4RV Publishing, LLC.

MISSIONARIES

Anderson, Dick. African Adventures. 2006. (Adventure Ser.). (ENG., Illus.). 96p. (J). pap. 8.99 *(978-1-85792-807-5(5),* 2e344661-25c6-4013-85cc-e144ff35da6d) Christian Focus Pubns. GBR. Dist: Bookmasters Distribution.

Benge, Janet & Benge, Geoff. Christian Heroes - Then & Now - C. T. Studd: No Retreat. 2005. (Christian Heroes Ser.). (ENG., Illus.). 192p. (YA). (gr. 4-7). pap. 9.99 *(978-1-57658-288-6(4))* YWAM Publishing.

—Christian Heroes - Then & Now - Florence Young: Mission Accomplished. 2005. (Christian Heroes Ser.). (ENG.). 183p. (YA). (gr. 4-7). pap. 9.99 *(978-1-57658-313-5(9))* YWAM Publishing.

—Christian Heroes - Then & Now - Ida Scudder: Healing Bodies, Touching Hearts. 2003. (Christian Heroes Ser.). (ENG.). 189p. (YA). pap. 9.99 *(978-1-57658-285-5(X))* YWAM Publishing.

—Christian Heroes - Then & Now - Lillian Trasher: The Greatest Wonder in Egypt. 2003. (Christian Heroes Ser.). (ENG.). 190p. (YA). pap. 9.99 *(978-1-57658-305-0(8))* YWAM Publishing.

—Christian Heroes - Then & Now - Rowland Bingham: Into Africa's Interior. 2003. (Christian Heroes Ser.). (Illus.). 181p. per. 8.99 *(978-1-57658-282-4(5))* YWAM Publishing.

—Heroes Cristianos de Ayer de Hoy - Peripecia en China: La vida de Hudson Taylor. 2004.Tr. of Christian Heroes - Then & Now - Hudson Taylor. (SPA.). 208p. pap. 6.99 *(978-1-57658-260-2(4))* YWAM Publishing.

—Heroes Cristianos de Ayer y de Hoy - la Intrepida Rescatadora: Amy Carmichael. 2004.Tr. of Christian Heroes: Then & Now - Amy Carmichael. (SPA.). 208p. pap. 6.99 *(978-1-57658-309-8(0))* YWAM Publishing.

—Jacob Deshazer: Forgive Your Enemies. 2009. (ENG.). 224p. (YA). pap. 9.99 *(978-1-57658-475-0(5))* YWAM Publishing.

—Klaus-Dieter John: Hope in the Land of the Incas. 2014. (Illus.). 216p. (J). pap. 9.99 *(978-1-57658-755-3(X))* YWAM Publishing.

Bodden, Valerie. To the Heart of Africa. 2011. (Illus.). 48p. (J). 35.65 *(978-1-60818-066-0(2),* Creative Education) Creative Co., The.

Brother Andrew, et al. God's Smuggler. Foley, Tim, illus. 2017. (ENG.). 224p. (J). pap. 9.99 *(978-0-8007-9805-5(8))* Chosen Bks.

Called to Serve: Celebrating Missionary Work Around the World. 2014. (Illus.). 112p. pap. 15.99 *(978-1-62108-667-3(4))* Covenant Communications, Inc.

Caughey, Ellen. Eric Liddell: Gold Medal Missionary. 2006. (Heros of the Faith Ser.). 206p. (YA). (gr. 8-12). per. 2.97 *(978-1-59789-115-8(0))* Barbour Publishing, Inc.

Edwards, Andrew & Thornton, Fleur. William Carey: The Story of a Country Boy & Shoe Mender Whose Big Dreams Took Him to India. 2005. (Footsteps of the Past Ser.). (Illus.). 32p. pap. 5.00 *(978-1-84625-012-5(9))* DayOne Pubns. GBR. Dist: Send The Light Distribution LLC.

Fitzpatrick, Anne. Mother Teresa. 2005. (Genius Ser.). (Illus.). 48p. (J). (gr. 5-9). lib. bdg. 21.95 *(978-1-58341-330-2(8),* Creative Education) Creative Co., The.

Gigliotti, Jim & dePaola, Tomie. Who Was Mother Teresa? Harrison, Nancy, illus. 2015. (Who Was? Ser.). (ENG.). 112p. (J). (gr. 3-7). 5.99 *(978-0-448-48299-6(1),* Grosset & Dunlap) Penguin Young Readers Group.

Glavich, Mary Kathleen. Blessed Teresa of Calcutta: Missionary of Charity. Kiwak, Barbara, tr. Kiwak, Barbara, illus. 2003. (Encounter the Saints Ser.: Vol. 17). 136p. (J). pap. 7.95 *(978-0-8198-1160-8(2),* 332-024) Pauline Bks. & Media.

Haluska, David. Jesus Loves Trucks. Ford, Emily, illus. 2014. 32p. (J). 7.99 *(978-0-8280-2719-9(6))* Review & Herald Publishing Assn.

Harkins, Susan Sales & Harkins, William H. The Life & Times of Father Jacques Marquette. 2008. (Profiles in American History Ser.). (Illus.). 48p. (J). (gr. 4-8). lib. bdg. 29.95 *(978-1-58415-528-7(0))* Mitchell Lane Pubs., Inc.

M
N
O

Harness, Cheryl. The Tragic Tale of Narcissa Whitman & a Faithful History of the Oregon Trail. Harness, Cheryl, illus. 2006. (Cheryl Harness Histories Ser.). (ENG., Illus.). 144p. (J). (gr. 5-9). 16.95 *(978-0-7922-5920-6(3)*, National Geographic Children's Bks.) National Geographic Society.

Harrison, Paul. Mother Teresa. 2017. (ENG., Illus.). 32p. (J). (gr. 4-6). pap. 6.99 *(978-0-7502-9877-3(4)*, Wayland) Hachette Children's Group GBR. Dist: Hachette Bk. Group.

Howat, Irene. James Chalmers: The Rainmaker's Friend. 2006. (Torchbearers Ser.). (ENG., Illus.). 160p. (J). (gr. 4-7). per. 8.99 *(978-1-84550-154-9(3)*, 46847407-f773-4975-8670-3794f74a682d) Christian Focus Pubns. GBR. Dist: Bookmasters Distribution.

—Jim Elliot: He Is No Fool... 2013. (Torchbearers Ser.). (ENG., Illus.). 160p. (J). per. 8.99 *(978-1-84550-064-1(4)*, a4eb1307-0211-43b6-b3a6-2e9f0acf080d) Christian Focus Pubns. GBR. Dist: Bookmasters Distribution.

Ishkanian, Charlotte. Best Ever Mission Stories: Kids in Action Around the World. 2008. (J). 5.97 *(978-0-8163-2263-3(5))* Pacific Pr. Publishing Assn.

Jay, Ruth Johnson. Mary Slessor: Missionary to Calabar. 2006. (Illus.). 143p. (J). *(978-1-56265-077-3(7))* Accelerated Christian Education, Inc.

Kelly, Terri B. Mary Slessor: Missionary Mother. 2014. (Illus.). 164p. (J). *(978-1-60682-630-0(1))* BJU Pr.

Kidder, Tracy. Mountains Beyond Mountains (Adapted for Young People) The Quest of Dr. Paul Farmer, a Man Who Would Cure the World. 2014. (ENG.). (YA). (gr. 7). lib. bdg. 19.60 ***(978-1-68065-029-7(7))*** Perfection Learning Corp.

Kidder, Tracy & French, Michael. Mountains Beyond Mountains (Adapted for Young People) The Quest of Dr. Paul Farmer, a Man Who Would Cure the World. 2014. (ENG.). 288p. (YA). (gr. 7). pap. 9.99 *(978-0-385-74319-8(X)*, Ember) Random Hse. Children's Bks.

Klaus, Sandra. Surrounded by Headhunters. Date not set. (ARA.). (J). (gr. 2-7). pap. *(978-1-890940-03-4(8))* Gospel Missionary Union.

Langley, Judy. God's World & Me from A to Z. Coker, Carla, illus. 2004. 32p. (gr. -1). 8.99 *(978-1-56309-367-8(7))* New Hope Pubs.

Leidenfrost, Lisa. At the Edge of the Village: Musings of a Missionary Wife. 2004. Orig. Title: African Sketches. (ENG., Illus.). 212p. (YA). pap. 17.00 *(978-1-59128-017-0(6))* Canon Pr.

MacKenzie, Catherine. Amy Carmichael - Can Brown Eyes Be Made Blue? Ammassari, Rita, illus. 2011. (Little Lights Ser.). (ENG.). 24p. (J). (gr. -1-2). 7.99 *(978-1-84550-108-2(X)*, 91ca3a79-be4d-488e-9c3f-283c9f77bf68) Christian Focus Pubns. GBR. Dist: Bookmasters Distribution.

—Could Somebody Pass the Salt? Ammassari, Rita, illus. 2012. (Little Lights Ser.). (ENG.). 24p. (J). (gr. 4-7). 7.99 *(978-1-84550-111-2(X)*, fc99de78-abc4-46d1-ad2d-579b7f21235e) Christian Focus Pubns. GBR. Dist: Bookmasters Distribution.

Martin, Mildred A. Missionary Stories with the Millers. Burkholder, Edith, illus. 2009. 208p. (J). *(978-1-884377-17-4(3))*; pap. *(978-1-884377-16-7(5))* Green Pastures Pr.

Mattews, Basil. Livingstone: The Pathfinder. 2003. (ENG.). 112p. (YA). pap. 9.95 *(978-0-923309-86-2(1))* Hartland Pubns.

McNeil, Niki, et al. HOCPP 1096 Missionaries to Know. 2006. spiral bd. 21.00 *(978-1-60308-096-5(1))* In the Hands of a Child.

Meloche, Renee. Heroes for Young Readers - Hudson Taylor: Friend of China. Pollard, Bryan, illus. 2004. (ENG.). 32p. (J). 8.99 *(978-1-57658-234-3(5))* YWAM Publishing.

Miller, William. Tales of Persia: Missionary Stories from Islamic Iran. Van Patten, Bruce, illus. 2005. 163p. per. 9.99 *(978-0-87552-615-7(2))* P & R Publishing.

Nelson, Robin. Mother Teresa: A Life of Caring. (Pull Ahead Books-Biographies Ser.). (Illus.). 32p. 2007. (ENG.). (gr. k-3). pap. 7.95 *(978-0-8225-6433-1(5))* 2006. (J). (gr. 3-7). lib. bdg. 22.60 *(978-0-8225-6384-6(3)*, Lerner Pubns.) Lerner Publishing Group.

Otfinoski, Steven. David Livingstone: Deep in the Heart of Africa. 2006. (Great Explorations Ser.). (Illus.). 79p. (J). (gr. 3-7). lib. bdg. 32.79 *(978-0-7614-2226-6(9)*, Benchmark Bks.) Marshall Cavendish Corp.

Petrie, Kristin. Marquette & Jolliet, 1 vol. 2007. (Explorers Set 2 Ser.). (ENG., Illus.). 32p. (gr. 4-7). 27.07 *(978-1-59679-745-1(2)*, Checkerboard Library) ABDO Publishing Co.

Reymond, Robert L. Paul, Missionary Theologian: A Survey of His Missionary Labours & Theology. 2006. (ENG., Illus.). 640p. 29.99 *(978-1-85792-497-8(5)*, 4f6c4fe5-c6c9-413f-b275-d3a21f0ca0b0, Mentor) Christian Focus Pubns. GBR. Dist: Bookmasters Distribution.

Robinson, Virgil E. Curse of the Cannibals. 2011. (Illus.). 126p. per. 11.95 *(978-1-57258-355-9(X))* TEACH Services, Inc.

Slavicek, Louise Chipley. Mother Teresa: Caring for the World's Poor. 2007. (Modern Peacemakers Ser.). (Illus.). 113p. (YA). (gr. 9-12). lib. bdg. 30.00 *(978-0-7910-9433-4(2))* Facts On File, Inc.

Sullivan, Anne Marie. Mother Teresa: Religious Humanitarian. 2013. (People of Importance Ser.: 21). (Illus.). 32p. (J). (gr. 4-18). 19.95 *(978-1-4222-2853-1(3))* Mason Crest.

—Mother Theresa: Religious Humanitarian. 2004. (Great Names Ser.). (Illus.). 32p. (J). (gr. 3-18). lib. bdg. 19.95 *(978-1-59084-142-6(5))* Mason Crest.

Tan, Joyce. Finding the Lord's ELect: How Missionaries can Tract Fruitfully. 2004. per. 12.95 *(978-0-9746016-0-1(8))* Eclectic Dragon Pr.

Toliver, Gwen. Seed Sowers: Gospel-Planting Adventures. 2012. 180p. (gr. -1). 30.95 *(978-1-4497-7132-4(7))*; pap. 13.95 *(978-1-4497-7130-0(0))* Author Solutions, Inc. (WestBow Pr.).

Valentine, Emily. Mother Teresa: With a Discussion of Compassion. 2004. (Values in Action Ser.). (J). *(978-1-59203-070-5(X))* Learning Challenge, Inc.

Vogel, Cara Lynn. The Lottie & Annie Upside-down Book. Adkins, Loretta B., illus. 2003. 16p. (J). 8.99 *(978-1-56309-627-3(7))* Woman's Missionary Union.

Walsh, Kay. John Paton - South Sea Island Rescue. 2005. (Trailblazers Ser.). (ENG.). 160p. (J). mass mkt. 8.99 *(978-1-85792-852-5(0)*, 19477cb3-06d2-420c-a2a4-07fe90bdf166) Christian Focus Pubns. GBR. Dist: Bookmasters Distribution.

Wilder, M. L. Missionary Annuls: Memoir of Robert Moffat. 2003. (ENG.). 64p. (YA). pap. 8.95 *(978-0-923309-88-6(8))* Hartland Pubns.

Williams, Laura E. Father Damien. Kofsky, Kristen, illus. 2009. (ENG.). 60p. (J). (gr. 4). pap. *(978-1-59700-757-3(9))* Island Heritage Publishing.

MISSIONARIES—FICTION

Allison, Carol. Missionary Adventures: Stories for Boys & Girls. 2011. 94p. 38.95 *(978-1-258-08225-3(X))* Literary Licensing, LLC.

Bruner, Roger & Bruner, Kristi Rae. Found in Translation: An Unforgettable Mission Trip Where Faith, Obedience, & Forgiveness Intersect. 2011. (Altered Hearts Ser.: 1). (ENG.). 368p. (YA). (gr. 9-12). pap. 9.99 *(978-1-60260-961-7(6)*, Barbour Bks.) Barbour Publishing, Inc.

The Captain, His Daughter, & Their Discovery. 2007. 48p. pap. 6.50 *(978-0-8341-2296-3(0)*, 083-412-2960) Beacon Hill Pr. of Kansas City.

The Case of the Secret Box. 2007. 56p. pap. 7.75 *(978-0-8341-2288-8(X)*, 083-412-288X) Beacon Hill Pr. of Kansas City.

Eareckson Tada, Joni & Jensen, Steve. The Mission Adventure. 2005. (Darcy & Friends Ser.). 143p. (gr. 3-6). pap. 5.99 *(978-1-58134-257-4(8)*, Crossway Bibles) Crossway.

Eby, Wes. Jungle Jeopardy. 2006. 56p. 7.75 *(978-0-8341-2228-4(6))* Beacon Hill Pr. of Kansas City.

Forbes, Dillon. Careful Enough? 2008. (YA). 8.99 *(978-1-59166-835-0(2))* BJU Pr.

Haislip, Phyllis Hall. Lottie's Courage: A Contraband Slave's Story. 2003. (Illus.). 120p. (J). pap. 7.95 *(978-1-57249-311-7(9)*, White Mane Kids) White Mane Publishing Co., Inc.

Hardy, LeAnne. Between Two Worlds: A Novel. 2003. 160p. (J). pap. 7.99 *(978-0-8254-2793-0(2))* Kregel Pubns.

Hering, Marianne. In Fear of the Spear. 2016. (AIO Imagination Station Bks.: 17). (ENG.). 144p. (J). pap. 4.99 *(978-1-58997-804-1(8))* Focus on the Family Publishing.

Howat, Irene. On His Majesty's Service. 2008. (Trailblazers Ser.). (ENG.). 176p. (J). (gr. 4-9). per. 8.99 *(978-1-84550-259-1(0)*, bea45fc4-969e-4e89-84fe-2abf3d4baa6d) Christian Focus Pubns. GBR. Dist: Bookmasters Distribution.

Hudson, Bonnie Rose. The Hidden Village. 2017. (J). ***(978-1-62856-311-5(7))*** BJU Pr.

MacKenzie, Catherine. Gladys Aylward - Are You Going to Stop? 2013. (Little Lights Ser.). (ENG., Illus.). 24p. (J). 7.99 *(978-1-78191-161-7(4)*, cfd6d604-97c6-4c41-889d-ab61929b782a) Christian Focus Pubns. GBR. Dist: Bookmasters Distribution.

McHugh, Michael. Giant of the Western Trail: Father Peter de Smet. Dougherty, Charles L., illus. 2011. 186p. 42.95 *(978-1-258-05887-6(1))* Literary Licensing, LLC.

Moffett, Slyvia. The Missionary Kids Adventure Series: Bo. 2006. 48p. pap. 16.95 *(978-1-4241-2854-9(4))* PublishAmerica, Inc.

Nogar, Anna M. & Lamadrid, Enrique R. Sisters in Blue: Sor María de Ágreda Comes to New Mexico = Hermanas de Azul: Sor María de Ágreda Viene a Nuevo México. Córdova, Amy, illus. 2017. (SPA & ENG.). 88p. (J). ***(978-0-8263-5821-9(7))*** Univ. of New Mexico Pr.

Palmer, Viola. The Man in the Green Jeep. 2006. (ENG.). 144p. pap. *(978-0-929292-61-8(8)*, 800-747-0738) Hannibal Bks.

Riordan, Robert. Medicine for Wildcat: A Story of the Friendship between a Menominee Indian & Frontier Priest Samuel Mazzuchelli. 2006. (Illus.). 132p. (YA). per. 14.95 *(978-0-9774934-0-1(7))* Sinsinawa Dominicans, Inc.

Singleton, Linda Joy. Melissa's Mission Impossible/Mail Order Monster: Twin Spins. 2005. (Twin Spins Ser.: 10). (ENG.). 168p. (YA). per. 10.95 *(978-0-7599-1009-6(X))* Hard Shell Word Factory.

Smith, Robert F. Bitten: A Romantic Comedy. 2008. (YA). pap. *(978-1-59038-904-1(2))* Deseret Bk. Co.

Snowballs & Coconuts. 2006. 56p. pap. 7.75 *(978-0-8341-2295-6(2)*, 083-412-2952) Beacon Hill Pr. of Kansas City.

St. John, Patricia. Secret of the Fourth Candle. rev. ed. 2003. (Illus.). 94p. 6.49 *(978-1-85999-511-2(X))* Scripture Union GBR. Dist: Gabriel Resources.

Stewart, Jennifer J. Close Encounters of a Third World Kind. 2004. (ENG.). 128p. (J). (gr. 4-6). tchr. ed. 16.95 *(978-0-8234-1850-3(2))* Holiday Hse., Inc.

—Close Encounters of a Third-World Kind. 2008. (ENG., Illus.). 181p. (J). (gr. 3-7). 6.95 *(978-0-8234-2161-9(9))* Holiday Hse., Inc.

White, Paul. Jungle Doctor Looks for Trouble. 2009. (Flamingo Fiction 9-13s Ser.). (ENG., Illus.). 160p. (J). pap. 8.99 *(978-1-84550-499-1(2)*, 9302ad19-8b28-4030-be88-ef9afc9f3a6c) Christian Focus Pubns. GBR. Dist: Bookmasters Distribution.

—Jungle Doctor Operates. 2009. (Flamingo Fiction 9-13s Ser.). (ENG., Illus.). 160p. (J). pap. 8.99 *(978-1-84550-500-4(X)*, 5b5acc8e-b6fe-4477-b9ac-b1a8ea9426ea) Christian Focus Pubns. GBR. Dist: Bookmasters Distribution.

—Jungle Doctor to the Rescue. 2009. (Flamingo Fiction 9-13s Ser.). (ENG., Illus.). 176p. (J). pap. 8.99 *(978-1-84550-516-5(6)*, 052662e3-f01a-4a40-9e4d-88634018ee06) Christian Focus Pubns. GBR. Dist: Bookmasters Distribution.

Williamson, Denise J. River of Danger. 2008. (J). 8.99 *(978-1-59166-854-1(9))* BJU Pr.

—Silent Road to Rescue. 2008. (J). 8.99 *(978-1-59166-852-7(2))* BJU Pr.

Wilson, Heather Gemmen. Lydia Barnes & the Blood Diamond Treasure. 2007. (Global Warning Ser.). 159p. (J). (gr. 3-7). per. 7.99 *(978-0-89827-350-2(1))* Wesleyan Publishing Hse.

—Lydia Barnes & the Escape from Shark Bay. 2008. 160p. (J). 9.99 *(978-0-89827-352-6(8))* Wesleyan Publishing Hse.

Youngberg, Norma R. Jungle Thorn. 2010. (Illus.). 132p. reprint ed. per. 11.95 *(978-1-57258-157-9(3)*, 945-6024) TEACH Services, Inc.

Zaugg, Sandra L. Hidden Notes & High Seas. 2005. (Illus.). 95p. (J). *(978-0-8163-2052-3(7))* Pacific Pr. Pubns.

—The Man in the Blue Skirt. 2005. (Illus.). 95p. (J). pap. *(978-0-8163-2055-4(1))* Pacific Pr. Pubns.

—A Prayer for Mother. 2005. (Illus.). 95p. (J). *(978-0-8163-2056-1(X))* Pacific Pr. Pubns.

MISSIONS

see also Missionaries

also names of churches, denominations, religious orders, etc. with the subdivision Missions, e.g. Catholic Church—Missions; etc.

Abbink, Emily. Monterey Bay Area Missions. 2007. (Exploring California Missions Ser.). (ENG., Illus.). 64p. (gr. 4-7). lib. bdg. 27.93 *(978-0-8225-0887-8(7)*, Lerner Pubns.) Lerner Publishing Group.

Anderson, Zachary. Discovering Mission Nuestra Señora de la Soledad. 2014. (California Missions Ser.). 48p. (J). (gr. 4-6). 31.36 *(978-1-62713-079-0(9))* Cavendish Square Publishing.

Arnéz, Lynda. Father Junipero Serra: Founder of the California Missions. 2015. (Exceptional Latinos Ser.). (ENG.). 24p. (J). (gr. 3-4). pap. 9.35 *(978-0-7660-6710-3(6))* Enslow Pubs., Inc.

Behrens, June. Central Coast Missions in California. 2007. (Exploring California Missions Ser.). (Illus.). 64p. (J). lib. bdg. 27.93 *(978-0-8225-0897-7(4)*, Lerner Pubns.) Lerner Publishing Group.

Benge, Janet & Benge, Geoff. Christian Heroes - Then & Now - Rowland Bingham: Into Africa's Interior. 2003. (Christian Heroes Ser.). (Illus.). 181p. per. 8.99 *(978-1-57658-282-4(5))* YWAM Publishing.

Bert, Ruth J. Everyone Called Her Sister Sarah. Westbeld, Kristine, illus. 2004. (ENG.). 32p. (J). (gr. -1-3). pap. 4.99 *(978-1-928915-62-1(0))* Evangel Publishing Hse.

Blackwell, Jodi. Fundamentals: Secret Mission Children's Pack. (J). (gr. 1-6). *(978-0-633-05795-4(9))* LifeWay Christian Resources.

Brother Andrew, et al. God's Smuggler. Foley, Tim, illus. 2017. (ENG.). 224p. (J). pap. 9.99 *(978-0-8007-9805-5(8))* Chosen Bks.

Brower, Pauline. Inland Valleys Missions in California. 2007. (Exploring California Missions Ser.). (ENG., Illus.). 64p. (gr. 4-7). lib. bdg. 27.93 *(978-0-8225-0899-1(0)*, Lerner Pubns.) Lerner Publishing Group.

Ching, Jacqueline. Mission San Fernando Rey de Espana. 2004. (Missions of California Ser.). 64p. (J). lib. bdg. 26.50 *(978-0-8239-5893-1(0)*, PowerKids Pr.) Rosen Publishing Group, Inc., The.

—Mission San Rafael Arcangel. 2003. (Missions of California Ser.). 64p. (J). 26.50 *(978-0-8239-5886-3(8)*, PowerKids Pr.) Rosen Publishing Group, Inc., The.

—Mission Santa Ines. (Missions of California Ser.). 64p. 2009. (gr. 4-4). 58.50 *(978-1-60854-042-6(1))* 2004. (J). lib. bdg. 26.50 *(978-0-8239-5894-8(9))* Rosen Publishing Group, Inc., The. (PowerKids Pr.).

Crouch, Cheryl. Trouble in East Timor. 2010. (Illus.). 56p. (J). *(978-0-8341-2488-2(2))* Beacon Hill Pr. of Kansas City.

Draper, Allison Stark. Mission San Fransisco de Solano. 2003. (Missions of Californiatm Ser.). (Illus.). 64p. (J). (gr. 4-18). 26.50 *(978-0-8239-5884-9(1))* Rosen Publishing Group, Inc., The.

—Mission San Juan Bautista. 2004. (Missions of California Ser.). 64p. (J). lib. bdg. 26.50 *(978-0-8239-5879-5(5)*, PowerKids Pr.) Rosen Publishing Group, Inc., The.

Eby, Wes. Coban Treasure Hunt. 2010. (Illus.). 56p. (J). *(978-0-8341-2489-9(0))* Beacon Hill Pr. of Kansas City.

Edgar, Kathleen J. & Edgar, Susan E. Mission San Carlos Borromeo Del Rio Carmelo. 2003. (Missions of Californiatm Ser.). (Illus.). 64p. (YA). (gr. 4-7). 26.50 *(978-0-8239-5890-0(6))* Rosen Publishing Group, Inc., The.

—Mission San Diego de Alcala. 2004. (Missions of California Ser.). 64p. (J). lib. bdg. 26.50 *(978-0-8239-5885-6(X)*, PowerKids Pr.) Rosen Publishing Group, Inc., The.

—Mission San Francisco de Asis. 2003. (Missions of Californiatm Ser.). (Illus.). 64p. (J). (gr. 4-18). 26.50 *(978-0-8239-5887-0(6))* Rosen Publishing Group, Inc., The.

—Mission San Miguel Arcangel. 2004. (Missions of California Ser.). 64p. (J). lib. bdg. 26.50 *(978-0-8239-5896-2(5)*, PowerKids Pr.) Rosen Publishing Group, Inc., The.

Gendell, Megan. Spanish Missions of California. 2010. (True Book(tm), a — Spanish Missions Ser.). (Illus.). 48p. (J). (gr. 2-5). 31.00 *(978-0-531-20577-8(0))* Scholastic Library Publishing.

—The Spanish Missions of California. 2010. (True Book Ser.). (ENG.). 48p. (J). (gr. 3-5). pap. 6.95 *(978-0-531-21240-0(8)*, Children's Pr.) Scholastic Library Publishing.

—The Spanish Missions of Texas. 2010. (True Book(tm), a — Spanish Missions Ser.). (ENG.). 48p. (J). (gr. 2-5). 31.00 *(978-0-531-20580-8(0))*; (Illus.). pap. 6.95 *(978-0-531-21243-1(2))* Scholastic Library Publishing.

Grate, Gina. Project Noah. 2006. 32p. 4.50 *(978-0-8341-2231-4(6))* Nazarene Publishing Hse.

Haluska, David. Jesus Loves Trucks. Ford, Emily, illus. 2014. 32p. (J). 7.99 *(978-0-8280-2719-9(6))* Review & Herald Publishing Assn.

Hare, Eric B. Jungle Heroes & Other Stories. 2005. (Illus.). 106p. (J). 9.99 *(978-0-8163-2063-9(2))* Pacific Pr. Publishing Assn.

Herrera, Matthew D. History Guide to Old Mission San Luis Obispo de Tolosa. 2003. (Illus.). 77p. 9.95 *(978-0-9723720-1-5(6))* Tixlini Scriptorium, Inc.

Jingling, Kathy, ed. Bernabe y su Gran Mision por Cristo. Oyola, Milta, tr. from ENG. Tobar, Malena, illus. 2011.Tr. of Barnabas & his Great Mission for Christ. (SPA.). 191p. (J). spiral bd. 7.00 *(978-1-931984-41-6(7)*, 2002-00S1) Faith & Action Team.

Langley, Judy. God's World & Me from A to Z. Coker, Carla, illus. 2004. 32p. (gr. -1). 8.99 *(978-1-56309-367-8(7))* New Hope Pubs.

Lemke, Nancy. Southern Coast Missions in California. 2007. (Exploring California Missions Ser.). (ENG., Illus.). 64p. (gr. 4-7). lib. bdg. 27.93 *(978-0-8225-1935-5(6)*, Lerner Pubns.) Lerner Publishing Group.

Lilly, Melinda. Misiones Espanolas (Spanish Missions) Capaldi, Gina, illus. 2005. (Lecturas Historicas Norteamericanas (Reading American Histor Ser.). 24p. (J). (gr. 3-7). lib. bdg. 22.79 *(978-1-59515-638-9(0))* Rourke Educational Media.

Lyon, Robin. The Spanish Missions of Arizona. 2010. (True Book(tm), a — Spanish Missions Ser.). 48p. (J). (gr. 2-5). 31.00 *(978-0-531-20576-1(2))*; (ENG.). pap. 6.95 *(978-0-531-21239-4(4))* Scholastic Library Publishing.

—Spanish Missions of New Mexico. 2010. (True Book(tm), a — Spanish Missions Ser.). (ENG.). 48p. (J). (gr. 2-5). 31.00 *(978-0-531-20579-2(7))* Scholastic Library Publishing.

—The Spanish Missions of New Mexico. 2010. (True Book Ser.). (ENG.). 48p. (J). pap. 6.95 *(978-0-531-21242-4(4)*, Children's Pr.) Scholastic Library Publishing.

MacMillan, Dianne M. Los Angeles Area Missions. 2007. (Exploring California Missions Ser.). (Illus.). 64p. (J). lib. bdg. 27.93 *(978-0-8225-0898-4(2)*, Lerner Pubns.) Lerner Publishing Group.

Margaret, Amy. Mission San Buenaventura. 2003. (Missions of Californiatm Ser.). (Illus.). 64p. (J). (gr. 4-18). 26.50 *(978-0-8239-5888-7(4))* Rosen Publishing Group, Inc., The.

—Mission San Jose de Guadalupe. 2004. (Missions of California Ser.). 64p. (J). lib. bdg. 26.50 *(978-0-8239-5897-9(3)*, PowerKids Pr.) Rosen Publishing Group, Inc., The.

—Mission Santa Barbara. (Missions of California Ser.). 64p. (gr. 4-4). 2009. 58.50 *(978-1-60854-037-2(5)*, PowerKids Pr.) 2003. (Illus.). (J). 26.50 *(978-0-8239-5880-1(9))* Rosen Publishing Group, Inc., The.

—Mission Santa Clara de Asis. (Missions of California Ser.). 64p. (gr. 4-4). 2009. 58.50 *(978-1-60854-038-9(3)*, PowerKids Pr.) 2003. (Illus.). (J). 26.50 *(978-0-8239-5883-2(3))* Rosen Publishing Group, Inc., The.

Margaret, Amy & Nuñes, Sofia. Discovering Mission Santa Clara de Asis. 2014. (California Missions Ser.). (Illus.). 48p. (J). (gr. 4-6). lib. bdg. 31.36 *(978-1-62713-067-7(5))* Cavendish Square Publishing.

McGinty, Alice B. Mission San Gabriel Arcangel. 2003. (Missions of Californiatm Ser.). (Illus.). 64p. (J). (gr. 4-18). 26.50 *(978-0-8239-5892-4(2))* Rosen Publishing Group, Inc., The.

La Mision (The Mission) Quarter 2, Level 3. (Caminando con Jesus (Walking with Jesus) Series A). (SPA.). (J). stu. ed. 3.50 *(978-0-570-05150-3(9))* Concordia Publishing Hse.

Munson, Jared. Courageous Witness: A Teenager Shares Jesus. 2003. (ENG., Illus.). 88p. pap. 8.95 *(978-0-8309-1069-4(7))* Herald Publishing Hse.

Nelson, Libby. California Missions Projects & Layouts. 2007. (Exploring California Missions Ser.). (Illus.). 112p. (J). lib. bdg. 27.93 *(978-0-8225-7950-2(2)*, Lerner Pubns.) Lerner Publishing Group.

Nussbaum, Ben. Junipero Serra: A Spanish Missionary. 2017. (Primary Source Readers Ser.). (Illus.). 32p. (gr. 4-4). 9.99 ***(978-1-4258-3235-3(0))*** Teacher Created Materials, Inc.

Ostrow, Kim. Mission Nuestra Senora de la Soledad. 2003. (Missions of Californiatm Ser.). (Illus.). 64p. (J). (gr. 4-18). 26.50 *(978-0-8239-5882-5(5))* Rosen Publishing Group, Inc., The.

—Mission Santa Cruz. (Missions of California Ser.). 64p. 2009. (gr. 4-4). 58.50 *(978-1-60854-041-9(3))* 2004. (J). lib. bdg. 26.50 *(978-0-8239-5878-8(7))* Rosen Publishing Group, Inc., The. (PowerKids Pr.).

Ostrow, Kim & Nuñes, Sofia. Discovering Mission Santa Cruz. 2014. (California Missions Ser.). (Illus.). 48p. (J). (gr. 4-6). lib. bdg. 31.36 *(978-1-62713-070-7(5))* Cavendish Square Publishing.

Peckham, Lori. Guide's Greatest Mission Stories. 2009. (J). *(978-0-8280-2501-0(0))* Review & Herald Publishing Assn.

People of the California Missions. (Illus.). (J). (gr. k-5). 151.50 *(978-0-8239-7263-0(1))* Rosen Publishing Group, Inc., The.

Perritano, John. Spanish Missions. 2010. (True Book(tm), a — Spanish Missions Ser.). (Illus.). 48p. (J). (gr. 2-5). 31.00 *(978-0-531-20575-4(4))*; pap. 6.95 *(978-0-531-21238-7(6))* Scholastic Library Publishing.

Price, Matt. The Mystery of the Ancient Anchor. Ettinger, Dorris, illus. 2010. 56p. (J). *(978-0-8341-2490-5(4))* Beacon Hill Pr. of Kansas City.

Primeros pasitos misioneros (First Steps, Spanish) 2004. pap. 12.99 *(978-1-56309-930-4(6))* Woman's Missionary Union.

Quantrell, Angie. I Can Do It! Lollar, Cathy, illus. 2003. 9.99 *(978-1-56309-626-6(9))* Woman's Missionary Union.

Quasha, Jennifer. Mission San Luis Rey de Francia. 2004. (Missions of California Ser.). 64p. (J). lib. bdg. 26.50 *(978-0-8239-5895-5(7)*, PowerKids Pr.) Rosen Publishing Group, Inc., The.

Roberts, Helen M. Miguel & the Pirates: A Tale of Mission Santa Cruz. Lawrence, Muriel, illus. 2011. 28p. 35.95 *(978-1-258-02882-4(4))* Literary Licensing, LLC.

Serafin, Kim. Mission San Antonio de Padua. 2003. (Missions of Californiatm Ser.). (Illus.). 64p. (J). (gr. 4-18). 26.50 *(978-0-8239-5891-7(4))* Rosen Publishing Group, Inc., The.

Suben, Eric. The Spanish Missions of Florida. 2010. (True Book(tm), a — Spanish Missions Ser.). 48p. (J). (gr. 2-5). 31.00 *(978-0-531-20578-5(9))*; (gr. 3-5). pap. 6.95 *(978-0-531-21241-7(6))* Scholastic Library Publishing.

Swinford, Betty. Missionary Stories from Around the World. 2005. (ENG., Illus.). 187p. (J). (gr. 4-7). per. 9.99 *(978-1-84550-042-9(3)*, Christian Focus) Christian Focus Pubns. GBR. Dist: Send The Light Distribution LLC.

Thompson, Gare. When the Mission Padre Came to the Rancho: The Early California Adventures of Rosalinda & Simon Delgado. 2004. (I Am American Ser.). (ENG., Illus.). 40p. (J). (gr. 3-7). pap. 6.99 *(978-0-7922-6945-8(4)*, National Geographic Children's Bks.) National Geographic Society.

Thompson, Gare & National Geographic Learning Staff. Missions & Ranchos. 2007. (Reading Expeditions Ser.). (ENG., Illus.). 40p. (J). pap. 19.95 *(978-0-7922-4548-3(2))* CENGAGE Learning.

Weber, Matt. California's Missions: From A to Z. 2010. (ENG.). 60p. (J). (gr. 2-4). 12.95 *(978-0-9841931-9-6(7))* 121 Pubns.

White, Tekla. San Francisco Bay Area Missions. 2007. (Exploring California Missions Ser.). (ENG., Illus.). 64p. (gr. 4-7). lib. bdg. 27.93 *(978-0-8225-0900-4(8)*, Lerner Pubns.) Lerner Publishing Group.

Williams, Jack S. Indians of the California Mission Frontier. 2009. (People of the California Missions Ser.). 64p. (gr. 4-4). 58.50 *(978-1-60851-157-0(X)*, PowerKids Pr.) Rosen Publishing Group, Inc., The.

—Padres of the California Mission Frontier. 2009. (People of the California Missions Ser.). 64p. (gr. 4-4). 58.50 *(978-1-60851-158-7(8)*, PowerKids Pr.) Rosen Publishing Group, Inc., The.

—Sailors, Merchants, & Muleteers of the California Mission Frontier. 2009. (People of the California Missions Ser.). 64p. (gr. 4-4). 58.50 *(978-1-60851-159-4(6),* PowerKids Pr.) Rosen Publishing Group, Inc., The.

—Soldiers & Their Families of the California Mission Frontier. 2009. (People of the California Missions Ser.). 64p. (gr. 4-4). 58.50 *(978-1-60851-160-0(X),* PowerKids Pr.) Rosen Publishing Group, Inc., The.

—Townspeople & Ranchers of the California Mission Frontier. 2009. (People of the California Missions Ser.). 64p. (gr. 4-4). 58.50 *(978-1-60851-161-7(8),* PowerKids Pr.) Rosen Publishing Group, Inc., The.

Williams, Jack S. & Davis, Thomas L. Padres of the California Mission Frontier. 2004. (People of the California Missions Ser.). (Illus.). 64p. (J). lib. bdg. 26.50 *(978-0-8239-6283-9(0),* PowerKids Pr.) Rosen Publishing Group, Inc., The.

—Soldiers & Their Families of the California Mission Frontier. 2004. (People of the California Missions Ser.). (Illus.). 64p. (J). lib. bdg. 26.50 *(978-0-8239-6285-3(7))* Rosen Publishing Group, Inc., The.

—Townspeople & Ranchers of the California Mission Frontier. 2004. (People of the California Missions Ser.). (Illus.). 64p. (J). lib. bdg. 26.50 *(978-0-8239-6284-6(9),* PowerKids Pr.) Rosen Publishing Group, Inc., The.

Williamson, Nancy. 52 Ways to Teach Missions. 2004. (Fifty-Two Ways Ser.). (Illus.). 64p. (J). (gr. -1-7). pap. 9.95 *(978-0-937282-67-0(7),* RB36169) Rainbow Pubs. & Legacy Pr.

WorldVenture 1 Activity Book for Girls in Action Grade 1. 2004. pap. 4.99 *(978-1-56309-628-0(5))* Woman's Missionary Union.

WorldVenture 2 Activity Book for Girls in Action Grade 2. 2003. pap. 4.99 *(978-1-56309-629-7(3))* Woman's Missionary Union.

WorldVenture 3 Activity Book for Girls in Action Grade 3. 2003. pap. 4.99 *(978-1-56309-630-3(7))* Woman's Missionary Union.

WorldVenture 4 Activity Book for Girls in Action Grade 4. 2003. pap. 4.99 *(978-1-56309-631-0(5))* Woman's Missionary Union.

WorldVenture 5 Activity Book for Girls in Action Grade 5. 2003. pap. 4.99 *(978-1-56309-632-7(3))* Woman's Missionary Union.

WorldVenture 6 Activity Book for Girls in Action Grade 6. 2003. pap. 4.99 *(978-1-56309-633-4(1))* Woman's Missionary Union.

WorldVenture Guide for Leaders of Grades 1-6. 2003. pap. 8.99 *(978-1-56309-634-1(X))* Woman's Missionary Union.

MISSISSIPPI

Brown, Jonatha A. & Ruffin, Frances E. Mississippi. 2006. (Portraits of the States Ser.). (Illus.). 32p. (gr. 2-6). pap. 10.50 *(978-0-8368-4689-8(3));* lib. bdg. 26.00 *(978-0-8368-4670-6(2))* Stevens, Gareth Publishing LLLP. (Gareth Stevens Learning Library).

Brown, Vanessa. Mississippi. 2009. (Bilingual Library of the United States of America Ser.). (ENG & SPA.). 32p. (gr. 2-2). 47.90 *(978-1-60853-369-5(7),* Editorial Buenas Letras) Rosen Publishing Group, Inc., The.

—Mississippi. Brusca, Maria Cristina, tr. 2005. (Bilingual Library of the United States of America Ser.: Set 2). (ENG & SPA., Illus.). 32p. (J). (gr. 3-6). lib. bdg. 25.25 *(978-1-4042-3089-7(0))* Rosen Publishing Group, Inc., The.

Dell, Pamela. Mississippi. 2014. (America the Beautiful Ser.: 3). (ENG.). 144p. (J). lib. bdg. 40.00 *(978-0-531-24891-1(7))* Scholastic Library Publishing.

Dill, Pamela Wescovich. Katrina's Rainbow: The Miracle of the Storm Crosses. 2006. (Illus.). 42p. (J). 17.99 *(978-1-59879-302-4(0))* Lifevest Publishing, Inc.

Figueroa, Acton. Mississippi: The Magnolia State. 2003. (World Almanac Library of the States). (Illus.). 48p. (gr. 4-9). pap. 14.05 *(978-0-8368-5323-0(7));* lib. bdg. 31.00 *(978-0-8368-5152-6(8))* Stevens, Gareth Publishing LLLP. (Gareth Stevens Learning Library).

Foran, Jill. Mississippi. 2011. (Guide to American States Ser.). (Illus.). 48p. (YA). (gr. 3-6). 29.99 *(978-1-61690-796-9(7))* Weigl Pubs., Inc.

Gaines, Ann Graham. Mississippi. 2007. (It's My State! Ser.). (Illus.). 80p. (J). (gr. 3-7). lib. bdg. 21.95 *(978-0-7614-2214-3(5))* Marshall Cavendish GBR. Dist: Marshall Cavendish Corp.

Hoena, Blake. Mississippi. 2013. (Exploring the States Ser.). (ENG., Illus.). 32p. (gr. 3-7). lib. bdg. 26.95 *(978-1-62617-023-0(1),* Blastoff! Readers) Bellwether Media.

Kuedee, Jaycee. How to Draw Mississippi's Sights & Symbols. 2009. (Kid's Guide to Drawing America Ser.). 32p. (gr. k-k). 50.50 *(978-1-61511-073-5(9),* PowerKids Pr.) Rosen Publishing Group, Inc., The.

Marsh, Carole. The Magnificent Mississippi Coloring Book. 2004. (Mississippi Experience! Ser.). (Illus.). 32p. (J). (gr. k-2). pap. 3.95 *(978-0-7933-9559-0(3))* Gallopade International.

—Mississippi Big Activity Book. 2004. (Mississippi Experience! Ser.). (Illus.). 96p. (J). (gr. 2-6). pap. 9.95 *(978-0-7933-9558-3(5))* Gallopade International.

—Mississippi Current Events Projects: 30 Cool, Activities, Crafts, Experiments & More for Kids to Do to Learn about Your State! 2003. (Mississippi Experience Ser.). 32p. (gr. k-8). pap. 5.95 *(978-0-635-02043-7(2),* Marsh, Carole Bks.) Gallopade International.

—The Mississippi Experience Pocket Guide. 2004. (Mississippi Experience! Ser.). (Illus.). 96p. (J). (gr. 3-8). pap. 6.95 *(978-0-7933-9554-5(2))* Gallopade International.

—Mississippi Geography Projects: 30 Cool, Activities, Crafts, Experiments & More for Kids to Do to Learn about Your State! 2003. (Mississippi Experience Ser.). 32p. (gr. k-5). pap. 5.95 *(978-0-635-01843-4(8),* Marsh, Carole Bks.) Gallopade International.

—Mississippi Government Projects: 30 Cool, Activities, Crafts, Experiments & More for Kids to Do to Learn about Your State! 2003. (Mississippi Experience Ser.). 32p. (gr. k-5). pap. 5.95 *(978-0-635-01943-1(4),* Marsh, Carole Bks.) Gallopade International.

—Mississippi Jeopardy. 2004. (Mississippi Experience! Ser.). (Illus.). 32p. (J). (gr. 3-8). pap. 7.95 *(978-0-7933-9556-9(9))* Gallopade International.

—Mississippi "Jography" A Fun Run Thru Our State! 2004. (Mississippi Experience! Ser.). (Illus.). 32p. (J). (gr. 3-8). pap. 7.95 *(978-0-7933-9557-6(7))* Gallopade International.

—Mississippi People Projects: 30 Cool, Activities, Crafts, Experiments & More for Kids to Do to Learn about Your State! 2003. (Mississippi Experience Ser.). 32p. (gr. k-5). pap. 5.95 *(978-0-635-01993-6(0),* Marsh, Carole Bks.) Gallopade International.

—Mississippi Symbols & Facts Projects: 30 Cool, Activities, Crafts, Experiments & More for Kids to Do to Learn about Your State! 2003. (Mississippi Experience Ser.). 32p. (gr. k-5). pap. 5.95 *(978-0-635-01893-9(4),* Marsh, Carole Bks.) Gallopade International.

—My First Book about Mississippi. 2004. (Mississippi Experience! Ser.). (Illus.). 32p. (J). (gr. k-4). pap. 7.95 *(978-0-7933-9555-2(0))* Gallopade International.

The Mississippi. 2011. (River Journey Ser.). (ENG.). 48p. (YA). (gr. 5-8). 27.95 *(978-1-4488-6015-9(6),* Rosen Reference) Rosen Publishing Group, Inc., The.

Murray, Julie. Mississippi. 1 vol. 2006. (United States Ser.). (ENG., Illus.). 32p. (gr. 2-4). 27.07 *(978-1-59197-683-7(9),* Buddy Bks.) ABDO Publishing Co.

Naden, Corinne J. & Blue, Rose. Mississippi: A MyReportLinks.com Book. 2003. (States Ser.). (Illus.). 48p. (J). lib. bdg. 25.26 *(978-0-7660-5144-7(7),* MyReportLinks.com Bks.) Enslow Pubs., Inc.

Putnam, Richelle & Aycock, John. The Inspiring Life of Eudora Welty. 2014. Orig. Title: The Inspiring Life of Eudora Welty. (ENG., Illus.). 144p. (gr. 4-7). pap. 16.99 *(978-1-62619-000-9(3),* History Pr., The) Arcadia Publishing.

Ready, Anna. Mississippi. 2nd exp. rev. ed. 2003. (Hello U. S. A. Ser.). (Illus.). 84p. (J). (gr. 3-6). 25.26 *(978-0-8225-4109-7(2),* Lerner Pubns.) Lerner Publishing Group.

Shirley, David & Kummer, Patricia K. Mississippi. 2nd rev. ed. 2007. (Celebrate the States Ser.). 144p. (gr. 6). lib. bdg. 42.79 *(978-0-7614-2717-9(1),* Benchmark Bks.) Marshall Cavendish Corp.

Shofner, Shawndra. Mississippi. 2008. (This Land Called America Ser.). 32p. (YA). (gr. 3-6). 22.95 *(978-1-58341-649-5(8))* Creative Co., The.

Trueit, Trudi Strain. Mississippi. 2007. (Rookie Read-About Geography Ser.). (Illus.). 31p. (J). (gr. 1-2). 20.50 *(978-0-531-12572-4(6),* Children's Pr.) Scholastic Library Publishing.

Wilson, Cristi. Just Because. Wilson, Cristi, illus. l.t. ed. 2006. (Illus.). 24p. (J). (gr. -1-3). per. 10.99 *(978-1-59879-251-5(2))* Lifevest Publishing, Inc.

MISSISSIPPI—FICTION

Armistead, John. The Return of Gabriel. Gregory, Fran, illus. 2004. 218p. (gr. 3-8). 17.45 *(978-0-7569-3460-6(5))* Perfection Learning Corp.

Bomgaars, Sharon. The Best Clubhouse Ever. 2009. 232p. pap. 14.49 *(978-1-4259-9306-1(0))* AuthorHouse.

Brook, Henry, retold by. Tom Sawyer. 2008. (Usborne Classics Retold Ser.). 160p. (J). pap. 4.99 *(978-0-7945-2063-2(4),* Usborne) EDC Publishing.

Chris, Crowe. Mississippi Trial 1955. 2014. (ENG.). 240p. (YA). (gr. 7-12). 10.24 *(978-1-63245-211-5(1))* Lectorum Pubns., Inc.

Cook, Kristi. Magnolia. 2014. (ENG., Illus.). 336p. (YA). (gr. 9). 17.99 *(978-1-4424-8535-8(3));* pap. 10.99 *(978-1-4424-8534-1(5))* Simon Pulse. (Simon Pulse).

Crowe, Chris. Mississippi Trial 1955. 2003. (ENG.). 240p. (YA). (gr. 7-18). 5.99 *(978-0-14-250192-4(1),* Speak) Penguin Young Readers Group.

—The Mississippi Trial 1955. 2003. (gr. 7-12). lib. bdg. 16.00 *(978-0-613-86522-7(7),* Turtleback) Turtleback Bks.

Curry, Kenneth. The Legend of the Dancing Trees: An African American Folk Tale. 2007. 111p. (J). per. 14.95 *(978-0-9798364-0-4(9))* Curry Brothers Publishing Group.

Curry, Kenneth, et al. The Legend of the Dancing Tees Teachers Resource: The Legend of the Dancing Trees. 2007.Tr. of Teachers Resource. per. 19.95 *(978-0-9798364-1-1(7))* Curry Brothers Publishing Group.

Darlington, Edgar. The Circus Boys on the Mississippi. 2007. 116p. per. *(978-1-4068-4235-7(4))* Echo Library.

Darlington, Edgar B. P. The Circus Boys on the Mississippi. 2005. 27.95 *(978-1-4218-1023-2(9));* 220p. pap. 12.95 *(978-1-4218-1123-9(5))* 1st World Publishing, Inc. (1st World Library - Literary Society).

Delashmit, Margaret V. Thief! 2012. 148p. (gr. 4-6). pap. 12.99 *(978-1-4624-0348-6(4),* Inspiring Voices) Author Solutions, Inc.

Dill, Margo L. Finding My Place: One Girl's Strength at Vicksburg. 2012. (ENG.). 202p. (J). pap. 8.95 *(978-1-57249-408-4(5),* White Mane Kids) White Mane Publishing Co., Inc.

Downing, Johnette. Down in Mississippi, 1 vol. Zecca, Katherine, illus. 2016. (ENG.). 32p. (J). 16.99 *(978-1-4556-2098-2(X))* Pelican Publishing Co., Inc.

Edgin, Brenda. Little Winston & His Big Adventures in Natchez: New Home near the Woods. 2011. 16p. 12.99 *(978-1-4567-3639-2(6))* AuthorHouse.

Ernst, Kathleen. Ghosts of Vicksburg. 2003. (White Main Kids Ser.: 13). (Illus.). 180p. (J). pap. 8.95 *(978-1-57249-322-3(4),* White Mane Kids) White Mane Publishing Co., Inc.

Falls, Kat. Inhuman. 2013. (ENG.). 384p. (J). (gr. 7). 17.99 *(978-0-545-37099-8(X),* Scholastic Pr.) Scholastic, Inc.

Gamble, Adam & Jasper, Mark. Good Night Mississippi. Veno, Joe, illus. 2015. (Good Night Our World Ser.). (ENG.). 20p. (J). (— 1). bds. 9.95 *(978-1-60219-221-8(9))* Good Night Bks.

Gibson, B. W. Extra Innings: The Diamond Thieves. 2014. 152p. pap. 14.95 *(978-1-4918-5663-5(7))* AuthorHouse.

Herwick Rice, Dona & Paris, Stephanie. Sal Fink, 1 vol. 2009. (Building Fluency Through Reader's Theater Ser.). (ENG.). 24p. (J). (gr. 2-4). pap. 6.99 *(978-1-4333-0995-3(5))* Teacher Created Materials, Inc.

Higgins, M. G. Finding Apeman. 2015. (Gravel Road Ser.). (YA). lib. bdg. 20.80 *(978-0-606-37210-7(5))* Turtleback Bks.

Horn, Shannon. Pirates of the Mississippian: The Adventures of Jerry & Draco. 2012. 24p. pap. 17.99 *(978-1-4772-6991-6(6))* AuthorHouse.

Jacobs, Lily. The Littlest Bunny in Mississippi: An Easter Adventure. Dunn, Robert, illus. 2015. (ENG.). 32p. (J). (-3). 9.99 *(978-1-4926-1123-3(9),* Sourcebooks Jabberwocky) Sourcebooks, Inc.

James, Eric. A Halloween Scare in Mississippi. Le Ray, Marina, illus. 2015. (ENG.). 32p. (J). (-5). 9.99 *(978-1-4926-2382-3(2),* 9781492623823, Sourcebooks Jabberwocky) Sourcebooks, Inc.

—Santa's Sleigh Is on Its Way to Mississippi: A Christmas Adventure. Dunn, Robert, illus. 2016. (ENG.). 32p. (J). (-2). 12.99 *(978-1-4926-4337-1(8),* 9781492643371, Sourcebooks Jabberwocky) Sourcebooks, Inc.

Johnson, Angela. I Dream of Trains. Long, Loren, illus. 2003. (ENG.). 32p. (J). (gr. k-2). 18.99 *(978-0-689-82609-2(5),* Simon & Schuster Bks. For Young Readers) Simon & Schuster Bks. For Young Readers.

Key, Watt. Hideout. 2017. (ENG.). 320p. (J). 16.99 *(978-0-374-30482-9(3),* 9780374304829, Farrar, Straus & Giroux (BYR)) Farrar, Straus & Giroux.

Masters, Susan Rowan. Night Journey to Vicksburg. Killcoyne, Hope L., ed. Smith, Duane A., illus. 2003. (Adventures in America Ser.). 74p. (gr. 4). 14.95 *(978-1-893110-30-4(3))* Silver Moon Pr.

McDougal-Littell Publishing Staff. Literature Connections English: Roll of Thunder, Hear My Cry. 2004. (McDougal Littell Literature Connections Ser.). (ENG.). 288p. (gr. 8-8). stu. ed. 16.90 *(978-0-395-77530-1(2),* 2-80099) Great Source Education Group, Inc.

McMullan, Margaret. How I Found the Strong: A Civil War Story. 2006. (ENG.). 144p. (YA). (gr. 7-12). reprint ed. mass mkt. 5.99 *(978-0-553-49492-1(9),* Laurel Leaf) Random Hse. Children's Bks.

Mellor, Colleen Kelly. Grandpa & the Truck Book 2. Irwin, Dana M., illus. 2012. 34p. pap. 9.99 *(978-0-9856770-2-2(3))* truckerkidzPr.

Murphy, Julie. Ramona Blue. (YA). (gr. 8). 2018. (ENG.). 448p. pap. 9.99 ***(978-0-06-241836-4(X))*** 2017. 432p. 17.99 *(978-0-06-241835-7(1))* HarperCollins Pubs.

P.A.W. My Summer Road Trip. 2012. 28p. pap. 15.99 *(978-1-4691-5077-2(8))* Xlibris Corp.

Rand, Johnathan. American Chillers #25 Mississippi Megalodon. 2008. 208p. (J). pap. 5.99 *(978-1-893699-33-5(1))* AudioCraft Publishing, Inc.

Rinaldi, Ann. My Vicksburg. 2011. (ENG.). 160p. (YA). (gr. 7). pap. 11.95 *(978-0-547-55000-8(6))* Houghton Mifflin Harcourt Publishing Co.

Robinson, Gary. Little Brother of War. 2013. (PathFinders Ser.). (ENG.). 113p. (YA). pap. 9.95 *(978-1-939053-02-2(1),* 7th Generation) Book Publishing Co.

Rodman, Mary Ann. Yankee Girl. 2008. (ENG.). 240p. (J). (gr. 4-6). pap. 9.99 *(978-0-312-53576-6(7),* 9780312535766) Square Fish.

Rubright, Lynn. Mama's Window. Smith, Duane, illus. 2005. 89p. (J). 16.95 *(978-1-57480-160-6(0))* Lee & Low Bks., Inc.

Scattergood, Augusta. Glory Be. (ENG.). 208p. (J). (gr. 3-7). 2014. pap. 6.99 *(978-0-545-33181-4(1))* 2012. 16.99 *(978-0-545-33180-7(3))* Scholastic, Inc. (Scholastic Pr.).

Silvano, Wendi. Love Is All Around Mississippi. Czernichowska, Joanna, illus. 2016. (ENG.). 32p. (J). (-6). 12.99 *(978-1-4926-2936-8(7),* Sourcebooks Jabberwocky) Sourcebooks, Inc.

Smallman, Steve. Santa Is Coming to Mississippi. Dunn, Robert, illus. 2013. (ENG.). 32p. (J). (-3). 9.99 *(978-1-4022-9015-2(2),* Sourcebooks Jabberwocky) Sourcebooks, Inc.

Taylor, Mildred D. Roll of Thunder, Hear My Cry. 2004. 276p. (gr. 4-8). reprint ed. pap. 10.00 *(978-0-7567-7955-9(3))* DIANE Publishing Co.

—Roll of Thunder, Hear My Cry. 40th anniv. ed. 2016. (ENG., Illus.). 304p. (J). (gr. 3-7). 19.99 *(978-1-101-99388-0(X),* Dial Bks) Penguin Young Readers Group.

Telgemeier, Raina. Drama. 2012. (ENG., Illus.). 240p. (J). (gr. 5-9). 24.99 *(978-0-545-32698-8(2));* pap. 10.99 *(978-0-545-32699-5(0))* Scholastic, Inc. (Graphix).

Tingle, Tim. Crossing Bok Chitto: A Choctaw Tale of Friendship & Freedom. Bridges, Jeanne Rorex, illus. (ENG.). 40p. (J). 2008. (gr. 2-7). pap. 8.95 *(978-1-933693-20-0(7))* 2006. (gr. 1-8). 17.95 *(978-0-938317-77-7(6))* Cinco Puntos Pr.

Twain, Mark, pseud. Adventures of Huckleberry Finn. Powell, Eric, illus. 2012. (ENG.). 276p. 19.99 *(978-1-61377-086-3(3),* 9781613770863) Idea & Design Works, LLC.

—The Adventures of Tom Sawyer. Corvino, Lucy, illus. 2005. (Classic Starts(tm) Ser.). (ENG.). 160p. (J). (gr. 2-4). 6.95 *(978-1-4027-1216-6(2))* Sterling Publishing Co., Inc.

—Tom Sawyer, 1 vol. Mullarkey, Lisa, illus. 2010. (Calico Illustrated Classics Ser.: No. 1). (ENG.). 112p. (J). (gr. 3-6). 27.07 *(978-1-60270-704-7(9))* Magic Wagon.

—Tom Sawyer. 2009. 196p. (gr. 4-7). pap. 12.99 *(978-1-934941-63-8(8))* Red & Black Pubs.

Vander Zee, Ruth. Mississippi Morning. Cooper, Floyd, illus. 2004. 32p. (J). 16.00 *(978-0-8028-5211-3(4))* Eerdmans, William B. Publishing Co.

Vaught, Susan. Footer Davis Probably Is Crazy. Reinhardt, Jennifer Black, illus. 2015. (ENG.). 240p. (J). (gr. 5-9). 16.99 *(978-1-4814-2276-5(6),* Simon & Schuster Bks. For Young Readers) Simon & Schuster Bks. For Young Readers.

—Things Too Huge to Fix by Saying Sorry. 2016. (ENG., Illus.). 352p. (J). (gr. 5-9). 16.99 *(978-1-4814-2279-6(0),* Simon & Schuster Bks. For Young Readers) Simon & Schuster Bks. For Young Readers.

—Things Too Huge to Fix by Saying Sorry. 2017. (ENG.). 368p. (J). (gr. 5-9). pap. 7.99 ***(978-1-4814-2280-2(4),*** Simon & Schuster/Paula Wiseman Bks.) Simon & Schuster/Paula Wiseman Bks.

Waller, Linda. Hard Road to Manhood: I Ain't No Snitch. 2010. 128p. pap. 10.99 *(978-1-4490-6892-9(8))* AuthorHouse.

Wiles, Deborah. The Aurora County All-Stars. (ENG., Illus.). 256p. (J). 2009. (gr. 2-5). pap. 7.99 *(978-0-15-206626-0(8))* 2007. (gr. 5-7). 16.00 *(978-0-15-206068-8(5))* Houghton Mifflin Harcourt Publishing Co.

—Love, Ruby Lavender. 2005. (ENG., Illus.). 240p. (J). (gr. 2-5). reprint ed. pap. 7.99 *(978-0-15-205478-6(2))* Houghton Mifflin Harcourt Publishing Co.

—Love, Ruby Lavender. 2004. 216p. (J). (gr. 3-7). pap. 36.00 incl. audio *(978-0-8072-2096-2(5),* Listening Library) Random Hse. Audio Publishing Group.

Wiles, Deborah. Revolution. (Sixties Trilogy Ser.: 2). (ENG.). 544p. (J). (gr. 3-7). 2017. pap. 8.99 ***(978-0-545-10608-5(7))*** 2014. (Illus.). 19.99 *(978-0-545-10607-8(9),* Scholastic Pr.) Scholastic, Inc.

Woodson, Jacqueline. Beneath a Meth Moon: An Elegy. 2013. (ENG.). 240p. (YA). (gr. 7). pap. 8.99 *(978-0-14-242392-9(0),* Speak) Penguin Young Readers Group.

MISSISSIPPI—HISTORY

Aretha, David. Freedom Summer. 2007. (Civil Rights Movement Ser.). (Illus.). 128p. (J). (gr. 3-7). lib. bdg. 27.95 *(978-1-59935-059-2(9))* Reynolds, Morgan Inc.

—The Murder of Emmett Till. 2007. (Civil Rights Movement Ser.). (Illus.). 160p. (J). (gr. 3-7). lib. bdg. 27.95 *(978-1-59935-057-8(2))* Reynolds, Morgan Inc.

Barton, Chris. The Amazing Age of John Roy Lynch. Tate, Don, illus. 2015. (ENG.). 50p. (J). 17.00 *(978-0-8028-5379-0(X),* Eerdmans Bks For Young Readers) Eerdmans, William B. Publishing Co.

Casil, Amy Sterling. Mississippi: Past & Present. 2010. (United States: Past & Present Ser.). (ENG.). 48p. (YA). pap. 11.75 *(978-1-4358-9512-6(6));* lib. bdg. 29.25 *(978-1-4358-9485-3(5))* Rosen Publishing Group, Inc., The. (Rosen Reference).

Coleman, Miriam. Mississippi: The Magnolia State. 2010. (Our Amazing States Ser.). (ENG.). 24p. (J). pap. 8.25 *(978-1-4488-0738-3(7));* lib. bdg. 22.60 *(978-1-4488-0653-9(4))* Rosen Publishing Group, Inc., The. (PowerKids Pr.).

Fiorelli, June Estep. Fannie Lou Hamer: A Voice for Freedom. 2004. (Avisson Young Adult Ser.). (Illus.). 117p. (J). pap. 19.95 *(978-1-888105-62-9(3))* Avisson Pr., Inc.

Foran, Jill. Mississippi: The Magnolia State. 2016. (J). *(978-1-4896-4887-7(9))* Weigl Pubs., Inc.

Gaines, Ann. Mississippi. 2014. (J). lib. bdg. *(978-1-62712-239-9(7))* Cavendish Square Publishing.

Gaines, Ann & Waring, Kerry Jones. Mississippi. 2016. (ENG., Illus.). 80p. (J). 34.21 *(978-1-62713-241-1(4))* Cavendish Square Publishing.

Lichter, Nick. The Road of Souls: Reflections on the Mississippi. 2004. (Illus.). 150p. per. 14.95 *(978-0-9758615-0-9(6))* Wing Dam Pr.

Marsh, Carole. Exploring Mississippi Through Project-Based Learning: Geography, History, Government, Economics & More. 2016. (Mississippi Experience Ser.). (ENG.). (J). pap. 9.99 *(978-0-635-12348-0(7))* Gallopade International.

—I'm Reading about Mississippi. 2014. (Mississippi Experience Ser.). (ENG., Illus.). (J). pap., pap. 8.99 *(978-0-635-11299-6(X))* Gallopade International.

—Mississippi History Projects: 30 Cool, Activities, Crafts, Experiments & More for Kids to Do to Learn about Your State! 2003. (Mississippi Experience Ser.). 32p. (gr. k-5). pap. 5.95 *(978-0-635-01793-2(8),* Marsh, Carole Bks.) Gallopade International.

McDowell, Pamela. Mississippi: The Magnolia State. 2012. (J). *(978-1-61913-367-9(9));* pap. *(978-1-61913-368-6(7))* Weigl Pubs., Inc.

Mills, Jordan. Mississippi. 2016. (States Ser.). (ENG., Illus.). 32p. (gr. 3-4). lib. bdg. 27.32 *(978-1-5157-0411-9(4))* Next Page Pr., The.

Murray, Julie. Mississippi, 1 vol. 2012. (Explore the United States Ser.). (ENG.). 32p. (J). (gr. 2-5). lib. bdg. 28.50 *(978-1-61783-362-5(2),* Big Buddy Bks.) ABDO Publishing Co.

Ready, Anna. Mississippi. 2013. (J). lib. bdg. 25.26 *(978-0-7613-4540-4(X),* Lerner Pubns.) Lerner Publishing Group.

Shoulders, Michael. 1 Mississippi 2 Mississippi: A Mississippi Number Book. Anderson, Rick, illus. 2004. (Count Your Way Across the U. S. A. Ser.). (ENG.). 40p. (J). 16.95 *(978-1-58536-188-5(7))* Sleeping Bear Pr.

Smith, Rich. Mississippi, 1 vol. 2009. (United States Ser.). (ENG., Illus.). 48p. (YA). (gr. 2-5). 27.07 *(978-1-60453-659-1(4))* ABDO Publishing Co.

Somervill, Barbara A. Mississippi. 2009. (From Sea to Shining Sea, Second Ser.). (ENG.). 80p. (J). pap. 7.95 *(978-0-531-21134-2(7),* Children's Pr.) Scholastic Library Publishing.

Taylor, Mildred D. Roll of Thunder, Hear My Cry (Puffin Modern Classics) 25th rev. ed. 2014. (Puffin Modern Classics Ser.). (ENG.). 288p. (J). 12.24 *(978-1-63245-097-5(6))* Lectorum Pubns., Inc.

Wright, Simeon & Boyd, Herb. Simeon's Story: An Eyewitness Account of the Kidnapping of Emmett Till. 2011. (ENG.). 160p. (J). (gr. 7). pap. 12.95 *(978-1-56976-819-8(6),* Hill, Lawrence Bks.) Chicago Review Pr., Inc.

Yasuda, Anita. What's Great about Mississippi? 2015. (Our Great States Ser.). (ENG., Illus.). 32p. (J). (gr. 2-5). pap. 7.95 *(978-1-4677-6084-3(6));* lib. bdg. 26.60 *(978-1-4677-3860-6(3),* Lerner Pubns.) Lerner Publishing Group.

Ziff, John. Gulf States: Alabama, Louisiana, Mississippi, Vol. 19. 2015. (Let's Explore the States Ser.). (Illus.). 64p. (J). (gr. 5). 23.95 *(978-1-4222-3324-5(3))* Mason Crest.

MISSISSIPPI RIVER

Adil, Janeen R. Mississippi River. 2013. (J). *(978-1-62127-475-9(6));* pap. *(978-1-62127-481-0(0))* Weigl Pubs., Inc.

—The Mississippi River: The Largest River in the United States. 2004. (Natural Wonders of the U. S. A. Ser.). (Illus.). 32p. (J). (gr. 3-6). per. 9.95 *(978-1-59036-163-4(6));* lib. bdg. 26.00 *(978-1-59036-041-5(9))* Weigl Pubs., Inc.

Anastasio, Dina. Where Is the Mississippi River? Hammond, Ted, illus. 2017. (Where Is? Ser.). (ENG.). 112p. (J). (gr. 3-7). 5.99 ***(978-0-515-15824-3(0));*** lib. bdg. 15.99 ***(978-0-515-15826-7(7))*** Penguin Young Readers Group. (Penguin Workshop).

Bauer, Marion Dane. The Mighty Mississippi. Wallace, John, illus. 2007. (Wonders of America Ser.). (ENG.). 32p. (J). (gr. -1-1). pap. 3.99 *(978-0-689-86950-1(9),* Simon Spotlight) Simon Spotlight.

Bechtold, Phyliss. Seymour Bluffs & the Legend of the Piasa Bird. 2007. 26p. 9.95 *(978-0-9728532-8-6(6))* New Horizons Christian Ctr.

Crompton, Samuel Willard. Robert de la Salle. 2009. (Great Explorers Ser.). (Illus.). 112p. (J). (gr. 6-12). 30.00 *(978-1-60413-419-3(4),* Chelsea Hse.) Facts On File, Inc.

Donaldson-Forbes, Jeff. La Salle. 2009. (Primary Source Library of Famous Explorers Ser.). 24p. (gr. 4-4). 42.50

MNO

(978-1-60854-129-4(0), PowerKids Pr.) Rosen Publishing Group, Inc., The.

Green, Jen. The Mississippi River. 2003. (Rivers of North America Ser.). (Illus.). 32p. (gr. 2-6). lib. bdg. 26.00 (978-0-8368-3757-5(6), Gareth Stevens Learning Library) Stevens, Gareth Publishing LLLP.

Harkins, Susan Sales & Harkins, William H. The Life & Times of Father Jacques Marquette. 2008. (Profiles in American History Ser.). (Illus.). 48p. (J). (gr. 4-8). lib. bdg. 29.95 (978-1-58415-528-7(0)) Mitchell Lane Pubs., Inc.

Johnson, Robin. The Mississippi: America's Mighty River. 2010. (Rivers Around the World Ser.). (ENG., Illus.). 32p. (J). (gr. 5-8). pap. (978-0-7787-7467-9(8)); lib. bdg. (978-0-7787-7444-0(9)) Crabtree Publishing Co.

Jordan, Shirley. Benjamin Brown & the Great Steamboat Race. Kemly, Kathleen, illus. 2011. (History Speaks: Picture Books Plus Reader's Theater Ser.). 48p. pap. 56.72 (978-0-7613-7630-9(5)); (ENG.). (gr. 2-4). pap. 9.95 (978-0-7613-6133-6(2)) Lerner Publishing Group.

Larson, Paul Cliff & Larson, Pamela All. Mississippi Escapade: Reliving the Grand Excursion Of 1854. 2004. (Illus.). 128p. (J). (gr. 3-7). pap. 17.95 (978-1-890434-64-9(7)) Afton Historical Society Pr.

Manning, Paul. The Mississippi. 2014. (River Adventures Ser.). (J). lib. bdg. 31.35 (978-1-59920-916-6(0)) Black Rabbit Bks.

Marsico, Katie. The Mississippi River. 2013. (Explorer Library: Social Studies Explorer Ser.). (ENG.). 32p. (J). (gr. 4-8). 28.50 (978-1-62431-011-9(7), 202495); pap. 14.21 (978-1-62431-035-5(4), 202497) Cherry Lake Publishing.

McNeese, Tim. The Mississippi River. 2004. (Rivers in American Life & Times Ser.). (Illus.). 120p. (C). (gr. 9-13). 32.50 (978-0-7910-7723-8(3), Chelsea Hse.) Facts On File, Inc.

O'Neal, Claire. The Mississippi River. 2012. (J). lib. bdg. 29.95 (978-1-61228-296-1(2)) Mitchell Lane Pubs., Inc.

Payment, Simone. La Salle: Claiming the Mississippi River for France. 2009. (Library of Explorers & Exploration Ser.). 112p. (gr. 5-8). 66.50 (978-1-60853-610-8(6), Rosen Reference) Rosen Publishing Group, Inc., The.

Petrie, Kristin. Marquette & Jolliet, 1 vol. 2007. (Explorers Set 2 Ser.). (ENG., Illus.). 32p. (gr. 4-7). 27.07 (978-1-59679-745-1(2), Checkerboard Library) ABDO Publishing Co.

—La Salle, 1 vol. 2007. (Explorers Set 2 Ser.). (ENG., Illus.). 32p. (gr. 4-7). 27.07 (978-1-59679-750-5(9), Checkerboard Library) ABDO Publishing Co.

Simon, Charnan. The Mighty Mississippi. 2004. (Geography of the World Ser.). (ENG., Illus.). 32p. (J). (gr. 3-6). 28.50 (978-1-59296-339-3(0), 200270) Child's World, Inc., The.

Vaughn, Royce, illus. Seymour Bluffs & the Legend of the Piasa Bird. 2006. 24p. (J). pap. 9.95 (978-0-9728538-2-8(0)) Amica Publishing.

Vieira, Linda. The Mighty Mississippi: The Life & Times of America's Greatest River. Bond, Higgins, illus. 2005. (J). (978-7-80802-789-7(8)) Walker & Co.

Waldman, Neil. Voyages: Reminiscences of Young Abe Lincoln. 2009. (ENG., Illus.). 32p. (J). (gr. 5-9). 16.95 (978-1-59078-471-6(5), Calkins Creek) Boyds Mills Pr.

Young, Jeff C. Hernando de Soto: Spanish Conquistador in the Americas. 2009. (Great Explorers of the World Ser.). (Illus.). 112p. (J). (gr. 7-12). lib. bdg. 33.27 (978-1-59845-104-7(9)) Enslow Pubs., Inc.

Youngblood, Wayne. Mark Twain along the Mississippi. 2006. (In the Footsteps of American Heroes Ser.). (Illus.). 64p. (gr. 5-12). pap. 14.05 (978-0-8368-6435-9(2)); lib. bdg. 34.00 (978-0-8368-6430-4(1)) Stevens, Gareth Publishing LLLP. (Gareth Stevens Secondary Library).

Zelenyi, Alexander & Zelenyj, Alexander. Marquette & Jolliet: Quest for the Mississippi. 2006. (In the Footsteps of Explorers Ser.). (ENG., Illus.). 32p. (J). (gr. 4-7). pap. (978-0-7787-2467-4(0)); lib. bdg. (978-0-7787-2431-5(X)) Crabtree Publishing Co.

Zronik, John Paul. Sieur de la Salle: New World Adventurer. 2005. (In the Footsteps of Explorers Ser.). (ENG., Illus.). 32p. (J). (gr. 4-5). pap. (978-0-7787-2449-0(2)) Crabtree Publishing Co.

MISSISSIPPI RIVER—FICTION

Aaron, Chester. An American Ghost. 2011. (YA). pap. (978-1-936144-28-0(X)) Zumaya Pubns. LLC.

Altsheler, Joseph A. The Free Rangers. 2007. (Young Trailers Ser.: Vol. 5). 244p. reprint ed. per. 14.45 (978-1-60424-038-2(5), Book Jungle) Standard Pubns., Inc.

—The Free Rangers: A Story of the Early Days along the Mississippi. 2005. (Young Trailers Ser.: Vol. 5). (J). reprint ed. 29.95 (978-1-4218-1477-3(3)); 312p. pap. 14.95 (978-1-4218-1577-0(X)) 1st World Publishing, Inc. (1st World Library - Literary Society).

—The Free Rangers: A Story of the Early Days along the Mississippi. 2009. (Young Trailers Ser.: Vol. 4). 294p. (J). reprint ed. 27.99 (978-1-60512-311-0(0)); pap. 14.99 (978-1-60512-411-7(7)) Akasha Publishing, LLC. (Akasha Classics).

—The Free Rangers: A Story of the Early Days along the Mississippi. (Young Trailers Ser.: Vol. 5). (J). reprint ed. 26.95 (978-0-8488-1237-9(9)) Amereon Ltd.

—The Free Rangers: A Story of the Early Days along the Mississippi. (Young Trailers Ser.: Vol. 5). (J). 2008. 280p. 28.99 (978-0-554-27117-0(6)) 2008. 280p. 25.99 (978-0-554-36420-9(4)) 2007. (ENG.). 278p. (gr. 4-7). reprint ed. pap. 23.99 (978-1-4346-2560-1(5)) 2010. (ENG.). 382p. (gr. 4-7). reprint ed. pap. 33.75 (978-1-176-61076-7(7)) 2007. (ENG.). 254p. reprint ed. pap. 21.99 (978-1-4346-2518-2(4)) Creative Media Partners, LLC.

—The Free Rangers: A Story of the Early Days along the Mississippi. 2006. (Young Trailers Ser.: Vol. 5). (J). reprint ed. pap. (978-1-4065-0811-6(X)) Dodo Pr.

—The Free Rangers: A Story of the Early Days along the Mississippi. 2006. (Young Trailers Ser.: Vol. 5). reprint ed. pap. (978-1-4068-0743-1(5)) Echo Library.

—The Free Rangers: A Story of the Early Days along the Mississippi. 2010. (Young Trailers Ser.: Vol. 5). (J). 170p. pap. 13.87 (978-1-152-24703-1(4)); 162p. (gr. 4-7). reprint ed. pap. 19.99 (978-1-4432-1506-0(6)) General Bks. LLC.

—The Free Rangers: A Story of the Early Days along the Mississippi. (Young Trailers Ser.: Vol. 5). (J). 2010. 232p. pap. (978-1-4076-1356-7(1)) 2012. 388p. (gr. 4-7). reprint ed. pap. (978-1-290-66522-3(2)) HardPr.

—The Free Rangers: A Story of the Early Days along the Mississippi. 2012. (Young Trailers Ser.: Vol. 5). 220p. (J). (gr. 4-7). pap. 14.95 (978-1-60444-735-4(4)) IndoEuropeanPublishing.com.

—The Free Rangers: A Story of the Early Days along the Mississippi. (Young Trailers Ser.: Vol. 5). (J). reprint ed. 2010. 248p. (gr. 4-7). 33.56 (978-1-169-30153-5(3)) 2010. 248p. (gr. 4-7). pap. 21.56 (978-1-162-69513-6(7)) 2010. 41.95 (978-1-161-46378-1(X)) 2004. pap. 1.99 (978-1-4192-6302-6(1)) 2004. pap. 26.95 (978-1-4191-6302-9(7)) Kessinger Publishing, LLC.

—The Free Rangers: A Story of the Early Days along the Mississippi. 2012. (Young Trailers Ser.: Vol. 5). 256p. (J). (gr. 4-7). reprint ed. (978-3-8491-6283-2(4)); pap. (978-3-8491-5398-4(3)) Tredition GmbH.

Black, Deirdre. River Run. 2012. (After the Dust Settled Ser.). (ENG.). 120p. (YA). (gr. 6-12). pap. 7.95 (978-0-8225-7274-9(5), Darby Creek); lib. bdg. 27.93 (978-0-7613-8326-0(3)) Lerner Publishing Group.

Cockrum, James L. Short Boat on a Long River. Sansevero, Tony, illus. 2013. 180p. (YA). pap. 14.95 (978-0-9768586-1-4(4)) Pangloss Publishing.

Dubisch, Mike, illus. The Haunted Cabin Mystery. 2009. (Boxcar Children Graphic Novels Ser.: 9). (ENG.). 32p. (J). (gr. 1-5). pap. 6.99 (978-0-8075-3180-8(4)) Whitman, Albert & Co.

Ely, Scott. The Elephant Mountains, 1 vol. 2011. (ENG.). 216p. (J). (gr. 8-12). lib. bdg. 19.95 (978-1-55469-406-8(X)) Orca Bk. Pubs. USA.

Helgerson, Joseph. Horns & Wrinkles. Ceccoli, Nicoletta, illus. 2008. (ENG.). 240p. (J). (gr. 5-7). pap. 6.99 (978-0-618-98178-6(0)) Houghton Mifflin Harcourt Publishing Co.

Horender, Philip M. The Mighty Maximilian: Samuel Clemens's Traveling Companion, 1 vol. Wolek, Guy, illus. 2013. (Maximilian P. Mouse, Time Traveler Ser.). (ENG.). 112p. (J). (gr. 3-6). lib. bdg. 27.07 (978-1-61641-960-8(1), Calico Chapter Bks) Magic Wagon.

Howard, Annabelle. Keelboat Annie: An American Tall Tale. 2006. (J). pap. (978-1-4108-6169-6(4)) Benchmark Education Co.

Hugger, M. A. Danny Malloy & His Mississippi River Samurai. 2008. 132p. 21.95 (978-0-595-49382-1(3)); pap. 11.95 (978-0-595-48462-1(X)) iUniverse, Inc.

Lawson, Jessica. The Actual & Truthful Adventures of Becky Thatcher. Bruno, Iacopo, illus. 2014. (ENG.). 224p. (J). (gr. 3-7). 16.99 (978-1-4814-0150-0(5), Simon & Schuster Bks. For Young Readers) Simon & Schuster Bks. For Young Readers.

Marsh, Carole. The Mystery on the Mighty Mississippi. 2009. (Real Kids, Real Places Ser.). (Illus.). 146p. (J). lib. bdg. 18.99 (978-0-635-07001-2(4), Marsh, Carole Mysteries) Gallopade International.

Meigs, Cornelia & Holm, Jennifer L. Swift Rivers. Orr, Forrest W., illus. 2004. (Newbery Honor Book Ser.). (ENG.). 288p. (YA). (gr. 5). pap. 8.99 (978-0-8027-7703-4(1), 9780802777034, Bloomsbury USA Childrens) Bloomsbury Publishing USA.

Meyer, L. A. Mississippi Jack: Being an Account of the Further Waterborne Adventures of Jacky Faber, Midshipman, Fine Lady, & the Lily of the West. 2nd ed. 2010. (Bloody Jack Adventures Ser.: 5). (ENG., Illus.). 624p. (J). (gr. 7). pap. 8.99 (978-0-15-206632-1(2)) Houghton Mifflin Harcourt Publishing Co.

Miller, Bobbi. Big River's Daughter. 2013. (ENG.). 224p. (J). (gr. 2-7). 16.95 (978-0-8234-2752-9(8)) Holiday Hse., Inc.

Publishing, Racehorse & Twain, Mark. Classics to Color: Adventures of Huckleberry Finn. 2016. (ENG., Illus.). 80p. (J). (gr. 1-6). pap. 8.99 (978-1-944686-99-4(1), Racehorse Publishing) Skyhorse Publishing Co., Inc.

Rathborne, St. George. The House Boat Boys; or, Drifting down to the Sunny South. 2007. 108p. per. (978-1-4068-3747-6(4)) Echo Library.

Ross, Patrick. Runt River Rat's Wild Ride, 1 vol. Burcham, David, illus. 2010. 24p. 24.95 (978-1-4512-0067-6(6)) PublishAmerica, Inc.

Rouzer, Walter. Rebel Stone & the Ghost Whisperers. 2009. 304p. 28.95 (978-0-595-51192-1(9)) iUniverse, Inc.

Stevermer, Caroline & Collin, Francesca. River Rats. 2005. (ENG., Illus.). 320p. (YA). (gr. 7-12). pap. 19.95 (978-0-15-205554-7(1)) Houghton Mifflin Harcourt Publishing Co.

Twain, Mark, pseud. The Adventures of Huckleberry Finn. Andreasen, Dan, illus. 2006. (Classic Starts(tm) Ser.). (ENG.). 160p. (J). (gr. 2-4). 6.95 (978-1-4027-2499-2(3)) Sterling Publishing Co., Inc.

—The Adventures of Huckleberry Finn. 96p. (J). pap. 4.95 (978-0-7910-4108-6(5), Chelsea Hse.) Facts On File, Inc.

—The Adventures of Huckleberry Finn. Andreasen, Dan, illus. 2010. (Classic Starts(tm) Ser.). (ENG.). 160p. (J). (gr. 2-4). cd-rom 9.95 (978-1-4027-7355-6(2)) Sterling Publishing Co., Inc.

—The Adventures of Huckleberry Finn: With a Discussion of Friendship. Lauter, Richard, tr. Lauter, Richard, illus. 2003. (Values in Action Illustrated Classics Ser.). (J). (978-1-59203-042-2(4)) Learning Challenge, Inc.

—The Adventures of Tom Sawyer: A Song for Aunt Polly. Bates, Amy, illus. 2008. (Easy Reader Classics Ser.). (ENG.). 32p. (gr. -1-3). lib. bdg. 24.21 (978-1-59961-334-5(4)) Spotlight.

—The Adventures of Tom Sawyer: With a Discussion of Imagination. Butterfield, Ned, illus. 2003. (Values in Action Illustrated Classics Ser.). 190p. (J). (978-1-59203-027-9(0)) Learning Challenge, Inc.

—Las Aventuras de Huckleberry Finn. de Atauri, Ines & de Atauri, Juan Diaz, eds. 2006. (Clasicos Juveniles Ser.).Tr. of Adventures of Huckleberry Finn. (SPA., Illus.). 359p. pap. 17.95 (978-84-263-5252-1(9)) Vives, Luis Editorial (Edelvives) ESP. Dist: Lectorum Pubns., Inc.

—Tom Sawyer. 2005. 264p. 28.95 (978-1-4218-0768-3(8), 1st World Library - Literary Society) 1st World Publishing, Inc.

—Tom Sawyer. 2006. (Classic Retelling Ser.). (Illus.). 224p. (YA). (gr. 8-12). (978-0-618-12053-6(X), 2-00218) Holt McDougal.

—Tom Sawyer. 2004. reprint ed. pap. 1.99 (978-1-4192-5166-5(X)) Kessinger Publishing, LLC.

—Tom Sawyer. (Young Collector's Illustrated Classics Ser.). (Illus.). 192p. (J). (gr. 3-7). 9.95 (978-1-56156-453-8(2)) Kidsbooks, LLC.

—Tom Sawyer. (Coleccion Clasicos de la Juventud). (SPA., Illus.). 220p. (J). 12.95 (978-84-7189-029-0(1), ORT310) Ortells, Alfredo Editorial S.L. ESP. Dist: Continental Bk. Co., Inc.

Vaughn, Royce, illus. Seymour Bluffs & Robert Wadlow, the Tallest Man in the World: A Story about Diversity & Tolerance. 2007. 28p. (J). 12.95 (978-0-9728538-4-2(7)) Amica Publishing.

Wang, Jack, et al. Mark Twain's the Adventures of Huckleberry Finn. 2016. (ENG., Illus.). 24p. (J). (gr. -1 — 1). bds. 9.95 (978-1-4521-5249-3(7)) Chronicle Bks. LLC.

Warner, Gertrude Chandler. The Haunted Cabin Mystery, 1 vol. Bloodworth, Mark, illus. 2010. (Boxcar Children Graphic Novels Ser.). (ENG.). 32p. (J). (gr. 2-5). 28.50 (978-1-60270-717-7(0)) ABDO Publishing Co.

Wynne, Sarah & Clark, Katie. River Royals: Master the Mississippi. 2014. (ENG., Illus.). 32p. (J). 19.95 (978-1-939055-71-2(7), 011fd19b-d6ae-4840-a0eb-8b2b0a698ba0) Bright Sky Pr.

MISSISSIPPI RIVER VALLEY

see also Middle West

Aretha, David. La Salle: French Explorer of the Mississippi. 2009. (Great Explorers of the World Ser.). (Illus.). 112p. (J). (gr. 7-12). lib. bdg. 33.27 (978-1-59845-098-9(0)) Enslow Pubs., Inc.

Cefrey, Holly. The Pinckney Treaty: America Wins the Right to Travel the Mississippi River. 2009. (Life in the New American Nation Ser.). 32p. (gr. 4-4). 47.90 (978-1-61514-286-6(X)) Rosen Publishing Group, Inc., The.

Donaldson-Forbes, Jeff. Jacques Marquette & Louis Jolliet. 2009. (Primary Source Library of Famous Explorers Ser.). 24p. (gr. 4-4). 42.50 (978-1-60854-127-0(4), PowerKids Pr.) Rosen Publishing Group, Inc., The.

Dougherty, Terri. Admiral David Farragut: "Full Speed Ahead!" 2011. (J). (978-1-59556-041-4(6)); pap. (978-1-59556-047-6(5)) OTTN Publishing.

Hazleton, Amie. Sieur de la Salle: An Explorer of the Great West. 2017. (World Explorers Ser.). (ENG., Illus.). 32p. (gr. 3-4). lib. bdg. 27.32 (978-1-5157-4206-7(7)) Capstone Press of Coughlan Cos.

Larkin, Tanya. Jacques Marquette & Louis Jolliet: Explorers of the Mississippi. 2009. (Library of Explorers & Exploration Ser.). 112p. (gr. 5-8). 66.50 (978-1-60853-608-5(4), Rosen Reference) Rosen Publishing Group, Inc., The.

Manning, Paul. The Mississippi. 2014. (River Adventures Ser.). (J). lib. bdg. 31.35 (978-1-59920-916-6(0)) Black Rabbit Bks.

Owens, L. L. A Journey with Sieur de la Salle. 2017. (Primary Source Explorers Ser.). (ENG.). 40p. (J). (gr. 3-5). 30.65 (978-1-5124-0775-4(5)) Lerner Publishing Group.

River Lake Press. An Osprey Summer. 2010. (Illus.). 32p. (J). 17.95 (978-0-615-36951-8(0)) River Lake Pr.

MISSISSIPPI RIVER VALLEY—HISTORY

Felsing, Dean E. New Orleans or Sunk! 2011. 64p. (gr. -1). pap. 13.95 (978-1-4582-0092-1(2), Abbott Pr.) Author Solutions, Inc.

Larson, Paul Cliff & Larson, Pamela All. Mississippi Escapade: Reliving the Grand Excursion Of 1854. 2004. (Illus.). 128p. (J). (gr. 3-7). pap. 17.95 (978-1-890434-64-9(7)) Afton Historical Society Pr.

Peppas, Lynn. Why Sieur de La Salle Matters to Texas. 2014. (Illus.). 32p. (J). lib. bdg. 26.25 (978-1-4777-0917-7(7)) Rosen Publishing Group, Inc., The.

MISSOURI

Alter, Judy. Missouri: A MyReportLinks.com Book. 2003. (States Ser.). (Illus.). 48p. (J). (gr. 4-10). lib. bdg. 25.26 (978-0-7660-5127-0(7), MyReportLinks.com Bks.) Enslow Pubs., Inc.

Barile, Mary Collins. J. Milton Turner; an American Hero. Guest, Peggy, illus. 2013. 52p. 24.95 (978-0-9889643-0-3(9)) MathisJones Communications, LLC.

Boekhoff, P. M. Missouri. 2005. (Portraits of the States Ser.). (Illus.). 32p. (gr. 2-6). pap. 10.50 (978-0-8368-4647-8(8)); lib. bdg. 26.00 (978-0-8368-4628-7(1)) Stevens, Gareth Publishing LLLP. (Gareth Stevens Learning Library).

Discover the Missouri River KIDS Activity Booklet. 2003. (J). pap. (978-1-888631-20-3(1)) Project WET Foundation.

Evdokimoff, Natasha. Missouri. 2011. (Guide to American States Ser.). (Illus.). 48p. (YA). (gr. 3-6). 29.99 (978-1-61690-797-6(5)); (J). (978-1-61690-473-9(9)) Weigl Pubs., Inc.

Kavanaugh, Dorothy. Central Mississippi River Basin: Arkansas, Iowa, Missouri, Vol. 19. 2015. (Let's Explore the States Ser.). (Illus.). 64p. (J). (gr. 5). lib. bdg. 23.95 (978-1-4222-3321-4(9)) Mason Crest.

Kuedee, Jaycee. How to Draw Missouri's Sights & Symbols. 2009. (Kid's Guide to Drawing America Ser.). 32p. (gr. k-k). 50.50 (978-1-61511-074-2(7), PowerKids Pr.) Rosen Publishing Group, Inc., The.

Lago, Mary Ellen & Karnovsky, Susan. Missouri. 2003. (From Sea to Shining Sea Ser.: 2). (ENG., Illus.). 80p. (J). 30.50 (978-0-516-22390-2(9), Children's Pr.) Scholastic Library Publishing.

Lowe, Pamela Fleming. Missouri Then & Now. 2004. (ENG., Illus.). 240p. (J). pap., stu. ed., act. bk. ed. 18.00 (978-0-8262-1540-6(8)); 184p. pap., tchr. ed., act. bk. ed. 25.00 (978-0-8262-1539-0(4)) Univ. of Missouri Pr.

Marsh, Carole. The Big Missouri Reproducible Big Activity Book. 2004. (Missouri Experience! Ser.). (Illus.). 128p. (J). (gr. 2-6). per. 9.95 (978-0-7933-9574-3(7)) Gallopade International.

—The Magnificant Missouri Coloring Book. 2004. (Missouri Experience! Ser.). (Illus.). 32p. (J). (gr. k-2). pap. 3.95 (978-0-7933-9575-0(5)) Gallopade International.

—Missouri Current Events Projects: 30 Cool, Activities, Crafts, Experiments & More for Kids to Do to Learn about Your State! 2003. (Missouri Experience Ser.). 32p. (gr. k-8). pap. 5.95 (978-0-635-02044-4(0), Marsh, Carole Bks.) Gallopade International.

—Missouri Geography Projects: 30 Cool, Activities, Crafts, Experiments & More for Kids to Do to Learn about Your State! 2003. (Missouri Experience Ser.). 32p. (gr. k-5). pap. 5.95 (978-0-635-01844-1(6), Marsh, Carole Bks.) Gallopade International.

—Missouri Government Projects: 30 Cool, Activities, Crafts, Experiments & More for Kids to Do to Learn about Your State! 2003. (Missouri Experience Ser.). 32p. (gr. k-5). pap. 5.95 (978-0-635-01944-8(2), Marsh, Carole Bks.) Gallopade International.

—Missouri Jeopardy! Answers & Questions about Our State! 2004. (Missouri Experience! Ser.). (Illus.). 32p. (J). (gr. 3-8). pap. 7.95 (978-0-7933-9572-9(0)) Gallopade International.

—Missouri "Jography" A Fun Run Thru Our State! 2004. (Missouri Experience! Ser.). (Illus.). 32p. (J). (gr. 3-8). pap. 7.95 (978-0-7933-9573-6(9)) Gallopade International.

—Missouri People Projects: 30 Cool, Activities, Crafts, Experiments & More for Kids to Do to Learn about Your State! 2003. (Missouri Experience Ser.). 32p. (gr. k-5). pap. 5.95 (978-0-635-01994-3(9), Marsh, Carole Bks.) Gallopade International.

—Missouri Symbols & Facts Projects: 30 Cool, Activities, Crafts, Experiments & More for Kids to Do to Learn about Your State! 2003. (Missouri Experience Ser.). 32p. (gr. k-5). pap. 5.95 (978-0-635-01894-6(2), Marsh, Carole Bks.) Gallopade International.

—My First Book about Missouri. 2004. (Missouri Experience! Ser.). (Illus.). 32p. (J). (gr. k-4). pap. 7.95 (978-0-7933-9571-2(2)) Gallopade International.

Mills, Jordan. Missouri. 2016. (States Ser.). (ENG., Illus.). 32p. (gr. 3-4). lib. bdg. 27.32 (978-1-5157-0412-6(2)) Next Page Pr., The.

Murray, Julie. Missouri, 1 vol. 2006. (Buddy Book Ser.). (ENG., Illus.). 32p. (gr. 2-4). 27.07 (978-1-59197-684-4(7), Buddy Bks.) ABDO Publishing Co.

Obregon, Jose Maria. Missouri. Brusca, Maria Cristina, tr. 2005. (Bilingual Library of the United States of America Ser.: Set 2). (ENG & SPA., Illus.). 32p. (J). (gr. 3-6). lib. bdg. 25.25 (978-1-4042-3090-3(4)) Rosen Publishing Group, Inc., The.

Obregón, José María. Missouri. 2009. (Bilingual Library of the United States of America Ser.). (SPA.). 32p. (gr. 2-2). 47.90 (978-1-60853-370-1(0), Editorial Buenas Letras) Rosen Publishing Group, Inc., The.

Sanders, Doug. Missouri. 2004. (It's My State! Ser.). (Illus.). 80p. (J). (gr. 3-7). lib. bdg. 27.07 (978-0-7614-1822-1(9), Benchmark Bks.) Marshall Cavendish Corp.

Taylor-Butler, Christine. Missouri. 2005. (Rookie Read-About Geography Ser.). (ENG., Illus.). 32p. (J). (gr. 1-2). lib. bdg. 20.50 (978-0-516-25258-2(5), Children's Pr.) Scholastic Library Publishing.

—The Missouri River. 2006. (Rookie Read-About Geography Ser.). (ENG., Illus.). 32p. (J). (gr. 1-2). lib. bdg. 20.50 (978-0-516-25037-3(X), Children's Pr.) Scholastic Library Publishing.

Wimmer, Teresa. Missouri. 2008. (This Land Called America Ser.). 32p. (YA). (gr. 3-6). 22.95 (978-1-58341-650-1(1)) Creative Co., The.

Young, Judy. Show Me the Number: A Missouri Number Book. Young, Ross, illus. rev. ed. 2007. (State Counting Ser.). (ENG.). 40p. (J). (gr. 1-7). 17.95 (978-1-58536-156-4(9)) Sleeping Bear Pr.

MISSOURI—FICTION

Brauning, Kate. How We Fall. 2014. (ENG.). 304p. (YA). 17.99 (978-1-4405-8179-3(7), Simon Pulse) Simon Pulse.

Ciocca, Donna. Tavern Tales. 2005. 136p. per. 14.95 (978-0-9747361-3-6(9)) Oak Manor Publishing, Inc.

Coleman, Roger. The Pope & the Snowman: A Christmas Tale. 2009. (Illus.). 108p. 23.99 (978-1-4490-1128-4(4)); pap. 12.49 (978-1-4490-1127-7(6)) AuthorHouse.

Crofford, Emily. When the River Ran Backward. (Adventures in Time Ser.). (gr. 4-8). 2005. (Illus.). 84p. 15.95 (978-1-57505-305-9(5)) 2003. 80p. (J). pap. 6.95 (978-1-57505-488-9(4)) Lerner Publishing Group.

Cutler, Jane. Susan Marcus Bends the Rules. 2014. (ENG.). 112p. (J). (gr. 3-7). pap. 16.95 (978-0-8234-3047-5(2)) Holiday Hse., Inc.

Dalton, Sherry A. Do Indians Eat Soup? 2011. 32p. pap. 24.95 (978-1-4560-7463-0(6)) America Star Bks.

Doty, Kathryn Adams. Wild Orphan. 2006. (ENG.). 144p. (gr. 3-7). per. 14.95 (978-1-889020-20-4(6)) Edinborough Pr.

Figley, Marthy Rhodes & Figley, Marty Rhodes. The Night the Chimneys Fell. Marschall, Felicia, illus. 2011. 48p. (J). pap. 6.95 (978-0-7613-3939-7(6), First Avenue Editions) Lerner Publishing Group.

Figley, Marty Rhodes. The Night the Chimneys Fell. Marschall, Felicia, illus. 2011. (On My Own History Ser.). 48p. (J). pap. 39.62 (978-0-7613-7622-4(4), First Avenue Editions) Lerner Publishing Group.

—The Night the Chimneys Fell. Marshall, Felicia, illus. 2009. (On My Own History Ser.). (ENG.). 48p. (gr. 2-4). 25.26 (978-0-8225-7894-9(8)) Lerner Publishing Group.

Fleischner, Jennifer. Nobody's Boy. 2006. (ENG., Illus.). 112p. (gr. 4). per. 12.95 (978-1-883982-58-4(8)) Missouri Historical Society Pr.

Ford, Laura. Buster Brown & Tige in Misfit Heroes. 2004. (Illus.). 320p. 19.95 (978-1-881554-28-8(7)) Skyward Publishing Co.

Gilfert, Shirley Tankersley. The Other Side of Jordan: A Story of the Underground Railroad. 2007. 140p. 21.95 (978-0-595-70289-3(9)); per. 11.95 (978-0-595-46274-2(X)) iUniverse, Inc.

Gratton, Tessa. Blood Magic. 2011. (YA). pap. (978-0-375-86486-5(5)) Random Hse. Children's Bks.

Grippando, James. Leapholes. 2006. (ENG.). 176p. (YA). (gr. 8-17). 15.95 (978-1-59031-666-5(5)) American Bar Assn.

H., Yves & Hermann. Manhattan Beach 1957. 2003. (Illus.). 56p. (YA). (gr. 11-18). 12.95 (978-1-931724-23-4(7)) Diamond Select Toys & Collectibles.

Hart, Alison. Emma's River, 1 vol. Bachem, Paul, illus. 2010. (ENG.). 160p. (J). (gr. 2-5). 12.95 (978-1-56145-524-9(5), Peachtree Junior) Peachtree Pubs.

Hubbard, Crystal. Alive & Unharmed. 2013. 164p. (J). pap. 12.95 (978-1-60043-144-9(5)) Parker Publishing Inc.

Hughes, Dean. As Wide As the River. 2005. 156p. (J). pap. (978-1-59038-450-3(4)) Deseret Bk. Co.

—Facing the Enemy. 2005. (Illus.). 153p. (J). pap. (978-1-59038-449-7(0)) Deseret Bk. Co.

—Under the Same Stars. 2005. viii, 152p. (J). pap. (978-1-59038-448-0(2)) Deseret Bk. Co.

Jackson, Louise A. Exiled! From Tragedy to Triumph on the Missouri Frontier. 2007. (Illus.). 235p. (YA). (gr. 7-9). per. 16.95 (978-1-57168-948-1(6), Eakin Pr.) Eakin Pr.

Jacobs, Lily. The Littlest Bunny in Missouri: An Easter Adventure. Dunn, Robert, illus. 2015. (ENG.). 32p. (J). (-3). 9.99 (978-1-4926-1126-4(3), Sourcebooks Jabberwocky) Sourcebooks, Inc.

James, Eric. A Halloween Scare in Missouri. Le Ray, Marina, illus. 2015. (ENG.). 32p. (J). (-5). 9.99 (978-1-4926-2383-0(0), 9781492623830, Sourcebooks Jabberwocky) Sourcebooks, Inc.

—Santa's Sleigh Is on Its Way to Missouri. Dunn, Robert, illus. 2015. (ENG.). 32p. (J). (-2). 12.99 (978-1-4926-2759-3(3), Sourcebooks Jabberwocky) Sourcebooks, Inc.

Johnson, Annabel. A Rock Candy Dream. 2009. 140p. 22.49 (978-1-4389-4233-9(8)); pap. 11.99 (978-1-4389-4234-6(6)) AuthorHouse.

Johnson, Deanna. Blarron Creek Chronicles. 2009. 108p. 23.49 (978-1-4389-5580-3(4)) AuthorHouse.

Jude, Sarah. The May Queen Murders. 2017. (ENG.). 304p. (YA). (gr. 9). pap. 9.99 (978-0-544-93725-3(2), HMH Books For Young Readers) Houghton Mifflin Harcourt Publishing Co.

Katcher, Brian. Almost Perfect. 2010. (ENG.). 368p. (YA). (gr. 9). pap. 9.99 (978-0-385-73665-7(7), Delacorte Bks. for Young Readers) Random Hse. Children's Bks.

—Playing with Matches. 2009. (ENG.). 304p. (YA). (gr. 9). mass mkt. 8.99 (978-0-385-73545-2(6), Laurel Leaf) Random Hse. Children's Bks.

Klise, Kate. Grounded. 2013. (ENG.). 224p. (J). (gr. 4-8). pap. 8.99 (978-0-312-55591-7(1), 9780312555917) Square Fish.

—Homesick. 2012. (ENG.). 192p. (J). (gr. 5-9). 16.99 (978-1-250-00842-8(5), 9781250008428) Feiwel & Friends.

Lane, M. j. & Lane, M. J. Where in the World Is Snickers? 2011. 42p. pap. 19.99 (978-0-557-81843-3(5)) Lulu Pr., Inc.

Lawson, Jessica. The Actual & Truthful Adventures of Becky Thatcher. Bruno, Iacopo, illus. 2014. (ENG.). 224p. (J). (gr. 3-7). 16.99 (978-1-4814-0150-0(5), Simon & Schuster Bks. For Young Readers) Simon & Schuster Bks. For Young Readers.

MacBride, Roger Lea. Little Farm in the Ozarks. 2007. (Little House Ser.). 157p. (J). (gr. 2-5). per. 5.99 (978-0-06-114810-1(5), Harper Trophy) HarperCollins Pubs.

Mackall, Dandi Daley. A Girl Named Dan. Graef, Renee, illus. 2008. (ENG.). 32p. (J). (gr. k-6). 16.95 (978-1-58536-351-3(0)) Sleeping Bear Pr.

—The Secrets of Tree Taylor. 2014. (ENG.). 288p. (J). (gr. 5). 16.99 (978-0-375-86897-9(6), Knopf Bks. for Young Readers) Random Hse. Children's Bks.

May, Gary L. The Wilkins Family Farm, 1 vol. Monks, Christian, illus. 2009. 75p. pap. 19.95 (978-1-4489-2605-3(X)) America Star Bks.

McCaughrean, Geraldine. The Glorious Adventures of the Sunshine Queen. 2011. 336p. (J). (gr. 5). 16.99 (978-0-06-200806-0(4)) HarperCollins Pubs.

McKissack, Patricia C. A Friendship for Today. 2008. 172p. (J). pap. (978-0-545-06563-4(1)) Scholastic, Inc.

Meyer, Franklyn. More Me & Caleb Again. 2008. (Illus.). 191p. (J). 16.95 (978-0-9789388-2-6(8)) Hester Publishing.

Milford, Kate. The Boneshaker. Offermann, Andrea, illus. 2011. (ENG.). 384p. (J). (gr. 5-7). pap. 7.99 (978-0-547-55004-6(9)) Houghton Mifflin Harcourt Publishing Co.

Moonshower, Candie. The Legend of Zoey. 2007. (ENG.). 224p. (J). (gr. 3-7). 6.99 (978-0-440-23924-6(9), Yearling) Random Hse. Children's Bks.

Mulford, Carolyn. The Feedsack Dress. 2007. (YA). per. 7.95 (978-0-9713497-4-2(6)) Cave Hollow Pr.

Neighbors, Jolene. Nobody's Dog. 2010. 107p. pap. 14.95 (978-1-4327-5957-5(4)) Outskirts Pr., Inc.

Nelson, Karen, creator. Crystal Brave: Literature Theme Unit. 2012. (Illus.). 48p. spiral bd. 19.99 (978-1-930584-02-0(4)) Progreso Publishing Group , LLC.

Nitz, Kristin Wolden. Suspect, 1 vol. 2010. (ENG.). 224p. (YA). (gr. 7-11). 16.95 (978-1-56145-543-0(1)) Peachtree Pubs.

O'Neill, Elizabeth. Alfred Visits Missouri. 2008. 24p. (J). pap. 12.00 (978-0-9799121-4-6(8)) Global Business Information Strategies, Inc.

Papa's Gold. 2013. 196p. pap. 11.97 (978-0-9851274-4-2(9)) Pen-L Publishing.

Publishing, Racehorse & Twain, Mark. Classics to Color: Adventures of Huckleberry Finn. 2016. (ENG., Illus.). 80p. (J). (gr. 1-6). pap. 8.99 (978-1-944686-99-4(1), Racehorse Publishing) Skyhorse Publishing Co., Inc.

Sargent, Daina. Missouri: Teamwork. Lenoir, Jane, illus. l.t. ed. 2004. (Double Trouble Ser.). 48p. (J). pap. 10.95 (978-1-59381-127-3(6)); lib. bdg. 23.60 (978-1-59381-126-6(8)) Ozark Publishing.

Silvano, Wendi. Love Is All Around Missouri. Czernichowska, Joanna, illus. 2016. (ENG.). 32p. (J). (-6). 12.99 (978-1-4926-2937-5(5), Sourcebooks Jabberwocky) Sourcebooks, Inc.

—Love Is All Around St. Louis. Czernichowska, Joanna, illus. 2016. (ENG.). 32p. (J). (-6). 12.99 (978-1-4926-2962-7(6), Sourcebooks Jabberwocky) Sourcebooks, Inc.

Smallman, Steve. Santa Is Coming to Jefferson City. Dunn, Robert, illus. 2014. (ENG.). 32p. (J). (-3). 9.99 (978-1-4926-0766-3(5), Sourcebooks Jabberwocky) Sourcebooks, Inc.

—Santa Is Coming to Missouri. Dunn, Robert, illus. 2013. (ENG.). 32p. (J). (-3). 9.99 (978-1-4022-8809-8(3), Sourcebooks Jabberwocky) Sourcebooks, Inc.

Stuber, Barbara. Crossing the Tracks. (ENG.). 272p. (YA). (gr. 7). 2011. pap. 8.99 (978-1-4169-9704-7(0)) 2010. 16.99 (978-1-4169-9703-0(2)) McElderry, Margaret K. Bks. (McElderry, Margaret K. Bks.).

Tarshis, Lauren. I Survived the Joplin Tornado 2011. 2015. (I Survived Ser.: 12). (ENG.). 112p. (J). (gr. 2-5). pap. 4.99 (978-0-545-65848-5(9), Scholastic Paperbacks) Scholastic, Inc.

Tate, Eleanora E. The Minstrel's Melody. 2009. (Mysteries Through Time Ser.). 176p. (gr. 4-8). (YA). pap. 15.25 (978-1-60754-180-6(7)); (Illus.). (J). 31.95 (978-1-60754-179-0(3)) Windmill Bks.

Twain, Mark, pseud. The Adventures of Huckleberry Finn. Andreasen, Dan, illus. 2010. (Classic Starts(tm) Ser.). (ENG.). 160p. (J). (gr. 2-4). cd-rom 9.95 (978-1-4027-7355-6(2)) Sterling Publishing Co., Inc.

—The Adventures of Huckleberry Finn: With a Discussion of Friendship. Lauter, Richard, tr. Lauter, Richard, illus. 2003. (Values in Action Illustrated Classics Ser.). (J). (978-1-59203-042-2(4)) Learning Challenge, Inc.

—The Adventures of Tom Sawyer. Ingpen, Robert R., illus. 2010. (Sterling Illustrated Classics Ser.). (ENG.). 240p. (J). (gr. 5-18). 19.95 (978-1-4027-6762-3(5)) Sterling Publishing Co., Inc.

—The Adventures of Tom Sawyer. Corvino, Lucy, illus. 2005. (Classic Starts(tm) Ser.). (ENG.). 160p. (J). (gr. 2-4). 6.95 (978-1-4027-1216-6(2)) Sterling Publishing Co., Inc.

—The Adventures of Tom Sawyer: A Song for Aunt Polly. Bates, Amy, illus. 2008. (Easy Reader Classics Ser.). (ENG.). 32p. (gr. -1-3). lib. bdg. 24.21 (978-1-59961-334-5(4)) Spotlight.

—The Adventures of Tom Sawyer: With a Discussion of Imagination. Butterfield, Ned, illus. 2003. (Values in Action Illustrated Classics Ser.). 190p. (J). (978-1-59203-027-9(0)) Learning Challenge, Inc.

—Las Aventuras de Huckleberry Finn. de Atauri, Ines & de Atauri, Juan Diaz, eds. 2006. (Clasicos Juveniles Ser.).Tr. of Adventures of Huckleberry Finn. (SPA., Illus.). 359p. pap. 17.95 (978-84-263-5252-1(9)) Vives, Luis Editorial (Edelvives) ESP. Dist: Lectorum Pubns., Inc.

—Tom Sawyer. 2005. 264p. 28.95 (978-1-4218-0768-3(8), 1st World Library - Literary Society) 1st World Publishing, Inc.

—Tom Sawyer. 2008. (Bring the Classics to Life Ser.). (Illus.). 72p. (gr. 2-12). pap., act. bk. ed. 10.95 (978-0-931334-29-0(2), EDCTR-202B) EDCON Publishing Group.

—Tom Sawyer. 2006. (Classic Retelling Ser.). (Illus.). 224p. (YA). (gr. 8-12). (978-0-618-12053-6(X), 2-00218) Holt McDougal.

—Tom Sawyer. 2004. reprint ed. pap. 1.99 (978-1-4192-5166-5(X)) Kessinger Publishing, LLC.

—Tom Sawyer. (Young Collector's Illustrated Classics Ser.). (Illus.). 192p. (J). (gr. 3-7). 9.95 (978-1-56156-453-8(2)) Kidsbooks, LLC.

—Tom Sawyer, 1 vol. Mullarkey, Lisa, illus. 2010. (Calico Illustrated Classics Ser.: No. 1). (ENG.). 112p. (J). (gr. 3-6). 27.07 (978-1-60270-704-7(9)) Magic Wagon.

—Tom Sawyer. (Coleccion Clasicos de la Juventud). (SPA., Illus.). 220p. (J). 12.95 (978-84-7189-029-0(1), ORT310) Ortells, Alfredo Editorial S.L. ESP. Dist: Continental Bk. Co., Inc.

—Tom Sawyer. 2009. 196p. (gr. 4-7). pap. 12.99 (978-1-934941-63-8(8)) Red & Black Pubs.

—Tom Sawyer. 2003. (Timeless Classics Ser.). (SPA., Illus.). 95p. (J). (gr. 5-8). pap. 12.95 (978-84-372-2235-6(4)) Santillana USA Publishing Co., Inc.

Wang, Jack, et al. Mark Twain's the Adventures of Huckleberry Finn. 2016. (ENG., Illus.). 24p. (J). (gr. -1 — 1). bds. 9.95 (978-1-4521-5249-3(7)) Chronicle Bks. LLC.

Webster, Amye. Shell's Journey. 2013. 162p. pap. 9.99 (978-0-9891510-2-3(6)) Zebra Ginkgo.

Whaley, John Corey. Noggin. 2015. (ENG., Illus.). 368p. (YA). (gr. 9). pap. 12.99 (978-1-4424-5873-4(9), Atheneum Bks. for Young Readers) Simon & Schuster Children's Publishing.

The Year We Sailed the Sun. 2015. (ENG., Illus.). 432p. (J). (gr. 3-7). 17.99 (978-0-689-85827-7(2), Atheneum/Richard Jackson Bks.) Simon & Schuster Children's Publishing.

MISSOURI—HISTORY

Bennett, Michelle & Hart, Joyce. Missouri. 2nd rev. ed. 2009. (Celebrate the States 10 Ser.). 144p. (gr. 6). 42.79 (978-0-7614-4727-6(X)) Marshall Cavendish Corp.

Blashfield, Jean F. Missouri (Revised Edition) 2014. (America the Beautiful, Third Ser. (Revised Edition) Ser.). (ENG.). 144p. (J). lib. bdg. 40.00 (978-0-531-28282-3(1)) Scholastic Library Publishing.

Bullard, Lisa. The Gateway Arch. 2009. (Lightning Bolt Books (tm) — Famous Places Ser.). (ENG.). 32p. (gr. k-2). 26.60 (978-0-8225-9406-2(4), Lerner Pubns.) Lerner Publishing Group.

Cruz, Ginny Wilson. E Is for Ellisville. 2011. (Illus.). (J). pap. (978-0-615-55095-4(9)) Pioneer Poet Publishing.

Evdokimoff, Natasha. Missouri: The Show Me State. 2016. (J). (978-1-4896-4890-7(9)) Weigl Pubs., Inc.

Gamble, Adam & Jasper, Mark. Good Night Missouri. Veno, Joe, illus. 2013. (Good Night Our World Ser.). (ENG.). 20p. (J). (— 1). bds. 9.95 (978-1-60219-077-1(1)) Good Night Bks.

Jackson, Robert. Meet Me in St. Louis: A Trip to the 1904 World's Fair. 2004. (ENG., Illus.). 144p. (J). (gr. 3-18). 17.99 (978-0-06-009267-2(X)) HarperCollins Pubs.

Jerome, Kate B. Lucky to Live in Missouri. 2017. (Arcadia Kids Ser.). (ENG., Illus.). 32p. (J). 16.99 **(978-0-7385-2788-8(2))** Arcadia Publishing.

—The Wise Animal Handbook Missouri. 2017. (Arcadia Kids Ser.). (ENG., Illus.). 32p. (J). 16.99 **(978-0-7385-2828-1(5))** Arcadia Publishing.

Koontz, Robin Michal. What's Great about Missouri? 2015. (ENG., Illus.). 32p. (J). (gr. 2-5). 26.65 (978-1-4677-3883-5(2)) Lerner Publishing Group.

Lago, Mary Ellen. Missouri. 2008. (ENG., Illus.). 80p. (J). pap. 7.95 (978-0-531-20809-0(5), Children's Pr.) Scholastic Library Publishing.

Lusted, Marcia Amidon. Missouri: The Show-Me State. 2010. (Our Amazing States Ser.). (Illus.). 24p. (J). pap. 8.25 (978-1-4358-9796-0(X)); lib. bdg. 22.60 (978-1-4358-9351-1(4)) Rosen Publishing Group, Inc., The. (PowerKids Pr.).

Marsh, Carole. Exploring Missouri Through Project-Based Learning: Geography, History, Government, Economics & More. 2016. (Missouri Experience Ser.). (ENG.). (J). pap. 9.99 (978-0-635-12349-7(5)) Gallopade International.

—Missouri History Projects: 30 Cool, Activities, Crafts, Experiments & More for Kids to Do to Learn about Your State! 2003. (Missouri Experience Ser.). 32p. (gr. k-5). pap. 5.95 (978-0-635-01794-9(6), Marsh, Carole Bks.) Gallopade International.

McDowell, Pamela. Missouri: The Show Me State. 2012. (J). (978-1-61913-369-3(5)); pap. (978-1-61913-370-9(9)) Weigl Pubs., Inc.

McManus, Donald. Emmett Kelly: The Greatest Clown on Earth. 2014. (ENG., Illus.). 48p. (J). lib. bdg. 24.00 (978-1-61248-120-3(5)) Truman State Univ. Pr.

McVicker, Maryellen. Joseph Kinney: Steamboat Captain. Hare, John, illus. 2014. (ENG.). 48p. (J). lib. bdg. 24.00 (978-1-61248-116-6(7)) Truman State Univ. Pr.

Missouri, Our Home Program Kit: All program components for Missouri, Our Home, 1 vol. 2009. 129.95 (978-1-4236-0721-2(X)) Gibbs Smith, Publisher.

Murray, Julie. Missouri, 1 vol. 2012. (Explore the United States Ser.). (ENG.). 32p. (J). (gr. 2-5). lib. bdg. 28.50 (978-1-61783-363-2(0), Big Buddy Bks.) ABDO Publishing Co.

Ollhoff, Jim. Missouri, 1 vol. 2009. (United States Ser.). (ENG., Illus.). 48p. (YA). (gr. 2-5). 27.07 (978-1-60453-660-7(8)) ABDO Publishing Co.

Ripley County Historical Society (Ripley County, Mo.) Staff, contrib. by. Ripley County, Missouri: History & Heritage. 2007. (Illus.). 176p. (978-0-9773198-5-5(7)) Acclaim Pr., Inc.

Roza, Greg. Missouri: Past & Present. 2010. (United States: Past & Present Ser.). (ENG., Illus.). 48p. (J). pap. 11.75 (978-1-4358-8490-8(6)); lib. bdg. 29.25 (978-1-4358-3520-7(4)) Rosen Publishing Group, Inc., The. (Rosen Reference).

Sanders, Doug. Missouri. 2014. (J). lib. bdg. (978-1-62712-240-5(0)) Cavendish Square Publishing.

Sanders, Doug & Boehme, Gerry. Missouri. 2016. (ENG., Illus.). 80p. (J). 34.21 (978-1-62713-244-2(9)) Cavendish Square Publishing.

Schultz, James Willard. Floating on the Missouri: 100 Years after Lewis & Clark. 2003. 152p. per. 19.95 (978-1-931832-15-1(3), 18667872363) Riverbend Publishing.

Sipperley, Keli. St. Louis Gateway Arch. 2014. (ENG.). 32p. (gr. 3-6). 32.79 (978-1-62717-742-9(6)) Rourke Educational Media.

St. Louis Union Station: A City Within a City. 2003. 19.95 (978-0-9748109-0-4(8)) Market 1 Group Inc.

Turninelly, Nancy. Missy the Show-Me Mule: A Story about Missouri, 1 vol. Doucet, Bob, illus. 2011. (Fact & Fable: State Stories Set 3 Ser.). (ENG.). 24p. (J). (gr. -1-2). 25.65 (978-1-61714-682-4(X)) ABDO Publishing Co.

Young, Judy & Wargin, Kathy-jo. Little Missouri. Urban, Helle, illus. 2012. (My Little State Ser.). (ENG.). 20p. (J). bds. 9.95 (978-1-58536-206-6(9)) Sleeping Bear Pr.

Young, Judy Dockrey. The Missouri Reader. Darnell, Kate, illus. 2010. (Readers Ser.). (ENG.). 96p. (J). 12.95 (978-1-58536-437-4(1)) Sleeping Bear Pr.

MISSOURI VALLEY

McNeese, Tim. The Missouri River. 2004. (Rivers in American Life & Times Ser.). (Illus.). 120p. (C). (gr. 9-13). 32.50 (978-0-7910-7724-5(1), Chelsea Hse.) Facts On File, Inc.

MITCHELL, MARIA, 1818-1889

Anderson, Dale. Maria Mitchell. 2003. (Women in Science Ser.). (Illus.). 112p. (gr. 6-12). 30.00 (978-0-7910-7249-3(5), Chelsea Hse.) Facts On File, Inc.

Butzer, Anna. Maria Mitchell, 1 vol. 2014. (Great Women in History Ser.). (ENG.). 24p. (gr. k-1). pap. 6.29 (978-1-4914-0542-0(2), Pebble Bks.) Capstone Press of Coughlan Cos.

Gormley, Beatrice. Maria Mitchell: The Soul of an Astronomer. 2004. (Illus.). 166p. (J). pap. 12.00 (978-0-8028-5264-9(5)) Eerdmans, William B. Publishing Co.

MITCHELL, WILLIAM, 1879-1936

Miller, Roger G. Billy Mitchell: Evangelist of Airpower. 2007. (Illus.). 152p. (J). (gr. 10-18). lib. bdg. 25.95 (978-1-59556-025-4(4)) OTTN Publishing.

MIXED MARRIAGE

see Intermarriage

MOBILES (SCULPTURE)

French, Cathy. Make an Animal Mobile & Haz un móvil de Animales: 6 English, 6 Spanish Adaptations. 2011. (SPA & ENG.). (J). 75.00 net. (978-1-4108-5619-7(4)) Benchmark Education Co.

MOBS

see Riots

MOCKINGBIRDS

Amim, Aife. A Bird Watcher's Guide to Mockingbirds. 2017. (Backyard Bird Watchers Ser.). 32p. (J). (gr. 2-3). pap. 10.50 **(978-1-5382-0319-4(7))** Stevens, Gareth Publishing LLLP.

Lunis, Natalie. Mockingbird: Noisy Mimic. 2011. (Animal Loudmouths: Noisy Animals Ser.). 24p. (YA). (gr. k-3). lib. bdg. 22.61 (978-1-61772-277-6(4)) Bearport Publishing Co., Inc.

Swisher, Dianne. To Save a Mockingbird. 2013. 32p. pap. (978-1-77097-049-6(5)) FriesenPress.

MODEL CAR RACING

Mercer, Bobby. The Racecar Book: Build & Race Mousetrap Cars, Dragsters, Tri-Can Haulers & More. 2013. (Science in Motion Ser.). (ENG., Illus.). 216p. (J). (gr. 4). pap. 14.95 (978-1-61374-714-8(4)) Chicago Review Pr., Inc.

Thorne, Troy. Getting Started in Pinewood Derby: Step-by-Step Workbook to Building Your First Car. 2011. (ENG., Illus.). 96p. pap. 12.95 (978-1-56523-617-2(3), 6172) Fox Chapel Publishing Co., Inc.

MODELING

see also Sculpture—Technique; Soap Sculpture

Bienik, Stella. Sculpting with Clay: Reason with Shapes & Their Attributes. 2014. (Math Masters: Geometry Ser.). 24p. (J). (gr. 2-3). 23.60 (978-1-4777-6444-2(5)); (ENG.). pap. 8.25 (978-1-4777-4906-7(3)) Rosen Publishing Group, Inc., The. (Rosen Classroom).

Cuxart, Bernadette. Spooky Characters: Easy-To-Follow Clay-Making Projects in Simple Steps. 2013. (Modeling Clay Bks.). (ENG.). 36p. (J). (gr. k-4). pap. 6.99 (978-1-4380-0358-0(7)) Barron's Educational Series, Inc.

Diamond, Cheryl. Model: A Memoir. 2008. (ENG., Illus.). 368p. (YA). (gr. 9-18). pap. 11.99 (978-1-4169-5904-5(1), Simon Pulse) Simon Pulse.

Fernandes, Kim. Gifts to Make with Crayola Model Magic, Incl. modelling material.Tr. of Surprises a Modeler avec Model Magic de Crayola. (FRE., Illus.). 32p. (J). 12.99 (978-0-590-24760-3(3)) Scholastic, Inc.

Fontichiaro, Kristin & Thomas, AnnMarie P. Squishy Circuits. 2014. (21st Century Skills Innovation Library: Makers As Innovators Ser.). (ENG., Illus.). 32p. (J). (gr. 4-8). 28.50 (978-1-63137-775-4(2), 205343) Cherry Lake Publishing.

Frankish, Lorraine. 30 Fun Ways to Learn with Clay & Squishy Stuff. 2011. (30 Fun Ways to Learn Ser.). (ENG.). 80p. (gr. -1-k). pap. 12.95 (978-0-87659-371-4(6), Gryphon House Inc) Gryphon Hse., Inc.

Hammonds, Heather. Modellieren MIT Knete. 2005. (GER., Illus.). 64p. (J). (978-3-937495-94-1(0)) Mud Puddle, Inc.

Henry, Sally. Clay Modeling. 2009. (Make Your Own Art Ser.). (ENG., Illus.). 32p. (gr. 2-6). pap. 11.75 (978-1-4358-2641-0(8), PowerKids Pr.) Rosen Publishing Group, Inc., The.

Llimós, Anna. Earth-Friendly Clay Crafts in 5 Easy Steps. 2013. (Earth-Friendly Crafts in 5 Easy Steps Ser.). 32p. (J). (gr. 3-4). pap. 7.95 (978-1-4644-0309-5(0), Enslow Elementary) Enslow Pubs., Inc.

Llimós Plomer, Anna. Earth-Friendly Clay Crafts in 5 Easy Steps. 2013. (Earth-Friendly Crafts in 5 Easy Steps Ser.). (Illus.). 32p. (J). lib. bdg. 23.94 (978-0-7660-4189-9(1)) Enslow Pubs., Inc.

Morris, Ting & Morris, Neil. Dinosaurs. Levy, Ruth & Cowne, Joanne, illus. 2006. (Sticky Fingers Ser.). 32p. (J). lib. bdg. 28.50 (978-1-59771-029-9(6)) Sea-To-Sea Pubns.

Newell, Keith. Models. 2005. (Art & Craft Skills (Sea-to-Sea) Ser.). (Illus.). 32p. (J). (gr. 3-6). lib. bdg. 27.10 (978-1-932889-85-7(X), 1247657) Sea-To-Sea Pubns.

Petelinsek, Kathleen. Modeling Clay Creations. Petelinsek, Kathleen, illus. 2014. (How-To Library). (ENG., Illus.). 32p. (J). (gr. 3-6). 28.50 (978-1-63137-783-9(3), 205375) Cherry Lake Publishing.

Ryall, Jeanette. Clay Art. 2012. (Awesome Art Ser.). (ENG., Illus.). 32p. (J). (gr. 3-6). 26.50 (978-1-4488-8085-0(8)); pap. 11.75 (978-1-4488-8138-3(2)) Windmill Bks.

Speechley, Greta. Step-by-Step Clay Modelling. 2004. (Step-by-Step Children's Crafts Ser.). (Illus.). 32p. pap. 7.95 (978-0-85532-914-3(9), 9149) Midpoint Trade Bks., Inc.

MODELS (PERSONS)

ABDO Publishing Company Staff. Essential Lives Set 7. 2011. (Essential Lives Set 7 Ser.: 8). (ENG., Illus.). 112p. (J). (gr. 6-12). lib. bdg. 285.12 (978-1-61783-000-6(3), Essential Library) ABDO Publishing Co.

Beker, Jeanne. Strutting It! The Grit Behind the Glamour. 2011. (ENG., Illus.). 78p. (J). (gr. 5-18). pap. 17.95 (978-1-77049-224-0(0), Tundra Bks.) Tundra Bks. CAN. Dist: Penguin Random Hse. LLC.

Berne, Emma Carlson. Paris & Nicky Hilton. (Pop Culture Ser.). (Illus.). 64p. (YA). (gr. 3-7). 2008. lib. bdg. 22.95 (978-1-4222-0204-3(6)) 2007. pap. 7.95 (978-1-4222-0358-3(1)) Mason Crest.

Davidson, Amy. Elle Fanning. 2012. (Rising Stars Ser.). (Illus.). 32p. (J). (gr. 3-6). 25.25 (978-1-4339-7280-5(8)); pap. 10.50 (978-1-4339-7281-2(6)) Stevens, Gareth Publishing LLLP.

—Kendall Jenner. 2012. (Rising Stars Ser.). (Illus.). 32p. (J). (gr. 3-6). 25.25 (978-1-4339-7288-1(3)); pap. 10.50 (978-1-4339-7289-8(1)) Stevens, Gareth Publishing LLLP.

Diamond, Cheryl. Model: A Memoir. 2008. (ENG., Illus.). 368p. (YA). (gr. 9-18). pap. 11.99 (978-1-4169-5904-5(1), Simon Pulse) Simon Pulse.

Dougherty, Terri. Tyra Banks. 2009. (People in the News Ser.). (Illus.). 128p. (YA). (gr. 7-12). 33.95 (978-1-4205-0161-2(5)) Cengage Gale.

Franks, Katie. I Want to Be a Supermodel. 2007. 28p. (gr. 3-7). pap. 21.25 (978-1-4358-3834-5(3), PowerKids Pr.) Rosen Publishing Group, Inc., The.

Hibbert, Clare & Hachette Children's Group. Fashion Model: Find Out How the Top Fashion Models Made It! 2012. (Celeb Ser.). (Illus.). 32p. (gr. 4-6). lib. bdg. 28.50 (978-1-59771-331-3(7)) Sea-To-Sea Pubns.

Hill, Anne E. Tyra Banks: From Supermodel to Role Model. 2009. (Gateway Biographies Ser.). (ENG.). 48p. (gr. 4-8). 26.60 (978-1-57505-949-5(5)) Lerner Publishing Group.

James, Kelle. Smile for the Camera: A Memoir. (ENG.). 400p. (YA). (gr. 9). 2011. pap. 9.99 (978-1-4424-0624-7(0)) 2010. 16.99 (978-1-4424-0623-0(2)) Simon & Schuster Bks. For Young Readers. (Simon & Schuster Bks. For Young Readers).

Parker, Vic. Inspiring Others, 1 vol. 2012. (Kids Making a Difference Ser.). (ENG.). 48p. (gr. 3-5). lib. bdg. 32.65 (978-1-4329-6502-0(6), NA-h) Heinemann-Raintree.

Rissman, Rebecca. Role Models, 1 vol. 2011. (Families Ser.). (ENG., Illus.). 24p. (gr. -1-1). 22.65 (978-1-4329-4660-9(9)); pap. 6.29 (978-1-4329-4668-5(4)) Heinemann-Raintree. (Acorn).

Schwartz, Heather. Zendaya: Capturing the Stage, Screen, & Modeling Scene. 2014. (Pop Culture Bios Ser.). (ENG., Illus.). 32p. (gr. 3-6). pap. 7.95 (978-1-4677-4548-2(0)) Lerner Publishing Group.

Schwartz, Heather E. Zendaya: Capturing the Stage, Screen, & Modeling Scene. 2014. (Pop Culture Bios Ser.). (ENG., Illus.). 32p. (J). (gr. 3-6). lib. bdg. 26.60 (978-1-4677-3673-2(2), Lerner Pubns.) Lerner Publishing Group.

Superwomen Role Models. 2016. (Superwomen Role Models Ser.). 32p. (gr. 4-3). 157.50 (978-1-4994-1888-0(4)); pap. 70.50 (978-1-4994-2461-4(2)) Rosen Publishing Group, Inc., The. (PowerKids Pr.).

Sutherland, Adam. Being a Model. 2012. (On the Radar: Awesome Jobs Ser.). (ENG., Illus.). 32p. (gr. 4-8). lib. bdg. 26.60 (978-0-7613-7782-5(4), Lerner Pubns.) Lerner Publishing Group.

Tobey, Cheryl. Choosing a Career as a Model. 2009. (World of Work Ser.). 64p. (gr. 5-5). 58.50 (978-1-60854-322-9(6)) Rosen Publishing Group, Inc., The.

Todd, Anne M. Tyra Banks. 2009. (Women of Achievement Ser.). (Illus.). 120p. (gr. 6-12). 35.00 (978-1-60413-462-9(3), Chelsea Hse.) Facts On File, Inc.

Torres, Jennifer. Paris Hilton. 2005. (Blue Banner Biography Ser.). (Illus.). 32p. (J). (gr. 4-8). lib. bdg. 25.70 (978-1-58415-382-5(2)) Mitchell Lane Pubs., Inc.

Woodcock, Sandra, et al. Being a Model. 2005. (ENG., Illus.). 32p. pap. (978-0-340-74716-2(1)) Cambridge Univ. Pr.

Zakarin, Debra Mostow. Who's Your Superstar BFF? 2010. 112p. pap. 4.95 (978-1-60747-775-4(0), Pickwick Pr.) Phoenix Bks., Inc.

—Who's Your Superstar Soul Mate? 2010. 112p. pap. 4.95 (978-1-60747-776-1(9), Pickwick Pr.) Phoenix Bks., Inc.

MODELS (PERSONS)—FICTION

Axelsson, Carina. Model Undercover: London. 2016. (Model Undercover Ser.: 3). (ENG.). 368p. (J). (gr. 5-8). pap. 6.99

(978-1-4926-2088-4(2), Sourcebooks Jabberwocky) Sourcebooks, Inc.

—Model Undercover: New York. 2015. (Model Undercover Ser.: 2). (ENG.). 320p. (J). (gr. 4-8). pap. 6.99 *(978-1-4926-0785-4(1),* Sourcebooks Jabberwocky) Sourcebooks, Inc.

Baker, Ken. How I Got Skinny, Famous, & Fell Madly in Love. 2014. (ENG.). 272p. (YA). (gr. 2-17). pap. 9.95 *(978-0-7624-5014-5(2),* Running Pr. Kids) Running Pr. Bk. Pubs.

Banks, Tyra. Modelland. 2011. 569p. (YA). (gr. 7). 17.99 *(978-0-375-97259-1(5),* Delacorte Pr) Random House Publishing Group.

Bell, Taryn. In the Spotlight. 2010. (ENG.). 256p. pap. 8.99 *(978-0-545-21444-5(0))* Scholastic, Inc.

Bennardo, Charlotte & Zaman, Natalie. Blonde Ops. 2014. (ENG.). 288p. (YA). (gr. 7). 17.99 *(978-1-250-03039-9(0),* 9781250030399, St. Martin's Griffin) St. Martin's Pr.

Bennett, Sophia. The Look. 2013. (J). (ENG.). 336p. (gr. 7). 17.99 *(978-0-545-46438-3(2)); (978-0-545-46439-0(0))* Scholastic, Inc. (Chicken Hse., The).

Berk, Sheryl & Berk, Carrie. Model Madness. 2017. (Fashion Academy Ser.: 4). (ENG.). 192p. (J). (gr. 5-8). pap. 7.99 *(978-1-4926-4496-5(X),* 9781492644965, Sourcebooks Jabberwocky) Sourcebooks, Inc.

Cabot, Meg. Airhead. (Airhead Ser.: 1). (ENG.). 352p. (J). (gr. 7). 2009. pap. 9.99 *(978-0-545-04054-9(X))* 2008. 16.99 *(978-0-545-04052-5(3))* Scholastic, Inc.

—Being Nikki. (Airhead Ser.: 2). (ENG.). 352p. (J). 2010. (gr. 3-7). pap. 9.99 *(978-0-545-04058-7(2))* 2009. (gr. 7-18). 16.99 *(978-0-545-04056-3(6))* Scholastic, Inc.

Carlson, Melody. New York Debut, 1 vol. 2014. (Carter House Girls Ser.). (ENG.). 224p. (YA). pap. 9.99 *(978-0-310-74779-6(1))* Zondervan.

Chambers, Veronica. Plus. 2010. (ENG.). 272p. (YA). (gr. 7-18). 8.99 *(978-1-59514-165-1(0),* Razorbill) Penguin Young Readers Group.

Cross, Gillian. Where I Belong. 2011. (ENG., Illus.). 256p. (J). (gr. 5-18). 17.95 *(978-0-8234-2332-3(8))* Holiday Hse., Inc.

Cross, Julie & Perini, Mark. You Before Anyone Else. 2016. (ENG.). 400p. (YA). (gr. 8-12). pap. 10.99 *(978-1-4926-0492-1(5),* 9781492604921) Sourcebooks, Inc.

Dessen, Sarah. Just Listen. 2008. (ENG.). 400p. (YA). (gr. 7-18). 10.99 *(978-0-14-241097-4(7),* Speak) Penguin Young Readers Group.

—Just Listen. 2007. 20.00 *(978-0-7569-8270-6(7))* Perfection Learning Corp.

—Just Listen. 2008. 22.10 *(978-1-4178-2016-0(0),* Turtleback) Turtleback Bks.

Dionne, Erin. Models Don't Eat Chocolate Cookies. 2009. (ENG.). 256p. (J). (gr. 3-7). pap. 6.99 *(978-0-8037-3296-4(1),* Dial Bks) Penguin Young Readers Group.

Hughes, Alison. Poser, 1 vol. 2013. (ENG.). 168p. (J). (gr. 4-7). pap. 9.95 *(978-1-4598-0147-9(4))* Orca Bk. Pubs. USA.

Hyde, Lara. Mosquito Bites. 2009. 132p. 21.95 *(978-0-595-51697-1(1));* pap. 11.95 *(978-0-595-52079-4(0))* iUniverse, Inc.

Keene, Carolyn. Model Suspect: Book Three in the Model Mystery Trilogy. 2009. (Nancy Drew (All New) Girl Detective Ser.: 38). (ENG.). 160p. (J). (gr. 3-7). pap. 5.99 *(978-1-4169-7841-1(0),* Aladdin) Simon & Schuster Children's Publishing.

Macaraeg, Diane. Last Meal. 2008. 132p. pap. *(978-3-639-03548-3(8))* AV Akademikerverlag GmbH & Co. KG.

The Model, 6 vols., Pack. (Chiquilibros Ser.). (gr. k-1). 23.00 *(978-0-7635-0426-7(2))* Rigby Education.

Osborne, Jill. Riley Mae & the Sole Fire Safari, 1 vol. 2014. (Faithgirlz / the Good News Shoes Ser.). (ENG.). 256p. (J). pap. 7.99 *(978-0-310-74283-8(8))* Zonderkidz.

Paige, D. M. Size 0. 2015. (Opportunity Ser.). (ENG.). 120p. (YA). (gr. 6-12). 34.65 *(978-1-4677-6017-1(X),* Lerner Digital) Lerner Publishing Group.

Perini, Mark & Cross, Julie. Halfway Perfect. 2015. (ENG.). 384p. (YA). (gr. 8-12). pap. 9.99 *(978-1-4022-9719-9(X),* 9781402297199) Sourcebooks, Inc.

Peschke, Marci. Fashion Queen. Mourning, Tuesday, illus. 2015. (Kylie Jean Ser.). (ENG.). 112p. (gr. 2-3). 8.95 *(978-1-4795-5881-0(8),* Kylie Jean) Picture Window Bks.

Rayban, Chloe. Models Move on to Starring Roles. 137p. pap. *(978-0-340-71428-7(X))* Hodder & Stoughton.

—Skin Deep, Vol. 2. 138p. pap. *(978-0-340-71429-4(8))* Hodder & Stoughton.

Simon, Coco. Emma, Smile & Say Cupcake! 2012. (Cupcake Diaries: 11). (ENG.). 160p. (J). (gr. 3-7). pap. 6.99 *(978-1-4424-5398-2(2),* Simon Spotlight) Simon Spotlight.

—Emma, Smile & Say "Cupcake!" 2014. (Cupcake Diaries: 11). (ENG., Illus.). 160p. (J). (gr. 3-7). 17.99 *(978-1-4424-9611-8(8),* Simon Spotlight) Simon Spotlight.

—Emma's Not-So-Sweet Dilemma. 2014. (Cupcake Diaries: 23). lib. bdg. 17.20 *(978-0-606-36102-6(2))* Turtleback Bks.

Simone, Ni-Ni & Abrams, Amir. Heels, Heartache & Headlines. 2017. (Hollywood High Ser.: 5). (ENG.). 288p. (YA). (gr. 9). pap. 9.95 *(978-0-7582-8856-1(5),* K-Teen/Dafina) Kensington Publishing Corp.

Slater, David Michael. Ned Breaks His Heart, 1 vol. Brooks, S. G., illus. 2009. (David Michael Slater Set 2 Ser.). (ENG.). 32p. (gr. -1-4). 28.50 *(978-1-60270-657-6(3),* Looking Glass Library) ABDO Publishing Co.

Smale, Holly. Geek Girl. 2015. (Geek Girl Ser.: 1). 384p. (YA). (gr. 8). 17.99 *(978-0-06-233357-5(7),* HarperTeen) HarperCollins Pubs.

—Geek Girl: Model Misfit. 2016. (Geek Girl Ser.: 2). 416p. (YA). (gr. 8). pap. 9.99 *(978-0-06-233361-2(5),* HarperTeen) HarperCollins Pubs.

—Geek Girl: Picture Perfect. 2016. (Geek Girl Ser.: 3). 416p. (YA). (gr. 8). 17.99 *(978-0-06-233363-6(1),* HarperTeen) HarperCollins Pubs.

Smith, Lucky Blue. Stay Golden. 2016. (ENG., Illus.). 240p. (YA). (gr. 9). 18.99 *(978-1-5247-1876-3(9),* Random Hse. Bks. for Young Readers) Random Hse. Children's Bks.

Vail, Rachel. Gorgeous. (Avery Sisters Trilogy Ser.: 2). (ENG.). (YA). (gr. 8). 2010. 304p. pap. 9.99 *(978-0-06-089048-3(7))* 2009. 288p. 16.99 *(978-0-06-089046-9(0))* HarperCollins Pubs.

MODELS (PERSONS)—VOCATIONAL GUIDANCE

Franks, Katie. I Want to Be a Supermodel. 2009. (Dream Jobs Ser.). 24p. (gr. 2-3). 42.50 *(978-1-61512-212-7(5),* PowerKids Pr.) Rosen Publishing Group, Inc., The.

Freese, Susan M. Fashion, 1 vol. 2011. (Inside the Industry Ser.). (ENG., Illus.). 112p. (J). (gr. 6-12). lib. bdg. 35.64 *(978-1-61714-800-2(8),* Essential Library) ABDO Publishing Co.

O'Donnell, Kerri. Careers in Modeling. (Career Resource Library). 192p. (gr. 7-12). 2009. 63.90 *(978-1-60853-400-5(6))* 2005. (Illus.). (YA). lib. bdg. 34.60 *(978-0-8239-3183-5(8))* Rosen Publishing Group, Inc., The.

Prescott, Sheri. How to Be a Super Model: A Guide to Inner Beauty. 2004. 237p. (YA). per. 14.99 *(978-1-58930-129-0(3))* Selah Publishing Group, LLC.

Tobey, Cheryl. Choosing a Career as a Model. 2005. (World of Work Ser.). (Illus.). 64p. (YA). (gr. 7-12). lib. bdg. 31.95 *(978-0-8239-3243-6(5))* Rosen Publishing Group, Inc., The.

MODELS, FASHION

see Models (Persons)

MODELS, MECHANICAL

see Machinery—Models

MODELS AND MODELMAKING

see also subdivision Models under types of objects, e.g. Automobiles—Models; Machinery—Models; and phrase headings for types of models

Ashman, Iain. Egyptian Mummy. 2004. (Cut-Out Models Ser.). (Illus.). 32p. (J). pap. 9.95 *(978-0-7945-0255-3(5),* Usborne) EDC Publishing.

Beck, Esther & Doudna, Kelly. Im on the Trail to Learn about Scale!, 1 vol. 2007. (Science Made Simple Ser.). (ENG., Illus.). 24p. (J). (gr. k-3). lib. bdg. 24.21 *(978-1-59928-592-4(4),* SandCastle) ABDO Publishing Co.

Beecroft, Simon & Fry, Jason. The Visual Dictionary. rev. exp. ed. 2014. (ENG.). 144p. (J). (gr. 3-7). lib. bdg. 21.99 *(978-1-4654-2136-4(X),* DK Children) Dorling Kindersley Publishing, Inc.

Campodonica, Carol A. How Congress Works. Miller, Bondell, ed. Anderson, Bill, illus. Uni Photo Picture Agency Staff, photos by. Date not set. (J). (gr. 4-5). pap. *(978-0-9648488-9-4(9))* Buzzard Pr. International.

—How to Build a California Mission: Santa Barbara, 20 vols. Wardup, Shirley et al, eds. Sousa, Jay, photos by. Date not set. (How to Build a California Mission Ser.). (Illus.). (J). (gr. 4-5). pap. *(978-0-9648488-3-2(X))* Buzzard Pr. International.

—How to Build a California Mission: Santa Cruz, 20 vols. Weber, Francis J. et al, eds. Anderson, Bill, illus. Anderson, Jay, photos by. Date not set. (How to Build a California Mission Ser.). (J). (gr. 4-5). pap. *(978-0-9648488-5-6(6))* Buzzard Pr. International.

Cryan, Mary Beth. Standups! at Work: 8 Easy-To-Make Models! 2013. (ENG.). 16p. (J). (gr. 2-5). pap. 9.99 *(978-0-486-49132-5(3))* Dover Pubns., Inc.

—Standups! Presidents: 8 Easy-To-Make Models! 2013. (ENG.). 16p. (J). (gr. 2-5). pap. 9.99 *(978-0-486-49131-8(5))* Dover Pubns., Inc.

Dorling Kindersley Publishing Staff. LEGO Star Wars Character Encyclopedia: Updated & Expanded: Updated & Expanded. 2015. (ENG., Illus.). 288p. (J). (gr. 3-7). 18.99 *(978-1-4654-3550-7(6),* DK Children) Dorling Kindersley Publishing, Inc.

Dorling Kindersley Publishing Staff & Lipkowitz, Daniel. LEGO Ideas Book. 2011. (ENG.). 200p. (J). (gr. 2-5). 24.99 *(978-0-7566-8606-2(7),* DK Children) Dorling Kindersley Publishing, Inc.

Dorling Kindersley Publishing Staff & Taylor, Victoria. Super-Villains Level 2. 2013. (DK Readers Ser.). (ENG., Illus.). 32p. (J). (gr. 1-3). pap. 3.99 *(978-1-4654-0176-2(8),* DK Children) Dorling Kindersley Publishing, Inc.

Dorling Kindersley Publishing Staff, et al. The Visual Dictionary. rev. exp. ed. 2014. (ENG.). 144p. (J). (gr. 3-7). 21.99 *(978-1-4654-1921-7(7),* DK Children) Dorling Kindersley Publishing, Inc.

Dyer, Janice. Get into Dioramas & Models. 2016. (Get-Into-It Guides). (ENG.). 32p. (J). (gr. 3-6). *(978-0-7787-2640-1(1))* Crabtree Publishing Co.

Elsmore, Warren. Brick History: A Brick History of the World in LEGO(r). 2016. (ENG., Illus.). 256p. pap. 18.99 *(978-1-4380-0754-0(X))* Barron's Educational Series, Inc.

Felix, Rebecca. Cool Construction & Building Blocks: Crafting Creative Toys & Amazing Games, 1 vol. 2016. (Cool Toys & Games Ser.). (ENG., Illus.). 32p. (J). (gr. 3-6). lib. bdg. 28.50 *(978-1-68078-047-5(6),* Checkerboard Library) ABDO Publishing Co.

French, Cathy. Make an Island & Haz una Isla: 6 English, 6 Spanish Adaptations. 2011. (ENG & SPA.). (J). 75.00 net. *(978-1-4108-5632-6(1))* Benchmark Education Co.

Gillon, Edmund V., Jr. Cut & Assemble a Victorian Cottage: An H-O Scale Model. 2017. (ENG., Illus.). 16p. (J). (gr. 2-8). pap. 9.95 *(978-0-486-27311-2(3))* Dover Pubns., Inc.

Henry, Sally. Clay Modeling. 2009. (Make Your Own Art Ser.). (Illus.). 32p. (J). (gr. 3-6). lib. bdg. 26.50 *(978-1-4358-2508-6(X),* PowerKids Pr.) Rosen Publishing Group, Inc., The.

Hugo, Simon. 365 Things to Do with LEGO Bricks. 2016. (ENG.). 256p. (J). (gr. 1-4). 24.99 *(978-1-4654-5302-0(4),* DK Children) Dorling Kindersley Publishing, Inc.

Ives, Rob. Castle Attack: Make Your Own Medieval Battlefield. De Quay, John Paul, illus. 2016. (Tabletop Wars Ser.). (ENG.). 32p. (J). (gr. 3-6). 26.65 *(978-1-5124-0639-9(2))* Lerner Publishing Group.

Kerley, Barbara. The Dinosaurs of Waterhouse Hawkins: An Illuminating History of Mr. Waterhouse Hawkins, Artist & Lecturer. Selznick, Brian, illus. 2011. (J). (gr. 2-5). 18.95 *(978-0-545-19703-8(1));* 29.95 *(978-0-545-19697-0(3))* Weston Woods Studios, Inc.

Kingloff, Amanda. Project Kid - Crafts That Go! 60 Imaginative Projects That Fly, Sail, Race, & Dive. 2016. (ENG., Illus.). 272p. (J). pap. 19.95 *(978-1-57965-683-6(8))* Artisan.

Lipkowitz, Daniel. Dark Side. 2014. (ENG.). 96p. (J). (gr. 1-4). 16.99 *(978-1-4654-1897-5(0),* DK Children) Dorling Kindersley Publishing, Inc.

Lipkowitz, Daniel & Dorling Kindersley Publishing Staff. LEGO Ideas Book. 2011. (ENG., Illus.). 200p. *(978-1-4053-5067-9(9))* Dorling Kindersley.

Marrewa, Jennifer. Making a Model with Solid Figures. 2008. (Math in Our World - Level 2 Ser.). 24p. (gr. 1-4). pap. 8.15 *(978-0-8368-9014-3(0));* (Illus.). lib. bdg. 22.00 *(978-0-8368-9005-1(1))* Stevens, Gareth Publishing LLLP. (Weekly Reader Leveled Readers).

—Vamos a Hacer una Maqueta con Figuras Solidas. 2008. (Las Matemáticas en Nuestro Mundo Ser.). (SPA.). 24p. (gr. 1-4). pap. 8.15 *(978-0-8368-9032-7(9));* (Illus.). lib. bdg. 22.00 *(978-0-8368-9023-5(X))* Stevens, Gareth Publishing LLLP. (Weekly Reader Leveled Readers).

Miller, Reagan. Engineers Build Models. 2013. (ENG., Illus.). 24p. (J). *(978-0-7787-0093-7(3));* pap. *(978-0-7787-0100-2(X))* Crabtree Publishing Co.

Models. (Jump Ser.). (Illus.). 36p. (J). (gr. 2-6). pap. *(978-1-882210-36-7(0))* Action Publishing, Inc.

Nelson, Libby. California Missions Projects & Layouts. 2007. (Exploring California Missions Ser.). (Illus.). 112p. (J). lib. bdg. 27.93 *(978-0-8225-7950-2(2),* Lerner Pubns.) Lerner Publishing Group.

Radford, Tracey. Make Your Own Zoo: 35 Projects for Kids Using Everyday Cardboard Packaging. Turn Your Recycling into a Zoo! 2015. (ENG., Illus.). 128p. (J). (gr. 3-11). pap. 19.95 *(978-1-78249-256-6(9),* CICO Books) Ryland Peters & Small GBR. Dist: WIPRO.

Rothrock, Megan H. The Lego Adventure, Vol. 3. 2015. (ENG., Illus.). 192p. (gr. 5). 24.95 *(978-1-59327-610-2(9))* No Starch Pr., Inc.

—The LEGO Adventure Book Vol. 2: Spaceships, Pirates, Dragons & More! 2013. (ENG., Illus.). 196p. (gr. 5). 24.95 *(978-1-59327-512-9(9),* 9781593275129) No Starch Pr., Inc.

Smith, A. G. Cut & Make a Human Skeleton. 2011. (Dover Children's Activity Bks.). (ENG., Illus.). 16p. (J). (gr. 4-8). pap. 7.99 *(978-0-486-26124-9(7))* Dover Pubns., Inc.

Stadler, Charlotte. Making Patterns. 2011. (Early Connections Ser.). (J). *(978-1-61672-640-9(7))* Benchmark Education Co.

Sturm, Jeanne. Understanding Models. 2009. (ENG., Illus.). 48p. (gr. 4-8). pap. 10.95 *(978-1-60694-528-5(9))* Rourke Educational Media.

Zuravicky, Orli. Exploring Pyramids Around the World: Making Models of Geometric Solids. 2009. (PowerMath Ser.). (ENG., Illus.). 32p. (gr. 4-5). pap. 10.00 *(978-0-8239-8908-9(9),* PowerKids Pr.) Rosen Publishing Group, Inc., The.

MODERN CIVILIZATION

see Civilization, Modern

MODERN HISTORY

see History, Modern

MODERNISM (ART)

Carter, David A. & Diaz, James. You Call That Art?! Learn about Modern Sculpture & Make Your Own. 2014. (ENG., Illus.). 48p. (J). (gr. 3-7). 24.95 *(978-1-4197-1307-1(8),* Abrams Bks. for Young Readers) Abrams, Inc.

Fitzpatrick, Anne. Late Modernism. 2005. (Movements in Art Ser.). (Illus.). 48p. (YA). (gr. 5-9). lib. bdg. 21.95 *(978-1-58341-348-7(0))* Creative Co., The.

—Late Modernism: Movements in Art. 2015. (Illus.). 80p. (J). *(978-1-60818-534-4(6),* Creative Education) Creative Co., The.

Gillingham, Sara. In My Den. Siminovich, Lorena, illus. 2009. (ENG.). 12p. (J). (gr. -1 — 1). bds. 8.99 *(978-0-8118-7053-5(7))* Chronicle Bks. LLC.

Gunderson, Jessica. Realism: Movements in Art. 2015. (Illus.). 80p. (J). *(978-1-60818-535-1(4),* Creative Education) Creative Co., The.

Hardy, Rachael. Cézanne, Vol. 7. 2015. (Great Artists Collection). (Illus.). 64p. (J). (gr. 7). lib. bdg. 23.95 *(978-1-4222-3257-6(3))* Mason Crest.

Kallen, Stuart A. Postmodern Art. 2008. (Eye on Art Ser.). (ENG., Illus.). 112p. (YA). (gr. 7-10). lib. bdg. 34.80 *(978-1-4205-0075-2(9),* LML02109-242079, Lucent Bks.) Cengage Gale.

Minond, Edgardo. Drac, Tell Us about Modernism. (SPA.). 80p. *(978-84-96137-13-4(9))* A. Asppan, S.L. Distribuidora Internacional de Libros y Revistas.

Orme, Helen. Body Art. 2011. (Fact to Fiction Grafx Ser.). (ENG., Illus.). 36p. (J). (gr. 4-7). lib. bdg. 17.45 *(978-1-61384-017-7(9))* Perfection Learning Corp.

Riggs, Kate. What Is Modernism? 2016. (Artworld Ser.). 24p. (J). (ENG.). (gr. 2-4). pap. 9.99 *(978-1-62832-225-5(X),* Creative Paperbacks); (Illus.). *(978-1-60818-627-3(X),* Creative Education) Creative Co., The.

Robinson, Shannon. Cubism: Movements in Art. 2015. (Illus.). 80p. (J). *(978-1-60818-531-3(1),* Creative Education) Creative Co., The.

MOGUL EMPIRE

Shirodkar, Suhag. Captured in Miniature. 2010. (ENG.). 56p. 16.95 *(978-0-944142-61-5(3))* Mapin Publishing Pvt. Ltd IND. Dist: National Bk. Network.

MOHAMMED, PROPHET, -632

see Muhammad, Prophet, -632

MOHAMMEDAN ART

see Islamic Art

MOLDS (BOTANY)

Kittinger, Jo S., et al. Un Aliento de Esperanza. Galey, Chuck, illus. 2013. (SPA.). (J). *(978-1-61438-868-5(7))* American Bar Assn.

Viegas, Jennifer. Fungi & Molds. 2004. (Germs: the Library of Disease-Causing Organisms Ser.). (Illus.). 48p. (gr. 7-12). lib. bdg. 29.25 *(978-0-8239-4492-7(1))* Rosen Publishing Group, Inc., The.

Viegas, Jennifer & Baum, Margaux. Fungi & Molds. 2016. (Germs: Disease Causing Organisms Ser.). 48p. (J). (gr. 5-5). pap. 11.75 *(978-1-4777-8840-0(9),* Rosen Reference) Rosen Publishing Group, Inc., The.

MOLECULAR BIOCHEMISTRY

see Molecular Biology

MOLECULAR BIOLOGY

Hamilton, Janet. James Watson: Solving the Mystery of DNA. 2004. (Nobel Prize-Winning Scientists Ser.). (Illus.). 104p. (J). lib. bdg. 27.94 *(978-0-7660-2258-4(7))* Enslow Pubs., Inc.

Olsen, Alana. A Day at Work with a Molecular Biologist, 01 vols., 1. 2016. (Super STEM Careers Ser.). (ENG., Illus.). 24p. (J). pap. 8.25 *(978-1-5081-4410-6(9),* PowerKids Pr.) Rosen Publishing Group, Inc., The.

Phelan, Glen. Double Helix: The Quest to Uncover the Structure of DNA. 2006. (Science Quest Ser.). (Illus.). 64p. (J). (gr. 5-9). 17.95 *(978-0-7922-5541-3(0));* lib. bdg. 25.90 *(978-0-7922-5542-0(9))* National Geographic Society. (National Geographic Children's Bks.).

MOLECULAR BIOPHYSICS

see Molecular Biology

MOLECULES

Aloian, Molly. Atoms & Molecules. 2008. (Why Chemistry Matters Ser.). (ENG., Illus.). 32p. (J). (gr. 3-7). pap. *(978-0-7787-4247-0(4))* Crabtree Publishing Co.

Bodden, Valerie. Proteins. 2015. (J). *(978-1-60818-511-5(7),* Creative Education) Creative Co., The.

Gardner, Robert. Atoms & Molecules Experiments Using Ice, Salt, Marbles, & More: One Hour or Less Science Experiments. 2012. (Last-Minute Science Projects Ser.). 48p. (J). (gr. 5-18). 25.27 *(978-0-7660-3961-2(7))* Enslow Pubs., Inc.

Gish, Melissa. Temperature. 2005. (My First Look at Science Ser.). (Illus.). 24p. (J). (gr. k-3). lib. bdg. 15.95 *(978-1-58341-375-3(8),* Creative Education) Creative Co., The.

Gratzer, Walter. Giant Molecules: From Nylon to Nanotubes. 2009. (ENG., Illus.). 176p. (J). 24.95 *(978-0-19-955002-9(6))* Oxford Univ. Pr., Inc.

Hall, Linley Erin. DNA & RNA. 2010. (Understanding Genetics Ser.). (ENG.). 80p. (YA). lib. bdg. 33.25 *(978-1-4358-9532-4(0))* Rosen Publishing Group, Inc., The.

Jackson, Tom. The Basics of Atoms & Molecules. 2013. (Core Concepts Ser.). 96p. (YA). (gr. 7-12). 34.60 *(978-1-4777-2715-7(9))* Rosen Publishing Group, Inc., The.

Juettner, Bonnie. Molecules. 2004. (Kidhaven Science Library). (ENG., Illus.). 48p. (J). (gr. 4-7). 27.50 *(978-0-7377-2076-1(X))* Cengage Gale.

Lepora, Nathan. Inside Atoms & Molecules. 2010. (Invisible Worlds Ser.). 48p. (gr. 4). 28.50 *(978-0-7614-4192-2(1))* Marshall Cavendish GBR. Dist: Marshall Cavendish Corp.

Manning, Phillip. Atoms, Molecules, & Compounds. 2007. (Essential Chemistry Ser.). (Illus.). 137p. (YA). (gr. 7-12). lib. bdg. 35.00 *(978-0-7910-9534-8(7))* Facts On File, Inc.

Maurer, Tracy Nelson. Atoms & Molecules. 2012. (ENG.). 24p. (gr. 4-5). pap. 8.95 *(978-1-61810-239-3(7))* Rourke Educational Media.

Monroe, Tilda. What Do You Know about Atoms & Molecules? 2010. (20 Questions: Physical Science Ser.). (ENG.). 24p. (J). pap. 8.25 *(978-1-4488-1223-3(2),* PowerKids Pr.); (YA). (gr. 2-5). lib. bdg. 22.60 *(978-1-4488-0669-0(0))* Rosen Publishing Group, Inc., The.

Saunders, Nigel. Exploring Atoms & Molecules. 2007. (Exploring Physical Science Ser.). (Illus.). 48p. (J). (gr. 4-7). lib. bdg. 26.50 *(978-1-4042-3750-6(X),* Rosen Reference) Rosen Publishing Group, Inc., The.

Slade, Suzanne. Looking at Atoms & Molecules. 2006. (Library of Physical Sciences). (Illus.). 24p. (J). (gr. 3-7). lib. bdg. 21.25 *(978-1-4042-3419-2(5),* PowerKids Pr.) Rosen Publishing Group, Inc., The.

—Scientific Instruments for Studying Atoms & Molecules. 2007. (Library of Physical Sciences). (ENG., Illus.). 24p. (gr. 4-8). pap. 7.05 *(978-1-4042-2166-6(2),* PowerKids Pr.) Rosen Publishing Group, Inc., The.

—States of Matter. 2007. (Library of Physical Sciences). (ENG., Illus.). 24p. (gr. 4-8). pap. 7.05 *(978-1-4042-2163-5(8),* PowerKids Pr.) Rosen Publishing Group, Inc., The.

Woodford, Chris & Clowes, Martin. Atoms & Molecules: Investigating the Building Blocks of Matter. 2012. (Scientific Pathways Ser.). (ENG., Illus.). 48p. (J). (gr. 5-8). lib. bdg. 27.95 *(978-1-4488-7196-4(4),* Rosen Reference) Rosen Publishing Group, Inc., The.

MOLES (ANIMALS)

George, Jean Craighead. Winter Moon. 2003. (J). (gr. 3-7). 20.75 *(978-0-8446-7244-1(0))* Smith, Peter Pub., Inc.

Owings, Lisa. Star-Nosed Mole. 2014. (Extremely Weird Animals Ser.). (ENG., Illus.). 24p. (J). (gr. 3-8). lib. bdg. 25.95 *(978-1-62617-078-0(9),* Pilot Bks.) Bellwether Media.

Perkins, Wendy. Star-Nosed Moles. 2017. (Weird & Unusual Animals Ser.). (ENG.). 24p. (gr. 1-4). 20.95 **(978-1-68151-161-0(4))** Amicus Publishing.

Riggs, Kate. Moles. (In My Backyard Ser.). (Illus.). 24p. (J). 2017. (ENG.). (gr. 1-3). pap. 8.99 *(978-1-62832-296-5(9),* Creative Paperbacks) 2016. *(978-1-60818-700-3(4),* Creative Education) Creative Co., The.

Savage, Stephen. Mole. 2009. (Animal Neighbors Ser.). 32p. (gr. k-5). pap. 10.60 *(978-1-4042-4566-2(9),* Rosen Classroom); (Illus.). (J). lib. bdg. 25.25 *(978-1-4358-4989-1(2),* PowerKids Pr.) Rosen Publishing Group, Inc., The.

Webster, Christine. Les Condylures étoilés: Les Animaux du Canada. Karvonen, Tanjah, tr. from ENG. 2011. (FRE.). 24p. (gr. 3-6). *(978-1-77071-416-8(2))* Weigl Educational Pubs. Ltd.

—Star-Nosed Mole. 2010. (Illus.). 24p. *(978-1-55388-665-5(8));* pap. *(978-1-55388-666-2(6))* Weigl Educational Pubs. Ltd.

MOLES (ANIMALS)—FICTION

Armo, Nancy. A Friend for Mole, 1 vol. Armo, Nancy, illus. 2016. (ENG., Illus.). 32p. (J). (gr. -1-k). 16.95 *(978-1-56145-865-3(1))* Peachtree Pubs.

Bailey, Arthur Scott. The Tale of Grandfather Mole. 2005. reprint ed. pap. 20.95 *(978-0-7661-9549-3(X))* Kessinger Publishing, LLC.

Bedford, David. Mole's Babies. Beardshaw, Rosalind, illus. 2012. (ENG.). 32p. (J). *(978-1-58925-108-3(3));* pap. *(978-1-58925-435-0(X))* Tiger Tales.

Caballero, Erica. Mount Mole. 2006. pap. 10.00 *(978-1-4257-2301-9(2))* Xlibris Corp.

Choi, SeoYun. Let's Be Friends. Furukawa, Masumi, illus. rev. ed. 2014. (MySELF Bookshelf Ser.). (ENG.). 32p. (J). (gr. k-2). pap. 11.94 *(978-1-60357-658-1(4));* lib. bdg. 25.27 *(978-1-59953-649-1(8))* Norwood Hse. Pr.

Conchie, Kathryn. I Am a Mole, & I Live in a Hole. Top That Publishing Staff, ed. Howarth, Daniel, illus. 2008. (Story Book Ser.). 12p. (J). (gr. -1). *(978-1-84666-575-2(2),* Tide Mill Pr.) Top That! Publishing PLC.

Duckers, John. The Amazing Adventures of the Silly Six. 2013. (Illus.). 188p. pap. *(978-1-78148-626-9(3))* Grosvenor Hse. Publishing Ltd.

Eaton, Maxwell, III. The Flying Beaver Brothers & the Mud-Slinging Moles. 2013. (Flying Beaver Brothers Ser.). (ENG., Illus.). 96p. (J). (gr. 1-4). pap. 7.99 *(978-0-449-81019-4(4),* Knopf Bks. for Young Readers) Random Hse. Children's Bks.

—The Flying Beaver Brothers & the Mud-Slinging Moles. 2013. (Flying Beaver Brothers Ser.: 3). lib. bdg. 17.20 *(978-0-606-32233-1(7),* Turtleback) Turtleback Bks.

Ehlert, Lois. Holey Moley. Ehlert, Lois, illus. 2015. (ENG., Illus.). 40p. (J). (gr. -1-3). 17.99 *(978-1-4424-9301-8(1),* Beach Lane Bks.) Beach Lane Bks.

Emmett, Jonathan. The Best Gift of All. Cabban, Vanessa, illus. 2008. (ENG.). 32p. (J). (gr. -1-2). 15.99 *(978-0-7636-3860-3(9))* Candlewick Pr.

Erlbruch, Wolf & Holzwarth, Werner. The Story of the Little Mole Who Knew It was None of His Business: Plop Up Edition. 2007. *(978-0-7322-8697-2(2))* HarperCollins Pubs. Australia.

Fagan, Cary. Danny, Who Fell in a Hole. 1 vol. Pavlovic, Milan, illus. 2013. (ENG.). 96p. (J). 14.95 *(978-1-55498-311-7(8))* Groundwood Bks. CAN. Dist: Publishers Group West (PGW).

—Danny, Who Fell in a Hole. 2013. 84p. pap. *(978-1-4596-6456-2(6))* ReadHowYouWant.com, Ltd.

Gates, Susan. Mole Who was Scared of the Dark. Breakespeare, Andrew, illus. 2005. (ENG.). 24p. (J). lib. bdg. 23.65 *(978-1-59646-710-1(X))* Dingles & Co.

Grahame, Kenneth. The Wind in the Willows. Ingpen, Robert R., illus. 2012. (Sterling Illustrated Classics Ser.). (ENG.). 224p. (J). (gr. 2-8). 19.95 *(978-1-4027-8283-1(7))* Sterling Publishing Co., Inc.

—The Wind in the Willows. Iosa, Ann, illus. 2003. 32p. (J). *(978-0-7607-3214-4(0))* Barnes & Noble, Inc.

Hahnl, John. Pocket & Toast, 1 vol. Hahnl, Olivia, illus. 2010. 40p. 24.95 *(978-1-4489-8425-1(4))* PublishAmerica, Inc.

Haile, Matthew. Worms Is Fool. 2010. (Illus.). 88p. pap. 10.49 *(978-1-4520-1956-7(8))* AuthorHouse.

Hillenbrand, Jane. What a Treasure! Hillenbrand, Will, illus. 2006. (ENG.). 24p. (J). (gr. -1-3). 16.95 *(978-0-8234-1896-1(0))* Holiday Hse., Inc.

—What a Treasure! Hillenbrand, Will, illus. 2017. (ENG.). 24p. (J). (gr. -1-1). bds. 7.99 *(978-0-8234-3763-4(9))* Holiday Hse., Inc.

Hillenbrand, Will. All for a Dime! A Bear & Mole Story. (ENG.). 32p. (J). (gr. -1-1). 2016. 7.99 *(978-0-8234-3684-2(5))* 2015. (Illus.). 16.95 *(978-0-8234-2946-2(6))* Holiday Hse., Inc.

—Kite Day: A Bear & Mole Story. Hillenbrand, Will, illus. (ENG., Illus.). 32p. (J). 2013. pap. 6.99 *(978-0-8234-2758-1(7))* 2012. 16.95 *(978-0-8234-1603-5(8))* Holiday Hse., Inc.

—Off We Go! A Bear & Mole Story. 2013. (Bear & Mole Ser.). (ENG., Illus.). 32p. (J). (gr. -1-1). 16.95 *(978-0-8234-2520-4(7))* Holiday Hse., Inc.

—Spring Is Here. Hillenbrand, Will, illus. 2012. (ENG., Illus.). 32p. (J). pap. 7.99 *(978-0-8234-2431-3(6))* Holiday Hse., Inc.

Holzwarth, Werner. The Story of the Little Mole Who Knew It Was None of His Business. Erlbruch, Wolf, illus. 2012. (ENG.). 24p. (J). (gr. -1-2). bds. 17.99 *(978-1-84365-132-1(7),* Pavilion Children's Books) Pavilion Bks. GBR. Dist: Independent Pubs. Group.

Holzwarth, Werner & Erlbruch, Wolf. The Story of the Little Mole Who Went in Search of Whodunit. 2007. (ENG., Illus.). (J). (gr. -1-5). 24p. 15.95 *(978-0-8109-1641-8(X),* Abrams Bks. for Young Readers); 22p. 10.95 *(978-0-8109-4457-2(X),* Abrams Image) Abrams, Inc.

Honigsberg, Peter Jan. Armful of Memories. Morse, Tony, illus. 2004. 32p. 17.95 *(978-1-57143-089-2(X))* RDR Bks.

—Pillow of Dreams. Morse, Tony, illus. 2004. 32p. (gr. k-4). 17.95 *(978-1-57143-076-2(8))* RDR Bks.

Jenkins, Amanda. Why Mole Lives Underground: A Folktale from Peru. 2006. (J). pap. *(978-1-4108-7160-2(6))* Benchmark Education Co.

Jonell, Lynne. Bravemole. 2004. (Illus.). (J). (gr. k-3). spiral bd. *(978-0-616-14579-1(9))* Canadian National Institute for the Blind/Institut National Canadien pour les Aveugles.

Little Mole Boxed Book & Toy Set. 2013. (ENG., Illus.). 24p. (J). (gr. -1-2). 22.99 *(978-1-84365-217-5(X),* Pavilion) Pavilion Bks. GBR. Dist: Independent Pubs. Group.

Maloney, Peter. A Bump on the Head. 2003. (Just Schoolin' Around Ser.). (Illus.). 32p. (J). pap. *(978-0-439-39520-5(8))* Scholastic, Inc.

Owen, Chris. Hairy Mole the Pirate 1. 2007. (Hairy Mole the Pirate Ser.). (ENG., Illus.). 82p. pap. *(978-1-84167-562-6(8))* Ransom Publishing Ltd.

Pearce, Philippa. The Little Gentleman. Pohrt, Tom, illus. 2004. 208p. (J). (gr. 3-18). lib. bdg. 16.89 *(978-0-06-073161-8(3))* HarperCollins Pubs.

Pearce, Philippa & Pearl, Matthew. The Little Gentleman, 3 vols. unabr. ed. 2005. (J). 55.75 *(978-1-4193-3601-0(0),* 42047) Recorded Bks., Inc.

Pilcher, Steve. Pixar Animation Studio Artist Showcase over There. Pilcher, Steve, illus. 2014. (Pixar Animation Studios Artist Showcase Ser.). (ENG., Illus.). 40p. (J). (gr. -1-k). 17.99 *(978-1-4231-4793-0(6))* Hyperion Bks. for Children.

Pochocki, Ethel & Mosher, Barry. The Mushroom Man, 1 vol. 2006. (ENG., Illus.). 32p. (gr. 2-6). reprint ed. 7.95 *(978-0-88448-278-9(2),* 884278) Tilbury Hse. Pubs.

Quattlebaum, Mary. Mighty Mole & Super Soil. Wallace, Chad, illus. 2015. (ENG.). 32p. (J). (gr. k-4). 16.95 *(978-1-58469-538-7(2))* Dawn Pubns.

Said Mouse to Mole. 2005. (J). per. 8.95 *(978-1-59566-139-5(5))* QEB Publishing Inc.

Santillo, LuAnn. Mole. Santillo, LuAnn, ed. 2003. (Half-Pint Kids Readers Ser.). (Illus.). 7p. (J). (gr. -1-1). pap. *(978-1-59256-111-7(X))* Half-Pint Kids, Inc.

—Rose. Santillo, LuAnn, ed. 2003. (Half-Pint Kids Readers Ser.). (Illus.). 7p. (J). (gr. -1-1). pap. 1.00 *(978-1-59256-101-8(2))* Half-Pint Kids, Inc.

Sargent, Dave & Sargent, Pat. Molly's Journey: I'm Getting Older, 15 vols., Vol. 19. Huff, Jeanie, illus. 2nd rev. ed. 2003. (Animal Pride Ser.: 19). 42p. (J). pap. 10.95 *(978-1-56763-796-0(5));* lib. bdg. 20.95 *(978-1-56763-795-3(7))* Ozark Publishing.

Schwartz, Roslyn. The Complete Adventures of the Mole Sisters. Schwartz, Roslyn, illus. 2004. (ENG., Illus.). 168p. (J). (gr. -1-k). 19.95 *(978-1-55037-883-2(X),* 9781550378832) Annick Pr., Ltd. CAN. Dist: Publishers Group West (PGW).

—The Mole Sisters & the Fairy Ring. Schwartz, Roslyn, illus. 2003. (Mole Sisters Ser.). (ENG., Illus.). 32p. (J). (gr. -1-k). 14.95 *(978-1-55037-819-1(8),* 9781550378191); 3rd ed. pap. 5.95 *(978-1-55037-818-4(X),* 9781550378184) Annick Pr., Ltd. CAN. Dist: Publishers Group West (PGW).

—The Mole Sisters & the Way Home. Schwartz, Roslyn, illus. 2003. (Mole Sisters Ser.). (ENG., Illus.). 32p. (J). (gr. -1-k). 14.95 *(978-1-55037-821-4(X),* 9781550378214); 3rd ed. pap. 5.95 *(978-1-55037-820-7(1),* 9781550378207) Annick Pr., Ltd. CAN. Dist: Publishers Group West (PGW).

Warnes, Tim. Warning! Do Not Touch! Warnes, Tim, illus. 2016. (ENG., Illus.). 32p. (J). (gr. -1-2). 16.99 *(978-1-68010-013-6(0))* Tiger Tales.

Wheeler, Lisa. One Dark Night. Bates, Ivan, illus. 2006. (ENG.). 32p. (J). (gr. -1-3). reprint ed. pap. 6.99 *(978-0-15-205888-3(5))* Houghton Mifflin Harcourt Publishing Co.

Yaccarino, Dan. Morris Mole. Yaccarino, Dan, illus. 2017. (Illus.). 40p. (J). (gr. -1-3). 17.99 *(978-0-06-241107-5(1))* HarperCollins Pubs.

Yee, Wong Herbert. Abracadabra! Magic with Mouse & Mole. 2010. (Mouse & Mole Story Ser.). (ENG., Illus.). 48p. (J). (gr. -1-3). pap. 3.99 *(978-0-547-40621-3(5))* Houghton Mifflin Harcourt Publishing Co.

—A Brand-New Day with Mouse & Mole. (Mouse & Mole Story Ser.). (ENG., Illus.). 48p. (J). (gr. 1-4). 2012. pap. 3.99 *(978-0-547-72209-2(5))* 2008. 15.00 *(978-0-618-96676-9(5))* Houghton Mifflin Harcourt Publishing Co.

—A Brand-New Day with Mouse & Mole. 2012. (Green Light Readers — Level 3 Ser.). lib. bdg. 13.55 *(978-0-606-24437-4(9),* Turtleback) Turtleback Bks.

—Fine Feathered Friends. Yee, Wong Herbert, illus. 2011. (Mouse & Mole Story Ser.). (ENG., Illus.). 48p. (J). (gr. 1-4). pap. 3.99 *(978-0-547-51977-7(X))* Houghton Mifflin Harcourt Publishing Co.

—Mouse & Mole, a Winter Wonderland. Yee, Wong Herbert, illus. 2011. (Mouse & Mole Story Ser.). (ENG., Illus.). 48p. (J). (gr. 1-4). pap. 3.99 *(978-0-547-57697-8(8))* Houghton Mifflin Harcourt Publishing Co.

—Mouse & Mole, Fine Feathered Friends. Yee, Wong Herbert, illus. 2009. (Mouse & Mole Story Ser.). (ENG., Illus.). 48p. (J). (gr. 1-4). 15.00 *(978-0-547-15222-6(1))* Houghton Mifflin Harcourt Publishing Co.

—A Perfect Halloween. 2011. (Mouse & Mole Story Ser.). (ENG., Illus.). 48p. (J). (gr. 1-4). 14.99 *(978-0-547-55152-4(5))* Houghton Mifflin Harcourt Publishing Co.

—Secret Valentine. Yee, Wong Herbert, illus. 2013. (Mouse & Mole Story Ser.). (ENG., Illus.). 48p. (J). (gr. 1-4). 15.99 *(978-0-547-88719-7(1))* Houghton Mifflin Harcourt Publishing Co.

—Upstairs Mouse, Downstairs Mole. 12th ed. 2007. (Mouse & Mole Story Ser.). (ENG., Illus.). 48p. (J). (gr. -1-3). 3.99 *(978-0-618-91586-6(9))* Houghton Mifflin Harcourt Publishing Co.

MOLLUSKS

see also Shells

Berger, Melvin & Berger, Gilda. Shellfish. 2013. (Illus.). 16p. (J). pap. *(978-0-545-35172-0(3))* Scholastic, Inc.

Bishop, Celeste. Slimy Slugs. 2015. (Icky Animals! Small & Gross Ser.). (ENG., Illus.). 24p. (J). (gr. 1-1). pap. 8.25 *(978-1-4994-0713-6(0),* PowerKids Pr.) Rosen Publishing Group, Inc., The.

Bodden, Valerie. Creepy Creatures: Slugs. 2013. (Creepy Creatures Ser.). (ENG., Illus.). 24p. (J). (gr. 1-3). pap. 8.99 *(978-0-89812-796-6(3),* Creative Paperbacks) Creative Co., The.

—Slugs. 2013. (Illus.). 24p. (J). 25.65 *(978-1-60818-233-6(9),* Creative Education) Creative Co., The.

Boothroyd, Jennifer. Shells. 2011. (First Step Nonfiction / Body Coverings Ser.). pap. 33.92 *(978-0-7613-8610-0(6));* (ENG.). 24p. pap. 6.95 *(978-0-7613-7630-3(8));* (ENG., Illus.). 24p. lib. bdg. 23.93 *(978-0-7613-5788-9(2))* Lerner Publishing Group.

Borgert-Spaniol, Megan. Slugs. 2016. (Creepy Crawlies Ser.). (ENG., Illus.). 24p. (J). (gr. k-3). lib. bdg. 25.95 *(978-1-62617-301-9(X),* Blastoff! Readers) Bellwether Media.

Cerullo, Mary M. Giant Squid: Searching for a Sea Monster, 1 vol. Roper, Clyde F. E., photos by. 2012. (Smithsonian Ser.). (ENG., Illus.). 48p. (gr. 4-5). pap. 8.95 *(978-1-4296-8023-3(7))* Capstone Press of Coughlan Cos.

—Giant Squid: Searching for a Sea Monster. 2012. (Smithsonian Ser.). (ENG.). 48p. (gr. 4-5). pap. 53.70 *(978-1-4296-8523-8(9))* Capstone Press of Coughlan Cos.

—Giant Squid: Searching for a Sea Monster, 1 vol. Roper, Clyde F. E., photos by. 2012. (Smithsonian Ser.). (ENG., Illus.). 48p. (gr. 4-5). lib. bdg. 29.32 *(978-1-4296-7541-3(1))* Capstone Press of Coughlan Cos.

Gravel, Élise. The Slug. (Disgusting Critters Ser.). (ENG., Illus.). 32p. (J). (gr. 1-4). 2016. pap. 5.99 *(978-1-77049-656-9(4))* 2014. 10.99 *(978-1-77049-655-2(6))* Tundra Bks. CAN. (Tundra Bks.). Dist: Penguin Random Hse. LLC.

Gray, Susan H. Nudibranch. 2014. (21st Century Skills Library: Exploring Our Oceans Ser.). (ENG., Illus.). 32p. (J). (gr. 3-6). 28.50 *(978-1-63188-021-6(7),* 205491) Cherry Lake Publishing.

Gross, Miriam J. The Sea Slug: Nudibranchs. 2009. (Weird Sea Creatures Ser.). 24p. (gr. 3-3). 42.50 *(978-1-60854-757-9(4),* PowerKids Pr.) Rosen Publishing Group, Inc., The.

Himmelman, John. Basic Illustrated Guide to Frogs, Snakes, Bugs, & Slugs. 2013. (Basic Illustrated Ser.). (ENG., Illus.). 104p. pap. 10.95 *(978-0-7627-8259-8(5),* Falcon Guides) Globe Pequot Pr., The.

Hopkins, Therese. Shells. 2009. (Home Sweet Home Ser.). (J). (gr. k-2). 24p. pap. 8.25 *(978-1-4358-3070-7(9),* PowerKids Pr.); lib. bdg. 22.60 *(978-1-4358-2696-0(5))* Rosen Publishing Group, Inc., The.

Jones, Tammy. At the Shore. 2009. (Sight Word Readers Set A Ser.). (J). 3.49 net. *(978-1-60719-137-7(7))* Newmark Learning LLC.

Lewis, Brenda Ralph. Crabs & Mollusks. 2006. (Nature's Monsters: Water Creatures Ser.). (Illus.). 32p. (J). (gr. 2-6). lib. bdg. 26.00 *(978-0-8368-6176-1(0),* Gareth Stevens Learning Library) Stevens, Gareth Publishing LLLP.

Lunis, Natalie. Slimy Sea Slugs. 2016. (No Backbone! Marine Invertebrates Ser.). (ENG.). 24p. (J). (gr. k-3). pap. 7.95 ***(978-1-944998-78-3(0))*** Bearport Publishing Co., Inc.

McNeil, Niki, et al. HOCPP 1103 Mollusks. 2006. spiral bd. 19.00 *(978-1-60308-103-0(8))* In the Hands of a Child.

Metz, Lorijo. Discovering Clams. 2012. (Along the Shore Ser.). (Illus.). 24p. (J). (gr. k-3). lib. bdg. 22.60 *(978-1-4488-4994-9(2))* Rosen Publishing Group, Inc., The.

Miller, Sara Swan. Secret Lives of Seashell Dwellers. 2010. (Secret Lives Ser.). 48p. (gr. 4). 29.93 *(978-0-7614-4228-8(6))* Marshall Cavendish Corp.

Morgan, Emily R. Next Time You See a Seashell. 2012. (Next Time You See Ser.). (ENG., Illus.). 32p. (J). (gr. k-5). pap. 12.95 *(978-1-936959-15-0(1))* National Science Teachers Assn.

Newman, Mark. Sooper Yooper: Environmental Defender. Heckman, Mark, illus. 2010. 48p. (J). 17.95 *(978-1-933272-26-9(0))* Thunder Bay Pr.

Petersen, Christine. Pearls, 1 vol. 2013. (Earth's Treasures Ser.). (ENG.). 32p. (J). (gr. 3-6). lib. bdg. 27.07 *(978-1-61783-873-6(X),* Checkerboard Library) ABDO Publishing Co.

Prezant, Fran Pollock & Marshak, Laura E. Dr. Vermeij's Conch Quest. 2010. 36p. 15.99 *(978-1-4490-9199-6(7))* AuthorHouse.

Rajczak, Michael. Attack of the Zebra Mussels. 2016. (Animal Invaders: Destroying Native Habitats Ser.). 00024p. (J). pap. 8.15 ***(978-1-4824-5683-7(4))*** Stevens, Gareth Publishing LLLP.

Richardson, Joy. Mollusks. 2005. (Variety of Life Ser.). (Illus.). 32p. (gr. 1-4). lib. bdg. 26.00 *(978-0-8368-4507-5(2),* Gareth Stevens Learning Library) Stevens, Gareth Publishing LLLP.

Robb, Jackie & Stringle, Berny. The Story of Slug. Duncan, Karen & Stringle, Sam, illus. 2004. (Bang on the Door Ser.). 32p. (YA). pap. *(978-1-85602-317-7(6),* Pavilion Children's Books) Pavilion Bks.

Rockwood, Leigh. Slugs Are Gross! 2010. (Creepy Crawlies Ser.). (Illus.). 24p. (gr. k-2). (YA). 22.60 *(978-1-4488-0704-8(2));* (J). pap. 8.25 *(978-1-4488-1369-8(7),* PowerKids Pr.) Rosen Publishing Group, Inc., The.

Salzmann, Mary Elizabeth. What Has a Shell?, 1 vol. 2007. (Creature Features Ser.). (ENG., Illus.). 24p. (gr. -1-3). 25.65 *(978-1-59928-871-0(0),* Super SandCastle) ABDO Publishing Co.

Smalley, Carol. A Project Guide to Sponges, Worms, & Mollusks. 2010. (Life Science Projects for Kids Ser.). (Illus.). 48p. (J). (gr. 4-8). lib. bdg. 29.95 *(978-1-58415-876-9(X))* Mitchell Lane Pubs., Inc.

Trueit, Trudi Strain. Slugs, Snails, & Worms. 2013. 32p. (J). (gr. 6-9). 28.50 *(978-1-60870-247-3(2))* Cavendish Square Publishing.

—Slugs, Snails & Worms. 2013. (Backyard Safari 2 Ser.). 32p. (J). (gr. 6-9). pap. 10.58 *(978-1-62712-030-2(0))* Cavendish Square Publishing.

White, Nancy. Creeping Land Snails. 2009. (No Backbone! Ser.). (Illus.). 24p. (J). (gr. k-3). lib. bdg. 21.28 *(978-1-59716-753-6(3))* Bearport Publishing Co., Inc.

World Book, Inc Staff, contrib. by. Mollusks & Similar Sea Creatures. 2009. (J). *(978-0-7166-0407-5(8))* World Bk., Inc.

Zoehfeld, Kathleen Weidner. What Lives in a Shell? Davie, Helen K., illus. 2015. (Let's-Read-And-Find-Out Science 1 Ser.). (ENG.). 32p. (J). (gr. -1-3). pap. 6.99 *(978-0-06-238196-5(2))* HarperCollins Pubs.

MONACO

Hintz, Martin. Monaco. 2004. (Enchantment of the World Ser.). (ENG., Illus.). 144p. (YA). (gr. 5-9). 39.00 *(978-0-516-24251-4(2))* Scholastic Library Publishing.

King, David C. Monaco. 2007. (Cultures of the World Ser.). 144p. (gr. 6). lib. bdg. 42.79 *(978-0-7614-2567-0(5),* Benchmark Bks.) Marshall Cavendish Corp.

MONARCHS

see Kings, Queens, Rulers, etc.

MONASTERIES

see also Monasticism and Religious Orders

Anderson, Dale. Monks & Monasteries in the Middle Ages. 2005. (World Almanac Library of the Middle Ages). 48p. (gr. 5-12). pap. 14.05 *(978-0-8368-5906-5(5));* (Illus.). lib. bdg. 31.00 *(978-0-8368-5897-6(2))* Stevens, Gareth Publishing LLLP. (Gareth Stevens Secondary Library).

Jovinelly, Joann. The Crafts & Culture of a Medieval Monastery. 2009. (Crafts & Cultures of the Middle Ages Ser.). 48p. (gr. 5-5). 58.50 *(978-1-61512-056-7(4),* Rosen Reference) Rosen Publishing Group, Inc., The.

Jovinelly, Joann & Netelkos, Jason. The Crafts & Culture of a Medieval Monastery. 2006. (Crafts & Cultures of the Middle Ages Ser.). (Illus.). 48p. (J). (gr. 4-8). lib. bdg. 29.25 *(978-1-4042-0759-2(7))* Rosen Publishing Group, Inc., The.

MONASTIC ORDERS

see Monasticism and Religious Orders

MONASTICISM AND RELIGIOUS ORDERS

see also Monasteries

Anderson, Dale. Monks & Monasteries in the Middle Ages. 2005. (World Almanac Library of the Middle Ages). 48p. (gr. 5-12). pap. 14.05 *(978-0-8368-5906-5(5));* (Illus.). lib. bdg. 31.00 *(978-0-8368-5897-6(2))* Stevens, Gareth Publishing LLLP. (Gareth Stevens Secondary Library).

Ficocelli, Elizabeth. Where Do Priests Come From? Wirrenga, Shannon, illus. 2010. (J). pap. 7.99 *(978-0-9844864-0-3(2))* Bezalel Bks.

Grube, Edward C. Martin Luther. White, Deborah J., illus. 2012. (Hero of Faith Ser.). (ENG.). 58p. (J). pap. 7.99 *(978-0-7586-3075-9(1))* Concordia Publishing Hse.

Jain, Manoj. Mahavira: The Hero of Nonviolence. Demi, illus. 2014. (ENG.). 28p. (J). (gr. k-4). 17.95 *(978-1-937786-21-2(8),* Wisdom Tales) World Wisdom, Inc.

Lee, Puck Hee. The Wizard Monk of Kamayut & Six Other True Stories. 2005. 48p. per. 10.00 *(978-1-4134-8216-4(3))* Xlibris Corp.

Rivera, Sheila. Dalai Lama: A Life of Compassion. 2007. (Pull Ahead Books-Biographies Ser.). (ENG., Illus.). 32p. (gr. k-3). pap. 7.95 *(978-0-8225-6435-5(1))* Lerner Publishing Group.

Senker, Cath. The Dalai Lama. 2017. (ENG., Illus.). 32p. (J). (gr. 4-6). pap. 12.99 ***(978-1-5263-0180-2(6),*** Wayland) Hachette Children's Group GBR. Dist: Hachette Bk. Group.

Young, Patricia A. The Holy Monks of Mt. Athos. Young, Patricia A., illus. l.t. ed. 2005. (Illus.). 28p. (J). 10.00 *(978-0-913026-49-6(2));* 20.00 *(978-0-913026-24-3(7))* St. Nectarios Pr.

MONASTICISM AND RELIGIOUS ORDERS—FICTION

Bogart, Jo Ellen. The White Cat & the Monk: A Retelling of the Poem Pangur Bán, 1 vol. Smith, Sydney, illus. 2016. (ENG.). 32p. (J). (gr. -1-3). 18.95 *(978-1-55498-780-1(6))* Groundwood Bks. CAN. Dist: Publishers Group West (PGW).

Costanza, Stephen, illus. Smudge & the Book of Mistakes: A Christmas Story. 2012. (ENG.). 48p. (J). (gr. 1-5). 17.95 *(978-1-58536-483-1(5))* Sleeping Bear Pr.

Flusfeder, David. John the Pupil. 2015. 240p. 24.99 *(978-0-06-233918-8(4))* HarperCollins Pubs.

Fusco, John. Little Monk & the Mantis: A Bug, a Boy, & the Birth of a Kung Fu Legend. Lugo, Patrick, illus. 2012. (ENG.). 32p. (J). (gr. -1-3). 16.95 *(978-0-8048-4221-1(3))* Tuttle Publishing.

Leslie, Emma. The Martyr's Victory: A Story of Danish England. Stacey, W., illus. 2007. 300p. 24.95 *(978-1-934671-08-5(8));* per. 14.95 *(978-1-934671-09-2(6))* Salem Ridge Press LLC.

Maguire, Gregory. Egg & Spoon. 2014. (ENG., Illus.). 496p. (YA). (gr. 7). 17.99 *(978-0-7636-7220-1(3))* Candlewick Pr.

Millen, C. M. The Ink Garden of Brother Theophane. Wisnewski, Andrea, illus. 2010. (ENG.). 32p. (J). (gr. k-3). 17.95 *(978-1-58089-179-0(9))* Charlesbridge Publishing, Inc.

Nelson, Marilyn. Snook Alone. Ering, Timothy Basil, illus. 2010. (ENG.). 48p. (J). (gr. -1-3). 16.99 *(978-0-7636-2667-9(8))* Candlewick Pr.

Padma, T. V. The Cleverest Thief. 2008. (Story Cove Ser.). (ENG., Illus.). 32p. (J). (gr. -1-3). pap. 4.95 *(978-0-87483-882-4(7))* August Hse. Pubs., Inc.

Smucker, Anna Egan. Brother Giovanni's Little Reward. Hall, Amanda, illus. 2015. (ENG.). 34p. (J). 17.00 *(978-0-8028-5420-9(6),* Eerdmans Bks For Young Readers) Eerdmans, William B. Publishing Co.

Smyth, Bethinna & Winkelmann, Rachele. The Sleepy Monk. 2012. 34p. pap. 16.95 *(978-1-105-43625-3(X))* Lulu.com GBR. Dist: Lulu Pr., Inc.

Thompson, Ricki. City of Cannibals. 2010. (ENG.). 269p. (YA). (gr. 9-12). 18.95 *(978-1-59078-623-9(8),* Front Street) Boyds Mills Pr.

MONDAY, ANTHONY (FICTITIOUS CHARACTER)—FICTION

Bellairs, John. The Mansion in the Mist. Gorey, Edward, illus. 2004. (Anthony Monday Ser.: No. 4). (ENG.). 176p. (J). (gr. 3-7). 6.99 *(978-0-14-240262-7(1),* Puffin Books) Penguin Young Readers Group.

MONET, CLAUDE, 1840-1926

Aston, Paul, tr. Claude Monet. Kutschbach, Doris, illus. 2006. (ENG.). 32p. (J). (gr. 1-4). 8.95 *(978-3-7913-3713-5(0))* Prestel Verlag GmbH & Co KG. DEU. Dist: Penguin Random Hse. LLC.

Björk, Christina. Linnea in Monet's Garden. Sandin, Joan, tr. Anderson, Lena, illus. 2012. (ENG.). 48p. (J). (-3). 16.99 *(978-1-4022-7729-0(6),* Sourcebooks Jabberwocky) Sourcebooks, Inc.

Carvalho de Magalhaes, Roberto. Claude Monet. 2005. (Great Artists Ser.). (Illus.). 40p. (J). (gr. 5). per. 7.95 *(978-1-59270-050-9(0))* Enchanted Lion Bks., LLC.

Connolly, Sean & Monet, Claude. Claude Monet. 2004. (Lives of the Artists Ser.). (Illus.). 48p. (gr. 5-12). pap. 14.05 *(978-0-8368-5655-2(4));* lib. bdg. 31.00 *(978-0-8368-5650-7(3))* Stevens, Gareth Publishing LLLP. (Gareth Stevens Secondary Library).

Danneberg, Julie. Monet Paints a Day. Heimerl, Caitlin, illus. 2012. (ENG.). 32p. (J). (gr. 1-4). 15.95 *(978-1-58089-240-7(X))* Charlesbridge Publishing, Inc.

Danneberg, Julie & Monet, Claude. Monet Paints a Day. Heimerl, Caitlin, illus. 2012. (J). pap. 15.95 *(978-1-58089-241-4(8))* Charlesbridge Publishing, Inc.

De Magalhaes, Roberto Carvalho. Claude Monet. 2003. (Great Artists Ser.). (Illus.). 40p. (J). 15.95 *(978-1-59270-009-7(8))* Enchanted Lion Bks., LLC.

Elschner, Géraldine. Where Is the Frog? A Children's Book Inspired by Claude Monet. Girel, Stephane, illus. 2013. (ENG.). 32p. (J). (gr. -1-3). 14.95 *(978-3-7913-7139-9(8))* Prestel Verlag GmbH & Co KG. DEU. Dist: Penguin Random Hse. LLC.

Kallen, Stuart A. Claude Monet. 2008. (Eye on Art Ser.). (ENG., Illus.). 112p. (YA). (gr. 7-10). lib. bdg. 34.80 *(978-1-4205-0074-5(0),* LML02109-242078, Lucent Bks.) Cengage Gale.

Klein, Adam G. Claude Monet, 1 vol. 2007. (Great Artists Set 2 Ser.). (ENG., Illus.). 32p. (gr. -1-3). 27.07 *(978-1-59679-732-1(0),* Checkerboard Library) ABDO Publishing Co.

Krieg, Katherine. Claude Monet. Morrow, J. T., illus. 2014. (World's Greatest Artists Ser.). (ENG.). 24p. (J). (gr. 2-5). 28.50 *(978-1-62687-348-3(8),* 207188) Child's World, Inc., The.

Lomberg, Michelle. Claude Monet. 2016. (Illus.). 32p. (J). *(978-1-4896-4619-4(1))* Weigl Pubs., Inc.

Merberg, Julie & Bober, Suzanne. A Picnic with Monet. 2003. (Mini Masters Ser.: MINI). (ENG., Illus.). 22p. (J). (gr. -1-7). bds. 6.99 *(978-0-8118-4046-0(8))* Chronicle Bks. LLC.

Nichols, Catherine. Claude Monet. (Primary Source Library of Famous Artists Ser.). 32p. 2009. (gr. 3-4). 42.50 *(978-1-60854-100-3(2))* 2006. (Illus.). (J). (gr. -1-3). lib. bdg. 23.95 *(978-1-4042-2761-3(X))* Rosen Publishing Group, Inc., The. (PowerKids Pr.).

Pappworth, Sara. The Life & Art of Claude Monet. Ryn, Aude van, illus. 2016. (Lives of Great Artists Ser.). 00080p. (J). (gr. 8-8). 35.75 *(978-1-4994-6584-6(X))* Rosen Publishing Group, Inc., The.

Rodriguez, Susan & Monet, Claude. Travels with Monet: Travel in the Artist's Footsteps. 2010. (ENG.). 32p. (J). 15.95 *(978-1-56290-664-1(X))* Crystal Productions.

Sánchez, Consuelo. Claudet Monet. 2005. (SPA.). 132p. (YA). *(978-958-30-1869-5(4))* Panamericana Editorial.

M
N
O

Spence, David. The Impressionists: Monet, Cezanne, Renoir, Degas. 2010. (ENG.). 128p. (J). (gr. 4-7). pap. 12.95 (978-1-84696-217-2(X), TickTock Books) Octopus Publishing Group GBR. Dist: Independent Pubs. Group.

Venezia, Mike. Claude Monet. Venezia, Mike, illus. rev. ed. 2014. (Getting to Know the World's Greatest Artists Ser.). (ENG., Illus.). 40p. (J). lib. bdg. 29.00 (978-0-531-21979-9(8)) Scholastic Library Publishing.

—Claude Monet (Revised Edition) 2014. (Getting to Know the World's Greatest Artists Ser.). (ENG., Illus.). 40p. (J). pap. 7.95 (978-0-531-22540-0(2)) Scholastic Library Publishing.

Waldron, Ann. Who Was Claude Monet? Harrison, Nancy & Marchesi, Stephen, illus. 2009. (Who Was? Ser.). (ENG.). 112p. (J). (gr. 3-7). pap. 5.99 (978-0-448-44985-2(4), Grosset & Dunlap) Penguin Young Readers Group.

—Who Was Claude Monet? 2009. (Who Was... ? Ser.). lib. bdg. 16.00 (978-0-606-04028-0(5), Turtleback) Turtleback Bks.

Whiting, Jim. Claude Monet. 2007. (Art Profiles for Kids Ser.). (Illus.). 48p. (YA). (gr. 4-7). lib. bdg. 29.95 (978-1-58415-563-8(9)) Mitchell Lane Pubs., Inc.

Wood, Alix. Claude Monet. 2013. (Artists Through the Ages Ser.). (ENG., Illus.). 32p. (J). (gr. 3-6). pap. 10.00 (978-1-61533-627-2(3)); lib. bdg. 25.25 (978-1-61533-620-3(6)) Windmill Bks.

MONET, CLAUDE, 1840-1926—FICTION

Anholt, Laurence. The Magical Garden of Claude Monet. (Anholt's Artists Books for Children Ser.). (ENG., Illus.). 32p. (J). 2007. (gr. -1-3). (978-0-7641-3855-3(3)) 2003. 16.99 (978-0-7641-5574-1(1)) Barron's Educational Series, Inc.

Mayhew, James. Katie & the Waterlily Pond. Mayhew, James, illus. 2015. (Katie Ser.). (ENG., Illus.). 32p. (J). (gr. -1-k). pap. 10.99 (978-1-4083-3245-0(0)) Hodder & Stoughton GBR. Dist: Hachette Bk. Group.

Mullarkey, Lisa & Mullarkey, John. Monet Changes Mediums, 1 vol. Bernard, Courtney, illus. 2015. (ENG.). 128p. (J). (978-1-62402-089-6(5)) Magic Wagon.

MONETARY QUESTION

see Money

MONEY

see also Banks and Banking; Coins; Credit; Gold; Mints; Paper Money

ABDO Publishing Company Staff & Doudna, Kelly. Dollars & Cents, Set. 2003. (Dollars & Cents Set 3 Ser.: 4). (ENG.). 24p. (J). (gr. k-3). lib. bdg. 96.84 (978-1-57765-910-5(4), SandCastle) ABDO Publishing Co.

ABDO Publishing Company Staff & Molter, Carey. Dollars & Cents, Set. 2003. (Dollars & Cents Set 2 Ser.: 6). (ENG.). 24p. (J). (gr. k-3). lib. bdg. 145.26 (978-1-57765-909-9(0), SandCastle) ABDO Publishing Co.

—Dollars & Cents Set 1, 1 vol. 2003. (Dollars & Cents Set 1 Ser.: 6). (ENG.). 24p. (J). (gr. k-3). lib. bdg. 145.26 (978-1-57765-883-2(3), SandCastle) ABDO Publishing Co.

Adler, David A. Money Madness. Miller, Edward, illus. 2009. (ENG.). 32p. (J). (gr. -1-3). pap. 7.99 (978-0-8234-2272-2(0)) Holiday Hse., Inc.

—Money Math: Addition & Subtraction. Miller, Edward, illus. 2017. (ENG.). 32p. (J). 17.95 **(978-0-8234-3698-9(5))** Holiday Hse., Inc.

Adler, David A. Prices! Prices! Prices! Why They Go up & Down. Miller, Edward, illus. (ENG.). 32p. (J). 2016. 7.99 (978-0-8234-3574-6(1)) 2015. (gr. 1-5). 17.95 (978-0-8234-3293-6(9)) Holiday Hse., Inc.

Alaina, Maria. Counting Money, 1 vol. (Wonder Readers Next Steps: Math Ser.). (ENG.). (gr. -1-1). 2013. 20p. 22.65 (978-1-4765-2366-8(5)) 2011. 16p. pap. 35.94 (978-1-4296-8081-3(4)) 2011. 32p. pap. 5.99 (978-1-4296-7801-8(1)) Capstone Press of Coughlan Cos. (Wonder Readers).

Anderson, Jill. Money Math with Sebastian Pig & Friends at the Farmer's Market. Amy Huntington, illus. 2013. (Math Fun with Sebastian Pig & Friends! Ser.). 32p. (J). (gr. k-3). pap. 7.95 (978-0-7660-5983-2(9), Enslow Elementary) Enslow Pubs., Inc.

—Money Math with Sebastian Pig & Friends at the Farmer's Market. Huntington, Amy, illus. 2009. (Math Fun with Sebastian Pig & Friends! Ser.). 32p. (J). (gr. k-3). lib. bdg. 23.94 (978-0-7660-3364-1(3)) Enslow Pubs., Inc.

Ayers, Amy. Using Money at the Lemonade Stand. 2007. (Math in Our World Ser.). 24p. (gr. 1-2). pap. 8.15 (978-0-8368-8481-4(7), Weekly Reader Leveled Readers) Stevens, Gareth Publishing LLLP.

Bailey, Diane. Top 10 Secrets for Creating & Sticking to a Budget Successfully. 2013. (Illus.). 64p. (YA). (gr. 7-12). 31.95 (978-1-4488-9360-7(7)); pap. 77.70 (978-1-4488-9370-6(4)); pap. 12.95 (978-1-4488-9369-0(0)) Rosen Publishing Group, Inc., The.

Bailey, Gerry. World Money. Beech, Mark, illus. 2015. (How Money Works). (ENG.). 64p. (J). (gr. 4-6). pap. 15.93 **(978-1-68404-071-1(X))** Norwood Hse. Pr.

—Your Money. Beech, Mark, illus. 2015. (How Money Works). (ENG.). 64p. (J). (gr. 4-6). pap. 15.93 **(978-1-68404-072-8(8))** Norwood Hse. Pr.

Bailey, Gerry & Law, Felicia. World Money. Beech, Mark, illus. 2015. (How Money Works). (ENG.). 64p. (J). (gr. 4-6). lib. bdg. 29.27 (978-1-59953-720-7(6)) Norwood Hse. Pr.

—Your Money. Beech, Mark, illus. 2015. (How Money Works). (ENG.). 64p. (J). (gr. 4-6). lib. bdg. 29.27 (978-1-59953-718-4(4)) Norwood Hse. Pr.

Bateman, Katherine R. The Young Investor: Projects & Activities for Making Your Money Grow. 2nd ed. 2010. (ENG., Illus.). 144p. (J). (gr. 4). pap. 14.95 (978-1-56976-546-3(4)) Chicago Review Pr., Inc.

Benchmark Education Company, LLC Staff, compiled by. Money: Theme Set. 2006. (J). 105.00 (978-1-4108-7077-3(4)) Benchmark Education Co.

Berger, Melvin. Round & Round the Money Goes. (Discovery Readers Ser.). (ENG.). 48p. (J). pap. 3.95 (978-0-8249-5310-2(X), Ideal Pubns.) Worthy Publishing.

Berne, Stanley. Legal Tender - Or - It's All About Money! 2003. 160p. (YA). pap. 40.00 (978-0-913844-27-4(6)) Rising Tide Pr.

Berry, Rob & Duey, Kathleen. The Smart Kids Allowance System: Step-by-Step Money Management Guidebook. Bartholomew, illus. Date not set. (Family Skill Builders Ser.). (J). (gr. k-6). pap. 9.95 (978-1-883761-34-9(4)) Family Life Productions.

Boritzer, Etan. What Is Money? West, Jennifer, illus. 2006. 40p. (J). pap. 6.95 (978-0-9762743-3-9(7)) Lane, Veronica Bks.

—What Is Money? 2006. (What Is? Ser.). (Illus.). 40p. (J). 14.95 (978-0-9762743-2-2(9)) Lane, Veronica Bks.

Bullard, Lisa. Ella Earns Her Own Money. Moran, Michael, illus. 2013. (Cloverleaf Books — Money Basics Ser.). (ENG.). 24p. (gr. k-2). lib. bdg. 23.93 (978-1-4677-0761-9(9), Millbrook Pr.) Lerner Publishing Group.

—Kyle Keeps Track of Cash. Byrne, Mike, illus. 2013. (Cloverleaf Books — Money Basics Ser.). (ENG.). 24p. (gr. k-2). pap. 6.95 (978-1-4677-1510-2(7)); lib. bdg. 23.93 (978-1-4677-0762-6(7)) Lerner Publishing Group. (Millbrook Pr.).

Burstein, John. Dollars & Sense: Developing Good Money Habits. 2010. (ENG., Illus.). 32p. (J). pap. (978-0-7787-4810-6(3)); lib. bdg. (978-0-7787-4794-9(8)) Crabtree Publishing Co.

Burton, Margie, et al. Our Money. 2011. (Early Connections Ser.). (J). (978-1-61672-502-0(8)) Benchmark Education Co.

—Sorting My Money. 2011. (Early Connections Ser.). (J). (978-1-61672-538-9(9)) Benchmark Education Co.

—Sorting My Money & Clasificar mi Dinero: 6 English, 6 Spanish Adaptations. 2011. (J). spiral bd. 75.00 net. (978-1-4108-5630-2(5)) Benchmark Education Co.

Byrd, Josiah. Makayla's Birthday Money! Work with Money. 2014. (Math Masters: Measurement & Data Ser.). 24p. (J). (gr. 2-3). 23.60 (978-1-4777-6407-7(0)); (ENG.). pap. 8.25 (978-1-4777-4822-0(9)) Rosen Publishing Group, Inc., The. (Rosen Classroom).

Carson-Dellosa Publishing Staff. Time & Money. 2006. (ENG., Illus.). 54p. (gr. k-3). 2.99 (978-0-7696-6480-4(6), Brighter Child) Carson-Dellosa Publishing, LLC.

Cartogna, Eileen. Fun at the Fair: Learning Subtraction Facts To 10. 2009. (Math for the REAL World Ser.). 12p. (gr. 1-2). pap. 5.90 (978-0-8239-8846-4(5), Rosen Classroom) Rosen Publishing Group, Inc., The.

Catel, Patrick. Graphing Money, 1 vol. 2010. (Real World Data Ser.). (ENG., Illus.). 32p. (gr. 3-5). lib. bdg. 29.99 (978-1-4329-2618-2(7), NA-h) Heinemann-Raintree.

—Money & Trade, 1 vol. 2011. (Understanding Money Ser.). (ENG.). 48p. (gr. 3-5). pap. 9.95 (978-1-4329-4642-5(0)); 33.32 (978-1-4329-4635-7(8)) Heinemann-Raintree. (Heinemann InfoSearch).

Cernek, Kim. Build-a-Skill Instant Books Time & Money. Faulkner, Stacey, ed. Campbell, Jenny & Tom, Darcy, illus. 2007. (J). 4.99 (978-1-59198-417-7(3)) Creative Teaching Pr., Inc.

Chatzky, Jean. Not Your Parents' Money Book: Making, Saving, & Spending Your Own Money. Jenkins, Ward & Haya, Erwin, illus. 2010. (ENG.). 176p. (J). (gr. 5-9). pap. 12.99 (978-1-4169-9472-5(6), Simon & Schuster Bks. For Young Readers) Simon & Schuster Bks. For Young Readers.

Chizuwa, Masayuki, illus. My Book of Money Counting Coins: Ages 5, 6, 7. 2007. 80p. (J). (gr. -1-3). per. 7.95 (978-1-933241-42-5(X)) Kumon Publishing North America, Inc.

—My Book of Money Counting Dollars & Cents: Ages 6, 7, 8. 2007. 80p. (J). (gr. -1-3). per. 7.95 (978-1-933241-43-2(8)) Kumon Publishing North America, Inc.

Cleary, Brian. A Dollar, a Penny, How Much & How Many? Gable, Brian, illus. 2014. (Math Is CATegorical (r) Ser.). (ENG.). 32p. (gr. k-3). pap. 6.95 (978-1-4677-2629-0(X), Millbrook Pr.) Lerner Publishing Group.

Cleary, Brian P. A Dollar, a Penny, How Much & How Many? Gable, Brian, illus. 2012. (Math Is CATegorical (r) Ser.). (ENG.). 32p. (gr. k-3). lib. bdg. 16.95 (978-0-8225-7882-6(4), Millbrook Pr.) Lerner Publishing Group.

Clifford, Tim. American Coins & Bills. 2008. (Study of Money Ser.). (Illus.). 32p. (YA). (gr. 3-6). 28.50 (978-1-60472-402-8(1)) Rourke Educational Media.

—Paying Without Money. 2008. (Illus.). 32p. (J). 28.50 (978-1-60472-407-3(2)) Rourke Educational Media.

Cohen, Marina. Money Problems. 2010. (ENG.). 24p. (J). (978-0-7787-6782-4(5)); pap. (978-0-7787-6791-6(4)) Crabtree Publishing Co.

Coins & Money. 2015. (Coins & Money Ser.). (ENG.). 24p. (J). (gr. 1-1). pap., pap., pap. 297.00 (978-1-4994-1276-5(2), PowerKids Pr.) Rosen Publishing Group, Inc., The.

Connolly, Sean. Money & Credit. 2010. (World Economy Explained Ser.). 48p. (YA). (gr. 7-12). 35.65 (978-1-60753-081-7(3)) Amicus Publishing.

—Money & Credit. 2012. (Illus.). 48p. (gr. 6-10). pap. 9.95 (978-1-926722-79-5(5)) Saunders Bk. Co. CAN. Dist: RiverStream Publishing.

Cooper, Jason. Department of the Treasury. 2007. (ENG., Illus.). 24p. (gr. 2-5). 28.50 (978-1-60472-123-2(5)) Rourke Educational Media.

Coss, Lauren. Let's Sort Money. 2014. (21st Century Basic Skills Library: Sorting Ser.). (ENG.). 24p. (J). (gr. k-3). 22.79 (978-1-63137-633-7(0), 205315) Cherry Lake Publishing.

Cribb, Joe. DK Eyewitness Books: Money. 2016. (DK Eyewitness Bks.). (ENG., Illus.). 72p. (J). (gr. 3-7). pap. 9.99 (978-1-4654-5178-1(1), 1405885, DK Children) Dorling Kindersley Publishing, Inc.

Croke, Liam & Naik, Anita. I'm Broke! The Money Handbook. 2009. (Really Useful Handbooks Ser.). (ENG., Illus.). 48p. (J). (gr. 5-11). pap. (978-0-7787-4402-3(7)); lib. bdg. (978-0-7787-4389-7(6)) Crabtree Publishing Co.

Dalton, Julie. Counting Money. 2006. (Rookie Read-About Math Ser.). (ENG., Illus.). 32p. (J). (gr. 1-2). per. 5.95 (978-0-516-25361-9(1), Children's Pr.) Scholastic Library Publishing.

—Making Change at the Fair. 2006. (Rookie Read-About Math Ser.). (ENG., Illus.). 32p. (J). (gr. 1-2). lib. bdg. 20.50 (978-0-516-24960-5(6), Children's Pr.) Scholastic Library Publishing.

Daniels, Kathryn. A Bluestocking Guide - the Money Mystery: Based on Richard J. Maybury's book the Money Mystery. Williams, Jane A., ed. 2004. (Bluestocking Guide Ser.). (ENG.). 31p. (YA). pap. 8.95 (978-0-942617-49-8(5)) Bluestocking Pr.

DaSilva-Gordon, Maria. Top 10 Secrets for Making Money & Even More Money. 2013. 64p. (YA). (gr. 7-12). 31.95 (978-1-4488-9359-1(3)); pap. 12.95 (978-1-4488-9373-7(9)); pap. 77.70 (978-1-4488-9374-4(7)) Rosen Publishing Group, Inc., The.

Deen, Marilyn. Dollars & Cents, 1 vol. 2011. (Wonder Readers: Mathematics Ser.). (ENG.). (gr. -1-2). 20p. lib. bdg. 22.65 (978-1-4296-8630-3(8)); 32p. pap. 5.99 (978-1-4296-7915-2(8)); 16p. pap. 35.94 (978-1-4296-8084-4(9)) Capstone Press of Coughlan Cos. (Wonder Readers).

Donovan, Sandy. Budgeting. 2005. (How Economics Works). (ENG., Illus.). 48p. (gr. 4-6). lib. bdg. 25.26 (978-0-8225-2665-0(4), Lerner Pubns.) Lerner Publishing Group.

Dorling Kindersley Publishing Staff. Heads up Money. 2017. (Heads Up Ser.). (ENG.). 160p. (YA). (gr. 5-12). 12.99 (978-1-4654-5626-7(0), DK Children) Dorling Kindersley Publishing, Inc.

—Money Math, Third Grade. 2016. (ENG.). 60p. (J). (gr. 2-4). pap. 6.99 (978-1-4654-5121-7(8), DK Children) Dorling Kindersley Publishing, Inc.

Doudna, Kelly. Let's Add Bills. 2003. (Dollars & Cents Set 3 Ser.). (ENG., Illus.). 24p. (J). (gr. k-3). lib. bdg. 24.21 (978-1-57765-898-6(1), SandCastle) ABDO Publishing Co.

—Let's Add Coins. 2003. (Dollars & Cents Set 3 Ser.). (ENG., Illus.). 24p. (J). (gr. k-3). lib. bdg. 24.21 (978-1-57765-896-2(5), SandCastle) ABDO Publishing Co.

—Let's Add Money. 2003. (Dollars & Cents Set 3 Ser.). (ENG., Illus.). 24p. (J). (gr. k-3). lib. bdg. 24.21 (978-1-57765-900-6(7), SandCastle) ABDO Publishing Co.

—Let's Subtract Bills. 2003. (Dollars & Cents Set 3 Ser.). (ENG., Illus.). 24p. (J). (gr. k-3). lib. bdg. 24.21 (978-1-57765-899-3(X), SandCastle) ABDO Publishing Co.

—Let's Subtract Coins. 2003. (Dollars & Cents Set 3 Ser.). (ENG., Illus.). 24p. (J). (gr. k-3). lib. bdg. 24.21 (978-1-57765-897-9(3), SandCastle) ABDO Publishing Co.

—Let's Subtract Money. 2003. (Dollars & Cents Set 3 Ser.). (ENG., Illus.). 24p. (J). (gr. k-3). lib. bdg. 24.21 (978-1-57765-901-3(5), SandCastle) ABDO Publishing Co.

Douglas, Vincent & Blevins, Wiley. Money, 6, Set. 2004. (Phonics Readers Books 37-72 Ser.). (ENG.). 8p. (gr. k-1). pap. 35.70 (978-0-7368-4052-1(4), Phonics Readers) Capstone Press of Coughlan Cos.

Dowdy, Penny. Money. 2008. (My Path to Math Ser.). (ENG., Illus.). 24p. (J). (gr. k-3). pap. (978-0-7787-4360-6(8)); lib. bdg. (978-0-7787-4342-2(X)) Crabtree Publishing Co.

Duke, Shirley. Money Counts. 2012. (ENG.). 24p. (gr. -1-1). pap. 8.95 (978-1-61810-209-6(5)) Rourke Educational Media.

Dyer, Wayne. It's Not What You've Got! Lessons for Kids on Money & Abundance. Budnick, Stacy Heller & Heller Budnick, Stacy, illus. 2007. (ENG.). 32p. (gr. -1-3). 15.99 (978-1-4019-1850-7(6)) Hay Hse., Inc.

Einspruch, Andrew. The Money System. 2012. (Money Sense Ser.). (Illus.). 32p. (gr. 4-6). lib. bdg. 28.50 (978-1-59920-429-1(0)) Black Rabbit Bks.

Endres, Hollie J. How Much Money? (Yellow Umbrella Fluent Level Ser.). (ENG.). 16p. (gr. k-1). 2016. pap. 6.29 (978-1-5157-3689-9(X)) 2005. pap. 35.70 (978-0-7368-5325-5(1)) Capstone Press of Coughlan Cos. (Yellow Umbrella Bks.).

Fan, Daphne. Money Champ: Teaching Kids about Money Management. 2010. 144p. pap. 57.95 (978-1-4327-4990-3(0)) Outskirts Pr., Inc.

Fay, Gail. Using Money, 1 vol. 2011. (Understanding Money Ser.). (ENG.). 48p. (gr. 3-5). pap. 9.95 (978-1-4329-4641-8(2)); 33.32 (978-1-4329-4634-0(X)) Heinemann-Raintree. (Heinemann InfoSearch).

Feldman, Jean R. & Karapetkova, Holly. Found a Penny (Tune, Found a Peanut) Lap Book. 2010. (ENG., Illus.). 16p. (gr. -1-k). 9.95 (978-1-61590-204-0(X)) Rourke Educational Media.

First, Rachel. What's It Worth? Fun with Coins & Bills, 1 vol. 2016. (Math Beginnings Ser.). (ENG., Illus.). 24p. (J). (gr. k-3). 24.21 (978-1-62403-937-9(5)) ABDO Publishing Co.

Fitzgerald, Lee. Pennies! 2015. (Coins & Money Ser.). (ENG., Illus.). 24p. (J). (gr. 1-1). 23.60 (978-1-4994-0502-6(2), PowerKids Pr.) Rosen Publishing Group, Inc., The.

Flash Kids Editors, ed. Time & Money: Grade 1 (Flash Skills) 2010. (Flash Skills Ser.). (ENG.). 64p. (J). pap. 3.95 (978-1-4114-3450-9(1), Spark Publishing Group) Sterling Publishing Co., Inc.

Fradin, Dennis Brindell & Fradin, Judith Bloom. Spending. 2010. (Money Smart Ser.). 64p. (gr. 4). 32.79 (978-1-60870-126-1(3)) Marshall Cavendish Corp.

Godfrey, Neale S. A Money Adventure: Earning, Saving, Spending, Sharing: Primary Home-School Kit. 2003. (One & Only Common Sense/ents Ser.). 44.50 (978-0-7652-2451-4(8)) Modern Curriculum Pr.

Graham, Roland. Making Money. 2003. (Real Readers - Upper Emergent Ser.). (ENG., Illus.). 12p. (gr. 1-2). pap. 5.90 (978-0-8239-6358-4(6)) Rosen Publishing Group, Inc., The.

Greenes, Carol, et al. Time & Money. 2003. (Illus.). 60p. (J). (gr. -1-3). 16.95 (978-0-7690-0004-6(5)) Seymour, Dale Pubns.

Gregoire, Maryellen. Ganar Dinero (Making Money) 2012. (Wonder Readers Spanish Emergent Ser.). (SPA.). 16p. (gr. -1-1). pap. 35.94 (978-1-62065-572-6(1)) Capstone Press of Coughlan Cos.

—Making Money. 2012. (Wonder Readers Emergent Level Ser.). (ENG.). (gr. -1-1). 16p. pap. 35.94 (978-1-4296-9206-9(5)); 32p. pap. 5.99 (978-1-4296-9196-3(4)) Capstone Press of Coughlan Cos. (Wonder Readers).

Guy, Pauline. Let's Count. 2004. 24p. (J). (gr. -1). 15.99 (978-0-9744205-6-1(5)) Golden Eagle Publishing Hse., Inc.

Hall, Margaret. Money. 2016. (Earning, Saving, Spending Ser.). (ENG.). 32p. (gr. 1-3). pap. 7.99 (978-1-4846-3642-8(2), NA-h) Heinemann-Raintree.

Hamilton, Robert M. Dimes! 2015. (Coins & Money Ser.). (ENG., Illus.). 24p. (J). (gr. 1-1). 23.60 (978-1-4994-0498-2(0), PowerKids Pr.) Rosen Publishing Group, Inc., The.

Harman, Hollis Page. Money Sense for Kids. 2nd ed. 2004. (ENG., Illus.). 192p. (J). pap. 14.99 (978-0-7641-2894-3(9)) Barron's Educational Series, Inc.

Heos, Bridget. Counting Change. Longhi, Katya, illus. 2015. (Math World Ser.). 24p. (J). lib. bdg. 27.10 (978-1-60753-462-4(2)) Amicus Publishing.

Hicer, Nancy. Pennies, Nickles, & Dimes. 2015. (Rosen REAL Readers: STEM & STEAM Collection). (ENG.). 8p. pap. 5.46 (978-1-4994-9723-6(7), Rosen Classroom) Rosen Publishing Group, Inc., The.

The History of Money. pap. 12.95 (978-89-314-3702-7(1)) Youngjin.com Publishing Co., Ltd. KOR. Dist: Transition Vendor.

Hollander, Barbara. Money Matters: An Introduction to Economics. 2010. (Global Marketplace Ser.). (ENG.). 56p. (gr. 6-9). 34.65 (978-1-4329-3929-8(7), NA-h) Heinemann-Raintree.

—Top 10 Secrets for Spending Your Money Wisely. 2013. (Student's Guide to Financial Empowerment Ser.). (Illus.). 64p. (YA). (gr. 7-12). pap. 77.70 (978-1-4488-9381-2(X)); pap. 12.95 (978-1-4488-9380-5(1)) Rosen Publishing Group, Inc., The.

—What Are Saving & Spending? 2016. (Let's Find Out! Ser.). (ENG.). 32p. (J). (gr. 3-2). lib. bdg. 24.45 (978-1-68048-405-2(2)) Rosen Publishing Group, Inc., The.

Hollander, Barbara & Gottfried Hollander, Barbara. Top 10 Secrets for Spending Your Money Wisely. 2013. (Illus.). 64p. (YA). (gr. 7-12). 31.95 (978-1-4488-9361-4(5)) Rosen Publishing Group, Inc., The.

Hollander, Barbara Gottfried. Bitcoins: Navigating Open Source Currency, 1 vol. 2015. (ENG.). 48p. (YA). 30.25 (978-1-4777-7930-9(2), Rosen Reference) Rosen Publishing Group, Inc., The.

Houghton, Gillian. Cash & ATMs. 2009. (Invest Kids Ser.). 24p. (gr. 2-5). (ENG., Illus.). (J). pap. 8.25 (978-1-4358-3206-0(X)); 42.50 (978-1-61513-611-7(8)); (J). lib. bdg. 22.60 (978-1-4358-2771-4(6)) Rosen Publishing Group, Inc., The. (PowerKids Pr.).

—How Credit Cards Work. 2009. (Invest Kids Ser.). (Illus.). 24p. (J). (gr. 2-5). (ENG.). pap. 8.25 (978-1-4358-3208-4(6)); lib. bdg. 22.60 (978-1-4358-2773-8(2)) Rosen Publishing Group, Inc., The. (PowerKids Pr.).

Hunt, Darleen L. Dog's Dollars: Patterns. Komarck, Michael, illus. 2003. (Sherman's Math Corner Ser.). (J). (gr. -1-3). (978-1-929591-08-4(X)) Reading Rock, Inc.

James, Jack. How to Let Your Parents Raise a Millionaire: A Kid-to-Kid View on How to Make Money Make a Difference & Have Fun Doing Both. 2012. (ENG.). 115p. pap. 14.95 (978-1-61448-248-2(9)) Morgan James Publishing.

Jones, Patrick. My Dog-Walking Business: Work with Money, 1 vol. 2015. (InfoMax Common Core Math Readers Ser.). (ENG.). 24p. (J). pap. 8.25 (978-1-4777-4750-6(8), Rosen Classroom) Rosen Publishing Group, Inc., The.

Joy, Berry. Help Me Good about Being Greedy. 2009. 32p. 7.95 (978-1-60577-109-0(0)) Berry, Joy Enterprises.

Junior Library of Money, 14 vols., Set. Incl. Earning Money: Jobs. Fischer, James. pap. 9.95 (978-1-4222-1882-2(1)); Entrepreneurship. Simons, Rae. pap. 9.95 (978-1-4222-1883-9(X)); Guide to Teaching Young Adults about Money. Simons, Rae. pap. 9.95 (978-1-4222-1884-6(8)); Investing Money. Thompson, Helen. pap. 9.95 (978-1-4222-1885-3(6)); Money & Relationships. Simons, Rae. pap. 9.95 (978-1-4222-1886-0(4)); Planning for Your Education. Fischer, James. pap. 9.95 (978-1-4222-1887-7(2)); Power to Do Good: Money & Charity. Fischer, James. pap. 9.95 (978-1-4222-1888-4(0)); Sustainable Lifestyles in a Changing Economy. Simons, Rae. pap. 9.95 (978-1-4222-1890-7(2)); 64p. (YA). (gr. 7-18). 2010. 2011. Set pap. 139.30 (978-1-4222-1878-5(3)) Mason Crest.

Kemper, Bitsy. Budgeting, Spending & Saving. 2015. (Searchlight Books (tm) — How Do We Use Money? Ser.). (ENG., Illus.). 40p. (J). (gr. 3-5). pap. 8.99 (978-1-4677-6105-5(2)); lib. bdg. 27.99 (978-1-4677-5228-2(2)) Lerner Publishing Group. (Lerner Pubns.).

—Budgeting, Spending, & Saving. 2015. (Searchlight Books (tm) — How Do We Use Money? Ser.). (ENG., Illus.). 40p. (gr. 3-5). 39.99 (978-1-4677-8914-1(3), Lerner Digital) Lerner Publishing Group.

—Earning Income. 2015. (Searchlight Books (tm) — How Do We Use Money? Ser.). (ENG., Illus.). 40p. (gr. 3-5). 39.99 (978-1-4677-8915-8(1), Lerner Digital); (J). pap. 8.99 (978-1-4677-6107-9(9), Lerner Pubns.); (J). lib. bdg. 27.99 (978-1-4677-5227-5(4), Lerner Pubns.) Lerner Publishing Group.

—Growing Your Money. 2015. (Searchlight Books (tm) — How Do We Use Money? Ser.). (ENG., Illus.). 40p. (gr. 3-5). 39.99 (978-1-4677-8916-5(X), Lerner Digital); (J). pap. 8.99 (978-1-4677-6108-6(7), Lerner Pubns.); (J). lib. bdg. 27.99 (978-1-4677-5230-5(4), Lerner Pubns.) Lerner Publishing Group.

Knowles, Amy. Working in a School Store. 2013. (Rosen Readers Ser.). (ENG.). 24p. (J). (gr. 3-4). pap. 8.25 (978-1-4777-2539-9(3)); pap. 49.50 (978-1-4777-2540-5(7)) Rosen Publishing Group, Inc., The. (Rosen Classroom).

Kompelien, Tracy. I Know about Money, It Is So Funny!, 1 vol. 2007. (Math Made Fun Ser.). (ENG., Illus.). 24p. (J). (gr. k-3). lib. bdg. 24.21 (978-1-59928-527-6(4), SandCastle) ABDO Publishing Co.

Kravitz, Robert J. A Collector's Guide to Fractional Currency: The Pocket Change of the Union Soldier. collector's ed. 2003. (Illus.). 262p. pap. 29.95 (978-0-918501-46-2(6), RK-2003, Archives Pr.) Media Assocs.

Kulp, Donald. Money Puppies: America's #1 Money Management Book for Kids. 2010. 36p. pap. 14.99 (978-1-4490-8977-1(1)) AuthorHouse.

Kummer, Patricia K. Currency. 2006. (Inventions That Shaped the World Ser.). (Illus.). 80p. (gr. 5-8). 19.95 (978-0-7569-6856-4(9)) Perfection Learning Corp.

Larson, Jennifer S. What Is Money, Anyway? Why Dollars & Coins Have Value. 2010. (Lightning Bolt Books — Exploring Economics Ser.). (ENG., Illus.). 32p. (gr. k-2). pap. 7.95 (978-0-7613-5668-4(1)); lib. bdg. 26.60 (978-0-7613-3915-1(9)) Lerner Publishing Group.

Lawrence, Lane & Ridgway, Tom. Buying Goods & Services. 2011. (J). 77.70 (978-1-4488-4751-8(6), Rosen Reference); (J). pap. 12.95 (978-1-4488-4719-8(2), Rosen Reference); (YA). (gr. 5-9). lib. bdg. 31.95 (978-1-4488-4715-0(X)) Rosen Publishing Group, Inc., The.

Linde, Barbara M. A Shopping Trip: Learning to Add Dollars & Cents up to $10. 00 Without Regrouping. 2009. (Math for the REAL World Ser.). 16p. (gr. 2-3). pap. 7.05

(978-0-8239-8900-3(3), Rosen Classroom) Rosen Publishing Group, Inc., The.

Llewellyn, Claire. My Money Choices. Gordon, Mike, illus. 2016. (Your Money Ser.). 00024p. (J). (gr. 1-1). pap. 8.25 (978-1-4994-8191-4(8), Windmill Bks.) Rosen Publishing Group, Inc., The.

—Saving My Money. Gordon, Mike, illus. 2016. (Your Money Ser.). 00024p. (J). (gr. 1-1). pap. 8.25 (978-1-4994-8194-5(2), Windmill Bks.) Rosen Publishing Group, Inc., The.

—Spending My Money. Gordon, Mike, illus. 2016. (Your Money Ser.). 00024p. (J). (gr. 1-1). pap. 8.25 (978-1-4994-8197-6(7), Windmill Bks.) Rosen Publishing Group, Inc., The.

—What Is Money? Gordon, Mike, illus. 2016. (Your Money Ser.). 00024p. (J). (gr. 1-1). pap. 8.25 (978-1-4994-8200-3(0), Windmill Bks.) Rosen Publishing Group, Inc., The.

Loughran, Donna. Carnival Coins: How Will We Count Our Money? 2013. (iMath Ser.). (Illus.). 24p. (J). (gr. k-2). pap. 11.94 (978-1-60357-491-4(3)); lib. bdg. 21.27 (978-1-59953-552-4(1)) Norwood Hse. Pr.

Make Money Now! 2013. (Make Money Now! Ser.). 80p. (YA). (gr. 7-12). 232.75 (978-1-4488-9396-6(8)) Rosen Publishing Group, Inc., The.

Maloof, Torrey. Money Matters: What's It Worth? Financial Literacy (Grade 3) 2017. (Mathematics Readers Ser.). (Illus.). 32p. (gr. 3-3). 8.99 **(978-1-4807-5806-3(X))** Teacher Created Materials, Inc.

Marks, Jennifer L. Clasificar Dinero/Sorting Money, 1 vol. 2012. (Vamos a Ordenar / Sorting Ser.). (ENG, SPA & MUL., Illus.). 32p. (gr. 1-2). lib. bdg. 27.32 (978-1-4296-8255-8(8), A+ Bilingue/Bilingual) Capstone Press of Coughlan Cos.

Marks, Jennifer L. & Bruning, Matt. Clasificar/Sorting. 2012. (Vamos a Ordenar / Sorting Ser.). (MUL.). 32p. (gr. 1-2). lib. bdg. 81.96 (978-1-4296-8256-5(6), A+ Bilingue/Bilingual) Capstone Press of Coughlan Cos.

Marrewa, Jennifer. Using Money on a Shopping Trip. 2008. (Math in Our World - Level 2 Ser.). 24p. (gr. 1-4). pap. 8.15 (978-0-8368-9013-6(2), Weekly Reader Leveled Readers) Stevens, Gareth Publishing LLLP.

—Using Money on a Shopping Trip. McKinley, Kay, photos by. 2008. (Math in Our World: Level 2 Ser.). (Illus.). 24p. (gr. 1-4). lib. bdg. 22.00 (978-0-8368-9004-4(3), Weekly Reader Leveled Readers) Stevens, Gareth Publishing LLLP.

—Vamos a Usar Dinero en un Viaje de Compras. McKinley, Kay, photos by. 2008. (Matemáticas en Nuestro Mundo - Nivel 2 (Math in Our World - Level 2) Ser.). (SPA., Illus.). 24p. (gr. 1-4). lib. bdg. 22.00 (978-0-8368-9022-8(1), Weekly Reader Leveled Readers) Stevens, Gareth Publishing LLLP.

—Vamos a USAR DINERO en un Viaje de Compras. 2008. (Las Matemáticas en Nuestro Mundo Ser.). (SPA.). 24p. (gr. 1-4). pap. 8.15 (978-0-8368-9031-0(0), Weekly Reader Leveled Readers) Stevens, Gareth Publishing LLLP.

Marsico, Katie. Shopping Trip Math. 2014. (Math Everywhere! Ser.). (Illus.). 32p. (gr. 3-4). (J). lib. bdg. 26.60 (978-1-4677-1884-4(X), Lerner Pubns.); pap. 7.95 (978-1-4677-4515-4(4)) Lerner Publishing Group.

—What Is Money? 2015. (21st Century Skills Library: Real World Math Ser.). (ENG., Illus.). 32p. (J). (gr. 4-7). 29.93 (978-1-63362-579-2(6), 206500) Cherry Lake Publishing.

Mason, Paul. Frauds & Counterfeits. 2010. (Solve It with Science Ser.). (YA). (gr. 5-9). 34.25 (978-1-59920-329-4(4)) Black Rabbit Bks.

Matheson, Murdoch H. Building Wealth for Teens: Answers to Questions Teens Care About. 2007. 116p. 24.65 (978-1-4251-2358-1(9)) Trafford Publishing.

Mathews, Janice. Happy Jack: How Much Stuff Is Enough? 2014. (Stewardship Jack Ser.: Vol. 4). (ENG., Illus.). 30p. (J). (gr. 3-7). 7.99 (978-0-8280-2786-1(2)) Review & Herald Publishing Assn.

McGillian, Jamie Kyle. The Kids' Money Book. Phillips, Ian, illus. 2006. 96p. (J). (gr. 4-8). reprint ed. 18.00 (978-0-7567-9900-7(7)) DIANE Publishing Co.

Mckenna, James & Glista, Jeannine. How to Turn $100 Into $1,000,000: Earn! Invest! Save! 2016. lib. bdg. 24.45 (978-0-606-37953-3(3)) Turtleback Bks.

McKenna, James, et al. How to Turn $100 Into $1,000,000: A Kid's Guide to Earning, Saving, & Investing. 2016. (ENG., Illus.). 144p. (J). (gr. 4-8). pap. 12.95 (978-0-7611-8080-7(X)) Workman Publishing Co., Inc.

McManus, Lori. Money Through History, 1 vol. 2011. (Understanding Money Ser.). (ENG., Illus.). 48p. (gr. 3-5). pap. 9.95 (978-1-4329-4643-2(9), Heinemann InfoSearch) Heinemann-Raintree.

Meachen Rau, Dana. Gastando el dinero (Spending Money) 2010. (Dinero y los Bancos (Money & Banks) Ser.). (SPA., Illus.). 24p. (gr. 2-5). pap. 8.15 (978-1-4339-3724-8(7)) Stevens, Gareth Publishing LLLP.

—Spending Money. 2010. (Money & Banks Ser.). (Illus.). 24p. (gr. 2-5). pap. 8.15 (978-1-4339-3390-5(X)) Stevens, Gareth Publishing LLLP.

Minden, Cecilia. What Is Money? 2009. (21st Century Skills Library: Real World Math Ser.). (ENG.). 32p. (gr. 4-8). lib. bdg. 29.93 (978-1-60279-312-5(3), 200208) Cherry Lake Publishing.

Molter, Carey. A Dime = 10 Cents, 1 vol. 2003. (Dollars & Cents Set 1 Ser.). (ENG., Illus.). 24p. (J). (gr. k-3). lib. bdg. 24.21 (978-1-57765-884-9(1)) ABDO Publishing Co.

—A Dollar = $1.00, 1 vol. 2003. (Dollars & Cents Set 1 Ser.). (ENG., Illus.). 24p. (J). (gr. k-3). lib. bdg. 24.21 (978-1-57765-885-6(X)) ABDO Publishing Co.

—A Half-Dollar = 50 Cents, 1 vol. 2003. (Dollars & Cents Set 1 Ser.). (ENG., Illus.). 24p. (J). (gr. k-3). lib. bdg. 24.21 (978-1-57765-886-3(8), SandCastle) ABDO Publishing Co.

—How Much Is $10. 00?, 1 vol. 2003. (Dollars & Cents Set 2 Ser.: Level II). (ENG., Illus.). 24p. (J). (gr. k-3). lib. bdg. 24.21 (978-1-57765-894-8(9), SandCastle) ABDO Publishing Co.

—How Much Is $1.00?, 1 vol. 2003. (Dollars & Cents Set 2 Ser.). (ENG., Illus.). 24p. (J). (gr. k-3). lib. bdg. 24.21 (978-1-57765-892-4(2), SandCastle) ABDO Publishing Co.

—How Much Is $100. 00?, 1 vol. 2003. (Dollars & Cents Set 2 Ser.). (ENG., Illus.). 24p. (J). (gr. k-3). lib. bdg. 24.21 (978-1-57765-893-1(0), SandCastle) ABDO Publishing Co.

—How Much Is $20. 00?, 1 vol. 2003. (Dollars & Cents Set 2 Ser.). (ENG., Illus.). 24p. (J). (gr. k-3). lib. bdg. 24.21 (978-1-57765-895-5(7), SandCastle) ABDO Publishing Co.

—How Much Is $5. 00?, 1 vol. 2003. (Dollars & Cents Set 2 Ser.). (ENG., Illus.). 24p. (J). (gr. k-3). lib. bdg. 24.21 (978-1-57765-891-7(4), SandCastle) ABDO Publishing Co.

—How Much Is $50.00?, 1 vol. 2003. (Dollars & Cents Set 2 Ser.). (ENG., Illus.). 24p. (J). (gr. k-3). lib. bdg. 24.21 (978-1-57765-890-0(6), SandCastle) ABDO Publishing Co.

—A Nickel = 5 Cents, 1 vol. 2003. (Dollars & Cents Set 1 Ser.). (ENG., Illus.). 24p. (J). (gr. k-3). lib. bdg. 24.21 (978-1-57765-887-0(6), SandCastle) ABDO Publishing Co.

—A Penny = 1 Cent, 1 vol. 2003. (Dollars & Cents Set 1 Ser.). (ENG., Illus.). 24p. (J). (gr. k-3). lib. bdg. 24.21 (978-1-57765-888-7(4), SandCastle) ABDO Publishing Co.

—A Quarter= 25 cents, 1 vol. 2003. (Dollars & Cents Set 1 Ser.: Level I). (ENG.). 24p. (J). (gr. k-3). lib. bdg. 24.21 (978-1-57765-889-4(2), SandCastle) ABDO Publishing Co.

Moneta. The Journey to the Money Tree. 2009. (Illus.). 28p. pap. 12.49 (978-1-4389-1499-2(7)) AuthorHouse.

Money. 2004. (Illus.). lib. bdg. 7.95 (978-0-8225-5257-4(4)) Lerner Publishing Group.

Money - Set 2: Dollars that Add Up. 2005. (J). spiral bd. 19.90 (978-0-9770248-5-8(7)) Sidedoor Publishing LLC.

Money Skills for Kids. 2017. (Money Skills for Kids Ser.). 32p. (gr. 10-10). 131.25 **(978-1-4994-3402-6(2))**; pap. 50.00 **(978-1-5081-5431-0(7))** Rosen Publishing Group, Inc., The. (PowerKids Pr.).

Mooney, Carla. Understanding Credit. 2015. (Searchlight Books (tm) — How Do We Use Money? Ser.). (ENG., Illus.). 40p. (J). (gr. 3-5). pap. 8.99 (978-1-4677-6106-2(0)); lib. bdg. 27.99 (978-1-4677-5229-9(0)) Lerner Publishing Group. (Lerner Pubns.).

Morgan, Elizabeth. Nickels! 2015. (Coins & Money Ser.). (ENG., Illus.). 24p. (J). (gr. 1-1). 23.60 (978-1-4994-0501-9(4), PowerKids Pr.) Rosen Publishing Group, Inc., The.

Morgan, Sally. Earth's Energy Sources. 2011. (Earth Cycles Ser.). 32p. (YA). (gr. 3-6). lib. bdg. 28.50 (978-1-59920-522-9(X)) Black Rabbit Bks.

Moriarty, J. T. The Birth of American Capitalism: The Growth of American Banks. 2004. (America's Industrial Society in the 19th Century Ser.). (Illus.). 32p. (gr. 5-8). pap. 10.00 (978-0-8239-4280-0(5)) Rosen Publishing Group, Inc., The.

Morrison, Jessica. Saving. 2017. (J). **(978-1-5105-1947-3(5))** SmartBook Media, Inc.

Mototsune, Kat. Money: Deal with It or Pay the Price, 1 vol. Geoffroi, Remie, illus. 2007. (Lorimer Deal with It Ser.). (ENG.). 32p. (J). (gr. 4-6). pap. 12.95 (978-1-55028-958-9(6), 9781550289589) Lorimer, James & Co., Ltd., Pubs. CAN. Dist: Casemate Pubs. & Bk. Distributors, LLC.

Murphy, Patricia J. Earning Money. 2005. (How Economics Works). (Illus.). 48p. (J). (gr. 3-7). lib. bdg. 25.26 (978-0-8225-2149-5(0), Lerner Pubns.) Lerner Publishing Group.

Nelson, Sandi. A Fly on the Wall Street. Beckstrand, Jared, illus. 2013. 23p. (J). 19.99 (978-1-938690-29-7(X)) Salem Author Services.

Norwood, R. Edward. Kids under$Tanding Money. 2009. 48p. pap. 19.95 (978-1-4389-4053-3(X)) AuthorHouse.

Nourigat, Paul. Why Is There Money? A Facinating Journey Through the Evolution of Money. Schofield, Angela, illus. 2011. (ENG.). 36p. (J). pap. 11.29 (978-1-936872-00-8(5)) FarBeyond Publishing LLC.

Orr, Tamra. Money Matters: A Kid's Guide to Money, 5 vols., Set. Incl. Budgeting Tips for Kids. lib. bdg. 29.95 (978-1-58415-644-4(9)); Coins & Other Currency. lib. bdg. 29.95 (978-1-58415-640-6(6)); Kid's Guide to Earning Money. lib. bdg. 29.95 (978-1-58415-643-7(0)); Kid's Guide to Stock Market Investing. lib. bdg. 29.95 (978-1-58415-642-0(2)); Savings Tips for Kids. lib. bdg. 29.95 (978-1-58415-641-3(4)); (Illus.). 48p. (YA). (gr. 3-6). 2008. 2008. Set lib. bdg. 149.75 (978-1-58415-645-1(7)) Mitchell Lane Pubs., Inc.

Outram, Richard. The Adventures of Exokid & the Teachings of Money. Kapatos, Elizabeth, illus. 2009. 36p. pap. 12.95 (978-1-59858-898-9(2)) Dog Ear Publishing, LLC.

Pellittiere II, Michael. GROW MONEY - A Kid's Guide to Saving & Investing. 2007. 60p. (YA). pap. 10.40 (978-0-615-14589-1(2)) Dakota Assocs., Inc.

—GROW MONEY II - A Teenager's Guide to Saving & Investing. 2008. 118p. (YA). pap. 11.42 (978-0-615-18343-5(3)) Dakota Assocs., Inc.

Penn, M. W. Counting Money!, 1 vol. 2012. (Pebble Math Ser.). (ENG.). 24p. (gr. k-1). pap. 6.29 (978-1-4296-7875-9(5)); pap. 35.70 (978-1-4296-8308-1(2)); lib. bdg. 21.99 (978-1-4296-7562-8(4)) Capstone Press of Coughlan Cos. (Pebble Bks.).

Phillips Mba, Nancy. The Zela Wela Kid: Build a Bank. 2010. 36p. pap. 15.75 (978-1-4490-7413-5(8)) AuthorHouse.

Pistoia, Sara. Money. 2016. (J). (978-1-4896-5113-6(6)) Weigl Pubs., Inc.

Prior, Jennifer Overend & Prior, Jennifer. Time & Money: 14 Reproducible Games That Help Struggling Learners Practice & Really Master Basic Time & Money Skills. 2007. (Math Games to Master Basic Skills Ser.). (ENG., Illus.). 48p. pap. 10.99 (978-0-439-55414-5(4), Teaching Resources) Scholastic, Inc.

Quin, Caroline. Shopping. 2004. (Activities for 3-5 Year Olds Ser.). (Illus.). 32p. pap. 11.00 (978-1-897675-58-6(5)) Brilliant Pubns. GBR. Dist: Parkwest Pubns., Inc.

Rau, Dana Meachen. Gastar el Dinero. 2010. (Dinero y los Bancos Ser.). (SPA., Illus.). 24p. (J). (gr. 2-5). lib. bdg. 22.00 (978-1-4339-3723-1(9)) Stevens, Gareth Publishing LLLP.

—Spending Money. 2010. (Money & Banks Ser.). (Illus.). 24p. (J). (gr. 2-5). lib. bdg. 22.00 (978-1-4339-3389-9(6)) Stevens, Gareth Publishing LLLP.

Rauen, Amy. Usamos Dinero en el Puesto de Limonada. 2007. (Las matimaticas en nuestro mundo (Spanish- Math in Our World) Ser.). (SPA.). 24p. (gr. 1-2). pap. 8.15 (978-0-8368-8499-9(X), Weekly Reader Leveled Readers) Stevens, Gareth Publishing LLLP.

Rauen, Amy & Ayers, Amy. Usamos Dinero en el Puesto de Limonada. Pickering, Russell, photos by. 2007. (Matemáticas en Nuestro Mundo (Math in Our World) Ser.). (SPA., Illus.). 24p. (gr. 1-2). lib. bdg. 22.00 (978-0-8368-8490-6(6), Weekly Reader Leveled Readers) Stevens, Gareth Publishing LLLP.

—Using Money at the Lemonade Stand. Pickering, Russell, photos by. 2007. (Math in Our World Ser.). (Illus.). 24p. (gr. 1-2). lib. bdg. 22.00 (978-0-8368-8472-2(8), Weekly Reader Leveled Readers) Stevens, Gareth Publishing LLLP.

Reeves, Diane Lindsey. Career Ideas for Kids Who Like Math & Money. Bond, Nancy, illus. 2nd rev. ed. 2007. (Career Ideas for Kids Ser.). 208p. (gr. 4-9). 32.95 (978-0-8160-6545-5(4), Ferguson Publishing Co.); per. 16.95 (978-0-8160-6546-2(2), Checkmark Bks.) Facts On File, Inc.

Reina, Mary. Learn about Money. 2015. (Money & You Ser.). (ENG.). 24p. (gr. k-1). lib. bdg. 21.99 (978-1-4914-2084-3(7), Pebble Bks.) Capstone Press of Coughlan Cos.

—Make Money Choices. 2015. (Money & You Ser.). (ENG.). 24p. (gr. k-1). pap. 5.95 (978-1-4914-2300-4(5), Pebble Bks.) Capstone Press of Coughlan Cos.

—Money & You. 2015. (Money & You Ser.). (ENG.). 24p. (gr. k-1). lib. bdg. 87.96 (978-1-4914-2569-5(5), Pebble Bks.) Capstone Press of Coughlan Cos.

Roberson, Erin. All about Money. 2005. (Rookie Read-About Math Ser.). (ENG., Illus.). 32p. (J). (gr. 1-2). pap. 5.95 (978-0-516-24672-7(0), Children's Pr.) Scholastic Library Publishing.

Roderick, Stacey & Warwick, Ellen. Centsibility: The Planet Girl Guide to Money. Melnychuk, Monika, illus. 2008. (Planet Girl Ser.). (ENG.). 80p. (J). (gr. 5-9). 12.95 (978-1-55453-208-7(6)) Kids Can Pr., Ltd. CAN. Dist: Hachette Bk. Group.

Roper, Dawn. 30 Fun Ways to Learn about Time & Money. 2011. (30 Fun Ways to Learn Ser.). (ENG.). 80p. (gr. -1-k). pap. 12.95 (978-0-87659-370-7(8), Gryphon House Inc) Gryphon Hse., Inc.

Rose, Simon. Loonies: Canadian Icons. 2010. (Illus.). 24p. (978-1-77071-579-0(7)); pap. (978-1-77071-586-8(X)) Weigl Educational Pubs. Ltd.

Rowe, Brooke. What Kind of Spender Are You? 2015. 32p. (J). (978-1-63470-040-5(6)) Cherry Lake Publishing.

Roy, Jennifer Rozines & Roy, Gregory. Money at the Store. 2007. (J). pap. 6.99 (978-0-7614-3385-9(6)) 2006. (Illus.). 32p. (gr. 2-7). lib. bdg. 29.93 (978-0-7614-2264-8(1), Benchmark Bks.) Marshall Cavendish Corp.

Rumsch, BreAnn. Money Matters, 1 vol. 2012. (Economy in Action! Ser.). (ENG.). 32p. (J). (gr. 3-6). lib. bdg. 27.07 (978-1-61783-489-9(0), Checkerboard Library) ABDO Publishing Co.

Russell, Solveig Paulson. From Barter to Gold: The Story of Money. Cary, illus. 2011. 66p. 36.95 (978-1-258-01865-8(9)) Literary Licensing, LLC.

Salzmann, Mary Elizabeth. Money for Clothes, 1 vol. 2010. (Your Piggy Bank: A Guide to Spending & Saving for Kids! Ser.). (ENG.). 24p. (J). (gr. k-3). 27.07 (978-1-61641-027-8(2)) Magic Wagon.

—Money for Entertainment, 1 vol. 2010. (Your Piggy Bank: A Guide to Spending & Saving for Kids! Ser.). (ENG., Illus.). 24p. (J). (gr. k-3). 27.07 (978-1-61641-028-5(0)) Magic Wagon.

—Money for Food, 1 vol. 2010. (Your Piggy Bank: A Guide to Spending & Saving for Kids! Ser.). (ENG.). 24p. (J). (gr. k-3). 27.07 (978-1-61641-029-2(9)) Magic Wagon.

—Money for Hobbies, 1 vol. 2010. (Your Piggy Bank: A Guide to Spending & Saving for Kids! Ser.). (ENG.). 24p. (J). (gr. k-3). 27.07 (978-1-61641-030-8(2)) Magic Wagon.

—Money for School, 1 vol. 2010. (Your Piggy Bank: A Guide to Spending & Saving for Kids! Ser.). (ENG.). 24p. (J). (gr. k-3). 27.07 (978-1-61641-031-5(0)) Magic Wagon.

—Money for Toys, 1 vol. 2010. (Your Piggy Bank: A Guide to Spending & Saving for Kids! Ser.). (ENG.). 24p. (J). (gr. k-3). 27.07 (978-1-61641-032-2(9)) Magic Wagon.

School Zone Interactive Staff. Time, Money & Fractions. rev. ed. 2004. (ENG.). 64p. (J). (gr. k-2). 15.99 (978-1-58947-832-9(0)) School Zone Publishing Co.

School Zone Staff. Time & Money. 2004. (ENG.). 56p. (J). 2.79 (978-1-58947-990-6(4)) School Zone Publishing Co.

School Zone Staff, ed. Time & Money. 2005. (ENG.). 26p. (J). (gr. 1-2). pap. 3.79 (978-1-58947-788-9(X)) School Zone Publishing Co.

—Time, Money & Fractions. 2003. (ENG.). (J). (gr. 1-2). cd-rom 19.99 (978-1-58947-930-2(0)) School Zone Publishing Co.

Schuh, Mari. Counting Money. 2015. (Money Matters Ser.). (ENG., Illus.). 24p. (J). (gr. k-3). lib. bdg. 25.95 (978-1-62617-245-6(5), Blastoff! Readers) Bellwether Media.

—Earning Money. 2015. (Money Matters Ser.). (ENG., Illus.). 24p. (J). (gr. k-3). lib. bdg. 25.95 (978-1-62617-246-3(3), Blastoff! Readers) Bellwether Media.

—Spending Money. 2015. (Money Matters Ser.). (ENG., Illus.). 24p. (J). (gr. k-3). lib. bdg. 25.95 (978-1-62617-248-7(X), Blastoff! Readers) Bellwether Media.

—Types of Money. 2015. (Money Matters Ser.). (ENG., Illus.). 24p. (J). (gr. k-3). lib. bdg. 25.95 (978-1-62617-249-4(8), Blastoff! Readers) Bellwether Media.

Schwartz, Heather E. Save Wisely. 2015. (Money Smarts Ser.). (ENG., Illus.). 32p. (J). (gr. 2-4). 19.95 (978-1-60753-794-6(X)) Amicus Publishing.

Seba, Jaime A. Smashing the Stereotypes: What Does It Mean to Be Gay, Lesbian, Bisexual, or Transgender? 2009. (Gallup's Guide to Modern Gay, Lesbian, & Transgender Lifestyle Ser.). 64p. (YA). (gr. 7-18). pap. 9.95 (978-1-4222-1874-7(0)) Mason Crest.

Seuling, Barbara. There Are Millions of Millionaires: And Other Freaky Facts About Earning, Saving, & Spending. Haugen, Ryan, illus. 2010. (Freaky Facts Ser.). 40p. pap. 0.35 (978-1-4048-6550-1(0), Nonfiction Picture Bks.) Picture Window Bks.

Sherman, Jill. Money: What You Need to Know. 2017. (Fact Files Ser.). (ENG.). 24p. (gr. 1-2). lib. bdg. 25.32 **(978-1-5157-8120-2(8)**, First Facts) Capstone Press of Coughlan Cos.

Siegel, Randy. One Proud Penny. Bloch, Serge, illus. 2017. (ENG.). 40p. (J). 17.99 (978-1-62672-235-4(8), 9781626722354) Roaring Brook Pr.

Sieplinga, Drew. Paint Your Own Piggy Bank. 2007. (Illus.). 32p. (J). (978-0-545-02112-8(X)) Scholastic, Inc.

Silbert, Jack. Honest Abe's Funny Money Book. 2012. (Illus.). 32p. (978-0-545-36740-0(9)) Scholastic, Inc.

Simons, Rae. All about Money: The History, Culture, & Meaning of Modern Finance. 2010. (Junior Library of Money). 64p. (YA). (gr. 7-18). lib. bdg. 22.95 (978-1-4222-1760-3(4)) Mason Crest.

—Money & Relationships. 2010. (Junior Library of Money). 64p. (YA). (gr. 7-18). pap. 9.95 (978-1-4222-1886-0(4)); lib. bdg. 22.95 (978-1-4222-1767-2(1)) Mason Crest.

—Spending Money. 2010. (Junior Library of Money). 64p. (YA). (gr. 7-18). lib. bdg. 22.95 (978-1-4222-1770-2(1)) Mason Crest.

St. Germain, Mark. Three Cups: Teaching Children How to Save, Spend & Be Charitable with Money Is As Easy As 1, 2, 3. Willy, April, illus. 2007. (ENG.). 28p. (J). pap. 10.00 (978-0-9794563-0-5(4)) Three Cups, LLC.

Stanley, Joseph. Half-Dollars! 2015. (Coins & Money Ser.). (ENG., Illus.). 24p. (J). (gr. 1-1). 23.60 (978-1-4994-0500-2(6), PowerKids Pr.) Rosen Publishing Group, Inc., The.

Steck-Vaughn Staff. At-Home Workbooks: Money. 2004. (Illus.). pap., wbk. ed. 5.99 (978-0-7398-8537-6(5)) Steck-Vaughn.

Sterling, Kristin. Money. 2008. pap. 22.95 (978-0-8225-9361-4(0)); (ENG.). 8p. (gr. -1-1). pap. 4.95 (978-0-8225-8848-1(X)) Lerner Publishing Group.

Stuart, Carrie. Kinds of Coins: Learning the Values of Pennies, Nickels, Dimes & Quarters. 2009. (Math for the REAL World Ser.). 12p. (gr. 1-2). pap. 5.90 (978-0-8239-8862-4(7), Rosen Classroom) Rosen Publishing Group, Inc., The.

Studio 2B Focus - On the Money. 2004. (YA). (978-0-88441-687-6(9)) Girl Scouts of the USA.

Suen, Anastasia. Downloading & Online Shopping Safety & Privacy. 2013. (21st Century Safety & Privacy Ser.). (Illus.). 64p. (J). (gr. 5-8). 31.95 (978-1-4488-9571-7(5)); pap. 12.95 (978-1-4488-9582-3(0)); pap. 77.70 (978-1-4488-9583-0(9)) Rosen Publishing Group, Inc., The.

Summers, Portia. Adding Coins & Bills. 2016. (Value of Money Ser.). 24p. (J). (gr. 2-1). pap. 9.35 (978-0-7660-7693-8(8)) Enslow Pubs., Inc.

—Counting Coins & Bills. 2016. (Value of Money Ser.). (Illus.). 24p. (J). (gr. 2-1). pap. 9.35 (978-0-7660-7700-3(4)) Enslow Pubs., Inc.

—Subtracting Coins & Bills. 2016. (Value of Money Ser.). 24p. (J). (gr. 2-1). pap. 9.35 (978-0-7660-7720-1(9)) Enslow Pubs., Inc.

—What Is Money? 2016. (Value of Money Ser.). (Illus.). 24p. (J). (gr. 2-1). pap. 9.35 (978-0-7660-7715-7(2)) Enslow Pubs., Inc.

—Word Problems with Money. 2016. (Value of Money Ser.). (Illus.). 24p. (J). (gr. 2-1). pap. 9.35 (978-0-7660-7707-2(1)) Enslow Pubs., Inc.

Sundance/Newbridge LLC Staff. Dollars & Cents. 2004. (Reading PowerWorks Ser.). (gr. 1-3). 37.50 (978-0-7608-8964-0(3)); pap. 6.10 (978-0-7608-8965-7(1)) Sundance/Newbridge Educational Publishing.

Swain, Cynthia. I Have a Coin. 2006. (Early Explorers Ser.). (J). pap. (978-1-4108-6040-8(X)) Benchmark Education Co.

Sylvester, Kevin & Hlinka, Michael. Follow Your Money: Who Gets It, Who Spends It, Where Does It Go? Sylvester, Kevin, illus. 2nd ed. 2013. (ENG., Illus.). 60p. (J). (gr. 5-12). 24.95 (978-1-55451-481-6(9), 9781554514816); pap. 14.95 (978-1-55451-480-9(0), 9781554514809) Annick Pr., Ltd. CAN. Dist: Publishers Group West (PGW).

Thayer, Tanya. Counting Money. 2005. (First Step Nonfiction Ser.). (Illus.). 24p. (gr. k-2). lib. bdg. 17.27 (978-0-8225-1258-5(0)) Lerner Publishing Group.

Thomas, Keltie. The Kids Guide to Money Cent$ MacEachern, Stephen, tr. MacEachern, Stephen, illus. 2004. (ENG.). 56p. (J). 8.95 (978-1-55337-391-9(X)); (gr. 4-6). 8.95 (978-1-55337-390-2(1)) Kids Can Pr., Ltd. CAN. Dist: Hachette Bk. Group.

Thompson, Helen. Investing Money. 2010. (Junior Library of Money). 64p. (YA). (gr. 7-18). pap. 9.95 (978-1-4222-1885-3(6)); lib. bdg. 22.95 (978-1-4222-1766-5(3)) Mason Crest.

—Understanding Credit. 2010. (Junior Library of Money). 64p. (YA). (gr. 7-18). lib. bdg. 22.95 (978-1-4222-1772-6(8)) Mason Crest.

Thouin, Juanita. Get Your Wallet On: The Money Quiz for High School Grads. 2003. 97p. (YA). per. 6.49 (978-0-9740641-0-9(6)) Daisy Publishing.

The Value of Money. 2016. (Value of Money Ser.). 24p. (gr. 2-1). pap. 56.10 (978-0-7660-7988-5(0)); lib. bdg. 135.60 (978-0-7660-7491-0(9)) Enslow Pubs., Inc.

Vickers, Rebecca. 101 Ways to Be Smart about Money. 2011. (101 Ser.). (ENG.). 56p. (gr. 5-9). pap. 9.95 (978-1-4109-4382-8(8), NA-r) Heinemann-Raintree.

Wallach, Jonah M. & Tattersall, Clare. Money & Banking. 2011. (J). 77.70 (978-1-4488-4752-5(4), Rosen Reference); (J). pap. 12.95 (978-1-4488-4720-4(6), Rosen Reference); (YA). (gr. 5-9). lib. bdg. 31.95 (978-1-4488-4713-6(3)) Rosen Publishing Group, Inc., The.

Weston Woods Staff, creator. If You Made a Million. 2011. 38.75 (978-0-439-84579-3(3)) 2004. (J). 29.95 (978-1-55592-134-7(5)) Weston Woods Studios, Inc.

White, Billy. Kids & Money. 2009. pap. (978-1-61623-010-4(X)) Independent Pub.

Whitehead, William. Country Money. Beech, Mark, illus. 2015. (How Money Works). (ENG.). 64p. (J). (gr. 4-6). pap. 15.93 **(978-1-68404-069-8(8))** Norwood Hse. Pr.

Whitehead, William. Family Money. Beech, Mark, illus. 2015. (How Money Works). (ENG.). 64p. (J). (gr. 4-6). lib. bdg. 29.27 (978-1-59953-717-7(6)); pap. 15.93 **(978-1-68404-070-4(1))** Norwood Hse. Pr.

Whitehead, William, et al. Country Money. Beech, Mark, illus. 2015. (How Money Works). (ENG.). 64p. (J). (gr. 4-6). lib. bdg. 29.27 (978-1-59953-719-1(2)) Norwood Hse. Pr.

Williams, Deborah. Nickels & Pennies. Gedeon, Gloria, illus. l.t. ed. 2005. (ENG.). 12p. (gr. k-1). pap. 7.95 (978-1-879835-87-0(8), Kaeden Bks.) Kaeden Corp.

Williams, Rozanne Lanczak. Learning about Coins. Jarrett, Michael, photos by. 2004. (I Can Do Math Ser.). (Illus.). 24p. (gr. k-3). lib. bdg. 22.00 (978-0-8368-4110-7(7), Gareth Stevens Learning Library) Stevens, Gareth Publishing LLLP.

Wingard-Nelson, Rebecca. How Many Pennies Make a Dollar? 2009. (I Like Money Math! Ser.). (Illus.). 24p. (J). pap. 7.95 (978-0-7660-3656-7(1), Enslow Elementary); (gr. 1-3). lib. bdg. 22.60 (978-0-7660-3141-8(1)) Enslow Pubs., Inc.

—I Can Add Bills & Coins. 2009. (I Like Money Math! Ser.). (Illus.). 24p. (J). pap. 7.95 (978-0-7660-3657-4(X), Enslow Elementary); (gr. 1-3). lib. bdg. 22.60 (978-0-7660-3143-2(8)) Enslow Pubs., Inc.

—I Can Count Money. 2009. (I Like Money Math! Ser.). (Illus.). 24p. (J). pap. 7.95 (978-0-7660-3658-1(8), Enslow Elementary); (gr. 1-3). lib. bdg. 22.60 (978-0-7660-3142-5(X)) Enslow Pubs., Inc.
—I Can Do Money Word Problems. 2009. (I Like Money Math! Ser.). (Illus.). 24p. (J). pap. 7.95 (978-0-7660-3659-8(6), Enslow Elementary); (gr. 1-3). lib. bdg. 22.60 (978-0-7660-3145-6(4)) Enslow Pubs., Inc.
—I Can Name Bills & Coins. 2009. (I Like Money Math! Ser.). (Illus.). 24p. (J). pap. 7.95 (978-0-7660-3660-4(X), Enslow Elementary); (gr. 1-3). lib. bdg. 22.60 (978-0-7660-3140-1(3)) Enslow Pubs., Inc.
—I Can Subtract Bills & Coins. 2009. (I Like Money Math! Ser.). (Illus.). 24p. (J). pap. 7.95 (978-0-7660-3661-1(8), Enslow Elementary); (gr. 1-3). lib. bdg. 22.60 (978-0-7660-3144-9(6)) Enslow Pubs., Inc.
Woolf, Alex. You Wouldn't Want to Live Without Money! Antram, David, illus. 2015. (You Wouldn't Want to Live Without... Ser.). (ENG.). 32p. (J). lib. bdg. 29.00 (978-0-531-21926-3(7), Watts, Franklin) Scholastic Library Publishing.
Worth, Bonnie. One Cent, Two Cents, Old Cent, New Cent: All about Money. Ruiz, Aristides & Mathieu, Joseph, illus. 2008. (Cat in the Hat's Learning Library). (ENG.). 48p. (J). (gr. -1-3). 9.99 (978-0-375-82881-2(8), Random Hse. Bks. for Young Readers) Random Hse. Children's Bks.
Yearling, Tricia & Summers, Portia. One Dollar: How Many Pennies? 2016. (Value of Money Ser.). (Illus.). 24p. (J). (gr. 2-1). pap. 9.35 (978-0-7660-7685-3(7)) Enslow Pubs., Inc.
Your Money. 2016. (Your Money Ser.). 00024p. (J). (gr. 1-1). 98.40 (978-1-4994-8137-2(3), Windmill Bks.) Rosen Publishing Group, Inc., The.
Zedeker, Rose Ross. Wealth in Biblical Times. 2009. (Money at its Best: Millionaires of the Old Testament Ser.). 112p. (YA). (gr. 7-12). 24.95 (978-1-4222-0477-1(4)) Mason Crest.

MONEY—FICTION

Anna. The Magic Money Tree. 2009. (Illus.). 20p. pap. 15.49 (978-1-4389-0472-6(X)) AuthorHouse.
Atchley, Dalton. If I Had a Million Dollars. 2012. 20p. pap. 17.99 (978-1-4772-7934-2(2)) AuthorHouse.
Auseon, Andrew. Funny Little Monkey. 2006. (ENG., Illus.). 312p. (YA). (gr. 9-12). pap. 17.99 (978-0-15-205413-7(8)) Houghton Mifflin Harcourt Publishing Co.
Barks, Carl, et al. Uncle Scrooge #389. 2009. 64p. pap. 7.99 (978-1-60360-089-7(2)) Gemstone Publishing, Inc.
Belgue, Nancy. Casey Little, Yo-Yo Queen, 1 vol. 2005. (Orca Young Readers Ser.). (ENG., Illus.). 128p. (J). (gr. 3-6). per. 5.95 (978-1-55143-357-8(5)) Orca Bk. Pubs. USA.
Bhakta, Sanjini. My Life as a Dollar Bill. 2010. 28p. pap. 12.95 (978-1-4520-6152-8(1)) AuthorHouse.
Blume, Judy. Double Fudge. 2007. (ENG.). 240p. (J). (gr. 3-7). 7.99 (978-0-14-240878-0(6), Puffin Books) Penguin Young Readers Group.
—Double Fudge. 2004. (Fudge Ser.). 160p. (J). (gr. 3-7). pap. 36.00 incl. audio (978-0-8072-2036-8(1), Listening Library) Random Hse. Audio Publishing Group.
—Double Fudge. 2013. pap. (978-0-439-58549-1(X), Scholastic) Scholastic, Inc.
—Double Fudge. 2007. (Fudge Bks.: 5). lib. bdg. 18.40 (978-1-4177-8371-7(0), Turtleback) Turtleback Bks.
Bohrer, Maddie. Penny's Penny Puzzle. 2010. 24p. pap. 11.49 (978-1-4490-6477-8(9)) AuthorHouse.
Boyce, Frank Cottrell. Millions. 2005. 247p. (gr. 3-7). 19.00 (978-0-7569-5439-0(8)) Perfection Learning Corp.
Boyce, Frank Cottrell & Boyce, Frank Cottrell. Millions. 6. Lenton, Steven, illus. 2nd unabr. ed. 2008. (ENG.). 272p. 15.95 (978-0-330-45084-3(0), Macmillan) Pan Macmillan GBR. Dist: Trans-Atlantic Pubns., Inc.
Brandeis, Batsheva. Faiga Finds the Way. Levitas, Alexander, illus. 2005. (Fun to Read Book Ser.). 120p. (J). pap. 9.95 (978-1-929628-28-5(5)) Hachai Publishing.
Brian, Kate, pseud. Invitation Only. 2009. (Private Ser.: No. 2). (ENG.). 272p. (YA). pap. 9.99 (978-1-4169-9947-8(7), Simon & Schuster Bks. For Young Readers) Simon & Schuster Bks. For Young Readers.
Bricker, Chris. The Leaping Frogs of Calameris County. 2006. 48p. pap. 16.95 (978-1-4241-2408-4(5)) PublishAmerica, Inc.
Brisson, Pat. Benny's Pennies. 2014. 17.00 (978-1-63419-688-8(0)) Perfection Learning Corp.
Burke, Patrick J. Getting Your First Allowance. Severino, Philip, illus. 2008. 28p. pap. 24.95 (978-1-60441-882-8(6)) America Star Bks.
Caletti, Deb. The Fortunes of Indigo Skye. 2009. (ENG.). 320p. (YA). (gr. 7). pap. 9.99 (978-1-4169-1008-4(5), Simon Pulse) Simon Pulse.
Callaghan, Cindy. Lost in Hollywood. 2016. (Mix Ser.). (ENG., Illus.). 240p. (J). (gr. 4-8). pap. 7.99 (978-1-4814-6571-7(6), Aladdin) Simon & Schuster Children's Publishing.
Chad Borrows Money. l.t. ed. 2003. (Illus.). 16p. (J). ring bd. 15.95 (978-0-9722829-6-3(3)) Red Carpet Publishing.
Child, Lauren. But I've Used All My Pocket Change. 2012. (Charlie & Lola Ser.). (ENG.). 32p. (J). (gr. -1-k). 16.99 (978-0-8037-3728-0(9), Dial Bks) Penguin Young Readers Group.
Christelow, Eileen. Five Little Monkeys Play Hide & Seek. 2010. (Five Little Monkeys Story Ser.). (ENG., Illus.). 40p. (J). (gr. -1-3). pap. 6.99 (978-0-547-33787-6(6)) Houghton Mifflin Harcourt Publishing Co.
Clark, Clara Gillow. Secrets of Greymoor. 2009. (ENG., Illus.). 176p. (J). (gr. 5). 15.99 (978-0-7636-3249-6(X)) Candlewick Pr.
Cleave, Brenda. The Money Tree. 2010. 40p. pap. 18.99 (978-1-4490-7468-5(5)) AuthorHouse.
Coe, Mary E. Willy: the Best Christmas Gift Ever. 2008. 127p. 25.95 (978-0-557-02890-0(6)); pap. 10.95 (978-1-4357-1627-8(2)) Lulu Pr., Inc.
—Willy: the Best Christmas Gift Ever a Children's Book. 2009. 95p. pap. 9.95 (978-0-557-09420-2(8)) Lulu Pr., Inc.
—Willy: the Best Christmas Gift Ever A Children's Book. 2009. 55p. pap. 9.95 (978-0-557-08687-0(6)) Lulu Pr., Inc.
Collins, Nancy A. Vamps. 2008. (Vamps Ser.: 1). (ENG.). 256p. (YA). (gr. 9-18). pap. 8.99 (978-0-06-134917-1(8), HarperTeen) HarperCollins Pubs.
Costain, Meredith. Kids for Hire. Dale, Rae, illus. 2004. iv, 36p. (J). pap. (978-0-7608-6748-8(8)) Sundance/Newbridge Educational Publishing.
Curtis, Christopher Paul. Mr. Chickee's Funny Money. 2007. (ENG.). 160p. (J). (gr. 3-7). 6.99 (978-0-440-22919-3(7), Yearling) Random Hse. Children's Bks.
Daniels, Dominique. Mike & the Bike: Money Doesn't Grow on Trees. 2010. (Illus.). 20p. pap. 13.50 (978-1-4490-1768-2(1)) AuthorHouse.
The Darling of Wall Street. 2005. (J). pap. (978-0-9744863-1-4(0)) Paulus Publishing.
D'Arruda, Kim. A Day to Play. 2007. (Illus.). 32p. (J). 14.95 (978-0-9777993-2-9(8)) Financial Safari Pr.
deRubertis, Barbara. Deena y su centavo de la Suerte. Holub, Joan & Fisher, Cynthia, illus. 2007. (Math Matters Ser.). (SPA.). 32p. (J). (gr. -1-3). pap. 5.95 (978-1-57565-249-8(8)) Kane Press, Inc.
—Deena Y Su Centavo de la Suerte; Deena's Lucky Penny. 2008. pap. 34.95 (978-1-58013-756-0(3)) Kane Press, Inc.
Deutsch, Tehilla. Dollars & Sense. Zimmer, Glenn, illus. 2012. 36p. (J). 12.95 (978-1-929628-65-0(X)) Hachai Publishing.
Dharma Publishing Staff. Heart of Gold: The Story about the Power of Generosity. 2010. (ENG.). 36p. (gr. -1-7). pap. 8.95 (978-0-89800-601-8(5)) Dharma Publishing.
Driscoll, Laura. Sally's Big Save. Wummer, Amy, illus. 2006. (Social Studies Connects). 32p. (J). (gr. -1-3). pap. 5.95 (978-1-57565-164-4(5)) Kane Press, Inc.
Dussling, Jennifer. Fair Is Fair! Palmisciano, Diane, illus. 2003. (Math Matters Ser.). (ENG.). 32p. (J). (gr. 1-3). pap. 5.95 (978-1-57565-131-6(9)) Kane Press, Inc.
—Lo Justo Es Justo; Fair Is Fair. 2008. pap. 34.95 (978-1-58013-785-0(7)) Kane Press, Inc.
Dussling, Jennifer A. Lo Justo Es Justo! Palmisciano, Diane, illus. 2008. (Math Matters en Espanol Ser.). (SPA.). 32p. (J). (gr. -1-3). pap. 5.95 (978-1-57565-269-6(2)) Kane Press, Inc.
Earnest Took It with Him. 2005. (J). 12.95 (978-0-9762679-0-4(X)) Birdsall, Bonnie Thomas.
Elliott, Zetta. Melena's Jubilee, 1 vol. Boyd, Aaron, illus. 2016. (ENG.). 32p. (gr. -1-5). 16.95 (978-0-88448-443-1(2), 884443) Tilbury Hse. Pubs.
Espinoza, Vicki. Donnie Dollar. 2008. 38p. pap. 16.78 (978-0-557-01616-7(9)) Lulu Pr., Inc.
Ferguson, Gloria. Fair Money. 2012. 62p. 19.95 (978-1-4626-3037-0(5)) America Star Bks.
Flake, Sharon G. Money Hungry. Disney Press Staff, illus. rev. ed. 2007. (ENG.). 192p. (J). (gr. 5-9). pap. 8.99 (978-1-4231-0386-8(6), Jump at the Sun) Hyperion Bks. for Children.
Fox, Jeannine. Feeding Penny Pig. 2009. 32p. (J). 14.95 (978-0-9841589-1-1(X)) Mincing Mockingbird, The.
Friedman, Laurie. In Business with Mallory. Pollak, Barbara, illus. 2007. (Mallory Ser.: 5). (ENG.). 160p. (J). (gr. 2-5). per. 5.95 (978-0-8225-6561-1(7), First Avenue Editions) Lerner Publishing Group.
Gallagher, Diana G. Advice about Work & Play: Claudia Cristina Cortez Uncomplicates Your Life. Garvey, Brann, illus. 2010. (Claudia Cristina Cortez Ser.). (ENG.). 80p. (gr. 2-3). pap. 6.10 (978-1-4342-2253-4(5)); 26.65 (978-1-4342-1908-4(9)) Stone Arch Bks. (Claudia Cristina Cortez).
Gilmore, Grace. The Lucky Wheel. Brown, Petra, illus. 2015. (Tales from Maple Ridge Ser.: 2). (ENG.). 128p. (J). (gr. k-4). pap. 5.99 (978-1-4814-2627-5(3), Little Simon) Little Simon.
Gottesfeld, Jeff. Too Many Dogs, 1 vol. 2015. (Red Rhino Ser.). (ENG.). 68p. (J). (gr. 4-6). pap. 7.95 (978-1-62250-951-5(X)) Saddleback Educational Publishing, Inc.
Grandpa. The Beginning of Meet the Müsh-Mice: (a Visit to the North Pole) 2012. 34p. 29.95 (978-1-4626-9377-1(6)) America Star Bks.
Groenewald, Catherine. Jingle-Jingle in My Pocket. 2011. (ENG.). 16p. (J). (gr. 2-4). pap. 7.95 (978-1-77009-832-9(1)) Jacana Media ZAF. Dist: Independent Pubs. Group.
Hapka, Catherine, pseud & Bloomberg, Georgina. My Favorite Mistake: An a Circuit Novel. 2012. (a Circuit Ser.). (ENG.). 256p. (YA). pap. 9.99 (978-1-59990-642-3(2), 9781599906423, Bloomsbury USA Childrens) Bloomsbury Publishing USA.
Hargreaves, Roger. Mr. Stingy. 2011. (Mr. Men & Little Miss Ser.). (ENG.). 32p. (J). (gr. -1-2). mass mkt. 4.99 (978-0-8431-9959-8(8), Price Stern Sloan) Penguin Young Readers Group.
Harris, Ted. Catney Reid Who Needs Money? (978-0-9744597-5-2(5)) Brown Books Publishing Group.
Haskins, Lori. No Money? No Problem! Nez, John A., illus. 2004. (Social Studies Connects). 32p. (J). (gr. k-2). pap. 5.95 (978-1-57565-141-5(6)) Kane Press, Inc.
Hill, Joyce. A Penny in My Pocket. 2007. 220p. 27.95 (978-0-9795818-0-9(X)); pap. 14.95 (978-0-9795818-1-6(8)) Mushgush Pr.
Holub, Joan & Williams, Suzanne. Medusa the Rich. 2015. (Goddess Girls Ser.: 16). lib. bdg. 18.40 (978-0-606-36309-9(2)) Turtleback Bks.
Horowitz, Anthony. The Switch. 2010. (ENG.). 192p. (J). (gr. 5-18). 7.99 (978-0-14-241547-4(2), Puffin Books) Penguin Young Readers Group.
Houran, Lori Haskins. Money Doesn't Grow on Mars: Self-Control. Warrick, Jessica, illus. 2017. (How to Be an Earthling (r) Ser.: 8). (ENG.). 64p. (gr. 1-3). 34.65 (978-1-57565-854-4(2)); (J). lib. bdg. 22.65 (978-1-57565-846-9(1)) Kane Press, Inc.
Houran, Lori Haskins. Money Doesn't Grow on Mars: Self-Control. Warrick, Jessica, illus. 2017. (How to Be an Earthling (r) Ser.: 8). (ENG.). 64p. (J). (gr. 1-3). 6.99 (978-1-57565-850-6(X)) Kane Press, Inc.
Jackson, Keith. I Forgot My Lunch Money. 2009. 32p. pap. 12.99 (978-1-4389-9006-8(1)) AuthorHouse.
Jacobs, Sheila. Jake Earns A Treat: A Life & Money Book. 2011. 24p. 11.99 (978-1-4567-3001-7(0)) AuthorHouse.
—Jake Saves the Day: A Life & Money Book. 2011. 24p. 11.99 (978-1-4520-9929-3(4)) AuthorHouse.
Julie Marie. The Adventures of Fred the Five Pound Note. 2009. (Illus.). 52p. pap. 10.49 (978-1-4389-4921-5(9)) AuthorHouse.
Karapetkova, Holly & Picou, Lin. Ouch! Stitches. Reese, Bob, illus. 2011. (ENG.). 24p. (gr. 1-2). pap. 8.95 (978-1-61236-023-2(8)) Rourke Educational Media.
Lee, Kathy. Phoebe's Fortune. 2003. 128p. 6.49 (978-1-85999-700-0(7)) Scripture Union GBR. Dist: Gabriel Resources.
Leedy, Loreen. The Monster Money Book. Leedy, Loreen, illus. 2005. (ENG., Illus.). 32p. (J). (gr. k-3). pap. 6.95 (978-0-8234-1558-8(9)) Holiday Hse., Inc.
Little, Robert. Jamaal's Lucky Day. Fitzpatrick, Audrey, illus. 2003. 32p. (J). (gr. 2-6). 15.95 (978-0-9701863-4-8(7)) Relde Publishing.
Locurto, Ian N. The Christmas Penny. 2010. 20p. 11.99 (978-1-4490-7100-4(7)) AuthorHouse.
Lorimer, Janet. Look to the Light, 1 vol. unabr. ed. 2010. (Q Reads Ser.). (ENG.). 32p. (YA). (gr. 9-12). pap. 6.95 (978-1-61651-193-7(1)) Saddleback Educational Publishing, Inc.
The Lost Money. 2005. (Georgie Giraffe Set 1 Ser.). (J). 7.33 (978-1-932570-37-3(3)) Pioneer Valley Bks.
Mackey, Lori. Money Mama & the Three Little Pigs. 2004. (Illus.). 48p. (J). 19.95 (978-0-9744570-2-4(7)) P4K Publishing.
Mallon, Lynn & Marshall, Jennifer. It Pays to Be Honest. 2010. 28p. pap. 11.95 (978-1-60594-440-1(8), Llumina Pr.) Aeon Publishing Inc.
Man-Kong, Mary. Learning to Save (Barbie) 2016. (Pictureback(R) Ser.). (ENG., Illus.). 16p. (J). (gr. -1-2). 4.99 (978-0-553-53921-9(3), Random Hse. Bks. for Young Readers) Random Hse. Children's Bks.
Manushkin, Fran. Piggy Bank Problems, 1 vol. Lyon, Tammie, illus. 2013. (Katie Woo Ser.). (ENG.). 32p. (gr. k-2). pap. 5.95 (978-1-4048-8048-1(8)); lib. bdg. 21.32 (978-1-4048-7654-5(5)) Picture Window Bks.
Manzo, Christopher. Oliver Brightside: You Don't Want That Penny. Adams, Lisa, illus. 2016. (ENG.). 36p. (J). 16.95 (978-0-9963756-4-1(3)) All About Kids Publishing.
Marie, Tina. Isabella Learns the Value of Money. 2011. 24p. pap. 12.95 (978-1-4567-4537-0(9)) AuthorHouse.
Matthews, Steve. Lord Grott of Grott Hall. 2015. (ENG.). 61p. (J). (gr. 2-3). mass mkt. 10.95 (978-1-78554-268-8(0), 4e62726f-2944-495d-b6d7-3f986cb7e57f) Austin, Stan AUS. Dist: Bookmasters Distribution.
May, Eleanor. Albert Helps Out: Counting Money. Melmon, Deborah, illus. 2017. (Mouse Math (r) Ser.). (ENG.). 32p. (gr. -1-1). 7.95 (978-1-57565-860-5(7)) Kane Press, Inc.
—Albert Helps Out: Counting Money. Melmon, Deborah, illus. 2017. (Mouse Math (r) Ser.). (ENG.). 32p. (gr. -1-1). lib. bdg. 22.65 (978-1-57565-857-5(7)); 34.65 (978-1-57565-863-6(1)) Kane Press, Inc.
Mayer, Mercer. Just a Little Luck. Mayer, Mercer, illus. 2011. (Little Critter Ser.). (ENG., Illus.). 24p. (J). (gr. -1-2). pap. 3.99 (978-0-06-147800-0(8), HarperFestival) HarperCollins Pubs.
—Just Saving My Money. Mayer, Mercer, illus. 2010. (My First I Can Read Ser.). (ENG., Illus.). 32p. (J). (gr. -1-3). pap. 3.99 (978-0-06-083557-6(5)) HarperCollins Pubs.
Mazer, Anne. That's the Way the Cookie Crumbles. 2005. (Amazing Days of Abby Hayes Ser.: Bk. 16). (Illus.). 119p. (J). (gr. 3-7). 12.65 (978-0-7569-6480-1(6)) Perfection Learning Corp.
McDougall, Jill. Jinxed! 2008. (Lightning Strikes Ser.). 96p. (J). pap. (978-1-921150-59-3(9)) Walker Bks. Australia Pty, Ltd.
McGreal, Pat & McGreal, Carol. Uncle Scrooge #385. 2008. 64p. pap. 7.99 (978-1-60360-062-0(0)) Gemstone Publishing, Inc.
McGreal, Pat, et al. Uncle Scrooge #390. 2009. 64p. pap. 7.99 (978-1-60360-090-3(6)) Gemstone Publishing, Inc.
McLeod, Cinders. Earn It! McLeod, Cinders, illus. 2017. (ENG., Illus.). 32p. (J). (-k). 16.99 (978-0-399-54444-6(5), Nancy Paulsen Books) Penguin Young Readers Group.
McQueen, Amelia. A Penny for Your Thoughts. 2010. 56p. pap. 23.99 (978-1-4490-8046-4(4)) AuthorHouse.
Medina, Meg. Tia Isa Quiere un Carro. Munoz, Claudio, illus. 2012.Tr. of Tia Isa Wants a Car. (SPA.). 32p. (J). (gr. -1-2). pap. 6.99 (978-0-7636-5751-2(4)) Candlewick Pr.
—Tia Isa Quiere un Carro. 2012.Tr. of Tia Isa Wants a Car. (SPA.). lib. bdg. 17.20 (978-0-606-23801-4(8), Turtleback) Turtleback Bks.
—Tia Isa Wants a Car. Munoz, Claudio, illus. 2016. (ENG.). 32p. (J). (gr. -1-2). 6.99 (978-0-7636-5752-9(2)) Candlewick Pr.
—Tia Isa Wants a Car. Muñoz, Claudio, illus. 2011. (ENG.). 32p. (J). (gr. -1-2). 15.99 (978-0-7636-4156-6(1)) Candlewick Pr.
Milway, Katie Smith. One Hen: How One Small Loan Made a Big Difference. Fernandes, Eugenie, illus. 2008. (CitizenKid Ser.). (ENG.). 32p. (J). (gr. 3-7). 18.95 (978-1-55453-028-1(8)) Kids Can Pr., Ltd. CAN. Dist: Hachette Bk. Group.
El Mono Azul. (Fantasmas de Fear Street Coleccion). (SPA.). (YA). (gr. 5-8). pap. 7.95 (978-950-04-2022-8(8), EM10965) Emecé Editores S.A. ARG. Dist: Planeta Publishing Corp., Lectorum Pubns., Inc.
Moonjar, ed. Conversations to Go - Money. 2005. 36p. 9.95 (978-0-9724282-5-5(9)) Moonjar, LLC.
—Noom & Raj Start Business. 2005. 36p. 19.95 (978-0-9724282-2-4(4)) Moonjar, LLC.
National Geographic Learning Staff. The Magic Money Box. 2012. (ENG., Illus.). 16p. (C). (gr. k-2). pap. 5.95 (978-1-57471-009-0(5)) National Geographic School Publishing, Inc.
Paige, D. M. Chart Topper. 2013. (Opportunity Ser.). (ENG.). 112p. (YA). (gr. 6-12). pap. 7.95 (978-1-4677-1493-8(3)); lib. bdg. 27.93 (978-1-4677-1370-2(8)) Lerner Publishing Group. (Darby Creek).
Parker, John. Sucked In. 2008. (Lightning Strikes Ser.). 96p. (J). pap. (978-1-921150-62-3(9)) Walker Bks. Australia Pty, Ltd.
Pascal, Francine. Dinero Desaparecido. Orig. Title: Jessica & the Money Mix-Up. (SPA.). (J). 6.95 (978-84-272-3600-4(X)) Molino, Editorial ESP. Dist: AIMS International Bks., Inc.
Paulsen, Gary. The Tent: A Parable in One Sitting. 2006. (ENG., Illus.). 96p. (YA). (gr. 7-12). pap. 7.95 (978-0-15-205833-3(8)) Houghton Mifflin Harcourt Publishing Co.
—The Tent: A Parable in One Sitting. 2006. 86p. (gr. 7-12). 15.95 (978-0-7569-6891-5(7)) Perfection Learning Corp.
Postgate, Oliver. Noggin & the Money. Firmin, Peter, illus. 2017. (Noggin the Nog Ser.: 7). (ENG.). 48p. (J). (gr. 1-3). 8.99 (978-1-4052-8143-0(X)) Egmont Bks., Ltd. GBR. Dist: Independent Pubs. Group.
Pujol, Miquel, et al. Uncle Scrooge #388. 2009. 64p. pap. 7.99 (978-1-60360-088-0(4)) Gemstone Publishing, Inc.
Ramsey, Dave. Careless at the Carnival: Junior Discovers Spending. Ramsey, Marshall, illus. 2003. 26p. (J). 7.95 (978-0-9726323-1-7(X)) Ramsey Pr.
—Dave Ramsey's 6 Kids Books Boxed Set. 2005. (J). 39.95 (978-0-9774895-8-9(2)) Ramsey Pr.
—My Fantastic Fieldtrip: Junior Discovers Saving. Ramsey, Marshall, illus. 2003. 26p. (J). 7.95 (978-0-9726323-3-1(6)) Ramsey Pr.
Reitz, Theresa, et al. The Money Tree: A Financial Book for Children. 2009. (Illus.). 52p. pap. 22.95 (978-1-4327-3653-8(1)) Outskirts Pr., Inc.
RIGBY. The Moneybag: a Tale from Korea: Third Grade Big Books. 2003. (Rigby on Our Way to English Ser.). (ENG.). 24p. (gr. 3-3). pap. 50.70 (978-0-7578-4214-6(3)) Rigby Education.
Riley, Andy. King Flashypants & the Evil Emperor. Riley, Andy, illus. 2017. (King Flashypants Ser.). (ENG., Illus.). 224p. (J). 13.99 (978-1-62779-809-9(9), 9781627798099, Holt, Henry & Co. Bks. For Young Readers) Holt, Henry & Co.
Rochester, Mary Frances. The Turquoise Monkey. 2010. 48p. pap. 17.99 (978-1-4490-7260-5(7)) AuthorHouse.
Rogers, Ramona. Buck & Penny. 2013. 26p. pap. 9.99 (978-0-9894748-9-4(5)) Mindstir Media.
Rose, Simon. Les Loonies: Les Emblèmes Canadiens. McMann, Julie, tr. from ENG. 2011. (FRE.). 24p. (YA). (gr. 2-4). (978-1-77071-409-0(X)) Weigl Educational Pubs. Ltd.
Roy, Ron. The Talking T. Rex. Gurney, John Steven, illus. 2003. (to Z Mysteries Ser.: 20). (gr. 3-6). lib. bdg. 14.75 (978-0-613-85127-5(7), Turtleback) Turtleback Bks.
—Trouble at the Treasury. Bush, Timothy, illus. 2006. (Capital Mysteries Ser.: No. 7). (ENG.). 96p. (J). (gr. 1-4). per. 4.99 (978-0-375-83969-6(0), Random Hse. Bks. for Young Readers) Random Hse. Children's Bks.
Roza, Greg. A Piggy Bank for Pedro. 2006. (Neighborhood Readers Ser.). (ENG.). 8p. (gr. -1-3). pap. 5.15 (978-1-4042-5714-6(4), Rosen Classroom) Rosen Publishing Group, Inc., The.
Sabo-Western, Deborah. Peter Penny: Discovers the Gift. 2007. (ENG.). 46p. pap. 15.99 (978-1-4196-8115-8(X)) CreateSpace Independent Publishing Platform.
Sadler, Marilyn & Bollen, Roger. Money, Money, Honey Bunny! 2006. (Bright & Early Books(R) Ser.). (ENG., Illus.). 36p. (J). (gr. -1-k). 9.99 (978-0-375-83370-0(6), Random Hse. Bks. for Young Readers) Random Hse. Children's Bks.
Santillo, LuAnn. Digging for Clams. Santillo, LuAnn, ed. 2003. (Half-Pint Kids Readers Ser.). (Illus.). 7p. (J). (gr. -1-1). pap. (978-1-59256-092-9(X)) Half-Pint Kids, Inc.
Schraff, Anne E. Second Chances. 2013. (Urban Underground — Harriet Tubman High School Ser.). (YA). lib. bdg. 20.80 (978-0-606-31584-5(5), Turtleback) Turtleback Bks.
Scraper, Katherine. Tag Sale Today. 2005. (J). pap. (978-1-4108-4210-7(X)) Benchmark Education Co.
Shannon Simmons. The Community Club: #1 Aubrey & the Fight for Life. 2009. 112p. pap. 10.95 (978-1-4401-7616-6(7)) iUniverse, Inc.
Siems, Thomas F. The Dangerous Pet. 2009. 48p. pap. 21.99 (978-1-4415-3454-5(7)) Xlibris Corp.
Simmons, Michael. Pool Boy. 2005. 164p. (gr. 7). 17.95 (978-0-7569-5064-4(3)) Perfection Learning Corp.
Singleton, Linda Joy. Cash Kat, 1 vol. Wald, Christina, illus. 2016. (ENG & SPA.). 32p. (J). (gr. k-3). 17.95 (978-1-62855-728-2(1)) Arbordale Publishing.
—Elena Efectivo, 1 vol. Wald, Christina, illus. 2016. (SPA.). 32p. (J). (gr. k-3). pap. 9.95 (978-1-62855-742-8(7)) Arbordale Publishing.
Slater, Jean M. Monkey Business: At the Market. Slater, Jean M., illus. 2003. (Illus.). 10p. (J). bds. 16.00 (978-0-9743149-4-5(3)) Slater Software. Inc.
Slater, Teddy & Scholastic, Inc. Staff. Nine Bright Pennies. Lewis, Stephen, illus. 2005. (Number Tales Ser.). (ENG.). 16p. (J). (gr. -1-1). pap. 2.99 (978-0-439-69020-1(X)) Scholastic, Inc.
Sparks, Candi. Max Gets It!, 4 vols. William, Graf, illus. 2008. (Can I Have Some Money? Ser.: Vol. 3). (ENG.). 32p. (J). pap. (978-0-9789445-1-3(8)) Sparks Fly.
—Of Course You Can! Educating Children about Money. Graf, William, illus. 2006. (Can I Have Some Money? Ser.). pap. 11.99 (978-0-9789445-0-6(X)) Sparks Fly.
Sparks, Candi & Sparks, Kelvin. Lemonade Sold Out: Can I Have Some Money? (No. 5) 2015. (Can I Have Some Money? Ser.: 5). (ENG., Illus.). 34p. (J). (gr. 1-8). pap. 12.98 (978-0-9789445-9-9(3)) Sparks Fly.
Sparks, Candi, et al. Nacho Money. Bill, Graf, illus. 2012. (Can I Have Some Money? Ser.). 36p. pap. 11.99 (978-0-9789445-6-8(9)) Sparks Fly.
Standish, Burt L. Dick Merriwell's Marked Money. Rudman, Jack, ed. 2003. (Frank Merriwell Ser.). pap. 9.95 (978-0-8373-9100-7(8)) Merriwell, Frank Inc.
Strasser, Todd. For Money & Love. 2007. (Mob Princess Ser.: 1). (ENG.). 208p. (YA). (gr. 9-18). pap. 19.99 (978-1-4169-3533-9(9), Simon Pulse) Simon Pulse.
Suddard, Lisa. Money Grows with Bees. Cabrillo, Cinthya, illus. 2009. 24p. pap. 14.95 (978-1-4251-8673-9(4)) Trafford Publishing.
Sundaram, Siddhartha & Raghuraman, Renuka S. Horace Leclaire & His Bottles of Air. Raghuraman, Savitri, illus. 2008. 36p. pap. 9.99 (978-1-935105-03-9(5)) Avid Readers Publishing Group.
Thompson, David. The Nine Clues of Christmas, 1 vol. 2009. 172p. pap. 24.95 (978-1-60813-410-6(5)) America Star Bks.
Toole, Spencer. Selena Saves Money: Checking Your Work. 2017. (Computer Science for the Real World Ser.). 16p. (gr. 7-8). pap. 7.95 (978-1-5383-5214-4(1), Rosen Classroom) Rosen Publishing Group, Inc., The.
Tyrrell, Helen. Nora & the Dancing Horse. 2003. 231p. (J). pap. 14.95 (978-0-7414-1349-9(3)) Infinity Publishing.
Van Draanen, Wendelin. Sammy Keyes & the Cold Hard Cash. 2010. (Sammy Keyes Ser.: Bk. 12). (ENG.). 320p. (J). (gr. 5-7). 8.99 (978-0-440-42113-9(6), Yearling) Random Hse. Children's Bks.
Watson Dubisch, Carolyn. The Horribles. 2010. 73p. pap. 16.96 (978-0-557-35938-7(4)) Lulu Pr., Inc.
Whitby, Adele. Kay's Story 1934. 2015. (Secrets of the Manor Ser.: 6). (ENG., Illus.). 160p. (J). (gr. 3-7). pap. 6.99 (978-1-4814-2755-5(5), Simon Spotlight) Simon Spotlight.

Williams, Shannon. Where Does Money Come From? Book One of Money Matters for Children. 2013. 20p. pap. 13.77 *(978-1-4907-0551-4(1))* Trafford Publishing.

Williams, Vera B. A Chair for My Mother. Williams, Vera B., illus. 25th anniv. ed. 2007. (Reading Rainbow Bks.). (ENG., Illus.). 32p. (J). (gr. -1-3). pap. 7.99 *(978-0-688-04074-1(8),* Greenwillow Bks.) HarperCollins Pubs.

Williams, Zachary. The Lost Nickel. 2006. (Neighborhood Readers Ser.). (ENG.). 8p. (gr. -1-3). pap. 5.15 *(978-1-4042-5786-3(1),* Rosen Classroom) Rosen Publishing Group, Inc., The.

Zajac, Kristen K. El Primo de Ebeneezer. Houdeshell, Jennifer Thomas, illus. 2011. 20p. pap. 10.95 *(978-1-61633-164-1(X))* Guardian Angel Publishing, Inc.

MONEY—HISTORY

Adler, David A. Money Madness. Miller, Edward, III, illus. 2009. (ENG.). 32p. (J). (gr. -1-3). 17.95 *(978-0-8234-1474-1(4))* Holiday Hse., Inc.

Brasch, Nicolas. The Invention of Money. 2013. (Discovery Education: Discoveries & Inventions Ser.). 32p. (J). (gr. 3-6). pap. 60.00 *(978-1-4777-1509-3(6));* pap. 10.00 *(978-1-4777-1508-6(8));* lib. bdg. 25.25 *(978-1-4777-1333-4(6))* Rosen Publishing Group, Inc., The. (PowerKids Pr.).

Furgang, Kathy. National Geographic Kids Everything Money: A Wealth of Facts, Photos, & Fun! 2013. (National Geographic Kids Everything Ser.). (ENG., Illus.). 64p. (J). (gr. 3-7). lib. bdg. 25.90 *(978-1-4263-1027-0(7),* National Geographic Children's Bks.) National Geographic Society.

Furgang, Kathy & National Geographic Kids Staff. Everything Money: A Wealth of Facts, Photos, & Fun! 2013. (National Geographic Kids Everything Ser.). (ENG., Illus.). 64p. (J). (gr. 3-7). pap. 12.95 *(978-1-4263-1026-3(9),* National Geographic Children's Bks.) National Geographic Society.

Gregory, Helen. We Need Money, 1 vol. 2011. (Wonder Readers Early Level Ser.). (ENG.). (gr. -1-1). 32p. pap. 5.99 *(978-1-4296-7808-7(9));* 16p. pap. 35.94 *(978-1-4296-8201-5(9))* Capstone Press of Coughlan Cos. (Wonder Readers).

Housel, Debra J. ¡Cómpralo! Historia Del Dinero. 2017. (TIME for Kids en Español - Level 3 Ser.). (SPA.). 32p. (gr. 3-3). lib. bdg. 31.99 ***(978-1-5157-5188-5(0))*** Time for Kids Inc AUS. Dist: Capstone Pub.

Housel, Debra J. & Rice, Dona. Buy It! History of Money, 1 vol. 2nd rev. ed. 2014. (TIME for KIDS(r) Nonfiction Readers Ser.). (ENG., Illus.). 32p. (J). (gr. 3-3). pap. 25.96 *(978-1-4807-1090-0(3))* Shell Educational Publishing.

Housel, Debra J. & Rice, Dona Herwick. Buy It! History of Money, 1 vol. 2nd rev. ed. 2012. (Nonfiction Readers Ser.). (ENG.). 32p. (J). (gr. 3-3). pap. 8.99 *(978-1-4333-3681-2(2))* Teacher Created Materials, Inc.

Jenkins, Martin. The History of Money: From Bartering to Banking. Kitamura, Satoshi, illus. 2014. (ENG.). 64p. (J). (gr. 4-7). 16.99 *(978-0-7636-6763-4(3))* Candlewick Pr.

Meachen Rau, Dana. The History of Money. 2010. (Money & Banks Ser.). (Illus.). 24p. (gr. 2-5). pap. 8.15 *(978-1-4339-3381-3(0))* Stevens, Gareth Publishing LLLP.

Rau, Dana Meachen. The History of Money. 2010. (Money & Banks Ser.). (Illus.). 24p. (J). (gr. 2-5). lib. bdg. 22.00 *(978-1-4339-3380-6(2))* Stevens, Gareth Publishing LLLP.

Resnick, Abraham. Money. 2009. 136p. pap. 18.95 *(978-1-4401-1318-5(1))* iUniverse, Inc.

Tiner, John. The Story of in God We Trust: Discovering Our Nations Heritage. 2003. (Discovering Our Nation's Heritage Ser.). (Illus.). 48p. (J). 9.99 *(978-0-89051-392-7(9),* 303-090) Master Bks.

Vox, Everett. The U. S. Mint: The History of U. S. Money. 2017. (Landmarks of Democracy: American Institutions Ser.). 24p. (J). (gr. 7-8). pap. 8.25 ***(978-1-5081-6101-1(1),*** PowerKids Pr.) Rosen Publishing Group, Inc., The.

MONEY-MAKING PROJECTS FOR CHILDREN

see Moneymaking Projects

MONEY, PAPER

see Paper Money

MONEY RAISING

see Fund Raising

MONEYMAKING PROJECTS

Antill, Sara. 10 Ways I Can Earn Money. 2012. (I Can Make a Difference Ser.). (ENG., Illus.). 24p. (J). (gr. 2-5). pap. 8.25 *(978-1-4488-6371-6(6));* lib. bdg. 22.60 *(978-1-4488-6206-1(X))* Rosen Publishing Group, Inc., The. (PowerKids Pr.).

Bochner, Arthur, et al. The New Totally Awesome Business Book for Kids. 3rd rev. ed. 2007. (New Totally Awesome Ser.: 2). (ENG., Illus.). 192p. (gr. 7-9). per. 11.99 *(978-1-55704-757-1(X),* William Morrow Paperbacks) HarperCollins Pubs.

Bradley, Kathleen E. Making Money Grow, 1 vol. 2nd rev. ed. 2013. (Nonfiction Readers Ser.). (ENG.). 64p. (J). (gr. 5-5). pap. 10.99 *(978-1-4333-4908-9(6));* (Illus.). pap. 31.96 *(978-1-4333-7431-9(5))* Teacher Created Materials, Inc.

Bullard, Lisa. Ella Earns Her Own Money. Moran, Mike, illus. 2013. (Cloverleaf Books — Money Basics Ser.). (ENG.). 24p. (gr. k-2). pap. 6.95 *(978-1-4677-1511-9(5),* Millbrook Pr.) Lerner Publishing Group.

—Ella Earns Her Own Money. Moran, Michael, illus. 2013. (Cloverleaf Books — Money Basics Ser.). (ENG.). 24p. (gr. k-2). lib. bdg. 23.93 *(978-1-4677-0761-9(9),* Millbrook Pr.) Lerner Publishing Group.

—Kyle Keeps Track of Cash. Byrne, Mike, illus. 2013. (Cloverleaf Books — Money Basics Ser.). (ENG.). 24p. (gr. k-2). pap. 6.95 *(978-1-4677-1510-2(7));* lib. bdg. 23.93 *(978-1-4677-0762-6(7))* Lerner Publishing Group. (Millbrook Pr.).

Carlson Berne, Emma. Run Your Own Babysitting Business, 1 vol., 1. 2014. (Young Entrepreneurs Ser.). (ENG.). 32p. (J). (gr. 4-6). 26.25 *(978-1-4777-2922-9(4),* PowerKids Pr.) Rosen Publishing Group, Inc., The.

—Run Your Own Bake Sale. 2014. (Young Entrepreneurs Ser.). 32p. (J). (gr. 4-6). pap. 10.00 *(978-1-4777-3007-2(9));*1. (ENG.). 26.25 *(978-1-4777-2918-2(6))* Rosen Publishing Group, Inc., The. (PowerKids Pr.).

—Run Your Own Car Wash. 2014. (Young Entrepreneurs Ser.). 32p. (J). (gr. 4-6). pap. 10.00 *(978-1-4777-3009-6(5));*1. (ENG.). 26.25 *(978-1-4777-2920-5(8))* Rosen Publishing Group, Inc., The. (PowerKids Pr.).

—Run Your Own Yard-Work Business. 2014. (Young Entrepreneurs Ser.). 32p. (J). (gr. 4-6). pap. 10.00 *(978-1-4777-3010-2(9));*1. (ENG.). 26.25 *(978-1-4777-6125-0(X))* Rosen Publishing Group, Inc., The. (PowerKids Pr.).

Daly, Ruth. Dog Walker. 2017. (J). ***(978-1-4896-6086-2(0),*** AV2 by Weigl) Weigl Pubs., Inc.

Eliot, Matthew. The Kid Millionaire. 2016. (ENG.). 128p. (J). (gr. 3). pap. 12.95 *(978-1-60433-653-5(6),* Applesauce Pr.) Cider Mill Pr. Bk. Pubs., LLC.

Gagne, Tammy. Start Your Petsitting Service. 2017. (Build Your Business Ser.). (ENG.). 32p. (gr. 3-4). lib. bdg. 27.99 ***(978-1-5157-6689-6(6))*** Capstone Press of Coughlan Cos.

Hagler, Gina. Money-Making Opportunities for Teens Who Are Artistic. 2013. (Make Money Now! Ser.). (Illus.). 80p. (YA). (gr. 7-12). lib. bdg. 33.25 *(978-1-4488-9387-4(9))* Rosen Publishing Group, Inc., The.

Hansen, Mark Victor. The Richest Kids in America: How They Earn It, How They Spend It, How You Can Too. 2009. (ENG.). 168p. pap. 14.99 *(978-0-9819709-0-5(7))* Hansen House Publishing, Inc.

Henneberg, Susan. Money-Making Opportunities for Teens Who Like Working with Kids. 2013. (Make Money Now! Ser.). (Illus.). 80p. (YA). (gr. 7-12). lib. bdg. 33.25 *(978-1-4488-9385-0(2))* Rosen Publishing Group, Inc., The.

Jacobson, Ryan. Get a Job Helping Others. Cannell, Jon, illus. 2014. (You're in Business! Ser.). 40p. (J). (gr. 5-9). lib. bdg. 27.93 *(978-1-4677-3836-1(0),* Lerner Pubns.) Lerner Publishing Group.

—Get a Job Making Stuff to Sell. Cannell, Jon, illus. 2014. (You're in Business! Ser.). 40p. (J). (gr. 5-9). lib. bdg. 27.93 *(978-1-4677-3837-8(9),* Lerner Pubns.) Lerner Publishing Group.

Kiefer, Jeanne. Jobs for Kids: A Smart Kid's Q & A Guide. Green, Anne Canevari, illus. 2003. (Single Titles Ser.). 112p. (gr. 5-8). lib. bdg. 25.90 *(978-0-7613-2611-3(1),* Millbrook Pr.) Lerner Publishing Group.

Leavitt, Amie Jane. How to Create Digital Portfolios for Collaborative Projects. 2017. (Project Learning Using Digital Portfolios Ser.). 64p. (gr. 12-12). 34.45 ***(978-1-5081-7524-7(1),*** Rosen Young Adult) Rosen Publishing Group, Inc., The.

—Start Your Yard Work Business. 2017. (Build Your Business Ser.). (ENG.). 32p. (gr. 3-4). lib. bdg. 27.99 ***(978-1-5157-6692-6(6))*** Capstone Press of Coughlan Cos.

Marsico, Katie. Money Math. 2015. (ENG., Illus.). 32p. (J). (gr. 3-4). 26.65 *(978-1-4677-8579-2(2),* Lerner Pubns.) Lerner Publishing Group.

Money Matters: A Kid's Guide to Money, 6 vols., Set. 2010. (J). (gr. 3-6). lib. bdg. 179.70 *(978-1-58415-835-6(2))* Mitchell Lane Pubs., Inc.

Murphy, Patricia J. Earning Money. 2005. (How Economics Works). (Illus.). 48p. (J). (gr. 3-7). lib. bdg. 25.26 *(978-0-8225-2149-5(0),* Lerner Pubns.) Lerner Publishing Group.

Orr, Tamra. A Kid's Guide to Earning Money. 2008. (Money Matters Ser.). (Illus.). 48p. (YA). (gr. 3-6). lib. bdg. 29.95 *(978-1-58415-643-7(0))* Mitchell Lane Pubs., Inc.

Rancic, Bill. Beyond the Lemonade Stand: Starting Small to Make It Big! 2006. (ENG., Illus.). 176p. (J). (gr. 3-7). pap. 6.99 *(978-1-59514-111-8(1),* Razorbill) Penguin Young Readers Group.

Reynolds, Mattie. Kids Making Money: An Introduction to Financial Literacy. 2013. (Start Smart: Money Ser.). (Illus.). 24p. (gr. k-2). (J). lib. bdg. 17.95 net. *(978-1-937529-41-3(X));* (ENG., pap. 5.95 *(978-1-937529-37-6(1))* Red Chair Pr.

Scheunemann, Pam. Cool Jobs for Handy Helpers: Ways to Make Money Doing Home Services, 1 vol. 2011. (Cool Kid Jobs Ser.). (ENG.). 32p. (gr. 3-6). 28.50 *(978-1-61613-195-1(0),* Checkerboard Library) ABDO Publishing Co.

—Cool Jobs for Kids Who Like Kids: Ways to Make Money Working with Children, 1 vol. 2011. (Cool Kid Jobs Ser.). (ENG.). 32p. (gr. 3-6). 28.50 *(978-1-61613-196-8(9),* Checkerboard Library) ABDO Publishing Co.

—Cool Jobs for Super Sales Kids: Ways to Make Money Selling Stuff, 1 vol. 2011. (Cool Kid Jobs Ser.). (ENG.). 32p. (gr. 3-6). 28.50 *(978-1-61613-197-5(7),* Checkerboard Library) ABDO Publishing Co.

—Cool Jobs for Yard-Working Kids: Ways to Make Money Doing Yard Work, 1 vol. 2011. (Cool Kid Jobs Ser.). (ENG.). 32p. (gr. 3-6). 28.50 *(978-1-61613-198-2(5),* Checkerboard Library) ABDO Publishing Co.

—Cool Jobs for Young Entertainers: Ways to Make Money Putting on an Event, 1 vol. 2011. (Cool Kid Jobs Ser.). (ENG.). 32p. (gr. 3-6). 28.50 *(978-1-61613-199-9(3),* Checkerboard Library) ABDO Publishing Co.

—Cool Jobs for Young Pet Lovers: Ways to Make Money Caring for Pets, 1 vol. 2011. (Cool Kid Jobs Ser.). (ENG.). 32p. (gr. 3-6). 28.50 *(978-1-61613-200-2(0),* Checkerboard Library) ABDO Publishing Co.

Swanson, Jennifer A. Smart Strategies for Turning an Idea into a Product or Service. 2014. (Financial Security & Life Success for Teens Ser.). 80p. (YA). (gr. 7-12). 34.25 *(978-1-4777-7634-6(6))* Rosen Publishing Group, Inc., The.

Tangerine Press Staff & Scholastic, Inc. Staff, contrib. by. Kid Biz. 2004. (Illus.). 62p. (J). *(978-0-439-69986-0(X))* Scholastic, Inc.

Thornton, J. D. How to Make Money. 2006. (Illus.). 92p. (J). pap. *(978-0-545-07195-6(X))* Scholastic, Inc.

MONEYMAKING PROJECTS—FICTION

Adler, David A. Danny's Doodles: the Dog Biscuit Breakfast. 2015. (Danny's Doodles Ser.: 3). (ENG.). 144p. (J). (gr. 2-5). 14.99 *(978-1-4926-1668-9(0),* Sourcebooks Jabberwocky) Sourcebooks, Inc.

Bair, Sheila. Isabel's Car Wash. Stead, Judy, illus. 2012. (J). 34.28 *(978-1-61913-118-7(8))* Weigl Pubs., Inc.

—Isabel's Car Wash. Stead, Judy, illus. 2011. (ENG.). 32p. (J). (gr. 1-3). 6.99 *(978-0-8075-3653-7(9))* Whitman, Albert & Co.

Banim, Lisa. In the Doghouse. 2005. 124p. (J). lib. bdg. 16.92 *(978-1-4242-0685-8(5))* Fitzgerald Bks.

Barrows, Annie. Ivy + Bean: No News Is Good News. Blackall, Sophie, illus. 2012. (Ivy & Bean Ser.). (ENG.). 144p. (J). (gr. 1-5). pap. 5.99 *(978-1-4521-0781-3(5))* Chronicle Bks. LLC.

—Ivy + Bean No News Is Good News. Blackall, Sophie, illus. 2011. (Ivy & Bean Ser.: IVYB). (ENG.). 128p. (J). (gr. 1-5). 14.99 *(978-0-8118-6693-4(9))* Chronicle Bks. LLC.

Barrows, Annie & Blackall, Sophie. Ivy + Bean, 1 vol. 2011. (Ivy & Bean Ser.). (ENG., Illus.). 128p. (J). (gr. 1-4). 24.21 *(978-1-59961-928-6(8))* Spotlight.

Belford, Bibi. Canned & Crushed. 2015. (ENG.). 192p. (J). (gr. 2-7). 14.99 *(978-1-63220-435-6(5),* Sky Pony Pr.) Skyhorse Publishing Co., Inc.

Benton, Jim. Dumbness Is a Dish Best Served Cold. Benton, Jim, illus. 2016. (Dear Dumb Diary Ser.). (ENG., Illus.). 224p. (J). (gr. 3-7). 12.99 *(978-0-545-93228-8(9),* Scholastic Pr.) Scholastic, Inc.

Best, Cari. Sally Jean, the Bicycle Queen. Davenier, Christine, illus. 2006. (ENG.). 32p. (J). (gr. -1-3). 17.99 *(978-0-374-36386-4(2),* 9780374363864, Farrar, Straus & Giroux (BYR)) Farrar, Straus & Giroux.

Birdsall, Jeanne. The Penderwicks in Spring. 2015. (Penderwicks Ser.). (ENG.). 352p. (J). (gr. 3-7). 16.99 *(978-0-375-87077-4(6),* Knopf Bks. for Young Readers) Random Hse. Children's Bks.

Bloom, Steve. The Stand-In. 2016. (ENG.). 360p. (YA). (gr. 8-12). 18.99 *(978-1-5124-1023-5(3));* 38.65 *(978-1-5124-1121-8(3),* Carolrhoda Lab™) Lerner Publishing Group.

Bowe, Julie. Dance Fever. 2017. (Victoria Torres, Unfortunately Average Ser.). (ENG.). 160p. (gr. 4-4). lib. bdg. 26.65 *(978-1-4965-3819-2(6))* Stone Arch Bks.

Bradman, Tony. Jack & the Bean Snacks, 1 vol. Warburton, Sarah, illus. (After Happily Ever After Ser.). (ENG.). 56p. (gr. 2-3). 2014. pap. 5.05 *(978-1-4342-7964-4(2))* 2009. 25.32 *(978-1-4342-1305-1(6))* Stone Arch Bks. (After Happily Ever After).

Branford, Anna. Violet Mackerel's Brilliant Plot. Allen, Elanna, illus. 2012. (Violet Mackerel Ser.). (ENG.). 112p. (J). (gr. 1-5). 15.99 *(978-1-4424-3585-8(2));* pap. 5.99 *(978-1-4424-3586-5(0))* Simon & Schuster Children's Publishing. (Atheneum Bks. for Young Readers).

Carlson, Melody. Raising Faith, 1 vol. 2016. (Faithgirlz / Girls of Harbor View Ser.). (ENG.). 272p. (J). pap. 9.99 *(978-0-310-75375-9(9))* Zonderkidz.

Clements, Andrew. Lunch Money. Selznick, Brian, illus. 2007. (ENG.). 240p. (J). (gr. 3-7). pap. 7.99 *(978-0-689-86685-2(2),* Atheneum Bks. for Young Readers) Simon & Schuster Children's Publishing.

—Lunch Money. 2007. 17.20 *(978-1-4177-8116-4(5),* Turtleback) Turtleback Bks.

Clifton, Lutricia. Immortal Max. Sheban, Chris, illus. 2014. (ENG.). 192p. (J). (gr. 3-7). 16.95 *(978-0-8234-3041-3(3))* Holiday Hse., Inc.

Cobb, Amy. Notes from a Pro, 1 vol. Cattish, Anna, illus. 2015. (ENG.). 112p. (J). *(978-1-62402-075-9(5))* Magic Wagon.

Conford, Ellen. A Job for Jenny Archer. Palmisciano, Diane & Brooks, Erik, illus. 2006. (ENG.). 80p. (J). (gr. 1-4). per. 13.99 *(978-0-316-01484-7(2))* Little, Brown Bks. for Young Readers.

—What's Cooking, Jenny Archer? Palmisciano, Diane & Brooks, Erik, illus. 2006. (ENG.). 80p. (J). (gr. 1-4). per. 13.99 *(978-0-316-01488-5(5))* Little, Brown Bks. for Young Readers.

conrad, catherine. The Lemonade Stand. 2008. (Illus.). 32p. (J). lib. bdg. 16.99 *(978-0-9799065-0-3(4))* Banana Pr.

Cossanteli, Veronica. The Extincts. Muradov, Roman, illus. 2016. (ENG.). 240p. (J). 16.99 *(978-1-62779-403-9(4),* 9781627794039, Holt, Henry & Co. Bks. For Young Readers) Holt, Henry & Co.

Davies, Jacqueline. The Lemonade War. (Lemonade War Ser.: 1). (ENG.). 192p. (J). (gr. 2-5). 2009. pap. 7.99 *(978-0-547-23765-7(0))* 2007. (Illus.). 16.99 *(978-0-618-75043-6(6))* Houghton Mifflin Harcourt Publishing Co.

Deriso, C. H. Elisabeth & the Unwanted Advice. 2016. (Babysitter Chronicles Ser.). (ENG., Illus.). 160p. (gr. 4-7). lib. bdg. 26.65 *(978-1-4965-2757-8(7))* Stone Arch Bks.

Deriso, Christine Hurley. Elisabeth & the Unwanted Advice. 2016. (Babysitter Chronicles Ser.). (ENG., Illus.). 160p. (gr. 4-7). pap. 6.95 *(978-1-4914-8864-5(6))* Stone Arch Bks.

deRubertis, Barbara. Walter Warthog's Wonderful Wagon. Alley, R. W., illus. 2011. (Animal Antics A to Z Ser.). 32p. (J). (ENG.). pap. 7.95 *(978-1-57565-348-8(6));* lib. bdg. 22.60 *(978-1-57565-356-3(7))* Kane Press, Inc.

deRubertis, Barbara & DeRubertis, Barbara. Walter Warthog's Wonderful Wagon. Alley, R. W., illus. 2012. (Animal Antics A to Z Ser.). 32p. (J). (gr. 2 — 1). cd-rom 7.95 *(978-1-57565-416-4(4))* Kane Press, Inc.

Dowell, Frances O'Roark. Blasts Off! McDaniels, Preston, illus. 2011. (From the Highly Scientific Notebooks of Phineas L. MacGuire Ser.). (ENG.). 224p. (J). (gr. 3-7). pap. 7.99 *(978-1-4424-2204-9(1),* Atheneum Bks. for Young Readers) Simon & Schuster Children's Publishing.

—Sam the Man & the Chicken Plan. Bates, Amy June, illus. 2017. (Sam the Man Ser.: 1). (ENG.). 144p. (J). (gr. 1-4). pap. 6.99 *(978-1-4814-4067-7(5))* Simon & Schuster Children's Publishing.

—Sam the Man & the Chicken Plan. 2016. (Sam the Man Ser.: 1). (ENG., Illus.). 128p. (J). (gr. 1-4). 15.99 *(978-1-4814-4066-0(7))* Simon & Schuster Children's Publishing.

Doyle, Bill. Attack of the Shark-Headed Zombie. Altman, Scott, illus. 2011. (Stepping Stone Book Ser.). (ENG.). 112p. (J). (gr. 1-4). 4.99 *(978-0-375-86675-3(2),* Random Hse. Bks. for Young Readers) Random Hse. Children's Bks.

Draper, Sharon M. The Backyard Animal Show. Watson, Jesse Joshua, illus. 2012. (Clubhouse Mysteries Ser.: 5). (ENG.). 128p. (J). (gr. 3-7). pap. 5.99 *(978-1-4424-5022-6(3),* Aladdin) Simon & Schuster Children's Publishing.

—The Backyard Animal Show. Watson, Jesse Joshua, illus. 2012. (Clubhouse Mysteries Ser.: 5). (ENG.). 128p. (J). (gr. 3-7). 15.99 *(978-1-4424-5023-3(1),* Simon & Schuster/Paula Wiseman Bks.) Simon & Schuster/Paula Wiseman Bks.

—Stars & Sparks on Stage. Watson, Jesse Joshua, illus. 2012. (Clubhouse Mysteries Ser.: 6). (ENG.). 144p. (J). (gr. 3-7). pap. 5.99 *(978-1-4424-5457-6(1),* Aladdin) Simon & Schuster Children's Publishing.

—Stars & Sparks on Stage. Watson, Jesse Joshua, illus. 2012. (Clubhouse Mysteries Ser.: 6). (ENG.). 144p. (J). (gr. 3-7). 15.99 *(978-1-4424-5459-0(8),* Simon & Schuster/Paula Wiseman Bks.) Simon & Schuster/Paula Wiseman Bks.

Eggleton, Jill. The Ice-Cream Machine. Pye, Trevor, illus. 2003. (Rigby Sails Early Ser.). (ENG.). 16p. (gr. 1-2). pap. 6.95 *(978-0-7578-8728-4(7))* Houghton Mifflin Harcourt Publishing Co.

Elliott, David. The Cool Crazy Crickets to the Rescue. Meisel, Paul, illus. 2010. (ENG.). 48p. (J). (gr. 1-4). 5.99 *(978-0-7636-4658-5(X))* Candlewick Pr.

Frazier, Sundee T. Cleo Edison Oliver in Persuasion Power. 2017. (ENG.). 256p. (J). (gr. 3-7). 16.99 *(978-0-545-82239-8(4),* Levine, Arthur A. Bks.) Scholastic, Inc.

Freeman, Marcia S. Catfish & Spaghetti. Stock, Rose, illus. 2013. (Maupin House Ser.). (ENG.). 48p. (gr. 3-5). pap. 4.50 *(978-0-929895-21-5(5))* Maupin Hse. Publishing.

Friedman, Laurie. In Business with Mallory. Pollak, Barbara, illus. (Mallory Ser.: 5). (ENG.). 160p. (J). (gr. 2-5). 2007. per. 5.95 *(978-0-8225-6561-1(7),* First Avenue Editions) 2006. 15.95 *(978-1-57505-925-9(8),* Carolrhoda Bks.) Lerner Publishing Group.

Graff, Lisa. The Life & Crimes of Bernetta Wallflower: The Pros & Cons. 2015. (ENG.). 288p. (J). (gr. 3-7). 7.99 *(978-0-14-751675-6(7),* Puffin Books) Penguin Young Readers Group.

Green, D. L. Kaitlyn & the Competition. 2016. (Babysitter Chronicles Ser.). (ENG.). 160p. (gr. 4-7). pap. 6.95 *(978-1-4914-8861-4(1))* Stone Arch Bks.

—Zeke Meeks vs the No-Fun Fund-Raiser, 1 vol. Alves, Josh, illus. 2013. (Zeke Meeks Ser.). (ENG.). 128p. (gr. 2-2). lib. bdg. 22.65 *(978-1-4048-7640-8(5),* Zeke Meeks) Picture Window Bks.

Greene, Stephanie. Owen Foote, Money Man. Weston, Martha, illus. 2003. 88p. (gr. 2-4). 14.95 *(978-0-7569-1559-9(7))* Perfection Learning Corp.

Greenwald, Tommy. Charlie Joe Jackson's Guide to Making Money. Coovert, J. P., illus. 2014. (Charlie Joe Jackson Ser.: 4). (ENG.). 208p. (J). (gr. 4-7). 13.99 *(978-1-59643-840-8(1),* 9781596438408) Roaring Brook Pr.

Gutman, Dan. The Get Rich Quick Club. (ENG.). 128p. (J). 2006. (gr. 3-7). pap. 5.99 *(978-0-06-053442-4(7))* 2004. 15.99 *(978-0-06-053440-0(0))* HarperCollins Pubs.

—Mrs. Master Is a Disaster! 2017. (My Weirdest School Ser.: 8). lib. bdg. 14.75 ***(978-0-606-40078-7(8))*** Turtleback Bks.

Gutman, Dan. My Weirdest School #8: Mrs. Master Is a Disaster! Paillot, Jim, illus. 2017. (My Weirdest School Ser.: 8). 112p. (J). (gr. 1-5). pap. 4.99 *(978-0-06-242933-9(7))* HarperCollins Pubs.

Hambrick, Sharon. Tommy's Race. Manning, Maurie J., illus. 2004. (Fig Street Kids Ser.). 95p. (J). (gr. 1-2). 7.49 *(978-1-59166-286-0(9))* BJU Pr.

Hartinger, Brent. Project Sweet Life. 2009. (J). lib. bdg. 17.89 *(978-0-06-082412-9(3));* (ENG.). 288p. (YA). (gr. 8-18). 16.99 *(978-0-06-082411-2(5))* HarperCollins Pubs. (HarperTeen).

Haugaard, Kay. No Place. 2nd ed. 2007. (ENG., Illus.). 140p. (J). (gr. 2-8). per. 6.95 *(978-1-57131-675-2(2))* Milkweed Editions.

Hawkins, Aaron. The Year Money Grew on Trees. 2011. (ENG.). 304p. (J). (gr. 5-7). pap. 6.99 *(978-0-547-57716-6(8))* Houghton Mifflin Harcourt Publishing Co.

Heine, Theresa & Barefoot Books Staff. Chandra's Magic Light. Gueyfier, Judith, illus. 2013. (J). 16.99 *(978-1-84686-493-3(3))* Barefoot Bks., Inc.

Hepler, Heather. Frosted Kisses. 2015. (ENG.). 272p. (J). (gr. 7). 17.99 *(978-0-545-79055-0(7))* Scholastic, Inc.

Holm, Jennifer L. Full of Beans. 2016. (ENG.). 208p. (J). (gr. 3-7). 16.99 *(978-0-553-51036-2(3));* lib. bdg. 19.99 *(978-0-553-51037-9(1))* Random Hse. Children's Bks. (Random Hse. Bks. for Young Readers).

Holm, Jennifer L. & Holm, Matthew. Bad Babysitter. Holm, Jennifer L. & Holm, Matthew, illus. 2015. (Babymouse Ser.: 19). (ENG., Illus.). 96p. (J). (gr. 2-5). pap. 6.99 *(978-0-307-93162-7(5),* Random Hse. Bks. for Young Readers) Random Hse. Children's Bks.

Hooks, Gwendolyn. The Pet Wash: A Pet Club Story, 1 vol. Byrne, Mike, illus. 2011. (Pet Club Ser.). (ENG.). 32p. (gr. 1-2). pap. 6.25 *(978-1-4342-3054-6(6));* lib. bdg. 22.65 *(978-1-4342-2514-6(3))* Stone Arch Bks.

Jakubowski, Michele. Big Dog Decisions, 1 vol. Montalto, Luisa, illus. 2014. (Sidney & Sydney Ser.). (ENG.). 128p. (gr. 1-3). 25.32 *(978-1-4795-5226-9(7))* Picture Window Bks.

Jenkins, Emily. Lemonade in Winter: A Book about Two Kids Counting Money. Karas, G. Brian, illus. 2012. (ENG.). 40p. (J). (gr. -1-2). 16.99 *(978-0-375-85883-3(0),* Schwartz & Wade Bks.) Random Hse. Children's Bks.

Johnson, Peter. The Amazing Adventures of John Smith, Jr. Aka Houdini. 2012. (ENG.). 176p. (J). (gr. 3-7). 16.99 *(978-0-06-198890-5(1))* HarperCollins Pubs.

—The Amazing Adventures of John Smith, Jr. AKA Houdini. 2014. (ENG.). 192p. (J). (gr. 3-7). pap. 6.99 *(978-0-06-198891-2(X))* HarperCollins Pubs.

Jones, Jen. Dog Days for Delaney. Franco, Paula, illus. 2014. (Sleepover Girls Ser.). (ENG.). 128p. (gr. 3-5). 22.65 *(978-1-4342-9756-3(X))* Stone Arch Bks.

—Lissa & the Fund-Raising Funk: # 3, 1 vol. 2012. (Team Cheer Ser.). (ENG.). 112p. (gr. 4-4). pap. 7.19 *(978-1-4342-4251-8(X),* Team Cheer) Stone Arch Bks.

Kelly, Katy. Melonhead & the We-Fix-It Company. Johnson, Gillian, illus. 2014. (Melonhead Ser.). (ENG.). 240p. (J). (gr. 3-7). 6.99 *(978-0-307-92970-9(1),* Yearling) Random Hse. Children's Bks.

Kennedy, Marlane. The Dog Days of Charlotte Hayes. 2009. (ENG., Illus.). 240p. (J). (gr. 3-7). 15.99 *(978-0-06-145241-3(6),* Greenwillow Bks.) HarperCollins Pubs.

Krulik, Nancy. World's Worst Wedgie. Blecha, Aaron, illus. 2010. (George Brown, Class Clown Ser.: 3). (ENG.). 128p. (J). (gr. 2-4). pap. 5.99 *(978-0-448-45369-9(X),* Grosset & Dunlap) Penguin Young Readers Group.

Lindman, Maj. Flicka, Ricka, Dicka Go to Market. Lindman, Maj, illus. 2012. (ENG., Illus.). 32p. (J). (gr. -1-3). 9.99 *(978-0-8075-2478-7(6));* (gr. k-3). 9.99 *(978-0-8075-2479-4(4))* Whitman, Albert & Co.

Lubar, David. Meltdown Madness. Loveridge, Matt, illus. 2013. (Looniverse Ser.: 2). (ENG.). 96p. (J). (gr. 1-3). 15.99

MNO

(978-0-545-49603-2(9)); pap. 4.99 (978-0-545-49604-9(7)) Scholastic, Inc.
—Meltdown Madness. 2013. (Looniverse Ser.: 2). lib. bdg. 14.75 (978-0-606-31983-6(2), Turtleback) Turtleback Bks.
Luper, Eric. Jeremy Bender vs. the Cupcake Cadets. 2011. (ENG.). 240p. (J). (gr. 3-7). 16.99 (978-0-06-201512-9(5)) HarperCollins Pubs.
Margolis, Leslie. Monkey Business. (Annabelle Unleashed Ser.). (ENG.). 224p. (YA). (gr. 3-6). 2015. pap. 7.99 (978-1-61963-799-3(5), 9781619637993) 2014. 16.99 (978-1-61963-393-3(0), 9781619633933) Bloomsbury Publishing USA. (Bloomsbury USA Childrens).
May, Eleanor. Albert Helps Out: Counting Money. Melmon, Deborah, illus. 2017. (Mouse Math (r) Ser.). (ENG.). 32p. (gr. -1-1). 7.95 (978-1-57565-860-5(7)) Kane Press, Inc.
—Albert Helps Out: Counting Money. Melmon, Deborah, illus. 2017. (Mouse Math (r) Ser.). (ENG.). 32p. (gr. -1-1). lib. bdg. 22.65 (978-1-57565-857-5(7)) Kane Press, Inc.
McDonald, Megan. Stink & the Midnight Zombie Walk. Reynolds, Peter H., illus. 2013. (Stink Ser.: 7). (ENG.). 160p. (J). (gr. 1-4). 12.99 (978-0-7636-6394-0(8)); pap. 4.99 (978-0-7636-6422-0(7)) Candlewick Pr.
—Stink & the Midnight Zombie Walk. 2013. (Stink Ser.: 7). lib. bdg. 14.75 (978-0-606-31586-9(1), Turtleback) Turtleback Bks.
McKay, Hilary. The Exiles at Home. 2007. (ENG.). 208p. (J). (gr. 3-7). pap. 12.95 (978-1-4169-6729-3(X), McElderry, Margaret K. Bks.) McElderry, Margaret K. Bks.
Messner, Kate. Marty McGuire Has Too Many Pets! Floca, Brian, illus. 2015. (Marty Mcguire Ser.). (ENG.). 176p. (J). (gr. -1-3). pap. 5.99 (978-0-545-53560-1(3), Scholastic Pr.) Scholastic, Inc.
Metz, Melinda. Bri's Big Crush. 2016. (Babysitter Chronicles Ser.). (ENG.). 160p. (gr. 4-7). lib. bdg. 26.65 (978-1-4965-2756-1(9), 1400591) Stone Arch Bks.
Morgan, Alex. Hat Trick. 2015. (Kicks Ser.). (ENG., Illus.). 128p. (J). (gr. 3-7). 16.99 (978-1-4814-5096-6(4), Simon & Schuster Bks. For Young Readers) Simon & Schuster Bks. For Young Readers.
Mullarkey, Lisa. The Artsy Fartsy Auction: Book 8, 1 vol. Harris, Phyllis, illus. 2012. (Katharine the Almost Great Ser.). (ENG.). 80p. (J). (gr. 1-4). 27.07 (978-1-61641-829-8(X)) Magic Wagon.
—Uses Her Common Cents, 1 vol. Harris, Phyllis, illus. 2009. (Katharine the Almost Great Ser.: No. 1). (ENG.). 80p. (J). (gr. 1-4). 27.07 (978-1-60270-579-1(8)) Magic Wagon.
Nesbit, E. Story of the Treasure Seekers. 2006. pap. (978-1-4068-3507-6(2)) Echo Library.
—The Story of the Treasure Seekers: Being the Adventures of the Bastable Children in Search of a Fortune. 2007. (ENG.). 150p. pap. 18.99 (978-1-4346-5163-1(0)); 170p. pap. 21.99 (978-1-4346-5164-8(9)) Creative Media Partners, LLC.
—The Story of the Treasure Seekers: Being the Adventures of the Bastable Children in Search of A Fortune. l.t. ed. 2005. 288p. pap. (978-1-84637-207-0(0)) Echo Library.
Nolen, Jerdine. Pitching in for Eubie. Lewis, E. B., illus. 2007. (ENG.). 32p. (J). (gr. k-3). 16.99 (978-0-688-14917-8(0), Amistad) HarperCollins Pubs.
O'Connor, Jane. Fancy Nancy & the Fabulous Fashion Boutique. Glasser, Robin Preiss, illus. 2010. (Fancy Nancy Ser.). 32p. (J). (gr. -1-3). (ENG.). 17.99 (978-0-06-123592-4(X)); lib. bdg. 18.89 (978-0-06-123593-1(8)) HarperCollins Pubs.
Olson, Gretchen. Call Me Hope. 2008. (ENG.). 288p. (J). (gr. 3-7). pap. 5.99 (978-0-316-01239-3(4)) Little, Brown Bks. for Young Readers.
O'Neal, Shaquille. Little Shaq. Taylor, Theodore, illus. 2015. 73p. (J). (978-1-68119-119-5(9)) Bloomsbury Pr.
—Little Shaq. Taylor, Theodore, III, illus. 2015. (ENG.). 80p. (J). (gr. k-2). 9.99 (978-1-61963-721-4(9), 9781619637214, Bloomsbury USA Childrens) Bloomsbury Publishing USA.
O'Neill, Alexis & Sanchez, Enrique O. Estela's Swap, 1 vol. 2005. (ENG., Illus.). 32p. (J). (gr. -1-3). pap. 9.95 (978-1-60060-253-5(3)) Lee & Low Bks., Inc.
Orme, Helen. Who's Who? 2008. (Siti's Sisters Ser.). (ENG., Illus.). 36p. pap. (978-1-84167-687-6(X)) Ransom Publishing Ltd.
Parish, Herman. Amelia Bedelia Means Business. Avril, Lynne, illus. (Amelia Bedelia Ser.). (ENG.). (J). (gr. 1-5). 2015. 320p. 12.99 (978-0-06-240367-4(2)) 2013. 160p. 15.99 (978-0-06-209497-1(1)) 2013. 149p. pap. 5.99 (978-0-06-209496-4(3)) HarperCollins Pubs. (Greenwillow Bks.).
—Amelia Bedelia Means Business. Avril, Lynne, illus. 2013. (Amelia Bedelia Chapter Book Ser.: 1). (J). lib. bdg. 14.75 (978-0-606-27137-0(6), Turtleback) Turtleback Bks.
Patterson, James & Tebbetts, Chris. Middle School: Dog's Best Friend. Tejido, Jomike, illus. 2016. (Middle School: Book 8 Ser.: 8). (ENG.). 256p. (J). (gr. 3-7). 13.99 (978-0-316-34954-3(2), Jimmy Patterson) Little Brown & Co.
Paulsen, Gary. Flat Broke: The Theory, Practice & Destructive Properties of Greed. (ENG.). 128p. (J). (gr. 3-7). 2012. pap. 6.99 (978-0-375-86612-8(4), Yearling) 2011. 12.99 (978-0-385-74002-9(6), Lamb, Wendy Bks.) Random Hse. Children's Bks.
—Lawn Boy. 2009. (ENG.). 96p. (J). (gr. 3-7). 5.99 (978-0-553-49465-5(1), Yearling) Random Hse. Children's Bks.
Peschke, Marci. Cupcake Queen. Mourning, Tuesday, illus. (Kylie Jean Ser.). (ENG.). 112p. (gr. 2-3). 2015. pap. 5.95 (978-1-4795-6753-9(1)) 2013. 8.95 (978-1-4048-8102-0(6)) 2013. lib. bdg. 22.65 (978-1-4048-7580-7(8)) Picture Window Bks. (Kylie Jean).
—Fashion Queen. Mourning, Tuesday, illus. 2015. (Kylie Jean Ser.). (ENG.). 112p. (gr. 2-3). 8.95 (978-1-4795-5881-0(8), Kylie Jean) Picture Window Bks.
Pett, Mark. The Girl & the Bicycle. Pett, Mark, illus. 2014. (ENG., Illus.). 40p. (J). 17.99 (978-1-4424-8319-4(9), Simon & Schuster Bks. For Young Readers) Simon & Schuster Bks. For Young Readers.
Reichert, Paul. The Lemonade Ripple: A Sweet Story of Kindness & Charity. 2012. (ENG., Illus.). 40p. (J). (gr. -1-k). 12.95 (978-1-61608-701-2(3), 608701, Sky Pony Pr.) Skyhorse Publishing Co., Inc.
Rey, H. A. Lemonade Stand. 2016. (Curious George TV Tie-In Early Reader Ser.). lib. bdg. 13.55 (978-0-606-37993-9(2)) Turtleback Bks.
Salisbury, Graham. The Zippy Fix. Rogers, Jacqueline, illus. 2010. (Calvin Coconut Ser.). (ENG.). 176p. (J). (gr. 3-7). pap. 6.99 (978-0-375-84601-4(8), Yearling) Random Hse. Children's Bks.
Scraper, Katherine. The Yard Sale. 2006. (Early Explorers Ser.). (J). pap. (978-1-4108-6043-9(4)) Benchmark Education Co.
Simon, Coco. Emma: Lights! Camera! Cupcakes! 2014. (Cupcake Diaries: 19). lib. bdg. 17.20 (978-0-606-35437-0(9)) Turtleback Bks.
—Emma on Thin Icing. 2013. (Cupcake Diaries: 3). (ENG., Illus.). 160p. (J). (gr. 3-7). 15.99 (978-1-4424-7492-5(0), Simon Spotlight) Simon Spotlight.
—Emma on Thin Icing. 2011. (Cupcake Diaries: 3). lib. bdg. 17.20 (978-0-606-23734-5(8), Turtleback) Turtleback Bks.
Spinelli, Eileen. Miss Fox's Class Earns a Field Trip. Kennedy, Anne, illus. 2012. (J). (978-1-61913-122-4(6)) Weigl Pubs., Inc.
—Miss Fox's Class Earns a Field Trip, 1 vol. Kennedy, Anne, illus. 2010. (Miss Fox's Class Ser.). (ENG.). 32p. (J). (gr. 1-3). 16.99 (978-0-8075-5169-1(4)) Whitman, Albert & Co.
Temairik, Jaime. Alice & Lucy Will Work for Bunk Beds. Temairik, Jaime, illus. 2016. (ENG., Illus.). 40p. (J). (gr. -1-k). 16.99 (978-1-4847-0816-3(4)) Disney Publishing Worldwide.
Terrell, Brandon. Above, 1 vol. Cano, Fernando, illus. 2013. (Tony Hawk: Live2Skate Ser.). (ENG.). 72p. (gr. 4-5). pap. 5.95 (978-1-4342-6186-1(7)); (gr. 3-4). pap. 35.70 (978-1-4342-6266-0(9), Tony Hawk's 900 Revolution); (gr. 4-5). lib. bdg. 25.32 (978-1-4342-4084-2(3)) Stone Arch Bks.
Updale, Eleanor. Johnny Swanson. 2012. (ENG.). 384p. (J). (gr. 3-7). 8.99 (978-0-385-75228-2(8), Yearling) Random Hse. Children's Bks.
Viorst, Judith. Lulu Walks the Dogs. Smith, Lane, illus. 2012. (ENG.). 160p. (J). (gr. 1-5). 16.99 (978-1-4424-3579-7(8), Atheneum Bks. for Young Readers) Simon & Schuster Children's Publishing.
—Lulu Walks the Dogs. 2014. (Lulu Ser.: 2). lib. bdg. 18.40 (978-0-606-35438-7(7)) Turtleback Bks.
Wells, Rosemary. Max's Bunny Business. 2008. (Max & Ruby Ser.). (ENG., Illus.). 32p. (J). (gr. -1-k). 15.99 (978-0-670-01105-6(3), Viking Books for Young Readers) Penguin Young Readers Group.
Weston, Robert Paul. Blues for Zoey. 2015. (ENG.). 312p. (YA). pap. 9.99 (978-0-7387-4340-0(2), Flux) North Star Editions.
Wiggins, Thalia. Greg's Game Dilemma, 1 vol. Tate, Don, illus. 2012. (Making Choices: the Mcnair Cousins Ser.). (ENG.). 64p. 27.07 (978-1-61641-632-4(7), Calico Chapter Bks) Magic Wagon.
Willson, Sarah. Pet Peeves! Nez, John A., illus. 2005. (Social Studies Connects). 32p. (J). pap. 5.95 (978-1-57565-149-1(1)) Kane Press, Inc.
Winston, Sherri. President of the Whole Sixth Grade. 2015. (ENG.). 320p. (J). (gr. 3-7). 17.00 (978-0-316-37723-2(6)) Little Brown & Co.
Wisler, Joelle. Ariana Gold. 2016. (What's Your Dream? Ser.). (ENG., Illus.). 96p. (gr. 3-4). lib. bdg. 25.32 (978-1-4965-3442-2(5)) Capstone Press of Coughlan Cos.

MONGOLIA

Adamson, Heather. Mongolia. 2016. (Exploring Countries Ser.). (ENG., Illus.). 32p. (J). (gr. 3-7). lib. bdg. 26.95 (978-1-62617-344-6(3), Blastoff! Readers) Bellwether Media.
Aloian, Molly. The Gobi Desert. 2012. (ENG.). 32p. (J). (978-0-7787-0710-3(5)); (Illus.). pap. (978-0-7787-0718-9(0)) Crabtree Publishing Co.
Bjorklund, Ruth. Mongolia. 2016. (Enchantment of the World(tm) Ser.). (ENG., Illus.). 144p. (J). lib. bdg. 40.00 (978-0-531-21884-6(8), Children's Pr.) Scholastic Library Publishing.
Graves, Sue. Meet Erdene. 2004. (ENG.). 24p. (J). (gr. 2-2). pap. 10.92 (978-0-7652-5189-3(2), Celebration Pr.) Pearson Schl.
Harper, Judith E. Unique Places. 2005. (Real Deal Ser.). (Illus.). 32p. (J). pap. (978-0-7608-9635-8(6)) Sundance/Newbridge Educational Publishing.
Joo, Mi-hwa. Where the Winds Meet: Mongolia. Cowley, Joy, ed. Oh, Lee, illus. 2015. (Global Kids Storybooks Ser.). (ENG.). 32p. (gr. 1-4). 26.65 (978-1-925246-29-2(9)); 7.99 (978-1-925246-55-1(8)); 26.65 (978-1-925246-03-2(5)) ChoiceMaker Pty. Ltd., The AUS. (Big and SMALL). Dist: Lerner Publishing Group.
—Where the Winds Meet: Mongolia. Cowley, Joy, ed. Lee, Oh, illus. 2015. (Global Kids Storybooks Ser.). (ENG.). 32p. (J). (gr. 1-4). pap. 7.99 (978-1-925233-49-0(9)) Lerner Publishing Group.
Montgomery, Sy. Saving the Ghost of the Mountain: An Expedition among Snow Leopards in Mongolia. Bishop, Nic, illus. Bishop, Nic, photos by. 2012. (Scientists in the Field Ser.). (ENG.). 80p. (J). (gr. 5-7). pap. 9.99 (978-0-547-72734-9(8)) Houghton Mifflin Harcourt Publishing Co.
Pang, Guek Cheng. Mongolia. 2nd rev. ed. 2009. (Cultures of the World 18 Ser.). 144p. (gr. 6). 42.79 (978-0-7614-4849-5(7)) Marshall Cavendish GBR. Dist: Marshall Cavendish Corp.

MONGOLIA—FICTION

Dahl, Michael. Dragon in the Desert, 1 vol. Vue, Tou, illus. (Dragonblood Ser.). (ENG.). 40p. (gr. 1-3). 2010. pap. 6.25 (978-1-4342-2309-8(4)) 2009. 23.99 (978-1-4342-1260-3(2)) Stone Arch Bks. (Zone Bks.).
Service, Pamela F. Alien Expedition. 2010. pap. 33.92 (978-0-7613-6958-5(9)) Lerner Publishing Group.
—Alien Expedition. Gorman, Mike, illus. (Alien Agent Ser.: 3). (ENG.). 160p. (J). (gr. 4-6). 2009. 16.95 (978-0-8225-8870-2(6))No. 3. 2010. pap. 5.95 (978-0-7613-5249-5(X)) Lerner Publishing Group. (Carolrhoda Bks.).
Stilton, Geronimo. Valley of the Giant Skeletons. 2008. (Illus.). 111p. (J). lib. bdg. 15.38 (978-1-4242-4303-7(3)) Fitzgerald Bks.
—Valley of the Giant Skeletons. 2008. (Geronimo Stilton Ser.). (Illus.). 110p. (gr. 2-5). 17.00 (978-0-7569-8805-0(5)) Perfection Learning Corp.
—Valley of the Giant Skeletons. 2008. (Geronimo Stilton Ser.: 32). (ENG., Illus.). 128p. (J). (gr. 2-5). pap. 7.99 (978-0-545-02132-6(4), Scholastic Paperbacks) Scholastic, Inc.
—Valley of the Giant Skeletons. 2008. (Geronimo Stilton Ser.: 32). lib. bdg. 18.40 (978-1-4364-2713-5(4)) Turtleback Bks.
Wilson, Diane Lee. I Rode a Horse of Milk White Jade. 2010. (ENG.). 272p. (J). (gr. 4-10). pap. 9.99 (978-1-4022-4027-0(9), Sourcebooks Jabberwocky) Sourcebooks, Inc.

MONGOLIA—HISTORY—FICTION

Hotchkiss, Gerald G. Emily in Kara Koto: A Young Girl's Adventure in Mongolia. 2014. (J). pap. (978-1-63293-013-2(7)) Sunstone Pr.

MONGOLISM

see Down Syndrome

MONGOLS

Bodden, Valerie. Great Warriors: Mongols. 2014. (Great Warriors Ser.). (ENG.). 24p. (J). (gr. 1-3). pap. 9.99 (978-1-62832-068-8(0), Creative Paperbacks) Creative Co., The.
Boeheme, Gerry. Genghis Khan. 2017. (J). **(978-1-5026-2787-2(6))** Cavendish Square Publishing.
Demi. Genghis Khan, 0 vols. 2009. (ENG.). 64p. (J). (gr. 3-7). 19.99 (978-0-7614-5547-9(7), 9780761455479, Amazon Children's Publishing) Amazon Publishing.
Harrison, Kathryn. Mongols on the Silk Road: Trade, Transportation, & Cross-Cultural Exchange in the Mongol Empire. 2016. (Mongols Ser.). 64p. (J). (gr. 6-6). pap. 12.95 (978-1-4994-6370-5(7)) Rosen Publishing Group, Inc., The.
Kent, Zachary. Genghis Khan: Invincible Ruler of the Mongol Empire. 2007. (Rulers of the Middle Ages Ser.). (Illus.). 160p. (YA). (gr. 6-12). lib. bdg. 35.94 (978-0-7660-2715-2(5)) Enslow Pubs., Inc.
Knight, P. V. Genghis Khan: Fierce Mongolian Conqueror. 2016. (History's Most Murderous Villains Ser.). (Illus.). 32p. (J). (gr. 5-4). pap. 10.50 (978-1-4824-4790-3(8)) Stevens, Gareth Publishing LLLP.
Krull, Kathleen. Kubla Khan: The Emperor of Everything. Byrd, Robert, illus. 2010. (ENG.). 48p. (J). (gr. 3-7). 17.99 (978-0-670-01114-8(2), Viking Books for Young Readers) Penguin Young Readers Group.
Matthews, Rupert. Mongols. 2015. (History's Fearless Fighters Ser.). (ENG., Illus.). 48p. (J). (gr. 5-6). pap. 14.05 (978-1-4824-3169-8(6)) Stevens, Gareth Publishing LLLP.
Reynolds, Jan. Mongolia. 2007. (Vanishing Cultures Ser.). (ENG., Illus.). 32p. (J). (gr. 4-7). 10.95 (978-1-60060-130-9(8)); 16.95 (978-1-60060-145-3(6)) Lee & Low Bks., Inc.
Rice, Earle, Jr. Empire in the East: The Story of Genghis Khan. 2005. (World Leaders Ser.). (Illus.). 160p. (gr. 3-7). 28.95 (978-1-931798-62-4(1)) Reynolds, Morgan Inc.
Sepahban, Lois. Mongol Warriors. 2015. (Ancient Warriors Ser.). (ENG.). 32p. (J). (gr. 2-5). 28.50 (978-1-63143-756-4(9), 208588) Child's World, Inc., The.
Watson, Galadriel Findlay. Mongols. 2013. (J). (978-1-62127-509-1(4)) 2013. (J). pap. (978-1-62127-513-8(2)) 2005. 32p. pap. 9.95 (978-1-59036-257-0(8)) 2004. (Illus.). 32p. (J). lib. bdg. 26.00 (978-1-59036-220-4(9)) Weigl Pubs., Inc.
Zelenyj, Alexander. Marco Polo: Overland to China. 2005. (In the Footsteps of Explorers Ser.). (ENG., Illus.). 32p. (J). (gr. 4-5). pap. (978-0-7787-2453-7(0)) Crabtree Publishing Co.

MONGOLS—FICTION

Boyce, Frank Cottrell. The Unforgotten Coat. Hunter, Carl & Heney, Clare, illus. Hunter, Carl & Heney, Clare, photos by. 2011. (ENG.). 112p. (J). (gr. 3-7). 16.99 (978-0-7636-5729-1(8)) Candlewick Pr.
—The Unforgotten Coat. 2011. (Playaway Children Ser.). (ENG.). (J). (gr. 4-7). 39.99 (978-1-4558-4539-2(6)) Findaway World, LLC.
Jones Yang, Dori. Daughter of Xanadu. 2012. (ENG.). 352p. (YA). (gr. 7). pap. 9.99 (978-0-385-73924-5(9), Ember) Random Hse. Children's Bks.
McCaughrean, Geraldine. The Kite Rider. 2003. (Illus.). 320p. (YA). (gr. 8-18). pap. 8.99 (978-0-06-441091-5(9), HarperTeen) HarperCollins Pubs.

MONGOLS—HISTORY

Behnke, Alison. The Conquests of Genghis Khan. 2008. (Pivotal Moments in History Ser.). (ENG., Illus.). 160p. (gr. 9-12). lib. bdg. 38.60 (978-0-8225-7519-1(1)) Lerner Publishing Group.
Bodden, Valerie. Mongols (Great Warriors) 2013. 24p. pap. (978-1-60818-468-2(4)) Creative Co., The.
Brian, Dittmar. Mongol Warriors. 2012. (History's Greatest Warriors Ser.). (ENG., Illus.). 24p. (J). (gr. 3-7). lib. bdg. 25.95 (978-1-60014-746-3(1), Torque Bks.) Bellwether Media.
Burgan, Michael. Empire of the Mongols, Revised Edition. 2nd rev. ed. 2009. (Great Empires of the Past Ser.). (Illus.). 160p. (gr. 6-12). 35.00 (978-1-60413-163-5(2)) Facts On File, Inc.
Helget, Nicole Lea. Mongols. 2012. (Fearsome Fighters Ser.). (Illus.). 48p. (J). (gr. 5-12). 23.95 (978-1-60818-184-1(7), Creative Education) Creative Co., The.
Medina, Nico. Who Was Genghis Khan? Thomson, Andrew & Harrison, Nancy, illus. 2014. (Who Was? Ser.). (ENG.). 112p. (J). (gr. 3-7). pap. 5.99 (978-0-448-48260-6(6), Grosset & Dunlap) Penguin Young Readers Group.
The Mongols. 2016. (Mongols Ser.). 64p. (gr. 6-6). 241.15 (978-1-4777-8554-6(X)); pap. 90.65 (978-1-4994-6425-2(8)) Rosen Publishing Group, Inc., The. (Rosen Young Adult).
Nardo, Don. Genghis Khan & the Mongol Empire. 2010. (World History Ser.). (ENG.). 128p. 34.95 (978-1-4205-0326-5(X), Lucent Bks.) Cengage Gale.
Whiting, Jim. The Life & Times of Genghis Khan. 2005. (Biography from Ancient Civilizations Ser.). (Illus.). 48p. (J). (gr. 4-8). lib. bdg. 29.95 (978-1-58415-348-1(2)) Mitchell Lane Pubs., Inc.
Worth, Richard. The Great Empire of China & Marco Polo in World History. 2003. (In World History Ser.). (Illus.). 112p. (J). lib. bdg. 26.60 (978-0-7660-1939-3(X)) Enslow Pubs., Inc.

MONGOOSES

Bodden, Valerie. Amazing Animals: Meerkats. 2017. (Amazing Animals Ser.). (ENG.). 24p. (J). (gr. 1-3). pap. 8.99 **(978-1-62832-364-1(7)**, Creative Paperbacks) Creative Co., The.
Bodden, Valerie. Meerkats. 2017. (J). (978-1-60818-756-0(X), Creative Education) Creative Co., The.
Borgert-Spaniol, Megan. Mongooses. 2013. (Animal Safari Ser.). (ENG., Illus.). 24p. (J). (gr. k-3). lib. bdg. 25.95 (978-1-60014-912-2(X), Blastoff! Readers) Bellwether Media.
Gish, Melissa. Meercats. 2016. (Living Wild Ser.). (ENG.). 48p. (J). (gr. 5-9). pap. 12.00 (978-1-62832-170-8(9), Creative Paperbacks) Creative Co., The.
Gregory, Josh. Meerkats. 2016. (Nature's Children Ser.). (ENG., Illus.). 48p. (J). pap. 6.95 (978-0-531-22519-6(4), Children's Pr.) Scholastic Library Publishing.
Halfmann, Janet. Mongoose. 2004. (Nature's Predators Ser.). (ENG., Illus.). 48p. (J). 27.50 (978-0-7377-2622-0(9), Greenhaven Pr., Inc.) Cengage Gale.
Meerkat Chat, 6 vols., Pack. (Story Steps Ser.). (gr. k-2). 32.00 (978-0-7635-9850-1(X)) Rigby Education.
Somervill, Barbara. Small Indian Mongoose. 2010. (21st Century Skills Library: Animal Invaders Ser.). (ENG.). 32p. (gr. 4-8). lib. bdg. 28.50 (978-1-60279-630-0(0), 200336) Cherry Lake Publishing.

MONGOOSES—FICTION

Bannerman, Helen. The Story of Little Black Mingo (Illustr. 2006. pap. (978-1-4065-0770-6(9)) Dodo Pr.
Cameron, Wade. Melvin the Mischievious Mongoose First Day of School. 2012. 28p. pap. 18.65 (978-1-4797-0270-1(6)) Xlibris Corp.
Facey, Paulet. Tom-Tom & the Punch Bowl of Irish Moss. 2012. 24p. pap. 15.99 (978-1-4797-3908-0(1)) Xlibris Corp.
Gill, Patricia. Pabi, Beega & the Mongoose Monster. 2009. 28p. pap. 14.99 (978-1-4490-2566-3(8)) AuthorHouse.
Holzwarth, Werner. I Wish I Were A... Jeschke, Stefanie, illus. 2013. (ENG.). 40p. (J). (gr. -1-k). 16.95 (978-1-62087-993-1(X), 620993, Sky Pony Pr.) Skyhorse Publishing Co., Inc.
Jones, Gareth P. Ninja Meerkats (#7) the Ultimate Dragon Warrior. Finlayson, Luke, illus. 2014. (Ninja Meerkats Ser.: 7). (ENG.). 128p. (J). (gr. 2-4). pap. 5.99 (978-1-250-04665-9(3), 9781250046659) Square Fish.
Kipling, Rudyard. Rikki-Tikki-Tavi. Jones, Chuck, illus. 2006. (ENG.). 32p. (J). (gr. -1-3). 8.95 (978-0-8249-6597-6(3), Ideal Pubns.) Worthy Publishing.
—Rikki-Tikki-Tavi & Toomai of the Elephants. 2008. (Unabridged Classics (in Audio) Ser.). (J). pap. 36.00 incl. audio compact disk (978-1-58472-431-5(5), In Audio) Sound Room Pubs., Inc.
Kipling, Rudyard & Pinkney, Jerry. Rikki-Tikki-Tavi. Pinkney, Jerry, illus. 2004. (ENG., Illus.). 48p. (J). (gr. -1-3). reprint ed. pap. 6.99 (978-0-06-058785-7(7)) HarperCollins Pubs.
—Rikki-Tikki-Tavi. 2004. (Illus.). (gr. -1-3). 17.00 (978-0-7569-3250-3(5)) Perfection Learning Corp.
Miller, Mark. Meerkats Don't Fly. Butterfield, Cathy, illus. 2007. (J). (978-0-9794393-0-8(2)) Good Turn Publishing.
Mongoose, Mongoose, Stop! Don't Run. 2004. (J). 11.95 (978-0-931548-65-9(9)) Island Heritage Publishing.
Smithey, Donna. Nichisan & the Ancient Ones. 2012. 36p. pap. 24.99 (978-1-62419-240-1(8)) Salem Author Services.
Tyler, William H. Who Let the Mongoose Loose? 2011. 48p. pap. 18.41 (978-1-4269-5694-2(0)) Trafford Publishing.
Watt, Fiona. That's Not My Meerkat. 2015. (Touchy-Feely Board Bks.). (ENG.). 10p. (J). 9.99 (978-0-7945-3599-5(2), Usborne) EDC Publishing.
Weston Woods Staff, creator. Rikki-Tikki-Tavi. 2011. 18.95 (978-0-439-72977-2(7)); 38.75 (978-0-439-72979-6(3)) Weston Woods Studios, Inc.

MONITOR (IRONCLAD)

Abnett, Dan. The Monitor Versus the Merrimac: Ironclads at War. Verma, Dheeraj, illus. 2007. (Graphic Battles of the Civil War Ser.). (ENG.). 48p. (YA). (gr. 4-7). lib. bdg. 31.95 (978-1-4042-0778-3(3)) Rosen Publishing Group, Inc., The.
Brager, Bruce L. The Monitor vs. the Merrimack. 2003. (Great Battles Through the Ages Ser.). (Illus.). 112p. (gr. 6-12). 30.00 (978-0-7910-7439-8(0), Chelsea Hse.) Facts On File, Inc.
O'Brien, Patrick. Duel of the Ironclads: The Monitor vs. the Virginia. 2003. (Illus.). 40p. (J). (gr. 1-5). 18.85 (978-0-8027-8843-6(2)) Walker & Co.
Thompson, Gare. Civil War Battleship: The Monitor. Day, Larry, illus. 2003. (Penguin Young Readers, Level 4 Ser.). (ENG.). 48p. (J). (gr. 3-4). mass mkt. 3.99 (978-0-448-43245-8(5), Penguin Young Readers) Penguin Young Readers Group.

MONITOR (IRONCLAD)—FICTION

Aviation Staff. Iron Thunder: The Battle Between the Monitor & the Merrimac. 2009. (ENG.). 208p. (J). (gr. 3-7). pap. 7.99 (978-1-4231-0518-3(4)) Hyperion Pr.

MONKEYS

see also Baboons

Aloian, Molly & Kalman, Bobbie. Endangered Monkeys. rev. ed. 2007. (Earth's Endangered Animals Ser.). (ENG., Illus.). 32p. (J). (gr. 1-5). pap. (978-0-7787-1908-3(1)) Crabtree Publishing Co.
—Les Singes. 2010. (FRE., Illus.). 32p. (J). pap. 9.95 (978-2-89579-288-8(7)) Bayard Canada Livres CAN. Dist: Crabtree Publishing Co.
Barnard, Edward S. & Wilsdon, Christina. Monkeys. 2009. (Amazing Animals Ser.). 48p. (J). (gr. 2-6). pap. 10.50 (978-1-4339-2026-4(3), Gareth Stevens Learning Library); (YA). (gr. 3-6). lib. bdg. 28.00 (978-0-8368-9109-6(0)) Stevens, Gareth Publishing LLLP.
Bodden, Valerie. Amazing Animals: Monkeys. 2011. (Amazing Animals Ser.). (ENG.). 24p. (J). (gr. 1-3). pap. 8.99 (978-0-89812-742-3(4), Creative Paperbacks) Creative Co., The.
—Monkeys. 2010. (Amazing Animals Ser.). 24p. (J). (gr. -1-3). 16.95 (978-1-58341-808-6(3), Creative Education) Creative Co., The.
Borgert-Spaniol, Megan. Spider Monkeys. 2014. (Animal Safari Ser.). (ENG., Illus.). 24p. (J). (gr. k-3). lib. bdg. 25.95 (978-1-62617-064-3(9), Blastoff! Readers) Bellwether Media.
Bowman, Lucy. Monkeys. Cooper, Jenny & King, Sue, illus. 2011. (Beginner's Nature Ser.). 32p. (J). ring bd. 4.99 (978-0-7945-2978-9(X), Usborne) EDC Publishing.
Brownlee, Christen. Beware of (Prairie) Dog! A Pet Swap Goes Viral. 2011. (J). pap. (978-0-545-32805-0(5)) Scholastic, Inc.
Bustos, Eduardo & Rodriguez, Lucho. Going Ape! 2012. (ENG., Illus.). 24p. (J). (gr. k-3). 9.95 (978-1-77049-282-0(8), Tundra Bks.) Tundra Bks. CAN. Dist: Penguin Random Hse. LLC.
Daly, Ruth. Mandrills. 2014. (J). (978-1-4896-2882-4(7)) Weigl Pubs., Inc.

De la Bédoyère, Camilla. Monkeys & Apes. 2014. (Animal Q & A Ser.). (Illus.). 24p. (J). (gr. k-3). lib. bdg. 23.60 *(978-1-4777-9190-5(6))* Windmill Bks.

Dennard, Deborah. Apes & Monkeys. McGee, John F., illus. 2003. (Our Wild World Ser.). (ENG.). 192p. (J). (gr. 2-5). 16.95 *(978-1-55971-863-9(3))* Cooper Square Publishing Llc.

Dunn, Joeming & Dunn, Ben. Albert II: The 1st Monkey in Space, 1 vol. 2011. (Famous Firsts: Animals Making History Ser.). (ENG., Illus.). 32p. (YA). (gr. 3-6). 28.50 *(978-1-61641-637-9(8))* Magic Wagon.

Dunn, Mary R. Pygmy Marmosets, 1 vol. 2013. (Monkeys Ser.). (ENG.). 24p. (gr. k-1). lib. bdg. 26.65 *(978-1-62065-107-0(6),* Pebble Plus) Capstone Press of Coughlan Cos.

—Spider Monkeys, 1 vol. 2013. (Monkeys Ser.). (ENG.). 24p. (gr. k-1). lib. bdg. 26.65 *(978-1-62065-104-9(1),* Pebble Plus) Capstone Press of Coughlan Cos.

—Tamarin Monkeys, 1 vol. 2013. (Monkeys Ser.). (ENG.). 24p. (gr. k-1). lib. bdg. 26.65 *(978-1-62065-105-6(X),* Pebble Plus) Capstone Press of Coughlan Cos.

Dyan, Penelope. The Comeback Kids — Book 9 — the Barbary Macaques of Gibraltar. Weigand, John D., photos by. 2012. (Illus.). 36p. pap. 14.95 *(978-1-61477-036-7(0))* Bellissima Publishing, LLC.

Franchino, Vicky. Spider Monkeys. 2014. (Nature's Children Ser.). (ENG.). 48p. (J). lib. bdg. 28.00 *(978-0-531-21229-5(7))* Scholastic Library Publishing.

Ganeri, Anita. Howler Monkey, 1 vol. 2010. (Day in the Life: Rain Forest Animals Ser.). (ENG.). 24p. (gr. k-2). 23.32 *(978-1-4329-4113-0(5));* pap. 6.79 *(978-1-4329-4124-6(0))* Heinemann-Raintree. (Heinemann Read & Learn).

Gillenwater, Chadwick. Howler Monkeys, 1 vol. 2012. (South American Animals Ser.). (ENG.). 24p. (gr. k-1). lib. bdg. 26.65 *(978-1-4296-7589-5(6),* Pebble Plus) Capstone Press of Coughlan Cos.

Gish, Melissa. Monkeys. 2009. (Living Wild Ser.). (Illus.). 48p. (J). 22.95 *(978-1-58341-740-9(0),* Creative Education) Creative Co., The.

Glaser, Rebecca Stromstad. Monkeys Swing. 2016. (ENG., Illus.). 16p. (J). (gr. -1 — 1). bds. 7.99 *(978-1-68152-072-8(9))* Amicus.

Gosman, Gillian. Howler Monkeys. 2012. (Illus.). 24p. (J). 49.50 *(978-1-4488-5172-0(6),* PowerKids Pr.); pap. 8.25 *(978-1-4488-5171-3(8),* PowerKids Pr.); lib. bdg. 22.60 *(978-1-4488-5019-8(3))* Rosen Publishing Group, Inc., The.

—Proboscis Monkeys. 2012. (Illus.). 24p. (J). 49.50 *(978-1-4488-5184-3(X),* PowerKids Pr.); (J). pap. 8.25 *(978-1-4488-5183-6(1),* PowerKids Pr.); (YA). lib. bdg. 22.60 *(978-1-4488-5024-2(X))* Rosen Publishing Group, Inc., The.

—Rhesus Monkeys. 2012. (Illus.). 24p. (J). 49.50 *(978-1-4488-5182-9(3),* PowerKids Pr.); (J). pap. 8.25 *(978-1-4488-5181-2(5),* PowerKids Pr.); (YA). lib. bdg. 22.60 *(978-1-4488-5023-5(1))* Rosen Publishing Group, Inc., The.

—Spider Monkeys. 2012. (J). 49.50 *(978-1-4488-5174-4(2),* PowerKids Pr.); (Illus.). 24p. (J). pap. 8.25 *(978-1-4488-5173-7(4),* PowerKids Pr.); (Illus.). 24p. (YA). lib. bdg. 22.60 *(978-1-4488-5020-4(7))* Rosen Publishing Group, Inc., The.

—Tamarins. 2012. (Illus.). 24p. (J). 49.50 *(978-1-4488-5176-8(9),* 1329354, PowerKids Pr.); pap. 8.25 *(978-1-4488-5175-1(0),* 1329354, PowerKids Pr.); lib. bdg. 22.60 *(978-1-4488-5021-1(5),* 1329354) Rosen Publishing Group, Inc., The.

Gray, Susan H. Spider Monkey. 2015. (21st Century Skills Library: Exploring Our Rainforests Ser.). (ENG., Illus.). 32p. (J). (gr. 3-6). 29.93 *(978-1-63188-980-6(X),* 205832) Cherry Lake Publishing.

Green, John. Monkeys & Apes Coloring Book. 2013. (Dover Nature Coloring Book Ser.). (ENG., Illus.). 48p. (J). (gr. 3-12). pap. 4.99 *(978-0-486-25798-3(3))* Dover Pubns., Inc.

Greenwall, Jessica & Brooks, Felicity. First Sticker Book Monkeys. 2013. (First Sticker Bks). 16p. (J). pap. 6.99 *(978-0-7945-3288-8(8),* Usborne) EDC Publishing.

Gregory, Josh. Monkeys. 2012. (J). pap. *(978-0-531-21079-6(0));* lib. bdg. *(978-0-531-20904-2(0))* Children's Pr., Ltd.

Guidone, Julie. Monkeys. 2009. (Animals That Live in the Rain Forest Ser.). 24p. (gr. -1-3). (J). lib. bdg. 22.60 *(978-1-4339-0024-2(6));* pap. 8.15 *(978-1-4339-0106-5(4))* Stevens, Gareth Publishing LLLP. (Weekly Reader Leveled Readers).

—Monkeys; Monos. 2009. (Animals That Live in the Rain Forest/Animales de la selva Ser.). (SPA & ENG.). 24p. (J). (gr. -1-3). pap. 8.15 *(978-1-4339-0113-3(7));* lib. bdg. 22.60 *(978-1-4339-0063-1(7))* Stevens, Gareth Publishing LLLP. (Weekly Reader Leveled Readers).

Hardyman, Robyn. Apes & Monkeys. 2008. (World of Animals Ser.). 32p. (gr. 2-5). 31.35 *(978-1-933834-37-5(4))* Brown Bear Bks.

Herrington, Lisa M. Monkeys & Apes. 2015. (Rookie Read-About(tm) Science: What's the Difference? Ser.). (ENG., Illus.). 32p. (J). lib. bdg. 25.00 *(978-0-531-21486-2(9),* Children's Pr.) Scholastic Library Publishing.

Hewett, Richard, illus. & photos by. A Monkey Baby Grows Up. Hewett, Richard, photos by. Hewett, Joan, photos by. 2004. (Baby Animals Ser.). 32p. (J). (gr. k-3). lib. bdg. 21.27 *(978-1-57505-199-4(0))* Lerner Publishing Group.

Hoff, Mary King. Monkeys. 2005. (Wild World of Animals (Creative Education) Ser.). (Illus.). 32p. (J). (gr. 2-5). lib. bdg. 18.95 *(978-1-58341-352-4(9),* Creative Education) Creative Co., The.

Howell, Laura. Monkeys Sticker Book. 2011. (Spotter's Guides Sticker Book Ser.). 24p. (J). pap. 6.99 *(978-0-7945-3004-4(4),* Usborne) EDC Publishing.

Ikids Staff. 10 Little Monkeys. King, Travis, illus. 2009. (ENG.). 20p. (J). (gr. -1-k). 14.99 *(978-1-58476-938-5(6))* Innovative Kids.

Jackson, Tom. Monkeys: Baboons, Macaques, Mandrills, Lemurs & Other Primates, All Shown in More Than 180 Enticing Pictures. 2016. (ENG., Illus.). 64p. 12.99 *(978-1-86147-497-1(0),* Armadillo) Anness Publishing GBR. Dist: National Bk. Network.

Jones, Teresa Chin. Tales of the Monkey King. Harris, Miki, illus. 2008. (J). *(978-1-881896-30-2(7))* Pacific View Pr.

Jordan, Apple. Guess Who Grabs. 2nd rev. ed. 2011. (Bookworms 2nd Edition: Guess Who Ser.). (Illus.). 24p. (J). (gr. k-2). 21.36 *(978-1-60870-426-2(2))* Marshall Cavendish Corp.

Kalman, Bobbie. Les Singes et Autres Primates. Sjonger, Rebecca, illus. 2012. (FRE.). 32p. (J). pap. 9.95 *(978-2-89579-440-0(5))* Bayard Canada CAN. Dist: Crabtree Publishing Co.

Klutz Editors, ed. Fuzzy Little Monkeys. 2009. (ENG.). 12p. (J). (gr. -1). 9.95 *(978-1-59174-646-1(9),* Chicken Socks) Klutz.

Kralovansky, Susan. Monkey or Ape?, 1 vol. 2014. (This or That? Ser.). (ENG.). 24p. (gr. 5-10). lib. bdg. 25.65 *(978-1-62403-287-5(7),* Super SandCastle) ABDO Publishing Co.

Kuskowski, Alex. Monkeys, 1 vol. 2014. (Zoo Animals Ser.). (ENG.). 24p. (J). (gr. k-3). lib. bdg. 24.21 *(978-1-62403-273-8(7),* SandCastle) ABDO Publishing Co.

Lindeen, Mary. Monkeys. 2013. (ENG., Illus.). 24p. (J). lib. bdg. 25.65 *(978-1-62031-065-6(1))* Jump! Inc.

Lunde, Darrin P. Monkey Colors. Wynne, Patricia J., illus. 2012. (ENG.). 32p. (J). (gr. -1-2). 15.95 *(978-1-57091-741-7(8));* pap. 7.99 *(978-1-57091-742-4(6))* Charlesbridge Publishing, Inc.

Lunis, Natalie. Howler Monkey: Super Loud. 2011. (Animal Loudmouths: Noisy Animals Ser.). 24p. (J). (gr. k-3). lib. bdg. 22.61 *(978-1-61772-276-9(6))* Bearport Publishing Co., Inc.

Lynette, Rachel. Squirrel Monkeys. 2013. (Jungle Babies of the Amazon Rain Forest Ser.). 24p. (J). (gr. -1-3). lib. bdg. 21.32 *(978-1-61772-757-3(1))* Bearport Publishing Co., Inc.

Macken, JoAnn Early. Monkeys: Los Monos. 2004. (Animals I See at the Zoo/ Animales que veo en el zoologico (bilingual) Ser.). (SPA., Illus.). 24p. (gr. k-3). pap. 8.15 *(978-0-8368-4388-0(6),* Weekly Reader Leveled Readers) Stevens, Gareth Publishing LLLP.

—Monkeys (Los Monos) 2004. (Animals I See at the Zoo/Animales que Veo en el Zoológico Ser.). (SPA., Illus.). 24p. (gr. k-3). lib. bdg. 22.00 *(978-0-8368-4383-5(5),* Weekly Reader Leveled Readers) Stevens, Gareth Publishing LLLP.

Markle, Sandra. The Great Monkey Rescue: Saving the Golden Lion Tamarins. 2015. (ENG., Illus.). 40p. (gr. 4-6). 30.65 *(978-1-4677-8850-2(3),* Millbrook Pr.) Lerner Publishing Group.

Marshall, Deb. Orangutans. 2014. (J). *(978-1-4896-2886-2(X))* Weigl Pubs., Inc.

McCarthy, Cecilia Pinto. Monkeys. 2013. (Monkeys Ser.). (ENG.). 24p. (gr. k-1). lib. bdg. 159.90 *(978-1-62065-110-0(6),* Pebble Plus) Capstone Press of Coughlan Cos.

McDaniel, Melissa. Monkeys. 2003. (Animals Animals Ser.). (Illus.). 48p. (gr. 3-18). lib. bdg. 29.93 *(978-0-7614-1615-9(3))* Marshall Cavendish Corp.

Meister, Cari. Do You Really Want to Meet a Monkey? Fabbri, Daniele, illus. 2015. (Do You Really Want to Meet... ? Ser.). 24p. (J). 27.10 *(978-1-60753-456-3(8))* Amicus Publishing.

Moldovo, Eustacia. Baby Monkeys at the Zoo. 2015. (J). *(978-0-7660-6597-0(9));* (ENG., Illus.). 24p. (gr. -1-1). pap. 9.35 *(978-0-7660-7073-8(5))* Enslow Pubs., Inc.

Monkey. 2004. (Peek-A-Boo Coloring Pads Ser.). 48p. (J). act. bk. ed. 3.99 *(978-1-85997-393-6(0))* Byeway Bks.

Monkey. (Buggy Buddies Ser.). (Illus.). (J). (gr. -1). bds. *(978-1-56021-353-6(1),* 204) W.J. Fantasy, Inc.

Monkeys. 2008. 96p. *(978-1-4075-1151-1(3))* Parragon, Inc.

Moore Niver, Heather. When Monkeys Laugh. 2017. (Animal Emotions Ser.). 32p. (J). (gr. 3-3). pap. 10.52 ***(978-0-7660-8861-0(8));*** lib. bdg. 25.27 ***(978-0-7660-8619-7(4))*** Enslow Pubs., Inc.

Murray, Julie. Monkeys, 1 vol. 2005. (Animal Kingdom Set Ii Ser.). (ENG., Illus.). 24p. (gr. k-4). 25.65 *(978-1-59197-326-3(0),* Buddy Bks.) ABDO Publishing Co.

National Geographic Kids Staff & Neuman, Susan B. National Geographic Readers: Hang on Monkey! 2014. (Readers Ser.). (ENG.). 24p. (J). (-k). pap. 3.99 *(978-1-4263-1755-2(7),* National Geographic Children's Bks.) National Geographic Society.

Neme, Laurel. Orangutan Houdini. Kelleher, Kathie, illus. 2014. (ENG.). 32p. (J). (gr. 1-2). 17.95 *(978-1-59373-153-3(1))* Bunker Hill Publishing, Inc.

Neuman, Susan B. Hang on, Monkey! (1 Hardcover/1 CD) 2017. (National Geographic Kids Ser.). (ENG.). (J). 29.95 ***(978-1-4301-2641-6(8))*** Live Oak Media.

—Hang on, Monkey! (1 Paperback/1 CD) 2017. (National Geographic Kids Ser.). (ENG.). (J). pap. 19.95 ***(978-1-4301-2640-9(X))*** Live Oak Media.

—Hang on, Monkey! (4 Paperbacks/1 CD), 4 vols. 2017. (National Geographic Kids Ser.). (ENG.). (J). pap., pap. 31.95 ***(978-1-4301-2642-3(6))*** Live Oak Media.

Nickel, Bonnie. Those Mischievous Monkeys. 2012. (Those Amazing Animals Ser.). (ENG.). 56p. (J). lib. bdg. 14.95 *(978-1-56164-510-7(9))* Pineapple Pr., Inc.

—Those Mischievous Monkeys. Weaver, Steve, illus. 2012. (Those Amazing Animals Ser.). (ENG.). 56p. (J). pap. 9.95 *(978-1-56164-509-1(5))* Pineapple Pr., Inc.

Owen, Ruth. Mischievous Monkeys. 2012. (Eye to Eye with Animals Ser.). (ENG., Illus.). 32p. (J). (gr. k-5). 25.25 *(978-1-4488-8071-3(8));* pap. 10.00 *(978-1-4488-8107-9(2))* Windmill Bks.

Owings, Lisa. Proboscis Monkey. 2014. (Extremely Weird Animals Ser.). (ENG., Illus.). 24p. (J). (gr. 3-8). lib. bdg. 25.95 *(978-1-62617-077-3(0),* Pilot Bks.) Bellwether Media.

Parramon Staff & Costa-Pau, Rosa. Gorilas. 2006. (SPA.). 32p. (J). (gr. 2-3). 10.40 *(978-84-342-2733-0(9),* PR33932) Parramon Ediciones S.A. ESP. Dist: Lectorum Pubns., Inc.

Pelusey, Michael & Pelusey, Jane. Apes & Monkeys. 2008. (Zoo Animals Ser.). 32p. (gr. 2-3). lib. bdg. 18.56 *(978-0-7614-3144-2(6),* Benchmark Bks.) Marshall Cavendish Corp.

Phillips, Dee. Spider Monkey. 2013. (Science Slam: Treed-Animal Life in the Trees Ser.). 24p. (J). (gr. -1-3). lib. bdg. 23.93 *(978-1-61772-912-6(4))* Bearport Publishing Co., Inc.

Priddy, Roger. Monkey. 2015. (Animal Buddies Ser.). (ENG., Illus.). 8p. (J). (gr. -1 — 1). bds. 5.99 *(978-0-312-51853-0(6),* 9780312518530, Priddy Bks.) St. Martin's Pr.

Pyers. Sail Main5 Monkeys, Diverse Animals. 2003. (Rigby Sails Ser.). (ENG.). 32p. (gr. 5-5). pap. 9.50 *(978-0-7578-8019-3(3))* Rigby Education.

Rabe, Tish. Can You See a Chimpanzee? All about Primates. Ruiz, Aristides & Mathieu, Joe, illus. 2014. (Cat in the Hat's Learning Library). (ENG.). 48p. (J). (gr. k-3). lib. bdg. 13.99 *(978-0-375-97074-0(6),* Random Hse. Bks. for Young Readers) Random Hse. Children's Bks.

Redmond, Ian. Gorilas. Anderson, Peter & Brightling, Geoff, illus. 2003. (SPA.). 64p. 14.95 *(978-84-372-2323-0(7))* Altea, Ediciones, S.A. - Grupo Santillana ESP. Dist: Santillana USA Publishing Co., Inc.

Riggs, Kate. Monkeys. 2012. (Seedlings Ser.). 24p. (J). (gr. -1-3). 15.95 *(978-1-60818-278-7(9),* Creative Education) Creative Co., The.

—Seedlings: Monkeys. 2013. (Seedlings Ser.). (ENG.). 24p. (J). (gr. -1-k). pap. 7.99 *(978-0-89812-785-0(8),* Creative Paperbacks) Creative Co., The.

Ryndak, Rob. Monkeys. 2015. (Jungle Animals Ser.). (ENG., Illus.). 24p. (J). (gr. k-k). 22.60 *(978-1-4824-1752-4(9))* Stevens, Gareth Publishing LLLP.

Sayre, April Pulley. Meet the Howlers! Miller, Woody, illus. 2010. (ENG.). 32p. (J). (gr. -1-2). 16.95 *(978-1-57091-733-2(7));* pap. 7.95 *(978-1-57091-734-9(5))* Charlesbridge Publishing, Inc.

Schreiber, Anne. Monkeys. 2013. (Readers Ser.). (ENG.). 32p. (J). (gr. k-3). pap. 3.99 *(978-1-4263-1106-2(0),* National Geographic Children's Bks.) National Geographic Society.

—National Geographic Readers: Monkeys. 2013. (Readers Ser.). (ENG.). 32p. (J). (gr. k-3). lib. bdg. 13.90 *(978-1-4263-1107-9(9),* National Geographic Children's Bks.) National Geographic Society.

Schreiber, Anne, et al. National Geographic Readers: Cutest Animals Collection. 2014. (Readers Ser.). (ENG.). 128p. (J). (gr. k-3). pap. 7.99 *(978-1-4263-1522-0(8),* National Geographic Children's Bks.) National Geographic Society.

Schuetz, Kari. Baby Monkeys. 2013. (Super Cute! Ser.). (ENG., Illus.). 24p. (J). (gr. k-3). lib. bdg. 25.95 *(978-1-60014-929-0(4),* Blastoff! Readers) Bellwether Media.

Sebe, Masayuki. 100 Hungry Monkeys!, 0 vols. Sebe, Masayuki, illus. 2014. (ENG., Illus.). 24p. (J). (gr. -1-2). 16.95 *(978-1-77138-045-4(4))* Kids Can Pr., Ltd. CAN. Dist: Hachette Bk. Group.

Steffora, Tracey. Animal Math: Comparing & Measuring, 1 vol. 2014. (Animal Math Ser.). (ENG.). 32p. (gr. -1-1). 29.99 *(978-1-4846-0062-7(2),* NA-h) Heinemann-Raintree.

—Measuring with Monkeys, 1 vol. 2013. (Animal Math Ser.). (ENG.). 24p. (gr. -1-1). 22.65 *(978-1-4329-7560-9(9));* pap. 6.95 *(978-1-4329-7567-8(6))* Heinemann-Raintree. (NA-h).

Stewart, Melissa. New World Monkeys. 2007. (Nature Watch Ser.). (ENG., Illus.). 48p. (J). (gr. 4-8). lib. bdg. 27.93 *(978-0-8225-6765-3(2),* Lerner Pubns.) Lerner Publishing Group.

Thatcher, Henry. Mandrills & Marmosets, 1 vol., 1. 2014. (Big Animals, Small Animals Ser.). (ENG.). 32p. (J). (gr. k-5). 26.25 *(978-1-4777-6118-2(7),* PowerKids Pr.) Rosen Publishing Group, Inc., The.

Throp, Claire. Monkeys, 1 vol. 2012. (Living in the Wild: Primates Ser.). (ENG.). 48p. (gr. 3-6). lib. bdg. 33.32 *(978-1-4329-5865-7(8),* Heinemann InfoSearch) Heinemann-Raintree.

Turner, Sarah Elizabeth. The Littlest Monkey, 1 vol. 2010. (ENG., Illus.). 32p. (J). (gr. -1-3). pap. 9.95 *(978-1-55039-174-9(7))* Sono Nis Pr. CAN. Dist: Orca Bk. Pubs. USA.

Twine, Alice. Monkeys. (Baby Animals Ser.). 24p. 2009. (gr. 1-1). 42.50 *(978-1-61511-493-1(9),* PowerKids Pr.) 2007. (Illus.). (J). (gr. -1-3). lib. bdg. 22.60 *(978-1-4042-3775-9(5))* Rosen Publishing Group, Inc., The.

—Monkeys/Monos. 2009. (Baby Animals/Animales bebé Ser.). (SPA.). 24p. (gr. 1-1). 42.50 *(978-1-61511-505-1(6),* Editorial Buenas Letras) Rosen Publishing Group, Inc., The.

—Monkeys/Monos. Obregon, Jose Maria, tr. 2007. (Baby Animals / Animales Bebé Ser.). (ENG & SPA., Illus.). 24p. (J). (gr. -1-3). lib. bdg. 22.60 *(978-1-4042-7635-2(1),* Editorial Buenas Letras) Rosen Publishing Group, Inc., The.

Wildlife Education, Ltd Staff, contrib. by. Monkeys. 2006. (Critters Up Close Ser.). (Illus.). (J). bds. 5.95 *(978-1-932396-15-7(2))* Wildlife Education, Ltd.

Williams, Zella. Howler Monkeys & Other Latin America Monkeys: Monos Aulladores y Otros Monos de Latino América. 2009. (Animals of Latin America / Animales de Latinoamérica Ser.). (SPA & ENG., Illus.). 24p. (J). pap. 8.25 *(978-1-4358-3384-5(8));* (gr. 1-3). lib. bdg. 22.60 *(978-1-4042-8127-1(4))* Rosen Publishing Group, Inc., The. (PowerKids Pr.).

Wilsdon, Christina. Monkeys. 2007. (J). *(978-1-59939-134-2(1),* Reader's Digest Young Families, Inc.) Studio Fun International.

Yasuda, Anita. Gibbons. 2014. (J). *(978-1-4896-2874-9(6))* Weigl Pubs., Inc.

—Monkey King: A Chinese Monkey Spirit Myth. 2014. (Short Tales Chinese Myths Ser.). 32p. (J). (gr. 3-6). lib. bdg. 24.21 *(978-1-62402-032-2(1),* Short Tales) Magic Wagon.

Zabludoff, Marc. Monkeys. 2007. (Animalways Ser.). (Illus.). 104p. (gr. 6-3). lib. bdg. 24.95 *(978-0-7614-2535-9(7),* Benchmark Bks.) Marshall Cavendish Corp.

MONKEYS—FICTION

Ackerman, Arlene. Glimmer de Gloop de Monkey Face: The Elf Named Pee-U & What He Knew. 2003. pap. 8.00 *(978-0-8059-6031-0(7))* Dorrance Publishing Co., Inc.

Adams, Ben. Chico Plays Hide & Seek. Cameron, Craig, illus. 2013. (Googly Eyes Ser.). (ENG.). 12p. (J). (gr. -1-k). bds. 6.99 *(978-1-84322-280-4(9),* Armadillo) Anness Publishing GBR. Dist: National Bk. Network.

Ainsworth, Kimberly. Little Monkey. Berg, Michelle, illus. 2008. (Little Green Bks.). (ENG.). 8p. (J). (gr. -1 — 1). 9.99 *(978-1-4169-6175-8(5),* Little Simon) Little Simon.

Alderfer, Lauren. Mindful Monkey, Happy Panda. MacLean, Kerry Lee, illus. 2011. (ENG.). 32p. (J). (gr. -1-3). 16.95 *(978-0-86171-683-8(3))* Wisdom Pubns.

Allen, Jonathan. Banana! Allen, Jonathan, illus. 2006. (Illus.). 32p. (J). pap. *(978-1-905417-02-5(0))* Boxer Bks., Ltd.

Amato, Mary. Missing Monkey! Jenkins, Ward, illus. 2014. (Good Crooks Ser.: Bk. 1). (ENG.). 128p. (J). (gr. 2-4). 4.99 *(978-1-60684-509-7(8));* 14.99 *(978-1-60684-396-3(6))* Lerner Publishing Group. (Darby Creek).

Anderson, Airlie. Momo & Snap. 2013. (Child's Play Library). (ENG., Illus.). 32p. (J). *(978-1-84643-603-1(6))* Child's Play International Ltd.

Anderson, R. P., et al. Happy Easter, Curious George. Young, Mary O'Keefe, illus. 2010. (Curious George Ser.). (ENG.). 24p. (J). (gr. -1-3). 9.99 *(978-0-547-04825-3(4))* Houghton Mifflin Harcourt Publishing Co.

Anholt, Laurence. A Kiss Like This. Anholt, Catherine, illus. 2009. (ENG.). 32p. (J). (gr. -1-1). pap. 7.95 *(978-1-84507-862-1(4),* Frances Lincoln) Quarto Publishing Group UK GBR. Dist: Hachette Bk. Group.

Anthony, David & Clasman, Charles David. Heroes A2Z #13: (Heroes a to Z): Monkey Monster Truck. Blakeslee, Lys, illus. 2012. 128p. (J). mass mkt. 4.99 *(978-0-9846528-1-5(7))* Sigil Publishing.

Ariel, A. D. The Tricky Monkey. 2016. (Spring Forward Ser.). (J). (gr. 2). *(978-1-4900-9441-0(5))* Benchmark Education Co.

Arnold, Audrey. Elkin's Tail. 2012. (Illus.). 52p. pap. 27.45 *(978-1-4772-2180-8(8))* AuthorHouse.

Auerbach, Adam. Monkey Brother. Auerbach, Adam, illus. 2017. (ENG., Illus.). 40p. (J). 17.99 *(978-1-62779-600-2(2),* 9781627796002, Holt, Henry & Co. Bks. For Young Readers) Holt, Henry & Co.

Award, Anna, et al. Monkey & the Fishermen & the Donkey in the Pond. 2014. (ENG.). 24p. (J). pap. 6.95 *(978-1-84135-956-4(4))* Award Pubns. Ltd. GBR. Dist: Parkwest Pubns., Inc.

Aylesworth, Jim. Naughty Little Monkeys. Cole, Henry, illus. 2006. (ENG.). 32p. (J). (gr. -1-2). reprint ed. 6.99 *(978-0-14-240562-8(0),* Puffin Books) Penguin Young Readers Group.

AZ Books, creator. Fidget Monkey. 2012. (Curious Eyes Ser.). (ENG., Illus.). 12p. (J). (gr. -1 — 1). bds. 12.95 *(978-1-61889-103-7(0))* AZ Bks. LLC.

Baltazar, Art & Aureliani, Franco. Monkey Metropolis!, 1 vol. Baltazar, Art, illus. 2013. (Superman Family Adventures Ser.). (ENG., Illus.). 32p. (gr. 1-2). 22.60 *(978-1-4342-4791-9(0))* Stone Arch Bks.

Banana-Tail. 2003. lib. bdg. 13.95 *(978-0-9727681-0-8(6))* Active Media Publishing, LLC.

Barragan, Sophia & Barragan, Ivy. Susana Banana the Fantastic Figure Skater. 2008. 32p. pap. 12.99 *(978-1-4389-0169-5(0))* AuthorHouse.

Barton, John. The Monkey Boy That Stood Up. 2012. (Illus.). 24p. pap. 19.82 *(978-1-4685-8581-0(9))* AuthorHouse.

Beard, Alex. Monkey See, Monkey Draw. 2011. (ENG., Illus.). 48p. (J). (gr. k-2). 17.95 *(978-0-8109-8970-2(0),* Abrams Bks. for Young Readers) Abrams, Inc.

Bell, Cece. Sock Monkey Boogie-Woogie. Bell, Cece, illus. 2015. (ENG., Illus.). 32p. (J). (gr. -1-3). 14.00 *(978-0-7636-7758-9(2))* Candlewick Pr.

—Sock Monkey Rides Again. Bell, Cece, illus. 2015. (ENG., Illus.). 32p. (J). (gr. -1-3). 14.00 *(978-0-7636-7760-2(4))* Candlewick Pr.

—Sock Monkey Takes a Bath. Bell, Cece, illus. 2015. (ENG., Illus.). 32p. (J). (gr. -1-3). 14.00 *(978-0-7636-7759-6(0))* Candlewick Pr.

Bentley, Douglas W. What Will It Take for a Toad to Kiss a Monkey: The Adventures of Princess Gracie & Prince Wallaby. Bentley, Julia Faye, illus. 2008. 52p. per. 24.95 *(978-1-4137-8849-5(1))* America Star Bks.

Benton, Lynne. The Sad Princess. Catling, Andy, illus. 2009. (Tadpoles Ser.). (ENG.). 24p. (J). (gr. k-2). pap. *(978-0-7787-3903-6(1))* Crabtree Publishing Co.

Beobi & the Magic Coloring Book A Visit to the Doctor. 2005. (J). 3.99 *(978-0-9743847-3-3(9))* Cohn, Tricia.

Beobi & the Magic Coloring Book Funland. 2006. (Illus.). 24p. (J). 3.99 *(978-0-9743847-7-1(1))* Cohn, Tricia.

Berenstain, Jan & Berenstain, Mike. The Berenstain Bears' Baby Easter Bunny. Berenstain, Jan & Berenstain, Mike, illus. 2008. (Berenstain Bears Ser.). (ENG., Illus.). 16p. (J). (gr. -1-1). pap. 6.99 *(978-0-06-057420-8(8),* HarperFestival) HarperCollins Pubs.

Beth, Libby. There's a Rainbow in the Mud. 2013. 52p. pap. 23.04 *(978-1-4669-9641-0(2))* Trafford Publishing.

Blackford, Andy. The Hungry Little Monkey. 2011. (Tadpoles Ser.). (ENG., Illus.). 24p. (J). (gr. k-2). lib. bdg. *(978-0-7787-0581-9(1));* pap. *(978-0-7787-0592-5(7))* Crabtree Publishing Co.

Blanks, Morgan Georgia. The Desert Island. 2008. 52p. pap. 20.49 *(978-1-4343-9006-6(3))* AuthorHouse.

Bloom, C. P. The Monkey & the Bee. Raymundo, Peter, illus. 2015. (Monkey Goes Bananas Ser.). (ENG.). 40p. (J). (gr. -1-2). 14.95 *(978-1-4197-0886-2(4),* Abrams Bks. for Young Readers) Abrams, Inc.

—The Monkey Goes Bananas. Raymundo, Peter, illus. 2014. (Monkey Goes Bananas Ser.). (ENG.). 40p. (J). (gr. k-2). 14.95 *(978-1-4197-0885-5(6),* Abrams Bks. for Young Readers) Abrams, Inc.

Boldt, Claudia. Melvin: The Luckiest Monkey in the World. 2013. (ENG., Illus.). 32p. (J). (gr. -1-k). 14.95 *(978-1-84976-086-7(1))* Tate Publishing, Ltd. GBR. Dist: Abrams, Inc.

Brian, Janeen. Maya Monkey, 1 vol. rev. ed. 2013. (Fiction Readers Ser.). (ENG., Illus.). 20p. (J). (gr. 1-1). pap. 15.96 *(978-1-4807-1142-6(X));* pap. 4.99 *(978-1-4333-5486-1(1))* Shell Educational Publishing.

Briley, Jennifer Lenore. Justin's Journey. 2008. 48p. pap. 16.95 *(978-1-60672-150-6(X))* America Star Bks.

Brimner, Larry Dane. Monkey Math. Kulka, Joe, illus. 2007. (Rookie Reader Skill Set Ser.). (ENG.). 32p. (J). (gr. k-2). pap. 4.95 *(978-0-531-13850-2(X))* Scholastic Library Publishing.

Brooks, Susie. Five Silly Monkeys. Tarbett, Debbie, illus. 2009. (ENG.). 14p. (J). (gr. k — 1). bds. 9.99 *(978-0-545-10222-3(7),* Cartwheel Bks.) Scholastic, Inc.

Brown, Alan James. Michael & the Monkey King. 2008. 180p. pap. 16.95 *(978-1-4092-0241-7(0))* Lulu Pr., Inc.

Brown, Marc. Monkey: Not Ready for Kindergarten. 2015. (ENG., Illus.). 32p. (J). (gr. -1-2). 12.99 *(978-0-553-49658-1(1),* Knopf Bks. for Young Readers) Random Hse. Children's Bks.

—Monkey: Not Ready for the Baby. 2016. (ENG., Illus.). 32p. (J). (gr. -1-2). 16.99 *(978-1-101-93327-5(5),* Knopf Bks. for Young Readers) Random Hse. Children's Bks.

Brown, Marc. Monkey: Not Ready for the Baby. 2017. (ENG.). 32p. (J). (gr. -1-2). 5.99 ***(978-0-399-55781-1(4),*** Dragonfly Bks.) Random Hse. Children's Bks.

Browne, Paula. El Cumpleanos de la Mona. Isabel, Isaias, tr. Browne, Paula, illus. 2004. (Paca, la Macaca Ser.). (SPA., Illus.). 20p. pap. 4.95 *(978-85-7416-214-0(0))* Callis Editora Ltda BRA. Dist: Independent Pubs. Group.

—Paca, la macaca en la Cocina. Isabel, Isaias, tr. Browne, Paula, illus. 2004. (Paca, la Macaca Ser.). (SPA., Illus.). 20p. pap. 4.95 *(978-85-7416-210-2(8))* Callis Editora Ltda BRA. Dist: Independent Pubs. Group.

—Paca, la Macaca va al Mercado. Isabel, Isaias, tr. Browne, Paula, illus. 2004. (Paca, la Macaca Ser.). (Illus.). 20p. pap. 4.95 *(978-85-7416-215-7(9))* Callis Editora Ltda BRA. Dist: Independent Pubs. Group.

—Que Desbarajuste, Paca. Isabel, Isaias, tr. Browne, Paula, illus. 2004. (Paca, la Macaca Ser.). (Illus.). 20p. pap. 6.95 *(978-85-7416-211-9(6))* Callis Editora Ltda BRA. Dist: Independent Pubs. Group.

Bruton, W., illus. The Dogs' Grand Dinner Party. 2011. (American Antiquarian Society Ser.). (ENG.). 16p. (gr. 1). 24.95 *(978-1-4290-9738-3(8))* Applewood Bks.

Burson, Ronda Pfohl. Monk-Monk the Monkey. 2010. 20p. 10.49 *(978-1-4520-0351-1(3))* AuthorHouse.

Campbell, Shirlene. Ook Ook the Monkey. 2013. 24p. pap. 24.95 *(978-1-63004-355-1(9))* America Star Bks.

Capucilli, Alyssa Satin. Monkey Play. 2012. (Step into Reading Ser.). (ENG., Illus.). 32p. (J). (gr. -1-1). pap. 3.99 *(978-0-375-86993-8(X)*, Random Hse. Bks. for Young Readers) Random Hse. Children's Bks.

Catalanotto, Peter. Monkey & Robot. Catalanotto, Peter, illus. (ENG., Illus.). 64p. (J). (gr. 1-4). 2014. pap. 5.99 *(978-1-4424-2979-6(8)*, Atheneum Bks. for Young Readers) 2013. 12.99 *(978-1-4424-2978-9(X)*, Atheneum/Richard Jackson Bks.) Simon & Schuster Children's Publishing.

—More of Monkey & Robot. Catalanotto, Peter, illus. 2014. (ENG., Illus.). 64p. (J). (gr. 1-4). 15.99 *(978-1-4424-5251-0(X)*, Atheneum/Richard Jackson Bks.) Simon & Schuster Children's Publishing.

Chamberlain, Nick. The Adventures of Papillon. 2008. 176p. pap. 15.95 *(978-1-60290-092-9(2))* OakTara Publishing Group LLC.

Chapman, Linda. Mr Monkey & the Fairy Tea Party. Hearn, Sam, illus. 2016. (Early Reader Ser.). (ENG.). 64p. (J). (gr. k-2). 6.99 *(978-1-4440-1552-2(4)*, Orion Children's Bks.) Hachette Children's Group GBR. Dist: Hachette Bk. Group.

Charles, Faustin. The Selfish Crocodile Book of Words. Terry, Michael, illus. 2012. (Selfish Crocodile Ser.). (ENG.). 12p. (J). (gr. -1-k). bds. 10.99 *(978-1-4088-1452-9(8)*, 9781408814529, Bloomsbury USA Childrens) Bloomsbury Publishing USA.

Charlesworth, Liza & Scholastic, Inc. Staff. Monkey's Missing Bananas. Sexton, Brenda, illus. 2005. (Number Tales Ser.). (ENG.). 16p. (J). (gr. -1-1). pap. 2.99 *(978-0-439-69032-4(3))* Scholastic, Inc.

Chen, Wei Dong. The Expulsion of Sun Wu Kong. Peng, Chao, illus. 2013. (Monkey King Ser.: 7). 176p. (YA). (gr. 6-12). lib. bdg. 29.27 *(978-89-94208-75-6(5))* Lerner Publishing Group.

—Fight to the Death. Peng, Chao, illus. 2013. (Monkey King Ser.: 11). 176p. (YA). (gr. 6-12). lib. bdg. 29.27 *(978-89-94208-79-4(8))* Lerner Publishing Group.

—The Lost Children. Peng, Chao, illus. 2013. (Monkey King Ser.: 12). 176p. (YA). (gr. 6-12). lib. bdg. 29.27 *(978-89-94208-80-0(1))* Lerner Publishing Group.

—Monkey King: Birth of the Stone Monkey. Peng, Chao, illus. 2012. (Monkey King Ser.: 1). (ENG.). 176p. (gr. 5-8). lib. bdg. 29.27 *(978-89-94208-69-5(0))* JR Comics KOR. Dist: Lerner Publishing Group.

—Monkey King: Enemies & a New Friend. Peng, Chao, illus. 2012. (Monkey King Ser.: 4). (ENG.). 176p. (gr. 5-8). lib. bdg. 29.27 *(978-89-94208-72-5(0))* JR Comics KOR. Dist: Lerner Publishing Group.

—Monkey King: Journey to the West. Peng, Chao, illus. 2012. (Monkey King Ser.: 3). (ENG.). 176p. (gr. 5-8). lib. bdg. 29.27 *(978-89-94208-71-8(2))* JR Comics KOR. Dist: Lerner Publishing Group.

—Monkey King: The Bane of Heaven. Peng, Chao, illus. 2012. (Monkey King Ser.: 2). (ENG.). 176p. (gr. 5-8). lib. bdg. 29.27 *(978-89-94208-70-1(4))* JR Comics KOR. Dist: Lerner Publishing Group.

—Monkey King: The Sacred Tree. Peng, Chao, illus. 2012. (Monkey King Ser.: 6). (ENG.). 176p. (gr. 5-8). lib. bdg. 29.27 *(978-89-94208-74-9(7))* JR Comics KOR. Dist: Lerner Publishing Group.

—Monkey King: Three Trials. Peng, Chao, illus. 2012. (Monkey King Ser.: 5). (ENG.). 176p. (gr. 5-8). lib. bdg. 29.27 *(978-89-94208-73-2(9))* JR Comics KOR. Dist: Lerner Publishing Group.

—The Realm of the Infant King. Peng, Chao, illus. 2013. (Monkey King Ser.: 10). 176p. (YA). (gr. 6-12). lib. bdg. 29.27 *(978-89-94208-78-7(X))* Lerner Publishing Group.

—The Stolen Kingdom. Peng, Chao, illus. 2013. (Monkey King Ser.: 9). 176p. (YA). (gr. 6-12). lib. bdg. 29.27 *(978-89-94208-77-0(1))* Lerner Publishing Group.

—Treasures of the Mountain Kings. Peng, Chao, illus. 2013. (Monkey King Ser.: 8). 176p. (YA). (gr. 6-12). lib. bdg. 29.27 *(978-89-94208-76-3(3))* Lerner Publishing Group.

Cheng'en, Wu. Journey to the West. Chiang, Shirley, illus. 2013. (Chinese Classics Ser.). (ENG.). 64p. pap. 6.95 *(978-1-906230-34-0(X))* Real Reads Ltd. GBR. Dist: Casemate Pubs. & Bk. Distributors, LLC.

Chin, Oliver. The Year of the Monkey: Tales from the Chinese Zodiac. Ono, Kenji, illus. 2015. (Tales from the Chinese Zodiac Ser.: 11). (ENG & CHI.). 36p. (J). (gr. -1). 15.95 *(978-1-59702-118-0(0))* Immedium.

Chojnowski, Bryan. Muffin Time: Origins. 2005. 98p. pap. 25.01 *(978-1-4116-4440-3(9))* Lulu Pr., Inc.

Choldenko, Gennifer. Putting the Monkeys to Bed. Davis, Jack E., illus. 2015. (ENG.). 32p. (J). (gr. -1-k). 16.99 *(978-0-399-24623-4(1)*, G.P. Putnam's Sons Books for Young Readers) Penguin Young Readers Group.

Christelow, Eileen. Cinco Monitos Colección de Oro. 2012. (Five Little Monkeys Story Ser.). (ENG & SPA., Illus.). 192p. (J). (gr. -1-3). 11.99 *(978-0-547-74593-0(1))* Houghton Mifflin Harcourt Publishing Co.

—Cinco Monitos Hacen un Pastel de Cumpleanos. 2014. (Five Little Monkeys Story Ser.).Tr. of Five Little Monkeys Bake a Birthday Cake. (ENG & SPA., Illus.). 30p. (J). (— 1). bds. 7.99 *(978-0-544-08899-3(9)*, HMH Books For Young Readers) Houghton Mifflin Harcourt Publishing Co.

—Cinco Monitos Sin Nada Que Hacer. 2014. (Five Little Monkeys Story Ser.).Tr. of Five Little Monkeys with Nothing to Do. (ENG & SPA., Illus.). 32p. (J). (— 1). bds. 7.99 *(978-0-544-08889-4(1)*, HMH Books For Young Readers) Houghton Mifflin Harcourt Publishing Co.

—Five Little Monkeys Bake a Birthday Cake. 2005. (Five Little Monkeys Story Ser.). (ENG., Illus.). 32p. (J). (gr. -1-3). pap. 6.99 *(978-0-618-49648-8(3))* Houghton Mifflin Harcourt Publishing Co.

—Five Little Monkeys Go Shopping. 2012. (Five Little Monkeys Story Ser.). lib. bdg. 17.20 *(978-0-606-23990-5(1)*, Turtleback) Turtleback Bks.

—Five Little Monkeys Jump in the Bath. 2012. (Five Little Monkeys Story Ser.). (ENG., Illus.). 20p. (J). (gr. k — 1). bds. 7.99 *(978-0-547-87527-9(4))* Houghton Mifflin Harcourt Publishing Co.

—Five Little Monkeys Jumping on the Bed Big Book. 2006. (Five Little Monkeys Story Ser.). (ENG., Illus.). 32p. (J). (gr. -1-3). 26.99 *(978-0-618-83682-6(9))* Houghton Mifflin Harcourt Publishing Co.

—Five Little Monkeys Jumping on the Bed Lap Board Book. 2008. (Five Little Monkeys Story Ser.). (ENG., Illus.). 30p. (J). (gr. -1 — 1). bds. 12.99 *(978-0-547-13176-4(3))* Houghton Mifflin Harcourt Publishing Co.

—Five Little Monkeys Play Hide & Seek. 2010. (Five Little Monkeys Story Ser.). lib. bdg. 17.20 *(978-0-606-14479-7(X)*, Turtleback) Turtleback Bks.

—Five Little Monkeys Reading in Bed. 2011. (Five Little Monkeys Story Ser.). (ENG., Illus.). 40p. (J). (gr. -1-3). 16.99 *(978-0-547-38610-2(9))* Houghton Mifflin Harcourt Publishing Co.

—Five Little Monkeys Set for Costco 2005. 2006. (J). bds. 0.01 *(978-0-618-73326-2(4)*, Clarion Bks.) Houghton Mifflin Harcourt Trade & Reference Pubs.

—Five Little Monkeys Sitting in a Tree. 2014. (Five Little Monkeys Story Ser.). (ENG & SPA., Illus.). 28p. (J). (— 1). bds. 7.99 *(978-0-544-30218-1(4)*, HMH Books For Young Readers) Houghton Mifflin Harcourt Publishing Co.

—Five Little Monkeys Sitting in a Tree Book & CD. 1 vol. 2007. (Five Little Monkeys Story Ser.). (ENG., Illus.). 32p. (J). (gr. -1-3). 10.99 *(978-0-618-85284-0(0))* Houghton Mifflin Harcourt Publishing Co.

—Five Little Monkeys Storybook Treasury. 2009. (Five Little Monkeys Story Ser.). (ENG., Illus.). 192p. (J). (gr. -1-3). 11.99 *(978-0-547-23873-9(8))* Houghton Mifflin Harcourt Publishing Co.

—Five Little Monkeys Travel Activity Kit. 2010. (Five Little Monkeys Story Ser.). (ENG., Illus.). 64p. (J). (gr. -1-3). 12.99 *(978-0-547-25879-9(8))* Houghton Mifflin Harcourt Publishing Co.

—Five Little Monkeys Trick-Or-Treat. 2013. (Five Little Monkeys Story Ser.). (ENG., Illus.). 40p. (J). (gr. -1-3). 16.99 *(978-0-547-85893-7(0))* Houghton Mifflin Harcourt Publishing Co.

—Five Little Monkeys Wash the Car. 2004. (Five Little Monkeys Story Ser.). (ENG., Illus.). 40p. (J). (gr. -1-3). 6.99 *(978-0-618-48602-1(X))* Houghton Mifflin Harcourt Publishing Co.

—Jumping on the Bed. 2017. (Five Little Monkeys Story Ser.). (ENG., Illus.). 30p. (J). (gr. -1 — 1). bds. 8.99 *(978-0-547-51075-0(6)*, HMH Books For Young Readers) Houghton Mifflin Harcourt Publishing Co.

Chuslo-Shur, Lauren, ed. The Golden Friendship. 2012. (ENG.). (J). pap. *(978-1-4675-4581-5(3))* Independent Pub.

Claiborn, Trevor M. The Monkey & the Forbidden Fruit. 2012. 112p. pap. 34.99 *(978-1-4772-0987-5(5))* AuthorHouse.

Clarke, Jane. How to Feed Your Cheeky Monkey. Birkett, Georgie, illus. 2017. 16p. (J). bds. 8.99 *(978-1-61067-497-3(9))* Kane Miller.

Cleveland, Rob. The Clever Monkey: A Folktale from West Africa. Hoffmire, Baird, illus. 2006. (Story Cove Ser.). (ENG.). 32p. (J). (gr. -1-3). pap. 4.95 *(978-0-87483-801-5(0))* August Hse. Pubs., Inc.

Cohn, Tricia L. Beobi & the Magic Coloring Book ABC First Words. 2003. (J). *(978-0-9743847-0-2(4))* Cohn, Tricia.

conrad, catherine. The Lemonade Stand. 2008. (Illus.). 32p. (J). lib. bdg. 16.99 *(978-0-9799065-0-3(4))* Banana Pr.

Cornell, Kevin. Mojo the Sock Monkey. 2005. 48p. (YA). pap. 15.99 *(978-1-4116-5713-7(6))* Lulu Pr., Inc.

Courtauld, Sarah. Monkeys Internet-Referenced. 2009. (First Reading Level 3 Ser.). 48p. (J). 6.99 *(978-0-7945-2290-2(4)*, Usborne) EDC Publishing.

Crenshaw, Glenda. Friends of the Enchanted Forest: How they Save Christmas. 2011. 28p. pap. 15.47 *(978-1-4520-0512-6(5))* AuthorHouse.

Curry, Kenneth. Priscilla & the Talking Monkey. 2007. (Illus.). 22p. (J). 10.95 *(978-0-9798364-6-6(8))* Curry Brothers Publishing Group.

Dahl, Roald. The Giraffe, the Pelly & Me. 2009. (Orig.). (gr. 3-6). 18.40 *(978-0-8085-9436-9(2)*, Turtleback) Turtleback Bks.

Dahl, Roald & Fitt, Matthew. The Eejits. Blake, Quentin, illus. 2006. (ENG.). 96p. (J). (gr. 1-7). pap. 7.99 ***(978-1-84502-097-2(9))*** Black and White Publishing Ltd. GBR. Dist: Independent Pubs. Group.

Dale, Jay. Big Green Crocodile, 1 vol. Hancock, Anna, illus. 2012. (Engage Literacy Blue Ser.). (ENG.). 32p. (gr. k-2). pap. 5.99 *(978-1-4296-8984-7(6)*, Engage Literacy) Capstone Press of Coughlan Cos.

—Min Monkey, 1 vol. Hancock, Anna, illus. 2012. (Engage Literacy Red Ser.). (ENG.). 32p. (gr. k-2). pap. 5.99 *(978-1-4296-8944-1(7)*, Engage Literacy) Capstone Press of Coughlan Cos.

—Up Here, 1 vol. Hancock, Anna, illus. 2012. (Engage Literacy Magenta Ser.). (ENG.). 32p. (gr. k-2). pap. 5.99 *(978-1-4296-8862-8(9)*, Engage Literacy) Capstone Press of Coughlan Cos.

de Brunhoff, Jean. Babar & Zephir. de Brunhoff, Jean, illus. 2005. (Illus.). 38p. (J). (gr. k-4). reprint ed. 16.00 *(978-0-7567-8935-0(4))* DIANE Publishing Co.

de la Mare, Walter. The Three Mulla-Mulgars. 2011. 196p. pap. 14.95 *(978-1-60664-560-4(9))* Rodgers, Alan Bks.

—The Three Mulla-Mulgars (The Three Royal Monkeys) Lathrop, Dorothy P., illus. 2013. (ENG.). 288p. (J). (gr. 3-6). pap. 12.95 *(978-0-486-49380-0(6))* Dover Pubns., Inc.

Deacon, Melissa. I Have a Monkey in My Tub! 2011. 32p. pap. 24.95 *(978-1-4626-2001-2(9))* America Star Bks.

Dean, James. Pete the Cat & the Bad Banana. Dean, James, illus. 2014. (My First I Can Read Ser.). (ENG., Illus.). 32p. (J). (gr. -1-3). pap. 3.99 *(978-0-06-230382-0(1))* HarperCollins Pubs.

Derdowski, Chad. All Robots Must Die: Nacho-Geddon. 2013. 187p. (J). pap. 7.99 *(978-1-933925-50-9(7)*, Agent of Danger) Komikwerks, LLC.

Deutsch, David. In Search of the Little People. l.t. ed. 2005. (Illus.). 60p. (J). per. 13.95 *(978-1-59879-013-9(7))* Lifevest Publishing, Inc.

Dharma Publishing Staff. The Monkey King: A Story about Compassion & Leadership. 2nd ed. 2013. (ENG.). 36p. (gr. -1-7). pap. 8.95 *(978-0-89800-495-3(0))* Dharma Publishing.

DiCamillo, Kate. Great Joy. Ibatoulline, Bagram, illus. 2010. (ENG.). 32p. (J). (gr. -1-3). 8.99 *(978-0-7636-4996-8(1))* Candlewick Pr.

Dixon, Chuck. Way of the Rat Traveler, Vol. 1. 2003. (Way of the Rat Traveler Ser.). (Illus.). 160p. (YA). pap. 9.95 *(978-1-59314-032-8(0))* CrossGeneration Comics, Inc.

Do, Kim-Thu, tr. from ENG. Tang Monk Disciples Monkey King: English/Vietnamese. Ma, Wenhai, illus. 2005. (Adventures of Monkey King Ser.: No. 3). (ENG & VIE.). 32p. (J). 16.95 *(978-1-57227-087-9(X))* Pan Asia Pubns. (USA), Inc.

Dockery, L. D. Michael Monkey Saves the Day. 2012. 30p. pap. 19.99 *(978-1-4772-6898-8(7))* AuthorHouse.

Dodd, Emma. More & More. Dodd, Emma, illus. 2014. (ENG., Illus.). 24p. (J). (-k). 12.99 *(978-0-7636-7543-1(1)*, Templar) Candlewick Pr.

Dombey, Elizabeth & Muldrow, Diane. How Do Penguins Play? Walker, David, illus. 2011. (Little Golden Book Ser.). (ENG.). 24p. (J). (gr. -1-k). 4.99 *(978-0-375-86501-5(2)*, Golden Bks.) Random Hse. Children's Bks.

Donaldson, Julia. Night Monkey, Day Monkey. Richards, Lucy, illus. 2016. (ENG.). 26p. (J). (gr. -1-k). bds. 10.99 *(978-1-4052-8334-2(3))* Egmont Bks., Ltd. GBR. Dist: Independent Pubs. Group.

—Where's My Mom? Scheffler, Axel, illus. 2008. (ENG.). 32p. (J). (gr. -1-2). 18.99 *(978-0-8037-3228-5(7)*, Dial Bks) Penguin Young Readers Group.

Donaldson, Julia & Richards, Lucy. Night Monkey, Day Monkey. 2012. (ENG., Illus.). 32p. (J). (gr. -1-k). pap. 10.99 *(978-0-7497-4893-7(1))* Egmont Bks., Ltd. GBR. Dist: Independent Pubs. Group.

Dong Chen, Wei. Band of Brothers. Peng, Chao, illus. 2013. (Monkey King Ser.: 18). (ENG.). 176p. (gr. 6-12). pap. 9.99 *(978-89-94208-63-3(1))* JR Comics KOR. Dist: Lerner Publishing Group.

—The Dual. Peng, Chao, illus. 2013. (Monkey King Ser.: 14). (ENG.). 176p. (gr. 6-12). pap. 9.99 *(978-89-94208-59-6(3))* JR Comics KOR. Dist: Lerner Publishing Group.

—Expulsion of Sun Wu. Peng, Chao, illus. 2013. (Monkey King Ser.: 7). (ENG.). 176p. (YA). (gr. 6-12). pap. 9.99 *(978-89-94208-51-0(8))* Lerner Publishing Group.

—Fanning the Flames. Peng, Chao, illus. 2013. (Monkey King Ser.: 15). (ENG.). 176p. (gr. 6-12). pap. 9.99 *(978-89-94208-60-2(7))* JR Comics KOR. Dist: Lerner Publishing Group.

—Fight to the Death. Peng, Chao, illus. 2013. (Monkey King Ser.: 11). (ENG.). 176p. (YA). (gr. 6-12). pap. 9.99 *(978-89-94208-56-5(9))* Lerner Publishing Group.

—Golden Temple. Peng, Chao, illus. 2013. (Monkey King Ser.: 16). (ENG.). 176p. (gr. 6-12). pap. 9.99 *(978-89-94208-61-9(5))* JR Comics KOR. Dist: Lerner Publishing Group.

—The Journey Ends. Peng, Chao, illus. 2013. (Monkey King Ser.: 20). (ENG.). 176p. (gr. 6-12). pap. 9.99 *(978-89-94208-65-7(8))* JR Comics KOR. Dist: Lerner Publishing Group.

—Lost Children. Peng, Chao, illus. 2013. (Monkey King Ser.: 12). (ENG.). 176p. (YA). (gr. 6-12). pap. 9.99 *(978-89-94208-57-2(7))* Lerner Publishing Group.

—Masters & Disciples. Peng, Chao, illus. 2013. (Monkey King Ser.: 19). (ENG.). 176p. (gr. 6-12). pap. 9.99 *(978-89-94208-64-0(X))* JR Comics KOR. Dist: Lerner Publishing Group.

—Realm of Infant King. Peng, Chao, illus. 2013. (Monkey King Ser.: 10). (ENG.). 176p. (YA). (gr. 6-12). pap. 9.99 *(978-89-94208-54-1(2))* Lerner Publishing Group.

—The Seven Sisters. Peng, Chao, illus. 2013. (Monkey King Ser.: 17). (ENG.). 176p. (gr. 6-12). pap. 9.99 *(978-89-94208-62-6(3))* JR Comics KOR. Dist: Lerner Publishing Group.

—Stolen Kingdom. Peng, Chao, illus. 2013. (Monkey King Ser.: 9). (ENG.). 176p. (YA). (gr. 6-12). pap. 9.99 *(978-89-94208-53-4(4))* Lerner Publishing Group.

—Treasures of the Mountain Kings. Peng, Chao, illus. 2013. (Monkey King Ser.: 8). (ENG.). 176p. (YA). (gr. 6-12). pap. 9.99 *(978-89-94208-52-7(6))* Lerner Publishing Group.

—Trust & Temptation. Peng, Chao, illus. 2013. (Monkey King Ser.: 13). (ENG.). 176p. (gr. 6-12). pap. 9.99 *(978-89-94208-58-9(5))* JR Comics KOR. Dist: Lerner Publishing Group.

Dong Chen, Wei & Peng, Chao. Bane of Heaven. 2012. (Monkey King Ser.: 2). (ENG., Illus.). 176p. (gr. 5-8). pap. 9.99 *(978-89-94208-46-6(1))* JR Comics KOR. Dist: Lerner Publishing Group.

—Birth of Stone Monkey. 2012. (Monkey King Ser.: 1). (ENG., Illus.). 176p. (gr. 5-8). pap. 9.99 *(978-89-94208-45-9(3))* JR Comics KOR. Dist: Lerner Publishing Group.

—Enemies & New Friend. 2012. (Monkey King Ser.: 4). (ENG., Illus.). 176p. (gr. 5-8). pap. 9.99 *(978-89-94208-48-0(8))* JR Comics KOR. Dist: Lerner Publishing Group.

—Journey to the West. 2012. (Monkey King Ser.: 3). (ENG., Illus.). 176p. (gr. 5-8). pap. 9.99 *(978-89-94208-47-3(X))* JR Comics KOR. Dist: Lerner Publishing Group.

—Sacred Tree. 2012. (Monkey King Ser.: 6). (ENG., Illus.). 176p. (gr. 5-8). pap. 9.99 *(978-89-94208-50-3(X))* JR Comics KOR. Dist: Lerner Publishing Group.

—Three Trials. 2012. (Monkey King Ser.: 5). (ENG., Illus.). 176p. (gr. 5-8). pap. 9.99 *(978-89-94208-49-7(6))* JR Comics KOR. Dist: Lerner Publishing Group.

Don't Let the Monkey Drive! 2004. (J). 10.95 *(978-0-9761350-1-2(9))* Murphey, Hiromi.

Dorling Kindersley Publishing Staff. Playtime. 2016. (Skills for Starting School Ser.). (ENG.). 18p. (J). (-k). 13.99 *(978-1-4654-5132-3(3)*, DK Children) Dorling Kindersley Publishing, Inc.

Drake, Christina M. Milo the Monkey. 2013. 88p. *(978-1-4602-2323-9(3))* FriesenPress.

Driscoll, Laura & Rey, H. A. Curious George at the Baseball Game. Hines, Anna Grossnickle, illus. 2006. (Curious George Ser.). (ENG.). 24p. (J). (gr. -1-3). pap. 4.99 *(978-0-618-66375-0(4))* Houghton Mifflin Harcourt Publishing Co.

Driscoll, Laura, et al. Curious George at the Baseball Game. Hines, Anna Grossnickle, illus. 2006. (Curious George Ser.). (ENG.). 24p. (J). (gr. -1-3). 13.99 *(978-0-618-66374-3(6))* Houghton Mifflin Harcourt Publishing Co.

Duckett, Brenda. Jeffrey & the blue Monkey. 2005. 32p. (J). spiral bd. 14.99 *(978-1-4116-5504-1(4))* Lulu Pr., Inc.

Durango, Julia. Cha-Cha Chimps. Taylor, Eleanor, illus. 2006. (ENG.). 32p. (J). (gr. -1-3). 17.99 *(978-0-689-86456-8(6)*, Simon & Schuster Bks. For Young Readers) Simon & Schuster Bks. For Young Readers.

Durant, Alan. I Love You Little Monkey. 2003. 32p. (J). *(978-0-7534-5555-5(2))* Kingfisher Publications, plc.

—I Love You, Little Monkey. McEwen, Katharine, illus. 2007. (ENG.). 32p. (J). (gr. -1-1). 15.99 *(978-1-4169-2481-4(7)*, Simon & Schuster Bks. For Young Readers) Simon & Schuster Bks. For Young Readers.

Elliot, Rachel. Monkey. East, Jacqueline, illus. 2009. (Wiggle-Waggles Ser.). (ENG.). 8p. (J). (gr. -1). bds. 4.99 *(978-0-7641-6238-1(1))* Barron's Educational Series, Inc.

Elliott, George. The Boy Who Loved Bananas. Krystoforski, Andrej, illus. 2005. 32p. (J). (gr. -1-2). 15.95 *(978-1-55337-744-3(3))* Kids Can Pr., Ltd. CAN. Dist: Hachette Bk. Group.

Elliott, Stacey "Sissy". What Kind of Bread Does a Monkey Eat ? 2011. 28p. pap. 15.99 *(978-1-4628-5921-4(6))* Xlibris Corp.

Emerson, Carl. Speed up, Sammy the Tree Sloth!, 1 vol. Trover, Zachary, illus. 2007. (Animal Underdogs Ser.). (ENG.). 32p. (gr. -1-3). 28.50 *(978-1-60270-019-2(2)*, Looking Glass Library) ABDO Publishing Co.

Erickson, John R. The Case of the Monkey Burglar. Holmes, Gerald L., illus. 2011. (Hank the Cowdog Ser.: No. 48). (ENG.). 129p. (J). (gr. 3-6). pap. 5.99 *(978-1-59188-148-3(X))* Maverick Bks., Inc.

—Hank the Cowdog & Monkey Business. Holmes, Gerald L., illus. 2011. (Hank the Cowdog Ser.). (ENG.). 110p. (J). (gr. 3-6). pap. 5.99 *(978-1-59188-114-8(5))* Maverick Bks., Inc.

Esphyr, Slobodkina & Slobodkina. Caps for Sale: A Tale of a Peddler, Some Monkeys & Their Monkey Business. 2014. (Reading Rainbow Bks). (ENG.). 48p. (J). 11.24 *(978-1-63245-155-2(7))* Lectorum Pubns., Inc.

Evans, Leah Beth. A Different Kind of Hero. Gedrich, Colleen, illus. 2007. 40p. (J). per. 14.95 *(978-0-9795045-2-5(X))* Tribute Bks.

Farkas, Steven E. Annie Pooh, Princess Pup, Monkey Shines. 2012. 40p. pap. 20.99 *(978-1-4772-9484-0(8))* AuthorHouse.

Fiani, M. A Cat Named Monkey. 2008. 24p. pap. 14.99 *(978-1-4389-1966-9(2))* AuthorHouse.

Find the Monkey. 2005. (J). *(978-0-9767179-2-8(1))* ABC Development, Inc.

Fitch, Sheree. There Were Monkeys in My Kitchen. braille ed. 2004. (Illus.). (J). (gr. k-3). spiral bd. *(978-0-616-01639-8(5))* Canadian National Institute for the Blind/Institut National Canadien pour les Aveugles.

Five Monkeys. 8p. (J). *(978-0-8136-3516-3(0))* Modern Curriculum Pr.

Foreman, Michael. Can't Catch Me! 2013. (Silver Tales Ser.). (ENG., Illus.). 28p. (J). (gr. -1-1). pap. *(978-1-74352-442-8(0))* Hinkler Bks. Pty, Ltd.

Fournier, Elizabeth. Sailboat Dreams: Monkey Island. 2012. 16p. pap. 15.99 *(978-1-4772-7670-9(X))* AuthorHouse.

Fox, Alex. Windsock Wesley & His Wild & Wonderful Weather MacHine, Living in Cloud. Bazzoni, Lainie M. A., illus. 2010. 48p. pap. 16.50 *(978-1-60911-873-0(1)*, Eloquent Bks.) Strategic Book Publishing & Rights Agency (SBPRA).

Fox, Mem. Two Little Monkeys. Barton, Jill, illus. 2012. (ENG.). 32p. (J). (gr. -1-3). 16.99 *(978-1-4169-8687-4(1)*, Beach Lane Bks.) Beach Lane Bks.

Franco, Betsy. Double Play: Monkeying Around with Addition. Cushman, Doug, illus. 2011. (ENG.). 32p. (J). (gr. -1-2). 15.99 *(978-1-58246-384-1(0)*, Tricycle Pr.) Random Hse. Children's Bks.

Freeman, Tina, illus. Ten Little Monkeys. 2004. (Classic Books with Holes Giant Board Book Ser.). (ENG.). 16p. (J). bds. *(978-0-85953-450-5(2))* Child's Play International Ltd.

Gail, Becky. How the Little White Monkey Became a Woman. 2008. 19p. pap. 24.95 *(978-1-60563-471-5(9))* America Star Bks.

Galloway, Ginger. Jasper. Zemke, Deborah, illus. 2003. (Books for Young Learners). (ENG.). 16p. (J). 5.75 net. *(978-1-57274-539-1(8)*, 2457, Bks. for Young Learners) Owen, Richard C. Pubs., Inc.

Garis, Howard Roger. Curly & Floppy Twistytail. 2005. 26.95 *(978-1-4218-1461-2(7))*; 164p. pap. 11.95 *(978-1-4218-1561-9(3))* 1st World Publishing, Inc. (1st World Library - Literary Society).

—Curly & Floppy Twistytail. 2004. reprint ed. pap. 19.95 *(978-1-4191-1479-3(4))*; pap. 1.99 *(978-1-4192-1479-0(9))* Kessinger Publishing, LLC.

—Umboo, the Elephant. 2005. 26.95 *(978-1-4218-0956-4(7))*; 132p. pap. 10.95 *(978-1-59540-656-9(5))* 1st World Publishing, Inc. (1st World Library - Literary Society).

Gates, Josephine Scribner. Nannette & the baby Monkey. 2007. (Illus.). 50p. (J). lib. bdg. 59.00 *(978-1-60304-020-4(X))* Dollworks.

Gill, Raj. A Monkey Ate My Pancakes. 2013. (ENG.). 34p. pap. 10.95 *(978-1-927005-28-6(0))* Burman Books, Inc. CAN. Dist: Innovative Logistics.

Gillingham, Sara. In My Jungle. Siminovich, Lorena, illus. 2011. (ENG.). 12p. (J). (gr. -1 — 1). bds. 8.99 *(978-0-8118-7716-9(7))* Chronicle Bks. LLC.

Graves, Keith. Second Banana. 2015. (ENG., Illus.). 32p. (J). (gr. 2-5). 17.99 *(978-1-59643-883-5(5)*, 9781596438835) Roaring Brook Pr.

Gravett, Emily. Monkey & Me. Gravett, Emily, illus. 2008. (ENG., Illus.). 32p. (J). (gr. -1-3). 17.99 *(978-1-4169-5457-6(0)*, Simon & Schuster Bks. For Young Readers) Simon & Schuster Bks. For Young Readers.

Greco, Francesca. Cyril the Mandrill, 1 vol. 2004. (ENG., Illus.). 32p. (J). (gr. -1 — 1). 16.95 *(978-1-932065-92-3(X))* Star Bright Bks., Inc.

Greene, Rhonda Gowler. Mail Monkeys. Bender, Robert, illus. 2006. (J). pap. *(978-1-58669-217-9(8))* Childcraft Education Corp.

Hager, Mickey. Clarence Duntz & the Monkey Spell. 2010. 62p. pap. 11.33 *(978-0-557-14381-8(0))* Lulu Pr., Inc.

Haidar, Hanna. Earl's Big Adventure in Costa Rica. Newton, Kimberly, illus. 2nd ed. 2012. 22p. (J). *(978-0-9800975-2-8(5))* Old Silver Pr.

—Earl's Big Adventure in Japan. Newton, Kimberly, illus. 2012. 26p. (J). *(978-0-9800975-1-1(7))* Old Silver Pr.

Hall, Bureda Ann Greathouse. Stories of My Little Blue Monkey. 2007. (Illus.). 32p. (J). pap. 15.00 *(978-0-8059-7397-6(4))* Dorrance Publishing Co., Inc.

Hall, Jennifer. Reginald's Broken Arm. 2008. 28p. pap. 16.95 *(978-1-4343-7532-2(3))* AuthorHouse.

Hamburg, Jennifer. Monkey & Duck Quack Up! Fotheringham, Edwin, illus. 2015. (ENG.). 32p. (J). (gr. -1-3). 17.99 *(978-0-545-64514-0(X),* Scholastic Pr.) Scholastic, Inc.

Hamilton, Linda. The Big-Hearted Monkey & the Crocodile. 2005. (J). *(978-1-933248-01-1(7))* World Quest Learning.

Hammersiough, Jane. Langur Monkey's Day. Buelt, Laura, illus. 2005. (Wild Reading Adventures! Ser.). (ENG.). 36p. (J). (gr. -1-2). 9.95 *(978-1-59249-144-5(8),* PS7156); 2.95 *(978-1-59249-143-8(X),* S7156) Soundprints.

—Langur Monkey's Day. Buelt, Laura, tr. Buelt, Laura, illus. 2005. (Wild Reading Adventures! Ser.). (ENG.). 36p. (J). (gr. -1-2). 15.95 *(978-1-59249-141-4(3),* B7106); pap. 6.95 *(978-1-59249-142-1(1),* S7106) Soundprints.

—Langur Monkey's Day. Buelt, Laura, illus. 2005. (Wild Reading Adventures! Ser.). (ENG.). 32p. (J). (gr. -1-2). 19.95 *(978-1-59249-221-3(5),* BC7106); 8.95 *(978-1-59249-222-0(3),* SC7106) Soundprints.

Hammersiough, Jane & Smithsonian Institution Staff. Langur Monkey's Day. Buelt, Laura, illus. rev. ed. 2008. (ENG.). 24p. (J). (gr. -1-3). 4.99 *(978-1-59249-706-5(3),* Little Soundprints) Soundprints.

Hana's Year: Evaluation Guide. 2006. (J). *(978-1-55942-408-0(7))* Witcher Productions.

Hansell, Robin. Mason & Monkey's Big Adventure. 2013. 52p. pap. 23.99 *(978-1-4808-0254-4(9))* Archway Publishing.

Hanson, Anders. Monkey Business, 1 vol. Chawla, Neena, illus. 2006. (Animal Tales Ser.). 24p. (J). (gr. k-3). (ENG.). lib. bdg. 24.21 *(978-1-59679-951-6(X),* SandCastle); pap. 48.42 *(978-1-59679-952-3(8))* ABDO Publishing Co.

Hapka, Catherine, pseud & Rey, H. A. Curious George's Dinosaur Discovery. Hines, Anna Grossnickle, illus. 2006. (Curious George Ser.). (ENG.). 24p. (J). (gr. -1-3). pap. 4.99 *(978-0-618-66377-4(0))* Houghton Mifflin Harcourt Publishing Co.

Harris, Stephanie C. The Wonders of Monkey Mac! 2009. 302p. pap. 15.95 *(978-1-60693-257-5(8),* Eloquent Bks.) Strategic Book Publishing & Rights Agency (SBPRA).

Hasany, Syed M. Stop the Train, Monkey! 2013. 28p. pap. 16.09 *(978-1-4669-7792-1(2))* Trafford Publishing.

Hascamp, Steve, illus. Eight Silly Monkeys. 2006. (ENG.). 18p. (J). 9.95 *(978-1-58117-186-0(2),* Intervisual/Piggy Toes) Bendon, Inc.

Haskamp, Steve, illus. Five Silly Monkeys. 2006. (ENG.). 12p. (J). bds. 14.95 *(978-1-58117-264-5(8),* Intervisual/Piggy Toes) Bendon, Inc.

—Ocho Monitos. 2005.Tr. of Eight Silly Monkeys. (SPA & ENG.). 18p. (J). 9.95 *(978-1-58117-334-5(2),* Intervisual/Piggy Toes) Bendon, Inc.

Haskamp, Steven, illus. Eight Silly Monkeys. 2007. (ENG.). 18p. (J). (gr. -1-3). bds. 15.95 *(978-1-58117-577-6(9),* Intervisual/Piggy Toes) Bendon, Inc.

—Five Silly Monkeys. 2006. (ENG.). 12p. (J). (gr. -1-k). 12.95 *(978-1-58117-460-1(8),* Intervisual/Piggy Toes) Bendon, Inc.

Heck, Ed. Monkey Lost. 2005. (Illus.). 32p. (J). 15.95 *(978-0-689-04633-9(2),* Milk & Cookies) ibooks, Inc.

Hevesi, Rachel. I Am a Monkey. Tyson, Liz, illus. 2008. 44p. pap. *(978-1-906210-75-5(6))* Grosvenor Hse. Publishing Ltd.

—Peppy - a Long Way from Home. Parathian, Hannah, illus. 2008. 48p. pap. *(978-1-906210-76-2(4))* Grosvenor Hse. Publishing Ltd.

Higginson, Sheila Sweeny & Disney Book Group Staff. Bubble Trouble. Disney Storybook Artists Staff & Disney Storybook Art Team, illus. 2013. (ENG.). 24p. (J). (gr. -1-k). pap. 4.99 *(978-1-4231-6454-8(7))* Disney Pr.

Hodgson, Jesse. Pongo. 2013. (ENG., Illus.). 32p. (J). (gr. -1-2). 16.95 *(978-1-909263-09-3(5))* Flying Eye Bks. GBR. Dist: Consortium Bk. Sales & Distribution.

Holden, Pam. The Flying Monkey, 6 pack. East, Jacqueline, illus. 2009. (Red Rocket Readers Ser.). (ENG.). 16p. (gr. -1-1). pap. *(978-1-877363-29-0(4),* Red Rocket Readers) Flying Start Bks.

—Max Monkey, 6 pack. East, Jacqueline, illus. 2009. (Red Rocket Readers Ser.). (ENG.). 16p. (gr. -1-1). pap. *(978-1-877363-24-5(3),* Red Rocket Readers) Flying Start Bks.

Hood, Sue. Monkey Business. Chapman, Susan, illus. 2005. (J). bds. *(978-1-890647-17-9(9))* TOMY International, Inc.

Horn, Neithard. Evi, My Little Monkey: A Good Night Book for You & for Grown-ups, Too, 1 vol. 2011. (ENG., Illus.). 32p. (J). 16.99 *(978-0-7643-3827-4(7),* 9780764338274, Schiffer Publishing Ltd) Schiffer Publishing, Ltd.

Horne, Constance. Emily Carr's Woo. Calvert, Lissa, illus. 2005. (ENG.). 72p. (J). pap. 9.95 *(978-0-88982-149-1(6))* Oolichan Bks. CAN. Dist: Univ. of Toronto Pr.

Horowitz, Dave. A Monkey among Us. Horowitz, Dave, illus. 2004. (Illus.). 40p. (J). (gr. -1-1). 14.99 *(978-0-06-054335-8(3),* HarperFestival) HarperCollins Pubs.

Houghton Mifflin Harcourt Publishing Company Staff & Rey, H. A. Start Your Engines 5-Minute Stories. 2014. (5-Minute Stories Ser.). (ENG., Illus.). 224p. (J). (gr. -1-3). 12.99 *(978-0-544-15881-8(4),* HMH Books For Young Readers) Houghton Mifflin Harcourt Publishing Co.

Howell, Gill. Tortoise & the Baboon. Woody, illus. 2004. (ENG.). 16p. (J). lib. bdg. 23.65 *(978-1-59646-686-9(3))* Dingles & Co.

Hudson, Charlotte & Gormley, Greg. Monkey Words. 2003. (ENG., Illus.). 32p. (J). 19.99 *(978-0-370-32636-8(9))* Random Hse. GBR. Dist: Independent Pubs. Group.

Hutcheson, John C. Tom Finch's Monkey. 2004. reprint ed. pap. 1.99 *(978-1-4192-9041-1(X))*; pap. 15.95 *(978-1-4191-9041-4(5))* Kessinger Publishing, LLC.

Idiaghe, Efosa Francis. A Day of a Monkey: Tricky the Monkey. 2012. 20p. pap. 13.77 *(978-1-4669-4158-8(8))* Trafford Publishing.

ImageBooks Staff. Little Monkey. Put, Klaartje van der, illus. 2013. (Little Finger Puppet Board Bks.). (ENG.). 12p. (J). (gr. -1 — 1). bds. 6.99 *(978-1-4521-1250-3(9))* Chronicle Bks. LLC.

Inches, Alison. Súper Bebés! Miller, Victoria, illus. 2006. (Dora la Exploradora Ser.). (SPA.). 24p. (J). (gr. -1-3). pap. 3.99 *(978-1-4169-2461-6(2),* Libros Para Ninos) Libros Para Ninos.

Jarvis. Fred Forgets. Jarvis, illus. 2016. (Illus.). 32p. (J). (gr. -1-3). 17.99 *(978-0-06-234916-3(3))* HarperCollins Pubs.

Jenkins, Henry A. The Adventures of Monkey Squirrel & Frogman: Sand Trap. 2009. 16p. pap. 8.49 *(978-1-4343-7827-9(6))* AuthorHouse.

Jin, Susie Lee, illus. It's Bedtime for Little Monkeys. 2010. (ENG.). 5p. (J). bds. 5.99 *(978-0-7369-2832-8(4))* Harvest Hse. Pubs.

Johnson, Myrna. Let's Take a Hike. 2013. (ENG., Illus.). 32p. (gr. -1-1). pap. 13.95 *(978-1-936205-79-0(3))* Austin, Stephen F. State Univ. Pr.

Jones, David. Baboon. 2007. (ENG.). 176p. (J). (gr. 5-9). 21.95 *(978-1-55451-054-2(6),* 9781554510542); 4th ed. pap. 11.95 *(978-1-55451-053-5(8),* 9781554510535) Annick Pr., Ltd. CAN. Dist: Publishers Group West (PGW).

Jones, Gareth P. The Eye of the Monkey. Finlayson, Luke, illus. 2013. (Ninja Meerkats Ser.: 2). (ENG.). 128p. (J). (gr. 2-4). pap. 5.99 *(978-1-250-01665-2(7),* 9781250016652) Square Fish.

Jordan, Apple. Baboons! (Disney Junior: the Lion Guard) RH Disney, illus. 2017. (Little Golden Book Ser.). (ENG.). 24p. (J). (-k). 4.99 *(978-0-7364-3563-5(8),* Golden/Disney) Random Hse. Children's Bks.

Jordan, Christina. I Wish I Were a Howler Monkey, 1 vol. Utomo, Gabhor, illus. 2011. (I Wish I Were ... Ser.). (ENG.). 24p. (J). (gr. k-3). 28.50 *(978-1-61641-657-7(2))* Magic Wagon.

Jordan, Mark. Courage the Monkey. 2006. (Illus.). 40p. (J). 13.95 *(978-0-9717013-7-3(7))* Decere Publishing.

Joy, Eliza. The Blue Monkey. 2012. (Illus.). 12p. pap. 18.30 *(978-1-4685-8265-9(8))* AuthorHouse.

Juhasz, Mike. Posey & Mosey Go Camping. Juhasz, Brenda, illus. 2008. 16p. pap. 24.95 *(978-1-60610-258-9(3))* America Star Bks.

Juliette, the Modern Art Monkey: Individual Title Six-Packs. (Bookweb Ser.). 32p. (gr. 5-18). 34.00 *(978-0-7635-3776-0(4))* Rigby Education.

Kamau, G. How Porcupine Got His Spines. 2004. (Illus.). 26p. pap. *(978-9966-25-168-8(5))* Heinemann Kenya, Limited (East African Educational Publishers Ltd E.A.E.P.) KEN. Dist: Michigan State Univ. Pr.

Kann, Victoria. Pinkalicious & the Pinkatastic Zoo Day. 2012. (Pinkalicious I Can Read Ser.). (J). lib. bdg. 13.55 *(978-0-606-26527-0(9),* Turtleback) Turtleback Bks.

Kelsey-Livin, Barbara. The Monkey & the Frog. 2012. 30p. 24.95 *(978-1-4626-6161-9(0))* America Star Bks.

Kienzle, Jackie. It's a Monkey's Life. 2011. (J). 32p. 31.99 *(978-1-4568-4353-3(2))*; 36p. pap. 21.99 *(978-1-4568-4352-6(4))* Xlibris Corp.

Kitunga, Demere. Lupompo & the Baby Monkey. 2004. (Illus.). 36p. pap. *(978-9987-411-21-4(5))* E & D Ltd TZA. Dist: Michigan State Univ. Pr.

Koller, Jackie French. One Monkey Too Many. Munsinger, Lynn, illus. 2003. (ENG.). 32p. (J). (gr. -1-3). pap. 7.99 *(978-0-15-204764-1(6))* Houghton Mifflin Harcourt Publishing Co.

Kramer, Adam. Monkey of the Month, 1 vol. Kramer, David, illus. 2012. (ENG.). 40p. (J). 16.99 *(978-0-7643-4156-4(1),* 9780764341564) Schiffer Publishing, Ltd.

Kravetz, Nathan. A Monkey's Tale. 2012. 64p. (gr. 4-6). pap. 8.95 *(978-1-4759-5825-6(0))* iUniverse, Inc.

Kulling, Monica. When Emily Carr Met Woo, 1 vol. Griffiths, Dean, illus. 2014. (ENG.). 32p. (J). (gr. k-4). 17.95 *(978-1-927485-40-8(1))* Pajama Pr. CAN. Dist: Ingram Publisher Services.

Ladybird. Anansi Helps a Friend, Level 1. 2016. (Ladybird Readers Ser.). (ENG.). 16p. (J). (gr. 2-4). pap., act. bk. ed. 5.99 *(978-0-241-25420-2(5))* Penguin Bks., Ltd. GBR. Dist: Independent Pubs. Group.

Laird, Elizabeth & Davison, Roz. Jungle School. Sim, David, illus. 2006. (Green Bananas Ser.). (ENG.). 48p. (J). (gr. -1-3). *(978-0-7787-1042-4(4))*; lib. bdg. *(978-0-7787-1026-4(2))* Crabtree Publishing Co.

Landstrom, Lena. A Hippo's Tale. Sandin, Joan, tr. from SWE. 2007. (Illus.). 32p. (J). (gr. -1-1). 15.00 *(978-91-29-66603-8(1))* R & S Bks. SWE. Dist: Macmillan.

Lansky, Bruce. Monkey See, Monkey Do at the Zoo. Wummer, Amy, illus. 2010. 10p. (J). bds. 6.99 *(978-1-4169-9317-9(7))* Meadowbrook Pr.

LaReau, Kara. Rocko & Spanky Call It Quits. LaReau, Jenna, illus. 2008. (Rocko & Spanky Ser.). 40p. (J). 16.00 *(978-0-15-216611-3(4))* Harcourt Children's Bks.

Law, Felicia & Way, Steve. Castaway Code: Sequencing in Action. Law, Felicia et al, illus. 2010. (Mandrill Mountain Math Mysteries Ser.). 32p. (J). (gr. 2-6). 22.60 *(978-1-60754-817-1(8))*; pap. 10.55 *(978-1-60754-822-5(4))* Windmill Bks.

—Crocodile Teeth: Geometric Shapes in Action. Spoor, Mike & Mostyn, David, illus. 2010. (Mandrill Mountain Math Mysteries Ser.). 32p. (J). (gr. 2-6). 22.60 *(978-1-60754-816-4(X))*; pap. 10.55 *(978-1-60754-821-8(6))* Windmill Bks.

—Mirage in the Mist: Measurement in Action. Spoor, Mike & Mostyn, David, illus. 2010. (Mandrill Mountain Math Mysteries Ser.). 32p. (J). (gr. 2-6). pap. 10.55 *(978-1-60754-823-2(2))* Windmill Bks.

—Mirage in the Mist: Measurements in Action. Spoor, Mike & Mostyn, David, illus. 2010. (Mandrill Mountain Math Mysteries Ser.). 32p. (J). (gr. 2-6). 22.60 *(978-1-60754-818-8(6))* Windmill Bks.

—The Mystery of Nine: Number Place & Value in Action. Spoor, Mike & Mostyn, David, illus. 2010. (Mandrill Mountain Math Mysteries Ser.). 32p. (J). (gr. 2-6). 22.60 *(978-1-60754-819-5(4))*; pap. 10.55 *(978-1-60754-824-9(0))* Windmill Bks.

—A Storm at Sea: Sorting, Mapping, & Grids in Action. Spoor, Mike & Mostyn, David, illus. 2010. (Mandrill Mountain Math Mysteries Ser.). 32p. (J). (gr. 2-6). 22.60 *(978-1-60754-815-7(1))*; pap. 10.55 *(978-1-60754-820-1(8))* Windmill Bks.

Lawati, A. The Jungle Adventure of Chimpoo. 2011. 40p. pap. 21.99 *(978-1-4634-2921-8(5))* AuthorHouse.

Leatham, Alan D. Four Cats, Five Monkeys, Absurd Birds & Other Fanciful Stuff. 2006. 108p. pap. 19.95 *(978-1-4241-0692-9(3))* America Star Bks.

Lee, Karen. Mushy Mashed Bananas. Lee, Karen, illus. 2012. (Illus.). 24p. pap. *(978-1-4602-0136-7(1))* FriesenPress.

Lehrhaupt, Adam. Warning: Do Not Open This Book! Forsythe, Matthew, illus. 2013. (ENG.). 40p. (J). (gr. -1-3). 17.99 *(978-1-4424-3582-7(8),* Simon & Schuster Bks. For Young Readers) Simon & Schuster Bks. For Young Readers.

Lemonade Zoo Monkeys. 2006. (Illus.). 33p. (YA). 10.95 *(978-0-9765321-2-5(3))* Taven Hill Studio.

Lewis, J. Patrick. That's What Friends Are For. Denise, Christopher, illus. 2012. (I Am A Reader! Ser.). (ENG.). 40p. (gr. k-3). pap. 3.99 *(978-1-58536-687-3(0))* Sleeping Bear Pr.

—Tugg & Teeny. Denise, Christopher, illus. 2011. (I am a Reader Ser.). (ENG.). 40p. (J). (gr. k-2). pap. 3.99 *(978-1-58536-685-9(4))*; Bk. 1. lib. bdg. 9.95 *(978-1-58536-514-2(9))* Sleeping Bear Pr.

—Tugg & Teeny: That's What Friends Are For. Denise, Christopher, illus. 2012. (I Am A Reader! Ser.). (ENG.). 40p. (gr. k-3). lib. bdg. 9.95 *(978-1-58536-516-6(5))* Sleeping Bear Pr.

—Tugg & Teeny - Jungle Suprises, Bk. 2. Denise, Christopher, illus. 2011. (I am a Reader Ser.). (ENG.). 40p. (J). (gr. k-2). lib. bdg. 9.95 *(978-1-58536-515-9(7))* Sleeping Bear Pr.

—Tugg & Tweeny - Jungle Surprises, Bk. 2. Denise, Christopher, illus. 2011. (I am a Reader Ser.). (ENG.). 40p. (J). (gr. k-2). pap. 3.99 *(978-1-58536-686-6(2))* Sleeping Bear Pr.

Lindgren, Astrid. Do You Know Pippi Longstocking? Dyssegaard, Elisabeth Kallick, tr. Nyman, Ingrid, illus. 2005. 32p. (J). pap. 4.95 *(978-91-29-66203-0(6))* R & S Bks. SWE. Dist: Macmillan.

Little Monkey & Friends. (Flocked Soft-to-Touch Board Ser.). 5p. bds. *(978-1-4054-9504-2(9))* Parragon, Inc.

Lloyd, Sam R. Yummy Yummy! Food for My Tummy. Tickle, Jack, illus. 2004. 32p. (J). tchr. ed. 15.95 *(978-1-58925-035-2(4))* Tiger Tales.

Lonczak, Heather Suzanne. Mookey the Monkey Gets over Being Teased. Ramsey, Marcy Dunn, illus. 2006. 32p. (J). (gr. -1-3). 9.95 *(978-1-59147-480-7(9))*; 14.95 *(978-1-59147-479-1(5))* American Psychological Assn. (Magination Pr.).

Lopez, Maria Lorena. The Bird's Party, Birds in the Tropical Dry Forest. 2009. 28p. pap. 13.00 *(978-1-60860-156-1(0),* Eloquent Bks.) Strategic Book Publishing & Rights Agency (SBPRA).

Lucas, David. Peanut. Lucas, David, illus. 2008. (ENG., Illus.). 32p. (J). (gr. k-k). 15.99 *(978-0-7636-3925-9(7))* Candlewick Pr.

Lumry, Amanda & Hurwitz, Laura. Operation Orangutan. 2007. (Adventures of Riley (Unnumberd) Ser.). (Illus.). 36p. (J). (gr. -1-3). 18.95 *(978-0-9748411-7-5(X))* Eaglemont Pr.

Ma, Wenhai, illus. Tang Monk Disciples Monkey King. 2005. (Adventures of Monkey King Ser.: No. 3). 32p. (J). 16.95 *(978-1-57227-084-8(5))* Pan Asia Pubns. (USA), Inc.

—Tang Monk Disciples Monkey King: English/Chinese. 2005. (Adventures of Monkey King Ser.: No. 3). (ENG & CHI.). 32p. (J). 16.95 *(978-1-57227-086-2(1))* Pan Asia Pubns. (USA), Inc.

Mackall, Dandi Daley. No, No Noah!, 1 vol. Kucharik, Elena, illus. 2007. (ENG.). 26p. (gr. -1-k). bds. 6.99 *(978-1-4003-1007-4(5))* Nelson, Thomas Inc.

MacLeod, Jennifer Tzivia. Yossi & the Monkeys: A Shavuot Story. Waisman, Shirley, illus. 2017. (ENG.). 32p. (gr. -1-3). 17.99 *(978-1-4677-8932-5(1),* Kar-Ben Publishing) Lerner Publishing Group.

Madison, Paul. The Purple Monkey. 2012. (Illus.). 32p. pap. 17.25 *(978-1-4669-3909-7(5))* Trafford Publishing.

Malone, D. L. 52 Purple Monkeys. 2009. 24p. pap. 24.95 *(978-1-60749-085-2(4))* America Star Bks.

Margaret. Curious George im Schokolade. 20.95 *(978-3-8157-2329-6(9))* Coppenrath, F. Verlag KG DEU. Dist: Distribooks, Inc.

—Curious George und der Lastwa. 20.95 *(978-3-8157-2327-2(2))* Coppenrath, F. Verlag KG DEU. Dist: Distribooks, Inc.

—Curious George und der Seltsa. 20.95 *(978-3-8157-2330-2(2))* Coppenrath, F. Verlag KG DEU. Dist: Distribooks, Inc.

—Curious George und die Hundelb. 20.95 *(978-3-8157-2328-9(0))* Coppenrath, F. Verlag KG DEU. Dist: Distribooks, Inc.

Marinaro, Stacy. Treasure Monkey. 2008. 32p. pap. 15.95 *(978-1-4357-2840-0(8))* Lulu Pr., Inc.

Maroulis, Danielle. Monk in the Trunk. 2011. 24p. (gr. 1-2). pap. 13.99 *(978-1-4634-0598-4(7))* AuthorHouse.

Martin, Alison J. Charlie, the Brave Monkey. Martin, Alison J., illus. 2013. (Illus.). 24p. pap. 13.97 *(978-1-62516-155-0(7),* Strategic Bk. Publishing) Strategic Book Publishing & Rights Agency (SBPRA).

Martin, Bill & Sampson, Michael R. Spunky Little Monkey. Won, Brian, illus. 2017. (ENG.). 32p. (J). (gr. -1-k). 17.99 *(978-0-545-77643-1(0),* Scholastic Pr.) Scholastic, Inc.

Mason, Albert. Ooshu the Monkey Escapes from the Zoo. 2009. 40p. pap. 16.99 *(978-1-4389-0974-5(8))* AuthorHouse.

Mason, Albert D. Ooshu & Dorothy's Cricket. 2011. 36p. pap. 15.99 *(978-1-4567-1667-7(0))* AuthorHouse.

McBrayer, Cassidy. You Can, Toucan! You Can. 2008. 20p. pap. 15.95 *(978-1-4327-1132-0(6))* Outskirts Pr., Inc.

McCarroll, Barbara. Tongue Turning Tales for the Classroom. Godfrey, Arthur Dwayne, illus. 2008. 36p. pap. 24.95 *(978-1-60703-254-0(6))* America Star Bks.

McDermott, Gerald. Monkey: A Trickster Tale from India. (ENG., Illus.). 32p. (J). (gr. -1-3). 2014. pap. 7.99 *(978-0-544-33918-7(5),* HMH Books For Young Readers) 2011. 16.99 *(978-0-15-216596-3(7))* Houghton Mifflin Harcourt Publishing Co.

Mcevoy, Ariane. Little Monkey Learns to Share. 2012. 28p. pap. 15.99 *(978-1-4691-5830-3(2))* Xlibris Corp.

McKenna, Mark, creator. Banana Tail's Tales & Activities. 2006. (Illus.). (J). 4.95 *(978-0-9727681-5-4(4))* McKenna, Mark.

McKenna, Mark, et al, illus. Banana Tail. 2003. 32p. (J). 12.95 *(978-0-9727681-3-9(0))* Active Media Publishing, LLC.

McNeil, Niki, et al. HOCPP 1069 Curious George Rides a Bike. 2006. spiral bd. 15.50 *(978-1-60308-069-9(4))* In the Hands of a Child.

Meek, Nora. Sniffing for Democracy. 2004. (J). per. *(978-0-9753852-0-3(8))* PM, INK.

Menard, Michele R. The Canopy House - Lost among the Stars. 2013. 38p. pap. 13.95 *(978-0-9887969-4-2(5))* Four Menards, The.

—The Canopy House - Vol 2- Gus & Ester Meet the Neighbors. 2013. 34p. pap. 12.50 *(978-0-9891734-1-4(0))* Four Menards, The.

Metzger, Steve. Dancing Clock. Nez, John Abbott, illus. 2011. (ENG.). 32p. 12.95 *(978-1-58925-100-7(8))*; (J). pap. 7.95 *(978-1-58925-429-9(5))* Tiger Tales.

Milgrim, David. See Otto. Milgrim, David, illus. 2016. (Adventures of Otto Ser.). (ENG., Illus.). 32p. (J). (gr. -1-k). pap. 3.99 *(978-1-4814-6796-4(4),* Simon Spotlight) Simon Spotlight.

—Swing Otto Swing! Milgrim, David, illus. 2005. (Ready-to-Read Ser.). (Illus.). (J). (gr. -1-k). 11.65 *(978-0-7569-6497-9(0))* Perfection Learning Corp.

Mitchell, Stan R. Oskar & Myer at the Lake. 2013. 24p. pap. 24.95 *(978-1-63000-414-9(6))* America Star Bks.

Mommy, Tell Me a Story about What Daddy Does. 2nd ed. 2013. 32p. pap. 13.99 *(978-0-9855699-6-9(4))* Richer Life, LLC.

Moncure, Jane Belk. What Do You Say When a Monkey Acts This Way? A Book about Manners. Gallagher-Cole, Memie, illus. 2013. (Magic Castle Readers Ser.). (ENG.). 32p. (J). (gr. -1-2). 25.64 *(978-1-62323-590-1(1),* 206325) Child's World, Inc., The.

A Monkey Ate My Homework. 2007. 32p. pap. 4.50 *(978-0-8341-2287-1(1),* 083-412-2871) Beacon Hill Pr. of Kansas City.

Monkey Business. 2005. (J). 4.95 *(978-1-59792-015-5(0))* F.A.S.T. Learning LLC.

Monkey Girl Staff. Jay Travels to the U S A. 2012. 20p. pap. 17.99 *(978-1-4685-4778-8(X))* AuthorHouse.

Monkeys: Individual Title, 6 packs. (Sails Literacy Ser.). 16p. (gr. k-18). 27.00 *(978-0-7635-4405-8(1))* Rigby Education.

Monkeys Can't Cook! 2004. (J). 10.95 *(978-0-9761350-3-6(5))* Murphey, Hiromi.

Monkeys Can't Fly! 2004. (J). 10.95 *(978-0-9761350-2-9(7))* Murphey, Hiromi.

Monkey's Friends: Individual Title Six-Packs. (Literatura 2000 Ser.). (gr. 1-2). 28.00 *(978-0-7635-0098-6(4))* Rigby Education.

Monkey's Shoes: 3-in-1 Package. (Sails Literacy Ser.). 24p. (gr. k-18). 57.00 *(978-0-7578-3201-7(6))* Rigby Education.

Monkey's Shoes: Big Book Only. (Sails Literacy Ser.). 24p. (gr. k-18). 27.00 *(978-0-7635-6987-7(9))* Rigby Education.

Monks, Lydia. Mungo Monkey Goes on a Train. 2015. (ENG., Illus.). 14p. (J). (gr. -1-k). 13.99 *(978-1-4052-6910-0(3))* Egmont Bks., Ltd. GBR. Dist: Independent Pubs. Group.

—Mungo Monkey Goes to School. 2014. (ENG., Illus.). 14p. (J). (gr. -1-k). 13.99 *(978-1-4052-6909-4(X))* Egmont Bks., Ltd. GBR. Dist: Independent Pubs. Group.

Monks, Lydia, illus. Mungo Monkey Has a Birthday Party. 2014. (ENG.). 14p. (J). (gr. -1). 12.99 *(978-1-4052-6866-0(2))* Egmont Bks., Ltd. GBR. Dist: Independent Pubs. Group.

Monroe, Chris. Monkey with a Tool Belt. Monroe, Chris, illus. 2008. (Carolrhoda Picture Bks.). (ENG., Illus.). 32p. (J). (gr. -1-2). lib. bdg. 16.95 *(978-0-8225-7631-0(7),* Carolrhoda Bks.) Lerner Publishing Group.

—Monkey with a Tool Belt & the Maniac Muffins. Monroe, Chris, illus. 2016. (ENG., Illus.). 32p. (gr. -1-2). (J). 17.99 *(978-1-4677-2155-4(7))*; 35.99 *(978-1-4677-9562-3(3))* Lerner Publishing Group. (Carolrhoda Bks.).

—Monkey with a Tool Belt & the Noisy Problem. Monroe, Chris, illus. 2009. (Carolrhoda Picture Bks.). (ENG., Illus.). 32p. (J). (gr. -1-2). 16.95 *(978-0-8225-9247-1(9))* Lerner Publishing Group.

—Monkey with a Tool Belt & the Seaside Shenanigans. Monroe, Chris, illus. 2011. (Carolrhoda Picture Books Ser.). (ENG., Illus.). 32p. (J). (gr. -1-2). lib. bdg. 16.95 *(978-0-7613-5616-5(9),* Carolrhoda Bks.) Lerner Publishing Group.

Moorthy, Anita. Monkey's Drum. Sarkar, Soumitro, illus. 2003. (ENG.). 24p. pap. 3.99 *(978-81-86211-15-1(2))* Penguin Publishing Group.

Morimoto, Diana. Max, He Likes it that Way, 1 vol. 2010. 24p. pap. 24.95 *(978-1-4489-6851-0(8))* PublishAmerica, Inc.

Morrel Disbrow, Corlyss. Ran's Upside-Down Day. 2012. 20p. pap. 24.95 *(978-1-4626-8368-0(1))* America Star Bks.

Morris, Dudley. Mike the Monk. 2011. 58p. 36.95 *(978-1-258-02967-8(7))* Literary Licensing, LLC.

Morrow, Tara Jaye. Just Mommy & Me. Bratun, Katy, illus. 2004. 32p. (J). 13.89 *(978-0-06-000725-6(7))* HarperCollins Pubs.

Munro, Rosemary. The Adventures of Fidget the Monkey. 2017. (ENG., Illus.). (gr. 1-2). pap. ***(978-1-78222-509-6(9))*** Paragon Publishing, Rothersthorpe.

Myers, Martha. Nibbles, the Mostly Mischievous Monkey. 2003. (Julius & Friends Ser.: Vol. 10). (Illus.). 91p. (J). 6.99 *(978-0-8163-1947-3(2))* Pacific Pr. Publishing Assn.

Myers, Walter Dean. Looking for the Easy Life. Harper, Lee, illus. 2011. (Looking at Other Countries Ser.). (ENG.). 40p. (J). (gr. -1-3). 16.99 *(978-0-06-054375-4(2))* HarperCollins Pubs.

Na, Il Sung, illus. The Opposite Zoo. 2016. (ENG.). 24p. (J). (-k). 16.99 *(978-0-553-51127-7(0),* Knopf Bks. for Young Readers) Random Hse. Children's Bks.

Napoli, Donna Jo & Johnston, Shelagh. Hotel Jungle. Spengler, Kenneth, tr. Spengler, Kenneth, illus. 2004. 33p. (J). 15.95 *(978-1-59336-002-3(9))*; pap. *(978-1-59336-003-0(7))* Mondo Publishing.

Neff, Ethel Maxine. Sally: The Runaway Monkey. 2004. (Illus.). 42p. (J). 5.99 *(978-0-8163-2062-2(4))* Pacific Pr. Publishing Assn.

Nyirenda, Vukani G. The Wise Old Tortoise & the Monkey. 2011. 24p. pap. 15.99 *(978-1-4568-9133-6(2))* Xlibris Corp.

Olshan, Matthew. The Flown Sky, 1. 2007. (Illus.). 352p. 19.95 *(978-0-9789391-0-6(7))* Chacmool Pr.

Opie, David, illus. Monkey & the Engineer. 2007. 24p. (J). 14.95 *(978-0-9793972-6-4(X))* JD Publishing.

Osterhold, Jared, illus. Olivia Claus. 2010. (Olivia TV Tie-In Ser.). (ENG.). 24p. (J). (gr. -1-1). 16.99 *(978-1-4424-0662-9(3),* Simon Spotlight) Simon Spotlight.

Ovani, Germano, illus. The Monkey King. 2007. (Young Reading Series 1 Gift Bks). 47p. (J). (gr. -1-3). 8.99 *(978-0-7945-1593-5(2),* Usborne) EDC Publishing.

Pankratz, Justin, illus. Blue Monkey. 2003. (J). 5.95 *(978-0-9742637-0-0(2))* Pankratz Creations.

Papp, Robert, illus. Monkey Trouble. 2011. (Boxcar Children Mysteries Ser.: 127). (ENG.). 128p. (J). (gr. 1-5). pap. 5.99 *(978-0-8075-5240-7(2))* Whitman, Albert & Co.

—Monkey Trouble. 2011. (Boxcar Children Mysteries Ser.: 127). (ENG.). 128p. (J). (gr. 1-5). lib. bdg. 14.99 *(978-0-8075-5239-1(9))* Whitman, Albert & Co.

Parker, Emma. The Monkey in the Tree. 2010. (Illus.). pap. *(978-1-877547-91-1(3))* First Edition Ltd.

—What a Hullabaloo. 2010. 20p. pap. *(978-1-877561-32-0(0))* First Edition Ltd.

Passen, Lisa. Monkey Mountain. 2013. 234p. pap. 14.99 *(978-1-60820-880-7(X))* MLR Pr., LLC.

Patricelli, Leslie. Be Quiet, Mike! 2011. (ENG., Illus.). 40p. (J). (gr. -1-2). 14.99 *(978-0-7636-4477-2(3))* Candlewick Pr.

Paul & Lady Jan. Mako in My Backyard. Beeson, Jan, illus. 2013. 34p. pap. 12.99 *(978-0-9890482-3-1(3))* Beeson, Jan.

Paul Frank Industries & Gillingham, Sara. I Love Color: A Paul Frank Book. 2011. (ENG.). 10p. (J). (gr. -1 — 1). bds. 8.99 *(978-1-4521-0222-1(8))* Chronicle Bks. LLC.

Peet, Mal & Graham, Elspeth. Cloud Tea Monkeys. Wijngaard, Juan, illus. 2010. (ENG.). 56p. (J). (gr. -1-3). 17.99 *(978-0-7636-4453-6(6))* Candlewick Pr.

Pepper, Lily. Bananas. 2012. (Illus.). 20p. pap. 19.82 *(978-1-4772-1964-5(1))* AuthorHouse.

Perez, Monica, et al. Curious George Builds a Home. 2006. (Curious George Ser.). (ENG., Illus.). 24p. (J). (gr. -1-3). 4.99 *(978-0-618-72395-9(1))* Houghton Mifflin Harcourt Publishing Co.

Phillipps, J. C. Monkey Ono. 2013. (ENG., Illus.). 40p. (J). (gr. -1-k). 16.99 *(978-0-670-78505-6(9),* Viking Books for Young Readers) Penguin Young Readers Group.

Phillips, Clifton. Ten Spunky Monkeys. Jung, Shirley, illus. 2007. 32p. (J). 8.99 *(978-0-9797106-4-3(2))* Avid Readers Publishing Group.

Phillips, Dee & Ticktock Media, Ltd. Staff. What Do Monkeys Do? 2009. (What Do Animals Do? Ser.). (ENG.). 5p. (J). (gr. k — 1). bds. 4.95 *(978-1-84696-960-7(3),* TickTock Books) Octopus Publishing Group GBR. Dist: Independent Pubs. Group.

Pilkey, Dav. Mighty Robot vs. the Mecha-Monkeys from Mars. Santat, Dan, illus. 2014. (Ricky Ricotta Ser.: 4). (ENG.). 144p. (J). (gr. -1-3). pap. 5.99 *(978-0-545-63012-2(6))* Scholastic, Inc.

Popper, Garry. Scary Monkeys: Going Ape. Forshaw, John, illus. 2004. 48p. 9.00 *(978-1-84161-014-6(3))* Ravette Publishing, Ltd. GBR. Dist: Parkwest Pubns., Inc.

Porter, Matthew. Monkey World ABC. 2012. (ENG., Illus.). 26p. (J). 8.95 *(978-1-927018-07-1(2))* Simply Read Bks. CAN. Dist: Ingram Publisher Services.

Posner-Sanchez, Andrea. Bubble-Rific! RH Disney Staff, illus. 2014. (Little Golden Book Ser.). (ENG.). 24p. (J). (-k). 4.99 *(978-0-7364-3236-8(1),* Golden/Disney) Random Hse. Children's Bks.

Poulin, Andrée. Monkey in the Mud. Eudes-Pascal, Elisabeth, illus. 2009. (Rainy Day Readers Ser.). 32p. (J). (gr. -1-3). pap. 10.55 *(978-1-60754-371-8(0))* Windmill Bks.

Poulin, Andrée. Monkey in the Mud. Eudes-Pascal, Elisabeth, illus. 2009. (Rainy Day Readers Ser.). 32p. (J). (gr. -1-3). 22.60 *(978-1-60754-370-1(2))* Windmill Bks.

Powell, Richard. Mandy Monkey. Rhodes, Katie, illus. 2004. (Fuzzy Friends Ser.). 10p. (J). 7.95 *(978-1-58925-720-7(0))* Tiger Tales.

Priddy, Roger. Little Friends: Little Monkey. 2015. (Little Friends Ser.). (ENG., Illus.). 10p. (J). (gr. -1 — 1). bds. 8.99 *(978-0-312-51779-3(3),* 9780312517793, Priddy Bks.) St. Martin's Pr.

Prouty, Krista. George Monkeys Around, 1 vol. 2010. 42p. 24.95 *(978-1-4489-4936-6(X))* PublishAmerica, Inc.

Pulford, Elizabeth. Finding Monkey Moon. Wilkinson, Kate, illus. 2015. (ENG.). 32p. (J). (gr. -1-2). 15.99 *(978-0-7636-6777-1(3))* Candlewick Pr.

Quigley, Michael. A Monkey's Riddle. 2013. 24p. pap. 24.95 *(978-1-63000-506-1(1))* America Star Bks.

Rabelo-Beacroft, Katia. The Grumpy Monkey Who Only Eats Bananas. 2012. 28p. pap. 16.10 *(978-1-4669-3957-8(5))* Trafford Publishing.

Ramoutar, Tagore. Brownie the Monkey Visits the Zoo. Cline, Ian, photos by. 2012. (Illus.). 38p. pap. *(978-1-907837-48-7(5))* Longshot Ventures, Ltd.

Rao, Sirish. Monkey Photo. Chitrakar, Swarna, illus. 2010. (ENG.). 32p. (J). (gr. -1-1). *(978-81-907546-2-0(9))* Tara Publishing.

Rathmann, Peggy. Buenas Noches, Gorila. Mayobre, Maria Francisca, tr. from ENG. Rathmann, Peggy, illus. 2004. (SPA., Illus.). 36p. (gr. k). 12.99 *(978-980-257-265-6(9))* Ekare, Ediciones VEN. Dist: Lectorum Pubns., Inc.

Redlich, Ben. Who Flung Dung? 2013. (ENG., Illus.). 28p. (J). (gr. -1-k). 16.95 *(978-1-62087-543-8(8),* 620543, Sky Pony Pr.) Skyhorse Publishing Co., Inc.

Rempt, Fione. Rico the Brave Sock Monkey. 2013. (Little Golden Book Ser.). (ENG., Illus.). 24p. (J). (-k). 4.99 *(978-0-375-86504-6(7),* Golden Bks.) Random Hse. Children's Bks.

Renier Nash, Oliver. The Primate Puzzle: A tale of two friends & the missing long-nosed Monkeys. 2009. 272p. pap. 15.49 *(978-1-4490-3099-5(8))* AuthorHouse.

Rey, H. A. Apple Harvest: Curious about Harvest Time. 2012. (Curious George TV Tie-In 8x8 Ser.). lib. bdg. 13.55 *(978-0-606-23984-4(7),* Turtleback) Turtleback Bks.

—Awake-Asleep Cloth Book & Door Hanger. 2010. (Curious Baby Curious George Ser.). (ENG., Illus.). 4p. (J). (gr. -1 — 1). 8.99 *(978-0-547-23897-5(5))* Houghton Mifflin Harcourt Publishing Co.

—Builds a Home. 2011. (Curious George Ser.). (ENG., Illus.). 24p. (J). (gr. -1-3). 6.99 *(978-0-547-59410-1(0))* Houghton Mifflin Harcourt Publishing Co.

—Builds a Tree House. 2017. (Curious George Ser.). (SPA & ENG., Illus.). 24p. (J). (gr. -1-3). 12.99 *(978-0-544-97461-6(1),* HMH Books For Young Readers) Houghton Mifflin Harcourt Publishing Co.

—Builds an Igloo. 2013. (Curious George Ser.). (ENG., Illus.). 24p. (J). (gr. -1-3). pap. 3.99 *(978-0-544-09666-0(5))* Houghton Mifflin Harcourt Publishing Co.

—C. G. Fish, Rides. (ENG., Illus.). bds., bds., bds. 95.20 *(978-0-618-13189-1(2))* Houghton Mifflin Harcourt Publishing Co.

—Car Wash. 2013. (Curious George Ser.). (ENG., Illus.). 24p. (J). (gr. -1-3). pap. 3.99 *(978-0-547-94086-1(6))* Houghton Mifflin Harcourt Publishing Co.

—Curious about Christmas. 2011. (Curious Baby Curious George Ser.). (ENG., Illus.). 12p. (J). (gr. k — 1). bds. 8.99 *(978-0-547-58841-4(0))* Houghton Mifflin Harcourt Publishing Co.

—Curious George a Home for Honeybees (CGTV Early Reader) 2014. (Curious George Ser.). (ENG., Illus.). 24p. (J). (gr. -1-3). 12.99 *(978-0-544-23777-3(3),* HMH Books For Young Readers) Houghton Mifflin Harcourt Publishing Co.

—Curious George & the Dump Truck. 2010. (Curious George Ser.). (ENG., Illus.). 24p. (J). (gr. -1-3). pap. 4.99 *(978-0-547-50425-4(X))* Houghton Mifflin Harcourt Publishing Co.

—Curious George & the Hot Air Balloon. 2011. (Curious George Ser.). (ENG., Illus.). 24p. (J). (gr. -1-3). pap. 4.99 *(978-0-547-54745-9(5))* Houghton Mifflin Harcourt Publishing Co.

—Curious George & the Ice Cream Surprise. 2011. (Curious George Ser.). (ENG., Illus.). 24p. (J). (gr. -1-3). 13.99 *(978-0-547-24284-2(0));* pap. 4.99 *(978-0-547-24285-9(9))* Houghton Mifflin Harcourt Publishing Co.

—Curious George Apple Harvest. 2012. (Curious George Ser.). (ENG., Illus.). 24p. (J). (gr. -1-3). pap. 4.99 *(978-0-547-51705-6(X))* Houghton Mifflin Harcourt Publishing Co.

—Curious George at the Baseball Game (Jorge el Curioso en el Partido de Beisbol) 2011. (Curious George Ser.). (SPA & ENG., Illus.). 24p. (J). (gr. -1-3). pap. 4.99 *(978-0-547-51500-7(6))* Houghton Mifflin Harcourt Publishing Co.

—Curious George at the Park. Meyer, Emily, ed. 2010. (Curious George Ser.). (ENG., Illus.). 10p. (J). (gr. -1 — 1). bds. 6.99 *(978-0-547-24300-9(6))* Houghton Mifflin Harcourt Publishing Co.

—Curious George Builds a Tree House (CGTV Reader) 2017. (Curious George Ser.). (ENG., Illus.). 24p. (J). (gr. -1-3). pap. 3.99 *(978-0-544-86704-8(1),* HMH Books For Young Readers) Houghton Mifflin Harcourt Publishing Co.

—Curious George Builds an Igloo (CGTV Reader) 2013. (Curious George Ser.). (ENG., Illus.). 24p. (J). (gr. -1-3). 12.99 *(978-0-544-09570-0(7))* Houghton Mifflin Harcourt Publishing Co.

—Curious George Car Wash. 2013. (Curious George Ser.). (ENG., Illus.). 24p. (J). (gr. -1-3). 12.99 *(978-0-544-03251-4(9))* Houghton Mifflin Harcourt Publishing Co.

—Curious George Classic Collection. 2015. (Curious George Ser.). (ENG., Illus.). 416p. (J). (gr. -1-3). 39.99 *(978-0-544-56239-4(9),* HMH Books For Young Readers) Houghton Mifflin Harcourt Publishing Co.

—Curious George Cleans Up. Canetti, Yanitzia, tr. 2007. (Curious George Ser.). (SPA & ENG., Illus.). 24p. (J). (gr. -1-3). mass mkt. 3.99 *(978-0-618-89687-5(2))* Houghton Mifflin Harcourt Publishing Co.

—Curious George Discovers Germs (Science Storybook) 2015. (Curious George Ser.). (ENG., Illus.). 32p. (J). (gr. -1-3). 6.99 *(978-0-544-43066-2(2),* HMH Books For Young Readers) Houghton Mifflin Harcourt Publishing Co.

—Curious George Discovers the Ocean (Science Storybook) 2015. (Curious George Ser.). (ENG., Illus.). 32p. (J). (gr. -1-3). 6.99 *(978-0-544-43065-5(4),* HMH Books For Young Readers) Houghton Mifflin Harcourt Publishing Co.

—Curious George Discovers the Rainbow (Science Storybook) 2015. (Curious George Ser.). (ENG., Illus.). 32p. (J). (gr. -1-3). 6.99 *(978-0-544-43068-6(9),* HMH Books For Young Readers) Houghton Mifflin Harcourt Publishing Co.

—Curious George Discovers the Senses. 2015. (Curious George Ser.). (ENG., Illus.). 32p. (J). (gr. -1-3). 6.99 *(978-0-544-50023-5(7),* HMH Books For Young Readers) Houghton Mifflin Harcourt Publishing Co.

—Curious George Discovers the Sun (Science Storybook) 2015. (Curious George Ser.). (ENG., Illus.). 32p. (J). (gr. -1-3). 6.99 *(978-0-544-43067-9(0),* HMH Books For Young Readers) Houghton Mifflin Harcourt Publishing Co.

—Curious George Farm to Table (CGTV 8x8) 2016. (Curious George Ser.). (ENG., Illus.). 24p. (J). (gr. -1-3). 12.99 *(978-0-544-65220-0(7),* HMH Books For Young Readers) Houghton Mifflin Harcourt Publishing Co.

—Curious George Flies a Kite. 2004. (J). (gr. k-3). spiral bd. *(978-0-616-01770-8(7));* spiral bd. *(978-0-616-01771-5(5))* Canadian National Institute for the Blind/Institut National Canadien pour les Aveugles.

—Curious George Grows a Garden. 2012. (Curious George Ser.). (ENG., Illus.). 48p. (J). (gr. -1-3). pap. 4.99 *(978-0-547-64304-5(7))* Houghton Mifflin Harcourt Publishing Co.

—Curious George Harvest Hoedown (CGTV 8 X 8) 2017. (Curious George Ser.). (ENG., Illus.). 24p. (J). (gr. -1-3). 12.99 ***(978-1-328-69596-3(4),*** HMH Books For Young Readers) Houghton Mifflin Harcourt Publishing Co.

—Curious George Haunted Halloween. 2014. (Curious George Ser.). (ENG., Illus.). 24p. (J). (gr. -1-3). pap. 3.99 *(978-0-544-32079-6(4),* HMH Books For Young Readers) Houghton Mifflin Harcourt Publishing Co.

—Curious George Home Run (Jorge el Curioso el Jonrón) 2012. (Curious George Ser.). (ENG & SPA., Illus.). 24p. (J). (gr. -1-3). pap. 3.99 *(978-0-547-69114-5(9))* Houghton Mifflin Harcourt Publishing Co.

—Curious George Learns the Alphabet, 1 vol. 2009. (Curious George Ser.). (ENG., Illus.). 80p. (J). (gr. -1-3). audio compact disk 10.99 *(978-0-618-95966-2(1))* Houghton Mifflin Harcourt Publishing Co.

—Curious George Learns to Count from 1 To 100. 2011. (Curious George Ser.). (ENG., Illus.). 80p. (J). (gr. -1-3). pap. 8.99 *(978-0-547-13841-1(5))* Houghton Mifflin Harcourt Publishing Co.

—Curious George Magnetic Maze Book. 2012. (Curious George Ser.). (ENG., Illus.). 10p. (J). (gr. -1-3). 12.99 *(978-0-547-64302-1(0))* Houghton Mifflin Harcourt Publishing Co.

—Curious George Makes Maple Syrup (CGTV 8x8) 2014. (Curious George Ser.). (ENG., Illus.). 24p. (J). (gr. -1-3). 12.99 *(978-0-544-10494-5(3))* Houghton Mifflin Harcourt Publishing Co.

—Curious George Makes Pancakes, 1 vol. Rey, Margret, illus. 2008. (Curious George Ser.). (ENG.). 24p. (gr. -1-3). lib. bdg. 24.21 *(978-1-59961-417-5(0))* Spotlight.

—Curious George Parade Day. 2011. (Curious George Ser.). (ENG., Illus.). 14p. (J). (gr. -1 — 1). bds. 7.99 *(978-0-547-47282-9(X))* Houghton Mifflin Harcourt Publishing Co.

—Curious George Pat-A-Cake. 2011. (Curious George Ser.). (ENG., Illus.). 8p. (J). (gr. k — 1). bds. 9.99 *(978-0-547-51689-9(4))* Houghton Mifflin Harcourt Publishing Co.

—Curious George Plants a Tree. Wilcox, Mary, ed. 2010. (Curious George Ser.). (ENG., Illus.). 24p. (J). (gr. -1-3). pap. 4.99 *(978-0-547-29776-7(9))* Houghton Mifflin Harcourt Publishing Co.

—Curious George Plants a Tree. 2009. (Curious George Ser.). (ENG., Illus.). 32p. (J). (gr. -1-3). 14.99 *(978-0-547-15087-1(3))* Houghton Mifflin Harcourt Publishing Co.

—Curious George Saves His Pennies. 2013. (Curious George Ser.). (ENG., Illus.). 32p. (J). (gr. -1-3). 12.99 *(978-0-547-63231-5(2))* Houghton Mifflin Harcourt Publishing Co.

—Curious George Tool Time (CGTV Board Book) 2013. (Curious George Ser.). (ENG., Illus.). 12p. (J). (gr. -1 — 1). bds. 6.99 *(978-0-547-96818-6(3))* Houghton Mifflin Harcourt Publishing Co.

—Curious George's 5-Minute Stories. 2013. (Curious George Ser.). (ENG., Illus.). 192p. (J). (gr. -1-3). 12.99 *(978-0-544-10793-9(4))* Houghton Mifflin Harcourt Publishing Co.

—Curious George's Dump Truck. 2014. (Curious George Ser.). (ENG., Illus.). 12p. (J). (— 1). bds. 8.99 *(978-0-544-14686-0(7),* HMH Books For Young Readers) Houghton Mifflin Harcourt Publishing Co.

—Curious George's Fire Truck. 2014. (Curious George Ser.). (ENG., Illus.). 12p. (J). (— 1). bds. 8.99 *(978-0-544-14709-6(X),* HMH Books For Young Readers) Houghton Mifflin Harcourt Publishing Co.

—Curious George's Train (mini Movers Shaped Board Books) 2014. (Curious George Ser.). (ENG., Illus.). 12p. (J). (— 1). bds. 8.99 *(978-0-544-32074-1(3),* HMH Books For Young Readers) Houghton Mifflin Harcourt Publishing Co.

—Dinosaur Tracks. 2011. (Curious George Ser.). (ENG., Illus.). 24p. (J). (gr. -1-3). pap. 3.99 *(978-0-547-43888-7(5))* Houghton Mifflin Harcourt Publishing Co.

—¡Eres Curioso Todo el Tiempo! 2012. (Curious George Ser.).Tr. of Curious You on Your Way! (ENG & SPA.). 32p. (J). (gr. -1-3). 9.99 *(978-0-547-79368-9(5))* Houghton Mifflin Harcourt Publishing Co.

—Feliz Navidad, Jorge el Curioso. Young, Mary O'Keefe, illus. 2012. (Curious George Ser.).Tr. of Merry Christmas, Curious George. (ENG & SPA.). 32p. (J). (gr. -1-3). 10.99 *(978-0-547-74503-9(6))* Houghton Mifflin Harcourt Publishing Co.

—Get Well, Curious George. 2017. (Curious George Ser.). (ENG., Illus.). 24p. (J). (gr. -1-3). 14.99 ***(978-0-544-97750-1(5),*** HMH Books For Young Readers) Houghton Mifflin Harcourt Publishing Co.

—Happy Halloween. 2008. (Curious George Ser.). (ENG., Illus.). 14p. (J). (gr. -1 — 1). bds. 7.99 *(978-0-618-91952-9(X))* Houghton Mifflin Harcourt Publishing Co.

—Happy St. Patrick's Day. 2014. (Curious George Ser.). (ENG., Illus.). 14p. (J). (— 1). bds. 7.99 *(978-0-544-08888-7(3))* Houghton Mifflin Harcourt Publishing Co.

—Happy Thanksgiving. 2010. (Curious George Ser.). (ENG., Illus.). 14p. (J). (gr. -1 — 1). bds. 7.99 *(978-0-547-13106-1(2))* Houghton Mifflin Harcourt Publishing Co.

—Happy Valentine's Day. Young, Mary O'Keefe, illus. 2011. (Curious George Ser.). (ENG.). 14p. (J). (gr. -1-3). 8.99 *(978-0-547-13107-8(0))* Houghton Mifflin Harcourt Publishing Co.

—Home Run. 2012. (Curious George Ser.). (ENG., Illus.). 24p. (J). (gr. -1-3). pap. 3.99 *(978-0-547-69118-3(1))* Houghton Mifflin Harcourt Publishing Co.

—Hooray for Halloween, Curious George. 2016. (Curious George Ser.). (ENG., Illus.). 24p. (J). (gr. -1-3). 9.99 *(978-0-544-69956-4(4),* HMH Books For Young Readers) Houghton Mifflin Harcourt Publishing Co.

—Jorge el Curioso en el Partido de Beisbol. 2011. (Curious George Ser.).Tr. of Curious George at the Baseball Game. (SPA & ENG., Illus.). 24p. (J). (gr. -1-3). 12.99 *(978-0-547-54746-6(3))* Houghton Mifflin Harcourt Publishing Co.

—Jorge el Curioso Huellas de Dinosaurio. 2011. (Curious George Ser.). (ENG & SPA., Illus.). 24p. (J). (gr. -1-3). pap. 3.99 *(978-0-547-55798-4(1))* Houghton Mifflin Harcourt Publishing Co.

—Jorge el Curioso Siembra Una Semilla. Zappy, Erica, ed. Canetti, Yanitzia, tr. 2007. (Curious George Ser.). (ENG & SPA., Illus.). 24p. (J). (gr. -1-3). mass mkt. 3.99 *(978-0-618-89688-2(0))* Houghton Mifflin Harcourt Publishing Co.

—Jorge el Curioso Va a una Fiesta de Disfraces/Curious George Goes to a Costume Party (Bilingual) 2012. (Curious George Ser.). (ENG & SPA., Illus.). 24p. (J). (gr. -1-3). pap. 3.99 *(978-0-547-86575-1(9))* Houghton Mifflin Harcourt Publishing Co.

—Jorge el Curioso Visita el Acuario. 2010. (Curious George Ser.).Tr. of Curious George at the Aquarium. (ENG & SPA., Illus.). 24p. (J). (gr. -1-3). pap. 4.99 *(978-0-547-29963-1(X))* Houghton Mifflin Harcourt Publishing Co.

—My Curious World. 2009. (Curious Baby Curious George Ser.). (ENG., Illus.). 10p. (J). (gr. -1 — 1). 14.99 *(978-0-547-21520-4(7))* Houghton Mifflin Harcourt Publishing Co.

—My Favorite Things. 2011. (Curious Baby Curious George Ser.). (ENG., Illus.). 14p. (J). (gr. -1 — 1). bds. 8.99 *(978-0-547-42893-2(6))* Houghton Mifflin Harcourt Publishing Co.

—The Perfect Carrot. 2010. (Curious George Ser.). (ENG., Illus.). 24p. (J). (gr. -1-3). pap. 3.99 *(978-0-547-24299-6(9))* Houghton Mifflin Harcourt Publishing Co.

—Sweet Dreams, Curious George. (Curious George Ser.). (ENG., Illus.). 24p. (J). (gr. -1-3). 2016. 4.99 *(978-0-544-50321-2(X),* HMH Books For Young Readers) 2013. 9.99 *(978-0-544-03880-6(0))* Houghton Mifflin Harcourt Publishing Co.

—Three Tales for a Winter's Night. 2012. (Curious George Ser.). (ENG., Illus.). 72p. (J). (gr. -1-3). pap. 7.99 *(978-0-547-83936-3(7))* Houghton Mifflin Harcourt Publishing Co.

—Time for School. 2011. (Curious George Ser.). (ENG., Illus.). 16p. (J). (gr. -1-3). 5.99 *(978-0-547-42230-5(X))* Houghton Mifflin Harcourt Publishing Co.

—Visits the Library / Jorge el Curioso Va a la Biblioteca. 2011. (Curious George Ser.). (ENG & SPA., Illus.). 24p. (J). (gr. -1-3). pap. 3.99 *(978-0-547-55075-6(8))* Houghton Mifflin Harcourt Publishing Co.

—Windy Delivery. 2014. (Curious George Ser.). (ENG., Illus.). 24p. (J). (gr. -1-3). 12.99 *(978-0-544-32075-8(1));* pap. 4.99 *(978-0-544-32076-5(X))* Houghton Mifflin Harcourt Publishing Co. (HMH Books For Young Readers).

Rey, H. A. & Berger, Sholem. [Dzshordzsh der Naygeriker/Fun H. A. Rey; Yidish, Sholem Berger] George der Naygeriker. 2005. (YID., Illus.). 57p. (J). *(978-0-9726939-2-9(0))* Twenty-fourth Street Bks, LLC.

Rey, H. A. & Hapka, Catherine. Merry Christmas, Curious George (with Stickers) Young, Mary O'Keefe, illus. 2017. (Curious George Ser.). (ENG.). 24p. (J). (gr. -1-3). pap. 5.99 ***(978-1-328-69558-1(1),*** HMH Books For Young Readers) Houghton Mifflin Harcourt Publishing Co.

Rey, H. A. & Houghton Mifflin Company Staff. Bigger & Smaller. 2007. (Curious George Ser.). (ENG., Illus.). 12p. (J). (gr. -1 — 1). bds. 6.99 *(978-0-618-73760-4(X))* Houghton Mifflin Harcourt Publishing Co.

Rey, H. A. & Margaret. Curious George Visits the Dentist. 2014. (Curious George Ser.). (ENG., Illus.). 24p. (J). (gr. -1-3). 13.99 *(978-0-544-14611-2(5),* HMH Books For Young Readers) Houghton Mifflin Harcourt Publishing Co.

Rey, H. A. & Rey, Margret. Big Book of Adventures: 12 Beginning Readers in One. 2013. (Curious George Ser.). (ENG., Illus.). 296p. (J). (gr. -1-3). 15.99 *(978-0-544-08463-6(2))* Houghton Mifflin Harcourt Publishing Co.

—Cecily G. & the 9 Monkeys. 2007. (Curious George Ser.). (ENG., Illus.). 48p. (J). (gr. -1-3). 16.00 *(978-0-618-80066-7(2))* Houghton Mifflin Harcourt Publishing Co.

—Cecily G. & the 9 Monkeys. 2009. (Curious George Ser.). (ENG., Illus.). 48p. (J). (gr. -1-3). pap. 6.99 *(978-0-618-99794-7(6),* HMH Books For Young Readers) Houghton Mifflin Harcourt Publishing Co.

—Circus Act. 2008. (Curious George Ser.). (ENG., Illus.). 16p. (J). (gr. -1-3). 5.99 *(978-0-618-99909-5(4))* Houghton Mifflin Harcourt Publishing Co.

—The Complete Adventures of Curious George. 2005. (J). (gr. -1-k). 30.00 *(978-0-618-64550-3(0))* Houghton Mifflin Harcourt Trade & Reference Pubs.

—The Complete Adventures of Curious George: 75th Anniversary Edition. 75th ed. 2016. (Curious George Ser.). (ENG., Illus.). 432p. (J). (gr. -1-3). 34.99 *(978-0-544-64448-9(4),* HMH Books For Young Readers) Houghton Mifflin Harcourt Publishing Co.

—Curious George & the Dump Truck, 1 vol. 2008. (Curious George Ser.). (ENG., Illus.). 24p. (gr. -1-3). lib. bdg. 24.21 *(978-1-59961-410-6(3))* Spotlight.

—Curious George & the Firefighters, 1 vol. 2008. (Curious George Ser.). (ENG., Illus.). 24p. (gr. -1-3). lib. bdg. 24.21 *(978-1-59961-411-3(1))* Spotlight.

—Curious George & the Pizza Party. 2013. (Curious George Ser.). (ENG., Illus.). 24p. (J). (gr. -1-3). pap. 4.99 *(978-0-544-10988-9(0))* Houghton Mifflin Harcourt Publishing Co.

—Curious George & the Pizza Party. Shalleck, Alan J., ed. 2010. (Curious George Ser.). (ENG., Illus.). 24p. (J). (gr. -1-3). 13.99 *(978-0-547-23211-9(X))* Houghton Mifflin Harcourt Publishing Co.

—Curious George & the Puppies. 2007. (Curious George Ser.). (ENG., Illus.). 24p. (J). (gr. -1-3). audio compact disk 10.99 *(978-0-618-80065-0(4))* Houghton Mifflin Harcourt Publishing Co.

—Curious George at the Aquarium. Hines, Anna Grossnickle, illus. 2007. (Curious George Ser.). (ENG.). 24p. (J). (gr. -1-3). 13.99 *(978-0-618-80067-4(0))* Houghton Mifflin Harcourt Publishing Co.

—Curious George at the Aquarium. 2014. (Curious George Ser.). (ENG., Illus.). 24p. (J). (gr. -1-3). pap. 4.99 *(978-0-544-17674-4(X))* Houghton Mifflin Harcourt Publishing Co.

—Curious George Goes to a Bookstore. 2014. (Curious George Ser.). (ENG., Illus.). 32p. (J). (gr. -1-3). 13.99 *(978-0-544-32073-4(5),* HMH Books For Young Readers) Houghton Mifflin Harcourt Publishing Co.

—Curious George Goes to a Movie, 1 vol. 2008. (Curious George Ser.). (ENG., Illus.). 24p. (gr. -1-3). lib. bdg. 24.21 *(978-1-59961-415-1(4))* Spotlight.

—Curious George Goes to the Zoo. 2014. (Curious George Ser.). (ENG., Illus.). 24p. (J). (gr. -1-3). 4.99 *(978-0-544-11000-7(5))* Houghton Mifflin Harcourt Publishing Co.

—Curious George in the Snow, 1 vol. 2008. (Curious George Ser.). (ENG., Illus.). 24p. (gr. -1-3). lib. bdg. 24.21 *(978-1-59961-416-8(2))* Spotlight.

—Curious George Learns the Alphabet. 50th ed. 2013. (Curious George Ser.). (ENG., Illus.). 80p. (J). (gr. -1-3). 12.99 (978-0-544-10523-2(0)) Houghton Mifflin Harcourt Publishing Co.
—Curious George Makes Maple Syrup. 2014. (Curious George Ser.). (ENG., Illus.). 24p. (J). (gr. -1-3). pap. 3.99 (978-0-544-03252-1(7)) Houghton Mifflin Harcourt Publishing Co.
—Curious George Saves His Pennies. 2014. (Curious George Ser.). (ENG., Illus.). 24p. (J). (gr. -1-3). pap. 4.99 (978-0-547-81853-5(X)) Houghton Mifflin Harcourt Publishing Co.
—Curious George Says Thank You. 2012. (Curious George Ser.). (ENG., Illus.). 24p. (J). (gr. -1-3). pap. 4.99 (978-0-547-81852-8(1)) Houghton Mifflin Harcourt Publishing Co.
—Curious George Says Thank You. 2012. (Curious George 8x8 Ser.). lib. bdg. 14.75 (978-0-606-26601-7(1), Turtleback) Turtleback Bks.
—Curious George Stories to Share. 2011. (Curious George Ser.). (ENG., Illus.). 208p. (J). (gr. -1-3). 10.99 (978-0-547-59529-0(8)) Houghton Mifflin Harcourt Publishing Co.
—Curious George Super Sticker Coloring Book. 2008. (Curious George Ser.). (ENG., Illus.). 64p. (J). (gr. -1-3). 12.99 (978-0-618-99877-7(2)) Houghton Mifflin Harcourt Publishing Co.
—Curious George Takes a Job. 2007. (Curious George Ser.). (ENG., Illus.). 48p. (J). (gr. -1-3). audio compact disk 10.99 (978-0-618-72406-2(0)) Houghton Mifflin Harcourt Publishing Co.
—Curious George the Boat Show. 2008. (Curious George Ser.). (ENG., Illus.). 24p. (J). (gr. -1-3). pap. 3.99 (978-0-618-89196-2(X)) Houghton Mifflin Harcourt Publishing Co.
—Curious George Visits the Library. Weston, Martha, illus. 2013. (Curious George Ser.). (ENG.). 24p. (J). (gr. -1-3). pap. 4.99 (978-0-544-11450-0(7)) Houghton Mifflin Harcourt Publishing Co.
—Curious George's Dream, 1 vol. 2008. (Curious George Ser.). (ENG., Illus.). 24p. (gr. -1-3). lib. bdg. 24.21 (978-1-59961-420-5(0)) Spotlight.
—Curious George's First Day of School, 1 vol. 2008. (Curious George Ser.). (ENG., Illus.). 24p. (gr. -1-3). lib. bdg. 24.21 (978-1-59961-421-2(9)) Spotlight.
—Dog Show. 2007. (Curious George Ser.). (ENG., Illus.). 24p. (J). (gr. -1-3). 3.99 (978-0-618-72397-3(8)) Houghton Mifflin Harcourt Publishing Co.
—George O Curioso. pap. 23.95 (978-85-336-0916-7(7)) Livraria Martins Editora BRA. Dist: Distribooks, Inc.
—Goes to the Beach. 2014. (Curious George Ser.). (ENG., Illus.). 24p. (J). (gr. -1-3). pap. 4.99 (978-0-544-25001-7(X), HMH Books For Young Readers) Houghton Mifflin Harcourt Publishing Co.
—Happy Hanukkah. 2012. (Curious George Ser.). (ENG., Illus.). 14p. (J). (gr. k — 1). bds. 7.99 (978-0-547-75731-5(X)) Houghton Mifflin Harcourt Publishing Co.
—Home Run. 2012. (Curious George TV Tie-In Early Reader Ser.). lib. bdg. 13.55 (978-0-606-23985-1(5), Turtleback) Turtleback Bks.
—Jorge el Curioso Encuentra Trabajo. Canetti, Yanitzia, tr. 2003. (Curious George Ser.).Tr. of Curious George Takes a Job. (SPA & ENG., Illus.). 48p. (J). (gr. -1-3). pap. 7.99 (978-0-618-33600-5(1)) Houghton Mifflin Harcourt Publishing Co.
—Librarian for a Day. 2012. (Curious George TV Tie-In Early Reader Ser.). lib. bdg. 13.55 (978-0-606-26602-4(X), Turtleback) Turtleback Bks.
—Plays Mini Golf. 2008. (Curious George Ser.). (ENG., Illus.). 24p. (J). (gr. -1-3). pap. 3.99 (978-0-618-99986-6(8)) Houghton Mifflin Harcourt Publishing Co.
—Roller Coaster. 2007. (Curious George Ser.). (ENG., Illus.). 24p. (J). (gr. -1-3). pap. 3.99 (978-0-618-80040-7(9)) Houghton Mifflin Harcourt Publishing Co.
—Seasons. 2008. (Curious George Ser.). (ENG., Illus.). 10p. (J). (gr. -1 — 1). bds. 6.99 (978-0-618-99848-7(9)) Houghton Mifflin Harcourt Publishing Co.
—The Surprise Gift. gif. ed. 2008. (Curious George Ser.). (ENG., Illus.). 24p. (J). (gr. -1-3). pap. 4.99 (978-0-618-99864-7(0)) Houghton Mifflin Harcourt Publishing Co.
—Three Tales for a Winter's Night. 2012. (Curious George TV Tie-In 8x8 Ser.). lib. bdg. 18.40 (978-0-606-26603-1(8), Turtleback) Turtleback Bks.
Rey, H. A. & Rey, Margret, illus. Curious George's ABCs. 2003. (J). bds. 9.95 (978-0-618-27708-7(0)) Houghton Mifflin Harcourt Trade & Reference Pubs.
—Curious George's Are You Curious? 2003. (J). bds. 9.95 (978-0-618-27710-0(2)) Houghton Mifflin Harcourt Trade & Reference Pubs.
—Curious George's Opposites. 2003. (J). bds. 9.95 (978-0-618-27709-4(9)) Houghton Mifflin Harcourt Trade & Reference Pubs.
Rey, H. A. & Young, Mary OKeefe. Ready for School. 2017. (Curious George Ser.). (ENG., Illus.). 14p. (J). (— 1). bds. 7.99 (978-0-544-93120-6(3), HMH Books For Young Readers) Houghton Mifflin Harcourt Publishing Co.
Rey, H. A., et al. Curious George & the Firefighters. 2007. (Curious George Ser.). (ENG., Illus.). 24p. (J). (gr. -1-3). bds. 11.99 (978-0-618-89194-8(3)) Houghton Mifflin Harcourt Publishing Co.
—Curious George Discovery Day. 2007. (Curious George Ser.). (ENG., Illus.). 14p. (J). (gr. k — 1). bds. 13.95 (978-0-618-73761-1(8)) Houghton Mifflin Harcourt Publishing Co.
—The Donut Delivery. 2007. (Curious George Ser.). (ENG., Illus.). 24p. (J). (gr. -1-3). 4.99 (978-0-618-73757-4(X)) Houghton Mifflin Harcourt Publishing Co.
—The Kite. 2007. (Curious George Ser.). (ENG., Illus.). 24p. (J). (gr. -1-3). 3.99 (978-0-618-72396-6(X)) Houghton Mifflin Harcourt Publishing Co.
—Merry Christmas, Curious George. Young, Mary O'Keefe, illus. 2012. (Curious George Ser.). (ENG.). 32p. (J). (gr. -1-3). 9.99 (978-0-547-76054-4(X)) Houghton Mifflin Harcourt Publishing Co.
Rey, Margret. Margret & H. A. Rey's Curious George Goes Camping. Vipah Interactive, illus. 2015. 24p. pap. 4.00 (978-1-61003-550-7(X)) Center for the Collaborative Classroom.
Rey, Margret & Rey, H. A. Curious George & the Hot Air Balloon, 1 vol. 2008. (Curious George Ser.). (ENG., Illus.). 24p. (gr. -1-3). lib. bdg. 24.21 (978-1-59961-412-0(X)) Spotlight.
—Curious George at the Aquarium. 2014. (Curious George 8x8 Ser.). lib. bdg. 14.75 (978-1-4177-9792-9(4), Turtleback) Turtleback Bks.
—Curious George Feeds the Animals, 1 vol. 2008. (Curious George Ser.). (ENG., Illus.). 24p. (gr. -1-3). lib. bdg. 24.21 (978-1-59961-413-7(8)) Spotlight.
—Curious George Goes Camping, 1 vol. 2007. (Read along Book & CD Ser.). (ENG., Illus.). 24p. (J). (gr. -1-3). audio compact disk 10.99 (978-0-618-73764-2(2)) Houghton Mifflin Harcourt Publishing Co.
—Curious George Goes Camping, 1 vol. 2008. (Curious George Ser.). (ENG., Illus.). 24p. (gr. -1-3). lib. bdg. 24.21 (978-1-59961-414-4(6)) Spotlight.
—Curious George Goes to an Ice Cream Shop. Rey, Margret, ed. 2011. (Curious George 8x8 Ser.). (gr. -1-2). lib. bdg. 14.75 (978-0-8335-3957-1(4), Turtleback) Turtleback Bks.
—Curious George Goes to the Beach. 2014. (Curious George 8x8 Ser.). (gr. k-3). lib. bdg. 13.55 (978-0-613-21392-9(0), Turtleback) Turtleback Bks.
—Curious George Goes to the Hospital, 1 vol. 2008. (Curious George Ser.). (ENG., Illus.). 48p. (J). (gr. -1-3). audio compact disk 10.95 (978-0-618-80063-6(8)) Houghton Mifflin Harcourt Publishing Co.
—Curious George Takes a Train, 1 vol. 2008. (Curious George Ser.). (ENG., Illus.). 24p. (gr. -1-3). lib. bdg. 24.21 (978-1-59961-418-2(9)) Spotlight.
—Curious George's First Day of School. Hines, Anna Grossnickle, illus. 2005. (Curious George Ser.). (ENG.). 24p. (J). (gr. -1-3). 13.99 (978-0-618-60563-7(0)); pap. 4.99 (978-0-618-60564-4(9)) Houghton Mifflin Harcourt Publishing Co.
—Curious George's First Day of School. Vipah Interactive Staff, illus. 2005. (Read along Book & CD Ser.). (ENG.). 24p. (J). (gr. -1-3). audio compact disk 10.99 (978-0-618-60565-1(7)) Houghton Mifflin Harcourt Publishing Co.
—Feeds the Animals, 1 vol. Vipah Interactive Staff, illus. 2005. (Read along Book & CD Ser.). (ENG.). 24p. (J). (gr. -1-3). audio compact disk 10.99 (978-0-618-60387-9(5)) Houghton Mifflin Harcourt Publishing Co.
—Makes Pancakes. 2008. (Curious George Ser.). (ENG., Illus.). 24p. (J). (gr. -1-3). audio compact disk 10.95 (978-0-618-99727-5(X)) Houghton Mifflin Harcourt Publishing Co.
—The New Adventures of Curious George. Vipah Interactive Staff, illus. 2006. (Curious George Ser.). (ENG.). 208p. (J). (gr. -1-3). 10.99 (978-0-618-66373-6(8)) Houghton Mifflin Harcourt Publishing Co.
—The Puppies. 2006. (Curious George Ser.). (ENG., Illus.). 24p. (J). (gr. -1 — 1). bds. 11.99 (978-0-618-77241-4(3)) Houghton Mifflin Harcourt Publishing Co.
—Takes a Train. Weston, Martha, illus. 2010. (Curious George Ser.). (ENG.). 24p. (J). (gr. -1-3). pap. 4.99 (978-0-547-50424-7(1)) Houghton Mifflin Harcourt Publishing Co.
Riccio, Nina M. Five Kids & a Monkey, 3 vols., Set. Blair, Beth L., illus. (J). (gr. 2-6). 23.85 (978-0-9653955-3-3(7)) Creative Attic, Inc., The.
Rickett, Sally. Minky the Shoebox Monkey - a Little Monkey with a Long Way to Go. 2010. 54p. pap. 17.95 (978-1-60860-625-2(2), Strategic Bk. Publishing) Strategic Book Publishing & Rights Agency (SBPRA).
Rigo, L., illus. Little Monkey. 2011. (Look at Me Bks.). 10p. (J). bds. 7.99 (978-0-7641-6428-6(7)) Barron's Educational Series, Inc.
Risco, Elle D. Dora Had a Little Lamb. Savitsky, Steve, illus. 2007. (Dora the Explorer Ser.). (J). (gr. -1-2). 11.65 (978-0-7569-8294-2(4)) Perfection Learning Corp.
Roberts, Daniel. Three Funky Monkeys. 2011. 36p. pap. 16.99 (978-1-4634-4732-8(9)) AuthorHouse.
Roberts, In Pursuit of the Curious Bangle J. In Pursuit of the Curious Bangle. 2010. 170p. pap. 14.50 (978-1-4457-7210-3(8)) Lulu Pr., Inc.
Robertson, Jean. Monkey Business. Dufalla, Anita, illus. 2012. (ENG.). 24p. (gr. 2-3). pap. 8.95 (978-1-61810-322-2(9)) Rourke Educational Media.
Rohrer, Kim. The Adventures of Little Dooey: The Doctor. 2012. 24p. pap. 9.95 (978-0-9848050-7-5(9), Little Creek Bks.) Jan-Carol Publishing, INC.
Roland, Timothy. Monkey Me & the Golden Monkey. Roland, Timothy, illus. 2014. (Monkey Me Ser.: 1). (ENG., Illus.). 96p. (J). (gr. 1-3). pap. 4.99 (978-0-545-55976-8(6)) Scholastic, Inc.
—Monkey Me & the Golden Monkey. 2014. (Monkey Me Ser.: 1). lib. bdg. 14.75 (978-0-606-35354-0(2)) Turtleback Bks.
—Monkey Me & the New Neighbor. 2014. (Monkey Me Ser.: 3). lib. bdg. 14.75 (978-0-606-35360-1(7)) Turtleback Bks.
—Monkey Me & the Pet Show. 2014. (Monkey Me Ser.: 2). (ENG.). 96p. (J). (gr. 1-3). 15.99 (978-0-545-55981-2(2)) Scholastic, Inc.
—Monkey Me & the Pet Show. 2014. (Monkey Me Ser.: 2). lib. bdg. 14.75 (978-0-606-35359-5(3)) Turtleback Bks.
—Monkey Me & the School Ghost. 2014. (Illus.). 90p. (J). (978-1-4844-3840-4(X)) Scholastic, Inc.
—Monkey Me & the School Ghost. 2014. (Monkey Me Ser.: 4). lib. bdg. 14.75 (978-0-606-36053-1(0)) Turtleback Bks.
—The Pet Show. 2014. (Monkey Me Ser.: 2). (ENG.). 96p. (J). (gr. 1-3). pap. 4.99 (978-0-545-55980-5(4)) Scholastic, Inc.
Rosano, John. Molly Monkey. 2008. (Illus.). (J). 14.95 (978-1-60131-013-2(7)) Big Tent Bks.
Rosario, Joann. Bitty Witty Witty Witty Monkey! Rosario, Joann, illus. 2004. (Illus.). 10p. (J). pap. 10.00 (978-0-9758746-9-1(1), 1246169) J.G.R. Enterprises.
Ross, Patrick. Oliver: The Great Escape. Burcham, David, illus. 2009. 34p. pap. 24.95 (978-1-60749-151-4(6)) America Star Bks.
Rothstein, Arminio & Brixler, Andreas. TOBY & TOBIAS: Die Abenteuer aus dem ZIRKUS HABAKUK. 2010. 134p. pap. 14.90 (978-3-8391-0292-3(8)) Bks. on Demand.
Roy, Ron. Mystery at the Washington Monument. Bush, Timothy, illus. 2007. (Capital Mysteries Ser.: No. 8). 87p. (gr. 1-4). 15.00 (978-0-7569-7845-7(9)) Perfection Learning Corp.
—Mystery at the Washington Monument. Bush, Timothy, illus. 2007. (Capital Mysteries Ser.: No. 8). (ENG.). 96p. (J). (gr. 1-4). per. 4.99 (978-0-375-83970-2(4), Random Hse. Bks. for Young Readers) Random Hse. Children's Bks.
Ruberto, Carolyn. There Was a Monkey. 2012. (Illus.). 40p. pap. 22.88 (978-1-4772-4570-5(7)) AuthorHouse.
Rylant, Cynthia. The Case of the Missing Monkey. Karas, G. Brian, illus. 2003. (I Can Read Level 2 Ser.: No. 1). (ENG.). 48p. (J). (gr. k-3). pap. 3.99 (978-0-06-444306-7(X), Greenwillow Bks.) HarperCollins Pubs.
—The Case of the Missing Monkey. Karas, G. Brian, illus. 2003. (High-Rise Private Eyes Ser.: No. 1). (J). 25.95 incl. audio (978-1-59112-194-7(9)); pap. 29.95 incl. audio (978-1-59112-195-4(7)) Live Oak Media.
—The Case of the Missing Monkey. Karas, G. Brian, illus. 2003. (High-Rise Private Eyes Ser.: 1). 46p. (J). (gr. 1-17). 13.55 (978-0-613-44194-0(X), Turtleback) Turtleback Bks.
Sandusky, Thomas & Hill, Kathy. Spidy the Spider Monkey. Johnson, Gretchen, illus. 2009. 32p. pap. 12.95 (978-0-9823002-5-1(5)) Peppertree Pr., The.
Santat, Dan. The Guild of Geniuses. 2004. (ENG., Illus.). 40p. (J). (gr. -1-3). 17.99 (978-0-439-43096-8(8), Levine, Arthur A. Bks.) Scholastic, Inc.
Saunders, Len. Spunky the Monkey: An Adventure in Exercise. 2010. 32p. pap. 14.95 (978-1-4389-3991-9(4)) AuthorHouse.
Sayles, Kristi. Jacob's Monkey-the Trouble with Lying. 2005. 38p. (J). pap. 10.29 (978-1-4116-6429-6(9)) Lulu Pr., Inc.
Schaefer, Carole Lexa. Monkey & Elephant. Bernstein, Galia, illus. 2013. (Candlewick Sparks Ser.). (ENG.). 48p. (J). (gr. k-4). pap. 3.99 (978-0-7636-6261-5(5)) Candlewick Pr.
—Monkey & Elephant & a Secret Birthday Surprise. Bernstein, Galia, illus. (Candlewick Sparks Ser.). (ENG.). 48p. (J). (gr. k-4). 2016. pap. 3.99 (978-0-7636-8744-1(8)) 2015. 14.99 (978-0-7636-6131-1(7)) Candlewick Pr.
—Monkey & Elephant & the Babysitting Adventure. Bernstein, Galia, illus. 2016. (ENG.). 48p. (J). (gr. k-4). 14.99 (978-0-7636-6535-7(5)) Candlewick Pr.
—Monkey & Elephant Get Better. Bernstein, Galia, illus. (Candlewick Sparks Ser.). (ENG.). 48p. (J). (gr. k-4). 2014. pap. 3.99 (978-0-7636-7180-8(0)) 2013. 14.99 (978-0-7636-4841-1(8)) Candlewick Pr.
—Monkey & Elephant Go Gadding. Bernstein, Galia, illus. 2015. (Candlewick Sparks Ser.). (ENG.). 48p. (J). (gr. k-4). pap. 3.99 (978-0-7636-8030-5(3)) Candlewick Pr.
Schweizer, Chris. Tricky Monkey Tales. Thomas, Chad, illus. 2011. (Tricky Journeys Ser.: 6). (ENG.). (J). (gr. 2-4). pap. 39.62 (978-0-7613-8630-8(0)); 64p. pap. 6.95 (978-0-7613-7860-0(X));No. 6. 64p. lib. bdg. 27.93 (978-0-7613-6611-9(3)) Lerner Publishing Group.
Scott, Nathan Kumar. Mangoes & Bananas. Balaji, T., illus. 2nd ed. 2006. (ENG.). 32p. (J). (978-81-86211-06-9(3)) Temmen, Edition, Horst Temmen.
Sehgal, Kabir & Sehgal, Surishtha. A Bucket of Blessings. Tsong, Jing Jing, illus. 2014. (ENG.). 32p. (J). (gr. -1-3). 17.99 (978-1-4424-5870-3(4), Beach Lane Bks.) Beach Lane Bks.
Sexton, Jessa R. Mobert's Irish Experience. Sexton, Jessa R., photos by. 2012. (Illus.). 34p. pap. 10.00 (978-0-9860150-3-8(2)) O'More Publishing.
Shanghai Animation Studio Staff & Tang, Sanmu. An Attempt to Scoop up the Moon. Ying, Wu, tr. from CHI. 2010. (Favorite Children's Ser.). (ENG., Illus.). 32p. (J). (gr. -1-3). pap. 5.95 (978-1-60220-971-8(5)) BetterLink Pr., Inc.
—Monkey Makes Havoc in Heaven. Xiaozhen, Wu, tr. from CHI. 2010. (Favorite Children's Ser.). (ENG., Illus.). 32p. (J). (gr. -1-3). pap. 5.95 (978-1-60220-974-9(X)) BetterLink Pr., Inc.
Shannon, Carol. Dusky Langurs at the Zoo. 2013. 40p. pap. 16.95 (978-1-4525-1014-9(8), Balboa Pr.) Author Solutions, Inc.
Shepard, Aaron. The Monkey King: A Superhero Tale of China, Retold from the Journey to the West. 2008. (Ancient Fantasy Ser.: 4). (J). 50p. lib. bdg. 15.00 (978-0-938497-40-0(5)); 44p. lib. bdg. 6.00 (978-0-938497-41-7(3)) Shepard Pubns. (Skyhook Pr.).
Shipton, Paul. Get the Fruit! Dunton, Trevor, illus. 2004. (Collins Big Cat Ser.). (ENG.). 24p. (J). (gr. -1-k). pap. 5.99 (978-0-00-718529-0(4)) HarperCollins Pubs. Ltd. GBR. Dist: Independent Pubs. Group.
Shoopman, Jim. Cowboy Zack & the Monkey from the Muggletown Zoo. 2013. 50p. pap. 13.98 (978-0-9887836-2-1(2)) Taylor and Seale Publishing, LLC.
Shreve, Steve. Monkey Island: Or the Advantage of Opposable Thumbs. Shreve, Steve, illus. 2010. (Adventures of Charlie Ser.). (Illus.). 32p. pap. (978-0-237-54288-7(9)) Evans Brothers, Ltd.
Sierra, Judy. What Time Is It, Mr. Crocodile? Cushman, Doug, illus. 2007. (ENG.). 32p. (J). (gr. -1-3). pap. 7.99 (978-0-15-205850-0(8)) Houghton Mifflin Harcourt Publishing Co.
Silberman, Dani. The Three Monkey Brothers. 2009. 28p. pap. 14.50 (978-1-60860-366-4(0), Eloquent Bks.) Strategic Book Publishing & Rights Agency (SBPRA).
Sithole, Thelma. The Little Monkey & the Crocodile. Montague, Christine, illus. 2007. 32p. per. 12.00 (978-1-59858-204-8(6)) Dog Ear Publishing, LLC.
—Little Shoko & the Crocodile. Holmes, Rebecca, illus. 2007. 36p. per. 12.00 (978-1-59858-330-4(1)) Dog Ear Publishing, LLC.
Skinner, J. C. Ringo & the Fruit Tree. 2008. 24p. pap. 24.95 (978-1-60441-028-0(0)) America Star Bks.
Slack, Michael H. & Slack, Mike. Monkey Truck. Slack, Michael H. & Slack, Mike, illus. 2011. (ENG., Illus.). 32p. (J). (gr. -1 — 1). 12.99 (978-0-8050-8878-6(4), 9780805088786, Holt, Henry & Co. Bks. For Young Readers) Holt, Henry & Co.
Slater Iii, John D. The Monkey & the Dragon Meet. 2009. 28p. pap. 12.99 (978-1-4389-4353-4(9)) AuthorHouse.
Slobodkina, Esphyr. Caps for Sale. Slobodkina, Esphyr, illus. 75th ed. 2015. (Reading Rainbow Bks.). (ENG., Illus.). 32p. (J). (gr. -1-3). bds. 8.99 (978-0-06-147453-8(3), HarperFestival) HarperCollins Pubs.
—Caps for Sale: A Tale of a Peddler, Some Monkeys & Their Monkey Business. Slobodkina, Esphyr, illus. 2008. (Young Scott Bks.). (Illus.). 48p. (J). (gr. -1-3). lib. bdg. 17.89 (978-0-06-025778-1(4)) HarperCollins Pubs.
Slobodkina, Esphyr & Sayer, Ann Marie Mulhearn. Caps for Sale & the Mindful Monkeys. Slobodkina, Esphyr, illus. 2017. (Illus.). 48p. (J). (gr. -1-3). 17.99 **(978-0-06-249988-2(2))** HarperCollins Pubs.
Slobodkina, Esphyr & Sayer, Ann Marie Mulhearn. More Caps for Sale: Another Tale of Mischievous Monkeys. Slobodkina, Esphyr, illus. (Illus.). 40p. (J). (gr. -1-3). 2017. pap. 8.99 (978-0-06-249957-8(2)) 2015. (ENG., 18.99 (978-0-06-240545-6(4)) HarperCollins Pubs.
Slobodkina, Esphyr & Slobodkina. Caps for Sale: A Tale of a Peddler, Some Monkeys & Their Monkey Business. Slobodkina, Esphyr, illus. 2015. (Young Scott Bks.). (ENG., Illus.). 48p. (J). (gr. -1-3). 17.99 (978-0-201-09147-2(X)); 75th ed. pap. 7.99 (978-0-06-443143-9(6)) HarperCollins Pubs.
Slobodkina, Esphyr & Slobodkina, E. Caps for Sale. 2015. (J). (gr. k-3). 17.20 (978-0-8085-2604-9(9), Turtleback) Turtleback Bks.
Smalley, Roger, adapted by. The Big-Hearted Monkey & the Lion. 2005. (J). (978-1-933248-02-8(5)) World Quest Learning.
Smart, Jamie. Bunny vs. Monkey. Smart, Jamie, illus. 2016. (ENG., Illus.). 64p. (J). (gr. 2-5). pap. 7.99 (978-0-545-86184-7(5), Graphix) Scholastic, Inc.
Smart, Kimberly. A New Home for Gabril. 2008. 32p. 15.95 (978-1-4357-0762-7(1)) Lulu Pr., Inc.
Smith, Carrie. Jumping Monkeys: Lap Book Edition. Daubney, Kate, illus. 2016. (My First Reader's Theater Tales Ser.). (J). (gr. k). (978-1-5021-5507-8(9)) Benchmark Education Co.
—Jumping Monkeys: Small Book Edition. Daubney, Kate, illus. 2016. (My First Reader's Theater Tales Ser.). (J). (gr. k). (978-1-5021-5512-2(5)) Benchmark Education Co.
Smith, Holly C. Tyler the Monkey & Andy the Mouse. 2012. 28p. (-18). pap. 24.95 (978-1-4626-9501-0(9)) America Star Bks.
Smith, Leone. Jasmine Finds a Doctor. Smith, Marcelle, illus. 2011. 30p. pap. 12.50 (978-1-61204-042-4(X), Strategic Bk. Publishing) Strategic Book Publishing & Rights Agency (SBPRA).
Smith, Todd Aaron. The Average Monkey. Smith, Todd Aaron, illus. 2003. (Higby the Monkey Ser.). (Illus.). 32p. (J). pap. 4.97 (978-1-58660-857-6(6)) Barbour Publishing, Inc.
—Higby Throws a Fit. Smith, Todd Aaron, illus. 2003. (Higby the Monkey Ser.). (Illus.). 32p. (J). pap. 4.97 (978-1-58660-858-3(4)) Barbour Publishing, Inc.
Snyder, Vicki & West, Lois. Lighten up Lenny. Kam, Mike, illus. 2005. (J). (978-0-9773187-0-4(2)) Snyder, Vicki.
Soderberg, Erin. Monkey See, Monkey Zoo. Francis, Guy, illus. 2010. (ENG.). 160p. (YA). (gr. 2-4). pap. 5.99 (978-1-59990-558-7(2), 9781599905587, Bloomsbury USA Childrens) Bloomsbury Publishing USA.
Sonnebom, Scott. The Good, the Bad, & the Monkeys, 1 vol. Bradley, Jessica, illus. 2013. (Comics Land Ser.). (ENG.). 32p. (gr. k-2). 7.95 (978-1-4342-6283-7(9)); lib. bdg. 25.32 (978-1-4342-4945-6(X)) Stone Arch Bks.
Southard, Patricia. Captain Andre's Adventure in the Sky. 2008. 27p. pap. 24.95 (978-1-4241-8613-6(7)) America Star Bks.
Spoor, Mike, illus. Desperate Measures: Units of Measurement in Action. 2010. (Mandrill Mountain Math Mysteries Ser.). (ENG.). 32p. (J). (gr. 2-6). pap. 10.55 (978-1-60754-925-3(5)) Windmill Bks.
—Desperate Measures: Units of Measurement in Action. 2010. (Mandrill Mountain Math Mysteries Ser.). (ENG.). 32p. (J). (gr. 2-6). lib. bdg. 22.60 (978-1-60754-920-8(4)) Windmill Bks.
—The Emperor's Guards: Concepts of Time. 2010. (Mandrill Mountain Math Mysteries Ser.). (ENG.). 32p. (J). (gr. 2-6). pap. 10.55 (978-1-60754-927-7(1)); lib. bdg. 22.60 (978-1-60754-922-2(0)) Windmill Bks.
—The Emperor's Last Command: Problem-solving in Action. 2010. (Mandrill Mountain Math Mysteries Ser.). (ENG.). 32p. (J). (gr. 2-6). pap. 10.55 (978-1-60754-928-4(X)) Windmill Bks.
—The Emperor's Last Command: Problem-Solving in Action. 2010. (Mandrill Mountain Math Mysteries Ser.). (ENG.). 32p. (J). (gr. 2-6). lib. bdg. 22.60 (978-1-60754-923-9(9)) Windmill Bks.
—The Hidden Valley: Reasoning in Action. 2010. (Mandrill Mountain Math Mysteries Ser.). (ENG.). 32p. (J). (gr. 2-6). pap. 10.55 (978-1-60754-924-6(7)); lib. bdg. 22.60 (978-1-60754-919-2(0)) Windmill Bks.
—Lightning Flash: Probability in Action. 2010. (Mandrill Mountain Math Mysteries Ser.). (ENG.). 32p. (J). (gr. 2-6). pap. 10.55 (978-1-60754-926-0(3)); lib. bdg. 22.60 (978-1-60754-921-5(2)) Windmill Bks.
Stephens, Sarah. Midway Monkey Madness, 1 vol. Baltazar, Art, illus. 2011. (DC Super-Pets Ser.). (ENG.). 56p. (gr. 2-2). pap. 4.95 (978-1-4048-6619-5(1)); lib. bdg. 23.99 (978-1-4048-6305-7(2)) Picture Window Bks. (DC Super-Pets).
Stiles, Erinn. The Monkey & the Rainbow. 2012. 36p. pap. 20.99 (978-1-4772-6918-3(5)) AuthorHouse.
Stiles, Martha Bennett. Sailing to Freedom. 2014. (ENG.). 256p. (J). (gr. 3-7). pap. 6.99 (978-1-250-03991-0(6), 9781250039910) Square Fish.
Stilton, Thea. Thea Stilton & the Prince's Emerald. 2012. (Thea Stilton Ser.: 12). lib. bdg. 19.65 (978-0-606-26534-8(1), Turtleback) Turtleback Bks.
Stockland, Patricia M. Anthill Home Repair, 1 vol. Haugen, Ryan, illus. 2008. (Safari Friends Ser.). (ENG.). 32p. (gr. -1-3). 28.50 (978-1-60270-082-6(6), Looking Glass Library) ABDO Publishing Co.
—The Big Banana Hunt, 1 vol. Haugen, Ryan, illus. 2008. (Safari Friends Ser.). (ENG.). 32p. (gr. -1-3). 28.50 (978-1-60270-083-3(4), Looking Glass Library) ABDO Publishing Co.
—Clean up the Watering Hole!, 1 vol. Haugen, Ryan, illus. 2008. (Safari Friends Ser.). (ENG.). 32p. (gr. -1-3). 28.50 (978-1-60270-084-0(2), Looking Glass Library) ABDO Publishing Co.
—Peanut Picking, 1 vol. Haugen, Ryan, illus. 2008. (Safari Friends Ser.). (ENG.). 32p. (gr. -1-3). 28.50 (978-1-60270-085-7(0), Looking Glass Library) ABDO Publishing Co.

MNO

—Stop the Grassfires!, 1 vol. Haugen, Ryan, illus. 2008. (Safari Friends Ser.). (ENG.). 32p. (gr. -1-3). 28.50 *(978-1-60270-086-4(9)*, Looking Glass Library) ABDO Publishing Co.

—Tiger Toothache, 1 vol. Haugen, Ryan, illus. 2008. (Safari Friends Ser.). (ENG.). 32p. (gr. -1-3). 28.50 *(978-1-60270-087-1(7)*, Looking Glass Library) ABDO Publishing Co.

Strasser, Stephanie. Blue Bananas. 2010. 28p. pap. 12.49 *(978-1-4490-5327-7(0))* AuthorHouse.

Studio Mouse Staff. Five Little Monkeys: And Other Counting Rhymes. Elliott, Rebecca et al, illus. rev. ed. 2007. (ENG.). 24p. (J). (gr. -1-k). 4.99 *(978-1-59069-608-8(5))* Studio Mouse LLC.

Sturm, James, illus. Birdsong: a Story in Pictures: TOON Level 1. 2016. (ENG.). 60p. (J). (gr. k). 12.95 *(978-1-935179-94-8(2))* TOON Books / RAW Junior, LLC.

Stycznski, Gary. The Animals of Greenback Valley: The Magic Card. 2009. 32p. pap. 24.95 *(978-1-59858-930-6(X))* Dog Ear Publishing, LLC.

Subrina. Jacko the Monkey. 2013. 16p. pap. 24.95 *(978-1-63000-145-2(7))* America Star Bks.

Tabares, Veronica. Monkeys on an Island. Tabares, Bridgitt, illus. 2012. 32p. (J). pap. 14.50 *(978-1-60916-005-0(3))* Sun Break Publishing.

Tagge, Mark. The Coma & Convulsion Club: The Retreat. 2008. 112p. pap. 13.99 *(978-1-4259-7221-9(7))* AuthorHouse.

Tang, Youshan, illus. The Magical Monkey King: Mischief in Heaven. 2004. (J). (gr. 2-5). 113p. 14.95 *(978-1-885008-24-4(4))*; 32p. per. 8.95 *(978-1-885008-25-1(2))* Lee & Low Bks., Inc. (Shen's Bks.).

Tao, Ted. The Monkey King & the Book of Death. 2008. (ENG., Illus.). 200p. (YA). pap. 7.99 *(978-1-930655-01-0(0))* Golden Peach Publishing.

Tay-Audouard, L. K. Monkey King: A Classic Chinese Tale for Children. 2017. (ENG., Illus.). 32p. (J). (gr. -1-3). 9.95 *(978-0-8048-4840-4(8))* Tuttle Publishing.

Taylor, Sean. Mojo & Weeza & the New Hat: Band 04/Blue. Mosedale, Julian, illus. 2007. (Collins Big Cat Ser.). (ENG.). 16p. (J). (gr. -1-1). pap. 5.99 *(978-0-00-718662-4(2))* HarperCollins Pubs. Ltd. GBR. Dist: Independent Pubs. Group.

Tekavec, Heather. Manners Are Not for Monkeys. Huyck, David, illus. 2016. (ENG.). 32p. (J). (gr. -1-2). 16.95 *(978-1-77138-051-5(9))* Kids Can Pr., Ltd. CAN. Dist: Hachette Bk. Group.

Terada, Junzo. Animal Friends: Swimming Hole Party! 2017. (ENG., Illus.). 10p. (J). bds. 9.99 *(978-1-4521-4983-7(6))* Chronicle Bks. LLC.

Thompson, Kim Mitzo. Five Little Monkeys Jumping on the Bed. Girouard, Patrick, illus. 2010. (Padded Board Book W/CD Ser.). 8p. (J). (gr. k-2). bds. 10.99 incl. audio compact disk *(978-1-59922-581-4(6))* Twin Sisters IP, LLC.

Thomson, Sarah L. Quick, Little Monkey! Judge, Lita, illus. 2016. (ENG.). 32p. (J). (gr. -1-2). 16.95 *(978-1-62979-100-5(8))* Boyds Mills Pr.

Thottam, Meena, adapted by. Monkey Do as Monkey Does. 2006. (J). 3.95 *(978-0-9776917-0-8(5)*, Curcumin Bks.) Davlaw Press.

Tidwell, Mae B. & Hancock, Vicki. Kyle Wants to Be a Monkey, 1 vol. 2009. 24p. pap. 24.95 *(978-1-60749-751-6(4))* America Star Bks.

Top That! Playtime Shapes (large Version) Parry, Jo, illus. 2007. 10p. (J). (gr. -1). *(978-1-84666-555-4(8)*, Tide Mill Pr.) Top That! Publishing PLC.

Top That!, creator. Animals with Martha the Monkey. 2012. (Learn with Magnets Ser.). (ENG., Illus.). 10p. (gr. -1-k). *(978-1-84956-670-4(4))* Top That! Publishing PLC.

Toral, Miguel A. Babu Goes Back to the Zoo. 2009. 32p. pap. 15.70 *(978-1-4389-6330-3(0))* AuthorHouse.

Towe, H.P. Mr. Monkey Sees & Mr. Monkey Do. 2013. 24p. pap. 14.93 *(978-1-4669-8760-9(X))* Trafford Publishing.

Twinn, A. Ten Little Monkeys: Jumping on the Bed. Freeman, Tina, illus. 2007. (Classic Books with Holes 8x8 with CD Ser.). (ENG.). 16p. (J). (gr. -1-1). pap. incl. audio compact disk *(978-1-904550-67-9(3))* Child's Play International Ltd.

Ufer, David A. The Giraffe Who Was Afraid of Heights, 1 vol. Carlson, Kirsten, illus. 2006. (ENG.). 32p. (J). (gr. -1-3). 15.95 *(978-0-9768823-0-5(2))* Arbordale Publishing.

Uncle Chuck. The Monkey Puzzle Tree. 2011. 32p. pap. 24.95 *(978-1-4560-6992-6(6))* America Star Bks.

Valentine, Victoria. The Cutest Little Duckie. Tucker, Amanda, illus. 2007. 80p. (J). per. 15.00 *(978-0-9723493-4-5(0)*, Water Forest Pr.) Skyline Pubn.

van Galen, Maggie. The Adventures of Keeno & Ernest: The Diamond Mine. 2013. (ENG.). 28p. (J). 19.95 *(978-1-4787-1812-3(9))* Outskirts Pr., Inc.

Verano, Vladimir, illus. The Prince, the Demon King, & the Monkey Warrior. 2011. (ENG.). 96p. (J). (gr. 3-6). pap. 9.95 *(978-1-934159-30-9(1))* ThingsAsian Pr.

Vickery-Bharadwaj, Janice. Valentino & His Friends: It's Magic! 2012. 28p. pap. 12.99 *(978-1-4691-7709-0(9))* Xlibris Corp.

Viselman, Kenn. I Love You Bunches. 2004. (Illus.). 28p. 14.98 *(978-0-9722361-0-2(4))* Viselman, Kenn Presents...

Vorster, Nicola. A Monkeys' Wedding. 2012. (Illus.). 24p. pap. 21.35 *(978-1-4772-3126-5(9))* AuthorHouse.

Wang, Margaret. Monkey Tumbles. Elliott, Rebecca, illus. 2007. (ENG.). 10p. (gr. -1-k). bds. 9.95 *(978-1-58117-501-1(9)*, Intervisual/Piggy Toes) Bendon, Inc.

Watt, Fiona. That's Not My Monkey. 2008. (Touchy-Feely Board Bks). 10p. (J). bds. 7.99 *(978-0-7945-2178-3(9)*, Usborne) EDC Publishing.

Weaver, Greg & Weaver, Allie. Mickey the Monkey Makes a Friend. 2013. 24p. pap. 24.95 *(978-1-63000-802-4(8))* America Star Bks.

Wehrmeijer, Annelien. Noah & Dexter. van de Liejgraaf, Deborah, illus. 2014. (My Best Friend & Me Ser.). (ENG.). 10p. (J). (gr. -1 — 1). bds. 6.99 *(978-0-7641-6662-4(X))* Barron's Educational Series, Inc.

Weiss, Fred G. Mag-Nan-I-Mous Monkey & Gerald Giraffe. 2013. 28p. 18.99 *(978-0-9898820-5-7(5))* Mindstir Media.

Wert, Yijin, tr. The Little Monkey King's Journey: Retold in English & Chinese. Jian, Li, illus. 2012. (ENG & CHI.). 48p. (J). (gr. -1-3). 16.95 *(978-1-60220-981-7(2))* BetterLink Pr., Inc.

Weston Woods Staff, creator. Curious George Rides a Bike. 2004. (J). 38.75 *(978-1-55592-819-3(6))*; 18.95 *(978-1-55592-802-5(1))* Weston Woods Studios, Inc.

Whitfield, Peter. Up & Down. Bevington, Nancy, illus. 2005. (Zen Tails Ser.). (ENG.). 28p. (J). (gr. -1-3). 15.95 *(978-1-894965-22-4(1))* Simply Read Bks. CAN. Dist: Ingram Publisher Services.

Wiley. The Extraordinary Adventures of Ordinary Basil: Island of the Volcano Monkeys. 2007. (Ordinary Basil Ser.). (J). pap. *(978-0-439-86133-5(0))* Blue Sky Pr.

Wilkerson, Dawn. Katie & Katoa Travel down the River. 2009. 48p. pap. 16.95 *(978-1-61582-862-3(1))* America Star Bks.

Williams, Emma Louise. What's That Smell Monkey? williams, Emma Louise, illus. 2012. 12p. pap. 7.99 *(978-1-939076-07-6(2))* Wiggies, Piggy.

Williams, Rozanne Lanczak. Monkey in the Story Tree. Hanke, Karen, illus. 2006. (Learn to Write Ser.). 8p. (J). (gr. k-2). pap. 3.49 *(978-1-59198-282-1(0)*, 6176) Creative Teaching Pr., Inc.

—Monkey in the Story Tree. Maio, Barbara & Faulkner, Stacey, eds. Hanke, Karen, illus. 2006. (J). per. 6.99 *(978-1-59198-333-0(9))* Creative Teaching Pr., Inc.

Williams, Suzanne. Ten Naughty Little Monkeys. Watts, Suzanne, illus. 2007. 32p. (J). (gr. -1-3). lib. bdg. 17.89 *(978-0-06-059905-8(7))* HarperCollins Pubs.

Wilson. Keely, Ivy, & Me. 2009. 28p. pap. 14.99 *(978-1-4389-7219-0(9))* AuthorHouse.

Wissman, Celeste Farris. When I Teach My Monkey How to Dance. 2012. 24p. pap. 17.99 *(978-1-4772-6035-7(8))* AuthorHouse.

Wolf, Justin. The Adventures of Silly Monkey & Jack. 2011. 20p. (gr. 1-2). pap. 12.99 *(978-1-4567-6452-4(7))* AuthorHouse.

Wood, Deanna Plummer. Whenever Monkeys Move Next Door, 1 volume. 2005. (Illus.). 24p. (J). pap. 8.50 *(978-0-9762935-1-4(X))* Perkins Crawford.

Woodward, Joanie. Seven Little Monkeys. Woodward, Joanie, illus. 2005. (Illus.). 40p. (J). per. *(978-0-9754676-4-0(6))* Yeoman Hse.

Wurge, B. B. Squiggle. 2009. (LeapKids Ser.). (ENG., Illus.). 152p. (J). (gr. 2-7). pap. 9.95 *(978-0-9815148-9-5(8))* Leapfrog Pr.

Yerrid, Gable. Marley's Treasure. Fitzgerald, Jennifer, illus. 2007. 28p. (J). (gr. -1-3). 15.95 *(978-0-9767442-6-9(0))* Yorkville Pr.

Yunger, Joshua. Hippo & Monkey. 2012. (Adventures of Hippo & Monkey Ser.: 1). (ENG., Illus.). 48p. (J). (gr. 1-3). 19.95 *(978-1-59373-107-6(8))* Bunker Hill Publishing, Inc.

Zajac, Kristen J. Ebeneezer's Cousin. Houdeshell, Jennifer T., illus. 2010. 20p. pap. 10.95 *(978-1-61633-045-3(7))* Guardian Angel Publishing, Inc.

Zajac, Kristen K. Ebeneezer's Cousin. Houdeshell, Jennifer Thomas, illus. 2013. 24p. 19.95 *(978-1-61633-440-6(1))* Guardian Angel Publishing, Inc.

Zana, Brian. Maurice Tries New Foods. 2012. 24p. pap. 15.99 *(978-1-4797-1430-8(5))* Xlibris Corp.

Ziefert, Harriet. Monkey's Noisy Jungle. Newton, Jill, illus. 2007. bds. 7.95 *(978-1-59354-598-7(3))* Blue Apple Bks.

Zoehfeld, Kathleen Weidner & Rey, H. A. Curious You on Your Way! 2008. (Curious George Ser.). (ENG., Illus.). 32p. (J). (gr. -1-3). 12.95 *(978-0-618-91975-8(9))* Houghton Mifflin Harcourt Publishing Co.

Zur Muehlen, Nersel. Monkey in the Mirror. Sanchez, Sara, illus. 2012. 56p. pap. 14.95 *(978-0-9829224-2-2(6))* BPM Research LLC.

Zvetkoff, Kathleen Charnes. The Adventures of Willy the Monkey. 2008. 40p. pap. *(978-0-9784909-5-9(9))* Soul Asylum Poetry.

MONKS

see Monasticism and Religious Orders

MONOLOGUES

Here are entered collections of monologues.

Bauman, Elizabeth. Private Stories: Monologues for Young Actors Ages 8 to 16 & the Seven Key Questions to Unlock Your Imagination. 2007. (ENG.). 152p. per. 10.95 *(978-0-87910-341-5(8)*, 0879103418, Limelight Editions) Leonard, Hal Corp.

Bolton, Martha. Humorous Monologues. Behr, Joyce, illus. 2003. 128p. (J). (gr. 2-7). 19.00 *(978-0-8069-6750-9(1))* Sterling Publishing Co., Inc.

Dabrowski, Kristen. My Second Monologue Book: Famous & Historical People: 100 Monologues for Young Children. 2008. (My First Acting Ser.). (Illus.). 112p. (J). (gr. 1-8). pap. 11.95 *(978-1-57525-601-6(0))* Smith & Kraus Pubs., Inc.

—My Third Monologue Book: 100 Monologues about Places near & Far. 2008. 112p. (J). (gr. 1-8). pap. 11.95 *(978-1-57525-602-3(9))* Smith & Kraus Pubs., Inc.

—Teens Speak, Girls Ages 13 to 15: Sixty Original Character Monologues. 2005. (Kids Speak Ser.). 80p. pap. 11.95 *(978-1-57525-412-8(3))* Smith & Kraus Pubs., Inc.

—The Ultimate Audition Book for Middle School Actors Volume IV: 111 One-Minute Monologues: the Rich, the Famous, the Historical, Vol. 4. 2008. (Young Actors Ser.: Vol. IV). 160p. (J). pap. 11.95 *(978-1-57525-579-8(0))* Smith & Kraus Pubs., Inc.

—111 One-Minute Monologues: The Ultimate Monologue Book for Middle School Actors, Vol. 3. 2004. (Ultimate Monologue Book for Middle School Actors Ser.: Vol. 1). 136p. (J). pap. 11.95 *(978-1-57525-419-7(0))* Smith & Kraus Pubs., Inc.

Depner, Mary. Smart Monologues: Vocabulary Building Monologues for Teens & Young Adults. 2012. (ENG.). (YA). pap. 9.95 *(978-1-4675-3844-2(2))* Independent Pub.

Fife, Stephen, et al, eds. One on One: Playing with a Purpose - Monologues for Kids 7-14. 2013. (ENG.). 248p. pap. 16.99 *(978-1-55783-841-4(0)*, 1557838410, Applause Theatre & Cinema) Leonard, Hal Corp.

Gaddis, Alisha. Kids' Comedic Monologues That Are Actually Funny. 2016. (ENG.). 208p. pap. 14.99 *(978-1-4950-1176-4(3)*, 1495011763, Applause Theatre & Cinema) Leonard, Hal Corp.

—Teen Boys Comedic Monologues That Are Actually Funny. 2015. (ENG.). 216p. pap. 14.99 *(978-1-4803-9679-1(6)*, 1480396796, Applause Theatre & Cinema) Leonard, Hal Corp.

—Teen Girls' Comedic Monologues That Are Actually Funny. 2015. (ENG.). 208p. pap. 14.99 *(978-1-4803-9680-7(X)*, 148039680X) Leonard, Hal Corp.

Haehnel, Alan. Remotely Related: Comedy Monologue. 2003. (YA). pap. 4.50 *(978-1-932404-05-0(8)*, 273) Brooklyn Pubs.

Howard, Vernon. Monologues for Teens. Landes, William-Alan, ed. unabr. ed. 2003. (Illus.). 120p. (J). pap. 15.00 *(978-0-88734-666-8(9))* Players Pr., Inc.

Jelliroll. Echo Booming Monologues. 2007. per. 11.95 net. *(978-1-60402-529-3(8))* Independent Pub.

Johansen, Mila. 50 Scenes to Go: And 20 Monologues to Show. 2003. (Illus.). 160p. (YA). (gr. 4-12). pap. 25.00 *(978-0-88734-933-1(1))* Players Pr., Inc.

Lamedman, Debbie. The Ultimate Audition Book for Teens Vol. II: 111 Monologues from Classical Theater, 2 Minutes & Under. 2006. 11.95 *(978-1-57525-458-6(1))* Smith & Kraus Pubs., Inc.

—The Ultimate Audition Book for Teens Vol. III: 111 Monologues from Classical Literature, 2 Minutes & Under, VIII. 2006. (ENG.). (J). 11.95 *(978-1-57525-459-3(X))* Smith & Kraus Pubs., Inc.

—The Ultimate Audition Book for Teens IV: 111 One Minute Monologues. 2003. (Ultimate Audition Book for Teens Ser.: Vol. 4). viii, 117p. (J). 11.95 *(978-1-57525-353-4(4))* Smith & Kraus Pubs., Inc.

McCormick, Kimberly A. Hey, Girlfriend: Seventy-five monologues for Girls, 1 vol. 2009. (ENG.). 160p. (YA). (gr. 9-18). pap. 15.95 *(978-1-56608-162-7(9))* Meriwether Publishing, Ltd.

Meadows, Kelly. The Dating Game: Comedy Monologue. 2003. (YA). pap. 4.50 *(978-1-932404-06-7(6)*, 274) Brooklyn Pubs.

Mercanti, J. V. In Performance: Contemporary Monologues for Teens. 2015. (ENG.). 200p. pap. 16.99 *(978-1-4803-9661-6(3)*, 1480396613, Applause Theatre & Cinema) Leonard, Hal Corp.

Milstein, Janet. Winners Competition Series: Award-Winning, Custom-Made, 90-Second Comic Monologues Ages 13-18, Vol. 3. 2008. 96p. (YA). pap. 14.95 *(978-1-57525-614-6(2))* Smith & Kraus Pubs., Inc.

—Winners Competition Series Volume I: Award-winning, Custom-made, 60-Second Comic Monologues Ages 4-12. 2008. 96p. (J). pap. *(978-1-57525-612-2(6))* Smith & Kraus Pubs., Inc.

Muir, Kerry. Childsplay: A Collection of Scenes & Monologues for Children, 1 vol. Johnson, Kris, photos by. 2004. (ENG., Illus.). 260p. (Orig.). (gr. -1-18). pap. 16.99 *(978-0-87910-188-6(1)*, 0879101881, Limelight Editions) Leonard, Hal Corp.

Roddy, Ruth Mae. More Minute Monologues for Kids: Contemporary Scene-Study Pieces for Kids. 2005. 57p. (J). pap. 9.95 *(978-0-940669-57-4(9))* Dramaline Pubns.

Stevens, Chambers. Magnificent Monologues for Kids 2: More Kids' Monologues for Every Occasion! 2008. (Hollywood 101 Ser.). 79p. (J). (gr. k-7). pap. 14.95 *(978-1-883995-14-0(0))* Sandcastle Publishing.

Surface, Mary Hall. More Short Scenes & Monologues for Middle School Students: Inspired by Literature, Social Studies, & Real Life. 2007. (Young Actors Ser.). 207p. (J). (gr. 3-7). pap. 11.95 *(978-1-57525-560-6(X))* Smith & Kraus Pubs., Inc.

Young, Rebecca. 102 Great Monologues: A versatile collection of monologues & duologues for student Actors, 1 vol. 2010. (ENG.). 154p. (J). pap. 16.95 *(978-1-56608-171-9(8))* Meriwether Publishing, Ltd.

MONOPLANES

see Airplanes

MONROE, JAMES, 1758-1831

Gross, Miriam. How to Draw the Life & Times of James Monroe. (Kid's Guide to Drawing the Presidents of the United States of America Ser.). 2009. 32p. (gr. 4-4). 50.50 *(978-1-61511-149-7(2)*, PowerKids Pr.) 2006. (YA). (gr. 2-5). 26.50 *(978-1-4042-2982-2(5))* Rosen Publishing Group, Inc., The.

Gunderson, Megan M. James Monroe, 1 vol. 2009. (United States Presidents Ser.). (ENG., Illus.). 40p. (YA). (gr. 3-6). 27.07 *(978-1-60453-467-2(2))* ABDO Publishing Co.

Hinman, Bonnie. James Monroe. 2017. (Premier Presidents Ser.). (ENG.). 24p. (J). (gr. 1-4). lib. bdg. 27.07 *(978-1-5038-1647-3(8)*, 211490) Child's World, Inc., The.

Kelley, K. C. James Monroe: The 5th President. 2016. (First Look at America's Presidents Ser.). (ENG., Illus.). 24p. (J). (gr. -1-3). 17.95 *(978-1-944102-64-7(7))* Bearport Publishing Co., Inc.

Levy, Debbie. James Monroe. 2005. (Presidential Leaders Ser.). (Illus.). 112p. (J). 29.27 *(978-0-8225-0824-3(9)*, Lerner Pubns.) Lerner Publishing Group.

Lusted, Marcia Amidon. Revolution & the New Nation: 1750-Early 1800s. 2007. (Presidents of the United States Ser.). (Illus.). 48p. (J). (gr. 4-7). lib. bdg. 29.05 *(978-1-59036-739-1(1))*; per. 10.95 *(978-1-59036-740-7(5))* Weigl Pubs., Inc.

Marcovitz, Hal. James Monroe. 2004. (Childhoods of the Presidents Ser.). (Illus.). 48p. (J). (gr. 4-18). lib. bdg. 17.95 *(978-1-59084-283-6(9))* Mason Crest.

Naden, Corinne J. & Blue, Rose. James Monroe. 2008. (Presidents & Their Times Ser.). 96p. (gr. 6-18). lib. bdg. 34.21 *(978-0-7614-2838-1(0)*, Benchmark Bks.) Marshall Cavendish Corp.

Venezia, Mike. James Monroe. Venezia, Mike, illus. 2005. (Getting to Know the U. S. Presidents Ser.). (ENG., Illus.). 32p. (J). (gr. 3-4). pap. 7.95 *(978-0-516-27479-9(1)*, Children's Pr.) Scholastic Library Publishing.

MONROE DOCTRINE

Alagna, Magdalena. The Monroe Doctrine: An End to European Colonies in America. (Life in the New American Nation Ser.). 32p. 2009. (gr. 4-4). 47.90 *(978-1-61514-285-9(1))* 2004. (Illus.). (gr. 5-8). pap. 10.00 *(978-0-8239-4258-9(9))* Rosen Publishing Group, Inc., The.

Renehan, Edward J., Jr. The Monroe Doctrine: The Cornerstone of American Foreign Policy. 2007. (Milestones in American History Ser.). (Illus.). 128p. (YA). (gr. 7-12). 35.00 *(978-0-7910-9353-5(0))* Facts On File, Inc.

MONSTERS

see also Dragons; Dwarfs; Giants

Abbott, Simon, illus. Learn to Draw: Monsters. 2011. (Learn to Draw Ser.). (ENG.). 24p. (J). (gr. k-2). pap. 6.95 *(978-1-84898-200-0(3)*, TickTock Books) Octopus Publishing Group GBR. Dist: Independent Pubs. Group.

ABDO Publishing Company Staff. Creatures of Legend. 2014. (Creatures of Legend Ser.: 6). (ENG.). 48p. (gr. 3-6). lib. bdg. 196.74 *(978-1-62403-149-6(8))* ABDO Publishing Co.

Altmann, Scott. Vampire Mazes. 2011. (Dover Children's Activity Bks.). (ENG., Illus.). 48p. (J). (gr. 3-4). pap. 4.99 *(978-0-486-47922-4(6))* Dover Pubns., Inc.

Anderson, Holly Lynn. Unexplained Monsters & Cryptids. 2015. (J). *(978-1-61900-071-1(7))* Eldorado Ink.

Ard, Catherine. Origami Monsters. 2015. (Amazing Origami Ser.). (ENG.). 32p. (J). (gr. 2-3). 26.60 *(978-1-4824-2201-6(8))* Stevens, Gareth Publishing LLLP.

Aunt Darla. There's a Monster under the Captain's Bed!!! Erik's Monster. Petersen, Darla & Shields, Erik P., illus. Date not set. 32p. 16.00 *(978-0-9658926-1-2(1))* Poet Tree Pubns.

Beaumont, Steve. Drawing Legendary Monsters, 6 vols., Set. Incl. Drawing Dragons: And Other Cold-Blooded Creatures. lib. bdg. 26.50 *(978-1-4488-3324-5(8))*; Drawing Griffins & Other Winged Wonders. lib. bdg. 26.50 *(978-1-4488-3253-8(5))*; Drawing the Kraken & Other Sea Monsters. lib. bdg. 26.50 *(978-1-4488-3252-1(7))*; Drawing the Minotaur & Other Demihumans. lib. bdg. 26.50 *(978-1-4488-3250-7(0))*; Drawing Unicorns & Other Mythical Beasts. lib. bdg. 26.50 *(978-1-4488-3251-4(9))*; Drawing Werewolves & Other Gothic Ghouls. 26.50 *(978-1-4488-3254-5(3))*; (J). (gr. 3-6). (Drawing Legendary Monsters Ser.). (Illus.). 32p. 2011. Set lib. bdg. 151.50 *(978-1-4488-3267-5(5)*, PowerKids Pr.) Rosen Publishing Group, Inc., The.

BeaverSimon. FANTASTIC CREATURES: MONSTERS, MERMAIDS, AND WILD MEN BEGINNING BOOK WITH ONLINE ACCESS. 2014. (ENG.). 24p. (J). pap. 9.50 *(978-1-107-69637-2(2))* Cambridge Univ. Pr.

Becker, Helaine. Monster Science: Could Monsters Survive (and Thrive!) in the Real World? McAndrew, Phil, illus. 2016. (ENG.). 96p. (J). (gr. 3-7). 18.95 *(978-1-77138-054-6(3))* Kids Can Pr., Ltd. CAN. Dist: Hachette Bk. Group.

Bergin, Mark. Ghosts & Ghouls. 2012. (It's Fun to Draw Ser.). (Illus.). 32p. (J). (gr. k-3). lib. bdg. 26.50 *(978-1-61533-600-5(1))* Windmill Bks.

—Monsters. 2012. (It's Fun to Draw Ser.). (Illus.). 32p. (J). (gr. k-3). lib. bdg. 26.50 *(978-1-61533-601-2(X))* Windmill Bks.

Bernhardt, Carolyn. Gila Monster: Venomous Desert Dweller. 2017. (Illus.). 32p. (J). **(978-1-68079-773-2(5))** ABDO Publishing Co.

Blade, Adam. A to Z of Beasts. 2016. (Beast Quest Ser.). (ENG., Illus.). 208p. (J). (gr. 2-17). 8.99 *(978-1-4083-3839-1(4)*, Orchard Bks.) Hachette Children's Group GBR. Dist: Hachette Bk. Group.

—The Book of Beasts. 2015. (Beast Quest Ser.). (ENG., Illus.). 128p. (J). (gr. 2-4). pap. 8.99 *(978-1-4083-1137-0(2)*, Orchard Bks.) Hachette Children's Group GBR. Dist: Hachette Bk. Group.

Bradley, Timothy. The Science of Monsters (Grade 6) 2016. (TIME for KIDS(r) Nonfiction Readers Ser.). (Illus.). 64p. (J). (gr. 6-6). 10.99 *(978-1-4938-3607-9(2))* Teacher Created Materials, Inc.

Bradley, Timothy J. The Science of Monsters. 2016. (Time for Kids Nonfiction Readers Ser.). (ENG.). (J). (gr. 5-8). lib. bdg. 22.10 **(978-0-606-39543-4(1))** Turtleback Bks.

Bradley, Timothy J. Strange but True: Bizarre Animals, 1 vol. 2nd rev. ed. 2012. (Nonfiction Readers Ser.). (ENG.). 48p. (J). (gr. 4-4). pap. 9.99 *(978-1-4333-4861-7(6))* Teacher Created Materials, Inc.

Brassey, Richard. Nessie the Loch Ness Monster. 2010. (ENG., Illus.). 24p. (gr. k-2). pap. 9.99 *(978-1-4440-0056-6(X)*, Orion Children's Bks.) Hachette Children's Group GBR. Dist: Hachette Bk. Group.

Braun, Eric. The Truth about Ogres, 1 vol. Tenney, Shawna J. C., illus. 2010. (Fairy-Tale Superstars Ser.). (ENG.). 32p. (gr. 1-3). lib. bdg. 27.32 *(978-1-4048-6159-6(9))* Picture Window Bks.

Brett, Flora. Get to Know Gila Monsters. 2015. (Get to Know Reptiles Ser.). (ENG.). 24p. (gr. 1-2). lib. bdg. 25.32 *(978-1-4914-2061-4(8))* Capstone Press of Coughlan Cos.

Brinker, Spencer. Odd or Even in a Monstrous Season. 2015. (Illus.). 32p. (J). lib. bdg. *(978-1-62724-331-5(3))* Bearport Publishing Co., Inc.

Brown, Marcy & Haley, Dennis. We Both Read Bilingual Edition-The Well-Mannered Monster/el Monstruo Debuenos Modales. Raglin, Tim, illus. 2011. (ENG & SPA.). 44p. (J). pap. 4.99 *(978-1-60115-044-8(X))* Treasure Bay, Inc.

Brown, Marcy, et al. The Well-Mannered Monster: Monstruo de Buenos Modales. Raglin, Tim, illus. 2010. 41p. (J). *(978-1-60115-043-1(1))* Treasure Bay, Inc.

Calcium Staff, contrib. by. The Monsters & Creatures of Greek Mythology, 1 vol. 2011. (Ancient Greek Mythology Ser.). (ENG.). 64p. (gr. 5-7). lib. bdg. 33.99 *(978-0-7565-4481-2(5)*, CPB Grades 4-8) Compass Point Bks.

Caldwell, Stella. Beastworld. 2016. (ENG., Illus.). 80p. (J). (gr. 3). 19.95 *(978-1-78312-106-9(8))* Carlton Kids GBR. Dist: Sterling Publishing Co., Inc.

Cheatham, Mark. Gremlins!, 1 vol., 1. 2014. (Jr. Graphic Monster Stories Ser.). (ENG.). 24p. (J). (gr. 3-6). 26.25 *(978-1-4777-6215-8(9)*, PowerKids Pr.) Rosen Publishing Group, Inc., The.

Chmielewski, Gary. The Ghost Zone: Jokes, Riddles, Tongue Twisters & Daffynitions. Caputo, Jim, illus. rev. ed. 2009. (Funny Zone Ser.). (ENG.). 24p. (J). (gr. 2-4). lib. bdg. 22.60 *(978-1-59953-297-4(2))* Norwood Hse. Pr.

Christopher, Neil. Those That Cause Fear, 1 vol. Arnaktauyok, Germaine, illus. 2016. (ENG.). 40p. (J). (gr. 2-4). 16.95 *(978-1-77227-085-3(7))* Inhabit Media Inc. CAN. Dist: Independent Pubs. Group.

Clark, Willow. Gila Monster! 2010. (Animal Danger Zone Ser.). (ENG.). 24p. (J). (gr. k-3). lib. bdg. 22.60 *(978-1-60754-960-4(3))*; (Illus.). pap. 8.15 *(978-1-60754-966-6(2))* Windmill Bks.

Collins, Terry Lee & Weakland, Mark Andrew. Scooby-Doo! & the Truth Behind Zombies. 2016. (Illus.). 24p. (J). *(978-1-4062-8894-0(2))* Capstone Press of Coughlan Cos.

—Scooby Doo Unmasks the Truth Behind Sea Monsters. 2016. (Illus.). 24p. (J). *(978-1-4062-8898-8(5))* Capstone Press of Coughlan Cos.

Cox, Barbara & Forbes, Scott. Beyond the Grave, Vol. 1. 2014. (Creepy Chronicles Ser.). (ENG., Illus.). 32p. (J). (gr. 5-6). 26.60 *(978-1-4824-0226-1(2))* Stevens, Gareth Publishing LLLP.

—Maniacal Monsters & Bizarre Beasts, Vol. 1. 2014. (Creepy Chronicles Ser.). (ENG., Illus.). 32p. (J). (gr. 5-6). 26.60 *(978-1-4824-0236-0(X))* Stevens, Gareth Publishing LLLP.

—Spooky Spirits & Creepy Creatures, Vol. 1. 2014. (Creepy Chronicles Ser.). (ENG., Illus.). 32p. (J). (gr. 5-6). 26.60 *(978-1-4824-0243-8(2))* Stevens, Gareth Publishing LLLP.

—Wicked Waters, Vol. 1. 2014. (Creepy Chronicles Ser.). (ENG.). 32p. (J). (gr. 5-6). 26.60 *(978-1-4824-0262-9(9))* Stevens, Gareth Publishing LLLP.

Curran, Bob. Frankenstein & Other Man-Made Monsters. 2013. (Haunted: Ghosts & the Paranormal Ser.). (Illus.). 208p. (YA). (gr. 7-12). 37.25 *(978-1-4777-0679-4(8))* Rosen Publishing Group, Inc., The.

The Dangerous Book of Monsters. 2015. (ENG., Illus.). 176p. (J). 16.99 *(978-1-4059-2003-2(3)*, 9781405920032) Penguin Bks., Ltd. GBR. Dist: Diamond Comic Distributors, Inc.

Devadasan, Rashmi Ruth. Kumari Loves a Monster: Kumariyin Ratcaca Katalan. Shyam, illus. 2010. (TAM & ENG.). 52p. pap. 17.95 *(978-93-80636-01-6(6))* Blaft Pubns.

Dicker, Katie. Mysterious Creatures. 2015. (Mystery! Ser.). 24p. (gr. 3-6). 28.50 *(978-1-62588-202-8(5))* Black Rabbit Bks.

Diker, Katie. Mysterious Creatures. 2015. (ENG., Illus.). 24p. (J). pap. 8.95 *(978-1-77092-233-4(4))* RiverStream Publishing.

Dinosaurs & Monsters. Date not set. (Illus.). 64p. (J). 2.98 *(978-1-4054-0448-8(5))* Parragon, Inc.

Doeden, Matt. Real-World Dragons, 1 vol. Pellegrino, Rich, illus. 2013. (World of Dragons Ser.). (ENG.). 32p. (gr. 1-2). lib. bdg. 26.65 *(978-1-62065-146-9(7)*, Blazers) Capstone Press of Coughlan Cos.

Dorling Kindersley Publishing Staff. Children's Book of Mythical Beasts & Magical Monsters. 2011. (ENG.). 144p. (J). (gr. 2-5). 24.99 *(978-0-7566-8605-5(9)*, DK Children) Dorling Kindersley Publishing, Inc.

Dorling Kindersley Publishing Staff & Hardie, Eric. Monster High Character Encyclopedia. 2016. (ENG., Illus.). 208p. (J). (gr. 2-4). 16.99 *(978-1-4654-5092-0(0)*, DK Children) Dorling Kindersley Publishing, Inc.

—Ultimate Sticker Collection: Monster High. 2016. (Ultimate Sticker Collections). (ENG.). 96p. (J). (gr. 2-4). pap. 12.99 *(978-1-4654-5140-8(4)*, DK Children) Dorling Kindersley Publishing, Inc.

Drake, Ernest. The Monsterology Handbook: A Practical Course in Monsters. Steer, Dugald A., ed. 2009. (Ologies Ser.). (ENG., Illus.). 80p. (J). (gr. 4-7). 12.99 *(978-0-7636-4622-6(9))* Candlewick Pr.

Edwards, Katie. Myths & Monsters: Secrets Revealed. Mendez, Simon, illus. 2004. 29p. (J). pap. 6.95 *(978-1-57091-582-6(2))* Charlesbridge Publishing, Inc.

Elder, Jeremy. Monsters Destroyed My City! Stained Glass Coloring Book. 2011. (Dover Stained Glass Coloring Book Ser.). (ENG., Illus.). 32p. (J). (gr. 2-5). pap. 6.99 *(978-0-486-47910-1(2))* Dover Pubns., Inc.

Eliot, Hannah. Monsters Are Real! And Other Fun Facts. Spurgeon, Aaron, illus. 2016. (Did You Know? Ser.). (ENG.). 32p. (J). (gr. -1-3). pap. 6.99 *(978-1-4814-6781-0(6)*, Little Simon) Little Simon.

Emberley, Edward R. Ed Emberley's Drawing Book of Weirdos. 2005. (ENG., Illus.). 32p. (J). (gr. 2-17). per. 7.00 *(978-0-316-78971-4(2))* Little, Brown Bks. for Young Readers.

Famous Movie Monsters, 8 Bks., Set. 2005. (YA). 212.00 *(978-1-4042-0377-8(X))* Rosen Publishing Group, Inc., The.

Feldman, Thea. Monsters: Myth or Fact? 2015. (Discover More Readers Level 2 Ser.). lib. bdg. 13.55 *(978-0-606-37758-4(1))* Turtleback Bks.

Flowerpot Press, creator. Monsters Coloring Book. 2013. (Sockheadz Ser.). (ENG., Illus.). 72p. (J). (gr. -1-3). 4.99 *(978-1-77093-545-7(2))* Flowerpot Pr.

Freedman, Claire. Monstersaurus. Cort, Ben, illus. 2013. (J). *(978-1-4351-4952-6(1))* Barnes & Noble, Inc.

Frisch, Aaron. That's Spooky: Zombies. 2013. (That's Spooky Ser.). (ENG., Illus.). 24p. (J). (gr. 1-3). pap. 7.99 *(978-0-89812-808-6(0)*, Creative Paperbacks) Creative Co., The.

Gale Editor & Redmond, Shirley Raye, eds. Golem. 2011. (Monsters Ser.). (Illus.). 48p. (YA). (gr. 7-12). lib. bdg. 30.45 *(978-0-7377-5866-5(X))* Cengage Gale.

Ganeri, Anita. Gila Monster, 1 vol. 2011. (Day in the Life: Desert Animals Ser.). (ENG., Illus.). 24p. (gr. k-2). pap. 6.79 *(978-1-4329-4781-1(8)*, Heinemann Read & Learn) Heinemann-Raintree.

Ganeri, Anita & West, David. Creatures of Myths & Legends. 2012. (J). 70.50 *(978-1-4488-5235-2(8))*; pap. 11.75 *(978-1-4488-5234-5(X))*; lib. bdg. 26.50 *(978-1-4488-5198-0(X))* Rosen Publishing Group, Inc., The. (PowerKids Pr.).

—Supernatural Creatures. 2012. (Illus.). 32p. 70.50 *(978-1-4488-5233-8(1))*; pap. 11.75 *(978-1-4488-5232-1(3))*; lib. bdg. 26.50 *(978-1-4488-5197-3(1))* Rosen Publishing Group, Inc., The. (PowerKids Pr.).

Gilpin, Rebecca. Monster Things to Make & Do. Harrison, Erica et al, illus. Allman, Howard, photos by. 2006. (Usborne Activities Ser.). 32p. (J). (gr. -1-3). pap. 6.99 *(978-0-7945-1354-2(9)*, Usborne) EDC Publishing.

Goddu, Krystyna Pora. Sea Monsters: From Kraken to Nessie. 2017. (Monster Mania Ser.). (ENG., Illus.). 32p. (J). (gr. 2-5). 26.65 *(978-1-5124-2593-2(1))* Lerner Publishing Group.

Goddu, Krystyna Poray. Movie Monsters: From Godzilla to Frankenstein. 2017. (Monster Mania Ser.). (ENG.). 32p. (J). (gr. 2-5). 12.99 ***(978-1-5124-3824-6(3))***; 39.99 ***(978-1-5124-3825-3(1))***; (Illus.). 39.99 ***(978-1-5124-2816-2(7))*** Lerner Publishing Group. (Lerner Pubns.).

—Sea Monsters: From Kraken to Nessie. 2017. (Monster Mania Ser.). (ENG.). 32p. (J). (gr. 2-5). 12.99 ***(978-1-5124-3827-7(8))***; 39.99 ***(978-1-5124-2817-9(5))***; 39.99 ***(978-1-5124-3828-4(6))*** Lerner Publishing Group. (Lerner Pubns.).

Godfrey, Linda S. Lake & Sea Monsters. 2008. (Mysteries, Legends, & Unexplained Phenomena Ser.). (Illus.). 128p. (YA). (gr. 7-12). 29.95 *(978-0-7910-9393-1(X))* Facts On File, Inc.

Gray, Peter. Monsters. (Drawing Manga Ser.). 32p. 2009. (gr. 4-4). 50.50 *(978-1-61512-200-4(1))* 2006. (Illus.). (YA). (gr. 3-6). lib. bdg. 26.50 *(978-1-4042-3331-7(8))* Rosen Publishing Group, Inc., The.

Greatest Movie Monsters. 2015. (Greatest Movie Monsters Ser.). (ENG.). 48p. (J). (gr. 5-6). pap., pap., pap. 82.25 *(978-1-4994-3679-2(3)*, Rosen Central) Rosen Publishing Group, Inc., The.

Green, Barry & Green, Dan. How to Draw 101 Monsters. 2003. (How to Draw 101 ... Ser.). (ENG., Illus.). 48p. (J). (gr. k). pap. 4.99 *(978-1-84229-742-1(2))* Top That! Publishing PLC GBR. Dist: Independent Pubs. Group.

Greene, Janice. Strange but True, 1 vol., Bk. 5. unabr. ed. 2011. (Strange but True Ser.). (ENG.). 75p. (YA). (gr. 9-12). pap. 8.95 *(978-1-61651-769-4(7))* Saddleback Educational Publishing, Inc.

—Strange but True Book 1, 1 vol. unabr. ed. 2011. (Strange but True Ser.). (ENG.). 76p. (YA). (gr. 9-12). pap. 8.95 *(978-1-61651-765-6(4))* Saddleback Educational Publishing, Inc.

Guiley, Rosemary Ellen & Dennett, Preston E. Bigfoot, Yeti, & Other Ape-Men. 2008. (Mysteries, Legends, & Unexplained Phenomena Ser.). (Illus.). 152p. (YA). (gr. 7-12). 29.95 *(978-0-7910-9386-3(7))* Facts On File, Inc.

Hall, Brianna. Hair-Raising Monster Stories, 1 vol. 2013. (Scared! Ser.). (ENG.). 32p. (gr. 3-4). 27.99 *(978-1-4296-9982-2(5)*, Snap Bks.) Capstone Press of Coughlan Cos.

Hall, Brianna, et al. Scared! 2013. (Scared! Ser.). (ENG.). 32p. (gr. 3-4). lib. bdg. 111.96 *(978-1-4296-9962-4(0)*, Snap Bks.) Capstone Press of Coughlan Cos.

Halls, Kelly Milner, et al. Tales of the Cryptids: Mysterious Creatures That May or May Not Exist. 2006. (ENG., Illus.). 72p. (J). (gr. 5-12). 18.95 *(978-1-58196-049-5(2)*, Darby Creek) Lerner Publishing Group.

Hamilton, S. L. Beasts. 2010. (Xtreme Monsters Ser.). 32p. (gr. 3-9). 27.07 *(978-1-61613-467-9(4)*, A&D Xtreme) ABDO Publishing Co.

Hamilton, Sue. Creatures of the Abyss, 1 vol. 2007. (Unsolved Mysteries Ser.). (ENG.). 32p. (gr. 3-7). 27.07 *(978-1-59928-836-9(2)*, Abdo & Daughters) ABDO Publishing Co.

—Monsters, 1 vol. 2007. (World of Horror Ser.). (ENG.). 32p. (gr. 4-8). 27.07 *(978-1-59928-771-3(4)*, Abdo & Daughters) ABDO Publishing Co.

—Monsters of Mystery, 1 vol. 2007. (Unsolved Mysteries Ser.). (ENG.). 32p. (gr. 3-7). 27.07 *(978-1-59928-835-2(4)*, Abdo & Daughters) ABDO Publishing Co.

Hanson, Anders & Mann, Elissa. Biggest, Baddest Book of Monsters, 1 vol. 2012. (Biggest, Baddest Books for Boys Ser.). (ENG.). 24p. (J). (gr. k-4). lib. bdg. 25.65 *(978-1-61783-407-3(6)*, Super SandCastle) ABDO Publishing Co.

Harris, John. My Monster Notebook. Todd, Mark, illus. 2011. (ENG.). 48p. (J). (gr. 3-18). 16.95 *(978-1-60606-050-6(3)*, J. Paul Getty Museum) Getty Pubns.

Harrison, Paul. Sea Monsters. 2008. (Up Close Ser.). (Illus.). 24p. (J). (gr. 3-7). lib. bdg. 25.25 *(978-1-4042-4224-1(4)*, PowerKids Pr.) Rosen Publishing Group, Inc., The.

Hawkins, John. Bigfoot & Other Monsters. 2012. (Mystery Hunters Ser.). (ENG., Illus.). 32p. (J). (gr. 4-6). pap. 10.60 *(978-1-4488-6445-4(3))*; lib. bdg. 25.25 *(978-1-4488-6431-7(3))* Rosen Publishing Group, Inc., The. (PowerKids Pr.).

Herbst, Judith. Monsters. (Unexplained Ser.). (ENG., Illus.). 48p. (gr. 5-12). 2005. pap. 8.95 *(978-0-8225-2408-3(2)*, Lerner Pubns.) 2004. lib. bdg. 26.60 *(978-0-8225-1626-2(8))* Lerner Publishing Group.

Hile, Kevin. Centaur. 2008. (Monsters Ser.). (ENG., Illus.). 48p. (YA). (gr. 4-7). lib. bdg. 30.45 *(978-0-7377-4042-4(6)*, LML02109-240009) Cengage Gale.

Hisao, Sato, des. Monsters. 2016. (ENG., Illus.). 56p. (J). (gr. 2-6). pap. 14.95 *(978-1-78067-794-1(4))* King, Laurence Publishing GBR. Dist: Hachette Bk. Group.

Holland, Simon. A Miscellany of Magical Beasts. Wyatt, David et al, illus. 2016. (ENG.). 48p. (J). 17.99 *(978-1-68119-430-1(9)*, 9781681194301, Bloomsbury USA Childrens) Bloomsbury Publishing USA.

Hunter, Llyn. A Little Book of Monsters. Hunter, Llyn, illus. 2007. (Illus.). 32p. (J). 7.95 *(978-0-9776419-0-1(2)*, 0-9776419-0-2) Bobcat Publishing.

Jango-Cohen, Judith. Real-Life Sea Monsters. 2009. pap. 40.95 *(978-0-7613-4820-7(4))* Lerner Publishing Group.

Jeffrey, Gary. Ogres. 2011. (Graphic Mythical Creatures Ser.). 24p. (J). (gr. 3-5). pap. 8.15 *(978-1-4339-6039-0(7)*, Gareth Stevens Learning Library); lib. bdg. 23.95 *(978-1-4339-6037-6(0))* Stevens, Gareth Publishing LLLP.

—Sea Monsters. 2011. (Graphic Mythical Creatures Ser.). (Illus.). 24p. (J). (gr. 3-5). pap. 8.15 *(978-1-4339-6043-7(5)*, Gareth Stevens Learning Library); lib. bdg. 23.95 *(978-1-4339-6041-3(9))* Stevens, Gareth Publishing LLLP.

Jensen Shaffer, Jody, et al. Monster Science. Gervasio & Aón, Carlos, illus. 2013. (Monster Science Ser.). (ENG.). 32p. (gr. 3-4). lib. bdg. 214.55 *(978-1-4296-9933-4(7)*, Graphic Library) Capstone Press of Coughlan Cos.

Jones, Jen. The Girls Guide to Zombies: Everything Vital about These Undead Monsters. 2010. (Girls' Guides to Everything Unexplained Ser.). (ENG.). 32p. (gr. 3-4). lib. bdg. 27.99 *(978-1-4296-5455-5(4)*, Snap Bks.) Capstone Press of Coughlan Cos.

Kelley, Gerald. M Is for Monster: A Fantastic Creatures Alphabet. 2014. (ENG., Illus.). 32p. (J). (gr. 2-5). 16.99 *(978-1-58536-818-1(0)*, 203669) Sleeping Bear Pr.

Kelly, Sophia. What a Beast! A Look-It-Up Guide to the Monsters & Mutants of Mythology. 2009. (Mythlopedia Ser.). (ENG.). 128p. (J). (gr. 5-9). pap. 13.95 *(978-1-60631-060-1(7)*, Watts, Franklin) Scholastic Library Publishing.

Klutz Editors. Monsters. Date not set. (Illus.). 40p. (J). 3.98 *(978-1-4054-0175-3(3))* Parragon, Inc.

Kraken: Fact or Fiction? 2010. (Creature Scene Investigation: the Science of Cryptozoology Ser.). (Illus.). 112p. (J). (gr. 5-8). 32.95 *(978-0-7910-9780-9(3)*, Chelsea Hse.) Facts On File, Inc.

Krensky, Stephen. The Bogeyman. 2008. pap. 52.95 *(978-0-8225-9891-6(4))* 2007. (ENG., Illus.). 48p. (gr. 4-7). lib. bdg. 26.60 *(978-0-8225-6760-8(1)*, Lerner Pubns.) Lerner Publishing Group.

—Creatures from the Deep. 2007. (Monster Chronicles Ser.). (ENG., Illus.). 48p. (gr. 4-7). lib. bdg. 26.60 *(978-0-8225-6761-5(X)*, Lerner Pubns.) Lerner Publishing Group.

—Frankenstein. 2005. (Monster Chronicles Ser.). (Illus.). 48p. (J). (gr. 3-7). lib. bdg. 26.60 *(978-0-8225-5923-8(4))* Lerner Publishing Group.

—Monster Chronicles Set II: Complete Library. 2008. pap. 263.95 *(978-1-58013-617-4(6))* Lerner Publishing Group.

—Monster Chronicles Set II Classroom Library. 2008. pap. 43.95 *(978-0-8225-8981-5(8))* Lerner Publishing Group.

Krohn, Katherine. Encountering Bigfoot: Eyewitness Accounts, 1 vol. Byers, Michael, illus. 2014. (Eyewitness to the Unexplained Ser.). (ENG.). 32p. (gr. 3-4). 30.65 *(978-1-4914-0243-6(1)*, Graphic Library) Capstone Press of Coughlan Cos.

Lake, G. G. Take Your Pick of Monster Encounters. 2017. (Take Your (Equally Horrible) Pick! Ser.). (ENG., Illus.). 32p. (gr. 1-2). pap. 7.95 *(978-1-5157-4476-4(0))*; lib. bdg. 26.65 *(978-1-5157-4472-6(8))* Capstone Press of Coughlan Cos. (Blazers).

Leblanc, Catherine. My Monster-Mashing. Garrigue, Roland, illus. 2016. (ENG.). 80p. (J). (gr. -1). pap., act. bk. ed. 14.99 *(978-1-60887-710-2(8))* Insight Editions.

Lew, Kristi. Monsters, Beasts, & Demons in America. 2011. (America's Supernatural Secrets Ser.). (ENG.). 48p. (YA). (gr. 5-8). pap. 11.75 *(978-1-4488-5584-1(5))*; lib. bdg. 29.25 *(978-1-4488-5532-2(2))* Rosen Publishing Group, Inc., The. (Rosen Reference).

Linde, Barbara M. & Benchmark Education Co. Staff. Monsters among Us? 2014. (Text Connections Ser.). (J). (gr. 6). *(978-1-4900-1519-4(1))* Benchmark Education Co.

Llenas, Anna. The Color Monster: A Pop-Up Book of Feelings. 2015. (ENG., Illus.). 20p. (J). (gr. -1-2). 19.95 *(978-1-4549-1729-8(6))* Sterling Publishing Co., Inc.

Loch Ness Monster: Fact or Fiction? 2010. (Creature Scene Investigation: the Science of Cryptozoology Ser.). (ENG., Illus.). 112p. (gr. 5-8). 32.95 *(978-0-7910-9779-3(X)*, Chelsea Hse.) Facts On File, Inc.

Lorimer, Janet. Strange but True Book 2, 1 vol. unabr. ed. 2011. (Strange but True Ser.). (ENG.). 75p. (YA). (gr. 9-12). pap. 8.95 *(978-1-61651-766-3(2))* Saddleback Educational Publishing, Inc.

—Strange but True Book 3, 1 vol. unabr. ed. 2011. (Strange but True Ser.). (ENG.). 76p. (YA). (gr. 9-12). pap. 8.95 *(978-1-61651-767-0(0))* Saddleback Educational Publishing, Inc.

—Strange but True Book 4, 1 vol. unabr. ed. 2011. (Strange but True Ser.). (ENG.). 76p. (YA). (gr. 9-12). pap. 8.95 *(978-1-61651-768-7(9))* Saddleback Educational Publishing, Inc.

Lynette, Rachel. The Abominable Snowman. 2007. (Monsters Ser.). (ENG., Illus.). 48p. (gr. 4-7). lib. bdg. 35.20 *(978-0-7377-3448-5(5)*, LML02109-225254) Cengage Gale.

Macdonald, Fiona. The Amazing History of Monsters: Discover Creatures Beyond Your Wildest Imagination in over 300 Exciting Pictures. 2016. (ENG., Illus.). 64p. (J). (gr. -1-12). 12.99 *(978-1-86147-744-6(9)*, Armadillo) Anness Publishing GBR. Dist: National Bk. Network.

—Murderous Mythical Creatures. 2010. (Top 10 Worst Ser.). (Illus.). 32p. (J). (gr. 3-6). (ENG.). pap. 10.50 *(978-1-4339-4083-5(3))*; lib. bdg. 26.60 *(978-1-4339-4082-8(5))* Stevens, Gareth Publishing LLLP. (Gareth Stevens Learning Library).

Macken, JoAnn Early. Gila Monsters. 2nd rev. ed. 2009. (Animals That Live in the Desert Ser.). (ENG.). 24p. (J). (gr. -1-3). pap. 8.15 *(978-1-4339-2449-1(8))*; lib. bdg. 22.60 *(978-1-4339-1951-0(6))* Stevens, Gareth Publishing LLLP. (Weekly Reader Leveled Readers).

—Gila Monsters;Monstruos de Gila. 2nd rev. ed. 2009. (Animals That Live in the Desert/Animales del desierto Ser.). (ENG & SPA.). 24p. (J). (gr. -1-3). pap. 8.15 *(978-1-4339-2457-6(9))*; lib. bdg. 22.60 *(978-1-4339-2062-2(X))* Stevens, Gareth Publishing LLLP. (Weekly Reader Leveled Readers).

The Making of a Monster: Vampires & Werewolves, 9 vols., Set. Incl. Ancient Werewolves & Vampires: The Roots of the Teeth. Bennett, Adelaide. (Illus.). pap. 9.95 *(978-1-4222-1955-3(0))*; Dracula & Beyond: Famous Vampires & Werewolves in Literature & Film. Indovino, Shaina Carmel. (Illus.). pap. 9.95 *(978-1-4222-1956-0(9))*; Fighting the Fangs: A Guide to Vampires & Werewolves. Martin, Nicholas. (Illus.). pap. 9.95 *(978-1-4222-1957-7(7))*; Global Legends & Lore: Vampires & Werewolves Around the World. Bennett, Adelaide. pap. 9.95 *(978-1-4222-1963-8(1))*; Howling at the Moon: Vampires & Werewolves in the New World. Etingoff, Kim. (Illus.). pap. 9.95 *(978-1-4222-1958-4(5))*; Pop Monsters: The Modern-Day Craze for Vampires & Werewolves. Sanna, Emily. pap. 9.95 *(978-1-4222-1959-1(3))*; Psychology of Our Dark Side: Humans' Love Affair with Vampires & Werewolves. Stewart, Sheila. (Illus.). pap. 9.95 *(978-1-4222-1960-7(7))*; Science of the Beast: The Facts Behind the Fangs. Etingoff, Kim. (Illus.). pap. 9.95 *(978-1-4222-1961-4(5))*; Transylvania & Beyond: Vampires & Werewolves in Old Europe. Indovino, Shaina Carmel. pap. 9.95 *(978-1-4222-1962-1(3))*; 64p. (YA). (gr. 7-18). 2010. 2011. Set pap. 89.55 *(978-1-4222-1954-6(2))*; Set lib. bdg. 206.55 *(978-1-4222-1801-3(5))* Mason Crest.

March, Julia. Monster Battles. 2016. (DK Reader Level 3 Ser.). lib. bdg. 13.55 *(978-0-606-38228-1(3))* Turtleback Bks.

Marsico, Katie. Undead Monsters: From Mummies to Zombies. 2017. (Monster Mania Ser.). (ENG.). 32p. (J). (gr. 2-5). 12.99 ***(978-1-5124-3830-7(8))***, Lerner Pubns.); 39.99 ***(978-1-5124-2818-6(3)***, Lerner Pubns.); 39.99 ***(978-1-5124-3831-4(6)***, Lerner Pubns.); (Illus.). 26.65 *(978-1-5124-2594-9(X))* Lerner Publishing Group.

Mayer, Kirsten. Meet the Ghouls Character Guidebook. 2014. (ENG., Illus.). 96p. (J). (gr. 3-7). 9.99 *(978-0-316-28361-8(4))* Little, Brown Bks. for Young Readers.

—Monster High: Create-A-Monster Design Lab Sticker Book. 2015. (ENG., Illus.). 96p. (J). (gr. k-17). pap. 12.99 *(978-0-316-33746-5(3))* Little, Brown Bks. for Young Readers.

McCollum, Sean, et al. Monster Handbooks. 2015. (Monster Handbooks Ser.). (ENG.). 32p. (gr. 3-4). 111.96 *(978-1-4914-6664-3(2)*, Edge Bks.) Capstone Press of Coughlan Cos.

McKerley, Jennifer Guess. The Kraken. 2007. (Monsters Ser.). (ENG., Illus.). 48p. (YA). (gr. 4-7). lib. bdg. 30.45 *(978-0-7377-3531-4(7))* Cengage Gale.

McNab, Chris. Mythical Monsters: The Scariest Creatures from Legends, Books, & Movies. 2006. (Illus.). 95p. (J). *(978-0-439-85479-5(2))* Scholastic, Inc.

Miles, Liz. Sea Monsters. 2015. (Danger! Dinosaurs Ser.). (ENG.). 32p. (J). (gr. 4-5). pap. 10.50 *(978-1-4824-3045-5(2))* Stevens, Gareth Publishing LLLP.

Mokele-Mbembe: Fact or Fiction? 2010. (Creature Scene Investigation: the Science of Cryptozoology Ser.). (ENG., Illus.). 104p. (gr. 5-8). 32.95 *(978-0-7910-9781-6(1)*, Chelsea Hse.) Facts On File, Inc.

Monster Hunting. 2016. (Monster Hunting Ser.). 00088p. (YA). (gr. 8-8). 148.40 *(978-1-4994-6570-9(X)*, Rosen Young Adult) Rosen Publishing Group, Inc., The.

Monsters! Set 2. 2016. (Monsters! Ser.). 32p. (gr. 2-1). pap. 63.00 *(978-1-4824-5292-1(8))*; lib. bdg. 159.60 *(978-1-4824-4609-8(X))* Stevens, Gareth Publishing LLLP.

Morey, Allan. 12 Terrifying Monsters. 2017. (Scary & Spooky Ser.). (ENG., Illus.). 32p. (J). (gr. 3-6). 21.95 *(978-1-63235-297-2(4))* Pr. Room Editions LLC.

Morpurgo, Michael. Beowulf. Foreman, Michael, illus. 2015. (ENG.). 160p. (J). (gr. 3-7). pap. 6.99 *(978-0-7636-7297-3(1))* Candlewick Pr.

Mortensen, Lori. Sphinx. 2007. (Monsters Ser.). (ENG., Illus.). 48p. (J). (gr. 3-5). lib. bdg. 27.50 *(978-0-7377-3633-5(X)*, Kidhaven) Cengage Gale.

Murray, Laura K. Are They Real?: Chupacabra. 2017. (Are They Real? Ser.). (ENG., Illus.). 24p. (J). (gr. 1-3). pap. 8.99 ***(978-1-62832-370-2(1)***, Creative Paperbacks) Creative Co., The.

—Are They Real?: Loch Ness Monster. 2017. (Are They Real? Ser.). (ENG., Illus.). 24p. (J). (gr. 1-3). pap. 8.99 ***(978-1-62832-372-6(8)***, Creative Paperbacks) Creative Co., The.

Murray, Laura K. Chupacabra. 2017. (Illus.). 24p. (J). *(978-1-60818-762-1(4)*, Creative Education) Creative Co., The.

My Big Creepy Sticker. 2003. (Illus.). 48p. (J). 5.98 *(978-1-4054-1218-6(6))* Parragon, Inc.

Mysterious Monsters. 2014. (Mysterious Monsters Ser.). 32p. (J). (gr. 3-6). 157.50 *(978-1-4777-7094-8(1))*; pap. 60.00 *(978-1-4777-7234-8(0))* Rosen Publishing Group, Inc., The. (PowerKids Pr.).

Namm, Diane. Monsters! Chambliss, Maxie, illus. 2003. (My First Reader Ser.). (ENG.). 32p. (J). 18.50 *(978-0-516-22933-1(8)*, Children's Pr.) Scholastic Library Publishing.

Nardo, Don. Martians. 2007. (Monsters Ser.). (ENG., Illus.). 48p. (gr. 4-7). lib. bdg. 35.20 *(978-0-7377-3639-7(9))* Cengage Gale.

Nichols, Catherine. Mysterious Creatures: A Chapter Book. 2005. (True Tales Ser.). (ENG., Illus.). 48p. (J). (gr. 2-4). lib. bdg. 22.50 *(978-0-516-25182-0(1)*, Children's Pr.) Scholastic Library Publishing.

O'Hearn, Michael. Monster Wars. Moffet, Patricia et al, illus. 2011. (Monster Wars Ser.). (ENG.). 32p. (gr. 3-4). pap. 190.80 *(978-1-4296-7270-2(6))*; lib. bdg. 111.96 *(978-1-4296-6524-7(6))* Capstone Press of Coughlan Cos. (Edge Bks.).

—Sea Monsters vs. Dragons: Showdown of the Legends, 1 vol. Altmann, Scott, illus. 2011. (Monster Wars Ser.). (ENG.). 32p. (gr. 3-4). pap. 7.95 *(978-1-4296-7263-4(3))*; pap. 47.70 *(978-1-4296-7264-1(1))*; lib. bdg. 27.99 *(978-1-4296-6523-0(8))* Capstone Press of Coughlan Cos. (Edge Bks.).

Olson, Gillia M. A Monster Alphabet: The ABCs of Screams! Loram, James, illus. 2016. (Alphabet Connection Ser.). (ENG.). 32p. (gr. k-1). lib. bdg. 27.32 *(978-1-4795-6887-1(2))* Picture Window Bks.

O'Meara, Stephen James. Are You Afraid Yet? The Science Behind Scary Stuff. Kaposy, Jeremy, illus. 2009. (ENG.). 80p. (J). (gr. 4-7). 17.95 *(978-1-55453-294-0(9))*; pap. 9.95 *(978-1-55453-295-7(7))* Kids Can Pr., Ltd. CAN. Dist: Hachette Bk. Group.

Ornoth, Tyler. Handbook to Bigfoot, Nessie, & Other Unexplained Creatures. 2016. (Paranormal Handbooks Ser.). (ENG., Illus.). 32p. (gr. 3-4). lib. bdg. 27.99 *(978-1-5157-1311-1(3)*, Edge Bks.) Capstone Press of Coughlan Cos.

Onn, Aidan. A Field Guide to Monsters & Mythical Beings. Hodgson, Rob, illus. 2017. (Magma for Laurence King Ser.). (ENG.). 56p. (J). (gr. 1-4). 17.99 ***(978-1-78627-067-2(6))*** King, Laurence Publishing GBR. Dist: Hachette Bk. Group.

Owen, Ruth. Half-Human Monsters & Other Fiends. 2013. (Not near Normal: the Paranormal Ser.). 32p. (J). (gr. 3-8). lib. bdg. 26.60 *(978-1-61772-725-2(3))* Bearport Publishing Co., Inc.

Page, Jason. Ghosts & Monsters. 2008. (Factastic Journey Ser.). (Illus.). 32p. (J). (gr. k-7). pap. 8.95 *(978-1-59905-240-3(7))* Saddleback Educational Publishing, Inc.

Peabody, Erin. Bigfoot. Rivas, Victor, illus. 2017. (Behind the Legend Ser.: 2). (ENG.). 128p. (J). (gr. 3-7). pap. 9.99 ***(978-1-4998-0425-6(3))*** Little Bee Books Inc.

Peabody, Erin. The Loch Ness Monster. Rivas, Victor, illus. 2017. (Behind the Legend Ser.: 1). (ENG.). 128p. (J). (gr. 3-7). pap. 9.99 ***(978-1-4998-0423-2(7))*** Little Bee Books Inc.

Pearce, Q. L. Mothman. 2010. (Mysterious Encounters Ser.). (ENG., Illus.). 48p. (J). 29.00 *(978-0-7377-5037-9(5)*, 1313769, Kidhaven) Cengage Gale.

Peebles, Alice. Demons & Dragons. Chilvers, Nigel, illus. 2015. (Mythical Beasts Ser.). (ENG.). 32p. (J). (gr. 3-6). pap. 7.99 *(978-1-4677-7651-6(3)*, Lerner Pubns.) Lerner Publishing Group.

—Mighty Mutants. Chilvers, Nigel, illus. 2015. (Mythical Beasts Ser.). (ENG.). 32p. (J). (gr. 3-6). lib. bdg. 26.65 *(978-1-4677-6343-1(8))* Lerner Publishing Group.

Peterson, Megan Cooley. Super Scary Monsters. 2016. (Super Scary Stuff Ser.). (ENG., Illus.). 24p. (gr. 1-2). lib. bdg. 25.32 *(978-1-5157-0277-1(4))* Capstone Press of Coughlan Cos.

Peterson, Megan Cooley & Rustad, Martha E. H. Encountering Chupacabra & Other Cryptids: Eyewitness Accounts, 1 vol. Stevens, Matt, illus. 2014. (Eyewitness to the Unexplained Ser.). (ENG.). 32p. (gr. 3-4). 30.65 *(978-1-4914-0242-9(3)*, Graphic Library) Capstone Press of Coughlan Cos.

Peterson, Megan Cooley, et al. Eyewitness to the Unexplained, 1 vol. 2014. (Eyewitness to the Unexplained Ser.). (ENG.). 32p. (gr. 3-4). 122.60 *(978-1-4914-0246-7(6)*, Graphic Library) Capstone Press of Coughlan Cos.

Pipe, Jim. Monsters. 2013. (Twilight Realm Ser.). (Illus.). 32p. (J). (gr. 4-6). 26.60 *(978-1-4339-8755-7(4))*; pap. 10.50 *(978-1-4339-8756-4(2))* Stevens, Gareth Publishing LLLP. (Gareth Stevens Learning Library).

Polydoros, Lori. Top 10 Mythical Creatures, 1 vol. 2012. (Top 10 Unexplained Ser.). (ENG.). 32p. (gr. 1-2). 26.65 *(978-1-4296-7640-3(X)*, Blazers) Capstone Press of Coughlan Cos.

Random House. Elmo's ABC Song (Sesame Street) 2015. (Pictureback(R) Ser.). (ENG., Illus.). 24p. (J). (gr. -1-2). pap. 4.99 *(978-0-553-53672-0(9)*, Random Hse. Bks. for Young Readers) Random Hse. Children's Bks.

Rau, Dana Meachen. Monsters. 2010. (Bookworms Chapter Books: for Real? Ser.). 24p. (gr. 2-3). 22.79 *(978-0-7614-4863-1(2))* Marshall Cavendish GBR. Dist: Marshall Cavendish Corp.

Raum, Elizabeth. Gila Monsters. 2015. (Lizards Ser.). (Illus.). 32p. (J). 28.50 *(978-1-60753-486-0(X))* Amicus Publishing.

Redmond, Shirley Raye. Bunyips. 2011. (Monsters Ser.). (ENG., Illus.). 48p. (gr. 4-8). lib. bdg. 35.20 *(978-0-7377-5919-8(4))* Cengage Gale.

—The Jersey Devil. 2009. (Monsters Ser.). (ENG., Illus.). 48p. (gr. 4-7). lib. bdg. 35.20 *(978-0-7377-4407-1(3)*, LML02109-245408) Cengage Gale.

Riggs, Kate. Magical Creatures. 2013. (Happily Ever After Ser.). (ENG., Illus.). 24p. (J). (gr. k-3). 25.65 *(978-1-60818-242-8(8)*, Creative Education) Creative Co., The.

Rivkin, Jennifer. Searching for el Chupacabra. 2014. (Mysterious Monsters Ser.). (Illus.). 32p. (J). (gr. 3-6). 26.25 *(978-1-4777-7113-6(1)*, PowerKids Pr.) Rosen Publishing Group, Inc., The.

—Searching for the Wendigo. 2014. (Mysterious Monsters Ser.). (Illus.). 32p. (J). (gr. 3-6). lib. bdg. 26.25 *(978-1-4777-7117-4(4)*, PowerKids Pr.) Rosen Publishing Group, Inc., The.

Roberts, Steven. Chupacabras! 2012. (Jr. Graphic Monster Stories Ser.). (ENG., Illus.). 24p. (J). (gr. 3-6). 25.25 *(978-1-4488-7902-1(7))*; pap. 10.60 *(978-1-4488-8002-7(5))* Rosen Publishing Group, Inc., The. (PowerKids Pr.).

Ross, Dave. The Not-so-Scary Monster Handbook: Halloween. Ross, Dave, illus. 2003. (Illus.). (J). 135.44 *(978-0-06-055492-7(4))* HarperCollins Pubs.

Rowe, Brooke. What Monster Are You Most Like? 2016. (Illus.). 32p. (J). *(978-1-63470-511-0(4))* Cherry Lake Publishing.

Russ, John Paul. The Monster Hunters' Survival Guide. Brusha, Joe, ed. 2011. (ENG., Illus.). 176p. (YA). pap. 12.99 *(978-0-9827507-8-0(1)*, 9780982750780) Zenescope Entertainment.

Satyr. 2008. (Monsters Ser.). (Illus.). 48p. (gr. 4-8). 26.20 *(978-0-7377-4083-7(3)*, Kidhaven) Cengage Gale.

Sautter, A. J. Discover Dragons, Giants, & Other Deadly Fantasy Monsters. 2017. (All about Fantasy Creatures Ser.). (ENG.). 32p. (gr. 1-2). lib. bdg. 26.65 ***(978-1-5157-6839-5(2)***, Blazers) Capstone Press of Coughlan Cos.

—Discover Orcs, Boggarts, & Other Nasty Fantasy Creatures. 2017. (All about Fantasy Creatures Ser.). (ENG.). 32p. (gr. 1-2). lib. bdg. 26.65 ***(978-1-5157-6837-1(6)***, Blazers) Capstone Press of Coughlan Cos.

—A Field Guide to Dragons, Trolls, & Other Dangerous Monsters, 1 vol. Ashcroft, Colin Michael et al, illus. 2014. (Fantasy Field Guides). (ENG.). 32p. (gr. 3-4). lib. bdg. 27.99 *(978-1-4914-0691-5(7))* Capstone Press of Coughlan Cos.

—A Field Guide to Goblins, Gremlins, & Other Wicked Creatures, 1 vol. Ashcroft, Colin Michael et al, illus. 2014. (Fantasy Field Guides). (ENG.). 32p. (gr. 3-4). lib. bdg. 27.99 *(978-1-4914-0689-2(5))* Capstone Press of Coughlan Cos.

Savery, Annabel. Monsters. 2012. (It's Amazing Ser.). (Illus.). 32p. (gr. 3-6). lib. bdg. 31.35 *(978-1-59920-689-9(7))* Black Rabbit Bks.

Scholastic, Inc. Staff, contrib. by. Monsters: Myth or Fact (Scholastic Discover More Reader, Level 2) 2015. (Scholastic Discover More Reader, Level 2 Ser.). (ENG.). 32p. (J). (gr. 1-3). pap. 3.99 *(978-0-545-83946-4(7)*, Scholastic Reference) Scholastic, Inc.

Schulte, Mary. Dover Demon. 2009. (Mysterious Encounters Ser.). (ENG., Illus.). 48p. (J). 29.00 *(978-0-7377-4570-2(3)*, Greenhaven Pr., Inc.) Cengage Gale.

—Sirens. 2007. (Monsters Ser.). (ENG., Illus.). 48p. (gr. 4-7). lib. bdg. 35.20 *(978-0-7377-3451-5(5))* Cengage Gale.

Scrace, Carolyn. Drawing Monsters. 2016. (Art Works). 32p. (gr. 2-6). 31.35 *(978-1-62588-346-9(3)*, Smart Apple Media) Black Rabbit Bks.

Sertori, J. M. Monsters. 2006. (Unexplained Ser.). (Illus.). 36p. (gr. 3-6). lib. bdg. 26.00 *(978-0-8368-6266-9(X)*, Gareth Stevens Learning Library) Stevens, Gareth Publishing LLLP.

Shaffer, Jody Jensen, et al. Monster Science. Gervasio et al, illus. 2013. (Monster Science Ser.). (ENG.). 32p. (gr. 3-4). lib. bdg. 61.30 *(978-1-4296-9932-7(9)*, Graphic Library) Capstone Press of Coughlan Cos.

Shea, Therese. Real-Life Monsters? 2015. (History's Mysteries Ser.). (ENG., Illus.). 32p. (J). (gr. 4-5). pap. 10.50 *(978-1-4824-2094-4(5))* Stevens, Gareth Publishing LLLP.

Shea, Therese. Was Dr. Frankenstein Real? 2017. (J). ***(978-0-7660-9198-6(8))*** Enslow Pubs., Inc.

Stowell, Louie. The Usborne Big Book of Big Monsters. Fiorin, Fabiano, illus. 2013. (Usborne Big Book Of... Ser.). (ENG.). 16p. (J). (gr. -1-3). 14.99 *(978-0-7945-3025-9(7)*, Usborne) EDC Publishing.

Summers, Portia & Rau, Dana Meachen. Are Monsters Real? 2016. (I Want to Know Ser.). (Illus.). 32p. (J). pap. 10.52 *(978-0-7660-8244-1(X))* Enslow Pubs., Inc.

Tallarico, Tony, Sr. & Drawing Staff. Drawing & Cartooning Monsters: A Step-by-Step Guide for the Aspiring Monster-Maker. 2010. (Dover How to Draw Ser.). (ENG., Illus.). 96p. (J). (gr. 3-6). pap. 6.99 *(978-0-486-47278-2(7))* Dover Pubns., Inc.

Taylor, Trace. Wheels. Taylor, Trace, illus. 2012. (1-3Y Getting Around Ser.). (ENG., Illus.). 16p. (J). pap. 5.99 *(978-1-61406-201-1(3))* American Reading Co.

Top That Publishing, ed. Mixed up Monsters. 2007. 144p. pap. *(978-1-84666-405-2(5))* Top That! Publishing PLC.

Top That Publishing Staff, ed. Funny Monsters. 2005. 12p. *(978-1-84510-734-5(9))* Top That! Publishing PLC.

Townsend, John. Strange Creatures. 2010. (Amazing Mysteries Ser.). (YA). (gr. 3-6). 28.50 *(978-1-59920-365-2(0))* Black Rabbit Bks.

Trantham, Cary. The Monster of Lake Champlain. 2012. 24p. pap. 17.99 *(978-1-4772-4907-9(9))* AuthorHouse.

Turner, Tracy. Beasts & Monsters. 2015. (Head-To-Head Ser.). (ENG., Illus.). 24p. (gr. 3-8). 28.50 *(978-1-62588-153-3(3))* Black Rabbit Bks.

Vallejo-Nagera, Alejandra. Los Cazadores de Monstruos. Guerrero, Andres, illus.Tr. of Monsters Hunters. (SPA.). 31p. (J). (gr. k-1). 8.95 *(978-1-58986-549-5(9))* Santillana USA Publishing Co., Inc.

Watt, Fiona. Monster Doodles. 2010. (Doodle Cards Ser.). 50p. (J). 9.99 *(978-0-7945-2550-7(4)*, Usborne) EDC Publishing.

—Spooky Things to Make & Do. 2012. (Activity Bks). 34p. (J). pap. 6.99 *(978-0-7945-1863-9(X)*, Usborne) EDC Publishing.

Weakland, Mark & Collins, Terry. Scooby-Doo! Unmasks Monsters: The Truth Behind Zombies, Werewolves, & Other Spooky Creatures. Cornia, Christian et al, illus. 2015. (ENG.). 144p. (gr. 1-2). pap. 9.95 *(978-1-62370-216-8(X))* Capstone Press of Coughlan Cos.

Weakland, Mark & Jensen Shaffer, Jody. Monster Science. Gervasio et al, illus. 2013. (Monster Science Ser.). (ENG.). 32p. (gr. 3-4). pap. 15.90 *(978-1-62065-824-6(0)*, Graphic Library) Capstone Press of Coughlan Cos.

Weakland, Mark, et al. Monster Science. Gervasio & Aón, Carlos, illus. 2013. (Monster Science Ser.). (ENG.). 32p. (gr. 3-4). pap. 63.60 *(978-1-62065-825-3(9))*; pap. 381.60 *(978-1-62065-826-0(7))* Capstone Press of Coughlan Cos. (Graphic Library).

Weakland, Mark Andrew & Collins, Terry Lee. Scooby Doo Unmasks the Truth Behind Mummies. 2016. (Illus.). 24p. (J). *(978-1-4062-8897-1(7))* Capstone Press of Coughlan Cos.

—Scooby Doo Unmasks the Truth Behind Vampires. 2016. (Illus.). 24p. (J). *(978-1-4062-8895-7(0))* Capstone Press of Coughlan Cos.

—Scooby Doo Unmasks the Truth Behind Werewolves. 2016. (Illus.). 24p. (J). *(978-1-4062-8896-4(9))* Capstone Press of Coughlan Cos.

West, David & Ganeri, Anita. Giants & Ogres. West, David & Ganeri, Anita, illus. 2010. (Dark Side Ser.). (Illus.). 32p. (J). (ENG.). pap. 10.50 *(978-1-4488-1568-5(1))*; lib. bdg. 26.50 *(978-1-61531-898-8(4))* Rosen Publishing Group, Inc., The. (PowerKids Pr.).

Whatmore, Candace. Monsters Coloring Book. 2012. (Coloring Bks). 32p. (J). pap. 5.99 *(978-0-7945-3195-9(4)*, Usborne) EDC Publishing.

Whelon, Chuck. Alien Invasion! Stickers. 2010. (Dover Little Activity Books Stickers Ser.). (ENG., Illus.). 4p. (J). (gr. k-3). 1.99 *(978-0-486-47234-8(5))* Dover Pubns., Inc.

—Create Your Own Monsters Sticker Activity Book. 2010. (Dover Little Activity Books Stickers Ser.). (ENG., Illus.). 4p. (J). (gr. 1-4). pap. 1.99 *(978-0-486-47515-8(8))* Dover Pubns., Inc.

Whiting, Jim. Scary Monsters. 2010. (Really Scary Stuff Ser.). (ENG.). 24p. (gr. 1-2). lib. bdg. 25.32 *(978-1-4296-3968-2(7)*, First Facts) Capstone Press of Coughlan Cos.

Whitmore, Andrew. How to Build a Monster. 2007. 96p. (J). *(978-1-4207-0727-4(2))* Sundance/Newbridge Educational Publishing.

Wright, Shannon. Dinosaurs & Monsters Coloring Book. 2013. (ENG.). 38p. 13.00 *(978-1-62884-683-6(6)*, Baby Professor (Education Kids)) Speedy Publishing LLC.

Yomtov, Nelson. Tracking Sea Monsters, Bigfoot, & Other Legendary Beasts, 1 vol. 2010. (Unexplained Phenomena Ser.). (ENG.). 48p. (gr. 3-4). lib. bdg. 31.99 *(978-1-4296-4817-2(1))* Capstone Press of Coughlan Cos.

Young, Judy. The Hidden Bestiary of Marvelous, Mysterious, & (Maybe Even) Magical Creatures. Filippucci, Laura Francesca, illus. 2009. (ENG.). 32p. (J). (gr. 1-4). 16.95 *(978-1-58536-433-6(9)*, 1299753) Sleeping Bear Pr.

Zenko, Darren. Field Notes for Monsters, 1 vol. 2009. (ENG.). 208p. pap. 14.95 ***(978-1-896124-38-4(0)***, 1896124380) Dragon Hill Publishing CAN. Dist: Lone Pine Publishing USA.

Zourelias, Diana. Monster Bugs. 2010. (Dover Nature Coloring Book Ser.). (ENG.). 32p. (J). (gr. 1-5). pap. 3.99 *(978-0-486-47673-5(1))* Dover Pubns., Inc.

MONSTERS—FICTION

Abbott, Tony. In the Ice Caves of Krog. Adams, Gil & Jessell, Tim, illus. 2003. (Secrets of Droon Ser.: No. 20). 114p. (J). (gr. 2-5). 12.65 *(978-0-7569-3940-3(2))* Perfection Learning Corp.

Abdo Publishing. Monster on the Loose, 1 vol. 2013. (Monster on the Loose Ser.: 4). (ENG.). 32p. (J). (gr. -1-4). lib. bdg. 114.00 *(978-1-61641-930-1(X)*, Looking Glass Library) Magic Wagon.

ABDO Publishing Company Staff. Story Time for Little Monsters. 2014. (Story Time for Little Monsters Ser.: 4). 24p. (J). (gr. -1-4). lib. bdg. 108.28 *(978-1-62402-019-3(4)*, Looking Glass Library) Magic Wagon.

Accord Publishing Staff. Trucks: A Mini Animotion Book. 2013. (ENG.). 14p. (J). bds. 5.99 *(978-1-4494-3558-5(0))* Andrews McMeel Publishing.

Accord Publishing Staff & Stone, Kate. One Spooky Night: A Halloween Adventure. 2011. (ENG.). 36p. (J). pap. 11.99 *(978-1-4494-0330-0(1))* Andrews McMeel Publishing.

Adams, Leonard. Two Girls & Two Monsters. 2008. 48p. pap. 7.95 *(978-0-557-01456-9(5))* Lulu Pr., Inc.

Al Mehairi, Maitha. Sally Ride's Adventure: The Dangerous Sea Monster Zelurius. 2013. 24p. pap. 20.21 *(978-1-4669-3538-9(3))* Trafford Publishing.

Albo, Pablo. The Glutton. 2007. (ENG., Illus.). 48p. (J). 18.95 *(978-84-96788-91-6(1))* OQO, Editora ESP. Dist: Baker & Taylor Bks.

Alfau, Georgette. Alfred & Alex & the Toy Eating Monster. 2009. 16p. 18.95 *(978-0-557-15276-6(3))* Lulu Pr., Inc.

Ameet Studio Staff. The Book of Monsters. 2016. (LEGO NEXO Knights Ser.). (ENG.). 96p. (J). (gr. 2-5). 12.99 *(978-1-338-03488-2(X))* Scholastic, Inc.

Americo, Tiago. Monsters. 2016. (First Sticker Story Fun Ser.). (ENG.). 30p. (J). (gr. -1-k). pap. 9.99 ***(978-1-5098-0673-7(3))*** Pan Macmillan GBR. Dist: Independent Pubs. Group.

Anaya, Rudolfo. ChupaCabra & the Roswell UFO. 2008. (ENG.). 144p. (YA). (gr. 9-18). 9.95 *(978-0-8263-4469-4(0))* Univ. of New Mexico Pr.

—Curse of the ChupaCabra. 2013. (ENG.). 176p. (YA). pap. 19.95 *(978-0-8263-4115-0(2))* Univ. of New Mexico Pr.

Anderson, Al. Adventures with Bingo Borden. Agora Publications Staff, tr. Kurzyca, Krystyna Emilia, illus. 2010. 77p. (J). pap. 9.50 *(978-1-887250-46-7(8))* Agora Pubns., Inc.

Anderson, Brian & Anderson, Liam. Monster Chefs. Anderson, Brian, illus. 2014. (ENG., Illus.). 32p. (J). (gr. -1-2). 16.99 *(978-1-59643-808-8(8)*, 9781596438088) Roaring Brook Pr.

Anderson, Shel. Spoofaloof's Adventures: Rainy Day Fun. Anderson, Shauna, illus. 2008. 52p. pap. 22.50 *(978-1-4389-1689-7(2))* AuthorHouse.

Andreae, Giles. Morris the Mankiest Monster. McIntyre, Sarah, illus. 2011. (ENG.). 32p. (J). (gr. -1-k). pap. 14.95 *(978-0-552-55935-5(0))* Transworld Publishers Ltd. GBR. Dist: Independent Pubs. Group.

Anthony, David & David, Charles. Heroes A2Z #2: (Heroes a to Z): Bowling over Halloween: Bowling over Halloween. Blakeslee, Lys, illus. 2007. (Heroes A2Z Ser.). 128p. (J). pap. 4.99 *(978-0-9728461-9-6(0))* Sigil Publishing.

Arabadjis, Heather. Monster Mas. 2013. 34p. pap. 11.95 *(978-1-4575-2493-6(7))* Dog Ear Publishing, LLC.

Armenteros, Sarah. Emma & the Mashed Potato Monster. 2009. (ENG., Illus.). 44p. (J). 18.99 *(978-1-59092-384-9(7))* Blue Forge Pr.

Armstrong-Ellis, Carey F. I Love You More Than Moldy Ham. 2015. (ENG., Illus.). 32p. (J). (gr. -1-3). 14.95 *(978-1-4197-1646-1(8)*, Abrams Bks. for Young Readers) Abrams, Inc.

Armstrong-Ellis, Carey F. Ten Creepy Monsters. (ENG., Illus.). 32p. (J). (gr. k-2). 2017. pap. 4.95 ***(978-1-4197-2741-2(9))*** 2012. 15.95 *(978-1-4197-0433-8(8))* Abrams, Inc. (Abrams Bks. for Young Readers).

Armstrong, K. L. & Marr, M. A. Loki's Wolves. (Blackwell Pages Ser.: 1). (ENG.). (J). (gr. 3-7). 2014. 374p. pap. 8.99 *(978-0-316-20497-2(8))* 2013. (Illus.). 358p. 17.00 *(978-0-316-20496-5(X))* Little, Brown Bks. for Young Readers.

—Odin's Ravens. 2014. (Blackwell Pages Ser.: 2). (ENG., Illus.). 342p. (J). (gr. 3-7). 17.00 *(978-0-316-20498-9(6))* Little, Brown Bks. for Young Readers.

Arnold, Caroline. The Terrible Hodag & the Animal Catchers. Sandford, John, illus. 2006. (ENG.). 34p. (J). (gr. k-7). 15.95 *(978-1-59078-166-1(X))* Boyds Mills Pr.

Arnold, Tedd. Fly Guy & the Frankenfly. 2013. (Fly Guy Ser.: 13). (ENG., Illus.). 32p. (J). (gr. -1-3). 6.99 *(978-0-545-49328-4(5)*, Cartwheel Bks.) Scholastic, Inc.

—Fly Guy & the Frankenfly. 2013. (Fly Guy Ser.: 13). lib. bdg. 17.20 *(978-0-606-32440-3(2)*, Turtleback) Turtleback Bks.

Atteberry, Kevan. Bunnies!!! Atteberry, Kevan, illus. 2015. (ENG., Illus.). 32p. (J). (gr. -1-3). 12.99 *(978-0-06-230783-5(5))* HarperCollins Pubs.

Atteberry, Kevan. I Love You More Than the Smell of Swamp Gas. Atteberry, Kevan, illus. 2017. (Illus.). 40p. (J). (gr. -1-3). 17.99 ***(978-0-06-240871-6(2))*** HarperCollins Pubs.

Auerbach, Annie. Scooby-Doo in the Coolsville Contraption Contest, 1 vol. 2016. (Scooby-Doo! Set 3 Ser.). (ENG., Illus.). 32p. (J). (gr. k-4). lib. bdg. 24.21 *(978-1-61479-409-7(X))* Spotlight.

Austin, Mike. Monsters Love Colors. Austin, Mike, illus. 2013. (ENG., Illus.). 40p. (J). (gr. -1-3). 15.99 *(978-0-06-212594-1(X))* HarperCollins Pubs.

Avila, Kat. Hanako Loves Monsters. 2008. 32p. 14.98 *(978-1-4357-0188-5(7))* Lulu Pr., Inc.

Awdry, W. Thomas & the Monster (Thomas & Friends) 2014. (Color Plus Chunky Crayons Ser.). (ENG.). 48p. (J). (gr. -1-2). pap. 3.99 *(978-0-385-38511-4(0)*, Golden Bks.) Random Hse. Children's Bks.

AZ Books Staff. Terribly Funny Monsters. Shumovich, Nadezhda, ed. 2012. (Terribly Funny Monsters Ser.). (ENG.). 10p. (J). (gr. -1-1). bds. 15.95 *(978-1-61889-133-4(2))* AZ Bks. LLC.

AZ Books Staff & Evans, Olivia. Haunted Castle. Shumovich, Nadezhda, ed. 2012. (Terribly Funny Monsters Ser.). (ENG., Illus.). 10p. (J). bds. 15.95 *(978-1-61889-134-1(0))* AZ Bks. LLC.

Babbitt, Natalie. El Cerro del Abismo. 2003.Tr. of Knee-Knock Rise. (SPA., Illus.). 128p. (J). (gr. 3-5). *(978-84-236-3420-0(5)*, ED0964) Edebé ESP. Dist: Lectorum Pubns., Inc.

Bach, Annie. Monster Party! 2014. (ENG., Illus.). 32p. (J). (gr. -1-k). 9.95 *(978-1-4549-1051-0(8))* Sterling Publishing Co., Inc.

Bader, Bonnie. 100 Monsters in My School. Hendrix, Bryan, illus. 2003. (All Aboard Math Reader Ser.). 48p. (gr. -1-3). 14.00 *(978-0-7569-1648-0(8))* Perfection Learning Corp.

Baghdasaryan, Rouzanna. The Dark. Morchiladze, Manana, illus. 2007. 32p. (J). (POL & ENG.). pap. 12.95 *(978-1-60195-096-3(9))*; (ARA & ENG.). pap. 12.95 *(978-1-60195-086-4(1))* International Step by Step Assn.

Bailey, Catherine. Mind Your Monsters. Vidal, Oriol, illus. 2015. (ENG.). 40p. (J). (gr. -1-2). 14.95 *(978-1-4549-1103-6(4))* Sterling Publishing Co., Inc.

Bailey City Monsters. 2005. (J). *(978-1-59564-798-6(8))* Steps To Literacy, LLC.

Balian, Lorna. The Aminal, 1 vol. Balian, Lorna & Balian, Lecia, illus. 2005. (ENG.). 48p. (J). 17.95 *(978-1-59572-006-1(5))* Star Bright Bks., Inc.

—Leprechauns Never Lie, 1 vol. Balian, Lorna, illus. 2004. (ENG., Illus.). 32p. (J). 14.95 *(978-1-932065-37-4(7))* Star Bright Bks., Inc.

Ballarini, Joe. A Babysitter's Guide to Monster Hunting #1. To, Vivienne, illus. 2017. (Babysitter's Guide to Monsters Ser.: 1). 352p. (J). (gr. 3-7). 13.99 *(978-0-06-243783-9(6)*, Tegen, Katherine Bks) HarperCollins Pubs.

Balmer, Fred. Festus & the Monster. Newcomb, Kristene, illus. 2004. 27p. (J). per. 6.95 *(978-0-9760790-2-6(X))* Folsom Fallies Pr.

Balmes, Santi. I Will Fight Monsters for You. Lyona, illus. 2015. (ENG.). 32p. (J). (gr. -1-3). 16.99 *(978-0-8075-9056-0(8))* Whitman, Albert & Co.

Balsley, Tilda & Fischer, Ellen. Shalom Everybodeee! Leigh, Tom, illus. 2016. (ENG.). 24p. (gr. -1-2). 16.99 *(978-0-7613-7558-6(9)*, Kar-Ben Publishing) Lerner Publishing Group.

Baltazar, Art, et al. Trouble in the Arena!, 1 vol. Brizuela, Dario, illus. 2014. (Green Lantern: the Animated Ser.). (ENG.). 32p. (gr. 2-3). 22.60 *(978-1-4342-4787-2(2))* Stone Arch Bks.

Bardugo, Leigh. Ruin & Rising. 2014. (Grisha Trilogy: Vol. 3). (ENG., Illus.). 432p. (YA). (gr. 7-12). 19.99 *(978-0-8050-9461-9(X)*, 9780805094619, Holt, Henry & Co. Bks. For Young Readers) Holt, Henry & Co.

—Shadow & Bone. 2012. (Shadow & Bone Trilogy Ser.: 1). (ENG.). 368p. (YA). (gr. 7-12). 19.99 *(978-0-8050-9459-6(8)*, 9780805094596, Holt, Henry & Co. Bks. For Young Readers) Holt, Henry & Co.

—Shadow & Bone. 2013. (Shadow & Bone Trilogy Ser.: 1). (ENG.). 416p. (YA). (gr. 7-12). pap. 10.99 *(978-1-250-02743-6(8)*, 9781250027436) Square Fish.

—Shadow & Bone. 2013. (Grisha Trilogy Ser.: 1). (YA). lib. bdg. 22.10 *(978-0-606-31903-4(4)*, Turtleback) Turtleback Bks.

—Siege & Storm. 2013. (Shadow & Bone Trilogy Ser.: 2). (ENG., Illus.). 448p. (YA). (gr. 7). 19.99 *(978-0-8050-9460-2(1)*, 9780805094602, Holt, Henry & Co. Bks. For Young Readers) Holt, Henry & Co.

—Siege & Storm. 2014. (Shadow & Bone Trilogy Ser.: 2). (ENG.). 496p. (YA). (gr. 7). pap. 10.99 *(978-1-250-04443-3(X)*, 9781250044433) Square Fish.

Bargiel, Nina G. & Amsterdam, Shane. Fintastic Friends Forever. 2016. (Illus.). 32p. (J). ***(978-1-5182-1661-9(7))*** Little Brown & Co.

Barnard, Sarah. The Map & the Stone. 2nd ed. 2010. (Illus.). 142p. pap. 16.95 *(978-0-9556887-2-0(8))* Ethics Trading GBR. Dist: Lulu Pr., Inc.

Barnett, Mac. Rules of the House. Myers, Matt, illus. 2016. (ENG.). 48p. (J). (gr. -1-k). 17.99 *(978-1-4231-8516-1(1))* Disney Publishing Worldwide.

Barnett, Susanne. Pink & the Mystery of the Stable Room Monster. 2012. 34p. pap. 19.99 *(978-1-4772-0921-9(2))* AuthorHouse.

Baruzzi, Agnese, illus. Hungry, Hungry Monsters. 2016. (ENG.). 26p. (J). (gr. -1). pap. 5.99 *(978-1-62686-678-2(3)*, Silver Dolphin Bks.) Readerlink Distribution Services, LLC.

Bass, Guy. The Ghost of Grotteskew, 1 vol. Williamson, Pete, illus. 2014. (Stitch Head Ser.). (ENG.). 208p. (gr. 3-4). 10.95 *(978-1-62370-030-0(2))* Capstone Young Readers of Coughlan Cos.

—The Pirate's Eye, 1 vol. Williamson, Pete, illus. 2013. (Stitch Head Ser.). (ENG.). 208p. (gr. 3-4). 10.95 *(978-1-62370-008-9(6))* Capstone Young Readers of Coughlan Cos.

—The Spider's Lair. Williamson, Pete, illus. 2015. (Stitch Head Ser.). (ENG.). 208p. (gr. 3-4). 10.95 *(978-1-62370-192-5(9))* Capstone Young Readers of Coughlan Cos.

—Stitch Head, 1 vol. Williamson, Pete, illus. 2013. (Stitch Head Ser.). (ENG.). 192p. (gr. 3-4). 10.95 *(978-1-62370-007-2(8))* Capstone Young Readers of Coughlan Cos.

Bataille Lange, Nikki. Extreme Monsters Joke Book. Stuby, Tim, illus. gif. ed. 2005. 95p. (J). (gr. 2-5). per. 3.99 *(978-1-57791-181-4(4))* Brighter Minds Children's Publishing.

Batchelor, Love. Mean Mo & the Christmas Star. 2013. (ENG., Illus.). (J). (gr. -1-3). pap. 9.95 *(978-1-62086-461-6(4))* Mascot Bks., Inc.

Baumgarten, Josephine & Baumgarten, Michael. My Baby Monsters & I went to the Park. 2005. 32p. pap. 14.99 *(978-1-4116-6348-0(9))* Lulu Pr., Inc.

Bayham, Dalan J. The Loch Ness Monster Incident - Junior Explorers Society Episode 2. 2007. 160p. pap. 12.95 *(978-1-4303-2291-7(8))* Lulu Pr., Inc.

Beacham, Travis, et al. Tales from Year Zero. 2013. (Pacific Rim Ser.). (ENG., Illus.). 128p. (gr. 8-17). 24.99 *(978-0-7851-5394-8(2))* Legendary Comics.

Beaty, Andrea. Hush, Baby Ghostling. Lemaître, Pascal, illus. 2009. (ENG.). 32p. (J). (gr. -1-3). 14.99 *(978-1-4169-2545-3(7)*, McElderry, Margaret K. Bks.) McElderry, Margaret K. Bks.

Beaudoin, Sean. The Infects. 2012. (ENG., Illus.). 384p. (YA). (gr. 9). 16.99 *(978-0-7636-5947-9(9))* Candlewick Pr.

Beck, Scott. Monster Sleepover! 2009. (ENG., Illus.). 32p. (J). (gr. k-2). 15.95 *(978-0-8109-4059-8(0)*, Abrams Bks. for Young Readers) Abrams, Inc.

Bee, William. Worst in Show. Hindley, Kate, illus. 2015. (ENG.). 40p. (J). (gr. -1-2). 15.99 *(978-0-7636-7318-5(8))* Candlewick Pr.

Bell, Braden. Penumbras. 2013. (Middle School Magic Ser.). (ENG.). 305p. (J). (gr. 3-7). 14.99 *(978-1-4621-1220-3(X)*, Sweetwater Bks.) Cedar Fort, Inc./CFI Distribution.

Bellin, Joshua David. Survival Colony 9: Forget the Past Fight to Stay Alive. 2015. (ENG., Illus.). 336p. (YA). (gr. 9). pap. 10.99 *(978-1-4814-0355-9(9)*, McElderry, Margaret K. Bks.) McElderry, Margaret K. Bks.

Bemis, John Claude. Out of Abaton, Book 2 Lord of Monsters. 2017. (Out of Abaton Ser.). (ENG.). 320p. (J). (gr. 3-7). 16.99 *(978-1-4847-0741-8(9))* Hyperion Bks. for Children.

Benjamin, Paul. Monsters, Inc: Laugh Factory. Mebberson, Amy, illus. 2010. (ENG.). 112p. (J). pap. 9.99 *(978-1-60886-508-6(8))* Boom! Studios.

Benjamin, Paul & Rosa, Don. Monsters, Inc: Laugh Factory. Mebberson, Amy & Rosa, Don, illus. 2010. (ENG.). 112p. (J). 24.99 *(978-1-60886-533-8(9))* Boom! Studios.

Bennett, Veronica. Angelmonster. 2006. (ENG.). 240p. (YA). (gr. 9-12). 15.99 *(978-0-7636-2994-6(4))* Candlewick Pr.

Bently, Peter. The Zingy Zapper: Practise Phonics with Non-Words. Beedie, Duncan, illus. 2016. (Monsters' Nonsense Ser.). (ENG.). 24p. (J). (gr. -1-2). 14.95 *(978-1-60992-912-1(8)*, Wide Eyed Editions) Quarto Publishing Group UK GBR. Dist: Hachette Bk. Group.

Benton, Jim. Five Stinky Socks: A Counting Book. 2015. (ENG.). 16p. (J). (— 1). bds. 5.99 *(978-0-545-64784-7(3)*, Cartwheel Bks.) Scholastic, Inc.

—Lunch Walks among Us. Benton, Jim, illus. (Franny K. Stein, Mad Scientist Ser.: 1). (ENG., Illus.). 112p. (J). (gr. 2-5). 2004. mass mkt. 5.99 *(978-0-689-86295-3(4))* 2003. 16.99

(978-0-689-86291-5(1)) Simon & Schuster Bks. For Young Readers. (Simon & Schuster Bks. For Young Readers).
—Lunch Walks among Us. 1 vol. Benton, Jim, illus. 2011. (Franny K. Stein, Mad Scientist Ser.). (ENG., Illus.). 112p. (gr. 3-6). 24.21 (978-1-59961-817-3(6)) Spotlight.
—Lunch Walks among Us. Benton, Jim, illus. 2004. (Franny K. Stein, Mad Scientist Ser.: 1). (Illus.). 102p. (gr. 2-5). lib. bdg. 16.00 (978-1-4176-4054-6(5), Turtleback) Turtleback Bks.
Berger, Samantha. Monster's New Undies. Carpenter, Tad, illus. 2017. (ENG.). 40p. (J). (gr. -1-k). 16.99 **(978-0-545-87973-6(6)**, Orchard Bks.) Scholastic, Inc.
Berglin, Ruth. Dear Big, Mean, Ugly Monster. DiRocco, Carl, illus. 2006. 40p. (J). (gr. -1-7). 14.95 (978-1-58760-072-2(2), Child & Family Pr.) Child Welfare League of America, Inc.
Berlan, Kathryn. Andrew's Amazing Monsters. 2013. (ENG., Illus.). 32p. (J). (gr. -1-3). 16.99 (978-1-4814-2160-7(3), Atheneum Bks. for Young Readers) Simon & Schuster Children's Publishing.
Bernoudy, Jasmine L. The Horrible Monster. 2012. 38p. pap. 9.99 (978-0-9858378-0-8(2)) Blu Phi'er Publishing, LLC.
Berrios, Frank. Rootin' Tootin' Racetrack! (Blaze & the Monster Machines) Foley, Niki, illus. 2017. (Little Golden Book Ser.). (ENG.). 24p. (J). (-k). 4.99 **(978-1-5247-1668-4(5)**, Golden Bks.) Random Hse. Children's Bks.
Berrios, Frank. Welcome to the Monster Dome! (Blaze & the Monster Machines) Random House, illus. 2017. (Tabbed Board Book Ser.). (ENG.). 16p. (J). (— 1). bds. 7.99 (978-0-399-55838-2(1), Random Hse. Bks. for Young Readers) Random Hse. Children's Bks.
Berry, Julie. Secondhand Charm. 2010. (ENG.). 352p. (YA). (gr. 5-8). 16.99 (978-1-59990-511-2(6), 9781599905112, Bloomsbury USA Childrens) Bloomsbury Publishing USA.
Berry, Julie & Gardner, Sally Faye. The Rat Brain Fiasco. 2010. (Splurch Academy Ser.: 1). (ENG.). 208p. (J). (gr. 3-7). pap. 6.99 (978-0-448-45359-0(2), Grosset & Dunlap) Penguin Young Readers Group.
Bick, Ilsa J. White Space, Bk. 1. 2014. (Dark Passages Ser.: Bk. 1). (ENG.). 560p. (J). (gr. 9). 18.99 (978-1-60684-419-9(9)) Lerner Publishing Group.
Bicknell, Joanna & Page, Nick. Finger Friends Tickle Monsters. Saunders, Katie, illus. 2007. (Finger Puppet Books Ser.). 12p. (gr. -1). bds. (978-1-84610-427-5(0)) Make Believe Ideas.
Billam, Rosemary. The Mud Monster. Remphry, Martin, illus. 2008. (Reading Corner Ser.). (ENG.). 24p. (J). (gr. k-2). pap. 6.99 (978-0-7496-7695-7(7), Franklin Watts) Hachette Children's Group GBR. Dist: Hachette Bk. Group.
Billings, Tirrea. The Monster in the Basement. 2010. 12p. pap. 10.99 (978-1-4490-2817-6(9)) AuthorHouse.
Biro, Val. Gumdrop & the Monster. (Illus.). 32p. (J). (978-0-340-71446-1(8)) Hodder & Stoughton.
—Gumdrop & the Monster. (Illus.). 32p. (J). pap. 11.99 (978-0-340-71447-8(6)) Hodder & Stoughton GBR. Dist: Trafalgar Square Publishing.
Bissett, Josie. Boogie Monster. Atteberry, Kevan J., illus. 2011. 36p. (J). (gr. -1-3). 16.95 (978-1-935414-10-0(0)) Compendium, Inc., Publishing & Communications.
Black, Holly & DiTerlizzi, Tony. The Spiderwick. DiTerlizzi, Tony, illus. 2009. (Spiderwick Chronicles Ser.). (ENG., Illus.). 608p. (J). (gr. 3-7). 29.99 (978-1-4169-8685-0(5), Simon & Schuster Bks. For Young Readers) Simon & Schuster Bks. For Young Readers.
Black, Tara. That's Not the Monster We Ordered. Fairgray, Richard & Jones, Terry, illus. 2016. (ENG.). 32p. (J). (gr. -1-k). 16.99 (978-1-5107-1136-5(8), Sky Pony Pr.) Skyhorse Publishing Co., Inc.
Blade, Adam. Anoret: The First Beast. 2014. (Beast Quest Ser.: 12). (ENG., Illus.). 192p. (J). (gr. 2-4). pap. 5.99 (978-1-4083-2410-3(5)) Hodder & Stoughton GBR. Dist: Hachette Bk. Group.
—Arax: The Soul Stealer. 2016. (Beast Quest Ser.). (ENG., Illus.). 80p. (J). (gr. k-17). pap. 5.99 (978-1-4083-3922-0(6), Orchard Bks.) Hachette Children's Group GBR. Dist: Hachette Bk. Group.
—Arax: The Soul Stealer. 2014. (Beast Quest Ser.). (ENG., Illus.). 192p. (J). (gr. 2-4). pap. 5.99 (978-1-4083-0382-5(5)) Hodder & Stoughton GBR. Dist: Hachette Bk. Group.
—Battle of the Beasts: Ferno vs Epos. 2014. (Beast Quest Ser.: 1). (ENG., Illus.). 192p. (J). (gr. 2-4). pap. 5.99 (978-1-4083-1867-6(9)) Hodder & Stoughton GBR. Dist: Hachette Bk. Group.
—Brutus: The Hound of Horror. 2014. (Beast Quest Ser.: 63). (ENG., Illus.). 144p. (J). (gr. 2-4). pap. 5.99 (978-1-4083-1843-0(1)) Hodder & Stoughton GBR. Dist: Hachette Bk. Group.
—Carnivora: The Winged Scavenger. 2015. (Beast Quest Ser.). (ENG., Illus.). 144p. (J). (gr. 2-4). pap. 5.99 (978-1-4083-0734-2(0)) Hodder & Stoughton GBR. Dist: Hachette Bk. Group.
—Convol: The Cold-Blooded Brute. 2015. (Beast Quest Ser.). (ENG., Illus.). 144p. (J). (gr. 2-4). pap. 5.99 (978-1-4083-0729-8(4)) Hodder & Stoughton GBR. Dist: Hachette Bk. Group.
—Creta: The Winged Terror. 2016. (Beast Quest Ser.). (ENG., Illus.). 80p. (J). (gr. k-17). pap. 5.99 (978-1-4083-3924-4(2), Orchard Bks.) Hachette Children's Group GBR. Dist: Hachette Bk. Group.
—Creta the Winged Terror. 2014. (Beast Quest Ser.: 5). (ENG., Illus.). 192p. (J). (gr. 2-4). pap. 5.99 (978-1-4083-0735-9(9)) Hodder & Stoughton GBR. Dist: Hachette Bk. Group.
—The Dagger of Doom. 2014. (Beast Quest Ser.). (ENG., Illus.). 128p. (J). (gr. 2-4). 5.99 (978-1-4083-1406-7(1)) Hodder & Stoughton GBR. Dist: Hachette Bk. Group.
—The Dark Cauldron. 2014. (Beast Quest Ser.). (ENG., Illus.). 112p. (J). (gr. 2-4). pap. 5.99 (978-1-4083-0943-8(2)) Hodder & Stoughton GBR. Dist: Hachette Bk. Group.
—Deep Dive #4: Kraya the Blood Shark. 2013. (Deep Dive Ser.: 4). (ENG.). 128p. (J). (gr. 2-5). pap. 4.99 (978-0-545-42770-8(3), Scholastic Paperbacks) Scholastic, Inc.
—Doomskull Bk. 60: The King of Fear. 2014. (Beast Quest Ser.: 60). (ENG., Illus.). 128p. (J). (gr. 2-4). pap. 5.99 (978-1-4083-1523-1(8)) Hodder & Stoughton GBR. Dist: Hachette Bk. Group.
—Drogan: The Jungle Menace. 2016. (Beast Quest Ser.). (ENG., Illus.). 144p. (J). (gr. 2-4). pap. 5.99 (978-1-4083-4295-4(2), Orchard Bks.) Hachette Children's Group GBR. Dist: Hachette Bk. Group.
—Elko: Lord of the Sea. 2014. (Beast Quest Ser.: 61). (ENG., Illus.). 128p. (J). (gr. 2-4). 5.99 (978-1-4083-1841-6(5)) Hodder & Stoughton GBR. Dist: Hachette Bk. Group.
—Ellik: The Lightning Horror. 2015. (Beast Quest Ser.). (ENG., Illus.). 144p. (J). (gr. 2-4). pap. 5.99 (978-1-4083-0733-5(2)) Hodder & Stoughton GBR. Dist: Hachette Bk. Group.
—Falkor: The Coiled Terror. 2017. (Beast Quest Ser.). (ENG., Illus.). 192p. (J). (gr. 2-4). pap. 5.99 (978-1-4083-4297-8(9), Orchard Bks.) Hachette Children's Group GBR. Dist: Hachette Bk. Group.
—Falra Bk. 82: The Snow Phoenix. 2016. (Beast Quest Ser.). (ENG., Illus.). 144p. (J). (gr. 2-4). pap. 5.99 (978-1-4083-2923-8(9), Orchard Bks.) Hachette Children's Group GBR. Dist: Hachette Bk. Group.
—Flaymar: The Scorched Blaze. 2014. (Beast Quest Ser.: 64). (ENG., Illus.). 144p. (J). (gr. 2-4). pap. 5.99 (978-1-4083-1844-7(X)) Hodder & Stoughton GBR. Dist: Hachette Bk. Group.
—The Ghost Warrior. 2016. (Beast Quest Ser.). (ENG., Illus.). 192p. (J). (gr. 2-4). pap. 5.99 (978-1-4083-3497-3(6), Orchard Bks.) Hachette Children's Group GBR. Dist: Hachette Bk. Group.
—Grashkor: The Beast Guard. 2015. (Beast Quest Ser.: 9). (ENG., Illus.). 192p. (J). (gr. 2-4). pap. 5.99 (978-1-4083-1517-0(3)) Hodder & Stoughton GBR. Dist: Hachette Bk. Group.
—Gryph: The Feathered Fiend. 2016. (Beast Quest Ser.). (ENG., Illus.). 144p. (J). (gr. 2-17). pap. 5.99 (978-1-4083-4076-9(3), Orchard Bks.) Hachette Children's Group GBR. Dist: Hachette Bk. Group.
—Hellion: The Fiery Foe. 2015. (Beast Quest Ser.). (ENG., Illus.). 144p. (J). (gr. 2-4). pap. 5.99 (978-1-4083-0730-4(8)) Hodder & Stoughton GBR. Dist: Hachette Bk. Group.
—Kanis: The Shadow Hound. 2016. (Beast Quest Ser.). (ENG., Illus.). 144p. (J). (gr. 2-17). pap. 5.99 (978-1-4083-3994-7(3), Orchard Bks.) Hachette Children's Group GBR. Dist: Hachette Bk. Group.
—Karixa: The Diamond Warrior. 2016. (Beast Quest Ser.). (ENG., Illus.). 144p. (J). (gr. 2-4). pap. 5.99 (978-1-4083-4309-8(6), Orchard Bks.) Hachette Children's Group GBR. Dist: Hachette Bk. Group.
—Koba: Ghoul of the Shadows. 2015. (Beast Quest Ser.: 78). (ENG., Illus.). 128p. (J). (gr. 2-4). pap. 5.99 (978-1-4083-2407-3(5)) Hodder & Stoughton GBR. Dist: Hachette Bk. Group.
—Koraka: The Winged Assassin. 2014. (Beast Quest Ser.: 51). (ENG., Illus.). 128p. (J). (gr. 2-4). pap. 5.99 (978-1-4083-1318-3(9)) Hodder & Stoughton GBR. Dist: Hachette Bk. Group.
—Korvax: The Sea Dragon. 2017. (Beast Quest Ser.). (ENG., Illus.). 144p. (J). (gr. 2-4). 5.99 **(978-1-4083-4313-5(4)**, Orchard Bks.) Hachette Children's Group GBR. Dist: Hachette Bk. Group.
—Kragos & Kildor: The Two-Headed Demon. 2016. (Beast Quest Ser.). (ENG., Illus.). 80p. (J). (gr. 2-4). pap. 5.99 (978-1-4083-3514-7(X), Orchard Bks.) Hachette Children's Group GBR. Dist: Hachette Bk. Group.
—Kragos & Kildor: The Two-Headed Demon. 2014. (Beast Quest Ser.: 4). (ENG., Illus.). 192p. (J). (gr. 2-4). pap. 5.99 (978-1-4083-0436-5(8)) Hodder & Stoughton GBR. Dist: Hachette Bk. Group.
—Krestor: The Crushing Terror. 2015. (Beast Quest Ser.). (ENG., Illus.). 144p. (J). (gr. 2-4). pap. 5.99 (978-1-4083-0731-1(6)) Hodder & Stoughton GBR. Dist: Hachette Bk. Group.
—Krytor: The Blood Bat. 2016. (Beast Quest Ser.). (ENG., Illus.). 144p. (J). (gr. 2-4). pap. 5.99 (978-1-4083-4086-8(0), Orchard Bks.) Hachette Children's Group GBR. Dist: Hachette Bk. Group.
—Kyrax: The Metal Warrior. 2017. (Beast Quest Ser.). (ENG., Illus.). 192p. (J). (gr. 2-17). 5.99 (978-1-4083-4299-2(5), Orchard Bks.) Hachette Children's Group GBR. Dist: Hachette Bk. Group.
—Linka Bk. 76: The Sky Conqueror. 2015. (Beast Quest Ser.: 76). (ENG., Illus.). 128p. (J). (gr. 2-4). pap. 5.99 (978-1-4083-2405-9(9)) Hodder & Stoughton GBR. Dist: Hachette Bk. Group.
—Lustor: The Acid Dart. 2014. (Beast Quest Ser.: 57). (ENG., Illus.). 128p. (J). (gr. 2-4). pap. 5.99 (978-1-4083-1520-0(3)) Hodder & Stoughton GBR. Dist: Hachette Bk. Group.
—Minos: The Demon Bull. 2014. (Beast Quest Ser.: 50). (ENG., Illus.). 128p. (J). (gr. 2-4). pap. 5.99 (978-1-4083-1317-6(0)) Hodder & Stoughton GBR. Dist: Hachette Bk. Group.
—Mortaxe: The Skeleton Warrior. 2016. (Beast Quest Ser.). (ENG., Illus.). 80p. (J). (gr. k-17). pap. 5.99 (978-1-4083-4182-7(4), Orchard Bks.) Hachette Children's Group GBR. Dist: Hachette Bk. Group.
—Noctila: The Death Owl. 2014. (Beast Quest Ser.: 55). (ENG., Illus.). 128p. (J). (gr. 2-4). pap. 5.99 (978-1-4083-1518-7(1)) Hodder & Stoughton GBR. Dist: Hachette Bk. Group.
—Okko: The Sand Monster. 2016. (Beast Quest Ser.). (ENG., Illus.). 144p. (J). (gr. 2-17). pap. 5.99 (978-1-4083-4082-0(8), Orchard Bks.) Hachette Children's Group GBR. Dist: Hachette Bk. Group.
—The Pirate's Curse. 2016. (Beast Quest Ser.). (ENG., Illus.). 144p. (J). (gr. 2-4). pap. 5.99 (978-1-4083-1840-9(7)) Hodder & Stoughton GBR. Dist: Hachette Bk. Group.
—Plexor: The Raging Reptile. 2016. (Beast Quest Ser.). (ENG., Illus.). 144p. (J). (gr. 2-4). pap. 5.99 (978-1-4083-3491-1(7), Orchard Bks.) Hachette Children's Group GBR. Dist: Hachette Bk. Group.
—Quagos the Armoured Beetle. 2016. (Beast Quest Ser.). (ENG., Illus.). 144p. (J). (gr. 2-4). pap. 5.99 (978-1-4083-3493-5(3), Orchard Bks.) Hachette Children's Group GBR. Dist: Hachette Bk. Group.
—Quarg: The Stone Dragon. 2017. (Beast Quest Ser.). (ENG., Illus.). 144p. (J). (gr. 2-4). 5.99 **(978-1-4083-4311-1(8)**, Orchard Bks.) Hachette Children's Group GBR. Dist: Hachette Bk. Group.
—Raffkor Bk. 79: The Stampeding Brute. 2016. (Beast Quest Ser.). (ENG., Illus.). 144p. (J). (gr. 2-4). pap. 5.99 (978-1-4083-2920-7(4), Orchard Bks.) Hachette Children's Group GBR. Dist: Hachette Bk. Group.
—Ravira: Ruler of the Underworld. 2016. (Beast Quest Ser.). (ENG., Illus.). 80p. (J). (gr. k-2). pap. 5.99 (978-1-4083-4184-1(0), Orchard Bks.) Hachette Children's Group GBR. Dist: Hachette Bk. Group.
—Ronak: The Toxic Terror. 2016. (Beast Quest Ser.). (ENG., Illus.). 144p. (J). (gr. 2-17). pap. 5.99 (978-1-4083-3996-1(X), Orchard Bks.) Hachette Children's Group GBR. Dist: Hachette Bk. Group.
—Saurex the Silent Creeper. 2016. (Beast Quest Ser.). (ENG., Illus.). 144p. (J). (gr. 2-17). pap. 5.99 (978-1-4083-4084-4(4), Orchard Bks.) Hachette Children's Group GBR. Dist: Hachette Bk. Group.
—Sepron vs Narga. 2015. (Beast Quest Ser.: 3). (ENG., Illus.). 192p. (J). (gr. 2-4). pap. 5.99 (978-1-4083-2409-7(1)) Hodder & Stoughton GBR. Dist: Hachette Bk. Group.
—Serpio: The Slithering Shadow. 2014. (Beast Quest Ser.: 65). (ENG., Illus.). 144p. (J). (gr. 2-4). pap. 5.99 (978-1-4083-1845-4(8)) Hodder & Stoughton GBR. Dist: Hachette Bk. Group.
—Shamani: The Raging Flame. 2014. (Beast Quest Ser.: 56). (ENG., Illus.). 128p. (J). (gr. 2-4). pap. 5.99 (978-1-4083-1519-4(X)) Hodder & Stoughton GBR. Dist: Hachette Bk. Group.
—Silver: The Wild Terror. 2014. (Beast Quest Ser.: 52). (ENG., Illus.). 128p. (J). (gr. 2-4). pap. 5.99 (978-1-4083-1319-0(7)) Hodder & Stoughton GBR. Dist: Hachette Bk. Group.
—Skolo: The Bladed Monster. 2016. (Beast Quest Ser.). (ENG., Illus.). 192p. (J). (gr. 2-4). pap. 5.99 (978-1-4083-2930-6(1), Orchard Bks.) Hachette Children's Group GBR. Dist: Hachette Bk. Group.
—Skurik Bk. 73: The Forest Demon. 2015. (Beast Quest Ser.: 73). (ENG., Illus.). 128p. (J). (gr. 2-4). pap. 5.99 (978-1-4083-2402-8(4)) Hodder & Stoughton GBR. Dist: Hachette Bk. Group.
—Slivka: The Cold-Hearted Curse. 2015. (Beast Quest Ser.: 75). (ENG., Illus.). 128p. (J). (gr. 2-4). pap. 5.99 (978-1-4083-2404-2(0)) Hodder & Stoughton GBR. Dist: Hachette Bk. Group.
—Soara: The Stinging Spectre. 2016. (Beast Quest Ser.). (ENG., Illus.). 144p. (J). (gr. 2-4). pap. 5.99 (978-1-4083-4088-2(7), Orchard Bks.) Hachette Children's Group GBR. Dist: Hachette Bk. Group.
—Solix Bk. 89: The Deadly Swarm. 2016. (Beast Quest Ser.). (ENG., Illus.). 144p. (J). (gr. 2-17). pap. 5.99 (978-1-4083-3988-6(9), Orchard Bks.) Hachette Children's Group GBR. Dist: Hachette Bk. Group.
—Spikefin: The Water King. 2014. (Beast Quest Ser.: 53). (ENG., Illus.). 128p. (J). (gr. 2-4). pap. 5.99 (978-1-4083-1320-6(0)) Hodder & Stoughton GBR. Dist: Hachette Bk. Group.
—Strytor the Skeleton Dragon. 2017. (Beast Quest Ser.). (ENG., Illus.). 144p. (J). (gr. 2-4). 5.99 **(978-1-4083-4317-3(7)**, Orchard Bks.) Hachette Children's Group GBR. Dist: Hachette Bk. Group.
—Styro: The Snapping Brute. 2016. (Beast Quest Ser.). (ENG., Illus.). 144p. (J). (gr. 2-17). pap. 5.99 (978-1-4083-3986-2(2), Orchard Bks.) Hachette Children's Group GBR. Dist: Hachette Bk. Group.
—Targro: The Arctic Menace. 2015. (Beast Quest Ser.: 74). (ENG., Illus.). 128p. (J). (gr. 2-4). pap. 5.99 (978-1-4083-2403-5(2)) Hodder & Stoughton GBR. Dist: Hachette Bk. Group.
—Tarrok the Blood Spike. 2014. (Beast Quest Ser.: 62). (ENG., Illus.). 144p. (J). (gr. 2-4). pap. 5.99 (978-1-4083-1842-3(3)) Hodder & Stoughton GBR. Dist: Hachette Bk. Group.
—Tauron: The Pounding Fury. 2014. (Beast Quest Ser.: 66). (ENG., Illus.). 144p. (J). (gr. 2-4). pap. 5.99 (978-1-4083-1846-1(6)) Hodder & Stoughton GBR. Dist: Hachette Bk. Group.
—Tecton: The Armoured Giant. 2014. (Beast Quest Ser.: 59). (ENG., Illus.). 128p. (J). (gr. 2-4). pap. 5.99 (978-1-4083-1522-4(X)) Hodder & Stoughton GBR. Dist: Hachette Bk. Group.
—Tempra: Thee Time Stealer. 2016. (Beast Quest Ser.). (ENG., Illus.). 192p. (J). (gr. 2-4). pap. 5.99 (978-1-4083-4078-3(X), Orchard Bks.) Hachette Children's Group GBR. Dist: Hachette Bk. Group.
—The Ultimate Story Collection. 2016. (Beast Quest Ser.). (ENG., Illus.). 384p. (J). (gr. 2-4). 16.99 (978-1-4083-4547-4(1), Orchard Bks.) Hachette Children's Group GBR. Dist: Hachette Bk. Group.
—Thoron: The Living Storm. 2016. (Beast Quest Ser.). (ENG., Illus.). 144p. (J). (gr. 2-17). pap. 5.99 (978-1-4083-4080-6(1), Orchard Bks.) Hachette Children's Group GBR. Dist: Hachette Bk. Group.
—Tikron Bk. 81: The Jungle Master. 2016. (Beast Quest Ser.). (ENG., Illus.). 144p. (J). (gr. 2-4). pap. 5.99 (978-1-4083-2922-1(0), Orchard Bks.) Hachette Children's Group GBR. Dist: Hachette Bk. Group.
—Torpix: The Twisting Serpent. 2014. (Beast Quest Ser.: 54). (ENG., Illus.). 128p. (J). (gr. 2-4). pap. 5.99 (978-1-4083-1321-3(9)) Hodder & Stoughton GBR. Dist: Hachette Bk. Group.
—Ursus Bk. 49: The Clawed Roar. 2014. (Beast Quest Ser.: 49). (ENG., Illus.). 128p. (J). (gr. 2-4). pap. 5.99 (978-1-4083-1316-9(2)) Hodder & Stoughton GBR. Dist: Hachette Bk. Group.
—Vedra & Krimon: Twin Beasts of Avantia. 2015. (Beast Quest Ser.). (ENG., Illus.). 80p. (J). (gr. 2-4). pap. 5.99 (978-1-4083-3500-0(X)) Hodder & Stoughton GBR. Dist: Hachette Bk. Group.
—Vermok: The Spiteful Scavenger. 2015. (Beast Quest Ser.: 77). (ENG., Illus.). 128p. (J). (gr. 2-4). pap. 5.99 (978-1-4083-2406-6(7)) Hodder & Stoughton GBR. Dist: Hachette Bk. Group.
—Vetrix the Poison Dragon. 2017. (Beast Quest Ser.). (ENG., Illus.). 144p. (J). (gr. 2-4). 5.99 **(978-1-4083-4315-9(0)**, Orchard Bks.) Hachette Children's Group GBR. Dist: Hachette Bk. Group.
—Viktor: The Deadly Archer. 2015. (Beast Quest Ser.: 11). (ENG., Illus.). 192p. (J). (gr. 2-4). pap. 5.99 (978-1-4083-2408-0(3)) Hodder & Stoughton GBR. Dist: Hachette Bk. Group.
—Vislak Bk. 80: The Slithering Serpent. 2016. (Beast Quest Ser.). (ENG., Illus.). 144p. (J). (gr. 2-4). pap. 5.99 (978-1-4083-2921-4(2), Orchard Bks.) Hachette Children's Group GBR. Dist: Hachette Bk. Group.
—Voltrex: The Two-Headed Octopus. 2014. (Beast Quest Ser.: 58). (ENG., Illus.). 144p. (J). (gr. 2-4). pap. 5.99 (978-1-4083-1521-7(1)) Hodder & Stoughton GBR. Dist: Hachette Bk. Group.
—Wardok the Sky Terror. 2016. (Beast Quest Ser.). (ENG., Illus.). 144p. (J). (gr. 2-4). pap. 5.99 (978-1-4083-3487-4(9), Orchard Bks.) Hachette Children's Group GBR. Dist: Hachette Bk. Group.
—Xerik: The Bone Cruncher. 2016. (Beast Quest Ser.). (ENG., Illus.). 144p. (J). (gr. 2-4). pap. 5.99 (978-1-4083-3489-8(5), Orchard Bks.) Hachette Children's Group GBR. Dist: Hachette Bk. Group.
—Yakorix: The Ice Bear. 2016. (Beast Quest Ser.). (ENG., Illus.). 192p. (J). (gr. 2-4). pap. 5.99 (978-1-4083-3495-9(X), Orchard Bks.) Hachette Children's Group GBR. Dist: Hachette Bk. Group.
Blance, Ellen. Monstruo, 12 bks., Set. Incl. Monstruo Compre un Animalito. Cook, Ann. 1.98 (978-0-8372-3482-3(4)); Monstruo Encuentra Trabajo. Cook, Tony. 1.98 (978-0-8372-3485-4(9)); Monstruo, la Senorita Monstruo y el Paseo en Bicicleta. Cook, Tony. 1.98 (978-0-8372-3488-5(3)); Monstruo Recorre la Ciudad. Cook, Tony. 1.98 (978-0-8372-3490-8(5)); Monstruo Va a la Playa. Cook, Tony. 1.98 (978-0-8372-3479-3(4)); Monstruo Va Al Circo. Cook, Tony. 1.98 (978-0-8372-3483-0(2)); Monstruo Va Al Hospital. Cook, Tony. 1.98 (978-0-8372-3489-2(1)); Monstruo y el Muro. Cook, Tony. 1.98 (978-0-8372-3487-8(5)); Monstruo y la Galleta de Sorpresa. Cook, Tony. 1.98 (978-0-8372-3486-1(7)); Monstruo y la Liquidacion de Juguetes. Cook, Tony. 1.98 (978-0-8372-3480-9(8)); Plan de la Senorita Monstruo. Cook, Tony. 1.98 (978-0-8372-3481-6(6)); Senorita Monstruo Ayuda. Cook, Tony. 1.98 (978-0-8372-3484-7(0)); (J). (Illus.). Set pap. 215.00 (978-0-8372-3493-9(X)) Bowmar/Noble Pubs.
Blance, Ellen & Cook, Ann. Monstruo Compre un Animalito. (J). 1.98 (978-0-8372-3482-3(4)) Bowmar/Noble Pubs.
Blance, Ellen & Cook, Tony. Lady Monster Has a Plan. Date not set. (Illus.). 40p. pap. 129.15 (978-0-582-19312-3(5)) Addison-Wesley Longman, Ltd. GBR. Dist: Trans-Atlantic Pubns., Inc.
—Lady Monster Helps Out. Date not set. (Illus.). 32p. pap. 129.15 (978-0-582-19302-4(8)) Addison-Wesley Longman, Ltd. GBR. Dist: Trans-Atlantic Pubns., Inc.
—Monster & Magic Umbrella. Date not set. (Illus.). 16p. pap. 129.15 (978-0-582-18593-7(9)) Addison-Wesley Longman, Ltd. GBR. Dist: Trans-Atlantic Pubns., Inc.
—Monster & Surprise Cookie. Date not set. (Illus.). 38p. pap. 129.15 (978-0-582-19308-6(7)) Addison-Wesley Longman, Ltd. GBR. Dist: Trans-Atlantic Pubns., Inc.
—Monster at School. Date not set. (Illus.). 24p. pap. 129.15 (978-0-582-18597-5(1)) Addison-Wesley Longman, Ltd. GBR. Dist: Trans-Atlantic Pubns., Inc.
—Monster Buys a Pet. Date not set. (Illus.). 40p. pap. 129.15 (978-0-582-19311-6(7)) Addison-Wesley Longman, Ltd. GBR. Dist: Trans-Atlantic Pubns., Inc.
—Monster Cleans His House. Date not set. (Illus.). 16p. pap. 129.15 (978-0-582-18590-6(4)) Addison-Wesley Longman, Ltd. GBR. Dist: Trans-Atlantic Pubns., Inc.
—Monster Comes to the City. Date not set. (Illus.). 16p. pap. 129.15 (978-0-582-18588-3(2)) Addison-Wesley Longman, Ltd. GBR. Dist: Trans-Atlantic Pubns., Inc.
—Monster Gets a Job. Date not set. (Illus.). 40p. pap. 129.15 (978-0-582-19307-9(9)) Addison-Wesley Longman, Ltd. GBR. Dist: Trans-Atlantic Pubns., Inc.
—Monster Goes Around Town. Date not set. (Illus.). 38p. pap. 129.15 (978-0-582-19309-3(5)) Addison-Wesley Longman, Ltd. GBR. Dist: Trans-Atlantic Pubns., Inc.
—Monster Goes to Circus. Date not set. (Illus.). 32p. pap. 129.15 (978-0-582-19304-8(4)) Addison-Wesley Longman, Ltd. GBR. Dist: Trans-Atlantic Pubns., Inc.
—Monster Goes to School. Date not set. (Illus.). 24p. pap. 129.15 (978-0-582-18596-8(3)) Addison-Wesley Longman, Ltd. GBR. Dist: Trans-Atlantic Pubns., Inc.
—Monster Goes to the Beach. Date not set. (Illus.). 40p. pap. 129.15 (978-0-582-19306-2(0)) Addison-Wesley Longman, Ltd. GBR. Dist: Trans-Atlantic Pubns., Inc.
—Monster Goes to the Hospital. Date not set. (Illus.). 40p. pap. 129.15 (978-0-582-19305-5(2)) Addison-Wesley Longman, Ltd. GBR. Dist: Trans-Atlantic Pubns., Inc.
—Monster Goes to the Zoo. Date not set. (Illus.). 24p. pap. 129.15 (978-0-582-18599-9(8)) Addison-Wesley Longman, Ltd. GBR. Dist: Trans-Atlantic Pubns., Inc.
—Monster Looks for a House. Date not set. (Illus.). 16p. pap. 129.15 (978-0-582-18589-0(0)) Addison-Wesley Longman, Ltd. GBR. Dist: Trans-Atlantic Pubns., Inc.
—Monster Looks for Friend. Date not set. (Illus.). 16p. pap. 129.15 (978-0-582-18591-3(2)) Addison-Wesley Longman, Ltd. GBR. Dist: Trans-Atlantic Pubns., Inc.
—Monster Meets Lady Monster. Date not set. (Illus.). 16p. pap. 129.15 (978-0-582-18592-0(0)) Addison-Wesley Longman, Ltd. GBR. Dist: Trans-Atlantic Pubns., Inc.
—Monster on the Bus. Date not set. (Illus.). 24p. pap. 129.15 (978-0-582-18595-1(5)) Addison-Wesley Longman, Ltd. GBR. Dist: Trans-Atlantic Pubns., Inc.
—Monstruo Encuentra Trabajo. (J). 1.98 (978-0-8372-3485-4(9)) Bowmar/Noble Pubs.
—Monstruo, la Senorita Monstruo y el Paseo en Bicicleta. (J). 1.98 (978-0-8372-3488-5(3)) Bowmar/Noble Pubs.
—Monstruo Recorre la Ciudad. (J). 1.98 (978-0-8372-3490-8(5)) Bowmar/Noble Pubs.
—Monstruo Va a la Playa. (J). 1.98 (978-0-8372-3479-3(4)) Bowmar/Noble Pubs.
—Monstruo Va Al Circo. (J). 1.98 (978-0-8372-3483-0(2)) Bowmar/Noble Pubs.
—Monstruo Va Al Hospital. (J). 1.98 (978-0-8372-3489-2(1)) Bowmar/Noble Pubs.
—Monstruo y el Muro. (J). 1.98 (978-0-8372-3487-8(5)) Bowmar/Noble Pubs.
—Monstruo y la Galleta de Sorpresa. (J). 1.98 (978-0-8372-3486-1(7)) Bowmar/Noble Pubs.
—Monstruo y la Liquidacion de Juguetes. (J). 1.98 (978-0-8372-3480-9(8)) Bowmar/Noble Pubs.
—El Plan de la Senorita Monstruo. (J). 1.98 (978-0-8372-3481-6(6)) Bowmar/Noble Pubs.

—La Senorita Monstruo Ayuda. (J). 1.98 *(978-0-8372-3484-7(0))* Bowmar/Noble Pubs.

Bledsoe, C. L. The Necro-Files. 2013. 174p. pap. 10.99 *(978-1-939194-93-0(8))* Etopia Pr.

Bloom, Ira. Hearts & Other Body Parts. 2017. (ENG.). 352p. (J). (gr. 9). 17.99 *(978-1-338-03073-0(6),* Scholastic Pr.) Scholastic, Inc.

Blume, Rebecca. A Really, Really, Scary Monster Story! Koji, Jeanette, illus. l.t. ed. 2006. 32p. (J). 24.95 *(978-0-9785427-0-2(3))* Liberty Artists Management.

Bobet, Leah. An Inheritance of Ashes. (ENG.). 400p. (YA). (gr. 7). 2016. pap. 9.99 *(978-0-544-81322-9(7),* HMH Books For Young Readers) 2015. 17.99 *(978-0-544-28111-0(X))* Houghton Mifflin Harcourt Publishing Co.

Bogel, Rachel Anne. A Ride on the Monster's Back. Greenfelder, Jill, illus. 2008. 28p. pap. 15.99 *(978-1-59858-752-4(8))* Dog Ear Publishing, LLC.

Bolger, Kevin. Zombiekins 2. Blecha, Aaron, illus. 2011. (J). 10.99 *(978-1-59514-432-4(3),* Razorbill) Penguin Publishing Group.

Bond, Gwenda & Rowe, Chistopher. The Lost Legacy. Thomas, Glenn, illus. 2017. (Supernormal Sleuthing Service Ser.: 1). 416p. (J). (gr. 3-7). 16.99 *(978-0-06-245994-7(5),* Greenwillow Bks.) HarperCollins Pubs.

Bonniol, Magali. El Ogro De Mariuchi. 2003. (SPA.). 40p. *(978-84-8470-112-5(3))* Corimbo, Editorial S.L.

Bottner, Barbara & Kruglik, Gerald. Pish & Posh Wish for Fairy Wings. Bottner, Barbara, illus. 2007. (I Can Read Level 2 Ser.). (ENG., Illus.). 48p. (J). (gr. k-3). pap. 3.99 *(978-0-06-051421-1(3),* Tegen, Katherine Bks) HarperCollins Pubs.

Boucher, Sarah E. Becoming Beauty: A Retelling of Beauty & the Beast. 2014. 249p. (YA). pap. 15.99 *(978-1-4621-1455-9(5))* Cedar Fort, Inc./CFI Distribution.

Boutte, Brock. Gris-Gris & the Cypress Tree: Louisiana. 2012. (ENG.). (J). pap. 17.95 *(978-1-4675-4497-9(3))* Independent Pub.

Bouwman, H. M. A Crack in the Sea. 2017. (ENG., Illus.). 368p. (J). (gr. 5). 16.99 *(978-0-399-54519-1(0),* G.P. Putnam's Sons Books for Young Readers) Penguin Young Readers Group.

Bowen, Carl. Jak & the Magic Nano-Beans: a Graphic Novel. Lozano, Omar, illus. 2016. (Far Out Fairy Tales Ser.). (ENG.). 40p. (gr. 3-4). lib. bdg. 25.32 *(978-1-4965-2510-9(8),* Far Out Fairy Tales) Stone Arch Bks.

Boyd, Colin. The Bath Monster. Ross, Tony, illus. 2016. (ENG.). 32p. (J). (gr. -1-3). 17.99 *(978-1-5124-0426-5(8))* Lerner Publishing Group.

Boylan, Jennifer Finney. Falcon Quinn & the Black Mirror. Dorman, Brandon, illus. (Falcon Quinn Ser.: 1). (ENG.). (J). (gr. 5-9). 2011. 512p. pap. 7.99 *(978-0-06-172834-1(9))* 2010. 496p. 16.99 *(978-0-06-172832-7(2))* HarperCollins Pubs. (Tegen, Katherine Bks).

—Falcon Quinn & the Crimson Vapor. 2011. (Falcon Quinn Ser.: 2). (ENG.). 384p. (J). (gr. 5-9). 16.99 *(978-0-06-172835-8(7),* Tegen, Katherine Bks) HarperCollins Pubs.

Bradford, Arthur & Webster, Chuck. 43 Monsters. 2015. (ENG., Illus.). 88p. 18.95 *(978-1-933149-92-9(2))* Manic D Pr.

Brallier, Max. Galactic Hot Dogs 2: The Wiener Strikes Back. Maguire, Rachel & Kelley, Nichole, illus. 2016. (Galactic Hot Dogs Ser.: 2). (ENG.). 288p. (J). (gr. 3-7). 13.99 *(978-1-4814-2496-7(3),* Aladdin) Simon & Schuster Children's Publishing.

Brallier, Max. The Last Kids on Earth. Holgate, Douglas, illus. (J). 2017. pap. ***(978-0-425-28872-6(2))*** 2016. (Last Kids on Earth Ser.: Vol. 2). (ENG.). (gr. 3-7). 13.99 *(978-0-670-01662-4(4))* 2015. (Last Kids on Earth Ser.: 1). (ENG.). 240p. (gr. 3-7). 13.99 *(978-0-670-01661-7(6))* Penguin Young Readers Group. (Viking Books for Young Readers).

Brege, K. B. All Isn't Well in Roswell! 2005. (Mick Morris Myth Solver Ser.: No. 1). (Illus.). 188p. (J). pap. 6.99 *(978-0-9774119-0-0(7))* Team B Creative LLC.

—Bigfoot... Big Trouble! 2006. (Mick Morris Myth Solver Ser.: No. 2). (J). pap. 6.99 *(978-0-9774119-1-7(5))* Team B Creative LLC.

Brendler, Carol. Not Very Scary. Pizzoli, Greg, illus. 2014. (ENG.). 40p. (J). (gr. -1-1). 12.99 *(978-0-374-35547-0(9),* 9780374355470, Farrar, Straus & Giroux (BYR)) Farrar, Straus & Giroux.

Brennan-Nelson, Denise. He's Been a Monster All Day. Moore, Cyd, illus. 2013. (ENG.). 32p. (J). (gr. -1-1). 14.99 *(978-1-58536-827-3(X),* 202363) Sleeping Bear Pr.

Bridgman, Rae. Kingdom of Trolls: A Middlegate Book. 2010. (Illus.). 287p. (J). pap. 15.00 *(978-0-9864974-1-4(X))* Sybertooth, Inc. CAN. Dist: Lightning Source, Inc.

Bright, J. E. & Sutton, Laurie S. Wonder Woman vs. Circe, 1 vol. Vecchio, Luciano, illus. 2013. (DC Super Heroes Ser.). (ENG.). 56p. (gr. 2-3). lib. bdg. 26.65 *(978-1-4342-6014-7(3))* Stone Arch Bks.

Bright, Rachel. Love Monster. (ENG., Illus.). 32p. (J). (gr. -1 — 1). 2014. bds. 7.99 *(978-0-374-30186-6(7),* 9780374301866) 2013. 16.99 *(978-0-374-34646-1(1),* 9780374346461) Farrar, Straus & Giroux. (Farrar, Straus & Giroux (BYR)).

—Love Monster & the Last Chocolate. 2015. (ENG., Illus.). 32p. (J). (gr. -1-k). 17.99 *(978-0-374-34690-4(9),* 9780374346904, Farrar, Straus & Giroux (BYR)) Farrar, Straus & Giroux.

—Love Monster & the Perfect Present. 2014. (ENG., Illus.). 32p. (J). (gr. -1-k). 17.99 *(978-0-374-34648-5(8),* 9780374346485, Farrar, Straus & Giroux (BYR)) Farrar, Straus & Giroux.

—Love Monster & the Scary Something. 2016. (ENG., Illus.). 32p. (J). 17.99 *(978-0-374-34691-1(7),* 9780374346911, Farrar, Straus & Giroux (BYR)) Farrar, Straus & Giroux.

Briley, Randy. Mr Underneath. 2013. 134p. pap. 12.99 *(978-0-9896269-0-3(3))* Raven Mad Studios.

Brittain, Bill. The Wizards & the Monster. Date not set. 96p. (J). (gr. 2-5). pap. 4.25 *(978-0-06-442003-7(5))* HarperCollins Pubs.

Bronson, Bill. Bill Bronson's Guide to Monsters, 1 vol. 2010. 24p. pap. 24.95 *(978-1-4489-6111-5(4))* PublishAmerica, Inc.

Brooks, Felicity. Jason & the Argonauts. Humphreys, Graham, illus. 2005. 144p. (J). pap. 4.95 *(978-0-7945-0275-1(X),* Usborne) EDC Publishing.

Brown, Bruce. Mwumba. O'Reilly, Sean Patrick, ed. 2011. (Illus.). 48p. (J). pap. 7.95 *(978-1-897548-03-5(6))* Arcana Studio, Inc.

Brown, Marcy & Haley, Dennis. We Both Read-the Well-Mannered Monster. Raglin, Tim, illus. 2006. (We Both Read Ser.). 40p. (J). (gr. -1-4). 7.99 *(978-1-891327-65-0(8))* Treasure Bay, Inc.

—We Both Read-The Well-Mannered Monster. Raglin, Tim, illus. 2006. (We Both Read Ser.). 44p. (J). (gr. -1-4). pap. 4.99 *(978-1-891327-66-7(6))* Treasure Bay, Inc.

Brown, Mick. From Round about Midnight until about Five! 2012. 60p. pap. 27.45 *(978-1-4772-2701-5(6))* AuthorHouse.

Brown, Monica. Marisol Mcdonald & the Monster: Marisol Mcdonald y el Monstruo. Palacios, Sara, illus. 2016. (Marisol Mcdonald Ser.). (ENG & SPA.). 32p. (J). (gr. k-3). 18.95 *(978-0-89239-326-8(2))* Lee & Low Bks., Inc.

Brown, Peter. My Teacher Is a Monster! (No, I Am Not.) 2014. (ENG., Illus.). 40p. (J). (gr. -1-3). 18.99 *(978-0-316-07029-4(7))* Little, Brown Bks. for Young Readers.

Bruchac, Joseph. The Dark Pond. Comport, Sally Wern, illus. 2005. 142p. (gr. 5-9). 17.00 *(978-0-7569-5436-9(3))* Perfection Learning Corp.

—Dark Pond. Comport, Sally Wern, illus. 2005. (ENG.). 160p. (J). (gr. 5-18). pap. 6.99 *(978-0-06-052998-7(9))* HarperCollins Pubs.

—Night Wings. Comport, Sally Wern, illus. 2009. (ENG.). 208p. (J). (gr. 3-7). 15.99 *(978-0-06-112318-4(8))* HarperCollins Pubs.

Brunell, Heather. Bedtime Monster. Adamson, Bonnie, illus. 2010. (ENG.). 32p. (J). (gr. -1-12). lib. bdg. 16.95 *(978-1-934960-03-5(9),* Raven Tree Pr.,Csi) Continental Sales, Inc.

—Bedtime Monster/A Dormir, Monstruito! Del Risco, Eida & de la Vega, Eida, trs. 2010. (ENG & SPA., Illus.). 32p. (J). (gr. -1-3). pap. 7.95 *(978-1-932748-81-9(4),* Raven Tree Pr.,Csi) Continental Sales, Inc.

—Bedtime Monster/A Dormir, Monstruito! de la Vega, Eida, tr. Adamson, Bonnie, illus. 2010. (ENG & SPA.). 32p. (J). (gr. -1-3). lib. bdg. 16.95 *(978-1-932748-80-2(6),* Raven Tree Pr.,Csi) Continental Sales, Inc.

Bryan, Ashley. Can't Scare Me! Bryan, Ashley, illus. 2013. (ENG., Illus.). 40p. (J). (gr. -1-3). 16.99 *(978-1-4424-7657-8(5),* Atheneum Bks. for Young Readers) Simon & Schuster Children's Publishing.

Buchanan, Nelda. The Hall Closet Light. 2009. 36p. (J). pap. 13.95 *(978-1-4327-4584-4(0))* Outskirts Pr., Inc.

Buchanan, Pendella. Layers. 2011. (Illus.). 16p. pap. 12.52 *(978-1-4567-8749-3(7))* AuthorHouse.

Buckley, Michael. The Fairy-Tale Detectives. Ferguson, Peter, illus. 2005. (ENG.). 288p. (J). (gr. 3-7). 16.95 *(978-0-8109-5925-5(9),* Abrams Bks. for Young Readers) Abrams, Inc.

—The Fairy-Tale Detectives. (Sisters Grimm Ser.: 1). (J). 2008. 81.45 *(978-1-4361-0398-5(3))* 2007. 214.75 *(978-1-4193-6197-5(X))* 2007. 1.25 *(978-1-4193-6193-7(7))* 2006. 71.75 *(978-1-4193-6198-2(8))* 2006. 86.75 *(978-1-4193-8749-4(9))* 2006. 74.75 *(978-1-4193-6196-8(1))* 2006. 89.75 *(978-1-4193-8747-0(2))* Recorded Bks., Inc.

—The Fairy-Tale Detectives: And the Unusual Suspects. Ferguson, Peter, illus. 2012. 580p. (J). *(978-1-4351-4487-3(2),* Amulet Bks.) Abrams, Inc.

—The Problem Child. Ferguson, Peter, illus. 2006. (Sisters Grimm Ser.). (ENG.). 320p. (J). (gr. 3-7). 16.95 *(978-0-8109-4914-0(8),* Amulet Bks.) Abrams, Inc.

—The Sisters Grimm: The Fairy-Tale Detectives. Ferguson, Peter, illus. 10th anniv. ed. 2017. (Sisters Grimm Ser.). (ENG.). 288p. (J). (gr. 3-7). pap. 8.95 *(978-1-4197-2005-5(8),* Amulet Bks.) Abrams, Inc.

Burch, Sharon. Freddie the Frog & the Bass Clef Monster. Harris, Tiffany, illus. 2010. (ENG.). 44p. (gr. -1-4). 24.99 incl. audio compact disk *(978-0-9747454-8-0(0),* 0974745480) Mystic Publishing.

Burfoot, Ella. Betty & the Yeti. 2nd ed. 2013. (ENG., Illus.). 32p. (J). (gr. -1-k). pap. 11.99 *(978-0-330-51117-9(3))* Pan Macmillan GBR. Dist: Independent Pubs. Group.

—Louie & the Monsters. Burfoot, Ella, illus. 2005. (Illus.). 32p. (J). (gr. -1-2). 6.95 *(978-1-58925-395-7(7))* Tiger Tales.

Butterworth, MyLinda. The Monster Run. Day, Linda S., ed. Mercer, Matthew, illus. l.t. ed. 2004. 32p. (J). (gr. -1-3). 14.95 *(978-1-890905-23-1(2),* Writers Collective, The) Day to Day Enterprises.

Byng, Georgia. Molly Moon & the Monster Music. 2013. (Molly Moon Ser.: 6). (ENG.). 320p. (J). (gr. 3-7). 16.99 *(978-0-06-166163-1(5))* HarperCollins Pubs.

Captain Underpants & the Tyrannical Retaliation of the Turbo Toilet 2000. 2014. (Captain Underpants Ser.: Bk. 11). (ENG., Illus.). 224p. (J). (gr. 2-5). 9.99 *(978-0-545-50490-4(2))* Scholastic, Inc.

Carbone, Courtney. Lights Out! (Marvel: Mighty Avengers) Spaziante, Patrick, illus. 2016. (Little Golden Book Ser.). (ENG.). 24p. (J). (-k). 4.99 *(978-0-307-97658-1(0),* Golden Bks.) Random Hse. Children's Bks.

Card, Melanie. Ward Against Darkness. 2013. (Necromancer Ser.: 2). (ENG.). 326p. (YA). (gr. 7). pap. 9.99 *(978-1-62061-303-0(4),* 9781620613030) Entangled Publishing, LLC.

Carter, Jimmy. The Little Baby Snoogle- Fleejer. Carter, Amy, illus. 2014. (ENG.). 24p. (J). 19.95 *(978-1-55728-671-0(X))* Univ. of Arkansas Pr.

Cavaliere, Katrina. Mom! There's a Monster under My Bed! 2008. 24p. per. 24.95 *(978-1-60441-066-2(3))* America Star Bks.

Cazet, Denys. Minnie & Moo Meet Frankenswine. Cazet, Denys, illus. 2004. (Readalongs for Beginning Readers Ser.). (Illus.). 28.95 incl. audio compact disk *(978-1-59112-876-2(5))*; (J). 25.95 incl. audio *(978-1-59112-262-3(7))*; (J). pap. 29.95 incl. audio *(978-1-59112-263-0(5))* Live Oak Media.

—Minnie & Moo Meet Frankenswine, 4 bks. 2004. (Readalongs for Beginning Readers Ser.). (Illus.). 48p. (J). (gr. -1-2). pap. 31.95 incl. audio compact disk *(978-1-59112-877-9(3))* Live Oak Media.

Cerasini, Marc. Godzilla Saves America: A Monster Showdown In 3-D! Morgan, Tom & Mounts, Paul, illus. 2006. 20p. (J). (gr. k-4). reprint ed. 12.00 *(978-1-4223-5409-4(1))* DIANE Publishing Co.

Chalifoux, Lisa M. Bravery Is like Love. Perras, Marielle, illus. 2009. 24p. pap. 10.99 *(978-1-4269-0942-9(X))* Trafford Publishing.

Chandler, Elizabeth. Monsters Are We. 2011. 28p. pap. 15.99 *(978-1-4628-8485-8(7))* Xlibris Corp.

Chapman, Linda. Max's Amazing Models. Jevons, Chris, illus. 2017. (Reading Ladder Ser.). (ENG.). 48p. (J). (gr. k-2). pap. 7.99 ***(978-1-4052-7823-2(4))*** Egmont Bks., Ltd. GBR. Dist: Independent Pubs. Group.

Chartrand, Lili. Taming Horrible Harry. Ouriou, Susan, tr. from FRE. Rogé, illus. 2006. (ENG.). 32p. (J). (gr. -1-3). 16.95 *(978-0-88776-772-2(9),* Tundra Bks.) Tundra Bks. CAN. Dist: Penguin Random Hse. LLC.

Chase, L. P. Elliot Stone & the Mystery of the Summer Vacation Sea Monster. DiRocco, Carl, illus. 2011. (ENG.). 165p. (J). pap. 8.99 *(978-0-9792918-7-6(9))* Blue Marlin Pubns.

Cheverton, Mark. Monsters in the Mist. 2017. (Mystery of Entity303 Ser.: 2). lib. bdg. 20.85 ***(978-0-606-40313-9(2))*** Turtleback Bks.

Child, Lauren. Ruby Redfort Take Your Last Breath. Child, Lauren, illus. 2013. (Ruby Redfort Ser.: 2). (ENG., Illus.). 432p. (J). (gr. 5-9). 16.99 *(978-0-7636-5468-9(X))* Candlewick Pr.

Childs, Tera Lynn. Sweet Legacy. 2013. (Sweet Venom Ser.: 3). (ENG.). 384p. (YA). (gr. 8). 17.99 *(978-0-06-200185-6(X),* Tegen, Katherine Bks) HarperCollins Pubs.

—Sweet Shadows. (Sweet Venom Ser.: 2). (ENG.). (YA). (gr. 8). 2013. 352p. pap. 9.99 *(978-0-06-200184-9(1))* 2012. 336p. 17.99 *(978-0-06-200183-2(3))* HarperCollins Pubs. (Tegen, Katherine Bks).

—Sweet Venom. (Sweet Venom Ser.: 1). (ENG.). (YA). (gr. 8). 2012. 384p. pap. 9.99 *(978-0-06-200182-5(5))* 2011. 352p. 17.99 *(978-0-06-200181-8(7))* HarperCollins Pubs. (Tegen, Katherine Bks).

Chin, Oliver. Welcome to Monster Isle. Miracola, Jeff, illus. 2008. (ENG.). 36p. (J). (gr. -1-3). 15.95 *(978-1-59702-016-9(8))* Immedium.

Christensen, Gerda. Troll Peter Discovers the Bog-Woman's Secret & Other Stories. 2010. 40p. pap. 18.27 *(978-1-4251-8822-1(2))* Trafford Publishing.

Christian, Mary Blount. Swamp Monsters. Brown, Marc, illus. 48p. (J). (gr. 1-2). pap. 3.99 *(978-0-8072-1355-1(1),* Listening Library) Random Hse. Audio Publishing Group.

Cimorelli, Amber. There Are Monsters Here! Galante, Ashley, illus. 2013. 40p. pap. 24.95 *(978-1-62709-064-3(9))* America Star Bks.

Cioffi, Dom, illus. Digby & the Lake Monster. l.t. ed. 2006. 36p. (J). per. *(978-0-9745931-0-4(9))* Vermont Bookworks.

Clark, Platte F. Good Ogre. 2015. (Bad Unicorn Trilogy Ser.: 3). (ENG., Illus.). 384p. (J). (gr. 3-7). 17.99 *(978-1-4424-5018-9(5),* Aladdin) Simon & Schuster Children's Publishing.

Clark, Simon P. Tell the Story to Its End. 2015. (ENG., Illus.). 208p. (YA). (gr. 7). 18.99 *(978-1-250-06675-6(1),* 9781250066756, St. Martin's Griffin) St. Martin's Pr.

Clarke, Justine & Baysting, Arthur. Gobbledygook Is Eating a Book. 2016. (ENG.). 32p. (J). (gr. -1-2). 13.99 ***(978-0-14-350693-5(5))*** Random Hse. Australia AUS. Dist: Independent Pubs. Group.

Class P3 in Scoil Chiarain Staff. 10 Scary Monsters. 2007. (ENG., Illus.). 32p. (J). pap. 12.95 *(978-1-84717-002-6(1))* O'Brien Pr., Ltd., The IRL. Dist: Dufour Editions, Inc.

Claybourne, Anna. Adventures of Ulysses. 2005. 144p. (J). pap. 4.95 *(978-0-7945-0322-2(5),* Usborne) EDC Publishing.

Clocktowerhill Research & Publishing Group. Loyd & Boyd & the Slug Monster of Webster County. 2011. (ENG., Illus.). 104p. (J). 12.99 *(978-0-9832130-0-0(3),* Lucas Violet) Clocktower Hill Research & Publishing Group, LLC.

Cohen, Caron Lee. Broom, Zoom! Ruzzier, Sergio, illus. 2010. (ENG.). 32p. (J). (gr. -1-3). 14.99 *(978-1-4169-9113-7(1),* Simon & Schuster Bks. For Young Readers) Simon & Schuster Bks. For Young Readers.

Cole, Lisa. Chessie of the Chesapeake Bay. Cole, Lisa, illus. 2011. (Illus.). 110p. pap. 9.95 *(978-1-936343-94-2(0))* Peppertree Pr., The.

Cole, Quinn. Alphabet Puke: Monsters' Medicine A-Z. Eubanks, Charles, illus. 2013. 32p. pap. 6.99 *(978-1-936214-94-5(6))* Wyatt-MacKenzie Publishing.

Collier, Kevin Scott. Professor Horace, Cryptozoologist. Collier, Kevin Scott, illus. 2008. (Illus.). 20p. pap. 9.95 *(978-1-935137-14-6(X))* Guardian Angel Publishing, Inc.

Collins, Terry & Weakland, Mark. Unmasking Monsters with Scooby-Doo! Cornia, Christian et al, illus. 2015. (Unmasking Monsters with Scooby-Doo! Ser.). (ENG.). 24p. (gr. 1-2). lib. bdg. 155.94 *(978-1-4914-1797-3(8))* Capstone Press of Coughlan Cos.

Colloredo, Sabino. Hercules. Ferrari, Antongionata, illus. 2009. (Hotel Olympus Ser.). 128p. (J). (gr. 3-6). 31.95 *(978-1-60754-708-2(2))* Windmill Bks.

Conley, Jennise M. I Think There's a Monster under My Bed! 2013. 28p. 9.99 *(978-1-61061-972-1(2))* My Three Sisters Publishing.

Connolly, MarcyKate. Monstrous. Young, Skottie, illus. (J). (gr. 3-7). 2016. 448p. pap. 7.99 *(978-0-06-227272-0(1))* 2015. (ENG.). 432p. 16.99 *(978-0-06-227271-3(3))* HarperCollins Pubs.

—Monstrous. 2016. (J). lib. bdg. 18.40 *(978-0-606-38136-9(8))* Turtleback Bks.

Connor, David. Archie & Billy in Monster Cave. 2011. (Illus.). 40p. 18.68 *(978-1-4567-7308-3(9))* AuthorHouse.

Constantin, Pascale, illus. Little Monster. 2007. (I'm Going to Read(r) Ser.). (ENG.). 28p. (J). (gr. -1-k). pap. 3.95 *(978-1-4027-2078-9(5))* Sterling Publishing Co., Inc.

Cooper, Susan. The Boggart & the Monster. Rayyan, Omar & Dillon, Julie, illus. 2004. (Boggart Ser.). (ENG.). 224p. (J). (gr. 3-7). pap. 7.99 *(978-0-689-86931-0(2),* McElderry, Margaret K. Bks.) McElderry, Margaret K. Bks.

Corentin, Philippe. Papa! (SPA.). 32p. *(978-84-95150-38-7(7))* Corimbo, Editorial S.L.

—Papa. 2003. (SPA.). (J). (gr. -1-k). 19.99 *(978-84-8470-094-4(1))* Corimbo, Editorial S.L. ESP. Dist: Lectorum Pubns., Inc.

Corey, Shana. Monster Parade. Terry, Will, illus. 2009. (Step into Reading Ser.). (ENG.). 24p. (J). (gr. -1-1). 3.99 *(978-0-375-85638-9(2),* Random Hse. Bks. for Young Readers) Random Hse. Children's Bks.

corjanjamnic. Angels on Earth, 1 vol. 2010. 48p. pap. 16.95 *(978-1-4512-0050-8(1))* America Star Bks.

Cornell, Kevin. Go to Sleep, Monster! Cornell, Kevin, illus. 2016. (Illus.). 32p. (J). (gr. -1-3). 17.99 *(978-0-06-234915-6(5))* HarperCollins Pubs.

Cornish, D. M. Foundling. Cornish, D. M., illus. 2007. (Monster Blood Tattoo Ser.). (Illus.). 434p. (gr. 7-12). 20.00 *(978-0-7569-7957-7(9))* Perfection Learning Corp.

Cosgrove, Stephen. Snugg N. Flitter: Facing Your Fears. Arroyo, Fian, illus. 2004. (J). *(978-1-58804-377-1(0))* P C I Education.

Costi, Vincent. The Planet of the Gargand. Smith, Anne & Smith, Owen, trs. from FRE. Elyum Studio, illus. 2014. (Little Prince Ser.: 15). (ENG.). 48p. (J). (gr. 4-8). lib. bdg. 26.60 *(978-0-7613-8765-7(X),* Graphic Universe™) Lerner Publishing Group.

Côté, Geneviève. Mr. King's Things. Côté, Geneviève, illus. 2012. (Mr. King Ser.). (ENG., Illus.). 32p. (J). (gr. -1-2). 16.95 *(978-1-55453-700-6(2))* Kids Can Pr., Ltd. CAN. Dist: Hachette Bk. Group.

Cotter, Bill. Don't Push the Button! 2013. (ENG., Illus.). 32p. (J). (-3). 16.99 *(978-1-4022-8746-6(1),* Sourcebooks Jabberwocky) Sourcebooks, Inc.

—Don't Touch This Book! 2016. (ENG., Illus.). (J). 28p. bds. 6.99 *(978-1-4926-4804-8(3),* 9781492648048); 32p. 16.99 *(978-1-4926-3224-5(4),* 9781492632245) Sourcebooks, Inc. (Sourcebooks Jabberwocky).

Cotton, Katie. Ten Monsters in the Bed. Blecha, Aaron, illus. 2015. (ENG.). 24p. (J). (gr. -1-k). 12.99 *(978-1-4998-0067-8(3))* Little Bee Books Inc.

Coville, Bruce. Always October. 2012. (ENG.). 384p. (J). (gr. 3-7). 16.99 *(978-0-06-089095-7(9))* HarperCollins Pubs.

—The Mischief Monster. Coville, Katherine, illus. 2008. (Moongobble & Me Ser.: Bk. 4). (ENG.). 80p. (J). (gr. 1-5). pap. 5.99 *(978-1-4169-0808-1(0),* Aladdin) Simon & Schuster Children's Publishing.

—The Monster's Ring. Coville, Katherine, illus. 2008. (Magic Shop Book Ser.: 1). (ENG.). 128p. (J). (gr. 5-7). pap. 6.99 *(978-0-15-206442-6(7))* Houghton Mifflin Harcourt Publishing Co.

—The Naughty Nork. Coville, Katherine, illus. 2009. (Moongobble & Me Ser.). (ENG.). 128p. (J). (gr. 1-5). pap. 6.99 *(978-1-4169-0810-4(2),* Aladdin) Simon & Schuster Children's Publishing.

Cowley, Joy. Meanies in the House Big Book. 2010. 48.25 *(978-1-60559-251-0(X))* Hameray Publishing Group, Inc.

Cox, Steve, illus. Is That You, Monster? Check Inside the Secret Pockets If You Dare! 2013. (ENG.). 22p. (J). (gr. -1-1). 12.99 *(978-0-7641-6608-2(5))* Barron's Educational Series, Inc.

Cranch, Christopher. The Last of the Huggermuggers. 2004. reprint ed. pap. 15.95 *(978-1-4191-6876-5(2))* Kessinger Publishing, LLC.

Cranch, Christopher Pierce. The Last of the Huggermuggers. 2004. reprint ed. pap. 1.99 *(978-1-4192-6876-2(7))* Kessinger Publishing, LLC.

Crayon, Paula. Mittens in the Attic. 2010. 40p. pap. 18.99 *(978-1-4520-9218-8(4))* AuthorHouse.

Crider, Mike. Mike Gonzo & the Sewer Monster. 2012. (ENG., Illus.). 144p. (J). (gr. 3-7). pap. 8.99 *(978-1-4424-8127-5(7),* Simon & Schuster/Paula Wiseman Bks.) Simon & Schuster/Paula Wiseman Bks.

—Mike Gonzo & the UFO Terror. 2012. (ENG., Illus.). 128p. (J). (gr. 3-7). pap. 7.99 *(978-1-4424-8129-9(3),* Simon & Schuster/Paula Wiseman Bks.) Simon & Schuster/Paula Wiseman Bks.

Crimi, Carolyn. Boris & Bella. Grimly, Gris, illus. 2006. (ENG.). 32p. (J). (gr. -1-3). reprint ed. pap. 7.99 *(978-0-15-205900-2(8))* Houghton Mifflin Harcourt Publishing Co.

—Where's My Mummy? Manders, John, illus. 2008. (ENG.). 32p. (J). (gr. -1-3). 15.99 *(978-0-7636-3196-3(5))* Candlewick Pr.

Crosby, June. A Monster in the Attic. Chapman, Michelle, illus. 2011. 16p. pap. 24.95 *(978-1-4560-6959-9(4))* America Star Bks.

Crow, Kristyn. Bedtime at the Swamp. Pamintuan, Macky, illus. 2008. (ENG.). 32p. (J). (gr. -1-1). 16.99 *(978-0-06-083951-2(1))* HarperCollins Pubs.

Crow, Marilee & Foster, Jack. Once There Was a Monster. 2012. 20p. pap. 9.95 *(978-1-61633-331-7(6))* Guardian Angel Publishing, Inc.

Crow, Nosy. Pip & Posy: the Scary Monster. Scheffler, Axel, illus. 2014. (Pip & Posy Ser.). (ENG.). 24p. (J). (-k). bds. 6.99 *(978-0-7636-7231-7(9),* Nosy Crow) Candlewick Pr.

Crowley, James. Monsterland. 2017. (ENG.). 384p. (J). (gr. 5). 16.99 *(978-0-399-17589-3(X),* G.P. Putnam's Sons Books for Young Readers) Penguin Young Readers Group.

Crownberry, Ethan. The Willies. 2012. 80p. pap. 8.95 *(978-1-300-00798-2(2))* Lulu Pr., Inc.

—The Willies. 2012. 80p. pap. 10.95 *(978-0-557-96056-9(8))* Lulu.com GBR. Dist: Lulu Pr., Inc.

Cua, Marcus Loo. How the Hungry T-Rex Got Fixed. 2012. 24p. pap. 28.03 *(978-1-4653-9643-3(8))* Xlibris Corp.

Cuccia, Ronni. Maria & the Monster. 2010. 16p. 10.99 *(978-1-4520-8966-9(3))* AuthorHouse.

Culpepper, Karen. The Homework Monster. 2011. 32p. (J). 23.95 *(978-0-9765641-2-6(2))* Rai Publishing.

Cummings, Pat. Ananse & the Monster. (Illus.). (YA). 16.99 *(978-0-8050-7782-7(0))* Holt, Henry & Co.

Cummings, Troy. Attack of the Shadow Smashers. 2013. (Notebook of Doom Ser.: 3). (ENG.). 96p. (J). (gr. 1-3). pap. 4.99 *(978-0-545-55297-4(4))* Scholastic, Inc.

—Attack of the Shadow Smashers. 2013. (Notebook of Doom Ser.: 3). lib. bdg. 14.75 *(978-0-606-32369-7(4),* Turtleback) Turtleback Bks.

—Charge of the Lightning Bugs. Cummings, Troy, illus. 2015. (Notebook of Doom Ser.: 8). (ENG., Illus.). 96p. (J). (gr. 1-3). 15.99 *(978-0-545-79554-8(0))*; pap. 4.99 *(978-0-545-79555-5(9))* Scholastic, Inc.

—Chomp of the Meat-Eating Vegetables. 2014. (Notebook of Doom Ser.: 4). (ENG.). 96p. (J). (gr. 1-3). 15.99 *(978-0-545-55300-1(8))*; (Illus.). pap. 4.99 *(978-0-545-55299-8(0))* Scholastic, Inc.

—Chomp of the Meat-Eating Vegetables. 2014. (Notebook of Doom Ser.: 4). lib. bdg. 14.75 *(978-0-606-35362-5(3))* Turtleback Bks.

—Day of the Night Crawlers. 2013. (Notebook of Doom Ser.: 2). (ENG.). 96p. (J). (gr. 1-3). 15.99 *(978-0-545-49324-6(2))*; pap. 4.99 *(978-0-545-49325-3(0))*; E-Book *(978-0-545-49327-7(7))* Scholastic, Inc.

—Day of the Night Crawlers. 2013. (Notebook of Doom Ser.: 2). lib. bdg. 14.75 *(978-0-606-32368-0(6)*, Turtleback) Turtleback Bks.

—Flurry of the Snombies. 2015. (Notebook of Doom Ser.: 7). (ENG., Illus.). 96p. (J). (gr. 1-3). 15.99 *(978-0-545-79551-7(6))*; pap. 4.99 *(978-0-545-79550-0(8))* Scholastic, Inc.

—March of the Vanderpants. 2017. (Notebook of Doom — Branches Ser.: 12). lib. bdg. 14.75 ***(978-0-606-40192-0(X))*** Turtleback Bks.

—March of the Vanderpants - A Branches Book. Cummings, Troy, illus. 2017. (Notebook of Doom Ser.: 12). (ENG., Illus.). 96p. (J). (gr. 1-3). pap. 4.99 ***(978-1-338-03452-3(9))***; lib. bdg. 15.99 ***(978-1-338-03453-0(7))*** Scholastic, Inc.

—The Notebook of Doom #6: Pop of the Bumpy Mummy (a Branches Book) - Library Edition. 2014. (Notebook of Doom Ser.: 6). (ENG.). 96p. (J). (gr. 1-3). 15.99 *(978-0-545-69899-3(5))* Scholastic, Inc.

—The Notebook of Doom Collection, Bks. 1-3. Cummings, Troy, illus. 2016. (Notebook of Doom Ser.). (ENG., Illus.). 288p. (J). (gr. 1-3). pap. 9.99 *(978-1-338-10199-7(4))* Scholastic, Inc.

—Pop of the Bumpy Mummy. Cummings, Troy, illus. 2014. (Notebook of Doom Ser.: 6). (ENG., Illus.). 96p. (J). (gr. 1-3). pap. 4.99 *(978-0-545-69898-6(7))* Scholastic, Inc.

—Pop of the Bumpy Mummy. 2014. (Notebook of Doom Ser.: 6). lib. bdg. 14.75 *(978-0-606-36339-6(4))* Turtleback Bks.

—Rise of the Balloon Goons. 2013. (Notebook of Doom Ser.: 1). (ENG., Illus.). 96p. (J). (gr. 1-3). 15.99 *(978-0-545-49322-2(6))*; pap. 4.99 *(978-0-545-49323-9(4))* Scholastic, Inc.

—Rumble of the Coaster Ghost. Cummings, Troy, illus. 2016. (Notebook of Doom Ser.: 9). (ENG., Illus.). 96p. (J). (gr. 1-3). pap. 4.99 *(978-0-545-86497-8(6))* Scholastic, Inc.

—Snap of the Super-Goop: A Branches Book. Cummings, Troy, illus. 2016. (Notebook of Doom Ser.: 1). (ENG., Illus.). 96p. (J). (gr. 1-3). 15.99 *(978-0-545-86500-5(X))* Scholastic, Inc.

—Snap of the Super-Goop - A Branches Book. Cummings, Troy, illus. 2016. (Notebook of Doom Ser.: 1). (ENG., Illus.). 96p. (J). (gr. 1-3). pap. 4.99 *(978-0-545-86499-2(2))* Scholastic, Inc.

—Sneeze of the Octo-Schnozz: a Branches Book (the Notebook of Doom #11) 2016. (Notebook of Doom Ser.: 11). (ENG.). 96p. (J). (gr. 1-3). pap. 4.99 *(978-1-338-03448-6(0))* Scholastic, Inc.

—Whack of the P-Rex. 2014. (Notebook of Doom Ser.: 5). (ENG.). 96p. (J). (gr. 1-3). pap. 4.99 *(978-0-545-69895-5(2))* Scholastic, Inc.

Cunliffe, John. Postman Pat & the Beast of Greendale, Bk. 12. (Illus.). 32p. (J). *(978-0-340-67816-9(X))* Hodder & Stoughton.

Cusack, Dale. Grace & the Drawl. 2008. (Illus.). 169p. pap. 11.95 *(978-1-4357-0926-3(8))* Lulu Pr., Inc.

Cuyler, Margery. Monster Mess! Schindler, S. D., illus. 2008. (ENG.). 32p. (J). (gr. -1-1). 14.99 *(978-0-689-86405-6(1)*, McElderry, Margaret K. Bks.) McElderry, Margaret K. Bks.

Czajak, Paul. Monster Needs a Christmas Tree. Grieb, Wendy, illus. 2014. (Monster & Me Ser.). (ENG.). 32p. (J). (-k). 16.95 *(978-1-938063-46-6(5)*, Mighty Media Kids) Mighty Media Pr.

—Monster Needs a Costume. Grieb, Wendy, illus. (Monster & Me Ser.). (ENG.). 32p. (J). (-k). 2014. 6.99 *(978-1-938063-38-1(4))* 2013. 16.95 *(978-1-938063-09-1(0))* Mighty Media Pr. (Mighty Media Kids).

—Monster Needs a Party. Grieb, Wendy, illus. 2015. (Monster & Me Ser.). (ENG.). 32p. (J). (-k). 16.95 *(978-1-938063-55-8(4)*, Mighty Media Kids) Mighty Media Pr.

—Monster Needs His Sleep. Grieb, Wendy, illus. 2014. (Monster & Me Ser.). (ENG.). 32p. (J). (-k). 16.95 *(978-1-938063-26-8(0)*, Mighty Media Kids) Mighty Media Pr.

—Monster Needs Your Vote. Grieb, Wendy, illus. 2015. (Monster & Me Ser.). (ENG.). 32p. (J). (gr. -1-3). 16.95 *(978-1-938063-63-3(5)*, Mighty Media Kids) Mighty Media Pr.

Dadey, Debbie. Great Green Gator Graduation. Lucas, Margeaux, illus. 2006. (Swamp Monster in Third Grade Ser.). 58p. (J). pap. *(978-0-439-79401-5(3))* Scholastic, Inc.

Dadey, Debbie & Jones, Marcia Thornton. Monsters Don't Scuba Dive. (Adventures of the Bailey School Kids Ser.: No. 14). (FRE., Illus.). 80p. (J). (gr. 2-4). pap. 5.99 *(978-0-590-24550-0(3))* Scholastic, Inc.

Dahl, Michael. Dark Tower Rising, 1 vol. Kovar, Ben, illus. 2012. (Troll Hunters Ser.). (ENG.). 112p. (gr. 2-3). lib. bdg. 25.32 *(978-1-4342-3308-0(1)*, Troll Hunters) Stone Arch Bks.

—Dungeon of Seven Dooms, 1 vol. 2011. (Good vs Evil Ser.). (ENG.). 48p. (gr. 1-2). lib. bdg. 23.99 *(978-1-4342-2091-2(5)*, Good vs Evil) Stone Arch Bks.

—Fallen Star, 1 vol. Kovar, Ben, illus. 2012. (Troll Hunters Ser.). (ENG.). 112p. (gr. 2-3). lib. bdg. 25.32 *(978-1-4342-3310-3(3)*, Troll Hunters) Stone Arch Bks.

—In One Ear, Out the Other, 1 vol. Omia-Blanco, Miguel, illus. 2010. (Monster Street Ser.). (ENG.). 32p. (gr. 1-2). lib. bdg. 23.99 *(978-1-4048-6068-1(1)*, Monster Street) Picture Window Bks.

—Inkfoot, 1 vol. Kendall, Bradford, illus. 2010. (Return to the Library of Doom Ser.). (ENG.). 72p. (gr. 1-3). 23.99 *(978-1-4342-2146-9(6)*, Zone Bks.) Stone Arch Bks.

—The Lava Crown, 1 vol. Kovar, Ben, illus. 2012. (Troll Hunters Ser.). (ENG.). 112p. (gr. 2-3). lib. bdg. 25.32 *(978-1-4342-3309-7(X)*, Troll Hunters) Stone Arch Bks.

—The Library Claw: And Other Scary Tales. Bonet, Xavier, illus. 2017. (Michael Dahl's Really Scary Stories Ser.). (ENG.). 72p. (gr. 2-3). lib. bdg. 25.32 ***(978-1-4965-4902-0(3))*** Stone Arch Bks.

—Maze Monster. Catling, Andy, illus. 2016. (Igor's Lab of Fear Ser.). (ENG.). 40p. (gr. 1-3). lib. bdg. 23.99 *(978-1-4965-3528-3(6))* Stone Arch Bks.

—The Monster in the Mailbox: And Other Scary Tales. Bonet, Xavier, illus. 2016. (Michael Dahl's Really Scary Stories Ser.). (ENG.). 72p. (gr. 2-3). lib. bdg. 25.32 *(978-1-4965-3771-3(8))* Stone Arch Bks.

—Monster Street, Set. Omia-Blanco, Miguel, illus. Incl. Cold Feet. lib. bdg. 23.99 *(978-1-4048-6070-4(3))*; In One Ear, Out the Other. lib. bdg. 23.99 *(978-1-4048-6068-1(1))*; Two Heads Are Better Than One. lib. bdg. 23.99 *(978-1-4048-6067-4(3))*; (gr. 1-2). (Monster Street Ser.). (ENG., Illus.). 32p. 2010. Set lib. bdg. 71.97 *(978-1-4048-6352-1(4)*, Monster Street) Picture Window Bks.

—Skyfall, 1 vol. Kovar, Ben, illus. 2012. (Troll Hunters Ser.). (ENG.). 112p. (gr. 2-3). lib. bdg. 25.32 *(978-1-4342-3307-3(3)*, Troll Hunters) Stone Arch Bks.

—The Spine Tingler. Evergreen, Nelson, illus. 2015. (Library of Doom: the Final Chapters Ser.). (ENG.). 40p. (gr. 1-3). 23.99 *(978-1-4342-9680-1(6))* Stone Arch Bks.

—Troll Hunters, 1 vol. Kovar, Ben, illus. 2012. (Troll Hunters Ser.). (ENG.). 320p. (gr. 4-4). 12.95 *(978-1-4342-4590-8(X))* Stone Arch Bks.

—Two Heads Are Better Than One, 1 vol. Omia-Blanco, Miguel, illus. 2010. (Monster Street Ser.). (ENG.). 32p. (gr. 1-2). lib. bdg. 23.99 *(978-1-4048-6067-4(3)*, Monster Street) Picture Window Bks.

Dahl, Roald. The Minpins. 2009. (ENG.). 32p. (J). (gr. 1-3). pap. 7.99 *(978-0-14-241474-3(3)*, Puffin Books) Penguin Young Readers Group.

Daisy, April. The Monster's in My Room. Daisy, April, illus. 2005. (Illus.). (J). per. 7.95 *(978-1-59466-048-1(4)*, Little Ones) Port Town Publishing.

d'Allancé, Mireille. Vaya Rabieta.Tr. of What A Tantrum! (SPA.). 32p. (J). *(978-84-95150-89-9(1))* Corimbo, Editorial S.L. ESP. Dist: Lectorum Pubns., Inc.

Dambrot, Marc. The Destined: A Hero's Calling. 2008. 116p. pap. 19.95 *(978-1-60474-792-8(7))* America Star Bks.

Daneshvari, Gitty. Ghoulfriends Forever. 2012. (ENG., Illus.). 272p. (J). (gr. 3-7). 12.99 *(978-0-316-22249-5(6))* Little, Brown Bks. for Young Readers.

—Ghoulfriends 'Til the End. 2014. (Monster High Ghoulfriends Ser.: 4). (ENG., Illus.). 256p. (J). (gr. 3-7). 13.99 *(978-0-316-22251-8(8))* Little, Brown Bks. for Young Readers.

—The Ghouls Rule Boxed Set, Set. 2013. (ENG., Illus.). 816p. (J). (gr. 3-7). 39.00 *(978-0-316-32361-1(6))* Little, Brown Bks. for Young Readers.

—Monster High: Ghoulfriends the Ghoul-It-Yourself Book. 2014. (Monster High Ghoulfriends Ser.: 4.5). (ENG., Illus.). 240p. (J). (gr. 3-7). 13.99 *(978-0-316-28222-2(7))* Little, Brown Bks. for Young Readers.

Daniels, Donna. What Do Monsters Do Tonight? 2009. (Illus.). 24p. pap. 11.49 *(978-1-4389-2650-6(2))* AuthorHouse.

Darke, J. A. Do Not Watch. Evans, Neil, illus. 2016. (Spine Shivers Ser.). (ENG.). 128p. (gr. 3-4). lib. bdg. 26.65 *(978-1-4965-3071-4(3))* Stone Arch Bks.

Darrows, Eva. The Awesome. 2015. (ENG.). 352p. (YA). (gr. 10). pap. 9.99 *(978-1-78108-324-6(X)*, Ravenstone) Rebellion GBR. Dist: Simon & Schuster, Inc.

David, Lawrence. The Invasion of the Shag Carpet Creature. Gott, Barry, illus. 2004. (Horace Splattly Ser.). 151p. (J). (gr. 4-7). 12.65 *(978-0-7569-2818-6(4))* Perfection Learning Corp.

Davidson, Danica. The Armies of Herobrine: An Unofficial Overworld Adventure, Book Five. 2016. (Unofficial Overworld Adventure Ser.). (ENG.). 112p. (J). (gr. 1-7). pap. 7.99 *(978-1-5107-1620-9(3)*, Sky Pony Pr.) Skyhorse Publishing Co., Inc.

—Escape from the Overworld. 2015. (Unofficial Overworld Adventure Ser.). (ENG.). 112p. (J). (gr. 1-7). pap. 7.99 *(978-1-63450-103-3(9)*, Sky Pony Pr.) Skyhorse Publishing Co., Inc.

Davis, Daniel M. & Davis, Dawna Jo. Klawberry: Good Girl. Bad World. McClellan, Sara, ed. ltd. ed. 2007. (Illus.). per. 20.00 *(978-0-9774173-3-9(6))* Steam Crow Pr.

Davis, Eleanor. Stinky. 2008. (ENG., Illus.). 40p. (J). (gr. -1-3). 12.95 *(978-0-9799238-4-5(0))* TOON Books / RAW Junior, LLC.

Dawson, Brianog Brady & Nolan, Alan. Danny Brown & the Monster Toothbrush. Connor, Michael, illus. 2017. (ENG.). 64p. (J). 10.00 ***(978-1-84717-880-0(4))*** O'Brien Pr., Ltd., The IRL. Dist: Dufour Editions, Inc.

Dayan, Linda Marcos. El Monstruo Graciopeo. Nepomniachi, Leonid, illus. (Barril Sin Fondo Ser.). (SPA.). (J). (gr. 3-5). pap. *(978-968-6465-60-0(X))* Casa de Estudios de Literatura y Talleres Artisticos Amaquemecan A.C. MEX. Dist: Lectorum Pubns., Inc.

Deadman, Ron & Gifford, Griselda. The Goat Monster & Other Stories, 4 vols. 2014. (ENG.). 128p. pap. 46.00 *(978-0-17-402427-9(4))* Oxford Univ. Pr., Inc.

Dean, Denise. Under Tommy's Bed: A Tommy Maloney Book. 2011. 40p. pap. 24.95 *(978-1-4560-7293-3(5))* America Star Bks.

del Toro, Guillermo & Kraus, Daniel. Trollhunters. Murray, Sean, illus. (Trollhunters Ser.). (ENG.). 320p. (YA). (gr. 7-12). 2016. pap. 9.99 ***(978-1-368-01218-8(3)***, 1380291) 2015. 18.99 *(978-1-4231-2598-3(3)*, 1380291) Hyperion Bks. for Children.

Delaney, Joseph. A New Darkness. 2014. (ENG.). 352p. (YA). (gr. 8). 17.99 *(978-0-06-233453-4(0)*, Greenwillow Bks.) HarperCollins Pubs.

—Slither, Bk. 11. (Last Apprentice Ser.). (ENG.). (YA). (gr. 8). 2014. 432p. pap. 9.99 *(978-0-06-219235-6(3))* 2013. 416p. 17.99 *(978-0-06-219234-9(5))* HarperCollins Pubs. (Greenwillow Bks.).

Delporte, Peyo, et al. The Smurfs & the Howlibird. 2011. (Smurfs Graphic Novels Ser.). (ENG., Illus.). 56p. (J). (gr. 2-5). 10.99 *(978-1-59707-261-8(3)*, 9781597072618) Papercutz.

Denise, Anika. Monster Trucks. Wragg, Nate, illus. 2016. 32p. (J). (gr. -1-3). 17.99 *(978-0-06-234522-6(2))* HarperCollins Pubs.

Depken, Kristen L. Monster Magic! (Shimmer & Shine) Aikins, David, illus. 2017. (Big Golden Book Ser.). (ENG.). 48p. (J). (gr. -1-2). 9.99 ***(978-1-5247-1671-4(5)***, Golden Bks.) Random Hse. Children's Bks.

DePrisco, Dorothea. Maximus the Monster Roars NO! 2009. (ENG.). 12p. 7.95 *(978-1-58117-915-6(4)*, Intervisual/Piggy Toes) Bendon, Inc.

Derejko-Viinikka, Jennifer. Marko & the Monster. 2008. 28p. pap. 12.49 *(978-1-4389-2898-2(X))* AuthorHouse.

Derek the Ghost Staff. Monsters on the March. Fischer, Scott M., illus. 2012. (Scary School Ser.: 2). (ENG.). 256p. (J). (gr. 3-7). 15.99 *(978-0-06-196095-6(0))* HarperCollins Pubs.

Deutsch, Stacia. Disney Fairies - Legend of the Neverbeast: The Chapter Book. 2015. (ENG.). 96p. (J). (gr. 3-7). pap. 4.99 *(978-0-316-28353-3(3))* Little, Brown Bks. for Young Readers.

Dhami, Narinder. Monster under the Stairs. Spoor, Mike, illus. 2005. (ENG.). 24p. (J). lib. bdg. 23.65 *(978-1-59646-718-7(5))* Dingles & Co.

Di Stiso, Robin Rountree. Cyber Monsters. 2008. 16p. pap. 19.00 *(978-1-4389-1354-4(0))* AuthorHouse.

DiCicco, Sue, illus. Totally Monster: Best Friends. 2013. (Totally Monsters Ser.). (ENG.). 14p. (J). 12.95 *(978-1-60710-643-2(4)*, Silver Dolphin Bks.) Readerlink Distribution Services, LLC.

—Totally Monster: Feelings. 2013. (Totally Monsters Ser.). (ENG.). 14p. (J). (gr. -1). 12.95 *(978-1-60710-644-9(2)*, Silver Dolphin Bks.) Readerlink Distribution Services, LLC.

Dickerson, Sharon. Jessica & the Tangle Monster. 2003. (J). pap. 9.00 *(978-0-8059-5991-8(2))* Dorrance Publishing Co., Inc.

Dickinson, Rebecca. Over in the Hollow. Britt, Stephanie, illus. 2009. (ENG.). 36p. (J). (gr. -1-2). 15.99 *(978-0-8118-5035-3(8))* Chronicle Bks. LLC.

Dillon, Elena. Breathe. 2013. 190p. pap. 9.99 *(978-0-9886353-2-6(1))* Dillon, Elena.

Dilloway, Margaret. Momotaro Xander & the Dream Thief. Yoon, Choong, illus. 2017. (Momotaro Ser.). (ENG.). 336p. (J). (gr. 3-7). 16.99 *(978-1-4847-2488-0(7))* Hyperion Bks. for Children.

—Momotaro Xander & the Lost Island of Monsters. Yoon, Choong, illus. 2017. (Momotaro Ser.). (ENG.). 336p. (J). (gr. 3-7). pap. 6.99 *(978-1-4847-4681-3(3))* Hyperion Bks. for Children.

Dimpel, Matt. The War of the Serpent Swords. 2011. 230p. pap. 24.95 *(978-1-4626-3169-8(X))* PublishAmerica, Inc.

Dipucchio, Kelly. Monster Makeovers. Pham, LeUyen, illus. 2006. (J). *(978-0-7868-5181-2(3))* Hyperion Bks. for Children.

Disney & Fox, Jennifer. Meet Nyx the Scout Fairy. 2015. (Passport to Reading Level 1 Ser.). (ENG., Illus.). 32p. (J). (gr. -1-1). pap. 3.99 *(978-0-316-28352-6(5))* Little, Brown Bks. for Young Readers.

Disney Book Group & Scollon, Bill. World of Reading: Henry Hugglemonster the Huggleball Game: Level Pre-1. Disney Storybook Art Team, illus. 2015. (World of Reading Ser.). (ENG.). 32p. (J). (gr. -1-k). pap. 3.99 *(978-1-4847-0253-6(0))* Disney Pr.

Disney Book Group Staff & Higginson, Sheila Sweeny. Henry Hugglemonster Daddo in Charge. Disney Storybook Art Team, illus. 2015. (ENG.). 12p. (J). (gr. -1-k). bds. 7.99 *(978-1-4847-0642-8(0))* Disney Pr.

—Henry Hugglemonster Pet Party. Disney Storybook Artists Staff & Disney Storybook Art Team, illus. 2014. (ENG.). 24p. (J). (gr. -1-k). pap. 4.99 *(978-1-4847-0263-5(8))* Disney Pr.

—Henry Hugglemonster Welcome to Roarsville. Disney Storybook Artists Staff, illus. 2014. (ENG.). 24p. (J). (gr. -1-k). pap. 4.99 *(978-1-4847-0264-2(6))* Disney Pr.

Disney Editors. Scaring Lessons. 2013. (Step into Reading Level 2 Ser.). lib. bdg. 13.55 *(978-0-606-31923-2(9)*, Turtleback) Turtleback Bks.

Disney Pixar Staff. Big Monsters on Campus. 2013. (Picture Viewer Ser.: 1). (ENG.). 32p. (J). (gr. k-2). 15.99 *(978-0-7944-2743-6(X))* Reader's Digest Assn., Inc., The.

Disney Storybook Art Team, illus. Legend of the Neverbeast. 2015. (Read-Along Storybook & CD Ser.). (ENG.). 32p. (J). (gr. 1-3). pap. 6.99 *(978-1-4847-1075-3(4))* Disney Pr.

—Moana Read-Along Storybook & CD. 2016. (Read-Along Storybook & CD Ser.). (ENG.). 32p. (J). (gr. 1-3). pap. 6.99 *(978-1-4847-4361-4(X))* Disney Pr.

—Monsters, Inc. 2012. (Read-Along Storybook & CD Ser.). (ENG.). 32p. (J). (gr. -1 — 1). pap. 6.99 *(978-1-4231-4259-1(4))* Disney Pr.

Dixon, Amy. Maurice the Unbeastly. Mountford, Karl James, illus. 2017. (ENG.). 32p. (J). (gr. -1). 16.95 ***(978-1-4549-1953-7(1))*** Sterling Publishing Co., Inc.

Dixon, Andy. Star Quest. Brooks, Felicity, ed. Harris, Nick, illus. 2006. (Usborne Fantasy Puzzle Bks.). 32p. (YA). (gr. 7). lib. bdg. 15.99 *(978-1-58086-906-5(8)*, Usborne) EDC Publishing.

d'Lacey, Chris. Alexander's Army. 2015. (UFiles Ser.: 2). (ENG.). 304p. (J). (gr. 3-7). 16.99 *(978-0-545-60880-0(5)*, Scholastic Pr.) Scholastic, Inc.

Doan, Janet Mailan. A Monster Stole My Chickens! 2012. 28p. pap. 16.09 *(978-1-4669-6468-6(5))* Trafford Publishing.

Docherty, Thomas. Big Scary Monster. Docherty, Thomas, illus. 2010. (ENG., Illus.). 40p. (J). (gr. -1-2). 15.99 *(978-0-7636-4787-2(X)*, Templar) Candlewick Pr.

Dodd, Lynley. Zachary Quack Minimonster. Dodd, Lynley, illus. 2006. (Gold Star First Readers Ser.). (Illus.). 32p. (gr. -1-3). lib. bdg. 23.00 *(978-0-8368-6187-7(6)*, Gareth Stevens Learning Library) Stevens, Gareth Publishing LLLP.

Doherty, Gillian. 1001 MonsterThings to Spot. 2008. (1001 Things to Spot Ser.). 32p. (J). 9.99 *(978-0-7945-2091-5(X)*, Usborne) EDC Publishing.

Donaldson, Connie & Polinko, Les. The Ganorch under the Porch. Polinko, Les, illus. 2013. (Illus.). 36p. pap. 9.95 *(978-0-9836682-3-7(X))* Hearthstone Rose.

Donaldson, Julia. The Gruffalo. Harris, Ben, tr. from ENG. Scheffler, Axel, illus. 2012. (LAT, SPA & ENG.). 32p. (J). (gr. -1-2). 19.99 *(978-0-230-75932-9(7))* Pan Macmillan GBR. Dist: Independent Pubs. Group.

—The Gruffalo. Scheffler, Axel, illus. (ENG.). (J). (gr. -1-2). 2006. 32p. pap. 7.99 *(978-0-14-240387-7(3)*, Puffin Books) 2005. 26p. bds. 8.99 *(978-0-8037-3047-2(0)*, Dial Bks) Penguin Young Readers Group.

—The Gruffalo. Scheffler, Axel, illus. 2005. (ENG.). 32p. (J). (gr. -1-2). 17.99 *(978-0-8037-3109-7(4)*, Dial Bks) Penguin Young Readers Group.

—The Gruffalo. 2006. lib. bdg. 18.40 *(978-0-606-23141-1(2)*, Turtleback) Turtleback Bks.

Donato, Cindy. Monsters! Monsters! 2004. 33p. pap. 24.95 *(978-1-4137-3221-4(6))* PublishAmerica, Inc.

Donnanna. Jamie & the Cheesy Foot Monster. 2010. (Illus.). 44p. pap. 16.99 *(978-1-4490-9785-1(5))* AuthorHouse.

Dooley, Larry. A Peanut Butter & Monster Sandwich. Grzelak, Kyle, illus. 2013. 24p. pap. 12.95 *(978-1-61493-206-2(9))* Peppertree Pr., The.

Dorling Kindersley Publishing Staff. LEGO Nexo Knights: Stop the Monsters! 2017. (DK Reader Level 1 Ser.). lib. bdg. 13.55 ***(978-0-606-39896-1(1))*** Turtleback Bks.

Dormer, Frank W. Socksquatch. Dormer, Frank W., illus. 2010. (ENG., Illus.). 32p. (J). (gr. -1-3). 14.99 *(978-0-8050-8952-3(7)*, 9780805089523, Holt, Henry & Co. Bks. For Young Readers) Holt, Henry & Co.

Dowding, Philippa. The Gargoyle in My Yard. 2009. (Lost Gargoyle Ser.: 1). (ENG.). 128p. (J). (gr. 4-7). pap. 9.99 *(978-1-894917-82-7(0)*, Napoleon & Co.) Dundurn CAN. Dist: Ingram Publisher Services.

—Myles & the Monster Outside. 2015. (Weird Stories Gone Wrong Ser.: 2). (ENG., Illus.). 128p. (J). pap. 9.99 *(978-1-4597-2943-8(9))* Dundurn CAN. Dist: Ingram Publisher Services.

Dower, Laura. The Beast with 1000 Eyes. Schlafman, Dave, illus. 2009. (Monster Squad Ser.: 3). (ENG.). 144p. (J). (gr. 3-7). pap. 5.99 *(978-0-448-44914-2(5)*, Grosset & Dunlap) Penguin Young Readers Group.

—Return of Mega Mantis. Schlafman, Dave, illus. 2009. (Monster Squad Ser.: 2). (ENG.). 144p. (J). (gr. 2-4). pap. 5.99 *(978-0-448-44913-5(7)*, Grosset & Dunlap) Penguin Young Readers Group.

—They Came from Planet Q. Schlafman, Dave, illus. 2010. (Monster Squad Ser.: 4). (ENG.). 144p. (J). (gr. 2-4). pap. 5.99 *(978-0-448-44915-9(3)*, Grosset & Dunlap) Penguin Young Readers Group.

Doyle, Bill. The Werewolf at Home Plate. Lee, Jared D., illus. 2012. (Scream Team Ser.: 1). (ENG.). 96p. (J). (gr. 2-5). pap. 4.99 *(978-0-545-34198-1(1)*, Scholastic Paperbacks) Scholastic, Inc.

Dozier, Kamilah. The Monster Named Fear. 2012. 68p. pap. 26.00 *(978-1-4772-9148-1(2))* AuthorHouse.

Dracula. (J). 9.95 *(978-1-56156-373-9(0))* Kidsbooks, LLC.

Drago, Ty. Queen of the Dead. Williams, Eric L., illus. 2012. (ENG.). 432p. (J). (gr. 5-8). pap. 7.99 *(978-1-4022-7557-9(9)*, Sourcebooks Jabberwocky) Sourcebooks, Inc.

Drake, Ernest. Monsterology: The Complete Book of Monstrous Creatures. Steer, Dugald A., ed. Carrel, Douglas, illus. 2008. (Ologies Ser.). (ENG.). 32p. (J). (gr. 3-7). 24.99 *(978-0-7636-3940-2(0))* Candlewick Pr.

Drescher, Henrik. Pat the Beastie: A Pull-and-Poke Book. Drescher, Henrik, illus. 2009. (ENG., Illus.). 11p. (J). (gr. -1-3). bds. 11.95 *(978-0-7611-5610-9(0)*, 15610) Workman Publishing Co., Inc.

—Simon's Book. 2006. (ENG., Illus.). 32p. (J). (gr. -1-1). *(978-1-59692-135-1(8))* MacAdam/Cage Publishing, Inc.

Du Lac, Leo J. Dogfish on the Moon: Santa Claus & the Flying Carpet 2. Baker, David, illus. 2012. 26p. 24.95 *(978-1-4560-1036-2(0))* America Star Bks.

Dube, Tory. A Trixi, a Shmoop & a Monster. Vasilevsky, Marina, illus. 2013. 32p. 19.99 *(978-0-9886193-1-9(8))* Dube, Tory.

Dube, Tory Lee. A Trixi, a Shmoop & a Monster. 2013. 32p. pap. 9.99 *(978-0-9886193-0-2(X))* Dube, Tory.

Dubos, Delphine. The Planet of Tear-Eaters. Smith, Anne & Smith, Owen, trs. from FRE. Élyum Studio, illus. 2014. (Little Prince Ser.: 13). (ENG.). 48p. (J). (gr. 4-8). lib. bdg. 26.60 *(978-0-7613-8763-3(3)*, Graphic Universe™) Lerner Publishing Group.

Duddle, Jonny. The Pirate Cruncher. Duddle, Jonny, illus. 2010. (ENG., Illus.). 38p. (J). (gr. -1-2). 15.99 *(978-0-7636-4876-3(0)*, Templar) Candlewick Pr.

Duerr, Doug. The Adventures of Jazz & Elliott: The Love Ness Monster. 2012. (ENG.). 37p. (J). pap. 14.95 *(978-1-4327-7746-3(7))* Outskirts Pr., Inc.

Durant, Alan. Billy Monster's Daymare. Collins, Ross, illus. 2008. 32p. (J). (gr. -1-2). pap. 6.95 *(978-1-58925-412-1(0))* Tiger Tales.

Durham, Paul. Fork-Tongue Charmers. Antonsson, Petur, illus. 2015. (Luck Uglies Ser.: 2). (ENG.). 416p. (J). (gr. 3-7). 16.99 *(978-0-06-227153-2(9))* HarperCollins Pubs.

—The Luck Uglies. Antonsson, Petur, illus. 2014. (Luck Uglies Ser.: 1). (ENG.). 400p. (J). (gr. 3-7). 16.99 *(978-0-06-227150-1(4))* HarperCollins Pubs.

Dussling, Jennifer. In a Dark, Dark House. Jones, Davy, illus. Date not set. (All Aboard Reading Ser.). 32p. (J). (gr. -1-k). pap. *(978-0-448-40974-0(7)*, Grosset & Dunlap) Penguin Publishing Group.

Dye, Troy & Kelesides, Tom. Goblin Chronicles 01A. 2008. (YA). 3.50 *(978-0-9801314-0-6(5))* Ape Entertainment.

—Goblin Chronicles #1B. 2008. (YA). 3.50 *(978-0-9801314-1-3(3))* Ape Entertainment.

—Goblin Chronicles #2A. 2008. (Illus.). 32p. (J). 3.50 *(978-0-9801314-2-0(1))* Ape Entertainment.

—Goblin Chronicles #2B. 2008. (Illus.). 32p. (J). 3.50 *(978-0-9801314-3-7(X))* Ape Entertainment.

Eaton, Deborah. Canciones de Monstruos. Translations.com Staff, tr. from ENG. Handelman, Dorothy, photos by. 2007. (Lecturas para niños de verdad - Nivel 2 (Real Kids Readers - Level 2) Ser.).Tr. of Monster Songs. (SPA., Illus.). 32p. (gr. k-3). per. 5.95 *(978-0-8225-7803-1(4))* Lerner Publishing Group.

Ecton, Emily. Night of the Living Lawn Ornaments. 2009. (ENG.). 240p. (J). (gr. 3-7). pap. 5.99 *(978-1-4169-6451-3(7)*, Aladdin) Simon & Schuster Children's Publishing.

Edwards, Elizabeth Marshall. How Parker James Got the Monsters Out from under His Bed. 2012. 20p. pap. 24.95 *(978-1-4626-6796-3(1))* America Star Bks.

Edwards, Jason. Will Allen & the Great Monster Detective: Chronicles of the Monster Detective Agency Volume 1. Friedman, Jeffrey, illus. l.t. ed. 2007. (Chronicles of the Monster Detective Agency Ser.: 1). (ENG.). 96p. (J). (gr. 2-6). per. 5.95 *(978-0-9789512-0-7(4))* Rogue Bear Pr.

Eifrig, Kate. Scary Monster. Graves, Dennis, illus. 2003. (ENG.). 8p. (gr. k-1). pap. 7.95 *(978-1-879835-29-0(0)*, Kaeden Bks.) Kaeden Corp.

Emberley, Ed. Bye-Bye, Big Bad Bullybug! Emberley, Ed, illus. 2007. (ENG., Illus.). 32p. (J). (gr. -1-3). 14.99 *(978-0-316-01762-6(0))* Little, Brown Bks. for Young Readers.

—Nighty Night, Little Green Monster. 2013. (ENG.). 32p. (J). (gr. -1-1). 9.99 (978-0-316-21041-6(2)) Little, Brown Bks. for Young Readers.

Emberley, Rebecca & Emberley, Ed. Ten Little Beasties. Emberley, Rebecca & Emberley, Ed, illus. 2011. (ENG., Illus.). 32p. (J). (gr. -1-1). 12.99 (978-1-59643-627-5(1), 9781596436275) Roaring Brook Pr.

Emerson, Carl. Monster Boy & the Classroom Pet, 1 vol. Levin, Lon, illus. 2008. (Monster Boy Ser.). (ENG.). 32p. (gr. -1-4). 28.50 (978-1-60270-234-9(9), Looking Glass Library) ABDO Publishing Co.

—Monster Boy & the Halloween Parade, 1 vol. Levin, Lon, illus. 2010. (Monster Boy Set 2 Ser.). (ENG.). 32p. (J). (gr. k-3). 28.50 (978-1-60270-777-1(4)) ABDO Publishing Co.

—Monster Boy & the Scary Scouts, 1 vol. Levin, Lon, illus. 2010. (Monster Boy Set 2 Ser.). (ENG.). 32p. (J). (gr. k-3). 28.50 (978-1-60270-778-8(2)) ABDO Publishing Co.

—Monster Boy at the Library, 1 vol. Levin, Lon, illus. 2008. (Monster Boy Ser.). (ENG.). 32p. (gr. -1-4). 28.50 (978-1-60270-235-6(7), Looking Glass Library) ABDO Publishing Co.

—Monster Boy's Art Project, 1 vol. Levin, Lon, illus. 2010. (Monster Boy Set 2 Ser.). (ENG.). 32p. (J). (gr. k-3). 28.50 (978-1-60270-780-1(4)) ABDO Publishing Co.

—Monster Boy's Field Trip, 1 vol. Levin, Lon, illus. 2008. (Monster Boy Ser.). (ENG.). 32p. (gr. -1-4). 28.50 (978-1-60270-236-3(5), Looking Glass Library) ABDO Publishing Co.

—Monster Boy's First Day of School, 1 vol. Levin, Lon, illus. 2008. (Monster Boy Ser.). (ENG.). 32p. (gr. -1-4). 28.50 (978-1-60270-237-0(3), Looking Glass Library) ABDO Publishing Co.

—Monster Boy's Gym Class, 1 vol. Levin, Lon, illus. 2010. (Monster Boy Set 2 Ser.). (ENG.). 32p. (J). (gr. k-3). 28.50 (978-1-60270-781-8(2)) ABDO Publishing Co.

—Monster Boy's School Lunch, 1 vol. Levin, Lon, illus. 2008. (Monster Boy Ser.). (ENG.). 32p. (gr. -1-4). 28.50 (978-1-60270-238-7(1), Looking Glass Library) ABDO Publishing Co.

—Monster Boy's Soccer Game, 1 vol. Levin, Lon, illus. 2008. (Monster Boy Ser.). (ENG.). 32p. (gr. -1-4). 28.50 (978-1-60270-239-4(X), Looking Glass Library) ABDO Publishing Co.

—Monster Boy's Valentine, 1 vol. Levin, Lon, illus. 2010. (Monster Boy Set 2 Ser.). (ENG.). 32p. (J). (gr. k-3). 28.50 (978-1-60270-782-5(0)) ABDO Publishing Co.

Emmett, Jonathan. Let's Read! Monsters: An Owner's Guide. Oliver, Mark, illus. 2014. (Let's Read! Ser.). (ENG.). 32p. (J). (gr. k-2). pap. 7.99 (978-1-4472-3697-9(1)) Pan Macmillan GBR. Dist: Independent Pubs. Group.

Enderle, Dotti & McWilliam, Howard. Ghost Detectors Book 12: Monsters!, 1 vol. 2012. (Ghost Detectors Ser.). (ENG., Illus.). 80p. (J). (gr. 2-5). 27.07 (978-1-61641-628-7(9)) Magic Wagon.

Ering, Timothy Basil. The Story of Frog Belly Rat Bone. Ering, Timothy Basil, illus. 2013. (ENG., Illus.). 48p. (J). (gr. -1-3). 17.99 (978-0-7636-6661-3(0)) Candlewick Pr.

Escondete y Grita, Vol. II. (Fantasmas de Fear Street Coleccion: No. 1). (SPA.). (J). (gr. 4-7). pap. 7.95 (978-950-04-1999-4(8), EM4474) Emecé Editores S.A. ARG. Dist: Planeta Publishing Corp., Lectorum Pubns., Inc.

Eugenio, Johnny. Lil' Jordan's 9 Holes of Fear. 2009. (Illus.). 32p. (J). (gr. -1). 16.95 (978-1-60747-703-7(3)) Phoenix Bks., Inc.

—Lil Jordan's 9 Holes of Fear. 2009. 48p. (J). 11.95 (978-1-60747-706-8(8)) Phoenix Bks., Inc.

Evans, Angela. A Monster Can Be Friendly. 2012. 28p. pap. 32.70 (978-1-4797-3645-4(7)) Xlibris Corp.

Evans, Dustin, illus. A Medieval Mess, 1 vol. 2013. (Mystical Pencil Ser.). (ENG.). 32p. (J). (gr. 3-6). 28.50 (978-1-61641-928-8(8)) Magic Wagon.

Fahnestock, Todd. The Wishing World. 2016. (ENG.). 224p. (J). 17.99 (978-0-7653-8588-8(0), 9780765385888, Starscape) Doherty, Tom Assocs., LLC.

Fantastik, B. Save the Sleepless Slumbernots! Valentine, M. K., illus. 2013. 32p. (978-1-4602-2777-0(8)) FriesenPress.

Farrey, Brian. The Vengekeep Prophecies. Helquist, Brett, illus. 2013. (Vengekeep Prophecies Ser.: 1). (ENG.). 416p. (J). (gr. 3-7). pap. 7.99 (978-0-06-204929-2(1)) HarperCollins Pubs.

Feaster, Raven Joye Raye. Merrileggs of Macon County. 2011. 72p. (gr. -1). pap. 10.75 (978-1-4567-6971-0(5)) AuthorHouse.

Feldman, Thea & Upton, Rachael. Scare-ific Secrets. 2015. (ENG., Illus.). 96p. (J). (gr. 1-3). 9.99 (978-0-7944-3481-6(9), Reader's Digest Children's Bks.) Studio Fun International.

Fields, Jan. Chase the Chupacabra, 1 vol. Brundage, Scott, illus. 2014. (Monster Hunters Ser.). (ENG.). 80p. (J). (gr. 8-12). 27.07 (978-1-62402-044-5(5)) Magic Wagon.

—Hunt the Ozark Howler, 1 vol. Brundage, Scott, illus. 2016. (ENG.). 80p. (J). lib. bdg. (978-1-62402-152-7(2)) Magic Wagon.

—Meet the Mothman, 1 vol. Brundage, Scott, illus. 2016. (ENG.). 80p. (J). lib. bdg. (978-1-62402-153-4(0)) Magic Wagon.

—Search for Bigfoot, 1 vol. Brundage, Scott, illus. 2014. (Monster Hunters Ser.). (ENG.). 80p. (J). (gr. 8-12). 27.07 (978-1-62402-046-9(1)) Magic Wagon.

—Spot the Swamp Lizard Man, 1 vol. Brundage, Scott, illus. 2016. (ENG.). 80p. (J). lib. bdg. (978-1-62402-154-1(9)) Magic Wagon.

—Tame Tahoe Tessie, 1 vol. Brundage, Scott, illus. 2014. (Monster Hunters Ser.). (ENG.). 80p. (J). (gr. 8-12). 27.07 (978-1-62402-047-6(X)) Magic Wagon.

—Track the Turtle Lake Monster, 1 vol. Brundage, Scott, illus. 2016. (ENG.). 80p. (J). lib. bdg. (978-1-62402-155-8(7)) Magic Wagon.

La Fiesta Monstruosa, 6 Pks. (Chiquilibros Ser.). (SPA.). (gr. k-1). 23.00 (978-0-7635-8600-3(5)) Rigby Education.

Finn, Perdita. Monster High. 2015. (ENG.). 576p. (J). (gr. 3-7). 24.00 (978-0-316-30125-1(6)) Little, Brown Bks. for Young Readers.

—Monster High - Haunted. 2015. (ENG., Illus.). 144p. (J). (gr. 3-7). pap. 5.99 (978-0-316-37739-3(2)) Little, Brown Bks. for Young Readers.

—Monster High: Electrified: the Deluxe Junior Novel. 2017. (ENG.). 144p. (J). (gr. 3-7). 9.99 **(978-0-316-54826-7(X))** Little, Brown Bks. for Young Readers.

—Monster High: Electrified: the Junior Novel. 2017. (ENG.). 144p. (J). (gr. 3-7). pap. 6.99 **(978-0-316-54836-6(7))** Little, Brown Bks. for Young Readers.

Fisher, Sam. The Midnight Door. 2015. (Scare Scape Ser.: 2). (ENG.). 352p. (J). (gr. 3-7). 12.99 (978-0-545-52163-5(7), Scholastic Pr.) Scholastic, Inc.

Fletcher, Tom. There's a Monster in Your Book, 4 vols. 2017. (ENG.). (J). 71.96 **(978-0-525-50216-6(5)**, Random Hse. Bks. for Young Readers) Random Hse. Children's Bks.

—There's a Monster in Your Book. Abbott, Greg, illus. 2017. (ENG.). 32p. (J). (gr. -1-2). 17.99 **(978-1-5247-6456-2(6)**, Random Hse. Bks. for Young Readers) Random Hse. Children's Bks.

Fliess, Sue. Goblin Hood. Thibodeau, Piper, illus. 2016. (ENG.). 32p. (J). (gr. -1-k). pap. 3.99 (978-0-448-48933-9(3), Grosset & Dunlap) Penguin Young Readers Group.

Flitcroft, Jean. The Loch Ness Monster. 2014. (Cryptid Files Ser.: No. 1). 192p. (J). (gr. 4-8). lib. bdg. 27.93 (978-1-4677-2602-3(8), Darby Creek) Lerner Publishing Group.

—The Pacific Giants. 2014. (Cryptid Files Ser.: No. 3). 240p. (gr. 4-8). (J). lib. bdg. 27.93 (978-1-4677-3266-6(4)); (ENG.). (YA). pap. 7.95 (978-1-4677-3485-1(3)) Lerner Publishing Group. (Darby Creek).

Fodi, Lee Edward. Kendra Kandlestar & the Crack in Kazah. 2011. (Illus.). 294p. (J). pap. 8.95 (978-1-61254-019-1(8)) Brown Books Publishing Group.

—Kendra Kandlestar & the Crack in Kazah. Fodi, Lee Edward, illus. 2011. (ENG., Illus.). 282p. (J). (gr. 4-7). 16.95 (978-1-61254-018-4(X)) Brown Books Publishing Group.

Fontes, Justine & Fontes, Ron. Casebook: The Loch Ness Monster. 2009. (Top Secret Graphica Mysteries Ser.). (Illus.). 48p. (YA). (gr. 2-6). 29.25 (978-1-60754-602-3(7)); pap. 11.75 (978-1-60754-600-9(0)) Windmill Bks.

Fourniea, Stephanie. Are You a Monster When You Eat. 2011. 24p. pap. 12.29 (978-1-4634-2958-4(4)) AuthorHouse.

Fox-Smith, Angela. The Clock-Mess Monster. 2011. 32p. pap. 24.95 (978-1-4560-5723-7(5)) America Star Bks.

Fred, Anthony. Fred & Anthony Meet the Heinie Goblins from the Black Lagoon. Primavera, Elise, illus. rev. ed. 2008. 128p. 14.99 (978-0-7868-3681-9(4)) Hyperion Bks. for Children.

Fredrickson, Lane. Monster Trouble. Robertson, Michael, illus. 2015. (ENG.). 32p. (J). (gr. -1-2). 14.95 (978-1-4549-1345-0(2)) Sterling Publishing Co., Inc.

Freedman, Claire. Dragon Jelly. Hendra, Sue, illus. 2015. (ENG.). 32p. (J). (gr. k-3). 14.99 (978-1-61963-682-8(4), 9781619636828, Bloomsbury USA Childrens) Bloomsbury Publishing USA.

—The Monster of the Woods! Julian, Russell, illus. 2013. (ENG.). 32p. (J). pap. (978-0-545-51571-9(8), Cartwheel Bks.) Scholastic, Inc.

—The Monster of the Woods!/By Claire Freedman & Russell Julian. Julian, Russell, illus. 2013. (J). (978-0-545-56837-1(4), Cartwheel Bks.) Scholastic, Inc.

—Spider Sandwiches. Hendra, Sue, illus. 2014. (ENG.). 32p. (J). (gr. k-3). 14.99 (978-1-61963-364-3(7), 9781619633643, Bloomsbury USA Childrens) Bloomsbury Publishing USA.

Freese, Thomas & Riddell, Fran. Halloween Sleepwalker, 1 vol. 2013. (ENG., Illus.). 64p. (J). 16.99 (978-0-7643-4399-5(8), 9780764343995) Schiffer Publishing, Ltd.

Freidman, Mel. The Blue Moon Effect. Smith, Eric, illus. gif. ed. 2005. (Extreme Monsters Ser.). 96p. (J). (gr. 2-5). per. 3.99 (978-1-57791-178-4(4)) Brighter Minds Children's Publishing.

French, Vivian. The Snow Dragon. Fisher, Chris, illus. 2003. (ENG.). 32p. (J). pap. 11.99 (978-0-552-54595-2(3)) Transworld Publishers Ltd. GBR. Dist: Trafalgar Square Publishing.

Froman, Annabelle. Beezeur. 2013. 34p. pap. 9.95 (978-0-9842053-1-8(4)) Breathless Vintage Enterprises.

Fujikawa, Brian. The Adventures of Bibole, Ri: The CURSE of the WEREMOUSE. 2012. 52p. pap. 18.41 (978-1-4669-3547-1(2)) Trafford Publishing.

Funari-Willever, Lisa. Theres A Kid under My Bed (Cj) 2008. 40p. 12.95 (978-0-9760469-4-3(6)) Franklin Mason Pr.

Funke, Cornelia. Ruffleclaw. Latsch, Oliver, tr. from GER. 2015. (ENG., Illus.). 112p. (J). (gr. 2-5). 12.99 (978-0-385-37550-4(6), Random Hse. Bks. for Young Readers) Random Hse. Children's Bks.

Gaiman, NEil. The Dangerous Alphabet. Grimly, Gris, illus. (ENG.). 32p. (J). (gr. k). 2010. pap. 6.99 (978-0-06-078335-8(4)) 2008. 17.99 (978-0-06-078333-4(8)) HarperCollins Pubs.

Galindo, Claudia. It's Bedtime, Cucuy!/A la Cama, Cucuy. Pluecker, John, tr. from ENG. Coombs, Jonathan, illus. 2008. (SPA & ENG.). 32p. (J). (gr. -1-2). 16.95 (978-1-55885-491-8(6), Piñata Books) Arte Publico Pr.

Galindo, Claudia & Pluecker, John. Do You Know the Cucuy? Conoces Al Cucuy? Coombs, Jonathan, illus. 2008. (SPA & ENG.). 32p. (J). (gr. -1-2). 16.95 (978-1-55885-492-5(4), Piñata Books) Arte Publico Pr.

Gall, Chris. Substitute Creacher. 2011. (ENG., Illus.). 40p. (J). (gr. -1-3). 16.99 (978-0-316-08915-9(X)) Little, Brown Bks. for Young Readers.

Gamble, Adam & Jasper, Mark. Good Night Little Monsters. Kelly, Cooper, illus. 2017. (Good Night Our World Ser.). (ENG.). 20p. (J). (gr. -1 — 1). bds. 9.95 **(978-1-60219-489-2(0))** Good Night Bks.

Gamble, Paul. The Monster's Daughter. 2017. (Ministry of SUITs Ser.: 2). (ENG.). 384p. (J). 16.99 (978-1-250-07683-0(8), 9781250076830) Feiwel & Friends.

Garza, Xavier. Juan & the Chupacabras/Juan y el Chupacabras. Ward, April, illus. 2006. (ENG & SPA.). 32p. (J). (gr. -1-2). 16.95 (978-1-55885-454-3(1), Piñata Books) Arte Publico Pr.

Gates, Susan. The Pumpkin Monster Blue Band. Sua, Laura, illus. 2016. (Cambridge Reading Adventures Ser.). (ENG.). 16p. pap. 6.56 (978-1-316-60576-9(0)) Cambridge Univ. Pr.

Geoghegan, Adrienne. There's a Wardrobe in My Monster! Johnson, Adrian, illus. 2003. (Picture Bks.). 32p. (J). (gr. -1-3). 15.95 (978-1-57505-414-8(0), Carolrhoda Bks.) Lerner Publishing Group.

Gerrold, David, et al. Wickeder. Parker, Rick et al, illus. 2010. (Tales from the Crypt Graphic Novels Ser.). (ENG.). 64p. (J). (gr. 5-12). pap. 6.99 (978-1-59707-215-1(X), 9781597072151); 10.99 (978-1-59707-216-8(8), 9781597072168) Papercutz.

Gervais, Ricky. Flanimals Pop-Up. Steen, Rob, illus. 2010. (ENG.). 14p. (J). (gr. k-4). 19.99 (978-0-7636-4781-0(0)) Candlewick Pr.

Giangregorio, Kimberly A. The Smelly Shoe. O'Toole, Julianne, illus. 2012. 24p. pap. 24.95 (978-1-4626-9387-0(3)) America Star Bks.

Gibala-Broxholm, Scott. Maddie's Monster Dad, 0 vols. Gibala-Broxholm, Scott, illus. 2011. (ENG., Illus.). 40p. (J). (gr. -1-3). 16.99 (978-0-7614-5846-3(8), 9780761458463, Amazon Children's Publishing) Amazon Publishing.

Gibson, James E. & Gibson, Sylvia Scott. Treetoe the Space Monster, 1 vol. Gibson, Gregory V., illus. 2010. 28p. 24.95 (978-1-4489-4896-3(7)) PublishAmerica, Inc.

Gilchrist, J. Into the Land of Nede. 2010. 108p. (gr. 4-6). 20.95 (978-1-4502-5433-5(0)); pap. 10.95 (978-1-4502-5432-8(2)) iUniverse, Inc.

Gill, Jacqueline Paske. The Monster in the Basement. Gill, Jacqueline Paske, illus. 2011. (Illus.). 32p. pap. 12.95 (978-1-61493-003-7(1)) Peppertree Pr., The.

Gilligan, Shannon. The Lake Monster Mystery. Newton, Keith, illus. 2009. (Dragonlarks Ser.). 80p. (J). (gr. k-3). pap. 7.99 (978-1-933390-60-4(3)) Chooseco LLC.

Gilman, Charles. Teacher's Pest. 2013. (Tales from Lovecraft Middle School Ser.: 3). (ENG., Illus.). 176p. (YA). (gr. 4-7). 13.99 (978-1-59474-614-7(1)) Quirk Bks.

Gold, Gina. Monster High: Voltageous Adventure! 2017. (ENG., Illus.). 32p. (J). (gr. -1-3). pap. 3.99 **(978-0-316-54793-2(X))** Little, Brown Bks. for Young Readers.

Golden Books & Dwight, Revena. The Together Book. Bradfield, Roger, illus. 2017. (Little Golden Book Ser.). (ENG.). 24p. (J). (-k). 4.99 **(978-1-5247-1978-4(1)**, Golden Bks.) Random Hse. Children's Bks.

Golden Books Staff. Danger from the Deep. 2009. (Deluxe Coloring Book Ser.). (ENG., Illus.). 96p. (J). (gr. -1-2). pap. 3.99 (978-0-375-85328-9(6), Golden Bks.) Random Hse. Children's Bks.

Goldthorpe, Jake. Mommy! Daddy! Help! There's a Monster in My Room! 2008. 28p. pap. 15.99 (978-1-4363-7114-8(7)) Xlibris Corp.

Gollub, Matthew. Ten Oni Drummers. Stone, Kazuko G., illus. 2013. (JPN & ENG.). 32p. (J). (gr. -1-3). 16.95 (978-1-58430-011-3(6)) Lee & Low Bks., Inc.

—Ten Oni Drummers. Stone, Kazuko G., illus. 2017. (J). (978-1-889910-51-2(1)) Tortuga Pr.

Gómez Cerdá, Alfredo. El Monstruo y la Bibliotecaria. 4th ed. (SPA., Illus.). 62p. (J). (gr. 3-5). (978-84-279-3456-6(4), NG1580) Noguer y Caralt Editores, S. A. ESP. Dist: Lectorum Pubns., Inc.

Gonzalez, L. M. R. Gifts Lucy. The Terrible Monster. 2008. 52p. pap. 24.93 (978-1-4357-5500-0(6)) Lulu Pr., Inc.

Goodhart, Pippa. Little Monster & the Spooky Party. Sharratt, Nick, illus. 2016. (ENG.). 16p. (J). (gr. -1-k). 12.99 **(978-1-4052-7742-6(4))** Egmont Bks., Ltd. GBR. Dist: Independent Pubs. Group.

Goodwin, Vincent. Call of Cthulhu, 1 vol. 2014. (Graphic Horror Set 3 Ser.). (ENG., Illus.). 32p. (J). (gr. 5-8). lib. bdg. 28.50 (978-1-62402-014-8(3), Graphic Planet) Magic Wagon.

—Wendigo, 1 vol. 2014. (Graphic Horror Set 3 Ser.). (ENG.). 32p. (J). (gr. 5-8). lib. bdg. 28.50 (978-1-62402-018-6(6), Graphic Planet) Magic Wagon.

Gorey, Edward. The Wuggly Ump. Gorey, Edward, illus. 2007. (Illus.). 32p. 12.95 (978-0-7649-4192-4(5), A142) Pomegranate Communications, Inc.

Gos & Peyo. The Astrosmurf. 2011. (Smurfs Graphic Novels Ser.). (ENG., Illus.). 56p. (J). (gr. 2-5). 10.99 (978-1-59707-251-9(6), 9781597072519) Papercutz.

Gos, Charles & Peyo. The Astrosmurf. 2011. (Smurfs Graphic Novels Ser.). (ENG., Illus.). 56p. (J). (gr. 2-5). pap. 5.99 (978-1-59707-250-2(8), 9781597072502) Papercutz.

Graham, Alastair. Full Moon Soup. 2007. (Illus.). 32p. (J). (gr. k-3). 12.95 (978-1-905417-54-4(3)) Boxer Bks., Ltd. GBR. Dist: Sterling Publishing Co., Inc.

Graham, Oakley. Monster Mayhem. Wilson, Jessica, illus. 2016. (Doodle Wars Ser.). (ENG.). 100p. (J). (gr. k-3). pap. 12.99 (978-1-84956-731-2(X)) Top That! Publishing PLC GBR. Dist: Independent Pubs. Group.

Graham, Richard. Jack y el Monstruo. Varley, Susan, illus. (Cotton Cloud Ser.). (SPA.). 32p. (J). (gr. 1-3). (978-84-7722-680-2(6)) Timun Mas, Editorial S.A. ESP. Dist: Lectorum Pubns., Inc.

Grandma. There Is a Vampire in Our Cellar: Adventures of Butterfly Nectar Meadows. 2008. 20p. pap. 24.95 (978-1-60813-128-0(9)) America Star Bks.

Grant, Michael. Monster. 2017. (Gone Ser.: 7). 432p. (YA). (gr. 9). 18.99 **(978-0-06-246784-3(0)**, Tegen, Katherine Bks) HarperCollins Pubs.

Gratz, Alan. The Dragon Lantern: A League of Seven Novel. 2015. (League of Seven Ser.: 2). (ENG., Illus.). 336p. (J). (gr. 5-9). 17.99 (978-0-7653-3823-5(8), 9780765338235, Starscape) Doherty, Tom Assocs., LLC.

—The League of Seven. Helquist, Brett, illus. 2015. (League of Seven Ser.: 1). (ENG.). 352p. (J). (gr. 5-9). pap. 9.99 (978-0-7653-3825-9(4), 9780765338259, Starscape) Doherty, Tom Assocs., LLC.

Grau, Sheila. Dr. Critchlore's School for Minions. Sutphin, Joe, illus. (Dr. Critchlore's School for Minions Ser.). (ENG.). (J). (gr. 3-7). 2016. 304p. pap. 7.95 (978-1-4197-2029-1(5)) 2015. 288p. 14.95 (978-1-4197-1370-5(1)) Abrams, Inc. (Amulet Bks.).

—Dr. Critchlore's School for Minions: Polar Distress. Sutphin, Joe, illus. 2017. (Dr. Critchlore's School for Minions Ser.). (ENG.). 288p. (J). (gr. 3-7). 14.95 (978-1-4197-2294-3(8), Amulet Bks.) Abrams, Inc.

Grau, Sheila & Sutphin, Joe. Dr. Critchlore's School for Minions: Gorilla Tactics. 2016. (Dr. Critchlore's School for Minions Ser.). (ENG., Illus.). 304p. (J). (gr. 3-7). 14.95 (978-1-4197-1371-2(X), Amulet Bks.) Abrams, Inc.

Gravel, Elise. I Want a Monster! Gravel, Elise, illus. 2016. (Illus.). 40p. (J). (gr. -1-3). 17.99 (978-0-06-241533-2(6), Tegen, Katherine Bks) HarperCollins Pubs.

Graves, Judith. Second Skin. 2011. 280p. (J). pap. 16.99 (978-1-61603-006-3(2)) Leap Bks.

—Under My Skin. Cox, Val, illus. 2010. 328p. (YA). (gr. 8-18). pap. 16.99 (978-1-61603-000-1(3)) Leap Bks.

Graves, Keith. The Monsterator. 2014. (ENG., Illus.). 40p. (J). (gr. 2-5). 17.99 (978-1-59643-855-2(X), 9781596438552) Roaring Brook Pr.

Gray, Kes. Nelly, the Monster Sitter. Hanson, Stephen, illus. 2009. (ENG.). 272p. (J). (gr. 3-7). 8.99 (978-1-59514-259-7(2), Razorbill) Penguin Young Readers Group.

Green, Andi. The Lonely Little Monster. 2007. (WorryWoo Monsters Ser.). (Illus.). 68p. (J). 14.99 (978-0-9792860-0-1(X)) Monsters in My Head, LLC, The.

—The Monster in the Bubble. 2009. (WorryWoo Monsters Ser.). 68p. (J). 14.99 (978-0-9792860-2-5(6)) Monsters in My Head, LLC, The.

—The Monster Who Couldn't Decide. 2010. (WorryWoo Monsters Ser.). 98p. (J). 14.99 (978-0-9792860-3-2(4)) Monsters in My Head, LLC, The.

Green, K. C. Regular Show Vol. 1. 2014. lib. bdg. 26.95 (978-0-606-35467-7(0)) Turtleback Bks.

Green, Margaret. Monster High: Fierce Friends. 2017. (Passport to Reading Level 2 Ser.). (ENG., Illus.). 32p. (J). (gr. -1-3). pap. 3.99 **(978-0-316-54838-0(3))** Little, Brown Bks. for Young Readers.

Greenwell, Jessica. Noisy Monsters. Wildish, Lee, illus. 2010. (Busy Sounds Board Bks). 10p. (J). bds. 18.99 (978-0-7945-2769-3(8), Usborne) EDC Publishing.

Gross, Kimberley & Gross, Kaiya. The Multiplication Monster. Gross, Sanai, illus. 2013. 84p. pap. 10.95 (978-0-9886402-3-8(6)) G.E. Bks.

Grossmann-Hensel, Katharina. Papa is a Pirate. Grossmann-Hensel, Katharina, illus. 2009. (ENG., Illus.). 32p. (J). (gr. -1-3). 16.95 (978-0-7358-2237-5(9)) North-South Bks., Inc.

Groves. Pond Monster, Bk. 5A. Date not set. (Illus.). 16p. (J). pap. 129.15 (978-0-582-18796-2(6)) Addison-Wesley Longman, Ltd. GBR. Dist: Trans-Atlantic Pubns., Inc.

Grunberg, Greg. Nightmare Escape. Turnbloom, Lucas, illus. 2016. (Dream Jumper Ser.: 1). (ENG.). 208p. (J). (gr. 3-7). 24.99 (978-0-545-82603-7(9), Graphix) Scholastic, Inc.

Gunhus, Jeff. Jack Templar & the Monster Hunter Academy. 2013. 330p. pap. 12.95 (978-0-9884259-4-1(7)) Seven Guns Pr.

—Jack Templar Monster Hunter. 2012. 196p. pap. 10.95 (978-0-9884259-0-3(4)) Seven Guns Pr.

Gutierrez, Rochelle. Dear Monster. 2010. 16p. pap. 8.95 (978-1-4490-7281-0(X)) AuthorHouse.

Haber, Tiffany Strelitz. The Monster Who Lost His Mean. Edmunds, Kirstie, illus. 2012. (ENG.). 40p. (J). (gr. -1-3). 17.99 (978-0-8050-9375-9(3), 9780805093759, Holt, Henry & Co. Bks. For Young Readers) Holt, Henry & Co.

Haesche, Richard Paul, Sr. The Magic of the Leprechaun. 2007. (ENG.). 182p. (YA). (978-0-9798536-3-0(X)) Kreative X-Pressions Pubns.

Haggarty, Holly. Summer Dragons. 2007. (ENG.). 176p. (J). (gr. 3-18). per. 9.95 (978-1-894917-52-0(9), Napoleon & Co.) Dundurn CAN. Dist: Ingram Publisher Services.

Hahn, Molly. Under the Sneep Tree: The Wamboozling of a Village. 2009. pap. (978-1-61623-907-7(7)) Independent Pub.

Hale, Bruce. Curse of the Were-Hyena: A Monstertown Mystery. Hale, Bruce, illus. 2016. (Monstertown Mysteries Ser.). (ENG., Illus.). 220p. (J). (gr. 3-7). 14.99 (978-1-4847-1325-9(7)) Disney Pr.

—Monsters on the Loose! A Seek & Solve Mystery! Garbot, Dave, illus. 2013. (ENG.). 32p. (J). (gr. -1-3). 7.99 (978-0-06-223706-4(3)) HarperCollins Pubs.

—Mutant Mantis Lunch Ladies! 2017. (Monstertown Mysteries Ser.). (ENG.). 208p. (J). (gr. 3-7). 14.99 (978-1-4847-1324-2(9)) Disney Pr.

Hale, Shannon & Hale, Dean. The Princess in Black. Pham, LeUyen, illus. (Princess in Black Ser.). (ENG.). 96p. (J). (gr. k-3). 2015. pap. 6.99 (978-0-7636-7888-3(0)) 2014. 14.99 (978-0-7636-6510-4(X)) Candlewick Pr.

—The Princess in Black. 2015. (Princess in Black Ser.: 1). lib. bdg. 17.20 (978-0-606-36863-6(9)) Turtleback Bks.

—The Princess in Black & the Hungry Bunny Horde. Pham, LeUyen, illus. 2016. (Princess in Black Ser.: 3). (ENG.). (J). (gr. k-3). 96p. pap. 6.99 (978-0-7636-9089-2(9)); 85p. 14.99 (978-0-7636-6513-5(4)) Candlewick Pr.

—The Princess in Black & the Hungry Bunny Horde. Pham, LeUyen, illus. 2016. (Princess in Black Ser.: 3). (ENG.). 85p. (J). (gr. k-3). 17.20 (978-0-606-39109-2(6)) Turtleback Bks.

Hale, Shannon & Hale, Dean. The Princess in Black & the Mysterious Playdate. Pham, LeUyen, illus. 2017. (Princess in Black Ser.: 5). (ENG.). 96p. (J). (gr. k-3). 14.99 **(978-0-7636-8826-4(6))** Candlewick Pr.

Hall, Michael. Frankencrayon. Hall, Michael, illus. 2016. (Illus.). 40p. (J). (gr. -1-3). 17.99 (978-0-06-225211-1(9)); lib. bdg. 18.89 (978-0-06-225212-8(7)) HarperCollins Pubs. (Greenwillow Bks.).

Hamilton, John. Mission to Mars, 6 bks. Incl. Mariner Missions to Mars. 32p. (gr. 5). 1998. 27.07 (978-1-56239-828-6(8), Abdo & Daughters); (Illus.). Set lib. bdg. 136.68 o.p. (978-1-57765-258-8(4), Abdo & Daughters) ABDO Publishing Co.

Hansen, Justin LaRocca. Monster Hunter. 2012. (ENG., Illus.). 32p. (J). (gr. -1-k). 16.95 (978-1-61608-968-9(7), 608968, Sky Pony Pr.) Skyhorse Publishing Co., Inc.

Hardin, J. R. Kalvin the Kudzu Monster. 2010. 76p. (J). pap. 8.95 (978-1-4502-5764-0(X)) iUniverse, Inc.

Harris, Abaghoul. Monster High Drop Dead Diary. 2011. (ENG.). 192p. (J). (gr. 7-17). 12.99 (978-0-316-18661-2(9), Poppy) Little, Brown Bks. for Young Readers.

Harris, Christine. Undercover Girl #5: Twisted. 2007. (ENG.). 136p. (J). per. 10.95 (978-1-59594-151-0(7), Wingspan Pr.) WingSpan Publishing.

Harris, M. S. Ed Rebecca a. & Harris, M. S. Ed. Megan's Monster. Lee, Joe, illus. 2009. 28p. pap. 15.00 (978-1-4490-2822-0(5)) AuthorHouse.

Harrison, Lisi. Back & Deader Than Ever. 2013. (Monster High Ser.: 4). (ENG.). 256p. (YA). (gr. 7-17). pap. 9.99 (978-0-316-18667-4(8), Poppy) Little, Brown Bks. for Young Readers.

—The Ghoul Next Door. (Monster High Ser.: 2). (ENG.). 256p. (YA). (gr. 7-17). 2012. pap. 8.99 *(978-0-316-18666-7(X))* 2011. 16.99 *(978-0-316-09911-0(2))* Little, Brown Bks. for Young Readers. (Poppy).

—Monster High. 2010. (SPA.). 448p. (YA). (gr. 8-12). mass mkt. 19.99 *(978-607-11-0641-4(9))* Aguilar, Altea, Taurus, Alfaguara, S.A. de C.V MEX. Dist: Two Rivers Distribution.

—Monster High. (Monster High Ser.: 1). (ENG.). 272p. (YA). (gr. 7-17). 2011. pap. 8.99 *(978-0-316-17621-7(4))* 2010. 16.99 *(978-0-316-09918-9(X))* Little, Brown Bks. for Young Readers. (Poppy).

—Monster High. 2011. (Monster High Ser.: 1). (YA). lib. bdg. 19.65 *(978-0-606-23459-7(4),* Turtleback) Turtleback Bks.

—Monster High: the Scary Cute Collection. 2013. (Monster High Ser.). (ENG.). 1056p. (J). (gr. 7-17). pap. 38.00 *(978-0-316-24908-9(4),* Poppy) Little, Brown Bks. for Young Readers.

—Monster High: Where There's a Wolf, There's a Way. 2011. (Monster High Ser.: 3). (ENG., Illus.). 256p. (YA). (gr. 7-17). 17.99 *(978-0-316-09919-6(8),* Poppy) Little, Brown Bks. for Young Readers.

—Where There's a Wolf, There's a Way. 2012. (Monster High Ser.: 3). (ENG., Illus.). 272p. (YA). (gr. 7-17). pap. 9.99 *(978-0-316-18668-1(6),* Poppy) Little, Brown Bks. for Young Readers.

Hart, Caryl. There's a Monster in My Fridge: With Fun Split Pages. Allwright, Deborah, illus. 2016. (ENG.). 24p. (J). (gr. -1-2). pap. 7.99 *(978-1-4380-0824-0(4))* Barron's Educational Series, Inc.

Hartley Bellows, Carol. Icey. 2009. 32p. pap. 14.99 *(978-1-4389-4475-3(6))* AuthorHouse.

Harvey, Keith & Beard, Lauren. Say Please, Louise! A Story of a Little Girl With Monstrous Manners. 2015. (ENG., Illus.). 24p. pap. 8.99 *(978-1-84135-921-2(1))* Award Pubns. Ltd. GBR. Dist: Parkwest Pubns., Inc.

Hawkins, Colin & Hawkins, Jacqui. Snap! Snap! 2005. (ENG., Illus.). 32p. (J). pap. 7.99 *(978-1-4052-1099-7(0))* Egmont Bks., Ltd. GBR. Dist: Trafalgar Square Publishing.

Hawkins, Rachel. School Spirits. 2014. (Hex Hall Novel Ser.). (ENG.). 304p. (YA). (gr. 7-12). pap. 9.99 *(978-1-4231-4850-0(9))* Hyperion Bks. for Children.

—School Spirits. 2013. (Hex Hall Novel Ser.). (ENG.). 304p. (YA). (gr. 7-12). 17.99 *(978-1-4231-4849-4(5))* Hyperion Pr.

Hawley, Kelvin, illus. My Things, 6 Packs. (Sails Literacy Ser.). 16p. (gr. k-18). 27.00 *(978-0-7635-4395-2(0))* Rigby Education.

—The Vacation: Individual Title Six-Packs. (Sails Literacy Ser.). 16p. (gr. k-18). 27.00 *(978-0-7635-4434-8(5))* Rigby Education.

Hawthorn, Phillip & Tyler, Jenny. There's A Monster in My House. 2007. 16p. (J). 9.99 *(978-0-7945-1567-6(3),* Usborne) EDC Publishing.

Hayes, Terri. The Day the Blue Puff Trees Bloomed. 2011. 36p. pap. 24.95 *(978-1-4560-6096-1(1))* America Star Bks.

Hellisen, Cat. Beastkeeper. 2015. (ENG.). 208p. (YA). (gr. 7-9). 16.99 *(978-0-8050-9980-5(8),* Holt, Henry & Co. Bks. For Young Readers) Holt, Henry & Co.

Helm, Julie G. The Lost Monster Tales. Cary, Debbi, illus. 2010. 212p. pap. 14.49 *(978-1-4490-3823-6(9))* AuthorHouse.

Herman, Gail. Boo on the Loose (Disney/Pixar Monsters, Inc.) Tilley, Scott, illus. 2012. (Step into Reading Ser.). (ENG.). 32p. (J). (gr. -1-1). pap. 3.99 *(978-0-7364-2860-6(7),* RH/Disney) Random Hse. Children's Bks.

—Scooby-Doo in the Lighthouse Mystery, 1 vol. 2016. (Scooby-Doo! Set 3 Ser.). (ENG., Illus.). 32p. (J). (gr. k-4). lib. bdg. 24.21 *(978-1-61479-410-3(3))* Spotlight.

Hernández, Gabriel, et al. Slappy's Tales of Horror. Roman, Dave et al, illus. 2015. 171p. (J). ***(978-0-545-87203-4(0),*** Graphix) Scholastic, Inc.

Hewitt, Franz. Monster Doctor, M. D. 2010. 40p. pap. 18.49 *(978-0-557-53188-2(8))* Lulu Pr., Inc.

Hibbs, Sasha. Black Amaranth. 2013. 286p. pap. *(978-1-77130-526-6(6))* Evernight Publishing.

Hickey, Laura L. What's in the Woods. 2012. 84p. pap. 19.95 *(978-1-4626-9025-1(4))* America Star Bks.

Hiebert, Elfrieda H. & Juel, Connie. My Monster & Me. (Little Book Practice Reader). (J). *(978-0-8136-0677-4(2))* Modern Curriculum Pr.

Higesanbon. Mo Mo Mo Mo Monster: Mon Monster. 2011. 56p. pap. 34.95 *(978-1-4327-4149-5(7))* Outskirts Pr., Inc.

Higgins, F. E. The Lunatic's Curse. 2011. (ENG.). 352p. (J). (gr. 5-9). 29.99 *(978-0-312-56682-1(4),* 9780312566821) Feiwel & Friends.

Higgins, Jim. The Enchanted Nursery: Nessie's Friends. 2008. 24p. pap. 11.49 *(978-1-4343-8993-0(6))* AuthorHouse.

Higginson, Sheila Sweeny. Henry Loves Beckett. 2014. (J). lib. bdg. 14.75 *(978-0-606-35907-8(9))* Turtleback Bks.

Hill, Andrew G. The Song of the Seraphim. 2009. 196p. pap. 13.95 *(978-1-60860-194-3(3),* Strategic Bk. Publishing) Strategic Book Publishing & Rights Agency (SBPRA).

Hines-Stephens, Sarah & Harper, Benjamin. Bug Girl. Syed, Anoosha, illus. 2017. (Bug Girl Ser.). (ENG.). 304p. (J). 14.99 *(978-1-250-10661-2(3),* 9781250106612) Imprint IND. Dist: Macmillan.

Hiti, Samuel. Waga's Big Scare. Hiti, Samuel, illus. 2012. (Carolrhoda Picture Bks.). (ENG., Illus.). 32p. (J). (gr. k-3). lib. bdg. 16.95 *(978-0-7613-5622-6(3))* Lerner Publishing Group.

Hodgkinson, Leigh. The Big Monster Snorey Book. Hodgkinson, Leigh, illus. 2016. (ENG., Illus.). (J). (gr. -1-2). 16.99 *(978-0-7636-8660-4(3),* Nosy Crow) Candlewick Pr.

Hodgman, Ann. Monsters Dance. Wood, Hannah, illus. 2013. (ENG.). 16p. (J). (gr. -1). bds. 8.95 *(978-1-58925-627-9(1))* Tiger Tales.

Hoena, Blake. Monster Heroes, 4 vols. Bardin, Dave, illus. 2016. (Monster Heroes Ser.). (ENG.). 32p. (gr. 1-2). 85.28 *(978-1-4965-3770-6(X))* Stone Arch Bks.

—Witch's Brew. Bardin, Dave, illus. 2016. (Monster Heroes Ser.). (ENG.). 32p. (gr. 1-2). lib. bdg. 21.32 *(978-1-4965-3756-0(4))* Stone Arch Bks.

Hoena, Blake & Hoena, Blake A. The Ghost Trap. Bardin, Dave, illus. 2016. (Monster Heroes Ser.). (ENG.). 32p. (gr. 1-2). lib. bdg. 21.32 *(978-1-4965-3757-7(2))* Stone Arch Bks.

—Vampires & Veggies. Bardin, Dave, illus. 2016. (Monster Heroes Ser.). (ENG.). 32p. (gr. 1-2). lib. bdg. 21.32 *(978-1-4965-3755-3(6))* Stone Arch Bks.

—Zombies & Meatballs. Bardin, Dave, illus. 2016. (Monster Heroes Ser.). (ENG.). 32p. (gr. 1-2). lib. bdg. 21.32 *(978-1-4965-3754-6(8))* Stone Arch Bks.

Holcomb, Carrie E., ed. Monster Nation JR. 2007. (Illus.). 32p. (J). per. 6.99 *(978-0-696-23688-4(5))* Meredith Bks.

Holm, Matthew & Follett, Jonathan. Marvin & the Moths. 2016. (ENG.). 352p. (J). (gr. 3-7). 16.99 *(978-0-545-87674-2(5),* Scholastic Pr.) Scholastic, Inc.

Holmqvist, Carin. African Tales. 2010. 64p. pap. 28.70 *(978-0-557-18184-1(4))* Lulu Pr., Inc.

Hook. Wrinkled Crinkled Grapes: A Purple Monster. 2007. 52p. per. 8.95 *(978-0-595-42310-1(8))* iUniverse, Inc.

Hopper, Karyn. There's a Monster in My Opu. 2006. (Illus.). 24p. (J). 11.95 *(978-1-57306-244-2(8))* Bess Pr., Inc.

Houghton Mifflin Harcourt Publishing Company Staff & Rey, H. A. Start Your Engines 5-Minute Stories. 2014. (5-Minute Stories Ser.). (ENG., Illus.). 224p. (J). (gr. -1-3). 12.99 *(978-0-544-15881-8(4),* HMH Books For Young Readers) Houghton Mifflin Harcourt Publishing Co.

Howard, Kate. Goosebumps the Movie: Night of the Living Monsters. 2015. (ENG.). 48p. (J). (gr. 2-5). pap. 4.99 *(978-0-545-82254-1(8))* Scholastic, Inc.

Howard, Kate, adapted by. Fright Knight! 2016. 71p. (J). ***(978-1-4844-8023-6(6))*** Scholastic, Inc.

Howland, Ashley. Ghostnapped. 2009. 64p. pap. 9.99 *(978-1-60860-145-5(5),* Strategic Bk. Publishing) Strategic Book Publishing & Rights Agency (SBPRA).

Huber, Randolph. Monsters from the ID. 2007. 48p. per. 16.95 *(978-1-4241-4682-6(8))* PublishAmerica, Inc.

Huckerby, Mark & Ostler, Nick. Defender of the Realm. 2017. (ENG.). 320p. (J). (gr. 3-7). 17.99 *(978-0-545-93666-8(7),* Scholastic Pr.) Scholastic, Inc.

Hull, Claudia. Procrastimonsters! They're Everywhere. Mikle, Toby, illus. 2012. 44p. pap. 15.95 *(978-1-257-64007-2(0))* Shalako Pr.

Hulme-Cross, Benjamin. The Marsh Demon. Evergreen, Nelson, illus. 2015. (Dark Hunter Ser.). (ENG.). 64p. (J). (gr. 4-8). 17.32 *(978-1-4677-8658-4(6))* Lerner Publishing Group.

Huneke, Amanda. A Monster at School, 1 vol. Wolek, Guy, illus. 2013. (Monster on the Loose Ser.). (ENG.). 32p. (J). (gr. -1-4). 28.50 *(978-1-61641-931-8(8))* Magic Wagon.

—A Monster in the Park, 1 vol. Wolek, Guy, illus. 2013. (Monster on the Loose Ser.). (ENG.). 32p. (J). (gr. -1-4). 28.50 *(978-1-61641-932-5(6))* Magic Wagon.

—A Monster on the Bus, 1 vol. Wolek, Guy, illus. 2013. (Monster on the Loose Ser.). (ENG.). 32p. (J). (gr. -1-4). 28.50 *(978-1-61641-933-2(4))* Magic Wagon.

—A Monster on the Loose, 1 vol. Wolek, Guy, illus. 2013. (Monster on the Loose Ser.). (ENG.). 32p. (J). (gr. -1-4). 28.50 *(978-1-61641-934-9(2))* Magic Wagon.

Hunter, Erin & Jolley, Dan. Warrior's Return, 3 vols. Barry, James L., illus. 2008. (Warriors Manga Ser.: No. 3). (ENG.). 112p. (J). (gr. 3-7). pap. 6.99 *(978-0-06-125233-4(6))* HarperCollins Pubs.

Hutchins, M. K. Drift, 1 vol. 2014. (ENG.). 352p. (YA). 19.95 *(978-1-62014-145-8(0))* Lee & Low Bks., Inc.

Huws, Emily. Anghenfil O Joc. 2005. (WEL., Illus.). 24p. pap. *(978-0-86174-164-9(1))* Drake Educational Assocs. Ltd.

Hyman, Jack G. Breakfast with the Birds. 2013. 216p. pap. 15.99 *(978-1-4525-8453-9(2),* Balboa Pr.) Author Solutions, Inc.

I Am Working, 6 Packs. (Sails Literacy Ser.). 16p. (gr. k-18). 27.00 *(978-0-7635-4407-2(8))* Rigby Education.

I Like Jam: Individual Title, 6 Packs. (Sails Literacy Ser.). 16p. (gr. k-18). 27.00 *(978-0-7635-4440-9(X))* Rigby Education.

If You're Gonna be a Monster do it Right. 2005. (YA). per. *(978-1-59872-088-4(0))* Instant Pub.

In the Mud, Pk. 6. (Sails Literacy Ser.). 16p. (gr. k-18). 27.00 *(978-0-7635-4428-7(0))* Rigby Education.

Inches, Alison. I Can Save the Earth! One Little Monster Learns to Reduce, Reuse, & Recycle. Garofoli, Viviana, illus. 2008. (Little Green Bks.). (ENG.). 24p. (J). (gr. -1-1). pap. 3.99 *(978-1-4169-6789-7(3),* Little Simon) Little Simon.

—I'm Not Little! Thomas, Glenn, illus. 2017. (ENG.). 32p. (J). (gr. -1-3). 16.99 *(978-1-4998-0377-8(X))* Little Bee Books Inc.

Inkpen, Mick. Kipper's Monster. 2008. (ENG., Illus.). 32p. (J). (gr. -1-12). pap. 10.99 *(978-0-340-93208-7(2))* Hodder & Stoughton GBR. Dist: Hachette Bk. Group.

Inzana, Ryan. Ichiro. (ENG., Illus.). 288p. (YA). (gr. 7). 2014. pap. 12.99 *(978-0-547-61789-3(5),* HMH Books For Young Readers) 2012. 24.99 *(978-0-547-25269-8(2))* Houghton Mifflin Harcourt Publishing Co.

Jacks, C. S. The Adventures of Pisten Billy: Pisten Billy Makes the Grade! 2010. 32p. pap. 12.99 *(978-1-4520-6624-0(8))* AuthorHouse.

Jahangiri, Holly. Trockle. 2008. (Illus.). 32p. (J). 18.99 *(978-0-9797513-2-5(2))* 4RV Publishing, LLC.

Jane, Pamela. Little Goblins Ten. Jane, Pamela & Manning, Jane, illus. 2011. (ENG.). 32p. (J). (gr. -1-3). 16.99 *(978-0-06-176798-2(0))* HarperCollins Pubs.

—Monster Mischief. Rosenberry, Vera, illus. 2014. (ENG.). 32p. (J). (gr. -1-2). 16.99 *(978-1-4814-2535-3(8),* Atheneum Bks. for Young Readers) Simon & Schuster Children's Publishing.

Janese, Julie. The Little Booger Book. 2009. 24p. pap. 11.49 *(978-1-4490-0310-4(9))* AuthorHouse.

Jay, Stacey. Of Beast & Beauty. 2014. (ENG.). 400p. (YA). (gr. 9). pap. 9.99 *(978-0-385-74321-1(1),* Ember) Random Hse. Children's Bks.

Jinks, Catherine. How to Catch a Bogle. Watts, Sarah, illus. 2014. (How to Catch a Bogle Ser.: 1). (ENG.). 336p. (J). (gr. 5-7). pap. 7.99 *(978-0-544-33627-8(5),* HMH Books For Young Readers) Houghton Mifflin Harcourt Publishing Co.

—The Last Bogler. (How to Catch a Bogle Ser.: 3). (ENG.). 336p. (J). (gr. 5-7). 2017. pap. 7.99 *(978-0-544-81309-0(X))* 2016. (Illus.). 16.99 *(978-0-544-08696-8(1))* Houghton Mifflin Harcourt Publishing Co. (HMH Books For Young Readers).

—A Plague of Bogles. 2015. (How to Catch a Bogle Ser.: 2). (ENG.). 336p. (J). (gr. 5-7). pap. 6.99 *(978-0-544-54067-5(0));* (Illus.). 16.99 *(978-0-544-08747-7(X))* Houghton Mifflin Harcourt Publishing Co. (HMH Books For Young Readers).

JJ Rabbit & the Monster: Level K, 6 vols. 128p. (gr. 2-3). 49.95 *(978-0-7699-0981-3(7))* Shortland Pubns. (U. S. A.) Inc.

Jobling, Curtis. The Beast of Bone Creek. 2016. (Max Helsing: Monster Hunter Ser.: 2). (ENG., Illus.). 304p. (J). (gr. 5). 16.99 *(978-0-451-47480-3(5),* Viking Books for Young Readers) Penguin Young Readers Group.

John, Jory. I Will Chomp You! Shea, Bob, illus. 2015. (ENG.). 40p. (J). (gr. -1-2). 20.99 *(978-0-385-38987-7(6),* Random Hse. Bks. for Young Readers) Random Hse. Children's Bks.

—Quit Calling Me a Monster! Shea, Bob, illus. 2016. (ENG.). 40p. (J). (gr. -1-2). 17.99 *(978-0-385-38990-7(6),* Random Hse. Bks. for Young Readers) Random Hse. Children's Bks.

Johnson, James A. The Beast & the Backpack. 2009. 64p. pap. 8.95 *(978-1-4401-5390-7(6))* iUniverse, Inc.

Johnson, Vickey L. The Monster Mix-Up. 2003. (Illus.). (J). pap. 9.00 *(978-0-8059-6125-6(9))* Dorrance Publishing Co., Inc.

Jolby, illus. Monsters under Bridges. 2013. (ENG.). 32p. (J). (gr. -1-3). 16.99 *(978-1-57061-856-7(9),* Little Bigfoot) Sasquatch Bks.

Judge, Chris. The Snow Beast. Judge, Chris, illus. 2015. (ENG., Illus.). 32p. (J). (gr. -1-3). 17.99 *(978-1-4677-9313-1(2))* Andersen Pr. GBR. Dist: Lerner Publishing Group.

Juncar, Nicola. The Legend of Thornton Wood. 2012. 238p. pap. *(978-1-78176-184-7(1))* FeedARead.com.

Jungman, Ann. Vlad the Drac Returns. 2006. (Vlad the Drac Ser.). (Illus.). 123p. (J). pap. 6.95 *(978-1-903015-34-6(0))* Barn Owl Bks, London GBR. Dist: Independent Pubs. Group.

—Vlad the Drac Superstar. Thompson, George, illus. 2006. (Vlad the Drac Ser.). 122p. (J). (gr. 2-4). pap. 6.95 *(978-1-903015-45-2(6))* Barn Owl Bks, London GBR. Dist: Independent Pubs. Group.

Juster, Norton. The Odious Ogre. Feiffer, Jules, illus. 2010. (ENG.). 32p. (J). (gr. -1-2). 17.95 *(978-0-545-16202-9(5),* Di Capua, Michael) Scholastic, Inc.

Kander, Beth & Kenyon, Bret. Glubbery Gray, the Knight-Eating Beast, 1 vol. Labbé, Jesse, illus. 2010. (ENG.). 40p. (J). (gr. k-3). 17.99 *(978-1-58980-867-6(3))* Pelican Publishing Co., Inc.

Kaplan, Bruce Eric. Monsters Eat Whiny Children. Kaplan, Bruce Eric, illus. 2010. (ENG., Illus.). 40p. (J). (gr. -1-3). 17.99 *(978-1-4169-8689-8(8),* Simon & Schuster Bks. For Young Readers) Simon & Schuster Bks. For Young Readers.

Kasza, Keiko. Los Secretos de Abuelo Sapo. (SPA., Illus.). (J). (gr. 1-3). *(978-958-04-3624-9(X),* NR7688) Norma S.A.

Katz, Welwyn Wilton. Beowulf, 1 vol. Gal, Laszlo, illus. 2nd ed. 2007. (ENG.). 96p. (J). (gr. 4-7). 17.95 *(978-0-88899-807-1(4))* Groundwood Bks. CAN. Dist: Publishers Group West (PGW).

Keane, Dave. First Day Frights. Keane, Dave, illus. 2012. (I Can Read Level 2 Ser.). (ENG., Illus.). 32p. (J). (gr. -1-3). pap. 3.99 *(978-0-06-085475-1(8))* HarperCollins Pubs.

—Monster School: First Day Frights. Keane, Dave, illus. 2012. (I Can Read Level 2 Ser.). (ENG., Illus.). 32p. (J). (gr. -1-3). 16.99 *(978-0-06-085476-8(6))* HarperCollins Pubs.

—Monster School: The Spooky Sleepover. Keane, Dave, illus. 2014. (I Can Read Level 2 Ser.). (ENG., Illus.). 32p. (J). (gr. -1-3). pap. 3.99 *(978-0-06-085477-5(4))* HarperCollins Pubs.

Keaton, Kelly. A Beautiful Evil. (ENG.). (YA). (gr. 9). 2013. 320p. pap. 11.99 *(978-1-4424-0928-6(2))* 2012. 304p. 17.99 *(978-1-4424-0927-9(4))* Simon Pulse. (Simon Pulse).

—Darkness Becomes Her. (ENG.). (YA). (gr. 9). 2012. 320p. pap. 9.99 *(978-1-4424-0925-5(8))* 2011. 288p. 16.99 *(978-1-4424-0924-8(X))* Simon Pulse. (Simon Pulse).

Keller, Joy. Monster Trucks. Saburi, Misa, illus. 2017. (ENG.). 32p. (J). 16.99 *(978-1-62779-617-0(7),* 9781627796170, Holt, Henry & Co. Bks. For Young Readers) Holt, Henry & Co.

Kelley, Jane. Octo-Man & the Headless Monster. 2017. (Escapades of Clint Mccool Ser.: 1). lib. bdg. 16.00 ***(978-0-606-40109-8(1))*** Turtleback Bks.

Kenner, Crystal R. The King of All Tickle Bugs & Other Stories. 2011. (Illus.). 124p. (gr. -1). pap. 10.95 *(978-1-4502-9466-9(9))* iUniverse, Inc.

Kennis, Don. Monsters Have Big Feet. Gowens, Kyle & Richmond, Bob, illus. 2006. (J). per. 8.95 *(978-0-9788553-0-7(2))* Guppy Publishing LLC.

Kent, Jaden. #2: Attack of the Stinky Fish Monster! Bodnaruk, Iryna, illus. 2017. (Ella & Owen Ser.: 2). (ENG.). 112p. (J). (gr. 1-3). pap. 5.99 *(978-1-4998-0369-3(9))* Little Bee Books Inc.

Kessler, Liz. Emily Windsnap & the Monster from the Deep. Gibb, Sarah, illus. 2012. (Emily Windsnap Ser.: 2). (ENG.). 240p. (J). (gr. 3-7). pap. 5.99 *(978-0-7636-6018-5(3))* Candlewick Pr.

—Emily Windsnap & the Monster from the Deep. 2012. (Emily Windsnap Ser.: 2). lib. bdg. 16.00 *(978-0-606-25573-8(7),* Turtleback) Turtleback Bks.

—Emily Windsnap: Two Magical Mermaid Tales. Gibb, Sarah, illus. 2014. (Emily Windsnap Ser.). (ENG.). 464p. (J). (gr. 3-7). pap. 9.99 *(978-0-7636-7452-6(4))* Candlewick Pr.

—Four Sparkling Underwater Adventures. Gibb, Sarah & Ledwidge, Natacha, illus. 2012. (Emily Windsnap Ser.). (ENG.). (J). (gr. 3-7). pap. 23.96 *(978-0-7636-6295-0(X))* Candlewick Pr.

Ketteman, Helen. Goodnight, Little Monster, 0 vols. Leick, Bonnie, illus. 2010. (ENG.). 32p. (J). (gr. -1-3). 16.99 *(978-0-7614-5683-4(X),* 9780761456834, Amazon Children's Publishing) Amazon Publishing.

Kettle, Jenny. Monster Hunting. 2011. 24p. pap. 15.99 *(978-1-4568-2857-8(6))* Xlibris Corp.

Kibuishi, Kazu. The Stonekeeper. 2008. (Amulet Ser.: 1). (ENG., Illus.). 192p. (J). (gr. 3-7). 24.99 *(978-0-439-84680-6(3));* pap. 12.99 *(978-0-439-84681-3(1))* Scholastic, Inc. (Graphix).

Kilgore, Lee. The Mr. Munch Adventures: Six Short Stories, 1 vol. 2010. 73p. pap. 19.95 *(978-1-4489-2876-7(1))* America Star Bks.

King, Aby. Lupo & the Lost Pirate of Kensington Palace Lupo & the Lost Pirate of Kensington Palace. 2016. (Lupo Ser.). (ENG., Illus.). 240p. (J). (gr. 4-17). pap. 7.99 *(978-1-4449-2157-1(6))* Hachette Children's Group GBR. Dist: Hachette Bk. Group.

King, Jane. The Monster Bash. 2013. (Ghoul School Ser.: 3). (ENG., Illus.). 80p. (J). (gr. 1-4). pap. 13.99 *(978-1-4814-2164-5(6),* Simon & Schuster/Paula Wiseman Bks.) Simon & Schuster/Paula Wiseman Bks.

King, Jeremy Jordan. In Stone: A Grotesque Faerie Tale. 2012. (ENG.). 264p. (gr. 7). pap. 11.95 *(978-1-60282-761-5(3))* Bold Strokes Bks.

King, Trey. Halloween Rescue! Wang, Sean, illus. 2013. (Lego City Ser.). (ENG.). 24p. (J). (gr. -1-3). 4.99 *(978-0-545-51572-6(6))* Scholastic, Inc.

Kingsley, Ron D. Stories from the Life of Ronnie Kaye: Monsters. 2013. (ENG.). 125p. (YA). pap. 8.95 *(978-1-4787-1121-6(3))* Outskirts Pr., Inc.

Kirk, David. Truckeroo School. Kirk, David, illus. 2017. (ENG., Illus.). 40p. (J). 17.99 *(978-1-250-01690-4(8),* 9781250016904) Feiwel & Friends.

Kirkland, Justin B. Jb Pumpernikel vs the Sock Monster. 2013. 74p. pap. 5.50 *(978-0-615-81456-8(5))* KIRKLAND, JUSTIN B.

Kishimoto, Masashi. Naruto: Chapter Book, Vol. 13. Kishimoto, Masashi, illus. 2010. (ENG., Illus.). 80p. (J). pap. 4.99 *(978-1-4215-3043-7(0))* Viz Media.

A Kiss for Jake. 2008. (Jake Flocked Board Ser.). 8p. bds. *(978-1-4075-1816-9(X))* Parragon, Inc.

Kleinberg, Naomi. Elmo's Monster Mash. Moroney, Christopher, illus. 2010. (ENG.). 12p. (J). (gr. k — 1). 4.99 *(978-0-375-85804-8(0),* Random Hse. Bks. for Young Readers) Random Hse. Children's Bks.

Kleinberg, Naomi. Who's Hiding (Sesame Street) 2017. (Pictureback(R) Ser.). (ENG., Illus.). 16p. (J). (gr. -1-2). pap. 5.99 ***(978-1-5247-1634-9(0),*** Random Hse. Bks. for Young Readers) Random Hse. Children's Bks.

Klemer, Amy Wade. The Scary Snake Monster. 2003. (Illus.). 16p. (J). pap. 8.00 *(978-0-9729216-1-9(3))* ABCDMoon Publishing.

Kleven, Elisa. A Monster in the House. 2013. 34p. 16.99 *(978-1-62352-036-6(3));* pap. 9.99 *(978-1-62352-041-0(X))* IntoPrint Publishing LLC.

Kline, Spencer. The Adventures of Fujimori-San. Brown, E. Jackie, illus. 2010. 20p. 12.99 *(978-1-4520-6275-4(7))* AuthorHouse.

Kloepfer, John. Monsters Unleashed. Oliver, Mark, illus. (Monsters Unleashed Ser.: 1). (J). (gr. 3-7). 2018. 224p. pap. 6.99 ***(978-0-06-229031-1(2))*** 2017. 208p. 16.99 ***(978-0-06-229030-4(4))*** HarperCollins Pubs.

Klug, Eric. The Monster in My Closet. Klug, Eric, illus. 2007. (Illus.). 32p. (J). (gr. -1-3). 15.95 *(978-1-60108-007-3(7))* Red Cygnet Pr.

Klutz Editors & Rose, Amber. Monsters. 2009. (Hammond Undercover Ser.). 72p. (J). (gr. 3-7). pap. 13.99 *(978-0-8416-1497-0(0))* Hammond World Atlas Corp.

Knight, Andrew. The Monster in the Loch. (Thumbprint Mysteries Ser.). 32.86 *(978-0-8092-0411-3(8))* McGraw-Hill/Contemporary.

Knudsen, Michelle. Marilyn's Monster. Phelan, Matt, illus. (ENG.). 40p. (J). (gr. -1-3). 2017. 6.99 *(978-0-7636-9301-5(4))* 2015. 16.99 *(978-0-7636-6011-6(6))* Candlewick Pr.

—Marilyn's Monster. Phelan, Matt, illus. 2017. (ENG.). (J). (gr. -1-3). lib. bdg. 17.20 ***(978-0-606-39844-2(9))*** Turtleback Bks.

Kochalka, James. The Happy Apples, Bk. 3. 2009. (Johnny Boo Ser.: 3). (ENG., Illus.). 40p. (J). (gr. 2-5). 9.95 *(978-1-60309-041-4(X),* 9781603090414) Top Shelf Productions.

Koller, Jackie French. No Such Thing. Lewin, Betsy, illus. 2012. (ENG.). 32p. (J). (gr. k-2). pap. 7.95 *(978-1-59078-911-7(3))* Boyds Mills Pr.

Krackow, Eric T. The Lollipop Monster, 1 vol. 2011. (ENG., Illus.). 64p. (J). 16.99 *(978-0-7643-3773-4(4),* 9780764337734, Schiffer Publishing Ltd) Schiffer Publishing, Ltd.

—The Lollipop Monster's Christmas, 1 vol. 2014. (ENG., Illus.). 64p. (J). (gr. 5-8). 16.99 *(978-0-7643-4743-6(8),* 9780764347436) Schiffer Publishing, Ltd.

Kretzer, Joyce B. Shane & the Jackadoo: A Butcher Hollow Fantasy. 2008. 24p. pap. 11.49 *(978-1-4389-1894-5(1))* AuthorHouse.

Kropp, Joseph P. Nathan Meets His Monsters. Johnston, Phillip, illus. 2012. 34p. 16.95 *(978-1-890905-59-0(3));* pap. 9.95 *(978-1-890905-58-3(5))* Day to Day Enterprises.

Kropp, Paul. Behind the Door. 2007. (HIP Edge Ser.). (Illus.). 112p. (YA). (gr. 7-12). pap. *(978-1-897039-26-7(3))* High Interest Publishing (HIP).

Kubler, Annie. Wheels on the Bus, 15 vols. 2005. (ENG, SPA & MUL., Illus.). 14p. (J). bds. *(978-1-84444-979-8(3))* Mantra Lingua.

—Wheels on the Bus, 15 vols. Kubler, Annie, illus. 2005. (ENG, SOM & MUL., Illus.). 14p. (J). bds. *(978-1-84444-978-1(5))* Mantra Lingua.

—Wheels on the Bus, 15 vols. 2005. (Illus.). 14p. (J). (POR, ENG & MUL.). bds. *(978-1-84444-977-4(7));* (PAN, ENG & MUL., bds. *(978-1-84444-976-7(9))* Mantra Lingua.

—Wheels on the Bus, 15 vols. Kubler, Annie, illus. 2005. (Illus.). 14p. (J). (ENG, FRE & MUL.). bds. *(978-1-84444-974-3(2));* (ARA, ENG & MUL., bds. *(978-1-84444-970-5(X));* (CHI, ENG & MUL., bds. *(978-1-84444-973-6(4));* (ENG, CHI & MUL., bds. *(978-1-84444-972-9(6));* (BEN, ENG & MUL., bds. *(978-1-84444-971-2(8));* (ENG, TUR & MUL., bds. *(978-1-84444-980-4(7));* (ENG, HIN & MUL., bds. *(978-1-84444-975-0(0));* (URD, ENG & MUL., bds. *(978-1-84444-981-1(5))* Mantra Lingua.

Kutner, Merrily. The Zombie Nite Cafe. Long, Ethan, illus. 2007. (ENG.). 32p. (J). (gr. -1-3). 16.95 *(978-0-8234-1963-0(0))* Holiday Hse., Inc.

Labatt, Mary. Lake Monster Mix-Up. Rioux, Jo-Anne, illus. 2009. (Sam & Friends Mystery Ser.). (ENG.). 96p. (J). (gr. 2-5). 7.95 *(978-1-55337-302-5(2));* 16.95 *(978-1-55337-822-8(9))* Kids Can Pr., Ltd. CAN. Dist: Hachette Bk. Group.

Lagonegro, Melissa. Monster Games. RH Disney Staff, illus. 2013. (Step into Reading Ser.). (ENG.). 32p. (J). (gr. -1-1). 3.99 *(978-0-7364-3106-4(3),* RH/Disney) Random Hse. Children's Bks.

—Monster Games. 2013. (Step into Reading Level 1 Ser.). lib. bdg. 13.55 *(978-0-606-32208-9(6),* Turtleback) Turtleback Bks.

—Monsters Get Scared of the Dark, Too (Disney/Pixar Monsters, Inc.) Random House Disney Staff, illus. 2013. (Pictureback(R) Ser.). (ENG.). 16p. (J). (gr. -1-2). 4.99

M
N
O

(978-0-7364-3056-2(3), RH/Disney) Random Hse. Children's Bks.

L'Allier, Peter Wesley Thomas. Rotten Robbie & the Legend of Wanabinoo. 2006. (Illus.). 215p. 18.95 (978-0-9724022-8-6(4)) TangleTown Media Inc.

Landgraf, James, Jr. Monsters Monsters Go Away. Warrick, Jessica, illus. 2008. 40p. (J). 8.99 (978-0-9819283-0-2(7)) Makdan Publishing.

Landis, David. Papercuttables. 2017. (ENG.). 80p. (J). (gr. 1-3). pap. 8.99 (978-0-545-83488-9(0), Cartwheel Bks.) Scholastic, Inc.

Langridge, Roger. The Muppet Show Comic Book - Muppet Mash. Langridge, Roger, illus. 2011. (Muppet Show Ser.). (Illus.). 128p. pap. 9.99 (978-1-60886-611-3(4)) Boom! Studios.

Langrish, Katherine. Troll Fell. 2004. (Illus.). 272p. (J). (gr. 5-18). lib. bdg. 16.89 (978-0-06-058305-7(3)) HarperCollins Pubs.

Lara, Sahai. My Loveable Little Monster. Hunt, Jim, illus. 2011. 22p. (J). pap. 5.99 (978-0-615-48221-7(X)) SNL Publishing.

LaRochelle, David. Monster & Son. Chou, Joey, illus. 2016. (ENG.). 32p. (J). (gr. -1 — 1). 16.99 (978-1-4521-2937-2(1)) Chronicle Bks. LLC.

Lawrence, Dionne L. The Story of Her?! 2012. 28p. (-18). pap. 16.95 (978-1-62709-253-1(6)) America Star Bks.

Layne, Steven L. My Brother Dan's Delicious, 1 vol. Galey, Chuck, illus. 2003. (ENG.). 32p. (J). (gr. k-3). 16.99 (978-1-58980-071-7(0)) Pelican Publishing Co., Inc.

Lazar, Tara. The Monstore. Burks, James, illus. 2013. (ENG.). 32p. (J). (gr. -1-2). 16.99 (978-1-4424-2017-5(0), Aladdin) Simon & Schuster Children's Publishing.

Lcg. The Pencil Monster! 2011. 28p. pap. 14.95 (978-0-557-94993-9(9)) Lulu Pr., Inc.

LeBow, Michael. Sally Salli & the Case of the Tic Monster: A Book for Kids Who Tic. Barnett, Thora, illus. 2013. 75p. (J). pap. 18.95 (978-1-59630-060-6(4)) Science & Humanities Pr.

Leedy, Loreen. The Monster Money Book. Leedy, Loreen, illus. 2005. (ENG., Illus.). 32p. (J). (gr. k-3). pap. 6.95 (978-0-8234-1558-8(9)) Holiday Hse., Inc.

Lemmens, Riske. A Box Full of Monsters. 2004. (Illus.). 26p. (J). (978-1-85269-852-2(7)); (978-1-85269-842-3(X)); (978-1-85269-837-9(3)); (978-1-85269-827-0(6)); (978-1-85269-847-8(0)) Mantra Lingua.

Lemmens, Riske & Dutta, Kunal, texts. A Box Full of Monsters: Kutia Plot Me Monstra. 2004. (Illus.). 25p. (J). (978-1-85269-822-5(5)) Mantra Lingua.

Lester, Helen. The Loch Mess Monster. Munsinger, Lynn, illus. 2014. (ENG.). 32p. (J). (gr. -1-3). 16.99 (978-0-544-09990-6(7), HMH Books For Young Readers) Houghton Mifflin Harcourt Publishing Co.

Lettrick, Robert. The Murk. Disney Storybook Art Team, illus. 2015. (ENG.). 320p. (J). (gr. 5-9). 16.99 (978-1-4231-8695-3(8)) Hyperion Bks. for Children.

Leuck, Laura. Goodnight, Baby Monster. Date not set. 32p. (J). (gr. -1-1). pap. 4.99 (978-0-06-443723-3(X)) HarperCollins Pubs.

—Jeepers Creepers: A Monstrous ABC. Parkins, David, illus. 2003. (ENG.). 32p. (J). (gr. -1-7). 15.95 (978-0-8118-3509-1(X), 53408263) Chronicle Bks. LLC.

—My Creature Teacher. Nash, Scott, illus. 2004. (ENG.). 32p. (J). (gr. -1-1). 15.99 (978-0-06-029694-0(1)) HarperCollins Pubs.

—Santa Claws. Grimly, Gris, illus. 2006. (ENG.). 32p. (J). (gr. -1-3). 16.95 (978-0-8118-4992-0(9)) Chronicle Bks. LLC.

Levis, Caron. Stuck with the Blooz. Davis, Jon, illus. 2012. (ENG.). 40p. (J). (gr. -1-3). 16.99 (978-0-547-74560-2(5)) Houghton Mifflin Harcourt Publishing Co.

Lewman, David. Monster Mayhem! (Teenage Mutant Ninja Turtles) Golden Books, illus. 2017. (Big Golden Book Ser.). (ENG.). 48p. (J). (gr. -1-2). 9.99 **(978-1-5247-1670-7(7)**, Golden Bks.) Random Hse. Children's Bks.

—Truck or Treat! (Blaze & the Monster Machines) Fruchter, Jason, illus. 2017. (Big Golden Book Ser.). (ENG.). 48p. (J). (gr. -1-2). 9.99 **(978-1-5247-1669-1(3)**, Golden Bks.) Random Hse. Children's Bks.

Light, Steven. Have You Seen My Monster? Light, Steve, illus. 2015. (ENG.). 48p. (J). (-k). 16.99 (978-0-7636-7513-4(X)) Candlewick Pr.

Lightburn, Ron. Frankenstink! A Cautionary Tale. 2015. (ENG., Illus.). 32p. (J). (gr. -1-3). 17.99 (978-1-77049-694-1(7), Tundra Bks.) Tundra Bks. CAN. Dist: Penguin Random Hse. LLC.

Lijewski, Christy. Next Exit, Vol. 1. 2006. (ENG., Illus.). 168p. (YA). pap. 12.95 (978-1-59362-037-0(3), 9781593620370) Slave Labor Bks.

Lindner, Brooke. Dance with Brobee! 2012. (Yo Gabba Gabba! Ser.). (ENG.). 12p. (J). (gr. -1-1). bds. 5.99 (978-1-4424-5445-3(8), Simon Spotlight) Simon Spotlight.

Lindquist, K. Margaret. Tyler Poncho's Amalgamated Menagerie. 2010. 62p. pap. 24.00 (978-0-557-31419-5(4)) Lulu Pr., Inc.

Lindquist, Kaeti. Tyler Poncho's Amalgamated Menagerie. 2011. 56p. pap. 25.00 (978-0-557-99490-8(X)) Lulu Pr., Inc.

Link, Kelly. Pretty Monsters. 2010. (ENG., Illus.). 416p. (YA). (gr. 7-18). 9.99 (978-0-14-241672-3(X), Speak) Penguin Young Readers Group.

Little, Awen. Sid y Bwystfil Bwyta Sanau. 2009. (WEL., Illus.). 32p. pap. 14.49 (978-1-4389-2711-4(8)) AuthorHouse.

Llanes, Adrian & Llanes, Christi. There's a Monster in My Closet. 2011. 28p. pap. 12.03 (978-1-4634-4054-1(5)) AuthorHouse.

Llewellyn, Sam. The Well Between the Worlds. 2010. (Lyonesse Ser.: 1). (ENG.). 368p. (J). (gr. 3-7). 7.99 (978-0-439-93470-1(2), Scholastic Paperbacks) Scholastic, Inc.

Lloyd, A. Wallis. Das Monster-Musical. 2013. 32p. pap. (978-3-944704-02-9(9)) Nothnagle, Alan. Edition Graugans.

Lloyd, Alicia. When the Monsters Are Quiet. Rottinger, Amy, illus. 2013. 26p. pap. 11.95 (978-1-61244-219-8(6)) Halo Publishing International.

Lonely Sea Monster. 2007. per. (978-1-59916-155-6(9)) Printing Systems.

Long, Ethan. Fright Club. 2015. (ENG., Illus.). 32p. (J). (gr. -1-2). 16.99 (978-1-61963-337-7(X), 9781619633377, Bloomsbury USA Childrens) Bloomsbury Publishing USA.

Longson, D. M. The Scunner. 2009. 32p. pap. 21.50 (978-1-4092-6995-3(7)) Lulu Pr., Inc.

Look Out for Space Monster. 2003. (Spaceboy Set 1 Ser.). (J). 7.33 (978-1-932570-04-5(7)) Pioneer Valley Bks.

Lorey, Dean. Monster Law. 2009. 304p. 10.99 (978-0-06-134048-2(0)) HarperCollins Pubs.

Loma, Balian. The Aminal, 1 vol. Loma, Balian & Lecia, Balian, illus. 2012. (ENG.). 48p. (J). pap. 7.95 (978-1-59572-363-5(3)) Star Bright Bks., Inc.

Louis, Robb. Monster in the Moat. 2011. (Illus.). 44p. (gr. -1). pap. 18.46 (978-1-4567-4053-5(9)) AuthorHouse.

Lubar, David. The Bully Bug: A Monsterrific Tale. 2014. (Monsterrific Tales Ser.). (ENG., Illus.). 144p. (J). (gr. 3-7). 24.99 (978-0-7653-3082-6(2), 9780765330826, Starscape) Doherty, Tom Assocs., LLC.

—The Gloomy Ghost. 2014. (Monsterrific Tales Ser.). (ENG., Illus.). 144p. (J). (gr. 3-7). 15.99 (978-0-7653-3080-2(6), 9780765330802, Starscape) Doherty, Tom Assocs., LLC.

Lund, Deb. Monsters on Machines. Neubecker, Robert, illus. 2017. (ENG.). 40p. (J). (gr. -1-3). pap. 6.99 (978-0-544-92783-4(4), HMH Books For Young Readers) Houghton Mifflin Harcourt Publishing Co.

—Monsters on Machines. Neubecker, Robert, illus. 2017. (ENG.). (J). (gr. -1-3). lib. bdg. 17.20 **(978-0-606-39815-2(5))** Turtleback Bks.

Lunetta, Demitria. In the After. 2013. (In the After Ser.: 1). (ENG.). 464p. (YA). (gr. 8). 17.99 (978-0-06-210545-5(0), HarperTeen) HarperCollins Pubs.

Lurie, Susan & Stine, R. L. Monster Survival Guide. 2015. (ENG., Illus.). 96p. (J). (gr. 3-8). pap. 7.99 (978-0-545-82126-1(6)) Scholastic, Inc.

Maberry, Jonathan. The Orphan Army. 2015. (Nightsiders Ser.: 1). (ENG., Illus.). 400p. (J). (gr. 3-7). 16.99 (978-1-4814-1575-0(1), Simon & Schuster Bks. For Young Readers) Simon & Schuster Bks. For Young Readers.

—The Orphan Army. 2016. (Nightsiders Ser.: 1). lib. bdg. 18.40 (978-0-606-38959-4(8)) Turtleback Bks.

—Vault of Shadows. (Nightsiders Ser.: 2). (ENG.). 464p. (J). (gr. 3-7). 2017. pap. 8.99 (978-1-4814-1579-8(4)) 2016. (Illus.). 16.99 (978-1-4814-1578-1(6)) Simon & Schuster Bks. For Young Readers. (Simon & Schuster Bks. For Young Readers).

MacDonald, Ross. Henry's Hand. 2013. (ENG., Illus.). 48p. (J). (gr. k-2). 17.95 (978-1-4197-0527-4(X), Abrams Bks. for Young Readers) Abrams, Inc.

MacHale, D. J. The Monster Princess. Boiger, Alexandra, illus. 2010. (ENG.). 40p. (J). (gr. -1-1). 17.99 (978-1-4169-4809-4(0), Aladdin) Simon & Schuster Children's Publishing.

Maggiore, Lisa. Ava the Monster Slayer. Felten, Ross, illus. 2015. (ENG.). 32p. (J). (gr. -1-k). 16.99 (978-1-63450-151-4(9), Sky Pony Pr.) Skyhorse Publishing Co., Inc.

Magoon, Scott. The Boy Who Cried Bigfoot! Magoon, Scott, illus. 2013. (ENG., Illus.). 48p. (J). (gr. -1-3). 17.99 (978-1-4424-1257-6(7), Simon & Schuster Bks. For Young Readers) Simon & Schuster/Paula Wiseman Bks.

Mahoney, Daniel J. Monstergarten. Kaminsky, Jef, illus. 2013. (ENG.). 40p. (J). (gr. -1-k). 16.99 (978-1-250-01441-2(7), 9781250014412) Feiwel & Friends.

Mahoney, Daniel J., illus. I See a Monster. 2008. (ENG.). 12p. (J). bds. 5.95 (978-1-58117-729-9(1), Intervisual/Piggy Toes) Bendon, Inc.

Manceau, Édouard, illus. Tickle Monster. 2015. (ENG.). 32p. (J). (gr. -1-k). 14.95 (978-1-4197-1731-4(6)) Abrams, Inc.

Mangum, James A. & Spires, Sidney. The Fairy the Chupacabra & Those Marfa Lights: A West Texas Fable. Mangum, James A., illus. 2008. (Illus.). 32p. (J). 17.95 (978-0-9798391-5-3(7)) Hardy, John M. Publishing Co.

Manning, Matthew K. Mystery of the Mist Monster. Neely, Scott, illus. 2016. (Scooby-Doo Comic Chapter Bks.). (ENG.). 88p. (gr. 3-7). pap. 5.95 (978-1-4965-3590-0(1)); lib. bdg. 27.32 (978-1-4965-3586-3(3)) Capstone Press of Coughlan Cos.

Mardani, Parisa. Nathan Sees a Monster But... . 2012. 16p. pap. 15.99 (978-1-4685-9405-8(2)) AuthorHouse.

Markell, Denis. Hush, Little Monster. Iwai, Melissa, illus. 2012. (ENG.). 32p. (J). (gr. -1-1). 9.99 (978-1-4424-4195-8(X), Little Simon) Little Simon.

Marriott, Zoë. The Name of the Blade. 2014. (ENG.). 368p. (YA). (gr. 7). 16.99 (978-0-7636-6957-7(1)) Candlewick Pr.

Marsh, Mike. The Grumblies Set a Trap. Jain, Priti, illus. 2012. 24p. pap. (978-0-9878019-2-0(9)) Yellow Toadstool Pr.

Marsh, Robert. Monster & Me, 1 vol. Percival, Tom, illus. 2009. (Monster & Me Ser.). (ENG.). 40p. (gr. 1-3). lib. bdg. 23.99 (978-1-4342-1589-5(X), Graphic Sparks) Stone Arch Bks.

—Monster in the Outfield, 1 vol. Percival, Tom, illus. 2009. (Monster & Me Ser.). (ENG.). 40p. (gr. 1-3). lib. bdg. 23.99 (978-1-4342-1590-1(3), Graphic Sparks) Stone Arch Bks.

—Monster Moneymaker, 1 vol. Percival, Tom, illus. 2010. (Monster & Me Ser.). (ENG.). 40p. (gr. 1-3). lib. bdg. 23.99 (978-1-4342-1891-9(0), Graphic Sparks) Stone Arch Bks.

Marsh, Sarah Glenn. Fear the Drowning Deep. 2016. (ENG.). 312p. (YA). (gr. 6). 16.99 (978-1-5107-0348-3(9), Sky Pony Pr.) Skyhorse Publishing Co., Inc.

Martín Anguita, Carmen & Carmen, Martín Anguita. Cuando Llega la Noche. Cortazar, Alicia Canas, illus. 2008. (SPA.). 32p. (J). 10.99 (978-84-241-5400-4(2)) Everest Editora ESP. Dist: Lectorum Pubns., Inc.

Martin, Benjamin. Samurai Awakening. 2012. (ENG.). 320p. (J). (gr. 7-12). 17.99 (978-4-8053-1228-5(9)) Tuttle Publishing.

—Samurai Awakening: (Samurai Awakening Book 1) 2016. (ENG.). 320p. (J). (gr. 7-12). 8.99 (978-0-8048-4737-7(1)) Tuttle Publishing.

Martin, Nicole. The Werewolf. 2006. 146p. pap. 14.99 (978-1-4120-8802-2(X)) Trafford Publishing.

Martin, Paul & Boisteau, Manu. Runaway Zombie! #8, 8 vols. 2011. (Monster Manor Ser.). (Illus.). 96p. (J). (gr. 3-6). 24.21 (978-1-59961-889-0(3)) Spotlight.

Martin, Paul, et al. Beatrice's Spells: #3, 3 vols. 2011. (Monster Manor Ser.). (Illus.). 96p. (J). (gr. 3-6). 24.21 (978-1-59961-884-5(2)) Spotlight.

—Count Snobula Vamps It Up: #6, 6 vols. 2011. (Monster Manor Ser.). (Illus.). 96p. (J). (gr. 3-6). 24.21 (978-1-59961-887-6(7)) Spotlight.

—Horror Gets Slimed: #5, 5 vols. 2011. (Monster Manor Ser.). (Illus.). 96p. (J). (gr. 3-6). 24.21 (978-1-59961-886-9(9)) Spotlight.

—Sally Gets Silly: #7, 7 vols. 2011. (Monster Manor Ser.). (Illus.). 96p. (J). (gr. 3-6). 24.21 (978-1-59961-888-3(5)) Spotlight.

—Wolf Man Stu Bites Back: #4, 4 vols. 2011. (Monster Manor Ser.). (Illus.). 96p. (J). (gr. 3-6). 24.21 (978-1-59961-885-2(0)) Spotlight.

Marts, Doreen Mulryan, illus. Even Monsters Say Good Night. 2015. (ENG.). 32p. (gr. -1-2). 14.95 (978-1-62370-256-4(9)) Capstone Young Readers of Coughlan Cos.

Marvel Book Group & Behling, Steve. Marvel Monsters Unleashed: the Gruesome Gorgilla! Marvel Press Artist, (IL, illus. 2017. (Marvel Monsters Unleashed! Ser.). (ENG.). 176p. (J). (gr. 3-7). pap. 6.99 **(978-1-368-00248-6(X)**, Marvel Pr.) Disney Publishing Worldwide.

Matharu, Taran. The Battlemage. 2017. (Summoner Trilogy Ser.: bk.3). (ENG., Illus.). 384p. (YA). 18.99 **(978-1-250-07632-8(3)**, 9781250076328) Feiwel & Friends.

Mathis, Kate. Moon over Monsters. 2013. 318p. pap. 12.95 (978-0-9819789-9-4(1)) PowWow Publishing.

Mattel. Monster High Diaries: Lagoona Blue & the Big Sea Scarecation. 2016. (Monster High Diaries: 3). (ENG.). 160p. (J). (gr. 3-7). 9.99 (978-0-316-30080-3(2)) Little, Brown Bks. for Young Readers.

—Monster High: Great Scarrier Reef 8x8. 2016. (ENG., Illus.). 24p. (J). (gr. -1-3). pap. 3.99 (978-0-316-30127-5(2)) Little, Brown Bks. for Young Readers.

—Monster High: Great Scarrier Reef Reader. 2016. (Passport to Reading Level 3 Ser.). (ENG., Illus.). 32p. (J). (gr. -1-3). pap. 3.99 (978-0-316-30130-5(2)) Little, Brown Bks. for Young Readers.

—Monster High: Great Scarrier Reef: the Deluxe Junior Novel. 2016. (ENG.). 144p. (J). (gr. 3-7). 9.99 (978-0-316-27046-5(6)) Little, Brown Bks. for Young Readers.

—Monster High: the Skultimate Sticker Book. 2014. (ENG., Illus.). 96p. (J). (gr. k-17). pap. 12.99 (978-0-316-27706-8(1)) Little, Brown Bks. for Young Readers.

Mattel & Finn, Pedita. Monster High: Boo York, Boo York: the Junior Novel. 2015. (ENG., Illus.). 160p. (J). (gr. 3-7). pap. 5.99 (978-0-316-30119-0(1)) Little, Brown Bks. for Young Readers.

Mattel & Finn, Perdita. Monster High: Boo York, Boo York: Catty Noir Finds Her Voice. 2015. (Passport to Reading Level 3 Ser.). (ENG., Illus.). 32p. (J). (gr. -1-3). pap. 3.99 (978-0-316-30116-9(7)) Little, Brown Bks. for Young Readers.

Mattel Inc. Staff & Finn, Perdita. Ever after High. 2016. (ENG., Illus.). 32p. (J). (gr. -1-3). pap. 3.99 (978-0-316-35677-0(8)) Little, Brown Bks. for Young Readers.

—Monster High: Boo York, Boo York: Welcome to Boo York. 2015. (ENG., Illus.). 24p. (J). (gr. -1-3). pap. 3.99 (978-0-316-30115-2(9)) Little, Brown Bks. for Young Readers.

Matthews, John. Henry Hunter & the Beast of Snagov: Henry Hunter Series #1. 2016. (Henry Hunter Ser.). (ENG., Illus.). 240p. (J). (gr. 2-7). 15.99 (978-1-5107-1038-2(8), Sky Pony Pr.) Skyhorse Publishing Co., Inc.

May, R. B. Charlie Finds a Friend. 2010. 32p. pap. 12.99 (978-1-4490-6913-1(4)) AuthorHouse.

Mayer, Kirsten. Monster High: Ghoul Spirit: A Monster High Doodle Book. GONZALES, Chuck, illus. 2013. (ENG.). 128p. (J). (gr. 1-17). 12.99 (978-0-316-24655-2(7)) Little, Brown Bks. for Young Readers.

Mayer, Mercer. Mercer Mayer's Little Monster Fun & Learn Book. 2011. (Classic Collectible Ser.: 2). (ENG.). 96p. (J). (gr. -1-3). 12.95 (978-1-60746-419-8(5), Premiere) FastPrncil, Inc.

—Mercer Mayer's Little Monster Home School & Work Book. 2012. (Classic Collectible Ser.: 3). (ENG.). 96p. (J). 12.95 (978-1-60746-945-2(6), Premiere) FastPrncil, Inc.

—Mercer Mayer's Little Monster Word Book with Mother Goose. 2012. (Classic Collectible Ser.: 4). (ENG.). 96p. (J). 12.95 (978-1-60746-688-8(0), Premiere) FastPrncil, Inc.

Mayer, Meyer. Il y a un cauchemar dans Mon. pap. 16.95 (978-2-07-054814-9(7)) Gallimard, Editions FRA. Dist: Distribooks, Inc.

McCann, Jesse Leon. Scooby-Doo & the Fishy Phantom, 1 vol. Duendes Del Sur Staff, illus. 2012. (Scooby-Doo! Set 2 Ser.: No. 2). (ENG.). 24p. (J). (gr. k-3). lib. bdg. 24.21 (978-1-59961-866-1(4)) Spotlight.

McCarty, Peter. The Monster Returns. McCarty, Peter, illus. 2012. (Jeremy & the Monster Ser.). (ENG., Illus.). 40p. (J). (gr. -1-1). 16.99 (978-0-8050-9030-7(4), 9780805090307, Holt, Henry & Co. Bks. For Young Readers) Holt, Henry & Co.

McCurry, Meryl. The Seamonster's Back. 2005. (J). per. 8.99 (978-0-9764690-4-9(9)) Professional Publishing Hse. LLC.

McDermott, Tom. Otis Steele & the Taileebone: A Southern Tall Tale, 1 vol. Crosby, Jeff, illus. 2013. (ENG.). 32p. (J). (gr. k-2). 16.99 (978-1-4556-1736-4(9)) Pelican Publishing Co., Inc.

McDonald, Ann-Eve. There are No Such Thing as Monsters. 2004. (J). (978-0-9770158-4-9(X)) BeachWalk Bks. Inc.

McDonnell, Patrick. The Monsters' Monster. 2012. (ENG., Illus.). 40p. (J). (gr. -1-3). 17.00 (978-0-316-04547-6(0)) Little Brown & Co.

McElligott, Matthew. Even Monsters Need Haircuts. McElligott, Matthew, illus. (ENG., Illus.). (J). 2015. 30p. (gr. -1-2). bds. 6.99 (978-0-8027-3839-4(7), 9780802738394) 2012. 40p. (gr. k-8). pap. 8.99 (978-0-8027-2801-2(4), 9780802728012) Bloomsbury Publishing USA. (Bloomsbury USA Childrens).

McGee, Warner, illus. Monster Halloween Party. 2007. (Backyardigans Ser.). (ENG.). 14p. (J). (gr. -1-k). bds. 6.99 (978-1-4169-3435-6(9), Simon Spotlight/Nickelodeon) Simon Spotlight/Nickelodeon.

McGrath, Raymond, illus. The Moon: Individual Title Six-Packs. (Sails Literacy Ser.). 16p. (gr. k-18). 27.00 (978-0-7635-4426-3(4)) Rigby Education.

McHale, Remme. No Place for Niappy. 2010. 28p. pap. 12.85 (978-1-4490-6900-1(2)) AuthorHouse.

Mcintyre, Mel. The Legend of Lumpus & Ogols. McQuillan, David, illus. 2009. 28p. pap. 10.95 (978-1-935137-96-2(4)) Guardian Angel Publishing, Inc.

McIsaac, Meaghan. The Boys of Fire & Ash. 2015. (ENG.). 336p. (J). (gr. 5). 19.99 (978-0-375-99167-7(0), Delacorte Bks. for Young Readers) Random Hse. Children's Bks.

McKee. Two Monsters. Date not set. 25p. (J). pap. (978-0-05-004546-6(6)) Addison-Wesley Longman, Inc.

McKee, David. Elmer & the Monster. McKee, David, illus. 2014. (Illus.). 32p. (J). (gr. -1-3). 16.95 (978-1-4677-4200-9(7)) Lerner Publishing Group.

—Not Now, Bernard. 2015. (ENG., Illus.). 32p. (J). (gr. -1-k). pap. 10.99 (978-1-78344-290-4(5)); 35th ed. 24.99 (978-1-78344-298-0(0)) Andersen Pr. GBR. Dist: Independent Pubs. Group.

—Three Monsters. 2007. (ENG., Illus.). 32p. (J). (gr. -1-7). 14.95 (978-1-59354-121-7(X), Handprint Bks.) Chronicle Bks. LLC.

McKee, David & Mckee, David. Tres Monstruos. 2006. (SPA., Illus.). 24p. (J). (gr. -1-2). (978-980-257-317-2(5)) Ekare, Ediciones.

McKenna, James. The Mind Traveller. 2013. 212p. pap. (978-0-9569723-8-5(1)) Lone Cloud Publishing.

McKissack, Patricia C. & Moss, Onawumi Jean. Precious & the Boo Hag. Brooker, Kyrsten, illus. 2005. (ENG.). 40p. (J). (gr. -1-3). 17.99 (978-0-689-85194-0(4), Atheneum Bks. for Young Readers) Simon & Schuster Children's Publishing.

McKown, Martha. The Adventures of Zingway, the Monster. 2011. 28p. 12.03 (978-1-4567-1087-3(7)) AuthorHouse.

McNamee, Graham. Bonechiller. 2012. (ENG.). 304p. (YA). (gr. 7). pap. 9.99 (978-0-307-97593-5(2), Ember) Random Hse. Children's Bks.

McNish, Cliff. Silver World. 2008. (ENG.). 248p. (J). (gr. 4-7). pap. 6.95 (978-1-58013-879-6(9), First Avenue Editions) Lerner Publishing Group.

McShane, Pol. Return to Animal Land: The Adventures of Johnny & Joey. 2007. 132p. (J). per. 10.95 (978-0-595-45804-2(1)) iUniverse, Inc.

Medina, Andre, illus. Meet the Monsters. 2015. (Hotel Transylvania 2 Ser.). (ENG.). 16p. (J). (gr. -1-3). pap. 5.99 (978-1-4814-4802-4(1), Simon Spotlight) Simon Spotlight.

Meister, Cari. Moopy el Monstruo Subterráneo/Moopy the Underground Monster. Heck, Claudia M., tr. from ENG. Messner, Dennis, illus. 2012. (Los Amigos Monstruos/Monster Friends Ser.). (SPA & MUL.). 32p. (gr. 2-3). lib. bdg. 22.65 (978-1-4342-3785-9(0), Bilingual Stone Arch Readers) Stone Arch Bks.

—Moopy on the Beach, 1 vol. Messner, Dennis, illus. 2010. (Monster Friends Ser.). (ENG.). 32p. (gr. 2-3). pap. 6.25 (978-1-4342-2304-3(3)); lib. bdg. 22.65 (978-1-4342-1874-2(0)) Stone Arch Bks.

—Moopy the Underground Monster, 1 vol. Messner, Dennis, illus. 2009. (Monster Friends Ser.). (ENG.). 32p. (gr. 2-3). 22.65 (978-1-4342-1630-4(6)); pap. 6.25 (978-1-4342-1745-5(0)) Stone Arch Bks.

—Ora - El Monstruo Marino. Heck, Claudia M., tr. from ENG. Messner, Dennis, illus. 2012. (Los Amigos Monstruos/Monster Friends Ser.).Tr. of Ora - The Sea Monster. (MUL & SPA.). 32p. (gr. 2-3). lib. bdg. 22.65 (978-1-4342-3784-2(2), Bilingual Stone Arch Readers) Stone Arch Bks.

—Ora - The Sea Monster. Messner, Dennis, illus. 2009. (Monster Friends Ser.). (ENG.). 32p. (gr. 2-3). pap. 6.25 (978-1-4342-1746-2(9)) Stone Arch Bks.

—Ora at the Monster Contest, 1 vol. Messner, Dennis, illus. 2010. (Monster Friends Ser.). (ENG.). 32p. (gr. 2-3). pap. 6.25 (978-1-4342-2305-0(1)); lib. bdg. 22.65 (978-1-4342-1875-9(9)) Stone Arch Bks.

—Ora the Sea Monster. Messner, Dennis, illus. 2009. (Monster Friends Ser.). (ENG.). 32p. (gr. 2-3). 22.65 (978-1-4342-1631-1(4)) Stone Arch Bks.

—Snorp: The City Monster. Messner, Dennis, illus. 2009. (Monster Friends Ser.). (ENG.). 32p. (gr. 2-3). 22.65 (978-1-4342-1632-8(2)); pap. 6.25 (978-1-4342-1747-9(7)) Stone Arch Bks.

—Snorp el Monstruo de la Ciudad/Snorp the City Monster, 1 vol. Heck, Claudia M., tr. from ENG. Messner, Dennis, illus. 2012. (Los Amigos Monstruos/Monster Friends Ser.). (MUL & SPA.). 32p. (gr. 2-3). lib. bdg. 22.65 (978-1-4342-3783-5(4), Bilingual Stone Arch Readers) Stone Arch Bks.

—Snorp on the Slopes, 1 vol. Messner, Dennis, illus. 2010. (Monster Friends Ser.). (ENG.). 32p. (gr. 2-3). pap. 6.25 (978-1-4342-2306-7(X)); lib. bdg. 22.65 (978-1-4342-1873-5(2)) Stone Arch Bks.

—Three Claws in the City, 1 vol. Messner, Dennis, illus. 2010. (Monster Friends Ser.). (ENG.). 32p. (gr. 2-3). pap. 6.25 (978-1-4342-2307-4(8)); lib. bdg. 22.65 (978-1-4342-1872-8(4)) Stone Arch Bks.

—Three Claws the Mountain Monster. Messner, Dennis, illus. 2009. (Monster Friends Ser.). (ENG.). 32p. (gr. 2-3). 22.65 (978-1-4342-1633-5(0)); pap. 6.25 (978-1-4342-1748-6(5)) Stone Arch Bks.

Meomi (Firm) Staff, contrib. by. The Octonauts & the Only Lonely Monster. 2006. (Octonauts Ser.). (ENG., Illus.). 36p. (J). (gr. -1-3). 15.95 (978-1-59702-005-3(2)) Immedium.

Merritt, Kory. The Dreadful Fate of Jonathan York. 2015. (ENG.). 128p. (J). pap. 9.99 (978-1-4494-7100-2(5)) Andrews McMeel Publishing.

Messner, Kate. Sea Monster & the Bossy Fish. Rash, Andy, illus. 2013. (ENG.). 40p. (J). (gr. -1-k). 16.99 (978-1-4521-1253-4(3)) Chronicle Bks. LLC.

—Sea Monster's First Day. Rash, Andy, illus. 2011. (ENG.). 36p. (J). (gr. -1-3). 16.99 (978-0-8118-7564-6(4)) Chronicle Bks. LLC.

Metzger, Steve. This Is the House That Monsters Built. Lee, Jared D., illus. 2016. (ENG.). 32p. (J). (gr. -1-k). 9.99 (978-0-545-61112-1(1)) Scholastic, Inc.

Meyer, Linda. The Kid in My Closet. Roberts, Miranda, illus. 2008. (ENG.). 32p. (J). pap. 12.95 (978-1-887542-94-4(9)) Book Pubs. Network.

Michalczewski, Raime. Monsters of a Different Color: Being Different Is Beautiful. 2011. 36p. pap. 18.99 (978-1-4567-2769-7(9)) AuthorHouse.

Michelle, Nelson-Schmidt. Jonathan James & Whatif Monster. Michelle, Nelson-Schmidt, illus. 2012. (ENG., Illus.). (J). 12.99 (978-1-61067-131-6(7)) Kane Miller.

Milgrim, David. Some Monsters Are Different. Milgrim, David, illus. 2013. (ENG., Illus.). 36p. (J). (gr. -1-k). 16.99

(978-0-8050-9519-7(5), 9780805095197, Holt, Henry & Co. Bks. For Young Readers) Holt, Henry & Co.
Miller, Kelly Hufnagle. The Monster in the Washer. 2012. 48p. pap. 21.99 (978-1-4772-5187-4(1)) AuthorHouse.
Millsaps, Grace & Murphy, Ryan. You Wouldn't Like Me Without My Coffee. Marin, Danny, illus. 2014. (ENG.). 40p. (J). (gr. k-2). 17.95 (978-0-9904093-0-4(9)) Millfree Mursaps Media.
Milway, Alex. Terror of the Deep: Armed, Dangerous & Covered in Fur! Milway, Alex, illus. 2013. (ENG., Illus.). 256p. (J). pap. 5.99 (978-1-61067-075-3(2)) Kane Miller.
Mongredien, Sue. Harry & the Monster. East, Nick, illus. 2013. (ENG.). 32p. (J). (gr. -1-k). 14.99 (978-1-58925-146-5(6)) Tiger Tales.
Monster at the End of This Book. 2009. (ENG.). 24p. 14.99 (978-1-74181-222-0(4), Ideal Pubns.) Worthy Publishing.
A Monster House: Individual Title Six-Packs. (Sails Literacy Ser.). 16p. (gr. k-18). 27.00 (978-0-7635-4385-3(3)) Rigby Education.
The Monster Next Door, Level 2. 2016. (Ladybird Readers Ser.). (ENG.). 48p. (J). (gr. 2-4). pap. 9.99 (978-0-241-25444-8(2)) Penguin Bks., Ltd. GBR. Dist: Independent Pubs. Group.
The Monster of Mirror Mountain: Individual Title Six-Packs. (Literatura 2000 Ser.). (gr. 2-3). 33.00 (978-0-7635-0231-7(6)) Rigby Education.
Monster Party: Individual Title Six-Packs. (Chiquilibros Ser.). (gr. k-1). 23.00 (978-0-7635-0422-9(X)) Rigby Education.
Monster Stories. 2003. 256p. (J). 5.98 (978-1-4054-1008-3(6)) Parragon, Inc.
Monstrata, Nessi. Monster High Diaries, Set. 2016. (Monster High Diaries). (ENG.). 768p. (J). (gr. 3-7). 50.00 (978-0-316-27353-4(8)) Little, Brown Bks. for Young Readers.
—Monster High Diaries: Clawdeen Wolf & the Freaky-Fabulous Fashion Show. 2016. (Monster High Diaries: 4). (ENG., Illus.). 160p. (J). (gr. 3-7). 9.99 (978-0-316-30078-0(0)) Little, Brown Bks. for Young Readers.
—Monster High Diaries: Cleo & the Creeperific Mummy Makeover. 2016. (Monster High Diaries: 5). (ENG.). 160p. (J). (gr. 3-7). 9.99 (978-0-316-26636-9(1)) Little, Brown Bks. for Young Readers.
—Monster High Diaries: Draculaura & the New Stepmomster. 2015. (Monster High Diaries: 1). (ENG.). 160p. (J). (gr. 3-7). 9.99 (978-0-316-30084-1(5)) Little, Brown Bks. for Young Readers.
—Monster High Diaries: Frankie Stein & the New Ghoul in School. 2015. (Monster High Diaries: 2). (ENG., Illus.). 160p. (J). (gr. 3-7). 9.99 (978-0-316-30094-0(2)) Little, Brown Bks. for Young Readers.
El monstruo de Montespejo: Individual Title Six-Packs. (Literatura 2000 Ser.). (SPA.). (gr. 2-3). 33.00 (978-0-7635-1265-1(6)) Rigby Education.
Montgomery, R. A. The Abominable Snowman Peguy, Laurence, illus. 2006. (Choose Your Own Adventure Ser.). 144p. (J). (gr. 4-8). per. 6.99 (978-1-933390-01-7(8), CHCL01) Chooseco LLC.
Montoya, Martha, creator. Cenando con el Monstruo: Take-Home. 2005. (Los Kitos Ser.). (SPA.). (YA). (gr. 1-3). 15.00 (978-0-8215-8813-0(3)) Sadlier, William H. Inc.
Moore, Ashley L. The Story of Princess K. 2012. 20p. pap. 24.95 (978-1-4626-6800-7(3)) America Star Bks.
Moore, Julianne. Best Friends Forever. Pham, LeUyen, illus. 2017. (Step into Reading Ser.). (ENG.). 32p. (J). (gr. -1-1). 15.99 (978-0-375-97369-7(9), Random Hse. Bks. for Young Readers) Random Hse. Children's Bks.
Moore, Nicholas & Murton, Gareth. Princess Lydia & the wailing Monster. 2008. 32p. pap. 18.95 (978-1-4092-4993-1(X)) Lulu Pr., Inc.
Morales, Yuyi. Niño: Wrestles the World. Morales, Yuyi, illus. 2013. (ENG., Illus.). 40p. (J). (gr. -1-3). 17.99 (978-1-59643-604-6(2), 9781596436046) Roaring Brook Pr.
Morpurgo, Michael. Gentle Giant. Foreman, Michael, illus. 2006. 28p. (J). (gr. k-4). reprint ed. pap. 12.00 (978-1-4223-5667-8(1)) DIANE Publishing Co.
Morris, Garvin. Dump Dog. Morris, Garvin, illus. (Illus.). (J). 2008. 32p. pap. 6.95 (978-1-60108-022-6(0)) 2007. 40p. (gr. -1-2). 15.95 (978-1-60108-012-7(3)) Red Cygnet Pr.
Morris, Jennifer E. The Sea Monster. 2014. (Scholastic Reader Level 1 Ser.). (Illus.). (J). lib. bdg. 13.55 (978-0-606-36046-3(8)) Turtleback Bks.
Morrissey, Dean & Krensky, Stephen. The Monster Trap. Morrissey, Dean, illus. 2004. (Illus.). 40p. (J). lib. bdg. 17.89 (978-0-06-052499-9(5)) HarperCollins Pubs.
Mortensen, Lori. The Missing Monster Card, 1 vol. Simard, Remy, illus. 2010. (My First Graphic Novel Ser.). (ENG.). 32p. (gr. k-2). pap. 6.25 (978-1-4342-2284-8(5)); lib. bdg. 24.65 (978-1-4342-1888-9(0)) Stone Arch Bks. (My First Graphic Novel).
Moser, Lisa. The Monster in the Backpack. Jones, Noah Z., illus. 2013. (Candlewick Sparks Ser.). (ENG.). 40p. (J). (gr. k-4). pap. 3.99 (978-0-7636-6643-9(2)) Candlewick Pr.
Moulton, Courtney Allison. Wings of the Wicked. 2012. (Angelfire Ser.: 2). (ENG.). 528p. (YA). (gr. 9). 17.99 (978-0-06-200236-5(8), Tegen, Katherine Bks) HarperCollins Pubs.
Munch. 2015. (ENG., Illus.). 24p. (J). (gr. k-4). 7.99 (978-1-85733-731-0(X)); 19.99 (978-1-85733-732-7(8)) Lerner Publishing Group.
Murphy, Jill. All for One. 2004. (Illus.). (J). (gr. -1-2). spiral bd. (978-0-616-14591-3(8)); spiral bd. (978-0-616-14592-0(6)) Canadian National Institute for the Blind/Institut National Canadien pour les Aveugles.
Murphy, Rose. Monster Mayhem. Arthur, Jenny, illus. 2011. (Pat & Sound Stories Ser.). (ENG.). 12p. (gr. -1). 14.95 (978-1-61524-497-3(2), Intervisual/Piggy Toes) Bendon, Inc.
Murphy, Stuart J. Percy Plays It Safe. 2010. (I See I Learn Ser.). (ENG., Illus.). 32p. (J). (gr. -1-k). pap. 6.95 (978-1-58089-453-1(4)) Charlesbridge Publishing, Inc.
Murray, Diana. Ned the Knitting Pirate. Lammle, Leslie, illus. 2016. (ENG.). 40p. (J). 16.99 (978-1-59643-890-3(8), 9781596438903) Roaring Brook Pr.
My Boyfriend Is a Monster, 4 vols., Set. Incl. I Love Him to Pieces. Tsang, Evonne. Görrissen, Janina, illus. 29.27 (978-0-7613-6004-9(2)); Made for Each Other. Storrie, Paul D. Cowgur, Eldon, illus. 29.27 (978-0-7613-5601-1(0)); No. 3. My Boyfriend Bites. Jolley, Dan. Martinez, Alitha E., illus. 29.27 (978-0-7613-5599-1(5)); No. 4. Under His Spell. Croall, Marie P. Park, Hyeondo, illus. 29.27 (978-0-7613-5602-8(9)); 128p. (YA). (gr. 7-12). 2011. Set lib. bdg. 117.08 (978-0-7613-5598-4(7), Graphic Universe™) Lerner Publishing Group.
My Monster Friends, 6 Packs. (Literatura 2000 Ser.). (gr. 1-2). 28.00 (978-0-7635-0102-0(6)) Rigby Education.
Myers, Walter Dean. Monster. l.t. ed. 2005. 231p. pap. 10.95 (978-0-7862-7363-8(1), Large Print Pr.) Thorndike Pr.
Naifeh, Ted. Courtney Crumrin Volume 4: Monstrous Holiday Special Edition: Monstrous Holiday Special Edition. 2013. (ENG., Illus.). 128p. (YA). 24.99 (978-1-934964-92-7(1), 9781934964927) Oni Pr., Inc.
Namm, Diane. Monsters! 2004. (My First Reader Ser.). (ENG.). 32p. (J). (gr. k-1). pap. 3.95 (978-0-516-24635-2(6), Children's Pr.) Scholastic Library Publishing.
Nelson-Schmidt, Michelle. Jonathan James & the Whatif Monster. Nelson-Schmidt, Michelle, illus. 2013. (ENG., Illus.). 32p. (J). pap. 6.99 (978-1-61067-118-7(X)) Kane Miller.
—Jonathan James & the Whatif Monster. 2013. (ENG., Illus.). (J). 26.99 (978-1-61067-194-1(5)) Kane Miller.
Nemmers, Lee. No Monsters Here! A Bedtime Shadow Book. Zschock, Martha Day, illus. 2015. (ENG.). 7p. (J). 12.99 (978-1-4413-1833-6(X), 9781441318336) Peter Pauper Pr. Inc.
Nesbitt, Kenn. Believe It or Not, My Brother Has a Monster! Slonim, David, illus. 2015. (ENG.). 32p. (J). (gr. k-2). 16.99 (978-0-545-65059-5(3), Cartwheel Bks.) Scholastic, Inc.
Ness, Patrick. A Monster Calls: Inspired by an Idea from Siobhan Dowd. (ENG.). 240p. (YA). (gr. 7). 2016. pap. 9.99 (978-0-7636-9215-5(8)) 2015. pap. 12.00 (978-0-7636-8081-7(8)) Candlewick Pr.
—A Monster Calls: Inspired by an Idea from Siobhan Dowd. Kay, Jim, illus. (ENG.). 224p. (YA). (gr. 7). 2013. pap. 12.00 (978-0-7636-6065-9(5)) 2011. 16.99 (978-0-7636-5559-4(7)) Candlewick Pr.
—A Monster Calls: Inspired by an Idea from Siobhan Dowd. 2011. (Playaway Children Ser.). (YA). (gr. 7-12). 54.99 (978-1-4558-4499-9(3)) Findaway World, LLC.
—A Monster Calls: Inspired by an Idea from Siobhan Dowd. 2013. lib. bdg. 23.30 (978-0-606-31603-3(5), Turtleback) Turtleback Bks.
Neubecker, Robert. Too Many Monsters! A Halloween Counting Book. Neubecker, Robert, illus. 2010. (ENG., Illus.). 26p. (J). (gr. -1-k). bds. 7.99 (978-1-4424-0172-3(9), Little Simon) Little Simon.
Neuman, M. Robert. Clawing & Scratching & Thumping About. 2013. 30p. pap. 9.99 (978-0-9898820-0-2(4)) Mindstir Media.
Newmann, Ed, illus. Marvin Monster's Big Date. 2007. (ENG.). 32p. (J). (gr. -1-3). 6.95 (978-0-9792371-4-0(9)) Keene Publishing.
—Marvin Monster's Teacher Jitters. 2006. (ENG.). 48p. (J). (gr. 4-7). per. 6.95 (978-0-9766805-3-6(X)) Keene Publishing.
Ngo, Lap. The Teaser Monster. Ngo, illus. 2012. 24p. (J). 11.99 (978-0-9838321-9-5(6)) Higher Ground Pr.
Nickel, Scott. Attack of the Mutant Lunch Lady. Smith, Andy J., illus. 2008. (Graphic Sparks Ser.). (ENG.). 40p. (gr. 1-3). per. 5.95 (978-1-4342-0501-8(0), Graphic Sparks) Stone Arch Bks.
—Attack of the Mutant Lunch Lady: A Buzz Beaker Brainstorm, 1 vol. Smith, Andy J., illus. 2008. (Buzz Beaker Brainstorm Ser.). (ENG.). 40p. (gr. 1-3). lib. bdg. 23.99 (978-1-4342-0451-6(0), Graphic Sparks) Stone Arch Bks.
Night, P. J. The Terror Behind the Mask. 2014. (You're Invited to a Creepover Ser.: 19). (ENG., Illus.). 160p. (J). (gr. 3-7). pap. 6.99 (978-1-4814-0460-0(1), Simon Spotlight) Simon Spotlight.
—The Terror Behind the Mask. 2014. (Creepover Ser.: 19). lib. bdg. 17.20 (978-0-606-35797-5(1)) Turtleback Bks.
—There's Something Out There, 1 vol. 2013. (You're Invited to a Creepover Ser.). (ENG.). 160p. (J). (gr. 3-6). lib. bdg. 24.21 (978-1-61479-064-8(7), Essential Library) ABDO Publishing Co.
—There's Something Out There. 2011. (You're Invited to a Creepover Ser.: 5). (ENG.). 160p. (J). (gr. 3-7). pap. 6.99 (978-1-4424-4148-4(8), Simon Spotlight) Simon Spotlight.
Noble, Ron. Letter Beasties. 2013. 34p. 19.95 (978-1-4575-1931-4(3)); pap. 12.95 (978-1-4575-1893-5(7)) Dog Ear Publishing, LLC.
Nolan, Lucy. The Lizard Man of Crabtree County, 1 vol. Kastner, Jill, illus. 2003. (ENG.). 32p. (J). (gr. 1-4). pap. 5.95 (978-0-7614-5144-0(7)) Marshall Cavendish Corp.
Noll, Amanda. Hey, That's My Monster! McWilliam, Howard, illus. 2016. (ENG.). 32p. (J). (gr. k-2). 17.95 (978-1-936261-37-6(5)) Flashlight Pr.
—I Need My Monster. McWilliam, Howard, illus. 2009. (I Need My Monster Ser.). (ENG.). 32p. (J). (gr. k-3). 16.95 (978-0-9799746-2-5(3)) Flashlight Pr.
Nordling, Lee. Andrew the Seeker. Roberts, Scott, illus. 2017. (Game for Adventure Ser.). (ENG.). 32p. (J). (gr. k-3). 25.32 (978-1-5124-1330-4(5), Graphic Universe™) Lerner Publishing Group.
Norton, Andre. The Monster's Legacy. Lee, Jody A., illus. 2017. (ENG.). 160p. (YA). (gr. 7). pap. 13.99 **(978-1-5344-1247-7(6)**, Atheneum Bks. for Young Readers) Simon & Schuster Children's Publishing.
Novotny-Hunter, Jana. My Tail's Not Tired. Bowles, Paula, illus. 2017. (Child's Play Library). (ENG.). 32p. (J). **(978-1-84643-985-8(X))**; pap. **(978-1-84643-986-5(8))** Child's Play International Ltd.
Nuhfer, Heather. Hopes & Screams. 2014. (Monster High Ser.). (ENG., Illus.). 112p. (J). (gr. 3-7). pap. 10.00 (978-0-316-25433-5(9)) Little, Brown Bks. for Young Readers.
Numberman, Neil. Do Not Build a Frankenstein! Weaver, Brian M., illus. 2009. (ENG.). 40p. (J). (gr. -1-3). 16.99 (978-0-06-156816-9(3), Greenwillow Bks.) HarperCollins Pubs.
O'Hearn, Kate. The Flame of Olympus. 2012. (Pegasus Ser.: 1). (ENG.). 400p. (J). (gr. 3-7). 17.99 (978-1-4424-4409-6(6), Simon & Schuster/Paula Wiseman Bks.) Simon & Schuster/Paula Wiseman Bks.
OHora, Zachariah. The Not So Quiet Library. 2016. (ENG., Illus.). 40p. (J). (-k). 17.99 (978-0-8037-4140-9(5), Dial Bks) Penguin Young Readers Group.
Olander, Johan. A Field Guide to Monsters: Googly-Eyed Wart Floppers, Shadow-Casters, Toe-Eaters, & Other Creatures, 0 vols. 2010. (ENG.). 64p. (J). (gr. 3-7). pap. 7.99 (978-0-7614-5728-2(3), 9780761457282, Amazon Children's Publishing) Amazon Publishing.
Onion Head Monster Attacks. 2007. (YA). per. 12.95 (978-0-9793676-0-1(3)) Friedrich, Paul.
Onion Head Monster Attacks (XL) 2006. per. 19.99 (978-0-9793676-3-2(8)) Friedrich, Paul.
Onion Head Monster Bombastic. 2007. (YA). per. 12.95 (978-0-9793676-1-8(1)) Friedrich, Paul.
Onion Head Monster Catastrophic. 2007. per. 11.99 (978-0-9793676-2-5(X)) Friedrich, Paul.
O'Reilly, Sean. The Abominable Snow Kid, 1 vol. 2012. (Mighty Mighty Monsters Ser.). (ENG.). 48p. (gr. 2-3). lib. bdg. 23.99 (978-1-4342-3892-4(X)) Stone Arch Bks.
—Abominable Snow Kid. 2013. (Mighty Mighty Monsters Ser.). (ENG., Illus.). 48p. (gr. 2-3). pap. 6.10 (978-1-4342-4227-3(7)) Stone Arch Bks.
—The Gremlin's Curse, 1 vol. 2012. (Mighty Mighty Monsters Ser.). (ENG.). 48p. (gr. 2-3). lib. bdg. 23.99 (978-1-4342-3894-8(6)) Stone Arch Bks.
—Gremlin's Curse. 2013. (Mighty Mighty Monsters Ser.). (ENG., Illus.). 48p. (gr. 2-3). pap. 6.10 (978-1-4342-4228-0(5)) Stone Arch Bks.
—Hide & Shriek!, 1 vol. Arcana Studio Staff, illus. 2011. (Mighty Mighty Monsters Ser.). (ENG.). 48p. (gr. 2-3). pap. 6.10 (978-1-4342-3417-9(7)) Stone Arch Bks.
—Hide & Shriek!, 1 vol. 2010. (Mighty Mighty Monsters Ser.). (ENG., Illus.). 48p. (gr. 2-3). lib. bdg. 23.99 (978-1-4342-2148-3(2)) Stone Arch Bks.
—Homesick Witch, 1 vol. (Mighty Mighty Monsters Ser.). (ENG., 48p. (gr. 2-3). 2013. Illus.). pap. 6.10 (978-1-4342-4225-9(0)) 2012. lib. bdg. 23.99 (978-1-4342-3893-1(8)) Stone Arch Bks.
—The King of Halloween Castle, 1 vol. 2010. (Mighty Mighty Monsters Ser.). (ENG., Illus.). 48p. (gr. 2-3). lib. bdg. 23.99 (978-1-4342-2150-6(4)) Stone Arch Bks.
—Lost in Spooky Forest, 1 vol. 2010. (Mighty Mighty Monsters Ser.). (ENG.). 48p. (gr. 2-3). lib. bdg. 23.99 (978-1-4342-2149-0(0)) Stone Arch Bks.
—Mighty Mighty Monsters. 2013. (Mighty Mighty Monsters Ser.). (ENG.). 48p. (gr. 2-3). pap. 23.80 (978-1-4342-4364-5(8)); pap. 73.20 (978-1-4342-6144-1(1)) Stone Arch Bks.
—Mighty Mighty Monsters, Set. Incl. Hide & Shriek! Arcana Studio Staff, contrib. by. (Illus.). lib. bdg. 23.99 (978-1-4342-2148-3(2)); King of Halloween Castle. Arcana Studio Staff, contrib. by. (Illus.). lib. bdg. 23.99 (978-1-4342-2150-6(4)); Lost in Spooky Forest. Arcana Studio Staff, contrib. by. lib. bdg. 23.99 (978-1-4342-2149-0(0)); Monster Mansion. Arcana Studio Staff, contrib. by. lib. bdg. 23.99 (978-1-4342-2152-0(0)); My Missing Monster. Arcana Studio Staff, contrib. by. lib. bdg. 23.99 (978-1-4342-2153-7(9)); New Monster in School. Arcana Studio, Arcana, illus. lib. bdg. 23.99 (978-1-4342-2151-3(2)); (gr. 2-3). (Mighty Mighty Monsters Ser.). (ENG.). 48p. 2010. Set lib. bdg. 143.94 (978-1-4342-2672-3(7)) Stone Arch Bks.
—The Missing Mummy, 1 vol. Arcana Studio Staff, illus. 2012. (Mighty Mighty Monsters Ser.). (ENG.). 48p. (gr. 2-3). pap. 6.10 (978-1-4342-4609-7(4)) Stone Arch Bks.
—The Missing Mummy, 1 vol. 2011. (Mighty Mighty Monsters Ser.). (ENG.). 48p. (gr. 2-3). lib. bdg. 23.99 (978-1-4342-3218-2(2)) Stone Arch Bks.
—Monster Beach, 1 vol. 2011. (Mighty Mighty Monsters Ser.). (ENG.). 48p. (gr. 2-3). lib. bdg. 23.99 (978-1-4342-3217-5(4)) Stone Arch Bks.
—Monster Beach, 1 vol. Arcana Studio Staff, illus. 2012. (Mighty Mighty Monsters Ser.). (ENG.). 48p. (gr. 2-3). pap. 6.10 (978-1-4342-4608-0(6)) Stone Arch Bks.
—The Monster Crooks, 1 vol. 2011. (Mighty Mighty Monsters Ser.). (ENG.). 48p. (gr. 2-3). lib. bdg. 23.99 (978-1-4342-3216-8(6)) Stone Arch Bks.
—The Monster Crooks, 1 vol. Arcana Studio Staff, illus. 2012. (Mighty Mighty Monsters Ser.). (ENG.). 48p. (gr. 2-3). pap. 6.10 (978-1-4342-4610-3(8)) Stone Arch Bks.
—Monster Mansion, 1 vol. 2010. (Mighty Mighty Monsters Ser.). (ENG.). 48p. (gr. 2-3). lib. bdg. 23.99 (978-1-4342-2152-0(0)) Stone Arch Bks.
—My Missing Monster, 1 vol. 2010. (Mighty Mighty Monsters Ser.). (ENG.). 48p. (gr. 2-3). lib. bdg. 23.99 (978-1-4342-2153-7(9)) Stone Arch Bks.
—New Monster in School, 1 vol. Arcana Studio, Arcana, illus. 2010. (Mighty Mighty Monsters Ser.). (ENG.). 48p. (gr. 2-3). lib. bdg. 23.99 (978-1-4342-2151-3(2)) Stone Arch Bks.
—The Scare Fair, 1 vol. 2011. (Mighty Mighty Monsters Ser.). (ENG.). 48p. (gr. 2-3). lib. bdg. 23.99 (978-1-4342-3220-5(4)) Stone Arch Bks.
—The Scare Fair, 1 vol. Arcana Studio Staff, illus. 2012. (Mighty Mighty Monsters Ser.). (ENG.). 48p. (gr. 2-3). pap. 6.10 (978-1-4342-4611-0(6)) Stone Arch Bks.
—Science Fair Nightmare, 1 vol. (Mighty Mighty Monsters Ser.). (ENG., 48p. (gr. 2-3). 2013. Illus.). pap. 6.10 (978-1-4342-4226-6(9)) 2012. lib. bdg. 23.99 (978-1-4342-3891-7(1)) Stone Arch Bks.
—The Toy Snatcher, 1 vol. Arcana Studio Staff, illus. 2012. (Mighty Mighty Monsters Ser.). (ENG.). 48p. (gr. 2-3). pap. 6.10 (978-1-4342-4612-7(4)) Stone Arch Bks.
—The Toy Snatcher, 1 vol. 2011. (Mighty Mighty Monsters Ser.). (ENG.). 48p. (gr. 2-3). lib. bdg. 23.99 (978-1-4342-3221-2(2)) Stone Arch Bks.
—The Wolfboy's Wish, 1 vol. 2011. (Mighty Mighty Monsters Ser.). (ENG.). 48p. (gr. 2-3). lib. bdg. 23.99 (978-1-4342-3219-9(0)) Stone Arch Bks.
—The Wolfboy's Wish, 1 vol. Arcana Studio Staff, illus. 2012. (Mighty Mighty Monsters Ser.). (ENG.). 48p. (gr. 2-3). pap. 6.10 (978-1-4342-4613-4(2)) Stone Arch Bks.
Orsi, Tea. Tinker Bell & the Legend of the NeverBeast. 2015. (Disney Fairies Graphic Novels Ser.: 17). (J). lib. bdg. 18.40 (978-0-606-37295-4(4)) Turtleback Bks.
Ortas, Rachel. The Messy Monster Book. 2014. (ENG., Illus.). 96p. (J). (gr. -1-3). 19.95 (978-1-84976-105-5(1)) Tate Publishing, Ltd. GBR. Dist: Abrams, Inc.
O'Ryan, Ray. Monsters in Space! Jack, Colin, illus. 2013. (Galaxy Zack Ser.: 4). (ENG.). 128p. (J). (gr. k-2). 16.99 (978-1-4424-6721-7(5)); pap. 5.99 (978-1-4424-6718-7(5)) Little Simon. (Little Simon).
—Monsters in Space! 2013. (Galaxy Zack Ser.: 4). lib. bdg. 16.00 (978-0-606-32460-1(7), Turtleback) Turtleback Bks.
Otoshi, Kathryn. Simon & the Sock Monster. 2004. (ENG., Illus.). 36p. (J). 16.95 (978-0-9723946-1-1(3)) KO Kids Bks.
Page, Terry. The Saddest Centaur. Page, Terry, illus. (Illus.). 24p. (J). (gr. 2-6). pap. 4.00 (978-1-887864-68-8(7)); lib. bdg. 7.00 (978-1-887864-36-7(9)) Boo Bks., Inc.
Paiva, Johannah Gilman. Is There a Monster in My Closet? Long, Paulette Rich, illus. 2014. (ENG.). 32p. (J). (gr. -1-3). 7.99 (978-1-4867-0002-8(0)) Flowerpot Children's Pr. Inc. CAN. Dist: Cardinal Pubs. Group.
Paquette, Ammi-Joan. Ghost in the House. Record, Adam, illus. (ENG.). (J). (gr. -1-2). 2015. 20p. 9.99 (978-0-7636-7622-3(5)) 2013. 32p. 15.99 (978-0-7636-5529-7(5)) Candlewick Pr.
Parish, Alex. Peter & the Flying Sergeant. 2009. 30p. 21.50 (978-0-9561613-0-7(8)) Parish, Alex GBR. Dist: Lulu Pr., Inc.
Parish, Peggy. No More Monsters for Me! 2003. 22.95 (978-0-673-75926-9(1)) Celebration Pr.
Park, Barbara. Junie B. Jones Has a Monster under Her Bed. unabr. ed. 2004. (Junie B. Jones Ser.: No. 8). 69p. (J). (gr. k-3). pap. 17.00 incl. audio (978-0-8072-0644-7(X), Listening Library) Random Hse. Audio Publishing Group.
Parnell, Fran. The Barefoot Book of Monsters! Fatus, Sophie, illus. 2003. (ENG.). 64p. (J). 19.99 (978-1-84148-178-4(5)) Barefoot Bks., Inc.
Parnell, Fran & Fatus, Sophie. Grim, Grunt & Grizzle-Tail: A Story from Chile. Fatus, Sophie, illus. 2013. (Monster Stories Ser.: 6). (ENG., Illus.). 48p. (J). (gr. 1-4). pap. 8.99 (978-1-84686-910-5(2)) Barefoot Bks., Inc.
—Rona Long-Teeth: A Story from Tahiti. Fatus, Sophie, illus. 2013. (Monster Stories Ser.: 5). (ENG., Illus.). 48p. (J). (gr. 1-5). pap. 8.99 (978-1-84686-908-2(0)) Barefoot Bks., Inc.
Parton, Matthew R. My Closet Monster Ate My Homework, 1 vol. 2009. (ENG.). 30p. 24.95 (978-1-60836-184-7(5)) America Star Bks.
The Party, 6 Packs. (Sails Literacy Ser.). 16p. (gr. k-18). 27.00 (978-0-7635-4414-0(0)) Rigby Education.
Patricelli, Leslie. The Patterson Puppies & the Midnight Monster Party. Patricelli, Leslie, illus. 2010. (ENG., Illus.). 32p. (J). (gr. -1-k). 14.99 (978-0-7636-3243-4(0)) Candlewick Pr.
Patten, E. J. The Legend Thief. Rocco, John, illus. (Hunter Chronicles Ser.: 2). (ENG.). 384p. (J). (gr. 3-7). 2014. pap. 7.99 (978-1-4424-2036-6(7)) 2013. 16.99 (978-1-4424-2035-9(9)) Simon & Schuster Bks. For Young Readers. (Simon & Schuster Bks. For Young Readers).
—Return to Exile. Rocco, John, illus. (Hunter Chronicles Ser.: 1). (ENG.). 512p. (J). (gr. 3-7). 2013. pap. 7.99 (978-1-4424-2033-5(2)) 2011. 16.99 (978-1-4424-2032-8(4)) Simon & Schuster Bks. For Young Readers. (Simon & Schuster Bks. For Young Readers).
Patterson, Rebecca. The Pirate House. 2013. (Illus.). (J). (978-1-4351-4762-1(6)) Barnes & Noble, Inc.
Pavanello, Roberto. The Thing in the Sewers, 1 vol. Zeni, Marco, tr. from ITA. Pisapia, Blasco & Brughera, Pamela, illus. 2012. (Echo & the Bat Pack Ser.). (ENG.). 128p. (gr. 2-3). 9.95 (978-1-4342-4247-1(1)); 25.32 (978-1-4342-3824-5(5), Echo & the Bat Pack) Stone Arch Bks.
Payne, M. D. Fartsunami. Dockery, Amanda, illus. 2013. (Monster Juice Ser.: 2). (ENG.). 192p. (J). (gr. 3-7). pap. 5.99 (978-0-448-46227-1(3), Grosset & Dunlap) Penguin Young Readers Group.
—Fear the Barfitron. Dockery, Amanda, illus. 2013. (Monster Juice Ser.: 1). (ENG.). 192p. (J). (gr. 3-7). pap. 5.99 (978-0-448-46226-4(5), Grosset & Dunlap) Penguin Young Readers Group.
Pearce, Jackson. Fathomless. 2013. (Fairy Tale Retelling Ser.). (ENG.). 320p. (YA). (gr. 10-17). pap. 8.99 (978-0-316-20777-5(2)) Little, Brown Bks. for Young Readers.
Pell, Jason. Woody & the Noble. O'Reilly, Sean Patrick, ed. 2011. (Illus.). 80p. (YA). pap. 14.95 (978-1-926914-33-6(3)) Arcana Studio, Inc.
Peretti, Frank E. The Cooper Kids Adventure Series. 2004. (Cooper Kids Adventure Ser.). (gr. 5-7). 23.96 (978-0-89107-901-9(7)) Crossway.
Perro Monstruoso. (Fantasmas de Fear Street Coleccion). (SPA.). (YA). (gr. 5-8). pap. 7.95 (978-950-04-1930-7(0), EM0316) Emecé Editores S.A. ARG. Dist: Planeta Publishing Corp., Lectorum Pubns., Inc.
Peter Pauper Press, Inc., creator. Teddy the Terrible. 2017. (ENG.). (J). 16.99 **(978-1-4413-2318-7(X))** Peter Pauper Pr. Inc.
Peters, Anna. The Friendly Rubbish Monsters. 2011. 92p. pap. 10.00 (978-1-60911-878-5(2), Eloquent Bks.) Strategic Book Publishing & Rights Agency (SBPRA).
Petracca, C. A. B. The Chronicles of Petr The. 2005. 208p. per. 14.95 (978-1-59858-012-9(4)) Dog Ear Publishing, LLC.
Petty, J. T. & Pope, Paul. The Fall of the House of West. Rubin, David, illus. 2015. 157p. (J). **(978-1-5182-0095-3(8)**, First Second Bks.) Roaring Brook Pr.
Peyo, et al. The Smurfs & the Howlibird. 2011. (Smurfs Graphic Novels Ser.). (ENG., Illus.). 56p. (J). (gr. 2-5). pap. 5.99 (978-1-59707-260-1(5), 9781597072601) Papercutz.
Pfister, Marcus. Rainbow Fish & the Sea Monsters' Cave. 2015. (Rainbow Fish Ser.). (ENG., Illus.). 32p. (J). pap. 9.95 (978-3-314-01733-9(2)) North-South Bks., Inc.
Pike, Christopher, pseud. Monstre de l'Armoire.Tr. of Spooksville. (FRE.). (J). pap. 12.95 (978-2-266-08418-5(6)) Presses Pocket FRA. Dist: Distribooks, Inc.
—The Secret of Ka. 2011. (ENG.). 416p. (YA). (gr. 7). pap. 8.99 (978-0-547-57729-6(X)) Houghton Mifflin Harcourt Publishing Co.
Pilkey, Dav. Dogzilla. Pilkey, Dav, illus. 2014. (Illus.). 32p. pap. 7.00 (978-1-61003-187-5(3)) Center for the Collaborative Classroom.
—Dogzilla. 2003. (ENG., Illus.). 32p. (J). (gr. -1-3). pap. 5.95 (978-0-15-204949-2(5)) Houghton Mifflin Harcourt Publishing Co.
—Dragon's Merry Christmas. 2003. (Dragon's Tales Ser.: Bk. 3). (ENG.). 48p. (J). (gr. -1-3). pap. 5.99 (978-0-439-54848-9(9), Orchard Bks.) Scholastic, Inc.

Pixar, told to. Monsters University Look & Find. 2013. 24p. (J). (gr. 1-3). 7.99 (978-1-4127-9649-1(0), ce47602a-38de-4bb7-82b3-69fb3502ef5d) Phoenix International Publications, Inc.

—Monsters University Play a Sound. 2013. (Illus.). 24p. (J). (gr. 1-3). 12.98 (978-1-4508-1607-6(X), 0e9ec920-3cca-43ee-9d08-a87cc2047168) Phoenix International Publications, Inc.

Poblocki, Dan. The Haunting of Gabriel Ashe. (ENG.). 288p. (J). (gr. 5-9). 2015. pap. 7.99 (978-0-545-40271-2(9)) 2013. 16.99 (978-0-545-40270-5(0)) Scholastic, Inc. (Scholastic Pr.).

—The Stone Child. 2010. (ENG.). 288p. (J). (gr. 3-7). pap. 7.99 (978-0-375-84255-9(1), Yearling) Random Hse. Children's Bks.

Pollock, Hal. Meet the Brittles: In Monstermania. 2009. (ENG.). 32p. (J). (gr. -1-3). 15.95 (978-1-59687-858-7(4)) IBks., Inc.

—Monster at the Bat. 2009. (ENG.). 32p. (J). (gr. 4-7). 15.95 (978-1-59687-884-6(3)) IBks., Inc.

—Monster for President. Parisi, Anthony, illus. 2008. 28p. 14.95 (978-0-9816554-1-3(6)) Esquire Publishing, Inc.

Pollock, Tom. The Glass Republic. 2016. (Skyscraper Throne Ser.: 2). (ENG.). 448p. (YA). (gr. 7-9). pap. 14.99 (978-1-68144-348-5(1), Jo Fletcher Books) Quercus NA.

Pope, Paul & Petty, J. T. The Rise of Aurora West. Rubín, David, illus. 2014. (Battling Boy Ser.). (ENG.). 160p. (J). (gr. 5-12). pap. 9.99 (978-1-62672-009-1(6), 9781626720091, First Second Bks.) Roaring Brook Pr.

Posner-Sanchez, Andrea. Fang-Tastic! (Disney Junior: Henry Hugglemonster) Laguna, Fabio & Gallego, James, illus. 2015. (Little Golden Book Ser.). (ENG.). 24p. (J). (-k). 4.99 (978-0-7364-3348-8(1), Golden/Disney) Random Hse. Children's Bks.

—The Hugglefish (Disney Junior: Henry Hugglemonster) Laguna, Fabio & Gallego, James, illus. 2015. (Little Golden Book Ser.). (ENG.). 24p. (J). (-k). 4.99 (978-0-7364-3360-0(0), Golden/Disney) Random Hse. Children's Bks.

—Monster Time (Disney/Pixar Monsters, Inc.) Tilley, Scott & Becker, Ken, illus. 2013. (Nifty Lift-And-Look Ser.). (ENG.). 12p. (J). (-k). bds. 5.99 (978-0-7364-3060-9(1), RH/Disney) Random Hse. Children's Bks.

—Monsters in a Box (Disney/Pixar Monsters University) Random House Disney Staff, illus. 2013. (Friendship Box Ser.). (ENG.). 48p. (J). (— 1). bds. 10.99 (978-0-7364-2989-4(1), RH/Disney) Random Hse. Children's Bks.

Pratchett, Terry. A Hat Full of Sky. (Tiffany Aching Ser.: 2). (YA). (gr. 8). 2015. (ENG.). 400p. pap. 9.99 (978-0-06-243527-9(2)) 2004. 288p. 17.99 (978-0-06-058660-7(5)) HarperCollins Pubs.

—A Hat Full of Sky. 2005. 407p. (gr. 7). 19.00 (978-0-7569-5126-9(7)) Perfection Learning Corp.

—A Hat Full of Sky. 2005. (Discworld Ser.: 32). 407p. (YA). 19.65 (978-1-4177-2658-5(X), Turtleback) Turtleback Bks.

Preller, James. Swamp Monster. Bruno, Iacopo, illus. 2015. (Scary Tales Ser.: 6). (ENG.). 96p. (J). (gr. 2-5). 15.99 (978-1-250-04097-8(3), 9781250040978) Feiwel & Friends.

Priddy, Roger. Spooky Bus. 2013. (Shaped Board Bks.). (ENG., Illus.). 6p. (J). (gr. -1-k). bds. 6.99 (978-0-312-51618-5(5), 9780312516185, Priddy Bks.) St. Martin's Pr.

Primavera, Elise. Fred & Anthony Meet the Heinie Goblins from the Black Lagoon. Primavera, Elise, illus. rev. ed. 2008. (ENG., Illus.). 128p. (J). (gr. 2-4). pap. 4.99 (978-0-7868-3682-6(2)) Hyperion Bks. for Children.

Primavera, Elise & Arevamirp, Esile. Fred & Anthony Escape from the Netherworld. Primavera, Elise, illus. 2007. (ENG., Illus.). 128p. (J). (gr. 2-6). pap. 4.99 (978-0-7868-3678-9(4)) Hyperion Pr.

Proctor, Darrell. The Cigarette Monster. 2006. (J). pap. 8.00 (978-0-8059-6790-6(7)) Dorrance Publishing Co., Inc.

Publications International Ltd. Staff. My 1St Look & Find Disney Pixar Friends & Heroes. 2007. 18p. (J). 9.98 (978-1-4127-6848-1(9), PIL Kids) Publications International, Ltd.

Publications International Ltd. Staff, ed. Busy Little Monster. 2010. 14p. (J). bds. 10.98 (978-1-60553-125-0(1), PIL Kids) Publications International, Ltd.

—Elmo Goes to the Doctor. 2010. 14p. (J). bds. 16.98 (978-1-4127-4609-0(4)) Phoenix International Publications, Inc.

—Full Moon Monster Madness (Look & Find) 2010. 24p. (J). 7.98 (978-1-4508-0154-6(4)) Publications International, Ltd.

—Monsters Can Share. 2010. 20p. bds. 10.98 (978-1-60553-464-0(1), PIL Kids) Publications International, Ltd.

—Potty Time for Monsters. 2011. 14p. (J). bds. 17.98 (978-1-4508-0572-8(8)) Phoenix International Publications, Inc.

—Sesame Street: Monsters in the Bathroom. 2009. 18p. (J). bds. 10.98 (978-1-4127-1734-2(5), PIL Kids) Publications International, Ltd.

—Sesame Street Happy Birthday to You. 2013. 12p. (J). bds. 9.98 (978-1-4508-6159-5(8), 0fc64c9f-9454-4eb3-b56f-9c42ccb72c61) Phoenix International Publications, Inc.

Punter, Russell. Monsters, Stories Of. 2004. (Young Reading Series One Ser.). 48p. (J). (gr. 2-18). pap. 5.95 (978-0-7945-0757-2(3), Usborne) EDC Publishing.

Quinn, Jordan. Sea Monster! McPhillips, Robert, illus. 2014. (Kingdom of Wrenly Ser.: 3). (ENG.). 128p. (J). (gr. k-4). pap. 5.99 (978-1-4814-0072-5(X), Little Simon) Little Simon.

R. Dixon, Jackie. Gilroy the Fairy Collector. 2015. (ENG.). 369p. (J). (gr. 4-6). mass mkt. 11.95 (978-1-78455-407-1(3), ef247b99-9022-425a-8ff9-42e8f9da0689) Austin, Stan AUS. Dist: Bookmasters Distribution.

The Race Car: Individual Title Six-Packs. (Sails Literacy Ser.). 16p. (gr. k-18). 27.00 (978-0-7635-4438-6(8)) Rigby Education.

Ralph, Brian. Cave In. 2013. (ENG., Illus.). 96p. (J). (gr. 7-12). pap. 14.95 (978-1-77046-094-2(2), 9781770460942) Drawn & Quarterly Pubns. CAN. Dist: Macmillan.

Ramos, Mario. A La Cama, Monstruito! (SPA.). 32p. (J). 16.95 (978-84-8470-007-4(0)) Corimbo, Editorial S.L. ESP. Dist: Lectorum Pubns., Inc., Distribooks, Inc.

Rand, Johnathan. Amer Ch Double Thrillers. 2010. 256p. pap. 6.99 (978-1-893699-26-7(9)) AudioCraft Publishing, Inc.

Rand, Jonathan. Michigan Chillers #14 Bionic Bats Bay City. 2007. 208p. (J). pap. 5.99 (978-1-893699-65-6(X)) AudioCraft Publishing, Inc.

Randall, Thomas & Golden, Christopher. Spirits of the Noh. 2011. (ENG.). 272p. (YA). (gr. 7-18). pap. 9.99 (978-1-59990-251-7(6), 9781599902517, Bloomsbury USA Childrens) Bloomsbury Publishing USA.

Rao, Lisa. Don't Bite Your Friends! 2009. (Yo Gabba Gabba! Ser.). (ENG.). 10p. (J). (gr. -1-2). 8.99 (978-1-4169-9014-7(3), Simon Spotlight) Simon Spotlight.

Rasheed, M. Monsters 101, Book One. 2007. 152p. pap. 15.00 (978-1-4303-2946-6(7)) Lulu Pr., Inc.

Raughley, Sarah. Fate of Flames. 2016. (Effigies Ser.: 1). (ENG., Illus.). 368p. (YA). (gr. 9). 17.99 (978-1-4814-6677-6(1), Simon Pulse) Simon Pulse.

Really Scary Stuff [Capstone Sole Source]. 2010. (Really Scary Stuff Ser.). 24p. lib. bdg. 95.96 (978-1-4296-5877-5(0), First Facts) Capstone Press of Coughlan Cos.

Reasoner, Charles & Wood, Steven. Little Monster. 2015. (Charles Reasoner Halloween Bks.). (ENG., Illus.). 12p. (gr. -1 — 1). bds. 5.99 (978-1-4795-8502-1(5)) Picture Window Bks.

Redbank, Tennant. The Secret Sea Monster. 2016. (Barbie Chapters Ser.). (ENG., Illus.). 64p. (J). (gr. 1-4). 5.99 (978-1-101-93844-7(7), Random Hse. Bks. for Young Readers) Random Hse. Children's Bks.

Reed, Len. Monsters at My Bed. 2011. 16p. (gr. 1-2). pap. 8.49 (978-1-4567-6786-0(0)) AuthorHouse.

Regan, Patrick. The Marvelous Monsters Talent Show. Bonson, Tom, illus. 2014. (J). (978-1-4351-5617-3(X), Blackbirch Pr., Inc.) Barnes & Noble, Inc.

Reida, Sarah Schauerte. Monsterville: a Lissa Black Production. 2016. (ENG.). 368p. (J). (gr. 2-7). 16.99 (978-1-5107-0733-7(6), Sky Pony Pr.) Skyhorse Publishing Co., Inc.

Reidy, Hannah. Crazy Creature Colors. Mackie, Clare, illus. 2003. (Crazy Creatures Ser.). 26p. (J). pap. (978-1-84089-221-5(8)) Zero to Ten, Ltd.

—Crazy Creatures Counting. Mackie, Clare, illus. 2003. (Crazy Creatures Ser.). 26p. (J). pap. (978-1-84089-220-8(X)) Zero to Ten, Ltd.

Reilly, Michael. Monster Sandwich. 2009. 50p. (J). pap. 31.99 (978-1-4415-0056-4(1)) Xlibris Corp.

Reiner, Carl. Tell Me A Scary Story... but Not Too Scary. 2009. (ENG.). (J). (gr. 1-3). 18.95 incl. lp (978-1-59687-926-3(2)) IBks., Inc.

Reschke, Kathleen. Monsters in My Basement. 2009. 72p. pap. 24.99 (978-1-4389-5793-7(9)) AuthorHouse.

Rex, Adam. Frankenstein Takes the Cake. 2012. (ENG., Illus.). 48p. (J). (gr. 1-4). pap. 7.99 (978-0-547-85062-7(X)) Houghton Mifflin Harcourt Publishing Co.

Rex, Michael. Goodnight Goon: A Petrifying Parody. Rex, Michael, illus. 2012. (ENG., Illus.). 30p. (J). (gr. -1 — 1). bds. 6.99 (978-0-399-26011-7(0), G.P. Putnam's Sons Books for Young Readers) Penguin Publishing Group.

—Goodnight Goon: A Petrifying Parody. Rex, Michael, illus. 2008. (ENG., Illus.). 32p. (J). (gr. -1-k). 15.99 (978-0-399-24534-3(0), G.P. Putnam's Sons Books for Young Readers) Penguin Young Readers Group.

Reynolds, Aaron. Here Comes Destructosaurus! Tankard, Jeremy, illus. 2014. (ENG.). 32p. (J). (gr. -1-k). 16.99 (978-1-4521-2454-4(X)) Chronicle Bks. LLC.

RH Disney. The Frozen Monster (Disney Frozen) RH Disney, illus. 2017. (Pictureback(R) Ser.). (ENG., Illus.). 24p. (J). (gr. -1-2). pap. 4.99 **(978-0-7364-3729-5(0)**, RH/Disney) Random Hse. Children's Bks.

RH Disney. Quest for the Heart. RH Disney, illus. 2016. (Step into Reading Ser.). (ENG., Illus.). 32p. (J). (gr. -1-1). lib. bdg. 12.99 (978-0-7364-8226-4(1), RH/Disney) Random Hse. Children's Bks.

RH Disney Staff. M Is for Monster (Disney/Pixar Monsters, Inc.) RH Disney Staff, illus. 2014. (Little Golden Book Ser.). (ENG., Illus.). 24p. (J). (-k). 3.99 (978-0-7364-3170-5(5), Golden/Disney) Random Hse. Children's Bks.

—Monster Hide-and-Seek. RH Disney Staff, illus. 2013. (Glow-In-the-Dark Board Book Ser.). (ENG., Illus.). 12p. (J). (-k). bds. 6.99 (978-0-7364-3032-6(6), Golden/Disney) Random Hse. Children's Bks.

—Monsters, Inc. Little Golden Book (Disney/Pixar Monsters, Inc.) RH Disney Staff, illus. 2012. (Little Golden Book Ser.). (ENG., Illus.). 24p. (J). (-k). 4.99 (978-0-7364-2799-9(6), Golden/Disney) Random Hse. Children's Bks.

—Monsters University Little Golden Book (Disney/Pixar Monsters University) RH Disney Staff, illus. 2013. (Little Golden Book Ser.). (ENG., Illus.). 24p. (J). (-k). 3.99 (978-0-7364-3034-0(2), Golden/Disney) Random Hse. Children's Bks.

—Scaring Lessons. RH Disney Staff, illus. 2013. (Step into Reading Ser.). (ENG., Illus.). 32p. (J). (gr. -1-1). 3.99 (978-0-7364-3035-7(0), RH/Disney) Random Hse. Children's Bks.

RH Disney Staff, illus. Disney/Pixar Little Golden Book Library (Disney/Pixar), 5 vols. 2014. (ENG.). 24p. (J). (-k). 19.95 (978-0-7364-3163-7(2), Golden/Disney) Random Hse. Children's Bks.

Rhoden, Chris J. B. How Niseag Became a Legend in Scoti. 2008. 48p. pap. 23.99 (978-1-4343-5461-7(X)) AuthorHouse.

Ricci, Christine. Legend Hunters! McGee, Warner, illus. 2007. (Backyardigans Ser.: 9). (ENG.). 24p. (J). (gr. -1-2). pap. 3.99 (978-1-4169-4058-6(8), Simon Spotlight/Nickelodeon) Simon Spotlight/Nickelodeon.

Rice, Morgan. A Charge of Valor. 2013. (Sorcerer's Ring Ser.: 6). 250p. (YA). pap. 14.99 (978-1-939416-18-6(3), Morgan Rice) Morgan Rice Bks.

Richards, Dan. The Problem with Not Being Scared of Kids. Neubecker, Robert, illus. 2015. (ENG.). 32p. (J). (gr. -1-3). 16.95 (978-1-62979-102-9(4)) Boyds Mills Pr.

—The Problem with Not Being Scared of Monsters. Neubecker, Robert, illus. 2014. (ENG.). 32p. (J). (gr. -1-3). 15.95 (978-1-62091-024-5(1)) Boyds Mills Pr.

Riddell, Chris. The Emperor of Absurdia. 3rd ed. 2007. (ENG., Illus.). 32p. (J). (gr. -1-k). pap. 11.99 (978-1-4050-9028-5(6)) Pan Macmillan GBR. Dist: Independent Pubs. Group.

Riddle, Mark. Margarash. Miller, Tim, illus. 2016. (ENG.). 48p. (J). (gr. -1-3). 17.95 (978-1-59270-216-9(3)) Enchanted Lion Bks., LLC.

Rideau, Nicole. What Is a Pookalaka? 2009. 28p. pap. 13.99 (978-1-4389-2275-1(2)) AuthorHouse.

Ridley, R. W. Dèlon City: Book Two of the Oz Chronicles. 2006. (YA). per. 9.99 (978-0-9792067-0-2(7)) Middlebury Hse. Publishing.

Riordan, Rick. The Battle of the Labyrinth, Bk. 4. (Percy Jackson & the Olympians Ser.). (ENG.). (J). (gr. 5-9). 2009. 400p. pap. 7.99 (978-1-4231-0149-9(9)) 2008. 384p. 17.99 (978-1-4231-0146-8(4)) Hyperion Pr.

—The Battle of the Labyrinth. 2011. 9.68 (978-0-7848-3442-8(3), Everbind) Marco Bk. Co.

—The Battle of the Labyrinth. l.t. ed. 2008. (Percy Jackson & the Olympians Ser.: Bk. 4). (ENG.). 462p. (J). (gr. 4-7). 23.95 (978-1-4104-1018-4(8)) Thorndike Pr.

—The Battle of the Labyrinth. 2009. (Percy Jackson & the Olympians Ser.: 4). (J). lib. bdg. 18.40 (978-0-606-02158-6(2), Turtleback) Turtleback Bks.

—The Demigod Diaries. 2012. (ENG.). 256p. (YA). (gr. 5-9). 12.99 (978-1-4231-6300-8(1)) Hyperion Pr.

—The Demigod Files. James, Steve, illus. 2009. (ENG.). 160p. (J). (gr. 5-6). 12.99 (978-1-4231-2166-4(X)) Hyperion Pr.

—Demigods & Magicians: Percy & Annabeth Meet the Kanes. 2016. (ENG.). 224p. (J). (gr. 3-7). 14.99 (978-1-4847-3278-6(2)) Hyperion Bks. for Children.

—The Last Olympian, Bk. 5. (Percy Jackson & the Olympians Ser.). (ENG.). (J). (gr. 5-9). 2011. 432p. pap. 7.99 (978-1-4231-0150-5(2)) 5th ed. 2009. 400p. 17.99 (978-1-4231-0147-5(2)) Hyperion Pr.

—The Lost Hero. 2011. (Heroes of Olympus Ser.: Bk. 1). (ENG.). 576p. pap. 9.99 (978-1-4231-5537-9(8)) Disney Pr.

—The Lost Hero. 2010. (Heroes of Olympus Ser.). (ENG.). 576p. (YA). (gr. 5-9). pap. 12.00 (978-1-4231-4265-2(9)) Hyperion Bks. for Children.

—The Lost Hero. (Heroes of Olympus Ser.). (ENG.). (J). (gr. 5-9). 2012. 592p. pap. 9.99 (978-1-4231-1346-1(2)) 2010. 576p. 19.99 (978-1-4231-1339-3(X)) Hyperion Pr.

—The Lost Hero. l.t. ed. 2010. (Heroes of Olympus Ser.: Bk. 1). (ENG.). 708p. 23.99 (978-1-4104-3359-6(5)) Thorndike Pr.

—The Lost Hero. 2012. (Heroes of Olympus Ser.: 1). (J). lib. bdg. 20.85 (978-0-606-23615-7(5), Turtleback) Turtleback Bks.

—Percy Jackson & the Olympians, Set. 2010. (ENG.). 1744p. (J). (gr. 5-17). 89.99 (978-1-4231-4189-1(X)) Hyperion Pr.

—Percy Jackson & the Olympians. l.t. ed. 2009. (Percy Jackson & the Olympians Ser.). (ENG.). 485p. (YA). 23.95 (978-1-4104-1678-0(X)) Thorndike Pr.

—Percy Jackson & the Olympians. 2011. (Percy Jackson & the Olympians Ser.: 5). (J). lib. bdg. 18.40 (978-0-606-10567-5(0), Turtleback) Turtleback Bks.

—The Sea of Monsters, Bk. 2. 2nd rev. ed. 2006. (Percy Jackson & the Olympians Ser.: Bk. 2). (ENG.). 288p. (J). (gr. 5-9). 17.99 (978-0-7868-5686-2(6)) Disney Publishing Worldwide.

—The Sea of Monsters. 2011. 9.68 (978-0-7848-3440-4(7), Everbind) Marco Bk. Co.

—The Son of Neptune. (Heroes of Olympus Ser.: Bk. 2). (ENG.). (J). (gr. 5-9). 2013. 560p. pap. 9.99 (978-1-4231-4199-0(7)) 2011. (Illus.). 544p. 19.99 (978-1-4231-4059-7(1)) Hyperion Pr.

—The Son of Neptune. l.t. ed. 2011. (Heroes of Olympus Ser.: Bk. 2). (ENG.). 616p. 23.99 (978-1-4104-4122-5(9)) Thorndike Pr.

—The Son of Neptune. 2013. (Heroes of Olympus Ser.: 2). (J). lib. bdg. 20.85 (978-0-606-31759-7(7), Turtleback) Turtleback Bks.

—The Son of Neptune: The Graphic Novel. 2017. (Heroes of Olympus Ser.). (ENG.). 192p. (J). (gr. 5-9). 21.99 (978-1-4847-1621-2(3)) Disney Pr.

—The Titan's Curse, Bk. 3. rev. ed. 2007. (Percy Jackson & the Olympians Ser.: Bk. 3). (ENG.). 320p. (J). (gr. 5-9). 17.99 (978-1-4231-0145-1(6)) Disney Publishing Worldwide.

—The Titan's Curse. 2008. (Percy Jackson & the Olympians Ser.: No. 3). 312p. (J). lib. bdg. 20.00 (978-1-4242-4710-3(1)) Fitzgerald Bks.

—The Titan's Curse, Bk. 3. 2008. (Percy Jackson & the Olympians Ser.). (ENG.). 352p. (J). (gr. 5-9). pap. 7.99 (978-1-4231-0148-2(0)) Hyperion Pr.

—The Titan's Curse. 2011. 9.68 (978-0-7848-3441-1(5), Everbind) Marco Bk. Co.

—The Titan's Curse. l.t. rev. ed. 2007. (Percy Jackson & the Olympians Ser.: 3). (ENG.). 402p. (gr. 5-9). 23.95 (978-0-7862-9701-6(8)) Thorndike Pr.

Riordan, Rick & Venditti, Robert. The Sea of Monsters. Futaki, Attila & Gaspar, Tamas, illus. 2013. (Percy Jackson & the Olympians Ser.). (ENG.). 128p. (J). (gr. 5-9). 19.99 (978-1-4231-4529-5(1)); pap. 12.99 (978-1-4231-4550-9(X)) Hyperion Pr.

—The Titan's Curse. Futaki, Attila & Guilhaumond, Gregory, illus. 2013. (Percy Jackson & the Olympians Ser.). (ENG.). 128p. (J). (gr. 5-9). pap. 14.99 (978-1-4231-4551-6(8)) Hyperion Pr.

—The Titan's Curse. 2013. (Percy Jackson & the Olympians Graphic Novels Ser.: 3). (J). lib. bdg. 26.95 (978-0-606-32286-7(8), Turtleback) Turtleback Bks.

Rioux, Jo. The Golden Twine. Rioux, Jo, illus. 2012. (Cat's Cradle Ser.: 1). (ENG., Illus.). 112p. (J). (gr. 4-7). 9.95 (978-1-55453-637-5(5)) Kids Can Pr., Ltd. CAN. Dist: Hachette Bk. Group.

Ritter, William. Beastly Bones. (Jackaby Ser.: 2). (ENG.). (YA). (gr. 8-12). 2016. 320p. pap. 9.95 (978-1-61620-636-9(5)) 2015. 304p. 17.95 (978-1-61620-354-2(4)) Algonquin Bks. of Chapel Hill.

—Beastly Bones. 2016. (Jackaby Ser.: 2). lib. bdg. 20.80 (978-0-606-39017-0(0)) Turtleback Bks.

Rivas, Spelile & Plascencia, Amira. No Time for Monsters/No Hay Tiempo para Monstruos. Cervantes, Valeria, illus. 2010. (SPA & ENG.). 32p. (J). (gr. -1-3). 16.95 (978-1-55885-445-1(2)) Arte Publico Pr.

Roach. Frogosaurus vs. the Bog Monster. 2013. (Monstrous Stories Ser.: 3). lib. bdg. 14.75 (978-0-606-32002-3(4), Turtleback) Turtleback Bks.

—Monstrous Stories #1: Night of the Zombie Goldfish. 2013. (Monstrous Stories Ser.). (ENG.). 64p. (J). (gr. 2-5). pap. 4.99 (978-0-545-42554-4(9), Scholastic Paperbacks) Scholastic, Inc.

—Night of the Zombie Goldfish. 2013. (Monstrous Stories Ser.: 1). lib. bdg. 14.75 (978-0-606-31523-4(3), Turtleback) Turtleback Bks.

Robberecht, Thierry. Superhero School. Goossens, Philippe, illus. 2012. (ENG.). 30p. (J). (gr. -1-k). 16.95 (978-1-60537-140-5(8)) Cobblestone Publishing Co.

Roberts, Chris. A Mcspooky Halloween. 2006. (J). pap. 9.00 (978-0-8059-7196-5(3)) Dorrance Publishing Co., Inc.

Roberts, Daniel. Harrison & His Dinosaur Robot & the Purple Spotted Sea Monster. 2012. 36p. pap. 20.99 (978-1-4772-6979-4(7)) AuthorHouse.

Roberts, Jeyn. Dark Inside. (ENG.). (YA). (gr. 9). 2012. 352p. pap. 10.99 (978-1-4424-2352-7(8)) 2011. 336p. 17.99 (978-1-4424-2351-0(X)) Simon & Schuster Bks. For Young Readers. (Simon & Schuster Bks. For Young Readers).

—Rage Within. (ENG., 368p. (YA). (gr. 9). 2013. Illus.). pap. 9.99 (978-1-4424-2355-8(2)) 2012. 17.99 (978-1-4424-2354-1(4)) Simon & Schuster Bks. For Young Readers. (Simon & Schuster Bks. For Young Readers).

Roberts, Rachel. The Warlock Diaries Omnibus. Shiei, illus. 2010. (Avalon: Web of Magic Ser.). (ENG.). 304p. (J). (gr. 3-6). pap. 11.99 (978-1-934876-88-6(7), 9781934876886) Seven Seas Entertainment, LLC.

Robico. My Little Monster 2. 2014. (My Little Monster Ser.). (ENG., Illus.). 176p. (YA). (gr. 9). pap. 10.99 (978-1-61262-598-0(3)) Kodansha America, Inc.

Robinson, Brenda. A Monster Came to Our House. 2013. 40p. pap. 16.46 (978-1-4669-9569-7(6)) Trafford Publishing.

Robinson, Gary. Paranormal: A Billy Buckhorn Supernatural Adventure. 2014. (PathFinders Ser.). (ENG.). 147p. (J). pap. (978-1-939053-08-4(0)) Book Publishing Co.

Robinson, Keith. Valley of Monsters. 2013. 212p. pap. (978-0-9843906-6-3(9)) Roxby Media Ltd.

Robinson, Mark. Vile: A Cautionary Tale for Little Monsters. Horne, Sarah, illus. 2011. (ENG.). 32p. (J). (gr. k-2). 14.99 (978-0-7459-6254-2(8)) Lion Hudson PLC GBR. Dist: Independent Pubs. Group.

Robinson, Nicola. The Monster Machine. Robinson, Nicola, illus. 2013. (ENG., Illus.). 32p. (J). (gr. -1-k). pap. 8.99 (978-1-84365-200-7(5), Pavilion) Pavilion Bks. GBR. Dist: Independent Pubs. Group.

Rockwood, Roy. The Wizard of the Se. 2008. 124p. 23.95 (978-1-60664-931-2(0)); pap. 10.95 (978-1-60664-051-7(8)) Aegypan.

Rodda, Emily. The Golden Door. 2012. (ENG.). 272p. (J). (gr. 3-7). 16.99 (978-0-545-42990-0(0), Scholastic Pr.) Scholastic, Inc.

—The Silver Door. 2013. (Illus.). (J). 278p. pap. (978-0-545-42993-1(5)); (ENG., 288p. (gr. 3-7). 16.99 (978-0-545-42992-4(7)) Scholastic, Inc. (Scholastic Pr.).

—The Third Door. 2013. (J). pap. (978-0-545-42995-5(1), Scholastic Pr.) Scholastic, Inc.

Rodriguez, Lourdes. Mandy, Princess of la la Land: The Green Monster. 2013. 52p. pap. 24.99 (978-1-4817-0077-1(4)) AuthorHouse.

Rogers, Kirsteen. Monsters Sticker Book. 2012. (Sticker Activity Book Ser.). 34p. (J). pap. 8.99 (978-0-7945-3325-0(6), Usborne) EDC Publishing.

Rogers, Michelle Elizabeth. The Adventures of Brutus & Baby: A Haunted Halloween. Collier, Kevin Scott, illus. 2010. 50p. pap. 16.50 (978-1-60860-592-7(2), Eloquent Bks.) Strategic Book Publishing & Rights Agency (SBPRA).

Rosenbaum, Andria Warmflash. Big Sister, Little Monster. Fotheringham, Edwin, illus. 2017. (ENG.). 40p. (J). (gr. -1-3). 17.99 **(978-0-545-83192-5(X)**, Scholastic Pr.) Scholastic, Inc.

Rotellar, Carlos. Little Red Monster: Tales of Monica. 2009. 24p. pap. 11.49 (978-1-4490-2812-1(8)) AuthorHouse.

Rozum, John & Pope, Robert. Scooby-Doo & the Monster of a Thousand Faces!, 1 vol. 2012. (Scooby-Doo Graphic Novels Ser.: No. 2). (ENG., Illus.). 24p. (J). (gr. 2-5). 24.21 (978-1-59961-916-3(4)) Spotlight.

Rubin, Adam. Big Bad Bubble. Salmieri, Daniel, illus. (ENG.). 40p. (J). (gr. -1-3). 2017. pap. 7.99 (978-0-544-92782-7(6), HMH Books For Young Readers) 2014. 16.99 (978-0-544-04549-1(1)) Houghton Mifflin Harcourt Publishing Co.

Rudden, Dave. Knights of the Borrowed Dark. (Knights of the Borrowed Dark Ser.: 1). (ENG.). (J). (gr. 5). 2017. 400p. 7.99 **(978-0-553-52300-3(7)**, Yearling) 2016. 384p. 16.99 (978-0-553-52297-6(3), Random Hse. Bks. for Young Readers) Random Hse. Children's Bks.

Ruiz, Rachel. When Penny Met POTUS. Manwill, Melissa A., illus. 2016. (Fiction Picture Bks.). (ENG.). 32p. (gr. 2-3). lib. bdg. 27.99 (978-1-5158-0218-1(3), Fiction Picture Bks.) Picture Window Bks.

Russell, Shane. Phloomp! 2010. (ENG.). 158p. pap. (978-1-84748-759-9(9)) Athena Pr.

Ryan, John. Pugwash & the Sea Monster. fac. ed. 2009. (ENG., Illus.). 32p. (J). (gr. -1-2). 16.95 (978-1-84507-888-1(8), Frances Lincoln) Quarto Publishing Group UK GBR. Dist: Hachette Bk. Group.

Salter, Charlotte. The Bone Snatcher. 2017. (ENG.). 352p. (J). (gr. 5-9). 16.99 (978-0-399-18634-9(4), Dial Bks) Penguin Young Readers Group.

Saracino, Luciano & Bernatene, Poly. The Monster Diaries. Bernatene, Poly, illus. 2009. (Illus.). 32p. (J). 15.99 (978-1-60010-502-9(5), Worthwhile Bks.) Idea & Design Works, LLC.

Sargent, Dave, et al. Grubby: (Smutty Olive Grullo) Have a Good Disposition, 30 vols., Vol. 31. 2003. (Saddle up Ser.: Vol. 31). (Illus.). 42p. (J). lib. bdg. 23.60 (978-1-56763-691-8(8)) Ozark Publishing.

Sauer, Tammi. Mostly Monsterly. Magoon, Scott, illus. 2010. (ENG.). 40p. (J). (gr. -1-3). 17.99 (978-1-4169-6110-9(0), Simon & Schuster/Paula Wiseman Bks.) Simon & Schuster/Paula Wiseman Bks.

Savage, J. Scott. Evil Twins. Holgate, Doug, illus. (Case File 13 Ser.: 3). (ENG.). (J). (gr. 3-7). 2015. 288p. pap. 6.99 (978-0-06-213338-0(1)) 2014. 272p. 14.99 (978-0-06-213337-3(3)) HarperCollins Pubs.

Sazaklis, John. Goat on a Boat, 1 vol. Bradley, Jessica, illus. 2013. (Comics Land Ser.). (ENG.). 32p. (gr. k-2). 7.95 (978-1-4342-6282-0(0)); lib. bdg. 25.32 (978-1-4342-4944-9(1)) Stone Arch Bks.

Schaefer, Lola M. Frankie Stein, 0 vols. Atteberry, Kevan, illus. 2009. (ENG.). 34p. (J). (gr. k-3). pap. 6.99 *(978-0-7614-5608-7(2)*, 9780761456087, Amazon Children's Publishing) Amazon Publishing.

—Frankie Stein Starts School, 0 vols. Atteberry, Kevan, illus. 2010. (ENG.). 32p. (J). (gr. k-3). 15.99 *(978-0-7614-5656-8(2)*, 9780761456568, Amazon Children's Publishing) Amazon Publishing.

Schauer, M. RIP, M. D. Vosburg, M., illus. 2010. (ENG.). 88p. pap. 12.99 *(978-1-60699-369-9(0)*, 699369) Fantagraphics Bks.

Schmitz, James H. The Other Likeness. 2011. 30p. 14.95 *(978-1-4638-9904-2(1))* Rodgers, Alan Bks.

Schneider, Josh. Bedtime Monsters. 2013. (ENG., Illus.). 32p. (J). (gr. -1-3). 16.99 *(978-0-544-00270-8(9))* Houghton Mifflin Harcourt Publishing Co.

Schnitzlein, Danny. The Monster Who Ate My Peas, 1 vol. Faulkner, Matt, illus. 2010. (ENG.). 32p. (J). pap. 7.95 *(978-1-56145-533-1(4))* Peachtree Pubs.

—The Monster Who Did My Math, 1 vol. Mayer, Bill, illus. (ENG.). 32p. (J). 2012. pap. 7.95 *(978-1-56145-668-0(3))* 2007. 16.95 *(978-1-56145-420-4(6))* Peachtree Pubs.

—Trick or Treat on Monster Street, 1 vol. Faulkner, Matt, illus. 2008. (ENG.). 32p. (J). (gr. k-3). 16.95 *(978-1-56145-465-5(6))* Peachtree Pubs.

Scholastic & Howard, Kate. Fright Knight!, Bk. 2. 2016. (LEGO NEXO Knights Ser.). (ENG.). 80p. (J). (gr. 2-5). pap. 4.99 *(978-0-545-92555-6(X))* Scholastic, Inc.

Scholastic, Inc. Staff. Scooby-Doo: Frankencreepy Movie Reader. 2014. (Scooby Doo Reader Ser.). lib. bdg. 13.55 *(978-0-606-36270-2(3))* Turtleback Bks.

Scholastic, Inc. Staff & Schmidt, Rebecca L. The Power of the Fortrex. 2016. (Scholastic Reader, Level 2 Ser.: 1). (ENG.). 32p. (J). (gr. 1-3). pap. 3.99 *(978-0-545-93338-4(2))* Scholastic, Inc.

Scholastic, Inc. Staff & Stine, R. L. Write Your Fright. 2011. (Goosebumps Horrorland Ser.). (ENG.). 64p. 12.99 *(978-0-545-33295-8(8)*, Scholastic Paperbacks) Scholastic, Inc.

Scholastic, Inc. Staff & West, Tracey. Graduation Day, Bk. 1. 2016. (LEGO NEXO Knights Ser.). (ENG.). 80p. (J). (gr. 2-5). pap. 4.99 *(978-0-545-92554-9(1))* Scholastic, Inc.

Schopp, Bernice Frances. The Legend of Moon-Goblin Town. 2012. 32p. pap. 21.99 *(978-1-4771-4475-6(7))* Xlibris Corp.

Scollon, Bill. Moshi Monsters Super Search. 2013. (Supersearch Ser.: 1). (ENG.). 96p. (J). (gr. 1-3). pap. 8.99 *(978-0-7944-2928-7(9))* Reader's Digest Assn., Inc., The.

Seagle, Steven T. Camp Midnight. 2016. lib. bdg. 29.40 *(978-0-606-37808-6(1))* Turtleback Bks.

—Frankie Stein. 2010. (ENG., Illus.). 48p. 14.99 *(978-1-60706-191-5(0)*, 9781607061915) Image Comics.

The Secret of the Monster Book, 6 vols., Vol. 2. (Woodland Mysteriestm Ser.). 133p. (gr. 3-7). 42.50 *(978-0-7802-7933-9(6))* Wright Group/McGraw-Hill.

Send-up, Maurice. Where the Mild Things Are: A Very Meek Parody. Leick, Bonnie, illus. 2009. (ENG.). 40p. (J). (gr. -1-3). 16.99 *(978-1-4169-9551-7(X)*, Simon & Schuster Bks. For Young Readers) Simon & Schuster Bks. For Young Readers.

Sendak, Maurice. Donde Viven los Monstruos. 2003. (SPA., Illus.). 40p. (J). (gr. k-3). 12.95 *(978-84-372-2185-4(4))* Altea, Ediciones, S.A. - Grupo Santillana ESP. Dist: Santillana USA Publishing Co., Inc.

—Where the Wild Things Are. Sendak, Maurice, illus. 25th anniv. ed. 2012. (ENG., Illus.). 48p. (J). (gr. -1-3). 18.95 *(978-0-06-025492-6(0))*; pap. 8.95 *(978-0-06-443178-1(9))* HarperCollins Pubs.

—Where the Wild Things Are. 2010. (HEB., Illus.). 38p. (J). *(978-965-07-1793-3(5))* Keter Publishing Hse.

—Where the Wild Things Are. (J). pap. 12.95 incl. audio Weston Woods Studios, Inc.

Sendak, Maurice & LaFleur, Richard A. Ubi Fera Sunt: Fabula Ed Picturae. 2015. (LAT.). (J). pap. 24.00 *(978-0-86516-831-2(8))* Bolchazy-Carducci Pubs.

Sensel, Joni. The Garbage Monster. Bivins, Christopher, illus. 2003. 24p. (J). (gr. -1-18). 14.95 *(978-0-9701195-2-0(6))* Dream Factory Bks.

Seroney, Kibny'aanko Arap. Cheebtabuut, Blue Berries & the Monsters Den. 2013. 36p. pap. *(978-1-909204-28-7(5))* BookPublishingWorld.

SFX Fantasy. Tween Tales - Robots, Dragons & the Interworld Machine. 2007. 131p. pap. 12.99 *(978-1-4303-2546-8(1))* Lulu Pr., Inc.

Shankman, Ed. Champ & Me by the Maple Tree. O'Neill, Dave, illus. 2010. (Shankman & O'Neill Ser.). (ENG.). 32p. (gr. -1-3). 14.95 *(978-0-9819430-5-3(5)*, Commonwealth Editions) Applewood Bks.

Shapiro D., Brian. Plaquetooth. 2008. 28p. pap. 13.99 *(978-1-4343-8913-8(8))* AuthorHouse.

Sharp, Michael. Vayda Jayne Bean - Vanilla. Van Tine, Laura, illus. 2007. 20p. (J). (gr. -1-3). pap. *(978-0-9780969-5-3(9))* Avatar Pubns., Inc.

Shelley, Mary. Frankenstein. Barr, Ken, illus. 2005. (Reader's Workshop Ser.). (ENG.). 80p. (C). pap. 17.95 *(978-0-7362-2793-3(8))* CENGAGE Learning.

—Frankenstein. Akib, Jamel, illus. 2006. (Classic Starts(tm) Ser.). (ENG.). 160p. (J). (gr. 2-4). 6.95 *(978-1-4027-2666-8(X))* Sterling Publishing Co., Inc.

—Frankenstein. 2009. (Foundation Classics Ser.). (Illus.). 56p. (J). (gr. 5-9). lib. bdg. 27.95 *(978-1-60754-848-5(8))* Windmill Bks.

—Frankenstein, 1 vol. Ho, Jason, illus. 2007. (Graphic Horror Ser.). (ENG.). 32p. (gr. 4-7). 28.50 *(978-1-60270-059-8(1)*, Graphic Planet- Fiction) ABDO Publishing Co.

—Frankenstein. 2014. (Differentiated Timeless Classics Ser.). (ENG.). 80p. (YA). (gr. 9-12). 12.95 *(978-1-62250-717-7(7))* Saddleback Educational Publishing, Inc.

—Frankenstein. abr. ed. 2010. (Dover Classic Stories Coloring Book Ser.). (ENG.). 48p. (J). (gr. 3-8). pap. 4.99 *(978-0-486-47415-1(1))* Dover Pubns., Inc.

—Frankenstein: With a Discussion of Tolerance. Clift, Eva, tr. Clift, Eva, illus. 2003. (Values in Action Illustrated Classics Ser.). (J). *(978-1-59203-048-4(3))* Learning Challenge, Inc.

—Gris Grimly's Frankenstein. Grimly, Gris, illus. 2013. (ENG.). 208p. (YA). (gr. 8). 24.99 *(978-0-06-186297-7(5))* HarperCollins Pubs.

—Gris Grimly's Frankenstein. Grimly, Gris, illus. 2015. (ENG.). 208p. (YA). (gr. 8). pap. 16.99 *(978-0-06-186298-4(3))* HarperCollins Pubs.

Shelley, Mary, et al. Frankenstein. 2004. (ENG.). 112p. pap. 20.00 *(978-0-582-82301-3(3))* Pearson Education, Ltd. GBR. Dist: Trans-Atlantic Pubns., Inc.

Sherrill, Rusty & Miers, Doug. Kid Nitro & the Sinister Slorp. Sherrill, Cathy, ed. Sherrill, Rusty, illus. 2007. (Illus.). 273p. (YA). per. 14.95 *(978-0-9787729-0-1(3))* RS Art Studio.

Shiels, Tony "Doc". Monstrum! a Wizard's Tale. 2011. 148p. pap. *(978-1-905723-55-3(5))* CFZ Pr.

Shook, Karl. The Family Thing. 2004. 166p. (YA). pap. 12.95 *(978-0-595-31121-7(0))* iUniverse, Inc.

Shopping, 6 Packs. (Sails Literacy Ser.). 16p. (gr. k-18). 27.00 *(978-0-7635-4422-5(1))* Rigby Education.

Shoshan, Beth. Mess Monsters at Christmas. 2009. 24p. (J). pap. 6.99 *(978-1-60010-560-9(2)*, Worthwhile Bks.) Idea & Design Works, LLC.

Shreve, Steve. The Bogey Man: Or a Good Argument for Not Picking Your Nose. Shreve, Steve, illus. 2010. (Adventures of Charlie Ser.). (Illus.). 32p. pap. *(978-0-237-54287-0(0))* Evans Brothers, Ltd.

Siciari, Theresa. The Pond Behind Grandmother's House. 2007. 32p. per. 24.95 *(978-1-4137-8597-5(2))* America Star Bks.

Sierra, Judy. Thelonius Monster's Sky-High Fly Pie. 2010. (ENG.). 40p. (J). (gr. -1-3). pap. 7.99 *(978-0-375-85949-6(7)*, Dragonfly Bks.) Random Hse. Children's Bks.

Sierra, Sergio A. & Shelley, Mary. Frankenstein by Mary Shelley. Ribas, Meritxell, illus. 2012. (Dark Graphic Novels Ser.). 96p. (J). (gr. 5-9). 31.94 *(978-0-7660-4084-7(4))* Enslow Pubs., Inc.

Sill, Cathryn. About Mollusks: A Guide for Children, 1 vol. Sill, John, illus. 2008. (About... Ser.). (ENG.). 40p. (J). (gr. k-3). pap. 7.95 *(978-1-56145-406-8(0))* Peachtree Pubs.

Simon, Francesca. Horrid Henry & the Abominable Snowman. 2010. (Horrid Henry Ser.). lib. bdg. 17.20 *(978-0-606-14063-8(8)*, Turtleback) Turtleback Bks.

Simonson, Louise. Battling Bigfoot. Elston, James W., illus. 2007. (Extreme Monsters Ser.). 94p. (J). (gr. 2-5). per. 3.99 *(978-1-57791-275-0(6)*, Penny Candy Pr.) Brighter Minds Children's Publishing.

—Meet Mr. Hydeous, Vol. 3. Elston, James W., illus. gif. ed. 2006. (Extreme Monsters Ser.). 96p. (J). per. 3.99 *(978-1-57791-255-2(1))* Brighter Minds Children's Publishing.

—Monster Magic, 1 vol. Schoening, Dan, illus. (Wonder Woman Ser.). (ENG.). 56p. (gr. 2-3). 2013. pap. 4.95 *(978-1-4342-2260-2(8))* 2010. lib. bdg. 26.65 *(978-1-4342-1884-1(8))* Stone Arch Bks. (DC Super Heroes).

—What's with Wulf? Elston, James W., illus. gif. ed. 2005. (Extreme Monsters Ser.). 96p. (J). (gr. 2-5). per. 3.99 *(978-1-57791-179-1(2))* Brighter Minds Children's Publishing.

Sinden, David, et al. Sea Monsters & Other Delicacies. Duddle, Jonny, illus. 2009. (Awfully Beastly Business Ser.: 2). (ENG.). 208p. (J). (gr. 3-7). 9.99 *(978-1-4169-8650-8(2)*, Aladdin) Simon & Schuster Children's Publishing.

Singlehurst, Naomi. Grandpa, What's That Sound in the Middle of the Night? Ellen Koski, Rachel, ed. Jamieson, Victoria, illus. 2008. (ENG.). 32p. (J). (gr. k-2). 14.95 *(978-1-930650-24-4(8))* mTrellis Publishing, Inc.

Sirowy, Alexandra. The Creeping: If You Hunt for Monsters, You'll Find Them. 2015. (ENG., Illus.). 400p. (YA). (gr. 7). 17.99 *(978-1-4814-1886-7(6))* Simon & Schuster Children's Publishing.

Sisler, Celeste & Fox, Jennifer. Meet Fawn. 2015. (Passport to Reading Level 1 Ser.). (ENG., Illus.). 32p. (J). (gr. -1-3). pap. 3.99 *(978-0-316-28350-2(9))* Little, Brown Bks. for Young Readers.

Sisler, Stephanie. Matthews Monsters, a Creative Comprehensive Exercise. Grzelak, Kyle, illus. 2011. 32p. pap. 12.95 *(978-1-61493-015-0(5))* Peppertree Pr., The.

—One Bright Monster. Holcomb, Nicholas, illus. 2012. 36p. pap. 12.95 *(978-1-61493-124-9(0))* Peppertree Pr., The.

Skovron, Jon. Man Made Boy. (ENG.). 384p. (YA). (gr. 7). 2015. pap. 10.99 *(978-0-14-242743-9(8)*, Speak) 2013. 17.99 *(978-0-670-78620-6(9)*, Viking Books for Young Readers) Penguin Young Readers Group.

Skrutskie, Emily. The Abyss Surrounds Us. 2016. (ENG., Illus.). 288p. (YA). pap. 11.99 *(978-0-7387-4691-3(6)*, Flux) North Star Editions.

—The Abyss Surrounds Us. 2016. lib. bdg. 23.30 *(978-0-606-38499-5(5))* Turtleback Bks.

Skye, obert. Batneezer. Skye, obert, illus. 2016. (Creature from My Closet Ser.: 6). (ENG., Illus.). 208p. (J). 13.99 *(978-1-62779-163-2(9)*, 9781627791632, Holt, Henry & Co. Bks. For Young Readers) Holt, Henry & Co.

—Lord of the Hat. Skye, obert, illus. 2015. (Creature from My Closet Ser.: 5). (ENG., Illus.). 256p. (J). (gr. 4-7). 13.99 *(978-1-62779-162-5(0)*, 9781627791625, Holt, Henry & Co. Bks. For Young Readers) Holt, Henry & Co.

—Pinocula. Skye, obert, illus. 2013. (Creature from My Closet Ser.: 3). (ENG., Illus.). 256p. (J). (gr. 4-7). 12.99 *(978-0-8050-9689-7(2)*, 9780805096897, Holt, Henry & Co. Bks. For Young Readers) Holt, Henry & Co.

—Potterwookiee. Skye, obert, illus. 2012. (Creature from My Closet Ser.: 2). (ENG., Illus.). 256p. (J). (gr. 4-7). 13.99 *(978-0-8050-9451-0(2)*, 9780805094510, Holt, Henry & Co. Bks. For Young Readers) Holt, Henry & Co.

—Wonkenstein. Skye, obert, illus. 2011. (Creature from My Closet Ser.: 1). (ENG.). 240p. (J). (gr. 4-7). 12.99 *(978-0-8050-9268-4(4)*, 9780805092684, Holt, Henry & Co. Bks. For Young Readers) Holt, Henry & Co.

—Wonkenstein. Skye, obert, illus. 2015. (Creature from My Closet Ser.: 1). (ENG., Illus.). 256p. (J). (gr. 4-7). pap. 6.99 *(978-1-250-01022-3(5)*, 9781250010223) Square Fish.

Slade, Arthur. Monsterology: Fabulous Lives of the Creepy, the Revolting, & the Undead. Mah, Derek, illus. 2005. (ENG.). 96p. (J). (gr. 4-7). pap. 8.95 *(978-0-88776-714-2(1)*, Tundra Bks.) Tundra Bks. CAN. Dist: Penguin Random Hse. LLC.

Slater, David Michael. Milo & the Monster, 1 vol. Ebbeler, Jeff, illus. 2009. (David Michael Slater Set 2 Ser.). (ENG.). 32p. (gr. -1-4). 28.50 *(978-1-60270-656-9(5)*, Looking Glass Library) ABDO Publishing Co.

Slonim, David. I Loathe You. Slonim, David, illus. 2012. (ENG., Illus.). 24p. (J). (gr. -1-2). 15.99 *(978-1-4424-2244-5(0)*, Aladdin) Simon & Schuster Children's Publishing.

Smith, Alexander Gordon. Hellfighters. 2016. (Devil's Engine Ser.: 2). (ENG.). 320p. (YA). 18.99 *(978-0-374-30172-9(7)*, 9780374301729, Farrar, Straus & Giroux (BYR)) Farrar, Straus & Giroux.

—Hellraisers. 2015. (Devil's Engine Ser.: 1). (ENG.). 352p. (YA). (gr. 7). 17.99 *(978-0-374-30169-9(7)*, 9780374301699, Farrar, Straus & Giroux (BYR)) Farrar, Straus & Giroux.

Smith, Caighlan. Children of Icarus. 2016. (ENG.). 312p. (gr. 9-10). 16.95 *(978-1-63079-057-8(5))* Switch Pr.

Smith, Clete Barrett. Magic Delivery. Dziekan, Michal, illus. 2014. (ENG.). 288p. (J). (gr. 3-7). 16.99 *(978-1-4231-6597-2(7))* Hyperion Bks. for Children.

Smith, James J. Mikey's Monster. 2013. (Step into Reading Level 4 Ser.). lib. bdg. 13.55 *(978-0-606-32223-2(X)*, Turtleback) Turtleback Bks.

Smith, James J. & James, Hollis. Mikey's Monster (Teenage Mutant Ninja Turtles) Spaziante, Patrick, illus. 2013. (Step into Reading Ser.). (ENG.). 48p. (J). (gr. k-3). 3.99 *(978-0-449-81826-8(8)*, Random Hse. Bks. for Young Readers) Random Hse. Children's Bks.

Smith, Lisa R. There's a Monster in My Washing MacHine. 2012. 20p. pap. 13.00 *(978-1-4357-6497-2(8))* Lulu Pr., Inc.

Snider, Brandon T. The Attack of the Movie Monsters. 2015. (Transformers 8x8 Ser.). (J). lib. bdg. 14.75 *(978-0-606-37514-6(7))* Turtleback Bks.

—Transformers Rescue Bots: The Attack of the Humungado. 2015. (ENG., Illus.). 24p. (J). (gr. -1-3). pap. 4.99 *(978-0-316-30171-8(X))* Little, Brown Bks. for Young Readers.

Snow, Alan. Here Be Monsters! Snow, Alan, illus. (Ratbridge Chronicles Ser.: 1). (ENG., Illus.). 544p. (J). (gr. 3-9). 2007. per. 9.99 *(978-0-689-87048-4(5))* 2006. 17.95 *(978-0-689-87047-7(7))* Simon & Schuster Children's Publishing. (Atheneum Bks. for Young Readers).

—Worse Things Happen at Sea! A Tale of Pirates, Poison, & Monsters. Snow, Alan, illus. 2014. (Ratbridge Chronicles Ser.: 2). (ENG., Illus.). 352p. (J). (gr. 3-9). pap. 9.99 *(978-0-689-87050-7(7)*, Atheneum Bks. for Young Readers) Simon & Schuster Children's Publishing.

Snow, Jeff. Beasts in the Closet. Snow, Jeff, illus. 2006. (Illus.). 32p. (J). 17.95 *(978-1-932362-11-4(8))* Snowbound Pr., Inc.

Soderberg, Erin. Puppy Pirates #5: Search for the Sea Monster. 2016. (Puppy Pirates Ser.). (ENG., Illus.). 96p. (J). (gr. 1-4). 4.99 *(978-1-101-93776-1(9)*, Random Hse. Bks. for Young Readers) Random Hse. Children's Bks.

Soman, David. The Monster Next Door. 2016. (ENG., Illus.). 40p. (J). (-k). 17.99 *(978-0-525-42783-4(X)*, Dial Bks) Penguin Young Readers Group.

Something Is There & Other Stories: Individual Title Six-Pack. (Story Steps Ser.). (gr. k-2). 48.00 *(978-0-7635-9828-0(3))* Rigby Education.

Sonneborn, Scott. Feet First. Banks, Timothy, illus. 2014. (Frankenstein Journals). (ENG.). 80p. (gr. 2-3). 22.65 *(978-1-4342-8999-5(0))* Stone Arch Bks.

—The Frankenstein Journals, 1 vol. Banks, Timothy, illus. 2014. (Frankenstein Journals). (ENG.). 160p. (gr. 2-3). 9.95 *(978-1-4342-9130-1(8))* Stone Arch Bks.

—The Frankenstein Journals: Guts or Bust. Banks, Timothy, illus. 2015. (Frankenstein Journals). (ENG.). 160p. (gr. 2-3). 9.95 *(978-1-4965-0223-0(X))* Stone Arch Bks.

—I for an Eye. Banks, Timothy, illus. 2014. (Frankenstein Journals). (ENG.). 80p. (gr. 2-3). 22.65 *(978-1-4342-9000-7(X))* Stone Arch Bks.

—A Pain in the Butt. Banks, Timothy, illus. 2015. (Frankenstein Journals). (ENG.). 80p. (gr. 2-3). 22.65 *(978-1-4965-0222-3(1))* Stone Arch Bks.

Soo, Kean. Jellaby, 1 vol. 2014. (Jellaby Ser.). (ENG.). 184p. (gr. 4-6). 55.98 *(978-1-4342-9601-6(6))* Stone Arch Bks.

—The Lost Monster. 2014. (Jellaby Ser.). (ENG.). 160p. (gr. 4-8). 27.99 *(978-1-4342-9195-0(2))* Stone Arch Bks.

—Monster in the City. 2014. (Jellaby Ser.). (ENG., Illus.). 184p. (gr. 4-8). pap. 12.95 *(978-1-4342-6421-3(1))* Stone Arch Bks.

Sowder, G. Wesley & Sowder, Joseph, told to. Hunter-Lee & the Toy Monster: Book One. 2008. 48p. pap. 16.95 *(978-1-60703-137-6(X))* America Star Bks.

Space Monster Saves the Day. 2007. (Spaceboy Chapter Ser.). (J). per. 7.67 *(978-1-932570-61-8(6))* Pioneer Valley Bks.

Spaht-Gill, Janie. Monster Stew. Reese, Bob, illus. (J). 5.95 *(978-0-89868-307-3(6))* ARO Publishing Co.

Spinale, Wendy. Umberland. 2017. (Everland Ser.: 2). (ENG.). 288p. (J). (gr. 7). 17.99 ***(978-0-545-95318-4(9)**, Scholastic Pr.)* Scholastic, Inc.

Spotswood, Jessica. A Tyranny of Petticoats. 2016. (ENG.). 368p. (YA). (gr. 9). 17.99 *(978-0-7636-7848-7(1))* Candlewick Pr.

Spradlin, Michael P. Feeding Frenzy. 2013. (Illus.). 167p. (J). *(978-0-545-62200-4(X))* Scholastic, Inc.

—Killer Species #3: Out for Blood. 2014. (Killer Species Ser.: 3). (ENG.). 192p. (J). (gr. 3-7). pap. 5.99 *(978-0-545-50676-2(X)*, Scholastic Paperbacks) Scholastic, Inc.

—Menace from the Deep. 2013. (Illus.). 225p. (J). *(978-0-545-56366-6(6))* Scholastic, Inc.

—Out for Blood. 2014. 168p. (J). pap. *(978-0-545-67523-9(5))* Scholastic, Inc.

—Out for Blood. 2014. (Killer Species Ser.: 3). lib. bdg. 16.00 *(978-0-606-35398-4(4))* Turtleback Bks.

—Ultimate Attack. 2014. (Killer Species Ser.: 4). lib. bdg. 16.00 *(978-0-606-35853-8(6))* Turtleback Bks.

Spurr, Elizabeth. Monsters, Mind Your Manners! Scales, Simon, illus. 2012. (J). 34.28 *(978-1-61913-124-8(2))* Weigl Pubs., Inc.

Stanford, Cody L. Sinews of the Heart. 2013. 186p. pap. 10.99 *(978-1-62757-059-6(4))* Storm Moon Pr., LLC.

Stanley, John. Melvin Monster, 3 vols., Vol. 2. 2010. (John Stanley Library). (ENG., Illus.). 112p. 24.95 *(978-1-77046-003-4(9)*, 9781770460034) Drawn & Quarterly Pubns. CAN. Dist: Macmillan.

Staunton, Ted. Morgan & the Dune Racer. Slavin, Bill, illus. 2011. (Formac First Novels Ser.). (ENG.). 64p. (J). (gr. 2-3). 14.95 *(978-0-88780-966-8(9)*, 9780887809668); pap. 5.95 *(978-0-88780-965-1(0)*, 9780887809651) Formac Publishing Co., Ltd. CAN. Dist: Casemate Pubs. & Bk. Distributors, LLC.

—Morgan on Ice, 1 vol. Slavin, Bill, illus. 2013. (Formac First Novels Ser.). (ENG.). 56p. (J). (gr. 2-3). 14.95 *(978-1-4595-0289-5(2)*, 9781459502895); pap. 5.95 *(978-1-4595-0290-1(6)*, 9781459502901) Formac Publishing Co., Ltd. CAN. Dist: Casemate Pubs. & Bk. Distributors, LLC.

Steele, Michael Anthony. Monster Mutt Madness. Jeralds, Scott, illus. 2017. (Scooby-Doo! Beginner Mysteries Ser.). (ENG.). 112p. (gr. 2-3). lib. bdg. 22.65 ***(978-1-4965-4767-5(5))*** Capstone Press of Coughlan Cos.

Steer, Dugald A. Snappy Little Halloween. Matthews, Derek, illus. 2004. 20p. (J). (gr. k-4). reprint ed. 13.00 *(978-0-7567-7403-5(9))* DIANE Publishing Co.

Steig, William. Shrek! Steig, William, illus. 20th anniv. ed. 2010. (ENG., Illus.). 40p. (J). (gr. -1-3). 18.99 *(978-0-374-36879-1(1)*, 9780374368791, Farrar, Straus & Giroux (BYR)) Farrar, Straus & Giroux.

—Shrek! Steig, William, illus. 2003. (Illus.). (J). (gr. -1-2). pap. 35.95 incl. audio compact disk *(978-1-59112-551-8(0))* Live Oak Media.

—Shrek!, Set. Steig, William, illus. unabr. ed. 2009. (ENG., Illus.). (J). (gr. -1-3). 9.99 *(978-1-4272-0827-9(1)*, 9781427208279) Macmillan Audio.

—Shrek! 2008. (Illus.). (gr. -1-3). 17.00 *(978-1-60686-207-0(3))* Perfection Learning Corp.

—Shrek! Steig, William, illus. 2008. (ENG., Illus.). 32p. (J). (gr. -1-3). pap. 7.99 *(978-0-312-38449-4(1)*, 9780312384494) Square Fish.

—Shrek! 2008. (J). (gr. -1-2). 18.40 *(978-0-7857-2221-2(1)*, Turtleback) Turtleback Bks.

Stein, Mathilde. Monstersong. Van Der Linden, Gerdien, illus. 2007. (ENG.). 32p. (J). (gr. -1-3). 15.95 *(978-1-932425-90-1(X))* Lemniscaat USA.

Stephens, John. The Black Reckoning. 2015. (Books of Beginning Ser.). (ENG.). 432p. (J). (gr. 3-7). 17.99 *(978-0-375-86872-6(0)*, Knopf Bks. for Young Readers) Random Hse. Children's Bks.

—The Emerald Atlas. (Books of Beginning Ser.). (ENG.). (J). (gr. 3-7). 2012. 448p. 7.99 *(978-0-375-87271-6(X)*, Yearling) 2011. 432p. 17.99 *(978-0-375-86870-2(4)*, Knopf Bks. for Young Readers) Random Hse. Children's Bks.

—The Emerald Atlas. Lt. ed. 2012. (Books of Beginning Ser.). (ENG.). 548p. (J). (gr. 4-7). 23.99 *(978-1-4104-4234-5(9))* Thorndike Pr.

—The Fire Chronicle. 2012. (Illus.). 437p. (J). *(978-0-449-81015-6(1))* Knopf, Alfred A. Inc.

—The Fire Chronicle. (Books of Beginning Ser.). (ENG.). 448p. (J). (gr. 3-7). 2013. 7.99 *(978-0-375-87272-3(8)*, Yearling) 2012. (Illus.). 17.99 *(978-0-375-86871-9(2)*, Knopf Bks. for Young Readers) Random Hse. Children's Bks.

Stephenson, Susan. Monster Maddie. Snider, K. C., illus. 2010. 20p. pap. 10.95 *(978-1-61633-027-9(9))* Guardian Angel Publishing, Inc.

Steps To Literacy Staff, compiled by. Beast Quest Collection Grades 2-5: Class Pack (6 Titles, 6 Each) 2010. (ENG.). (J). pap. 170.75 *(978-1-60923-616-8(5))* Steps To Literacy, LLC.

—Beast Quest Collection Grades 2-5: Variety Pack (6 Titles, 1 Each) 2010. (ENG.). (J). pap. 29.90 *(978-1-60923-615-1(7))* Steps To Literacy, LLC.

—Percy Jackson & the Olympians Series: Variety Pack (5 Titles, 1 Each) 2010. (J). pap. 39.95 *(978-1-60923-745-5(5))* Steps To Literacy, LLC.

Sterner, Wendy L. Seymore Monster. 2008. 32p. pap. 24.95 *(978-1-60441-748-7(X))* America Star Bks.

Steve, Behling. Marvel Monsters Unleashed: Beware the Glop! Marvel Press Artist Staff, illus. 2017. (Marvel Monsters Unleashed! Ser.). (ENG.). 176p. (J). (gr. 3-7). pap. 6.99 ***(978-1-368-00247-9(1)**, Marvel Pr.)* Disney Publishing Worldwide.

Stevens, Lynda. The Lawn Monster: A Book to Help Kids Learn to Be Brave. 2012. 44p. pap. 21.99 *(978-1-4771-0291-6(4))* Xlibris Corp.

Stewart, Dianne. Who's Afraid of the Dark? Rankin, Joan, illus. 2012. (ENG.). 32p. (J). (gr. k-2). pap. 6.95 *(978-1-4314-0118-5(8))* Jacana Media ZAF. Dist: Independent Pubs. Group.

Stewart, Joel. Dexter Bexley & the Big Blue Beastie. Stewart, Joel, illus. 2007. (ENG., Illus.). 32p. (J). (gr. -1-3). 16.95 *(978-0-8234-2068-1(X))* Holiday Hse., Inc.

—Dexter Bexley & the Big Blue Beastie on the Road. 2010. (ENG., Illus.). 32p. (J). (gr. -1-3). pap. 16.95 *(978-0-8234-2292-0(5))* Holiday Hse., Inc.

Stewart, Yale. Alien Superman!, 1 vol. Stewart, Yale, illus. 2014. (Amazing Adventures of Superman! Ser.). (ENG., Illus.). 32p. (gr. k-2). lib. bdg. 25.32 *(978-1-4795-5733-2(1)*, DC Super Heroes) Stone Arch Bks.

Stilton, Geronimo. Meet Me in Horrorwood. 2011. (Creepella Von Cacklefur Ser.: 2). (ENG., Illus.). 128p. (J). (gr. 2-5). pap. 7.99 *(978-0-545-30743-7(0)*, Scholastic Paperbacks) Scholastic, Inc.

—Meet Me in Horrorwood. 2011. (Geronimo Stilton — Creepella Von Cacklefur Ser.: 2). (Illus.). 112p. (J). lib. bdg. 18.40 *(978-0-606-22947-0(7)*, Turtleback) Turtleback Bks.

—Return of the Vampire. 2012. (Geronimo Stilton — Creepella Von Cacklefur Ser.: 4). lib. bdg. 18.40 *(978-0-606-26180-7(X)*, Turtleback) Turtleback Bks.

Stimson, James. Thirteen O'Clock. Stimson, James, illus. 2005. (ENG., Illus.). 40p. (J). (gr. -1-2). 15.95 *(978-0-8118-4839-8(6))* Chronicle Bks. LLC.

Stine, R. L. Claws! 2011. (Goosebumps Hall of Horrors Ser.: 1). (ENG.). 160p. (J). (gr. 3-7). pap. 6.99 *(978-0-545-28933-7(5)*, Scholastic Paperbacks) Scholastic, Inc.

—Creature Teacher: The Final Exam. 2014. (Goosebumps Most Wanted Ser.: 6). (ENG.). 160p. (J). (gr. 3-7). pap. 6.99 *(978-0-545-62773-3(7)*, Scholastic Paperbacks) Scholastic, Inc.

—Creep from the Deep. 2008. (Goosebumps HorrorLand Ser.: No. 2). 137p. (gr. 4-7). 17.00 *(978-0-7569-8815-9(2))* Perfection Learning Corp.

—Don't Stay up Late: A Fear Street Novel. 2015. (Fear Street Ser.). (ENG.). 304p. (YA). (gr. 7-12). 17.99 *(978-1-250-05162-2(2)*, 9781250051622, St. Martin's Griffin) St. Martin's Pr.

—Dr. Maniac vs. Robby Schwartz. 2008. (Goosebumps Horrorland Ser.: 5). (ENG.). 160p. (J). (gr. 3-7). pap. 6.99 *(978-0-439-91873-2(1),* Scholastic Paperbacks) Scholastic, Inc.
—Fear Street Super Thriller: Party Games & Don't Stay up Late. 2015. (Fear Street Ser.). (ENG.). 592p. (YA). (gr. 7-12). pap. 11.99 *(978-1-250-07693-9(5),* 9781250076939, St. Martin's Griffin) St. Martin's Pr.
—Here Comes the Shaggedy. 2016. (Goosebumps: Most Wanted Ser.: 9). (ENG., Illus.). 160p. (J). (gr. 3-7). pap. 6.99 *(978-0-545-82547-4(4),* Scholastic Paperbacks) Scholastic, Inc.
—Here Comes the Shaggedy. 2016. (Goosebumps Most Wanted Ser.: 9). (Illus.). 140p. (J). lib. bdg. 17.20 *(978-0-606-38587-9(8))* Turtleback Bks.
—The Horror at Chiller House. 2011. (Goosebumps Horrorland Ser.: 19). (ENG.). 160p. (J). (gr. 3-7). pap. 6.99 *(978-0-545-16200-5(9),* Scholastic Paperbacks) Scholastic, Inc.
—How to Be a Vampire. 2011. (R. L. Stine's Ghosts of Fear Street Ser.). (ENG.). 128p. (J). (gr. 3-7). pap. 6.99 *(978-1-4424-2760-0(4),* Aladdin) Simon & Schuster Children's Publishing.
—Little Shop of Hamsters. 2010. 160p. (J). (Goosebumps Horrorland Ser.: 14). (ENG.). (gr. 3-7). 6.99 *(978-0-545-16195-4(9),* Scholastic Paperbacks); pap. 2.99 *(978-1-4071-1635-8(5))* Scholastic, Inc.
—Little Shop of Hamsters. 2010. (Goosebumps HorrorLand Ser.: 14). lib. bdg. 17.20 *(978-0-606-10559-0(X),* Turtleback) Turtleback Bks.
—Monster Blood. 2008. (Classic Goosebumps Ser.: 3). (ENG.). 144p. (J). (gr. 3-7). 6.99 *(978-0-545-03520-0(1),* Scholastic Paperbacks) Scholastic, Inc.
—Monster Blood for Breakfast! 2008. (Goosebumps Horrorland Ser.: 3). (ENG.). 144p. (J). (gr. 3-7). pap. 6.99 *(978-0-439-91871-8(5),* Scholastic Paperbacks) Scholastic, Inc.
—My Friends Call Me Monster. 2009. (Goosebumps Horrorland Ser.: 7). (ENG.). 160p. (J). (gr. 3-7). 6.99 *(978-0-439-91875-6(8),* Scholastic Paperbacks) Scholastic, Inc.
—Revenge of the Lawn Gnomes. 2011. (Classic Goosebumps Ser.: 19). (ENG.). 160p. (J). (gr. 3-7). pap. 6.99 *(978-0-545-29835-3(0),* Scholastic Paperbacks) Scholastic, Inc.
—Revenge of the Living Dummy. 2008. (Goosebumps HorrorLand Ser.: No. 1). 128p. (J). (gr. 4-7). 13.65 *(978-0-7569-8816-6(0))* Perfection Learning Corp.
—Revenge of the Living Dummy. 2008. (Goosebumps HorrorLand Ser.: 1). 128p. (gr. 4-7). lib. bdg. 17.20 *(978-1-4178-1891-4(3),* Turtleback) Turtleback Bks.
—Say Cheese - And Die Screaming! 2009. (Goosebumps Horrorland Ser.: 8). (ENG.). 160p. (J). (gr. 3-7). 6.99 *(978-0-439-91876-3(6),* Scholastic Paperbacks) Scholastic, Inc.
—A Shocker on Shock Street. 2015. (Goosebumps Ser.: 23). lib. bdg. 17.20 *(978-0-606-37064-6(1))* Turtleback Bks.
—Werewolf of Fever Swamp. 2009. (Classic Goosebumps Ser.: 11). (ENG.). 160p. (J). (gr. 3-7). 6.99 *(978-0-545-15886-2(9),* Scholastic Paperbacks) Scholastic, Inc.
—You Can't Scare Me! 2010. (Classic Goosebumps Ser.: 17). (ENG.). 160p. (J). (gr. 3-7). pap. 6.99 *(978-0-545-17796-2(0),* Scholastic Paperbacks) Scholastic, Inc.
Stine, R. L. & Brown, Marc. The Little Shop of Monsters. 2015. (ENG., Illus.). 40p. (J). (gr. -1-3). 17.00 *(978-0-316-36983-1(7))* Little Brown & Co.
Stone, Jon. The Monster at the End of This Book. Smollin, Michael, illus. (Little Golden Board Book Ser.). (ENG.). (J). 2015. 26p. (— 1). bds. 7.99 *(978-0-553-50873-4(3))* 2004. 32p. (gr. -1-2). 8.99 *(978-0-375-82913-0(X))* Random Hse. Children's Bks. (Golden Bks.).
Storrie, Paul D. Made for Each Other, 2 vols. Cowgur, Eldon, illus. 2011. (My Boyfriend Is a Monster Ser.: 2). (ENG.). 128p. (YA). (gr. 7-12). 29.27 *(978-0-7613-5601-1(0))* Lerner Publishing Group.
—#02 Made for Each Other. Cowgur, Eldon, illus. 2011. (My Boyfriend Is a Monster Ser.). 128p. (YA). pap. 56.72 *(978-0-7613-7604-0(6),* Graphic Universe™) Lerner Publishing Group.
Strachan, Linda. Hamish Mchaggis & the Search for the Loch Ness Monster. Collins, Sally J., illus. 2005. 32p. (J). pap. 9.00 *(978-0-9546701-5-3(9))* GW Publishing GBR. Dist: Wilson & Assocs.
Stumpe, Jennifer. Aunt Jo Jo's Magical Gifts: Amazing Underwater Adventure. 2011. 32p. (gr. 1-2). pap. 14.95 *(978-1-4567-3160-1(2))* AuthorHouse.
Suarez, Sergio Lopez. Huakala! a los Miedos. Suarez, Sergio Lopez, illus. 2003. (SPA., Illus.). 32p. (J). (gr. k-3). 9.95 *(978-968-19-0556-9(3))* Aguilar, Altea, Taurus, Alfaguara, S.A. de C.V MEX. Dist: Santillana USA Publishing Co., Inc.
Survival Colony 9. 2014. (ENG., Illus.). 336p. (YA). (gr. 9). 18.99 *(978-1-4814-0354-2(0),* McElderry, Margaret K. Bks.) McElderry, Margaret K. Bks.
Tadjo, Veronique. Mamy Wata & the Monster, 8 vols. 2005. (ARA, ENG, VIE, CHI & BEN., Illus.). 24p. (J). pap. 9.95 *(978-1-84059-264-1(8))* Milet Publishing.
Tagg, Christine. Who Will You Meet on Scary Street? Nine Pop-up Nightmares! Fuge, Charles, illus. 2004. 20p. (J). reprint ed. 15.00 *(978-0-7567-8003-6(9))* DIANE Publishing Co.
Tamura, Mitsuhisa & Fujita, Kazuhiro. BakéGyamon, Vol. 1. 2009. (ENG.). 200p. (J). pap. 7.99 *(978-1-4215-1793-3(0))* Viz Media.
—BakéGyamon, Vol. 2. 2009. (ENG.). 200p. (J). pap. 7.99 *(978-1-4215-1794-0(9))* Viz Media.
Taplin, Sam. This Is My Monster. Furukawa, Masumi, illus. 2008. (Noisy Touchy-Feely Board Bks). 10p. (J). bds. 16.99 *(978-0-7945-2353-4(6),* Usborne) EDC Publishing.
Tatulli, Mark. Desmond Pucket & the Cloverfield Junior High Carnival of Horrors. 2016. (Desmond Pucket Ser.: 3). (ENG., Illus.). 240p. (J). 13.99 *(978-1-4494-6628-2(1))* Andrews McMeel Publishing.
—Desmond Pucket & the Mountain Full of Monsters. 2015. (ENG.). 240p. (J). pap. 9.99 *(978-1-4494-7140-8(4))* Andrews McMeel Publishing.
—Desmond Pucket & the Mountain Full of Monsters. 2015. (Desmond Pucket Ser.: 2). lib. bdg. 20.85 *(978-0-606-38232-8(1))* Turtleback Bks.
—Desmond Pucket Makes Monster Magic. (ENG.). 240p. (J). 2015. pap. 9.99 *(978-1-4494-7139-2(0))* 2013. (Desmond Pucket Ser.: 1). 13.99 *(978-1-4494-3548-6(3))* Andrews McMeel Publishing.
—Desmond Pucket Makes Monster Magic. 2015. (Desmond Pucket Ser.: 1). lib. bdg. 20.85 *(978-0-606-38231-1(3))* Turtleback Bks.
Tatulli, Mark, et al. Lio: "There's a Monster in My Socks" 2012. (Lio Ser.: 7). (ENG., Illus.). 224p. (J). pap. 9.99 *(978-1-4494-2304-9(3))* Andrews McMeel Publishing.
Tavares, Victor, illus. Beauty & the Beast. 2007. (Usborne Young Reading: Series Two Ser.). 63p. (J). 8.99 *(978-0-7945-1456-3(1),* Usborne) EDC Publishing.
Tayler, Amber. What Do Monsters Look Like? Birth, Ryan, illus. 2009. 36p. pap. 11.25 *(978-1-935125-51-8(6))* Robertson Publishing.
Taylor, Greg. Killer Pizza. 2011. (ENG.). 368p. (YA). (gr. 5-9). pap. 10.99 *(978-0-312-67485-4(6),* 9780312674854) Square Fish.
—Killer Pizza: the Slice. 2012. (ENG.). 368p. (YA). (gr. 5-9). pap. 10.99 *(978-1-250-00478-9(0),* 9781250004789) Square Fish.
Taylor, Phillip J. Brian, His Granddad & the Cup of Ages. 2012. 310p. pap. *(978-1-78003-422-5(9))* Pen Pr. Pubs., Ltd.
Taylor, Sean. I Want to Be in a Scary Story. Jullien, Jean, illus. 2017. (ENG.). 32p. (J). (-k). 15.99 ***(978-0-7636-8953-7(X))*** Candlewick Pr.
Taylor, Sean. When a Monster Is Born. Sharratt, Nick, illus. 2011. (ENG.). 32p. (J). (gr. -1-1). pap. 6.99 *(978-0-312-55348-7(X),* 9780312553487) Square Fish.
Testa, Susan L. Myra the House Cat & the Garbage Can Monster. 2011. 44p. pap. 24.95 *(978-1-4560-4887-7(2))* America Star Bks.
Thaler, Mike. Black Lagoon, 6 vols., Set. Lee, Jared, illus. Incl. Gym Teacher from the Black Lagoon. lib. bdg. 24.21 *(978-1-59961-794-7(3));* Librarian from the Black Lagoon. lib. bdg. 24.21 *(978-1-59961-795-4(1));* Music Teacher from the Black Lagoon. lib. bdg. 24.21 *(978-1-59961-796-1(X));* Principal from the Black Lagoon. lib. bdg. 24.21 *(978-1-59961-797-8(8));* School Nurse from the Black Lagoon. lib. bdg. 24.21 *(978-1-59961-798-5(6));* Teacher from the Black Lagoon. lib. bdg. 24.21 *(978-1-59961-799-2(4));* (gr. -1-2). (Black Lagoon Set 1 Ser.: 6). (ENG., Illus.). 32p. 2011. Set lib. bdg. 145.26 *(978-1-59961-793-0(5))* Spotlight.
—Meatloaf Monster from the School Cafeteria. Lee, Jared D., illus. 2012. (J). pap. *(978-0-545-48570-8(3))* Scholastic, Inc.
—The School Carnival from the Black Lagoon. Lee, Jared, illus. 2005. 64p. (J). pap. *(978-0-439-80075-4(7))* Scholastic, Inc.
—The School Carnival from the Black Lagoon, 1 vol. Lee, Jared, illus. 2012. (Black Lagoon Adventures Ser.: No. 2). (ENG.). 64p. (J). (gr. 2-5). 24.21 *(978-1-59961-962-0(8))* Spotlight.
—The Secret Santa from the Black Lagoon. Lee, Jared D., illus. 2014. 64p. (J). *(978-0-545-78519-8(7))* Scholastic, Inc.
—The Thanksgiving Day from the Black Lagoon. Lee, Jared, illus. 2009. 64p. (J). *(978-0-545-16812-0(0))* Scholastic, Inc.
—Valentine's Day from the Black Lagoon, 1 vol. 2014. (Black Lagoon Adventures Set 3 Ser.). (ENG.). 64p. (J). (gr. 3-6). lib. bdg. 24.21 *(978-1-61479-209-3(7))* Spotlight.
There's a Monster under the Sheets. 2004. (J). pap. 8.00 *(978-0-8059-6461-5(4))* Dorrance Publishing Co., Inc.
Thomas, Colleen. No Monster Here. 2009. *(978-1-61584-910-9(6))* Independent Pub.
Thomassie, Tynia. Feliciana Meets d'Loup Garou: A Cajun Tall Tale, 1 vol. Smith, Cat Bowman, illus. 2005. (ENG.). 32p. (J). (gr. k-3). 16.99 *(978-1-58980-287-2(X))* Pelican Publishing Co., Inc.
Thompson, Jill. The Revenge of Jimmy. 2006. (Illus.). 48p. pap. 9.95 *(978-1-57989-071-1(7))* Sirius Entertainment, Inc.
—Scary Godmother. 2005. (Illus.). 48p. pap. 9.95 *(978-1-57989-070-4(9))* Sirius Entertainment, Inc.
Thompson, Jill, creator. Scary Godmother: The Mystery Date. 2004. (Illus.). 48p. pap. 9.95 *(978-1-57989-072-8(5))* Sirius Entertainment, Inc.
Thomson, Malcolm. Saga of the Vegvisir. 2012. (Illus.). 68p. pap. 32.03 *(978-1-4772-4741-9(6))* AuthorHouse.
Ticktock Media, Ltd. Staff. The Unexplained: Encounters with Ghosts, Monsters, & Aliens. 2008. (ENG.). 96p. (J). (gr. 2-4). pap. 9.95 *(978-1-84696-807-5(0),* TickTock Books) Octopus Publishing Group GBR. Dist: Independent Pubs. Group.
Tillworth, Mary. Big Monster, Little Monster. Random House Disney Staff, illus. 2014. (Step into Reading Ser.). (ENG.). 24p. (J). (gr. -1-1). 3.99 *(978-0-7364-3094-4(6),* RH/Disney) Random Hse. Children's Bks.
Tillworth, Mary. Spark Bug Rescue! (Blaze & the Monster Machines) Aikins, Dave, illus. 2017. (Pictureback(R) Ser.). (ENG.). 16p. (J). (gr. -1-2). pap. 5.99 ***(978-1-5247-1717-9(7),*** Random Hse. Bks. for Young Readers) Random Hse. Children's Bks.
Titan Books Staff, et al. Monsters vs. Aliens: the M Files. Dalton, Alex & Laguna, Fabio, illus. 2009. (ENG.). 48p. pap. 4.95 *(978-1-84856-281-3(0),* Titan Bks.) Titan Bks. Ltd. GBR. Dist: Penguin Random Hse. LLC.
Tombo. The Magic Nickel: A Fable about an Unhappy Salesman, a Sad Retired Person, & an Invisible Monster. 2012. 26p. pap. 16.99 *(978-1-4624-0280-9(1),* Inspiring Voices) Author Solutions, Inc.
Top That Publishing Staff, ed. Mini Monsters. 2005. (Illus.). 24p. pap. *(978-1-84510-159-6(6))* Top That! Publishing PLC.
Toreeva, Natalia G. Greg & the Sea Monster. 2011. 34p. pap. 14.50 *(978-1-61204-332-6(1),* Eloquent Bks.) Strategic Book Publishing & Rights Agency (SBPRA).
Torres, J., et al. Monster Zit!, 1 vol. 2014. (Teen Titans GO! Ser.). (ENG., Illus.). 32p. (gr. 2-3). 22.60 *(978-1-4342-9213-1(4))* Stone Arch Bks.
Toufexis, George. Monster Mall Activity Book. 2013. (Dover Children's Activity Bks.). (ENG.). 48p. (J). (gr. 3-8). pap. 4.99 *(978-0-486-49962-8(6))* Dover Pubns., Inc.
—MONSTER MASH-Up — Rise of the Predators. 2014. (ENG., Illus.). 48p. (J). (gr. 4). pap. 4.99 *(978-0-486-49224-7(9))* Dover Pubns., Inc.
—Monster Matrix Activity Book. 2013. (Dover Children's Activity Bks.). (ENG.). 48p. (J). (gr. 3-8). pap. 4.99 *(978-0-486-49963-5(4))* Dover Pubns., Inc.
ToyBox Innovations, creator. Disney's Monsters, Inc. Read-along. 2006. (Disney's Read Along Ser.). (ENG., Illus.). 24p. (J). pap. *(978-0-7634-2175-5(8))* Walt Disney Records.
Trapani, Iza. Gabe & Goon. Trapani, Iza, illus. 2016. (ENG., Illus.). 32p. (J). (gr. -1-1). lib. bdg. 16.95 *(978-1-58089-640-5(5))* Charlesbridge Publishing, Inc.
Trayer, Edward H. Struggles of Felicity Brady: Articulus Quest. 2005. (YA). per. 14.95 *(978-1-59571-091-8(4))* Word Association Pubs.
Tremblay, Carole. Floop in the Dark. Beshwaty, Steve, illus. 2009. (Floop Ser.). 24p. (J). (gr. -1-k). 22.60 *(978-1-60754-341-1(9));* pap. 8.15 *(978-1-60754-342-8(7))* Windmill Bks.
Troupe, Thomas Kingsley. The Big Hairy Secret, 1 vol. Gilpin, Stephen, illus. 2013. (Furry & Flo Ser.). (ENG.). 128p. (gr. 2-3). 8.95 *(978-1-62370-033-1(7));* lib. bdg. 25.32 *(978-1-4342-3858-0(X))* Stone Arch Bks.
—Furry & Flo, 1 vol. (Furry & Flo Ser.). (ENG.). 128p. (gr. 2-3). 2014. 101.28 *(978-1-4342-6400-8(9))* 2013. 50.64 *(978-1-4342-6348-3(7))* Stone Arch Bks.
—The Misplaced Mummy, 1 vol. Gilpin, Stephen, illus. 2014. (Furry & Flo Ser.). (ENG.). 128p. (gr. 2-3). 25.32 *(978-1-4342-6396-4(7))* Stone Arch Bks.
—The Skeletons in City Park, 1 vol. Gilpin, Stephen, illus. 2014. (Furry & Flo Ser.). (ENG.). 128p. (gr. 2-3). 25.32 *(978-1-4342-6397-1(5))* Stone Arch Bks.
—The Solemn Golem. Gilpin, Stephen, illus. 2015. (Furry & Flo Ser.). (ENG.). 128p. (gr. 2-3). lib. bdg. 25.32 *(978-1-4342-9646-7(6))* Stone Arch Bks.
Tulien, Sean & Hoena, Blake. The Not-So-Helpless Princess. Cunyat, Pol, illus. 2016. (Thud & Blunder Ser.). (ENG.). 56p. (gr. 2-4). pap. 4.95 *(978-1-4965-3222-0(8));* lib. bdg. 23.99 *(978-1-4965-3218-3(X))* Stone Arch Bks.
Tuxford, Jenny & Brazier, Jenny. Fredd Boggitt & the Loch Ness Monster. 2009. 152p. pap. 11.99 *(978-1-4389-9593-9(8))* AuthorHouse.
Twin Sister Produtions & Shepherd, Jodie. Sesame Street Big Red Riding Hood. 2010. (J). (gr. k-2). 14.99 *(978-1-59922-635-4(9))* Twin Sisters IP, LLC.
Twin Sister Produtions Staff & Shepherd, Jodie. Sesame Street Big Red Riding Hood. 2010. (J). (gr. k-2). 14.99 *(978-1-59922-526-5(3))* Twin Sisters IP, LLC.
Tyrrell, Colm. Snow Day. 2015. (Illus.). 32p. (J). *(978-1-5182-0102-8(4))* Disney Publishing Worldwide.
Tyrrell, Melissa. Beauty & the Beast. McMullen, Nigel, illus. 2005. (Fairytale Friends Ser.). 12p. (J). bds. 5.95 *(978-1-58117-153-2(6),* Intervisual/Piggy Toes) Bendon, Inc.
Uram, Maggie. Good Night Good Knight. 2004. (Illus.). 39p. (J). per. *(978-1-932077-38-4(3))* Athena Pr.
V, Vasanthi. The Toy-Gobbling Monster. Lee, Anais, illus. 2013. (ENG.). (J). 14.95 *(978-1-62086-330-5(8))* Mascot Bks., Inc.
Valentino, Serena & Disney Book Group Staff. The Beast Within: A Tale of Beauty's Prince. Disney Storybook Artists Staff & Disney Storybook Art Team, illus. 2014. (Villains Ser.). (ENG.). 224p. (J). (gr. 5-9). 16.99 *(978-1-4231-5912-4(8))* Disney Pr.
Vallejo-Nagera, Alejandra. Los Cazadores de Monstruos.Tr. of Monsters Hunters. (SPA.). 32p. (J). 10.95 *(978-84-204-4955-5(5))* Ediciones Alfaguara ESP. Dist: Santillana USA Publishing Co., Inc.
Van Dusen, Chris. Hattie & Hudson. Van Dusen, Chris, illus. 2017. (ENG., Illus.). 40p. (J). (gr. -1-3). 16.99 *(978-0-7636-6545-6(2))* Candlewick Pr.
Van Hout, Mies. Friends. 2013. (ENG., Illus.). 32p. (J). (gr. -1). 17.95 *(978-1-935954-23-1(7),* 9781935954231) Lemniscaat USA.
Van Lente, Fred, et al. Tales from the Crypt. Todd, Mort et al, illus. 2009. (Tales from the Crypt Graphic Novels Ser.: 6). (ENG.). 96p. (J). (gr. 5-12). 12.95 *(978-1-59707-137-6(4),* 9781597071376) Papercutz.
Vana, Dan. Joey & the Magic Dream Pillow. Ware, Quinton, illus. 2013. 20p. pap. 24.95 *(978-1-4626-7872-3(6))* America Star Bks.
VanRiper, Gary & VanRiper, Justin. Legend of the Lake Monster. 2009. (Adirondack Kids Ser.: Vol. 9). 96p. (J). (gr. 2-7). pap. 9.95 *(978-0-9707044-9-8(6))* Adirondack Kids Pr.
Varley, Dax. Graveyard Dirt. Proctor, Jon, illus. 2016. (ENG.). 48p. (J). lib. bdg. *(978-1-62402-158-9(1))* Magic Wagon.
—Hideout. Proctor, Jon, illus. 2016. (ENG.). 48p. (J). lib. bdg. 28.50 *(978-1-62402-157-2(3))* Magic Wagon.
Vega, Danielle & Loftin, Nikki. Survive the Night. 2015. (DUT & ENG.). 272p. (YA). (gr. 9). 17.99 *(978-1-59514-724-0(1),* Razorbill) Penguin Young Readers Group.
Vega, Denise. If Your Monster Won't Go to Bed. OHora, Zachariah, illus. 2017. (ENG.). 40p. (J). (gr. -1-2). 17.99 *(978-0-553-49655-0(7),* Knopf Bks. for Young Readers) Random Hse. Children's Bks.
Velhuijs, Max. The Kind-Hearted Monster. 2015. (ENG., Illus.). 64p. (J). 19.95 *(978-0-7358-4107-9(1))* North-South Bks., Inc.
Venditti, Robert & Riordan, Rick. The Sea of Monsters. 2013. (Percy Jackson & the Olympians Graphic Novels Ser.: 2). (J). lib. bdg. 24.50 *(978-0-606-23611-9(2),* Turtleback) Turtleback Bks.
—The Titan's Curse. Futaki, Attila & Guilhaumond, Gregory, illus. 2013. (Percy Jackson & the Olympians Ser.). (ENG.). 128p. (J). (gr. 5-9). 19.99 *(978-1-4231-4530-1(5))* Disney Pr.
Verano, Vladimir, illus. The Prince, the Demon King, & the Monkey Warrior. 2011. (ENG.). 96p. (J). (gr. 3-6). pap. 9.95 *(978-1-934159-30-9(1))* ThingsAsian Pr.
Vere, Ed. Bedtime for Monsters. Vere, Ed, illus. 2012. (ENG., Illus.). 32p. (J). (gr. -1-k). 14.99 *(978-0-8050-9509-8(8),* 9780805095098, Holt, Henry & Co. Bks. For Young Readers) Holt, Henry & Co.
—A Dormir, Monstruos! 2012. (SPA.). 32p. (J). (gr. -1-1). pap. 21.99 *(978-84-261-3890-3(X))* Juventud, Editorial ESP. Dist: Lectorum Pubns., Inc.
Vernick, Audrey. Unlike Other Monsters. Jack, Colin, illus. 2016. (ENG.). 48p. (J). (gr. -1-k). 16.99 *(978-1-4231-9959-5(6))* Disney Pr.
Viguié, Debbie. The Fall of Candy Corn, 1 vol. 2008. (Sweet Seasons Novel Ser.). (ENG.). 224p. (YA). (gr. 8-11). pap. 9.99 *(978-0-310-71559-7(8))* Zondervan.
Villarreal, Jennifer. The Monster under My Bed. 2008. 20p. pap. 13.50 *(978-1-4389-0371-2(5))* AuthorHouse.
Villeneuve, Anne. Loula & Mister the Monster. Villeneuve, Anne, illus. 2015. (Loula Ser.). (ENG., Illus.). 32p. (J). (gr. -1-2). 16.95 *(978-1-77138-326-4(7))* Kids Can Pr., Ltd. CAN. Dist: Hachette Bk. Group.
Waisanen, Emily. The Book Monster. Konecny, John, illus. 2012. 24p. pap. 8.99 *(978-1-937165-25-3(6))* Orange Hat Publishing.
Wallace, Adam. How to Catch a Monster. Elkerton, Andy, illus. 2017. (ENG.). 40p. (J). (-3). 10.99 ***(978-1-4926-4894-9(9),*** Sourcebooks Jabberwocky) Sourcebooks, Inc.
Wallace, Lizzie. My Sister's Turning into a Monster. 2011. (Illus.). 20p. 10.96 *(978-1-4520-9930-9(8))* AuthorHouse.
Walton, Rick. Frankenstein. Hale, Nathan, illus. 2012. (ENG.). 48p. (J). (gr. -1-3). 14.99 *(978-0-312-55366-1(8),* 9780312553661) Feiwel & Friends.
—10 Little Monsters Go to San Fransisco. Smiley, Jess Smart, illus. 2015. (ENG.). 32p. (J). 16.95 *(978-1-942672-99-9(3))* Familius LLC.
—10 Little Monsters Visit Oregon. Smiley, Jess Smart, illus. 2014. (ENG.). 32p. (J). 16.95 *(978-1-939629-29-6(2),* 9781939629296) Familius LLC.
—10 Little Monsters Visit Washington. Smiley, Jess Smart, illus. 2015. (ENG.). 32p. (J). 16.95 *(978-1-942672-98-2(5))* Familius LLC.
Wang, Andrea. The Nian Monster. Chau, Alina, illus. 2016. (ENG.). 32p. (J). (gr. -1-3). 16.99 *(978-0-8075-5642-9(4))* Whitman, Albert & Co.
Ward, Nick. Another Rumpus. Ward, Nick, illus. 2015. (ENG., Illus.). 24p. (J). (gr. -1-3). 7.99 *(978-1-85733-728-0(X))* Lerner Publishing Group.
Ward-Showers, Latanya. Could It Be a Monster in the Attic? 2013. 24p. pap. 17.99 *(978-1-4817-0542-4(3))* AuthorHouse.
Warren, Celia. A Big Surprise, 4 vols. 2005. (Read On (QEB) Ser.). (Illus.). 24p. (J). (gr. 1-4). lib. bdg. 15.95 *(978-1-59566-092-3(5))* QEB Publishing Inc.
Washer, S. N. The Wingate Adventures: Our New Friends. 2006. 164p. pap. 11.95 *(978-1-59800-510-3(3))* Outskirts Pr., Inc.
Watson Dubisch, Carolyn. The Horribles. 2010. 73p. pap. 16.96 *(978-0-557-35938-7(4))* Lulu Pr., Inc.
Watson, Michael. Search, Secrets, & Spies. 2011. 32p. pap. 13.00 *(978-1-61204-357-9(7),* Strategic Bk. Publishing) Strategic Book Publishing & Rights Agency (SBPRA).
Watt, Fiona. That's Not My Monster. Wells, Rachel, illus. 2004. 10p. (J). 7.99 *(978-0-7945-0818-0(9),* Usborne) EDC Publishing.
Watters, Shannon & Stevenson, Noelle. Band Together. 2016. (Lumberjanes Ser.: 5). lib. bdg. 26.95 *(978-0-606-39484-0(2))* Turtleback Bks.
Wayne, Matt. Panic of the Composite Creatures. Suriano, Andy & Davis, Dan W., illus. 2012. (Batman: the Brave & the Bold Ser.). (ENG.). 32p. (gr. 2-3). lib. bdg. 22.60 *(978-1-4342-4545-8(4))* Stone Arch Bks.
Webb, Rita. Tears. 2012. 350p. pap. 12.99 *(978-0-615-51355-3(7))* Robot Playground, Inc.
Weigand, Jessica. I Have a Monster under My Bed. 2009. 20p. pap. 10.49 *(978-1-4389-7503-0(1))* AuthorHouse.
Weinberg, Jennifer Liberts. Happy Birthday, Mike! 2014. (Step into Reading Level 2 Ser.). lib. bdg. 13.55 *(978-0-606-36006-7(9))* Turtleback Bks.
—Happy Birthday, Mike! (Disney/Pixar Monsters, Inc.) RH Disney Staff, illus. 2014. (Step into Reading Ser.). (ENG.). 32p. (J). (gr. -1-1). 3.99 *(978-0-7364-3198-9(5),* RH/Disney) Random Hse. Children's Bks.
Weiner, Jennifer. The Littlest Bigfoot. 2017. (Littlest Bigfoot Ser.: 1). (ENG.). 352p. (J). (gr. 3-7). pap. 7.99 ***(978-1-4814-7075-9(2),*** Aladdin) Simon & Schuster Children's Publishing.
—The Littlest Bigfoot. Mulvanny, Sara, illus. 2016. (Littlest Bigfoot Ser.: 1). (ENG.). 304p. (J). (gr. 3-7). 16.99 *(978-1-4814-7074-2(4),* Aladdin) Simon & Schuster Children's Publishing.
—The Littlest Bigfoot. 2017. lib. bdg. 18.40 ***(978-0-606-40206-4(3))*** Turtleback Bks.
Weiss, Ellen. Whatever You Do, I Love You. Williams, Sam, illus. 2010. (ENG.). 16p. (J). (gr. -1 — 1). bds. 7.99 *(978-1-4424-0809-8(X),* Little Simon) Little Simon.
Wellington, Stanley. Where Monsters Hide. 2003. 223p. (YA). per. 16.95 *(978-1-59196-384-4(2))* 2nd ed. 2004. 237p. per. 17.95 *(978-1-59196-481-0(4))* Instant Pub.
West, David. Ten of the Best Monster Stories. 2014. (ENG., Illus.). 24p. (J). *(978-0-7787-0783-7(0))* Crabtree Publishing Co.
West, Robert. Attack of the Spider Bots, 1 vol. 2008. (Star-Fighters of Murphy Street Ser.). (ENG., Illus.). 160p. (J). (gr. 4-7). pap. 6.99 *(978-0-310-71426-2(5))* Zonderkidz.
West, Tracey. More Monsters, More Problems. 2016. (LEGO NEXO Knights Ser.). (ENG.). 80p. (J). (gr. 2-5). pap. 4.99 *(978-1-338-03804-0(4))* Scholastic, Inc.
Weyn, Suzanne. Dr. Frankenstein's Daughters. 2013. (ENG.). 256p. (J). (gr. 7). 17.99 *(978-0-545-42533-9(6),* Scholastic Pr.) Scholastic, Inc.
Wheeler, Kim. Even More Adventures of Jonny Plumb. 2013. 186p. pap. *(978-0-7552-1570-6(2),* Bright Pen) Authors OnLine, Ltd.
Wheeler, Lisa. Boogie Knights. Siegel, Mark, illus. 2008. (ENG.). 40p. (J). (gr. -1-3). 16.99 *(978-0-689-87639-4(4),* Atheneum/Richard Jackson Bks.) Simon & Schuster Children's Publishing.
—Even Monsters Need to Sleep. Van Dusen, Chris, illus. 2017. 32p. (J). (gr. -1-3). 17.99 *(978-0-06-236640-5(8))* HarperCollins Pubs.
Where the Wild Things Are. 2005. (J). *(978-1-59564-831-0(3))* Steps To Literacy, LLC.
Whitesides, Tyler. Curse of the Broomstaff. 2013. (Janitors Ser.: 3). (ENG., Illus.). 384p. (J). (gr. 5). 18.99 *(978-1-60907-605-4(2),* Shadow Mountain) Shadow Mountain Publishing.
—Heroes of the Dustbin. 2015. (Janitors Ser.: Bk. 5). (Illus.). vii, 408p. (J). 18.99 *(978-1-62972-065-4(8),* Shadow Mountain) Deseret Bk. Co.
—Janitors. 2011. (Janitors Ser.: Bk. 1). pap. 34.99 *(978-1-60908-075-4(0));* (J). 17.99 *(978-1-60908-056-3(4))* Deseret Bk. Co.

—Janitors. 2012. (Janitors Ser.: 1). (ENG., Illus.). 320p. (J). (gr. 5). pap. 7.99 *(978-1-60907-065-6(8)*, Shadow Mountain) Shadow Mountain Publishing.
—Secrets of New Forest Academy. 2013. (Janitors Ser.: 2). (ENG., Illus.). 368p. (J). (gr. 5). pap. 8.99 *(978-1-60907-546-0(3)*, Shadow Mountain) Shadow Mountain Publishing.
—Strike of the Sweepers. 2014. (Janitors Ser.: 4). (ENG., Illus.). 400p. (J). (gr. 5). 18.99 *(978-1-60907-907-9(8)*, Shadow Mountain) Shadow Mountain Publishing.
Whiting, Jim. Really Scary Stuff, 4 vols., Set. Incl. Scary Ghosts. lib. bdg. 25.32 *(978-1-4296-3967-5(9))*; Scary Monsters. lib. bdg. 25.32 *(978-1-4296-3968-2(7))*; Scary Places. lib. bdg. 25.32 *(978-1-4296-3970-5(9))*; (gr. 1-2). (Really Scary Stuff Ser.). (ENG.). 24p. 2010. Set lib. bdg. 75.96 *(978-1-4296-4417-4(6)*, First Facts) Capstone Press of Coughlan Cos.
Whitten, A. J. The Well. 2009. (ENG., Illus.). 336p. (YA). (gr. 7-18). pap. 18.95 *(978-0-547-23229-4(2))* Houghton Mifflin Harcourt Publishing Co.
Wigger, Sherry. Scary Stories for Brave Kids, 1 vol. 2009. 73p. pap. 16.95 *(978-1-61582-308-6(5))* PublishAmerica, Inc.
Wilden, Beverley. Who Said Monsters Don't Exist? 2010. (Illus.). 32p. pap. 12.99 *(978-1-4490-7313-8(1))* AuthorHouse.
Willems, Mo. Leonardo, the Terrible Monster. Willems, Mo, illus. 2005. (ENG., Illus.). 48p. (J). (gr. -1-k). 17.99 *(978-0-7868-5294-9(1))* Hyperion Pr.
Willems, Mo. Sam, the Most Scaredy-Cat Kid in the Whole World. Willems, Mo, illus. 2017. (ENG., Illus.). 48p. (J). (gr. -1-k). 17.99 ***(978-1-368-00214-1(5))*** Hyperion Bks. for Children.
Willems, Mo, narrated by. Leonardo, the Terrible Monster. 2011. (Illus.). (J). (gr. -1-3). 29.95 *(978-0-439-02766-3(7)*, WHCD801) Weston Woods Studios, Inc.
Williams, Harland, illus. The Kid with Too Many Nightmares. 2004. (J). *(978-0-8431-1582-6(3)*, Price Stern Sloan) Penguin Publishing Group.
Williams, Kristen. Sheepy Sue & the Bedtime Blues. 2012. 28p. pap. 12.95 *(978-1-105-48819-1(5))* Lulu.com GBR. Dist: Lulu Pr., Inc.
Williams, Rozanne Lanczak. Little Monster Becomes an Author. Hefferan, Rob, illus. 2006. (Learn to Write Ser.). 16p. (J). (gr. k-2). pap. 3.49 *(978-1-59198-300-2(2)*, 6192) Creative Teaching Pr., Inc.
—Little Monster Becomes an Author. Maio, Barbara, ed. Hefferan, Rob, illus. 2006. (J). per. 8.99 *(978-1-59198-349-1(5))* Creative Teaching Pr., Inc.
Williams, Tim & Williams, Tony. Timmy's Bedtime: A Monster Bear Tale. 2011. 28p. pap. 12.50 *(978-1-61204-171-1(X)*, Eloquent Bks.) Strategic Book Publishing & Rights Agency (SBPRA).
Williams, Walter. A Monster for Tea. Williams, Walter, illus. 2013. (ENG., Illus.). 32p. (J). (gr. -1-2). 17.99 *(978-0-9890698-3-0(4))* Fernwood & Hedges Bks.
Williamson, Joshua. Sketch Monsters Book 1: Escape of the Scribbles: Escape of the Scribbles. 2011. (ENG., Illus.). 40p. 12.99 *(978-1-934964-69-9(7)*, 9781934964699) Oni Pr., Inc.
Willis, Jeanne. La Tormenta Monstruosa. (Cotton Cloud Ser.). (SPA.). (J). (gr. 1-3). pap. *(978-84-480-0180-3(X))* Timun Mas, Editorial S.A. ESP. Dist: Lectorum Pubns., Inc.
Wilson, A. c. & Wilson, A. C. Ambersil - the Legacy of Mr Harrison. 2011. 496p. pap. *(978-1-908105-45-5(3))* Grosvenor Hse. Publishing Ltd.
Wilson-Timmons, Karen & Dubois, Marie Thérèse. Agha the Eight-Mile Monster. rev. ed. 2012. (ENG., Illus.). 32p. (J). (gr. -1). 16.99 *(978-1-60887-124-7(X))* Mandala Publishing.
Wilson, W. Shane. The sprite Adventure. 2010. 97p. pap. 12.99 *(978-0-557-42603-4(0))* Lulu Pr., Inc.
Windsor, Herbert C. The Colour Monster. 2009. (Illus.). 32p. pap. 12.99 *(978-1-4490-1056-0(3))* AuthorHouse.
Windsor, M. L. Jack Death. Ewald, Chris, illus. 2016. (ENG.). 165p. (J). (gr. 2-7). 12.99 *(978-1-939547-28-6(8))* Creston Bks.
Winick, Judd. Saving the Whole Wide World. 2016. (Hilo Ser.: 2). (ENG., Illus.). 208p. (J). (gr. 3-7). 16.99 *(978-0-385-38624-1(9))*;Bk. 2. 13.99 *(978-0-385-38623-4(0))* Random Hse. Children's Bks. (Random Hse. Bks. for Young Readers).
Winthrop, Elizabeth. Maia & the Monster Baby. Haley, Amanda, illus. 2012. (ENG.). 32p. (J). 16.95 *(978-0-8234-2518-1(5))* Holiday Hse., Inc.
Wohnoutka, Mike. Little Puppy & the Big Green Monster. Wohnoutka, Mike, illus. 2014. (ENG., Illus.). 32p. (J). (gr. -1-k). 16.95 *(978-0-8234-3064-2(2))* Holiday Hse., Inc.
Wong, Angi Ma. Who Ate My Socks? 2005. (Illus.). 32p. (J). 11.98 *(978-1-928753-00-1(0))* Pacific Heritage Bks.
Wormell, Chris. Molly & the Night Monster. Wormell, Chris, illus. 2011. (ENG., Illus.). 32p. (J). (gr. -1-k). pap. 9.99 *(978-1-86230-185-6(9)*, Red Fox) Random House Children's Books GBR. Dist: Independent Pubs. Group.
—The Sea Monster. Wormell, Chris, illus. 2005. (ENG., Illus.). 32p. (J). (gr. k-2). pap. 12.99 *(978-0-09-945147-1(6)*, Red Fox) Random House Children's Books GBR. Dist: Independent Pubs. Group.
Wrecks, Billy. Green Lantern vs. the Meteor Monster! Random House Staff, illus. 2011. (Pictureback Ser.). (ENG.). 24p. (J). (gr. -1-2). pap. 3.99 *(978-0-375-87297-6(3)*, Random Hse. Bks. for Young Readers) Random Hse. Children's Bks.
—Monster Madness! (DC Super Friends) Random House Staff, illus. 2011. (Pictureback Ser.). (ENG.). 16p. (J). (gr. -1-2). pap. 3.99 *(978-0-375-87230-3(2)*, Random Hse. Bks. for Young Readers) Random Hse. Children's Bks.
Wrecks, Billy & Shealy, Dennis. T. Rex Trouble! Random House Staff et al, illus. 2011. (Step into Reading Ser.). (ENG.). 32p. (J). (gr. -1-1). pap. 3.99 *(978-0-375-86777-4(5)*, Random Hse. Bks. for Young Readers) Random Hse. Children's Bks.
Wreggelsworth, Irene. Help, Children! - The Monsters Kidnapped Santa Claus: Bilingual Book in English & Spanish. Piccione, Dana, illus. 2010. (ENG.). 120p. pap. 26.99 *(978-1-4537-1272-6(0))* CreateSpace Independent Publishing Platform.
Wright, Terry. The One-Eyed Monster. 2006. 48p. pap. 16.95 *(978-1-4241-3696-4(2))* PublishAmerica, Inc.
X, Sulayman. King of Storms. 2016. (Five Kingdoms Ser.: Vol. 2). (ENG., Illus.). (YA). 29.99 ***(978-1-63533-038-0(6)***, Harmony Ink Pr.) Dreamspinner Pr.
Yancey, Rick. The Curse of the Wendigo. 2011. (Monstrumologist Ser.: 2). (ENG.). 464p. (YA). (gr. 9). pap. 12.99 *(978-1-4169-8451-1(8)*, Simon & Schuster Bks. For Young Readers) Simon & Schuster Bks. For Young Readers.
—The Final Descent. 2013. (Monstrumologist Ser.: 4). (ENG., Illus.). 320p. (YA). (gr. 9). 18.99 *(978-1-4424-5153-7(X)*, Simon & Schuster Bks. For Young Readers) Simon & Schuster Bks. For Young Readers.
—The Isle of Blood. (Monstrumologist Ser.: 3). (ENG.). 560p. (YA). (gr. 9). 2012. pap. 12.99 *(978-1-4169-8453-5(4))* 2011. (Illus.). 18.99 *(978-1-4169-8452-8(6))* Simon & Schuster Bks. For Young Readers. (Simon & Schuster Bks. For Young Readers).
—The Monstrumologist. (Monstrumologist Ser.: 1). (ENG.). (YA). (gr. 9). 2010. 464p. pap. 11.99 *(978-1-4169-8449-8(6))* 2009. 448p. 21.99 *(978-1-4169-8448-1(8))* Simon & Schuster Bks. For Young Readers. (Simon & Schuster Bks. For Young Readers).
—The Monstrumologist Collection: Monstrumologist; Curse of the Wendigo; Isle of Blood; Final Descent. 2014. (Monstrumologist Ser.). (ENG., Illus.). 1808p. (YA). (gr. 9). pap. 46.99 *(978-1-4814-3012-8(2)*, Simon & Schuster Bks. For Young Readers) Simon & Schuster Bks. For Young Readers.
Yarlett, Emma, illus. Nibbles: The Book Monster. 2016. (J). *(978-1-61067-467-6(7))* Kane Miller.
Yohn-Rhodes, Phyllis. The Monster. 2005. (Special Kids of Sharon Ser.). (ENG., Illus.). 34p. (J). (gr. -1-3). per. 15.99 *(978-1-4134-8516-5(2))* Xlibris Corp.
Yolen, Jane. Creepy Monsters, Sleepy Monsters. Murphy, Kelly, illus. 2013. (ENG.). 32p. (J). (gr. -1-2). 5.99 *(978-0-7636-6283-7(6))* Candlewick Pr.
—Romping Monsters, Stomping Monsters. Murphy, Kelly, illus. 2013. (ENG.). 32p. (J). (gr. -1-2). 14.99 *(978-0-7636-5727-7(1))* Candlewick Pr.
Yolen, Jane & Stemple, Adam. The Hostage Prince. 2014. (Seelie Wars Ser.). (ENG.). 256p. (J). (gr. 3-7). pap. 7.99 *(978-0-14-242234-2(7)*, Puffin Books) Penguin Young Readers Group.
Yorinks, Arthur. Maurice Sendak's Seven Little Monsters: Hide & Seek. 6th rev. ed. 2004. 24p. (J). pap. 3.99 *(978-0-7868-1780-1(1))* Hyperion Pr.
—Maurice Sendak's Seven Little Monsters: Take a Hike. 5th rev. ed. 2004. 24p. (J). pap. 3.99 *(978-0-7868-1779-5(8))* Hyperion Pr.
Young, Billy. Teddy the Bear. 2007. 27p. 19.95 *(978-1-84799-068-6(1))* Lulu Pr., Inc.
Young, Laurie. I See a Monster! Mahoney, Daniel J., illus. 2007. (Touch & Feel Ser.). 12p. (gr. -1-k). 15.95 *(978-1-58117-574-5(4)*, Intervisual/Piggy Toes) Bendon, Inc.
Yovanoff, Brenna. The Replacement. 2011. (ENG.). 368p. (YA). (gr. 7-18). 8.99 *(978-1-59514-381-5(5)*, Razorbill) Penguin Young Readers Group.
Zappa, Ahmet. Because I'm Your Dad. Santat, Dan, illus. 2013. (ENG.). 32p. (J). (gr. -1-k). 15.99 *(978-1-4231-4774-9(X))* Disney Pr.
—Because I'm Your Dad. Santat, Dan, illus. 2016. (ENG.). 32p. (J). (gr. -1-k). bds. 7.99 *(978-1-4847-2661-7(8))* Hyperion Bks. for Children.
Zenz, Aaron. Monsters Go Night-Night. 2016. (ENG., Illus.). 32p. (J). (gr. -1-k). 12.95 *(978-1-4197-1653-9(0)*, Abrams Appleseed) Abrams, Inc.
Zimet, Sara Goodman. The Monster Solution. Parish, Shannon, illus. 2005. 32p. (J). 16.95 *(978-0-9645159-1-8(1)*, 1245168) Discovery Pr. Pubns., Inc.
Zindel, Paul. Loch. 2005. 209p. (YA). (gr. 7-12). 13.65 *(978-0-7569-6001-8(0))* Perfection Learning Corp.
Zornow, Jeff. Werewolf, 1 vol. Zornow, Jeff, illus. 2007. (Graphic Horror Ser.). (ENG., Illus.). 32p. (gr. 3-7). 28.50 *(978-1-60270-062-8(1)*, Graphic Planet- Fiction) ABDO Publishing Co.
Zucker, Jonny. Mission 1: Game On. Woodman, Ned, illus. 2013. (Max Flash Ser.: 1). (ENG.). 144p. (gr. 2-5). pap. 7.95 *(978-1-4677-1465-5(8))*; lib. bdg. 27.93 *(978-1-4677-1207-1(8))* Lerner Publishing Group. (Darby Creek).
—Mission 5: Subzero. Woodman, Ned, illus. 2013. (Max Flash Ser.: 5). (ENG.). 144p. (gr. 2-5). pap. 7.95 *(978-1-4677-1481-5(X))*; lib. bdg. 27.93 *(978-1-4677-1212-5(4))* Lerner Publishing Group. (Darby Creek).
Zuckerman, Heather. A Monster Named Criney Who Makes Kids Whiney. Delice, Shelly Meredith, illus. 2005. 32p. (J). (gr. -1-3). 15.95 *(978-0-9744307-0-6(6))* Merry Lane Pr.

MONSTROSITIES

see Monsters

MONTANA

Alt, David D. & Hyndman, Donald W. Roadside Geology of Montana. rev. ed. (Roadside Geology Ser.). (Illus.). 435p. (J). (gr. 4). pap. 20.00 *(978-0-87842-202-9(1)*, 212) Mountain Pr. Publishing Co., Inc.
Alter, Judy. Montana: A MyReportLinks.com Book. 2003. (States Ser.). (Illus.). 48p. (J). lib. bdg. 25.26 *(978-0-7660-5136-2(6)*, MyReportLinks.com Bks.) Enslow Pubs., Inc.
Bailer, Darice. What's Great about Montana? 2014. (Our Great States Ser.). (ENG.). 32p. (gr. 2-5). lib. bdg. 26.60 *(978-1-4677-3387-8(3)*, Lerner Pubns.) Lerner Publishing Group.
Bakker, Robert T. Raptor Pack. Skrepnick, Michael, illus. 2003. (Step into Reading Ser.). (ENG.). 48p. (J). (gr. 2-4). pap. 3.99 *(978-0-375-82303-9(4)*, Random Hse. Bks. for Young Readers) Random Hse. Children's Bks.
Bennett, Clayton & Mead, Wendy. Montana. 2nd rev. ed. 2009. (Celebrate the States 11 Ser.). 144p. (gr. 6). 42.79 *(978-0-7614-4731-3(8))* Marshall Cavendish Corp.
Bjorklund, Ruth. Montana. 2013. (It's My State 2nd Ed 5 Ser.). 80p. (J). (gr. 4-8). pap. 17.64 *(978-1-62712-100-2(5))* Cavendish Square Publishing.
Brown, Jonatha A. Montana. 2006. (Portraits of the States Ser.). 32p. (gr. 2-6). pap. 10.50 *(978-0-8368-4719-2(9))*; (Illus.). lib. bdg. 26.00 *(978-0-8368-4702-4(4))* Stevens, Gareth Publishing LLLP. (Gareth Stevens Learning Library).
Brown, Vanessa. Montana. 2009. (Bilingual Library of the United States of America Ser.). (SPA.). 32p. (gr. 2-2). 47.90 *(978-1-60853-371-8(9)*, Editorial Buenas Letras) Rosen Publishing Group, Inc., The.
—Montana. Brusca, Maria Cristina, tr. from ENG. 2006. (Bilingual Library of the United States of America Ser.: Set 2). (ENG & SPA., Illus.). 32p. (J). (gr. 3-6). lib. bdg. 25.25 *(978-1-4042-3091-0(2))* Rosen Publishing Group, Inc., The.
Bruchac, Joseph. Buffalo Song. Farnsworth, Bill, illus. 2008. (J). Lee & Low Bks., Inc.
Collard, Sneed B., III. B Is for Big Sky Country. Yardley, Joanna, illus. 2003. (Discover America State by State Ser.). (ENG.). 40p. (J). 17.95 *(978-1-58536-098-7(8))* Sleeping Bear Pr.
Hirschmann, Kris. Montana: The Treasure State. 2003. (World Almanac Library of the States). (Illus.). 48p. (gr. 4-9). pap. 14.05 *(978-0-8368-5324-7(5))*; lib. bdg. 31.00 *(978-0-8368-5153-3(6))* Stevens, Gareth Publishing LLLP. (Gareth Stevens Learning Library).
Kuedee, Jaycee. How to Draw Montana's Sights & Symbols. 2009. (Kid's Guide to Drawing America Ser.). 32p. (gr. k-k). 50.50 *(978-1-61511-075-9(5)*, PowerKids Pr.) Rosen Publishing Group, Inc., The.
LaDoux, Rita. Montana. 2012. (J). lib. bdg. 25.26 *(978-0-7613-4542-8(6)*, Lerner Pubns.) Lerner Publishing Group.
Lawson, Cheri. Chip the Buffalo: Based on a True Story. Lawson, J., illus. Beemtsen, Tammy, photos by. 2006. 32p. (J). lib. bdg. 14.95 *(978-1-930580-61-9(4)*, Luminary Media Group) Pine Orchard, Inc.
Marsh, Carole. Montana Current Events Projects: 30 Cool, Activities, Crafts, Experiments & More for Kids to Do to Learn about Your State! 2003. (Montana Experience Ser.). 32p. (gr. k-5). pap. 5.95 *(978-0-635-02045-1(9)*, Marsh, Carole Bks.) Gallopade International.
—Montana Geography Projects: 30 Cool, Activities, Crafts, Experiments & More for Kids to Do to Learn about Your State! 2003. (Montana Experience Ser.). 32p. (gr. k-5). pap. 5.95 *(978-0-635-01845-8(4)*, Marsh, Carole Bks.) Gallopade International.
—Montana Government Projects: 30 Cool, Activities, Crafts, Experiments & More for Kids to Do to Learn about Your State! 2003. (Montana Experience Ser.). 32p. (gr. k-5). pap. 5.95 *(978-0-635-01945-5(0)*, Marsh, Carole Bks.) Gallopade International.
—Montana People Projects: 30 Cool, Activities, Crafts, Experiments & More for Kids to Do to Learn about Your State! 2003. (Montana Experience Ser.). 32p. (gr. k-5). pap. 5.95 *(978-0-635-01995-0(7)*, Marsh, Carole Bks.) Gallopade International.
—Montana Symbols & Facts Projects: 30 Cool, Activities, Crafts, Experiments & More for Kids to Do to Learn about Your State! 2003. (Montana Experience Ser.). 32p. (gr. k-5). pap. 5.95 *(978-0-635-01895-3(0)*, Marsh, Carole Bks.) Gallopade International.
McLuskey, Krista. Montana. 2011. (Guide to American States Ser.). (Illus.). 48p. (YA). (gr. 3-6). 29.99 *(978-1-61690-798-3(3))* Weigl Pubs., Inc.
Murray, Julie. Montana, 1 vol. 2006. (Buddy Book Ser.). (ENG., Illus.). 32p. (gr. 2-4). 27.07 *(978-1-59197-685-1(5)*, Buddy Bks.) ABDO Publishing Co.

MONTANA—FICTION

Andrews, Neva. Stormy & Stub. 2008. 108p. pap. 10.95 *(978-0-595-52854-7(6)*, iUniverse, Inc.) iUniverse, Inc.
Aureliani, Franco. Dino-Mike! Aureliani, Franco, illus. 2015. (Dino-Mike! Ser.). (ENG., Illus.). 128p. (gr. 1-3). lib. bdg. 101.28 *(978-1-4965-0311-4(2)*, Dino-Mike!) Stone Arch Bks.
—Dino-Mike & the T. Rex Attack. Aureliani, Franco, illus. 2015. (Dino-Mike! Ser.). (ENG., Illus.). 128p. (gr. 1-3). lib. bdg. 25.32 *(978-1-4342-9627-6(X))* Stone Arch Bks.
Brammer, Deb. Moose. 2007. 132p. (YA). (gr. 8-12). per. 8.99 *(978-1-59166-722-3(4))* BJU Pr.
Bryant, Annie. Ghost Town. 2009. (Beacon Street Girls Ser.: 11). (ENG.). 240p. (J). (gr. 4-8). pap. 7.99 *(978-1-4169-6441-4(X)*, Aladdin) Simon & Schuster Children's Publishing.
Charles L. Wilson. The Search Is On: The Wild Adventures of Lester & Dora. 2009. 200p. 24.99 *(978-1-4269-1813-1(5))*; pap. 14.99 *(978-1-4269-1812-4(7))* Trafford Publishing.
Collard, Sneed B., III. Dog Sense, 1 vol. (ENG.). 192p. (J). (gr. 3-7). 2008. pap. 7.95 *(978-1-56145-460-0(5))* 2005. 14.95 *(978-1-56145-351-1(X))* Peachtree Pubs.
—Flash Point, 1 vol. (ENG.). 256p. (YA). 2011. (gr. 5-9). pap. 7.95 *(978-1-56145-577-5(6))* 2006. (Illus.). (gr. 7-18). 16.95 *(978-1-56145-385-6(4))* Peachtree Pubs.
—The Governor's Dog Is Missing. 2011. (Slate Stephens Mysteries Ser.). 176p. (J). (gr. 4-6). 16.00 *(978-0-9844460-1-8(X))* Bucking Horse Bks.
Danforth, Emily M. The Miseducation of Cameron Post. (ENG.). 480p. (YA). (gr. 9). 2013. pap. 9.99 *(978-0-06-202057-4(9))* 2012. 17.99 *(978-0-06-202056-7(0))* HarperCollins Pubs.
Davis, Trisha. Wildfire! 2011. 112p. (gr. 4-6). 20.95 *(978-1-4620-1615-0(4))*; pap. 10.95 *(978-1-4620-1616-7(2))* iUniverse, Inc.
Eberhard, Phyllis Lunde Brees. Little Miss Neat-As-A-Pin. Jacoby, Nickolina Dye, illus. 2007. (J). *(978-0-9722741-7-3(0))* Publishing Factory, The.
Ellison, Laura. Hard Rock, Hard Times: Coming of Age in Butte Montana, 1911-1917. 2005. 195p. (YA). per. *(978-0-9722217-7-1(8))* Horse Creek Pubns.
Fames, Catherine. Snowblind. 2004. 108p. (J). *(978-1-59166-329-4(6))* BJU Pr.
Ficklin, Jonene H. Orinoco Intrigue. 2005. (YA). 14.95 *(978-0-9761188-1-7(5))* Victor's Crown Publishing.
Franco, Franco. Dino-Mike! Franco, Franco, illus. 2015. (Dino-Mike! Ser.). (ENG., Illus.). 128p. (gr. 1-3). pap. 23.80 *(978-1-4965-2233-7(8)*, Dino-Mike!) Stone Arch Bks.
Gavila, Robert. Nisha: Montana. 2004. (YA). 2.25 *(978-0-9748466-0-6(0))* Gavila Publishing.
A Gift to Share. 2005. (J). 17.00 *(978-0-9721457-1-8(0))* Silent Moon Bks.
Gilliland, Hap. Alone in the Wilderness. 2003. (Illus.). 160p. (YA). (gr. 6-10). pap. 14.95 *(978-0-87961-257-3(6))* Naturegraph Pubs., Inc.
Hill, Janet Muirhead. The Horse & the Crow: A Miranda & Starlight Story. 2015. (ENG.). 268p. (J). pap. 13.00 *(978-1-937849-27-6(9))* Raven Publishing Inc. of Montana.
Hipp, Diane. Stuart the Donkey: A Tale of His Tail. Hill, T. J., illus. 2010. 52p. pap. 21.99 *(978-1-4520-3420-1(6))* AuthorHouse.
Hodder, Beth. The Ghost of Schafer Meadows. 2007. (J). per. 7.99 *(978-0-9793963-0-4(1))* Grizzly Ridge Publishing.
—Stealing the Wild. 2010. 166p. (J). pap. 11.95 *(978-0-9793963-1-1(X))* Grizzly Ridge Publishing.
Inglis, Lucy. Crow Mountain. 2016. (ENG.). 368p. (YA). (gr. 9). 17.99 *(978-0-545-90407-0(2)*, Chicken Hse., The) Scholastic, Inc.
Ingold, Jeanette. The Big Burn: Teddy Roosevelt & the Fire That Saved America. 2003. (Illus.). 301p. (YA). (gr. 8-12). 14.60 *(978-0-7569-4283-0(7))* Perfection Learning Corp.
—Hitch. 2006. (ENG., Illus.). 288p. (YA). (gr. 7-12). pap. 7.99 *(978-0-15-205619-3(X))* Houghton Mifflin Harcourt Publishing Co.
—Mountain Solo. 2005. (ENG.). 320p. (YA). (gr. 7-12). pap. 15.95 *(978-0-15-205358-1(1))* Houghton Mifflin Harcourt Publishing Co.
Ingold, Jeanette & Egan, Timothy. The Big Burn: Teddy Roosevelt & the Fire That Saved America. 2003. (ENG., Illus.). 320p. (YA). (gr. 7-12). pap. 6.95 *(978-0-15-204924-9(X))* Houghton Mifflin Harcourt Publishing Co.
Jacobs, Lily. The Littlest Bunny in Montana: An Easter Adventure. Dunn, Robert, illus. 2015. (ENG.). 32p. (J). (-3). 9.99 *(978-1-4926-1129-5(8)*, Sourcebooks Jabberwocky) Sourcebooks, Inc.
James, Eric. A Halloween Scare in Montana. Le Ray, Marina, illus. 2015. (ENG.). 32p. (J). (-5). 9.99 *(978-1-4926-2384-7(9)*, 9781492623847, Sourcebooks Jabberwocky) Sourcebooks, Inc.
—Santa's Sleigh Is on Its Way to Montana: A Christmas Adventure. Dunn, Robert, illus. 2016. (ENG.). 32p. (J). (-2). 12.99 *(978-1-4926-4338-8(6)*, 9781492643388, Sourcebooks Jabberwocky) Sourcebooks, Inc.
Johnson, Terry Lynn. Falcon Wild. 2017. (ENG.). 176p. (J). (gr. 5). lib. bdg. 16.99 ***(978-1-58089-788-4(6))*** Charlesbridge Publishing, Inc.
Kevtherev. Riddle Tails: The Golden Fruit. 2012. 28p. pap. 30.70 *(978-1-4634-0617-2(7))* AuthorHouse.
Konigsberg, Bill. The Porcupine of Truth. 2015. (ENG.). 336p. (J). (gr. 9). 17.99 *(978-0-545-64893-6(9))* Scholastic, Inc.
Krovatin, Christopher. Mountain of Bones. (Gravediggers Ser.: 1). (ENG.). (J). (gr. 3-7). 2013. 352p. pap. 6.99 *(978-0-06-207741-7(4))* 2012. 336p. 16.99 *(978-0-06-207740-0(6))* HarperCollins Pubs. (Tegen, Katherine Bks).
Larson, Kirby. Hattie Big Sky. (ENG.). (YA). (gr. 7-7). 2008. 304p. 7.99 *(978-0-385-73595-7(2)*, Yearling) 2007. 320p. pap. 8.99 *(978-0-440-23941-3(9)*, Ember) Random Hse. Children's Bks.
—Hattie Big Sky. l.t. ed. 2007. (Literacy Bridge Young Adult Ser.). 381p. (YA). (gr. 7-12). 23.95 *(978-0-7862-9697-2(6))* Thorndike Pr.
Lemna, Don. Out in Left Field. Collins, Matt, illus. 2013. (ENG.). 217p. (J). pap. 7.99 *(978-0-8234-2766-6(8))* Holiday Hse., Inc.
—When the Sergeant Came Marching Home. (ENG.). 208p. (J). (gr. 3-7). 2009. pap. 7.95 *(978-0-8234-2211-1(9))* 2008. (Illus.). 17.95 *(978-0-8234-2083-4(3))* Holiday Hse., Inc.
Lenz, Dave. Jack Crow: Indian Healer. 2014. (J). *(978-0-9801744-7-2(3))* Barnhardt & Ashe Publishing, Inc.
Maynard, Joyce. The Cloud Chamber. 2006. (ENG.). 288p. (YA). (gr. 7-7). pap. 13.99 *(978-1-4169-2699-3(2)*, Simon Pulse) Simon Pulse.
McMann, Lisa. Cryer's Cross. 2011. (ENG.). 256p. (YA). (gr. 9). pap. 9.99 *(978-1-4169-9482-4(3)*, Simon Pulse) Simon Pulse.
Meddaugh, Susan. Martha & Skits Out West. 2011. (Martha Speaks Ser.). (ENG., Illus.). 96p. (J). (gr. 1-4). pap. 5.99 *(978-0-547-21074-2(4))* Houghton Mifflin Harcourt Publishing Co.
Melton, Marcia. The Boarding House. Doran, Fran, illus. 2012. 153p. (J). pap. 12.00 *(978-1-937849-03-0(1))* Raven Publishing Inc. of Montana.
—Joe Henry's Journey. 2014. (Illus.). 169p. (J). pap. 12.00 *(978-1-937849-20-7(1))* Raven Publishing Inc. of Montana.
Miller, Paula. One-Eyed Jack. Forrest, Chris, illus. (J). 2007. (ENG.). 133p. (gr. 2-7). pap. 8.95 *(978-0-9769417-0-5(8))* 2006. 144p. 13.95 *(978-0-9718348-8-0(1))* Blooming Tree Pr.
O'Neill, Elizabeth. Alfred Visits Montana. 2009. 24p. pap. 12.00 *(978-0-9822288-6-9(4))* Global Business Information Strategies, Inc.
Out of the Blue. 2014. (J). pap. *(978-0-8163-5016-2(7))* Pacific Pr. Publishing Assn.
Palmer, Robin. Girl vs. Superstar, Bk. 1. 2010. (Yours Truly, Lucy B. Parker Ser.: 1). (ENG.). 224p. (J). (gr. 5-18). 6.99 *(978-0-14-241500-9(6)*, Puffin Books) Penguin Young Readers Group.
Philips, Fleur. Crumble. 2013. 168p. (YA). pap. 8.99 *(978-0-9889299-0-6(2))* Philips, Fleur.
Piper, William Bowman. Giraffe of Montana, Volume 1, 1. 2005. (Giraffe of Montana Ser.). (Illus.). 152p. (J). 19.95 *(978-0-9763359-4-8(8)*, 0-9763359) Little Pemberley Pr.
—Giraffe of Montana, Volume 3. 2007. (Giraffe of Montana Ser.). (Illus.). 144p. (J). 19.95 *(978-0-9763359-6-2(4))* Little Pemberley Pr.
Porter, Pamela. Sky, 1 vol. Gerber, Mary Jane, illus. 2005. (ENG.). 88p. (J). (gr. 3-5). pap. 9.95 *(978-0-88899-607-7(1)*, Libros Tigrillo) Groundwood Bks. CAN. Dist: Publishers Group West (PGW).
Sanderson, Nancy. Summer of the Painted Horse. 2009. 188p. pap. 14.49 *(978-1-4490-2312-6(6))* AuthorHouse.
Sargent, Dave & Sargent, Pat. Sweetpea: (Purple Corn Welsh) Be Happy, 30 vols., Vol. 58. Lenoir, Jane, illus. 2003. (Saddle up Ser.: Vol. 58). 42p. (J). pap. 10.95 *(978-1-56763-816-5(3))*; lib. bdg. 23.60 *(978-1-56763-815-8(5))* Ozark Publishing.
Schaaf, Ron. BearClaw: Finding Courage Within. 2007. (J). *(978-0-9787555-1-5(0))* Hickory Tales Publishing.
Seidler, Tor. Firstborn. Sheban, Chris, illus. 2015. (ENG.). 240p. (J). (gr. 4-9). 16.99 *(978-1-4814-1017-5(2)*, Atheneum

MNO

Bks. for Young Readers) Simon & Schuster Children's Publishing.
Silvano, Wendi. Love Is All Around Montana. Czernichowska, Joanna, illus. 2016. (ENG.). 32p. (J). (-6). 12.99 *(978-1-4926-2938-2(3)*, Sourcebooks Jabberwocky) Sourcebooks, Inc.
Smallman, Steve. Santa Is Coming to Bozeman. Dunn, Robert, illus. 2013. (ENG.). 32p. (J). (-3). 9.99 *(978-1-4022-9045-9(4)*, Sourcebooks Jabberwocky) Sourcebooks, Inc.
—Santa Is Coming to Missoula. Dunn, Robert, illus. 2015. (ENG.). 32p. (J). (-3). 9.99 *(978-1-4926-2656-5(2)*, Sourcebooks Jabberwocky) Sourcebooks, Inc.
—Santa Is Coming to Montana. Dunn, Robert, illus. 2013. (ENG.). 32p. (J). (-3). 9.99 *(978-1-4022-9018-3(7)*, Sourcebooks Jabberwocky) Sourcebooks, Inc.
Smith, Michael. Thomas the T. Rex: The Journey of a Young Dinosaur to Los Angeles. Roski, Gayle Garner, illus. 2011. (J). *(978-0-9832278-4-7(5))* East West Discovery Pr.
Smith, Michael & Roski, Gayle Garner. Thomas the T. Rex: The Journey of a Young Dinosaur to Los Angeles. Roski, Gayle Garner, illus. 2011. (SPA & ENG., Illus.). (J). *(978-0-9832278-2-3(9))* East West Discovery Pr.
Solberg, Jessica. First Dog: Unleashed in the Montana Capital. Rath, Robert, illus. 2007. 40p. (J). (gr. 2-4). 17.95 *(978-1-56037-425-1(X))* Farcountry Pr.
Stine, Faye. Wolf: A Story of the Wild. 2012. (ENG.). 64p. pap. 10.95 *(978-1-4787-2054-6(9))* Outskirts Pr., Inc.
Swinger-Ellbogen, Sue. Campfire Kids, 1 vol. 2010. 54p. pap. 16.95 *(978-1-4489-5493-3(2))* America Star Bks.
Thomas, Jeanne Taylor. Kerry Mcdaniels & the Cave. 2012. (ENG.). 276p. pap. 18.95 *(978-1-4327-7296-3(1))* Outskirts Pr., Inc.
Yep, Laurence. When the Circus Came to Town. Wang, Suling, illus. 2004. 112p. (J). (gr. 3-5). 13.65 *(978-0-7569-2969-5(5))* Perfection Learning Corp.

MONTANA—HISTORY

Bailer, Darice. What's Great about Montana? 2014. (Our Great States Ser.). (ENG., Illus.). 32p. (gr. 2-5). pap. 7.95 *(978-1-4677-4537-6(5))* Lerner Publishing Group.
Bjorklund, Ruth & Todras, Ellen H. Montana. 2013. 80p. (J). (gr. 4-8). 31.36 *(978-0-7614-7999-4(6))* Cavendish Square Publishing.
Bjorklund, Ruth, et al. Montana. 2016. (ENG., Illus.). 80p. (J). 34.21 *(978-1-62713-204-6(X))* Cavendish Square Publishing.
Blake, Kevin. Deadly Mine: Libby, Montana. 2017. (Eco-Disasters Ser.). (ENG.). 32p. (J). (gr. 2-7). 19.95 ***(978-1-68402-222-9(3))*** Bearport Publishing Co., Inc.
Collard, Sneed B., III. The World Famous Miles City Bucking Horse Sale. 2010. 64p. 18.00 *(978-0-9844460-0-1(1))* Bucking Horse Bks.
Gamble, Adam. Good Night Montana. 2013. (Good Night Our World Ser.). (ENG., Illus.). 20p. (J). (— 1). bds. 9.95 *(978-1-60219-080-1(1))* Good Night Bks.
Jerome, Kate B. Lucky to Live in Montana. 2017. (Arcadia Kids Ser.). (ENG., Illus.). 32p. (J). 16.99 ***(978-0-7385-2803-8(X))*** Arcadia Publishing.
—The Wise Animal Handbook Montana. 2017. (Arcadia Kids Ser.). (ENG., Illus.). 32p. (J). 16.99 ***(978-0-7385-2829-8(3))*** Arcadia Publishing.
Jones, Donald M., photos by. Buffalo Country: America's National Bison Range. 2005. (Illus.). 72p. per. 14.95 *(978-1-931832-56-4(0)*, 8667872363) Riverbend Publishing.
Kopp, Megan. Montana: The Treasure State. 2012. (J). *(978-1-61913-371-6(7))*; pap. *(978-1-61913-372-3(5))* Weigl Pubs., Inc.
Lusted, Marcia Amidon. Montana: The Treasure State. 2010. (Our Amazing States Ser.). (ENG.). 24p. (J). pap. 8.25 *(978-1-4488-0758-1(1))*; lib. bdg. 22.60 *(978-1-4488-0662-1(3))* Rosen Publishing Group, Inc., The. (PowerKids Pr.).
Marsh, Carole. Exploring Montana Through Project-Based Learning: Geography, History, Government, Economics & More. 2016. (Montana Experience Ser.). (ENG.). (J). pap. 9.99 *(978-0-635-12350-3(9))* Gallopade International.
—I'm Reading about Montana. 2014. (Montana Experience Ser.). (ENG., Illus.). (J). pap., pap. 8.99 *(978-0-635-11301-6(5))* Gallopade International.
—Montana History Projects: 30 Cool, Activities, Crafts, Experiments & More for Kids to Do to Learn about Your State! 2003. (Montana Experience Ser.). 32p. (gr. k-5). pap. 5.95 *(978-0-635-01795-6(4)*, Marsh, Carole Bks.) Gallopade International.
McLuskey, Krista. Montana: The Treasure State. 2016. (J). *(978-1-4896-4893-8(3))* Weigl Pubs., Inc.
Merrill-Maker, Andrea. Montana: People & Their Stories. 2004. (Illus.). 371p. (J). 32.09 *(978-0-913205-28-0(1))* Sage Hill Pubs., LLC.
Mills, Jordan. Montana. 2016. (States Ser.). (ENG., Illus.). 32p. (gr. 3-4). lib. bdg. 27.32 *(978-1-5157-0413-3(0))* Next Page Pr., The.
Montana History Notebook Map. 2004. (J). *(978-0-9759433-6-6(7))* Maps For Kids Inc.
Murray, Julie. Montana, 1 vol. 2012. (Explore the United States Ser.). (ENG.). 32p. (J). (gr. 2-5). lib. bdg. 28.50 *(978-1-61783-364-9(9)*, Big Buddy Bks.) ABDO Publishing Co.
Ollhoff, Jim. Montana, 1 vol. 2009. (United States Ser.). (ENG., Illus.). 48p. (YA). (gr. 2-5). 27.07 *(978-1-60453-661-4(6))* ABDO Publishing Co.
Patent, Dorothy Hinshaw. The Call of the Osprey. Muñoz, William, illus. Muñoz, William, photos by. 2015. (Scientists in the Field Ser.). (ENG.). 80p. (J). (gr. 5-7). 18.99 *(978-0-544-23268-6(2)*, HMH Books For Young Readers) Houghton Mifflin Harcourt Publishing Co.
Peterson, Sheryl. Montana. 2009. (This Land Called America Ser.). 32p. (YA). (gr. 3-6). 19.95 *(978-1-58341-779-9(6))* Creative Co., The.
Porterfield, Jason. Montana: Past & Present. 2010. (United States: Past & Present Ser.). (ENG.). 48p. (YA). pap. 11.75 *(978-1-4358-9513-3(4))*; lib. bdg. 29.25 *(978-1-4358-9486-0(3))* Rosen Publishing Group, Inc., The. (Rosen Reference).
Solberg, Jessica L. First Dog: Unleashed in the Montana Capitol. Rath, Robert, illus. 2007. (J). 11.95 *(978-1-56037-419-0(5))* Farcountry Pr.
Stein, R. Conrad. Montana (Revised Edition) 2014. (America the Beautiful, Third Ser. (Revised Edition) Ser.). (ENG.). 144p. (J). lib. bdg. 40.00 *(978-0-531-28283-0(X))* Scholastic Library Publishing.
Westcott, Jim. Upper Plains: Montana, North Dakota, South Dakota, Vol. 19. 2015. (Let's Explore the States Ser.). (Illus.). 64p. (J). (gr. 5). 23.95 *(978-1-4222-3336-8(7))* Mason Crest.
Williams, Judith M. Montana. 2009. (From Sea to Shining Sea, Second Ser.). (ENG.). 80p. (J). pap. 7.95 *(978-0-531-21135-9(5)*, Children's Pr.) Scholastic Library Publishing.

MONTEREY (CALIF.)

Abbink, Emily. Monterey Bay Area Missions. 2007. (Exploring California Missions Ser.). (ENG., Illus.). 64p. (gr. 4-7). lib. bdg. 27.93 *(978-0-8225-0887-8(7)*, Lerner Pubns.) Lerner Publishing Group.

MONTEREY (CALIF.)—FICTION

Collins, Yvonne & Rideout, Sandy. The Black Sheep. 2007. 348p. (J). *(978-1-4287-4665-7(X))* Hyperion Pr.

MONTESSORI, MARIA, 1870-1952

Bach, Nancy. Maria Montessori & Her Quiet Revolution: A Picture Book about Maria Montessori & Her School Method. Lätti, Leo, illus. 2013. 24p. pap. *(978-1-938712-10-4(2))* Roxby Media Ltd.
Sharpe, Paula A. Maria Montessori. Ward, Patricia R. & Pigford, Grady A., illus. 2010. 51p. (J). *(978-1-892142-47-4(3))* Cedar Tree Bks.

MONTEZUMA II, EMPEROR OF MEXICO, 1480-1520

Conklin, Wendy. Moctezuma: Aztec Ruler, 1 vol. 2007. (Primary Source Readers Ser.). (ENG.). 32p. (J). (gr. 4-4). pap. 8.99 *(978-0-7439-0457-5(5))* Shell Educational Publishing.
Green, Carl R. Cortés: Conquering the Powerful Aztec Empire. 2010. (Great Explorers of the World Ser.). (Illus.). 112p. (J). (gr. 7-12). 33.27 *(978-1-59845-099-6(9))* Enslow Pubs., Inc.
Schulz, Elizabeth. Montezuma II. 2017. (J). ***(978-1-5026-2789-6(2))*** Cavendish Square Publishing.

MONTEZUMA, CARLOS, 1866-1923

Capaldi, Gina. A Boy Named Beckoning: The True Story of Dr. Carlos Montezuma, Native American Hero. Capaldi, Gina, illus. 2008. (Exceptional Social Studies Titles for Intermediate Grades). (ENG., Illus.). 32p. (J). (gr. 3-6). lib. bdg. 16.95 *(978-0-8225-7644-0(9))* Lerner Publishing Group.

MONTGOLFIER, JOSEPH MICHEL, 1740-1810

Lowery, Lawrence F. Up, Up in a Balloon. 2013. (I Wonder Why Ser.). (ENG., Illus.). 36p. (J). (gr. k-3). pap. 11.95 *(978-1-938946-14-1(6))* National Science Teachers Assn.

MONTGOMERY, L. M. (LUCY MAUD), 1874-1942

Kjelle, Marylou Morano. L. M. Montgomery. 2005. (Who Wrote That? Ser.). (Illus.). 112p. (gr. 6-12). lib. bdg. 35.00 *(978-0-7910-8234-8(2)*, Chelsea Hse.) Facts On File, Inc.
MacLeod, Elizabeth. Lucy Maud Montgomery. Mantha, John, illus. 2008. (ENG.). 32p. (J). (gr. 1-3). 14.95 *(978-1-55453-055-7(5))*; pap. 3.95 *(978-1-55453-056-4(3))* Kids Can Pr., Ltd. CAN. Dist: Hachette Bk. Group.
Wallner, Alexandra. Lucy Maud Montgomery. Wallner, Alexandra, illus. 2006. (ENG., Illus.). 32p. (J). (gr. -1-3). 16.95 *(978-0-8234-1549-6(X))* Holiday Hse., Inc.

MONTGOMERY (ALA.)—RACE RELATIONS

Aretha, David. The Story of Rosa Parks & the Montgomery Bus Boycott in Photographs. 2014. (Story of the Civil Rights Movement in Photographs Ser.). 48p. (J). 25.27 *(978-0-7660-4234-6(0))* Enslow Pubs., Inc.
Banting, Erinn. Rosa Parks. 2005. (Great African American Women for Kids Ser.). (Illus.). 24p. (J). (gr. 2-3). lib. bdg. 26.00 *(978-1-59036-336-2(1))*; (gr. 3-7). per. 8.95 *(978-1-59036-342-3(6))* Weigl Pubs., Inc.
Bjornlund, Lydia. Rosa Parks & the Montgomery Bus Boycott. 2007. (Lucent Library of Black History Ser.). (ENG., Illus.). 128p. (gr. 8-12). lib. bdg. 39.40 *(978-1-4205-0010-3(4)*, Lucent Bks.) Cengage Gale.
Brandt, Keith & Mattern, Joanne. Rosa Parks: Freedom Rider. Griffith, Gershom, illus. 2006. 54p. (J). pap. *(978-0-439-66045-7(9))* Scholastic, Inc.
Brown, Jonatha A. Rosa Parks. 2005. (People We Should Know Ser.). (Illus.). 24p. (gr. 1-4). pap. 8.15 *(978-0-8368-4755-0(5))*; (ENG & SPA., pap. 8.15 *(978-0-8368-4769-7(5))*; (ENG & SPA., lib. bdg. 22.00 *(978-0-8368-4762-8(8))*; lib. bdg. 22.00 *(978-0-8368-4748-2(2))* Stevens, Gareth Publishing LLLP. (Weekly Reader Leveled Readers).
Connors, Kathleen. The Life of Rosa Parks, Vol. 1. 2014. (Famous Lives Ser.). (ENG.). 24p. (J). (gr. 1-2). 22.60 *(978-1-4824-0419-7(2))* Stevens, Gareth Publishing LLLP.
Dubowski, Cathy East. Rosa Parks: Don't Give In! 2005. (Defining Moments Ser.). (Illus.). 32p. (J). (gr. 2-5). lib. bdg. 25.27 *(978-1-59716-078-0(4))* Bearport Publishing Co., Inc.
Edwards, Pamela Duncan. The Bus Ride That Changed History: The Story of Rosa Parks. Shanahan, Danny, illus. 2009. (ENG.). 32p. (J). (gr. -1-3). pap. 6.99 *(978-0-547-07674-4(6))* Houghton Mifflin Harcourt Publishing Co.
Fine, Edith Hope. Rosa Parks: Meet a Civil Rights Hero. 2004. (Meeting Famous People Ser.). (Illus.). 32p. (J). lib. bdg. 23.94 *(978-0-7660-2099-3(1))* Enslow Pubs., Inc.
Fradin, Dennis Brindell. The Montgomery Bus Boycott. 2009. (Turning Points in U. S. History Ser.). 48p. (gr. 3-18). 31.36 *(978-0-7614-4258-5(8))* Marshall Cavendish Corp.
Freedman, Russell. Freedom Walkers: The Story of the Montgomery Bus Boycott. (ENG., Illus.). 112p. (J). 2009. (gr. 3-7). pap. 14.95 *(978-0-8234-2195-4(3))* 2006. (gr. 5-10). 18.95 *(978-0-8234-2031-5(0))* Holiday Hse., Inc.
Giovanni, Nikki. Rosa. Collier, Bryan, illus. rev. ed. 2005. (ENG.). 40p. (J). (gr. -1-3). 17.99 *(978-0-8050-7106-1(7)*, 9780805071061, Holt, Henry & Co. Bks. For Young Readers) Holt, Henry & Co.
—Rosa. Collier, Bryan, illus. 2007. (ENG.). 40p. (J). (gr. -1-3). per. 8.99 *(978-0-312-37602-4(2)*, 9780312376024) Square Fish.
—Rosa. Collier, Bryan, illus. 2011. (J). (gr. 2-5). 29.95 *(978-0-545-04261-1(5))* Weston Woods Studios, Inc.
Hoose, Phillip. Claudette Colvin: Twice Toward Justice. 2010. (ENG., Illus.). 160p. (YA). (gr. 8-12). pap. 9.99 *(978-0-312-66105-2(3)*, 9780312661052) Square Fish.
Hull, Mary. Rosa Parks: Civil Rights Leader. 2nd rev. ed. 2006. (Black Americans of Achievement Ser.). (Illus.). 122p. (YA). (gr. 7-12). lib. bdg. 35.00 *(978-0-7910-9523-2(1))* Facts On File, Inc.
Hull, Mary & Gelfand, Dale Evva. Rosa Parks. 2nd rev. ed. 2008. (Black Americans of Achievement: Legacy Edition Ser.). 128p. (gr. 6-12). pap. 11.95 *(978-1-60413-325-7(2)*, Checkmark Bks.) Facts On File, Inc.
Hurt, Avery Elizabeth. Rosa Parks: Civil Rights Activist. 2017. (J). ***(978-1-5383-8105-2(2))*** Rosen Publishing Group, Inc., The.
Kishel, Ann-Marie. Rosa Parks: A Life of Courage. 2006. (Pull Ahead Books-Biographies Ser.). (ENG., Illus.). 32p. (gr. k-3). lib. bdg. 22.60 *(978-0-8225-3478-5(9)*, Lerner Pubns.) Lerner Publishing Group.
—Rosa Parks: Una Vida de Valentia. Translations.com Staff, tr. 2006. (Libros para Avanzar-Biografías (Pull Ahead Books-Biographies) Ser.). (ENG & SPA., Illus.). 32p. (gr. k-3). lib. bdg. 22.60 *(978-0-8225-6239-9(1))* Lerner Publishing Group.
Kittinger, Jo S. Rosa's Bus: The Ride to Civil Rights. Walker, Steven, illus. 2010. (ENG.). 40p. (J). (gr. 2-4). 17.95 *(978-1-59078-722-9(6))* Boyds Mills Pr.
Mara, Wil. Rosa Parks. (Rookie Biographies Ser.). (ENG., Illus.). 32p. (J). (gr. 1-2). 2004. pap. 4.95 *(978-0-516-27916-9(5))* 2007. pap. 4.95 *(978-0-531-12592-2(0))* Scholastic Library Publishing. (Children's Pr.).
—Rosa Parks: Mother of the Civil Rights Movement. 2014. (Rookie Biographies(r) Ser.). (ENG.). 32p. (J). pap. 5.95 *(978-0-531-21204-2(1))* Scholastic Library Publishing.
Marsico, Katie. The Montgomery Bus Boycott: Milestone of the Civil Rights Movement. 2011. (Perspectives on 3 Ser.). (Illus.). 112p. (J). (gr. 7). 39.93 *(978-1-60870-447-7(5))* Marshall Cavendish Corp.
McDonough, Yona Zeldis. Who Was Rosa Parks? Harrison, Nancy & Marchesi, Stephen, illus. 2010. (Who Was? Ser.). (ENG.). 112p. (J). (gr. 3-7). pap. 5.99 *(978-0-448-45442-9(4)*, Grosset & Dunlap) Penguin Young Readers Group.
Meltzer, Brad. I Am Rosa Parks. Eliopoulos, Christopher, illus. 2014. (Ordinary People Change World Ser.). (ENG.). 40p. (J). (gr. -1-k). 14.99 *(978-0-8037-4085-3(9)*, Dial Bks) Penguin Publishing Group.
Miller, Connie Colwell. Rosa Parks & the Montgomery Bus Boycott, 1 vol. Kalal, Dan, illus. 2006. (Graphic History Ser.). (ENG.). 32p. (gr. 3-4). per. 8.10 *(978-0-7368-9658-0(9)*, Graphic Library) Capstone Press of Coughlan Cos.
Miller, Jake. The Montgomery Bus Boycott: Integrating Public Buses. (Library of the Civil Rights Movement Ser.). 24p. 2009. (gr. 3-3). 42.50 *(978-1-60853-895-9(8))* 2004. (Illus.). (J). lib. bdg. 22.60 *(978-0-8239-6251-8(2))* Rosen Publishing Group, Inc., The. (PowerKids Pr.).
Mis, Melody S. Meet Rosa Parks. 2009. (Civil Rights Leaders Ser.). 24p. (gr. 2-3). 42.50 *(978-1-61511-855-7(1)*, PowerKids Pr.) Rosen Publishing Group, Inc., The.
Morris, Roz. Rosa Parks: Mother of the Civil Rights Movement. 2003. (Alabama Roots Biography Ser.). (Illus.). 109p. (J). *(978-1-878561-57-2(X))* Seacoast Publishing, Inc.
O'Hern, Kerri & Walsh, Frank. The Montgomery Bus Boycott. 2006. (Graphic Histories Ser.). (Illus.). 32p. (gr. 5-8). pap. 10.50 *(978-0-8368-6257-7(0))* Stevens, Gareth Publishing LLLP.
Pingry, Patricia A. Meet Rosa Parks. Walker, Steven, illus. 2008. (ENG.). 32p. (J). (gr. k-3). per. 7.99 *(978-0-8249-5578-6(1)*, Ideal Pubns.) Worthy Publishing.
Rinaldo, Denise. Rosa Parks: With a Discussion of Courage. 2003. (Values in Action Ser.). (J). *(978-1-59203-061-3(0))* Learning Challenge, Inc.
Ringgold, Faith. If a Bus Could Talk: The Story of Rosa Parks. Ringgold, Faith, illus. 2003. (ENG., Illus.). 32p. (J). (gr. k-4). pap. 7.99 *(978-0-689-85676-1(8)*, Aladdin) Simon & Schuster Children's Publishing.
Schraff, Anne E. Rosa Parks: Tired of Giving In. 2005. (African-American Biography Library). (Illus.). 128p. (J). (gr. 6-12). lib. bdg. 33.27 *(978-0-7660-2463-2(6))* Enslow Pubs., Inc.
Sepahban, Lois. 12 Incredible Facts about the Montgomery Bus Boycott. 2015. (Turning Points in US History Ser.). (ENG., Illus.). 32p. (J). (gr. 3-5). *(978-1-63235-132-6(3)*, 12-Story Library) Pr. Room Editions LLC.
Shone, Rob. Rosa Parks: The Life of a Civil Rights Heroine. 2009. (Graphic Nonfiction Biographies Ser.). (ENG.). 48p. (YA). (gr. 4-5). 58.50 *(978-1-61513-026-9(8)*, Rosen Reference) Rosen Publishing Group, Inc., The.
—Rosa Parks: The Life of a Civil Rights Heroine. Spender, Nick, illus. 2007. (Graphic Nonfiction Biographies Ser.). (ENG.). 48p. (J). (gr. 4-7). lib. bdg. 31.95 *(978-1-4042-0864-3(X))* Rosen Publishing Group, Inc., The.
—Rosa Parks: The Life of a Civil Rights Heroine. Spender, Nik, illus. 2007. (Graphic Biographies Ser.). (ENG.). 48p. (gr. 5-8). pap. 14.05 *(978-1-4042-0927-5(1))* Rosen Publishing Group, Inc., The.
Summer, L. S. Rosa Parks. 2009. (Journey to Freedom Ser.). (ENG., Illus.). 32p. (J). (gr. 4-7). 29.93 *(978-1-60253-133-8(1)*, 200399) Child's World, Inc., The.
Tieck, Sarah. Rosa Parks, 1 vol. 2006. (Buddy Book Ser.). (ENG., Illus.). 32p. (gr. -1-3). 27.07 *(978-1-59679-788-8(6)*, Buddy Bks.) ABDO Publishing Co.
Time for Kids Editors. Rosa Parks: Civil Rights Pioneer. 2007. (Time for Kids Biographies Ser.). (Illus.). 44p. (gr. 2-4). 14.00 *(978-0-7569-8110-5(7))* Perfection Learning Corp.
Vaughn, Wally G. & Davis, Mattie Campbell, eds. The Selma Campaign, 1963-1965: The Decisive Battle of the Civil Rights Movement. 2006. (ENG., Illus.). 244p. pap. 19.95 *(978-0-912469-44-7(7))* Majority Pr., The.
Walsh, Frank. The Montgomery Bus Boycott. 2003. (Landmark Events in American History Ser.). (Illus.). 48p. (gr. 5-12). pap. 14.05 *(978-0-8368-5403-9(9)*, Gareth Stevens Secondary Library) Stevens, Gareth Publishing LLLP.
Weidt, Maryann N. Rosa Parks. (History Maker Bios Ser.). (Illus.). (J). 2004. 48p. pap. 8.95 *(978-0-8225-4805-8(4))* 2003. 47p. 26.60 *(978-0-8225-4673-3(6))* Lerner Publishing Group. (Lerner Pubns.).
Weston Woods Staff, creator. Rosa. 2011. 38.75 *(978-0-545-14963-1(0))*; 18.95 *(978-0-545-14962-4(2))* Weston Woods Studios, Inc.
Wheeler, Jill C. Rosa Parks, Set II. 2003. (Breaking Barriers Ser.). 64p. (gr. 3-8). 27.07 *(978-1-57765-640-1(7)*, Abdo & Daughters) ABDO Publishing Co.
Whiting, Jim. Rosa Parks. 2007. (What's So Great About... ? Ser.). (Illus.). 32p. (YA). (gr. 2-4). lib. bdg. 25.70 *(978-1-58415-573-7(6))* Mitchell Lane Pubs., Inc.

MONTHS

Brode, Robyn. April;abril. 2009. (Months of the Year/Meses del año Ser.). (ENG & SPA.). 24p. (J). (gr. -1-3). pap. 8.15 *(978-1-4339-2109-4(X)*, Weekly Reader Leveled Readers) Stevens, Gareth Publishing LLLP.
—April/Abril. 2009. (Months of the Year/Meses del año Ser.). (ENG & SPA.). 24p. (J). (gr. -1-3). lib. bdg. 22.00 *(978-1-4339-1932-9(X)*, Weekly Reader Leveled Readers) Stevens, Gareth Publishing LLLP.
—August;agosto. 2009. (Months of the Year/Meses del año Ser.). (ENG & SPA.). 24p. (J). (gr. -1-3). pap. 8.15 *(978-1-4339-2113-1(8)*, Weekly Reader Leveled Readers) Stevens, Gareth Publishing LLLP.
—August/Agosto. 2009. (Months of the Year/Meses del año Ser.). (ENG & SPA.). 24p. (J). (gr. -1-3). lib. bdg. 22.00 *(978-1-4339-1936-7(2)*, Weekly Reader Leveled Readers) Stevens, Gareth Publishing LLLP.
—December;diciembre. 2009. (Months of the Year/Meses del año Ser.). (ENG & SPA.). 24p. (J). (gr. -1-3). pap. 8.15 *(978-1-4339-2117-9(0)*, Weekly Reader Leveled Readers) Stevens, Gareth Publishing LLLP.
—December/Diciembre. 2009. (Months of the Year/Meses del año Ser.). (ENG & SPA.). 24p. (J). (gr. -1-3). lib. bdg. 22.00 *(978-1-4339-1940-4(0)*, Weekly Reader Leveled Readers) Stevens, Gareth Publishing LLLP.
—February;febrero. 2009. (Months of the Year/Meses del año Ser.). (ENG & SPA.). 24p. (J). (gr. -1-3). pap. 8.15 *(978-1-4339-2107-0(3)*, Weekly Reader Leveled Readers) Stevens, Gareth Publishing LLLP.
—February/Febrero. 2009. (Months of the Year/Meses del año Ser.). (ENG & SPA.). 24p. (J). (gr. -1-3). lib. bdg. 22.00 *(978-1-4339-1930-5(3)*, Weekly Reader Leveled Readers) Stevens, Gareth Publishing LLLP.
—January;enero. 2009. (Months of the Year/Meses del año Ser.). (ENG & SPA.). 24p. (J). (gr. -1-3). pap. 8.15 *(978-1-4339-2106-3(5)*, Weekly Reader Leveled Readers) Stevens, Gareth Publishing LLLP.
—January/Enero. 2009. (Months of the Year/Meses del año Ser.). (ENG & SPA.). 24p. (J). (gr. -1-3). lib. bdg. 22.00 *(978-1-4339-1929-9(X)*, Weekly Reader Leveled Readers) Stevens, Gareth Publishing LLLP.
—July;julio. 2009. (Months of the Year/Meses del año Ser.). (ENG & SPA.). 24p. (J). (gr. -1-3). pap. 8.15 *(978-1-4339-2112-4(X)*, Weekly Reader Leveled Readers) Stevens, Gareth Publishing LLLP.
—July/Julio. 2009. (Months of the Year/Meses del año Ser.). (ENG & SPA.). 24p. (J). (gr. -1-3). lib. bdg. 22.00 *(978-1-4339-1935-0(4)*, Weekly Reader Leveled Readers) Stevens, Gareth Publishing LLLP.
—June;junio. 2009. (Months of the Year/Meses del año Ser.). (ENG & SPA.). 24p. (J). (gr. -1-3). pap. 8.15 *(978-1-4339-2111-7(1)*, Weekly Reader Leveled Readers) Stevens, Gareth Publishing LLLP.
—June/Junio. 2009. (Months of the Year/Meses del año Ser.). (ENG & SPA.). 24p. (J). (gr. -1-3). lib. bdg. 22.00 *(978-1-4339-1934-3(6)*, Weekly Reader Leveled Readers) Stevens, Gareth Publishing LLLP.
—March;marzo. 2009. (Months of the Year/Meses del año Ser.). (ENG & SPA.). 24p. (J). (gr. -1-3). pap. 8.15 *(978-1-4339-2108-7(1)*, Weekly Reader Leveled Readers) Stevens, Gareth Publishing LLLP.
—March/Marzo. 2009. (Months of the Year/Meses del año Ser.). (ENG & SPA.). 24p. (J). (gr. -1-3). lib. bdg. 22.00 *(978-1-4339-1931-2(1)*, Weekly Reader Leveled Readers) Stevens, Gareth Publishing LLLP.
—November;noviembre. 2009. (Months of the Year/Meses del año Ser.). (ENG & SPA.). 24p. (J). (gr. -1-3). pap. 8.15 *(978-1-4339-2116-2(2)*, Weekly Reader Leveled Readers) Stevens, Gareth Publishing LLLP.
—November/Noviembre. 2009. (Months of the Year/Meses del año Ser.). (ENG & SPA.). 24p. (J). (gr. -1-3). lib. bdg. 22.00 *(978-1-4339-1939-8(7)*, Weekly Reader Leveled Readers) Stevens, Gareth Publishing LLLP.
—October. 2nd rev. ed. 2009. (Months of the Year Ser.). 24p. (J). (gr. -1-3). pap. 8.15 *(978-1-4339-2103-2(0))*; lib. bdg. 22.00 *(978-1-4339-1926-8(5))* Stevens, Gareth Publishing LLLP. (Weekly Reader Leveled Readers).
—October;octubre. 2009. (Months of the Year/Meses del año Ser.). (ENG & SPA.). 24p. (J). (gr. -1-3). pap. 8.15 *(978-1-4339-2115-5(4)*, Weekly Reader Leveled Readers) Stevens, Gareth Publishing LLLP.
—October/Octubre. 2009. (Months of the Year/Meses del año Ser.). (ENG & SPA.). 24p. (J). (gr. -1-3). lib. bdg. 22.00 *(978-1-4339-1938-1(9)*, Weekly Reader Leveled Readers) Stevens, Gareth Publishing LLLP.
—September;septiembre. 2009. (Months of the Year/Meses del año Ser.). (ENG & SPA.). 24p. (J). (gr. -1-3). pap. 8.15 *(978-1-4339-2114-8(6)*, Weekly Reader Leveled Readers) Stevens, Gareth Publishing LLLP.
—September/Septiembre. 2009. (Months of the Year/Meses del año Ser.). (ENG & SPA.). 24p. (J). (gr. -1-3). lib. bdg. 22.00 *(978-1-4339-1937-4(0)*, Weekly Reader Leveled Readers) Stevens, Gareth Publishing LLLP.
Brode, Robyn & Nations, Susan. April. 2nd rev. ed. 2009. (Months of the Year Ser.). (ENG.). 24p. (J). (gr. -1-3). pap. 8.15 *(978-1-4339-2097-4(2))*; lib. bdg. 22.00 *(978-1-4339-1920-6(6))* Stevens, Gareth Publishing LLLP. (Weekly Reader Leveled Readers).
—August. 2nd rev. ed. 2009. (Months of the Year Ser.). (ENG.). 24p. (J). (gr. -1-3). pap. 8.15 *(978-1-4339-2101-8(4))*; lib. bdg. 22.00 *(978-1-4339-1924-4(9))* Stevens, Gareth Publishing LLLP. (Weekly Reader Leveled Readers).
—February. 2nd rev. ed. 2009. (Months of the Year Ser.). (ENG.). 24p. (J). (gr. -1-3). pap. 8.15 *(978-1-4339-2095-0(6))*; lib. bdg. 22.00 *(978-1-4339-1918-3(4))* Stevens, Gareth Publishing LLLP. (Weekly Reader Leveled Readers).
—January. 2nd rev. ed. 2009. (Months of the Year Ser.). (ENG.). 24p. (J). (gr. -1-3). pap. 8.15 *(978-1-4339-2094-3(8))*; lib. bdg. 22.00

(978-1-4339-1917-6(6)) Stevens, Gareth Publishing LLLP. (Weekly Reader Leveled Readers).
—July. 2nd rev. ed. 2009. (Months of the Year Ser.). (ENG.). 24p. (J). (gr. -1-3). pap. 8.15 *(978-1-4339-2100-1(6))*; lib. bdg. 22.00 *(978-1-4339-1923-7(0))* Stevens, Gareth Publishing LLLP. (Weekly Reader Leveled Readers).
—June. 2nd rev. ed. 2009. (Months of the Year Ser.). (ENG.). 24p. (J). (gr. -1-3). pap. 8.15 *(978-1-4339-2099-8(9))*; lib. bdg. 22.00 *(978-1-4339-1922-0(2))* Stevens, Gareth Publishing LLLP. (Weekly Reader Leveled Readers).
—March. 2nd rev. ed. 2009. (Months of the Year Ser.). (ENG.). 24p. (J). (gr. -1-3). pap. 8.15 *(978-1-4339-2096-7(4))*; lib. bdg. 22.00 *(978-1-4339-1919-0(2))* Stevens, Gareth Publishing LLLP. (Weekly Reader Leveled Readers).
—May. 2nd rev. ed. 2009. (Months of the Year Ser.). (ENG.). 24p. (J). (gr. -1-3). pap. 8.15 *(978-1-4339-2098-1(0))*; lib. bdg. 22.00 *(978-1-4339-1921-3(4))* Stevens, Gareth Publishing LLLP. (Weekly Reader Leveled Readers).
—November. 2nd rev. ed. 2009. (Months of the Year Ser.). (ENG.). 24p. (J). (gr. -1-3). pap. 8.15 *(978-1-4339-2104-9(9))*; lib. bdg. 22.00 *(978-1-4339-1927-5(3))* Stevens, Gareth Publishing LLLP. (Weekly Reader Leveled Readers).
—September. 2nd rev. ed. 2009. (Months of the Year Ser.). (ENG.). 24p. (J). (gr. -1-3). pap. 8.15 *(978-1-4339-2102-5(2))*; lib. bdg. 22.00 *(978-1-4339-1925-1(7))* Stevens, Gareth Publishing LLLP. (Weekly Reader Leveled Readers).
Clark, Claire. How Long Is a Month? 2012. (Calendar Ser.). (ENG.). 24p. (gr. k-1). pap. 41.70 *(978-1-4296-8335-7(X)*, Pebble Plus) Capstone Press of Coughlan Cos.
Cohn, Scott. One Wolf Howls, 1 vol. Detwiler, Susan, illus. 2009. (ENG.). 32p. (J). (gr. -1-3). 16.95 *(978-1-934359-92-1(0))* Arbordale Publishing.
Gürth, Per-Henrik. Canada All Year. Gürth, Per-Henrik, illus. 2011. (ENG., Illus.). 32p. (J). (gr. -1-1). 14.95 *(978-1-55453-709-9(6))* Kids Can Pr., Ltd. CAN. Dist: Hachette Bk. Group.
Havercroft, Elizabeth. A Year in the World of Dinosaurs. 2008. (Time Goes By Ser.). (ENG.). (gr. k-2). pap. 39.62 *(978-0-7613-4714-9(3))*; (Illus.). 24p. lib. bdg. 22.60 *(978-1-58013-548-1(X))* Lerner Publishing Group.
Hunt, Darleen L. Bob's Busy Year: Months of the Year. Komarck, Michael, illus. 2003. (Sherman's Math Corner Ser.). (J). (gr. -1-3). *(978-1-929591-03-9(9))* Reading Rock, Inc.
Kelley, K. C. April. Ostrom, Bob, illus. 2014. (Twelve Magic Months Ser.). (ENG.). 24p. (J). (gr. k-3). 27.07 *(978-1-62687-362-9(3)*, 207202) Child's World, Inc., The.
—August. Ostrom, Bob, illus. 2014. (Twelve Magic Months Ser.). (ENG.). 24p. (J). (gr. k-3). 27.07 *(978-1-62687-363-6(1)*, 207203) Child's World, Inc., The.
—December. Ostrom, Bob, illus. 2014. (Twelve Magic Months Ser.). (ENG.). 24p. (J). (gr. k-3). 27.07 *(978-1-62687-364-3(X)*, 207204) Child's World, Inc., The.
—February. Ostrom, Bob, illus. 2014. (Twelve Magic Months Ser.). (ENG.). 24p. (J). (gr. k-3). 27.07 *(978-1-62687-365-0(8)*, 207205) Child's World, Inc., The.
—January. Ostrom, Bob, illus. 2014. (Twelve Magic Months Ser.). (ENG.). 24p. (J). (gr. k-3). 27.07 *(978-1-62687-366-7(6)*, 207206) Child's World, Inc., The.
—July. Ostrom, Bob, illus. 2014. (Twelve Magic Months Ser.). (ENG.). 24p. (J). (gr. k-3). 27.07 *(978-1-62687-367-4(4)*, 207207) Child's World, Inc., The.
—June. Ostrom, Bob, illus. 2014. (Twelve Magic Months Ser.). (ENG.). 24p. (J). (gr. k-3). 27.07 *(978-1-62687-368-1(2)*, 207208) Child's World, Inc., The.
—March. Ostrom, Bob, illus. 2014. (Twelve Magic Months Ser.). (ENG.). 24p. (J). (gr. k-3). 27.07 *(978-1-62687-369-8(0)*, 207209) Child's World, Inc., The.
—May. Ostrom, Bob, illus. 2014. (Twelve Magic Months Ser.). (ENG.). 24p. (J). (gr. k-3). 27.07 *(978-1-62687-370-4(4)*, 207210) Child's World, Inc., The.
—November. Ostrom, Bob, illus. 2014. (Twelve Magic Months Ser.). (ENG.). 24p. (J). (gr. k-3). 27.07 *(978-1-62687-371-1(2)*, 207211) Child's World, Inc., The.
—October. Ostrom, Bob, illus. 2014. (Twelve Magic Months Ser.). (ENG.). 24p. (J). (gr. k-3). 27.07 *(978-1-62687-372-8(0)*, 207212) Child's World, Inc., The.
—September. Ostrom, Bob, illus. 2014. (Twelve Magic Months Ser.). (ENG.). 24p. (J). (gr. k-3). 27.07 *(978-1-62687-373-5(9)*, 207213) Child's World, Inc., The.
Kesselring, Mari. April, 1 vol. Dumm, Brian Caleb, illus. 2009. (Months of the Year Ser.). (ENG.). 24p. (gr. -1-2). 27.07 *(978-1-60270-631-6(X)*, Looking Glass Library- Nonfiction) Magic Wagon.
—August, 1 vol. Collier-Morales, Roberta, illus. 2009. (Months of the Year Ser.). (ENG.). 24p. (gr. -1-2). 27.07 *(978-1-60270-635-4(2)*, Looking Glass Library- Nonfiction) Magic Wagon.
—December, 1 vol. Billin-Frye, Paige, illus. 2009. (Months of the Year Ser.). (ENG.). 24p. (gr. -1-2). 27.07 *(978-1-60270-639-2(5)*, Looking Glass Library- Nonfiction) Magic Wagon.
—February, 1 vol. Billin-Frye, Paige, illus. 2009. (Months of the Year Ser.). (ENG.). 24p. (gr. -1-2). 27.07 *(978-1-60270-629-3(8)*, Looking Glass Library- Nonfiction) Magic Wagon.
—January, 1 vol. Billin-Frye, Paige, illus. 2009. (Months of the Year Ser.). (ENG.). 24p. (gr. -1-2). 27.07 *(978-1-60270-628-6(X)*, Looking Glass Library- Nonfiction) Magic Wagon.
—July, 1 vol. Collier-Morales, Roberta, illus. 2009. (Months of the Year Ser.). (ENG.). 24p. (gr. -1-2). 27.07 *(978-1-60270-634-7(4)*, Looking Glass Library- Nonfiction) Magic Wagon.
—June, 1 vol. Collier-Morales, Roberta, illus. 2009. (Months of the Year Ser.). (ENG.). 24p. (gr. -1-2). 27.07 *(978-1-60270-633-0(6)*, Looking Glass Library- Nonfiction) Magic Wagon.
—March, 1 vol. Dumm, Brian Caleb, illus. 2009. (Months of the Year Ser.). (ENG.). 24p. (gr. -1-2). 27.07 *(978-1-60270-630-9(1)*, Looking Glass Library- Nonfiction) Magic Wagon.
—May, 1 vol. Dumm, Brian Caleb, illus. 2009. (Months of the Year Ser.). (ENG.). 24p. (gr. -1-2). 27.07 *(978-1-60270-632-3(8)*, Looking Glass Library- Nonfiction) Magic Wagon.
—Months of the Year, 12 vols., Set. Incl. April. Dumm, Brian Caleb, illus. 27.07 *(978-1-60270-631-6(X))*; August. Collier-Morales, Roberta, illus. 27.07 *(978-1-60270-635-4(2))*; December. Billin-Frye, Paige, illus. 27.07 *(978-1-60270-639-2(5))*; February. Billin-Frye, Paige, illus. 27.07 *(978-1-60270-629-3(8))*; January. Billin-Frye, Paige, illus. 27.07 *(978-1-60270-628-6(X))*; July. Collier-Morales, Roberta, illus. 27.07 *(978-1-60270-634-7(4))*; June. Collier-Morales, Roberta, illus. 27.07 *(978-1-60270-633-0(6))*; March. Dumm, Brian Caleb, illus. 27.07 *(978-1-60270-630-9(1))*; May. Dumm, Brian Caleb, illus. 27.07 *(978-1-60270-632-3(8))*; November. Rooney, Ronnie, illus. 27.07 *(978-1-60270-638-5(7))*; October. Rooney, Ronnie, illus. 27.07 *(978-1-60270-637-8(9))*; September. Rooney, Ronnie, illus. 27.07 *(978-1-60270-636-1(0))*; (gr. -1-2). (Months of the Year Ser.). 24p. 2009. 324.84 *(978-1-60270-627-9(1)*, Looking Glass Library- Nonfiction) Magic Wagon.
—November, 1 vol. Rooney, Ronnie, illus. 2009. (Months of the Year Ser.). (ENG.). 24p. (gr. -1-2). 27.07 *(978-1-60270-638-5(7)*, Looking Glass Library- Nonfiction) Magic Wagon.
—October, 1 vol. Rooney, Ronnie, illus. 2009. (Months of the Year Ser.). (ENG.). 24p. (gr. -1-2). 27.07 *(978-1-60270-637-8(9)*, Looking Glass Library- Nonfiction) Magic Wagon.
—September, 1 vol. Rooney, Ronnie, illus. 2009. (Months of the Year Ser.). (ENG.). 24p. (gr. -1-2). 27.07 *(978-1-60270-636-1(0)*, Looking Glass Library- Nonfiction) Magic Wagon.
Mitten, Luana K. Mi Calendario: Los Meses Del Año/My Calendar: Months of the Year. 2008. (SPA & ENG., Illus.). 24p. (J). 22.79 *(978-1-60472-492-9(7))* Rourke Educational Media.
Morris, Sheila L. Sweet Baby's Fun Months of the Year. 2013. 16p. pap. 9.99 *(978-1-61897-424-2(6)*, Strategic Bk. Publishing) Strategic Book Publishing & Rights Agency (SBPRA).
Nikola-lisa, W. Till Year's Good End. Manson, Christopher, illus. 2009. (ENG.). 36p. (J). (gr. 1-4). 12.99 *(978-1-4424-0225-6(3)*, Atheneum Bks. for Young Readers) Simon & Schuster Children's Publishing.
Randolph, Joanne. All about A Months/Los Meses. Brusca, Maria Cristina, tr. 2007. (It's about Time / Los Libros Del Tiempo Ser.). (SPA., Illus.). 24p. (J). (gr. k-2). lib. bdg. 22.60 *(978-1-4042-7628-4(9))* Rosen Publishing Group, Inc., The.
—All about the Months. (It's about Time Ser.). 24p. 2009. (gr. 1-1). 42.50 *(978-1-61513-632-2(0)*, PowerKids Pr.) 2007. (Illus.). (J). (gr. k-2). lib. bdg. 22.60 *(978-1-4042-3769-8(0))* Rosen Publishing Group, Inc., The.
—All about the Months/Los Meses. 2009. (It's about Time/Los libros del tiempo Ser.). (SPA.). 24p. (gr. 1-1). 42.50 *(978-1-61513-628-5(2)*, Editorial Buenas Letras) Rosen Publishing Group, Inc., The.
Scheunemann, Pam. Time to Learn about Weeks & Months, 1 vol. 2008. (Time Ser.). (ENG., Illus.). 24p. (J). (gr. k-3). lib. bdg. 24.21 *(978-1-60453-020-9(0))* ABDO Publishing Co.
Steffora, Tracey. Meses del Año. 2011. (Medir el Tiempo Ser.). (SPA.). 24p. (gr. -1-1). 22.65 *(978-1-4329-5631-8(0))*; pap. 6.29 *(978-1-4329-5638-7(8))* Heinemann-Raintree. (Bellota).
—Months of the Year, 1 vol. 2011. (Measuring Time Ser.). (ENG.). 24p. (gr. -1-1). 22.65 *(978-1-4329-4905-1(5)*, Acorn) Heinemann-Raintree.
Twelve Magic Months (Set), 12 vols. 2014. (Twelve Magic Months Ser.). (ENG.). (J). (gr. k-3). 324.84 *(978-1-60973-167-0(0)*, 208282) Child's World, Inc., The.

MONTHS—FICTION

Barner, Bob. Parade Day: Marching Through the Calendar Year. 2003. (ENG., Illus.). 32p. (J). (gr. k-3). tchr. ed. 16.95 *(978-0-8234-1690-5(9))* Holiday Hse., Inc.
Bauer, Marion Dane. In Like a Lion, Out Like a Lamb. McCully, Emily Arnold, illus. 2011. (ENG.). 32p. (J). (gr. -1-3). 16.95 *(978-0-8234-2238-8(0))* Holiday Hse., Inc.
Blackstone, Stella. Jump into January. Carluccio, Maria, illus. 2004. 32p. (J). 15.99 *(978-1-84148-629-1(9))* Barefoot Bks., Inc.
—On y Danse les Saisons. Carluccio, Maria, illus. 2016. (FRE.). (J). pap. *(978-1-78285-298-8(0))* Barefoot Bks., Inc.
—Skip Through the Seasons. Carluccio, Maria, illus. 2009. (ENG.). 32p. (J). 16.99 *(978-1-84686-293-9(0))* Barefoot Bks., Inc.
Blackstone, Stella & Carluccio, Maria. Un Recorrido Por Las Estaciones. Carluccio, Maria, illus. 2009. (SPA., Illus.). 32p. (J). (gr. -1-2). pap. 7.99 *(978-1-84686-291-5(4))* Barefoot Bks., Inc.
—Skip Through the Seasons. Carluccio, Maria, illus. 2006. (Seek-and-Find Bks.). (ENG., Illus.). 32p. (J). (gr. -1-k). 7.99 *(978-1-905236-71-8(9))* Barefoot Bks., Inc.
Gravett, Emily. The Rabbit Problem. Gravett, Emily, illus. 2010. (ENG., Illus.). 32p. (J). (gr. -1-3). 17.99 *(978-1-4424-1255-2(0)*, Simon & Schuster Bks. For Young Readers) Simon & Schuster Bks. For Young Readers.
Inkpen, Mick. One Year with Kipper. 2015. (ENG., Illus.). 32p. (J). (gr. -1-k). pap. 10.99 *(978-1-4449-1820-5(6))* Hodder & Stoughton GBR. Dist: Hachette Bk. Group.
Martin, Bill, Jr. The Turning of the Year. Shed, Greg, illus. 2007. (ENG.). 28p. (J). (gr. -1-3). pap. 6.99 *(978-0-15-204555-5(4))* Houghton Mifflin Harcourt Publishing Co.
Menge, Dawn & Rhoades, Heath. Queen Vernita Meets Sir HeathyBean the Astronomer. 2010. 33p. (J). pap. 19.95 *(978-1-4327-3120-5(3))* Outskirts Pr., Inc.
Moncure, Jane Belk. Here We Go 'Round the Year: A Book about the Months. Billin-Frye, Paige, illus. 2013. (Magic Castle Readers Ser.). (ENG.). 32p. (J). (gr. -1-2). 25.64 *(978-1-62323-582-6(0)*, 206318) Child's World, Inc., The.
Parker, Sandy. What Month Is It? Hofner, Cathy, illus. l.t. ed. 2004. 32p. 15.95 *(978-0-9643462-5-3(7)*, Just Think Bks.) Canary Connect Pubns.
Rylant, Cynthia & Siegel, Mark. Long Night Moon. Siegel, Mark, illus. 2004. (ENG., Illus.). 32p. (J). (gr. -1-3). 17.99 *(978-0-689-85426-2(9)*, Simon & Schuster Bks. For Young Readers) Simon & Schuster Bks. For Young Readers.
Scelsa, Greg. Months of the Year. Faulkner, Stacey, ed. Fulcher, Roz, illus. 2006. (J). pap. 2.99 *(978-1-59198-320-0(7))* Creative Teaching Pr., Inc.
Tudor, Tasha. Around the Year. Tudor, Tasha, illus. 2004. (ENG., Illus.). 64p. (J). (gr. -1-3). 7.99 *(978-0-689-87350-8(6)*, Aladdin) Simon & Schuster Children's Publishing.
Walsh, Susanne. My Very Favorite Time of Year: Featuring the Whimsy Kids. 2007. 34p. pap. 24.95 *(978-1-4241-9090-4(8))* America Star Bks.

MONTHS—POETRY

Leduc, Émilie. All Year Round, 1 vol. Tanaka, Shelley, tr. from FRE. 2015. (ENG., Illus.). 36p. (J). (-k). 16.95 *(978-1-55498-411-4(4))* Groundwood Bks. CAN. Dist: Publishers Group West (PGW).
Livingston, Myra Cohn. Calendar. Hillenbrand, Will, illus. 2007. (ENG.). 32p. (J). (gr. -1-3). 16.95 *(978-0-8234-1725-4(5))* Holiday Hse., Inc.
Weston Woods Staff, creator. Chicken Soup with Rice. 2004. (J). 18.95 *(978-1-55592-801-8(3))* Weston Woods Studios, Inc.

MONTICELLO (VA.)

Chew, Elizabeth V. A Day at Monticello. Elliott, Mark, illus. 2014. (ENG.). 56p. (J). (gr. 3-7). 18.95 *(978-1-4197-0541-0(5)*, Abrams Bks. for Young Readers) Abrams, Inc.
Tieck, Sarah. Monticello, 1 vol. 2008. (All Aboard America Ser.). (ENG.). 24p. (J). (gr. 1-4). 25.65 *(978-1-59928-937-3(7))* ABDO Publishing Co.

MONTREAL (QUEBEC)

Rowe, Percy & Coster, Patience. Montreal. 2004. (Great Cities of the World Ser.). (Illus.). 48p. (gr. 5-12). lib. bdg. 31.00 *(978-0-8368-5039-0(4)*, Gareth Stevens Secondary Library) Stevens, Gareth Publishing LLLP.

MONTREAL (QUEBEC)—FICTION

Bayle, B. J. Perilous Passage. 2007. (ENG.). 184p. (YA). (gr. k-7). pap. 11.99 *(978-1-55002-689-4(5)*, Sandcastle Bks.) Dundurn CAN. Dist: Ingram Publisher Services.
Gamble, Adam. Good Night Montreal. Kelly, Cooper, illus. 2007. (Good Night Our World Ser.). (ENG.). 20p. (J). (gr. k — 1). bds. 9.95 *(978-1-60219-012-2(7))* Good Night Bks.
Goodwin, Catherine. Seeking Shelter. 2006. (ENG., Illus.). 156p. (J). per. *(978-1-55380-033-0(8))* Ronsdale Pr.
Kimmel, Elizabeth Cody. Suddenly Supernatural 4: Crossing Over. 2011. (Suddenly Supernatural Ser.: 4). (ENG.). 256p. (J). (gr. 3-7). pap. 5.99 *(978-0-316-13345-6(0))* Little, Brown Bks. for Young Readers.
Launier, Veronique. Deliverance. 2014. (Hearts of Stone Ser.: 2). (ENG.). 288p. (YA). pap. 9.99 *(978-0-7387-3075-2(0)*, Flux) Llewellyn Pubns.
Polak, Monique. Finding Elmo, 1 vol. 2007. (Orca Currents Ser.). (ENG.). (J). (gr. 5-9). 112p. lib. bdg. 14.95 *(978-1-55143-688-3(4))*; 128p. per. 9.95 *(978-1-55143-686-9(8))* Orca Bk. Pubs. USA.
—Pyro, 1 vol. 2012. (Orca Currents Ser.). (ENG.). 128p. (J). (gr. 5-9). pap. 9.95 *(978-1-4598-0228-5(4))*; lib. bdg. 16.95 *(978-1-4598-0229-2(2))* Orca Bk. Pubs. USA.
—Straight Punch, 1 vol. 2014. (ENG.). 256p. (YA). (gr. 8-12). pap. 12.95 *(978-1-4598-0391-6(4))* Orca Bk. Pubs. USA.
Schwartz, Ellen. Yossi's Goal, 1 vol. 2006. (Orca Young Readers Ser.). (ENG., Illus.). 144p. (J). (gr. 3-6). per. 6.95 *(978-1-55143-492-6(X))* Orca Bk. Pubs. USA.
Zweig, Eric. Fever Season. 2009. (ENG.). 256p. (YA). (gr. 4-18). pap. 10.99 *(978-1-55488-432-2(2)*, Dundurn Pr.) Dundurn CAN. Dist: Ingram Publisher Services.

MONUMENTS

see also Pyramids

Bryant, Tamera. We Remember: State Monuments & Historic Sites. 2004. (ZB Reads Trio Books). (Illus.). iii, 43p. (gr. 3-5). pap., tchr. ed. 4.50 *(978-0-7367-1783-0(8))* Zaner-Bloser, Inc.
Chapman, Tony. Buildings, Bridges, & Landmarks: a Complete History. 2016. (ENG., Illus.). 118p. pap. 19.99 *(978-1-62686-556-3(6)*, Thunder Bay Pr.) Readerlink Distribution Services, LLC.
Ferry, Joseph. Vietnam Veterans Memorial: Remembering a Generation & a War. Moreno, Barry, ed. 2014. (Patriotic Symbols of America Ser.: 20). 48p. (J). (gr. 4-18). lib. bdg. 20.95 *(978-1-4222-3136-4(4))* Mason Crest.
Gabriel, Luke. Mount Rushmore. 2014. (United States Landmarks Ser.). (ENG.). 24p. (J). (gr. 1-4). 27.07 *(978-1-62323-955-8(9)*, 206730) Child's World, Inc., The.
Gamble, Adam & Jasper, Mark. Good Night Statue of Liberty. Kelly, Cooper, illus. 2017. (Good Night Our World Ser.). (ENG.). 20p. (J). (gr. -1 — 1). bds. 9.95 ***(978-1-60219-429-8(7))*** Good Night Bks.
Gilmore, Frederic. The Lincoln Memorial. 2014. (United States Landmarks Ser.). (ENG.). 24p. (J). (gr. 1-4). 27.07 *(978-1-62323-957-2(5)*, 206732) Child's World, Inc., The.
—The Washington Monument. 2014. (United States Landmarks Ser.). (ENG.). 24p. (J). (gr. 1-4). 27.07 *(978-1-62323-959-6(1)*, 206734) Child's World, Inc., The.
Gray, Leon. Solving the Mysteries of Stonehenge. 2008. (Digging into History Ser.). 32p. (gr. 4-18). lib. bdg. 29.93 *(978-0-7614-3110-7(1)*, Benchmark Bks.) Marshall Cavendish Corp.
Hargrove, Julia. Bostons Trail to Freedom. 2003. (Historic Monuments Ser.). (Illus.). 48p. (J). (gr. 4-8). pap. 6.95 *(978-1-57310-403-6(5))* Teaching & Learning Co.
Henzel, Cynthia Kennedy. Stonehenge, 1 vol. 2011. (Troubled Treasures: World Heritage Sites Ser.). (ENG., Illus.). 32p. (YA). (gr. 3-6). 27.07 *(978-1-61613-567-6(0))* ABDO Publishing Co.
Hoobler, Dorothy & Hoobler, Thomas. Where Is the Taj Mahal? 2017. (Where Is... ? Ser.). lib. bdg. 16.00 ***(978-0-606-39777-3(9))*** Turtleback Bks.
Jango-Cohen, Judith. Mount Rushmore. 2010. pap. 45.32 *(978-0-7613-6990-5(2))* Lerner Publishing Group.
Kelley, True. Where Is Stonehenge? Hinderliter, John & Groff, David, illus. 2016. (Where Is... ? Ser.). (ENG.). 112p. (J). (gr. 3-7). 16.00 *(978-0-606-39317-1(X))* Turtleback Bks.
Malam, John. Stone Circles: Discover Stone, Bronze & Iron Age Britain. 2016. (Prehistoric Adventures Ser.). (ENG., Illus.). 32p. (J). (gr. 2-4). 17.99 *(978-0-7502-9583-3(X)*, Wayland) Hachette Children's Group GBR. Dist: Hachette Bk. Group.
Mattern, Joanne. The Alamo. 2014. (ENG.). 32p. (gr. 3-6). 32.79 *(978-1-62717-740-5(X))* Rourke Educational Media.
—Mount Rushmore. 2014. (ENG.). 32p. (gr. 3-6). 32.79 *(978-1-62717-741-2(8))* Rourke Educational Media.
—National Mall. 2014. (ENG.). 32p. (gr. 3-6). 32.79 *(978-1-62717-739-9(6))* Rourke Educational Media.
Moriarty, Siobhan. Visit the Statue of Liberty. 2012. (Landmarks of Liberty Ser.). (ENG., Illus.). 24p. (J). (gr. 2-5). pap. 8.15 *(978-1-4339-6402-2(3)*, Gareth Stevens Learning Library); lib. bdg. 22.60 *(978-1-4339-6400-8(7))* Stevens, Gareth Publishing LLLP.
National Geographic Learning Staff. Famous Landmarks, Level 3. 2011. (World Windows Ser.). (ENG.). 16p. stu. ed. 9.95 *(978-1-133-56616-8(2))* Cengage Heinle.
Niver, Heather Moore. 20 Fun Facts about US Monuments. 2013. (Fun Fact File: US History! Ser.). 32p. (J). (gr. 3-6). pap. 63.00 *(978-1-4339-9210-0(8))*; pap. 10.50 *(978-1-4339-9209-4(4))* Stevens, Gareth Publishing LLLP.
Niver, Heather Moore & Moore Niver, Heather. 20 Fun Facts about US Monuments. 2013. 32p. (J). (gr. 3-6). 25.25 *(978-1-4339-9208-7(6))* Stevens, Gareth Publishing LLLP.
O'connor, Jim. Where Is the Colosseum? 2017. (Where Is... ? Ser.). lib. bdg. 16.00 ***(978-0-606-39776-6(0))*** Turtleback Bks.
O'Donnell, Kerri. The Great Wall of China. 2009. (Reading Room Collection 2 Ser.). 24p. (gr. 3-4). 42.50 *(978-1-60851-994-1(5)*, PowerKids Pr.) Rosen Publishing Group, Inc., The.
Owings, Lisa. Stonehenge. 2015. (Unexplained Mysteries Ser.). (ENG., Illus.). 24p. (J). (gr. 3-7). lib. bdg. 25.95 *(978-1-62617-204-3(8)*, Epic Bks.) Bellwether Media.
Phillips, Cynthia & Priwer, Shana. Ancient Monuments. 2009. (ENG., Illus.). 115p. (C). (gr. 6-18). lib. bdg. 158.00 *(978-0-7656-8123-2(4)*, Y181320) Routledge.
Prior, Jennifer. America's Man-Made Landmarks. rev. ed. 2014. (Primary Source Readers Content & Literacy Ser.). (ENG., Illus.). 32p. (gr. 3-3). pap. 8.99 *(978-1-4333-7370-1(X))* Teacher Created Materials, Inc.
Putnam, Jeff. National Monuments: Events & Times. 2004. (ZB Reads Trio Books). (Illus.). iii, 75p. (gr. 4-6). pap. 5.00 *(978-0-7367-1787-8(0))* Zaner-Bloser, Inc.
—National Monuments: Nature. 2004. (ZB Reads Trio Books). (Illus.). iii, 92p. (gr. 4-6). pap. 5.00 *(978-0-7367-1788-5(9))* Zaner-Bloser, Inc.
Ridley, Sarah. Remembering the Fallen of the First World War. 2016. (ENG., Illus.). 48p. (J). (gr. 6-11). 18.99 *(978-1-4451-4250-0(3)*, Franklin Watts) Hachette Children's Group GBR. Dist: Hachette Bk. Group.
Riggs, Kate. Stonehenge. 2009. (Places of Old Ser.). 24p. (J). (gr. 1-5). lib. bdg. 24.25 *(978-1-58341-711-9(7)*, Creative Education) Creative Co., The.
—Taj Mahal. 2009. (Places of Old Ser.). 24p. (J). (gr. 1-5). lib. bdg. 24.25 *(978-1-58341-712-6(5)*, Creative Education) Creative Co., The.
Scholastic, Inc. Staff & Keenan, Sheila. O, Say Can You See? America's Symbols, Landmarks, & Important Words. Boyajian, Ann, illus. 2007. (ENG.). 64p. (J). (gr. -1-3). pap. 6.99 *(978-0-439-59360-1(3)*, Scholastic Nonfiction) Scholastic, Inc.
Schwartz, Heather E. & Salzano, Tammi. Around the World: An Amazing World. 2009. (Illus.). 48p. (J). pap. *(978-0-545-17229-5(2))* Scholastic, Inc.
Scott, Dan. Big Buildings of the Ancient World. 2015. (Inside Eye Ser.). (Illus.). 32p. (gr. 3-6). 31.35 *(978-1-906370-75-6(3))* Book Hse. GBR. Dist: Black Rabbit Bks.
Silate, Jennifer. The Statue of Liberty. (Primary Sources of American Symbols Ser.). 24p. 2009. (gr. 3-3). 42.50 *(978-1-60851-510-3(9)*, PowerKids Pr.) 2006. (Illus.). (J). (gr. -1-3). lib. bdg. 22.60 *(978-1-4042-2696-8(6))* Rosen Publishing Group, Inc., The.
Sipperley, Keli. St. Louis Gateway Arch. 2014. (ENG.). 32p. (gr. 3-6). 32.79 *(978-1-62717-742-9(6))* Rourke Educational Media.
—The White House. 2014. (ENG.). 32p. (gr. 3-6). 32.79 *(978-1-62717-744-3(2))* Rourke Educational Media.
Weil, Ann. The World's Most Amazing Monuments, 1 vol. 2011. (Landmark Top Tens Ser.). (ENG.). 32p. (gr. 3-5). pap. 8.29 *(978-1-4109-4247-0(3)*, Raintree Perspectives) Heinemann-Raintree.
World Book, Inc Staff, contrib. by. The Mysteries of Stonehenge. 2014. (J). *(978-0-7166-2667-1(5))* World Bk., Inc.
Yasuda, Anita. The 12 Most Amazing American Monuments & Symbols. 2014. (ENG., Illus.). 32p. (J). *(978-1-63235-009-1(2))* Pr. Room Editions LLC.

MONUMENTS, NATURAL

see Natural Monuments

MONUMENTS—UNITED STATES

Ashley, Susan. Mount Rushmore. 2004. (Weekly Reader Early Learning Library). (Illus.). 24p. (gr. 1-4). pap. 8.15 *(978-0-8368-4149-7(2))*; lib. bdg. 22.00 *(978-0-8368-4142-8(5))* Stevens, Gareth Publishing LLLP. (Weekly Reader Leveled Readers).
—The Washington Monument. 2004. (Weekly Reader Early Learning Library). (Illus.). 24p. (gr. 1-4). pap. 8.15 *(978-0-8368-4151-0(4))*; lib. bdg. 22.00 *(978-0-8368-4144-2(1))* Stevens, Gareth Publishing LLLP. (Weekly Reader Leveled Readers).
Cain, Marie Mowery. Monumental America. 2013. (Big Books, Red Ser.). (ENG & SPA., Illus.). 16p. pap. 33.00 *(978-1-59246-224-7(3))* Big Books, by George!
Demarest, Chris L. Arlington: The Story of Our Nation's Cemetery. Demarest, Chris L., illus. 2010. (ENG., Illus.). 32p. (J). (gr. 1-5). 18.99 *(978-1-59643-517-9(8)*, 9781596435179) Roaring Brook Pr.
Dickerson, Joy E. Pack & Go. 2004. (ZB Reads Trio Books). (Illus.). iii, 75p. (gr. 3-5). pap. 5.00 *(978-0-7367-1785-4(4))* Zaner-Bloser, Inc.
Eggers, Dave. Her Right Foot. Ojala, Eiko & Harris, Shawn, illus. 2017. (ENG.). 104p. (J). (gr. k-3). 19.99 ***(978-1-4521-6281-2(6))*** Chronicle Bks. LLC.
Ferry, Joseph. The Jefferson Memorial. 2004. (American Symbols & Their Meanings Ser.). (Illus.). 48p. (J). (gr. 4-18). lib. bdg. 19.95 *(978-1-59084-034-4(8))* Mason Crest.
—Jefferson Memorial: A Monument to Greatness. Moreno, Barry, ed. 2014. (Patriotic Symbols of America Ser.: 20). 48p. (J). (gr. 4-18). lib. bdg. 20.95 *(978-1-4222-3125-8(9))* Mason Crest.

M
N
O

—The Vietnam Veterans Memorial. 2004. (American Symbols & Their Meanings Ser.). (Illus.). 48p. (J). (gr. 4-18). lib. bdg. 19.95 *(978-1-59084-039-9(9))* Mason Crest.

Foran, Jill. Statues & Monuments. 2004. (American Symbols Ser.). (Illus.). 24p. (J). (gr. 4-7). per. 8.95 *(978-1-59036-178-8(4))* Weigl Pubs., Inc.

Gunderson, Jessica, et al. Monumental History, 1 vol. 2014. (Monumental History Ser.). (ENG.). 32p. (gr. 3-4). 109.28 *(978-1-4914-0207-8(5),* Fact Finders) Capstone Press of Coughlan Cos.

Healy, Nick. The Statue of Liberty. 2003. (J). pap. *(978-1-58417-117-1(0));* lib. bdg. *(978-1-58417-054-9(9))* Lake Street Pubs.

Jango-Cohen, Judith. Mount Rushmore. 2003. (Pull Ahead Books-American Symbols Ser.). (ENG., Illus.). 32p. (gr. k-3). pap. 7.95 *(978-0-8225-3755-7(9));* lib. bdg. 22.60 *(978-0-8225-3801-1(6))* Lerner Publishing Group.

Kasson, Joseph E. The Making of the Star of Texas. 2003. (Illus.). 32p. (J). lib. bdg. 14.95 *(978-0-9729435-8-1(7))* Kasson Publishing.

Lavelett, Lucille. Through the Years at Monument, Colorado, 1 Vol. 5th ed. 2004. (Illus.). 168p. (YA). per. *(978-0-9755989-0-0(2))* Palmer Lake Historical Society.

Lindeen, Mary. History Rocks!, 1 vol. (Wonder Readers: Social Studies). (ENG.). (gr. -1-2). 2012. 20p. lib. bdg. 22.65 *(978-1-4296-9614-2(1))* 2011. 32p. pap. 5.99 *(978-1-4296-7927-5(1))* 2011. 16p. pap. 35.94 *(978-1-4296-8262-6(0))* Capstone Press of Coughlan Cos. (Wonder Readers).

Marcovitz, Hal. Liberty Bell: Let Freedom Ring. 2015. (Illus.). 48p. (J). *(978-1-4222-3117-3(8))* Mason Crest.

Nelson, Kristin L. The Lincoln Memorial. 2003. (Pull Ahead Books-American Symbols Ser.). (ENG., Illus.). 32p. (gr. k-3). pap. 7.95 *(978-0-8225-3761-8(3))* Lerner Publishing Group.

—The Washington Monument. (Lightning Bolt Bks.). 32p. (gr. k-2). 2010. (Illus.). (J). lib. bdg. 25.26 *(978-0-7613-6019-3(0),* Lerner Pubns.) 2010. (ENG.). pap. 7.95 *(978-0-7613-6053-7(0))* 2003. (ENG.). pap. 7.95 *(978-0-8225-3759-5(1))* 2003. (ENG., Illus.). lib. bdg. 22.60 *(978-0-8225-0250-0(X))* Lerner Publishing Group.

RJF Publishing Staff & Hankins, Chelsey. The Gateway Arch. 2009. (Symbols of American Freedom Ser.). 48p. (gr. 4-6). 30.00 *(978-1-60413-513-8(1),* Chelsea Clubhouse) Facts On File, Inc.

Rowell, Rebecca. The 12 Most Amazing American Natural Wonders. 2014. (ENG.). 32p. (J). *(978-1-63235-011-4(4))* Pr. Room Editions LLC.

Stein, R. Conrad. The Oklahoma City National Memorial. 2003. (Cornerstones of Freedom Ser.). (ENG., Illus.). 48p. (YA). (gr. 4-7). 26.00 *(978-0-516-24205-7(9))* Scholastic Library Publishing.

Trumbauer, Lisa. Set in Stone. 2005. (Yellow Umbrella Fluent Level Ser.). (ENG.). 16p. (gr. k-1). pap. 35.70 *(978-0-7368-5308-8(1),* Yellow Umbrella Bks.) Capstone Press of Coughlan Cos.

Wachtel, Roger. The Tomb of the Unknown Soldier. 2003. (Cornerstones of Freedom Ser.). (ENG., Illus.). 48p. (YA). (gr. 4-7). 26.00 *(978-0-516-24215-6(6))* Scholastic Library Publishing.

Yasuda, Anita. The 12 Most Amazing American Monuments & Symbols. 2015. (ENG., Illus.). 32p. (J). pap. 9.95 *(978-1-63235-069-5(6))* RiverStream Publishing.

MOODY, JUDY (FICTITIOUS CHARACTER)—FICTION

Jones, Lucinda. Moody: What Moody Likes to Do. 2010. 28p. pap. 15.99 *(978-1-4535-3794-7(5))* Xlibris Corp.

McDonald, Megan. Around the World in 8 1/2 Days. 2007. (Judy Moody Ser.: 7). (SPA.). (J). 1.25 *(978-1-4281-3376-1(3))* Recorded Bks., Inc.

—Around the World in 8 1/2 Days. Reynolds, Peter H., illus. 2010. (Judy Moody Ser.: 7). (ENG.). 176p. (J). (gr. 1-4). 15.99 *(978-0-7636-4864-0(7))* Candlewick Pr.

—Around the World in 8 1/2 Days. 2010. (Judy Moody Ser.: 7). lib. bdg. 16.00 *(978-0-606-12349-5(0),* Turtleback) Turtleback Bks.

—Around the World in 8 1/2 Days, Bk. 7. Reynolds, Peter H., illus. 2010. (Judy Moody Ser.: 7). (ENG.). 176p. (J). (gr. 1-4). pap. 5.99 *(978-0-7636-4863-3(9))* Candlewick Pr.

—Doctora Judy Moody. Reynolds, Peter H., illus. 2005. (SPA.). 74p. (J). (gr. 3-5). per. 7.95 *(978-1-59820-034-8(8))* Ediciones Alfaguara ESP. Dist: Two Rivers Distribution.

—Girl Detective. Reynolds, Peter H., illus. (Judy Moody Ser.: 9). (ENG.). 192p. (J). (gr. 1-4). 2011. pap. 5.99 *(978-0-7636-4349-2(1))*Bk. 9. 2010. 15.99 *(978-0-7636-3450-6(6))* Candlewick Pr.

—Jessica Finch in Pig Trouble. Madrid, Erwin, illus. 2014. (Judy Moody Ser.: 1). (ENG.). 64p. (J). (gr. -1-1). 12.99 *(978-0-7636-5718-5(2));* pap. 4.99 *(978-0-7636-7027-6(8))* Candlewick Pr.

—Jessica Finch in Pig Trouble. 2014. (Judy Moody & Friends Ser.). (Illus.). 60p. (J). lib. bdg. 14.75 *(978-0-606-35162-1(0))* Turtleback Bks.

—Judy Moody. 2010. (Judy Moody Ser.: 1). lib. bdg. 16.00 *(978-0-606-12330-3(X),* Turtleback) Turtleback Bks.

—Judy Moody & Stink: The Mad, Mad, Mad, Mad Treasure Hunt. Reynolds, Peter H., illus. 2009. (Judy Moody Ser.: No. 2). (ENG.). 128p. (J). (gr. 1-4). 14.99 *(978-0-7636-3962-4(1))* Candlewick Pr.

—Judy Moody & Stink in the School's Out Collection. Reynolds, Peter H., illus. 2015. (Judy Moody Ser.). (ENG.). (J). (gr. 1-4). pap. 19.97 *(978-0-7636-8018-3(4))* Candlewick Pr.

—Judy Moody & Stink: the Big Bad Blackout. Reynolds, Peter H., illus. 2015. (Judy Moody Ser.). (ENG.). 144p. (J). (gr. 1-4). pap. 6.99 *(978-0-7636-7665-0(9))* Candlewick Pr.

—Judy Moody & Stink: the Wishbone Wish. Reynolds, Peter H., illus. 2015. (Judy Moody Ser.). (ENG.). 128p. (J). (gr. 1-4). 14.99 *(978-0-7636-7206-5(8))* Candlewick Pr.

—Judy Moody & the Bucket List. Reynolds, Peter H., illus. 2017. (Judy Moody Ser.: 13). (ENG.). 176p. (J). (gr. 1-4). pap. 5.99 ***(978-0-7636-9759-4(1))*** Candlewick Pr.

—Judy Moody & the Not Bummer Summer. Reynolds, Peter H., illus. movie tie-in ed. (Judy Moody Ser.: Bk. 10). (ENG.). (J). (gr. 1-4). 2011. 128p. pap. 5.99 *(978-0-7636-5351-4(9))*Bk. 10. 2012. 208p. 15.99 *(978-0-7636-5711-6(5))*Bk. 10. 2012. 208p. pap. 5.99 *(978-0-7636-5710-9(7))* Candlewick Pr.

—Judy Moody & the Not Bummer Summer. 2012. (Judy Moody Ser.: 10). lib. bdg. 16.00 *(978-0-606-23800-7(X),* Turtleback) Turtleback Bks.

—Judy Moody Esta de Mal Humor, de Muy Mal Humor. Mendoza Garcia, Isabel, tr. Reynolds, Peter H., illus. 2004. (SPA.). 160p. (J). (gr. 3-5). pap. 7.95 *(978-1-59437-816-4(9))* Ediciones Alfaguara ESP. Dist: Two Rivers Distribution.

—Judy Moody Goes to Hollywood: Behind the Scenes with Judy Moody & Friends. Reynolds, Peter H. & Candlewick Press Staff, illus. 2011. (Judy Moody Ser.). (ENG.). 160p. (J). (gr. 1-4). 14.99 *(978-0-7636-5551-8(1))* Candlewick Pr.

—Judy Moody, Mood Martian. Reynolds, Peter H., illus. 2014. (Judy Moody Ser.: 12). (ENG.). 208p. (J). (gr. 1-4). 15.99 *(978-0-7636-6698-9(X))* Candlewick Pr.

—Judy Moody Saves the World! Reynolds, Peter H., illus. 2010. (Judy Moody Ser.: 3). (ENG.). 160p. (J). (gr. 1-4). 15.99 *(978-0-7636-4860-2(4))* Candlewick Pr.

—Judy Moody Saves the World! 2010. (Judy Moody Ser.: 3). lib. bdg. 16.00 *(978-0-606-12340-2(7),* Turtleback) Turtleback Bks.

—Judy Moody se Vuelve Famosa! Mendoza Garcia, Isabel, tr. Reynolds, Peter H., illus. 2004. (SPA.). 340p. (J). (gr. 3-5). pap. 7.95 *(978-1-59437-817-1(7))* Ediciones Alfaguara ESP. Dist: Two Rivers Distribution.

—Judy Moody's Best Mood Ever Coloring & Activity Book. Reynolds, Peter H., illus. 2011. (Judy Moody Ser.). (ENG.). 32p. (J). (gr. -1-2). pap. 3.99 *(978-0-7636-5707-9(7))* Candlewick Pr.

—Judy Moody's Mini-Mysteries & Other Sneaky Stuff for Super-Sleuths. Reynolds, Peter H., illus. 2012. (Judy Moody Ser.). (ENG.). 96p. (J). (gr. 1-4). pap. 4.99 *(978-0-7636-5941-7(X))* Candlewick Pr.

—Mad Rad. Reynolds, Peter H., illus. 2012. (Judy Moody Ser.: Bks. 7-9). (ENG.). (J). (gr. 1-4). pap. 17.97 *(978-0-7636-5410-8(8))* Candlewick Pr.

—Mood Martian. Reynolds, Peter H., illus. 2015. (Judy Moody Ser.). (ENG.). 208p. (J). (gr. 1-4). pap. 5.99 *(978-0-7636-8015-2(X))* Candlewick Pr.

—Rocky Zang in the Amazing Mr. Magic. 2014. (Judy Moody & Friends Ser.). lib. bdg. 14.75 *(978-0-606-35163-8(9))* Turtleback Bks.

—Stink Moody in Master of Disaster. Madrid, Erwin, illus. 2015. (Judy Moody Ser.: 5). (ENG.). 64p. (J). (gr. -1-1). 12.99 *(978-0-7636-7218-8(1))* Candlewick Pr.

—Triple Pet Trouble. Madrid, Erwin, illus. 2015. (Judy Moody Ser.: 6). (ENG.). 64p. (J). (gr. -1-1). 12.99 *(978-0-7636-7443-4(5))* Candlewick Pr.

—Twice as Moody. Reynolds, Peter H., illus. 2011. (Judy Moody Ser.). (ENG.). 304p. (J). (gr. 1-4). pap. 8.99 *(978-0-7636-5740-6(9))* Candlewick Pr.

—Was in a Mood. Reynolds, Peter H., illus. 2010. (Judy Moody Ser.: 1). (ENG.). 160p. (J). (gr. 1-4). 15.99 *(978-0-7636-4850-3(7))* Candlewick Pr.

—The Wishbone Wish. Reynolds, Peter H., illus. 2016. (Judy Moody & Stink Ser.: 4). (ENG.). 116p. (J). (gr. 1-4). lib. bdg. 18.40 *(978-0-606-39093-4(6))* Turtleback Bks.

McDonald, Megan & Michalak, Jamie. The Poop Picnic. Reynolds, Peter H. & Candlewick Press Staff, illus. 2011. (Judy Moody Ser.). (ENG.). 48p. (J). (gr. k-3). pap. 3.99 *(978-0-7636-5553-2(8))* Candlewick Pr.

Michalak, Jamie. Judy Moody & the Thrill Points Race. Candlewick Press Staff, illus. 2011. (Judy Moody Ser.). (ENG.). 48p. (J). (gr. k-3). pap. 3.99 *(978-0-7636-5552-5(X))* Candlewick Pr.

MOON, LOTTIE, 1840-1912

Meloche, Renee. Heroes for Young Readers - Lottie Moon: A Generous Offering. Pollard, Bryan, illus. 2004. (Heroes for Young Readers Ser.). (ENG.). 32p. (J). 8.99 *(978-1-57658-243-5(4))* YWAM Publishing.

Vogel, Cara Lynn. The Lottie & Annie Upside-down Book. Adkins, Loretta B., illus. 2003. 16p. (J). 8.99 *(978-1-56309-627-3(7))* Woman's Missionary Union.

MOON, MOLLY (FICTITIOUS CHARACTER)—FICTION

Byng, Georgia. Molly Moon Detiene el Mundo. 2004. (SPA.). 358p. (gr. 5-8). 18.99 *(978-84-348-9610-9(9))* SM Ediciones ESP. Dist: Lectorum Pubns., Inc.

—Molly Moon, Micky Minus, & the Mind Machine. (Molly Moon Ser.: 4). (ENG.). (J). (gr. 3-7). 2008. 416p. pap. 7.99 *(978-0-06-075038-1(3))* 2007. 384p. 16.99 *(978-0-06-075036-7(7))* HarperCollins Pubs.

—Molly Moon Stops the World. (J). 2004. (Illus.). 384p. 16.99 *(978-0-06-051410-5(8))* 2005. (Molly Moon Ser.: 2). (ENG.). 416p. (gr. 3-7). reprint ed. pap. 7.99 *(978-0-06-051415-0(9))* HarperCollins Pubs.

—Molly Moon Viaja a Traes del Tiempo. Crispin, Maria Dolores, tr. 2005. (SPA.). 350p. *(978-84-675-0570-2(2))* SM Ediciones.

—Molly Moon y el Increible Libro. 2003. (SPA.). 349p. (J). 18.99 *(978-84-348-9076-3(3))* SM Ediciones ESP. Dist: Lectorum Pubns., Inc.

—Molly Moon's Hypnotic Time Travel Adventure. (ENG.). 400p. (J). 2006. (Molly Moon Ser.: 3). (gr. 3-7). pap. 7.99 *(978-0-06-075034-3(0))* 2005. (Illus.). 16.99 *(978-0-06-075032-9(4))* HarperCollins Pubs.

—Molly Moon's Hypnotic Time-Travel Adventure. 2005. (Illus.). 400p. (J). lib. bdg. 18.89 *(978-0-06-075033-6(2))* HarperCollins Pubs.

—Molly Moon's Incredible Book of Hypnotism. 2003. 135.92 *(978-0-06-057217-4(5))* 2003. (Molly Moon Ser.: 1). (Illus.). 384p. (J). (gr. 3-7). 17.99 *(978-0-06-051406-8(X))* 2004. (Molly Moon Ser.: 1). (ENG., Illus.). 384p. (J). (gr. 3-7). reprint ed. pap. 7.99 *(978-0-06-051409-9(4))* HarperCollins Pubs.

MOON

see also Tides

Adams, Alison. Our Moon. 2011. (Early Connections Ser.). (J). *(978-1-61672-531-0(1))* Benchmark Education Co.

Adamson, Thomas K. The Moon [Scholastic]. 2011. (Exploring the Galaxy Ser.). 24p. pap. 0.50 *(978-1-4296-6289-5(1),* Pebble Plus) Capstone Press of Coughlan Cos.

Alexander, Richard. Exploring the Moon. 2017. (J). ***(978-1-5345-2249-7(2),*** KidHaven Publishing) Greenhaven Publishing LLC.

Allyn, Daisy. The Moon: Earth's Satellite. 2010. (Our Solar System Ser.). 24p. (J). (gr. k-3). (ENG.). pap. 8.15 *(978-1-4339-3831-3(6));* (Illus.). lib. bdg. 22.60 *(978-1-4339-3830-6(8))* Stevens, Gareth Publishing LLLP.

Anderson, Michael. Earth & Its Moon. 2011. lib. bdg. 31.70 *(978-1-61530-515-5(7))* Rosen Publishing Group, Inc., The.

Ashby, Ruth. The Earth & Its Moon. 2003. (New Solar System Ser.). (J). lib. bdg. 28.50 *(978-1-58340-287-0(X))* Black Rabbit Bks.

Ashley, Michele. Why Does the Moon Look Different? 2014. (Little Books of Answers: Level e Ser.). (Illus.). 16p. (gr. k-2). pap. 7.95 *(978-1-927136-46-1(6))* Three Crows Media NZL. Dist: RiverStream Publishing.

Asimov, Isaac & Hantula, Richard. La Luna. Porras, Carlos & D'Andrea, Patricia, trs. from ENG. 2003. (Isaac Asimov's Biblioteca del Universo del Siglo XXI).Tr. of Moon. (SPA., Illus.). 32p. (gr. 2-6). lib. bdg. 26.00 *(978-0-8368-3855-8(6),* Gareth Stevens Learning Library) Stevens, Gareth Publishing LLLP.

Aspen-Baxter, Linda. La Luna, with Code. 2012. (Mirando Al Cielo Ser.). (SPA., Illus.). 24p. (J). (gr. k-2). lib. bdg. 27.13 *(978-1-61913-214-6(1),* AV2 by Weigl) Weigl Pubs., Inc.

Beaton, Kathryn. The Moon Changes Shape. 2015. (Tell Me Why Library). (ENG., Illus.). 24p. (J). (gr. 2-5). 27.07 *(978-1-63362-000-1(X),* 205912) Cherry Lake Publishing.

BeaverSimon. A LIGHT IN THE NIGHT: THE MOON BEGINNING BOOK WITH ONLINE ACCESS. 2014. (ENG.). 24p. (J). pap. 9.50 *(978-1-107-64756-5(8))* Cambridge Univ. Pr.

Biard, Philippe, et al. Moon. Biard, Philippe, illus. 2012. (ENG., Illus.). 34p. (J). (gr. k-3). pap. 11.99 *(978-1-85103-366-9(1))* Moonlight Publishing, Ltd. GBR. Dist: Independent Pubs. Group.

Bowman, Donna H. What Is the Moon Made Of? And Other Questions Kids Have about Space, 1 vol. Lubach, Peter, illus. (Kids' Questions Ser.). (ENG.). 24p. (gr. 1-2). 2011. pap. 7.49 *(978-1-4048-6726-0(0))* 2009. lib. bdg. 26.65 *(978-1-4048-5529-8(7))* Picture Window Bks.

Branley, Franklyn M. The Moon Seems to Change. Emberley, Barbara & Ed, illus. 2015. (Let's-Read-And-Find-Out Science 2 Ser.). (ENG.). 32p. (J). (gr. -1-3). pap. 6.99 *(978-0-06-238206-1(3))* HarperCollins Pubs.

Bredeson, Carmen. What Is the Moon? 2008. (I Like Space! Ser.). (Illus.). 32p. (J). (gr. 1-3). lib. bdg. 23.94 *(978-0-7660-2946-0(8),* Enslow Elementary) Enslow Pubs., Inc.

Brinkman, Patricia. Discover the Moon. 2006. (J). pap. *(978-1-4108-6478-9(2))* Benchmark Education Co.

—The Moon. 2006. (J). pap. *(978-1-4108-6475-8(8))* Benchmark Education Co.

Buckley, James & Bader, Bonnie. The Moon. 2016. (Smithsonian Ser.). (ENG., Illus.). 48p. (J). (gr. 3-4). 3.99 *(978-0-448-49020-5(X),* Penguin Young Readers) Penguin Young Readers Group.

Cain, Marie Mowery. A Trip to the Moon. 2013. (Big Books, Red Ser.). (ENG & SPA., Illus.). 16p. pap. 33.00 *(978-1-59246-211-7(1))* Big Books, by George!

Carlin, Lydia. The Moon. 2007. (Illus.). 16p. (J). 3.95 *(978-0-545-00732-0(1))* Scholastic, Inc.

Carroll, Jillian. Zoom Around a Moon. 2003. (J). pap. *(978-1-58417-241-3(X));* lib. bdg. *(978-1-58417-240-6(1))* Lake Street Pubs.

Carson, Mary Kay. Far-Out Guide to the Moon. 2010. (Far-Out Guide to the Solar System Ser.). (Illus.). 48p. (J). pap. 8.95 *(978-1-59845-184-9(7),* Enslow Elementary) Enslow Pubs., Inc.

Carson, Mary Kay & Library Association Staff. Far-Out Guide to the Moon. 2010. (Far-Out Guide to the Solar System Ser.). 48p. (J). (gr. 2-5). 25.27 *(978-0-7660-3189-0(6))* Enslow Pubs., Inc.

Chrismer, Melanie. The Moon. 2008. (Scholastic News Nonfiction Readers Ser.). (ENG., Illus.). 24p. (J). (gr. 1-2). pap. 6.95 *(978-0-531-14764-1(9))* Scholastic Library Publishing.

Clark, Claire & Shaskan, Trisha Speed. How Long Is a Month?, 1 vol. 2012. (Calendar Ser.). (ENG.). 24p. (gr. k-1). lib. bdg. 26.65 *(978-1-4296-7593-2(4),* Pebble Plus) Capstone Press of Coughlan Cos.

Cole, Joanna & Capeci, Anne. Takes a Moonwalk. Bracken, Carolyn, illus. 2007. (Magic School Bus Science Reader Ser.). (ENG.). 32p. (J). (gr. -1-3). per. 4.99 *(978-0-439-68400-2(5))* Scholastic, Inc.

Courgeon, Rémi. Many Moons: A Fun Guide to Learning about Moon Phases. 2017. (ENG., Illus.). 32p. (J). (gr. -1-1). 16.95 *(978-1-63322-298-4(5),* Walter Foster Jr) Quarto Publishing Group USA.

Crabtree Editors & Miller, Reagan. The Moon. 2012. (Journey Through Space Ser.). (ENG.). 24p. (J). (gr. 3-6). lib. bdg. *(978-0-7787-5306-3(9))* Crabtree Publishing Co.

Crelin, Bob. Faces of the Moon. Evans, Leslie, illus. 2009. (ENG.). 40p. (J). (gr. 1-4). 16.95 *(978-1-57091-785-1(X))* Charlesbridge Publishing, Inc.

Dale, Jay. To the Moon, 1 vol. Dybing, Michelle, illus. 2012. (Wonder Words Ser.). (ENG.). 32p. (gr. k-2). pap. 5.99 *(978-1-4296-8904-5(8),* Engage Literacy) Capstone Press of Coughlan Cos.

DeCristofano, Carolyn Cinami. The Sun & the Moon. Morley, Taia, illus. 2016. (Let's-Read-And-Find-Out Science 1 Ser.). 40p. (J). (gr. -1-3). pap. 6.99 *(978-0-06-233803-7(X))* HarperCollins Pubs.

deMarin, Layne. The Moon Book, 1 vol. 2011. (Wonder Readers: Science Ser.). (ENG.). (gr. -1-2). 20p. lib. bdg. 22.65 *(978-1-4296-8636-5(7));* 32p. pap. 5.99 *(978-1-4296-7942-8(5));* 16p. pap. 35.94 *(978-1-4296-8169-8(1))* Capstone Press of Coughlan Cos. (Wonder Readers).

DeYoe, Aaron. Moons, 1 vol. 2015. (ENG., Illus.). 24p. (J). *(978-1-62403-743-6(7))* ABDO Publishing Co.

Di Piazza, Domenica. NASA Computer Scientist Margaret Hamilton. 2017. (STEM Trailblazer Bios Ser.). (ENG.). 32p. (J). (gr. 2-5). 26.65 ***(978-1-5124-3450-7(7))*** Lerner Publishing Group.

Dickmann, Nancy. Exploring Planet Earth & the Moon. 2015. (Spectacular Space Science Ser.). (ENG., Illus.). 48p. (J). (gr. 5-6). 30.25 *(978-1-4994-3625-9(4),* Rosen Central) Rosen Publishing Group, Inc., The.

Dils, Tracey E. Around the Moon 1,2,3: A Space Counting Book. 2015. (1, 2, 3... Count with Me Ser.). (ENG., Illus.). 24p. (J). (gr. k-2). 19.95 *(978-1-60753-714-4(1))* Amicus Publishing.

Dyson, Laurence. Journey to the Moon, 1 vol. 2014. (Spotlight on Space Science Ser.). (ENG.). 32p. (J). (gr. 5-5). pap. 11.75 *(978-1-4994-0373-2(9),* PowerKids Pr.) Rosen Publishing Group, Inc., The.

Eckart, Edana. Watching the Moon. 2004. (Wel-Watching Nature Ser.). (Illus.). 24p. (J). 19.00 *(978-0-516-27598-7(4),* Children's Pr.) Scholastic Library Publishing.

Feinstein, Stephen. The Moon: A MyReportLinks. com Book. 2005. (Solar System Ser.). (Illus.). 48p. (J). lib. bdg. 26.60 *(978-0-7660-5306-9(7),* MyReportLinks.com Bks.) Enslow Pubs., Inc.

Gardner, Robert. Far-Out Science Projects about Earth's Sun & Moon. LaBaff, Tom, illus. 2007. (Rockin' Earth Science Experiments Ser.). 48p. (J). (gr. 3-4). lib. bdg. 25.27 *(978-0-7660-2736-7(8),* Enslow Elementary) Enslow Pubs., Inc.

—Science Fair Projects about the Sun & the Moon. 2016. (Hands-On Science Ser.). 48p. (J). pap. 11.70 *(978-0-7660-8215-1(6))* Enslow Pubs., Inc.

Gendell, Megan & Connolly, Rachel. Your Home in Space: Everything You Wanted to Know about Earth, the Sun, & the Moon. 2008. (Illus.). 32p. (J). *(978-0-545-04457-8(X))* Scholastic, Inc.

Gibbons, Gail, et al. The Moon Book. Gibbons, Gail, illus. 2003. (Avenues Ser.). (ENG., Illus.). 32p. (C). (gr. k-3). 12.95 *(978-0-8234-1364-5(0))* National Geographic School Publishing, Inc.

Goldstein, Margaret J. The Moon. 2005. (Pull Ahead Bks.). (Illus.). 32p. (gr. 2-4). lib. bdg. 22.60 *(978-0-8225-4658-0(2))* Lerner Publishing Group.

Graham, Ian. Our Moon. 2015. (Space Ser.). (Illus.). 24p. (gr. 3-6). lib. bdg. 28.50 *(978-1-62588-209-7(2))* Black Rabbit Bks.

Haelle, Tara. Seasons, Tides, & Lunar Phases. 2016. (Let's Explore Science Ser.). (ENG., Illus.). 48p. (gr. 5-8). 35.64 *(978-1-68191-395-7(X))* Rourke Educational Media.

Harman, Alice. Moon, 01 vols., 1. 2016. (Fact Finders: Space Ser.). (ENG., Illus.). 24p. (J). pap. 8.25 *(978-1-5081-9129-2(8),* Windmill Bks.) Rosen Publishing Group, Inc., The.

HB Staff. Let's Visit the Moon. 97th ed. 2003. (Signatures Ser.). (gr. 1-18). pap. 19.20 *(978-0-15-308181-1(3))* Harcourt Schl. Pubs.

Hicks, Terry Allan. Earth & the Moon. 2009. (Space!). 64p. (gr. 5-18). lib. bdg. 32.79 *(978-0-7614-4254-7(5))* Marshall Cavendish Corp.

Hill, Christina. Earth's Moon, 1 vol. 2015. (Science Readers: Content & Literacy Ser.). (ENG., Illus.). 32p. (gr. 3-3). pap. 8.99 *(978-1-4807-4651-0(7))* Teacher Created Materials, Inc.

Howard, Fran. The Moon, 1 vol. 2008. (Universe Ser.). (ENG.). 32p. (gr. k-4). 27.07 *(978-1-59928-929-8(6),* Buddy Bks.) ABDO Publishing Co.

Hutmacher, Kimberly. The Night Sky. 2012. (ENG.). 24p. (gr. 3-4). pap. 8.95 *(978-1-61810-225-6(7))* Rourke Educational Media.

Hutson, Matt. The Inside Story of the Moon. 2006. (J). 7.80 *(978-1-933798-05-9(X))* Sally Ride Science.

Jefferis, David. The Moon: Earth's Neighbor. 2008. (Exploring Our Solar System Ser.). (ENG., Illus.). 32p. (J). (gr. 3-7). pap. *(978-0-7787-3747-6(0))* Crabtree Publishing Co.

Kissock, Heather. Moon. 2011. (J). *(978-1-61690-600-9(6));* *(978-1-61690-954-3(4))* Weigl Pubs., Inc.

Koontz, Robin. Hide & Seek Moon: The Moon Phases, 1 vol. Davidson, Chris, illus. 2011. (First Graphics: Nature Cycles Ser.). (ENG.). 24p. (gr. 1-2). pap. 6.29 *(978-1-4296-6229-1(8));* pap. 35.70 *(978-1-4296-6398-4(7))* Capstone Press of Coughlan Cos.

Koontz, Robin Michal. Hide & Seek Moon: The Moon Phases, 1 vol. Davidson, Chris, illus. 2010. (First Graphics: Nature Cycles Ser.). (ENG.). 24p. (gr. 1-2). 23.99 *(978-1-4296-5365-7(5))* Capstone Press of Coughlan Cos.

Lawrence, Ellen. The Moon: Our Neighbor in Space. 2013. (Zoom into Space Ser.). 24p. (J). (gr. -1-3). lib. bdg. 23.93 *(978-1-909673-08-3(0))* Ruby Tuesday Books Limited GBR. Dist: Bearport Publishing Co., Inc.

Lilly, Melinda. Sun & Moon. Thompson, Scott M., photos by. 2005. (Rourke Discovery Library). (Illus.). 24p. (J). (gr. 1-4). lib. bdg. 14.95 *(978-1-59515-405-7(1),* 1244276) Rourke Educational Media.

Lipschultz, Wes. All about the Moon. 2009. (Reading Room Collection 2 Ser.). 24p. (gr. 3-4). 42.50 *(978-1-60851-955-2(4),* PowerKids Pr.) Rosen Publishing Group, Inc., The.

Llewellyn, Claire. The Moon. 2003. (Starters Ser.). 24p. (J). lib. bdg. 21.35 *(978-1-58340-260-3(8))* Black Rabbit Bks.

Lockhart, Barbara M. Circle the Moon. Grunden, Kimberly, illus. 2008. 24p. pap. 10.95 *(978-1-934246-96-2(4))* Peppertree Pr., The.

Lockyer, John. The Moon. 2015. (ENG., Illus.). 16p. (-2). pap. *(978-1-77654-140-9(5),* Red Rocket Readers) Flying Start Bks.

Lucas, Debra. Our Moon. 2005. (Yellow Umbrella Fluent Level Ser.). (ENG., Illus.). 16p. (gr. k-1). pap. 35.70 *(978-0-7368-5296-8(4),* Yellow Umbrella Bks.) Capstone Press of Coughlan Cos.

Lundgren, Julie K. Moon: Earth's Satellite. 2014. (ENG.). 24p. (gr. k-3). 28.50 *(978-1-62717-725-2(6))* Rourke Educational Media.

Malam, John. Man Walks on the Moon. 2003. (Dates with History Ser.). 45p. (J). lib. bdg. 28.50 *(978-1-58340-407-2(4))* Black Rabbit Bks.

Maloof, Torrey. Earth & Moon, 1 vol. (Science Readers: Content & Literacy Ser.). (ENG., Illus.). 24p. (gr. 1-1). 2015. pap. 22.96 *(978-1-4938-1158-8(4))* 2014. pap. 8.99 *(978-1-4807-4571-1(5))* Teacher Created Materials, Inc.

Mattern, Joanne. Our Moon, 1 vol. (Solar System & Beyond Ser.). (ENG., 32p. (gr. 3-4). 2011. lib. bdg. 8.10 *(978-1-4296-6239-0(5))* 2011. pap. 47.70 *(978-1-4296-6408-0(8))* 2010. lib. bdg. 27.32 *(978-1-4296-5394-7(9))* Capstone Press of Coughlan Cos. (Fact Finders).

McNeil, Niki, et al. The Moon. 2007. (In the Hands of a Child: Project Pack Continent Study Ser.). (Illus.). 73p. spiral bd. 16.50 *(978-1-60308-100-9(3))* In the Hands of a Child.

McNulty, Faith. If You Decide to Go to the Moon. Kellogg, Steven, illus. 2010. (Rise & Shine Ser.). (ENG.). 48p. (C). (gr.

-1-3). 30.95 *(978-0-590-48359-9(5))* National Geographic School Publishing, Inc.
Meachen Rau, Dana. Night Light: A Book about the Moon, 1 vol. Shea, Denise, illus. 2005. (Amazing Science: Exploring the Sky Ser.). (ENG.). 24p. (gr. k-4). lib. bdg. 26.65 *(978-1-4048-1136-2(2))* Picture Window Bks.
Metebole, Mattie. The Lunar Cycle: Phases of the Moon. 2009. (Amazing Science Ser.). 24p. (gr. 3-3). 42.50 *(978-1-61511-330-9(4)*, PowerKids Pr.) Rosen Publishing Group, Inc., The.
Michele, Tracey. The Moon. 2011. (Learn-Abouts Ser.). (Illus.). 16p. (J). pap. 7.95 *(978-1-59920-625-7(0))* Black Rabbit Bks.
Milbourne, Anna. On the Moon. 2004. (On the Moon Ser.). 24p. (J). 9.95 *(978-0-7945-0617-9(8)*, Usborne) EDC Publishing.
Miller, Derek L. Earth, Sun, & Moon: Cyclic Patterns of Lunar Phases, Eclipses, & the Seasons. 2016. (Space Systems Ser.). 112p. (J). 42.79 *(978-1-5026-2291-4(2))* Cavendish Square Publishing.
Miller, Ron. Earth & the Moon. 2003. (Worlds Beyond Ser.). (Illus.). 96p. (gr. 7-18). lib. bdg. 27.93 *(978-0-7613-2358-7(9)*, Twenty-First Century Bks.) Lerner Publishing Group.
Mitchell, Melanie S. Moon. 2004. (First Step Nonfiction). (ENG., Illus.). 24p. (gr. k-2). lib. bdg. 23.93 *(978-0-8225-0188-6(0))* Lerner Publishing Group.
—The Moon. 2004. (First Step Nonfiction). (ENG., Illus.). 24p. (gr. k-2). pap. 6.95 *(978-0-8225-3591-1(2))* Lerner Publishing Group.
The Moon. 2nd rev. ed. 2008. (New Solar System Ser.). 32p. (YA). (gr. 3-6). 23.00 *(978-1-60413-207-6(8))* Facts On File, Inc.
Moon, Walt K. Let's Explore the Moon. 2017. (Bumba Books (tm) — a First Look at Space Ser.). (ENG.). 24p. (J). (gr. -1-1). 25.32 ***(978-1-5124-3346-3(2))*** Lerner Publishing Group.
Mora, Pat. The Night the Moon Fell: A Maya Myth, 1 vol. Domi, Carlos, illus. 2009. (ENG.). 32p. (J). (gr. k-k). pap. 6.95 *(978-0-88899-938-2(0))* Groundwood Bks. CAN. Dist: Publishers Group West (PGW).
—La Noche Que Se Cayó la Luna. Domi, illus. 2009. (SPA.). 32p. (J). (gr. k-k). pap. 6.95 *(978-0-88899-963-4(1))* Groundwood Bks. CAN. Dist: Publishers Group West (PGW).
Morgan, Emily R. Next Time You See the Moon. 2014. (Next Time You See Ser.). (ENG.). 32p. (J). (gr. k-5). pap. 12.95 *(978-1-938946-33-2(2))* National Science Teachers Assn.
—La Próxima Vez Que Veas la Luna. 2016. (Next Time You See Ser.). (SPA.). 32p. (J). (gr. 2-4). pap. 12.95 *(978-1-68140-286-4(6))* National Science Teachers Assn.
Nagelhout, Ryan. What Is a Moon? 2014. (Let's Find Out! Ser.). 32p. (J). (gr. 3-6). 23.45 *(978-1-62275-466-3(2))* Rosen Publishing Group, Inc., The.
—20 Fun Facts about the Moon. 2014. (Fun Fact File: Space! Ser.). 32p. (J). (gr. 2-5). 25.25 *(978-1-4824-1018-1(4))* Stevens, Gareth Publishing LLLP.
Nelson, Robin. El Cielo de Noche (the Night Sky) 2012. (Mi Primer Paso Al Mundo Real - Descubriendo Los Ciclos de la Naturaleza (First Step Nonfiction - Discovering Nature's Cycles) Ser.). (Illus.). 24p. (gr. k-2). (ENG & SPA.). pap. 6.95 *(978-0-7613-9360-3(9))*; (SPA., lib. bdg. 23.93 *(978-0-7613-9341-2(2))* Lerner Publishing Group. (Ediciones Lerner).
—The Night Sky. 2010. pap. 33.92 *(978-0-7613-6917-2(1))*; (ENG.). 24p. pap. 6.95 *(978-0-7613-5683-7(5))*; (ENG., Illus.). 24p. lib. bdg. 23.93 *(978-0-7613-4577-0(9))* Lerner Publishing Group.
Nuestro Satelite: La Luna. (SPA.). (J). 10.00 *(978-84-342-1811-6(9))* Parramon Ediciones S.A. ESP. Dist: Distribuidora Norma, Inc.
Olien, Rebecca. Exploring the Moon. 2007. (Objects in the Sky Ser.). (Illus.). 24p. (J). (gr. 3-7). lib. bdg. 22.60 *(978-1-4042-3466-6(7)*, PowerKids Pr.) Rosen Publishing Group, Inc., The.
Olson, Gillia M. Phases of the Moon, 1 vol. Miller, Jo, illus. 2006. (Patterns in Nature Ser.). (ENG.). 24p. (gr. k-1). 24.65 *(978-0-7368-6340-7(0)*, Pebble Plus) Capstone Press of Coughlan Cos.
O'Mara, Genevieve. The Lunar Cycle: Phases of the Moon. 2009. (Real Life Readers Ser.). 24p. (gr. 3-4). pap. 8.25 *(978-1-4358-0002-1(8)*, Rosen Classroom); (J). (gr. 2-5). lib. bdg. 22.60 *(978-1-4358-2973-2(5)*, PowerKids Pr.) Rosen Publishing Group, Inc., The.
Orme, Helen & Orme, David. Let's Explore the Moon. 2007. (Space Launch! Ser.). (Illus.). 24p. (gr. 1-4). pap. 8.15 *(978-0-8368-8128-8(1))*; lib. bdg. 23.00 *(978-0-8368-7943-8(0))* Stevens, Gareth Publishing LLLP. (Gareth Stevens Learning Library).
Orr, Tamra. I Spy in the Sky the Moon. 2011. (Randy's Corner Ser.). (Illus.). 32p. (J). (gr. k-3). lib. bdg. 25.70 *(978-1-58415-973-5(1))* Mitchell Lane Pubs., Inc.
Oxlade, Chris. Earth & Its Moon. 2007. (Earth & Space Ser.). (Illus.). 48p. (YA). (gr. 5-9). lib. bdg. 29.25 *(978-1-4042-3734-6(8))* Rosen Publishing Group, Inc., The.
—The Moon, 1 vol. 2012. (Astronaut Travel Guides). (ENG.). 48p. (gr. 3-6). pap. 9.95 *(978-1-4109-4581-5(2)*, NA-r) Heinemann-Raintree.
—The Moon, 1 vol. Edwards, Jeff, illus. 2012. (Astronaut Travel Guides). (ENG.). 48p. (gr. 3-6). lib. bdg. 32.65 *(978-1-4109-4572-3(3)*, NA-r) Heinemann-Raintree.
—The Moon. 2010. (Eye on Space Ser.). 24p. (J). pap. 8.25 *(978-1-61532-546-7(8)*, PowerKids Pr.); (ENG.). lib. bdg. 22.60 *(978-1-61532-541-2(7))* Rosen Publishing Group, Inc., The.
Paris, Stephanie. 20th Century: Race to the Moon, 1 vol. 2nd rev. ed. 2013. (Nonfiction Readers Ser.). (ENG.). 64p. (J). (gr. 5-5). pap. 10.99 *(978-1-4333-4899-0(3))*; (Illus.). pap. 31.96 *(978-1-4333-7422-7(6))* Teacher Created Materials, Inc.
Peters, Elisa. The Moon. 2012. (PowerKids Readers: the Universe Ser.). (ENG., Illus.). 24p. (J). (gr. k-2). pap. 8.25 *(978-1-4488-7466-8(1))*; lib. bdg. 22.60 *(978-1-4488-7386-9(X))* Rosen Publishing Group, Inc., The. (PowerKids Pr.).
—The Moon: La Luna. 2012. (PowerKids Readers: the Universe / el universo Ser.). (SPA & ENG., Illus.). 24p. (J). (gr. k-2). lib. bdg. 22.60 *(978-1-4488-7822-2(5)*, PowerKids Pr.) Rosen Publishing Group, Inc., The.
Phelan, Glen. Earth, Sun, Moon. 2007. (Reading Expeditions Ser.). (ENG., Illus.). 32p. (J). pap. 17.95 *(978-0-7922-4573-5(3))* CENGAGE Learning.
Podesto, Martine. The Moon. 2008. (My Science Notebook Ser.). (Illus.). 104p. (YA). (gr. 5-9). lib. bdg. 31.00 *(978-0-8368-9215-4(1))* Stevens, Gareth Publishing LLLP.
Portillo, Athena Yvette. Sun & Moon. 2007. (Illus.). 32p. (J). pap. 8.00 *(978-0-8059-7278-8(1))* Dorrance Publishing Co., Inc.
Portman, Michael. Where Did the Moon Come From? 2013. (Space Mysteries Ser.). (Illus.). 32p. (J). (gr. 2-5). 25.25 *(978-1-4339-8277-4(3))*; pap. 10.50 *(978-1-4339-8278-1(1))* Stevens, Gareth Publishing LLLP. (Gareth Stevens Learning Library).
Reilly, Carmel. The Moon. 2011. (Sky Watching Ser.). 32p. (gr. 2-4). 28.50 *(978-1-60870-581-8(1))* Marshall Cavendish Corp.
Rice, Clay. Mama, Let's Make a Moon. 2013. 32p. 16.95 *(978-1-938301-05-6(6))*; (ENG.). (J). 16.95 *(978-1-938301-06-3(4))* Familius LLC.
Riley, Peter. Earth, Moon & Sun. 2007. (Essential Science/Watts Ser.). (Illus.). 32p. (YA). (gr. 3-6). lib. bdg. 28.50 *(978-1-59920-025-5(2))* Black Rabbit Bks.
Robbins, Dean. Margaret & the Moon: How Margaret Hamilton Saved the First Lunar Landing. Knisley, Lucy, illus. 2017. (ENG.). 40p. (J). (gr. -1-3). 17.99 *(978-0-399-55185-7(9)*, Knopf Bks. for Young Readers) Random Hse. Children's Bks.
Roca, Núria, et al. The Moon. 2014. (Solar System Ser.). (ENG., Illus.). 36p. (J). (gr. -1-2). pap. 7.99 *(978-1-4380-0476-1(1))* Barron's Educational Series, Inc.
Rushworth, Gary. Our Solar System the Moon: Set Of 6. 2011. (Navigators Ser.). (J). pap. 44.00 net. *(978-1-4108-6221-1(6))* Benchmark Education Co.
—Our Solar System: the Moon: Text Pairs. 2008. (Bridges/Navigators Ser.). (J). (gr. 3). 89.00 *(978-1-4108-8370-4(1))* Benchmark Education Co.
Rustad, Martha E. H. Does the Sun Sleep? Noticing Sun, Moon, & Star Patterns. Conger, Holli, illus. 2015. (ENG.). 24p. (J). (gr. k-2). 25.32 *(978-1-4677-8560-0(1)*, Millbrook Pr.) Lerner Publishing Group.
—La Luna. 2010. (En el Espacio/Out in Space Ser.).Tr. of Moon. (SPA, ENG & MUL.). 24p. (gr. k-1). lib. bdg. 21.99 *(978-1-4296-5340-4(X))* Capstone Press of Coughlan Cos.
—La Luna/the Moon, 1 vol. 2012. (En el Espacio/Out in Space Ser.). (MUL & SPA.). 24p. (gr. k-1). pap. 5.95 *(978-1-4296-8552-8(2))*; pap. 35.70 *(978-1-4296-8553-5(0))* Capstone Press of Coughlan Cos.
—The Moon. (Space Ser.). (ENG., Illus.). 24p. (gr. k-1). 2016. lib. bdg. 21.99 *(978-1-4914-8323-7(7))* 2008. pap. 6.29 *(978-1-4296-2811-2(1)*, 1284181) Capstone Press of Coughlan Cos. (Pebble Bks.).
—The Moon [Scholastic]: Revised Edition. 2009. (Out in Space Ser.). 24p. (gr. k-1). pap. 2.50 *(978-1-4296-4048-0(0)*, Pebble Bks.) Capstone Press of Coughlan Cos.
Ryback, Carol. The Moon. 2006. (In the Sky Ser.). (Illus.). 24p. (gr. 1-4). pap. 8.15 *(978-0-8368-6348-2(8))*; lib. bdg. 22.00 *(978-0-8368-6343-7(7))* Stevens, Gareth Publishing LLLP. (Weekly Reader Leveled Readers).
Salas, Laura Purdie. If You Were the Moon. Kim, Jaime, illus. 2017. (ENG.). 32p. (gr. k-2). (J). 19.99 *(978-1-4677-8009-4(X))*; 30.65 ***(978-1-5124-2838-4(8))*** Lerner Publishing Group. (Millbrook Pr.).
Sasek, Miroslav. This Is the Way to the Moon. 2009. (ENG., Illus.). 64p. (J). (gr. 2-12). 17.95 *(978-0-7893-1842-8(3))* Universe Publishing.
Sawyer, J. Clark. Nuestra Luna: El Objeto MÁS Brillante Del Cielo Nocturno. 2015. (Fuera de Este Mundo Ser.). (SPA., Illus.). 24p. (J). (gr. -1-3). lib. bdg. 23.93 *(978-1-62724-594-4(4))* Bearport Publishing Co., Inc.
—Our Moon: Brightest Object in the Night Sky. 2015. (Out of This World Ser.). (ENG.). 24p. (J). (gr. -1-3). lib. bdg. 23.93 *(978-1-62724-570-8(7))* Bearport Publishing Co., Inc.
Sexton, Colleen. The Moon. 2010. (Exploring Space Ser.). (ENG., Illus.). 24p. (J). (gr. k-3). lib. bdg. 25.95 *(978-1-60014-401-1(2)*, Blastoff! Readers) Bellwether Media.
Seymour, Arlene. The Moon Book: A Lunar Pop-up Celebration. Seymour, Arlene, illus. 2004. (Illus.). 14p. (YA). (gr. k-4). reprint ed. 22.00 *(978-0-7567-7645-9(7))* DIANE Publishing Co.
Simon, Seymour. The Moon. rev. ed. 2003. (ENG., Illus.). 32p. (J). (gr. 2-6). 19.99 *(978-0-689-83563-6(9))*, Simon & Schuster Bks. For Young Readers) Simon & Schuster Bks. For Young Readers.
Slade, Suzanne. The Phases of the Moon. 2009. (Cycles in Nature Ser.). 24p. (gr. 3-3). 42.50 *(978-1-61512-115-1(3)*, PowerKids Pr.) Rosen Publishing Group, Inc., The.
Sohn, Emily & Harter, Adam. Sun, Moon, & Stars: A Cosmic Case. 2011. (iScience Readers Ser.). 32p. (J). (gr. 3-4). lib. bdg. 22.60 *(978-1-59953-421-3(5))* Norwood Hse. Pr.
Sparrow, Giles. Destination the Moon. 32p. (J). 2010. (Illus.). pap. 10.00 *(978-1-4358-3465-1(8))* 2009. (ENG.). lib. bdg. 25.25 *(978-1-4358-3445-3(3))* Rosen Publishing Group, Inc., The. (PowerKids Pr.).
Stewart, Melissa. Why Does the Moon Change Shape? 2008. (Tell Me Why, Tell Me How Ser.). (Illus.). 32p. (YA). (gr. 3-18). lib. bdg. 29.93 *(978-0-7614-2921-0(2)*, Benchmark Bks.) Marshall Cavendish Corp.
Storad, Conrad J. Day & Night. 2011. (ENG., Illus.). 24p. (gr. k-1). pap. 8.95 *(978-1-61741-926-3(5))* Rourke Educational Media.
Taylor-Butler, Christine. The Moon. 2014. (True Book(tm), A — Space Ser.). (ENG.). 48p. (J). lib. bdg. 31.00 *(978-0-531-21154-0(1))* Scholastic Library Publishing.
Tomecek, Steve. Moon. Guida, Liisa Chauncy, illus. 2008. (Jump into Science Ser.). (ENG.). 32p. (J). (gr. -1-3). 6.95 *(978-1-4263-0250-3(9)*, National Geographic Children's Bks.) National Geographic Society.
—Moon. Guida, Liisa C., illus. 2005. (Jump into Science Ser.). (ENG.). 32p. (J). (gr. -1-3). 16.95 *(978-0-7922-8304-1(X)*, National Geographic Children's Bks.) National Geographic Society.
—Moon. Guida, Liisa Chauncy, illus. 2005. (Jump into Science Ser.). (ENG.). 32p. (J). (gr. -1-3). 16.95 *(978-0-7922-5123-1(7)*, National Geographic Children's Bks.) National Geographic Society.
Turnbull, Stephanie. Sun, Moon & Stars. Chen, Kuo Kang & Mayer, Uwe, illus. 2006. (Beginners Nature: Level 2 Ser.). 32p. (J). (gr. 1-3). 4.99 *(978-0-7945-1399-3(9)*, Usborne) EDC Publishing.
Waxman, Laura Hamilton. The Moon. 2010. (Early Bird Astronomy Ser.). (ENG.). 48p. (gr. 2-5). lib. bdg. 26.60 *(978-0-7613-3872-7(1))*; (Illus.). pap. 8.95 *(978-0-7613-4983-9(9)*, 1306462, Lerner Pubns.) Lerner Publishing Group.
Wilkins, Mary-Jane. The Moon. 2017. (Fast Track: Our Solar System Ser.). 24p. (gr. k-3). 28.50 ***(978-1-78121-365-0(8))*** Brown Bear Bks.
Wishinsky, Frieda. Could We Live on the Moon? 2004. (ENG., Illus.). 24p. (J). (gr. 2-2). pap. 10.92 *(978-0-7652-5178-7(7)*, Celebration Pr.) Pearson Schl.
World Book, contrib. by. Earth & Earth's Moon. 2nd ed. 2007. (World Book's Solar System & Space Exploration Library). (Illus.). 64p. (J). *(978-0-7166-9512-7(X))* World Bk., Inc.
World Book, Inc Staff, contrib. by. Earth & Earth's Moon. (J). 2010. *(978-0-7166-9540-0(5))* 2006. 63p. *(978-0-7166-9503-5(0))* World Bk., Inc.
Zimmerman, W. Our Colorful Moon: Beautiful Images to Energize & Delight. 2007. 40p. per. 18.27 *(978-1-934840-04-7(1))* Nimble Bks. LLC.

MOON—EXPLORATION

Adamson, Thomas K. Apollo 11 Moon Landing: An Interactive Space Exploration Adventure. 2016. (You Choose: Space Ser.). (ENG., Illus.). 112p. (gr. 3-4). lib. bdg. 31.99 *(978-1-4914-8103-5(X)*, You Choose Bks.) Capstone Press of Coughlan Cos.
—Do You Really Want to Visit the Moon? Fabbri, Daniele, illus. 2013. (Do You Really Want to Visit... ? Ser.). (ENG.). 24p. (gr. 1-4). 27.10 *(978-1-60753-197-5(6))* Amicus Publishing.
—The First Moon Landing, 1 vol. Purcell, Gordon & Beatty, Terry, illus. 2006. (Graphic History Ser.). (ENG.). 32p. (gr. 3-4). per. 8.10 *(978-0-7368-9654-2(6)*, Graphic Library) Capstone Press of Coughlan Cos.
Alexander, Richard. Exploring the Moon. 2017. (J). ***(978-1-5345-2249-7(2)***, KidHaven Publishing) Greenhaven Publishing LLC.
Allien Cave Explorers: Meet NASA Inventor William "Red" Whittaker & His Team's. 2017. (J). ***(978-0-7166-6163-4(2))*** World Bk., Inc.
Baker, David & Kissock, Heather. Living on the Moon. 2009. (Exploring Space Ser.). (Illus.). 32p. (J). (gr. 2-4). lib. bdg. 26.00 *(978-1-60596-021-0(7))* Weigl Pubs., Inc.
—Moon Base: Exploring Space. 2009. (Exploring Space Ser.). (Illus.). 32p. (J). (gr. 2-4). pap. 9.95 *(978-1-60596-022-7(5))* Weigl Pubs., Inc.
Bredeson, Carmen & Dyson, Marianne. Exploring the Moon. 2015. (Launch into Space! Ser.). (ENG.). 32p. (J). (gr. 3-4). pap. 10.52 *(978-0-7660-6821-6(8))* Enslow Pubs., Inc.
Bredeson, Carmen, et al. Exploring the Moon. 2015. (Launch into Space! Ser.). (ENG., Illus.). 32p. (J). (gr. 3-4). 25.27 *(978-0-7660-6823-0(4))* Enslow Pubs., Inc.
Close, Edward. Moon Missions, 1 vol., 1. 2014. (Discovery Education: Earth & Space Science Ser.). (ENG.). 32p. (gr. 3-6). 26.25 *(978-1-4777-6178-6(0)*, PowerKids Pr.) Rosen Publishing Group, Inc., The.
Dyer, Alan. Mission to the Moon. 2009. (ENG., Illus.). 80p. (J). (gr. 3-7). 19.99 *(978-1-4169-7935-7(2)*, Simon & Schuster Bks. For Young Readers) Simon & Schuster Bks. For Young Readers.
Dyson, Marianne J. Home on the Moon: Living on a Space Frontier. 2003. (ENG., Illus.). 64p. (J). (gr. 3-7). 18.95 *(978-0-7922-7193-2(9)*, National Geographic Children's Bks.) National Geographic Society.
Glatzer, Jenna. The Exploration of the Moon. 2004. (Exploration & Discovery Ser.). (Illus.). 64p. (YA). (gr. 5-18). lib. bdg. 19.95 *(978-1-59084-048-1(8))* Mason Crest.
Jefferis, David & Irvine, Mat. Return to the Moon. 2007. (Humans in Space Ser.). (ENG., Illus.). 32p. (J). (gr. 4-7). lib. bdg. *(978-0-7787-3103-0(0))*; pap. *(978-0-7787-3117-7(0))* Crabtree Publishing Co.
Morris, Neil. Who Traveled to the Moon?, 1 vol. 2014. (Primary Source Detectives Ser.). (ENG.). 64p. (gr. 7-8). lib. bdg. 35.99 *(978-1-4329-9605-5(3))* Heinemann-Raintree.
Olien, Rebecca. Exploring the Moon. 2009. (Objects in the Sky Ser.). 24p. (gr. 3-3). 42.50 *(978-1-60851-140-2(5)*, PowerKids Pr.) Rosen Publishing Group, Inc., The.
Owen, Ruth. The Moon. 2013. (Explore Outer Space Ser.). 32p. (J). (gr. 3-6). pap. 60.00 *(978-1-61533-760-6(1))*; pap. 10.00 *(978-1-61533-759-0(8))*; lib. bdg. 25.25 *(978-1-61533-721-7(0))* Windmill Bks.
Scott, Elaine. Our Moon: New Discoveries about Earth's Closest Companion. 2016. (ENG., Illus.). 72p. (J). (gr. 5-7). 18.99 *(978-0-547-48394-8(5)*, Clarion Bks.) Houghton Mifflin Harcourt Trade & Reference Pubs.
Shepherd, Jodie. To the Moon! Byrne, Mike, illus. 2017. (Cloverleaf Books (tm) — Space Adventures Ser.). (ENG.). 24p. (J). (gr. k-2). 25.32 *(978-1-5124-2536-9(2))*; 6.99 ***(978-1-5124-3894-9(4))***; 38.65 ***(978-1-5124-3893-2(6))***; 38.65 ***(978-1-5124-2833-9(7))*** Lerner Publishing Group. (Millbrook Pr.).
Stefoff, Rebecca. Space Race: An Interactive Space Exploration Adventure. 2016. (You Choose: Space Ser.). (ENG.). 112p. (gr. 3-4). lib. bdg. 31.99 *(978-1-4914-8101-1(3)*, You Choose Bks.) Capstone Press of Coughlan Cos.
Wilkinson, Philip. Spacebusters. 2012. (DK Reader Level 3 Ser.). lib. bdg. 13.55 *(978-0-606-26544-7(9)*, Turtleback) Turtleback Bks.

MOON—EXPLORATION—FICTION

Anderson, M. T. Feed. 2004. 320p. (J). (gr. 7-18). pap. 38.00 incl. audio *(978-1-4000-9022-8(9)*, Listening Library) Random Hse. Audio Publishing Group.
Hillert, Margaret. Up, up, & Away. Spinks, Scott, illus. 2016. (BeginningtoRead Ser.). (ENG.). 32p. (J). (gr. -1-2). pap. 11.94 *(978-1-60357-947-6(8))* Norwood Hse. Pr.
Montgomery, Anson. Moon Quest. Semionov, Vladimir, illus. 2008. (Choose Your Own Adventure Ser.: No. 26). 144p. (J). (gr. 2-7). pap. 6.99 *(978-1-933390-26-0(3))* Chooseco LLC.
Newbery, Linda. Andie's Moon. 2009. (Historical House Ser.). 208p. (YA). (gr. 5-18). pap. 5.99 *(978-0-7945-2333-6(1)*, Usborne) EDC Publishing.
Palmer, S. Y. May's Moon. 2015. (ENG.). 184p. (J). (gr. -1-12). pap. 11.95 *(978-1-78279-780-7(7)*, Our Street Bks.) Hunt, John Publishing Ltd. GBR. Dist: National Bk. Network.
Rockwood, Roy. Lost on the Moon. 2008. 132p. 24.95 *(978-1-60664-737-0(7))* Rodgers, Alan Bks.
Verne, Jules. From the Earth to the Moon. 2008. (Bring the Classics to Life Ser.). (ENG., Illus.). 72p. (gr. 4-12). pap., act. bk. ed. 10.95 *(978-1-55576-181-3(X)*, EDCTR-407B) EDCON Publishing Group.

MOON—FICTION

Ackerman, Jill. Hey, Diddle Diddle! Berg, Michelle, illus. 2011. (Little Scholastic Ser.). (ENG.). 6p. (J). (gr. k — 1). 12.99 *(978-0-545-35113-3(8)*, Cartwheel Bks.) Scholastic, Inc.
Akers, Darla G. The Man, the Moon, & the Star. 2008. 24p. per. 24.95 *(978-1-60474-030-1(2))* PublishAmerica, Inc.
Allen, Page. Madison's Descent: A Child's Journey. (Illus.). (J). 2006. pap. 25.00 *(978-0-9752516-2-1(7))* 2004. lib. bdg. 60.00 *(978-0-9752516-1-4(9))* Otis & Randolph Pr.
Almond, David. The Boy Who Climbed into the Moon. Dunbar, Polly, illus. 2010. (ENG.). 128p. (J). (gr. 3-7). 15.99 *(978-0-7636-4217-4(7))* Candlewick Pr.
Andersen, D. R. Why the Moon Changes in the Night Sky. 2005. (J). pap. *(978-1-4108-4190-2(1))* Benchmark Education Co.
Anderson, M. T. Feed. 2012. (ENG., Illus.). 320p. (YA). (gr. 9). pap. 8.99 *(978-0-7636-6262-2(3))* Candlewick Pr.
Artus, William. The King on the Moon. 2008. 32p. pap. 20.95 *(978-1-4092-3044-1(9))* Lulu Pr., Inc.
Asch, Frank. Happy Birthday, Moon. Asch, Frank, illus. 2014. (Moonbear Ser.). (ENG., Illus.). 32p. (J). (gr. -1-3). 7.99 *(978-1-4424-9400-8(X)*, Aladdin) Simon & Schuster Children's Publishing.
—Mooncake. Asch, Frank, illus. 2014. (Moonbear Ser.). (ENG., Illus.). 32p. (J). (gr. -1-3). 7.99 *(978-1-4424-9403-9(4)*, Aladdin) Simon & Schuster Children's Publishing.
—Moondance. Asch, Frank, illus. 2014. (Moonbear Ser.). (ENG., Illus.). 32p. (J). (gr. -1-3). 17.99 *(978-1-4424-6659-3(6)*, Aladdin) Simon & Schuster Children's Publishing.
—Moongame. Asch, Frank, illus. 2014. (Moonbear Ser.). (ENG., Illus.). 32p. (J). (gr. -1-3). 7.99 *(978-1-4424-9406-0(9)*, Aladdin) Simon & Schuster Children's Publishing.
Asch, Frank & Asch, Frank. Happy Birthday, Moon. Asch, Frank & Asch, Frank, illus. 2005. (Stories to Go! Ser.). (ENG., Illus.). 32p. (J). 4.99 *(978-1-4169-0307-9(0)*, Simon & Schuster/Paula Wiseman Bks.) Simon & Schuster/Paula Wiseman Bks.
Astro, Ian. Moon School. 2006. (Neighborhood Readers Ser.). (ENG.). 16p. (gr. 1-3). pap. 6.50 *(978-1-4042-7196-8(1)*, Rosen Classroom) Rosen Publishing Group, Inc., The.
Banks, Kate. And If the Moon Could Talk. Hallensleben, Georg, illus. 2005. (ENG.). 40p. (J). (gr. -1-1). reprint ed. per. 7.99 *(978-0-374-43558-5(8)*, 9780374435585, Farrar, Straus & Giroux (BYR)) Farrar, Straus & Giroux.
Bean, Raymond. Journey to the Moon. 2016. (Out of This World Ser.). (ENG., Illus.). 112p. (gr. 2-5). lib. bdg. 32.65 *(978-1-4965-3616-7(9))* Out of this World GBR. Dist: Capstone Pub.
Belle, Deborah A. The Day the Sun Called Out Sick!!! Collenberger, Chris, illus. 2013. 30p. pap. 12.99 *(978-0-9853406-0-5(6))* Scribez, Scarebz & Vibez.
Bencivengo, Mary Ann. The Man in the Moon. 2011. 56p. pap. *(978-1-77067-302-1(4))* FriesenPress.
Bennett, Jeffrey. Max Goes to the Moon: A Science Adventure with Max the Dog. Okamoto, Alan, illus. 2nd ed. 2012. (Science Adventures with Max the Dog Ser.). (ENG.). 32p. (J). (gr. 2-4). 15.00 *(978-1-937548-20-9(1))* Big Kid Science.
Bennett, Jeffrey, et al. Max Goes to Jupiter: A Science Adventure with Max the Dog. Carroll, Michael, illus. 2008. (Science Adventures with Max the Dog Ser.). (ENG.). 32p. (J). (gr. 2-4). 16.95 *(978-0-9721819-3-8(8))* Big Kid Science.
Berggren, Jeff. My Moon Lagoon. Hansen, Tammy A., ed. Berggren, Jeff, illus. 2007. (Illus.). (J). per. 14.95 *(978-0-9755033-1-7(6))* Deep Dish Design.
Bewley, Elizabeth. The Moon Followed Me Home. Furukawa, Masumi, illus. 2007. (ENG.). 6p. (J). (gr. -1-3). 12.95 *(978-1-58117-598-1(1)*, Intervisual/Piggy Toes) Bendon, Inc.
Biviano, David J. True Moon. 2009. 36p. pap. 17.95 *(978-1-4490-1693-7(6))* AuthorHouse.
Black, Robert A. Lunar Pioneers. 2008. 280p. (YA). pap. 14.99 *(978-1-59092-397-9(9))* Blue Forge Pr.
Bolden, Tonya. Beautiful Moon: A Child's Prayer. Velasquez, Eric, illus. 2014. (ENG.). 32p. (J). (gr. k-2). 16.95 *(978-1-4197-0792-6(2)*, Abrams Bks. for Young Readers) Abrams, Inc.
Bonnell, Kris. The Happy Moon. 2006. (J). pap. 5.95 *(978-1-933727-30-1(6))* Reading Reading Bks., LLC.
Bootsma, Verner. Talking to the Moon. LaGrange, Tiffany, illus. 2007. 32p. per. 12.95 *(978-1-934246-70-2(0))* Peppertree Pr., The.
Boyce, Frank Cottrell. Chitty Chitty Bang Bang over the Moon. Berger, Joe, illus. 2015. (Chitty Chitty Bang Bang Ser.). (ENG.). 304p. (J). (gr. 4-7). pap. 6.99 *(978-0-7636-7666-7(7))* Candlewick Pr.
Branson, Terri. Tyler on the Moon. Taylor, Chet, illus. Lt. ed. 24p. (J). 2005. lib. bdg. 24.95 *(978-0-9765786-2-8(X))* 2004. 18.99 *(978-0-9755888-2-6(6))* Dragonfly Publishing, Inc.
Brickwood, L. M. Children of the Moon. 2007. 216p. pap. 14.95 *(978-1-920153-03-8(9))* Zulu Planet Pubs. ZAF. Dist: APG Sales & Distribution Services.
Brière-Haquet, Alice. Peter & the Moon, 1 vol. Chauffrey, Celia, illus. 2012. (Big Picture Book Ser.). (ENG.). 48p. (J). (gr. k). 16.95 *(978-2-7338-1940-1(2))* Auzou, Philippe Editions FRA. Dist: Consortium Bk. Sales & Distribution.
Bronn, Charles Heil. The Sun, the Moon, & the Gardener's Son. Kami, Y. Z., illus. 2006. 30p. (J). (gr. 4-12). reprint ed. 16.00 *(978-1-4223-5222-9(6))* DIANE Publishing Co.
Brooks. Mary Will Not Watch Moon. Date not set. 32p. (J). (gr. -1-1). 14.99 *(978-0-06-024491-0(7))* HarperCollins Pubs.
—Mary Will Not Watch the Moon. Date not set. 32p. (J). (gr. -1-1). lib. bdg. 15.89 *(978-0-06-024492-7(5))* HarperCollins Pubs.
Brown, Betisa Garagozlu. Sister Sun & Sister Moon. 2012. 28p. pap. 13.95 *(978-1-4525-4635-3(5))* Balboa Pr.

MNO

Brown, Margaret Wise. Buenas Noches, Luna, 1 vol. Mlawer, Teresa, tr. from ENG. Hurd, Clement, illus. 2006.Tr. of Goodnight Moon. (SPA.). 32p. (J). (gr. -1-3). 17.99 *(978-0-06-026214-3(1),* HC0528, Rayo) HarperCollins Pubs.

—Goodnight Moon 1 2 3: A Counting Book. Hurd, Clement, illus. 2008. (ENG.). 30p. (J). (gr. -1-k). bds. 8.99 *(978-0-06-112597-3(0),* HarperFestival) HarperCollins Pubs.

—Goodnight Moon 123 Lap Edition. Hurd, Clement, illus. 2008. (ENG.). 30p. (J). (gr. -1 — 1). bds. 12.99 *(978-0-06-166755-8(2),* HarperFestival) HarperCollins Pubs.

—Goodnight Moon Classic Library: Contains Goodnight Moon, the Runaway Bunny, & My World. Hurd, Clement, illus. 2011. (ENG.). 32p. (J). (gr. -1-1). 14.99 *(978-0-06-199823-2(0))* HarperCollins Pubs.

—Over the Moon: Goodnight Moon, the Runaway Bunny, & My World. Hurd, Clement, illus. 2006. (ENG.). 108p. (J). (gr. -1-1). 19.99 *(978-0-06-076162-2(8))* HarperCollins Pubs.

Brown, Margaret Wise & Brown, Wise M. Buenas Noches, Luna, 1 vol. Mlawer, Teresa, tr. from ENG. Hurd, Clement, illus. 2006. (Trophy Picture Bks.).Tr. of Goodnight Moon. (SPA.). 32p. (J). (gr. -1-3). pap. 7.99 *(978-0-06-443416-4(8),* HC0527) HarperCollins Pubs.

Brown-Wood, Janay. Imani's Moon. Mitchell, Hazell, illus. 2014. (ENG.). 32p. (J). (gr. 1-4). pap. 7.95 *(978-1-934133-58-3(2),* Mackinac Island Press, Inc.) Charlesbridge Publishing, Inc.

Byrne, Barbara. Megan's Moon. 2004. 18p. 14.87 *(978-1-4116-1008-8(3))* Lulu Pr., Inc.

Carle, Eric. Coccinelle Mal Lune. pap. 18.95 *(978-2-87142-287-7(7))* Mijade Editions BEL. Dist: Distribooks, Inc.

Carrington, Samala. Sally Sunshine Mandy Moon. 2011. 20p. (gr. -1). pap. 12.99 *(978-1-4567-6708-2(9))* AuthorHouse.

Carroll, James Christopher. The Boy & the Moon. Carroll, James Christopher, illus. 2010. (ENG., Illus.). 32p. (J). (gr. 1-4). 19.99 *(978-1-58536-521-0(1),* 202209) Sleeping Bear Pr.

Casado, Alicia & Casado, Dami. La Luna. 2005. (Yo Te Hablare De... Ser.). (SPA., Illus.). 14p. (J). per., bds. 8.99 *(978-84-272-7386-3(X))* Molino, Editorial ESP. Dist: Santillana USA Publishing Co., Inc.

Castelli, Jeanette. Los Gatos en la Luna/the Cats on the Moon. Santana, Andrea, illus. 2005. (Bilingual Collection). (SPA.). 51p. (J). (gr. k-2). *(978-958-30-1767-4(1))* Panamericana Editorial.

Chafe, Justin. Bunny Rabbit on the Moon. 2007. (Illus.). 28p. (J). 14.95 *(978-0-9787660-0-9(8))* Baboosic Enterprises, LLC.

Christenson, Lisa & Christenson, Emme Jo. Who Ate the Moon? Christenson, Lisa & Christenson, Emme Jo, illus. 2006. (Illus.). (J). per. *(978-0-9725311-2-2(2),* Pickled Eggs Press (TM)) Lisa Loucks Christenson Publishing, LLC.

Cole, Rachael. City Moon. Gomez, Blanca, illus. 2017. (ENG.). 40p. (J). (gr. -1-2). lib. bdg. 20.99 ***(978-0-553-49708-3(1),*** Schwartz & Wade Bks.) Random Hse. Children's Bks.

Conway, David. Shine Moon Shine. Kolanovic, Dubravka, illus. 2008. 32p. (J). (gr. -1-2). 15.95 *(978-1-58925-073-4(7))* Tiger Tales.

Cooper, Floyd. Max & the Tag-Along Moon. Cooper, Floyd, illus. (ENG., Illus.). 32p. (J). (gr. -1-2). 2015. pap. 8.99 *(978-0-14-751546-9(7),* Puffin Books) 2013. 16.99 *(978-0-399-23342-5(3),* Philomel Bks.) Penguin Young Readers Group.

Craft, Mahlon. Christmas Moon. Craft, K. Y., illus. 2003. 32p. (J). 15.95 *(978-1-58717-056-0(6));* lib. bdg. *(978-1-58717-057-7(4))* Chronicle Bks. LLC. (SeaStar Bks.).

Cundiff, Joe. Fly to the Moon on a Witch's Broom. 2013. (ENG.). 34p. (J). pap. 15.95 *(978-1-4787-2306-6(8))* Outskirts Pr., Inc.

Curtis, Carolyn. I Took the Moon for a Walk. Jay, Alison, illus. (ENG.). 32p. (J). 2012. (gr. -1-2). 8.99 *(978-1-84148-803-5(8))* 2004. 16.99 *(978-1-84148-611-6(6))* Barefoot Bks., Inc.

Curtis, Carolyn, et al. Lleve a la Luna a Pasear. Jay, Alison, illus. 2014. (SPA.). 32p. (J). (gr. -1-2). pap. 8.99 *(978-1-78285-084-7(8))* Barefoot Bks., Inc.

Dabell, John. Moon People. 2011. 266p. pap. *(978-1-908105-66-0(6))* Grosvenor Hse. Publishing Ltd.

Dale, Penny. Dinosaur Rocket! Dale, Penny, illus. 2015. (ENG., Illus.). 32p. (J). (-k). 15.99 *(978-0-7636-7999-6(2),* Nosy Crow) Candlewick Pr.

Danilo, Roberto. Mylene & the Moon. 2011. 24p. pap. 12.99 *(978-1-4634-1196-1(0))* AuthorHouse.

Danziger, Paula. This Place Has No Atmosphere. 2006. (ENG.). 240p. (J). (gr. 5-18). 8.99 *(978-0-14-240680-9(5),* Puffin Books) Penguin Young Readers Group.

de Brunhoff, Laurent. Babar Raconte la Course a la Lune. (Babar Ser.). (FRE., Illus.). 48p. (J). (gr. -1-3). 19.95 *(978-0-7859-8820-5(3))* French & European Pubns., Inc.

de Lint, Charles. Wolf Moon. 2004. (ENG., Illus.). 256p. (Orig.). (YA). (gr. 7-18). 6.99 *(978-0-14-240077-7(7),* Firebird) Penguin Young Readers Group.

Delessert, Etienne. Moon Theater. 2010. (ENG.). 32p. (J). (gr. 1-3). 17.95 *(978-1-56846-208-0(5),* Creative Editions) Creative Co., The.

Dillon, Jana. Lucky O'Leprechaun in School, 1 vol. Dillon, Jana, illus. 2003. (Lucky o'Leprechaun Ser.). (ENG., Illus.). 32p. (J). (gr. k-3). 16.99 *(978-1-58980-035-9(4))* Pelican Publishing Co., Inc.

Dorling Kindersley Publishing Staff. Good Night, Baby Moon. 2017. (ENG.). 12p. (J). (-k). bds. 12.99 ***(978-1-4654-6307-4(0),*** DK Children) Dorling Kindersley Publishing, Inc.

Duffy, Carol Ann. The Tear Thief. Ceccoli, Nicoletta, illus. 2007. (ENG.). 32p. (J). (gr. -1-3). 16.99 *(978-1-84686-045-4(8))* Barefoot Bks., Inc.

Duffy, Carol Ann & Stevenson, Juliet. The Tear Thief. Ceccoli, Nicoletta, illus. 2011. (ENG.). 32p. (J). (gr. k-4). 9.99 *(978-1-84686-622-7(7))* Barefoot Bks., Inc.

Dyan, Penelope. I Am the Moon. 2011. 34p. pap. 11.95 *(978-1-935630-91-3(1))* Bellissima Publishing, LLC.

Eastridge, Jim. Gregory & the Moon. 2008. 12p. pap. 24.95 *(978-1-4241-9008-9(8))* America Star Bks.

Ehlert, Lois. Moon Rope. 2003. Orig. Title: Un Lazo a la Luna. (SPA & ENG.). (gr. k-3). lib. bdg. 18.40 *(978-0-613-70661-2(7),* Turtleback) Turtleback Bks.

Eubanks-Adkison, Eufa. When the Moon Was Born, 1 vol. Spinks, Stefphany (Snider), illus. 2010. 16p. 24.95 *(978-1-4512-1367-6(0))* PublishAmerica, Inc.

Farias, Juan. Los Caminos de la Luna. (SPA., Illus.). 96p. (J). *(978-84-207-8293-5(9))* Grupo Anaya, S.A. ESP. Dist: Lectorum Pubns., Inc.

Farnol, Jeffery. Money Moon. 2006. pap. 13.95 *(978-1-4218-3066-7(3))* 1st World Publishing, Inc.

Farrell, Darren. Stop Following Me, Moon! 2016. (ENG., Illus.). 40p. (J). (-k). 17.99 *(978-0-8037-4159-1(6),* Dial Bks) Penguin Young Readers Group.

Fischer, Kelly. The Moon Throws a Birthday Party. Duckworth, Michelle, illus. 2011. (ENG.). 32p. (J). 19.50 *(978-1-58385-237-8(9))* ktf-writers-studio.

Fletcher, Ralph. Hello, Harvest Moon. Kiesler, Kate, illus. 2017. (ENG.). 32p. (J). (gr. -1-3). pap. 7.99 ***(978-1-328-74049-6(8),*** HMH Books For Young Readers) Houghton Mifflin Harcourt Publishing Co.

Fletcher, Ralph J. & Fletcher, Ralph. Hello, Harvest Moon. Kiesler, Kate, illus. 2003. (ENG.). 32p. (J). (gr. -1-3). 17.99 *(978-0-618-16451-6(0))* Houghton Mifflin Harcourt Publishing Co.

Fluharty, Kristi & Fluharty, T. Lively. Fool Moon Rising. Fluharty, Kristi & Fluharty, T. Lively, illus. 2009. (Illus.). 40p. (J). 16.99 *(978-1-4335-0682-6(3))* Crossway.

Foley, Greg. Willoughby & the Moon. Foley, Greg, illus. 2010. (ENG., Illus.). 40p. (J). (gr. -1-2). 18.99 *(978-0-06-154753-9(0))* HarperCollins Pubs.

Foster, Marilyn. Moon Tricks. Vega, Alison, illus. 2012. 48p. pap. *(978-1-77097-960-4(3))* FriesenPress.

Franco, Franco. Dino-Mike & the Lunar Showdown. Franco, Franco & Garcia, Eduardo, illus. 2016. (Dino-Mike! Ser.). (ENG.). 128p. (gr. 1-3). lib. bdg. 25.32 *(978-1-4965-2492-8(6),* Dino-Mike!) Stone Arch Bks.

Froud, Brian, illus. Chelsea Morning. 2004. 32p. (J). *(978-0-689-03593-7(4),* Milk & Cookies) ibooks, Inc.

Galliez, Roxane Marie. Give Me Moon. Delanssay, Cathy, illus. 2009. 44p. (J). (gr. -1-3). 14.99 *(978-0-8416-7138-6(9))* Hammond World Atlas Corp.

Galloway, Emily Ledford. Nimby the Cloud. 2008. 32p. pap. 24.95 *(978-1-60441-779-1(X))* America Star Bks.

García, Cristina. The Dog Who Loved the Moon. Serra, Sebastia, illus. 2011. (ENG.). 32p. (J). (gr. -1-3). 16.99 *(978-1-4424-3089-1(3),* Atheneum Bks. for Young Readers) Simon & Schuster Children's Publishing.

Gardner, Sally. Maggot Moon. Crouch, Julian, illus. (ENG.). 288p. (YA). (gr. 7). 2014. pap. 8.99 *(978-0-7636-7169-3(X))* 2013. 16.99 *(978-0-7636-6553-1(3))* Candlewick Pr.

Gayatri Stein, Mari. Puddle Moon. 2010. (ENG., Illus.). 32p. 17.95 *(978-0-9793840-0-4(1),* Riverwood Bks.) White Cloud Pr.

Gerstein, Mordicai. How to Bicycle to the Moon to Plant Sunflowers: A Simple but Brilliant Plan in 24 Easy Steps. Gerstein, Mordicai, illus. 2013. (ENG., Illus.). 40p. (J). (gr. -1-2). 16.99 *(978-1-59643-512-4(7),* 9781596435124) Roaring Brook Pr.

Gibbs, Stuart. Space Case. 2015. (Moon Base Alpha Ser.). (ENG., Illus.). 368p. (J). (gr. 3-7). pap. 7.99 *(978-1-4424-9487-9(5),* Simon & Schuster Bks. For Young Readers) Simon & Schuster Bks. For Young Readers.

—Space Case. 2015. (Moon Base Alpha Ser.: 1). lib. bdg. 18.40 *(978-0-606-37883-3(9))* Turtleback Bks.

—Spaced Out. (Moon Base Alpha Ser.). (ENG.). (J). (gr. 3-7). 2017. 368p. pap. 7.99 *(978-1-4814-2337-3(1))* 2016. (Illus.). 352p. 17.99 *(978-1-4814-2336-6(3))* Simon & Schuster Bks. For Young Readers. (Simon & Schuster Bks. For Young Readers).

—Spaced Out. 2017. (Moon Base Alpha Ser.: 2). lib. bdg. 18.40 ***(978-0-606-39762-9(0))*** Turtleback Bks.

Gill, Michael. Mitsuki. 2008. 32p. pap. 19.99 *(978-1-4363-0938-7(7))* Xlibris Corp.

Golde, Justin F. Yes, My Dear, Alligators Do Belong on the Moon. 2012. 24p. pap. 11.50 *(978-1-62212-188-5(0),* Strategic Bk. Publishing) Strategic Book Publishing & Rights Agency (SBPRA).

Graham, Judith A. The Didley-Doo's, 1 vol. 2009. 36p. pap. 24.95 *(978-1-60836-035-2(0))* America Star Bks.

Griffith, Helen V. Moonlight. Dronzek, Laura, illus. 2012. (ENG.). 32p. (J). (gr. -1-k). 16.99 *(978-0-06-203285-0(2),* Greenwillow Bks.) HarperCollins Pubs.

Guess What the Moon Saw? Individual Title Six-Packs. (gr. -1-2). 23.00 *(978-0-7635-8807-6(5))* Rigby Education.

Guettier, Nancy. Jude's Moon. Walsh, Tina, illus. (ENG.). 32p. (gr. -1-4). 2015. 19.95 *(978-1-63047-725-7(7))* 2014. pap. 9.95 *(978-1-61448-964-1(5))* Morgan James Publishing.

Gutierrez, Lorna. Hello, Mr. Moon. Watkins, Laura, illus. 2016. (J). ***(978-1-4351-6412-3(1))*** Barnes & Noble, Inc.

Haaji. Black Moon. 2004. 176p. per. 15.00 *(978-0-9747017-2-1(6))* Neshee Pubn.

Handa, Nimret. Good Night Stories. 2004. (Illus.). 20p. (J). *(978-81-291-0373-4(7))* Rupa & Co.

Hanford, Juliana. Werewolf Moon. Pillo, Cary, illus. 2009. (Science Solves It! Complete Set Ser.). 32p. (J). (gr. k-7). pap. 5.95 *(978-1-57565-291-7(9))* Kane Press, Inc.

Hano, Patricia. Tyler Meets the Moon. 2010. 28p. pap. 11.99 *(978-1-60911-189-2(3),* Eloquent Bks.) Strategic Book Publishing & Rights Agency (SBPRA).

Hanson, Anders. Night Owl, 1 vol. Haberstroh, Anne, illus. 2006. (Animal Tales Ser.). 24p. (J). (gr. k-3). (ENG.). lib. bdg. 24.21 *(978-1-59679-953-0(6),* SandCastle); pap. 48.42 *(978-1-59679-954-7(4))* ABDO Publishing Co.

Hanson, Robert. Bluey & the Great Spirit Moon. 2013. 48p. pap. 17.45 *(978-1-4525-0845-0(3))* Balboa Pr.

Harley, Bill. Bear's All-Night Party. Ferreira, Melissa, illus. 2005. (ENG.). 32p. (J). (gr. -1-2). 15.95 *(978-0-87483-572-4(0))* August Hse. Pubs., Inc.

Harstad, Johan. 172 Hours on the Moon. 2013. (ENG.). 384p. (J). (gr. 8-17). pap. 10.99 *(978-0-316-18289-8(3))* Little, Brown Bks. for Young Readers.

Harstad, Johan & Chace, Tara. 172 Hours on the Moon. 2012. (ENG.). 368p. (gr. 7-17). 17.99 *(978-0-316-18288-1(5))* Little Brown & Co.

Hawthorne, Rachel. Full Moon. 2009. (Dark Guardian Ser.: 2). (ENG.). 272p. (YA). (gr. 9-18). pap. 8.99 *(978-0-06-170956-2(5),* HarperTeen) HarperCollins Pubs.

Hayes, Vicki C. Home Planet, 1 vol. 2015. (Red Rhino Ser.). (ENG.). 72p. (J). (gr. 3-6). mass mkt. 7.95 *(978-1-62250-966-9(8))* Saddleback Educational Publishing, Inc.

Heather Rose Brabant. The Moon Princess. 2009. 20p. pap. 11.95 *(978-1-4389-2980-4(3))* AuthorHouse.

Heimdallson, Freydis, et al. Kindertales: Stories Old & New for the Children of the Folk. 2008. 100p. pap. 19.50 *(978-1-4357-2563-8(8))* Lulu Pr., Inc.

Heller, Janet Ruth. How the Moon Regained Her Shape, 1 vol. Hodson, Ben, illus. 2006. (ENG.). 32p. (J). (gr. 1-5). 15.95 *(978-0-9764943-4-8(5))* Arbordale Publishing.

Hendrick-Lockyer, Veronica. Moon Boy. 2013. 18p. pap. *(978-1-84903-209-4(2))* Schiel & Denver Publishing Ltd.

Henkes, Kevin. Kitten's First Full Moon. Henkes, Kevin, illus. (ENG., Illus.). (J). (gr. -1 — 1). 2015. 34p. bds. 8.99 *(978-0-06-241710-7(X))* 2004. 40p. 17.99 *(978-0-06-058828-1(4))* HarperCollins Pubs. (Greenwillow Bks.).

—La Primera Luna Llena de Gatita, 1 vol. Henkes, Kevin, illus. 2006. Orig. Title: Kitten's First Full Moon. (SPA., Illus.). 40p. (J). (gr. -1-2). 17.99 *(978-0-06-087223-6(3))* HarperCollins Pubs.

Heo, Yumi, illus. Sun & Moon Have a Tea Party. 2016. (J). *(978-0-385-39033-0(5),* Schwartz & Wade Bks.) Random Hse. Children's Bks.

Hergé. Destination Moon.Tr. of Objectif Lune. (J). (gr. 3-8). ring bd. 19.95 *(978-0-8288-5026-1(7));* (Illus.). 62p. 19.95 *(978-0-8288-5027-8(5))* French & European Pubns., Inc.

—Objectif Lune.Tr. of Destination Moon. (FRE., Illus.). (J). (gr. 7-9). ring bd. 19.95 *(978-0-8288-5051-3(8))* French & European Pubns., Inc.

—On a Marche sur la Lune. (Tintin Ser.).Tr. of Explorers on the Moon. (FRE.). (J). pap. 21.95 *(978-2-203-00116-9(X))* Casterman, Editions FRA. Dist: Distribooks, Inc.

—On a Marche sur la Lune.Tr. of Explorers on the Moon. (FRE., Illus.). (J). (gr. 7-9). ring bd. 19.95 *(978-0-8288-5053-7(4))* French & European Pubns., Inc.

Hija del Sol y de Luna (Daughter of Sun & Moon) (SPA.). 24p. (J). 4.95 *(978-84-246-1610-6(3))* La Galera, S.A. Editorial ESP. Dist: AIMS International Bks., Inc.

Hillert, Margaret. Up, up, & Away. Spinks, Scott, illus. 2016. (BeginningtoRead Ser.). (ENG.). 32p. (J). (gr. 1-2). 22.60 *(978-1-59953-806-8(7))* Norwood Hse. Pr.

Holland, Trish. Lasso the Moon. Petrone, Valeria, illus. 2005. (Little Golden Book Ser.). (ENG.). 24p. (J). (gr. -1-2). 4.99 *(978-0-375-83289-5(0),* Golden Bks.) Random Hse. Children's Bks.

Holmes-Merritt, Angela. LINK Fairflies & Fairies. 2008. 36p. 17.50 *(978-0-615-17415-0(9))* AngiesInk.

Hooten, K. J. The Egg Nanny Tales. 2008. 98p. pap. 19.95 *(978-1-60563-722-8(X))* America Star Bks.

Hopkins, Lee Bennett. Full Moon & Star. Hall, Marcellus, illus. 2011. (ENG.). 32p. (J). (gr. -1-k). 16.95 *(978-1-4197-0013-2(8),* Abrams Bks. for Young Readers) Abrams, Inc.

Hopkins, Leslie. A World Apart. 2012. 20p. pap. 17.99 *(978-1-4772-6783-7(2))* AuthorHouse.

Horácek, Petr. The Mouse Who Ate the Moon. Horácek, Petr, illus. 2014. (ENG., Illus.). 32p. (J). (gr. -1-2). 15.99 *(978-0-7636-7059-7(6))* Candlewick Pr.

Hosford, Kate. Big Birthday. Clifton-Brown, Holly, illus. 2012. (Carolrhoda Picture Bks.). (ENG.). 32p. (J). (gr. k-2). lib. bdg. 16.95 *(978-0-7613-5410-9(7))* Lerner Publishing Group.

Hughes, Ann. Kaitlyn & the Moonman. 2008. (Illus.). 56p. pap. *(978-1-84748-470-3(0))* Athena Pr.

Hunter, R. C. Moon Kids. 2010. 64p. pap. 11.99 *(978-1-4490-7846-1(X))* AuthorHouse.

Ikeda, Daisaku. The Princess & the Moon. McCraughrean, Geraldine, tr. from JPN. Wildsmith, Brian, illus. 2013. 6.95 *(978-1-935523-58-1(9))* World Tribune Pr.

Ikin, Susan. Alex & the Night-tide Dragon. 2010. (Illus.). 68p. pap. 18.95 *(978-1-4461-4894-5(7))* Lulu Pr., Inc.

Inkpen, Mick. Ploo & the Terrible Gnobbler. 2003. (ENG., Illus.). 32p. (J). (gr. -1-k). 17.99 *(978-0-340-85573-7(8))* Hodder & Stoughton GBR. Dist: Hachette Bk. Group.

Isadora, Rachel. Mr. Moon. Date not set. (J). 15.99 *(978-0-06-029821-0(9));* lib. bdg. 16.89 *(978-0-06-029822-7(7))* HarperCollins Pubs.

Ishwaran, Wobine. A Journey into Space: Kary to the Moon. 2008. 24p. pap. 11.49 *(978-1-4343-6717-4(7))* AuthorHouse.

Jackson, Bridgett. The Monster on the Moon: Book Three of Tales from the Creek. 2009. 40p. pap. 18.49 *(978-1-4389-3540-9(4))* AuthorHouse.

Jay, Alison & Curtis, Carolyn. I Took the Moon for a Walk. 2008. (ENG., Illus.). 32p. (J). (gr. -1-2). 14.99 *(978-1-84686-200-7(0))* Barefoot Bks., Inc.

Jeffers, Dawn. Beautiful Moon. Leick, Bonnie, illus. 2009. (ENG.). 32p. (J). (gr. -1-3). 16.95 *(978-1-934960-05-9(5),* Raven Tree Pr.,Csi) Continental Sales, Inc.

Jeffers, Oliver. The Way Back Home. Jeffers, Oliver, illus. 2008. (ENG., Illus.). 32p. (J). (gr. -1-3). 17.99 *(978-0-399-25074-3(3),* Philomel Bks.) Penguin Young Readers Group.

Jennerich, Douglas Todd. My Little Half-Moon. Berube, Kate, illus. 2017. (ENG.). 32p. (J). (gr. k-3). 16.99 *(978-0-399-16901-4(6),* G.P. Putnam's Sons Books for Young Readers) Penguin Young Readers Group.

Jones, Alexandra. Moon Magic. 2012. 28p. pap. 21.99 *(978-1-4771-3995-0(8))* Xlibris Corp.

Joyce, William. The Man in the Moon. Joyce, William, illus. 2011. (Guardians of Childhood Ser.). (ENG., Illus.). 56p. (J). (gr. -1-3). 17.99 *(978-1-4424-3041-9(9));* 200.00 *(978-1-4424-4357-0(X))* Simon & Schuster Children's Publishing. (Atheneum Bks. for Young Readers).

—The Sandman. Joyce, William, illus. 2012. (Guardians of Childhood Ser.). (ENG., Illus.). 48p. (J). (gr. -1-3). 17.99 *(978-1-4424-3042-6(7),* Atheneum Bks. for Young Readers) Simon & Schuster Children's Publishing.

Joyce, William & Geringer, Laura. Nicholas St. North & the Battle of the Nightmare King, Bk. 1. Joyce, William, illus. 2011. (Guardians Ser.: 1). (ENG., Illus.). 240p. (J). (gr. 2-6). 15.99 *(978-1-4424-3048-8(6),* Atheneum Bks. for Young Readers) Simon & Schuster Children's Publishing.

Kalz, Jill. Tuckerbean on the Moon, 1 vol. Mahan, Benton, illus. 2009. (Read-It! Readers: Adventures of Tuckerbean Ser.). (ENG.). 24p. (gr. -1-3). 21.32 *(978-1-4048-5234-1(4),* Easy Readers) Picture Window Bks.

Kemble, Mai S. The Moon & the Night Sweeper. Kemble, Mai S., illus. 2008. (Illus.). (J). pap. 6.95 *(978-1-60108-023-3(9))* Red Cygnet Pr.

Kemble, Mai S., illus. The Moon & the Night Sweeper. 2007. 30p. (J). (gr. -1-2). 15.95 *(978-1-60108-013-4(1))* Red Cygnet Pr.

Kherdian, David. Come Back, Moon. Hogrogian, Nonny, illus. 2013. (ENG.). 32p. (J). (gr. -1-3). 16.99 *(978-1-4424-5887-1(9),* Beach Lane Bks.) Beach Lane Bks.

Kim, Cecil. Little Moon's Christmas: Imagination - Objects. Cowley, Joy, ed. Horácek, Petr, illus. 2015. (Step up - Creative Thinking Ser.). (ENG.). 32p. (J). (gr. -1-2). 26.65 *(978-1-925186-39-0(3))* Lerner Publishing Group.

King, Thomas. Coyote Sings to the Moon. Wales, Johnny, illus. 2008. (ENG.). 36p. (J). pap. *(978-1-55263-868-2(5))* Magma.

Kitze, Carrie A. We See the Moon. Jinshan Painting Academy, illus. l.t. ed. 2003. 32p. (J). (gr. -1-3). 16.95 *(978-0-9726244-0-4(6))* EMK Pr.

Koksal, Erin. Bedtime for Abbie. 2010. 23p. (J). pap. 11.95 *(978-1-4327-5693-2(1))* Outskirts Pr., Inc.

Komai, Asuka, illus. October Moon. 2009. (J). *(978-1-60108-017-2(4))* Red Cygnet Pr.

Koren, Robert. The Moon in the Man. 2010. 28p. pap. 15.99 *(978-1-4535-3946-0(8))* Xlibris Corp.

Kraatz, Jeramey. The Moon Platoon. 2017. (Space Runners Ser.: 1). 352p. (J). (gr. 3-7). 16.99 *(978-0-06-244597-1(9))* HarperCollins Pubs.

Krans, Kim. Whose Moon Is That? 2017. (ENG., Illus.). 48p. (J). (gr. -1-2). 17.99 *(978-1-101-93227-8(9),* Random Hse. Bks. for Young Readers) Random Hse. Children's Bks.

Krilanovich, Nadia. Moon Child. Sayles, Elizabeth, illus. 2010. (ENG.). 32p. (J). (gr. -1-2). 15.99 *(978-1-58246-325-4(5),* Tricycle Pr.) Random Hse. Children's Bks.

Krouskop, Adrienne. The Bakers Moon. 2013. 24p. pap. 10.50 *(978-1-938743-92-4(X))* Reimann Bks.

Lamar, Gail Renfroe. Moon of the Wishing Night. Mask, Cynthia, illus. 2004. 32p. (J). 17.95 *(978-1-57966-047-5(9),* River City Kids) River City Publishing.

Landry, Leo. Space Boy. Landry, Leo, illus. 2007. (ENG., Illus.). 32p. (J). (gr. -1-3). 16.99 *(978-0-618-60568-2(1))* Houghton Mifflin Harcourt Publishing Co.

Lascurain, Anna. Apollo in the Moon House. 2006. Orig. Title: The Moonboy. (J). per. 7.99 *(978-0-9769612-3-9(7))* Darker Intentions Pr.

Lemieux, Jean. Toby Shoots for Infinity. Cummins, Sarah, tr. from FRE. Casson, Sophie, illus. 2005. (Formac First Novels Ser.: 55). (ENG.). 64p. (J). (gr. 2-5). 14.95 *(978-0-88780-685-8(6),* 9780887806858) Formac Publishing Co., Ltd. CAN. Dist: Casemate Pubs. & Bk. Distributors, LLC.

—Toby Shoots for Infinity, 1 vol. Cummins, Sarah, tr. from FRE. Casson, Sophie, illus. 2005. (Formac First Novels Ser.: 55). (ENG.). 64p. (J). (gr. 2-5). 4.95 *(978-0-88780-684-1(8),* 9780887806841) Formac Publishing Co., Ltd. CAN. Dist: Casemate Pubs. & Bk. Distributors, LLC.

Lin, Grace. Starry River of the Sky. (ENG., Illus.). (J). (gr. 3-7). 2014. 320p. pap. 10.99 *(978-0-316-12597-0(0))* 2012. 304p. 17.99 *(978-0-316-12595-6(4))* Little, Brown Bks. for Young Readers.

—Starry River of the Sky. 2014. (J). lib. bdg. 20.85 *(978-0-606-32277-5(9),* Turtleback) Turtleback Bks.

—Thanking the Moon: Celebrating the Mid-Autumn Moon Festival. 2010. (ENG.). 32p. (J). (gr. -1-2). 16.99 *(978-0-375-86101-7(7),* Knopf Bks. for Young Readers) Random Hse. Children's Bks.

—Where the Mountain Meets the Moon. 2009. (ENG., Illus.). 288p. (J). (gr. 3-7). 18.99 *(978-0-316-11427-1(8))* Little Brown & Co.

—Where the Mountain Meets the Moon. 2011. (ENG., Illus.). 320p. (J). (gr. 3-7). pap., pap. 10.99 *(978-0-316-03863-8(6))* Little, Brown Bks. for Young Readers.

—Where the Mountain Meets the Moon. 2011. (ENG., Illus.). 278p. (gr. 4-7). 19.00 *(978-1-61383-087-1(4))* Perfection Learning Corp.

—Where the Mountain Meets the Moon. 2011. (J). lib. bdg. 22.10 *(978-0-606-16233-3(X),* Turtleback) Turtleback Bks.

Lin, Grace, illus. Star Baby. 2017. (J). ***(978-0-316-40448-8(9))*** Little Brown & Co.

Longstreet, Olivia. Edgar's Moon. 2011. 24p. pap. 15.99 *(978-1-4568-6524-5(2))* Xlibris Corp.

Lopez, Sixto. Snarloff Duwaki's Adventures. 2011. 24p. pap. 24.95 *(978-1-4626-2557-4(6))* America Star Bks.

The Lotus Caves. 2014. (ENG., Illus.). 288p. (J). (gr. 4-8). pap. 7.99 *(978-1-4814-1837-9(8),* Aladdin) Simon & Schuster Children's Publishing.

The Lotus Caves. 2014. (ENG., Illus.). 288p. (J). (gr. 4-8). 17.99 *(978-1-4814-1838-6(6),* Simon & Schuster/Paula Wiseman Bks.) Simon & Schuster/Paula Wiseman Bks.

Loveridge, Pamela. The Man in the Moon. 2012. 28p. pap. 32.70 *(978-1-4797-5423-6(4))* Xlibris Corp.

Lowe, Tom. Louie the Loon & the Moon. Leadlove, Ben, illus. 2011. 28p. pap. 11.00 *(978-1-61170-030-5(2))* Robertson Publishing.

Mackin, Joan Marie. It's Just the Moon. 2004. (J). pap. 9.00 *(978-0-8059-6315-1(4))* Dorrance Publishing Co., Inc.

MacLachlan, Patricia. The Moon's Almost Here. dePaola, Tomie, illus. 2016. (ENG.). 32p. (J). (gr. -1-3). 17.99 *(978-1-4814-2062-4(3),* McElderry, Margaret K. Bks.) McElderry, Margaret K. Bks.

Madison's Descent: A Child's Journey. collector's ed. 2004. (J). 75.00 *(978-0-9752516-0-7(0))* Otis & Randolph Pr.

Maher, Mickle Brandt. Master Stitchum & the Moon. Dousias, Spiro, illus. 2003. (J). 19.99 *(978-1-932188-01-1(0))* Bollix Bks.

Mai, Lily. Bertie Boom's Trip to the Moon. 2010. (Illus.). 20p. 12.49 *(978-1-4520-1379-4(9))* AuthorHouse.

Martin-Duttmann, Robin. Zoo on the Moon. 2013. 24p. pap. 12.97 *(978-1-62212-735-1(8),* Strategic Bk. Publishing) Strategic Book Publishing & Rights Agency (SBPRA).

Martin, Gina. Mother Moon: Magic Pool in the Sky. 2008. 28p. pap. 12.49 *(978-1-4389-0138-1(0))* AuthorHouse.

MaryAnn, Aunt. Spooky Journey down Riverside Drive the Night of the Full Moon. 2010. 40p. pap. 15.95 *(978-0-557-31081-4(4))* Lulu Pr., Inc.

McCann, Jesse L., et al. Bad Moon Rising, 1 vol. 2014. (Krypto the Superdog Ser.). (ENG., Illus.). 32p. (gr. 1-2). 22.60 *(978-1-4342-6475-6(0))* Stone Arch Bks.

McCarty, Peter. Moon Plane. McCarty, Peter, illus. 2006. (ENG., Illus.). 40p. (J). (gr. -1-1). 18.99 *(978-0-8050-7943-2(2)*, 9780805079432, Holt, Henry & Co. Bks. For Young Readers) Holt, Henry & Co.

McCluire, Brian D. The Sun & the Moon. 2006. (Illus.). 36p. (J). 14.95 *(978-1-933426-09-9(8))* Universal Flag Publishing.

McKellop, Holly R. To the Moon. 2012. 32p. pap. 24.95 *(978-1-4626-8034-4(8))* America Star Bks.

McKinnon, Yolanda Amos. Why Is the Moon Following Me? 2012. 24p. pap. 15.99 *(978-1-4771-3081-0(0))* Xlibris Corp.

Meschenmoser, Sebastian. Mr. Squirrel & the Moon. 2015. (ENG., Illus.). 48p. (J). 18.95 *(978-0-7358-4156-7(X))* North-South Bks., Inc.

Micchelli, Lauren. The Snootzytime Adventures of Maddie & Murphy - to the Moon & Back. 2015. (ENG., Illus.). 40p. (J). pap. 14.95 *(978-1-62287-843-7(4))* First Edition Design eBook Publishing.

Milbourne, A. & Wells, R. Mouse on the Moon. 2004. (Touchy-Feely Board Bks.). (Illus.). 10p. (J). (gr. -1-18). 4.95 *(978-0-7945-0163-1(X)*, Usborne) EDC Publishing.

Miller, Jules, illus. When Night Became Day. 2015. (ENG.). 32p. (J). (gr. -1-k). 16.95 *(978-1-62914-632-4(3)*, Sky Pony Pr.) Skyhorse Publishing Co., Inc.

Mindler, Jason. Giralon. 2003. 122p. (YA). 20.95 *(978-0-595-74854-9(6))*; pap. 10.95 *(978-0-595-28581-5(3))* iUniverse, Inc. (Writers Club Pr.).

Moon Stories. 2004. (YA). 11.95 *(978-0-9752801-1-9(2))* Beres, Nancy.

Morrissey, Dean & Krensky, Stephen. The Crimson Comet. Morrissey, Dean, illus. 2006. (Illus.). 32p. (J). (gr. k-4). 17.89 *(978-0-06-008070-9(1))* HarperCollins Pubs.

Mortensen, Lori. Cindy Moo. Mack, Jeff, illus. 2012. (ENG.). 32p. (J). (gr. -1-2). 16.99 *(978-0-06-204393-1(5))* HarperCollins Pubs.

Murphy, Bobby. Ted the Turtle's Trip to the Moon. 2013. 24p. pap. 11.50 *(978-1-62212-431-2(6)*, Strategic Bk. Publishing) Strategic Book Publishing & Rights Agency (SBPRA).

Murray, Joe. Who Asked the Moon to Dinner? 2015. (ENG., Illus.). 100p. (gr. 4-7). pap. 16.95 *(978-0-9676061-8-7(7))* Tallfellow Pr.

Mutuku, E. M. When the Sun Challenged the Moon. 2012. 20p. pap. 15.50 *(978-1-4634-4718-2(3))* AuthorHouse.

My Trip to the Moon. 2004. (J). ring bd. 4.50 *(978-0-9762740-0-1(0)*, Flat Kids) Smart Smiles Co., The.

Neira, Elsy. The Kid That Flew to the Moon: El niño que volo a la Luna. 2011. 40p. pap. *(978-1-4269-6986-7(4))* Trafford Publishing (UK) Ltd.

Nickel, Scott. Blastoff to the Secret Side of the Moon!, 1 vol. Bradley, Jessica, illus. 2013. (Comics Land Ser.). (ENG.). 32p. (gr. k-2). 7.95 *(978-1-4342-4273-0(0))*; lib. bdg. 25.32 *(978-1-4342-4031-6(2))* Stone Arch Bks.

Oddo, Joanne. The Strawberry Moon. 2004. (Illus.). 24.99 *(978-1-4134-5075-0(X))* Xlibris Corp.

Ofanansky, Allison. New Month, New Moon. Alpern, Eliyahu, photos by. 2014. (ENG., Illus.). 32p. (J). (gr. -1-2). 16.95 *(978-1-4677-1945-2(5)*, Kar-Ben Publishing) Lerner Publishing Group.

Olker, Constance. The Punctuation Pals Go to the Moon. 2005. (Illus.). (J). 64p. per. 24.95 *(978-1-933449-13-5(6))*; per. 19.95 *(978-0-9761289-6-0(9))* Nightengale Pr.

Orobosa-Ogbeide, Kathryn. The Boy & the Moon. 2012. 12p. pap. 12.68 *(978-1-4669-1894-8(2))* Trafford Publishing.

Orsi, Tea & Panaro, Carlo. Tinker Bell & the Lost Treasure. Razzi, Manuela et al, illus. 2013. (Disney Fairies Ser.: 12). (ENG.). 64p. (J). (gr. 1-6). pap. 7.99 *(978-1-59707-428-5(4)*, 9781597074285) Papercutz.

Overton, Lou Ann. Thank You, Moon. 2013. 24p. pap. 12.45 *(978-1-4908-0030-1(1)*, WestBow Pr.) Author Solutions, Inc.

Palazzolo, Gail M. Mommy, How Can We Catch the Moon? 2008. 15p. pap. 24.95 *(978-1-60672-864-2(4))* America Star Bks.

Paraskevas, Michael. Mr. Moon. 2016. (ENG., Illus.). 40p. (J). (gr. -1-2). 17.99 *(978-0-399-54992-2(7)*, Crown Books For Young Readers) Random Hse. Children's Bks.

Pearce, Clemency. Frangoline & the Midnight Dream. Elliott, Rebecca, illus. 2011. (ENG.). 32p. (J). (gr. -1-k). 16.99 *(978-0-545-31426-8(7)*, Chicken Hse., The) Scholastic, Inc.

Pearle, Ida. The Moon Is Going to Addy's House. 2015. (ENG., Illus.). 32p. (J). (gr. -1-k). 17.99 *(978-0-8037-4054-9(9)*, Dial Bks) Penguin Young Readers Group.

Petrone, Catherine. Moon Worms. 2010. 27p. (J). pap. 12.95 *(978-1-4327-1477-2(5))* Outskirts Pr., Inc.

Plunkett, Windyann. Fiddle Me a Riddle & Bring Me the Moon. Davidson, Mary, illus. 2011. 24p. pap. 24.95 *(978-1-4626-3920-5(8))* America Star Bks.

Porter, Pamela. Yellow Moon, Apple Moon, 1 vol. James, Matt, illus. 2008. (ENG.). 32p. (J). (gr. k — 1). 17.95 *(978-0-88899-809-5(0))* Groundwood Bks. CAN. Dist: Publishers Group West (PGW).

Posnock, Michael A. The Adventures of Wilbur the Wave. 2013. 44p. pap. 17.99 *(978-1-4808-0132-5(1))* Archway Publishing.

Potts, Molly. The Falling Moon. 2012. 26p. 24.95 *(978-1-4626-6596-9(9))* America Star Bks.

Reed, Lynn Rowe. Swim to the Moon. 2009. 32p. pap. 12.99 *(978-1-4389-4980-2(4))* AuthorHouse.

Reeve, Rosie. Lullaby Moon. Reeve, Rosie, illus. 2010. (ENG., Illus.). 20p. (J). (gr. k — 1). bds. 8.99 *(978-0-545-21146-8(8)*, Cartwheel Bks.) Scholastic, Inc.

Rex, Adam. Moonday. Rex, Adam, illus. 2013. (ENG., Illus.). 40p. (J). (gr. -1-2). 16.99 *(978-1-4231-1920-3(7))* Disney Pr.

Reynolds, Paul. To the Moon! Reynolds, Peter H., illus. 2017. (ENG.). 48p. (J). (gr. 1-4). pap. 4.99 ***(978-1-58089-680-1(4))*** Charlesbridge Publishing, Inc.

Reynolds, Paul A. Sydney & Simon: To the Moon & Beyond! Reynolds, Peter H., illus. 2017. (ENG.). 48p. (J). (gr. 1-4). lib. bdg. 12.99 *(978-1-58089-679-5(0))* Charlesbridge Publishing, Inc.

Robinson, Hilary. Over the Moon. Abbott, Jane, illus. 2009. (Tadpoles Ser.). (ENG.). 24p. (J). (gr. k-2). pap. *(978-0-7787-3899-2(X))*; lib. bdg. *(978-0-7787-3868-8(X))* Crabtree Publishing Co.

Rosario, Joann. Where Did Sabrina Go? Rosario, Joann, illus. 2004. (Illus.). 13p. (J). (gr. -1-5). pap. 10.00 *(978-0-9758746-1-5(6))* J.G.R. Enterprises.

Ross, Daisy T. Ty & the Moon. 2012. 80p. pap. 25.25 *(978-1-4772-6950-3(9))* AuthorHouse.

Routley, Becky. Moon Golf. 2009. (Illus.). 28p. pap. 12.49 *(978-1-4490-4713-9(0))* AuthorHouse.

Rustgi, Jennifer. A Moon of My Own, 1 vol. White, Ashley, illus. 2016. (ENG.). 32p. (J). (gr. k-4). 16.95 *(978-1-58469-572-1(2))* Dawn Pubns.

Ryan, Karlene Kay. Genevieve & the Moon. Johnson, Meredith, illus. 2013. 34p. pap. 9.99 *(978-0-9888843-3-5(X))* Ryan, Karlene Kay Author.

Rylant, Cynthia & Siegel, Mark. Long Night Moon. Siegel, Mark, illus. 2004. (ENG., Illus.). 32p. (J). (gr. -1-3). 17.99 *(978-0-689-85426-2(9)*, Simon & Schuster Bks. For Young Readers) Simon & Schuster Bks. For Young Readers.

Saikia, Mayur, illus. Anansi & His Children. 2010. (J). *(978-1-60617-139-4(9))* Teaching Strategies, LLC.

Samuels, Gregory Robert. Mommy, Where Does Everything Come From? Brennan, Craig, illus. 2008. 11p. pap. 24.95 *(978-1-60610-437-8(3))* America Star Bks.

Scillian, Devin. Cosmo's Moon. Braught, Mark, illus. 2003. (ENG.). 40p. (J). (gr. 1-4). 15.95 *(978-1-58536-123-6(2)*, 201986) Sleeping Bear Pr.

Scott, Janine. Mars Mouse. Wood, Hannah, illus. 2009. (Treasure Chest Readers Ser.). 24p. (J). (gr. -1-2). pap. 8.15 *(978-1-60754-677-1(9))*; lib. bdg. 22.60 *(978-1-60754-676-4(0))* Windmill Bks.

Shanghai Animation Studio Staff & Tang, Sanmu. An Attempt to Scoop up the Moon. Ying, Wu, tr. from CHI. 2010. (Favorite Children's Ser.). (ENG., Illus.). 32p. (J). (gr. -1-3). pap. 5.95 *(978-1-60220-971-8(5))* BetterLink Pr., Inc.

Sharpe, Jemima. Mr Moon Wakes Up. Sharpe, Jemima, illus. 2016. (Child's Play Library). (ENG., Illus.). 32p. (J). *(978-1-84643-694-9(X))* Child's Play International Ltd.

Shoshan, Beth. Little Rabbit Waits for the Moon. Peel, Stephanie, illus. 2013. (J). *(978-1-4351-4802-4(9))* Barnes & Noble, Inc.

Sills, Elizabeth & Patrice, Elena. Nana Star. Saker, Linda, illus. 2007. 32p. (J). (gr. -1-3). 15.95 *(978-0-9753843-5-0(X))* ee publishing & productions, inc.

—Nana Star & the Moonman. Saker, Linda, illus. 2008. 32p. (J). (gr. -1-3). 15.95 *(978-0-9753843-6-7(8))* ee publishing & productions, inc.

Silverman, Erica. Let's Go to the Moon. Golden, Jess, illus. 2017. (Green Light Readers Level 2 Ser.). (ENG.). 32p. (J). (gr. -1-3). 12.99 *(978-0-544-86760-4(2)*, HMH Books For Young Readers) Houghton Mifflin Harcourt Publishing Co.

Simon, Francesca. Hello, Moon! Cort, Ben, illus. 2014. (ENG.). 32p. (J). (gr. -1-k). 16.99 *(978-0-545-64795-3(9)*, Orchard Bks.) Scholastic, Inc.

Simon, Mary Manz. God Made the Moon. Walkley, Lizzie, illus. 2016. (J). *(978-0-8249-1981-8(5)*, Ideal Pubns.) Worthy Publishing.

Sinke, Janet Mary. Priscilla Mcdoodlenut Doodle Mcmae Asks, Why? Pennington, Craig, illus. 2007. 40p. (J). 17.95 *(978-0-9742732-8-0(7))* My Grandma & Me Pubs.

Smith, Buckley. Moonsailors. Smith, Buckley, illus. 2007. (ENG., Illus.). 40p. (J). (gr. -1-7). 14.95 *(978-0-937822-95-1(7))* WoodenBoat Pubns.

Smith, Richard G. When the Moon Fell Down. Date not set. 32p. (J). (gr. -1-18). pap. 4.99 *(978-0-06-443550-5(4))* HarperCollins Pubs.

Smith, Rosemarie. Meet the Bubblechomps - & the Bubblechomps Go Skiing. 2010. (Illus.). 36p. pap. *(978-1-907652-00-4(0))* Grosvenor Hse. Publishing Ltd.

Soetoro-Ng, Maya. Ladder to the Moon. Morales, Yuyi, illus. (ENG.). 48p. (J). (gr. -1-3). 2017. 7.99 *(978-0-7636-9343-5(X))* 2011. 16.99 *(978-0-7636-4570-0(2))* Candlewick Pr.

—Ladder to the Moon with CD. Morales, Yuyi, illus. 2012. (ENG.). 48p. (J). (gr. -1-3). 19.99 *(978-0-7636-6006-2(X))* Candlewick Pr.

Solner Heimer, Patricia. Li'l Earth. Solner Heimer, Patricia, illus. 2010. (Illus.). 32p. (J). (gr. k-4). 15.99 *(978-0-9844453-0-1(7))* Maple Road Publishing, Inc.

Sonneborn, Scott. Moon Bandits. Cavallaro, Mike & DC Comics Staff, illus. 2013. (Man of Steel Ser.). (ENG.). 88p. (gr. 2-3). 26.65 *(978-1-4342-4093-4(2))* Stone Arch Bks.

—The Moon Bandits. Cavallaro, Mike, illus. 2013. (Man of Steel Ser.). (ENG.). 88p. (gr. 2-3). pap. 5.95 *(978-1-4342-4223-5(4))* Stone Arch Bks.

Space Case. 2014. (Moon Base Alpha Ser.). (ENG., Illus.). 352p. (J). (gr. 3-7). 17.99 *(978-1-4424-9486-2(7)*, Simon & Schuster Bks. For Young Readers) Simon & Schuster Bks. For Young Readers.

The Spotted Moon & Deputy KC: Chase the Big Orange Ball. 2008. (J). spiral bd. *(978-0-9793930-3-7(5))* Dandelion Publishing.

St. Romain, Rose Anne. Moon's Cloud Blanket. Waites, Joan C., illus. 2003. 32p. (J). 15.95 *(978-1-56554-922-7(8))* Pelican Publishing Co., Inc.

Steadman, Ralph. Flowers for the Moon. 2004. (Illus.). 42p. 100.00 *(978-0-9760742-0-5(6))* Sylph Pubns.

Steinmann, Donna. Hello, Grand Mamoon! Guion, Tamara, illus. 2005. 32p. (J). 16.95 *(978-0-9663286-4-6(7))* EarthTime Pubns.

Stokholm, Susan Mary. Between a Shadow & the Moon. 2010. 252p. pap. 14.49 *(978-1-4520-1752-5(2))* AuthorHouse.

Sutherland, Suzanne. Under the Dusty Moon. 2016. (ENG.). 272p. (YA). pap. 14.99 *(978-1-4597-3202-5(2))* Dundurn CAN. Dist: Ingram Publisher Services.

Swarbrick, David E. Peggy's Play House. 2011. 24p. pap. 24.95 *(978-1-4626-1989-4(4))* America Star Bks.

Tara, Stephanie. I'll Follow the Moon. Fodi, Lee Edward, illus. 2005. 40p. (J). 20.95 *(978-1-933285-13-9(3))* Brown Books Publishing Group.

Taylor, Rosemary. Eddie's Rocket Adventure. 2011. 28p. pap. 13.54 *(978-1-4670-2537-9(2))* AuthorHouse.

Torgerson, Scotty Delray. Jacob Goes to the Moon. 2nd l.t. ed. 2005. (Illus.). 32p. (J). 10.00 *(978-0-9767116-0-5(5))* Torgerson Meadows Publishing.

Udry, Janice May. The Moon Jumpers. Sendak, Maurice, illus. 2013. (Sendak Reissues Ser.). (ENG.). 32p. (J). (gr. -1-3). 17.95 *(978-0-06-028460-2(9))* HarperCollins Pubs.

Ungerer, Tomi. El Hombre de la Luna. (SPA., Illus.). 40p. (J). (gr. k-2). 7.95 *(978-84-204-3746-0(8)*, AF0456) Santillana USA Publishing Co., Inc.

—El Hombre de la Luna. Ungerer, Tomi, illus. 2003. (Picture Books Collection). (SPA., Illus.). 40p. (J). (gr. k-3). pap. 10.95 *(978-968-19-0661-0(6))* Santillana USA Publishing Co., Inc.

van Genechten, Guido. Moon Is Sad. 2010. (ENG.). 12p. (J). (gr. k — 1). bds. 8.95 *(978-1-60537-048-4(7))* Clavis Publishing.

Veil, Karney. Sun & Moon Play Hide & Seek: A Children's Story. 2012. 24p. (-18). pap. 24.95 *(978-1-4626-9401-3(2))* America Star Bks.

Vere, Ed. Max at Night. 2016. (Max Ser.: 2). (ENG.). 32p. (J). (-2). 16.99 *(978-1-4926-3296-2(1)*, 9781492632962, Sourcebooks Jabberwocky) Sourcebooks, Inc.

Waller, C. L. Lady Sun & the Man in the Moon. 2008. 16p. per. 24.95 *(978-1-4241-8670-9(6))* America Star Bks.

Walton, Ann. The Tale of Sun & Moon. Hinrichsen, Tamsin, illus. 2010. (ENG.). 32p. (J). (gr. k-2). 11.95 *(978-1-77009-705-6(8))* Jacana Media ZAF. Dist: Independent Pubs. Group.

Ward, Helen. Moon Dog. 2005. (Illus.). 40p. (J). *(978-1-84011-864-3(4))* Templar Publishing.

Wartko, Karen J. I Know My Daddy Works on the Moon. 2004. (J). lib. bdg. 17.95 *(978-0-9748979-0-5(6))* Spreeda Publishing.

Weston Woods Staff, creator. Happy Birthday Moon. 2004. 29.95 *(978-1-55592-842-1(0))*; (J). 18.95 *(978-1-55592-805-6(6))*; (J). 38.75 *(978-1-55592-822-3(6))* Weston Woods Studios, Inc.

—Kitten's First Full Moon. 2011. 29.95 *(978-0-545-37422-4(7))* Weston Woods Studios, Inc.

Williams, John Joseph. The Frightened Garden. 2013. 98p. (J). pap. *(978-1-78299-167-0(0))* FeedARead.com.

Wilson, Land. Sofia's Dream. O'Malley, Judy, ed. Cornelison, Sue, illus. 2010. (ENG.). 40p. (J). (gr. -1-2). 18.95 *(978-0-9829938-1-1(1))* March 4th, Inc.

Yakola, Carrie. Full Moon Maxi. 2008. 36p. pap. 19.99 *(978-1-4343-3966-9(1))* AuthorHouse.

Yankey, Lindsey. Sun & Moon. 2015. (ENG., Illus.). 32p. (J). (gr. -1-3). 16.95 *(978-1-927018-60-6(9))* Simply Read Bks. CAN. Dist: Ingram Publisher Services.

Young, Katharine Anne. Grandmother Moon & Roy G Biv: A Colorful Bedtime Story for All Ages. EXPLORE the AMAZING SECRETS of COLOR. 2009. 72p. pap. 23.49 *(978-1-4389-7844-4(8))* AuthorHouse.

Zumwalt, Susan. Shine on Me. 2007. 16p. per. 24.95 *(978-1-4241-8836-9(9))* America Star Bks.

MOON, VOYAGES TO

see Space Flight to the Moon

MOON PROBES

see Lunar Probes

MOORE, HENRY, 1898-1986

O'Reilly, Sally. Henry Moore. 2003. (Artists in Their Time Ser.). (ENG., Illus.). 48p. (J). 24.00 *(978-0-531-12241-9(7)*, Watts, Franklin) Scholastic Library Publishing.

MOORISH ART

see Islamic Art

MOORS (PEOPLE)

see Muslims

MOORS (WETLANDS)—FICTION

Overington, Marcus. Lost on Bodmin Moor. 2012. (Illus.). 50p. pap. *(978-1-909039-36-0(5))* Legend Pr.

MOOSE

Arnold, Caroline. A Moose's World, 1 vol. Arnold, Caroline, illus. 2010. (Caroline Arnold's Animals Ser.). (ENG., Illus.). 24p. (gr. k-2). lib. bdg. 27.99 *(978-1-4048-5742-1(7))* Picture Window Bks.

Borgert-Spaniol, Megan. Moose. 2015. (North American Animals Ser.). (ENG., Illus.). 24p. (J). (gr. k-3). lib. bdg. 25.95 *(978-1-62617-260-9(9)*, Blastoff! Readers) Bellwether Media.

Carr, Aaron. Moose. 2014. (Illus.). 24p. (J). *(978-1-62127-212-0(5))* Weigl Pubs., Inc.

Doudna, Kelly. It's a Baby Moose!, 1 vol. 2008. (Baby Mammals Ser.). (ENG., Illus.). 24p. (J). (gr. k-3). lib. bdg. 24.21 *(978-1-60453-026-1(X))* ABDO Publishing Co.

Estigarribia, Diana. Moose. 2005. (Animals Animals Ser.). (Illus.). 48p. (gr. 3-7). lib. bdg. 29.93 *(978-0-7614-1870-2(9)*, Benchmark Bks.) Marshall Cavendish Corp.

Gannij, Joan. Elusive Moose. Beaton, Clare, illus. (ENG.). (J). (gr. -1-k). 2011. 32p. pap. 7.99 *(978-1-84686-075-1(X))* 2007. 24p. 7.99 *(978-1-84686-001-0(6))* Barefoot Bks., Inc.

Gannij, Joan & Grannij, Joan. Elusive Moose. 2006. (Hide-and-Seek Books (Barefoot Books) Ser.). (ENG., Illus.). 32p. (J). (gr. -1-3). 15.99 *(978-1-905236-75-6(1))* Barefoot Bks., Inc.

Gish, Melissa. Living Wild - Moose. (Living Wild Ser.). (Illus.). (J). 2011. (ENG.). 48p. (gr. 4-7). pap. 12.00 *(978-0-89812-556-6(1)*, Creative Paperbacks) 2010. 46p. (gr. 5-18). 23.95 *(978-1-58341-973-1(X)*, Creative Education) Creative Co., The.

Gregory, Josh. Moose. 2015. (ENG., Illus.). 48p. (J). lib. bdg. *(978-0-531-21393-3(5)*, Orchard Bks.) Scholastic, Inc.

Hemstock, Annie. Moose, 1 vol. 2012. (North American Animals Ser.). (ENG.). 24p. (gr. k-1). pap. 7.29 *(978-1-4296-7924-4(7))*; pap. 41.70 *(978-1-4296-8360-9(0))*; lib. bdg. 26.65 *(978-1-4296-7705-9(8))* Capstone Press of Coughlan Cos. (Pebble Plus).

Krauskopf, Sharma. Moose Family Close Up. Holdsworth, Henry, photos by. 2007. (Illus.). 28p. per. *(978-0-9543367-4-5(7))* Scottish Radiance Pubns.

Lawrence, Ellen. Enormous Ears & Soft Brown Hair (Moose) 2015. (Whose Little Baby Are You? Ser.). (ENG.). 24p. (J). (gr. -1-3). lib. bdg. 23.93 *(978-1-910549-18-6(5))* Bearport Publishing Co., Inc.

Love, Pamela. A Moose's Morning. Sochor, Lesia, illus. 2007. (ENG.). 32p. (J). (gr. -1-3). 15.95 *(978-0-89272-733-9(0))* Down East Bks.

Macken, JoAnn Early. Moose. 2nd rev. ed. 2009. (Animals That Live in the Forest Ser.). (ENG., Illus.). 24p. (J). (gr. -1-3). pap. 8.15 *(978-1-4339-2480-4(3))*; lib. bdg. 22.60 *(978-1-4339-2404-0(8))* Stevens, Gareth Publishing LLLP.

—Moose;Alces. 2nd rev. ed. 2009. (Animals That Live in the Forest/Animales del bosque Ser.). (SPA & ENG.). 24p. (J). (gr. -1-3). lib. bdg. 22.60 *(978-1-4339-2436-1(6)*, Weekly Reader Leveled Readers) Stevens, Gareth Publishing LLLP.

Magby, Meryl. Moose. 2012. (American Animals Ser.). (ENG., Illus.). 24p. (J). (gr. k-3). lib. bdg. 22.60 *(978-1-4488-6183-5(7))*; pap. 8.25 *(978-1-4488-6325-9(2)*, PowerKids Pr.) Rosen Publishing Group, Inc., The.

Meister, Cari. Do You Really Want to Meet a Moose? Fabbri, Daniele, illus. 2015. (Do You Really Want to Meet ... ? Ser.). (ENG.). 24p. (J). (gr. 1-3). 19.95 *(978-1-60753-736-6(2))* Amicus Publishing.

Mihaly, Christy. Moose. 2017. (Animals of North America (paperback) Ser.). (ENG.). 32p. (J). (gr. 3-5). pap. 9.95 ***(978-1-63517-091-7(5)***, Focus Readers) North Star Editions.

The Moose, 6 vols. (gr. 4-18). 39.95 *(978-0-7368-8500-3(5))* Red Brick Learning.

Owen, Ruth. Moose, 1. 2014. (Dr. Bob's Amazing World of Animals Ser.). (ENG.). 32p. (J). (gr. k-5). pap. 11.75 *(978-1-4777-9037-3(3))*; lib. bdg. 27.50 *(978-1-4777-9036-6(5))* Rosen Publishing Group, Inc., The. (Windmill Bks.).

Owings, Lisa. Moose Attack. 2012. (Animal Attacks Ser.). (ENG., Illus.). 24p. (J). (gr. 3-7). lib. bdg. 25.95 *(978-1-60014-788-3(7)*, Torque Bks.) Bellwether Media.

Riggs, Kate. Amazing Animals: Moose. 2012. (Amazing Animals Ser.). (ENG., Illus.). 24p. (J). (gr. 1-3). pap. 8.99 *(978-0-89812-696-9(7)*, Creative Paperbacks) Creative Co., The.

—Moose. 2012. 24p. (J). 25.65 *(978-1-60818-111-7(1)*, Creative Education) Creative Co., The.

Rogers, Amy B. Moose, 01 vols., 1. 2016. (North America's Biggest Beasts Ser.). (ENG., Illus.). 24p. (J). pap. 8.25 *(978-1-5081-4296-6(3)*, PowerKids Pr.) Rosen Publishing Group, Inc., The.

Schuetz, Kristin. Moose. 2014. (Backyard Wildlife Ser.). (ENG.). 24p. (J). (gr. k-3). lib. bdg. 25.95 *(978-1-60014-969-6(3)*, Blastoff! Readers) Bellwether Media.

Shea, Mary Molly. Massive Moose. 2016. (Cutest Animals... That Could Kill You! Ser.). (Illus.). 24p. (J). (gr. 3-2). 22.60 *(978-1-4824-4913-6(7))* Stevens, Gareth Publishing LLLP.

Stewart, Anne. I Saw a Moose Today. 2007. (Illus.). 32p. (J). (gr. 1-2). 12.95 *(978-0-9766264-6-6(2))* Raven Productions, Inc.

Terp, Gail. Moose. 2017. (Wild Animal Kingdom Ser.). (ENG., Illus.). 32p. (J). (gr. 3-7). 31.35 ***(978-1-68072-053-2(8)***, Bolt) Black Rabbit Bks.

Winnick, Nick. Moose. 2010. (Backyard Animals Ser.). (Illus.). 24p. (gr. 2-4). (J). pap. 11.95 *(978-1-60596-947-3(8))*; (YA). lib. bdg. 25.70 *(978-1-60596-946-6(X))* Weigl Pubs., Inc.

MOOSE—FICTION

Ayton, Shalanna. The Adventures of Missy the Moose. 2009. 68p. pap. 26.99 *(978-1-4389-7827-7(8))* AuthorHouse.

Bakos, Lisa M. Too Many Moose! Chambers, Mark, illus. 2016. (ENG.). 40p. (J). (-4). 16.99 *(978-1-4926-0935-3(8)*, 9781492609353, Sourcebooks Jabberwocky) Sourcebooks, Inc.

Bardhan-Quallen, Sudipta. Duck, Duck, Moose! Jones, Noah Z., illus. 2014. (ENG.). 32p. (J). (gr. -1-k). 16.99 *(978-1-4231-7110-2(1))* Hyperion Bks. for Children.

Beckhorn, Susan Williams. Moose Eggs: Or, Why Moose Has Flat Antlers. Stevens, Helen, illus. 2007. (ENG.). 32p. (J). (gr. -1-3). 15.95 *(978-0-89272-689-9(X))* Down East Bks.

—Moose Power! Muskeg Saves the Day. Huntington, Amy, illus. 2010. (ENG.). 40p. (J). (gr. -1-3). 16.95 *(978-0-89272-762-9(4))* Down East Bks.

Bingham, Kelly. Circle, Square, Moose. Zelinsky, Paul O., illus. 2014. (ENG.). 48p. (J). (gr. -1-3). 17.99 *(978-0-06-229003-8(7)*, Greenwillow Bks.) HarperCollins Pubs.

—Z Is for Moose. Zelinsky, Paul O., illus. 2012. 32p. (J). (gr. -1-2). (ENG.). 16.99 *(978-0-06-079984-7(6))*; lib. bdg. 17.89 *(978-0-06-079985-4(4))* HarperCollins Pubs. (Greenwillow Bks.).

Blizzard on Moose Mountain. 2007. (J). pap. *(978-0-9794542-0-2(4))* Battat, Inc.

Bourgeois, Paulette. Franklin's New Friend. Clark, Brenda, illus. (Franklin Ser.). (ENG.). 32p. (J). (gr. -1-3). *(978-1-55074-363-0(5))* Kids Can Pr., Ltd.

—Franklin's New Friend. 2004. (Illus.). (J). (gr. k-3). spiral bd. *(978-0-616-01590-2(9))*; spiral bd. *(978-0-616-01591-9(7))* Canadian National Institute for the Blind/Institut National Canadien pour les Aveugles.

Briggs, Kelly Paul. Lighthouse Lullaby. 2008. (ENG., Illus.). 32p. (J). (gr. -1-17). pap. 9.95 *(978-0-89272-549-6(4))* Down East Bks.

Brightwood, Laura, illus. Red Hat / Blue Hat. Brightwood, Laura, . 2006. (J). *(978-0-9779290-5-4(1))* 3-C Institute for Social Development.

Calmenson, Stephanie. There Are No Moose on This Island, 1 vol. Thermes, Jennifer, illus. 2013. (ENG.). 32p. (J). 17.95 *(978-1-934031-34-6(8)*, a2b39bfc-ad16-4e21-bc2e-5db5168164a8) Islandport Pr., Inc.

Carlson, Amanda. Sultenfuss Moose's Lost Slipper. 2006. 26p. 18.03 *(978-1-4116-7729-6(3))* Lulu Pr., Inc.

Carpenter, Chad. Morry Moose's Time-Traveling Outhouse Adventure. 2013. (ENG.). 48p. (J). pap. 12.95 *(978-1-62343-163-1(8))* Willow Creek Pr., Inc.

Casanova, Mary. Moose Tracks. l.t. ed. 2004. (LRS Large Print Cornerstone Ser.). 117p. (J). lib. bdg. 27.95 *(978-1-58118-117-3(5))* LRS.

—Moose Tracks. 2nd ed. 2010. (J). *(978-0-9793444-3-5(3))* Quercus Pr.

Chapman, Karean. The Adventures of Northern the Moose & a Dragon Named Zeus. Ciesinka, Izabela, illus. 2010. 38p. pap. 12.95 *(978-1-935268-44-4(9))* Halo Publishing International.

Charron, Ashley. Hello Green Mountains: It's a Soggy Spring. 2013. (ENG.). 26p. (J). 21.95 *(978-1-4787-0803-2(4))* Outskirts Pr., Inc.

The Chocolate Moose. 2007. (Illus.). 48p. (J). per. 13.00 *(978-0-9767189-5-6(2))* Better Day Publishing LLC.

Chronicle Books Staff & ImageBooks Staff. Little Moose: Finger Puppet Book. Put, Klaartje van der, illus. 2015. (ENG.). 12p. (J). (gr. -1 — 1). bds. 6.99 *(978-1-4521-4231-9(9))* Chronicle Bks. LLC.

Claflin, Willy. The Little Moose Who Couldn't Go to Sleep. Stimson, James, illus. 2014. (ENG.). 36p. audio compact disk 18.95 (978-1-939160-67-6(7)) August Hse. Pubs., Inc.

—Rapunzel & the Seven Dwarfs: A Maynard Moose Tale. Stimson, James, illus. 2011. (ENG.). 33p. (J). (gr. -1-3). 18.95 (978-0-87483-914-2(9)) August Hse. Pubs., Inc.

—The Uglified Ducky. Stimson, James, illus. 2011. (ENG.). 32p. (J). (gr. -1-3). pap. 9.95 (978-0-87483-953-1(X)) August Hse. Pubs., Inc.

Clarke, Jacqueline A. Moose's Loose Tooth. McNally, Bruce, illus. 2003. (J). (978-0-439-41183-7(1)) Scholastic, Inc.

Cook, Sherry & Johnson, Terri. Mary Motion, 26 vols. Kuhn, Jesse, illus. l.t. ed. 2006. (Quirkles — Exploring Phonics through Science Ser.: 13). 32p. (J). 7.99 (978-1-933815-12-1(4), Quirkles, The) Creative 3, LLC.

Cook, Terry. A Moose at the Bus Stop. Cook, Terry, illus. 2013. (Illus.). 24p. pap. 10.95 (978-1-61633-378-2(2)) Guardian Angel Publishing, Inc.

Custard, Stefanie. The Story of Baby Moose Joe. 2008. (Illus.). 32p. pap. 20.99 (978-1-4343-9138-4(8)) AuthorHouse.

Derrick, Patricia & Sibbett, Joyce. Montgomery the Moose Can Shake His Caboose. Martinez, J-P Loppo, illus. 2007. 32p. (J). (gr. -1). 18.95 incl. audio compact disk (978-1-933818-18-4(2)) Animalations.

deRubertis, Barbara. Maxwell Moose's Mountain Monster. Alley, R. W., illus. 2011. (Animal Antics A to Z Ser.). 32p. (J). pap. 45.32 (978-0-7613-7659-0(3)); (ENG.). lib. bdg. 22.60 (978-1-57565-334-1(6)); (ENG.). (gr. -1-3). pap. 7.95 (978-1-57565-325-9(7)) Kane Press, Inc.

deRubertis, Barbara & DeRubertis, Barbara. Maxwell Moose's Mountain Monster. Alley, R. W., illus. 2012. (Animal Antics A to Z Ser.). 32p. (J). (gr. 2 — 1). cd-rom 7.95 (978-1-57565-406-5(7)) Kane Press, Inc.

Dixon, Karen S. Alexander the Moose. Crouch, Frances, illus. 2004. 23p. pap. 24.95 (978-1-4137-3626-7(2)) PublishAmerica, Inc.

Dyan, Penelope. Ba-Ba-Ba-Bad — -The Story of One Mean Moose. Dyan, Penelope, illus. 2012. (Illus.). 34p. pap. 11.95 (978-1-61477-053-4(0)) Bellissima Publishing, LLC.

—Molly Moose Is on the Loose. Dyan, Penelope, illus. 2012. (Illus.). 34p. pap. 11.95 (978-1-61477-025-1(5)) Bellissima Publishing, LLC.

Engelhardt. Efficient Use of School Build. 2013. (Fesler-Lampert Minnesota Heritage Ser.). (ENG.). 128p. pap. 9.95 (978-0-8166-9019-0(7)) Univ. of Minnesota Pr.

Evans, Sarah. The Moose, the Flea, the Fly. 2007. 16p. pap. 24.95 (978-1-4241-8533-7(5)) America Star Bks.

Fraggalosch, Audrey. Let's Explore, Moose! Forest, Crista, illus. 2005. (ENG.). 32p. (J). (gr. -1-1). pap. 3.95 (978-1-59249-151-3(0), S2017) Soundprints.

Fraggolosch, Audrey. Northern Refuge: A Story of a Canadian Boreal Forest. Fraggalosch, Crista, illus. 2005. (Soundprints' Wild Habitats Ser.). (ENG.). 36p. (J). (gr. 1-4). 8.95 (978-1-59249-100-1(6), SC7012) Soundprints.

Gauthier, Pamela. The Adventures of Bernie the Moose: Bernie Meets Marla. 2009. 20p. pap. 10.49 (978-1-4490-3019-3(X)) AuthorHouse.

Greene, Stephanie. Moose Crossing, 0 vols. Mathieu, Joe, illus. 2010. (Moose & Hildy Ser.: 0). (ENG.). 64p. (J). (gr. 1-2). pap. 9.99 (978-0-7614-5699-5(6), 9780761456995, Amazon Children's Publishing) Amazon Publishing.

—Moose's Big Idea, 0 vols. Mathieu, Joe, illus. 2010. (Moose & Hildy Ser.: 0). (ENG.). 64p. (J). (gr. 1-4). pap. 6.99 (978-0-7614-5698-8(8), 9780761456988, Amazon Children's Publishing) Amazon Publishing.

—Pig Pickin', 0 vols. Mathieu, Joe, illus. 2013. (Moose & Hildy Ser.). (ENG.). 68p. (J). (gr. -1-3). pap. 9.99 (978-1-4778-1684-4(4), 9781477816844, Amazon Children's Publishing) Amazon Publishing.

—The Show-Off, 0 vols. Mathieu, Joe, illus. 2007. (Moose & Hildy Ser.: 0). (ENG.). 64p. (J). (gr. 1-4). lib. bdg. 14.99 (978-0-7614-5374-1(1), 9780761453741, Amazon Children's Publishing) Amazon Publishing.

Haseley, Dennis. The Invisible Moose. Kellogg, Steven, illus. 2008. (ENG.). 40p. (J). (gr. -1-3). pap. 6.99 (978-0-14-241066-0(7), Puffin Books) Penguin Young Readers Group.

Hatch, Thomas. Larry the Moose. 2009. 32p. pap. 15.99 (978-1-4389-8533-6(9)) AuthorHouse.

Hoff, Syd. Santa's Moose. Hoff, Syd, illus. 2017. (I Can Read Level 1 Ser.). (Illus.). 32p. (J). (gr. -1-3). 16.99 **(978-0-06-264308-7(8))**; pap. 3.99 **(978-0-06-264307-0(X))** HarperCollins Pubs.

Horowitz, Dave. Duck Duck Moose. Horowitz, Dave, illus. 2009. (ENG., Illus.). 32p. (J). (gr. k-3). 16.99 (978-0-399-24782-8(3), G.P. Putnam's Sons Books for Young Readers) Penguin Young Readers Group.

Hulet, Paul. Bruce the Moose Is on the Loose. 2009. (Illus.). 36p. (gr. -1-7). pap. 13.95 (978-1-60860-473-9(X), Strategic Bk. Publishing) Strategic Book Publishing & Rights Agency (SBPRA).

Jeffers, Oliver. This Moose Belongs to Me. Jeffers, Oliver, illus. 2012. (ENG., Illus.). 32p. (J). (gr. -1-2). 17.99 (978-0-399-16103-2(1), Philomel Bks.) Penguin Young Readers Group.

Kaiser, Lori. Megan the Moody Moose. Kaiser, Lori, illus. 2013. (Illus.). 26p. pap. (978-0-9883770-5-9(5)) Roxby Media Ltd.

Kaut, Joy. Matilda Moose Learns about Being Unique. 2013. 32p. pap. 13.95 (978-1-4497-9362-3(2), WestBow Pr.) Author Solutions, Inc.

Kawecki, Daniel. The Mad Moose. 2009. 32p. pap. 13.00 (978-1-60693-888-1(6), Eloquent Bks.) Strategic Book Publishing & Rights Agency (SBPRA).

Kellogg, Catherine Berry. The Moose Who Ate My Fort: Stories from Bella Sage. 2008. 36p. pap. 24.95 (978-1-60441-696-1(3)) America Star Bks.

Kerns, Kim A. Moose on the Loose: Moose Capades Book 1. 2011. 21p. (J). pap. 6.99 (978-0-615-40229-1(1)) KAK.

Larsen, Jill. There's a Moose on the Loose Coloring Book. 2004. (J). pap. 4.99 (978-0-9755200-0-0(8)) Kids, Critters & Country Publishing.

Lindwall, Erika. The Moose & the Goose. Lindwall, Erika, illus. 2013. (Illus.). 32p. pap. 11.95 (978-1-940728-01-8(0), Simple Faith Bks.) Sunrise Mountain Bks.

Macy-Mills, Phyllis. Murphy Moose & Garrett Goose. Russell, Kay, illus. 2003. (J). spiral bd. (978-1-932303-48-3(0), Llumina Pr.) Aeon Publishing Inc.

Majestic's Search. 2004. (J). (978-0-615-12544-2(1)) Jadenaila Publishing.

Martin, Ruth. The Little Moose. Boey, Stephanie, illus. 2008. (ENG.). 35p. (J). (978-1-55168-332-4(6)) Fenn, H. B. & Co., Ltd.

McArthur, Cathy E. The Story of Chris Moose, 1 vol. Stutz, Chris, illus. 2009. 24p. pap. 24.95 (978-1-4489-0928-5(7)) America Star Bks.

McClaine, Jamie. Have You Ever Seen a Moose Brushing His Teeth? Willy, April, illus. 2003. (ENG.). 24p. (J). (gr. -1). 18.95 (978-0-9709533-2-2(1)) J A F S, Inc.

Messy Moose: Take-Home Book. 2005. (Emergent Library: Vol. 2). (YA). (gr. -1-1). 12.60 (978-0-8215-7251-1(2)) Sadlier, William H. Inc.

Miller, Janie Evans. How Randy the Moose Turned His Frown Upside Down. 2013. 50p. pap. 23.95 (978-1-4908-0936-6(8), WestBow Pr.) Author Solutions, Inc.

Mooney, Silk Waters. Puka the Moose. 2006. (YA). 24.95 (978-0-9776608-1-0(8)) Silk Waters Mooney.

Morgan, Roxy. Melvin the Moose & Mr. Bluefish. 2007. (Illus.). 35p. (J). lib. bdg. 18.95 (978-0-9768052-4-3(3)) New Century Publishing, LLC.

Mott, Chuck. The Hannukah Moose. 2009. 48p. pap. 19.99 (978-1-4490-4974-4(5)) AuthorHouse.

Munsch, Robert. Moose! Martchenko, Michael, illus. 2015. 28p. (J). pap. **(978-0-545-82631-0(4))** Scholastic, Inc.

Nelson-Schmidt, Michelle. Bob Is a Unicorn. Nelson-Schmidt, Michelle, illus. 2014. (ENG., Illus.). 28p. (J). 14.99 (978-1-61067-155-2(4)) Kane Miller.

Northcutt, Allen. The Legend of Chris Moose: The Most Beautiful Moose in the World. 2012. (ENG.). 48p. (J). 17.95 (978-1-938462-01-6(7)) Old Stone Pr.

Numeroff, Laura Joffe. If You Give a Moose a Matzoh. Date not set. (J). pap. (978-0-06-443558-1(X)) HarperCollins Pubs.

—If You Give a Moose a Muffin. Bond, Felicia, illus. Date not set. (J). bds. 6.99 (978-0-694-01426-2(5)) HarperCollins Pubs.

—If You Give a Moose a Muffin: Book & Doll. Bond, Felicia, illus. Date not set. (J). 19.99 (978-0-694-01421-7(4)) HarperCollins Pubs.

—Moose Stroller Songs. Bond, Felicia, illus. Date not set. (J). 9.99 (978-0-694-01424-8(9)) HarperCollins Pubs.

Oldland, Nicholas. Making the Moose Out of Life. Oldland, Nicholas, illus. (Life in the Wild Ser.). (ENG., Illus.). 32p. (J). (gr. -1-2). 2015. pap. 7.95 (978-1-55453-627-6(8)) 2010. 16.95 (978-1-55453-580-4(8)) Kids Can Pr., Ltd. CAN. Dist: Hachette Bk. Group.

Palatini, Margie. Moosestache. 32p. pap. (978-0-7868-1497-8(7)) Hyperion Bks. for Children.

Plourde, Paulette. Smitty Moose, Petey & Me - Episode One, the Witch. Golen, Jessica, illus. l.t. ed. 2005. 32p. (J). per. 9.95 (978-1-59879-038-2(2)) Lifevest Publishing, Inc.

Raschka, Chris. Moosey Moose. 2014. (Thingy Things Ser.). (ENG., Illus.). 24p. (J). (gr. -1-k). 6.95 (978-1-4197-1202-9(0), Abrams Appleseed) Abrams, Inc.

Rayner, Catherine. Ernest, the Moose Who Doesn't Fit. Rayner, Catherine, illus. 2010. (ENG., Illus.). 32p. (J). (gr. -1-1). 18.99 (978-0-374-32217-5(1), 9780374322175, Farrar, Straus & Giroux (BYR)) Farrar, Straus & Giroux.

Rea, Monique. Toulouse the Moose. 2003. (J). 3.50 (978-1-891030-30-7(2)) Paragon Agency, The.

—Toulouse the Moose & the Mystery Guests. 2012. 34p. pap. 13.99 (978-0-9788926-4-7(X)) Trails of Discovery.

Rea, Monique F. The Original Story of Toulouse the Moose & His Friends: Book & CD. 2007. (J). (978-0-9788926-2-3(3)) Trails of Discovery.

—Toulouse the Moose Coloring Book. 2007. (J). (978-0-9788926-3-0(1)) Trails of Discovery.

Restrepo, Bettina. Moose & Magpie, 1 vol. Rogers, Sherry, illus. 2009. (ENG.). 32p. (J). (gr. -1-3). pap. 8.95 (978-1-60718-042-5(1)) Arbordale Publishing.

Restrepo, Bettina & Rogers, Sherry. Moose & Magpie, 1 vol. 2009. (ENG., Illus.). 32p. (J). (gr. -1-3). 16.95 (978-1-934359-97-6(1)) Arbordale Publishing.

Rivard, Erin. Agattu: The Alaskan Caribou. 2013. (J). pap. 9.95 (978-1-59433-344-6(0)) Publication Consultants.

Robinson, Fiona. The Useful Moose: A Truthful, Moose-Full Tale. 2004. (ENG., Illus.). 32p. (J). (gr. -1-3). 15.95 (978-0-8109-4925-6(3)) Abrams, Inc.

Root, Phyllis. Looking for a Moose. Cecil, Randy, illus. 2008. (ENG.). 40p. (J). (gr. -1-2). pap. 6.99 (978-0-7636-3885-6(4)) Candlewick Pr.

Rosoff, Meg. Moose Baby. Ercolini, David, illus. 2017. (J). **(978-0-399-16664-8(5)**, Putnam Juvenile) Penguin Publishing Group.

Rouncville, Bibi. Sea Bugs & Moose Eggs. 2009. 52p. pap. 9.50 (978-1-4357-4004-4(1)) Lulu Pr., Inc.

Savage, Doug. Laser Moose & Rabbit Boy. 2016. (ENG.). 144p. (J). pap. 9.99 (978-1-4494-7094-4(7)) Andrews McMeel Publishing.

Scaling, Sam T. Marv the Moose Is on the Loose. Stanley, Susan, illus. 2012. 32p. (J). (978-0-9798806-4-3(5)) STS Publishing.

Schwartz, Corey Rosen & Gomez, Rebecca J. What about Moose? Yamaguchi, Keika, illus. 2015. (ENG.). 40p. (J). (gr. -1-3). 17.99 (978-1-4814-0496-9(2), Atheneum Bks. for Young Readers) Simon & Schuster Children's Publishing.

Scott, Joanna I. Stanley the Moose: Book One of the Woodsie Tails Series. 2009. (Illus.). 40p. (J). 19.95 net. (978-0-9795678-1-0(5)) Cherakota Publishing.

Shankman, Ed. I Met a Moose in Maine One Day. O'Neill, Dave, illus. 2008. (Shankman & O'Neill Ser.). (ENG.). 32p. (J). (gr. -1-3). 14.95 (978-1-933212-77-7(2), Commonwealth Editions) Applewood Bks.

Skrentny, Jan. The Christmas Moose. 2008. 36p. pap. 18.95 (978-1-4389-2807-4(6)) AuthorHouse.

Spinelle, Nancy Louise. El Diente Flojo Del Alce (6 Pack) Gedeon, Gloria, illus. 2011.Tr. of Moose's Loose Tooth. (SPA.). 16p. (gr. k-2). pap. (978-1-61181-166-7(X), Kaeden Bks.) Kaeden Corp.

—Moose's Loose Tooth. Gedeon, Gloria, illus. l.t. ed. 2005. (ENG.). 16p. (gr. k-2). pap. 7.95 (978-1-57874-032-1(0), Kaeden Bks.) Kaeden Corp.

Stihler, Cherie B. The Cabin That Moose Built. Trammell, Jeremiah, illus. 2006. (Paws IV Ser.). (ENG.). 32p. (J). (gr. -1-2). pap. 10.99 (978-1-57061-446-0(6), Little Bigfoot) Sasquatch Bks.

Swinney, Kay. Marty Moose & the Mystical Reunion, 1 vol. 2009. 73p. pap. 19.95 (978-1-61546-867-6(6)) America Star Bks.

Turner, Tracie & Dyson, Kyree. The Adventures of Kyree the Chocolate Moose. 2013. 20p. pap. 24.95 (978-1-62709-178-7(5)) America Star Bks.

VanRiper, Gary & VanRiper, Justin. Mystery of the Missing Moose. 2007. (Adirondack Kids Ser.: Vol. 7). 77p. (J). (gr. 2-7). pap. 9.95 (978-0-9707044-7-4(X), ADK7) Adirondack Kids Pr.

Wargin, Kathy-jo. Moose on the Loose. Bendall-Brunello, John, illus. 2009. (ENG.). 32p. (J). (gr. k-6). 15.95 (978-1-58536-427-5(4)) Sleeping Bear Pr.

William H. Sadlier Staff. Messy Moose. 2005. (Emergent Library: Vol. 2). (gr. -1-1). 24.00 net. (978-0-8215-8921-2(0)) Sadlier, William H. Inc.

Wilson, Karma. Moose Tracks! Davis, Jack E., illus. 2006. (ENG.). 32p. (J). (gr. -1-2). 17.99 (978-0-689-83437-0(3), McElderry, Margaret K. Bks.) McElderry, Margaret K. Bks.

Womack, Rowena. Yellowstone Moose. 2013. 28p. pap. 13.95 (978-1-61160-597-6(0)) Whiskey Creek Restorations.

Yellowstone Moose. 2004. (Illus.). (J). spiral bd. 9.95 (978-0-9754913-1-7(8), Gap Tooth Publishing) Charles River Pr.

Yoon, Salina. Found. Yoon, Salina, illus. 2014. (ENG., Illus.). 40p. (J). (gr. -1-1). 14.99 (978-0-8027-3559-1(2), 9780802735591, Bloomsbury USA Childrens) Bloomsbury Publishing USA.

MORAL EDUCATION

ABDO Publishing Company Staff & Salzmann, Mary Elizabeth. Building Character, Set. 2003. (Building Character Ser.: 3). (ENG.). (J). (gr. k-3). lib. bdg. 72.63 (978-1-57765-824-5(8), SandCastle) ABDO Publishing Co.

Aguilera, Dana, et al. Character in Motion! Real Life Stories Series 5th Grade Student Workbook. 2006. 68p. (J). per. 5.95 (978-0-9765722-8-2(1)) Positively for Kids, Inc.

Bakhtiar, Laleh. Islamic Ethics: An Interfaith Perspective: Grade 2: the Moral Education Series. 2005. 32p. (J). pap., pupil's gde. ed. 4.95 net. (978-1-56744-722-4(8)) Kazi Pubns., Inc.

—Islamic Ethics: An Interfaith Perspective: Grade 3: the Moral Education Textbook Series. 2005. 32p. (J). 4.95 net. (978-1-56744-723-1(6)) Kazi Pubns., Inc.

—Islamic Ethics: An Interfaith Perspective: the Moral Education Textbook Series. 2005. (Islamic Books for Children). 32p. (J). pupil's gde. ed. 4.95 net. (978-1-56744-721-7(X)) Kazi Pubns., Inc.

Bergstrom, Amy, et al. The Seventh Generation: Native Students Speak about Finding the Good Path. 2003. 300p. (YA). (gr. 7-12). pap. 25.00 (978-1-880785-25-6(0)) ERIC Clearinghouse on Rural Education & Small Schls.

Boritzer, Etan. What Is Right? Sale, Graham, illus. l.t. ed. 2005. (What Is? Ser.). 40p. (J). (gr. k-5). pap. 6.95 (978-0-9762743-0-8(2)) Lane, Veronica Bks.

Brooks, Diane L. Readings & Activities for Character Education. 220p. (YA). (gr. 4-18). ring bd. 69.95 (978-0-8126-7550-4(9)) Cricket Bks.

Carson-Dellosa Publishing Staff, compiled by. Daily Character Education Activities, Grades 2 - 3: 180 Lessons for Each Day of the School Year. 2004. (ENG.). 64p. (gr. 2-3). pap. 9.99 (978-0-88724-206-9(5), CD-0066) Carson-Dellosa Publishing, LLC.

—Daily Character Education Activities, Grades 4 - 5: 180 Lessons for Each Day of the School Year. 2004. (ENG.). 64p. (gr. 4-5). pap. 9.99 (978-0-88724-207-6(3), CD-0067) Carson-Dellosa Publishing, LLC.

Character Ed Says Courtesy Is Contagious. 2006. (J). 4.95 (978-1-55548-055-4(1), 676) Human Relations Media.

Character Ed Says Honesty Counts. 2006. (J). 4.95 (978-1-55548-057-8(8), 678) Human Relations Media.

Character Ed Says Keep Your Cool. 2006. (J). 4.95 (978-1-55548-056-1(X), 677) Human Relations Media.

Clifford, Kathleen & Uy, Meqan Black. Great Lives, Vital Lessons: A Character Education Curriculum Resource for Grades 5-8. Bohlin, Karen E. & Lerner, Bernice, eds. 2005. (gr. 5-8). pap. 19.95 (978-1-892056-41-2(0)) Character Development Group, Inc,.

Deroche, Ed, et al. Character: A Guide for Middle Grade Students. 2004. (ENG.). 176p. pap., wbk. ed. 9.95 (978-1-55864-152-5(1), JIST Life) JIST Publishing.

Donovan, Sandy. Does My Voice Count? A Book about Citizenship. 2014. (Show Your Character Ser.). (ENG., Illus.). 32p. (gr. 1-3). lib. bdg. 26.60 (978-1-4677-1366-5(X), Lerner Pubns.) Lerner Publishing Group.

Dunagan, Cindy. Journaling Toward Moral Excellence Volume Four for Young Adults: A Character Building Workbook of 100 Thought-Provoking Questions to Help the Young Discover the Value of Moral Strength. 2004. (Journaling Toward Moral Excellence Ser.: Vol. 4). 107p. (YA). (gr. 11-18). 11.95 (978-0-9759871-3-1(5)) Straight Paths Pr.

—Journaling Toward Moral Excellence Volume One for Young Writers. 2004. (Journaling Toward Moral Excellence Ser.: Vol. 1). 107p. (J). (gr. 1-4). 11.95 (978-0-9759871-0-0(0)) Straight Paths Pr.

—Journaling Toward Moral Excellence Volume Three for Teenagers: A Character Building Workbook of 100 Thought-Provoking Questions to Help the Young Discover the Value of Moral Strength. 2004. (Journaling Toward Moral Excellence Ser.: Vol. 3). 107p. (YA). (gr. 8-10). 11.95 (978-0-9759871-2-4(7)) Straight Paths Pr.

—Journaling Toward Moral Excellence Volume Two for Pre-Teens Vol. 2: A Character Building Workbook of 100 Thought-Provoking Questions to Help the Young Discover the Value of Moral Strength. 2004. (Journaling Toward Moral Excellence Ser.: Vol. 2). 107p. (J). (gr. 5-7). 11.95 (978-0-9759871-1-7(9)) Straight Paths Pr.

Everyday Character Education, 12 vols., Set. 2005. (Everyday Character Education Ser.). (ENG., Illus.). 24p. (gr. 1-2). 49.30 (978-0-7368-4410-9(4), First Facts) Capstone Press of Coughlan Cos.

Handley, Rod, et al. Team Studies on Character: Inspiration for Life & Sports. 2004. (YA). pap. 6.99 (978-1-929478-65-1(8)) Cross Training Publishing.

It's Good 2b Good Staff & Zerner, Sandra. It's Good 2B Good: Why It's Not Bad to Be Good. 2011. (ENG., Illus.). 106p. (J). pap. 12.95 (978-0-615-51275-4(5)) It's Good 2B Good LLC.

Keuss, Jeff & Sloth, Lia. Character in Motion! Athlete Series. 2006. (Illus.). 136p. (YA). per. 5.95 (978-0-9765722-0-6(6)) Positively for Kids, Inc.

Lang, Carol, et al. Character in Motion! Real Life Stories Series 3rd Grade Student Workbook. 2006. 63p. (J). per. 5.95 (978-0-9765722-9-9(X)) Positively for Kids, Inc.

Lewis, Barbara A. What Do You Stand For? For Teens: A Guide to Building Character. Espeland, Pamela, ed. 2005. (ENG., Illus.). 288p. (YA). (gr. 5-9). pap. 19.99 (978-1-57542-029-5(5)) Free Spirit Publishing, Inc.

—What Do You Stand For? - For Kids: A Guide to Building Character. Lisovskis, Marjorie, ed. 2005. (ENG., Illus.). 176p. (J). (gr. 3-7). pap. 14.99 (978-1-57542-174-2(7)) Free Spirit Publishing, Inc.

Lewis, Barbara A. & Free Spirit Publishing Staff. What Do You Stand For? Character Building. 2006. (ENG., Illus.). 60p. (gr. 1-6). 13.99 (978-1-57542-217-6(4)) Free Spirit Publishing, Inc.

MacAdam, Lea. You & the Rules in Your Family. 2005. (Family Matters Ser.). (Illus.). 48p. (YA). (gr. 5-8). lib. bdg. 29.25 (978-0-8239-3350-1(4)) Rosen Publishing Group, Inc., The.

Merino, Noël. Should Character Be Taught in School? 2010. (At Issue Ser.). (ENG.). 128p. (gr. 10-12). 39.40 (978-0-7377-4890-1(7)); pap. 27.80 (978-0-7377-4891-8(5), Greenhaven Pr., Inc.) Cengage Gale.

Miller, Marie-Therese & Banas, Sharon L. Managing Responsibilities. 2009. (Character Education Ser.). (Illus.). 136p. (gr. 6-12). 35.00 (978-1-60413-124-6(1), Chelsea Hse.) Facts On File, Inc.

Munroe, Terri, et al. Rachel's Challenge: A Columbine Legacy Student Workbook. 2006. (YA). per. 5.95 (978-0-9765722-4-4(9)) Positively for Kids, Inc.

Murphy, John Paul. Watt's Special Purpose. 2012. 20p. pap. 17.99 (978-1-4685-5344-4(5)) AuthorHouse.

Murray, Amy. The Character & Career Connection. 2005. (Illus.). 76p. (J). per. 19.95 (978-1-931636-45-2(1)) National Ctr. For Youth Issues.

Perez, Claire M. & Fox, Mary. Peacemakers: The New Generation Practical Group Activities for Grades 6-8. 2003. (Illus.). 76p. (YA). (gr. 6-8). pap. 20.00 (978-1-893757-32-5(3), E T Nedder) Paulist Pr.

Small, Mary. Caring: A Book about Caring, 1 vol. Previn, Stacey, illus. 2005. (Way to Be! Ser.). (ENG.). 24p. (gr. k-2). lib. bdg. 26.65 (978-1-4048-1049-5(8)) Picture Window Bks.

Stein, Lee. Generation Communication: For Teens Who Want to Get Ahead in the World. 2011. 60p. (YA). per. 9.99 (978-0-9786663-1-6(3)) Paradoxical Pr., The.

Stephens, Wayne. Building Character Through Music - Elementary Song Book. 2004. spiral bd. 39.95 (978-1-892056-32-0(1)) Character Development Group, Inc,.

—Building Character Through Music - High School Song Book. 2004. (YA). spiral bd. 39.95 (978-1-892056-36-8(4)) Character Development Group, Inc,.

Tracy, Jean. Character Building on BackTalk Street. 2004. 110p. (J). spiral bd. 25.00 (978-0-9749244-0-3(7)) KidsDiscuss.com.

Turner, Dale. Free to Be. Summer, Angel, ed. Smart, Ross, illus. 2003. 112p. (J). (gr. k-5). 16.95 (978-1-892696-28-1(2)) High Tide Pr.

Wiley, Lori. Character Education Activities. 2004. (Illus.). 176p. (J). per. 9.95 (978-1-55864-154-9(8), K1548, KIDSRIGHTS) JIST Publishing.

MORAL EDUCATION—FICTION

Adeleke, Abraham Ajibade. Beauty Contest in the Animal Kingdom. 2011. 40p. pap. 16.46 (978-1-4269-5773-4(4)) Trafford Publishing.

Brezenoff, Steve. Cheaters, 1 vol. Pinelli, Amerigo, illus. 2013. (Ravens Pass Ser.). (ENG.). 96p. (gr. 2-3). lib. bdg. 25.32 (978-1-4342-4616-5(7)) Stone Arch Bks.

Cr. Adventures of Jenni & Jake. 2011. 28p. pap. 12.99 (978-1-4568-8677-6(0)) Xlibris Corp.

Farnsworth-Simpson, Patricia Ann. Stories to Thrill & Delight. 2008. 142p. pap. 12.95 (978-1-4357-3275-9(8)) Lulu Pr., Inc.

Ferrin, Wendy Wakefield. Germs on Their Fingers! Tono, Lucia, tr. Broyles, Beverly Ashley, illus. 2003.Tr. of Germenes en Tus Manos! (SPA & ENG.). 64p. (J). (gr. 1-7). 17.95 (978-0-9703632-1-3(4)); pap. 12.95 (978-0-9703632-0-6(6)) Wakefield Connection, The.

Hamilton, Elizabeth L. Christopher Cat's Character Club. 2003. (Character Critters Ser.: No. 1). (Illus.). 32p. (J). (gr. -1-3). per. 5.95 (978-0-9713749-2-8(9), Character-in-Action) Quiet Impact, Inc.

—Cubby Bear's Big Responsibility. 2004. (Character Critters Ser.: No. 8). (Illus.). 32p. (J). per. 5.95 (978-0-9754629-4-2(6), Character-in-Action) Quiet Impact, Inc.

—Date with Responsibility. 2004. (Character-in-Action Ser.: No. 2). (Illus.). 384p. (YA). per. 19.95 (978-0-9713749-0-4(2), Character-in-Action) Quiet Impact, Inc.

—Georgey Giraffe's Giant Respect: Character Critter Series #6. 2004. (Character Critters Ser.: No. 6). (Illus.). 32p. (J). per. 5.95 (978-0-9754629-1-1(1), Character-in-Action) Quiet Impact, Inc.

—Jeremy Rabbit's Honesty Pie. 2003. (Character Critters Ser.: No. 2). (Illus.). 32p. (J). (gr. -1-3). per. 5.95 (978-0-9713749-5-9(3), Character-in-Action) Quiet Impact, Inc.

—Little Zoh's Submissive Trunk. 2003. (Character Critters Ser.: No. 3). (Illus.). 32p. (J). (gr. -1-3). per. 5.95 (978-0-9713749-9-7(6), Character-in-Action) Quiet Impact, Inc.

—Lost on Superstition Mountain. 2004. (Character Mystery Ser.: No. 3). (Illus.). 144p. (J). per. 9.95 (978-0-9754629-5-9(4), Character-in-Action) Quiet Impact, Inc.

—Mystery at Lake Cachuma. 2003. (Character Mystery Ser.: No. 1). (Illus.). 114p. (J). (gr. 3-6). per. 9.95 (978-0-9713749-4-2(5), Character-in-Action) Quiet Impact, Inc.

—Pandora Puppy's Caring Circle. 2004. (Character Critters Ser.: No. 5). (Illus.). 32p. (J). per. 5.95 (978-0-9754629-0-4(3), Character-in-Action) Quiet Impact, Inc.

—Pansy Pig's Patience Pit. 2004. (Character Critters Ser.: No. 7). (Illus.). 32p. (J). per. 5.95 *(978-0-9754629-3-5(8)*, Character-in-Action) Quiet Impact, Inc.
—Stinky Skunk's Self-Control. 2004. (Character Critters Ser.: No. 4). (Illus.). 32p. (J). (gr. -1-3). per. 5.95 *(978-0-9713749-6-6(1)*, Character-in-Action) Quiet Impact, Inc.
—Surprise at Pearl Harbor. 2004. (Character Mystery Ser.: No. 2). (Illus.). 144p. (J). per. 9.95 *(978-0-9754629-2-8(X)*, Character-in-Action) Quiet Impact, Inc.
Harvey, Sharon M. Virginia's Travel Basket. 2008. 76p. pap. 10.95 *(978-1-4327-3424-4(5))* Outskirts Pr., Inc.
Henry, Heather French. What Freedom Means to Me: A Flag Day Story. Henry, Heather French, illus. 2004. (Claire's Holiday Adventures Ser.). (Illus.). 32p. (J). (gr. k-4). (ENG.). 15.95 *(978-0-9706341-2-2(9)*, 1231611); pap. 8.95 *(978-0-9706341-9-1(6))* Cubbie Blue Publishing.
Knisley, Lucy. Heart: Seed Snow Circuit. 2007. 20p. pap. 10.00 *(978-0-9789427-7-9(9)*, Epigraph Bks.) Monkfish Bk. Publishing Co.
Mbonu, Ngozi Elizabeth. Tatiana. Taylor, Kristen Michelle, illus. 2013. (ENG.). (J). 14.95 *(978-1-62086-307-7(3))* Mascot Bks., Inc.
Miller, Jay. Opal, Herby, & Squeaky. 2008. 44p. pap. 18.99 *(978-1-4389-1808-2(9))* AuthorHouse.
Minnie & Minnie. The Science Playground: Fun with Science Concepts & Nature. 2009. 48p. pap. 24.99 *(978-1-4389-3466-2(1))* AuthorHouse.
Montgomery, Arch. Hank. 2003. 171p. (YA). 19.95 *(978-1-890862-22-0(3))* Bancroft Pr.
Olsen EdS, Marci. Lessons to Live by: Character Building Books for School-Age Children. 2008. 52p. pap. 24.95 *(978-1-60474-501-6(0))* America Star Bks.

MORAL PHILOSOPHY
see Ethics

MORALITY
see Ethics

MORALS
see Behavior; Ethics

MORE, THOMAS, SIR, SAINT, 1478-1535
Crompton, Samuel Willard. Thomas More: And His Struggles of Conscience. 2005. (Makers of the Middle Ages & Renaissance Ser.). (Illus.). 152p. (J). (gr. 5-8). lib. bdg. 32.95 *(978-0-7910-8636-0(4)*, Chelsea Hse.) Facts On File, Inc.
Hobbes, Emma. Thomas More & Utopia. 2016. (J). lib. bdg. *(978-1-68048-551-6(2))* Rosen Publishing Group, Inc., The.
Wallace, Susan Helen & Jablonski, Patricia E. Saint Thomas More: Courage, Conscience, & the King. Lachuk, Dani, illus. 2014. (ENG.). 144p. (J). pap. 8.95 *(978-0-8198-9021-4(9))* Pauline Bks. & Media.

MORGAN, DANIEL, 1736-1802
Gallagher, Jim. Daniel Morgan: Fighting Frontiersman. 2006. (J). pap. *(978-1-59556-020-9(3))*; (Illus.). 88p. (gr. 5-11). lib. bdg. 23.95 *(978-1-59556-015-5(7))* OTTN Publishing.
Solesbee, Mary Ann. Sal & Amanda Take Morgan's Victory March to the Battle of Cowpens. Waters, Tony, illus. 2014. Orig. Title: Sal & Amanda Take Morgan's Victory March to the Battle of Cowpens. (ENG.). 128p. pap. 12.99 *(978-1-62619-279-9(0)*, History Pr., The) Arcadia Publishing.

MORGAN, HENRY, SIR, 1635-1688
Hamilton, Sue L. Henry Morgan. 1 vol. 2007. (Pirates! Ser.). (ENG., Illus.). 32p. (gr. 4-8). 27.07 *(978-1-59928-760-7(9)*, Abdo & Daughters) ABDO Publishing Co.
Sullivan, Laura L. Sir Henry Morgan. 2015. (J). lib. bdg. *(978-1-62713-308-1(9))* Cavendish Square Publishing.
Weintraub, Aileen. Henry Morgan: 17th-Century Buccaneer. 2009. (Library of Pirates Ser.). 24p. (gr. 3-3). 42.50 *(978-1-60853-812-6(5)*, PowerKids Pr.) Rosen Publishing Group, Inc., The.

MORMONS AND MORMONISM
Andersen, Susan. Nephi Breaks His Bow. 2009. 20p. pap. 5.95 *(978-1-60641-115-5(2))* Deseret Bk. Co.
Bagley, Val. Gospel Truths from the Book of Mormon. 2004. (Seek & Ye Shall Find Flap Book Ser.). (Illus.). (J). bds. 13.95 *(978-1-59156-279-5(1))* Covenant Communications, Inc.
Bagley, Val Chadwick, illus. I Will Follow God's Plan for Me. 2004. (J). *(978-1-59156-579-6(0))* Covenant Communications.
Bagley, Val Chadwick & Mullins, Amy. My Favorite Stories from the Book of Mormon. 2007. (Carry-Along Lift-The-Flap Book Ser.). (Illus.). (J). *(978-1-59811-385-3(2))* Covenant Communications.
Barnes, Kathleen. I Love to See the Temple Reprint. 2009. 32p. pap. 8.95 *(978-1-60641-112-4(8))* Deseret Bk. Co.
—Sacrament Time. 2009. 32p. pap. 9.95 *(978-1-60641-113-1(6))* Deseret Bk. Co.
Bernice, Janet. Tiny Talks: I Will Follow God's Plan for Me, Vol. 5. 2004. (J). pap. 7.95 *(978-1-55517-815-4(4))* Cedar Fort, Inc./CFI Distribution.
Bowman, David. The Great Plan of Happiness. 2010. (J). 15.99 *(978-1-59955-451-8(8))* Cedar Fort, Inc./CFI Distribution.
—The Great Plan of Happiness. 2010. (J). *(978-1-60641-637-2(5))* Deseret Bk. Co.
—Who's Your Hero? Boxed Set of Five Books. 2009. pap. 45.95 *(978-1-60641-152-0(7))* Deseret Bk. Co.
—Who's Your Hero? Vol. 1: Book of Mormon Stories Applied to Children, Vol. 1. 2006. (Illus.). 74p. (J). pap. 15.95 *(978-1-59038-573-9(X))* Deseret Bk. Co.
—Who's Your Hero? Vol. 2: Book of Mormon Stories Applied to Children. Bowman, David, illus. 2006. (Illus.). 80p. (J). pap. 14.95 *(978-1-59038-691-0(4))* Deseret Bk. Co.
—Who's Your Hero? Vol. 4: Book of Mormon Stories Applied to Children. 2008. 80p. pap. 14.95 *(978-1-59038-928-7(X))* Deseret Bk. Co.
Bowman, David, illus. Beyond Bethlehem: A Book of Mormon Christmas. 2008. 32p. (J). pap. 11.95 *(978-1-59038-991-1(3))* Deseret Bk. Co.
Brown, Toni Sorenson. Heroes of the Book of Mormon. 2004. bds. 10.95 *(978-1-59156-056-2(X))* Covenant Communications, Inc.
Buck, Deanna. My First Articles of Faith BK. 2008. 32p. pap. 6.95 *(978-1-59038-931-7(X))* Deseret Bk. Co.
—My First Church HIST Stories. 2008. 32p. pap. 8.95 *(978-1-60641-078-3(4))* Deseret Bk. Co.
Buck, Deanna Draper. My First Book of Temples. Nelson, Casey, illus. 2012. 28p. (J). bds. 15.99 *(978-1-60907-158-5(1))* Deseret Bk. Co.
Bytheway, John. Are Your Standards Fences or Guardrails? 2003. (Illus.). xiv, 97p. (J). pap. *(978-1-57008-990-9(6))* Deseret Bk. Co.
Carnesecca, Michele. How Does the Holy Ghost Make Me Feel? Xanthos, Carol, illus. 2010. 44p. *(978-1-60641-245-9(0))* Deseret Bk. Co.
Christensen, Laurel. LYFSGUD: If God Sent You a Text Message. 2009. (J). *(978-1-60641-108-7(X))* Deseret Bk. Co.
Coltrane, R. Book of Mormon Adventures. 2017. (ENG.). (J). (gr. -1-2). 14.99 ***(978-1-4621-2089-5(X))*** Cedar Fort, Inc./CFI Distribution.
Craner, Ben, tr. & illus. I Can Be a Missionary, Too. Craner, Ben, illus. 2003. (J). *(978-1-57008-965-7(5))* Deseret Bk. Co.
Daybell, Chad. The Aaronic Priesthood: Seven Principles That Will Make This Power a Part of Your Daily Life. Murray, Rhett E., illus. 2003. 100p. (YA). pap. 8.95 *(978-1-55517-717-1(4)*, 77174) Cedar Fort, Inc./CFI Distribution.
—Book of Mormon Numbers. Bonham, Bob, illus. 2004. (J). bds. 8.95 *(978-1-55517-755-3(7)*, 77557) Cedar Fort, Inc./CFI Distribution.
Dean, Arlan. The Mormon Pioneer Trail: From Nauvoo, Illinois to the Great Salt Lake, Utah. 2009. (Famous American Trails Ser.). 24p. (gr. 3-3). 42.50 *(978-1-61512-488-6(8)*, PowerKids Pr.) Rosen Publishing Group, Inc., The.
Dobson, Cynthia Lund. I'm Trying to Be Like Jesus. Dewey, Simon, illus. 2010. (J). 19.99 *(978-1-60641-846-8(7))* Deseret Bk. Co.
Doxey, Heidi. Tiny Talks, Volume 15. 2014. pap. 8.99 *(978-1-4621-1511-2(X)*, Horizon Pubs.) Cedar Fort, Inc./CFI Distribution.
—1, 2, 3 with Nephi & Me! Konopasek, Emily, illus. 2015. 9.99 *(978-1-4621-1636-2(1)*, Horizon Pubs.) Cedar Fort, Inc./CFI Distribution.
Durrant, George D. Seven Years Old & Preparing for Baptism. 2007. (Illus.). 68p. (J). pap. 7.95 *(978-1-932898-74-3(3))* Spring Creek Bk. Co.
Eden, Kristena. Book of Mormon 1-2-3s. Silvestri, Linda, illus. 2016. (ENG.). (J). 14.99 *(978-1-4621-1651-5(5))* Cedar Fort, Inc./CFI Distribution.
Eden, Kristena. Prophet Joseph's 1-2-3s. Silvestri, Linda, illus. 2016. (ENG.). (gr. -1-1). 14.99 *(978-1-4621-1949-3(2))* Cedar Fort, Inc./CFI Distribution.
Encyclopaedia Britannica, Inc. Staff, compiled by. Brigham Young. 2008. 49.95 *(978-1-59339-525-4(6))* Encyclopaedia Britannica, Inc.
Gibby, Shauna. Heroic Stories from the Book of Mormon: A Flashlight Discovery Book. Nelson, Casey, illus. 2017. (J). 16.99 *(978-1-62972-319-8(3))* Deseret Bk. Co.
Gowans, Floyd W. Covenant Verses: The Book of Mormon. 2004. 276p. (YA). per. 19.95 *(978-1-58982-160-6(2)*, Millennial Mind Publishing) American Bk. Publishing Group.
Gudmundson, C. J. When I Take the Sacrament, I Remember Jesus. Tenney, Shawna J. C., illus. 2012. (J). *(978-1-62108-020-6(X))* Covenant Communications, Inc.
Hall, Annalisa. The Holy Ghost Is Like a Blanket. Egbert, Corey, illus. 2014. 12.99 *(978-1-4621-1419-1(9)*, Horizon Pubs.) Cedar Fort, Inc./CFI Distribution.
—I Want to Be Baptized. Egbert, Corey, illus. 2015. (J). 10.99 *(978-1-4621-1670-6(1)*, Horizon Pubs.) Cedar Fort, Inc./CFI Distribution.
Johnson, Alice W. & Warner, Allison H. Believe & You're There When Lehi Left Jerusalem. Harston, Jerry, illus. 2010. (J). *(978-1-60641-246-6(9))* Deseret Bk. Co.
Krishna, McArthur & Spalding, Bethany Brady. Girls Who Choose God: Stories of Strong Women from the Book of Mormon. Peterson, Kathleen, illus. 2015. (J). 18.99 *(978-1-62972-101-9(8))* Deseret Bk. Co.
Madsen, Susan Arrington. I Walked to Zion: True Stories of Young Pioneers on the Mormon Trail. 2008. 192p. pap. 9.95 *(978-1-59038-930-0(1))* Deseret Bk. Co.
Marsh, Dilleen, tr. & illus. What Happens When People Die? Marsh, Dilleen, illus. 2003. (J). 12.95 *(978-1-57008-954-1(X))* Deseret Bk. Co.
McKellar, Tyler. Book of Mormon Family Reader. Burr, Dan, illus. 2017. 24.99 ***(978-1-62972-334-1(7))*** Deseret Bk. Co.
Millett, Melanie. Teeny Tiny Talks: Junior Primary: I Will Follow God's Plan for Me, Vol. 1. Millett, Melanie, illus. 2004. (Illus.). (J). per. 12.95 *(978-1-55517-778-2(6)*, Cedar Fort, Inc.) Cedar Fort, Inc./CFI Distribution.
Morton, William A. From Plowboy to Mormon Prophet Being a Short History of Joseph Smith for Children. Ramsey, L. A., illus. 2004. reprint ed. pap. 30.95 *(978-1-4179-6860-2(5))* Kessinger Publishing, LLC.
Mullins, Amy. I'm Reverent When- Bagley, Val Chadwick, illus. 2005. ("Move-About" Book Ser.). (J). *(978-1-59156-951-0(6))* Covenant Communications.
Naden, Corinne J. & Blue, Rose. Mormonism. 2004. (Illus.). 112p. (J). 29.95 *(978-1-59018-452-3(1)*, Lucent Bks.) Cengage Gale.
Newell, Karmel H. Come Follow Me: A Child's Guide to Faith, Hope, & Charity. Smith, Mary Ann Free, illus. 2003. (J). 16.95 *(978-1-57008-809-4(8)*, Bookcraft, Inc.) Deseret Bk. Co.
Oaks, Kristen M. My Home Can Be a Holy Place. Burr, Dan, illus. 2015. (J). 18.99 *(978-1-62972-099-9(2))* Deseret Bk. Co.
Oaks, Kristen M. & Phillips, JoAnn. The Testimony Glove. Burr, Dan, illus. 2010. (J). (gr. -1-4). 17.99 *(978-1-60641-151-3(9))* Deseret Bk. Co.
Oaks, Robert C. Believe! Helping Youth Learn to Trust in the Lord. 2003. (Illus.). xiii, 126p. (J). pap. 14.95 *(978-1-59038-203-5(X))* Deseret Bk. Co.
Olsen, Bevan Lloyd. The Littlest Nephite in Nephi & the Brass Plates. Miller, Rebecca, illus. 2008. 14p. (J). (gr. 3-7). 15.99 *(978-1-59955-087-9(3))* Cedar Fort, Inc./CFI Distribution.
Palmer, Alison. Simply Singing Time. 2009. 96p. (J). pap. 8.99 *(978-0-88290-970-7(3))* Cedar Fort, Inc./CFI Distribution.
Poelman, Heidi. I Can Love Like Jesus. 2017. (ENG., Illus.). (J). (gr. -1-2). 14.99 ***(978-1-4621-1940-0(9))*** Cedar Fort, Inc./CFI Distribution.
Pruett, Jason. Seek & Find: Book of Mormon Stories (Board Book) 2017. (ENG., Illus.). (gr. -1). bds. 12.99 ***(978-1-4621-2099-4(7))*** Cedar Fort, Inc./CFI Distribution.
Pruett, Jason. Seek & Find Book of Mormon Stories. 2015. 14.99 *(978-1-4621-1528-0(4)*, Horizon Pubs.) Cedar Fort, Inc./CFI Distribution.
Rich, J. Milton. Heavenly Fathers Plan of Salvation Coloring Book. Knaupp, Andrew & Koford, Adam, illus. 2003. 108p. (J). per. 7.95 *(978-0-9726670-2-9(4))* Rich Publishing.
Richards, Claude. The Temple Letters: A Rewarding Path to Happiness on Earth & Everlasting Treasures in Heaven. 2011. 228p. 46.95 *(978-1-258-05537-0(6))* Literary Licensing, LLC.
Rostrom, Laura Lee. My First Book of Mormon Activity Book, Vol. 1. 2011. 64p. pap. 3.99 *(978-1-59955-957-5(9))* Cedar Fort, Inc./CFI Distribution.
Rowley, Deborah Pace. White Dresses: A Baptism Keepsake for Girls. Hodson, Jewel, illus. 2006. 32p. (J). 16.99 *(978-1-59038-632-3(9))* Deseret Bk. Co.
—White Shirts: A Baptism Keepsake for Boys. Call, Brian, illus. 2006. 32p. (J). 16.99 *(978-1-59038-633-0(7))* Deseret Bk. Co.
Sanford, William R. & Green, Carl R. Brigham Young: Courageous Mormon Leader. 2012. (Courageous Heroes of the American West Ser.). (Illus.). 48p. (J). pap. 8.95 *(978-1-4644-0089-6(X))*; (gr. 5-18). 22.60 *(978-0-7660-4004-5(6))* Enslow Pubs., Inc.
Setzer, Lee Ann. I Am a Child of God. Harmon, Glenn, illus. 2007. (Tiny Talks Ser.). 74p. (J). per. 7.99 *(978-1-59955-076-3(8))* Cedar Fort, Inc./CFI Distribution.
—I Am Ready for Baptism. 2006. 30p. (J). pap. 4.99 *(978-1-55517-944-1(4))* Cedar Fort, Inc./CFI Distribution.
—Tiny Talks: My Savior, Jesus Christ, Vol. 10. 2009. 86p. (J). pap. 8.99 *(978-1-59955-375-7(9))* Cedar Fort, Inc./CFI Distribution.
—Tiny Talks #6: I will Trust in Heavenly Father & His Son, Jesus Christ-Their Promises are Sure, Vol. 6. 2005. (J). pap. 7.99 *(978-1-55517-889-5(8))* Cedar Fort, Inc./CFI Distribution.
Staker, Sara. My Baptism Keepsake. 2009. (Illus.). (J). *(978-1-59811-837-7(4))* Covenant Communications, Inc.
Turley, Richard & Littke, Lael. Stories from the Life of Joseph Smith. 2008. 192p. pap. 16.95 *(978-1-60641-080-6(6))* Deseret Bk. Co.
Turley, Richard E. & Littke, Lael. Stories from the Life of Joseph Smith. 2003. (Illus.). viii, 184p. (J). *(978-1-57008-915-2(9))* Deseret Bk. Co.
Wells, Anita. Nephi, Nephi, the Scriptures Are True. Anderson, Neal, illus. 2004. 32p. (J). (gr. -1-2). 17.95 *(978-1-59038-307-0(9))* Deseret Bk. Co.

MORMONS AND MORMONISM—FICTION
Andersen, C. B. The Book of Mormon Sleuth Vol. 3: The Hidden Path. 2003. ix, 214p. (J). pap. *(978-1-57008-988-6(4))* Deseret Bk. Co.
—The Forgotten Treasure. 2004. 215p. (J). pap. *(978-1-59038-314-8(1))* Deseret Bk. Co.
—The Secret Mission. 2008. (J). *(978-1-59038-906-5(9))* Deseret Bk. Co.
Bateman, Anya. I Just Got a Letter from Allyson Pringle. 2008. 256p. (YA). pap. 15.95 *(978-1-60641-028-8(8))* Deseret Bk. Co.
—The Makeover of James Orville Wickenbee. 2007. 262p. (J). pap. *(978-1-59038-707-8(4))* Deseret Bk. Co.
Bell, Michele Ashman. Dragon's Jaw: A Heart-Pounding Adventure. 2005. 241p. (J). *(978-1-59156-880-3(3))* Covenant Communications.
Bennett, Carolyn Hart. Seven Sisters: The Voyage. 2008. 232p. 25.95 *(978-0-595-51213-3(5))*; pap. 15.95 *(978-0-595-52242-2(4))* iUniverse, Inc.
Bessey, Siân Ann. Uprising in Samoa: A Novel. 2004. 178p. (J). *(978-1-59156-890-2(0))* Covenant Communications.
Bowman, David. Who's Your Hero? Vol. 3: Book of Mormon Stories Applied to Children. 2007. 80p. pap. 14.95 *(978-1-59038-759-7(7))* Deseret Bk. Co.
Boyack, Merrilee. The Mismatched Nativity. Tenney, Shawna J. C., illus. 2016. (J). 18.99 *(978-1-62972-239-9(1))* Deseret Bk. Co.
Brown, Toni Sorenson. I Can't Go to Church. Jolley, Mack, illus. 2005. (J). *(978-1-59156-270-2(8))* Covenant Communications.
C. Larene Hall. Martha's Freedom Train. 2009. 100p. pap. 10.49 *(978-1-4389-7977-9(0))* AuthorHouse.
Call, Brian D., tr. & illus. Sarah's Cloud. Call, Brian D., illus. 2003. (J). 15.95 *(978-1-57008-955-8(8))* Deseret Bk. Co.
Cannon, A. E. Charlotte's Rose. 2011. (ENG., Illus.). 256p. (J). (gr. 4). pap. 9.95 *(978-1-60781-141-1(3))* Univ. of Utah Pr.
Condie, Ally. Being Sixteen. 2010. (YA). *(978-1-60641-233-6(7))* Deseret Bk. Co.
—First Day. 2007. 304p. (YA). pap. 15.95 *(978-1-59038-775-7(9))* Deseret Bk. Co.
—Reunion. 2008. 288p. (YA). pap. 15.95 *(978-1-59038-989-8(1))* Deseret Bk. Co.
—Yearbook. 2006. 208p. (YA). pap. 14.95 *(978-1-59038-690-3(6))* Deseret Bk. Co.
Crane, Cheri J. Moment of Truth: A Novel. 2005. 238p. (YA). *(978-1-59156-727-1(0))* Covenant Communications.
Durrant, George D. Shakespeare's Best Work: A Novel of Unexpected Family Ties & Uncommon Faith. 2003. 130p. pap. 10.95 *(978-1-55517-709-6(3)*, 77093) Cedar Fort, Inc./CFI Distribution.
Evans, Loralee. The King's Heir. 2006. 287p. (YA). (gr. 8-12). per. 18.99 *(978-1-55517-865-9(0)*, Bonneville Bks.) Cedar Fort, Inc./CFI Distribution.
Fechner, Maggie. Growing Up Gracie. 2010. 240p. pap. 15.99 *(978-1-59955-453-2(4))* Cedar Fort, Inc./CFI Distribution.
Ficklin, Jonene H. The Garden Gate. 2005. (YA). 14.95 *(978-0-9761188-2-4(3))* Victor's Crown Publishing.
From the Dust #1: The Last King of Judah. 2012. (ENG.). pap. 14.99 *(978-0-9859884-1-8(X))* Spider Comics.
Gavin, Sherrie. Baptism & Boomerangs. 2015. (Illus.). (J). 14.99 *(978-1-4621-1681-2(7))* Cedar Fort, Inc./CFI Distribution.
Greene, Michele Dominguez. Keep Sweet. (ENG.). 224p. (YA). (gr. 9). 2011. pap. 9.99 *(978-1-4424-0977-4(0))* 2010. 16.99 *(978-1-4169-8681-2(2))* Simon Pulse. (Simon Pulse).
Harman, Debbie G. My Baptism: The Best Day Ever. 2007. (Illus.). 31p. (J). *(978-1-59156-564-2(2))* Covenant Communications.
Heimerdinger, Chris. Escape from Zarahemla. 2011. 263p. (YA). pap. *(978-1-60861-539-1(1))* Covenant Communications.
—Kingdoms & Conquerors: A Novel. 2005. 434p. (YA). *(978-1-59156-740-0(8))* Covenant Communications.
—Tower of Thunder Vol. 9: A Novel. 2004. (Tennis Shoes Adventure Ser.). 406p. pap. 14.95 *(978-1-59156-177-4(9))* Covenant Communications, Inc.
Hughes, Dean. As Wide As the River. 2005. 156p. (J). pap. *(978-1-59038-450-3(4))* Deseret Bk. Co.
—Under the Same Stars. 2005. viii, 152p. (J). pap. *(978-1-59038-448-0(2))* Deseret Bk. Co.
Hulet, Debra. Independence Rock. 2011. 208p. pap. 13.99 *(978-1-59955-441-9(0)*, Bonneville Bks.) Cedar Fort, Inc./CFI Distribution.
Johnson, Alice W. & Warner, Allison H. Believe & You're There When Amon Was a Missionary. Harston, Jerry, illus. 2010. (J). *(978-1-60641-247-3(7))* Deseret Bk. Co.
Johnson-Choong, Shelly. A Light to Come Home By. 2nd unabr. ed. 2004. 212p. (C). reprint ed. pap. 12.95 *(978-1-932280-52-4(9)*, 80529) Granite Publishing & Distribution.
Kearns, Ann. Dell's Discovery. 2006. 108p. (YA). per. 9.95 *(978-0-9710696-6-4(2))* Jorlan Publishing, Inc.
Littke, Lael. Searching for Selene. 2003. 203p. (J). pap. 13.95 *(978-1-59038-179-3(3))* Deseret Bk. Co.
Luce, Willard. Jerry Lindsey: Explorer to the San Juan. Collett, Farrell R., illus. 2011. 88p. 38.95 *(978-1-258-07330-5(7))* Literary Licensing, LLC.
Mangum, Kay Lynn. When the Bough Breaks. 2007. 352p. (YA). pap. 15.95 *(978-1-59038-748-1(1))* Deseret Bk. Co.
Millett, Melanie. CTR Boy. 2006. (Illus.). (J). *(978-1-59811-062-3(4))* Covenant Communications.
Monson, Marianne. The Enchanted Tunnel Vol. 3: Journey to Jerusalem. Burr, Dan, illus. 2011. (J). (gr. 3-6). pap. 7.99 *(978-1-60908-068-6(8))* Deseret Bk. Co.
—The Enchanted Tunnel Vol. 4: Wandering in the Wilderness. Burr, Dan, illus. 2011. 85p. (YA). (gr. 3-6). pap. 7.99 *(978-1-60908-069-3(6))* Deseret Bk. Co.
—Escape from Egypt. 2010. (J). *(978-1-60641-670-9(7))* Deseret Bk. Co.
Nelson, Wendy Watson. The Not Even Once Club: My Promise to Heavenly Father. Dorman, Brandon, illus. 2013. 18.99 *(978-1-60907-337-4(1))* Deseret Bk. Co.
Norton, Tamra. Comfortable in My Own Genes: A Novel. 2004. 175p. pap. 15.95 *(978-1-55517-772-0(7))* Cedar Fort, Inc./CFI Distribution.
—Molly Mormon? Myth or Me? 2011. (Illus.). 170p. (YA). pap. 11.99 *(978-1-55517-606-8(2)*, Bonneville Bks.) Cedar Fort, Inc./CFI Distribution.
Parker, Emma Rae. Papa's Book of Mormon Christmas. 2015. (Illus.). (J). 14.99 *(978-1-4621-1741-3(4))* Cedar Fort, Inc./CFI Distribution.
Peterson, David. 10 Days Until Forever. 2011. 32p. 14.99 *(978-1-59955-266-8(3)*, Bonneville Bks.) Cedar Fort, Inc./CFI Distribution.
Pike, Kenneth & Stewart, Isaac. Jacob's Journal of Doom: Confessions of an Almost-Deacon. 2012. (J). 14.99 *(978-1-60907-016-8(X))* Deseret Bk. Co.
Rowley, Deborah. The Miracle of the Wooden Shoes. 2008. 32p. (J). 18.95 *(978-1-59038-990-4(5))* Deseret Bk. Co.
Rowley, Deborah Pace. Easter Walk: A Treasure Hunt for the Real Meaning of Easter. Burr, Dan, illus. 2010. (J). *(978-1-60641-055-4(5))* Deseret Bk. Co.
Savage, Jeffrey S. The Fourth Nephite: Return to Palmyra, Bk. 2. 2011. audio compact disk 29.99 *(978-1-60908-073-0(4))* Deseret Bk. Co.
Sebra, Diane. Making Mountains Out of Moles. 2003. 120p. pap. 9.95 *(978-1-55517-712-6(3)*, 77123) Cedar Fort, Inc./CFI Distribution.
Setzer, Lee Ann. Sariah McDuff: Primary Program Diva. Officer, Robyn, illus. 2004. 61p. (J). pap. 4.95 *(978-1-55517-786-7(7))* Cedar Fort, Inc./CFI Distribution.
Smith, Robert F. Bitten: A Romantic Comedy. 2008. (YA). pap. *(978-1-59038-904-1(2))* Deseret Bk. Co.
Sorenson, Toni. I Will Go, I Will Do: A Book of Mormon Story. 2008. (Illus.). (J). *(978-1-59811-627-4(4))* Covenant Communications.
Sume, Lori Anne, illus. Sorry, Sorry, Sorry: Learning to Choose the Right. 2004. (J). bds. 9.95 *(978-1-59156-298-6(8))* Covenant Communications, Inc.
Talley, Rebecca Cornish. Heaven Scent. 2008. 229p. (gr. 8-12). pap. 15.99 *(978-1-59955-100-5(4))* Cedar Fort, Inc./CFI Distribution.
Thompson, Michelle. Taming the Wind. 2010. 176p. pap. 12.99 *(978-1-59955-379-5(1))* Cedar Fort, Inc./CFI Distribution.
Weyland, Jack. As Always, Dave. 2008. 320p. (YA). pap. 15.95 *(978-1-59038-849-5(6))* Deseret Bk. Co.
Wiles, Patricia. Early-Morning Cemetery: A Novel. 2006. 243p. (YA). pap. *(978-1-59811-077-7(2))* Covenant Communications.
—The Final Farewell: A Novel. 2007. 246p. (J). *(978-1-59811-353-2(4))* Covenant Communications.
Wood, Holly J. Invaluable. 2011. (YA). pap. 14.99 *(978-1-60908-835-4(2))* Deseret Bk. Co.
Yates, Alma J. Sammy's Song: A Novel. 2005. 272p. (J). *(978-1-59156-945-9(1))* Covenant Communications.

MOROCCO
Beardsley, Kurt. Under Saharan Skies. 2004. (Illus.). 96p. per. 25.00 *(978-0-9761103-0-9(X)*, 1000) International Vaquero Productions.
Blauer, Ettagale & Lauré, Jason. Morocco. 2015. (ENG., Illus.). 144p. (J). lib. bdg. *(978-0-531-21696-5(9)*, Orchard Bks.) Scholastic, Inc.
Cassanos, Lynda Cohen. Morocco. 2010. (Major Muslim Nations Ser.). 128p. (YA). (gr. 5-18). lib. bdg. 25.95 *(978-1-4222-1391-9(9))* Mason Crest.
Fordyce, Deborah. Welcome to Morocco. 2004. (Welcome to My Country Ser.). (Illus.). 48p. (gr. 2-5). lib. bdg. 27.00 *(978-0-8368-2561-9(6))* Stevens, Gareth Publishing LLLP.
Raabe, Emily. A Primary Source Guide to Morocco. (Countries of the World). 24p. 2009. (gr. 2-3). 42.50 *(978-1-61512-040-6(8))* 2005. (Illus.). lib. bdg. 22.60 *(978-1-4042-2755-2(5))* Rosen Publishing Group, Inc., The. (PowerKids Pr.).

Seward, Pat & Hargraves, Orin. Morocco. 2nd rev. ed. 2005. (Cultures of the World Ser.). (Illus.). 144p. (J). (gr. 6-10). lib. bdg. 42.79 *(978-0-7614-2051-4(7),* Benchmark Bks.) Marshall Cavendish Corp.

U. S. A. Global Investment Center Staff. Morocco Customs, Trade Regulations & Procedures Handbook. 2003. (World Investment & Business Library). pap. 99.95 *(978-0-7397-5590-7(0))* International Business Pubns., USA.

MOROCCO—FICTION

Baker, Jeannie. Mirror. Baker, Jeannie, illus. 2010. (ENG., Illus.). 48p. (J). (gr. k-4). 18.99 *(978-0-7636-4848-0(5))* Candlewick Pr.

Brodien-Jones, Christine. The Scorpions of Zahir. Murphy, Kelly, illus. 2012. (ENG.). 384p. (J). (gr. 5). 17.99 *(978-0-385-73933-7(8),* Delacorte Bks. for Young Readers) Random Hse. Children's Bks.

Coatsworth, Elizabeth. The White Horse. Sewell, Helen, illus. 2006. (Sally (Bethlehem Books) Ser.). 169p. (J). (gr. 5-7). per. 11.95 *(978-1-883937-86-7(8))* Bethlehem Bks.

Demetrios, Heather. Blood Passage. 2016. (Dark Caravan Cycle Ser.: 2). (ENG.). 512p. (YA). (gr. 8). 17.99 *(978-0-06-231859-6(4))* HarperCollins Pubs.

Dixon, Ken. Cobweb Jack & the Sacred Khunjar. 2009. 210p. pap. 28.50 *(978-1-4092-8919-7(2))* Lulu Pr., Inc.

Feuerman, Ruchama King. The Mountain Jews & the Mirror. Kosec, Polona & Calderon, Marcela, illus. 2015. (ENG.). 32p. (J). (gr. k-4). 7.99 *(978-1-4677-3896-5(4),* Kar-Ben Publishing) Lerner Publishing Group.

Feuman, Ruchama. The Mountain Jews & the Mirror. Calderon, Marcela & Kosec, Polona, illus. 2015. (ENG.). 32p. (J). (gr. k-4). 17.99 *(978-1-4677-3894-1(8),* Kar-Ben Publishing) Lerner Publishing Group.

Friedman, J. S. Casablanca. Beatrice, Chris, illus. 2013. (Maurice's Valises: Moral Tails in an Immoral World Ser.: Vol. 3). (ENG.). 45p. (J). (gr. k-4). pap. *(978-94-91613-09-8(X))* Mouse Prints Pr.

Klaus, Sandra. Mustafas Geheimnis: Ein Moslemischer Junge auf der Suche nach Gott. Date not set.Tr. of Mustapha's Secret - A Muslim Boy's Search to Know God. (GER., Illus.). (J). (gr. 2-7). pap. *(978-0-9617490-6-4(7))* Gospel Missionary Union.

—Tainata na Mustapha. Date not set.Tr. of Mustapha's Secret. (BUL.). (J). (gr. 2-7). pap. *(978-1-890940-04-1(6))* Gospel Missionary Union.

Laurie, Victoria. Oracles of Delphi Keep. 2010. (Oracles of Delphi Keep Ser.). (ENG.). 576p. (J). (gr. 3-7). 7.99 *(978-0-440-42258-7(2),* Yearling) Random Hse. Children's Bks.

O'Neill, Joe. Legends of the Rif, bk. 3. Addicott, Sara & Walton, Bedelia C., eds. 2015. (Red Hand Adventures Ser.: 3). (ENG., Illus.). 311p. (gr. 3-7). pap. 9.95 *(978-0-9851969-8-1(X))* Blacklock Nature Photography.

Peterson, Will. The Burning. 2009. (Triskellion Ser.: 2). (ENG., Illus.). 480p. (YA). (gr. 9-18). 16.99 *(978-0-7636-4223-5(1))* Candlewick Pr.

Tóth-Jones, Dee S. The Street Cats of Marrakech. Stevenson, Seline, illus. 2013. 34p. pap. *(978-1-908794-08-6(9))* Chiaroscuro Bks.

Turk, Evan. The Storyteller. Turk, Evan, illus. 2016. (ENG., Illus.). 48p. (J). (gr. -1-3). 18.99 *(978-1-4814-3518-5(3))* Simon & Schuster Children's Publishing.

MOROCCO—HISTORY

Hunter, Nick. Morocco, 1 vol. 2012. (Countries Around the World Ser.). (ENG.). 48p. (gr. 3-6). lib. bdg. 33.32 *(978-1-4329-6105-3(5),* NA-h) Heinemann-Raintree.

Kavanaugh, Dorothy. Morocco. 2012. (J). *(978-1-4222-2227-0(6))* Mason Crest.

—Morocco. Rotberg, Robert I., ed. 2012. (Evolution of Africa's Major Nations Ser.). (Illus.). 88p. (J). (gr. 7). 22.95 *(978-1-4222-2199-0(7))* Mason Crest.

Leavitt, Amie Jane. We Visit Morocco. 2012. (J). lib. bdg. 33.95 *(978-1-61228-306-7(3))* Mitchell Lane Pubs., Inc.

Nelson, Robin. Morocco. 2011. (Country Explorers Ser.). (ENG., Illus.). 48p. (J). (gr. 2-4). lib. bdg. 29.27 *(978-0-7613-6419-1(6))* Lerner Publishing Group.

Seward, Pat, et al. Morocco. 2016. (Cultures of the World (r) Ser.). (Illus.). 144p. (J). (gr. 5-5). 47.07 *(978-1-5026-1699-9(8))* Cavendish Square Publishing.

Sheen, Barbara, ed. Foods of Morocco. 2011. (Taste of Culture Ser.). (Illus.). 64p. (J). lib. bdg. 30.45 *(978-0-7377-5865-8(1),* Kidhaven) Cengage Gale.

Simmons, Walter. Morocco. 2012. (Exploring Countries Ser.). (ENG., Illus.). 32p. (J). (gr. 3-7). lib. bdg. 26.95 *(978-1-60014-731-9(3),* Blastoff! Readers) Bellwether Media.

MORPHOLOGY

see Anatomy; Anatomy, Comparative; Biology

MORRISON, TONI, 1931-

Burton, Zisca Isabel. Bloom's How to Write about Toni Morrison. 2008. (Bloom's How to Write about Literature Ser.). 212p. (C). (gr. 9-12). 45.00 *(978-0-7910-9548-5(7),* Chelsea Hse.) Facts On File, Inc.

Crayton, Lisa A. Reading & Interpreting the Works of Toni Morrison. 2016. (Lit Crit Guides). (ENG., Illus.). 152p. (J). (gr. 8-8). lib. bdg. 39.93 *(978-0-7660-7352-4(1))* Enslow Pubs., Inc.

Hinds, Maurene J. How to Analyze the Works of Toni Morrison, 1 vol. 2012. (Essential Critiques Set 3 Ser.). (ENG.). 112p. (J). (gr. 6-12). lib. bdg. 35.64 *(978-1-61783-458-5(0),* Essential Library) ABDO Publishing Co.

Kramer, Barbara. Toni Morrison: A Biography of a Nobel Prize-Winning Writer. 2013. (African-American Icons Ser.). 104p. (J). (gr. 6-12). pap. 10.95 *(978-1-59845-392-8(0))* Enslow Pubs., Inc.

Watson, Galadriel Findlay. Toni Morrison. 2005. (Great African American Women for Kids Ser.). (Illus.). 24p. (J). (gr. 2-3). lib. bdg. 24.45 *(978-1-59036-334-8(5))* Weigl Pubs., Inc.

MORSE, SAMUEL FINLEY BREESE, 1791-1872

Davis, Lynn. Samuel Morse, 1 vol. 2016. (ENG., Illus.). 24p. (J). *(978-1-62403-725-2(9))* ABDO Publishing Co.

Seidman, David & Williams, Keith. Samuel Morse & the Telegraph, 1 vol. Whigham, Rod & Barnett, Charles, III, illus. 2007. (Inventions & Discovery Ser.). (ENG.). 32p. (gr. 3-4). pap. 8.10 *(978-0-7368-7898-2(X),* Graphic Library) Capstone Press of Coughlan Cos.

Seidman, David, et al. Samuel Morse & the Telegraph, 1 vol. Whigham, Rod, illus. 2007. (Inventions & Discovery Ser.). (ENG.). 32p. (gr. 3-4). 30.65 *(978-0-7368-6846-4(1),* Graphic Library) Capstone Press of Coughlan Cos.

Zannos, Susan. Samuel Morse & the Telegraph. 2004. (Uncharted, Unexplored, & Unexplained Ser.). (Illus.). 48p. (J). (gr. 4-8). lib. bdg. 29.95 *(978-1-58415-269-9(9))* Mitchell Lane Pubs., Inc.

MORTUARY CUSTOMS

see Funeral Rites and Ceremonies

MOSAICS

The American Mosaic: Immigration Today. 2014. (American Mosaic: Immigration Today Ser.). 24p. (J). (gr. 3-6). 141.60 *(978-1-4777-6653-8(7),* PowerKids Pr.) Rosen Publishing Group, Inc., The.

Harris, Nathaniel. Mosaics. 2016. (ENG., Illus.). 32p. (J). (gr. 4-6). pap. 11.99 *(978-0-7502-9440-9(X),* Wayland) Hachette Children's Group GBR. Dist: Hachette Bk. Group.

—Mosaics. 2009. (Stories in Art Ser.). (Illus.). 30p. (J). (gr. 4-8). lib. bdg. 26.50 *(978-1-4042-4438-2(7),* PowerKids Pr.) Rosen Publishing Group, Inc., The.

Henry, Sally & Cook, Trevor. Making Mosaics. 2010. (Make Your Own Art Ser.). (Illus.). 32p. (J). pap. 11.75 *(978-1-4488-1617-0(3));* (gr. 3-6). 26.50 *(978-1-4488-1585-2(1))* Rosen Publishing Group, Inc., The. (PowerKids Pr.).

Mazurkiewicz, Jessica. 3-D Coloring Book — Mosaic Madness. 2011. (Dover 3-D Coloring Book Ser.). (ENG., Illus.). 32p. (J). (gr. 3-5). pap. 5.99 *(978-0-486-48104-3(2))* Dover Pubns., Inc.

Mosaics: Creative Tiled Projects. 2013. (Kits for Kids Ser.). (ENG., Illus.). 64p. (J). (gr. 1-7). *(978-1-77132-052-8(4))* SpiceBox Products Ltd.

MOSCOW (RUSSIA)

Goldsworthy, Steve. Kremlin. 2014. (Illus.). 24p. (J). *(978-1-62127-464-3(0))* Weigl Pubs., Inc.

Mason Crest. Moscow, Vol. 8. 2016. (Major World Cities Ser.: Vol. 8). (ENG., Illus.). 48p. (J). (gr. 5-8). 20.95 *(978-1-4222-3542-3(4))* Mason Crest.

Maule, David. What Makes a Place Special? Moscow, Egypt, Australia. 2014. (ENG., Illus.). 24p. (J). pap. 9.50 *(978-1-107-63317-9(6))* Cambridge Univ. Pr.

Steele, Philip. Moscow. 2003. (Great Cities of the World Ser.). (Illus.). 48p. (gr. 5-12). lib. bdg. 31.00 *(978-0-8368-5024-6(6),* Gareth Stevens Secondary Library) Stevens, Gareth Publishing LLLP.

Tolstikova, Dasha. A Year Without Mom, 1 vol. 2015. (ENG., Illus.). 176p. (J). (gr. 4-9). 19.95 *(978-1-55498-692-7(3))* Groundwood Bks. CAN. Dist: Publishers Group West (PGW).

MOSCOW (RUSSIA)—FICTION

Angel, Ido. Vipo in Moscow: The Siberian Tiger Is Hungry! 2015. (AV2 Animated Storytime Ser.). (ENG.). (J). lib. bdg. 29.99 *(978-1-4896-3914-1(4),* AV2 by Weigl) Weigl Pubs., Inc.

Brodsky, Slava. Funny Children's Stories (in Russian - Smeshnye detskie Rasskazy) 2007. (RUS.). 144p. pap. 8.76 *(978-0-615-16120-4(0))* Manhattan Academia.

Davey, Owen. Laika: Astronaut Dog. Davey, Owen, illus. 2013. (ENG., Illus.). 32p. (J). (gr. k-3). 15.99 *(978-0-7636-6822-8(2),* Templar) Candlewick Pr.

Evans, Connie. Sasha & Babushka: A Story of Russia. Schpitalnik, Vladimir, illus. (Make Friends Around the World Ser.). (ENG.). 32p. (J). (gr. k-3). 8.95 *(978-1-59249-446-0(3),* SC8007) Soundprints.

Evans, Cornelia & Shpitalnik, Vladimir. Sasha & Babushka: A Story of Russia. 2005. (Make Friends Around the World Ser.). (ENG., Illus.). 32p. (J). (gr. k-3). 19.95 *(978-1-59249-445-3(5),* BC8007) Soundprints.

Friedman, J. S. The Micetro of Moscow. Beatrice, Chris, illus. 2013. (Maurice's Valises: Moral Tails in an Immoral World Ser.: Vol. 2). (ENG.). 37p. (J). (gr. k-4). pap. *(978-94-91613-06-7(5))* Mouse Prints Pr.

Grant, Myrna. Ivan & the Daring Escape. 2006. (Flamingo Fiction 9-13s Ser.). (ENG., Illus.). 144p. (J). (gr. 4-7). per. 6.99 *(978-1-84550-132-7(2),* 24be2b87-de69-4377-8a1b-bc7b2ad8cd87) Christian Focus Pubns. GBR. Dist: Bookmasters Distribution.

—Ivan & the Moscow Circus. 2006. (Flamingo Fiction 9-13s Ser.). (ENG., Illus.). 160p. (J). (gr. 4-7). per. 6.99 *(978-1-84550-135-8(7),* 4a6719e2-1a18-4f7c-9b8f-fed8a960777e) Christian Focus Pubns. GBR. Dist: Bookmasters Distribution.

Lane, Andrew. Black Ice. 2013. (Sherlock Holmes: the Legend Begins Ser.: 3). (ENG.). 288p. (YA). (gr. 7-12). 17.99 *(978-0-374-38769-3(9),* 9780374387693, Farrar, Straus & Giroux (BYR)) Farrar, Straus & Giroux.

—Black Ice. 2013. (Sherlock Holmes: the Legend Begins Ser.: 3). (ENG.). 304p. (YA). (gr. 7-12). pap. 11.99 *(978-1-250-03654-4(2),* 9781250036544) Square Fish.

Pyron, Bobbie. The Dogs of Winter. 2014. (ENG.). 320p. (J). (gr. 5-9). pap. 7.99 *(978-0-545-39931-9(9),* Levine, Arthur A. Bks.) Scholastic, Inc.

Shpitalnik, Vladimir & Evans, Connie. Sasha & Babushka: A Story of Russia. 2005. (Make Friends Around the World Ser.). (ENG., Illus.). 32p. (J). (gr. k-3). pap. 6.95 *(978-1-59249-444-6(7),* S8007) Soundprints.

Shpitalnik, Vladimir & Evans, Cornelia. Sasha & Babushka: A Story of Russia. 2005. (Make Friends Around the World Ser.). (ENG., Illus.). 32p. (J). (gr. k-3). 15.95 *(978-1-59249-443-9(9),* B8007) Soundprints.

MOSES (BIBLICAL LEADER)

The Adventures of Moses: A Bible Story to Color. (Illus.). 16p. (J). pap. 1.50 *(978-0-87162-849-7(X),* E6023) Warner Pr., Inc.

Andrews, Jackie. Moses in the Bulrushes. de Klerk, Roger, illus. 2012. (ENG.). 24p. (J). 8.50 *(978-1-84135-807-9(X))* Award Pubns. Ltd. GBR. Dist: Parkwest Pubns., Inc.

Award, Anna. Moses in the Bulrushes: See the Picture & Say the Word. 2012. (ENG., Illus.). 24p. (J). pap. 6.50 *(978-1-84135-602-0(6))* Award Pubns. Ltd. GBR. Dist: Parkwest Pubns., Inc.

B&H Kids Editorial Staff. Moses. Conger, Holli, illus. 2016. (Little Words Matter(tm) Ser.). (ENG.). 24p. (J). (gr. -1 — 1). bds. 8.99 *(978-1-4336-8650-4(3),* B&H Kids) B&H Publishing Group.

Bader, Joanne. Moses & the Long Walk. von der Sterre, Johanna, illus. 2006. 16p. (J). 1.99 *(978-0-7586-0874-1(8))* Concordia Publishing Hse.

Blyton, Enid. Moses in the Bulrushes: See the Picture & Say the Word. 2012. (ENG.). 24p. (J). pap. 9.95 *(978-1-84135-747-8(2))* Award Pubns. Ltd. GBR. Dist: Parkwest Pubns., Inc.

Bower, Gary. The Hurry-Up Exit from Egypt. Chotiner, Barbara, illus. 2017. (Faith That God Built Book Ser.). (ENG.). 32p. (J). 14.99 *(978-1-4964-1745-9(3))* Tyndale Hse. Pubs.

Dietrich, Julie. Tiny Baby Moses. Clark, Bill, illus. 2003. (Arch Bks.). (ENG.). 16p. (J). (gr. k-4). 1.99 *(978-0-570-07581-3(5))* Concordia Publishing Hse.

Fernandez, Francisco. Moises. Osorio, Sergio, illus. 2005. (Historia de la Biblia Ser.). (SPA.). 64p. (J). pap. 4.70 *(978-970-643-875-1(0))* Selector, S.A. de C.V. MEX. Dist: Lectorum Pubns., Inc.

Fogle, Robin. Baby Moses Coloring Book. 2007. (Illus.). 16p. (J). pap. 1.89 *(978-1-59317-189-6(7))* Warner Pr., Inc.

Frank, Penny. Let My People Go! 2nd rev. ed. (ENG., Illus.). 24p. pap. 2.99 *(978-0-7459-4108-0(7),* Lion Books) Lion Hudson PLC GBR. Dist: Trafalgar Square Publishing.

—The Princess & the Baby. 2nd rev. ed. (ENG., Illus.). 24p. pap. 2.99 *(978-0-7459-4107-3(9),* Lion Books) Lion Hudson PLC GBR. Dist: Trafalgar Square Publishing.

Gallaudet, Thomas H. Scripture Biography for the Young: Vol. 3 - Moses Part 1. 2009. 224p. pap. 18.00 *(978-1-59925-235-3(X))* Solid Ground Christian Bks.

—Scripture Biography for the Young: Vol. 4 - Moses Part 2. 2009. 276p. pap. 20.00 *(978-1-59925-236-0(8))* Solid Ground Christian Bks.

Gamblin, Rose Tooley. Baby Moses. 2007. (J). *(978-0-8127-0466-2(5))* Autumn Hse. Publishing Co.

Holder, Jennifer. God Said & Moses Led. Munger, Nancy, illus. 2014. (Happy Day Ser.). (ENG.). 16p. (J). pap. 2.49 *(978-1-4143-9483-1(7))* Tyndale Hse. Pubs.

Hyatt, Greg. Moses & the Bronze Snake. 2008. (Arch Bks.). (Illus.). 16p. (J). (gr. k-4). pap. 1.99 *(978-0-7586-1456-8(X))* Concordia Publishing Hse.

Jules, Jacqueline & Hechtkopf, Jacqueline. Miriam in the Desert. Ugliano, Natascia, illus. 2010. (Bible Ser.). (ENG.). 32p. (J). (gr. k-3). 17.95 *(978-0-7613-4494-0(2));* pap. 8.95 *(978-0-7613-4496-4(9))* Lerner Publishing Group. (Kar-Ben Publishing).

Koralek, Jenny. The Moses Basket. Baynes, Pauline, illus. 2004. 32p. (J). 16.00 *(978-0-8028-5251-9(3))* Eerdmans, William B. Publishing Co.

Kovacs, Victoria. Miriam/Daniel Flip-Over Book. Krome, Mike & Ryley, David, illus. 2015. (Little Bible Heroes(tm) Ser.). (ENG.). 32p. (J). (gr. k-2). pap. 3.99 *(978-1-4336-8717-4(8),* B&H Kids) B&H Publishing Group.

Lafond, Pascale. The Story of Moses. Flowerpot Press, ed. 2012. (Illus.). 32p. (J). *(978-1-77093-388-0(3))* Flowerpot Children's Pr. Inc.

Lashbrook, Marilyn. Who Needs a Boat? Britt, Stephanie McFetridge, illus. 2012. 32p. (J). pap. 8.00 *(978-1-935014-39-3(0))* Hutchings, John Pubs.

Mackenzie, Carine. Moses: God's Leader. 2013. (Bible Time Ser.). (ENG.). 32p. (J). pap. 3.99 *(978-1-84550-381-9(3),* dd4bb926-7d6d-4143-9766-5b10686d2926) Christian Focus Pubns. GBR. Dist: Bookmasters Distribution.

—Moses the Child: Kept by God. Kennedy, Graham, illus. 2008. (Bible Alive Ser.). (ENG.). 24p. (J). 3.99 *(978-1-84550-330-7(9),* 156cef3d-f530-4fe2-b8ac-a56d9fd08ef1) Christian Focus Pubns. GBR. Dist: Bookmasters Distribution.

MacKenzie, Carine. Moses the Leader: Used by God. Kennedy, Graham, illus. 2008. (Bible Alive Ser.). (ENG.). 24p. (J). 3.99 *(978-1-84550-332-1(5),* e4e8286f-94a0-4e13-9832-038525bb82a2) Christian Focus Pubns. GBR. Dist: Bookmasters Distribution.

Mackenzie, Carine. Moses the Shepherd: Chosen by God. Kennedy, Graham, illus. 2008. (Bible Alive Ser.). (ENG.). 24p. (J). 3.99 *(978-1-84550-331-4(7),* 018499d7-3c39-4c05-b67c-092fea1603a3) Christian Focus Pubns. GBR. Dist: Bookmasters Distribution.

—Moses the Traveller: Guided by God. Kennedy, Graham, illus. 2008. (Bible Alive Ser.). (ENG.). 24p. (J). 3.99 *(978-1-84550-333-8(3),* be99525d-a728-4d19-be2a-89c99cdb04f2) Christian Focus Pubns. GBR. Dist: Bookmasters Distribution.

Mahany, Patricia Shely. Baby Moses in a Basket. Grant, Margret, illus. 2013. (Happy Day Ser.). (ENG.). 16p. (J). pap. 2.49 *(978-1-4143-9297-4(4))* Tyndale Hse. Pubs.

Martin, Oscar, Jr., creator. The Story of Moses I.t. ed. 2003. (Illus.). 25p. (J). E-Book 19.95 incl. cd-rom *(978-0-9748416-2-5(5))* Build Your Story.

Miller, Mary R. Moses, the Meekest Man. Higgins, Tabitha & Shirk, Linda, illus. 2016. 32p. (J). ***(978-0-7399-2536-2(9))*** Rod & Staff Pubs., Inc.

Moises (Moses) (Divertidas Historias Biblicas para Ninos Ser.). (SPA.). (J). 3.49 *(978-0-7899-0597-0(3),* 496644) Editorial Unilit.

Moses Bible Sticker Book. 2003. (Illus.). 16p. (J). 2.98 *(978-1-4054-1557-6(6))* Parragon, Inc.

Moses: God's Man of the Hour — Activity Book. 2005. pap. 1.69 *(978-1-59317-109-4(9))* Warner Pr., Inc.

Nolan, Allia Zobel. Moses' Big Adventure. Cox, Steve, illus. 2004. 12p. (J). bds. 10.99 *(978-0-8254-5521-6(9))* Kregel Pubns.

Pingry, Patricia A. The Story of the Ten Commandments. 2011. (Little Bible Bks). 22p. (J). (gr. -1-k). bds. 6.99 *(978-0-8249-1855-2(X),* Ideal Pubns.) Worthy Publishing.

—The Story of the Ten Commandments. Venturi-Pickett, Stacy, illus. (ENG.). (J). 2008. 32p. (gr. k-3). pap. 3.99 *(978-0-8249-5554-0(4))* 2006. 26p. (gr. -1-3). bds. 10.95 *(978-0-8249-6656-0(2))* Worthy Publishing. (Ideal Pubns.).

Powell Smith, Brendan. Baby Moses: The Brick Bible for Kids. 2016. (Brick Bible for Kids Ser.). (ENG., Illus.). 32p. (J). (gr. -1-k). 12.99 *(978-1-5107-1266-9(6),* Sky Pony Pr.) Skyhorse Publishing Co., Inc.

Priddy, Roger & Priddy Books Staff. The Story of Moses. 2012. (ENG., Illus.). 12p. (J). (gr. -1 — 1). bds. 4.95 *(978-0-312-51455-6(7),* 9780312514556, Priddy Bks.) St. Martin's Pr.

Roberts, Catrin, et al. Mawredd Mawr Moses! 16 Sesiwn Beiblaidd Ar Gyfer Clwb Plant Neu'r Ysgol Sul. 2005. (WEL., Illus.). 76p. pap. *(978-1-85994-034-1(X))* Cyhoeddiadau'r Gair.

Stowell, Gordon. Y Ddihangfa Anhygoel! Llyfr Drysfa Beiblaidd. Davies, Aled, ed. Wyn, Delyth, tr. Richardson-Jones, Tessa, illus. 2005. (WEL.). 12p. *(978-1-85994-469-1(8))* Cyhoeddiadau'r Gair.

Thomas, Sylvia A. Moses & the Exodus from Egypt. 2012. 34p. pap. 19.99 *(978-1-61904-669-6(5))* Salem Author Services.

Van Der Veer, Andrew. Bible Lessons for Juniors, Book 1: Creation Through Moses. 2007. 88p. (J). 6.00 *(978-1-60178-012-6(5))* Reformation Heritage Bks.

Whiting, Jim. The Life & Times of Moses. 2005. (Biography from Ancient Civilizations Ser.). (Illus.). 48p. (J). (gr. -1-7). lib. bdg. 29.95 *(978-1-58415-340-5(7))* Mitchell Lane Pubs., Inc.

Zondervan Bibles Staff. Moses & the King, 1 vol. Pulley, Kelly, illus. 2009. (I Can Read! / the Beginner's Bible Ser.). (ENG.). 32p. (J). pap. 3.99 *(978-0-310-71800-0(7))* Zonderkidz.

Zondervan Staff. Baby Moses & the Princess, 1 vol. Pulley, Kelly, illus. 2009. (I Can Read! / the Beginner's Bible Ser.). (ENG.). 32p. (J). pap. 3.99 *(978-0-310-71767-6(1))* Zonderkidz.

—Moses, God's Brave Servant, 1 vol. Jones, Dennis G., illus. 2010. (I Can Read! / Dennis Jones Ser.). (ENG.). 32p. (J). (gr. -1-2). pap. 3.99 *(978-0-310-71882-6(1))* Zonderkidz.

—Moses Leads the People, 1 vol. Miles, David, illus. 2014. (I Can Read! / Adventure Bible Ser.). (ENG.). 32p. (J). pap. 3.99 *(978-0-310-73236-5(0))* Zondervan.

MOSES (BIBLICAL LEADER)—FICTION

Adler, David A. Brothers in Egypt. abr. ed. (Prince of Egypt Ser.). (ENG.). 64p. pap. *(978-0-582-36482-0(5))* Addison-Wesley Longman, Inc.

Baby Moses. 2005. (J). bds. 5.99 *(978-0-9753127-9-7(0))* Family Bks. at Home.

Booth, Bradley. Escape from Egypt. 2009. (J). pap. 11.99 *(978-0-8163-2305-0(4))* Pacific Pr. Publishing Assn.

—Plagues in the Palace. 2006. 159p. (J). 10.99 *(978-0-8163-2143-8(4))* Pacific Pr. Publishing Assn.

CrossStaff Publishing, creator. The Ten Commandments Movie Coloring Book, Part 2. 2007. (Epic Stories of the Bible Ser.). (Illus.). 32p. (J). (gr. -1-3). 5.99 *(978-0-9743876-3-5(0))* CrossStaff Publishing.

Lester, Julius. Pharaoh's Daughter: A Novel of Ancient Egypt. 2009. (ENG., Illus.). 192p. (J). (gr. 7). pap. 6.99 *(978-0-15-206662-8(4))* Houghton Mifflin Harcourt Publishing Co.

Monson, Marianne. Escape from Egypt. 2010. (J). *(978-1-60641-670-9(7))* Deseret Bk. Co.

Rothero, C. Moses in the Bulrushes. 2005. (See & Say Storybook Ser.). (Illus.). 20p. (J). 5.95 *(978-965-483-008-9(6),* Devora Publishing) Simcha Media Group.

MOSES, GRANDMA, 1860-1961

Klein, Adam G. Grandma Moses, 1 vol. 2007. (Great Artists Set 2 Ser.). (ENG., Illus.). 32p. (J). (gr. -1-3). 27.07 *(978-1-59679-737-6(1),* Checkerboard Library) ABDO Publishing Co.

Kopp, Megan. Grandma Moses. 2016. (Illus.). 32p. (J). *(978-1-4896-4621-7(3))* Weigl Pubs., Inc.

Stephens, Pamela. Dropping in on Grandma Moses. McNeill, Jim, illus. 2008. 32p. (J). 15.95 *(978-1-56290-598-9(8))* Crystal Productions.

Venezia, Mike. Grandma Moses. Venezia, Mike, illus. 2004. (Getting to Know the World's Greatest Artists Ser.). (ENG., Illus.). 32p. (J). (gr. 3-4). pap. 6.95 *(978-0-516-27913-8(0),* Children's Pr.) Scholastic Library Publishing.

Wallner, Alexandra, tr. & illus. Grandma Moses. Wallner, Alexandra, illus. 2004. (ENG.). 32p. (J). (gr. k-3). tchr. ed. 16.95 *(978-0-8234-1538-0(4))* Holiday Hse., Inc.

MOSLEM ART

see Islamic Art

MOSQUITOES

Carr, Aaron. Mosquitoes. 2014. (J). *(978-1-4896-3200-5(X))* Weigl Pubs., Inc.

Dessen, Maci. Look Out for the Mosquito! 2015. (Surprisingly Scary! Ser.). (ENG.). 24p. (J). (gr. 2-3). 23.60 *(978-1-4994-0942-0(7),* PowerKids Pr.) Rosen Publishing Group, Inc., The.

DiConsiglio, John. Bitten! Mosquitoes Infect New York. 2011. (J). *(978-0-545-32807-4(1))* Scholastic, Inc.

Diconsiglio, John. Blood Suckers! Deadly Mosquito Bites. 2007. (24/7: Science Behind the Scenes Ser.). (ENG., Illus.). 64p. (J). (gr. 9-12). 29.00 *(978-0-531-12070-5(8));* pap. 7.95 *(978-0-531-17529-3(4))* Scholastic Library Publishing. (Watts, Franklin).

Doudna, Kelly. Mischievous Mosquitoes, 1 vol. 2012. (Bug Bks.). (ENG.). 24p. (J). (gr. k-3). 24.21 *(978-1-61783-193-5(X),* SandCastle) ABDO Publishing Co.

Goldish, Meish. Bloodthirsty Mosquitoes. 2008. (No Backbone! Ser.). (Illus.). 24p. (J). (gr. k-3). lib. bdg. 21.28 *(978-1-59716-585-3(9))* Bearport Publishing Co., Inc.

Hansen, Grace. Mosquitoes, 1 vol. 2014. (Insects Ser.). (ENG.). 24p. (J). (gr. 4-8). lib. bdg. 28.50 *(978-1-62970-041-0(X))* ABDO Publishing Co.

Hansen, Grace, et al. Mosquitos. 2015. (Insectos Ser.). (SPA., Illus.). 24p. (J). (gr. k-1). pap. 7.95 *(978-1-4966-0481-1(4))* Capstone Classroom.

Hunt, Santana. Bloodsucking Mosquitoes. 2016. (Real-Life Vampires Ser.). (ENG., Illus.). 24p. (J). (gr. 2-3). pap. 8.15 *(978-1-4824-3955-7(7))* Stevens, Gareth Publishing LLLP.

Kalman, Bobbie. El Ciclo de Vida del Mosquito. 2005. (Serie Ciclos de Vida Ser.). (SPA., Illus.). 32p. (J). lib. bdg. *(978-0-7787-8667-2(6));* (gr. 1-7). pap. *(978-0-7787-8713-6(3))* Crabtree Publishing Co.

—The Life Cycle of a Mosquito. 2003. (Life Cycle Ser.). (ENG., Illus.). 32p. (J). pap. *(978-0-7787-0695-3(8))* Crabtree Publishing Co.

—Les Moustiques. Briere, Marie-Josee, tr. from ENG. 2006. (Petit Monde Vivant Ser.). (FRE., Illus.). 32p. (J). (gr. -1-3). pap. 9.95 *(978-2-89579-077-8(9))* Bayard Canada Livres CAN. Dist: Crabtree Publishing Co.

Kravetz, Jonathan. Mosquitoes. (Gross Bugs Ser.). 24p. 2009. (gr. 3-4). 42.50 *(978-1-61513-229-4(5))* 2006. (Illus.). (J). lib. bdg. 22.60 *(978-1-4042-3044-6(0))* Rosen Publishing Group, Inc., The. (PowerKids Pr.).

Lew, Kristi. Mosquito-Borne Illnesses. 2009. (Health Alert 6 Ser.). 64p. (gr. 4). 32.79 *(978-0-7614-3980-6(3))* Marshall Cavendish GBR. Dist: Marshall Cavendish Corp.

Markle, Sandra. Mosquitoes. 2008. pap. 52.95 *(978-1-58013-284-8(7))* Lerner Publishing Group.

—Mosquitoes: Tiny Insect Troublemakers. 2008. (Insect World Ser.). (ENG., Illus.). 48p. (gr. 4-8). lib. bdg. 27.93 *(978-0-8225-7299-2(0),* Lerner Pubns.) Lerner Publishing Group.

Mitchell, Kirstin. Madame Anopheles. 2008.Tr. of Seòora Anopheles. (Illus.). 26p. (J). pap. 20.00 *(978-0-9816301-0-6(3))* Alexander, Raine.

Murray, Julie. Mosquitos, 1 vol. 2003. (Animal Kingdom Ser.). (ENG.). 24p. (gr. k-4). 25.65 *(978-1-57765-723-1(3),* Buddy Bks.) ABDO Publishing Co.

Orr, Tamra B. Understanding Insects. 2014. (Explorer Library: Follow the Clues Ser.). (ENG., Illus.). 32p. (J). (gr. 4-8). 28.50 *(978-1-62431-783-5(9),* 203328) Cherry Lake Publishing.

Piehl, Janet. Flying Mosquitoes. 2006. (Pull Ahead Bks.). (Illus.). 32p. (J). (gr. 3-7). lib. bdg. 22.60 *(978-0-8225-5932-0(3),* Lerner Pubns.); (ENG., (gr. k-3). per. 7.95 *(978-0-8225-6508-6(0),* First Avenue Editions) Lerner Publishing Group.

Reher, Matt. The Life of a Mosquito. 2016. (2G Bugs Ser.). (ENG., Illus.). 24p. (J). pap. 5.99 *(978-1-63437-503-0(3))* American Reading Co.

—Mosquito Moms. 2016. (2G Bugs Ser.). (ENG., Illus.). 24p. (J). pap. 5.99 *(978-1-63437-510-8(6))* American Reading Co.

Richter, Abigail. Deadly Mosquitoes. 2011. (Small but Deadly Ser.). (Illus.). 24p. (J). (gr. 2-5). pap. 8.15 *(978-1-4339-5740-6(X));* lib. bdg. 22.60 *(978-1-4339-5738-3(8))* Stevens, Gareth Publishing LLLP. (Gareth Stevens Learning Library).

Rustad, Martha E. H. Mosquitoes. 2007. (World of Insects Ser.). (ENG., Illus.). 24p. (J). (gr. k-3). lib. bdg. 25.95 *(978-1-60014-078-5(5))* Bellwether Media.

Schuh, Mari. Mosquitoes. 2014. (Illus.). 24p. (J). lib. bdg. 25.65 *(978-1-62031-085-4(6),* Bullfrog Bks.) Jump! Inc.

Scott, Jane Beecher. The Amazing Mosquito Bridge Secret. Scott, Jane Beecher, ed. Scott, Jane Beecher, illus. Scott, Jane Beecher, photos by. 5th ed. 2004. (Illus.). 32p. (J). (gr. k-12). 12.95 *(978-0-9763077-0-9(7))* Beecher Scott.

Siy, Alexandra. Mosquito Bite. Kunkel, Dennis, illus. (ENG.). 32p. (J). (gr. 2-5). 2006. pap. 7.95 *(978-1-57091-592-5(X))* 2005. 16.95 *(978-1-57091-591-8(1))* Charlesbridge Publishing, Inc.

Somervill, Barbara A. Mosquitoes: Hungry for Blood. (Bloodsuckers Ser.). 24p. (gr. 2-3). 2009. 42.50 *(978-1-61511-635-5(4),* PowerKids Pr.) 2007. (Illus.). (J). lib. bdg. 22.60 *(978-1-4042-3802-2(6))* Rosen Publishing Group, Inc., The.

Walker, Sally M. Mosquitoes. 2008. (Early Bird Nature Books Ser.). (Illus.). 48p. (J). (gr. 2-5). 26.60 *(978-0-8225-1375-9(7))* Lerner Publishing Group.

Webster, Christine. Mosquitoes. 2009. (Backyard Animals Ser.). (Illus.). 24p. (J). (gr. 3-5). pap. 8.95 *(978-1-60596-087-6(X));* lib. bdg. 24.45 *(978-1-60596-086-9(1))* Weigl Pubs., Inc.

MOTELS

see Hotels, Motels, etc.

MOTHER AND CHILD

see also Mothers and Daughters; Mothers and Sons

April, Elyse. Ready to Wean: The Return of the Dangling Red Earrings. Iverson, Diane, illus. 2012. (Family & World Health / We Like To Ser.). (ENG.). 32p. (J). pap. 9.95 *(978-1-935387-30-5(8))* Hohm Pr.

Barry, Ron & Fitzgerald, Paula. Me 'n Mom: A Keepsake Scrapbook Journal. Sharp, Chris, illus. 2009. (ENG.). 33p. pap. 14.99 *(978-0-8249-1435-6(X),* Ideal Pubns.) Worthy Publishing.

Berry, Joy. I Love Mommies & Daddies. Regan, Dana, illus. 2010. (Teach Me About Ser.). (ENG.). 20p. (J). (gr. k — 1). pap. 5.99 *(978-1-60577-001-7(9))* Berry, Joy Enterprises.

Catt, Thessaly. My Mom. 2010. (My Family Ser.). (ENG.). 24p. (J). pap. 8.25 *(978-1-4488-1490-9(1));* lib. bdg. 22.60 *(978-1-4488-1462-6(6))* Rosen Publishing Group, Inc., The. (PowerKids Pr.).

—My Mom(Mi Mamá) 2010. (My Family / Mi Familia Ser.). (SPA & ENG.). 24p. lib. bdg. 22.60 *(978-1-4488-0717-8(4),* PowerKids Pr.) Rosen Publishing Group, Inc., The.

D'Costa, Jasmine. Real Justice: Branded a Baby Killer: The Story of Tammy Marquardt. 2015. (Lorimer Real Justice Ser.). (ENG., Illus.). 120p. (YA). (gr. 9-12). pap. 12.95 *(978-1-4594-0993-4(0))* Lorimer, James & Co., Ltd., Pubs. CAN. Dist: Casemate Pubs. & Bk. Distributors, LLC.

D'Costa, Jasmine Anita Yvette. Branded a Baby Killer: The Story of Tammy Marquardt. 2016. (Lorimer Real Justice Ser.). (ENG.). 120p. (YA). (gr. 9-12). lib. bdg. 27.99 *(978-1-4594-0994-1(9),* 9781459409941) Lorimer, James & Co., Ltd., Pubs. CAN. Dist: Casemate Pubs. & Bk. Distributors, LLC.

Dicker, Katie. My Mum. 2017. (Popcorn: Families Ser.). (ENG., Illus.). 24p. (J). (gr. k-2). pap. 10.99 *(978-0-7502-8882-8(5),* Wayland) Hachette Children's Group GBR. Dist: Hachette Bk. Group.

Elkus, Julie. Cuando Mi Mama Me Lee/When My Mama Reads to Me. Fagin, Cristina, tr. from ENG. Nunez, Jose Luis, illus. 2005. (SPA & ENG.). 24p. (J). (gr. -1-3). 8.95 *(978-1-933197-06-7(4))* Orange Frazer Pr.

Gamble, Adam & Jasper, Mark. Good Night Mommy. Kelly, Cooper, illus. 2015. (Good Night Our World Ser.). (ENG.). 20p. (J). (— 1). bds. 9.95 *(978-1-60219-230-0(8))* Good Night Bks.

Gervais, Josephine. Mommies Are Protecting Their Children. 2013. 20p. pap. 24.95 *(978-1-62709-538-9(1))* America Star Bks.

—Mommies Are Special People. 2013. 24p. pap. 24.95 *(978-1-62709-537-2(3))* America Star Bks.

Greven, Alec. How to Talk to Moms. Acedera, Kei, illus. 2009. (ENG.). 48p. (J). (gr. 1-5). 9.99 *(978-0-06-171001-8(6),* Collins) HarperCollins Pubs.

Horlacher, Bill & Horlacher, Kathy. I'm Glad I'm Your Mother. Johnson, Meredith, illus. 2013. (Happy Day Ser.). (ENG.). 16p. (J). pap. 2.49 *(978-1-4143-9292-9(3))* Tyndale Hse. Pubs.

Jackson, Toneal M. Four Girls: A Lot of Choices. 2011. 40p. pap. 24.95 *(978-1-4560-8518-6(2))* PublishAmerica, Inc.

Jenner, Caryn. My Mum. 2017. (Family World Ser.). (ENG., Illus.). 24p. (J). (gr. k-2). pap. 9.99 *(978-1-4451-5223-3(1),* Franklin Watts) Hachette Children's Group GBR. Dist: Hachette Bk. Group.

Legg, Brook. The Healing Rhythms of Home: 30 Days of Devotion for the Homeschool Mom. 2012. 74p. pap. 9.95 *(978-1-4497-5587-4(9),* WestBow Pr.) Author Solutions, Inc.

L'Heureux, Christine. Caillou: I Love You. Brignaud, Pierre, illus. 2012. (Hand in Hand Ser.). (ENG.). 24p. (J). (gr. -1-k). 5.95 *(978-2-89450-860-2(3))* Caillouet, Gerry.

Liles, Rebecca. My Mommy's a Soldier, 2 bks. 2003. (Illus.). 16p. (J). 4.99 *(978-0-9744346-1-2(2))* Rebecca's Bks.

Lindsay, Jeanne Warren & Brunelli, Jean. Nurturing Your Newborn: Young Parents' Guide to Baby's First Month. 2nd ed. 2006. (Illus.). 96p. (J). pap. *(978-1-932538-38-0(0))* Morning Glory Pr., Inc.

Moore, M. Meet My Mom: Learning the M Sound. 2009. (PowerPhonics Ser.). 24p. (gr. 1-1). 39.90 *(978-1-60851-459-5(5),* PowerKids Pr.) Rosen Publishing Group, Inc., The.

Moore-Mallinos, Jennifer & Roca, Nuria. Mom Has Cancer! Fabrega, Marta, illus. 2008. (Let's Talk about It Ser.). (ENG.). 32p. (J). (gr. -1-2). pap. 7.99 *(978-0-7641-4074-7(4))* Barron's Educational Series, Inc.

Moulton, Alison. When Mommy Is Home with Me. Beckett, Kinsey, illus. 2017. (J). 14.99 ***(978-1-4622-0093-1(1),*** Horizon Pubs.) Cedar Fort, Inc./CFI Distribution.

Neumann, Rachel. Baby Present. 2016. (ENG., Illus.). 22p. (J). (gr. -1 — 1). bds. 9.95 *(978-1-941529-24-9(0))* Parallax Pr.

Newell, Cheri Cameron. An Angel Just Like You. 2012. (ENG.). (J). pap. *(978-1-4675-5356-8(5))* Independent Pub.

Nilsen, Anna. My Mum's Best. Dodd, Emma, illus. 2011. 24p. bds. *(978-1-84089-679-4(5))* Zero to Ten, Ltd.

Page, Liza & Innovative Kids Staff. Mommies & Babies. Larrañaga, Ana Martín, illus. 2008. (ENG.). 12p. (J). (gr. -1 — 1). bds. 5.99 *(978-1-58476-656-8(5))* Innovative Kids.

Parr, Todd. The Mommy Book. 2016. (ENG., Illus.). 20p. (J). (gr. -1 — 1). bds. 6.99 *(978-0-316-33774-8(9))* Little, Brown Bks. for Young Readers.

Rhatigan, Joe. Hey Diddle Diddle. O'Kif, Alejandro, illus. 2017. (Classic Nursery Rhymes Retold Ser.). (ENG.). 32p. (J). (gr. -1-k). 12.95 *(978-1-63322-161-1(X),* Moondance) Quarto Publishing Group USA.

Richmond, Marianne. Thank You Mom. 2004. (Illus.). 40p. (YA). 7.95 *(978-0-9741465-6-0(0),* Marianne Richmond Studios, Inc.) Sourcebooks, Inc.

Riehle, Mary Ann McCabe. M Is for Mom: A Child's Alphabet. Ellison, Chris, illus. 2009. (ENG.). 32p. (J). (gr. k-6). 17.95 *(978-1-58536-458-9(4))* Sleeping Bear Pr.

Schaefer, Lola M. Mothers. Saunders-Smith, Gail, ed. rev. ed. 2008. (Families Ser.). (ENG., Illus.). 24p. (gr. k-1). 21.99 *(978-1-4296-1227-2(4));* per. 6.29 *(978-1-4296-1756-7(X))* Capstone Press of Coughlan Cos. (Pebble Bks.).

Silva Escalera, Manuel. Ale y Su Estrellit. 2009. 80p. pap. 26.49 *(978-1-4490-2217-4(0))* AuthorHouse.

Snead, Kathi. My Mom Has a Job. Grove, Christine, illus. 2004. (J). *(978-0-9747385-0-5(6))* City of Manassas Department of Social Services.

Staehli, Melissa. I Love You to the Moon. 2011. 28p. pap. 11.95 *(978-1-935268-88-8(0))* Halo Publishing International.

Steigemeyer, Julie. Mommy Promises. Ong, Wilson, illus. 2008. 32p. pap. 7.49 *(978-0-7586-1479-7(9))* Concordia Publishing Hse.

Tobel, Susan Von. Mei-Ling's Forever Mommy. 2012. 40p. pap. 21.99 *(978-1-4691-2578-7(1))* Xlibris Corp.

Washburn, Sandi. Good Night, Grandma. Roehler, Yvonne Fetig, illus. 2009. (ENG.). 16p. (J). 17.95 *(978-1-934367-09-4(5))* Growing Art Pr.

Why Mom Deserves a Diamond(r) 2012 Anthology - A Gift of Love. 2012. 39.95 *(978-1-891665-46-2(4))* Moon Over Mountains Publishing (M.O.M.).

MOTHER AND CHILD—FICTION

Abbott, Donna. Cjam, the Unique Camel. 2008. 24p. pap. 24.95 *(978-1-60610-228-2(1))* America Star Bks.

Abegg, Rainbow. Mom, Are You There? 2004. (Illus.). (J). *(978-1-59156-437-9(9))* Covenant Communications.

Allan, Delores. Magical Moments with Roy & Toni: Have You Hugged Your Mother Today. 2012. 24p. pap. 17.99 *(978-1-4685-7584-2(8))* AuthorHouse.

Alvarez, Miguel, et al. Why, Mommy!!, 1 vol. Pastrovicchio, Lorenzo, illus. 2009. 17p. pap. 24.95 *(978-1-60749-429-4(9))* America Star Bks.

Anastas, Margaret. Mommy's Best Kisses. Winter, Susan, illus. 2008. (ENG.). 34p. (J). (gr. -1-k). bds. 6.99 *(978-0-06-124130-7(X),* HarperFestival) HarperCollins Pubs.

Andreae, Giles. I Love My Mommy. Dodd, Emma, illus. 2013. (ENG.). 26p. (J). (gr. -1-k). bds. 6.99 *(978-1-4231-6825-6(9))* Hyperion Pr.

Appelt, Kathi. Oh My Baby, Little One. Dyer, Jane, illus. 2006. (ENG.). 32p. (J). (gr. -1 — 1). pap. 3.99 *(978-0-15-206031-2(6))* Houghton Mifflin Harcourt Publishing Co.

Armstrong-Ellis, Carey F. I Love You More Than Moldy Ham. 2015. (ENG., Illus.). 32p. (J). (gr. -1-3). 14.95 *(978-1-4197-1646-1(8),* Abrams Bks. for Young Readers) Abrams, Inc.

Arnosky, Jim. Babies in the Bayou. Arnosky, Jim, illus. 2010. (ENG., Illus.). 32p. (J). (gr. -1-k). pap. 6.99 *(978-0-14-241463-7(8),* Puffin Books) Penguin Young Readers Group.

Ashman, Linda. Mama's Day. Ormerod, Jan, illus. 2011. (ENG.). 32p. (J). (gr. -1-1). pap. 16.99 *(978-1-4424-5233-6(1),* Simon & Schuster Bks. For Young Readers) Simon & Schuster Bks. For Young Readers.

—Rock-a-Bye Romp. Mulazzani, Simona, illus. 2016. (ENG.). 36p. (J). (— 1). 16.99 *(978-0-399-17150-5(9),* Nancy Paulsen Books) Penguin Young Readers Group.

Ashman, Linda & Airgood, Ellen. Little Baby Buttercup. Byun, You, illus. 2015. (ENG.). 32p. (J). (— 1). 16.99 *(978-0-399-16763-8(3),* Nancy Paulsen Books) Penguin Young Readers Group.

Asper-Smith, Sarah. I Would Tuck You In. Watley, Mitchell, illus. 2014. (ENG.). 20p. (J). (— 1). bds. 9.99 *(978-1-57061-944-1(1),* Little Bigfoot) Sasquatch Bks.

Aspinall, Sarah. Penguins Love Colors. Aspinall, Sarah, illus. 2016. (ENG., Illus.). 40p. (J). (gr. -1-k). 17.99 *(978-0-545-87654-4(0),* Blue Sky Pr., The) Scholastic, Inc.

Aspinall, Sarah. Penguins Love Their ABC's. Aspinall, Sarah, illus. 2017. (ENG., Illus.). 40p. (J). (gr. -1-k). 17.99 ***(978-1-338-13420-9(5),*** Blue Sky Pr., The) Scholastic, Inc.

Atkinson, Olympia J. Kendahl's Plans. 2010. 24p. 11.99 *(978-1-4490-8371-7(4))* AuthorHouse.

Averbeck, Jim. Oh No, Little Dragon! Averbeck, Jim, illus. 2012. (ENG., Illus.). 40p. (J). (gr. -1-1). 14.99 *(978-1-4169-9545-6(5),* Atheneum Bks. for Young Readers) Simon & Schuster Children's Publishing.

Bagley, Jessixa. Boats for Papa. 2015. (ENG., Illus.). 40p. (J). (gr. -1-2). 17.99 *(978-1-62672-039-8(8),* 9781626720398) Roaring Brook Pr.

Bailey, Melissa. Well, for Goodness Sake Little Jake. 2009. 24p. pap. 11.50 *(978-1-60693-675-7(1),* Eloquent Bks.) Strategic Book Publishing & Rights Agency (SBPRA).

Baker, Liza. I Love You Because You're You. McPhail, David, illus. 2008. (ENG.). (J). (gr. -1-k). bds. 8.99 *(978-0-545-02931-5(7),* Cartwheel Bks.) Scholastic, Inc.

Ballard, George Anne. Flowers along the Way. Ballard, George Anne & Bolton, Georgia Helen, illus. 2012. 26p. pap. 12.00 *(978-0-9855312-2-5(3))* Bolton Publishing LLC.

Balsley, Tilda. Soo's Boo-Boos: She's Got 10! McNicholas, Shelagh, illus. 2013. (ENG.). 32p. (J). (gr. -1-2). 12.95 *(978-1-58925-128-2(0))* Tiger Tales.

Banks, Kate. Close Your Eyes. Hallensleben, Georg, illus. 2015. (ENG.). 36p. (J). (gr. -1-1). bds. 7.99 *(978-0-374-30101-9(8),* 9780374301019, Farrar, Straus & Giroux (BYR)) Farrar, Straus & Giroux.

Barcelo, François. My Mommy's Hands. Mongeau, Marc, illus. 2009. (My First Stories Ser.). 24p. (J). (gr. -1-3). 22.60 *(978-1-60754-362-6(1));* pap. 8.15 *(978-1-60754-365-7(6))* Windmill Bks.

Bardhan-Quallen, Sudipta. Chicks Run Wild. Jenkins, Ward, illus. 2011. (ENG.). 32p. (J). (gr. -1-1). 15.99 *(978-1-4424-0673-5(9),* Simon & Schuster Bks. For Young Readers) Simon & Schuster Bks. For Young Readers.

—Rutabaga Boo! Adamson, Bonnie, illus. 2017. (ENG.). 40p. (J). (gr. -1-3). 15.99 *(978-1-4814-2461-5(0))* Simon & Schuster Children's Publishing.

Baron, Michael & Aronica, Lou. A Winter Discovery. 2011. (ENG.). 60p. pap. 4.99 *(978-1-61188-027-4(0))* Story Plant, The.

Bauer, Marion Dane. Grandmother's Song. Rossi, Pamela, illus. 2007. (ENG.). 32p. (J). (gr. -1-3). 10.99 *(978-1-4169-6849-8(0),* Simon & Schuster/Paula Wiseman Bks.) Simon & Schuster/Paula Wiseman Bks.

Beaty, Andrea. Hush, Baby Ghostling. Lemaître, Pascal, illus. 2009. (ENG.). 32p. (J). (gr. -1-3). 14.99 *(978-1-4169-2545-3(7),* McElderry, Margaret K. Bks.) McElderry, Margaret K. Bks.

Beek, Rosheena. Mommy Says! Maye, Warren L., illus. 2nd ed. 2013. (ENG.). 24p. pap. *(978-1-927750-20-9(2))* Bermuda National Trust.

Berenstain, Jan & Berenstain, Mike. We Love Our Mom! 2012. (Berenstain Bears Ser.). (J). lib. bdg. 13.55 *(978-0-606-23578-5(7),* Turtleback) Turtleback Bks.

Bergren, Lisa T. How Big Is God? Bryant, Laura J., illus. 2008. (HarperBlessings Ser.). (ENG.). 32p. (J). (gr. -1-2). 10.99 *(978-0-06-113174-5(1))* HarperCollins Pubs.

Berry, Ron. Where Is Mommy? Smart Kids Publishing Staff, ed. 2009. (ENG.). 20p. (J). bds. 7.99 *(978-0-8249-1404-2(X),* Ideal Pubns.) Worthy Publishing.

Bertram, Debbie & Bloom, Susan. The Best Place to Read. 2007. lib. bdg. 18.40 *(978-1-4177-9097-5(0),* Turtleback) Turtleback Bks.

Best, Cari. If I Could Drive, Mama. Shin, Simone, illus. 2016. (ENG.). 40p. (J). 17.99 *(978-0-374-30205-4(7),* 9780374302054, Farrar, Straus & Giroux (BYR)) Farrar, Straus & Giroux.

Billingsley, Franny. Big Bad Bunny. Karas, G. Brian, illus. 2008. (ENG.). 40p. (J). (gr. k-3). 17.99 *(978-1-4169-0601-8(0),* Atheneum/Richard Jackson Bks.) Simon & Schuster Children's Publishing.

Bland, Nick. Some Moms. 2017. (ENG., Illus.). 24p. (J). (gr. -1-1). 9.95 *(978-0-7624-6200-1(0),* Running Pr.) Running Pr. Bk. Pubs.

Bloncourt, Nelson & Botero, Fernando. Botero: Paintings & Works on Paper. Polyansky, Nikita, illus. 2013. (ENG.). 252p. 125.00 *(978-0-9881745-1-1(0))* Glitterati, Inc.

Bloom, Susan & Bertram, Debbie. The Best Place to Read. Garland, Michael, illus. 2007. (ENG.). 32p. (J). (gr. -1-2). pap. 7.99 *(978-0-375-83757-9(4),* Dragonfly Bks.) Random Hse. Children's Bks.

Bonnell, Kris. Presents for Mom. 2007. (J). pap. 6.95 *(978-1-933727-61-5(6))* Reading Reading Bks., LLC.

Bourguignon, Laurence. Heart in the Pocket. D'heur, Valérie, illus. 2008. 26p. (J). (gr. -1-3). 16.50 *(978-0-8028-5343-1(9))* Eerdmans, William B. Publishing Co.

Bower, Gary. Mommy Love. Bower, Jan, illus. 2012. (Little Lovable Board Bks.). (ENG.). 16p. (J). bds. 8.50 *(978-0-9845236-0-3(X))* Storybook Meadow Publishing.

Bowman, Crystal. Mommy, May I Hug the Fish?, 1 vol. Christensen, Donna, illus. 2009. (I Can Read! / ¡Yo Sé Leer! Ser.).Tr. of Mamá, Puedo Abrazar Al Pez? (ENG & SPA.). 32p. (J). pap. 3.99 *(978-0-310-71868-0(6))* Vida Pubs.

Braun, Sebastien. I Love My Mommy Board Book. Braun, Sebastien, illus. 2017. (Illus.). 26p. (J). (gr. -1 — 1). bds. 7.99 *(978-0-06-256424-5(2),* Tegen, Katherine Bks) HarperCollins Pubs.

Bravi, Soledad. Mommy, Pick Me Up. 2016. (ENG., Illus.). 40p. (J). 17.99 *(978-0-374-30268-9(5),* 9780374302689, Farrar, Straus & Giroux (BYR)) Farrar, Straus & Giroux.

Brewer, Sarah. Our New Garden. Brewer, Sarah & Brewer, Dean, illus. 2013. 20p. pap. 24.95 *(978-1-63004-768-9(6))* America Star Bks.

Brill, Calista. Little Wing Learns to Fly. Bell, Jennifer A., illus. 2016. (Little Wing Ser.). 32p. (J). (gr. -1-3). 17.99 *(978-0-06-236033-5(7))* HarperCollins Pubs.

Brown, Jo. Where's My Mommy? Brown, Jo, illus. 2006. (Storytime Board Bks.). (Illus.). 18p. (J). (gr. -1-3). bds. 6.95 *(978-1-58925-795-5(2))* Tiger Tales.

Brown, Palmer. Something for Christmas. Brown, Palmer, illus. 2011. (ENG., Illus.). 40p. (J). (gr. -1-2). 12.95 *(978-1-59017-462-3(3),* NYR Children's Collection) New York Review of Bks., Inc., The.

Brown, Ruby. Cuddles for Mommy. Macnaughton, Tina, illus. 2016. (ENG.). 32p. (J). (gr. -1-3). 16.99 *(978-1-4998-0203-0(X))* Little Bee Books Inc.

Brown, Toni Sorenson. I Can't Go to Church. Jolley, Mack, illus. 2005. (J). *(978-1-59156-270-2(8))* Covenant Communications.

Browne, Anthony. My Mom. Browne, Anthony, illus. 2009. (ENG., Illus.). 32p. (J). (gr. k-3). pap. 7.99 *(978-0-374-40026-2(1),* 9780374400262) Square Fish.

Browne, Susan Chalker. Freddy's Day at the Races, 1 vol. Rose, Hilda, illus. 2008. (ENG.). 32p. (J). (gr. 1-8). 10.95 *(978-1-897174-36-4(5))* Creative Bk. Publishing CAN. Dist: Orca Bk. Pubs. USA.

Bruno, Debra. Petey's Tale: A Story of Survival Inspired by Actual Events. 2010. 28p. pap. 12.49 *(978-1-4490-6597-3(X))* AuthorHouse.

Buller, Jon & Schade, Susan. I Love You, Good Night: Lap Edition. Pons, Bernadette, illus. 2013. (ENG.). 28p. (J). (gr. -1 — 1). bds. 12.99 *(978-1-4424-8539-6(6),* Little Simon) Little Simon.

Bunting, Eve. Pirate Boy. Fortenberry, Julie, illus. (ENG.). 32p. (J). (gr. -1-2). 2012. pap. 7.99 *(978-0-8234-2546-4(0))* 2011. 16.95 *(978-0-8234-2321-7(2))* Holiday Hse., Inc.

—Tweak Tweak. Ruzzier, Sergio, illus. 2011. (ENG.). 40p. (J). (gr. -1-3). 14.99 *(978-0-618-99851-7(9))* Houghton Mifflin Harcourt Publishing Co.

Burden-Evans, Patricia. A Steep Mountain to Climb. 2008. 151p. pap. 9.95 *(978-0-615-15120-5(5))* Burden-Evans, Patricia.

Burlingham, Abi. All Grown Up. Everitt-Stewart, Andy, illus. 2009. (Stories to Grow with Ser.). 24p. (J). (gr. -1-2). 22.60 *(978-1-60754-469-2(5));* pap. 8.15 *(978-1-60754-470-8(9))* Windmill Bks.

Burnett, Frances Hodgson. Esmeralda, Mère Giraud's Little Daughter, Little Saint Elizabeth & Other Stories: A Collection of Short Stories by Frances Hodgson Burnett. 2012. 378p. *(978-1-78139-164-8(5))* Benediction Classics.

Burroughs, Denise. The Story of the Day You Were Born. 2012. 28p. pap. 16.00 *(978-1-4772-4547-7(2))* AuthorHouse.

Buzzeo, Toni. Stay Close to Mama. Wohnoutka, Mike, illus. 2012. (ENG.). 32p. (J). (gr. -1-k). 15.99 *(978-1-4231-3482-4(6))* Hyperion Pr.

Byrne, Jean Livingstone. Legends of Newgrange. 2014. 54p. pap. 12.99 *(978-1-84386-818-7(0))* Vanguard Pr.

Cabrera, Jane. Mommy, Carry Me Please! Cabrera, Jane, illus. 2008. (Jane Cabrera Board Bks.). (ENG., Illus.). 24p. (J). (gr. -1-k). bds. 6.95 *(978-0-8234-2131-2(7))* Holiday Hse., Inc.

—There Was an Old Woman Who Lived in a Shoe. (ENG.). 32p. (J). (gr. -1-k). 2017. 6.99 *(978-0-8234-3771-9(X))* 2016. (Illus.). 16.95 *(978-0-8234-3554-8(7))* Holiday Hse., Inc.

Calaf, Monica. You, Me & the Breast. Fuentes, Mikel, illus. 2012. (ENG.). 40p. (J). (gr. -1-12). pap. 9.99 *(978-1-905177-52-3(6))* Pinter & Martin Ltd. GBR. Dist: National Bk. Network.

Calhoun, Megan. Oscar the Pig: Mommy Goes to Work. 2008. 32p. 18.50 *(978-0-615-25193-6(5))* Silly String Media.

Capucilli, Alyssa Satin. My Mom & Me. Mitchell, Susan, illus. 2009. (ENG.). 16p. (J). (gr. -1-1). 7.99 *(978-1-4169-5829-1(0),* Little Simon) Little Simon.

Carlisle, Kelly. My Mommy Is A Rocker. 2007. (Illus.). 21p. (J). lib. bdg. *(978-0-9795046-2-4(7))* Kwist, Karla.

Carlstrom, Nancy White. Mama, Will It Snow Tonight? Tong, Paul, illus. 2009. (ENG.). 32p. (J). (gr. k-3). 16.95 *(978-1-59078-562-1(2))* Boyds Mills Pr.

Carpenter, Donna. A Triple Treat. 2007. (Illus.). 20p. (J). 14.95 *(978-0-9793987-0-4(3))* DFC Pubs.

Carrick, Carol. Mothers Are Like That. Carrick, Paul, illus. 2007. (ENG.). 32p. (J). (gr. k — 1). 5.95 *(978-0-618-75241-6(2))* Houghton Mifflin Harcourt Publishing Co.

Catherine, Maria. Time Together, 1 vol. 2014. (Time Together Ser.). (ENG.). 32p. (gr. -1-2). pap. 15.90 *(978-1-4795-4822-4(7),* Fiction Picture Bks.) Picture Window Bks.

—Time Together: Me & Mom, 1 vol. Campion, Pascal, illus. 2014. (Time Together Ser.). (ENG.). 32p. (gr. -1-2). 8.95 *(978-1-4795-2252-1(X),* Fiction Picture Bks.) Picture Window Bks.

Cavaliere, Lisa. Lainey Lemonade's Cupcake Parade. 2008. 32p. pap. 24.95 *(978-1-60474-860-4(5))* America Star Bks.

Chaffin, Dawn Marie. My Love. 2010. 20p. 11.99 *(978-1-4520-0031-2(X))* AuthorHouse.

Chamberlin, Ann. Dumpling. 2012. (Illus.). 32p. pap. 21.99 *(978-1-4691-6313-0(6))* Xlibris Corp.

Chichester Clark, Emma. My Baby Sister. Chichester Clark, Emma, illus. 2009. (Humber & Plum Ser.: 2). (ENG., Illus.). 32p. (J). (gr. -1-k). 9.99 *(978-0-00-727324-9(X),* HarperCollins Children's Bks.) HarperCollins Pubs. Ltd. GBR. Dist: HarperCollins Pubs.

Childress, Story. Momma, What's Love?, 1 vol. 2010. 28p. 24.95 *(978-1-61546-067-0(5))* PublishAmerica, Inc.

Choclate-Brown, Honey. Mama never told Me. 2005. (J). 9.95 *(978-0-9765467-0-2(1))* Creative Bk. Pubs.

Chou, Yih-fen. Mimi Tidies Up. Chen, Zhiyuan, illus. 2011. (J). *(978-0-9845523-6-8(7))* Heryin Publishing Corp.

Christelow, Eileen. Five Little Monkeys Reading in Bed. 2011. (Five Little Monkeys Story Ser.). (ENG., Illus.). 40p. (J). (gr. -1-3). 16.99 *(978-0-547-38610-2(9))* Houghton Mifflin Harcourt Publishing Co.

Cinderella. 2005. 124p. 26.95 *(978-1-4218-0600-6(2),* 1st World Library - Literary Society) 1st World Publishing, Inc.

Clark, Amy. Mom Just Said No! 2012. 28p. pap. 21.99 *(978-1-4691-5104-5(9))* Xlibris Corp.

Clark, Danell. Daisy. Irwin, April, illus. 2008. 28p. pap. 11.95 *(978-1-59858-642-8(4))* Dog Ear Publishing, LLC.

Clark, Sally. Where's My Hug? Corke, Estelle, illus. 2015. (J). *(978-0-8249-1952-8(1),* Ideal Pubns.) Worthy Publishing.

Cline, H. R. Just Mommy & Me. 2009. 16p. pap. 9.95 *(978-1-4389-3879-0(9))* AuthorHouse.

Cobb, Amy. First Chair, 1 vol. Cattish, Anna, illus. 2015. (ENG.). 112p. (J). *(978-1-62402-074-2(7))* Magic Wagon.

Collier, Kelly L. Mommy, Why am I Different? 2011. 16p. (gr. 1-2). pap. 10.99 *(978-1-4634-0357-7(7))* AuthorHouse.

Collum, Karen. Blow Me a Kiss. Geddes, Serena, illus. 2012. (J). *(978-1-4351-4513-9(5))* Barnes & Noble, Inc.

M N O

Conroy, Christine. Mama Wants a Llam. 2012. 16p. pap. 15.99 *(978-1-4772-1605-7(7))* AuthorHouse.

Cook, Jessica & Stephens, Michael. What If Mommy Took a Vacation? 2011. 28p. pap. 13.99 *(978-1-4634-3601-8(7))* AuthorHouse.

Cook, Kajsa. Discoveries in the Shriver Family Attic: How a Woman & Her Children Dealt with the Battle of Gettysburg. 2009. (Illus.). 122p. (J). (gr. 4-8). pap. 8.95 *(978-1-57249-398-8(4)*, White Mane Kids) White Mane Publishing Co., Inc.

Cooley, Judy. I Want to Be a Mommy. 2012. (Illus.). (J). 17.99 *(978-1-60908-910-8(3))* Deseret Bk. Co.

Cooper, Bernice Soroka. The Little Elf-Frog. 2012. 24p. pap. 17.99 *(978-1-4772-9525-0(9))* AuthorHouse.

Corderoy, Tracey. I Want My Mommy! Edgson, Alison, illus. 2014. (ENG.). 32p. (J). (gr. -1-3). mass mkt. 3.99 *(978-1-58925-453-4(8))* Tiger Tales.

Cousins, Lucy. Hooray for Fish! Cousins, Lucy, illus. (ENG., Illus.). (J). (— 1). 2008. 34p. bds. 8.99 *(978-0-7636-3918-1(4))* 2005. 40p. 16.99 *(978-0-7636-2741-6(0))* Candlewick Pr.

Couteaud, Cheryl. A Monster for Halloween. Couteaud, Cheryl, illus. 2009. (Illus.). 24p. pap. 10.96 *(978-1-4251-8563-3(0))* Trafford Publishing.

Craver, Marcella Marino. Joey Daring, Caring, & Curious. Lew-Vriethoff, Joanne, illus. 2014. (J). *(978-1-4338-1652-9(0))*; pap. *(978-1-4338-1653-6(9))* American Psychological Assn. (Magination Pr.).

Crimi, Carolyn. Where's My Mummy? Manders, John, illus. (ENG.). 32p. (J). (gr. -1-3). 2009. 7.99 *(978-0-7636-4337-9(8))* 2008. 15.99 *(978-0-7636-3196-3(5))* Candlewick Pr.

Crosby, June. A Monster in the Attic. Chapman, Michelle, illus. 2011. 16p. pap. 24.95 *(978-1-4560-6959-9(4))* America Star Bks.

Crumbaugh, David. The Primrose Kids. 2006. 81p. pap. 16.95 *(978-1-4241-3250-8(9))* PublishAmerica, Inc.

Dahl, Michael. Bear Says Thank You, 1 vol. Vidal, Oriol, illus. 2011. (Hello Genius Ser.). (ENG.). 20p. (gr. 1-2). bds. 7.99 *(978-1-4048-6786-4(4))* Picture Window Bks.

—Penguin Misses Mom. Vidal, Oriol, illus. 2016. (Hello Genius Ser.). (ENG.). 20p. (gr. 1-2). bds. 7.99 *(978-1-4795-8739-1(7))* Picture Window Bks.

Dalmatian Press Staff. Mommy, Is That You? 2008. (ENG.). 5p. bds. 4.95 *(978-1-58117-714-5(3)*, Intervisual/Piggy Toes) Bendon, Inc.

Darling, Helen. Hide-n-seek Monday. Glickstein, Jennifer, ed. Sona and Jacob, illus. 2007. (J). 10.00 *(978-0-9797674-0-1(7))* My Darling-Tots Pubns.

Dauphin, Lili. I Will Fly Again: The Restavek. 2007. 284p. 29.95 *(978-0-9748329-9-9(5))* MiraQuest.

Davis, Terrance. Mom & Me. 2012. 24p. (-18). pap. 24.95 *(978-1-4626-9502-7(7))* America Star Bks.

De Blumenthal, Verra X. K. Folk Tales from the Russian. 2008. 88p. pap. 8.95 *(978-1-60664-152-1(2))* Aegypan.

de Las Casas, Dianne. Mama's Bayou, 1 vol. Stone-Barker, Holly, illus. 2010. (ENG.). 32p. (J). (gr. k-k). 16.99 *(978-1-58980-787-7(1))* Pelican Publishing Co., Inc.

Deflitch, Jennifer L. Where Do You Go? 2013. 24p. pap. 24.95 *(978-1-62709-307-1(9))* America Star Bks.

Dena. Happi Baby, Happi Mommy. 2011. (Happi Baby Ser.). (ENG., Illus.). 12p. (J). (— 1). bds. 6.99 *(978-0-375-87399-7(6)*, Random Hse. Bks. for Young Readers) Random Hse. Children's Bks.

dePaola, Tomie. My Mother Is So Smart. dePaola, Tomie, illus. (ENG., Illus.). 32p. (J). (gr. -1-k). 2013. pap. 6.99 *(978-0-14-242536-7(2)*, Puffin Books) 2010. 16.99 *(978-0-399-25442-0(0)*, G.P. Putnam's Sons Books for Young Readers) Penguin Young Readers Group.

Derrick, David G., Jr. Animals Don't, So I Won't! 2012. (ENG., Illus.). 36p. (J). (gr. -1-3). 15.95 *(978-1-59702-029-9(X))* Immedium.

Deshmukh, Manisha. Chinu's Day Out. 2008. 24p. pap. 11.49 *(978-1-4389-0601-0(3))* AuthorHouse.

Dewdney, Anna. Llama Llama - Birthday Party! Dewdney, Anna, illus. 2013. (Llama Llama Ser.). (ENG., Illus.). 16p. (J). (gr. -1-k). 6.99 *(978-0-448-45880-9(2)*, Grosset & Dunlap) Penguin Young Readers Group.

—Llama Llama Holiday Drama. 2010. (Llama Llama Ser.). (ENG.). 40p. (J). (gr. -1-k). 17.99 *(978-0-670-01161-2(4)*, Viking Books for Young Readers) Penguin Young Readers Group.

—Llama Llama Home with Mama. 2011. (Llama Llama Ser.). (ENG.). 32p. (J). (gr. -1-k). 17.99 *(978-0-670-01232-9(7)*, Viking Books for Young Readers) Penguin Young Readers Group.

—Llama Llama Mad at Mama. Dewdney, Anna, illus. 2007. (Llama Llama Ser.). (ENG., Illus.). 40p. (J). (gr. -1-k). 17.99 *(978-0-670-06240-9(5)*, Viking Books for Young Readers) Penguin Young Readers Group.

—Llama Llama Mad at Mama. 2009. (Illus.). (J). *(978-0-545-15933-3(4))* Scholastic, Inc.

—Llama Llama Red Pajama. Dewdney, Anna, illus. (Llama Llama Ser.). (ENG., Illus.). 40p. (J). (gr. -1-k). 2014. 25.00 *(978-0-451-46990-8(9))* 2005. 17.99 *(978-0-670-05983-6(8))* Penguin Young Readers Group. (Viking Books for Young Readers).

—Llama Llama Red Pajama, 6 vols., Pack. gif. ed. 2014. (ENG.). (J). 107.94 *(978-0-451-47544-2(5)*, Viking Books for Young Readers) Penguin Young Readers Group.

—Llama Llama Red Pajama. *(978-0-439-90665-4(2))*; 2006. lp *(978-0-439-90679-1(2))* Scholastic, Inc.

Di Santo, Melina. Mel & her Magic Journey. 2010. (Illus.). 32p. 14.49 *(978-1-4490-6889-9(8))* AuthorHouse.

Diaz, Cynthia. Sunny & Cubby's Real Life: ... Venturing Through Darkness. 2012. 24p. pap. 14.93 *(978-1-4669-4316-2(5))* Trafford Publishing.

Diesen, Deborah. Bloom. Lundquist, Mary, illus. 2017. (ENG.). 32p. (J). 16.99 *(978-0-374-30250-4(2)*, 9780374302504, Farrar, Straus & Giroux (BYR)) *Farrar, Straus & Giroux*.

Dodd, Emma. Happy. Dodd, Emma, illus. 2015. (Emma Dodd's Love You Bks.). (ENG., Illus.). 24p. (J). (-k). 12.99 *(978-0-7636-8008-4(7)*, Nosy Crow) Candlewick Pr.

—When I Grow Up. Dodd, Emma, illus. 2015. (Emma Dodd's Love You Bks.). (ENG., Illus.). 24p. (J). (-k). 12.99 *(978-0-7636-7985-9(2)*, Templar) Candlewick Pr.

—Wish. Dodd, Emma, illus. 2015. (Emma Dodd's Love You Bks.). (ENG., Illus.). 24p. (J). (-k). 12.99 *(978-0-7636-8009-1(5)*, Nosy Crow) Candlewick Pr.

Doman, Regina. Angel in the Waters. Hatke, Ben, illus. 2004. 48p. (J). (gr. -1-3). pap. 6.95 *(978-1-928832-81-2(4))* Sophia Institute Pr.

—Mi Angelito en Las Aguas. Hatke, Ben, illus. 2006. (SPA.). 40p. (J). (gr. -1-3). pap. 6.95 *(978-1-933184-22-7(1))* Sophia Institute Pr.

Driscoll, Laura & Disney Book Group Staff. I Love You, My Bunnies. Tyminski, Lori et al, illus. 2008. (ENG.). 24p. (J). (gr. -1-k). pap. 3.99 *(978-1-4231-2095-7(7))* Disney Pr.

Dunrea, Olivier. It's Snowing! Dunrea, Olivier, illus. 2009. (ENG., Illus.). 32p. (J). (gr. -1-1). pap. 6.99 *(978-0-312-60216-1(2)*, 9780312602161) Square Fish.

Dyan, Penelope. A New Bag! Dyan, Penelope, illus. 2012. (Illus.). 34p. pap. 11.95 *(978-1-61477-054-1(9))* Bellissima Publishing, LLC.

Earhardt, Ainsley & Cristaldi, Kathryn. Take Heart, My Child: A Mother's Dream. Kim, Jaime, illus. 2016. (ENG.). 32p. (J). (gr. -1-3). 18.99 *(978-1-4814-6622-6(4)*, Aladdin) Simon & Schuster Children's Publishing.

Edwards, Christine. The Charmed Enchanted Book. 2010. 24p. pap. 16.49 *(978-1-4490-7091-5(4))* AuthorHouse.

Egan, Kate. Kate & Nate Are Running Late! Yaccarino, Dan, illus. 2012. (ENG.). 36p. (J). (gr. k-2). 16.99 *(978-1-250-00080-4(7)*, 9781250000804) Feiwel & Friends.

Enriquez, Lucy Rivas. Dj's Lullaby: A Mother's Love Song. 2013. (ENG.). 26p. (J). pap. 12.95 *(978-1-4787-1148-3(5))* Outskirts Pr., Inc.

Feeney, Tatyana. Small Bunny's Blue Blanket. 2013. (ENG.). 24p. (J). (— 1). bds. 6.99 *(978-0-385-75363-0(2)*, Knopf Bks. for Young Readers) Random Hse. Children's Bks.

Felts, C. C. My Best Friend Mommy. 2008. 12p. pap. 24.95 *(978-1-60703-671-5(1))* America Star Bks.

Fernandez, Texanna. My Mighty Mother. 2010. 16p. pap. 9.00 *(978-1-4490-5409-0(9))* AuthorHouse.

Fleming, Denise. Sleepy, Oh So Sleepy. Fleming, Denise, illus. 2010. (ENG., Illus.). 32p. (J). (gr. -1-k). 16.99 *(978-0-8050-8126-8(7)*, 9780805081268, Holt, Henry & Co. Bks. For Young Readers) Holt, Henry & Co.

Fleuriel, Allison. Are You Done Sleeping? 2006. (J). pap. 16.00 *(978-0-8059-7115-6(7))* Dorrance Publishing Co., Inc.

Freedman, Claire. Goodnight, Sleep Tight! Tyger, Rory, illus. 2013. (ENG.). 32p. (J). (gr. -1). pap. 3.99 *(978-1-58925-440-4(6))* Tiger Tales.

—My Precious Little Bear. Scott, Gavin, illus. 2011. (ENG.). 20p. (J). (gr. k — 1). bds. 8.99 *(978-0-545-27432-6(X)*, Cartwheel Bks.) Scholastic, Inc.

Freedman, Claire, et al. Me & My Mommy: By My Side, Little Panda/Just for You!/Big Bear, Little Bear/the Most Precious Thing/Little Bear's Special Wish/My Mommy & Me. Tyger, Rory et al, illus. 2014. (ENG.). (J). (gr. -1). 11.99 *(978-1-58925-449-7(X))* Tiger Tales.

Frey, Cathy. Muttin's Puttins. 2010. 24p. pap. 13.99 *(978-1-4490-6753-3(0))* AuthorHouse.

Friester, Paul. Owl Howl Board Book. Goossens, Philippe, illus. 2nd rev. ed. 2016. (ENG.). 26p. (J). bds. 8.95 *(978-0-7358-4234-2(5))* North-South Bks., Inc.

Frost, Adam. Run! The Elephant Weighs a Ton! Chambers, Mark, illus. 2012. (ENG.). 128p. (J). (gr. -1-k). pap. 8.99 *(978-1-4088-2707-9(7)*, 9781408827079, Bloomsbury USA Childrens) Bloomsbury Publishing USA.

Fuenmayor, Morella & popular, Tradición. Estaba la Pajara Pinta. 2011. (SPA.). 14p. (J). (gr. -1-k). pap. 8.99 *(978-980-257-026-3(5))* Ekare, Ediciones VEN. Dist: Lectorum Pubns., Inc.

Furrow, Rebecca. You Grew in My Heart: An Adoption Story. 2012. 32p. pap. 16.95 *(978-1-4497-6064-9(3)*, WestBow Pr.) Author Solutions, Inc.

Gabriel, Andrea. My Favorite Bear. 2014. 32p. pap. 8.00 *(978-1-61003-310-7(8))* Center for the Collaborative Classroom.

Gaichies, Sarah. Mirabelle the Lost Kitten. 2010. (Illus.). 76p. pap. 24.99 *(978-1-4490-5593-6(1))* AuthorHouse.

Galindo, Renata. My New Mom & Me. 2016. (ENG., Illus.). 32p. (J). (gr. -1-2). 19.99 *(978-0-553-52135-1(7)*, Schwartz & Wade Bks.) Random Hse. Children's Bks.

Galvin, Laura. I Love My Mommy. 2009. (I Love My... Ser.). (ENG., Illus.). 16p. (J). 12.95 *(978-1-59249-801-7(9))* Soundprints.

Galvin, Laura, told to. I Love My Mommy. 2007. (ENG., Illus.). 16p. (J). (gr. -1-k). bds. 6.95 *(978-1-59249-730-0(6))* Soundprints.

Galvin, Laura G. & Galvin, Laura. I Love My Mommy (with Download) 2011. (ENG.). 16p. (J). *(978-1-60727-345-5(4))* Soundprints.

Galvin, Laura Gates. Baby Koala & Mommy. 2007. (Baby Animals Ser.). (ENG., Illus.). 16p. (gr. -1-k). 6.95 *(978-1-59249-744-7(6))* Soundprints.

Gaylord, Laurel Porter. Quiero a Mi Mama Porque. Wolff, Ashley, illus. 2004.Tr. of I Love My Mommy Because. (SPA & ENG.). 22p. (J). (gr. -1 — 1). bds. 6.99 *(978-0-525-47248-3(7)*, Dutton Books for Young Readers) Penguin Young Readers Group.

Georges, Theodore K. Forever in My Arms. 2011. 28p. pap. 13.99 *(978-1-4634-1494-8(3))* AuthorHouse.

Gessner, Kati. What Do You See When You Look at Me. 2012. 32p. pap. 19.99 *(978-1-4772-2106-8(9))* AuthorHouse.

Gibby, Bayne. You Mean the World to Me. Walker, David, illus. 2013. (ENG.). 16p. (J). (gr. -1-k). bds. 8.99 *(978-0-545-40570-6(X)*, Cartwheel Bks.) Scholastic, Inc.

Gliori, Debi. Dragon's Extraordinary Egg. 2014. (ENG., Illus.). 32p. (J). (gr. -1-3). 17.99 *(978-0-8027-3759-5(5)*, 9780802737595, Bloomsbury USA Childrens) Bloomsbury Publishing USA.

Goode, Molly. Mama Loves. McCue, Lisa, illus. 2015. (Step into Reading Ser.). (ENG.). 32p. (J). (gr. -1-1). 4.99 *(978-0-553-53896-0(9)*, Random Hse. Bks. for Young Readers) Random Hse. Children's Bks.

Gore, Leonid. Mommy, Where Are You? Gore, Leonid, illus. 2009. (ENG., Illus.). 32p. (J). (gr. -1-2). 16.99 *(978-1-4169-5505-4(4)*, Atheneum Bks. for Young Readers) Simon & Schuster Children's Publishing.

Gray, Susannah. Gotta See Nathan! Jones, Nathan, illus. 2012. 20p. pap. 15.00 *(978-1-4575-1315-2(3))* Dog Ear Publishing, LLC.

Green, Jose. Castro's Diary. 2004. 174p. pap. 24.95 *(978-1-4137-4556-6(3))* America Star Bks.

Griffune, Donna L. I Love You with My Heart. 2007. 44p. (J). pap. 8.99 *(978-1-59092-391-7(X))* Blue Forge Pr.

Gummelt, Donna & Melchiorre, Dondino. Your Name Is Mud. Wall, Randy Hugh, ed. Varela, Carmen, tr. Varela, Juan D., illus. l.t. ed. 2006.Tr. of Tu nombre es Mud. 34p. (J). 14.95 *(978-0-9764798-3-3(4))* Story Store Collection Publishing.

Halfmann, Janet. Good Night, Little Sea Otter, 1 vol. Williams, Wish, illus. (ENG.). (J). 2012. 24p. 15.95 *(978-1-59572-277-5(7))* 2010. 32p. (gr. -1-3). pap. 5.95 *(978-1-59572-254-6(8))* Star Bright Bks., Inc.

—Good Night, Little Sea Otter (Burmese Karen/English), 1 vol. Williams, Wish, illus. 2012. (KAR & ENG.). 24p. (J). 5.95 *(978-1-59572-371-0(4))* Star Bright Bks., Inc.

—Good Night, Little Sea Otter (Burmese/English), 1 vol. Williams, Wish, illus. 2012. (ENG.). 24p. (J). pap. 5.95 *(978-1-59572-370-3(6))* Star Bright Bks., Inc.

—Good Night, Little Sea Otter (Hmong/English), 1 vol. Williams, Wish, illus. 2012. (ENG.). 24p. (J). pap. 5.95 *(978-1-59572-365-9(X))* Star Bright Bks., Inc.

—Good Night, Little Sea Otter (Portuguese/English), 1 vol. Williams, Wish, illus. 2012. (ENG.). 24p. (J). pap. 5.95 *(978-1-59572-359-8(5))* Star Bright Bks., Inc.

—Good Night, Little Sea Otter (Spanish/English), 1 vol. Williams, Wish, illus. 2012. (ENG.). 32p. (J). pap. 5.95 *(978-1-59572-347-5(1))* Star Bright Bks., Inc.

Hall, Annalisa. Momma, i hold You. 2009. 32p. pap. 7.99 *(978-0-557-05470-1(2))* Lulu Pr., Inc.

Hall, Pamela. Miss You Like Crazy. Bell, Jennifer A., illus. 2014. (ENG.). 32p. (J). (gr. -1-3). 15.99 *(978-1-933718-91-0(9))* Tanglewood Pr.

Hallensleben, Georg & Gutman, Anne. Mommy Snuggles. 2017. (ENG., Illus.). 14p. (J). (gr. -1 — 1). bds. 5.99 *(978-1-4521-5822-8(3))* Chronicle Bks. LLC.

Hallinan, P. K. My Mommy & I. 2005. (ENG., Illus.). 32p. (J). (gr. k-3). pap. 3.95 *(978-0-8249-5520-5(X)*, Ideal Pubns.) Worthy Publishing.

Hamilton, Clarice. Special Delivery. 2010. 16p. 12.50 *(978-1-4520-4199-5(7))* AuthorHouse.

Hao, K. T. Where's My Mommy? Toni, Alessandra, illus. 2008. (ENG.). 32p. (J). (gr. -1). 15.95 *(978-1-933327-40-2(5))* Purple Bear Bks., Inc.

—Where's My Mommy? Toni, Alessandra, illus. 2008. (ENG.). 32p. (J). (gr. -1). 16.50 *(978-1-933327-41-9(3))* Purple Bear Bks., Inc.

Hardesty, Michael. Who Made the Sun, Mommy? 2011. 28p. 15.95 *(978-1-4520-7721-5(5))* AuthorHouse.

Hardin, Melinda. Hero Mom. Langdo, Bryan, illus. 2013. 24p. pap. 12.99 *(978-1-4778-6645-0(0))* Amazon Publishing.

Harms, Carol. What If? 2010. 20p. 10.49 *(978-1-4520-8463-3(7))* AuthorHouse.

Hart, Linda. When Mummy Says. 2009. (Illus.). 32p. pap. 18.99 *(978-1-4490-1291-5(4))* AuthorHouse.

Harvey Mph, Janera P. What Mommy Does. Utley, J. Stacy, illus. 2012. 24p. pap. 24.95 *(978-1-4560-4180-9(0))* America Star Bks.

Haughey, Jennifer. NOT a Stupid Baby Book: Top Secret: Boys Only! 2010. (ENG.). 26p. pap. 9.25 *(978-1-4505-1212-1(7))* CreateSpace Independent Publishing Platform.

Haughton, Chris. Little Owl Lost. Haughton, Chris, illus. 2010. (ENG., Illus.). 32p. (J). (gr. -1-k). 14.99 *(978-0-7636-5022-3(6))* Candlewick Pr.

Hayes, Geoffrey. Patrick in a Teddy Bear's Picnic & Other Stories. 2011. (ENG., Illus.). 32p. (J). (gr. -1-3). 12.95 *(978-1-935179-09-2(8))* TOON Books / RAW Junior, LLC.

Heath, Paulette Powell. In the Mist. 2012. 24p. pap. 15.99 *(978-1-4797-4354-4(2))* Xlibris Corp.

Henkes, Kevin. Words of Stone. 2005. (ENG.). 160p. (J). (gr. 3-7). reprint ed. pap. 6.99 *(978-0-06-078230-6(7)*, Greenwillow Bks.) HarperCollins Pubs.

Hicks, Constance. Florabelle Bunny & the Sparrow. 2011. 24p. pap. 12.99 *(978-1-4490-9969-5(6))* AuthorHouse.

Higgins, M. G. Trouble in the City. Taylor, Jo, illus. 2016. (Sibling Split Ser.). (ENG.). 112p. (gr. 2-3). lib. bdg. 25.32 *(978-1-4965-2591-8(4))* Stone Arch Bks.

Hodgman, Ann. That's My Mommy! Logan, Laura, illus. 2013. (ENG.). 22p. bds. *(978-1-58925-645-3(X))* Tiger Tales.

Huber, Mike. Mama's Gloves. Cowman, Joseph, illus. 2014. (ENG.). 32p. (gr. -1). 15.95 *(978-1-60554-210-2(5))* Redleaf Pr.

Huether, Michael & Huether, Amy. Ju Ju & the Sunblock. 2012. 32p. pap. 10.95 *(978-1-60494-729-8(2))* Wheatmark, Inc.

Hwang, Sun-mi. The Hen Who Dreamed She Could Fly. 2013. lib. bdg. 28.20 *(978-0-606-35094-5(2)*, Turtleback) Turtleback Bks.

I Love You, Mommy. 2008. (I Love... Ser.). 32p. *(978-1-4075-0856-6(3))* Parragon, Inc.

ImageBooks Staff. Snow Baby Finger Puppet Book. 2011. (Little Finger Puppet Board Bks.). (ENG.). 12p. (J). (gr. -1 — 1). bds. 6.99 *(978-1-4521-0220-7(1))* Chronicle Bks. LLC.

Ivey, Pamela. Mom! I'm Special I Am Fearfully & Wonderfully Made! 2011. 28p. pap. 12.99 *(978-1-4634-3830-2(3))* AuthorHouse.

Iwai, Melissa. Soup Day. Iwai, Melissa, illus. 2010. (ENG., Illus.). 40p. (J). (gr. -1-k). 15.99 *(978-0-8050-9004-8(5)*, 9780805090048, Holt, Henry & Co. Bks. For Young Readers) Holt, Henry & Co.

Jenkins, T. L. On the Bed & off the Bed. 2009. 28p. pap. 12.49 *(978-1-4389-2648-3(0))* AuthorHouse.

Jensen, Bonnie Rickner. God Loves Mommy & Me, 1 vol. 2017. (ENG., Illus.). 20p. (J). bds. 9.99 *(978-0-7180-9178-1(7))* Nelson, Thomas Inc.

Jeram, Anita. Bunny My Honey. Jeram, Anita, illus. 2009. (ENG., Illus.). 22p. (J). (gr. k-k). bds. 7.99 *(978-0-7636-4645-5(8))* Candlewick Pr.

Johnson, Wyletta. Your Precious Eyes. 2013. 16p. pap. 9.99 *(978-0-9897168-3-3(X))* Mindstir Media.

Joyce, Melanie. I Love You Because ... Lovsin, Polona, illus. 2016. (ENG.). 24p. (J). (gr. -1-1). 16.99 *(978-1-4998-0212-2(9))* Little Bee Books Inc.

Katz, Karen. Mommy Hugs. Katz, Karen, illus. 2007. (Classic Board Bks.). (ENG., Illus.). 32p. (J). (gr. -1 — 1). bds. 7.99 *(978-1-4169-4121-7(5)*, Little Simon) Little Simon.

—Mommy Hugs. Katz, Karen, illus. 2006. (ENG., Illus.). 32p. (J). (gr. -1-3). 17.99 *(978-0-689-87772-8(2)*, McElderry, Margaret K. Bks.) McElderry, Margaret K. Bks.

—Mommy Hugs: Lap Edition. Katz, Karen, illus. 2010. (ENG., Illus.). 26p. (J). (gr. -1 — 1). bds. 12.99 *(978-1-4424-0791-6(3)*, Little Simon) Little Simon.

Katz, Susan B. My Mama Earth. Launay, Melissa, illus. 2012. (ENG.). 24p. (J). 16.99 *(978-1-84686-418-6(6))* Barefoot Bks., Inc.

—My Mama Hung the World for Me. Newey, Gail, illus. 2009. (J). *(978-1-84686-269-4(8))* Barefoot Bks., Inc.

Kaus, Cathy. The Bean Bandit, 1 vol. 2010. 24p. 24.95 *(978-1-4489-2202-4(X))* PublishAmerica, Inc.

Keller, Holly. Miranda's Beach Day. Keller, Holly, illus. 2009. (Illus.). 32p. (J). (gr. -1). lib. bdg. 18.89 *(978-0-06-158300-1(6))*; (ENG., 17.99 *(978-0-06-158298-1(0))* HarperCollins Pubs. (Greenwillow Bks.).

Kelley, Louise. Stretch the Giraffe. 2012. 32p. pap. 19.99 *(978-1-4772-2161-7(1))* AuthorHouse.

Kelly, Mij. The Bump. Allan, Nicholas, illus. 2012. (ENG.). 32p. (J). *(978-1-58925-107-6(5))* Tiger Tales.

Ketteman, Helen. Goodnight, Little Monster, 0 vols. Leick, Bonnie, illus. 2010. (ENG.). 32p. (J). (gr. -1-3). 16.99 *(978-0-7614-5683-4(X)*, 9780761456834, Amazon Children's Publishing) Amazon Publishing.

—If Beaver Had a Fever, 0 vols. O'Malley, Kevin, illus. 2011. (ENG.). 32p. (J). (gr. -1-3). 16.99 *(978-0-7614-5951-4(0)*, 9780761459514, Amazon Children's Publishing) Amazon Publishing.

Keys, Dalen. Just a Quilt? Sponaugle, Kim, illus. 2nd ed. 2012. (ENG.). 32p. (J). 16.00 *(978-1-886068-56-8(9))* Fruitbearer Publishing, LLC.

Kimla, Lenka J. I Love My Mommy. Golds, Alexandra Kimla, illus. 2008. 22p. pap. 24.95 *(978-1-60703-126-0(4))* America Star Bks.

King, Frances. The Roundabout Boy. 2012. 28p. pap. 16.50 *(978-1-4772-8059-1(6))* AuthorHouse.

Kingsbury, Karen. Let's Go on a Mommy Date, 1 vol. Andreasen, Dan, illus. 2008. (ENG.). 32p. (J). (gr. -1-3). 15.99 *(978-0-310-71214-5(9))* Zonderkidz.

Kirchner, Janette. I Love You So Much. 2011. 20p. pap. 24.95 *(978-1-4137-5952-5(1))* America Star Bks.

Kleinberg, Naomi. Elmo's Mommy. Womble, Louis, illus. 2012. (ENG.). 12p. (J). (gr. k-k). bds. 4.99 *(978-0-307-92967-9(1)*, Random Hse. Bks. for Young Readers) Random Hse. Children's Bks.

Klise, Kate. Little Rabbit & the Meanest Mother on Earth. Klise, M. Sarah, illus. (ENG.). 32p. (J). (gr. -1-3). 2015. 6.99 *(978-0-544-45611-2(4)*, HMH Books For Young Readers) 2010. 17.99 *(978-0-15-206201-9(7))* Houghton Mifflin Harcourt Publishing Co.

Knapman, Timothy. Soon. Benson, Patrick, illus. 2015. (ENG.). 33p. (J). (-k). 16.99 *(978-0-7636-7478-6(8))* Candlewick Pr.

Konrad, Marla Stewart. Just Like You: Beautiful Babies Around the World, 1 vol. Wang, Lin, illus. 2010. (ENG.). 32p. (J). (gr. -1-2). 15.99 *(978-0-310-71478-1(8))* Zonderkidz.

—Mom & Me. 2009. (Early Reader Ser.). (ENG., Illus.). 24p. (J). (gr. -1-2). 12.95 *(978-0-88776-866-8(0)*, Tundra Bks.) Tundra Bks. CAN. Dist: Penguin Random Hse. LLC.

Kroll, Steve. Nina in That Makes Me Mad!, 1 vol. 2013. (Toon Bks). (ENG.). 36p. (J). (gr. 1-2). lib. bdg. 27.07 *(978-1-61479-153-9(8))* Spotlight.

Kuskin, Karla. A Boy Had a Mother Who Bought Him a Hat. Hawkes, Kevin, illus. 2010. (ENG.). 32p. (J). (gr. -1-3). 16.99 *(978-0-06-075330-6(7))* HarperCollins Pubs.

La Coccinella. Look & See: Mommy, Where Are You? 2014. (Look & See! Ser.). (ENG., Illus.). 24p. (J). (gr. -1 — 1). bds. 6.95 *(978-1-4549-0615-5(4))* Sterling Publishing Co., Inc.

Laible, Steve William, ed. Dandylion. Berry, VacieAnna, illus. 2012. (ENG.). 38p. (J). pap. 9.95 *(978-0-9844784-6-0(9)*, Empire Holdins - Literary Division for Young Readers) Kodel Group, LLC, The.

Lampson, Rosalie. Give Mom a Minute. 2009. 32p. pap. 13.99 *(978-1-4490-1407-0(0))* AuthorHouse.

The Land Beyond Forever. 2006. 25.00 *(978-0-9785570-0-3(X))* Three Sisters Publishing Hse., Ltd.

Landers, Gail J. Late for the Race. 2008. 24p. pap. 24.95 *(978-1-60441-371-7(9))* America Star Bks.

LaPoint, Crystal Godfrey. When My Mommy Cries: A Story to Help Families Cope with Sadness. Eldridge, Crystal, illus. 2012. (ENG.). 32p. (gr. k-6). pap. 19.99 *(978-1-4525-4241-6(4)*, 7529fdad-44ef-45a0-9351-f4e3e18c4d7c, Balboa Pr.) Author Solutions, Inc.

Lawson-Miller, Barb. I Love Mommy Because... 2004. (Illus.). 14p. bds. *(978-0-9688553-1-7(8))* Barbamel Bks., Inc.

Lee, Calee M. I Love You! Tharp, Tricia, illus. 2013. 32p. pap. 9.99 *(978-1-62395-471-0(1))* Xist Publishing.

Lee, Spike & Lee, Tonya Lewis. Please, Baby, Please. Nelson, Kadir, illus. 2007. (Classic Board Bks.). (ENG.). 32p. (J). (gr. -1-k). bds. 7.99 *(978-1-4169-4911-4(9)*, Little Simon) Little Simon.

Lewis, Anne Margaret. The Runaway Mitten. Zenz, Aaron, illus. 2015. (ENG.). 40p. (J). (gr. -1-k). 15.99 *(978-1-63450-213-9(2)*, Sky Pony Pr.) Skyhorse Publishing Co., Inc.

—The Runaway Pumpkin. Zenz, Aaron, illus. 2015. (ENG.). 40p. (J). (gr. -1-k). 15.99 *(978-1-63450-214-6(0)*, Sky Pony Pr.) Skyhorse Publishing Co., Inc.

Lewis, Paeony. I'll Always Love You. Ives, Penny, illus. (J). 2013. (ENG.). 32p. pap. *(978-1-58925-441-1(4))* 2008. 12p. (gr. -1-3). bds. 7.95 *(978-1-58925-833-4(9))* Tiger Tales.

Ling, Nancy Tupper. The Story I'll Tell, 1 vol. Lanan, Jessica, illus. 2015. (ENG.). 32p. (J). (gr. 3-3). 17.95 *(978-1-62014-160-1(4))* Lee & Low Bks., Inc.

Link, Amy. My Mommy Wears a Wig. 2009. 16p. pap. 17.95 *(978-1-4490-0218-3(8))* AuthorHouse.

The Little Saguaro. 2007. (YA). pap. 15.95 *(978-1-886679-37-5(1))* Arizona Sonora Desert Museum Pr.

Litton, Jonathan. I Love My Mommy. Galloway, Fhiona, illus. 2016. (My Little World Ser.). (ENG.). 16p. (J). (gr. -1-k). bds. 7.99 *(978-1-58925-216-5(0))* Tiger Tales.

Lois, Lowry. Son. (ENG.). 400p. (YA). (gr. 7). 2014. pap. 9.99 *(978-0-544-33625-4(9)*, HMH Books For Young Readers) 2012. (Giver Quartet Ser.: 4). 17.99 *(978-0-547-88720-3(5))* Houghton Mifflin Harcourt Publishing Co.

—Son. l.t. ed. 2013. (Giver Quartet Ser.). (ENG.). 422p. 23.99 *(978-1-4104-5448-5(7))* Thorndike Pr.
—Son. 2014. (Giver Quartet Ser.: 4). lib. bdg. 20.85 *(978-0-606-35979-5(6))* Turtleback Bks.
Lombardi, Kristine A. Lovey Bunny. 2015. (Lovey Bunny Ser.). (ENG., Illus.). 32p. (J). (gr. -1-2). 14.95 *(978-1-4197-1485-6(6)*, Abrams Bks. for Young Readers) Abrams, Inc.
Lomp, Stephan. Mamasaurus. 2016. (ENG., Illus.). 40p. (J). (gr. -1-k). 16.99 *(978-1-4521-4424-5(9))* Chronicle Bks. LLC.
Looper, Grace W. Great-Grandpa's Hidden Treasure. 2006. (YA). pap. *(978-1-933523-18-7(2))* Bella Rosa Bks.
Love, Judy. Praise Be & Rainbows. 2006. 51p. pap. 16.95 *(978-1-4241-0333-1(9))* PublishAmerica, Inc.
Ltd Mommy Loves/Mommy Kisses. 2005. (J). bds. 11.90 *(978-0-8118-9934-5(9))* Chronicle Bks. LLC.
Luebs, Robin. Please Pick Me up, Mama! Luebs, Robin, illus. 2009. (ENG., Illus.). 40p. (J). (gr. -1-k). 15.99 *(978-1-4169-7977-7(8)*, Beach Lane Bks.) Beach Lane Bks.
MacLachlan, Patricia. Lala Salama: A Tanzanian Lullaby. Zunon, Elizabeth, illus. 2011. (ENG.). 32p. (J). (gr. -1-2). 16.99 *(978-0-7636-4747-6(0))* Candlewick Pr.
Maltese, John. I Love You the Most. 2009. 33p. pap. 16.40 *(978-0-557-09465-3(8))* Lulu Pr., Inc.
Mariam, Sahra Mire - Umm. I Love Making Mummy Happy. 2011. (Illus.). 28p. pap. 15.99 *(978-1-4628-9341-6(4))* Xlibris Corp.
Marino, Gianna. Meet Me at the Moon. 2012. (ENG.). 32p. (J). (gr. -1-k). 16.99 *(978-0-670-01313-5(7)*, Viking Books for Young Readers) Penguin Young Readers Group.
Marr, Melissa & Airgood, Ellen. Bunny Roo, I Love You. White, Teagan, illus. 2015. (ENG.). 32p. (J). (gr. -1 — 1). 16.99 *(978-0-399-16742-3(0)*, Nancy Paulsen Books) Penguin Young Readers Group.
Marsh, Laura F. Big Enough. 2009. (Mama Mirabelle Ser.). (ENG., Illus.). 24p. (J). (gr. -1-2). pap. 3.99 *(978-1-4263-0432-3(3))*; lib. bdg. 11.90 *(978-1-4263-0433-0(1))* National Geographic Society. (National Geographic Children's Bks.).
—What's in a Tail? 2009. (Mama Mirabelle Ser.). (ENG., Illus.). 24p. (J). (gr. -1-2). lib. bdg. 11.90 *(978-1-4263-0431-6(5)*, National Geographic Children's Bks.) National Geographic Society.
Martin, Bill, Jr. Baby Bear, Baby Bear, What Do You See? Carle, Eric, illus. (Brown Bear & Friends Ser.). (ENG.). (J). (gr. -1-k). 2014. 28p. bds. 12.99 *(978-0-8050-9949-2(2)*, 9780805099492) 2011. 40p. 8.99 *(978-0-8050-9291-2(9)*, 9780805092912) 2009. 28p. bds. 7.99 *(978-0-8050-8990-5(X)*, 9780805089905) 2007. 32p. 17.99 *(978-0-8050-8336-1(7)*, 9780805083361) Holt, Henry & Co. (Holt, Henry & Co. Bks. For Young Readers).
—Baby Bear, Baby Bear, What Do You See? 10th Anniversary Edition with Audio CD. Carle, Eric, illus. 2016. (Brown Bear & Friends Ser.). (ENG.). 32p. (J). 19.99 *(978-1-62779-731-3(9)*, 9781627797313, Holt, Henry & Co. Bks. For Young Readers) Holt, Henry & Co.
—Baby Bear, Baby Bear, What Do You See? Big Book. Carle, Eric, illus. 2011. (Brown Bear & Friends Ser.). (ENG.). 32p. (J). (gr. -1-k). pap. 27.99 *(978-0-8050-9345-2(1)*, 9780805093452, Holt, Henry & Co. Bks. For Young Readers) Holt, Henry & Co.
McBratney, Sam. I Love It When You Smile. Fuge, Charles, illus. 2012. 32p. (J). (gr. -1-3). 9.99 *(978-0-06-222133-9(7))* HarperCollins Pubs.
McCloskey, Robert. Blueberries for Sal, 1 vol. 2010. (Puffin Storytime Ser.). (ENG.). 15p. (J). (gr. -1-k). 9.99 *(978-0-14-241643-3(6)*, Puffin Books) Penguin Young Readers Group.
—Blueberries for Sal. (J). (gr. -1-k). pap. 12.95 incl. audio. 2004. 29.95 *(978-1-55592-841-4(2))*; 2004. (J). 38.75 *(978-1-55592-816-2(1))*; 2004. (J). 18.95 *(978-1-55592-799-8(8))* Weston Woods Studios, Inc.
McCourt, Lisa. Goodnight, Stinky Face. Moore, Cyd, illus. 2016. (ENG.). 32p. (J). (— 1). bds. 6.99 *(978-0-545-90592-3(3)*, Cartwheel Bks.) Scholastic, Inc.
—Happy Halloween, Stinky Face. Moore, Cyd, illus. 2011. (ENG.). 32p. (J). (gr. k — 1). bds. 6.99 *(978-0-545-28542-1(9)*, Cartwheel Bks.) Scholastic, Inc.
—I Love You, Stinky Face. Moore, Cyd, illus. 2009. (ENG.). (J). (gr. -1-3). 18.95 *(978-0-545-11944-3(8))* Scholastic, Inc.
—I Miss You. Moore, Cyd, illus. 2014. (Stinky Face Ser.). (ENG.). 32p. (J). (gr. -1 — 1). bds. 6.99 *(978-0-545-74848-3(8)*, Cartwheel Bks.) Scholastic, Inc.
—Merry Christmas, Stinky Face. Moore, Cyd, illus. 2016. (ENG.). 32p. (J). (— 1). 3.99 *(978-1-338-02919-2(3)*, Cartwheel Bks.) Scholastic, Inc.
—You Can Do It, Stinky Face! Moore, Cyd, illus. 2016. (ENG.). 32p. (J). (— 1). bds. 6.99 *(978-0-545-80648-0(8)*, Cartwheel Bks.) Scholastic, Inc.
McCue, Lisa. HideAway Hedgehog & the Magical Rainbow. 2015. (HideAway Pets Bks.). (ENG., Illus.). 26p. (J). (gr. -1-2). 9.95 *(978-1-4549-1602-4(8))* Sterling Publishing Co., Inc.
McDaniel, Lurlene. Losing Gabriel: a Love Story. 2017. (ENG.). 336p. (YA). (gr. 7). pap. 9.99 ***(978-0-385-74422-5(6)***, Ember) Random Hse. Children's Bks.
McDonald, Megan. Baya, Baya, Lulla-By-a. Rosenberry, Vera, illus. 2014. (ENG.). 32p. (J). (gr. -1-1). 16.99 *(978-1-4814-2533-9(1)*, Atheneum Bks. for Young Readers) Simon & Schuster Children's Publishing.
McDonnell, Patrick. Art. 2006. (ENG., Illus.). 48p. (J). (gr. -1-3). 17.99 *(978-0-316-11491-2(X))* Little, Brown Bks. for Young Readers.
—Art. 2011. (J). (gr. -1-3). 29.95 *(978-0-545-10697-9(4))* Weston Woods Studios, Inc.
Mcdoogle, Farrah. A Sweet Surprise for Mom. 2015. (Olivia 8x8 Ser.). lib. bdg. 13.55 *(978-0-606-36319-8(X))* Turtleback Bks.
Mcghee, Alison. Someday. Reynolds, Peter H., illus. 2015. (ENG.). 42p. (J). bds. 9.99 *(978-1-4814-6012-5(9)*, Little Simon) Little Simon.
—Someday. 2014. pap. 29.95 *(978-0-545-79756-6(X))* Scholastic, Inc.
—Someday. Reynolds, Peter H., illus. 2007. (ENG.). 40p. (J). (gr. -1-3). 16.99 *(978-1-4169-2811-9(1)*, Atheneum Bks. for Young Readers) Simon & Schuster Children's Publishing.
—Someday. Reynolds, Peter H., illus. 2008. (J). (gr. -1-2). 29.95 incl. audio compact disk *(978-0-8045-4200-5(7))*; 27.95 incl. audio *(978-0-8045-6975-0(4))* Spoken Arts, Inc.
McGinty, Alice B. Eliza's Kindergarten Surprise, 0 vols. Speir, Nancy, illus. 2013. (ENG.). 34p. (J). (gr. k-3). pap. 9.99 *(978-1-4778-1683-7(6)*, 9781477816837, Amazon Children's Publishing) Amazon Publishing.
McGowen, Julie. Virginia's Voyage. 2007. 48p. per. 16.95 *(978-1-4241-6672-5(1))* America Star Bks.
McKoin, Cathy Taylor. Little Pup Finds a Home! 2009. 28p. pap. 15.99 *(978-1-4415-3407-1(5))* Xlibris Corp.
McMullan, Kate. Mamas' Kisses. Nyeu, Tao, illus. 2017. (ENG.). 40p. (J). (-k). 16.99 *(978-0-525-42832-9(1)*, Dial Bks) Penguin Young Readers Group.
McPhail, David. I Promise. 2017. (ENG., Illus.). 40p. (J). (gr. -1-3). 16.99 *(978-0-316-29787-5(9))* Little Brown & Co.
Meade, L. A Little Mother to the Others. 2006. pap. 36.99 *(978-1-4219-7036-3(8))* IndyPublish.com.
Mellor, Christie. You Look Fine, Really. 2010. (ENG.). 256p. 22.99 *(978-0-06-123825-3(2)*, Morrow, William & Co.) HarperCollins Pubs.
Melmed, Laura Krauss. Before We Met. Tsong, Jing Jing, illus. 2016. (ENG.). 32p. (J). (gr. -1-3). 17.99 *(978-1-4424-4156-9(9)*, Beach Lane Bks.) Beach Lane Bks.
Mendelsohn, Jeffrey. Grumpalina. 2012. (ENG.). 30p. (J). 25.95 *(978-1-4327-7830-9(7))* Outskirts Pr., Inc.
Merrick, Laurie K. Mama, Don't! Eremeyev, Margarita, illus. 2008. 20p. per. 24.95 *(978-1-4241-9868-9(2))* America Star Bks.
Miller, Victoria, illus. Flowers for Mami Unicorn! 2010. (Dora the Explorer Ser.). (ENG.). 24p. (J). (gr. -1-2). pap. 3.99 *(978-1-4169-9064-2(X)*, Simon Spotlight/Nickelodeon) Simon Spotlight/Nickelodeon.
Milligan, Domino. The Sandman. Spiller, Michael, illus. 2008. 16p. pap. 24.95 *(978-1-60703-728-6(9))* America Star Bks.
Milord, Susan. If I Could. Denise, Christopher, illus. 2009. (ENG.). 32p. (J). (gr. k-k). 15.99 *(978-0-7636-4342-3(4))* Candlewick Pr.
Mitton, Tony. The Somethingosaur. Ayto, Russell, illus. 2014. (ENG.). 32p. (J). 17.99 *(978-0-00-758395-9(8)*, HarperCollins Children's Bks.) HarperCollins Pubs. Ltd. GBR. Dist: HarperCollins Pubs.
Mommy You're My Hero. 2nd ed. 2005. (J). bds. 12.99 *(978-0-9729264-3-0(7)*, Books for Brats) Little Redhaired Girl Publishing, Inc.
Moneer, Simi. Once upon a Time: Part (1) 2012. (Illus.). 92p. pap. 35.08 *(978-1-4685-0353-1(7))* AuthorHouse.
Monreal, Jeannie. What Will I Be? Asked Little Miss Christina Magee. 2010. 30p. pap. 12.99 *(978-1-60860-791-4(7)*, Eloquent Bks.) Strategic Book Publishing & Rights Agency (SBPRA).
Moore, Diane. Aniville Tales Presents: O. C.'s Big Lesson. 2009. 15p. (J). pap. 12.95 *(978-1-4327-3630-9(2))* Outskirts Pr., Inc.
Moore, Julianne. My Mom Is a Foreigner, but Not to Me. So, Meilo, illus. 2013. (ENG.). 40p. (J). (gr. k-3). 16.99 *(978-1-4521-0792-9(0))* Chronicle Bks. LLC.
Moore, Rita M. Big Bell Goes Shopping. 2005. (J). pap. 8.00 *(978-0-8059-6514-8(9))* Dorrance Publishing Co., Inc.
Morgan, Cythia. The Day I Met You & You Met Me! Cable, Annette, illus. 2008. 32p. pap. 5.95 *(978-0-9802497-0-5(8))* King'S Land Pr. Inc.
Morgan, Mary. Pip Sits. 2017. (I Like to Read(r) Ser.). (ENG., Illus.). 24p. (J). (gr. -1-3). 14.95 *(978-0-8234-3676-7(4))* Holiday Hse., Inc.
—Sleep Tight, Little Mouse. Morgan, Mary, illus. 2015. (ENG., Illus.). 32p. (J). (gr. -1-2). bds. 6.99 *(978-0-553-49829-5(0)*, Knopf Bks. for Young Readers) Random Hse. Children's Bks.
Morris, C. J. The Stone Children. 2005. (YA). per. 13.95 *(978-1-58597-314-9(9))* Leathers Publishing.
Morris, Deborah K. Here I Am Look at Me! Morris, Douglas, illus. 2010. 36p. pap. 13.95 *(978-1-60911-739-9(5)*, Eloquent Bks.) Strategic Book Publishing & Rights Agency (SBPRA).
Moses, Antoinette. The Girl at the Window. 2007. (Cambridge English Readers Ser.). (ENG., Illus.). 32p. pap. 8.50 *(978-0-521-70585-1(1))* Cambridge Univ. Pr.
Mukherjee, Aiswarya & S., Bijan, illus. My Family! ABCs with Keesha. 2011. (J). pap. 2.99 *(978-0-9767273-9-2(0))* Dodi Pr.
Muldrow, Diane & Golden Books Staff. Where Do Giggles Come From? Kennedy, Anne, illus. 2011. (Little Golden Book Ser.). (ENG.). 24p. (J). (gr. -1-2). 4.99 *(978-0-375-86133-8(5)*, Golden Bks.) Random Hse. Children's Bks.
Munsch, Robert. Love You Forever Pop-Up Edition. McGraw, Sheila, illus. 2017. (ENG.). 14p. (J). (gr. -1-1). 24.95 ***(978-1-77085-965-4(9)***, 9781770859654) Firefly Bks., Ltd.
Murphy, Mary. Are You My Mommy? Murphy, Mary, illus. 2015. (ENG., Illus.). 16p. (J). (gr. -1 — 1). bds. 6.99 *(978-0-7636-7372-7(2))* Candlewick Pr.
—A Kiss Like This. Murphy, Mary, illus. 2012. (ENG., Illus.). 32p. (J). (gr. k-k). 12.99 *(978-0-7636-6182-3(1))* Candlewick Pr.
Murphy, Mary Elizabeth. I Kissed the Baby! Murphy, Mary Elizabeth, illus. 2004. (ENG., Illus.). 24p. (J). (— 1). bds. 6.99 *(978-0-7636-2443-9(8))* Candlewick Pr.
Nethaway, Misty. I Know My Mommy Loves Me. 2008. 17p. pap. 24.95 *(978-1-60672-475-0(4))* America Star Bks.
Nia, Nikki. Mommy's Love. 2007. 19.95 *(978-0-9792151-0-0(2))* Global Pr.
Numeroff, Laura Joffe & Munsinger, Lynn. Nighty-Night, Cooper. Munsinger, Lynn, illus. 2013. (ENG., Illus.). 32p. (J). (gr. -1-3). 16.99 *(978-0-547-40205-5(8))* Houghton Mifflin Harcourt Publishing Co.
O'Connor, Crystal Ball. Gift/ Book Combo. Hollinger, Valerie Bunch, illus. 2005. (J). 25.00 *(978-0-9774038-0-6(7))* Monarch Pubs.
—Jake & the Migration of the Monarch. Hollinger, Valerie Bunch, illus. 2005. 32p. (J). 17.95 *(978-0-615-12659-3(6))* Monarch Pubs.
—Jake y la Migraci'on de la Monarca. Brenes-Sotela, Guillermo J. & Quave, Gloria Martinez, trs. from ENG. Hollinger, Valerie Bunch, illus. 2005. (SPA.). (J). 17.95 *(978-0-9774038-2-0(3))* Monarch Pubs.
Oelschlager, Vanita. A Tale of Two Mommies. Blanc, Mike, illus. 2011. (ENG.). 40p. (J). (gr. -1-3). 15.95 *(978-0-9826366-4-0(0))*; pap. 8.95 *(978-0-9826366-7-1(9))* VanitaBooks.
Ohlin, Nancy. Beauty. 2013. (ENG., Illus.). 208p. (YA). (gr. 7). pap. 9.99 *(978-1-4424-7265-5(0)*, Simon Pulse) Simon Pulse.
Osterhold, Jared, illus. Cooks up a Surprise. 2011. (Olivia TV Tie-In Ser.). (ENG.). 24p. (J). (gr. -1-2). pap. 3.99 *(978-1-4424-1384-9(0)*, Simon Spotlight) Simon Spotlight.
Ostermann, Riley. So Big. 2009. 24p. pap. 12.00 *(978-1-60693-970-3(X)*, Eloquent Bks.) Strategic Book Publishing & Rights Agency (SBPRA).
Palazzolo, Gail M. Mommy, How Can We Catch the Moon? 2008. 15p. pap. 24.95 *(978-1-60672-864-2(4))* America Star Bks.
Parragon Staff, ed. Corderito. 2010. pap. 5.95 *(978-1-4054-4914-4(4))* Parragon, Inc.
Patricelli, Leslie. Tubby. Patricelli, Leslie, illus. 2010. (Leslie Patricelli Board Bks.). (ENG., Illus.). 28p. (J). (— 1). bds. 6.99 *(978-0-7636-4567-0(2))* Candlewick Pr.
Pauly, Natalie. Mommy Mayhem. 2009. (Illus.). 28p. pap. 13.99 *(978-1-4389-6254-2(1))* AuthorHouse.
Pendleton, Claudette M. I'm Mommy's Little Helper. Scott, Christopher L., illus. 2012. 46p. 24.95 *(978-1-4626-9303-0(2))* America Star Bks.
Penn, Audrey. Chester Raccoon & the Acorn Full of Memories. Gibson, Barbara L., illus. 2009. (Kissing Hand Ser.). (ENG.). 32p. (J). (gr. -1-3). 16.95 *(978-1-933718-29-3(3))* Tanglewood Pr.
—A Pocket Full of Kisses. Gibson, Barbara Leonard, illus. 2004. (New Child & Family Press Titles Ser.). 32p. (gr. -1-1). 16.95 *(978-0-87868-894-4(3)*, 8943, Child & Family Pr.) Child Welfare League of America, Inc.
—A Pocket Full of Kisses. Gibson, Barbara Leonard, illus. 2006. (Kissing Hand Ser.). (ENG.). 32p. (J). (gr. -1-3). 16.95 *(978-1-933718-02-6(1))* Tanglewood Pr.
Perlman, Willa. Pocket Kisses. McDonald, Jill, illus. 2011. (ENG.). 14p. (J). (gr. -1-17). 7.99 *(978-0-316-07787-3(9))* Little, Brown Bks. for Young Readers.
Peterson, Willa. It's a Mommy Day! 2011. 28p. pap. 13.99 *(978-1-4634-3592-9(4))* AuthorHouse.
Phyllarry (Rittmueller), Kathryn. Beauregart the Bear. 2009. (ENG., Illus.). 64p. (J). 12.95 *(978-0-943972-80-0(9))* Homestead Publishing.
Pick Me up, Mama! 2014. (ENG., Illus.). 34p. (J). (gr. -1-k). bds. 5.99 *(978-1-4814-1633-7(2)*, Little Simon) Little Simon.
Pignataro, Anna. Our Love Grows. 2016. (ENG.). 24p. (J). (-4). 16.99 *(978-1-4926-3418-8(2)*, 9781492634188, Sourcebooks Jabberwocky) Sourcebooks, Inc.
Pitts, Daphne. What Makes God Laugh. 2012. 30p. 25.99 *(978-1-62419-299-9(8))*; pap. 15.99 *(978-1-62419-298-2(X))* Salem Author Services.
Platt, Cynthia. Little Bit of Love. Whitty, Hannah, illus. 2011. (ENG.). 32p. (J). (gr. -1-2). pap. 7.95 *(978-1-58925-426-8(0))* Tiger Tales.
—A Little Bit of Love. Whitty, Hannah, illus. 2011. (ENG.). 32p. (J). (gr. -1-2). 15.95 *(978-1-58925-095-6(8))* Tiger Tales.
Polacco, Patricia. Mommies Say Shhh! Polacco, Patricia, illus. 2007. (ENG., Illus.). 32p. (J). (gr. -1 — 1). bds. 6.99 *(978-0-399-24720-0(3)*, Philomel Bks.) Penguin Young Readers Group.
Potvin, Amy K. I Miss Daddy. 2009. 28p. pap. 13.99 *(978-1-4259-1705-0(4))* AuthorHouse.
Propaganda, Amanda. People Flavors. 2006. (Illus.). (J). 6.00 *(978-1-60149-000-1(3))* Punkin Pr.
Publications International Ltd. Staff, creator. Mother Goose. 2007. (Pop-up Treasury Ser.). (Illus.). 16p. (J). (gr. -1-3). 12.98 *(978-1-4127-8833-5(1))* Publications International, Ltd.
Quintart, Natalie. Mama Bear. Blanchart, Stephanie, illus. 2005. (Tiger Tales Ser.). 32p. (J). (gr. -1-2). 6.95 *(978-1-58925-394-0(9))* Tiger Tales.
Raab, Brigitte. Mama, I Can't Sleep. Olten, Manuela, illus. 2012. (ENG.). 32p. (J). (gr. -1-k). 16.95 *(978-1-61608-965-8(2)*, 608965, Sky Pony Pr.) Skyhorse Publishing Co., Inc.
Racek, Jennifer. Cadberry's Letters. 2008. 33p. 13.90 *(978-1-4357-0566-1(1))* Lulu Pr., Inc.
Ramos, Angelica. If My Mommy Was an Octopus. 2008. 12p. pap. 24.95 *(978-1-60563-821-8(8))* PublishAmerica, Inc.
Rankin, Joan E. First Day. Rankin, Joan E., illus. 2007. (ENG., Illus.). 32p. (J). (gr. -1-2). 10.99 *(978-1-4169-6848-1(2)*, Simon & Schuster/Paula Wiseman Bks.) Simon & Schuster/Paula Wiseman Bks.
Raquel, Israel & Sissom, Carol. Help Mommy Clean-Up! 2006. (Help Mommy Clen-Up! Ser.: Vol. 1). (Illus.). 16p. (J). mass mkt. 7.99 *(978-1-4243-2034-9(8))* Independent Publisher Services.
Reed, Jennifer Bond. That's a Lot of Love. Houdeshell, Jennifer Thomas, illus. 2011. 16p. pap. 9.95 *(978-1-61633-172-6(0))* Guardian Angel Publishing, Inc.
Rex, Michael. Runaway Mummy: A Petrifying Parody. 2012. (ENG.). 32p. (J). (gr. -1-k). pap. 6.99 *(978-0-14-242121-5(9)*, Puffin Books) Penguin Young Readers Group.
—The Runaway Mummy: A Petrifying Parody. 2012. lib. bdg. 17.20 *(978-0-606-26086-2(2)*, Turtleback) Turtleback Bks.
Reyes, S. L. Mommy Does a Lot So I Want to Too, 1 vol. Taylor, Amber, illus. 2010. 30p. 24.95 *(978-1-4489-5420-9(7))* PublishAmerica, Inc.
Reynolds, Alison. Why I Love My Mom. Geddes, Serena, illus. 2015. (ENG.). 22p. (J). (gr. -1-1). 9.99 *(978-1-4998-0020-3(7))* Little Bee Books Inc.
Richards, Dan. Can One Balloon Make an Elephant Fly? Newman, Jeff, illus. 2016. (ENG.). 40p. (J). (gr. -1-3). 17.99 *(978-1-4424-5215-2(3))* Simon & Schuster Bks. For Young Readers.
Richards, Dawn. My Mommy Is Magic. Massey, Jane, illus. 2015. (ENG.). 32p. (J). (gr. -1-k). 8.99 *(978-0-7641-6757-7(X))* Barron's Educational Series, Inc.
Richmond, Marianne. Oh, the Things My Mom Will Do. 2013. (ENG., Illus.). 32p. (J). (-2). 9.99 *(978-1-4022-8215-7(X)*, 9781402282157); 16.99 *(978-1-4022-8233-1(8))* Sourcebooks, Inc. (Sourcebooks Jabberwocky).
Richmond, Marianne R. I Wished for You: An Adoption Story. 2008. (ENG., Illus.). 40p. (J). (gr. -1-3). 15.95 *(978-1-934082-06-5(6)*, Marianne Richmond Studios, Inc.) Sourcebooks, Inc.
—You Are My Wish Come True. 2008. (ENG., Illus.). 40p. (J). (gr. -1-3). 15.95 *(978-1-934082-25-6(2)*, Marianne Richmond Studios, Inc.) Sourcebooks, Inc.
Riebel, Jessica Mire. Katrina & the Rinky-Dink Sewing Machine. Herpin, K. K., illus. 2008. 32p. pap. 24.95 *(978-1-60813-545-5(4))* America Star Bks.
Rigo, L. Little Cow. 2011. (Look at Me Bks.). (ENG., Illus.). 10p. (J). bds. 7.99 *(978-0-7641-6446-0(5))* Barron's Educational Series, Inc.
—Little Owl. 2011. (Look at Me Bks.). (ENG., Illus.). 10p. (J). bds. 8.99 *(978-0-7641-6447-7(3))* Barron's Educational Series, Inc.
—Little Pony. 2011. (Look at Me Bks.). (ENG., Illus.). 10p. (J). bds. 8.99 *(978-0-7641-6448-4(1))* Barron's Educational Series, Inc.
—Little Reindeer. 2011. (Look at Me Bks.). (ENG., Illus.). 10p. (J). bds. 7.99 *(978-0-7641-6450-7(3))* Barron's Educational Series, Inc.
Rigo, L., illus. Little Duckling. 2011. (Look at Me Bks.). 10p. (J). bds. 7.99 *(978-0-7641-6425-5(2))* Barron's Educational Series, Inc.
—Little Elephant. 2011. (Look at Me Bks.). 10p. (J). bds. 8.99 *(978-0-7641-6426-2(0))* Barron's Educational Series, Inc.
—Little Lamb. 2011. (Look at Me Bks.). 10p. (J). (gr. -1). bds. 7.99 *(978-0-7641-6427-9(9))* Barron's Educational Series, Inc.
—Little Monkey. 2011. (Look at Me Bks.). 10p. (J). bds. 7.99 *(978-0-7641-6428-6(7))* Barron's Educational Series, Inc.
Rinker, Sherri Duskey. Silly Wonderful You. McDonnell, Patrick, illus. 2016. 40p. (J). (gr. -1-3). 17.99 *(978-0-06-227105-1(9))* HarperCollins Pubs.
Ritchie, Kate. I Just Couldn't Wait to Meet You. Somerville, Hannah, illus. 2015. (ENG.). 32p. (J). (-k). 22.99 *(978-0-85798-970-3(7))* Random Hse. Australia AUS. Dist: Independent Pubs. Group.
Robaard, Jedda, illus. A Little Book about Me & My Mom. 2014. (ENG.). 24p. (J). (gr. 1-5). 7.99 *(978-0-7641-6671-6(9))* Barron's Educational Series, Inc.
Robert, Nadine. Joseph Fipps. Godbout, Geneviève, illus. 2014. (ENG.). 64p. (J). (gr. -1-2). 16.95 *(978-1-59270-117-9(5))* Enchanted Lion Bks., LLC.
Romano, Melissa. Mama, Lions Don't Listen. 2008. 24p. pap. 11.99 *(978-1-4343-9907-6(9))* AuthorHouse.
Romeo, Fran & Romeo, Fran. Once upon A Dream. 2007. (ENG., Illus.). 18p. 14.99 *(978-0-8249-5901-2(9)*, Ideal Pubns.) Worthy Publishing.
Ron, Berry. Mommy Do You Love Me. 2009. (ENG.). 20p. bds. 5.99 *(978-0-8249-1422-6(8)*, Ideal Pubns.) Worthy Publishing.
Root, Phyllis. Big Momma Makes the World. Oxenbury, Helen, illus. 2007. (ENG.). 48p. (J). (gr. -1-3). pap. 7.99 *(978-0-7636-2600-6(7))* Candlewick Pr.
—Flip, Flap, Fly! A Book for Babies Everywhere. Walker, David, illus. 2011. (ENG.). 32p. (J). (gr. -1 — 1). bds. 6.99 *(978-0-7636-5325-5(X))* Candlewick Pr.
Roper, Shannon L. Mommy's Garden. 2012. 26p. 24.95 *(978-1-4626-5327-0(8))* America Star Bks.
Rose, Deborah Lee. Someone's Sleepy. Andreasen, Dan, illus. 2013. (ENG.). 32p. (J). (gr. -1-k). 16.95 *(978-1-4197-0539-7(3)*, Abrams Bks. for Young Readers) Abrams, Inc.
Rosland, Linsey. How Much Do I Love You? 2012. 20p. pap. 14.99 *(978-1-4567-4880-7(7))* AuthorHouse.
Roth, Carol. Will You Still Love Me? Howarth, Daniel, illus. 2011. (ENG.). 16p. (J). (gr. -1 — 1). bds. 7.99 *(978-0-8075-9116-1(5))* Whitman, Albert & Co.
Roth, Kapra Lynn. The Healing Bugs. 2008. 24p. pap. 24.95 *(978-1-60703-169-7(8))* America Star Bks.
Russell, B. M. My Friend Bianca. 2010. 32p. 13.95 *(978-1-4497-0168-0(X)*, WestBow Pr.) Author Solutions, Inc.
Ryder, Joanne. Bear of My Heart. Moore, Margie, illus. 2009. (ENG.). 32p. (J). (gr. -1 — 1). bds. 9.99 *(978-1-4169-5472-9(4)*, Little Simon) Little Simon.
Sagendorph, Jean. Starry Night, Hold Me Tight. Siebold, Kim, illus. 2015. (ENG.). 18p. (J). (gr. -1-17). bds. 6.95 *(978-0-7624-5853-0(4)*, Running Pr. Kids) Running Pr. Bk. Pubs.
Sakai, Komako. The Snow Day. 2009. (J). pap. *(978-0-545-01322-2(4)*, Levine, Arthur A. Bks.) Scholastic, Inc.
Sala, Laurenne. You Made Me a Mother. Glasser, Robin Preiss, illus. 2016. 32p. (J). (gr. -1-3). 15.99 *(978-0-06-235886-8(3))* HarperCollins Pubs.
Salzano, Tammi. I Love You Just the Way You Are. Grey, Ada, illus. 2014. (ENG.). 32p. (J). (gr. -1-3). 16.99 *(978-1-58925-161-8(X))* Tiger Tales.
Samuels, Gregory Robert. Mommy, Where Does Everything Come From? Brennan, Craig, illus. 2008. 11p. pap. 24.95 *(978-1-60610-437-8(3))* America Star Bks.
Sandau, Carol E. Prairie Patchwork. 2012. 88p. (gr. 4-6). pap. 9.95 *(978-1-4759-4807-3(7))* iUniverse, Inc.
Sands, Monty. King of Nine Mile Canyon. 2008. 124p. 11.99 *(978-0-615-25788-4(7))* Sands, Monty.
Sanna, Francesca. The Journey. Sanna, Francesca, illus. 2016. (ENG., Illus.). 48p. (J). (gr. -1-2). 17.95 *(978-1-909263-99-4(0))* Flying Eye Bks. GBR. Dist: Consortium Bk. Sales & Distribution.
Schad, Kristine. Do You Love Me Best? Timmons, Gayle, illus. 2007. 40p. (J). lib. bdg. 23.95 *(978-1-58374-156-6(9))* Chicago Spectrum Pr.
Schulz, Kathy. I Need a Little Help. Iosa, Ann, illus. 2011. (Rookie Ready to Learn — All about Me! Ser.). 32p. (J). (gr. -1-k). lib. bdg. 25.00 *(978-0-531-26526-0(9)*, Children's Pr.) Scholastic Library Publishing.
—Necesito una Ayudita. Iosa, Ann, illus. 2011. (Rookie Ready to Learn Español Ser.). (SPA.). 32p. (J). pap. 5.95 *(978-0-531-26782-0(2))*; lib. bdg. 23.00 *(978-0-531-26114-9(X))* Scholastic Library Publishing. (Children's Pr.).
Scott, Ann Herbert. En Las Piernas de Mamá. Coalson, Glo, illus. 2007.Tr. of On Mother's Lap. (SPA & ENG.). 14p. (J). (gr. k — 1). bds. 5.95 *(978-0-618-75247-8(1))* Houghton Mifflin Harcourt Publishing Co.
Seif Simpson, Martha. What NOT to Give Your Mom on Mother's Day, 0 vols. 2013. (ENG.). 24p. (J). (gr. -1-2). 12.99 *(978-1-4778-1647-9(X)*, 9781477816479, Amazon Children's Publishing) Amazon Publishing.

M
N
O

Senir, Mirik & Shubow, Mary Jane. When I First Held You: A Lullaby from Israel. 2009. (J). lib. bdg. 17.95 *(978-0-7613-5096-5(9)*, Kar-Ben Publishing) Lerner Publishing Group.

Sewell, Jaime. When Mommy Went on Strike. 2010. 28p. pap. 15.49 *(978-1-4490-8726-5(4))* AuthorHouse.

Shaffer, Jennifer. I Want to Play! 2012. 26p. 24.95 *(978-1-4626-5779-7(6))* America Star Bks.

Shanghai Animation Studio Staff & Tang, Sanmu. Tadpoles Looking for Their Mother. Xiaozhen, Wu, tr. from CHI. 2010. (Favorite Children's Ser.). (ENG., Illus.). 32p. (J). (gr. -1-3). pap. 5.95 *(978-1-60220-972-5(3))* BetterLink Pr., Inc.

Shaw, Stephanie. Piece by Piece. Daigneault, Sylvie, illus. 2017. (ENG.). 32p. (J). (gr. 1-4). 16.99 ***(978-1-58536-999-7(3)***, 204318) Sleeping Bear Pr.

Shea, Bob. Dinosaur vs. Mommy. Shea, Bob, illus. 2015. (Dinosaur vs. Book Ser.). (ENG., Illus.). 40p. (J). (gr. -1-k). 16.99 *(978-1-4231-6086-1(X))* Hyperion Bks. for Children.

Sheehy-Culhane, Roisin. WHEN MAMA GOES to WORK: DEVIN's STORY. 2006. (ENG.). 32p. per. 19.99 *(978-1-4257-0596-1(0))* Xlibris Corp.

Shepherd, Melissa L. On Mother's Day. 2012. 24p. pap. 14.93 *(978-1-4669-1165-9(4))* Trafford Publishing.

Sherwood, Mary Marth. The History of Lucy Clare. 2004. reprint ed. pap. 15.95 *(978-1-4191-6620-4(4))* Kessinger Publishing, LLC.

Sherwood, Mary Martha. The History of Lucy Clare. 2004. reprint ed. pap. 1.99 *(978-1-4192-6620-1(9))* Kessinger Publishing, LLC.

Sigmon-Heck, Christina. A Smile for Only You! 2012. 24p. 24.95 *(978-1-4626-6197-8(1))* America Star Bks.

Sills, Kathy & Sills, Karen. Feelings, Feelings, Feelings. 2012. 19p. 19.00 *(978-1-4349-8743-3(4)*, RoseDog Bks.) Dorrance Publishing Co., Inc.

Silva, Abbey. She Came to Heal. 2008. 136p. pap. 11.50 *(978-1-4389-1086-4(X))* AuthorHouse.

Simons, Paulina. I Love My Baby Because... Thomas, Cassia, illus. 2015. (ENG.). 24p. (J). 17.99 *(978-0-00-810211-1(2)*, HarperCollins Children's Bks.) HarperCollins Pubs. Ltd. GBR. Dist: HarperCollins Pubs.

—Poppet Gets Two Big Brothers. Thomas, Cassia, illus. 2015. (ENG.). 32p. (J). 17.99 *(978-0-00-811041-3(7)*, HarperCollins Children's Bks.) HarperCollins Pubs. Ltd. GBR. Dist: HarperCollins Pubs.

Skougaard, Shari. Grumpy Goo, I Love You. 2009. 24p. pap. 13.50 *(978-1-60860-454-8(3)*, Eloquent Bks.) Strategic Book Publishing & Rights Agency (SBPRA).

Sliwerski, Jessica Reid. Cancer Hates Kisses. Song, Mika, illus. 2017. (ENG.). 40p. (J). (-k). 17.99 ***(978-0-7352-2781-1(0)***, Dial Bks) Penguin Young Readers Group.

Smith, Andrea Neile. Who Aiden Was. 2012. 38p. pap. 14.95 *(978-1-60594-879-9(9))* Aeon Publishing Inc.

Smith, Joye. What Does It Mean to Be Poor? 2005. (Illus.). 30p. (J). 8.99 *(978-1-56309-880-2(6))* Woman's Missionary Union.

Smith, Maggie. And I Have You: A Book of Mothers & Babies. 2017. (ENG.). 32p. (J). (gr. -1-2). 17.99 *(978-0-553-51019-5(3)*, Knopf Bks. for Young Readers) Random Hse. Children's Bks.

Smith, Rosie. My Mom's the Best. Whatley, Bruce, illus. 2013. (J). *(978-0-545-60361-4(7))* Scholastic, Inc.

—My Mom's the Best. Whatley, Bruce, illus. 2017. (ENG.). 24p. (J). (gr. -1). bds. 6.95 ***(978-1-4549-2480-7(2))*** Sterling Publishing Co., Inc.

Smith, Sarah, illus. Where's My Mommy? 2009. (J). *(978-0-7607-8404-4(3))* Barnes & Noble, Inc.

Soffer, Allison & Sarnoff, Allison. Apple Days: A Rosh Hashanah Story. McMahon, Bob, illus. 2014. (ENG.). 32p. (J). (gr. -1-2). 7.95 *(978-1-4677-1204-0(3)*, Kar-Ben Publishing) Lerner Publishing Group.

Soffer, Allison Sarnoff. Apple Days: A Rosh Hashanah Story. McMahon, Bob, illus. 2014. (ENG.). 32p. (J). (gr. -1-2). 17.95 *(978-1-4677-1203-3(5))* Lerner Publishing Group.

Sperring, Mark. The Shape of My Heart. Paterson, Alys, illus. (ENG.). 32p. (J). 2015. (gr. -1). bds. 7.99 *(978-1-68119-017-4(6)*, 9781681190174) 2012. lib. bdg. 15.89 *(978-1-59990-963-9(4)*, 9781599909639) 2012. (gr. -1-k). 16.99 *(978-1-59990-962-2(6)*, 9781599909622) Bloomsbury Publishing USA. (Bloomsbury USA Childrens).

Spinelli, Eileen. I Like Noisy, Mom Likes Quiet. Halverson, Lydia, illus. 2006. (ENG.). 32p. (J). (gr. -1-3). 8.95 *(978-0-8249-5517-5(X)*, 1256103, Ideal Pubns.) Worthy Publishing.

—Two to Cuddle. Logan, Laura, illus. 2009. (ENG.). 20p. (J). bds. 6.99 *(978-0-8249-1824-8(X)*, Ideal Pubns.) Worthy Publishing.

Spinelli, Jerry. Mama Seeton's Whistle. 2015. (ENG., Illus.). 40p. (J). (gr. -1-3). 17.00 *(978-0-316-12217-7(3))* Little, Brown Bks. for Young Readers.

Spooner, Carol. I Love You Best. 2012. 24p. pap. 24.95 *(978-1-4626-5803-9(2))* America Star Bks.

Stanwood, Jane. Squeak's Bus Company. 2008. 28p. per. 11.95 *(978-1-4327-1964-7(5))* Outskirts Pr., Inc.

Stein, David Ezra. Pouch! Stein, David Ezra, illus. 2010. (Rise & Shine Ser.). (ENG., Illus.). 32p. (C). (gr. -1-k). 25.95 *(978-0-399-25051-4(4))* National Geographic School Publishing, Inc.

—Pouch! Stein, David Ezra, illus. 2012. (ENG., Illus.). 32p. (J). (gr. -1 — 1). bds. 7.99 *(978-0-399-25738-4(1)*, Nancy Paulsen Books) Penguin Young Readers Group.

Stevens, Jennifer. Love You More. 2013. 24p. pap. 24.95 *(978-1-63004-655-2(8))* America Star Bks.

Stewart, Shawna. Amazing Tails of Zomber Doodles & Buttons, 1 vol. 2010. 30p. pap. 24.95 *(978-1-4489-7913-4(7))* PublishAmerica, Inc.

Stone, Julia. Little Bear's Sparkly Christmas. Muss, Angela, illus. 2014. (ENG.). 6p. (J). (gr. -1-k). 8.99 *(978-0-7459-6262-7(9))* Lion Hudson PLC GBR. Dist: Independent Pubs. Group.

Stott, Ann. Always. Phelan, Matt, illus. 2008. (ENG.). 32p. (J). (gr. k-k). 15.99 *(978-0-7636-3232-8(5))* Candlewick Pr.

—I'll Be There. Phelan, Matt, illus. 2011. (ENG.). 32p. (J). (gr. -1-2). 14.99 *(978-0-7636-4711-7(X))* Candlewick Pr.

Stram, Dawn. Fat Ladies Shouldn't Have Orange Hair! 2011. 56p. pap. 31.99 *(978-1-4568-5804-9(1))* Xlibris Corp.

Streltski, Mies & Hartog, Arnold. Woobie Dreams Hc. 2006. (ENG., Illus.). 32p. (J). 16.95 *(978-1-59249-554-2(0))* Soundprints.

Summer, Laura LeClair. Mommy will always come Home. White, Kathy, illus. 2006. 35p. (J). per. 24.95 *(978-1-4276-0158-2(5))* Aardvark Global Publishing.

Sundaram, Renuka. Sammy, the Galapagos Sea Lion. 2011. 32p. pap. 15.00 *(978-1-61286-015-2(X))* Avid Readers Publishing Group.

Sutherland, Eileen. Mom & the Polka-Dot Boo-Boo: A Gentle Story Explaining Breast Cancer to a Young Child. Sutherland, Eileen & Sutherland, Maggie, illus. 2007. (ENG.). 24p. (J). (gr. -1-k). 14.95 *(978-0-944235-87-4(5)*, 9780944235874) American Cancer Society, Inc.

Sutton, Jane. What's up with This Chicken?, 1 vol. Welling, Peter, illus. 2015. (ENG.). 32p. (J). (gr. k-3). 16.99 *(978-1-4556-2085-2(8))* Pelican Publishing Co., Inc.

Swain, Cynthia. The Birthday Flowers. 2006. (Early Explorers Ser.). (J). pap. *(978-1-4108-6025-5(6))* Benchmark Education Co.

Swinburne, Stephen R. Safe in a Storm. Bell, Jennifer, illus. 2016. (J). *(978-0-545-66987-0(1))*; (ENG.). 32p. (gr. -1-k). 10.99 *(978-0-545-86792-4(4))* Scholastic, Inc.

Tafuri, Nancy. Five Little Chicks. Tafuri, Nancy, illus. 2011. (Classic Board Bks.). (ENG., Illus.). 34p. (J). (gr. -1 — 1). bds. 7.99 *(978-1-4424-0722-0(0)*, Little Simon) Little Simon.

—Five Little Chicks. Tafuri, Nancy, illus. 2006. (ENG., Illus.). 32p. (J). (gr. -1-3). 16.99 *(978-0-689-87342-3(5)*, Simon & Schuster Bks. For Young Readers) Simon & Schuster Bks. For Young Readers.

—Whose Chick Are You? Tafuri, Nancy, illus. 2007. (ENG., Illus.). 40p. (J). (gr. -1-k). 16.99 *(978-0-06-082514-0(6)*, Greenwillow Bks.) HarperCollins Pubs.

Thiel Annie. The Playdate Kids Dakota's Mom Goes to the Hospital 2ED 2007. 2007. 32p. 12.95 *(978-1-933721-30-9(8))*; pap. 6.95 *(978-1-933721-26-2(X))* Playdate Kids Publishing.

Thiel, Annie & Fanning, Tena. Dakota Gets Lost. Edwards, William M., illus. 2007. (Playdate Kids: Let's Be Friends! Ser.). 27p. (J). (gr. -1-3). per. 6.95 *(978-1-933721-20-0(0))* Playdate Kids Publishing.

Thomas Nelson Publishing Staff. Mommy Loves You So Much, 1 vol. Parry, Jo, illus. 2015. (ENG.). 20p. (J). bds. 9.99 *(978-0-529-12338-1(X))* Nelson, Thomas Inc.

Thomas, Pam. Mamarswpial. 2005. (WEL., Illus.). 128p. pap. *(978-0-86243-360-4(6))* Y Lolfa.

Thompson, Lauren. Leap Back Home to Me. Cordell, Matthew, illus. 2011. (ENG.). 32p. (J). (gr. -1-1). 17.99 *(978-1-4169-0664-3(9)*, McElderry, Margaret K. Bks.) McElderry, Margaret K. Bks.

—Mouse's First Spring. Erdogan, Buket, illus. 2012. (Classic Board Bks.). (ENG.). 34p. (J). (gr. -1-3). bds. 7.99 *(978-1-4424-3431-8(7)*, Little Simon) Little Simon.

Thomson, Sarah L. Cub's Big World. Cepeda, Joe, illus. 2013. (ENG.). 32p. (J). (gr. -1-3). 16.99 *(978-0-544-05739-5(2))* Houghton Mifflin Harcourt Publishing Co.

Thuma, Chris. Cigarette Sue. 2008. 24p. per. 12.95 *(978-1-59858-561-2(4))* Dog Ear Publishing, LLC.

Todorov, Boriana & Todorov, Vladimir. Oliver's Tantrums. 2013. (ENG., Illus.). 34p. (J). (gr. k-4). 16.95 *(978-1-897476-67-3(1))* Simply Read Bks. CAN. Dist: Ingram Publisher Services.

Tomey, Ingrid. The Queen of Dreamland. 2004. 179p. (YA). (gr. 6-10). reprint ed. 15.00 *(978-0-7567-7151-5(X))* DIANE Publishing Co.

Tompert, Ann & Lister, Ralph. Little Fox Goes to the End of the World, 0 vols. Bryant, Laura J., illus. 2010. (ENG.). 32p. (J). (gr. -1-2). 16.99 *(978-0-7614-5703-9(8)*, 9780761457039, Amazon Children's Publishing) Amazon Publishing.

Toms, Kate. I Udderly Love You. 2009. (Kate Toms Ser.). (Illus.). 26p. (gr. -1). bds. 7.99 *(978-1-84610-990-4(6))* Make Believe Ideas GBR. Dist: Nelson, Thomas Inc.

—I Udderly Love You! 2007. (Kate Toms Ser.). (Illus.). 26p. (gr. -1). bds. 7.95 *(978-1-84610-460-2(2))* Make Believe Ideas GBR. Dist: Nelson, Thomas Inc.

Top That Publishing Staff, ed. Who's My Mommy. 2005. 12p. bds. *(978-1-84510-067-4(0))* Top That! Publishing PLC.

Torres, Jos A. & Torres, Jose A. Joey Kanga Roo: Plays the Trumpet. 2009. 36p. pap. 15.99 *(978-1-4389-7434-7(5))* AuthorHouse.

The Trail of the Wooden Horse. 2007. 32p. pap. 4.50 *(978-0-8341-2284-0(7)*, 083-412-2847) Beacon Hill Pr. of Kansas City.

Umrigar, Thrity & Chen, Ziyue. When I Carried You in My Belly. 2017. (ENG., Illus.). 40p. (J). (gr. -1-3). 16.99 *(978-0-7624-6058-8(X)*, Running Pr.) Running Pr. Bk. Pubs.

Vagnozzi, Barbara, illus. Jack & the Beanstalk. 2007. (Flip-Up Fairy Tales Ser.). (ENG.). 24p. (J). (gr. -1-2). audio compact disk *(978-1-84643-086-2(0))* Child's Play International Ltd.

van Genechten, Guido. Because I Love You So Much. 2006. (Illus.). 12p. (J). (gr. -1-3). 15.95 *(978-1-58925-794-8(4))* Tiger Tales.

—Mommies & Their Babies. 2012. (Black & White Ser.). (ENG.). 20p. (J). (gr. k — 1). bds. 9.95 *(978-1-60537-109-2(2))* Cobblestone Publishing Co.

Van Laan, Nancy. Scrubba Dub. Pons, Bernadette, illus. 2008. (ENG.). 32p. (J). (gr. -1-1). 8.99 *(978-1-4169-7859-6(3)*, Simon & Schuster/Paula Wiseman Bks.) Simon & Schuster/Paula Wiseman Bks.

Van, Muon. The Little Tree. Adinolfi, JoAnn, illus. 2015. (ENG.). 32p. (J). (gr. -1). 16.95 *(978-1-939547-19-4(9))* Creston Bks.

Velde, Marie. Laundry Day. 2007. (Illus.). (J). bds. 22.95 *(978-1-933156-17-0(1)*, Visikid Bks.) GSVQ Publishing.

Vella, Sylvia. It's Okay to Tell. 2011. 28p. 13.59 *(978-1-4567-1912-8(2))* AuthorHouse.

Verburg, Bonnie. The Kiss Box. Cole, Henry, illus. 2011. (ENG.). 32p. (J). (gr. -1-k). 16.99 *(978-0-545-11284-0(2)*, Orchard Bks.) Scholastic, Inc.

Vernick, Audrey & Scanlon, Liz Garton. Bob, Not Bob! Cordell, Matthew, illus. 2017. (ENG.). 40p. (J). (gr. -1-k). 17.99 *(978-1-4847-2302-9(3))* Disney Pr.

Vision, David, et al. My Very Breast Friend. Alcantara, Ignacio, illus. 2009. (ENG.). 40p. 17.00 *(978-0-9659538-5-6(8))* Vitally Important.

Voskoboinikov, Valery & Linnamagi, Anne. The Icicle. 2007. (POL & ENG., Illus.). 32p. (J). pap. 16.95 *(978-1-60195-100-7(0))* International Step by Step Assn.

Waddell, Martin. Owl Babies. Benson, Patrick, illus. 2015. (ENG.). 22p. (J). (— 1). bds. 6.99 *(978-0-7636-7961-3(5))* Candlewick Pr.

—Owl Babies. Benson, Patrick, illus. 2017. (ENG.). 32p. (J). (gr. -1-2). 16.99 ***(978-0-7636-9519-4(X))*** Candlewick Pr.

—Owl Babies Book & Toy Gift Set. Benson, Patrick, illus. 2016. (ENG.). (J). (-k). bds. 15.99 *(978-0-7636-8898-1(3))* Candlewick Pr.

—Owl Babies: Candlewick Storybook Animations. Benson, Patrick, illus. 2008. (Candlewick Storybook Animations Ser.). (ENG.). 32p. (J). (gr. k-k). 14.99 *(978-0-7636-3538-1(3))* Candlewick Pr.

Walker, Anna. Hurry up, Alfie! 2016. (ENG., Illus.). 24p. (J). (gr. -1-3). 14.99 *(978-0-544-58654-3(9))* Houghton Mifflin Harcourt Publishing Co.

—I Love My Mom. Walker, Anna, illus. 2010. (ENG., Illus.). 32p. (J). (gr. -1-1). 9.99 *(978-1-4169-8318-7(X)*, Simon & Schuster Bks. For Young Readers) Simon & Schuster Bks. For Young Readers.

Walker, Susan Eileen. I Know the Quigglebush Heroes. 2008. 53p. pap. 16.95 *(978-1-60672-587-0(4))* America Star Bks.

Walsh, Ann. Horse Power, 1 vol. 2007. (Orca Currents Ser.). (ENG.). (J). (gr. 5-9). 128p. pap. 9.95 *(978-1-55143-881-8(X))*; 112p. lib. bdg. 14.95 *(978-1-55143-883-2(6))* Orca Bk. Pubs. USA.

Walters, Eric. Visions. 2011. (ENG.). 208p. (J). pap. *(978-1-55455-122-4(6))* Fitzhenry & Whiteside, Ltd.

Wan, Joyce. Are You My Mommy? 2014. (ENG.). 18p. (J). (gr. -1 — 1). bds. 6.99 *(978-0-545-54047-6(X)*, Cartwheel Bks.) Scholastic, Inc.

Weiss, Ellen. I Love You, Little Monster. Arnold, Ali, illus. 2012. (ENG.). 16p. (J). (gr. -1 — 1). bds. 7.99 *(978-1-4424-2850-8(3)*, Little Simon) Little Simon.

Wells, Jason. Why Children Should Listen to Their Mothers. 2013. 28p. pap. 24.95 *(978-1-62709-489-4(X))* America Star Bks.

Wells, Rosemary. Yoko Finds Her Way. 2014. (Yoko Book Ser.). (ENG.). 32p. (J). (gr. -1-k). 16.99 *(978-1-4231-6512-5(8))* Hyperion Pr.

Weninger, Brigitte & Tharlet, Eve. Davy Loves His Mommy. 2014. (ENG., Illus.). 32p. (J). (gr. k-3). 15.95 *(978-0-7358-4164-2(0))* North-South Bks., Inc.

Wheeler, Laura C. I'll Kiss You A Promise. 2010. 24p. pap. 12.99 *(978-1-4520-0790-8(X))* AuthorHouse.

White, Gloria. Something More Important. 2013. 24p. pap. *(978-1-4602-1115-1(4))* FriesenPress.

Wilhelm, Hans. Little Whale in Deep Trouble: A Story Inspired by a True Event. 2017. (ENG., Illus.). 32p. (J). (gr. -1-2). 9.99 *(978-0-7641-6851-2(7))* Barron's Educational Series, Inc.

Willis, Jeanne. Slug Needs a Hug! Ross, Tony, illus. 2015. (ENG.). 32p. (J). (gr. -1-3). 17.99 *(978-1-4677-9317-9(5))*; 17.99 *(978-1-4677-9309-4(4))* Lerner Publishing Group.

—Upside down Babies. Reynolds, Adrian, illus. 2014. (ENG.). 32p. (J). (gr. -1-3). 16.95 *(978-1-4677-3424-0(1))* Lerner Publishing Group.

Wilson, Karma. Mama Always Comes Home. Dyer, Brooke, illus. 2007. (ENG.). 32p. (J). (gr. -1-1). pap. 6.99 *(978-0-06-057507-6(7)*, Harper Trophy) HarperCollins Pubs.

—Mama, Why? Mendez, Simon, illus. 2011. (ENG.). 40p. (J). (gr. -1-2). 16.99 *(978-1-4169-4205-4(X)*, McElderry, Margaret K. Bks.) McElderry, Margaret K. Bks.

Wilson, Sarah. Moms Are the Best! 2014. (Spongebob Squarepants Step into Reading Ser.). lib. bdg. 13.55 *(978-0-606-35203-1(1))* Turtleback Bks.

Wilt, Gerri Ann, et al. My Little One: A Mother's Lullaby. Sargent, Shannon Marie, illus. 2008. (J). *(978-0-87839-299-5(8))* North Star Pr. of St. Cloud.

Winters, Kari-Lynn. On My Walk, 1 vol. Leist, Christina, illus. 2010. (ENG.). 32p. (J). (gr. k-1). 16.95 *(978-1-896580-61-6(0))* Tradewind Bks. CAN. Dist: Orca Bk. Pubs. USA.

Wolnik, Charlotte. The Chocolate Chip Ghost. 2008. 40p. pap. 24.95 *(978-1-4241-8896-3(2))* America Star Bks.

Wood, Audrey. The Birthday Queen. Wood, Don, illus. 2013. (ENG.). 32p. (J). (gr. -1-3). 17.99 *(978-0-545-41474-6(1)*, Blue Sky Pr., The) Scholastic, Inc.

Woodson, Jacqueline. Pecan Pie Baby. Blackall, Sophie, illus. (ENG.). 32p. (J). (gr. k-3). 2013. 7.99 *(978-0-14-751128-7(3)*, Puffin Books) 2010. 16.99 *(978-0-399-23987-8(1)*, G.P. Putnam's Sons Books for Young Readers) Penguin Young Readers Group.

Wright, Gina. My Mommy Has Breast Cancer. 2009. 32p. pap. 13.49 *(978-1-4490-2150-4(6))* AuthorHouse.

Wright, Velma. Fuzz, an Impatient Chick. 2010. 12p. 12.68 *(978-1-4269-3430-8(0))* Trafford Publishing.

Yellowknife, Jessica. Spring Break Adventure. 2011. 84p. pap. 11.11 *(978-1-4269-6952-2(X))* Trafford Publishing.

Young, Michael. Portrait of a Mother. 2011. 16p. pap. 2.99 *(978-1-59955-810-3(6)*, Bonneville Bks.) Cedar Fort, Inc./CFI Distribution.

Yum, Hyewon. The Twins' Little Sister. Yum, Hyewon, illus. 2014. (ENG., Illus.). 40p. (J). (gr. -1-1). 17.99 *(978-0-374-37973-5(4)*, 9780374379735, Farrar, Straus & Giroux (BYR)) Farrar, Straus & Giroux.

MOTHER GOOSE

Greenaway, Kate. Mother Goose Coloring Book. Perkins, Nancy, illus. 2013. (Dover Coloring Bks.). (ENG.). 48p. (J). (gr. -1-8). pap. 4.99 *(978-0-486-22883-9(5))* Dover Pubns., Inc.

Hysom, Dennis Joe & Walker, Christine. Wooleycat's Musical Rhyme Time Theater. 2003. (Wooleycat's Favorite Nursery Rhymes Ser.). (Illus.). (J). pap. *(978-1-889910-26-0(0))* Tortuga Pr.

—Wooleycat's Musical Theater. Walker, Christine, illus. 2003. (Wooleycat's Favorite Nursery Rhymes Ser.). (Illus.). 32p. (J). (gr. -1-2). 18.95 incl. audio compact disk *(978-1-889910-25-3(2))* Tortuga Pr.

Provensen, Alice & Provensen, Martin. The Golden Mother Goose. 2017. (ENG.). 72p. (J). (— 1). 15.99 ***(978-1-5247-1578-6(6))***; lib. bdg. 18.99 ***(978-1-5247-1579-3(4))*** Random Hse. Children's Bks. (Golden Bks.).

MOTHER GOOSE—SONGS AND MUSIC

Beall, Pamela Conn & Nipp, Susan Hagen. Wee Sing Mother Goose, 1 vol. Guida, Lisa & Klein, Nancy Spence, illus. 2006. (Wee Sing Ser.). (ENG.). 64p. (J). (gr. -1-2). 10.99 *(978-0-8431-0485-1(6)*, Price Stern Sloan) Penguin Young Readers Group.

MOTHERS

Ashford, Kathy. Around & Back Around Again: A Metaphor, 1 vol. 2010. 48p. pap. 16.95 *(978-1-4489-5883-2(0))* America Star Bks.

Auld, Mary. Mi Mama. Coffey, Colleen & Carrillo, Consuelo, trs. from ENG. 2004. (Conoce la Familia Ser.). (SPA., Illus.). 24p. (gr. k-3). lib. bdg. 22.00 *(978-0-8368-3932-6(3)*, Gareth Stevens Learning Library) Stevens, Gareth Publishing LLLP.

—My Mom. 2004. (Meet the Family Ser.). (Illus.). 24p. (gr. k-3). lib. bdg. 22.00 *(978-0-8368-3927-2(7)*, Gareth Stevens Learning Library) Stevens, Gareth Publishing LLLP.

Barbara, Diane & Donnier, Christine. Mom & Me: A Special Book for You & Your Mom to Fill in Together & Share with Each Other. 2004. (ENG., Illus.). 48p. (J). (gr. -1-3). 16.95 *(978-0-8109-4820-4(6))* Abrams, Inc.

Bedford, David & Worthington, Leonie. Mums. 2007. (Illus.). 16p. *(978-1-921049-78-1(2))* Little Hare Bks. AUS. Dist: HarperCollins Pubs. Australia.

Campbell, Carol P. & Orr, Tamra. Frequently Asked Questions about Teen Pregnancy. 2011. (FAQ: Teen Life Ser.). (J). lib. bdg. 31.95 *(978-1-4488-4627-6(7))* Rosen Publishing Group, Inc., The.

Catt, Thessaly. My Mom. 2010. (My Family Ser.). (ENG.). 24p. (J). pap. 8.25 *(978-1-4488-1490-9(1))*; lib. bdg. 22.60 *(978-1-4488-1462-6(6))* Rosen Publishing Group, Inc., The. (PowerKids Pr.).

—My Mom(Mi Mamá) 2010. (My Family / Mi Familia Ser.). (SPA & ENG.). 24p. lib. bdg. 22.60 *(978-1-4488-0717-8(4)*, PowerKids Pr.) Rosen Publishing Group, Inc., The.

Dicker, Katie. My Mum. 2017. (Popcorn: Families Ser.). (ENG., Illus.). 24p. (J). (gr. k-2). pap. 10.99 *(978-0-7502-8882-8(5)*, Wayland) Hachette Children's Group GBR. Dist: Hachette Bk. Group.

Edgehill, S. D. To Honor Thy Mother. 2003. 380p. (YA). mass mkt. 21.95 *(978-0-9744027-0-3(2))* Cahill Publishing.

Fisanick, Christina, ed. Working Women. 2007. (Opposing Viewpoints Ser.). (ENG., Illus.). 186p. (gr. 10-12). lib. bdg. 46.45 *(978-0-7377-3771-4(9)*, LML02109-234440, Greenhaven Pr., Inc.) Cengage Gale.

Gamble, Adam & Jasper, Mark. Good Night Mommy. Kelly, Cooper, illus. 2015. (Good Night Our World Ser.). (ENG.). 20p. (J). (— 1). bds. 9.95 *(978-1-60219-230-0(8))* Good Night Bks.

Gherman, Beverly. First Mothers. Downing, Julie, illus. 2012. (ENG.). 64p. (J). (gr. 1-4). 17.99 *(978-0-547-22301-8(3))* Houghton Mifflin Harcourt Publishing Co.

Greven, Alec. How to Talk to Moms. Acedera, Kei, illus. 2009. (ENG.). 48p. (J). (gr. 1-5). 9.99 *(978-0-06-171001-8(6)*, Collins) HarperCollins Pubs.

Halteman, Laverne K. Mommy Goes to Heaven. 2003. (Illus.). (J). *(978-0-87813-612-4(6))* Christian Light Pubns., Inc.

Hammerslough, Jane. Everything You Need to Know about Teen Motherhood. 2009. (Need to Know Library). 64p. (gr. 5-5). 58.50 *(978-1-60854-090-7(1))* Rosen Publishing Group, Inc., The.

Jeffries, Joyce. I Learn from My Mom. 2016. (Things I Learn Ser.). (Illus.). 24p. (J). (gr. 1-1). pap. 8.25 *(978-1-4994-2371-6(3)*, PowerKids Pr.) Rosen Publishing Group, Inc., The.

Jenner, Caryn. My Mum. 2017. (Family World Ser.). (ENG., Illus.). 24p. (J). (gr. k-2). pap. 9.99 *(978-1-4451-5223-3(1)*, Franklin Watts) Hachette Children's Group GBR. Dist: Hachette Bk. Group.

Moore, M. Meet My Mom: Learning the M Sound. 2009. (PowerPhonics Ser.). 24p. (gr. 1-1). 39.90 *(978-1-60851-459-5(5)*, PowerKids Pr.) Rosen Publishing Group, Inc., The.

Mothers. 7.50 *(978-0-8054-5972-2(3))* B&H Publishing Group.

Newkirk, Stephanie. I'm So Madd!!! 2009. 28p. pap. 12.99 *(978-1-4389-6022-7(0))* AuthorHouse.

Nilsen, Anna. My Mum's Best. Dodd, Emma, illus. 2011. 24p. bds. *(978-1-84089-679-4(5))* Zero to Ten, Ltd.

Numeroff, Laura Joffe. What Mommies Do Best; What Daddies Do Best. Munsinger, Lynn, illus. 2006. (ENG.). 40p. (J). (gr. -1-3). 4.99 *(978-0-689-84218-4(X)*, Simon & Schuster/Paula Wiseman Bks.) Simon & Schuster/Paula Wiseman Bks.

Parr, Todd. The Mommy Book. 2016. (ENG., Illus.). 20p. (J). (gr. -1 — 1). bds. 6.99 *(978-0-316-33774-8(9))* Little, Brown Bks. for Young Readers.

Poole, H. W. Teen Parents, Vol. 12. 2016. (Families Today Ser.). (Illus.). 48p. (J). (gr. 5). 20.95 *(978-1-4222-3624-6(2))* Mason Crest.

Raatma, Lucia. Mothers Are Part of a Family. 2017. (Our Families Ser.). (ENG.). 24p. (gr. k-1). lib. bdg. 21.99 ***(978-1-5157-7465-5(1)***, Pebble Bks.) Capstone Press of Coughlan Cos.

Riehle, Mary Ann McCabe. M Is for Mom: A Child's Alphabet. Ellison, Chris, illus. 2009. (ENG.). 32p. (J). (gr. k-6). 17.95 *(978-1-58536-458-9(4))* Sleeping Bear Pr.

Schaefer, Lola M. Mothers. Saunders-Smith, Gail, ed. rev. ed. 2008. (Families Ser.). (ENG., Illus.). 24p. (gr. k-1). 21.99 *(978-1-4296-1227-2(4))*; per. 6.29 *(978-1-4296-1756-7(X))* Capstone Press of Coughlan Cos. (Pebble Bks.).

Sourcebooks. To the Best Mom Ever! 2016. (Sealed with a Kiss Ser.: 0). (ENG.). 48p. (J). (gr. 1-4). pap. 7.99 *(978-1-4926-3329-7(1))* Sourcebooks, Inc.

Stewart, Kelsey. The Best for You. 2009. 24p. pap. 12.49 *(978-1-4490-0832-1(1))* AuthorHouse.

Stewart, Sheila. Sometimes My Mom Drinks Too Much. (Kids Have Troubles Too Ser.). (Illus.). 48p. (YA). (gr. 5-18). 2010. lib. bdg. 19.95 *(978-1-4222-1704-7(3))* 2009. pap. 7.95 *(978-1-4222-1917-1(8))* Mason Crest.

MOTHERS—FICTION

Alligator Books Staff & Fabiny, Sarah. Pip Puppy Looks for Mom. Hughes, Cathy, illus. 2012. (Squeaky Board Bks.). (ENG.). 18p. (J). bds. 4.99 *(978-0-7641-6482-8(1))* Barron's Educational Series, Inc.

Andreae, Giles. I Love My Mommy. Dodd, Emma, illus. 2013. (ENG.). 26p. (J). (gr. -1-k). bds. 6.99 *(978-1-4231-6825-6(9))* Hyperion Pr.

Armstrong, Rachel. Fair Folk in Knob's End. 2013. 274p. pap. 14.99 *(978-1-60820-851-7(6))* MLR Pr., LLC.

Arno, Ronni. Dear Poppy. 2016. (Mix Ser.). (ENG., Illus.). 256p. (J). (gr. 4-8). 17.99 *(978-1-4814-3760-8(7)*, Simon &

Schuster/Paula Wiseman Bks.) Simon & Schuster/Paula Wiseman Bks.

Balian, Lorna. Mother's Mother's Day. 1 vol. 2004. (ENG., Illus.). 32p. (J). 8.95 *(978-1-932065-39-8(3))* Star Bright Bks., Inc.

Banting, Celia. I Only Said I Didn't Want You Because I Was Terrified. 2006. (I Only Said Ser.: 4). 240p. (YA). pap. 14.99 *(978-0-9786648-3-1(3))* Wighita Pr.

Barber, Barbara E. Saturday at the New You. Rich, Anna, illus. 2013. (ENG.). 32p. (J). (gr. -1-3). reprint ed. pap. 9.95 *(978-1-880000-43-4(1))* Lee & Low Bks., Inc.

Barkow, Henriette. That's My Mum. Brazell, Derek, illus. 2004. 28p. (J). (ALB & ENG.). pap. *(978-1-85269-595-8(1))*; (ENG & YOR.). pap. *(978-1-84444-381-9(7))* Mantra Lingua.

Baskin, Nora Raleigh. All We Know of Love. 2008. (ENG., Illus.). 208p. (YA). (gr. 9). 16.99 *(978-0-7636-3623-4(1))* Candlewick Pr.

Bauer, Marion Dane. My Mother Is Mine. Elwell, Peter, illus. 2009. (Classic Board Bks.). (ENG.). 36p. (J). (gr. -1-k). bds. 7.99 *(978-1-4169-6090-4(2)*, Little Simon) Little Simon.

—My Mother Is Mine. Elwell, Peter, illus. 2004. (ENG.). 40p. (J). (gr. -1-k). reprint ed. 7.99 *(978-0-689-86695-1(X)*, Simon & Schuster Bks. For Young Readers) Simon & Schuster Bks. For Young Readers.

Beasley, Kate. Gertie's Leap to Greatness. Tamaki, Jillian, illus. 2016. (ENG.). 256p. (J). 16.99 *(978-0-374-30261-0(8)*, 9780374302610, Farrar, Straus & Giroux (BYR)) Farrar, Straus & Giroux.

Beha, Eileen. The Secrets of Eastcliff-by-the-Sea: The Story of Annaliese Easterling & Throckmorton, Her Simply Remarkable Sock Monkey. Wright, Sarah Jane, illus. 2015. (ENG.). 288p. (J). (gr. 3-7). pap. 8.99 *(978-1-4424-9841-9(2)*, Beach Lane Bks.) Beach Lane Bks.

Berenstain, Stan & Berenstain, Jan. The Berenstain Bears & the Mama's Day Surprise. 2004. (First Time Books Ser.). (ENG., Illus.). 32p. (J). (gr. -1-2). pap. 4.99 *(978-0-375-81132-6(X)*, Random Hse. Bks. for Young Readers) Random Hse. Children's Bks.

A Big Surprise for Mom. 2005. (J). per. *(978-0-9765950-1-4(X))* Carlson, Debra R.

Blackmore, Charlotte Lozano. Jeanettie Is Called Retard. 1 vol. Francis, Amber Rose, illus. 2010. 34p. 24.95 *(978-1-4489-4096-7(6))* PublishAmerica, Inc.

Bonnell, Kris. Mother Animals. 2007. (J). pap. 5.95 *(978-1-933727-49-3(7))* Reading Reading Bks., LLC.

Breathed, Berkeley. Mars Needs Moms! Breathed, Berkeley, illus. 2007. (ENG., Illus.). 40p. (J). (gr. k-3). 17.99 *(978-0-399-24736-1(X)*, Philomel Bks.) Penguin Young Readers Group.

Brez, Lisa. Hickerdoodle Gets Lost. l.t. ed. 2003. (Illus.). 32p. (J). per. 6.99 *(978-0-9743758-4-7(5))* Red Engine Pr.

Brezenoff, Steven. The Case of the Missing Mom. Weber, Lisa K., illus. 2016. (Museum Mysteries Ser.). (ENG.). 128p. (gr. 2-3). 26.65 *(978-1-4965-2517-8(5))* Stone Arch Bks.

Brisson, Pat. Sometimes We Were Brave. Brassard, France, illus. 2010. (ENG.). 32p. (J). (gr. k-2). 16.95 *(978-1-59078-586-7(X))* Boyds Mills Pr.

Brown, Rena Cherry. Otter Lee Brave. 1 vol. Maidment, Mikaila, illus. 2012. (ENG.). 48p. (J). 16.99 *(978-0-7643-4155-7(3)*, 9780764341557) Schiffer Publishing, Ltd.

Browne, Anthony. My Mom. Browne, Anthony, illus. 2009. (ENG., Illus.). 32p. (J). (gr. k-3). pap. 7.99 *(978-0-374-40026-2(1)*, 9780374400262) Square Fish.

Bruno, Cristina. The Mother Store. 2009. 52p. pap. 30.00 *(978-1-4389-2875-3(0))* AuthorHouse.

Buller, Jon & Schade, Susan. I Love You, Good Night. Pons, Bernadette, illus. 2006. (ENG.). 28p. (J). (gr. -1 — 1). bds. 7.99 *(978-0-689-86212-0(1)*, Little Simon) Little Simon.

Callen, Sharon. Happy Faces Leave Home. 1 vol. 2013. (Fiction Readers Ser.). (ENG., Illus.). 28p. (J). (gr. 2-2). pap. 6.99 *(978-1-4333-5560-8(4))* Shell Educational Publishing.

Cameron, Kristy. The Adventures of Herb the Wild Turkey - Herb Goes Camping. Shickle, Ian, illus. 2012. 38p. pap. *(978-0-9859790-0-3(3))* LP Publishing.

Carle, Eric, illus. I Love Mom with the Very Hungry Caterpillar. 2017. (World of Eric Carle Ser.). (ENG.). 32p. (J). (-k). 8.99 *(978-0-451-53346-3(1)*, Grosset & Dunlap) Penguin Young Readers Group.

Carlson, Nancy. Poor Carl. Carlson, Nancy, illus. 2012. (Nancy Carlson Picture Bks). (Illus.). 32p. (J). (gr. k-2). 56.72 *(978-0-7613-9305-4(6)*, Carolrhoda Bks.) Lerner Publishing Group.

Carpenter, Angie. Digewi Deer: The Tale of a Blind Deer. Berner Coble, Lynn, ed. 2013. 82p. (J). pap. 8.99 *(978-0-9846724-3-1(5))* Paws and Claws Publishing, LLC.

Casey, Dawn. The Children of Lir: A Celtic Legend. Mayo, Diana, illus. 2004. 32p. (J). pap. *(978-1-85269-872-0(1))*; pap. *(978-1-85269-868-3(3))*; pap. *(978-1-85269-867-6(5))*; pap. *(978-1-85269-858-4(6))*; pap. *(978-1-85269-897-3(7))*; pap. *(978-1-85269-818-8(7))*; pap. *(978-1-85269-823-2(3))*; pap. *(978-1-85269-828-7(4))*; pap. *(978-1-85269-838-6(1))*; pap. *(978-1-85269-843-0(8))*; pap. *(978-1-85269-873-7(X))*; pap. *(978-1-85269-878-2(0))*; pap. *(978-1-85269-887-4(X))*; pap. *(978-1-85269-892-8(6))*; pap. *(978-1-85269-863-8(2))*; pap. *(978-1-85269-853-9(5))*; pap. *(978-1-85269-848-5(9))* Mantra Lingua.

Cassidy, Yvonne. How Many Letters Are in Goodbye? 2016. (ENG.). 432p. (YA). pap. 11.99 *(978-0-7387-4745-3(9)*, Flux) North Star Editions.

Cebulski, Megan Elizabeth. The Brave Little Butterfly. 2008. 32p. pap. 24.95 *(978-1-60474-739-3(0))* America Star Bks.

Celcer, Irene. The Gift of Surrogacy. Gatto, Horacio, illus. 2007. (Hope & Will Have a Baby Ser.). 32p. (J). (gr. k-3). pap. 19.95 *(978-0-9755810-4-9(X)*, 9780975581049) Graphite Pr.

Chambers, Pamela G. My Mommy's Getting Married. Stewart, Muriel, illus. 2009. 32p. (gr. -1-3). 17.95 *(978-0-9799487-0-1(3))* Infinity Publishing Co.

Chang, Victoria. Is Mommy... ? Frazee, Marla, illus. 2015. (ENG.). 40p. (J). (gr. -1-k). 15.99 *(978-1-4814-0292-7(7)*, Beach Lane Bks.) Beach Lane Bks.

Cleary, Beverly. Emily's Runaway Imagination. Krush, Beth et al, illus. 2008. (Cleary Reissue Ser.). (ENG.). 288p. (J). (gr. 3-7). pap. 6.99 *(978-0-380-70923-6(6))* HarperCollins Pubs.

—Emily's Runaway Imagination. 221p. (J). (gr. 2-4). pap. 4.95 *(978-0-8072-1416-9(7)*, Listening Library) Random Hse. Audio Publishing Group.

Connor, Leslie. Waiting for Normal. (ENG.). (J). (gr. 5). 2010. 320p. pap. 6.99 *(978-0-06-089090-2(8))* 2008. 304p. 16.99 *(978-0-06-089088-9(6))* HarperCollins Pubs. (Tegen, Katherine Bks).

Cooper, Jennifer. Guardian Angel. 2009. 155p. pap. 12.87 *(978-0-557-09330-4(9))* Lulu Pr., Inc.

Corbett, Sue. 12 Again. 2007. (ENG.). 240p. (J). (gr. 5-18). 6.99 *(978-0-14-240729-5(1)*, Puffin Books) Penguin Young Readers Group.

Cosgrove, Stephen. Button Breaker. 2016. (Treasure Trolls Ser.). (ENG., Illus.). 32p. (J). (gr. k-4). pap. 7.95 *(978-1-941437-79-7(6))* Heritage Builders, LLC.

Cousins, Dave. 15 Days Without a Head. 2013. (ENG.). 312p. (YA). pap. 9.99 *(978-0-7387-3642-6(2)*, Flux) North Star Editions.

Crayon, Paula. An Angel in My Pocket. 2010. 44p. (J). pap. 17.99 *(978-1-4490-9921-3(1))* AuthorHouse.

Cronin, Doreen. M. O. M. (Mom Operating Manual) Cornell, Laura, illus. 2011. (ENG.). 56p. (J). (gr. -1-3). 16.99 *(978-1-4169-6150-5(X)*, Atheneum Bks. for Young Readers) Simon & Schuster Children's Publishing.

Curtis, Christopher Paul. Bucking the Sarge. 2006. (Readers Circle Ser.). (ENG.). 288p. (YA). (gr. 7-7). reprint ed. mass mkt. 6.99 *(978-0-440-41331-8(1)*, Laurel Leaf) Random Hse. Children's Bks.

Curtis, Jamie Lee. My Mommy Hung the Moon: A Love Story. Date not set. 32p. (J). (gr. -1-3). pap. 6.99 *(978-0-06-443696-0(9))* HarperCollins Pubs.

—My Mommy Hung the Moon: A Love Story. Cornell, Laura, illus. 2010. 40p. (J). (gr. -1-3). (ENG.). 16.99 *(978-0-06-029016-0(1))*; lib. bdg. 17.89 *(978-0-06-029017-7(X))* HarperCollins Pubs.

Cushman, Jean, et al. Little Golden Book Mommy Stories. Wilkin, Eloise & Meisel, Paul, illus. 2015. (Little Golden Book Favorites Ser.). (ENG.). 80p. (J). (-k). 6.99 *(978-0-385-39273-0(7)*, Golden Bks.) Random Hse. Children's Bks.

De Palma, Toni. Under the Banyan Tree. 2007. (ENG.). 192p. (YA). (gr. 7-18). 16.95 *(978-0-8234-1965-4(7))* Holiday Hse., Inc.

Dean, James. Rock On, Mom & Dad! Dean, James, illus. 2015. (Pete the Cat Ser.). (ENG., Illus.). 24p. (J). (gr. -1-3). pap. 6.99 *(978-0-06-230408-7(9)*, HarperFestival) HarperCollins Pubs.

—Rock on, Mom & Dad! Dean, James, illus. 2015. (Pete the Cat (HarperCollins) Ser.). (Illus.). (J). lib. bdg. 17.20 *(978-0-606-36490-4(0))* Turtleback Bks.

Deem, James M. 3 NBs of Julian Drew. 2004. (ENG.). 208p. (YA). (gr. 7-18). pap. 13.95 *(978-0-618-43907-2(2))* Houghton Mifflin Harcourt Publishing Co.

Dixon, Heather. Entwined. 2012. (ENG.). 480p. (YA). (gr. 8). pap. 9.99 *(978-0-06-200104-7(3)*, Greenwillow Bks.) HarperCollins Pubs.

Dodd, Christina. Back to School Mom, 18 Copies. 2003. mass mkt. 128.88 *(978-0-06-056267-0(6))* HarperCollins Pubs.

Dorsey, Angela & Miller, Marina. Sun Chaser. 2012. 112p. pap. *(978-1-927100-21-9(6))* Enchanted Pony Bks.

Dowley, Ruth. Hard Rock. 2006. (ENG.). 160p. (J). (gr. 4-7). pap. 9.99 *(978-1-84270-467-7(2))* Andersen Pr. GBR. Dist: Independent Pubs. Group.

Downing, Julie. Where Is My Mommy? Downing, Julie, illus. 2003. (ENG., Illus.). 32p. (J). (gr. -1-18). 15.99 *(978-0-688-17824-6(3))* HarperCollins Pubs.

Doyle, Roddy. Her Mother's Face. Blackwood, Freya, illus. 2008. (J). pap. *(978-0-439-81502-4(9)*, Levine, Arthur A. Bks.) Scholastic, Inc.

Dukes, Alicia. Ms. Mabel's Fables. 2010. 94p. pap. 42.20 *(978-0-557-31374-7(0))* Lulu Pr., Inc.

Duncan, Alice Faye. Honey Baby Sugar Child. Keeter, Susan, illus. 2005. (ENG.). 32p. (J). (gr. -1-1). 17.99 *(978-0-689-84678-6(9)*, Simon & Schuster Bks. For Young Readers) Simon & Schuster Bks. For Young Readers.

Dunn, Pintip. The Darkest Lie. 2016. viii, 292p. (YA). **(978-1-5182-2703-5(1)**, Kensington Bks.) Kensington Publishing Corp.

Dyan, Penelope. Baylee's Giraffes! Sometimes Only a Giraffe Will Do. Dyan, Penelope, illus. 2013. (Illus.). 34p. pap. 11.95 *(978-1-61477-085-5(9))* Bellissima Publishing, LLC.

Eastman, P. D. Are You My Mother? (Big Bright & Early Board Book Ser.). (ENG., Illus.). (J). (— 1). 2015. 24p. bds. 6.99 *(978-0-553-49680-2(8))* 2005. 8p. 16.99 *(978-0-375-81599-7(6))* Random Hse. Children's Bks. (Random Hse. Bks. for Young Readers).

—Are You My Mother?/¿Eres Tú Mi Mamá? 2016. (ENG & SPA., Illus.). 72p. (J). (gr. 1-4). 16.99 *(978-0-553-53990-5(6)*, Random Hse. Bks. for Young Readers) Random Hse. Children's Bks.

—¿Eres Tú Mi Mamá? (Are You My Mother?) 2016. (Beginner Books(R) Ser.). (ENG & SPA., Illus.). 72p. (J). (gr. 1-4). 9.99 *(978-0-553-53989-9(2)*, Random Hse. Bks. for Young Readers) Random Hse. Children's Bks.

Edge, Christopher. The Many Worlds of Albie Bright. 2017. (ENG.). 176p. (J). (gr. 4-7). 16.99 ***(978-1-5247-1357-7(0))***; lib. bdg. 19.99 ***(978-1-5247-1359-1(7))*** Random Hse. Children's Bks. (Delacorte Bks. for Young Readers).

Eldridge, Sherrie. Forever Fingerprints: An Amazing Discovery for Adopted Children. Williams, Rob, illus. 2014. (ENG.). 32p. 15.95 *(978-1-84905-778-3(8)*, 3057) Kingsley, Jessica Pubs. GBR. Dist: Macmillan Distribution Ltd.

Erhard, Lorie. Mama's Many Hats. Kalis, Jennifer, illus. 2014. (ENG.). 32p. (J). 18.99 *(978-0-9914701-4-3(1))* Bumble Bee Bks.

Evans, Stephanie. Steven James: I Just Can't Pay Attention. 2011. 28p. 12.03 *(978-1-4567-2707-9(9))* AuthorHouse.

Finley, Martha. Elsie's Motherhood. 2006. 29.95 *(978-1-4218-2995-1(9))*; pap. 14.95 *(978-1-4218-3095-7(7))* 1st World Publishing, Inc.

—Elsie's Motherhood. l.t. ed. 2007. 286p. pap. 23.99 *(978-1-4264-8102-4(0))* Creative Media Partners, LLC.

—Elsie's Motherhood, Vol. 5. 320p. (gr. 7-12). pap. 5.95 *(978-1-58182-068-3(2)*, Cumberland Hse.) Sourcebooks, Inc.

Flaherty, Kathleen Marion. An Octopus Named Mom. Donehey, Jennifer Caulfield, illus. 2012. (ENG.). 32p. (J). 16.95 *(978-0-9767276-8-2(4))* Three Bean Pr.

The Flower Pot Bunnies Return. 2006. (J). *(978-0-9755390-2-6(7))* Fifth Ave Pr.

Fontinalis. The Far Shore. 2011. 76p. pap. 6.99 *(978-1-61667-309-3(5))* Raider Publishing International.

Frantz, Donna. Silly Gilly Gil - Gay L-U-V. Evans, Gabriel, illus. 2013. 30p. pap. *(978-1-921883-38-5(3)*, MBS Pr.) Pick-a-Woo Woo Pubs.

Fruisen, Catherine Myler. My Mother's Pearls. 2005. (Illus.). 32p. (J). pap. 5.95 *(978-1-59572-005-4(7))* Star Bright Bks., Inc.

Fusco, Kimberly Newton. Tending to Grace. 2005. 175p. (gr. 7-12). 16.50 *(978-0-7569-5478-9(9))* Perfection Learning Corp.

Gabriel, Andrea. My Favorite Bear. Gabriel, Andrea, illus. 2004. (ENG., Illus.). 32p. (J). (-k). pap. 7.95 *(978-1-58089-039-7(3))* Charlesbridge Publishing, Inc.

Gantos, Jack. The Love Curse of the Rumbaughs. 2008. (ENG.). 192p. (YA). (gr. 9-12). pap. 14.99 *(978-0-312-38052-6(6)*, 9780312380526) Square Fish.

Garner, Em. Contaminated. (ENG.). 336p. (J). (gr. 7). 2014. pap. 9.99 *(978-1-60684-542-4(X))* 2013. 17.99 *(978-1-60684-354-3(0))* Lerner Publishing Group. (Carolrhoda Lab™).

Gay, Michel. El Cochecito. 2003. (SPA.). 68p. *(978-84-8470-084-5(4))* Corimbo, Editorial S.L.

George, Mindy Lee. These Hands. Hagan, Donell, illus. 2013. 30p. pap. *(978-0-9878208-4-6(2))* Catching Rainbows.

Glaser, P. H. Chrystallia & the Source of Light. 2011. (Illus.). 196p. (J). 18.99 *(978-1-60832-232-9(7))* Greenleaf Book Group.

Glines, Abbi. After the Game: A Field Party Novel. 2017. (YA). **(978-1-5344-0168-6(7)**, Simon Pulse) Simon Pulse.

Graves, Annie. Frankenkids. 2015. (Nightmare Club Ser.: 5). (ENG., Illus.). 64p. (J). (gr. 2-5). pap. 6.99 *(978-1-4677-6043-0(9))* Lerner Publishing Group.

Greban, Quentin. Mommy, I Love You. 2007. (ENG., Illus.). 32p. (J). (gr. -1-3). 15.99 *(978-1-59687-184-7(9))* IBks., Inc.

Gutman, Anne & Hallensleben, Georg. Mommy Hugs. 2003. (ENG., Illus.). 14p. (J). (gr. -1-7). bds. 5.95 *(978-0-8118-3916-7(8))* Chronicle Bks. LLC.

Haddix, Margaret Peterson. Escape from Memory. (ENG.). (YA). (gr. 7). 2012. 272p. pap. 8.99 *(978-1-4424-4602-1(1))* 2003. (Illus.). 224p. 17.99 *(978-0-689-85421-7(8))* Simon & Schuster Bks. For Young Readers. (Simon & Schuster Bks. For Young Readers).

—Takeoffs & Landings. 2004. 201p. (gr. 5-9). 17.00 *(978-0-7569-4255-7(1))* Perfection Learning Corp.

Hallinan, P. K. We're Very Good Friends, My Mother & I. 24p. (J). 7.95 *(978-0-8249-5373-7(8))*; 5.95 *(978-0-8249-5374-4(6))* Worthy Publishing. (Ideal Pubns.).

Hardin, Melinda. Hero Mom. 0 vols. Langdo, Bryan, illus. 2013. (ENG.). 24p. (J). (gr. -1-3). 12.99 *(978-1-4778-1645-5(3)*, 9781477816455, Amazon Children's Publishing) Amazon Publishing.

Harding, Susan. Here I Am! 2008. 20p. pap. 24.95 *(978-1-60474-093-6(0))* America Star Bks.

Harrington, Claudia. My Two Moms. 1 vol. Persico, Zoe, illus. 2016. (ENG.). 32p. (J). *(978-1-62402-110-7(7))* Magic Wagon.

Harris, Kandi. Princess, the Future Queen: A Mother's Guidance. Rippon, Jor-El, illus. l.t. ed. 2006. 32p. (J). bds. 12.99 *(978-0-9770331-1-9(2))* Harris, K Publishing, Inc.

Harvey, Jacqueline. The Sound of the Sea. Crossett, Warren, illus. 2005. 32p. (J). *(978-0-7344-0742-9(4)*, Lothian Children's Bks.) Hachette Australia.

Hill, Nancy. If Body Parts Could Grow on Trees. 2010. 32p. pap. 12.99 *(978-1-4520-0661-1(X))* AuthorHouse.

Hill, Tara Theresa. What Can You Do with Two Mommies? 2012. 40p. pap. 18.00 *(978-1-105-50649-9(5))* Lulu Pr., Inc.

Hodgman, Ann. That's My Mommy! Logan, Laura, illus. 2013. (ENG.). 22p. bds. *(978-1-58925-645-3(X))* Tiger Tales.

Hodkin, Faith. What Was My Mother Thinking? Militello, Joy, illus. 2013. (J). 22.95 *(978-1-933420-02-8(2))* Ravenwood Studios.

Hopkins, Ellen. Fallout. (ENG., (YA). (gr. 9). 2013. Illus.). 720p. pap. 12.99 *(978-1-4424-7180-1(8))* 2010. 672p. 18.99 *(978-1-4169-5009-7(5))* McElderry, Margaret K. Bks. (McElderry, Margaret K. Bks.).

Hutchins, Pat. Where, Oh Where, Is Rosie's Chick? 2016. (ENG., Illus.). 32p. (J). (gr. -1-3). 17.99 *(978-1-4814-6071-2(4)*, Simon & Schuster Bks. For Young Readers) Simon & Schuster Bks. For Young Readers.

Jafa, Manorama. My Mother Taught Me Origami (English) 2013. (ENG.). 16p. pap. 4.95 *(978-93-5036-109-2(4))* Ratna Sagar Pvt. Ltd. IND. Dist: Midpoint Trade Bks., Inc.

Jahn-Clough, Lisa. Country Girl, City Girl. 2009. (ENG.). 192p. (YA). (gr. 7). pap. 12.95 *(978-0-547-22322-3(6))* Houghton Mifflin Harcourt Publishing Co.

Jessica Hoel. Adam B Brave. Samantha Nowak, illus. 2009. 20p. pap. 12.49 *(978-1-4389-3240-8(5))* AuthorHouse.

Jimenez, Angeles. Macarena la Anguila. Gil, Sabina, illus. 2004. 26p. pap. 8.00 *(978-84-931888-0-1(8))* Editorial Brief ESP. Dist: Independent Pubs. Group.

Johansson, Cecilia, illus. Just Like Mommy. 2006. (ENG.). 16p. (J). (gr. -1 — 1). bds. 7.99 *(978-1-4169-1218-7(5)*, Little Simon) Little Simon.

Johnson, Gerald J. J. Betty, the Chubby Butterfly. Miltenberger, Jeri and Dave, illus. 2011. 24p. pap. 24.95 *(978-1-4489-3990-9(9))* America Star Bks.

Jones, Kelly. Mama. Kewley, Ken, illus. 2004. 32p. (J). *(978-0-9745930-0-5(1))* Stunt Publishing.

Jordan, Deloris. Did I Tell You I Love You Today? Evans, Shane W., illus. 2004. (ENG.). 32p. (J). (gr. -1-3). 18.99 *(978-0-689-85271-8(1)*, Simon & Schuster/Paula Wiseman Bks.) Simon & Schuster/Paula Wiseman Bks.

Kane, Kimberly Brougham. Every Time You Call Me Mommy-an Adoption Blessing. 2007. 32p. 16.50 *(978-0-615-17610-9(0))* Kane, Kimberly Brougham.

Kasza, Keiko. A Mother for Choco. 2003. (ENG.). 30p. (J). (gr. -1 — 1). bds. 7.99 *(978-0-399-24191-8(4)*, G.P. Putnam's Sons Books for Young Readers) Penguin Young Readers Group.

Kelley, Khris. Ringo the Helpful Raccoon. Crisenbery, Casey, illus. 2012. 38p. (J). 14.95 *(978-1-937406-70-7(9))* Mascot Bks., Inc.

Kephart, Beth. Nothing but Ghosts. 2009. (ENG.). 288p. (J). (gr. 8-18). 17.99 *(978-0-06-166796-1(X)*, HarperTeen) HarperCollins Pubs.

Kilgore, Mary & Kilgore, Mitchell. Where Is My Mommy? Coping When a Parent Leaves (and Doesn't Come Back) Pillo, Cary, illus. 2010. (ENG.). 32p. (J). (gr. -1-4). pap. 12.95 *(978-1-884734-46-5(4))* Parenting Pr., Inc.

Kormos, Lawrence A. There Is A Place I Go. 2007. (Illus.). (J). *(978-1-55452-245-3(5))* Essence Publishing.

—What Is Love Mama? 2007. (Illus.). (J). *(978-1-55452-190-6(4))* Essence Publishing.

Krivinskas, Carol Italiano. Barnyard Babies to the Rescue. 2008. 20p. pap. 13.95 *(978-1-4327-2183-1(6))* Outskirts Pr., Inc.

Lake, Mary. Piccolo. Collier, Kevin Scott, illus. 2007. 25p. (J). (gr. -1-3). 14.99 *(978-1-59879-358-1(6))* Lifevest Publishing, Inc.

Lee, Marie Myung-Ok. Somebody's Daughter. 2006. (ENG.). 280p. per. 21.00 *(978-0-8070-8389-5(5)*, Beacon Pr.) Beacon Pr.

Leeson, Christine. Just for You! Ellis, Andy, illus. 2008. (Tiger Tales Ser.). 24p. (J). (gr. -1-2). pap. 6.95 *(978-1-58925-408-4(2))* Tiger Tales.

Leicht, Martin & Neal, Isla. The World Forgot. 2015. 279p. (YA). pap. *(978-1-4424-2967-3(4)*, Simon & Schuster Bks. For Young Readers) Simon & Schuster Bks. For Young Readers.

Lewis, Carolyn. Hairy Beary Book Two Bk. 2,Vol. 2: The Great Waterfall, 3 bks. DeVince, James, ed. Porcheron, Tammy, illus. 2003. (Hairy Beary Ser.: 2). 42p. (J). pap. 9.95 *(978-0-9712641-1-3(2))* J M D's Business Services.

Lewis-Long, Carla. Why I'm So Special: A Book about Surrogacy. 2010. 44p. pap. 19.95 *(978-1-4389-9656-1(X))* AuthorHouse.

Lewis, Stewart. The Secret Ingredient. 2013. (ENG.). 256p. (YA). (gr. 7). 17.99 *(978-0-385-74331-0(9)*, Delacorte Bks. for Young Readers) Random Hse. Children's Bks.

—You Have Seven Messages. 2012. (ENG.). 304p. (YA). (gr. 7). pap. 9.99 *(978-0-385-74029-6(8)*, Ember) Random Hse. Children's Bks.

Lindsay, Maud. More Mother Stories. Sanborn, F. C. & Railton, Fanny, illus. 2008. 160p. pap. 9.95 *(978-1-59915-168-7(5))* Yesterday's Classics.

Litz, Amanda. Sam & Pam Can & You Can Too! We Can Help Our Mom. Garcia, Cynthia, illus. 2011. 32p. (J). pap. 3.99 *(978-0-9841496-1-2(9))* Traveler's Trunk Publishing LLC.

Love, Mary. Mama's House. 2005. 44p. per. 23.99 *(978-1-4257-0254-0(6))* Xlibris Corp.

Lowell, Pamela. Returnable Girl. 0 vols. 2009. (ENG.). 240p. (J). (gr. 8-12). pap. 9.99 *(978-0-7614-5592-9(2)*, 9780761455929, Amazon Children's Publishing) Amazon Publishing.

—Returnable Girl. 2006. 229p. (YA). (gr. 8-12). 16.99 *(978-0-7614-5317-8(2))* Marshall Cavendish Corp.

Lyga, Barry. Goth Girl Rising. 2011. (ENG.). 400p. (YA). (gr. 9). pap. 8.99 *(978-0-547-40308-3(9))* Houghton Mifflin Harcourt Publishing Co.

Lyons, Belinda. Meet My Air Force Mommy. 2008. 20p. pap. 24.95 *(978-1-60563-673-3(8))* America Star Bks.

Mac, Carrie. Charmed. 1 vol. 2004. (Orca Soundings Ser.). (ENG.). 128p. (YA). (gr. 8-12). pap. 9.95 *(978-1-55143-321-9(4))* Orca Bk. Pubs. USA.

Mack, Dinah. Mommy, Look What I Can Do! 2013. (Look What I Can Do Ser.). (ENG.). 14p. (J). (— 1). bds. 10.95 *(978-1-60537-169-6(6))* Cobblestone Publishing Co.

MacLachlan, Patricia. More Perfect Than the Moon. 2004. (Sarah, Plain & Tall Ser.). 96p. (J). (gr. 3-5). 14.99 *(978-0-06-027558-7(8)*, Cotler, Joanna Books) HarperCollins Pubs.

Magden, Loretta. The Treetop Bird Family. Barringer, J. M., illus. 2007. 28p. (J). 15.95 *(978-0-9788771-0-1(1))* Level Green Bks.

Martin, Ann M. Here Today. 2005. 308p. (gr. 5-9). 18.00 *(978-0-7569-5104-7(6))* Perfection Learning Corp.

—Here Today. 2005. (ENG.). 336p. (J). (gr. 3-7). pap. 7.99 *(978-0-439-57945-2(7)*, Scholastic Paperbacks) Scholastic, Inc.

McAllister, Angela. My Mom Has X-Ray Vision. Smith, Alex T., illus. 2011. (ENG.). 32p. (J). (gr. -1-2). 15.95 *(978-1-58925-097-0(4))* Tiger Tales.

McCourt, Lisa. I Love You, Stinky Face. Moore, Cyd, illus. (ENG.). (J). 2004. 16p. (gr. 3-7). bds. 6.99 *(978-0-439-63572-1(1))* 2003. 32p. (gr. -1 — 1). pap. 6.99 *(978-0-439-63469-4(5))* Scholastic, Inc.

McCue, Lisa. My First Mother Goose. 2009. (Carry along Bks.). (ENG., Illus.). 20p. (J). (gr. -1-k). bds. 14.99 *(978-0-7944-1931-8(3)*, Reader's Digest Children's Bks.) Studio Fun International.

McDaniel, Lurlene. Mother, Please Don't Die. 2005. (ENG.). 128p. (Orig.). (YA). (gr. 7-12). per. 4.99 *(978-1-58196-028-0(X)*, Darby Creek) Lerner Publishing Group.

Mceldowney, Connie. Josiah's Journey. 2009. 34p. pap. 12.99 *(978-1-4490-0489-7(X))* AuthorHouse.

McIntosh, Kenneth. The Trickster's Image: Forensic Art. 2009. (J). pap. 24.95 *(978-1-4222-1452-7(4))* 2007. (Illus.). 144p. (YA). (gr. 8-12). pap. 9.95 *(978-1-4222-0873-1(7))* Mason Crest.

—The Trickster's Image: Forensic Art, 3 vols. Miller, Justin, illus. 2007. (Crime Scene Club Ser.). 144p. (YA). (gr. 9-12). lib. bdg. 24.95 *(978-1-4222-0249-4(6))* Mason Crest.

McRee Turner, Amber. Sway. 2013. (ENG.). 320p. (J). (gr. 4-7). pap. 6.99 *(978-1-4231-3784-9(1))* Hyperion Pr.

Melmed, Laura Krauss. I Love You As Much... Board Book & Picture Frame. 2003. (Illus.). 22p. (J). (gr. -1-2). 12.99 *(978-0-06-008659-6(9)*, HarperFestival) HarperCollins Pubs.

Messaoudi, Michele. My Mum Is a Wonder. Peckham, Ruth, illus. 2016. (ENG.). 24p. (J). (gr. -1). 8.95 *(978-0-86037-298-1(7))* Kube Publishing Ltd. GBR. Dist: Consortium Bk. Sales & Distribution.

Metcalf, Paula. My Mummy. Barnard, Lucy, illus. 2015. (ENG.). 24p. (J). (-1). bds. 9.99 *(978-1-4472-7699-9(X))* Pan Macmillan GBR. Dist: Independent Pubs. Group.

Metz, Melinda & Burns, Laura J. Crave, Bk. 1. 2010. (ENG.). 288p. (YA). (gr. 9-18). pap. 9.99 *(978-1-4424-0816-6(2)*, Simon & Schuster Bks. For Young Readers) Simon & Schuster Bks. For Young Readers.

Miller, Constances. Mommy Always Comes Back. 2011. 28p. pap. 16.99 *(978-1-257-13201-0(6))* Lulu Pr., Inc.

M
N
O

Mogk, Matt. That's Not Your Mommy Anymore: A Zombie Tale. Wells, Aja, illus. 2011. (ENG.). 32p. pap. 10.00 (978-1-56975-926-4(X)) Ulysses Pr.

Mom Dresses Up. 2003. (Mom & Dad Ser.). (J). 7.33 (978-1-58453-254-5(8)) Pioneer Valley Bks.

Moore, Julianne. My Mom Is a Foreigner, but Not to Me. So, Meilo, illus. 2013. (ENG.). 40p. (J). (gr. k-3). 16.99 (978-1-4521-0792-9(0)) Chronicle Bks. LLC.

Moore, Karen. Mommy Loves Me. Stanley, Mandy, illus. gif. ed. 2005. 10p. (J). (gr. -1-1). per., bds. 6.99 (978-1-57791-182-1(2)) Brighter Minds Children's Publishing.

Moore, Mel. Mother's Little Helper. 2006. (Illus.). 16p. (J). per. (978-0-9775919-5-4(6)) Carpe Diem Publishing.

Moses, Shelia P. Joseph. (ENG.). (YA). (gr. 7). 2010. 208p. pap. 8.99 (978-1-4169-9442-8(4)) 2008. (Illus.). 176p. 16.99 (978-1-4169-1752-6(7)) McElderry, Margaret K. Bks. (McElderry, Margaret K. Bks.).

—Joseph's Grace. 2011. (ENG.). 160p. (YA). (gr. 7-18). 16.99 (978-1-4169-3942-9(3), McElderry, Margaret K. Bks.) McElderry, Margaret K. Bks.

Moundlic, Charlotte. The Scar. Tallec, Olivier, illus. 2011. (ENG.). 32p. (J). (gr. k-4). 14.99 (978-0-7636-5341-5(1)) Candlewick Pr.

Muñoz, Isabel. Just Like Mom. Mazali, Gustavo, illus. 2005. 22p. (J). pap. (978-0-439-78844-1(7)) Scholastic, Inc.

Munsch, Robert. I'm So Embarrassed! 2007. (J). 12.65 (978-0-7569-7624-8(3)) Perfection Learning Corp.

Murphy, Jill. Five Minutes' Peace. Murphy, Jill, illus. 2012. (ENG., Illus.). 24p. (J). (gr. -1 — 1). bds. 7.99 (978-0-399-25707-0(1), G.P. Putnam's Sons Books for Young Readers) Penguin Young Readers Group.

My Big Book of Beginner Books about Me. 2011. (Beginner Books(R) Ser.). (ENG., Illus.). 208p. (J). (gr. -1-2). 16.99 (978-0-307-93183-2(8), Random Hse. Bks. for Young Readers) Random Hse. Children's Bks.

My Mom Is Great. (My Great Relatives... Ser.). 32p. (J). (978-1-84250-577-9(7), Bright Sparks) Parragon, Inc.

My Stepmother: Individual Title Six-Packs. (gr. -1-2). 27.00 (978-0-7635-9466-4(0)) Rigby Education.

Naylor, Phyllis Reynolds. Alice on Her Way. 2006. (Alice McKinley Ser.: No. 17). 322p. (gr. 9-12). 17.00 (978-0-7569-6909-7(3)) Perfection Learning Corp.

—Polo's Mother. Daniel, Alan, illus. 2006. (ENG.). 176p. (J). (gr. 3-7). pap. 6.99 (978-0-689-87404-8(9), Atheneum Bks. for Young Readers) Simon & Schuster Children's Publishing.

Nitz, Kristin Wolden. Suspect, 1 vol. 2010. (ENG.). 224p. (YA). (gr. 7-11). 16.95 (978-1-56145-543-0(1)) Peachtree Pubs.

Njenga, Wamoro P. Wow, What a Mama!! Webber, Penny, illus. 2012. 58p. pap. 13.70 (978-0-9827461-2-7(1)) Prop-Abilities Inc.

Old Mother Hubbard: 6 Small Books. (gr. k-2). 23.00 (978-0-7635-8496-2(7)) Rigby Education.

Olsen, Sylvia. The Girl with a Baby, 1 vol. 2003. (ENG.). 208p. (YA). (gr. 7-12). pap. 9.95 (978-1-55039-142-8(9)) Sono Nis Pr. CAN. Dist: Orca Bk. Pubs. USA.

O'Maley, Elizabeth. By Freedom's Light. 2009. 188p. (J). 15.95 (978-0-87195-273-8(4)); pap. 7.95 (978-0-87195-274-5(2)) Indiana Historical Society.

Painter, Grace. The Harry Bear Story. Kacer, Stephen, illus. 2011. 28p. pap. 24.95 (978-1-4626-3327-2(7)) America Star Bks.

Paratore, Coleen Murtagh. Catching the Sun. 2010. (J). (978-0-618-45780-9(1)) Houghton Mifflin Harcourt Publishing Co.

Parker, Amy. A Night Night Prayer, 1 vol. Pedler, Caroline, illus. 2014. (Night Night Ser.). (ENG.). 20p. (J). bds. 9.99 (978-1-4003-2431-6(9)) Nelson, Thomas Inc.

Paschalis, Juli. Druan O Mam! 2005. (WEL., Illus.). 16p. pap. (978-0-86174-149-6(8)) Drake Educational Assocs. Ltd.

Petty, J. T. & Pope, Paul. The Fall of the House of West. Rubín, David, illus. 2015. 157p. (J). **(978-1-5182-0095-3(8)**, First Second Bks.) Roaring Brook Pr.

Phillips, Dee. Baby's Day. 2009. (Flip Flap Fun Bks.). (ENG.). 5p. (J). (gr. -1-k). bds. 5.95 (978-1-84696-087-1(8), TickTock Books) Octopus Publishing Group GBR. Dist: Independent Pubs. Group.

Podos, Rebecca. The Mystery of Hollow Places. 2016. 304p. (YA). (gr. 9). 17.99 (978-0-06-237334-2(X)) HarperCollins Pubs.

Polacco, Patricia. In Our Mothers' House. Polacco, Patricia, illus. 2009. (ENG., Illus.). 48p. (J). (gr. 1-3). 17.99 (978-0-399-25076-7(X), Philomel Bks.) Penguin Young Readers Group.

Potter, Ellen. The Kneebone Boy. 2011. (ENG.). 304p. (J). (gr. 4-7). pap. 8.99 (978-0-312-67432-8(5), 9780312674328) Square Fish.

Pullman, Philip. Sally y el Tigre en el Pozo. 2003. (SPA.). 512p. (YA). 16.95 (978-84-95618-49-8(4), Umbriel) Ediciones Urano S. A. ESP. Dist: Spanish Pubs., LLC.

Ramljak, Marijan. Are You My Mommy? 2009. (Look for Me Bks.). (Illus.). (J). bds. 9.99 (978-1-934650-65-3(X)) Just For Kids Pr., LLC.

Ramos, Angelica. If My Mommy Was an Octopus. 2008. 12p. pap. 24.95 (978-1-60563-821-8(8)) PublishAmerica, Inc.

Random House & Wilson, Sarah. Moms Are the Best! (SpongeBob SquarePants) Random House, illus. 2014. (Step into Reading Ser.). (ENG., Illus.). 32p. (J). (gr. -1-1). 3.99 (978-0-385-37499-6(2), Random Hse. Bks. for Young Readers) Random Hse. Children's Bks.

Random House Staff & Wilson, Sarah. Moms Are the Best! (SpongeBob SquarePants) Random House Staff, illus. 2014. (Step into Reading Ser.). (ENG., Illus.). 32p. (J). (gr. -1-1). lib. bdg. 12.99 (978-0-385-37500-9(X), Random Hse. Bks. for Young Readers) Random Hse. Children's Bks.

Reagan, Jean. How to Raise a Mom. Wildish, Lee, illus. 2017. (ENG.). 32p. (J). (gr. -1-3). 17.99 (978-0-553-53829-8(2), Knopf Bks. for Young Readers) Random Hse. Children's Bks.

Reid-Tulloch, Joseth. Manu's Special Day. 2012. 16p. pap. 14.99 (978-1-4520-9150-1(1)) AuthorHouse.

Reinhardt, Dana. A Brief Chapter in My Impossible Life. 2007. (ENG.). 256p. (YA). (gr. 9-12). pap. 8.99 (978-0-375-84691-5(3), Ember) Random Hse. Children's Bks.

Revell, Mike. Stormwalker. 2016. (ENG.). 304p. (J). (gr. 5-9). 16.99 (978-1-68144-493-2(3)) Quercus NA.

Richter, Bernd & Richter, Susan. The Little Bear Who Didn't Want to Hibernate. Green, Sue, illus. 2003. 42p. pap. 9.95 (978-1-931353-10-6(7)) Saddle Pal Creations, Inc.

Richter, Jutta. The Summer of the Pike. Brailovsky, Anna, tr. from GER. Buchholz, Quint, illus. 2006. (ENG.). 132p. (J). (gr. 2-8). 16.95 (978-1-57131-671-4(X)); (gr. 8-12). per. 6.95 (978-1-57131-672-1(8)) Milkweed Editions.

Rigby Education Staff. Old Mother Big Book. (gr. k-2). 21.00 (978-0-7635-2408-1(5)) Rigby Education.

Ringgold, Robyn. My Mom Hugs Trees. Vasudevan, Vidya, illus. 2006. 24p. (J). per. 15.95 (978-0-9785326-1-1(9)) Solar Publishing LLC.

Rinker, Sherri Duskey. Silly Wonderful You. McDonnell, Patrick, illus. 2016. 40p. (J). (gr. -1-3). 17.99 (978-0-06-227105-1(9)) HarperCollins Pubs.

Ritchie, Kate. I Just Couldn't Wait to Meet You. Somerville, Hannah, illus. 2015. (ENG.). 32p. (J). (-k). 22.99 (978-0-85798-970-3(7)) Random Hse. Australia AUS. Dist: Independent Pubs. Group.

Robaard, Jedda. If My Mom Were a Bird. 2015. (ENG., Illus.). 40p. (J). (gr. -1-2). 14.99 (978-1-4998-0021-0(5)) Little Bee Books Inc.

Roberts, Pauline. Oh! I Wish. Bates, Lindsey E. & Wiggan, Desmond, illus. 2012. 24p. pap. 9.95 (978-0-9848243-3-5(2)) Beckham Pubns. Group, Inc.

Rollins, Ellie. Zip. 2013. (ENG.). 336p. (J). (gr. 3-7). pap. 7.99 (978-1-59514-571-0(0), Razorbill) Penguin Young Readers Group.

Rosenberg, Natascha & Kempter, Christa. When Mama Can't Sleep. 2011. (ENG., Illus.). 24p. (J). (gr. -1 — 1). 6.95 (978-0-7358-4015-7(6)) North-South Bks., Inc.

Ruby, Laura. Play Me. 2009. (ENG.). 336p. (YA). (gr. 9). pap. 9.99 (978-0-06-124329-5(9), HarperTeen) HarperCollins Pubs.

Rushton, Rosie. Just Don't Make a Scene, Mum! 2005. 224p. (J). pap. 5.99 (978-0-7868-5186-7(4)) Hyperion Bks. for Children.

Ryan, Darlene & Fernández, Queta. De Nadie Mas, 1 vol. 2008. (Spanish Soundings Ser.). (SPA.). 112p. (YA). (gr. 8-12). pap. 9.95 (978-1-55143-969-3(7)) Orca Bk. Pubs. USA.

Ryan, Nancy. The Bookworm & His New Book. 2012. 32p. pap. 24.95 (978-1-4626-6492-4(X)) America Star Bks.

Sala, Laurenne. You Made Me a Mother. Glasser, Robin Preiss, illus. 2016. 32p. (J). (gr. -1-3). 15.99 (978-0-06-235886-8(3)) HarperCollins Pubs.

Salan, Felipe Lopez, illus. Jack & the Beanstalk. 2006. (ENG.). 32p. (J). (gr. -1). 15.95 (978-1-933327-11-2(1)) Purple Bear Bks., Inc.

Sanderson, Brandon. Alcatraz Versus the Knights of Crystallia. 2016. (Alcatraz Versus the Evil Librarians Ser.: 3). (ENG.). 320p. (J). 16.99 (978-0-7653-7898-9(1), 9780765378989, Starscape) Doherty, Tom Assocs., LLC.

Sappenfield, Heather. Life at the Speed of Us. 2016. (ENG.). 384p. (YA). pap. 11.99 (978-0-7387-4730-9(0), Flux) North Star Editions.

Sautereau, Francois. La Extrana Navidad de Jonas.Tr. of Jonas's Extraordinary Christmas. (SPA.). 92p. (YA). (gr. 5-8). (978-84-279-3163-3(8), NG3472) Noguer y Caralt Editores, S. A. ESP. Dist: Lectorum Pubns., Inc.

Say, Allen. Tree of Cranes. Say, Allen, illus. 2009. (ENG., Illus.). 32p. (J). (gr. -1-3). pap. 7.99 (978-0-547-24830-1(X)) Houghton Mifflin Harcourt Publishing Co.

Schreiber, Hannah & Hartsock, Conner. One in a Buzzillion. Foster, Jack, illus. 2011. 16p. pap. 9.95 (978-1-61633-154-2(2)) Guardian Angel Publishing, Inc.

Scott, Kieran. This Is So Not Happening. 2013. (He's So/She's So Trilogy Ser.). (ENG., Illus.). 320p. (YA). (gr. 7). pap. 9.99 (978-1-4169-9956-0(6), Simon & Schuster Bks. For Young Readers) Simon & Schuster Bks. For Young Readers.

The Secrets of Eastcliff-By-the-Sea: The Story of Annaliese Easterling & Throckmorton, Her Simply Remarkable Sock Monkey. 2014. (ENG., Illus.). 288p. (J). (gr. 3-7). 16.99 (978-1-4424-9840-2(4), Beach Lane Bks.) Beach Lane Bks.

Setterington, Ken. Mom & Mum Are Getting Married!, 1 vol. Priestley, Alice, illus. 2004. (ENG.). 24p. (J). (gr. -1-3). 15.95 (978-1-896764-84-9(3)) Second Story Pr. CAN. Dist: Orca Bk. Pubs. USA.

Shahan, Sherry. Death Mountain, 1 vol. (ENG.). 176p. (YA). (gr. 5-9). 2007. pap. 7.95 (978-1-56145-428-0(1)) 2005. 15.95 (978-1-56145-353-5(6)) Peachtree Pubs.

Shanahan, Lisa. My Mom Tarzan. Guthridge, Bettina, illus. 2008. (ENG.). 32p. (J). (gr. -1-3). (978-1-59692-239-6(7)) MacAdam/Cage Publishing, Inc.

Shaw, Susan. Safe. 2007. (ENG.). 176p. (YA). (gr. 9-18). pap. 14.00 (978-0-525-47829-4(9), Dutton Books for Young Readers) Penguin Young Readers Group.

Silberberg, Alan. Milo: Sticky Notes & Brain Freeze. Silberberg, Alan, illus. (ENG., Illus.). 288p. (J). (gr. 4-8). 2011. pap. 7.99 (978-1-4169-9431-2(9)) 2010. 15.99 (978-1-4169-9430-5(0)) Simon & Schuster Children's Publishing. (Aladdin).

Simmons, Jane. Come On. 2005. (Daisy Ser.). (Illus.). (Orig.). (J). (ARA, ENG, VIE, CHI & BEN.). 36p. pap. 11.95 (978-1-84059-217-7(6)); (VIE, ENG, CHI, ARA & BEN., 3p. (gr. -1-1). pap. 11.95 (978-1-84059-183-5(8)); (URD, ENG, VIE, CHI & ARA., 36p. (gr. -1-1). pap. 11.95 (978-1-84059-182-8(X)) Milet Publishing.

Sinclair, Gardine. Keira at Stageschool. 2013. 186p. (J). pap. (978-1-78299-387-2(8)) FeedARead.com.

Sitomer, Alan Lawrence. Daddies Do It Different. Carter, Abby, illus. 2012. (ENG.). 40p. (J). (gr. -1 — 1). 16.99 (978-1-4231-3315-5(3)) Hyperion Pr.

Skougaard, Shari. Grumpy Goo, I Love You. 2009. 24p. pap. 13.50 (978-1-60860-454-8(3), Eloquent Bks.) Strategic Book Publishing & Rights Agency (SBPRA).

Smith, Roland. Independence Hall. (I, Q Ser.: Bk. 1). (ENG., 312p. (gr. 5-9). 2009. Illus.). (J). 15.95 (978-1-58536-468-8(1)) 2008. (YA). pap. 8.95 (978-1-58536-325-4(1)) Sleeping Bear Pr.

Smith, Rosie. My Mom's the Best. Whatley, Bruce, illus. 2013. (J). (978-0-545-60361-4(7)) Scholastic, Inc.

—My Mom's the Best. Whatley, Bruce, illus. 2017. (ENG.). 24p. (J). (gr. -1). bds. 6.95 **(978-1-4549-2480-7(2))** Sterling Publishing Co., Inc.

Smucker, Shawn. The Day the Angels Fell. 2017. (ENG.). 320p. (YA). 17.99 **(978-0-8007-2849-6(1))** Revell.

Snead, Kathi. My Mom Has a Job. Christine, Grove, illus. 2004. (J). (978-0-9747385-1-2(4)) City of Manassas Department of Social Services.

Somper, Justin. Black Heart. 2010. (Vampirates Ser.: 4). (ENG.). 512p. (J). (gr. 3-7). pap. 8.99 (978-0-316-02088-6(5)) Little, Brown Bks. for Young Readers.

Sparks, Favre. The Ugly Brown Cup. 2013. 12p. pap. 9.00 (978-1-62516-468-1(8), Strategic Bk. Publishing) Strategic Book Publishing & Rights Agency (SBPRA).

St. Anthony, Jane. Grace above All. 2015. (Fesler-Lampert Minnesota Heritage Ser.). (ENG.). 176p. pap. 9.95 (978-0-8166-9814-1(7)) Univ. of Minnesota Pr.

Stevens, Rob. Would the Real Stanley Carrot Please Stand Up? 2015. (ENG.). 272p. (J). (gr. 4-6). pap. 12.99 **(978-1-78344-228-7(X))** Andersen Pr. GBR. Dist: Independent Pubs. Group.

Stevenson, Robin. Escape Velocity, 1 vol. 2011. (ENG.). 240p. (YA). (gr. 8-12). pap. 12.95 (978-1-55469-866-0(9)) Orca Bk. Pubs. USA.

Stewart, Kiera. Fetching. 2012. (ENG.). 304p. (YA). (gr. 5-9). pap. 7.99 (978-1-4231-4245-4(4)) Hyperion Pr.

Sutton, Michelle. It's Not about Him. 2012. (Second Glances Ser.). (ENG.). 228p. pap. 12.99 (978-0-9838836-0-9(2)) Sword of the Spirit Publishing.

Swanson, A. M. Momma's Biscuits. 2010. 19p. (J). pap. 14.95 (978-1-4327-4699-5(5)) Outskirts Pr., Inc.

Tamaro, Susanna. Castello Dei Sogni Storie Che. pap. 18.95 (978-88-04-50610-2(5)) Mondadori ITA. Dist: Distribooks, Inc.

Tara, Stephanie Lisa. Eliza's Forever Trees. Walton, Alex, illus. 2012. 290p. (J). pap. 9.99 net. (978-1-61254-067-2(8)) Brown Books Publishing Group.

Tarver, Whitney B. When Mommy Went Back to Work. 2011. 20p. (gr. 1-2). pap. 13.95 (978-1-4269-6833-4(7)) Trafford Publishing.

Tattum, Stephan. Mom. 2005. (J). 4.95 (978-1-59792-006-3(1)) F.A.S.T. Learning LLC.

Tayleur, Karen. Famous (Scholastic) The Awesome Life of David Mortimore Baxter. Garvey, Brann, illus. 2009. (David Mortimore Baxter Ser.). 88p. pap. 0.80 (978-1-4342-2503-0(8), David Mortimore Baxter) Stone Arch Bks.

Thomson, Sarah L. Mercy: The Last New England Vampire, 1 vol. 2011. (ENG.). 178p. (J). pap. 16.95 (978-1-934031-36-0(4), 9caae975-eeb4-4b56-8673-b3abbf16fc2f) Islandport Pr., Inc.

Toon, Paige. The Accidental Life of Jessie Jefferson. 2016. (Jessie Jefferson Novels Ser.: 1). (ENG.). 336p. (J). pap. 9.99 (978-1-4711-4582-7(4), Simon & Schuster Children's) Simon & Schuster, Ltd. GBR. Dist: Simon & Schuster, Inc.

Trilling, Richard J. Still More Stories of Stephanie & Friends: Volume 3 in the Stephanie Series. 2011. 72p. pap. 21.00 (978-1-61204-546-7(4), Strategic Bk. Publishing) Strategic Book Publishing & Rights Agency (SBPRA).

Tucker, Mark. Super Phil & the Missing Mom. Patete, Christine, illus. 2003. 24p. (J). 4.50 (978-1-882440-01-6(3)) God's World Pubns. Inc.

Ungerer, Tomi. No Kiss for Mother. 2012. (ENG., Illus.). 48p. (gr. -1-1). 16.95 (978-0-7148-6475-4(7)) Phaidon Pr., Inc.

van Genechten, Guido. Porque Te Quiero Tanto. 2003. (SPA., Illus.). 28p. (J). (gr. k-3). 15.95 (978-970-29-0912-5(0)) Santillana USA Publishing Co., Inc.

Van Slyke, Rebecca. Mom School. Burris, Priscilla, illus. 2015. (ENG.). 32p. (J). (gr. -1-2). 16.99 (978-0-385-38892-4(6), Doubleday Bks. for Young Readers) Random Hse. Children's Bks.

Waddell, Martin. Owl Babies. (Illus.). 25p. (J). (CHI, ENG, URD, TUR & VIE.). (978-1-85430-343-1(0), 93441); (ENG, VIE, URD, TUR & CHI., (978-1-85430-348-6(1), 93442) Little Tiger Pr. Group.

Walsh, Joanna. I Love Mom. Abbot, Judi, illus. 2014. (ENG.). 32p. (J). (gr. -1-3). 16.99 (978-1-4814-2808-8(X), Simon & Schuster/Paula Wiseman Bks.) Simon & Schuster/Paula Wiseman Bks.

Walton, Rick. Frankenstein's Fright Before Christmas. Hale, Nathan, illus. 2014. (ENG.). 32p. (J). (gr. -1-3). 16.99 (978-0-312-55367-8(6), 9780312553678) Feiwel & Friends.

Weatherly, L. A. Watcher. 2012. (Stoke Books Titles Ser.). (ENG.). 64p. (YA). (gr. 8-12). pap. 6.95 (978-1-78112-106-1(0)); lib. bdg. 22.60 (978-1-78112-107-8(9)) Lerner Publishing Group.

Webb, Holly. Rose & the Silver Ghost. 2015. (Rose Ser.: 4). (ENG.). 224p. (J). (gr. 3-6). pap. 6.99 (978-1-4926-0433-4(X), Sourcebooks Jabberwocky) Sourcebooks, Inc.

Webster, Michelle B. The Christmas of Miracles. 2004. 136p. per. 12.95 (978-0-9753117-0-7(0)) Four Sonkist Angels.

Wells, Rosemary. La Estupenda Mama de Roberta. (SPA.). (J). 16.95 (978-84-372-1612-6(5)) Santillana USA Publishing Co., Inc.

Werlin, Nancy. Impossible. 2011. 11.04 (978-0-7848-3488-6(1), Everbind) Marco Bk. Co.

—Impossible. 2009. (ENG.). 384p. (YA). (gr. 7-18). 9.99 (978-0-14-241491-0(3), Speak) Penguin Young Readers Group.

White, Ruth. Belle Prater's Boy. unabr. ed. 2004. 196p. (J). (gr. 5-9). pap. 38.00 incl. audio (978-0-8072-8682-1(6), YA234SP, Listening Library) Random Hse. Audio Publishing Group.

Willard, Renee. The Mama Who Didn't Work. 2012. 48p. pap. 24.95 (978-1-4626-6930-1(1)) America Star Bks.

Williams-Garcia, Rita. One Crazy Summer. 2009. (KOR.). 272p. (J). pap. (978-89-7199-494-8(0)) Dolbegae Publishing Co.

—One Crazy Summer. (J). (gr. 4-7). 2011. (ENG.). 240p. pap. 7.99 (978-0-06-076090-8(7)) 2010. (ENG.). 224p. 16.99 (978-0-06-076088-5(5)) 2010. 224p. lib. bdg. 16.89 (978-0-06-076089-2(3)) HarperCollins Pubs. (Amistad).

—One Crazy Summer. (J). 2011. 1.25 (978-1-4498-2201-9(0)) 2010. 69.75 (978-1-4498-2197-5(9)) 2010. 67.75 (978-1-4498-2199-9(5)) Recorded Bks., Inc.

—One Crazy Summer. 2011. (J). lib. bdg. 17.20 (978-0-606-23555-6(8), Turtleback) Turtleback Bks.

Williams, Jane. Heeey Ma. Date not set. (Illus.). 40p. (J). (gr. -1-1). pap. 5.99 (978-0-06-443601-4(2)) HarperCollins Pubs.

Williams, Vera B. A Chair for My Mother. Williams, Vera B., illus. 25th anniv. ed. 2007. (Reading Rainbow Bks.). (ENG., Illus.). 32p. (J). (gr. -1-3). pap. 7.99 (978-0-688-04074-1(8), Greenwillow Bks.) HarperCollins Pubs.

—Un Sillón para Mi Mamá, 1 vol. Marcuse, Aida E., tr. Williams, Vera B., illus. 25th anniv. ed. 2007. (SPA & ENG., Illus.). 32p. (J). (gr. -1-3). reprint ed. pap. 6.99 (978-0-688-13200-2(6), MR5678) HarperCollins Pubs.

Wilson, Sarah. Moms Are the Best! 2014. (Spongebob Squarepants Step into Reading Ser.). lib. bdg. 13.55 (978-0-606-35203-1(1)) Turtleback Bks.

Wolff, Virginia Euwer. Make Lemonade. 2006. (ENG.). 208p. (YA). (gr. 5-9). pap. 8.99 (978-0-8050-8070-4(8), 9780805080704) Square Fish.

Woodson, J. L. Superwoman's Child: Son of a Single Mother. Malone, Susan Mary, ed. 2005. 204p. pap. 14.95 (978-0-9754130-8-1(2)) Macro Publishing Group.

Xinran, Xinran & Mother's Bridge of Love Staff. Motherbridge of Love. Masse, Josée, illus. 2013. (ENG.). 32p. (J). (gr. k-3). 7.99 (978-1-78285-040-3(6)) Barefoot Bks., Inc.

Yeh, Kat. The Truth about Twinkie Pie. 2015. (J). (978-0-316-23671-3(3)) Little Brown & Co.

Young, Andrew. The Giving Mother. 2006. (J). (978-1-933554-36-5(3)) Primordia.

MOTHERS—POETRY

Grover, Lorie Ann. Loose Threads. 2007. (ENG.). 304p. (J). (gr. 4-7). pap. 14.95 (978-1-4169-5562-7(3), McElderry, Margaret K. Bks.) McElderry, Margaret K. Bks.

Morgan, Gaby. I Love My Mum. 2015. (ENG., Illus.). 96p. (J). (gr. 2). pap. 8.99 (978-1-4472-8044-6(X)) Pan Macmillan GBR. Dist: Independent Pubs. Group.

MOTHERS AND DAUGHTERS

Biestman, Margot. Grammie Stories: True Stories about People Living in the Real World. 2009. (YA). audio compact disk (978-0-936865-06-5(7)) Pergot Pr.

Cammarata, Jan. Karli's Kritters. 2009. 20p. pap. 12.00 (978-1-4389-6726-4(8)) AuthorHouse.

Falligant, Erin, ed. Just Mom & Me: The Tear-Out, Punch-Out, Fill-Out Book of Fun for Girls & Their Moms. Peterson, Stacy, illus. 2008. (ENG.). 96p. (J). (gr. 4-7). spiral bd. 10.95 (978-1-59369-340-4(0)) American Girl Publishing, Inc.

Florian, Melanie. A Day with Mommy. Florian, Melanie, illus. 2010. (Sticker Stories Ser.). (ENG., Illus.). 16p. (J). (gr. -1-2). pap. 5.99 (978-0-448-45342-2(8), Grosset & Dunlap) Penguin Young Readers Group.

Fowler, Leona. I Don't Want to Be Grumpy Anymore! Martins, Ann-Kathrin & Fowler, Romana, illus. 2011. 19p. (J). 12.95 (978-1-58909-804-6(8)) Bookstand Publishing.

Guipre, Jewel Moreland. Dance with Me. 2012. 32p. 24.95 (978-1-4560-6044-2(9)) America Star Bks.

Harper, Lisa. You Belong to Me Little One. 2011. 16p. (gr. -1). pap. 8.99 (978-1-4634-1371-2(8)) AuthorHouse.

Khalifé, Fatima & Mouazen, Deema. If Your Mom Was... . What Will You Do? 2012. 28p. pap. 19.99 (978-1-4772-6951-0(7)) AuthorHouse.

McDonald, Stacy. Raising Maidens of Virtue: A Study of Feminine Loveliness for Mothers & Daughters. 2004. (Illus.). 226p. (YA). 18.00 (978-0-9743390-1-6(6)) Bks. on the Path.

Noonan, Helen. Mom Let Me Be Me. 2009. 28p. pap. 15.95 (978-1-4389-7414-9(0)) AuthorHouse.

Polacco, Patricia. Betty Doll. 2004. 18.00 (978-0-7569-3208-4(4)) Perfection Learning Corp.

Summer Rogers Martin. Kaylea Grows Up: Mommy & Me Days. Debi Rogers, illus. 2009. 20p. pap. 10.99 (978-1-4389-5908-5(7)) AuthorHouse.

Tolstikova, Dasha. A Year Without Mom, 1 vol. 2015. (ENG., Illus.). 176p. (J). (gr. 4-9). 19.95 (978-1-55498-692-7(3)) Groundwood Bks. CAN. Dist: Publishers Group West (PGW).

Yoon, Nicola. Everything, Everything. 2017. (ENG.). 336p. (YA). (gr. 7). pap. 10.99 **(978-1-5247-6960-4(6)**, Ember) Random Hse. Children's Bks.

Zweber, Rhonda. Mommy's Hats. 2009. 36p. pap. 18.50 (978-1-60860-204-9(4), Eloquent Bks.) Strategic Book Publishing & Rights Agency (SBPRA).

MOTHERS AND DAUGHTERS—FICTION

Acorn, Alesa. Diary of the Beloved Book One: The Hidden. 2011. 512p. 31.95 (978-1-4634-0276-1(7)) AuthorHouse.

Adams, Thomas J. My Mommy Went to Sea Today. 2012. 16p. pap. 15.99 (978-1-4772-8476-6(1)) AuthorHouse.

Adewoyin, Beverly. Inside the Mommie Pond. 2013. (ENG.). 28p. (J). pap. 11.95 (978-1-4327-9703-4(4)) Outskirts Pr., Inc.

Adhikary, Anita B. My Daughters Are Smart! D Is for Daughters & S Is for Smart. Russo, Blythe, illus. 2014. (ENG.). 24p. (J). (gr. -1-3). 14.95 (978-1-62086-429-6(0)) Mascot Bks., Inc.

The Adventures of Molly. 2004. pap. 13.95 (978-1-59526-180-9(X)) Aeon Publishing Inc.

Afandalor, Indu. Mooooooom, Do You Love Me? 2012. 28p. pap. 15.50 (978-1-4670-7132-1(3)) AuthorHouse.

Airgood, Ellen. The Education of Ivy Blake. 2015. (ENG.). 240p. (J). (gr. 5). 16.99 (978-0-399-16278-7(X), Nancy Paulsen Books) Penguin Young Readers Group.

Albert, Lisa. Mercy Lily. 2011. (ENG.). 240p. (YA). pap. 9.95 (978-0-7387-2699-1(0), Flux) North Star Editions.

Alegre, Mari. Destiny. 2011. 174p. 29.99 (978-1-4568-2040-4(0)); pap. 19.99 (978-1-4568-2039-8(7)) Xlibris Corp.

Alegria, Malin. Estrella's Quinceañera. (ENG.). (YA). (gr. 7-18). 2007. 288p. pap. 10.99 (978-0-689-87810-7(9)) 2006. (Illus.). 272p. 15.99 (978-0-689-87809-1(5)) Simon & Schuster Bks. For Young Readers. (Simon & Schuster Bks. For Young Readers).

Alexander, Jill S. The Sweetheart of Prosper County. 2010. (ENG.). 240p. (YA). (gr. 7-12). pap. 18.99 (978-0-312-54857-5(5), 9780312548575) Square Fish.

Alexander, R. C. Unfamiliar Magic. 2011. (ENG.). 368p. (J). (gr. 3-7). pap. 8.99 (978-0-375-85855-0(5), Yearling) Random Hse. Children's Bks.

Alexander, William. A Properly Unhaunted Place. Murphy, Kelly, illus. 2017. (ENG.). 192p. (J). (gr. 3-7). 16.99 **(978-1-4814-6915-9(0)**, McElderry, Margaret K. Bks.) McElderry, Margaret K. Bks.

Alexandria, Shalayne. Nyville High No. 2: Mother May I. 2007. 130p. (YA). pap. 10.00 (978-0-9786180-4-9(1)) 5 Muses Publishing.

Alfonsi, Alice, adapted by. 'Rents: Lizzie Mcguire. 2005. 134p. (J). lib. bdg. 16.92 (978-1-4242-0689-6(8)) Fitzgerald Bks.

Almond, David. My Name Is Mina. (ENG.). 304p. (J). 2012. (gr. 5). 6.99 (978-0-375-87327-0(9), Yearling) 2011. (gr. 3-7). 15.99 (978-0-385-74073-9(5), Delacorte Bks. for Young Readers) Random Hse. Children's Bks.

Altieri, Maria. Mom, Tell Me a Story. 2012. 20p. pap. 24.95 (978-1-62709-702-4(3)) America Star Bks.

Ambatchew, Daniel. Mimi Mystery. 2012. (Illus.). 39p. pap. 10.95 (978-9988-647-83-4(2)) Sub-Saharan Pubs. & Traders GHA. Dist: African Bks. Collective, Ltd.

Amelia Asks Why... Book of Fun. 2007. (J). 1.09 (978-0-9726075-7-5(9)) EPI Bks.

Anderson, Jessica Lee. Calli. 2011. (ENG.). 198p. (J). (gr. 6). 16.95 (978-1-57131-702-5(3)); pap. 8.00 (978-1-57131-699-8(X)) Milkweed Editions.

Anselmo, Robert Louis. We're All Different & yet Still the Same. l.t. ed. 2006. (Illus.). 22p. (J). 14.99 (978-1-59879-107-5(9)); per. 9.99 (978-1-59879-088-7(9)) Lifevest Publishing, Inc.

Appelt, Kathi. Keeper. Hall, August, illus. (ENG.). (J). (gr. 3-7). 2012. 432p. pap. 8.99 (978-1-4169-5061-5(3)) 2010. 416p. 17.99 (978-1-4169-5060-8(5)) Simon & Schuster Children's Publishing. (Atheneum Bks. for Young Readers).

Arno, Ronni. Dear Poppy. 2016. (Mix Ser.). (ENG., Illus.). 256p. (J). (gr. 4-8). pap. 7.99 (978-1-4814-3759-2(3), Aladdin) Simon & Schuster Children's Publishing.

Arnold, David. Mosquitoland. 2015. (ENG.). 352p. (YA). (gr. 7). 17.99 (978-0-451-47077-5(X), Viking Books for Young Readers) Penguin Young Readers Group.

Arnold, Elana K. Infandous. 2015. (ENG.). 200p. (YA). (gr. 8-12). 18.99 (978-1-4677-3849-1(2)) Lerner Publishing Group.

Aschermann, Kurt. Bj & the Amazing Doctor Directions. 2008. 172p. pap. 11.99 (978-1-4343-7708-1(3)) AuthorHouse.

AZ Books, creator. Lamb Searches for Her Mom. 2012. (Plush Baby Ser.). (ENG., Illus.). 10p. (J). (gr. -1 — 1). 11.95 (978-1-61889-218-8(5)) AZ Bks. LLC.

Babbitt, Kelli. You Grew in My Heart Instead. 2008. 36p. pap. 24.95 (978-1-60474-981-6(4)) America Star Bks.

Bachorz, Pam. Drought. 2011. (ENG.). 400p. (gr. 7-18). 17.99 (978-1-60684-016-0(9)) Lerner Publishing Group.

Baier, Hiltrud. Greta in Schweden. 2009. 114p. pap. (978-3-8391-2523-6(5)) Books on Demand GmbH.

Baker, Andrea. Worlds Apart: Leah. 2013. 284p. pap. 14.99 (978-0-9892854-3-8(X)) Taylor Street Publishing LLC.

Banks, Lynne Reid. Uprooted - A Canadian War Story. 2015. (ENG.). 336p. (J). pap. 8.99 (978-0-00-813235-4(6), HarperCollins Children's Bks.) HarperCollins Pubs. Ltd. GBR. Dist: HarperCollins Pubs.

Banks, Taylor. Rock Princess. 2009. 102p. pap. 15.99 (978-1-4415-4288-5(4)) Xlibris Corp.

Baratz-Logsted, Lauren. Secrets of My Suburban Life. 2008. (ENG.). 240p. (YA). (gr. 9-18). pap. 7.99 (978-1-4169-2525-5(2), Simon Pulse) Simon Pulse.

Bardsley-Sirois, Lois. Katherine's Winter Garden. 2012. 24p. pap. 12.99 (978-1-4525-6269-8(5)) Balboa Pr.

Barkow, Henriette. Buri & the Maroow. Finlay, Lizzie, illus. 2004. (ENG & FRE.). 24p. (J). pap. (978-1-85269-583-5(8)) Mantra Lingua.

Barnhart, Judy. Sand Angels in the Snow. 2007. 68p. per. 8.95 (978-0-595-45154-8(3)) iUniverse, Inc.

Barr, Barbara Jean. My Mom Inside My Pocket, 1 vol. Stutz, Chris, illus. 2010. 16p. 24.95 (978-1-4489-5704-0(4)) America Star Bks.

Barry, Debra R. Debbie's Eyes. Tessier, Beth Marie, photos by. 2011. (Illus.). 32p. pap. 24.95 (978-1-4560-5272-0(1)) America Star Bks.

Baskin, Nora Raleigh. Ruby on the Outside. 2015. (ENG., Illus.). 176p. (J). (gr. 3-7). 18.99 (978-1-4424-8503-7(5), Simon & Schuster Bks. For Young Readers) Simon & Schuster Bks. For Young Readers.

Bateson, Catherine. The Boyfriend Rules of Good Behavior. 2006. (ENG.). 192p. (YA). (gr. 8-12). 16.95 (978-0-8234-2026-1(4)) Holiday Hse., Inc.

Bauer, Joan. Almost Home. (ENG.). (J). (gr. 5). 2013. 288p. pap. 7.99 (978-0-14-242748-4(9), Puffin Books) 2012. 272p. 16.99 (978-0-670-01289-3(0), Viking Books for Young Readers) Penguin Young Readers Group.

Beale, Fleur. The Boy in the Olive Grove. 2013. 368p. pap. (978-1-4596-5723-6(3)) ReadHowYouWant.com, Ltd.

—I Am Not Esther. 2013. 246p. pap. (978-1-4596-5748-9(9)) ReadHowYouWant.com, Ltd.

Bedford, David A. Angela. 2009. 190p. 25.50 (978-1-60860-755-6(0), Eloquent Bks.) Strategic Book Publishing & Rights Agency (SBPRA).

Bell, Clare. Ratha's Challenge. 2011. (Named Ser.: Bk. 4). (ENG.). 252p. (YA). pap. 14.95 (978-0-9745603-9-7(1)) Imaginator Pr.

Bell, Hilari. Sword of Waters. Willis, Drew, illus. 2009. (Shield, Sword, & Crown Ser.: 2). (ENG.). 384p. (J). (gr. 3-7). pap. 6.99 (978-1-4169-0597-4(9), Aladdin) Simon & Schuster Children's Publishing.

—Sword of Waters, No. 2. Willis, Drew, illus. 2008. (Shield, Sword, & Crown Ser.: 2). (ENG.). 368p. (J). (gr. 3-7). 16.99 (978-1-4169-0596-7(0), Simon & Schuster/Paula Wiseman Bks.) Simon & Schuster/Paula Wiseman Bks.

Bendinger, Jessica. The Seven Rays. 2010. (ENG.). 336p. (YA). (gr. 9). pap. 9.99 (978-1-4169-3840-8(0), Simon & Schuster Bks. For Young Readers) Simon & Schuster Bks. For Young Readers.

Bennett, Kelly. Your Daddy Was Just Like You. Walker, David, illus. 2010. (ENG.). 32p. (J). (gr. -1-k). 16.99 (978-0-399-25258-7(4), G.P. Putnam's Sons Books for Young Readers) Penguin Young Readers Group.

Berke, Lindsey Jensen. Am I Pretty? 2013. 28p. 22.99 (978-1-4808-0106-6(2)); pap. 16.99 (978-1-4808-0108-0(9)) Archway Publishing.

Bernal, Estela. Can You See Me Now? 2014. (ENG.). (YA). pap. 10.95 (978-1-55885-783-4(4), Piñata Books) Arte Publico Pr.

Bernard, Margaret Mitchell. Kate & the Family Tree. Duncan, Shirley, ed. Ciesinska, Izabela, illus. 2009. 24p. pap. 14.99 (978-1-4251-7408-8(6)) Trafford Publishing.

Black, Amber. A Day with Miss Sassy. 2008. 16p. pap. 24.95 (978-1-60610-338-8(5)) PublishAmerica, Inc.

Blake, Ashley Herring. How to Make a Wish. 2017. (ENG.). 336p. (YA). (gr. 9). 17.99 (978-0-544-81519-3(X), HMH Books For Young Readers) Houghton Mifflin Harcourt Publishing Co.

Blanchard, Amy Ella. A Sweet Little Maid. 2007. (ENG.). 120p. pap. 18.99 (978-1-4264-9546-5(3)); 132p. pap. 19.99 (978-1-4264-9927-2(2)) Creative Media Partners, LLC.

Bliss, Barbara. Abigail Elliot & the Dollhouse Family. 2008. (ENG.). 258p. pap. 9.99 (978-1-4196-7615-4(6)) CreateSpace Independent Publishing Platform.

Blocker, Ariel S. Beauty in Me. 2012. 24p. pap. 12.45 (978-1-4497-6363-3(4), WestBow Pr.) Author Solutions, Inc.

Blue Moon. 2014. (Dead City Ser.: 2). (ENG., Illus.). 336p. (J). (gr. 4-8). pap. 7.99 (978-1-4424-4132-3(1), Aladdin) Simon & Schuster Children's Publishing.

Blume, Lesley M. M. Tennyson. 2009. (ENG.). 240p. (J). (gr. 3-7). 7.99 (978-0-440-24061-7(1), Yearling) Random Hse. Children's Bks.

Blythe, Carolita. Revenge of a Not-So-Pretty Girl. 2013. (ENG.). 336p. (YA). (gr. 7). 19.99 (978-0-375-99081-6(X), Delacorte Bks. for Young Readers) Random Hse. Children's Bks.

Bonnell, Kris. We Like the Beach. 2007. (J). pap. 5.95 (978-1-933727-55-4(1)) Reading Reading Bks., LLC.

Bonnett-Rampersaud, Louise. Bubble & Squeak, 1 vol. Banta, Susan, illus. 2006. (ENG.). 24p. (J). (gr. -1-2). 14.99 (978-0-7614-5310-9(5)) Marshall Cavendish Corp.

Bosworth, Jennifer. The Killing Jar. 2016. (ENG.). 352p. (YA). 17.99 (978-0-374-34137-4(0), 9780374341374, Farrar, Straus & Giroux (BYR)) Farrar, Straus & Giroux.

Boudreau, Helene. Real Mermaids Don't Hold Their Breath. 2012. (ENG.). 240p. (J). (gr. 4-8). pap. 9.99 (978-1-4022-6446-7(1), Sourcebooks Jabberwocky) Sourcebooks, Inc.

Bowe, Julie. Birthday Glamour! 2015. (Victoria Torres, Unfortunately Average Ser.). (ENG.). 160p. (gr. 4-4). lib. bdg. 26.65 (978-1-4965-0533-0(6)) Stone Arch Bks.

Bowsher, Melodie. My Lost & Found Life. 2006. (ENG.). 320p. (YA). (gr. 9-13). 16.95 (978-1-58234-736-3(0), 9781582347363, Bloomsbury USA Childrens) Bloomsbury Publishing USA.

Braxton-Smith, Ananda. Merrow. 2016. (ENG.). 240p. (YA). (gr. 9). 16.99 (978-0-7636-7924-8(0)) Candlewick Pr.

Brewer, Melanie. Sweep Away the Bad Day. 2009. 20p. pap. 12.99 (978-1-4490-1605-0(7)) AuthorHouse.

Britt, Paige. The Lost Track of Time. 2016. (ENG.). 320p. (J). (gr. 3-7). pap. 9.99 (978-0-545-53813-8(0), Scholastic Pr.) Scholastic, Inc.

Broberg, Janel. Catie the Cute, Curious & Sometimes Crooked Caterpillar. 2012. 24p. pap. 12.00 (978-1-61170-073-2(6)) Robertson Publishing.

Brothers, Marilee. Moonstone. 2008. 236p. (YA). pap. 14.95 (978-0-9802453-4-9(6), Bell Bridge Bks.) BelleBks., Inc.

Brown, Teri. Born of Illusion. 2013. (ENG.). 384p. (YA). (Born of Illusion Ser.: 1). (gr. 8). 17.99 (978-0-06-218754-3(6)); pap. 9.99 (978-0-06-227720-6(0)) HarperCollins Pubs.

Brucke, Candice Yarbray. Night-Night Town. 2009. 28p. pap. 15.00 (978-1-4389-7467-5(1)) AuthorHouse.

Bruha, Ginger. Lilly's Breakfast Time. 2004. 20p. pap. 24.95 (978-1-4137-3133-0(3)) PublishAmerica, Inc.

Bryant, Cathy. The Doctor Said I Have Leukemi. Bunker, Thomas, illus. 2012. 24p. pap. 24.95 (978-1-4560-6929-2(2)) America Star Bks.

Buckley, Michael. Once upon a Crime. Ferguson, Peter, illus. 2007. (ENG.). 288p. (J). (gr. 2-8). 16.95 (978-0-8109-1610-4(X), Amulet Bks.) Abrams, Inc.

Budhos, Marina. Tell Us We're Home. 2011. (ENG.). 320p. (YA). (gr. 7). pap. 9.99 (978-1-4424-2128-8(2), Atheneum Bks. for Young Readers) Simon & Schuster Children's Publishing.

Bullen, Alexandra. Wishful Thinking. 2011. (ENG.). 256p. (J). (gr. 9-9). 17.99 (978-0-545-13907-6(4)) Scholastic, Inc.

Burian, Natalka. Welcome to the Slipstream. 2017. (ENG., Illus.). 272p. (YA). (gr. 9-12). 17.99 (978-1-5072-0075-9(7), Simon Pulse) Simon Pulse.

Burkart, Tammy Jayne. Lillie, 1 vol. 2009. 48p. pap. 16.95 (978-1-60813-680-3(9)) America Star Bks.

Burrell, Carol klio. Secret Diary. Neel, Julien, illus. 2012. (Lou! Ser.: 1). (ENG.). 48p. (J). (gr. 6-9). lib. bdg. 27.93 (978-0-7613-8776-3(5), Graphic Universe™) Lerner Publishing Group.

—Summertime Blues. Neel, Julien, illus. 2012. (Lou! Ser.: 2). (ENG.). 48p. (J). (gr. 6-9). lib. bdg. 27.93 (978-0-7613-8777-0(3), Graphic Universe™) Lerner Publishing Group.

Bush, Rosetta Bowman. My Name Is Violet. 2013. 20p. pap. 24.95 (978-1-63000-515-3(0)) America Star Bks.

By Kaleena Ma. Glasses for Me? Oh No! Dawn Phillips, illus. 2009. 40p. pap. 18.49 (978-1-4389-5418-9(2)) AuthorHouse.

Cala, C. J. Mother Dandy's Nonmalmani. 2011. 58p. pap. 6.95 (978-1-257-37974-3(7)) Lulu Pr., Inc.

Caletti, Deb. The Queen of Everything. Greenberg, Anne, ed. 2008. (ENG.). 352p. (YA). (gr. 7-12). pap. 8.99 (978-1-4169-5781-2(2), Simon Pulse) Simon Pulse.

—The Six Rules of Maybe. (ENG.). (YA). (gr. 7). 2011. 352p. pap. 9.99 (978-1-4169-7971-5(9)) 2010. 336p. 16.99 (978-1-4169-7969-2(7)) Simon Pulse. (Simon Pulse).

Callender, Simone. Rosa's Paw-Paw Tree: An inspiring tale about a daughter's deep love for her Mother. Downer, Romeo, illus. 2011. 24p. pap. 8.99 (978-1-4575-0596-6(7)) Dog Ear Publishing, LLC.

Cameron, Ann. The Secret Life of Amanda K. Woods. 2014. (ENG.). 208p. (J). (gr. 5-9). pap. 6.99 (978-1-250-04419-8(7), 9781250044198) Square Fish.

Campbell-Fells. Blue Ribbon Girls. 2005. 145p. pap. 13.95 (978-0-7414-2593-5(9)) Infinity Publishing.

Carey, Janet Lee. Dragon's Keep. 2007. 302p. (J). (978-1-4287-3929-1(7)) Harcourt Trade Pubs.

—Dragon's Keep. 2008. (ENG., Illus.). 320p. (YA). (gr. 7-18). pap. 7.95 (978-0-15-206401-3(X)) Houghton Mifflin Harcourt Publishing Co.

Carlson, Melody. A Not-So-Simple Life. 2008. (Diary of a Teenage Girl Ser.: Bk. 14). (ENG.). 256p. (YA). (gr. 7). pap. 14.99 (978-1-60142-117-3(6), Multnomah) Doubleday Religious Publishing Group, The.

Carlson, Nancy. It's Going to Be Perfect! Carlson, Nancy, illus. 2012. (Nancy Carlson Picture Bks). (Illus.). 32p. (J). (gr. k-2). (ENG.). 9.95 (978-0-7613-8944-6(X)); 56.72 (978-0-7613-9299-6(8)) Lerner Publishing Group. (Carolrhoda Bks.).

Carlstrom, Nancy White. It's Your First Day of School, Annie Claire. Moore, Margie, illus. 2009. (ENG.). 32p. (J). (gr. k-2). 16.95 (978-0-8109-4057-4(4), Abrams Bks. for Young Readers) Abrams, Inc.

Carney, Mary Lou. The Treasure Rock. 2009. 32p. 14.00 (978-0-687-64537-4(9)) Abingdon Pr.

Carter, Nikki. Step to This. 2009. (ENG., Illus.). 240p. (YA). (gr. 9). 9.95 (978-0-7582-3439-1(2), K-Teen/Dafina) Kensington Publishing Corp.

Carter, Olivia. Through My Eyes, Book One: Jake. 2013. (ENG.). 235p. (YA). (gr. 7). pap. 10.95 (978-1-935089-63-6(3)) Acacia Publishing, Inc.

Carttar, Debra. Picturing Lucy. 2010. pap. 14.95 (978-0-7414-6195-7(1)) Infinity Publishing.

The Case of the Secret Box. 2007. 56p. pap. 7.75 (978-0-8341-2288-8(X), 083-412-288X) Beacon Hill Pr. of Kansas City.

Cassidy, Cathy. Dizzy. 2005. (ENG.). 272p. (J). (gr. 3-7). 6.99 (978-0-14-240474-4(8), Puffin Books) Penguin Young Readers Group.

Castro, Edmund Lee. Crystal & Her Flying Adventure. 2010. 44p. 16.99 (978-1-4490-6867-7(7)) AuthorHouse.

—Crystal & the Not-So-Scary Night. 2008. 36p. pap. 24.95 (978-1-60672-236-7(0)) America Star Bks.

Chang, Hae-Kyung. Oh No, School! Bisaillon, Josée, illus. 2014. 30p. (J). (978-1-4338-1333-7(5), Magination Pr.) American Psychological Assn.

Chappas, Bess. Kiki & the Red Shoes. Branam, Sandy, illus. 2007. (J). 17.99 (978-1-60131-012-5(9)) Big Tent Bks.

Charles, Bob. A Trip to the Market & una visita al Mercado: 6 English, 6 Spanish Adaptations. 2011. (ENG & SPA.). (J). 75.00 net. (978-1-4108-5642-5(9)) Benchmark Education Co.

Charrier, Lisa. Oh My, Oh No! Domergue, Agnes, illus. 2014. (ENG.). 32p. (-k). 15.95 (978-0-7624-5409-9(1), Running Pr. Kids) Running Pr. Bk. Pubs.

Cheever, Karen J. The Tuck-In: (a Child's Event) 2012. 24p. (-18). pap. 17.99 (978-1-4772-7546-7(0)) AuthorHouse.

Chen, Justina. Nothing but the Truth (And a Few White Lies) 2007. (Justina Chen Novel Ser.). (ENG.). 256p. (J). (gr. 7-17). per. 9.99 (978-0-316-01131-0(2)) Little, Brown Bks. for Young Readers.

Cheng, Andrea. Brushing Mom's Hair. Wong, Nicole, illus. 2009. (ENG.). 64p. (J). (gr. 5-8). 17.95 (978-1-59078-599-7(1), Front Street) Boyds Mills Pr.

Chew, Ruth. Witch's Broom. 2015. (Matter-Of-Fact Magic Book Ser.). (ENG., Illus.). 144p. (J). (gr. 2-5). pap. 5.99 (978-0-449-81578-6(1), Random Hse. Bks. for Young Readers) Random Hse. Children's Bks.

Clare, Cassandra. The Mortal Instruments: City of Bones; City of Ashes; City of Glass; City of Fallen Angels; City of Lost Souls; City of Heavenly Fire. 2014. (Mortal Instruments Ser.). (ENG., Illus.). 3248p. (YA). (gr. 9). 137.99 (978-1-4814-4296-1(1), McElderry, Margaret K. Bks.) McElderry, Margaret K. Bks.

Clark, Kristin Elizabeth. Jess, Chunk, & the Road Trip to Infinity. 2016. (ENG.). 272p. (YA). 17.99 (978-0-374-38006-9(6), 9780374380069, Farrar, Straus & Giroux (BYR)) Farrar, Straus & Giroux.

Clark, Kristina. The Great Adventures of Ella: The Magic Desk. 2010. 28p. 12.95 (978-1-4520-2412-7(X)) AuthorHouse.

Clark, M. H. T. L. C. 2015. 36p. 16.95 (978-1-938298-42-4(X)) Compendium, Inc., Publishing & Communications.

Clark Sherryl Staff. Bone Song. 2008. (Cutting Edge Ser.). (ENG.). 200p. pap. (978-1-84167-751-4(5)) Ransom Publishing Ltd.

Clarke, E. J. Oakwing: A Fairy's Tale. 2017. (Oakwing Ser.: 1). (ENG., Illus.). 192p. (J). (gr. 2-6). 16.99 **(978-1-4814-8191-5(6)**, Aladdin) Simon & Schuster Children's Publishing.

—Oakwing: A Fairy's Tale. 2017. (J). pap. **(978-1-4814-8190-8(8)**, Simon & Schuster/Paula Wiseman Bks.) Simon & Schuster/Paula Wiseman Bks.

Clavette, Taylor. Shapeshifter's Mark. 2012. 168p. (gr. 10-12). pap. 12.95 (978-1-4697-9264-4(8)) iUniverse, Inc.

Clow, Alexine. Jenny's Dreams. Clow, Alexine, illus. 2010. (Illus.). 20p. pap. 10.95 (978-1-936051-89-2(3)) Peppertree Pr., The.

Coates, Angel J. Mommy Loves No ! 2008. (Illus.). 48p. pap. 19.95 (978-1-4343-8642-7(2)) AuthorHouse.

Cochran, Cheryl. The Mini Message Man & the Great Candy Caper. Cochran, Christina, illus. 2011. 40p. pap. 24.95 (978-1-4560-7565-1(9)) America Star Bks.

Cochrane, Mick. The Girl Who Threw Butterflies. 2010. (ENG.). 192p. (J). (gr. 3-7). 6.99 (978-0-375-84610-6(7), Yearling) Random Hse. Children's Bks.

Cohn, Rachel. Shrimp, 7 vols. 2005. (YA). 171.75 (978-1-4193-5253-9(9)) Recorded Bks., Inc.

—Shrimp. 2006. (ENG.). 352p. (YA). (gr. 7-12). reprint ed. pap. 6.99 (978-0-689-86613-5(5), Simon & Schuster Bks. For Young Readers) Simon & Schuster Bks. For Young Readers.

Coker, Rachel. Interrupted: A Life Beyond Words, 1 vol. 2013. (ENG.). 256p. (YA). pap. 9.99 (978-0-310-72810-8(X)) Zondervan.

Connors, Faith Raymond. Love, Midgie. Connors, Tracy D., ed. 2008. (ENG., Illus.). 308p. pap. 12.95 (978-0-9640138-1-0(9), 9780964013810) BelleAire Pr.

Cooney, Caroline B. The Lost Songs. 2013. (ENG.). 256p. (YA). (gr. 7). pap. 8.99 (978-0-385-73967-2(2), Ember) Random Hse. Children's Bks.

Cooper, Abby. Bubbles. 2017. (ENG.). 272p. (J). 16.99 (978-0-374-30290-0(1), 9780374302900, Farrar, Straus & Giroux (BYR)) Farrar, Straus & Giroux.

Cornwell, Betsy. Mechanica. 2016. lib. bdg. 19.65 (978-0-606-37999-1(1)) Turtleback Bks.

Cowling, Chani. Cookie Baker, Sweet & Sour. 2008. 24p. pap. 24.95 (978-1-60703-021-8(7)) America Star Bks.

Cox, Tracey M. Angels Do That. Movshina, Marina, illus. 2012. 16p. pap. 9.95 (978-1-61633-299-0(9)) Guardian Angel Publishing, Inc.

Coyle, Carmela Lavigna. Do Princesses Wear Hiking Boots? Gordon, Mike & Gordon, Carl, illus. 2003. (ENG.). 32p. (J). (gr. -1-2). 15.95 (978-0-87358-828-7(2)) Cooper Square Publishing Llc.

Crosby, Sherry. A Bad Case of the Grownies. 2012. 28p. pap. 16.09 (978-1-4669-3554-9(5)) Trafford Publishing.

Crossan, Sarah. Apple & Rain. (ENG.). 352p. (YA). 2016. pap. 9.99 (978-1-68119-073-0(7), 9781681190730) 2015. (gr. 7). 17.99 (978-1-61963-690-3(5), 9781619636903) Bloomsbury Publishing USA. (Bloomsbury USA Childrens).

CRUTCHFIELD, Shannon. Arion's Way. 2010. 10p. 11.50 (978-0-557-54457-8(2)) Lulu Pr., Inc.

Cunningham, Laura Shaine & Cunningham, Laura S. The Midnight Diary of Zoya Blume. 2005. 176p. (J). (gr. 3-18). 15.99 (978-0-06-072259-3(2), Geringer, Laura Book) HarperCollins Pubs.

Dagg, Carole Estby. The Year We Were Famous. 2011. (ENG.). 256p. (YA). (gr. 7-18). 17.99 (978-0-618-99983-5(3)) Houghton Mifflin Harcourt Publishing Co.

Daines, Ellie. Shine Izzy Shine. 2015. (ENG.). 224p. (J). 12.99 (978-1-84939-529-8(2)) Andersen Pr. GBR. Dist: Independent Pubs. Group.

Dale, Jay. Our Baby, 1 vol. Everitt-Stewart, Andrew, illus. 2012. (Engage Literacy Green Ser.). (ENG.). 32p. (gr. k-2). pap. 5.99 (978-1-4296-9023-2(2), Engage Literacy) Capstone Press of Coughlan Cos.

Dale, Katie. Mumnesia. 2016. (ENG.). 272p. (J). (gr. 4-6). pap. 9.99 **(978-1-5098-1070-3(6))** Pan Macmillan GBR. Dist: Independent Pubs. Group.

Damico, Gina. Hellhole. 2015. (ENG.). 368p. (YA). (gr. 9). 17.99 (978-0-544-30710-0(0), HMH Books For Young Readers) Houghton Mifflin Harcourt Publishing Co.

Danticat, Edwidge. Mama's Nightingale: A Story of Immigration & Separation. Staub, Leslie, illus. 2015. (ENG.). 32p. (J). (gr. k-3). 17.99 (978-0-525-42809-1(7), Dial Bks) Penguin Young Readers Group.

Danziger, Paula. Amber Brown Is Green with Envy. 2014. (Amber Brown Ser.: 9). (ENG., Illus.). 176p. (J). (gr. 2-5). pap. 5.99 (978-0-14-242699-9(7), Puffin Books) Penguin Young Readers Group.

—Amber Brown Is Green with Envy. Ross, Tony, illus. 2004. (Amber Brown Ser.: No. 9). 151p. (J). (gr. 2-5). 12.65 (978-0-7569-2978-7(4)) Perfection Learning Corp.

—Amber Brown Wants Extra Credit. Ross, Tony, illus. 2008. (Amber Brown Ser.: 4). (ENG.). 144p. (J). (gr. 2-5). 5.99 (978-0-14-241049-3(7), Puffin Books) Penguin Young Readers Group.

Dao, Cindy. Mama? 2005. (Illus.). 36p. (J). per. 8.99 (978-1-932338-79-9(9)) Lifevest Publishing, Inc.

Darrows, Eva. The Awesome. 2015. (ENG.). 352p. (YA). (gr. 10). pap. 9.99 (978-1-78108-324-6(X), Ravenstone) Rebellion GBR. Dist: Simon & Schuster, Inc.

Dauphin, Lili. I Will Fly Again: The Restavek. 2007. 284p. per. 18.95 (978-0-9748329-8-2(7)) MiraQuest.

Davenport, Jennifer. Anna Begins. 2008. (ENG.). 150p. 21.95 (978-0-930773-83-0(7)) Black Heron Pr.

David, Kate. Murphy & the Magical Hat. 2012. (ENG.). 26p. (J). 18.95 (978-1-4327-8582-6(6)) Outskirts Pr., Inc.

Davis, Chasta. Maggie's Little Strawberry, 1 vol. 2010. 20p. pap. 24.95 (978-1-4489-5486-5(X)) PublishAmerica, Inc.

Davis, Jacky & Soman, David. Ladybug Girl & Her Mama. Soman, David, illus. 2013. (Ladybug Girl Ser.). (ENG., Illus.). 14p. (J). (gr. -1 — 1). bds. 5.99 (978-0-8037-3891-1(9), Dial Bks) Penguin Young Readers Group.

Dawn, Sasha. Splinter. 2017. (ENG.). 304p. (YA). (gr. 8-12). 18.99 (978-1-5124-1151-5(5)); 9.99 **(978-1-5124-3434-7(5)**, Carolrhoda Lab™); 38.65 **(978-1-5124-2695-3(4)**, Carolrhoda Lab™); 38.65 **(978-1-5124-3435-4(3)**, Carolrhoda Lab™) Lerner Publishing Group.

Deal-Trainor, Carol. Marilee: A Manatee's First Journey to the Springs. 2008. 48p. pap. 16.95 (978-1-60563-660-3(6)) America Star Bks.

Deaver, Julie Reece. The Night I Disappeared. 2012. (ENG.). 256p. (YA). (gr. 7). pap. 12.99 (978-1-4424-7298-3(7), Simon Pulse) Simon Pulse.

Dee, Barbara. Trauma Queen. 2011. (Mix Ser.). (ENG.). 272p. (J). (gr. 4-8). pap. 6.99 (978-1-4424-0923-1(1), Aladdin) Simon & Schuster Children's Publishing.

Delaney, Mark. Pepperland, 1 vol. 2007. (ENG.). 224p. (YA). (gr. 7-18). pap. 7.95 (978-1-56145-402-0(8)) Peachtree Pubs.

Delmonte, Ellis. Miracle Girl. 2007. (ENG.). 208p. (YA). per. (978-0-9555096-4-3(5)) Hawkwood Bks.

DeNomme, Donna & Proctor, Tina. Ophelia's Oracle: Discovering the Healthy, Happy, Self-aware, & Competant Girl in the Mirror. 2009. (YA). pap. 16.95 (978-1-61539-958-1(5)) Independent Pub.

Deriso, Christine Hurley. Talia Talk. 2009. 184p. (J). pap. (978-0-375-84496-6(1), Delacorte Pr) Random House Publishing Group.

Devlin, Calla. Right Where You Left Me. 2017. (ENG., Illus.). 256p. (YA). (gr. 9). 17.99 **(978-1-4814-8699-6(3)**, Atheneum Bks. for Young Readers) Simon & Schuster Children's Publishing.

Devlin, Calla. Tell Me Something Real. 2016. (ENG., Illus.). 304p. (YA). (gr. 9). 17.99 (978-1-4814-6115-3(X), Atheneum Bks. for Young Readers) Simon & Schuster Children's Publishing.

Diesen, Deborah. Catch a Kiss. McLeod, Kris Aro, illus. 2016. (ENG.). 32p. (J). (gr. k-2). 15.99 (978-1-58536-961-4(6), 204037) Sleeping Bear Pr.

Dixon, Linda A. Cupcakes for Cristina! 2010. 16p. 9.99 (978-1-4520-6650-9(7)) AuthorHouse.

Dodd, Kelly. Gregarious Gabby & Her Gabbyful Life: Moving Day. 2011. 28p. 13.59 (978-1-4567-2890-8(3)) AuthorHouse.

Dolamore, Jaclyn. Dark Metropolis. 2014. (ENG., Illus.). 304p. (YA). (gr. 7-12). 17.99 (978-1-4231-6332-9(X)) Hyperion Bks. for Children.

Dorros, Arthur. Mama & Me. Gutierrez, Rudy, illus. 2011. (ENG & SPA.). 32p. (J). (gr. -1-3). 16.99 (978-0-06-058160-2(3), Rayo) HarperCollins Pubs.

Doty, Kathryn Adams. Wild Orphan. 2006. (ENG.). 144p. (gr. 3-7). per. 14.95 (978-1-889020-20-4(6)) Edinborough Pr.

Dougherty, Meghan. Woe of Jade Doe. Birnbach, Alece, illus. 2015. (Dorothy's Derby Chronicles Ser.: 2). (ENG.). 288p. (J). (gr. 4-7). pap. 6.99 (978-1-4926-0147-0(0), Sourcebooks Jabberwocky) Sourcebooks, Inc.

Dower, Laura. Gabi & the Great Big Bakeover. Lazuli, Lilly, illus. 160p. 2017. (J). (978-1-4747-2213-1(X)) 2016. (ENG.). (gr. 4-5). lib. bdg. 26.65 (978-1-4965-3119-3(1)) Stone Arch Bks.

Downham, Jenny. Unbecoming. (ENG.). 384p. (J). (gr. 9-9). 2017. pap. 9.99 ***(978-1-338-16072-7(9))*** 2016. 17.99 *(978-0-545-90717-0(9))* Scholastic, Inc.

Doyle, Roddy. A Greyhound of a Girl. 2013. (ENG.). 224p. (YA). (gr. 3-7). pap. 7.95 *(978-1-4197-0798-8(1),* Amulet Bks.) Abrams, Inc.

Dube, Pierrette. How to Become a Perfect Princess in Five Days. Melanson, Luc, illus. 2009. (Rainy Day Readers Ser.). 32p. (J). (gr. -1-3). 22.60 *(978-1-60754-376-3(1))* Windmill Bks.

Duble, Kathleen Benner. The Sacrifice. 2007. (ENG.). 224p. (J). (gr. 5-9). pap. 7.99 *(978-0-689-87651-6(3),* McElderry, Margaret K. Bks.) McElderry, Margaret K. Bks.

Dubrule, Jackie. Miranda, God & the Park. Swope, Brenda, illus. 2011. 32p. pap. 24.95 *(978-1-4560-0966-3(4))* America Star Bks.

Durgan, Lori Origer. The Little Scrub Lady. 2012. 28p. pap. 15.99 *(978-1-4797-4259-2(7))* Xlibris Corp.

Dyan, Penelope. Introducing Fabulous Marie, a Girl with a Good Head on Her Shoulders. Dyan, Penelope, illus. 2009. (Illus.). 44p. pap. 11.95 *(978-1-935118-55-8(2))* Bellissima Publishing, LLC.

—Lovely Libby. Dyan, Penelope, illus. 2010. (Illus.). 34p. pap. 11.95 *(978-1-935630-28-9(8))* Bellissima Publishing, LLC.

Dyer, Hadley. Johnny Kellock Died Today. 2007. (ENG.). 192p. (J). mass mkt. 6.92 ***(978-0-00-639534-8(1),*** Harper Trophy) HarperCollins Pubs.

Easton, Kelly. To Be Mona. (ENG.). 224p. (YA). (gr. 7). 2009. pap. 7.99 *(978-1-4169-0055-9(1))* 2008. 16.99 *(978-1-4169-0054-2(3))* McElderry, Margaret K. Bks. (McElderry, Margaret K. Bks.).

Egan, Catherine. The Unmaking, 1 vol. 2013. (Last Days of Tian Di Ser.: 2). (ENG.). 248p. (J). (gr. 4-6). pap. 12.95 *(978-1-55050-559-7(9))* Coteau Bks. CAN. Dist: Orca Bk. Pubs. USA.

Ehrlich, Amy. Joyride. 2008. (ENG., Illus.). 256p. (YA). (gr. 7). pap. 8.99 *(978-0-7636-2321-0(0))* Candlewick Pr.

Eilrich, Dinah Kay. Teeny Tessie's Big Baking Adventure. 2009. 28p. pap. 13.99 *(978-1-4490-2277-8(4))* AuthorHouse.

Eisenberg, Kristy. When I Grow Up. Joslin, Irene, illus. 2009. 28p. pap. 12.49 *(978-1-4389-0183-1(6))* AuthorHouse.

Ekster, Carol Gordon. Before I Sleep I Say Thank You. Rojas, Mary, illus. 2015. (J). 14.95 *(978-0-8198-1225-4(0))* Pauline Bks. & Media.

Ellis, Amanda & Block, Maggie. Jwenlapaix in the Bateyes. 2009. 52p. pap. 24.00 *(978-1-4389-4391-6(1))* AuthorHouse.

Erlich, Bev. Pink Roses Everywhere. gif. ed. 2004. (Illus.). 64p. (J). 14.95 *(978-0-9743913-0-4(1))* Snojoy Publishing.

Ernst, Kathleen. Whistler in the Dark. 2009. (Mysteries Through Time Ser.). 144 - 176p. (J). (gr. 4-8). 31.95 *(978-1-60754-429-6(6));* pap. 15.25 *(978-1-60754-432-6(6))* Windmill Bks.

Evetts-Secker, Josephine. Mother & Daughter Tales. Cann, Helen, illus. 2011. (ENG.). 40p. (J). 21.99 *(978-1-84686-572-5(7))* Barefoot Bks., Inc.

Farish, Terry. The Good Braider, 0 vols. 2014. (ENG.). 224p. (YA). (gr. 9-12). pap. 9.99 *(978-1-4778-1628-8(3),* 9781477816288, Amazon Children's Publishing) Amazon Publishing.

Feiffer, Kate. My Mom Is Trying to Ruin My Life. Goode, Diane, illus. 2009. (ENG.). 32p. (J). (gr. -1-3). 18.99 *(978-1-4169-4100-2(2),* Simon & Schuster/Paula Wiseman Bks.) Simon & Schuster/Paula Wiseman Bks.

Fenderson, Shani. Mommy, Why Is the Sky So Blue? Fenderson, David, illus. 2009. 24p. pap. 24.95 *(978-1-60749-550-5(3))* America Star Bks.

Ferrier, Charlotte. Little Red Riding Hood. 2016. (Fairytale Cottages Ser.). (ENG.). 12p. (J). (gr. -1-k). bds. 8.99 *(978-0-7641-6818-5(5))* Barron's Educational Series, Inc.

Fessler, Jennifer. Precious Is Worried. 2008. 16p. 11.30 *(978-0-615-24258-3(8))* Twin Sisters Publishing Co.

Filigenzi, Courtney & Bersani, Shennen. Let My Colors Out. Bersani, Shennen, illus. 2009. (ENG., Illus.). 16p. (J). (gr. -1-k). pap. 11.95 *(978-1-60443-011-0(7),* 1604430117) American Cancer Society, Inc.

Fisher, Annabelle. The Secret Destiny of Pixie Piper. Andrewson, Natalie, illus. 2016. (Pixie Piper Ser.: 1). 320p. (J). (gr. 3-7). 16.99 *(978-0-06-239377-7(4),* Greenwillow Bks.) HarperCollins Pubs.

Fisher, Rusty. Littlest Vampire's Story, 1 vol. 2014. (Story Time for Little Monsters Ser.). (ENG., Illus.). 24p. (J). (gr. -1-4). lib. bdg. 27.07 *(978-1-62402-020-9(8),* Looking Glass Library) Magic Wagon.

—Littlest Werewolf's Story, 1 vol. 2014. (Story Time for Little Monsters Ser.). (ENG.). 24p. (J). (gr. -1-4). lib. bdg. 27.07 *(978-1-62402-021-6(6),* Looking Glass Library) Magic Wagon.

—Littlest Witch's Story, 1 vol. 2014. (Story Time for Little Monsters Ser.). (ENG., Illus.). 24p. (J). (gr. -1-4). lib. bdg. 27.07 *(978-1-62402-022-3(4),* Looking Glass Library) Magic Wagon.

—Littlest Zombie's Story, 1 vol. 2014. (Story Time for Little Monsters Ser.). (ENG.). 24p. (J). (gr. -1-4). lib. bdg. 27.07 *(978-1-62402-023-0(2),* Looking Glass Library) Magic Wagon.

Fitzmaurice, Kathryn. Destiny, Rewritten. 2015. (ENG.). 368p. (J). (gr. 3-7). pap. 6.99 *(978-0-06-162503-9(5),* Tegen, Katherine Bks) HarperCollins Pubs.

Fixmer, Elizabeth. Down from the Mountain. 2015. (ENG.). 288p. (YA). (gr. 8-12). 16.99 *(978-0-8075-8370-8(7))* Whitman, Albert & Co.

Flinn, Alex. Diva. 2013. (ENG.). 304p. (YA). (gr. 9). pap. 9.99 *(978-0-06-212434-0(X))* 2007. (ENG.). 288p. (J). (gr. 9-12). pap. 8.99 *(978-0-06-056846-7(1),* HarperTeen) 2006. 263p. (YA). (gr. 7-12). 16.99 *(978-0-06-056843-6(7),* HarperTeen) 2006. 263p. (YA). (gr. 7-12). lib. bdg. 18.89 *(978-0-06-056845-0(3),* HarperTeen) HarperCollins Pubs.

Floyd, Brandi. Alex's Choice. 2012. 38p. 24.95 *(978-1-4626-6028-5(2))* America Star Bks.

Fonner, Deborah K. An Extra Ordinary Day. VonBokel, Jan, illus. 2012. 24p. 19.95 *(978-1-4327-8342-6(4))* Outskirts Pr., Inc.

Fox, Mem. This & That. Horacek, Judy, illus. 2017. (ENG.). 32p. (J). (gr. -1-k). 17.99 *(978-1-338-03780-7(3),* Scholastic Pr.) Scholastic, Inc.

Frederick, Heather Vogel. The Complete Mother-Daughter Book Club Collection: The Mother-Daughter Book Club; Much Ado about Anne; Dear Pen Pal; Pies & Prejudice; Home for the Holidays; Wish You Were Eyre. 2013. (Mother-Daughter Book Club Ser.). (ENG., Illus.). 2320p. (YA). (gr. 4-7). pap. 47.99 *(978-1-4424-9843-3(9),* Simon & Schuster Bks. For Young Readers) Simon & Schuster Bks. For Young Readers.

—Dear Pen Pal. (Mother-Daughter Book Club Ser.). (ENG.). (J). (gr. 4-7). 2010. 432p. pap. 7.99 *(978-1-4424-0848-7(0))* 2009. 416p. 16.99 *(978-1-4169-7430-7(X))* Simon & Schuster Bks. For Young Readers. (Simon & Schuster Bks. For Young Readers).

—Home for the Holidays. (Mother-Daughter Book Club Ser.). (ENG.). (J). (gr. 4-9). 2012. 384p. pap. 8.99 *(978-1-4424-0686-5(0))* 2011. 352p. 18.99 *(978-1-4424-0685-8(2))* Simon & Schuster Bks. For Young Readers. (Simon & Schuster Bks. For Young Readers).

—The Mother-Daughter Book Club. (Mother-Daughter Book Club Ser.). (ENG.). (J). 2008. 288p. (gr. 4-7). pap. 7.99 *(978-1-4169-7079-8(7))* 2007. (Illus.). 256p. (gr. 5-7). 17.99 *(978-0-689-86412-4(4))* Simon & Schuster Bks. For Young Readers. (Simon & Schuster Bks. For Young Readers).

—Much Ado about Anne. (Mother-Daughter Book Club Ser.). (ENG., Illus.). (J). (gr. 4-7). 2009. 352p. pap. 7.99 *(978-1-4169-8269-2(8))* 2008. 336p. 15.99 *(978-0-689-85566-5(4))* Simon & Schuster Bks. For Young Readers. (Simon & Schuster Bks. For Young Readers).

—Pies & Prejudice. (Mother-Daughter Book Club Ser.). (ENG.). (J). (gr. 4-7). 2011. 400p. pap. 8.99 *(978-1-4424-2019-9(7))* 2010. 384p. 15.99 *(978-1-4169-7431-4(8))* Simon & Schuster Bks. For Young Readers. (Simon & Schuster Bks. For Young Readers).

—Wish You Were Eyre. 2013. (Mother-Daughter Book Club Ser.). (ENG.). 480p. (J). (gr. 4-9). pap. 7.99 *(978-1-4424-3065-5(6),* Simon & Schuster Bks. For Young Readers) Simon & Schuster Bks. For Young Readers.

Freer, Dave. Cuttlefish. 2012. (ENG.). 299p. (YA). (gr. 7). 16.95 *(978-1-61614-625-2(7))* Prometheus Bks., Pubs.

Frenette, Bethany. Burn Bright. 2014. (Dark Star Ser.). (ENG.). 352p. (YA). (gr. 7-12). 17.99 *(978-1-4231-4666-7(2))* Hyperion Bks. for Children.

—Dark Star. 2013. (Dark Star Ser.). (ENG.). 384p. (YA). (gr. 7-12). pap. 9.99 *(978-1-4231-4853-1(3))* Hyperion Pr.

Friedman, Aimee. Two Summers. 2016. (ENG.). 368p. (J). (gr. 7). 17.99 *(978-0-545-51807-9(5))* Scholastic, Inc.

Friend, Natasha. For Keeps. 2011. (ENG.). 272p. (YA). (gr. 7-18). 7.99 *(978-0-14-241846-8(3),* Speak) Penguin Young Readers Group.

Froemming, Kaylee. My Mama's Hair Is Everywhere: It just won't go Away!! 2008. 12p. pap. 8.49 *(978-1-4389-0385-9(5))* AuthorHouse.

Furniss, Clare. The Year of the Rat. 2015. (ENG.). 304p. (YA). (gr. 7). pap. 10.99 *(978-1-4814-2100-3(X),* McElderry, Margaret K. Bks.) McElderry, Margaret K. Bks.

Galang, M. Evelina. Angel de la Luna & the 5th Glorious Mystery. 2013. (ENG.). 304p. (J). (gr. 6). pap. 12.00 *(978-1-56689-333-6(X))* Coffee Hse. Pr.

Galante, Cecilia. The Summer of May. Carpenter, Tad, illus. (ENG.). 256p. (J). (gr. 4-8). 2012. pap. 6.99 *(978-1-4169-8304-0(X))* 2011. 16.99 *(978-1-4169-8023-0(7))* Simon & Schuster/Paula Wiseman Bks. (Simon & Schuster/Paula Wiseman Bks.).

Gardner, Sally. I, Coriander. 2007. (ENG., Illus.). 288p. (J). (gr. 5-18). 7.99 *(978-0-14-240763-9(1),* Puffin Books) Penguin Young Readers Group.

Garnett, Tarreka. The Sleepover. Damon Danielson, illus. 2013. 32p. pap. 14.97 *(978-1-62212-249-3(6),* Strategic Bk. Publishing) Strategic Book Publishing & Rights Agency (SBPRA).

Garton, Carol. Isabella Barella. 2013. (ENG.). 300p. (YA). 32.95 *(978-1-4787-1339-5(9));* pap. 17.95 *(978-1-4787-1490-3(5))* Outskirts Pr., Inc.

Gayton, Sam. The Adventures of Lettie Peppercorn. Bernatene, Poly, illus. 2016. (ENG.). 304p. (J). (gr. 3-7). 16.99 *(978-1-4814-4769-0(6),* McElderry, Margaret K. Bks.) McElderry, Margaret K. Bks.

Gelenius, Deb. My Mom, My Teacher. 2013. 28p. pap. 11.95 *(978-1-61244-135-1(1))* Halo Publishing International.

Gerber, Alyson. Braced. 2017. (ENG.). 304p. (J). (gr. 3-7). 16.99 *(978-0-545-90214-4(2))* Scholastic, Inc.

Giff, Patricia Reilly. Jubilee. (ENG.). 160p. (J). (gr. 3-7). 2017. 6.99 ***(978-0-385-74489-8(7),*** Yearling) 2016. 16.99 *(978-0-385-74486-7(2),* Lamb, Wendy Bks.) Random Hse. Children's Bks.

Gillis, Jennifer Blizin. What Do You Say? Losa, Ann, illus. 2006. (Reader's Clubhouse Level 2 Reader Ser.). (ENG.). 24p. (J). (gr. 1-4). pap. 3.99 *(978-0-7641-3298-8(9))* Barron's Educational Series, Inc.

Glocke, Robin. Tiny Fish. 2006. 56p. pap. 16.95 *(978-1-4241-3777-0(2))* PublishAmerica, Inc.

Goerzen, Christy. The Big Apple Effect, 1 vol. 2014. (Orca Currents Ser.). (ENG.). 136p. (J). (gr. 5-9). pap. 9.95 *(978-1-4598-0738-9(3))* Orca Bk. Pubs. USA.

—Farmed Out, 1 vol. 2011. (Orca Currents Ser.). (ENG.). 128p. (J). (gr. 5-9). pap. 9.95 *(978-1-55469-910-0(X));* lib. bdg. 16.95 *(978-1-55469-911-7(8))* Orca Bk. Pubs. USA.

Gomes, Filomena. My Mom Loves Me More Than Sushi. Spires, Ashley, illus. 2006. 24p. (J). pap. *(978-1-897187-13-5(0))* Second Story Pr.

—My Mom Loves Me More Than Sushi, 1 vol. Spires, Ashley, illus. 2006. (ENG.). 32p. (J). (gr. -1-3). 15.95 *(978-1-897187-09-8(2))* Second Story Pr. CAN. Dist: Orca Bk. Pubs. USA.

Gonzalez, Noni. Dream of Wings. Gonzalez, Tom, illus. 2013. (ENG.). 40p. (J). pap. 9.99 *(978-1-939337-20-7(8));* 14.99 *(978-1-939337-71-9(2))* Telemachus Pr., LLC.

Grant, Michael & Applegate, Katherine. Eve & Adam. 2013. (ENG.). 304p. (YA). (gr. 8-12). pap. 9.99 *(978-1-250-03419-9(1),* 9781250034199) Square Fish.

Graves, Sue. A Cake for Dinner. 2011. (Tadpoles Ser.: No. 26). (ENG., Illus.). 24p. (J). (gr. k-3). pap. *(978-0-7787-0583-3(8))* Crabtree Publishing Co.

Gray, Dianne & Gray, Dianne E. Holding up the Earth. 2006. (ENG.). 210p. (J). (gr. 5-7). pap. 12.95 *(978-0-618-73747-5(2))* Houghton Mifflin Harcourt Publishing Co.

Gray, Kes. Daisy & the Trouble with Life. Sharratt, Nick & Parsons, Garry, illus. 2007. (Daisy Ser.: 12). (ENG.). 240p. (J). (gr. 2-4). pap. 11.95 *(978-1-86230-167-2(0),* Red Fox) Random House Children's Books GBR. Dist: Independent Pubs. Group.

Gray, Kristin L. Vilonia Beebe Takes Charge. 2017. (ENG., Illus.). 208p. (J). (gr. 3-7). 16.99 *(978-1-4814-5842-9(6),* Simon & Schuster/Paula Wiseman Bks.) Simon & Schuster/Paula Wiseman Bks.

Greathouse, Cindy. Sophie the Missing Bunny. 2011. 20p. pap. 24.95 *(978-1-4489-5607-4(2))* America Star Bks.

Greenacres, Levi. Mommy's New Tattoo: A Bedtime Story for People, 1 vol. 2013. (ENG., Illus.). 32p. 16.99 *(978-0-7643-4389-6(0),* 9780764343896) Schiffer Publishing, Ltd.

Greene, Bette. The Drowning of Stephan Jones. 2012. 220p. pap. 9.99 *(978-0-9834681-3-4(3))* Greene & Sandell.

Greenwald, Lisa. My Life in Pink & Green. (Pink & Green Ser.). (ENG.). (gr. 3-7). 2010. 288p. (J). pap. 7.95 *(978-0-8109-8984-9(0))* 2009. 272p. (YA). 17.95 *(978-0-8109-8352-6(4))* Abrams, Inc. (Amulet Bks.).

Grimes, Nikki. Poems in the Attic. Zunon, Elizabeth, illus. 2015. (ENG.). 48p. (J). 19.95 *(978-1-62014-027-7(6))* Lee & Low Bks., Inc.

Guest, Jacqueline. Dream Racer, 1 vol. 2006. (Lorimer SideStreets Ser.). (ENG.). 136p. (YA). (gr. 9-12). 16.95 *(978-1-55028-945-9(4),* 9781550289459); 9.95 *(978-1-55028-942-8(X),* 9781550289428) Lorimer, James & Co., Ltd., Pubs. CAN. Dist: Casemate Pubs. & Bk. Distributors, LLC.

Gummer, Chiele. A Family of Geese. 2013. 34p. pap. 16.95 *(978-1-4808-0026-7(0))* Archway Publishing.

Gunning, Monica. A Shelter in Our Car. Pedlar, Elaine, illus. 2013. (ENG.). 32p. (J). pap. 9.95 *(978-0-89239-308-4(4),* Children's Book Press) Lee & Low Bks., Inc.

Gurevich, Margaret. Made to Measure. Hagel, Brooke, illus. 2016. (Chloe by Design Ser.). (ENG.). 96p. (gr. 5-8). lib. bdg. 25.32 *(978-1-4965-3262-6(7))* Stone Arch Bks.

Gurtler, Janet. Shyanna's Song. Wood, Katie, illus. 2015. (Mermaid Kingdom Ser.). (ENG.). 96p. (gr. 3-5). lib. bdg. 23.99 *(978-1-4342-9693-1(8))* Stone Arch Bks.

Hackl, Jo. Smack Dab in the Middle of Maybe. 2017. (J). ***(978-0-399-55738-5(5))*** Random Hse., Inc.

Haddix, Margaret Peterson. Full Ride. (ENG.). (YA). (gr. 7). 2014. 368p. pap. 12.99 *(978-1-4424-4279-5(4))* 2013. 352p. 16.99 *(978-1-4424-4278-8(6))* Simon & Schuster Bks. For Young Readers. (Simon & Schuster Bks. For Young Readers).

Hahn, Mary Downing. Deep & Dark & Dangerous. 2008. (ENG.). 192p. (J). (gr. 5-7). pap. 7.99 *(978-0-547-07645-4(2))* Houghton Mifflin Harcourt Publishing Co.

—Deep & Dark & Dangerous: A Ghost Story. 2007. (ENG.). 192p. (J). (gr. 5-7). 16.99 *(978-0-618-66545-7(5))* Houghton Mifflin Harcourt Publishing Co.

—Tallahassee Higgins. 2007. (ENG.). 192p. (J). (gr. 5-7). pap. 6.95 *(978-0-618-75246-1(3))* Houghton Mifflin Harcourt Publishing Co.

Halahmy, Miriam. Behind Closed Doors. 2017. (ENG.). 208p. (J). (gr. 9). 16.95 *(978-0-8234-3641-5(1));* ***(978-0-8234-3792-4(2))*** Holiday Hse., Inc.

Hale, Marian. The Goodbye Season. 2009. (ENG.). 288p. (YA). (gr. 7-12). 16.99 *(978-0-8050-8855-7(5),* 9780805088557, Holt, Henry & Co. Bks. For Young Readers) Holt, Henry & Co.

Hamilton, Deborah E. Why are You my Mother? A Mother's Response to Her Adopted Daughter. Andrules, Jamie L., illus. 2006. (J). 9.99 net. *(978-0-9789202-0-3(1))* Dreams Due Media Group, Inc.

Harlow, Joan Hiatt. The Watcher. 2015. (ENG.). 304p. (J). (gr. 3-7). pap. 6.99 *(978-1-4424-2912-3(7),* McElderry, Margaret K. Bks.) McElderry, Margaret K. Bks.

Harmon, Michael. Brutal. 2011. (ENG.). 240p. (YA). (gr. 9). pap. 8.99 *(978-0-440-23995-6(8),* Knopf Bks. for Young Readers) Random Hse. Children's Bks.

Harper, Charise Mericle. Dreamer, Wisher, Liar. 2014. (ENG.). 352p. (J). (gr. 3-7). 16.99 *(978-0-06-202675-0(5))* HarperCollins Pubs.

Harrington, Claudia. My Two Moms, 1 vol. Persico, Zoe, illus. 2016. (ENG.). 32p. (J). *(978-1-62402-110-7(7))* Magic Wagon.

Harrington, Janine. Soul Sister. 2012. 244p. pap. *(978-1-78176-139-7(6))* FeedARead.com.

Harris, Angela. Night Light. 2008. 28p. pap. 12.95 *(978-1-4389-1971-3(9))* AuthorHouse.

Harris, Annaka. I Wonder. Rowe, John, illus. 2013. (ENG.). 32p. (J). 16.95 *(978-1-940051-04-8(5))* Four Elephants Pr.

Harris, Dee. I Am Not a Hippopotamus, I Am a Little Girl, Book. Bohart, Lisa, illus. 2011. 24p. pap. 12.95 *(978-1-61493-005-1(8))* Peppertree Pr., The.

Harris, Teresa E. The Perfect Place. 2014. (ENG.). 272p. (J). (gr. 5-7). 17.99 *(978-0-547-25519-4(5))* Houghton Mifflin Harcourt Publishing Co.

Harrison, Emma. Toe the Line: A Rival High Novel. 2008. (YA). *(978-1-4114-0526-4(9),* Spark Publishing Group) Sterling Publishing Co., Inc.

Harrold, A. F. The Imaginary. Gravett, Emily, illus. 2015. (ENG.). 240p. (YA). (gr. 3-6). 16.99 *(978-0-8027-3811-0(7),* 9780802738110, Bloomsbury USA Childrens) Bloomsbury Publishing USA.

Hartman, Carrie. Child of Mine. 2007. (ENG., Illus.). 32p. (J). lib. bdg. 11.99 *(978-1-934277-12-6(6))* Mam Green Publishing, Inc.

Haydel, Catherine. Uno the Cat & Hurricane Katrina. 2006. 18.00 *(978-0-8059-7341-9(9))* Dorrance Publishing Co., Inc.

Haydu, Corey Ann. Rules for Stealing Stars. 2015. (ENG.). 336p. (J). (gr. 3-7). 16.99 *(978-0-06-235271-2(7),* Tegen, Katherine Bks) HarperCollins Pubs.

Hayes-Knoll, Carolyn. Ista Cante. 2004. (Illus.). 32p. (J). *(978-0-9755646-6-0(8))* Westview Publishing Co., Inc.

Heasley, Gwendolyn. Don't Call Me Baby. 2014. (ENG.). 304p. (YA). (gr. 8). pap. 9.99 *(978-0-06-220852-1(7),* HarperTeen) HarperCollins Pubs.

Heller, Maryellen. My Big Sister's First Day of School. Soman, David, illus. 2009. (J). *(978-0-8037-3246-9(5),* Dial) Penguin Publishing Group.

Henderson, Susan Sinclair. Penelope's Journey Home. 2013. 48p. pap. 9.99 *(978-1-4908-0420-0(X),* WestBow Pr.) Author Solutions, Inc.

Henig, Sherry. Sara Makes Her Mother Proud & Learns Good Behavior: A Children's Book. 2nd ed. 2006. per. 6.95 *(978-0-9777203-2-3(2))* Brenner Publishing, LLC.

Hepler, Heather. Frosted Kisses. 2015. (ENG.). 272p. (J). (gr. 7). 17.99 *(978-0-545-79055-0(7))* Scholastic, Inc.

Hermes, Patricia. You Shouldn't Have to Say GoodBye: It's Hard Losing the Person You Love The Most. 2008. (ENG.). 128p. (J). (gr. 4-7). pap. 8.99 *(978-1-4022-1325-0(5),* Sourcebooks Jabberwocky) Sourcebooks, Inc.

Hernandez, Jo Ann Yolanda. The Throwaway Piece. 2006. 246p. (J). (gr. 6). per. 9.95 *(978-1-55885-353-9(7),* Piñata Books) Arte Publico Pr.

Herring, Bruce D. The Wizard of Wonderland, 1 vol. 2010. 192p. pap. 24.95 *(978-1-4489-5844-3(X))* America Star Bks.

Hibbs, Lisa. Allie Doogledorf & the Mighty Mess. 2009. 36p. pap. 21.99 *(978-1-4500-0777-1(5))* Xlibris Corp.

Hichens, Joanne. Stained. 2008. (Cutting Edge Ser.). (ENG.). 200p. pap. *(978-1-84167-715-6(9))* Ransom Publishing Ltd.

Hill, Tara Theresa. What Can You Do with Two Mommies? 2012. 40p. pap. 18.00 *(978-1-105-50649-9(5))* Lulu Pr., Inc.

Hillyer, Brenda L. Mystery in the Marsh. 2008. 48p. pap. 16.95 *(978-1-60703-784-2(X))* America Star Bks.

Hines, Thomas, illus. The Bubble Machine. lt. ed. 2003. 26p. (J). per. *(978-1-887636-02-5(1))* Creative Writing & Publishing Co.

Hirota, Denise. The Circus Poster. 2011. 58p. pap. 9.99 *(978-1-60911-292-9(X),* Eloquent Bks.) Strategic Book Publishing & Rights Agency (SBPRA).

Hobbs, Valerie. Carolina Crow Girl. 2013. 146p. pap. 12.95 *(978-1-62352-008-3(8))* IntoPrint Publishing LLC.

Hoffman, Diana / Lynne. Lighting the Earth. Brough, Karen, illus. 2014. 34p. (J). 23.95 *(978-0-9891296-4-0(0),* Aurora Books) Eco-Justice Pr., LLC.

Holcomb, T. Toot-Toot & Her Troubles: Name Calling. 2008. 12p. pap. 24.95 *(978-1-60563-472-2(7))* America Star Bks.

Hollyer, Belinda. River Song. 2008. (ENG.). 198p. (J). (gr. 3-7). 16.95 *(978-0-8234-2149-7(X))* Holiday Hse., Inc.

Holmes, Kathryn. How It Feels to Fly. 2016. 368p. (YA). (gr. 8). 17.99 *(978-0-06-238734-9(0),* HarperTeen) HarperCollins Pubs.

Holub, Joan. Be Patient, Pandora! Patricelli, Leslie, illus. 2014. (Mini Myths Ser.). (ENG.). 24p. (J). (gr. -1 — 1). bds. 6.95 *(978-1-4197-0951-7(8),* Abrams Appleseed) Abrams, Inc.

Hoover, P. J. Solstice. 2013. (ENG.). 384p. (YA). (gr. 8). 17.99 *(978-0-7653-3469-5(0),* Tor Teen) Doherty, Tom Assocs., LLC.

Howard, A. G. Splintered. 2013. (Splintered Ser.). (ENG., Illus.). 384p. (YA). (gr. 9-17). 17.95 *(978-1-4197-0428-4(1),* Amulet Bks.) Abrams, Inc.

—Splintered. 2014. (Splintered Ser.: 1). (J). lib. bdg. 19.60 *(978-0-606-35235-2(X))* Turtleback Bks.

—Unhinged. (Splintered Ser.). (ENG.). (YA). (gr. 9-17). 2015. 416p. pap. 9.99 *(978-1-4197-1373-6(6))* 2014. 400p. 17.95 *(978-1-4197-0971-5(2))* Abrams, Inc. (Amulet Bks.).

—Unhinged. 2015. (Splintered Ser.: 2). (J). lib. bdg. 19.60 *(978-0-606-36565-9(6))* Turtleback Bks.

Howard, J. J. That Time I Joined the Circus. 2013. (ENG.). 272p. (J). (gr. 7). 17.99 *(978-0-545-43381-5(9))* Scholastic, Inc.

Hubbard, Amanda & Hubbard, Mandy. Everything but the Truth. 2015. (If Only... Ser.). (ENG.). 288p. (YA). (gr. 7). 17.99 *(978-1-61963-659-0(X),* 9781619636590, Bloomsbury USA Childrens) Bloomsbury Publishing USA.

Hunt, Lynda Mullaly. One for the Murphys. (ENG.). (J). (gr. 5). 2013. 256p. pap. 7.99 *(978-0-14-242652-4(0),* Puffin Books) 2012. 288p. 16.99 *(978-0-399-25615-8(6),* Nancy Paulsen Books) Penguin Young Readers Group.

Hurwitz, Laura. Disappear Home. 2015. (ENG.). 256p. (J). (gr. 8-12). 16.99 *(978-0-8075-2468-8(9))* Whitman, Albert & Co.

Hyde, Catherine Ryan. Jumpstart the World. 2011. (ENG.). 192p. (YA). (gr. 9). pap. 7.99 *(978-0-375-86626-5(4),* Ember) Random Hse. Children's Bks.

Hysen, Sylvia. A Very Dairy Christmas. 2005. 290p. 24.95 *(978-0-9763365-6-3(1))* 1st Impression Publishing.

Ibbotson, Eva. The Star of Kazan. Hawkes, Kevin, illus. 2006. (ENG.). 416p. (J). (gr. 3-7). reprint ed. 8.99 *(978-0-14-240582-6(5),* Puffin Books) Penguin Young Readers Group.

Inglis, Lucy. City of Halves. 2015. (ENG.). 368p. (J). (gr. 7). 17.99 *(978-0-545-82958-8(5),* Chicken Hse., The) Scholastic, Inc.

Jackson, Everett E. Kimme Meets Squirrelly D. 2008. 28p. pap. 16.95 *(978-1-4389-0971-4(3))* AuthorHouse.

Jacobs, John. I Wanna Be. 2006. (Illus.). 144p. 9.95 *(978-0-9774659-6-5(9))* Cameo Pubns., LLC.

Jahn-Clough, Lisa. Me, Penelope. 2009. (ENG.). 208p. (YA). (gr. 9). pap. 12.99 *(978-0-547-07632-4(0))* Houghton Mifflin Harcourt Publishing Co.

Jalonen, Riitta. Tundra Mouse Mountain. Ledgard, J. M., tr. from FIN. Louhi, Kristiina, illus. 2006. (Picture books from around the World Seri Ser.). (ENG.). 56p. (J). (gr. k-2). 20.95 *(978-1-905341-05-4(9))* WingedChariot Pr. GBR. Dist: Independent Pubs. Group.

James, Debra & James, Jessica. The Social Pyramid. 2010. 57p. pap. 7.50 *(978-0-557-40789-7(3))* Lulu Pr., Inc.

Janice Turner & Colleen Connelly. Colleen Goes to the Farmer's Market. Ron Frazier, photos by. 2009. (Illus.). 20p. pap. 12.49 *(978-1-4389-6085-2(9))* AuthorHouse.

Jansen, Karen. The Coming of an Astronaut. 2009. 68p. pap. 9.99 *(978-1-60911-076-5(5),* Eloquent Bks.) Strategic Book Publishing & Rights Agency (SBPRA).

Jefferson, Coretta Carte. Beautiful Lizzie. 2012. 24p. pap. 24.95 *(978-1-4626-8988-0(4))* America Star Bks.

Johnson, Andrea N. Mommy & Me. 2013. 20p. pap. 24.95 *(978-1-4626-9892-9(1))* America Star Bks.

Johnson, Christine. Claire de Lune. (ENG.). (YA). (gr. 7). 2011. 368p. pap. 9.99 *(978-1-4424-0766-4(2))* 2010. 352p. 16.99 *(978-1-4169-9182-3(4))* Simon Pulse. (Simon Pulse).

—Nocturne. (ENG.). (YA). (gr. 7). 2012. 384p. pap. 9.99 *(978-1-4424-0777-0(8))* 2011. 368p. 16.99 *(978-1-4424-0776-3(X))* Simon Pulse. (Simon Pulse).

Johnson, D. C. & Turner, Sandra. Let's Be Friends. Johnson, D. C. & Johnson, Darnell, illus. 2007. (J). per. 9.95 *(978-1-933556-66-6(8))* Publishers' Graphics, L.L.C.

Johnston, Wayne M. North Fork. 2016. (ENG.). 210p. (YA). (gr. 7-12). pap. 14.95 *(978-1-936364-20-6(4))* Black Heron Pr.
Jones, Callie Carol Rodgers. A Good Cry. 2013. 20p. pap. 17.99 *(978-1-4772-9414-7(7))* AuthorHouse.
Jones, Carrie. Flying. 2016. (Flying Ser.: 1). (ENG.). 256p. (YA). 17.99 *(978-0-7653-3657-6(X)*, 9780765336576, Tor Teen) Doherty, Tom Assocs., LLC.
Jones, Jen. Maren's New Family. Franco, Paula, illus. 2015. (Sleepover Girls Ser.). (ENG.). 128p. (gr. 3-5). lib. bdg. 22.65 *(978-1-4965-0540-8(9))* Stone Arch Bks.
Jones M.A., Yvette. I Know I Love You. 2008. 36p. pap. 24.95 *(978-1-60474-474-3(X))* America Star Bks.
Jones, Patrick. Freedom Flight. 2015. (ENG.). 112p. (YA). (gr. 6-12). lib. bdg. 27.99 *(978-1-4677-8051-3(0)*, Darby Creek) Lerner Publishing Group.
—Outburst. 2014. (Alternative Ser.). (ENG.). 104p. (YA). (gr. 6-12). lib. bdg. 27.93 *(978-1-4677-3901-6(4))* Lerner Publishing Group.
—Outburst. 2014. (Alternative Ser.). (ENG.). 104p. (YA). (gr. 6-12). pap. 7.95 *(978-1-4677-4484-3(0)*, Darby Creek) Lerner Publishing Group.
—Raising Heaven. 2015. (J). 9.99 *(978-1-4677-7697-4(1))*; (ENG.). 96p. (gr. 6-12). lib. bdg. 27.99 *(978-1-4677-5802-4(7))* Lerner Publishing Group.
Joosse, Barbara M. Mama, Do You Love Me?, Set. Lavallee, Barbara, illus. 2017. (ENG.). 62p. (J). (gr. -1 — 1). bds. 14.99 ***(978-1-4521-6612-4(9))*** Chronicle Bks. LLC.
—Mama, Do You Love Me? 2014. (J). lib. bdg. 18.40 *(978-0-606-35289-5(9))* Turtleback Bks.
Joseph, Danielle. Pure Red. 2011. (ENG.). 240p. (YA). pap. 9.95 *(978-0-7387-2743-1(1)*, Flux) North Star Editions.
—Shrinking Violet. 2009. (ENG.). 320p. pap. 19.99 *(978-1-4165-9696-7(8)*, MTV Bks.) MTV Books.
June, Kimberly. It's No Fun Sucking Your Thumb. 2012. 28p. pap. 15.99 *(978-1-4691-8228-5(9))* Xlibris Corp.
Kadohata, Cynthia. Outside Beauty. (ENG.). (YA). (gr. 7). 2009. 288p. pap. 8.99 *(978-1-4169-9818-1(7))* 2008. (Illus.). 272p. 16.99 *(978-0-689-86575-6(9))* Simon & Schuster Children's Publishing. (Atheneum Bks. for Young Readers).
Kalmbach, Nicole. Lilly J, What Did I Say? 2011. 20p. 10.03 *(978-1-4520-9318-5(0))* AuthorHouse.
Kamata, Suzanne. Gadget Girl: The Art of Being Invisible. 2013. (ENG., Illus.). 256p. (YA). pap. 14.95 *(978-1-936846-38-2(1))* GemmaMedia.
Kanady, Mary Ellen Murdock. Mommy & Me. 2008. (Illus.). 32p. (J). pap. 8.00 *(978-0-8059-7728-8(7))* Dorrance Publishing Co., Inc.
Kann, Victoria. Pinkalicious & the Perfect Present. Kann, Victoria, illus. 2014. (I Can Read Level 1 Ser.). (ENG., Illus.). 32p. (J). (gr. -1-3). 16.99 *(978-0-06-218789-5(9))*; pap. 3.99 *(978-0-06-218788-8(0))* HarperCollins Pubs.
Karandeev, Oleg. Dmitri II: The Kind Storyteller Book Two of Five. Ciesinska, Izabela, illus. 2007. 76p. (YA). per. 15.95 *(978-0-9793944-3-0(0))* Digi-Tall Media.
Katies Choice. 2005. (YA). per. *(978-1-59872-217-8(4))* Instant Pub.
Kats, Jewel. Snow White's Seven Patches: A Vitiligo Fairy Tale. Goodfellow, Dan, illus. 2013. 40p. (J). pap. 14.95 *(978-1-61599-206-5(5))* Loving Healing Pr., Inc.
Katschke, Judy. I Love My Mami! Aikins, Dave, illus. 2006. (Dora the Explorer Ser.: 9). (ENG.). 24p. (J). (gr. -1-k). pap. 3.99 *(978-1-4169-0650-6(9)*, Simon Spotlight/Nickelodeon) Simon Spotlight/Nickelodeon.
Kay, Sjoukje & Kay, Sjoukje. The Donut Yogi. Vita, Ariela, illus. 2007. (ENG.). 32p. (J). 2.50 *(978-0-9789698-1-3(2))* Kay, Sjoukje.
Kearns, Zannah & Quarto Generic Staff. No Use Crying. 2012. (ENG.). 320p. (J). (gr. 7-9). pap. 8.99 *(978-1-84780-214-9(1)*, Frances Lincoln) Quarto Publishing Group UK GBR. Dist: Hachette Bk. Group.
Kelso, Mary Jean. Birds in the Flower Basket. Hammond, Julie, illus. 2012. 26p. 19.95 *(978-1-61633-343-0(X))* Guardian Angel Publishing, Inc.
Kelso, Mary Jean & Hammond, Julie. Birds in the Flower Basket. 2012. 26p. pap. 11.95 *(978-1-61633-344-7(8))* Guardian Angel Publishing, Inc.
Kenneally, Miranda. Stealing Parker. 2012. (Hundred Oaks Ser.: Bk. 2). (ENG.). 256p. (YA). (gr. 7-12). pap. 10.99 *(978-1-4022-7187-8(5))* Sourcebooks, Inc.
Kennedy, Marlane. Me & the Pumpkin Queen. 2009. (ENG.). 192p. (J). (gr. 3-7). pap. 5.99 *(978-0-06-114024-2(4)*, Greenwillow Bks.) HarperCollins Pubs.
Kent, Trilby. Stones for My Father. 2011. (ENG.). 176p. (YA). (gr. 5-18). 19.95 *(978-1-77049-252-3(6)*, Tundra Bks.) Tundra Bks. CAN. Dist: Penguin Random Hse. LLC.
Keonna-E'nea. Momzilla, 1 vol. Joane', E'nea, illus. 2009. 18p. pap. 24.95 *(978-1-60749-607-6(0))* America Star Bks.
Kephart, Beth. House of Dance. 2010. (ENG.). 272p. (J). (gr. 8). pap. 10.99 *(978-0-06-142930-9(9))* 2008. 263p. (YA). (gr. 7-18). lib. bdg. 17.89 *(978-0-06-142929-3(5))* HarperCollins Pubs. (HarperTeen).
Kew, Trevor. Trading Goals, 1 vol. 2009. (Lorimer Sports Stories Ser.). (ENG.). 144p. (J). (gr. 4-8). 16.95 *(978-1-55277-425-0(2)*, 9781552774250) Lorimer, James & Co., Ltd., Pubs. CAN. Dist: Casemate Pubs. & Bk. Distributors, LLC.
Kimmel, Elizabeth Cody. Suddenly Supernatural 4: Crossing Over. 2011. (Suddenly Supernatural Ser.: 4). (ENG.). 256p. (J). (gr. 3-7). pap. 5.99 *(978-0-316-13345-6(0))* Little, Brown Bks. for Young Readers.
—Suddenly Supernatural: Scaredy Kat. 2010. (Suddenly Supernatural Ser.: 2). (ENG.). 272p. (J). (gr. 3-7). pap. 5.99 *(978-0-316-08745-2(9))* Little, Brown Bks. for Young Readers.
—Suddenly Supernatural: School Spirit. 2010. (Suddenly Supernatural Ser.: 1). (ENG.). 336p. (J). (gr. 3-7). pap. 7.99 *(978-0-316-07821-4(2))* Little, Brown Bks. for Young Readers.
Kirby, Jessi. Golden. (ENG.). 288p. (YA). (gr. 7). 2014. pap. 9.99 *(978-1-4424-5218-3(8))* 2013. 16.99 *(978-1-4424-5216-9(1))* Simon & Schuster Bks. For Young Readers. (Simon & Schuster Bks. For Young Readers).
Kirby, Matthew J. The Arctic Code. 2015. (Dark Gravity Sequence Ser.: 1). (ENG.). 336p. (J). (gr. 3-7). 16.99 *(978-0-06-222487-3(5))* HarperCollins Pubs.
Kittredge, Caitlin. The Mirrored Shard: the Iron Codex Book Three. 2013. (Iron Codex Ser.). (ENG.). 304p. (YA). (gr. 7). 17.99 *(978-0-385-73833-0(1)*, Delacorte Bks. for Young Readers) Random Hse. Children's Bks.
Klein, Alina. Rape Girl. 2012. 132p. (YA). 18.95 *(978-1-60898-123-6(1))*; pap. 9.95 *(978-1-60898-124-3(X))* namelos llc.
Kletter, Kerry. The First Time She Drowned. 2016. (ENG.). 352p. (YA). (gr. 9). 17.99 *(978-0-399-17103-1(7)*, Philomel Bks.) Penguin Young Readers Group.
Knight, Andrew. Dead Beckoning. (Thumbprint Mysteries Ser.). 32.86 *(978-0-8092-0421-2(5))* McGraw-Hill/Contemporary.
Knowles, Johanna. Pearl. 2011. (ENG.). 224p. (YA). (gr. 7-12). 16.99 *(978-0-8050-9207-3(2)*, 9780805092073, Holt, Henry & Co. Bks. For Young Readers) Holt, Henry & Co.
Korelitz, Jean Hanff. Interference Powder, 0 vols. 2006. (ENG.). 146p. (J). (gr. 4-7). pap. 7.99 *(978-0-7614-5275-1(3)*, 9780761452751, Amazon Children's Publishing) Amazon Publishing.
Krulik, Nancy. Tip-Top Tappin' Mom!, 31 vols. John and Wendy Staff, illus. 2009. (Katie Kazoo, Switcheroo Ser.: 31). (ENG.). 80p. (J). (gr. 2-4). pap. 4.99 *(978-0-448-45041-4(0)*, Grosset & Dunlap) Penguin Young Readers Group.
Kuipers, Alice. Lost for Words. 2010. 224p. (YA). (gr. 8-18). 16.99 *(978-0-06-142922-4(8)*, HarperTeen) HarperCollins Pubs.
Kulper, Kendall. Salt & Storm. 2014. (YA). *(978-0-316-40456-3(X))* Little Brown & Co.
Lacámara, Laura. Floating on Mama's Song: Flotando con la Canción de Mamá. Morales, Yuyi, illus. 2010. (SPA & ENG.). 32p. (J). (gr. -1-2). 16.99 *(978-0-06-084368-7(3)*, Tegen, Katherine Bks) HarperCollins Pubs.
LaChanze. Little Diva. Pinkney, Brian, illus. 2010. (ENG.). 32p. (J). (gr. -1-3). 16.99 *(978-0-312-37010-7(5)*, 9780312370107) Feiwel & Friends.
LaFaye, A. Nissa's Place. 2010. (ENG.). 256p. (J). (gr. 2-8). pap. 8.00 *(978-1-57131-697-4(3))* Milkweed Editions.
—The Year of the Sawdust Man. 2008. (ENG.). 224p. (J). (gr. 2-8). pap. 6.95 *(978-1-57131-679-0(5))* Milkweed Editions.
Laird, Chynna. Dark Water. 2012. 166p. pap. *(978-1-926997-76-6(X))* Imajin Bks.
Lake, Nick. There Will Be Lies. 2015. (ENG.). 464p. (YA). (gr. 9-12). 17.99 *(978-1-61963-440-4(6)*, 9781619634404, Bloomsbury USA Childrens) Bloomsbury Publishing USA.
Lambert, Mary E. Family Game Night & Other Catastrophes. 2017. (ENG.). 256p. (J). (gr. 3-7). 16.99 *(978-0-545-93198-4(3)*, Scholastic Pr.) Scholastic, Inc.
Lambert, Susan Dodd. Clarence the Clam. Modugno, Tina, illus. 2013. 28p. pap. 6.95 *(978-0-9883893-5-9(5))* Borgo Publishing.
Lanagan, Margo. Tender Morsels. 2010. (ENG.). 464p. (YA). (gr. 9-18). pap. 11.99 *(978-0-375-84305-1(1)*, Ember) Random Hse. Children's Bks.
Lane, Dakota. The Orpheus Obsession. 2008. (ENG., Illus.). 288p. (YA). (gr. 9). pap. 8.99 *(978-0-06-074175-4(9)*, HarperTeen) HarperCollins Pubs.
Lasky, Kathryn. Before I Was Your Mother. Pham, LeUyen, illus. 2007. (ENG.). 40p. (J). (gr. -1-3). pap. 6.99 *(978-0-15-205842-5(7))* Houghton Mifflin Harcourt Publishing Co.
—Escape. 2014. (Horses of the Dawn Ser.: 1). (ENG.). 240p. (J). (gr. 3-7). 16.99 *(978-0-545-39716-2(2)*, Scholastic Pr.) Scholastic, Inc.
—The Escape. 2014. (Horses of the Dawn Trilogy Ser.: 1). lib. bdg. 17.20 *(978-0-606-36034-0(4))* Turtleback Bks.
—Horses of the Dawn #1: the Escape. 2014. (Horses of the Dawn Ser.: 1). (ENG.). 240p. (J). (gr. 3-7). pap. 6.99 *(978-0-545-39730-8(8)*, Scholastic Pr.) Scholastic, Inc.
Lasota, Mary. Kitty Piper, Angel Cat, Book 3, A Surprise for Ashley. 2011. 48p. (gr. 1-2). pap. 11.66 *(978-1-4634-1031-5(X))* AuthorHouse.
Laurie, Cook, illus. Amelia Asks Why. 2007. (J). 3.99 *(978-0-9726075-4-4(4))* EPI Bks.
Laurie, Victoria. When. 2015. (ENG.). 336p. (YA). (gr. 7-12). 17.99 *(978-1-4847-0008-2(2))* Hyperion Pr.
Lawless, Freda. Shauna's Chance. 2013. 24p. pap. 24.95 *(978-1-62709-601-0(9))* America Star Bks.
Lawson, Jessica. Under the Bottle Bridge. 2017. (ENG., Illus.). 352p. (J). (gr. 3-7). 16.99 ***(978-1-4814-4842-0(0)***, Simon & Schuster Bks. For Young Readers) Simon & Schuster Bks. For Young Readers.
Lawson, Kate. Mum's the Word. 2011. (ENG.). 400p. 14.99 *(978-1-84756-052-0(0)*, Avon Bks.) HarperCollins Pubs.
Leavitt, Caroline. Girls in Trouble: A Novel. 2005. (ENG.). 368p. pap. 22.99 *(978-0-312-33973-9(9)*, 9780312339739, St. Martin's Griffin) St. Martin's Pr.
Lee, Kyanna Shanae. Stepdad? No Thanks...! 2008. 60p. pap. 19.95 *(978-1-60563-422-7(0))* America Star Bks.
Lee, P. Janet. Ella Elephant: And Her Fear of Mice. 2007. (ENG., Illus.). 36p. (J). per. 15.95 *(978-1-59800-713-8(0))* Outskirts Pr., Inc.
Lemon, Emily. Little Hands. 2012. 24p. pap. 15.99 *(978-1-4771-4875-4(2))* Xlibris Corp.
Leonard, Marcia. Mi Día de Campamento. Translations.com Staff, tr. from ENG. Handelman, Dorothy, photos by. 2007. (Lecturas para niños de Verdad - Nivel 1 (Real Kids Readers - Level 1) Ser.).Tr. of My Camp-Out. (SPA., Illus.). 32p. (gr. k-2). per. 5.95 *(978-0-8225-7798-0(4)*, Ediciones Lerner) Lerner Publishing Group.
—Mi Día de Campamento; My Camp Out. 2008. pap. 34.95 *(978-0-8225-9496-3(X))* Lerner Publishing Group.
Leszczynski, Diana. Fern Verdant & the Silver Rose. 2009. (Playaway Children Ser.). (J). 59.99 *(978-1-4332-7708-5(5))* Findaway World, LLC.
Liggett, Kim. Blood & Salt. 2015. (ENG.). 352p. (YA). (gr. 9-12). 17.99 *(978-0-399-16648-8(3)*, G.P. Putnam's Sons Books for Young Readers) Penguin Young Readers Group.
Liner, Robin. Your Own Little Silly Mcgilly. Rogers, Madalyn V., illus. 2013. 38p. pap. 9.99 *(978-0-9910342-0-8(1))* East Stream Group, LLC.
Lisa Catanzarite. What the World Is Like to Bea Moore: Dear Santa. 2009. 60p. pap. 16.43 *(978-1-4269-2115-5(2))* Trafford Publishing.
Little, Cynthia. Mom's Imaginary Child. 2008. pap. *(978-0-9747707-2-7(8))* Sleepless Warrior Publishing.
Little, Kimberley Griffiths. Circle of Secrets. 2011. 326p. (J). *(978-0-545-38523-7(7)*, Scholastic Pr.) Scholastic, Inc.
—The Healing Spell. 2010. (ENG.). 368p. (J). (gr. 3-7). 17.99 *(978-0-545-16559-4(8)*, Scholastic Pr.) Scholastic, Inc.
Liu, Liana. The Memory Key. 2015. (ENG.). 368p. (YA). (gr. 8). 17.99 *(978-0-06-230664-7(2)*, HarperTeen) HarperCollins Pubs.
Lloyd, Natalie. A Snicker of Magic. (ENG.). 320p. (J). (gr. 3-7). 2015. pap. 6.99 *(978-0-545-55273-8(7))* 2014. 16.99 *(978-0-545-55270-7(2))* Scholastic, Inc. (Scholastic Pr.).
—A Snicker of Magic. 2015. lib. bdg. 17.20 *(978-0-606-37089-9(7))* Turtleback Bks.
Lloyd, Natalie, et al. A Snicker of Magic. 2014. (ENG.). mass mkt. *(978-0-545-68447-7(1))* Scholastic, Inc.
Long, Hayley. Lottie Biggs Is Not Tragic. 2014. (ENG.). 272p. (YA). (gr. 7). pap. 10.99 *(978-1-4472-6555-9(6))* Pan Macmillan GBR. Dist: Independent Pubs. Group.
Lopresti, Kirsten. Bright Coin Moon: A Novel. 2014. (ENG.). 272p. (J). (gr. 6). 16.95 *(978-1-62914-751-2(6)*, Sky Pony Pr.) Skyhorse Publishing Co., Inc.
Lord, Emery. The Names They Gave Us. 2017. (ENG.). 400p. (YA). 17.99 *(978-1-61963-958-4(0)*, 9781619639584, Bloomsbury USA Childrens) Bloomsbury Publishing USA.
Lorimer, Janet. The Mystery Quilt, 1 vol. unabr. ed. 2010. (Q Reads Ser.). (ENG.). 32p. (YA). (gr. 9-12). pap. 6.95 *(978-1-61651-183-8(4))* Saddleback Educational Publishing, Inc.
Love, D. Anne. Semiprecious. (ENG.). 304p. (J). (gr. 5-9). 2009. pap. 6.99 *(978-0-689-87389-8(1))* 2006. (Illus.). 17.99 *(978-0-689-85638-9(5))* McElderry, Margaret K. Bks. (McElderry, Margaret K. Bks.).
Lovett, Louise Sheppa, illus. A Happy Day. Lovett, Louise Sheppa, . 2008. 32p. (J). 18.50 *(978-0-9793419-0-8(6))* Tish & Co. LLC.
Lowe, Natasha. The Courage of Cat Campbell. 2015. (Poppy Pendle Ser.). (ENG., Illus.). 288p. (J). (gr. 3-7). 16.99 *(978-1-4814-1870-6(X)*, Simon & Schuster/Paula Wiseman Bks.) Simon & Schuster/Paula Wiseman Bks.
Ludwig, Elisa. Pretty Sly. 2014. (Pretty Crooked Trilogy Ser.: 2). (ENG.). 336p. (YA). (gr. 8). 17.99 *(978-0-06-206609-1(9)*, Tegen, Katherine Bks) HarperCollins Pubs.
—Pretty Wanted. 2015. (Pretty Crooked Trilogy Ser.: 3). (ENG.). 336p. (YA). (gr. 8). 17.99 *(978-0-06-206612-1(9)*, Tegen, Katherine Bks) HarperCollins Pubs.
Lyon, George Ella. No Dessert Forever! Catalanotto, Peter, illus. 2006. (ENG.). 40p. (J). (gr. k-4). 17.99 *(978-1-4169-0385-7(2)*, Atheneum/Richard Jackson Bks.) Simon & Schuster Children's Publishing.
Maciel, Amanda. Lucky Girl. 2017. 320p. (YA). (gr. 9). 17.99 *(978-0-06-230533-6(6))* HarperCollins Pubs.
Mack, Winnie. After All, You're Callie Boone. 2013. (ENG.). 192p. (J). (gr. 4-7). pap. 14.99 *(978-1-250-02735-1(7)*, 9781250027351) Square Fish.
Mackler, Carolyn. Guyaholic. 2009. (ENG., Illus.). 192p. (YA). (gr. 9). pap. 7.99 *(978-0-7636-2801-7(8))* Candlewick Pr.
MacLachlan, Patricia. More Perfect Than the Moon. 2005. 16.00 *(978-0-7569-5437-6(1))* Perfection Learning Corp.
Maddox, Jake. Power Play. 2016. (Jake Maddox JV Girls Ser.). (ENG.). 96p. (gr. 3-4). lib. bdg. 25.99 *(978-1-4965-3673-0(8))* Stone Arch Bks.
—Taekwondo Clash. 2016. (Jake Maddox JV Ser.). (ENG.). 96p. (gr. 3-4). lib. bdg. 25.99 *(978-1-4965-3981-6(8))* Stone Arch Bks.
Madonia, Kristen-Paige. Fingerprints of You. 2013. (ENG., Illus.). 272p. (YA). (gr. 9). pap. 9.99 *(978-1-4424-2921-5(6)*, Simon & Schuster Bks. For Young Readers) Simon & Schuster Bks. For Young Readers.
—Fingerprints of You. Ribera, Terry, illus. 2012. (ENG.). 272p. (YA). (gr. 9). 16.99 *(978-1-4424-2920-8(8))*, Simon & Schuster Bks. For Young Readers) Simon & Schuster Bks. For Young Readers.
Madrigal, Antonio Hernandez. Erandi's Braids. dePaola, Tomie, illus. 2015. 32p. pap. 7.00 *(978-1-61003-530-9(5))* Center for the Collaborative Classroom.
Maguire, Gregory. Matchless: An Illumination of Hans Christian Andersen's Classic the Little Match Girl. 2010. (ENG., Illus.). 112p. pap. 12.99 *(978-0-06-200482-6(4)*, Harper Paperbacks) HarperCollins Pubs.
Man-Kong, Mary. Barbie in a Mermaid Tale. Golden Books Staff, illus. 2010. (Little Golden Book Ser.). (ENG.). (J). (gr. -1-2). 24p. 4.99 *(978-0-375-85733-1(8)*, Golden Bks.); 16p. pap. 3.99 *(978-0-375-85735-5(4)*, Random Hse. Bks. for Young Readers) Random Hse. Children's Bks.
Mancini, Kristen Belmont. A Bunny Named Boo. 2011. 24p. pap. 24.95 *(978-1-4269-7640-7(2))* Trafford Publishing (UK) Ltd.
Manushkin, Fran. Katie's Happy Mother's Day. Lyon, Tammie, illus. 2015. (Katie Woo Ser.). (ENG.). 32p. (gr. k-2). 21.32 *(978-1-4795-6179-7(7))* Picture Window Bks.
Marchese, Allison Marie. Patty's Best Friend. 2008. (Illus.). 16p. (J). 7.00 *(978-0-8059-7533-8(0))* Dorrance Publishing Co., Inc.
Marciniak, Christine. Lights, Camera, Ali! 2013. 232p. pap. 13.99 *(978-1-61271-214-7(2))* Zumaya Pubns. LLC.
Marie, Jessica. Keeping Broken Promises, 1 vol. 2010. 182p. pap. 24.95 *(978-1-4489-5273-1(5))* America Star Bks.
Marino, Andy. The Door. 2014. (ENG.). 304p. (J). (gr. 3-7). 17.99 *(978-0-545-55137-3(4)*, Scholastic Pr.) Scholastic, Inc.
Marler, Jerilyn. Lily Hates Goodbyes. Stoltenberg, Nathan, illus. 2012. 32p. pap. 6.95 *(978-1-936214-78-5(4))* Wyatt-MacKenzie Publishing.
Marlow, Herb. A Long Way Home. l.t. ed. 2003. (Illus.). 14p. (J). 19.95 *(978-1-893595-35-4(8))* Four Seasons Bks., Inc.
Marr, Kendra Lynn. I Was Rufus. 2013. 20p. pap. 24.95 *(978-1-4626-9917-9(0))* America Star Bks.
Marrone, Amanda. The Shape-Shifter's Curse. 2010. (Magic Repair Shop Ser.: 2). (ENG.). 240p. (J). (gr. 3-7). pap. 5.99 *(978-1-4169-9034-5(8)*, Aladdin) Simon & Schuster Children's Publishing.
Marshall, Linda Elovitz. Rainbow Weaver/Tejedora del Arcoíris. Chavarri, Elisa, illus. 2016. (ENG & SPA.). 40p. (J). (gr. 1-4). 18.95 *(978-0-89239-374-9(2))* Lee & Low Bks., Inc.
Martin, Ann M. Family Tree Book Three: Best Kept Secret. 2014. (ENG.). 224p. (J). (gr. 3-7). 16.99 *(978-0-545-35944-3(9)*, Scholastic Pr.) Scholastic, Inc.
—The Long Way Home. 2013. (Family Tree Ser.: 2). (ENG.). 224p. (J). (gr. 3-7). 16.99 *(978-0-545-35943-6(0)*, Scholastic Pr.) Scholastic, Inc.
Martin-Fluet, Marie T. The Fairies' Century Celebration. 2011. 40p. pap. 18.62 *(978-1-4567-2477-1(0))* AuthorHouse.
Martinez, Jessica. Virtuosity. (ENG.). (YA). (gr. 9). 2012. 320p. pap. 9.99 *(978-1-4424-2053-3(7))* 2011. 304p. 16.99 *(978-1-4424-2052-6(9))* Simon Pulse. (Simon Pulse).
Marts, Doreen Mulryan, illus. Even Monsters Say Good Night. 2015. (ENG.). 32p. (gr. -1-2). 14.95 *(978-1-62370-256-4(9))* Capstone Young Readers of Coughlan Cos.
Mason-Black, Jennifer. Devil & the Bluebird. 2016. (ENG.). 336p. (J). (gr. 8-17). 17.95 *(978-1-4197-2000-0(7)*, Amulet Bks.) Abrams, Inc.
Mason, Christopher. Little Bunny Comfy Pants. 2011. 20p. pap. 24.95 *(978-1-4626-0900-0(7))* America Star Bks.
Mathieu, Jennifer. Moxie. 2017. (YA). pap. ***(978-1-250-10426-7(2))*** Roaring Brook Pr.
Mathis, Tabitha. The Princess & the Tyger. 2012. 28p. pap. 24.95 *(978-1-4626-8265-2(0))* America Star Bks.
Mathisen, Michael. Abby & the Helping Mommy. Estill, Amy, illus. 2009. 28p. pap. 13.99 *(978-1-4389-5327-4(5))* AuthorHouse.
Matuszak, Pat. Simone's Secret, 2, Bk 2. 2009. (Angel Light Ser.: 2). (ENG.). 192p. (gr. 11). pap. 12.99 *(978-0-89957-876-7(4))* AMG Pubs.
Mayhew, Julie. Red Ink. 2016. (ENG.). 320p. (YA). (gr. 9). 16.99 *(978-0-7636-7731-2(0))* Candlewick Pr.
Mazer, Norma Fox. Missing Pieces. 2007. (ENG., Illus.). 160p. (YA). (gr. 7-12). pap. 11.95 *(978-0-15-206271-2(8))* Houghton Mifflin Harcourt Publishing Co.
Mazurick, Shannon K. Gemm: The Search for the Gem. 2011. 24p. pap. 15.00 *(978-1-4634-4265-1(3))* AuthorHouse.
McCahan, Erin. I Now Pronounce You Someone Else. 2010. (ENG.). 272p. (J). (gr. 7-18). 16.99 *(978-0-545-08818-3(6)*, Levine, Arthur A. Bks.) Scholastic, Inc.
McCormick, Michelle. Priscilla Willa, Party Planner: Night at the Haunted Hotel. 2013. (ENG.). 108p. (YA). pap. 9.95 *(978-1-4787-0890-2(5))* Outskirts Pr., Inc.
McDaniel, Lurlene. Garden of Angels. 2005. 272p. (gr. 7). 16.50 *(978-0-7569-5756-8(7))* Perfection Learning Corp.
McDonnell, Margot. Torn to Pieces. 2010. (ENG.). 272p. (YA). (gr. 7). pap. 8.99 *(978-0-385-73557-5(X)*, Delacorte Bks. for Young Readers) Random Hse. Children's Bks.
McDoogle, Farrah. A Sweet Surprise for Mom. Osterhold, Jared, illus. 2015. (Olivia TV Tie-In Ser.). (ENG.). 24p. (J). (gr. -1-2). pap. 3.99 *(978-1-4814-2763-0(6)*, Simon Spotlight) Simon Spotlight.
McElreath, Kim. Pouring in Love. l.t. ed. 2005. (Illus.). 30p. (J). 13.95 *(978-0-9769271-0-5(1))* McElreath, K.M.
McElroy, Lisa Tucker. Love, Lizzie: Letters to a Military Mom. Paterson, Diane, illus. (ENG.). 32p. (J). (gr. 1-3). 2009. pap. 6.99 *(978-0-8075-4778-6(6))* 2005. lib. bdg. 16.99 *(978-0-8075-4777-9(8))* Whitman, Albert & Co.
McGee, Pamela M. Keri. Miller, Dawn Ellen, illus. 2012. 20p. pap. 24.95 *(978-1-4626-8593-6(5))* America Star Bks.
—Keri: Dandelions. Miller, Dawn Ellen, illus. 2012. 24p. pap. 24.95 *(978-1-4626-9977-3(4))* America Star Bks.
—Keri: The Wedding. Miller, Dawn Ellen, illus. 2013. 20p. pap. 24.95 *(978-1-63004-171-7(6))* America Star Bks.
McGinnis, Mindy. Not a Drop to Drink. (ENG.). (YA). (gr. 9). 2014. 352p. pap. 9.99 *(978-0-06-219851-8(3))* 2013. 320p. 17.99 *(978-0-06-219850-1(5))* HarperCollins Pubs. (Tegen, Katherine Bks).
McGrath, Liz & Quick, Barbara. Even More/Todavía Más. de la Vega, Eida, tr. from ENG. McGrath, Liz, illus. 2004.Tr. of Todavía Más. (SPA & ENG., Illus.). 32p. (J). (gr. -1-3). 16.95 *(978-0-9720192-8-6(6)*, 626999, Raven Tree Pr.,Csi) Continental Sales, Inc.
McKenny, Stephanie L. Pearls of My Own. 2012. 102p. pap. 10.00 *(978-0-9705008-5-4(8))* J & J Publishing Co.
McKenzie, Paige. The Haunting of Sunshine Girl. (ENG.). 2016. 320p. (gr. 7-10). pap. 9.99 *(978-1-60286-302-6(4))* 2015. (Haunting of Sunshine Girl Ser.: Bk. 1). 304p. (YA). 16.00 *(978-1-60286-272-2(9))* Perseus Bks. Group. (Weinstein Bks.).
McLachlan, Jenny. Love Bomb. 2016. (Ladybirds Ser.: 2). (ENG.). 208p. (YA). 16.99 *(978-1-250-06149-2(0)*, 9781250061492) Feiwel & Friends.
Meade, L. T. A Little Mother to the Others. 2007. (ENG.). 216p. pap. 20.99 *(978-1-4346-1019-5(5))*; 244p. pap. 22.99 *(978-1-4346-1223-6(6))* Creative Media Partners, LLC.
Meldrum, Christina. Madapple. 2010. (ENG.). 416p. (YA). (gr. 9-18). pap. 10.99 *(978-0-375-85177-3(1))*, Knopf Bks. for Young Readers) Random Hse. Children's Bks.
Mentyka, Sharon. Chasing at the Surface. 2016. (ENG., Illus.). 228p. (J). pap. 12.99 *(978-1-943328-60-4(9)*, West Winds Pr.) Graphic Arts Ctr. Publishing Co.
Micinilio, Leanne Plein. Tia's Troubles: The First in a series of Tia's Adventures. 2011. 40p. pap. 16.99 *(978-1-4490-4695-8(9))* AuthorHouse.
Mickelson, Marcia. The Huaca. 2013. (J). pap. 16.99 *(978-1-4621-1190-9(4)*, Horizon Pubs.) Cedar Fort, Inc./CFI Distribution.
Miller-Johnston, Renee. Double Trouble for Courtney Logan Kennedy, 1 vol. 2009. 88p. pap. 19.95 *(978-1-60836-384-1(8))* America Star Bks.
Miller, Kymberly. My Mommy's Having a Baby. 2012. 36p. (-18). pap. 18.99 *(978-1-4772-8660-9(8))* AuthorHouse.
Miller, Mary Beth. Aimee. 2005. 276p. (gr. 9-12). 17.00 *(978-0-7569-6303-3(6))* Perfection Learning Corp.
Mills, Wendy. Positively Beautiful. (ENG.). 368p. (YA). 2016. pap. 9.99 *(978-1-68119-025-9(7)*, 9781681190259) 2015. (gr. 9). 17.99 *(978-1-61963-341-4(8)*, 9781619633414) Bloomsbury Publishing USA. (Bloomsbury USA Childrens).
Mincin, Sabrina. Catching a Shooting Star. 2012. 28p. pap. 12.95 *(978-1-4575-0862-2(1))* Dog Ear Publishing, LLC.
Minix, Holly. What Does Mommy Do at Night? 2009. 68p. pap. 25.00 *(978-1-60693-705-1(7)*, Strategic Bk. Publishing) Strategic Book Publishing & Rights Agency (SBPRA).
Miranda, Megan. The Safest Lies. (ENG.). 368p. (YA). (gr. 9). 2017. pap. 9.99 ***(978-0-553-53754-3(7)***, Ember) 2016. 17.99 *(978-0-553-53751-2(2)*, Crown Books For Young Readers) Random Hse. Children's Bks.
Mitchell, Rae. Anna's Wish. 2009. 24p. pap. 13.50 *(978-1-60860-441-8(1)*, Eloquent Bks.) Strategic Book Publishing & Rights Agency (SBPRA).
Molesworth & Molesworth, Mary Louisa S. Rosy. 2008. 120p. pap. 9.95 *(978-1-60664-226-9(X))* Rodgers, Alan Bks.
Monnar, Alberto. The Girl & the Mirror. Weiner, Linda, ed. Morton, Lisa, illus. 2008. per. 14.99 *(978-0-9768035-8-4(5))* Readers Are Leaders U.S.A., Inc.

MNO

Monstrata, Nessi. Monster High Diaries: Cleo & the Creeperific Mummy Makeover. 2016. (Monster High Diaries: 5). (ENG.). 160p. (J). (gr. 3-7). 9.99 (978-0-316-26636-9(1)) Little, Brown Bks. for Young Readers.

Montijo, Rhode. Gum Luck. Montijo, Rhode, illus. 2017. (Gum Girl Novel Ser.). (ENG., Illus.). 160p. (J). (gr. 1-3). 14.99 (978-1-4231-6117-2(3)) Hyperion Bks. for Children.

Moore, Meredith. I Am Her Revenge. 2015. (ENG.). 336p. (YA). (gr. 7). 17.99 (978-1-59514-782-0(9), Razorbill) Penguin Young Readers Group.

Morgan, Phillip. Abused, Alone & Forsaken: Mommy, Don't Leave Me. 2009. 212p. pap. 24.95 (978-1-4489-2733-3(1)) America Star Bks.

Morrissey, Donna. What Beautiful Mistake Did You Make Today? 2012. 24p. pap. 13.95 (978-1-4772-5669-5(5)) AuthorHouse.

Moulton, Erin E. Keepers of the Labyrinth. 2015. (ENG., Illus.). 304p. (YA). (gr. 7-12). 17.99 (978-0-399-16459-0(6), Philomel Bks.) Penguin Publishing Group.

Mullarkey, Lisa. Major Mama Drama, 1 vol. Harris, Phyllis, illus. 2009. (Katharine the Almost Great Ser.: No. 1). (ENG.). 80p. (J). (gr. 1-4). 27.07 (978-1-60270-580-7(1)) Magic Wagon.

Mummy's Little Girl. (Daddy's / Mommy's Ser.). 32p. (978-1-4054-9458-8(1)) Parragon, Inc.

Muñoz, Isabel. Just Like Mom. Mazali, Gustavo, illus. 2005. 22p. (J). pap. (978-0-439-78844-1(7)) Scholastic, Inc.

Mureddu, R. The Laundromat. 2011. 96p. pap. 19.95 (978-1-4560-8389-2(9)) America Star Bks.

Murray, Victoria Christopher. Aaliyah. 2009. (Divas Ser.). (ENG.). 208p. pap. 14.99 (978-1-4165-6351-8(2), Gallery Bks.) Gallery Bks.

Myers, Lily. This Impossible Light. 2017. (ENG.). 352p. (YA). (gr. 7). 17.99 (978-0-399-17372-1(2), Philomel Bks.) Penguin Young Readers Group.

Myracle, Lauren. The Forgetting Spell. 2017. (Wishing Day Ser.: 2). 352p. (J). (gr. 3-7). 16.99 (978-0-06-234209-6(6), Tegen, Katherine Bks) HarperCollins Pubs.

Napoli, Donna Jo. Zel. 2005. 240p. (J). (gr. 5-9). 21.00 (978-0-8446-7278-6(5), 3593) Smith, Peter Pub., Inc.

Nation, Kay. Jamie Learns to Love. 2006. pap. 10.00 (978-1-4257-0534-3(0)) Xlibris Corp.

Neel, Julien. Down in the Dumps. Neel, Julien, illus. 2012. (Lou! Ser.: 3). (ENG., Illus.). 48p. (J). (gr. 6-9). pap. 8.95 (978-0-8225-9165-8(0), Graphic Universe™) Lerner Publishing Group.

—The Perfect Summer. Neel, Julien, illus. 2012. (Lou! Ser.: 4). (ENG., Illus.). 48p. (J). (gr. 6-9). pap. 8.95 (978-0-8225-9169-6(3), Graphic Universe™) Lerner Publishing Group.

—Secret Diary. Neel, Julien, illus. 2012. (Lou! Ser.). (Illus.). 48p. (J). (gr. 4-8). pap. 51.02 (978-0-7613-9285-9(8)); (ENG., (gr. 6-9). pap. 8.95 (978-0-7613-8868-5(0)) Lerner Publishing Group. (Graphic Universe™).

—Summertime Blues. Neel, Julien, illus. 2012. (Lou! Ser.). (Illus.). 48p. (J). (gr. 4-8). pap. 51.02 (978-0-7613-9286-6(6)); (ENG., (gr. 6-9). pap. 8.95 (978-0-7613-8869-2(9)) Lerner Publishing Group. (Graphic Universe™).

Neel, Julien & Burrell, Carol klio. Down in the Dumps. Neel, Julien, illus. 2012. (Lou! Ser.: 3). (ENG., Illus.). 48p. (J). (gr. 6-9). lib. bdg. 27.93 (978-0-7613-8779-4(X), Graphic Universe™) Lerner Publishing Group.

—The Perfect Summer. Neel, Julien, illus. 2012. (Lou! Ser.: 4). (ENG., Illus.). 48p. (J). (gr. 6-9). lib. bdg. 27.93 (978-0-7613-8780-0(3), Graphic Universe™) Lerner Publishing Group.

Newman, Lesléa. Heather Has Two Mommies. Cornell, Laura, illus. 2015. (ENG.). 32p. (J). (gr. -1-2). 16.99 (978-0-7636-6631-6(9)) Candlewick Pr.

—Just Like Mama. Gorton, Julia, illus. 2010. (ENG.). 32p. (J). (gr. k-2). 15.95 (978-0-8109-8393-9(1), Abrams Bks. for Young Readers) Abrams, Inc.

Nickles, Clay & Ayres, Ella. Ali's Treasure. l.t. ed. 2005. (Illus.). 38p. (J). per. 16.95 (978-1-59879-006-1(4)) Lifevest Publishing, Inc.

Nielsen-Fernlund, Susin. The Magic Beads. Cote, Genevieve, illus. 2007. (ENG.). 32p. (J). (gr. -1-3). 16.95 (978-1-894965-47-7(7)) Simply Read Bks. CAN. Dist: Ingram Publisher Services.

Nix, Josef. My Mama's War. 2009. 104p. pap. 9.99 (978-1-60860-666-5(X), Strategic Bk. Publishing) Strategic Book Publishing & Rights Agency (SBPRA).

Nona Theresa Perez - Bayanin. The Birth of Nadia Mei. 2012. 24p. pap. 15.99 (978-1-4771-0387-6(2)) Xlibris Corp.

Norac, Carl. My Mummy Is Magic. Godon, Ingrid, illus. 2006. (ENG.). 32p. (J). (gr. 3-6). pap. 14.95 (978-1-4050-9023-0(5), Macmillan) Pan Macmillan GBR. Dist: Trans-Atlantic Pubns., Inc.

Noyes, Deborah. Angel & Apostle. 2007. (ENG.). 304p. per. 14.95 (978-1-932961-29-4(1)) Unbridled Bks.

Oakes, Cory Putman. Witchtown. 2017. (ENG.). 320p. (YA). (gr. 7). 17.99 (978-0-544-76557-3(5), HMH Books For Young Readers) Houghton Mifflin Harcourt Publishing Co.

Oakes, Stephanie. The Arsonist. 2017. (ENG.). 496p. (YA). (gr. 7). 17.99 **(978-0-8037-4071-6(9)**, Dial Bks) Penguin Young Readers Group.

Oates, Joyce Carol. Freaky Green Eyes. 2005. 341p. (YA). 15.65 (978-0-7569-6308-8(7)) Perfection Learning Corp.

O'Brien, Claudia Moore. My Mom's Apron. Friar, Joanne, illus. 2005. (ENG.). 12p. (J). 5.75 (978-1-57274-753-1(6), 2772, Bks. for Young Learners) Owen, Richard C. Pubs., Inc.

Ofelia, Dumas Lachtman. Big Enough Bastante Grande. Enrique, Sanchez, illus. 2008. 32p. (J). pap. 7.95 (978-1-55885-239-6(5)) Arte Publico Pr.

Oliver, Jan. Heart of Fire. 2009. 176p. pap. 18.95 (978-1-4092-6660-0(5)) Lulu Pr., Inc.

Olson, Gretchen. Call Me Hope. 2008. (ENG.). 288p. (J). (gr. 3-7). pap. 5.99 (978-0-316-01239-3(4)) Little, Brown Bks. for Young Readers.

One Last Garden. 2006. (J). per. 10.95 (978-1-933505-20-6(6)) Quantum Manifestations Publishing.

O'Reilly, Jane. The Secret of Goldenrod. 2016. (ENG.). (gr. 3-6). 328p. (J). 17.99 (978-1-5124-0135-6(8)); 376p. 35.99 (978-1-5124-0894-2(8)) Lerner Publishing Group. (Carolrhoda Bks.).

Ormerod, Jan. Lizzie Nonsense. 2006. (Illus.). 32p. pap. (978-1-877003-93-6(X)) Little Hare Bks. AUS. Dist: HarperCollins Pubs. Australia.

Paoline, Dyann. Cecilia's Fitness Adventure. 2011. 24p. pap. 15.75 (978-1-4634-0797-1(1)) AuthorHouse.

Paratore, Coleen Murtagh. The Wedding Planner's Daughter. McGregor, Barbara, illus. 2006. (Wedding Planner's Daughter Ser.). (ENG.). 208p. (J). (gr. 3-8). reprint ed. pap. 6.99 (978-1-4169-1854-7(X), Simon & Schuster Bks. For Young Readers) Simon & Schuster Bks. For Young Readers.

Parish, Herman. Amelia Bedelia by the Yard. Avril, Lynne, illus. 2016. (I Can Read Level 1 Ser.). 32p. (J). (gr. -1-3). pap. 3.99 (978-0-06-233427-5(1), Greenwillow Bks.) HarperCollins Pubs.

—Amelia Bedelia Chalks It Up! Avril, Lynne, illus. 2014. (I Can Read Level 1 Ser.). (ENG.). 32p. (J). (gr. -1-3). 16.99 (978-0-06-233422-0(0), Greenwillow Bks.) HarperCollins Pubs.

—Amelia Bedelia Chalks One Up. Avril, Lynne, illus. 2014. (I Can Read Level 1 Ser.). (ENG.). 32p. (J). (gr. -1-3). pap. 3.99 (978-0-06-233421-3(2), Greenwillow Bks.) HarperCollins Pubs.

—Amelia Bedelia Chalks One Up. 2014. (Amelia Bedelia: I Can Read! Ser.). (J). lib. bdg. 13.55 (978-0-606-35947-4(8)) Turtleback Bks.

Pascal, Francine. Falsas Apariencias. Orig. Title: Jumping to Conclusions. (SPA., Illus.). 128p. (J). 6.95 (978-84-272-3794-0(4)) Molino, Editorial ESP. Dist: AIMS International Bks., Inc.

Patron, Susan. Maybe Yes, Maybe No, Maybe Maybe. Halpin, Abigail, illus. 2009. (ENG.). 128p. (J). (gr. 3-5). pap. 5.99 (978-1-4169-6176-5(3), Atheneum Bks. for Young Readers) Simon & Schuster Children's Publishing.

Patterson, Valerie O. The Other Side of Blue. 2011. (ENG.). 240p. (YA). (gr. 7). pap. 13.99 (978-0-547-55215-6(7)) Houghton Mifflin Harcourt Publishing Co.

Paul, Dominique. The Possibility of Fireflies. 2007. (ENG.). 224p. (YA). (gr. 8-12). pap. 8.99 (978-1-4169-1311-5(4), Simon & Schuster Bks. For Young Readers) Simon & Schuster Bks. For Young Readers.

Peakler, Nicole Danette. Tayno Ti & the Legend of the Coqui. 2012. 28p. 24.95 (978-1-4626-5940-1(3)) America Star Bks.

Pearce, Valarie. When Mommy Needs a Timeout. Johnson, Meredith, illus. 2012. 26p. pap. 10.99 (978-0-9843111-5-6(7)) ImaRa Publishing.

Peet, Mal & Graham, Elspeth. Cloud Tea Monkeys. Wijngaard, Juan, illus. 2010. (ENG.). 56p. (J). (gr. -1-3). 17.99 (978-0-7636-4453-6(6)) Candlewick Pr.

Perelman-Bernstein, Helen. Feel the Noise! Tips & Tricks to Rockin' Camp. 2009. (ENG.). 40p. (J). 4.99 (978-1-4231-2219-7(4)) Disney Pr.

Peterka, Edward S. Zoe Isabella Goes to the Zoo. 2011. 32p. pap. 12.77 (978-1-4520-0305-4(X)) AuthorHouse.

Peterson, Lois J. Three Good Things, 1 vol. 2015. (Orca Currents Ser.). (ENG.). 144p. (J). (gr. 5-9). pap. 9.95 (978-1-4598-0985-7(8)) Orca Bk. Pubs. USA.

Pfoutz, Sally. Missing Person. 2009. 192p. (gr. 7-18). pap. 12.95 (978-1-4401-5108-8(3)) iUniverse, Inc.

Philbin, Joanna. The Daughters Take the Stage. 2011. (Daughters Ser.: 3). (ENG.). 304p. (J). (gr. 7-17). pap. 8.99 (978-0-316-04908-5(5), Poppy) Little, Brown Bks. for Young Readers.

Phillips, Gin. The Hidden Summer. 2014. (ENG.). 208p. (J). (gr. 5). pap. 7.99 (978-0-14-242568-8(0), Puffin Books) Penguin Young Readers Group.

Phillips, Linda Vigen. Crazy. 2014. (ENG.). 320p. (YA). pap. 9.00 (978-0-8028-5437-7(0), Eerdmans Bks For Young Readers) Eerdmans, William B. Publishing Co.

Pickett, Anola. Whisper Island. 2013. (ENG.). 235p. (J). (gr. 3-7). pap. 14.99 (978-1-4621-1167-1(X), Sweetwater Bks.) Cedar Fort, Inc./CFI Distribution.

Picoult, Jodi & van Leer, Samantha. Between the Lines. (ENG., Illus.). 368p. (YA). (gr. 7). 2013. pap. 12.99 (978-1-4516-3581-2(8)) 2012. 19.99 (978-1-4516-3575-1(3)) Atria/Emily Bestler Bks. (Atria/Emily Bestler Bks.).

Pierres, Marianne De. Serious Sas & Messy Magda. Bridgen, Rachel Annie, illus. 2013. 32p. pap. (978-1-909423-04-6(1)) Bks. to Treasure.

Pierro, Rita. A Horse in the House, 1 vol. French, David, illus. 2009. 29p. pap. 24.95 (978-1-60836-410-7(0)) America Star Bks.

Polsky, Sara. This Is How I Find Her. (ENG.). 272p. (YA). (gr. 8-12). 2015. pap. 9.99 (978-0-8075-7880-3(0)) 2013. 16.99 (978-0-8075-7877-3(0)) Whitman, Albert & Co.

Ponnay, Brenda & Ponnay, Brenda. Secret Agent Josephine in Paris. 2013. 32p. pap. 9.99 (978-1-62395-552-6(1)) Xist Publishing.

Ponti, James. Dead City. (Dead City Ser.: 1). (ENG., Illus.). (J). (gr. 4-8). 2013. 304p. pap. 7.99 (978-1-4424-4130-9(5)) 2012. 288p. 17.99 (978-1-4424-4129-3(1)) Simon & Schuster Children's Publishing. (Aladdin).

Porter, Gene Stratton-. A Girl of the Limberlost. 2011. 266p. pap. 17.99 (978-1-61279-071-8(2)) Publishing in Motion.

Posner, Richard. Sparrows Flight. 2014. (ENG.). 222p. (J). (gr. 7-10). pap. 14.95 (978-1-59077-316-1(0)) Evans, M. & Co., Inc.

Poston, Karen. A Baby for Mabel & Frederick. 2005. 20p. (J). 11.28 (978-1-4116-6024-3(2)) Lulu Pr., Inc.

Potter, Dawn. Isobel's Tree. 2010. 16p. pap. 9.99 (978-1-60860-966-6(9), Eloquent Bks.) Strategic Book Publishing & Rights Agency (SBPRA).

Powers, J. L. This Thing Called the Future. 2011. (FRS & ENG.). 208p. (J). (gr. 7-11). 16.95 (978-1-933693-95-8(9)) Cinco Puntos Pr.

Pressler, Mirjam. Malka. Murdoch, Brian, tr. 2005. 280p. (YA). (gr. 7-12). 13.65 (978-0-7569-5217-4(4)) Perfection Learning Corp.

Price, M. J. The Skin I'm In. 2013. 32p. pap. 24.95 (978-1-63000-967-0(9)) America Star Bks.

Promise, 1 vol. 2014. (Faerieground Ser.). (ENG., Illus.). 96p. (gr. 1-3). lib. bdg. 23.99 (978-1-4342-9188-2(X)) Stone Arch Bks.

Prose, Francine. Touch. 2010. (ENG.). 272p. (YA). (gr. 9). pap. 8.99 (978-0-06-137519-4(5), HarperTeen) HarperCollins Pubs.

Puentes, Christina. On the Way to Granny's House. 2005. 28p. per. 17.32 (978-1-4134-3612-9(9)) Xlibris Corp.

Pullman, Philip. Le Miroir d'Ambre. (FRE.). pap. 18.95 (978-2-07-054376-2(5)) Gallimard, Editions FRA. Dist: Distribooks, Inc.

Pyles, Mary Kay. Rise & Shine Rosie. 2013. 134p. pap. 11.95 (978-0-9887836-9-0(X)) Taylor and Seale Publishing, LLC.

Quirk, Katie. A Girl Called Problem. 2013. (ENG., Illus.). 256p. (J). pap. 8.50 (978-0-8028-5404-9(4), Eerdmans Bks For Young Readers) Eerdmans, William B. Publishing Co.

Rahlens, Holly-Jane. Prince William, Maximilian Minsky, & Me. 2007. (ENG.). 320p. (YA). (gr. 7-11). per. 7.99 (978-0-7636-3299-1(6)) Candlewick Pr.

Rando, Licia. The Warmest Place of All. Jewett, Anne, illus. 2009. (ENG.). 32p. (J). (gr. -1-k). 16.95 (978-0-9792035-8-9(9)) Pleasant St. Pr.

Random House Staff. I Love My Mami! (Dora the Explorer) Random House Staff & Aikins, Dave, illus. 2013. (Step into Reading Ser.). (ENG.). 24p. (J). (gr. -1-1). pap. 3.99 (978-0-449-81439-0(4), Random Hse. Bks. for Young Readers) Random Hse. Children's Bks.

Rao, Sandhya. My Mother's Sari. Sabnani, Nina, illus. 2009. (ENG.). 28p. (J). (gr. -1-3). 7.95 (978-0-7358-2233-7(6)) North-South Bks., Inc.

Ratcliffe-Kitchingman, Linda. Lindylou in I Hate Porridge. 2012. 32p. pap. 8.99 (978-1-62419-173-2(8)) Salem Author Services.

Ratliff, Lana. A Blanket Full of Blessings. 2012. 32p. 29.99 (978-1-62230-245-1(1)); pap. 19.99 (978-1-62230-244-4(3)) Salem Author Services.

Raymundo, Peter. Third Grade Mermaid. 2017. (ENG.). 208p. (J). (gr. 1-3). 12.99 (978-0-545-91816-9(2), Scholastic Pr.) Scholastic, Inc.

Reed, Amy. Over You. (ENG., Illus.). (YA). (gr. 9). 2014. 336p. pap. 9.99 (978-1-4424-5697-6(3)) 2013. 320p. 16.99 (978-1-4424-5696-9(5)) Simon Pulse. (Simon Pulse).

Reeves, Dia. Bleeding Violet. 2010. (ENG.). 480p. (YA). (gr. 9). pap. 20.99 (978-1-4169-8619-5(7), Simon Pulse) Simon Pulse.

Reichert, Amy. Take Your Mama to Work Today. Boiger, Alexandra, illus. 2012. (ENG.). 40p. (J). (gr. -1-8). 16.99 (978-1-4169-7095-8(9), Atheneum Bks. for Young Readers) Simon & Schuster Children's Publishing.

Reiser, Lynn. Tortillas & Lullabies. Hart, Rebecca, tr. Valientes, Corazones, illus. 2008. (Rise & Shine Ser.).Tr. of Tortillas y Cancioncitas. (SPA & ENG.). 48p. (J). (gr. -1-3). pap. 6.99 (978-0-06-089185-5(8), Greenwillow Bks.) HarperCollins Pubs.

Renfrew, Regan. Orphans of the Heart: A Young Girl & a Paint Filly Heal Each Other's Broken Hearts. 2013. (ENG.). 163p. (YA). pap. 12.95 (978-1-4787-1686-0(X)) Outskirts Pr., Inc.

Resau, Laura. The Indigo Notebook. 2010. (ENG.). 336p. (YA). (gr. 7). pap. 9.99 (978-0-375-84524-6(0), Ember) Random Hse. Children's Bks.

—The Ruby Notebook. 2012. (ENG.). 384p. (YA). (gr. 7). pap. 9.99 (978-0-375-84525-3(9), Ember) Random Hse. Children's Bks.

Reschke, Kathleen. Grandma, Mommy & Me. 2010. 20p. pap. 12.95 (978-1-4490-5550-9(8)) AuthorHouse.

Return to the Crows, 1 vol. 2014. (Faerieground Ser.). (ENG., Illus.). 96p. (gr. 1-3). lib. bdg. 23.99 (978-1-4342-9187-5(1)) Stone Arch Bks.

Rice, Luanne. The Beautiful Lost. 2017. (ENG.). 304p. (J). (gr. 7). 18.99 **(978-1-338-11107-1(8))** Scholastic, Inc.

Richards, Katherine. My Favorite Run. Fieldhouse, Vicky, illus. 2013. (ENG.). 32p. (J). 16.99 (978-0-9895095-2-7(4)) Fit Kids Publishing.

Rim, Sujean. Birdie's Big-Girl Hair. 2014. (Birdie Ser.). (ENG., Illus.). 40p. (J). (gr. -1-3). 17.00 (978-0-316-22791-9(9)) Little Brown & Co.

Rim, Sujean, illus. Birdie's Big-Girl Shoes. 2009. (Birdie Ser.). (ENG.). 40p. (J). (gr. -1-3). 17.99 (978-0-316-04470-7(9)) Little, Brown Bks. for Young Readers.

Rinaldi, Ann. The Family Greene. 2011. (ENG.). 256p. (YA). (gr. 7). pap. 14.95 (978-0-547-57723-4(0)) Houghton Mifflin Harcourt Publishing Co.

Rivers, Karen. Finding Ruby Starling. 2014. (ENG.). 304p. (J). (gr. 4-7). 17.99 (978-0-545-53479-6(8), Levine, Arthur A. Bks.) Scholastic, Inc.

Rivers, Phoebe. Yesterday & Today. 2013. (Saranormal Ser.: 11). (ENG., Illus.). 160p. (J). (gr. 3-7). 15.99 (978-1-4424-8962-2(6)); pap. 5.99 (978-1-4424-8961-5(8)) Simon Spotlight. (Simon Spotlight).

Roash, Riki. Mom, I Can Sleep in My Bed Tonight! 2013. 24p. pap. 24.95 (978-1-4626-8255-3(3)) America Star Bks.

Robinson, Kathleen Marie. Snowflake Sandwiches. 2007. 15p. pap. 24.95 (978-1-4241-8620-4(X)) America Star Bks.

Rodgers, Mary. Freaky Friday. 2005. 176p. (YA). (gr. 5-9). 21.25 (978-0-8446-7273-1(4), 3588) Smith, Peter Pub., Inc.

Rosenthal, Amy Krouse. Bedtime for Mommy. Pham, LeUyen, illus. 2010. (ENG.). 32p. (J). (gr. -1-k). 16.99 (978-1-59990-341-5(5), 9781599903415, Bloomsbury USA Childrens) Bloomsbury Publishing USA.

Roske, Melissa. Kat Greene Comes Clean. 2017. (ENG.). 224p. (J). (gr. 4-7). lib. bdg. 16.99 (978-1-58089-776-1(2)) Charlesbridge Publishing, Inc.

Ross, Tony. I Want My Mom! Ross, Tony, illus. 2012. (Andersen Press Picture Bks). (ENG., Illus.). 32p. (J). (gr. -1-3). 16.95 (978-1-4677-0318-5(4)) Lerner Publishing Group.

Rubi, Nicholas. My Mom's Not Cool. Maia, Chavez Larkin, illus. 2008. 24p. (J). per. 12.95 (978-0-9776906-4-0(4)) Blueline Publishing.

Ruby, Laura. Lily's Ghosts. 2005. (Illus.). 258p. (J). (gr. 5-9). 13.65 (978-0-7569-5115-3(1)) Perfection Learning Corp.

Rundell, Katherine. The Wolf Wilder. 2015. (ENG., Illus.). 240p. (J). (gr. 3-7). 16.99 (978-1-4814-1942-0(0), Simon & Schuster Bks. For Young Readers) Simon & Schuster Bks. For Young Readers.

Russo, Angela B. Beautiful. 2013. 28p. pap. 24.95 (978-1-62709-040-7(1)) America Star Bks.

Ryder, Joanne & Ryder. My Mother's Voice. Catalanotto, Peter, illus. 2006. (ENG.). 32p. (J). (gr. -1-3). 16.99 (978-0-06-029509-7(0)) HarperCollins Pubs.

Sackier, Shelley. Dear OPL. 2015. (ENG.). 240p. (J). (gr. 5-8). pap. 7.99 (978-1-4926-0859-2(9), 9781492608592) Sourcebooks, Inc.

Salma, Hammad. I am Beautiful. 2007. (Illus.). 20p. (J). mass mkt. (978-0-9787849-9-7(5)) Lucent Interpretations, LLC.

Salter, Sydney. My Big Nose & Other Natural Disasters. 2009. (ENG., Illus.). 352p. (J). (gr. 7-18). pap. 19.95 (978-0-15-206643-7(8)) Houghton Mifflin Harcourt Publishing Co.

Sanchez, Jenny Torres. Because of the Sun. 2017. (ENG.). 272p. (YA). (gr. 7). 17.99 (978-0-399-55145-1(X), Delacorte Pr.) Random Hse. Children's Bks.

Sand-Eveland, Cyndi. A Tinfoil Sky. (ENG., Illus.). (YA). (gr. 5). 2014. 216p. pap. 9.99 (978-1-77049-510-4(X)) 2012. 218p. 17.95 (978-1-77049-277-6(1)) Tundra Bks. CAN. (Tundra Bks.). Dist: Penguin Random Hse. LLC.

Satterfield, Barbara. Answer Why for Mee Mee. 2004. (Illus.). 32p. (J). pap. 11.50 (978-0-9748715-1-6(6), 314-004) Vision Harmony Publishing.

Sauer, Tammi. Dear Jack. 2004. 164p. (YA). mass mkt. 6.99 (978-0-9753367-0-0(3)) Onstage Publishing, LLC.

Scanlon, Liz Garton. The Great Good Summer. 2015. (ENG., Illus.). 224p. (J). (gr. 3-7). 16.99 (978-1-4814-1147-9(0), Beach Lane Bks.) Beach Lane Bks.

Schantz, Sarah Elizabeth. Fig. 2016. (ENG.). 352p. (YA). (gr. 9). pap. 10.99 (978-1-4814-2359-5(2), McElderry, Margaret K. Bks.) McElderry, Margaret K. Bks.

Schena, Maghan. When I Grow Up. 2011. (ENG.). 18p. (J). pap. 11.95 (978-1-4327-8203-0(7)) Outskirts Pr., Inc.

Schindler, Holly. A Blue So Dark. 2010. (ENG.). 288p. (YA). (gr. 9-18). pap. 11.99 (978-0-7387-1926-9(9), Flux) North Star Editions.

Schnell, Selynn. The Backpack Jungle. 2011. 48p. pap. 16.95 (978-1-4560-3332-3(8)) America Star Bks.

Schoettler, Joan. Good Fortune in a Wrapping Cloth. Lanan, Jessica, illus. 2011. (ENG.). (J). 17.95 (978-1-885008-40-4(6), Shen's Bks.) Lee & Low Bks., Inc.

Schrader, Margaret. Green Knee-High Farm. Schrader, Kimberly, illus. 2009. 28p. pap. 12.95 (978-1-60844-000-9(1)) Dog Ear Publishing, LLC.

Schraff, Anne. The Fairest, 1 vol. unabr. ed. 2011. (Urban Underground Ser.). (ENG.). 179p. (YA). (gr. 9-12). pap. 9.95 (978-1-61651-007-7(2)) Saddleback Educational Publishing, Inc.

Schraff, Anne E. Misjudged. 2014. (Urban Underground — Cesar Chavez High School Ser.). (YA). lib. bdg. 20.80 (978-0-606-35589-6(8)) Turtleback Bks.

Schröder, Monika. Be Light Like a Bird. 2016. (ENG.). 240p. (gr. 3-7). lib. bdg. 14.95 (978-1-62370-749-1(8)) Capstone Young Readers of Coughlan Cos.

—Be Light Like a Bird. 2016. (Middle-Grade Novels Ser.). (ENG.). 240p. (gr. 4-7). 26.65 (978-1-4965-3301-2(1)) Stone Arch Bks.

Schroeder, Lisa. The Bridge from Me to You. 2014. (ENG.). 336p. (J). (gr. 7). 17.99 (978-0-545-64601-7(4)) Scholastic, Inc.

—It's Raining Cupcakes. (ENG., Illus.). 208p. (J). (gr. 3-7). 2011. pap. 6.99 (978-1-4169-9085-7(2)) 2010. 17.99 (978-1-4169-9084-0(4)) Simon & Schuster Children's Publishing. (Aladdin).

—My Secret Guide to Paris. (ENG.). 224p. (J). (gr. 3-7). 2016. pap. 6.99 (978-0-545-70810-4(9)) 2015. 16.99 (978-0-545-70808-1(7), Scholastic Pr.) Scholastic, Inc.

Schumacher, Julie. The Unbearable Book Club for Unsinkable Girls. 2013. (ENG.). 240p. (YA). (gr. 7). pap. 8.99 (978-0-375-85127-8(5), Ember) Random Hse. Children's Bks.

Scott, Elizabeth. Stealing Heaven. 2009. (ENG.). 336p. (YA). (gr. 8). pap. 8.99 (978-0-06-112282-8(3), HarperTeen) HarperCollins Pubs.

Selby, Vicki L. Sleepy Sierra & the Great Blanket Adventure. 2011. 20p. (gr. 1-2). pap. 11.32 (978-1-4567-3099-4(1)) AuthorHouse.

Selfors, Suzanne. Kiss & Spell. 2015. (Ever after High Ser.: Bk. 2). (ENG., Illus.). 224p. (J). (gr. 3-7). 13.99 (978-0-316-40131-9(5)) Little, Brown Bks. for Young Readers.

Sepetys, Ruta. Out of the Easy. 2013. (ENG.). 352p. (YA). (gr. 9). 17.99 (978-0-399-25692-9(X), Philomel Bks.) Penguin Young Readers Group.

Sharenow, Robert. My Mother the Cheerleader. 2009. (ENG.). 320p. (YA). (gr. 8). pap. 9.99 (978-0-06-114898-9(9), HarperTeen) 2007. 304p. (J). (gr. 7-18). 16.99 (978-0-06-114896-5(2), Geringer, Laura Book) 2007. 304p. (J). (gr. 7-18). lib. bdg. 17.89 (978-0-06-114897-2(0), Geringer, Laura Book) HarperCollins Pubs.

Shaw, Laura. Priscilla & the Big Red Ball, 1 vol. Shaw, Yvonne, illus. 2009. 19p. pap. 24.95 (978-1-60749-523-9(6)) America Star Bks.

Shaw, Susan. Black-Eyed Suzie. 2007. (ENG.). 176p. (J). (gr. 6-9). pap. 9.95 (978-1-59078-533-1(9), Front Street) Boyds Mills Pr.

Shemin, Craig. Families Are Forever. McCoy, John, illus. 2006. 34p. (J). (gr. -1-2). 16.95 (978-0-9728666-6-8(3)) As Simple As That Publishing.

Sherrard, Valerie. Searching for Yesterday: A Shelby Belgarden Mystery. 2008. (ENG.). 224p. (YA). (gr. 6-10). pap. 12.99 (978-1-55002-788-4(3), Boardwalk Bks.) Dundurn CAN. Dist: Ingram Publisher Services.

Shimizu, Michio. Ding Dong. McLaughlin, Sako, tr. Yamamoto, Matsuko, illus. 2009. 32p. 14.95 (978-1-74126-440-1(5)) R.I.C. Pubns. AUS. Dist: SCB Distributors.

Shofner, Corabel. Almost Paradise. 2017. (ENG.). 304p. (J). 16.99 (978-0-374-30378-5(9), 9780374303785, Farrar, Straus & Giroux (BYR)) Farrar, Straus & Giroux.

Shulman, Dee. On Stage in America. 2012. (My Totally Secret Diary Ser.). (ENG., Illus.). 144p. (J). (gr. 2-4). pap. 12.99 (978-1-86230-423-9(8), Red Fox) Random House Children's Books GBR. Dist: Independent Pubs. Group.

Silverthorne, Judith. The Secret of the Stone House, 1 vol. 2005. (From Many Peoples Ser.). (ENG., Illus.). 224p. (J). (gr. 4-7). pap. 7.95 (978-1-55050-325-8(1)) Coteau Bks. CAN. Dist: Orca Bk. Pubs. USA.

Simmons, Kristen. Article 5. 2012. (Article 5 Ser.: 1). (ENG.). 368p. (YA). (gr. 8-12). 17.99 (978-0-7653-2958-5(1), 9780765329585, Tor Teen) Doherty, Tom Assocs., LLC.

Simner, Janni Lee. Secret of the Three Treasures. 2006. (ENG.). 160p. (YA). (gr. 8-12). 16.95 (978-0-8234-1914-2(2)) Holiday Hse., Inc.

Simon, Sandy. Sylvie. 2012. 16p. pap. 15.99 (978-1-4772-4899-7(4)) AuthorHouse.

Simone, Ni-Ni & Abrams, Amir. Lights, Love, & Lip Gloss. 2014. (Hollywood High Ser.: 4). (ENG., Illus.). 240p. (YA). (gr. 13). pap. 9.95 *(978-0-7582-8854-7(9)*, K-Teen) Kensington Publishing Corp.
Sinclair, Mehded Maryam. When Wings Expand. 2013. (ENG., Illus.). 150p. (J). (gr. 5-9). pap. 9.95 *(978-0-86037-499-2(8))* Kube Publishing Ltd. GBR. Dist: Consortium Bk. Sales & Distribution.
Singleton, Paul. Sometimes Mama's Just Like That. 2013. 30p. pap. 17.99 *(978-0-578-13425-3(X))* Drinking Gourd Pr.
Sinois, Latrice J. You Are My Sunshine. 2012. 20p. pap. 17.99 *(978-1-4772-5731-9(4))* AuthorHouse.
Slegers, Liesbet. Laura Ayuda a Su Mama/ Laura Helps Her Mom. 2008. 28p. 10.95 *(978-84-263-6492-0(6))* Vives, Luis Editorial (Edelvives) ESP. Dist: Baker & Taylor Bks.
Smith, Rosemary. Three Wishes for Maddy. 2012. 48p. pap. 10.00 *(978-1-61204-798-0(X)*, Strategic Bk. Publishing) Strategic Book Publishing & Rights Agency (SBPRA).
Snyder, Laurel. Seven Stories Up. 2015. (ENG.). 240p. (J). (gr. 3-7). 6.99 *(978-0-375-87326-3(0)*, Yearling) Random Hse. Children's Bks.
Soda, Cynthia. Lolly's Basement Crawlies. 2011. 28p. (gr. 1-2). pap. 13.59 *(978-1-4567-4562-2(X))* AuthorHouse.
Sonnenblick, Jordan. Falling over Sideways. (ENG.). 272p. (J). (gr. 7). 2017. pap. 9.99 ***(978-0-545-86325-4(2))*** 2016. 17.99 *(978-0-545-86324-7(4)*, Scholastic Pr.) Scholastic, Inc.
Soo, Kean. The Lost Monster. 2014. (Jellaby Ser.). (ENG., Illus.). 160p. (gr. 4-8). pap. 12.95 *(978-1-4342-6420-6(3))* Stone Arch Bks.
Sorrells, Walter. Club Dread. 2007. (Hunted Ser.). (ENG.). 272p. (YA). (gr. 7-18). 8.99 *(978-0-14-240904-6(9)*, Puffin Books) Penguin Young Readers Group.
—Fake ID. 2007. (Hunted Ser.). (ENG.). 336p. (YA). (gr. 7-18). 9.99 *(978-0-14-240762-2(3)*, Puffin Books) Penguin Young Readers Group.
Spalding, Amy. The Reece Malcolm List. 2013. (ENG.). 352p. (YA). (gr. 8). pap. 9.99 *(978-1-62061-240-8(2)*, 9781620612408) Entangled Publishing, LLC.
Speaker, Cathy. The Road Home. Rosteck, Rachel, illus. 2012. (ENG.). 45p. (J). pap. 15.95 *(978-1-4327-9146-9(X))* Outskirts Pr., Inc.
Springer, Nancy. Possessing Jessie. 2010. (ENG.). 128p. (YA). (gr. 7-18). pap. 16.95 *(978-0-8234-2259-3(3))* Holiday Hse., Inc.
Spyri, Johanna. Gritli's Children. 2006. 144p. (gr. 4-7). per. 11.95 *(978-1-59818-921-6(2))*; 24.95 *(978-1-59818-413-6(X))* Aegypan.
St. Anthony, Jane. The Summer Sherman Loved Me. 2015. (Fesler-Lampert Minnesota Heritage Ser.). (ENG.). 144p. pap. 9.95 *(978-0-8166-9815-8(5))* Univ. of Minnesota Pr.
Stamm, Linda J. Phoebe's Family: A Story about Egg Donation. Clipp, Joan, illus. 2015. (J). pap. *(978-0-9755810-7-0(4))* Graphite Pr.
Stamm, Linda J. Scarlett's Story: A Tale about Embryo Donation. Clipp, Joan, illus. 2017. (J). pap. ***(978-1-938313-17-2(8))*** Graphite Pr.
Stan, Jaskiel, illus. Families are Forever Learning & Activity Guide. 2007. 20p. (J). 9.95 *(978-0-9728666-2-0(0))* As Simple As That Publishing.
Staniszewski, Anna. Once upon a Cruise: a Wish Novel. 2016. (ENG.). 256p. (J). (gr. 3-7). pap. 6.99 *(978-0-545-87986-6(8)*, Scholastic Paperbacks) Scholastic, Inc.
Stanley, Shalanda. Drowning Is Inevitable. 2015. (ENG.). 288p. (YA). (gr. 9). 17.99 *(978-0-553-50828-4(8)*, Knopf Bks. for Young Readers) Random Hse. Children's Bks.
Steffen, Tim. Mom's Cup of Coffee: The (Incr)Edible Adventures of Allie Quirk. 2012. (Illus.). 65p. (J). pap. *(978-0-9779518-5-7(5))* Cardinal Pr.
Stern, A. J. Fashion Frenzy. Marts, Doreen Mulryan, illus. 2011. (Frankly, Frannie Ser.: 6). (ENG.). 128p. (J). (gr. 1-3). pap. 5.99 *(978-0-448-45544-0(7)*, Grosset & Dunlap) Penguin Young Readers Group.
Sternberg, Julie. Bedtime at Bessie & Lil's. Gudeon, Adam, illus. 2015. (ENG.). 32p. (J). (gr. -1-2). 16.95 *(978-1-59078-934-6(2))* Boyds Mills Pr.
Stevenson, Robin. Impossible Things, 1 vol. 2008. (ENG.). 192p. (J). (gr. 4-8). pap. 8.95 *(978-1-55143-736-1(8))* Orca Bk. Pubs. USA.
Stirling, Tricia. When My Heart Was Wicked. 2015. (ENG.). 192p. (J). (gr. 9). 17.99 *(978-0-545-69573-2(2)*, Scholastic Pr.) Scholastic, Inc.
Stiverson, Charlotte L. Nellie's Walk. Aitken, Kati, illus. 2016. (J). *(978-1-935864-62-2(9))* Oncology Nursing Society.
Stone, Heather Duffy. Over the Tracks. 2015. (ENG.). 96p. (YA). (gr. 6-12). 27.99 *(978-1-4677-5711-9(X))* Lerner Publishing Group.
Stone, Jade. Whispering Willow Woods. 2005. 73p. pap. 19.95 *(978-1-4137-4264-0(5))* America Star Bks.
Stone, Laura. Little Lulu Learns a Lesson. 2010. 34p. pap. 16.95 *(978-0-557-33222-9(2))* Lulu Pr., Inc.
Stone, Phoebe. Paris for Two. 2016. (ENG.). 272p. (J). (gr. 3-7). 16.99 *(978-0-545-44362-3(8)*, Levine, Arthur A. Bks.) Scholastic, Inc.
Stone, Summer. Lobster Trips. 2012. 24p. pap. 16.50 *(978-1-4772-9130-6(X))* AuthorHouse.
Stratton-Porter, Gene. A Girl of the Limberlost. Benda, Wladyslaw T., illus. 2005. reprint ed. pap. 38.95 *(978-0-7661-9424-3(8))* Kessinger Publishing, LLC.
—A Girl of the Limberlost. 2006. 336p. (YA). 21.95 *(978-1-934169-30-8(7))*; pap. 10.95 *(978-1-934169-31-5(5))* Norilana Bks.
—Wonder, Hope, Love, & Loss: The Selected Novels of Gene Stratton-Porter. 2015. (ENG.). 784p. (gr. 6). pap. 17.99 *(978-1-63220-320-5(0)*, Sky Pony Pr.) Skyhorse Publishing Co., Inc.
Stringam, Jean. How Not to Cry in Public. 2013. 390p. pap. 16.99 *(978-0-9855540-1-9(0))* Dollison Road Bks.
Struyk-Bonn, Chris. Nice Girls Endure. 2016. (ENG.). 256p. (gr. 9-12). 16.95 *(978-1-63079-047-9(8))* Switch Pr.
Stuart, Carrie. Lenore's Chores. 2006. (Neighborhood Readers Ser.). (ENG.). 8p. (gr. 1-3). pap. 5.15 *(978-1-4042-6823-4(5)*, Rosen Classroom) Rosen Publishing Group, Inc., The.
Suchy, Julianne. Leaf Me Alone. 2009. 36p. pap. 13.95 *(978-1-60693-300-8(0)*, Eloquent Bks.) Strategic Book Publishing & Rights Agency (SBPRA).
Sudo, Kumiko. Coco-Chan's Kimono. Sudo, Kumiko, illus. 2010. (ENG., Illus.). 32p. (J). (gr. k-2). 16.95 *(978-1-933308-26-5(5))* Breckling Pr.
Suma, Nova Ren. Fade Out. 2012. (ENG.). 288p. (YA). (gr. 7). pap. 9.99 *(978-1-4169-7565-6(9)*, Simon Pulse) Simon Pulse.
Summy, Barrie. I So Don't Do Famous. 2012. (ENG.). 304p. (J). (gr. 5). 7.99 *(978-0-385-73791-3(2)*, Yearling) Random Hse. Children's Bks.
—I So Don't Do Makeup. 2011. (ENG.). 288p. (J). (gr. 3-7). 7.99 *(978-0-385-73789-0(0)*, Yearling) Random Hse. Children's Bks.
—I So Don't Do Mysteries. 2009. (ENG.). 288p. (J). (gr. 3-7). 6.99 *(978-0-385-73603-9(7)*, Yearling) Random Hse. Children's Bks.
—I So Don't Do Spooky. 2010. (ENG.). 304p. (J). (gr. 3-7). 7.99 *(978-0-385-73605-3(3)*, Yearling) Random Hse. Children's Bks.
Supplee, Suzanne. Artichoke's Heart. 2009. (ENG.). 288p. (YA). (gr. 7-18). 8.99 *(978-0-14-241427-9(1)*, Speak) Penguin Young Readers Group.
Sutton, Katisha Barner. Caring & Sharing. 2011. 26p. pap. 12.50 *(978-1-60976-177-6(4)*, Strategic Bk. Publishing) Strategic Book Publishing & Rights Agency (SBPRA).
Sweeney, Joyce. Waiting for June, 0 vols. 2006. (ENG.). 158p. (YA). (gr. 10-12). pap. 7.99 *(978-0-7614-5329-1(6)*, 9780761453291, Amazon Children's Publishing) Amazon Publishing.
Sydor, Colleen. My Mother Is a French Fry & Further Proof of My Fuzzed-Up Life. 2008. (ENG.). 256p. (J). (gr. 7-9). pap. 8.95 *(978-1-55453-184-4(5))* Kids Can Pr., Ltd. CAN. Dist: Hachette Bk. Group.
Symons, Brandy. Lemonade Kisses. 2009. 24p. pap. 12.95 *(978-1-4389-7251-0(2))* AuthorHouse.
Tait, Elena. Mommy Why Wasn't I at Your Wedding? 2009. 24p. pap. 11.49 *(978-1-4389-5426-4(3))* AuthorHouse.
Taylor, Kim. Cissy Funk. Date not set. 224p. (YA). (gr. 5-18). mass mkt. 4.99 *(978-0-06-440880-6(9))* HarperCollins Pubs.
Telma, Tante. Telma's Day at Magens Bay. 2012. 16p. pap. 15.99 *(978-1-4772-7776-8(5))* AuthorHouse.
Templeton, Donna L. Mother's Surprise. Berlinger, Nancy A., illus. 2009. (ENG.). 32p. (J). pap. 9.99 *(978-0-9764336-6-8(4))* MJS Publishing Group LLC.
The Calaiacovo Family. The Amazing Adventures of Ruby & Rubette: San Francisco. 2010. 32p. pap. 14.49 *(978-1-4490-6948-3(7))* AuthorHouse.
Thomas, Chericia. Buffy the Football Player. 2010. 20p. 12.49 *(978-1-4490-9708-0(1))* AuthorHouse.
Thomas, Shelley Moore. Secrets of Selkie Bay. 2015. (ENG.). 208p. (J). (gr. 3-7). 15.99 *(978-0-374-36749-7(3)*, 9780374367497, Farrar, Straus & Giroux (BYR)) Farrar, Straus & Giroux.
Tilly, Meg. First Time, 1 vol. 2008. (Orca Soundings Ser.). (ENG.). (YA). (gr. 8-12). 128p. pap. 9.95 *(978-1-55143-944-0(1))*; 112p. 16.95 *(978-1-55143-946-4(8))* Orca Bk. Pubs. USA.
Tinsley, Helen. Me & My Grandma: A Story for Children about AIDS. 2012.Tr. of 32. (Illus.). 34p. (J). pap. 14.95 *(978-1-937622-21-3(5)*, Nefu Bks.) Africana Homestead Legacy Pubs., Inc.
Townley, Roderick. A Bitter Magic. 2015. (ENG.). 304p. (J). (gr. 4-7). 16.99 *(978-0-449-81649-3(4)*, Knopf Bks. for Young Readers) Random Hse. Children's Bks.
Tracey, Rhian. True Colours. 2007. (ENG.). 272p. (J). (gr. 4-7). per. 11.95 *(978-0-7475-8941-9(0))* Bloomsbury Publishing Plc GBR. Dist: Independent Pubs. Group.
Train, Mary. Time for the Fair. Hayes, Karel, illus. 2005. (ENG.). 28p. (J). (gr. k-17). 15.95 *(978-0-89272-694-3(6))* Down East Bks.
Turninelly, Nancy. Horse Shoes. Nobens, C. A., illus. 2006. (Fact & Fiction Ser.). 24p. (J). pap. 48.42 *(978-1-59679-944-8(7))* ABDO Publishing Co.
—Los Zapatos de la Potranca, 1 vol. Nobens, C. A., illus. 2007. (Cuentos de Animales Ser.). (SPA & ENG.). 24p. (J). (gr. k-3). lib. bdg. 24.21 *(978-1-59928-677-8(7)*, SandCastle) ABDO Publishing Co.
Turner, Juliette. That's Not Hay in My Hair, 1 vol. 2016. (ENG.). 240p. (J). pap. 8.99 *(978-0-310-73244-0(1))* Zonderkidz.
Turner, Nicci. Milky's Story, 1 vol. 2010. 18p. pap. 24.95 *(978-1-4489-6808-4(9))* PublishAmerica, Inc.
Unsworth, Tania. Brightwood. 2016. (ENG.). 272p. (J). (gr. 4-7). 16.95 *(978-1-61620-330-6(7))* Algonquin Bks. of Chapel Hill.
Updale, Eleanor. Johnny Swanson. 2012. (ENG.). 384p. (J). (gr. 3-7). 8.99 *(978-0-385-75228-2(8)*, Yearling) Random Hse. Children's Bks.
V., Patti. My Na Na Stories. 2005. 18.00 *(978-0-8059-9806-1(3))* Dorrance Publishing Co., Inc.
Vail, Rachel. Brilliant. 2011. (Avery Sisters Trilogy Ser.: 3). (ENG., Illus.). 256p. (YA). (gr. 8). pap. 8.99 *(978-0-06-089051-3(7))* HarperCollins Pubs.
—Please, Please, Please. 2014. (Friendship Ring Ser.: 2). (ENG.). 176p. (J). (gr. 5). pap. 7.99 *(978-0-14-751119-5(4)*, Puffin Books) Penguin Young Readers Group.
Van Draanen, Wendelin. Sammy Keyes & the Hollywood Mummy. 2008. (Sammy Keyes Ser.: Bk. 6). (J). 64.99 *(978-1-60640-641-0(8))* Findaway World, LLC.
—Sammy Keyes & the Showdown in Sin City. 2013. (Sammy Keyes Ser.: Bk. 16). (ENG.). 304p. (J). (gr. 5). pap. 7.99 *(978-0-307-93061-3(0)*, Yearling) Random Hse. Children's Bks.
van Genechten, Guido. Kangaroo Christine. van Genechten, Guido, illus. 2005. (Illus.). 24p. (J). (gr. 3-7). pap. 6.95 *(978-1-58925-396-4(5))* Tiger Tales.
Van Winkle, Amy. The Flower Fairy, 1 vol. 2010. 13p. pap. 24.95 *(978-1-61582-729-9(3))* PublishAmerica, Inc.
Vande Velde, Vivian & Bash, Barbara. The Book of Mordred. 2007. (ENG.). 352p. (YA). (gr. 7-12). pap. 8.99 *(978-0-618-80916-5(3))* Houghton Mifflin Harcourt Publishing Co.
Vander Zee, Ruth. Always with You. Himler, Ronald, illus. 2008. (ENG.). 32p. (J). (gr. -1-3). 17.00 *(978-0-8028-5295-3(5)*, Eerdmans Bks For Young Readers) Eerdmans, William B. Publishing Co.
Vaughn, Trudy D. Bugs Beware My Mom Doesn't Care! 2012. 24p. pap. 10.95 *(978-1-4497-3635-4(1)*, WestBow Pr.) Author Solutions, Inc.
Velásquez, Gloria. Rudy's Memory Walk. 2009. (Roosevelt High School Ser.). 140p. (YA). (gr. 6-18). pap. 9.95 *(978-1-55885-593-9(9))* Arte Publico Pr.
Verdi, Jessica. The Summer I Wasn't Me. 2014. (ENG.). 352p. (YA). (gr. 7-12). pap. 9.99 *(978-1-4022-7788-7(1)*, 9781402277887) Sourcebooks, Inc.
Vernick, Shirley Reva. The Black Butterfly. 2014. (ENG.). 226p. (J). 19.95 *(978-1-935955-79-5(9))* Cinco Puntos Pr.
Vescovi, Laura A. Good Morning Sleepyhead. 2004. 15.95 *(978-0-9763219-0-3(4))* Vescovi, Laura.
Vita. Head in the Clouds. 2004. (Illus.). 108p. pap. 44.50 *(978-0-9760062-0-6(0))* Magic Woman Pubns.
Wait for Me. 2007. 169p. (gr. 4-7). 18.00 *(978-0-7569-7959-1(5))* Perfection Learning Corp.
Waldman, Debby & Feutl, Rita. Room Enough for Daisy, 1 vol. Revell, Cindy, illus. 2011. (ENG.). 32p. (J). (gr. -1-3). 19.95 *(978-1-55469-255-2(5))* Orca Bk. Pubs. USA.
Walker, D. S. Delightfully Different. 2010. 160p. (gr. -1). 22.95 *(978-1-4502-6051-0(9))*; pap. 12.95 *(978-1-4502-6050-3(0))* iUniverse, Inc.
Wallace, Carey. The Ghost in the Glass House. 2014. (ENG.). 240p. (YA). (gr. 7). pap. 13.99 *(978-0-544-33618-6(6)*, HMH Books For Young Readers) Houghton Mifflin Harcourt Publishing Co.
Wallace, Karen. Mirror, Mirror, 1 vol. Brett, Cathy, illus. 2013. (Start Reading Ser.). (ENG.). 24p. (gr. k-1). pap. 7.95 *(978-1-4765-4117-4(5))* Capstone Press of Coughlan Cos.
Walsh, Ann. Flower Power. 2006. (Orca Currents Ser.). 107p. (gr. 5-9). 19.95 *(978-0-7569-6874-8(7))* Perfection Learning Corp.
Warren, Cathy. Saturday Belongs to Sara. 2013. (ENG., Illus.). 48p. (J). (gr. -1-3). 13.99 *(978-1-4814-2146-1(8)*, Simon & Schuster Bks. For Young Readers) Simon & Schuster Bks. For Young Readers.
Watson, Stephanie Elaine. Elvis & Olive: Super Detectives. 2010. (ENG.). 288p. (J). (gr. 3-7). 15.99 *(978-0-545-15148-1(1)*, Scholastic Pr.) Scholastic, Inc.
Watts, Julia. Revived Spirits. 2011. (ENG.). 170p. (J). (gr. 7). pap. 8.95 *(978-0-9831032-2-6(4)*, BeanPole Bks.) Harren Communications, LLC.
Weber, Lori. Tattoo Heaven, 1 vol. 2005. (Lorimer SideStreets Ser.). (ENG.). 168p. (YA). (gr. 9-12). 16.95 *(978-1-55028-903-9(9)*, 9781550289039); 9.95 *(978-1-55028-902-2(0)*, 9781550289022) Lorimer, James & Co., Ltd., Pubs. CAN. Dist: Casemate Pubs. & Bk. Distributors, LLC.
Weeks, Sarah. Pie. 2013. (ENG.). 192p. (J). (gr. 3-7). pap. 6.99 *(978-0-545-27012-0(X)*, Scholastic Paperbacks) Scholastic, Inc.
—So B. It. 2009. 9.00 *(978-0-7848-3326-1(5)*, Everbind) Marco Bk. Co.
—So B. It. 2005. 17.00 *(978-0-7569-5112-2(7))* Perfection Learning Corp.
—So B. It. 2007. (J). 1.25 *(978-1-4193-7988-8(7))* Recorded Bks., Inc.
Weeks, Sarah & Weeks. So B. It. (ENG.). (J). (gr. 5). 2005. 288p. pap. 7.99 *(978-0-06-441047-2(1))* 2004. 256p. 16.99 *(978-0-06-623622-3(3))* HarperCollins Pubs.
Welch, Jenna Evans. Love & Gelato. (ENG., Illus.). 400p. (YA). (gr. 7). 2017. pap. 10.99 ***(978-1-4814-3255-9(9))*** 2016. 17.99 *(978-1-4814-3254-2(0))* Simon Pulse. (Simon Pulse).
Welsh, Kenneth Wilbur. Magic Chalk. 2011. 16p. pap. 12.00 *(978-1-4520-6078-1(9))* AuthorHouse.
Wessel-Estes, Pam. A Quilt & a Home. 2012. 36p. pap. 14.95 *(978-1-4575-1489-0(3))*; 24.95 *(978-1-4575-1490-6(7))* Dog Ear Publishing, LLC.
West, Kasie. The Distance Between Us. 2013. (ENG.). 320p. (YA). (gr. 8). pap. 9.99 *(978-0-06-223565-7(6)*, HarperTeen) HarperCollins Pubs.
Whincup, Sara. The St John's Cross Spider. Yapsangco, Kenn, illus. 2015. (ENG.). 28p. (J). pap. 28.22 *(978-1-5035-0985-6(0))* Xlibris Corp.
White, Amy Brecount. Forget-Her-Nots. 2010. (ENG.). 384p. (YA). (gr. 8-18). 16.99 *(978-0-06-167298-9(X)*, Greenwillow Bks.) HarperCollins Pubs.
White, Kathryn. Ruby's School Walk. Latimer, Miriam, illus. 2010. (ENG.). 32p. (J). (gr. -1-2). 16.99 *(978-1-84686-275-5(2))* Barefoot Bks., Inc.
Whittemore, Jo. Colonial Madness. 2015. (ENG., Illus.). 240p. (J). (gr. 4-8). 17.99 *(978-1-4814-0508-9(X)*, Aladdin) Simon & Schuster Children's Publishing.
Wiggin, Kate Douglas. Polly Oliver's Problem. 2007. 108p. per. 9.95 *(978-1-60312-369-3(5))*; 22.95 *(978-1-60312-707-3(0))* Aegypan.
Williams, Carol Lynch. Glimpse. 2010. (ENG.). 496p. (YA). (gr. 9-18). 16.99 *(978-1-4169-9730-6(X)*, Simon & Schuster/Paula Wiseman Bks.) Simon & Schuster/Paula Wiseman Bks.
—Signed, Skye Harper. 2014. (ENG., Illus.). 304p. (YA). (gr. 7). 17.99 *(978-1-4814-0032-9(0)*, Simon & Schuster/Paula Wiseman Bks.) Simon & Schuster/Paula Wiseman Bks.
Williams, Carol Lynch & Gregg, L. B. Glimpse. Gregg, Anna, photos by. 2012. (ENG., Illus.). 512p. (YA). (gr. 9). pap. 12.99 *(978-1-4169-9731-3(8)*, Simon & Schuster/Paula Wiseman Bks.) Simon & Schuster/Paula Wiseman Bks.
Williams-Garcia, Rita. Catching the Wild Waiyuuzee. Reed, Mike, illus. 2007. (ENG.). 32p. (J). (gr. -1-1). 12.99 *(978-1-4169-6141-3(0)*, Simon & Schuster/Paula Wiseman Bks.) Simon & Schuster/Paula Wiseman Bks.
Williams, Jamie L. Mommy's Little Helper, 1 vol. 2010. 26p. 24.95 *(978-1-4512-9232-9(5))* PublishAmerica, Inc.
Williams, Lori Aurelia. Broken China. 2006. (ENG., Illus.). 272p. (YA). (gr. 7-12). reprint ed. mass mkt. 7.99 *(978-1-4169-1618-5(0)*, Simon Pulse) Simon Pulse.
Williams, Marilyn & Caspersen, Barbara. Peggy & Barbie on the Farm. 2013. 24p. pap. 24.95 *(978-1-63004-043-7(6))* America Star Bks.
Williams, Rozanne Lanczak. How Can I Get a Pet? Reid, Mick, illus. 2006. (Learn to Write Ser.). 8p. (J). (gr. k-2). pap. *(978-1-59198-290-6(1)*, 6184) Creative Teaching Pr., Inc.
—How Can I Get a Pet? Maio, Barbara & Faulkner, Stacey, eds. Reid, Mick, illus. 2006. (J). per. 6.99 *(978-1-59198-363-7(0))* Creative Teaching Pr., Inc.
Williams, Shanica. Amy Goes Shopping for School. 2012. 16p. pap. 15.99 *(978-1-4772-1360-5(0))* AuthorHouse.
Willis, Meredith Sue. Meli's Way. 2015. 178p. (YA). *(978-1-932727-15-9(9))* Montemayor Pr.
Wilson, Annette. K'Nyah's Big Celebration. 2012. 28p. pap. 24.95 *(978-1-4626-9925-4(1))* America Star Bks.
Wilson, Jacqueline. The Story of Tracy Beaker. Sharratt, Nick, illus. 2004. (ENG.). 133p. 16.00 *(978-0-7569-3205-3(X))* Perfection Learning Corp.
Winston, Sherri. The Sweetest Sound. 2017. (ENG.). 272p. (J). (gr. 3-7). 17.99 *(978-0-316-30295-1(3))* Little Brown & Co.
Wittlinger, Ellen. Blind Faith. 2007. (ENG.). 304p. (YA). (gr. 7-12). pap. 9.99 *(978-1-4169-4906-0(2)*, Simon & Schuster Bks. For Young Readers) Simon & Schuster Bks. For Young Readers.
Wolf, Elaine. Camp. 2012. (ENG.). 256p. (YA). (gr. 6-17). 16.95 *(978-1-61608-657-2(2)*, 608657, Sky Pony Pr.) Skyhorse Publishing Co., Inc.
Wood, Gail. Lizzie & the Big Lake Mystery. 2015. (Illus.). ix, 93p. (J). pap. *(978-1-57249-416-9(6)*, White Mane Kids) White Mane Publishing Co., Inc.
Woodson, Jacqueline. Show Way. Talbott, Hudson, illus. 2005. (ENG.). 48p. (J). (gr. -1-3). 17.99 *(978-0-399-23749-2(6)*, G.P. Putnam's Sons Books for Young Readers) Penguin Young Readers Group.
Wormell, Chris. Molly & the Night Monster. Wormell, Chris, illus. 2011. (ENG., Illus.). 32p. (J). (gr. -1-k). pap. 9.99 *(978-1-86230-185-6(9)*, Red Fox) Random House Children's Books GBR. Dist: Independent Pubs. Group.
Wrede, Patricia C. Snow White & Rose Red. 2009. (ENG.). 288p. (YA). (gr. 7-18). 8.99 *(978-0-14-241121-6(3)*, Firebird) Penguin Young Readers Group.
Wunder, Wendy. The Probability of Miracles. 2012. (ENG., Illus.). 336p. (YA). (gr. 9). pap. 9.99 *(978-1-59514-480-5(3)*, Razorbill) Penguin Young Readers Group.
Wyeth, Sharon Dennis. The Granddaughter Necklace. Ibatoulline, Bagram, illus. (J). 2013. (ENG.). 32p. (gr. -1-3). 18.99 *(978-0-545-08125-2(4))* 2012. pap. *(978-0-545-23983-7(4))* Scholastic, Inc. (Levine, Arthur A. Bks.).
Ye, Ting-Xing. Throwaway Daughter. 2004. (ENG.). 320p. (J). (gr. 7). mass mkt. 9.99 *(978-0-7704-2921-8(1)*, Seal Bks.) Penguin Random House Canada Young Readers CAN. Dist: Penguin Random Hse. LLC.
Yee, Lisa. Absolutely Maybe. 2009. (ENG.). 288p. (J). (gr. 7-18). 16.99 *(978-0-439-83844-3(4)*, Levine, Arthur A. Bks.) Scholastic, Inc.
Yohalem, Eve. Escape under the Forever Sky. (ENG.). 2011. 219p. (YA). (gr. 4-7). pap. 7.99 *(978-0-8118-7874-6(0))* 2009. 224p. (J). (gr. 5-17). 16.99 *(978-0-8118-6653-8(X))* Chronicle Bks. LLC.
Young, Ruth. Aunty Marmalade. 2009. 218p. pap. 13.78 *(978-1-60693-893-5(2)*, Eloquent Bks.) Strategic Book Publishing & Rights Agency (SBPRA).
Younge-Ullman, Danielle. Everything Beautiful Is Not Ruined. 2017. (ENG.). 368p. (YA). (gr. 9). 17.99 *(978-0-425-28759-0(9)*, Viking Books for Young Readers) Penguin Young Readers Group.
Zabel, Vivian. I Like Pink. Nielson, Ginger, illus. 2013. 28p. pap. 12.99 *(978-0-9889617-1-5(7))* 4RV Publishing, LLC.
Zarr, Sara. How to Save a Life. 2012. (ENG.). 368p. (YA). (gr. 7-17). pap. 10.99 *(978-0-316-03605-4(6))* Little, Brown Bks. for Young Readers.
Zerza, Safoora Z. Sophia V. Is Flower Girl. 2012. 24p. pap. 17.99 *(978-1-4685-5136-5(1))* AuthorHouse.
Zimmerman, Diana S. Kandide & the Secret of the Mists. Gadd, Maxine, illus. 2008. (Calabiyau Chronicles Ser.: Bk. 1). 296p. (YA). (gr. 5-18). 17.99 *(978-0-9794328-3-5(9))*;Bk. 1. 289p. (J). (gr. 4-7). pap. 9.99 *(978-0-9794328-2-8(0))* Noesis Publishing.
Zimmerman, Mary Joyce. Just Four. 2005. (Illus.). 32p. (gr. -1-5). 2.70 *(978-0-7399-2340-5(4)*, 2779) Rod & Staff Pubs., Inc.
Zirin, David. My Name Is Erica Montoya de la Cruz. White, DeBorah, illus. 2005. (ENG.). 16p. (J). 5.75 *(978-1-57274-732-6(3)*, 2779, Bks. for Young Learners) Owen, Richard C. Pubs., Inc.
Zolotow, Charlotte. Say It! Voake, Charlotte, illus. 2015. (ENG.). 32p. (J). (-k). 15.99 *(978-0-7636-8115-9(6))* Candlewick Pr.
1, 2, 3 Happy Family. 2005. (J). bds. *(978-0-9769910-2-1(0))* Terrific Twins LLC.

MOTHERS AND SONS

Anderson, Nancy. My Mother Helps Me with Homework. 2016. (Rosen REAL Readers: Social Studies Nonfiction / Fiction: Family, Community, & the World Ser.). 8p. (gr. 1-k). pap. 5.46 *(978-1-5081-2284-5(9)*, Rosen Classroom) Rosen Publishing Group, Inc., The.
Cargile, Phillip & Miss Cheryl. The Wagon Man: The Untold Story of the Go-Burn Kids. 2009. 54p. pap. 16.95 *(978-1-60703-939-6(7))* America Star Bks.
Hoge, Robert. Ugly. Robinson, Keith, illus. 2016. (ENG.). 208p. (J). (gr. 3-7). 16.99 *(978-0-425-28775-0(0)*, Viking Books for Young Readers) Penguin Young Readers Group.
Lynch, Chris. Angry Young Man. 2012. (ENG.). 192p. (YA). (gr. 7). pap. 10.99 *(978-1-4424-5419-4(9)*, Simon & Schuster Bks. For Young Readers) Simon & Schuster Bks. For Young Readers.
My Mom Is Great. 2008. (My Great Relatives... Ser.). 32p. *(978-1-4075-0860-3(1))* Parragon, Inc.

MOTHERS AND SONS—FICTION

Acampora, Paul. How to Avoid Extinction. 2016. (ENG.). 208p. (J). (gr. 3-7). 16.99 *(978-0-545-89906-2(0)*, Scholastic Pr.) Scholastic, Inc.
Acevedo, Ari. Juan Bobo Sends the Pig to Mass. Wrenn, Tom, illus. 2008. (Story Cove Ser.). (SPA & ENG.). 24p. (J). (gr. -1-3). pap. 4.95 *(978-0-87483-883-1(5))* August Hse. Pubs., Inc.
Addison, George R. Iii. When Mom Came Home. 2012. 32p. pap. 21.99 *(978-1-4691-6406-9(X))* Xlibris Corp.
Akiona, Micalynn. My Mom Can Do Anything. 2011. 28p. pap. 15.99 *(978-1-4568-2006-0(0))* Xlibris Corp.
Alan E. And Lisa J. Laird. Cows Can Be Scary. 2009. 40p. pap. 18.49 *(978-1-4389-8150-5(3))* AuthorHouse.
Alger, Horatio. Herbert Carter's Legacy. 2006. pap. *(978-1-4065-0710-2(5))* Dodo Pr.
—Herbert Carter's Legacy: Or, the Inventor's Son. I.t. ed. 2007. (ENG.). 188p. pap. 21.99 *(978-1-4346-5068-9(5))* Creative Media Partners, LLC.

MNO

Alger Jr. Horatio Staff. Andy Grants Pluck. rev. ed. 2006. 312p. 29.95 *(978-1-4218-1762-0(4))*; pap. 14.95 *(978-1-4218-1862-7(0))* 1st World Publishing, Inc. (1st World Library - Literary Society).

—Do & Dare. rev. ed. 2006. 272p. 28.95 *(978-1-4218-1757-6(8))*; pap. 13.95 *(978-1-4218-1857-3(4))* 1st World Publishing, Inc. (1st World Library - Literary Society).

—Herbert Carter's Legacy. rev. ed. 2006. 264p. 28.95 *(978-1-4218-1756-9(X))*; pap. 13.95 *(978-1-4218-1856-6(6))* 1st World Publishing, Inc. (1st World Library - Literary Society).

Anderson, Alice. Danny Be Good! 2012. 24p. pap. 17.99 *(978-1-4685-6433-4(1))* AuthorHouse.

Anderson, Jane. Inspector Insector. 2005. (J). pap. *(978-1-4108-4196-4(0))* Benchmark Education Co.

Ankhnu Feaster, Teraab & Campbell, Rochelle. The Magic Seeds. 2009. 42p. pap. 19.25 *(978-1-4490-0784-3(8))* AuthorHouse.

Appelt, Kathi. When Otis Courted Mama. Szekeres, Cyndy & McElmurry, Jill, illus. 2015. (ENG.). 40p. (J). (gr. -1-3). 16.99 *(978-0-15-216688-5(2))*, HMH Books For Young Readers) Houghton Mifflin Harcourt Publishing Co.

Armand, Glenda. Love Twelve Miles Long. Bootman, Colin, illus. (ENG.). 32p. (J). 2015. pap. 9.95 *(978-1-62014-254-7(6))* 2013. 17.95 *(978-1-60060-245-0(2))* Lee & Low Bks., Inc.

Arrington, R. Region. Billy Buckins & the Pirates Map, 1 vol. 2010. 64p. pap. 19.95 *(978-1-4512-2087-2(1))* America Star Bks.

Ashley, Bernard. Aftershock. 2011. (ENG.). 144p. (J). (gr. 4-7). pap. 8.95 *(978-1-84780-055-8(6))*, Frances Lincoln Children's Bks.) Quarto Publishing Group UK GBR. Dist: Hachette Bk. Group.

Ashley, Sharon. I Wish I Could See. 2013. 24p. pap. 24.95 *(978-1-4626-9700-7(3))* America Star Bks.

Asim, Jabari. Boy of Mine. Pham, LeUyen, illus. 2010. (ENG.). 20p. (J). (gr. -1 — 1). bds. 6.99 *(978-0-316-73577-3(9))* Little, Brown Bks. for Young Readers.

Auch, M. J. Wing Nut. 2008. (ENG.). 256p. (J). (gr. 5-9). pap. 14.99 *(978-0-312-38420-3(3))*, 9780312384203) Square Fish.

Baggett, Shirley Reed. Adventures of Bandit: A Little Racoon Goes into the Forbidden Forest. 2011. 16p. (gr. 1-2). pap. 9.99 *(978-1-4567-6575-0(2))* AuthorHouse.

Baker, Liza. I Love You Because You're You (a StoryPlay Book) McPhail, David, illus. 2016. (ENG.). 32p. (J). (gr. -1-k). 5.99 *(978-0-545-94527-1(5))*, Cartwheel Bks.) Scholastic, Inc.

Ball, Jacqueline A. Timmy's My Hero, Who's Yours? 2007. 36p. per. 24.95 *(978-1-4137-0063-3(2))* America Star Bks.

Banerjee, Anjali. The Silver Spell. Fiegenshuh, Emily, illus. 2005. (Knights of the Silver Dragon Ser.: Bk. 8). 174p. (J). *(978-1-4156-1645-1(0))*, Mirrorstone) Wizards of the Coast.

Banks, Lynne Reid. The Indian in the Cupboard. 2010. (Indian in the Cupboard Ser.). (ENG.). 240p. (J). (gr. 3-7). 6.99 *(978-0-375-84753-0(7))*, Yearling) Random Hse. Children's Bks.

Banting, Celia. I Only Said I Had No Choice. 2006. (I Only Said Ser.). (Illus.). 202p. (YA). pap. 14.99 *(978-0-9766648-0-0(9))* Wighita Pr.

Barchers, Suzanne I. Read with Gus, 1 vol. 2011. (Targeted Phonics Ser.). (ENG.). 16p. (J). (gr. k-2). pap. 5.99 *(978-1-4333-2420-8(2))* Teacher Created Materials, Inc.

Barnes, John. Tales of the Madman Underground. 2011. (ENG.). 544p. (YA). (gr. 9-18). 9.99 *(978-0-14-241702-7(5))*, Speak) Penguin Young Readers Group.

Barry, Debra R. Brady Pickles. 2011. 32p. pap. 24.95 *(978-1-4626-3716-4(7))* America Star Bks.

—Let's Go to the Market. 2012. 28p. pap. 24.95 *(978-1-4626-8533-2(1))* America Star Bks.

Bates, Melinda. Nick Pricer: An American Heir. 2012. 88p. 19.95 *(978-1-4697-8478-6(5))*; pap. 9.95 *(978-1-4697-8476-2(9))* iUniverse, Inc.

Bean, Jonathan. Big Snow. Bean, Jonathan, illus. 2013. (ENG., Illus.). 32p. (J). (gr. -1-1). 16.99 *(978-0-374-30696-0(6))*, 9780374306960, Farrar, Straus & Giroux (BYR)) Farrar, Straus & Giroux.

Bell, Liz. Mohawk, Fro or Crew, It Is up to You. 2011. 24p. pap. 24.95 *(978-1-4626-3196-4(7))* America Star Bks.

Benavides, Desiree. Little Henry's Adventures: Henry's Trip to the Supermarket. 2008. 24p. pap. 24.95 *(978-1-60563-011-3(X))* America Star Bks.

Benjamin, Rick A. The Hunt for Lost Treasure, 1 vol. 2010. 56p. pap. 16.95 *(978-1-4489-6417-8(2))* America Star Bks.

Benwell, Sarah. The Last Leaves Falling. 2015. (ENG., Illus.). 368p. (YA). (gr. 9). 17.99 *(978-1-4814-3065-4(3))* Simon & Schuster Children's Publishing.

Bernstein, David D. The Enchanted Rope. 2010. 25p. (J). pap. 13.95 *(978-1-4327-5175-3(1))* Outskirts Pr., Inc.

Bevan, Lizzie. Never Far When in My Heart. 2013. (ENG., Illus.). 31p. (J). pap. 15.95 *(978-1-4787-1027-1(6))* Outskirts Pr., Inc.

Bilan Hochenberg, Nerissa. Mommy Works. Bilan, Edgar, illus. 2013. 24p. pap. *(978-1-4602-2602-5(X))* FriesenPress.

Bird, Jodi Stirz. Going on a Tree Hunt: A Tree Identification Book for Young Children. 2011. 28p. (gr. 1-2). pap. 14.99 *(978-1-4490-8308-3(0))* AuthorHouse.

Bishop, Brandy. The Christmas Mice, 1 vol. 2010. 30p. 24.95 *(978-1-4489-4438-5(4))* PublishAmerica, Inc.

Blackall, Sophie. Are You Awake? Blackall, Sophie, illus. 2011. (ENG., Illus.). 40p. (J). (gr. -1-k). 12.99 *(978-0-8050-7858-9(4))*, 9780805078589, Holt, Henry & Co. Bks. For Young Readers) Holt, Henry & Co.

Blackmon, Rodney Allan. A Kitten Named Buddy: Buddy Goes Outside. 2013. 20p. pap. 24.95 *(978-1-62709-677-5(9))* America Star Bks.

Blake, Colleen H. Robley. Don't You Wish Your Momma Could Cook Like Mine? Jennings, Randy, illus. 2012. 40p. pap. 16.97 *(978-1-61204-876-5(5))*, Strategic Bk. Publishing) Strategic Book Publishing & Rights Agency (SBPRA).

Blake, Jocelyn. Mama Is on an Airplane. Blake, Jocelyn, illus. 2006. (Illus.). (J). per. 9.99 *(978-0-9790572-0-5(5))* Kreativ Kaos.

Blevins, Wiley. Jack & the Bloody Beanstalk. Cox, Steve, illus. 2016. (Scary Tales Retold Ser.). (ENG.). 24p. (gr. k-3). lib. bdg. 23.99 *(978-1-63440-099-2(2))* Red Chair Pr.

Boles, Rhonda G. Why Does the Sun Set, Mommy? 2009. 24p. pap. 10.99 *(978-1-4389-8112-3(0))* AuthorHouse.

Bombaci, James J. The Million Dollar Dog. 2010. 32p. pap. 14.99 *(978-1-4490-4936-2(2))* AuthorHouse.

Bradford, Wade. Why Do I Have to Make My Bed? van der Sterre, Johanna, illus. 2011. (ENG.). 32p. (J). (gr. -1-2). 16.99 *(978-1-58246-327-8(1))*, Tricycle Pr.) Random Hse. Children's Bks.

Bradley, A. M. Finnegan's Magic Sunglasses. 2013. 24p. pap. 24.95 *(978-1-62709-814-4(3))* America Star Bks.

Bratcher, Shirley Kay. Tudy Goes to the Zoo. 2013. 24p. pap. 24.95 *(978-1-4626-9560-7(4))* America Star Bks.

—Tudy Won't Count - Three. 2012. 16p. pap. 24.95 *(978-1-4626-8886-9(1))* America Star Bks.

Broach, Elise. When Dinosaurs Came with Everything. Small, David, illus. 2007. (ENG.). 40p. (J). (gr. -1-3). 17.99 *(978-0-689-86922-8(3))*, Atheneum Bks. for Young Readers) Simon & Schuster Children's Publishing.

Buckle, J. A. Half My Facebook Friends Are Ferrets, 1 vol. 2014. (ENG.). 224p. (gr. 9-12). 16.95 *(978-1-63079-000-4(1))* Switch Pr.

Cakal, Kimberly. Today I Hugged a Porcupine. 2007. 20p. per. 24.95 *(978-1-4241-8561-0(0))* America Star Bks.

Cali, Davide. Piano, Piano. Rivers, Randi, tr. from FRE. Heliot, Eric, illus. 2007. 28p. (J). (gr. 4-7). 15.95 *(978-1-58089-191-2(8))* Charlesbridge Publishing, Inc.

Campbell, Suzy. Pennies for Christmas, 1 vol. 2010. 24p. 24.95 *(978-1-4512-0553-4(8))* PublishAmerica, Inc.

Carr, Kathy. Granny, Where Did My Mommy Go? 2008. 24p. pap. 24.95 *(978-1-60610-324-1(5))* America Star Bks.

Castillo, Elizabeth. Jaden Christian. 2012. 24p. pap. 24.95 *(978-1-4626-7624-8(3))* America Star Bks.

Childers, Amy. You're My Boy! 2011. 36p. (gr. -1). pap. 17.95 *(978-1-4567-5514-0(5))* AuthorHouse.

Christie, Douglas, Jr. Dougie Goes to School. 2009. 32p. (J). pap. 16.50 *(978-0-9794827-7-9(1))* Infinite Love Publishing.

Ciccone, Tiziana & Linardi, Franca. No More Peanut Butter, Daniel! Bucci, Gino, illus. 2012. 36p. pap. 13.95 *(978-1-61897-718-2(0))*, Strategic Bk. Publishing) Strategic Book Publishing & Rights Agency (SBPRA).

Clements, Andrew. Because Your Mommy Loves You. Alley, R. W., illus. 2012. (ENG.). 32p. (J). (gr. -1-3). 16.99 *(978-0-547-25522-4(5))* Houghton Mifflin Harcourt Publishing Co.

Clifton, Lutricia. Freaky Fast Frankie Joe. (ENG.). 272p. (J). 2013. pap. 7.99 *(978-0-8234-2867-0(2))* 2012. 16.95 *(978-0-8234-2367-5(0))* Holiday Hse., Inc.

Coleman, Candace. Zubie the Lightning Bug - I Want to Remember Your Thoughts. 2006. (J). 15.99 *(978-0-9774998-0-9(4))* Parent Brigade Company, The.

Colfer, Eoin. Artemis Fowl, 3 vols., Set. 2010. (Artemis Fowl Ser.). (ENG.). 944p. (J). (gr. 5-17). 19.99 *(978-1-4231-3681-1(0))* Disney Pr.

—Artemis Fowl. (Artemis Fowl Ser.: Bk. 1). (FRE.). pap. 34.95 *(978-2-07-054681-7(0))* Gallimard, Editions FRA. Dist: Distribooks, Inc.

—Artemis Fowl. rev. ed. 2009. (Artemis Fowl Ser.). (ENG.). 304p. (J). (gr. 5-9). pap. 8.99 *(978-1-4231-2452-8(9))* Hyperion Pr.

—Artemis Fowl. (Artemis Fowl Ser.: Bk. 1). pap. 34.95 *(978-88-04-49788-2(2))* Mondadori ITA. Dist: Distribooks, Inc.

—Artemis Fowl. (Artemis Fowl Ser.: 1). (YA). 2007. 1.25 *(978-1-4193-6020-6(5))* 2006. 52.75 *(978-1-4193-6023-7(X))* 2006. 54.75 *(978-1-4193-6021-3(3))* 2006. 54.75 *(978-1-4193-6026-8(4))* 2006. 132.75 *(978-1-4193-6022-0(1))* 2005. 56.75 *(978-1-4193-6024-4(8))* Recorded Bks., Inc.

—Artemis Fowl. 2009. (Artemis Fowl Ser.: 1). (J). (gr. 5-8). lib. bdg. 19.65 *(978-0-613-60637-0(X))*, Turtleback) Turtleback Bks.

—Artemis Fowl. Feldmann, Claudia, tr. (Artemis Fowl Ser.: Bk. 1). (GER.). pap. 24.95 *(978-3-548-60320-9(3))* Ullstein-Taschenbuch-Verlag DEU. Dist: Distribooks, Inc.

—Artemis Fowl: El Mundo Subterráneo. 2013. (Vintage Espanol Ser.: Bk. 1). (SPA.). 288p. (YA). (gr. 5). pap. 9.95 *(978-0-345-80418-1(X))*, Vintage Espanol) Knopf Doubleday Publishing Group.

—EL MUNDO SUBTERRÁNEO (ARTEMIS FOWL 1) (Artemis Fowl Ser.: Bk. 1). (SPA.). 288p. pap. *(978-84-8441-115-4(X))*, MO31567) Grijalbo Mondadori, S.A.-Montena.

Colfer, Eoin & Donkin, Andrew. Artemis Fowl. Rigano, Giovanni & Lamanna, Paolo, illus. 2007. (Artemis Fowl Ser.). (ENG.). 112p. (J). (gr. 5-9). 18.99 *(978-0-7868-4881-2(2))*; pap. 12.99 *(978-0-7868-4882-9(0))* Hyperion Pr.

—The Eternity Code. Rigano, Giovanni & Lamanna, Paolo, illus. 2013. (Artemis Fowl Ser.: 3). (ENG.). 112p. (J). (gr. 5-9). 19.99 *(978-1-4231-4527-1(5))* Hyperion Pr.

Connell, Julie. The Adventures of Cutie Pie & Mr. Squishy. 2008. 12p. pap. 24.95 *(978-1-60703-826-9(9))* America Star Bks.

Cooley, Judy. Mom Says I Can. 2008. (Illus.). 32p. (J). (gr. -1-3). lib. bdg. 17.95 *(978-1-59038-872-3(0))*, Shadow Mountain) Shadow Mountain Publishing.

Cooper & the Enchanted Metal Detector. 2013. (ENG.). 250p. (J). pap. 9.95 *(978-1-60898-150-2(9))* namelos llc.

Corbett, Sue. Free Baseball. 2008. (ENG.). 160p. (J). (gr. 3-7). 6.99 *(978-0-14-241080-6(2))*, Puffin Books) Penguin Young Readers Group.

Cornish, Linda Sowa Young. Pong's Birthday Journey. 2006. (J). pap. 15.00 *(978-0-8059-6993-1(4))* Dorrance Publishing Co., Inc.

Craig, Joni. A Shoulder for Oscar. Haddad-Hamwi, Louise, illus. 2013. 40p. pap. 11.95 *(978-0-9887836-6-9(5))* Taylor and Seale Publishing, LLC.

D'Agata, Tabatha Jean. Storm Tunes: Yes, I Can Read! Nature Series, Book 2. Lineberger, Judy, illus. 2006. (Yes, I Can Read! Ser.: Bk. 2). 30p. (J). pap. 6.95 *(978-1-934138-02-1(9))* Bouncing Ball Bks., Inc.

Davis, Ashley. The Big Storm. 2006. (Neighborhood Readers Ser.). (ENG.). 16p. (gr. 1-3). pap. 6.50 *(978-1-4042-7192-0(9))*, Rosen Classroom) Rosen Publishing Group, Inc., The.

deGroat, Diane. Happy Birthday to You, You Belong in a Zoo. deGroat, Diane, illus. 2007. (Gilbert & Friends Ser.). (Illus.). (gr. -1-3). 17.00 *(978-0-7569-8108-2(5))* Perfection Learning Corp.

Denman, K. L. La Cache: (Stuff We All Get), 1 vol. 2012. (FRE.). 128p. (J). (gr. 5-9). pap. 9.95 *(978-1-4598-0314-5(0))* Orca Bk. Pubs. USA.

Dieterle, Amber. Will You Miss Me? 2008. 14p. pap. 24.95 *(978-1-60672-485-9(1))* PublishAmerica, Inc.

d'Lacey, Chris. A Crown of Dragons. 2016. (UFiles Ser.: 3). (ENG.). 320p. (J). (gr. 3-7). 16.99 *(978-0-545-60883-1(X))*, Scholastic Pr.) Scholastic, Inc.

—A Dark Inheritance. 2014. (UFiles Ser.). (ENG.). 304p. (J). (gr. 3-7). 16.99 *(978-0-545-60876-3(7))*, Scholastic Pr.) Scholastic, Inc.

—UFiles #1: a Dark Inheritance. 2014. (UFiles Ser.: 1). (ENG.). 304p. (J). (gr. 3-7). pap. 7.99 *(978-0-545-60878-7(3))*, Scholastic Paperbacks) Scholastic, Inc.

Dodd, Emma. Together. Dodd, Emma, illus. 2016. (Emma Dodd's Love You Bks.). (ENG., Illus.). 24p. (J). (-k). 12.99 *(978-0-7636-8940-7(8))*, Nosy Crow) Candlewick Pr.

Downes, Patrick. Come Home, Angus. Kulikov, Boris, illus. 2016. (ENG.). 32p. (J). (gr. -1-k). 17.99 *(978-0-545-59768-5(4))* Scholastic, Inc.

Duff, Justin. Alex Goes Apple Picking. 2012. 32p. pap. 21.99 *(978-1-4771-2845-9(X))* Xlibris Corp.

Duksta, Laura. I Love You More. Keesler, Karen, illus. (ENG.). (J). 2009. 24p. bds. 6.99 *(978-1-4022-2460-7(5))* 2007. 34p. 16.99 *(978-1-4022-1126-3(0))* Sourcebooks, Inc. (Sourcebooks Jabberwocky).

—Te Quiero Más. Keesler, Karen, illus. 2013. (ENG & SPA.). 24p. (J). bds. 6.99 *(978-1-4022-8177-8(3))*, Sourcebooks Jabberwocky) Sourcebooks, Inc.

Duley, Wayla C. Strawberry Soup & Other Crazy Things. 2013. 28p. pap. 24.95 *(978-1-63000-952-6(0))* America Star Bks.

Edwards, Carol. Jacy Meets Betsy: Jacy's Search for Jesus Book 2. Frey, Daniel, illus. 2006. 32p. (J). 15.95 *(978-0-9755314-1-9(7))* Majestic Publishing, LLC.

Elizabeth Arkward Newton. The Little Boy Who Wished God Had Not Given Him a Brain: Big Momma Books. 2009. 36p. pap. 18.99 *(978-1-4389-0133-6(X))* AuthorHouse.

Espinoza, Olivia G. Jay-Dylan's Cat & Fish. 2011. 24p. (gr. -1). pap. 14.39 *(978-1-4567-5119-7(0))* AuthorHouse.

Eugster, Rachel. The Pocket Mommy. Goldsmith, Tom, illus. 2013. (ENG.). 32p. (J). (gr. -1-1). 16.95 *(978-1-77049-300-1(X))*, Tundra Bks.) Tundra Bks. CAN. Dist: Penguin Random Hse. LLC.

Feeney, Tatyana. Little Owl's Orange Scarf. (ENG.). (J). (— 1). 2015. 28p. bds. 6.99 *(978-0-553-49673-4(5))* 2013. 32p. 16.99 *(978-0-449-81411-6(4))* Random Hse. Children's Bks. (Knopf Bks. for Young Readers).

Feiffer, Jules. I'm Not Bobby! Feiffer, Jules, illus. 2006. (Illus.). 28p. (J). (gr. k-4). reprint ed. 16.00 *(978-0-7567-9853-6(1))* DIANE Publishing Co.

Fitch, Sheree. One More Step, 1 vol. 2006. (Orca Soundings Ser.). (ENG.). 112p. (YA). (gr. 8-12). 14.95 *(978-1-55143-554-1(3))* Orca Bk. Pubs. USA.

Fleming, Chula. Spooky Old Tree, 1 vol. 2010. 26p. pap. 24.95 *(978-1-4489-9166-2(8))* PublishAmerica, Inc.

Fogg, K. L. Serpent Tide. 2006. 16.95 *(978-1-59156-861-2(7))* Covenant Communications, Inc.

Ford, J. One in Four. 2007. pap. *(978-1-84747-173-4(0))* Chipmunkapublishing.

French, Simon. Where in the World, 1 vol. 2008. (ENG.). 208p. (J). (gr. 3-7). pap. 7.95 *(978-1-56145-443-3(5))* Peachtree Pubs.

Friend, Gaythel Boggs & Miller, Dalton. Foundation of a Clown, 1 vol. 2010. 58p. pap. 19.95 *(978-1-4489-8253-0(7))* America Star Bks.

Furniss, Alice. The Happiest Mommy Ever. 2009. (Illus.). 32p. (J). 17.95 *(978-1-60641-056-1(3))* Deseret Bk. Co.

Garcia, Cindy Booth. Rat-a-Tat-Tat Not That!, 1 vol. 2010. 22p. 24.95 *(978-1-4489-7425-2(9))* PublishAmerica, Inc.

González, Rigoberto. Antonio's Card: La Tarjeta de Antonio. Álvarez, Cecilia, illus. 2016. (ENG & SPA.). (J). pap. 9.95 *(978-0-89239-387-9(4))*, Children's Book Press) Lee & Low Bks., Inc.

Goode, Diane. The Most Perfect Spot. Goode, Diane, illus. 2006. (ENG., Illus.). 32p. (J). (gr. -1-3). 16.99 *(978-0-06-072697-3(0))* HarperCollins Pubs.

Gooding-Alber, Karry. Red Shoelace, 1 vol. 2010. 16p. pap. 24.95 *(978-1-4489-6255-6(2))* America Star Bks.

Gorbachev, Valeri. Pizza-Pie Snowman. 2016. (ENG., Illus.). 32p. (J). 16.95 *(978-0-8234-3654-5(3))* Holiday Hse., Inc.

Graham, Frederick. Why Me? 2008. 98p. pap. 13.95 *(978-1-4303-1628-2(4))* Lulu Pr., Inc.

Grant, Vicki. Res Judicata, 1 vol. 2008. (ENG.). 184p. (YA). (gr. 7-12). pap. 9.95 *(978-1-55143-940-2(9))* Orca Bk. Pubs. USA.

Green, D. L. Zeke Meeks vs the Mother's Day Meltdown. Alves, Josh, illus. 2015. (Zeke Meeks Ser.). (ENG.). 128p. (gr. 2-2). 22.65 *(978-1-4795-2168-5(X))*, Zeke Meeks) Picture Window Bks.

Green, Tim. Lost Boy. (J). (gr. 3-7). 2016. 320p. pap. 6.99 *(978-0-06-231709-4(1))* 2015. (ENG.). 304p. 16.99 *(978-0-06-231708-7(3))* HarperCollins Pubs.

Grimshaw, Luke. Sniffle, Sneeze, Cough... Back Off!, 1 vol. Brzozowski, Christina, illus. 2010. 22p. 24.95 *(978-1-4512-1034-7(5))* America Star Bks.

Grossman, David. The Hug. Schoffman, Stuart, tr. Rovner, Michal, illus. 2013. (ENG.). 32p. (gr. 4-13). 19.95 *(978-1-4683-0273-8(6))*, 460273) Overlook Pr., The.

Gutman, Dan. Abner & Me. 2007. (Baseball Card Adventures Ser.). (ENG., Illus.). 176p. (J). (gr. 5-9). pap. 5.99 *(978-0-06-053445-5(1))* HarperCollins Pubs.

—Abner & Me. 2007. (Baseball Card Adventures Ser.). (Illus.). 166p. (gr. 5-9). 16.00 *(978-0-7569-7920-1(X))* Perfection Learning Corp.

Hall, Christina. Can Checkers Come Too? Hall, Lowell, illus. 2011. 36p. pap. 24.95 *(978-1-4560-7753-2(8))* America Star Bks.

Hamilton, S. J. The Cat's Eye View. 2012. 186p. pap. 24.95 *(978-1-4626-6056-8(8))* America Star Bks.

Hanington, John G. The Adventures of Quick Fox. 2006. (ENG.). 92p. per. 9.95 *(978-0-7414-3223-0(4))* Infinity Publishing.

Hanning, Jacob. Mommy's Little Helper: That's Me. 2012. 28p. pap. 24.95 *(978-1-4626-5649-3(8))* America Star Bks.

Hansen, MaryAnn Shelley. Sam the Second. 2010. 32p. 14.49 *(978-1-4520-2408-0(1))* AuthorHouse.

Harel, Moshe. Elf Prince. 2012. (ENG.). 258p. pap. *(978-965-550-089-9(6))* Contento De Semrik.

Harris, Angela L. Mommy What Is a Ceo? Chapman, Debbie, illus. 2013. 32p. pap. 10.00 *(978-0-615-62527-0(4))* ALHsiccesslines.

Hazelton, Tanya & Bonanni, Constance. Ian's Golden Passage. 2009. 168p. pap. 9.99 *(978-1-935105-33-6(7))* Avid Readers Publishing Group.

HB Staff. My Wild Woolly. 97th ed. 2003. (First-Place Reading Ser.). (gr. 1-18). pap. 16.50 *(978-0-15-308163-7(5))* Harcourt Schl. Pubs.

Heaney Dunn, John, illus. The Little Red House with No Doors & No Windows & A Star Inside. 2011. 25p. (J). pap. 15.95 *(978-1-58909-915-9(X))* Bookstand Publishing.

Hest, Amy. Don't You Feel Well, Sam? Jeram, Anita, illus. 2007. (Sam Bks.). (ENG.). 32p. (J). (gr. -1-k). 4.99 *(978-0-7636-2408-8(X))* Candlewick Pr.

Hill, Eric. Spot Loves His Mommy. Hill, Eric, illus. 2006. (Spot Ser.). (ENG., Illus.). 14p. (J). (gr. -1 — 1). bds. 5.99 *(978-0-399-24511-4(1))*, Warne) Penguin Young Readers Group.

Hillert, Margaret. The Magic Beans. Zaman, Farida, illus. 2016. (BeginningtoRead Ser.). (ENG.). 32p. (J). (gr. -1-2). pap. 11.94 *(978-1-60357-910-0(9))* Norwood Hse. Pr.

Himes, Rachel. Princess & the Peas. Himes, Rachel, illus. 2017. (ENG., Illus.). 32p. (J). (gr. k-3). 16.99 *(978-1-58089-718-1(5))* Charlesbridge Publishing, Inc.

Hiris, Monica. Just Like Mom. Sierra, Holly, illus. 2005. (ENG.). 8p. (gr. k-1). pap. 7.95 *(978-1-57874-088-8(6))*, Kaeden Bks.) Kaeden Corp.

Hoover, Paulette. What's That Lump in Your Bed? 2011. 28p. pap. 21.95 *(978-1-4567-1859-6(2))* AuthorHouse.

Howe, James. Also Known As Elvis. (Misfits Ser.). (ENG., Illus.). (J). (gr. 5-9). 2015. 304p. pap. 7.99 *(978-1-4424-4511-6(4))* 2014. 288p. 16.99 *(978-1-4424-4510-9(6))*, Atheneum Bks. for Young Readers) Simon & Schuster Children's Publishing.

Hughes, Shirley. Alfie Gets in First. Hughes, Shirley, illus. 2009. (Alfie Ser.). (ENG., Illus.). 32p. (J). (gr. -1-k). pap. 9.99 *(978-1-86230-783-4(0))*, Red Fox) Random House Children's Books GBR. Dist: Independent Pubs. Group.

Hunter, Skillman "Kim". El Becerrito en Valle Grande. Ritthaler, Sarah Pilcher, tr. Sundstrom, Mary, illus. 2006.Tr. of Little Cow in Valle Grande. (SPA & ENG.). 32p. (J). (gr. -1-k). 16.95 *(978-0-8263-4044-3(X))* Univ. of New Mexico Pr.

Iacovone, Lauren Marie. Here Lies Thomas Crawford, 1 vol. 2010. 252p. pap. 27.95 *(978-1-61582-690-2(4))* America Star Bks.

Jacobson, Jennifer Richard. Small as an Elephant. 2011. (ENG., Illus.). 288p. (J). (gr. 4-7). 15.99 *(978-0-7636-4155-9(3))* Candlewick Pr.

Jasper, J. J. When I Grow Up. Bullock, Brad, illus. 2003. 16p. (J). *(978-0-9727279-8-3(1))* Pine Hill Graphics.

Jenkins, Amanda & Benchmark Education Co., LLC. The Secret Life of Wally Smithers. Fagan, Martin, illus. 2014. (Text Connections Ser.). (J). (gr. 3). *(978-1-4509-9656-3(6))* Benchmark Education Co.

Jennings, Sharon. Bearcub & Mama. Watt, Mélanie, illus. 2007. (ENG.). 32p. (J). (gr. -1-2). 6.95 *(978-1-55453-162-2(4))* Kids Can Pr., Ltd. CAN. Dist: Hachette Bk. Group.

Johnson, Gail. Chasing the Sun. 2009. 40p. pap. 17.99 *(978-1-4389-2192-1(6))* AuthorHouse.

Johnson, Gerald J. J. A Boy Called Tiny Tim. 2013. 20p. pap. 24.95 *(978-1-62709-865-6(8))* America Star Bks.

Jonell, Lynne. The Sign of the Cat. 2015. (ENG., Illus.). 368p. (J). (gr. 3-7). 16.99 *(978-0-8050-9683-5(3))*, 9780805096835, Holt, Henry & Co. Bks. For Young Readers) Holt, Henry & Co.

—The Sign of the Cat. 2016. (J). lib. bdg. 18.40 *(978-0-606-39559-5(8))* Turtleback Bks.

Judd, Christopher M. Bearable Moments. 2005. (J). 16.95 *(978-0-9766666-1-5(8))* Arcadian Hse.

Judd-Leisten, Betty. Tell It for a Toll, Toll It for a Tale. 2005. 102p. per. 7.95 *(978-1-59824-057-3(9))* E-BookTime LLC.

Jue, Thea. Remember the Love. Lenz, Mary, illus. 2013. 36p. pap. 13.95 *(978-0-9827753-3-2(4))* Interdimensional Pr.

Kaufman, Sashi. The Other Way Around. 288p. (YA). (gr. 8-12). 2017. (ENG.). pap. 9.99 ***(978-1-5124-8177-8(7)***, Carolrhoda Bks.) 2014. 17.95 *(978-1-4677-0262-1(5))* Lerner Publishing Group.

Keeley, Holly M. The Journey of a Grape. 2009. 20p. pap. 12.49 *(978-1-4490-3060-5(2))* AuthorHouse.

Kelley, Maria Felicia. Buz Words: Discovering Words in Pairs. Kelley, Maria Felicia, illus. 2007. (Illus.). 32p. (J). (gr. -1-3). 14.95 *(978-0-9650918-1-7(3))* April Arts Press & Productions.

Kenyon, Sherrilyn. Infinity, Vol. 1. Ahn, JiYoung, illus. 2013. (Dark-Hunters Ser.: 1). (ENG.). 240p. (gr. 11-17). 13.00 *(978-0-316-19053-4(5))*, Yen Pr.) Orbit.

—Infinity. (Chronicles of Nick Ser.: 1). (ENG.). 480p. (YA). (gr. 7-18). 2011. pap. 11.99 *(978-0-312-60304-5(5))*, 9780312603045) 2010. 19.99 *(978-0-312-59907-2(2))*, 9780312599072) St. Martin's Pr. (St. Martin's Griffin).

Kim, HoJeong. Kanga & Anger. Kim, SookKyeong, illus. rev. ed. 2014. (MySELF Bookshelf Ser.). (ENG.). 32p. (J). (gr. k-2). pap. 11.94 *(978-1-60357-652-9(5))*; lib. bdg. 25.27 *(978-1-59953-643-9(9))* Norwood Hse. Pr.

Kingsbury, Karen. Whatever You Grow up to Be, 1 vol. Docampo, Valeria, illus. rev. ed. 2014. (ENG.). 32p. (J). 15.99 *(978-0-310-71646-4(2))* Zonderkidz.

Knudson, Mike & Wilkinson, Steve. Bases Loaded. 2011. (Raymond & Graham Ser.). (ENG.). 160p. (J). (gr. 3-7). 6.99 *(978-0-14-241751-5(3))*, Puffin Books) Penguin Young Readers Group.

Koertge, Ronald. Where the Kissing Never Stops. 2005. (ENG.). 256p. (YA). (gr. 9-18). per. 6.99 *(978-0-7636-2696-9(1))* Candlewick Pr.

Kraatz, Jeramey. The Cloak Society. (Cloak Society Ser.: 1). (ENG.). (J). (gr. 3-7). 2013. 304p. pap. 6.99 *(978-0-06-209548-0(X))* 2012. 288p. 16.99 *(978-0-06-209547-3(1))* HarperCollins Pubs.

Kropp, Paul. Winner! *(978-1-897039-31-1(X))* High Interest Publishing (HIP).

Krosoczka, Jarrett J. Good Night, Monkey Boy. Krosoczka, Jarrett J., illus. 2013. (ENG., Illus.). 32p. (J). (-k). bds. 6.99

(978-0-449-81323-2(1), Knopf Bks. for Young Readers) Random Hse. Children's Bks.
Kumara, Mark. The Tr-Youth Truth: Knowledge, Apprehens. 2005. (Illus.). 206p. pap. 24.75 (978-1-4120-6960-1(2)) Trafford Publishing.
Kuracka, Vicki. When the Sun Sleeps. 2010. 16p. pap. 9.99 (978-1-60911-509-8(0), Eloquent Bks.) Strategic Book Publishing & Rights Agency (SBPRA).
Kurstedt, Rosanne. And I Thought about You. Carletta-Vietes, Lisa, illus. 2012. (J). 14.95 (978-1-937406-65-3(2)) Mascot Bks., Inc.
LaFaye, A. Walking Home to Rosie Lee. Shepherd, Keith D., illus. 2011. (ENG.). 32p. (J). (gr. 1-6). 16.95 (978-1-933693-97-2(5)) Cinco Puntos Pr.
Lagrou, Patrick. Born among the Dolphins. 2008. (Born among the Dolphins Ser.: 1). (ENG & DUT.). 154p. (J). (gr. 3-18). 19.95 (978-1-60537-022-4(3)) Clavis Publishing.
LaRochelle, David. The Best Pet of All. Wakiyama, Hanako, illus. 2009. (ENG.). 32p. (J). (gr. -1-k). pap. 7.99 (978-0-14-241272-5(4), Puffin Books) Penguin Young Readers Group.
Lawrence, D. H. The Rocking-Horse Winner. 2010. (Illus.). 40p. (J). 19.95 (978-1-58341-924-3(1), Creative Education) Creative Co., The.
Le Verrier, Renee & Frank, Samuel. A Treasure Hunt for Mama & Me: Helping Children Cope with Parental Illness. Taylor, Adam, illus. 2013. (Let's Talk Ser.). (ENG.). 48p. (J). (gr. -1-2). 9.95 (978-0-88282-436-9(8)) New Horizon Pr. Pubs., Inc.
Leonard, Marcia. Pantalones Nuevos, No! Handelman, Dorothy, photos by. 2005.Tr. of No New Pants! (Illus.). 32p. (J). (ENG & SPA.). (gr. -1-1). pap. 4.99 (978-0-8225-3297-2(2)); (SPA., (gr. 1-1). per. 5.95 (978-0-8225-3296-5(4), Ediciones Lerner) Lerner Publishing Group.
Lerangis, Peter. The Code. 2004. (Spy X Ser.: No. 1). 139p. (Orig.). (J). (978-0-439-70242-3(9)) Scholastic, Inc.
Licciardi, Paula. Wasting Calvin's Time. 2006. 9.00 (978-0-8059-8138-4(1)) Dorrance Publishing Co., Inc.
Lloyd, A. Wallis. Das Monster-Musical. 2013. 32p. pap. (978-3-944704-02-9(9)) Nothnagle, Alan. Edition Graugans.
Lopez, Lorraine. Call Me Henri. 2012. (ENG.). 242p. pap. 19.95 (978-0-8101-2893-4(4)) Curbstone Pr.
Lord, Pia. The Day the Sun Went Out. 2012. 30p. 24.95 (978-1-4626-6797-0(X)) America Star Bks.
Lundebrek, Amy & Rich, Anna. Under the Night Sky, 1 vol. 2008. (ENG., Illus.). 32p. (J). (gr. 3-6). 16.95 (978-0-88448-297-0(9), 884297) Tilbury Hse. Pubs.
Lupica, Mike. The Batboy. 2011. (ENG.). 272p. (J). (gr. 5-18). 7.99 (978-0-14-241782-9(3), Puffin Books) Penguin Young Readers Group.
—The Batboy. 2011. lib. bdg. 18.40 (978-0-606-15352-2(7), Turtleback) Turtleback Bks.
Magaziner, Lauren. The Only Thing Worse Than Witches. 2014. (ENG.). 272p. (J). (gr. 3-7). 16.99 (978-0-8037-3918-5(4), Dial Bks) Penguin Young Readers Group.
Mahy, Margaret. The Man Whose Mother Was a Pirate. Chamberlain, Margaret, illus. 2013. (Early Reader Ser.). (ENG.). 64p. (J). (gr. k-2). pap. 7.99 (978-1-4440-0925-5(7), Orion Children's Bks.) Hachette Children's Group GBR. Dist: Hachette Bk. Group.
Mai, Resa. Toy for Chantelle. 2007. 32p. per. 12.95 (978-1-59858-338-0(7)) Dog Ear Publishing, LLC.
Mankell, Henning. Journey to the End of the World. 2011. (Joel Gustafson Stories Ser.: No. 4). (ENG.). 208p. (YA). (gr. 7). pap. 7.99 (978-0-385-73498-1(0), Delacorte Bks. for Young Readers) Random Hse. Children's Bks.
Mannion, Mary. Roaring Rory. Fitzgerald, Brian, illus. 2010. 68p. pap. (978-1-907276-63-7(7)) Lapwing Pubns.
Marcotte, David A. Be Wary of Strangers. 2005. (ENG., Illus.). 36p. per. 14.95 (978-1-932672-47-3(8)) Outskirts Pr., Inc.
Mardani, Parisa. Nathan Sees a Monster But... . 2012. 16p. pap. 15.99 (978-1-4685-9405-8(2)) AuthorHouse.
Marr, Nikki. Marty Misbehaves. 2008. 40p. pap. 17.99 (978-1-4389-3171-5(9)) AuthorHouse.
Marshall, Peter, et al. Nate Donovan: Revolutionary Spy. 2007. 208p. (J). pap. 9.99 (978-0-8054-4394-3(0), B&H Bks.) B&H Publishing Group.
Martin, Brian. The Gold of Angel Island. McDonald, Kim, illus. 2007. 46p. (J). (978-0-9798059-0-5(2)) Lunchbox Stories Inc.
Mayer, Mercer. Just Me & My Mom. 2014. (Little Critter Ser.). lib. bdg. 14.75 (978-0-606-35555-1(3)) Turtleback Bks.
Mayo, Jason. Do Witches Make Fishes? 2010. 36p. pap. 16.99 (978-1-4520-6944-9(1)) AuthorHouse.
McAllister, Angela. My Mom Has X-Ray Vision. Smith, Alex T., illus. 2011. (ENG.). 32p. (J). (gr. -1-2). 15.95 (978-1-58925-097-0(4)); pap. 7.95 (978-1-58925-428-2(7)) Tiger Tales.
McC, Meg. Goodnap, Brewer, 1 vol. 2010. 32p. 24.95 (978-1-4512-1447-5(2)) PublishAmerica, Inc.
McClure, Brian D. The Bubble. 2006. (Illus.). 64p. (J). 14.95 (978-1-933426-05-1(5)) Universal Flag Publishing.
McCourt, Lisa. I Love You, Stinky Face. Moore, Cyd, illus. 2009. (ENG.). (J). (gr. -1-3). 9.99 (978-0-545-11757-9(7)) Scholastic, Inc.
—I Miss You, Stinky Face. Moore, Cyd, illus. 2009. (ENG.). (J). (gr. -1-3). 9.95 (978-0-545-13849-9(3)) Scholastic, Inc.
McCullough, Myrina D. Feet. Schafrath, Ty, illus. 2013. 28p. pap. 15.00 (978-0-9847740-1-2(7)) Systems Group, Inc., The.
McFadden, Jennifer. Rusty My Playful Cat. 2010. 24p. pap. 11.49 (978-1-4490-5101-3(4)) AuthorHouse.
McKinty, Adrian. The Lighthouse Land. 2006. (ENG., Illus.). 200p. (YA). (gr. 6-10). 16.95 (978-0-8109-5480-9(X)) Abrams, Inc.
Mencio, Anna. The Day the Wind Changed. 2012. 24p. pap. 28.03 (978-1-4691-8232-2(7)) Xlibris Corp.
Minarik, Else Holmelund. Little Bear. Sendak, Maurice, illus. 2003. (I Can Read Level 1 Ser.). (ENG.). 64p. (J). (gr. k-3). pap. 3.95 (978-0-06-444004-2(4)) HarperCollins Pubs.
—Little Bear. 2003. (Little Bear: I Can Read! Ser.). (J). (gr. k-3). lib. bdg. 13.55 (978-0-8085-2618-6(9), Turtleback) Turtleback Bks.
—Osito. Aguilar, Joaquina, tr. Sendak, Maurice, illus. 2003. (Infantil Alfaguara Ser.: 25).Tr. of Little Bear. (SPA.). 60p. (J). (gr. k-3). pap. 8.95 (978-84-204-3044-7(7), AF1346) Santillana USA Publishing Co., Inc.
Mitchell, Mary Esther. The Adventures of Timmy Gills. 2005. (J). pap. 20.00 (978-0-8059-9660-9(5), RoseDog Bks.) Dorrance Publishing Co., Inc.
Mohamoud, Ashlee. Brown Is Beautiful, 1 vol. 2010. 18p. 24.95 (978-1-4512-0064-5(1)) PublishAmerica, Inc.
Mommy Has a Tattoo. 2006. (GER, ITA & SPA., Illus.). 32p. (J). (gr. 3-7). 16.95 (978-0-9770232-7-1(3)) Mommy Has Tattoos.
Moon, Adam. The Fuzzle. 2007. (J). per. 7.95 (978-1-934345-28-3(8)) SouthWest Pubns.
Morgenroth, Kate. Jude. 2006. (ENG., Illus.). 288p. (YA). (gr. 7-12). reprint ed. mass mkt. 7.99 (978-1-4169-1267-5(3), Simon Pulse) Simon Pulse.
Moritz, S. Dianne & Mitchell, Hazel. 1, 2, 3 ... by the Sea. 2013. (ENG., Illus.). 36p. (J). pap. 6.99 (978-1-935279-94-5(7)) Kane Miller.
Mosby, Pamela. I'm So Angry. Brever, Amy, illus. 2013. 28p. pap. 7.99 (978-0-9886272-4-6(8)) Brothers N Publishing Corp.
Mosel, Arlene. Tikki Tikki Tembo Book & CD Storytime Set. Lent, Blair, illus. unabr. ed. 2012. (ENG.). (J). 12.99 (978-1-4272-3211-3(3), 9781427232113) Macmillan Audio.
Mowry, Jess. Skeleton Key. 2007. 280p. (YA). pap. 14.99 (978-1-59092-353-5(7)) Blue Forge Pr.
Mrazovic, Ivan. Phobias - Crash Course. 2010. 48p. pap. 20.99 (978-0-557-38257-6(2)) Lulu Pr., Inc.
Munson, Kayla, illus. Night Night. 2013. (ENG.). 34p. (J). pap. 12.95 **(978-0-9821956-3-5(X))** Fleur De Lis Publishing, LLC.
Muse, Ludi. My Day at the Park. 2007. 32p. per. 13.95 (978-1-4259-6563-1(6)) AuthorHouse.
Myers, Jason. Blazed. 2014. (ENG., Illus.). 528p. (YA). (gr. 11-11). pap. 11.99 (978-1-4424-8721-5(6), Simon Pulse) Simon Pulse.
Nelson, N. A. Bringing the Boy Home. 2008. (ENG.). 224p. (J). (gr. 3-7). 16.99 (978-0-06-088698-1(6)) HarperCollins Pubs.
Ness, Patrick. A Monster Calls: Inspired by an Idea from Siobhan Dowd. (ENG.). 240p. (YA). (gr. 7). 2016. pap. 9.99 (978-0-7636-9215-5(8)) 2015. pap. 12.00 (978-0-7636-8081-7(8)) Candlewick Pr.
—A Monster Calls: Inspired by an Idea from Siobhan Dowd. Kay, Jim, illus. (ENG.). 224p. (YA). (gr. 7). 2013. pap. 12.00 (978-0-7636-6065-9(5)) 2011. 16.99 (978-0-7636-5559-4(7)) Candlewick Pr.
—A Monster Calls: Inspired by an Idea from Siobhan Dowd. 2011. (Playaway Children Ser.). (YA). (gr. 7-12). 54.99 (978-1-4558-4499-9(3)) Findaway World, LLC.
—A Monster Calls: Inspired by an Idea from Siobhan Dowd. 2013. lib. bdg. 23.30 (978-0-606-31603-3(5), Turtleback) Turtleback Bks.
Newman, Lesléa. Donovan's Big Day. Dutton, Mike, illus. 2011. (ENG.). 32p. (J). (gr. -1-2). 15.99 (978-1-58246-332-2(8), Tricycle Pr.) Random Hse. Children's Bks.
Nicolas, Stephanie. A Forged Report Card. 2004. (J). pap. 8.00 (978-0-8059-6420-2(7)) Dorrance Publishing Co., Inc.
Nielsen, Kelli & Benham, Kelly. You Will Always Be My Son. 2009. 36p. pap. 13.95 (978-1-60844-018-4(4)) Dog Ear Publishing, LLC.
Nielsen, Susin. Word Nerd. (ENG.). (J). (gr. 4-7). 2010. 264p. pap. 12.95 (978-0-88776-990-0(X)) 2008. 256p. 18.95 (978-0-88776-875-0(X)) Tundra Bks. CAN. (Tundra Bks.). Dist: Penguin Random Hse. LLC.
Norris, Gayle A. Bed Bug, 1 vol. 2009. 23p. pap. 24.95 (978-1-60836-088-8(1)) America Star Bks.
Northrop, Michael. The Final Kingdom. 2016. (TombQuest Ser.: 5). (ENG.). 192p. (J). (gr. 3-7). 16.99 (978-0-545-87111-2(5)); 12.99 (978-0-545-72342-8(6)) Scholastic, Inc. (Scholastic Pr.).
—The Stone Warriors. 2015. (TombQuest Ser.: 4). (ENG.). 192p. (J). (gr. 3-7). 12.99 (978-0-545-72341-1(8)); 16.99 (978-0-545-87108-2(5)) Scholastic, Inc. (Scholastic Pr.).
Ochsner, Gina. The Hidden Letters of Velta B. 2017. (ENG.). 320p. pap. 14.99 (978-0-544-70304-9(9)) Houghton Mifflin Harcourt Publishing Co.
Odezi, Jesse. Little Sunny & the Giants: The World's Greatest. 2012. 76p. pap. 30.00 (978-1-4669-0270-1(1)) Trafford Publishing.
Olvera, Jillann. Christian's Lullaby. 2006. 29p. pap. 24.95 (978-1-4241-1909-7(X)) PublishAmerica, Inc.
Osterweil, Adam. Cooper & the Enchanted Metal Detector. 2013. (ENG.). 250p. (J). 18.95 (978-1-60898-149-6(5)) namelos llc.
Panagopoulos, Janie Lynn. Mark of the Bear Claw. 2007. 224p. (J). pap. 8.95 (978-0-938682-83-7(0)) River Road Pubns., Inc.
Pastis, Stephan. Timmy Failure: the Book You're Not Supposed to Have. Pastis, Stephan, illus. 2016. (Timmy Failure Ser.). (ENG., Illus.). 304p. (J). (gr. 3-7). 14.99 (978-0-7636-9004-5(X)) Candlewick Pr.
Patron, Susan. Lucky for Good. McGuire, Erin, illus. 2012. (ENG.). 224p. (J). (gr. 3-7). pap. 6.99 (978-1-4169-9059-8(3), Atheneum Bks. for Young Readers) Simon & Schuster Children's Publishing.
—Lucky for Good. McGuire, Erin K., illus. 2011. (ENG.). 224p. (J). (gr. 3-7). 16.99 (978-1-4169-9058-1(5), Atheneum Bks. for Young Readers) Simon & Schuster Children's Publishing.
Paul, J. D. The Little Lost Dog, 1 vol. 2010. 12p. pap. 24.95 (978-1-4489-9251-5(6)) PublishAmerica, Inc.
Paulsen, Gary. The Glass Cafe or, the Stripper & the State: How My Mother Started a War with the System That Made Us Kind of Rich & a Little Bit Famous. 2004. 99p. (J). 13.65 (978-0-7569-3105-6(3)) Perfection Learning Corp.
Pavón, Mar. Could It Happen to Anyone? 2011. (ENG., Illus.). 32p. (J). (gr. k-2). 16.95 (978-84-15241-03-4(8)) D P & G Military Pubs.
Pen, Chenda. Dara Learns How to Ride a Bike! An Autism Story. 2010. 24p. pap. 14.99 (978-1-4490-6943-8(6)) AuthorHouse.
Penn, Audrey. Un Beso en Mi Mano. Harper, Ruth E. & Leak, Nancy M., illus. 2006. (Kissing Hand Ser.). (SPA & ENG.). 32p. (J). (gr. -1-3). 16.95 (978-1-933718-01-9(3)) Tanglewood Pr.
—The Kissing Hand. Gibson, Barbara Leonard, illus. 2014. (Kissing Hand Ser.). (ENG.). 14p. (J). (-k). bds. 7.99 (978-1-933718-77-4(3)) Tanglewood Pr.
—The Kissing Hand. Harper, Ruth E. & Leak, Nancy M., illus. 2007. (Kissing Hand Ser.). (ENG.). 32p. (J). (gr. -1-3). 28.95 (978-1-933718-07-1(2)); 12.95 (978-1-933718-10-1(2)) Tanglewood Pr.
Penn, Audrey, et al, illus. The Kissing Hand. 2010. 23.05 (978-0-7569-9299-6(0)) Natl Bk. Network.
Pennington, Norma C. & Schuller, Sheldon V. The Unopened Gift, 1 vol. 2010. 18p. 24.95 (978-1-4489-7670-6(7)) PublishAmerica, Inc.
Pentz, Jane A. Horatio's Magical Journeys - the Secret. 2007. 108p. pap. 10.00 (978-1-892426-11-6(0)) LMA Publishing.
Perry, Fred. Grossery Games. 2012. (ENG., Illus.). 128p. (J). (gr. 4-7). pap. 10.99 (978-0-9850925-5-9(6), 9780985092559) Antarctic Pr., Inc.
—Playing Dead. 2012. (ENG., Illus.). 128p. (J). pap. 10.99 (978-0-9850925-4-2(8), 9780985092542) Antarctic Pr., Inc.
Pham, LeUyen. All the Things I Love about You. Pham, LeUyen, illus. 2010. (ENG., Illus.). 40p. (J). (gr. -1-3). 14.99 (978-0-06-199029-8(9)) HarperCollins Pubs.
Pick, Alice. Jamey's Promise, 1 vol. 2009. 61p. pap. 19.95 (978-1-61582-547-9(9)) America Star Bks.
Pignataro, Anna. Mama, Will I Be Yours Forever? Pignataro, Anna, illus. 2013. (ENG., Illus.). 32p. (J). (gr. -1-k). pap. 4.99 (978-0-545-46074-3(3), Cartwheel Bks.) Scholastic, Inc.
—Mama, Will You Hold My Hand? Pignataro, Anna, illus. 2010. (ENG., Illus.). 32p. (J). (gr. -1-k). pap. 4.99 (978-0-545-16986-8(0), Cartwheel Bks.) Scholastic, Inc.
Poh, Jennie. Herbie's Big Adventure. Poh, Jennie, illus. 2016. (Fiction Picture Bks.). (ENG., Illus.). 40p. (J). (gr. 1-2). lib. bdg. 23.32 (978-1-5158-0234-1(5), Fiction Picture Bks.) Picture Window Bks.
Powell, Randy. Tribute to Another Dead Rock Star. 2003. (ENG.). 224p. (YA). (gr. 7-12). pap. 14.99 (978-0-374-47968-8(2), Sunburst) Farrar, Straus & Giroux.
Prevost, Jeanne. It's Raining Cats & Cats! Hansen, Amelia, illus. 2008. (ENG.). 24p. (J). (gr. k-2). 16.95 (978-0-940719-06-4(1)) Gryphon Pr., The.
Prince Apple Head Humpledink. 2006. 38p. (J). 13.68 (978-1-4116-7232-1(1)) Lulu Pr., Inc.
Quiller-Couch, Arthur Thomas. Naughts & Crosses. 2009. 188p. 26.95 (978-1-60664-671-7(0)) Rodgers, Alan Bks.
Quiller-Couch, Arthur Thomas & Q. Naughts & Crosses. 2009. 188p. pap. 13.95 (978-1-60664-299-3(5)) Rodgers, Alan Bks.
Rahnama, Seyed Javad. Minty Ear. 2011. (Illus.). 20p. pap. 14.11 (978-1-4567-8188-0(X)) AuthorHouse.
Ramdayal, Mia. Learning How to Fly. 2012. 28p. pap. 15.99 (978-1-4691-5897-6(3)) Xlibris Corp.
Ramsey, Jo. Nail Polish & Feathers. 2016. (ENG., Illus.). (YA). (gr. 9-12). 24.99 **(978-1-63533-050-2(5))** 2013. 210p. pap. 14.99 (978-1-62798-088-3(1)) Dreamspinner Pr. (Harmony Ink Pr.).
Randall, Rommie. Mommy's Little Boy. (Daddy's / Mommy's Ser.). 32p. (978-1-4054-9457-1(3)) Parragon, Inc.
Reedy, Trent. Divided We Fall. 2014. (Divided We Fall Ser.: 1). (ENG.). 384p. (J). (gr. 9). pap. 9.99 (978-0-545-54368-2(1)); 17.99 (978-0-545-54367-5(3)) Scholastic, Inc. (Levine, Arthur A. Bks.).
Renero, Joaquin. The Enchanted Scrapbook: Welcome to the Wilburton Society. 2011. 320p. 29.95 (978-1-4502-6140-1(X)); pap. 19.95 (978-1-4502-6138-8(8)) iUniverse, Inc.
Reynolds, Aaron. Back of the Bus. Cooper, Floyd, illus. 2013. (ENG.). 32p. (J). (gr. 1-3). 8.99 (978-0-14-751058-7(9), Puffin Books) Penguin Young Readers Group.
Rhodes, Terry. Marley's Big Day. 2008. 16p. pap. 24.95 (978-1-60474-947-2(4)) America Star Bks.
Richardson, Tom. Dominic Is Strong. 2005. (Illus.). 26p. (J). lib. bdg. 16.95 (978-1-932338-99-7(3)) Lifevest Publishing, Inc.
Ringo, Mary Lou. That's Not Fair. 2012. 28p. pap. 24.95 (978-1-4626-5153-5(4)) America Star Bks.
Rivera, Veronica. Mommy's Little Helper. 2012. 32p. pap. 17.49 (978-1-4691-9026-6(5)) Xlibris Corp.
Robert, Nadine. Joseph Fipps. Godbout, Geneviève, illus. 2014. (ENG.). 64p. (J). (gr. -1-2). 16.95 (978-1-59270-117-9(5)) Enchanted Lion Bks., LLC.
Rockliff, Mara. Me & Momma & Big John. Low, William, illus. 2012. (ENG.). 32p. (J). (gr. -1-2). 16.99 (978-0-7636-4359-1(9)) Candlewick Pr.
Romagnoli, L. M. Memories of Me, 1 vol. 2009. 22p. pap. 24.95 (978-1-60836-084-0(9)) America Star Bks.
Rossell, Judith. Oliver. Rossell, Judith, illus. 2012. (ENG., Illus.). 32p. (J). (gr. -1-2). 16.99 (978-0-06-202210-3(5)) HarperCollins Pubs.
Rudolph, Shaina & Royer, Danielle. All My Stripes: A Story for Children with Autism. Zivoin, Jennifer, illus. 2014. (J). pap. (978-1-4338-1917-9(1), Magination Pr.) American Psychological Assn.
Ruth, Greg. Coming Home. Ruth, Greg, illus. 2014. (ENG., Illus.). 32p. (J). (gr. -1-2). 16.99 (978-1-250-05547-7(4), 9781250055477) Feiwel & Friends.
Ryan, Pam Muñoz. Yo, Naomi León. 2005. (SPA.). 272p. (J). (gr. 3-7). pap. 6.99 (978-0-439-75572-6(7), Scholastic en Espanol) Scholastic, Inc.
Ryan, Patrick. In Mike We Trust. 2009. 321p. (J). lib. bdg. 17.89 (978-0-06-085814-8(1), HarperTeen) HarperCollins Pubs.
Rylant, Cynthia. A Kindness. Date not set. (Sky Bks.). 104p. pap. 54.75 (978-0-582-08106-2(8)) Addison-Wesley Longman, Ltd. GBR. Dist: Trans-Atlantic Pubns., Inc.
Sabo, J. Mamma's Boy. 2012. 30p. 24.95 (978-1-4626-6928-8(X)) America Star Bks.
Samuel, Lynette M. Mommy's Hat. Capps, Leigh, illus. 2005. (J). per. (978-0-9727703-3-0(X)) P.R.A. Publishing.
Sateren, Shelley Swanson. Max & Zoe Celebrate Mother's Day, 1 vol. Sullivan, Mary, illus. 2012. (Max & Zoe Ser.). (ENG.). 32p. (gr. k-2). lib. bdg. 21.32 (978-1-4048-6214-2(5), Max & Zoe) Picture Window Bks.
Saunders, Brianna. The Magic Marble. 2013. 32p. pap. 24.95 (978-1-63004-598-2(5)) America Star Bks.
Sawyer, Louise. Mother's Storybook Signs, Vol. 1. 2004. (YA). spiral bd. 19.95 (978-0-9719842-0-2(4)) Martin & Brothers.
Schmidt, Shawntay. Invincible Me. Du Pont, Brittany, illus. 2013. 24p. pap. 8.99 (978-1-937165-61-1(2)) Orange Hat Publishing.
Scholastic, Inc. Staff. My Mommy. 2014. (Peppa Pig Ser.). (ENG.). 16p. (J). (gr. -1-k). bds. 7.99 (978-0-545-46804-6(3)) Scholastic, Inc.
Schraff, Anne. To Be a Man. 2011. (Urban Underground — Harriet Tubman High School Ser.). (YA). lib. bdg. 20.80 (978-0-606-14815-3(9), Turtleback) Turtleback Bks.
Scraper, Katherine. The Yard Sale. 2006. (Early Explorers Ser.). (J). pap. (978-1-4108-6043-9(4)) Benchmark Education Co.
Seghetti, Nancy & Esseveld, Nelson. The Day Mom Quit. 2009. 36p. pap. 16.99 (978-1-4389-2168-6(3)) AuthorHouse.
Sexauer, Donald E. The Standoff & Kramer Too! 2012. 24p. pap. 12.56 (978-1-4669-4577-7(X)) Trafford Publishing.
Shea, John & Harmon, Michael B. A Kid from Southie. 2011. 240p. (YA). (gr. 9-18). 16.95 (978-1-934813-53-9(2)) Westside Bks.
Shutz, Ashley. Little Ricky Roo. 2012. 28p. 24.95 (978-1-4512-6491-3(7)) America Star Bks.
Smith, Andrew Christopher John. Soi. 2009. (Illus.). 40p. pap. 16.99 (978-1-4490-3591-4(4)) AuthorHouse.
Smith, Dan. Boy X. 2017. (J). **(978-1-338-17150-1(X))** Scholastic, Inc.
Smith, Latoya K. My Favorite Trey. 2009. 24p. pap. 11.49 (978-1-4490-4220-2(1)) AuthorHouse.
Smucker, Shawn. The Day the Angels Fell. 2017. (ENG.). 320p. (YA). 17.99 **(978-0-8007-2849-6(1))** Revell.
Solomon, Enid. Toby Visits Mommy: A Book for Children Who See Their Parents Only During Scheduled Visitations. 2010. 32p. pap. 13.25 (978-1-4490-0683-9(3)) AuthorHouse.
Sonnenblick, Jordan. The Secret Sheriff of Sixth Grade. 2017. (ENG.). 208p. (J). (gr. 4-7). 16.99 **(978-0-545-86320-9(1),** Scholastic Pr.) Scholastic, Inc.
Sprenger, Luke. Sommer in Canvas Bay. 2008. 92p. pap. 13.95 (978-1-4092-3213-1(1)) Lulu Pr., Inc.
Stanley, Dan. Danny the Fisherman, 1 vol. LaRue, Athena Mariah, illus. 2010. 46p. 24.95 (978-1-4512-9695-2(9)) PublishAmerica, Inc.
Star, Eloney. Heavy Duty Trucker. 2007. 28p. (J). per. 7.99 (978-1-59879-287-4(3)) Lifevest Publishing, Inc.
Stinson, Kathy & Petricic, Dusan. The Man with the Violin. 2016. (ENG., Illus.). 32p. (J). (gr. k-3). pap. 9.95 (978-1-55451-564-6(5)) Annick Pr., Ltd. CAN. Dist: Publishers Group West (PGW).
Stultz, Janice. Harry Turnaround. 2012. 24p. pap. 15.99 (978-1-4691-7141-8(4)) Xlibris Corp.
Sullivan, Paula. Todd's Box. Westcott, Nadine Bernard, illus. 2004. (J). (gr. -1-1). 11.60 (978-0-7569-5629-5(3)) Perfection Learning Corp.
Suter, Lorenzo. TrYouth Truth Knowledge Apprehension Cog. 2005. (Illus.). 206p. 27.55 (978-1-4122-0095-0(4)) Trafford Publishing.
Swain, Cynthia. No, Tim! 2006. (Early Explorers Ser.). (J). pap. (978-1-4108-6029-3(9)) Benchmark Education Co.
Taylor, Brigid. How I Turn My Mom into a Monster! 2009. 16p. pap. 9.95 (978-1-4389-9755-1(8)) AuthorHouse.
Thomas, Alease Allen. Bobby Jones of Beardsley Terrace. 2006. 18.00 (978-0-8059-9829-0(2)) Dorrance Publishing Co., Inc.
Thompson, Mary G. Wuftoom. 2013. (ENG.). 256p. (YA). (gr. 7). pap. 8.99 (978-0-544-02247-8(5)) Houghton Mifflin Harcourt Publishing Co.
Tommasi, Michael Richard. Stinky Mcgee. 2008. 16p. pap. 9.95 (978-1-4343-6004-5(0)) AuthorHouse.
Torres, Jose A. Joey Kanga Roo: First Day of School. 2009. 36p. pap. 15.99 (978-1-4389-3964-3(7)) AuthorHouse.
Travis, Allison J. Bundy. One More Wake Up: With Faith All Things Are Possible-Even Surviving the Loss of a Loved One. 2012. 34p. 24.95 (978-1-4626-5862-6(8)) America Star Bks.
Truly Blessed Ink. I Know You Won't Forget. Jordan, Carol, illus. 2007. (ENG.). 40p. (J). 16.95 (978-0-9789066-1-0(6)) Square Circle Pr. LLC.
Tulloch, Scott. Willy's Mum. 2008. (Illus.). 32p. pap. (978-1-86950-682-7(0)) HarperCollins Pubs. Australia.
Turnbull-Kennedy, Tiffany. No School for Evil Eraser! 2011. (Illus.). 48p. pap. 16.59 (978-1-4634-3965-1(2)) AuthorHouse.
Tyburski, Kimberly. Pesty Boy. 2011. 24p. pap. 15.99 (978-1-4628-9302-7(3)) Xlibris Corp.
Underwood, Deborah. Pirate Mom. Gilpin, Stephen, illus. 2006. (Step into Reading Ser.: Vol. 3). (ENG.). 48p. (J). (gr. k-3). per. 3.99 (978-0-375-83323-6(4), Random Hse. Bks. for Young Readers) Random Hse. Children's Bks.
Varley, Dax. The Crow. Proctor, Jon, illus. 2016. (ENG.). 48p. (J). lib. bdg. (978-1-62402-160-2(3)) Magic Wagon.
—Graveyard Dirt. Proctor, Jon, illus. 2016. (ENG.). 48p. (J). lib. bdg. (978-1-62402-158-9(1)) Magic Wagon.
—The Locket. Proctor, Jon, illus. 2016. (ENG.). 48p. (J). lib. bdg. (978-1-62402-159-6(X)) Magic Wagon.
Vernick, Audrey. Screaming at the Ump. 2014. (ENG.). 272p. (J). (gr. 5-7). 16.99 (978-0-544-25208-0(X), Clarion Bks.) Houghton Mifflin Harcourt Trade & Reference Pubs.
Villareal, Ray. Don't Call Me Hero. 2011. (J). pap. 10.95 (978-1-55885-711-7(7), Piñata Books) Arte Publico Pr.
Wallace, Nancy Elizabeth. Shells! Shells! Shells!, 0 vols. 2013. (ENG.). 40p. (J). (gr. k-3). pap. 9.99 (978-1-4778-1679-0(8), 9781477816790, Amazon Children's Publishing) Amazon Publishing.
Walter, Chris. Tell Your Dreams to Me. 2008. 32p. pap. 14.95 (978-1-4389-0162-6(3)) AuthorHouse.
Walters, Celeste. Deception. 2005. 288p. (YA). pap. (978-0-7022-3527-6(X)) Univ. of Queensland Pr.
Ward Appleton's Pancakes a Special Way. 2005. 10.95 (978-0-9754779-6-0(X)) Chosen Word Publishing.
Weatherall, Barry. Jay & the Worm Save the Day. 2005. 40p. 14.28 (978-1-4116-4717-6(3)) Lulu Pr., Inc.
Weatherford, Carole Boston. In Your Hands. Pinkney, Brian, illus. 2017. (ENG.). 32p. (J). (gr. -1-3). 17.99 **(978-1-4814-6293-8(8))** Simon & Schuster Children's Publishing.
Weiner, Brian. Toad Catchers' Creek. Weintraub, Claudia & Frederick, Robin, eds. Cannon, Martin, illus. 2005. 40p. (J). lib. bdg. 17.99 (978-1-932949-58-2(5)) Illusion Factory, The.
Welsh, Karen Leis. Eh, Spaghetti You Say? 2012. 36p. pap. 20.99 (978-1-4772-0473-3(3)) AuthorHouse.

Wheelwright, Ryan. Olivar & the Forbidden Plum Patch. 2011. 21p. (J). pap. 11.95 (978-1-4327-6689-4(9)) Outskirts Pr., Inc.

Whitten, A. J. The Well. 2009. (ENG., Illus.). 336p. (YA). (gr. 7-18). pap. 18.95 (978-0-547-23229-4(2)) Houghton Mifflin Harcourt Publishing Co.

Wilderness, Dale. Drift in Your Pillow's Eyes. 2013. pap. 9.95 (978-1-59433-155-8(3)) Publication Consultants.

Williams, Tova. The Boy Who Did Not Want to Read, 1 vol. Suggs, Aisha, illus. 2010. 36p. pap. 24.95 (978-1-4489-5705-7(2)) PublishAmerica, Inc.

Williamson, Jennifer. Timmy the Tow Truck, 6 vols. Williamson, Alan, 8th, illus. 2005. 28p. (J). pap. (978-0-9771678-1-4(X)) Theee Hole Punch Publishing.

Willis, Jeanne. Cottonball Colin. Ross, Tony, illus. 2008. 26p. (J). (gr. -1-4). 16.00 (978-0-8028-5331-8(5), Eerdmans Bks For Young Readers) Eerdmans, William B. Publishing Co.

Wilson, N. D. Leepike Ridge. 2008. (ENG., Illus.). 256p. (J). (gr. 3-7). 6.99 (978-0-375-83874-3(0), Yearling) Random Hse. Children's Bks.

Wood, Courtney. Just the Way It Was. 2013. 28p. pap. 19.99 (978-1-4817-0734-3(5)) AuthorHouse.

Wood, Frank. Little Ray's Trip to the Doctor. 2012. 58p. pap. 40.00 (978-1-60746-263-7(X)) FastPrncil, Inc.

Woodson, Jacqueline. From the Notebooks of Melanin Sun. 2011. 9.68 (978-0-7848-3512-8(8)) 2009. 7.84 (978-0-7848-2356-9(1)) Marco Bk. Co. (Everbind).

—From the Notebooks of Melanin Sun. 2010. (ENG.). 176p. (J). (gr. 5-18). 7.99 (978-0-14-241641-9(X), Puffin Books) Penguin Young Readers Group.

—From the Notebooks of Melanin Sun. 2003. (Point Ser.). (ENG.). 141p. (YA). (gr. 7). 13.65 (978-0-7807-7292-2(X)) Perfection Learning Corp.

Young, Candice June. My Name Is Wes & My Mema Has Ms. 2013. 24p. pap. 24.95 (978-1-4137-7777-2(5)) America Star Bks.

Yum, Hyewon. Mom, It's My First Day of Kindergarten!, 1 vol. Yum, Hyewon, illus. 2012. (ENG., Illus.). 36p. (J). (gr. -1-2). 16.99 (978-0-374-35004-8(3), 9780374350048, Farrar, Straus & Giroux (BYR)) Farrar, Straus & Giroux.

—Puddle. 2016. (ENG., Illus.). 40p. (J). 16.99 (978-0-374-31695-2(3), 9780374316952, Farrar, Straus & Giroux (BYR)) Farrar, Straus & Giroux.

Zolotow, Charlotte. The Seashore Book. Minor, Wendell, illus. 2004. (Reading Rainbow Bks.). (gr. -1-3). 17.00 (978-0-7569-4234-2(9)) Perfection Learning Corp.

Zolotow, Charlotte & Minor, Wendell. The Seashore Book. 2017. (ENG., Illus.). 32p. (J). (-k). lib. bdg. 16.99 (978-1-58089-787-7(8)) Charlesbridge Publishing, Inc.

MOTHER'S DAY

Day, Erin. Happy Mother's Day! 2016. (Celebrations Ser.). 00024p. (J). (gr. 1-1). pap. 8.25 (978-1-4994-2765-3(4), PowerKids Pr.) Rosen Publishing Group, Inc., The.

Erlbach, Arlene & Erlbach, Herb. Fun Mother's Day Crafts. 2015. (Kid Fun Holiday Crafts! Ser.). 32p. (J). (gr. 3-4). 23.94 (978-0-7660-6245-0(7)) Enslow Pubs., Inc.

Erlbach, Arlene & Erlbach, Herbert. Fun Mother's Day Crafts. 2015. (Kid Fun Holiday Crafts! Ser.). 32p. (J). (gr. 3-4). pap. 7.95 (978-0-7660-6246-7(5), Enslow Elementary) Enslow Pubs., Inc.

—Mother's Day Crafts. 2005. (Fun Holiday Crafts Kids Can Do! Ser.). (Illus.). 32p. (J). lib. bdg. 23.94 (978-0-7660-2348-2(6), Enslow Elementary) Enslow Pubs., Inc.

Florian, Melanie. A Day with Mommy. Florian, Melanie, illus. 2010. (Sticker Stories Ser.). (ENG., Illus.). 16p. (J). (gr. -1-2). pap. 5.99 (978-0-448-45342-2(8), Grosset & Dunlap) Penguin Young Readers Group.

Fowler, Eleri. My Mother, My Heart. Fowler, Eleri, illus. 2016. (Illus.). 96p. (J). (gr. -1). pap. 15.99 (978-0-06-247938-9(5)) HarperCollins Pubs.

Gilpin, Rebecca. Things to Make for Mother's Day. Figg, Non, illus. 2004. (ENG.). 32p. (J). pap. 8.95 (978-0-7945-0693-3(3), Usborne) EDC Publishing.

Heinrichs, Ann. Mother's Day. Alley, R. W., illus. 2013. (Holidays & Celebrations Ser.). (ENG.). 32p. (J). (gr. k-3). 27.07 (978-1-62323-510-9(3), 206284) Child's World, Inc., The.

Honoring Mothers. 7.50 (978-0-8054-5928-9(6)) B&H Publishing Group.

Miller, Reagan. Mother's Day & Other Family Days. 2010. (Celebrations in My World Ser.). (ENG.). 32p. (J). (gr. k-3). pap. (978-0-7787-4937-0(1)); lib. bdg. (978-0-7787-4930-1(4)) Crabtree Publishing Co.

Nelid, Piper. Mother's Day with My Moms, 01 vols., 1. 2016. (Rosen REAL Readers: Social Studies Nonfiction / Fiction: Family, Community, & the World Ser.). (ENG.). 8p. (J). pap. 5.46 (978-1-5081-1647-9(4), Rosen Classroom) Rosen Publishing Group, Inc., The.

Ross, Kathy. All New Crafts for Mother's Day & Father's Day. Holm, Sharon Lane, illus. 2007. (All New Holiday Crafts for Kids Ser.). (ENG.). 48p. (gr. k-3). per. 7.95 (978-0-8225-6368-6(1), First Avenue Editions) Lerner Publishing Group.

—All New Holiday Crafts for Mother's & Father's Day. Holm, Sharon Lane, illus. 2007. (All New Holiday Crafts for Kids Ser.). (ENG.). 48p. (gr. k-3). lib. bdg. 25.26 (978-0-8225-6367-9(3), Millbrook Pr.) Lerner Publishing Group.

Watson, Michael C., frwd. Why Mom Deserves a Diamond(r) -Twelve Years of Love: Twelve Years of Love. 2005. 144p. (YA). lib. bdg. 29.95 (978-1-891665-35-6(9)) Moon Over Mountains Publishing (M.O.M.).

Williams, Colleen Madonna Flood. My Adventure on Mother's Day. 2007. 44p. (J). 8.99 (978-1-59092-552-2(1)) Blue Forge Pr.

York, M. J. It's Mother's Day! 2017. (Welcome, Spring! Ser.). (ENG.). 24p. (J). (gr. -1-2). lib. bdg. 27.07 (978-1-5038-1653-4(2), 211506) Child's World, Inc., The.

MOTHER'S DAY—FICTION

Berenstain, Jan & Berenstain, Mike. We Love Our Mom! 2012. (Berenstain Bears Ser.). (J). lib. bdg. 13.55 (978-0-606-23578-5(7), Turtleback) Turtleback Bks.

Berenstain, Mike. The Berenstain Bears Mother's Day Blessings, 1 vol. 2016. (Berenstain Bears/Living Lights Ser.). (ENG., Illus.). 24p. (J). pap. 3.99 (978-0-310-74869-4(0)) Zonderkidz.

Berenstain, Mike. Mother's Day Blessings. 2016. (Illus.). (J). **(978-1-4844-6294-2(7))** Zonderkidz.

Britt, Paige. The Lost Track of Time. White, Lee, illus. 2015. (ENG.). 320p. (J). (gr. 3-7). 17.99 (978-0-545-53812-1(2), Scholastic Pr.) Scholastic, Inc.

Disney Book Group Staff & Hapka, Catherine. Me & Our Mom. Disney Storybook Art Team, illus. 2015. (ENG.). 24p. (J). (gr. -1-k). pap. 4.99 (978-1-4847-0688-6(9)) Disney Pr.

González, Rigoberto. Antonio's Card: La Tarjeta de Antonio. Álvarez, Cecilia, illus. 2016. (ENG & SPA.). (J). pap. 9.95 (978-0-89239-387-9(4), Children's Book Press) Lee & Low Bks., Inc.

González, Rigoberto & Alvarez, Cecilia Concepcion. Antonio's Card/la Tarjeta de Antonio. 2013. (ENG & SPA., Illus.). 32p. (J). 17.95 (978-0-89239-204-9(5)) Lee & Low Bks., Inc.

Grambling, Lois G. T. Rex & the Mother's Day Hug. Davis, Jack E., illus. (ENG.). 32p. (J). (gr. -1-1). 2011. pap. 6.99 (978-0-06-053128-7(2)) 2008. 16.99 (978-0-06-053126-3(6)) HarperCollins Pubs. (Tegen, Katherine Bks).

Green, D. L. Zeke Meeks vs the Mother's Day Meltdown. Alves, Josh, illus. 2015. (Zeke Meeks Ser.). (ENG.). 128p. (gr. 2-2). 22.65 (978-1-4795-2168-5(X), Zeke Meeks) Picture Window Bks.

Hapka, Catherine, pseud. Sofia the First: Our Mother's Day Surprise. 2015. (Sofia the First Ser.). (Illus.). 24p. (J). lib. bdg. 14.75 (978-0-606-35913-9(3)) Turtleback Bks.

Hillert, Margaret. Happy Mother's Day, Dear Dragon. Starfall Education, illus. 2005. (ENG.). 32p. (J). pap. (978-1-59577-023-3(2)) Starfall Education.

Kann, Victoria. Mother's Day Surprise. Kann, Victoria, illus. 2015. (Pinkalicious Ser.). (ENG., Illus.). 24p. (J). (gr. -1-3). pap. 6.99 (978-0-06-224587-8(2), HarperFestival) HarperCollins Pubs.

Kleinberg, Naomi. Elmo's Mommy. Womble, Louis, illus. 2012. (ENG.). 12p. (J). (gr. k-k). bds. 4.99 (978-0-307-92967-9(1), Random Hse. Bks. for Young Readers) Random Hse. Children's Bks.

Knudsen, Michelle. Mother's Day Ribbons. Wallace, John, illus. 2005. (ENG.). 12p. (J). bds. 6.99 (978-0-689-86381-3(0), Little Simon) Little Simon.

Lampson, Rosalie. Give Mom a Minute. 2009. 32p. pap. 13.99 (978-1-4490-1407-0(0)) AuthorHouse.

Manushkin, Fran. Katie Woo Tries Something New. Lyon, Tammie, illus. 2015. (Katie Woo Ser.). (ENG.). 96p. (gr. k-2). pap. 4.95 (978-1-4795-6182-7(7)) Picture Window Bks.

—Katie's Happy Mother's Day. Lyon, Tammie, illus. 2015. (Katie Woo Ser.). (ENG.). 32p. (gr. k-2). 21.32 (978-1-4795-6179-7(7)) Picture Window Bks.

May, Eleanor. The Best Mother's Day Ever. Pilz, M. H., illus. 2010. (Social Studies Connects Ser.). 32p. (J). (gr. 1-3). pap. 5.95 (978-1-57565-299-3(4)) Kane Press, Inc.

McClatchy, Lisa. Eloise's Mother's Day Surprise. Lyon, Tammie, illus. 2009. (Eloise Ser.). (ENG.). 32p. (J). (gr. -1-1). pap. 3.99 (978-1-4169-7889-3(5), Simon Spotlight) Simon Spotlight.

McDonald, Kirsten. The Yummy Mistake. Meza, Erika, illus. 2016. (ENG.). 32p. (J). (978-1-62402-145-9(X)) Magic Wagon.

O'Connor, Jane. Fancy Nancy's Marvelous Mother's Day Brunch. Glasser, Robin Preiss, illus. 2011. (Fancy Nancy Ser.). (ENG.). 16p. (J). (gr. -1-3). pap. 6.99 (978-0-06-170380-5(X), HarperFestival) HarperCollins Pubs.

Pratt, Laura. La Fête des Mères: Les Célébrations Canadiennes. Karvonen, Tanjah, tr. from ENG. 2011. (FRE.). 24p. (gr. k-3). (978-1-77071-398-7(0)) Weigl Educational Pubs. Ltd.

Remkiewicz, Frank. Gus Makes a Gift. 2012. (Scholastic Reader Pre-Level 1 Ser.). (ENG., Illus.). 24p. (J). (gr. k-1). pap. 3.99 (978-0-545-24469-5(2), Cartwheel Bks.) Scholastic, Inc.

Ricci, Christine. I Love My Abuela! Miller, Victoria, illus. 2009. (Dora the Explorer Ser.: 28). (ENG.). 24p. (J). pap. 3.99 (978-1-4169-6866-5(0), Simon Spotlight/Nickelodeon) Simon Spotlight/Nickelodeon.

Rylant, Cynthia. Henry & Mudge & the Funny Lunch. Bracken, Carolyn, illus. 2005. (Henry & Mudge Ready-To-Read Ser.: 24). 40p. (gr. k-2). lib. bdg. 13.55 (978-1-4176-7107-6(6), Turtleback) Turtleback Bks.

Schiffer, Miriam B. Stella Brings the Family. Clifton-Brown, Holly, illus. 2015. (ENG.). 36p. (J). (gr. k-3). 16.99 (978-1-4521-1190-2(1)) Chronicle Bks. LLC.

Seif Simpson, Martha. What NOT to Give Your Mom on Mother's Day, 0 vols. 2013. (ENG.). 24p. (J). (gr. -1-2). 12.99 (978-1-4778-1647-9(X), 9781477816479, Amazon Children's Publishing) Amazon Publishing.

Spinelli, Eileen. I Like Noisy, Mom Likes Quiet. Halverson, Lydia, illus. 2006. (ENG.). 32p. (J). (gr. -1-3). 8.95 (978-0-8249-5517-5(X), 1256103, Ideal Pubns.) Worthy Publishing.

Stone Arch Books. Mother's Day & Father's Day, 1 vol. Nguyen, Dustin, illus. 2014. (Batman: Li'l Gotham Ser.). (ENG.). 32p. (gr. 2-3). 22.60 (978-1-4342-9221-6(5)) Stone Arch Bks.

Temple, Bob. The Day Mom Finally Snapped, 1 vol. Harpster, Steve, illus. 2006. (Graphic Sparks Ser.). (ENG.). 40p. (gr. 1-3). 23.99 (978-1-59889-038-9(7), Graphic Sparks) Stone Arch Bks.

Warne. A Present for Mom. 2015. (Peter Rabbit Animation Ser.). (ENG., Illus.). 32p. (J). (gr. -1-k). 3.99 (978-0-7232-9568-6(9), Warne) Penguin Young Readers Group.

Weninger, Brigitte & Tharlet, Eve. Davy Loves His Mommy. 2014. (ENG., Illus.). 32p. (J). (gr. k-3). 15.95 (978-0-7358-4164-2(0)) North-South Bks., Inc.

Wiseman, Blaine. La Fête des Pères: Les Célébrations Canadiennes. Karvonen, Tanjah, tr. from ENG. 2011. (FRE.). 24p. (gr. k-3). (978-1-77071-396-3(4)) Weigl Educational Pubs. Ltd.

MOTHS

see also Butterflies; Caterpillars; Silkworms

Adams, Alison. Butterflies & Moths. 2011. (Early Connections Ser.). (J). (978-1-61672-629-4(6)) Benchmark Education Co.

Bishop, Nic. Butterflies & Moths. Bishop, Nic, photos by. 2009. (Nic Bishop Ser.). (ENG., Illus.). 48p. (J). (gr. -1-3). 17.99 (978-0-439-87757-2(1)) Scholastic, Inc.

Bodden, Valerie. Creepy Creatures: Moths. 2014. (Creepy Creatures Ser.). (ENG.). 24p. (J). (gr. 1-3). pap. 7.99 (978-0-89812-937-3(0), Creative Paperbacks) Creative Co., The.

—Moths. 2014. (J). (978-1-60818-358-6(0), Creative Education) Creative Co., The.

Braun, Eric. Lookin' for Light: Science Adventures with Manny the Origami Moth, 1 vol. Christoph, Jamey, illus. 2014. (Origami Science Adventures Ser.). (ENG.). 24p. (gr. 3-4). lib. bdg. 27.32 (978-1-4795-2186-9(8)) Picture Window Bks.

Carr, Aaron. Moths. 2014. (J). (978-1-4896-1044-7(8)); (978-1-4896-1042-3(1)) Weigl Pubs., Inc.

Coleman, Miriam. Moths Drink Tears!, 1 vol., 1. 2014. (Disgusting Animal Dinners Ser.). (ENG.). 24p. (J). (gr. k-5). 23.60 (978-1-4777-2883-3(X), PowerKids Pr.) Rosen Publishing Group, Inc., The.

Dorling Kindersley Publishing Staff. Butterfly & Moth. 2012. (DK Eyewitness Bks.). (ENG., Illus.). 72p. (J). (gr. 3-7). 16.99 (978-0-7566-9298-8(9), DK Children) Dorling Kindersley Publishing, Inc.

Farndon, John. Butterflies & Moths: A Comprehensive Guide to the Brief But BrilliantLives of These Fascinating Creatures, With over 200 Pictures. 2015. (ENG., Illus.). 64p. (J). (gr. -1-k). 12.99 (978-1-86147-407-0(5), Armadillo) Anness Publishing GBR. Dist: National Bk. Network.

Helget, Nicole. Moths. 2007. (Bugbooks Ser.). (Illus.). 24p. (J). (gr. -1-3). lib. bdg. 24.25 (978-1-58341-543-6(2), Creative Education) Creative Co., The.

Herrington, Lisa M. Butterflies & Moths. 2015. (Rookie Read-About(tm) Science: What's the Difference? Ser.). (ENG., Illus.). 32p. (J). lib. bdg. 25.00 (978-0-531-21485-5(0), Children's Pr.) Scholastic Library Publishing.

Kralovansky, Susan. Moth or Butterfly?, 1 vol. 2014. (This or That? Ser.). (ENG.). 24p. (gr. 5-10). lib. bdg. 25.65 (978-1-62403-288-2(5), Super SandCastle) ABDO Publishing Co.

Lockwood, Sophie. Moths. 2007. (World of Insects Ser.). (ENG., Illus.). 40p. (J). (gr. 3-6). 31.36 (978-1-59296-824-4(4), 200977) Child's World, Inc., The.

Lundgren, Julie K. Butterflies & Moths. 2010. (ENG., Illus.). 24p. (gr. 1-4). pap. 8.95 (978-1-61590-547-8(2)) Rourke Educational Media.

Macken, JoAnn Early. The Life Cycle of a Moth. 2006. (Things with Wings Ser.). (Illus.). 24p. (gr. k-3). pap. 8.15 (978-0-8368-6391-8(7)); lib. bdg. 22.00 (978-0-8368-6384-0(4)) Stevens, Gareth Publishing LLLP. (Weekly Reader Leveled Readers).

Markle, Sandra. Luna Moths. 2008. pap. 52.95 (978-1-58013-283-1(9)) Lerner Publishing Group.

—Luna Moths: Masters of Change. 2008. (Insect World Ser.). (ENG., Illus.). 48p. (gr. 4-8). lib. bdg. 27.93 (978-0-8225-7302-9(4), Lerner Pubns.) Lerner Publishing Group.

Mitchell, Susan K. Biggest vs. Smallest Things with Wings. 2010. (Biggest vs. Smallest Animals Ser.). (Illus.). 24p. (J). 22.60 (978-0-7660-3578-2(6), Enslow Elementary) Enslow Pubs., Inc.

Moth. 2003. (J). 36.95 (978-0-8136-9268-5(7)); 38.95 (978-0-8136-4161-4(6)) Modern Curriculum Pr.

Orenstein, Ronald. Weird Butterflies & Moths. Marent, Thomas, photos by. 2016. (ENG., Illus.). 64p. (J). (gr. 5-8). pap. 9.95 (978-1-77085-814-5(8), 9781770858145) Firefly Bks., Ltd.

Reagan, Naomi. Butterflies & Moths: Represent & Interpret Data. 2014. (Rosen Common Core Math Readers Ser.). (ENG., Illus.). 24p. (J). (gr. 3-4). pap. 8.25 (978-1-4777-4901-2(2), Rosen Classroom) Rosen Publishing Group, Inc., The.

Rustad, Martha E. H. Magnificent Moths. 2017. (Bugs Are Beautiful! Ser.). (ENG., Illus.). 32p. (gr. 1-2). lib. bdg. 27.32 (978-1-5157-4499-3(X), Aplus Bks.) Capstone Press of Coughlan Cos.

Sajjad, Mohammad. Insecticide Resistance Management in Tomato Fruit Borer. 2011. 232p. pap. (978-3-8443-8248-8(8)) Lap Lambert Academic Publishing GmbH & Co. KG.

Schuh, Mari. Moths. 2014. (Illus.). 24p. (J). lib. bdg. 25.65 (978-1-62031-086-1(4), Bullfrog Bks.) Jump! Inc.

Silverman, Buffy. Can You Tell a Butterfly from a Moth? 2011. (Lightning Bolt Books (tm) — Animal Look-Alikes Ser.). (ENG.). 32p. (gr. k-2). pap. 7.95 (978-0-7613-7844-0(8)); (Illus.). lib. bdg. 26.60 (978-0-7613-6731-4(4)) Lerner Publishing Group.

—Can You Tell A Butterfly from A Moth? 2011. (Animal Look-Alikes Ser.). pap. 45.32 (978-0-7613-8383-3(2)) Lerner Publishing Group.

Stewart, Melissa. Butterfly or Moth? How Do You Know? 2011. (Which Animal Is Which? Ser.). (Illus.). 24p. (J). (gr. k-18). pap. 7.95 (978-1-59845-235-8(5), Enslow Elementary); lib. bdg. 22.60 (978-0-7660-3678-9(2)) Enslow Pubs., Inc.

Upgrade kit dsm-3 Butterflies&moths. (J). 2004. (978-1-59242-526-6(7)) 2003. (978-1-59242-409-2(0)) Delta Education, LLC.

MOTION

see also Force and Energy; Mechanics; Speed

Angliss, Sarah, et al. Hands-On Science: Forces & Motion. 2013. (Hands-On Science Ser.). (ENG., Illus.). 32p. (J). (gr. 2-5). pap. 7.99 (978-0-7534-6972-9(3), 9780753469729, Kingfisher) Roaring Brook Pr.

Ballard, Carol. Exploring Forces & Movement. 2008. (How Does Science Work? Ser.). (Illus.). 32p. (J). (gr. 3-7). lib. bdg. 26.50 (978-1-4042-4277-7(5)) Rosen Publishing Group, Inc., The.

Benchmark Education Company. Newton & His Laws (Teacher Guide) 2005. (978-1-4108-4670-9(9)) Benchmark Education Co.

—Objects in Motion (Teacher Guide) 2005. (978-1-4108-4663-1(6)) Benchmark Education Co.

—The Three Laws of Motion (Teacher Guide) 2005. (978-1-4108-4677-8(6)) Benchmark Education Co.

Benchmark Education Company, LLC Staff, compiled by. Bodies in Motion & Body Systems. 2005. spiral bd. 225.00 (978-1-4108-5824-5(3)) Benchmark Education Co.

—Forces & Motion. 2006. spiral bd. 330.00 (978-1-4108-7014-8(6)) 2006. (J). 178.00 (978-1-4108-7030-8(8)) 2005. (J). spiral bd. 265.00 (978-1-4108-5760-6(3)) Benchmark Education Co.

—Forces & Motion: Theme Set. 2006. (J). 183.00 (978-1-4108-7146-6(0)) Benchmark Education Co.

—Science Theme: Forces & Motion. 2005. spiral bd. 115.00 (978-1-4108-5312-7(8)) Benchmark Education Co.

Biskup, Agnieszka. The Gripping Truth about Forces & Motion. Lum, Bernice, illus. 2012. (LOL Physical Science Ser.). (ENG.). 32p. (gr. 3-4). pap. 47.70 (978-1-4296-9299-1(5), Fact Finders); pap. 8.10 (978-1-4296-9298-4(7)); lib. bdg. 27.32 (978-1-4296-8601-3(4)) Capstone Press of Coughlan Cos.

—The Powerful World of Energy with Max Axiom, Super Scientist, 1 vol. 2009. (Graphic Science Ser.). (ENG.). 32p. (gr. 3-4). pap. 8.10 (978-1-4296-3450-2(2), Graphic Library) Capstone Press of Coughlan Cos.

—Super Cool Forces & Motion Activities with Max Axiom. Baez, Marcelo, illus. 2015. (Max Axiom Science & Engineering Activities Ser.). (ENG.). 32p. (gr. 3-4). lib. bdg. 30.65 (978-1-4914-2079-9(0), Graphic Library) Capstone Press of Coughlan Cos.

Blanche, Lynn. What Makes It Go? 2005. (IOpeners Ser.). (Illus.). 8p. (J). pap. 7.56 (978-0-7652-5138-1(8)) Celebration Pr.

Bonnet, Robert L. & Keen, Dan. Home Run! Science Projects with Baseball & Softball. 2009. (Score! Sports Science Projects Ser.). (Illus.). 104p. (J). (gr. 5-9). lib. bdg. 33.27 (978-0-7660-3365-8(1)) Enslow Pubs., Inc.

Boothroyd, Jennifer. Give it A Push! Give it A Pull! 2010. pap. 45.32 (978-0-7613-6931-8(7)) Lerner Publishing Group.

—Give It a Push! Give It a Pull! A Look at Forces. 2010. (Lightning Bolt Books (tm) — Exploring Physical Science Ser.). (ENG., Illus.). 32p. (gr. k-2). lib. bdg. 26.60 (978-0-7613-5431-4(X)) Lerner Publishing Group.

—Many Ways to Move. 2010. pap. 45.32 (978-0-7613-6932-5(5)) Lerner Publishing Group.

—Many Ways to Move: A Look at Motion. 2010. (Lightning Bolt Books (tm) — Exploring Physical Science Ser.). (ENG.). 32p. (gr. k-2). pap. 7.95 (978-0-7613-6060-5(3)); (Illus.). lib. bdg. 26.60 (978-0-7613-5434-5(4)) Lerner Publishing Group.

Bortz, Fred. Laws of Motion & Isaac Newton. 2013. (Revolutionary Discoveries of Scientific Pioneers Ser.). (Illus.). 80p. (J). (gr. 7-12). 33.25 (978-1-4777-1808-7(7)) Rosen Publishing Group, Inc., The.

Brannon, Barbara. Discover Motion. 2005. (J). pap. (978-1-4108-5126-0(5)) Benchmark Education Co.

—Discover the Laws of Motion. 2005. (J). pap. (978-1-4108-5128-4(1)) Benchmark Education Co.

Bug, Amy L. Forces & Motion. 2008. (Physics in Action Ser.). 134p. (YA). (gr. 9-12). 35.00 (978-0-7910-8931-6(2)) Facts On File, Inc.

Carlson Berne, Emma. Speeding! Mechanical Energy. 2013. (Energy Everywhere Ser.). (ENG., Illus.). 24p. (J). (gr. 3-6). 22.60 (978-1-4488-9651-6(7)); pap. 8.25 (978-1-4488-9760-5(2)) Rosen Publishing Group, Inc., The. (PowerKids Pr.).

Chiang, Mona. Isaac Newton & His Laws of Motion: Text Pairs. 2008. (Bridges/Navigators Ser.). (J). (gr. 6). 94.00 (978-1-4108-8442-8(2)) Benchmark Education Co.

Claybourne, Anna. Forces & Motion. 2016. (Mind Webs Ser.). (ENG., Illus.). 32p. (J). (gr. 4-6). pap. 11.99 (978-0-7502-8983-2(X), Wayland) Hachette Children's Group GBR. Dist: Hachette Bk. Group.

—Pushes & Pulls. 2012. (Illus.). 24p. (gr. k-4). pap. 7.95 (978-1-926853-59-8(8)) Saunders Bk. Co. CAN. Dist: RiverStream Publishing.

Close, Edward. Force & Motion, 1 vol., 1. 2014. (Discovery Education: How It Works). (ENG.). 32p. (gr. 3-6). 26.25 (978-1-4777-6317-9(1), PowerKids Pr.) Rosen Publishing Group, Inc., The.

Cobb, Vicki. Whirlers & Twirlers: Science Fun with Spinning. Haefele, Steve, illus. 2007. (Science Fun with Vicki Cobb Ser.). (J). (gr. 4-7). per. 7.95 (978-0-8225-7025-7(4), First Avenue Editions) Lerner Publishing Group.

Dicker, Katie. Forces & Motion. 2010. (Sherlock Bones Looks at Physical Science Ser.). (ENG.). 32p. (YA). (gr. 3-6). lib. bdg. 25.25 (978-1-61533-211-3(1)) Windmill Bks.

Duke, Shirley. Forces & Motion at Work. 2011. (ENG., Illus.). 48p. (gr. 4-6). pap. 10.95 (978-1-61741-990-4(7)) Rourke Educational Media.

Evans Ogden, Lesley J. Forces & Motion. 2011. (J). (gr. 4-6). pap. 12.95 (978-1-61690-733-4(9), AV2 by Weigl); (Illus.). 24p. (gr. 3-6). 27.13 (978-1-61690-729-7(0)) Weigl Pubs., Inc.

—Studying Forces & Motion. 2016. (Illus.). 24p. (J). (978-1-5105-1124-8(5)) SmartBook Media, Inc.

Ferrie, Chris. Newtonian Physics for Babies. 2017. (Baby University Ser.: 0). (ENG., Illus.). 24p. (J). bds. 9.99 **(978-1-4926-5620-3(8)**, Sourcebooks Jabberwocky) Sourcebooks, Inc.

Fiedler, Julie. Learning about Force & Motion with Graphic Organizers. 2007. (Graphic Organizers in Science Ser.: Vol. 3). (ENG., Illus.). 24p. (J). (gr. 3-7). lib. bdg. 22.60 (978-1-4042-3410-9(1)) Rosen Publishing Group, Inc., The.

Frisch-Schmoll, Joy. Motion & Movement. 2008. (Simple Science Ser.). (Illus.). 24p. (J). (gr. -1). lib. bdg. 24.25 (978-1-58341-578-8(5), Creative Education) Creative Co., The.

Frost, Adriana. Making Things Move: Force & Motion. 2013. (InfoMax Readers Ser.). (ENG.). 24p. (J). (gr. 2-3). pap. 49.50 (978-1-4777-2336-4(6)); (Illus.). pap. 8.25 (978-1-4777-2335-7(8)) Rosen Publishing Group, Inc., The. (Rosen Classroom).

Funk, Tara. Newton & His Laws. 2005. (J). pap. (978-1-4108-4622-8(9)) Benchmark Education Co.

—Objects in Motion. 2005. (J). pap. (978-1-4108-4615-0(6)) Benchmark Education Co.

—The Three Laws of Motion. 2005. (J). pap. (978-1-4108-4629-7(6)) Benchmark Education Co.

Gardner, Robert. The Physics of Sports Science Projects. 2013. (Exploring Hands-On Science Projects Ser.). 128p. (J). (gr. 5-12). pap. 10.95 (978-1-4644-0222-7(1)); lib. bdg. 27.94 (978-0-7660-4146-2(8)) Enslow Pubs., Inc.

Gianopoulos, Andrea & Barnett, Charles, III. Isaac Newton & the Laws of Motion, 1 vol. Miller, Phil, illus. 2007. (Inventions & Discovery Ser.). (ENG.). 32p. (gr. 3-4). pap. 8.10 (978-0-7368-7899-9(8), 1264949, Graphic Library) Capstone Press of Coughlan Cos.

Gianopoulos, Andrea & Barnett III, Charles. Isaac Newton & the Laws of Motion [Scholastic]. Miller, Phil, illus. 2010. (Inventions & Discovery Ser.). 32p. pap. 0.45 *(978-1-4296-5969-7(6),* Capstone Interactive Library) Capstone Digital.

Glass, Maya. The Jumping Book. 2004. (Let's Get Moving Ser.). (Illus.). 24p. (J). (gr. k-1). lib. bdg. 22.60 *(978-1-4042-2513-8(7),* Editorial Buenas Letras) Rosen Publishing Group, Inc., The.

—The Jumping Book/Saltar. Brusca, Maria Cristina, tr. from ENG. 2004. (Let's Get Moving / Diviértete en Movimiento Ser.). (ENG & SPA., Illus.). 24p. (J). (gr. k-1). lib. bdg. 22.60 *(978-1-4042-7513-3(4),* Editorial Buenas Letras) Rosen Publishing Group, Inc., The.

Goodstein, Madeline P. Goal! Science Projects with Soccer. 2009. (Score! Sports Science Projects Ser.). (Illus.). 104p. (J). (gr. 5-9). lib. bdg. 33.27 *(978-0-7660-3106-7(3))* Enslow Pubs., Inc.

Graham, Stella. Forces & Motion at the Playground. 2009. (Real Life Readers Ser.). 16p. (gr. 2-3). pap. 7.05 *(978-1-4358-0057-1(5),* Rosen Classroom) Rosen Publishing Group, Inc., The.

Gray, Leon. Forces & Motion. 2013. (Physical Science Ser.). 48p. (J). (gr. 4-6). pap. 84.30 *(978-1-4339-9506-4(9));* pap. 14.05 *(978-1-4339-9505-7(0));* (ENG., Illus.). lib. bdg. 31.95 *(978-1-4339-9504-0(2))* Stevens, Gareth Publishing LLLP.

Gray, Susan H. Experiments with Motion. 2011. (True Bk Ser.). (ENG., Illus.). 48p. (J). pap. 6.95 *(978-0-531-26646-5(X));* lib. bdg. 29.00 *(978-0-531-26346-4(0))* Scholastic Library Publishing. (Children's Pr.).

Grudzina, Rebecca. Motion. 2017. (Text Connections Guided Close Reading Ser.). (J). (gr. k). *(978-1-4900-1763-1(1))* Benchmark Education Co.

Haber-Schaim, Uri, et al. Force, Motion, & Energy Assessment Package. 2003. pap. *(978-1-882057-15-3(5),* SCI-777-3393) Science Curriculum, Inc.

Hewitt, Sally. Amazing Forces & Movement. 2007. (Amazing Science Ser.). (ENG.). 32p. (J). pap. *(978-0-7787-3625-7(3))* Crabtree Publishing Co.

—Forces & Motion. (Illus.). 32p. (YA). (gr. 2-18). lib. bdg. 27.10 *(978-1-932333-32-9(0))* Chrysalis Education.

Higgins, Nadia. Marvelous Motion, 1 vol. Ricci, Andres Martinez, illus. 2008. (Science Rocks Ser.). (ENG.). 32p. (gr. -1-4). 28.50 *(978-1-60270-278-3(0),* 1287326, Looking Glass Library- Nonfiction) Magic Wagon.

—Marvelous Motion CD+Book. Martinez Ricci, Andres, illus. 2010. (Science Rocks! Set 2 CD+Book Ser.). 32p. lib. bdg. 54.14 incl. cd-rom *(978-1-60270-993-5(9))* ABDO Publishing Co.

—Marvelous Motion Site CD+Book. Martinez Ricci, Andres, illus. 2010. (Science Rocks! Set 2 Site CD+Book Ser.). 32p. lib. bdg. 84.14 incl. cd-rom *(978-1-61641-010-0(8))* ABDO Publishing Co.

Hirsch, Rebecca. Science Lab: Motion & Forces. 2011. (Explorer Library: Language Arts Explorer Ser.). (ENG.). 32p. (gr. 4-8). 28.50 *(978-1-61080-205-5(5),* 201186); pap. 14.21 *(978-1-61080-294-9(2),* 201216) Cherry Lake Publishing.

Hoffmann, Sara. Going from Here to There. 2012. (First Step Nonfiction - Balance & Motion Ser.). (ENG., Illus.). 8p. (gr. -1-1). pap. 4.95 *(978-1-4677-0516-5(0),* Lerner Pubns.) Lerner Publishing Group.

—Spinning. 2012. (First Step Nonfiction - Balance & Motion Ser.). (ENG., Illus.). 8p. (gr. -1-1). pap. 4.95 *(978-1-4677-0513-4(6),* Lerner Pubns.) Lerner Publishing Group.

Holt, Rinehart and Winston Staff. Holt Science & Technology Chapter 5: Physical Science: Matter in Motion. 5th ed. 2004. (Illus.). pap. 12.86 *(978-0-03-030376-0(1))* Holt McDougal.

Holzweiss, Kristina. Amazing Makerspace DIY Movers. 2017. (True Book — MakerSpace Projects Ser.). (ENG.). 48p. (J). lib. bdg. 31.00 ***(978-0-531-23847-9(4),*** Children's Pr.) Scholastic Library Publishing.

Housel, Debra J. Motion, 1 vol. rev. ed. 2014. (Science Readers: Content & Literacy Ser.). (ENG.). 32p. (gr. 2-2). pap. 8.99 *(978-1-4807-4607-7(X))* Teacher Created Materials, Inc.

Hyde, Natalie. Changing Direction. 2014. (ENG., Illus.). 24p. (J). *(978-0-7787-0528-4(5))* Crabtree Publishing Co.

—Pushing & Pulling. 2014. (ENG., Illus.). 24p. (J). *(978-0-7787-0529-1(3))* Crabtree Publishing Co.

—What Is Motion? 2014. (ENG., Illus.). 24p. (J). *(978-0-7787-0527-7(7))* Crabtree Publishing Co.

Ives, Rob. Fun Experiments with Forces & Motion: Hovercrafts, Rockets, & More. Sassin, Eva, illus. 2017. (Amazing Science Experiments Ser.). (ENG.). (J). (gr. 3-6). lib. bdg. 26.65 ***(978-1-5124-3217-6(2))*** Lerner Publishing Group.

Jonath, Leslie & Nash, Josh. On the Go. 2010. (ENG., Illus.). 12p. (J). (gr. -1). 9.99 *(978-0-7407-9800-9(6))* Andrews McMeel Publishing.

Jones, Tammy. I Go! 2009. (Sight Word Readers Set A Ser.). (J). 3.49 net. *(978-1-60719-143-8(1))* Newmark Learning LLC.

Juettner, Bonnie. Motion. 2004. (KidHaven Science Library). (ENG., Illus.). 48p. (J). (gr. 4-7). 27.50 *(978-0-7377-1536-1(7),* Greenhaven Pr., Inc.) Cengage Gale.

Kelley, Jennifer. Ways Things Move. 2006. (Science Leveled Readers Ser.). (ENG., Illus.). 8p. (gr. k-k). pap. 5.40 *(978-0-15-365319-3(1))* Harcourt Schl. Pubs.

Kelly, Lynne. Simple Concepts in Physics: Motion. (Illus.). (J). (gr. 3-6). pap. *(978-1-875739-35-6(1))* Wizard Bks.

Kenney, Karen Latchana. The Science of Race Cars: Studying Forces & Motion, 1 vol. 2016. (Science in Action Ser.). (ENG., Illus.). 32p. (J). (gr. 3-6). 27.07 *(978-1-62403-963-8(4))* ABDO Publishing Co.

Kook, Ima. Newton's Laws: They Tell How Things Move. 2008. (Illus.). 24p. (J). pap. 12.00 *(978-1-892298-24-9(4))* Abique Pub.

Kuskowski, Alex. Science Experiments with Gravity & Motion, 1 vol. 2013. (More Super Simple Science Ser.). (ENG.). 32p. (gr. k-4). lib. bdg. 27.07 *(978-1-61783-850-7(0),* Super SandCastle) ABDO Publishing Co.

Lawrence, Debbie & Lawrence, Richard. Machines & Motion: God's Design for the Physical World. 2005. (Illus.). 160p. per. *(978-0-9725365-9-2(0))* Boarding House Publishing.

Lawrence, Ellen. Motion. 2013. (Science Slam: FUN-Damental Experiments Ser.). 24p. (J). (gr. -1-3). lib. bdg. 23.93 *(978-1-61772-739-9(3))* Bearport Publishing Co., Inc.

Llewellyn, Claire. And Everyone Shouted, Pull! A First Look at Forces & Motion. Abel, Simone, illus. 2004. (First Look: Science Ser.). (ENG.). 32p. (gr. -1-2). 26.65 *(978-1-4048-0656-6(3))* Picture Window Bks.

—Forces & Movement. 2010. (Start-Up Connections Ser.). (ENG., Illus.). 24p. (J). (gr. 2-4). pap. 14.99 *(978-0-237-54172-9(6))* Evans Brothers, Ltd. GBR. Dist: Independent Pubs. Group.

Macken, JoAnn Early. Toys. 2010. (Everyday Science Ser.). 24p. (J). (gr. k-3). 25.65 *(978-1-60753-017-6(1))* Amicus Publishing.

Manolis, Kay. Motion. 2008. (First Science Ser.). (ENG., Illus.). 24p. (J). (gr. 2-5). lib. bdg. 25.95 *(978-1-60014-225-3(7))* Bellwether Media.

—Motion. 2011. (Blastoff! Readers Ser.). 24p. (J). pap. 5.95 *(978-0-531-28458-2(1),* Children's Pr.) Scholastic Library Publishing.

Marsico, Katie. Key Discoveries in Physical Science. 2015. (Science Discovery Timelines Ser.). (ENG., Illus.). 48p. (J). (gr. 6-8). pap. 8.99 *(978-1-4677-6160-4(5));* lib. bdg. 30.65 *(978-1-4677-5785-0(3))* Lerner Publishing Group. (Lerner Pubns.).

Mason, Adrienne. Move It! Motion, Forces & You. Dávila, Claudia, illus. 2005. (Primary Physical Science Ser.). (ENG.). 32p. (J). (gr. -1-2). pap. 7.95 *(978-1-55337-759-7(1))* Kids Can Pr., Ltd. CAN. Dist: Hachette Bk. Group.

McNeilly, Linden. What's Your Potential? The Energy of Motion. 2016. (Let's Explore Science Ser.). (ENG., Illus.). 48p. (gr. 5-8). 35.64 *(978-1-68191-394-0(1))* Rourke Educational Media.

Monroe, Tilda. What Do You Know about Forces & Motion? 2010. (20 Questions: Physical Science Ser.). (ENG.). 24p. (J). pap. 8.25 *(978-1-4488-1254-7(2),* PowerKids Pr.); (gr. 2-5). lib. bdg. 22.60 *(978-1-4488-0673-7(9))* Rosen Publishing Group, Inc., The.

Motion & Force: Integrated Physics & Chemistry / Algebra I Instructional Unit. 2003. (Region IV ESC Resources for Mathematics & Science Ser.). stu. ed., per. *(978-1-932524-69-7(X))* Region IV Education Service Ctr.

Motion & Forces. 2011. (Science Made Simple Ser.). (ENG.). 64p. (YA). pap. 12.95 *(978-1-4488-2240-9(8))* Rosen Publishing Group, Inc., The.

Murphy, Brian. Movement. 2004. (Experiment with Ser.). (SPA., Illus.). 32p. (J). (gr. 2-5). 9.95 *(978-1-58728-248-5(8),* Two-Can Publishing) T&N Children's Publishing.

Murray, Julie. Motion, 1 vol. 2006. (First Science - 12 Titles Ser.). (ENG., Illus.). 24p. (gr. k-4). 25.65 *(978-1-59679-829-8(7),* Buddy Bks.) ABDO Publishing Co.

Nelson, Robin. Cómo Se Mueven Las Cosas. Translations.com Staff, tr. from ENG. 2007. (Mi Primer Paso Al Mundo Real - Fuerzas y Movimiento (First Step Nonfiction - Forces & Motion) Ser.). (SPA., Illus.). 24p. (gr. k-2). lib. bdg. 23.93 *(978-0-8225-7811-6(5),* Ediciones Lerner) Lerner Publishing Group.

—Ways Things Move. (Forces & Motion Ser.). (Illus.). (J). 2005. 22p. pap. 5.95 *(978-0-8225-5300-7(7))* 2004. 24p. lib. bdg. 18.60 *(978-0-8225-5136-2(5))* Lerner Publishing Group.

Newton, Joan. Gravity in Action: Roller Coasters! 2009. (Real Life Readers Ser.). 24p. (gr. 3-4). pap. 8.25 *(978-1-4358-0008-3(7),* Rosen Classroom); (J). (gr. 2-5). lib. bdg. 22.60 *(978-1-4358-2976-3(X),* PowerKids Pr.) Rosen Publishing Group, Inc., The.

Nsrc. Science & Technology for Children Books: Motion & Design. 2004. (Illus.). 64p. (J). *(978-1-933008-03-5(2))* Smithsonian Science Education Ctr. (SSEC).

O'Donnell, Kerri. Sir Isaac Newton: Using the Laws of Motion to Solve Problems. (Math for the Real World Ser.). 32p. 2009. (ENG., Illus.). (gr. 6-7). pap. 10.00 *(978-1-4042-6079-5(X))* 2009. (gr. 5-5). 47.90 *(978-1-60851-366-6(1),* PowerKids Pr.) 2006. (Illus.). (YA). (gr. 5-9). lib. bdg. 25.25 *(978-1-4042-3363-8(6))* Rosen Publishing Group, Inc., The.

O'Leary, Denyse. What Are Newton's Laws of Motion? 2010. (Shaping Modern Science Ser.). (ENG.). 64p. (J). (gr. 5-8). pap. *(978-0-7787-7207-1(1))* Crabtree Publishing Co.

Orr, Tamra. Motion & Forces. 2011. (Science Made Simple Ser.). (Illus.). 64p. (YA). (gr. 5-8). lib. bdg. 31.95 *(978-1-4488-1232-5(1))* Rosen Publishing Group, Inc., The.

Oxlade, Chris. Forces & Motion: An Investigation. 2008. (Science Investigations Ser.). (Illus.). 32p. (YA). (gr. 4-7). lib. bdg. 26.50 *(978-1-4042-4283-8(X))* Rosen Publishing Group, Inc., The.

—Simple Experiments with Inclined Planes. 2013. (Science Experiments with Simple Machines Ser.). 32p. (J). (gr. k-3). 26.50 *(978-1-61533-752-1(0));* pap. 70.50 *(978-1-61533-822-1(5));* pap. 11.75 *(978-1-61533-821-4(7))* Windmill Bks.

Pamplona, Alberto Hernández. A Visual Guide to Energy & Movement. 2017. (Visual Exploration of Science Ser.). 96p. (J). (gr. 12-13). 37.10 ***(978-1-5081-7582-7(9),*** Rosen Young Adult) Rosen Publishing Group, Inc., The.

Petersen, Kristen. Understanding the Laws of Motion. 2015. (J). lib. bdg. *(978-1-62713-427-9(1))* Cavendish Square Publishing.

Peterson, Megan Cooley. Scooby-Doo! a Science of Forces & Motion Mystery: The Rogue Robot. 2016. (Scooby-Doo Solves It with S. T. E. M. Ser.). (ENG., Illus.). 32p. (gr. 3-4). 27.99 *(978-1-5157-2590-9(1))* Capstone Press of Coughlan Cos.

Phelan, Glen. Forces & Motion in Sports: Set Of 6. 2011. (Navigators Ser.). (J). pap. 50.00 net. *(978-1-4108-5088-1(9))* Benchmark Education Co.

—Forces & Motion on Earth: Set Of 6. 2011. (Navigators Ser.). (J). pap. 50.00 net. *(978-1-4108-5087-4(0))* Benchmark Education Co.

—Introduction to Energy. 2007. (Nonfiction Reading & Writing Workshops Ser.). (ENG., Illus.). 32p. (J). pap. 17.95 *(978-0-7922-4580-3(6))* CENGAGE Learning.

—Invisible Force: The Quest to Define the Laws of Motion. 2006. (Science Quest Ser.). (ENG., Illus.). 64p. (J). (gr. 5-9). 17.95 *(978-0-7922-5539-0(9),* National Geographic Children's Bks.) National Geographic Society.

—Newton's Laws. 2007. (Reading Expeditions Ser.). (ENG., Illus.). 32p. (J). pap. 17.95 *(978-0-7922-4584-1(9))* CENGAGE Learning.

Rand, Casey. Forces & Motion. 2016. (Sci-Hi: Physical Science Ser.). (ENG.). 48p. (gr. 4-4). pap. 8.99 *(978-1-4109-8633-7(0),* Sci-Hi) Heinemann-Raintree.

Rowell, Rebecca. Forces & Motion Through Infographics. Dean, Venitia, illus. 2013. (Super Science Infographics Ser.). (ENG.). 32p. (gr. 3-5). (J). lib. bdg. 26.60 *(978-1-4677-1291-0(4),* Lerner Pubns.); pap. 8.95 *(978-1-4677-1591-1(3))* Lerner Publishing Group.

Royston, Angela. Forces: Pushes & Pulls. 2012. (Science Corner Ser.). (Illus.). 24p. (J). (gr. 1-4). lib. bdg. 22.60 *(978-1-4488-5292-5(7))* Rosen Publishing Group, Inc., The.

—Looking at Forces & Motion: How Do Things Move? 2008. (Looking at Science: How Things Change Ser.). (Illus.). 32p. (J). (gr. 3-7). lib. bdg. 23.94 *(978-0-7660-3089-3(X),* Enslow Elementary) Enslow Pubs., Inc.

—Race That Bike! Forces in Vehicles. 2015. (Feel the Force Ser.). (ENG., Illus.). 48p. (gr. 3-6). 33.32 *(978-1-4846-2599-6(4))* Heinemann-Raintree.

—Win That Sprint! Forces in Sport. 2015. (Feel the Force Ser.). (ENG., Illus.). 48p. (gr. 3-6). 33.32 *(978-1-4846-2597-2(8))* Heinemann-Raintree.

Science & Technology for Children Books, Motion & Design Set, 8 vols. 2004. (Illus.). 64p. (J). *(978-1-933008-15-8(6))* Smithsonian Science Education Ctr. (SSEC).

Science Stories Foss Spanish Balance & Motion EA CR05. 2005. (J). *(978-1-59242-582-2(8))* Delta Education, LLC.

Sheehan, Thomas F. Playground Science. 2005. (ENG.). 24p. (gr. k-3). pap. 8.95 *(978-1-62717-235-6(1))* Rourke Educational Media.

Silverman, Buffy. Pull It, Push It. 2012. (ENG.). 24p. (gr. 3-4). pap. 8.95 *(978-1-61810-229-4(X))* Rourke Educational Media.

Silverstein, Alvin, et al. Forces & Motion. 2008. (Science Concepts, Second Ser.). (ENG., Illus.). 112p. (gr. 6-8). lib. bdg. 31.93 *(978-0-8225-7514-6(0))* Lerner Publishing Group.

Sohn, Emily. Experiments in Forces & Motion with Toys & Everyday Stuff. 2015. (Fun Science Ser.). (ENG., Illus.). 24p. (gr. 1-2). lib. bdg. 25.32 *(978-1-4914-5032-1(0))* Capstone Press of Coughlan Cos.

Sohn, Emily & Brennan, Joseph. Balance & Motion: Toying with Gravity. 2011. (iScience Readers Ser.). 24p. (J). (gr. k-2). lib. bdg. 21.27 *(978-1-59953-405-3(3))* Norwood Hse. Pr.

Solway, Andrew. Exploring Forces & Motion. 2007. (Exploring Physical Science Ser.). (Illus.). 48p. (YA). (gr. 5-9). lib. bdg. 26.50 *(978-1-4042-3747-6(X))* Rosen Publishing Group, Inc., The.

Spilsbury, Richard & Spilsbury, Louise. What Are Forces & Motion? Exploring Science with Hands-on Activities. 2008. (In Touch with Basic Science Ser.). (Illus.). 32p. (J). (gr. 3-4). lib. bdg. 23.94 *(978-0-7660-3095-4(4),* Enslow Elementary) Enslow Pubs., Inc.

Stille, Darlene R. Motion: Push & Pull, Fast & Slow. Boyd, Sheree, tr. Boyd, Sheree, illus. 2004. (Amazing Science Ser.). (ENG.). 24p. (gr. k-4). 26.65 *(978-1-4048-0250-6(9))* Picture Window Bks.

—El Movimiento: Tira y Empuja, Rápido y Despacio. Robledo, Sol, tr. from ENG. Boyd, Sheree, illus. 2007. (Ciencia Asombrosa Ser.). (SPA.). 24p. (gr. k-4). lib. bdg. 26.65 *(978-1-4048-3222-0(X))* Picture Window Bks.

Sullivan, Laura L. What Is Motion? 2016. (Unseen Science Ser.). (ENG., Illus.). 32p. (J). (gr. 3-3). pap. 10.58 *(978-1-5026-0914-4(2))* Cavendish Square Publishing.

Troupe, Thomas Kingsley. Are Bowling Balls Bullies? Learning about Forces & Motion with the Garbage Gang. Toye, Derek, illus. 2015. (Garbage Gang's Super Science Questions Ser.). (ENG.). 24p. (gr. k-2). lib. bdg. 26.65 *(978-1-4795-7057-7(5))* Picture Window Bks.

Uttley, Colin. Experiments with Force & Motion. 2010. (Cool Science Ser.). (Illus.). 32p. (J). (gr. 5-6). pap. 10.50 *(978-1-4339-3460-5(4));* lib. bdg. 28.00 *(978-1-4339-3459-9(0),* 1309302) Stevens, Gareth Publishing LLLP. (Gareth Stevens Learning Library).

Wadsworth, Pamela. Golwg Gyntaf Ar Bethau'n Symud. 2005. (WEL., Illus.). 24p. pap. *(978-1-85596-252-1(7))* Dref Wen.

Waters, Jennifer. All Kinds of Motion, 1 vol. 2010. (Physical Science Ser.). (ENG.). 24p. (gr. k-1). lib. bdg. 26.65 *(978-1-4296-6607-7(2),* Pebble Plus) Capstone Press of Coughlan Cos.

Way, Jennifer. The Hopping Book. 2004. (Let's Get Moving Ser.). (Illus.). 24p. (J). (gr. k-1). lib. bdg. 22.60 *(978-1-4042-2514-5(5),* PowerKids Pr.) Rosen Publishing Group, Inc., The.

—The Hopping Book/Brincar en un Pie. Brusca, Maria Cristina, tr. from ENG. 2004. (Let's Get Moving / Diviértete en Movimiento Ser.). (ENG & SPA., Illus.). 24p. (J). (gr. k-1). lib. bdg. 22.60 *(978-1-4042-7514-0(2),* Powerstart Pr.) Rosen Publishing Group, Inc., The.

Weakland, Mark. Zombies & Forces & Motion, 1 vol. Gervasio, illus. 2011. (Monster Science Ser.). (ENG.). 32p. (gr. 3-4). lib. bdg. 30.65 *(978-1-4296-6577-3(7),* Graphic Library) Capstone Press of Coughlan Cos.

Weir, Jane. Investigating Forces & Motion, 1 vol. 2007. (Science Readers Ser.). (ENG.). 32p. (J). (gr. 4-4). pap. 8.99 *(978-0-7439-0573-2(3))* Shell Educational Publishing.

What Makes It Move? KinderFacts Individual Title Six-Packs. (Kinderstarters Ser.). 8p. (gr. -1-1). 21.00 *(978-0-7635-8755-0(9))* Rigby Education.

Whitehouse, Patty. Moving Machines. 2006. (Construction Forces Discovery Library). (Illus.). 24p. (J). (gr. k-2). lib. bdg. 22.79 *(978-1-60044-192-9(0))* Rourke Educational Media.

Whiting, Jim. The Science of Hitting a Home Run: Forces & Motion in Action. 2010. (Action Science Ser.). (ENG.). 32p. (gr. 3-4). pap. 47.70 *(978-1-4296-5076-2(1),* Fact Finders) Capstone Press of Coughlan Cos.

World Book, Inc Staff, contrib. by. Learning about Energy, Forces, & Motion. 2011. (J). *(978-0-7166-0233-0(4))* World Bk., Inc.

Zuravicky, Orli. The Galloping Book. 2004. (Let's Get Moving Ser.). (Illus.). 24p. (J). (gr. k-1). lib. bdg. 22.60 *(978-1-4042-2517-6(X),* PowerKids Pr.) Rosen Publishing Group, Inc., The.

—The Galloping Book/Trotar. De Leon, Mauricio Velzaquez, tr. from ENG. 2004. (Let's Get Moving / Diviértete en Movimiento Ser.). (ENG & SPA., Illus.). 24p. (J). (gr. k-1). lib. bdg. 22.60 *(978-1-4042-7517-1(7),* Editorial Buenas Letras) Rosen Publishing Group, Inc., The.

—The Skipping Book: Avanzar a Saltitos. Brusca, Maria C., tr. from ENG. 2004. (Let's Get Moving / Diviértete en Movimiento Ser.). (ENG & SPA., Illus.). 24p. (J). (gr. -1-1). lib. bdg. 22.60 *(978-1-4042-7515-7(0),* Powerstart Pr.) Rosen Publishing Group, Inc., The.

MOTION PICTURE CARTOONS

see Animated Films

MOTION PICTURE INDUSTRY

ABDO Publishing Company Staff. Essential Critiques Set 2, 1 vol. 2011. (Essential Critiques Set 2 Ser.: 8). (ENG., Illus.). 112p. (J). (gr. 6-12). lib. bdg. 285.12 *(978-1-61783-086-0(0),* Essential Library) ABDO Publishing Co.

Albert, Lisa Rondinelli. So You Want to Be a Film or TV Actor? 2008. (Careers in Film & Television Ser.). (Illus.). 128p. (J). (gr. 3-7). lib. bdg. 33.27 *(978-0-7660-2741-1(4))* Enslow Pubs., Inc.

Brown, Don. Mack Made Movies. Brown, Don, illus. 2008. (Illus.). (J). (gr. 2-5). 25.95 incl. audio compact disk *(978-1-4301-0432-2(5));* pap. 16.95 incl. audio *(978-1-4301-0431-5(7))* Live Oak Media.

Burgan, Michael. Ronald Reagan. 2011. 128p. pap. 14.99 *(978-0-7566-7739-8(4))* Dorling Kindersley Publishing, Inc.

Careers in Focus: Animation. 2010. (Careers in Focus Ser.). (Illus.). 208p. (J). (gr. 6-12). 32.95 *(978-0-8160-8015-1(1),* Ferguson Publishing Co.) Facts On File, Inc.

Cartlidge, Cherese. Leonardo Dicaprio. Gale, ed. 2011. (People in the News Ser.). (ENG.). 128p. (gr. 7-10). lib. bdg. 39.40 *(978-1-4205-0427-9(4),* Lucent Bks.) Cengage Gale.

Downing, Todd. Filmmaking. 2010. (Master This! Ser.). (ENG.). 32p. (J). lib. bdg. 25.25 *(978-1-61532-597-9(2),* PowerKids Pr.) Rosen Publishing Group, Inc., The.

Espejo, Roman. The Film Industry. 2009. (Opposing Viewpoints Ser.). (ENG., Illus.). (gr. 10-12). 224p. 48.80 *(978-0-7377-4364-7(6),* LML02109-245373); 240p. (YA). 29.45 *(978-0-7377-4363-0(8),* LML02109-245355) Cengage Gale. (Greenhaven Pr., Inc.).

Facts on File, Inc. Staff. Movies. 2012. (Discovering Careers Ser.). (Illus.). 112p. (gr. 4-9). 24.95 *(978-0-8160-8058-8(5),* Ferguson Publishing Co.) Facts On File, Inc.

Garza, Sarah. Action! Making Movies, 1 vol. 2nd rev. ed. 2013. (Nonfiction Readers Ser.). (ENG., Illus.). 64p. (J). (gr. 5-5). pap. 31.96 *(978-1-4333-7448-7(X))* Teacher Created Materials, Inc.

Gosling, Maureen, et al. You Can Be a Woman Movie Maker. l.t. ed. 2003. (Illus.). 80p. (J). 19.95 incl. DVD *(978-1-880599-64-8(3));* pap. 14.95 incl. DVD *(978-1-880599-63-1(5))* Cascade Pass, Inc.

Great Filmmakers. 2014. (Great Filmmakers Ser.). 80p. (YA). (gr. 8-11). 188.16 *(978-1-62713-134-6(5))* Cavendish Square Publishing.

Hahn, Don. The Alchemy of Animation: Making an Animated Film in the Modern Age. 3rd ed. 2008. (Disney Editions Deluxe (Film) Ser.). (ENG., Illus.). 144p. (YA). (gr. 5-9). pap. 19.99 *(978-1-4231-0476-6(5),* Disney Editions) Disney Pr.

Hammelef, Danielle S. Behind the Glamour. 2017. (Behind the Glamour Ser.). (ENG.). 64p. (gr. 4-5). 125.28 *(978-1-5157-4900-4(2))* Capstone Press of Coughlan Cos.

—Behind-The-Scenes Movie Careers. 2017. (Behind the Glamour Ser.). (ENG.). 64p. (gr. 4-5). lib. bdg. 31.32 *(978-1-5157-4899-1(5))* Capstone Press of Coughlan Cos.

Hindman, Susan. Working at a Movie Theater. 2011. (21st Century Junior Library: Careers Ser.). (ENG.). 24p. (gr. 2-5). lib. bdg. 25.64 *(978-1-60279-979-0(2),* 200948) Cherry Lake Publishing.

Johnson, Marlys H. Careers in the Movies. 2005. (Career Resource Library). (Illus.). 192p. (YA). (gr. 7-12). lib. bdg. 34.60 *(978-0-8239-3186-6(2))* Rosen Publishing Group, Inc., The.

Kennon, Michou. Queen Latifah. 2011. (Hip-Hop Headliners Ser.). (Illus.). 32p. (J). (gr. 3-8). lib. bdg. 25.25 *(978-1-4339-4808-4(7))* Stevens, Gareth Publishing LLLP.

Kushner, Jill Menkes. Johnny Depp: Movie Megastar. 2009. (Hot Celebrity Biographies Ser.). (Illus.). 48p. (J). (gr. 5-9). lib. bdg. 25.27 *(978-0-7660-3567-6(0))* Enslow Pubs., Inc.

Mapua, Jeff. Lana Wachowski. 2016. (Transgender Pioneers Ser.). 112p. (J). (gr. 6-6). 37.10 *(978-1-5081-7160-7(2))* Rosen Publishing Group, Inc., The.

Mullins, Matt. Special Effects Technician. 2011. (21st Century Skills Library: Cool Arts Careers Ser.). (ENG.). 32p. (gr. 4-8). lib. bdg. 28.50 *(978-1-61080-134-8(2),* 201146) Cherry Lake Publishing.

One Direction Staff. One Direction: Meet One Direction. 2013. (Illus.). 64p. (J). (gr. 3-7). pap. 10.99 *(978-0-06-228362-7(6))* HarperCollins Pubs.

Rauf, Don & Vescia, Monique. Hollywood. 2016. (Bright Futures Press: Choose Your Own Career Adventure Ser.). (ENG., Illus.). 32p. (J). (gr. 4-6). 29.93 *(978-1-63471-911-7(5),* 208965) Cherry Lake Publishing.

Scholastic, Inc. Staff. The Hunger Games Official Illustrated Movie Companion. 2012. (Illus.). 158p. (YA). lib. bdg. 31.80 *(978-0-606-23704-8(6),* Turtleback) Turtleback Bks.

Schuman, Michael A. Halle Berry: A Biography of an Oscar-Winning Actress. 2013. (African-American Icons Ser.). 104p. (J). (gr. 6-12). pap. 10.95 *(978-1-59845-396-6(3))* Enslow Pubs., Inc.

Skogen, Jenny. Film. 2014. (Urban Entrepreneurs Ser.). (gr. 3-8). pap. 8.99 *(978-1-61570-872-7(3))* Scobre Pr. Corp.

Spinner, Stephanie. Who Is Steven Spielberg? Mather, Daniel & Harrison, Nancy, illus. 2013. (Who Was? Ser.). (ENG.). 112p. (J). (gr. 3-7). 5.99 *(978-0-448-47935-4(4),* Grosset & Dunlap) Penguin Young Readers Group.

Svitil, Torene & Dunkleburger, Amy. So You Want to Work in Set Design, Costuming, or Make-Up? 2008. (Careers in Film & Television Ser.). (Illus.). 128p. (J). (gr. 6-9). lib. bdg. 33.27 *(978-0-7660-2740-4(6))* Enslow Pubs., Inc.

Vander Hook, Sue. Steven Spielberg: Groundbreaking Director, 1 vol. 2009. (Essential Lives Set 4 Ser.). (ENG., Illus.). 112p. (J). (gr. 6-12). lib. bdg. 35.64 *(978-1-60453-704-8(3))* ABDO Publishing Co.

Zannos, Susan. Ron Howard. l.t. ed. 2003. (Billboard Biography Ser.). (Illus.). 32p. (J). (gr. 3-8). lib. bdg. 25.70 *(978-1-58415-185-2(4))* Mitchell Lane Pubs., Inc.

M
N
O

MOTION PICTURE INDUSTRY—FICTION

Baron, Jeff. Sean Rosen Is Not for Sale. (ENG.). 384p. (J). (gr. 3-7). 2015. pap. 6.99 *(978-0-06-218751-2(1))* 2014. 16.99 *(978-0-06-218750-5(3))* HarperCollins Pubs. (Greenwillow Bks.).

Bentley, Sue. Star of the Show, 4 vols. Swan, Angela & Farley, Andrew, illus. 2009. (Magic Puppy Ser.: 4). (ENG.). 128p. (J). (gr. 1-3). pap. 5.99 *(978-0-448-45047-6(X)*, Grosset & Dunlap) Penguin Young Readers Group.

Boné, Thomas H., illus. The Teacher Who Would Not Retire Becomes a Movie Star. 2012. (J). *(978-0-9792918-6-9(0))* Blue Marlin Pubns.

Brouwer, Sigmund. Scarlet Thunder, 1 vol. 2008. (Orca Sports Ser.). (ENG.). 176p. (YA). (gr. 6-10). pap. 9.95 *(978-1-55143-911-2(5))* Orca Bk. Pubs. USA.

Castellucci, Cecil. Boy Proof. (ENG.). 208p. (YA). (gr. 9-18). 2005. 15.99 *(978-0-7636-2333-3(4))* 2006. reprint ed. per. 8.99 *(978-0-7636-2796-6(8))* Candlewick Pr.

—Boy Proof, 4 vols. 2005. (YA). 62.75 *(978-1-4193-5131-0(1))* Recorded Bks., Inc.

Caveney, Philip. Night on Terror Island. 2013. (ENG.). 240p. (J). (gr. 4-6). pap. 12.99 *(978-1-84939-270-9(6))* Andersen Pr. GBR. Dist: Independent Pubs. Group.

Coleman, Rowan. Film Star. 2011. (ENG., Illus.). 320p. (J). (gr. 6-9). pap. 11.99 *(978-0-00-719039-3(5))* HarperCollins Pubs. Ltd. GBR. Dist: HarperCollins Pubs.

—Shooting Star. 2011. (ENG.). 256p. (J). (gr. 6-9). pap. 9.99 *(978-0-00-725812-3(7))* HarperCollins Pubs. Ltd. GBR. Dist: HarperCollins Pubs.

Doctorow, Cory. Pirate Cinema. 2012. (ENG.). 384p. (YA). (gr. 8-13). 19.99 *(978-0-7653-2908-0(5)*, 9780765329080, Tor Teen) Doherty, Tom Assocs., LLC.

Gensler, Sonia. Ghostlight. 2015. (ENG.). 256p. (J). (gr. 3-7). 16.99 *(978-0-553-52214-3(0)*, Knopf Bks. for Young Readers) Random Hse. Children's Bks.

Gentry, Brad. The Hollywood Princess. 2009. 40p. pap. 20.99 *(978-1-4490-3545-7(0))* AuthorHouse.

Handford, Martin. Where's Waldo? in Hollywood. Handford, Martin, illus. deluxe ed. 2013. (Where's Waldo? Ser.). (ENG., Illus.). 32p. (J). (gr. k-4). 16.99 *(978-0-7636-4527-4(3))* Candlewick Pr.

Hapka, Catherine, pseud. Rio 2: Vacation in the Wild. 2014. (I Can Read Level 2 Ser.). (ENG.). 32p. (J). (gr. -1-3). pap. 3.99 *(978-0-06-228499-0(1))* HarperCollins Pubs.

Hare, Mimi & Naylor, Clare. The First Assistant: A Continuing Tale from Behind the Hollywood Curtain. 2007. (ENG.). 288p. (gr. 12-18). 14.00 *(978-0-452-28836-2(3)*, Plume) Penguin Publishing Group.

Harrison, Emma. That's a Wrap: A Rival High Novel. 2008. (YA). *(978-1-4114-0527-1(7)*, Spark Publishing Group) Sterling Publishing Co., Inc.

Hill, Donna. In My Bedroom. 2005. (ENG., Illus.). 272p. pap. 19.99 *(978-0-312-30727-1(6)*, 9780312307271, St. Martin's Griffin) St. Martin's Pr.

John, Antony. Imposter. 2015. (ENG.). 320p. (YA). (gr. 7). 17.99 *(978-0-8037-4124-9(3)*, Dial Bks) Penguin Young Readers Group.

Keene, Carolyn. Movie Madness. Francis, Peter, illus. 2016. (Nancy Drew Clue Book Ser.: 5). (ENG.). 96p. (J). (gr. 1-4). 16.99 *(978-1-4814-5821-4(3)*, Simon & Schuster/Paula Wiseman Bks.) Simon & Schuster/Paula Wiseman Bks.

—A Script for Danger. 2015. (Nancy Drew Diaries: 10). (ENG., Illus.). 192p. (J). (gr. 3-7). 6.99 *(978-1-4814-3810-0(7)*, Aladdin) Simon & Schuster Children's Publishing.

Klise, Kate. Hollywood, Dead Ahead. Klise, M. Sarah, illus. (43 Old Cemetery Road Ser.: 5). (ENG.). 144p. (J). (gr. 2-5). 2014. pap. 6.99 *(978-0-544-33661-2(5)*, HMH Books For Young Readers) 2013. 15.99 *(978-0-547-85283-6(5))* Houghton Mifflin Harcourt Publishing Co.

LaCour, Nina. Everything Leads to You. 2014. (ENG.). 272p. (YA). (gr. 9). 17.99 *(978-0-525-42588-5(8)*, Dutton Books for Young Readers) Penguin Young Readers Group.

Lombardo, Constance. Stunt Cat to the Stars. Lombardo, Constance, illus. 2015. (Mr. Puffball Ser.: 1). (ENG., Illus.). 240p. (J). (gr. 3-7). 12.99 *(978-0-06-232065-0(3))* HarperCollins Pubs.

Mata, Julie. Kate Walden Directs: Bride of Slug Man. 2015. (ENG., Illus.). 288p. (J). (gr. 3-7). 16.99 *(978-1-4231-9460-6(8))* Disney Pr.

McAlpine, Gordon. Once upon a Midnight Eerie. Zuppardi, Sam, illus. 2015. (Misadventures of Edgar & Allan Poe Ser.: 2). (ENG.). 208p. (J). (gr. 3-7). 6.99 *(978-0-14-242349-3(1)*, Puffin Books) Penguin Young Readers Group.

—Once upon a Midnight Eerie: Book #2. Zuppardi, Sam, illus. 2014. (Misadventures of Edgar & Allan Poe Ser.: 2). (ENG.). 192p. (J). (gr. 3-7). 16.99 *(978-0-670-78493-6(1)*, Viking Books for Young Readers) Penguin Young Readers Group.

McCully, Emily Arnold. Strongheart: The World's First Movie Star Dog. McCully, Emily Arnold, illus. 2014. (ENG., Illus.). 40p. (J). (gr. -1-3). 17.99 *(978-0-8050-9448-0(2)*, 9780805094480, Holt, Henry & Co. Bks. For Young Readers) Holt, Henry & Co.

Movie Mayhem. 2012. (Hardy Boys (All New) Undercover Brothers Ser.: 39). (ENG.). 176p. (J). (gr. 3-7). pap. 5.99 *(978-1-4424-0260-7(1)*, Aladdin) Simon & Schuster Children's Publishing.

Movie Menace. 2011. (Hardy Boys (All New) Undercover Brothers Ser.: 37). (ENG.). 176p. (J). (gr. 3-7). pap. 5.99 *(978-1-4424-0258-4(X)*, Aladdin) Simon & Schuster Children's Publishing.

Nielsen, Susin. Dear George Clooney: Please Marry My Mom. 2012. (ENG., Illus.). 232p. (J). (gr. 5-9). 10.95 *(978-1-77049-295-0(X)*, Tundra Bks.) Tundra Bks. CAN. Dist: Penguin Random Hse. LLC.

Salisbury, Graham. Extra Famous. Rogers, Jacqueline, illus. 2014. (Calvin Coconut Ser.). (ENG.). 176p. (J). (gr. 2-5). pap. 6.99 *(978-0-307-93075-0(0)*, Yearling) Random Hse. Children's Bks.

Schraff, Anne. The Lost, 1 vol. unabr. ed. 2011. (Urban Underground Ser.). (ENG.). 198p. (YA). (gr. 9-12). pap. 9.95 *(978-1-61651-585-0(6))* Saddleback Educational Publishing, Inc.

Umminger, Alison. American Girls. 2016. (ENG.). 304p. (YA). 17.99 *(978-1-250-07500-0(9)*, 9781250075000) Flatiron Bks.

MOTION PICTURE MUSIC

Horn, Geoffrey M. Movie Soundtracks & Sound Effects. 2006. (Making Movies Ser.). (Illus.). 32p. (gr. 5-8). lib. bdg. 26.00 *(978-0-8368-6839-5(0))* Stevens, Gareth Publishing LLLP.

Toybox Innovations, creator. Disney's Enchanted. 2007. (Disney's Read along Collection). (Illus.). 24p. (J). (gr. -1-3). pap. *(978-0-7634-2197-7(9))* Walt Disney Records.

MOTION PICTURE PLAYS

Rowling, J. K. Fantastic Beasts & Where to Find Them: The Original Screenplay. 2016. (ENG.). (J). (gr. 3). 304p. 24.99 *(978-1-338-10906-1(5)*, Scholastic Pr.); 224p. 27.99 *(978-1-338-13208-3(3)*, Levine, Arthur A. Bks.) Scholastic, Inc.

—Fantastic Beasts & Where to Find Them: The Original Screenplay. 2016. lib. bdg. 39.15 *(978-0-606-39668-4(3))* Turtleback Bks.

MOTION PICTURES

Adams, Colleen. Jake Gyllenhaal. 2009. (Stars in the Spotlight Ser.). 32p. (gr. 4-4). 47.90 *(978-1-60853-202-5(X)*, PowerKids Pr.) Rosen Publishing Group, Inc., The.

—Orlando Bloom. (Stars in the Spotlight Ser.). 32p. (gr. 4-4). 2009. 47.90 *(978-1-60853-205-6(4)*, PowerKids Pr.) 2006. (Illus.). (YA). lib. bdg. 25.25 *(978-1-4042-3517-5(5))* Rosen Publishing Group, Inc., The.

Anniss, Matthew. Create Your Own Movie or TV Show. 2016. (Media Genius Ser.). (ENG.). 48p. (gr. 5-8). lib. bdg. 33.32 *(978-1-4109-8110-3(X))* Heinemann-Raintree.

Apel, Melanie. Cool Careers Without College for Film & Television Buffs. 2008. (Cool Careers Without College Ser.). (Illus.). 144p. (YA). (gr. 7-12). lib. bdg. 35.95 *(978-1-4042-1429-3(1))* Rosen Publishing Group, Inc., The.

Beecroft, Simon. Pirates ... & Worse! Dorling Kindersley Publishing Staff, ed. 2009. (Star Wars: the Clone Wars DK Readers Ser.). lib. bdg. 13.55 *(978-0-606-07064-5(8)*, Turtleback) Turtleback Bks.

Beecroft, Simon & Saunders, Catherine. Join the Rebels. 2010. (DK Readers Ser.). (ENG.). 32p. (J). (gr. 1-3). 3.99 *(978-0-7566-6313-1(X)*, DK Children) Dorling Kindersley Publishing, Inc.

Bell, Elisa. Sleepover Movie Scrapbook. 2004. (Illus.). 48p. (J). *(978-0-439-66058-7(0))* Scholastic, Inc.

Benjamin, Daniel. American Life & Movies from the Ten Commandments to Twilight. 2013. (Pop Culture in American Life Ser.). 112p. (YA). (gr. 7-12). pap. 19.99 *(978-1-62712-121-7(8))* Cavendish Square Publishing.

Blofield, Robert. How to Make a Movie in 10 Easy Lessons: Learn How to Write, Direct, & Edit Your Own Film Without a Hollywood Budget. 2015. (Super Skills Ser.). (ENG.). 64p. (J). (gr. 3-7). spiral bd. 12.95 *(978-1-63322-012-6(5))* Quarto Publishing Group USA.

Bodden, Valerie. How to Analyze the Films of George Lucas, 1 vol. 2011. (Essential Critiques Set 2 Ser.). (ENG., Illus.). 112p. (J). (gr. 6-12). lib. bdg. 35.64 *(978-1-61783-087-7(9))* ABDO Publishing Co.

BookSource Staff, compiled by. Who Saved the Galaxy? 2012. (Star Wars DK Readers Level 1 Ser.). lib. bdg. 13.55 *(978-0-606-26677-2(1)*, Turtleback) Turtleback Bks.

Bradley, Timothy. History of Monster Movies (Grade 6) 2016. (TIME for KIDS(r) Nonfiction Readers Ser.). (Illus.). 48p. (J). (gr. 6-6). pap. 9.99 *(978-1-4938-3596-6(3))* Teacher Created Materials, Inc.

Bradley, Timothy J. History of Monster Movies. 2016. (Time for Kids Nonfiction Readers Ser.). (ENG.). (J). (gr. 5-8). lib. bdg. 20.85 ***(978-0-606-39532-8(6))*** Turtleback Bks.

A Brief Guide for the High School Moviemaker. 2003. 56p. (YA). per. *(978-0-9753076-0-1(6))* Kerr, Alex.

Bringle, Jennifer. Vampires in Film & Television. 2011. 77.70 *(978-1-4488-2236-2(X)*, Rosen Reference); pap. 12.95 *(978-1-4488-2229-4(7)*, Rosen Reference); (YA). (gr. 5-9). lib. bdg. 31.95 *(978-1-4488-1226-4(7))* Rosen Publishing Group, Inc., The.

Brodie, Ian. Cameras in Narnia: How the Lion, the Witch & the Wardrobe Came to Life. 2005. (Illus.). 72p. (J). pap. *(978-1-86950-580-6(8))* HarperCollins Pubs. New Zealand.

Buckley, Annie. Making Movies. 2006. (Reading Rocks! Ser.). (ENG., Illus.). 32p. (J). (gr. 2-5). 28.50 *(978-1-59296-746-9(9)*, 200731) Child's World, Inc., The.

—Movies. 2008. (21st Century Skills Innovation Library: Innovation in Entertainment Ser.). (ENG.). 32p. (gr. 4-8). lib. bdg. 28.50 *(978-1-60279-222-7(4)*, 200153) Cherry Lake Publishing.

Buller, Laura. What Is a Wookiee? 2015. (DK Readers Ser.). (ENG., Illus.). 48p. (Orig.). (J). (gr. k-4). pap. 3.99 *(978-1-4654-3386-2(4)*, DK Children) Dorling Kindersley Publishing, Inc.

Candlewick Press & Barba, Rick. Fantastic Beasts & Where to Find Them. 2016. (ENG.). 48p. (J). (gr. 5). 19.99 *(978-0-7636-9590-3(4))* Candlewick Pr.

Capek, Michael. Zorro. 2017. 25.70 *(978-1-61228-972-4(X))* Mitchell Lane Pubs., Inc.

Carlton Books & Rowlands, Caroline. Jurassic World: Where Dinosaurs Come to Life. 2015. (IExplore Ser.). (ENG., Illus.). 32p. (J). (gr. 3). 12.95 *(978-1-78312-156-4(4))* Carlton Kids GBR. Dist: Sterling Publishing Co., Inc.

Casey, Joe & Saunders, Catherine. Darth Maul: Sith Apprentice. 2012. (Star Wars DK Readers Level 4 Ser.). lib. bdg. 13.55 *(978-0-606-26563-8(5)*, Turtleback) Turtleback Bks.

Chambers, Jo. Making Movies. 2007. (Trackers-Math Ser.). (gr. 2-5). pap. 5.00 *(978-1-59055-932-1(0))* Pacific Learning, Inc.

Chambers, Mary & Meinking, Mary. Who Rolls Through Fire? Working on a Movie Set. 2010. (Wild Work Ser.). (ENG., Illus.). 32p. (gr. 1-2). 29.99 *(978-1-4109-3850-3(6)*, Read Me!) Heinemann-Raintree.

Chapman, Patricia. The Bible in the Hunger Games: A "Bibleizing" Study Guide. Kyle, Margaret, illus. 2012. (ENG.). 52p. (J). (gr. 17-17). pap. 9.95 *(978-1-77064-565-3(9))* Wood Lake Publishing, Inc. CAN. Dist: Westminster John Knox Pr.

El Cine. (Coleccion Biblioteca Visual).Tr. of Cinema. (SPA.). (YA). (gr. 5-8). 14.95 *(978-84-372-3767-1(X))* Altea, Ediciones, S.A. - Grupo Santillana ESP. Dist: Lectorum Pubns., Inc.

Clare, John. Braveheart. 2009. (Hodder History: Concepts & Processes Ser.). (Illus.). 48p. pap. 23.50 *(978-0-340-95771-4(9))* Hodder Education Group GBR. Dist: Trans-Atlantic Pubns., Inc.

Clark, Katie. Animal Actors. 2013. (We Work! Animals with Jobs Ser.). (Illus.). 24p. (J). (gr. -1-3). lib. bdg. 21.32 *(978-1-61772-897-6(7))* Bearport Publishing Co., Inc.

Collins, Suzanne, et al. The Official Illustrated Movie Companion. 2012. (Hunger Games Ser.). (ENG., Illus.). 160p. (J). (gr. 7). pap. 18.99 *(978-0-545-42290-1(6))* Scholastic, Inc.

Connolly, Sean. Movies & Video. 2010. 34.25 *(978-1-59920-346-1(4))* Black Rabbit Bks.

Corporate Contributor Staff & Johnson, Robin. The Economics of Making a Movie. 2013. (ENG.). 48p. (J). *(978-0-7787-7971-1(8))*; pap. *(978-0-7787-7976-6(9))* Crabtree Publishing Co.

Croce, Nicholas. The History of Film. 2015. (Britannica Guide to the Visual & Performing Arts Ser.). (ENG., Illus.). 128p. (YA). (gr. 9-10). 45.00 *(978-1-68048-076-4(6)*, Britannica Educational Publishing) Rosen Publishing Group, Inc., The.

Davis, Robin & Starr, Lara. Wookiee Pies, Clone Scones, & Other Galactic Goodies. 2012. (ENG., Illus.). 64p. (J). (gr. -1-17). 22.99 *(978-1-4521-0466-9(2))* Chronicle Bks. LLC.

Disney Enterprises Inc., Staff. Finding Dory: Including Dory, Nemo, Marlin, & All Your Favorite Characters! Loter, John, illus. 2017. (Learn to Draw Favorite Characters: Expanded Edition Ser.). (ENG.). 64p. (J). (gr. 3-5). 33.32 *(978-1-942875-18-5(5))* Quarto Publishing Group USA.

Disney Publishing Creative Development (Firm) Staff, et al, contrib. by. Learn to Draw Disney/Pixar Toy Story: Featuring Favorite Characters from Toy Story 2 & Toy Story 3! 2010. (Learn to Draw Favorite Characters Ser.). 32p. (J). (gr. k-3). 28.50 *(978-1-936309-00-9(9))* Quarto Publishing Group USA.

Disney Storybook Artists Staff, contrib. by. Disney/Pixar Cars: Learn to Draw. 2015. (Learn to Draw Favorite Characters: Expanded Edition Ser.). (ENG., Illus.). 64p. (gr. k-5). 33.32 *(978-1-939581-44-0(3))* Quarto Publishing Group USA.

—Learn to Draw Disney/Pixar Brave. 2015. (Learn to Draw Favorite Characters: Expanded Edition Ser.). (ENG., Illus.). 64p. (J). (gr. k-5). 33.32 *(978-1-939581-45-7(1))* Quarto Publishing Group USA.

—Learn to Draw Plus Disney Pixar Toy Story: Featuring Favorite Characters from Toy Story 2 & Toy Story 3! 2012. (J). *(978-1-936309-69-6(6))* Quarto Publishing Group USA.

Donovan, Sandy. Movies & TV Top Tens. 2014. (Entertainment's Top 10 Ser.). (ENG., Illus.). 32p. (gr. 5-8). lib. bdg. 26.60 *(978-1-4677-3840-8(9)*, Lerner Pubns.) Lerner Publishing Group.

Dorling Kindersley Publishing Staff. Ahsoka in Action! 2012. (Star Wars: The Clone Wars DK Readers Ser.). lib. bdg. 13.55 *(978-0-606-31472-5(5)*, Turtleback) Turtleback Bks.

—The Batman Movie. 2016. (Ultimate Sticker Collections). (ENG.). 96p. (J). (gr. 1-4). pap. 12.99 *(978-1-4654-5632-8(5)*, DK Children) Dorling Kindersley Publishing, Inc.

—Bounty Hunters for Hire, Level 2. 2013. (DK Readers Ser.). (ENG.). 32p. (J). (gr. 1-3). pap. 3.99 *(978-1-4654-1017-7(1)*, DK Children) Dorling Kindersley Publishing, Inc.

—Can You Spot a Jedi? 2014. (DK Readers Ser.). (ENG., Illus.). 32p. (J). (gr. k-4). 14.99 *(978-1-4654-1681-0(1))*; pap. 3.99 *(978-1-4654-1680-3(3))* Dorling Kindersley Publishing, Inc. (DK Children).

—Disney Frozen. 2014. (ENG., Illus.). 104p. (J). (gr. k-k). 19.99 *(978-1-4654-3447-0(X)*, DK Children) Dorling Kindersley Publishing, Inc.

—Disney Pixar Cars 3. 2017. (Ultimate Sticker Bks.). (ENG.). 16p. (J). (gr. k-4). pap. 6.99 ***(978-1-4654-5560-4(4)***, DK Children) Dorling Kindersley Publishing, Inc.

—Disney Pixar Cars 3: the Essential Guide. 2017. (ENG.). 64p. (J). (gr. 1-4). 12.99 ***(978-1-4654-5559-8(0)***, DK Children) Dorling Kindersley Publishing, Inc.

—Disney Pixar Finding Nemo: the Essential Guide, 2nd Edition. 2016. (ENG.). 64p. (J). (gr. 1-4). pap. 8.99 *(978-1-4654-4923-8(X)*, DK Children) Dorling Kindersley Publishing, Inc.

—Disney Zootopia. 2016. (ENG.). 16p. (J). (gr. 1-4). pap. 6.99 *(978-1-4654-4429-5(7)*, DK Children) Dorling Kindersley Publishing, Inc.

—Disney Zootopia: The Essential Guide. 2016. (ENG., Illus.). 64p. (J). (gr. 1-4). 12.99 *(978-1-4654-4428-8(9)*, DK Children) Dorling Kindersley Publishing, Inc.

—Frozen: The Essential Guide. 2013. (ENG.). 64p. (J). (gr. k-4). 12.99 *(978-1-4654-1404-5(5)*, DK Children) Dorling Kindersley Publishing, Inc.

—Inside Out. 2015. (Ultimate Sticker Bks.). (ENG.). 16p. (J). (gr. k-4). pap. 6.99 *(978-1-4654-3532-3(8)*, DK Children) Dorling Kindersley Publishing, Inc.

—Mysteries of the Jedi. 2011. (ENG., Illus.). 96p. (J). (gr. 2-5). 12.99 *(978-0-7566-7197-6(3)*, DK Children) Dorling Kindersley Publishing, Inc.

—Star Wars: Jedi Battles. 2013. (DK Adventures Ser.). lib. bdg. 16.00 *(978-0-606-35319-9(4))* Turtleback Bks.

—Star Wars: Sith Wars. 2013. (DK Adventures Ser.). lib. bdg. 16.00 *(978-0-606-35320-5(8))* Turtleback Bks.

—Star Wars Character Encyclopedia. 2011. 208p. pap. *(978-0-7566-8885-1(X))* Dorling Kindersley Publishing, Inc.

Dorling Kindersley Publishing Staff, ed. Star Wars. 2004. (Ultimate Sticker Bks.). (ENG.). 16p. (J). (gr. k-3). pap. 6.99 *(978-0-7566-0764-7(7)*, DK Children) Dorling Kindersley Publishing, Inc.

Dorling Kindersley Publishing Staff & Bray, Adam. Star Wars Rebels the Visual Guide. 2014. (ENG.). 128p. (J). (gr. 3-7). 16.99 *(978-1-4654-2080-0(0)*, DK Children) Dorling Kindersley Publishing, Inc.

Dorling Kindersley Publishing Staff & Dolan, Hannah. The Lego Movie - Essential Guide. 2013. (ENG.). 64p. (J). (gr. k-4). 12.99 *(978-1-4654-1700-8(1)*, DK Children) Dorling Kindersley Publishing, Inc.

Dorling Kindersley Publishing Staff & Dowsett, Elizabeth. Revenge of the Sith, Level 3. 2013. (DK Readers Ser.). (ENG.). 48p. (J). (gr. 2-4). pap. 3.99 *(978-1-4654-0869-3(X)*, DK Children) Dorling Kindersley Publishing, Inc.

Dorling Kindersley Publishing Staff & Dubowski, Cathy East. Ahsoka in Action!, Level 1. 2012. (DK Readers Ser.). (ENG., Illus.). 32p. (J). (gr. k-4). pap. 3.99 *(978-1-4654-0583-8(6)*, DK Children) Dorling Kindersley Publishing, Inc.

Dorling Kindersley Publishing Staff & East Dubowski, Cathy. Ahsoka in Action! 2012. (DK Readers Ser.). (ENG., Illus.). 32p. (J). (gr. k-4). 14.99 *(978-1-4654-0584-5(4)*, DK Children) Dorling Kindersley Publishing, Inc.

—Masters of the Force. 2012. (DK Readers Ser.). (ENG.). 32p. (J). (gr. -1-1). pap. 3.99 *(978-1-4654-0585-2(2)*, DK Children) Dorling Kindersley Publishing, Inc.

Dorling Kindersley Publishing Staff & Fentiman, David. The LEGO Movie. 2013. (Ultimate Sticker Collections). (ENG.). 96p. (J). (gr. 1-4). pap. 12.99 *(978-1-4654-1701-5(X)*, DK Children) Dorling Kindersley Publishing, Inc.

Dorling Kindersley Publishing Staff & Harper, Benjamin. Feel the Force! 2011. (DK Readers Ser.). (ENG.). 48p. (J). (gr. 2-4). 3.99 *(978-0-7566-7126-6(4)*, DK Children) Dorling Kindersley Publishing, Inc.

Dorling Kindersley Publishing Staff & Kent, Lindsay. Ultimate Duels, Level 4. 2011. (DK Readers Ser.). (ENG.). 48p. (J). (gr. 3-7). 3.99 *(978-0-7566-8263-7(0)*, DK Children) Dorling Kindersley Publishing, Inc.

Dorling Kindersley Publishing Staff & Miller-Zarneke, Tracey. The LEGO(r) Batman Movie: the Making of the Movie. 2017. (ENG.). 200p. (J). (gr. 5-12). 24.99 *(978-1-4654-5661-8(9)*, DK Children) Dorling Kindersley Publishing, Inc.

Dorling Kindersley Publishing Staff & Saunders, Catherine. The Legendary Yoda, Level 3. 2013. (DK Readers Ser.). (ENG., Illus.). 48p. (J). (gr. 2-4). pap. 3.99 *(978-1-4654-0184-7(9)*, DK Children) Dorling Kindersley Publishing, Inc.

Dorling Kindersley Publishing Staff & Stock, Lisa. Battle for Naboo. 2012. (DK Readers Ser.). (ENG.). 48p. (J). (gr. 2-4). 3.99 *(978-0-7566-9008-3(0)*, DK Children) Dorling Kindersley Publishing, Inc.

Dorling Kindersley Publishing Staff & Wallace, Daniel. Battle for the Galaxy. 2011. (ENG., Illus.). 96p. (J). (gr. 2-5). 12.99 *(978-0-7566-7315-4(1)*, DK Children) Dorling Kindersley Publishing, Inc.

Dorling Kindersley Publishing Staff & Windham, Ryder. Star Wars: the Ultimate Visual Guide: The Ultimate Visual Guide. 2012. (ENG., Illus.). 200p. (J). (gr. 5-12). 24.99 *(978-0-7566-9248-3(2)*, DK Children) Dorling Kindersley Publishing, Inc.

Dorling Kindersley Publishing Staff, et al. Darth Maul Sith Apprentice. 2012. (DK Readers Ser.). (ENG.). 48p. (J). (gr. 3-7). 3.99 *(978-0-7566-8866-0(3)*, DK Children) Dorling Kindersley Publishing, Inc.

Downey, Glen R. & Malara, Maria. The 10 Hottest Hollywood Cars. 2007. 14.99 *(978-1-55448-526-0(6))* Scholastic Library Publishing.

Drake, Carol. The 10 Best Movies from Books. 2007. (J). 14.99 *(978-1-55448-463-8(4))* Scholastic Library Publishing.

Dunkleberger, Amy. So You Want to Be a Film or TV Director? 2007. (Careers in Film & Television Ser.). (Illus.). 128p. (J). (gr. 6-9). lib. bdg. 33.27 *(978-0-7660-2738-1(4))* Enslow Pubs., Inc.

—So You Want to Be a Film or TV Screenwriter? 2007. (Careers in Film & Television Ser.). (Illus.). 128p. (J). (gr. 6-9). lib. bdg. 33.27 *(978-0-7660-2645-2(0))* Enslow Pubs., Inc.

Dunn, Mary R. I Want to Make Movies. 2009. (Dream Jobs Ser.). 24p. (gr. 2-3). 42.50 *(978-1-61512-216-5(8)*, PowerKids Pr.); (Illus.). (YA). lib. bdg. 22.60 *(978-1-4042-4473-3(5))* Rosen Publishing Group, Inc., The.

—Quiero Hacer Películas. 2009. (Trabajos de ensueño (Dream Jobs) Ser.). (SPA.). 24p. pap. 8.25 *(978-1-4358-3429-3(1))*; (Illus.). (J). (gr. 2-4). lib. bdg. 22.60 *(978-1-4042-8155-4(X))* Rosen Publishing Group, Inc., The. (PowerKids Pr.).

Eboch, M. M. History of Film, 1 vol. 2014. (Essential Library of Cultural History Ser.). (ENG., Illus.). 112p. (J). (gr. 6-12). lib. bdg. 35.64 *(978-1-62403-554-8(X)*, Essential Library) ABDO Publishing Co.

Editors of Topix Media Lab. The Force Awakens: The Official Lucas Collector's Edition. 2016. (Nonfiction - Young Adult Ser.). (ENG., Illus.). 96p. (YA). (gr. 6-12). 33.22 *(978-1-5124-1791-3(2)*, Twenty-First Century Bks.) Lerner Publishing Group.

Egan, Kate, et al. The World of the Hunger Games. 2012. (ENG., Illus.). 192p. (J). (gr. 7-7). 17.99 *(978-0-545-42512-4(3))* Scholastic, Inc.

Elish, Dan. Screenplays. 2011. (Craft of Writing Ser.). 96p. (gr. 6). 34.21 *(978-1-60870-501-6(3))* Marshall Cavendish Corp.

Elish, Dan & Benjamin, Daniel. American Life & Movies from the Ten Commandments to Twilight. 2013. 112p. (YA). (gr. 7-12). 35.64 *(978-1-60870-921-2(3))* Cavendish Square Publishing.

Facts on File, Inc. Staff. Movies. 2012. (Discovering Careers Ser.). (Illus.). 112p. (gr. 4-9). 24.95 *(978-0-8160-8058-8(5)*, Ferguson Publishing Co.) Facts On File, Inc.

Fields, Jan. Asking Questions about How Hollywood Movies Get Made. 2015. (21st Century Skills Library: Asking Questions about Media Ser.). (ENG., Illus.). 32p. (J). (gr. 4-8). pap. 14.21 *(978-1-63362-504-4(4)*, 206861) Cherry Lake Publishing.

Firth, Melissa. Behind the Scenes at a Movie Set. 2014. (VIP Tours Ser.). 48p. (J). (gr. 4-6). 31.36 *(978-1-62713-025-7(X))* Cavendish Square Publishing.

Fiscus, James W. Meet King Kong. 2004. (Famous Movie Monsters Ser.). (Illus.). 48p. lib. bdg. 29.25 *(978-1-4042-0270-2(6))* Rosen Publishing Group, Inc., The.

Franks, Katie. I Want to Be a Movie Star. (Dream Jobs Ser.). 24p. (gr. 2-3). 2009. 42.50 *(978-1-61512-207-3(9)*, PowerKids Pr.) 2007. (Illus.). (YA). lib. bdg. 22.60 *(978-1-4042-3619-6(8))* Rosen Publishing Group, Inc., The.

Garza, Sarah. ¡Acción! Filmando Películas. 2016. (TIME for Kids en Español - Level 5 Ser.). (SPA.). 64p. (gr. 5-5). lib. bdg. 31.99 *(978-1-5157-2942-6(7))* Time for Kids Inc AUS. Dist: Capstone Pub.

—Action! Making Movies, 1 vol. 2nd rev. ed. 2013. (TIME for KIDS(r) Nonfiction Readers Ser.). (ENG.). 64p. (J). (gr. 5-5). pap. 10.99 *(978-1-4333-4949-2(3))* Teacher Created Materials, Inc.

Gitlin, Martin. Tyler Perry: A Biography of a Movie Mogul. 2014. (African-American Icons Ser.). 104p. (J). lib. bdg. 27.94 *(978-0-7660-4241-4(3))* Enslow Pubs., Inc.

Glassbourg, Michael. Learn to Speak Film: A Guide to Creating, Promoting & Screening Your Movies. Kulak, Jeff & Owlkids Books Inc. Staff, illus. 2013. (Learn to Speak Ser.). (ENG.). 96p. (J). (gr. 4-8). pap. 14.95 *(978-1-926973-85-2(2)*, Owlkids) Owlkids Bks. Inc. CAN. Dist: Publishers Group West (PGW).

Goddu, Krystyna Poray. Movie Monsters: From Frankenstein to Godzilla. 2017. (Monster Mania Ser.). (ENG.). 32p. (J). (gr. 2-5). 26.65 *(978-1-5124-2591-8(5))* Lerner Publishing Group.

Grabham, Tim, et al. Movie Maker: The Ultimate Guide to Making Films. Parsons, Garry, illus. 2010. (ENG.). 48p. (J). (gr. 3-7). 19.99 *(978-0-7636-4949-4(X))* Candlewick Pr.

Greatest Movie Monsters. 2015. (Greatest Movie Monsters Ser.). (ENG.). 48p. (J). (gr. 5-6). pap., pap., pap. 493.50 *(978-1-4777-8622-2(8),* Rosen Central) Rosen Publishing Group, Inc., The.

Green, Julie. Super Smart Information Strategies: Shooting Video to Make Learning Fun. 2010. (Explorer Library: Information Explorer Ser.). (ENG.). 32p. (gr. 4-8). lib. bdg. 28.50 *(978-1-60279-955-4(5),* 200635) Cherry Lake Publishing.

Green, Naima. Meet Frankenstein. (Famous Movie Monsters Ser.). 48p. 2009. (gr. 6-6). 53.00 *(978-1-61512-529-6(9))* 2004. (Illus.). lib. bdg. 29.25 *(978-1-4042-0268-9(4))* Rosen Publishing Group, Inc., The.

Green, Sara. Star Wars. 2017. (Brands We Know Ser.). (ENG., Illus.). 24p. (J). (gr. 3-8). lib. bdg. 25.95 ***(978-1-62617-656-0(6),*** Pilot Bks.) Bellwether Media.

Greenberger, Robert. Meet Godzilla. 2004. (Famous Movie Monsters Ser.). (Illus.). 48p. lib. bdg. 29.25 *(978-1-4042-0269-6(2))* Rosen Publishing Group, Inc., The.

Gulko, Candace S. Film. 2010. (Career Launcher Ser.). 176p. (C). (gr. 9). 34.95 *(978-0-8160-7959-9(5),* Ferguson Publishing Co.); pap. 14.95 *(978-0-8160-7981-0(1),* Checkmark Bks.) Facts On File, Inc.

Hamen, Susan E. How to Analyze the Films of James Cameron, 1 vol. 2011. (Essential Critiques Set 2 Ser.). (ENG., Illus.). 112p. (J). (gr. 6-12). lib. bdg. 35.64 *(978-1-61783-088-4(7))* ABDO Publishing Co.

—How to Analyze the Films of the Coen Brothers, 1 vol. 2012. (Essential Critiques Set 3 Ser.). (ENG.). 112p. (J). (gr. 6-12). 35.64 *(978-1-61783-454-7(8))* ABDO Publishing Co.

Harland, Joan & Timmons, Nick. As Film Studies. 2006. (ENG., Illus.). 240p. (YA). pap. 49.50 *(978-0-7487-9030-2(6))* Nelson Thornes Ltd. GBR. Dist: Trans-Atlantic Pubns., Inc.

Harmon, Daniel E. Werewolves. 2015. (Greatest Movie Monsters Ser.). (ENG., Illus.). 48p. (J). (gr. 5-6). 30.25 *(978-1-4994-3521-4(5),* Rosen Central) Rosen Publishing Group, Inc., The.

Hermansson, Casie. How to Analyze the Films of Clint Eastwood, 1 vol. 2012. (Essential Critiques Set 3 Ser.). (ENG.). 112p. (J). (gr. 6-12). lib. bdg. 35.64 *(978-1-61783-453-0(X),* Essential Library) ABDO Publishing Co.

—Parental Guidance Ratings. 2013. (Hot Topics in Media EBook Ser.). (ENG.). 48p. (J). pap. 15.64 *(978-1-61783-784-5(9));* (gr. 3-6). lib. bdg. 32.79 *(978-1-61783-734-0(2))* ABDO Publishing Co.

Hibbert, Clare & Hachette Children's Books Staff. Movie Star: Find Out How Your Favorite Movie Stars Made It! 2012. (Celeb Ser.). (Illus.). 32p. (gr. 4-6). lib. bdg. 28.50 *(978-1-59771-332-0(5))* Sea-To-Sea Pubns.

Hill, Mary. Let's Go to a Movie. 2004. (Welcome Bks.). (ENG.). 24p. (J). (gr. -1-2). pap. 4.95 *(978-0-516-25917-8(2),* Children's Pr.) Scholastic Library Publishing.

Hofer, Charles. Meet Dracula. (Famous Movie Monsters Ser.). 48p. 2009. (gr. 6-6). 53.00 *(978-1-61512-528-9(0))* 2004. (Illus.). 29.25 *(978-1-4042-0267-2(6))* Rosen Publishing Group, Inc., The.

Holzer, Harold. Lincoln: How Abraham Lincoln Ended Slavery in America - A Companion Book for Young Readers to the Steven Spielberg Film. 2012. (ENG.). 240p. 16.99 *(978-0-06-226509-8(1))* HarperCollins Pubs.

Horn, Geoffrey M. Writing, Producing, & Directing Movies. 2006. (Making Movies Ser.). (Illus.). 32p. (gr. 5-8). lib. bdg. 26.00 *(978-0-8368-6841-8(2))* Stevens, Gareth Publishing LLLP.

Howard, Kate. The Lego Movie: Junior Novel. 2013. lib. bdg. 16.00 *(978-0-606-35406-6(9))* Turtleback Bks.

Indovino, Shaina Carmel. Dracula & Beyond: Famous Vampires & Werewolves in Literature & Film. 2010. (Making of a Monster Ser.). (Illus.). 64p. (YA). (gr. 7-18). pap. 9.95 *(978-1-4222-1956-0(9));* lib. bdg. 22.95 *(978-1-4222-1803-7(1))* Mason Crest.

Jantner, Janos, illus. Drawing Horror-Movie Monsters. 2013. (How to Draw Monsters Ser.). (ENG.). 32p. (J). (gr. 3-6). 26.50 *(978-1-4777-0308-3(X));* pap. 11.75 *(978-1-4777-0338-0(1))* Rosen Publishing Group, Inc., The. (PowerKids Pr.).

Johnson, Marlys. Careers in the Movies. 2009. (Career Resource Library). 192p. (gr. 7-12). 63.90 *(978-1-60853-406-7(5))* Rosen Publishing Group, Inc., The.

Jones, Bruce Patrick. Action Stars Paper Dolls. Jones, Bruce Patrick, illus. 2010. (Dover Celebrity Paper Dolls Ser.). (ENG., Illus.). 32p. (J). (gr. 3-5). pap. 9.99 *(978-0-486-47606-3(5))* Dover Pubns., Inc.

Jones, Sarah. Film. 2003. (Media Wise Ser.). (Illus.). 64p. (J). lib. bdg. 28.50 *(978-1-58340-256-6(X))* Black Rabbit Bks.

Kassnoff, David. Transformers, Robots, & Cyborgs. 2015. (Greatest Movie Monsters Ser.). (ENG., Illus.). 48p. (J). (gr. 5-6). 30.25 *(978-1-4994-3529-0(0),* Rosen Central) Rosen Publishing Group, Inc., The.

Kinney, Jeff. How Greg Heffley Went To Hollywood. 2012. (Diary of a Wimpy Kid Ser.). (ENG., Illus.). 256p. (J). (gr. 3-7). 15.95 *(978-1-4197-0642-4(X),* Amulet Bks.) Abrams, Inc.

Kinney, Jeff. The Wimpy Kid Movie Diary: The Next Chapter (The Making of the Long Haul) 2017. (ENG., Illus.). 208p. (J). (gr. 3-7). 16.95 ***(978-1-4197-2752-8(4),*** Amulet Bks.) Abrams, Inc.

Krasner, Barbara. The 12 Most Influential Movies of All Times. 2018. (ENG.). 32p. (gr. 3-6). 31.35 ***(978-1-63235-410-5(1),*** 12-Story Library) Pr. Room Editions LLC.

La Bella, Laura. Drones & Entertainment. 2016. (Inside the World of Drones Ser.). 00064p. (J). (gr. 7-7). 34.45 *(978-1-5081-7339-7(7))* Rosen Publishing Group, Inc., The.

Lace, William W. Blacks in Film. 2008. (Lucent Library of Black History Ser.). (ENG., Illus.). 104p. (J). (gr. 7-10). 34.80 *(978-1-4205-0084-4(8),* 1284137, Lucent Bks.) Cengage Gale.

Larson, Jeff. FX! Lighting & Sound. 2017. (Time for Kids Nonfiction Readers Ser.). lib. bdg. 22.10 ***(978-0-606-40269-9(1))*** Turtleback Bks.

Lee, Sun Hee Teresa. How to Analyze the Films of Tim Burton, 1 vol. 2011. (Essential Critiques Set 2 Ser.). (ENG., Illus.). 112p. (J). (gr. 6-12). lib. bdg. 35.64 *(978-1-61783-089-1(5))* ABDO Publishing Co.

Little Sparrow. 2004. pap. 9.99 *(978-0-307-14298-6(1))* Random Hse., Inc.

Lockyer, John & Holden, Pam. Making a Movie, 6 pack. 2009. (Red Rocket Readers Ser.). (ENG., Illus.). 16p. (gr. 2-2). pap. *(978-1-877435-50-8(3),* Red Rocket Readers) Flying Start Bks.

Loh-Hagan, Virginia. Sound Effects Artist. 2015. (Illus.). 32p. (J). pap. *(978-1-63470-056-6(2))* Cherry Lake Publishing.

Margles, Samantha. Star Wars: Science Fair Book. 2013. lib. bdg. 20.85 *(978-0-606-32399-4(6),* Turtleback) Turtleback Bks.

Markegard, Blake. John Cena. 2017. (John Cena Ser.). 24p. (J). (gr. 3-7). pap. 7.99 ***(978-1-61891-244-2(5),*** Epic Bks.) Bellwether Media.

Matthews, John. DVDs. 2008. (21st Century Skills Library: Global Products Ser.). (ENG., Illus.). 32p. (gr. 4-8). lib. bdg. 28.50 *(978-1-60279-253-1(4),* 200120) Cherry Lake Publishing.

McAlpine, Margaret. Working in Film & Television. 2004. (My Future Career Ser.). (Illus.). 64p. (gr. 3-7). lib. bdg. 27.00 *(978-0-8368-4237-1(5),* Gareth Stevens Learning Library) Stevens, Gareth Publishing LLLP.

Mead, Richelle. Vampire Academy. movie tie-in ed. 2013. (Vampire Academy Ser.: 1). (ENG.). 352p. (YA). (gr. 7). pap. 10.99 *(978-1-59514-360-0(2),* Razorbill) Penguin Publishing Group.

Miller, Connie Colwell. Movie Animals. 2013. (Animals with Jobs Ser.). (ENG.). 32p. (gr. 1-4). 28.50 *(978-1-60753-379-5(0))* Amicus Publishing.

Mooney, Carla. STEM Jobs in Movies. 2014. (ENG.). 48p. (gr. 4-8). 35.64 *(978-1-62717-701-6(9))* Rourke Educational Media.

Morgan, Kathryn. Zombies. 2015. (Greatest Movie Monsters Ser.). (ENG., Illus.). 48p. (J). (gr. 5-6). 30.25 *(978-1-4994-3545-0(2),* Rosen Central) Rosen Publishing Group, Inc., The.

Morina, Barbara, concept. Films, a Movie Lover's Journal: Journals Unlimited. 2003. (Write It down Ser.). (Illus.). 200p. 19.95 *(978-1-892033-34-5(8))* Journals Unlimited, Inc.

Mosqueda, Olga T. & Tucker, Marianne, illus. Learn to Draw Plus Disney Winnie the Pooh. 2012. (J). *(978-1-936309-68-9(8))* Quarto Publishing Group USA.

Mullins, Matt. Scriptwriter. 2011. (21st Century Skills Library: Cool Arts Careers Ser.). (ENG.). 32p. (gr. 4-8). lib. bdg. 28.50 *(978-1-61080-135-5(0),* 201148) Cherry Lake Publishing.

Murdico, Suzanne J. Meet the Blob. 2004. (Famous Movie Monsters Ser.). (Illus.). 48p. lib. bdg. 29.25 *(978-1-4042-0271-9(4))* Rosen Publishing Group, Inc., The.

Murphy, Maggie. Johnny Depp. 2011. (Movie Superstars Ser.). (Illus.). 32p. (J). pap. 10.00 *(978-1-4488-2721-3(3),* PowerKids Pr.) Rosen Publishing Group, Inc., The.

—Movie Superstars, 6 vols., Set. Incl. Johnny Depp. 25.25 *(978-1-4488-2566-0(0));* Megan Fox. lib. bdg. 25.25 *(978-1-4488-2567-7(9));* Reese Witherspoon. lib. bdg. 25.25 *(978-1-4488-2568-4(7));* Shia Labeouf. 25.25 *(978-1-4488-2563-9(6));* Taylor Lautner. lib. bdg. 25.25 *(978-1-4488-2564-6(4));* Zoe Saldana. lib. bdg. 25.25 *(978-1-4488-2565-3(2));* (J). (gr. 4-6). (Movie Superstars Ser.). (Illus.). 32p. 2011. Set lib. bdg. 143.70 *(978-1-4488-2907-1(0),* PowerKids Pr.) Rosen Publishing Group, Inc., The.

Naha, Ed. The Ten Commandments Movie Storybook. 2007. (Epic Stories of the Bible Ser.). (Illus.). 77p. (J). (gr. -1-3). 14.99 *(978-0-9743876-4-2(9))* CrossStaff Publishing.

Niver, Heather Moore. Dracula & Other Vampires. 2015. (Greatest Movie Monsters Ser.). (ENG., Illus.). 48p. (J). (gr. 5-6). 30.25 *(978-1-4994-3525-2(8),* Rosen Central) Rosen Publishing Group, Inc., The.

O'Neill, Joseph. Movie Director. 2009. (21st Century Skills Library: Cool Careers Ser.). (ENG.). 32p. (gr. 4-8). lib. bdg. 28.50 *(978-1-60279-499-3(5),* 200310) Cherry Lake Publishing.

Parish, James Robert. Steven Spielberg, Filmmaker. 2003. (Ferguson Career Biographies Ser.). (Illus.). 160p. (gr. 6-12). 25.00 *(978-0-8160-5481-7(9),* Ferguson Publishing Co.) Facts On File, Inc.

Patz, Deborah S. Write! Shoot! Edit! The Complete Guide for Teen Filmmakers. 2017. (ENG.). 210p. (YA). pap. 23.95 *(978-1-61593-264-1(X))* Wiese, Michael Productions.

Pelusey, Michael & Pelusey, Jane. Film & Television. 2005. (Media Ser.). (Illus.). 32p. (gr. 5-8). lib. bdg. 21.95 *(978-0-7910-8802-9(2),* Chelsea Hse.) Facts On File, Inc.

Perritano, John. The Science of Movies, 1 vol. 2017. (Red Rhino Nonfiction Ser.). (ENG.). 60p. (J). (gr. 3-8). pap. 8.95 ***(978-1-68021-050-7(5))*** Saddleback Educational Publishing, Inc.

Perritano, Johnrau Dana M. The Science of Movies. 2017. (Red Rhino Nonfiction Ser.). (J). lib. bdg. 19.60 ***(978-0-606-39892-3(9))*** Turtleback Bks.

Pipe, Jim. Make a Movie! 2013. (Find Your Talent Ser.). 32p. (gr. 5-8). 28.50 *(978-1-84858-573-7(X))* Arcturus Publishing GBR. Dist: Black Rabbit Bks.

Pollack, Pam & Meg Belviso. Who Is George Lucas? 2014. (Who Is... ? Ser.). (Illus.). 105p. (J). lib. bdg. 16.00 *(978-0-606-35690-9(8))* Turtleback Bks.

Pollack, Pamela D. & Belviso, Meg. Who Was Alfred Hitchcock? 2014. (Who Was... ? Ser.). lib. bdg. 14.75 *(978-0-606-36176-7(6))* Turtleback Bks.

Pratt, Mary K. How to Analyze the Films of Quentin Tarantino, 1 vol. 2010. (Essential Critiques Set 1 Ser.). (ENG., Illus.). 112p. (J). (gr. 6-12). lib. bdg. 35.64 *(978-1-61613-529-4(8),* 1315565, Essential Library) ABDO Publishing Co.

Price, Roger & Stern, Leonard. Star Wars Mad Libs. 2008. (Star Wars Ser.). (ENG.). 48p. (J). (gr. 3-7). 4.99 *(978-0-8431-3271-7(X),* Mad Libs) Penguin Young Readers Group.

Quijano, Jonathan. Make Your Movie. 2012. (Make Your Movie Ser.). (ENG.). 48p. (gr. 3-4). lib. bdg. 127.96 *(978-1-4296-8223-7(X))* Capstone Press of Coughlan Cos.

—Make Your Own Action Thriller, 1 vol. 2012. (Make Your Movie Ser.). (ENG.). 48p. (gr. 3-4). lib. bdg. 31.99 *(978-1-4296-7529-1(2))* Capstone Press of Coughlan Cos.

—Make Your Own Comedy, 1 vol. 2012. (Make Your Movie Ser.). (ENG.). 48p. (gr. 3-4). lib. bdg. 31.99 *(978-1-4296-7530-7(6))* Capstone Press of Coughlan Cos.

—Make Your Own Horror Movie, 1 vol. 2012. (Make Your Movie Ser.). (ENG., Illus.). 48p. (gr. 3-4). lib. bdg. 31.99 *(978-1-4296-7528-4(4))* Capstone Press of Coughlan Cos.

Revenson, Jody. J. K. Rowling's Wizarding World: the Dark Arts: a Movie Scrapbook. 2017. (J. K. Rowling's Wizarding World Ser.). (ENG.). 48p. (J). (gr. 5). 19.99 ***(978-0-7636-9591-0(2))*** Candlewick Pr.

Revenson, Jody. Movie Magic: Extraordinary People & Fascinating Places. 2016. (J. K. Rowling's Wizarding World Ser.). (ENG.). 96p. (J). (gr. 5). 29.99 *(978-0-7636-9582-8(3))* Candlewick Pr.

Reynolds, Mike. How to Analyze the Films of Spike Lee, 1 vol. 2010. (Essential Critiques Set 1 Ser.). (ENG.). 112p. (J). (gr. 6-12). lib. bdg. 35.64 *(978-1-61613-530-0(1),* Essential Library) ABDO Publishing Co.

Richards, Andrea. Girl Director: A How-to-Guide for the First-Time, Flat-Broke Filmmaker (and Videomaker) (ENG., Illus.). 106p. (YA). pap. 17.95 *(978-1-931497-00-8(1))* Girl Pr., Inc.

Riordan, Rick. Percy Jackson & the Olympians. 2010. (Percy Jackson & the Olympians Ser.). (ENG., Illus.). 156p. (J). (gr. 5-9). 12.99 *(978-1-4231-2171-8(6))* Hyperion Pr.

Saunders, Catherine. Are Ewoks Scared of Stormtroopers? 2013. (Star Wars DK Readers Level 1 Ser.). lib. bdg. 13.55 *(978-0-606-35205-5(8))* Turtleback Bks.

Scholastic. Harry Potter - Ron Weasley: Cinematic Guide. 2016. (ENG.). 64p. (J). (gr. 2-5). 8.99 *(978-1-338-11674-8(6))* Scholastic, Inc.

—Harry Potter: Boxed Set: Cinematic Guide. 2016. (ENG.). (J). (gr. 2-5). 35.96 *(978-1-338-13250-2(4))* Scholastic, Inc.

Scholastic & Fry, Jason. Darth Vader Sith Lord. Martinez, Randy, illus. 2017. (Backstories Ser.: 6). (ENG.). 128p. (J). (gr. 3-7). pap. 5.99 *(978-1-338-02982-6(7))* Scholastic, Inc.

Scholastic & Glass, Calliope. Princess Leia Royal Rebel. 2016. (Backstories Ser.: 7). (ENG., Illus.). 128p. (J). (gr. 3-7). pap. 5.99 *(978-1-338-02980-2(0))* Scholastic, Inc.

Scholastic, Inc. Staff, contrib. by. The World of Harry Potter: Harry Potter Poster Book. 2011. (Illus.). 125p. (J). pap. *(978-0-545-31482-4(8))* Scholastic, Inc.

Scholastic, Inc. Staff & Brooks, Riley. Edward or Jacob? Quick Quizzes for Fans of the Twilight Saga. 2010. (ENG., Illus.). 96p. (J). (gr. 3-7). pap. 5.99 *(978-0-545-24842-6(6))* Scholastic, Inc.

Seder, Rufus Butler. Star Wars: A Scanimation Book - 11 Iconic Scenes from a Galaxy Far, Far Away... 2010. (Scanimation Ser.). (ENG., Illus.). 13p. (gr. k-12). 14.95 *(978-0-7611-5846-2(4),* 15846) Workman Publishing Co., Inc.

Segall, Miriam. Career Building Through Digital Moviemaking. (Digital Career Building Ser.). 64p. 2009. (gr. 6-6). 58.50 *(978-1-61512-164-9(1))* 2007. (Illus.). (YA). (gr. 7-12). lib. bdg. 29.25 *(978-1-4042-1945-8(5))* Rosen Publishing Group, Inc., The.

Seibert, Brian. Jerome Robbins. 2005. (Library of American Choreographers Ser.). (Illus.). 48p. (J). (gr. k-3). lib. bdg. 29.25 *(978-1-4042-0448-5(2))* Rosen Publishing Group, Inc., The.

Seife, Emily & Collins, Suzanne. The Hunger Games - Tribute Guide. 2012. (Hunger Games Ser.). (ENG., Illus.). 128p. (J). (gr. 7). pap. 7.99 *(978-0-545-45782-8(3),* Scholastic Pr.) Scholastic, Inc.

Shea, Therese. Godzilla. 2015. (Greatest Movie Monsters Ser.). (ENG., Illus.). 48p. (J). (gr. 5-6). 30.25 *(978-1-4994-3533-7(9),* Rosen Central) Rosen Publishing Group, Inc., The.

Slaby, Nette. Movies I've Seen. 2006. 65p. (J). per. *(978-0-9774118-5-6(0))* SLABYPRESS.

Small, Cathleen. Frankenstein's Monster. 2016. (Creatures of Fantasy Ser.). (ENG., Illus.). 64p. (J). (gr. 6-6). lib. bdg. 34.21 *(978-1-5026-0936-6(3))* Cavendish Square Publishing.

Smith, Kath. Let's Make a Movie. Dodd, Emma, illus. 2003. (ENG.). 32p. (J). *(978-1-84089-190-4(4))* Zero to Ten, Ltd.

Somervill, Barbara. Actor. 2011. (21st Century Skills Library: Cool Arts Careers Ser.). (ENG.). 32p. (gr. 4-8). lib. bdg. 28.50 *(978-1-61080-129-4(6),* 201136) Cherry Lake Publishing.

Spencer, Liv. Love Bites: The Unofficial Saga of Twilight. 2010. (ENG., Illus.). 203p. (YA). (gr. 7). pap. *(978-1-55022-930-1(3))* Filmer Ltd.

Star Wars in 100 Scenes. 2014. (ENG.). 208p. (J). (gr. 2-5). 18.99 *(978-1-4654-2012-1(6),* DK Children) Dorling Kindersley Publishing, Inc.

Stewart, Mark. Movie Blockbusters. 2009. (Ultimate 10: Entertainment Ser.). (ENG.). 48p. (J). (gr. 4-8). pap. 10.50 *(978-1-4339-2211-4(8));* (YA). (gr. 5-9). lib. bdg. 31.00 *(978-0-8368-9163-8(5))* Stevens, Gareth Publishing LLLP.

—Movie Characters. 2009. (Ultimate 10: Entertainment Ser.). (ENG.). 48p. (J). (gr. 4-8). pap. 10.50 *(978-1-4339-2212-1(6));* (YA). (gr. 5-9). lib. bdg. 31.00 *(978-0-8368-9164-5(3))* Stevens, Gareth Publishing LLLP.

Stoller, Bryan Michael. Smartphone Movie Maker. 2017. (ENG.). (J). 22.99 *(978-0-7636-9411-1(8))* Candlewick Pr.

Sublette, Guen. Here's Lookin' at Lizzie. *(978-0-312-32669-2(6))* St. Martin's Pr.

Die Theatre der Welt.Tr. of Theater of the World. (GER., Illus.). (YA). 31.95 *(978-3-411-09061-7(8))* Bibliographisches Institut & F. A. Brockhaus AG DEU. Dist: Continental Bk. Co., Inc.

Thomas, William. Movie Stunt Worker. 2010. (Benchmark Rockets: Dirty & Dangerous Jobs Ser.). 32p. (J). (gr. 3-6). 28.50 *(978-0-7614-4(-8?)* ...

Tieck, Sarah. Jennifer Lawrence: Star of the Hunger Games, 1 vol. 2013. (Big Buddy Biographies Set 9 Ser.). (ENG.). 32p. (J). (gr. 2-5). lib. bdg. 28.50 *(978-1-61783-751-7(2),* Big Buddy Bks.) ABDO Publishing Co.

Tolkien, J. R. R. Como Se Hizo el Senor de los Anillos. 2003. (Lord of the Rings Ser.). (SPA., Illus.). 192p. (J). 14.95 *(978-84-450-7414-5(8))* Minotauro Ediciones ESP. Dist: Planeta Publishing Corp.

—Guia de Fotos. 2003. (Lord of the Rings Ser.). (SPA., Illus.). 48p. (J). 7.95 *(978-84-450-7415-2(6))* Minotauro Ediciones ESP. Dist: Planeta Publishing Corp.

Tougas, Shelley. Girls Star! Amazing Tales of Hollywood's Leading Ladies, 1 vol. 2014. (Girls Rock! Ser.). (ENG.). 64p. (gr. 4-5). lib. bdg. 34.65 *(978-1-4765-4057-3(8))* Capstone Press of Coughlan Cos.

Triumph Books Staff. Hilary Duff: Total Hilary, Metamorphosis, Lizzie McGuire. . . & More. 2003. (Illus.). 80p. pap. 9.95 *(978-1-57243-625-1(5))* Triumph Bks.

Tucker, Marianne & Phillipson, Andy, illus. Learn to Draw Plus Disney Pixar Cars. 2012. *(978-1-936309-70-2(X))* Quarto Publishing Group USA.

Valentine, Emily. Steven Spielberg: With a Discussion of Imagination. 2004. (Values in Action Biographies Ser.). (J). *(978-1-59203-072-9(6))* Learning Challenge, Inc.

Valle, Suzette. 101 Movies to See Before You Grow Up. 2017. (101 Ser.). (ENG., Illus.). 144p. (J). (gr. 3-5). lib. bdg. 33.32 ***(978-1-942875-15-4(0),*** Walter Foster Jr) Quarto Publishing Group USA.

Valle, Suzette. 101 Movies to See Before You Grow Up: Be Your Own Movie Critic-the Must-See Movie List for Kids. 2015. (101 Things Ser.). (ENG.). 144p. (J). (gr. 3-7). pap. 12.95 *(978-1-63322-043-0(5),* Walter Foster Jr) Quarto Publishing Group USA.

Vander Hook, Sue. How to Analyze the Roles of Paul Newman, 1 vol. 2010. (Essential Critiques Set 1 Ser.). (ENG.). 112p. (J). (gr. 6-12). lib. bdg. 35.64 *(978-1-61613-532-4(8),* Essential Library) ABDO Publishing Co.

Vaz, Mark Cotta. The Twilight Saga Breaking Dawn Pt. 1: The Official Illustrated Movie Companion. 2011. (ENG., Illus.). 144p. (J). (gr. 7-17). pap., pap. 18.99 *(978-0-316-13411-8(2))* Little, Brown Bks. for Young Readers.

Wallace, Daniel & Dorling Kindersley Publishing Staff. Batman - The World of the Dark Knight. 2012. (ENG., Illus.). 200p. (J). (gr. 1-4). 24.99 *(978-0-7566-9249-0(0),* DK Children) Dorling Kindersley Publishing, Inc.

Wessling, Katherine. Backstage at a Movie Set. 2003. (High Interest Bks.). (ENG., Illus.). 48p. (J). (gr. 7-12). pap. 6.95 *(978-0-516-24387-0(X),* Children's Pr.) Scholastic Library Publishing.

West, Tracey. Robin to the Rescue!, Level 2. 2016. (LEGO Batman Movie Ser.). (ENG.). 32p. (J). (gr. 1-3). pap. 4.99 *(978-1-338-11214-6(7))* Scholastic, Inc.

Whos Who at the Zoo. 2004. pap. 9.99 *(978-0-307-14272-6(8))* Random Hse., Inc.

Willian, Michael. The Essential It's a Wonderful Life Film Guidebook: A scene by scene look at a holiday Classic. 2004. (Illus.). 140p. per. 15.95 *(978-0-9762429-0-1(7))* Kerpluggo Bks. LLC.

Willoughby, Nick. Digital Filmmaking for Kids for Dummies. 2015. (For Kids for Dummies Ser.). (ENG., Illus.). 336p. pap. 29.99 *(978-1-119-02740-9(3),* For Dummies) Wiley, John & Sons, Inc.

Woog, Adam. Vampires in the Movies. 2010. (Vampire Library). (Illus.). 80p. (J). (gr. 7-12). lib. bdg. 26.95 *(978-1-60152-135-4(9))* ReferencePoint Pr., Inc.

Wooley, John & Price, Michael H. The Big Book of Biker Flicks: 40 of the Best Motorcycle Movies of All Times, 1. 2005. (Illus.). 168p. pap. 24.95 *(978-1-930709-45-4(5))* HAWK Publishing Group.

Wright, Greg. Peter Jackson in Perspective: The Power Behind Cinema's the Lord of the Rings: A Look at Hollywood's Take on Tolkien's Epic Tale. 2004. 212p. per. 13.95 *(978-0-9759577-0-7(8))* Hollywood Jesus Bks.

Wyss, Johann. The Swiss Family Robinson, 1 vol. 2010. (Illustrated Classics Ser.). (ENG., Illus.). 64p. (YA). (gr. 9-12). per. 9.95 *(978-1-56254-938-1(3))* Saddleback Educational Publishing, Inc.

Zahed, Ramin. J. K. Rowling's Wizarding World: Movie Magic Volume Two: Curious Creatures. 2017. (J. K. Rowling's Wizarding World Ser.). (ENG.). 104p. (J). (gr. 5). 29.99 ***(978-0-7636-9583-5(1))*** Candlewick Pr.

MOTION PICTURES—BIOGRAPHY

see also Actors and Actresses

Abrams, Dennis. Gregory Hines. 2008. (Black Americans of Achievement Ser.). (Illus.). 98p. (gr. 6-12). lib. bdg. 35.00 *(978-0-7910-9718-2(8),* Chelsea Hse.) Facts On File, Inc.

Adams, Colleen. Keira Knightley. 2009. (Stars in the Spotlight Ser.). 32p. (gr. 4-4). 47.90 *(978-1-60853-203-2(8),* PowerKids Pr.) Rosen Publishing Group, Inc., The.

—Kelly Clarkson. 2009. (Stars in the Spotlight Ser.). 32p. (gr. 4-4). 47.90 *(978-1-60853-204-9(6),* PowerKids Pr.) Rosen Publishing Group, Inc., The.

Allen, Amy Ruth. Queen Latifah: From Jersey Girl to Superstar. 2012. (USA TODAY Lifeline Biographies Ser.). (ENG., Illus.). 112p. (gr. 6-12). lib. bdg. 34.60 *(978-0-7613-4234-2(6))* Lerner Publishing Group.

Arrazola, Amaia & Sanchez Vegara, Isabel. Audrey Hepburn. 2017. (Little People, Big Dreams Ser.). (ENG.). 32p. (J). (gr. k-3). 14.99 ***(978-1-78603-053-5(5),*** Frances Lincoln Children's Bks.) Quarto Publishing Group UK GBR. Dist: Hachette Bk. Group.

Bjornlund, Lydia D. Angelina Jolie. 2010. (Modern Role Models Ser.). (Illus.). 64p. (YA). (gr. 7-12). 22.95 *(978-1-4222-0504-4(5))* Mason Crest.

Boshier, Rosa. Ronald Reagan: 40th US President, 1 vol. 2013. (Essential Lives Set 8 Ser.). (ENG.). 112p. (J). (gr. 6-12). lib. bdg. 35.64 *(978-1-61783-895-8(0),* Essential Library) ABDO Publishing Co.

Brown, Don. Mack Made Movies. Brown, Don, illus. 2008. (Illus.). (J). (gr. 2-5). 25.95 incl. audio compact disk *(978-1-4301-0432-2(5));* pap. 16.95 incl. audio *(978-1-4301-0431-5(7));* pap. 39.95 incl. audio compact disk *(978-1-4301-0436-0(8));*Set. pap. 37.95 incl. audio *(978-1-4301-0433-9(3))* Live Oak Media.

Brown, Jonatha A. Steven Spielberg. 2005. (People We Should Know Ser.). 24p. (gr. 1-4). (SPA.). pap. 8.15 *(978-0-8368-4592-1(7),* GHS33828); (Illus.). pap. 8.15 *(978-0-8368-4476-4(9));* (Illus.). lib. bdg. 22.00 *(978-0-8368-4469-6(6))* Stevens, Gareth Publishing LLLP. (Weekly Reader Leveled Readers).

Currie, Cherie & O'Neill, Tony. Neon Angel: A Memoir of a Runaway. 2010. (ENG.). 368p. 24.99 *(978-0-06-196135-9(3))* HarperCollins Pubs.

Dakers, Diane. Oprah Winfrey: Media Legend & Inspiration to Millions. 2015. (Crabtree Groundbreaker Biographies Ser.). (ENG., Illus.). 112p. (J). (gr. 5-8). *(978-0-7787-2559-6(6))* Crabtree Publishing Co.

Davidson, Amy. Elle Fanning. 2012. (Rising Stars Ser.). (Illus.). 32p. (J). (gr. 3-6). 25.25 *(978-1-4339-7280-5(8));* pap. 10.50 *(978-1-4339-7281-2(6))* Stevens, Gareth Publishing LLLP.

MNO

—Keke Palmer. 2012. (Rising Stars Ser.). (Illus.). 32p. (J). (gr. 3-6). 25.25 (978-1-4339-7287-4(5)); pap. 10.50 (978-1-4339-7284-3(0)) Stevens, Gareth Publishing LLLP.
Demuth, Patricia Brennan. Who Was Charlie Chaplin? Copeland, Gregory, illus. 2016. (Who Was? Ser.). (ENG.). 112p. (J). (gr. 3-7). lib. bdg. 15.99 (978-0-399-54241-1(8), Grosset & Dunlap) Penguin Young Readers Group.
Doeden, Matt. Johnny Depp: Hollywood Rebel. 2011. (USA TODAY Lifeline Biographies Ser.). (ENG., Illus.). 112p. (gr. 6-12). lib. bdg. 34.60 (978-0-7613-6420-7(X), 1322549) Lerner Publishing Group.
—Will Smith. 2007. (Illus.). 112p. (J). pap. 9.95 (978-0-8225-7064-6(5)) Lerner Publishing Group.
Dougherty, Terri. Jennifer Lopez. 2007. (Twentieth Century Most Influential Hispanics Ser.). (ENG., Illus.). 128p. (YA). (gr. 7-12). 34.80 (978-1-4205-0021-9(X)) Cengage Gale.
Edge, Laura Bufano. Steven Spielberg: Director of Blockbuster Films. 2008. (People to Know Today Ser.). (Illus.). 128p. (J). (gr. k-6). lib. bdg. 33.27 (978-0-7660-2888-3(7)) Enslow Pubs., Inc.
Fleischman, Sid. Sir Charlie: Chaplin, the Funniest Man in the World. 2010. (ENG.). 288p. (J). (gr. 4-18). 19.99 (978-0-06-189640-8(3), Greenwillow Bks.) HarperCollins Pubs.
Flor Ada, Alma & Campoy, F. Isabel, contrib. by. Pasos. (Literature Collection of Puertas Al Sol Ser.).Tr. of Steps. (SPA.). 32p. (J). (gr. k-6). pap. 13.95 (978-1-59437-704-4(9)) Santillana USA Publishing Co., Inc.
—Voces. (Literature Collection of Puertas Al Sol Ser.).Tr. of Voices. (SPA.). 32p. (J). (gr. k-6). pap. 13.95 (978-1-59437-707-5(3)) Santillana USA Publishing Co., Inc.
Ford, Carin T. Walt Disney: Meet the Cartoonist. 2003. (Meeting Famous People Ser.). (Illus.). 32p. (J). (gr. 1-4). lib. bdg. 23.94 (978-0-7660-1857-0(1)) Enslow Pubs., Inc.
Gagne, Tammy. What It's Like to Be Cameron Diaz. 2012. (SPA & ENG., Illus.). 32p. (J). lib. bdg. 25.70 (978-1-61228-323-4(3)) Mitchell Lane Pubs., Inc.
Galaxy of Superstars. 2005. (Galaxy of Superstars Ser.). (gr. 6-12). 375.00 (978-0-7910-9145-6(7), Chelsea Hse.) Facts On File, Inc.
Gale Editor, ed. Jennifer Hudson. 2011. (People in the News Ser.). (Illus.). 128p. (YA). (gr. 7-12). lib. bdg. 33.95 (978-1-4205-0607-5(2)) Cengage Gale.
Gogerly, Liz. Film Stars. 2012. (Celebrity Secrets Ser.). (ENG., Illus.). 24p. (J). (gr. 5-8). pap. 8.25 (978-1-4488-7084-4(4)); lib. bdg. 22.60 (978-1-4488-7037-0(2)) Rosen Publishing Group, Inc., The. (PowerKids Pr.).
Gold, Susan Dudley. Kathryn Bigelow. 2014. (Great Filmmakers Ser.). 80p. (YA). (gr. 8-11). lib. bdg. 35.64 (978-1-62712-939-8(1)) Cavendish Square Publishing.
—Sofia Coppola. 2014. (Great Filmmakers Ser.). 80p. (YA). (gr. 8-11). lib. bdg. 35.64 (978-1-62712-945-9(6)) Cavendish Square Publishing.
González, Juan Carlos. Francois Truffaut -una vida hecha Cine. 2005. (SPA.). 150p. (YA). (978-958-30-1686-8(1)) Panamericana Editorial.
Gosling, Maureen, et al. You Can Be a Woman Movie Maker. l.t. ed. 2003. (Illus.). 80p. (J). 19.95 incl. DVD (978-1-880599-64-8(3)); pap. 14.95 incl. DVD (978-1-880599-63-1(5)) Cascade Pass, Inc.
Graziano, Jim. Johnny Depp. 2008. (Pop Culture Ser.). (Illus.). 64p. (YA). (gr. 3-7). lib. bdg. 22.95 (978-1-4222-0200-5(3)) Mason Crest.
Hart, Haley. I (Heart) Zac Efron. 2010. 144p. (YA). (gr. 7-18). pap. 4.95 (978-1-60747-707-5(6), Dove Books and Audio) Phoenix Bks., Inc.
Hasday, Judy L. Extraordinary People in the Movies. 2003. (Extraordinary People Ser.). (ENG., Illus.). 288p. (J). (gr. 6-18). 40.00 (978-0-516-22348-3(8), Children's Pr.) Scholastic Library Publishing.
Henricks, Dana. George Clooney. (Sharing the American Dream Ser.). 64p. (YA). (gr. 7-12). 2009. 22.95 (978-1-4222-0600-3(9)) 2007. pap. 9.95 (978-1-4222-0741-3(2)) Mason Crest.
Heppermann, Christine. Whitney Houston: Recording Artist & Actress, 1 vol. 2012. (Lives Cut Short Set 2 Ser.). (ENG.). 112p. (J). (gr. 6-12). lib. bdg. 35.64 (978-1-61783-544-5(7), Essential Library) ABDO Publishing Co.
Herringshaw, DeAnn. Dorothy Dandridge: Singer & Actress, 1 vol. 2011. (Essential Lives Set 6 Ser.). (ENG., Illus.). 112p. (J). (gr. 6-12). lib. bdg. 35.64 (978-1-61714-779-1(6), Essential Library) ABDO Publishing Co.
Jenks, Andrew. Andrew Jenks: My Adventures as a Young Filmmaker. 2013. (ENG.). 224p. (J). (gr. 7). 19.99 (978-0-545-41727-3(9), Scholastic Pr.) Scholastic, Inc.
Johns, Michael-Anne. School Cool. 2009. (Illus.). 48p. (J). (978-0-545-15901-2(6)) Scholastic, Inc.
Johnson, Robin. Kristen Stewart. 2010. (Superstars! Ser.). (ENG.). 32p. (J). (gr. 3-6). lib. bdg. (978-0-7787-7248-4(9)) Crabtree Publishing Co.
—Robert Pattinson. 2010. (Superstars! Ser.). (ENG., Illus.). 32p. (J). (gr. 3-6). lib. bdg. (978-0-7787-7251-4(9)) Crabtree Publishing Co.
Kushner, Jill Menkes. Johnny Depp: Movie Megastar. 2009. (Hot Celebrity Biographies Ser.). (Illus.). 48p. (J). (gr. 5-9). pap. 8.95 (978-0-7660-3631-4(6), Enslow Elementary) Enslow Pubs., Inc.
Latinos in the Limelight. 2005. (Latinos in the Limelight Ser.). (gr. 5-8). 165.00 (978-0-7910-8728-2(X), Chelsea Hse.) Facts On File, Inc.
Lawrence, Katherine. Jean-Claude Van Damme. 2009. (Martial Arts Masters Ser.). 112p. (gr. 5-5). 63.90 (978-1-61514-373-3(4)) Rosen Publishing Group, Inc., The.
Lee, T. S. The Stephen Spielberg Story: The First Stephen Spielberg Comic Biography. 2010. 177p. (J). pap. 14.95 (978-0-9819542-7-1(8)) DASANBOOKS.
Lenburg, Jeff. John Lasseter. 2012. (Legends of Animation Ser.). (Illus.). 136p. (gr. 6-12). 34.95 (978-1-60413-840-5(8), Chelsea Hse.) Facts On File, Inc.
Lewis, J. Patrick. Michelangelo's World. 2008. (ENG., Illus.). 40p. (J). (gr. 1-3). 17.95 (978-1-56846-167-0(4), Creative Editions) Creative Co., The.
Lunzer, Lee. Betty Grable Paper Dolls. Lunzer, Lee, illus. 2007. (ENG., Illus.). 16p. pap. 12.00 (978-0-9790668-7-0(5)) Paper Studio Pr.
Lynette, Rachel. Tim Burton: Filmmaker. 2006. (Inventors & Creators Ser.). (ENG., Illus.). 64p. (J). (gr. 4-8). lib. bdg. 28.75 (978-0-7377-3556-7(2), LML02109-227405, Greenhaven Pr., Inc.) Cengage Gale.
MacKay, Jennifer. James Cameron. Greenhaven Press Editors, ed. 2013. (People in the News Ser.). (ENG., Illus.). 128p. (gr. 7-10). lib. bdg. 39.40 (978-1-4205-0885-7(7), Lucent Bks.) Cengage Gale.
Madan, Fredric C. Greer Garson Paper Dolls. Madan, Fredric C. & Ernst, Clara, illus. 2007. (ENG.). 16p. pap. 12.00 (978-0-9790668-6-3(7)) Paper Studio Pr.
Magid, Jennifer. Angelina Jolie. 2008. (Today's Superstars). 32p. (YA). (gr. 4-7). lib. bdg. 31.95 (978-0-8368-9234-5(8)) Stevens, Gareth Publishing LLLP.
Mara, Wil. Clint Eastwood. 2014. (Great Filmmakers Ser.). 80p. (YA). (gr. 8-11). lib. bdg. 35.64 (978-1-62712-948-0(0)) Cavendish Square Publishing.
—James Cameron. 2014. (Great Filmmakers Ser.). 80p. (YA). (gr. 8-11). lib. bdg. 35.64 (978-1-62712-951-0(0)) Cavendish Square Publishing.
—Peter Jackson. 2014. (Great Filmmakers Ser.). (Illus.). 80p. (YA). (gr. 8-11). lib. bdg. 35.64 (978-1-62712-942-8(1)) Cavendish Square Publishing.
—Steven Spielberg. 2014. (Great Filmmakers Ser.). 80p. (YA). (gr. 8-11). lib. bdg. 35.64 (978-1-62712-936-7(7)) Cavendish Square Publishing.
—Steven Spielberg. 2005. (Rookie Biographies Ser.). (ENG., Illus.). 32p. (J). (gr. 1-2). 20.50 (978-0-516-21842-7(5), Children's Pr.) Scholastic Library Publishing.
Marcovitz, Hal. Madonna: Entertainer. 2010. (Women of Achievement Ser.). 128p. (gr. 6-12). 35.00 (978-1-60413-859-7(9), Chelsea Hse.) Facts On File, Inc.
—Owen & Luke Wilson. 2007. (Popular Culture: A View from the Paparazzi Ser.). (Illus.). 64p. (YA). (gr. 3-7). pap. 7.95 (978-1-4222-0365-1(4)) Mason Crest.
Markegard, Blake. John Cena. 2014. (Wrestling Superstars Ser.). (ENG.). 24p. (J). (gr. 3-7). 25.95 (978-1-62617-141-1(6), Epic Bks.) Bellwether Media.
Marx, Christy. Jet Li. 2009. (Martial Arts Masters Ser.). 112p. (gr. 5-5). 63.90 (978-1-61514-374-0(2)) Rosen Publishing Group, Inc., The.
—The Wachowski Brothers: Creators of the Matrix. 2009. (Famous Families Ser.). 48p. (gr. 5-5). 53.00 (978-1-61512-511-1(6)) Rosen Publishing Group, Inc., The.
Mattern, Joanne. Keke Palmer. 2010. (Robbie Reader Ser.). (Illus.). 32p. (J). (gr. 2-5). lib. bdg. 25.70 (978-1-58415-896-7(4)) Mitchell Lane Pubs., Inc.
—Tyler Perry. 2012. (J). lib. bdg. 25.70 (978-1-61228-334-0(9)) Mitchell Lane Pubs., Inc.
Miller, Diane Disney & Miller, Diane D. Walt Disney: His Life in Pictures. 2009. (ENG.). 64p. (YA). (gr. 3-17). 14.95 (978-1-4231-2105-3(8)) Disney Pr.
Miller, Kat. I Love Robert Pattinson. 2010. (Fan Club Ser.). (ENG.). 24p. (gr. 3-6). lib. bdg. 22.60 (978-1-61533-057-7(7)); (Illus.). (J). pap. 8.15 (978-1-61533-058-4(5)) Windmill Bks.
Mills, Clifford W. Ang Lee. 2009. (Asian Americans of Achievement Ser.). (Illus.). 120p. (J). (gr. 7-12). 35.00 (978-1-60413-566-4(2)) Facts On File, Inc.
Mingo, Norman. Alice Faye Paper Dolls: Glamorous Movie Star Paper Dolls & Costumes. Mingo, Norman & Ernst, Clara, illus. 2007. 8p. pap. 12.00 (978-0-9795053-0-0(5)) Paper Studio Pr.
—Bette Davis Paper Dolls. Taliadoros, Jenny, ed. Mingo, Norman & Ernst, Clara, illus. 2007. (ENG.). 16p. pap. 12.00 (978-0-9790668-2-5(4)) Paper Studio Pr.
—Deanna Durbin Paper Dolls. Mingo, Norman & Emt, Clara, illus. 2007. 16p. pap. 12.00 (978-0-9790668-5-6(9)) Paper Studio Pr.
—Rita Hayworth Paper Dolls. Taliadoros, Jenny, ed. Mingo, Norman & Ernst, Clara, illus. 2006. 16p. pap. 12.00 (978-0-9790668-0-1(8)) Paper Studio Pr.
Mochizuki, Ken. Be Water, My Friend: The Early Years of Bruce Lee. Lee, Dom, illus. 2014. (ENG.). 32p. (J). pap. 9.95 (978-1-62014-164-9(7)) Lee & Low Bks., Inc.
Murphy, Maggie. Johnny Depp. 2011. (Movie Superstars Ser.). (Illus.). 32p. (J). (gr. 4-6). 25.25 (978-1-4488-2566-0(0), PowerKids Pr.) Rosen Publishing Group, Inc., The.
—Miley Cyrus: Rock Star. 2010. (Young & Famous Ser.). 24p. (J). (ENG.). (gr. 3-6). 22.60 (978-1-4488-0643-0(7)); (Illus.). pap. 8.85 (978-1-4488-1799-3(4), PowerKids Pr.) Rosen Publishing Group, Inc., The.
—Reese Witherspoon. 2011. (Movie Superstars Ser.). (Illus.). 32p. (J). pap. 10.00 (978-1-4488-2725-1(6)); (gr. 4-6). lib. bdg. 25.25 (978-1-4488-2568-4(7)) Rosen Publishing Group, Inc., The. (PowerKids Pr.).
Nagle, Jeanne. Jennifer Hudson. 2008. (Who's Your Idol? Ser.). (Illus.). 48p. (J). (gr. 3-7). lib. bdg. 29.25 (978-1-4042-1372-2(4)) Rosen Publishing Group, Inc., The.
Nelson, Maria. Robert Pattinson. 2011. (Rising Stars Ser.). 32p. (J). (gr. 3-6). pap. 10.50 (978-1-4339-5900-4(3)); lib. bdg. 25.25 (978-1-4339-5898-4(8)) Stevens, Gareth Publishing LLLP.
Norwich, Grace. Daniel Radcliffe: No Ordinary Wizard. 2008. (ENG.). 128p. (J). (gr. 4-9). pap. 5.99 (978-1-4169-6771-2(0), Simon Spotlight) Simon Spotlight.
Orr, Tamra. Robert Pattison. 2010. (Blue Banner Biography Ser.). (Illus.). 32p. (YA). (gr. 4-7). lib. bdg. 25.70 (978-1-58415-905-6(7)) Mitchell Lane Pubs., Inc.
Owings, Lisa. Marilyn Monroe: Hollywood Icon, 1 vol. 2012. (Lives Cut Short Set 2 Ser.). (ENG.). 112p. (J). (gr. 6-12). lib. bdg. 35.64 (978-1-61783-481-3(5)) ABDO Publishing Co.
Parish, James Robert. Jim Henson: Puppeteer & Filmmaker. 2006. (Ferguson Career Biographies Ser.). (Illus.). 138p. (gr. 6-12). 25.00 (978-0-8160-5834-1(2), Ferguson Publishing Co.) Facts On File, Inc.
Parvis, Sarah. Taylor Lautner. 2010. (ENG.). 80p. 5.99 (978-0-7407-9962-4(2)) Andrews McMeel Publishing.
Peppas, Lynn. Zac Efron. 2010. (Superstars! Ser.). (ENG., Illus.). 32p. (J). (gr. 3-6). lib. bdg. (978-0-7787-7254-5(3)) Crabtree Publishing Co.
Pollack, Pamela D. & Belviso, Meg. Who Is George Lucas? Hammond, Ted & McVeigh, Kevin, illus. 2014. (Who Was? Ser.). (ENG.). 112p. (J). (gr. 3-7). 5.99 (978-0-448-47947-7(8), Grosset & Dunlap) Penguin Young Readers Group.
—Who Was Alfred Hitchcock? Moore, Jonathan & Harrison, Nancy, illus. 2014. (Who Was? Ser.). (ENG.). 112p. (J). (gr. 3-7). pap. 4.99 (978-0-448-48237-8(1), Grosset & Dunlap) Penguin Young Readers Group.
Powers, Tom. Steven Spielberg. (Just the Facts Biographies Ser.). (Illus.). 112p. 2004. (ENG.). (gr. 5-12). 27.93 (978-0-8225-2473-1(2)) 2003. (J). (gr. 6-18). pap. 7.95 (978-0-8225-9694-3(6)) Lerner Publishing Group.
Richardson, Adele D. The Story of Disney. 2003. (Built for Success Ser.). (Illus.). 48p. (J). 19.95 (978-1-58340-291-7(8)) Black Rabbit Bks.
Sapet, Kerrily. Halle Berry. (Transcending Race in America Ser.). (Illus.). 64p. (J). 2010. (gr. 4-8). 22.95 (978-1-4222-1612-5(8)) 2009. (gr. 5-18). pap. 9.95 (978-1-4222-1626-2(8)) Mason Crest.
—Halle Berry: Academy Award®Winning Actress. 2012. (Transcending Race Ser.). 64p. (J). (gr. 5). 22.95 (978-1-4222-2729-9(4)) Mason Crest.
Schuman, Michael. Halle Berry: A Biography of an Oscar-Winning Actress. 2013. (African-American Icons Ser.). 104p. (J). (gr. 6-12). lib. bdg. 27.94 (978-0-7660-3993-3(5)) Enslow Pubs., Inc.
Schuman, Michael A. Angelina Jolie: Celebrity with Heart. 2010. (Celebrities with Heart Ser.). (Illus.). 128p. (J). pap. 10.95 (978-1-59845-203-7(7)) Enslow Pubs., Inc.
—Halle Berry: Beauty Is Not Just Physical. 2006. (African-American Biography Library). (Illus.). 112p. (J). (gr. 6-12). lib. bdg. 33.27 (978-0-7660-2467-0(9)) Enslow Pubs., Inc.
—Robert Pattinson: Shining Star. 2011. (Hot Celebrity Biographies Ser.). (Illus.). 48p. (J). (gr. 5-18). pap. 8.95 (978-1-59845-284-6(3)); lib. bdg. 25.27 (978-0-7660-3872-1(6)) Enslow Pubs., Inc.
Seibert, Brian. Jerome Robbins. 2005. (Library of American Choreographers Ser.). (Illus.). 48p. (J). (gr. k-3). lib. bdg. 29.25 (978-1-4042-0448-5(2)) Rosen Publishing Group, Inc., The.
Sheen, Barbara. J. J. Abrams. 2015. (People in the News Ser.). (ENG., Illus.). 128p. (J). (gr. 7-10). 39.40 (978-1-4205-1249-6(8), Lucent Bks.) Cengage Gale.
Shields, Clarissa & O'Shea, Mick. Beyond District 12: The Stars of the Hunger Games. 2012. (ENG., Illus.). 160p. pap. 16.95 (978-0-85965-487-6(7)) Plexus Publishing, Ltd. GBR. Dist: Publishers Group West (PGW).
Simoni, Suzanne. Fantastic Female Filmmakers, 1 vol. 2008. (Women's Hall of Fame Ser.). (ENG., Illus.). 120p. (J). (gr. 5-8). pap. 10.95 (978-1-897187-36-4(X)) Second Story Pr. CAN. Dist: Orca Bk. Pubs. USA.
Snyder, Gail. Jake Gyllenhaal. 2008. (Pop Culture Ser.). (Illus.). 64p. (YA). (gr. 3-7). lib. bdg. 22.95 (978-1-4222-0203-6(8)) Mason Crest.
Spence, Kelly. Emma Stone. 2015. (ENG., Illus.). 32p. (J). (978-0-7787-8078-6(3)) Crabtree Publishing Co.
Spencer, Liv. The Miranda Cosgrove & iCarly Spectacular! Unofficial & Unstoppable. 2010. (ENG., Illus.). 142p. (J). (gr. 4-7). pap. (978-1-55022-929-5(X)) Filmer Ltd.
Spinner, Stephanie. Who Is Steven Spielberg? 2013. (Who Is... ? Ser.). lib. bdg. 16.00 (978-0-606-34157-8(9), Turtleback) Turtleback Bks.
Stair, Nancy L. Michelle Yeoh. 2009. (Martial Arts Masters Ser.). 112p. (gr. 5-5). 63.90 (978-1-61514-375-7(0)) Rosen Publishing Group, Inc., The.
Stone, Adam. John Cena. 2011. (Pro Wrestling Champions Ser.). (ENG., Illus.). 24p. (J). (gr. 3-7). lib. bdg. 25.95 (978-1-60014-636-7(8), Torque Bks.) Bellwether Media.
Stone, Amy. Jackie Chan. 2007. (Today's Superstars). (Illus.). 32p. (gr. 5-8). lib. bdg. 31.95 (978-0-8368-7648-2(2)) Stevens, Gareth Publishing LLLP.
—Jim Carrey. 2007. (Today's Superstars). (Illus.). 32p. (gr. 5-8). lib. bdg. 31.95 (978-0-8368-8197-4(4)) Stevens, Gareth Publishing LLLP.
Sutcliffe, Jane & Walt Disney Company Staff. Walt Disney. 2009. (History Maker Biographies Ser.). (gr. 3-6). 26.60 (978-1-58013-704-1(0), Lerner Pubns.) Lerner Publishing Group.
Taliadoros, Jenny, ed. Doris Day Paper Dolls. 2007. (ENG., Illus.). 16p. pap. 12.00 (978-0-9790668-4-9(0)) Paper Studio Pr.
Thomas, William David. Johnny Depp. 2007. (Today's Superstars). (Illus.). 32p. (gr. 5-8). lib. bdg. 31.95 (978-0-8368-7650-5(4)) Stevens, Gareth Publishing LLLP.
Tieck, Sarah. Jaden Smith: Talented Actor, 1 vol. 2011. (Big Buddy Biographies Set 6 Ser.). (ENG., Illus.). 32p. (J). (gr. 2-5). 28.50 (978-1-61714-707-4(9)) ABDO Publishing Co.
—Johnny Depp: Famous Actor, 1 vol. 2009. (Big Buddy Biographies Set 3 Ser.). (ENG., Illus.). 32p. (J). (gr. 2-5). 28.50 (978-1-60453-707-9(8)) ABDO Publishing Co.
—Liam Hemsworth: Star of the Hunger Games, 1 vol. 2013. (Big Buddy Biographies Set 9 Ser.). (ENG.). 32p. (J). (gr. 2-5). lib. bdg. 28.50 (978-1-61783-749-4(0), Big Buddy Bks.) ABDO Publishing Co.
—Taylor Lautner: Star of Twilight, 1 vol. 2011. (Big Buddy Biographies Set 6 Ser.). (ENG., Illus.). 32p. (J). (gr. 2-5). 28.50 (978-1-61714-704-3(4)) ABDO Publishing Co.
Toler, Pamela D. Matt Damon. 2012. (Role Model Entertainers Ser.). 64p. (J). (gr. 7). 22.95 (978-1-4222-2718-3(9)) Mason Crest.
Torres, Jennifer. Kate Hudson. 2005. (Blue Banner Biography Ser.). (Illus.). 32p. (J). (gr. 3-8). lib. bdg. 25.70 (978-1-58415-381-8(4)) Mitchell Lane Pubs., Inc.
Tracy, Kathleen. Johnny Depp. 2007. (Blue Banner Biography Ser.). (Illus.). 32p. (J). (gr. 4-7). lib. bdg. 25.70 (978-1-58415-614-7(7)) Mitchell Lane Pubs., Inc.
Uschan, Michael V. Halle Berry. 2012. (People in the News Ser.). (ENG., Illus.). 128p. (gr. 7-10). lib. bdg. 39.40 (978-1-4205-0817-8(2), Lucent Bks.) Cengage Gale.
Uschan, Michael V., ed. Tyler Perry. 2010. (People in the News Ser.). (ENG.). 96p. (YA). (gr. 7-12). 33.95 (978-1-4205-0309-8(X)) Cengage Gale.
Valliant, Regina. Judy Garland Cut-Out Dolls. Valliant, Regina & Lunzer, Lee, illus. 2007. (ENG.). 16p. pap. 12.00 (978-0-9790668-9-4(1)) Paper Studio Pr.
Watson, Stephanie. Heath Ledger: Talented Actor, 1 vol. 2010. (Lives Cut Short Set 1 Ser.). (ENG.). 112p. (J). (gr. 6-12). lib. bdg. 35.64 (978-1-60453-789-5(2)) ABDO Publishing Co.
Weber, Terri Smith. Halle Berry: Fighting for First. 2003. (J). pap. (978-0-9740180-8-9(2)); lib. bdg. (978-0-9740180-7-2(4)) Panda Publishing, L.L.C. (Bios for Kids).
White, Katherine. The Wayans Brothers. 2009. (Famous Families Ser.). 48p. (gr. 5-5). 53.00 (978-1-61512-512-8(4)) Rosen Publishing Group, Inc., The.
Williams, Mel. Stars in the Arena: Meet the Hotties of the Hunger Games. 2012. (ENG.). 48p. (YA). (gr. 7). pap. 9.99 (978-1-4424-5363-0(X), Simon Pulse) Simon Pulse.
Yasuda, Anita. James Cameron. 2010. (Remarkable People Ser.). (Illus.). 24p. (J). (gr. 4-6). pap. 11.95 (978-1-61690-176-9(4)); lib. bdg. 25.70 (978-1-61690-175-2(6)) Weigl Pubs., Inc.
—Johnny Depp. 2012. (J). 27.13 (978-1-61913-536-9(1)) Weigl Pubs., Inc.
—Mike Meyers. 2012. (J). (978-1-61913-587-1(6)); pap. (978-1-61913-593-2(0)) Weigl Pubs., Inc.
Yoo, Paula & Wang, Lin. Shining Star: The Anna May Wong Story. 2016. (ENG., Illus.). 32p. (J). (gr. 1-4). pap. 9.95 (978-1-62014-257-8(0)) Lee & Low Bks., Inc.

MOTION PICTURES—FICTION

Abela, Deborah. Hollywood. O'Connor, George, illus. 2007. (Spy Force Ser.: 4). (ENG.). 240p. (J). (gr. 3-7). pap. 10.99 (978-1-4169-3969-6(5), Aladdin) Simon & Schuster Children's Publishing.
Acton, Vanessa. Director's Cut. 2016. (Atlas of Cursed Places Ser.). (ENG.). 104p. (YA). (gr. 6-12). lib. bdg. 26.65 (978-1-5124-1324-3(0), Darby Creek) Lerner Publishing Group.
Appelt, Kathi. Bat Jamboree. Sweet, Melissa, illus. 2004. 17.00 (978-0-7569-4074-4(5)) Perfection Learning Corp.
Appleton, Victor. The Moving Picture Boys at Panama: Stirring Adventures along the Great Canal. 2007. (ENG.). 140p. pap. 18.99 (978-1-4346-2170-2(7)); 152p. pap. 21.99 (978-1-4346-2230-3(4)) Creative Media Partners, LLC.
—The Moving Picture Boys on the Coast or Showing up the Perils of the Deep. 2004. reprint ed. pap. 24.95 (978-1-4179-1612-2(5)) Kessinger Publishing, LLC.
—Tom Swift & his Wizard Camera. 2005. 26.95 (978-1-4218-1507-7(9)); 196p. pap. 11.95 (978-1-4218-1607-4(5)) 1st World Publishing, Inc. (1st World Library - Literary Society).
—Tom Swift & His Wizard Camera: Or Thrilling Adventures While Taking Moving Pictu. l.t. ed. 2007. (ENG.). 148p. pap. 19.99 (978-1-4346-1579-4(0)) Creative Media Partners, LLC.
—Tom Swift & His Wizard Camera or Thril. 2006. pap. (978-1-4065-0912-0(4)) Dodo Pr.
Ashworth, Sherry. Close-Up. 2006. (ENG.). 256p. (J). (gr. 7). pap. 11.95 (978-1-4169-0474-8(3), Simon & Schuster Children's) Simon & Schuster, Ltd. GBR. Dist: Simon & Schuster, Inc.
Beecroft, Simon. R2-D2 & Friends. 2008. (Star Wars DK Readers Level 2 Ser.). (Illus.). 32p. lib. bdg. 13.55 (978-1-4364-5044-7(6), Turtleback) Turtleback Bks.
Bernard, Cecilia. Inside Divergent: The Initiate's World. 2014. (ENG., Illus.). 144p. (J). (gr. 8). pap. 9.99 (978-0-06-231560-1(9), Tegen, Katherine Bks) HarperCollins Pubs.
Blume, Lesley M. M. The Wondrous Journals of Dr. Wendell Wellington Wiggins. Foote, David, illus. 2013. (ENG.). 256p. (J). (gr. 3-7). pap. 7.99 (978-0-375-87218-1(3), Knopf Bks. for Young Readers) Random Hse. Children's Bks.
Bracegirdle, P. J. Sinister Scenes. (Joy of Spooking Ser.). (ENG.). 320p. (J). (gr. 3-7). 2012. pap. 6.99 (978-1-4169-3421-9(9)) 2011. 15.99 (978-1-4169-3420-2(0)) McElderry, Margaret K. Bks. (McElderry, Margaret K. Bks.).
Bryant, Annie. Maeve on the Red Carpet. 2009. (Beacon Street Girls Ser.: No. 3). (ENG.). 240p. (J). (gr. 4-8). pap. 6.99 (978-1-4169-6432-2(0), Aladdin) Simon & Schuster Children's Publishing.
Carlson, Bryce. Wall- E: Out There. Luthi, Morgan, illus. 2010. (ENG.). 112p. (J). (gr. 3-6). pap. 9.99 (978-1-60886-568-0(1)) Boom! Studios.
Castellucci, Cecil. Boy Proof. (ENG.). 208p. (YA). (gr. 9-18). 2005. 15.99 (978-0-7636-2333-3(4)) 2006. reprint ed. per. 8.99 (978-0-7636-2796-6(8)) Candlewick Pr.
Cheaney, J. B. I Don't Know How the Story Ends. 2015. (ENG.). 288p. (J). (gr. 4-7). 16.99 (978-1-4926-0944-5(7), 9781492609445, Sourcebooks Jabberwocky) Sourcebooks, Inc.
Conford, Ellen. Annabel the Actress Starring in Camping It Up. Andriani, Renee W., illus. 2005. (Annabel the Actress Ser.). 60p. (J). (gr. 2-5). 11.65 (978-0-7569-5555-7(6)) Perfection Learning Corp.
—Annabel the Actress Starring in Camping It Up. Andriani, Renee W., illus. 2013. (ENG.). 64p. (J). (gr. 2-5). pap. 13.99 (978-1-4814-0147-0(5), Simon & Schuster Bks. For Young Readers) Simon & Schuster Bks. For Young Readers.
—Annabel the Actress Starring in Just a Little Extra. Andriani, Renee W., illus. 2013. (ENG.). 64p. (J). (gr. 4-6). pap. 13.99 (978-1-4814-0148-7(3), Simon & Schuster Bks. For Young Readers) Simon & Schuster Bks. For Young Readers.
Costain, Meredith. Stella & the Movie Star. McGowan, Shane, illus. 2015. (Legends in Their Own Lunchbox Ser.). (ENG.). 56p. (gr. 2-3). pap. 7.99 (978-1-4966-0261-9(7), Legends in Their Own Lunchbox) Capstone Classroom.
Cousins, Lucy. Maisy Goes to the Movies. 2014. (Maisy First Experiences Ser.). lib. bdg. 17.20 (978-0-606-35156-0(6)) Turtleback Bks.
—Maisy Goes to the Movies: A Maisy First Experiences Book. Cousins, Lucy, illus. 2014. (Maisy Ser.). (ENG., Illus.). 32p. (J). (gr. -1-2). 6.99 (978-0-7636-7237-9(8)) Candlewick Pr.
Cowley, Joy. Meanies Night Out. 2009. pap. 8.25 (978-1-60559-229-9(3)) Hameray Publishing Group, Inc.
Darke, J. A. Do Not Watch. Evans, Neil, illus. 2016. (Spine Shivers Ser.). (ENG.). 128p. (gr. 3-4). lib. bdg. 26.65 (978-1-4965-3071-4(3)) Stone Arch Bks.
Dessen, Sarah. The Moon & More. 2013. (ENG.). 384p. (J). (gr. 7). 19.99 (978-0-670-78560-5(1), Viking Books for Young Readers) Penguin Young Readers Group.
Devine, Eric. Press Play. 2014. (ENG.). 368p. (YA). (gr. 3-17). pap. 9.95 (978-0-7624-5512-6(8), Running Pr. Kids) Running Pr. Bk. Pubs.
Dewin, Howie. Jem & the Holograms Movie Handbook. 2015. (ENG.). 64p. (J). (gr. 2-5). pap. 5.99 (978-0-545-90881-8(7)) Scholastic, Inc.
Dixon, Franklin W. Deception on the Set. 2015. (Hardy Boys Adventures Ser.: 8). (ENG., Illus.). 128p. (J). (gr. 3-7). pap.

6.99 *(978-1-4814-1406-7(2),* Aladdin) Simon & Schuster Children's Publishing.
Doctorow, Cory. Pirate Cinema. 2013. (ENG.). 384p. (YA). (gr. 7). pap. 9.99 *(978-0-7653-2909-7(3),* 9780765329097, Tor Teen) Doherty, Tom Assocs., LLC.
Dolby, Tom. Secret Society. 2011. (ENG.). 368p. (YA). (gr. 8). pap. 8.99 *(978-0-06-172163-2(8),* Tegen, Katherine Bks) HarperCollins Pubs.
Dorling Kindersley Publishing Staff. The Adventures of C-3PO. 2014. (Star Wars DK Readers Level 2 Ser.). lib. bdg. 13.55 *(978-0-606-35324-3(0))* Turtleback Bks.
Dorling Kindersley Publishing Staff & Beecroft, Simon. Clone Wars, Level 3: Yoda in Action! 2009. (DK Readers Ser.). (ENG.). 48p. (J). (gr. 2-4). pap. 3.99 *(978-0-7566-4514-4(X),* DK Children) Dorling Kindersley Publishing, Inc.
Dorling Kindersley Publishing Staff & Dolan, Hannah. Phantom Menace. 2012. (DK Readers Ser.). (ENG.). 32p. (J). (gr. 1-3). 14.99 *(978-0-7566-8692-5(X),* DK Children) Dorling Kindersley Publishing, Inc.
—The Phantom Menace, Level 2. 2012. (DK Readers Ser.). (ENG.). 32p. (J). (gr. 1-3). 3.99 *(978-0-7566-8693-2(8),* DK Children) Dorling Kindersley Publishing, Inc.
Dorling Kindersley Publishing Staff & Scott, Heather. The Clone Wars - Forces of Darkness, Level 3. 2009. (DK Readers Ser.). (ENG.). 48p. (J). (gr. 2-4). pap. 3.99 *(978-0-7566-5201-2(4),* DK Children) Dorling Kindersley Publishing, Inc.
—Jedi in Training. 2009. (DK Readers Ser.). (ENG.). 32p. (J). (gr. 1-3). pap. 3.99 *(978-0-7566-5199-2(9),* DK Children) Dorling Kindersley Publishing, Inc.
Dower, Laura. They Came from Planet Q. Schlafman, Dave, illus. 2010. (Monster Squad Ser.: 4). (ENG.). 144p. (J). (gr. 2-4). pap. 5.99 *(978-0-448-44915-9(3),* Grosset & Dunlap) Penguin Young Readers Group.
Edge, Christopher. Shadows of the Silver Screen. 2014. (Penelope Tredwell Mysteries Ser.: 2). (ENG.). 256p. (J). (gr. 3-7). 16.99 *(978-0-8075-7319-8(1))* Whitman, Albert & Co.
Encyclopaedia Britannica, Inc. Staff, compiled by. How the Elephant Got His Trunk. 2008. 49.95 *(978-1-59339-556-8(6))* Encyclopaedia Britannica, Inc.
Enderle, Dotti & McWilliam, Howard. Ghost Detectors Book 12: Monsters!, 1 vol. 2012. (Ghost Detectors Ser.). (ENG., Illus.). 80p. (J). (gr. 2-5). 27.07 *(978-1-61641-628-7(9))* Magic Wagon.
Fox, Hugh. Wobbley Zombies. 2004. 64p. (J). per. 5.95 *(978-1-930648-80-7(4))* Goose River Pr.
Frost, Michael. Movie Mission: Book Two in the Deathstalker Trilogy. 2011. (Hardy Boys (All New) Undercover Brothers Ser.: 38). (ENG.). 176p. (J). (gr. 3-7). pap. 5.99 *(978-1-4424-0266-9(0),* Aladdin) Simon & Schuster Children's Publishing.
Gaiman, Neil. Mirrormask. McKean, Dave, illus. 2005. (ENG.). 80p. (J). (gr. 5). 16.99 *(978-0-06-082109-8(4))* HarperCollins Pubs.
Gorgas, Paula Blais. Little Lost Leprechaun. 2006. (Illus.). 24p. (J). lib. bdg. 24.95 *(978-0-9778651-4-7(2))* Dragonfly Publishing, Inc.
Grabenstein, Chris. Beach Party Surf Monkey. Allen, Brooke A., illus. 2017. (Welcome to Wonderland Ser.: 2). (ENG.). 320p. (J). (gr. 3-7). 13.99 *(978-0-553-53610-2(9),* Random Hse. Bks. for Young Readers) Random Hse. Children's Bks.
Grace, N. B. Lights, Camera, Action! 14th ed. 2009. (ENG.). 128p. (J). pap. 4.99 *(978-1-4231-1609-7(7))* Disney Pr.
Greenwald, Tommy. Pete Milano's Guide to Being a Movie Star. Roher, Rebecca, illus. 2016. (ENG.). 256p. (J). 13.99 *(978-1-62672-167-8(X),* 9781626721678) Roaring Brook Pr.
Hamilton, Sable. Free Spirit. 2015. (Stardust Stables Ser.). (ENG.). 160p. (gr. 3-6). lib. bdg. 22.65 *(978-1-4342-9792-1(6))* Stone Arch Bks.
—A Star Is Born. 2015. (Stardust Stables Ser.). (ENG.). 160p. (gr. 3-6). lib. bdg. 22.65 *(978-1-4342-9790-7(X))* Stone Arch Bks.
—Stardust Stables. 2015. (Stardust Stables Ser.). (ENG.). 160p. (gr. 3-6). lib. bdg. 67.95 *(978-1-4965-0112-7(8),* Stardust Stables) Stone Arch Bks.
—Wildfire. 2015. (Stardust Stables Ser.). (ENG.). 160p. (gr. 3-6). lib. bdg. 22.65 *(978-1-4342-9791-4(8))* Stone Arch Bks.
Handford, Martin. Where's Waldo? in Hollywood. 2007. (Where's Waldo? Ser.). (Illus.). 24p. (gr. 4-7). lib. bdg. 18.40 *(978-1-4178-2425-0(5),* Turtleback) Turtleback Bks.
Harrison, Lisi. Dial L for Loser. 2008. (Clique Novels Ser.). 268p. 20.00 *(978-1-60686-291-9(X))* Perfection Learning Corp.
Hartinger, Brent. Split Screen: Attack of the Soul-Sucking Brain Zombies; Bride of the Soul-Sucking Brain Zombies. 2007. 304p. (YA). (gr. 9-12). lib. bdg. 17.89 *(978-0-06-082409-9(3),* HarperTeen) HarperCollins Pubs.
Harvey, Jacqueline. Clementine Rose & the Movie Magic. 2015. (Clementine Rose Ser.: 9). (ENG., Illus.). 128p. (J). (gr. 1-3). pap. 8.99 *(978-0-85798-518-7(3))* Random Hse. Australia AUS. Dist: Independent Pubs. Group.
Hicks, Barbara Jean & Disney Book Group Staff. A Sister More Like Me. Disney Storybook Artists Staff et al, illus. 2013. (ENG.). 32p. (J). (gr. 1-3). 15.99 *(978-1-4231-7014-3(8))* Disney Pr.
Holm, Jennifer L. & Holm, Matthew. Babymouse Tales from the Locker Presents Lights, Camera, Messy Whiskers. 2017. (Babymouse Tales from the Locker Ser.: 1). (ENG., Illus.). 208p. (J). (gr. 3-7). 13.99 *(978-0-399-55438-4(6),* Random Hse. Bks. for Young Readers) Random Hse. Children's Bks.
—Fear the Amoeba. Holm, Jennifer L. & Holm, Matthew, illus. 2014. (Squish Ser.: No. 6). (ENG., Illus.). 96p. (J). (gr. 2-5). 12.99 *(978-0-307-98303-9(X));*No. 6. pap. 6.99 *(978-0-307-98302-2(1))* Random Hse. Children's Bks. (Random Hse. Bks. for Young Readers).
Hope, Laura Lee. The Moving Picture Girls at Oak Farm: Or, Queer Happenings While Taking Rural Plays. 2007. (ENG.). 140p. pap. 18.99 *(978-1-4346-3488-7(4));* 154p. pap. 21.99 *(978-1-4346-3489-4(2))* Creative Media Partners, LLC.
—The Moving Picture Girls under the Palms: Or Lost in the Wilds of Florida. 2007. 140p. pap. 18.99 *(978-1-4346-0717-1(8));* (ENG.). 158p. pap. 21.99 *(978-1-4346-0777-5(1))* Creative Media Partners, LLC.
Jones, Buck. Buck Jones Rangers-Cowboys Collection. 2011. 68p. 36.95 *(978-1-258-07141-7(X))* Literary Licensing, LLC.
Kaplan-Taylor, Maeve. At the Movies with Maeve. 2004. (Illus.). 36p. (J). 3.99 *(978-0-9746587-4-2(X),* Beacon Street Girls) B*tween Productions, Inc.
Keene, Carolyn. Movie Madness. Francis, Peter, illus. 2016. (Nancy Drew Clue Book Ser.: 5). (ENG.). 96p. (J). (gr. 1-4). pap. 5.99 *(978-1-4814-5820-7(5),* Aladdin) Simon & Schuster Children's Publishing.
Kidd, Ronald. The Year of the Bomb. 2009. (ENG.). 208p. (YA). (gr. 7). pap. 5.99 *(978-1-4169-9625-5(7));* 16.99 *(978-1-4169-5892-5(4))* Simon & Schuster Bks. For Young Readers. (Simon & Schuster Bks. For Young Readers).
—Year of the Bomb. 2009. 208p. 5.99 *(978-1-4169-9504-3(8))* Studio Fun International.
Kinney, Jeff. Double Down. 2016. (Diary of a Wimpy Kid Ser.: Bk. 11). (ENG., Illus.). 224p. (J). (gr. 3-7). 13.95 *(978-1-4197-2344-5(8));* E-Book 12.56 *(978-1-61312-992-0(0))* Abrams, Inc. (Amulet Bks.).
—Double Down. 2016. (Diary of a Wimpy Kid Ser.: 11). (J). lib. bdg. 25.70 *(978-0-606-38998-3(9))* Turtleback Bks.
Krulik, Nancy. It's Snow Joke. John and Wendy Staff, illus. 2006. (Katie Kazoo, Switcheroo Ser.: 22). (ENG.). 80p. (J). (gr. 2-4). pap. 3.99 *(978-0-448-44396-6(1),* Grosset & Dunlap) Penguin Young Readers Group.
Kyi, Tanya Lloyd. Anywhere but Here. 2013. (ENG., Illus.). 320p. (YA). (gr. 9). 17.99 *(978-1-4424-8070-4(X));* pap. 9.99 *(978-1-4424-8069-8(6))* Simon Pulse. (Simon Pulse).
Lasky, Kathryn. The Extra. 2013. (ENG.). 320p. (YA). (gr. 7). 16.99 *(978-0-7636-3972-3(9))* Candlewick Pr.
Magorian, Michelle. Just Henry. 2015. (ENG.). 720p. (J). (gr. 5-7). pap. 12.99 *(978-1-4052-7695-5(9))* Egmont Bks., Ltd. GBR. Dist: Independent Pubs. Group.
Martinusen-Coloma, Cindy. Ruby Unscripted, 1 vol. 2009. (ENG.). 272p. (YA). (gr. 7-18). pap. 12.99 *(978-1-59554-356-1(2))* Nelson, Thomas Inc.
Mass, Wendy. Finally. 2011. (ENG.). 304p. (J). (gr. 3-7). pap. 6.99 *(978-0-545-05243-6(2),* Scholastic Paperbacks) Scholastic, Inc.
Mata, Julie. Kate Walden Directs: Bride of Slug Man. 2016. (Kate Walden Directs Ser.). (ENG.). 288p. (J). (gr. 3-7). pap. 6.99 *(978-1-4847-4746-9(1))* Hyperion Bks. for Children.
—Night of the Zombie Chickens. 2014. (Kate Walden Ser.). (ENG., Illus.). 288p. (J). (gr. 3-7). 16.99 *(978-1-4231-9459-0(4))* Hyperion Bks. for Children.
McDonald, Megan. Judy Moody Goes to Hollywood: Behind the Scenes with Judy Moody & Friends. Reynolds, Peter H. & Candlewick Press Staff, illus. 2011. (Judy Moody Ser.). (ENG.). 160p. (J). (gr. 1-4). 14.99 *(978-0-7636-5551-8(1))* Candlewick Pr.
McFarlane, Susannah. Drama Queen: EJ12 Girl Hero. 2017. (Illus.). 128p. (J). pap. 5.99 *(978-1-61067-509-3(6))* Kane Miller.
McKean, Dave. Mirrormask. McKean, Dave, illus. 2005. (Illus.). 80p. (J). lib. bdg. 17.89 *(978-0-06-082110-4(8))* HarperCollins Pubs.
Morgan, Melissa J. Extra Credit. 2009. (Camp Confidential Ser.: 22). (ENG.). 160p. (J). (gr. 4-7). pap. 4.99 *(978-0-448-45216-6(2),* Grosset & Dunlap) Penguin Young Readers Group.
Morrill, Lauren. My Unscripted Life. 2016. (ENG.). 288p. (YA). (gr. 7). 17.99 *(978-0-553-49801-1(0),* Delacorte Pr.) Random Hse. Children's Bks.
Movie Menace. 2011. (Hardy Boys (All New) Undercover Brothers Ser.: 37). (ENG.). 176p. (J). (gr. 3-7). pap. 5.99 *(978-1-4424-0258-4(X),* Aladdin) Simon & Schuster Children's Publishing.
Mullarkey, Lisa. A Filming Fiasco, 1 vol. Franco, Paula, illus. 2016. (ENG.). 112p. (J). lib. bdg. *(978-1-62402-164-0(6))* Magic Wagon.
Paige, D. M. Box-Office Smash. (Opportunity Ser.). (ENG.). 112p. (YA). (gr. 6-12). 2015. 34.65 *(978-1-4677-6012-6(9),* Lerner Digital) 2013. pap. 7.95 *(978-1-4677-1494-5(1),* Darby Creek) 2013. lib. bdg. 27.93 *(978-1-4677-1371-9(6),* Darby Creek) Lerner Publishing Group.
Pauley, Kimberly. Cat Girl's Day Off, 1 vol. 2012. (ENG.). 336p. (YA). 17.95 *(978-1-60060-883-4(3),* Tu Bks.) Lee & Low Bks., Inc.
Pfeffer, Susan Beth. Revenge of the Aztecs. 2004. 118p. (J). lib. bdg. 16.92 *(978-1-4242-0763-3(0))* Fitzgerald Bks.
Pflugfelder, Bob & Hockensmith, Steve. Nick & Tesla's Special Effects Spectacular: A Mystery with Animatronics, Alien Makeup, Camera Gear, & Other Movie Magic You Can Make Yourself! 2015. (Nick & Tesla Ser.: 5). (ENG.). 256p. (J). (gr. 4-7). 12.95 *(978-1-59474-760-1(1))* Quirk Bks.
Poulsen, David A. The Hunk Machine. 2nd rev. ed. 2007. (Salt & Pepper Chronicles). (ENG.). 160p. (J). (gr. 4-7). 6.95 *(978-1-55263-723-4(9))* Leaf Storm Pr.
Rey. Vive le Cinema. 16.95 *(978-2-09-250166-5(6))* Nathan, Fernand FRA. Dist: Distribooks, Inc.
Rippin, Sally. The Night Fright. Fukuoka, Aki, illus. 2015. 43p. (J). *(978-1-61067-451-5(0))* Kane Miller.
—The Night Fright: Billie B Brown. Fukuoka, Aki, illus. 2016. (ENG.). 48p. (J). pap. 4.99 *(978-1-61067-391-4(3))* Kane Miller.
Ruditis, P. J. Love, Hollywood Style. 2013. (Romantic Comedies Ser.). (ENG., Illus.). 272p. (YA). (gr. 7). pap. 13.99 *(978-1-4814-1539-2(5),* Simon Pulse) Simon Pulse.
Saxon, Victoria. Big Trouble in Little Rodentia. 2016. (Illus.). (J). ***(978-1-5182-0883-6(5))*** Random House Children's Books.
Scholastic, Inc. Staff & Rusu, Meredith. Lights, Camera, Shopkins! 2016. (Shopkins Ser.: 2). (ENG.). 24p. (J). (gr. -1-3). pap. 4.99 *(978-0-545-94041-2(9))* Scholastic, Inc.
Shaler, Robert. The Boy Scouts with the Motion Picture P. 2005. pap. 21.95 *(978-1-885529-59-6(7))* Stevens Publishing.
Shan, Darren, pseud. Slawter. 2007. (ENG.). 240p. (J). (gr. 10-17). pap. 10.99 *(978-0-316-01388-8(9))* Little, Brown Bks. for Young Readers.
Shaw, Tucker. Oh Yeah, Audrey! 2014. (ENG., Illus.). 256p. (YA). (gr. 8-17). 16.95 *(978-1-4197-1223-4(3),* Amulet Bks.) Abrams, Inc.
Sheldon, Dyan. Confessions of a Teenage Hollywood Star. 2007. (ENG., Illus.). 208p. (YA). (gr. 7-12). per. 7.99 *(978-0-7636-3408-7(5))* Candlewick Pr.
Sortland, Bjorn. The Dream Factory Starring Anna & Henry. Christianson, Emily V. & Hedin, Robert, trs. from NOR. Elling, Lars, illus. 2003. (Picture Bks.). 40p. (J). (gr. -1-3). 15.95 *(978-0-87614-009-3(6),* Carolrhoda Bks.) Lerner Publishing Group.
Star Wars Villains. 2011. (Illus.). (J). *(978-0-545-28664-0(6))* Scholastic, Inc.
Steel, Danielle. Pretty Minnie in Hollywood. Valiant, Kristi, illus. 2016. (ENG.). 32p. (J). (gr. -1-2). 17.99 *(978-0-553-53755-0(5),* Doubleday Bks. for Young Readers) Random Hse. Children's Bks.
Stern, J. David, et al. Eloise in Hollywood. Enik, Ted, illus. 2006. (Eloise Ser.). (ENG.). 70p. (J). (gr. -1-3). 19.99 *(978-0-689-84289-4(9),* Simon & Schuster Bks. For Young Readers) Simon & Schuster Bks. For Young Readers.
Stevens, Mark. Tailspin Tommy: The Mystery of the Midnight Patrol. Beebe, Robb, illus. 2011. 226p. 44.95 *(978-1-258-10164-0(5))* Literary Licensing, LLC.
Stevenson, Steve. The Hollywood Intrigue #9. Turconi, Stefano, illus. 2015. (Agatha: Girl of Mystery Ser.: 9). (ENG.). 144p. (J). (gr. 3-7). 5.99 *(978-0-448-48680-2(6),* Grosset & Dunlap) Penguin Young Readers Group.
Stilton, Thea. Thea Stilton & the Hollywood Hoax. 2016. (Thea Stilton Ser.: 23). lib. bdg. 18.40 *(978-0-606-38799-6(4))* Turtleback Bks.
Stine, R. L. A Midsummer Night's Scream. 2013. (ENG.). 256p. (YA). (gr. 7). 17.99 *(978-1-250-02434-3(X),* 9781250024343) Feiwel & Friends.
Stone, Danika & Goble, Karin. All the Feels. 2016. (ENG., Illus.). 336p. (YA). pap. 9.99 *(978-1-250-08409-5(1),* 9781250084095) Feiwel & Friends.
Strand, Jeff. The Greatest Zombie Movie Ever. 2016. (ENG.). 272p. (YA). (gr. 6-12). pap. 10.99 *(978-1-4926-2814-9(X),* 9781492628149) Sourcebooks, Inc.
Strange, Jason. To Wake the Dead, 1 vol. Parks, Phil, illus. 2011. (Jason Strange Ser.). (ENG.). 72p. (gr. 2-3). pap. 6.25 *(978-1-4342-3094-2(5));* 25.32 *(978-1-4342-2963-2(7))* Stone Arch Bks.
Struyk-Bonn, Chris. Nice Girls Endure. 2016. (ENG.). 256p. (gr. 9-12). 16.95 *(978-1-63079-047-9(8))* Switch Pr.
Suma, Nova Ren. Fade Out. 2012. (ENG.). 288p. (YA). (gr. 7). pap. 9.99 *(978-1-4169-7565-6(9),* Simon Pulse) Simon Pulse.
Tashjian, Janet. My Life as a Stuntboy. Tashjian, Jake, illus. 2011. (My Life Ser.: 2). (ENG.). 272p. (J). (gr. 4-7). 15.99 *(978-0-8050-8904-2(7),* 9780805089042, Holt, Henry & Co. Bks. For Young Readers) Holt, Henry & Co.
—My Life as a Stuntboy. Tashjian, Jake, illus. 2015. (My Life Ser.: 2). (ENG.). 288p. (J). (gr. 4-7). pap. 7.99 *(978-1-250-01038-4(1),* 9781250010384) Square Fish.
Tillworth, Mary. Movie Night Magic! (Shimmer & Shine) Aikins, David, illus. 2016. (Step into Reading Ser.). (ENG.). 24p. (J). (gr. -1-1). 4.99 *(978-1-101-93704-4(1),* Random Hse. Bks. for Young Readers) Random Hse. Children's Bks.
Victor, Appleton. Tom Swift & His Wizard Camera: Or Thrilling Adventures While Taking Moving Pictu. 2007. (ENG.). 132p. pap. 18.99 *(978-1-4346-1485-8(9))* Creative Media Partners, LLC.
Wheeler, Shannon & Torres, J. Wall E Vol. 1: Recharge. Luthi, Morgan, illus. 2010. (ENG.). 112p. (J). 24.99 *(978-1-60886-554-3(1))* Boom! Studios.
Wheeler, Shannon, et al. Wall-E Vol. 1: Recharge. Luthi, Morgan & Barks, Carl, illus. 2010. (ENG.). 112p. (J). pap. 9.99 *(978-1-60886-512-3(6))* Boom! Studios.
Wilsdon, Christina. Lights! Action! California! Hockerman, Dennis, illus. 2006. 26p. (J). 7.99 *(978-1-59939-009-3(4))* Cornerstone Pr.

MOTION PICTURES—PLAY WRITING
see Motion Picture Plays

MOTION PICTURES IN EDUCATION
Fernandez, Elizabeth. Screenwriting & Directing for Secondary Schools. 2010. 181p. pap. 68.95 *(978-1-4452-9245-8(9))* Lulu Pr., Inc.

MOTOR BOATS
see Motorboats

MOTOR BUSES
see Buses

MOTOR CARS
see Automobiles

MOTOR COURTS
see Hotels, Motels, etc.

MOTOR CYCLES
see Motorcycles

MOTOR SPORTS
see also Automobile Racing
2004. (Machines at Work Ser.). 24p. (J). (gr. -1-3). lib. bdg. 21.36 Child's World, Inc., The.
ABDO Publishing Company Staff. Inside the Speedway. 2014. (Inside the Speedway Ser.: 6). (ENG.). 48p. (J). (gr. 3-6). lib. bdg. 163.95 *(978-1-62403-401-5(2),* SportsZone) ABDO Publishing Co.
Adamson, Thomas K. Freestyle Motocross. 2010. (Dirt Bike World Ser.). (ENG.). 32p. (gr. 1-2). pap. 47.70 *(978-1-4296-5707-5(3),* Blazers) Capstone Press of Coughlan Cos.
—Motocross Racing. 2010. (Dirt Bike World Ser.). (ENG.). 32p. (gr. 1-2). pap. 47.70 *(978-1-4296-5706-8(5),* Blazers) Capstone Press of Coughlan Cos.
Carney, Larry. Jeff Gordon. PC Treasures Staff, ed. Houghton, Chris & Morrison, Jeff, illus. 2009. (Nascar Drivers Coloring/Sticker Book Ser.). (ENG.). 96p. (J). pap. 6.95 *(978-1-60072-162-5(1))* PC Treasures, Inc.
Carr, Aaron. Motocross. 2013. (Deportes de Moda Ser.). (SPA., Illus.). 24p. (J). (gr. k-2). lib. bdg. 27.13 *(978-1-62127-629-6(5),* AV2 by Weigl) Weigl Pubs., Inc.
Crawford, Cindy. Drag Racing Basics: Christmas Tree to Finish Line Has Something for All Drag Racing Enthusiasts. 2003. (ENG., Illus.). 168p. pap. 24.95 *(978-0-929758-22-0(6),* 0929758226) Beeman Jorgensen, Inc.
Gifford, Clive. The Inside Story of Motorsports. 2011. (Sports World Ser.). (YA). (gr. 5-9). lib. bdg. 29.25 *(978-1-4488-4848-5(2))* Rosen Publishing Group, Inc., The.
—Motorsports. 2016. (Great Sporting Events Ser.). (ENG., Illus.). 32p. (J). (gr. 4-6). pap. 11.99 *(978-1-4451-4963-9(X),* Franklin Watts) Hachette Children's Group GBR. Dist: Hachette Bk. Group.
Hoblin, Paul & Hueller, Patrick. Tractor Pulling: Tearing It Up. 2014. (Dirt & Destruction Sports Zone Ser.). (ENG., Illus.). 32p. (gr. 4-8). lib. bdg. 26.60 *(978-1-4677-2123-3(9),* Lerner Pubns.) Lerner Publishing Group.
Hurley, Michael. Racing, 1 vol. 2013. (Fantastic Sports Facts Ser.). (ENG.). 32p. (gr. 1-3). pap. 8.29 *(978-1-4109-5112-0(X));* lib. bdg. 29.99 *(978-1-4109-5105-2(7))* Heinemann-Raintree. (Read Me!).
Kirkpatrick, Rob. Dale Earnhardt Jr. NASCAR Road Racer/Piloto de NASCAR. 2004. (Hot Shots / Grandes Idolos Ser.).Tr. of Piloto de NASCAR. (ENG & SPA., Illus.). 24p. (J). (gr. 3-6). 22.60 *(978-1-4042-7540-9(1),* Editorial Buenas Letras) Rosen Publishing Group, Inc., The.
Mapua, Jeff. Extreme Motorsports. 2015. (Sports to the Extreme Ser.). (ENG., Illus.). 48p. (J). (gr. 5-6). 30.25 *(978-1-4994-3549-8(5),* Rosen Central) Rosen Publishing Group, Inc., The.
Mason, Paul. Motorcycles. 2010. (Motorsports Ser.). 32p. (J). (gr. 3-6). 28.50 *(978-1-60753-121-0(6))* Amicus Publishing.
Mezzanotte, Jim. Supermoto. 2006. (Motorcycle Racing: the Fast Track Ser.). (Illus.). 24p. (gr. 5-8). lib. bdg. 23.00 *(978-0-8368-6426-7(3));* (SPA., lib. bdg. 23.00 *(978-0-8368-6444-1(1),* Gareth Stevens Learning Library) Stevens, Gareth Publishing LLLP.
Parker, Steve. On the Race Track. 2010. (J). 28.50 *(978-1-59920-287-7(5))* Black Rabbit Bks.
PC Treasures Staff, ed. Jimmie Johnson, Vol. 48. 2009. (Nascar Drivers Coloring/Sticker Book Ser.). (ENG., Illus.). 96p. (J). 6.95 *(978-1-60072-161-8(3))* PC Treasures, Inc.
Tyson, Carolee. Factory Ride. 2004. 198p. (YA). per. 6.99 *(978-0-9754459-0-7(1))* Pumpkin Ridge Publishing.
Weber, M. Wild Moments on Dirt Bikes. 2017. (Wild Moments of Motorsports Ser.). (ENG.). 32p. (gr. 3-4). lib. bdg. 27.99 ***(978-1-5157-7406-8(6),*** Edge Bks.) Capstone Press of Coughlan Cos.
Woods, Bob. Snowmobile Racers. 2010. (Kid Racers Ser.). (Illus.). 48p. (J). pap. 8.95 *(978-0-7660-3756-4(8));* (gr. 5-9). 25.27 *(978-0-7660-3487-7(9))* Enslow Pubs., Inc.

MOTOR TRUCKS
see Trucks

MOTORBOAT RACING
Bach, Rachel. The Boat Race. 2017. (Let's Race Ser.). (ENG., Illus.). 16p. (J). (gr. -1-1). pap. 7.99 *(978-1-68152-130-5(X))* Amicus.
—The Boat Race. 2016. (Let's Race Ser.). (ENG., Illus.). 16p. (J). (gr. k-3). 17.95 *(978-1-60753-911-7(X))* Amicus Publishing.
Bullard, Lisa. Powerboats. 2004. (Pull Ahead Bks.). (ENG., Illus.). 32p. (gr. k-2). (J). pap. 6.95 *(978-0-8225-9921-0(X));* lib. bdg. 22.60 *(978-0-8225-0744-4(7))* Lerner Publishing Group.
Ertle-Rickard, Stephen. Powerboat Race. 2008. (321 Go! Ser.). (ENG., Illus.). 36p. pap. *(978-1-84167-786-6(8))* Ransom Publishing Ltd.
Gigliotti, Jim. Powerboat Racing. 2012. (Extreme Sports Ser.). (ENG., Illus.). 32p. (J). (gr. 2-5). lib. bdg. 28.50 *(978-1-60973-181-6(6),* 201129) Child's World, Inc., The.
Hauenstein, Michael. Speedboat Racers. 2010. (Kid Racers Ser.). (Illus.). 48p. (J). pap. 8.95 *(978-0-7660-3755-7(X));* (gr. 5-9). 25.27 *(978-0-7660-3485-3(2))* Enslow Pubs., Inc.
Hetrick, Hans. Hydroplanes, 1 vol. 2010. (Full Throttle Ser.). (ENG.). 32p. (gr. 3-4). lib. bdg. 27.99 *(978-1-4296-4753-3(1),* Edge Bks.) Capstone Press of Coughlan Cos.
—Sport Bikes, 1 vol. 2010. (Full Throttle Ser.). (ENG.). 32p. (gr. 3-4). lib. bdg. 27.99 *(978-1-4296-4751-9(5),* Edge Bks.) Capstone Press of Coughlan Cos.
Hofer, Charles. Speedboats. (World's Fastest Machines Ser.). 24p. 2009. (gr. 2-3). 42.50 *(978-1-60854-856-9(2))* 2008. (Illus.). (J). (gr. 3-7). lib. bdg. 22.60 *(978-1-4042-4176-3(0))* Rosen Publishing Group, Inc., The. (PowerKids Pr.).
MacArthur, Collin. Inside a Speedboat. 2014. (Life in the Fast Lane Ser.). 48p. (J). (gr. 4-6). 31.36 *(978-1-62713-037-0(3))* Cavendish Square Publishing.

MOTORBOAT RACING—FICTION
Farber, E. S. Operation Fireball. Beene, Jason, illus. 2014. (Fish Finelli Ser.). (ENG.). 172p. (J). (gr. 3-7). 15.99 *(978-1-4521-1083-7(2))* Chronicle Bks. LLC.
Kay, Ross. The Go Ahead Boys & the Racing Motor-Boat. 2007. 176p. per. *(978-1-4065-1858-0(1))* Dodo Pr.
—Go Ahead Boys & the Racing Motorboat. 2007. (ENG.). 154p. pap. 19.99 *(978-1-4264-3551-5(7));* 176p. pap. 21.99 *(978-1-4264-3606-2(8))* Creative Media Partners, LLC.

MOTORBOATS
Bullard, Lisa. Powerboats. 2004. (Pull Ahead Bks.). (ENG., Illus.). 32p. (gr. k-2). (J). pap. 6.95 *(978-0-8225-9921-0(X));* lib. bdg. 22.60 *(978-0-8225-0744-4(7))* Lerner Publishing Group.
Eason, Sarah. How Does a Powerboat Work? 2010. (How Does It Work? Ser.). 32p. (J). (gr. 3-6). lib. bdg. 26.00 *(978-1-4339-3474-2(4));* (Illus.). pap. 10.50 *(978-1-4339-3475-9(2))* Stevens, Gareth Publishing LLLP. (Gareth Stevens Learning Library).
Gabrielson, Curt. Kinetic Contraptions: Build a Hovercraft, Airboat, & More with a Hobby Motor. 2010. (ENG., Illus.). 192p. (J). (gr. 7-18). pap. 16.95 *(978-1-55652-957-3(0))* Chicago Review Pr., Inc.
Gigliotti, Jim. Personal Watercraft. 2012. (Extreme Sports Ser.). (ENG., Illus.). 32p. (J). (gr. 2-5). lib. bdg. 28.50 *(978-1-60973-180-9(8),* 201128) Child's World, Inc., The.
—Powerboat Racing. 2012. (Extreme Sports Ser.). (ENG., Illus.). 32p. (J). (gr. 2-5). lib. bdg. 28.50 *(978-1-60973-181-6(6),* 201129) Child's World, Inc., The.
Hamilton, John. Hydroplanes. 2012. (Speed Zone Ser.). 32p. (J). (gr. 3-9). lib. bdg. 27.07 *(978-1-61783-528-5(5),* A&D Xtreme) ABDO Publishing Co.
Hofer, Charles. Speedboats. 2009. (World's Fastest Machines Ser.). 24p. (gr. 2-3). 42.50 *(978-1-60854-856-9(2),* PowerKids Pr.) Rosen Publishing Group, Inc., The.
Jacobson, Bob. Ole Evinrude & His Outboard Motor. 2009. (Badger Biographies Ser.). (ENG., Illus.). 78p. (J). (gr. 3-7). pap. 12.95 *(978-0-87020-420-3(3))* Wisconsin Historical Society.
MacArthur, Collin. Inside a Speedboat. 2014. (Life in the Fast Lane Ser.). 48p. (J). (gr. 4-6). 31.36 *(978-1-62713-037-0(3))* Cavendish Square Publishing.
McClellan, Ray & Finn, Denny Von. Hydroplanes. 2008. (Cool Rides Ser.). (ENG., Illus.). 24p. (J). (gr. 3-7). lib. bdg. 25.95 *(978-1-60014-211-6(7))* Bellwether Media.

M
N
O

Riggs, Kate. Seedlings: Speedboats. 2015. (Seedlings Ser.). (ENG.). 24p. (J). (gr. -1-1). pap. 6.99 *(978-1-62832-123-4(7),* Creative Paperbacks) Creative Co., The.

—Speedboats. 24p. (J). 2015. *(978-1-60818-523-8(0))* 2010. (gr. -1-3). 16.95 *(978-1-58341-915-1(2))* Creative Co., The. (Creative Education).

Tieck, Sarah. Speedboats, 1 vol. 2009. (Amazing Vehicles Ser.). (ENG., Illus.). 32p. (gr. 2-5). 28.50 *(978-1-60453-544-0(X),* Big Buddy Bks.) ABDO Publishing Co.

Von Finn, Denny. Powerboats. 2009. (World's Fastest Ser.). (ENG., Illus.). 24p. (J). (gr. 3-7). lib. bdg. 25.95 *(978-1-60014-282-6(6),* Torque Bks.) Bellwether Media.

Werther, Scott P. Powerboats: Lanchas Motorizadas. 2004. (Extreme Machines / Máquinas Extremas Ser.). (SPA & ENG., Illus.). 24p. (J). (gr. 3-6). lib. bdg. 22.60 *(978-0-8239-6890-9(1),* Editorial Buenas Letras) Rosen Publishing Group, Inc., The.

—Powerboats / Lanchas Motorizadas. 2009. (Extreme Machines / Máquinas extremas Ser.). (ENG & SPA.). 24p. (gr. 1-2). 42.50 *(978-1-61512-448-0(9),* Editorial Buenas Letras) Rosen Publishing Group, Inc., The.

MOTORCYCLES

ABDO Publishing Company Staff. Xtreme Motorcycles. 2014. (Xtreme Motorcycles Ser.: 6). (ENG.). 32p. (gr. 3-9). lib. bdg. 162.42 *(978-1-62403-216-5(8),* Abdo & Daughters) ABDO Publishing Co.

Adamson, Thomas K. Motocross Freestyle. 2015. (Extreme Sports Ser.). (ENG., Illus.). 24p. (J). (gr. 3-7). lib. bdg. 25.95 *(978-1-62617-275-3(7),* Epic Bks.) Bellwether Media.

Aloian, Molly. Motorcycles. 2011. (ENG.). 32p. (J). lib. bdg. *(978-0-7787-2730-9(0));* (Vehicles on the Move Ser.: No. 16). pap. *(978-0-7787-2737-8(8))* Crabtree Publishing Co.

Aloian, Molly, contrib. by. Les Motocyclettes. 2011. (FRE.). 32p. (J). pap. *(978-2-89579-490-5(1))* Crabtree Publishing Co.

Armentrout, David & Armentrout, Patricia. Dirt Bikes. 2005. (Motorcycle Mania Ser.). (Illus.). 24p. (J). (gr. 3-6). lib. bdg. 27.07 *(978-1-59515-453-8(1),* 1244371) Rourke Educational Media.

—Sportbikes. 2005. (Motorcycle Mania Ser.). (Illus.). 24p. (J). (gr. 3-6). lib. bdg. 27.07 *(978-1-59515-456-9(6),* 1244375) Rourke Educational Media.

—Stunts, Tricks, & Jumps. 2007. (Motorcycle Mania (High Interest) Ser.). (Illus.). 24p. (J). (gr. 3-7). lib. bdg. 27.07 *(978-1-60044-591-0(8))* Rourke Educational Media.

Bailey, Diane. Yamaha: Sport Racing Legend. 2013. (Motorcycles: a Guide to the World's Best Bikes Ser.). (Illus.). 48p. (J). (gr. 5-8). 29.95 *(978-1-4777-1859-9(1));* pap. 70.50 *(978-1-4777-1879-7(6));* pap. 11.75 *(978-1-4777-1878-0(8))* Rosen Publishing Group, Inc., The. (Rosen Reference).

Bailey, Katharine. Sport Bikes. rev. ed. 2007. (Automania! Ser.). (ENG., Illus.). 32p. (J). (gr. 4-7). pap. *(978-0-7787-3035-4(2))* Crabtree Publishing Co.

Barnes, Pete. Harley & the Davidsons: Motorcycle Legends. 2007. (Badger Biographies Ser.). (ENG., Illus.). 112p. (J). (gr. 4-8). per. 12.95 *(978-0-87020-380-0(0))* Wisconsin Historical Society.

Barrington, Richard. Ducati: High Performance Italian Racer. 2013. (Motorcycles: a Guide to the World's Best Bikes Ser.). (Illus.). 48p. (J). (gr. 5-8). 29.95 *(978-1-4777-1856-8(7));* pap. 11.75 *(978-1-4777-1870-4(2));* pap. 70.50 *(978-1-4777-1871-1(0))* Rosen Publishing Group, Inc., The. (Rosen Reference).

Belcher, Andrew. Motorcycles Turquoise Band. 2016. (Cambridge Reading Adventures Ser.). (ENG.). 24p. pap. 7.19 *(978-1-107-57624-7(5))* Cambridge Univ. Pr.

Bender, Lionel. Cars & Motorcycles. 2006. (J). *(978-1-59389-262-3(4))* Chrysalis Education.

Beyer, Mark. Motocicletas Del Pasado. 2004. (Transporte Ayer y Hoy (Transportation Through the Ages) Ser.). (SPA & ENG., Illus.). 24p. (J). (gr. 3-6). lib. bdg. 22.60 *(978-0-8239-6854-1(5),* Editorial Buenas Letras) Rosen Publishing Group, Inc., The.

—Motocicletas del pasado (Motorcycles of the Past) 2009. (transporte ayer y hoy (Transportation Through the Ages) Ser.). 24p. (gr. 1-2). 42.50 *(978-1-61512-255-4(9),* Editorial Buenas Letras) Rosen Publishing Group, Inc., The.

—Motorcycles of the Past. 2009. (Transportation Through the Ages Ser.). 24p. (gr. 1-1). 42.50 *(978-1-60854-589-6(X),* PowerKids Pr.) Rosen Publishing Group, Inc., The.

Blaine, Victor. Mi Patineta / My Scooter, 1 vol. 2015. (¡Mírame, Ahí Voy! / Watch Me Go! Ser.). (ENG & SPA., Illus.). 24p. (J). 23.60 *(978-1-4994-0288-9(0),* 1384314, PowerKids Pr.) Rosen Publishing Group, Inc., The.

Bodensteiner, Peter. Choppers. 2017. (Gearhead Garage Ser.). (ENG., Illus.). 32p. (gr. 3-7). 31.35 ***(978-1-68072-028-0(7))*** Black Rabbit Bks.

—Sport Bikes. 2017. (Gearhead Garage Ser.). (ENG., Illus.). 32p. (gr. 3-7). 31.35 ***(978-1-68072-034-1(1))*** Black Rabbit Bks.

Brooklyn, Billie. Motorcycle Racing, 1 vol. 2015. (ENG., Illus.). 32p. (J). lib. bdg. 26.25 *(978-1-4994-0158-5(2),* PowerKids Pr.) Rosen Publishing Group, Inc., The.

Brown, Roland & Scarborough, Kate. Hot Bikes. 2012. (Fast Facts Ser.). 32p. (gr. 4-6). pap. 28.50 *(978-1-59771-326-9(0))* Sea-To-Sea Pubns.

Bullard, Lisa. Supercross Motorcycles. 2006. (Pull Ahead Books-Mighty Movers Ser.). (ENG., Illus.). 32p. (gr. k-3). pap. 7.95 *(978-0-8225-5898-9(X),* First Avenue Editions) Lerner Publishing Group.

Cain, Patrick G. BMX Street. 2013. (Extreme Summer Sports Zone Ser.). (ENG., Illus.). 32p. (gr. 4-8). pap. 8.95 *(978-1-4677-1080-6(0))* Lerner Publishing Group.

—BMX Vert. 2013. (Extreme Summer Sports Zone Ser.). (ENG., Illus.). 32p. (gr. 4-8). pap. 8.95 *(978-1-4677-1081-7(4));* lib. bdg. 26.60 *(978-1-4677-0750-3(3),* Lerner Pubns.) Lerner Publishing Group.

—Moto X Best Trick. 2013. (Extreme Summer Sports Zone Ser.). (ENG., Illus.). 32p. (gr. 4-8). pap. 8.95 *(978-1-4677-1082-4(2));* lib. bdg. 26.60 *(978-1-4677-0752-7(X),* Lerner Pubns.) Lerner Publishing Group.

—Moto X Freestyle. 2013. (Extreme Summer Sports Zone Ser.). (ENG., Illus.). 32p. (gr. 4-8). pap. 8.95 *(978-1-4677-1083-1(0));* lib. bdg. 26.60 *(978-1-4677-0753-4(8),* Lerner Pubns.) Lerner Publishing Group.

Capstone Press. Dirt Bike World, 1 vol. 2010. (Dirt Bike World Ser.). (ENG.). 32p. lib. bdg. 101.28 *(978-1-4296-5931-4(9),* Blazers) Capstone Press of Coughlan Cos.

Castellano, Peter. Motocross. 2015. (Daredevil Sports Ser.). (ENG., Illus.). 32p. (J). (gr. 1-1). lib. bdg. 25.25 *(978-1-4824-2985-5(3))* Stevens, Gareth Publishing LLLP.

Cerato, Mattia & Sexton, Brenda. Easy-to-Draw Vehicles. Cerato, Mattia & Sexton, Brenda, illus. 2011. (You Can Draw Ser.). (ENG., Illus.). 48p. (gr. 1-2). pap. 5.19 *(978-1-4048-7058-1(X))* Picture Window Bks.

Ciovacco, Justine. All about Motorcycles. 2016. (Let's Find Out! Ser.). 32p. (J). (gr. 3-2). lib. bdg. 24.45 *(978-1-68048-441-0(9))* Rosen Publishing Group, Inc., The.

Clark, Willow. Motorcycles on the Move. 2010. (Transportation Station Ser.). (Illus.). 24p. (J). pap. 8.25 *(978-1-4358-9758-8(7));* (gr. 2-5). lib. bdg. 22.60 *(978-1-4358-9335-1(2))* Rosen Publishing Group, Inc., The. (PowerKids Pr.).

Colson, Rob. Motorbikes. 2013. (Ultimate Machines Ser.). (ENG., Illus.). 24p. (J). (gr. 3-6). 22.60 *(978-1-4777-0066-2(8));* pap. 8.25 *(978-1-4777-0117-1(6))* Rosen Publishing Group, Inc., The. (PowerKids Pr.).

Crabtree Editors & Stuckey, Rachel. Ride It Bmx. 2012. (Sports Starters Ser.). (ENG., Illus.). 32p. (J). (gr. 1-4). lib. bdg. *(978-0-7787-3150-4(2))* Crabtree Publishing Co.

David, Jack. Choppers. 2007. (Motorcycles Ser.). (ENG., Illus.). 24p. (J). (gr. 3-7). lib. bdg. 25.95 *(978-1-60014-131-7(5))* Bellwether Media.

—Cruisers. 2007. (Motorcycles Ser.). (ENG., Illus.). 24p. (J). (gr. 3-7). lib. bdg. 25.95 *(978-1-60014-132-4(3))* Bellwether Media.

—Enduro Motorcycles. 2007. (Motorcycles Ser.). (ENG., Illus.). 24p. (J). (gr. 3-7). lib. bdg. 25.95 *(978-1-60014-133-1(1))* Bellwether Media.

—Harley-Davidson Motorcycles. 2007. (Motorcycles Ser.). (ENG., Illus.). 24p. (J). (gr. 3-7). lib. bdg. 25.95 *(978-1-60014-134-8(X))* Bellwether Media.

—Motocross Cycles. 2008. (Cool Rides Ser.). (ENG., Illus.). 24p. (J). (gr. 3-7). lib. bdg. 25.95 *(978-1-60014-152-2(8))* Bellwether Media.

—Motocross Racing. 2007. (Action Sports Ser.). (ENG., Illus.). 24p. (J). (gr. 3-7). lib. bdg. 25.95 *(978-1-60014-124-9(2))* Bellwether Media.

—Supercross Racing. 2008. (Action Sports Ser.). (ENG., Illus.). 24p. (J). (gr. 3-7). lib. bdg. 25.95 *(978-1-60014-200-0(1))* Bellwether Media.

—Touring Motorcycles. 2007. (Motorcycles Ser.). (ENG., Illus.). 24p. (J). (gr. 3-7). lib. bdg. 25.95 *(978-1-60014-136-2(6))* Bellwether Media.

David West. Motorcycle. 2006. (Illus.). 32p. (J). pap. *(978-1-4109-2561-9(7))* Steck-Vaughn.

Davidson, Jean. My Daddy Makes the Best Motorcycles in the Whole Wide World, the Harley-Davidson. Hammerquist, Theresa, illus. 2004. (J). 16.95 *(978-1-930596-26-9(X))* Amherst Pr.

Dayton, Connor. Choppers. 2007. (Motorcycles Made for Speed / Motocicletas a Toda Velocidad Ser.). (Illus.). 24p. (J). (gr. 2-5). (SPA.). lib. bdg. 22.60 *(978-1-4042-7612-3(2));* lib. bdg. 22.60 *(978-1-4042-3654-7(6))* Rosen Publishing Group, Inc., The.

—Cool Bikes. 2007. (Motorcycles: Made for Speed Ser.). (Illus.). 24p. (J). (gr. 2-5). lib. bdg. 22.60 *(978-1-4042-3655-4(4))* Rosen Publishing Group, Inc., The.

—Cool Bikes/Motos Cool. Alaman, Eduardo, tr. 2007. (Motorcycles Made for Speed / Motocicletas a Toda Velocidad Ser.). (SPA., Illus.). 24p. (J). (gr. 2-5). lib. bdg. 22.60 *(978-1-4042-7613-0(0))* Rosen Publishing Group, Inc., The.

—Dirt Bikes. 2007. (Motorcycles: Made for Speed Ser.). (Illus.). 24p. (J). (gr. 2-5). lib. bdg. 22.60 *(978-1-4042-3652-3(X))* Rosen Publishing Group, Inc., The.

—Dirt Bikes. Alaman, Eduardo, tr. 2007. (Motorcycles Made for Speed / Motocicletas a Toda Velocidad Ser.). (SPA., Illus.). 24p. (J). (gr. 2-5). lib. bdg. 22.60 *(978-1-4042-7610-9(6))* Rosen Publishing Group, Inc., The.

—Motorcycles: Made for Speed, 6 bks., Set. Incl. Choppers. lib. bdg. 22.60 *(978-1-4042-3654-7(6));* Cool Bikes. lib. bdg. 22.60 *(978-1-4042-3655-4(4));* Dirt Bikes. lib. bdg. 22.60 *(978-1-4042-3652-3(X));* Street Bikes. lib. bdg. 22.60 *(978-1-4042-3656-1(2));* Superbikes. lib. bdg. 22.60 *(978-1-4042-3653-0(8));* Tricks with Bikes. lib. bdg. 22.60 *(978-1-4042-3657-8(0));* (Illus.). 24p. (J). (gr. 2-5). 2007. 2007. Set lib. bdg. 127.50 *(978-1-4042-3604-2(X))* Rosen Publishing Group, Inc., The.

—Street Bikes. 2007. (Motorcycles: Made for Speed Ser.). (Illus.). 24p. (J). (gr. 2-5). lib. bdg. 22.60 *(978-1-4042-3656-1(2))* Rosen Publishing Group, Inc., The.

—Street Bikes/Motos de Calle. Alaman, Eduardo, tr. 2007. (Motorcycles Made for Speed / Motocicletas a Toda Velocidad Ser.). (SPA., Illus.). 24p. (J). (gr. 2-5). lib. bdg. 22.60 *(978-1-4042-7614-7(9))* Rosen Publishing Group, Inc., The.

—Superbikes. 2007. (Motorcycles: Made for Speed Ser.). (Illus.). 24p. (J). (gr. 2-5). lib. bdg. 22.60 *(978-1-4042-3653-0(8))* Rosen Publishing Group, Inc., The.

—Superbikes. Alaman, Eduardo, tr. 2007. (Motorcycles Made for Speed / Motocicletas a Toda Velocidad Ser.). (SPA., Illus.). 24p. (J). (gr. 2-5). lib. bdg. 22.60 *(978-1-4042-7611-6(4))* Rosen Publishing Group, Inc., The.

—Tricks with Bikes/Trucos con la Moto. Alaman, Eduardo, tr. from ENG. 2007. (Motorcycles Made for Speed / Motocicletas a Toda Velocidad Ser.). (SPA., Illus.). 24p. (J). (gr. 2-5). lib. bdg. 22.60 *(978-1-4042-7615-4(7))* Rosen Publishing Group, Inc., The.

Dinmont, Kerry. Motorcycles on the Go. 2016. (Bumba Books (tm) — Machines That Go Ser.). (ENG.). 24p. (J). (gr. -1-1). 25.32 *(978-1-5124-1446-2(8))* Lerner Publishing Group.

Dinmont, Kerry & Granat, Annette. Motocicletas en Acción. 2017. (Bumba Books (tm) en Español — Máquinas en Acción (Machines That Go) Ser.). (SPA., Illus.). 24p. (J). (gr. -1-1). 25.32 *(978-1-5124-2879-7(5))* Lerner Publishing Group.

Dirt Bike World. 2010. (Dirt Bike World Ser.). (ENG.). 32p. (gr. 1-2). pap. 190.80 *(978-1-4296-5712-9(X),* Blazers) Capstone Press of Coughlan Cos.

Doeden, Matt. Choppers. 2008. pap. 52.95 *(978-1-58013-661-7(3));* (ENG., Illus.). 48p. (gr. 4-7). lib. bdg. 26.60 *(978-0-8225-7288-6(5))* Lerner Publishing Group.

—Supercross. 2010. (Dirt Bike World Ser.). (ENG.). 32p. (gr. 1-2). pap. 47.70 *(978-1-4296-5708-2(1),* Blazers) Capstone Press of Coughlan Cos.

Dowds, Alan. High-Speed Superbikes. 2006. (Cool Wheels Ser.). (Illus.). 32p. (gr. 2-6). lib. bdg. 26.00 *(978-0-8368-6826-5(9),* Gareth Stevens Learning Library) Stevens, Gareth Publishing LLLP.

Dubowski, Mark. Superfast Motorcycles. 2005. (Ultimate Speed Ser.). (Illus.). 32p. (J). (gr. 3-6). lib. bdg. 25.27 *(978-1-59716-081-0(4))* Bearport Publishing Co., Inc.

Eagen, Rachel. Street Bikes. rev. ed. 2007. (Automania! Ser.). (ENG., Illus.). 32p. (J). (gr. 4-7). pap. *(978-0-7787-3036-1(0))* Crabtree Publishing Co.

Enz, Tammy. Batmobiles & Batcycles: The Engineering Behind Batman's Vehicles, 1 vol. 2014. (Batman Science Ser.). (ENG.). 32p. (gr. 3-4). 27.32 *(978-1-4765-3940-9(5),* DC Super Heroes) Stone Arch Bks.

—Building Vehicles That Roll. 2017. (Young Engineers Ser.). (ENG., Illus.). 32p. (gr. 1-2). lib. bdg. 27.32 *(978-1-4846-3748-7(8),* Heinemann First Library) Heinemann-Raintree.

Finn, Denny Von. Drag Racing Motorcycles. 2011. (World's Fastest Ser.). (ENG., Illus.). 24p. (J). (gr. 3-7). lib. bdg. 25.95 *(978-1-60014-586-5(8),* Torque Bks.) Bellwether Media.

—Racing Motorcycles. 2009. (World's Fastest Ser.). (ENG., Illus.). 24p. (J). (gr. 3-7). lib. bdg. 25.95 *(978-1-60014-291-8(5),* Torque Bks.) Bellwether Media.

Franchino, Vicky. Motorcycles. 2008. (21st Century Skills Innovation Library: Innovation in Transportation Ser.). (ENG., Illus.). 32p. (gr. 4-8). lib. bdg. 28.50 *(978-1-60279-238-8(0),* 200168) Cherry Lake Publishing.

Franks, Katie. Choppers. 2009. (Motorcycles: Made for Speed Ser.). 24p. (gr. 1-1). 42.50 *(978-1-61514-676-5(8),* PowerKids Pr.); (ENG & SPA.). 42.50 *(978-1-61514-670-3(9),* Editorial Buenas Letras) Rosen Publishing Group, Inc., The.

—Cool Bikes. 2009. (Motorcycles: Made for Speed Ser.). 24p. (gr. 1-1). 42.50 *(978-1-61514-677-2(6),* PowerKids Pr.) Rosen Publishing Group, Inc., The.

—Cool Bikes/Motos Cool. 2009. (Motorcycles Made for Speed/Motocicletas a toda velocidad Ser.). (ENG & SPA.). 24p. (gr. 1-1). 42.50 *(978-1-61514-671-0(7),* Editorial Buenas Letras) Rosen Publishing Group, Inc., The.

—Dirt Bikes. 2009. (Motorcycles Made for Speed/Motocicletas a toda velocidad Ser.). 24p. (gr. 1-1). (ENG & SPA.). 42.50 *(978-1-61514-672-7(5),* Editorial Buenas Letras); 42.50 *(978-1-61514-678-9(4),* PowerKids Pr.) Rosen Publishing Group, Inc., The.

—Street Bikes. 2009. (Motorcycles: Made for Speed Ser.). 24p. (gr. 1-1). 42.50 *(978-1-61514-679-6(2),* PowerKids Pr.) Rosen Publishing Group, Inc., The.

—Street Bikes/Motos de Calle. 2009. (Motorcycles Made for Speed/Motocicletas a toda velocidad Ser.). (ENG & SPA.). 24p. (gr. 1-1). 42.50 *(978-1-61514-673-4(3),* Editorial Buenas Letras) Rosen Publishing Group, Inc., The.

—Superbikes. 2009. (Motorcycles Made for Speed/Motocicletas a toda velocidad Ser.). 24p. (gr. 1-1). (ENG & SPA.). 42.50 *(978-1-61514-674-1(1),* Editorial Buenas Letras); 42.50 *(978-1-61514-680-2(6),* PowerKids Pr.) Rosen Publishing Group, Inc., The.

—Tricks with Bikes. 2009. (Motorcycles: Made for Speed Ser.). 24p. (gr. 1-1). 42.50 *(978-1-61514-681-9(4),* PowerKids Pr.) Rosen Publishing Group, Inc., The.

—Tricks with Bikes/Trucos con la Moto. 2009. (Motorcycles Made for Speed/Motocicletas a toda velocidad Ser.). (ENG & SPA.). 24p. (gr. 1-1). 42.50 *(978-1-61514-675-8(X),* Editorial Buenas Letras) Rosen Publishing Group, Inc., The.

Freeman, Gary. Motocross. 2012. (To the Limit Ser.). (ENG., Illus.). 32p. (J). (gr. 5-8). pap. 10.00 *(978-1-4488-7062-2(3));* lib. bdg. 25.25 *(978-1-4488-7027-1(5))* Rosen Publishing Group, Inc., The. (PowerKids Pr.).

Gibbs, Lynne. Mega Book of Motorcycles. 2003. (Illus.). 32p. (YA). pap. *(978-1-903954-57-7(6),* Pavilion Children's Books) Pavilion Bks.

Gifford, Clive. Ducati. 2009. (Red-Hot Bikes Ser.). (YA). (gr. 2-5). 28.50 *(978-1-59771-135-7(7))* Sea-To-Sea Pubns.

—Motorbikes. 2012. (ENG.). 24p. (J). lib. bdg. *(978-0-7787-7475-4(9));* (Illus.). pap. *(978-0-7787-7480-8(5))* Crabtree Publishing Co.

Gillespie, Leslie. Motorcycles. 2011. (Discovery Adventures Ser.). 80p. (J). pap. 8.99 *(978-0-7945-2565-1(2),* Usborne) EDC Publishing.

Glover, David & Glover, Penny. Motorcycles in Action. 2008. (On the Go Ser.). (Illus.). 24p. (J). (gr. 3-7). lib. bdg. 22.60 *(978-1-4042-4311-8(9),* PowerKids Pr.) Rosen Publishing Group, Inc., The.

Goodman, Susan E. Motorcycles! Doolittle, Michael, illus. 2007. (Step into Reading Ser.). (ENG.). 48p. (J). (gr. k-3). per. 3.99 *(978-0-375-84116-3(4),* Random Hse. Bks. for Young Readers) Random Hse. Children's Bks.

Graham, Ian. Bikes. 2017. (Mighty Machines Ser.). (ENG., Illus.). 24p. (J). (gr. -1-2). pap. 5.95 *(978-1-77085-849-7(0),* 9781770858497) Firefly Bks., Ltd.

—Motorcycles. 2015. (Wonderwise Ser.). (Illus.). 32p. (gr. 2-6). 31.35 *(978-1-62588-360-5(9))* Black Rabbit Bks.

Graham, Ian & Salariya, David. Super Bikes. Hewetson, N. J., illus. 2014. (Time Shift Speed Ser.). 32p. (gr. 3-6). 31.35 ***(978-1-908973-96-2(X))*** Book Hse. GBR. Dist: Black Rabbit Bks.

Gunston, Bill Tudor & Parker, Steve. Fasten Your Seatbelt! Mind-Boggling Machines. 2010. (ENG.). 96p. (J). (gr. 2-4). pap. 9.95 *(978-1-84696-205-9(6),* TickTock Books) Octopus Publishing Group GBR. Dist: Independent Pubs. Group.

Hanson, Anders. Let's Go by Motorcycle, 1 vol. 2008. (Let's Go Ser.). (ENG., Illus.). 24p. (J). (gr. k-3). lib. bdg. 24.21 *(978-1-59928-901-4(6),* SandCastle) ABDO Publishing Co.

Harrison, Paul. Superbikes. 2013. (Illus.). 32p. (J). *(978-1-84858-563-8(2))* Arcturus Pubs., Inc.

Hatter, Hilda E. Bananas & Balloons: Inspirational Stories of Motorcycling Adventures. 2004. 307p. (YA). per. 15.99 *(978-0-9761167-0-7(7))* TIGO & Co.

Hawkins, Clyde. Harley Davidson, Vol. 8. 2015. (Classic Cars & Bikes Collection). (Illus.). 64p. (J). (gr. 7). lib. bdg. 23.95 *(978-1-4222-3280-4(8))* Mason Crest.

Hill, David. Speed King: Burt Munro, the World's Fastest Indian. 2016. (ENG., Illus.). 32p. (J). 17.99 ***(978-0-14-350722-2(2))*** Penguin Group New Zealand, Ltd. NZL. Dist: Independent Pubs. Group.

Hill, Lee Sullivan. Motorcycles. 2004. (Pull Ahead Books-Mighty Movers Ser.). (ENG., Illus.). 32p. (gr. k-3). pap. 7.95 *(978-0-8225-9924-1(4));* lib. bdg. 22.60 *(978-0-8225-0695-9(5))* Lerner Publishing Group.

—Motorcycles on the Move. 2011. (Lightning Bolt Books Vroom-Vroom Ser.). 32p. pap. 45.32 *(978-0-7613-7619-4(4));* (ENG., Illus.). lib. bdg. 26.60 *(978-0-7613-6026-1(3))* Lerner Publishing Group.

Hill, Lee Sullivan & Hill, Lee Sullivan. Motorcycles on the Move. 2011. (Lightning Bolt Books Vroom-Vroom Ser.). (ENG.). 32p. (gr. k-2). pap. 7.95 *(978-0-7613-7112-0(5))* Lerner Publishing Group.

Hobbs, Mike. Superbikes, Vol. 8. 2015. (Classic Cars & Bikes Collection). (Illus.). 64p. (J). (gr. 7). lib. bdg. 23.95 *(978-1-4222-3282-8(4))* Mason Crest.

Hofer, Charles. Motorcycles. 2008. (World's Fastest Machines Ser.). (Illus.). 24p. (J). (gr. 3-7). lib. bdg. 22.60 *(978-1-4042-4177-0(9),* PowerKids Pr.) Rosen Publishing Group, Inc., The.

Holter, James. Dirt Bike Racers. 2010. (Kid Racers Ser.). (Illus.). 48p. (J). (gr. 5-9). 25.27 *(978-0-7660-3483-9(6))* Enslow Pubs., Inc.

Johnson, Ben. Motocross. 2008. (Crabtree Contact Ser.). (ENG., Illus.). 32p. (J). (gr. 3-7). pap. *(978-0-7787-3786-5(1));* lib. bdg. *(978-0-7787-3764-3(0))* Crabtree Publishing Co.

Kamberg, Mary-Lane. Kawasaki: World's Fastest Bike. 2013. (Motorcycles: a Guide to the World's Best Bikes Ser.). 48p. (J). (gr. 5-8). pap. 11.75 *(978-1-4777-1874-2(5),* Rosen Reference) Rosen Publishing Group, Inc., The.

Katirgis, Jane & Holter, James. Racing Dirt Bikes. 2017. (J). ***(978-0-7660-9275-4(5))*** Enslow Pubs., Inc.

Kawasaki: World's Fastest Bike. 2013. (Motorcycles: a Guide to the World's Best Bikes Ser.). 48p. (J). (gr. 5-8). pap. 70.50 *(978-1-4777-1875-9(3),* Rosen Reference) Rosen Publishing Group, Inc., The.

Lacey, Saskia. How to Build a Motorcycle: An off-Road Adventure of Mechanics, Teamwork, & Friendship. Sodomka, Martin, illus. 2016. (Technical Tales Ser.). (ENG.). 64p. (J). (gr. 1-3). 14.95 *(978-1-63322-057-7(5))* Quarto Publishing Group USA.

Levy, Janey. Freestyle Motocross. (Motocross Ser.). 32p. 2009. (gr. 4-5). 47.90 *(978-1-61514-662-8(8))* 2007. (Illus.). (J). (gr. 3-7). lib. bdg. 25.25 *(978-1-4042-3694-3(5))* Rosen Publishing Group, Inc., The. (PowerKids Pr.).

—Motocross. 2007. (gr. 3-7). 36p. pap. 23.95 *(978-1-4358-3836-9(X));* (Illus.). 32p. (J). lib. bdg. 25.25 *(978-1-4042-3692-9(9))* Rosen Publishing Group, Inc., The. (PowerKids Pr.).

—Motocross, 6 bks., Set. Incl. Freestyle Motocross. lib. bdg. 25.25 *(978-1-4042-3694-3(5));* lib. bdg. 25.25 *(978-1-4042-3692-9(9));* Motocross Races. lib. bdg. 25.25 *(978-1-4042-3696-7(1));* Motocross Superstars. lib. bdg. 25.25 *(978-1-4042-3695-0(3));* Motocross Tricks. lib. bdg. 25.25 *(978-1-4042-3697-4(X));* Supercross. lib. bdg. 25.25 *(978-1-4042-3693-6(7));* (Illus.). 32p. (J). (gr. 3-7). 2007., PowerKids Pr. 2007. Set lib. bdg. 143.70 *(978-1-4042-3611-0(2))* Rosen Publishing Group, Inc., The.

—Motocross Races. 2007. (Motocross Ser.). (Illus.). 32p. (J). (gr. 3-7). lib. bdg. 25.25 *(978-1-4042-3696-7(1),* PowerKids Pr.) Rosen Publishing Group, Inc., The.

—Motocross Superstars. 2007. (Motocross Ser.). (Illus.). 32p. (J). (gr. 3-7). lib. bdg. 25.25 *(978-1-4042-3695-0(3),* PowerKids Pr.) Rosen Publishing Group, Inc., The.

—Motocross Tricks. 2007. (Motocross Ser.). (Illus.). 32p. (J). (gr. 3-7). lib. bdg. 25.25 *(978-1-4042-3697-4(X),* PowerKids Pr.) Rosen Publishing Group, Inc., The.

—Supercross. (Motocross Ser.). 32p. 2009. (gr. 4-5). 47.90 *(978-1-61514-669-7(5))* 2007. (Illus.). (J). (gr. 3-7). lib. bdg. 25.25 *(978-1-4042-3693-6(7))* Rosen Publishing Group, Inc., The. (PowerKids Pr.).

Louck, Cheryl. The ABC's of Motocross. Zielinski, Dave, photos by. 2003. (Illus.). 24p. (J). per. 14.95 *(978-0-9744230-0-5(9))* Louck, Cheryl.

Lusted, Marcia Amidon. The Science of Motorcycle Racing, 1 vol. 2014. (Science of Speed Ser.). (ENG.). 48p. (gr. 3-4). lib. bdg. 31.99 *(978-1-4765-3912-6(X))* Capstone Press of Coughlan Cos.

Macken, JoAnn Early. Bike Riding. 2005. (After-School Fun Ser.). (Illus.). 24p. (gr. k-3). lib. bdg. 21.00 *(978-0-8368-4512-9(9),* Weekly Reader Leveled Readers) Stevens, Gareth Publishing LLLP.

Mahaney, Ian F. Travis Pastrana: Motorcross Champion. 2005. (Extreme Sports Biographies Ser.). (Illus.). 24p. (J). 22.60 *(978-1-4042-2748-4(2),* PowerKids Pr.) Rosen Publishing Group, Inc., The.

Mara, Wil. Extreme Motocross. 2013. (Sports on the Edge 2 Ser.). 48p. (J). (gr. 4-8). pap. 12.93 *(978-1-62712-132-3(3))* Cavendish Square Publishing.

Marshall, Jane. Superbikes. 2013. (Wild Rides Ser.). 32p. (gr. 2-4). *(978-1-84898-621-3(1),* TickTock Books) Octopus Publishing Group.

Mason, Paul. Dirt Biking: The World's Most Remarkable Dirt Bike Rides & Techniques, 1 vol. 2011. (Passport to World Sports Ser.). (ENG.). 32p. (gr. 3-4). lib. bdg. 27.99 *(978-1-4296-6878-1(4),* Edge Bks.) Capstone Press of Coughlan Cos.

—Motorcycles. 2010. (Motorsports Ser.). 32p. (J). (gr. 3-6). 28.50 *(978-1-60753-121-0(6))* Amicus Publishing.

Mattern, Joanne. Staying Safe on My Bike. 2007. (Safety First Ser.). (Illus.). 24p. (gr. k-3). pap. 8.15 *(978-0-8368-7801-1(9));* lib. bdg. 22.00 *(978-0-8368-7794-6(2))* Stevens, Gareth Publishing LLLP. (Weekly Reader Leveled Readers).

—Staying Safe on My Bike/La Seguridad en Mi Bicicleta. 2007. (Safety First / la Seguridad Es lo Primero Ser.). (SPA., Illus.). 24p. (gr. k-3). lib. bdg. 22.00 *(978-0-8368-8059-5(5),* Weekly Reader Leveled Readers) Stevens, Gareth Publishing LLLP.

McClellan, Ray. SuperMoto. 2008. (Action Sports Ser.). (ENG., Illus.). 24p. (J). (gr. 3-7). lib. bdg. 25.95 *(978-1-60014-144-7(7))* Bellwether Media.

Mezzanotte, Jim. Motocross. 2006. (Motorcycle Racing: the Fast Track Ser.). (Illus.). 24p. (gr. 5-8). lib. bdg. 23.00 *(978-0-8368-6423-6(9))* Stevens, Gareth Publishing LLLP.

—Superbike. 2006. (Motorcycle Racing: the Fast Track Ser.). (Illus.). 24p. (gr. 5-8). pap. 8.15 *(978-0-8368-6573-8(1))*; lib. bdg. 23.00 *(978-0-8368-6424-3(7))* Stevens, Gareth Publishing LLLP.

—Supercross. 2006. (Motorcycle Racing: the Fast Track Ser.). (Illus.). 24p. (gr. 5-8). lib. bdg. 23.00 *(978-0-8368-6425-0(5))* Stevens, Gareth Publishing LLLP.

—Supermoto. 2006. (Motorcycle Racing: the Fast Track Ser.). (Illus.). 24p. (gr. 5-8). pap. 8.15 *(978-0-8368-6575-2(8))* Stevens, Gareth Publishing LLLP.

Mitton, Tony. Marvelous Motorcycles. Parker, Ant, illus. 2016. (Amazing Machines Ser.). (ENG.). 24p. 9.99 *(978-0-7534-7292-7(9)*, 9780753472927, Kingfisher) Roaring Brook Pr.

Morey, Allan. Motorcycles. 2014. (Illus.). 24p. (J). lib. bdg. 25.65 *(978-1-62031-103-5(8)*, Bullfrog Bks.) Jump! Inc.

Motor Bike. 2004. (Press-Out & Build Ser.). (Illus.). 24p. (J). per. *(978-1-84229-724-7(4))* Top That! Publishing PLC.

Motorcycles: a Guide to the World's Best Bikes: A Guide to the World's Best Bikes. 2013. (Motorcycles: a Guide to the World's Best Bikes Ser.). 48p. (J). (gr. 5-8). 179.70 *(978-1-4777-1867-4(2))*; pap. 70.50 *(978-1-4777-7801-2(2))*; pap. 423.00 *(978-1-4777-7800-5(4))* Rosen Publishing Group, Inc., The. (Rosen Reference).

Mr Mcdoodle & His Scooter: 3-in-1 Package. (Sails Literacy Ser.). 24p. (gr. 2-18). 57.00 *(978-0-7578-6831-3(2))* Rigby Education.

Mr Mcdoodle & His Scooter: Big Book Only. (Sails Literacy Ser.). 24p. (gr. 2-18). 27.00 *(978-0-7578-6819-1(3))* Rigby Education.

Nix, Harvey. How to Ride a Bike: My Very First Learn-To Book. 2006. 92p. 14.95 *(978-0-944353-22-6(3))* Rivendell Bk. Factory.

Nixon, James. Motocross Champion. 2017. (How to Be a Champion Ser.). (ENG., Illus.). 32p. (J). (gr. 4-6). 17.99 *(978-1-4451-3629-5(5)*, Franklin Watts) Hachette Children's Group GBR. Dist: Hachette Bk. Group.

—Motorcycles. 2010. (Machines on the Move Ser.). 32p. (J). 28.50 *(978-1-60753-060-2(0))* Amicus Publishing.

—Motorcycles. 2012. (Illus.). 32p. (gr. 1-3). pap. 8.95 *(978-1-926722-70-2(1))* Saunders Bk. Co. CAN. Dist: RiverStream Publishing.

Norman, Tony. Motorbike Racing. 2006. (Action Sports Ser.). (Illus.). 32p. (gr. 3-6). lib. bdg. 26.00 *(978-0-8368-6368-0(2)*, Gareth Stevens Learning Library) Stevens, Gareth Publishing LLLP.

Norris, Ashley P. Watson. The World's Fastest Motorcycles. 2016. (World Record Breakers Ser.). (ENG., Illus.). 32p. (gr. 3-4). lib. bdg. 27.99 *(978-1-4914-8178-3(1)*, Edge Bks.) Capstone Press of Coughlan Cos.

Omoth, Tyler. Building a Motorcycle, 1 vol. 2014. (See How It's Made Ser.). (ENG.). 32p. (gr. 1-2). lib. bdg. 26.65 *(978-1-4765-3977-5(4)*, Blazers) Capstone Press of Coughlan Cos.

Oxlade, Chris. Motorcycles. (Mighty Machines Ser.). (Illus.). (gr. 4-7). 2009. 31p. (J). pap. 7.95 *(978-1-59920-255-6(7))* 2007. 32p. (YA). lib. bdg. 28.50 *(978-1-59920-041-5(4))* Black Rabbit Bks.

—Motorcycles. 2009. (How Machines Work Ser.). (Illus.). 32p. (J). (gr. -1-3). pap. *(978-1-897563-44-1(2))* Saunders Bk. Co.

—Motorcycles Inside & Out. 2009. (Machines Inside Out Ser.). (ENG., Illus.). 32p. (J). (gr. 4-6). pap. 10.00 *(978-1-4358-2942-8(5)*, PowerKids Pr.); (YA). (gr. 3-6). lib. bdg. 25.25 *(978-1-4358-2864-3(X))* Rosen Publishing Group, Inc., The.

Parker, Steve. Cars Trucks & Bikes. 2010. (How It Works Ser.). (Illus.). 40p. (J). (gr. 3-18). lib. bdg. 19.95 *(978-1-4222-1792-4(2)*, 1317905) Mason Crest.

Perritano, John. American MX: From Backwater to World Leaders. 2008. (MXplosion! Ser.). (ENG., Illus.). 32p. (J). (gr. 3-7). pap. *(978-0-7787-3999-6(9))*; (gr. 4-7). lib. bdg. *(978-0-7787-3986-9(4))* Crabtree Publishing Co.

—Motocross Racing. 2015. (ENG.). 48p. (gr. 3-6). 35.64 *(978-1-63430-442-9(X))* Rourke Educational Media.

—Mx Bikes: Evolution from Primitive Street Machines to State of the Art Off-Road Machines. 2008. (MXplosion! Ser.). (ENG., Illus.). 32p. (J). (gr. 3-7). pap. *(978-0-7787-4001-8(3))*; lib. bdg. *(978-0-7787-3988-3(0))* Crabtree Publishing Co.

Peterson, Blaire & Peterson, Brent. The Bike Race. 2013. (Rosen Math Readers Ser.). (ENG.). 24p. (J). (gr. 1-2). pap. 8.25 *(978-1-4777-2022-6(7)*, Rosen Classroom) Rosen Publishing Group, Inc., The.

Peterson, Brent. The Bike Race: Add Within 20. 2013. (Rosen Math Readers Ser.). (ENG.). 24p. (J). (gr. 1-2). pap. 49.50 *(978-1-4777-2023-3(5)*, Rosen Classroom) Rosen Publishing Group, Inc., The.

Polydoros, Lori. Dirt Bike Racing, 1 vol. 2013. (Super Speed Ser.). (ENG.). 32p. (gr. 1-2). 26.65 *(978-1-4765-0120-8(3)*, Blazers) Capstone Press of Coughlan Cos.

—Dirt Bikes, 1 vol. 2010. (Full Throttle Ser.). (ENG.). 32p. (gr. 3-4). lib. bdg. 27.99 *(978-1-4296-3940-8(7)*, Edge Bks.) Capstone Press of Coughlan Cos.

—Motocross Greats. 2011. (Best of the Best Ser.). (ENG.). 32p. (gr. 1-2). pap. 47.70 *(978-1-4296-7250-4(1))*; lib. bdg. 26.65 *(978-1-4296-6499-8(1))* Capstone Press of Coughlan Cos. (Blazers).

Raby, Philip & Nix, Simon. Motorbikes. 2005. (Need for Speed Ser.). (Illus.). 32p. (J). (gr. 3-5). pap. 7.95 *(978-0-8225-9854-1(X))* Lerner Publishing Group.

Riggs, Kate. Motorcycles. (J). 2015. *(978-1-60818-522-1(2))* 2010. 24p. (gr. -1-3). 16.95 *(978-1-58341-914-4(4))* 2007. (Illus.). 24p. (gr. -1-3). lib. bdg. 24.25 *(978-1-58341-528-3(9))* Creative Co., The. (Creative Education).

—Seedlings: Motorcycles. 2015. (Seedlings Ser.). (ENG.). 24p. (J). (gr. -1-1). pap. 7.99 *(978-1-62832-122-7(9)*, Creative Paperbacks) Creative Co., The.

Rosenberg, Aaron. Kick Scooters: Techniques & Tricks. 2009. (Rad Sports: Techniques & Tricks Ser.). 48p. (gr. 5-8). 53.00 *(978-1-60851-934-7(1)*, Rosen Reference) Rosen Publishing Group, Inc., The.

Roza, Greg. Harley-Davidson: An All-American Legend. 2013. (Motorcycles: a Guide to the World's Best Bikes Ser.). (Illus.). 48p. (J). (gr. 5-8). 29.95 *(978-1-4777-1855-1(9))*; pap. 11.75 *(978-1-4777-1872-8(9))*; pap. 70.50 *(978-1-4777-1873-5(7))* Rosen Publishing Group, Inc., The. (Rosen Reference).

Ruck, Colleen. Motorcycles. 2011. (My Favorite Machines Ser.). 24p. (gr. 2-5). 28.50 *(978-1-59920-676-9(5))* Black Rabbit Bks.

Sautter, Aaron. How to Draw Amazing Motorcycles, 1 vol. Smith, Tod, illus. 2007. (Drawing Cool Stuff Ser.). (ENG.). 32p. (gr. 3-4). 27.99 *(978-1-4296-0073-6(X)*, Edge Bks.) Capstone Press of Coughlan Cos.

Savage, Jeff. Choppers, 1 vol. 2010. (Full Throttle Ser.). (ENG.). 32p. (gr. 3-4). lib. bdg. 27.99 *(978-1-4296-3939-2(3)*, Edge Bks.) Capstone Press of Coughlan Cos.

—James Stewart. 2008. pap. 40.95 *(978-0-8225-9286-0(X))* Lerner Publishing Group.

—Motorcycles. collector's ed. 2005. (Race Car Legends Ser.). (Illus.). 80p. (YA). (gr. 5-9). lib. bdg. 25.00 *(978-0-7910-8695-7(X))* Facts On File, Inc.

—Travis Pastrana. 2006. (Amazing Athletes Ser.). (Illus.). 32p. (J). (gr. 2-5). per. 5.95 *(978-0-8225-3433-4(9)*, First Avenue Editions) Lerner Publishing Group.

Scheff, Matt. Dirt Bikes, 1 vol. 2014. (Speed Machines Ser.). (ENG., Illus.). 32p. (J). (gr. 3-6). lib. bdg. 27.07 *(978-1-62403-609-5(0)*, SportsZone) ABDO Publishing Co.

—Superbikes, 1 vol. 2014. (Speed Machines Ser.). (ENG., Illus.). 32p. (J). (gr. 3-6). lib. bdg. 27.07 *(978-1-62403-615-6(5)*, SportsZone) ABDO Publishing Co.

Schuh, Mari. Motorcycles. 2017. (Transportation Ser.). (ENG.). 24p. (gr. k-1). lib. bdg. 21.99 ***(978-1-5157-7303-0(5)**, Pebble Bks.)* Capstone Press of Coughlan Cos.

Sharkey, Alex. Classic Bikes, Vol. 8. 2015. (Classic Cars & Bikes Collection). (Illus.). 64p. (J). (gr. 7). lib. bdg. 23.95 *(978-1-4222-3277-4(8))* Mason Crest.

Shofner, Shawndra. How It Happens at the Motorcycle Plant. Wolfe, Bob & Wolfe, Diane, photos by. 2006. (How It Happens Ser.). (Illus.). 32p. (J). (gr. 2-5). lib. bdg. 19.95 *(978-1-881508-99-1(4))* Oliver Pr., Inc.

Stealey, Bryan. Motorcross. 2009. (Racing Mania Ser.). 48p. (gr. 4-18). lib. bdg. 31.36 *(978-0-7614-4386-5(X))* Marshall Cavendish Corp.

Streissguth, Thomas. Mini Bikes. 2008. (Motorcycles Ser.). (ENG., Illus.). 24p. (J). (gr. 3-7). lib. bdg. 25.95 *(978-1-60014-155-3(2))* Bellwether Media.

—Off-Road Motorcycles. 2008. (Motorcycles Ser.). (ENG., Illus.). 24p. (J). (gr. 3-7). lib. bdg. 25.95 *(978-1-60014-156-0(0))* Bellwether Media.

—Pocket Bikes. 2008. (Motorcycles Ser.). (ENG., Illus.). 24p. (J). (gr. 3-7). lib. bdg. 25.95 *(978-1-60014-157-7(9))* Bellwether Media.

—Scooters. 2008. (Motorcycles Ser.). (ENG., Illus.). 24p. (J). (gr. 3-7). lib. bdg. 25.95 *(978-1-60014-158-4(7))* Bellwether Media.

—Standard Motorcycles. 2008. (Motorcycles Ser.). (ENG., Illus.). 24p. (J). (gr. 3-7). lib. bdg. 25.95 *(978-1-60014-159-1(5))* Bellwether Media.

—Trials Bikes. 2008. (Motorcycles Ser.). (ENG., Illus.). 24p. (J). (gr. 3-7). lib. bdg. 25.95 *(978-1-60014-160-7(9))* Bellwether Media.

Stuckey, Rachel. Ride It Bmx. 2012. (ENG., Illus.). 32p. (J). pap. *(978-0-7787-3161-0(8))* Crabtree Publishing Co.

Taylor, Trace. Bikes. Taylor, Trace, illus. 2008. (1-3Y Getting Around Ser.). (ENG., Illus.). 24p. (J). (gr. k-2). pap. 5.99 *(978-1-59301-465-0(1))* American Reading Co.

Tieck, Sarah. Choppers, 1 vol. 2011. (Amazing Vehicles Set 2 Ser.). (ENG., Illus.). 32p. (J). (gr. 2-5). 28.50 *(978-1-61714-695-4(1))* ABDO Publishing Co.

—Dirt Bikes, 1 vol. 2009. (Amazing Vehicles Ser.). (ENG., Illus.). 32p. (J). (gr. 2-5). 28.50 *(978-1-60453-540-2(7)*, Big Buddy Bks.) ABDO Publishing Co.

—Superbikes, 1 vol. 2011. (Amazing Vehicles Set 2 Ser.). (ENG., Illus.). 32p. (J). (gr. 2-5). 28.50 *(978-1-61714-700-5(1))* ABDO Publishing Co.

Tiner, John Hudson. Motorcycles. (Illus.). 32p. 2004. pap. 8.95 *(978-0-89812-389-0(5)*, Creative Paperbacks) 2003. (J). lib. bdg. 18.95 *(978-1-58341-285-5(9)*, Creative Education) Creative Co., The.

Townsend, John. Cars & Motorcycles, 1 vol. 2011. (Sci-Hi: Science & Technology Ser.). (ENG., Illus.). 48p. (gr. 4-4). pap. 9.95 *(978-1-4109-4278-4(3)*, Sci-Hi) Heinemann-Raintree.

Tudhope, Simon. Build Your Own Motorcycles Sticker Book. 2015. (Build Your Own Sticker Bks.). (ENG.). 24+10p. (J). (gr. k-5). pap. 8.99 *(978-0-7945-3546-9(1)*, Usborne) EDC Publishing.

West, David. Motorcycles. 2015. (Mechanic Mike's Machines (continuation) Ser.). (Illus.). 24p. (gr. k-3). 27.10 *(978-1-62588-064-2(2))* Black Rabbit Bks.

Wiseman, Blaine. MotoX. 2010. (Record Breakers Ser.). (Illus.). 24p. (YA). (gr. 3-6). lib. bdg. 27.13 *(978-1-61690-115-8(2))*; (J). (gr. 4-6). pap. 12.95 *(978-1-61690-116-5(0))* Weigl Pubs., Inc.

Woods, Bob. Motocross History: From Local Scrambling to World Championship MX to Freestyle. 2008. (MXplosion! Ser.). (ENG., Illus.). 32p. (J). (gr. 3-7). pap. *(978-0-7787-4000-1(5))*; lib. bdg. *(978-0-7787-3987-6(2))* Crabtree Publishing Co.

—Smokin' Motorcycles. 2014. (Fast Wheels! Ser.). 48p. (J). (gr. 4-9). pap. 8.95 *(978-1-62285-086-0(6))* Enslow Pubs., Inc.

Worms, Penny. Motorcycles. 2016. (Motormania Ser.). 32p. (gr. 2-7). 31.35 *(978-1-59920-996-8(9)*, Smart Apple Media) Black Rabbit Bks.

Young, Jeff C. Motorcycles: The Ins & Outs of Superbikes, Choppers, & Other Motorcycles. 2010. (Rpm Ser.). (ENG.). 48p. (gr. 3-4). pap. 59.70 *(978-1-4296-5127-1(X))* Capstone Press of Coughlan Cos.

Zobel, Derek. Motorcycles. 2009. (Mighty Machines Ser.). (ENG., Illus.). 24p. (J). (gr. k-3). lib. bdg. 25.95 *(978-1-60014-269-7(9))* Bellwether Media.

Zuehlke, Jeffrey. Motorcycle Road Racing. 2009. pap. 52.95 *(978-0-7613-4792-7(5))* Lerner Publishing Group.

—Supercross. 2008. pap. 52.95 *(978-1-58013-709-6(1))* Lerner Publishing Group.

MOTORCYCLES—FICTION

Appleton, Victor. Tom Swift & his Motor-Cycle. 2005. 26.95 *(978-1-4218-1502-2(8))*; 192p. pap. 11.95 *(978-1-4218-1602-9(4))* 1st World Publishing, Inc. (1st World Library - Literary Society).

—Tom Swift & His Motor Cycle. 2004. reprint ed. pap. 1.99 *(978-1-4192-8459-5(2))* Kessinger Publishing, LLC.

—Tom Swift & His Motor-Cycle, Tom Swift & His Motor-Boat, Tom Swift & His Airship. 2007. 292p. per. 12.99 *(978-1-60459-097-5(1))* Wilder Pubns., Corp.

—Tom Swift & His MotorCycle. 2006. pap. *(978-1-4068-0727-1(3))* Echo Library.

—Tom Swift & His MotorCycle or Fun and. 2006. pap. *(978-1-4065-0905-2(1))* Dodo Pr.

Aronson, Jeff & Aronson, Miriam. Little Mike & Maddie's Black Hill's Adventure. Aronson, Jeff & Zephyr, Jay, illus. 2007. 33p. (J). 16.00 *(978-0-9795302-1-0(0)*, CrumbGobbler Pr.) Downtown Wetmore Pr.

—Little Mike & Maddie's First Motorcycle Ride. Aronson, Jeff & Zephyr, Jay, illus. 2007. 32p. (J). 16.00 *(978-0-9795302-0-3(2)*, CrumbGobbler Pr.) Downtown Wetmore Pr.

Billet, Marion, illus. Scooter Bug. 2014. (Whizzy Wheels Ser.). (ENG.). 10p. (J). (gr. -1-k). bds. 9.99 *(978-1-4472-5763-9(4))* Pan Macmillan GBR. Dist: Independent Pubs. Group.

Blake, Quentin. Mrs. Armitage, Queen of the Road. Blake, Quentin, illus. 2003. (ENG., Illus.). 32p. (J). (gr. k-3). 15.95 *(978-1-56145-287-3(4))* Peachtree Pubs.

The Box. 2012. (ENG.). 30p. (J). (gr. -1-k). 16.95 *(978-1-60537-134-4(3))* Cobblestone Publishing Co.

Burger, Kyle. The Adventures of Buddy the Motocross Bike: Buddy Learns about Confidence. 2012. 32p. pap. 19.99 *(978-1-4685-0609-9(9))* AuthorHouse.

Caldwell, Bruce. Sidecar Scooter. Hayward, Charlie O., illus. 2008. 32p. (J). pap. 9.95 *(978-0-9792612-9-9(5))* Blue Gate Bks.

Charles, Norma. Chasing a Star. 2009. (ENG., Illus.). 182p. (YA). (gr. 5-8). pap. *(978-1-55380-077-4(X))* Ronsdale Pr.

Choyce, Lesley. Reckless, 1 vol. 2010. (Orca Currents Ser.). (ENG.). (gr. 5-9). 128p. (J). pap. 9.95 *(978-1-55469-223-1(7))*; 112p. (YA). lib. bdg. 16.95 *(978-1-55469-224-8(5))* Orca Bk. Pubs. USA.

Christopher, Matt. Dirt Bike Racer. 2007. (New Matt Christopher Sports Library). 152p. (J). (gr. 4-6). lib. bdg. 26.60 *(978-1-59953-113-7(5))* Norwood Hse. Pr.

—Dirt Bike Runaway. 2008. (New Matt Christopher Sports Library). 176p. (J). (gr. 4-6). lib. bdg. 26.60 *(978-1-59953-215-8(8))* Norwood Hse. Pr.

Davidson, Jean. My Grandma Rides a Harley: She's Cool! Bauknecht, Julie, illus. 2007. (J). *(978-1-930596-79-5(0))* Amherst Pr.

Davis, Terry. If Rock & Roll Were a Machine. 2015. (ENG., Illus.). 256p. (YA). (gr. 7). pap. 10.99 *(978-1-4814-5632-6(6)*, Simon & Schuster Bks. For Young Readers) Simon & Schuster Bks. For Young Readers.

Duff, Ms. Michelle Ann. Five Cats, One Dog, a Motorcycle & a Lady in a Hot Pink Jacket. 2012. 146p. pap. *(978-0-9685706-7-8(4))* Mad8 Publishing.

Hofmeyr, David. Stone Rider. 2015. (ENG., Illus.). 336p. (YA). (gr. 7). 18.99 *(978-0-385-74473-7(0)*, Delacorte Pr.) Random Hse. Children's Bks.

Jamiol, Paul. Bikers Are Animals: A Children's Book on Motorcycling. Habib, Linda, ed. 2009. 38p. pap. 14.95 *(978-1-60844-232-4(2))* Dog Ear Publishing, LLC.

—Bikers Are Animals 4: Working & Riding. 2013. (Illus.). 38p. pap. 14.95 *(978-1-4575-2323-6(X))* Dog Ear Publishing, LLC.

Jones, Christianne C. Secret Scooter, 1 vol. Sullivan, Mary, illus. 2009. (My First Graphic Novel Ser.). (ENG.). 32p. (gr. k-2). 24.65 *(978-1-4342-1619-9(5)*, My First Graphic Novel) Stone Arch Bks.

Kertell, Lynn Maslen. I Can Ride! Hendra, Sue, illus. 2012. (Scholastic Reader Level 1 Ser.). (ENG.). 32p. (J). (gr. -1-3). pap. 3.99 *(978-0-545-38272-4(6))* Scholastic, Inc.

Kirkpatrick, Brenna. My Motorcycle & Me: A Trip in the Mountains. 2011. 28p. pap. 14.56 *(978-1-4634-0469-7(7))* AuthorHouse.

Lagonegro, Melissa. The Spooky Sound. Cohee, Ron, illus. 2010. (Step into Reading Ser.). (ENG.). 32p. (J). (gr. k-3). pap. 3.99 *(978-0-7364-2664-0(7)*, RH/Disney) Random Hse. Children's Bks.

Link, C. Edward. The Little Motorcycle. Serfass, Jim, illus. 2004. (J). 9.95 *(978-0-9749615-0-7(7))* Roadracing World Publishing, Inc.

Maddox, Jake. Motocross Double-Cross. Tiffany, Sean, illus. 2007. (Jake Maddox Sports Stories Ser.). (ENG.). 72p. (gr. 2-3). pap. 5.95 *(978-1-59889-897-2(3))*; lib. bdg. 25.32 *(978-1-59889-845-3(0))* Stone Arch Bks.

Matson, Carole. Jesus Loves Dirt Bikes Too!! 2009. 33p. pap. 15.40 *(978-0-557-15092-2(2))* Lulu Pr., Inc.

Meadows, Michelle. Traffic Pups. Andreasen, Dan, illus. 2011. (ENG.). 32p. (J). (gr. -1-3). 15.99 *(978-1-4169-2485-2(X)*, Simon & Schuster Bks. For Young Readers) Simon & Schuster Bks. For Young Readers.

Messner, Kate. Rolling Thunder. Ruth, Greg, illus. 2017. (ENG.). 32p. (J). (gr. -1-3). 17.99 *(978-0-545-47012-4(9)*, Scholastic Pr.) Scholastic, Inc.

Mount, Jill. The Mystery of the Dirty Bike. 2005. 9.00 *(978-0-8059-9778-1(4))* Dorrance Publishing Co., Inc.

Nelson, Scott. Patch the Porcupine & the Bike Shop Job. Nelson, Scott, illus. 2004. (Illus.). 28p. (J). 14.95 *(978-0-9745715-3-9(9))* KRBY Creations, LLC.

O'Malley, Kevin. Once upon a Cool Motorcycle Dude. O'Malley, Kevin et al, illus. 2005. (ENG.). 32p. (J). (gr. 1-5). 16.99 *(978-0-8027-8947-1(1)*, 9780802789471, Bloomsbury USA Childrens) Bloomsbury Publishing USA.

Pakalne, Violeta. A Motorcyclist Croaker Lee. 2010. 80p. pap. 29.49 *(978-1-4520-9578-3(7))* AuthorHouse.

Parker, John. Sucked In. 2008. (Lightning Strikes Ser.). 96p. (J). pap. *(978-1-921150-62-3(9))* Walker Bks. Australia Pty, Ltd.

Quigley, Daniel. A Face Full of Wind. 2003. 106p. (YA). pap. 10.95 *(978-0-7414-1798-5(7))* Infinity Publishing.

Ralphson, G. Harvey. Boy Scouts on Motorcycles. 2007. 100p. per. *(978-1-4068-3731-5(8))* Echo Library.

Randolph, Robert. Their Very Own Bike, 1 vol. 2010. 28p. 24.95 *(978-1-4489-8322-3(3))* PublishAmerica, Inc.

Roy, James. Queasy Rider. 2008. (Lightning Strikes Ser.). 96p. (J). pap. *(978-1-921150-57-9(2))* Walker Bks. Australia Pty, Ltd.

Siebert, Diane. Motorcycle Song. Jenkins, Leonard, illus. Date not set. 32p. (J). (gr. -1-3). 5.99 *(978-0-06-443632-8(2))* HarperCollins Pubs.

Strange, David. Why Grandpa Rides a Harley. 2005. 16.95 *(978-0-9772771-0-0(0))* Cherry Tree Pr. LLC.

Togden, Ra Chel. The Legendary Rabbit of Death - Volume One [Paperback]. 2013. 108p. pap. *(978-1-898185-27-7(1))* Aro Bks. worldwide.

Walters, Celeste. The Glass Mountain. 2003. 280p. (YA). pap. *(978-0-7022-3297-8(1))* Univ. of Queensland Pr.

MOTORING

see Automobile Travel

MOTORS

see Electric Motors; Engines

MOTT, LUCRETIA, 1793-1880

Marsico, Katie. Lucretia Mott: Abolitionist & Women's Rights Leader, 1 vol. 2008. (Essential Lives Set 2 Ser.). (ENG., Illus.). 112p. (J). (gr. 6-12). lib. bdg. 35.64 *(978-1-60453-039-1(1))* ABDO Publishing Co.

MOUNDS AND MOUND BUILDERS

see also Excavations (Archaeology)

Anthony, David. Who Were the Mound Builders? 2013. (Rosen Readers Ser.). (ENG.). 24p. (J). (gr. 3-4). pap. 8.25 *(978-1-4777-2623-5(3))*; pap. 49.50 *(978-1-4777-2624-2(1))* Rosen Publishing Group, Inc., The. (Rosen Classroom).

Rosebrough, Amy & Malone, Bobbie. Water Panthers, Bears, & Thunderbirds: Exploring Wisconsin's Effigy Mounds. 2003. (New Badger History Ser.). (ENG., Illus.). 48p. (J). (gr. 4-7). pap. 9.95 *(978-0-87020-357-2(6))* Wisconsin Historical Society.

Steele, Kris. Journey to Cahokia. Steele, Kris, illus. (Illus.). 32p. (Orig.). (J). (gr. 4-6). pap. 4.95 *(978-1-881563-02-0(2))* Cahokia Mounds Museum Society.

MOUNT RUSHMORE NATIONAL MEMORIAL (S.D.)

Ashley, Susan. Mount Rushmore. 2004. (Weekly Reader Early Learning Library). (Illus.). 24p. (gr. 1-4). pap. 8.15 *(978-0-8368-4149-7(2))*; lib. bdg. 22.00 *(978-0-8368-4142-8(5))* Stevens, Gareth Publishing LLLP. (Weekly Reader Leveled Readers).

Bauer, Marion Dane. Mount Rushmore. Wallace, John, illus. 2007. (Wonders of America Ser.). (ENG.). 32p. (J). (gr. -1-1). pap. 3.99 *(978-1-4169-3477-6(4)*, Simon Spotlight) Simon Spotlight.

Eldridge, Alison & Eldridge, Stephen. Mount Rushmore: An American Symbol. 2012. (All about American Symbols Ser.). 24p. (J). (gr. -1-1). (Illus.). pap. 7.95 *(978-1-4644-0049-0(0)*, Enslow Elementary); 22.60 *(978-0-7660-4060-1(7))* Enslow Pubs., Inc.

Falk, Laine. What Is Mount Rushmore? 2009. (Scholastic News Nonfiction Readers Ser.). 24p. (J). (gr. 1-2). (ENG.). pap. 6.95 *(978-0-531-22427-4(9))*; (Illus.). 22.00 *(978-0-531-21090-1(1))* Scholastic Library Publishing.

Goldsworthy, Kaite. Mount Rushmore with Code. 2012. (AV2 American Icons Ser.). (ENG., Illus.). 24p. (J). pap. 12.95 *(978-1-61913-302-0(4))*; lib. bdg. 27.13 *(978-1-61913-079-1(3))* Weigl Pubs., Inc. (AV2 by Weigl).

Gunderson, Jessica. Mount Rushmore: Myths, Legends, & Facts, 1 vol. 2014. (Monumental History Ser.). (ENG., Illus.). 32p. (gr. 3-4). lib. bdg. 27.32 *(978-1-4914-0203-0(2))* Capstone Press of Coughlan Cos.

Hahn, Laura. Mount Rushmore: Memorial to Our Greatest Presidents. Moreno, Barry, ed. 2014. (Patriotic Symbols of America Ser.: 20). 48p. (J). (gr. 4-18). lib. bdg. 20.95 *(978-1-4222-3128-9(3))* Mason Crest.

Jango-Cohen, Judith. Mount Rushmore. (Lightning Bolt Bks.). (gr. k-2). 2010. (Illus.). 32p. (J). lib. bdg. 25.26 *(978-0-7613-6021-6(2)*, Lerner Pubns.) 2010. pap. 45.32 *(978-0-7613-6990-5(2))* 2010. (ENG.). 32p. pap. 7.95 *(978-0-7613-6049-0(2))* 2003. (ENG., Illus.). 32p. pap. 7.95 *(978-0-8225-3755-7(9))* 2003. (ENG., Illus.). 32p. lib. bdg. 22.60 *(978-0-8225-3801-1(6))* Lerner Publishing Group.

Kelley, True. Where Is Mount Rushmore? 2015. (Where Is... ? Ser.). lib. bdg. 16.00 *(978-0-606-36589-5(3))* Turtleback Bks.

Kelley, True & dePaola, Tomie. Where Is Mount Rushmore? Groff, David & Hinderliter, John, illus. 2015. (Where Is? Ser.). (ENG.). 112p. (J). (gr. 3-7). 5.99 *(978-0-448-48356-6(4)*, Grosset & Dunlap) Penguin Young Readers Group.

Kenney, Karen Latchana. Mount Rushmore, 1 vol. Hunt, Judith A., illus. 2011. (Our Nation's Pride Set 2 Ser.). (ENG.). 32p. (J). (gr. 1-4). 28.50 *(978-1-61641-153-4(8))* Magic Wagon.

Koestler-Grack, Rachel A. Mount Rushmore, 1 vol. 2005. (American Moments Ser.). (ENG., Illus.). 48p. (gr. 4-8). 27.07 *(978-1-59197-936-4(6)*, Abdo & Daughters) ABDO Publishing Co.

Mattern, Joanne. Mount Rushmore. 2014. (ENG.). 32p. (gr. 3-6). 32.79 *(978-1-62717-741-2(8))* Rourke Educational Media.

Mojica, Barbara Ann. Little Miss History Travels to Mount Rushmore. Mojica, Victor Ramon, illus. 2012. 36p. pap. 13.95 *(978-0-9885030-0-7(X))* eugenus STUDIOS.

Murray, Julie. Mount Rushmore, 1 vol. 2003. (Buddy Book Ser.). (ENG., Illus.). 24p. (gr. k-4). 25.65 *(978-1-57765-667-8(9)*, Buddy Bks.) ABDO Publishing Co.

O'Mara, Mary. Visit Mount Rushmore. 2012. (Landmarks of Liberty Ser.). (ENG.). 24p. (J). (gr. 2-5). pap. 8.15 *(978-1-4339-6390-2(6)*, Gareth Stevens Learning Library); lib. bdg. 22.60 *(978-1-4339-6388-9(4))* Stevens, Gareth Publishing LLLP.

Patrick, Jean L. S. Face to Face with Mount Rushmore. Patrick, Jean L. S. & Fancy, Patrick, illus. 2008. (J). *(978-0-9798823-1-9(1))* Mount Rushmore Bookstores.

—Who Carved the Mountain? The Story of Mount Rushmore. Graef, Renee, illus. 2005. 37p. (J). 16.99 *(978-0-9752617-4-3(6))* Mount Rushmore Bookstores.

Riggs, Kate. Mount Rushmore. 2009. (Now That's Big Ser.). 24p. (J). (gr. 1-5). lib. bdg. 24.25 *(978-1-58341-705-8(2)*, Creative Education) Creative Co., The.

RJF Publishing Staff & Thomas, William David. Mount Rushmore. 2009. (Symbols of American Freedom Ser.). (Illus.). 48p. (J). (gr. 4-6). 30.00 *(978-1-60413-515-2(8)*, Chelsea Clubhouse) Facts On File, Inc.

The Seasons of Mount Rushmore Coloring Book. 2006. (J). *(978-0-9752617-4-0(0))* Mount Rushmore Bookstores.

Troupe, Thomas Kingsley. Mount Rushmore, 1 vol. Skeens, Matthew, illus. 2009. (American Symbols Ser.). (ENG.). 24p.

MNO

(gr. 1-2). lib. bdg. 26.65 *(978-1-4048-5168-9(2))* Picture Window Bks.

MOUNT VERNON (VA.: ESTATE)

Dyan, Penelope. This Is the House George Built! a Kid's Guide to Mount Vernon. Weigand, John D., photos by. 2009. (Illus.). 44p. pap. 11.95 *(978-1-935118-83-1(8))* Bellissima Publishing, LLC.

Rinaldi, Ann. Sarah's Ground. 2012. (ENG.). 192p. (YA). (gr. 7). pap. 9.99 *(978-1-4424-8107-7(2)*, Simon & Schuster Bks. For Young Readers) Simon & Schuster Bks. For Young Readers.

Thomas, Peggy. Farmer George Plants a Nation. Johnson, Layne, illus. 2013. (ENG.). 40p. (J). (gr. 4-6). pap. 7.95 *(978-1-62091-029-0(2)*, Calkins Creek) Boyds Mills Pr.

MOUNTAIN CLIMBING

see Mountaineering

MOUNTAIN LIFE—SOUTHERN STATES

Santella, Andrew. Mountain Men. 2003. (Cornerstones of Freedom Ser.). (ENG., Illus.). 48p. (YA). (gr. 4-7). 26.00 *(978-0-516-24216-3(4))* Scholastic Library Publishing.

MOUNTAIN LIFE—SOUTHERN STATES—FICTION

Bare, Bart. Girl. 2010. 188p. (YA). pap. 11.95 *(978-0-9825396-4-4(9))* Canterbury Hse. Publishing, Ltd.

Spyri, Johanna. Heidi. Marks, Alan, illus. 2006. 63p. (J). (gr. 2). 8.99 *(978-0-7945-1237-8(2)*, Usborne) EDC Publishing.

MOUNTAINEERING

Alcraft, Rob. Everest Ice Climbers. 2017. (ENG.). 48p. (J). pap. 8.99 ***(978-0-00-820887-5(5))*** HarperCollins Pubs. Ltd. GBR. Dist: Independent Pubs. Group.

Athans, Sandra K. Secrets of the Sky Caves: Danger & Discovery on Nepal's Mustang Cliffs. 2014. (ENG., Illus.). 64p. (gr. 4-8). lib. bdg. 33.27 *(978-1-4677-0016-0(9)*, Millbrook Pr.) Lerner Publishing Group.

Benjamin, Daniel. Extreme Rock Climbing. 2013. (Sports on the Edge 2 Ser.). 48p. (J). (gr. 4-8). pap. 12.93 *(978-1-62712-133-0(1))*; (Illus.). 29.93 *(978-1-60870-223-7(5))* Cavendish Square Publishing.

Bodden, Valerie. To the Top of Mount Everest. 2011. (Great Expeditions (Creative Education) Ser.). (Illus.). 48p. (J). (gr. 5-8). lib. bdg. 34.25 *(978-1-60818-070-7(0)*, Creative Education) Creative Co., The.

Brown, Alex. Mountain Adventures. 2009. (Difficult & Dangerous Ser.). (J). 28.50 *(978-1-59920-157-3(7))* Black Rabbit Bks.

—Mountain Adventures. 2009. (Difficult & Dangerous Ser.). (Illus.). 32p. (J). pap. *(978-1-897563-25-0(6))* Saunders Bk. Co.

Champion, Neil. Rock Climbing. 2009. (Get Outdoors Ser.). (Illus.). 32p. (ENG.). (J). pap. 10.00 *(978-1-4358-3051-6(2)*, PowerKids Pr.); (YA). (gr. 4-7). lib. bdg. 25.25 *(978-1-4358-3043-1(1))* Rosen Publishing Group, Inc., The.

—Wild Rock: Climbing & Mountaineering. 2013. (Illus.). 32p. (J). lib. bdg. 28.50 *(978-1-59920-807-7(5))* Black Rabbit Bks.

Chapman, Simon. In the Himalayas. Chapman, Simon, illus. 2005. (Illus.). 103p. (J). lib. bdg. 20.00 *(978-1-4242-0626-1(X))* Fitzgerald Bks.

Cleare, John. Epic Climbs. 2011. (Illus.). 64p. (J). (gr. 3-6). 19.99 *(978-0-7534-6473-1(X))* Larousse Kingfisher Chambers, Inc.

Cohn, Jessica. Mountain Climbing. 2013. (Incredibly Insane Sports Ser.). (Illus.). 48p. (J). (gr. 4-6). 31.95 *(978-1-4339-8830-1(5)*, Gareth Stevens Learning Library) Stevens, Gareth Publishing LLLP.

Dean, Cynthia A. Rock Climbing: Making It to the Top. 2005. (High Five Reading - Blue Ser.). (ENG., Illus.). 48p. (gr. 3-4). per. 9.00 *(978-0-7368-5745-1(1)*, High Five Reading (RBL)) Capstone Press of Coughlan Cos.

Dickmann, Nancy. Mount Everest, 1 vol. 2012. (Explorer Tales Ser.). (ENG.). 32p. (gr. 1-3). 29.99 *(978-1-4109-4783-3(1)*, Read Me!) Heinemann-Raintree.

Doeden, Matt. Can You Survive Extreme Mountain Climbing? An Interactive Survival Adventure, 1 vol. 2012. (You Choose: Survival Ser.). (ENG., 112p. (gr. 3-4). Illus.). pap. 6.95 *(978-1-4296-9478-0(5))*; pap. 41.70 *(978-1-4296-9479-7(3))*; (Illus.). lib. bdg. 31.99 *(978-1-4296-8583-2(2))* Capstone Press of Coughlan Cos. (You Choose Bks.).

Dugan, Christine. Defying Gravity! Rock Climbing, 1 vol. 2nd rev. ed. 2013. (Nonfiction Readers Ser.). (ENG., Illus.). 48p. (J). (gr. 4-4). pap. 29.96 *(978-1-4807-1106-8(3))* Shell Educational Publishing.

—Defying Gravity! Rock Climbing, 1 vol. 2nd rev. ed. 2012. (TIME for KIDS(r) Nonfiction Readers Ser.). (ENG.). 48p. (J). (gr. 4-4). pap. 9.99 *(978-1-4333-4830-3(6))* Teacher Created Materials, Inc.

—¡Desafiando la Gravedad! Escalada en Roca. 2017. (TIME for Kids en Español - Level 4 Ser.). (SPA., Illus.). 48p. (gr. 4-4). lib. bdg. 31.99 *(978-1-5157-5135-9(X))* Time for Kids Inc AUS. Dist: Capstone Pub.

Endres, Hollie. Rock Climbing. 2007. (Action Sports Ser.). (ENG., Illus.). 24p. (J). (gr. 3-7). lib. bdg. 25.95 *(978-1-60014-127-0(7))* Bellwether Media.

Fandel, Jennifer. Rock Climbing. 2007. (Active Sports Ser.). (Illus.). 24p. (J). (gr. -1-3). lib. bdg. 24.25 *(978-1-58341-468-2(1)*, Creative Education) Creative Co., The.

Follett, Katherine. One Giant Leap. 2004. (Reader's Theater Ser.). (J). pap. *(978-1-4108-1147-9(6))* Benchmark Education Co.

Fowler Hicks, Ginny. Mountain Star: A Story about a Mountaineer That Will Teach You How to Draw a Star! Fowler, Charlie, photos by. 2008. (Illus.). 24p. (J). 18.95 *(978-0-9763309-3-6(8))* Mountain World Media LLC.

Frisch-Schmoll, Joy. Rock Climbing. 2017. (J). *(978-1-60818-689-1(X)*, Creative Education) Creative Co., The.

Genereux, Andy. Yamnuska Rock: The Crown Jewel of Canadian Rockies Traditional Climbing, 1 vol. 2010. (ENG., Illus.). 320p. pap. *(978-1-894765-74-9(5))* RMB Rocky Mountain Bks.

Goldish, Meish. Lost on a Mountain. 2015. (Illus.). 32p. (J). lib. bdg. *(978-1-62724-292-9(9))* Bearport Publishing Co., Inc.

Graf, Mike. Rock Climbing. 2004. (Illus.). 56p. pap. 9.00 *(978-0-7891-6043-0(9))*; (J). (gr. 4-7). lib. bdg. 17.95 *(978-0-7569-1385-4(3))* Perfection Learning Corp.

Green, Sara. Mountain Climbing. 2013. (Outdoor Adventures Ser.). (ENG., Illus.). 24p. (J). (gr. 3-8). lib. bdg. 25.95 *(978-1-60014-892-7(1)*, Pilot Bks.) Bellwether Media.

Helfand, Lewis. Conquering Everest: The Lives of Edmund Hillary & Tenzing Norgay. Tayal, Amit, illus. 2011. (Campfire Graphic Novels Ser.). (ENG.). 96p. (YA). (gr. 5-12). pap. 12.99 *(978-93-80741-24-6(3)*, Campfire) Steerforth Pr.

Herman, Gail & Amatrula, Michele. Climbing Everest (Totally True Adventures) 2015. (Totally True Adventures Ser.). (ENG., Illus.). 112p. (J). (gr. 2-5). 4.99 *(978-0-553-50986-1(1)*, Random Hse. Bks. for Young Readers) Random Hse. Children's Bks.

Hyde, Natalie. Conquering Everest. 2013. (ENG., Illus.). 48p. (J). pap. *(978-0-7787-1175-9(7))* Crabtree Publishing Co.

Iversen, Sandra. A Day on the Mountain. 2010. (Quick60 Factual Bks.). (ENG., Illus.). 12p. (J). pap. *(978-1-77540-220-6(7))* Iversen Publishing Ltd.

Jankowski, Emily. Reaching Everest's Summit. 2015. (Incredible True Adventures Ser.). (ENG., Illus.). 32p. (J). (gr. 3-4). pap. 10.50 *(978-1-4824-2046-3(5))* Stevens, Gareth Publishing LLLP.

Johnson, Robin. Conquering Everest. 2013. (ENG., Illus.). 48p. (J). *(978-0-7787-1167-4(6))* Crabtree Publishing Co.

Kalman, Bobbie & Crossingham, John. Extreme Climbing. 2003. (Extreme Sports No Limits! Ser.). (ENG., Illus.). 32p. (J). pap. *(978-0-7787-1717-1(8))*; lib. bdg. *(978-0-7787-1671-6(6))* Crabtree Publishing Co.

Loh-Hagan, Virginia. Extreme Mountain Climbing. 2016. (Nailed It! Ser.). (ENG., Illus.). 32p. (J). (gr. 4-8). 29.93 *(978-1-63470-491-5(6)*, 207695) Cherry Lake Publishing.

—Extreme Rock Climbing. 2015. (Illus.). 32p. (J). *(978-1-63470-020-7(1))* Cherry Lake Publishing.

Luke, Andrew. Mountain Sports. 2017. (Illus.). 48p. (J). ***(978-1-4222-3707-6(9))*** Mason Crest.

McFee, Shane. Rock Climbing. (Living on the Edge Ser.). 24p. (gr. 2-3). 2009. 42.50 *(978-1-61514-297-2(5)*, PowerKids Pr.) 2008. (Illus.). (J). lib. bdg. 22.60 *(978-1-4042-4220-3(1))* Rosen Publishing Group, Inc., The.

Mountaineering Adventures, 6 vols. (gr. 4-18). 39.95 *(978-0-7368-9029-8(7))* Red Brick Learning.

Oxlade, Chris. Mountain Rescue, 1 vol. 2012. (Heroic Jobs Ser.). (ENG., Illus.). 32p. (gr. 1-2). lib. bdg. 29.99 *(978-1-4109-4357-6(7)*, Read Me!) Heinemann-Raintree.

—Rock Climbing. 2003. (Extreme Sports Ser.). (ENG., Illus.). 32p. (gr. 3-6). lib. bdg. 22.60 *(978-0-8225-1240-0(8))* Lerner Publishing Group.

Publishers, Wayland & Newland, Sonya. Climbing the Himalayan Mountains. 2016. (Travelling Wild Ser.). (ENG., Illus.). 32p. (J). (gr. 4-6). 17.99 *(978-0-7502-9864-3(2)*, Wayland) Hachette Children's Group GBR. Dist: Hachette Bk. Group.

Randall, Jory. My Day in the Mountains. 2009. (Kid's Life! Ser.). 24p. (J). (ENG.). pap. 8.25 *(978-1-4358-2471-3(7))*; (Illus.). lib. bdg. 22.60 *(978-1-4042-8076-2(6))* Rosen Publishing Group, Inc., The. (PowerKids Pr.).

Rapparlie, Leslie & Wurdinger, Scott. Rock Climbing. 2006. (Adventure Sports Ser.). (Illus.). 48p. (YA). (gr. 5-9). lib. bdg. 21.95 *(978-1-58341-394-4(4))* Creative Co., The.

Romero, Jordan. No Summit Out of Sight: The True Story of the Youngest Person to Climb the Seven Summits. 2014. (ENG., Illus.). 368p. (YA). (gr. 7). 18.99 *(978-1-4767-0962-8(9)*, Simon & Schuster Bks. For Young Readers) Simon & Schuster Bks. For Young Readers.

Salkeld, Audrey. Climbing Everest: Tales of Triumph & Tragedy on the World's Highest Mountain. 2003. (ENG., Illus.). 128p. (J). (gr. 5). 21.00 *(978-0-7922-5105-7(9)*, National Geographic Children's Bks.) National Geographic Society.

Scherer, Glenn & Library. True Mountain Rescue Stories. 2010. (True Rescue Stories Ser.). 48p. (J). lib. bdg. 22.60 *(978-0-7660-3572-0(7))* Enslow Pubs., Inc.

Schindler, John. Rock Climbing. 2005. (Extreme Sports Ser.). (Illus.). 24p. (gr. 2-5). pap. 8.15 *(978-0-8368-4548-8(X))*; lib. bdg. 23.00 *(978-0-8368-4541-9(2))* Stevens, Gareth Publishing LLLP. (Gareth Stevens Learning Library).

ShackletonCaroline. TRAPPED! THE ARON RALSTON STORY HIGH INTERMEDIATE BOOK WITH ONLINE ACCESS. 2014. (ENG., Illus.). 28p. (J). pap. 9.50 *(978-1-107-66998-7(7))* Cambridge Univ. Pr.

Shea, Therese. Rock & Ice Climbing. 2015. (Sports to the Extreme Ser.). (ENG., Illus.). 48p. (J). (gr. 5-6). 30.25 *(978-1-4994-3557-3(6)*, Rosen Central) Rosen Publishing Group, Inc., The.

Sheehan, Robert. Conquering Mount Everest. 2013. (Discovery Education: Sensational True Stories Ser.). (ENG., Illus.). 32p. (J). (gr. 3-6). pap. 10.00 *(978-1-4777-0109-6(5))*; lib. bdg. 25.25 *(978-1-4777-0062-4(5))* Rosen Publishing Group, Inc., The. (PowerKids Pr.).

Shone, Rob. Defying Death in the Mountains. Spender, Nick, illus. 2010. (Graphic Survival Stories Ser.). 48p. (YA). 58.50 *(978-1-61532-901-4(3)*, Rosen Reference) Rosen Publishing Group, Inc., The.

—Defying Death in the Mountains. Spender, Nik, illus. 2010. (Graphic Survival Stories Ser.). 48p. (YA). (ENG.). pap. 14.05 *(978-1-61532-866-6(1))*; (gr. 5-8). 31.95 *(978-1-4358-3532-0(8))* Rosen Publishing Group, Inc., The. (Rosen Reference).

Skreslet, Laurie & MacLeod, Elizabeth. To the Top of Everest. 2003. (ENG., Illus.). 56p. (J). (gr. 3-6). 9.95 *(978-1-55074-814-7(9))* Kids Can Pr., Ltd. CAN. Dist: Hachette Bk. Group.

Spilsbury, Louise. How to Survive on a Mountain. 2012. (Tough Guides). (ENG., Illus.). 32p. (J). (gr. 4-6). pap. 10.00 *(978-1-4488-7936-6(1))*; lib. bdg. 25.25 *(978-1-4488-7871-0(3))* Rosen Publishing Group, Inc., The. (PowerKids Pr.).

Taylor-Butler, Christine. Sacred Mountain: Everest. 2009. (ENG., Illus.). 48p. (J). (gr. 2-7). 19.95 *(978-1-60060-255-9(X))* Lee & Low Bks., Inc.

Teitelbaum, Michael. Rock Climbing. 2007. (21st Century Skills Library: Healthy for Life Ser.). (ENG.). 32p. (gr. 4-8). lib. bdg. 28.50 *(978-1-60279-014-8(0)*, 200031) Cherry Lake Publishing.

Thomas, William David. Mountain Rescuer. 2008. (Cool Careers Ser.). 32p. (gr. 5-8). pap. 10.50 *(978-0-8368-9328-1(X))*; lib. bdg. 26.00 *(978-0-8368-9195-9(3))* Stevens, Gareth Publishing LLLP.

Tomljanovic, Tatiana. Rock Climbing. (J). 2013. *(978-1-62127-359-2(8))* 2013. pap. *(978-1-62127-365-3(2))* 2007. (Illus.). 24p. (gr. 4-7). lib. bdg. 24.45 *(978-1-59036-667-7(0))* 2007. (Illus.). 24p. (gr. 4-7). per. 8.95 *(978-1-59036-668-4(9))* Weigl Pubs., Inc.

Turnbull, Stephanie. Rock Climbing. 2016. (Adventure Sports Ser.). 24p. (gr. 2-6). 28.50 *(978-1-62588-386-5(2)*, Smart Apple Media) Black Rabbit Bks.

Weil, Ann. Mountain Disasters, 1 vol. unabr. ed. 2012. (Disasters Ser.). (ENG.). 92p. (YA). (gr. 9-12). 8.95 *(978-1-61651-932-2(0))* Saddleback Educational Publishing, Inc.

Weingarten, A. J. Rock Climbing. 2012. (Great Outdoors Ser.). (Illus.). 24p. (J). (gr. 2-5). pap. 8.15 *(978-1-4339-7108-2(9))*; lib. bdg. 22.60 *(978-1-4339-7107-5(0))* Stevens, Gareth Publishing LLLP.

Weintraub, Aileen. Mount Everest: The Highest Mountain. 2009. (Great Record Breakers in Nature Ser.). 24p. (gr. 3-4). 42.50 *(978-1-61513-181-5(7)*, PowerKids Pr.) Rosen Publishing Group, Inc., The.

—Rock Climbing. 2003. (High Interest Bks.). (ENG., Illus.). 48p. (J). 24.50 *(978-0-516-24319-1(5)*, Children's Pr.); (YA). (gr. 7-12). pap. 6.95 *(978-0-516-24381-8(0)*, Watts, Franklin) Scholastic Library Publishing.

Whiting, Jim. Ultra Running with Scott Jurek. 2006. (Extreme Sports Ser.). (Illus.). 32p. (J). (gr. 1-4). lib. bdg. 25.70 *(978-1-58415-484-6(5))* Mitchell Lane Pubs., Inc.

Willet, Edward. Rock Sport Climbing: Techniques & Tricks. 2009. (Rad Sports: Techniques & Tricks Ser.). 48p. (gr. 5-8). 53.00 *(978-1-60851-936-1(8)*, Rosen Reference) Rosen Publishing Group, Inc., The.

Willett, Edward. Rock Sport Climbing. 2005. (Rad Sports: Techniques & Tricks Ser.). (Illus.). 48p. (YA). (gr. 5-8). lib. bdg. 29.25 *(978-0-8239-3847-6(6))* Rosen Publishing Group, Inc., The.

York, M. J. Rock Climbing. 2014. (Great Outdoors Ser.). (ENG.). 24p. (J). (gr. 2-5). 28.50 *(978-1-62687-333-9(X)*, 207173) Child's World, Inc., The.

Young, Jeff C. Belaying the Line: Mountain, Rock, & Ice Climbing, 1 vol. 2011. (Adrenaline Adventure Ser.). (ENG., Illus.). 32p. (YA). (gr. 3-6). 27.07 *(978-1-61613-547-8(6))* ABDO Publishing Co.

MOUNTAINEERING—BIOGRAPHY

see Mountaineers

MOUNTAINEERING—FICTION

Baillie, Helen. The Azura Stones. 2007. 212p. (YA). per. 18.00 *(978-1-58982-374-7(5)*, Bedside Bks.) American Bk. Publishing Group.

Barwin, Steven. Rock Dogs, 1 vol. 2009. (Lorimer Sports Stories Ser.). (ENG.). 104p. (J). (gr. 4-8). 16.95 *(978-1-55277-028-3(1)*, 9781552770283); 8.95 *(978-1-55277-027-6(3)*, 9781552770276) Lorimer, James & Co., Ltd., Pubs. CAN. Dist: Casemate Pubs. & Bk. Distributors, LLC.

Birdseye, Tom. Storm Mountain. 2010. (ENG.). 256p. (J). (gr. 3-7). 16.95 *(978-0-8234-2130-5(9))* Holiday Hse., Inc.

Borgenicht, David, et al. The Worst-Case Scenario: Everest - You Decide How to Survive! Labat, Yancey, illus. 2011. (Worst Case Scenario Ser.). (ENG.). 208p. (J). (gr. 4-5). 12.99 *(978-0-8118-7123-5(1))* Chronicle Bks. LLC.

Coleman, K. R. Deadman Anchor. 2016. (Atlas of Cursed Places Ser.). (ENG.). 112p. (YA). (gr. 6-12). lib. bdg. 26.65 *(978-1-5124-1326-7(7)*, Darby Creek) Lerner Publishing Group.

Curlin, Tera. Pat's Mountain, 1 vol. 2010. 16p. 24.95 *(978-1-4489-4356-2(6))* PublishAmerica, Inc.

Dale, Jay. I Go Up, 1 vol. Gulliver, Amanda, illus. 2012. (Engage Literacy Magenta Ser.). (ENG.). 32p. (gr. k-2). pap. 5.99 *(978-1-4296-8832-1(7)*, Engage Literacy) Capstone Press of Coughlan Cos.

Doyle, Bill & Borgenicht, David. Everest: You Decide How to Survive! 2015. (WorstCase Scenario Ultimate Adventure Ser.). (ENG., Illus.). 204p. (gr. 3-8). 47.10 *(978-1-59920-978-4(0))* Black Rabbit Bks.

Dunn, Joeming. Mountain Top Mystery, No. 15. Dunn, Ben, illus. 2010. (Boxcar Children Graphic Novels Ser.: 15). (ENG.). 32p. (J). (gr. 1-5). pap. 6.99 *(978-0-8075-5294-0(1))* Whitman, Albert & Co.

Fawcett, Heather. Even the Darkest Stars. 2017. (Even the Darkest Stars Ser.: 1). 432p. (YA). (gr. 8). 17.99 ***(978-0-06-246338-8(1))*** HarperCollins Pubs.

Fuerst, Jeffrey B. Bear Went over the Mountain. Oliver, Mark, illus. 2010. (Rising Readers Ser.). (J). 3.49 *(978-1-60719-686-0(7))* Newmark Learning LLC.

Jones, V. M. Out of Reach, 0 vols. unabr. ed. 2013. (ENG.). 272p. (J). (gr. 7-9). pap. 9.99 *(978-1-4778-1705-6(0)*, 9781477817056, Amazon Children's Publishing) Amazon Publishing.

Korman, Gordon. Everest Book One: the Contest. 2012. (Everest Ser.). (ENG.). 144p. (J). (gr. 3-7). pap. 6.99 *(978-0-545-39232-7(2))* Scholastic, Inc.

—Everest Book Three: the Summit. 2012. (Everest Ser.). (ENG.). 160p. (J). (gr. 3-7). pap. 6.99 *(978-0-545-39234-1(9))* Scholastic, Inc.

Lasher, Kathy. Heinrich Streudleman Climbs Mt. Baker. 2010. 32p. pap. 14.49 *(978-1-4520-2090-7(6))* AuthorHouse.

Mantell, Paul. Mountain Bike Mania. 2005. (Sports Classics IV Ser.). 151p. (J). lib. bdg. 15.00 *(978-1-59054-764-9(0))* Fitzgerald Bks.

Monroy, Eva. Little Mountain. 2004. (J). pap. 8.00 *(978-0-8059-6535-3(1))* Dorrance Publishing Co., Inc.

Montgomery, R. A. The Abominable Snowman Peguy, Laurence, illus. 2006. (Choose Your Own Adventure Ser.). 144p. (J). (gr. 4-8). per. 6.99 *(978-1-933390-01-7(8)*, CHCL01) Chooseco LLC.

Myers, Edward. Climb or Die. 2nd ed. 2016. 154p. (J). pap. *(978-1-932727-12-8(4))* Montemayor Pr.

—Solos en la Montaña. 2016. (SPA.). 157p. (J). pap. *(978-1-932727-18-0(3))* Montemayor Pr.

Newman, Gwill York. Bingo Bear Was Here: A Toy Bear's Climb to the Top of Africa's Highest Mountain. Babcock, Jeff, illus. 2003. 48p. (J). pap. 8.95 *(978-0-86534-395-5(0))* Sunstone Pr.

Orme, Helen. Wet! 2008. (Siti's Sisters Ser.). (ENG., Illus.). 36p. pap. *(978-1-84167-688-3(8))* Ransom Publishing Ltd.

Paulsen, Gary & Roberts, Esyllt Nest. Craig y Diafol. 2005.Tr. of Devil's Wall. (WEL.). 64p. pap. *(978-0-86381-684-0(3))* Gwasg Carreg Gwalch.

Simpson, Joe & Bembibre, Cecilia. Tocando el Vacío. 2014. (SPA., Illus.). 64p. pap., stu. ed. 13.75 incl. audio compact disk *(978-84-9848-133-4(3))* Edinumen, Editorial ESP. Dist: Cambridge Univ. Pr.

Smelcer, John. Savage Mountain. 2015. (ENG., Illus.). 160p. (J). (gr. 6). pap. 12.00 *(978-1-935248-65-1(0))* Leapfrog Pr.

Smith, Roland. The Edge. 2015. (Peak Marcello Adventure Ser.). (ENG.). 240p. (YA). (gr. 7). 17.99 *(978-0-544-34122-7(8)*, HMH Books For Young Readers) Houghton Mifflin Harcourt Publishing Co.

—The Edge. 2016. (Peak Marcello Adventure Ser.). (ENG.). 240p. (YA). (gr. 7). pap. 7.99 *(978-0-544-81354-0(5)*, HMH Books For Young Readers) Houghton Mifflin Harcourt Publishing Co.

Smith, Roland, et al. Peak. 2008. (Peak Marcello Adventure Ser.). (ENG., Illus.). 256p. (YA). (gr. 7). pap. 7.99 *(978-0-15-206268-2(8))* Houghton Mifflin Harcourt Publishing Co.

Sterling, James Milton. Willy the Mountain Climber. 2012. 32p. pap. 24.95 *(978-1-4626-8242-3(1))* America Star Bks.

Stilton, Geronimo. I'm Too Fond of My Fur! Wolf, Matt, illus. 2004. (Geronimo Stilton Ser.: No. 4). 116p. (J). lib. bdg. 10.00 *(978-1-4242-0698-8(7))* Fitzgerald Bks.

—Mighty Mount Kilimanjaro. 2010. (Geronimo Stilton Ser.: 41). (ENG.). 128p. (J). (gr. 2-5). 7.99 *(978-0-545-10371-8(1)*, Scholastic Paperbacks) Scholastic, Inc.

VanRiper, Gary & VanRiper, Justin. Islands in the Sky. 2005. (Adirondack Kids Ser.: Vol. 5). 78p. (J). (gr. 2-7). pap. 9.95 *(978-0-9707044-5-0(3))* Adirondack Kids Pr.

MOUNTAINEERS

Bodden, Valerie. To the Top of Mount Everest. (Great Expeditions Ser.). (Illus.). 48p. (J). 2012. (ENG.). (gr. 4-7). pap. 12.00 *(978-0-89812-668-6(1))* 2011. (gr. 5-8). lib. bdg. 34.25 *(978-1-60818-070-7(0))* Creative Co., The. (Creative Education).

Burleigh, Robert. Tiger of the Snows: Tenzing Norgay: the Boy Whose Dream Was Everest. Young, Ed, illus. 2010. (ENG.). 40p. (J). (gr. 2-5). 16.99 *(978-1-4424-2192-9(4)*, Atheneum Bks. for Young Readers) Simon & Schuster Children's Publishing.

Crompton, Samuel Willard. Sir Edmund Hillary. 2009. (Great Explorers Ser.). (Illus.). 112p. (J). (gr. 6-12). 30.00 *(978-1-60413-420-9(8)*, Chelsea Hse.) Facts On File, Inc.

Elish, Dan. Edmund Hillary: First to the Top. 2006. (Great Explorations Ser.). (Illus.). 80p. (J). (gr. 3-7). lib. bdg. 32.79 *(978-0-7614-2224-2(2)*, Benchmark Bks.) Marshall Cavendish Corp.

Hyde, Natalie. Conquering Everest. 2013. (ENG., Illus.). 48p. (J). pap. *(978-0-7787-1175-9(7))* Crabtree Publishing Co.

Iversen, Sandra. A Day on the Mountain. 2010. (Quick60 Factual Bks.). (ENG., Illus.). 12p. (J). pap. *(978-1-77540-220-6(7))* Iversen Publishing Ltd.

Johnson, Robin. Conquering Everest. 2013. (ENG., Illus.). 48p. (J). *(978-0-7787-1167-4(6))* Crabtree Publishing Co.

Jones, Brenn. Learning about Teamwork from the Lives of Sir Edmund Hillary & Tenzing Norgay. 2009. (Character Building Book Ser.). 24p. (gr. 2-3). 42.50 *(978-1-60854-968-9(2)*, PowerKids Pr.) Rosen Publishing Group, Inc., The.

Rolfe, Helen Y. & Rolfe, Helen. Women Explorers: 100 Years of Mountain Adventure. 2007. (Amazing Stories Ser.). (ENG., Illus.). 96p. (J). (gr. 4-5). pap. 9.95 *(978-1-55439-709-9(X)*, 9781554397099) Lorimer, James & Co., Ltd., Pubs. CAN. Dist: Casemate Pubs. & Bk. Distributors, LLC.

Romero, Jordan. No Summit Out of Sight: The True Story of the Youngest Person to Climb the Seven Summits. 2014. (ENG., Illus.). 368p. (YA). (gr. 7). 18.99 *(978-1-4767-0962-8(9)*, Simon & Schuster Bks. For Young Readers) Simon & Schuster Bks. For Young Readers.

—No Summit Out of Sight: The True Story of the Youngest Person to Climb the Seven Summits. 2015. lib. bdg. 24.50 *(978-0-606-37139-1(7))* Turtleback Bks.

Trussell-Cullen, Alan. Edmund Hillary. 2009. pap. 13.25 *(978-1-60559-058-5(4))* Hameray Publishing Group, Inc.

Whipple, Heather. Hillary & Norgay: To the Top of Mount Everest. 2007. (In the Footsteps of Explorers Ser.). (ENG., Illus.). 32p. (J). (gr. 3-7). lib. bdg. *(978-0-7787-2418-6(2))*; pap. *(978-0-7787-2454-4(9))* Crabtree Publishing Co.

Yomtov, Nel. Amelia Earhart Flies Across the Atlantic. 2015. (Extraordinary Explorers Ser.). (ENG., Illus.). 24p. (J). (gr. 3-7). lib. bdg. 29.95 *(978-1-62617-290-6(0)*, Black Sheep) Bellwether Media.

—Edmund Hillary Reaches the Top of Everest. 2015. (Extraordinary Explorers Ser.). (ENG., Illus.). 24p. (J). (gr. 3-7). lib. bdg. 29.95 *(978-1-62617-291-3(9)*, Black Sheep) Bellwether Media.

MOUNTAINS

see also Mountaineering; Volcanoes

also names of mountain ranges, e.g. Rocky Mountains; etc.

Adams, Alison. Mountains. 2011. (Early Connections Ser.). (J). *(978-1-61672-644-7(X))* Benchmark Education Co.

Aleshire, Peter. Mountains. 2008. (Extreme Earth Ser.). (Illus.). 144p. (gr. 6-12). 35.00 *(978-0-8160-5918-8(7))* Facts On File, Inc.

Anderson, Sheila. Mountains. (First Step Nonfiction - Landforms Ser.). (gr. k-2). 2015. (ENG., Illus.). 24p. 23.99 *(978-1-5124-1043-3(8)*, Lerner Pubns.) 2008. pap. 34.95 *(978-0-8225-9937-1(6))* 2008. (ENG.). 24p. pap. 6.95 *(978-0-8225-8605-0(3))* 2008. (ENG., Illus.). 24p. lib. bdg. 23.93 *(978-0-8225-8590-9(1)*, Lerner Pubns.) Lerner Publishing Group.

Arden, Carolyn. Mountains & Valleys. 2009. (Restless Earth Ser.). (Illus.). 112p. (YA). (gr. 5-9). 35.00 *(978-0-7910-9707-6(2))* Facts On File, Inc.

Arnold, Quinn M. Mountains. 2016. (Illus.). 24p. (J). *(978-1-60818-742-3(X)*, Creative Education) Creative Co., The.

Atwal, Shalini. Mighty U. S. Mountains. 2013. (InfoMax Readers Ser.). (ENG.). 24p. (J). (gr. 3-4). pap. 8.25 *(978-1-4777-2485-9(0))*; pap. 49.50 *(978-1-4777-2486-6(9))* Rosen Publishing Group, Inc., The. (Rosen Classroom).

Bailey, Gerry. Trapped on the Rock. 2014. (ENG., Illus.). 32p. (J). *(978-0-7787-0433-1(5))* Crabtree Publishing Co.

Banting, Erinn. Mountains. 2016. (Illus.). 32p. (J). *(978-1-5105-0873-6(2))* SmartBook Media, Inc.
—Mountains. (J). 2013. (Illus.). 32p. 28.55 *(978-1-61913-073-9(4))* 2013. (Illus.). 32p. 13.95 *(978-1-61913-236-8(2))* 2006. (Illus.). 32p. (gr. 3-7). lib. bdg. 26.00 *(978-1-59036-444-4(9))* 2006. 9.95 *(978-1-59036-445-1(7))* Weigl Pubs., Inc.
Barber, Nicola. Mountain Homes. 2007. (Homes Around the World Ser.). (ENG., Illus.). 32p. (J). (gr. 3-7). pap. *(978-0-7787-3557-1(5))* Crabtree Publishing Co.
Barnes, Julia. 101 Facts about Mountains. 2003. (One Hundred One Facts about Our World Ser.). (Illus.). 32p. (gr. 1-4). lib. bdg. 26.00 *(978-0-8368-3708-7(6))*, Gareth Stevens Learning Library) Stevens, Gareth Publishing LLLP.
Benduhn, Tea. Living in Mountains. 2007. (Life on the Edge Ser.). 24p. (gr. 1-4). pap. 8.15 *(978-0-8368-8347-3(0))*; (Illus.). lib. bdg. 22.00 *(978-0-8368-8342-8(X))* Stevens, Gareth Publishing LLLP. (Weekly Reader Leveled Readers).
Best, B. J. How Are Mountains Formed? 2017. (J). pap. 16.95 ***(978-1-5026-2545-8(8))*** Cavendish Square Publishing.
Bodden, Valerie. Mountains. 2006. (Our World Ser.). (Illus.). 24p. (J). (gr. -1-3). lib. bdg. 16.95 *(978-1-58341-463-7(0))*, Creative Education) Creative Co., The.
Braidich, Shelby. What Is a Mountain? 2008. (Real Readers - Upper Emergent Ser.). (ENG., Illus.). 12p. (gr. 1-2). pap. 5.90 *(978-0-8239-8122-9(3))* Rosen Publishing Group, Inc., The.
Callery, Sean. Mountain. (Lifecycles Ser.). (ENG., Illus.). 32p. (J). (gr. 2-5). 2013. 6.99 *(978-0-7534-7076-3(4))*, 9780753470763) 2012. 12.99 *(978-0-7534-6810-4(7))*, 9780753468104) Roaring Brook Pr. (Kingfisher).
Carlson Berne, Emma. Hills. 2009. (Geography Zone: Landforms Ser.). 24p. (gr. 2-3). 42.50 *(978-1-61512-710-8(0))*, PowerKids Pr.) Rosen Publishing Group, Inc., The.
Casado, Dami & Casado, Alicia. Las Montanas. 2005. (Yo Te Hablare De... Ser.). (SPA., Illus.). 14p. (J). per., bds. 8.99 *(978-84-272-7388-7(6))* Molino, Editorial ESP. Dist: Santillana USA Publishing Co., Inc.
Chambers, Catherine. Stickmen's Guide to Mountains & Valleys in Layers. Dean, Venitia & de Quay, John Paul, illus. 2016. (Stickmen's Guides to This Incredible Earth Ser.). (ENG.). 32p. (J). (gr. 3-6). 26.65 *(978-1-5124-0618-4(X))* Lerner Publishing Group.
Clarke, Penny. Scary Creatures of the Mountains. 2008. (Scary Creatures Ser.). (ENG.). 32p. (J). 27.00 *(978-0-531-21748-1(5))*, Watts, Franklin) Scholastic Library Publishing.
Claybourne, Anna. Mountains. 2004. (Geography Fact Files Ser.). (Illus.). (J). lib. bdg. 28.50 *(978-1-58340-426-3(0))* Black Rabbit Bks.
Cole, Melissa S. Mountain. 2003. (Wild America Habitats Ser.). (Illus.). 24p. (J). 21.20 *(978-1-56711-806-3(2))*, Blackbirch Pr., Inc.) Cengage Gale.
Frankston, Evan. Mountains & Valleys: What's the Difference? 2013. (InfoMax Readers Ser.). (ENG.). 24p. (J). (gr. 3-4). pap. 49.50 *(978-1-4777-2464-4(8))*; (Illus.). pap. 8.25 *(978-1-4777-2463-7(X))* Rosen Publishing Group, Inc., The. (Rosen Classroom).
Freedman, Jeri. Land Formation: The Shifting, Moving, Changing Earth: The Creation of Mountains. 2009. (J). 77.70 *(978-1-4358-5599-1(X))*; (ENG.). 64p. (YA). pap. 12.95 *(978-1-4358-5598-4(1))*; (ENG., Illus.). 64p. (YA). (gr. 5-9). lib. bdg. 31.95 *(978-1-4358-5300-3(8))* Rosen Publishing Group, Inc., The.
Gaff, Jackie. I Wonder Why Mountains Have Snow on Top: And Other Questions about Mountains. 2017. (I Wonder Why Ser.). (ENG.). 32p. (J). pap. 6.99 *(978-0-7534-7361-0(5))*, 9780753473610, Kingfisher) Roaring Brook Pr.
Gamble, Adam, et al. Good Night Mountains. 2013. (Good Night Our World Ser.). (ENG., Illus.). 26p. (J). (— 1). bds. 9.95 *(978-1-60219-090-0(9))* Good Night Bks.
Ganeri, Anita. Cliff Climbers, 1 vol. 2011. (Landform Adventurers Ser.). (ENG.). 32p. (gr. 1-2). 29.99 *(978-1-4109-4138-1(8))*, Read Me!) Heinemann-Raintree.
—Exploring Habitats, with Benjamin Blog & His Inquisitive Dog, 1 vol. 2014. (Exploring Habitats with Benjamin Blog & His Inquisitive Dog Ser.). (ENG.). 32p. (gr. 1-3). lib. bdg. 179.94 *(978-1-4329-8781-7(X))*, NA-h) Heinemann-Raintree.
—Exploring Mountains: A Benjamin Blog & His Inquisitive Dog Investigation, 1 vol. 2014. (Exploring Habitats with Benjamin Blog & His Inquisitive Dog Ser.). (ENG.). 32p. (gr. 1-3). lib. bdg. 29.99 *(978-1-4329-8776-3(3))*, NA-h) Heinemann-Raintree.
Gill, Shelley. Up on Denali: Alaska's Wild Mountain. Cartwright, Shannon, illus. 2006. (Paws IV Ser.). (ENG.). 32p. (J). (gr. -1-2). pap. 10.99 *(978-1-57061-365-4(6))*, Little Bigfoot) Sasquatch Bks.
Gordon, Sharon. At Home on the Mountain. 2005. (Bookworms Ser.). (SPA., Illus.). 32p. (J). (gr. 3-7). lib. bdg. *(978-0-7614-1961-7(6))*, Benchmark Bks.) Marshall Cavendish Corp.
—At Home on the Mountain/Mi Casa en la Montana. 2006. (Bookworms Ser.). (ENG & SPA., Illus.). 32p. (gr. k-2). lib. bdg. 15.95 *(978-0-7614-2455-0(5))* Marshall Cavendish Corp.
—Mi Casa en la Montana. 2006. (Bookworms Ser.). (SPA & ENG., Illus.). 32p. (gr. k-2). lib. bdg. 15.95 *(978-0-7614-2376-8(1))* Marshall Cavendish Corp.
Great Mountain Ranges. (Illus.). (J). (gr. k-5). 127.50 *(978-0-8239-6995-1(9))* Rosen Publishing Group, Inc., The.
Green, Emily K. Mountains. 2011. (Blastoff! Readers Ser.). 24p. (J). pap. 5.95 *(978-0-531-26031-9(3))*, Children's Pr.) Scholastic Library Publishing.
Green, Jen. Mountains. 2011. (Geography Wise Ser.). (Illus.). 32p. (YA). (gr. 2-5). lib. bdg. 26.50 *(978-1-4488-3281-1(0))* Rosen Publishing Group, Inc., The.
—Mountains Around the World. 2009. (Geography Now! Ser.). (ENG., Illus.). 32p. (J). (gr. 4-6). pap. 10.00 *(978-1-4358-2955-8(7))*, PowerKids Pr.); (YA). (gr. 3-6). lib. bdg. 26.50 *(978-1-4358-2869-8(0))* Rosen Publishing Group, Inc., The.
Hewitt, Sally. Mountains. 2010. (Starting Geography Ser.). 32p. (J). (gr. 2-5). 28.50 *(978-1-60753-127-2(5))* Amicus Publishing.
Hicks, Terry Allan. How Do Mountains Form? 2009. (Tell Me Why, Tell Me How Ser.). 32p. (gr. 3-5). 29.93 *(978-0-7614-3992-9(7))* Marshall Cavendish Corp.
Holland, Gini. I Live in the Mountains. 2004. (Where I Live Ser.). (Illus.). 24p. (gr. k-3). lib. bdg. 22.00 *(978-0-8368-4081-0(X))*, Weekly Reader Leveled Readers) Stevens, Gareth Publishing LLLP.
—I Live in the Mountains/Vivo en las Montañas. Coffey, Colleen & Carrillo, Consuelo, trs. 2004. (Weekly Reader Early Learning Library). (ENG & SPA., Illus.). 24p. (gr. k-3). lib. bdg. 22.00 *(978-0-8368-4129-9(8))*, Weekly Reader Leveled Readers) Stevens, Gareth Publishing LLLP.
Howard, Fran. Mountains, 1 vol. 2006. (Habitats Ser.). (ENG., Illus.). 32p. (J). (gr. -1-3). lib. bdg. 27.07 *(978-1-59679-780-2(0))*, Buddy Bks.) ABDO Publishing Co.
Hutmacher, Kimberly M. Mountains, 1 vol. 2010. (Natural Wonders Ser.). (ENG., 24p. (gr. k-1). Illus.). pap. 7.29 *(978-1-4296-5590-3(9))*; pap. 41.70 *(978-1-4296-5591-0(7))*; lib. bdg. 26.65 *(978-1-4296-5004-5(4))* Capstone Press of Coughlan Cos. (Pebble Plus).
Hynes, Margaret. Discover Science: Mountains. (Discover Science Ser.). (ENG.). 56p. (J). 2017. pap. 7.99 *(978-0-7534-7335-1(6))*, 9780753473351) 2012. (Illus.). (gr. -1-3). 9.99 *(978-0-7534-6835-7(2))*, 9780753468357) Roaring Brook Pr. (Kingfisher).
Jeffries, Joyce. Mountains of the United States. 2013. (Rosen Readers Ser.). (ENG.). 24p. (J). (gr. 3-4). pap. 49.50 *(978-1-4777-2472-9(9))*; pap. 8.25 *(978-1-4777-2471-2(0))* Rosen Publishing Group, Inc., The. (Rosen Classroom).
Jennings, Terry J. Massive Mountains. 2009. (Amazing Planet Earth Ser.). 32p. (gr. 4-7). 31.35 *(978-1-59920-370-6(7))* Black Rabbit Bks.
Kalman, Bobbie. Earth's Mountains. 2008. (Looking at Earth Ser.). (ENG., Illus.). 32p. (J). (gr. 1-4). pap. *(978-0-7787-3217-4(7))*; lib. bdg. *(978-0-7787-3207-5(X))* Crabtree Publishing Co.
—Las Montañas de la Tierra. 2009. (SPA.). 32p. (J). *(978-0-7787-8238-4(7))*; pap. *(978-0-7787-8255-1(7))* Crabtree Publishing Co.
—Where on Earth Are Mountains? 2014. (ENG., Illus.). 32p. (J). *(978-0-7787-0501-7(3))* Crabtree Publishing Co.
Labrecque, Ellen. Earth's Last Frontiers, 1 vol. 2014. (Earth's Last Frontiers Ser.). (ENG.). 32p. (gr. 1-3). lib. bdg. 119.96 *(978-1-4109-6181-5(8))*, Read Me!) Heinemann-Raintree.
—Living on a Mountain. 2015. (Places We Live Ser.). (ENG., Illus.). 32p. (gr. 1-3). 27.32 *(978-1-4846-0806-7(2))*, Heinemann First Library) Heinemann-Raintree.
—Mountain Tops, 1 vol. 2014. (Earth's Last Frontiers Ser.). (ENG.). 32p. (gr. 1-3). lib. bdg. 29.99 *(978-1-4109-6179-2(6))*, Read Me!) Heinemann-Raintree.
Le Tord, Bijou. A Mountain Is to Climb. Le Tord, Bijou, illus. Date not set. (Illus.). 40p. (J). 5.99 *(978-0-06-443591-8(1))* HarperCollins Pubs.
Levin, Judy. Life at a High Altitude. (Life in Extreme Environments Ser.). 64p. (gr. 5-8). 2009. 53.00 *(978-1-61514-268-2(1))* 2004. (Illus.). (J). lib. bdg. 31.95 *(978-0-8239-3987-9(1))* Rosen Publishing Group, Inc., The. (Rosen Reference).
Levy, Janey. Discovering Mountains. (World Habitats Ser.). 32p. 2009. (gr. 4-5). 47.90 *(978-1-60854-835-4(X))*, PowerKids Pr.) 2007. (Illus.). (YA). (gr. 3-6). lib. bdg. 25.25 *(978-1-4042-3785-8(2))* Rosen Publishing Group, Inc., The.
Lonely Planet Publications Staff. Lonely Planet Let's Explore... Mountains, 1 vol. 2017. (Lonely Planet Kids Ser.). (ENG., Illus.). 60p. (J). pap. 9.99 *(978-1-78657-315-5(6))*, 5401) Lonely Planet Pubns.
Macken, JoAnn Early. Montañas. 2006. (Conoces la Tierra? Geografía del mundo (Where on Earth? World Geography) Ser.). (ENG & SPA., Illus.). 24p. (gr. 1-4). pap. 8.15 *(978-0-8368-6553-0(7))*, Weekly Reader Leveled Readers) Stevens, Gareth Publishing LLLP.
—Montanas. 2006. (Conoces la Tierra? Geografía del mundo (Where on Earth? World Geography) Ser.). (ENG & SPA., Illus.). 24p. (gr. 1-4). lib. bdg. 22.00 *(978-0-8368-6546-2(4))*, Weekly Reader Leveled Readers) Stevens, Gareth Publishing LLLP.
—Mountains. 2006. (Where on Earth? World Geography Ser.). (Illus.). 24p. (gr. 1-4). lib. bdg. 22.00 *(978-0-8368-6395-6(X))*, Weekly Reader Leveled Readers) Stevens, Gareth Publishing LLLP.
Marsico, Katie. Mountains. 2009. (21st Century Skills Library: Real World Math Ser.). (ENG.). 32p. (gr. 4-8). lib. bdg. 28.50 *(978-1-60279-492-4(8))*, 200316) Cherry Lake Publishing.
Masterson, Josephine. The Big Hill. 2015. (Rosen REAL Readers: STEM & STEAM Collection). (ENG.). 8p. pap. 5.46 *(978-1-4994-9683-3(4))*, Rosen Classroom) Rosen Publishing Group, Inc., The.
Maynard, Charles W. The Appalachians. 2004. (Great Mountain Ranges of the World Ser.). (Illus.). 24p. (YA). (gr. 3-6). lib. bdg. 22.60 *(978-0-8239-6695-0(X))* Rosen Publishing Group, Inc., The.
—The Ural Mountains. (Great Mountain Ranges of the World Ser.). 24p. 2009. (gr. 3-3). 42.50 *(978-1-61513-172-3(8))* 2004. (Illus.). (J). lib. bdg. 22.60 *(978-0-8239-6699-8(2))* Rosen Publishing Group, Inc., The. (PowerKids Pr.).
McCurry, Kristin. Mountain Babies. 2006. (Animal Babies Ser.). (ENG., Illus.). 22p. (J). (gr. -1 — 1). bds. 5.95 *(978-1-55971-940-7(0))* Cooper Square Publishing Llc.
Minden, Cecilia. Mountains. 2010. (21st Century Basic Skills Library: the World Around Us Ser.). (ENG.). 24p. (gr. k-3). lib. bdg. 22.79 *(978-1-60279-860-1(5))*, 200586) Cherry Lake Publishing.
Mis, Melody S. Exploring Mountains. 2009. (Geography Zone: Landforms Ser.). 24p. (J). (gr. 2-4). pap. 8.25 *(978-1-4358-3113-1(6))*; (gr. 2-3). 42.50 *(978-1-61512-704-7(6))*; (Illus.). (J). lib. bdg. 22.60 *(978-1-4358-2715-8(5))* Rosen Publishing Group, Inc., The. (PowerKids Pr.).
Morley, Catherine Weyerhaeuser. Where Do Mountains Come from, Momma? 2012. (Illus.). (J). *(978-0-87842-582-2(9))* Mountain Pr. Publishing Co., Inc.
Nadeau, Isaac. Mountains. (Library of Landforms Ser.). 24p. (gr. 3-4). 2009. 42.50 *(978-1-60853-727-3(7))*, PowerKids Pr.) 2006. (Illus.). (J). lib. bdg. 22.60 *(978-1-4042-3127-6(7))* Rosen Publishing Group, Inc., The.
Northcott, Richard. In the Mountains. Geatches, Hazel, ed. 2013. (ENG.). 40p. pap. 9.38 *(978-0-19-464687-1(4))* Oxford Univ. Pr., Inc.
O'DellKathryn. SURVIVAL GUIDE: LOST IN THE MOUNTAINS LOW INTERMEDIATE BOOK WITH ONLINE ACCESS. 2014. (ENG.). 28p. (J). pap. 9.50 *(978-1-107-64328-4(7))* Cambridge Univ. Pr.
Oxlade, Chris. Mountains, 1 vol. (Learning about Landforms Ser.). (ENG., 2014. Illus.). 32p. (gr. 1-3). lib. bdg. 27.32 *(978-1-4329-9536-2(7))*, Heinemann First Library) 2013. 48p. (gr. 3-6). 29.99 *(978-1-4109-5430-5(7))*, NA-r) 2013. 48p. (gr. 3-6). pap. 8.95 *(978-1-4109-5437-4(4))*, NA-r) Heinemann-Raintree.
Pyers, Greg. Biodiversity of Alpine Regions. 2011. (Biodiversity 2 Ser.). 32p. (gr. 4). 28.50 *(978-1-60870-528-3(5))* Marshall Cavendish Corp.
Randall, Jory. My Day in the Mountains. 2009. (Kid's Life! Ser.). 24p. (J). (ENG.). pap. 8.25 *(978-1-4358-2471-3(7))*; (Illus.). lib. bdg. 22.60 *(978-1-4042-8076-2(6))* Rosen Publishing Group, Inc., The. (PowerKids Pr.).
Rau, Dana Meachen. On the Mountain. 2007. (J). pap. 6.99 *(978-0-7614-3310-1(4))* Marshall Cavendish Corp.
Richardson, Gillian. Mountain Extremes. 2008. (Extreme Nature Ser.). (ENG., Illus.). 32p. (J). (gr. 2-3). pap. *(978-0-7787-4520-4(1))*; lib. bdg. *(978-0-7787-4503-7(1))* Crabtree Publishing Co.
Riggs, Kate & Arnold, Quinn M. Mountains. 2017. (Seedlings Ser.). (ENG., Illus.). 24p. (J). (gr. k-2). pap. 7.99 *(978-1-62832-338-2(8))*, Creative Paperbacks) Creative Co., The.
Rissman, Rebecca. Living & Nonliving in the Mountains, 1 vol. 2013. (Is It Living or Nonliving? Ser.). (ENG.). 24p. (gr. k-2). 23.32 *(978-1-4109-5385-8(8))*; pap. 6.95 *(978-1-4109-5392-6(0))* Heinemann-Raintree.
Roumanis, Alexis. Mountains. 2014. (Illus.). 24p. (J). *(978-1-4896-3010-0(4))* Weigl Pubs., Inc.
Samuel, Nigel. The 10 Mightiest Mountains. 2007. (Illus.). (J). 14.99 *(978-1-55448-509-3(6))* Scholastic Library Publishing.
Sill, Cathryn P. & Sill, Cathryn P. About Habitats-Mountains, 1 vol. Sill, John & Sill, John, illus. 2009. (About Habitats Ser.). (ENG.). 48p. (J). (gr. -1-2). 16.95 *(978-1-56145-469-3(9))* Peachtree Pubs.
Snedden, Robert. Protecting Mountain Habitats. 2005. (Protecting Habitats Ser.). (Illus.). 32p. (gr. 4-7). lib. bdg. 26.00 *(978-0-8368-4991-2(4))*, Gareth Stevens Learning Library) Stevens, Gareth Publishing LLLP.
Somervill, Barbara A. The Timeworn Urals. 2004. (Geography of the World Ser.). (ENG., Illus.). 32p. (J). (gr. 3-6). 28.50 *(978-1-59296-335-5(8))*, 200267) Child's World, Inc., The.
Staub, Frank. America's Mountains. 2003. (Illus.). 48p. (J). (gr. 2-6). 16.95 *(978-1-59034-870-3(2))*; *(978-1-59034-872-7(9))* Mondo Publishing.
Taylor, Chad. Our Community Is in the Mountains. 2016. (Rosen REAL Readers: Social Studies Nonfiction / Fiction: Family, Community, & the World Ser.). 8p. (gr. 1-k). pap. 5.46 *(978-1-5081-2299-9(7))*, Rosen Classroom) Rosen Publishing Group, Inc., The.
Thomson, Ruth. Mountains. 2012. (Geography Corner Ser.). (ENG., Illus.). 24p. (J). (gr. k-3). 21.25 *(978-1-4488-6617-5(0))*, PowerKids Pr.) Rosen Publishing Group, Inc., The.
Tull, Mary. Mountains. 2007. (Reading Expeditions Ser.). (ENG., Illus.). 32p. (J). pap. 17.95 *(978-0-7922-4562-9(8))* CENGAGE Learning.
Waldron, Melanie. Mountains, 1 vol. 2012. (Habitat Survival Ser.). (ENG.). 32p. (gr. 2-4). pap. 8.29 *(978-1-4109-4606-5(1))*, Raintree Perspectives) Heinemann-Raintree.
Watson, Galadriel Findlay. Mount Kilimanjaro. 2008. (Natural Wonders Ser.). (Illus.). 32p. (J). (gr. 5-6). pap. 9.95 *(978-1-59036-935-7(1))* Weigl Pubs., Inc.
Waxman, Laura Hamilton. Life on a Mountain. 2016. (Biomes Alive! Ser.). (ENG., Illus.). 24p. (J). (gr. k-3). lib. bdg. 25.95 *(978-1-62617-319-4(2))*, Blastoff! Readers) Bellwether Media.
Weatherly, Myra. The Lure of Mountain Peaks. 2004. (Geography of the World Ser.). (ENG., Illus.). 32p. (J). (gr. 3-6). 28.50 *(978-1-59296-333-1(1))*, 200264) Child's World, Inc., The.
Webster, Christine. K2. 2008. (Natural Wonders Ser.). 32p. (J). (gr. 5-6). lib. bdg. 26.00 *(978-1-59036-938-8(6))*; (Illus.). pap. 9.95 *(978-1-59036-939-5(4))* Weigl Pubs., Inc.
Wilkes, Angela. Wild Places: Combined Volume. 2009. (Explainers Ser.). 96p. (J). pap. 12.99 *(978-0-7945-2499-9(0))*, Usborne) EDC Publishing.
Woods, Michael & Woods, Mary B. Seven Natural Wonders of Africa. 2009. (Seven Wonders Ser.). (ENG., Illus.). 80p. (gr. 5-8). lib. bdg. 33.26 *(978-0-8225-9071-2(9))* Lerner Publishing Group.
World Book, Inc Staff, contrib. by. Mountains, Deserts, & Grasslands. 2008. 64p. (J). *(978-0-7166-1403-6(0))* World Bk., Inc.
World Book, Inc Staff, contrib. by. Nature's Skyscrapers. 2017. (J). ***(978-0-7166-3368-6(X))*** World Bk., Inc.
Zoehfeld, Kathleen Weidner. How Mountains Are Made. Hale, James Graham, illus. 2015. (Let's-Read-And-Find-Out Science 2 Ser.). (ENG.). 32p. (J). (gr. -1-3). pap. 6.99 *(978-0-06-238203-0(9))* HarperCollins Pubs.
—How Mountains Are Made. 2015. (Let's Read & Find Out Science Stage 2 Ser.). (J). lib. bdg. 17.20 *(978-0-606-37637-2(2))* Turtleback Bks.
Zolty, Howard. Mountain View A through Z. A Colorful Reader for Children of All Ages. 2006. 28p. 14.99 *(978-1-4116-5708-3(X))* Lulu Pr., Inc.

MOUNTIES

see Royal Canadian Mounted Police

MOURNING CUSTOMS

see Funeral Rites and Ceremonies

MOUSE

see Mice

MOUTH ORGAN

see Harmonica

MOVIES

see Motion Pictures

MOVING, HOUSEHOLD

Amos, Janine. Moving. 2009. (Changes Ser.). (Illus.). 32p. (J). (gr. k-2). 22.60 *(978-1-60754-487-6(3))*; (gr. 2-5). pap. 10.55 *(978-1-60754-488-3(1))* Windmill Bks.
Barber, Nicola. Moving to a New House. 2009. (Big Day! Ser.). 24p. (J). (gr. k-2). (ENG., Illus.). pap. 8.25 *(978-1-4358-2897-1(6))*; 22.60 *(978-1-4358-2841-4(0))* Rosen Publishing Group, Inc., The. (PowerKids Pr.).
Berry, Joy. Good Answers to Tough Questions about Moving. 2009. (ENG.). 52p. (J). (gr. k-7). pap. 7.95 *(978-1-60577-503-6(7))* Berry, Joy Enterprises.
—Good Answers to Tough Questions Moving. Bartholomew, illus. 2010. (Good Answers to Tough Questions Ser.). (ENG.). 48p. (J). (gr. k-7). pap. 7.99 *(978-1-60577-508-1(8))* Berry, Joy Enterprises.
Civardi, Anne. Moving House Sticker Book. 2009. (First Experiences Sticker Bks). 18p. (J). pap. 6.99 *(978-0-7945-2430-2(3))*, Usborne) EDC Publishing.
Davis, Gabriel. The Moving Book: A Kids' Survival Guide. Dennen, Sue, illus. 2nd ed. 2008. 160p. (J). spiral bd. 22.95 *(978-0-912301-92-1(9))* First Bks.
Glasser, Debbie & Schenck, Emily. New Kid, New Scene: A Guide to Moving & Switching Schools. 2011. (Illus.). 112p. (J). 14.95 *(978-1-4338-1039-8(5))*; pap. 9.95 *(978-1-4338-1038-1(7))* American Psychological Assn. (Magination Pr.).
Guillain, Charlotte. Coping with Moving Away, 1 vol. 2011. (Real Life Issues Ser.). (ENG.). 48p. (gr. 6-8). 32.65 *(978-1-4329-4764-4(8))* Heinemann-Raintree.
Lott, Ruth. BK's Big Move Across the Country: From Philadelphia to Los Angeles. 2012. (Illus.). 104p. (J). *(978-1-58982-846-9(1))*, Millennial Mind Publishing) American Bk. Publishing Group.
McAneney, Caitlin. Moving, 1 vol. 2015. (ENG.). 24p. (J). pap. 8.25 *(978-1-4777-5801-4(1))*, PowerKids Pr.) Rosen Publishing Group, Inc., The.
A New House. 2004. (J). pap. 6.95 *(978-0-9760646-0-2(X))* Grape Elephant MarketPr.
Parker, Steve & Parker, Vic. Moving, 1 vol. 2011. (Growing Up Ser.). (ENG.). 24p. (gr. k-2). 23.32 *(978-1-4329-4800-9(8))*, Heinemann Read & Learn) Heinemann-Raintree.
Petersen, Christine. The Smart Kid's Guide to Moving. Rooney, Ronnie, illus. 2014. (Smart Kid's Guide to Everyday Life Ser.). (ENG.). 32p. (J). (gr. 2-5). 28.50 *(978-1-62687-345-2(3))*, 207185) Child's World, Inc., The.
Rober, Harold. Moving Day. 2017. (Bumba Books (tm) — Fun Firsts Ser.). (ENG.). 24p. (J). (gr. -1-1). 12.99 ***(978-1-5124-3687-7(9))***; 38.65 ***(978-1-5124-2747-9(0))***; 38.65 ***(978-1-5124-3686-0(0))*** Lerner Publishing Group. (Lerner Pubns.).
Rober, Harold T. Moving Day. 2017. (Bumba Books (tm) — Fun Firsts Ser.). (ENG., Illus.). 24p. (J). (gr. -1-1). 25.32 *(978-1-5124-2551-2(6))* Lerner Publishing Group.
Sportelli-Rehak, Angela. Moving Again Mom! Hinlicky, Gregg, illus. (J). 2004. (Uncle Sam's Kids Ser.: Bk. 2). 40p. (gr. -1-7). pap. 7.95 *(978-0-9714515-0-6(8))* 2003. (gr. k-7). pap. *(978-0-9714515-3-7(2))* Abidenme Bks.
—Uncle Sam's Kids: Moving Again Mom. Hinlicky, Gregg, illus. 2004. (Uncle Sam's Kids Ser.: Bk. 2). 40p. (gr. k-6). 16.95 *(978-0-9714515-2-0(4))* Abidenme Bks.

MOVING, HOUSEHOLD—FICTION

Absolutely Truly: A Pumpkin Falls Mystery. 2014. (Pumpkin Falls Mystery Ser.). (ENG., Illus.). 368p. (J). (gr. 3-7). 17.99 *(978-1-4424-2972-7(0))*, Simon & Schuster Bks. For Young Readers) Simon & Schuster Bks. For Young Readers.
Acampora, Paul. Rachel Spinelli Punched Me in the Face. 2013. (ENG.). 192p. (J). (gr. 3-7). pap. 8.99 *(978-1-250-01669-0(X))*, 9781250016690) Square Fish.
Albright, Lauren. Exit Strategy. 2017. (Max Ser.). (ENG., Illus.). 176p. (J). (gr. 4-8). 16.99 ***(978-1-4814-7912-7(1))***, Aladdin) Simon & Schuster Children's Publishing.
Allen, Nancy. Amazing Grace: A Kentucky Girl with Gumption During World War II. 2014. Orig. Title: Amazing Grace: a Kentucky Girl with Gumption During World War II. (ENG., Illus.). 160p. (gr. 4-7). pap. 14.99 *(978-1-62619-405-2(X))*, History Pr., The) Arcadia Publishing.
Almond, David. Skellig. 2009. 9.14 *(978-0-7848-2973-8(X))*, Everbind) Marco Bk. Co.
Amato, Mary. Invisible Lines. Caparo, Antonio, illus. 2011. (ENG.). 336p. (gr. 5). 7.99 *(978-1-60684-187-7(4))*, Carolrhoda Bks.) Lerner Publishing Group.
Anderson, Laurie Halse. Helping Hands. 2013. (Vet Volunteers Ser.: 15). (ENG.). 144p. (J). (gr. 3-7). pap. 6.99 *(978-0-14-241677-8(0))*, Puffin Books) Penguin Young Readers Group.
—New Beginnings #13, 13 vols. 2012. (Vet Volunteers Ser.: 13). (ENG.). 192p. (J). (gr. 3-7). 6.99 *(978-0-14-241675-4(4))*, Puffin Books) Penguin Young Readers Group.
Archer, Jennifer. Through Her Eyes. 2012. (ENG.). 400p. (YA). (gr. 8). pap. 9.99 *(978-0-06-183459-2(9))*, HarperTeen) HarperCollins Pubs.
Arnaldo, Monica. Arto's Big Move. 2014. (ENG., Illus.). 40p. (J). (gr. -1-3). 17.95 *(978-1-77147-066-7(6))*, Owlkids) Owlkids Bks. Inc. CAN. Dist: Publishers Group West (PGW).
Arno, Ronni. Dear Poppy. 2016. (Mix Ser.). (ENG., Illus.). 256p. (J). (gr. 4-8). pap. 7.99 *(978-1-4814-3759-2(3))*, Aladdin) Simon & Schuster Children's Publishing.
—Dear Poppy. 2016. (Mix Ser.). (ENG., Illus.). 256p. (J). (gr. 4-8). 17.99 *(978-1-4814-3760-8(7))*, Simon & Schuster/Paula Wiseman Bks.) Simon & Schuster/Paula Wiseman Bks.
Arnold, Elana K. Far from Fair. 2016. (ENG.). 240p. (J). (gr. 5-7). 16.99 *(978-0-544-60227-4(7))*, HMH Books For Young Readers) Houghton Mifflin Harcourt Publishing Co.
—The Question of Miracles. 2016. (ENG.). 256p. (J). (gr. 5-7). pap. 6.99 *(978-0-544-66852-2(9))*, HMH Books For Young Readers) Houghton Mifflin Harcourt Publishing Co.
Atkinson, Elizabeth. From Alice to Zen & Everyone in Between. (gr. 4-7). 2013. (ENG.). 248p. (J). pap. 9.95 *(978-1-4677-0861-6(5))*, Carolrhoda Bks.) 2008. 247p. (YA). 16.95 *(978-0-8225-7271-8(0))* Lerner Publishing Group.
Auch, M. J. Wing Nut. 2008. (ENG.). 256p. (J). (gr. 5-9). pap. 14.99 *(978-0-312-38420-3(3))*, 9780312384203) Square Fish.
Bagley, Jessixa. Before I Leave. 2016. (ENG., Illus.). 40p. (J). 17.99 *(978-1-62672-040-4(1))*, 9781626720404) Roaring Brook Pr.

M
N
O

Banks, Kate & Sheldrake, Rupert. Boy's Best Friend. 2015. (ENG.). 224p. (J). (gr. 3-7). 15.99 *(978-0-374-38008-3(2),* 9780374380083, Farrar, Straus & Giroux (BYR)) Farrar, Straus & Giroux.

Banks, Lynne Reid. The Mystery of the Cupboard. Newsom, Tom, illus. 2004. (Indian in the Cupboard Ser.: No. 4). (ENG.). 256p. (J). (gr. 4-18). pap. 6.99 *(978-0-380-72013-2(2))* HarperCollins Pubs.

Barnes, Jennifer Lynn. The Fixer. (ENG.). (YA). 2016. 400p. pap. 9.99 *(978-1-61963-598-2(4),* 9781619635982) 2015. 384p. (gr. 7). 17.99 *(978-1-61963-594-4(1),* 9781619635944) Bloomsbury Publishing USA. (Bloomsbury USA Childrens).

Barnett, Mac & John, Jory. The Terrible Two. Cornell, Kevin, illus. (Terrible Two Ser.). (ENG.). (J). (gr. 3-7). 2016. 224p. 13.95 *(978-1-4197-1680-5(8),* Amulet Bks.) 2016. pap. 7.95 *(978-1-4197-1925-7(4))* 2015. 224p. 13.95 *(978-1-4197-1491-7(0),* Amulet Bks.) Abrams, Inc.

—The Terrible Two. 2017. (Terrible Two Ser.: 1). lib. bdg. 18.40 ***(978-0-606-40723-6(5))***; lib. bdg. 18.40 ***(978-0-606-40724-3(3))*** Turtleback Bks.

Barshaw, Ruth McNally. New Kid in School. Barshaw, Ruth McNally, illus. 2013. (Ellie Mcdoodle Diaries). (ENG., Illus.). 192p. (YA). (gr. 3-6). 12.99 *(978-1-61963-174-8(1),* 9781619631748, Bloomsbury USA Childrens) Bloomsbury Publishing USA.

Bateson, Catherine. Stranded in Boringsville. (ENG.). 144p. (J). (gr. 5-9). 2007. pap. 6.95 *(978-0-8234-2113-8(9))* 2005. 16.95 *(978-0-8234-1969-2(X))* Holiday Hse., Inc.

Bauer, Joan. Soar. 2016. (ENG.). 304p. (J). (gr. 5). 16.99 *(978-0-451-47034-8(6),* Viking Books for Young Readers) Penguin Young Readers Group.

Beake, Lesley. Home Now. Littlewood, Karin, illus. 2007. 32p. (J). (ENG.). (gr. -1-3). pap. 6.95 *(978-1-58089-163-9(2))*; (gr. k-3). 16.95 *(978-1-58089-162-2(4))* Charlesbridge Publishing, Inc.

Bean, Raymond. First Family in Space. 2016. (Out of This World Ser.). (ENG., Illus.). 112p. (gr. 2-5). lib. bdg. 32.65 *(978-1-4965-3617-4(7))* Out of this World GBR. Dist: Capstone Pub.

Beiko, S. M. The Lake & the Library. l.t. ed. 2013. 542p. pap. *(978-1-4596-6871-3(5))* ReadHowYouWant.com, Ltd.

Bennett, Jenn. Alex, Approximately. 2017. (ENG., Illus.). 400p. (YA). (gr. 9). 17.99 *(978-1-4814-7877-9(X),* Simon Pulse) Simon Pulse.

Benson, Linda. Finding Chance. Lane, Nancy, illus. 2006. 112p. (J). *(978-1-59336-696-4(5))* Mondo Publishing.

Bentley, Sue. Chocolate Wishes #1. Swan, Angela, illus. 2013. (Magic Bunny Ser.: 1). (ENG.). 128p. (J). (gr. 1-3). pap. 5.99 *(978-0-448-46727-6(5),* Grosset & Dunlap) Penguin Young Readers Group.

—A Puzzle of Paws. 2014. (Magic Kitten Ser.: 12). lib. bdg. 14.75 *(978-0-606-35682-4(7))* Turtleback Bks.

—A Puzzle of Paws #12. Swan, Angela & Farley, Andrew, illus. 2014. (Magic Kitten Ser.: 12). (ENG.). 128p. (J). (gr. 1-3). 4.99 *(978-0-448-46795-5(X),* Grosset & Dunlap) Penguin Young Readers Group.

—Seaside Mystery. 2013. (Magic Kitten Ser.: 9). lib. bdg. 16.00 *(978-0-606-32121-1(7),* Turtleback) Turtleback Bks.

Benyo, Richard. The South Street Gang vs. the Coalcracker Cyclops. 2010. (ENG.). 151p. pap. 8.00 *(978-1-58966-208-7(3))* Univ. of Scranton Pr.

Berman, Ali. Misdirected: A Novel. 2014. (ENG., Illus.). 290p. (YA). (gr. 7). 18.95 *(978-1-60980-573-9(9),* Triangle Square) Seven Stories Pr.

Berry, Eileen M. Looking for Home. Manning, Maurie J., illus. 2006. 75p. (J). (gr. -1-3). per. *(978-1-59166-493-2(4))* BJU Pr.

Bietz, Barbara. The Sundown Kid. 2017. (ENG., Illus.). 32p. (J). (gr. k-2). pap. 8.95 *(978-1-939160-94-2(4))* August Hse. Pubs., Inc.

Binns, B. A. & McKenzie, C. Lee. The Princess of Las Pulgas. 2010. 334p. (YA). (gr. 8-18). 16.95 *(978-1-934813-44-7(3))* Westside Bks.

Birle, Pete. Locals Only. 2013. (Av2 Audio Chapter Bks.). (ENG.). 121p. (J). 27.13 *(978-1-62127-985-3(5),* AV2 by Weigl) Weigl Pubs., Inc.

Blabey, Aaron. Sunday Chutney. Blabey, Aaron, illus. 2009. (ENG., Illus.). 32p. (J). (gr. -1-k). 16.95 *(978-1-59078-597-3(5),* Front Street) Boyds Mills Pr.

Blackaby, Susan. Moving Day, 1 vol. Haugen, Ryan, illus. 2005. (Read-It! Readers Ser.). (ENG.). 24p. (gr. -1-3). 21.32 *(978-1-4048-1006-8(4),* Easy Readers) Picture Window Bks.

Blakemore, Megan Frazer. The Water Castle. 2014. (ENG.). 368p. (YA). (gr. 3-8). pap. 7.99 *(978-0-8027-3593-5(2),* 9780802735935, Bloomsbury USA Childrens) Bloomsbury Publishing USA.

Blevins, Wiley. I'm Not Moving! Cerato, Mattia, illus. 2014. (Family Snaps Ser.). (ENG.). 32p. (J). (gr. k-2). pap. 6.95 *(978-1-939656-64-3(8))* Red Chair Pr.

Blume, Judy. Starring Sally J. Freedman As Herself. 2014. (ENG., Illus.). (J). (gr. 3-7). 384p. 17.99 *(978-1-4814-1437-1(2))*; 400p. pap. 7.99 *(978-1-4814-1355-8(4))* Simon & Schuster Children's Publishing. (Atheneum Bks. for Young Readers).

Blythe, Daniel. Shadow Breakers. 2013. (J). *(978-0-545-47980-6(0))*; (ENG.). 256p. (gr. 5-9). 16.99 *(978-0-545-47979-0(7))* Scholastic, Inc. (Chicken Hse., The).

Border, Terry. Peanut Butter & Cupcake. Border, Terry, illus. 2014. (ENG., Illus.). 32p. (J). (gr. -1-2). 17.99 *(978-0-399-16773-7(0),* Philomel Bks.) Penguin Publishing Group.

Bottner, Barbara. Rosa's Room, 1 vol. Spiegel, Beth, illus. 2014. (ENG.). 32p. (J). (gr. -1-3). pap. 7.95 *(978-1-56145-776-2(0))* Peachtree Pubs.

—Rosa's Room, 1 vol. Spiegel, Beth, tr. Spiegel, Beth, illus. 2004. (ENG.). 32p. (J). (gr. k-3). 15.95 *(978-1-56145-302-3(1))* Peachtree Pubs.

Bowers, Tim. A New Home. 2003. (Green Light Readers Level 1 Ser.). (ENG., Illus.). 24p. (J). (gr. -1-3). pap. 3.95 *(978-0-15-204848-8(0))* Houghton Mifflin Harcourt Publishing Co.

Boyack, Merrilee. The Mismatched Nativity. Tenney, Shawna J. C., illus. 2016. (J). 18.99 *(978-1-62972-239-9(1))* Deseret Bk. Co.

Brandon, Anthony G. Moving Day. Yee, Wong Herbert, illus. 2005. (Green Light Readers Level 2 Ser.). (ENG.). 32p. (J). (gr. -1-3). pap. 3.95 *(978-0-15-205652-0(1))* Houghton Mifflin Harcourt Publishing Co.

Branford, Anna. Violet Mackerel's Personal Space. Allen, Elanna, illus. 2013. (Violet Mackerel Ser.). (ENG.). 128p. (J). (gr. 1-5). 15.99 *(978-1-4424-3591-9(7))*; pap. 5.99 *(978-1-4424-3592-6(5))* Simon & Schuster Children's Publishing. (Atheneum Bks. for Young Readers).

—Violet Mackerel's Possible Friend. Allen, Elanna, illus. 2014. (Violet Mackerel Ser.). (ENG.). 128p. (J). (gr. 1-5). 15.99 *(978-1-4424-9455-8(7),* Atheneum Bks. for Young Readers) Simon & Schuster Children's Publishing.

Braver, Vanita. Madison & the New Neighbors, 1 vol. Brown, Jonathan, illus. 2014. (ENG.). 32p. (J). 15.99 *(978-1-59572-686-5(1))* Star Bright Bks., Inc.

Brennan-Nelson, Denise. Willow & the Snow Day Dance. Moore, Cyd, illus. 2010. (ENG.). 32p. (J). (gr. k-6). lib. bdg. 16.95 *(978-1-58536-522-7(X))* Sleeping Bear Pr.

Brewer, Heather. The Cemetery Boys. 2015. (ENG.). 288p. (YA). (gr. 8). 17.99 *(978-0-06-230788-0(6),* HarperTeen) HarperCollins Pubs.

—The Cemetery Boys. 2016. 304p. (YA). (gr. 8). pap. 9.99 *(978-0-06-230789-7(4),* HarperTeen) HarperCollins Pubs.

—The Cemetery Boys. 2016. (YA). lib. bdg. 20.85 *(978-0-606-38741-5(2))* Turtleback Bks.

Brezenoff, Steve. Alley of Shadows, 1 vol. Martin, Cynthia, illus. 2008. (Vortex Bks.). (ENG.). 112p. (gr. 2-3). pap. 7.19 *(978-1-59889-922-1(8),* Vortex Bks.) Stone Arch Bks.

—No Place Like Home, 1 vol. Pinelli, Amerigo, illus. 2013. (Ravens Pass Ser.). (ENG.). 96p. (gr. 2-3). pap. 6.15 *(978-1-4342-6215-8(4))* Stone Arch Bks.

—No Place Like Home. 2013. (Ravens Pass Ser.). (ENG.). 96p. (gr. 2-3). pap. 35.70 *(978-1-4342-6292-9(8))* Stone Arch Bks.

—No Place Like Home, 1 vol. Pinelli, Amerigo, illus. 2013. (Ravens Pass Ser.). (ENG.). 96p. (gr. 2-3). lib. bdg. 25.32 *(978-1-4342-4615-8(9))* Stone Arch Bks.

Brian, Kate. Shadowlands. 2013. (Shadowlands Ser.). (ENG.). 352p. (YA). (gr. 9-17). pap. 9.99 *(978-1-4231-6525-5(X))* Hyperion Pr.

Brooks, Erik. Later, Gator! 2016. (ENG., Illus.). 40p. (J). (gr. -1). 14.95 *(978-1-4549-1816-5(0))* Sterling Publishing Co., Inc.

Brown, Gavin. Josh Baxter Levels Up. 2016. (ENG., Illus.). 192p. (J). (gr. 3-7). 12.99 *(978-0-545-77294-5(X),* Scholastic Pr.) Scholastic, Inc.

Brown, Jennifer. Life on Mars. 2014. (ENG.). 240p. (YA). (gr. 3-6). 16.99 *(978-1-61963-252-3(7),* 9781619632523, Bloomsbury USA Childrens) Bloomsbury Publishing USA.

Brown, Linda. An Unusual Hero. 2015. (ENG.). 171p. (J). (gr. 3-4). pap. 10.95 *(978-1-78455-392-0(1),* 6b50768c-de9d-47dc-989f-e46793d20877) Austin, Stan AUS. Dist: Bookmasters Distribution.

Buckingham, Royce. The Dead Boys. 2010. (ENG.). 208p. (J). (gr. 5-18). 16.99 *(978-0-399-25222-8(3),* G.P. Putnam's Sons Books for Young Readers) Penguin Young Readers Group.

Bullard, Lisa. Trick-or-Treat on Milton Street. Oeltjenbruns, Joni, illus. (Carolrhoda Picture Books Ser.). 32p. (J). 2004. (ENG.). (gr. k-4). pap. 6.95 *(978-1-57505-793-4(X))* 2003. (gr. -1-3). 15.95 *(978-1-57505-158-1(3),* Carolrhoda Bks.) Lerner Publishing Group.

Bundy, Tamara. Walking with Miss Millie. 2017. (ENG.). 240p. (J). (gr. 5). 16.99 ***(978-0-399-54456-9(9),*** Nancy Paulsen Books) Penguin Young Readers Group.

Burkhart, Jessica. Wild Hearts. 2015. (If Only... Ser.). (ENG.). 368p. (YA). (gr. 7). 17.99 *(978-1-61963-258-5(6),* 9781619632585, Bloomsbury USA Childrens) Bloomsbury Publishing USA.

Butler, Dori Hillestad. Sliding into Home, 1 vol. Casale, Paul, illus. 2003. (Peachtree Junior Publication Ser.). (ENG.). 192p. (J). (gr. 3-7). 14.95 *(978-1-56145-222-4(X))* Peachtree Pubs.

Buxbaum, Julie. Tell Me Three Things. (ENG.). (YA). (gr. 7). 2017. 352p. pap. 9.99 ***(978-0-553-53567-9(6),*** Ember) 2016. 336p. 17.99 *(978-0-553-53564-8(1),* Delacorte Pr.) 2016. 336p. lib. bdg. 20.99 *(978-0-553-53565-5(X),* Delacorte Pr.) Random Hse. Children's Bks.

Buyea, Rob. Mr. Terupt Falls Again. 2013. (ENG.). 384p. (J). (gr. 4-7). 7.99 *(978-0-307-93046-0(7),* Yearling) Random Hse. Children's Bks.

—Mr. Terupt Falls Again. 2013. lib. bdg. 18.40 *(978-0-606-32236-2(1),* Turtleback) Turtleback Bks.

Buzbee, Lewis. Steinbeck's Ghost. 2010. (ENG.). 368p. (J). (gr. 5-9). pap. 18.99 *(978-0-312-60211-6(1),* 9780312602116) Square Fish.

Byun, You. Dream Friends. Byun, You, illus. 2013. (ENG., Illus.). 32p. (J). (gr. -1-k). 16.99 *(978-0-399-25739-1(X),* Nancy Paulsen Books) Penguin Young Readers Group.

Cabot, Meg. Moving Day. 2009. (Allie Finkle's Rules for Girls Ser.: Bk. 1). (ENG.). 256p. (J). (gr. 3-7). 6.99 *(978-0-545-04041-9(8),* Scholastic Paperbacks) Scholastic, Inc.

—Moving Day. 2009. (Allie Finkle's Rules for Girls Ser.: 1). lib. bdg. 17.20 *(978-0-606-06818-5(X),* Turtleback) Turtleback Bks.

—The New Girl. 2008. (Allie Finkle's Rules for Girls Ser.: 2). (ENG.). 240p. (J). (gr. 3-7). 15.99 *(978-0-545-04049-5(3),* Scholastic Pr.) Scholastic, Inc.

Calhoun, Dia. After the River the Sun. Slater, Kate, illus. 2013. (ENG.). 368p. (J). (gr. 4-7). 16.99 *(978-1-4424-3985-6(8))* Simon & Schuster Children's Publishing.

Callaghan, Cindy. Sydney Mackenzie Knocks 'Em Dead. 2017. (ENG., Illus.). 256p. (J). (gr. 4-8). 17.99 *(978-1-4814-6569-4(4),* Simon & Schuster/Paula Wiseman Bks.) Simon & Schuster/Paula Wiseman Bks.

Calonita, Jen. Belles. 2012. (Belles Ser.: 1). (ENG.). 384p. (YA). (gr. 7-17). pap. 8.99 *(978-0-316-09112-1(X),* Poppy) Little, Brown Bks. for Young Readers.

Campbell, Isaiah. AbrakaPOW. 2016. (ENG., Illus.). 400p. (J). (gr. 3-7). 16.99 *(978-1-4814-2634-3(6),* Simon & Schuster Bks. For Young Readers) Simon & Schuster Bks. For Young Readers.

Carey, Janet Lee. The Double Life of Zoe Flynn. 2007. (ENG.). 240p. (J). (gr. 3-7). pap. 12.95 *(978-1-4169-6754-5(0),* Simon & Schuster/Paula Wiseman Bks.) Simon & Schuster/Paula Wiseman Bks.

Carlson, Nancy. My Best Friend Moved Away. Carlson, Nancy, illus. 2012. (Nancy Carlson Picture Bks). (Illus.). 32p. (J). (gr. k-2). 56.72 *(978-0-7613-9309-2(9))*; (ENG.). 9.95 *(978-0-7613-8954-5(7))* Lerner Publishing Group. (Carolrhoda Bks.).

Carmean, John. Moving Day: Adventures in Hogtown. l.t. ed. 2011. (ENG., Illus.). 33p. (J). pap. 16.99 *(978-0-9839799-1-3(X))* Carmean Productions LLC.

Cassidy, Cathy. Indigo Blue. 2006. (ENG.). 240p. (J). (gr. 5-18). 7.99 *(978-0-14-240703-5(8),* Puffin Books) Penguin Young Readers Group.

Chamberlin, Ann. Dumpling. 2012. (Illus.). 32p. pap. 21.99 *(978-1-4691-6313-0(6))* Xlibris Corp.

Chambliss Bertman, Jennifer. Book Scavenger. 2015. (Book Scavenger Ser.). (ENG., Illus.). 368p. (J). (gr. 4-9). 16.99 *(978-1-62779-115-1(9),* 9781627791151, Holt, Henry & Co. Bks. For Young Readers) Holt, Henry & Co.

—Book Scavenger. 2016. (Book Scavenger Ser.). (ENG.). 368p. (J). pap. 7.99 *(978-1-250-07980-0(2),* 9781250079800) Square Fish.

Chen, Justina. Return to Me. 2013. (ENG.). 352p. (YA). (gr. 7-17). 17.99 *(978-0-316-10255-1(5))* Little Brown & Co.

Cheng, Andrea. The Year of the Garden. Barton, Patrice, illus. 2017. (Anna Wang Novel Ser.: 5). (ENG.). 128p. (J). (gr. 1-4). 15.99 *(978-0-544-66444-9(2),* HMH Books For Young Readers) Houghton Mifflin Harcourt Publishing Co.

Christopher, Matt. The Extreme Team: Skateboard Moves. Leonard, David, illus. 2013. (Passport to Reading Level 3 Ser.: 1). (ENG.). 32p. (J). (gr. 1-4). 3.99 *(978-0-316-25230-0(1))* Little, Brown Bks. for Young Readers.

—Hot Shot. 2010. (ENG.). 128p. (J). (gr. 3-7). pap. 5.99 *(978-0-316-04482-0(2))* Little, Brown Bks. for Young Readers.

—One Smooth Move. Koelsch, Michael, illus. 2004. (ENG.). 64p. (J). (gr. 1-4). pap. 13.99 *(978-0-316-73749-4(6))* Little, Brown Bks. for Young Readers.

Civardi, Anne. Moving House. Bates, Michelle, ed. Cartwright, Stephen, illus. rev. ed. 2005. 16p. (J). (gr. -1-17). pap. 4.95 *(978-0-7945-1009-1(4),* Usborne) EDC Publishing.

Clark, Eleanor. Katie Sue: Heading West. 2007. (Eleanor Ser.: Bk. 3). 220p. 14.99 *(978-0-9788726-0-1(6))* HonorNet.

Clements, Andrew. Lost & Found. Elliott, Mark, illus. 2010. (ENG.). 192p. (J). (gr. 3-7). pap. 7.99 *(978-1-4169-0986-6(9),* Atheneum Bks. for Young Readers) Simon & Schuster Children's Publishing.

Coates, Charmian. Secret Staircase. 2011. (Illus.). 88p. pap. 27.76 *(978-1-4567-8715-8(2))* AuthorHouse.

Coben, Harlan. Shelter. (Mickey Bolitar Novel Ser.: 1). (ENG.). (YA). (gr. 7-18). 2011. 288p. 18.99 *(978-0-399-25650-9(4),* G.P. Putnam's Sons Books for Young Readers)Bk. 1. 2012. 336p. pap. 9.99 *(978-0-14-242203-8(7),* Speak) Penguin Young Readers Group.

—Shelter. l.t. ed. 2011. (Mickey Bolitar Ser.: Bk. 1). (ENG.). 354p. (J). (gr. 9-12). 23.99 *(978-1-4104-4365-6(5))* Thorndike Pr.

—Shelter. 2012. (Mickey Bolitar Ser.: 1). lib. bdg. 20.85 *(978-0-606-26669-7(0),* Turtleback) Turtleback Bks.

Cochrane, Ian. Shian & the Corryvreckan. 2013. (Illus.). 96p. pap. *(978-1-909465-09-1(7))* Cloister Hse. Pr., The.

Cody, Matthew. Powerless. 2011. (Supers of Noble's Green Ser.). (ENG.). 288p. (J). (gr. 3-7). 7.99 *(978-0-375-84489-8(9),* Yearling) Random Hse. Children's Bks.

Colasanti, Susane. So Much Closer. 2012. (ENG.). 272p. (YA). (gr. 7-18). pap. 8.99 *(978-0-14-242114-7(6),* Speak) Penguin Young Readers Group.

Colin, Beatrice & Pinto, Sara. My Invisible Sister. Pinto, Sara, illus. 2011. (ENG., Illus.). 128p. (YA). (gr. 3-6). pap. 6.99 *(978-1-59990-678-2(3),* 9781599906782, Bloomsbury USA Childrens) Bloomsbury Publishing USA.

Collard, Sneed B., III. Dog Sense, 1 vol. 2005. (ENG.). 192p. (J). (gr. 3-7). 14.95 *(978-1-56145-351-1(X))* Peachtree Pubs.

Conklin, Melanie. Counting Thyme. 2016. (ENG.). 320p. (J). (gr. 5). 16.99 *(978-0-399-17330-1(7),* G.P. Putnam's Sons Books for Young Readers) Penguin Young Readers Group.

Cook, Eileen. Unraveling Isobel. 2012. (ENG.). (YA). (gr. 9). 320p. pap. 9.99 *(978-1-4424-1328-3(X))*; 304p. 16.99 *(978-1-4424-1327-6(1))* Simon Pulse. (Simon Pulse).

Cornveau, Art. How I Got a Life & a Dog. 2012. (ENG.). 288p. (J). (gr. 3-7). pap. 7.95 *(978-1-4197-0015-6(4),* Amulet Bks.) Abrams, Inc.

—How I, Nicky Flynn, Finally Got a Life (And a Dog) 2010. (ENG.). 272p. (YA). (gr. 3-7). 16.95 *(978-0-8109-8298-7(6),* Amulet Bks.) Abrams, Inc.

—13 Hangmen. 2012. (ENG.). 352p. (J). (gr. 3-7). 17.95 *(978-1-4197-0159-7(2),* Amulet Bks.) Abrams, Inc.

Cosgrove, Stephen. Bee Double Bopp: Respecting Others. Arroyo, Fian, illus. 2004. (J). *(978-1-58804-350-4(9))* P C I Education.

Couloumbis, Audrey. Not Exactly a Love Story. 2014. (ENG.). 288p. (YA). (gr. 7). pap. 9.99 *(978-0-375-86606-7(X),* Ember) Random Hse. Children's Bks.

Cousins, Dave. Waiting for Gonzo. 2015. (ENG.). 288p. (YA). pap. 9.99 *(978-0-7387-4199-4(X),* Flux) North Star Editions.

Cox, Phil Roxbee. Mouse Moves House. Tyler, Jenny, ed. Cartwright, Stephen, illus. rev. ed. 2006. (Phonic Readers Ser.). 16p. (J). (gr. -1-3). pap. 6.99 *(978-0-7945-1507-2(X),* Usborne) EDC Publishing.

Crimi, Carolyn. The Louds Move In!, 1 vol. Dunnick, Regan, illus. 2006. (ENG.). 32p. (J). (gr. -1-3). 14.95 *(978-0-7614-5221-8(4))* Marshall Cavendish Corp.

Croza, Laurel. From There to Here, 1 vol. James, Matt, illus. 2014. (ENG.). 36p. (J). (gr. -1-2). 18.95 *(978-1-55498-365-0(7))* Groundwood Bks. CAN. Dist: Publishers Group West (PGW).

Cumbie, Patricia. Where People Like Us Live. 2008. 224p. (YA). (gr. 7-18). lib. bdg. 17.89 *(978-0-06-137598-9(5),* Geringer, Laura Book) HarperCollins Pubs.

Cumming, Hannah. The Red Boat. Cumming, Hannah, illus. 2012. (Child's Play Library). (ENG., Illus.). 32p. (J). *(978-1-84643-481-5(5))* Child's Play International Ltd.

Cutler, Jane. Susan Marcus Bends the Rules. 2014. (ENG.). 112p. (J). (gr. 3-7). pap. 16.95 *(978-0-8234-3047-5(2))* Holiday Hse., Inc.

Dagg, Carole Estby. Sweet Home Alaska. 2016. (ENG.). 304p. (J). (gr. 5). 16.99 *(978-0-399-17203-8(3),* Nancy Paulsen Books) Penguin Young Readers Group.

D'Amico, Carmela & D'Amico, Steven. Ella the Elegant Elephant. 2004. (ENG., Illus.). 56p. (J). (gr. -1-3). 17.99 *(978-0-439-62792-4(3),* Levine, Arthur A. Bks.) Scholastic, Inc.

Danielson, Diane K. There Is a Mouse That Is Haunting Our House. 2012. (ENG.). 28p. (J). pap. 14.99 *(978-0-9885157-0-3(9))* SDP Publishing.

Danziger, Paula. Amber Brown Is Green with Envy. 2014. (Amber Brown Ser.: 9). (ENG., Illus.). 176p. (J). (gr. 2-5). pap. 5.99 *(978-0-14-242699-9(7),* Puffin Books) Penguin Young Readers Group.

—Amber Brown Is Green with Envy. Ross, Tony, illus. 2004. (Amber Brown Ser.: No. 9). 151p. (J). (gr. 2-5). 12.65 *(978-0-7569-2978-7(4))* Perfection Learning Corp.

—Amber Brown Is Not a Crayon. Ross, Tony, illus. 2006. (Amber Brown Ser.: 1). (ENG.). 96p. (J). (gr. 2-5). 5.99 *(978-0-14-240619-9(8),* Puffin Books) Penguin Young Readers Group.

—Amber Brown Is Not a Crayon. (Amber Brown Ser.: No. 1). 80p. (J). (gr. 3-6). pap. 3.50 *(978-0-8072-1289-9(X),* Listening Library) Random Hse. Audio Publishing Group.

—This Place Has No Atmosphere. 2006. (ENG.). 240p. (J). (gr. 5-18). 8.99 *(978-0-14-240680-9(5),* Puffin Books) Penguin Young Readers Group.

Danziger, Paula & Martin, Ann M. P. S. Longer Letter Later. (Tara Starr & Elizabeth Ser.). 240p. (J). (gr. 3-5). pap. 4.99 *(978-0-8072-1537-1(6),* Listening Library) Random Hse. Audio Publishing Group.

Danziger, Paula & Mazer, Anne. Is Green with Envy. Ross, Tony, illus. 2004. (Amber Brown Ser.: 9). (ENG.). 160p. (J). (gr. 2-5). pap. 4.99 *(978-0-439-07171-0(2),* Scholastic Paperbacks) Scholastic, Inc.

Danziger, Paula, et al. Amber Brown Is on the Move. Lewis, Anthony, illus. 2014. (Amber Brown Ser.: 11). (ENG.). 192p. (J). (gr. 2-5). pap. 6.99 *(978-0-14-751223-9(9),* Puffin Books) Penguin Young Readers Group.

Daswani, Kavita. Lovetorn. 2012. (ENG.). 256p. (YA). (gr. 8). 17.99 *(978-0-06-167311-5(0),* HarperTeen) HarperCollins Pubs.

Dee, Barbara. Trauma Queen. 2011. (Mix Ser.). (ENG.). 272p. (J). (gr. 4-8). pap. 6.99 *(978-1-4424-0923-1(1),* Aladdin) Simon & Schuster Children's Publishing.

DeFelice, Cynthia C. Signal. 2011. (ENG.). 176p. (J). (gr. 5-8). pap. 8.99 *(978-0-312-61776-9(3),* 9780312617769) Square Fish.

Dellasega, Cheryl. Nugrl90, 0 vols. LaPierre, Karina, illus. 2007. (Bloggrls Ser.: 1). (ENG.). 192p. (YA). (gr. 7-11). pap. 9.99 *(978-0-7614-5396-3(2),* 9780761453963, Amazon Children's Publishing) Amazon Publishing.

Delton, Judy. Angel Bites the Bullet. Weber, Jill, illus. 2003. (ENG.). 144p. (J). (gr. 2-5). pap. 10.95 *(978-0-618-36920-1(1))* Houghton Mifflin Harcourt Publishing Co.

Demas, Corinne. Everything I Was. (Carolrhoda YA Ser.). (ENG.). 216p. (YA). (gr. 6-10). 2012. pap. 9.95 *(978-0-7613-9011-4(1))* 2011. 17.95 *(978-0-7613-7303-2(9))* Lerner Publishing Group. (Carolrhoda Lab™).

deRubertis, Barbara. Nina Nandu's Nervous Noggin. Alley, R. W., illus. 2011. (Animal Antics A to Z Ser.). 32p. (J). pap. 45.32 *(978-0-7613-7660-6(7))*; (ENG.). lib. bdg. 22.60 *(978-1-57565-335-8(4))*; (gr. -1-3). pap. 7.95 *(978-1-57565-326-6(5))* Kane Press, Inc.

deRubertis, Barbara & DeRubertis, Barbara. Nina Nandu's Nervous Noggin. Alley, R. W., illus. 2012. (Animal Antics A to Z Ser.). 32p. (J). (gr. 2 — 1). cd-rom 7.95 *(978-1-57565-407-2(5))* Kane Press, Inc.

DiCerto, Joseph J. The Wall People: In Search of a Home. 2014. (Illus.). 128p. (J). pap. 14.00 *(978-0-87842-633-1(7))* Mountain Pr. Publishing Co., Inc.

Dickson, Darnell G. Small Town, Big Dreams: A Dane Jordan Sports Novel. 2008. pap. 14.99 *(978-1-59955-229-3(9))* Cedar Fort, Inc./CFI Distribution.

Dinardo, Jeff. Bunny & Bird Are Best Friends: Making New Friends. Ho, Jannie, illus. 2014. (Funny Bone Readers: Being a Friend Ser.). 24p. (gr. -1-1). pap. 4.99 *(978-1-939656-02-5(8))* Red Chair Pr.

Dougherty, Meghan. Rise of the Undead Redhead. Bimbach, Alece, illus. 2014. (Dorothy's Derby Chronicles Ser.: 1). (ENG.). 256p. (J). (gr. 3-6). pap. 6.99 *(978-1-4022-9535-5(9),* Sourcebooks Jabberwocky) Sourcebooks, Inc.

Duckett, Brenda. Summit Lane. 2005. 79p. pap. 10.99 *(978-1-4116-3897-6(2))* Lulu Pr., Inc.

Dunham, Wendy. My Name Is River. 2015. (ENG.). 144p. (J). (gr. 2-7). pap. 7.99 *(978-0-7369-6461-6(4))* Harvest Hse. Pubs.

Earhart, Kristin. Welcome Home! Geddes, Serena, illus. 2015. (Marguerite Henry's Misty Inn Ser.: 1). (ENG.). 128p. (J). (gr. 2-5). 16.99 *(978-1-4814-1414-2(3),* Aladdin) Simon & Schuster Children's Publishing.

—Welcome Home! 2015. (Marguerite Henry's Misty Inn Ser.: 1). lib. bdg. 16.00 *(978-0-606-37126-1(5))* Turtleback Bks.

Elkeles, Simone. Better Than Perfect. 2014. (Wild Cards Ser.). (ENG.). 352p. (YA). (gr. 9). pap. 9.99 *(978-0-8027-3725-0(0),* 9780802737250, Bloomsbury USA Childrens) Bloomsbury Publishing USA.

Ellis, Sarah. Ben Says Goodbye. LaFave, Kim, illus. 2016. (ENG.). 32p. (J). (gr. -1-1). 16.95 *(978-1-927485-79-8(7))* Pajama Pr. CAN. Dist: Ingram Publisher Services.

Emmer, E. R. Me, Minerva & the Flying Flora. Huerta, Catherine, illus. 2nd rev. ed. 2003. (Going to Ser.). Orig. Title: Me, Minera & the Flying Car. (ENG.). 133p. (J). (gr. 4-8). pap. 6.95 *(978-1-893577-10-7(4))* Fruitbearer Publishing, LLC.

Engel, Christiane. We Are Moving: Louis & Bobo. Engel, Christiane, illus. 2007. (ENG., Illus.). 28p. (J). (gr. k-2). pap. 7.99 *(978-1-84458-375-1(9))* Pavilion Bks. GBR. Dist: Independent Pubs. Group.

English, Karen. Dog Days. Freeman, Laura, illus. 2014. (Carver Chronicles Ser.). (ENG.). 128p. (J). (gr. 1-4). pap. 5.99 *(978-0-544-33912-5(6),* HMH Books For Young Readers) Houghton Mifflin Harcourt Publishing Co.

Evans, Richard. If Only. 2015. (ENG., Illus.). 288p. (YA). (gr. 9). pap. 11.99 *(978-1-4814-4853-6(6),* Simon Pulse) Simon Pulse.

Faruqi, Reem & Lyon, Lea. Lailah's Lunchbox, 1 vol. 2015. (ENG., Illus.). 32p. (gr. 1-7). 16.95 *(978-0-88448-431-8(9),* 884431) Tilbury Hse. Pubs.

Feagan, Robert. Arctic Thunder. 2010. (ENG.). 288p. (YA). (gr. 7). pap. 12.99 *(978-1-55488-700-2(3))* Dundurn CAN. Dist: Ingram Publisher Services.

Fehlbaum, Beth. Big Fat Disaster. (ENG.). (YA). 2015. 286p. pap. 9.99 *(978-1-4405-9267-6(5))* 2014. 288p. 17.99 *(978-1-4405-7048-3(5))* Simon Pulse. (Simon Pulse).

Feinstein, John. The Walk On. 2015. (Triple Threat Ser.). (ENG.). 384p. (J). (gr. 5). pap. 7.99 *(978-0-385-75349-4(7),* Yearling) Random Hse. Children's Bks.

—The Walk On. 2015. (Triple Threat Ser.: 1). lib. bdg. 18.40 *(978-0-606-37704-1(2))* Turtleback Bks.

Ferrell, Miralee. A Horse for Kate. 2015. (Horses & Friends Ser.: 1). (ENG.). 208p. (J). pap. 7.99 *(978-0-7814-1114-1(9))* Cook, David C.

Figley, Marthy Rhodes & Figley, Marty Rhodes. The Night the Chimneys Fell. Marschall, Felicia, illus. 2011. 48p. (J). pap. 6.95 *(978-0-7613-3939-7(6),* First Avenue Editions) Lerner Publishing Group.

Figley, Marty Rhodes. The Night the Chimneys Fell. Marschall, Felicia, illus. 2011. (On My Own History Ser.). 48p. (J). pap. 39.62 *(978-0-7613-7622-4(4),* First Avenue Editions) Lerner Publishing Group.

—The Night the Chimneys Fell. Marshall, Felicia, illus. 2009. (On My Own History Ser.). (ENG.). 48p. (J). (gr. 2-4). 25.26 *(978-0-8225-7894-9(8))* Lerner Publishing Group.

Fleming, Candace. Lowji Discovers America. 2008. (ENG.). 160p. (J). (gr. 2-6). pap. 7.99 *(978-1-4169-5832-1(0),* Aladdin) Simon & Schuster Children's Publishing.

Fletcher, Ralph. Spider Boy. 2009. (ENG.). 192p. (J). (gr. 5-7). pap. 6.99 *(978-0-547-24820-2(2))* Houghton Mifflin Harcourt Publishing Co.

Flor, Ada Alma. My Name Is Maria Isabel. 2014. (ENG.). 64p. (J). (gr. 12-12). 9.24 *(978-1-63245-189-7(1))* Lectorum Pubns., Inc.

Foutz, Ian. Year of the Dragon. Miller, Madeline, illus. 2014. (J). ***(978-1-62086-634-4(X))*** Mascot Bks., Inc.

Frederick, Heather Vogel. Absolutely Truly. 2015. (Pumpkin Falls Mystery Ser.). (ENG., Illus.). 368p. (J). (gr. 3-7). pap. 7.99 *(978-1-4424-2973-4(9),* Simon & Schuster Bks. For Young Readers) Simon & Schuster Bks. For Young Readers.

French, Simon. Where in the World. 2008. 198p. *(978-1-921272-57-8(0))* Little Hare Bks. AUS. Dist: HarperCollins Pubs. Australia.

Friedland, Joyce, ed. Lizzie Bright & the Buckminster Boy: Novel-Ties Study Guide. 2007. 36p. pap. 16.95 *(978-0-7675-3558-8(8))* Learning Links Inc.

Friedman, Laurie. Back to School, Mallory. Schmitz, Tamara, illus. (Mallory Ser.: 2). (ENG.). 176p. (J). (gr. 2-5). 2005. per. 5.95 *(978-1-57505-865-8(0))* 2004. 15.95 *(978-1-57505-658-6(5))* Lerner Publishing Group.

—A Clases Otra Vez, Mallory. Anaya, Josefina, tr. from ENG. Schmitz, Tamara, illus. 2008. (Mallory en español (Mallory in Spanish) Ser.).Tr. of Back to School, Mallory. (SPA & ENG.). 176p. (J). (gr. 2-5). pap. 5.95 *(978-0-7613-3904-5(3))* Lerner Publishing Group.

—Mallory on the Move. Schmitz, Tamara, tr. Schmitz, Tamara, illus. 2004. (Mallory Ser.: 1). (ENG.). 160p. (J). (gr. 2-5). 15.95 *(978-1-57505-538-1(4))* Lerner Publishing Group.

—Mallory Se Muda. Schmitz, Tamara, illus. 2007. (Mallory en español (Mallory in Spanish) Ser.). (SPA.). 160p. (J). (gr. 4-7). per. 5.95 *(978-0-8225-7493-4(4),* Ediciones Lerner) Lerner Publishing Group.

Friend, Natasha. Where You'll Find Me. 2016. (ENG.). 272p. (YA). 16.99 *(978-0-374-30230-6(8),* 9780374302306, Farrar, Straus & Giroux (BYR)) Farrar, Straus & Giroux.

—Where You'll Find Me. 2017. (YA). lib. bdg. 20.85 ***(978-0-606-39591-5(1))*** Turtleback Bks.

Galante, Cecilia. Willowood. 2011. (ENG.). 288p. (J). (gr. 4-8). pap. 6.99 *(978-1-4169-8303-3(1),* Aladdin) Simon & Schuster Children's Publishing.

—Willowood. 2010. (ENG.). 272p. (J). (gr. 4-8). 16.99 *(978-1-4169-8022-3(9),* Simon & Schuster/Paula Wiseman Bks.) Simon & Schuster/Paula Wiseman Bks.

Gantos, Jack. The Follower. 2015. (ENG.). 224p. (YA). (gr. 7-10). 17.99 *(978-0-374-37995-7(5),* 9780374379957, Farrar, Straus & Giroux (BYR)) Farrar, Straus & Giroux.

Garrott, Dawn E. How Riley Tamed the Invisible Monster. 2008. (J). pap. *(978-0-87743-709-3(2))* Baha'i Publishing Trust, U.S.

Georgieva, Zoia. Herman the Earth Worm: Illustrated by Emma C. Van Dyke. 2008. pap. 18.00 *(978-0-8059-8630-3(8))* Dorrance Publishing Co., Inc.

Gibson, Marley. The Awakening. 2009. (ENG.). 352p. (YA). (gr. 7-18). pap. 19.99 *(978-0-547-15093-2(8))* Houghton Mifflin Harcourt Publishing Co.

—The Guidance. 2009. (ENG.). 320p. (YA). (gr. 7-18). pap. 16.95 *(978-0-547-15094-9(6))* Houghton Mifflin Harcourt Publishing Co.

—The Reason, Bk. 3. 2010. (ENG.). 240p. (YA). (gr. 7-18). pap. 8.99 *(978-0-547-15095-6(4))* Houghton Mifflin Harcourt Publishing Co.

Gier, Kerstin. Dream a Little Dream. Bell, Anthea, tr. from GER. 2015. (Silver Trilogy Ser.: 1). (ENG.). 336p. (YA). (gr. 7). 17.99 *(978-1-62779-027-7(6),* 9781627790277, Holt, Henry & Co. Bks. For Young Readers) Holt, Henry & Co.

Giff, Patricia Reilly. R My Name Is Rachel. 2012. (ENG.). 176p. (J). (gr. 4-7). pap. 6.99 *(978-0-440-42176-4(4),* Yearling) Random Hse. Children's Bks.

Glaser, Linda. Hannah's Way. Gustavson, Adam, illus. 2012. (Shabbat Ser.). 32p. (J). (gr. k-3). (ENG.). pap. 7.95 *(978-0-7613-5138-2(8));* lib. bdg. 17.95 *(978-0-7613-5137-5(X))* Lerner Publishing Group. (Kar-Ben Publishing).

Gleeson, Libby. Half a World Away. Blackwood, Freya, illus. 2007. (J). pap. *(978-0-439-88978-0(2),* Levine, Arthur A. Bks.) Scholastic, Inc.

Gonzalez, Gabriela & Triana, Gaby. Backstage Pass. 2004. (Illus.). 224p. (J). (gr. 7-18). 15.99 *(978-0-06-056017-1(7));* lib. bdg. 16.89 *(978-0-06-056018-8(5))* HarperCollins Pubs.

Gordon, Amy. Twenty Gold Falcons. (ENG.). 240p. (J). (gr. 3-7). 2012. pap. 8.99 *(978-0-8234-2656-0(4))* 2010. 16.95 *(978-0-8234-2252-4(6))* Holiday Hse., Inc.

Gownley, Jimmy. Amelia in into Graceland, 1 vol. 2013. (Amelia Rules! Set 2 Ser.). (ENG.). 36p. (J). (gr. 3-6). 24.21 *(978-1-61479-071-6(X))* Spotlight.

—Superheroes. Gownley, Jimmy, illus. 2011. (Amelia Rules! Ser.). (ENG., Illus.). 176p. (J). (gr. 2-7). 19.99 *(978-1-4424-4540-6(8),* Atheneum Bks. for Young Readers) Simon & Schuster Children's Publishing.

Grabenstein, Chris. The Crossroads. 2009. (Haunted Mystery Ser.: 1). (ENG.). 352p. (J). (gr. 3-7). 7.99 *(978-0-375-84698-4(0),* Yearling) Random Hse. Children's Bks.

Graff, Lisa. Double Dog Dare. (ENG.). (J). (gr. 3-7). 2013. 320p. pap. 7.99 *(978-0-14-242412-4(9),* Puffin Books) 2012. 304p. 16.99 *(978-0-399-25516-8(8),* Philomel Bks.) Penguin Young Readers Group.

Green, Tim. First Team. 2015. (ENG.). 352p. (J). (gr. 3-7). pap. 6.99 *(978-0-06-220876-7(4))* HarperCollins Pubs.

—First Team. 2014. (ENG.). 336p. (J). (gr. 3-7). 16.99 *(978-0-06-220875-0(6))* HarperCollins Pubs.

—First Team. 2015. (J). lib. bdg. 17.20 *(978-0-606-37616-7(X))* Turtleback Bks.

—New Kid. (ENG.). (J). (gr. 3-7). 2015. 336p. pap. 6.99 *(978-0-06-220873-6(X))* 2014. 320p. 16.99 *(978-0-06-220872-9(1))* HarperCollins Pubs.

Greene, Stephanie. Falling into Place. 2006. (ENG.). 128p. (J). (gr. 5-7). pap. 8.95 *(978-0-618-68928-6(1))* Houghton Mifflin Harcourt Publishing Co.

Greenwald, Lisa. Reel Life Starring Us. (ENG.). (YA). (gr. 3-7). 2013. 320p. pap. 7.95 *(978-1-4197-0426-0(5))* 2011. 304p. 16.95 *(978-1-4197-0026-2(X))* Abrams, Inc. (Amulet Bks.).

Griffith, Gretchen. When Christmas Feels Like Home. Farias, Carolina, illus. 2013. (ENG.). 32p. (J). (gr. -1-3). 16.99 *(978-0-8075-8872-7(5))* Whitman, Albert & Co.

Grimes, Nikki. Make Way for Dyamonde Daniel. Christie, R. Gregory, illus. (Dyamonde Daniel Book Ser.: 1). (ENG.). (J). (gr. 2-4). 2010. 112p. pap. 5.99 *(978-0-14-241555-9(3),* Puffin Books) 2009. 96p. 10.99 *(978-0-399-25175-7(6),* G.P. Putnam's Sons Books for Young Readers) Penguin Young Readers Group.

—Poems in the Attic. Zunon, Elizabeth, illus. 2015. (ENG.). 48p. (J). 19.95 *(978-1-62014-027-7(6))* Lee & Low Bks., Inc.

Gunnery, Sylvia. Out of Bounds. 2004. (Sports Stories Ser.). (ENG.). 104p. (J). (gr. 3-8). *(978-1-55028-827-8(X))* Lorimer, James & Co., Ltd., Pubs. CAN. Dist: Casemate Pubs. & Bk. Distributors, LLC.

Gurtler, Janet. Rachel's Worry. Wood, Katie, illus. 2016. (Mermaid Kingdom Ser.). (ENG.). 96p. (gr. 3-5). 23.99 *(978-1-4965-2607-6(4))* Stone Arch Bks.

Haight, Jessica & Robinson, Stephanie. The Secret Files of Fairday Morrow. Muradov, Roman, illus. 2015. (ENG.). 272p. (J). (gr. 4-7). 18.99 *(978-0-375-99182-0(4),* Delacorte Bks. for Young Readers) Random Hse. Children's Bks.

Hale, Marian. The Truth about Sparrows. 2007. (ENG.). 288p. (YA). (gr. 7-12). per. 9.99 *(978-0-312-37133-3(0),* 9780312371333) Square Fish.

Hall, Kirsten. My New Town. Suzan, Gerardo, illus. 2005. (My First Reader Ser.). (ENG.). 32p. (J). (gr. k-1). lib. bdg. 18.50 *(978-0-516-24877-6(4),* Children's Pr.) Scholastic Library Publishing.

Hallowell, George & Holub, Joan. Wagons Ho! Avril, Lynne, illus. 2011. (ENG.). 32p. (J). (gr. 1-3). 16.99 *(978-0-8075-8612-9(9))* Whitman, Albert & Co.

Hand, Cynthia. Unearthly. 2011. (Unearthly Ser.: 1). (ENG.). 464p. (YA). (gr. 8). pap. 9.99 *(978-0-06-199617-7(3),* HarperTeen) HarperCollins Pubs.

Harley, Bill. Night of the Spadefoot Toads, 1 vol. 2008. (ENG.). 192p. (J). (gr. 3-7). 15.95 *(978-1-56145-459-4(1))* Peachtree Pubs.

Harmon, Michael. Brutal. 2011. (ENG.). 240p. (YA). (gr. 9). pap. 8.99 *(978-0-440-23995-6(8),* Knopf Bks. for Young Readers) Random Hse. Children's Bks.

Harrington, Janice N. Going North. Lagarrigue, Jerome, illus. 2004. (ENG.). 40p. (J). (gr. k-3). 18.99 *(978-0-374-32681-4(9),* 9780374326814, Farrar, Straus & Giroux (BYR)) Farrar, Straus & Giroux.

Harris, Danielle. The Big Move to the Little House. 2013. 24p. pap. 24.95 *(978-1-4626-8725-1(3))* America Star Bks.

Hart, Melissa. Avenging the Owl. 2016. (ENG.). 224p. (J). (gr. 5-8). 15.99 *(978-1-63450-147-7(0),* Sky Pony Pr.) Skyhorse Publishing Co., Inc.

Haskins, Lori. Butterfly Fever. Smath, Jerry, illus. 2004. 31p. (J). lib. bdg. 20.00 *(978-1-4242-1087-9(9))* Fitzgerald Bks.

—Locura Por Las Mariposas (Butterfly Fever) Smath, Jerry, illus. 2009. (Science Solves It! (r) en Espanol Ser.). (SPA.). (gr. 1-3). pap. 33.92 *(978-0-7613-4799-6(2))* Lerner Publishing Group.

Haskins, Lori & Ramirez, Alma. Locura por las Mariposas. Smath, Jerry, illus. 2009. (Science Solves It! en Espanol Ser.). (SPA.). 32p. (J). (gr. 1-3). pap. 5.95 *(978-1-57565-284-9(6))* Kane Press, Inc.

Hatton, Jenny. Moving House. Rankin, Joan, illus. 2012. (Lucy Bks.). (ENG.). 32p. (J). (gr. -1-k). pap. 6.95 *(978-1-4314-0217-5(6))* Jacana Media ZAF. Dist: Independent Pubs. Group.

Hautman, Pete. The Big Crunch. 2011. (ENG.). 288p. (J). (gr. 7-8). 17.99 *(978-0-545-24075-8(1),* Scholastic Pr.) Scholastic, Inc.

Havill, Juanita. Jamaica's Blue Marker. O'Brien, Anne Sibley, illus. 2003. (ENG.). 32p. (J). (gr. -1-3). pap. 7.99 *(978-0-618-36917-1(1))* Houghton Mifflin Harcourt Publishing Co.

Hawes, Adrienne Hill. Moving Danielle. 2008. 22p. pap. 24.95 *(978-1-4241-4977-3(0))* America Star Bks.

Haxhia, Miranda. Andy's Cherry Tree. Deisadze, Zaur, illus. 2007. (POL & ENG.). 32p. (J). pap. 12.95 *(978-1-60195-094-9(2))* International Step by Step Assn.

Heasley, Gwendolyn. A Long Way from You. 2012. (Where I Belong Ser.: 2). (ENG.). 336p. (YA). (gr. 8). pap. 8.99 *(978-0-06-197885-2(X),* HarperTeen) HarperCollins Pubs.

—Where I Belong. 2011. (Where I Belong Ser.: 1). (ENG.). 304p. (YA). (gr. 8-18). pap. 9.99 *(978-0-06-197884-5(1),* HarperTeen) HarperCollins Pubs.

Hees, Miriam. The Adventures of Jilly & Brad: Noises in the Attic. Kinneman, D. Michael, illus. 2003. 128p. (J). pap. 5.95 *(978-0-9718348-4-2(9))* Blooming Tree Pr.

Hepler, Heather. The Cupcake Queen. 2010. (ENG.). 256p. (YA). (gr. 7-18). 7.99 *(978-0-14-241668-6(1),* Speak) Penguin Young Readers Group.

Herman, Gail. New Dog in Town. Nez, John, illus. 2006. (Social Studies Connects). 32p. (J). (gr. -1-3). pap. 5.95 *(978-1-57565-165-1(3))* Kane Press, Inc.

Hermes, Patricia. Emma Dilemma, the Nanny, & the Best Horse Ever, 0 vols. Carter, Abby, illus. 2013. (Emma Dilemma Ser.: 6). (ENG.). 144p. (J). (gr. 3-6). pap. 9.99 *(978-1-4778-1633-2(X),* 9781477816332, Amazon Children's Publishing) Amazon Publishing.

Heyne, Kara. The Locket's Secret. 2013. (ENG.). 162p. (J). pap. 8.95 *(978-0-8198-7484-9(1))* Pauline Bks. & Media.

Hill, Kirkpatrick. Bo at Iditarod Creek. Pham, LeUyen, illus. 2014. (ENG.). 288p. (J). (gr. 3-7). 15.99 *(978-0-8050-9352-0(4),* 9780805093520, Holt, Henry & Co. Bks. For Young Readers) Holt, Henry & Co.

Hill, Ryan. J P Trouble. 2012. 32p. pap. 12.95 *(978-1-886057-15-9(X))* Warren Publishing, Inc.

Hobbs, William. Leaving Protection. 2004. 192p. (J). (gr. 5-18). lib. bdg. 16.89 *(978-0-06-051632-1(1))* HarperCollins Pubs.

Hoberman, Mary Ann. Strawberry Hill. 2010. (ENG., Illus.). 240p. (J). (gr. 3-7). pap. 7.99 *(978-0-316-04135-5(1))* Little, Brown Bks. for Young Readers.

Hoffman, Mary. Bravo, Grace! 2011. (ENG.). 112p. (J). (gr. 3-7). 5.99 *(978-0-14-241850-5(1),* Puffin Books) Penguin Young Readers Group.

Hofmann-Maniyar, Ariane. Ice in the Jungle. Hofmann-Maniyar, Ariane, illus. 2015. (Child's Play Library). (ENG., Illus.). 32p. (J). *(978-1-84643-731-1(8))* Child's Play International Ltd.

Hofmann-Maniyar, Ariane, illus. Ice in the Jungle. 2015. (Child's Play Library). (ENG.). 32p. (J). pap. *(978-1-84643-730-4(X))* Child's Play International Ltd.

Hogan, Mary. The Serious Kiss. 2005. (ENG.). 256p. (YA). (gr. 8). pap. 7.99 *(978-0-06-072208-1(8),* HarperTeen); (gr. 7-18). 16.99 *(978-0-06-072206-7(1))* HarperCollins Pubs.

Holczer, Tracy. The Secret Hum of a Daisy. 2014. (ENG.). 320p. (J). (gr. 5). 16.99 *(978-0-399-16393-7(X),* G.P. Putnam's Sons Books for Young Readers) Penguin Young Readers Group.

Holt, Kimberly Willis. Navy Brat. Davenier, Christine, illus. 2011. (Piper Reed Ser.: 1). (ENG.). 176p. (J). (gr. 3-6). pap. 6.99 *(978-0-312-62548-1(0),* 9780312625481) Square Fish.

—Piper Reed, Forever Friend. Davenier, Christine, illus. 2012. (Piper Reed Ser.: 6). (ENG.). 160p. (J). (gr. 3-6). 15.99 *(978-0-8050-9008-6(8),* 9780805090086, Holt, Henry & Co. Bks. For Young Readers) Holt, Henry & Co.

—Piper Reed, Forever Friend. Davenier, Christine, illus. 2013. (Piper Reed Ser.: 6). (ENG.). 176p. (J). (gr. 3-6). pap. 6.99 *(978-1-250-02725-2(X),* 9781250027252) Square Fish.

Howland, Leila. Hello, Sunshine. 2017. (ENG.). 368p. (YA). (gr. 9-17). 17.99 ***(978-1-4847-2545-0(X))*** Hyperion Bks. for Children.

Hundal, Nancy. Kaleidoscopes & Butterfly Dreams. 2009. (ENG.). 112p. (YA). (gr. 5-9). pap. 12.95 *(978-0-88982-256-6(5))* Oolichan Bks. CAN. Dist: Univ. of Toronto Pr.

Hyde, Catherine Ryan. Jumpstart the World. 2011. (ENG.). 192p. (YA). (gr. 9). pap. 7.99 *(978-0-375-86626-5(4),* Ember) Random Hse. Children's Bks.

Inacio, Maria St. Katie's Big Move! 2013. 20p. pap. 17.99 *(978-1-4772-8703-3(5))* AuthorHouse.

Jakubowski, Michele. Best Friends Forever? Fekete, Hedi, illus. 2016. (Ashley Small & Ashlee Tall Ser.). (ENG.). 64p. (gr. 1-3). lib. bdg. 20.65 *(978-1-4795-9191-6(2))* Picture Window Bks.

—Brushes & Basketballs. Fekete, Hedi, illus. 2016. (Ashley Small & Ashlee Tall Ser.). (ENG.). 64p. (gr. 1-3). lib. bdg. 20.65 *(978-1-5158-0010-1(5))* Picture Window Bks.

James, Brian. Zombie Blondes. 2009. (ENG.). 256p. (YA). (gr. 7-12). pap. 8.99 *(978-0-312-57375-1(8),* 9780312573751) Square Fish.

Johnson, Amy Crane. Mason Moves Away. Mommaerts, Robb, illus. 2009. (ENG.). 32p. (J). (gr. 4-7). 16.95 *(978-1-934960-56-1(X),* Raven Tree Pr.,Csi) Continental Sales, Inc.

Johnson-Choong, Shelly. The Jewelry Box. 2nd ed. 2004. (YA). reprint ed. pap. 10.95 *(978-1-932260-40-1(5),* 80405) Granite Publishing & Distribution.

Johnson, Janet. The Last Great Adventure of the PB & J Society. 2016. (ENG.). 256p. (gr. 4-8). 12.95 *(978-1-62370-636-4(X))* Capstone Young Readers of Coughlan Cos.

Johnson, Lindsay Lee. Worlds Apart. 2005. (ENG.). 168p. (J). (gr. 6-9). 16.95 *(978-1-932425-28-4(4),* Lemniscaat) Boyds Mills Pr.

Jonell, Lynne. Hamster Magic. Dorman, Brandon, illus. 2012. (Magical Mix-Ups Ser.: 1). (ENG.). 112p. (J). (gr. 1-4). pap. 4.99 *(978-0-375-86616-6(7),* Random Hse. Bks. for Young Readers) Random Hse. Children's Bks.

Jordan, Sophie. Firelight. (Firelight Ser.: 1). (ENG.). (YA). (gr. 8). 2011. 352p. pap. 9.99 *(978-0-06-193509-1(3))* 2010. 336p. 16.99 *(978-0-06-193508-4(5))* HarperCollins Pubs.

Joseph, Bruchac. Eagle Song. 2014. (ENG.). 80p. (J). (gr. 12-12). 9.24 *(978-1-63245-103-3(4))* Lectorum Pubns., Inc.

Jukes, Mavis. The New Kid. (ENG.). 288p. (J). 2012. (gr. 4-7). 7.99 *(978-0-375-85367-8(7),* Yearling) 2011. (gr. 3-7). 14.99 *(978-0-375-85879-6(2),* Knopf Bks. for Young Readers) Random Hse. Children's Bks.

Jules, Jacqueline. What a Way to Start a New Year! A Rosh Hashanah Story. Stead, Judy, illus. 2013. (High Holidays Ser.). (ENG.). 24p. (J). (gr. -1-2). 7.95 *(978-0-7613-8117-4(1));* lib. bdg. 16.95 *(978-0-7613-8116-7(3))* Lerner Publishing Group. (Kar-Ben Publishing).

Juster, Norton. Neville. Karas, G. Brian, illus. 2011. (ENG.). 32p. (J). (gr. -1-3). 17.99 *(978-0-375-86765-1(1),* Schwartz & Wade Bks.) Random Hse. Children's Bks.

Keenan-Bolger, Andrew, et al. Jack & Louisa - Act 1. Webster, Kyle T., illus. 2015. (Jack & Louisa Ser.: 1). (ENG.). 240p. (J). (gr. 3-7). bds. 16.99 *(978-0-448-47839-5(0),* Grosset & Dunlap) Penguin Young Readers Group.

Kehret, Peg & the Cat, Pete. The Stranger Next Door. 2008. (Pete the Cat Ser.). (ENG.). 176p. (J). (gr. 3-7). 5.99 *(978-0-14-241248-0(1),* Puffin Books) Penguin Young Readers Group.

Kelley, Jane. The Girl Behind the Glass. 2012. (ENG.). 192p. (J). (gr. 4-7). pap. 6.99 *(978-0-375-86219-9(6),* Yearling) Random Hse. Children's Bks.

Kelly, Katy. Here's the Thing about Me. Rex, Adam, illus. 2006. (Lucy Rose Ser.). (ENG.). 160p. (J). (gr. 3-7). reprint ed. per. 6.99 *(978-0-440-42026-2(1),* Yearling) Random Hse. Children's Bks.

Kennedy, Pamela. Moving Day for Sam: A Story about Change. Petrov, Anton, illus. 2007. 32p. (J). (gr. -1-3). 8.99 *(978-0-8249-5558-8(7),* Ideal Pubns.) Worthy Publishing.

Kent, Rose. Rocky Road. 2012. (ENG.). 304p. (J). (gr. 3-7). 7.99 *(978-0-375-86345-5(1),* Yearling) Random Hse. Children's Bks.

Kimmel, Jordan L. The Magic Gown. 2007. (Illus.). 144p. (J). (gr. 3-6). pap. *(978-0-9785007-0-2(9))* Spring Tree Pr.

Kirby, Jessi. Moonglass. (ENG.). (YA). (gr. 7). 2012. 256p. pap. 9.99 *(978-1-4424-1695-6(5))* 2011. 240p. 16.99 *(978-1-4424-1694-9(7))* Simon & Schuster Bks. For Young Readers. (Simon & Schuster Bks. For Young Readers).

Kirby, Stan. Captain Awesome to the Rescue! O'Connor, George, illus. 2012. (Captain Awesome Ser.: 1). (ENG.). 128p. (J). (gr. k-2). 16.99 *(978-1-4424-4090-6(2));* pap. 5.99 *(978-1-4424-3561-2(5))* Little Simon. (Little Simon).

—Captain Awesome to the Rescue! 2012. (Captain Awesome Ser.: 1). lib. bdg. 16.00 *(978-0-606-26322-1(5),* Turtleback) Turtleback Bks.

Klein, Adria F. Tia Tape Measure & the Move, 1 vol. Rowland, Andrew, illus. 2012. (Tool School Ser.). (ENG.). 32p. (gr. 1-3). pap. 6.25 *(978-1-4342-4236-5(6));* lib. bdg. 22.65 *(978-1-4342-4023-1(1))* Stone Arch Bks.

Koponen, Libby. Blow Out the Moon. 2006. (ENG., Illus.). 224p. (gr. 8-17). per. 18.99 *(978-0-316-01480-9(X),* Tingley, Megan Bks.) Little, Brown Bks. for Young Readers.

Korman, Gordon. Pop. 272p. (YA). (gr. 8). 2011. pap. 9.99 *(978-0-06-174261-3(9))* 2009. 16.99 *(978-0-06-174228-6(7))* HarperCollins Pubs.

Kraus, Daniel. Rotters. 2012. (ENG.). 464p. (YA). (gr. 9). pap. 10.99 *(978-0-385-73858-3(7),* Ember) Random Hse. Children's Bks.

Krech, Bob & Krecht, R.J. Love Puppies & Corner Kicks. 2011. (ENG.). 224p. (J). (gr. 5-18). 7.99 *(978-0-14-241783-6(1),* Puffin Books) Penguin Young Readers Group.

Krishnaswami, Uma. The Grand Plan to Fix Everything. Halpin, Abigail, illus. (ENG.). (J). (gr. 3-7). 2013. 288p. pap. 8.99 *(978-1-4169-9590-6(0))* 2011. 272p. 16.99 *(978-1-4169-9589-0(7))* Simon & Schuster Children's Publishing. (Atheneum Bks. for Young Readers).

Krishnaswami, Uma & Bhabha, Shiraaz. The Closet Ghosts. Bhabha, Shiraaz, illus. 2013. (ENG., Illus.). 32p. (J). (gr. 2). 16.95 *(978-0-89239-208-7(8))* Lee & Low Bks., Inc.

Krulik, Nancy. Super Burp!, No. 1. Blecha, Aaron, illus. 2010. (George Brown, Class Clown Ser.: 1). (ENG.). 128p. (J). (gr. 2-4). pap. 5.99 *(978-0-448-45367-5(3),* Grosset & Dunlap) Penguin Young Readers Group.

Kurtz, Jane. Anna Was Here. 2013. (ENG.). 288p. (J). (gr. 3-7). 16.99 *(978-0-06-056493-3(8),* Greenwillow Bks.) HarperCollins Pubs.

—Lemon Sand. 2011. (J). lib. bdg. 17.89 *(978-0-06-056494-0(6),* Greenwillow Bks.) HarperCollins Pubs.

Lachtman, Ofelia Dumas. Pepita on Pepper Street/Pepita en la Calle Pepper. Monsivais, Maria Estela, tr. from ENG. Delange, Alex Pardo, illus. 2008. (SPA & ENG.). 32p. (J). (gr. -1-3). 16.95 *(978-1-55885-443-7(6),* Piñata Books) Arte Publico Pr.

—Pepita Packs Up: Pepita Empaca. Ventura, Gabriela Baeza, tr. from ENG. Delange, Alex Pardo, illus. 2005. 48p. (J). (gr. -1-k). lib. bdg. 16.95 *(978-1-55885-431-4(2),* Piñata Books) Arte Publico Pr.

LaFleur, Suzanne. Listening for Lucca. 2015. (ENG.). 240p. (J). (gr. 4-7). pap. 7.99 *(978-0-307-98030-4(8),* Yearling) Random Hse. Children's Bks.

Lahan, Tim. Nosyhood. 2016. (ENG., Illus.). 60p. (gr. -1). 16.95 *(978-1-938073-93-9(2))* McSweeney's Publishing.

Landgraf, James, Jr. Monsters Monsters Go Away. Warrick, Jessica, illus. 2008. 40p. (J). 8.99 *(978-0-9819283-0-2(7))* Makdan Publishing.

Léger, Diane Carmel. Emily Carr's Attic, 1 vol. Léger, Michael, illus. 2008. (ENG.). 32p. (J). (gr. -1-3). pap. 9.95 *(978-1-55143-958-7(1))* Orca Bk. Pubs. USA.

Liliom, Laura. You Are a Really Good Friend of Mine. Vagharshyan, Lilit, illus. 2007. 32p. (J). (ARA & ENG.). pap. 16.95 *(978-1-60195-310-0(0));* (POL & ENG.). pap. 16.95 *(978-1-60195-107-6(8))* International Step by Step Assn.

Lindbergh, Anne M. The People in Pineapple Place. 2011. (ENG.). 176p. (J). pap. 12.95 *(978-1-56792-411-4(5))* Godine, David R. Pub.

Ling, Nancy Tupper. Double Happiness. Chau, Alina, illus. 2015. (ENG.). 48p. (J). (gr. k-3). 16.99 *(978-1-4521-2918-1(5))* Chronicle Bks. LLC.

Littman, Sarah Darer. Life, After. 2010. (ENG.). 288p. (J). (gr. 7-18). 17.99 *(978-0-545-15144-3(9),* Scholastic Pr.) Scholastic, Inc.

Loe, Steve. The Hot Hurry of Mercurial Fleeting. 2016. (YA). pap. 9.99 *(978-0-88092-303-3(2))* Royal Fireworks Publishing Co.

Lord, Bette Bao. In the Year of the Boar & Jackie Robinson. Simont, Marc, illus. 2003. (ENG.). 176p. (J). (gr. 3-7). pap. 6.99 *(978-0-06-440175-3(8))* HarperCollins Pubs.

—In the Year of the Boar & Jackie Robinson. 2009. 8.32 *(978-0-7848-0826-9(0),* Everbind) Marco Bk. Co.

—In the Year of the Boar & Jackie Robinson. (J). 2008. 67.75 *(978-1-4281-8016-1(8))* 2004. 46.75 *(978-1-4025-9147-1(0))* Recorded Bks., Inc.

—In the Year of the Boar & Jackie Robinson. 2003. (J). (gr. 3-6). 16.00 *(978-0-8085-7599-3(6),* Turtleback) Turtleback Bks.

Lore, Pittacus. I Am Number Four. (YA). (gr. 9). 2016. (Lorien Legacies: the Lost Files Ser.). 416p. pap. 9.99 *(978-0-06-238771-4(5))* 2011. (Lorien Legacies Ser.: 1). (ENG.). 496p. pap. 9.99 *(978-0-06-196957-7(5))* 2010. (Lorien Legacies Ser.: 1). (ENG.). 448p. 17.99 *(978-0-06-196955-3(9))* 2011. (Lorien Legacies Ser.: 1). (ENG.). 496p. pap. 9.99 *(978-0-06-211655-0(X))* 2011. (Lorien Legacies Ser.: 1). (ENG.). 480p. 17.99 *(978-0-06-202624-8(0))* HarperCollins Pubs.

M
N
O

—I Am Number Four. 2009. (Lorien Legacies Ser.: Bk. 1). 11.04 *(978-0-7848-3715-3(5)*, Everbind) Marco Bk. Co.
—I Am Number Four. 2011. (I Am Number Four Ser.: Vol. 1). (ENG.). 440p. (gr. 9-12). 20.00 *(978-1-61383-207-3(9))* Perfection Learning Corp.
—I Am Number Four. 2011. (Lorien Legacies Ser.: 1). (YA). lib. bdg. 20.85 *(978-0-606-23545-7(0)*, Turtleback) Turtleback Bks.
—I Am Number Four: The Lost Files: Rebel Allies. 2015. (Lorien Legacies: the Lost Files Ser.). (ENG.). 416p. (YA). (gr. 9). pap. 9.99 *(978-0-06-236404-3(9))* HarperCollins Pubs.
—I Am Number Four: The Lost Files: Secret Histories. 2013. (Lorien Legacies: the Lost Files Ser.). (ENG.). 416p. (YA). (gr. 9). pap. 9.99 *(978-0-06-222367-8(4))* HarperCollins Pubs.
—Secret Histories. 2013. (Lorien Legacies: the Lost Files Ser.). (YA). lib. bdg. 20.85 *(978-0-606-31823-5(2)*, Turtleback) Turtleback Bks.
Lorenz, Albert. The Exceptionally, Extraordinarily Ordinary First Day of School. 2010. (ENG., Illus.). 32p. (J). (gr. 1-4). 15.95 *(978-0-8109-8960-3(3)*, Abrams Bks. for Young Readers) Abrams, Inc.
Lorenzi, Natalie Dias. Flying the Dragon. (ENG.). 240p. (J). (gr. 4-7). 2014. pap. 8.95 *(978-1-58089-435-7(6))* 2012. 16.95 *(978-1-58089-434-0(8))* Charlesbridge Publishing, Inc.
Lovelace, Maud Hart & Lovelace, M. Betsy-Tacy. 2007. (Betsy-Tacy Ser.). (J). (gr. 3-6). lib. bdg. 16.00 *(978-0-8335-1338-0(9)*, Turtleback) Turtleback Bks.
Lupica, Mike. Shoot-Out. (Comeback Kids Ser.). (ENG.). 176p. (J). (gr. 3-7). 2011. 6.99 *(978-0-14-241844-4(7)*, Puffin Books) 2010. 10.99 *(978-0-399-24718-7(1)*, Philomel Bks.) Penguin Young Readers Group.
—Shoot-Out, 1 vol. 2012. (Comeback Kids Ser.). (ENG.). 176p. (J). (gr. 4-8). lib. bdg. 27.07 *(978-1-59961-178-5(3))* Spotlight.
Luthardt, Kevin. When Edgar Met Cecil, 1 vol. Luthardt, Kevin, illus. 2013. (ENG., Illus.). 32p. (J). (gr. -1-3). 15.95 *(978-1-56145-706-9(X))* Peachtree Pubs.
Lynch, Chris. The Gravedigger's Cottage. 2004. (ENG.). 208p. (J). (gr. 7-18). 15.99 *(978-0-06-623940-8(0))* HarperCollins Pubs.
MacLachlan, Patricia. What You Know First. 2007. 17.00 *(978-0-7569-7908-9(0))* Perfection Learning Corp.
Macomber, Debbie & Carney, Mary Lou. The Yippy, Yappy Yorkie in the Green Doggy Sweater. Lambert, Sally Anne, illus. 2011. (ENG.). 32p. (J). (gr. -1-2). 16.99 *(978-0-06-165096-3(X))* HarperCollins Pubs.
Maddox, Jake. Beach Bully, 1 vol. Aburtov, illus. 2013. (Jake Maddox Sports Stories Ser.). (ENG.). 72p. (gr. 2-3). pap. 5.95 *(978-1-4342-6206-6(5))* Stone Arch Bks.
—Beach Bully. 2013. (Jake Maddox Sports Stories Ser.). (ENG.). 72p. (gr. 2-3). pap. 35.70 *(978-1-4342-6234-9(0))* Stone Arch Bks.
—Beach Bully, 1 vol. Aburtov, Jesus, illus. 2013. (Jake Maddox Sports Stories Ser.). (ENG.). 72p. (gr. 2-3). lib. bdg. 25.32 *(978-1-4342-5973-8(0))* Stone Arch Bks.
—Board Rebel. Tiffany, Sean, illus. 2007. (Jake Maddox Sports Stories Ser.). (ENG.). 72p. (gr. 2-3). pap. 5.95 *(978-1-59889-414-1(5))*; lib. bdg. 25.32 *(978-1-59889-319-9(X))* Stone Arch Bks.
—Dance Team Drama. 2016. (Jake Maddox JV Girls Ser.). (ENG.). 96p. (gr. 3-4). pap. 5.95 *(978-1-4965-3678-5(9))*; lib. bdg. 25.99 *(978-1-4965-3674-7(6))* Stone Arch Bks.
—El Rebelde de la Patineta, 1 vol. Heck, Claudia, tr. from ENG. Tiffany, Sean, illus. 2012. (Jake Maddox en Español Ser.). (SPA.). 72p. (gr. 2-3). 25.32 *(978-1-4342-3816-0(4))* Stone Arch Bks.
—Touchdown Triumph. Aburto, Jesus, illus. 2015. (Jake Maddox Sports Stories Ser.). (ENG.). 72p. (gr. 2-3). lib. bdg. 25.32 *(978-1-4965-0492-0(5))* Stone Arch Bks.
Madonia, Kristen-Paige. Fingerprints of You. 2013. (ENG., Illus.). 272p. (YA). (gr. 9). pap. 9.99 *(978-1-4424-2921-5(6)*, Simon & Schuster Bks. For Young Readers) Simon & Schuster Bks. For Young Readers.
—Fingerprints of You. Ribera, Terry, illus. 2012. (ENG.). 272p. (YA). (gr. 9). 16.99 *(978-1-4424-2920-8(8)*, Simon & Schuster Bks. For Young Readers) Simon & Schuster Bks. For Young Readers.
Magee, Wes. Blue, Where Are You? Suggs, Margaret, illus. 2007. (Flyers Ser.: 16). (ENG.). 64p. (J). pap. 9.95 *(978-1-84717-009-5(9))* O'Brien Pr., Ltd., The IRL. Dist: Dufour Editions, Inc.
Major, Kevin. The House of Wooden Santas, 1 vol. Pratt, Ned, photos by. gif. ed. 2004. (ENG., Illus.). 96p. (J). 34.95 *(978-0-88995-249-2(3))* Red Deer Pr. CAN. Dist: Fitzhenry & Whiteside, Ltd.
Malone, Nola. A Home. 2013. (ENG.). 28p. (J). (gr. -1-3). 14.99 *(978-1-4814-2128-7(X)*, Simon & Schuster Bks. For Young Readers) Simon & Schuster Bks. For Young Readers.
Mancusi, Mari. Gamer Girl. 2010. (ENG.). 256p. (YA). (gr. 7-18). 7.99 *(978-0-14-241509-2(X)*, Speak) Penguin Young Readers Group.
Manushkin, Fran. Moving Day, 1 vol. Lyon, Tammie, illus. 2010. (Katie Woo Ser.). (ENG.). 32p. (gr. k-2). pap. 5.95 *(978-1-4048-6059-9(2))*; lib. bdg. 21.32 *(978-1-4048-5733-9(8))* Picture Window Bks.
Marcionette, Jake. Just Jake. Villa, Victor Rivas, illus. 2014. (Just Jake Ser.: No. 1). (ENG.). 160p. (J). (gr. 3-7). 11.99 *(978-0-448-46692-7(9)*, Grosset & Dunlap) Penguin Young Readers Group.
Margolis, Leslie. Boys Are Dogs. 2008. (Annabelle Unleashed Ser.). (ENG., Illus.). 208p. (YA). (gr. 3-6). 15.99 *(978-1-59990-221-0(4)*, 9781599902210, Bloomsbury USA Childrens) Bloomsbury Publishing USA.
Marsden, Carolyn. The Gold-Threaded Dress. 2006. (ENG.). 80p. (J). (gr. 2-4). reprint ed. per. 6.99 *(978-0-7636-2993-9(6))* Candlewick Pr.
—The Gold-Threaded Dress. 2006. 73p. (gr. 2-4). 17.00 *(978-0-7569-6574-7(8))* Perfection Learning Corp.
Martin, Ann M. The Summer Before. 2010. (Baby-Sitters Club Ser.). (ENG.). 224p. (J). (gr. 3-7). 16.99 *(978-0-545-16093-3(6))* Scholastic, Inc.
—Welcome to Camden Falls. 2007. (Main Street Ser.: 1). (ENG., Illus.). 192p. (J). (gr. 3-7). 6.99 *(978-0-439-86879-2(3)*, Scholastic Paperbacks) Scholastic, Inc.
Martin, Rebecca. Joanna's Journey. Yoder, Laura & Weaver, Lisa, illus. 2006. 168p. (YA). pap. 9.99 *(978-1-933753-01-0(3))* Carlisle Pr.- Walnut Creek.
Martinusen-Coloma, Cindy. Ruby Unscripted, 1 vol. 2009. (ENG.). 272p. (YA). (gr. 7-18). pap. 12.99 *(978-1-59554-356-1(2))* Nelson, Thomas Inc.
Maturana, Andrea. Life Without Nico. Olea, Francisco Javier, illus. 2016. (ENG.). 40p. (J). (gr. -1-2). 16.95 *(978-1-77138-611-1(8))* Kids Can Pr., Ltd. CAN. Dist: Hachette Bk. Group.
Mayhall, Robin. He Loves Me, He Loves Me Not. Cella, Kristen & Tiede, Dirk, illus. 2013. (My Boyfriend Is a Monster Ser.: 7). (ENG.). 128p. (YA). (gr. 7-12). lib. bdg. 29.27 *(978-0-7613-6005-6(0)*, Graphic Universe™) Lerner Publishing Group.
—He Loves Me, He Loves Me Not. Cella, Kristen et al, illus. 2013. (My Boyfriend Is a Monster Ser.: 7). (ENG.). 128p. (YA). (gr. 7-12). pap. 9.95 *(978-0-7613-8548-6(7)*, Graphic Universe™) Lerner Publishing Group.
Mazer, Norma Fox. What I Believe. 2007. (ENG., Illus.). 176p. (J). (gr. 5-9). pap. 12.95 *(978-0-15-206283-5(1))* Houghton Mifflin Harcourt Publishing Co.
McDonald, Kirsten. The Nighttime Noise, 1 vol. Meza, Erika, illus. 2016. (Carlos & Carmen Ser.). (ENG.). 32p. (J). (gr. k-3). 27.07 *(978-1-62402-139-8(5))* Magic Wagon.
—The One-Tire House, 1 vol. Meza, Erika, illus. 2016. (Carlos & Carmen Ser.). (ENG.). 32p. (J). (gr. k-3). 27.07 *(978-1-62402-140-4(9))* Magic Wagon.
McDonald, Marion. The Missing Mom. McDonald, Marion & Brown, Marion, illus. 2012. 38p. pap. 9.00 *(978-1-4349-8628-3(4)*, RoseDog Bks.) Dorrance Publishing Co., Inc.
McGuirk, Leslie. The Moogees Move House. McGuirk, Leslie, illus. 2012. (ENG., Illus.). 32p. (J). (gr. -1-2). 14.99 *(978-0-7636-5558-7(9))* Candlewick Pr.
McKay, Hilary. Binny for Short. Player, Micah, illus. (ENG.). (J). (gr. 3-7). 2014. 320p. pap. 7.99 *(978-1-4424-8276-0(1))* 2013. 304p. 16.99 *(978-1-4424-8275-3(3))* McElderry, Margaret K. Bks. (McElderry, Margaret K. Bks.).
McKenzie, C. Lee. The Princess of Las Pulgas. 2010. (ENG.). (YA). *(978-1-934813-46-1(X))* Westside Bks.
McKinty, Adrian. Deviant. 2011. (ENG.). 368p. (YA). (gr. 9-17). 16.95 *(978-0-8109-8420-2(2)*, Amulet Bks.) Abrams, Inc.
McQuestion, Karen. Life on Hold, 0 vols. unabr. ed. 2011. (ENG.). 196p. (gr. 4-6). pap. 9.95 *(978-1-935597-27-8(2)*, 9781935597278, Skyscape) Amazon Publishing.
McVoy, Terra Elan. After the Kiss. (ENG.). (YA). (gr. 9). 2011. 416p. pap. 10.99 *(978-1-4424-0216-4(4))* 2010. 400p. 16.99 *(978-1-4424-0211-9(3))* Simon Pulse. (Simon Pulse).
Mead, Emi. Ryan Is Moving Away. 2009. 32p. pap. 12.99 *(978-1-4389-7226-8(1))* AuthorHouse.
Meltzer, Amy. A Mezuzah on the Door. Fried, Janice, illus. 2007. (Jewish Identity Ser.). 32p. (J). (gr. -1-3). (ENG.). 7.95 *(978-1-58013-251-0(0))*; 17.95 *(978-1-58013-249-7(9))* Lerner Publishing Group. (Kar-Ben Publishing).
Meres, Jonathan. May Contain Nuts. 2012. (ENG., Illus.). 304p. (J). (gr. 4-6). pap. 10.99 *(978-1-4083-1303-9(0))* Hodder & Stoughton GBR. Dist: Hachette Bk. Group.
Meyerhoff, Jenny. Green Thumbs-Up! Chatelain, Eva, illus. 2015. (Friendship Garden Ser.: 1). (ENG.). 176p. (J). (gr. 2-5). pap. 5.99 *(978-1-4814-3904-6(9)*, Aladdin) Simon & Schuster Children's Publishing.
Mills, Emma. This Adventure Ends. 2016. (ENG.). 320p. (YA). 17.99 *(978-1-62779-935-5(4)*, 9781627799355, Holt, Henry & Co. Bks. For Young Readers) Holt, Henry & Co.
Moore, Stephanie Perry. Enjoying True Peace, 1 vol. 2010. (Yasmin Peace Ser.: 5). (ENG.). 176p. pap. 6.99 *(978-0-8024-8606-6(1)*, Lift Every Voice) Moody Pubs.
—True Friends. 2005. (Carmen Browne Ser.: 1). (ENG.). 128p. (YA). pap. 6.99 *(978-0-8024-8172-6(8)*, Lift Every Voice) Moody Pubs.
Moser, Lisa. Kisses on the Wind. Brown, Kathryn, illus. 2009. (ENG.). 32p. (J). (gr. -1-2). 16.99 *(978-0-7636-3110-9(8))* Candlewick Pr.
Moss, Alexandra, pseud. Ellie's Chance to Dance. 2005. (Royal Ballet School Diaries: 1). (ENG.). 144p. (J). (gr. 3-7). mass mkt. 5.99 *(978-0-448-43535-0(7)*, Grosset & Dunlap) Penguin Young Readers Group.
Moss, Marissa. Amelia's Notebook. Moss, Marissa, illus. 2006. (Amelia Ser.). (ENG., Illus.). (J). 5.99 *(978-1-4169-1286-6(X))*; 40p. (gr. 2-5). 12.99 *(978-1-4169-0905-7(2))* Simon & Schuster/Paula Wiseman Bks. (Simon & Schuster/Paula Wiseman Bks.).
Moss, Peggy & Weber, Penny. One of Us, 1 vol. 2010. (ENG., Illus.). 32p. (gr. 1-7). 16.95 *(978-0-88448-322-9(3)*, 884322) Tilbury Hse. Pubs.
Mowry, Tia & Mowry, Tamera. Double Vision. 2015. (Twintuition Ser.: 1). (ENG.). 208p. (J). (gr. 3-7). 16.99 *(978-0-06-237286-4(6))* HarperCollins Pubs.
Munro, Sandie. Karlee's Other Family. 2006. 84p. pap. 8.95 *(978-1-60126-000-0(8))* Masthof Pr.
Murphy, Stuart J. Emma Hace Amigos. 2011. (I See I Learn Ser.). (SPA & ENG., Illus.). 32p. (J). (-k). 14.95 *(978-1-58089-482-1(8))*; pap. 6.95 *(978-1-58089-483-8(6))* Charlesbridge Publishing, Inc.
—Emma's Friendwich. 2010. (I See I Learn Ser.). (ENG., Illus.). 32p. (J). (gr. -1-k). 14.95 *(978-1-58089-450-0(X))* Charlesbridge Publishing, Inc.
Nelson, Marilyn. Pemba's Song. 2008. (ENG.). 112p. (J). (gr. 7-18). 16.99 *(978-0-545-02076-3(X)*, Scholastic Pr.) Scholastic, Inc.
Nicholls, Claire. In it to win it. 2011. 160p. (gr. 4-6). pap. 14.09 *(978-1-4567-7994-8(X))* AuthorHouse.
Noonan, Diana. The Old Things (Paperback) Copyright 2016. 2015. (ENG.). (gr. k-6). pap. 6.97 *(978-0-328-83269-9(3)*, Scott Foresman) Addison Wesley Schl.
Norfleet, Mary Crockett. Hand Me down House. Mallory, Edgar, illus. 2011. 98p. 38.95 *(978-1-258-07946-8(1))* Literary Licensing, LLC.
Numberman, Neil. Do Not Build a Frankenstein! Weaver, Brian M., illus. 2009. (ENG.). 40p. (J). (gr. -1-3). 16.99 *(978-0-06-156816-9(3)*, Greenwillow Bks.) HarperCollins Pubs.
Old Cat & the Kitten. 2014. (ENG., Illus.). 128p. (J). (gr. 3-7). pap. 6.99 *(978-1-4814-1938-3(2)*, Aladdin) Simon & Schuster Children's Publishing.
O'Malley, Elizabeth. By Freedom's Light. 2009. 188p. (J). 15.95 *(978-0-87195-273-8(4))*; pap. 7.95 *(978-0-87195-274-5(2))* Indiana Historical Society.
O'Neill, Joy. Why Do We Have to Move? 2013. (Illus.). 32p. pap. *(978-0-7552-1525-6(7)*, Bright Pen) Authors OnLine, Ltd.
O'Reilly, Jane. The Secret of Goldenrod. 2016. (ENG.). (gr. 3-6). 328p. (J). 17.99 *(978-1-5124-0135-6(8))*; 376p. 35.99 *(978-1-5124-0894-2(8))* Lerner Publishing Group. (Carolrhoda Bks.).
Orr, Wendy. Lost! - A Dog Called Bear. Boase, Susan, illus. 2011. (Rainbow Street Shelter Ser.: 1). (ENG.). 112p. (J). (gr. 2-5). pap. 5.99 *(978-0-8050-9381-0(8)*, 9780805093810, Holt, Henry & Co. Bks. For Young Readers) Holt, Henry & Co.
O'Ryan, Ray. Hello, Nebulon! Jack, Colin, illus. 2013. (Galaxy Zack Ser.: 1). (ENG.). 128p. (J). (gr. k-2). 16.99 *(978-1-4424-5387-6(7))*; pap. 5.99 *(978-1-4424-5386-9(9))* Little Simon. (Little Simon).
—Hello, Nebulon! 2013. (Galaxy Zack Ser.: 1). lib. bdg. 16.00 *(978-0-606-32442-7(9)*, Turtleback) Turtleback Bks.
O'Ryan, Ray & Jack, Colin. Hello, Nebulon!, 1 vol. 2015. (ENG.). 128p. *(978-1-61479-367-0(0))* ABDO Publishing Co.
Ostow, Micol. Amity. 2014. (ENG.). 362p. (J). (gr. 9). 18.99 *(978-1-60684-156-3(4)*, Carolrhoda Lab™) Lerner Publishing Group.
Palmer, Robin. Sealed with a Kiss, 2 vols., No. 2. 2010. (Yours Truly, Lucy B. Parker Ser.: 2). (ENG.). 224p. (J). (gr. 5-18). 6.99 *(978-0-14-241501-6(4)*, Puffin Books) Penguin Young Readers Group.
Paris, Harper. The Mystery of the Gold Coin. Calo, Marcos, illus. 2014. (Greetings from Somewhere Ser.: 1). (ENG.). 128p. (J). (gr. k-4). pap. 5.99 *(978-1-4424-9718-4(1)*, Little Simon) Little Simon.
Parker, David. My Best Friend Is Moving. Lucas, Margeaux, illus. 2007. (J). *(978-0-545-00389-6(X))* Scholastic, Inc.
Patrick, Cat. Revived. 2013. (ENG.). 368p. (YA). (gr. 7-17). pap. 10.99 *(978-0-316-09463-4(3))* Little, Brown Bks. for Young Readers.
Patron, Susan. Maybe Yes, Maybe No, Maybe Maybe. Halpin, Abigail, illus. 2009. (ENG.). 128p. (J). (gr. 3-5). pap. 5.99 *(978-1-4169-6176-5(3)*, Atheneum Bks. for Young Readers) Simon & Schuster Children's Publishing.
Payton, Belle. A Whole New Ball Game. 2014. (It Takes Two Ser.: 1). (ENG., Illus.). 160p. (J). (gr. 3-7). 16.99 *(978-1-4814-0642-0(6))*; pap. 6.99 *(978-1-4814-0641-3(8))* Simon Spotlight. (Simon Spotlight).
Peck, Richard. A Season of Gifts. 2010. (ENG.). 208p. (J). (gr. 5-18). 7.99 *(978-0-14-241729-4(7)*, Puffin Books) Penguin Young Readers Group.
Pennypacker, Sara. Meet the Dullards. Salmieri, Daniel, illus. 2015. (ENG.). 32p. (J). (gr. -1-3). 17.99 *(978-0-06-219856-3(4))* HarperCollins Pubs.
Percival, Tom. Herman's Letter. 2014. (ENG., Illus.). 32p. (J). (gr. -1-1). 17.99 *(978-1-61963-423-7(6)*, 9781619634237, Bloomsbury USA Childrens) Bloomsbury Publishing USA.
Perry, Hailey. On the Move. 2010. 188p. pap. 12.00 *(978-1-60844-428-1(7))* Dog Ear Publishing, LLC.
Phillips, Dee. Grind, 1 vol. unabr. ed. 2011. (Right Now! Ser.). (ENG., Illus.). 45p. (YA). (gr. 9-12). pap. 8.95 *(978-1-61651-250-7(4))* Saddleback Educational Publishing, Inc.
Phillips, Gin. A Little Bit of Spectacular. 2015. (ENG.). 176p. (J). (gr. 5). 16.99 *(978-0-8037-3837-9(4)*, Dial Bks) Penguin Young Readers Group.
Pike, Aprilynne. Life after Theft. 2013. (Life after Theft Ser.). (ENG.). 352p. (YA). (gr. 8). 17.99 *(978-0-06-199900-0(8)*, HarperTeen) HarperCollins Pubs.
Pirc, Jerri J. Kate & Caboodle. Smith, Jane, illus. 2015. pap. *(978-0-473-32583-1(7))* Pirc, Jerri J.
Plastow, Joan. Adventures of Joe. 2003. (Illus.). 68p. pap. *(978-1-84401-144-5(5))* Athena Pr.
Polacco, Patricia. The Graves Family. Polacco, Patricia, illus. 2006. (Illus.). (gr. k-3). 17.00 *(978-0-7569-6715-4(5))* Perfection Learning Corp.
Potter, Ellen. Otis Dooda: Strange but True. Heatley, David, illus. 2013. (Otis Dooda Ser.: 1). (ENG.). 240p. (J). (gr. 2-5). 13.99 *(978-1-250-01176-3(0)*, 9781250011763) Feiwel & Friends.
—Otis Dooda: Downright Dangerous. Heatley, David, illus. 2014. (Otis Dooda Ser.: 2). (ENG.). 240p. (J). (gr. 2-5). 13.99 *(978-1-250-01177-0(9)*, 9781250011770) Feiwel & Friends.
Preller, James. Bystander. 2011. (ENG.). 256p. (YA). (gr. 5-9). pap. 8.99 *(978-0-312-54796-7(X)*, 9780312547967) Square Fish.
—Home Sweet Horror. Bruno, Iacopo, illus. 2013. (Scary Tales Ser.: 1). (ENG.). 112p. (J). (gr. 2-5). pap. 5.99 *(978-1-250-01887-8(0)*, 9781250018878) Feiwel & Friends.
Prendergast, Gabrielle. Audacious, 1 vol. 2015. (ENG.). 336p. (YA). (gr. 8-12). pap. 12.95 *(978-1-4598-0264-3(0))* Orca Bk. Pubs. USA.
Quirk, Katie. A Girl Called Problem. 2013. (ENG., Illus.). 256p. (J). pap. 8.50 *(978-0-8028-5404-9(4)*, Eerdmans Bks For Young Readers) Eerdmans, William B. Publishing Co.
Randle, Kristen D. The Only Alien on the Planet. 2009. (ENG.). 240p. (YA). (gr. 7-12). pap. 11.99 *(978-1-4022-2669-4(1)*, 9781402226694, Sourcebooks Jabberwocky) Sourcebooks, Inc.
Random House Disney Staff. Inside Out (Disney/Pixar Inside Out) Batson, Alan, illus. 2016. (Little Golden Book Ser.). (ENG.). 24p. (J). (-k). 4.99 *(978-0-7364-3629-8(4)*, Golden/Disney) Random Hse. Children's Bks.
—Journey into the Mind. Random House Disney Staff, illus. 2015. (Step into Reading Ser.). (ENG., Illus.). 32p. (J). (gr. -1-1). 4.99 *(978-0-7364-3316-7(3)*, RH/Disney) Random Hse. Children's Bks.
—Rose & the Wish Thing. Magerl, Caroline, illus. 2016. (ENG.). 40p. (J). (gr. -1-2). 16.99 *(978-0-553-53617-1(6)*, Doubleday Bks. for Young Readers) Random Hse. Children's Bks.
Ransom, Candice. Seeing Sky-Blue Pink. 2007. (Exceptional Reading & Language Arts Titles for Intermediate Grades Ser.). 122p. (J). (gr. 4-7). 16.95 *(978-0-8225-7142-1(0)*, Carolrhoda Bks.) Lerner Publishing Group.
Reed, Ken. Sara's Big Challenge: Who's the Real Me? A Sara Thompson Sports Book. 2008. 188p. (J). pap. 9.95 *(978-1-4327-0624-1(1))* Outskirts Pr., Inc.
Reynolds, Alison. A Year with Marmalade. McKenzie, Heath, illus. 2013. (ENG.). 40p. (J). (gr. -1-1). 15.99 *(978-1-4424-8105-3(6)*, Little Simon) Little Simon.
Rhodes, O. K. & Spencer, Octavia. The Case of the Time-Capsule Bandit. To, Vivienne, illus. 2013. (Randi Rhodes, Ninja Detective Ser.: 1). (ENG.). 224p. (J). (gr. 3-7). 16.99 *(978-1-4424-7681-3(8)*, Simon & Schuster Bks. For Young Readers) Simon & Schuster Bks. For Young Readers.
Rim, Sujean. Chee-Kee: A Panda in Bearland. 2017. (ENG., Illus.). 40p. (J). (gr. -1-3). 17.99 *(978-0-316-40744-1(5))* Little Brown & Co.
Ripken, Cal, Jr. & Cowherd, Kevin. Super Slugger. 2013. (ENG.). 200p. (YA). (gr. 3-7). pap. 6.99 *(978-1-4231-4004-7(4))* Hyperion Pr.
Rivers, Phoebe. Ghost Town. 2012. (Saranormal Ser.: 1). (ENG.). 160p. (J). (gr. 3-7). pap. 5.99 *(978-1-4424-4038-8(4)*, Simon Spotlight) Simon Spotlight.
Ross, Tony. I Want to Go Home! Ross, Tony, illus. 2014. (Illus.). 32p. (J). (gr. -1-3). 16.95 *(978-1-4677-5095-0(6))* Lerner Publishing Group.
Rottman, S. L. Out of the Blue, 1 vol. (ENG.). 288p. (gr. 7-12). 2014. (J). pap. 9.95 *(978-1-56145-786-1(8))* 2009. (YA). 16.95 *(978-1-56145-499-0(0))* Peachtree Pubs.
Rouss, Sylvia A. Sammy Spider's New Friend. Kahn, Katherine, illus. 2012. (Kar-Ben Favorites Ser.). (ENG.). 32p. (J). (gr. -1-2). lib. bdg. 17.95 *(978-0-7613-6663-8(6)*, Kar-Ben Publishing) Lerner Publishing Group.
Rouss, Sylvia A. & Janus Kahn, Katherine. Sammy Spider's New Friend. 2012. (Kar-Ben Favorites Ser.). (ENG., Illus.). 32p. (J). (gr. -1-3). 7.95 *(978-0-7613-6664-5(4)*, Kar-Ben Publishing) Lerner Publishing Group.
Rowland, Patty. Marvelous Max, the Mansion Mouse. Rasmussen, Wendy, tr. Rasmussen, Wendy, illus. 2003. 32p. (J). 17.95 *(978-0-9649934-4-0(9))* Norfleet Pr., Inc.
Salisbury, Linda G. The Wild Women of Lake Anna: A Bailey Fish Adventure. 2005. (Illus.). 159p. (J). *(978-1-881539-37-7(7))* Tabby Hse. Bks.
Scattergood, Augusta. The Way to Stay in Destiny. 2015. (ENG.). 192p. (J). (gr. 3-7). 16.99 *(978-0-545-53824-4(6)*, Scholastic Pr.) Scholastic, Inc.
Schmidt, Gary D. Lizzie Bright & the Buckminster Boy. 2013. (ENG.). 224p. (J). (gr. 5-7). pap. 7.99 *(978-0-544-02279-9(3))* Houghton Mifflin Harcourt Publishing Co.
Schröder, Monika. Be Light Like a Bird. 2016. (ENG.). 240p. (gr. 3-7). lib. bdg. 14.95 *(978-1-62370-749-1(8))* Capstone Young Readers of Coughlan Cos.
—Be Light Like a Bird. 2016. (Middle-Grade Novels Ser.). (ENG.). 240p. (gr. 4-7). 26.65 *(978-1-4965-3301-2(1))* Stone Arch Bks.
Schultz, Jan Neubert. Firestorm. 2003. (Adventures in Time Ser.). 204p. (YA). (gr. 4-7). 15.95 *(978-0-87614-276-9(5)*, Carolrhoda Bks.) Lerner Publishing Group.
Scieszka, Jon. Spaceheadz. Prigmore, Shane, illus. (Spaceheadz Ser.: 1). (ENG.). (J). (gr. 2-5). 2010. 176p. 14.99 *(978-1-4169-7951-7(4))*Set. 2013. 864p. pap. 23.99 *(978-1-4424-9858-7(7))* Simon & Schuster Bks. For Young Readers. (Simon & Schuster Bks. For Young Readers).
—SPHDZ Book #1! Prigmore, Shane, illus. 2011. (Spaceheadz Ser.: 1). (ENG.). 192p. (J). (gr. 2-5). pap. 7.99 *(978-1-4424-1986-5(5)*, Simon & Schuster Bks. For Young Readers) Simon & Schuster Bks. For Young Readers.
—SPHDZ Book #2! Prigmore, Shane, illus. 2010. (Spaceheadz Ser.: 2). (ENG.). 240p. (J). (gr. 2-5). 14.99 *(978-1-4169-7953-1(0)*, Simon & Schuster Bks. For Young Readers) Simon & Schuster Bks. For Young Readers.
Scott, Elizabeth. Stealing Heaven. 2009. (ENG.). 336p. (YA). (gr. 8). pap. 8.99 *(978-0-06-112282-8(3)*, HarperTeen) HarperCollins Pubs.
Sedita, Francesco. Miss Popularity. 2007. 120p. (J). pap. *(978-0-545-00828-0(X))* Scholastic, Inc.
Seybold, Celisa. The Keys to Adventure. 2010. 62p. pap. 9.95 *(978-0-557-55086-9(6))* Lulu Pr., Inc.
Seyfert, Ella Maie. Amish Moving Day. Jones, Henrietta, illus. 2011. 132p. 40.95 *(978-1-258-01315-8(0))* Literary Licensing, LLC.
Sheinmel, Courtney. The Kindness Club. 2016. (Kindness Club Ser.). (ENG.). 224p. (J). 15.99 *(978-1-68119-091-4(5)*, 9781681190914, Bloomsbury USA Childrens) Bloomsbury Publishing USA.
Sheriff, Jeanne. Walkabout Kid. 2013. 172p. pap. 12.95 *(978-1-4787-2130-7(8))* Outskirts Pr., Inc.
Shreeve, Elizabeth. Oliver at the Window. McDonald, Candice Hartsough, illus. 2009. (ENG.). 32p. (J). (gr. -1-1). 16.95 *(978-1-59078-548-5(7)*, Front Street) Boyds Mills Pr.
Simpson, Lesley. The Purim Surprise. Church, Peter, illus. 2004. (Purim Ser.). 32p. (J). (gr. -1-3). pap. 6.95 *(978-1-58013-090-5(9)*, Kar-Ben Publishing) Lerner Publishing Group.
Slater, Teddy. Patty & the Pink Princesses. Springer, Sally, illus. 2007. (J). pap. *(978-0-439-89707-5(6))* Scholastic, Inc.
Sleator, William & Monticone, Ann. The Phantom Limb. 2011. (ENG.). 224p. (YA). (gr. 9-17). 16.95 *(978-0-8109-8428-8(8)*, Amulet Bks.) Abrams, Inc.
Smallman, Jeff. Stump's in the Cellar. 2008. 100p. pap. 13.95 *(978-0-557-03091-0(9))* Lulu Pr., Inc.
Smith, Heather. Baygirl, 1 vol. 2013. (ENG.). 288p. (YA). (gr. 8-12). pap. 12.95 *(978-1-4598-0274-2(8))* Orca Bk. Pubs. USA.
Soderberg, Erin & Munford, Rebecca. Welcome to Normal. 2013. (Quirks Ser.). (ENG., Illus.). 240p. (YA). (gr. 3-6). 13.99 *(978-1-59990-789-5(5)*, 9781599907895, Bloomsbury USA Childrens) Bloomsbury Publishing USA.
Sones, Sonya. One of Those Hideous Books Where the Mother Dies. (ENG., (YA). (gr. 7). 2013. Illus.). 288p. pap. 9.99 *(978-1-4424-9383-4(6))* 2005. 272p. reprint ed. pap. 7.99 *(978-1-4169-0788-6(2))* Simon & Schuster Bks. For Young Readers. (Simon & Schuster Bks. For Young Readers).
Sorenson, Margo. Aloha for Carol Ann. Burris, Priscilla, illus. 2011. 32p. (J). (gr. -1-3). pap. 8.95 *(978-1-60349-027-6(2)*, Marimba Bks.) Hudson Publishing Group, The.
Soup, Cuthbert. A Whole Nother Story. Timmins, Jeffrey Stewart, illus. 2010. (Whole Nother Story Ser.). (ENG.). 288p. (YA). (gr. 3-6). pap. 7.99 *(978-1-59990-518-1(3)*,

9781599905181, Bloomsbury USA Childrens) Bloomsbury Publishing USA.

Spiegelman, Nadja. Lost in NYC: A Subway Adventure. Sánchez, Sergio García, illus. 2015. (ENG.). 52p. (J). (gr. 2-7). 16.95 *(978-1-935179-81-8(0))* TOON Books / RAW Junior, LLC.

Spinelli, Jerry. Tooter Pepperday. 2004. (Stepping Stone Book Ser.). (ENG., Illus.). 96p. (J). (gr. 1-4). 3.99 *(978-0-679-84702-1(2)*, Random Hse. Bks. for Young Readers) Random Hse. Children's Bks.

Springer, Nancy. Somebody. 2009. (ENG.). 128p. (YA). (gr. 7-18). 16.95 *(978-0-8234-2099-5(X))* Holiday Hse., Inc.

Springstubb, Tricia. Mo Wren, Lost & Found. Ross, Heather, illus. 2011. (Fox Street Ser.: 2). (ENG.). 256p. (J). (gr. 3-7). 15.99 *(978-0-06-199039-7(6))* HarperCollins Pubs.

Stahler, David, Jr. Gathering of Shades. 2006. (ENG.). 256p. pap. *(978-0-06-052296-4(8))* HarperCollins Canada, Ltd.

—A Gathering of Shades. 2005. (ENG.). 304p. (J). 15.99 *(978-0-06-052294-0(1)*, HarperTeen) HarperCollins Pubs.

Stanley, Brenda. I Am Nuchu. 2010. 334p. (YA). (gr. 9-18). 16.95 *(978-1-934813-47-8(8))* Westside Bks.

Stanley, George E. Night Fires. 2009. (ENG.). 192p. (J). (gr. 3-7). 15.99 *(978-1-4169-7559-5(4)*, Simon & Schuster/Paula Wiseman Bks.) Simon & Schuster/Paula Wiseman Bks.

Stanley, George Edward. Night Fires. 2011. (ENG.). 192p. (J). (gr. 3-7). pap. 6.99 *(978-1-4169-1250-7(9)*, Simon & Schuster/Paula Wiseman Bks.) Simon & Schuster/Paula Wiseman Bks.

Stead, Philip C. Lenny & Lucy. Stead, Erin E., illus. 2015. (ENG.). 40p. (J). (gr. -1-2). 17.99 *(978-1-59643-932-0(7)*, 9781596439320) Roaring Brook Pr.

Stever, Karen Malloy. Jabin, the Talking Donkey: In Jerusalem. 2012. 24p. pap. 24.95 *(978-1-4626-8285-0(5))* America Star Bks.

Stine, R. L. First Evil. 2011. (Fear Street Cheerleaders Ser.: 1). (ENG.). 176p. (YA). (gr. 9). pap. 9.99 *(978-1-4424-3086-0(9)*, Simon Pulse) Simon Pulse.

—Here Comes the Shaggedy. 2016. (Goosebumps: Most Wanted Ser.: 9). (ENG., Illus.). 160p. (J). (gr. 3-7). pap. 6.99 *(978-0-545-82547-4(4)*, Scholastic Paperbacks) Scholastic, Inc.

—Here Comes the Shaggedy. 2016. (Goosebumps Most Wanted Ser.: 9). (Illus.). 140p. (J). lib. bdg. 17.20 *(978-0-606-38587-9(8))* Turtleback Bks.

Stockham, Jess, illus. Moving House! 2011. (Helping Hands Ser.). (ENG.). 24p. (J). *(978-1-84643-414-3(9))* Child's Play International Ltd.

Stromberg, Ronica. A Shadow in the Dark. 2009. (J). pap. *(978-0-88092-751-2(8))*; lib. bdg. *(978-0-88092-750-5(X))* Royal Fireworks Publishing Co.

Strow, Lorie. The Shimmers. 2011. 32p. pap. 21.99 *(978-1-4568-8133-7(7))* Xlibris Corp.

Suen, Anastasia. In the Big City. Myer, Ed, illus. 2012. (ENG.). 24p. (gr. k-1). pap. 8.95 *(978-1-61810-302-4(4))* Rourke Educational Media.

Sumner Johnson, Janet. The Last Great Adventure of the PB & J Society. 2016. (Middle-Grade Novels Ser.). (ENG.). 256p. (gr. 4-7). lib. bdg. 26.65 *(978-1-4965-2695-3(3))* Stone Arch Bks.

Tabby, Abigail. The KnitWits Make a Move! Wildish, Lee, illus. Frost, Michael, photos by. 2013. (ENG.). 32p. (J). (gr. -1-1). 14.99 *(978-1-4424-5342-5(7)*, Little Simon) Little Simon.

Tanaka, Shelley. Nobody Knows, 1 vol. 2012. (ENG.). 144p. (J). (gr. 4). 16.95 *(978-1-55498-140-3(9))* Groundwood Bks. CAN. Dist: Publishers Group West (PGW).

Telgemeier, Raina. Ghosts. Telgemeier, Raina, illus. 2016. (ENG., Illus.). 256p. (J). (gr. 3-7). 24.99 *(978-0-545-54061-2(5)*, Graphix) Scholastic, Inc.

Thomas, Kara. Little Monsters. 2017. (ENG.). 336p. (YA). (gr. 9). 17.99 ***(978-0-553-52149-8(7)***, Delacorte Pr.) Random Hse. Children's Bks.

Tillworth, Mary. Meet My Friends! (Dora & Friends) Aikins, David, illus. 2014. (Step into Reading Ser.). (ENG.). 24p. (J). (gr. -1-1). 3.99 *(978-0-385-38462-9(9)*, Random Hse. Bks. for Young Readers) Random Hse. Children's Bks.

Tolan, Stephanie S. Wishworks, Inc. Bates, Amy June, illus. 2011. (ENG.). 160p. (J). (gr. 2-5). pap. 5.99 *(978-0-545-03155-4(9)*, Levine, Arthur A. Bks.) Scholastic, Inc.

Tooke, Wes. Lucky: Maris, Mantle, & My Best Summer Ever. (ENG.). 192p. (J). (gr. 3-7). 2011. pap. 6.99 *(978-1-4169-8664-5(2))* 2010. 15.99 *(978-1-4169-8663-8(4))* Simon & Schuster Bks. For Young Readers. (Simon & Schuster Bks. For Young Readers).

Tregay, Sarah. Love & Leftovers. 2011. (ENG.). 448p. (YA). (gr. 8). 17.99 *(978-0-06-202358-2(6)*, Tegen, Katherine Bks) HarperCollins Pubs.

Tromly, Stephanie. Trouble Is a Friend of Mine. 2015. (ENG.). 336p. (YA). (gr. 7-12). 17.99 *(978-0-525-42840-4(2)*, Kathy Dawson Books) Penguin Young Readers Group.

Underwood, Deborah. Bad Bye, Good Bye. Bean, Jonathan, illus. 2014. (ENG.). 32p. (J). (gr. -1-3). 16.99 *(978-0-547-92852-4(1)*, HMH Books For Young Readers) Houghton Mifflin Harcourt Publishing Co.

Venditti, Robert. Attack of the Alien Horde. Higgins, Dusty, illus. 2015. (Miles Taylor & the Golden Cape Ser.: 1). (ENG.). 304p. (J). (gr. 4-7). 16.99 *(978-1-4814-0542-3(X))* Simon & Schuster, Inc.

Viguie, Debbie & Holder, Nancy. Unleashed. 2012. (Wolf Spring Chronicles Ser.). (ENG.). 400p. (YA). (gr. 7). pap. 9.99 *(978-0-385-74099-9(9)*, Ember) Random Hse. Children's Bks.

Villeneuve, Marie-Paule & Audet, Patrice. Qui a Enlevé Polka? 2004. (FRE., Illus.). 122p. (J). 8.95 *(978-2-922565-81-2(5))* Editions de la Paix CAN. Dist: World of Reading, Ltd.

Viorst, Judith. Alexander, Who's Not (Do You Hear Me? I Mean It!) Going to Move. Glasser, Robin Preiss, illus. 2015. 32p. pap. 9.00 *(978-1-61003-597-2(6))* Center for the Collaborative Classroom.

Vrabel, Beth. A Blind Guide to Stinkville. (ENG.). (J). (gr. 2-7). 2016. 280p. pap. 7.99 *(978-1-5107-0382-7(9))* 2015. 264p. 16.99 *(978-1-63450-157-6(8))* Skyhorse Publishing Co., Inc. (Sky Pony Pr.).

Vrettos, Adrienne Maria. Best Friends for Never. 2016. (ENG.). 240p. (J). (gr. 3-7). 16.99 *(978-0-545-56149-5(3)*, Scholastic Pr.) Scholastic, Inc.

Vries, Lizzette de & Vries, Cecile de. How the Tooth Mouse Met the Tooth Fairy. Suwannakit, Tul, illus. 2010. (J). 19.95 *(978-0-86715-507-5(8))* Quintessence Publishing Co., Inc.

Wade, Rebecca. The Whispering House. 2012. (ENG.). 272p. (J). (gr. 3-7). 16.99 *(978-0-06-077497-4(5)*, Tegen, Katherine Bks) HarperCollins Pubs.

Wallace, Ian. Mr. Kneebone's New Digs. Wallace, Ian, illus. (Illus.). (J). 16.95 *(978-0-88899-143-0(6))* Groundwood Bks. CAN. Dist: Publishers Group West (PGW).

Wallace, Rich. Southpaw. 2006. 105p. (J). lib. bdg. 15.38 *(978-1-4242-2166-0(8))* Fitzgerald Bks.

—Southpaw. 6th ed. 2007. (Winning Season Ser.). (ENG.). 128p. (J). (gr. 3-7). 5.99 *(978-0-14-240785-1(2)*, Puffin Books) Penguin Young Readers Group.

Watson, Philip & Ofiesh, Nicole. The Treasure Chest. 2011. 52p. 20.50 *(978-1-4269-5350-7(X))*; pap. 10.50 *(978-1-4269-5269-2(4))* Trafford Publishing.

Watt, Fiona. Complete Book of First Experiences. rev. ed. 2011. (First Experiences Ser.). 144p. (J). ring bd. 19.99 *(978-0-7945-2948-2(8)*, Usborne) EDC Publishing.

Watt, Mélanie. Augustine. Watt, Mélanie, illus. 2008. (ENG., Illus.). 32p. (J). (gr. -1-2). pap. 7.95 *(978-1-55453-268-1(X))* Kids Can Pr., Ltd. CAN. Dist: Hachette Bk. Group.

Watts, Jeri. A Piece of Home. Yum, Hyewon, illus. 2016. (ENG.). 32p. (J). (gr. k-3). 16.99 *(978-0-7636-6971-3(7))* Candlewick Pr.

Webster, Christy. Mom, Dad & Me. Random House Disney Staff, illus. 2016. (Step into Reading Ser.). (ENG.). 24p. (J). (gr. -1-1). lib. bdg. 12.99 *(978-0-7364-8238-7(5)*, RH/Disney) Random Hse. Children's Bks.

—Mom, Dad, & Me. Random House Disney Staff, illus. 2016. (Step into Reading Ser.). (ENG.). 24p. (J). (gr. -1-1). 4.99 *(978-0-7364-3536-9(0)*, RH/Disney) Random Hse. Children's Bks.

Weitzman, Jacqueline Preiss. Superhero Joe & the Creature Next Door. Barrett, Ron, illus. 2013. (ENG.). 32p. (J). (gr. -1-3). 16.99 *(978-1-4424-1268-2(2)*, Simon & Schuster Bks. For Young Readers) Simon & Schuster Bks. For Young Readers.

Welch, Ginger. The Dream Reader. 2012. 76p. 19.95 *(978-1-4626-7276-9(0))*; pap. 19.95 *(978-1-4626-8291-1(X))* America Star Bks.

Wenberg, Michael. Stringz. 2010. 216p. (YA). (gr. 6-10). 16.95 *(978-1-934813-33-1(8))* Westside Bks.

Wertheim, L. Jon & Moskowitz, Tobias J. The Rookie Bookie. (ENG., Illus.). 272p. (J). (gr. 3-7). 2015. pap. 7.00 *(978-0-316-24979-9(3))* 2014. 17.00 *(978-0-316-24981-2(5))* Little, Brown Bks. for Young Readers.

Wigington, Patti. Summer's Ashes. 2007. (ENG.). 208p. (gr. 8-12). per. 15.00 *(978-0-9766805-9-8(9))* Keene Publishing.

Williams, Sarah DeFord. Palace Beautiful. 2011. (ENG.). 240p. (J). (gr. 5-18). 6.99 *(978-0-14-241745-4(9)*, Puffin Books) Penguin Young Readers Group.

Wilson, Nathaniel. Jessie's Big Move. Shoopik, Marina, illus. 2010. (ENG.). 54p. (J). 16.95 *(978-0-9744935-7-2(0))* AllWrite Advertising & Publishing.

Winkler, Henry & Oliver, Lin. Zero to Hero. 2012. (Ghost Buddy Ser.: 1). (ENG.). 176p. (J). (gr. 3-7). pap. 5.99 *(978-0-545-29882-7(2)*, Scholastic Paperbacks) Scholastic, Inc.

Wolf, Maria. Black Dog. 2013. 12p. pap. 15.99 *(978-1-4817-0405-2(2))* AuthorHouse.

Wolfe, Jacqueline A. Megan Has to Move, 1 vol. Kouse, Patrick, illus. 2006. (Read-It! Readers Ser.). (ENG.). 32p. (gr. -1-3). 21.32 *(978-1-4048-1613-8(5)*, Easy Readers) Picture Window Bks.

Wong, Janet S. Homegrown House. Lewis, E. B., illus. 2009. (ENG.). 40p. (J). (gr. -1-3). 16.99 *(978-0-689-84718-9(1)*, McElderry, Margaret K. Bks.) McElderry, Margaret K. Bks.

Wood, Fiona. Six Impossible Things. 2015. (ENG.). 304p. (YA). (gr. 7-17). 18.00 *(978-0-316-24216-5(0))* Little Brown & Co.

—Six Impossible Things. 2016. (ENG.). 304p. (YA). (gr. 7-17). pap. 9.99 *(978-0-316-29941-1(3)*, Poppy) Little, Brown Bks. for Young Readers.

Yee, Wong Herbert. Did You See Chip? Ovresat, Laura, illus. 2004. (Green Light Readers Level 2 Ser.). (ENG.). 24p. (J). (gr. -1-3). pap. 3.95 *(978-0-15-205096-2(5))* Houghton Mifflin Harcourt Publishing Co.

Yeh, Kat. The Truth about Twinkie Pie. 2015. (J). *(978-0-316-23671-3(3))* Little Brown & Co.

Yelchin, Eugene & Kuryla, Mary. The Next Door Bear. Yelchin, Eugene & Kuryla, Mary, illus. 2011. (ENG., Illus.). 40p. (J). (gr. -1-3). 16.99 *(978-0-06-125925-8(X))* HarperCollins Pubs.

Yolen, Jane. Elsie's Bird. Small, David, illus. 2010. (ENG.). 40p. (J). (gr. k-3). 17.99 *(978-0-399-25292-1(4)*, Philomel Bks.) Penguin Young Readers Group.

Yoo, Paula. Lily's New Home. Ng-Benitez, Shirley, illus. 2016. (Confetti Kids Ser.). (ENG.). 32p. (J). (gr. -1-3). 14.95 *(978-1-62014-249-3(X))* Lee & Low Bks., Inc.

Young, Karen Romano. Doodlebug: A Novel in Doodles. 2012. (ENG., Illus.). 128p. (J). (gr. 3-7). pap. 7.99 *(978-1-250-01020-9(9)*, 9781250010209) Square Fish.

Ziegler, Jennifer. How Not to Be Popular. 2010. (ENG.). 348p. (YA). (gr. 7). mass mkt. 8.99 *(978-0-440-24024-2(7)*, Delacorte Bks. for Young Readers) Random Hse. Children's Bks.

Zink, Michelle. Lies I Told. 2015. (Lies I Told Ser.: 1). (ENG.). 352p. (YA). (gr. 8). pap. 9.99 *(978-0-06-232713-0(5)*, HarperTeen); 17.99 *(978-0-06-232712-3(7))* HarperCollins Pubs.

Zolotow, Charlotte. A Tiger Called Thomas. 2017. (J). *(978-1-4926-0171-5(3))* Sourcebooks, Inc.

50 Cent Staff. Playground. Akana, Lizzi, illus. 2012. (ENG.). 320p. (YA). (gr. 7). pap. 9.99 *(978-1-59514-478-2(1)*, Razorbill) Penguin Young Readers Group.

MOWGLI (FICTITIOUS CHARACTER)—FICTION

Disney Book Group, et al. Mowgli's Jungle Book: The Tale of a Man-Cub. Howell, Corin, illus. 2016. (ENG.). 336p. (J). (gr. 3-7). 12.99 *(978-1-4847-2579-5(4))* Disney Pr.

Kipling, Rudyard. The Jungle Book. Thorne, Jenny, illus. 2014. (ENG.). 48p. (J). (gr. k-5). pap. 7.99 *(978-1-84322-882-0(3)*, Armadillo) Anness Publishing GBR. Dist: National Bk. Network.

—The Jungle Book. Daily, Don, illus. 2014. (ENG.). 68p. (J). (gr. -1). 18.95 *(978-1-60433-475-3(4))* Cider Mill Pr. Bk. Pubs., LLC.

—The Jungle Book. 2010. 318p. (gr. 3-7). pap. 30.75 *(978-1-142-79715-7(5))* Creative Media Partners, LLC.

—The Jungle Book. Detmold, Edward J. & Detmold, Maurice, illus. 2010. (Calla Editions Ser.). (ENG.). 192p. 30.00 *(978-1-60660-009-2(5))* Dover Pubns., Inc.

—The Jungle Book. 2008. (Bring the Classics to Life Ser.). (ENG., Illus.). 72p. (gr. 1-12). pap., act. bk. ed. 10.95 *(978-1-55576-355-8(3)*, EDCTR-109B) EDCON Publishing Group.

—The Jungle Book. 2009. 122p. (gr. 3-7). pap. 19.99 *(978-1-4589-2084-3(4))* General Bks. LLC.

—The Jungle Book. Drake, W. H., Jr., illus. 2015. (Macmillan Classics Ser.). (ENG.). 320p. (J). (gr. 2-4). 17.99 *(978-1-4472-7307-3(9))* Pan Macmillan GBR. Dist: Independent Pubs. Group.

—The Jungle Book. Basford, Johanna, illus. 2013. (ENG.). 256p. (J). (gr. 4-7). pap. 10.99 *(978-0-09-957302-9(4))* Random Hse. GBR. Dist: Independent Pubs. Group.

—The Jungle Book. Ingpen, Robert R., illus. 2012. (Sterling Illustrated Classics Ser.). (ENG.). 192p. (J). (gr. 5-8). 19.95 *(978-1-4027-8284-8(5))* Sterling Publishing Co., Inc.

—The Jungle Books. 2013. (ENG.). 384p. (gr. 12). mass mkt. 5.95 *(978-0-451-41918-7(9)*, Signet) Penguin Publishing Group.

—Jungle Books. Nagai, Kaori, ed. 2013. (ENG.). 448p. (gr. 12). 11.00 *(978-0-14-119665-7(3)*, Penguin Classics) Penguin Publishing Group.

—The Jungle Books: The Mowgli Stories. Blau, Aljosha, illus. 2015. (ENG.). 240p. (J). 26.95 *(978-0-7358-4226-7(4))* North-South Bks., Inc.

Kipling, Rudyard & Ladybird Books Staff. The Jungle Book. Bernstein, Galia, illus. 2015. (Ladybird Classics Ser.). (ENG.). 72p. (J). (gr. 3-7). 8.99 *(978-1-4093-1358-8(1))* Penguin Bks., Ltd. GBR. Dist: Independent Pubs. Group.

Rowe, John, ed. The Jungle Book. (J). reprint ed. lib. bdg. 24.95 *(978-0-88411-819-0(3))* Amereon Ltd.

Thorne, Jenny, illus. The Jungle Book. 2016. (ENG.). 24p. pap. 7.99 *(978-1-86147-814-6(3)*, Armadillo) Anness Publishing GBR. Dist: National Bk. Network.

MOZART, WOLFGANG AMADEUS, 1756-1791

Allman, Barbara. Musical Genius: A Story about Wolfgang Amadeus Mozart. Hamlin, Janet, illus. 2004. (Creative Minds Biographies Ser.). (ENG.). 64p. (gr. 4-8). 22.60 *(978-1-57505-604-3(6))*; per. 8.95 *(978-1-57505-637-1(2))* Lerner Publishing Group.

Bailey, Gerry & Foster, Karen. Mozart's Wig. 2008. (Stories of Great People Ser.). (ENG., Illus.). 40p. (J). (gr. 3-6). pap. *(978-0-7787-3718-6(7))* Crabtree Publishing Co.

—Mozart's Wig. Noyes, Leighton & Radford, Karen, illus. 2008. (Stories of Great People Ser.). (ENG.). 40p. (J). (gr. 3-6). lib. bdg. *(978-0-7787-3696-7(2))* Crabtree Publishing Co.

Beth, Georgia. 18th Century Superstar: Mozart. 2017. (TIME for KIDS(r) Nonfiction Readers Ser.). (Illus.). 32p. (J). (gr. 7-7). pap. 8.99 *(978-1-4938-3631-4(5))* Teacher Created Materials, Inc.

—18th Century Superstar: Mozart. 2017. (Time for Kids Nonfiction Readers Ser.). lib. bdg. 19.65 ***(978-0-606-40268-2(3))*** Turtleback Bks.

Bodden, Valerie & Riggs, Kate. Wolfgang Amadeus Mozart. 2017. (Odysseys in Artistry Ser.). (ENG., Illus.). 80p. (J). (gr. 7-11). pap. 14.99 *(978-1-62832-318-4(3)*, Creative Paperbacks) Creative Co., The.

Brighton, Catherine. Mozart. 2004. (Illus.). 30p. (J). pap. *(978-1-84507-212-4(X))* ReiseArt Buchhandlung GmbH.

Cook, Diane. Wolfgang Amadeus Mozart: World-Famous Composer. (Illus.). 32p. (J). 2013. (People of Importance Ser.: 21). (gr. 4-18). 19.95 *(978-1-4222-2860-9(6))* 2004. (Great Names Ser.). (gr. 3-18). lib. bdg. 19.95 *(978-1-59084-159-4(X))* Mason Crest.

Cooke, Tim. Mozart. 2016. (Meet the Greats Ser.). 00048p. (J). pap. 14.05 ***(978-1-4824-5956-2(6))*** Stevens, Gareth Publishing LLLP.

Dunn, Mary. My Adventure with Mozart. 2006. 44p. (J). 8.99 *(978-1-59092-459-4(2))* Blue Forge Pr.

Kaufmann, Helen L. The Story of Mozart. Meadowcroft, Enid Lamonte, ed. Simon, Eric M., illus. 2011. 190p. 42.95 *(978-1-258-06631-4(9))* Literary Licensing, LLC.

Loria, Laura. Wolfgang Amadeus Mozart, 1 vol. 2015. (ENG.). 32p. (J). 23.45 *(978-1-62275-681-0(9)*, Britannica Educational Publishing) Rosen Publishing Group, Inc., The.

McDonough, Yona Zeldis. Who Was Wolfgang Amadeus Mozart? Robbins, Carrie, illus. 2003. (Who Was? Ser.). (ENG.). 112p. (J). (gr. 3-7). pap. 5.99 *(978-0-448-43104-8(1)*, Grosset & Dunlap) Penguin Young Readers Group.

—Who Was Wolfgang Amadeus Mozart? 2003. (Who Was... ? Ser.). (gr. 3-6). 16.00 *(978-0-613-61669-0(3)*, Turtleback) Turtleback Bks.

Murtagh, Ciaran. The Making of Mozart. 2017. (ENG., Illus.). 32p. (J). pap. 7.99 ***(978-0-00-820876-9(X))*** HarperCollins Pubs. Ltd. GBR. Dist: Independent Pubs. Group.

Riggs, Kate. Wolfgang Amadeus Mozart. (Illus.). (J). 2016. 80p. *(978-1-60818-722-5(5))* 2008. 48p. (gr. 4-7). lib. bdg. 22.95 *(978-1-58341-664-8(1))* Creative Co., The. (Creative Education).

Ross, Stewart. The Story of Wolfgang Amadeus Mozart. (Lifetimes Ser.). (Illus.). 48p. (J). lib. bdg. 28.50 *(978-1-931983-14-3(3))* Chrysalis Education.

Sís, Peter. Play, Mozart, Play! Sís, Peter, illus. 2006. (Illus.). 32p. (J). (gr. -1-3). 16.99 *(978-0-06-112181-4(9)*, Greenwillow Bks.) HarperCollins Pubs.

Stanley, Diane. Mozart: The Wonder Child - A Puppet Play in Three Acts. Stanley, Diane, illus. 2009. (ENG., Illus.). 48p. (J). (gr. 3-7). 17.99 *(978-0-06-072674-4(1)*, Collins) HarperCollins Pubs.

Summerer, Eric. Wolfgang Amadeus Mozart. 2006. 36p. pap. 21.25 *(978-1-4358-3796-6(7)*, PowerKids Pr.) Rosen Publishing Group, Inc., The.

Summerer, Eric Michael. Wolfgang Amadeus Mozart. (Primary Source Library of Famous Composers Ser.). 32p. 2009. (gr. 4-4). 42.50 *(978-1-60854-115-7(0))* 2006. (Illus.). (J). (gr. -1-3). lib. bdg. 21.25 *(978-1-4042-2772-9(5))* Rosen Publishing Group, Inc., The. (PowerKids Pr.).

Turner, Barrie Carson. Mozart. 2003. (Famous Childhoods Ser.). (Illus.). (J). lib. bdg. 24.25 *(978-1-59389-115-2(6))* Chrysalis Education.

Venezia, Mike. Wolfgang Amadeus Mozart (Revised Edition) 2017. (Getting to Know the World's Greatest Composers Ser.). (ENG.). 40p. (J). lib. bdg. 29.00 *(978-0-531-22058-0(3)*, Children's Pr.) Scholastic Library Publishing.

Weeks, Marcus. Mozart: The Boy Who Changed the World with His Music. 2007. (National Geographic World History Biographies Ser.). (ENG., Illus.). 64p. (J). (gr. 3-7). 17.95 *(978-1-4263-0002-8(6))*; lib. bdg. 27.90 *(978-1-4263-0003-5(4))* National Geographic Society. (National Geographic Children's Bks.).

—World History Biographies: Mozart: The Boy Who Changed the World with His Music. 2013. (National Geographic World History Biographies Ser.). (ENG., Illus.). 64p. (J). (gr. 3-7). pap. 7.99 *(978-1-4263-1451-3(5)*, National Geographic Children's Bks.) National Geographic Society.

MOZART, WOLFGANG AMADEUS, 1756-1791—FICTION

Muir, Sabine. Meeting Wolfie: A Story about Mozart. 2006. 129p. pap. 19.95 *(978-1-4241-3968-2(6))* PublishAmerica, Inc.

Stilton, Geronimo. Play It Again, Mozart! Cooper-McGuinness, Nanette, tr. 2011. (Geronimo Stilton Graphic Novels Ser.). (ENG., Illus.). 56p. (J). (gr. 2-6). 9.99 *(978-1-59707-276-2(1)*, 9781597072762) Papercutz.

Turnbull, Ann. Mary Ann & Miss Mozart. 2009. (Historical House Ser.). 166p. (YA). (gr. 5-18). pap. 5.99 *(978-0-7945-2332-9(3)*, Usborne) EDC Publishing.

MUDGE (FICTITIOUS CHARACTER)—FICTION

Henry & Mudge Book Set 800925, 6 vols. 2005. (J). pap. *(978-1-59794-090-0(9))* Environments, Inc.

The Henry & Mudge Collector's Set: Henry & Mudge; Henry & Mudge in Puddle Trouble; Henry & Mudge in the Green Time; Henry & Mudge under the Yellow Moon; Henry & Mudge in the Sparkle Days; Henry & Mudge & the Forever Sea. 2014. (Henry & Mudge Ser.). (ENG., Illus.). 280p. (J). (gr. k-2). pap. 15.99 *(978-1-4814-2147-8(6)*, Simon Spotlight) Simon Spotlight.

Rylant, Cynthia. Annie & Snowball & the Teacup Club. Stevenson, Suçie, illus. 2009. (Annie & Snowball Ser.: 3). (ENG.). 40p. (J). (gr. k-2). pap. 3.99 *(978-1-4169-1461-7(7)*, Simon Spotlight) Simon Spotlight.

—Henry & Mudge & a Very Merry Christmas. Stevenson, Suçie, illus. 2004. (Henry & Mudge Ser.: 25). (ENG.). 40p. (J). (gr. k-2). 16.99 *(978-0-689-81168-5(3)*, Simon Spotlight) Simon Spotlight.

—Henry & Mudge & Mrs. Hopper's House. Bracken, Carolyn, illus. (Henry & Mudge Ser.: 22). (ENG.). 40p. (J). (gr. k-2). 2004. pap. 3.99 *(978-0-689-83446-2(2))* 2003. 15.99 *(978-0-689-81153-1(5))* Simon Spotlight. (Simon Spotlight).

—Henry & Mudge & the Big Sleepover. Stevenson, Suçie & Stevenson, Suçie, illus. 2006. (Henry & Mudge Ser.: 28). (ENG.). 40p. (J). (gr. k-2). 16.99 *(978-0-689-81171-5(3)*, Simon Spotlight) Simon Spotlight.

—Henry & Mudge & the Big Sleepover, Bk. 28. Stevenson, Suçie, illus. 2007. (Henry & Mudge Ser.: 28). (ENG.). 40p. (J). (gr. k-2). pap. 3.99 *(978-0-689-83451-6(9)*, Simon Spotlight) Simon Spotlight.

—Henry & Mudge & the Great Grandpas. Stevenson, Suçie & Stevenson, Suçie, illus. 2005. (Henry & Mudge Ser.: 26). (ENG.). 40p. (J). (gr. k-2). 15.99 *(978-0-689-81170-8(5)*, Simon Spotlight) Simon Spotlight.

—Henry & Mudge & the Tumbling Trip. Bracken, Carolyn, illus. 2005. (Henry & Mudge Ser.: 27). (ENG.). 40p. (J). (gr. k-2). 16.99 *(978-0-689-81180-7(2)*, Simon Spotlight) Simon Spotlight.

—Puppy Mudge Has a Snack. Mones, Isidre, illus. 2004. (Puppy Mudge Ser.). (ENG.). 32p. (J). (gr. -1-k). pap. 3.99 *(978-0-689-86995-2(9)*, Simon Spotlight) Simon Spotlight.

Rylant, Cynthia & Bracken, Carolyn. Henry & Mudge & the Funny Lunch. Bracken, Carolyn, illus. 2004. (Henry & Mudge Ser.: 24). (ENG., Illus.). 40p. (J). (gr. k-2). 16.99 *(978-0-689-81178-4(0)*, Simon Spotlight) Simon Spotlight.

—Henry & Mudge & the Wild Goose Chase. 2004. (Henry & Mudge Ser.: 23). (ENG., Illus.). 40p. (J). (gr. k-2). pap. 3.99 *(978-0-689-83450-9(0)*, Simon Spotlight) Simon Spotlight.

—Henry & Mudge & the Wild Goose Chase. Bracken, Carolyn, illus. 2003. (Henry & Mudge Ser.: 23). (ENG., Illus.). 40p. (J). (gr. k-2). 16.99 *(978-0-689-81172-2(1)*, Simon Spotlight) Simon Spotlight.

MUHAMMAD, PROPHET, -632

Azm, Mohsen Abou El, illus. Muhammad: The Life of the Prophet - Based on Original Sources. adapted ed. 2014. (ENG.). 64p. pap. 6.95 *(978-1-906230-62-3(5))* Real Reads Ltd. GBR. Dist: Casemate Pubs. & Bk. Distributors, LLC.

Büyüksahin, Mehmet, et al. Khadija Bint Khuwaylid. 2016. (Age of Bliss Ser.). (ENG.). v, 80p. (J). (gr. 4-8). pap. 5.95 *(978-1-59784-375-1(X))* Tughra Bks.

Caglaroglu, Nurefsan. Night of Wonders, 6 vols. 2008. (ENG.). 16p. (J). (gr. 2-4). pap. 12.95 *(978-1-59784-126-9(9))* Tughra Bks.

Cohn, Jessica. Muhammad: Prophet of Islam, 1 vol. 2012. (Primary Source Readers Ser.). (ENG.). 32p. (J). (gr. 4-4). pap. 8.99 *(978-1-4333-5004-7(1))* Teacher Created Materials, Inc.

Haylamaz, Resit. Abu Bakr: The Pinnacle of Truthfulness. 2011. (ENG.). 175p. (gr. 8-11). pap. 8.95 *(978-1-59784-250-1(8))* Tughra Bks.

—Ali: Hero of Chivalry. 2011. (ENG.). 142p. pap. 9.95 *(978-1-59784-253-2(2))* Tughra Bks.

—The Luminous Life of Our Prophet. 2014. (ENG.). 365p. pap. 14.95 *(978-1-59784-310-2(5))* Tughra Bks.

—Zayd: The Rose That Bloomed in Captivity. 2011. (ENG.). 88p. (gr. 8-11). pap. 6.95 *(978-1-59784-247-1(8))* Tughra Bks.

Kaya, Rahime. Prophet Muhammad: The Seal of All Prophets. 2014. (ENG.). 229p. pap. 14.95 *(978-1-59784-309-6(1))* Tughra Bks.

Oral, Osman. I Believe in the Prophets. 2013. (J). *(978-1-59784-305-8(9))* Tughra Bks.

Öze, Özkan. I Wonder about the Prophet. Ayduz, Selma, tr. 2016. (ENG., Illus.). 143p. (J). pap. 10.95 *(978-0-86037-508-1(0))* Kube Publishing Ltd. GBR. Dist: Consortium Bk. Sales & Distribution.

Pike, E. Royston. Mohammed: Founder of the Religion of Islam. 2011. 134p. 40.95 *(978-1-258-00657-0(X))* Literary Licensing, LLC.

Tarantino, Mardijah Aldrich. Marvellous Stories from the Life of Muhammad. Murad, Khurram, ed. 2012. (ENG., Illus.). 120p.

MNO

(J). (gr. 2-7). pap. 8.95 *(978-0-86037-103-8(4))* Kube Publishing Ltd. GBR. Dist: Consortium Bk. Sales & Distribution.

MUHAMMAD ALI, 1942-

see Ali, Muhammad, 1942-2016

MUIR, JOHN, 1838-1914

Archer, Jules. To Save the Earth: The American Environmental Movement. 2016. (Jules Archer History for Young Readers Ser.). (ENG., Illus.). 200p. (J). (gr. 6). 16.99 *(978-1-63450-196-5(9),* Sky Pony Pr.) Skyhorse Publishing Co., Inc.

Danneberg, Julie. John Muir Wrestles a Waterfall. Hogan, Jamie, illus. 2015. (ENG.). 32p. (J). (gr. -1-3). lib. bdg. 16.95 *(978-1-58089-586-6(7))* Charlesbridge Publishing, Inc.

Elliot, Henry. John Muir: Protecting & Preserving the Environment. 2009. (Voices for Green Choices Ser.). (ENG., Illus.). 48p. (J). (gr. 5-9). pap. *(978-0-7787-4681-2(X))*; lib. bdg. *(978-0-7787-4668-3(2))* Crabtree Publishing Co.

Goldstein, Natalie. John Muir. 2011. (Conservation Heroes Ser.). (Illus.). 144p. (YA). (gr. 6-12). 35.00 *(978-1-60413-945-7(5),* Chelsea Hse.) Facts On File, Inc.

Koehler-Pentacoff, Elizabeth. John Muir & Stickeen: An Alaskan Adventure. Swanson, Karl W., illus. 2003. (Single Titles Ser.). 32p. (J). 14.95 *(978-0-7613-1997-9(2))* Lerner Publishing Group.

—John Muir & Stickeen: An Alaskan Adventure. Swanson, Karl, illus. 2003. (Single Titles Ser.). (ENG.). 32p. (J). (gr. 4-8). lib. bdg. 15.95 *(978-0-7613-2769-1(X),* Millbrook Pr.) Lerner Publishing Group.

Locker, Thomas. John Muir: America's Naturalist. 2010. (ENG.). 32p. (J). (gr. -1-3). pap. 12.95 *(978-1-55591-705-0(4))* Fulcrum Publishing.

Mara, Wil & National Geographic Learning Staff. John Muir. 2010. (Rise & Shine Ser.). (ENG., Illus.). 32p. (C). (gr. 1-2). pap. 8.95 *(978-0-516-27342-6(6))* National Geographic School Publishing, Inc.

Maynard, Charles W. John Muir: Naturalist & Explorer. (Famous Explorers of the American West Ser.). 24p. 2009. (gr. 3-4). 42.50 *(978-1-61512-504-3(3))* 2003. (Illus.). (J). lib. bdg. 22.60 *(978-0-8239-6291-4(1))* Rosen Publishing Group, Inc., The. (PowerKids Pr.).

Miller, Barbara Kiely. John Muir. 2007. (Grandes Personajes (Great Americans) Ser.). 24p. (gr. 1-4). (SPA.). pap. 8.15 *(978-0-8368-8339-8(X))*; lib. bdg. 22.00 *(978-0-8368-8318-3(7))*; (SPA.). lib. bdg. 22.00 *(978-0-8368-8332-9(2))* Stevens, Gareth Publishing LLLP. (Weekly Reader Leveled Readers).

National Geographic Learning Staff. The Mountain Man & the President. 2010. (ENG., Illus.). 48p. (C). (gr. 2-8). pap. 18.95 *(978-0-8114-8064-2(X))* National Geographic School Publishing, Inc.

Rosenstock, Barb. The Camping Trip That Changed America: Theodore Roosevelt, John Muir, & Our National Parks. Gerstein, Mordecai, illus. 2012. (ENG.). 32p. (J). (gr. 1-3). 17.99 *(978-0-8037-3710-5(6),* Dial Bks) Penguin Young Readers Group.

Wadsworth, Ginger. Camping with the President. Dugan, Karen, illus. 2009. (ENG.). 32p. (J). (gr. 4-18). 16.95 *(978-1-59078-497-6(9),* Calkins Creek) Boyds Mills Pr.

MULES

Goldish, Meish & Parkhurst, Anthony. Horses, Donkeys, & Mules in the Marines. 2012. (America's Animal Soldiers Ser.). 24p. (J). (gr. 1-6). lib. bdg. 23.93 *(978-1-61772-453-4(X))* Bearport Publishing Co., Inc.

Graubart, Norman D. Mules in American History. 2014. (How Animals Shaped History Ser.). (Illus.). 24p. (J). (gr. k-5). 23.60 *(978-1-4777-6769-6(X),* PowerKids Pr.) Rosen Publishing Group, Inc., The.

Schmid, Diana J. Samule the Worthless White Mule. 2009. 24p. pap. 12.49 *(978-1-4490-0032-5(0))* AuthorHouse.

MULES—FICTION

Buzel, Alita. The Adventures of Jedediah the Mule: Book One. 2010. 116p. 24.95 *(978-1-4520-4336-4(1))*; pap. 12.95 *(978-1-4520-4337-1(X))* AuthorHouse.

Grovet, Heather. Sarah Lee & a Mule Named Maybe. 2003. (Pathfinder Junior Book Club Ser.). 136p. (J). pap. 7.99 *(978-0-8280-1725-1(5),* 191-530) Review & Herald Publishing Assn.

Hodges, Meredith. Jasper: A Christmas Caper. Shields, Bonnie, illus. 2004. 85p. (J). 24.95 *(978-1-928624-20-2(0))* Lucky 3 Ranch, Inc.

—Jasper: A Fabulous Fourth. Shields, Bonnie, illus. 2006. 83p. (J). *(978-1-928624-24-0(3))* Lucky 3 Ranch, Inc.

—Jasper: The Story of a Mule. Shields, Bonnie, illus. 2003. 245p. (J). (gr. k-7). 39.95 *(978-0-9702309-8-0(2))* Lucky 3 Ranch, Inc.

Hopkinson, Deborah. From Slave to Soldier: Based on a True Civil War Story. Floca, Brian, illus. (Ready-To-Reads Ser.). (ENG.). 48p. (J). (gr. 1-3). 2007. pap. 3.99 *(978-0-689-83966-5(9))* 2005. 16.99 *(978-0-689-83965-8(0))* Simon Spotlight. (Simon Spotlight).

Huston, Donna. Mr. O'Toole, the Diabetic Mule. 2006. (J). spiral bd. 19.95 *(978-0-9771192-2-6(X))* Shayne Publishing.

Nash, Andy. Melinda & Her Mule: For Kids Blessed with a Strong Will. 2008. (J). *(978-0-8127-0453-2(3))* Autumn Hse. Publishing Co.

Rae Strawn, Evelyn. Moncho the Mule. 2010. 24p. 12.99 *(978-1-4389-8751-4(X))* AuthorHouse.

Root, Alice. A Job for Deirdre. 2010. 69p. pap. 24.70 *(978-0-557-23363-2(1))* Lulu Pr., Inc.

—What Is a Mule? 2010. 17p. 9.10 *(978-0-557-19648-7(5))* Lulu Pr., Inc.

Schmauss, Judy Kentor. Luke's Mule. Costello, Shawn, illus. 2006. (Reader's Clubhouse Level 2 Reader Ser.). (ENG.). 24p. (J). (gr. 1-4). pap. 3.99 *(978-0-7641-3297-1(0))* Barron's Educational Series, Inc.

Schroeder, Lisa. Charmed Life #4: Hannah's Bright Star. 2014. (Charmed Life Ser.: 4). (ENG.). 192p. (J). (gr. 3-7). pap. 5.99 *(978-0-545-60379-9(X),* Scholastic Paperbacks) Scholastic, Inc.

Sommer, Carl. Tied up in Knots(Enredados) Budwine, Greg, illus. 2009. (Another Sommer-Time Story Bilingual Ser.). (SPA & ENG.). 48p. (J). lib. bdg. 16.95 *(978-1-57537-169-6(3))* Advance Publishing, Inc.

Stroud, Bettye. Belle, the Last Mule at Gee's Bend: A Civil Rights Story. Holyfield, John, illus. 2016. (ENG.). (J). (gr. k-3). 7.99 *(978-0-7636-8769-4(3))* Candlewick Pr.

Stroud, Bettye & Ramsey, Calvin Alexander. Belle, the Last Mule at Gee's Bend: A Civil Rights Story. Holyfield, John, illus. 2011. (ENG.). 32p. (J). (gr. k-3). 16.99 *(978-0-7636-4058-3(1))* Candlewick Pr.

Wilson, Douglas. Maude, the Flop-Eared Mule. Fore, Elizabeth, illus. 2012. 38p. 24.95 *(978-1-4626-7455-8(0))* America Star Bks.

MULTICULTURAL EDUCATION

Alexander, Linda B. & Kwon, Nahyun, eds. Multicultural Programs for Tweens & Teens. 2010. 216p. pap. 50.00 *(978-0-8389-3582-8(6))* American Library Assn.

Padmanabhan, Manjula. I Am Different. 2011. (ENG., Illus.). 40p. (J). (gr. 1-4). 16.95 *(978-1-57091-639-7(X))* Charlesbridge Publishing, Inc.

Pugliano-Martin, Carol. Making Crafts from Around the World & Artesanías del Mundo: 6 English, 6 Spanish Adaptations. 2011. (ENG & SPA.). (J). 89.00 net. *(978-1-4108-5674-6(7))* Benchmark Education Co.

Schuman, Jo Miles. Art from Many Hands: Multicultural Art Projects. rev. ed. 2003. (ENG., Illus.). 304p. pap. 29.95 *(978-0-87192-593-0(1))* Davis Pubns., Inc.

Tabor, Nancy Maria Grande. Somos un Arco Iris (We Are a Rainbow) Tabor, Nancy Maria Grande, illus. 2006. (ENG & SPA., Illus.). 28p. (gr. -1-3). 17.95 *(978-0-7569-7027-7(X))* Perfection Learning Corp.

MULTICULTURAL EDUCATION—FICTION

Mycek-Wodecki, Anna. The Bilingual Dog. Abt, Diana, tr. Mycek-Wodecki, Anna, illus. 2008. (Minutka Ser.). (SPA & ENG., Illus.). 48p. (J). (gr. -1-k). 9.95 *(978-1-84059-509-3(4))* Milet Publishing.

—The Bilingual Dog/Iki Dilli Kopek. Erdogan, Fatih, tr. Mycek-Wodecki, Anna, illus. 2008. (Minutka Ser.). (TUR & ENG., Illus.). 48p. (J). (gr. -1-k). 9.95 *(978-1-84059-510-9(8))* Milet Publishing.

MULTICULTURALISM

Here are entered works on policies or programs that foster the preservation of different cultural identities, including customs, languages, and beliefs, within a unified society such as a state or nation.

Ajmera, Maya, et al. Healthy Kids. 2013. (ENG., Illus.). 32p. (J). (gr. -1-3). pap. 7.95 *(978-1-58089-437-1(2))*; lib. bdg. 17.95 *(978-1-58089-436-4(4))* Charlesbridge Publishing, Inc.

Anderson, Joanna. The Many People of America. 2012. (I'm an American Citizen Ser.). (ENG., Illus.). 24p. (J). (gr. 1-3). 22.60 *(978-1-4488-8591-6(4),* PowerKids Pr.) Rosen Publishing Group, Inc., The.

Behrens, Janice. We Are Alike, We Are Different. 2009. (Scholastic News Nonfiction Readers Ser.). (ENG.). 24p. (J). (gr. 1-2). pap. 6.95 *(978-0-531-21447-3(8),* Children's Pr.); lib. bdg. 22.00 *(978-0-531-21347-6(1))* Scholastic Library Publishing.

Fox, Mem. Whoever You Are. Staub, Leslie, illus. 2007.Tr. of Sé de¿it Mak Ó. (ENG.). 28p. (J). (gr. -1 — 1). bds. 6.95 *(978-0-15-206066-4(9))* Houghton Mifflin Harcourt Publishing Co.

Higgins, Melissa. We All Come from Different Cultures, 1 vol. 2012. (Celebrating Differences Ser.). (ENG.). 24p. (gr. k-1). 26.65 *(978-1-4296-7577-2(2))*; pap. 7.29 *(978-1-4296-7887-2(9))*; pap. 41.70 *(978-1-4296-8320-3(1))* Capstone Press of Coughlan Cos. (Pebble Plus).

Kerley, Barbara. A Cool Drink of Water. 2006. (Barbara Kerley Photo Inspirations Ser.). (ENG., Illus.). 32p. (J). (gr. -1-3). pap. 7.95 *(978-0-7922-5489-8(9),* National Geographic Children's Bks.) National Geographic Society.

Lewis, Wendy. Sabrina the Girl with A Hole in Her Heart. Lucas, Diane, illus. 2011. (ENG.). 34p. pap. 10.95 *(978-1-4663-3473-1(8))* CreateSpace Independent Publishing Platform.

Life Around the World. 2016. (Life Around the World Ser.). (ENG.). 24p. lib. bdg. 133.25 *(978-1-5157-5862-4(1),* Pebble Plus) Capstone Press of Coughlan Cos.

Loewen, Nancy & Skelley, Paula. People of the World. 2015. (Go Go Global Ser.). (ENG., Illus.). 32p. (gr. 1-2). lib. bdg. 27.32 *(978-1-4914-3920-3(3),* Aplus Bks.) Capstone Press of Coughlan Cos.

Marwah, Gauri. Tikki Tikki Tembo. 2013. 12p. pap. 7.95 *(978-1-4828-1424-8(2))* Partridge Pub.

McIntosh, Kenneth & Walker, Ida. Interpreting an Alien World: Youth with Cultural/Language Differences. 2007. (Helping Youth with Mental, Physical, & Social Challenges Ser.). (Illus.). 128p. (YA). (gr. 8-12). pap. 14.95 *(978-1-4222-0441-2(3))* Mason Crest.

Meet Our New Student, 12 vols., Set. 2008. (J). (gr. 1-5). lib. bdg. 359.40 *(978-1-58415-658-1(9))* Mitchell Lane Pubs., Inc.

Milord, Susan. Tales Alive! Donato, Michael A., illus. 2007. (ENG.). 128p. 16.99 *(978-0-8249-6804-5(2),* Ideal Pubns.) Worthy Publishing.

Multicultural Voices, 5 vols., Set. 2010. (Multicultural Voices Ser.). (gr. 6-12). 175.00 *(978-1-60413-963-1(3),* Chelsea Hse.) Facts On File, Inc.

Ogden, Charlie. Equality & Diversity. 2017. 32p. (J). ***(978-0-7787-3265-5(7))*** Crabtree Publishing Co.

Robins, Maureen Picard. One Land, Many Cultures. 2012. (ENG.). 24p. (gr. k-2). pap. 8.95 *(978-1-61810-276-8(1))* Rourke Educational Media.

Samuels, Barbara. Canada's Multicultural Society Today: Multiculturalism in Canada. 2011. 32p. (gr. 5-8). *(978-1-77071-706-0(4))*; pap. *(978-1-77071-709-1(9))* Weigl Educational Pubs. Ltd.

—Multiculturalism in Early Canada: Multiculturalism in Canada. 2011. 32p. (gr. 5-8). *(978-1-77071-704-6(8))* Weigl Educational Pubs. Ltd.

Schramm, Linda Anette. Don't Let the Ziglers into the Zoo! 2004. 31p. pap. 24.95 *(978-1-4137-1541-5(9))* PublishAmerica, Inc.

Teichmann, Iris. A Multicultural World. 2006. (Understanding Immigration Ser.). (Illus.). 44p. (YA). (gr. 5-9). lib. bdg. 31.35 *(978-1-58340-969-5(6))* Black Rabbit Bks.

Wachtel, Alan. Southeast Asian Americans. 2009. (New Americans Ser.). 80p. (gr. 5-8). 35.64 *(978-0-7614-4312-4(6))* Marshall Cavendish Corp.

MULTICULTURALISM—FICTION

Abrams, Douglas Carlton & Tutu, Desmond. God's Dream. Pham, LeUyen, illus. 2010. (ENG.). 32p. (J). (— 1). bds. 7.99 *(978-0-7636-4742-1(X))* Candlewick Pr.

Aunt Judy. Chickens on the Go! Chickens from different locations around the World. Aunt Judy, illus. 2nd ed. 2006. (Illus.). 40p. (J). pap. 7.00 *(978-0-9780693-0-8(7))* McEwen, Judith A.

Brown, Margaret Wise. Around the World We Go! 2013. (Illus.). (J). *(978-1-4351-4720-1(0))* Barnes & Noble, Inc.

Constantine, Cara J. I Can Choose to Be Happy. Barge III, John S., illus. 2012. 32p. 24.95 *(978-1-4626-4731-6(6))* America Star Bks.

Flake, Sharon G. The Skin I'm In. Disney Press Staff, illus. rev. ed. 2007. (ENG.). 176p. (J). (gr. 5-9). pap. 8.99 *(978-1-4231-0385-1(8),* Jump at the Sun) Hyperion Bks. for Children.

Gomes, Linda Nunes. Special Words: A Story about Multicultural Families & Their Pets. Levine, Lenora D., illus. 2007. (YA). per. 12.99 *(978-1-934400-02-9(5))* Rock Village Publishing.

Gonzales, Mark. Yo Soy Muslim. 2017. (ENG., Illus.). 32p. (J). (gr. -1-3). 17.99 ***(978-1-4814-8936-2(4),*** Simon & Schuster Bks. For Young Readers) Simon & Schuster Bks. For Young Readers.

Iyengar, Malathi Michelle. Romina's Rangoli. Wanardi, Jennifer, illus. 2007. (Romina's Rangoli Ser.). 32p. (J). (gr. -1-3). 16.95 *(978-1-885008-32-9(5),* Shen's Bks.) Lee & Low Bks., Inc.

Khan, Rukhsana, et al. Many Windows: Six Kids, Five Faiths, One Community. 2008. (ENG., Illus.). 88p. (J). (gr. 4-18). pap. 14.99 *(978-1-894917-56-8(1),* Napoleon & Co.) Dundurn CAN. Dist: Ingram Publisher Services.

Minaki, Christina. Zoe's Extraordinary Holiday Adventures, 1 vol. 2007. (ENG.). 116p. (J). (gr. 2-5). pap. 8.95 *(978-1-897187-26-5(2))* Second Story Pr. CAN. Dist: Orca Bk. Pubs. USA.

Murray, Victoria Christopher. Veronique. 2009. (Divas Ser.). (ENG., Illus.). 272p. pap. 11.00 *(978-1-4165-6350-1(4),* Gallery Bks.) Gallery Bks.

Murrell, Belinda. Lulu Bell & the Arabian Nights. 2015. (Lulu Bell Ser.). (ENG.). 96p. (J). (gr. 1-3). pap. 7.99 *(978-0-85798-558-3(2))* Random Hse. Australia AUS. Dist: Independent Pubs. Group.

Rodari, Gianni. One & Seven. Anglin, David, tr. from ITA. Alemagna, Beatrice, illus. 2005. (SPA.). 26p. (J). (gr. k-3). 17.95 *(978-0-9628720-6-8(7))* Iaconi, Mariuccia Bk. Imports.

Saunders, Sara. Swirly. Pierce, Matthew, illus. 2012. 32p. (J). 7.99 *(978-0-8280-2681-9(5))* Review & Herald Publishing Assn.

Selected Children's Stories - Multi Cultural, 3 bks. (Illus.). (J). lib. bdg. 38.85 *(978-1-56674-906-0(9))* Forest Hse. Publishing Co., Inc.

Smith, Charles R., Jr. I Am the World. 2013. (ENG., Illus.). 48p. (J). (gr. -1-2). 17.99 *(978-1-4424-2302-2(1))* Simon & Schuster Children's Publishing.

Suter, Lorenzo. TrYouth Truth Knowledge Apprehension Cog. 2005. (Illus.). 206p. 27.55 *(978-1-4122-0095-0(4))* Trafford Publishing.

Theo & the Sisters of Sage: From the Creator of We Are All the Same Inside. 2003. (We Are All the Same Inside Ser.: Vol. 3). (Illus.). 32p. (J). pap. 9.95 *(978-0-9718232-1-1(9))* T.I.M.M.-E. Co., Inc.

Tutu, Desmond & Abrams, Douglas Carlton. God's Dream. Pham, LeUyen, illus. 2008. (ENG.). 40p. (J). (gr. k-12). 17.99 *(978-0-7636-3388-2(7))* Candlewick Pr.

Winkler, Henry & Oliver, Lin. Holy Enchilada! Heyer, Carol et al, illus. 2004. (Hank Zipzer Ser.: 6). (ENG.). 160p. (J). (gr. 3-7). pap. 5.99 *(978-0-448-43353-0(2),* Grosset & Dunlap) Penguin Young Readers Group.

—The Zippity Zinger, 4 vols. Heitz, Tim, illus. 2004. (Hank Zipzer Ser.: 4). (ENG.). 160p. (J). (gr. 3-7). mass mkt. 5.99 *(978-0-448-43193-2(9),* Grosset & Dunlap) Penguin Young Readers Group.

MUMMIES

Ashman, Iain. Egyptian Mummy. 2004. (Cut-Out Models Ser.). (Illus.). 32p. (J). pap. 9.95 *(978-0-7945-0255-3(5),* Usborne) EDC Publishing.

Axelrod-Contrada, Joan. The Kids' Guide to Mummies, 1 vol. 2010. (Kids' Guides). (ENG.). 32p. (gr. 3-4). 27.99 *(978-1-4296-5441-8(4),* Edge Bks.) Capstone Press of Coughlan Cos.

Biskup, Agnieszka, et al. Uncovering Mummies: An Isabel Soto Archaeology Adventure. 2016. (Graphic Expeditions Ser.). (ENG., Illus.). 32p. pap. 8.10 *(978-1-5157-6190-7(8),* Graphic Library) Capstone Press of Coughlan Cos.

Bolton, Anne. Pyramids & Mummies. 2008. (ENG., Illus.). 32p. (J). (gr. 3-8). 21.99 *(978-1-4169-5873-4(8),* Simon & Schuster Bks. For Young Readers) Simon & Schuster Bks. For Young Readers.

Bower, Tamara. The Mummy-Makers of Egypt. 2016. (ENG., Illus.). 42p. (J). (gr. 2-5). 17.95 *(978-1-60980-600-2(X),* Triangle Square) Seven Stories Pr.

Burgan, Michael. Mummy Lairs. 2012. (Scary Places Ser.). 32p. (J). (gr. 4-8). lib. bdg. 25.27 *(978-1-61772-568-5(4))* Bearport Publishing Co., Inc.

Carney, Elizabeth. Mummies. 2009. (Readers Ser.). (ENG., Illus.). 32p. (J). (gr. k-3). 13.90 *(978-1-4263-0529-0(X))*; pap. 3.99 *(978-1-4263-0528-3(1))* National Geographic Society. (National Geographic Children's Bks.).

Cheatham, Mark. Mummies. 2012. (Jr. Graphic Monster Stories Ser.). (ENG.). 24p. (J). (gr. 3-6). pap. 10.60 *(978-1-4488-6409-6(7))*; lib. bdg. 25.25 *(978-1-4488-6225-2(6))* Rosen Publishing Group, Inc., The. (PowerKids Pr.).

Clarke, Penny. The Story of Mummies. 2013. (Illus.). 63p. (J). *(978-1-4351-5032-4(5))* Barnes & Noble, Inc.

Claybourne, Anna. Mummies Around the World. 2010. (Big Picture: People & Culture Ser.). (ENG.). 24p. (gr. 1-2). pap. 41.70 *(978-1-4296-5821-8(5),* First Facts) Capstone Press of Coughlan Cos.

Davis, Kenneth C. Don't Know Much about Mummies. Date not set. 48p. (J). pap. 5.99 *(978-0-06-443645-8(4))* HarperCollins Pubs.

Deem, James M. Bodies from the Ice: Melting Glaciers & the Recovery of the Past. 2008. (ENG., Illus.). 64p. (J). (gr. 5-7). 17.99 *(978-0-618-80045-2(X))* Houghton Mifflin Harcourt Publishing Co.

Dorling Kindersley Publishing Staff & Putnam, James. Mummy. 2009. (DK Eyewitness Bks.). (ENG., Illus.). 72p. (J). (gr. 3-7). 16.99 *(978-0-7566-4541-0(7),* DK Children) Dorling Kindersley Publishing, Inc.

Farndon, John. How to Live Like an Egyptian Mummy Maker. Campidelli, Maurizio, illus. 2016. (How to Live Like... Ser.). (ENG.). 32p. (J). (gr. 3-6). 26.65 *(978-1-5124-0629-0(5))* Lerner Publishing Group.

Fleury, Kevin. Mummies. (Up Close Ser.). 24p. (gr. 3-3). 2009. 47.90 *(978-1-60854-698-5(5))* 2007. (Illus.). (J). lib. bdg. 25.25 *(978-1-4042-3761-2(5))* Rosen Publishing Group, Inc., The. (PowerKids Pr.).

Frisch, Aaron. Mummies. 2013. 24p. (J). 25.65 *(978-1-60818-247-3(9),* Creative Education) Creative Co., The.

—That's Spooky: Mummies. 2013. (That's Spooky Ser.). (ENG.). 24p. (J). (gr. 1-3). pap. 7.99 *(978-0-89812-804-8(8),* Creative Paperbacks) Creative Co., The.

Ganeri, Anita. Mummies & Ancient Egypt. 2009. (History Explorers Ser.). (ENG.). 24p. (J). (gr. k-2). pap. 5.95 *(978-1-84696-210-3(2),* TickTock Books) Octopus Publishing Group GBR. Dist: Independent Pubs. Group.

Griffey, Harriet. Secrets of the Mummies. 2013. (DK Reader Level 4 Ser.). lib. bdg. 13.55 *(978-0-606-32438-0(0),* Turtleback) Turtleback Bks.

Griffey, Harriet & Dorling Kindersley Publishing Staff. Secrets of the Mummies, Level 4. 2013. (DK Readers Ser.). (ENG.). 48p. (J). (gr. 3-7). pap. 3.99 *(978-1-4654-0940-9(8),* DK Children) Dorling Kindersley Publishing, Inc.

Guiberson, Brenda Z. Mummy Mysteries: Tales from North America. Guiberson, Brenda Z., illus. 2013. (My Readers Ser.). (ENG., Illus.). 48p. (J). (gr. 1-3). pap. 3.99 *(978-1-250-01047-6(0),* 9781250010476) Square Fish.

Hall, Brianna. Mummies of Ancient Egypt. 2012. (Ancient Egyptian Civilization Ser.). (ENG.). 32p. (gr. 3-4). pap. 47.70 *(978-1-4296-8403-3(8))*; pap. 8.10 *(978-1-4296-7978-7(6))*; lib. bdg. 27.32 *(978-1-4296-7629-8(9))* Capstone Press of Coughlan Cos. (Fact Finders).

Hamilton, S. L. Mummies. 2010. (Xtreme Monsters Ser.). 32p. (gr. 3-9). 27.07 *(978-1-61613-469-3(0),* A&D Xtreme) ABDO Publishing Co.

Harrison, Paul. Uncovering Mummies & Other Mysteries of the Ancient World. 2010. (Extreme! Ser.). (ENG.). 32p. (gr. 3-4). pap. 47.70 *(978-1-4296-5117-2(2),* Fact Finders) Capstone Press of Coughlan Cos.

Hawass, Zahi. The Curse of the Pharaohs: My Adventures with Mummies. 2004. (ENG., Illus.). 160p. (J). (gr. 5). 29.90 *(978-0-7922-6963-2(2))*; 19.95 *(978-0-7922-6665-5(X))* National Geographic Society. (National Geographic Children's Bks.).

Keyes, Anna. Pharaohs, Pyramids Mummies & Faraones, pirámides y Momias: 6 English, 6 Spanish Adaptations. 2011. (ENG & SPA.). (J). 101.00 net. *(978-1-4108-5732-3(8))* Benchmark Education Co.

Knapp, Ron. Mummy Secrets Uncovered. 2011. (Bizarre Science Ser.). (Illus.). 48p. (J). (gr. 5-18). pap. 8.95 *(978-1-59845-222-8(3))*; lib. bdg. 25.27 *(978-0-7660-3670-3(7))* Enslow Pubs., Inc.

Knudsen, Shannon. I'M All Wrapped Up! - Meet a Mummy. Kurilla, Renee, illus. 2014. (Monster Buddies Ser.). (ENG.). 24p. (gr. k-2). lib. bdg. 23.93 *(978-0-7613-9188-3(6),* Millbrook Pr.) Lerner Publishing Group.

Krensky, Stephen. The Mummy. 2006. (Monster Chronicles Ser.). (Illus.). 48p. (J). (gr. 5-8). lib. bdg. 26.60 *(978-0-8225-5924-5(2),* Lerner Pubns.) Lerner Publishing Group.

Lace, William W. Mummification & Death Rituals of Ancient Egypt. 2012. (ENG., Illus.). 80p. (J). lib. bdg. *(978-1-60152-254-2(1))* ReferencePoint Pr., Inc.

MacDonald, Fiona. The Amazing History of Mummies & Tombs: Uncover the Secrets of the Egyptian Pyramids & Other Ancient Burial Sites, Shown in over 350 Exciting Pictures. 2016. (ENG., Illus.). 64p. (J). (gr. -1-12). 12.99 *(978-1-86147-735-4(X),* Armadillo) Anness Publishing GBR. Dist: National Bk. Network.

—The Egyptian Mummy. 2011. (History Detectives Ser.). (ENG.). 32p. (J). (gr. 4-7). spiral bd. 9.95 *(978-1-84898-186-7(4),* TickTock Books) Octopus Publishing Group GBR. Dist: Independent Pubs. Group.

MacDonald, Fiona & Millard, Anne. Mummies: Discover the Fascinating World of Mummies, Tombs, Mysterious Gods & Treasure Troves. 2010. (ENG., Illus.). 64p. (J). (gr. 4-7). pap. 12.99 *(978-1-84476-608-6(X))* Anness Publishing GBR. Dist: National Bk. Network.

Malam, John. Mummies. (Amazing History Ser.). (Illus.). (J). (gr. 2-6). 2009. 32p. pap. 7.95 *(978-1-59920-207-5(7))* 2008. pap. 28.50 *(978-1-59920-106-1(2))* Black Rabbit Bks.

—Mummies. 2010. (Remarkable Man & Beast Ser.). 48p. (J). (gr. 3-18). lib. bdg. 19.95 *(978-1-4222-1971-3(2))* Mason Crest.

—Mummies. 2015. (100 Facts You Should Know Ser.). (ENG., Illus.). 48p. (J). (gr. 4-5). lib. bdg. 31.95 *(978-1-4824-2177-4(1))* Stevens, Gareth Publishing LLLP.

Mason, Roger. Mummies - Mysteries of the Past. 2004. pap. 48.30 *(978-1-4109-0283-2(8))* Harcourt Schl. Pubs.

McCall, Henrietta. Egyptian Mummies. 2015. (ENG., Illus.). 32p. (J). pap. 9.95 *(978-1-910184-26-4(8))* RiverStream Publishing.

—Mummies. 2015. (Time Shift History Ser.). (Illus.). 32p. (gr. 3-6). 31.35 *(978-1-905638-41-3(8))* Book Hse. GBR. Dist: Black Rabbit Bks.

McNeil, Niki, et al. Egyptian Mummies. 2007. (In the Hands of a Child: Project Pack Continent Study Ser.). (Illus.). 52p. spiral bd. 12.50 *(978-1-60308-064-4(3))* In the Hands of a Child.

Momias. 2003. (Megabites Ser.). (SPA., Illus.). (J). pap. 8.95 *(978-0-9715256-6-5(8))* Planeta Publishing Corp.

Montgomery, Heather L. Mummies: Truth & Rumors. Doty, Eldon, illus. 2010. (Truth & Rumors Ser.). (ENG.). 32p. (gr. 3-4). lib. bdg. 27.99 *(978-1-4296-3950-7(4),* Edge Bks.) Capstone Press of Coughlan Cos.

Mummy Sticker Book. 2003. (Illus.). 16p. (J). 2.98 *(978-1-84273-122-2(X))* Parragon, Inc.

National Geographic Learning, National Geographic Learning. Secrets of the Mummies. 2005. (Reader's Workshop Ser.). (ENG.). (C). pap. 21.95 *(978-0-7362-2809-1(8))* National Geographic School Publishing, Inc.

O'Hearn, Michael. Zombies vs. Mummies: Clash of the Living Dead. Moffet, Patricia, illus. 2011. (Monster Wars Ser.). (ENG.). 32p. (gr. 3-4). pap. 47.70 *(978-1-4296-7268-9(4))*; lib. bdg. 27.99 *(978-1-4296-6520-9(3))* Capstone Press of Coughlan Cos. (Edge Bks.).

Ollhoff, Jim. Mummies, 1 vol. 2007. (World of Horror Ser.). (ENG.). 32p. (gr. 3-7). 27.07 *(978-1-59928-772-0(2)*, Abdo & Daughters) ABDO Publishing Co.

Orme, David. Mummies. 2007. (Trailblazers Ser.). (ENG., Illus.). 36p. pap. *(978-1-84167-427-8(3))* Ransom Publishing Ltd.

—Mummies. 2009. (Fact to Fiction Ser.). (Illus.). 36p. (J). 16.95 *(978-0-7569-9281-1(8))*; pap. 6.95 *(978-0-7891-7904-3(0))* Perfection Learning Corp.

Owen, Ruth. How to Make an Egyptian Mummy. 2015. (It's a Fact Ser.). (ENG.). 32p. (J). (gr. 3-6). lib. bdg. 26.60 *(978-1-909673-94-6(3))* Bearport Publishing Co., Inc.

Owings, Lisa. The Mummy's Curse. 2015. (Unexplained Mysteries Ser.). (ENG., Illus.). 24p. (J). (gr. 3-7). lib. bdg. 25.95 *(978-1-62617-203-6(X)*, Epic Bks.) Bellwether Media.

Rau, Dana Meachen. Mummies. 2010. (Bookworms Chapter Books: Surprising Science Ser.). 24p. (gr. 2-3). 22.79 *(978-0-7614-4869-3(1))* Marshall Cavendish Corp.

Shea, Therese. Mummies of Ancient Egypt. 2009. (Real Life Readers Ser.). 24p. (gr. 3-4). pap. 8.25 *(978-1-4358-0052-6(4)*, Rosen Classroom) Rosen Publishing Group, Inc., The.

Skillet, Helen. Mummies! Unwrapping the Secrets of Ancient Egypt. 2005. (YA). cd-rom *(978-1-4105-0411-1(5))* Johnston, Don Inc.

Sloan, Chris & Sloan, Christopher. Mummies: Tanned, Dried, Sealed, Drained, Frozen, Embalmed, Stuffed, Wrapped, & Smoked... & We're Dead Serious. 2010. (ENG., Illus.). 48p. (J). (gr. 3-7). 17.95 *(978-1-4263-0695-2(4)*, National Geographic Children's Bks.) National Geographic Society.

Sloan, Christopher. Mummies: Dried, Tanned, Sealed, Drained, Frozen, Embalmed, Stuffed, Wrapped, & Smoked... & We're Dead Serious. 2010. (ENG., Illus.). 48p. (J). (gr. 3-7). 26.90 *(978-1-4263-0696-9(2)*, National Geographic Children's Bks.) National Geographic Society.

Small, Cathleen. Mummies. 2016. (Creatures of Fantasy Ser.). (Illus.). 64p. (J). (gr. 6-6). 34.21 *(978-1-5026-1854-2(0))* Cavendish Square Publishing.

Stewart, David. Creepy Egyptian Mummies. 2010. (Top 10 Worst Ser.). (Illus.). 32p. (J). (gr. 3-6). (ENG.). pap. 10.50 *(978-1-4339-4080-4(9))*; lib. bdg. 26.60 *(978-1-4339-4079-8(5))* Stevens, Gareth Publishing LLLP. (Gareth Stevens Learning Library).

—You Wouldn't Want to... Be an Egyptian Mummy! Antram, David, illus. rev. ed. 2012. (ENG.). 32p. (J). lib. bdg. 29.00 *(978-0-531-27501-6(9))* Scholastic Library Publishing.

—You Wouldn't Want to Be an Egyptian Mummy! Disgusting Things You'd Rather Not Know. Antram, David, illus. rev. ed. 2012. (You Wouldn't Want to...: Ancient Civilization Ser.). (ENG.). 40p. (J). pap. 9.95 *(978-0-531-28026-3(8))* Scholastic Library Publishing.

Strom, Laura Layton. The Egyptian Science Gazette. 2008. (Illus.). 36p. (J). pap. *(978-0-531-18813-2(2))* Children's Pr., Ltd.

Taplin, Sam. Mummies & Pyramids. 2004. (Discovery Program Ser.). (Illus.). 48p. (J). pap. 8.95 *(978-0-7945-0317-8(9)*, Usborne); lib. bdg. 16.95 *(978-1-58086-479-4(1))* EDC Publishing.

Tieck, Sarah. Mummies, 1 vol. 2015. (ENG.). 32p. (J). *(978-1-62403-766-5(6))* ABDO Publishing Co.

Weakland, Mark Andrew & Collins, Terry Lee. Scooby Doo Unmasks the Truth Behind Mummies. 2016. (Illus.). 24p. (J). *(978-1-4062-8897-1(7))* Capstone Press of Coughlan Cos.

Wood, Alix. Mummification. Wood, Alix, illus. 2013. (Illus.). 32p. (J). (gr. 4-6). 26.60 *(978-1-4339-9588-0(3))*; pap. 63.00 *(978-1-4339-9590-3(5))*; pap. 10.50 *(978-1-4339-9589-7(1))* Stevens, Gareth Publishing LLLP.

Woog, Adam. Mummies. 2008. (Mysterious & Unknown Ser.). 104p. (YA). (gr. 7-12). lib. bdg. 25.95 *(978-1-60152-054-8(9))* ReferencePoint Pr., Inc.

MUMMIES—FICTION

Bosch, Pseudonymous. You Have to Stop This. (Secret Ser.: 5). (ENG.). (J). (gr. 3-7). 2012. 368p. pap. 8.99 *(978-0-316-07627-2(9))* 2011. 352p. 16.99 *(978-0-316-07626-5(0))* Little, Brown Bks. for Young Readers.

—You Have to Stop This. 2012. (Secret Ser.: 5). (J). lib. bdg. 18.45 *(978-0-606-26695-6(X)*, Turtleback) Turtleback Bks.

Bradman, Tony. The Mummy Family Find Fame. 2006. (Red Bananas Ser.). (ENG., Illus.). 48p. (J). (gr. -1-3). lib. bdg. *(978-0-7787-1076-9(9))* Crabtree Publishing Co.

—Surprise Party. Chatterton, Martin, illus. 2004. (Red Bananas Ser.). (ENG.). 48p. (J). (gr. k-2). pap. 5.99 *(978-1-4052-0756-0(6))* Egmont Bks., Ltd. GBR. Dist: Independent Pubs. Group.

Bradman, Tony & Chatterton, Martin. The Surprise Party. 2005. (Red Bananas Ser.). (ENG., Illus.). 48p. (J). (gr. 1-3). *(978-0-7787-1084-4(X))* Crabtree Publishing Co.

Branzei, Sylvia. Ickstory - Unraveling the Icky History of Mummies. Keely, Jack, illus. 2009. (Penguin Young Readers, Level 4 Ser.). (ENG.). 48p. (J). (gr. 3-4). mass mkt. 3.99 *(978-0-448-45033-9(X)*, Penguin Young Readers) Penguin Young Readers Group.

Brezenoff, Steve. The Mummy at Midnight. Prothero, Tiffany, illus. 2008. (Shade Bks.). (ENG.). 80p. (gr. 2-3). 25.32 *(978-1-4342-0797-5(8)*, Shade Bks.) Stone Arch Bks.

Bright, J. E. Savage Sands, 1 vol. Schoening, Dan, illus. 2011. (Green Lantern Ser.). (ENG.). 56p. (gr. 2-3). pap. 4.95 *(978-1-4342-3405-6(3))*; lib. bdg. 26.65 *(978-1-4342-2619-8(0))* Stone Arch Bks. (DC Super Heroes).

Bunting, Eve. Ballywhinney Girl. McCully, Emily Arnold, illus. 2012. (ENG.). 32p. (J). (gr. -1-3). 16.99 *(978-0-547-55843-1(0))* Houghton Mifflin Harcourt Publishing Co.

Chatterton, Martin & Bradman, Tony. The Surprise Party. Chatterton, Martin, illus. 2005. (Red Bananas Ser.). (ENG., Illus.). 48p. (J). lib. bdg. *(978-0-7787-1068-4(8))* Crabtree Publishing Co.

Classic Goosebumps & Stine, R. L. The Curse of the Mummy's Tomb. 2009. (Classic Goosebumps Ser.: 6). (ENG.). 160p. (J). (gr. 3-7). 6.99 *(978-0-545-03523-1(6)*, Scholastic Paperbacks) Scholastic, Inc.

Crimi, Carolyn. Where's My Mummy? Manders, John, illus. 2008. (ENG.). 32p. (J). (gr. -1-3). 15.99 *(978-0-7636-3196-3(5))* Candlewick Pr.

De Gieter, Lucien. The Evil Mummies. Spear, Luke, tr. from FRE. 2010. (Papyrus Ser.: 4). (ENG., Illus.). 46p. (J). (gr. 4-7). pap. 11.95 *(978-1-84918-027-6(X))* CineBook GBR. Dist: National Bk. Network.

Donbavand, Tommy. Claw of the Werewolf, Bk. 6. Cartoon Saloon Staff, illus. 2010. (Scream Street Ser.: 6). (ENG.). 128p. (J). (gr. 3-7). pap. 5.99 *(978-0-7636-4638-7(5))* Candlewick Pr.

—Claw of the Werewolf: Book 6, 1 vol. Cartoon Saloon, illus. 2012. (ENG.). 120p. (J). 24.21 *(978-1-59961-997-2(0)*, Chapter Bks.) Spotlight.

—Heart of the Mummy, Bk. 3. Cartoon Saloon Staff, illus. 2010. (Scream Street Ser.: 3). (ENG.). 128p. (J). (gr. 3-7). pap. 5.99 *(978-0-7636-4636-3(9))* Candlewick Pr.

—Heart of the Mummy: Book 3, 1 vol. Cartoon Saloon, illus. 2012. (ENG.). 120p. (J). 24.21 *(978-1-59961-994-1(6)*, Chapter Bks.) Spotlight.

—Skull of the Skeleton, Bk. 5. Cartoon Saloon Staff, illus. 2010. (Scream Street Ser.: 5). (ENG.). 128p. (J). (gr. 3-7). pap. 5.99 *(978-0-7636-4635-6(0))* Candlewick Pr.

—Skull of the Skeleton: Book 5, 1 vol. Cartoon Saloon, illus. 2012. (ENG.). 120p. (J). 24.21 *(978-1-59961-996-5(2)*, Chapter Bks.) Spotlight.

Duey, Kathleen. Time Soldiers - Mummy. Epstein, Eugene, illus. Gould, Robert, photos by. 2005. (Time Soldiers Ser.: 5). (ENG.). (J). (gr. k-2). 48p. 15.95 *(978-1-929945-50-4(7))*; 96p. per. 5.95 *(978-1-929945-57-3(4))* Big Guy Bks., Inc.

Ewert, Marcus. Mummy Cat. Brown, Lisa, illus. 2015. (ENG.). 48p. (J). (gr. 1-4). 16.99 *(978-0-544-34082-4(5)*, Clarion Bks.) Houghton Mifflin Harcourt Trade & Reference Pubs.

Feder, Jane. Spooky Friends. Downing, Julie, illus. 2013. (ENG.). 40p. (J). (gr. k-2). 16.99 *(978-0-545-47815-1(4)*, Scholastic Pr.) Scholastic, Inc.

—Spooky Friends, Level 2. Downing, Julie, illus. 2013. (Scholastic Reader Level 2 Ser.). (ENG.). 40p. (J). (gr. 1-2). pap. 3.99 *(978-0-545-47816-8(2)*, Scholastic Pr.) Scholastic, Inc.

Hawksley, Gerald. Mommies & Babies on the Farm. Calitri, Susan, illus. 2004. (J). bds. 11.99 *(978-1-890647-11-7(X))* TOMY International, Inc.

Howard, Lee. Scooby-Doo in Mummy Scares Best, 1 vol. 2016. (Scooby-Doo Comic Readers Ser.). (ENG.). 32p. (J). (gr. k-3). lib. bdg. 24.21 *(978-1-61479-455-4(3)*, Graphic Planet) Magic Wagon.

Howe, James. Howie Monroe & the Screaming Mummies of the Pharoah's Tomb II. 2004. (Tales from the House of Bunnicula Ser.). 112p. (J). (gr. 3-6). pap. 17.00 incl. audio *(978-1-4000-8635-1(3)*, Listening Library) Random Hse. Audio Publishing Group.

Jolley, Dan. Wrapped up in You. Nourigat, Natalie, illus. 2012. (My Boyfriend Is a Monster Ser.: 6). (ENG.). 128p. (YA). (gr. 7-12). pap. 9.95 *(978-0-8225-9425-3(0))*; lib. bdg. 29.27 *(978-0-7613-6856-4(6))* Lerner Publishing Group. (Graphic Universe™).

McBrier, Page. Abracadabra Tut. 2014. (ENG.). (J). pap. 9.99 *(978-0-9960794-0-2(8))* Palm Canyon Pr.

McCann, Jesse Leon. Scooby-Doo & Museum Madness, 1 vol. Duendes Del Sur Staff, illus. 2012. (Scooby-Doo! Set 2 Ser.: No. 2). (ENG.). 24p. (J). (gr. k-3). lib. bdg. 24.21 *(978-1-59961-867-8(2))* Spotlight.

Nesbit, Troy. The Indian Mummy Mystery, Vol. 2013. (Wilderness Mystery Ser.). (ENG., Illus.). 276p. (J). (gr. 3-7). pap. 12.95 *(978-1-58979-813-7(9))* Taylor Trade Publishing.

Night, P. J. Off the Wall. 2013. (You're Invited to a Creepover Ser.: 14). (ENG., Illus.). 160p. (J). (gr. 3-7). pap. 5.99 *(978-1-4424-7238-9(3)*, Simon Spotlight) Simon Spotlight.

O'Reilly, Sean. The Missing Mummy, 1 vol. Arcana Studio Staff, illus. 2012. (Mighty Mighty Monsters Ser.). (ENG.). 48p. (gr. 2-3). pap. 6.10 *(978-1-4342-4609-7(4))* Stone Arch Bks.

—The Missing Mummy, 1 vol. 2011. (Mighty Mighty Monsters Ser.). (ENG.). 48p. (gr. 2-3). lib. bdg. 23.99 *(978-1-4342-3218-2(2))* Stone Arch Bks.

Osborne, Mary Pope. Una Momia Al Amanecer. 2004. (Casa del Arbol Ser.: 3). (SPA.). (J). pap. 5.99 *(978-1-930332-51-5(3))* Lectorum Pubns., Inc.

—Una Momia en la Manana. 2003. (Magic Tree House Ser.: 3). (SPA.). (gr. 3-6). lib. bdg. 16.00 *(978-0-613-64609-3(6)*, Turtleback) Turtleback Bks.

—Mummies in the Morning. unabr. ed. 2004. (Magic Tree House Ser.: No. 3). 65p. (J). (gr. k-5). pap. 17.00 incl. audio *(978-0-8072-0332-3(7)*, Listening Library) Random Hse. Audio Publishing Group.

Pavanello, Roberto. King Tut's Grandmother, 1 vol. Zeni, Marco, tr. from ITA. Pisapia, Blasco & Brughera, Pamela, illus. 2012. (Echo & the Bat Pack Ser.). (ENG.). 128p. (gr. 2-3). 9.95 *(978-1-4342-4245-7(5))*; lib. bdg. 25.32 *(978-1-4342-3823-8(7)*, Echo & the Bat Pack) Stone Arch Bks.

Pekkalainen, Leena. Mummies, Monsters, & the Ship of Millions. 2017. (ENG., Illus.). 128p. pap. 18.95 **(978-977-416-851-2(8))** American Univ. in Cairo Pr.

Preller, James. Jigsaw Jones: the Case of the Mummy Mystery. 2017. (Jigsaw Jones Mysteries Ser.). (ENG., Illus.). 96p. (J). pap. 4.99 *(978-1-250-11082-4(3)*, 9781250110824) Feiwel & Friends.

Rex, Michael. Runaway Mummy: A Petrifying Parody. 2012. (ENG.). 32p. (J). (gr. -1-k). pap. 6.99 *(978-0-14-242121-5(9)*, Puffin Books) Penguin Young Readers Group.

—The Runaway Mummy: A Petrifying Parody. 2012. lib. bdg. 17.20 *(978-0-606-26086-2(2)*, Turtleback) Turtleback Bks.

Robbins, Trina. The Maltese Mummy. Page, Tyler, illus. 2011. (Chicagoland Detective Agency Ser.: 2). (ENG.). 64p. (gr. 4-8). 29.27 *(978-0-7613-4615-9(5))* Lerner Publishing Group.

Rogers, Kirsteen. Mummies & Pyramids: Internet-Linked. 2009. (Discovery Nature Ser.). 48p. (J). 6.99 *(978-0-7945-2239-1(4)*, Usborne) EDC Publishing.

Roy, Ron. The Missing Mummy. (A to Z Mystery Ser.: Vol. 13). (J). 11.32 *(978-0-7383-3465-3(0))* Booksource, The.

Schachner, Judy. Skippyjon Jones in Mummy Trouble. 2008. (Skippyjon Jones Ser.). (ENG.). 32p. (J). (gr. -1-k). pap. 6.99 *(978-0-14-241211-4(2)*, Puffin Books) Penguin Young Readers Group.

—Skippyjon Jones in Mummy Trouble. Schachner, Judy, illus. 2006. (Skippyjon Jones Ser.). (ENG., Illus.). 32p. (J). (gr. -1-k). 17.99 *(978-0-525-47754-9(3)*, Dutton Books for Young Readers) Penguin Young Readers Group.

—Skippyjon Jones in Mummy Trouble. 2009. (Skippyjon Jones Ser.). 17.00 *(978-1-60686-418-0(1))* Perfection Learning Corp.

Shreve, Steve. The Mummy: Or Another Great Use for Toilet Paper. 2010. (Adventures of Charlie Ser.). (Illus.). 32p. pap. *(978-0-237-54285-6(4))* Evans Brothers, Ltd.

Shultz, D. B. The World Adventures of Sahara the Mummy: The Magical Exploration of Ancient Egypt. 2012. 28p. pap. 17.99 *(978-1-4772-3310-8(5))* AuthorHouse.

Stilton, Geronimo. The Mummy with No Name. 2006. (Geronimo Stilton Ser.: 26). (ENG., Illus.). 128p. (J). (gr. 2-5). pap. 7.99 *(978-0-439-84117-7(8)*, Scholastic Paperbacks) Scholastic, Inc.

Stine, R. L. The Curse of the Mummy's Tomb. 2009. (Goosebumps Ser.: 6). lib. bdg. 17.20 *(978-0-606-00243-1(X)*, Turtleback) Turtleback Bks.

—Return of the Mummy. 2010. (Classic Goosebumps Ser.: 18). (ENG.). 160p. (J). (gr. 3-7). pap. 6.99 *(978-0-545-17794-8(4)*, Scholastic Paperbacks) Scholastic, Inc.

—Who's Your Mummy? 2009. (Goosebumps HorrorLand Ser.: No. 7). 160p. (J). pap. *(978-1-4071-0755-4(0))* Scholastic, Inc.

—Who's Your Mummy? 2009. (Goosebumps HorrorLand Ser.: 6). lib. bdg. 17.20 *(978-0-606-05328-0(X)*, Turtleback) Turtleback Bks.

Stoker, Bram. Mummy, 1 vol. Miroglio, Brian, illus. 2007. (Graphic Horror Ser.). (ENG.). 32p. (gr. 3-7). 28.50 *(978-1-60270-061-1(3)*, Graphic Planet- Fiction) ABDO Publishing Co.

Troupe, Thomas Kingsley. The Misplaced Mummy, 1 vol. Gilpin, Stephen, illus. 2014. (Furry & Flo Ser.). (ENG.). 128p. (gr. 2-3). 25.32 *(978-1-4342-6396-4(7))* Stone Arch Bks.

Voskuil, Hannah. Horus & the Curse of Everlasting Regret. 2016. (ENG.). 224p. (J). (gr. 3-7). 16.99 *(978-1-101-93333-6(X)*, Knopf Bks. for Young Readers) Random Hse. Children's Bks.

Widmark, Martin. The Mummy Mystery. Willis, Helena, illus. 2015. (Whodunit Detective Agency Ser.: 5). (ENG.). 80p. (J). (gr. 2-4). 5.99 *(978-0-448-48074-9(3)*, Grosset & Dunlap) Penguin Young Readers Group.

MUMPS

Colligan, L. H. Measles & Mumps. 2010. (Health Alert 7 Ser.). (Illus.). 64p. (J). (gr. 4-7). 32.79 *(978-0-7614-4819-8(5))* Marshall Cavendish Corp.

Hecht, Alan. Mumps. 2011. (Deadly Diseases & Epidemics Ser.). (J). 34.95 *(978-1-61753-019-7(0)*, Chelsea Hse.) Facts On File, Inc.

MUNICH (GERMANY)

Dyan, Penelope. The Big Clock! a Kid's Guide to Munich, Germany. Weigand, John D., photos by. 2013. (Illus.). 34p. pap. 11.95 *(978-1-61477-080-0(8))* Bellissima Publishing, LLC.

Sasek, M. This Is Munich. 2012. (ENG., Illus.). 64p. (J). (gr. k-12). 17.95 *(978-0-7893-2426-9(1))* Universe Publishing.

Sonneborn, Liz. Murder at the 1972 Olympics in Munich. 2009. (Terrorist Attacks Ser.). 64p. (gr. 5-5). 58.50 *(978-1-60853-308-4(5))* Rosen Publishing Group, Inc., The.

MUNICIPAL ADMINISTRATION

see Municipal Government

MUNICIPAL EMPLOYEES

see Civil Service; Municipal Government

MUNICIPAL ENGINEERING

see also Refuse and Refuse Disposal; Water-Supply

Porter, Esther. Peeking under the City. Lozano, Andres, illus. 2016. (What's Beneath Ser.). (ENG.). 32p. (gr. -1-3). lib. bdg. 27.32 *(978-1-4795-8665-3(X))* Picture Window Bks.

Ringstad, Arnold. Sewer Inspector. 2015. (Gross Jobs Ser.). (ENG.). 24p. (J). (gr. 2-5). 27.07 *(978-1-63143-691-8(0)*, 208526) Child's World, Inc., The.

MUNICIPAL GOVERNMENT

see also Cities and Towns; Public Administration

Attebury, Nancy Garhan. Out & about at City Hall. Trover, Zachary, illus. 2005. (Field Trips Ser.). (ENG.). 24p. (gr. -1-3). lib. bdg. 27.32 *(978-1-4048-1146-1(X))* Picture Window Bks.

Bozzo, Linda & Library. Community Helpers of the Past, Present, & Future. 2010. (Imagining the Future Ser.). (Illus.). 24p. (J). lib. bdg. 22.60 *(978-0-7660-3435-8(6)*, Enslow Elementary) Enslow Pubs., Inc.

Cuthbert, Megan & Siemens, Jared. City Hall. 2016. (J). **(978-1-5105-1881-0(9))** SmartBook Media, Inc.

Edwards, Clint. Show Me Community Helpers: My First Picture Encyclopedia, 1 vol. 2013. (My First Picture Encyclopedias Ser.). (ENG.). 32p. (gr. 1-2). 7.95 *(978-1-62065-918-2(2))*; lib. bdg. 27.32 *(978-1-62065-056-1(8))* Capstone Press of Coughlan Cos.

Goldsworthy, Steve. Municipal Government. 2010. (Illus.). 32p. *(978-1-55388-679-2(8))*; pap. *(978-1-55388-683-9(6))* Weigl Educational Pubs. Ltd.

Manning, Jack. The City Mayor, 1 vol. 2014. (Our Government Ser.). (ENG.). 24p. (gr. 1-2). 25.32 *(978-1-4914-0336-5(5)*, First Facts) Capstone Press of Coughlan Cos.

Muschal, Frank. Local Action. 2007. (21st Century Skills Library: Citizens & Their Governments Ser.). (ENG., Illus.). 32p. (gr. 4-8). lib. bdg. 28.50 *(978-1-60279-061-2(2)*, 200007) Cherry Lake Publishing.

Raatma, Lucia. Working at City Hall. 2011. (21st Century Junior Library: Careers Ser.). (ENG.). 24p. (gr. 2-5). lib. bdg. 25.64 *(978-1-60279-981-3(4)*, 200952) Cherry Lake Publishing.

Silate, Jennifer. Your Mayor: Local Government in Action. 2009. (Primary Source Library of American Citizenship Ser.). 32p. (gr. 5-5). 47.90 *(978-1-61511-237-1(5)*, Rosen Reference) Rosen Publishing Group, Inc., The.

MUNICIPALITIES

see Cities and Towns; Municipal Government

MUNITIONS

see Military Weapons

MUNOZ MARIN, LUIS, 1898-1980

Ebon Research Systems Staff. Dare to Be Vol. 4: Luis Munoz Marion. l.t. ed. 2003.Tr. of Atrevete Ser... Un Heroe Luis Munoz Marin. (ENG & SPA., Illus.). 14p. (J). 3.99 *(978-0-9648313-7-7(6))* Ebon Research Systems Publishing, LLC.

MURAL PAINTING AND DECORATION

see Cave Paintings; Mosaics

MURDER

see also Assassination

Allman, Toney. The Homicide Detective. 2009. (Crime Scene Investigations Ser.). (ENG., Illus.). 128p. (YA). (gr. 7-12). 35.45 *(978-1-4205-0109-4(7))* Cengage Gale.

—Poisoning. 2008. (Crime Scene Investigations Ser.). (ENG., Illus.). 128p. (gr. 7-10). lib. bdg. 40.40 *(978-1-4205-0064-6(3)*, LML02109-241678, Lucent Bks.) Cengage Gale.

Alphin, Elaine. An Unspeakable Crime: The Prosecution & Persecution of Leo Frank. 2014. (ENG., Illus.). 152p. (gr. 9-12). pap. 9.95 *(978-1-4677-4630-4(4)*, Carolrhoda Bks.) Lerner Publishing Group.

Anniss, Matt. Cold Cases. 2013. (Crime Science Ser.). (Illus.). 48p. (J). (gr. 4-8). pap. 14.05 *(978-1-4339-9477-7(1))*; pap. 84.30 *(978-1-4339-9478-4(X))*; (ENG., lib. bdg. 31.95 *(978-1-4339-9476-0(3))* Stevens, Gareth Publishing LLLP.

Dicker, Katie. Unsolved Crimes. 2015. (Mystery! Ser.). 24p. (gr. 3-6). 28.50 *(978-1-62588-205-9(X))* Black Rabbit Bks.

Faryon, Cynthia J. Real Justice: Guilty of Being Weird: The Story of Guy Paul Morin, 1 vol. 2012. (Lorimer Real Justice Ser.). (ENG., Illus.). 144p. (YA). (gr. 8-12). 18.95 *(978-1-4594-0093-1(3)*, 9781459400931); pap. 12.95 *(978-1-4594-0092-4(5)*, 9781459400924) Lorimer, James & Co., Ltd., Pubs. CAN. Dist: Casemate Pubs. & Bk. Distributors, LLC.

—Sentenced to Life at Seventeen: The Story of David Milgaard, 1 vol. 2012. (Lorimer Real Justice Ser.). (ENG., Illus.). 120p. (J). (gr. 8-12). 18.95 *(978-1-4594-0169-3(7)*, 9781459401693) Lorimer, James & Co., Ltd., Pubs. CAN. Dist: Casemate Pubs. & Bk. Distributors, LLC.

Heing, Bridey. Investigating Mass Shootings in the United States. 2017. (Terrorism in the 21st Century: Causes & Effects Ser.). 64p. (gr. 12-11). lib. bdg. 34.45 **(978-1-5081-7462-2(8)**, Rosen Young Adult) Rosen Publishing Group, Inc., The.

Heits, Rudolph T. Mass Murderers. 2013. (J). 34.98 *(978-1-61900-034-6(2))* Eldorado Ink.

Hinton, Kerry. The Trial of Sacco & Vanzetti: A Primary Source Account. 2009. (Great Trials of the Twentieth Century Ser.). 64p. (gr. 5-8). 58.50 *(978-1-61513-220-1(1))* Rosen Publishing Group, Inc., The.

Hoblin, Paul. The Boston Strangler, 1 vol. 2012. (Unsolved Mysteries (el) Ser.). (ENG.). 112p. (J). (gr. 6-12). lib. bdg. 35.64 *(978-1-61783-299-4(5)*, Essential Library) ABDO Publishing Co.

Houser, Aimee. Tragedy in Tucson: The Arizona Shooting Rampage, 1 vol. 2012. (Essential Events Set 8 Ser.). (ENG.). 112p. (J). (gr. 6-12). lib. bdg. 35.64 *(978-1-61783-312-0(6))* ABDO Publishing Co.

Innes, Brian. Serial Murders, Vol. 20. Gomez, Manny, ed. 2016. (Crime & Detection Ser.). (Illus.). 96p. (J). (gr. 7). 24.95 *(978-1-4222-3486-0(X))* Mason Crest.

Joyce, Jaime. Going Ballistic: Who Pulled the Trigger in a Gangland Massacre? 2011. (J). pap. *(978-0-545-32801-2(2))* Scholastic, Inc.

Latta, Sara L. Medical Serial Killers. 2016. (Psychology of Serial Killers Ser.). (ENG.). 128p. (J). (gr. 9-9). lib. bdg. 37.27 *(978-0-7660-7296-1(7))* Enslow Pubs., Inc.

Loker, Aleck. The Murder of Joseph Henry Ching: A Legend Examined. 2003. (Illus.). 28p. 6.00 *(978-1-928874-04-1(5))* Solitude Pr.

Miller, Sarah. The Borden Murders: Lizzie Borden & the Trial of the Century. 2016. (ENG., Illus.). 304p. (J). (gr. 5). 17.99 *(978-0-553-49808-0(8)*, Schwartz & Wade Bks.) Random Hse. Children's Bks.

Mitchell, Jeff. Young, Innocent & in Prison: The Story of Robert Baltovich, 1 vol. 2012. (Lorimer Real Justice Ser.). (ENG., Illus.). 128p. (YA). (gr. 8-12). 18.95 *(978-1-4594-0079-5(8)*, 9781459400795); pap. 12.95 *(978-1-4594-0078-8(X)*, 9781459400788) Lorimer, James & Co., Ltd., Pubs. CAN. Dist: Casemate Pubs. & Bk. Distributors, LLC.

Newton, Michael. Serial Killers. 2008. (Criminal Investigations Ser.). (Illus.). 120p. (J). (gr. 9-12). 35.00 *(978-0-7910-9411-2(1)*, Chelsea Hse.) Facts On File, Inc.

Orr, Tamra. Murder. 2008. (Man's Inhumanities Ser.). (YA). (gr. 7-12). 23.95 *(978-1-60217-977-6(8))* Erickson Pr.

Rogers, Kate. The Zodiac Killer: Terror in California. 2017. (J). **(978-1-5345-6085-7(8))** Greenhaven Publishing LLC.

Royston, Angela. Homicide. 2013. (Crime Science Ser.). (Illus.). 48p. (J). (gr. 4-8). pap. 14.05 *(978-1-4339-9493-7(3)*, 1358485); pap. 84.30 *(978-1-4339-9494-4(1)*, 1358485); (ENG., lib. bdg. 31.95 *(978-1-4339-9492-0(5)*, 1358485) Stevens, Gareth Publishing LLLP.

Schauer, Peter J. The People Behind Cult Murders. 2016. (Psychology of Mass Murderers Ser.). (Illus.). 144p. (J). (gr. 8-8). 37.27 *(978-0-7660-7610-5(5))* Enslow Pubs., Inc.

Stewart, Gail B. Cold Cases. Gale Editors, ed. 2010. (Crime Scene Investigations Ser.). (ENG.). 128p. (YA). (gr. 7-12). 35.45 *(978-1-4205-0323-4(5))* Cengage Gale.

Swan, Bill. Fourteen & Sentenced to Death: The Story of Steven Truscott, 1 vol. 2012. (Lorimer Real Justice Ser.). (ENG., Illus.). 152p. (YA). (gr. 8-12). 18.95 *(978-1-4594-0075-7(5)*, 9781459400757); pap. 12.95 *(978-1-4594-0074-0(7)*, 9781459400740) Lorimer, James & Co., Ltd., Pubs. CAN. Dist: Casemate Pubs. & Bk. Distributors, LLC.

Townsend, John. Unsolved Crimes. 2010. (Amazing Mysteries Ser.). (YA). (gr. 3-6). 28.50 *(978-1-59920-367-6(7))* Black Rabbit Bks.

Wolf, Allan. Who Killed Christopher Goodman? 2017. (ENG.). 288p. (YA). (gr. 9). 16.99 *(978-0-7636-5613-3(5))* Candlewick Pr.

Worth, Richard. Massacre at Virginia Tech: Disaster & Survival. 2008. (Deadly Disasters Ser.). (Illus.). 48p. (J). (gr. 5-9). lib. bdg. 25.27 *(978-0-7660-3274-3(4))* Enslow Pubs., Inc.

Wright, Simeon & Boyd, Herb. Simeon's Story: An Eyewitness Account of the Kidnapping of Emmett Till. 2011. (ENG.).

MNO

160p. (J). (gr. 7). pap. 12.95 (978-1-56976-819-8(6), Hill, Lawrence Bks.) Chicago Review Pr., Inc.

Yancey, Diane. Murder. 2006. (Crime Scene Investigations Ser.). (ENG., Illus.). 128p. (gr. 7-12). lib. bdg. 40.40 (978-1-59018-619-0(2)) Cengage Gale.

—The Zodiac Killer. 2008. (Crime Scene Investigations Ser.). (Illus.). 112p. (YA). (gr. 7-10). lib. bdg. 35.45 (978-1-4205-0063-9(5), LML02109-240733, Lucent Bks.) Cengage Gale.

MURDER—FICTION

Abrahams, Peter. Down the Rabbit Hole. 2006. (Echo Falls Mystery Ser.: 1). (ENG.). 448p. (J). (gr. 5-9). reprint ed. pap. 7.99 (978-0-06-073703-0(4)) HarperCollins Pubs.

—Into the Dark. 2009. (Echo Falls Mystery Ser.: 3). (ENG.). 352p. (J). (gr. 5-18). pap. 6.99 (978-0-06-073710-8(7)) HarperCollins Pubs.

Adler, Irene. The Dark Lady, 1 vol. Bruno, Iacopo, illus. 2014. (Sherlock, Lupin, & Me Ser.). (ENG.). 240p. (gr. 4-8). 12.95 (978-1-62370-040-9(X)) Capstone Young Readers of Coughlan Cos.

—The Mystery of the Scarlet Rose. McGuinness, Nanette, tr. from ITA. Bruno, Iacopo, illus. 2015. (Sherlock, Lupin, & Me Ser.). (ENG.). 256p. (gr. 4-8). lib. bdg. 26.65 (978-1-4342-6524-1(2)) Stone Arch Bks.

—The Soprano's Last Song, 1 vol. Iacopo, Bruno & Bruno, Iacopo, illus. 2014. (Sherlock, Lupin, & Me Ser.). (ENG.). 240p. (gr. 4-8). lib. bdg. 26.65 (978-1-4342-6522-7(6)) Stone Arch Bks.

Ahdieh, Renée. The Wrath & the Dawn. 2016. (Wrath & the Dawn Ser.). (ENG.). 432p. (YA). (gr. 7). pap. 10.99 (978-0-14-751385-4(5), Speak) Penguin Young Readers Group.

—The Wrath & the Dawn. 2016. lib. bdg. 22.10 (978-0-606-38849-8(4)) Turtleback Bks.

Ahdieh, Renée & McPike, Elizabeth. The Wrath & the Dawn. 2015. (Wrath & the Dawn Ser.). (ENG., Illus.). 416p. (YA). (gr. 7). 17.99 (978-0-399-17161-1(4), G.P. Putnam's Sons Books for Young Readers) Penguin Young Readers Group.

Alderson, Sarah. The Sound. 2014. (ENG., Illus.). 320p. (YA). (gr. 9). 17.99 (978-1-4424-9933-1(8), Simon Pulse) Simon Pulse.

Alender, Katie. Marie Antoinette, Serial Killer. 2014. (ENG.). 304p. (J). (gr. 7). pap. 9.99 (978-0-545-46810-7(8), Scholastic Paperbacks) Scholastic, Inc.

Alphin, Elaine Marie. Counterfeit Son. 2010. (ENG., Illus.). 192p. (YA). (gr. 9). pap. 7.99 (978-0-547-25853-9(4)) Houghton Mifflin Harcourt Publishing Co.

—The Perfect Shot. (Carolrhoda YA Ser.). (ENG.). 360p. (YA). (gr. 6-12). 2011. pap. 9.95 (978-0-7613-8138-9(4), Carolrhoda Lab™) 2005. 16.95 (978-1-57505-862-7(6), Carolrhoda Bks.) Lerner Publishing Group.

Anderson, Jennifer. Spider. 2013. 174p. pap. 10.99 (978-1-62237-146-4(1)) Turquoise Morning Pr.

Anderson, Natalie C. City of Saints & Thieves. 2017. (ENG.). 432p. (YA). (gr. 7). 18.99 (978-0-399-54758-4(4), G.P. Putnam's Sons Books for Young Readers) Penguin Young Readers Group.

Anderson, R. J. A Little Taste of Poison. 2016. (ENG., Illus.). 368p. (J). (gr. 4-7). 17.99 (978-1-4814-3774-5(7), Atheneum Bks. for Young Readers) Simon & Schuster Children's Publishing.

—A Pocket Full of Murder. 2015. (ENG., Illus.). 352p. (J). (gr. 4-7). 18.99 (978-1-4814-3771-4(2)) Simon & Schuster Children's Publishing.

Armstrong, Robert. Buyer Beware. 2016. (ENG.). 94p. (YA). (gr. 10-12). 10.95 (978-1-78554-474-3(8), c9488c0c-967c-408f-abd6-01a587eaeb62) Austin, Stan AUS. Dist: Bookmasters Distribution.

Avasthi, Swati. Chasing Shadows. Phillips, Craig, illus. 2015. (ENG.). 336p. (YA). (gr. 9). pap. 10.99 (978-0-375-86343-1(5), Ember) Random Hse. Children's Bks.

Axelrod, Amy & Axelrod, David. The Bullet Catch. 2015. (ENG.). 320p. (J). (gr. 5-9). 17.95 (978-0-8234-2858-8(3)) Holiday Hse., Inc.

Ballantyne, R. M. Blown to Bits; or, the Lonely Man of Rak. 2006. pap. (978-1-4065-0515-3(3)) Dodo Pr.

Ballesteros, Jason. Sideways. 2010. 145p. pap. 14.72 (978-0-557-28699-7(9)) Lulu Pr., Inc.

Baratz-Logsted, Lauren. The Twin's Daughter. (ENG.). (YA). 2014. 416p. (gr. 7-12). pap. 9.99 (978-1-59990-661-4(9), 9781599906614) 2010. 400p. (gr. 9-12). 16.99 (978-1-59990-513-6(2), 9781599905136) Bloomsbury Publishing USA. (Bloomsbury USA Childrens).

Barnes, Jennifer Lynn. All in. 2015. (Naturals Ser.: Bk. 3). (ENG.). 384p. (YA). (gr. 7-12). 17.99 (978-1-4847-1643-4(4)) Hyperion Bks. for Children.

Barrett, Jennifer. Lethal Delivery, Postage Prepaid. (Thumbprint Mysteries Ser.). 32.86 (978-0-8092-0425-0(8)) McGraw-Hill/Contemporary.

Berk, Josh. The Dark Days of Hamburger Halpin. 2011. (ENG.). 258p. (YA). (gr. 7). pap. 8.99 (978-0-375-84625-0(5), Ember) Random Hse. Children's Bks.

—Strike Three, You're Dead. 2014. (Lenny & the Mikes Ser.). (ENG.). 272p. (J). (gr. 3-7). 6.99 (978-0-307-93006-4(8), Yearling) Random Hse. Children's Bks.

Bick, Ilsa J. The Sin-Eater's Confession. Élyum Studio, illus. 2014. (ENG.). 296p. (YA). (gr. 9-12). pap. 9.95 (978-1-4677-3705-0(4), Carolrhoda Lab™) Lerner Publishing Group.

—The Sin-Eater's Confession. 2013. (ENG.). 296p. (YA). (gr. 9-12). 17.95 (978-0-7613-5687-5(8)) Lerner Publishing Group.

Blundell, Judy. Strings Attached. (ENG.). 320p. (J). (gr. 7). 2012. pap. 9.99 (978-0-545-22127-6(7), Scholastic Paperbacks) 2011. 17.99 (978-0-545-22126-9(9), Scholastic Pr.) Scholastic, Inc.

Boaz, Ashley. The Mystery of the Midnight Blaze. 2005. (J). (978-0-9761033-6-3(2)) Waldenhouse Pubs., Inc.

Bowler, Tim. Playing Dead. 2010. (Blade Ser.: 1). (ENG.). 256p. (YA). (gr. 9-18). 7.99 (978-0-14-241600-6(2), Speak) Penguin Young Readers Group.

Brambles, Lindsay. Becoming Darkness. 2015. (ENG.). 496p. 17.95 (978-1-63079-017-2(6)) Switch Pr.

Bray, Libba. The Diviners. 2012. 578p. (YA). 9.99 (978-0-316-23242-5(4)) Little Brown & Co.

—The Diviners. (Diviners Ser.: 1). (ENG.). (YA). (gr. 10-17). 2013. 496p. pap. 12.99 (978-0-316-12610-6(1)) 2012. 800p. 42.99 (978-0-316-22426-0(X)) Little, Brown Bks. for Young Readers.

—The Diviners. 2013. (Diviners Ser.: 1). (YA). lib. bdg. 24.50 (978-0-606-32284-3(1), Turtleback) Turtleback Bks.

Brewer, Amy J. The Mystery of Murder. 2012. 28p. pap. 16.95 (978-1-62709-595-2(0)) America Star Bks.

Brian, Kate. Shadowlands. 2013. (Shadowlands Ser.). (ENG.). 352p. (YA). (gr. 9-17). pap. 9.99 (978-1-4231-6525-5(X)) Hyperion Pr.

Brian, Kate, pseud. Ambition. 2008. (Private Ser.: No. 7). (ENG.). 288p. (YA). (gr. 9-18). pap. 12.99 (978-1-4169-5882-6(7), Simon & Schuster Bks. For Young Readers) Simon & Schuster Bks. For Young Readers.

—Confessions. 2009. (Private Ser.: No. 4). (ENG.). 240p. (YA). pap. 9.99 (978-1-4169-9949-2(3), Simon & Schuster Bks. For Young Readers) Simon & Schuster Bks. For Young Readers.

—Last Christmas: The Private Prequel. 2010. (Private Ser.). (ENG.). 288p. (YA). (gr. 9). pap. 9.99 (978-1-4169-1370-2(X), Simon & Schuster Bks. For Young Readers) Simon & Schuster Bks. For Young Readers.

—Ominous. 2011. (Private Ser.). (ENG.). 224p. (YA). (gr. 9-18). pap. 9.99 (978-1-4169-8472-6(0), Simon & Schuster Bks. For Young Readers) Simon & Schuster Bks. For Young Readers.

—Privilege. 2008. (Privilege Ser.: No. 1). (ENG.). 304p. (YA). (gr. 9-18). pap. 9.99 (978-1-4169-6759-0(1), Simon & Schuster Bks. For Young Readers) Simon & Schuster Bks. For Young Readers.

Bryant, Clive, ed. Sweeney Todd: The Demon Barber of Fleet Street. Shalvey, Declan et al, illus. 2012. (ENG.). 176p. pap. 16.95 (978-1-907127-10-6(0), Classical Comics, Ltd.); pap. 16.95 (978-1-907127-09-0(7), Classical Comics, Ltd.); (gr. 9). lib. bdg. 24.95 (978-1-907127-82-3(8)) Classical Comics GBR. Dist: Publishers Group West (PGW).

Bunce, Elizabeth C. Liar's Moon. 2011. (YA). pap. (978-0-545-13607-5(5)); (ENG.). 368p. (J). (gr. 7-7). 17.99 (978-0-545-13608-2(3)) Scholastic, Inc. (Levine, Arthur A. Bks.).

Burke, Morgan. Get It Started. 2010. (Party Room Ser.: 1). (ENG.). 272p. (J). (gr. 11). pap. 12.99 (978-1-4424-1420-4(0), Simon Pulse) Simon Pulse.

Butcher, Kristin. Return to Bone Tree Hill. 2009. (ENG.). 176p. (J). pap. 12.95 (978-1-897235-58-4(5)) Thistledown Pr., Ltd. CAN. Dist: Univ. of Toronto Pr.

Byars, Betsy. Death's Door. 2006. (Herculeah Jones Mystery Ser.). (ENG.). 144p. (J). (gr. 3-7). 6.99 (978-0-14-240565-9(5), Puffin Books) Penguin Young Readers Group.

—Tarot Says Beware. 2006. (Herculeah Jones Mystery Ser.). 151p. (gr. 3-7). 16.00 (978-0-7569-6737-6(6)) Perfection Learning Corp.

Cabot, Meg. Safe House - Sanctuary. 2011. (Vanished Ser.: Bks. 3 & 4). (ENG.). 512p. (YA). (gr. 7). pap. 12.99 (978-1-4424-0631-5(3), Simon Pulse) Simon Pulse.

Caletti, Deb. The Queen of Everything. Greenberg, Anne, ed. 2008. (ENG.). 352p. (YA). (gr. 7-12). pap. 8.99 (978-1-4169-5781-2(2), Simon Pulse) Simon Pulse.

Carey, Anna. Blackbird. 2014. (Blackbird Ser.: 1). (ENG.). 256p. (YA). (gr. 9). 17.99 (978-0-06-229973-4(5), HarperTeen) HarperCollins Pubs.

—Blackbird. 2015. (SPA.). 240p. (YA). (gr. 9-12). pap. 17.99 (978-987-612-909-1(0)) Lectorum Pubns., Inc.

—Deadfall. 2015. 256p. (J). pap. (978-0-06-242788-5(1)) HarperCollins Pubs.

—Deadfall: The Sequel to Blackbird. 2015. (Blackbird Ser.: 2). (ENG.). 256p. (YA). (gr. 9). 17.99 (978-0-06-229976-5(X), HarperTeen) HarperCollins Pubs.

Carey, Benedict. Poison Most Vial: A Mystery. 2012. (ENG.). 240p. (J). (gr. 3-7). 17.95 (978-1-4197-0031-6(6), Amulet Bks.) Abrams, Inc.

Carroll, Jenny, pseud. Safe House. 2011. (1-800-Where-R-You Ser.: 3). (ENG.). 272p. (YA). (gr. 9). pap. 12.99 (978-1-4424-3084-6(2), Simon Pulse) Simon Pulse.

Carroll, Jenny, pseud & Cabot, Meg. Darkest Hour. 2004. (Mediator Ser.: 4). (ENG.). 336p. (YA). (gr. 8-18). pap. 7.99 (978-0-06-072514-3(1), HarperTeen) HarperCollins Pubs.

Carter, Ally. All Fall Down. 2015. (Embassy Row Ser.: 1). (ENG.). 320p. (J). (gr. 7). 17.99 (978-0-545-65474-6(2), Scholastic Pr.) Scholastic, Inc.

—See How They Run (Embassy Row, Book 2) 2015. (Embassy Row Ser.: 2). (ENG.). 336p. (J). (gr. 7). 17.99 (978-0-545-65484-5(X), Scholastic Pr.) Scholastic, Inc.

—Take the Key & Lock Her Up. 2016. (Embassy Row Ser.: 3). (ENG.). 336p. (J). (gr. 7). 17.99 (978-0-545-65495-1(5), Scholastic Pr.) Scholastic, Inc.

Cassidy, Anne. Innocent. 2014. (ENG.). 192p. (YA). (gr. 7). pap. 8.99 (978-0-340-88200-9(X)) Hodder & Stoughton GBR. Dist: Hachette Bk. Group.

—Looking for JJ. 2009. (ENG., Illus.). 336p. (J). (gr. 7). pap. 20.95 (978-0-15-206638-3(1)) Houghton Mifflin Harcourt Publishing Co.

Cavallaro, Brittany. A Study in Charlotte. 2016. (Charlotte Holmes Novel Ser.: 1). 336p. (YA). (gr. 8). 17.99 (978-0-06-239890-1(3), Tegen, Katherine Bks) HarperCollins Pubs.

Chadwick, Robert. Vengeful Impulse. 2003. 70p. pap. 8.95 (978-0-595-27876-3(0)) iUniverse, Inc.

Chandler, Elizabeth. The Back Door of Midnight. 2010. (Dark Secrets Ser.: Vol. 5). (ENG.). 320p. (YA). (gr. 7-18). pap. 9.99 (978-1-4424-0626-1(7), Simon Pulse) Simon Pulse.

—Everlasting. (Kissed by an Angel Ser.). (ENG.). (YA). (gr. 7). 2013. 336p. pap. 9.99 (978-1-4424-0917-0(7)) 2012. 320p. 16.99 (978-1-4424-0921-7(5)) Simon Pulse. (Simon Pulse).

Chee, Traci. The Reader. (Sea of Ink & Gold Ser.: 1). (ENG.). 464p. (YA). (gr. 7). 2017. pap. 10.99 **(978-0-14-751805-7(9)**, Speak)Bk. 1. 2016. 19.99 (978-0-399-17677-7(2), G.P. Putnam's Sons Books for Young Readers) Penguin Young Readers Group.

—The Reader. 2017. (Sea of Ink & Gold Ser.: 1). lib. bdg. 22.10 **(978-0-606-40001-5(X))** Turtleback Bks.

Chima, Cinda Williams. The Sorcerer Heir. 2016. (Heir Chronicles Ser.). (ENG.). 560p. (J). (gr. 5-9). pap. 9.99 (978-1-4231-9475-0(6)) Hyperion Bks. for Children.

Choyce, Lesley. Rat, 1 vol. 2012. (Orca Soundings Ser.). (ENG.). 128p. (YA). (gr. 8-12). pap. 9.95 (978-1-4598-0300-8(0)); lib. bdg. 16.95 (978-1-4598-0301-5(9)) Orca Bk. Pubs. USA.

Clark, Melissa. Bear Witness: A Novel. 2015. (ENG.). 118p. pap. 13.00 (978-1-940716-75-6(6)) SparkPr. (a Bks.parks Imprint).

Coben, Harlan. Found. 2014. (Mickey Bolitar Novel Ser.: 3). (ENG.). 336p. (YA). (gr. 7). 18.99 (978-0-399-25652-3(0), G.P. Putnam's Sons Books for Young Readers) Penguin Young Readers Group.

—Seconds Away. (Mickey Bolitar Novel Ser.: 2). (ENG.). (YA). (gr. 7). 2012. 352p. 18.99 (978-0-399-25651-6(2), G.P. Putnam's Sons Books for Young Readers)Bk. 2. 2013. 368p. pap. 9.99 (978-0-14-242635-7(0), Speak) Penguin Young Readers Group.

—Seconds Away. l.t. ed. 2012. (Mickey Bolitar Ser.: 2). (ENG.). 396p. 23.99 (978-1-4104-5348-8(0)) Thorndike Pr.

—Seconds Away. 2013. (Mickey Bolitar Ser.: 2). lib. bdg. 20.85 (978-0-606-32141-9(1), Turtleback) Turtleback Bks.

Collins, Amberly & Collins, Brandilyn. Final Touch, 1 vol. 2010. (Rayne Tour Ser.). (ENG.). 224p. (YA). (gr. 8-11). pap. 9.99 (978-0-310-71933-5(X)) Zondervan.

Cooney, Caroline B. Enter Three Witches: A Story of Macbeth. l.t. ed. 2007. (Thorndike Literacy Bridge Young Adult Ser.). 343p. (YA). (gr. 8-12). 22.95 (978-0-7862-9889-1(8)) Thorndike Pr.

—No Such Person. (ENG.). 256p. (YA). (gr. 7). 2016. pap. 9.99 (978-0-385-74292-4(4), Ember) 2015. 17.99 (978-0-385-74291-7(6), Delacorte Pr.) 2015. lib. bdg. 20.99 (978-0-375-99084-7(4), Delacorte Pr.) Random Hse. Children's Bks.

Cooney, Caroline B. & Shakespeare, William. Enter Three Witches: A Story of Macbeth. 2007. 281p. (YA). pap. (978-0-545-01972-9(9)) Scholastic, Inc.

Cormier, Robert. Tenderness. 2004. 229p. 19.00 (978-0-7569-3636-5(5)) Perfection Learning Corp.

Cosimano, Elle & Carey, Janet Lee. Nearly Found. 2015. (Nearly Boswell Mysteries Ser.). (ENG.). 384p. (YA). (gr. 7-12). 17.99 (978-0-8037-3927-7(3), Kathy Dawson Books) Penguin Young Readers Group.

Crawford, Ann Fears. Keechee: The Witch of the Woods. 2005. (J). (978-1-931823-21-0(9)) Halcyon Pr.

Cray, Jordan. Shiver. 2009. (Danger. com Ser.: 9). (ENG.). 224p. (YA). (gr. 7). pap. 10.99 (978-1-4169-9853-2(5), Simon Pulse) Simon Pulse.

Cusick, Richie Tankersley. Starstruck. 2013. (ENG., Illus.). 240p. (YA). (gr. 7). pap. 15.99 (978-1-4814-0161-6(0), Simon Pulse) Simon Pulse.

Dawson, James. Hollow Pike. 2012. (ENG.). 320p. (YA). (gr. 7-17). 8.99 (978-1-78062-128-9(0), Orion Children's Bks.) Hachette Children's Group GBR. Dist: Hachette Bk. Group.

Dekker, James. Scum, 1 vol. 2008. (Orca Soundings Ser.). (ENG.). 112p. (YA). (gr. 8-12). pap. 9.95 (978-1-55143-924-2(7)) Orca Bk. Pubs. USA.

Dekker, James C. Scum, 1 vol. 2008. (Orca Soundings Ser.). (ENG.). 112p. (YA). (gr. 8-12). 16.95 (978-1-55143-926-6(3)) Orca Bk. Pubs. USA.

Derting, Kimberly. Body Finder. 2011. (Body Finder Ser.: 1). (ENG.). 352p. (YA). (gr. 9). pap. 9.99 (978-0-06-177983-1(0)) HarperCollins Pubs.

—Desires of the Dead. 2012. (Body Finder Ser.: 2). (ENG.). 384p. (YA). (gr. 9). pap. 8.99 (978-0-06-177986-2(5)) HarperCollins Pubs.

Devine, Eric. Look Past. 2016. (ENG.). 288p. (YA). (gr. 2-17). 16.95 (978-0-7624-5921-6(2), Running Pr. Kids) Running Pr. Bk. Pubs.

Devlin, Ivy. Low Red Moon. 2010. (ENG., Illus.). 256p. (YA). (gr. 7-18). 16.99 (978-1-59990-510-5(8), 9781599905105, Bloomsbury USA Childrens) Bloomsbury Publishing USA.

Dix, Catherine R. Rosetta Stones. 2009. (ENG.). 213p. pap. 14.95 (978-0-9798452-2-2(X)) Central Ave. Pr.

Dixon, Franklin W. Top Ten Ways to Die. 2006. 169p. (J). lib. bdg. 16.92 (978-1-4242-0390-1(2)) Fitzgerald Bks.

Dockter, Debra. Deadly Design. 2015. (ENG.). 368p. (YA). (gr. 7). 17.99 (978-0-399-17105-5(3), G.P. Putnam's Sons Books for Young Readers) Penguin Young Readers Group.

Doherty, Patrick. Cold Waves, Cold Blood. Warner, Christopher, ed. Struntz, D. J., photos by. 2015. (Illus.). 146p. (YA). (gr. 9-12). pap. 11.95 (978-0-9963756-3-4(5)) All About Kids Publishing.

Doller, Trish. The Devil You Know. 2015. (ENG.). 256p. (YA). (gr. 9). 17.99 (978-1-61963-416-9(3), 9781619634169, Bloomsbury USA Childrens) Bloomsbury Publishing USA.

Donnelly, Jennifer. A Northern Light. 2004. (ENG.). 416p. (YA). (gr. 9-12). reprint ed. pap. 9.99 (978-0-15-205310-9(7)) Houghton Mifflin Harcourt Publishing Co.

—A Northern Light. 2004. 396p. (gr. 9-12). 20.00 (978-0-7569-3614-3(4)) Perfection Learning Corp.

Dunlap, Susanne. The Musician's Daughter. (ENG.). (YA). (gr. 7). 2010. 352p. pap. 8.99 (978-1-59990-452-8(7), 9781599904528) 2009. 336p. 16.99 (978-1-59990-332-3(6), 9781599903323) Bloomsbury Publishing USA. (Bloomsbury USA Childrens).

Dunn, Pintip. Before Tomorrow. 2016. (ENG., Illus.). (YA). pap. 12.99 **(978-1-68281-336-2(3))** Entangled Publishing, LLC.

Durango, Julia. Sea of the Dead. 2009. (ENG.). 144p. (J). (gr. 3-7). 16.99 (978-1-4169-5778-2(2), Simon & Schuster Bks. For Young Readers) Simon & Schuster Bks. For Young Readers.

Efaw, Amy. After. 2010. (ENG.). 368p. (YA). (gr. 7-18). 8.99 (978-0-14-241590-0(1), Speak) Penguin Young Readers Group.

Electric Chair or Taser Fried: Malicious Murder; Good Cop, Bad Cop. 2004. (YA). per. 25.00 (978-0-9760909-0-8(2)) Yost-Haynes, Melissa.

Ellis, Kat. Breaker. 2016. (ENG.). 336p. (YA). (gr. 2-17). pap. 9.95 (978-0-7624-5908-7(5), Running Pr. Kids) Running Pr. Bk. Pubs.

Elston, Ashley. The Rules for Breaking. 2014. (Rules Ser.). (ENG.). 320p. (YA). (gr. 7-12). 16.99 (978-1-4231-6898-0(4)) Hyperion Bks. for Children.

Epstein, Robin. Hear. 2015. (ENG., Illus.). 272p. (YA). (gr. 9). 18.99 (978-1-61695-581-6(3), Soho Teen) Soho Pr., Inc.

Ewell, Katherine. Dear Killer. 2014. (ENG.). 368p. (YA). (gr. 8). 17.99 (978-0-06-225780-2(3)) HarperCollins Pubs.

Fahy, Thomas. Sleepless. 2010. (ENG.). 224p. (YA). (gr. 7). pap. 8.99 (978-1-4169-5902-1(5), Simon & Schuster Bks. For Young Readers) Simon & Schuster Bks. For Young Readers.

—The Unspoken. 2008. (ENG.). 176p. (YA). (gr. 7-18). 15.99 (978-1-4169-4007-4(3), Simon & Schuster Bks. For Young Readers) Simon & Schuster Bks. For Young Readers.

—The Unspoken. 2009. (ENG.). 256p. (YA). (gr. 7). mass mkt. 6.99 (978-1-4169-4008-1(1), Simon Pulse) Simon Pulse.

Fahy, Thomas Richard & Fahy, Thomas. Sleepless. 2009. (ENG.). 224p. (YA). (gr. 7-18). 15.99 (978-1-4169-5901-4(7), Simon & Schuster Bks. For Young Readers) Simon & Schuster Bks. For Young Readers.

Fama, Elizabeth. Monstrous Beauty. 2013. (ENG.). 352p. (YA). (gr. 7-12). pap. 9.99 (978-1-250-03425-0(6)) Square Fish.

Fantaskey, Beth. Jekel Loves Hyde. 2011. (ENG.). 288p. (YA). (gr. 9). pap. 8.99 (978-0-547-55027-5(8)) Houghton Mifflin Harcourt Publishing Co.

Ferguson, Alane. The Angel of Death. 2008. (Forensic Mystery Ser.). 258p. 17.00 (978-0-7569-8929-3(9)) Perfection Learning Corp.

Fiore, Kelly. Thicker Than Water. 2016. 320p. (YA). (gr. 9). 17.99 (978-0-06-232473-3(X), HarperTeen) HarperCollins Pubs.

Fisher, Linda C. A Will of Her Own. 2006. (YA). pap. (978-0-88092-641-6(4)); lib. bdg. (978-0-88092-640-9(6)) Royal Fireworks Publishing Co.

Flinn, Alex. Nothing to Lose. 2005. (ENG.). 304p. (YA). (gr. 9-12). pap. 8.99 (978-0-06-051752-6(2), HarperTeen) HarperCollins Pubs.

Forrest. Sign of Blood. (Thumbprint Mysteries Ser.). 32.86 (978-0-8092-0408-3(8)) McGraw-Hill/Contemporary.

Fredericks, Mariah. The Girl in the Park. 2013. (ENG.). 224p. (YA). (gr. 9). pap. 8.99 (978-0-449-81591-5(9), Ember) Random Hse. Children's Bks.

Frost, Heather. Guardians. 2013. (Seers - Trilogy Ser.: Vol. 3). (ENG.). 424p. (J). (gr. 8-12). pap. 17.99 (978-1-4621-1035-3(5), Sweetwater Bks.) Cedar Fort, Inc./CFI Distribution.

Giles, Gail. Right Behind You. 2008. (ENG.). 320p. (J). (gr. 10-17). pap. 10.99 (978-0-316-16637-9(5)) Little, Brown Bks. for Young Readers.

Girard, Geoffrey. Project Cain. 2013. (ENG., Illus.). 368p. (YA). (gr. 9). 17.99 (978-1-4424-7696-7(6), Simon & Schuster Bks. For Young Readers) Simon & Schuster Bks. For Young Readers.

Godfrey. Murder in the Shadows. (Thumbprint Mysteries Ser.). 32.86 (978-0-8092-0418-2(5)) McGraw-Hill/Contemporary.

Gonzalez, Christina Diaz. Moving Target. (ENG.). 256p. (J). (gr. 3-7). 2016. pap. 6.99 (978-0-545-77319-5(9)) 2015. 17.99 (978-0-545-77318-8(0)) Scholastic, Inc. (Scholastic Pr.).

Goodwin, Vincent. Moonlit Road, 1 vol. 2014. (Graphic Horror Set 3 Ser.). (ENG.). 32p. (J). (gr. 5-8). lib. bdg. 28.50 (978-1-62402-016-2(X), Graphic Planet) Magic Wagon.

Grabenstein, Chris. The Black Heart Crypt. 2012. (Haunted Mystery Ser.: 4). (ENG.). 336p. (J). (gr. 3-7). 7.99 (978-0-375-87301-0(5), Yearling) Random Hse. Children's Bks.

Gratz, Alan. Something Rotten. 2009. (ENG.). 224p. (YA). (gr. 7-18). 7.99 (978-0-14-241297-8(X), Puffin Books) Penguin Young Readers Group.

—Something Wicked. 2009. (ENG.). 288p. (YA). (gr. 7-18). 7.99 (978-0-14-241496-5(4), Puffin Books) Penguin Young Readers Group.

Gray, Clio. Peder & the Skincatcher. 2013. 188p. (J). pap. (978-1-78299-157-1(3)) FeedARead.com.

Gray, Keith. Ghosting. 2012. (Stoke Books Titles Ser.). (ENG.). 72p. (YA). (gr. 8-12). pap. 6.95 (978-1-78112-103-0(6)); lib. bdg. 22.60 (978-1-78112-104-7(4)) Lerner Publishing Group.

Green, Jacqueline. Secrets & Lies. 2014. (Truth or Dare Ser.: 2). (ENG.). 336p. (YA). (gr. 10-17). pap. 21.99 (978-0-316-22030-9(2), Poppy) Little, Brown Bks. for Young Readers.

Green, Ken. Not a Chance. (Thumbprint Mysteries Ser.). 32.86 (978-0-8092-0422-9(3)) McGraw-Hill/Contemporary.

Green, Risa. Projection. 2014. (ENG., Illus.). 286p. (YA). (gr. 9). pap. 9.99 (978-1-61695-454-3(X), Soho Teen) Soho Pr., Inc.

Grisham, John. Kid Lawyer. (Theodore Boone Ser.: 1). (ENG.). (J). (gr. 3-7). 2011. 288p. 8.99 (978-0-14-241722-5(X), Puffin Books) 2010. 272p. 16.99 (978-0-525-42384-3(2), Dutton Books for Young Readers) Penguin Young Readers Group.

—Kid Lawyer. l.t. ed. 2010. (Theodore Boone Ser.: Bk. 1). (ENG.). 278p. (J). 24.99 (978-1-4104-3050-2(2)) Thorndike Pr.

—Kid Lawyer. 2011. (Theodore Boone Ser.: 1). lib. bdg. 19.65 (978-0-606-23071-1(8), Turtleback) Turtleback Bks.

Groot, De. Black Moon. Spear, Luke, tr. from FRE. Rodrigue, illus. 2007. (Clifton Ser.: 4). (ENG.). 48p. (J). (gr. 4-7). pap. 9.99 (978-1-905460-30-4(9)) CineBook GBR. Dist: National Bk. Network.

Haas, Abigail. Dangerous Girls. (ENG., Illus.). 400p. (YA). (gr. 9). 2014. pap. 10.99 (978-1-4424-8660-7(0)) 2013. 16.99 (978-1-4424-8659-1(7)) Simon Pulse. (Simon Pulse).

Hahn, Mary Downing. Closed for the Season. 2010. (ENG.). 192p. (J). (gr. 5-7). pap. 6.99 (978-0-547-39853-2(0)) Houghton Mifflin Harcourt Publishing Co.

—Mister Death's Blue-Eyed Girls. (ENG.). 336p. (YA). (gr. 7). 2012. 16.99 (978-0-547-76062-9(0)) 2013. pap. 8.99 (978-0-544-02224-9(6)) Houghton Mifflin Harcourt Publishing Co.

Hainsworth, Emily. Take the Fall. 2016. 368p. (YA). (gr. 9). 17.99 (978-0-06-209422-3(X)) HarperCollins Pubs.

Hale, Kathleen. No One Else Can Have You. 2014. (Kippy Bushman Ser.). (ENG.). 384p. (YA). (gr. 9). 17.99 (978-0-06-221119-4(6)) HarperCollins Pubs.

Hammel, Sara. The Underdogs. 2016. (ENG.). 320p. (J). 16.99 (978-0-374-30161-3(1), 9780374301613, Farrar, Straus & Giroux (BYR)) Farrar, Straus & Giroux.

—The Underdogs. 2017. (J). lib. bdg. 18.40 **(978-0-606-39936-4(4))** Turtleback Bks.

Handwerk, Marina. Hey Cool, I've Never Seen a Teacher with His Head Cut off Before! 2007. 284p. per. 11.95 (978-1-4327-0332-5(3)) Outskirts Pr., Inc.

Hansen, Lynne & Bosco, Sally. AltDeath.com. 2004. 152p. (YA). pap. 9.00 (978-0-7599-4572-2(1)) Hard Shell Word Factory.

Harrington, K. A. Forget Me. 2014. (ENG.). 288p. (YA). (gr. 7). 17.99 (978-0-399-16529-0(0), G.P. Putnam's Sons Books for Young Readers) Penguin Young Readers Group.

Harrington, Kim. Clarity. (ENG.). 256p. (J). (gr. 9-9). 2012. pap. 8.99 (978-0-545-23051-3(9)) 2011. 16.99 (978-0-545-23050-6(0)) Scholastic, Inc.

—The Dead & Buried. 2013. (ENG.). 304p. (J). (gr. 7). 17.99 (978-0-545-33302-3(4)) Scholastic, Inc.

Hathaway, Jill. Slide. (Slide Ser.: 1). (ENG.). (YA). (gr. 9). 2013. 272p. pap. 9.99 (978-0-06-207796-7(1)) 2012. 256p. 17.99 (978-0-06-207790-5(2)) HarperCollins Pubs.

Henderson, Lauren. Kiss Me Kill Me. 2009. (ENG.). 272p. (YA). (gr. 9). pap. 8.99 (978-0-385-73488-2(3), Delacorte Pr.) Random Hse. Children's Bks.

Henn, Pamela. Nick & Slim: The Legend of the Falcon Mine. 2006. (Illus.). 472p. (YA). 19.95 (978-0-9760654-0-1(1)) White Wolf Studio, Inc.

Henry, April. Blood Will Tell. 2015. (Point Last Seen Ser.: 2). (ENG.). 272p. (YA). (gr. 7). 17.99 (978-0-8050-9853-2(4), 9780805098532, Holt, Henry & Co. Bks. For Young Readers) Holt, Henry & Co.

—The Body in the Woods. 2014. (Point Last Seen Ser.: 1). (ENG.). 272p. (YA). (gr. 7). 17.99 (978-0-8050-9852-5(6), 9780805098525, Holt, Henry & Co. Bks. For Young Readers) Holt, Henry & Co.

—The Girl I Used to Be. 2016. (ENG., Illus.). 240p. (YA). 17.99 (978-1-62779-332-2(1), 9781627793322, Holt, Henry & Co. Bks. For Young Readers) Holt, Henry & Co.

Herren, Greg. Sleeping Angel. 2011. (ENG.). 288p. (J). (gr. 7). pap. 13.95 (978-1-60282-214-6(X)) Bold Strokes Bks.

Herrick, Steven. Cold Skin. 2009. (ENG.). 279p. (YA). (gr. 9-18). 18.95 (978-1-59078-572-0(X), Front Street) Boyds Mills Pr.

Hill, William. Department Nineteen. 2012. (Department Nineteen Ser.: 1). (ENG.). 544p. (YA). (gr. 9). 9.99 (978-1-59514-485-0(4), Razorbill) Penguin Young Readers Group.

Hodkin, Michelle. The Retribution of Mara Dyer. 2014. (Mara Dyer Trilogy: Vol. 3). (ENG., Illus.). 480p. (YA). (gr. 9). 18.99 (978-1-4424-8423-8(3), Simon & Schuster Bks. For Young Readers) Simon & Schuster Bks. For Young Readers.

—The Unbecoming of Mara Dyer. (Mara Dyer Trilogy Ser.: 1). (ENG., Illus.). (YA). (gr. 9). 2012. 480p. pap. 12.99 (978-1-4424-2177-6(0)) 2011. 464p. 21.99 (978-1-4424-2176-9(2)) Simon & Schuster Bks. For Young Readers. (Simon & Schuster Bks. For Young Readers).

Hoffman, Mary. The Falconer's Knot: A Story of Friars, Flirtation & Foul Play. (ENG., Illus.). 304p. (YA). (gr. 7). 2008. pap. 7.99 (978-1-59990-229-6(X), 9781599902296) 2007. 16.95 (978-1-59990-056-8(4), 9781599900568) Bloomsbury Publishing USA. (Bloomsbury USA Childrens).

Hofmeyr, Dianne. Eye of the Moon. 2011. (ENG.). 336p. (J). (gr. 3-7). pap. 9.99 (978-1-4424-1188-3(0), Aladdin) Simon & Schuster Children's Publishing.

Hounam, Donald. A Dangerous Magic. 2017. (ENG.). 352p. (YA). (gr. 5-12). 17.99 **(978-1-5124-3232-9(6))** Lerner Publishing Group.

Ireland, Justina. Promise of Shadows. 2014. (ENG., Illus.). 384p. (YA). (gr. 9). 17.99 (978-1-4424-4464-5(9), Simon & Schuster Bks. For Young Readers) Simon & Schuster Bks. For Young Readers.

—Vengeance Bound. 2013. (ENG.). 320p. (YA). (gr. 9). 17.99 (978-1-4424-4462-1(2), Simon & Schuster Bks. For Young Readers) Simon & Schuster Bks. For Young Readers.

Jablonski, Carla. The Travelers, Bk. 1. 2009. (Pendragon: Before the War Ser.: 1). (ENG.). 256p. (J). (gr. 5-9). pap. 7.99 (978-1-4169-6522-0(X), Aladdin) Simon & Schuster Children's Publishing.

Johnson, Alaya Dawn. Detective Frankenstein. Ota, Yuko, illus. 2011. (Twisted Journeys Ser.: 17). (ENG.). 112p. (J). (gr. 4-7). pap. 45.32 (978-0-7613-7613-2(5)); pap. 7.95 (978-0-8225-8943-3(5)); lib. bdg. 27.93 (978-0-8225-8942-6(7)) Lerner Publishing Group. (Graphic Universe™).

Johnson, Maureen. The Madness Underneath. 2013. (Shades of London Ser.: 2). (ENG.). 304p. (YA). (gr. 7). pap. 9.99 (978-0-14-242754-5(3), Speak) Penguin Young Readers Group.

—The Name of the Star. (Shades of London Ser.: 1). (ENG.). (YA). (gr. 7). 2012. 400p. pap. 10.99 (978-0-14-242205-2(3), Speak) 2011. 368p. 16.99 (978-0-399-25660-8(1), G.P. Putnam's Sons Books for Young Readers) Penguin Young Readers Group.

Jones, Rob Lloyd. Wild Boy: The Real Life of the Savage of Aveyron. 2013. (ENG.). 304p. (J). (gr. 5). 16.99 (978-0-7636-6252-3(6)) Candlewick Pr.

Jordan, Sophie. Uninvited. (Uninvited Ser.: 1). (ENG.). (YA). (gr. 8). 2015. 400p. pap. 9.99 (978-0-06-223364-6(5)) 2014. 384p. 17.99 (978-0-06-223365-3(3)) HarperCollins Pubs. (HarperTeen).

Jude, Sarah. The May Queen Murders. 2016. (ENG.). 304p. (YA). (gr. 9). 17.99 (978-0-544-64041-2(1), HMH Books For Young Readers) Houghton Mifflin Harcourt Publishing Co.

Kam, Jennifer Wolf. Devin Rhodes Is Dead. 2014. (YA). (ENG.). 240p. (gr. 7). 16.95 (978-1-934133-59-0(0), Mackinac Island Press, Inc.); 228p. (978-1-60734-706-4(7)) Charlesbridge Publishing, Inc.

Khan, Joshua. Shadow Magic. Hibon, Ben, illus. 2016. (ENG.). 336p. (J). (gr. 3-7). 16.99 (978-1-4847-3272-4(3)) Hyperion Bks. for Children.

Kittscher, Kristen. The Tiara on the Terrace. 2016. 400p. (J). (gr. 3-7). 16.99 (978-0-06-222798-0(X)) HarperCollins Pubs.

Kollar, J. P. Three Tomato Brand. 2005. 127p. per. 12.95 (978-1-59879-076-4(5)) Lifevest Publishing, Inc.

Kraus, Daniel. The Death & Life of Zebulon Finch Vol. 2: Empire Decayed. 2016. (Zebulon Finch Ser.: 2). (ENG., Illus.). 784p. (YA). (gr. 9). 19.99 (978-1-4814-1142-4(X), Simon & Schuster Bks. For Young Readers) Simon & Schuster Bks. For Young Readers.

Kunze, Nansi. Kill the Music. l.t. ed. 2013. 330p. pap. (978-1-4596-6983-3(5)) ReadHowYouWant.com, Ltd.

Kyi, Tanya Lloyd. Truth. 2003. (YA). (gr. 7-18). pap. 7.95 (978-1-55143-235-9(8)) Orca Bk. Pubs. USA.

—Truth. 2004. (Orca Soundings Ser.). 108p. 19.95 (978-0-7569-4346-2(9)) Perfection Learning Corp.

Lane, Andrew. Black Ice. 2013. (Sherlock Holmes: the Legend Begins Ser.: 3). (ENG.). 288p. (YA). (gr. 7-12). 17.99 (978-0-374-38769-3(9), 9780374387693, Farrar, Straus & Giroux (BYR)) Farrar, Straus & Giroux.

—Black Ice. 2013. (Sherlock Holmes: the Legend Begins Ser.: 3). (ENG.). 304p. (YA). (gr. 7-12). pap. 11.99 (978-1-250-03654-4(2), 9781250036544) Square Fish.

—Death Cloud. 2012. (ENG.). (YA). (gr. 7-12). 64.99 (978-1-4272-2800-0(0)) Findaway World, LLC.

—Death Cloud. 2011. (Sherlock Holmes: the Legend Begins Ser.: 1). (ENG.). 336p. (YA). (gr. 7-12). pap. 10.99 (978-0-312-56371-4(X), 9780312563714) Square Fish.

—Death Cloud. l.t. ed. 2011. (Young Sherlock Holmes Ser.). 367p. 23.99 (978-1-4104-3971-0(2)) Thorndike Pr.

—Death Cloud. 2011. (Sherlock Holmes: the Legend Begins Ser.: 1). (YA). lib. bdg. 22.10 (978-0-606-23781-9(X), Turtleback) Turtleback Bks.

Latham, Jennifer. Dreamland Burning. 2017.Tr. of s. (ENG.). 384p. (YA). (gr. 9-17). 18.99 (978-0-316-38493-3(3)) Little, Brown Bks. for Young Readers.

Lawrence, Caroline. The Assassins of Rome. 2005. (Roman Mysteries Ser.). (Illus.). 161p. (J). (gr. 3-7). 14.65 (978-0-7569-5879-4(2)) Perfection Learning Corp.

—The Fugitive from Corinth. 2006. (ENG., Illus.). 240p. (gr. 7-9). pap. 10.99 (978-1-84255-515-6(4), Orion Children's Bks.) Hachette Children's Group GBR. Dist: Hachette Bk. Group.

Lee, Y. S. The Body at the Tower. 2010. (Agency Ser.: 2). (ENG., Illus.). 352p. (YA). (gr. 7-18). 16.99 (978-0-7636-4968-5(6)) Candlewick Pr.

—Rivals in the City. 2015. (Agency Ser.). (ENG.). 304p. (YA). (gr. 7). 16.99 (978-0-7636-5914-1(2)) Candlewick Pr.

—The Traitor in the Tunnel. 2012. (Agency Ser.: 3). (ENG., Illus.). 384p. (YA). (gr. 7). 16.99 (978-0-7636-5316-3(0)) Candlewick Pr.

Leonard, Julia Platt. Cold Case. Mauro, Tony, illus. 2011. (ENG.). 288p. (J). (gr. 3-7). 15.99 (978-1-4424-2009-0(X), Simon & Schuster/Paula Wiseman Bks.) Simon & Schuster/Paula Wiseman Bks.

Leonard, Niall. Crusher. 2013. (ENG.). 368p. (YA). (gr. 9). pap. 9.99 (978-0-385-74362-4(9), Ember) Random Hse. Children's Bks.

Lester, Julius. When Dad Killed Mom. 2003. (YA). (gr. 7-12). mass mkt. 6.95 (978-0-15-524698-0(4), Silver Whistle) Harcourt Trade Pubs.

—When Dad Killed Mom. 2003. (ENG.). 216p. (YA). (gr. 7-12). pap. 13.95 (978-0-15-204698-9(4)) Houghton Mifflin Harcourt Publishing Co.

Lindsey, Julie Anne. Deceived. 2013. (ENG.). 320p. (YA). 17.99 (978-1-4405-6389-8(6), Simon Pulse) Simon Pulse.

—Reinventing Chloe. 2013. 278p. pap. 13.99 (978-1-62237-152-5(6)) Turquoise Morning Pr.

Ludwig, Elisa. Pretty Wanted. 2015. (Pretty Crooked Trilogy Ser.: 3). (ENG.). 336p. (YA). (gr. 8). 17.99 (978-0-06-206612-1(9), Tegen, Katherine Bks) HarperCollins Pubs.

Lyga, Barry. I Hunt Killers. (ENG.). (YA). (gr. 10-17). 2014. 464p. mass mkt. 8.00 (978-0-316-28363-2(0)) 2013. 384p. pap. 10.00 (978-0-316-12583-3(0)) Little, Brown Bks. for Young Readers.

MacColl, Michaela. The Revelation of Louisa May. 2015. (ENG.). 272p. (J). (gr. 7-12). 16.99 (978-1-4521-3357-7(3)) Chronicle Bks. LLC.

MacGregor, Roy. Murder at the Winter Games, No. 18. 2004. (Screech Owls Ser.: No. 18). (ENG., Illus.). 128p. (YA). mass mkt. 4.95 (978-0-7710-5647-5(8), Screech Owls) McClelland & Stewart CAN. Dist: Penguin Random Hse. LLC.

MacGregor, Roy & MacGregor, Roy. The Complete Screech Owls, Vol. 4. 2006. (Complete Screech Owls Ser.). (ENG.). 488p. (J). (gr. 3-7). per. 15.95 (978-0-7710-5491-4(2), Screech Owls) McClelland & Stewart CAN. Dist: Penguin Random Hse. LLC.

Mackall, Dandi Daley. The Silence of Murder. 2012. (ENG.). 336p. (YA). (gr. 9). pap. 9.99 (978-0-375-87293-8(0), Ember) Random Hse. Children's Bks.

Maniscalco, Kerri. Stalking Jack the Ripper. (ENG., Illus.). (YA). (gr. 10-17). 2017. 352p. pap. 10.99 **(978-0-316-27351-0(1))** 2016. 336p. 18.99 (978-0-316-27349-7(X)) 2016. 464p. 20.99 (978-0-316-46428-4(7)) Little Brown & Co. (Jimmy Patterson).

Marsden, John. Hamlet. 2009. (ENG., Illus.). 240p. (YA). (gr. 9-18). 16.99 (978-0-7636-4451-2(X)) Candlewick Pr.

Mason, Simon. Running Girl. 2016. (ENG.). 432p. (J). (gr. 9). 18.99 (978-1-338-03642-8(4)) Scholastic, Inc.

Matthews. Death in the Desert. (Thumbprint Mysteries Ser.). 32.86 (978-0-8092-0416-8(9)) McGraw-Hill/Contemporary.

Maxwell, Susan. Good Red Herring. Simpson, Steve, illus. 2016. (ENG.). 304p. (YA). (gr. 7). pap. 12.99 (978-1-908195-93-7(2)) Little Island IRL. Dist: Independent Pubs. Group.

McCaughrean, Geraldine. Stories from Shakespeare. 2017. (ENG.). 176p. (J). (gr. 4-6). pap. 7.99 **(978-1-5101-0145-6(4)**, Orion Children's Bks.) Hachette Children's Group GBR. Dist: Hachette Bk. Group.

McClintock, Norah. Bang, 1 vol. 2007. (Orca Soundings Ser.). (ENG.). 112p. (YA). (gr. 8-12). per. 9.95 (978-1-55143-654-8(X)) Orca Bk. Pubs. USA.

—Change of Heart. 2013. (Robyn Hunter Mysteries Ser.: 7). (ENG.). 224p. (YA). (gr. 6-12). pap. 8.95 (978-1-4677-0701-5(5)); lib. bdg. 27.93 (978-0-7613-8317-8(4)) Lerner Publishing Group.

—Dead & Gone. 2014. (Mike & Riel Mysteries Ser.: No. 3). 224p. (YA). (gr. 6-12). lib. bdg. 27.93 (978-1-4677-2607-8(9)); (ENG.). pap. 8.95 (978-1-4677-2615-3(X)) Lerner Publishing Group. (Darby Creek).

—Dead Silence. 2014. (Mike & Riel Mysteries Ser.: No. 5). 240p. (YA). (gr. 6-12). lib. bdg. 27.93 (978-1-4677-2609-2(5)); (ENG.). pap. 8.95 (978-1-4677-2619-1(2)) Lerner Publishing Group. (Darby Creek).

—Guilty, 1 vol. 2012. (ENG.). 224p. (YA). (gr. 8-12). pap. 12.95 (978-1-55469-989-6(4)) Orca Bk. Pubs. USA.

—I, Witness, 1 vol. Deas, Mike, illus. 2012. (ENG.). 144p. (YA). (gr. 8-12). pap. 16.95 (978-1-55469-789-2(1)) Orca Bk. Pubs. USA.

—Tell. 2007. (Orca Soundings Ser.). 100p. (gr. 4-7). 19.95 (978-0-7569-8069-6(0)) Perfection Learning Corp.

—Truth & Lies. 2014. (Mike & Riel Mysteries Ser.: 2). (ENG.). 216p. (YA). (gr. 6-12). pap. 8.95 (978-1-4677-2613-9(3), Darby Creek) Lerner Publishing Group.

McDaniel, Lurlene. Raina's Story. 2006. (Angels in Pink Ser.). (ENG.). 208p. (YA). (gr. 7-12). mass mkt. 6.99 (978-0-440-23866-9(8), Laurel Leaf) Random Hse. Children's Bks.

McGill, Nichole. Girl #3. 2009. (ENG.). 224p. (YA). (gr. 7-18). pap. (978-1-55470-143-8(0)) Me to We.

McGowan, Anthony. The Knife That Killed Me. 2011. (ENG.). 224p. (YA). (gr. 9). pap. 8.99 (978-0-375-85516-0(5), Ember) Random Hse. Children's Bks.

McIntosh, Kenneth. Close-Up: Forensic Photography. 2009. (J). pap. 24.95 (978-1-4222-1455-8(9)) Mason Crest.

—Close-Up: Forensic Photography, 5 vols. Sanborn, Casey, illus. 2007. (Crime Scene Club Ser.: Bk. 5). 144p. (YA). (gr. 9-12). lib. bdg. 24.95 (978-1-4222-0251-7(8)) Mason Crest.

McKissack, Jenny & McKissack, Jennifer. Sanctuary. 2015. (ENG.). 320p. (J). (gr. 7). 17.99 (978-0-545-58758-7(1), Scholastic Pr.) Scholastic, Inc.

McManus, Karen M. One of Us Is Lying. 2017. (ENG.). 368p. (YA). (gr. 9). 17.99 **(978-1-5247-1468-0(2))**; lib. bdg. 20.99 **(978-1-5247-1469-7(0))** Random Hse. Children's Bks. (Delacorte Pr.).

McNamee, Graham. Defender. 2016. (ENG.). 240p. (YA). (gr. 9). 17.99 (978-0-553-49895-0(9), Lamb, Wendy Bks.) Random Hse. Children's Bks.

McNeil, Gretchen. Get Dirty. 2015. (Don't Get Mad Ser.). (ENG.). 384p. (YA). (gr. 8). pap. 9.99 (978-0-06-226087-1(1)) HarperCollins Pubs.

—Ten. 2013. (ENG.). 320p. (YA). (gr. 8). pap. 9.99 (978-0-06-211879-0(X)) HarperCollins Pubs.

McVoy, Terra Elan. Criminal. (ENG., (YA). (gr. 9). 2014. Illus.). 304p. pap. 9.99 (978-1-4424-2163-9(0)) 2013. 288p. 16.99 (978-1-4424-2162-2(2)) Simon Pulse. (Simon Pulse).

Medina, Meg. Burn Baby Burn. 2016. (ENG.). 320p. (YA). (gr. 9). 17.99 (978-0-7636-7467-0(2)) Candlewick Pr.

Meldrum, Christina. Madapple. 2010. (ENG.). 416p. (YA). (gr. 9-18). pap. 10.99 (978-0-375-85177-3(1), Knopf Bks. for Young Readers) Random Hse. Children's Bks.

Michaels, Rune. Genesis Alpha. 2007. (ENG.). 208p. (YA). (gr. 7-12). 23.80 (978-1-4287-4620-6(X), Follettbound) Follett School Solutions.

—Genesis Alpha. 2011. (ENG.). 224p. (YA). (gr. 7). pap. 8.99 (978-1-4169-6500-8(9), Atheneum Bks. for Young Readers) Simon & Schuster Children's Publishing.

Moldavsky, Goldy. Kill the Boy Band. (ENG.). 320p. (J). (gr. 9). 2017. pap. 9.99 (978-0-545-86750-4(9)) 2016. 17.99 (978-0-545-86747-4(9)) Scholastic, Inc.

—Kill the Boy Band. 2017. lib. bdg. 20.85 **(978-0-606-39701-8(9))** Turtleback Bks.

Moriarty, Chris. The Watcher in the Shadows. Geyer, Mark Edward, illus. (ENG.). 336p. (J). (gr. 5-7). 2014. pap. 7.99 (978-0-544-22776-7(X), HMH Books For Young Readers) 2013. 16.99 (978-0-547-46632-3(3)) Houghton Mifflin Harcourt Publishing Co.

Mussi, Sarah. The Door of No Return. (ENG.). 400p. (YA). (gr. 7). 2009. pap. 10.99 (978-1-4169-6825-2(3)) 2008. 17.99 (978-1-4169-1550-8(8)) McElderry, Margaret K. Bks. (McElderry, Margaret K. Bks.).

Myers, Walter Dean. Monster. Myers, Christopher, illus. 2004. (Monster Ser.). (ENG.). 304p. (YA). (gr. 8). reprint ed. pap. 9.99 (978-0-06-440731-1(4), Amistad) HarperCollins Pubs.

Naylor, Phyllis Reynolds. Saving Shiloh. unabr. ed. 2004. 137p. (J). (gr. 3-7). pap. 29.00 incl. audio (978-0-8072-0456-6(0), Listening Library) Random Hse. Audio Publishing Group.

Neal, Terry L. The Find It Club. 2007. 80p. per. 19.95 (978-1-4241-7490-4(2)) America Star Bks.

Nelson, Blake. Paranoid Park. 2008. (ENG.). 192p. (YA). (gr. 7-18). 6.99 (978-0-14-241156-8(6), Puffin Books) Penguin Young Readers Group.

Nelson, R. A. Breathe My Name. 2008. (ENG.). 320p. (YA). (gr. 7-18). 9.99 (978-1-59514-186-6(3), Razorbill) Penguin Young Readers Group.

Newsome, Richard. The Mask of Destiny. Duddle, Jonny, illus. 2013. 384p. (J). (gr. 3-7). pap. 6.99 (978-0-06-194495-6(5), Waldon Pond Pr.) HarperCollins Pubs.

Nixon & Brush. Champagne with a Corpse. (Thumbprint Mysteries Ser.). 32.86 (978-0-8092-0420-5(7)) McGraw-Hill/Contemporary.

Nixon, Joan Lowery. Nightmare. 2005. 166p. (gr. 5-7). 17.00 (978-0-7569-5239-6(5)) Perfection Learning Corp.

Nordin, Ruth Ann. Witness to a Murder. 2007. 140p. per. 11.95 (978-0-595-45089-3(X)) iUniverse, Inc.

Oakes, Stephanie. The Sacred Lies of Minnow Bly. 2015. (ENG.). 400p. (YA). (gr. 9). 17.99 (978-0-8037-4070-9(0), Dial Bks) Penguin Young Readers Group.

Oates, Joyce Carol. Freaky Green Eyes. 2003. 352p. (J). 16.99 (978-0-06-623759-6(9)) 2005. (ENG.). 368p. (YA). (gr. 8). reprint ed. pap. 9.99 (978-0-06-447348-4(1)) HarperCollins Pubs. (HarperTeen).

—Freaky Green Eyes. 2005. 341p. (YA). 15.65 (978-0-7569-6308-8(7)) Perfection Learning Corp.

O'Leary, Edward J. Murder in the I. R. S. 2003. (YA). per. 18.95 (978-0-9708590-9-9(0)) First Word Publishing, The.

Olsen, Nora. Maxine Wore Black. 2014. (ENG.). 264p. (J). (gr. 7). pap. 11.95 (978-1-62639-208-3(0)) Bold Strokes Bks.

Omololu, C. J. The Third Twin. 2015. (ENG.). 336p. (YA). (gr. 7). 20.99 (978-0-375-99171-4(9), Delacorte Pr.) Random Hse. Children's Bks.

O'Rourke, Tim. Flashes. 2015. (ENG.). 320p. (J). (gr. 9). 16.99 (978-0-545-82959-5(3)) Scholastic, Inc.

Patterson, James & Paetro, Maxine. Confessions: The Private School Murders. 2013. 422p. (YA). (978-0-316-24263-9(2)) Little Brown & Co.

—The Private School Murders. 2015. (Confessions Ser.: 2). (ENG.). 400p. mass mkt. 8.00 (978-1-4555-5946-6(6), Jimmy Patterson) Grand Central Publishing.

—The Private School Murders. (Confessions Ser.: 2). (ENG.). (YA). (gr. 7-17). 2014. 448p. pap. 10.00 (978-0-316-20764-5(0)) 2013. 448p. 18.00 (978-0-316-20765-2(9)) 2013. 480p. 22.00 (978-0-316-23992-9(5)) Little Brown & Co. (Jimmy Patterson).

—The Private School Murders. 2014. (Confessions Ser.: 2). (YA). lib. bdg. 20.85 (978-0-606-35945-0(1)) Turtleback Bks.

Peacock, Kathleen. Hemlock. (Hemlock Trilogy Ser.: 1). (ENG.). (YA). (gr. 9). 2013. 432p. pap. 9.99 (978-0-06-204866-0(X)) 2012. 416p. 17.99 (978-0-06-204865-3(1)) HarperCollins Pubs. (Tegen, Katherine Bks).

Pearsall, Shelley. Crooked River. 2007. 249p. (gr. 5-9). 17.00 (978-0-7569-7771-9(1)) Perfection Learning Corp.

Perez, Marlene. Dead Is Just a Dream. (Dead Is Ser.: 8). (ENG.). 176p. (YA). (gr. 7). 2014. pap. 7.99 (978-0-544-33634-6(8), HMH Books For Young Readers) 2013. 16.99 (978-0-544-10262-0(2)) Houghton Mifflin Harcourt Publishing Co.

—Dead Is Just a Dream. 2014. (Dead Is Ser.: 8). lib. bdg. 18.40 (978-0-606-35990-0(7)) Turtleback Bks.

Perkins, T. J. In the Grand Scheme of Things: A Kim & Kelly Mystery. 2007. (Illus.). 151p. (YA). 10.99 (978-0-9777538-4-0(0)) GumShoe Press.

Perkins, TJ. Fantasies Are Murder: A Kim & Kelly Mystery. novel ed. 2005. (Illus.). 148p. (YA). 10.99 (978-0-9777538-0-2(8)) GumShoe Press.

Pierce, Tamora. Magic Steps. 2006. (Circle Opens Ser.: No. 1). 264p. 18.00 (978-0-7569-6588-4(8)) Perfection Learning Corp.

Pike, Aprilynne. Sleep No More. 2014. (ENG.). 352p. (YA). (gr. 8). 17.99 (978-0-06-199903-1(2), HarperTeen) HarperCollins Pubs.

Porter, Tracey. Lark. 2011. (ENG.). 192p. (YA). (gr. 8-18). 15.99 (978-0-06-112287-3(4), HarperTeen) HarperCollins Pubs.

Price, Charlie. Dead Connection. 2008. (ENG.). 240p. (YA). (gr. 7). pap. 10.99 (978-0-312-37966-7(8), 9780312379667) Square Fish.

—Dead Investigation. 2015. (ENG.). 336p. (YA). (gr. 7). 18.99 (978-0-374-30227-6(8), 9780374302276, Farrar, Straus & Giroux (BYR)) Farrar, Straus & Giroux.

Priestley, Chris. Death & the Arrow: A Gripping Tale of Murder & Revenge. 2007. (Tom Marlowe Ser.). (ENG., Illus.). 240p. (YA). (gr. 7). per. 12.95 (978-0-552-55475-6(8)) Transworld Publishers Ltd. GBR. Dist: Independent Pubs. Group.

Project Cain. 2014. (ENG., Illus.). 384p. (YA). (gr. 9). pap. 11.99 (978-1-4424-7698-1(2), Simon & Schuster Bks. For Young Readers) Simon & Schuster Bks. For Young Readers.

Prophet, John M. Body in the Salt Marsh Boatyard: A Casey Miller Mystery. 2004. 162p. (YA). pap. 13.95 (978-0-595-30991-7(7), Mystery & Suspense Pr.) iUniverse, Inc.

Purdie, Kathryn. Burning Glass. (Burning Glass Ser.: 1). (YA). (gr. 9). 2017. 528p. pap. 9.99 (978-0-06-241237-9(X)) 2016. (Illus.). 512p. 17.99 (978-0-06-241236-2(1)) HarperCollins Pubs. (Tegen, Katherine Bks).

Quinn, Spencer, pseud. ARF - A Bowser & Birdie Novel. 2016. (ENG.). 304p. (J). (gr. 3-7). 16.99 (978-0-545-64334-4(1), Scholastic Pr.) Scholastic, Inc.

Ray, Michelle. Falling for Hamlet. 2012. (ENG.). 368p. (YA). (gr. 10-17). pap. 17.99 (978-0-316-10161-5(3), Poppy) Little, Brown Bks. for Young Readers.

Reeves, Amy Carol. Ripper. 2012. (Ripper Novel Ser.: 1). (ENG., Illus.). 360p. (YA). pap. 9.95 (978-0-7387-3072-1(6), Flux) North Star Editions.

Reeves, Dia. Slice of Cherry. 2011. (ENG.). (YA). (gr. 9). 528p. pap. 9.99 (978-1-4169-8621-8(9)); 512p. 16.99 (978-1-4169-8620-1(0)) Simon Pulse. (Simon Pulse).

Revis, Beth. Across the Universe. 2012. (Across the Universe Trilogy: Bk. 1). (ENG.). (YA). (gr. 7-12). 54.99 (978-1-61587-857-4(2), Penguin AudioBooks) Penguin Publishing Group.

—Across the Universe. 2011. (Across the Universe Ser.: Bk. 1). (ENG.). (YA). (gr. 9-18). 448p. 9.99 (978-1-59514-467-6(6)); 416p. 17.99 (978-1-59514-397-6(1)) Penguin Young Readers Group. (Razorbill).

—Across the Universe. 2011. (Across the Universe Trilogy: 1). lib. bdg. 20.85 (978-0-606-23139-8(0), Turtleback) Turtleback Bks.

Ritter, William. Ghostly Echoes: A Jackaby Novel. (Jackaby Ser.: 3). (ENG.). 352p. (YA). (gr. 8-12). 2017. pap. 9.95 **(978-1-61620-744-1(2))** 2016. 17.95 (978-1-61620-579-9(2)) Algonquin Bks. of Chapel Hill.

Ritter, William. Jackaby. (Jackaby Ser.: 1). (ENG.). 304p. (YA). (gr. 9-12). 2015. pap. 9.95 (978-1-61620-546-1(6)) 2014. 16.95 (978-1-61620-353-5(6), 73353) Algonquin Bks. of Chapel Hill.

Roberts, Willo Davis. Nightmare. 2012. (ENG.). 224p. (J). (gr. 5-9). pap. 10.99 (978-1-4424-7229-7(4), Atheneum Bks. for Young Readers) Simon & Schuster Children's Publishing.

Roecker, Lisa & Roecker, Laura. The Liar Society. 2011. (Liar Society Ser.: 1). (ENG.). 368p. (YA). (gr. 7-12). pap. 9.99 (978-1-4022-5633-2(7)) Sourcebooks, Inc.

Rogers, Anne. The magic rainbow large Print. 2008. 332p. pap. 30.95 (978-1-4092-3059-5(7)) Lulu Pr., Inc.

—The magic rainbow very large Print. 2008. 502p. pap. 39.50 (978-1-4092-3065-6(1)) Lulu Pr., Inc.

Safren, Hannah. Dive: The Life & Fight of Reba Tutt. 2013. (ENG.). 154p. pap. 15.00 (978-1-938912-28-3(4)) Write Bloody Publishing.

Salemi, Dianne K. The Caged Graves. 2014. (ENG.). 336p. (YA). (gr. 7). pap. 8.99 (978-0-544-33622-3(4), HMH Books For Young Readers) Houghton Mifflin Harcourt Publishing Co.

Samms, Olivia. Sketchy. 2013. pap. (978-1-4778-6650-4(7)) Amazon Publishing.

Sampson, Jeff. Vesper. 2011. (Deviants Ser.: 1). (ENG.). 304p. (YA). (gr. 8-18). 16.99 (978-0-06-199276-6(3)) HarperCollins Pubs.

—Vesper: A Deviants Novel. 2011. (Deviants Ser.: 1). (ENG.). 320p. (YA). (gr. 8). pap. 8.99 (978-0-06-199277-3(1)) HarperCollins Pubs.

Sanderson, Brandon. The Rithmatist. McSweeney, Ben, illus. 2014. (ENG.). 384p. (YA). (gr. 7). pap. 10.99 (978-0-7653-3844-0(0), 9780765338440, Tor Teen) Doherty, Tom Assocs., LLC.

—The Rithmatist. 2013. (ENG., Illus.). 384p. (YA). (gr. 7). 17.99 (978-0-7653-2032-2(0), 9780765320322, Tor Teen) Doherty, Tom Assocs., LLC.

—The Rithmatist. 2014. (YA). lib. bdg. 22.10 (978-0-606-38512-1(6)) Turtleback Bks.

Schraff, Anne. One of Us, 1 vol. unabr. ed. 2010. (Urban Underground Ser.). (ENG.). 180p. (YA). (gr. 9-12). pap. 9.95 *(978-1-61651-004-6(8))* Saddleback Educational Publishing, Inc.

—One of Us. 2010. (Urban Underground — Harriet Tubman High School Ser.). (YA). lib. bdg. 20.80 *(978-0-606-14267-0(3))*, Turtleback) Turtleback Bks.

Schrefer, Eliot. The Deadly Sister. 2010. (ENG.). 320p. (J). (gr. 7-18). 17.99 *(978-0-545-16574-7(1))*, Scholastic Pr.) Scholastic, Inc.

Scott, Kieran. What Waits in the Woods. 2017. (ENG.). 288p. (J). (gr. 7). pap. 9.99 ***(978-0-545-83763-7(4))*** Scholastic, Inc.

Selzer, Adam. Just Kill Me. 2016. (ENG., Illus.). 336p. (YA). (gr. 9). 17.99 *(978-1-4814-3494-2(2))*, Simon & Schuster Bks. For Young Readers) Simon & Schuster Bks. For Young Readers.

Sepetys, Ruta. Out of the Easy. 2013. (ENG.). 352p. (YA). (gr. 9). 17.99 *(978-0-399-25692-9(X))*, Philomel Bks.) Penguin Young Readers Group.

Shankman, Adam & Sullivan, Laura L. Murder among the Stars. 2017. (YA). pap. ***(978-1-4814-4791-1(2))***; (ENG., Illus.). 320p. (gr. 9). 17.99 ***(978-1-4814-4790-4(4))*** Simon & Schuster Children's Publishing. (Atheneum Bks. for Young Readers).

Sharpe, Tess. Far from You. 2014. (ENG.). 352p. (YA). (gr. 9-17). 17.99 *(978-1-4231-8462-1(9))* Hyperion Bks. for Children.

Shaw, Susan. Tunnel Vision. (ENG.). 272p. (YA). (gr. 7). 2012. pap. 8.99 *(978-1-4424-0840-1(5))* 2011. 16.99 *(978-1-4424-0839-5(1))* McElderry, Margaret K. Bks. (McElderry, Margaret K. Bks.).

Shaw Wolf, Jennifer. Dead Girls Don't Lie. 2013. 336p. pap. 17.99 *(978-0-8027-3450-1(2))* Walker & Co.

Sheehan, Judy. I Woke up Dead at the Mall. 2016. (ENG.). 288p. (YA). (gr. 7). 17.99 *(978-0-553-51246-5(3))*, Delacorte Pr.) Random Hse. Children's Bks.

Shepard, Sara. The Amateurs. 2016. (Amateurs Ser.). (ENG.). 320p. (YA). (gr. 9-17). 17.99 *(978-1-4847-4227-3(3))* Hyperion Bks. for Children.

—Cross My Heart, Hope to Die. 2013. (Lying Game Ser.: 5). (ENG.). 336p. (YA). (gr. 9). 17.99 *(978-0-06-212819-5(1))*, HarperTeen) HarperCollins Pubs.

—Deadly. 2014. (Pretty Little Liars Ser.: 14). (YA). lib. bdg. 20.85 *(978-0-606-35972-6(9))* Turtleback Bks.

—The Good Girls. 2015. (Perfectionists Ser.: 2). (ENG.). 368p. (YA). (gr. 9). 17.99 *(978-0-06-207452-2(0))*, HarperTeen); 341p. (J). *(978-0-06-239115-5(1))* HarperCollins Pubs.

—Hide & Seek. (YA). 2013. (Lying Game Ser.: 4). (ENG.). 320p. (gr. 9). pap. 10.99 *(978-0-06-186977-8(5))* 2012. (Lying Game Ser.: 4). (ENG.). 304p. (gr. 9). 17.99 *(978-0-06-186976-1(7))* 2012. (Lying Game Ser.: Bk. 4). 289p. 9.99 *(978-0-06-219369-8(4))* HarperCollins Pubs. (HarperTeen).

—The Lying Game. (Lying Game Ser.: 1). (ENG.). (YA). (gr. 9-18). 2011. 336p. pap. 10.99 *(978-0-06-186971-6(6))* 2010. 320p. 16.99 *(978-0-06-186970-9(8))* 2011. 336p. 16.99 *(978-0-06-211416-7(6))* HarperCollins Pubs. (HarperTeen).

—The Lying Game. 2011. (Lying Game (Quality) Ser.: Vol. 1). (ENG.). (YA). (gr. 9). lib. bdg. 20.60 ***(978-1-61383-667-5(8))*** Perfection Learning Corp.

—Never Have I Ever. (Lying Game Ser.: 2). (ENG.). (YA). (gr. 9). 2012. 336p. pap. 9.99 *(978-0-06-186973-0(2))* 2011. 320p. 16.99 *(978-0-06-186972-3(4))* HarperCollins Pubs. (HarperTeen).

—The Perfectionists. 2014. (Perfectionists Ser.: 1). (ENG.). 336p. (YA). (gr. 9). 17.99 *(978-0-06-207469-0(5))* HarperCollins Pubs.

—Seven Minutes in Heaven. 2014. (Lying Game Ser.: 6). (ENG.). 400p. (YA). (gr. 9). pap. 10.99 *(978-0-06-212823-2(X))*, HarperTeen) HarperCollins Pubs.

—Two Truths & a Lie. (Lying Game Ser.: 3). (ENG.). (YA). (gr. 9). 2013. 320p. pap. 9.99 *(978-0-06-186975-4(9))* 2012. 304p. 17.99 *(978-0-06-186974-7(0))* HarperCollins Pubs. (HarperTeen).

—Vicious. 2014. (Pretty Little Liars Ser.: 16). (ENG.). 352p. (YA). (gr. 9). 17.99 *(978-0-06-228704-5(4))* HarperCollins Pubs.

Shimko, Bonnie. You Know What You Have to Do, 0 vols. 2013. (ENG.). 240p. (YA). (gr. 9-12). 17.99 *(978-1-4778-1642-4(9))*, 9781477816424, Amazon Children's Publishing) Amazon Publishing.

Shusterman, Neal. Scythe. 2016. (Arc of a Scythe Ser.: 1). (ENG., Illus.). 448p. (YA). (gr. 7). 18.99 *(978-1-4424-7242-6(1))*, Simon & Schuster Bks. For Young Readers) Simon & Schuster Bks. For Young Readers.

Simmons, Ted. Diablo Creek. 2007. (ENG.). 168p. (YA). pap. *(978-0-9776958-7-4(5))* CyPress Pubns.

Sims, Guy A. & Myers, Walter Dean. Monster. Anyabwile, Dawud, illus. 2015. (Monster Ser.). (ENG.). 160p. (YA). (gr. 8). pap. 9.99 *(978-0-06-227499-1(6))* HarperCollins Pubs.

Singer, Nicky. The Innocent's Story. 2007. 220p. (YA). (gr. 7-18). 16.95 *(978-0-8234-2082-7(5))* Holiday Hse., Inc.

Singleton, Linda Joy. Fatal Charm. 2007. (Seer Ser.: 5). (ENG.). 384p. (YA). (gr. 7-12). per. 9.95 *(978-0-7387-1153-9(5))*, Flux) North Star Editions.

Sirowy, Alexandra. The Creeping: If You Hunt for Monsters, You'll Find Them. 2015. (ENG., Illus.). 400p. (YA). (gr. 7). 17.99 *(978-1-4814-1886-7(6))* Simon & Schuster Children's Publishing.

—The Telling. 2016. (ENG., Illus.). 400p. (YA). (gr. 7). 17.99 *(978-1-4814-1889-8(0))*, Simon & Schuster Bks. For Young Readers) Simon & Schuster Bks. For Young Readers.

Snicket, Lemony, pseud & Stookey, Nathaniel. The Composer Is Dead. Ellis, Carson, illus. 2009. (ENG.). 40p. (J). (gr. k-5). 17.99 *(978-0-06-123627-3(6))* HarperCollins Pubs.

Snyder, Zilpha Keatley. The Egypt Game. 2014. (ENG.). 240p. (J). (gr. 3-7). 11.24 *(978-1-63245-327-3(4))* Lectorum Pubns., Inc.

—The Egypt Game. Raible, Alton, illus. 2009. (ENG.). 240p. (J). (gr. 3-7). pap. 8.99 *(978-1-4169-9051-2(8))*, Atheneum Bks. for Young Readers) Simon & Schuster Children's Publishing.

Sorrells, Walter. Club Dread. 2007. (Hunted Ser.). (ENG.). 272p. (YA). (gr. 7-18). 8.99 *(978-0-14-240904-6(9))*, Puffin Books) Penguin Young Readers Group.

—Fake ID. 2007. (Hunted Ser.). (ENG.). 336p. (YA). (gr. 7-18). 9.99 *(978-0-14-240762-2(3))*, Puffin Books) Penguin Young Readers Group.

—First Shot. 2009. (ENG.). 288p. (YA). (gr. 7-18). 8.99 *(978-0-14-241421-7(2))*, Puffin Books) Penguin Young Readers Group.

—The Travelers, Bk. 2. 2009. (Pendragon: 2). (ENG.). 240p. (J). (gr. 5-9). pap. 6.99 *(978-1-4169-6523-7(8))*, Aladdin) Simon & Schuster Children's Publishing.

Sourcebooks. Twisted. 2016. (ENG.). 320p. (YA). (gr. 8-12). pap. 10.99 *(978-1-4926-3179-8(5))*, 9781492631798) Sourcebooks, Inc.

St. Claire, Roxanne. They All Fall Down. (ENG.). 352p. (YA). (gr. 7). 2016. pap. 9.99 *(978-0-385-74272-6(X))*, Ember) 2014. 17.99 *(978-0-385-74271-9(1))*, Delacorte Pr.) Random Hse. Children's Bks.

Stampler, Ann Redisch. How to Disappear. 2016. (ENG., Illus.). 416p. (YA). (gr. 9). 18.99 *(978-1-4814-4393-7(3))*, Simon Pulse) Simon Pulse.

Steiner. Murder Takes a Fast Track. (Thumbprint Mysteries Ser.). 32.86 *(978-0-8092-0417-5(7))* McGraw-Hill/Contemporary.

Stelmach, Orest. The Boy Who Stole from the Dead, 0 vols. 2014. (Nadia Tesla Ser.: 2). (ENG.). 366p. pap. 14.95 *(978-1-4778-0948-8(1))*, 9781477809488, Thomas & Mercer) Amazon Publishing.

Stevens, Bonnie. Fighting Chance. 2015. (ENG.). 326p. (YA). pap. 10.95 *(978-1-929345-14-4(3))* Poisoned Pen Pr.

Stevens, Robin. Murder Is Bad Manners. 2015. (Wells & Wong Mystery Ser.). (ENG., Illus.). 320p. (J). (gr. 5). 17.99 *(978-1-4814-2212-3(X))*, Simon & Schuster Bks. For Young Readers) Simon & Schuster Bks. For Young Readers.

—Poison Is Not Polite. 2016. (Wells & Wong Mystery Ser.). (ENG., Illus.). 336p. (J). (gr. 5). 17.99 *(978-1-4814-2215-4(4))*, Simon & Schuster Bks. For Young Readers) Simon & Schuster Bks. For Young Readers.

Stevenson, Steve. The Eiffel Tower Incident #5. Turconi, Stefano, illus. 2014. (Agatha: Girl of Mystery Ser.: 5). (ENG.). 144p. (J). (gr. 2-5). 6.99 *(978-0-448-46223-3(0))*, Grosset & Dunlap) Penguin Young Readers Group.

Stine, R. L. The Confession. 2005. (Fear Street Ser.: Bk. 39). 150p. (J). lib. bdg. 13.00 *(978-1-4242-1000-8(3))* Fitzgerald Bks.

—Fear Street Super Thriller: Party Games & Don't Stay up Late. 2015. (Fear Street Ser.). (ENG.). 592p. (YA). (gr. 7-12). pap. 11.99 *(978-1-250-07693-9(5))*, 9781250076939, St. Martin's Griffin) St. Martin's Pr.

—Midnight Games. 2005. (Fear Street Nights Ser.: No. 2). 183p. (YA). lib. bdg. 20.00 *(978-1-4242-1119-7(0))* Fitzgerald Bks.

—A Midsummer Night's Scream. 2013. (ENG.). 256p. (YA). (gr. 7). 17.99 *(978-1-250-02434-3(X))*, 9781250024343) Feiwel & Friends.

—A Midsummer Night's Scream. 2014. (ENG.). 256p. (YA). (gr. 7-12). pap. 10.99 *(978-1-250-04434-1(0))*, 9781250044341) Square Fish.

—When the Ghost Dog Howls. 2010. (Goosebumps Horrorland Ser.: 13). (ENG.). 160p. (J). (gr. 3-7). 6.99 *(978-0-545-16194-7(0))*, Scholastic Paperbacks) Scholastic, Inc.

Strange, Jason. 23 Crow's Perch, 1 vol. Evergreen, Nelson & Kendall, Bradford, illus. 2012. (Jason Strange Ser.). (ENG.). 72p. (gr. 2-3). pap. 6.25 *(978-1-4342-3885-6(7))*; lib. bdg. 25.32 *(978-1-4342-3297-7(2))* Stone Arch Bks.

Strohmeyer, Sarah. The Secrets of Lily Graves. 2014. (ENG.). 304p. (YA). (gr. 8). pap. 9.99 *(978-0-06-225960-8(1))* HarperCollins Pubs.

Summers, Tamara. Never Bite a Boy on the First Date. 2009. (ENG.). 288p. (YA). (gr. 9-18). pap. 5.99 *(978-0-06-172154-0(9))*, HarperTeen) HarperCollins Pubs.

Taylor, Kara. Prep School Confidential. 2013. (Prep School Confidential Novel Ser.: 1). (ENG.). 336p. (YA). (gr. 7). pap. 9.99 *(978-1-250-01759-8(9))*, 9781250017598, St. Martin's Griffin) St. Martin's Pr.

Terrill, Cristin. All Our Yesterdays. 2014. (All Our Yesterdays Ser.). (ENG.). 368p. (YA). (gr. 7-12). pap. 9.99 *(978-1-4231-8524-6(2))* Hyperion Bks. for Children.

—All Our Yesterdays. 2013. (All Our Yesterdays Ser.). (ENG.). 368p. (YA). (gr. 7-12). 17.99 *(978-1-4231-7637-4(5))* Hyperion Pr.

This Is How It Ends. 2014. (ENG., Illus.). 320p. (YA). (gr. 9). pap. 11.99 *(978-1-4814-0210-1(2))*, Simon Pulse) Simon Pulse.

Thomas, Kara. The Darkest Corners. (ENG.). (YA). (gr. 9). 2017. 352p. pap. 9.99 ***(978-0-553-52148-1(9))***, Ember) 2016. 336p. 17.99 *(978-0-553-52145-0(4))*, Delacorte Pr.) Random Hse. Children's Bks.

A Thousand Pieces of You. 2014. (Firebird Ser.: 1). (ENG.). 368p. (YA). (gr. 9). 17.99 *(978-0-06-227896-8(7))* HarperCollins Pubs.

Tims, Laura. Please Don't Tell. 2016. 336p. (YA). (gr. 8). 17.99 *(978-0-06-231732-2(6))*, HarperTeen) HarperCollins Pubs.

Turnage, Sheila. Three Times Lucky. (ENG.). (J). (gr. 5). 2013. 336p. pap. 7.99 *(978-0-14-242605-0(9))*, Puffin Books) 2012. 314p. 16.99 *(978-0-8037-3670-2(3))*, Dial Bks) Penguin Young Readers Group.

—Three Times Lucky. 2013. lib. bdg. 18.40 *(978-0-606-34168-4(4))*, Turtleback) Turtleback Bks.

Turner, Henry. Ask the Dark. (ENG.). 256p. (YA). (gr. 9). 2016. pap. 9.99 *(978-0-544-81353-3(7))*, HMH Books For Young Readers) 2015. 17.99 *(978-0-544-30827-5(1))*, Clarion Bks.) Houghton Mifflin Harcourt Publishing Co.

Vande Velde, Vivian. Magic Can Be Murder. 2009. (ENG.). 208p. (YA). (gr. 7). pap. 12.99 *(978-0-547-25872-0(0))* Houghton Mifflin Harcourt Publishing Co.

—Never Trust a Dead Man. 2008. (ENG., Illus.). 208p. (YA). (gr. 7). pap. 13.95 *(978-0-15-206448-8(6))* Houghton Mifflin Harcourt Publishing Co.

Vehlmann, Fabien. Green Manor Pt. 1: Assassins & Gentleman. Bodart, Denis, illus. 2008. (Expresso Collection). (ENG.). 56p. pap. 13.95 *(978-1-905460-53-3(8))* CineBook GBR. Dist: National Bk. Network.

Villani, Donna. The Capture of Art. 2008. 244p. pap. 14.95 *(978-1-60693-104-2(0))*, Eloquent Bks.) Strategic Book Publishing & Rights Agency (SBPRA).

Volponi, Paul. Rucker Park Setup. 2008. (ENG.). 160p. (YA). (gr. 7-18). 6.99 *(978-0-14-241207-7(4))*, Speak) Penguin Young Readers Group.

Walden, Mark. Rogue. (H. I. V. E. Ser.: 5). (ENG.). (J). (gr. 3-7). 2012. 320p. pap. 8.99 *(978-1-4424-1369-6(7))* 2011. 304p. 16.99 *(978-1-4424-2187-5(8))* Simon & Schuster Bks. For Young Readers. (Simon & Schuster Bks. For Young Readers).

Walkup, Jennifer. Second Verse. 2013. 270p. pap. 15.95 *(978-1-935462-87-3(3))*; (ENG.). 200p. (YA). (gr. 7-12). pap. 11.95 *(978-1-935462-85-9(7))* Luminis Bks., Inc.

Wallace, Becky. The Storyspinner. 2015. (Keepers' Chronicles Ser.). (ENG., Illus.). 432p. (YA). (gr. 9). 17.99 *(978-1-4814-0565-2(9))*, McElderry, Margaret K. Bks.) McElderry, Margaret K. Bks.

Wallace, Kali. Shallow Graves. (YA). (gr. 9). 2017. 384p. pap. 9.99 ***(978-0-06-236621-4(1))*** 2016. 368p. 17.99 *(978-0-06-236620-7(3))* HarperCollins Pubs. (Tegen, Katherine Bks).

Wallace, Rich. A Deadly Fall. Volpari, Daniela, illus. 2016. 48p. (J). *(978-1-62402-147-3(6))* Magic Wagon.

Warstler, Mary Lu. Michael's Angel, 1 vol. 2009. 227p. pap. 24.95 *(978-1-61546-723-5(8))* PublishAmerica, Inc.

Wasserman, Robin. The Book of Blood & Shadow. 2012. (ENG.). 448p. (YA). (gr. 7). 17.99 *(978-0-375-86876-4(3))*; lib. bdg. 20.99 *(978-0-375-96876-1(8))* Random Hse. Children's Bks. (Knopf Bks. for Young Readers).

—The Waking Dark. 2013. (ENG.). 464p. (YA). (gr. 9). 17.99 *(978-0-375-86877-1(1))*, Knopf Bks. for Young Readers) Random Hse. Children's Bks.

Waters, Daniel. Break My Heart 1,000 Times. 2013. (ENG., Illus.). 352p. (YA). (gr. 7-17). pap. 9.99 *(978-1-4231-2228-9(3))* Hyperion Pr.

Watt, Erin. Twisted Palace. 2016. (Royals Ser.: 3). (ENG.). 370p. (gr. 7-12). pap. 14.99 *(978-1-68230-506-5(6))*, EverAfter Romance) Diversion Publishing Corp.

Weber, Richard D. Elvis & Me. 2004. 511p. (YA). per. 17.41 *(978-1-4116-0549-7(7))* Lulu Pr., Inc.

Welch, Jim. Steven Stevens' Killer App. 2012. 232p. pap. 16.50 *(978-1-105-06310-7(0))* Lulu Pr., Inc.

Welshman, Kate. Anais Butt & the Hairy-Handed Gent. 2013. 164p. pap. 16.50 *(978-1-61213-187-0(5))* Writer's Coffee Shop, The.

Wennick, Elizabeth. Whatever Doesn't Kill You, 1 vol. 2013. (ENG.). 208p. (YA). (gr. 8-12). pap. 12.95 *(978-1-4598-0083-0(4))* Orca Bk. Pubs. USA.

Werlin, Nancy. Black Mirror. 2003. (ENG.). 256p. (YA). (gr. 7-12). 6.99 *(978-0-14-250028-6(3))*, Puffin Books) Penguin Young Readers Group.

Whiting, Sue. Portraits of Celina. 2015. (ENG.). 352p. 16.95 *(978-1-63079-024-0(9))* Switch Pr.

Wilcox. The Hidden Men. (Thumbprint Mysteries Ser.). 32.86 *(978-0-8092-0415-1(0))* McGraw-Hill/Contemporary.

Williams, Katie & Chronicle Books Staff. The Space Between Trees. 2010. (ENG.). 280p. (YA). (gr. 9-17). 17.99 *(978-0-8118-7175-4(4))* Chronicle Bks. LLC.

Wilson, John. Ghost Moon, 1 vol. 2011. (Desert Legend Trilogy Ser.: 2). (ENG.). 192p. (YA). (gr. 8-12). pap. 12.95 *(978-1-55469-879-0(0))* Orca Bk. Pubs. USA.

Winters, Cat. The Steep & Thorny Way. (ENG.). (YA). (gr. 8-17). 2017. 368p. pap. 9.99 ***(978-1-4197-2350-6(2))*** 2016. (Illus.). 352p. 17.95 *(978-1-4197-1915-8(7))* Abrams, Inc. (Amulet Bks.).

Wolf, Jennifer Shaw. Dead Girls Don't Lie. 2014. (ENG.). 368p. (YA). (gr. 9). pap. 9.99 *(978-0-8027-3753-3(6))*, 9780802737533, Bloomsbury USA Childrens) Bloomsbury Publishing USA.

Wynne-Jones, Tim. The Boy in the Burning House. braille ed. 2003. (J). (gr. 2). spiral bd. *(978-0-616-15275-1(2))* Canadian National Institute for the Blind/Institut National Canadien pour les Aveugles.

—The Boy in the Burning House. 2003. (ENG.). 224p. (J). (gr. 5-9). pap. 12.99 *(978-0-374-40887-9(4))*, 9780374408879, Farrar, Straus & Giroux (BYR)) Farrar, Straus & Giroux.

—The Boy in the Burning House, 1 vol. (ENG.). 232p. pap. 8.95 *(978-0-88899-500-1(8))* Groundwood Bks. CAN. Dist: Publishers Group West (PGW).

Yovanoff, Brenna. Paper Valentine. 2013. (ENG.). 320p. (YA). (gr. 7). 17.99 *(978-1-59514-599-4(0))*, Razorbill) Penguin Young Readers Group.

MURPHY, JIMMY, 1894-1924

Briggs, Raymond. Jimmy Murphy & the White Duesenberg. 2006. (Illus.). (J). *(978-0-9766683-0-5(0))* Racemaker Pr.

MURRY FAMILY (FICTITIOUS CHARACTER)—FICTION

L'Engle, Madeleine. Many Waters. 2007. (Wrinkle in Time Quintet Ser.: 3). (ENG.). 368p. (J). (gr. 5-9). per. 6.99 *(978-0-312-36857-9(7))*, 9780312368579) Square Fish.

—A Swiftly Tilting Planet. 228p. (YA). (gr. 5-18). pap. 5.50 *(978-0-8072-1495-4(7))*, Listening Library) Random Hse. Audio Publishing Group.

—A Swiftly Tilting Planet. 2007. (Wrinkle in Time Quintet Ser.: 4). (ENG.). 320p. (J). (gr. 5-9). per. 7.99 *(978-0-312-36856-2(9))*, 9780312368562) Square Fish.

—A Wind in the Door. 211p. (YA). (gr. 5-18). pap. 5.50 *(978-0-8072-1466-4(3))*, Listening Library) Random Hse. Audio Publishing Group.

—A Wind in the Door. 2007. (Wrinkle in Time Quintet Ser.: 2). (ENG.). 256p. (J). (gr. 5-9). per. 6.99 *(978-0-312-36854-8(2))*, 9780312368548) Square Fish.

—A Wrinkle in Time, 2 vols., Set. 20.00 *(978-0-89064-014-2(9))* National Assn. for Visually Handicapped.

—A Wrinkle in Time. 211p. (YA). (gr. 5-18). pap. 5.99 *(978-0-8072-1460-2(4))*, Listening Library) Random Hse. Audio Publishing Group.

—A Wrinkle in Time. l.t. ed. 2005. 273p. pap. 10.95 *(978-0-7862-7335-5(6))*, Large Print Pr.) Thorndike Pr.

MUSA, SULTAN OF MALI, ACTIVE 1324

Krasner, Barbara. Mansa Musa. 2016. (Silk Road's Greatest Travelers Ser.). 112p. (J). (gr. 6-6). 37.10 *(978-1-5081-7151-5(3))* Rosen Publishing Group, Inc., The.

Supples, Kevin & National Geographic Learning Staff. Mali. 2007. (Reading Expeditions Ser.). (ENG., Illus.). 24p. (J). pap. 14.95 *(978-0-7922-4539-1(3))* CENGAGE Learning.

Zamosky, Lisa. Mansa Musa: Leader of Mali, 1 vol. 2007. (Primary Source Readers Ser.). (ENG.). 32p. (J). (gr. 4-4). pap. 8.99 *(978-0-7439-0439-1(7))* Shell Educational Publishing.

MUSCLES

Abramovitz, Melissa. Muscular Dystrophy. 2008. (Diseases & Disorders Ser.). (ENG., Illus.). 104p. (YA). (gr. 7-10). lib. bdg. 34.95 *(978-1-4205-0073-8(2))*, LML02109-242077, Lucent Bks.) Cengage Gale.

Bailey, Jacqui. What Happens When You Move? 2009. 32p. (gr. k-5). pap. 10.60 *(978-1-4358-2617-5(5))*, Rosen Classroom) Rosen Publishing Group, Inc., The.

Ballard, Carol. The Skeleton & Muscles. 2005. (Exploring the Human Body Ser.). (ENG., Illus.). 32p. (J). (gr. 3-6). lib. bdg. 27.80 *(978-0-7377-3022-7(6))*, Greenhaven Pr., Inc.) Cengage Gale.

Beevor, Lucy. Understanding Our Muscles. 2017. (Brains, Body, Bones! Ser.). (ENG., Illus.). 32p. (gr. 3-5). lib. bdg. 30.65 *(978-1-4109-8581-1(4))*, Raintree Perspectives) Heinemann-Raintree.

Berger, Melvin & Berger, Gilda. Your Muscles. 2005. (Illus.). pap. *(978-0-439-77371-3(7))* Scholastic, Inc.

Biskup, Agnieszka. The Science Behind Superman's Strength. 2017. (Science Behind Superman Ser.). (ENG., Illus.). 24p. (gr. 1-2). lib. bdg. 25.32 *(978-1-5157-5099-4(X))*, DC Super Heroes) Stone Arch Bks.

—Stopping Runaway Trains: Superman & the Science of Strength. 2016. (Superman Science Ser.). (ENG., Illus.). 32p. (gr. 3-4). lib. bdg. 27.32 *(978-1-5157-0914-5(0))*, DC Super Heroes) Stone Arch Bks.

Biskup, Agnieszka & Enz, Tammy. Superman Science: The Real-World Science Behind Superman's Powers. 2017. (ENG., Illus.). 144p. (gr. 3-4). pap. 9.95 *(978-1-62370-702-6(1))*, DC Super Heroes) Stone Arch Bks.

Brett, Flora. Your Muscular System Works! 2015. (Your Body Systems Ser.). (ENG.). 24p. (gr. 1-2). lib. bdg. 25.32 *(978-1-4914-2065-2(0))* Capstone Press of Coughlan Cos.

Brynie, Faith Hickman. 101 Questions about Muscles: To Stretch Your Mind & Flex Your Brain. 2007. (101 Questions... Ser.). (ENG., Illus.). 176p. (gr. 7-12). lib. bdg. 30.60 *(978-0-8225-6380-8(0))* Lerner Publishing Group.

Burstein, John. The Mighty Muscular & Skeletal Systems: How Do My Bones & Muscles Work? 2009. (Slim Goodbody's Body Buddies Ser.). (ENG., Illus.). 32p. (J). (gr. 3-5). lib. bdg. *(978-0-7787-4419-1(1))* Crabtree Publishing Co.

—The Mighty Muscular-Skeletal System: How Do My Bones & Muscles Work? 2009. (Slim Goodbody's Body Buddies Ser.). (ENG., Illus.). 32p. (J). (gr. 3-5). pap. *(978-0-7787-4433-7(7))* Crabtree Publishing Co.

Canavan, Thomas. How Many Muscles Make Your Smile? Questions about Muscles & Movement. 2016. (Human Body FAQ Ser.). 00032p. (J). (gr. 3-3). pap. 10.00 *(978-1-4994-3166-7(X))*, PowerKids Pr.) Rosen Publishing Group, Inc., The.

Clark, Katie. A Tour of Your Muscular & Skeletal Systems. Jones, Chris B., illus. 2012. (First Graphics: Body Systems Ser.). (ENG.). 24p. (gr. 1-2). pap. 35.70 *(978-1-4296-9327-1(4))* Capstone Press of Coughlan Cos.

Colligan, L. H. Muscles. 2009. (Amazing Human Body 2 Ser.). 80p. (gr. 5). 34.21 *(978-0-7614-4038-3(0))* Marshall Cavendish Corp.

Farndon, John. Stickmen's Guide to Your Mighty Muscles & Bones. Dean, Venitia, illus. 2017. (Stickmen's Guides to Your Awesome Body Ser.). (ENG.). 32p. (J). (gr. 3-6). 26.65 ***(978-1-5124-3214-5(8))*** Lerner Publishing Group.

Fitzpatrick, Anne. The Muscles. 2003. (Illus.). 24p. (J). lib. bdg. 21.35 *(978-1-58340-309-9(4))* Black Rabbit Bks.

Gardner, Jane P. Take a Closer Look at Your Muscles. 2013. (Take a Closer Look Ser.). (ENG.). 24p. (J). (gr. 2-5). 28.50 *(978-1-62323-551-2(0))*, 206354) Child's World, Inc., The.

Gray, Susan H. The Muscular System. 2014. (Human Body Ser.). (ENG.). 24p. (J). (gr. 2-5). 28.50 *(978-1-62687-336-0(4))*, 207176) Child's World, Inc., The.

Green, Emily & Manolis, Kay. The Muscular System. 2009. (Body Systems Ser.). (ENG., Illus.). 24p. (J). (gr. 2-5). lib. bdg. 25.95 *(978-1-60014-244-4(3))* Bellwether Media.

Guillain, Charlotte. Nuestros Músculos, 1 vol. 2010. (Nuestros Cuerpos Ser.).Tr. of Our Muscles. (SPA.). 24p. (gr. -1-1). 22.65 *(978-1-4329-4298-4(0))*; pap. 6.29 *(978-1-4329-4307-3(3))* Heinemann-Raintree. (Bellota).

—Our Muscles, 1 vol. 2010. (Our Bodies Ser.). (ENG., Illus.). 24p. (gr. -1-1). 22.65 *(978-1-4329-3593-1(3))*; pap. 6.29 *(978-1-4329-3602-0(6))* Heinemann-Raintree. (Acorn).

Halvorson, Karin. Inside the Muscles, 1 vol. 2016. (Super Simple Body Set 2 Ser.). (ENG., Illus.). 32p. (J). (gr. k-4). 27.07 *(978-1-62403-940-9(5))* ABDO Publishing Co.

Houghton, Gillian. Muscles: The Muscular System. 2009. (Body Works Ser.). 24p. (gr. 2-3). 42.50 *(978-1-61511-645-4(1))*, PowerKids Pr.) Rosen Publishing Group, Inc., The.

—Muscles: the Muscular System. 2006. (Body Works Ser.). (Illus.). 24p. (YA). (gr. 2-5). lib. bdg. 22.60 *(978-1-4042-3475-8(6))* Rosen Publishing Group, Inc., The.

—The Muscular System. 2007. (How Your Body Works). (ENG., Illus.). 24p. (gr. 3-5). pap. 7.05 *(978-1-4042-2184-0(0))*, PowerKids Pr.) Rosen Publishing Group, Inc., The.

Ipcizade, Catherine. The Strongest Animals. 2011. (Extreme Animals Ser.). (ENG.). 24p. (gr. k-1). pap. 41.70 *(978-1-4296-6381-6(2))*, Pebble Plus) Capstone Press of Coughlan Cos.

Johnson, Rebecca L. The Muscular System. 2005. (Early Bird Body Systems Ser.). (Illus.). 48p. (J). (gr. 2-4). lib. bdg. 25.26 *(978-0-8225-1248-6(3))* Lerner Publishing Group.

—Muscular System. 2005. (Early Bird Body Systems Ser.). (ENG., Illus.). 48p. (gr. 2-5). pap. 7.95 *(978-0-8225-2520-2(8))*, Lerner Pubns.) Lerner Publishing Group.

—El Sistema Muscular. Translations.com Staff, tr. 2006. (Libros Sobre el Cuerpo Humano para Madrugadores Ser.).Tr. of Muscular System. (ENG & SPA., Illus.). 48p. (gr. 2-4). lib. bdg. 26.60 *(978-0-8225-6254-2(5))* Lerner Publishing Group.

—El Sistema Muscular (The Muscular System) 2007. (Libros Sobre el Cuerpo Humano para Madrugadores Ser.). (Illus.). 48p. (J). (gr. -1-3). per. 8.95 *(978-0-8225-6650-2(8))* Lerner Publishing Group.

Johnson, Rebecca L. & National Geographic Learning Staff. Bones & Muscles. 2007. (Reading Expeditions Ser.). (ENG.,

Illus.). 32p. (J). pap. 17.95 (978-0-7922-4585-8(7)) CENGAGE Learning.

Jordan, Apple & Rau, Dana Meachen. My Bones & Muscles. 2nd ed. 2013. 24p. (gr. 1-3). 21.36 (978-1-60870-433-0(5)) Cavendish Square Publishing.

Kenney, Karen Latchana. Strength Training for Teen Athletes: Exercises to Take Your Game to the Next Level, 1 vol. 2012. (Sports Training Zone Ser.). (ENG.). 48p. (gr. 4-5). pap. 8.19 (978-1-4296-8002-8(4)); lib. bdg. 31.99 (978-1-4296-7680-9(9)) Capstone Press of Coughlan Cos.

Kirk, Bill. Muscles Make Us Move. Ruble, Eugene, illus. 2011. 32p. pap. 10.95 (978-1-61633-134-4(8)) Guardian Angel Publishing, Inc.

Korb, Rena B. & Weinhaus, Anthony J. My Muscles, 1 vol. Simard, Remy, illus. 2010. (My Body Ser.). (ENG.). 32p. (J). (gr. k-3). 28.50 (978-1-60270-807-5(X)) Magic Wagon.

Leading Women 2. 2013. (Bookworms Fluent — My Body Ser.). (gr. 1-3). 239.58 (978-1-62712-000-5(9)) Cavendish Square Publishing.

Manolis, Kay. The Muscular System. 2009. (Blastoff! Readers Ser.). (ENG., Illus.). 24p. (J). (gr. k-3). 20.00 (978-0-531-21703-0(5), Children's Pr.) Scholastic Library Publishing.

Martin, Bobi. The Muscles in Your Body, 1 vol. 2015. (ENG.). 32p. (J). 23.45 (978-1-62275-651-3(7), Britannica Educational Publishing) Rosen Publishing Group, Inc., The.

Martin, Chia. The Art of Touch: A Massage Manual for Young People. 2015. (ENG., Illus.). 72p. (gr. 4-7). pap. 15.95 (978-0-934252-57-7(2)) Hohm Pr.

Meachen Rau, Dana. Huesos y Musculos: Que Hay Dentro de Mi? 2006. (Bookworms Ser.). (SPA & ENG., Illus.). 32p. (gr. 1-2). lib. bdg. 15.95 (978-0-7614-2401-7(6)) Marshall Cavendish Corp.

—My Bones & Muscles. 2004. (Bookworms Ser.). (ENG & SPA., Illus.). 32p. (gr. 1-2). 15.95 (978-0-7614-1777-4(X), Benchmark Bks.) Marshall Cavendish Corp.

—My Bones & Muscles/Huesos y Musculos. 2006. (Bookworms Ser.). (ENG & SPA., Illus.). 32p. (gr. 1-2). lib. bdg. 15.95 (978-0-7614-2479-6(2)) Marshall Cavendish Corp.

Murray, Julie. Strongest Animals, 1 vol. 2010. (That's Wild!: A Look at Animals Ser.). (ENG.). 32p. (J). (gr. 2-5). 28.50 (978-1-60453-981-3(X)) ABDO Publishing Co.

El Musculo, Organo de la Fuerza. (Coleccion Mundo Invisible).Tr. of How Are Muscles Work. (SPA.). (YA). (gr. 5-8). pap. 8.00 (978-958-04-3225-8(2)) Norma S.A. COL. Dist: Distribuidora Norma, Inc.

Musculo, Organo de la Fuerza. (SPA.). 88p. (J). 10.00 (978-84-342-1740-9(6)) Parramon Ediciones S.A. ESP. Dist: Distribuidora Norma, Inc.

Ollhoff, Jim. Muscles & Bones. 2012. (J). (978-1-61783-256-7(1)) ABDO Publishing Co.

Parker, Steve. How Do My Muscles Get Strong? Muscles & Exercise, 1 vol. 2011. (Inside My Body Ser.). (ENG.). 32p. (gr. 3-5). pap. 7.99 (978-1-4109-4028-5(4)); lib. bdg. 30.65 (978-1-4109-4017-9(9)) Heinemann-Raintree. (NA-r).

Petrie, Kristin. The Muscular System, 1 vol. 2007. (Human Body Ser.). (ENG., Illus.). 32p. (gr. 4-7). 27.07 (978-1-59679-711-6(8), Checkerboard Library) ABDO Publishing Co.

Rau, Dana Meachen. My Bones & Muscles. 2013. (Bookworms Fluent — My Body Ser.). 24p. (gr. 1-3). pap. 8.22 (978-1-62712-032-6(7)) Cavendish Square Publishing.

—My Bones & Muscles. 2014. (Illus.). 23p. (J). pap. (978-1-67212-032-6(2)) Musa Publishing.

Ross, Veronica. Muscles. 2004. (Body Ser.). (Illus.). 32p. (J). (gr. -1-3). lib. bdg. 27.10 (978-1-59389-166-4(0)) Chrysalis Education.

Rushworth, Gary. Body Systems: Set of 6: Skeletal & Muscular. 2011. (Navigators Ser.). (J). pap. (978-1-4108-5085-0(4)) Benchmark Education Co.

Shaffer, Jody Jensen. My Muscles. Alberini, Teresa, illus. 2015. (Inside My Body Ser.). (ENG.). 24p. (J). (gr. 1-3). 19.95 (978-1-60753-757-1(5)) Amicus Publishing.

Spilsbury, Louise & Spilsbury, Richard. The Science of the Skeleton & Muscles. 2017. (Flowchart Smart Ser.). 48p. (gr. 4-5). pap. 84.30 **(978-1-5382-0686-7(2))** Stevens, Gareth Publishing LLLP.

Thames, Susan. Our Muscles. 2007. (ENG., Illus.). 24p. (gr. k-1). per. 8.95 (978-1-60044-673-3(6)) Rourke Educational Media.

Tieck, Sarah. Muscular System, 1 vol. 2011. (Body Systems Ser.). (ENG., Illus.). 32p. (J). (gr. 2-5). lib. bdg. 27.07 (978-1-61613-499-0(2)) ABDO Publishing Co.

Treays, Rebecca. Understanding Your Muscles & Bones: Internet-Linked. Fox, Christyan, illus. rev. ed. 2006. (Usborne Science for Beginners Ser.). 32p. (J). (gr. 3-7). per. 7.99 (978-0-7945-0813-5(8), Usborne) EDC Publishing.

Williams, Ben. Look Inside: Your Skeleton & Muscles, 1 vol. 2nd rev. ed. 2013. (Nonfiction Readers Ser.). (ENG., Illus.). 28p. (J). (gr. 2-2). pap. 23.96 (978-1-4807-1056-6(3)) Shell Educational Publishing.

—Your Skeleton & Muscles, 1 vol. 2nd rev. ed. 2011. (Nonfiction Readers Ser.). (ENG.). 28p. (J). (gr. 2-2). pap. 6.99 (978-1-4333-3635-5(9)) Teacher Created Materials, Inc.

MUSEUMS

see also Art Museums

also names of countries, cities, etc. with the subdivision Galleries and Museums (e.g. United States—Galleries and Museums; etc.); and names of galleries and museums, e.g. New York Metropolitan Museum of Art

Andersen, Jill. My Favorite Museum. 2016. (Rosen REAL Readers: Social Studies Nonfiction / Fiction: Family, Community, & the World Ser.). 8p. (gr. 1-k). pap. 5.46 (978-1-5081-2266-1(0), Rosen Classroom) Rosen Publishing Group, Inc., The.

Bishop, Celeste. A Day at the Children's Museum. 2016. (Places in My Community Ser.). 00024p. (J). (gr. 1-1). pap. 8.25 (978-1-4994-2773-8(5), PowerKids Pr.) Rosen Publishing Group, Inc., The.

Bolden, Tonya. How to Build a Museum: Smithsonian's National Museum of African American History & Culture. 2016. (Smithsonian Ser.). (ENG., Illus.). 64p. (J). (gr. 5-7). 17.99 (978-0-451-47637-1(9), Viking Books for Young Readers) Penguin Young Readers Group.

Broom, Jenny. Animalium. Scott, Katie, illus. 2014. (Welcome to the Museum Ser.). (ENG.). 112p. (J). (gr. 3-7). 35.00 (978-0-7636-7508-0(3), Big Picture Press) Candlewick Pr.

Candlewick Press, Candlewick. The Louvre. McMenemy, Sarah, illus. 2014. (Panorama Pops Ser.). (ENG.). 64p. (J). (gr. k-4). 8.99 (978-0-7636-7506-6(7)) Candlewick Pr.

Clark, Rosalyn. A Visit to the Museum. 2017. (Bumba Books (tm) — Places We Go Ser.). (ENG.). 24p. (J). (gr. -1-1). 25.32 **(978-1-5124-3371-5(3))** Lerner Publishing Group.

Cooley Peterson, Megan. The National Air & Space Museum. 2017. (Smithsonian Field Trips Ser.). (ENG.). 32p. (gr. 3-4). lib. bdg. 27.99 **(978-1-5157-7974-2(2))** Capstone Press of Coughlan Cos.

—The National Museum of American History. 2017. (Smithsonian Field Trips Ser.). (ENG.). 32p. (gr. 3-4). lib. bdg. 27.99 **(978-1-5157-7976-6(9))** Capstone Press of Coughlan Cos.

Cuthbert, Megan & Siemens, Jared. Museum. 2016. (J). **(978-1-5105-1885-8(1))** SmartBook Media, Inc.

Ducatteau, Florence. A Day at the Museum. Peten, Chantal, illus. 2013. (Want to Know Ser.). (ENG.). 32p. (J). (gr. k-2). 16.95 (978-1-60537-142-9(4)) Cobblestone Publishing Co.

First Sticker Book Museums. 2017. (First Sticker Bks.). (ENG.). (J). pap. 6.99 **(978-0-7945-3999-3(8)**, Usborne) EDC Publishing.

Gloor, Elizabeth. The Cultural Institutions of New York City. 2011. (My Community Ser.). (ENG., Illus.). 12p. (gr. 2-2). pap. 6.95 (978-1-4488-5716-6(3), Rosen Classroom) Rosen Publishing Group, Inc., The.

Gorman, Jacqueline Laks. The Museum. 2005. (I Like to Visit Ser.). (Illus.). 24p. (gr. k-3). pap. 8.15 (978-0-8368-4460-3(2), Weekly Reader Leveled Readers) Stevens, Gareth Publishing LLLP.

—The Museum (El Museo) Acosta, Tatiana & Gutiérrez, Guillermo, trs. 2005. (I Like to Visit/Me Gusta Visitar Ser.). (SPA & ENG., Illus.). 24p. (gr. k-3). lib. bdg. 22.00 (978-0-8368-4597-6(8), Weekly Reader Leveled Readers) Stevens, Gareth Publishing LLLP.

—The Museum/El Museo. 2005. (I Like to Visit/ Me gusta visitar Ser.). (ENG & SPA., Illus.). 24p. (gr. k-3). pap. 8.15 (978-0-8368-4604-1(4), Weekly Reader Leveled Readers) Stevens, Gareth Publishing LLLP.

Gregory, Joy. The Field Museum of Natural History. 2014. (Illus.). 24p. (J). (978-1-4896-3252-4(2)) Weigl Pubs., Inc.

Guidone, Lisa M. What Happens at a Museum? 2008. (Where People Work Ser.). 24p. (gr. -1-3). (J). lib. bdg. 22.00 (978-0-8368-9276-5(3)); pap. 8.15 (978-0-8368-9375-5(1)) Stevens, Gareth Publishing LLLP. (Weekly Reader Leveled Readers).

Hayes, Amy. Discovering STEM at the Museum. 2015. (STEM in the Real World Ser.). (ENG., Illus.). 24p. (J). (gr. 2-3). pap. 8.25 (978-1-4994-0919-2(2), PowerKids Pr.) Rosen Publishing Group, Inc., The.

Hill, Mary. Let's Go to a Science Center. 2004. (Welcome Bks.). (ENG.). 24p. (J). (gr. -1-2). pap. 4.95 (978-0-516-25920-8(2), Children's Pr.) Scholastic Library Publishing.

Honey, Alison. My Ashmolean Discovery Book. 2010. (ENG., Illus.). 24p. (J). (gr. -1-3). pap. 9.95 (978-1-85444-242-0(2)) Ashmolean Museum GBR. Dist: National Bk. Network.

Hopper, Whitney. Time to Go to the Science Museum! Work with Time. 2014. (Math Masters: Measurement & Data Ser.). 24p. (J). (gr. 2-3). 23.60 (978-1-4777-6406-0(2)); (ENG.). pap. 8.25 (978-1-4777-4819-0(9)) Rosen Publishing Group, Inc., The. (Rosen Classroom).

Howse, Jennifer. The British Museum. 2014. (J). (978-1-4896-1186-4(X)) Weigl Pubs., Inc.

Howse, Jennifer. Museum Volunteer. 2016. (J). **(978-1-4896-5851-7(3))** Weigl Pubs., Inc.

Korrell, Emily B. Awesome Adventures at the Smithsonian: The Official Kids Guide to the Smithsonian Institution. 2013. (ENG., Illus.). 128p. (gr. 2-5). pap. 14.95 (978-1-58834-349-9(9), Smithsonian Bks.) Smithsonian Institution Scholarly Pr.

Kreisman, Rachelle. Things We Do: A Kids' Guide to Community Activity. Haggerty, Tim, illus. 2015. (Start Smart: Community Ser.). (ENG.). 32p. (gr. 1-3). 26.65 (978-1-937529-51-2(7)) Red Chair Pr.

Lee, Michelle. Guggenheim Museum. 2015. (How Did They Build That? Ser.). (ENG., Illus.). 32p. (gr. 3-8). 27.99 (978-1-62920-563-2(X)) Scobre Pr. Corp.

Lindeen, Carol K. What Is a Museum?, 6 vols., Set. 2004. (Phonics Readers Books 37-72 Ser.). (ENG.). 8p. (gr. k-1). pap. 35.70 (978-0-7368-4076-7(1), Phonics Readers) Capstone Press of Coughlan Cos.

Macken, JoAnn Early. The Dinosaur Museum. 2010. (My Community Ser.). 24p. (J). 25.65 (978-1-60753-023-7(6)) Amicus Publishing.

Margaret, Amy. George Bush Presidential Library. 2004. (Presidential Libraries Ser.). (Illus.). 24p. (J). lib. bdg. 22.60 (978-0-8239-6273-0(3), PowerKids Pr.) Rosen Publishing Group, Inc., The.

—Gerald R. Ford Library & Museum. 2004. (Presidential Libraries Ser.). (Illus.). 24p. (J). lib. bdg. 22.60 (978-0-8239-6270-9(9), PowerKids Pr.) Rosen Publishing Group, Inc., The.

Mark, Jan. The Museum Book: A Guide to Strange & Wonderful Collections. Holland, Richard, illus. (ENG.). 56p. (J). 2014. (gr. 2-5). 8.99 (978-0-7636-7500-4(8)) 2007. (gr. 3-7). 18.99 (978-0-7636-3370-7(4)) Candlewick Pr.

Markarian, Margie. Who Cleans Dinosaur Bones? Working at a Museum. 2010. (Wild Work Ser.). (ENG.). 32p. (gr. 1-2). pap. 8.29 (978-1-4109-3857-2(3), Read Me!) Heinemann-Raintree.

METROPOLITAN MUSEUM OF ART, Metropolitan Museum, compiled by. Nyc ABC. 2016. (ENG., Illus.). 60p. (J). (gr. -1-3). 4.98 (978-0-7893-2597-6(7), Rizzoli Universe Promotional Bks.) Rizzoli International Pubns., Inc.

Nelson, Jo. Historium. Wilkinson, Richard, illus. 2015. (Welcome to the Museum Ser.). (ENG.). 112p. (J). (gr. 3-7). 35.00 (978-0-7636-7984-2(4), Big Picture Press) Candlewick Pr.

Pioch, Marc. Art & Culture: Exploring the Louvre: Shapes (Grade 3) 2017. (Mathematics Readers Ser.). (Illus.). 32p. (J). (gr. 3-3). pap. 8.99 **(978-1-4807-5813-1(2))** Teacher Created Materials, Inc.

Quinlivan, Kelly. Science Museum Time! Work with Time, 1 vol. 2015. (InfoMax Common Core Math Readers Ser.). (ENG.). 24p. (J). pap. 8.25 (978-1-4777-4755-1(9), Rosen Classroom) Rosen Publishing Group, Inc., The.

Rissman, Rebecca. Going to a Museum, 1 vol. 2012. (World of Field Trips Ser.). (ENG.). 24p. (gr. -1-1). pap. 6.29 (978-1-4329-6076-6(8)); lib. bdg. 22.65 (978-1-4329-6067-4(9)) Heinemann-Raintree. (Acorn).

Ross, Tony. Let's Visit the Louvre Museum. 2012. (ENG., Illus.). 36p. (J). (gr. 2-6). pap. 11.99 (978-1-85103-230-3(4)) Moonlight Publishing, Ltd. GBR. Dist: Independent Pubs. Group.

Wells, Naomi. Stars at the Science Museum: What Will Happen? 2017. (Computer Science for the Real World Ser.). 12p. (gr. 6-7). pap. 7.05 **(978-1-5383-5152-9(8)**, Rosen Classroom) Rosen Publishing Group, Inc., The.

Wight, Karol. Paperweight Pals. 2012. (Illus.). 22p. (J). (978-0-87290-191-9(2)) Corning Museum of Glass.

Yenawine, Philip. Places. 2006. (Illus.). 22p. (J). (gr. 4-8). reprint ed. 15.00 (978-1-4223-5407-0(5)) DIANE Publishing Co.

MUSEUMS—FICTION

Adler, David A. Bones & the Dinosaur Mystery. Newman, Barbara Johansen, illus. 2005. (Jeffrey Bones Mystery Ser.: No. 4). 32p. (J). (978-0-670-05970-6(6), Viking Adult) Penguin Publishing Group.

—Bones & the Dinosaur Mystery, No. 4. Newman, Barbara Johansen, illus. 2009. (Bones Ser.: 4). (ENG.). 32p. (J). (gr. 1-3). mass mkt. 3.99 (978-0-14-241341-8(0), Penguin Young Readers) Penguin Young Readers Group.

Ali, Raydin. The Mystic Museum. 2010. 64p. pap. 12.00 (978-1-4269-1138-5(6)) Trafford Publishing.

Allison, Jennifer. The Dead Drop. 2010. (Gilda Joyce Ser.). (ENG.). 320p. (J). (gr. 5-18). 9.99 (978-0-14-241638-9(X), Puffin Books) Penguin Young Readers Group.

Aureliani, Franco. Dino-Mike & the Museum Mayhem. Aureliani, Franco, illus. 2015. (Dino-Mike! Ser.). (ENG., Illus.). 128p. (gr. 1-3). lib. bdg. 25.32 (978-1-4342-9628-3(8), Dino-Mike!) Stone Arch Bks.

Aureliani, Franco, illus. Dino-Mike & the Museum Mayhem. 2015. (J). lib. bdg. (978-1-4062-9391-3(1)) Stone Arch Bks.

Bailer, Darice. The Last Rail. 2011. (ENG.). 32p. (J). 9.95 (978-1-60727-173-4(7)) Soundprints.

—The Pony Express. Antonishak, Tom, illus. 3rd ed. 2003. (Soundprints' Read-and-Discover Ser.). (ENG.). 48p. (J). (gr. -1-3). pap. 3.95 (978-1-59249-019-6(0), S2008) Soundprints.

Bakewell, Lori. Savannah Adventure: Pirate's Treasure. 2007. 173p. (J). pap. 12.95 (978-0-9799473-9-1(1)) Tailwind Press.

Barkley, Callie. Liz's Night at the Museum. Bishop, Tracy, illus. 2016. (Critter Club Ser.: 15). (ENG.). 128p. (J). (gr. k-4). pap. 5.99 (978-1-4814-7164-0(3), Little Simon) Little Simon.

Battista, Mary Jane. Danny's Day at the Children's Museum. 2009. 24p. pap. 11.49 (978-1-4389-4396-1(2)) AuthorHouse.

The Battle of Bayport. 2014. (Hardy Boys Adventures Ser.: 6). (ENG., Illus.). 160p. (J). (gr. 3-7). 16.99 (978-1-4814-0007-7(X)); pap. 6.99 (978-1-4814-0006-0(1)) Simon & Schuster Children's Publishing. (Aladdin).

Brett, Jan. Mossy. Brett, Jan, illus. 2012. (ENG., Illus.). 32p. (J). (gr. -1-k). 18.99 (978-0-399-25782-7(9), G.P. Putnam's Sons Books for Young Readers) Penguin Young Readers Group.

Brezenoff, Steve. The Case of the Counterfeit Painting. Weber, Lisa K., illus. 2016. (Museum Mysteries Ser.). (ENG.). 128p. (gr. 2-3). pap. 6.95 (978-1-4965-2522-2(1), Museum Mysteries) Stone Arch Bks.

—The Case of the Soldier's Ghost. Weber, Lisa K., illus. 2016. (Museum Mysteries Ser.). (ENG.). 128p. (gr. 2-3). lib. bdg. 26.65 (978-1-4965-2519-2(1), Museum Mysteries) Stone Arch Bks.

—The Crook That Made Kids Cry, 1 vol. Calo, Marcos, illus. 2013. (Field Trip Mysteries Ser.). (ENG.). 88p. (gr. 2-3). pap. 6.10 (978-1-4342-6210-3(3)); lib. bdg. 25.32 (978-1-4342-5977-6(3)) Stone Arch Bks.

—Crook That Made Kids Cry. 2013. (Field Trip Mysteries Ser.). (ENG.). 88p. (gr. 2-3). pap. 35.70 (978-1-4342-6232-5(4)) Stone Arch Bks.

—Dinosaur That Disappeared. 2013. (Field Trip Mysteries Ser.). (ENG.). 88p. (gr. 2-3). pap. 35.70 (978-1-4342-6233-2(2)) Stone Arch Bks.

—Museum Mysteries. Weber, Lisa K., illus. 2015. (Museum Mysteries Ser.). (ENG.). 128p. (gr. 2-3). 106.60 (978-1-4965-0262-9(0), Museum Mysteries) Stone Arch Bks.

—The Outlaw from Outer Space: An Interactive Mystery Adventure. Calo, Marcos, illus. 2017. (You Choose Stories: Field Trip Mysteries Ser.). (ENG.). 112p. (gr. 3-7). lib. bdg. 32.65 (978-1-4965-2644-1(9)) Stone Arch Bks.

Brezenoff, Steven. The Case of the Haunted History Museum. Weber, Lisa K., illus. 2015. (Museum Mysteries Ser.). (ENG.). 128p. (gr. 2-3). lib. bdg. 26.65 (978-1-4342-9687-0(3)) Stone Arch Bks.

—The Case of the Missing Museum Archives. Weber, Lisa K., illus. 2015. (Museum Mysteries Ser.). (ENG.). 128p. (gr. 2-3). lib. bdg. 26.65 (978-1-4342-9688-7(1)) Stone Arch Bks.

—The Case of the Portrait Vandal. Weber, Lisa K., illus. 2015. (Museum Mysteries Ser.). (ENG.). 128p. (gr. 2-3). lib. bdg. 26.65 (978-1-4342-9685-6(7)) Stone Arch Bks.

—The Case of the Soldier's Ghost. Weber, Lisa K., illus. 2017. 120p. (J). pap. (978-1-4965-2531-4(0)) Stone Arch Bks.

—The Case of the Stolen Sculpture. Weber, Lisa K., illus. 2015. (Museum Mysteries Ser.). (ENG.). 128p. (gr. 2-3). lib. bdg. 26.65 (978-1-4342-9686-3(5)) Stone Arch Bks.

—The Case of the Stolen Space Suit. Weber, Lisa K., illus. 2016. (Museum Mysteries Ser.). (ENG.). 128p. (gr. 2-3). 26.65 (978-1-4965-2516-1(7)) Stone Arch Bks.

Brown, Marc. Arthur Lost in the Museum. 2005. (Step into Reading Ser.). (ENG., Illus.). 24p. (J). (gr. k-3). pap. 3.99 (978-0-375-82973-4(3), Random Hse. Bks. for Young Readers) Random Hse. Children's Bks.

Burke, Arlene Avery & Hamilton, Phyllis McAllister. Grandma's Fairy Tale Museum. 2009. 40p. pap. 21.99 (978-1-4415-0607-8(1)) Xlibris Corp.

Burroughs, Scott, illus. Fossil Frenzy. 2014. (Hardy Boys: the Secret Files Ser.: 14). (ENG.). 96p. (J). (gr. 1-4). pap. 5.99 (978-1-4424-9043-7(8), Aladdin) Simon & Schuster Children's Publishing.

Cairn, Barbara. Gatsby's Grand Adventure: Book 2 Renoir's the Apple Seller. Ruble, Eugene, illus. 2013. 16p. pap. 9.95 (978-1-61633-387-4(1)) Guardian Angel Publishing, Inc.

Cali, Davide & Chaud, Benjamin. A Funny Thing Happened at the Museum ... 2017. (ENG., Illus.). 44p. (J). (gr. 1-4). 12.99 (978-1-4521-5593-7(3)) Chronicle Bks. LLC.

Candlewick Press, Candlewick. Peppa Pig & the Day at the Museum. 2015. (Peppa Pig Ser.). (ENG., Illus.). 32p. (J). (-k). 12.99 (978-0-7636-8060-2(5), Candlewick Entertainment) Candlewick Pr.

Casad, Mary Brooke. Bluebonnet at the Ocean Star Museum, 1 vol. Vincent, Benjamin, Illus. 2012. (ENG.). 32p. (J). (gr. k-3). 16.99 (978-1-4556-1721-0(0)) Pelican Publishing Co., Inc.

Chambers, Mark, illus. Zach & Lucy & the Museum of Natural Wonders. 2016. (Zach & Lucy Ser.). (ENG.). 40p. (J). (gr. 1-3). pap. 3.99 (978-1-4814-3935-0(9), Simon Spotlight) Simon Spotlight.

Cousins, Lucy. Maisy Goes to the Museum. Cousins, Lucy, illus. 2009. (Maisy Ser.). (ENG., Illus.). 32p. (J). (gr. k-k). pap. 6.99 (978-0-7636-4370-6(X)) Candlewick Pr.

Crain, Kira. SEK Statton. 2009. (GER.). 136p. 29.95 (978-1-4092-6127-8(1)) Lulu Pr., Inc.

Cummings, Pat. Harvey Moon, Museum Boy. Cummings, Pat, illus. 2008. (Illus.). 32p. (J). (gr. -1-3). lib. bdg. 18.89 (978-0-06-057861-9(0)) HarperCollins Pubs.

Cummings, Troy. The Notebook of Doom #6: Pop of the Bumpy Mummy (a Branches Book) - Library Edition. 2014. (Notebook of Doom Ser.: 6). (ENG.). 96p. (J). (gr. 1-3). 15.99 (978-0-545-69899-3(5)) Scholastic, Inc.

—Pop of the Bumpy Mummy. Cummings, Troy, illus. 2014. (Notebook of Doom Ser.: 6). (ENG., Illus.). 96p. (J). (gr. 1-3). pap. 4.99 (978-0-545-69898-6(7)) Scholastic, Inc.

Czernecki, Stefan. Mystery at Midnight Museum. Date not set. 32p. (J). 14.99 (978-0-06-026199-3(4)) HarperCollins Pubs.

David Wiggles: Individual Title Six-Packs. (gr. -1-2). 27.00 (978-0-7635-9445-9(8)) Rigby Education.

Davis, Jacky. Ladybug Girl's Day Out with Grandpa. Soman, David, illus. 2017. (Ladybug Girl Ser.). (ENG.). 40p. (J). (-k). 17.99 (978-0-8037-4032-7(8), Dial Bks) Penguin Young Readers Group.

de Brunhoff, Laurent. Babar's Museum of Art, 65 vols. 2003. (ENG., Illus.). 48p. (J). (gr. -1-17). 19.99 (978-0-8109-4597-5(5)) Abrams, Inc.

Evans, Dustin, illus. Dinosaur Drama, 1 vol. 2013. (Mystical Pencil Ser.). (ENG.). 32p. (J). (gr. 3-6). 28.50 (978-1-61641-927-1(X)) Magic Wagon.

Evans, Michelle D. I Don't Belong in the Jungle. 2011. 20p. pap. 24.95 (978-1-4626-1382-3(9)) America Star Bks.

Floca, Brian. The Frightful Story of Harry Walfish. Floca, Brian, illus. 2004. (Illus.). 26p. (J). (gr. k-4). reprint ed. pap. (978-0-7567-7852-1(2)) DIANE Publishing Co.

Foxlee, Karen. Ophelia & the Marvelous Boy. 2014. (ENG.). 240p. (J). (gr. 3-7). 16.99 (978-0-385-75354-8(3), Knopf Bks. for Young Readers) Random Hse. Children's Bks.

Gannon, Nicholas. The Doldrums. 368p. (J). (gr. 3-7). 2017. pap. 7.99 **(978-0-06-232095-7(5))** 2015. (ENG., Illus.). 17.99 (978-0-06-232094-0(7)) HarperCollins Pubs. (Greenwillow Bks.).

Garcia, Marina, et al. Mateo de Paseo Por el Museo Del Prado. 2004. (SPA.). 42p. (J). 18.99 (978-84-8488-070-7(2)) Serres, Ediciones, S. L. ESP. Dist: Lectorum Pubns., Inc.

Garton, Sam. Otter in Space. Garton, Sam, illus. 2015. (ENG., Illus.). 32p. (J). (gr. -1-3). 16.99 (978-0-06-224776-6(X)) HarperCollins Pubs.

Gayle, Sharon Shavers. Emma's Escape: A Story of America's Underground Railroad. Velasquez, Eric, illus. 3rd ed. 2003. (Soundprints' Read-and-Discover Ser.). (ENG.). 48p. (J). (gr. -1-3). pap. 3.95 (978-1-59249-021-9(2), S2009) Soundprints.

Gilman, Grace. Dixie & the School Trip. 2012. (Dixie: I Can Read Ser.). (J). lib. bdg. 13.55 (978-0-606-26284-2(9), Turtleback) Turtleback Bks.

Goldin, David. Meet Me at the Art Museum: A Whimsical Look Behind the Scenes. 2012. (ENG., Illus.). 40p. (J). (gr. k-2). 19.95 (978-1-4197-0187-0(8), Abrams Bks. for Young Readers) Abrams, Inc.

Goldman, Leslie & Trenc, Milan. Night at the Museum. 2006. (ENG., Illus.). 144p. (J). (gr. 3-7). per. 4.99 (978-0-7641-3576-7(7)) Barron's Educational Series, Inc.

Gutierrez, Elisa. Picturescape. rev. ed. 2007. (ENG., Illus.). 40p. (J). (gr. -1-3). pap. 9.95 (978-1-894965-65-1(5)) Simply Read Bks. CAN. Dist: Ingram Publisher Services.

Gutman, Dan. My Weird School Goes to the Museum. Paillot, Jim, illus. 2016. 30p. (J). **(978-1-5182-2157-6(2))** Harper & Row Ltd.

—My Weird School Goes to the Museum. Paillot, Jim, illus. 2016. (I Can Read Level 2 Ser.). 32p. (J). (gr. -1-3). pap. 3.99 (978-0-06-236742-6(0)) HarperCollins Pubs.

Harrison, Zac. Frozen Enemies, 1 vol. 2013. (Hyperspace High Ser.). (ENG.). 288p. (gr. 4-8). 27.32 (978-1-4342-6307-0(X)) Stone Arch Bks.

Henry, James. The Cabinet of Curiosities. 2010. 240p. pap. 21.50 (978-0-9559851-0-2(2)) Blue Cat GBR. Dist: Lulu Pr., Inc.

Hergé. The Broken Ear. 2011. (Adventures of Tintin: Young Readers Edition Ser.). (ENG., Illus.). 96p. (J). (gr. 3-17). pap. 11.00 (978-0-316-13385-2(X)) Little, Brown Bks. for Young Readers.

Hosch, Amanda. Mabel Opal Pear & the Rules for Spying. Sluyterman van Langeweyde, Ira, illus. 2017. (Middle-Grade Novels Ser.). (ENG.). 272p. (gr. 4-7). lib. bdg. 26.65 **(978-1-4965-4051-5(4))** Stone Arch Bks.

Huffman, Mindy. Sofia Goes to the Science Museum: What Will Happen? 2017. (Computer Science for the Real World Ser.). 12p. (gr. 6-7). pap. 7.05 **(978-1-5383-5150-5(1)**, Rosen Classroom) Rosen Publishing Group, Inc., The.

Hunt, Elizabeth Singer. The Escape of the Deadly Dinosaur - USA. Williamson, Brian, illus. 2007. (Secret Agent Jack Stalwart Ser.: 1). (ENG.). 128p. (J). (gr. 1-4). per. 5.99 (978-1-60286-004-9(1), Weinstein Bks.) Perseus Bks. Group.

—The Mystery of the Mona Lisa, Bk. 3. Williamson, Brian, illus. 2007. (Secret Agent Jack Stalwart Ser.: 3). (ENG.). 128p. (J). (gr. 1-4). per. 5.99 (978-1-60286-001-8(7), Weinstein Bks.) Perseus Bks. Group.

Isaacson, Rick. The Magic Museum. 2013. 34p. pap. 19.95 (978-0-9844938-4-5(0)) Lexingford Publishing.

Jaggi, Harleen. Mystery at the Book Store. 2007. (J). per. (978-0-9790896-0-2(3)) Booksmart Pubns.

Jakubowski, Michele. The Professor's Discovery. Pinelli, Amerigo, illus. 2016. (Sleuths of Somerville Ser.). (ENG.). 144p. (gr. 4-6). lib. bdg. 25.99 *(978-1-4965-3177-3(9))* Stone Arch Bks.

—The Professor's Discovery. Pinelli, Amerigo, illus. 2017. (Sleuths of Somerville Ser.). (ENG.). 144p. (gr. 4-6). pap. 6.95 *(978-1-4965-3181-0(7))* Stone Arch Bks.

Jane, Pamela. Winky Blue Goes Wild! Tilley, Debbie, illus. 2003. 64p. (J). 13.95 *(978-1-59034-588-7(6))*; pap. *(978-1-59034-589-4(4))* Mondo Publishing.

Johnson, Shane, illus. OLIVIA Paints a Mural. 2011. (Olivia TV Tie-In Ser.). (ENG.). 12p. (J). (gr. -1-1). bds. 5.99 *(978-1-4424-1674-1(2)*, Simon Spotlight) Simon Spotlight.

Johnson-Simon. Anaya Visits the James E Lewis Museum of Art at Morgan State University. 2009. 40p. pap. 16.99 *(978-1-4490-1884-9(X))* AuthorHouse.

Keene, Carolyn. Butterfly Blues. Francis, Peter, illus. 2015. (Nancy Drew & the Clue Crew Ser.: 40). (ENG.). 96p. (J). (gr. 1-4). pap. 5.99 *(978-1-4814-1470-8(4)*, Aladdin) Simon & Schuster Children's Publishing.

Kelly, Katherine, text. Albert Bear & the Big Celebration. 2005. (J). 12.95 *(978-0-9773481-0-7(5))* Kelly, Katherine.

Kelly, Kathy & Feder, Debbie. Jelly Bean's Art Museum Adventure. 2012. 40p. pap. 20.99 *(978-1-4772-4828-7(5))* AuthorHouse.

Kenah, Katharine. The Best Seat in Second Grade. Carter, Abby, illus. 2006. (I Can Read Level 2 Ser.). (ENG.). 48p. (J). (gr. k-3). pap. 3.99 *(978-0-06-000736-2(2))* HarperCollins Pubs.

—The Best Seat in Second Grade. Carter, Abby, illus. 2006. (I Can Read Bks.). 48p. (J). (gr. -1-3). 11.65 *(978-0-7569-6979-0(4))* Perfection Learning Corp.

Kerr, P. B., pseud. The Day of the Djinn Warriors. 2008. (Children of the Lamp Ser.: 4). (ENG.). 400p. (J). (gr. 3-7). 7.99 *(978-0-439-93216-5(5)*, Scholastic Paperbacks) Scholastic, Inc.

Kientz, Chris & Hockensmith, Steve. The Wrong Wrights. Keane, John & Nielsen, Lee, illus. 2016. (Secret Smithsonian Adventures Ser.: 1). (ENG.). 64p. (J). (gr. 4-7). pap. 10.95 *(978-1-58834-541-7(6)*, Smithsonian Bks.) Smithsonian Institution Scholarly Pr.

Kirby, Stan. Captain Awesome & the Mummy's Treasure. O'Connor, George, illus. 2015. (Captain Awesome Ser.: 15). (ENG.). 128p. (J). (gr. k-4). pap. 5.99 *(978-1-4814-4438-5(7)*, Little Simon) Little Simon.

Kirk, Daniel. Library Mouse: A Museum Adventure. 2012. (ENG., Illus.). 32p. (J). (gr. k-2). 17.95 *(978-1-4197-0173-3(8)*, Abrams Bks. for Young Readers) Abrams, Inc.

Konigsburg, E. L. From the Mixed-up Files of Mrs. Basil E. Frankweiler. 2007. (Illus.). 74p. (J). pap. *(978-0-545-04173-7(2))* Scholastic, Inc.

—From the Mixed-up Files of Mrs. Basil E. Frankweiler. l.t. ed. 2005. 186p. pap. 10.95 *(978-0-7862-7358-4(5)*, Large Print Pr.) Thorndike Pr.

Krulik, Nancy. Don't Be Such a Turkey! John and Wendy Staff, illus. 2010. (Katie Kazoo, Switcheroo Ser.). (ENG.). 160p. (J). (gr. 2-4). pap. 4.99 *(978-0-448-45448-1(3)*, Grosset & Dunlap) Penguin Young Readers Group.

—No Bones about It. John and Wendy Staff, illus. 12th ed. 2004. (Katie Kazoo, Switcheroo Ser.: 12). (ENG.). 80p. (J). (gr. 2-4). pap. 3.99 *(978-0-448-43358-5(3)*, Grosset & Dunlap) Penguin Young Readers Group.

Kruse, Donald W. Jasper Has Left the Building! Crank, Donny, illus. 2013. 50p. pap. 12.95 *(978-1-59663-863-1(X)*, Castle Keep Pr.) Rock, James A. & Co. Pubs.

LaFevers, R. L. Theodosia & the Eyes of Horus. Tanaka, Yoko, illus. 2011. (ENG.). 384p. (J). (gr. 2-5). pap. 7.99 *(978-0-547-55011-4(1))* Houghton Mifflin Harcourt Publishing Co.

—Theodosia & the Serpents of Chaos. Tanaka, Yoko, illus. 2008. (ENG.). 352p. (J). (gr. 2-5). pap. 7.99 *(978-0-618-99976-7(0))* Houghton Mifflin Harcourt Publishing Co.

LaPorte, Tom. Hembree Heiroglyphs. 2008. 98p. pap. 9.42 *(978-1-4357-5970-1(2))* Lulu Pr., Inc.

Lattimore, Deborah Nourse. Mystery at Midnight Museum. Date not set. 32p. (J). 15.89 *(978-0-06-026202-0(8))* HarperCollins Pubs.

Lavette, Lavaille. The Adventures of Roopster Roux: That's Not Punny, 1 vol. Nguyen, Duke, ed. Kuon, Vuthy, illus. 2007. (Roupster Roux Ser.: Vol. 5). (ENG.). 32p. (J). (gr. 3-7). 16.95 *(978-1-58980-483-8(X))* Pelican Publishing Co., Inc.

Lehman, Barbara. Museum Trip. 2006. (ENG., Illus.). 40p. (J). (gr. -1-3). 16.99 *(978-0-618-58125-2(1))* Houghton Mifflin Harcourt Publishing Co.

Lemke, Donald. Batman Classic: Dino Dilemma. Tong, Andie, illus. 2017. (I Can Read Level 2 Ser.). 32p. (J). (gr. -1-3). pap. 3.99 ***(978-0-06-236091-5(4))*** HarperCollins Pubs.

Lithgow, John. The Carnival of the Animals. Kulikov, Boris, illus. 2004. (ENG.). 40p. (J). (gr. -1-3). 19.99 *(978-0-689-86721-7(2)*, Simon & Schuster Bks. For Young Readers) Simon & Schuster Bks. For Young Readers.

—Micawber. Payne, C. F., illus. 2005. (ENG.). 40p. (J). (gr. -1-3). reprint ed. 8.99 *(978-0-689-83542-1(6)*, Simon & Schuster Bks. For Young Readers) Simon & Schuster Bks. For Young Readers.

Loux, Matthew. The Time Museum. 2017. (Time Museum Ser.: 1). (ENG., Illus.). 256p. (J). pap. 14.99 *(978-1-59643-849-1(5)*, 9781596438491, First Second Bks.) Roaring Brook Pr.

—The Time Museum. 2017. (J). lib. bdg. 26.95 ***(978-0-606-40348-1(5))*** Turtleback Bks.

LUCAS, David. Christmas at the Toy Museum. LUCAS, David, illus. 2012. (ENG., Illus.). 32p. (J). (gr. -1-2). 15.99 *(978-0-7636-5868-7(5))* Candlewick Pr.

Marsh, Carole. The Mystery at Hollywood. 2011. (Carole Marsh Mysteries Ser.). (J). pap. 7.99 *(978-0-635-07959-6(3)*, Marsh, Carole Mysteries) Gallopade International.

—The Mystery of the Missing Dinosaurs. 2009. (Real Kids, Real Places Ser.). 146p. (J). 18.99 *(978-0-635-06995-5(4)*, Marsh, Carole Mysteries) Gallopade International.

Matyas, Diane. The Terrible Captain Jack Visits the Museum: Or A Guide of Museum Manners for Incorrigible Pirates & the Like. 2008. (Illus.). 24p. (J). *(978-0-9623017-2-8(8))* Noble Maritime Collection, The.

May, Eleanor. Lost in the Mouseum. Melmon, Deborah, illus. 2015. (Mouse Math (r) Ser.). (ENG.). 32p. (J). (gr. -1-1). 22.60 *(978-1-57565-643-4(4))* Kane Press, Inc.

Mayer, Mercer. Little Critter: My Trip to the Science Museum. Mayer, Mercer, illus. 2017. (Little Critter Ser.). (Illus.). 24p. (J). (gr. -1-3). pap. 3.99 *(978-0-06-147809-3(1)*, HarperFestival) HarperCollins Pubs.

Mayer, Mercer. My Trip to the Science Museum. 2017. (Little Critter Ser.). (J). lib. bdg. 13.55 ***(978-0-606-39625-7(X))*** Turtleback Bks.

Mayhew, James. Katie & the Dinosaurs. Mayhew, James, illus. 2014. (ENG., Illus.). 32p. (J). (gr. -1-k). 9.99 *(978-1-4083-3191-0(8))* Hodder & Stoughton GBR. Dist: Hachette Bk. Group.

—Katie & the Waterlily Pond. Mayhew, James, illus. 2015. (Katie Ser.). (ENG., Illus.). 32p. (J). (gr. -1-k). pap. 10.99 *(978-1-4083-3245-0(0))* Hodder & Stoughton GBR. Dist: Hachette Bk. Group.

—Katie's Picture Show. Mayhew, James, illus. 2014. (ENG., Illus.). 32p. (J). (gr. -1-k). 16.99 *(978-1-4083-3605-2(7))* Hodder & Stoughton GBR. Dist: Hachette Bk. Group.

McCann, Jesse Leon. Scooby-Doo & Museum Madness, 1 vol. Duendes Del Sur Staff, illus. 2012. (Scooby-Doo! Set 2 Ser.: No. 2). (ENG.). 24p. (J). (gr. k-3). lib. bdg. 24.21 *(978-1-59961-867-8(2))* Spotlight.

McClatchy, Lisa & Thompson, Kay. Eloise & the Dinosaurs. Lyon, Tammie Speer & Lyon, Tammie, illus. 2007. (Eloise Ser.). (ENG.). 32p. (J). (gr. -1-1). pap. 3.99 *(978-0-689-87453-6(7)*, Simon Spotlight) Simon Spotlight.

McKay, Sindy. We Both Read Bilingual Edition-Museum Day/Dia Del Museo. Johnson, Meredith, illus. 2015.Tr. of Dia Del Museo. (ENG & SPA.). 44p. (J). (gr. k-1). pap. 4.99 *(978-1-60115-064-6(4))* Treasure Bay, Inc.

Menchin, Scott. Grandma in Blue with Red Hat. Bliss, Harry, illus. 2015. (ENG.). 32p. (J). (gr. -1-3). 16.95 *(978-1-4197-1484-9(8)*, Abrams Bks. for Young Readers) Abrams, Inc.

Meredith-Markowitz, Susan. Charlie's Museum Adventure: Set Of 6. 2010. (Early Connections Ser.). (J). pap. 37.00 net. *(978-1-4108-1367-1(3))* Benchmark Education Co.

Messner, Kate. Fergus & Zeke. Ross, Heather, illus. 2017. (ENG.). 56p. (J). (gr. k-3). 14.99 *(978-0-7636-7846-3(5))* Candlewick Pr.

Metcalf, Dan. The Catacombs of Chaos: A Lottie Lipton Adventure. Panagarry, Rachelle, illus. 2017. (Adventures of Lottie Lipton Ser.). (ENG.). (J). (gr. 2-5). 80p. pap. 6.99 ***(978-1-5124-8185-3(8))***; lib. bdg. 25.32 ***(978-1-5124-8183-9(1))*** Lerner Publishing Group. (Darby Creek).

—The Curse of the Cairo Cat: A Lottie Lipton Adventure. Panagarry, Rachelle, illus. 2017. (Adventures of Lottie Lipton Ser.). (ENG.). (J). (gr. 2-5). 80p. pap. 6.99 ***(978-1-5124-8186-0(6))***; lib. bdg. 25.32 ***(978-1-5124-8179-2(3))*** Lerner Publishing Group. (Darby Creek).

—The Eagle of Rome: A Lottie Lipton Adventure. Panagarry, Rachelle, illus. 2017. (Adventures of Lottie Lipton Ser.). (ENG.). (J). (gr. 2-5). 80p. pap. 6.99 ***(978-1-5124-8187-7(4))***; lib. bdg. 25.32 ***(978-1-5124-8184-6(X))*** Lerner Publishing Group. (Darby Creek).

—The Egyptian Enchantment: A Lottie Lipton Adventure. Panagarry, Rachelle, illus. 2017. (Adventures of Lottie Lipton Ser.). (ENG.). (J). (gr. 2-5). 96p. pap. 6.99 ***(978-1-5124-8188-4(2))***; lib. bdg. 25.32 ***(978-1-5124-8182-2(3))*** Lerner Publishing Group. (Darby Creek).

—The Scroll of Alexandria: A Lottie Lipton Adventure. Panagarry, Rachelle, illus. 2017. (Adventures of Lottie Lipton Ser.). (ENG.). 80p. (J). (gr. 2-5). 25.32 ***(978-1-5124-8181-5(5))***; pap. 6.99 ***(978-1-5124-8189-1(0))*** Lerner Publishing Group. (Darby Creek).

—The Secrets of the Stone: A Lottie Lipton Adventure. Panagarry, Rachelle, illus. 2017. (Adventures of Lottie Lipton Ser.). (ENG.). 80p. (J). (gr. 2-5). 25.32 ***(978-1-5124-8180-8(7))***; pap. 6.99 ***(978-1-5124-8190-7(4))*** Lerner Publishing Group. (Darby Creek).

Munoz, Isabel. En el Museo. Mazali, Gustavo, illus. 2011. (Eric & Julieta Ser.).Tr. of At the Museum. (SPA & ENG.). 24p. (J). (gr. -1-3). pap. 3.99 *(978-0-545-34512-5(X)*, Scholastic en Espanol) Scholastic, Inc.

Museum Mayhem. 2014. (Nancy Drew & the Clue Crew Ser.: 39). (ENG., Illus.). 96p. (J). (gr. 1-4). pap. 5.99 *(978-1-4424-9967-6(2)*, Aladdin) Simon & Schuster Children's Publishing.

Nesbit, Sara E. Mary Wants to Be an Artist. 2009. 28p. pap. 12.49 *(978-1-4490-2609-7(5))* AuthorHouse.

Neubecker, Robert. Linus the Vegetarian T. Rex. Neubecker, Robert, illus. 2013. (ENG., Illus.). 40p. (J). (gr. -1-3). 16.99 *(978-1-4169-8512-9(3)*, Beach Lane Bks.) Beach Lane Bks.

Night, P. J. Off the Wall. 2013. (You're Invited to a Creepover Ser.: 14). (ENG., Illus.). 160p. (J). (gr. 3-7). pap. 5.99 *(978-1-4424-7238-9(3)*, Simon Spotlight) Simon Spotlight.

Nolan, Han. When We Were Saints. 2005. (ENG.). 312p. (YA). (gr. 7-12). pap. 15.95 *(978-0-15-205322-2(0))* Houghton Mifflin Harcourt Publishing Co.

Nord, Kristin Magnuson. Moosh & Grizzle. 2011. 28p. (gr. 1-2). 13.95 *(978-1-4269-6167-0(7))* Trafford Publishing.

O'Connor, Jane. Fancy Nancy at the Museum. Enik, Ted & Glasser, Robin Preiss, illus. 2008. (I Can Read Level 1 Ser.). (ENG.). 32p. (J). (gr. -1-3). 16.99 *(978-0-06-123608-2(X))*; pap. 3.99 *(978-0-06-123607-5(1))* HarperCollins Pubs.

O'Connor, Jane & Harper Collins / LeapFrog. Fancy Nancy at the Museum. Glasser, Robin Preiss, illus. 2008. (Fancy Nancy Ser.). (J). 13.99 *(978-1-59319-940-1(6))* LeapFrog Enterprises, Inc.

Oliver, Lauren & Chester, H. C. The Shrunken Head. Lacombe, Benjamin, illus. 2015. (Curiosity House Ser.: 1). (ENG.). 368p. (J). (gr. 3-7). 16.99 *(978-0-06-227081-8(8))* HarperCollins Pubs.

O'neal, Katherine Pebley. The Fume in the Tomb. Collins, Daryl, illus. 2004. 68p. (J). lib. bdg. 15.00 *(978-1-4242-0901-9(3))* Fitzgerald Bks.

O'Reilly, Sean. The Missing Mummy, 1 vol. Arcana Studio Staff, illus. 2012. (Mighty Mighty Monsters Ser.). (ENG.). 48p. (gr. 2-3). pap. 6.10 *(978-1-4342-4609-7(4))* Stone Arch Bks.

Orloff, Karen Kaufman. Nightlight Detective: Mystery at the Museum. Smith, Jamie, illus. 2013. 42p. spiral bd. 12.99 *(978-1-4413-1228-0(5))* Peter Pauper Pr. Inc.

Papademetriou, Lisa. Apartment 1986. 2017. 272p. (J). (gr. 3-7). 16.99 *(978-0-06-237108-9(8))* HarperCollins Pubs.

Parish, Herman. Amelia Bedelia's Backpack Bundle. Sweat, Lynn, illus. 2012. 192p. (J). *(978-1-4351-4392-0(2)*, Greenwillow Bks.) HarperCollins Pubs.

—Amelia Bedelia's Masterpiece. Sweat, Lynn, illus. (I Can Read Level 2 Ser.). (ENG.). 64p. (J). (gr. k-3). 2008. pap. 3.99 *(978-0-06-084357-1(8))* 2007. 16.99 *(978-0-06-084355-7(1))* HarperCollins Pubs. (Greenwillow Bks.).

Parsons, Tom. Pinky the Rat at the Brussels Sprout Museum. 2007. 194p. 27.76 *(978-1-4303-1538-4(5))* Lulu Pr., Inc.

Pavanello, Roberto. King Tut's Grandmother, 1 vol. Zeni, Marco, tr. from ITA. Pisapia, Blasco & Brughera, Pamela, illus. 2012. (Echo & the Bat Pack Ser.). (ENG.). 128p. (gr. 2-3). 9.95 *(978-1-4342-4245-7(5))*; lib. bdg. 25.32 *(978-1-4342-3823-8(7)*, Echo & the Bat Pack) Stone Arch Bks.

Perelstein, Jennifer. Who Moved the Masterpieces? A Visit to the Mcnay Art Museum. 2010. 30p. pap. 15.99 *(978-1-60844-585-1(2))* Dog Ear Publishing, LLC.

The Phantom of Nantucket. 2014. (Nancy Drew Diaries: 7). (ENG., Illus.). 192p. (J). (gr. 3-7). pap. 6.99 *(978-1-4814-0015-2(0)*, Aladdin) Simon & Schuster Children's Publishing.

Prime, D. Van al Museo. (Serie Sara y Pablo - Sarah & Paul Ser.: No. 5).Tr. of Go to the Museum. (SPA.). (J). 2.99 *(978-0-7899-0499-7(3)*, 498899) Editorial Unilit.

Prime, Derek. Sarah & Paul Go to the Museum: Discover about the Ten Commandments. 2006. (Sarah & Paul Ser.). (ENG., Illus.). 128p. (J). (gr. 2-5). per. 6.99 *(978-1-84550-161-7(6)*, 4451dd6e-e239-4e8a-b092-b7a203a1a9fe) Christian Focus Pubns. GBR. Dist: Bookmasters Distribution.

Pushker, Gloria Teles & Tarman, Mel. Toby Belfer Learns about Heroes & Martyrs, 1 vol. Henriquez, Emile, illus. 2009. (Toby Belfer Ser.). (ENG.). 128p. (J). (gr. 3-7). 14.95 *(978-1-58980-647-4(6))* Pelican Publishing Co., Inc.

Rau, Dana. Moon Walk. Buchs, Thomas, illus. 3rd ed. 2003. (Soundprints' Read-and-Discover Ser.). (ENG.). 48p. (J). (gr. -1-3). pap. 4.35 *(978-1-59249-015-8(8)*, S2006) Soundprints.

Rau, Dana Meachen. Moon Walk. Buchs, Thomas, illus. 2004. (Soundprints' Read-and-Discover Ser.). 48p. (gr. -1-3). 13.95 *(978-0-7569-3370-8(6))* Perfection Learning Corp.

Rey, H. A. Curious George Museum Mystery (CGTV 8x8) 2017. (Curious George Ser.). (ENG., Illus.). 24p. (J). (gr. -1-3). 12.99 *(978-0-544-85992-0(8)*, HMH Books For Young Readers) Houghton Mifflin Harcourt Publishing Co.

Richardson, Deborra. Treasures at the Museum. 2011. (Illus.). 64p. (J). pap. 5.99 *(978-0-9824945-1-6(3))* Elevator Group, The.

Rim, Sujean. Birdie's Happiest Halloween. 2016. (ENG., Illus.). 40p. (J). (gr. -1-3). 16.99 *(978-0-316-40746-5(1))* Little Brown & Co.

Ripley's Believe It or Not Editors. Haunted Hotel. 2011. (Ripley RBI Ser.). 128p. (J). pap. 4.99 *(978-1-893951-65-5(0))* Ripley Entertainment, Inc.

Rock, Zack. Homer Henry Hudson's Curio Museum. 2014. (ENG., Illus.). 32p. (J). (gr. 1-3). 18.99 *(978-1-56846-260-8(3)*, Creative Editions) Creative Co., The.

Rosen, Michael. You're Thinking about Doughnuts. Tisdall, Sarah, illus. 2006. 90p. (J). (gr. 2-4). per. 6.95 *(978-1-903015-03-2(0))* Barn Owl Bks, London GBR. Dist: Independent Pubs. Group.

Rosenberg, Aaron. Blackout: Danger in the Dark. 2016. (S. T. E. M. Squad Ser.). (ENG.). 224p. (J). (gr. 3-10). pap. 7.99 *(978-1-4380-0921-6(6))* Barron's Educational Series, Inc.

Rush, Barbara & Stratton, Jane. The Boat in the Attic. 2012. (ENG.). 30p. pap. 15.00 *(978-1-938002-02-1(4)*, Hummingbird World Media) Double Edge Pr.

Sagner, Sibel, et al. A Day at the Museum Blue Band. Pérez, Moni, illus. 2016. (Cambridge Reading Adventures Ser.). (ENG.). 16p. pap. 6.56 *(978-1-316-50320-1(8))* Cambridge Univ. Pr.

Sale, Carolyn. How to Read a Dinosaur & Other Museum Tales. Dubinsky, Lon, ed. 2004. (Illus.). 96p. *(978-1-895766-27-1(3)*, Pacific Educational Pr.) Univ. of British Columbia Pr.

Sally's Picture: Individual Title Six-Packs. (Literatura 2000 Ser.). (gr. 1-2). 28.00 *(978-0-7635-0108-2(5))* Rigby Education.

Sanders, Addie Meyer. I Don't Want to Go. l.t. ed. 2012. 43p. (J). pap. *(978-1-4596-3449-7(7))* ReadHowYouWant.com, Ltd.

Santopolo, Jill. The Nina, the Pinta, & the Vanishing Treasure. 2009. (Alec Flint Mystery Ser.: 1). (ENG.). 192p. (J). (gr. 2-5). pap. 6.99 *(978-0-439-90353-0(X)*, Scholastic Paperbacks) Scholastic, Inc.

Scholastic, Inc. Staff & King, Trey. Detective Chase McCain - Stop That Heist! Kiernan, Kenny, illus. 2013. (Lego City Ser.). (ENG.). 32p. (J). (gr. -1-3). pap. 3.99 *(978-0-545-49596-7(2))* Scholastic, Inc.

Scieszka, Jon. 2095. Smith, Lane, illus. 2004. (Time Warp Trio Ser.: 5). (ENG.). 80p. (J). (gr. 2-4). pap. 5.99 *(978-0-14-240044-9(0)*, Puffin Books) Penguin Young Readers Group.

—2095. Smith, Lane, illus. 2005. (Time Warp Trio Ser.: No. 5). 72p. (gr. 4-7). 15.00 *(978-0-7569-5989-0(6))* Perfection Learning Corp.

Seifert, Brandon. Disney Kingdoms: Seekers of the Weird. 2014. (ENG., Illus.). 120p. (J). (gr. -1-17). 24.99 *(978-0-7851-5452-5(3))* Marvel Worldwide, Inc.

Selznick, Brian. Wonderstruck. Selznick, Brian, illus. 2011. (ENG., Illus.). 640p. (J). (gr. 4-7). 29.99 *(978-0-545-02789-2(6)*, Scholastic Pr.); 300.00 *(978-0-545-38985-3(2))* Scholastic, Inc.

Shields, Kathleen J. Hamilton Troll Meets Dinosaurs. Klug, Leigh A. & Bryant, Carol W., illus. 6th ed. 2013. 36p. 14.00 *(978-0-9882745-5-6(8))* Erin Go Bragh Publishing.

Snyder, Karen. Mona Lisa's Makeover. LaGrange, Tiffany, illus. 2010. 24p. pap. 12.95 *(978-1-936343-15-7(0))* Peppertree Pr., The.

Steele, Michael Anthony. Night at the Museum: Secret of the Tomb. 3rd ed. 2014. (ENG.). 176p. (J). (gr. 3-7). pap. 5.99 *(978-1-4380-0524-9(5))* Barron's Educational Series, Inc.

Stine, R. L. Fright Knight & the Ooze: Twice Terrifying Tales. 2010. (R. L. Stine's Ghosts of Fear Street Ser.). (ENG.). 240p. (J). (gr. 3-7). pap. 6.99 *(978-1-4169-9135-9(2)*, Aladdin) Simon & Schuster Children's Publishing.

Stout, Shawn K. Penelope Crumb Never Forgets. Docampo, Valeria, illus. 2013. (Penelope Crumb Ser.: 2). (ENG.). 208p. (J). (gr. 2-5). pap. 5.99 *(978-0-14-751009-9(0)*, Puffin Books) Penguin Young Readers Group.

Strohm, Stephanie Kate. Pilgrims Don't Wear Pink. 2012. (ENG.). 208p. (YA). (gr. 7). pap. 8.99 *(978-0-547-56459-3(7))* Houghton Mifflin Harcourt Publishing Co.

Suen, Anastasia. Dino Hunt: A Robot & Rico Story. Laughead, Mike, illus. 2010. (Robot & Rico Ser.). (ENG.). 32p. (gr. 1-2). pap. 6.25 *(978-1-4342-2300-5(0))* Stone Arch Bks.

Teitelbaum, Michael. The Phantom Pharaoh. 2015. (Cold Whispers Ser.). (ENG., Illus.). 32p. (J). (gr. 2-6). lib. bdg. 26.60 *(978-1-62724-810-5(2))* Bearport Publishing Co., Inc.

Thomas, Debbie. Dead Hairy. MacDonald, Stella, illus. 2011. (ENG.). 256p. (J). pap. 14.95 *(978-1-85635-678-7(7))* Mercier Pr., Ltd., The IRL. Dist: Dufour Editions, Inc.

Town, Vicky. Mayhem in the Museum. 2013. 74p. pap. 9.99 *(978-1-61720-974-1(0))* Wilder Pubns., Corp.

Trenc, Milan. The Night at the Museum. 2006. (ENG., Illus.). 32p. (J). (gr. -1-2). pap. 6.99 *(978-0-7641-3631-3(3))* Barron's Educational Series, Inc.

Vajda, Tibor Timothy. The End of the World. 2008. 96p. pap. 9.95 *(978-0-595-52914-8(3))* iUniverse, Inc.

Verde, Susan. The Museum. Reynolds, Peter H., illus. 2013. (ENG.). 32p. (J). (gr. k-2). 16.95 *(978-1-4197-0594-6(6)*, Abrams Bks. for Young Readers) Abrams, Inc.

Waite, Judy. Digging for Dinosaurs. Parsons, Garry, illus. 2003. (Flying Foxes Ser.). (ENG.). 48p. (J). lib. bdg. *(978-0-7787-1483-5(7))* Crabtree Publishing Co.

Wallace, Nancy Elizabeth. Stars! Stars! Stars!, 0 vols. Wallace, Nancy Elizabeth, illus. 2009. (ENG., Illus.). 40p. (J). (gr. -1-3). 17.99 *(978-0-7614-5612-4(0)*, 9780761456124, Amazon Children's Publishing) Amazon Publishing.

Warner, Penny. The Code Busters Club, Case #4: the Mummy's Curse. 2014. (ENG., Illus.). 224p. (J). (gr. 3-7). 16.99 *(978-1-60684-459-5(8)*, Darby Creek) Lerner Publishing Group.

We Both Read-Museum Day. 2014. (Illus.). 44p. (J). 9.95 *(978-1-60115-265-7(5))*; pap. 4.99 *(978-1-60115-266-4(3))* Treasure Bay, Inc.

Wells, Helen. Cherry Ames, Companion Nurse. 2007. (Cherry Ames Nurse Stories Ser.). 224p. (J). (gr. 3-7). 14.95 *(978-0-8261-0431-1(2))* Springer Publishing Co., Inc.

Weston Woods Staff, creator. Norman the Doorman. 2011. 29.95 *(978-0-439-78648-5(7))* Weston Woods Studios, Inc.

Weyn, Suzanne. The Titanic Locket. 2014. (Hauntings: the Haunted Museum Ser.: 1). lib. bdg. 17.20 *(978-0-606-35809-5(9))* Turtleback Bks.

Whitney, Daisy. Starry Nights. (ENG.). (YA). (gr. 7). 2014. 304p. pap. 9.99 *(978-1-61963-436-7(8)*, 9781619634367) 2013. 288p. 17.99 *(978-1-61963-133-5(4)*, 9781619631335) Bloomsbury Publishing USA. (Bloomsbury USA Childrens).

Widmark, Martin. The Mummy Mystery. Willis, Helena, illus. 2015. (Whodunit Detective Agency Ser.: 5). (ENG.). 80p. (J). (gr. 2-4). 5.99 *(978-0-448-48074-9(3)*, Grosset & Dunlap) Penguin Young Readers Group.

Wilburn, Mary Lynne. Sam's Toy Museum. 2012. 24p. pap. 15.99 *(978-1-4653-4029-0(7))* Xlibris Corp.

Wilkins, James Francis. The Queen & Mr Brown: a Night in the Natural History Museum. 2016. (ENG., Illus.). 48p. (J). (gr. -1-2). 17.99 *(978-0-565-09376-1(2))* Natural History Museum Pubns. GBR. Dist: Independent Pubs. Group.

Young, Jessica. Art-Rageous. Secheret, Jessica, illus. 2015. (Finley Flowers Ser.). (ENG.). 128p. (gr. 2-3). 8.95 *(978-1-4795-5960-2(1)*, Finley Flowers) Picture Window Bks.

Zalben, Jane Breskin. Mousterpiece. Zalben, Jane Breskin, illus. 2012. (ENG., Illus.). 36p. (J). (gr. -1-2). 16.99 *(978-1-59643-549-0(6)*, 9781596435490) Roaring Brook Pr.

MUSHROOMS

see also Fungi

Bowers, A., et al. Mushrooms of the World with Pictures to Color. 2013. (Dover Nature Coloring Book Ser.). (ENG., Illus.). 48p. (J). (gr. 3-12). pap. 4.99 *(978-0-486-24643-7(4))* Dover Pubns., Inc.

Mushroom. 2003. stu. ed. 36.95 *(978-0-8136-9261-6(X))*; 38.95 *(978-0-8136-4122-5(5))* Modern Curriculum Pr.

Nelson, Cyndi. Rocky Mountain Mushrooms: Edible & Poisonous. 2nd rev. ed. 2007. (Illus.). 43p. pap. 7.95 *(978-1-55566-404-6(0)*, Johnson Bks.) Bower Hse.

Owings, Lisa. From Spore to Mushroom. 2017. (Start to Finish, Second Ser.). (ENG.). (J). (gr. k-3). 24p. 23.99 *(978-1-5124-3441-5(8))*; pap. 6.99 ***(978-1-5124-5626-4(8))*** Lerner Publishing Group.

Royston, Angela. El Hongo, 1 vol. 2010. (Ciclo de Vida Ser.). (SPA & ENG.). 32p. (gr. 1-3). 27.32 *(978-1-4329-4373-8(1))* Heinemann-Raintree.

MUSIAL, STAN, 1920-2013

Giglio, James N. Stan Musial: Baseball Hero. 2015. (ENG., Illus.). 48p. (J). pap. 24.00 *(978-1-61248-151-7(5))* Truman State Univ. Pr.

MUSIC

see also Church Music; Concerts; Jazz; Musicians; Singing; Sound

also Orchestral Music; Organ Music; Piano music; etc. and headings beginning with the words Music and Musical

Aksomitis, Linda. Downloading Music. 2007. (Issues That Concern You Ser.). (ENG., Illus.). 144p. (gr. 10-12). lib. bdg. 42.00 *(978-0-7377-3646-5(1))* Cengage Gale.

Albrecht, Sally K., et al. I Sing, You Sing, Too! 30 Echo Songs for Young Singers. 2008. (ENG.). 68p. pap. 44.95 *(978-0-7390-5257-0(8))* Alfred Publishing Co., Inc.

Albrecht, Sally K. & Althouse, Jay. I Sing, You Sing, Too! 30 Echo Songs for Young Singers. 2008. (ENG.). 68p. pap. 19.95 *(978-0-7390-5259-4(4))* Alfred Publishing Co., Inc.

Alfred Publishing Staff, et al. Classroom Music for Little Mozarts - The Big Music Book: 10 Sequential Lessons for Ages 4-6, Big Book. 2010. (Music for Little Mozarts Ser.: Bk

3). (ENG.). 24p. (J). pap. 49.95 *(978-0-7390-4564-0(4))* Alfred Publishing Co., Inc.

Aliki. ¡Musica! 2004. (SPA.). 28p. (J). (gr. k-3). 22.99 *(978-84-261-3343-4(6))* Juventud, Editorial ESP. Dist: Lectorum Pubns., Inc.

Allan, Delores. Magical Moments with Roy & Toni: The Magic of Music. 2011. 20p. pap. 11.99 *(978-1-4634-2686-6(0))* AuthorHouse.

Allman, Toney. Downloading Music. 2007. (Ripped from the Headlines Ser.). 64p. (J). (gr. 7-12). 23.95 *(978-1-60217-006-3(1))* Erickson Pr.

Ancona, George. Olé Flamenco! Ancona, George, photos by. 2010. (ENG., Illus.). 48p. (J). (gr. 2-6). 19.95 *(978-1-60060-361-7(0))* Lee & Low Bks., Inc.

Anniss, Matt. The Story of Techno & Dance Music. 2013. (Pop Histories Ser.). (Illus.). 32p. (gr. 4-7). 31.35 *(978-1-59920-967-8(5))* Black Rabbit Bks.

Anniss, Matthew. The Music Industry. 2016. (Music Scene Ser.). (ENG., Illus.). 48p. (J). (gr. 5-9). pap. 12.99 *(978-1-4451-3937-1(5)*, Franklin Watts) Hachette Children's Group GBR. Dist: Hachette Bk. Group.

Apostoli, Andrea, ed. What Great Music! Classical Selections to Hear & to See. Dufey, Alexandra, illus. 2011. (ENG.). 48p. (J). (-1). pap. 19.95 *(978-1-57999-841-7(0))* G I A Pubns., Inc.

Archuleta, Michael, concept. Mariachi Method Book for Vihuela. 2nd ed. 2005. (YA). 24.95 *(978-0-9675951-3-9(4))* Mixta Publishing Co.

Ardley, Neil. DK Eyewitness Books - Music. Dorling Kindersley Publishing Staff, ed. 2004. (DK Eyewitness Bks.). (ENG., Illus.). 72p. (J). (gr. 3-7). 16.99 *(978-0-7566-0709-8(4)*, DK Children) Dorling Kindersley Publishing, Inc.

—La Musica.Tr. of Music. (SPA.). 64p. (YA). (gr. 5-8). *(978-84-372-3711-4(4))* Altea, Ediciones, S.A. - Grupo Santillana.

Barber, Jill. Music Is for Everyone, 1 vol. Smith, Sydney, illus. 2014. (ENG.). 32p. (J). (gr. -1-3). 19.95 *(978-1-77108-150-4(3))* Nimbus Publishing, Ltd. CAN. Dist: Orca Bk. Pubs. USA.

Barden, Christine H., et al. Music for Little Mozarts Little Mozarts Perform the Nutcracker: 8 Favorites form Tchaikovsky's Nutcracker Suite. 2007. (Music for Little Mozarts Ser.). (ENG.). 24p. (J). pap. 7.95 *(978-0-7390-4822-1(8))* Alfred Publishing Co., Inc.

Baron, Jessica. Let's Make Music. 2008. (Real Readers - Upper Emergent Ser.). (ENG., Illus.). 12p. (gr. 1-2). pap. 5.90 *(978-0-8239-8193-9(2))* Rosen Publishing Group, Inc., The.

Bass Schule. 2004. (GER.). (YA). cd-rom *(978-1-891155-18-5(0))* EMedia Corp.

Ben-Hur, Roni Amos. Talk Jazz Guitar: A Comprehensive Collection of Be Bop Studies for the Aspiringand Professional Jazz Guitarist. 2004. 268p. (YA). pap. 34.00 net. *(978-0-9744943-1-9(3))* Bohobza Music.

Bennett, Paul. The Seven Harmonies of Music: A Field Guide, 1. 2004. (Illus.). 80p. ring bd. 19.95 *(978-0-9753599-0-7(8))* Music Awareness.

Bernard, Yves & Fredette, Nathalie. Le Guide de la Musique du Monde. 2004. (FRE., Illus.). 230p. (J). pap. *(978-2-89021-662-4(4))* Diffusion du livre Mirabel (DLM).

Between the Lions - Early Literacy Kit - Zoop! Zoop!, 1 cass., 1 bk. 2005. (Between the Lions Ser.). 36p. (J). VHS 29.95 *(978-1-59375-287-3(3)*, WG38653) WGBH Boston Video.

Billet, Marion, illus. I Love Music: My First Sound Book. 2016. (ENG.). 16p. (J). (gr. -1 — 1). 9.99 *(978-1-338-03261-1(5)*, Cartwheel Bks.) Scholastic, Inc.

Birthday Party Songs. (Twin Sisters Ser.). (J). 7.98 incl. audio. incl. audio NewSound, LLC.

Bissinger, Wendy & Wendy Bissinger. Sequenced Scale Studies for Cello. 2004. (Illus.). 108p. (J). spiral bd. *(978-0-9755624-0-6(1))* Boshu Pr.

Black, Dave. Alfred's Kid's Drum Course 1 Bk & Cd & Drum. 2005. (Kid's Drum Course Ser.: Bk 1). (ENG.). pap. 25.99 *(978-0-7390-3742-3(0))* Alfred Publishing Co., Inc.

Blair, Cathy. Music Baseball: Name That Style. 2005. act. bk. ed., instr.'s gde. ed. 29.95 *(978-0-89328-174-8(3)*, 30/2006H) Heritage Music Pr.

—Rhythm Rally! Level 1, Grades 3-5: Six Fun & Fast-Paced Rhythm Games in One! 2004. act. bk. ed. 29.95 *(978-0-89328-176-2(X)*, 30/1908H) Heritage Music Pr.

—Rhythm Rally! Level 2, Grades 5-7: Six Fun & Fast-Paced Rhythm Games in One! 2004. act. bk. ed. 29.95 *(978-0-89328-177-9(8)*, 30/1909H) Heritage Music Pr.

—Rhythms of the World: Discovering the Indigenous Rhythms of Africa, India, Cuba, & Brazil; Grades 5-8. 2005. 34.95 *(978-0-89328-173-1(5)*, 30/1989H) Heritage Music Pr.

Blending Music Styles Videotape: Videotape Packages. 2003. (Share the Music Ser.). (gr. 4-8). *(978-0-02-295486-4(4))* Macmillan/McGraw-Hill Schl. Div.

Boom, Tap-n-Play Bells & Boomwhackers. 2006. cd-rom 19.95 *(978-1-933260-16-7(5))* Vision Pubns.

Bowen, Meurig & Bowen, Rachel. The School of Music. Frost, Daniel, illus. 2017. (School Of Ser.). (ENG.). 96p. (J). (gr. 3-6). 19.99 *(978-1-84780-861-5(1)*, Wide Eyed Editions) Quarto Publishing Group UK GBR. Dist: Hachette Bk. Group.

Boytim, Joan Frey. Daffodils, Violets & Snowflakes: 24 Classical Songs for Young Women, Ages Ten to Mid-Teens. 2003. (ENG.). 88p. pap. 16.99 *(978-0-634-06212-4(3)*, 0634062123) Leonard, Hal Corp.

Boytim, Joan Frey, ed. Daffodils, Violets & Snowflakes: 24 Classical Songs for Young Women, Ages 10 to Mid-Teens. 2003. (ENG.). 88p. (gr. 5-18). pap. 16.99 *(978-0-634-06181-3(X)*, 063406181X) Leonard, Hal Corp.

Bryan, Colgan & Stang, Aaron, eds. Dream Theater: Awake. 2007. (ENG.). 160p. pap. 26.99 *(978-0-89724-608-8(X)*, 089724608X) Alfred Publishing Co., Inc.

Burch, Lynda S. Meet Me at the Park! Burch, Lynda S., photos by. 2005. (Illus.). 64p. (J). E-Book 6.00 incl. cd-rom *(978-1-933090-15-3(4))* Guardian Angel Publishing, Inc.

—Wicky Wacky Things that Go! Airplanes 1. Roberts, MarySue, photos by. 2004. (Illus.). 28p. (J). E-Book 9.95 incl. cd-rom *(978-1-933090-07-8(3))* Guardian Angel Publishing, Inc.

—Wicky Wacky Things that Go! Tractors. Burch, Lynda S., photos by. 2004. (Illus.). 28p. (J). E-Book 9.95 incl. cd-rom *(978-1-933090-09-2(X))* Guardian Angel Publishing, Inc.

—Wicky Wacky Things that Go! Trains 1. Burch, Lynda S., photos by. 2004. (Illus.). 16p. (J). E-Book 9.95 incl. cd-rom *(978-1-933090-02-3(2))* Guardian Angel Publishing, Inc.

—Wicky Wacky Things That Go! Trucks. Burch, Lynda S., photos by. 2004. (Illus.). 28p. (J). E-Book 9.95 incl. cd-rom *(978-1-933090-11-5(1))* Guardian Angel Publishing, Inc.

—Zoom Zoom Zoom Come Count with Me! Burch, Lynda S., photos by. 2005. (Illus.). 20p. (J). E-Book 6.00 incl. cd-rom *(978-1-933090-14-6(6))* Guardian Angel Publishing, Inc.

Can't Help Falling in Love. Date not set. 32p. 15.99 *(978-0-06-027796-3(3))* HarperCollins Pubs.

Carolus, Mario. Music for New Zealand, Years 9 & 10. 2013. (ENG.). pap., stu. ed. *(978-1-107-61206-8(3))* Cambridge Univ. Pr.

Casterline, L. C. The Sounds of Music. Yerkes, Lane, illus. 2004. (Picture Books/Quality Time Ser.). 16p. (gr. k-3). lib. bdg. 20.00 *(978-0-8368-4100-8(X)*, Gareth Stevens Learning Library) Stevens, Gareth Publishing LLLP.

Cefrey, Holly. Career Building Through Music, Video, & Software Mashups. 2009. (Digital Career Building Ser.). 64p. (gr. 6-6). 58.50 *(978-1-61512-169-4(2))* Rosen Publishing Group, Inc., The.

Celia, Shannon Casey. Nature's Music: Musical Colors Series 2003. (ENG., Illus.). 12p. (J). spiral bd. 10.95 *(978-1-931844-07-9(0)*, PP1019) Piano Pr.

Claudio, Abbado. Yo Sere Director de Orquesta. 2007. (SPA.). 48p. (J). (gr. 4-5). 23.99 *(978-84-8470-052-4(6))* Corimbo, Editorial S.L. ESP. Dist: Lectorum Pubns., Inc.

Compact Discs. 2003. (Share the Music Ser.). (gr. 2-18). *(978-0-02-295437-6(6))*; (gr. 3-18). *(978-0-02-295438-3(4))*; (gr. 4-18). *(978-0-02-295439-0(2))*; (gr. 5-18). *(978-0-02-295440-6(6))*; (gr. 7-18). *(978-0-02-295442-0(2))* Macmillan/McGraw-Hill Schl. Div.

Congratulations - Grade 1 Alto Sax & Piano. (YA). 9.95 *(978-1-85909-666-6(2)*, Warner Bros. Pubns.) Alfred Publishing Co., Inc.

Conley, Eddie And Uchenna. Team Conley: Elaykim's Life Lessons for the Love of Music. 2011. 28p. pap. 13.99 *(978-1-4634-0144-3(2))* AuthorHouse.

Creating Musical Moods Videotape: Videotape Packages. 2003. (Share the Music Ser.). (gr. 3-6). *(978-0-02-295484-0(8))* Macmillan/McGraw-Hill Schl. Div.

Croft, Malcolm. 5 Seconds of Summer - The Ultimate Fan Book: All You Need to Know about the World's Hottest New Boy Band! 2014. (ENG., Illus.). 48p. (J). (gr. 3-10). 9.99 *(978-0-7641-6761-4(8))* Barron's Educational Series, Inc.

Dale, Monica. Eurhythmics for Young Children: Six Lessons for Winter. 2003. (Illus.). 108p. pap. 24.95 *(978-0-9701416-1-3(0))* MusiKinesis.

Davidson, Susanna. Swan Lake with Music. 2012. (Picture Books with Music Ser.). 24p. (J). bds. 18.99 *(978-0-7945-3301-4(9)*, Usborne) EDC Publishing.

Derezinzki, Amelia. Star Turns: Dancing on Broadway. 2004. (Curtain Call Library of Dance Ser.). (Illus.). 48p. (J). (gr. 5-8). lib. bdg. 29.25 *(978-0-8239-4557-3(X)*, Rosen Reference) Rosen Publishing Group, Inc., The.

Diamond, Eileen. Let's Make Music Fun! Songs to Sing, Action Songs, Rounds & Songs with Percussion Instruments. (Let's Make Music Fun Ser.). 14.95 *(978-1-85909-417-4(1)*, Warner Bros. Pubns.) Alfred Publishing Co., Inc.

District License Package: Technology: Music with MIDI. 2003. (Share the Music Ser.). (gr. 1-18). *(978-0-02-295470-3(8))*; (gr. 2-18). *(978-0-02-295471-0(6))*; (gr. 3-18). *(978-0-02-295472-7(4))*; (gr. 4-18). *(978-0-02-295473-4(2))*; (gr. 5-18). *(978-0-02-295474-1(0))*; (gr. 6-18). *(978-0-02-295475-8(9))*; (gr. 7-18). *(978-0-02-295298-3(5))*; (gr. 8-18). *(978-0-02-295299-0(3))* Macmillan/McGraw-Hill Schl. Div.

Dorling Kindersley Publishing Staff. Children's Book of Music. 2010. (ENG., Illus.). 144p. (J). (gr. 3-7). 24.99 *(978-0-7566-6734-4(8)*, DK Children) Dorling Kindersley Publishing, Inc.

—Noisy Peekabook - Toot! Toot! 2013. (ENG., Illus.). 12p. (J). (gr. -1 — 1). bds. 12.99 *(978-1-4654-1068-9(6)*, DK Children) Dorling Kindersley Publishing, Inc.

Doug Smith's Classical Guitar Method, Reading Book 1: Introduction to the Natural Notes in the First Position. 2004. (J). 24.95 *(978-0-9729879-1-2(6))* Musictech College Pr.

EMedia Fortgeschrittene Gitarren Schule. 2004. (GER.). (YA). cd-rom *(978-1-891155-16-1(4))* EMedia Corp.

eMedia Klavier & Keyboard Einstieg. CD-ROM für Windows XP/ME/2000/NT/98//95 und Macintosh: Die ersten Schritte auf dem Klavier und Keyboard. 2004. (GER.). (YA). cd-rom *(978-1-891155-22-2(9))* EMedia Corp.

Emmer, Rae. Band: Banda. 2004. (School Activities / Actividades Escolares Ser.). (SPA & ENG., Illus.). 24p. (J). (gr. 1-4). lib. bdg. 22.60 *(978-0-8239-6902-9(9)*, 1213143) Rosen Publishing Group, Inc., The.

—Chorus. 2009. (School Activities Ser.). 24p. (gr. 1-1). 42.50 *(978-1-60852-996-4(7)*, PowerKids Pr.) Rosen Publishing Group, Inc., The.

—Chorus: Coro. 2004. (School Activities / Actividades Escolares Ser.). (SPA & ENG., Illus.). 24p. (J). (gr. 1-4). lib. bdg. 22.60 *(978-0-8239-6903-6(7)*, 1213163) Rosen Publishing Group, Inc., The.

—Chorus / Coro. 2009. (School Activities / Actividades escolares Ser.). (ENG & SPA.). 24p. (gr. 1-2). 42.50 *(978-1-60853-002-1(7)*, Editorial Buenas Letras) Rosen Publishing Group, Inc., The.

Espejo, Roman. What Is the Future of the Music Industry? 2008. (At Issue Ser.). (ENG., Illus.). 80-128p. (gr. 10-12). 24.45 *(978-0-7377-4111-7(2))*; pap. 34.45 *(978-0-7377-4110-0(4))* Cengage Gale. (Greenhaven Pr., Inc.).

Feierabend, John M. The Book of Beginning Circle Games: Let's Make a Circle. 2004. (First Steps in Music Ser.). (ENG., Illus.). 84p. (J). (gr. -1-2). pap. 14.95 *(978-1-57999-266-8(8)*, G-5878) G I A Pubns., Inc.

Feierabend, John M. & Kahan, Jane. The Book of Movement Exploration: Can You Move Like This? 2004. (First Steps in Music Ser.). (ENG., Illus.). 66p. (J). (gr. -1-2). pap. 14.95 *(978-1-57999-264-4(1)*, G-5876) G I A Pubns., Inc.

Feldstein, Sandy. Rhythm Party Guide. 2004. audio compact disk 24.95 *(978-1-932895-16-2(7))* PlayinTime Productions, Inc.

Feldstein, Sandy & Clark, Larry. Antiphony. 2004. (YA). pap. 40.00 *(978-1-932895-03-2(5))* PlayinTime Productions, Inc.

—Fanfare Minuet - Trombone/Baritone/Basson Solo with Piano Acc. 2005. (YA). pap. 9.95 incl. audio compact disk *(978-1-932895-53-7(1))* PlayinTime Productions, Inc.

—Fanfare Minuet -Trumpet/Baritone Solo with Piano Acc. 2005. (YA). pap. 9.95 incl. audio compact disk *(978-1-932895-51-3(5))* PlayinTime Productions, Inc.

—The Fifers. 2005. (YA). pap. 10.95 *(978-1-932895-81-0(7))* PlayinTime Productions, Inc.

—Honor March. 2005. (YA). pap. 40.00 *(978-1-932895-99-5(X))* PlayinTime Productions, Inc.

—Jupiter. 2004. (YA). pap. 40.00 *(978-1-932895-00-1(0))* PlayinTime Productions, Inc.

—Jupiter - Conductor's Score. 2004. (YA). pap. 6.00 *(978-1-932895-01-8(9))* PlayinTime Productions, Inc.

—Outback Rhapsody. 2004. (YA). pap. 40.00 *(978-1-932895-06-3(X))* PlayinTime Productions, Inc.

—Outback Rhapsody - Conductor's Score. 2004. (YA). pap. 8.00 *(978-1-932895-07-0(8))* PlayinTime Productions, Inc.

—Scherzando - Alto Sax/Bari. Sax Solo with Piano Acc. W/CD. 2005. (YA). pap. 9.95 *(978-1-932895-28-5(0))* PlayinTime Productions, Inc.

—Scherzando - Keyboard Percussion Solo with piano acc. W/CD. 2005. (YA). pap. 9.95 *(978-1-932895-34-6(5))* PlayinTime Productions, Inc.

—Scherzando - Snare Drum Solo with Piano Acc. W/CD. 2005. (YA). pap. 9.95 *(978-1-932895-35-3(3))* PlayinTime Productions, Inc.

—Scherzando - Trombone/Baritone/Bassoon Solo with Piano Acc. W/CD. 2005. (YA). pap. 9.95 *(978-1-932895-32-2(9))* PlayinTime Productions, Inc.

—Scherzando - Tuba Solo with Piano Acc. W/CD. 2005. (YA). pap. 9.95 *(978-1-932895-33-9(7))* PlayinTime Productions, Inc.

—Scherzando -Trumpet/Baritone Solo with Piano Acc. w/ CD. 2005. (YA). pap. 9.95 *(978-1-932895-30-8(2))* PlayinTime Productions, Inc.

—Scherzando Tenor Sax Solo with Piano Acc. W/CD. 2005. (YA). pap. 9.95 *(978-1-932895-29-2(9))* PlayinTime Productions, Inc.

—Sentinel. 2004. (YA). pap. 40.00 *(978-1-932895-10-0(8))* PlayinTime Productions, Inc.

—Sentinel - conductor's Score. 2004. (YA). pap. 6.00 *(978-1-932895-11-7(6))* PlayinTime Productions, Inc.

Feldstein, Sandy & Firth, Vic. Vic Firth/SandyFeldstein Percussion Series - complete Score. 2004. (YA). 24.95 *(978-1-932895-12-4(4))* PlayinTime Productions, Inc.

Gallina, Jill, et al. The Green Machine Team: A Mini-Musical to Recycle, Replenish, & Renew! 2008. (ENG.). 40p. pap. 49.99 *(978-1-4234-8618-3(8)*, 1423486188) Leonard, Hal Corp.

—Snoozy Snowflake: Singin' & Swingin' at the K-2 Chorale Series. 2011. (ENG.). 48p. pap. 49.99 *(978-1-4234-9891-9(7)*, 1423498917) Shawnee Pr., Inc.

Gameplan - Grade One: An Active Music Curriculum for Children. 2005. spiral bd. 80.00 net. *(978-0-9767650-0-4(4))* KiD Sounds.

Gardner, Jane P. Music Science, Vol. 11. Lewin, Russ, ed. 2015. (Science 24/7 Ser.). (Illus.). 48p. (J). (gr. 5). 20.95 *(978-1-4222-3412-9(6))* Mason Crest.

George, Francis. Mr G Clef & Friends. Wasvary, Marcia, illus. 2012. 32p. 24.95 *(978-1-4560-9642-7(7))* America Star Bks.

Gitarren Einstieg. 2004. (GER.). (YA). cd-rom *(978-1-891155-21-5(0))* EMedia Corp.

Godula, Ellen Kjelgaard & Godula, Brian. Queen Mab, Musical Verses Volume 3. 2007. (J). audio compact disk 16.99 *(978-0-9764109-3-5(1))* Pillar Rock Publishing.

Gordon, Edwin E. Am I Musical? Discover Your Musical Potential (Adults & Children Ages 7 & Up) 2004. (ENG., Illus.). 40p. pap. 18.95 *(978-1-57999-222-4(6)*, G-6092) G I A Pubns., Inc.

Grade: Gr 7 Te Share the Music 2000. 2003. (Share the Music Ser.). (gr. 7-18). *(978-0-02-295393-5(0))* Macmillan/McGraw-Hill Schl. Div.

Grade: Gr 8 CDs Share the Music 2000. 2003. (Share the Music Ser.). (gr. 8-18). *(978-0-02-295443-7(0))* Macmillan/McGraw-Hill Schl. Div.

Grade: Gr 8 Te Share the Music 2000. 2003. (Share the Music Ser.). (gr. 8-18). *(978-0-02-295394-2(9))* Macmillan/McGraw-Hill Schl. Div.

Graham, Roland. How We Make Music. 2003. (Real Readers Series: Level Blue Ser.). (ENG., Illus.). 12p. (gr. 1-2). pap. 5.90 *(978-0-8239-6355-3(1))* Rosen Publishing Group, Inc., The.

Gray, Susan H. Zebra Mussel. 2008. (21st Century Skills Library: Animal Invaders Ser.). (ENG.). 32p. (gr. 4-8). lib. bdg. 28.50 *(978-1-60279-111-4(2)*, 200113) Cherry Lake Publishing.

The Grey House Performing Arts Directory. 4th ed. 2004. 1,500p. 185.00 *(978-1-59237-023-8(3)*, Universal Reference Pubns.) Grey Hse. Publishing.

Hal Leonard Corp. Staff. Children's Songs for Ukulele Strummers. 2012. (ENG.). 56p. pap. 14.99 *(978-1-4768-1275-5(6)*, 1476812756) Leonard, Hal Corp.

Hal Leonard Corp. Staff, contrib. by. Experiencing Choral Music, Advanced Mixed: Grades 9-12. 2004. (Illus.). 281p. stu. ed., per. 30.61 *(978-0-07-861129-2(6)*, 9780078611292) Glencoe/McGraw-Hill.

Hal Leonard Corp. Staff, creator. Disney Movie Hits: Alto Sax. 2003. (ENG.). 20p. pap. 12.95 incl. audio compact disk *(978-0-634-00095-9(0)*, 0634000950) Leonard, Hal Corp.

—Disney Movie Hits: Cello. 2003. (ENG.). 20p. pap. 12.99 *(978-0-634-00101-7(9)*, 0634001019) Leonard, Hal Corp.

—Disney Movie Hits: Clarinet. 2003. (ENG.). 20p. pap. 12.99 *(978-0-634-00094-2(2)*, 0634000942) Leonard, Hal Corp.

—Disney Movie Hits: F Horn. 2003. (ENG.). 20p. pap. 12.99 *(978-0-634-00097-3(7)*, 0634000977) Leonard, Hal Corp.

—Disney Movie Hits: Trombone/Baritone. 2003. (ENG.). 20p. pap. 12.99 *(978-0-634-00098-0(5)*, 0634000985) Leonard, Hal Corp.

—Disney Movie Hits: Trumpet. 2003. (ENG.). 20p. pap. 12.99 *(978-0-634-00096-6(9)*, 0634000969) Leonard, Hal Corp.

—Disney Movie Hits: Viola. 2003. (ENG.). 20p. pap. 12.99 *(978-0-634-00100-0(0)*, 0634001000) Leonard, Hal Corp.

Hamilton, Jill. The Music Industry. 2009. (Introducing Issues with Opposing Viewpoints Ser.). (ENG.). 144p. (gr. 10-12). 42.00 *(978-0-7377-4339-5(5)*, Greenhaven Pr., Inc.) Cengage Gale.

Hapka, Catherine, pseud. Together We Can Do It. 2004. (Star Power Ser.: 4). (ENG.). 160p. (J). (gr. 4-8). pap. 4.99 *(978-0-689-86790-3(5)*, Aladdin) Simon & Schuster Children's Publishing.

Harding, James. From Wibbleton to Wobbleton: Adventures with the Elements of Music & Movement. Noyes, Eli, illus. 2014. (Pentatonic Press Integrated Learning Ser.: 3). (ENG.). 201p. pap. 32.00 *(978-0-9773712-5-9(5))* Pentatonic Pr.

Hemperly, Ilona K. & Nanni, Lyn. Koa'e Kea. (Illus.). (J). pap. 11.95 *(978-0-9639279-0-3(6))* Sunset Beach Music.

Hilderbrand, Karen Mitzo & Thompson, Kim Mitzo. Essential Preschool Skills. 2008. (J). 44.99 *(978-1-59922-321-6(X))* Findaway World, LLC.

Holl, Kristi. Shazam & Chris Barton, Philip Inghelbrecht, Dhiraj Mukherjee, & Avery Wang, 1 vol. 2015. (ENG., Illus.). 128p. (J). 35.60 *(978-1-4777-7925-5(6)*, Rosen Young Adult) Rosen Publishing Group, Inc., The.

Hopper, Jessica. The Girls' Guide to Rocking: How to Start a Band, Book Gigs, & Get Rolling to Rock Stardom. 2009. (ENG., Illus.). 288p. (J). (gr. 4-12). pap. 13.95 *(978-0-7611-5141-8(9)*, 15141) Workman Publishing Co., Inc.

Hull, Bunny. Dream a World: A Child's Journey to Self-Discovery Dreamer's Activity Kit. Saint-James, Synthia, illus. 2004. 24p. (J). 16.95 incl. cd-rom *(978-0-9721478-3-5(7))* BrassHeart Music.

Hyde, Heidi Smith. Mendel's Accordion. van der Sterre, Johanna, illus. 2007. 30p. (J). (gr. 3-7). lib. bdg. 16.95 *(978-1-58013-212-1(X)*, Kar-Ben Publishing) Lerner Publishing Group.

Im Kindergarten. 2005. (GER.). (J). pap. 14.25 *(978-3-411-09841-5(4))* Langenscheidt Publishing Group.

Introduction to the Computer in Music Videotape: Videotape Packages. 2003. (Share the Music Ser.). (gr. 3-8). *(978-0-02-295492-5(9))* Macmillan/McGraw-Hill Schl. Div.

Jackson, Tom. Music Technology. 2015. (Technology Timelines Ser.). (Illus.). 32p. (gr. 3-6). 31.35 *(978-1-78121-240-0(6))* Brown Bear Bks.

Kallen, Stuart A. The History of R&B & Soul Music. Greenhaven Press Editors, ed. 2013. (Music Library). (ENG., Illus.). 128p. (gr. 7-10). lib. bdg. 39.40 *(978-1-4205-0899-4(7))* Cengage Gale.

Kennedy, Steven. Crescent City Collection: Marimba Tunes from the Big Easy for Grades 4 - 8. Holl, Brent, ed. 2012. 40p. (J). spiral bd. 29.95 *(978-0-9832648-9-7(9))* Beatin' Path Pubns., LLC.

KociendaGenevieve. THE MAGIC OF MUSIC LOW INTERMEDIATE BOOK WITH ONLINE ACCESS. 2014. (ENG., Illus.). 24p. (J). pap. 9.50 *(978-1-107-66558-3(2))* Cambridge Univ. Pr.

Koopmans, Andy. The History of the Blues. 2005. (Music Library). (ENG., Illus.). 112p. (J). (gr. 4-7). lib. bdg. 33.45 *(978-1-59018-767-8(9)*, Lucent Bks.) Cengage Gale.

Krull, Kathleen. M Is for Music. Innerst, Stacy, illus. 2003. (ENG.). 56p. (J). (gr. -1-3). 17.00 *(978-0-15-201438-4(1))* Houghton Mifflin Harcourt Publishing Co.

Lach, William. Can You Hear It? 2006. (ENG., Illus.). 32p. (J). (gr. -1-5). 19.95 *(978-0-8109-5721-3(3)*, Abrams Bks. for Young Readers) Abrams, Inc.

Laing, Robin. The Whisky Muse: Collected & Introduced by Robin Laing. Dewar, Bob, illus. 2nd ed. 2003. (ENG.). 224p. per. 19.95 *(978-1-84282-041-4(9))* Luath Pr. Ltd. GBR. Dist: Midpoint Trade Bks., Inc.

Learn to Play the Recorder. 2004. (Fun Kits Ser.). (Illus.). 48p. (J). *(978-1-84229-730-8(9))* Top That! Publishing PLC.

Listening Map Transparencies. 2003. (Share the Music Ser.). (gr. k-18). *(978-0-02-295494-9(5))*; (gr. 1-18). *(978-0-02-295495-6(3))*; (gr. 2-18). *(978-0-02-295496-3(1))*; (gr. 3-18). *(978-0-02-295497-0(X))*; (gr. 4-18). *(978-0-02-295498-7(8))*; (gr. 5-18). *(978-0-02-295499-4(6))*; (gr. 6-18). *(978-0-02-295500-7(3))* Macmillan/McGraw-Hill Schl. Div.

Lorenz, Geoff, et al, creators. The Ultimate Music Game Book: Grades K-6+ 2005. (Illus.). 96p. spiral bd. 29.95 *(978-0-89328-031-4(3)*, 30/2013H) Heritage Music Pr.

Lorenz, Geoff & Vogt, Janet, creators. Music Out of a Hat, Grades 4-6: 7 Card Games for Classroom Fun! 2005. act. bk. ed. 39.95 *(978-0-89328-025-3(9)*, 30/2008H) Heritage Music Pr.

—Music Out of a Hat, Grades K-3: 7 Card Games for Classroom Fun! 2005. act. bk. ed. 39.95 *(978-0-89328-024-6(0)*, 30/2007H) Heritage Music Pr.

Lowe, Marilyn, et al. Music Moves for Two. 2004. (J). Bk. 1. 15.95 *(978-1-57999-347-4(8)*, G-6443)Bk. 2. 22p. 7.95 *(978-1-57999-348-1(6)*, G-6444) G I A Pubns., Inc.

MacGregor, Helen, et al. Roald Dahl's Cinderella: A Clock-Stopping Show-Stopping Musical, 1 vol. Eccles, Jane & Blake, Quentin, illus. 2008. (and C Black Musicals Ser.). (ENG.). 64p. (J). (gr. 2-6). pap. 42.95 incl. cd-rom ***(978-0-7136-8195-6(0))*** HarperCollins Pubs. Ltd. GBR. Dist: Independent Pubs. Group.

Maderna, Victoria & Stickers. Woodland Music Stickers. 2011. (Dover Little Activity Books Stickers Ser.). (ENG.). 4p. (J). (gr. k-3). pap. 1.50 *(978-0-486-48332-0(0))* Dover Pubns., Inc.

Maestro in the Making. 2006. cd-rom 24.95 *(978-1-933260-15-0(7))* Vision Pubns.

Making Music Videotape: Videotape Packages. 2003. (Share the Music Ser.). (gr. 4-8). *(978-0-02-295487-1(2))* Macmillan/McGraw-Hill Schl. Div.

Martin, Oscar, Jr., creator. History of Music I.t. ed. 2003. (Illus.). 25p. (J). E-Book 19.95 incl. cd-rom *(978-0-9748416-7-0(6))* Build Your Story.

Mason, Antony. Music. 2004. (Culture Encyclopedia Ser.). (Illus.). 40p. (YA). (gr. 5-18). lib. bdg. 19.95 *(978-1-59084-479-3(3))* Mason Crest.

McAlpine, Margaret. Working in Music & Dance. 2005. (My Future Career Ser.). (Illus.). 64p. (gr. 3-7). lib. bdg. 27.00 *(978-0-8368-4777-2(6)*, Gareth Stevens Learning Library) Stevens, Gareth Publishing LLLP.

McCarthy, John. Clap, Tap, Sing & Swing: Rockin' Kids Motor Skills. Gorenburg, Steve, ed. 2007. (ENG.). 48p. pap. 17.99 incl. audio compact disk *(978-0-9796229-0-8(5)*, 0979622905, Rock Hse. Method, The) Russell, Fred Publishing.

McGraw-Hill-Glencoe Staff. Experiencing Choral Music. 2004. (Experiencing Choral Music Intermediate Se Ser.). (ENG.,

M
N
O

Illus.). 256p. (gr. 7-9). stu. ed., per. 39.88 *(978-0-07-861114-8(8)*, 0078611148) McGraw-Hill Higher Education.

McGraw-Hill Staff. Experiencing Choral Music. 2004. (Experiencing Choral Music Intermediate Se Ser.). (ENG., Illus.). 235p. (gr. 6-12). stu. ed., per. 42.32 *(978-0-07-861111-7(3)*, 0078611113) McGraw-Hill Education.

—Experiencing Choral Music: Treble. 2004. (Experiencing Choral Music Proficient Se Ser.). (ENG., Illus.). 287p. (gr. 9-12). stu. ed., per. 42.32 *(978-0-07-861122-3(9)*, 0078611229) McGraw-Hill Higher Education.

—Experiencing Choral Music, Proficient Mixed Voices. 2004. (Experiencing Choral Music Proficient Se Ser.). (ENG., Illus.). 288p. (gr. 9-12). stu. ed., per. 42.32 *(978-0-07-861119-3(9)*, 0078611199) McGraw-Hill Higher Education.

—Experiencing Choral Music, Proficient Tenor Bass Voices. 2004. (Experiencing Choral Music Proficient Se Ser.). (ENG., Illus.). 263p. (gr. 9-12). stu. ed., per. 42.32 *(978-0-07-861125-4(3)*, 0078611253) McGraw-Hill Higher Education.

—Grade: Gr 4-8 Sound Perc. Video Share Music 2000. 2003. (Share the Music Ser.). (gr. 4-8). *(978-0-02-295485-7(6))* Macmillan/McGraw-Hill Schl. Div.

—Grade: Gr 6 Playing Guitar Share Music 2000. 2003. (Share the Music Ser.). (gr. 6-18). *(978-0-02-295406-2(6))* Macmillan/McGraw-Hill Schl. Div.

—Grade: Gr K CDs Share the Music 2000. 2003. (Share the Music Ser.). (gr. k-18). *(978-0-02-295435-2(X))* Macmillan/McGraw-Hill Schl. Div.

—Grade: Gr1 Cd(8) Share the Music. 2003. (Share the Music Ser.). (gr. 1-18). *(978-0-02-295436-9(8))* Macmillan/McGraw-Hill Schl. Div.

—Videocassette: Video Gr 3-6 Signing Share Music 2000. 2003. (Share the Music Ser.). (gr. 3-6). *(978-0-02-295480-2(5))* Macmillan/McGraw-Hill Schl. Div.

McGraw-Hill Staff, creator. Experiencing Choral Music Pt. 2 & 3: Unison. 2004. (Experiencing Choral Music Beginning Se Ser.). (ENG., Illus.). 261p. (gr. 6-12). stu. ed., per. 42.32 *(978-0-07-861104-9(0)*, 0078611040) McGraw-Hill Education.

McGraw-Hill Staff & McGraw-Hill Education Staff. Experiencing Choral Music, Intermediate Mixed Voices. 2004. (Experiencing Choral Music Intermediate Se Ser.). (ENG.). (gr. 6-12). pap., stu. ed. 42.32 *(978-0-07-861108-7(3)*, 0078611083) McGraw-Hill Education.

Michael, Judah Israel. The New Music. 2004. 60p. (YA). per. 12.95 *(978-1-59196-665-4(5))* Instant Pub.

MiDisaurus. 2003. (Technology: Music Ser.). (gr. 1-3). *(978-0-02-295557-1(7))*; *(978-0-02-295528-1(3))* Macmillan/McGraw-Hill Schl. Div.

The Mischievous Bugs. 2003. (J). pap., tchr. ed., act. bk. ed. 17.95 *(978-0-9722673-2-8(8))* Audrey Productions.

Mitchell, Loretta. Ready-to-Use Music Reading Activities Kit: A Complete Sequential Program for Use with Mallet & Keyboard Instruments. 2003. (Illus.). 228p. pap. 29.95 *(978-0-89328-156-4(5)*, 30/1801H) Heritage Music Pr.

Modern Music Masters, vols. 3, vol. 3. Incl. Reggae Poet: The Story of Bob Marley. Miller, Calvin Craig. 128p. (YA). (gr. 9-18). 2007. lib. bdg. 27.95 *(978-1-59935-071-4(8))*; Revolution: The Story of John Lennon. Duggleby, John. 176p. 2007. lib. bdg. 28.95 *(978-1-59935-034-9(3))*; Say It with Music: The Story of Irving Berlin. Furstinger, Nancy. 128p. (gr. 6-12). 2003. 28.95 *(978-1-931798-12-9(5))*; Spin: The Story of Michael Jackson. O'Keefe, Sherry. 144p. (YA). (gr. 6-9). 2011. 28.95 *(978-1-59935-134-6(X))*; Uh Huh! The Story of Ray Charles. Duggleby, John. 160p. (gr. 9-12). 2005. lib. bdg. 28.95 *(978-1-931798-65-5(6))*; (Illus.). 2010. Set lib. bdg. 92.85 *(978-1-59935-007-3(6))* Reynolds, Morgan Inc.

Moore, Shannon Baker. History of Music, 1 vol. 2014. (Essential Library of Cultural History Ser.). (ENG., Illus.). 112p. (J). (gr. 6-12). lib. bdg. 35.64 *(978-1-62403-555-5(8)*, Essential Library) ABDO Publishing Co.

Mueller, Todd & Boland, Hank. Soup du Jour (mus) 2003. (YA). (gr. 10). pap. 7.50 *(978-1-58342-179-6(3)*, SH7) Dramatic Publishing Co.

Music. Gr 1 Share the Music Pe. 2003. (Share the Music Ser.). (gr. 1-18). *(978-0-02-295563-2(1))* Macmillan/McGraw-Hill Schl. Div.

—Gr 6 Share the Music Pe. 2003. (Share the Music Ser.). (gr. 6-18). *(978-0-02-295568-7(2))* Macmillan/McGraw-Hill Schl. Div.

—Gr K-3 Stm Music & Moveme. 2003. (Share the Music Ser.). (gr. k-3). *(978-0-02-295482-6(1))* Macmillan/McGraw-Hill Schl. Div.

—Instrmnts of the Orch(Cd- 2003. (Share the Music Ser.). (gr. 1-8). *(978-0-02-295594-6(1))* Macmillan/McGraw-Hill Schl. Div.

—Instrmnts of the World(Cd. 2003. (Share the Music Ser.). (gr. 3-8). *(978-0-02-295595-3(X))* Macmillan/McGraw-Hill Schl. Div.

—Instrumental Sounds. 2003. (Share the Music Ser.). (gr. 1-8). incl. audio compact disk *(978-0-02-295596-0(8))* Macmillan/McGraw-Hill Schl. Div.

—Share the Music Big Book Grade 1. 2003. (Share the Music Ser.). (gr. 1-18). *(978-0-02-295384-3(1))* Macmillan/McGraw-Hill Schl. Div.

—Share the Music Big Book Grade 2. 2003. (Share the Music Ser.). (gr. 2-18). *(978-0-02-295385-0(X))* Macmillan/McGraw-Hill Schl. Div.

Music Ace. 2003. (Technology: Music Ser.). *(978-0-02-295318-8(3))*; *(978-0-02-295319-5(1))*; *(978-0-02-295327-0(2))*; *(978-0-02-295320-1(5))*; *(978-0-02-295328-7(0))*; *(978-0-02-295321-8(3))* Macmillan/McGraw-Hill Schl. Div.

Music Ace 2. 2003. (Technology: Music Ser.). *(978-0-02-295335-5(3))*; *(978-0-02-295334-8(5))*; *(978-0-02-295333-1(7))*; *(978-0-02-295336-2(1))*; *(978-0-02-295344-7(2))* Macmillan/McGraw-Hill Schl. Div.

Music Alive Magazine Classroom Set. 2003. (Share the Music Ser.). (gr. 6-8). *(978-0-02-295618-9(2))* Macmillan/McGraw-Hill Schl. Div.

Music Express Magazine Classroom Set. 2003. (Share the Music Ser.). (gr. k-6). *(978-0-02-295671-4(9))* Macmillan/McGraw-Hill Schl. Div.

Music Time. 1.85 *(978-0-7673-6158-3(X))*; 2005. 1.95 *(978-0-633-17857-4(8))*; 2005. 1.95 *(978-0-633-17659-4(1))*; 2004. 1.95 *(978-0-633-17464-4(5))*; 2004. 1.95 *(978-0-633-08665-7(7))*; 2004. 1.95 *(978-0-633-08415-8(8))*; 2004. 1.95 *(978-0-633-08163-8(9))*; 2003. 1.95 *(978-0-633-07791-4(7))* LifeWay Christian Resources.

Music Time. 2003. (Technology: Music Ser.). *(978-0-02-295245-7(4))*; *(978-0-02-295243-3(8))* Macmillan/McGraw-Hill Schl. Div.

Musica para todos Handbook: Additional Components. 2003. (Share the Music Ser.). (gr. k-2). *(978-0-02-295444-4(9))*; (gr. 3-6). *(978-0-02-295445-1(7))* Macmillan/McGraw-Hill Schl. Div.

Musical Expression Videotape: Videotape Packages. 2003. (Share the Music Ser.). (gr. 3-6). *(978-0-02-295483-3(X))* Macmillan/McGraw-Hill Schl. Div.

Musik. 3rd ed. (Duden-Schuelerduden Ser.). (GER.). 504p. (YA). *(978-3-411-05393-3(3))* Bibliographisches Institut & F. A. Brockhaus AG DEU. Dist: International Bk. Import Service, Inc.

Naji, Jamilla. Musical Storyland: A Sing-A-Long Book with Musical Disc. l.t. ed. 2004. (Illus.). 32p. (J). per. 19.99 *(978-0-9745568-0-2(7))* Worlds In Ink Publishing, Inc.

Ochs, Bill. The Clarke Learn-to-Play Tin Whistle Set: Includes Clarke Original D Tin Whistle on Blister Card: Book, Whistle & Compact Disc. 2003. (Illus.). 80p. audio compact disk 29.95 *(978-0-9727516-0-5(2))* Pennywhistler's Pr.

Okee Dokee Brothers, The. Can You Canoe? & Other Adventure Songs. Reese, Brandon, illus. 2016. (ENG.). 40p. (J). (gr. -1). 17.95 *(978-1-4549-1803-5(9))* Sterling Publishing Co., Inc.

Orchestrations for Orff Instruments. 2003. (Share the Music Ser.). (gr. 1-18). *(978-0-02-295407-9(4))*; (gr. 2-18). *(978-0-02-295408-6(2))*; (gr. 3-18). *(978-0-02-295409-3(0))*; (gr. 4-18). *(978-0-02-295410-9(4))*; (gr. 5-18). *(978-0-02-295411-6(2))*; (gr. 6-18). *(978-0-02-295412-3(0))* Macmillan/McGraw-Hill Schl. Div.

Patrick, Chris. Beyoncé & Destiny's Child. 2005. (Illus.). 122p. (J). *(978-0-439-80832-3(4))* Scholastic, Inc.

Penton. Masterpieces Set. 2003. (Baby's First Ser.). (ENG.). (J). 23.95 *(978-1-59125-335-8(7))* Penton Overseas, Inc.

—Sleep Little Baby Set. 2003. (Relaxation Ser.). (ENG.). (J). 23.95 *(978-1-59125-336-5(5))* Penton Overseas, Inc.

Performance Supplement Kit: Additional Components. 2003. (Share the Music Ser.). (gr. k-18). *(978-0-02-295664-6(6))*; (gr. 1-18). *(978-0-02-295665-3(4))*; (gr. 2-18). *(978-0-02-295666-0(2))*; (gr. 3-18). *(978-0-02-295667-7(0))*; (gr. 4-18). *(978-0-02-295668-4(9))*; (gr. 5-18). *(978-0-02-295669-1(7))*; (gr. 6-18). *(978-0-02-295670-7(0))* Macmillan/McGraw-Hill Schl. Div.

Perucca, Nancy Call & Evans, Renee Call. Sea Notes on the Keyboard: The Fast & Fun Way to Learn the Notes on the Keyboard! Perucca, Nancy Call, illus. 2004. (Illus.). 32p. (J). pap. 9.95 *(978-0-9748074-1-6(9))* Nancy's Artworks.

Playing the Recorder. 2003. (Share the Music Ser.). (gr. 3-18). *(978-0-02-295402-4(3))*; (gr. 4-18). *(978-0-02-295403-1(1))*; (gr. 5-18). *(978-0-02-295404-8(X))*; (gr. 6-18). *(978-0-02-295405-5(8))* Macmillan/McGraw-Hill Schl. Div.

Potter, Giselle, illus. C'mon an' Swing in My Tree! 2005. 14p. (J). bds. 16.95 incl. audio compact disk *(978-0-9763012-0-2(2))* Cow Heard Records.

Price, Roger & Stern, Leonard. Rock 'n' Roll Mad Libs. 2010. (Mad Libs Ser.). (ENG.). 48p. (J). (gr. 3-7). 4.99 *(978-0-8431-2695-2(7)*, Mad Libs) Penguin Young Readers Group.

Publications International Ltd. Staff, creator. Get Ready for Fun! 2007. (Sesame Street Music Works). (Illus.). 6p. (J). bds. 9.98 *(978-1-4127-8746-8(7))* Publications International, Ltd.

Publications International Ltd. Staff, ed. Nickelodeon(tm) Bubble Guppies(tm) Let's Rock! 2014. 12p. (J). bds. *(978-1-4508-7489-2(4)*, 1450874894) Publications International, Ltd.

—Xylophone Dora. 2010. 24p. (J). bds. 19.98 *(978-1-4127-4554-3(3))* Phoenix International Publications, Inc.

Pugliano-Martin, Carol. Around the World with Music: Set Of 6. 2010. (Early Connections Ser.). (J). pap. 37.00 net. *(978-1-4108-1081-6(X))* Benchmark Education Co.

Pupil Edition. 2003. (Share the Music Ser.). (gr. 2-18). *(978-0-02-295564-9(X))*; (gr. 3-18). *(978-0-02-295565-6(8))*; (gr. 4-18). *(978-0-02-295566-3(6))*; (gr. 5-18). *(978-0-02-295567-0(4))* Macmillan/McGraw-Hill Schl. Div.

Quill, Charlie. History of the Blues. 2009. (Reading Room Collection 2 Ser.). 24p. (gr. 3-4). 42.50 *(978-1-60851-968-2(6)*, PowerKids Pr.) Rosen Publishing Group, Inc., The.

Rands, Bernard. Concerto, No. 1. 2006. (ENG.). 92p. pap. 100.00 *(978-1-4234-0305-0(3)*, 1423403053) Schott Musik International GmbH & Co. KG DEU. Dist: Leonard, Hal Corp.

Ridgley, Sara & Mole, Gavin. Sing It & Say - France. (Illus.). 124p. 10.95 *(978-1-85909-301-6(9)*, Warner Bros. Pubns.) Alfred Publishing Co., Inc.

Ridgley, Sara, et al. Sing It & Say - Festivals. (Illus.). 128p. 10.95 *(978-1-85909-304-7(3)*, Warner Bros. Pubns.) Alfred Publishing Co., Inc.

Rigby Education Staff. Bingo. (Illus.). (J). suppl. ed. 20.00 *(978-0-7635-6473-5(7)*, 764737C99) Rigby Education.

Rodrigo, Joaquin. Concierto de Aranjuez. 2005. (ENG.). 80p. pap. 27.95 *(978-1-4234-0287-9(1)*, 1423402871) Schott Music Corp.

Rutland, Jonathan. Abracadabra Saxophone, 1 vol. 3rd ed. 2008. (Abracadabra Ser.). (ENG., Illus.). 72p. (J). pap., stu. ed. 15.95 incl. audio compact disk ***(978-1-4081-0529-0(2))*** HarperCollins Pubs. Ltd. GBR. Dist: Independent Pubs. Group.

Sanderson, Ana & White, Matthew. Roald Dahl's the Three Little Pigs: A Tail-Twistingly Treacherous Musical, 1 vol. Blake, Quentin, illus. 2007. (and C Black Musicals Ser.). (ENG.). 64p. (J). (gr. 2-6). pap. 42.95 incl. cd-rom ***(978-0-7136-8202-1(7))*** HarperCollins Pubs. Ltd. GBR. Dist: Independent Pubs. Group.

Scholastic, Inc. Staff. Clifford Musical Memory Games. 2004. (J). cd-rom 9.99 *(978-0-439-44355-5(5))* Scholastic, Inc.

Schwaeber, Barbie Heit. Alphabet of Music. Santillan, Jorge & Clark, Debbie, illus. 2011. (Alphabet Bks.). (ENG.). 40p. (J). (gr. -1-3). 9.95 *(978-1-60727-445-2(0))* Soundprints.

—Alphabet of Music. Clark, Debbie, illus. 2009. (ENG.). 40p. 9.95 *(978-1-59249-995-3(3))* Soundprints.

—Alphabet of Music. Santillan, Jorge, illus. 2008. (ENG.). 40p. (J). (gr. k-2). 15.95 *(978-1-59249-770-6(5))* Soundprints.

Schwartz, Betty Ann. What Makes Music? A Magic Ribbon Book. Turner, Dona, illus. 2005. (Stories to Share Ser.). 16p. (J). (gr. -1-3). act. bk. ed. 11.95 *(978-1-58117-139-6(0)*, Intervisual/Piggy Toes) Bendon, Inc.

Share Caribbean Music: Additional Components. 2003. (Share the Music Ser.). (gr. 3-5). incl. audio compact disk *(978-0-02-295598-4(4))* Macmillan/McGraw-Hill Schl. Div.

Share the Music Big Book. 2003. (Share the Music Ser.). (gr. k-18). *(978-0-02-295366-9(3))* Macmillan/McGraw-Hill Schl. Div.

Signing for Primary Grades Videotape: Videotape Packages. 2003. (Share the Music Ser.). (gr. k-2). *(978-0-02-295479-6(1))* Macmillan/McGraw-Hill Schl. Div.

Sing a Song Set 800867, 3 vols. 2005. (J). pap. *(978-1-59794-052-8(6))* Environments, Inc.

Site License Package: Technology: Music with MIDI. 2003. (Share the Music Ser.). (gr. 4-18). *(978-0-02-295467-3(8))*; (gr. 7-18). *(978-0-02-295237-2(3))*; (gr. 8-18). *(978-0-02-295238-9(1))* Macmillan/McGraw-Hill Schl. Div.

Smith, Douglas W. Doug Smith's Classical Guitar Method, Reading Book 2: Beginning Pieces for the First Position. 2004. (J). 24.95 *(978-0-9729879-2-9(4))* Musictech College Pr.

Spilsbury, Richard, et al. I'm in the Band, 1 vol. 2014. (I'm in the Band Ser.). (ENG.). 48p. (gr. 6-6). 133.28 *(978-1-4109-6727-5(1))* Heinemann-Raintree.

SRA Publications Staff. Grade: Gr 6 CDs Share the Music. 2003. (Share the Music Ser.). (gr. 6-18). *(978-0-02-295441-3(4))* Macmillan/McGraw-Hill Schl. Div.

Standard Package: Technology: Music with MIDI. 2003. (Share the Music Ser.). (gr. 4-18). *(978-0-02-295461-1(9))*; (gr. 7-18). *(978-0-02-295231-0(4))*; (gr. 8-18). *(978-0-02-295232-7(2))* Macmillan/McGraw-Hill Schl. Div.

Stephens, Wayne. Building Character Through Music - Elementary Song Book. 2004. spiral bd. 39.95 *(978-1-892056-32-0(1))* Character Development Group, Inc.

—Building Character Through Music - High School Song Book. 2004. (YA). spiral bd. 39.95 *(978-1-892056-36-8(4))* Character Development Group, Inc.

Sturm, Jeanne. MP3 Players. 2008. (Let's Explore Science Ser.). (Illus.). 48p. (J). (gr. 4-8). lib. bdg. 31.36 *(978-1-60472-332-8(7))* Rourke Educational Media.

Suen, Anastasia. Ipod & Electronics Visionary Tony Fadell. 2014. (STEM Trailblazer Bios Ser.). (ENG., Illus.). 32p. (gr. 2-5). lib. bdg. 26.60 *(978-1-4677-2456-2(4)*, Lerner Pubns.) Lerner Publishing Group.

Swain, Cynthia & Benchmark Education Co. Staff. Folksongs: The Music of My Life. 2014. (Text Connections Ser.). (J). (gr. 6). *(978-1-4900-1520-0(5))* Benchmark Education Co.

Syratt, Becky & Rumens-Syratt, Becky. The Batsford Book of Music for Children. 2016. (ENG., Illus.). 128p. (J). (gr. k-4). 14.95 *(978-1-84994-309-3(5)*, Batsford) Pavilion Bks. GBR. Dist: Sterling Publishing Co., Inc.

Television Themes Alto Sax. 13.95 incl. audio compact disk *(978-1-85909-718-2(9)*, Warner Bros. Pubns.) Alfred Publishing Co., Inc.

Television Themes Clarinet. 13.95 incl. audio compact disk *(978-1-85909-717-5(0)*, Warner Bros. Pubns.) Alfred Publishing Co., Inc.

Television Themes Flute. 13.95 incl. audio compact disk *(978-1-85909-716-8(2)*, Warner Bros. Pubns.) Alfred Publishing Co., Inc.

Theory for Young Musicians. (J). Bk. 1. *(978-0-7390-0232-2(5)*, 18513)Bk. 2. *(978-0-7390-0235-3(X)*, 18516) Alfred Publishing Co., Inc.

Thomson, Ryan J. Left Handed Fiddling for Beginners: A Teach Yourself Method, 1 bk, 1 CD. 2004. (Illus.). 22p. 22.95 *(978-0-931877-44-5(X))* Captain Fiddle Pubns.

Thyberg, Kathleen. Pianomouse's Musical Circus: Lesson Book 1, vols. , vol. 2. 2013. (ENG., Illus.). 72p. pap. 9.95 *(978-0-9889068-0-8(5))* Pianomouse Productions.

Tomaselli, Anthony. Play Guitar 1. 2003. cd-rom *(978-0-9714299-5-6(2))* I Save A Tree.

Turck, Mary C. Freedom Song: Young Voices & the Struggle for Civil Rights. 2008. (ENG., Illus.). 160p. (J). (gr. 4). pap. 18.95 *(978-1-55652-773-9(X))* Chicago Review Pr., Inc.

Turnbull, Elizabeth, ed. Music from the Romantic Era: Violin & Piano. 2004. (gr. 4-7). 19.95 *(978-0-8256-1843-7(6)*, BOE005012) Music Sales Corp.

Turner, Gary. Keyboard Method for Young Beginners, Book 1. Stewart, James, illus. 2006. (Young Beginner Giant Coloring Bks.). 48p. pap. incl. audio compact disk *(978-1-86469-097-2(6))* LearnToPlayMusic.com Pty Ltd.

—Recorder Method for Young Beginners, Book 1. Stewart, James, illus. 2006. (Young Beginner Giant Coloring Bks.). 36p. pap. *(978-1-86469-099-6(2))* LearnToPlayMusic.com Pty Ltd.

Umansky, Kaye & MacGregor, Helen. Three Rocking Crocs: Making Music with Traditional Stories. 2006. (Threes Ser.). (ENG., Illus.). 80p. (J). (gr. -1-k). pap. 22.95 ***(978-0-7136-7756-0(2))*** HarperCollins Pubs. Ltd. GBR. Dist: Independent Pubs. Group.

Wadsworth, Pamela. Golwg Gyntaf Ar Sain a Cherddoriaeth. 2005. (WEL., Illus.). 24p. pap. *(978-1-85596-247-7(0))* Dref Wen.

Wargin, Kathy-jo. M Is for Melody: A Music Alphabet. Larson, Katherine, illus. 2006. (Art & Culture Ser.). (ENG.). 40p. (J). (gr. 1-4). 16.95 *(978-1-58536-215-8(8)*, 202129) Sleeping Bear Pr.

—M Is for Melody: A Music Alphabet. Larson, Katherine, illus. rev. ed. 2006. (Art & Culture Ser.). (ENG.). 40p. (J). (gr. 1-4). pap. 9.99 *(978-1-58536-332-2(4)*, 202295) Sleeping Bear Pr.

Warner, Dennis. Beads on One String. 2004. (Illus.). 31p. (J). lib. bdg. 24.95 *(978-0-9747147-7-6(1))* MK Publishing.

Washburn, Sandi. Good Night, Grandma. Roehler, Yvonne Fetig, illus. 2009. (ENG.). 16p. (J). 17.95 *(978-1-934367-09-4(5))* Growing Art Pr.

Weeks, Sarah. Z Is for Zoe. Date not set. 32p. (J). (gr. -1-3). 15.99 *(978-0-06-028138-0(3))* HarperCollins Pubs.

Wu, Miriam, et al. Scaling the Tenor Clef Dragon: A Tenor Clef Workbook for Cellists. 2004. 28p. (J). 8.95 *(978-0-9755624-1-3(X))* Boshu Pr.

Yes I Can Staff. A Mariachi I'll Be. (J). stu. ed. 12.95 *(978-0-8136-4418-9(6))* Modern Curriculum Pr.

Zimmerman Rutledge, Jill S. Prom: The Big Night Out. 2017. (Nonfiction — Young Adult Ser.). (ENG.). 80p. (YA). (gr. 8-12). 19.99 ***(978-1-5124-3917-5(7))***; 53.32 ***(978-1-5124-3918-2(5))***; 53.32 ***(978-1-5124-2850-6(7))*** Lerner Publishing Group. (Twenty-First Century Bks.).

Zoo-phonics Music that Teaches. 2004. (J). cd-rom 19.95 *(978-1-886441-43-9(X))* Zoo-phonics, Inc.

MUSIC—ACOUSTICS AND PHYSICS

see also Sound

Allen, Kathy. The Science of a Rock Concert: Sound in Action. 2010. (Action Science Ser.). (ENG.). 32p. (gr. 3-4). pap. 47.70 *(978-1-4296-5075-5(3)*, Fact Finders) Capstone Press of Coughlan Cos.

Claybourne, Anna. The Science of a Guitar: The Science of Sound. 2009. (Science of... Ser.). (Illus.). 32p. (YA). (gr. 3-6). lib. bdg. 26.00 *(978-1-4339-0042-6(4))* Stevens, Gareth Publishing LLLP.

Flesch Connors, Abigail. Exploring the Science of Sounds: 100 Musical Activities for Young Children. 2017. (ENG.). (gr. 13). pap. 16.95 ***(978-0-87659-731-6(2)***, Gryphon House Inc) Gryphon Hse., Inc.

Jennings, Terry J. Sound. 2009. (J). 28.50 *(978-1-59920-275-4(1))* Black Rabbit Bks.

Kenney, Karen Latchana. The Science of Music: Discovering Sound, 1 vol. 2016. (Science in Action Ser.). (ENG., Illus.). 32p. (J). (gr. 3-6). 27.07 *(978-1-62403-962-1(6))* ABDO Publishing Co.

Music. 2010. (Experimenting with Everyday Science Ser.). (Illus.). 168p. (gr. 6-12). 35.00 *(978-1-60413-169-7(1)*, Chelsea Hse.) Facts On File, Inc.

Rowe, Brooke. Playing Musical Bottles. Bane, Jeff, illus. 2016. (My Early Library: My Science Fun Ser.). (ENG.). 24p. (J). (gr. k-1). 28.50 *(978-1-63471-028-2(2)*, 208192) Cherry Lake Publishing.

MUSIC, AMERICAN

Carlin, Richard, ed. American Popular Music, 8 vols., Set. 2005. (American Popular Music Ser.). 1042p. (gr. 6-12). 268.00 *(978-0-8160-5309-4(X))* Facts On File, Inc.

Kuzma, Gregory. On the Field from Denver, Colorado... the Blue Knights! One Member's Experience of the 1994 Summer National Tour. 2004. 206p. (YA). pap. 17.95 *(978-0-595-32278-7(6))* iUniverse, Inc.

Lindeen, Mary. Cool Latin Music: Create & Appreciate What Makes Music Great!, 1 vol. 2008. (Cool Music Ser.). (ENG., Illus.). 32p. (YA). (gr. 3-6). 28.50 *(978-1-59928-972-4(5))* ABDO Publishing Co.

MUSIC—ANALYSIS, APPRECIATION

see Music Appreciation

MUSIC—APPRECIATION

see Music Appreciation

MUSIC—BIOGRAPHY

see Musicians

MUSIC—DICTIONARIES

Krull, Kathleen. M Is for Music. Innerst, Stacy, illus. 2003. (ENG.). 56p. (J). (gr. -1-3). 17.00 *(978-0-15-201438-4(1))* Houghton Mifflin Harcourt Publishing Co.

—M Is for Music. Innerst, Stacy, illus. 2009. (ENG.). 48p. (J). (gr. -1-3). pap. 6.99 *(978-0-15-206479-2(6))* Houghton Mifflin Harcourt Publishing Co.

Munoz, Miguel. Diccionario Juvenil de Musica.Tr. of Children's Music Dictionary. (SPA.). (J). (gr. 3-5). pap. 11.20 *(978-958-33-1357-8(2))* Botero de Borrero, Beatriz & Martha Olga Botero de Gomez COL. Dist: Lectorum Pubns., Inc.

—Sonodiccionario: Asi Suenan los Instrumentos. (SPA.). (J). (gr. k-2). pap. 8.76 *(978-958-33-1556-5(7))* Botero de Borrero, Beatriz & Martha Olga Botero de Gomez COL. Dist: Lectorum Pubns., Inc.

MUSIC, DRAMATIC

see Opera

MUSIC—FICTION

Abdo, Kenny. Duck, Dive, Rock & Roll, 1 vol. Doucet, Bob, illus. 2013. (Haven't Got a Clue! Ser.). (ENG.). 80p. (J). (gr. 3-6). lib. bdg. 27.07 *(978-1-61641-952-3(0)*, Calico Chapter Bks) Magic Wagon.

Adoff, Arnold. Roots & Blues: A Celebration. Christie, R. Gregory, illus. 2011. (ENG.). 96p. (J). (gr. 5-7). 17.99 *(978-0-547-23554-7(2))* Houghton Mifflin Harcourt Publishing Co.

The Adventures of Max & Millie: At the Pond. 2003. (Illus.). 32p. (J). 8.95 *(978-0-9744427-0-9(4))* Music Bks. & Games.

Alexander, Carol. Percy Mogoo. 2012. 24p. pap. 15.99 *(978-1-4771-2359-1(8))* Xlibris Corp.

Alexander, William. Ghoulish Song. (ENG., Illus.). (J). (gr. 3-7). 2014. 192p. pap. 6.99 *(978-1-4424-2730-3(2))* 2013. 176p. 16.99 *(978-1-4424-2729-7(9))* McElderry, Margaret K. Bks. (McElderry, Margaret K. Bks.).

Anaya, Hector. Cuenta Cuenta. Moreno, Sergio, illus. 2nd rev. ed. 2005. (Castillo de la Lectura Verde Ser.). (SPA & ENG.). 184p. (J). (gr. -1-7). pap. 7.95 *(978-970-20-0135-5(8))* Castillo, Ediciones, S. A. de C. V. MEX. Dist: Macmillan.

Angus, John. Beautiful Music A Children's Concert. 2009. 21p. pap. 10.99 *(978-0-9716411-0-5(2))* APG Sales & Distribution Services.

Arkin, Alan. Cassie Loves Beethoven. l.t. ed. 2003. (Children's Large Print Ser.). 28.95 *(978-1-58118-108-1(6))* LRS.

AZ Books Staff. Merry Orchestra. Tulup, Natalia, ed. 2012. (Tra-La-la Ser.). (ENG.). 14p. (J). (-k). bds. 10.95 *(978-1-61889-056-6(5))* AZ Bks. LLC.

—Musical Animals. Tulup, Natalia, ed. 2012. (Tra-La-la Ser.). (ENG.). 14p. (J). (-k). bds. 10.95 *(978-1-61889-057-3(3))* AZ Bks. LLC.

—Musical Machines. Tulup, Natalia, ed. 2012. (Tra-La-la Ser.). (ENG.). 14p. (J). (-k). bds. 10.95 *(978-1-61889-055-9(7))* AZ Bks. LLC.

Ball, Marcia. Christmas Fais Do-Do. 2006. (Illus.). 36p. (J). per. 14.95 *(978-1-58939-972-3(2))* Virtualbookworm.com Publishing, Inc.

Banks, Steven. The Song That Never Ends. DePorter, Vince, illus. 2004. (Spongebob Squarepants Ser.). 32p. (J). (gr. k-2). 11.65 *(978-0-7569-5374-4(X))* Perfection Learning Corp.

Baron, Andrew, illus. El Pulpo Rex. 2003. (SPA.). (J). per. 17.95 *(978-0-9760348-1-0(6))* BaHart Pubns. / Eight Legs Publishing.

Bartlett, T. C. Tuba Lessons. Felix, Monique, illus. 2011. (ENG.). 32p. (J). (gr. 1-17). pap. 9.95

(978-0-89812-522-1(7), Creative Paperbacks) Creative Co., The.

Basore, Polly M. Santa's Stray in A Piano for Christmas. Williams, Carlene H., illus. 2005. 32p. (J). per. (978-0-9771749-1-1(3)) AngelBooks.

Becker, May R. Woodland Party. 2013. 10.95 (978-0-7414-8170-2(7)) Infinity Publishing.

—Woodland Party - Color. 2013. pap. 19.95 (978-0-7414-8171-9(5)) Infinity Publishing.

Bergen, Lara. Drama Queen. 2007. 164p. (J). pap. (978-0-545-03702-0(6)) Scholastic, Inc.

Black, Allyson. Fashion Face-off. Johnson, Shane L., illus. 2011. (Scarlett & Crimson Ser.). (ENG.). 112p. (J). (gr. 3-7). pap. 6.99 (978-1-4169-5937-3(8), Simon Spotlight) Simon Spotlight.

Bloom, Stephanie. The Drummer Who Lost His Beat. Keylon, Joe, illus. 2005. 40p. (J). lib. bdg. 16.95 (978-1-931969-47-5(7)) Bloom & Grow Bks.

Bonnett-Rampersaud, Louise. The Spring Un-Fair, 0 vols. 2015. (Secret Knock Club Ser.: 0). (ENG.). 112p. (J). (gr. 1-4). pap. 9.99 (978-0-7614-6326-9(7), 9780761463269, Amazon Children's Publishing) Amazon Publishing.

Brandt, Courney. A Fine Line. 2008. 164p. pap. 12.95 (978-0-595-52500-3(8)) iUniverse, Inc.

Brennah-Nelson, Denise. Maestro Stu Saves the Zoo. 2012. (ENG., Illus.). 32p. (J). 15.95 (978-1-58536-802-0(4)) Sleeping Bear Pr.

Brenner, Vida. The Magic Music Shop. Sharp, Mary, ed. Sharpnack, Joe, illus. 2013. 102p. pap. 12.95 (978-1-57216-094-1(2)) Penfield Bks.

Bronson, Matthew Shane & Bronson, Tammy Carter. Kaleidonotes & the Mixed-up Orchestra. Bronson, Tammy Carter, illus. 2nd rev. ed. 2003. (Illus.). 24p. (J). lib. bdg. 12.99 (978-0-9678167-6-0(9)) Bookaroos Publishing, Inc.

Burch, Sharon. Freddie the Frog & the Mysterious Wahooooo: 3rd Adventure: Tempo Island. 2010. (ENG.). 34p. 24.99 incl. audio compact disk (978-0-9747454-7-3(2), 0974745472) Mystic Publishing.

—Freddie the Frog & the Mysterious Wahooooo (DIGITAL EDITION) Digital Storybook with Step-By-Step Lessons for Interactive Whiteboard. 2015. (ENG.). 2p. pap. 29.99 (978-1-4950-1092-7(9), 1495010929) Leonard, Hal Corp.

Burch, Sharon, et al. Freddie the Frog & the Secret of Crater Island: 4th Adventure: Crater Island. 2010. (ENG.). 48p. 24.99 incl. audio compact disk (978-0-9747454-6-6(4), 0974745464) Mystic Publishing.

Byng, Georgia. Molly Moon & the Monster Music. 2013. (Molly Moon Ser.: 6). (ENG.). 320p. (J). (gr. 3-7). 16.99 (978-0-06-166163-1(5)) HarperCollins Pubs.

Cabrera, Jane. The 12 Days of Christmas. 2013. (ENG., Illus.). 32p. (J). (gr. -1-k). 16.95 (978-0-8234-2870-0(2)) Holiday Hse., Inc.

Caines-Floyd, Eydi. The Story of Wanton Desire. 2009. 64p. (J). pap. 26.49 (978-1-4389-3156-2(5)) AuthorHouse.

Campagne, Michelle & Gallant, Dany. Fabuleuse Melodie De. 2013. (FRE., Illus.). 44p. (J). (gr. -1-k). 16.95 (978-2-923163-30-7(3)) La Montagne Secrete CAN. Dist: Independent Pubs. Group.

La Cancion de Roldan. (SPA., Illus.). 160p. (YA). 11.95 (978-84-7281-076-1(3), AF1076) Auriga, Ediciones S.A. ESP. Dist: Continental Bk. Co., Inc.

Carolan, Joanna F. Old Makana Had a Taro Farm. Carolan, Joanna F., illus. 2008. (Illus.). 48p. 17.95 (978-0-9715333-9-4(3)) Banana Patch Pr.

Carr, Heather. The Jiggleworm. Carr, Greg, illus. 2005. 18p. (J). 21.95 incl. audio compact disk (978-0-9768450-0-3(8), Giggletins) Le Bk. Moderne, LLC.

Castonguay, Leo. Piper Peter. 2012. 44p. 24.95 (978-1-4626-8604-9(4)); pap. 24.95 (978-1-4626-8078-8(X)) America Star Bks.

Cattell, Bob & Agard, John. Butter-Finger. Smy, Pam, illus. 2006. (ENG.). 128p. (J). (gr. 2-17). per. 7.95 (978-1-84507-376-3(2), Frances Lincoln) Quarto Publishing Group UK GBR. Dist: Hachette Bk. Group.

Celenza, Anna Harwell. Bach's Goldberg Variations. Kitchel, JoAnn E., illus. 2016. (Once upon a Masterpiece Ser.). (ENG.). 32p. (J). (gr. 1-4). lib. bdg. 16.95 (978-1-58089-529-3(8)) Charlesbridge Publishing, Inc.

Chaviano, Daina. Pais de Dragones. 2003. (Fables & Legends Ser.). (SPA., Illus.). 136p. (J). 9.95 (978-84-239-6346-1(2), EC30627) Espasa Calpe, S.A. ESP. Dist: Planeta Publishing Corp., Lectorum Pubns., Inc.

Cheerios Counting Songs. 2004. (Illus.). (J). (978-0-7853-9953-7(4)) Publications International, Ltd.

Clark, Platte F. Good Ogre. 2015. (Bad Unicorn Trilogy Ser.: 3). (ENG., Illus.). 384p. (J). (gr. 3-7). 17.99 (978-1-4424-5018-9(5), Aladdin) Simon & Schuster Children's Publishing.

Clarkson, Kelly. River Rose & the Magical Lullaby. Hughes, Laura, illus. 2016. 32p. (J). (gr. -1-3). 18.99 (978-0-06-242756-4(3)) HarperCollins Pubs.

Clements, Andrew. The Last Holiday Concert. 2006. (ENG., Illus.). 176p. (J). (gr. 3-7). pap. 7.99 (978-0-689-84525-3(1), Atheneum Bks. for Young Readers) Simon & Schuster Children's Publishing.

—The Last Holiday Concert. rev. l.t. ed. 2007. (Literacy Bridge Middle Reader Ser.). 165p. (J). (gr. 3-7). 22.95 (978-0-7862-9374-2(8)) Thorndike Pr.

—Things Hoped For. 2008. (ENG.). 176p. (J). (gr. 5-18). 7.99 (978-0-14-241073-8(X), Puffin Books) Penguin Young Readers Group.

—Things Hoped For. 2008. 167p. (gr. 5-9). 17.00 (978-0-7569-8933-0(7)) Perfection Learning Corp.

—Things Hoped For. l.t. ed. 2008. (Thorndike Literacy Bridge Ser.). 207p. 23.95 (978-1-4104-0500-5(1)) Thorndike Pr.

Clifford the Best Helper. (Illus.). 10p. (J). bds. 9.98 (978-0-7853-9948-3(8), 7208900) Publications International, Ltd.

Cline, Thornton. The Amazing Incredible Shrinking Drums. 2017. (ENG.). 44p. pap. 9.99 **(978-1-57424-344-4(6)**, 1574243446) Centerstream Publishing.

Cole, Barbara H. Wash Day, 1 vol. Himler, Ronald, illus. 2004. (ENG.). 32p. (J). 15.95 (978-1-932065-36-7(9), 7187849112) Star Bright Bks., Inc.

Collins, Pat Lowery. Hidden Voices: The Orphan Musicians of Venice. 2009. (ENG., Illus.). 352p. (YA). (gr. 7). 17.99 (978-0-7636-3917-4(6)) Candlewick Pr.

Constantine, Clélia. The Planet of Music. Smith, Owen & Collins Smith, Anne, trs. ELyum Studio, illus. 2012. (Little Prince Ser.: 3). (ENG.). 56p. (J). (gr. 4-8). pap. 7.95 (978-0-8225-9424-6(2), Graphic Universe™) Lerner Publishing Group.

Cook, Jacqueline. The Little Bear Who Worried Too Much: Suzie Bear & the Music Festival. 2010. 32p. pap. 13.00 (978-1-60860-529-3(9), Strategic Bk. Publishing) Strategic Book Publishing & Rights Agency (SBPRA).

Coveleskie, Sally & Goodrich, Peter. Henry the Steinway Tours the World. Friedman, Laura, illus. 2005. (Henry the Steinway Ser.: 3). 32p. (J). (gr. -1-3). 15.95 (978-0-9729427-8-2(5)) Yorkville Pr.

Coveleskie, Sally & Peter, Goodrich. Henry the Steinway a Star Is Born. Friedman, Laura, illus. 2003. (Henry the Steinway Ser.: Vol. 2). 32p. (J). (gr. k-3). (978-0-9729427-1-3(8)) Yorkville Pr.

Coveleskie, Sally, et al. Henry the Steinway & the Piano Recital. Friedman, Laura, illus. 2003. (Henry the Steinway Ser.: Vol. 1). 32p. (J). (gr. k-3). (978-1-931721-05-9(X)) Bright Sky Pr.

Cowley, Joy. Miss Doll & Friends: Toy Music. Bordicchia, Gaia, illus. 2014. (ENG.). 8p. pap. (978-0-927244-59-6(4), Joy Cowley Club) Flying Start Bks.

Cowling, Douglas. Vivaldi's Ring of Mystery. Fernandez, Laura & Jacobson, Rick, illus. 2004. (ENG.). 44p. (J). (978-0-439-96904-8(2), North Winds Pr) Scholastic Canada, Ltd.

Cox, Judy. Ukulele Hayley. Haley, Amanda, illus. (ENG.). 96p. (J). (gr. 2-5). 2014. pap. 5.99 (978-0-8234-3190-8(8)) 2013. 16.95 (978-0-8234-2863-2(X)) Holiday Hse., Inc.

Cox, Steven. Justin's Very Own Drum. Saavedra, Anthony, illus. 2009. 24p. pap. 24.95 (978-1-60749-553-6(8)) America Star Bks.

Crew, Gary. Pig on the Titanic: A True Story. Whatley, Bruce, illus. 2005. 32p. (J). 15.99 (978-0-06-052305-3(0)) HarperCollins Pubs.

Culbertson, Kim. Songs for a Teenage Nomad. 2010. (ENG.). 256p. (YA). (gr. 7-12). pap. 12.99 (978-1-4022-4301-1(4)) Sourcebooks, Inc.

Daddy Saved the Day: Six-Pack. (Greetings Ser.: Vol. 3). 24p. (gr. 2-3). 31.00 (978-0-7635-9417-6(2)) Rigby Education.

d'Allancé, Mireille. No, No Y No! 2005. (SPA., Illus.). (J). 15.99 (978-84-8470-114-9(X)) Corimbo, Editorial S.L. ESP. Dist: Iaconi, Mariuccia Bk. Imports.

Dapre, Alan & Rooney, Ronnie. Brum Big Town Songs. 2004. (Illus.). 10p. (J). bds. (978-0-7853-9898-1(0)) Publications International, Ltd.

Decker, Tim. The Punk Ethic. Decker, Tim, illus. 2012. (ENG., Illus.). 188p. (YA). 18.95 (978-1-60898-120-5(7)); pap. 9.95 (978-1-60898-121-2(5)) namelos llc.

DeLand, M. Maitland. Busy Bees on Broadway. Martin, Lyn, illus. 2011. 32p. 15.95 (978-1-60832-063-9(4)) Greenleaf Book Group.

Delporte, Yvan. The Smurfs & the Magic Flute. Peyo, illus. 2010. (Smurfs Graphic Novels Ser.). (ENG.). 64p. (J). (gr. 2-5). pap. 5.99 (978-1-59707-208-3(7), 9781597072083) Papercutz.

Delporte, Yvan & Peyo. The Smurfs & the Magic Flute. 2010. (Smurfs Graphic Novels Ser.). (ENG., Illus.). 64p. (J). (gr. 2-5). 10.99 (978-1-59707-209-0(5), 9781597072090) Papercutz.

Demby, Kyri. Lori Biscuit, the Musical Detective: The Escape of Fortissimo. 2009. 24p. pap. 11.49 (978-1-4343-5223-1(4)) AuthorHouse.

Denman, K. L. Stuff We All Get, 1 vol. 2011. (Orca Currents Ser.). (ENG.). 128p. (J). (gr. 5-9). pap. 9.95 (978-1-55469-820-2(0)); lib. bdg. 16.95 (978-1-55469-821-9(9)) Orca Bk. Pubs. USA.

Desrosiers, Sylvie. Aimez-Vous la Musique? Sylvestre, Daniel, illus. 2004. (Roman Jeunesse Ser.). (FRE.). 96p. (J). (gr. 4-7). pap. (978-2-89021-709-6(4)) Diffusion du livre Mirabel (DLM).

Destiny, A. & Lenhard, Elizabeth. Our Song. 2015. 225p. (YA). (978-1-4424-8407-8(1), Simon Pulse) Simon Pulse.

Dimopoulos, Elaine. Material Girls. 2016. (ENG.). 336p. (YA). (gr. 9). pap. 8.99 (978-0-544-67173-7(2), HMH Books For Young Readers) Houghton Mifflin Harcourt Publishing Co.

Disney Book Club Staff. Disney Junior Music Player Storybook. 2013. (Music Player Storybook Ser.: 1). (ENG.). 32p. (J). (gr. -1-2). 19.99 (978-0-7944-3011-5(2)) Reader's Digest Assn., Inc., The.

Disney Frozen, Disney. Disney Frozen Music Player Storybook. 2015. (Music Player Storybook Ser.: 1). (ENG.). 32p. (J). (gr. -1-k). 24.99 (978-0-7944-3490-8(8)) Reader's Digest Assn., Inc., The.

Disney Junior, Disney. Disney Sofia the First Music Player Storybook. 2015. (Music Player Storybook Ser.: 1). (ENG.). 32p. (J). (gr. -1-2). 19.99 (978-0-7944-3357-4(X), Reader's Digest Children's Bks.) Studio Fun International.

Disney Storybook Artists Staff & Reader's Digest Staff. Disney Princess Music Player Storybook. 2013. (Music Player Storybook Ser.). (ENG.). 40p. (J). (gr. -1-3). 19.99 (978-0-7944-2804-4(5)) Reader's Digest Assn., Inc., The.

Donald, David R. Gogo's Song. 2012. 64p. (-18). pap. 15.99 (978-1-4797-1024-9(5)) Xlibris Corp.

Donegan, Noel & Donegan, Luz. The Hot-Headed Bassoon. 2013. (Magical Mozart & His Musical Ser.). (ENG.). 32p. (J). pap. 8.95 (978-1-84730-392-9(7)) Veritas Pubns. IRL. Dist: Dufour Editions, Inc.

—The Noisy Blue Drum. 2013. (Magical Mozart & His Musical Ser.). (ENG.). 32p. (J). pap. 8.95 (978-1-84730-391-2(9)) Veritas Pubns. IRL. Dist: Dufour Editions, Inc.

—The Sad Little Violin. 2013. (Magical Mozart & His Musical Ser.). (ENG.). 32p. (J). pap. 8.95 (978-1-84730-393-6(5)) Veritas Pubns. IRL. Dist: Dufour Editions, Inc.

Dowell, Frances O'Roark. Ten Miles Past Normal. 2011. (ENG.). 224p. (YA). (gr. 7-18). 16.99 (978-1-4169-9585-2(4), Atheneum Bks. for Young Readers) Simon & Schuster Children's Publishing.

Drachman, Eric. Ellison the Elephant. Muscarello, James, illus. 2005. (ENG.). 32p. (J). (gr. -1-2). 18.95 incl. audio compact disk (978-0-9703809-1-3(7)) Kidwick Bks.

Duchesne, Christiane. W Is for Wapiti! An Alphabet Songbook. Côté, Geneviève, illus. 2012. (ENG.). 48p. (J). (gr. -1-k). 16.95 (978-2-923163-83-3(4)) La Montagne Secrete CAN. Dist: Independent Pubs. Group.

Dyan, Penelope. The Musical Family — Sometimes a Song Says It All. Dyan, Penelope, illus. 2009. (Illus.). 42p. pap. 11.95 (978-1-935118-81-7(1)) Bellissima Publishing, LLC.

EarTwiggle's Adventure 1: Twiggle Book. 2004. (J). 1.99 (978-0-9762573-1-8(9)) Ear Twiggles Productions, Inc.

Elerya. One Step Higher: Piano Paradise Book II, 1 vol. 2009. 79p. pap. 16.95 (978-1-60749-477-5(9)) PublishAmerica, Inc.

Engle, Margarita. Drum Dream Girl: How One Girl's Courage Changed Music. López, Rafael, illus. 2015. (ENG.). 48p. (J). (gr. -1-3). 16.99 (978-0-544-10229-3(0), HMH Books For Young Readers) Houghton Mifflin Harcourt Publishing Co.

Evensen, Rachelle. Finn's Marching Band: A Story of Counting, Colors, & Playing Together. 2009. 32p. (J). 14.95 (978-0-8091-6749-4(2), Ambassador Bks.) Paulist Pr.

Ewing, Lynne. Motown Anthology. 2003. (ENG.). 96p. (J). 22.99 (978-0-7868-0854-0(3)) Hyperion Pr.

Federle, Tim. Better Nate Than Ever. (ENG., Illus.). (J). (gr. 4-8). 2014. 296p. pap. 7.99 (978-1-4424-4691-5(9)) 2013. 288p. 17.99 (978-1-4424-4689-2(7)) Simon & Schuster Bks. For Young Readers. (Simon & Schuster Bks. For Young Readers).

—Five, Six, Seven, Nate! 2014. (ENG., Illus.). 304p. (J). (gr. 5-9). 16.99 (978-1-4424-4693-9(5), Simon & Schuster Bks. For Young Readers) Simon & Schuster Bks. For Young Readers.

Fertig, Michael P. Musical Mystery Scooby Doo! McKee, Darren, illus. 2007. (Scooby Doo Ser.). (J). (gr. -1-3). 12.98 (978-1-4127-7429-1(2)) Publications International, Ltd.

Fischel, Ana. The Twelve Quests - Book 3, the Pied Piper's Flute. 2009. 158p. pap. (978-1-84923-875-5(8)) YouWriteOn.

Fishman, Linda Charles. The Little Girl Who Loves Music: Book Three of Grandma's Girls. 2012. 24p. pap. 17.99 (978-1-4772-6156-9(7)) AuthorHouse.

Fitzer, Robin. Summer Stories. 2008. 45p. pap. 24.95 (978-1-60563-742-6(4)) America Star Bks.

Fogelin, Adrian. The Big Nothing. (ENG.). 224p. (J). (gr. 3-7). 2006. pap. 7.95 (978-1-56145-388-7(9)) 2004. 15.95 (978-1-56145-326-9(9)) Peachtree Pubs.

Freeman, Don. Manuelo the Playing Mantis. 2006. (ENG., Illus.). 32p. (J). (gr. -1-2). reprint ed. pap. 6.99 (978-0-14-240560-4(4), Puffin Books) Penguin Young Readers Group.

French, Simon. Where in the World. 2008. 198p. (978-1-921272-57-8(0)) Little Hare Bks. AUS. Dist: HarperCollins Pubs. Australia.

Friedman, Laurie. Play It Again, Mallory. Kalis, Jennifer, illus. 2013. (Mallory Ser.: 20). (ENG.). 160p. (J). (gr. 2-5). 15.95 (978-0-7613-6075-9(1), Darby Creek) Lerner Publishing Group.

Friesel, Uwe. Tim, the Peacemaker. Wilkon, Jozef, illus. 32p. (J). (gr. -1-3). 13.95 (978-0-87592-052-8(7)) Scroll Pr., Inc.

Galvin, Laura Gates. If Cookie Had a Cookie. Wood, Damian, illus. 2009. (Sesame Street Read, Play & Go Ser.). 20p. (J). (gr. -1). 9.99 incl. audio compact disk (978-1-59069-867-9(3)) Studio Mouse LLC.

—I've Been Working on the Railroad. Brown, Dan, illus. 2008. (ENG.). 32p. (J). (gr. k-2). 14.95 (978-1-59249-771-3(3)); 8.95 (978-1-59249-772-0(1)) Soundprints.

—Musical Safari - Little Einsteins. 2009. (Little Einstein Audio Tales). (ENG.). 20p. (J). (gr. -1). 8.99 (978-1-59069-774-0(X)) Studio Mouse LLC.

Godinez, Flory. The Adventures of Max & Millie: The Notable Orchard. 2004. (Illus.). 32p. (J). 9.95 (978-0-9744427-1-6(2)) Music Bks. & Games.

Goembel, Ponder. Animal Fair, 0 vols. Goembel, Ponder, illus. 2010. (ENG., Illus.). 24p. (J). (gr. -1 — 1). 12.99 (978-0-7614-5642-1(2), 9780761456421, Amazon Children's Publishing) Amazon Publishing.

Gordon, Amy. The Gorillas of Gill Park. 2003. (ENG., Illus.). 256p. (J). (gr. 4-6). tchr. ed. 16.95 (978-0-8234-1751-3(4)) Holiday Hse., Inc.

Gray, Michael Loyd. King Biscuit. 2013. (J). pap. (978-1-938237-04-1(8)) Tempest Bk. Shop.

Gripe, Maria. Elvis Karlsson. Gripe, Harold, illus. 2003. (SPA.). 148p. (J). (gr. 3-5). pap. 9.95 (978-958-24-0181-8(8)) Santillana USA Publishing Co., Inc.

Haak, Harold H. The Mubox Bugs. l.t. ed. 2003. (Illus.). 20p. (J). 5.95 (978-1-931474-82-5(6)) Creative Teaching Assocs.

Hanson, Anders. Beetle Mania, 1 vol. 2007. (Critter Chronicles Ser.). (ENG., Illus.). 24p. (J). (gr. k-3). lib. bdg. 24.21 (978-1-59928-432-3(4), SandCastle) ABDO Publishing Co.

Harrison, John. Fergal Onions. 2005. (Illus.). 32p. pap. (978-0-7022-3481-1(8)) Univ. of Queensland Pr.

Hartman, Rachel. Seraphina. (ENG.). (YA). (gr. 7). 2014. 528p. pap. 10.99 (978-0-375-86622-7(1), Ember) 2012. 512p. lib. bdg. 20.99 (978-0-375-96656-9(0), Random Hse. Bks. for Young Readers) Random Hse. Children's Bks.

Harvey, Jeanne Walker. My Hands Sing the Blues: Romare Bearden's Childhood Journey, 0 vols. Zunon, Elizabeth, illus. 2011. (ENG.). 40p. (J). (gr. k-3). 17.99 (978-0-7614-5810-4(7), 9780761458104, Amazon Children's Publishing) Amazon Publishing.

Hayes, Mj. Emma's House of Sound. Robinson-Chavez, Kathryn A. & Madzel, D. E., illus. 2012. 80p. pap. 12.95 (978-0-9819634-4-0(7)) St. Augustine Pr.

Helguera, Luis Ignacio. Gracias a Johannes. Morales, Judith, illus. 2003. (SPA.). (978-968-494-086-4(6), CI5287) Centro de Informacion y Desarrollo de la Comunicacion y la Literatura MEX. Dist: Lectorum Pubns., Inc.

Heller, Sarah. Tinker Bell My Music MP3 Player: Storybook & Personal Music Player. 2008. (RD Innovative Book & Player Format Ser.). (ENG.). 36p. (YA). bds. 24.99 (978-0-7944-1673-7(X)) Reader's Digest Assn., Inc., The.

Henkes, Kevin. Penny & Her Song. Henkes, Kevin, illus. 2012. (I Can Read Level 1 Ser.). (Illus.). 32p. (J). (gr. -1-3). (ENG.). pap. 3.99 (978-0-06-208197-1(7)); (ENG., 12.99 (978-0-06-208195-7(0)); lib. bdg. 14.89 (978-0-06-208196-4(9)) HarperCollins Pubs. (Greenwillow Bks.).

—Penny & Her Song. 2012. (J). lib. bdg. 13.55 (978-0-606-26847-9(2), Turtleback) Turtleback Bks.

Herrera, Alberto. Músik: A Delightfully Harmonic Tale of the Origin of Music. 2012. 26p. 25.95 (978-1-4327-8807-0(8)) Outskirts Pr., Inc.

Hertz, Kellen. Tenney. 2017. (American Girl: Tenney Grant Ser.: 1). (ENG.). 192p. (J). (gr. 3-7). pap. 9.99 (978-1-338-11755-4(6)) Scholastic, Inc.

Hertz, Kellen. Tenney Shares the Stage. 2017. (American Girl: Tenney Grant Ser.: 3). (ENG.). 208p. (J). (gr. 3-7). pap. 9.99 **(978-1-338-11757-8(2))** Scholastic, Inc.

—Tenney Shares the Stage. 2017. (American Girl Contemporary Middle Grade Ser.: 3). lib. bdg. 20.85 **(978-0-606-40161-6(X))** Turtleback Bks.

Hoffman, Amalia. Klezmer Bunch. 2009. 36p. 15.95 (978-965-229-447-0(0)) Gefen Publishing Hse., Ltd ISR. Dist: Strauss Consultants.

Hoffman, Don & Palmer, Priscilla. Find Your Music. Dakins, Todd, illus. 2016. (ENG.). 32p. (J). (gr. -1-k). pap. 3.99 (978-1-943154-06-7(6)) Peek-A-Boo Publishing.

Hoffmann, Burton R. Millicent the Magnificent. du Houx, Emily C., illus. 2004. 64p. pap. 12.00 (978-1-882190-68-3(8)) Polar Bear & Co.

Holm, Jennifer L. & Holm, Matthew. The Musical. Holm, Jennifer L. & Holm, Matthew, illus. 2009. (Babymouse Ser.: 10). (ENG., Illus.). 96p. (J). (gr. 2-5). pap. 6.99 (978-0-375-84388-4(4)); lib. bdg. 12.99 (978-0-375-93791-0(9)) Random Hse. Children's Bks. (Random Hse. Bks. for Young Readers).

Houran, Lori Haskins. Too Many Cats. Mathieu, Joe, illus. 2009. (Step into Reading Ser.). (ENG.). 32p. (J). (gr. -1-1). pap. 3.99 (978-0-375-85197-1(6), Random Hse. Bks. for Young Readers) Random Hse. Children's Bks.

Howard, Ryan & Howard, Krystle. The Talent Show (Little Rhino #4) Madrid, Erwin, illus. 2016. (Little Rhino Ser.: 4). (ENG.). 112p. (J). (gr. 2-5). pap. 5.99 (978-1-338-05223-7(3), Scholastic Paperbacks) Scholastic, Inc.

Howie, Vicki. Silent Night. Kallai, Kriszta Nagy, illus. 2009. 32p. (J). (gr. -1). pap. 13.49 (978-0-7586-1779-8(8)) Concordia Publishing Hse.

Humble, Mark. Elmo Raps. 2009. (Sesame Street Step by Step Ser.). 10p. (J). (gr. -1). bds. 15.99 (978-1-59069-870-9(3)) Studio Mouse LLC.

Ibbitson, John. The Landing. 2008. (ENG.). 160p. (J). (gr. 7-9). 17.95 (978-1-55453-234-6(5)); pap. 7.95 (978-1-55453-238-4(8)) Kids Can Pr., Ltd. CAN. Dist: Hachette Bk. Group.

Jacobson, John & Huff, Mac. North Pole Musical: One Singular Sensational Holiday Revue. 2010. (Illus.). 72p. (J). pap. (978-1-4234-7661-0(1)) Leonard, Hal Corp.

James, Karim. The Kids Time to Rhyme: Read & Rhyme at the same Time. 2009. 16p. pap. 14.99 (978-1-4490-0424-8(5)) AuthorHouse.

Kalman, Esther. Tchaikovski Descubre America. 2003. (SPA., Illus.). 38p. (J). (gr. 3-5). 10.95 (978-1-58105-123-0(9), SAN1239) Santillana USA Publishing Co., Inc.

Katz, Alan. Where Did They Hide My Presents? Silly Dilly Christmas Songs. Catrow, David, illus. 2008. (ENG.). 32p. (J). (gr. -1-3). 6.99 (978-1-4169-6830-6(X), McElderry, Margaret K. Bks.) McElderry, Margaret K. Bks.

Kelly, Erin Entrada. Blackbird Fly. Peterschmidt, Betsy, illus. 2015. (ENG.). 304p. (J). (gr. 3-7). 16.99 (978-0-06-223861-0(2), Greenwillow Bks.) HarperCollins Pubs.

Kenneally, Miranda. Jesse's Girl. 2015. (Hundred Oaks Ser.: Bk. 6). (ENG.). 304p. (YA). (gr. 8-12). 16.99 (978-1-4022-8482-3(9), 9781402284823) Sourcebooks, Inc.

Kimmel, Eric A. The Three Cabritos, 0 vols. Gilpin, Stephen, illus. 2012. (ENG.). 32p. (J). (gr. -1-3). pap. 7.99 (978-0-7614-6309-2(7), 9780761463092, Amazon Children's Publishing) Amazon Publishing.

Kimpton, Paul & Kimpton, Ann Kaczkowski. Dog Tags: A Boy & His Bugle in America During WWII. 2012. (Adventures with Music Ser.: 2). (ENG.). 120p. (J). (gr. 4-7). pap. 8.95 (978-1-57999-882-0(8)) G I A Pubns., Inc.

—Summer of Firsts: WWII Is Ending, but the Music Adventures Are Just Beginning. 2013. (Adventures with Music Ser.: 3). (ENG., Illus.). 288p. (J). (gr. 4-7). pap. 8.95 (978-1-57999-972-8(7)) G I A Pubns., Inc.

Kirsch - Gambrell, Deneen. No Music for Mouseville. 2012. 32p. pap. 19.99 (978-1-4772-7151-3(1)) AuthorHouse.

Kirwan, Wednesday. Baby Loves to Rock! Kirwan, Wednesday, illus. 2013. (ENG., Illus.). 28p. (J). (gr. -1 — 1). bds. 5.99 (978-1-4424-5989-2(1), Little Simon) Little Simon.

Knight, Hilary. A Firefly in a Fir Tree: A Carol for Mice. Knight, Hilary, illus. 2004. (Illus.). 32p. (J). (gr. -1-3). lib. bdg. 15.89 (978-0-06-000992-2(6), Tegen, Katherine Bks) HarperCollins Pubs.

Kormos, Lawrence. It Happened One Night in the Barn. Purdy, Joanne, illus. 2007. 24p. (978-1-55452-192-0(0)) Essence Publishing.

Kristen, Judith. Once upon a Time in Liverpool. Cash, Eric, illus. 2012. 40p. pap. 15.95 (978-0-9849505-2-2(4)) Aquinas & Krone Publishing, LLC.

Krulik, Nancy. Hair Today, Gone Tomorrow!, 34 vols., No. 34. John and Wendy Staff, illus. 2010. (Katie Kazoo, Switcheroo Ser.: 34). (ENG.). 80p. (J). (gr. 2-4). pap. 3.99 (978-0-448-45231-9(6), Grosset & Dunlap) Penguin Young Readers Group.

Lacaille, Link. Roots, Rock, Rap & Reggae, 1 vol. 2009. 25p. pap. 24.95 (978-1-60836-930-0(7)) America Star Bks.

Langham, Tony. Creepy Crawly Calypso. Harter, Debbie, illus. 2004. (ENG.). 32p. (J). 16.99 (978-1-84148-699-4(X)) Barefoot Bks., Inc.

Langham, Tony & Harter, Debbie. Creepy Crawly Calypso. 2005. (ENG.). 32p. (J). pap. 9.99 (978-1-902283-46-3(5)) Barefoot Bks., Inc.

Lauture, Mireille B. Gade Yon Kado Remi Jwenn / Remi's Magical Gift: Mancy's Haitian Folktale Collection. 2012. 28p. pap. 16.99 (978-1-4685-5546-2(4)) AuthorHouse.

LeFlore, Lyah B. The World Is Mine. Warfield, D. L., illus. 2009. (Come Up Ser.). (ENG.). 304p. (YA). (gr. 9-18). pap. 8.99 (978-1-4169-7963-0(8), Simon Pulse) Simon Pulse.

Lewman, David. Drop the Beat! 2017. (Step into Reading Level 1 Ser.). lib. bdg. 14.75 **(978-0-606-40252-1(7))** Turtleback Bks.

Lies, Brian. Bats in the Band. Lies, Brian, illus. 2014. (Bat Book Ser.). (ENG., Illus.). 32p. (J). (gr. -1-3). 17.99 (978-0-544-10569-0(9), HMH Books For Young Readers) Houghton Mifflin Harcourt Publishing Co.

Lionni, Leo. Geraldine, the Music Mouse. Lionni, Leo, illus. 2016. (ENG., Illus.). 32p. (J). (gr. -1-2). 20.99

MNO

(978-0-394-94238-4(8)); 17.99 *(978-0-394-84238-7(3))* Random Hse. Children's Bks. (Knopf Bks. for Young Readers).

—Geraldine, the Music Mouse. 2009. (ENG., Illus.). 32p. (J). (gr. -1-2). pap. 7.99 *(978-0-375-85514-6(9)*, Dragonfly Bks.) Random Hse. Children's Bks.

Lipsyte, Robert. Yellow Flag. 2009. (ENG.). 256p. (YA). (gr. 8). pap. 9.99 *(978-0-06-055709-6(5)*, Tegen, Katherine Bks) HarperCollins Pubs.

Litchfield, David. The Bear & the Piano. 2016. (ENG., Illus.). 40p. (J). (gr. -1-3). 16.99 *(978-0-544-67454-7(5))* Houghton Mifflin Harcourt Publishing Co.

LOS MUSICOS DE BREMEN. 2004. (Caballo Alado Clásicos-Al Galope Ser.). (SPA & ENG., Illus.). 24p. (J). (gr. k-2). 7.95 *(978-84-7864-783-5(X))* Combel Editorial, S.A. ESP. Dist: Independent Pubs. Group.

Lowell, Sophia. Glee: Summer Break: An Original Novel. 2011. (Glee Ser.: 3). (ENG.). 224p. (YA). (gr. 10-17). pap., pap. 9.99 *(978-0-316-12360-0(9)*, Poppy) Little, Brown Bks. for Young Readers.

Lupton, Hugh. Tales of Wisdom & Wonder. Sharkey, Niamh, illus. 2008. (ENG.). 64p. (J). 19.99 *(978-1-84686-243-4(4))* Barefoot Bks., Inc.

MacHado, Ana Maria. Un Buen Coro. (Torre de Papel Ser.). (SPA., Illus.). (J). 7.95 *(978-958-04-4525-8(7)*, NR30643) Norma S.A. COL. Dist: Distribuidora Norma, Inc., Lectorum Pubns., Inc.

Madden, Kerry. Gentle's Holler. 2007. (Maggie Valley Ser.). 237p. (gr. 4-7). 17.00 *(978-0-7569-8090-0(9))* Perfection Learning Corp.

Maloney, Andrew. The Master Song. 2014. (Illus.). 352p. (YA). *(978-1-62911-176-6(7))* Whitaker Hse.

—Verse of Valor. 2015. 285p. (YA). *(978-1-62911-357-9(3))* Whitaker Hse.

Man-Kong, Mary. I Can Be a Rock Star. Golden Books Staff, illus. 2010. (Pictureback(R) Ser.). (ENG.). 16p. (J). (gr. -1-2). pap. 3.99 *(978-0-375-86545-9(4)*, Golden Bks.) Random Hse. Children's Bks.

Manning, Sarra. Guitar Girl. 2005. 217p. (gr. 9-12). 17.00 *(978-0-7569-5702-5(8))* Perfection Learning Corp.

Manushkin, Fran. Katie's Noisy Music. Lyon, Tammie, illus. 2015. (Katie Woo Ser.). (ENG.). 32p. (gr. k-2). 21.32 *(978-1-4795-5893-3(1))* Picture Window Bks.

Martin, Amy. Symphony City. 2011. (ENG., Illus.). 48p. (J). (gr. -1-4). 17.95 *(978-1-936365-39-5(1))* McSweeney's Publishing.

Mason-Black, Jennifer. Devil & the Bluebird. 2016. (ENG.). 336p. (J). (gr. 8-17). 17.95 *(978-1-4197-2000-0(7)*, Amulet Bks.) Abrams, Inc.

Mayer, Mercer. Just a Little Music. Mayer, Mercer, illus. 2009. (Little Critter Ser.). (ENG., Illus.). 24p. (J). (gr. -1-3). pap. 3.99 *(978-0-06-053962-7(3)*, HarperFestival) HarperCollins Pubs.

Mayerhofer, Felix. Horace the Great Harmonica King. MacFarlane, John, illus. 2006. 31p. (J). (gr. -1-7). per. 16.95 *(978-1-60002-255-5(3)*, 4313) Mountain Valley Publishing, LLC.

Mazer, Anne. It's Music to My Ears. 2005. (Amazing Days of Abby Hayes Ser.). (Illus.). 110p. (J). (gr. 3-7). 12.65 *(978-0-7569-5910-4(1))* Perfection Learning Corp.

McCanna, Tim. Barnyard Boogie! Black, Allison, illus. 2017. (ENG.). 24p. (gr. -1-k). 12.95 *(978-1-4197-2346-9(4)*, Abrams Appleseed) Abrams, Inc.

McGowan, Jayme. One Bear Extraordinaire. 2015. (ENG., Illus.). 32p. (J). (gr. -1-3). 16.95 *(978-1-4197-1654-6(9)*, Abrams Bks. for Young Readers) Abrams, Inc.

McKenzie, Tim A. Baxter Barret Brown's Cowboy Band. Atkinson, Elaine, illus. 2006. (ENG.). 28p. (gr. 2-4). 19.95 *(978-1-931721-77-6(7)*, a4a22ca5-3fa1-4c8b-8248-2efe0591d9b2) Bright Sky Pr.

Meadows, Daisy. Adele the Voice Fairy. 2013. (Rainbow Magic — the Superstar Fairies Ser.: 2). lib. bdg. 14.75 *(978-0-606-31514-2(4)*, Turtleback) Turtleback Bks.

—Alyssa the Star-Spotter Fairy. 2013. (Rainbow Magic — the Superstar Fairies Ser.: 6). lib. bdg. 14.75 *(978-0-606-31518-0(7)*, Turtleback) Turtleback Bks.

—Frankie the Makeup Fairy. 2013. (Rainbow Magic — the Superstar Fairies Ser.: 5). lib. bdg. 14.75 *(978-0-606-31517-3(9)*, Turtleback) Turtleback Bks.

—Jessie the Lyrics Fairy. 2013. (Rainbow Magic — the Superstar Fairies Ser.: 1). lib. bdg. 14.75 *(978-0-606-31513-5(6)*, Turtleback) Turtleback Bks.

Merveille, David. Juke Box. Merveille, David, illus. 2008. (ENG., Illus.). 48p. (J). (gr. 4-7). 9.99 *(978-1-933605-72-2(3))* Kane Miller.

Middlemiss, David. The Great Hamstini. Middlemiss, Laura B., illus. 2010. 108p. *(978-1-907211-18-8(7))* Grosvenor Hse. Publishing Ltd.

Middleton, William. The Chipmunk Jamboree. 2013. 24p. pap. 12.45 *(978-1-4624-0669-2(6)*, Inspiring Voices) Author Solutions, Inc.

Miller, Karl. Bongo Boy's Magical Drums. 2011. 72p. pap. 31.27 *(978-1-4567-7102-7(7))* AuthorHouse.

Miller, Sara. My Pod: Libro de Cuentos y Reproductor Personal de Musica. Peterson, Stacy & Maberry, Maranda, illus. 2007. (SPA.). 38p. (J). (gr. -1-3). *(978-970-718-495-4(7)*, Silver Dolphin en Español) Advanced Marketing, S. de R. L. de C. V.

Mit musik geht alles Besser. pap. 12.95 *(978-3-89748-676-8(8))* Dino Entertainment AG DEU. Dist: Distribooks, Inc.

Moss, Lloyd. Zin! Zin! Zin! A Violin. Priceman, Marjorie, illus. 2004. (gr. -1-3). 18.00 *(978-0-7569-1919-1(3))* Perfection Learning Corp.

—Zin! Zin! Zin! A Violin. Priceman, Marjorie, illus. 2005. (Stories to Go! Ser.). (ENG.). 32p. (J). (gr. -1-3). 4.99 *(978-1-4169-0838-8(2)*, Simon & Schuster/Paula Wiseman Bks.) Simon & Schuster/Paula Wiseman Bks.

Moulton, Mark Kimball. A Cricket's Carol. Blowers, Lisa, illus. 2004. 32p. (J). 14.95 *(978-0-8249-5488-6(2)*, Ideal Pubns.) Worthy Publishing.

Muller, Daniella L. Rumble, Rumble, Boom! 2009. 28p. pap. 12.99 *(978-1-4389-7710-2(7))* AuthorHouse.

Nall, Gail. Out of Tune. 2016. (Mix Ser.). (ENG., Illus.). 336p. (J). (gr. 4-9). 17.99 *(978-1-4814-5817-7(5)*, Simon & Schuster/Paula Wiseman Bks.) Simon & Schuster/Paula Wiseman Bks.

Newton, Jill, illus. Crash Bang Donkey! 2015. 32p. (J). *(978-1-4896-3858-8(X))* Weigl Pubs., Inc.

Norman, Tyler & Perez, Jose S. The Banjoman/El Hombre del Banjo. Perez, Jose S., illus. 2004. (ENG & SPA., Illus.). 32p. (J). 12.95 *(978-1-57072-292-9(7))* Overmountain Pr.

Nowlin, Laura. This Song Is (Not) for You. 2016. (ENG.). 240p. (YA). (gr. 8-12). pap. 9.99 *(978-1-4926-0290-3(6)*, 9781492602903) Sourcebooks, Inc.

Ode, Eric. Dan, the Taxi Man. Culotta, Kent, illus. 2012. (Picture Book Ser.). (ENG.). 32p. (J). 14.99 *(978-1-61067-072-2(8))* Kane Miller.

O'Neill, Richard & Quarmby, Katharine. Ossiri & the Bala Mengro. Tolson, Hannah, illus. 2017. (Child's Play Library). (ENG.). 32p. (J). *(978-1-84643-925-4(6))* Child's Play International Ltd.

Paige, D. M. Chart Topper. 2015. (Opportunity Ser.). (ENG.). 112p. (YA). (gr. 6-12). 34.65 *(978-1-4677-6014-0(5)*, Lerner Digital) Lerner Publishing Group.

Palonen, Jukka & Conrad, Tim. The Game Plan: A Kids' Musical about God's Master Plan for Each of Us. 2009. (ENG.). 96p. pap. 7.99 *(978-0-8341-7742-0(0)*, 9780834177420) Lillenas Publishing Co.

Parenteau Shirley, Shirley. Bears in a Band. Walker, David, illus. 2016. (ENG.). 32p. (J). (-k). 15.99 *(978-0-7636-8147-0(4))* Candlewick Pr.

Patrick, Wendy. When Passion Wins. 2012. 186p. (gr. 4-6). pap. 14.50 *(978-1-4669-7131-8(2))* Trafford Publishing.

Payne, C. C. Something to Sing About. 2008. (ENG.). 167p. (J). (gr. 4-7). pap. 8.50 *(978-0-8028-5344-8(7))* Eerdmans, William B. Publishing Co.

Payne, Sandy. Find Your Magic. Goodpaster, Nancy, illus. 2013. 50p. pap. 12.95 *(978-1-937508-16-6(1))* Bearhead Publishing, LLC.

Perelman, Helen. Heart to Heart. 2007. (High School Musical Stories from East High Ser.). 125p. (J). (gr. 3-7). 12.65 *(978-0-7569-8340-6(1))* Perfection Learning Corp.

Perez, Marlene. Dead Is a Killer Tune. 2012. (Dead Is Ser.: 7). lib. bdg. 18.40 *(978-0-606-26623-9(2)*, Turtleback) Turtleback Bks.

Pierpont, James Lord. Jingle Bells. Samuel, Janet, illus. 2014. 24p. (J). bds. 6.99 *(978-0-8249-1941-2(6)*, Ideal Pubns.) Worthy Publishing.

Plant, Marilyn. Trinka's Music Lessons. 2013. 48p. pap. *(978-1-4602-1273-8(8))* FriesenPress.

Politi, Leo. Pedro: The Angel of Olvera Street. 2009. (ENG., Illus.). 32p. 14.95 *(978-0-89236-990-4(6))* Oxford Univ. Pr., Inc.

Poulsen, David A. Jeremy's Song. 2004. 110p. (YA). pap. 3.99 *(978-1-55305-027-8(4))* Cygnet Publishing Group, Inc./Coolreading.com CAN. Dist: Orca Bk. Pubs. USA.

—Jeremy's Song. 2008. (Lawrence High Yearbook Ser.). (ENG.). 96p. (YA). (gr. 7-18). pap. *(978-1-55470-098-1(1))* Me to We.

Poupart, Jean-Marie. Des Pianos Qui S'Envolent. 2003. (Roman Jeunesse Ser.). (FRE.). 96p. (YA). (gr. 4-7). pap. *(978-2-89021-173-5(8))* Diffusion du livre Mirabel (DLM).

Powell, Amy. Hope Music. Farley, Katherine, illus. 2006. 32p. (J). (gr. -1-3). per. 12.00 *(978-0-9773608-4-0(9))* Shiny Red Ball Publishing.

Prinz, Yvonne. The Vinyl Princess. 2011. 336p. (J). pap. 8.99 *(978-0-06-171585-3(9)*, HarperTeen) 2009. (ENG.). 320p. (YA). (gr. 8-18). 16.99 *(978-0-06-171583-9(2))* HarperCollins Pubs.

Pritchett, Dylan. The First Music. Banks, Erin, illus. 2006. (ENG.). 32p. (J). (gr. -1-3). 16.95 *(978-0-87483-776-6(6))* August Hse. Pubs., Inc.

Publications International Ltd. Staff, creator. High School Musical: Let's Text. 2008. (High School Musical Ser.). (Illus.). 24p. (J). (gr. 4-7). 19.98 *(978-1-4127-7569-4(8))* Publications International, Ltd.

—Pooh Surprise Sing-along. 2007. (Surprise Mirror Book Ser.). (Illus.). (gr. -1-k). 15.98 *(978-1-4127-7418-5(7))* Publications International, Ltd.

Publications International Ltd. Staff, ed. Baby Einstein: Look, Listen, & Discover. 2010. 14p. (J). bds. 22.98 *(978-1-4127-4517-8(9)*, 1412745179) Phoenix International Publications, Inc.

—Barney Favorite Things. 2010. 12p. (J). bds. 10.98 *(978-1-4127-4465-2(2)*, PIL Kids) Publications International, Ltd.

—Hello Kitty I Love to Play Piano. 2013. 12p. (J). (gr. k-3). bds. 16.99 *(978-1-4508-6168-7(7)*, 3621dc87-b55b-4629-b450-4e32aa29210f) Phoenix International Publications, Inc.

—Look & Find Elmo. 2010. 24p. (J). 7.98 *(978-1-60553-766-5(7))* Phoenix International Publications, Inc.

—Musical Pop up Disney Princess. 2008. (SPA.). (J). 15.98 *(978-1-4127-8980-6(X))* Publications International, Ltd.

—Sesame Street (Musical Treasury) 2011. 40p. (J). bds. 15.98 *(978-1-4508-1081-4(0))* Publications International, Ltd.

Pugliano-Martin, Carol. The Very Mean King & el rey Malo: 6 English, 6 Spanish Adaptations. 2011. (ENG & SPA.). (J). 75.00 net. *(978-1-4108-5648-7(8))* Benchmark Education Co.

Quinn, Jordan. The Bard & the Beast. McPhillips, Robert, illus. 2015. (Kingdom of Wrenly Ser.: 9). (ENG.). 128p. (J). (gr. k-4). pap. 5.99 *(978-1-4814-4396-8(8)*, Little Simon) Little Simon.

Reader's Digest Staff. Disney Minnie - Take-Along Tunes: Music Player with 20 Tunes. 2013. (Take-Along Tunes Ser.). (ENG.). 32p. (J). (gr. -1-k). 19.99 *(978-0-7944-2553-1(4))* Reader's Digest Assn., Inc., The.

Rey, H. A. Curious George Harvest Hoedown (CGTV 8 X 8) 2017. (Curious George Ser.). (ENG., Illus.). 24p. (J). (gr. -1-3). 12.99 ***(978-1-328-69596-3(4)**, HMH Books For Young Readers) Houghton Mifflin Harcourt Publishing Co.

Rey, H. A. Music Play. 2009. (Curious Baby Curious George Ser.). (ENG., Illus.). 12p. (J). (gr. -1 — 1). bds. 8.99 *(978-0-547-23876-0(2))* Houghton Mifflin Harcourt Publishing Co.

Reynolds, Paul A. Sydney & Simon: Going Green! Reynolds, Paul A. & Reynolds, Peter H., illus. 2015. (Sydney & Simon Ser.). (ENG.). 48p. (J). (gr. 1-4). lib. bdg. 12.95 *(978-1-58089-677-1(4))* Charlesbridge Publishing, Inc.

Reynolds, Peter H. Playing from the Heart. Reynolds, Peter H., illus. 2016. (ENG., Illus.). 32p. (J). (gr. k-12). 15.00 *(978-0-7636-7892-0(9))* Candlewick Pr.

Richards, Chip & De Alessi, O. B. Flutes in the Garden. 2015. (ENG.). 68p. pap. 13.95 *(978-0-7387-4658-6(4))* Llewellyn Pubns.

Richardson, Bill. I Would Have Gone to Woodstock. 2007. 28p. (YA). per. 12.95 *(978-1-4327-1256-3(X))* Outskirts Pr., Inc.

Robinson, Fiona. What Animals Really Like. 2011. (ENG., Illus.). 24p. (J). (gr. k-2). 15.95 *(978-0-8109-8976-4(X)*, Abrams Bks. for Young Readers) Abrams, Inc.

Rodgers and Hammerstein Organization Staff & Lindsay and Crouse Staff. The Sound of Music: A Classic Collectible Pop-Up. Andreasen, Dan, illus. 2009. (ENG.). 14p. (J). (gr. -1-3). 34.99 *(978-1-4169-3655-8(6)*, Little Simon) Little Simon.

Rodman, Mercedes. My Blue Butterfly. 2012.Tr. of Mi Mariposa Azul. (SPA & ENG., Illus.). 64p. (J). pap. 19.95 *(978-0-9827146-7-6(X))* Vineyard Stories.

Rodriguez Ferrer, Janel. The Arts-Angels Track 1: Drawn to You. 2012. 252p. pap. 8.99 *(978-1-936214-91-4(1))* Wyatt-MacKenzie Publishing.

Rollins, Barbara B. Syncopated Summer. unabr. ed. 2006. (J). per. 9.95 *(978-1-932196-97-9(8))* WordWright.biz, Inc.

Romanelli, Serena. El Pequeno Coco. Lamas, Blanca Rosa, tr. from GER. de Beer, Hans, illus. 2004.Tr. of Kleiner Dodo was Spielst du?. (SPA.). 24p. (J). (gr. k-4). reprint ed. 16.00 *(978-0-7567-7707-4(0))* DIANE Publishing Co.

Rosenberg, Michael. The Little Lost Tune: More Adventures from Bendalot. 2010. 30p. pap. 13.00 *(978-1-60911-881-5(2)*, Eloquent Bks.) Strategic Book Publishing & Rights Agency (SBPRA).

Roth, Susan & Roth, Susan L. Do Re Mi: If You Can Read Music, Thank Guido D'Arezzo. Roth, Susan L., illus. 2007. (ENG., Illus.). 40p. (J). (gr. -1-3). 17.99 *(978-0-618-46572-9(3))* Houghton Mifflin Harcourt Publishing Co.

Roybal, Laura. Blood Brothers. Warner, Christopher, ed. 2015. 278p. (YA). (gr. 8-12). pap. 11.95 *(978-0-9963756-2-7(7))* All About Kids Publishing.

Russell, D. Z. The Amazing Adventures of Andy Owl: A Children's Guide to Understanding Music. Stone, John, illus. 2003. 34p. (J). per. 7.95 *(978-0-9725398-0-7(8))* World Famous Children's Bks.

Ryan, Pam Muñoz. Echo. 2015. (ENG., Illus.). 512p. (J). (gr. 5-9). 19.99 *(978-0-439-87402-1(5)*, Scholastic Pr.) Scholastic, Inc.

Santillo, LuAnn. The Tune. Santillo, LuAnn, ed. 2003. (Half-Pint Kids Readers Ser.). (Illus.). 7p. (J). (gr. -1-1). pap. 1.00 *(978-1-59256-102-5(0))* Half-Pint Kids, Inc.

Schram, Scott. The Last Noel: A Christmas Musical for Children. 2007. (ENG.). pap. 64.95 *(978-0-7390-4487-2(7))* Alfred Publishing Co., Inc.

Schreiber, Sam. Raise Your Voice. 2004. (Illus.). 187p. (J). pap. *(978-0-439-73083-9(X))* Scholastic, Inc.

Schulz, Charles M. A Charlie Brown Christmas: With Sound & Music. 2011. (ENG.). 48p. (J). (gr. -1-3). 22.95 *(978-0-7624-4005-4(8))* Running Pr. Bk. Pubs.

Sesame Street. Sesame Street Elmo's Musical Hugs. 2014. (Hugs Book Ser.: 5). (ENG.). 32p. (J). 19.99 *(978-0-7944-2862-4(2))* Reader's Digest Assn., Inc., The.

Shammas, Anna. Recorder Karate. Guiza, Victor, illus. 2012. 32p. pap. 8.95 *(978-0-9843869-2-5(0)*, Castlebridge Bks.) Big Tent Bks.

Shankman, Ed. The Bourbon Street Band Is Back. O'Neill, Dave, illus. 2011. (Shankman & O'Neill Ser.). (ENG.). 32p. (gr. -1-3). 14.95 *(978-1-933212-79-1(9)*, Commonwealth Editions) Applewood Bks.

Shefelman, Janice Jordan. Anna Maria's Gift. Papp, Robert, illus. 2011. (Stepping Stone Book Ser.). (ENG.). 112p. (J). (gr. 2-5). pap. 4.99 *(978-0-375-85882-6(2)*, Random Hse. Bks. for Young Readers) Random Hse. Children's Bks.

Sing with Your Baby. 2006. (ENG., Illus.). 36p. (gr. -1). 12.99 *(978-1-59069-494-7(5)*, 1P800) Studio Mouse LLC.

Spears, Rick. Black Metal Volume 3: Darkness Enthroned: Darkness Enthroned. 2014. (ENG., Illus.). 160p. (YA). pap. 11.99 *(978-1-934964-82-8(4)*, 9781934964828) Oni Pr., Inc.

St. Jean, Alan. The Legend of OinkADoodleMoo. St. Jean, Alan, ed. Krock, Libby Carruth, illus. 2013. 32p. 19.95 *(978-0-9777272-9-2(7))* Oren Village, LLC.

Staub, Leslie. Everybody Gets the Blues. Roth, R G, illus. 2012. (ENG.). 32p. (J). (gr. -1-3). 16.99 *(978-0-15-206300-9(5))* Houghton Mifflin Harcourt Publishing Co.

Staunton, Ted. Accord de Puissance: (Power Chord), 1 vol. 2012. (FRE.). 128p. (J). (gr. 5-9). pap. 9.95 *(978-1-4598-0311-4(6))* Orca Bk. Pubs. USA.

Steve Cormey. The Brothers Foot: A Hare Raising Story. Ronda Eden, illus. 2009. 56p. pap. 21.99 *(978-1-4389-4269-8(9))* AuthorHouse.

Stilton, Geronimo. Singing Sensation. 2009. (Geronimo Stilton Ser.: 39). lib. bdg. 18.40 *(978-0-606-00230-1(8)*, Turtleback) Turtleback Bks.

Stilwell, Norma Mintum. Making Beautiful Music. LaGrange, Tiffany, illus. 2011. 28p. pap. 14.95 *(978-1-936343-92-8(4))* Peppertree Pr., The.

Stinson, Kathy & Petricic, Dusan. The Man with the Violin. (ENG., Illus.). (J). (gr. k-3). 2016. 32p. pap. 9.95 *(978-1-55451-564-6(5))* 5th ed. 2013. 36p. 19.95 *(978-1-55451-565-3(3)*, 9781554515653) Annick Pr., Ltd. CAN. Dist: Publishers Group West (PGW).

Stone, Laura. Miss Clarissa & Her Musical Shoes. 2010. 32p. pap. 16.95 *(978-0-557-33226-7(5))* Lulu Pr., Inc.

Stuchner, Joan Betty. The Kugel Valley Klezmer Band. Row, Richard, illus. 2009. (PJ Library). (ENG.). 32p. (J). (gr. -1-3). pap. 7.95 *(978-1-56656-782-4(3)*, Crocodile Bks.) Interlink Publishing Group, Inc.

Studio Mouse Staff. Musical Fun: Colors & Patterns. rev. ed. 2008. (ENG., Illus.). 24p. (J). 4.99 *(978-1-59069-605-7(0))* Studio Mouse LLC.

Sullivan, Sarah. Passing the Music Down. Root, Barry, illus. 2011. (ENG.). 32p. (J). (gr. k-3). 17.99 *(978-0-7636-3753-8(X))* Candlewick Pr.

Supplee, Suzanne. Somebody Everybody Listens To. 2011. (ENG.). 288p. (YA). (gr. 7-18). 8.99 *(978-0-14-241886-4(2)*, Speak) Penguin Young Readers Group.

Tash, Sarvenaz. Three Day Summer. 2016. (ENG.). 320p. (YA). (gr. 7). pap. 10.99 *(978-1-4814-3932-9(4))* Simon & Schuster Children's Publishing.

Taylor, Je'. The Animal Dance. 2009. 32p. pap. 14.49 *(978-1-4490-2626-4(5))* AuthorHouse.

Taylor, Vincent. Cornbread Has a Bad Habit. 2007. (Illus.). 96p. (J). pap. 4.99 *(978-0-9704512-5-5(3))* TriEclipse, Inc.

Thaler, Mike. The Music Teacher from the Black Lagoon, 1 vol. Lee, Jared, illus. 2011. (Black Lagoon Set 1 Ser.: No. 1). (ENG.). 32p. (gr. -1-2). lib. bdg. 24.21 *(978-1-59961-796-1(X))* Spotlight.

The Library Fairy. The Magical Tree & Musical Wind. Faust, Laurie A., illus. 2008. 32p. pap. 16.95 *(978-1-59858-604-6(1))* Dog Ear Publishing, LLC.

Thomas, Maria Jose & Thomas, María José. !Bravo, Rosina! Muñoz, Claudio, illus. 2005. (SPA.). 48p. (J). (gr. -1-5). 10.40 *(978-980-257-242-7(X)*, EK33833) Ekare, Ediciones VEN. Dist: Lectorum Pubns., Inc.

Thomas, Terri. J Mac Is the Freestyle King! Sefcik, Wendy, illus. 2010. 38p. pap. 20.00 *(978-1-60844-453-3(8))* Dog Ear Publishing, LLC.

Thompson, Carol. Music. Thompson, Carol, illus. 2017. (Amazing Me! Ser.: 4). (ENG., Illus.). 12p. (J). (gr. k-k). bds. ***(978-1-84643-961-2(2))*** Child's Play International Ltd.

Thompson, Kate. The New Policeman. (Illus.). 2008. (New Policeman Trilogy Ser.: 1). (ENG.). 464p. (YA). (gr. 8-12). pap. 9.99 *(978-0-06-117429-2(7))* 2007. 448p. (J). (gr. 7-12). 16.99 *(978-0-06-117427-8(0))* HarperCollins Pubs. (Greenwillow Bks.).

—The New Policeman. pap. 1.00 *(978-1-4074-4550-2(2))* Recorded Bks., Inc.

Tibo, Gilles. Simon et la Musique. 2004.Tr. of Simon Makes Music. (FRE.). (J). (gr. -1-2). spiral bd. *(978-0-616-01845-3(2))* Canadian National Institute for the Blind/Institut National Canadien pour les Aveugles.

—Simon Makes Music. 2004. (J). (gr. -1-2). spiral bd. *(978-0-616-01793-7(6))*; spiral bd. *(978-0-616-01792-0(8))* Canadian National Institute for the Blind/Institut National Canadien pour les Aveugles.

Tomlinson, Heather. Aurelie: A Faerie Tale. 2010. (ENG.). 208p. (YA). (gr. 7-12). pap. 18.99 *(978-0-312-60275-8(8)*, 9780312602758) Square Fish.

Toon, Paige. All about the Hype. 2017. (Jessie Jefferson Novels Ser.: 3). (ENG.). 320p. (J). 9.99 *(978-1-4711-4610-7(3)*, Simon & Schuster Children's) Simon & Schuster, Ltd. GBR. Dist: Simon & Schuster, Inc.

Torgan, Keith & Siesel, Barbara. Green Golly & Her Golden Flute. Langelier-Lebeda, Suzanne, illus. 2013. 58p. pap. 19.99 *(978-1-936172-61-0(5))* Eifrig Publishing.

Traditional. Silent Night. Pulley, Kelly & Reed, Lisa, illus. 2014. (VeggieTales Book Ser.). 16p. (J). bds. 12.99 *(978-0-8249-1934-4(3)*, Ideal Pubns.) Worthy Publishing.

Trevayne, Emma. Chorus. 2014. (ENG.). 288p. (YA). (gr. 2-17). pap. 9.95 *(978-0-7624-4950-7(0)*, Running Pr. Kids) Running Pr. Bk. Pubs.

—Coda. 2013. (ENG.). 320p. (YA). (gr. 2-17). pap. 9.95 *(978-0-7624-4728-2(1)*, Running Pr. Kids) Running Pr. Bk. Pubs.

Urban, Linda. A Crooked Kind of Perfect. 2009. (ENG., Illus.). 224p. (J). (gr. 5-7). pap. 7.99 *(978-0-15-206608-6(X))* Houghton Mifflin Harcourt Publishing Co.

Van Dyne, Edith. Aunt Jane's Nieces Abroad. I.t. ed. 2007. (ENG.). 204p. pap. 22.99 *(978-1-4346-0259-6(1))* Creative Media Partners, LLC.

Velasquez, Eric. Grandma's Records. 2014. 32p. pap. 9.00 *(978-1-61003-346-6(9))* Center for the Collaborative Classroom.

—Grandma's Records. 2004. (Illus.). 32p. (J). (gr. k-3). 16.95 *(978-0-8027-8760-6(6))*; 17.85 *(978-0-8027-8761-3(4))* Walker & Co.

Velasquez, Eric & National Geographic Learning Staff. Grandma's Records. Velasquez, Eric, illus. 2004. (ENG., Illus.). 32p. (J). (gr. k-3). pap. 9.99 *(978-0-8027-7660-0(4)*, 9780802776600, Bloomsbury USA Childrens) Bloomsbury Publishing USA.

Vigneault, Gilles. Un Cadeau Pour Sophie: Conte et Chansons. Jorisch, Stéphane, illus. 2013. (FRE.). 40p. (J). (gr. k-2). 16.95 *(978-2-923163-38-3(9))* La Montagne Secrete CAN. Dist: Independent Pubs. Group.

Vipont, Elfrida. The Lark in the Morn. Freeman, T. R., illus. 2007. 196p. (YA). pap. 12.95 *(978-1-932350-22-7(5))* Bethlehem Bks.

Wallace, Suzanne. The Man Who Loved Violins. 2011. 28p. pap. 15.99 *(978-1-4568-7753-8(4))* Xlibris Corp.

Walton, O. F. Christie's Old Organ: A Little Boy's Journey to Find a Home of His Own. 2008. (Classic Stories Ser.). (ENG.). 176p. (J). (gr. 4-7). mass mkt. 7.99 *(978-1-85792-523-4(8)*, 5a46b3a9-187e-4c6b-b178-6593da9ecb66) Christian Focus Pubns. GBR. Dist: Bookmasters Distribution.

Watt, Fiona. Little Children's Christmas Music Book. 2012. (Little Children's Music Book Ser.). 24p. (J). bds. 18.99 *(978-0-7945-3328-1(0)*, Usborne) EDC Publishing.

—Sing-Along Christmas Carols. Bonnet, Rosalinde, illus. 2010. (Baby Board Books with CD Ser.). 10p. (J). bds. 14.99 incl. audio compact disk *(978-0-7945-2660-3(8)*, Usborne) EDC Publishing.

Watts, Leander. Beautiful City of the Dead. 2007. (ENG.). 256p. (YA). (gr. 7-12). pap. 14.99 *(978-0-618-59499-3(X))* Houghton Mifflin Harcourt Publishing Co.

Weidt, Maryann N. Daddy Played Music for the Cows. Sorensen, Henri, illus. 2nd ed. 2004. 32p. (J). pap. 7.95 *(978-0-89317-060-8(7)*, WW-0607, Windward Publishing) Finney Co., Inc.

Weinstone, David. Music Class Today! Vogel, Vin, illus. 2015. (ENG.). 40p. (J). (gr. -1 — 1). 17.99 *(978-0-374-35131-1(7)*, 9780374351311, Farrar, Straus & Giroux (BYR)) Farrar, Straus & Giroux.

Wekelo, Kerry. Audrey's Journey: Round & Round Yoga. 2012. 16p. pap. 15.99 *(978-1-4685-9645-8(4))* AuthorHouse.

Wells, Tina. Mixed Messages. (Mackenzie Blue Ser.: 4). (ENG.). (J). (gr. 3-7). 2013. 224p. pap. 6.99 *(978-0-06-158319-3(7))* 2010. 208p. 12.99 *(978-0-06-158317-9(0))* HarperCollins Pubs.

—The Secret Crush. Segawa, Michael, illus. 2009. (Mackenzie Blue Ser.: 2). (ENG.). 240p. (J). (gr. 3-7). 10.99 *(978-0-06-158311-7(1))* HarperCollins Pubs.

Wheeler, Lisa. Jazz Baby. Christie, R. Gregory, illus. 2007. (ENG.). 40p. (J). (gr. -1-3). 17.99 *(978-0-15-202522-9(7))* Houghton Mifflin Harcourt Publishing Co.
Where's Henry?, 6 Pack. (gr. k-1). 23.00 *(978-0-7635-8828-1(8))* Rigby Education.
Whitaker, Alecia. The Road to You. 2015. (Wildflower Ser.: 2). (ENG.). 352p. (YA). (gr. 7-17). 18.00 *(978-0-316-25140-2(2))* Sports Illustrated For Kids.
—The Way Back Home. 2016. (Wildflower Ser.: 3). (ENG.). 336p. (YA). (gr. 7-17). 17.99 *(978-0-316-25144-0(5)*, Poppy) Little, Brown Bks. for Young Readers.
Williams-Garcia, Rita. Clayton Byrd Goes Underground. Morrison, Frank, illus. 2017. 176p. (J). (gr. 3-7). 16.99 *(978-0-06-221591-8(4))*; (ENG.). E-Book *(978-0-06-221594-9(9))* HarperCollins Pubs. (Amistad).
Wilson, Budge. A Fiddle for Angus. Tooke, Susan, illus. 2006. (ENG.). 32p. (J). (gr. 1-4). pap. 13.95 *(978-0-88776-785-2(0)*, Tundra Bks.) Tundra Bks. CAN. Dist: Penguin Random Hse. LLC.
Winters, Ben H. The Secret Life of Ms. Finkleman. 2010. (ENG.). 256p. (J). (gr. 3-7). 16.99 *(978-0-06-196541-8(3))* HarperCollins Pubs.
Witte, Anna. El Fandango de Lola. Archer, Micha, illus. 2011. (SPA.). 32p. (J). (gr. k-5). 9.99 *(978-1-84686-359-2(7))* Barefoot Bks., Inc.
Yager, Fred. Sound from a Star: A Novel. 2011. 150p. (YA). 31.95 *(978-1-889262-90-1(0))* Hannacroix Creek Bks., Inc.
Zimelman, Nathan. Evening Song. Morrison, Cathy, illus. 2003. (Books for Young Learners). (ENG.). 12p. (J). 5.75 net. *(978-1-57274-536-0(3)*, 2741, Bks. for Young Learners) Owen, Richard C. Pubs., Inc.
Ziskind, Hélio & Duchesne, Christiane. Le Géant de la Forêt: Un Voyage Musical. Pratt, Pierre, illus. 2014. (FRE.). 48p. (J). (gr. k-2). 16.95 *(978-2-923163-36-9(2))* La Montagne Secrete CAN. Dist: Independent Pubs. Group.

MUSIC—HISTORY AND CRITICISM

Aliki. Ah, Music! Aliki, illus. (ENG., Illus.). 48p. (J). (gr. k-5). 2005. pap. 6.99 *(978-0-06-446236-5(6))* 2003. 17.99 *(978-0-06-028719-1(5))* HarperCollins Pubs.
Allen, Nancy Kelly. Happy Birthday: The Story of the World's Most Popular Song, 1 vol. Undercuffler, Gary, illus. 2010. (ENG.). 32p. (J). (gr. k-3). 16.99 *(978-1-58980-675-7(1))* Pelican Publishing Co., Inc.
Ancona, George. Mi Musica. 2006. (Somos Latinos (We Are Latinos) Ser.).Tr. of My Music. (SPA., Illus.). 32p. (J). (gr. 1-3). per. 8.95 *(978-0-516-25494-4(4)*, Children's Pr.) Scholastic Library Publishing.
Anderson, Jennifer Joline. How to Analyze the Music of Michael Jackson, 1 vol. 2011. (Essential Critiques Set 2 Ser.). (ENG., Illus.). 112p. (J). (gr. 6-12). lib. bdg. 35.64 *(978-1-61783-091-4(7))* ABDO Publishing Co.
Barlex, David & Wadsworth, Pamela. Rhagor Am Sain a Cherddoriaeth. 2005. (WEL., Illus.). 24p. pap. *(978-1-85596-240-8(3))* Dref Wen.
—Sain a Cherddoriaeth. 2005. (WEL., Illus.). 24p. pap. *(978-1-85596-239-2(X))* Dref Wen.
Basher, Simon & Green, Dan. Music. Basher, Simon, illus. 2011. (Basher Basics Ser.). (ENG., Illus.). 64p. (J). (gr. 3-7). pap. 7.99 *(978-0-7534-6595-0(7)*, 9780753465950, Kingfisher) Roaring Brook Pr.
Birkenshaw, Lois. Music for Fun, Music for Learning. 4th ed. 2006. (Illus.). 390p. per. 46.00 *(978-1-891278-43-3(6))* Barcelona Pubs.
Boone, Mary. Dizzy Gillespie. 2012. 48p. (J). (gr. 4-8). lib. bdg. 29.95 *(978-1-61228-272-5(5))* Mitchell Lane Pubs., Inc.
Buckley, Annie. Music. 2008. (21st Century Skills Innovation Library: Innovation in Entertainment Ser.). (ENG., Illus.). 32p. (gr. 4-8). lib. bdg. 28.50 *(978-1-60279-220-3(8)*, 200151) Cherry Lake Publishing.
Cameron, Andrea. The 10 Most Revolutionary Songs. 2008. 14.99 *(978-1-55448-493-5(6))* Scholastic Library Publishing.
Carr, Aaron. Blues. 2015. (J). *(978-1-4896-3573-0(4))* Weigl Pubs., Inc.
—Country. 2015. (J). *(978-1-4896-3577-8(7))* Weigl Pubs., Inc.
Ellis, Carol. Landmark Hip-Hop Hits. 2012. (Illus.). 64p. (J). pap. *(978-1-4222-2134-1(2))*; (gr. 4). 22.95 *(978-1-4222-2121-1(0))* Mason Crest.
Fullman, Joe. The Ultimate Guide to Music. 2016. (ENG., Illus.). 96p. (J). (gr. 3). 19.95 *(978-1-78312-091-8(6))* Carlton Kids GBR. Dist: Sterling Publishing Co., Inc.
Gershenson, Harold P. America the Musical 1900-2000: A Nation's History Through Music. Chesworth, Michael, illus. 2006. (J). *(978-1-58987-201-1(0))* Kindermusik International.
Greenhaven Press Editors & Kallen, Stuart A. The History of Country Music. 2012. (Music Library). (ENG., Illus.). 128p. (gr. 7-10). lib. bdg. 39.40 *(978-1-4205-0737-9(0))* Cengage Gale.
Guillain, Charlotte. Music: From the Voice to Electronica. 2010. (Timeline History Ser.). (ENG., Illus.). 32p. (gr. 3-5). 29.99 *(978-1-4329-3808-6(8)*, NA-h) Heinemann-Raintree.
Handyside, Chris. A History of Blues. 2006. (J). *(978-1-4109-1811-6(4))* Steck-Vaughn.
—A History of Country. 2006. (J). *(978-1-4109-1814-7(9))* Steck-Vaughn.
—A History of Soul & R&B. 2006. (J). *(978-1-4109-1816-1(5))* Steck-Vaughn.
Heyer, Sandra. True Stories Behind the Songs. 2010. (ENG.). 112p. (C). pap. 37.32 *(978-0-13-246804-6(2))* Prentice Hall, ESL Dept.
Hill, Z. B. Music & Musicians. 2014. (Art Today! Ser.: 10). 64p. (J). (gr. 7-18). 23.95 *(978-1-4222-3172-2(0))* Mason Crest.
Hyde, Heidi Smith. Mendel's Accordion. van der Sterre, Johanna, illus. 2007. (ENG.). 32p. (J). (gr. k-4). pap. 9.95 *(978-1-58013-214-5(6)*, Kar-Ben Publishing) Lerner Publishing Group.
Igus, Toyomi. I See the Rhythm of Gospel, 1 vol. Wood, Michele, illus. 2010. (ENG.). 40p. (J). (gr. 4-7). 16.99 *(978-0-310-71819-2(8))* Zonderkidz.
Kallen, Stuart A. Electronic Dance Music DJs. 2016. (ENG.). 80p. (YA). (gr. 5-12). *(978-1-60152-966-4(X))* ReferencePoint Pr., Inc.
—The History of Latin Music. 2006. (Music Library). (ENG., Illus.). 104p. (J). (gr. 3-7). lib. bdg. 34.45 *(978-1-59018-737-1(7)*, Lucent Bks.) Cengage Gale.
—The History of Reggae. 2005. (Music Library). (ENG., Illus.). 112p. (J). (gr. 4-7). lib. bdg. 33.45 *(978-1-59018-740-1(7)*, Lucent Bks.) Cengage Gale.
—The History of World Music. 2006. (Music Library). (ENG., Illus.). 112p. (YA). (gr. 7-10). lib. bdg. 33.45 *(978-1-59018-741-8(5)*, Lucent Bks.) Cengage Gale.
Kallen, Stuart A., ed. The History of American Pop. 2012. (Music Library). (Illus.). 128p. (J). (gr. 7-10). lib. bdg. 34.45 *(978-1-4205-0672-3(2))* Cengage Gale.
—The History of Classical Music. 2013. (Music Library). (ENG., Illus.). 128p. (J). (gr. 7-10). lib. bdg. 34.45 *(978-1-4205-0944-1(6)*, Lucent Bks.) Cengage Gale.
—The History of Latin Music. 2013. (Music Library). (ENG., Illus.). 128p. (gr. 7-10). lib. bdg. 34.45 *(978-1-4205-0947-2(0)*, Lucent Bks.) Cengage Gale.
—The History of Rock & Roll. 2012. (Music Library). (Illus.). 128p. (J). (gr. 7-10). lib. bdg. 34.45 *(978-1-4205-0694-5(3))* Cengage Gale.
Kaufmann, Helen L. The Story of Beethoven. Meadowcroft, Enid Lamonte, ed. Kredel, Fritz, illus. 2011. 192p. 42.95 *(978-1-258-10000-1(2))* Literary Licensing, LLC.
—The Story of Mozart. Meadowcroft, Enid Lamonte, ed. Simon, Eric M., illus. 2011. 190p. 42.95 *(978-1-258-06631-4(9))* Literary Licensing, LLC.
Kenney, Karen Latchana. Cool Reggae Music: Create & Appreciate What Makes Music Great!, 1 vol. 2008. (Cool Music Ser.). (ENG., Illus.). 32p. (YA). (gr. 3-6). 28.50 *(978-1-59928-973-1(3))* ABDO Publishing Co.
Killcoyne, Hope Lourie. The History of Music. 2015. (Britannica Guide to the Visual & Performing Arts Ser.). (ENG., Illus.). 128p. (J). (gr. 9-10). 45.00 *(978-1-68048-091-7(X)*, Britannica Educational Publishing) Rosen Publishing Group, Inc., The.
Killcoyne, Hope Lourie, ed. The History of Music. 2015. (Britannica Guide to the Visual & Performing Arts Ser.). (ENG.). 128p. (YA). (gr. 9-10). 90.00 *(978-1-68048-092-4(8)*, Britannica Educational Publishing) Rosen Publishing Group, Inc., The.
Kuhtz, Russell. Music: Techniques, Styles, Instruments, & Practice. 2016. (Britannica's Practical Guide to the Arts Ser.). 128p. (J). (gr. 10-10). lib. bdg. 36.25 *(978-1-68048-372-7(2)*, Britannica Educational Publishing) Rosen Publishing Group, Inc., The.
Lindeen, Mary. Cool Country Music: Create & Appreciate What Makes Music Great!, 1 vol. 2008. (Cool Music Ser.). (ENG.). 32p. (YA). (gr. 3-6). 28.50 *(978-1-59928-970-0(9))* ABDO Publishing Co.
Manzella, Teresa Ryan. How to Analyze the Music of Bob Dylan, 1 vol. 2011. (Essential Critiques Set 2 Ser.). (ENG., Illus.). 112p. (J). (gr. 6-12). lib. bdg. 35.64 *(978-1-61783-090-7(9))* ABDO Publishing Co.
Mendelson, Aaron. Gospel Grooves, Funky Drummers, & Soul Power. 2012. (American Music Milestones Ser.). (ENG., Illus.). 64p. (gr. 5-12). lib. bdg. 30.60 *(978-0-7613-4501-5(9))* Lerner Publishing Group.
Mills, Nathan & Wesolowski, Harriet. The Songs We Sing: Honoring Our Country. 2012. (Rosen Readers Ser.). (ENG., Illus.). 24p. (J). (gr. 1-2). pap. 8.25 *(978-1-4488-8821-4(2)*, Rosen Classroom) Rosen Publishing Group, Inc., The.
O'Brien, Eileen. The Usborne Story of Music. Danes, Emma & Hooper, Caroline, eds. Cuzik, David, illus. 2006. (Story of Music Ser.). 32p. (J). (gr. 4). lib. bdg. 15.99 *(978-1-58086-935-5(1)*, Usborne) EDC Publishing.
—The Usborne Story of Music. Danes, Emma, ed. Cuzik, David, illus. 2006. 32p. (J). (gr. 4-7). per. 7.99 *(978-0-7945-1403-7(0)*, Usborne) EDC Publishing.
Our Musical Past 16p. (YA). pap. 16.95 incl. audio *(978-0-88432-403-4(6)*, S11020) Pavilion Pubs.
Quill, Charles G. The History of the Blues. 2003. (Reading Room Collection 2 Ser.). (Illus.). 24p. (J). lib. bdg. 22.60 *(978-0-8239-3706-6(2))* Rosen Publishing Group, Inc., The.
Raum, Elizabeth. Song & Dance: A Journey Through Musical Theater. 2010. (Culture in Action Ser.). (ENG.). 32p. (gr. 3-6). 30.65 *(978-1-4109-3921-0(9)*, NA-r) Heinemann-Raintree.
Riggs, Kate. Classical Music. 2008. (World of Music Ser.). (Illus.). 24p. (J). (gr. -1). lib. bdg. 24.25 *(978-1-58341-564-1(5)*, Creative Education) Creative Co., The.
—Country Music. 2008. (World of Music Ser.). (Illus.). 24p. (J). (gr. -1). lib. bdg. 24.25 *(978-1-58341-565-8(3)*, Creative Education) Creative Co., The.
—Folk Music. 2008. (World of Music Ser.). (Illus.). 24p. (J). (gr. -1). lib. bdg. 24.25 *(978-1-58341-566-5(1)*, Creative Education) Creative Co., The.
Sachs, Lloyd. American Country: Bluegrass, Honky-Tonk, & Crossover Sounds. 2012. (American Music Milestones Ser.). (ENG.). 64p. (gr. 5-12). lib. bdg. 30.60 *(978-0-7613-4502-2(7))* Lerner Publishing Group.
Sombart, Elisabeth, et al. Doce Vidas para la Musica.Tr. of Twelve Composers. (SPA.). 118p. (J). 17.95 *(978-84-261-3115-7(8)*, JV11155) Juventud, Editorial ESP. Dist: Lectorum Pubns., Inc.
Turner, Cherie. Everything You Need to Know about the Riot Grrrl Movement: The Feminism of a New Generation. 2009. (Need to Know Library). 64p. (gr. 5-5). 58.50 *(978-1-60854-095-2(2))* Rosen Publishing Group, Inc., The.
Uschan, Michael V. The Blues. 2011. (Lucent Library of Black History Ser.). (ENG., Illus.). 128p. (gr. 7-10). lib. bdg. 39.40 *(978-1-4205-0658-7(7))* Cengage Gale.
Walker, Ida. Around the World. 2009. (Hip-Hop Ser.). (Illus.). 64p. (YA). (gr. 4-7). pap. 7.95 *(978-1-4222-0350-7(6))* Mason Crest.
Wargin, Kathy-jo. M Is for Melody: A Music Alphabet. Larson, Katherine, illus. 2006. (Art & Culture Ser.). (ENG.). 40p. (J). (gr. 1-4). 16.95 *(978-1-58536-215-8(8)*, 202129) Sleeping Bear Pr.
Wesolowski, Harriet. The Songs We Sing: Honoring Our Country. 2012. (I'm an American Citizen Ser.). (ENG., Illus.). 24p. (J). (gr. 1-3). 22.60 *(978-1-4488-8581-7(7)*, PowerKids Pr.) Rosen Publishing Group, Inc., The.
What Jazz & Blues Can I Play - Alto Sax. 20p. 6.95 *(978-1-85909-426-6(0)*, Warner Bros. Pubns.) Alfred Publishing Co., Inc.
Wheeler, Opal. Handel: at the Court of Kings. Greenwalt, Mary, illus. 2006. 166p. per. 13.95 *(978-1-933573-03-8(1)*, 4481) Zeezok Publishing, LLC.
Wheeler, Opal & Deucher, Sybil. Joseph Haydn: the Merry Little Peasant. Greenwalt, Mary, illus. 2005. 118p. per. 13.95 *(978-1-933573-00-7(7))* Zeezok Publishing, LLC.
Woog, Adam. The History of Gospel Music. Greenhaven Press Editors, ed. 2014. (Music Library). (ENG., Illus.). 128p. (gr. 7-10). lib. bdg. 39.40 *(978-1-4205-0945-8(4)*, Lucent Bks.) Cengage Gale.

MUSIC, INDIAN

see Indians of North America—Music

MUSIC—INSTRUCTION AND STUDY

see Music—Study and Teaching

MUSIC—NOTATION

see Musical Notation

MUSIC, POPULAR

see Popular Music

MUSIC, SACRED

see Church Music

MUSIC—STUDY AND TEACHING

Alfred Publishing Staff, et al. Kid's Guitar Course Movie & TV Songbook 1 & 2: 13 Fun Arrangements That Make Learning Even Easier! 2009. (Kid's Guitar Course Ser.). (ENG.). 24p. pap. 15.99 *(978-0-7390-6419-1(3))* Alfred Publishing Co., Inc.
Aruffo, Christopher, tr. We Hear & Play. 2005. (J). Vol. 1. 112p. ring bd. 44.95 *(978-0-9761435-2-9(6))* Vol. 2. 112p. ring bd. 44.95 *(978-0-9761435-3-6(4))* Vol. 3. ring bd. 49.95 *(978-0-9761435-4-3(2))* Acoustic Learning Inc.
Atlantic, Leonard. We Play Music! 2017. (Ways to Play Ser.). 24p. (gr. k-k). pap. 8.15 ***(978-1-4824-6349-1(0))*** Stevens, Gareth Publishing LLLP.
Barden, Christine H., et al. Music for Little Mozarts — Little Mozarts Go to Church, Bk 1-2: 10 Favorite Hymns, Spirituals & Sunday School Songs. 2008. (Music for Little Mozarts Ser.: Bk 1-2). (ENG.). 24p. (J). pap. 6.00 *(978-0-7390-5689-9(1))* Alfred Publishing Co., Inc.
—Music for Little Mozarts — Little Mozarts Go to Church, Bk 3-4: 10 Favorite Hymns, Spirituals & Sunday School Songs. 2008. (Music for Little Mozarts Ser.: Bk 3-4). (ENG.). 24p. (J). pap. 6.00 *(978-0-7390-5690-5(5))* Alfred Publishing Co., Inc.
Battaglia, Stephen. Mr. Mcsymphony's It's All about Classical Music. 2008. (ENG.). 32p. pap. 9.99 *(978-1-4196-8085-4(4))* CreateSpace Independent Publishing Platform.
—Mr. Mcsymphony's It's All about Jazz. 2008. (ENG.). 28p. pap. 9.99 *(978-1-4196-8086-1(2))* CreateSpace Independent Publishing Platform.
Blair, Peter, compiled by. Concert Ensembles for Everyone: Works for Instrumental Ensembles with Limited or Non-Traditional Instrumentation, Grades 3-4 (Alto Saxophone - WW 3 And 4) 2006. 8.95 *(978-0-89328-262-2(6))* Heritage Music Pr.
—Concert Ensembles for Everyone: Works for Instrumental Ensembles with Limited or Non-Traditional Instrumentation, Grades 3-4 (Bass - Tuba/Bass, Baritone Saxophone & Bass Clarinet) 2006. 8.95 *(978-0-89328-268-4(5))* Heritage Music Pr.
—Concert Ensembles for Everyone: Works for Instrumental Ensembles with Limited or Non-Traditional Instrumentation, Grades 3-4 (Clarinet A - WW 1 And 2) 2006. 8.95 *(978-0-89328-260-8(X))* Heritage Music Pr.
—Concert Ensembles for Everyone: Works for Instrumental Ensembles with Limited or Non-Traditional Instrumentation, Grades 3-4 (Clarinet B - WW 2 And 3) 2006. 8.95 *(978-0-89328-261-5(8))* Heritage Music Pr.
—Concert Ensembles for Everyone: Works for Instrumental Ensembles with Limited or Non-Traditional Instrumentation, Grades 3-4 (F Horn - Brass 3 And 4) 2006. 8.95 *(978-0-89328-266-0(9))* Heritage Music Pr.
—Concert Ensembles for Everyone: Works for Instrumental Ensembles with Limited or Non-Traditional Instrumentation, Grades 3-4 (Tenor Saxophone - WW 4 & Brass 4) 2006. 8.95 *(978-0-89328-263-9(4))* Heritage Music Pr.
—Concert Ensembles for Everyone: Works for Instrumental Ensembles with Limited or Non-Traditional Instrumentation, Grades 3-4 (Trombone/Baritone B. C. /Bassoon - Brass 4 & Bass) 2006. 8.95 *(978-0-89328-267-7(7))* Heritage Music Pr.
—Concert Ensembles for Everyone: Works for Instrumental Ensembles with Limited or Non-Traditional Instrumentation, Grades 3-4 (Trumpet A - Brass 1 And 2) 2006. 8.95 *(978-0-89328-264-6(2))* Heritage Music Pr.
—Concert Ensembles for Everyone: Works for Instrumental Ensembles with Limited or Non-Traditional Instrumentation, Grades 3-4 (Trumpet B - Brass 2 And 3) 2006. 8.95 *(978-0-89328-265-3(0))* Heritage Music Pr.
Brass, Alice. Orff Explorations: Classroom Projects in Music, Movement & Poetry. Sakhavarz, Nazy, illus. 2010. (ENG.). 80p. spiral bd. 20.00 *(978-1-896941-34-9(6))* Brass, Robin Studio, Inc. CAN. Dist: Midpoint Trade Bks., Inc.
Bridges, Doreen. Music, Young Children & You: A Parent-Teacher Guide to Music for 0 -5 Year Olds. (Illus.). 160p. (J). (gr. -1-k). pap. *(978-0-86806-530-4(7)*, Hale & Iremonger) GHR Pr., The.
Bridges, Madeline. Sing Together, Children. 2008. (J). mass mkt. 39.95 *(978-1-929187-21-8(1))* Choristers Guild.
Burch, Sharon. Sticks! 2013. (ENG.). 56p. pap. 29.99 incl. audio compact disk *(978-1-4803-4266-8(1)*, 1480342661) Shawnee Pr., Inc.
Burton, Leon H. & Kudo, Takeo. Soundplay: Understanding Music Through Creative Movement. 2006. (ENG., Illus.). 120p. pap. 50.00 incl. lp *(978-1-56545-130-8(9)*, 3003) Rowman & Littlefield Publishers, Inc.
Celik, Vladislav. You Too Can Play Piano & Organ Without Teacher, Vol. 1. (Music Instructional Ser.). (Illus.). 96p. (J). pap. 12.95 incl. audio *(978-0-9624062-1-8(X))* Music Institute of California.
Chadwick, Stephen. Complete Music Scheme for Primary Class Teachers: Age 10-11, 3 vols. 2nd ed. 2014. (Music Express Ser.). (ENG., Illus.). 64p. (J). (gr. 5-6). pap. 47.95 ***(978-1-4729-0022-7(7))*** HarperCollins Pubs. Ltd. GBR. Dist: Independent Pubs. Group.
Ciravolo, Tish. Everything a Girl Needs to Know Abut Playing Guitar! 2003. (Girl's Guitar Method Ser.: Bk 2). (ENG.). 40p. pap. 15.99 *(978-0-7390-3175-9(9)*, 21971) Alfred Publishing Co., Inc.
Coates, Dan. The Kids' Music Collection, Vol. 2. 2005. (ENG.). 124p. pap. 14.95 *(978-0-7579-3763-7(2)*, AFM0416) Alfred Publishing Co., Inc.
Concert Ensembles for Everyone: Works for Instrumental Ensembles with Limited or Non-Traditional Instrumentation, Grades 3-4 (Conductor's Score with CD) 2006. 29.95 *(978-0-89328-258-5(8))* Heritage Music Pr.
Dale, Monica. Eurhythmics for Young Children: Six Lessons for Spring. 2003. (Illus.). 90p. pap. 24.95 *(978-0-9701416-2-0(9))* MusiKinesis.
Dorling Kindersley Publishing Staff. Help Your Kids with Music. 2015. (Help Your Kids Ser.). (ENG.). 256p. 19.95 *(978-1-4654-3604-7(9)*, DK) Dorling Kindersley Publishing, Inc.
Dyke, Sylvie. Piano Music Made Easy. 2012. (Illus.). 28p. pap. *(978-1-78148-794-5(4))* Grosvenor Hse. Publishing Ltd.
Edwards, Linda Carol, et al. Music: A Way of Life for the Young Child. 5th ed. 2004. (ENG., Illus.). 288p. pap. 49.33 *(978-0-13-111676-4(2))* Prentice Hall PTR.
Flohr, John W. & Trollinger, Valerie L. Music in Elementary Education. 2010. (Illus.). xiii, 244p. *(978-0-205-76035-0(X))* Prentice Hall PTR.
Francis, Dale. The Quelbe Method: Music Fundamentals in Quelbe Ensembles. 2012. 256p. (gr. -1). pap. 27.95 *(978-1-4759-2684-2(7))* iUniverse, Inc.
Frostick, Richard. Sound Beginnings. 2003. (Faber Edition Ser.). (ENG., Illus.). 46p. pap. 10.25 *(978-0-571-51991-0(1))* Faber & Faber, Ltd. GBR. Dist: Alfred Publishing Co., Inc.
The Fundamental Guitar Method Book 2: The Science of Harmony. 2004. (YA). spiral bd. *(978-0-9771357-1-4(3))* Sound Craft Designs.
Gallina, Jill, et al. Oceans of Fun. 2011. (ENG.). 62p. pap. 64.99 *(978-1-61780-710-7(9)*, 1617807109); 64p. pap. 24.99 incl. audio compact disk *(978-1-61780-708-4(7)*, 1617807087) Shawnee Pr., Inc.
Hammond, Susan. Susan Hammond's Classical Kids: A New Music-Based Curriculum: Grades K-8. 2008. (Classical Kids Ser.). (J). (gr. -1-8). *(978-1-897166-42-0(7))* Children's Group, The.
Harris, Paul & Brewer, Mike. Improve Sight-Singing! Low/Medium Voice - Elementary level. 2003. (Faber Edition Ser.). (ENG.). 40p. (gr. 1-5). pap. 8.25 *(978-0-571-51766-4(8))* Faber & Faber, Ltd. GBR. Dist: Alfred Publishing Co., Inc.
Heritage & Almeida, Artie. Music Proficiency: Doggone Dynamics. 2005. ring bd. 14.95 *(978-0-89328-029-1(1))* Lorenz Corp., The.
Hooper, Caroline. Learn Songwriting. 2004. (Learn to Play Ser.). (Illus.). 48p. (YA). (gr. 1-18). lib. bdg. 17.95 *(978-1-58086-222-6(5))* EDC Publishing.
Kenney, Karen Latchana. Cool Reggae Music: Create & Appreciate What Makes Music Great!, 1 vol. 2008. (Cool Music Ser.). (ENG., Illus.). 32p. (YA). (gr. 3-6). 28.50 *(978-1-59928-973-1(3))* ABDO Publishing Co.
—Cool School Music: Fun Ideas & Activities to Build School Spirit, 1 vol. 2011. (Cool School Spirit Ser.). (ENG., Illus.). 32p. (J). (gr. 3-6). 28.50 *(978-1-61714-669-5(2)*, Checkerboard Library) ABDO Publishing Co.
Key Porter Books, creator. Music Play: Inspired Ways to Explore Music. rev. ed. 2007. (Gymboree Play & Music Ser.). (ENG., Illus.). 36p. (J). (gr. -1-2). bds. *(978-1-55263-964-1(9))* Magma.
Kurz, Ron. The Inner Music Experience. l.t. ed. 2003. 124p. (YA). 75.00 *(978-0-939829-07-1(X)*, Item#3) Kurz, Ron.
Lindeen, Mary. Cool Country Music: Create & Appreciate What Makes Music Great!, 1 vol. 2008. (Cool Music Ser.). (ENG.). 32p. (YA). (gr. 3-6). 28.50 *(978-1-59928-970-0(9))* ABDO Publishing Co.
—Cool Latin Music: Create & Appreciate What Makes Music Great!, 1 vol. 2008. (Cool Music Ser.). (ENG., Illus.). 32p. (YA). (gr. 3-6). 28.50 *(978-1-59928-972-4(5))* ABDO Publishing Co.
Lindeman, Carolynn. Musical Children: Engaging Children in Musical Experiences. 2010. (ENG.). 264p. (C). pap. 65.95 *(978-0-13-604384-3(4)*, Y204706) Routledge.
MacGregor, Helen. Complete Music Scheme for Primary Class Teachers: Age 9-10, 3 vols. 2nd ed. 2014. (Music Express Ser.). (ENG., Illus.). 64p. (J). (gr. 4-5). pap. 47.95 ***(978-1-4729-0021-0(9))*** HarperCollins Pubs. Ltd. GBR. Dist: Independent Pubs. Group.
—Complete Music Scheme for Primary Class Teachers, Age 7-8, 3 vols. 2nd ed. 2014. (Music Express Ser.). (ENG., Illus.). 64p. (J). (gr. 2-3). pap. 47.95 ***(978-1-4729-0019-7(7))*** HarperCollins Pubs. Ltd. GBR. Dist: Independent Pubs. Group.
—Complete Music Scheme for Primary Class Teachers, Age 8-9, 3 vols. 2nd ed. 2014. (Music Express Ser.). (ENG., Illus.). 64p. (J). (gr. 3-4). pap. 47.95 ***(978-1-4729-0020-3(0))*** HarperCollins Pubs. Ltd. GBR. Dist: Independent Pubs. Group.
Michael, Ted. So You Wanna Be a Superstar? The Ultimate Audition Guide. 2012. (ENG., Illus.). 152p. (J). (gr. -1-17). pap. 10.95 *(978-0-7624-4610-0(2)*, Running Pr. Kids) Running Pr. Bk. Pubs.
Mister C's Beginning Drums, Vol. 1. 2004. (Illus.). (J). spiral bd. 14.99 *(978-0-9755333-0-7(4))* Mister C Music.
Morgan, Jeanette, ed. Activate!: Music, Movement & More: The Music Magazine for Grades K-6. 2011. (Illus.). 84p. pap. 19.95 incl. audio compact disk *(978-0-89328-376-6(2))* Heritage Music Pr.
Moses, David & Sebba, Jane. Recorder Magic, 1 vol. 2003. (Recorder Magic Ser.). (ENG., Illus.). 32p. (J). pap. 11.95 incl. audio compact disk ***(978-0-7136-6581-9(5))*** HarperCollins Pubs. Ltd. GBR. Dist: Independent Pubs. Group.
Neelly, Linda Page. Musical ConverSings with Children. 2007. (Illus.). 161p. 79.00 *(978-1-60021-708-1(7))* Nova Science Pubs., Inc.
O'Brien, Eileen. Introduction to Music. Alaverdy, Melissa, illus. 2004. (ENG.). 96p. (J). 7.95 *(978-0-7945-0276-8(8)*, Usborne) EDC Publishing.
Parker, Ben. My First Keyboard - Learn to Play: Kids. 2013. (Illus.). 42p. pap. *(978-1-908707-15-4(1))* Kyle Craig Publishing.
—My First Recorder - Learn to Play: Kids. 2013. 38p. pap. *(978-1-908707-18-5(6))* Kyle Craig Publishing.
Parker, Kate & Parker, Zac. Nos Gusta Tocar Musica: We Like to Play Music. 2009. (SPA & ENG.). 32p. (J). pap. 10.95 *(978-1-890772-90-1(9))* Hohm Pr.
—We Like to Play Music. 2015. (ENG.). 32p. (J). pap. 9.95 *(978-1-890772-85-7(2))* Hohm Pr.

Phillips, Sarah. Play It! Recorder. 2005. (Play It! Ser.). (Illus.). 24p. (J). (gr. k-3). (978-1-905051-59-5(X)) Make Believe Ideas.

Price, Melissa. Luke & Lori's Musical Journey: Learning the Basic Elements of Music. Keren Weaver Graphics, illus. 2003. 48p. (J). spiral bd. (978-0-9747792-0-1(2)) Luke & Lori Bks.

Publications International Ltd. Staff, ed. Electronic Time for Learning: Music. 2011. 120p. (J). (978-1-4508-0260-4(5)) Publications International, Ltd.

—Princess Songs Play & Learn. 2010. 24p. (J). 12.98 (978-1-4508-0113-3(7)) Phoenix International Publications, Inc.

Purton, Michael. Show Me How: I Can Make Music. 2015. (ENG., Illus.). 48p. (J). (gr. -1-12). 7.99 (978-1-86147-297-7(8), Armadillo) Anness Publishing GBR. Dist: National Bk. Network.

Regan, Lisa & Anniss, Matt. Being a Dj. 2012. (On the Radar: Awesome Jobs Ser.). (ENG., Illus.). 32p. (gr. 4-8). lib. bdg. 26.60 (978-0-7613-7775-7(1), Lerner Pubns.) Lerner Publishing Group.

Rowsell, Cyrilla & Vinden, David. The Music Handbook, Level 2: Teaching Music Skills to Children Through Singing. Lamb, Karen, illus. 2012. (ENG.). 212p. (J). spiral bd. 59.95 incl. audio compact disk (978-1-84414-265-1(5), Jolly Learning) Jolly Learning, Ltd. GBR. Dist: American International Distribution Corp.

Scott, Daniel. Classical Greats: Easy Playalong for Recorder. 2003. (ENG., Illus.). 32p. pap. 14.95 incl. audio compact disk (978-0-7119-9144-6(8), 0711991448) Music Sales Corp.

Scott, Patricia, et al. Music Express Early Years Foundation Stage: Complete Music Scheme for Early Years Foundation Stage, 3 vols. 2nd ed. 2012. (Music Express Ser.). (ENG., Illus.). 88p. pap. 55.00 incl. audio compact disk **(978-1-4081-8707-4(8))** HarperCollins Pubs. Ltd. GBR. Dist: Independent Pubs. Group.

Snitkin, Harvey R. Practicing for Young Musicians: You Are Your Own Teacher. 2nd rev. ed. 2011. (Illus.). 153p. (Orig.). (gr. 4-18). pap. 14.95 (978-1-888732-00-9(8)) H M S Pubns., Inc.

Stultz, Marie. Innocent Sounds, Book II: Building Choral Tone & Artistry in Your Children's Choir. 2008. 240p. per. (978-0-944529-45-4(3)) Morning Star Music Pubs.

Sullivan, Erin Ash. Music Counts & Cálculos Musicales: 6 English, 6 Spanish Adaptations. 2011. (ENG & SPA.). (J). 89.00 net. (978-1-4108-5675-3(5)) Benchmark Education Co.

Tornquist, Carol. Music in Me - A Piano Method for Young Christian Students: Lesson (Reading Music) Level 5. 2007. (ENG.). 48p. pap. 8.95 (978-1-4234-1884-9(0), 1423418840) Leonard, Hal Corp.

Vogt, Janet. Music Brain Teasers. 2006. pap. 19.95 (978-0-89328-248-6(0)) Lorenz Corp., The.

Wedgwood, Pamela. Up-Grade Flute: Light Relief Between Grades. 2003. (Faber Edition: up-Grade! Ser.). (ENG.). (gr. 2). pap. 12.25 (978-0-571-51818-0(4)) Faber & Faber, Ltd. GBR. Dist: Alfred Publishing Co., Inc.

Whykes, Susan. Let's Practise: Be a Better Musician. 2009. 216p. pap. 14.49 (978-1-4389-2933-0(1)) AuthorHouse.

Young, Susan. Music 3-5. 2008. (Essential Guides for Early Years Practitioners Ser.). (ENG.). (C). 136p. 75.00 (978-0-415-43056-2(9), RU44504); 128p. 35.95 (978-0-415-43057-9(7), RU44505) Routledge.

MUSIC—THEORY

see Music Theory

MUSIC—VOCATIONAL GUIDANCE

Anniss, Matt. Start a Band! 2013. (Find Your Talent Ser.). (Illus.). 32p. (J). (gr. 5-8). 28.50 (978-1-84858-571-3(3)) Arcturus Publishing GBR. Dist: Black Rabbit Bks.

Barden, Christine H., et al. Little Mozarts Go to Hollywood, Pop Book 1 And 2: 10 Favorites from TV, Movies & Radio. Finn, Christine, illus. 2008. (Music for Little Mozarts Ser.: Bk 1-2). (ENG.). 24p. (J). pap. 8.99 (978-0-7390-5013-2(3)) Alfred Publishing Co., Inc.

Burling, Alexis. Working in Music. 2018. (ENG.). 32p. (gr. 3-6). **(978-1-63235-447-1(0),** 12-Story Library) Pr. Room Editions LLC.

Cefrey, Holly. Career Building Through Music, Video, & Software Mashups. 2008. (Digital Career Building Ser.). (Illus.). 64p. (YA). (gr. 8-12). lib. bdg. 31.95 (978-1-4042-1359-3(7)) Rosen Publishing Group, Inc., The.

Crossingham, John. Learn to Speak Music: A Guide to Creating, Performing, & Promoting Your Songs. Kulak, Jeff & Owlkids Books Inc. Staff, illus. 2009. (ENG.). 96p. (J). (gr. 3-8). pap. 22.95 (978-1-897349-65-6(3), Owlkids) Owlkids Bks. Inc. CAN. Dist: Publishers Group West (PGW).

Culp, Jennifer. Using Computer Science in Digital Music Careers. 2017. (Coding Your Passion Ser.). 80p. (gr. 12-12). 35.75 **(978-1-5081-7517-9(9),** Rosen Young Adult) Rosen Publishing Group, Inc., The.

Duke, Shirley. STEM Jobs in Music. 2014. (ENG., Illus.). 48p. (gr. 4-8). 35.64 (978-1-62717-699-6(3)) Rourke Educational Media.

Feierabend, John. First Steps in Music Vocal Development Kit. 2004. 21p. (J). 79.95 (978-1-57999-326-9(5), G-6400) G I A Pubns., Inc.

Guillain, Charlotte. Music, 1 vol. 2012. (Jobs If You Like... Ser.). (ENG.). 32p. (gr. 1-3). pap. 8.29 (978-1-4329-6820-5(3)); lib. bdg. 27.32 (978-1-4329-6809-0(2)) Heinemann-Raintree. (Heinemann First Library).

Harvey, M. A. Wannabes Pop Diva: For Girls Who Know What They Want to Be. 2004. (Illus.). 128p. (J). pap. (978-1-84458-049-1(0), Pavilion Children's Books) Pavilion Bks.

Hasan, Heather. How to Produce, Release, & Market Your Music. 2011. (Garage Bands Ser.). (ENG.). 64p. (YA). (gr. 5-8). pap. 12.95 (978-1-4488-5662-6(0)); lib. bdg. 31.95 (978-1-4488-5658-9(2)) Rosen Publishing Group, Inc., The.

Hill, Z. B. Music & Musicians. 2014. (Art Today! Ser.: 10). 64p. (J). (gr. 7-18). 23.95 (978-1-4222-3172-2(0)) Mason Crest.

Hinton, Kerry. Cool Careers Without College for Music Lovers. 2007. (Cool Careers Without College Ser.). (Illus.). 140p. (J). (gr. 4-7). lib. bdg. 33.25 (978-1-4042-1093-6(8)); (YA). (gr. 8-12). lib. bdg. 33.25 (978-1-4042-0872-8(0)) Rosen Publishing Group, Inc., The.

Liebman, Daniel & Liebman, Dan. I Want to Be a Musician. 2003. (I Want to Be Ser.). (ENG., Illus.). 24p. (J). (gr. -1-2). 14.95 (978-1-55297-760-6(9), 9781552977606); pap. 3.99 (978-1-55297-759-0(5), 9781552977590) Firefly Bks., Ltd.

—Quiero Ser Musico. 2003. (Quiero Ser.). (ENG & SPA., Illus.). 24p. (J). (gr. -1-2). pap. 5.99 (978-1-55297-761-3(7), 9781552977613) Firefly Bks., Ltd.

Miller, Connie Colwell. I'll Be a Musician. Baroncelli, Silvia, illus. 2016. (When I Grow Up Ser.). (ENG.). 24p. (J). (gr. k-3). 20.95 (978-1-60753-762-5(1)) Amicus Publishing.

Mooney, Carla. Cool Careers Without College for People Who Love Music. 2013. (New Cool Careers Without College Ser.). 144p. (YA). (gr. 7-12). 35.95 (978-1-4777-1819-3(2)) Rosen Publishing Group, Inc., The.

Parks, Peggy J. Musician. 2003. (Illus.). 48p. (J). 26.20 (978-0-7377-2067-9(0), Greenhaven Pr., Inc.) Cengage Gale.

Payment, Simone. Taking Your Band Online. 2011. (Garage Bands Ser.). (ENG.). 64p. (YA). (gr. 5-8). pap. 12.95 (978-1-4488-5664-0(7)); lib. bdg. 31.95 (978-1-4488-5660-2(4)) Rosen Publishing Group, Inc., The.

Reeves, Diane Lindsey. Career Ideas for Kids Who Like Music & Dance. 2nd rev. ed. 2007. (Career Ideas for Kids Ser.). 208p. (gr. 4-9). pap. 16.95 (978-0-8160-6538-7(1), Checkmark Bks.) Facts On File, Inc.

Roberts, Laura. Careers If You Like Music. 2017. (ENG.). 80p. (YA). (gr. 5-12). **(978-1-68282-138-1(2))** ReferencePoint Pr., Inc.

Somervill, Barbara. Musician. 2011. (21st Century Skills Library: Cool Arts Careers Ser.). (ENG.). 32p. (gr. 4-8). lib. bdg. 28.50 (978-1-61080-132-4(6), 201142) Cherry Lake Publishing.

Spaulding, Jeffrey & Gisnash, Sahara. Career Building Through Digital Sampling & Remixing. 2008. (Digital Career Building Ser.). (Illus.). 64p. (J). (gr. 3-7). lib. bdg. 31.95 (978-1-4042-1355-5(4)) Rosen Publishing Group, Inc., The.

MUSIC APPRECIATION

Adams, Dena C. & Clark, Claire D. This Is Music! Preschool, Vol 1: Itsy Bitsy Music, Book & CD. 2008. (This Is Music! Ser.: Vol 1). (ENG.). 224p. pap. 64.95 (978-0-7390-4723-1(X)) Alfred Publishing Co., Inc.

Ajmera, Maya & Derstine, Elise Hofer. Music Everywhere! Pon, Cynthia, illus. 2014. (ENG.). 32p. (J). (gr. -1-3). pap. 7.95 (978-1-57091-937-4(2)) Charlesbridge Publishing, Inc.

Baldwin, Lillian. Music for Young Listeners: The Blue Book. 2012. 128p. 40.95 (978-1-258-23857-5(8)); pap. 25.95 (978-1-258-24708-9(9)) Literary Licensing, LLC.

—Music for Young Listeners: The Crimson Book. 2012. 128p. 40.95 (978-1-258-23856-8(X)); pap. 25.95 (978-1-258-24709-6(7)) Literary Licensing, LLC.

Bernard, Yves & Fredette, Nathalie. Le Guide de la Musique du Monde. 2004. (FRE., Illus.). 230p. (J). pap. (978-2-89021-662-4(4)) Diffusion du livre Mirabel (DLM).

Buchanan, Fannie R. Magic Music Story Interpretations. 2006. (Illus.). pap. 21.95 (978-1-4286-5945-2(5)) Kessinger Publishing, LLC.

Gerhard, Ana. Listen to the Birds: An Introduction to Classical Music. Varela, Cecilia, illus. 2013. (ENG.). 48p. (J). (gr. 2-4). 16.95 (978-2-923163-89-5(3)) La Montagne Secrete CAN. Dist: Independent Pubs. Group.

Labrecque, Ellen. How Did That Get to My House? Music. 2009. (Community Connections: How Did That Get to My House? Ser.). (ENG.). 24p. (gr. 2-5). lib. bdg. 25.64 (978-1-60279-481-8(2), 200246) Cherry Lake Publishing.

Lindeen, Mary. Cool Classical Music: Create & Appreciate What Makes Music Great!, 1 vol. 2008. (Cool Music Ser.). (ENG.). 32p. (YA). (gr. 3-6). 28.50 (978-1-59928-969-4(5)) ABDO Publishing Co.

Parker, Kate & Parker, Zac. Nos Gusta Tocar Musica: We Like to Play Music. 2009. (SPA & ENG.). 32p. (J). pap. 10.95 (978-1-890772-90-1(9)) Hohm Pr.

—We Like to Play Music. 2015. (ENG.). 32p. (J). pap. 9.95 (978-1-890772-85-7(2)) Hohm Pr.

Persons, Marjorie Kiel. Themes to Remember, 3, Vol. 1. Nellis, Philip, illus. 2007. 124p. (J). lib. bdg. 31.95 incl. audio compact disk (978-0-9794947-0-3(2)) Classical Magic, Inc.

—Themes to Remember, Volume 2, Vol. 2. Nellis, Philip & Johnson, George Ann, illus. rev. ed. 2004. 128p. (J). lib. bdg. 31.95 (978-0-9675997-5-5(X)) Classical Magic, Inc.

MUSIC THEORY

Alexander, Dennis, et al. Alfred's Premier Piano Course: Lesson 3. 2007. (Premier Piano Course Ser.: Bk 3). (ENG., Illus.). 48p. pap. 8.99 (978-0-7390-4639-5(X)) Alfred Publishing Co., Inc.

—Alfred's Premier Piano Course: Performance 3. Manus, Morton, ed. 2007. (Alfred's Premier Piano Course Ser.). (Illus.). 32p. pap. 6.95 (978-0-7390-4743-9(4)) Alfred Publishing Co., Inc.

—Alfred's Premier Piano Course - Theory 3. Manus, Morton, ed. 2007. (Premier Piano Course Ser.: Bk 3). (ENG., Illus.). 32p. pap. 7.99 (978-0-7390-4750-7(7)) Alfred Publishing Co., Inc.

—Alfred's Premier Piano Course Assignment Book: Level 1A-6. Manus, Morton, ed. 2007. (Premier Piano Course Ser.). (ENG.). 80p. pap. 6.95 (978-0-7390-4877-1(5)) Alfred Publishing Co., Inc.

Biklou, Eliyana. Lady Treble & the Seven Notes. 2010. (ENG., Illus.). 32p. (J). (gr. -1-3). 16.95 (978-1-897476-21-5(3)) Simply Read Bks. CAN. Dist: Ingram Publisher Services.

Danes, E. Music Theory for Beginners. rev. ed. 2004. (ENG.). 48p. (J). pap. 8.95 (978-0-7945-0389-5(6)) EDC Publishing.

Danes, Emma. Music Theory for Beginners. Wood, Gerald, illus. 2006. (Music Theory Ser.). 48p. (J). (gr. 4). lib. bdg. 16.95 (978-1-58086-562-3(3)) EDC Publishing.

Day, Jonathan. The Politics of Navigation: Globalisation, Music & Composition. 2008. 180p. pap. (978-3-639-07208-2(1)) AV Akademikerverlag GmbH & Co. KG.

Sharp, M. Theory of Music for Young Musicians. 2013. 57p. reprint ed. lthr. 79.00 (978-0-7812-9322-8(7)) Reprint Services Corp.

MUSICAL APPRECIATION

see Music Appreciation

MUSICAL COMEDIES

see Musicals

MUSICAL CRITICISM

see Music—History and Criticism

MUSICAL EDUCATION

see Music—Study and Teaching

MUSICAL INSTRUCTION

see Music—Study and Teaching

MUSICAL INSTRUMENTS

see also Orchestra

also groups of instruments, e.g. Percussion Instruments; Stringed Instruments; Wind Instruments; etc.; also names of musical instruments, e.g. Drum; etc.

A. and C. Black Publishers Staff, et al. Abracadabra Cello Beginner, 1 vol. rev. ed. 2007. (Abracadabra Ser.). (ENG., Illus.). 32p. (J). pap. 11.95 incl. audio compact disk **(978-0-7136-9366-9(5))** HarperCollins Pubs. Ltd. GBR. Dist: Independent Pubs. Group.

Ackland, Nick. Bang! Bradley, Jennie, illus. 2016. (Baby Sparkler Ser.). (ENG.). 10p. (J). (gr. -1 — 1). bds. 5.99 (978-0-7641-6846-8(0)) Barron's Educational Series, Inc.

Almeida, Artie. Recorder Express (Soprano Recorder Method for Classroom or Individual Use) Soprano Recorder Method for Classroom or Individual Use, Book & CD. 2007. (ENG.). 48p. pap. 14.95 (978-0-7390-4726-2(4)) Alfred Publishing Co., Inc.

Amoroso, Cynthia & Noyed, Robert B. Trumpets. 2010. (Music Makers Ser.). (ENG., Illus.). 24p. (J). (gr. -1-2). 27.07 (978-1-60253-357-8(1), 200508) Child's World, Inc., The.

Baron, Jessica. Let's Make Music. 2008. (Real Readers - Upper Emergent Ser.). (ENG., Illus.). 12p. (gr. 1-2). pap. 5.90 (978-0-8239-8193-9(2)) Rosen Publishing Group, Inc., The.

Battaglia, Stephen. Mr. Mcsymphony's Musicians & their Instruments. 2008. (ENG.). 28p. pap. 9.99 (978-1-4196-8077-9(3)) CreateSpace Independent Publishing Platform.

Blair, Peter, compiled by. Concert Ensembles for Everyone: Works for Instrumental Ensembles with Limited or Non-Traditional Instrumentation, Grades 3-4 (Flute/Oboe - WW 1 And 2) 2006. 8.95 (978-0-89328-259-2(6)) Heritage Music Pr.

Blane, Francisco. I Can Play Music: Lap Book. 2009. (My First Reader's Theater Set B Ser.). (J). 28.00 (978-1-935441-03-8(5)) Benchmark Education Co.

Canetti, Yanitzia. ABeCedario Musical. 2010. (SPA.). 40p. (J). pap. 8.99 (978-1-59835-222-1(9), BrickHouse Education) Cambridge BrickHouse, Inc.

—Musical ABCs. 2010. 40p. (J). pap. 8.99 (978-1-59835-221-4(0), BrickHouse Education) Cambridge BrickHouse, Inc.

—Musical Colors/Colores Musicales: A World of Color. 2010. 24p. (J). pap. 6.99 (978-1-59835-267-2(9), BrickHouse Education) Cambridge BrickHouse, Inc.

Casterline, L. C. The Sounds of Music. Yerkes, Lane, illus. 2004. (Picture Books/Quality Time Ser.). 16p. (gr. k-3). lib. bdg. 20.00 (978-0-8368-4100-8(X), Gareth Stevens Learning Library) Stevens, Gareth Publishing LLLP.

Claudio, Abbado. Yo Sere Director de Orquesta. 2007. (SPA.). 48p. (J). (gr. 4-5). 23.99 (978-84-8470-052-4(6)) Corimbo, Editorial S.L. ESP. Dist: Lectorum Pubns., Inc.

Clyne, Margaret & Griffiths, Rachel. Let's Make Music. 2004. (ENG., Illus.). 16p. (J). (gr. 1-1). pap. 10.92 (978-0-7652-5155-8(8), Celebration Pr.) Pearson Schl.

Congratulations - Grade 1 Clarinet/Piano. (J). 9.95 (978-1-85909-667-3(0), Warner Bros. Pubns.) Alfred Publishing Co., Inc.

Congratulations- Grade 2 Alto Sax/Piano. 9.95 (978-1-85909-816-5(9), Warner Bros. Pubns.) Alfred Publishing Co., Inc.

Congratulations: Grade 2 Clarinet. (J). 9.95 (978-1-85909-814-1(2), Warner Bros. Pubns.) Alfred Publishing Co., Inc.

Congratulations: Grade 2 Flute. 9.95 (978-1-85909-815-8(0), Warner Bros. Pubns.) Alfred Publishing Co., Inc.

Coulthard, Emma. Recorder Wizard. 2005. (ENG.). 40p. pap. 8.95 incl. audio compact disk (978-0-8256-3338-6(9), 0825633389, Chester Music) Music Sales Corp.

D'Cruz, Anna-Marie. Make Your Own Musical Instruments. 2009. (Do It Yourself Projects! Ser.). 24p. (J). (gr. 3-5). (ENG., Illus.). pap. 9.40 (978-1-4358-2925-1(5), 1291887); lib. bdg. 25.25 (978-1-4358-2854-4(2)) Rosen Publishing Group, Inc., The. (PowerKids Pr.).

Deane-Pratt, Ade. Musical Instruments. 2012. (How Things Work Ser.). (Illus.). 32p. (J). (gr. 3-6). lib. bdg. 26.50 (978-1-4488-5280-2(3)) Rosen Publishing Group, Inc., The.

Dearling, Robert. Encyclopedia of Musical Instruments, 5 vols., Set. 2005. (Encyclopedia of Musical Instruments Ser.). (Illus.). 48p. (gr. 6-12). 91.80 (978-0-7910-6090-2(X), Chelsea Hse.) Facts On File, Inc.

Dobson, Jolie. Bang Bang Plink Plink. 2014. (Snappy Sounds Ser.). (ENG., Illus.). 22p. (J). (gr. -1 — 1). bds. 5.95 (978-1-77085-438-3(X), 9781770854383) Firefly Bks., Ltd.

Dorling Kindersley Publishing Staff. How to Play the Recorder. 2015. (ENG., Illus.). 64p. (J). (gr. 1-4). 9.99 (978-1-4654-3548-4(4), 1390246, DK Children) Dorling Kindersley Publishing, Inc.

Dyke, Sylvie. "Descant" Recorder Music Made Easy - Just for Little Fingers! 2013. 36p. pap. (978-1-78148-611-5(5)) Grosvenor Hse. Publishing Ltd.

Equipo Staff & Josephine, Paker. Las lautas Tienen Agujeros. 2003. (Enciclopedia Me Pregunto Por Que). (SPA., Illus.). 32p. (J). (gr. 3-5). 12.99 (978-84-241-1968-3(1), EV2041) Everest Editora ESP. Dist: Lectorum Pubns., Inc.

Faine, Edward Allan. Bebop Babies. 2003. (Illus.). 22p. (J). bds. 5.95 (978-0-9716911-3-1(4)) IM Pr.

Frogs Play Cellos. 2014. (Did You Know? Ser.). (ENG., Illus.). 32p. (J). (gr. -1-3). pap. 6.99 (978-1-4814-1425-8(9), Little Simon) Little Simon.

Froseth, James O. Alto Saxophone Home Helper First Lessons at School & at Home. 2005. 16p. 7.95 (978-1-57999-499-0(7), M574) G I A Pubns., Inc.

—Baritone BC Home Helper First Lessons at School & at Home. 2005. 16p. 7.95 (978-1-57999-505-8(5), M580) G I A Pubns., Inc.

—Bassoon Home Helper First Lessons at School & at Home. 2005. 16p. 7.95 (978-1-57999-498-3(9), M573) G I A Pubns., Inc.

—Clarinet Home Helper First Lessons at School & at Home. 2005. 16p. 7.95 (978-1-57999-496-9(2), M571) G I A Pubns., Inc.

George, Francis. Mr G Clef & Friends. Wasvary, Marcia, illus. 2012. 32p. 24.95 (978-1-4560-9642-7(7)) America Star Bks.

George, Gale. We're in the Band: Develop Understanding of Fractions & Numbers. 2014. (Rosen Common Core Math Readers Ser.). (ENG., Illus.). 24p. (J). (gr. 3-4). pap. 8.25 (978-1-4777-4927-2(6), Rosen Classroom) Rosen Publishing Group, Inc., The.

Graham, Roland. How We Make Music. 2003. (Real Readers Series: Level Blue Ser.). (ENG., Illus.). 12p. (gr. 1-2). pap. 5.90 (978-0-8239-6355-3(1)) Rosen Publishing Group, Inc., The.

Green, John. Musical Instruments Stained Glass Coloring Book. 2006. (Dover Stained Glass Coloring Book Ser.). (ENG., Illus.). 8p. (J). (gr. -1-5). pap. 1.50 (978-0-486-44936-4(X)) Dover Pubns., Inc.

Greenwood, Mark & Lessac, Frané. Drummer Boy of John John. 2006. (ENG., Illus.). 40p. (J). 18.95 (978-1-60060-652-6(0)) Lee & Low Bks., Inc.

Helenek, Sophie. My First Book MUSICAL INSTRUMENTS: GOLD Mom's Choice Awards Recipient. 2014. (My First Book Ser.). (ENG., Illus.). 16p. (J). (gr. -1 — 1). bds. 5.99 (978-0-9894505-2-2(X)) Nursery Bks.

Helsby, Genevieve. Those Amazing Musical Instruments! Your Guide to the Orchestra Through Sounds & Stories. 2007. (Naxos Bks.: 0). (ENG., Illus.). 176p. (J). (gr. 3-7). 24.99 (978-1-4022-0825-6(1), Sourcebooks Jabberwocky) Sourcebooks, Inc.

Holden, Pam. Musical Instruments. 2015. (ENG., Illus.). 16p. (-1). pap. (978-1-77654-116-4(2), Red Rocket Readers) Flying Start Bks.

Jackson, Jake. Chords for Kids Made Easy: Comprehensive Sound Links. 2016. (Music Made Easy Ser.). (ENG., Illus.). 256p. pap. 15.99 (978-1-78361-219-2(3), 9781783612192) Flame Tree Publishing GBR. Dist: Bookmasters Distribution.

Kallen, Stuart A. The Instruments of Music. 2013. (Music Library). (ENG., Illus.). 128p. (gr. 7-10). lib. bdg. 39.40 (978-1-4205-0946-5(2), Lucent Bks.) Cengage Gale.

Kenney, Karen Latchana. The Science of Music: Discovering Sound, 1 vol. 2016. (Science in Action Ser.). (ENG., Illus.). 32p. (J). (gr. 3-6). 27.07 (978-1-62403-962-1(6)) ABDO Publishing Co.

The Lac Hong Music Group: Six-Pack. (Greetings Ser.: Vol. 1). (gr. 3-5). 31.00 (978-0-7635-1750-2(X)) Rigby Education.

Landau, Elaine. Is the Flute for You? 2010. (Ready to Make Music Ser.). (ENG., Illus.). 40p. (gr. 4-6). lib. bdg. 27.93 (978-0-7613-5420-8(4), Lerner Pubns.) Lerner Publishing Group.

—Is the Saxophone for You? 2010. (Ready to Make Music Ser.). (ENG.). 40p. (gr. 4-6). lib. bdg. 27.93 (978-0-7613-5425-3(5), Lerner Pubns.) Lerner Publishing Group.

—Is the Trumpet for You? 2010. (Ready to Make Music Ser.). (ENG., Illus.). 40p. (gr. 4-6). lib. bdg. 27.93 (978-0-7613-5422-2(0), Lerner Pubns.) Lerner Publishing Group.

Langstaff, John & Wiseman, Ann Sayre. Making Music: Create & Play 70 Musical Instruments Using Stuff from Around Your House. 2003. (ENG., Illus.). 96p. (J). (gr. k-8). pap. 9.95 (978-1-58017-512-8(0), 67512) Storey Publishing, LLC.

Lawson, Julia & Goodman, Polly. Music. 2011. (Little Steps Ser.). (ENG., Illus.). 14p. (J). (gr. -1-k). bds. (978-1-84089-590-2(X)) Zero to Ten, Ltd.

Lemmerz, Claudia Baumgaertner. My Book about Musical Instruments. 2011. (ENG.). 64p. (J). 19.95 (978-0-9837585-3-2(0)) Touch the Music.

Martin, Iain C., illus. Complete Theory Fun Factory. 2004. (ENG.). 96p. pap. 27.99 (978-0-85162-181-4(3), 0851621813) Boosey & Hawkes, Inc.

Maybank, Chris & Wearing, Katie. Abracadabra Double Bass Beginner, 1 vol. rev. ed. 2007. (Abracadabra Ser.). (ENG., Illus.). 32p. (J). pap., stu. ed. 11.95 incl. audio compact disk **(978-0-7136-8163-5(2))** HarperCollins Pubs. Ltd. GBR. Dist: Independent Pubs. Group.

McGraw-Hill Interactive Recorder. 2003. (Share the Music Ser.). (gr. 3-6). cd-rom (978-0-02-295529-8(1)) Macmillan/McGraw-Hill Schl. Div.

McKean, Helen. Abracadabra Oboe: The Way to Learn Through Songs & Tunes, 1 vol. 3rd ed. 2008. (Abracadabra Ser.). (ENG., Illus.). 64p. (J). pap., stu. ed. 15.95 incl. audio compact disk **(978-1-4081-0528-3(4))** HarperCollins Pubs. Ltd. GBR. Dist: Independent Pubs. Group.

Michele, Tracey. Musical Instruments. 2011. (Learn-Abouts Ser.). (Illus.). 16p. (J). pap. 7.95 (978-1-59920-642-4(0)) Black Rabbit Bks.

Miles, Liz. Playing the Spoons & Other Curious Instruments, 1 vol. 2010. (Culture in Action Ser.). (ENG.). 32p. (gr. 3-6). 30.65 (978-1-4109-3917-3(0), NA-r) Heinemann-Raintree.

Milet Publishing Staff. Music. 2012. (My First Bilingual Book Ser.). (ENG, POL & POR., Illus.). 24p. (J). (gr. k — 1). bds. 7.99 (978-1-84059-724-0(0)); bds. 7.99 (978-1-84059-716-5(X)); bds. 7.99 (978-1-84059-718-9(6)) Milet Publishing.

—Music - English-Spanish. 2012. (My First Bilingual Book Ser.). (SPA & ENG., Illus.). 24p. (J). (gr. k — 1). bds. 7.99 (978-1-84059-728-8(3)) Milet Publishing.

—Music - My First Bilingual Book. 2012. (My First Bilingual Book Ser.). (ENG & POR., Illus.). 24p. (J). (gr. k — 1). bds. 7.99 (978-1-84059-725-7(9)); bds. 7.99 (978-1-84059-722-6(4)) Milet Publishing.

—La Musique. 2012. (My First Bilingual Book Ser.).Tr. of Music. (FRE & ENG., Illus.). 24p. (J). (gr. k — 1). bds. 7.99 (978-1-84059-720-2(8)) Milet Publishing.

—My First Bilingual Book-Music. 2012. (My First Bilingual Book Ser.). (ENG & BEN., Illus.). 24p. (J). (gr. k — 1). bds. 7.99 (978-1-84059-717-2(8)) Milet Publishing.

—My First Bilingual Book-Music (English-Farsi) 2012. (My First Bilingual Book Ser.). (ENG & PER., Illus.). 24p. (J). (gr. k — 1). bds. 7.99 (978-1-84059-719-6(4)) Milet Publishing.

—My First Bilingual Book-Music (English-German) 2012. (My First Bilingual Book Ser.). (ENG & GER., Illus.). 24p. (J). (gr. k — 1). bds. 7.99 (978-1-84059-721-9(6)) Milet Publishing.

—My First Bilingual Book-Music (English-Korean) 2012. (My First Bilingual Book Ser.). (ENG & KOR., Illus.). 24p. (J). (gr. k — 1). bds. 7.99 (978-1-84059-723-3(2)) Milet Publishing.

—My First Bilingual Book-Music (English-Russian) 2012. (My First Bilingual Book Ser.). (ENG & RUS., Illus.). 24p. (J). (gr. k — 1). bds. 7.99 (978-1-84059-726-4(7)) Milet Publishing.

—My First Bilingual Book-Music (English-Somali) 2012. (My First Bilingual Book Ser.). (ENG & SOM., Illus.). 24p. (J). (gr. k — 1). bds. 7.99 *(978-1-84059-727-1(5))* Milet Publishing.
—My First Bilingual Book-Music (English-Turkish) 2012. (My First Bilingual Book Ser.). (ENG & TUR., Illus.). 24p. (J). (gr. k — 1). bds. 7.99 *(978-1-84059-729-5(1))* Milet Publishing.
—My First Bilingual Book-Music (English-Urdu) 2012. (My First Bilingual Book Ser.). (ENG & URD., Illus.). 24p. (J). (gr. k — 1). bds. 7.99 *(978-1-84059-730-1(5))* Milet Publishing.
—My First Bilingual Book-Music (English-Vietnamese) 2012. (My First Bilingual Book Ser.). (ENG & VIE., Illus.). 24p. (J). (gr. k — 1). bds. 7.99 *(978-1-84059-731-8(3))* Milet Publishing.
Miller, Randy. The Fiddler's Throne: A Selection of 375 Tunes for Contra Dances, Sessions, & House Parties 2004. (Illus.). 246p. spiral bd. 25.00 *(978-0-9770530-1-8(6))* Miller, Randy.
Murphy, Maggie. High-Tech DIY Projects with Musical Instruments. 2014. (Maker Kids Ser.). (Illus.). 32p. (J). (gr. 3-6). pap. 70.50 *(978-1-4777-6661-3(8))* Rosen Publishing Group, Inc., The.
Music. Gr K-3 Stm Instrument Sou. 2003. (Share the Music Ser.). (gr. k-3). *(978-0-02-295481-9(3))* Macmillan/McGraw-Hill Schl. Div.
Music. 2010. (Experimenting with Everyday Science Ser.). (Illus.). 168p. (gr. 6-12). 35.00 *(978-1-60413-169-7(1),* Chelsea Hse.) Facts On File, Inc.
Niven, Felicia Lowenstein. Nifty Thrifty Music Crafts. Ponte, June, illus. 2007. (Nifty Thrifty Crafts for Kids Ser.). 32p. (J). (gr. 3-4). lib. bdg. 23.94 *(978-0-7660-2784-8(8),* 1264783, Enslow Elementary) Enslow Pubs., Inc.
Norgaard, Martin. Jazz Cello/Bass Wizard Junior, Book 2, 1 vol., Bk. 2. 2005. (ENG., Illus.). 64p. pap. 17.95 *(978-0-7866-6655-3(2),* 20869BCD) Mel Bay Pubns., Inc.
—Jazz Fiddle Wizard Junior, Book 2, 1 vol., Book. 2. 2005. (ENG., Illus.). 64p. 19.99 *(978-0-7866-6644-7(7),* 20726BCD) Mel Bay Pubns., Inc.
—Jazz Viola Wizard Junior, Book 2, 1 vol., Bk. 2. 2005. (ENG., Illus.). 64p. 17.95 *(978-0-7866-6653-9(6),* 20868BCD) Mel Bay Pubns., Inc.
Nunn, Daniel. Instruments & Music, 1 vol. 2011. (ENG.). 24p. (gr. -1-1). 25.99 *(978-1-4329-5487-1(3),* Acorn Read-Aloud) Heinemann-Raintree.
—Keyboards, 1 vol. 2011. (Instruments & Music Ser.). (ENG.). 24p. (gr. -1-1). pap. 6.29 *(978-1-4329-5066-8(5),* Acorn) Heinemann-Raintree.
O'Hara, Shelley. I Can IPod. 2005. (ENG., Illus.). 160p. (J). per. 12.99 *(978-0-7897-3527-0(X))* Que.
Parker, Ben. My First Keyboard - Learn to Play: Kids. 2013. (Illus.). 42p. pap. *(978-1-908707-15-4(1))* Kyle Craig Publishing.
—My First Recorder - Learn to Play: Kids. 2013. 38p. pap. *(978-1-908707-18-5(6))* Kyle Craig Publishing.
Passchier, Maja. Abracadabra Cello: The Way to Learn Through Songs & Tunes, 1 vol. 3rd ed. 2009. (Abracadabra Ser.). (ENG., Illus.). 64p. (J). pap. 15.95 incl. audio compact disk ***(978-1-4081-1462-9(3))*** HarperCollins Pubs. Ltd. GBR. Dist: Independent Pubs. Group.
Pollock, Malcolm. Abracadabra Flute: The Way to Learn Through Songs & Tunes, 1 vol. 3rd ed. 2008. (Abracadabra Ser.). (ENG., Illus.). 72p. (J). (gr. k-4). pap., stu. ed. 15.95 incl. audio compact disk ***(978-1-4081-0527-6(6))*** HarperCollins Pubs. Ltd. GBR. Dist: Independent Pubs. Group.
Purton, Michael. Show Me How: I Can Make Music. 2015. (ENG., Illus.). 48p. (J). (gr. -1-12). 7.99 *(978-1-86147-297-7(8),* Armadillo) Anness Publishing GBR. Dist: National Bk. Network.
Riggs, Kate. Making Music: Flute. 2014. (Making Music Ser.). (ENG.). 24p. (J). (gr. 1-3). pap. 9.99 *(978-0-89812-946-5(X),* Creative Paperbacks) Creative Co., The.
—Making Music: Trumpet. 2014. (Making Music Ser.). (ENG.). 24p. (J). (gr. 1-3). pap. 9.99 *(978-0-89812-949-6(4),* Creative Paperbacks) Creative Co., The.
Roberts, Gregory. Chin Music. 2007. 208p. (J). pap. 12.99 *(978-0-14-305573-0(9))* Penguin Publishing Group.
Rowe, Brooke. Playing Musical Bottles. Bane, Jeff, illus. 2016. (My Early Library: My Science Fun Ser.). (ENG.). 24p. (J). (gr. k-1). 28.50 *(978-1-63471-028-2(2),* 208192) Cherry Lake Publishing.
Roza, Greg. Getting the Most Out of Makerspaces to Make Musical Instruments. 2014. (Makerspaces Ser.). 64p. (J). (gr. 6-12). 32.95 *(978-1-4777-7823-4(3));* pap. 12.95 *(978-1-4777-7825-8(X));* pap. 77.70 *(978-1-4777-7826-5(8))* Rosen Publishing Group, Inc., The.
Rutland, Jonathan. Abracadabra Clarinet, 2 vols. 3rd ed. 2008. (ENG., Illus.). 72p. (J). pap., stu. ed. 15.95 incl. audio compact disk ***(978-1-4081-0530-6(6))*** HarperCollins Pubs. Ltd. GBR. Dist: Independent Pubs. Group.
—Abracadabra Saxophone, 1 vol. 3rd ed. 2008. (Abracadabra Ser.). (ENG., Illus.). 72p. (J). pap., stu. ed. 15.95 incl. audio compact disk ***(978-1-4081-0529-0(2))*** HarperCollins Pubs. Ltd. GBR. Dist: Independent Pubs. Group.
Saaf, Donald. The ABC Animal Orchestra. Saaf, Donald, illus. 2015. (ENG., Illus.). 40p. (J). (gr. -1 — 1). 16.99 *(978-0-8050-9072-7(X),* 9780805090727, Holt, Henry & Co. Bks. For Young Readers) Holt, Henry & Co.
Salzmann, Mary Elizabeth. What in the World Is a Flute?, 1 vol. 2012. (ENG.). 24p. 25.65 *(978-1-61783-205-5(7),* Super SandCastle) ABDO Publishing Co.
Schwartz, Betty Ann. What Makes Music? A Magic Ribbon Book. Turner, Dona, illus. 2005. (Stories to Share Ser.). 16p. (J). (gr. -1-3). act. bk. ed. 11.95 *(978-1-58117-139-6(0),* Intervisual/Piggy Toes) Bendon, Inc.
Sesame Workshop Staff, ed. My First Library Sesame Street: 12 Board Books. 2004. (Illus.). 120p. (J). bds. 10.98 *(978-1-4127-0515-8(0),* 7224100) Phoenix International Publications, Inc.
Shaskan, Trisha Speed. Around the World with the Percussion Family!, 1 vol. Meganck, Robert & Communication Design (Firm) Staff, illus. 2010. (Musical Families Ser.). (ENG.). 24p. (gr. 2-3). lib. bdg. 25.32 *(978-1-4048-6044-5(4))* Picture Window Bks.
—The Keyboard Family Takes Center Stage!, 1 vol. Meganck, Robert & Communication Design (Firm) Staff, illus. 2010. (Musical Families Ser.). (ENG.). 24p. (gr. 2-3). lib. bdg. 25.32 *(978-1-4048-6045-2(2))* Picture Window Bks.
Sherab, Chodzin & Langham, Tony. Creepy Crawly Calypso. 2012. (ENG., Illus.). 32p. (J). (gr. -1-2). 9.99 *(978-1-84686-828-3(9))* Barefoot Bks., Inc.
Sjonger, Rebecca. Maker Projects for Kids Who Love Music. 2016. (ENG., Illus.). 32p. (J). *(978-0-7787-2252-6(X))* Crabtree Publishing Co.
Smith, A. G. Little Mandalas Stained Glass Coloring Book. 2006. (Dover Stained Glass Coloring Book Ser.). (ENG., Illus.). 8p. (J). (gr. k-3). 1.99 *(978-0-486-44937-1(8))* Dover Pubns., Inc.
Smith, Erica. Making Music with Stringed Instruments. 2009. (Reading Room Collection 2 Ser.). 24p. (gr. 3-4). 42.50 *(978-1-60851-979-8(1),* PowerKids Pr.) Rosen Publishing Group, Inc., The.
Smith, Melanie. Beginner Cello Theory for Children, Book One, 1 vol. 2005. (ENG., Illus.). 84p. pap. 19.99 *(978-0-7866-7088-8(6),* 20451) Mel Bay Pubns., Inc.
Suzuki, Shinichi. Suzuki Cello School: Piano Accompaniment, Vol. 6. rev. ed. 2003. (Suzuki Cello School Ser.: Vol 6). (ENG., Illus.). 32p. (gr. 6-12). pap. 8.99 *(978-0-87487-271-2(5),* Warner Bros. Pubns.) Alfred Publishing Co., Inc.
Suzuki, Shinichi & Alfred Publishing Staff. Suzuki Cello School, Vol. 5. rev. ed. 2003. (Suzuki Cello School Ser.: Vol 5). (ENG., Illus.). 16p. (gr. k-12). pap. 7.99 *(978-0-87487-267-5(7),* Suzuki) Alfred Publishing Co., Inc.
Tarantino, Scott & Ruggiero, David. High Sticking: Xylophone & Marimba Pieces for Grades 4 - 8. 2011. 32p. (J). pap. 19.95 *(978-0-9832648-2-8(1))* Beatin' Path Pubns., LLC.
Verderosa, Laura. In the Band. 2010. (Sight Word Readers Ser.). (J). 3.49 *(978-1-60719-612-9(3))* Newmark Learning LLC.
Watt, Fiona. Little Children's Music Book. 2012. (Little Children's Music Book Ser.). 24p. (J). bds. 18.99 *(978-0-7945-3168-3(7),* Usborne) EDC Publishing.
Whykes, Susan. Let's Practise: Be a Better Musician. 2009. 216p. pap. 14.49 *(978-1-4389-2933-0(1))* AuthorHouse.
Witmer, Scott. Drums, Keyboards, & Other Instruments, 1 vol. 2009. (Rock Band Ser.). (ENG., Illus.). 32p. (YA). (gr. 4-7). 27.07 *(978-1-60453-690-4(X))* ABDO Publishing Co.

MUSICAL INSTRUMENTS—FICTION

Adair, Amy. Jay Jay's Special Delivery. 2003. (Illus.). (J). 15.98 *(978-0-7853-8625-4(4))* Publications International, Ltd.
Albee, Sarah. Max Can Fix That. Schick, Joel, illus. 2006. (Step-By-Step Readers Ser.). (J). pap. *(978-1-59939-055-0(8),* Reader's Digest Young Families, Inc.) Studio Fun International.
Barton, Chris. 88 Instruments. 2016. (ENG., Illus.). 32p. (J). (gr. -1-2). 17.99 *(978-0-553-53814-4(4),* Knopf Bks. for Young Readers) Random Hse. Children's Bks.
Bass, L. G. & Geringer, Laura. Boom Boom Go Away! Ibatoulline, Bagram, illus. 2010. (ENG.). 40p. (J). (gr. -1-1). 15.99 *(978-0-689-85093-6(X),* Atheneum Bks. for Young Readers) Simon & Schuster Children's Publishing.
Benator, Eileen. A Marching Band for Bears. Benator, Seth, illus. 2004. 32p. (J). lib. bdg. 15.95 *(978-0-9748478-5-6(2))* Lion's Tale Pr., LLC.
Blumberg, Margie. Avram's Gift. McGaw, Laurie, illus. (ENG.). 48p. 2005. (YA). pap. 11.95 *(978-0-9624166-3-7(0))* 2003. (J). (gr. 3-18). 15.95 *(978-0-9624166-2-0(2))* MB Publishing, LLC.
Blume, Lesley M. M. The Rising Star of Rusty Nail. 2009. (ENG.). 288p. (J). (gr. 3-7). 7.99 *(978-0-440-42111-5(X),* Yearling) Random Hse. Children's Bks.
Bowe, Julie. Face the Music. 2015. (Victoria Torres, Unfortunately Average Ser.). (ENG.). 160p. (gr. 4-4). pap. 5.95 *(978-1-4965-0538-5(7))* Stone Arch Bks.
Bunting, Eve. Hey Diddle Diddle. Fraser, Mary Ann, illus. 2011. (ENG.). 32p. (J). (gr. -1-k). 16.95 *(978-1-59078-768-7(4))* Boyds Mills Pr.
Cali, Davide. Piano, Piano. Rivers, Randi, tr. from FRE. Heliot, Eric, illus. 2007. 28p. (J). (gr. 4-7). 15.95 *(978-1-58089-191-2(8))* Charlesbridge Publishing, Inc.
Campagne, Michelle & Gallant, Dany. Fabuleuse Melodie De. 2013. (FRE., Illus.). 44p. (J). (gr. -1-k). 16.95 *(978-2-923163-30-7(3))* La Montagne Secrete CAN. Dist: Independent Pubs. Group.
Carlson, Nancy. Loudmouth George & the Cornet. rev. ed. 2004. (Carolrhoda Picture Books Ser.). (ENG., Illus.). 32p. (J). (gr. k-2). pap. 9.95 *(978-1-57505-725-5(5))* Lerner Publishing Group.
Castonguay, Leo. Piper Peter. 2012. 44p. 24.95 *(978-1-4626-8604-9(4))* America Star Bks.
Curtis, Gavin. The Bat Boy & His Violin. 2004. (Illus.). (J). (gr. k-3). spiral bd. *(978-0-616-07254-7(6))* Canadian National Institute for the Blind/Institut National Canadien pour les Aveugles.
Dagostino, Argus. Stop the Lute. 2010. 35p. pap. 20.00 *(978-0-557-24546-8(X))* Lulu Pr., Inc.
Donegan, Noel & Donegan, Luz. The Hot-Headed Bassoon. 2013. (Magical Mozart & His Musical Ser.). (ENG.). 32p. (J). pap. 8.95 *(978-1-84730-392-9(7))* Veritas Pubns. IRL. Dist: Dufour Editions, Inc.
—The Noisy Blue Drum. 2013. (Magical Mozart & His Musical Ser.). (ENG.). 32p. (J). pap. 8.95 *(978-1-84730-391-2(9))* Veritas Pubns. IRL. Dist: Dufour Editions, Inc.
—The Sad Little Violin. 2013. (Magical Mozart & His Musical Ser.). (ENG.). 32p. (J). pap. 8.95 *(978-1-84730-393-6(5))* Veritas Pubns. IRL. Dist: Dufour Editions, Inc.
Errico, Jessica / C. Grandpa's Magical Accordion. Star, Brenda, illus. 2007. 28p. (J). pap. 17.95 incl. cd-rom *(978-0-9800577-0-6(1))* Three Part Harmony LLC.
Falconer, Ian. Olivia Forms a Band. Falconer, Ian, illus. 2006. (ENG., Illus.). 50p. (J). (gr. -1-3). 18.99 *(978-1-4169-2454-8(X),* Atheneum Bks. for Young Readers) Simon & Schuster Children's Publishing.
Farmer, Zoe. Practice Makes Perfect. Farmer, Zoe, illus. 2007. (Illus.). 74p. (gr. -1-k). pap. *(978-1-58690-029-8(3))* Mould, Paul Publishing.
Forman, Gayle. Where She Went. l.t. ed. 2015. (If I Stay Ser.: BK.2). (ENG.). 288p. (YA). 23.99 *(978-1-4104-7562-6(X))* Cengage Gale.
—Where She Went. (If I Stay Ser.: BK.2). (ENG.). (YA). (gr. 9-18). 2012. 304p. 10.99 *(978-0-14-242089-8(1),* Speak) 2011. 272p. 17.99 *(978-0-525-42294-5(3),* Dutton Books for Young Readers) Penguin Young Readers Group.
—Where She Went. 2012. (If I Stay Ser.: BK.2). (YA). 21.00 *(978-1-61383-394-0(6))* Perfection Learning Corp.
—Where She Went. l.t. ed. 2015. (If I Stay Ser.: BK.2). (ENG.). 286p. (YA). pap. 12.99 *(978-1-59413-855-3(9),* Large Print Pr.) Thorndike Pr.
—Where She Went. 2012. (If I Stay Ser.: BK.2). (YA). lib. bdg. 22.10 *(978-0-606-23644-7(9),* Turtleback) Turtleback Bks.
Free Kazoos. 2003. *(978-0-375-88484-9(X))* Random Hse. Children's Bks.
Garriel, Barbara. I Know a Shy Fellow Who Swallowed a Cello. O'brien, John, illus. 2012. (ENG.). 32p. (J). (gr. k-2). pap. 6.95 *(978-1-59078-946-9(6))* Boyds Mills Pr.
Garriel, Barbara S. I Know a Shy Fellow Who Swallowed a Cello. O'brien, John, illus. 2004. (ENG.). 32p. (J). (gr. k-3). 17.95 *(978-1-59078-043-5(4))* Boyds Mills Pr.
George Trad. The Symph - in Search of Harmony. Beniamino Brady, illus. 2012. 38p. 30.50 *(978-1-61897-519-5(6),* Strategic Bk. Publishing) Strategic Book Publishing & Rights Agency (SBPRA).
Ginsberg, Mort. Ukey & His Magical Ukulele. 2008. 75p. pap. 19.95 *(978-1-60610-395-1(4))* America Star Bks.
Harris, Lee. Carla & the Great Talent Show. 2009. 80p. pap. 10.00 *(978-1-60860-515-6(9),* Strategic Bk. Publishing) Strategic Book Publishing & Rights Agency (SBPRA).
Haseley, Dennis. The Old Banjo. Gammell, Stephen, illus. 2013. (ENG.). 32p. (J). (gr. -1-3). 16.99 *(978-1-4424-8879-3(4),* Simon & Schuster Bks. For Young Readers) Simon & Schuster Bks. For Young Readers.
Hopman, Philip. Valentine & His Violin. 2012. (ENG., Illus.). 32p. (J). (gr. -1). 17.95 *(978-1-935954-17-0(2),* 9781935954170) Lemniscaat USA.
Keller, Jessica. Mia's Marvelous Musical Group. 2009. (Illus.). 64p. (gr. -1-3). pap. 26.99 *(978-1-4389-8160-4(0))* AuthorHouse.
Kenney, Cindy, et al. Frog Wars, 1 vol. 2005. (Big Idea Books / VeggieTown Values Ser.: Bk. 2). (ENG., Illus.). 32p. (J). pap. 3.99 *(978-0-310-70627-4(0))* Zonderkidz.
Laird, Judie. I Don't Want to Play the Piano! 2009. 20p. pap. 10.95 *(978-1-4490-1496-4(8))* AuthorHouse.
—Lori Takes Piano Lessons. 2009. 20p. pap. 10.95 *(978-1-4490-1205-2(1))* AuthorHouse.
Landon, Kristen. Life in the Pit. 2008. (ENG., Illus.). 248p. (YA). (gr. 5-13). pap. 8.95 *(978-1-933831-08-4(1))* Blooming Tree Pr.
Langham, Tony. Creepy Crawly Calypso. Harter, Debbie, illus. 2004. (ENG.). 32p. (J). 16.99 *(978-1-84148-699-4(X))* Barefoot Bks., Inc.
Langham, Tony & Harter, Debbie. Creepy Crawly Calypso. 2005. (ENG.). 32p. (J). pap. 9.99 *(978-1-902283-46-3(5))* Barefoot Bks., Inc.
Lilly, Sara. The Inseparables. 2015. (ENG.). 77p. (J). (gr. 3-4). mass mkt. 14.95 *(978-1-78455-920-5(2),* d4b15bff-7ea4-4131-af5d-e5ff708023ca) Austin, Stan AUS. Dist: Bookmasters Distribution.
Lithgow, John & Payne, C. F. The Remarkable Farkle McBride. 2003. (ENG., Illus.). 40p. (J). (gr. -1-3). pap. 7.99 *(978-0-689-83541-4(8),* Simon & Schuster Bks. For Young Readers) Simon & Schuster Bks. For Young Readers.
Manning, Sarra. Guitar Girl. 2003. (ENG.). 256p. (YA). pap. *(978-0-340-86071-7(5))* Hodder & Stoughton.
—Guitar Girl. 2005. (ENG.). 240p. (YA). (gr. 7-9). reprint ed. pap. 6.99 *(978-0-14-240318-1(0),* Speak) Penguin Young Readers Group.
Manushkin, Fran. Katie's Noisy Music. Lyon, Tammie, illus. 2015. (Katie Woo Ser.). (ENG.). 32p. (gr. k-2). 21.32 *(978-1-4795-5893-3(1))* Picture Window Bks.
Meadows, Daisy. Danni the Drum Fairy #4. 2010. (ENG.). 80p. (J). lib. bdg. 15.39 *(978-1-4242-4729-5(2))* Fitzgerald Bks.
—Fiona the Flute Fairy #3. 2010. (ENG.). 80p. (J). lib. bdg. 15.39 *(978-1-4242-4731-8(4))* Fitzgerald Bks.
—Maya the Harp Fairy #5. 2010. (ENG.). 80p. (J). lib. bdg. 15.39 *(978-1-4242-4732-5(2))* Fitzgerald Bks.
—Poppy the Piano Fairy #1. 2010. (ENG.). 80p. (J). lib. bdg. 15.39 *(978-1-4242-4733-2(0))* Fitzgerald Bks.
—Sadie the Saxophone Fairy #7. 2010. (ENG.). 80p. (J). lib. bdg. 15.39 *(978-1-4242-4734-9(9))* Fitzgerald Bks.
Megerdichian, Janet. Pine Needle Pedro. Adams, Allysa, illus. 2010. 36p. pap. 16.99 *(978-1-4520-4422-4(8))* AuthorHouse.
Montparker, Carol. Polly & the Piano. 2004. (ENG., Illus.). 40p. pap. 19.95 *(978-1-57467-093-6(X),* 157467093X, Amadeus Press) Leonard, Hal Corp.
Moss, Lloyd. Zin! Zin! Zin! A Violin. Priceman, Marjorie, illus. 2004. (gr. -1-3). 18.00 *(978-0-7569-1919-1(3))* Perfection Learning Corp.
—Zin! Zin! Zin! A Violin. 2004. 18.95 *(978-1-55592-118-7(3));* 29.95 *(978-1-55592-131-6(0));* 18.95 *(978-1-55592-118-7(3));* 38.75 *(978-1-55592-650-2(9))* Weston Woods Studios, Inc.
Mulder, Michelle. Out of the Box. 2011. 150p. (J). *(978-1-55469-329-0(2))* Orca Bk. Pubs.
—Out of the Box, 1 vol. 2011. (ENG.). 160p. (J). (gr. 4-7). pap. 9.95 *(978-1-55469-328-3(4))* Orca Bk. Pubs. USA.
Pellegata, Donna, illus. The Harp Mouse Chooses Her Home: The Adventure Begins. 2008. 24p. (J). pap. 6.95 *(978-0-9742174-1-3(7))* Heart & Harp LLC.
Perkins, Lynne Rae. The Cardboard Piano. Perkins, Lynne Rae, illus. 2008. (ENG., Illus.). 32p. (J). (gr. -1-2). 17.99 *(978-0-06-154265-7(2),* Greenwillow Bks.) HarperCollins Pubs.
pierSath, Chath. Sinat & the Instrument of the Heart: A Story of Cambodia. Nath, Vann & Pouriseth, Phal, illus. 2010. (Make Friends Around the World Ser.). (ENG.). 32p. (J). (gr. k-3). 9.95 *(978-1-60727-117-8(6));* 9.95 *(978-1-60727-098-0(6));* 9.95 *(978-1-60727-116-1(8));* 19.95 *(978-1-60727-097-3(8));* 16.95 *(978-1-60727-087-4(0));* pap. 6.95 *(978-1-60727-088-1(9))* Soundprints.
Potter, Debra, illus. I Am the Music Man. 2006. (Classic Books with Holes Big Book Ser.). (ENG.). 16p. (J). (gr. -1-3). *(978-1-84643-010-7(0))* Child's Play International Ltd.
Publications International Ltd. Staff. Dora PNO BK Follow Music. 2008. 10p. (J). 16.98 *(978-1-4127-8996-7(6),* PIL Kids) Publications International, Ltd.
Ray, Mary Lyn. A Violin for Elva. Tusa, Tricia, illus. 2015. (ENG.). 32p. (J). (gr. -1-3). 16.99 *(978-0-15-225483-4(8),* HMH Books For Young Readers) Houghton Mifflin Harcourt Publishing Co.
Richardson, Bill. The Aunts Come Marching. Nugent, Cynthia, illus. 2007. (ENG.). 32p. (J). (gr. -1-3). 15.95 *(978-1-55192-990-3(2))* Raincoast Bk. Distribution CAN. Dist: Publishers Group West (PGW).
Rovetch, L. Bob. I Need a Kazoot! Castillon, Carly, illus. 2006. (J). *(978-1-58987-055-0(7))* Kindermusik International.
Rumbley, Rose-Mary. Dear Santa: Thanks for the Piano. 2004. (Illus.). 46p. (J). pap. 8.95 *(978-1-57168-466-0(2))* Eakin Pr.
Rylant, Cynthia. The Case of the Puzzling Possum. Karas, G. Brian, illus. 2003. (High-Rise Private Eyes Ser.: No. 3). (J). (gr. -1-3). 25.95 incl. audio *(978-1-59112-198-5(1));* (gr. k-3). pap. 29.95 incl. audio *(978-1-59112-199-2(X))* Live Oak Media.
Seybold, Celisa. The Keys to Adventure. 2010. 62p. pap. 9.95 *(978-0-557-55086-9(6))* Lulu Pr., Inc.
Shahan, Sherry. The Jazzy Alphabet. Thelen, Mary, illus. 2006. 30p. (J). (gr. k-4). reprint ed. 16.00 *(978-1-4223-5730-9(9))* DIANE Publishing Co.
Smith, J. D. The Best Mariachi in the World/El Mejor Mariachi del Mundo. de la Vega, Eida, tr. Jones, Dani, illus. 2008. (ENG & SPA.). 32p. (J). (gr. 4-7). lib. bdg. 16.95 *(978-0-9770906-1-7(2),* Raven Tree Pr.,Csi) Continental Sales, Inc.
Snicket, Lemony, pseud & Stookey, Nathaniel. The Composer Is Dead. Ellis, Carson, illus. 2009. (ENG.). 40p. (J). (gr. k-5). 17.99 *(978-0-06-123627-3(6))* HarperCollins Pubs.
Stewart, Kymberly M. Play It Again, Rachel. 2003. 74p. (J). pap. 10.95 *(978-0-9740653-0-4(7))* Neema's Children Literature Assn., Inc.
Stilwell, Norma Minturn. Making Beautiful Music. LaGrange, Tiffany, illus. 2011. 28p. pap. 14.95 *(978-1-936343-92-8(4))* Peppertree Pr., The.
Studio Mouse Staff. Sesame Street My First Instrument. 2008. (ENG.). 24p. (J). (gr. -1). 4.99 *(978-1-59069-737-5(5))* Studio Mouse LLC.
Taylor, Lillian Webb. Santa's Musical Elves. 2009. 28p. pap. 12.25 *(978-1-60860-146-2(3),* Strategic Bk. Publishing) Strategic Book Publishing & Rights Agency (SBPRA).
Tripp, Paul. Tubby the Tuba. Cole, Henry, illus. 2006. (ENG.). 32p. (J). (gr. -1-3). 16.99 *(978-0-525-47717-4(9),* Dutton Books for Young Readers) Penguin Young Readers Group.
Urban, Linda. A Crooked Kind of Perfect. 2007. (ENG., Illus.). 224p. (J). (gr. 5-7). 16.00 *(978-0-15-206007-7(3))* Houghton Mifflin Harcourt Publishing Co.
Weston Woods Staff, creator. Dem Bones. 2004. 29.95 *(978-1-55592-702-8(5))* Weston Woods Studios, Inc.
Wilson, Budge. A Fiddle for Angus. Tooke, Susan, illus. 2006. (ENG.). 32p. (J). (gr. 1-4). pap. 13.95 *(978-0-88776-785-2(0),* Tundra Bks.) Tundra Bks. CAN. Dist: Penguin Random Hse. LLC.
Yoo, Paula. Good Enough. 2012. (ENG.). 336p. (YA). (gr. 8). pap. 7.99 *(978-0-06-079090-5(3),* HarperTeen) HarperCollins Pubs.
Zobel-Nolan, Allia. Animal Parade. Maddocks, Maria, illus. 2008. 10p. (J). (gr. -1). 12.95 *(978-1-932915-63-1(X))* Sandvik Innovations, LLC.

MUSICAL NOTATION

Biklou, Eliyana. Lady Treble & the Seven Notes. 2010. (ENG., Illus.). 32p. (J). (gr. -1-3). 16.95 *(978-1-897476-21-5(3))* Simply Read Bks. CAN. Dist: Ingram Publisher Services.
Collins, Kathleen. Music Math: Exploring Different Interpretations of Fractions. (Powermath Ser.). 32p. 2009. (ENG., Illus.). (J). (gr. 4-5). pap. 10.00 *(978-0-8239-8877-8(5))* 2009. (gr. 4-5). 47.90 *(978-1-60851-398-7(X))* 2004. (Illus.). (J). lib. bdg. 25.25 *(978-0-8239-8984-3(4))* Rosen Publishing Group, Inc., The. (PowerKids Pr.).
Yazbeck, Peter & Castano, Clara. Learning Cards(tm) Musical Symbols in Q&A Form, Secondary Level, 3 bks., Bk. 3. 2007. (Illus.). 150p. ring bd. 9.95 *(978-0-9785118-5-2(9))* CCRiddles.

MUSICALS

Children's Theatre Company Staff. Key Change: New Musicals for Young Audiences. Brosius, Peter & Adams, Elissa, eds. 2016. (ENG., Illus.). 296p. 70.00 *(978-0-8166-9809-7(0))* Univ. of Minnesota Pr.
Hal Leonard Corp. Staff, creator. Teaching Little Fingers to Play More Broadway Songs: Mid to Later Elementary Level. 2012. (ENG.). 32p. pap. 12.99 incl. audio compact disk *(978-1-4584-1768-8(9),* 1458417689) Willis Music Co.
Isenberg, Barbara. Making It Big: The Diary of a Broadway Musical. 2004. (ENG., Illus.). 214p. 25.00 *(978-0-87910-088-9(5),* 0879100885, Limelight Editions) Leonard, Hal Corp.
Marsico, Katie. How to Analyze the Works of Andrew Lloyd Webber, 1 vol. 2010. (Essential Critiques Set 1 Ser.). (ENG., Illus.). 112p. (J). (gr. 6-12). lib. bdg. 35.64 *(978-1-61613-533-1(6),* Essential Library) ABDO Publishing Co.
McMahon, James P. & Ryan, Nancy. Buttonbush. 2003. (Musicals Ser.). 55p. (Orig.). (J). (gr. k-7). pap. 10.00 *(978-0-88734-526-5(3))* Players Pr., Inc.
van Leer, Jake, et al. Over the Moon: A Musical Play. 2011. (ENG., Illus.). 240p. (YA). (gr. 7-18). pap. 15.99 *(978-1-4424-2132-5(0),* Simon Pulse) Simon Pulse.

MUSICIANS

see also African American Musicians; Composers; Pianists; Rap Musicians; Singers; Violinists

Aberback, Brian. Black Sabbath: Pioneers of Heavy Metal. 2010. (Rebels of Rock Ser.). (Illus.). 112p. (J). (gr. 7-18). pap. 10.95 *(978-1-59845-212-9(6))* Enslow Pubs., Inc.
Abrams, Dennis. Eminem. 2007. (Hip-Hop Stars Ser.). (Illus.). 103p. (YA). (gr. 7-12). lib. bdg. 30.00 *(978-0-7910-9479-2(0))* Facts On File, Inc.
Adams, Michelle Medlock. Tim Mcgraw. 2006. (Blue Banner Biography Ser.). (Illus.). 32p. (YA). (gr. 4-7). lib. bdg. 25.70 *(978-1-58415-501-0(9))* Mitchell Lane Pubs., Inc.
Alagna, Magdalena. Elvis Presley. 2009. (Rock & Roll Hall of Famers Ser.). 112p. (gr. 5-8). 63.90 *(978-1-60852-474-7(4),* Rosen Reference) Rosen Publishing Group, Inc., The.
Allen, Kathy, et al. Girls Rock! 2011. (Girls Rock! Ser.). (ENG.). 64p. (gr. 4-5). lib. bdg. 138.60 *(978-1-4765-0467-4(9))* Capstone Press of Coughlan Cos.
Allen, Richard, contrib. by. Charlie Parker Played Be Bop. 2003. (Illus.). (J). (gr. -1-2). pap. 35.95 incl. audio compact disk *(978-1-59112-602-7(9))* Live Oak Media.

MNO

—Mysterious Thelonious. abr. ed. 2003. (Illus.). (J). (gr. -1-2). audio compact disk 28.95 *(978-1-59112-422-1(0))* Live Oak Media.

Anderson, Jennifer Joline. John Lennon: Legendary Musician & Beatle, 1 vol. 2010. (Lives Cut Short Set 1 Ser.). (ENG.). 112p. (J). (gr. 6-12). lib. bdg. 35.64 *(978-1-60453-790-1(6))* ABDO Publishing Co.

Anderson, Kirsten. Who Is Elton John? Qiu, Joseph J. M.   & Harrison, Nancy, illus. 2016. (Who Was? Ser.). (ENG.). 112p. (J). (gr. 3-7). pap. 5.99 *(978-0-448-48846-2(9),* Grosset & Dunlap) Penguin Young Readers Group.

—Who Is Elton John? 2016. (Who Is... ? Ser.). lib. bdg. 16.00 *(978-0-606-38396-7(4))* Turtleback Bks.

Angel, Ann. Janis Joplin: Rise up Singing. 2010. (ENG., Illus.). 128p. (YA). (gr. 7-17). 24.95 *(978-0-8109-8349-6(4),* Amulet Bks.) Abrams, Inc.

Anniss, Matt. Music, Fashion, & Style. 2015. (Music Scene Ser.). (J). lib. bdg. 37.10 *(978-1-59920-912-8(8))* Black Rabbit Bks.

Anniss, Matthew. Music, Fashion & Style. 2016. (ENG., Illus.). 48p. (J). (gr. 5-9). pap. 12.99 *(978-1-4451-3940-1(5),* Franklin Watts) Hachette Children's Group GBR. Dist: Hachette Bk. Group.

Ashley, Susan. Yo-Yo Ma. 2004. (Trailblazers of the Modern World Ser.). (Illus.). 48p. (gr. 5-12). lib. bdg. 31.00 *(978-0-8368-5497-8(7),* Gareth Stevens Secondary Library) Stevens, Gareth Publishing LLLP.

Bailey, Ellen. One Dream, One Direction. 2012. (ENG.). 64p. (J). (gr. 3-7). pap. 9.99 *(978-1-4424-7308-9(8),* Aladdin) Simon & Schuster Children's Publishing.

Bailey, Ellen & Williams, Imogen. 5 Seconds of Summer: 100% Unofficial. 2014. (ENG., Illus.). 24p. (J). (gr. 3-7). pap. 7.99 *(978-1-4814-4365-4(8),* Aladdin) Simon & Schuster Children's Publishing.

Bailey, Tom. Hank Williams Sr: Country Music Legend. 2008. (Illus.). 104p. (J). *(978-1-59421-043-3(8))* Seacoast Publishing, Inc.

Ball, Heather. Magnificent Women in Music, 1 vol. 2006. (Women's Hall of Fame Ser.). (ENG., Illus.). 102p. (J). (gr. 4-8). pap. 10.95 *(978-1-897187-02-9(5))* Second Story Pr. CAN. Dist: Orca Bk. Pubs. USA.

Bankston, John. Jay-Z. l.t. ed. 2004. (Blue Banner Biography Ser.). (Illus.). 32p. (J). (gr. 3-8). lib. bdg. 25.70 *(978-1-58415-223-1(0))* Mitchell Lane Pubs., Inc.

—The Life & Times of Duke Ellington. 2004. (Masters of Music Ser.). (Illus.). 48p. (gr. 4-8). lib. bdg. 20.95 *(978-1-58415-248-4(6))* Mitchell Lane Pubs., Inc.

Battaglia, Stephen. Mr. Mcsymphony's Musicians & their Instruments. 2008. (ENG.). 28p. pap. 9.99 *(978-1-4196-8077-9(3))* CreateSpace Independent Publishing Platform.

Behnke, Alison. Death of a Dreamer: The Assassination of John Lennon. 2012. (Single Titles Ser.). (ENG.). 96p. (gr. 6-12). lib. bdg. 33.26 *(978-0-8225-9036-1(0),* Twenty-First Century Bks.) Lerner Publishing Group.

Bernard, Jan. Justin Bieber. 2012. (Stars of Today Ser.). (ENG.). 32p. (J). (gr. 2-5). 28.50 *(978-1-61473-291-4(4),* 205043) Child's World, Inc., The.

Beyer, Mark. Stevie Wonder. 2009. (Rock & Roll Hall of Famers Ser.). 112p. (gr. 5-8). 63.90 *(978-1-60852-475-4(2),* Rosen Reference) Rosen Publishing Group, Inc., The.

Blue Banner Biographies, 26 Bks, Set. (gr. 3-8). (Illus.). lib. bdg. *(978-1-58415-323-8(7));* 2005. (J). lib. bdg. 745.80 *(978-1-58415-412-9(8))* Mitchell Lane Pubs., Inc.

Bodden, Valerie. One Direction. 2015. (J). *(978-1-60818-497-2(8),* Creative Education) Creative Co., The.

Bolte, Mari. Rock Star Style: Fun Fashions You Can Sketch, 1 vol. Dahl, Sarah, illus. 2013. (Drawing Fun Fashions Ser.). (ENG.). 32p. (gr. 3-4). lib. bdg. 27.99 *(978-1-62065-036-3(3),* Snap Bks.) Capstone Press of Coughlan Cos.

Boone, Mary. Behind-The-Scenes Music Careers. 2017. (Behind the Glamour Ser.). (ENG., Illus.). 64p. (gr. 4-5). lib. bdg. 31.32 *(978-1-5157-4898-4(7))* Capstone Press of Coughlan Cos.

Bowe, Brian J. The Clash: Punk Rock Band. 2010. (Rebels of Rock Ser.). (Illus.). 112p. (J). pap. 10.95 *(978-1-59845-211-2(8))* Enslow Pubs., Inc.

—Judas Priest: Metal Gods. 2009. (Rebels of Rock Ser.). (Illus.). 112p. (J). (gr. 5-18). pap. 10.95 *(978-0-7660-3621-5(9));* (gr. 7-12). lib. bdg. 33.27 *(978-0-7660-3029-9(6))* Enslow Pubs., Inc.

—The Ramones: American Punk Rock Band. 2010. (Rebels of Rock Ser.). (Illus.). 128p. (J). (gr. 7-18). pap. 10.95 *(978-1-59845-213-6(4))* Enslow Pubs., Inc.

Braidich, Shelby. Faith Hill. 2010. (Country Music Stars Ser.). (Illus.). 32p. (J). (gr. 3-8). pap. 10.50 *(978-1-4339-3614-2(3));* lib. bdg. 25.25 *(978-1-4339-3613-5(5))* Stevens, Gareth Publishing LLLP.

Braun, Eric. Prince: The Man, the Symbol, the Music. 2017. (Gateway Biographies Ser.). (ENG.). 48p. (J). (gr. 4-8). 12.99 ***(978-1-5124-3861-1(8),*** Lerner Pubns.); 39.99 ***(978-1-5124-3860-4(X),*** Lerner Pubns.); (Illus.). 26.65 *(978-1-5124-3456-9(6));* 39.99 ***(978-1-5124-3457-6(4),*** Lerner Pubns.) Lerner Publishing Group.

Breguet, Amy. Yellowcard. 2009. (Contemporary Musicians & Their Music Ser.). 48p. (gr. 6-6). 53.00 *(978-1-61511-948-6(5))* Rosen Publishing Group, Inc., The.

Broadbent, Paul. Rock Stars. 2007. (Trackers-Math Ser.). (gr. 2-5). pap. 5.00 *(978-1-59055-939-0(8))* Pacific Learning, Inc.

Brooks, Riley. One Direction: Superstardom! 2013. (ENG., Illus.). 48p. (J). (gr. 3-7). pap. 4.99 *(978-0-545-59131-7(7))* Scholastic, Inc.

—Up Close! [25 of Your Fave Stars Inside!]. 2013. (Illus.). 48p. (J). pap. *(978-0-545-54126-8(3))* Scholastic, Inc.

Brooks, Riley & Hodgin, Molly. One Direction: Straight to the Top! 2012. (ENG., Illus.). 48p. (J). (gr. -1-3). pap. 4.99 *(978-0-545-49988-0(7))* Scholastic, Inc.

Brown, Risa. Blake Shelton. 2014. (Illus.). 32p. (J). 25.70 *(978-1-61228-641-9(0))* Mitchell Lane Pubs., Inc.

Buckley, Annie. Yo-Yo Ma. 2007. (21st Century Skills Library: Life Skills Biographies Ser.). (ENG., Illus.). 48p. (gr. 4-8). lib. bdg. 31.36 *(978-1-60279-077-3(9),* 200049) Cherry Lake Publishing.

Burling, Alexis. Pharrell Williams: Grammy-Winning Singer, Songwriter & Producer, 1 vol. 2014. (Contemporary Lives Set 4 Ser.). (ENG., Illus.). 112p. (J). (gr. 6-12). lib. bdg. 35.64 *(978-1-62403-549-4(3),* Essential Library) ABDO Publishing Co.

Burlingame, Jeff. Aerosmith: Hard Rock Superstars. 2010. (Rebels of Rock Ser.). (Illus.). 112p. (J). (gr. 7-18). pap. 10.95 *(978-1-59845-210-5(X))* Enslow Pubs., Inc.

—Taylor Swift: Music Superstar. 2011. (Hot Celebrity Biographies Ser.). (Illus.). 48p. (J). (gr. 5-18). pap. 8.95 *(978-1-59845-286-0(X))* Enslow Pubs., Inc.

Capaldi, Gina & Pearce, Q. L. Red Bird Sings: The Story of Zitkala-Sa, Native American Author, Musician, & Activist. Capaldi, Gina, illus. 2011. (Exceptional Social Studies Titles for Intermediate Grades). (ENG., Illus.). 32p. (J). (gr. 3-6). lib. bdg. 17.95 *(978-0-7613-5257-0(0))* Lerner Publishing Group.

Carlin, Richard. Folk. 2007. (American Popular Music Ser.). (Illus.). 304p. (gr. 6-12). per. 21.95 *(978-0-8160-7340-5(6),* Checkmark Bks.) Facts On File, Inc.

Chippendale, Lisa A. Yo-Yo Ma: A Cello Superstar Brings Music to the World. 2004. (People to Know Ser.). (Illus.). 112p. (J). lib. bdg. 26.60 *(978-0-7660-2286-7(2))* Enslow Pubs., Inc.

Christensen, Bonnie. Django: World's Greatest Jazz Guitarist. Christensen, Bonnie, illus. 2011. (ENG., Illus.). 32p. (J). (gr. k-4). pap. 8.99 *(978-1-59643-696-1(4),* 9781596436961) Roaring Brook Pr.

Christenson, Maren. Just Like Joan. 2011. 36p. pap. 15.14 *(978-1-4634-3848-7(6))* AuthorHouse.

Cline-Ransome, Lesa. Just a Lucky So & So: The Story of Louis Armstrong. Ransome, James E., illus. 2016. (ENG.). 32p. (J). 16.95 *(978-0-8234-3428-2(1))* Holiday Hse., Inc.

Cooke, C. W. & McCormack, Patrick. Pop Star - Fame. 2011. (ENG., Illus.). 96p. (YA). pap. 17.99 *(978-1-4507-4430-0(3))* Bluewater Productions, Inc.

Croft, Malcolm. One Direction in 3D: Unofficial & Unauthorised. 2015. (ENG., Illus.). 48p. (J). (gr. 4). 12.95 *(978-1-78097-564-1(3))* Carlton Bks., Ltd. GBR. Dist: Sterling Publishing Co., Inc.

Currie, Cherie & O'Neill, Tony. Neon Angel: A Memoir of a Runaway. 2010. (ENG.). 368p. 24.99 *(978-0-06-196135-9(3))* HarperCollins Pubs.

Da Coll, Ivar. Azucar! Da Coll, Ivar, illus. 2005. (SPA., Illus.). (J). 14.99 *(978-1-930332-65-2(3))* Lectorum Pubns., Inc.

Dakers, Diane. The Beatles: Leading the British Invasion. 2013. (ENG., Illus.). 112p. (J). pap. *(978-0-7787-1045-5(9))* Crabtree Publishing Co.

Dann, Sarah. Beyonce. 2013. (ENG., Illus.). 32p. (J). pap. *(978-0-7787-0039-5(9))* Crabtree Publishing Co.

Diver, Lucas. Pop Bios, 1 vol. 2014. (Pop Bios Ser.: 6). (ENG.). 24p. (J). (gr. 2-4). lib. bdg. 171.00 *(978-1-62970-723-5(6))* ABDO Publishing Co.

Doeden, Matt. Green Day: Keeping Their Edge. 2006. (Gateway Biographies Ser.). (ENG., Illus.). 48p. (gr. 4-8). lib. bdg. 26.60 *(978-0-8225-6390-7(8),* Lerner Pubns.) Lerner Publishing Group.

Dominguez, Angela. Sing, Don't Cry. Dominguez, Angela, illus. 2017. (ENG., Illus.). 40p. (J). 17.99 *(978-1-62779-839-6(0),* 9781627798396, Holt, Henry & Co. Bks. For Young Readers) Holt, Henry & Co.

Donovan, Sandy. Music & Theater Top Tens. 2014. (Entertainment's Top 10 Ser.). (Illus.). 32p. (J). (gr. 5-8). lib. bdg. 26.60 *(978-1-4677-3843-9(3),* Lerner Pubns.) Lerner Publishing Group.

Earl, C. F. Timbaland. 2012. (J). *(978-1-4222-2554-7(2));* (Illus.). 48p. (gr. 3-4). 19.95 *(978-1-4222-2528-8(3))* Mason Crest.

Edward, Herman. Pink Floyd. 2008. (Pop Rock Ser.). (Illus.). 64p. (YA). (gr. 3-7). lib. bdg. 22.95 *(978-1-4222-0214-2(3))* Mason Crest.

Eggleton, Jill. Up to the Challenge. 2007. (Connectors Ser.). (gr. 2-5). pap. *(978-1-877453-21-2(8))* Global Education Systems Ltd.

Elish, Dan. Louis Armstrong & the Jazz Age. 2005. (Cornerstones of Freedom Ser.). (ENG., Illus.). 48p. (YA). (gr. 4-7). 26.00 *(978-0-516-23629-2(6))* Scholastic Library Publishing.

Ellison, Katie. Who Was Bob Marley? 2017. (Who Was... ? Ser.). lib. bdg. 16.00 ***(978-0-606-40115-9(6))*** Turtleback Bks.

Flynn, Noa. The Who. 2008. (Pop Rock Ser.). (Illus.). 64p. (YA). (gr. 3-7). lib. bdg. 22.95 *(978-1-4222-0196-1(1))* Mason Crest.

Ford, Jeanne Marie. The 12 Most Influential Musicians of All Time. 2018. (ENG.). 32p. (gr. 3-6). 31.35 ***(978-1-63235-411-2(X),*** 12-Story Library) Pr. Room Editions LLC.

Forget, Thomas. The Rolling Stones. (Rock & Roll Hall of Famers Ser.). 112p. (gr. 5-8). 2009. 63.90 *(978-1-60852-478-5(7),* Rosen Reference) 2006. (Illus.). (YA). lib. bdg. 34.60 *(978-0-8239-3644-1(9))* Rosen Publishing Group, Inc., The.

Fyffe, Daniel. Indoor Percussion Ensembles & Drum Corps. 2009. (Team Spirit! Ser.). 64p. (gr. 6-6). 53.00 *(978-1-60853-270-4(4))* Rosen Publishing Group, Inc., The.

Gagne, Tammy. Darius Rucker. 2014. (Illus.). 32p. (J). (gr. 1-4). 25.70 *(978-1-61228-639-6(9))* Mitchell Lane Pubs., Inc.

Gallagher, James. The Beatles. 2008. (Pop Rock Ser.). (Illus.). 64p. (YA). (gr. 4-7). lib. bdg. 22.95 *(978-1-4222-0186-2(4))* Mason Crest.

Galletti, Barbara. A Baltimore Symphony Chorus Retrospective. 2004. (Illus.). 56p. pap. 24.00 *(978-0-9748737-0-1(5))* Galletti, Barbara.

Golio, Gary. Spirit Seeker: John Coltrane's Musical Journey. Gutierrez, Rudy, illus. 2012. (ENG.). 48p. (J). (gr. 5-7). 17.99 *(978-0-547-23994-1(7))* Houghton Mifflin Harcourt Publishing Co.

Greenwood, Mark & Lessac, Frané. Drummer Boy of John John. 2006. (ENG., Illus.). 40p. (J). 18.95 *(978-1-60060-652-6(0))* Lee & Low Bks., Inc.

Gregory, Peter. The Allman Brothers. 2008. (Pop Rock Ser.). (Illus.). 64p. (YA). (gr. 3-7). lib. bdg. 22.95 *(978-1-4222-0188-6(0))* Mason Crest.

—Queen. 2008. (Pop Rock Ser.). (Illus.). 64p. (YA). (gr. 4-7). lib. bdg. 22.95 *(978-1-4222-0193-0(7))* Mason Crest.

Hakit, Ruben. Keith Urban. 2010. (Country Music Stars Ser.). (Illus.). 32p. (J). (gr. 3-8). pap. 10.50 *(978-1-4339-3605-0(4));* lib. bdg. 25.25 *(978-1-4339-3604-3(6))* Stevens, Gareth Publishing LLLP.

Hetrick, Hans. The Rolling Stones: Pushing Rock's Boundaries. 2015. (Legends of Rock Ser.). (ENG., Illus.). 32p. (gr. 3-4). lib. bdg. 27.99 *(978-1-4914-1817-8(6))* Capstone Press of Coughlan Cos.

Hibbert, Clare & Hachette Children's Group. Pop Star - Celeb: Find Out How Your Favorite Pop Stars Made It! 2012. (Celeb Ser.). (Illus.). 32p. (gr. 4-6). lib. bdg. 28.50 *(978-1-59771-333-7(3))* Sea-To-Sea Pubns.

Hill, Susan. The Rolling Stones. (Unseen Archives Ser.). (Illus.). 384p. (YA). 29.95 *(978-0-7525-8971-8(7))* Parragon, Inc.

Hill, Z. B. Usher. 2012. (J). pap. *(978-1-4222-2557-8(7));* (Illus.). 48p. (gr. 3-4). 19.95 *(978-1-4222-2531-8(3))* Mason Crest.

—50 Cent. 2012. (J). pap. *(978-1-4222-2535-6(6));* (Illus.). 48p. (gr. 3-4). 19.95 *(978-1-4222-2509-7(7))* Mason Crest.

Hinman, Bonnie. John Legend. 2009. (Blue Banner Biography Ser.). (Illus.). 32p. (YA). (gr. 4-7). lib. bdg. 25.70 *(978-1-58415-774-8(7))* Mitchell Lane Pubs., Inc.

Hoffmann, Frank. Rhythm & Blues, Rap, & Hip-Hop. 2007. (American Popular Music Ser.). (Illus.). 352p. (gr. 6-12). per. 21.95 *(978-0-8160-7341-2(4),* Checkmark Bks.) Facts On File, Inc.

Holcomb, Mark. The Beach Boys. 2009. (Rock & Roll Hall of Famers Ser.). 112p. (gr. 5-8). 63.90 *(978-1-60852-476-1(0),* Rosen Reference) Rosen Publishing Group, Inc., The.

Hollow, Michele C. Grateful Dead: What a Long, Strange Trip It's Been. 2009. (Rebels of Rock Ser.). (Illus.). 104p. (J). (gr. 5-18). pap. 10.95 *(978-0-7660-3620-8(0));* (gr. 7-12). lib. bdg. 33.27 *(978-0-7660-3028-2(8))* Enslow Pubs., Inc.

Hood, Susan. Ada's Violin: The Story of the Recycled Orchestra of Paraguay. Comport, Sally Wern, illus. 2016. (ENG.). 40p. (J). (gr. -1-3). 17.99 *(978-1-4814-3095-1(5),* Simon & Schuster Bks. For Young Readers) Simon & Schuster Bks. For Young Readers.

—El Violín de Ada (Ada's Violin) La Historia de la Orquesta de Reciclados Del Paraguay. McConnell, Shelley, tr. from ENG. Comport, Sally Wern, illus. 2016. (SPA.). 40p. (J). (gr. -1-3). 17.99 *(978-1-4814-6657-8(7),* Simon & Schuster Bks. For Young Readers) Simon & Schuster Bks. For Young Readers.

Horn, Geoffrey M. Usher. 2005. (Today's Superstars). (Illus.). 32p. (gr. 5-8). lib. bdg. 31.95 *(978-0-8368-4235-7(9))* Stevens, Gareth Publishing LLLP.

Huston, Jennifer L. U2: Changing the World Through Rock 'n' Roll. 2015. (Legends of Rock Ser.). (ENG.). 32p. (gr. 3-4). lib. bdg. 27.99 *(978-1-4914-1818-5(4))* Capstone Press of Coughlan Cos.

Jeffrey, Laura S. Def Leppard: Arena Rock Band. 2010. (Rebels of Rock Ser.). (Illus.). 104p. (J). pap. 10.95 *(978-1-59845-208-2(8));* (gr. 7-12). 33.27 *(978-0-7660-3234-7(5))* Enslow Pubs., Inc.

—Pink Floyd: The Rock Band. 2009. (Rebels of Rock Ser.). (Illus.). 112p. (J). (gr. 7-12). lib. bdg. 33.27 *(978-0-7660-3030-5(X));* (gr. 5-18). pap. 10.95 *(978-0-7660-3622-2(7))* Enslow Pubs., Inc.

Johnson, Robin. The Jonas Brothers. 2010. (Superstars! Ser.). (ENG.). 32p. (J). (gr. 3-6). lib. bdg. *(978-0-7787-7247-7(0))* Crabtree Publishing Co.

—Robert Pattinson. 2010. (Superstars! Ser.). (ENG., Illus.). 32p. (J). pap. *(978-0-7787-7260-6(8))* Crabtree Publishing Co.

Josephson, Judith Pinkerton. Louis Armstrong. 2008. (History Maker Biographies Ser.). (Illus.). 47p. (J). (gr. 3-7). lib. bdg. 26.60 *(978-0-8225-7169-8(2),* Lerner Pubns.) Lerner Publishing Group.

Juzwiak, Rich. Lifehouse. 2009. (Contemporary Musicians & Their Music Ser.). 48p. (gr. 6-6). 53.00 *(978-1-61511-941-7(8))* Rosen Publishing Group, Inc., The.

Kallen, Stuart A. The Beatles. 2011. (Innovators Ser.). (ENG., Illus.). 48p. (gr. 4-8). lib. bdg. 34.60 *(978-0-7377-5868-9(6))* Cengage Gale.

—Bono. (Role Model Entertainers Ser.). (Illus.). 64p. (YA). 2010. (gr. 7-12). 22.95 *(978-1-4222-0499-3(5))* 2007. pap. 9.95 *(978-1-4222-0786-4(2))* Mason Crest.

Kamberg, Mary-Lane. Bono: Fighting World Hunger & Poverty. (Celebrity Activists Ser.). 112p. 2009. (gr. 8-8). 66.50 *(978-1-61511-828-1(4))* 2008. (Illus.). (YA). (gr. 7-12). lib. bdg. 34.60 *(978-1-4042-1760-7(6))* Rosen Publishing Group, Inc., The.

—Bono Fighting World Hunger & Poverty. l.t. ed. 2012. 188p. pap. *(978-1-4596-3374-2(1))* ReadHowYouWant.com, Ltd.

Keedle, Jayne. Jonas Brothers. 2009. (Today's Superstars Ser.). (ENG.). 48p. (J). (gr. 5-8). pap. 14.05 *(978-1-4339-2163-6(4));* lib. bdg. 31.95 *(978-1-4339-1970-1(2))* Stevens, Gareth Publishing LLLP.

Konieczny, Vladimir. Struggling for Perfection: The Story of Glenn Gould. Wysotski, Chrissie, illus. 2009. (Stories of Canada Ser.: 5). (ENG.). 104p. (J). (gr. 4-7). per. 18.99 *(978-1-894917-48-3(0),* Napoleon & Co.) Dundurn CAN. Dist: Ingram Publisher Services.

Kramer, Barbara. Mahalia Jackson: The Voice of Gospel & Civil Rights. 2003. (African-American Biographies Ser.). (Illus.). 128p. (J). lib. bdg. 26.60 *(978-0-7660-2115-0(7))* Enslow Pubs., Inc.

Krohn, Katherine. Michael Jackson: Ultimate Music Legend. 2015. (Gateway Biographies Ser.). (ENG., Illus.). 48p. (gr. 4-8). 34.65 *(978-1-4677-5976-2(7),* Lerner Digital) Lerner Publishing Group.

Krohn, Katherine E. Michael Jackson: Ultimate Music Legend. 2010. (Gateway Biographies Ser.). (ENG., Illus.). 48p. (gr. 4-8). lib. bdg. 26.60 *(978-0-7613-5762-9(9),* Lerner Pubns.) Lerner Publishing Group.

Krull, Kathleen. Lives of the Musicians: Good Times, Bad Times (and What the Neighbors Thought) Hewitt, Kathryn, illus. 2013. (Lives Of ... Ser.). (ENG.). 96p. (J). (gr. 5-7). pap. 8.99 *(978-0-544-23806-0(0))* Houghton Mifflin Harcourt Publishing Co.

La Bella, Laura. My Chemical Romance. 2009. (Contemporary Musicians & Their Music Ser.). 48p. (gr. 6-6). 53.00 *(978-1-61511-943-1(4))* Rosen Publishing Group, Inc., The.

Lajiness, Katie. One Direction, 1 vol. 2016. (Big Buddy Pop Biographies Ser.). (ENG., Illus.). 32p. (J). (gr. 2-5). lib. bdg. 28.50 *(978-1-68078-056-7(5),* Big Buddy Bks.) ABDO Publishing Co.

—5 Seconds of Summer, 1 vol. 2016. (Big Buddy Pop Biographies Ser.). (ENG., Illus.). 32p. (J). (gr. 2-5). lib. bdg. 28.50 *(978-1-68078-052-9(2),* Big Buddy Bks.) ABDO Publishing Co.

Leavitt, Amie Jane. Keith Urban. 2007. (Blue Banner Biography Ser.). (Illus.). 32p. (YA). (gr. 4-7). lib. bdg. 25.70 *(978-1-58415-619-2(8))* Mitchell Lane Pubs., Inc.

—What It's Like to Be the Jonas Brothers: Que Se Siente Al Ser Los Hermanos Jonas. Vega, Eida de la, tr. 2009. (What It's Like to Be/Que se Siente al Ser Ser.). (SPA & ENG., Illus.). 32p. (J). (gr. -1-2). 25.70 *(978-1-58415-842-4(5))* Mitchell Lane Pubs., Inc.

Liebman, Daniel & Liebman, Dan. I Want to Be a Musician. 2003. (I Want to Be Ser.). (ENG., Illus.). 24p. (J). (gr. -1-2). 14.95 *(978-1-55297-760-6(9),* 9781552977606); pap. 3.99 *(978-1-55297-759-0(5),* 9781552977590) Firefly Bks., Ltd.

—Quiero Ser Musico. 2003. (Quiero Ser.). (ENG & SPA., Illus.). 24p. (J). (gr. -1-2). pap. 5.99 *(978-1-55297-761-3(7),* 9781552977613) Firefly Bks., Ltd.

Loh-Hagan, Virginia. Band. 2016. (Illus.). 32p. (J). *(978-1-63470-498-4(3))* Cherry Lake Publishing.

Lommel, Cookie. Russell Simmons. 2007. (Hip-Hop Stars Ser.). (Illus.). 104p. (YA). (gr. 7-12). lib. bdg. 30.00 *(978-0-7910-9467-9(7))* Facts On File, Inc.

Lord, Michelle. A Song for Cambodia, 1 vol. Arihara, Shino, illus. 2008. (ENG.). 32p. (J). (gr. 1-6). 16.95 *(978-1-60060-139-2(1))* Lee & Low Bks., Inc.

Lord, Raymond. Usher. 2008. (Hip-Hop Ser.). (Illus.). 64p. (YA). (gr. 7-12). lib. bdg. 22.95 *(978-1-4222-0131-2(7))* Mason Crest.

Louie, Ai-Ling. Yo-Yo & Yeou-Cheng Ma, Finding Their Way: Amazing Asian Americans. Peng, Cathy, illus. 2012. (Biographies of Amazing Asian Americans Ser.: 2). (ENG.). 48p. (J). pap. 16.99 *(978-0-9787465-0-6(3))* Dragoneagle Pr.

Lusted, Marcia Amidon. One Direction: Breakout Boy Band. 2012. (Pop Culture Bios Ser.). (ENG., Illus.). 32p. (gr. 3-6). pap. 7.95 *(978-1-4677-0879-1(8));* lib. bdg. 26.60 *(978-1-4677-0877-7(1))* Lerner Publishing Group.

Markel, Rita J. & Poole, Rebecca. Jimi Hendrix. 2006. (Just the Facts Biographies Ser.). (ENG., Illus.). 112p. (gr. 5-12). 27.93 *(978-0-8225-3532-4(7),* Lerner Pubns.) Lerner Publishing Group.

Marlowe, Christie. Dj. 2013. (Earning $50,000 - $100,000 with a High School Diploma or Less Ser.: 14). 64p. (J). (gr. 7-18). 22.95 *(978-1-4222-2892-0(4))* Mason Crest.

Mattern, Joanne. Jonas Brothers. 2008. (Robbie Reader Ser.). (Illus.). 32p. (YA). (gr. 2-5). lib. bdg. 25.70 *(978-1-58415-721-2(6))* Mitchell Lane Pubs., Inc.

—Selena. 2011. (Blue Banner Biography Ser.). (Illus.). 32p. (YA). (gr. 4-7). lib. bdg. 25.70 *(978-1-61228-054-7(4))* Mitchell Lane Pubs., Inc.

Matthews, Sheelagh. Bono. 2007. (Remarkable People Ser.). (Illus.). 24p. (J). (gr. 3-7). pap. 8.95 *(978-1-59036-638-7(7));* lib. bdg. 24.45 *(978-1-59036-637-0(9))* Weigl Pubs., Inc.

McDonough, Yona Zeldis. Who Was Louis Armstrong? O'Brien, John A. & Harrison, Nancy, illus. 2004. (Who Was? Ser.). (ENG.). 112p. (J). (gr. 3-7). pap. 5.99 *(978-0-448-43368-4(0),* Grosset & Dunlap) Penguin Young Readers Group.

Medina, Tony. I & I: Bob Marley. Watson, Jesse Joshua, illus. 2009. (ENG.). 48p. (J). (gr. 3-6). 19.95 *(978-1-60060-257-3(6))* Lee & Low Bks., Inc.

Megastars, 6 vols., Set. Incl. Jonas Brothers. Orr, Tamra. 29.25 *(978-1-4358-3572-6(7),* Rosen Reference); Lady Gaga. Heos, Bridget. lib. bdg. 29.25 *(978-1-4358-3574-0(3));* Miley Cyrus. Bailey, Diane. lib. bdg. 29.25 *(978-1-4358-3573-3(5),* Rosen Reference); Pink. Sirota, Lyn. 29.25 *(978-1-4358-3577-1(8),* Rosen Reference); Rihanna. Heos, Bridget. lib. bdg. 29.25 *(978-1-4358-3576-4(X));* Taylor Swift. Cefrey, Holly. 29.25 *(978-1-4358-3575-7(1),* Rosen Reference); (YA). (gr. 5-8). 2011. (Megastars Ser.). (Illus.). 48p. 2011. Set lib. bdg. 159.00 *(978-1-4358-9418-1(9),* Rosen Reference) Rosen Publishing Group, Inc., The.

Micklos, John. Elvis Presley: "I Want to Entertain People" 2010. (American Rebels Ser.). 160p. (YA). (gr. 7-12). 35.94 *(978-0-7660-3382-5(1))* Enslow Pubs., Inc.

Milet Publishing Staff. Music. 2012. (My First Bilingual Book Ser.). (ENG & CHI., Illus.). 24p. (J). (gr. k — 1). bds. 7.99 *(978-1-84059-718-9(6));* bds. 7.99 *(978-1-84059-716-5(X))* Milet Publishing.

—Music - English-Spanish. 2012. (My First Bilingual Book Ser.). (SPA & ENG., Illus.). 24p. (J). (gr. k — 1). bds. 7.99 *(978-1-84059-728-8(3))* Milet Publishing.

—Music - My First Bilingual Book. 2012. (My First Bilingual Book Ser.). (ENG & POR., Illus.). 24p. (J). (gr. k — 1). bds. 7.99 *(978-1-84059-725-7(9));* bds. 7.99 *(978-1-84059-722-6(4))* Milet Publishing.

—La Musique. 2012. (My First Bilingual Book Ser.).Tr. of Music. (FRE & ENG., Illus.). 24p. (J). (gr. k — 1). bds. 7.99 *(978-1-84059-720-2(8))* Milet Publishing.

—My First Bilingual Book-Music. 2012. (My First Bilingual Book Ser.). (ENG & BEN., Illus.). 24p. (J). (gr. k — 1). bds. 7.99 *(978-1-84059-717-2(8))* Milet Publishing.

—My First Bilingual Book-Music (English-Farsi) 2012. (My First Bilingual Book Ser.). (ENG & PER., Illus.). 24p. (J). (gr. k — 1). bds. 7.99 *(978-1-84059-719-6(4))* Milet Publishing.

—My First Bilingual Book-Music (English-German) 2012. (My First Bilingual Book Ser.). (ENG & GER., Illus.). 24p. (J). (gr. k — 1). bds. 7.99 *(978-1-84059-721-9(6))* Milet Publishing.

—My First Bilingual Book-Music (English-Korean) 2012. (My First Bilingual Book Ser.). (ENG & KOR., Illus.). 24p. (J). (gr. k — 1). bds. 7.99 *(978-1-84059-723-3(2))* Milet Publishing.

—My First Bilingual Book-Music (English-Russian) 2012. (My First Bilingual Book Ser.). (ENG & RUS., Illus.). 24p. (J). (gr. k — 1). bds. 7.99 *(978-1-84059-726-4(7))* Milet Publishing.

—My First Bilingual Book-Music (English-Somali) 2012. (My First Bilingual Book Ser.). (ENG & SOM., Illus.). 24p. (J). (gr. k — 1). bds. 7.99 *(978-1-84059-727-1(5))* Milet Publishing.

—My First Bilingual Book-Music (English-Turkish) 2012. (My First Bilingual Book Ser.). (ENG & TUR., Illus.). 24p. (J). (gr. k — 1). bds. 7.99 *(978-1-84059-729-5(1))* Milet Publishing.

—My First Bilingual Book-Music (English-Urdu) 2012. (My First Bilingual Book Ser.). (ENG & URD., Illus.). 24p. (J). (gr. k — 1). bds. 7.99 *(978-1-84059-730-1(5))* Milet Publishing.

—My First Bilingual Book-Music (English-Vietnamese) 2012. (My First Bilingual Book Ser.). (ENG & VIE., Illus.). 24p. (J). (gr. k — 1). bds. 7.99 *(978-1-84059-731-8(3))* Milet Publishing.

Miller, Calvin Craig. Reggae Poet: The Story of Bob Marley. 2007. (Modern Music Masters Ser.). (Illus.). 128p. (YA). (gr.

9-18). lib. bdg. 27.95 *(978-1-59935-071-4(8))* Reynolds, Morgan Inc.

Miller, Heather. AC/DC: Hard Rock Band. 2009. (Rebels of Rock Ser.). (Illus.). 104p. (J). (gr. 5-18). pap. 10.95 *(978-0-7660-3623-9(5))*; (gr. 7-12). lib. bdg. 33.27 *(978-0-7660-3031-2(8))* Enslow Pubs., Inc.

—The Rolling Stones: The Greatest Rock Band. 2010. (Rebels of Rock Ser.). (Illus.). 112p. (J). pap. 10.95 *(978-1-59845-209-9(6))*; (gr. 7-12). 33.27 *(978-0-7660-3231-6(0))* Enslow Pubs., Inc.

Miller, Kat. I Love the Jonas Brothers. 2010. (Fan Club Ser.). (ENG.). 24p. (J). (gr. 3-6). lib. bdg. 22.60 *(978-1-61533-048-5(8))*; (Illus.). pap. 8.15 *(978-1-61533-049-2(6))* Windmill Bks.

Mitchell Lane Publishers Inc. Staff. Blue Banner Biographies-Child Stars. 2004. (Blue Banner Biography Ser.). (Illus.). (J). (gr. 3-8). lib. bdg. 179.90 *(978-1-58415-354-2(7))* Mitchell Lane Pubs., Inc.

—Masters of Music: The World's Greatest Composers, 24 vols., Set. 2003. (Illus.). (gr. 4-8). lib. bdg. 502.80 *(978-1-58415-318-4(0))* Mitchell Lane Pubs., Inc.

Mitchells, Brett. Dixie Chicks. 2009. (Contemporary Musicians & Their Music Ser.). 48p. (gr. 6-6). 53.00 *(978-1-61511-932-5(9))* Rosen Publishing Group, Inc., The.

Mooney, Melissa Duke & Print Mafia Staff. The ABCs of Rock. 2010. (ENG., Illus.). 32p. (J). (gr. k-12). 16.99 *(978-1-58246-293-6(3)*, Tricycle Pr.) Random Hse. Children's Bks.

Morreale, Marie. One Direction. 2014. (ENG.). 48p. (J). pap. 7.95 *(978-0-531-21271-4(8))*; lib. bdg. 29.00 *(978-0-531-21196-0(7))* Scholastic Library Publishing.

—Taylor Swift: Born to Sing! 2017. (Rookie Biographies(tm) Ser.). (ENG., Illus.). 32p. (J). lib. bdg. 25.00 *(978-0-531-22292-8(6)*, Children's Pr.) Scholastic Library Publishing.

—5 Seconds of Summer. 2015. (Real Bios Ser.). (ENG., Illus.). 48p. (J). pap. 7.95 *(978-0-531-21662-0(4)*, Children's Pr.) Scholastic Library Publishing.

Mour, Stanley I. Innovators of American Jazz. 2013. (Inspiring Collective Biographies Ser.). 112p. (J). (gr. 5-12). pap. 10.95 *(978-1-4644-0271-5(X))* Enslow Pubs., Inc.

Murphy, Maggie. The Jonas Brothers: Rock Stars. 2010. (Young & Famous Ser.). (ENG.). 24p. (J). (gr. 3-6). lib. bdg. 22.60 *(978-1-4488-0646-1(1))* Rosen Publishing Group, Inc., The.

—Taylor Swift: Country Music Star. 2010. (Young & Famous Ser.). (ENG.). 24p. (J). (gr. 3-6). lib. bdg. 22.60 *(978-1-4488-0645-4(3))* Rosen Publishing Group, Inc., The.

Nagle, Jeanne & Chippendale, Lisa A. Yo-Yo Ma: Grammy Award-Winning Cellist. 2016. (Influential Asians Ser.). 128p. (J). (gr. 7-6). 37.27 *(978-0-7660-7899-4(X))* Enslow Pubs., Inc.

Napoli, Tony. Justin Timberlake: Breakout Music Superstar. 2009. (Hot Celebrity Biographies Ser.). (Illus.). 48p. (J). (gr. 5-9). lib. bdg. 25.27 *(978-0-7660-3566-9(2))* Enslow Pubs., Inc.

Neimark, Anne E. Johnny Cash: A Twentieth-Century Life. 2007. (Up Close Ser.). (Illus.). 207p. (J). *(978-1-4287-3958-1(0)*, Viking Adult) Penguin Publishing Group.

Newkey-Burden, Chas. One Way Street: One Direction: The Story of Britain's Biggest Boy Band. 2012. (ENG.). 96p. (YA). (gr. 8-12). pap. *(978-1-907823-28-2(X))* Grange Communications Ltd.

Niver, Heather Moore. Taylor Swift: Singer & Songwriter. 2017. (J). pap. ***(978-0-7660-9057-6(4))*** Enslow Pubs., Inc.

O'Keefe, Sherry. Spin: The Story of Michael Jackson. 2011. (Modern Music Masters Ser.). (Illus.). 144p. (YA). (gr. 6-9). 28.95 *(978-1-59935-134-6(X))* Reynolds, Morgan Inc.

O'Mahony, John. Elton John. 2003. (World Musicmakers Ser.). (Illus.). 64p. (J). 26.20 *(978-1-56711-972-5(7)*, Blackbirch Pr., Inc.) Cengage Gale.

One Direction. One Direction: Where We Are - Our Band, Our Story - 100% Official. 2013. (Illus.). 288p. (J). (gr. 3-7). 21.99 *(978-0-06-221904-6(9))* HarperCollins Pubs.

—Who We Are: One Direction: Our Autobiography. 2014. (ENG., Illus.). 352p. 21.99 *(978-0-00-757731-6(1))* HarperCollins Pubs.

One Direction Staff. One Direction: A Year with One Direction. 2013. 64p. (J). (gr. 3-7). pap. 10.99 *(978-0-06-222317-3(8)*, HarperFestival) HarperCollins Pubs.

—One Direction: Meet One Direction. 2013. (Illus.). 64p. (J). (gr. 3-7). pap. 10.99 *(978-0-06-228362-7(6))* HarperCollins Pubs.

—One Direction: Where We Are: Our Band, Our Story: 100% Official. 2015. 288p. (J). (gr. 3-7). pap. 12.99 *(978-0-06-221905-3(7))* HarperCollins Pubs.

O'Shea, Mick. One Direction: No Limits. 2012. (ENG., Illus.). 128p. (gr. 3). pap. 12.95 *(978-0-85965-493-7(1))* Plexus Publishing, Ltd. GBR. Dist: Publishers Group West (PGW).

Parks, Peggy J. Musician. 2003. (Illus.). 48p. (J). 26.20 *(978-0-7377-2067-9(0)*, Greenhaven Pr., Inc.) Cengage Gale.

Patrick, James. Legend of the Delta Blues. 2010. (Inspiring Lives Ser.). 32p. (J). (gr. 5-8). lib. bdg. 25.25 *(978-1-4339-3619-7(4))*; (Illus.). pap. 10.50 *(978-1-4339-3620-3(8))* Stevens, Gareth Publishing LLLP.

Patton, Julie. Maximizing Your Studio's Potential: the Student Log Book: Skill Assessment & Progress Management Tools for the College-Level Musician. 2004. 200p. (C). stu. ed., spiral bd. 24.95 *(978-0-9762902-0-9(0))* Purple Lizard Pr. LLC.

Peppas, Lynn. M. I. A. 2010. (Superstars! Ser.). (ENG., Illus.). 32p. (J). (gr. 3-6). lib. bdg. *(978-0-7787-7249-1(7))* Crabtree Publishing Co.

—One Direction. 2013. (ENG., Illus.). 32p. (J). *(978-0-7787-1049-3(1))*; pap. *(978-0-7787-1053-0(X))* Crabtree Publishing Co.

Polark, Kelly. Rockabet: Classic Edition. Little, Kelli Ann, illus. 2013. 32p. pap. 10.49 *(978-0-9888462-0-3(9))* Big Smile Pr., LLC.

Polydoros, Lori, et al. The Best of the Best. 2012. (Best of the Best Ser.). (ENG.). 32p. (gr. 1-2). lib. bdg. 53.30 *(978-1-4296-9135-2(2)*, Blazers) Capstone Press of Coughlan Cos.

Pop Rock: Popular Rock Superstars of Yesterday & Today, 17 vols., Set. Incl. AC/DC. Schlesinger, Ethan. (gr. 3-7). lib. bdg. 22.95 *(978-1-4222-0183-1(X))*; Aerosmith. Schlesinger, Ethan. (gr. 3-7). lib. bdg. 22.95 *(978-1-4222-0184-8(8))*; Allman Brothers. Gregory, Peter. (gr. 3-7). lib. bdg. 22.95 *(978-1-4222-0188-6(0))*; Beatles. Gallagher, James. (gr. 4-7). lib. bdg. 22.95 *(978-1-4222-0186-2(4))*; Billy Joel. Schlesinger, Ethan. (gr. 3-7). lib. bdg. 22.95 *(978-1-4222-0185-5(6))*; Bob Marley & the Wailers. Waters, Rosa. (gr. 7-18). lib. bdg. 22.95 *(978-1-4222-0192-3(9))*; Bruce Springsteen. Simons, Rae. (gr. 4-7). lib. bdg. 22.95 *(978-1-4222-0187-9(2))*; Doors. Simons, Rae. (gr. 3-7). lib. bdg. 22.95 *(978-1-4222-0190-9(2))*; Elton John. Schlesinger, Ethan. (gr. 3-7). lib. bdg. 22.95 *(978-1-4222-0189-3(9))*; Grateful Dead. McIntosh, Kenneth. (gr. 4-7). lib. bdg. 22.95 *(978-1-4222-0191-6(0))*; Led Zeppelin. Schlesinger, Ethan. (gr. 3-7). lib. bdg. 22.95 *(978-1-4222-0212-8(7))*; Lynyrd Skynrd. Walker, Ida. (gr. 4-7). lib. bdg. 22.95 *(978-1-4222-0213-5(5))*; Pink Floyd. Edward, Herman. (gr. 3-7). lib. bdg. 22.95 *(978-1-4222-0214-2(3))*; Queen. Gregory, Peter. (gr. 4-7). lib. bdg. 22.95 *(978-1-4222-0193-0(7))*; Rolling Stones. Schlesinger, Ethan. (gr. 3-7). lib. bdg. 22.95 *(978-1-4222-0194-7(5))*; Who. Flynn, Noa. (gr. 3-7). lib. bdg. 22.95 *(978-1-4222-0196-1(1))*; (Illus.). 64p. (YA). 2008. 2007. Set lib. bdg. 390.15 *(978-1-4222-0182-4(1))* Mason Crest.

Pratt, Mary K. Michael Jackson: King of Pop, 1 vol. (Lives Cut Short Set 1 Ser.). 2010. (ENG.). 112p. (J). (gr. 6-12). lib. bdg. 35.64 *(978-1-60453-788-8(4))* 2011. (YA). (gr. 7-12). 71.36 *(978-1-61641-447-4(2)*, Essential Library) ABDO Publishing Co.

Rappaport, Doreen. John's Secret Dreams: The Life of John Lennon. Collier, Bryan, illus. 2016. (Big Words Ser.). (ENG.). 48p. (J). (gr. 1-3). pap. 8.99 *(978-1-4847-4962-3(6))* Hyperion Bks. for Children.

Raschka, Chris. Mysterious Thelonious. Raschka, Chris, illus. (Illus.). pap. 18.95 incl. audio compact disk *(978-1-59112-421-4(2))* Live Oak Media.

Rawson, Katherine. The Jonas Brothers. (J). 2010. pap. 9.40 *(978-1-4358-3402-6(X))* 2009. (Illus.). 24p. lib. bdg. 22.60 *(978-1-4042-8134-9(7))* Rosen Publishing Group, Inc., The.

—Taylor Swift. (J). 2010. pap. 9.40 *(978-1-4358-3410-1(0))* 2009. (Illus.). 24p. lib. bdg. 22.60 *(978-1-4042-8138-7(X))* Rosen Publishing Group, Inc., The. (PowerKids Pr.).

Reisfeld, Randi. This Is the Sound: The Best of Alternative Rock. 2011. (ENG.). 144p. (YA). (gr. 9). pap. 8.99 *(978-1-4424-3098-3(2)*, Simon Pulse) Simon Pulse.

Richards, Keith. Gus & Me: The Story of My Granddad & My First Guitar. Richards, Theodora, illus. 2014. (ENG.). 32p. (J). (gr. -1-1). 18.00 *(978-0-316-32065-8(X))* Little, Brown Bks. for Young Readers.

Robertson, Robbie, et al. Legends, Icons & Rebels: Music That Changed the World. (ENG., Illus.). (J). (gr. 4-7). 2016. 128p. pap. 18.99 *(978-1-101-91868-5(3))* 2013. 130p. 29.00 *(978-1-77049-571-5(1))* Tundra Bks. CAN. (Tundra Bks.). Dist: Penguin Random Hse. LLC.

Robertson, Sebastian. Rock & Roll Highway: The Robbie Robertson Story. Gustavson, Adam, illus. 2014. (ENG.). 40p. (J). (gr. 1-4). 17.99 *(978-0-8050-9473-2(3)*, 9780805094732, Holt, Henry & Co. Bks. For Young Readers) Holt, Henry & Co.

Robson, David. Prince: Singer-Songwriter, Musician, & Record Producer. (Transcending Race in America Ser.). 64p. (YA). 2010. (Illus.). (gr. 4-8). lib. bdg. 22.95 *(978-1-4222-1614-9(4))* 2009. (gr. 5-18). pap. 9.95 *(978-1-4222-1628-6(4))* Mason Crest.

Rock & Roll Hall of Famers: Set 2, 6 bks. Incl. Aretha Franklin. Rivera, Ursula. lib. bdg. 34.60 *(978-0-8239-3639-7(2))*; Beach Boys. Holcomb, Mark. lib. bdg. 34.60 *(978-0-8239-3643-4(0))*; Billie Holiday. Alagna, Magdalena. lib. bdg. 34.60 *(978-0-8239-3640-3(6))*; Elton John. White, Katherine. lib. bdg. 34.60 *(978-0-8239-3641-0(4))*; Rolling Stones. Forget, Thomas. lib. bdg. 34.60 *(978-0-8239-3644-1(9))*; (YA). (gr. 5-8). (Illus.). 112p. 2006. Set lib. bdg. 175.50 *(978-0-8239-3888-9(3))* Rosen Publishing Group, Inc., The.

Rosen, Steven & Steventon, John. History of Rock. 2009. (Crabtree Contact Ser.). (ENG., Illus.). 32p. (J). (gr. 6-8). pap. *(978-0-7787-3844-2(2))*; lib. bdg. *(978-0-7787-3823-7(X))* Crabtree Publishing Co.

Rubin, Susan Goldman. Music Was IT: Young Leonard Bernstein. 2015. (ENG., Illus.). 192p. (J). (gr. 4-7). pap. 12.95 *(978-1-58089-345-9(7))* Charlesbridge Publishing, Inc.

Saddleback Educational Publishing Staff. Jay-Z. 2013. (Hip-Hop Biographies (Saddleback Publishing) Ser.). (YA). lib. bdg. 23.25 *(978-0-606-31484-8(9)*, Turtleback) Turtleback Bks.

—Nicki Minaj. 2013. (Hip-Hop Biographies (Saddleback Publishing) Ser.). (YA). lib. bdg. 23.25 *(978-0-606-31487-9(3)*, Turtleback) Turtleback Bks.

—Pitbull. 2013. (Hip-Hop Biographies (Saddleback Publishing) Ser.). (YA). lib. bdg. 23.25 *(978-0-606-31488-6(1)*, Turtleback) Turtleback Bks.

Saddleback Educational Publishing Staff, ed. The Beatles, 1 vol. unabr. ed. 2008. (Graphic Biographies Ser.). (ENG., Illus.). 25p. (YA). (gr. 9-12). pap. 7.95 *(978-1-59905-216-8(4))* Saddleback Educational Publishing, Inc.

Sandler, Martin W. How the Beatles Changed the World. 2014. (ENG., Illus.). 176p. (J). (gr. 5-8). 20.99 *(978-0-8027-3565-2(7)*, 9780802735652, Bloomsbury USA Childrens) Bloomsbury Publishing USA.

Saucerman, Linda. Ozzy & Kelly Osbourne. 2004. (Famous Families Ser.). (Illus.). 48p. (J). lib. bdg. 29.25 *(978-1-4042-0262-7(5))* Rosen Publishing Group, Inc., The.

—Ozzy Osbourne & Kelly Osbourne. 2009. (Famous Families Ser.). 48p. (gr. 5-5). 53.00 *(978-1-61512-509-8(4))* Rosen Publishing Group, Inc., The.

Saulmon, Greg. Linkin Park. 2009. (Contemporary Musicians & Their Music Ser.). 48p. (gr. 6-6). 53.00 *(978-1-61511-942-4(6))* Rosen Publishing Group, Inc., The.

Schilling, Vincent. Native Musicians in the Groove, 1 vol. 2009. (Native Trailblazers Ser.). (ENG.). 132p. (YA). (gr. 5-10). pap. 9.95 *(978-0-9779183-4-8(3)*, 7th Generation) Book Publishing Co.

Schlesinger, Ethan. Billy Joel. (Pop Rock Ser.). (Illus.). 64p. (YA). (gr. 3-7). 2008. lib. bdg. 22.95 *(978-1-4222-0185-5(6))* 2007. pap. 7.95 *(978-1-4222-0315-6(8))* Mason Crest.

—Led Zeppelin. 2007. (Popular Rock Superstars of Yesterday & Today Ser.). (Illus.). 64p. (YA). (gr. 3-7). pap. 7.95 *(978-1-4222-0324-8(7))* Mason Crest.

—The Rolling Stones. 2008. (Pop Rock Ser.). (Illus.). 64p. (YA). (gr. 3-7). lib. bdg. 22.95 *(978-1-4222-0194-7(5))* Mason Crest.

Schlessinger Media Staff, prod. My Family from Japan. 2003. (Families Around the World Ser.). (J). (gr. k-4). pap., tchr. ed. 19.95 incl. VHS *(978-1-57225-644-6(3))* Schlessinger Media.

Schuman, Michael A. Bob Dylan: The Life & Times of an American Icon. 2003. (People to Know Ser.). (Illus.). 112p. (J). lib. bdg. 26.60 *(978-0-7660-2108-2(4))* Enslow Pubs., Inc.

—Led Zeppelin: Legendary Rock Band. 2009. (Rebels of Rock Ser.). (Illus.). 112p. (J). (gr. 7-12). lib. bdg. 33.27 *(978-0-7660-3026-8(1))* Enslow Pubs., Inc.

Schwartz, Heather. Little Mix: Singers with X-Tra Success. 2014. (Pop Culture Bios Ser.). (Illus.). 32p. (J). (gr. 3-6). lib. bdg. 26.60 *(978-1-4677-3668-8(6)*, Lerner Pubns.) Lerner Publishing Group.

Schwartz, Heather E. Justin Timberlake: From Mouseketeer to Megastar. 2015. (Pop Culture Bios Ser.). (ENG., Illus.). 32p. (J). (gr. 3-6). lib. bdg. 26.60 *(978-1-4677-5715-7(2)*, Lerner Pubns.) Lerner Publishing Group.

—Taylor Swift, 1 vol. 2012. (Star Biographies Ser.). (ENG., Illus.). 32p. (gr. 3-4). lib. bdg. 27.99 *(978-1-4296-4758-8(2)*, Snap Bks.) Capstone Press of Coughlan Cos.

—The Wanted: British Boy Band Sensation. 2013. (Pop Culture Bios Ser.). (ENG., Illus.). 32p. (J). (gr. 3-6). pap. 7.95 *(978-1-4677-1548-5(4))*; lib. bdg. 26.60 *(978-1-4677-1307-8(4)*, Lerner Pubns.) Lerner Publishing Group.

Shea, Mary Molly. Taylor Swift. 2010. (Country Music Stars Ser.). (Illus.). 32p. (J). (gr. 3-8). pap. 10.50 *(978-1-4339-3611-1(9))*; lib. bdg. 25.25 *(978-1-4339-3610-4(0))* Stevens, Gareth Publishing LLLP.

Shea, Therese. John Lee Hooker: King of the Blues. 2010. (Inspiring Lives Ser.). 32p. (J). (gr. 5-8). lib. bdg. 25.25 *(978-1-4339-3625-8(9))*; (Illus.). pap. 10.50 *(978-1-4339-3626-5(7))* Stevens, Gareth Publishing LLLP.

Sierra i Fabra, Jordi. John Lennon - Imagina que esto fue Real. 2005. (SPA.). 168p. (YA). *(978-958-30-1702-5(7))* Panamericana Editorial.

Simons, Rae. Bruce Springsteen. (Pop Rock Ser.). (Illus.). 64p. (YA). (gr. 4-7). 2008. lib. bdg. 22.95 *(978-1-4222-0187-9(2))* 2007. pap. 7.95 *(978-1-4222-0321-7(2))* Mason Crest.

—The Doors. 2008. (Pop Rock Ser.). (Illus.). 64p. (YA). (gr. 3-7). lib. bdg. 22.95 *(978-1-4222-0190-9(2))* Mason Crest.

Slavicek, Louise Chipley. Carlos Santana. 2006. (Great Hispanic Heritage Ser.). (Illus.). 112p. (gr. 6-12). lib. bdg. 35.00 *(978-0-7910-8844-9(8)*, Chelsea Hse.) Facts On File, Inc.

Sloate, Susan. Ray Charles: Find Another Way! 2006. (Defining Moments Ser.). (Illus.). 32p. (J). (gr. 2-5). lib. bdg. 25.27 *(978-1-59716-267-8(1))* Bearport Publishing Co., Inc.

Smith Weber, Terri. Dixie Chicks. 2004. (J). pap. *(978-0-9740180-9-6(0)*, Bios for Kids) Panda Publishing, L.L.C.

Sooner, Jeffrey. Rascal Flatts. 2010. (Country Music Stars Ser.). (Illus.). 32p. (J). (gr. 3-8). pap. 10.50 *(978-1-4339-3617-3(8))*; lib. bdg. 25.25 *(978-1-4339-3616-6(X)*, 1309366) Stevens, Gareth Publishing LLLP.

Spencer, Liv. Taylor Swift: Every Day Is a Fairytale - The Unofficial Story. 2010. (ENG., Illus.). 155p. (YA). (gr. 7-18). pap. *(978-1-55022-931-8(1))* Filmer Ltd.

Stark, William N., et al. Legends of Rock. 2015. (Legends of Rock Ser.). (ENG.). 32p. (gr. 3-4). lib. bdg. 111.96 *(978-1-4914-1819-2(2)*, Edge Bks.) Capstone Press of Coughlan Cos.

Steventon, John. DJing. 2009. (Crabtree Contact Ser.). (ENG., Illus.). 32p. (J). (gr. 6-8). pap. *(978-0-7787-3840-4(X))*; lib. bdg. *(978-0-7787-3819-0(1))* Crabtree Publishing Co.

Stewart, Mark. Music Legends. 2009. (Ultimate 10: Entertainment Ser.). (ENG.). 48p. (J). (gr. 4-8). pap. 10.50 *(978-1-4339-2213-8(4))*; (YA). (gr. 5-9). lib. bdg. 31.00 *(978-0-8368-9165-2(1))* Stevens, Gareth Publishing LLLP.

Subset 2: Masters of Music. (Illus.). 9p. (gr. 4-8). lib. bdg. *(978-1-58415-352-8(0))* Mitchell Lane Pubs., Inc.

Summerer, Eric Michael. Wolfgang Amadeus Mozart. 2006. (Primary Source Library of Famous Composers). (Illus.). 32p. (J). (gr. -1-3). lib. bdg. 21.25 *(978-1-4042-2772-9(5)*, PowerKids Pr.) Rosen Publishing Group, Inc., The.

Sutoski, Jennifer. Hedley. 2015. (Canadian Biographies Ser.). (ENG., Illus.). 24p. (gr. k-1). lib. bdg. 26.65 *(978-1-4914-7837-0(3)*, Pebble Plus) Capstone Press of Coughlan Cos.

Thomson, Cindy. Kenny Chesney. 2009. (Sharing the American Dream Ser.). 64p. (YA). (gr. 7-12). 22.95 *(978-1-4222-0594-5(0))* Mason Crest.

Tieck, Sarah. Daft Punk: Electronic Music Duo, 1 vol. 2014. (Big Buddy Biographies Set 12 Ser.). (ENG.). 32p. (J). (gr. 2-5). 28.50 *(978-1-62403-567-8(1))* ABDO Publishing Co.

—Jonas Brothers CD & Book. 2010. (Big Buddy Biographies CD+Book Ser.). 32p. (gr. 2-5). audio compact disk 57.00 *(978-1-61613-308-5(2)*, Big Buddy Bks.) ABDO Publishing Co.

—Jonas Brothers Site CD & Book. 2010. (Big Buddy Biographies Site CD+Book Ser.). 32p. (gr. 2-5). cd-rom 85.57 *(978-1-61613-280-4(9)*, Big Buddy Bks.) ABDO Publishing Co.

—Kacey Musgraves: Country Music Star, 1 vol. 2014. (Big Buddy Biographies Set 12 Ser.). (ENG.). 32p. (gr. 2-5). 28.50 *(978-1-62403-571-5(X))* ABDO Publishing Co.

—Michael Jackson: Music Legend, 1 vol. 2011. (Big Buddy Biographies Set 6 Ser.). (ENG., Illus.). 32p. (J). (gr. 2-5). 28.50 *(978-1-61714-703-6(6))* ABDO Publishing Co.

—Miranda Lambert: Country Music Star, 1 vol. 2011. (Big Buddy Biographies Set 7 Ser.). (ENG., Illus.). 32p. (J). (gr. 2-5). 28.50 *(978-1-61783-018-1(6))* ABDO Publishing Co.

—One Direction: Popular Boy Band, 1 vol. 2013. (Big Buddy Biographies Set 9 Ser.). (ENG.). 32p. (J). (gr. 2-5). lib. bdg. 28.50 *(978-1-61783-752-4(0)*, Big Buddy Bks.) ABDO Publishing Co.

—Taylor Swift: Country Music Star Site CD & Book. 2010. (Big Buddy Biographies Site CD+Book Ser.). 32p. (gr. 2-5). cd-rom 85.57 *(978-1-61613-283-5(3)*, Big Buddy Bks.) ABDO Publishing Co.

Tierney, Tom. Rock & Roll Legends of the 1950s Paper Dolls. 2007. (Dover Celebrity Paper Dolls Ser.). (ENG., Illus.). 32p. (J). (gr. 4-8). pap. 6.95 *(978-0-486-45660-7(9))* Dover Pubns., Inc.

Tougas, Shelley. Girls Rock! Amazing Tales of Women in Music, 1 vol. 2013. (Girls Rock! Ser.). (ENG.). 64p. (gr. 4-5). 34.65 *(978-1-4765-0234-2(X))* Capstone Press of Coughlan Cos.

Tougas, Shelley & Phillips, Jennifer. Girls Rock!, 1 vol. 2014. (Girls Rock! Ser.). (ENG.). 64p. (gr. 4-5). lib. bdg. 69.30 *(978-1-4765-4650-6(9))* Capstone Press of Coughlan Cos.

Trachtenberg, Martha P. Bono: Rock Star Activist. 2008. (People to Know Today Ser.). (Illus.). 128p. (J). (gr. 6-18). lib. bdg. 33.27 *(978-0-7660-2695-7(7))* Enslow Pubs., Inc.

Tracy, Kathleen. Gwen Stefani. 2006. (Blue Banner Biography Ser.). (Illus.). 32p. (YA). (gr. 4-7). lib. bdg. 25.70 *(978-1-58415-514-0(0))* Mitchell Lane Pubs., Inc.

—Mario. 2006. (Blue Banner Biography Ser.). (Illus.). 32p. (J). (gr. 3-8). lib. bdg. 25.70 *(978-1-58415-391-7(1))* Mitchell Lane Pubs., Inc.

—Orianthi. 2010. (Blue Banner Biography Ser.). (Illus.). 32p. (YA). (gr. 4-7). lib. bdg. 25.70 *(978-1-58415-913-1(8))* Mitchell Lane Pubs., Inc.

Triumph Books Staff. One Direction: Where We Are. 2014. (ENG.). 112p. (YA). (gr. 7). pap. 12.95 *(978-1-62937-019-4(3))* Triumph Bks.

—5 Seconds of Summer: She Looks So Perfect. 2014. (ENG.). 112p. (YA). (gr. 7). pap. 12.95 *(978-1-62937-069-9(X))* Triumph Bks.

Ungs, Tim. Paul McCartney & Stella McCartney. 2004. (Famous Families Ser.). (Illus.). 48p. (J). lib. bdg. 29.25 *(978-1-4042-0263-4(3))* Rosen Publishing Group, Inc., The.

—Paul Mccartney & Stella Mccartney. 2009. (Famous Families Ser.). 48p. (gr. 5-5). 53.00 *(978-1-61512-510-4(8))* Rosen Publishing Group, Inc., The.

Venezia, Mike. Beatles, the (Revised Edition) 2017. (Getting to Know the World's Greatest Composers Ser.). (ENG., Illus.). 40p. (J). lib. bdg. 29.00 *(978-0-531-22061-0(3)*, Children's Pr.) Scholastic Library Publishing.

—Duke Ellington (Revised Edition) 2017. (Getting to Know the World's Greatest Composers Ser.). (ENG.). 40p. (J). pap. 7.95 ***(978-0-531-23036-7(8))***; lib. bdg. 29.00 ***(978-0-531-22658-2(1))*** Scholastic Library Publishing. (Children's Pr.).

—Leonard Bernstein (Revised Edition) 2017. (Getting to Know the World's Greatest Composers Ser.). (ENG.). 40p. (J). pap. 7.95 ***(978-0-531-23034-3(1))***; lib. bdg. 29.00 ***(978-0-531-22656-8(5))*** Scholastic Library Publishing. (Children's Pr.).

Washburn, Kim. Beyond the Music: The Bono Story, 1 vol. rev. ed. 2013. (ZonderKidz Biography Ser.). (ENG.). 128p. (J). pap. 6.99 *(978-0-310-73838-1(5))* Zonderkidz.

Waters, Rosa. Bob Marley & the Wailers. (Pop Rock Ser.). (Illus.). 64p. (YA). 2008. (gr. 7-18). lib. bdg. 22.95 *(978-1-4222-0192-3(9))* 2007. pap. 7.95 *(978-1-4222-0317-0(4))* Mason Crest.

Watson, Cindy. Out of Darkness: The Jeff Healey Story. 2010. (ENG., Illus.). 144p. (YA). (gr. k-6). pap. 19.99 *(978-1-55488-706-4(2)*, 9781554887064) Dundurn CAN. Dist: Ingram Publisher Services.

Weintraub, Aileen. Kiss: I Wanna Rock & Roll All Night. 2009. (Rebels of Rock Ser.). (Illus.). 112p. (J). (gr. 7-12). lib. bdg. 33.27 *(978-0-7660-3027-5(X))* Enslow Pubs., Inc.

Wentzel, Jim. The Beatles. 2009. (Rock & Roll Hall of Famers Ser.). 112p. (gr. 5-8). 63.90 *(978-1-60852-477-8(9)*, Rosen Reference) Rosen Publishing Group, Inc., The.

Wheeler, Jill C. Faith Hill. 2003. (Star Tracks Ser.). (Illus.). 64p. (gr. 3-8). 27.07 *(978-1-57765-771-2(3)*, Abdo & Daughters) ABDO Publishing Co.

Wheeler, Opal & Deucher, Sybil. Sebastian Bach: the Boy from Thuringia. Greenwalt, Mary, illus. l.t. ed. 2005. 126p. per. 13.95 *(978-0-9746505-1-7(X)*, 4354) Zeezok Publishing, LLC.

White, Danny. One Direction: La Historia. 2nd ed. 2013. (Corazon Joven Ser.). (SPA., Illus.). 254p. (YA). pap. *(978-84-15579-15-1(2))* Akcent, Vydavatelstvi, Drahomir Rybnicek.

White, Katherine. Elton John. 2009. (Rock & Roll Hall of Famers Ser.). 112p. (gr. 5-8). 63.90 *(978-1-60852-473-0(6)*, Rosen Reference) Rosen Publishing Group, Inc., The.

Whiting, Jim. The Life & Times of Gilbert & Sullivan. 2004. (Masters of Music Ser.). (Illus.). 48p. (gr. 4-8). lib. bdg. 20.95 *(978-1-58415-276-7(1))* Mitchell Lane Pubs., Inc.

Wilcox, Christine. Justin Bieber. Greenaven Press Staff, ed. 2013. (People in the News Ser.). (ENG., Illus.). 128p. (gr. 7-10). lib. bdg. 39.40 *(978-1-4205-0756-0(7)*, Lucent Bks.) Cengage Gale.

Willett, Edward. Jimi Hendrix: Kiss the Sky. 2006. (American Rebels Ser.). (Illus.). 160p. (YA). (gr. 6-9). lib. bdg. 35.94 *(978-0-7660-2449-6(0))* Enslow Pubs., Inc.

Wilson, Rene. Kenny Chesney. 2010. (Country Music Stars Ser.). (Illus.). 32p. (J). (gr. 3-8). pap. 10.50 *(978-1-4339-3608-1(9))*; lib. bdg. 25.25 *(978-1-4339-3607-4(0))* Stevens, Gareth Publishing LLLP.

Winter, Jonah. Dizzy. Qualls, Sean, illus. 2006. (J). 16.99 *(978-0-439-50736-3(7)*, Levine, Arthur A. Bks.) Scholastic, Inc.

Wood, Ramona. The Goat Woman of Smackover: An Arkansas Legend. Wood, Ramona, . 2006. (Illus.). 32p. (J). 11.00 *(978-0-9758622-1-6(9))* ABC Pr.

Woog, Adam. Blake Shelton. 2015. (People in the News Ser.). (ENG., Illus.). 128p. (J). (gr. 7-10). 39.40 *(978-1-4205-1225-0(0)*, Lucent Bks.) Cengage Gale.

Wooten, Sara McIntosh. Tim McGraw. 2010. (Celebrities with Heart Ser.). (Illus.). 128p. (J). (gr. 7-12). 33.27 *(978-0-7660-3405-1(4))* Enslow Pubs., Inc.

—Tim McGraw: Celebrity with Heart. 2010. (Celebrities with Heart Ser.). (Illus.). 128p. (J). pap. 10.95 *(978-1-59845-207-5(X))* Enslow Pubs., Inc.

Worth, Richard. Yo-Yo Ma. 2007. (Asian Americans of Achievement Ser.). (Illus.). 119p. (YA). (gr. 7-12). lib. bdg. 35.00 *(978-0-7910-9270-5(4))* Facts On File, Inc.

Wyckoff, Edwin Brit. Electric Guitar Man: The Genius of les Paul. 2008. (Genius at Work! Great Inventor Biographies Ser.). (Illus.). 32p. (J). (gr. 3-7). lib. bdg. 23.94

M
N
O

(978-0-7660-2847-0(X), Enslow Elementary) Enslow Pubs., Inc.

Wyner, Zach. Music. 2014. (Urban Entrepreneurs Ser.). (gr. 3-8). pap. 8.99 *(978-1-61570-873-4(1))* Scobre Pr. Corp.

Yasuda, Anita. Taylor Swift. 2010. (Remarkable People Ser.). (Illus.). 24p. (J). (gr. 4-6). pap. 11.95 *(978-1-61690-158-5(6))*; lib. bdg. 25.70 *(978-1-61690-157-8(8))* Weigl Pubs., Inc.

Zimmerman, Robert K. Switchfoot. 2006. (Contemporary Musicians & Their Music Ser.). (Illus.). 48p. (YA). (gr. 5-9). lib. bdg. 29.25 *(978-1-4042-0709-7(0))* Rosen Publishing Group, Inc., The.

MUSICIANS, AFRICAN AMERICAN

see African American Musicians

MUSICIANS, BLACK

see African American Musicians

MUSICIANS—FICTION

Acampora, Paul. Rachel Spinelli Punched Me in the Face. 2013. (ENG.). 192p. (J). (gr. 3-7). pap. 8.99 *(978-1-250-01669-0(X)*, 9781250016690) Square Fish.

Alexander, Kwame. Acoustic Rooster & His Barnyard Band. Bowers, Tim, illus. 2011. (ENG.). 32p. (gr. k-5). lib. bdg. 15.95 *(978-1-58536-688-0(9))* Sleeping Bear Pr.

Alexander, Kwame & Hess, Mary Rand. Solo, 1 vol. 2017. (ENG.). 464p. (YA). 17.99 ***(978-0-310-76183-9(2))*** Blink.

Alger, Horatio. Phil the Fiddler. rev. ed. 2006. (ENG.). 224p. 27.95 *(978-1-4218-2091-0(9)*, 1st World Library - Literary Society) 1st World Publishing, Inc.

—Phil the Fiddler. 2006. pap. *(978-1-4068-0667-0(6))* Echo Library.

—The Young Musician. reprint ed. pap. 79.00 *(978-1-4047-3629-0(8))* Classic Textbooks.

—The Young Musician. 2006. pap. *(978-1-4068-0673-1(0))* Echo Library.

Alikhan, Salima. The Pied Piper of Austin, 1 vol. Alikhan, Salima, illus. 2009. (ENG., Illus.). 32p. (J). (gr. k-3). 16.99 *(978-1-58980-629-0(8))* Pelican Publishing Co., Inc.

Allison, Jennifer. The Ghost Sonata. 2008. (Gilda Joyce Ser.). (ENG.). 352p. (J). (gr. 3-7). 8.99 *(978-0-14-241232-9(5)*, Puffin Books) Penguin Young Readers Group.

Amato, Mary. Get Happy. (ENG.). 244p. (gr. 7-12). 2016. pap. 9.99 *(978-1-5124-2627-4(X)*, Carolrhoda Bks.) 2014. (J). 16.99 *(978-1-60684-522-6(5)*, Carolrhoda Lab™) Lerner Publishing Group.

—Guitar Notes. (ENG., Illus.). 304p. (J). (gr. 7). 2014. pap. 8.99 *(978-1-60684-503-5(9))* 2012. 16.99 *(978-1-60684-124-2(6))* Lerner Publishing Group. (Carolrhoda Lab™).

Andrews, Jesse. The Haters. (ENG.). 336p. (YA). (gr. 8-17). 2017. pap. 9.95 *(978-1-4197-2370-4(7))* 2016. 18.95 *(978-1-4197-2078-9(3))* Abrams, Inc. (Amulet Bks.).

—The Haters. 2017. (YA). lib. bdg. 20.80 ***(978-0-606-39688-2(8))*** Turtleback Bks.

Andrews, Julie. Simeon's Gift. 2003. (J). 169.90 *(978-0-06-056905-1(0))*; 169.90 *(978-0-06-056906-8(9))* HarperCollins Pubs. (Julie Andrews Collection).

Andrews, Julie & Hamilton, Emma Walton. Simeon's Gift. Spirin, Gennady, illus. 2006. 30p. (J). (gr. 4-8). reprint ed. 17.00 *(978-1-4223-5855-9(0))* DIANE Publishing Co.

—Simeon's Gift. Spirin, Gennady, illus. 2003. (Julie Andrews Collection). 40p. (J). 17.89 *(978-0-06-008915-3(6)*, Julie Andrews Collection) HarperCollins Pubs.

Andrews, Julie, et al. Simeon's Gift. Spirin, Gennady, illus. 2003. (Julie Andrews Collection). (ENG.). 40p. (J). (gr. k-4). 19.99 *(978-0-06-008914-6(8))* HarperCollins Pubs.

Armstrong, Samuel, illus. Gene Autry & the Lost Dogie. 2011. 30p. 35.95 *(978-1-258-02476-5(4))* Literary Licensing, LLC.

Asphyxia. The Grimstones Collection. Asphyxia, illus. 2015. (Grimstones Ser.). (ENG., Illus.). 488p. (J). (gr. 3-7). pap. 17.99 *(978-1-76011-391-9(3))* Allen & Unwin AUS. Dist: Independent Pubs. Group.

Auch, M. J. Guitar Boy. 2012. (ENG.). 288p. (J). (gr. 5-9). pap. 14.99 *(978-0-312-64124-5(9)*, 9780312641245) Square Fish.

Autry, Gene. Gene Autry & the Land Grab Mystery. 2011. 286p. 48.95 *(978-1-258-02327-0(X))* Literary Licensing, LLC.

Barretta, Gene. Zoola Palooza: A Book of Homographs. Barretta, Gene, illus. 2011. (ENG., Illus.). 40p. (J). (gr. k-3). 16.99 *(978-0-8050-9107-6(6)*, 9780805091076, Holt, Henry & Co. Bks. For Young Readers) Holt, Henry & Co.

Beaudoin, Sean. Wise Young Fool. 2013. (ENG.). 448p. (YA). (gr. 9-17). 18.00 *(978-0-316-20379-1(3))* Little, Brown Bks. for Young Readers.

Bell, Anthea, ed. & tr. The Bremen Town Musicians. Bell, Anthea, tr. Lai, Hsin-Shih, illus. 2007. 32p. (J). (gr. -1-3). 17.95 *(978-0-88010-583-5(6)*, Bell Pond Bks.) SteinerBooks, Inc.

Berlin, Eric. The Puzzler's Mansion: The Puzzling World of Winston Breen. (Puzzling World of Winston Breen Ser.: 3). (ENG.). (J). (gr. 3-7). 2013. 272p. pap. 7.99 *(978-0-14-242643-2(1)*, Puffin Books) 2012. 256p. 16.99 *(978-0-399-25697-4(0)*, G.P. Putnam's Sons Books for Young Readers) Penguin Young Readers Group.

Blake, Ashley Herring. How to Make a Wish. 2017. (ENG.). 336p. (YA). (gr. 9). 17.99 *(978-0-544-81519-3(X)*, HMH Books For Young Readers) Houghton Mifflin Harcourt Publishing Co.

Blume, Lesley M. M. The Rising Star of Rusty Nail. 2009. (ENG.). 288p. (J). (gr. 3-7). 7.99 *(978-0-440-42111-5(X)*, Yearling) Random Hse. Children's Bks.

Bodecker, N. M. The Lost String Quartet. 2016. (ENG., Illus.). 40p. (J). (gr. -1-3). 13.99 *(978-1-4814-8000-0(6)*, Atheneum Bks. for Young Readers) Simon & Schuster Children's Publishing.

Brezenoff, Steve. Brooklyn, Burning. 2011. (Carolrhoda YA Ser.). (ENG.). 208p. (YA). (gr. 9-12). 17.95 *(978-0-7613-7526-5(0)*, Carolrhoda Lab™) Lerner Publishing Group.

Brouwer, Sigmund. Rock the Boat, 1 vol. 2015. (Orca Limelights Ser.). (ENG.). 128p. (J). (gr. 6-9). pap. 9.95 *(978-1-4598-0455-5(4))* Orca Bk. Pubs. USA.

Burstein, Lisa. MIA & the Bad Boy. 2015. (ENG., Illus.). 220p. (J). pap. 14.99 *(978-1-943336-18-0(0))* Entangled Publishing, LLC.

Caine, Rachel, pseud. Kiss of Death, 8 vols. 2010. (Morganville Vampires Ser.: 8). (ENG.). 256p. (YA). (gr. 9-18). 6.99 *(978-0-451-22973-1(8)*, Berkley) Penguin Publishing Group.

—The Morganville Vampires, Vol. 4. 2011. (Morganville Vampires Ser.: Bks. 7-8). (ENG.). 464p. (YA). (gr. 9-18). 9.99 *(978-0-451-23426-1(X)*, Berkley) Penguin Publishing Group.

Caletti, Deb. Love Is All You Need: Wild Roses - The Nature of Jade. 2013. (ENG.). 608p. (YA). (gr. 7-7). pap. 11.99 *(978-1-4424-6636-4(7)*, Simon Pulse) Simon Pulse.

—Wild Roses. (ENG.). (YA). (gr. 7-12). 2008. 320p. pap. 8.99 *(978-1-4169-5782-9(0))* 2005. (Illus.). 304p. 15.95 *(978-0-689-86766-8(2))* Simon Pulse. (Simon Pulse).

Calmenson, Stephanie. Jazzmatazz! Degen, Bruce, illus. 2008. 32p. (J). (gr. -1). lib. bdg. 17.89 *(978-0-06-077290-1(5))* HarperCollins Pubs.

Calvani, Mayra. The Luthier's Apprentice. 2014. (ENG.). 184p. (J). pap. 15.95 *(978-1-60619-029-6(6))* Twilight Times Bks.

Camp Rock: Second Session: Super Special: under the Mistletoe (Camp Rock: Second Session) 2009. 256p. pap. 6.99 *(978-1-4231-2222-7(4))* Disney Pr.

Capetta, Amy Rose. Entangled. (ENG.). (YA). (gr. 9). 2014. 352p. pap. 9.99 *(978-0-544-33624-7(0)*, HMH Books For Young Readers) 2013. 336p. 17.99 *(978-0-544-08744-6(5))* Houghton Mifflin Harcourt Publishing Co.

Carlon, Mick. Riding on Duke's Train. 2011. (LeapKids Ser.). (ENG.). 160p. (J). (gr. k-7). pap. 9.95 *(978-1-935248-06-4(5))* Leapfrog Pr.

—Travels with Louis. 2012. (LeapKids Ser.). (ENG.). 240p. (J). (gr. 2-10). pap. 9.95 *(978-1-935248-35-4(9))* Leapfrog Pr.

Carter, Nikki. Doing My Own Thing. 2011. (ENG., Illus.). 240p. (YA). (gr. 9). 9.95 *(978-0-7582-5558-7(6)*, K-Teen/Dafina) Kensington Publishing Corp.

Castellucci, Cecil. Beige. (ENG., 320p. (YA). 2009. Illus.). (gr. 9). pap. 8.99 *(978-0-7636-4232-7(0))* 2007. (Illus.). (gr. 9-18). 16.99 *(978-0-7636-3066-9(7))* 2007. 25.66 *(978-1-4287-4767-8(2))* Candlewick Pr.

Christopher, Nicholas. The True Adventures of Nicolo Zen: A Novel. 2015. (ENG.). 288p. (YA). (gr. 7). pap. 9.99 *(978-0-375-86492-6(X)*, Ember) Random Hse. Children's Bks.

Cobb, Amy. Band Camp Rules. 2016. (Band Geeks Set 2 Ser.). (ENG., Illus.). (J). (gr. 3-6). lib. bdg. 27.07 ***(978-1-62402-172-5(7))*** ABDO Publishing Co.

Cobb, Amy. Notes from a Pro, 1 vol. Cattish, Anna, illus. 2015. (ENG.). 112p. (J). *(978-1-62402-075-9(5))* Magic Wagon.

Cosgrove, Stephen. Cricket Clickett: Finding Your Talents. Arroyo, Fian, illus. 2004. (J). *(978-1-58804-382-5(7))* P C I Education.

Cross, Mimi. Before Goodbye, 0 vols. 2016. (ENG.). 389p. (YA). (gr. 8-12). pap. 9.99 *(978-1-5039-4972-0(9)*, 9781503949720, Skyscape) Amazon Publishing.

Crow, Kristyn. Skeleton Cat. Krall, Dan, illus. 2012. (ENG.). 32p. (J). (gr. -1-3). pap. 6.99 *(978-0-545-15385-0(9)*, Scholastic Pr.) Scholastic, Inc.

—Skeleton Cat. 2012. lib. bdg. 17.20 *(978-0-606-26209-5(1)*, Turtleback) Turtleback Bks.

Crowley, Cath. A Little Wanting Song. 2011. (ENG.). 288p. (YA). (gr. 9). pap. 8.99 *(978-0-375-85449-1(5)*, Ember) Random Hse. Children's Bks.

Curtis, Marci Lyn. The One Thing. 2015. (ENG., Illus.). 336p. (YA). (gr. 7-12). 17.99 *(978-1-4847-0902-3(0))* Hyperion Bks. for Children.

Dachman, Adam. The Player Piano Mouse. Julich, Jenniffer, illus. 2008. 32p. (J). 14.99 *(978-0-9797794-0-4(5))* Player Piano Mouse Productions (PPMP).

Darden, Floyd. Drumdee makes a Drum. 2007. 15.95 *(978-1-59526-711-5(5))* Aeon Publishing Inc.

Davidson, Susanna. The Musicians of Bremen. Gordon, Mike & Gordon, Carl, illus. 2007. (Usborne First Reading: Level 3 Ser.). 48p. (J). 8.99 *(978-0-7945-1911-7(3)*, Usborne) EDC Publishing.

Dawn, Nyrae, et al. Out of Play. 2013. (Entangled Teen Ser.). (ENG.). 320p. (YA). pap. 9.99 *(978-1-62266-010-0(2)*, 9781622660100) Entangled Publishing, LLC.

Derubertis, Barbara. Xavier Ox's Xylophone Experiment. Alley, R. W., illus. 2011. (Animal Antics A to Z Set III Ser.). pap. 45.32 *(978-0-7613-8433-5(2))* Kane Press, Inc.

deRubertis, Barbara. Xavier Ox's Xylophone Experiment. Alley, R. W., illus. 2011. (Animal Antics A to Z Ser.). 32p. (J). (ENG.). pap. 7.95 *(978-1-57565-349-5(4))*; lib. bdg. 22.60 *(978-1-57565-357-0(5))* Kane Press, Inc.

deRubertis, Barbara & DeRubertis, Barbara. Xavier Ox's Xylophone Experiment. Alley, R. W., illus. 2012. (Animal Antics A to Z Ser.). 32p. (J). (gr. 2 — 1). cd-rom 7.95 *(978-1-57565-417-1(2))* Kane Press, Inc.

Deutsch, Stacia. The Book of Life Movie Novelization. 2014. (Book of Life Ser.). (ENG., Illus.). 144p. (J). (gr. 3-7). pap. 6.99 *(978-1-4814-2351-9(7)*, Simon Spotlight) Simon Spotlight.

DiCamillo, Kate. Great Joy. Ibatoulline, Bagram, illus. 2010. (ENG.). 32p. (J). (gr. -1-3). 8.99 *(978-0-7636-4996-8(1))* Candlewick Pr.

Dionne, Erin. Notes from an Accidental Band Geek. 2012. (ENG.). 304p. (J). (gr. 5). pap. 6.99 *(978-0-14-242247-2(9)*, Puffin Books) Penguin Young Readers Group.

Disney Book Group Staff. The Inside Scoop. Peake, Marilyn, ed. movie tie-in ed. 2009. (ENG.). 32p. (J). (gr. 1-4). pap. 3.99 *(978-1-4231-1819-0(7))* Disney Pr.

Donbavand, Tommy. Flesh of the Zombie, Bk. 4. Cartoon Saloon Staff, illus. 2010. (Scream Street Ser.: 4). (ENG.). 128p. (J). (gr. 3-7). pap. 5.99 *(978-0-7636-4637-0(7))* Candlewick Pr.

Donnelly, Jennifer. Revolution. 2011. (ENG.). 512p. (YA). (gr. 9). pap. 9.99 *(978-0-385-73764-7(5)*, Ember) Random Hse. Children's Bks.

Draper, Polly. Cry Wolff. 2007. 89p. (J). pap. *(978-0-545-02570-6(2))* Scholastic, Inc.

Dunlap Cather, Katherine. Boyhood Stories of Famous Men. 2013. 292p. pap. *(978-3-95507-921-5(X))* DOGMA. in Europäischer Hochschulverlag GmbH & Co. KG.

Dunlap, Susanne. The Musician's Daughter. (ENG.). (YA). (gr. 7). 2010. 352p. pap. 8.99 *(978-1-59990-452-8(7)*, 9781599904528) 2009. 336p. 16.99 *(978-1-59990-332-3(6)*, 9781599903323) Bloomsbury Publishing USA. (Bloomsbury USA Childrens).

Edwards, Pamela Duncan. The Leprechaun's Gold. Cole, Henry, illus. 2006. (ENG.). 40p. (J). (gr. -1-2). reprint ed. 6.99 *(978-0-06-443878-0(3)*, Tegen, Katherine Bks) HarperCollins Pubs.

Ehrhardt, Karen. This Jazz Man. Roth, R G, illus. 2006. (ENG.). 32p. (J). (gr. -1-3). 17.99 *(978-0-15-205307-9(7))* Houghton Mifflin Harcourt Publishing Co.

—This Jazz Man. Roth, R. G., illus. 2010. (J). (gr. 1-5). 28.95 incl. audio compact disk *(978-1-4301-0740-8(5))* Live Oak Media.

Enderle, Dotti. Book 15: Rock & Roll!, 1 vol. 2014. (Ghost Detectors Set 3 Ser.). (ENG., Illus.). 80p. (J). (gr. 2-5). lib. bdg. 27.07 *(978-1-62402-003-2(8)*, Calico Chapter Bks) Magic Wagon.

England, Linda. The Old Cotton Blues. Flavin, Teresa, illus. 2011. (ENG.). 32p. (J). (gr. -1-2). 14.99 *(978-1-4424-2945-1(3)*, McElderry, Margaret K. Bks.) McElderry, Margaret K. Bks.

Engle, Margarita. Drum Dream Girl: How One Girl's Courage Changed Music. López, Rafael, illus. 2015. (ENG.). 48p. (J). (gr. -1-3). 16.99 *(978-0-544-10229-3(0)*, HMH Books For Young Readers) Houghton Mifflin Harcourt Publishing Co.

FableVision. Spf 40. Reynolds, Peter H., illus. 2013. (Zebrafish Ser.). (ENG.). 128p. (J). (gr. 5-9). 19.99 *(978-1-4169-9708-5(3)*, Atheneum Bks. for Young Readers) Simon & Schuster Children's Publishing.

FableVision Staff. Spf 40. Reynolds, Peter H., illus. 2013. (Zebrafish Ser.). (ENG.). 128p. (J). (gr. 5-9). pap. 9.99 *(978-1-4169-9709-2(1)*, Atheneum Bks. for Young Readers) Simon & Schuster Children's Publishing.

Falconer, Ian. Olivia Forms a Band. Falconer, Ian, illus. 2006. (ENG., Illus.). 50p. (J). (gr. -1-3). 18.99 *(978-1-4169-2454-8(X)*, Atheneum Bks. for Young Readers) Simon & Schuster Children's Publishing.

Fannin, Cole. Gene Autry & the Golden Stallion. Hampton, John, illus. 2011. 284p. 48.95 *(978-1-258-02563-2(9))* Literary Licensing, LLC.

Ferron, Joanne. Luis Saves the Llama. 2012. (ENG.). 35p. (J). pap. 17.95 *(978-1-4327-7623-7(1))* Outskirts Pr., Inc.

Fisher, Catherine. The Oracle Betrayed. 2005. (Oracle Prophecies Ser.). (Illus.). 332p. (YA). (gr. 7-12). 14.65 *(978-0-7569-5269-3(7))* Perfection Learning Corp.

Fleming, Candace. Westward Ho, Carlotta! Catrow, David, illus. 2009. (ENG.). 36p. (J). (gr. -1-2). 10.99 *(978-1-4424-0218-8(0)*, Atheneum Bks. for Young Readers) Simon & Schuster Children's Publishing.

Fletcher, Steffi. Gene Autry. Crawford, Mel, illus. 2011. 32p. pap. 35.95 *(978-1-258-02476-7(9))* Literary Licensing, LLC.

Forman, Gayle. If I Stay. 2011. (If I Stay Ser.: BK.1). (YA). 10.36 *(978-0-7848-3573-9(X)*, Everbind) Marco Bk. Co.

—If I Stay. movie tie-in ed. 2014. (If I Stay Ser.: BK.1). (ENG.). 304p. (YA). (gr. 9). pap. 10.99 *(978-0-14-751453-0(3))* Penguin Publishing Group.

—If I Stay. (If I Stay Ser.: BK.1). (ENG.). (YA). (gr. 9-18). 2010. 320p. 10.99 *(978-0-14-241543-6(X)*, Speak) 2009. 208p. 17.99 *(978-0-525-42103-0(3)*, Dutton Books for Young Readers) 2014. 304p. 17.99 *(978-0-451-47464-3(3)*, Viking Books for Young Readers) Penguin Young Readers Group.

—If I Stay. 2010. (If I Stay Ser.: BK.1). (ENG.). 262p. (YA). (gr. 9-12). 18.45 *(978-1-60686-742-6(3))* Perfection Learning Corp.

—If I Stay. l.t. ed. 2014. (If I Stay Ser.: BK.1). (ENG.). (YA). 482p. 23.99 *(978-1-4104-7543-5(3))*; 480p. pap. 12.99 *(978-1-59413-814-0(1)*, Large Print Pr.) Thorndike Pr.

—If I Stay. 2010. (If I Stay Ser.: BK.1). (YA). lib. bdg. 22.10 *(978-0-606-14395-0(5)*, Turtleback) Turtleback Bks.

Fox, Paula. The Slave Dancer. unabr. ed. 2004. 152p. (J). (gr. 5-9). pap. 38.00 incl. audio *(978-0-8072-0458-0(7)*, Listening Library) Random Hse. Audio Publishing Group.

Frank, Lucy. Lucky Stars. 2014. (ENG.). 304p. (J). (gr. 5-9). pap. 14.99 *(978-1-4814-2901-6(9)*, Atheneum Bks. for Young Readers) Simon & Schuster Children's Publishing.

French, Simon. Where in the World, 1 vol. 2008. (ENG.). 208p. (J). (gr. 3-7). pap. 7.95 *(978-1-56145-443-3(5))* Peachtree Pubs.

Friedman, J. S. The Micetro of Moscow. Beatrice, Chris, illus. 2013. (Maurice's Valises: Moral Tails in an Immoral World Ser.: Vol. 2). (ENG.). 37p. (J). (gr. k-4). pap. *(978-94-91613-06-7(5))* Mouse Prints Pr.

Garcia, Kami & Stohl, Margaret. Dangerous Deception. 2015. (ENG.). 352p. (YA). (gr. 7-17). 19.00 *(978-0-316-37034-9(7))* Little Brown & Co.

Gershenson, Harold P. Freddy Flamingo & the Kindertown Five. Mills, Christopher, illus. 2005. 27p. (J). *(978-1-58987-070-3(0))* Kindermusik International.

Gillmor, Don. The Fabulous Song. Gay, Marie-Louise, illus. 2003. 32p. (J). pap. 7.95 *(978-1-929132-48-5(4))* Kane Miller.

Gillmor, Don, et al. The Fabulous Song. Gay, Marie-Louise, illus. 2006. (ENG.). 44p. (J). (gr. -1-2). 16.95 *(978-2-923163-17-8(6))* La Montagne Secrete CAN. Dist: Independent Pubs. Group.

Ginsberg, Mort. Ukey & His Magical Ukulele. 2008. 75p. pap. 19.95 *(978-1-60610-395-1(4))* America Star Bks.

Glines, Abbi. Bad for You. 2015. (Sea Breeze Ser.). (ENG., Illus.). 320p. (YA). (gr. 11). pap. 11.99 *(978-1-4814-2074-7(7)*, Simon Pulse) Simon Pulse.

—Breathe. 2013. (Sea Breeze Ser.). (ENG., Illus.). 352p. (YA). (gr. 11). 17.99 *(978-1-4424-8870-0(0))*; pap. 9.99 *(978-1-4424-8869-4(7))* Simon Pulse. (Simon Pulse).

—Breathe. 2011. 166p. (gr. 8-12). pap. 9.99 *(978-1-61798-004-6(8))* Wild Child Publishing.

—Misbehaving. 2014. (Sea Breeze Ser.). (ENG., Illus.). 352p. (YA). (gr. 11). 17.99 *(978-1-4814-0674-1(4))*; pap. 11.99 *(978-1-4814-0673-4(6))* Simon Pulse. (Simon Pulse).

Going, K. L. Fat Kid Rules the World. 2004. (ENG.). 224p. (YA). (gr. 7-18). reprint ed. pap. 9.99 *(978-0-14-240208-5(7)*, Speak) Penguin Young Readers Group.

Gollub, Matthew. Jazz Fly 2: The Jungle Pachanga. Hanke, Karen, illus. 2010. (J). 32p. (gr. -1-3). 17.95 incl. audio compact disk *(978-1-889910-44-4(9))*; *(978-1-889910-45-1(7))* Tortuga Pr.

Gonzalez, Gabriela & Triana, Gaby. Backstage Pass. 2004. (Illus.). 224p. (J). (gr. 7-18). 15.99 *(978-0-06-056017-1(7))*; lib. bdg. 16.89 *(978-0-06-056018-8(5))* HarperCollins Pubs.

Goodan, Till. Gene Autry & Raiders of the Range. 2011. 350p. 51.95 *(978-1-258-02137-5(4))* Literary Licensing, LLC.

Graham, Hilary Weisman. Reunited. 2013. (ENG., Illus.). 336p. (YA). (gr. 7). pap. 9.99 *(978-1-4424-0687-2(9)*, Simon & Schuster Bks. For Young Readers) Simon & Schuster Bks. For Young Readers.

Greene, Janice. The Dark Lady, 1 vol. unabr. ed. 2010. (Q Reads Ser.). (ENG.). 32p. (YA). (gr. 9-12). pap. 6.95 *(978-1-61651-215-6(6))* Saddleback Educational Publishing, Inc.

Greene, Kimberly. My Sister's a Pop Star. 2011. (My Sister's a Pop Star Ser.). 277p. (J). pap. 5.99 *(978-0-7945-2899-7(6)*, Usborne) EDC Publishing.

Grimm, Jacob & Grimm, Wilhelm K. The Bremen Town Musicians: A Tale about Working Together. Catalano, Dominic, illus. 2006. (Famous Fables Ser.). (J). *(978-1-59939-039-0(6)*, Reader's Digest Young Families, Inc.) Studio Fun International.

Grosso, Mike. I Am Drums. 2016. (ENG.). 256p. (J). (gr. 5-7). 16.99 *(978-0-544-70710-8(9))* Houghton Mifflin Harcourt Publishing Co.

Hamlisch, Marvin. Marvin Makes Music. Madsen, Jim, illus. 2012. (ENG.). 32p. (J). (gr. 1-3). 17.99 *(978-0-8037-3730-3(0)*, Dial Bks) Penguin Young Readers Group.

Hannigan, Paula & Accord Publishing Staff. Music Star. Slade, Christian, illus. 2011. (ENG.). 16p. (J). (gr. -1-3). 14.99 *(978-1-4494-0173-3(2))* Andrews McMeel Publishing.

Hanson, Anders. Beetle Mania, 1 vol. 2007. (Critter Chronicles Ser.). (ENG., Illus.). 24p. (J). (gr. k-3). lib. bdg. 24.21 *(978-1-59928-432-3(4)*, SandCastle) ABDO Publishing Co.

Haus, Jean. With the Band, 0 vols. 2014. (Luminescent Juliet Ser.: 3). (ENG.). 286p. (YA). (gr. 7-12). pap. 7.99 *(978-1-4778-4709-1(X)*, 9781477847091, Amazon Children's Publishing) Amazon Publishing.

Hedderwick, Mairi. Katie Morag & the Grand Concert. Hedderwick, Mairi, illus. 2010. (Katie Morag Ser.: 6). (ENG., Illus.). 32p. (J). (gr. k-2). pap. 12.99 *(978-1-84941-087-8(9)*, Red Fox) Random House Children's Books GBR. Dist: Independent Pubs. Group.

Heim, Robert. The Squeaking Earl. 2009. 32p. pap. 16.50 *(978-1-60693-711-2(1)*, Strategic Bk. Publishing) Strategic Book Publishing & Rights Agency (SBPRA).

Hillerman, Tony. Buster Mesquite's Cowboy Band. 2006. (J). reprint ed. lib. bdg. 14.95 *(978-0-914001-12-6(4))* Sidewinder Publishing LLC.

Hodgin, Molly. Tenney's Journal. 2017. (American Girl: Tenney Grant Ser.). (ENG.). 160p. (J). (gr. 3-7). 11.99 *(978-1-338-13704-0(2))* Scholastic, Inc.

Hoffman, Amalia. Klezmer Bunch. 2009. 36p. 15.95 *(978-965-229-447-0(0))* Gefen Publishing Hse., Ltd ISR. Dist: Strauss Consultants.

Huelin, Jodi. Alvin & the Chipmunks: Alvin's Easter Break. Artful Doodlers Limited Staff & Carzon, Walter, illus. 2014. (ENG.). 24p. (J). (gr. -1-3). pap. 3.99 *(978-0-06-225222-7(4)*, HarperFestival) HarperCollins Pubs.

Hughes, Mark Peter. Lemonade Mouth. movie tie-in ed. 2011. (ENG.). 352p. (YA). (gr. 7-7). pap. 8.99 *(978-0-385-74208-5(8)*, Ember) Random Hse. Children's Bks.

Hurd, Thacher. Mama Don't Allow. 2003. (Illus.). (J). (gr. -1-2). pap. 35.95 incl. audio compact disk *(978-1-59112-605-8(3))* Live Oak Media.

Hurd, Thacher & Hurd. Mama Don't Allow. Hurd, Thacher, illus. 25th anniv. ed. 2008. (Trophy Picture Bks.). (ENG., Illus.). 40p. (J). (gr. -1-3). pap. 6.99 *(978-0-06-443078-4(2))* HarperCollins Pubs.

Hurd, Thacher & Hurd, T. Mama Don't Allow. 2008. (Illus.). (J). (gr. -1-2). 17.20 *(978-0-8085-3698-7(2)*, Turtleback) Turtleback Bks.

Jackson, Ellen B. Cinnamon Brown & the Seven Dwarfs. Brown, Elbrite, illus. 2006. (J). *(978-0-670-06106-8(9)*, Viking Adult) Penguin Publishing Group.

Jackson, Jennifer. The Punkydoos Take the Stage. Andreasen, Dan, illus. 2014. (Punkydoos Book Ser.). (ENG.). 32p. (J). (gr. -1-k). 17.99 *(978-1-4231-4339-0(6))* Hyperion Bks. for Children.

Janover, Caroline D. Zipper: The Kid with ADHD. 2007. 172p. per. 12.95 *(978-0-595-47615-2(5)*, Backinprint.com) iUniverse, Inc.

Johnson, Angela. Violet's Music. Huliska-Beith, Laura & Laura, Huliska-beith, illus. 2004. (ENG.). 32p. (J). (gr. -1-3). 17.99 *(978-0-8037-2740-3(2)*, Dial Bks) Penguin Young Readers Group.

Johnson, Christine. The Gathering Dark. (ENG., (YA). (gr. 9). 2014. Illus.). 528p. pap. 9.99 *(978-1-4424-3904-7(1))* 2013. 512p. 16.99 *(978-1-4424-3903-0(3))* Simon Pulse. (Simon Pulse).

Kadence, Sam. Unicorns & Rainbow Poop. (J). 2016. (ENG., Illus.). 27.99 ***(978-1-63477-988-3(6)***, Harmony Ink Pr.) 2014. 246p. pap. *(978-1-63216-417-9(5))* Dreamspinner Pr.

Kamata, Suzanne. Screaming Divas. 2014. (ENG.). 208p. (YA). 17.99 *(978-1-4405-7279-1(8)*, Simon Pulse) Simon Pulse.

Kay, Verla. Civil War Drummer Boy. Day, Larry, illus. 2012. (ENG.). 32p. (J). (gr. 1-3). 16.99 *(978-0-399-23992-2(8)*, G.P. Putnam's Sons Books for Young Readers) Penguin Young Readers Group.

Keller, Jessica. Mia's Marvelous Musical Group. 2009. (Illus.). 64p. (gr. -1-3). pap. 26.99 *(978-1-4389-8160-4(0))* AuthorHouse.

Kerick, Mia. Intervention. 2016. (ENG., Illus.). (J). 24.99 ***(978-1-63533-036-6(X)***, Harmony Ink Pr.) Dreamspinner Pr.

Kerick, Mia. Intervention [Library Edition]. 2014. 230p. pap. 14.99 *(978-1-62798-336-5(8)*, Harmony Ink Pr.) Dreamspinner Pr.

Kerner, Charlotte. Blueprint. Crawford, Elizabeth D., tr. from GER. 2003. (Young Adult Fiction Ser.). 192p. (YA). (gr. 9-12). 16.95 *(978-0-8225-0080-3(9)*, Carolrhoda Bks.) Lerner Publishing Group.

Kimmel, Elizabeth Cody. Suddenly Supernatural: Scaredy Kat. 2010. (Suddenly Supernatural Ser.: 2). (ENG.). 272p. (J). (gr. 3-7). pap. 5.99 *(978-0-316-08745-2(9))* Little, Brown Bks. for Young Readers.

Kogler, Jennifer Anne. Ruby Tuesday. 2005. (ENG.). 320p. (J). (gr. 7-18). 15.99 *(978-0-06-073956-0(8))* HarperCollins Pubs.

Koosis, Lisa A. Resurrecting Sunshine. 2016. (ENG.). 320p. (YA). (gr. 8-12). 16.99 *(978-0-8075-6943-6(7))* Whitman, Albert & Co.

Krosoczka, Jarrett J. Punk Farm. (ENG.). 40p. (J). (gr. -1-2). 2010. pap. 7.99 *(978-0-440-41793-4(7)*, Dragonfly Bks.)

2005. (Illus.). 15.95 *(978-0-375-82429-6(4)*, Knopf Bks. for Young Readers) Random Hse. Children's Bks.

—Punk Farm on Tour. 2007. (ENG., Illus.). 40p. (J). (gr. -1-2). 15.99 *(978-0-375-83343-4(9)*, Knopf Bks. for Young Readers) Random Hse. Children's Bks.

Krulik, Nancy. She's Got the Beat. 2010. (Romantic Comedies Ser.). (ENG.). 320p. (YA). (gr. 9). pap. 14.99 *(978-1-4424-1419-8(7)*, Simon Pulse) Simon Pulse.

Leroux, Gaston. The Phantom of the Opera. Howell, Troy, illus. 2008. (Classic Starts(tm) Ser.). (ENG.). 160p. (J). (gr. 2-4). 6.95 *(978-1-4027-4580-5(X))* Sterling Publishing Co., Inc.

Lewis, Stewart. Stealing Candy. 2017. (ENG.). 288p. (YA). (gr. 8-12). pap. 10.99 *(978-1-4926-3888-9(9)*, 9781492638889) Sourcebooks, Inc.

Long, Loren. The Drummer Boy. Long, Loren, illus. 2008. (ENG., Illus.). 40p. (J). (gr. -1-k). 18.99 *(978-0-399-25174-0(X)*, Philomel Bks.) Penguin Young Readers Group.

—Drummer Boy. Long, Loren, illus. 2012. (ENG., Illus.). 40p. (J). (gr. -1-k). mass mkt. 7.99 *(978-0-14-242341-7(6)*, Puffin Books) Penguin Young Readers Group.

Malouf, Juman. The Trilogy of Two. 2015. (ENG.). 416p. (J). (gr. 5-7). 17.99 *(978-0-399-17114-7(2)*, G.P. Putnam's Sons Books for Young Readers) Penguin Young Readers Group.

Man-Kong, Mary. Star Power. Random House Staff, illus. 2012. (Step into Reading Ser.). (ENG.). 32p. (J). (gr. -1-1). pap. 3.99 *(978-0-307-93196-2(X)*, Random Hse. Bks. for Young Readers) Random Hse. Children's Bks.

—Star Power. 2012. (Barbie Step into Reading Level 2 Ser.). lib. bdg. 13.55 *(978-0-606-26550-8(3)*, Turtleback) Turtleback Bks.

Marchetta, Melina. The Piper's Son. (ENG.). 336p. (YA). (gr. 9). 2012. pap. 7.99 *(978-0-7636-6062-8(0))* 2011. (Illus.). 17.99 *(978-0-7636-4758-2(6))* Candlewick Pr.

Marino, Nan. Hiding Out at the Pancake Palace. 2013. (ENG.). 256p. (J). (gr. 3-7). 16.99 *(978-1-59643-753-1(7)*, 9781596437531) Roaring Brook Pr.

—Hiding Out at the Pancake Palace. 2014. (ENG.). 272p. (J). (gr. 3-7). pap. 7.99 *(978-1-250-04000-8(0)*, 9781250040008) Square Fish.

Martínez, Jessica. Virtuosity. (ENG.). (YA). (gr. 9). 2012. 320p. pap. 9.99 *(978-1-4424-2053-3(7))* 2011. 304p. 16.99 *(978-1-4424-2052-6(9))* Simon Pulse. (Simon Pulse).

Massenot, Véronique & Hie, Vanessa. The Three Musicians: A Children's Book Inspired by Pablo Picasso. 2013. (ENG., Illus.). 32p. (J). (gr. -1-3). 14.95 *(978-3-7913-7151-1(7))* Prestel Verlag GmbH & Co KG. DEU. Dist: Penguin Random Hse. LLC.

McCarry, Sarah. All Our Pretty Songs. 2013. (Metamorphoses Trilogy Ser.: 1). (ENG.). 240p. (YA). (gr. 8-12). pap. 9.99 *(978-1-250-02708-5(X)*, 9781250027085, St. Martin's Griffin) St. Martin's Pr.

McKenzie, Tim A. Baxter Barret Brown's Bass Fiddle. Shaw, Charles, illus. 2004. (ENG.). 24p. (J). (gr. 2-4). 19.95 *(978-1-931721-06-6(8))* Bright Sky Pr.

McRobb, Will & Viscardi, Chris. Battle of the Bands. 2007. 87p. (J). pap. *(978-0-545-02571-3(0))* Scholastic, Inc.

Milanes, Janelle. The Victoria in My Head. 2017. (ENG., Illus.). 400p. (YA). (gr. 7). 17.99 ***(978-1-4814-8089-5(8)**,* Simon Pulse) Simon Pulse.

Montano, Josie. Pop Starlets. 2005. (Illus.). 142p. pap. *(978-0-7344-0446-6(8)*, Lothian Children's Bks.) Hachette Australia.

Mutchnick, Brenda & Casden, Ron. A Noteworthy Tale. Penney, Ian, illus. 2004. 30p. (J). (gr. k-4). reprint ed. 19.00 *(978-0-7567-7654-1(6))* DIANE Publishing Co.

Myers, Walter Dean & Myers, Christopher. Jazz. Myers, Christopher, illus. 2006. (ENG., Illus.). 48p. (J). (gr. -1-3). 18.95 *(978-0-8234-1545-8(7))* Holiday Hse., Inc.

Nelson, Jandy. The Sky Is Everywhere. (ENG.). (YA). (gr. 9-18). 2011. 320p. 9.99 *(978-0-14-241780-5(7)*, Speak) 2010. 288p. 17.99 *(978-0-8037-3495-1(6)*, Dial Bks) Penguin Young Readers Group.

—The Sky Is Everywhere. 2011. (ENG., Illus.). 275p. (gr. 9-12). 19.00 *(978-1-61383-223-3(0))* Perfection Learning Corp.

Nichols, Travis. Matthew Meets the Man. 2012. (ENG., Illus.). 176p. (YA). (gr. 6-9). 24.99 *(978-1-59643-545-2(3)*, 9781596435452) Roaring Brook Pr.

Nickel, Barbara. Hannah Waters & the Daughter of Johann Sebastian Bach. 2006. (ENG., Illus.). 176p. (J). (gr. 7-18). 6.99 *(978-0-14-305079-7(6)*, Puffin Canada) Penguin Random House Canada Young Readers CAN. Dist: Penguin Random Hse. LLC.

Ohlin, Nancy. Consent. 2015. (ENG., Illus.). 288p. (YA). (gr. 9). 17.99 *(978-1-4424-6490-2(9)*, Simon Pulse) Simon Pulse.

Ostrander, P. Martin. P Martin Ostrander's Dangerous Four Series: Book #1. 2007. 112p. 20.95 *(978-0-595-68250-8(2))* iUniverse, Inc.

Parent, David D. Drummers Forward! Marching with Angels: The Exciting Tale of a Drummer Boy Serving with the First Vermont Brigade & His Adventures During the Americ. 2013. 188p. pap. 13.50 *(978-1-62516-582-4(X)*, Strategic Bk. Publishing) Strategic Book Publishing & Rights Agency (SBPRA).

Parker, Vic, compiled by. The Musicians of Bremen & Other Silly Stories. 2016. (Silly Stories Ser.). (ENG.). 40p. (J). (gr. 2-3). pap. 14.05 *(978-1-4824-4207-6(8))* Stevens, Gareth Publishing LLLP.

Parsons, Mark Huntley. Road Rash. 2015. (ENG.). 352p. (YA). (gr. 7). pap. 9.99 *(978-0-385-75345-6(4)*, Ember) Random Hse. Children's Bks.

Patricelli, Leslie. Be Quiet, Mike! 2011. (ENG., Illus.). 40p. (J). (gr. -1-2). 14.99 *(978-0-7636-4477-2(3))* Candlewick Pr.

Patten, Lewis B. Gene Autry & Arapaho War Drums. Hampton, John W., illus. 2011. 280p. 47.95 *(978-1-258-04495-4(1))* Literary Licensing, LLC.

—Gene Autry & the Ghost Riders. Bartram, Bob & Eggers, James, illus. 2011. 280p. 47.95 *(978-1-258-02621-9(X))* Literary Licensing, LLC.

Pearson, Maggie. The Pop Star Pirates. 2015. (Race Further with Reading Ser.). (ENG., Illus.). 48p. (J). *(978-0-7787-2089-8(6))* Crabtree Publishing Co.

Phillips, Dee. Scout. 1 vol. unabr. ed. 2011. (Right Now! Ser.). (ENG., Illus.). 45p. (YA). (gr. 9-12). pap. 8.95 *(978-1-61651-252-1(0))* Saddleback Educational Publishing, Inc.

Pinfold, Levi. The Django. Pinfold, Levi, illus. 2010. (ENG., Illus.). 40p. (J). (gr. k-4). 16.99 *(978-0-7636-4788-9(8)*, Templar) Candlewick Pr.

Potter, Debra, illus. I Am the Music Man. 2006. (Classic Books with Holes Big Book Ser.). (ENG.). 16p. (J). (gr. -1-3). *(978-1-84643-010-7(0))* Child's Play International Ltd.

Pratchett, Terry. The Amazing Maurice & His Educated Rodents. 2008. (Discworld Novels Ser.). 368p. (YA). (gr. 8-18). pap. 8.99 *(978-0-06-001235-9(8))* HarperCollins Pubs.

—The Amazing Maurice & His Educated Rodents. 2003. (ENG.). 340p. (gr. 7). 19.00 *(978-0-7569-1458-5(2))* Perfection Learning Corp.

—The Amazing Maurice & His Educated Rodents. 2008. (Discworld Ser.: 33). (YA). (gr. 5-8). 19.65 *(978-0-613-65757-0(8)*, Turtleback) Turtleback Bks.

Prendergast, Gabrielle. The Frail Days, 1 vol. 2015. (Orca Limelights Ser.). (ENG.). 128p. (J). (gr. 6-9). pap. 9.95 *(978-1-4598-0464-7(3))* Orca Bk. Pubs. USA.

Rainbird, Becky. Taking Notes. 2010. (Lucky Six Ser.: 3). (ENG., Illus.). 160p. (J). (gr. 4-7). pap. 6.99 *(978-1-4052-3944-8(1))* Egmont Bks., Ltd. GBR. Dist: Independent Pubs. Group.

Reel FX Inc. Staff, et al, illus. A Tale of Two Friends. 2014. (Book of Life Ser.). (ENG.). 32p. (J). (gr. k-2). pap. 3.99 *(978-1-4814-2573-5(0)*, Simon Spotlight) Simon Spotlight.

Ritter, John H. Under the Baseball Moon. 2008. (ENG., Illus.). 320p. (J). (gr. 5-18). 9.99 *(978-0-14-241090-5(X)*, Puffin Books) Penguin Young Readers Group.

—Under the Baseball Moon. 2008. (Illus.). 283p. (gr. 8-12). 17.00 *(978-0-7569-8934-7(5))* Perfection Learning Corp.

Rivers, Olivia. Tone Deaf. 2016. (ENG.). 288p. (YA). (gr. 8). 17.99 *(978-1-63450-707-3(X)*, Sky Pony Pr.) Skyhorse Publishing Co., Inc.

Robinson, Craig & Mansbach, Adam. Jake the Fake Keeps It Real. Knight, Keith, illus. 2017. (Jake the Fake Ser.: 1). (ENG.). 144p. (J). (gr. 3-7). 13.99 *(978-0-553-52351-5(1)*, Crown Books For Young Readers) Random Hse. Children's Bks.

Ross, Jeff. At Ease, 1 vol. 2015. (Orca Limelights Ser.). (ENG.). 144p. (J). (gr. 6-9). pap. 9.95 *(978-1-4598-0800-3(2))* Orca Bk. Pubs. USA.

Roy, Jennifer. Mindblind, 0 vols. unabr. ed. 2013. (ENG.). 254p. (J). (gr. 7-9). pap. 9.99 *(978-1-4778-1712-4(3)*, 9781477817124, Amazon Children's Publishing) Amazon Publishing.

Roy, Ron. The X'ed-Out X-Ray. Gurney, John Steven, illus. 2005. (to Z Mysteries Ser.: No. 24). (ENG.). 96p. (J). (gr. 1-4). 4.99 *(978-0-375-82481-4(2)*, Random Hse. Bks. for Young Readers) Random Hse. Children's Bks.

Rubens, Michael. The Bad Decisions Playlist. (ENG.). 304p. (YA). (gr. 9). 2017. pap. 9.99 ***(978-1-328-74208-7(3)**,* HMH Books For Young Readers) 2016. 17.99 *(978-0-544-09667-7(3))* Houghton Mifflin Harcourt Publishing Co.

Ryan, Tom. Totally Unrelated, 1 vol. 2013. (Orca Limelights Ser.). (J). (ENG.). 128p. (gr. 6-9). pap. 9.95 *(978-1-4598-0458-6(9))*; 120p. *(978-1-4598-0648-1(4))* Orca Bk. Pubs. USA.

Sachar, Louis. Small Steps. 2008. (ENG.). 288p. (YA). (gr. 7-9). pap. 9.99 *(978-0-385-73315-1(1)*, Ember) Random Hse. Children's Bks.

Schwabach, Karen. The Storm Before Atlanta. 2011. (ENG.). 320p. (J). (gr. 3-7). pap. 6.99 *(978-0-375-85867-3(9)*, Yearling) Random Hse. Children's Bks.

Seidler, Tor. Toes. Beddows, Eric, illus. 2004. 176p. (J). (gr. 3-18). (ENG.). 15.99 *(978-0-06-054099-9(0))*; lib. bdg. 16.89 *(978-0-06-054100-2(8))* HarperCollins Pubs. (Geringer, Laura Book).

Shahegh, Mahvash. The Green Musician. Ewart, Claire, illus. 2015. (ENG.). 36p. (J). (gr. k-3). 16.95 *(978-1-937786-42-7(0)*, Wisdom Tales) World Wisdom, Inc.

Shaskan, Trisha Speed. Punk Skunks. Shaskan, Stephen, illus. 2016. 40p. (J). (gr. -1-3). 17.99 *(978-0-06-236396-1(4))* HarperCollins Pubs.

Shlasko, Robert. Molly & the Sword Diamond, Donna, illus. 2004. 32p. (J). 15.95 *(978-0-9745077-4-3(1))* Jane & Street Pubs. Ltd.

Shoulders, Michael. Crossing the Dead Line: Stephen's Journey Through the Civil War. 2016. (ENG.). 384p. (YA). (gr. 4-7). 16.99 *(978-1-58536-951-5(9)*, 204098) Sleeping Bear Pr.

Singer, Marilyn. Miss Muffet, or What Came After. Litchfield, David, illus. 2016. (ENG.). 40p. (J). (gr. 1-4). 16.99 *(978-0-547-90566-2(1))* Houghton Mifflin Harcourt Publishing Co.

Skuse, C. J. Rockoholic. 2012. (YA). *(978-0-545-44251-0(6))*; (ENG.). 368p. (J). (gr. 9). 18.99 *(978-0-545-42960-3(9))* Scholastic, Inc.

Slater, Teddy. Four Fiddlers. Kennedy, Kelly, illus. 2005. (Number Tales Ser.). (ENG.). 16p. (J). (gr. -1-1). pap. 2.99 *(978-0-439-69008-9(0))* Scholastic, Inc.

Sluzhaev, Viktor, illus. The Lute Player: A Tale from Russia. 2013. (Tales of Honor Ser.). (ENG.). 32p. (J). (gr. 1-4). pap. 8.95 *(978-1-937529-59-8(2))*; lib. bdg. 26.60 *(978-1-937529-75-8(4))* Red Chair Pr.

Smith, J. D. The Best Mariachi in the World/El Mejor Mariachi del Mundo. de la Vega, Eida, tr. Jones, Dani, illus. 2008. (ENG & SPA.). 32p. (J). (gr. 4-7). lib. bdg. 16.95 *(978-0-9770906-1-7(2)*, Raven Tree Pr.,Csi) Continental Sales, Inc.

Smith-Ready, Jeri. Shade. (ENG.). (YA). (gr. 9). 2011. 336p. pap. 9.99 *(978-1-4169-9406-0(8))* 2010. 320p. 17.99 *(978-1-4169-9406-0(8))* Simon Pulse. (Simon Pulse).

—Shift. (ENG.). (YA). (gr. 9). 2012. 400p. pap. 9.99 *(978-1-4169-9409-1(2))* 2011. 384p. 17.99 *(978-1-4169-9408-4(4))* Simon Pulse. (Simon Pulse).

Smith, Roland. Independence Hall. (I, Q Ser.: Bk. 1). (ENG., 312p. (gr. 5-9). 2009. Illus.). (J). 15.95 *(978-1-58536-468-8(1))* 2008. (YA). pap. 8.95 *(978-1-58536-325-4(1))* Sleeping Bear Pr.

Smith, Roland & Spradlin, Michael P. The Windy City, Bk.5. 2014. (I, Q Ser.). (ENG.). 240p. (YA). (gr. 5-7). 9.99 *(978-1-58536-823-5(7)*, 202902) Sleeping Bear Pr.

Sonnenblick, Jordan. Are You Experienced? 2015. (YA). lib. bdg. 20.85 *(978-0-606-37592-4(9))* Turtleback Bks.

—Notes from the Midnight Driver. 2009. 265p. 18.00 *(978-1-60686-516-3(1))* Perfection Learning Corp.

—Notes from the Midnight Driver. 2007. (ENG.). 288p. (J). (gr. 7-12). pap. 9.99 *(978-0-439-75781-2(9)*, Scholastic Paperbacks) Scholastic, Inc.

Sorrells, Walter. Fake ID. 2007. (Hunted Ser.). (ENG.). 336p. (YA). (gr. 7-18). 9.99 *(978-0-14-240762-2(3)*, Puffin Books) Penguin Young Readers Group.

Spradlin, Michael P. & Smith, Roland. Alcatraz. 2014. (I, Q Ser.). (ENG.). 272p. (J). (gr. 5-7). 16.99 *(978-1-58536-826-6(1)*, 203667); pap. 9.99 *(978-1-58536-825-9(3)*, 203727) Sleeping Bear Pr.

Staunton, Ted. Power Chord, 1 vol. 2011. (Orca Currents Ser.). (ENG.). 128p. (J). (gr. 5-9). pap. 9.95 *(978-1-55469-903-2(7))*; lib. bdg. 16.95 *(978-1-55469-904-9(5))* Orca Bk. Pubs. USA.

Stern, A. J. Rocking Out! Marts, Doreen Mulryan, illus. 2012. (Frankly, Frannie Ser.: 8). (ENG.). 128p. (J). (gr. 1-3). 12.99 *(978-0-448-45751-2(2))*; pap. 4.99 *(978-0-448-45750-5(4))* Penguin Young Readers Group. (Grosset & Dunlap).

Stevenson, Chris. The Drum of Destiny. 2016. (Middle-Grade Novels Ser.). (ENG., Illus.). 224p. (gr. 4-7). lib. bdg. 26.65 *(978-1-4965-2673-1(2))* Stone Arch Bks.

Stiefvater, Maggie. Lament: The Faerie Queen's Deception. 2008. (Lament Novel Ser.: 1). (ENG., Illus.). 336p. (YA). (gr. 8-18). pap. 9.95 *(978-0-7387-1370-0(8)*, 1286181, Flux) North Star Editions.

Sugg, Zoe. Girl Online: On Tour. 2016. (ENG.). (Girl Online Book Ser.: 2). 368p. (gr. 7). pap. 11.99 *(978-1-5011-0034-5(3)*, Atria Bks.); (J). pap. 13.00 ***(978-1-5011-5958-9(5))*** Simon & Schuster.

—Girl Online - On Tour. 2015. (Girl Online Book Ser.: 2). (ENG., Illus.). 352p. (gr. 7-12). 17.99 *(978-1-5011-0033-8(5)*, Atria Bks.) Simon & Schuster.

Sullivan, Sarah. Passing the Music Down. Root, Barry, illus. 2011. (ENG.). 32p. (J). (gr. k-3). 17.99 *(978-0-7636-3753-8(X))* Candlewick Pr.

Tangerine, Tracey. Buddy Zooka: In the French Quarter & Beyond. 2010. (ENG.). 201p. (J). (gr. 7-12). pap. 16.00 *(978-0-9741995-8-0(3))* Chin Music Pr.

Tashjian, Janet. For What It's Worth. 2012. (ENG.). 288p. (YA). (gr. 7-12). 16.99 *(978-0-8050-9365-0(6)*, 9780805093650, Holt, Henry & Co. Bks. For Young Readers) Holt, Henry & Co.

Tate, Eleanora E. The Minstrel's Melody. 2009. (Mysteries Through Time Ser.). 176p. (gr. 4-8). (YA). pap. 15.25 *(978-1-60754-180-6(7))*; (Illus.). (J). 31.95 *(978-1-60754-179-0(3))* Windmill Bks.

Taylor, Debbie & Morrison, Frank. Sweet Music in Harlem, 1 vol. 2004. (ENG., Illus.). 32p. (J). 17.95 *(978-1-58430-165-3(1))* Lee & Low Bks., Inc.

Taylor, Debbie A. Sweet Music in Harlem. Morrison, Frank, illus. 2014. 32p. pap. 9.00 *(978-1-61003-220-9(9))* Center for the Collaborative Classroom.

Thompson, Kate. The Last of the High Kings. 2008. 323p. (YA). (gr. 7-18). lib. bdg. 17.89 *(978-0-06-117596-1(X)*, HarperTeen) HarperCollins Pubs.

Torres, Jennifer. Finding the Music, 1 vol. Alarcão, Renato, illus. 2015.Tr. of En Pos de la Música. (ENG & SPA.). 40p. (J). 18.95 *(978-0-89239-291-9(6))* Lee & Low Bks., Inc.

Townley, Roderick. Sky. 2010. (ENG.). 272p. (YA). (gr. 7). pap. 12.99 *(978-1-4423-3973-6(X)*, Atheneum Bks. for Young Readers) Simon & Schuster Children's Publishing.

Trine, Greg. The Grateful Fred. Montijo, Rhode, illus. 3rd rev. ed. 2006. (Melvin Beederman, Superhero Ser.: 3). (ENG.). 144p. (J). (gr. 2-5). pap. 8.99 *(978-0-8050-7922-7(X)*, 9780805079227) Square Fish.

Trout, Robert J. Drumbeat: The Story of a Civil War Drummer Boy. 2007. 190p. (J). (gr. 4-9). pap. 12.95 *(978-1-57249-390-2(9)*, White Mane Kids) White Mane Publishing Co., Inc.

Vagnozzi, Barbara. The Musicians of Bremen. 2007. (Flip-Up Fairy Tales Ser.). (ENG., Illus.). 24p. (J). (gr. 1-2). *(978-1-84643-115-9(8))* Child's Play International Ltd.

Vernick, Audrey. Teach Your Buffalo to Play Drums. Jennewein, Daniel, illus. 2011. (ENG.). 32p. (J). (gr. -1-3). 16.99 *(978-0-06-176253-6(9))* HarperCollins Pubs.

Walsh, Alice. A Gift of Music: Emile Benoit & His Fiddle, 1 vol. Butler, Geoff, illus. 2010. (ENG.). 32p. (J). (gr. k-5). 12.95 *(978-1-897174-52-4(7)*, Tuckamore Bks) Creative Bk. Publishing CAN. Dist: Orca Bk. Pubs. USA.

Weatherford, Carole Boston. Becoming Billie Holiday. Cooper, Floyd, illus. 2008. (ENG.). 120p. (YA). (gr. 9-18). 19.95 *(978-1-59078-507-2(X)*, Wordsong) Boyds Mills Pr.

Wells, Helen. Cherry Ames, Private Duty Nurse. 2006. (Cherry Ames Nurse Stories Ser.). 224p. (J). (gr. 3-7). 14.95 *(978-0-8261-0398-7(7))* Springer Publishing Co., Inc.

Wenberg, Michael. Stringz. 2010. 216p. (YA). (gr. 6-10). 16.95 *(978-1-934813-33-1(6))* Westside Bks.

Whitaker, Alecia. The Road to You. 2015. (Wildflower Ser.: 2). (ENG.). 352p. (YA). (gr. 7-17). 18.00 *(978-0-316-25140-2(2))* Sports Illustrated For Kids.

—The Way Back Home. 2016. (Wildflower Ser.: 3). (ENG.). 336p. (YA). (gr. 7-17). 17.99 *(978-0-316-25144-0(5)*, Poppy) Little, Brown Bks. for Young Readers.

Winters, Ben H. The Secret Life of Ms. Finkleman. 2011. (ENG.). 272p. (J). (gr. 3-7). pap. 5.99 *(978-0-06-196543-2(X))* HarperCollins Pubs.

Wolff, Virginia Euwer. The Mozart Season. 2007. (ENG.). 272p. (J). (gr. 6-8). per. 11.99 *(978-0-312-36745-9(7)*, 9780312367459) Square Fish.

Yoo, Paula. Good Enough. 2012. (ENG.). 336p. (YA). (gr. 8). pap. 7.99 *(978-0-06-079090-5(3)*, HarperTeen) HarperCollins Pubs.

Zepp, Gene W. Return of the Pied Piper of Hamelin. 2011. 48p. pap. 21.99 *(978-1-4628-7007-3(4))* Xlibris Corp.

MUSICIANS, NEGRO

see African American Musicians

MUSICIANS—UNITED STATES

Adams, Michelle Medlock. Kenny Chesney. 2006. (Blue Banner Biography Ser.). (Illus.). 32p. (YA). (gr. 4-7). lib. bdg. 25.70 *(978-1-58415-502-7(7)*, 1259607) Mitchell Lane Pubs., Inc.

Andrews, Troy. Trombone Shorty. Collier, Bryan, illus. 2015. (ENG.). 40p. (J). (gr. -1-3). 17.95 *(978-1-4197-1465-8(1)*, Abrams Bks. for Young Readers) Abrams, Inc.

Aretha Franklin: Singer. 2nd rev. ed. 2010. (Black Americans of Achievement Legacy Edition Ser.). (Illus.). 104p. (gr. 6-12). 35.00 *(978-1-60413-712-5(6))* Facts On File, Inc.

Azzarelli, Ally. Drake! Hip-Hop Celebrity. 2013. (Sizzling Celebrities Ser.). 48p. (J). (gr. 4-9). pap. 8.95 *(978-1-4644-0275-3(2))* Enslow Pubs., Inc.

Bankston, John. The Life & Times of Scott Joplin. 2004. (Masters of Music Ser.). (Illus.). 48p. (gr. 4-8). lib. bdg. 20.95 *(978-1-58415-270-5(2))* Mitchell Lane Pubs., Inc.

Bodden, Valerie. Carrie Underwood: Big Time. 2013. 21p. 23.09 *(978-1-60818-476-7(5))* Creative Co., The.

Boone, Mary. Dizzy Gillespie. 2012. 48p. (J). (gr. 4-8). lib. bdg. 29.95 *(978-1-61228-272-5(5))* Mitchell Lane Pubs., Inc.

—Ornette Coleman. 2012. (J). lib. bdg. 29.95 *(978-1-61228-268-8(7))* Mitchell Lane Pubs., Inc.

—Taylor Swift: Seeing Red. 2013. (Illus.). 96p. (J). pap. *(978-1-60078-902-1(1))* Triumph Bks.

Breguet, Amy. Yellowcard. 2006. (Contemporary Musicians & Their Music Ser.). (Illus.). 48p. (YA). (gr. 5-9). lib. bdg. 29.25 *(978-1-4042-0714-1(7))* Rosen Publishing Group, Inc., The.

Brooks, Riley. Taylor Swift: Fearless Star. 2010. (Illus.). 48p. (J). *(978-0-545-30382-8(6))* Scholastic, Inc.

Brown, Jim. Willie Nelson: Red Headed Stranger. 2014. (ENG., Illus.). 224p. (J). pap. 16.95 *(978-1-55082-255-7(1)*, Fox Music Bks.) Quarry Pr. CAN. Dist: SCB Distributors.

Brown, Monica. Tito Puente: Mambo King; Rey del Mambo. López, Rafael, illus. 2013. (ENG.). 32p. (J). (gr. -1-3). 17.99 *(978-0-06-122783-7(8)*, Rayo) HarperCollins Pubs.

Burlingame, Jeff. Taylor Swift: Music Superstar. 2011. (Hot Celebrity Biographies Ser.). (Illus.). 48p. (J). (gr. 5-9). lib. bdg. 25.27 *(978-0-7660-3870-7(X))* Enslow Pubs., Inc.

Burns, Kylie. Carrie Underwood. 2013. (ENG., Illus.). 32p. (J). *(978-0-7787-0024-1(0))*; pap. *(978-0-7787-0043-2(7))* Crabtree Publishing Co.

Cefrey, Holly. Taylor Swift. 2011. (Megastars Ser.). (Illus.). 48p. (YA). (gr. 5-8). 29.25 *(978-1-4358-3575-7(1)*, Rosen Reference) Rosen Publishing Group, Inc., The.

Christensen, Bonnie. Elvis: The Story of the Rock & Roll King. Christensen, Bonnie, illus. 2015. (ENG., Illus.). 32p. (J). (gr. 1-4). 17.99 *(978-0-8050-9447-3(4)*, 9780805094473, Holt, Henry & Co. Bks. For Young Readers) Holt, Henry & Co.

—Woody Guthrie: Poet of the People. Christensen, Bonnie, illus. 2009. (ENG., Illus.). 32p. (J). (gr. -1-2). pap. 7.99 *(978-0-553-11203-0(1)*, Dragonfly Bks.) Random Hse. Children's Bks.

Cline-Ransome, Lesa. Benny Goodman & Teddy Wilson: Taking the Stage As the First Black-and-White Jazz Band in History. Ransome, James E., illus. 2014. (ENG.). 32p. (J). (gr. 3-7). 16.95 *(978-0-8234-2362-0(X))* Holiday Hse., Inc.

Collins, Terry. Elvis: A Graphic Novel, 1 vol. Melcher, Michele, illus. (American Graphic Ser.). (ENG.). 32p. (gr. 3-4). 2011. pap. 8.10 *(978-1-4296-6266-6(2))* 2011. pap. 47.70 *(978-1-4296-6434-9(7))* 2010. lib. bdg. 30.65 *(978-1-4296-5476-0(7))* Capstone Press of Coughlan Cos. (Graphic Library).

—King of Pop: The Story of Michael Jackson, 1 vol. Byers, Michael, illus. 2012. (American Graphic Ser.). (ENG.). 32p. (gr. 3-4). pap. 8.10 *(978-1-4296-7994-7(8))*; 30.65 *(978-1-4296-6015-0(5))* Capstone Press of Coughlan Cos. (Graphic Library).

—Louis Armstrong: Jazz Legend, 1 vol. Pope, Richie, illus. 2012. (American Graphic Ser.). (ENG.). 32p. (gr. 3-4). pap. 8.10 *(978-1-4296-9336-3(3))*; lib. bdg. 30.65 *(978-1-4296-8622-8(7))* Capstone Press of Coughlan Cos. (Graphic Library).

Cupp, Tonya. Taylor Swift. 2015. (Illus.). 48p. (J). lib. bdg. *(978-1-62713-310-4(0))* Cavendish Square Publishing.

Currie-McGhee, L. K. Alicia Keys. 2012. (People in the News Ser.). (ENG.). 128p. 39.40 *(978-1-4205-0782-9(6)*, Lucent Bks.) Cengage Gale.

Dann, Sarah. Beyoncé. 2013. (ENG., Illus.). 32p. (J). *(978-0-7787-0019-7(4))* Crabtree Publishing Co.

Deans, Karen. Swing Sisters: The Story of the International Sweethearts of Rhythm. Cepeda, Joe, illus. 2015. (ENG.). 32p. (J). (gr. -1-3). 16.95 *(978-0-8234-1970-8(3))* Holiday Hse., Inc.

Dylan, Bob. Forever Young. Rogers, Paul, illus. 2008. (ENG.). 40p. (J). (gr. -1-4). 17.99 *(978-1-4169-5808-6(8)*, Atheneum Bks. for Young Readers) Simon & Schuster Children's Publishing.

Earl, C. F. Kanye West. 2012. (Superstars of Hip-Hop Ser.). (Illus.). 48p. (J). (gr. 3-4). 19.95 *(978-1-4222-2533-2(X))* Mason Crest.

Edgers, Geoff. Who Was Elvis Presley? O'brien, John, illus. 2007. (Who Was... ? Ser.). 105p. (gr. 2-5). 15.00 *(978-0-7569-8164-8(6))* Perfection Learning Corp.

Franke, Alfe. Julianne Hough. 2010. (Country Music Stars Ser.). (ENG.). 32p. (J). (gr. 3-8). pap. 10.50 *(978-1-4339-3933-4(9))*; lib. bdg. 25.25 *(978-1-4339-3932-7(0))* Stevens, Gareth Publishing LLLP.

—Miranda Lambert. 2010. (Country Music Stars Ser.). (ENG.). 32p. (J). (gr. 3-8). pap. 10.50 *(978-1-4339-3936-5(3))*; lib. bdg. 25.25 *(978-1-4339-3935-8(5))* Stevens, Gareth Publishing LLLP.

French, Holly. One Direction. 2015. (Pop Icons Ser.). (Illus.). 64p. (J). (gr. 7). lib. bdg. 23.95 *(978-1-4222-3249-1(2))* Mason Crest.

Frisch, Aaron. Taylor Swift. 2013. (Illus.). 24p. (J). 25.65 *(978-1-60818-333-3(5)*, Creative Education) Creative Co., The.

Giddens, Sandra. Chris Daughtry. (Who's Your Idol? Ser.). 48p. 2009. (gr. 5-5). 53.00 *(978-1-60854-786-9(8)*, Rosen Reference) 2008. (Illus.). (J). (gr. 3-7). lib. bdg. 29.25 *(978-1-4042-1371-5(6))* Rosen Publishing Group, Inc., The.

Gigliotti, Jim. Who Is Stevie Wonder? Marchesi, Stephen, illus. 2016. (Who Was? Ser.). (ENG.). 112p. (J). (gr. 3-7). lib. bdg. 15.99 *(978-0-399-54243-5(4)*, Grosset & Dunlap) Penguin Young Readers Group.

Gitlin, Martin. Chaz Bono. 2016. (Transgender Pioneers Ser.). 112p. (J). (gr. 6-6). 37.10 *(978-1-5081-7157-7(2))* Rosen Publishing Group, Inc., The.

Golio, Gary. Bird & Diz. Young, Ed, illus. 2015. (ENG.). 26p. (J). (gr. -1-3). 19.99 *(978-0-7636-6660-6(2))* Candlewick Pr.

—Jimi: Sounds Like a Rainbow - A Story of the Young Jimi Hendrix. Steptoe, Javaka, illus. 2010. (ENG.). 32p. (J). (gr. 1-4). 17.99 *(978-0-618-85279-6(4))* Houghton Mifflin Harcourt Publishing Co.

M
N
O

Gourley, Robbin. Talkin' Guitar: A Story of Young Doc Watson. 2015. (ENG., Illus.). 40p. (J). (gr. -1-3). 16.99 *(978-0-544-12988-7(1),* Clarion Bks.) Houghton Mifflin Harcourt Trade & Reference Pubs.

Griffiths, Katie. Beyoncé. 2017. (J). **(978-1-5026-2705-6(1))** Cavendish Square Publishing.

Hamilton, Toby G. Busta Rhymes. 2009. (Hip Hop (Mason Crest Paperback) Ser.). (Illus.). 64p. (YA). (gr. 4-7). pap. 7.95 *(978-1-4222-0333-0(6))* Mason Crest.

Hampton, Wilborn. Elvis Presley: A Twentieth Century Life. 2007. (ENG., Illus.). 192p. (YA). (gr. 7). 26.16 *(978-1-4287-4879-8(2))* Follett School Solutions.

Higgins, Melissa & Houser, Aimee. Taylor Swift: Country & Pop Superstar, 1 vol. 2012. (Contemporary Lives Set 1 Ser.). (ENG.). 112p. (J). (gr. 6-12). lib. bdg. 35.64 *(978-1-61783-327-4(4))* ABDO Publishing Co.

Higgins, Nadia. Bruno Mars: Pop Singer & Producer. 2012. (Pop Culture Bios Ser.). (ENG., Illus.). 32p. (gr. 3-6). pap. 7.95 *(978-1-4677-0235-5(8));* lib. bdg. 26.60 *(978-0-7613-4144-4(7),* Lerner Pubns.) Lerner Publishing Group.

Jacobson, Bob. Les Paul: Guitar Wizard. 2012. (Badger Biographies Ser.). (ENG., Illus.). 112p. (J). (gr. 4-6). pap. 12.95 *(978-0-87020-488-3(2))* Wisconsin Historical Society.

Janic, Susan & Thomas, Scott. Jonas Brothers Forever: The Unofficial Story of Kevin, Joe & Nick. 2009. (ENG., Illus.). 158p. (J). (gr. 4-7). pap. *(978-1-55022-851-9(X))* Filmer Ltd.

Jemaine, Bret. Sugarland. 2010. (Country Music Stars Ser.). (ENG.). 32p. (J). (gr. 3-8). pap. 10.50 *(978-1-4339-3939-6(8));* lib. bdg. 25.25 *(978-1-4339-3938-9(X))* Stevens, Gareth Publishing LLLP.

—Tim McGraw. 2010. (Country Music Stars Ser.). (ENG.). 32p. (J). (gr. 3-8). pap. 10.50 *(978-1-4339-3942-6(8));* lib. bdg. 25.25 *(978-1-4339-3941-9(X))* Stevens, Gareth Publishing LLLP.

The Jonas Brothers. 2011. (Megastars Ser.). (Illus.). 48p. (YA). pap. 11.75 *(978-1-4488-2258-4(0),* Rosen Reference) Rosen Publishing Group, Inc., The.

Kallen, Stuart A. Gwen Stefani. (Role Model Entertainers Ser.). (Illus.). 64p. (YA). 2010. (gr. 7-12). 22.95 *(978-1-4222-0510-5(X))* 2007. pap. 9.95 *(978-1-4222-0797-0(8))* Mason Crest.

Kawa, Katie & Cartlidge, Cherese. Taylor Swift: Superstar Singer. 2017. (People in the News Ser.). 104p. (J). (gr. 7-7). lib. bdg. 39.40 **(978-1-5345-6025-3(4),** Lucent Pr.) Greenhaven Publishing LLC.

Kelley, True. Who Is Dolly Parton? Harrison, Nancy et al, illus. 2014. (Who Was? Ser.). (ENG.). 112p. (J). (gr. 3-7). 5.99 *(978-0-448-47892-0(7),* Grosset & Dunlap) Penguin Young Readers Group.

Kohler, Dean Ellis & VanHecke, Susan. Rock 'n' Roll Soldier: A Memoir. 2009. (ENG.). 288p. (YA). (gr. 9-18). 17.99 *(978-0-06-124255-7(1),* HarperTeen) HarperCollins Pubs.

La Bella, Laura. My Chemical Romance. (Contemporary Musicians & Their Music Ser.). (Illus.). 48p. 2009. (ENG.). (gr. 7-12). pap. 11.75 *(978-1-4358-5126-9(9))* 2008. (J). lib. bdg. 29.25 *(978-1-4042-1818-5(1))* Rosen Publishing Group, Inc., The.

Lajiness, Katie. R5, 1 vol. 2016. (Big Buddy Pop Biographies Ser.). (ENG., Illus.). 32p. (J). (gr. 2-5). 28.50 *(978-1-68078-058-1(1))* ABDO Publishing Co.

—Riker Lynch, 1 vol. 2016. (Big Buddy Pop Biographies Ser.). (ENG., Illus.). 32p. (J). (gr. 2-5). 28.50 *(978-1-68078-054-3(9))* ABDO Publishing Co.

—Taylor Swift, 1 vol. 2016. (Big Buddy Pop Biographies Ser.). (ENG., Illus.). 32p. (J). (gr. 2-5). 28.50 *(978-1-68078-060-4(3))* ABDO Publishing Co.

Landau, Elaine. Beyoncé: R & B Superstar. 2012. (Pop Culture Bios Ser.). (ENG., Illus.). 32p. (gr. 3-6). pap. 7.95 *(978-1-4677-0234-8(X));* lib. bdg. 26.60 *(978-0-7613-4147-5(1),* Lerner Pubns.) Lerner Publishing Group.

Leavitt, Amie Jane. Bruno Mars. 2012. (Illus.). 32p. (J). lib. bdg. 25.70 *(978-1-61228-316-6(0))* Mitchell Lane Pubs., Inc.

—Toby Keith. 2008. (Blue Banner Biography Ser.). (Illus.). 32p. (YA). (gr. 4-7). lib. bdg. 25.70 *(978-1-58415-678-9(3))* Mitchell Lane Pubs., Inc.

Linde, Barbara M. Taylor Swift. 2010. (Today's Superstars Ser.). (ENG.). 48p. (J). (gr. 5-8). pap. 14.05 *(978-1-4339-4002-6(7));* lib. bdg. 31.95 *(978-1-4339-4001-9(9))* Stevens, Gareth Publishing LLLP.

Lusted, Marcia Amidon. Justin Timberlake: Musician, Actor, & Dancer, 1 vol. 2012. (Contemporary Lives Set 1 Ser.). (ENG.). 112p. (J). (gr. 6-12). lib. bdg. 35.64 *(978-1-61783-328-1(2))* ABDO Publishing Co.

Lynette, Rachel. Miles Davis. 2010. (Innovators Ser.). (Illus.). 64p. (J). 29.95 *(978-0-7377-5034-8(0),* Kidhaven) Cengage Gale.

Maccarry, Noel. Who Was Pete Seeger? 2017. (Who Was... ? Ser.). lib. bdg. 16.00 **(978-0-606-40116-6(4))** Turtleback Bks.

Magram, Clara. John Legend. (Pop Culture Ser.). (Illus.). 64p. (YA). (gr. 4-7). 2008. lib. bdg. 22.95 *(978-1-4222-0076-6(0))* 2007. pap. 7.95 *(978-1-4222-0360-6(3))* Mason Crest.

Mahin, Michael. Muddy: The Story of Blues Legend Muddy Waters. Turk, Evan, illus. 2017. (ENG.). 48p. (J). (gr. -1-3). 17.99 *(978-1-4814-4349-4(6))* Simon & Schuster Children's Publishing.

Marcovitz, Hal. Chris Daughtry. 2009. (Dream Big: American Idol Superstars Ser.). 64p. (YA). (gr. 5-18). 22.95 *(978-1-4222-1508-1(3));* pap. 9.95 *(978-1-4222-1595-1(4))* Mason Crest.

—Madonna: Entertainer. 2010. (Women of Achievement Ser.). 128p. (gr. 6-12). 35.00 *(978-1-60413-859-7(9),* Chelsea Hse.) Facts On File, Inc.

Markel, Rita J. Jimi Hendrix. 2003. (Biography Ser.). (Illus.). 112p. (YA). (gr. 6-18). pap. 7.95 *(978-0-8225-9697-4(0),* Carolrhoda Bks.) Lerner Publishing Group.

Marvis, Barbara. Day by Day with Beyonce. 2010. (Randy's Corner Ser.). (Illus.). 32p. (J). (gr. -1-2). lib. bdg. 25.70 *(978-1-58415-859-2(X))* Mitchell Lane Pubs., Inc.

Mattern, Joanne. Benny Goodman. 2012. (J). lib. bdg. 29.95 *(978-1-61228-269-5(5))* Mitchell Lane Pubs., Inc.

—Count Basie. 2012. (J). lib. bdg. 29.95 *(978-1-61228-270-1(9))* Mitchell Lane Pubs., Inc.

McDougall, Chros. Kurt Cobain: Alternative Rock Innovator, 1 vol. 2012. (Lives Cut Short Set 2 Ser.). (ENG.). 112p. (J). (gr. 6-12). 35.64 *(978-1-61783-480-6(7))* ABDO Publishing Co.

McIntosh, Kenneth. The Grateful Dead. 2008. (Pop Rock Ser.). (Illus.). 64p. (YA). (gr. 4-7). lib. bdg. 22.95 *(978-1-4222-0191-6(0))* Mason Crest.

McKissack, Patricia C. & McKissack, Fredrick L. Louis Armstrong: King of Jazz. 2013. (Famous African Americans Ser.). (Illus.). 24p. (J). (gr. k-18). 22.60 *(978-0-7660-4106-6(9));* pap. 7.95 *(978-1-4644-0200-5(0))* Enslow Pubs., Inc. (Enslow Elementary).

McNeese, Tim. Tito Puente. 2008. (Great Hispanic Heritage Ser.). (Illus.). 118p. (gr. 6-12). lib. bdg. 35.00 *(978-0-7910-9666-6(1),* Chelsea Hse.) Facts On File, Inc.

Mellark, Kat. Louis Armstrong: American Musician. 2013. (InfoMax Readers Ser.). (ENG.). 24p. (J). (gr. 2-3). pap. 49.50 *(978-1-4777-2429-3(X));* (Illus.). pap. 8.25 *(978-1-4777-2428-6(1))* Rosen Publishing Group, Inc., The. (Rosen Classroom).

Mitchells, Brett. The Dixie Chicks. 2008. (Contemporary Musicians & Their Music Ser.). (Illus.). 48p. (J). lib. bdg. 29.25 *(978-1-4042-1817-8(3))* Rosen Publishing Group, Inc., The.

—Dixie Chicks. 2009. (Contemporary Musicians & Their Music Ser.). (Illus.). 48p. (gr. 7-12). pap. 11.75 *(978-1-4358-5125-2(0),* Rosen Classroom) Rosen Publishing Group, Inc., The.

Mooney, Carla & Gale Editors. Jonas Brothers. 2009. (People in the News Ser.). (Illus.). 128p. (YA). (gr. 7-12). 33.95 *(978-1-4205-0236-7(0))* Cengage Gale.

Morganelli, Adrianna. Bruno Mars. 2013. (ENG., Illus.). 32p. (J). pap. *(978-0-7787-0041-8(0))* Crabtree Publishing Co.

Morreale, Marie. Ross Lynch. 2015. (ENG., Illus.). 48p. (J). lib. bdg. *(978-0-531-21573-9(3))* Children's Pr., Ltd.

—Taylor Swift. 2015. (ENG.). 48p. (J). pap. 7.95 *(978-0-531-21429-9(X),* Children's Pr.) Scholastic Library Publishing.

Mour, Stanley I. Innovators of American Jazz. 2013. (Inspiring Collective Biographies Ser.). 112p. (J). (gr. 5-18). 33.27 *(978-0-7660-4166-0(2))* Enslow Pubs., Inc.

Murphy, Maggie. The Jonas Brothers: Rock Stars. 2010. (Reading Power). (Illus.). 24p. (J). pap. 8.85 *(978-1-4488-1805-1(2),* PowerKids Pr.) Rosen Publishing Group, Inc., The.

—Taylor Swift: Country Music Star. 2010. (Reading Power). (Illus.). 24p. (J). pap. 8.85 *(978-1-4488-1803-7(6),* PowerKids Pr.) Rosen Publishing Group, Inc., The.

Napoli, Tony. Justin Timberlake: Breakout Music Superstar. 2009. (Hot Celebrity Biographies Ser.). (Illus.). 48p. (J). (gr. 5-9). pap. 8.95 *(978-0-7660-3632-1(4),* Enslow Elementary) Enslow Pubs., Inc.

Neimark, Anne E. Johnny Cash. 2008. (Up Close Ser.). (ENG., Illus.). 208p. (YA). (gr. 7-18). 7.99 *(978-0-14-241047-9(0),* Puffin Books) Penguin Young Readers Group.

Nelson, Robin. Taylor Swift: Country Pop Hit Maker. 2012. (Pop Culture Bios Ser.). (ENG., Illus.). 32p. (gr. 3-6). pap. 7.95 *(978-1-4677-0239-3(0));* lib. bdg. 26.60 *(978-0-7613-4143-7(9),* Lerner Pubns.) Lerner Publishing Group.

Nolan, Nina. Mahalia Jackson: Walking with Kings & Queens. Holyfield, John, illus. 2015. (ENG.). 32p. (J). (gr. -1-3). 17.99 *(978-0-06-087944-0(0))* HarperCollins Pubs.

O'Connor, Jim. Who Is Bob Dylan? Harrison, Nancy & O'brien, John, illus. 2013. (Who Was? Ser.). (ENG.). 112p. (J). (gr. 3-7). pap. 5.99 *(978-0-448-46461-9(6),* Grosset & Dunlap) Penguin Young Readers Group.

—Who Is Bob Dylan? 2013. (Who Is... ? Ser.). lib. bdg. 16.00 *(978-0-606-31685-9(X),* Turtleback) Turtleback Bks.

Old, Wendie C. The Life of Duke Ellington: Giant of Jazz. 2014. (Legendary African Americans Ser.). (Illus.). 96p. (J). (gr. 6-12). 27.94 *(978-0-7660-6127-9(2))* Enslow Pubs., Inc.

—The Life of Louis Armstrong: King of Jazz. 2014. (Legendary African Americans Ser.). (Illus.). 96p. (J). (gr. 6-12). 27.94 *(978-0-7660-6142-2(6))* Enslow Pubs., Inc.

Orr, Tamra. The Jonas Brothers. 2011. (Megastars Ser.). (Illus.). 48p. (YA). (gr. 5-8). 29.25 *(978-1-4358-3572-6(7),* Rosen Reference) Rosen Publishing Group, Inc., The.

—Louis Armstrong. 2012. (J). lib. bdg. 29.95 *(978-1-61228-264-0(4))* Mitchell Lane Pubs., Inc.

—Miles Davis. 2012. (J). lib. bdg. 29.95 *(978-1-61228-265-7(2))* Mitchell Lane Pubs., Inc.

Parker, Robert A. Piano Starts Here: The Young Art Tatum. Parker, Robert A., illus. 2016. (ENG., Illus.). 40p. (J). (gr. -1-3). 7.99 *(978-0-553-53392-7(4),* Dragonfly Bks.) Random Hse. Children's Bks.

Peppas, Lynn. Taylor Swift. 2010. (Superstars! Ser.). (ENG.). 32p. (J). (gr. 3-6). lib. bdg. *(978-0-7787-7252-1(7))* Crabtree Publishing Co.

Rajczak Nelson, Kristen. Bruno Mars: Singer & Songwriter. 2017. (Illus.). 24p. (J). pap. **(978-80-7660-784-2(1))** Enslow Pubs., Inc.

Rajczak Nelson, Kristen. China Anne McClain: Actress, Singer, & Songwriter. 2016. (Junior Biographies Ser.). 24p. (J). pap. 9.35 *(978-0-7660-8184-0(2))* Enslow Pubs., Inc.

Rau, Dana Meachen. Who Are the Rolling Stones? 2017. (Who Is... ? Ser.). lib. bdg. 16.00 **(978-0-606-39778-0(7))** Turtleback Bks.

Reef, Catherine. Leonard Bernstein & American Music. 2012. (Modern Music Masters Ser.). (gr. 7-12). 27.95 *(978-1-59935-125-4(0))* Reynolds, Morgan Inc.

Reusser, Kayleen. Day by Day with Taylor Swift. 2010. (Randy's Corner Ser.). (Illus.). 32p. (J). (gr. -1-2). lib. bdg. 25.70 *(978-1-58415-857-8(3))* Mitchell Lane Pubs., Inc.

—Taylor Swift. 2008. (Blue Banner Biography Ser.). (Illus.). 32p. (YA). (gr. 4-7). lib. bdg. 25.70 *(978-1-58415-675-8(9))* Mitchell Lane Pubs., Inc.

Rice, Earle. Charlie Parker. 2012. (J). lib. bdg. 29.95 *(978-1-61228-266-4(0))* Mitchell Lane Pubs., Inc.

Riddle, Sharon Kay & Sanders, Nancy/Ida. Tony Loved to Learn. Mendoza, Megan Elizabeth, illus. 2007. 32p. (J). pap. 15.00 *(978-0-9761583-6-3(1))* Olive Leaf Pubns.

Rivera, Ursula. Aretha Franklin. 2009. (Rock & Roll Hall of Famers Ser.). 112p. (gr. 5-8). 63.90 *(978-1-60852-467-9(1),* Rosen Reference) Rosen Publishing Group, Inc., The.

Roberts, Russell. Alicia Keys: Singer-Songwriter, Musician, Actress, & Producer. 2012. (Transcending Race Ser.). 64p. (J). (gr. 5). 22.95 *(978-1-4222-2727-5(8))* Mason Crest.

Roza, Greg. Bo Diddley: Rock-And-Roll All-Star. 2010. (Inspiring Lives Ser.). 32p. (J). (gr. 5-8). lib. bdg. 25.25 *(978-1-4339-3622-7(4));* (Illus.). pap. 10.50 *(978-1-4339-3623-4(2))* Stevens, Gareth Publishing LLLP.

Rubin, Laurie. Do You Dream in Color? Insights from a Girl Without Sight. 2012. (ENG., Illus.). 400p. (J). (gr. 7). pap. 18.95 *(978-1-60980-424-4(4),* Triangle Square) Seven Stories Pr.

Russell-Brown, Katheryn. Little Melba & Her Big Trombone. Morrison, Frank, illus. 2014. (ENG.). 40p. (J). 18.95 *(978-1-60060-898-8(1))* Lee & Low Bks., Inc.

Sabol, Stephanie. Who Is Bruce Springsteen? Copeland, Gregory, illus. 2016. (Who Was? Ser.). (ENG.). 112p. (J). (gr. 3-7). 5.99 *(978-0-448-48703-8(9),* Grosset & Dunlap) Penguin Young Readers Group.

Saddleback Educational Publishing Staff. Usher. 2013. (Hip-Hop Biographies (Saddleback Publishing) Ser.). (YA). lib. bdg. 23.25 *(978-0-606-31490-9(3),* Turtleback) Turtleback Bks.

Saddleback Educational Publishing Staff, ed. Elvis Presley, 1 vol. unabr. ed. 2008. (Graphic Biographies Ser.). (ENG., Illus.). 25p. (YA). (gr. 9-12). pap. 7.95 *(978-1-59905-221-2(0))* Saddleback Educational Publishing, Inc.

Sawyer, Sarah. Fall Out Boy. (Contemporary Musicians & Their Music Ser.). 48p. 2009. (ENG., Illus.). (gr. 7-12). pap. 11.75 *(978-1-4358-5127-6(7))* 2009. (gr. 6-6). 53.00 *(978-1-61511-935-6(3))* 2008. (Illus.). (J). lib. bdg. 29.25 *(978-1-4042-1819-2(X))* Rosen Publishing Group, Inc., The.

Schuman, Michael A. Beyonc: A Biography of a Legendary Singer. 2014. (African-American Icons Ser.). 104p. (J). lib. bdg. 27.94 *(978-0-7660-4230-8(8))* Enslow Pubs., Inc.

—Led Zeppelin: Legendary Rock Band. 2009. (Rebels of Rock Ser.). (Illus.). 112p. (J). (gr. 5-18). pap. 10.95 *(978-0-7660-3618-5(9))* Enslow Pubs., Inc.

Schwartz, Heather E. Justin Timberlake: From Mouseketeer to Megastar. 2015. (Pop Culture Bios Ser.). (ENG., Illus.). 32p. (J). (gr. 3-6). pap. 7.95 *(978-1-4677-6098-0(6),* Lerner Pubns.) Lerner Publishing Group.

Shea, Therese. Brad Paisley. 2010. (Country Music Stars Ser.). (ENG.). 32p. (J). (gr. 3-8). pap. 10.50 *(978-1-4339-3930-3(4));* lib. bdg. 25.25 *(978-1-4339-3929-7(0))* Stevens, Gareth Publishing LLLP.

—Toby Keith. 2010. (Country Music Stars Ser.). (ENG.). 32p. (J). (gr. 3-8). pap. 10.50 *(978-1-4339-3945-7(2));* lib. bdg. 25.25 *(978-1-4339-3944-0(4))* Stevens, Gareth Publishing LLLP.

—Usher. 2011. (Hip-Hop Headliners Ser.). (Illus.). 32p. (gr. 3-8). pap. 10.50 *(978-1-4339-4813-8(3));* (J). 25.25 *(978-1-4339-4812-1(5))* Stevens, Gareth Publishing LLLP.

Sheafer, Silvia Anne. The Life of Aretha Franklin: Queen of Soul. 2015. (Legendary African Americans Ser.). 96p. (J). (gr. 6-12). 27.94 *(978-0-7660-6225-2(2))* Enslow Pubs., Inc.

Spence, Kelly. Taylor Swift: Pop Music Superstar. 2016. (Leading Women Ser.). (Illus.). 112p. (J). (gr. 7-7). 39.93 *(978-1-5026-1991-4(1))* Cavendish Square Publishing.

Stark, William N. Aerosmith: Living the Rock 'n' Roll Dream. 2015. (Legends of Rock Ser.). (ENG.). 32p. (J). (gr. 3-4). lib. bdg. 27.99 *(978-1-4914-1815-4(X),* Edge Bks.) Capstone Press of Coughlan Cos.

Stine, Megan. Who Was Michael Jackson? 2015. (Who Was... ? Ser.). lib. bdg. 16.00 *(978-0-606-37559-7(7))* Turtleback Bks.

Stine, Megan & dePaola, Tomie. Who Was Michael Jackson? Qui, Joseph J. M., illus. 2015. (Who Was? Ser.). (ENG.). 112p. (J). (gr. 3-7). 5.99 *(978-0-448-48410-5(2),* Grosset & Dunlap) Penguin Young Readers Group.

Taylor Swift. 2011. (Megastars Ser.). (Illus.). 48p. (YA). pap. 11.75 *(978-1-4488-2261-4(0),* Rosen Reference) Rosen Publishing Group, Inc., The.

Tieck, Sarah. Blake Shelton: Country Music Star, 1 vol. 2013. (Big Buddy Biographies Set 9 Ser.). (ENG.). 32p. (J). (gr. 2-5). lib. bdg. 28.50 *(978-1-61783-754-8(7),* Big Buddy Bks.) ABDO Publishing Co.

—Bruno Mars: Popular Singer & Songwriter, 1 vol. 2012. (Big Buddy Biographies Ser.). (ENG.). 32p. (J). (gr. 2-5). 28.50 *(978-1-61783-226-0(X))* ABDO Publishing Co.

—Jonas Brothers: Singing Sensations, 1 vol. 2009. (Big Buddy Biographies Set 2 Ser.). (ENG., Illus.). 32p. (J). (gr. 2-5). 28.50 *(978-1-60453-549-5(0))* ABDO Publishing Co.

—Nat & Alex Wolff: Stars of Nickelodeon's the Naked Brothers Band, 1 vol. 2008. (Big Buddy Biographies Ser.). (ENG.). 32p. (J). (gr. 2-5). 28.50 *(978-1-60453-126-8(6))* ABDO Publishing Co.

—Taylor Swift: Country Music Star, 1 vol. 2009. (Big Buddy Biographies Set 3 Ser.). (ENG., Illus.). 32p. (J). (gr. 2-5). 28.50 *(978-1-60453-712-3(4))* ABDO Publishing Co.

—Taylor Swift: Country Music Star CD & Book. 2010. (Big Buddy Biographies CD+Book Ser.). 32p. (gr. 2-5). audio compact disk 57.00 *(978-1-61613-311-5(2),* Big Buddy Bks.) ABDO Publishing Co.

—Usher: Famous Singer, 1 vol. 2009. (Big Buddy Biographies Set 2 Ser.). (ENG., Illus.). 32p. (J). (gr. 2-5). 28.50 *(978-1-60453-551-8(2))* ABDO Publishing Co.

Torres, John A. Timbaland. 2008. (Blue Banner Biography Ser.). (Illus.). 32p. (YA). (gr. 4-7). lib. bdg. 25.70 *(978-1-58415-671-0(6))* Mitchell Lane Pubs., Inc.

Tracy, Kathleen. Chris Daughtry. 2007. (Blue Banner Biography Ser.). (Illus.). 32p. (YA). (gr. 4-7). lib. bdg. 25.70 *(978-1-58415-629-1(5))* Mitchell Lane Pubs., Inc.

Walker, Ida. Lynyrd Skynyrd. 2008. (Pop Rock Ser.). (Illus.). 64p. (YA). (gr. 4-7). lib. bdg. 22.95 *(978-1-4222-0213-5(5))* Mason Crest.

—Lynyrd Skynyrd. 2007. (Popular Rock Superstars of Yesterday & Today Ser.). (Illus.). 64p. (YA). (gr. 4-7). pap. 7.95 *(978-1-4222-0320-0(4))* Mason Crest.

Wallenfeldt, Jeff, ed. The Birth of Rock & Roll: Music in the 1950s Through the 1960s. 2012. (Popular Music Through the Decades Ser.). (ENG., Illus.). 240p. (J). (gr. 9-12). lib. bdg. 45.00 *(978-1-61530-906-1(3))* Rosen Publishing Group, Inc., The.

—The Birth of Rock & Roll: Music in the 1950S Through The 1960S. 2012. (Popular Music Through the Decades Ser.). (ENG., Illus.). 240p. (YA). (gr. 9-12). 90.00 *(978-1-61530-915-3(2))* Rosen Publishing Group, Inc., The.

Watson, Stephanie. Elvis Presley: Rock & Roll's King, 1 vol. 2012. (Lives Cut Short Set 2 Ser.). (ENG.). 112p. (J). (gr. 6-12). 35.64 *(978-1-61783-482-0(3))* ABDO Publishing Co.

Weatherford, Carole Boston. Before John Was a Jazz Giant: A Song of John Coltrane. Qualls, Sean, illus. 2008. (ENG.). 32p. (J). (gr. k-4). 17.99 *(978-0-8050-7994-4(7),* 9780805079944, Holt, Henry & Co. Bks. For Young Readers) Holt, Henry & Co.

Webster, Christine. The Jonas Brothers. 2009. (Remarkable People Ser.). (Illus.). 24p. (J). (gr. 4-6). pap. 8.95 *(978-1-60596-627-4(4));* lib. bdg. 24.45 *(978-1-60596-626-7(6))* Weigl Pubs., Inc.

Wells, Peggy Sue. Soulja Boy Tell 'Em. 2008. (Blue Banner Biography Ser.). (Illus.). 32p. (YA). (gr. 4-7). lib. bdg. 25.70 *(978-1-58415-676-5(7))* Mitchell Lane Pubs., Inc.

Winter, Jonah. How Jelly Roll Morton Invented Jazz. Mallett, Keith, illus. 2015. (ENG.). 32p. (J). (gr. k-3). 17.99 *(978-1-59643-963-4(7),* 9781596439634) Roaring Brook Pr.

Wyckoff, Edwin Brit. The Man Who Invented the Electric Guitar: The Genius of les Paul. 2013. (Genius Inventors & Their Great Ideas Ser.). (Illus.). 48p. (J). (gr. 3-18). 25.27 *(978-0-7660-4137-0(9));* pap. 8.95 *(978-1-4644-0207-4(8),* Enslow Elementary) Enslow Pubs., Inc.

Zimmerman, Robert. Switchfoot. 2009. (Contemporary Musicians & Their Music Ser.). 48p. (gr. 6-6). 53.00 *(978-1-61511-946-2(9))* Rosen Publishing Group, Inc., The.

MUSKOX

Flaherty, William & Niptanatiak, Allen. Muskox, 1 vol. Zhao, Amei & McLeod, Kagan, illus. 2016. (Animals Illustrated Ser.). (ENG.). 24p. (J). (gr. k-2). 15.95 *(978-1-77227-122-5(5))* Inhabit Media Inc. CAN. Dist: Independent Pubs. Group.

Markle, Sandra. Musk Oxen. (Animal Prey Ser.). 2008. (Illus.). 39p. (J). (gr. 3-7). per. 7.95 *(978-0-8225-6067-8(4),* First Avenue Editions) 2008. pap. 46.95 *(978-0-8225-9320-1(3))* 2007. (ENG., Illus.). 40p. (J). (gr. 3-6). lib. bdg. 25.26 *(978-0-8225-6064-7(X))* Lerner Publishing Group.

Owen, Ruth. Musk Oxen. 2013. (Polar Animals: Life in the Freezer Ser.). (ENG., Illus.). 32p. (J). (gr. k-5). pap. 10.00 *(978-1-4777-0225-3(3));* lib. bdg. 25.25 *(978-1-4777-0219-2(9))* Windmill Bks.

Patrick, Roman. Musk Oxen. 2010. (Animals That Live in the Tundra Ser.). (ENG.). 24p. (J). (gr. -1-3). pap. 8.15 *(978-1-4339-3903-7(7));* lib. bdg. 22.60 *(978-1-4339-3902-0(9))* Stevens, Gareth Publishing LLLP.

Pratt, Laura. Les Boelig;ufs Musqueacute;s: Les Animaux du Canada. Karvonen, Tanjah, tr. from ENG. 2011. (FRE.). 24p. (gr. 3-6). *(978-1-77071-414-4(6))* Weigl Educational Pubs. Ltd.

—Muskox. 2010. (Illus.). 24p. *(978-1-55388-668-6(2));* pap. *(978-1-55388-669-3(0))* Weigl Educational Pubs. Ltd.

MUSKOX—FICTION

Brown, Tricia. The Itchy Little Musk Ox. Dubac, Debra, illus. 2006. (ENG.). 32p. (J). (gr. -1-3). pap. 9.99 *(978-0-88240-614-5(0),* Alaska Northwest Bks.) Graphic Arts Ctr. Publishing Co.

Cabatingan, Erin. A Is for Musk Ox. Myers, Matthew, illus. 2012. (Musk Ox Ser.: 1). (ENG.). 40p. (J). (gr. k-2). 18.99 *(978-1-59643-676-3(X),* 9781596436763) Roaring Brook Pr.

—Musk Ox Counts. Myers, Matthew, illus. 2013. (Musk Ox Ser.: 2). (ENG.). 36p. (J). (gr. k-2). 16.99 *(978-1-59643-798-2(7),* 9781596437982) Roaring Brook Pr.

—The World According to Musk Ox. Myers, Matthew, illus. 2014. (Musk Ox Ser.: 3). (ENG.). 40p. (J). (gr. k-2). 17.99 *(978-1-59643-799-9(5),* 9781596437999) Roaring Brook Pr.

MUSKRATS

Lawrence, Ellen. Muskrat. 2016. (Swamp Things: Animal Life in a Wetland Ser.). (ENG.). 24p. (J). (gr. -1-3). 17.95 *(978-1-944102-55-5(8))* Bearport Publishing Co., Inc.

MUSKRATS—FICTION

Burgess, Thornton W. The Adventures of Jerry Muskrat. 2007. 108p. (gr. 2-5). per. 9.95 *(978-1-60312-336-5(9));* 22.95 *(978-1-60312-674-8(0))* Aegypan.

—The Adventures of Jerry Muskrat. 2006. pap. 9.95 *(978-1-59605-676-3(2),* Cosimo Classics) Cosimo, Inc.

—The Adventures of Jerry Muskrat. 2011. 108p. 23.95 *(978-1-4638-9564-8(X))* Rodgers, Alan Bks.

—Jerry Muskrat at Home. (J). 18.95 *(978-0-8488-0399-5(X))* Amereon Ltd.

Chaconas, Dori. The Babysitters. McCue, Lisa, illus. 2014. (Cork & Fuzz Ser.: 6). (ENG.). 32p. (J). (gr. 1-3). pap. 3.99 *(978-0-448-48050-3(6),* Penguin Young Readers) Penguin Young Readers Group.

—Best Friends No. 1. McCue, Lisa, illus. 2010. (Cork & Fuzz Ser.: 1). (ENG.). 32p. (J). (gr. 1-3). mass mkt. 3.99 *(978-0-14-241593-1(6),* Penguin Young Readers) Penguin Young Readers Group.

—The Collectors, 4 vols. McCue, Lisa, illus. 2010. (Cork & Fuzz Ser.: 4). (ENG.). 32p. (J). (gr. 1-3). mass mkt. 3.99 *(978-0-14-241714-0(9),* Penguin Young Readers) Penguin Young Readers Group.

—Cork & Fuzz. McCue, Lisa, illus. 2005. (Cork & Fuzz Ser.: 1). (ENG.). 32p. (J). (gr. 1-3). 13.99 *(978-0-670-03602-8(1),* Viking Books for Young Readers) Penguin Young Readers Group.

—Cork & Fuzz - The Collectors. McCue, Lisa, illus. 2008. (Cork & Fuzz Ser.: 4). (ENG.). 32p. (J). (gr. k-3). 13.99 *(978-0-670-06286-7(3),* Viking Books for Young Readers) Penguin Young Readers Group.

—Finders Keepers, 5 vols. McCue, Lisa, illus. 2011. (Cork & Fuzz Ser.: 5). (ENG.). 32p. (J). (gr. 1-3). mass mkt. 3.99 *(978-0-14-241869-7(2),* Penguin Young Readers) Penguin Young Readers Group.

—Good Sports. McCue, Lisa, illus. 2010. (Cork & Fuzz Ser.: 3). (ENG.). 32p. (J). (gr. 1-3). mass mkt. 3.99 *(978-0-14-241713-3(0),* Penguin Young Readers) Penguin Young Readers Group.

—Merry Merry Holly Holly. McCue, Lisa, illus. 2015. (Cork & Fuzz Ser.: 11). (ENG.). 32p. (J). (gr. -1-k). 16.99 *(978-0-451-47501-5(1),* Viking Books for Young Readers) Penguin Young Readers Group.

—Short & Tall No. 2, 2 vols. McCue, Lisa, illus. 2010. (Cork & Fuzz Ser.: 2). (ENG.). 32p. (J). (gr. 1-3). mass mkt. 3.99 *(978-0-14-241594-8(4),* Penguin Young Readers) Penguin Young Readers Group.

—Swimming Lesson, 7 vols. McCue, Lisa, illus. 2011. (Cork & Fuzz Ser.: 7). (ENG.). 32p. (J). (gr. 1-3). 13.99 *(978-0-670-01261-7(5),* Viking Books for Young Readers) Penguin Young Readers Group.

—The Swimming Lesson. McCue, Lisa, illus. 2014. (Cork & Fuzz Ser.: 7). (ENG.). 32p. (J). (gr. 1-3). pap. 3.99 *(978-0-448-48051-0(4),* Penguin Young Readers) Penguin Young Readers Group.

Chaconas, Dori & Bader, Bonnie. Spring Cleaning. McCue, Lisa, illus. 2015. (Cork & Fuzz Ser.: 10). (ENG.). 32p. (J). (gr. 1-3). 14.99 *(978-0-670-01686-0(1),* Penguin Young Readers) Penguin Young Readers Group.

—Wait a Minute. McCue, Lisa, illus. 2015. (Cork & Fuzz Ser.: 9). (ENG.). 32p. (J). (gr. 1-3). 3.99 *(978-0-14-750856-0(8),* Penguin Young Readers) Penguin Young Readers Group.

Garis, Howard Roger. Sammie & Susie Littletail. 2005. 182p. pap. 11.95 *(978-1-4218-1565-7(6),* 1st World Library - Literary Society) 1st World Publishing, Inc.

McSorley, Paul J. & Bearss, Patricia. The Adventures of Forealdo: Finding Millie. 2012. 34p. 24.95 *(978-1-4626-6721-5(X))* America Star Bks.

Savageau, Cheryl & Hynes, Robert. Muskrat Will Be Swimming, 1 vol. 2006. (ENG., Illus.). 32p. (gr. 3-7). 7.95 *(978-0-88448-280-2(4),* 884280) Tilbury Hse. Pubs.

MUSLIMS

Here are entered works on the community of believers in Islam. Works on the religion of which Muhammad is the prophet are entered under Islam.

Abdullah, Noorah Kathryn. What Do We Say... A Guide to Islamic Manners. 2nd ed. 2010. (ENG., Illus.). 24p. (J). (gr. -1-k). 8.95 *(978-0-86037-350-6(9))* Kube Publishing Ltd. GBR. Dist: Consortium Bk. Sales & Distribution.

Arab-American & Muslim Writers. 2010. (Multicultural Voices Ser.). (Illus.). 130p. (gr. 6-12). 35.00 *(978-1-60413-377-6(5),* Chelsea Hse.) Facts On File, Inc.

Blake, Philip. We Are Muslims. 2016. (ENG., Illus.). 32p. (J). (gr. 4-6). pap. 11.99 *(978-1-4451-3888-6(3),* Franklin Watts) Hachette Children's Group GBR. Dist: Hachette Bk. Group.

Demi, Barbara. Muhammad. Demi, Barbara, illus. 2003. (ENG., Illus.). 48p. (J). (gr. 2-5). 19.95 *(978-0-689-85264-0(9),* McElderry, Margaret K. Bks.) McElderry, Margaret K. Bks.

Diaz, Wendy Umm Uthman. Nuestros Oficios. 2012. (ENG.). (J). pap. 12.99 *(978-1-4675-3282-2(7))* Independent Pub.

Faust, Daniel R. Ibtihaj Muhammad: Muslim American Champion Fencer & Olympian. 2017. (Breakout Biographies Ser.). 32p. (gr. 9-10). 26.25 ***(978-1-5081-6060-1(0),*** PowerKids Pr.) Rosen Publishing Group, Inc., The.

Flatt, Lizann. Early Islamic Empires. 2013. (Life in the Early Islamic World Ser.). (ENG., Illus.). 48p. (J). pap. *(978-0-7787-2178-9(7))* Crabtree Publishing Co.

Gunderson, Jessica. A Biography of Malcolm X. Hayden, Seitu, illus. 2010. (American Graphic Ser.). (ENG.). 32p. (gr. 3-4). lib. bdg. 30.65 *(978-1-4296-5471-5(6),* Graphic Library) Capstone Press of Coughlan Cos.

—X: A Biography of Malcolm X. Hayden, Seitu, illus. 2011. (American Graphic Ser.). (ENG.). 32p. (gr. 3-4). pap. 8.10 *(978-1-4296-6267-3(0),* Graphic Library) Capstone Press of Coughlan Cos.

Hafiz, Dilara, et al. The American Muslim Teenager's Handbook. 2009. (ENG., Illus.). 192p. (YA). (gr. 7-18). pap. 13.99 *(978-1-4169-8578-5(6),* Atheneum Bks. for Young Readers) Simon & Schuster Children's Publishing.

Heiligman, Deborah & Yavari, Neguin. Celebrate Ramadan & Eid Al-Fitr: With Praying, Fasting, & Charity. 2009. (Holidays Around the World Ser.). (ENG., Illus.). 32p. (J). (gr. 1-4). 6.95 *(978-1-4263-0476-7(5),* National Geographic Children's Bks.) National Geographic Society.

Hodges, Rick. What Muslims Think, & How They Live. 2005. (Introducing Islam Ser.). (Illus.). 112p. (YA). lib. bdg. 24.95 *(978-1-59084-702-2(4))* Mason Crest.

Ismail, Vehbi. Muhammad: The Last Prophet. 2011. 190p. 42.95 *(978-1-258-03217-3(1))* Literary Licensing, LLC.

Kavanaugh, Dorothy. The Muslim World: An Overview. 2010. (World of Islam Ser.). (Illus.). 64p. (YA). (gr. 4-7). lib. bdg. 22.95 *(978-1-4222-0532-7(0))* Mason Crest.

Kemmetmueller, Donna Jean. My Muslim Friend: A Young Catholic Learns about Islam. Jacobsen, Laura, illus. 2006. 47p. (J). 15.95 *(978-0-8198-4844-4(1))* Pauline Bks. & Media.

Melman, Anna. Muslims in America. 2010. (World of Islam Ser.). (Illus.). 64p. (YA). (gr. 4-7). lib. bdg. 22.95 *(978-1-4222-0535-8(5))* Mason Crest.

Peppas, Lynn. Cultural Traditions in Iran. 2015. (ENG., Illus.). 32p. (J). *(978-0-7787-8061-8(9))* Crabtree Publishing Co.

Robert, Na'ima B. Mabrook! a World of Muslim Weddings. Adl, Shirin, illus. 2016. (ENG.). 32p. (J). (gr. -1-2). 17.99 *(978-1-84780-588-1(4),* Frances Lincoln Children's Bks.) Quarto Publishing Group UK GBR. Dist: Hachette Bk. Group.

Rowell, Rebecca & Llanas, Sheila Griffin. Malala Yousafzai: Education Activist, 1 vol. 2013. (Essential Lives Set 8 Ser.). (ENG., Illus.). 112p. (J). (gr. 6-12). lib. bdg. 35.64 *(978-1-61783-897-2(7),* Essential Library) ABDO Publishing Co.

Sanna, Ellyn. Gallup Guides for Youth Facing Persistent Prejudice Muslims. 2012. (Gallup Guides for Youth Facing Persistent Prejudice Ser.). 64p. (J). (gr. 7-8). 22.95 *(978-1-4222-2468-7(6))* Mason Crest.

—People with Mental & Physical Challenges. 2012. (Gallup Guides for Youth Facing Persistent Prejudice Ser.). 64p. (J). (gr. 7-8). 22.95 *(978-1-4222-2470-0(8))* Mason Crest.

Sears, Evelyn. Muslims & the West. 2005. (Introducing Islam Ser.). (Illus.). 112p. (YA). lib. bdg. 24.95 *(978-1-59084-700-8(8))* Mason Crest.

Shabazz, Ilyasah & Magoon, Kekla. X. 2016. (ENG.). 384p. (YA). (gr. 9). 19.65 *(978-0-606-39098-9(7))* Turtleback Bks.

Vietze, Andrew. The Life & Death of Malcolm X. 2017. (J). pap. ***(978-1-5383-8031-4(5),*** Rosen Young Adult) Rosen Publishing Group, Inc., The.

Wolny, Philip. Muslims Around the World Today. 2009. (Understanding Islam Ser.). 64p. (gr. 6-6). 58.50 *(978-1-60854-626-8(8))* Rosen Publishing Group, Inc., The.

Zaidi, Anbara. Muslims in America, Vol. 8. Pecastaing, Camille, ed. 2016. (Understanding Islam Ser.: Vol. 8). (ENG., Illus.). 112p. (J). (gr. 7-12). 25.95 *(978-1-4222-3676-5(5))* Mason Crest.

40 Hadiths for Children. 2014. (ENG., Illus.). 84p. (J). (gr. 3-7). pap. 8.95 *(978-1-59784-311-9(3))* Tughra Bks.

MUSLIMS, BLACK

see Black Muslims

MUSLIMS—FICTION

Abdel-Fattah, Randa. Does My Head Look Big in This? 2007. 360p. (YA). 25.66 *(978-1-4287-4610-7(2),* Follettbound) Follett School Solutions.

—Does My Head Look Big in This? 2008. (ENG.). 368p. (J). (gr. 7). pap. 9.99 *(978-0-439-92233-3(X),* Scholastic Paperbacks) Scholastic, Inc.

Abdel-Fattah, Randa. The Lines We Cross. 2017. (ENG.). 400p. (J). (gr. 7-7). 18.99 ***(978-1-338-11866-7(8),*** Scholastic Pr.) Scholastic, Inc.

Abdelsalam, Lisa. A Song for Me: A Muslim Holiday Story. Nielsen, Janet Marie, illus. 2006. 34p. (J). *(978-0-9755975-1-4(5))* Abdelsalam Corp.

Addasi, Maha. Time to Pray. Albitar, Nuha, tr. Gannon, Ned, illus. 2010. (ENG & ARA.). 32p. (J). (gr. 2-4). 17.95 *(978-1-59078-611-6(4))* Boyds Mills Pr.

Ali, Anila & Gottlieb, Karen. Mommy, Am I A? Seiders, Marian, illus. 2010. 28p. pap. 11.95 *(978-1-935105-45-9(0))* Avid Readers Publishing Group.

Ali, S. K. Saints, Misfits, Monsters, & Mayhem. 2017. (ENG., Illus.). 336p. (YA). (gr. 9). 18.99 ***(978-1-4814-9924-8(6),*** Salaam Reads) Simon & Schuster Bks. For Young Readers.

Barto, Linda iLham, illus. Where the Ghost Camel Grins: Muslim Fables for Families of All Faiths. 2009. (ENG.). 119p. (gr. 5). 19.95 *(978-1-879402-24-9(6))* Tahrike Tarsile Quran, Inc.

Bradbury, Jennifer. A Moment Comes. 2013. (ENG., Illus.). 288p. (YA). (gr. 7). 17.99 *(978-1-4169-7876-3(3))* Simon & Schuster Children's Publishing.

Budhos, Marina. Watched. 2016. (ENG.). 272p. (YA). (gr. 7). 17.99 *(978-0-553-53418-4(1),* Lamb, Wendy Bks.) Random Hse. Children's Bks.

Cunnane, Kelly. Deep in the Sahara. Hadadi, Hoda, illus. 2013. (ENG.). 40p. (J). (gr. -1-3). 17.99 *(978-0-375-87034-7(2),* Schwartz & Wade Bks.) Random Hse. Children's Bks.

Dhar, Lisa Jane. Aisha Goes in Search of Colour. Zulkifli, Azhari, illus. 2009. (ENG.). 32p. (J). (gr. k-2). 6.95 *(978-0-86037-472-5(6))* Kube Publishing Ltd. GBR. Dist: Consortium Bk. Sales & Distribution.

Doller, Trish. In a Perfect World. 2017. (ENG., Illus.). 304p. (YA). (gr. 7). 18.99 ***(978-1-4814-7988-2(1),*** Simon Pulse) Simon Pulse.

Faruqi, Reem & Lyon, Lea. Lailah's Lunchbox, 1 vol. 2015. (ENG., Illus.). 32p. (gr. 1-7). 16.95 *(978-0-88448-431-8(9),* 884431) Tilbury Hse. Pubs.

Gilani-Williams, Fawzia. Yaffa & Fatima: Shalom, Salaam. Fedele, Chiara, illus. 2017. (ENG.). 24p. (gr. -1-3). 17.99 *(978-1-4677-8938-7(0),* Kar-Ben Publishing) Lerner Publishing Group.

Gonzales, Mark. Yo Soy Muslim. 2017. (ENG., Illus.). 32p. (J). (gr. -1-3). 17.99 ***(978-1-4814-8936-2(4),*** Simon & Schuster Bks. For Young Readers) Simon & Schuster Bks. For Young Readers.

Hamed, Maissa. The Last Night of Ramadan. El Wakil, Mohamed, illus. 2007. (J). (gr. -1-3). *(978-0-88010-586-6(0),* Bell Pond Bks.) SteinerBooks, Inc.

Hayes, Rosemary. Mixing It. 2007. (ENG.). 192p. (J). (gr. 4-7). per. *(978-1-84507-495-1(5))* Rough Guides, Ltd.

—Payback. 2009. (ENG.). 208p. (J). (gr. 7-10). pap. 8.95 *(978-1-84507-935-2(3),* Frances Lincoln) Quarto Publishing Group UK GBR. Dist: Hachette Bk. Group.

Helwani, Najiyah Diana. Sophia's Journal: Time Warp 1857. 2008. (YA). per. *(978-0-9793577-2-5(1))* Muslim Writers Publishing.

Hingoro, Samira, creator. A Marriage Proposal. 2003. (YA). per. 12.95 *(978-0-9743167-0-3(9))* Faith Pubns.

Holm, M. S. How Mohammed Saved Miss Liberty: The Story of a Good Muslim Boy. 2008. (ENG., Illus.). 270p. (YA). (gr. 7-12). pap. 12.00 *(978-0-9796199-0-8(4),* Sentry Bks.) Great West Publishing.

Husain, Aliya. Neither This nor That. 2010. 260p. pap. 19.99 *(978-0-557-22302-2(4))* Lulu Pr., Inc.

Jalali, Reza. Moon Watchers: Shirin's Ramadan Miracle, 1 vol. Sibley O'Brien, Anne, illus. 2017. (ENG.). 32p. (gr. 1-7). pap. 8.95 *(978-0-88448-587-2(0),* 884587) Tilbury Hse. Pubs.

Jolin, Paula. In the Name of God. 2008. (ENG.). 224p. (YA). (gr. 9-12). pap. 18.99 *(978-0-312-38455-5(6),* 9780312384555) Square Fish.

Karim, Sheba. That Thing We Call a Heart. 2017. 288p. (YA). (gr. 8). 17.99 *(978-0-06-244570-4(7),* HarperTeen) HarperCollins Pubs.

Kayani, M. S. Assalamu Alaykum. Hewitt, Ibrahim, ed. Norridge, Terry, illus. 2nd ed. 2009. (ENG.). 22p. (J). (gr. -1-1). 8.95 *(978-0-86037-347-6(9))* Kube Publishing Ltd. GBR. Dist: Consortium Bk. Sales & Distribution.

Khan, Farheen. Ibrahim Khan & the Mystery of the Roaring Lion. 2010. (Ibrahim Khan Ser.). (ENG., Illus.). 56p. (J). (gr. 2-6). pap. 6.50 *(978-0-86037-467-1(X))* Kube Publishing Ltd. GBR. Dist: Consortium Bk. Sales & Distribution.

Khan, Hena. Amina's Voice. Dela Cruz, Abigail, illus. 2017. (ENG.). 208p. (J). (gr. 3-7). 16.99 *(978-1-4814-9206-5(3),* Salaam Reads) Simon & Schuster Bks. For Young Readers.

—Golden Domes & Silver Lanterns: A Muslim Book of Colors. Amini, Mehrdokht, illus. 2012. (ENG.). 32p. (J). (gr. -1-2). 17.99 *(978-0-8118-7905-7(4))* Chronicle Bks. LLC.

—The Night of the Moon: A Muslim Holiday Story. Paschkis, Julie, illus. 2008. (ENG.). 32p. (J). (gr. -1-3). 16.99 *(978-0-8118-6062-8(0))* Chronicle Bks. LLC.

Kimmel, Eric A. Hiss-S-S-S! 2012. (ENG.). 208p. (J). 17.95 *(978-0-8234-2415-3(4))* Holiday Hse., Inc.

Klaus, Sandra. Mustafas Geheimnis: Ein Moslemischer Junge auf der Suche nach Gott. Date not set.Tr. of Mustapha's Secret - A Muslim Boy's Search to Know God. (GER., Illus.). (J). (gr. 2-7). pap. *(978-0-9617490-6-4(7))* Gospel Missionary Union.

—Tainata na Mustapha. Date not set.Tr. of Mustapha's Secret. (BUL.). (J). (gr. 2-7). pap. *(978-1-890940-04-1(6))* Gospel Missionary Union.

Krantz, Hazel. In the Garden of the Caliph. 2012. 132p. (gr. 4-6). 23.14 *(978-1-4669-2888-6(3));* (J). pap. 13.14 *(978-1-4669-2886-2(7))* Trafford Publishing.

Laird, Elizabeth. Crusade. 2016. (ENG.). 400p. (J). (gr. 4-7). pap. 8.99 *(978-1-5098-0296-8(7))* Pan Macmillan GBR. Dist: Independent Pubs. Group.

Lat. Kampung Boy. Lat, illus. rev. ed. 2006. Orig. Title: The Kampung Boy. (ENG., Illus.). 144p. (YA). (gr. 7-8). pap. 19.99 *(978-1-59643-121-8(0),* 9781596431218, First Second Bks.) Roaring Brook Pr.

Lipp, Frederick. Fatima. Lindmark, Margaret, illus. 2006. 32p. (J). pap. *(978-1-59336-302-4(8))* Mondo Publishing.

Mahmoodian, Maryam. Muslim Teens In: Pitfalls & Pranks. 2008. (YA). per. 10.95 *(978-0-9793577-3-2(X))* Muslim Writers Publishing.

Marsden, Carolyn. The White Zone. (ENG.). 192p. (J). (gr. 4-8). 2014. pap. 9.95 *(978-1-4677-5177-3(4))* 2012. 17.95 *(978-0-7613-7383-4(7))* Lerner Publishing Group. (Carolrhoda Bks.).

Mills, Wendy. All We Have Left. (ENG.). 368p. (YA). 2017. pap. 9.99 *(978-1-68119-432-5(5),* 9781681194325) 2016. 17.99 *(978-1-61963-343-8(4),* 9781619633438) Bloomsbury Publishing USA. (Bloomsbury USA Childrens).

Mobin-Uddin, Asma. My Name Is Bilal. Kiwak, Barbara, illus. 2005. (ENG.). 32p. (J). (gr. 1-7). 16.95 *(978-1-59078-175-3(9))* Boyds Mills Pr.

Muhammad, Khaleel. Helping the Polonskys. 2013. (ENG., Illus.). 80p. (J). (gr. 2-6). pap. 8.95 *(978-0-86037-454-1(8))* Kube Publishing Ltd. GBR. Dist: Consortium Bk. Sales & Distribution.

Mullarkey, Lisa. A Feast of Fun, 1 vol. Franco, Paula, illus. 2016. (ENG.). 112p. (J). lib. bdg. *(978-1-62402-163-3(8))* Magic Wagon.

Munshey, Sana. We're off to Make 'Umrah. 2011. (ENG., Illus.). 32p. (J). (gr. -1-k). 10.95 *(978-0-86037-458-9(0))* Kube Publishing Ltd. GBR. Dist: Consortium Bk. Sales & Distribution.

Muschla, Gary Robert. The Sword & the Cross. 2009. (YA). lib. bdg. *(978-0-88092-471-9(3))* Royal Fireworks Publishing Co.

Nolan, Han. A Summer of Kings. 2006. 334p. (J). *(978-1-4156-7340-9(3))* Harcourt Trade Pubs.

O'Malley Cerra, Kerry. Just a Drop of Water. 2016. (ENG.). 320p. (J). (gr. 2-7). pap. 7.99 *(978-1-5107-1234-8(8),* Sky Pony Pr.) Skyhorse Publishing Co., Inc.

Paterson, Katherine. The Day of the Pelican. 2010. (ENG.). 160p. (J). (gr. 5-7). pap. 7.99 *(978-0-547-40627-5(4))* Houghton Mifflin Harcourt Publishing Co.

Perera, Anna. Guantanamo Boy. (ENG.). 352p. (YA). (gr. 8-12). 2012. 9.99 *(978-0-8075-3078-8(6))* 2011. 17.99 *(978-0-8075-3077-1(8))* Whitman, Albert & Co.

Pollock, Tom. The Glass Republic. 2016. (Skyscraper Throne Ser.: 2). (ENG.). 448p. (YA). (gr. 7-9). pap. 14.99 *(978-1-68144-348-5(1),* Jo Fletcher Books) Quercus NA.

Radwan, Hassan. Rashid & the Missing Body. 2010. (ENG., Illus.). 80p. (J). (gr. 2-6). pap. 5.95 *(978-0-86037-395-7(9))* Kube Publishing Ltd. GBR. Dist: Consortium Bk. Sales & Distribution.

Radwan, Hassan & Stratford, Stevan. Rashid & the Haupmann Diamond. 2010. (ENG., Illus.). 112p. (J). (gr. 2-6). pap. 6.50 *(978-0-86037-357-5(6))* Kube Publishing Ltd. GBR. Dist: Consortium Bk. Sales & Distribution.

Robert, Na'ima Bint. The Swirling Hijaab. Mistry, Nilesh, illus. 2004. 24p. (J). *(978-1-85269-910-9(8));* (BEN & ENG.). pap. *(978-1-85269-160-8(3));* (PER & ENG.). pap. *(978-1-85269-163-9(8));* (GER & ENG.). pap. *(978-1-85269-165-3(4));* (ITA & ENG.). pap. *(978-1-85269-167-7(0));* (URD & ENG.). pap. *(978-1-85269-143-1(3));* (ARA & ENG.). pap. *(978-1-85269-119-6(0));* (PAN & ENG.). pap. *(978-1-85269-178-3(6));* (POR & ENG.). pap. *(978-1-85269-179-0(4));* (SER & ENG.). pap. *(978-1-85269-180-6(8));* (SOM & ENG.). pap. *(978-1-85269-181-3(6));* (SPA & ENG.). pap. *(978-1-85269-182-0(4));* (TAM & ENG.). pap. *(978-1-85269-188-2(3));* (TUR & ENG.). pap. *(978-1-85269-189-9(1));* (CZE & ENG.). pap. *(978-1-85269-629-0(X))* Mantra Lingua.

Robert, Naima Bint, tr. The Swirling Hijaab: Le Foulard Qui Tourbillonne. Mistry, Nilesh, illus. 2004. (FRE & ENG.). 24p. (J). pap. *(978-1-85269-164-6(6))* Mantra Lingua.

Schaenen, Inda. All the Cats of Cairo. 2007. 225p. (J). (gr. -1-10). per. 8.95 *(978-0-9768126-5-4(7))* Brown Barn Bks.

Sharif, Medeia. Bestest. Ramadan. Ever. 2011. (ENG.). 312p. (YA). pap. 9.95 *(978-0-7387-2323-5(1),* Flux) North Star Editions.

Stolz, Joelle. The Shadows of Ghadames. Temerson, Catherine, tr. 2006. (ENG.). 128p. (J). (gr. 3-7). 5.99 *(978-0-440-41949-5(2),* Yearling) Random Hse. Children's Bks.

Stratton, Allan. Borderline. (ENG.). (YA). (gr. 8). 2012. 320p. pap. 9.99 *(978-0-06-145113-3(4))* 2010. (Illus.). 304p. 16.99 *(978-0-06-145111-9(8))* HarperCollins Pubs. (HarperTeen).

Ulker, Munise. Little Batul's Eid Celebration: The Most Pleasant Festival of Sacrifice. 2013. (ENG., Illus.). 32p. (J). (gr. -1-3). pap. 6.95 *(978-1-59784-294-5(X))* Tughra Bks.

Westlund, Emmaline. Fatim. 2012. 42p. pap. 16.95 *(978-1-4626-9660-4(0))* America Star Bks.

Worsham, Adria F. Max Celebrates Ramadan, 1 vol. Gallagher-Cole, Memie, illus. 2008. (Read-It! Readers: the Life of Max Ser.). (ENG.). 24p. (gr. -1-2). lib. bdg. 21.32 *(978-1-4048-4762-0(6),* Easy Readers) Picture Window Bks.

Youree, Barbara. Senegal Sleuths. 2006. 56p. 7.75 *(978-0-8341-2226-0(X))* Beacon Hill Pr. of Kansas City.

Zalben, Jane Breskin. A Moon for Moe & Mo. Quraishi, Mariam, illus. 2017. (J). lib. bdg. *(978-1-58089-727-3(4))* Charlesbridge Publishing, Inc.

Zia, Farhana. The Garden of My Imaan, 1 vol. (ENG.). (J). (gr. 3-6). 2016. 232p. pap. 7.95 *(978-1-56145-921-6(6))* 2013. 192p. 15.95 *(978-1-56145-698-7(5))* Peachtree Pubs.

MUSSOLINI, BENITO, 1883-1945

Benchmark Education Company. Three Twentieth Century Dictators (Teacher Guide) 2004. *(978-1-4108-2593-3(0))* Benchmark Education Co.

Ruby, India. Three Twentieth Century Dictators: Set Of 6. 2011. (Navigators Ser.). (J). pap. 50.00 net. *(978-1-4108-2578-0(7))* Benchmark Education Co.

MUSTELIDAE

Klobuchar, Lisa. Badgers & Other Mustelids. 2005. (World Book's Animals of the World Ser.). (Illus.). 64p. (J). *(978-0-7166-1265-0(8))* World Bk., Inc.

Morgan, Sally. The Weasel Family. 2004. (J). lib. bdg. *(978-1-59389-173-2(3))* Cherrytree Bks.

Paulsen, Rosalie. My Ferrets. 2009. 84p. pap. 19.95 *(978-1-4489-9257-7(5))* America Star Bks.

MUTATION (BIOLOGY)

see Evolution

MYCENAE (EXTINCT CITY)

Schlitz, Laura Amy. The Hero Schliemann: The Dreamer Who Dug up Troy. Byrd, Robert, illus. 2006. (ENG.). 80p. (J). (gr. 4-7). lib. bdg. 17.99 *(978-0-7636-2283-1(4))* Candlewick Pr.

MYCOLOGY

see Fungi

MYSTERY AND DETECTIVE STORIES

A. Gunderson, Jessica. Pick your Poison Apple. 2009. 187p. pap. 14.32 *(978-0-557-19188-6(2))* Lulu Pr., Inc.

Abdo, Kenny. All for a Game, 1 vol. Doucet, Bob, illus. 2013. (Haven't Got a Clue! Ser.). (ENG.). 80p. (J). (gr. 3-6). lib. bdg. 27.07 *(978-1-61641-950-9(4),* Calico Chapter Bks) Magic Wagon.

—Comic Relief, 1 vol. Doucet, Bob, illus. 2013. (Haven't Got a Clue! Ser.). (ENG.). 80p. (J). (gr. 3-6). lib. bdg. 27.07 *(978-1-61641-951-6(2),* Calico Chapter Bks) Magic Wagon.

—Duck, Dive, Rock & Roll, 1 vol. Doucet, Bob, illus. 2013. (Haven't Got a Clue! Ser.). (ENG.). 80p. (J). (gr. 3-6). lib. bdg. 27.07 *(978-1-61641-952-3(0),* Calico Chapter Bks) Magic Wagon.

—Give Me Liberty or Give Me Detention!, 1 vol. Doucet, Bob, illus. 2013. (Haven't Got a Clue! Ser.). (ENG.). 80p. (J). (gr. 3-6). lib. bdg. 27.07 *(978-1-61641-953-0(9),* Calico Chapter Bks) Magic Wagon.

—Psych-Out!, 1 vol. Doucet, Bob, illus. 2013. (Haven't Got a Clue! Ser.). (ENG.). 80p. (J). (gr. 3-6). lib. bdg. 27.07 *(978-1-61641-954-7(7),* Calico Chapter Bks) Magic Wagon.

—Triple Take, 1 vol. Doucet, Bob, illus. 2013. (Haven't Got a Clue! Ser.). (ENG.). 80p. (J). (gr. 3-6). lib. bdg. 27.07 *(978-1-61641-955-4(5),* Calico Chapter Bks) Magic Wagon.

Abdo Publishing. Scooby-Doo Mysteries Set 2, 1 vol. 2013. (Scooby-Doo Mysteries Set 2 Ser.: 6). (ENG.). 64p. (J). (gr. 3-6). lib. bdg. 145.26 *(978-1-61479-041-9(8),* Essential Library) ABDO Publishing Co.

—Scooby-Doo! Picture Clue Books, 1 vol. 2013. (Scooby-Doo! Picture Clue Bks.: 6). (ENG.). 24p. (J). (gr. -1-1). lib. bdg. 145.26 *(978-1-61479-034-1(5))* ABDO Publishing Co.

ABDO Publishing Company. Haven't Got a Clue! Set Of 6. 2013. (Haven't Got a Clue! Ser.: 6). 80p. (J). (gr. 3-6). lib. bdg. 162.42 *(978-1-61641-949-3(0),* Calico Chapter Bks) Magic Wagon.

ABDO Publishing Company Staff. Chet Gecko Mysteries - 10 Titles. 2008. (Chet Gecko Mystery Ser.). (J). 242.10 *(978-1-59961-460-1(X))* Spotlight.

—Nancy Drew - 4 Titles. 2005. (Nancy Drew Ser.). (ENG., Illus.). 88p. (gr. 3-8). 72.63 *(978-1-59961-056-6(6))* Spotlight.

—Nancy Drew & the Clue Crew - 4 Titles. 2007. (Nancy Drew & the Clue Crew Ser.). (ENG., Illus.). 80p. 96.84 *(978-1-59961-344-4(1))* Spotlight.

Abdul-Jabbar, Kareem. Streetball Crew Book One Sasquatch in the Paint. 2015. (Streetball Crew Ser.). (ENG.). 288p. (J). (gr. 3-7). pap. 7.99 *(978-1-4231-9254-1(0))* Hyperion Bks. for Children.

Abdul-Jabbar, Kareem & Obstfeld, Raymond. Sasquatch in the Paint. 2013. (Streetball Crew Ser.). (ENG.). 272p. (J). (gr. 3-7). 16.99 *(978-1-4231-7870-5(X))* Hyperion Pr.

The Abominable Snowman, 6 Vols., Pack. (Bookweb Ser.). 32p. (gr. 3-18). 34.00 *(978-0-7635-3935-1(X))* Rigby Education.

The Abominable Snowman Doesn't Roast Marshmallows, 6 bks., Pack. 2005. 96p. (J). pap. 3.99 *(978-0-439-86573-9(5))* Scholastic, Inc.

Abrahams, Peter. Behind the Curtain. 2007. (Echo Falls Mystery Ser.: 2). (ENG.). 400p. (J). (gr. 5-18). pap. 6.99 *(978-0-06-073706-1(9))* HarperCollins Pubs.

—Down the Rabbit Hole. 2006. (Echo Falls Mystery Ser.: 1). (ENG.). 448p. (J). (gr. 5-9). reprint ed. pap. 7.99 *(978-0-06-073703-0(4))* HarperCollins Pubs.

—Into the Dark. 2009. (Echo Falls Mystery Ser.: 3). (ENG.). 352p. (J). (gr. 5-18). pap. 6.99 *(978-0-06-073710-8(7))* HarperCollins Pubs.

Absolutely Truly: A Pumpkin Falls Mystery. 2014. (Pumpkin Falls Mystery Ser.). (ENG., Illus.). 368p. (J). (gr. 3-7). 17.99 *(978-1-4424-2972-7(0),* Simon & Schuster Bks. For Young Readers) Simon & Schuster Bks. For Young Readers.

Abuhamda, Nasser. 6 Tales of Adventure. 2009. 84p. pap. 14.95 *(978-1-59858-833-0(8))* Dog Ear Publishing, LLC.

Acker, Rick. The Lost Treasure of Fernando Montoya, Vol. 2. 2003. (Davis Detective Mysteries Ser.). 192p. (J). pap. 7.99 *(978-0-8254-2005-4(9))* Kregel Pubns.

Ackerman, Helen. Casper's Paper Caper. 2013. 36p. pap. 18.41 *(978-1-4669-7448-7(6))* Trafford Publishing.

Adam, Paul. Escape from Shadow Island. (ENG.). 304p. (J). (gr. 5). 2011. (Max Cassidy Ser.: Bk. 1). pap. 5.99 *(978-0-06-186325-7(4))* 2010. 16.99 *(978-0-06-186323-3(8))* HarperCollins Pubs. (Walden Pond Pr.).

Adams, Andy. The African Ivory Mystery: A Biff Brewster Mystery Adventure. 2011. 184p. 42.95 *(978-1-258-09296-2(4))* Literary Licensing, LLC.

—Mystery of the Ambush in Indi: A Biff Brewster Mystery. 2011. 180p. 42.95 *(978-1-258-09701-1(X))* Literary Licensing, LLC.

—Mystery of the Mexican Treasure: A Biff Brewster Mystery Adventure. 2011. 192p. 42.95 *(978-1-258-10141-1(6))* Literary Licensing, LLC.

Adappur, Georgekutty. Jack Batson & the Secret in the Manuscript. 2009. 142p. pap. 24.95 *(978-1-4489-8439-8(4))* America Star Bks.

Adler, David A. The Barking Treasure Mystery. Natti, Susanna, illus. 2005. (Cam Jansen Ser.: 19). (ENG.). 64p. (J). (gr. 2-5). 4.99 *(978-0-14-240319-8(9),* Puffin Books) Penguin Young Readers Group.

—The Basketball Mystery, 29 vols., No. 29. Allen, Joy, illus. 2010. (Cam Jansen Ser.: 29). (ENG.). 64p. (J). (gr. 2-5). 4.99 *(978-0-14-241671-6(1),* Puffin Books) Penguin Young Readers Group.

—Birthday Mystery. Natti, Susanna, illus. 2005. (Cam Jansen Ser.: 20). (ENG.). 64p. (J). (gr. 2-5). 4.99 *(978-0-14-240354-9(7),* Puffin Books) Penguin Young Readers Group.

—Bones & the Apple Pie Mystery. Newman, Barbara Johansen, illus. 2014. (Bones Ser.: 10). (ENG.). 32p. (J). (gr. 1-3). pap. 3.99 *(978-0-448-48231-6(2),* Penguin Young Readers) Penguin Young Readers Group.

M
N
O

—Bones & the Big Yellow Mystery, No. 1. Newman, Barbara Johansen, illus. 2008. (Bones Ser.: 1). (ENG.). 32p. (J). (gr. 1-3). mass mkt. 3.99 (978-0-14-241042-4(X), Penguin Young Readers) Penguin Young Readers Group.
—Bones & the Big Yellow Mystery. Newman, Barbara Johansen, illus. 2008. (Puffin Easy-to-Read Ser.). 32p. (gr. k-3). 14.00 (978-0-7569-8914-9(0)) Perfection Learning Corp.
—Bones & the Birthday Mystery, No. 5. Newman, Barbara Johansen, illus. 2009. (Bones Ser.: 5). (ENG.). 32p. (J). (gr. 1-3). mass mkt. 3.99 (978-0-14-241432-3(8), Penguin Young Readers) Penguin Young Readers Group.
—Bones & the Clown Mix-Up Mystery, No. 8. Newman, Barbara Johansen, illus. 2011. (Bones Ser.: 8). (ENG.). 32p. (J). (gr. 1-3). 3.99 (978-0-14-241825-3(0), Penguin Young Readers) Penguin Young Readers Group.
—Bones & the Cupcake Mystery, No. 3. Newman, Barbara Johansen, illus. 2008. (Bones Ser.: 3). (ENG.). 32p. (J). (gr. 1-3). mass mkt. 3.99 (978-0-14-241147-6(7), Penguin Young Readers) Penguin Young Readers Group.
—Bones & the Dinosaur Mystery. Newman, Barbara Johansen, illus. 2005. (Jeffrey Bones Mystery Ser.: No. 4). 32p. (J). (978-0-670-05970-6(6), Viking Adult) Penguin Publishing Group.
—Bones & the Dinosaur Mystery, No. 4. Newman, Barbara Johansen, illus. 2009. (Bones Ser.: 4). (ENG.). 32p. (J). (gr. 1-3). mass mkt. 3.99 (978-0-14-241341-8(0), Penguin Young Readers) Penguin Young Readers Group.
—Bones & the Dog Gone Mystery, No. 2. Newman, Barbara Johansen, illus. 2008. (Bones Ser.: 2). (ENG.). 32p. (J). (gr. 1-3). mass mkt. 3.99 (978-0-14-241043-1(8), Penguin Young Readers) Penguin Young Readers Group.
—Bones & the Dog Gone Mystery. Newman, Barbara Johansen, illus. 2008. (Puffin Easy-to-Read Ser.: Bk. 2). 32p. (gr. k-3). 14.00 (978-0-7569-8916-3(7)) Perfection Learning Corp.
—Bones & the Football Mystery. 2013. (Bones Ser.: 9). (ENG.). 32p. (J). (gr. 1-3). pap. 3.99 (978-0-448-47942-2(7), Penguin Young Readers) Penguin Young Readers Group.
—Bones & the Football Mystery. 2013. (Bones Penguin Young Readers Ser.: 9). lib. bdg. 13.55 (978-0-606-32450-2(X), Turtleback) Turtleback Bks.
—Bones & the Math Test. 2010. (Bones Penguin Young Readers Ser.: 6). lib. bdg. 13.55 (978-0-606-10585-9(9), Turtleback) Turtleback Bks.
—Bones & the Math Test Mystery. Newman, Barbara Johansen, illus. 2010. (Bones Ser.: 6). (ENG.). 32p. (J). (gr. 1-3). mass mkt. 3.99 (978-0-14-241519-1(7), Penguin Young Readers) Penguin Young Readers Group.
—Bones & the Roller Coaster Mystery, 7 vols. Newman, Barbara Johansen, illus. 2010. (Bones Ser.: 7). (ENG.). 32p. (J). (gr. 1-3). mass mkt. 3.99 (978-0-14-241687-7(8), Penguin Young Readers) Penguin Young Readers Group.
—Cam Jansen: The Mystery of the Babe Ruth Baseball. (Cam Jansen Ser.: No. 6). 57p. (J). (gr. 2-4). pap. 3.99 (978-0-8072-1347-6(0), Listening Library) Random Hse. Audio Publishing Group.
—Cam Jansen - The First Day of School Mystery, 22 vols. Natti, Susanna, illus. 2005. (Cam Jansen Ser.: 22). (ENG.). 64p. (J). (gr. 2-5). 4.99 (978-0-14-240326-6(1), Puffin Books) Penguin Young Readers Group.
—Cam Jansen - The Mystery Writer Mystery. Allen, Joy, illus. 27th ed. 2008. (Cam Jansen Ser.: 27). (ENG.). 64p. (J). (gr. 2-5). 4.99 (978-0-14-241194-0(9), Puffin Books) Penguin Young Readers Group.
—Cam Jansen - The Wedding Cake Mystery, 30 vols. Allen, Joy, illus. 2011. (Cam Jansen Ser.: 30). (ENG.). 64p. (J). (gr. 2-5). 4.99 (978-0-14-241958-8(3), Puffin Books) Penguin Young Readers Group.
—Cam Jansen & the Catnapping Mystery. Natti, Susanna, illus. 2005. (Cam Jansen Ser.). 58p. (gr. 2-5). 14.00 (978-0-7569-5045-3(7)) Perfection Learning Corp.
—Cam Jansen & the Graduation Day Mystery. 2012. (Cam Jansen Ser.: 31). (ENG.). 64p. (J). (gr. 2-5). pap. 4.99 (978-0-14-242208-3(8), Puffin Books) Penguin Young Readers Group.
—Cam Jansen & the Graduation Day Mystery. 2012. (Cam Jansen Ser.: 31). lib. bdg. 14.75 (978-0-606-26663-5(1), Turtleback) Turtleback Bks.
—Cam Jansen & the Joke House Mystery. Allen, Joy, illus. 2014. (Cam Jansen Ser.: 34). (ENG.). 64p. (J). (gr. 2-5). 14.99 (978-0-670-01262-6(9), Viking Books for Young Readers) Penguin Young Readers Group.
—Cam Jansen & the Millionaire Mystery. Allen, Joy, illus. 2013. (Cam Jansen Ser.: 32). (ENG.). 64p. (J). (gr. 2-5). pap. 4.99 (978-0-14-242747-7(0), Puffin Books) Penguin Young Readers Group.
—Cam Jansen & the Spaghetti Max Mystery. Allen, Joy, illus. (Cam Jansen Ser.: 33). (ENG.). 64p. (J). (gr. 2-5). 2014. pap. 4.99 (978-0-14-751232-1(8), Puffin Books) 2013. 14.99 (978-0-670-01260-2(2), Viking Books for Young Readers) Penguin Young Readers Group.
—Cam Jansen & the Sports Day Mysteries. Allen, Joy, illus. 2009. (Cam Jansen: A Super Special Ser.). 118p. 16.00 (978-1-60686-431-9(9)) Perfection Learning Corp.
—Cam Jansen & the Sports Day Mysteries: A Super Special. 2009. (Cam Jansen Ser.). lib. bdg. 16.00 (978-0-606-00110-6(7), Turtleback) Turtleback Bks.
—Cam Jansen the Sports Day Mysteries: A Super Special. Allen, Joy, illus. 2009. (Cam Jansen Ser.). (ENG.). 128p. (J). (gr. 2-5). 5.99 (978-0-14-241225-1(2), Puffin Books) Penguin Young Readers Group.
—The Catnapping Mystery, 18 vols. Natti, Susanna, illus. 2005. (Cam Jansen Ser.: 18). (ENG.). 64p. (J). (gr. 2-5). 4.99 (978-0-14-240289-4(3), Puffin Books) Penguin Young Readers Group.
—The Chocolate Fudge Mystery, 14 vols. Natti, Susanna, illus. 2004. (Cam Jansen Ser.: 14). (ENG.). 64p. (J). (gr. 2-5). 4.99 (978-0-14-240211-5(7), Puffin Books) Penguin Young Readers Group.
—Danny's Doodles: the Squirting Donuts. 2014. (Danny's Doodles Ser.: 2). (ENG.). 144p. (J). (gr. 2-5). 14.99 (978-1-4926-1401-2(7), Sourcebooks Jabberwocky) Sourcebooks, Inc.
—The Ghostly Mystery, Vol. 16. Natti, Susanna, illus. 2005. (Cam Jansen Ser.: 16). (ENG.). 64p. (J). (gr. 2-5). 4.99 (978-0-14-240287-0(7), Puffin Books) Penguin Young Readers Group.
—The Green School Mystery, No. 28. Allen, Joy, illus. 2009. (Cam Jansen Ser.: 28). (ENG.). 64p. (J). (gr. 2-5). 4.99 (978-0-14-241456-9(5), Puffin Books) Penguin Young Readers Group.
—The Mystery of Flight 427: Inside a Crash Investigation. Natti, Susanna, illus. 2004. (Cam Jansen Ser.: No. 12). 56p. (J). pap. (978-0-439-13384-5(X), Puffin) Penguin Publishing Group.
—The Mystery of Flight 54, 12 vols. Natti, Susanna, illus. 2004. (Cam Jansen Ser.: 12). (ENG.). 64p. (J). (gr. 2-5). 4.99 (978-0-14-240179-8(X), Puffin Books) Penguin Young Readers Group.
—The Mystery of the Carnival Prize, 9 vols. Natti, Susanna, illus. 2004. (Cam Jansen Ser.: 9). (ENG.). 64p. (J). (gr. 2-5). 4.99 (978-0-14-240018-0(1), Puffin Books) Penguin Young Readers Group.
—The Mystery of the Circus Clown, 7 vols. Natti, Susanna, illus. 2004. (Cam Jansen Ser.: 7). (ENG.). 64p. (J). (gr. 2-5). 4.99 (978-0-14-240016-6(5), Puffin Books) Penguin Young Readers Group.
—The Mystery of the Gold Coins, 5 vols. Natti, Susanna, illus. 2004. (Cam Jansen Ser.: 5). (ENG.). 64p. (J). (gr. 2-5). 4.99 (978-0-14-240014-2(9), Puffin Books) Penguin Young Readers Group.
—The Mystery of the Monkey House. Natti, Susanna, illus. 2004. (Cam Jansen Ser.: 10). (ENG.). 64p. (J). (gr. 2-5). 4.99 (978-0-14-240019-7(X), Puffin Books) Penguin Young Readers Group.
—The Mystery of the Monster Movie, 8 vols. Natti, Susanna, illus. 2004. (Cam Jansen Ser.: 8). (ENG.). 64p. (J). (gr. 2-5). 4.99 (978-0-14-240017-3(3), Puffin Books) Penguin Young Readers Group.
—The Mystery of the Stolen Corn Popper, 11 vols. Natti, Susanna, illus. 2004. (Cam Jansen Ser.: 11). (ENG.). 64p. (J). (gr. 2-5). 4.99 (978-0-14-240178-1(1), Puffin Books) Penguin Young Readers Group.
—The Mystery of the Stolen Diamonds. Natti, Susanna, illus. 2004. (Cam Jansen Ser.: 1). (ENG.). 64p. (J). (gr. 2-5). pap. 4.99 (978-0-14-240010-4(6), Puffin Books) Penguin Young Readers Group.
—The Mystery of the Television Dog, 4 vols. Natti, Susanna, illus. 2004. (Cam Jansen Ser.: 4). (ENG.). 64p. (J). (gr. 2-5). 4.99 (978-0-14-240013-5(0), Puffin Books) Penguin Young Readers Group.
—The Mystery of the U. F. O., 2 vols. Natti, Susanna, illus. 2004. (Cam Jansen Ser.: 2). (ENG.). 64p. (J). (gr. 2-5). 4.99 (978-0-14-240011-1(4), Puffin Books) Penguin Young Readers Group.
—Not Wanted by the Police. Franson, Leanne, illus. 2005. (Andy Russell Ser.: Bk. 5). (ENG.). 128p. (J). (gr. 1-4). pap. 5.99 (978-0-15-216719-6(6)) Houghton Mifflin Harcourt Publishing Co.
—The Scary Snake Mystery. Natti, Susanna, illus. 2005. (Cam Jansen Ser.: 17). (ENG.). 64p. (J). (gr. 2-5). 4.99 (978-0-14-240288-7(5), Puffin Books) Penguin Young Readers Group.
—The School Play Mystery. Natti, Susanna, illus. 2005. (Cam Jansen Ser.: 21). (ENG.). 64p. (J). (gr. 2-5). 4.99 (978-0-14-240355-6(5), Puffin Books) Penguin Young Readers Group.
—The Secret Service Mystery. Natti, Susanna, illus. 2008. (Cam Jansen Ser.: 26). (ENG.). 64p. (J). (gr. 2-5). 4.99 (978-0-14-241074-5(8), Puffin Books) Penguin Young Readers Group.
—The Secret Service Mystery. Natti, Susanna, illus. 2008. (Cam Jansen Ser.: Bk. 26). 57p. (J). (gr. 2-5). 11.65 (978-0-7569-8917-0(5)) Perfection Learning Corp.
—The Snowy Day Mystery, 24 vols. Natti, Susanna, illus. 2005. (Cam Jansen Ser.: 24). (ENG.). 64p. (J). (gr. 2-5). 4.99 (978-0-14-240417-1(9), Puffin Books) Penguin Young Readers Group.
—The Speedy Car Mystery, 16 vols. Natti, Susanna, illus. 2010. (Young Cam Jansen Ser.: 16). (ENG.). 32p. (J). (gr. 1-3). 14.99 (978-0-670-06143-3(3), Viking Books for Young Readers) Penguin Young Readers Group.
—The Summer Camp Mysteries. Allen, Joy, illus. 2007. (Cam Jansen Ser.). (ENG.). 128p. (J). (gr. 2-5). 5.99 (978-0-14-240742-4(9), Puffin Books) Penguin Young Readers Group.
—The Triceratops Pops Mystery, 15 vols. Natti, Susanna, illus. 2004. (Cam Jansen Ser.: 15). (ENG.). 64p. (J). (gr. 2-5). 4.99 (978-0-14-240206-1(0), Puffin Books) Penguin Young Readers Group.
—The Valentine Baby Mystery. Natti, Susanna, illus. 25th ed. 2006. (Cam Jansen Ser.: 25). (ENG.). 80p. (J). (gr. 2-5). 4.99 (978-0-14-240694-6(5), Puffin Books) Penguin Young Readers Group.
—Young Cam Jansen & the 100th Day of School, 15 vols. Natti, Susanna, illus. 2010. (Young Cam Jansen Ser.: 15). (ENG.). 32p. (J). (gr. 1-3). mass mkt. 3.99 (978-0-14-241685-3(1), Penguin Young Readers) Penguin Young Readers Group.
—Young Cam Jansen & the 100th Day of School Mystery, 15 vols. Natti, Susanna, illus. 2009. (Young Cam Jansen Ser.: 15). (ENG.). 32p. (J). (gr. 1-3). 13.99 (978-0-670-06172-3(7), Viking Books for Young Readers) Penguin Young Readers Group.
—Young Cam Jansen & the Circus Mystery. Natti, Susanna, illus. 2013. (Young Cam Jansen Ser.: 17). (ENG.). 32p. (J). (gr. 1-3). pap. 3.99 (978-0-448-46614-9(7), Penguin Young Readers) Penguin Young Readers Group.
—Young Cam Jansen & the Double Beach Mystery. Natti, Susanna, illus. 2003. (Young Cam Jansen Ser.: 8). (ENG.). 32p. (J). (gr. 1-3). mass mkt. 3.99 (978-0-14-250079-8(8), Penguin Young Readers) Penguin Young Readers Group.
—Young Cam Jansen & the Double Beach Mystery. Natti, Susanna, illus. 2003. (Young Cam Jansen — Penguin Young Readers Level 3 Ser.: 8). 30p. (gr. -1-3). lib. bdg. 13.55 (978-0-613-67477-5(4), Turtleback) Turtleback Bks.
—Young Cam Jansen & the Goldfish Mystery. Natti, Susanna, illus. (Young Cam Jansen Ser.: 19). (ENG.). 32p. (J). (gr. 1-3). 2014. pap. 3.99 (978-0-14-242224-3(X)) 2013. 14.99 (978-0-670-01259-6(9)) Penguin Young Readers Group. (Penguin Young Readers).
—Young Cam Jansen & the Knock, Knock Mystery. Natti, Susanna, illus. (Young Cam Jansen Ser.: 20). (ENG.). 32p. (J). (gr. 1-3). 2015. pap. 3.99 (978-0-14-242225-0(8)) 2014. 14.99 (978-0-670-01261-9(0)) Penguin Young Readers Group. (Penguin Young Readers).
—Young Cam Jansen & the Lions' Lunch Mystery. Natti, Susanna, illus. 2007. (Young Cam Jansen Ser.: 13). (ENG.). 32p. (J). (gr. 1-3). 13.99 (978-0-670-06171-6(9), Viking Books for Young Readers) Penguin Young Readers Group.
—Young Cam Jansen & the Lions' Lunch Mystery, No. 13. Natti, Susanna, illus. 2008. (Young Cam Jansen Ser.: 13). (ENG.). 32p. (J). (gr. 1-3). mass mkt. 3.99 (978-0-14-241176-6(0), Penguin Young Readers) Penguin Young Readers Group.
—Young Cam Jansen & the Magic Bird Mystery. Natti, Susanna, illus. 2013. (Young Cam Jansen Ser.: 18). (ENG.). 32p. (J). (gr. 1-3). pap. 3.99 (978-0-448-46613-2(9), Penguin Young Readers) Penguin Young Readers Group.
—Young Cam Jansen & the Molly Shoe Mystery, No. 14. Natti, Susanna, illus. 2009. (Young Cam Jansen Ser.: 14). (ENG.). 32p. (J). (gr. 1-3). mass mkt. 3.99 (978-0-14-241402-6(6), Penguin Young Readers) Penguin Young Readers Group.
—Young Cam Jansen & the New Girl Mystery. Natti, Susanna, illus. 2005. (Young Cam Jansen Ser.: 10). (ENG.). 32p. (J). (gr. 1-3). mass mkt. 3.99 (978-0-14-240353-2(9), Penguin Young Readers) Penguin Young Readers Group.
—Young Cam Jansen & the New Girl Mystery. Natti, Susanna, illus. 2005. (Young Cam Jansen Ser.: Bk. 10). 32p. (gr. k-2). 14.00 (978-0-7569-5522-9(X)) Perfection Learning Corp.
—Young Cam Jansen & the Speedy Car Mystery, 16 vols. Natti, Susanna, illus. 2011. (Young Cam Jansen Ser.: 16). (ENG.). 32p. (J). (gr. 1-3). mass mkt. 3.99 (978-0-14-241868-0(4), Penguin Young Readers) Penguin Young Readers Group.
—Young Cam Jansen & the Spotted Cat Mystery, No. 12. Natti, Susanna & Natti, S., illus. 2007. (Young Cam Jansen Ser.: 12). (ENG.). 32p. (J). (gr. 1-3). pap. 3.99 (978-0-14-241012-7(8), Penguin Young Readers) Penguin Young Readers Group.
—Young Cam Jansen & the Spotted Cat Mystery. Natti, Susanna, illus. 2007. (Young Cam Jansen (prebound) Ser.). 31p. (gr. -1-3). 14.00 (978-0-7569-8155-6(7)) Perfection Learning Corp.
—Young Cam Jansen & the Zoo Note Mystery. Natti, Susanna, illus. 2013. (Puffin Young Readers, L3 Ser.). (ENG.). 31p. (J). (gr. -1-3). pap. 3.99 (978-0-448-46633-0(3), Puffin) Penguin Publishing Group.
—Young Cam Jansen & the Zoo Note Mystery. Natti, Susanna, illus. 2004. (Young Cam Jansen Ser.: 9). (ENG.). 32p. (J). (gr. 1-3). mass mkt. 3.99 (978-0-14-240204-7(4), Penguin Young Readers) Penguin Young Readers Group.
Adler, Irene. The Cathedral of Fear. McGuinness, Nanette, tr. from ITA. Bruno, Iacopo, illus. 2015. (Sherlock, Lupin, & Me Ser.). (ENG.). 256p. (gr. 4-8). lib. bdg. 26.65 (978-1-4965-0490-6(9)) Stone Arch Bks.
—The Dark Lady, 1 vol. Bruno, Iacopo, illus. 2014. (Sherlock, Lupin, & Me Ser.). (ENG.). 240p. (gr. 4-8). 12.95 (978-1-62370-040-9(X)) Capstone Young Readers of Coughlan Cos.
—The Mystery of the Scarlet Rose. McGuinness, Nanette, tr. from ITA. Bruno, Iacopo, illus. 2015. (Sherlock, Lupin, & Me Ser.). (ENG.). 256p. (gr. 4-8). lib. bdg. 26.65 (978-1-4342-6524-1(2)) Stone Arch Bks.
—Sherlock, Lupin, & Me, 1 vol. Bruno, Iacopo, illus. 2014. (Sherlock, Lupin, & Me Ser.). (ENG.). 240p. (gr. 4-8). 53.30 (978-1-4342-9602-3(4)) Stone Arch Bks.
—The Soprano's Last Song, 1 vol. Iacopo, Bruno & Bruno, Iacopo, illus. 2014. (Sherlock, Lupin, & Me Ser.). (ENG.). 240p. (gr. 4-8). lib. bdg. 26.65 (978-1-4342-6522-7(6)) Stone Arch Bks.
Aili, Olivia. The Portrait Pathway. 2012. 62p. 19.95 (978-1-4626-7206-6(X)); pap. 12.99 (978-1-4626-7937-9(4)) America Star Bks.
Albin, Colin. Tom's Tales. 2013. 136p. pap. (978-1-78407-043-4(2)) FeedARead.com.
Alderson, Sarah. Out of Control. 2015. (ENG., Illus.). 320p. (J). (gr. 9). 17.99 (978-1-4814-2716-6(4), Simon Pulse) Simon Pulse.
Alender, Katie. Famous Last Words. 2014. (ENG.). 320p. (J). (gr. 7). 18.99 (978-0-545-63997-2(2)) Scholastic, Inc.
Alessio, Amy. Taking the High Ground. 2013. 128p. pap. 19.99 (978-1-940310-00-8(8)) 4RV Publishing, LLC.
Alexander, Heather. The Case of the Tattooed Cat. 2003. (New Adventures of Mary-Kate & Ashley Ser.). (Illus.). 83p. (J). (gr. 1-5). 12.65 (978-0-7569-5351-5(0)) Perfection Learning Corp.
—Wallace & Grace & the Cupcake Caper. Zarrin, Laura, illus. 2017. (Wallace & Grace Ser.). (ENG.). 80p. (J). 9.99 (978-1-68119-010-5(9), 9781681190105, Bloomsbury USA Childrens) Bloomsbury Publishing USA.
—Wallace & Grace Take the Case. Zarrin, Laura, illus. 2017. (Wallace & Grace Ser.). (ENG.). 80p. (J). 9.99 (978-1-61963-988-1(2), 9781619639881, Bloomsbury USA Childrens) Bloomsbury Publishing USA.
Alexander, Tracy. Alias. 2016. (ENG.). 304p. (YA). (gr. 9). pap. 8.99 (978-1-84812-444-8(9)) Bonnier Publishing GBR. Dist: Independent Pubs. Group.
—Hacked. 2016. (ENG.). 288p. (YA). (gr. 7). pap. 8.99 (978-1-84812-414-1(7)) Bonnier Publishing GBR. Dist: Independent Pubs. Group.
Alexander, Yvonne. Adventure in Autou. 2012. 230p. pap. 15.99 (978-1-62230-262-8(1)) Salem Author Services.
Alexandria, Vincent. Marvelous Martin: Case of the Freckle-Faced Bully. 2009. 64p. (J). (gr. 2-7). 7.95 (978-1-60349-015-3(9), Marimba Bks.) Hudson Publishing Group, The.
—Marvelous Marvin. 2009. 64p. 4.99 (978-1-60349-013-9(2), Marimba Bks.) Hudson Publishing Group, The.
Alfonsi, Alice. The Almost Invisible Cases. Harrington, Rich, illus. 2007. 96p. (J). (978-0-545-01585-1(5)) Scholastic, Inc.
—The Code Red Cases. Harrington, Rich, illus. 2006. 96p. (J). (978-0-439-91447-5(7)) Scholastic, Inc.
—The Playing Card Cases. Harrington, Rich, illus. 2007. 96p. (J). (978-0-545-01087-0(X)) Scholastic, Inc.
Alger, Horatio. The Store Boy. 2005. 256p. 28.95 (978-1-4218-0954-0(0), 1st World Library - Literary Society) 1st World Publishing, Inc.
—The Store Boy. 2007. (ENG.). 170p. pap. 19.99 (978-1-4264-4359-6(5)); 182p. pap. 21.99 (978-1-4264-4397-8(8)) Creative Media Partners, LLC.
—The Store Boy. 2006. pap. (978-1-4065-0722-5(9)) Dodo Pr.
—The Store Boy. 2007. 116p. per. (978-1-4068-1617-4(5)) Echo Library.
—Timothy Crump's Ward. 2005. 27.95 (978-1-4218-1451-3(X)); 220p. pap. 12.95 (978-1-4218-1551-0(6)) 1st World Publishing, Inc. (1st World Library - Literary Society).
Alice B. Emerson. Betty Gordon at Mountain Camp. l.t. ed. 2007. (ENG.). 148p. pap. 19.99 (978-1-4264-8096-6(2)) Creative Media Partners, LLC.
Alison, Hart. Spy on the Home Front. Jean-P, Tibbles, illus. 2005. (American Girls Collection). (ENG.). 176p. (J). 10.95 (978-1-58485-996-3(2), American Girl) American Girl Publishing, Inc.
Allen, Betsy. The Mystery of the Ruby Queens: Connie Blair Mystery Series. 2011. 192p. 42.95 (978-1-258-09539-0(4)) Literary Licensing, LLC.
—The Silver Secret: A Connie Blair Mystery. 2011. 184p. 42.95 (978-1-258-09883-4(0)) Literary Licensing, LLC.
Allen, Michelle. Grandma Nell's Basement. 2009. 24p. pap. 15.00 (978-1-4490-1551-0(4)) AuthorHouse.
Allen, Quincy. The Outdoor Chums at Cabin Point: Or the Golden Cup Mystery. 2007. (ENG.). 154p. pap. 19.99 (978-1-4346-3238-8(5)); 166p. pap. 21.99 (978-1-4346-3239-5(3)) Creative Media Partners, LLC.
Allison, Jennifer. The Dead Drop. (Gilda Joyce Ser.). (ENG.). 320p. (J). (gr. 5-18). 2010. 9.99 (978-0-14-241638-9(X), Puffin Books) 2009. 16.99 (978-0-525-47980-2(5), Dutton Books for Young Readers) Penguin Young Readers Group.
—The Ladies of the Lake. 2007. (Gilda Joyce Ser.). (ENG.). 352p. (J). (gr. 5-18). 9.99 (978-0-14-240907-7(3), Puffin Books) Penguin Young Readers Group.
Allison, John. Bad Machinery Vol. 3: The Case of the Simple Soul. 2014. (ENG., Illus.). 136p. (YA). pap. 19.99 (978-1-62010-193-3(9), 9781620101933) Oni Pr., Inc.
—Bad Machinery Volume 1 - Pocket Edition: The Case of the Team Spirit. 2017. (ENG., Illus.). 136p. (J). pap. 9.99 (**978-1-62010-387-6(7)**, 9781620103876) Oni Pr., Inc.
Allison, John. Bad Machinery Volume 2: The Case of the Good Boy. 2014. (ENG., Illus.). 136p. (YA). pap. 19.99 (978-1-62010-114-8(9), 9781620101148) Oni Pr., Inc.
Alpine, Rachele. A Void the Size of the World. 2017. (ENG., Illus.). 368p. (YA). (gr. 9). 17.99 (**978-1-4814-8571-5(7)**, Simon Pulse) Simon Pulse.
Altebrando, Tara. The Leaving. 2016. (ENG.). 432p. (YA). 17.99 (978-1-61963-803-7(7), 9781619638037, Bloomsbury USA Childrens) Bloomsbury Publishing USA.
Amato, Carol J. The Lost Treasure of the Golden Sun. 2005. 172p. (J). (978-0-9713756-3-5(1)) Stargazer Publishing Co.
—The Secret of Blackhurst Manor. 2017. (ENG.). 232p. (J). pap. 9.95 (978-1-933277-02-8(5)) Stargazer Publishing Co.
Amato, Mary. Edgar Allan's Official Crime Investigation Notebook. (ENG.). 176p. (J). 2011. pap. 6.99 (978-0-8234-2386-6(7)) 2010. (gr. 1-5). 16.95 (978-0-8234-2271-5(2)) Holiday Hse., Inc.
Anastasiu, Heather & Brown, Anne Greenwood. Girl Last Seen. 2016. (ENG.). 272p. (YA). (gr. 8-12). pap. 9.99 (978-0-8075-8141-4(0)) Whitman, Albert & Co.
Andersen, C. B. The Secret Mission. 2008. (J). (978-1-59038-906-5(9)) Deseret Bk. Co.
Anderson, Connie Kingrey. Toadies. 2013. (Creepers Mysteries Ser.: Bk. 2). (ENG.). 142p. (J). pap. 7.99 (978-1-935793-03-8(9)) Movies for the Ear, LLC.
Anderson, Janet. The Last Treasure. 2004. (ENG.). 272p. (J). (gr. 3-7). 8.99 (978-0-14-240217-7(6), Puffin Books) Penguin Young Readers Group.
Anderson, Jennifer. Spider. 2013. 174p. pap. 10.99 (978-1-62237-146-4(1)) Turquoise Morning Pr.
Anderson, Jessica. Mystery of the Pink Owl Flu. 2015. (ENG.). 64p. (gr. 3-6). 29.95 (978-1-63430-385-9(7)) Rourke Educational Media.
—Shaky, Breaky School Sleuth. 2015. (ENG.). 64p. (gr. 3-6). 29.95 (978-1-63430-387-3(3)) Rourke Educational Media.
Anderson, M. T. Agent Q, or the Smell of Danger! Cyrus, Kurt, illus. (Pals in Peril Tale Ser.). (ENG.). (J). (gr. 5-9). 2011. 320p. pap. 6.99 (978-1-4424-2640-5(3)) 2010. 304p. 16.99 (978-1-4169-8640-9(5)) Beach Lane Bks. (Beach Lane Bks.).
—The Clue of the Linoleum Lederhosen. Cyrus, Kurt, illus. 2010. (Pals in Peril Tale Ser.). (ENG.). (J). (gr. 5-9). 256p. 17.99 (978-1-4424-0697-1(6)); 272p. pap. 6.99 (978-1-4424-0702-2(6)) Beach Lane Bks. (Beach Lane Bks.).
—Jasper Dash & the Flame-Pits of Delaware. Cyrus, Kurt, illus. (Pals in Peril Tale Ser.). (ENG.). (J). (gr. 5-9). 2010. 448p. pap. 6.99 (978-1-4424-0838-8(3)) 2009. 432p. 16.99 (978-1-4169-8639-3(1)) Beach Lane Bks. (Beach Lane Bks.).
Anderson, Max Elliott. Mountain Cabin Mystery. 2004. (Tweener Press Adventure Ser.). (Illus.). 123p. (J). (gr. 3). per. 10.95 (978-0-9729256-3-1(5), Tweener Pr.) Baker Trittin Pr.
Anderson, R. J. A Little Taste of Poison. 2016. (ENG., Illus.). 368p. (J). (gr. 4-7). 17.99 (978-1-4814-3774-5(7), Atheneum Bks. for Young Readers) Simon & Schuster Children's Publishing.
—A Pocket Full of Murder. 2015. (ENG., Illus.). 352p. (J). (gr. 4-7). 18.99 (978-1-4814-3771-4(2)) Simon & Schuster Children's Publishing.
Ando, Yuma. Sherlock Bones. 2014. (Sherlock Bones Ser.). (ENG., Illus.). 200p. pap. 10.99 (978-1-61262-545-4(2)) Kodansha America, Inc.
—Sherlock Bones. Sato, Yuki, illus. (Sherlock Bones Ser.). (ENG.). 200p. Vol. 1. 2013. pap. 10.99 (978-1-61262-444-0(8)) Vol. 3. 2014. pap. 10.99 (978-1-61262-446-4(4)) Kodansha America, Inc.
—Sherlock Bones, Vol. 4. 2014. (Sherlock Bones Ser.). (ENG., Illus.). 200p. pap. 10.99 (978-1-61262-447-1(2)) Kodansha America, Inc.
Andrews, John. Beck's Missing Shoes. 2013. 28p. pap. 9.95 (978-1-4787-2524-4(9)) Outskirts Pr., Inc.
Angleberger, Tom. The Da Vinci Cold. 2016. (Inspector Flytrap Ser.: 1). (J). lib. bdg. 15.95 (978-0-606-38200-7(3)) Turtleback Bks.

—Horton Halfpott: Or, the Fiendish Mystery of Smugwick Manor - Or, the Loosening of M'Lady Luggertuck's Corset. 2011. (ENG., Illus.). 224p. (J). (gr. 3-7). 16.95 (978-0-8109-9715-8(0), Amulet Bks.) Abrams, Inc.
—Inspector Flytrap. Bell, Cece, illus. (Inspector Flytrap Ser.). (ENG.). 112p. (J). (gr. 1-4). 2017. 14.95 (978-1-4197-0956-2(9)) 2016. 14.95 (978-1-4197-0948-7(8)) 2016. 14.95 (978-1-4197-0955-5(0)) 2016. pap. 5.95 (978-1-4197-0965-4(8)) Abrams, Inc. (Amulet Bks.).
—The President's Mane Is Missing. 2016. (Inspector Flytrap Ser.: 2). (J). lib. bdg. 15.95 (978-0-606-38201-4(1)) Turtleback Bks.
Anyone's Guess Teen Kits: A Murderous Melodrama. 2004. 39.95 (978-1-932146-26-4(1), Upstart Bks.) Highsmith Inc.
Anza, Ana Luisa. El Misterio de la Casa Chueca (y el Bulto Color Mugre) The Mystery of the Crooked House. Escobar, Antonio Rocha, illus. rev. ed. 2006. (Castillo de la Lectura Naranja Ser.). (SPA & ENG.). 120p. (J). (gr. 4-7). pap. 7.95 (978-970-20-0200-0(1)) Castillo, Ediciones, S. A. de C. V. MEX. Dist: Macmillan.
Appleton, Victor. Moving Picture Boys at Panama. 2006. pap. (978-1-4065-0890-1(X)) Dodo Pr.
—The Moving Picture Boys on the Coast or Showing up the Perils of the Deep. 2004. reprint ed. pap. 24.95 (978-1-4179-1612-2(5)) Kessinger Publishing, LLC.
—Moving Picture Boys on the War Front or. 2006. pap. (978-1-4065-0891-8(8)) Dodo Pr.
Appleton, Victor & Appleton, Victor, II. On Top of the World. 2007. (Tom Swift, Young Inventor Ser.: 5). (ENG.). 160p. (J). (gr. 3-7). pap. 8.99 (978-1-4169-3643-5(2), Aladdin) Simon & Schuster Children's Publishing.
Archer, Jennifer. Through Her Eyes. 2012. (ENG.). 400p. (YA). (gr. 8). pap. 9.99 (978-0-06-183459-2(9), HarperTeen) HarperCollins Pubs.
Arensen, Shel. The Poison Arrow Tree. 2003. (Rugendo Rhino Ser.). (Illus.). 128p. (J). pap. 5.99 (978-0-8254-2041-2(5)) Kregel Pubns.
Armentrout, Jennifer L. Don't Look Back. 2014. (Novel Ser.: 1). (ENG.). 384p. (YA). (gr. 9-17). 16.99 (978-1-4231-7512-4(3)) Hyperion Bks. for Children.
Armstrong, Robert. Buyer Beware. 2016. (ENG.). 94p. (YA). (gr. 10-12). 10.95 (978-1-78554-474-3(8), c9488c0c-967c-408f-abd6-01a587eaeb62) Austin, Stan AUS. Dist: Bookmasters Distribution.
Arnett, Mindee. The Nightmare Dilemma. 2015. (Arkwell Academy Ser.: 2). (ENG.). 400p. (YA). (gr. 8-12). pap. 10.99 (978-0-7653-3337-7(6), 9780765333377, Tor Teen) Doherty, Tom Assocs., LLC.
Arnold, Chirley. Double Trouble: A Novel. 160p. (YA). pap. 7.95 (978-1-56236-454-0(5)) Aspen Bks.
Asad, Megan Emily. The Juggler's Journey. 2005. 144p. pap. 9.95 (978-0-7599-4470-1(9)) Hard Shell Word Factory.
Ashby, Freya Katrina. Summer at the Dunes: A Deirdre Carlisle Mystery. 2007. 108p. per. 9.95 (978-0-595-43663-7(3)) iUniverse, Inc.
Ashley, Bernard. Solitaire. 2012. (Fiction Ser.). 338p. (J). pap. 6.99 (978-0-7945-3031-0(1), Usborne) EDC Publishing.
Ashley, Elana. Splunkunio Splunkey Detective & Peacemaker Detective y Pacificador: Case One: The Missing Friendship Bracelet Caso Primero: El Brazalete de la Amistad Desaparecido. Nikolov, Stefan V., tr. Ashley, Elana, photos by. 2005. (SPA & ENG., Illus.). 32p. (J). (gr. k-3). 17.95 (978-0-9744812-1-0(1)) Dream Image Pr., LLC.
Ashton, Brodi. Diplomatic Immunity. 2016. 368p. (YA). (gr. 8). 17.99 (978-0-06-236856-0(7)) HarperCollins Pubs.
Ashton, Kenneth. Gale's Gold Ring: The Legend of Lincoln's Lost Gold. Ashton-Briggs, Shelley, illus. 2012. (ENG.). 198p. pap. 14.95 (978-1-4327-8224-5(X)) Outskirts Pr., Inc.
Askew, Kim & Helmes, Amy. Tempestuous. Mitchard, Jacquelyn, ed. 2014. (Twisted Lit Ser.). (ENG.). 224p. (YA). pap. 9.99 (978-1-4405-8283-7(1), Simon Pulse) Simon Pulse.
Atanacio, Frank. Aggravating Factors: From the Nick Barnum Sealed Case File a Nick Barnum Novel II. 2003. 128p. (YA). pap. 10.95 (978-0-595-26985-3(0), Writers Club Pr.) iUniverse, Inc.
Atkins, Ron. Abby & the Bicycle Caper. 2004. 48p. pap. 8.95 (978-0-595-30565-0(2)) iUniverse, Inc.
Atwater-Rhodes, Amelia. Midnight Predator. 2003. (Den of Shadows Ser.). (ENG.). 256p. (YA). (gr. 7). mass mkt. 6.99 (978-0-440-23797-6(1), Laurel Leaf) Random Hse. Children's Bks.
Auerbach, Annie. Scooby-Doo in the Coolsville Contraption Contest, 1 vol. 2016. (Scooby-Doo! Set 3 Ser.). (ENG., Illus.). 32p. (J). (gr. k-4). lib. bdg. 24.21 (978-1-61479-409-7(X)) Spotlight.
—Scooby-Doo in the Mystery Mansion, 1 vol. 2016. (Scooby-Doo! Set 3 Ser.). (ENG., Illus.). 32p. (J). (gr. k-4). lib. bdg. 24.21 (978-1-61479-411-0(1), 1401187) Spotlight.
Austin, Rikey. Captain's Treasure: Alice's Bear Shop. 2012. 28p. pap. (978-1-78092-149-5(7)) MX Publishing, Ltd.
Austin, Su. The Salterns House Mystery. 2013. 186p. pap. (978-1-78299-194-6(8)) FeedARead.com.
Avasthi, Swati. Chasing Shadows. Phillips, Craig, illus. 2013. (ENG.). 320p. (YA). (gr. 9). 17.99 (978-0-375-86342-4(7)); lib. bdg. 20.99 (978-0-375-96341-4(3)) Random Hse. Children's Bks. (Knopf Bks. for Young Readers).
Averbeck, Jim. A Hitch at the Fairmont. Bertozzi, Nick, illus. (ENG.). 416p. (J). (gr. 3-7). 2015. pap. 7.99 (978-1-4424-9448-0(4)) 2014. 16.99 (978-1-4424-9447-3(6), Atheneum Bks. for Young Readers) Simon & Schuster Children's Publishing.
Avi. City of Orphans. Ruth, Greg, illus. (ENG.). 368p. (J). (gr. 5-9). 2012. pap. 8.99 (978-1-4169-7108-5(4), Atheneum Bks. for Young Readers) 2011. 17.99 (978-1-4169-7102-3(5), Atheneum/Richard Jackson Bks.) Simon & Schuster Children's Publishing.
—Murder at Midnight. 2011. (ENG.). 256p. (J). (gr. 3-7). pap. 6.99 (978-0-545-08091-0(6), Scholastic Paperbacks) Scholastic, Inc.
—The Traitors' Gate. Raude, Karina, illus. (ENG.). 368p. (J). (gr. 5-8). 2010. pap. 7.99 (978-0-689-85336-4(X), Atheneum Bks. for Young Readers) 2007. 17.99 (978-0-689-85335-7(1), Atheneum/Richard Jackson Bks.) Simon & Schuster Children's Publishing.
—Wolf Rider. 2008. (ENG.). 208p. (YA). (gr. 7-12). mass mkt. 7.99 (978-1-4169-5444-6(9), Simon Pulse) Simon Pulse.
Awad, Shelley. The Greenhouse Kids: Dan Delion's Secret. Zonta, Rose, illus. 2009. 127p. (J). pap. (978-0-88887-379-8(4)) Borealis Pr.
Awdry, W. Blue Mountain Mystery. Golden Books, illus. 2012. (Little Golden Book Ser.). (ENG.). 24p. (J). (gr. k-k). 4.99 (978-0-307-97590-4(8), Golden Bks.) Random Hse. Children's Bks.
Awdry, Wilbert V. Blue Mountain Mystery. Stubbs, Tommy, illus. 2012. (Big Golden Book Ser.). (ENG.). 48p. (J). (gr. -1-2). 9.99 (978-0-307-93149-8(8), Golden Bks.) Random Hse. Children's Bks.
Axelrod, Amy & Axelrod, David. The Bullet Catch. 2015. (ENG.). 320p. (J). (gr. 5-9). 17.95 (978-0-8234-2858-8(3)) Holiday Hse., Inc.
Axelsson, Carina. Model Undercover: London. 2016. (Model Undercover Ser.: 3). (ENG.). 368p. (J). (gr. 5-8). pap. 6.99 (978-1-4926-2088-4(2), Sourcebooks Jabberwocky) Sourcebooks, Inc.
—Model Undercover: New York. 2015. (Model Undercover Ser.: 2). (ENG.). 320p. (J). (gr. 4-8). pap. 6.99 (978-1-4926-0785-4(1), Sourcebooks Jabberwocky) Sourcebooks, Inc.
—Paris. 2014. (Model Undercover Ser.: 1). (ENG.). 368p. (J). (gr. 4-7). pap. 6.99 (978-1-4022-8587-5(6), Sourcebooks Jabberwocky) Sourcebooks, Inc.
Ayres, Katherine. Under Copp's Hill. 2009. (Mysteries Through Time Ser.). 176p. (YA). (gr. 4-8). 31.95 (978-1-60754-185-1(8)); pap. 15.25 (978-1-60754-186-8(6)) Windmill Bks.
—Voices at Whisper Bend. 2009. (Mysteries Through Time Ser.). 176p. (YA). (gr. 4-8). 31.95 (978-1-60754-182-0(3)); pap. 15.25 (978-1-60754-183-7(1)) Windmill Bks.
Babbitt, Natalie. El Cerro del Abismo. 2003.Tr. of Knee-Knock Rise. (SPA., Illus.). 128p. (J). (gr. 3-5). (978-84-236-3420-0(5), ED0964) Edebé ESP. Dist: Lectorum Pubns., Inc.
—Goody Hall. Babbitt, Natalie, illus. 2007. (ENG., Illus.). 192p. (J). (gr. 3-7). per. 8.99 (978-0-312-36983-5(2), 9780312369835) Square Fish.
—Kneeknock Rise. Babbitt, Natalie, illus. 2007. (ENG., Illus.). 144p. (J). (gr. 3-7). per. 7.99 (978-0-312-37009-1(1), 9780312370091) Square Fish.
Baccalario, Pierdomenico. Century #3: City of Wind. Janeczko, Leah D., tr. from ITA. 2012. (Century Ser.: 3). (ENG., Illus.). 336p. (J). (gr. 5-8). 8.99 (978-0-375-85797-3(4), Yearling) Random Hse. Children's Bks.
—Dragon of Seas. Janeczko, Leah D., tr. from ITA. 2013. (Century Ser.: 4). (ENG.). 320p. (J). (gr. 3-7). 7.99 (978-0-375-85798-0(2), Yearling) Random Hse. Children's Bks.
—Star of Stone. Janeczko, Leah D., tr. 2011. (Century Ser.). (ENG.). 320p. (J). (gr. 3-7). 7.99 (978-0-375-85796-6(6), Yearling) Random Hse. Children's Bks.
Bacigalupi, Paolo. The Doubt Factory. 2016. (ENG.). 512p. (YA). (gr. 10-17). pap. 12.99 (978-0-316-22076-7(0)) Little, Brown Bks. for Young Readers.
Backman, Aidel, illus. & adapted by. The Money in the Honey. Backman, Aidel, adapted by. 2003. 32p. (J). 13.95 (978-0-8266-0030-1(1)) Merkos L'Inyonei Chinuch.
Backues, E. Sharol. Stories of a Dragonfly Spy, a Dog Named Droop & a Little Calf That Wondered Why? 2011. 28p. pap. 21.99 (978-1-4653-6343-5(2)) Xlibris Corp.
Badeaux, Dewey. Sam & Skully. Ball, Lauren, illus. 2013. 126p. pap. 12.99 (978-0-9884057-4-5(1)) Alligator Pr.
Baglio, Ben M. Help Find Honey! 2006. (Pet Finders Club Ser.: Vol. 10). (Illus.). 157p. (J). (978-0-439-87143-3(3)) Scholastic, Inc.
—Max Is Missing. 2005. (Pet Finders Club Ser.: Vol. 2). (Illus.). 126p. (J). pap. (978-0-439-68884-0(1)) Scholastic, Inc.
—Runaway Rascal. 2006. (Illus.). 157p. (J). (978-0-439-79250-9(9)) Scholastic, Inc.
—Vanishing Point. Ettlinger, Doris, illus. 2007. 158p. (J). pap. (978-0-439-87145-7(X)) Scholastic, Inc.
Bailey, Linda. How Can a Brilliant Detective Shine in the Dark?, No. 6. 2003. (Stevie Diamond Mystery Ser.). (ENG.). 200p. (J). (gr. 13-18). 14.95 (978-1-55074-896-3(3)) Kids Can Pr., Ltd. CAN. Dist: Hachette Bk. Group.
—What's a Serious Detective Like Me Doing in Such a Silly Movie? 2003. (Stevie Diamond Mystery Ser.). 192p. (YA). (978-1-55337-639-2(0)) Kids Can Pr., Ltd.
Bailey, Mary. Vhan Zeely & the Time Prevaricators. 2009. 192p. 25.50 (978-1-60693-477-7(5), Eloquent Bks.) Strategic Book Publishing & Rights Agency (SBPRA).
Bailie, Helen. The Azura Stones. 2007. 212p. (YA). per. 18.00 (978-1-58982-374-7(5), Bedside Bks.) American Bk. Publishing Group.
The Baker Street Bunch & the Missing Honeybees Mystery. 2005. (J). per. (978-0-9754241-5-5(7)) MiMar Publishing.
Balaban, Mariah. Scooby-Doo! & the Haunted Diner. 2010. (Illus.). 31p. (J). (978-0-545-20882-6(3)) Scholastic, Inc.
—Scooby-Doo & the Rotten Robot, 1 vol. Duendes Del Sur Staff, illus. 2012. (Scooby-Doo! Set 2 Ser.: No. 2). (ENG.). 24p. (J). (gr. k-3). lib. bdg. 24.21 (978-1-59961-868-5(0)) Spotlight.
—Scooby-Doo & the Scary Snowman, 1 vol. Duendes Del Sur Staff, illus. 2012. (Scooby-Doo! Set 2 Ser.: No. 2). (ENG.). 24p. (J). (gr. k-3). lib. bdg. 24.21 (978-1-59961-869-2(9)) Spotlight.
—Scooby-Doo & the Thanksgiving Terror, 1 vol. Duendes Del Sur Staff, illus. 2012. (Scooby-Doo! Set 2 Ser.: No. 2). (ENG.). 24p. (J). (gr. k-3). lib. bdg. 24.21 (978-1-59961-870-8(2)) Spotlight.
Balasubramanian, Lalitha. The Twins at the Ancient Villa, 1 vol. 2009. 48p. pap. 16.95 (978-1-61582-601-8(7)) America Star Bks.
Baldwin, Faith. Judy: A Story of Divine Corners. Beebe, Robb, illus. 2011. 264p. 47.95 (978-1-258-08877-4(0)) Literary Licensing, LLC.
Baldwin, Rich & Jones, Sandie. The Detective Company. Dawn, Baumer, illus. 2004. 183p. (YA). pap. 9.95 (978-0-9742920-0-7(1), 2001) Buttonwood Pr.
Balian, Lorna. Un Fiasco de Bruja, 1 vol. 2003.Tr. of Humbug Witch. (SPA., Illus.). 32p. (J). (gr. -1). pap. 4.95 (978-1-59572-011-5(1)) Star Bright Bks., Inc.
Ball, Duncan. An Eyeful of Emily. 2007. 336p. (978-0-7322-8568-5(2)) HarperCollins Pubs. Australia.
—Selby Supersnoop. Stomann, Allan, illus. 2003. 176p. (978-0-207-20005-2(X)) HarperCollins Pubs. Australia.
Balliett, Blue. The Calder Game. Helquist, Brett, illus. (ENG.). (J). (gr. 3-7). 2010. 416p. 7.99 (978-0-439-85208-1(0), Scholastic Paperbacks) 2008. 400p. 17.99 (978-0-439-85207-4(2), Scholastic Pr.) Scholastic, Inc.
—Chasing Vermeer. Helquist, Brett, illus. 2005. (ENG.). 288p. (J). (gr. 3-7). reprint ed. pap. 7.99 (978-0-439-37297-8(6)) Scholastic, Inc.
—The Danger Box. 2010. (ENG.). 320p. (J). (gr. 4-18). 16.99 (978-0-439-85209-8(9), Scholastic Pr.) Scholastic, Inc.
—Hold Fast. 2015. (ENG.). 288p. (J). (gr. 3-7). pap. 6.99 (978-0-545-29989-3(6), Scholastic Paperbacks) Scholastic, Inc.
—The Wright 3. Helquist, Brett, illus. 2008. 318p. (gr. 4-7). 18.00 (978-0-7569-8942-2(6)) Perfection Learning Corp.
—The Wright 3. Helquist, Brett, illus. 2007. (ENG.). 352p. (J). (gr. 3-7). pap. 7.99 (978-0-439-69368-4(3), Scholastic Paperbacks) Scholastic, Inc.
Balmer, Fred. Festus & the Hole in the Fence Gang. Newcomb, Kristene, illus. 2005. 33p. (J). per. 7.00 (978-0-9760790-3-3(8)) Folsom Fallies Pr.
—Festus & the Missing Bag of Feed. Newcomb, Kristene, illus. 2004. 26p. (J). per. 7.00 (978-0-9760790-0-2(3)) Folsom Fallies Pr.
Banim, Lisa. In the Doghouse. 2005. 124p. (J). lib. bdg. 16.92 (978-1-4242-0685-8(5)) Fitzgerald Bks.
Banim, Lisa & Minsky, Terri. The Case of the Kate Haters. 2005. (Illus.). 124p. (J). (978-1-4156-3927-6(2)) Disney Pr.
Banks, Lynne Reid. The Mystery of the Cupboard. Newsom, Tom, illus. 2004. (Indian in the Cupboard Ser.: No. 4). (ENG.). 256p. (J). (gr. 4-18). pap. 6.99 (978-0-380-72013-2(2)) HarperCollins Pubs.
—The Mystery of the Cupboard. (ENG., Illus.). 208p. pap. (978-0-00-714901-8(8)) HarperCollins Pubs. Ltd.
—The Mystery of the Cupboard. (Indian in the Cupboard Ser.: No. 4). 246p. (J). (gr. 4-7). pap. 4.99 (978-0-8072-1459-6(0), Listening Library) Random Hse. Audio Publishing Group.
Banyard, Jen. Riddle Gully Secrets. 2016. (Riddle Gully Ser.). (ENG.). 188p. (J). 9.95 (978-1-925163-95-7(4)) Fremantle Pr. AUS. Dist: Independent Pubs. Group.
Baratz-Logsted, Lauren. The Twin's Daughter. (ENG.). (YA). 2014. 416p. (gr. 7-12). pap. 9.99 (978-1-59990-661-4(9), 9781599906614) 2010. 400p. (gr. 9-12). 16.99 (978-1-59990-513-6(2), 9781599905136) Bloomsbury Publishing USA. (Bloomsbury USA Childrens).
Baratz-Logsted, Lauren, et al. Marcia's Madness. Weber, Lisa K., illus. 2010. (Sisters Eight Ser.: 5). (ENG.). 128p. (J). (gr. 1-4). pap. 5.99 (978-0-547-32864-5(8)) Houghton Mifflin Harcourt Publishing Co.
Barba, Rick. The Quantum Quandary. 2006. (Spy Gear Adventures Ser.: 3). (ENG.). 208p. (J). (gr. 3-7). pap. 10.99 (978-1-4169-0889-0(7), Aladdin) Simon & Schuster Children's Publishing.
Barbo, Maria S. Catnapped Caper, 1 vol. 2013. (Scooby-Doo! Picture Clue Bks.). (ENG.). 24p. (J). (gr. -1-1). lib. bdg. 24.21 (978-1-61479-035-8(3), Essential Library) ABDO Publishing Co.
Barbo, Maria S. & Preller, James. The Case of the Four-Leaf Clover. Smith, Jamie, illus. 2008. 104p. (J). pap. (978-0-545-03837-9(5)) Scholastic, Inc.
Barklem, Jill. La Escalera Secreta.Tr. of Secret Staircase. (SPA.). 30p. (J). 8.95 (978-84-233-2765-2(5)) Ediciones Destino ESP. Dist: Planeta Publishing Corp.
Barkley, Callie. Amy & the Missing Puppy. Riti, Marsha, illus. 2013. (Critter Club Ser.: 1). (ENG.). 128p. (J). (gr. k-2). 15.99 (978-1-4424-5770-6(8)); pap. 5.99 (978-1-4424-5769-0(4)) Little Simon. (Little Simon).
—Amy & the Missing Puppy. 2013. (Critter Club Ser.: 1). lib. bdg. 16.00 (978-0-606-27023-6(X), Turtleback) Turtleback Bks.
Barnes, Jennifer Lynn. All in. 2015. (Naturals Ser.: Bk. 3). (ENG.). 384p. (YA). (gr. 7-12). 17.99 (978-1-4847-1643-4(4)) Hyperion Bks. for Children.
—Bad Blood (the Naturals #4) ((the Naturals #4)) 2016. (Naturals Ser.). (ENG.). 384p. (YA). (gr. 7-12). 17.99 (978-1-4847-5732-1(7)) Hyperion Bks. for Children.
—Killer Instinct. 2015. (Naturals Ser.: Bk. 2). (ENG.). 400p. (YA). (gr. 9-17). pap. 9.99 (978-1-4231-7182-9(9)) Hyperion Bks. for Children.
—Killer Instinct. 2014. (Naturals Ser.: Bk. 2). (ENG.). 384p. (YA). (gr. 9-17). 17.99 (978-1-4231-6832-4(1)) Hyperion Pr.
—The Long Game: A Fixer Novel. (ENG.). 368p. (YA). 2017. pap. 9.99 (978-1-61963-599-9(2), 9781619635999) 2016. 17.99 (978-1-61963-596-8(8), 9781619635968) Bloomsbury Publishing USA. (Bloomsbury USA Childrens).
Barnes, Phil. My Teacher's a Spy! 2017. (ENG.). 66p. (J). pap. 10.95 (**978-1-78629-497-5(4)**, 050057eb-4aa0-4e8e-acb5-a4c22418a979) Austin, Stan AUS. Dist: Bookmasters Distribution.
Barnett, Angela. Mystic Grove. 2006. pap. 10.00 (978-1-4257-1912-8(0)) Xlibris Corp.
Barnett, Mac. The Case of the Case of Mistaken Identity. Rex, Adam, illus. (Brixton Brothers Ser.: 1). (ENG.). (J). (gr. 3-7). 2010. 208p. pap. 7.99 (978-1-4169-7816-9(X)) 2009. 192p. 15.99 (978-1-4169-7815-2(1)) Simon & Schuster Bks. For Young Readers. (Simon & Schuster Bks. For Young Readers).
—Danger Goes Berserk. Myers, Matthew, illus. (Brixton Brothers Ser.: 4). (ENG.). 256p. (J). (gr. 3-7). 2013. pap. 7.99 (978-1-4424-3978-8(5)) 2012. 17.99 (978-1-4424-3977-1(7)) Simon & Schuster Bks. For Young Readers. (Simon & Schuster Bks. For Young Readers).
—The Ghostwriter Secret. Rex, Adam, illus. (Brixton Brothers Ser.: 2). (ENG.). (J). (gr. 3-7). 2011. 256p. pap. 7.99 (978-1-4169-7818-3(6)) 2010. 240p. 17.99 (978-1-4169-7817-6(8)) Simon & Schuster Bks. For Young Readers. (Simon & Schuster Bks. For Young Readers).
—It Happened on a Train. Rex, Adam, illus. (Brixton Brothers Ser.: 3). (ENG.). (J). (gr. 3-7). 2012. 304p. pap. 7.99 (978-1-4169-7820-6(8)) 2011. 288p. 17.99 (978-1-4169-7819-0(4)) Simon & Schuster Bks. For Young Readers. (Simon & Schuster Bks. For Young Readers).
—Mysterious Case of Cases: The Case of the Case of Mistaken Identity - The Ghostwriter Secret - It Happened on a Train - Danger Goes Berserk. Rex, Adam & Myers, Matthew, illus. 2013. (Brixton Brothers Ser.). (ENG.). 1024p. (J). (gr. 3-7). pap. 29.99 (978-1-4424-9818-1(8), Simon & Schuster Bks. For Young Readers) Simon & Schuster Bks. For Young Readers.
Barnett, Mac, et al. The Clock Without a Face. Teplin, Scott & Rex, Adam, illus. 2010. (ENG.). 30p. (gr. 2-18). bds. 19.95 (978-1-934781-71-5(1)) McSweeney's Publishing.
Barnholdt, Lauren. Girl Meets Ghost. 2013. (Girl Meets Ghost Ser.: 1). (ENG.). 224p. (J). (gr. 4-9). 15.99 (978-1-4424-4246-7(8), Aladdin) Simon & Schuster Children's Publishing.
—The Harder the Fall. (Girl Meets Ghost Ser.: 2). (ENG., (J). (gr. 4-9). 2014. Illus.). 256p. pap. 7.99 (978-1-4424-2147-9(9)) 2013. 240p. 16.99 (978-1-4424-4247-4(6)) Simon & Schuster Children's Publishing. (Aladdin).
Barnickle, Angela. Miles Gardner & the Secret of Blissville: A Blissville Mystery Series. 2011. 128p. (gr. 4-6). 23.89 (978-1-4634-1675-1(X)); pap. 12.01 (978-1-4634-1676-8(8)) AuthorHouse.
Barr, Robert. The Clue of the Silver Spoons. 2004. reprint ed. pap. 1.99 (978-1-4192-5701-8(3)); pap. 15.95 (978-1-4191-5701-1(9)) Kessinger Publishing, LLC.
Barrett, Cheryl. Andy Goes Crab Fishin' 2010. 32p. pap. 12.99 (978-1-4490-7459-3(6)) AuthorHouse.
Barrett, Jennifer. Lethal Delivery, Postage Prepaid. (Thumbprint Mysteries Ser.). 32.86 (978-0-8092-0425-0(8)) McGraw-Hill/Contemporary.
Barrett, Tracy. The Beast of Blackslope. 2011. (Sherlock Files Ser.: 2). (ENG., Illus.). 192p. (J). (gr. 3-7). pap. 7.99 (978-0-312-65918-9(0), 9780312659189) Square Fish.
—The Case That Time Forgot. 2011. (Sherlock Files Ser.: 3). (ENG., Illus.). 176p. (J). (gr. 3-7). pap. 7.99 (978-0-312-56358-5(2), 9780312563585) Square Fish.
—The Missing Heir. 2012. (Sherlock Files Ser.: 4). (ENG., Illus.). 192p. (J). (gr. 3-7). pap. 8.99 (978-1-250-00480-2(2), 9781250004802) Square Fish.
—The Missing Heir. 2012. (Sherlock Files Ser.: 4). (J). lib. bdg. 19.65 (978-0-606-26131-9(1), Turtleback) Turtleback Bks.
Barriman, Lydia. The Runaway Puppy: A Mystery with Probability. Grutzik, Becky, illus. 2010. (Manga Math Mysteries Ser.: 8). (ENG.). 48p. (gr. 3-5). 29.27 (978-0-7613-4910-5(3)) Lerner Publishing Group.
—Thr Runaway Puppy: A Mystery with Probability. Grutzik, Becky, illus. 2011. (Manga Math Mysteries Ser.: 8). (ENG.). 46p. (gr. 3-5). pap. 6.95 (978-0-7613-8137-2(6), Graphic Universe™) Lerner Publishing Group.
—#8 the Runaway Puppy: A Mystery with Probability. Grutzik, Becky, illus. 2011. (Manga Math Mysteries Set II Ser.). pap. 39.62 (978-0-7613-8365-9(4), Graphic Universe™) Lerner Publishing Group.
Barron, T. A. The Heartlight Saga. 2014. (Adventures of Kate Ser.). (ENG.). 864p. (J). pap. 10.99 (978-0-14-751032-7(5), Puffin Books) Penguin Young Readers Group.
Barrows, Annie. Ivy + Bean + Me: A Fill-in-the-Blank Book. Blackall, Sophie, illus. 2014. (ENG.). 104p. (J). (gr. 3-9). 10.99 (978-1-4521-3729-2(3)) Chronicle Bks. LLC.
—Ivy + Bean Take the Case. Blackall, Sophie, illus. (ENG.). (J). (gr. 1-4). 2014. 136p. pap. 5.99 (978-1-4521-2871-9(5)) 2013. 128p. 14.99 (978-1-4521-0699-1(1)) Chronicle Bks. LLC.
—Ivy & Bean Take the Case. 2014. (Ivy & Bean Ser.: 10). (J). lib. bdg. 16.00 (978-0-606-36537-6(0)) Turtleback Bks.
Barry, Nick. Escape of the Terra-Cotta Soldiers: An Ethan Sparks Adventure. 2008. 180p. 23.95 (978-0-595-49365-4(3)); pap. 13.95 (978-0-595-45413-6(5)) iUniverse, Inc.
Bartlett, Philip A. Mystery of the Circle of Fire: A Roy Stover Story. 2011. 258p. 47.95 (978-1-258-09666-3(8)) Literary Licensing, LLC.
The Baseball Heroes, 6 vols. (Woodland Mysteriestm Ser.). 133p. (gr. 3-7). 42.50 (978-0-7802-7931-5(X)) Wright Group/McGraw-Hill.
Bates, Sonya. Topspin, 1 vol. 2013. (Orca Sports Ser.). (ENG.). 160p. (YA). (gr. 6-10). pap. 9.95 (978-1-4598-0385-5(X)) Orca Bk. Pubs. USA.
Bath, K. P. Flip Side. 2009. (YA). 16.99 (978-0-316-03836-2(9)) Little Brown & Co.
Battle, Craig. Max Finder Mystery Collected Casebook, Vol. 6. Pérez, Ramón, illus. 2012. (Max Finder Mystery Collected Casebook Ser.: 6). (ENG.). 96p. (J). (gr. 3-6). pap. 9.95 (978-1-926973-21-0(6), Owlkids) Owlkids Bks. Inc. CAN. Dist: Publishers Group West (PGW).
The Battle of Bayport. 2014. (Hardy Boys Adventures Ser.: 6). (ENG., Illus.). 160p. (J). (gr. 3-7). 16.99 (978-1-4814-0007-7(X)); pap. 6.99 (978-1-4814-0006-0(1)) Simon & Schuster Children's Publishing. (Aladdin).
Baucom, Ian. Through the Skylight. Gerard, Justin, illus. (ENG.). 400p. (J). (gr. 4-8). 2014. pap. 6.99 (978-1-4424-8167-1(6)) 2013. 17.99 (978-1-4169-1777-9(2)) Simon & Schuster Children's Publishing. (Atheneum Bks. for Young Readers).
Bauer, Joan. Tell Me. 2015. (ENG.). 288p. (J). (gr. 5). 7.99 (978-0-14-751314-4(6), Puffin Books) Penguin Young Readers Group.
Baum, L. Frank. Mary Louise in the Country. 2011. 188p. pap. 14.95 (978-1-4638-0069-7(X)) Rodgers, Alan Bks.
Baum, L. Frank & van Dyne, Edith. Mary Louise in the Country. 2011. 188p. 26.95 (978-1-4638-9605-8(0)) Rodgers, Alan Bks.
—Mary Louise Solves a Mystery. 2011. 140p. 24.95 (978-1-4638-9498-6(8)) Rodgers, Alan Bks.
Baumgartner, Edward Louis. Wabash Boy. 2011. 236p. (gr. 4-6). pap. 16.26 (978-1-4269-7615-5(1)) Trafford Publishing.
Baumgartner, John Robert. Like Losing Your Left Hand. 2011. 244p. pap. 24.95 (978-1-4560-4043-7(X)) America Star Bks.
Beard, Elizabeth. Liza & the Mysteries. 2004. 70p. (J). per. (978-1-59196-640-1(X)) Instant Pub.
Beatty, Scott. Murder in Mind, Vol. 4. Guice, Butch et al, illus. 2004. (Ruse Ser.: Vol. 4). 160p. (YA). pap. 15.95 (978-1-59314-047-2(9)) CrossGeneration Comics, Inc.
Beaufrand, M. J. Useless Bay. 2016. (ENG.). 240p. (YA). (gr. 8-17). 17.95 (978-1-4197-2138-0(0), Amulet Bks.) Abrams, Inc.
Beauregard, Lynda. Summer Camp Science Mysteries. Helmer, Der-Shing, illus. 2012. (Summer Camp Science Mysteries Ser.). (ENG.). 48p. (gr. 3-6). pap. 52.82 (978-0-7613-9272-9(6));Pack, Set. pap. 316.92

(978-0-7613-9273-6(4)) Lerner Publishing Group. (Graphic Universe™).

—Summer Camp Science Mysteries: Spring 2012 New Releases. Helmer, Der-Shing, illus. 2012. (Summer Camp Science Mysteries Ser.). 48p. (J). (gr. 3-6). lib. bdg. 117.08 *(978-0-7613-5688-2(6),* Graphic Universe™) Lerner Publishing Group.

—The Whispering Lake Ghosts: A Mystery about Sound. Torres, German, illus. 2013. (Summer Camp Science Mysteries Ser.: 6). (ENG.). 48p. (gr. 3-6). pap. 6.95 *(978-1-4677-0734-3(1),* Graphic Universe™) Lerner Publishing Group.

Beauvais, Clémentine. Gargoyles Gone AWOL. Horne, Sarah, illus. 2015. (Sesame Seade Mystery Ser.: 2). (ENG.). 208p. (J). (gr. 2-6). 16.95 *(978-0-8234-3205-9(X))* Holiday Hse., Inc.

—Scam on the Cam. Horne, Sarah, illus. 2016. (Sesame Seade Mystery Ser.: 3). (ENG.). 192p. (J). 16.95 *(978-0-8234-3630-9(6))* Holiday Hse., Inc.

—Sleuth on Skates. Horne, Sarah, illus. 2014. (Sesame Seade Mystery Ser.: 1). (ENG.). 224p. (J). (gr. 2-5). 16.95 *(978-0-8234-3197-7(5))* Holiday Hse., Inc.

Beauvais, Clementine, et al. Mystery & Mayhem. 2016. (ENG., Illus.). 320p. (J). (gr. 3-5). pap. 9.99 *(978-1-4052-8264-2(9))* Egmont Bks., Ltd. GBR. Dist: Independent Pubs. Group.

Beck, W. H. Malcolm at Midnight. Lies, Brian, illus. (ENG.). 272p. (J). (gr. 2-5). 2015. pap. 7.99 *(978-0-544-33666-7(6),* HMH Books For Young Readers) 2012. 16.99 *(978-0-547-68100-9(3))* Houghton Mifflin Harcourt Publishing Co.

—Malcolm under the Stars. Lies, Brian, illus. (ENG.). 272p. (J). (gr. 2-5). 2016. pap. 7.99 *(978-0-544-81312-0(X))* 2015. 16.99 *(978-0-544-39267-0(1))* Houghton Mifflin Harcourt Publishing Co. (HMH Books For Young Readers).

Beer, Henry, photos by. Girl Defective. 2015. (ENG., Illus.). 320p. (YA). (gr. 9). pap. 10.99 *(978-1-4424-9761-0(0))* Simon & Schuster Children's Publishing.

Behrens, Kathryn J. Breakdown. 2016. (Atlas of Cursed Places Ser.). (ENG.). 96p. (YA). (gr. 6-12). lib. bdg. 26.65 *(978-1-5124-1323-6(2),* Darby Creek) Lerner Publishing Group.

Behrens, Rebecca. Summer of Lost & Found. 2016. (ENG., Illus.). 288p. (J). (gr. 3-7). 16.99 *(978-1-4814-5896-2(5),* Aladdin) Simon & Schuster Children's Publishing.

Beil, Michael D. Lantern Sam & the Blue Streak Bandits. (ENG., Illus.). 288p. (J). (gr. 3-7). 2015. pap. 7.99 *(978-0-385-75320-3(9),* Yearling) 2014. 15.99 *(978-0-385-75317-3(9),* Knopf Bks. for Young Readers) Random Hse. Children's Bks.

—The Mistaken Masterpiece. 2011. (Red Blazer Girls Ser.). (ENG.). 320p. (J). (gr. 3-7). 16.99 *(978-0-375-86740-8(6),* Knopf Bks. for Young Readers) Random Hse. Children's Bks.

—The Red Blazer Girls. 2010. (Red Blazer Girls Ser.). (ENG.). 320p. (J). (gr. 3-7). 7.99 *(978-0-375-84303-7(5),* Yearling) Random Hse. Children's Bks.

—The Red Blazer Girls: the Mistaken Masterpiece. 2012. (Red Blazer Girls Ser.). (ENG.). 336p. (J). (gr. 5). 8.99 *(978-0-375-86494-0(6),* Yearling) Random Hse. Children's Bks.

—The Red Blazer Girls: the Secret Cellar. 2012. (Red Blazer Girls Ser.). (ENG., Illus.). 288p. (J). (gr. 5). 17.99 *(978-0-375-86741-5(4),* Knopf Bks. for Young Readers) Random Hse. Children's Bks.

—The Red Blazer Girls: the Vanishing Violin. 2011. (Red Blazer Girls Ser.). (ENG.). 336p. (J). (gr. 3-7). 8.99 *(978-0-375-85454-5(1),* Yearling) Random Hse. Children's Bks.

—The Secret Cellar. 2013. (Red Blazer Girls Ser.). (ENG., Illus.). 288p. (J). (gr. 5). pap. 8.99 *(978-0-375-86495-7(4),* Yearling) Random Hse. Children's Bks.

—Summer at Forsaken Lake. Kneen, Maggie, illus. 2013. (ENG.). 336p. (J). (gr. 5). pap. 8.99 *(978-0-375-86496-4(2),* Yearling) Random Hse. Children's Bks.

Beitia, Sara. The Last Good Place of Lily Odilon. 2010. (ENG.). 312p. (YA). (gr. 8-18). pap. 9.95 *(978-0-7387-2068-5(2),* Flux) North Star Editions.

Bell, Alex. Frozen Charlotte. 2016. (ENG.). 304p. (J). (gr. 7). 18.99 *(978-0-545-94108-2(3),* Scholastic Pr.) Scholastic, Inc.

Bell, Juliet. Kepler's Dream. 2013. (ENG.). 256p. (J). (gr. 5). pap. 6.99 *(978-0-14-242648-7(2),* Puffin Books) Penguin Young Readers Group.

Bellairs, John. The Chessmen of Doom (A Johnny Dixon Mystery: Book Seven) 2011. 114p. pap. 14.95 *(978-1-61756-348-5(X))* Open Road Integrated Media, Inc.

—The Curse of the Blue Figurine (A Johnny Dixon Mystery: Book One) 2011. 150p. pap. 15.95 *(978-1-61756-324-9(2))* Open Road Integrated Media, Inc.

—The Eyes of the Killer Robot (A Johnny Dixon Mystery: Book Five) 2011. 126p. pap. 14.95 *(978-1-61756-340-9(4))* Open Road Integrated Media, Inc.

—The Mummy, the Will, & the Crypt (A Johnny Dixon Mystery: Book Two) 2011. 126p. pap. 14.95 *(978-1-61756-328-7(5))* Open Road Integrated Media, Inc.

—The Secret of the Underground Room (A Johnny Dixon Mystery: Book Eight) 2011. 96p. pap. 14.95 *(978-1-61756-352-2(8))* Open Road Integrated Media, Inc.

—The Spell of the Sorcerer's Skull. Gorey, Edward, illus. 2004. 170p. (J). (gr. 4-7). 13.65 *(978-0-7569-4965-5(3))* Perfection Learning Corp.

—The Spell of the Sorcerer's Skull (A Johnny Dixon Mystery: Book Three) 2011. 124p. pap. 14.95 *(978-1-61756-332-4(3))* Open Road Integrated Media, Inc.

Bellingham, Brenda. La Maldicion del Cofre de Plata. (SPA.). (YA). 8.95 *(978-958-04-7079-3(0))* Norma S.A. COL. Dist: Distribuidora Norma, Inc.

Bellino, Sarah. The Little Miss Detectives: Case Number 1. 2012. 32p. pap. 14.51 *(978-1-4669-6867-7(2))* Trafford Publishing.

Benjamin, Ruth. The Lost Treasure of Chelton. 2004. viii, 170p. (J). 13.95 *(978-1-932443-02-8(9))* Judaica Pr., Inc., The.

—The Mysterious Lighthouse of Chelton. 2006. (ENG.). 160p. (J). 14.95 *(978-1-932443-57-8(6))* Judaica Pr., Inc., The.

Bennardo, Charlotte & Zaman, Natalie. Blonde Ops. 2014. (ENG.). 288p. (YA). (gr. 7). 17.99 *(978-1-250-03039-9(0),* 9781250030399, St. Martin's Griffin) St. Martin's Pr.

Bennett, Marcia Allen. Mystery at Saddlecreek. 2003. (Illus.). 162p. (J). pap. 12.95 *(978-1-57168-494-3(8),* Eakin Pr.) Eakin Pr.

Bennett, Marcia Allen & Eckhardt, Jason C. Mystery at Saddlecreek. 2004. (Illus.). 162p. (J). 17.95 *(978-1-57168-336-6(4),* Eakin Pr.) Eakin Pr.

Bennicke, Rune Brandt. The Mystery Hat. Jensen, Jakob Hjort, illus. 2014. (ENG.). 32p. (J). (gr. -1-k). 16.95 *(978-1-62914-621-8(8),* Sky Pony Pr.) Skyhorse Publishing Co., Inc.

Benoit, Charles. Cold Calls. (ENG.). (gr. 7). 2016. 304p. (YA). pap. 8.99 *(978-0-544-54121-4(9),* HMH Books For Young Readers) 2014. 288p. (J). 17.99 *(978-0-544-23950-0(4))* Houghton Mifflin Harcourt Publishing Co.

Benson, Amber. Among the Ghosts. Grace, Sina, illus. 2011. (ENG.). 256p. (J). (gr. 3-7). pap. 6.99 *(978-1-4169-9426-8(2),* Aladdin) Simon & Schuster Children's Publishing.

—Among the Ghosts. Grace, Sina, illus. 2010. (ENG.). 256p. (J). (gr. 3-7). 15.99 *(978-1-4169-9405-3(X),* Simon & Schuster/Paula Wiseman Bks.) Simon & Schuster/Paula Wiseman Bks.

Benyo, Richard. The South Street Gang vs. the Coalcracker Cyclops. 2010. (ENG.). 151p. pap. 8.00 *(978-1-58966-208-7(3))* Univ. of Scranton Pr.

Beresford, Elisabeth. The Great Cake Mystery. (Illus.). 16p. (J). (gr. k-6). pap. *(978-0-340-74672-1(6))* Hodder & Stoughton.

Berk, Josh. The Dark Days of Hamburger Halpin. 2011. (ENG.). 258p. (YA). (gr. 7). pap. 8.99 *(978-0-375-84625-0(5),* Ember) Random Hse. Children's Bks.

—Guy Langman, Crime Scene Procrastinator. 2013. (ENG.). 240p. (YA). (gr. 7). pap. 8.99 *(978-0-375-84627-4(1),* Ember) Random Hse. Children's Bks.

—Say It Ain't So. (Lenny & the Mikes Ser.). (ENG.). 288p. (J). (gr. 3-7). 2015. pap. 7.99 *(978-0-307-93007-1(6),* Yearling) 2014. 16.99 *(978-0-375-87009-5(1),* Knopf Bks. for Young Readers) Random Hse. Children's Bks.

—Strike Three, You're Dead. 2014. (Lenny & the Mikes Ser.). (ENG.). 272p. (J). (gr. 3-7). 6.99 *(978-0-307-93006-4(8),* Yearling) Random Hse. Children's Bks.

Berlin, Eric. The Potato Chip Puzzles. 2010. (Puzzling World of Winston Breen Ser.: 2). (ENG.). 272p. (J). (gr. 3-7). 7.99 *(978-0-14-241637-2(1),* Puffin Books) Penguin Young Readers Group.

—The Puzzler's Mansion: The Puzzling World of Winston Breen. (Puzzling World of Winston Breen Ser.: 3). (ENG.). (J). (gr. 3-7). 2013. 272p. pap. 7.99 *(978-0-14-242643-2(1),* Puffin Books) 2012. 256p. 16.99 *(978-0-399-25697-4(0),* G.P. Putnam's Sons Books for Young Readers) Penguin Young Readers Group.

—The Puzzling World of Winston Breen. 2009. (Puzzling World of Winston Breen Ser.: 1). (ENG.). 224p. (J). (gr. 3-7). pap. 7.99 *(978-0-14-241388-3(7),* Puffin Books) Penguin Young Readers Group.

Bern, Dave. Best Friends. 2006. 28p. pap. 9.95 *(978-1-4327-0036-2(7))* Outskirts Pr., Inc.

Bernard, Romily. Find Me. (Find Me Ser.: 1). (ENG.). (YA). (gr. 8). 2014. 336p. pap. 9.99 *(978-0-06-222904-5(4))* 2013. 320p. 17.99 *(978-0-06-222903-8(6))* HarperCollins Pubs. (HarperTeen).

—Remember Me. 2014. (Find Me Ser.: 2). (ENG.). 368p. (YA). (gr. 8). 17.99 *(978-0-06-222906-9(0),* HarperTeen) HarperCollins Pubs.

Berry, Julie. All the Truth That's in Me. 2014. (ENG.). 304p. (YA). (gr. 7). pap. 9.99 *(978-0-14-242730-9(6),* Speak) Penguin Young Readers Group.

—The Scandalous Sisterhood of Prickwillow Place. 2014. (ENG.). 368p. (J). (gr. 5-9). 15.99 *(978-1-59643-956-6(4),* 9781596439566) Roaring Brook Pr.

Betancourt, Jeanne. Penny & Pepper. Riley, Kellee, illus. 2011. (Scholastic Reader Level 3 Ser.). (ENG.). 48p. (J). (gr. 1-4). pap. 3.99 *(978-0-545-11508-7(6),* Cartwheel Bks.) Scholastic, Inc.

Bevins, Pegi & Doyle, Arthur Conan. Sherlock Holmes. 2003. (Retold Classics Anthologies Ser.). (Illus.). 282p. (J). pap. 9.99 *(978-0-7891-5931-1(7))* Perfection Learning Corp.

Bhagwat, B. R. Faster Fenay at Fort Pratapgad. Modak, Tejas, tr. 2013. 120p. 10.00 *(978-0-14-333201-5(5))* Penguin Group India IND. Dist: Penguin Publishing Group.

Bial, Raymond. Shadow Island: A Tale of Lake Superior. 2006. 172p. (J). (gr. 3-7). 18.95 *(978-1-883953-37-9(5));* per. 12.95 *(978-1-883953-36-2(7))* Great Lakes Literary, LLC. (Blue Horse Books).

Bichoman Vuelve de la Tumba. (Fantasmas de Fear Street Coleccion). (SPA.). (YA). (gr. 5-8). pap. 7.95 *(978-950-04-1718-1(9),* EM9292) Emecé Editores S.A. ARG. Dist: Planeta Publishing Corp., Lectorum Pubns., Inc.

Bick, Ilsa J. White Space, Bk. 1. 2014. (Dark Passages Ser.: Bk. 1). (ENG.). 560p. (J). (gr. 9). 18.99 *(978-1-60684-419-9(9))* Lerner Publishing Group.

Biedrzycki, David. Ace Lacewing: Bad Bugs Are My Business. Biedrzycki, David, illus. 2011. (ENG., Illus.). 44p. (J). (gr. k-4). pap. 8.95 *(978-1-57091-693-9(4))* Charlesbridge Publishing, Inc.

—Ace Lacewing, Bug Detective: Bad Bugs Are My Business. Biedrzycki, David, illus. 2009. (ENG., Illus.). 44p. (J). (gr. k-4). 16.95 *(978-1-57091-692-2(6))* Charlesbridge Publishing, Inc.

—Ace Lacewing, Bug Detective: The Big Swat. Biedrzycki, David, illus. 2010. (ENG., Illus.). 44p. (J). (gr. k-4). 16.95 *(978-1-57091-747-9(7))* Charlesbridge Publishing, Inc.

—Ace Lacewing Bug Detective: The Big Swat. Biedrzycki, David, illus. 2012. (ENG., Illus.). 44p. (J). (gr. k-4). pap. 8.95 *(978-1-57091-748-6(5))* Charlesbridge Publishing, Inc.

Bills, Randall N. Detective Mysteries. 2008. 92p. pap. 6.95 *(978-0-9796392-1-0(2))* Adventure Boys Inc.

Birch, Beverley. Rift. 2008. (ENG., Illus.). 224p. (YA). (gr. 7-18). pap. 9.95 *(978-1-4052-1589-3(5))* Egmont Bks., Ltd. GBR. Dist: Independent Pubs. Group.

Birney, Betty G. Mysteries According to Humphrey. 2013. (Humphrey Ser.: 8). (ENG.). 176p. (J). (gr. 3-7). pap. 5.99 *(978-0-14-242669-2(5),* Puffin Books) Penguin Young Readers Group.

—Mysteries According to Humphrey. 2013. (According to Humphrey Ser.: 8). lib. bdg. 16.00 *(978-0-606-31699-6(X),* Turtleback) Turtleback Bks.

Bishop, Mary Harelkin & Coteau Books Staff. Tunnels of Tyranny: A Fourth Moose Jaw Adventure, 1 vol. 2005. (Moose Jaw Adventure Ser.). (ENG.). 248p. (J). (gr. 4-7). pap. 7.95 *(978-1-55050-316-6(2))* Coteau Bks. CAN. Dist: Orca Bk. Pubs. USA.

Blackburn, Gary. Pickerel Lake, 1 vol. 2010. 220p. pap. 24.95 *(978-1-4489-4971-7(8))* America Star Bks.

Blackwell-Burke, Melissa & Kunkel, Kristen. The Messy Mystery. 2003. (J). spiral bd. 14.95 *(978-1-58605-958-3(0),* LeapFrog Schl. Hse.) LeapFrog Enterprises, Inc.

Blaine, John. The Blue Ghost Mystery: A Rick Brant Science Adventure Story. 2011. 188p. 42.95 *(978-1-258-09526-0(2))* Literary Licensing, LLC.

—The Caves of Fear: A Rick Brant Science Adventure Story. 2011. 220p. 44.95 *(978-1-258-09271-9(9))* Literary Licensing, LLC.

—The Egyptian Cat Mystery: A Rick Brant Science Adventure Story. 2011. 192p. 42.95 *(978-1-258-09449-2(5))* Literary Licensing, LLC.

—The Pirates of Shan: A Rick Brant Science Adventure Story. 2011. 190p. 42.95 *(978-1-258-10086-5(X))* Literary Licensing, LLC.

—The Scarlet Lake Mystery: A Rick Brant Science Adventure Story. 2011. 192p. 42.95 *(978-1-258-09823-0(7))* Literary Licensing, LLC.

—Smuggler's Reef: A Rick Brant Science Adventure Story. 2011. 220p. 44.95 *(978-1-258-04085-7(9))* Literary Licensing, LLC.

Blaine, John & Goodwin, Harold Leland. The Caves of Fear. 2011. 150p. 24.95 *(978-1-4638-9614-0(X));* pap. 13.95 *(978-1-4638-0073-4(8))* Rodgers, Alan Bks.

Blaisdell, Patty. The Haunted Shed, 1 vol. 2009. 32p. pap. 24.95 *(978-1-60836-674-3(X))* America Star Bks.

Blake-Garrett, Andrea. The Adventures of Izzy & Juju: Twin Detective Investigators (T. D. I.) 2012. 28p. pap. 19.99 *(978-1-4685-0683-9(8))* AuthorHouse.

Blakemore, Megan Frazer. The Spy Catchers of Maple Hill. 2014. (ENG.). 320p. (YA). (gr. 3-6). 16.99 *(978-1-61963-348-3(5),* 9781619633483, Bloomsbury USA Childrens) Bloomsbury Publishing USA.

Blankman, Anne. Conspiracy of Blood & Smoke. 2015. (ENG.). 416p. (YA). (gr. 8). 17.99 *(978-0-06-227884-5(3))* HarperCollins Pubs.

—Prisoner of Night & Fog. 2014. (ENG.). 416p. (YA). (gr. 8). 17.99 *(978-0-06-227881-4(9))* HarperCollins Pubs.

Bloodworth, Mark, illus. The Castle Mystery. 2010. (Boxcar Children Graphic Novels Ser.: 12). (ENG.). 32p. (J). (gr. 1-5). pap. 6.99 *(978-0-8075-1080-3(7))* Whitman, Albert & Co.

Bloom, Ira. Hearts & Other Body Parts. 2017. (ENG.). 352p. (J). (gr. 9). 17.99 *(978-1-338-03073-0(6),* Scholastic Pr.) Scholastic, Inc.

Blum, Paul. Alien Implants. 2007. (Extraordinary Files Ser.). (ENG., Illus.). 48p. (J). (gr. 4-7). pap. 11.99 *(978-1-84680-181-5(8))* Evans Brothers, Ltd. GBR. Dist: Independent Pubs. Group.

—Atlanta. 2007. (Extraordinary Files Ser.). (ENG., Illus.). 48p. (J). (gr. 4-7). pap. 11.99 *(978-1-84680-179-2(6))* Evans Brothers, Ltd. GBR. Dist: Independent Pubs. Group.

—Dawn of the Zombies. 2007. (Extraordinary Files Ser.). (ENG., Illus.). 48p. (J). (gr. 4-7). pap. 10.99 *(978-1-84680-250-8(4))* Evans Brothers, Ltd. GBR. Dist: Independent Pubs. Group.

—Day of Judgement. 2007. (Extraordinary Files Ser.). (ENG., Illus.). 48p. (J). (gr. 4-7). pap. 11.99 *(978-1-84680-251-5(2))* Evans Brothers, Ltd. GBR. Dist: Independent Pubs. Group.

—Gene Machine. 2007. (Extraordinary Files Ser.). (ENG., Illus.). 48p. (J). (gr. 4-7). pap. 10.99 *(978-1-84680-252-2(0))* Evans Brothers, Ltd. GBR. Dist: Independent Pubs. Group.

—Headless Ghost. 2007. (Extraordinary Files Ser.). (ENG., Illus.). 48p. (J). (gr. 4-7). pap. 10.99 *(978-1-84680-173-0(7))* Evans Brothers, Ltd. GBR. Dist: Independent Pubs. Group.

—Killer Robot. 2007. (Extraordinary Files Ser.). (ENG., Illus.). 48p. (J). (gr. 4-7). pap. 10.99 *(978-1-84680-178-5(8))* Evans Brothers, Ltd. GBR. Dist: Independent Pubs. Group.

—Puppet Master. 2007. (Extraordinary Files Ser.). (ENG., Illus.). 48p. (J). (gr. 4-7). pap. 10.99 *(978-1-84680-182-2(6))* Evans Brothers, Ltd. GBR. Dist: Independent Pubs. Group.

—Secrets & Lies. 2007. (Extraordinary Files Ser.). (ENG., Illus.). 48p. (J). (gr. 4-7). pap. 10.99 *(978-1-84680-249-2(0))* Evans Brothers, Ltd. GBR. Dist: Independent Pubs. Group.

—Sleep Walker. 2007. (Extraordinary Files Ser.). (ENG., Illus.). 48p. (J). (gr. 4-7). pap. 10.99 *(978-1-84680-174-7(5))* Evans Brothers, Ltd. GBR. Dist: Independent Pubs. Group.

—Spider Invasion. 2007. (Extraordinary Files Ser.). (ENG., Illus.). 48p. (J). (gr. 4-7). pap. 10.99 *(978-1-84680-183-9(4))* Evans Brothers, Ltd. GBR. Dist: Independent Pubs. Group.

—Werewolf Eclipse. 2007. (Extraordinary Files Ser.). (ENG., Illus.). 48p. (J). (gr. 4-7). pap. 10.99 *(978-1-84680-180-8(X))* Evans Brothers, Ltd. GBR. Dist: Independent Pubs. Group.

Blythe, Daniel. Shadow Breakers. 2013. (J). *(978-0-545-47980-6(0));* (ENG.). 256p. (gr. 5-9). 16.99 *(978-0-545-47979-0(7))* Scholastic, Inc. (Chicken Hse., The).

Blyton, Enid. The Adventure of the Strange Ruby. (Illus.). 128p. (J). pap. 5.95 *(978-0-09-958230-4(9))* Random Hse. GBR. Dist: Trafalgar Square Publishing.

—The Ragamuffin Mystery: A Barney Mystery. 2013. (ENG.). 199p. (J). pap. 9.99 *(978-1-84135-733-1(2))* Award Pubns. Ltd. GBR. Dist: Parkwest Pubns., Inc.

—The Rat-a-Tat Mystery. 2013. (ENG.). 220p. (J). pap. 9.99 *(978-1-84135-732-4(4))* Award Pubns. Ltd. GBR. Dist: Parkwest Pubns., Inc.

—The Rilloby Fair Mystery. 2013. (ENG.). 284p. (J). pap. 9.99 *(978-1-84135-729-4(4))* Award Pubns. Ltd. GBR. Dist: Parkwest Pubns., Inc.

—The Ring O' Bells Mystery. 2013. (ENG.). 276p. (J). pap. 9.99 *(978-1-84135-730-0(8))* Award Pubns. Ltd. GBR. Dist: Parkwest Pubns., Inc.

—The Rockingdown Mystery. 2013. (ENG.). 295p. (J). pap. 9.99 *(978-1-84135-728-7(6))* Award Pubns. Ltd. GBR. Dist: Parkwest Pubns., Inc.

—The Rubadub Mystery. 2013. (ENG.). 280p. (J). pap. 9.99 *(978-1-84135-731-7(6))* Award Pubns. Ltd. GBR. Dist: Parkwest Pubns., Inc.

—The Secret of Cliff Castle: 3 Great Adventure Stories. Downer, Maggie, illus. 2013. (ENG.). 288p. (J). 16.50 *(978-1-84135-588-7(7))* Award Pubns. Ltd. GBR. Dist: Parkwest Pubns., Inc.

—The Secret of the Lost Necklace: 3 Great Adventure Stories. Biro, Val, illus. 2013. (ENG.). 272p. (J). 16.50 *(978-1-84135-587-0(9))* Award Pubns. Ltd. GBR. Dist: Parkwest Pubns., Inc.

Boaz, Ashley. The Mystery of the Midnight Blaze. 2005. (J). *(978-0-9761033-6-3(2))* Waldenhouse Pubs., Inc.

Bodeen, S. A. The Fallout. 2014. (Compound Ser.: 2). (ENG.). 352p. (YA). (gr. 7-12). pap. 10.99 *(978-1-250-05078-6(2),* 9781250050786) Square Fish.

Bohannon, C. S. Spatula Boy: And the Secret of the Mysterious Old House. 2007. 52p. per. 16.95 *(978-1-4241-6956-6(9))* America Star Bks.

Bolger, Z. C. Danny Calloway & the Puzzle House. Robinson, Garrett, ed. Tallent, Alyssa, illus. 2013. 346p. 24.99 *(978-1-939698-01-2(3))* Story Road Publishing, Inc.

Bollback, Anthony G. Capture of the Twin Dragon. 2012. 152p. pap. 8.99 *(978-0-9849359-1-8(6))* Finding the Cause, LLC.

—Hijacked. 2012. 176p. pap. 8.99 *(978-0-9849359-5-6(9))* Finding the Cause, LLC.

—Mystery of the Counterfeit Money. 2012. 170p. (gr. 4-7). pap. 8.99 *(978-0-9849359-2-5(4))* Finding the Cause, LLC.

—Rescue at Cripple Creek. 2012. 178p. pap. 8.99 *(978-0-9849359-3-2(2))* Finding the Cause, LLC.

—Smugglers in Hong Kong. 2012. 156p. pap. 8.99 *(978-0-9849359-0-1(8))* Finding the Cause, LLC.

—The Tiger Shark Strikes Again. 2012. 172p. pap. 8.99 *(978-0-9849359-4-9(0))* Finding the Cause, LLC.

Bolling, Ruben. Ghostly Thief of Time: An EMU Club Adventure. 2015. (ENG., Illus.). 144p. (J). 12.99 *(978-1-4494-5710-5(X))* Andrews McMeel Publishing.

Bomback, Mark & Craze, Galaxy. Mapmaker. 2017. (ENG.). 272p. (YA). (gr. 9). pap. 10.99 *(978-1-61695-633-2(X),* Soho Teen) Soho Pr., Inc.

Bonar, Troy A. Safety = Caring. 2013. 28p. pap. 9.95 *(978-1-4787-0745-5(3))* Outside the Box Publishing, LLC.

Bond, Gwenda. Strange Alchemy. 2017. (ENG.). 336p. (gr. 9-12). 17.95 ***(978-1-63079-076-9(1))*** Switch Pr.

Bonham, T. J. Spi: The Case of the Dark Shadow. 2012. (ENG.). 112p. (J). pap. 12.99 *(978-0-7643-4132-8(4),* 9780764341328) Schiffer Publishing, Ltd.

Bonner, Anne. Intrigue at Pine Haven: Civil War in Florida. Akridge, Bill, illus. 2006. 220p. (YA). 12.95 net. *(978-1-878398-76-5(8),* Blue Note Bks.) Blue Note Pubns.

BookSource Staff, compiled by. Balloon Blow-Up. 2013. (Hardy Boys: Secret Files Ser.: 13). lib. bdg. 16.00 *(978-0-606-32328-4(7),* Turtleback) Turtleback Bks.

—The Great Coaster Caper. 2012. (Hardy Boys: Secret Files Ser.: 9). lib. bdg. 14.75 *(978-0-606-26321-4(7),* Turtleback) Turtleback Bks.

—Lights, Camera... Zombies! 2013. (Hardy Boys: Secret Files Ser.: 12). lib. bdg. 14.75 *(978-0-606-32033-7(4),* Turtleback) Turtleback Bks.

—Robot Rumble. 2013. (Hardy Boys: Secret Files Ser.: 11). lib. bdg. 16.00 *(978-0-606-27027-4(2),* Turtleback) Turtleback Bks.

Bosch, Pseudonymous. The Name of This Book Is Secret. (Secret Ser.: 1). (ENG.). 400p. (J). (gr. 3-7). 2008. pap. 8.99 *(978-0-316-11369-4(7))* 2015. 12.99 *(978-0-316-26502-7(0))* Little, Brown Bks. for Young Readers.

—The Name of This Book Is Secret. Ford, Gilbert, illus. rev. ed. 2007. (Secret Ser.: 1). (ENG.). 384p. (J). (gr. 3-7). 17.99 *(978-0-316-11366-3(2))* Little, Brown Bks. for Young Readers.

—The Name of This Book Is Secret. 2009. 18.00 *(978-1-60686-518-7(8))* Perfection Learning Corp.

—The Name of This Book Is Secret. 2008. (Secret Ser.: 1). (J). lib. bdg. 19.65 *(978-1-4178-2975-0(3),* Turtleback) Turtleback Bks.

—The Secret Series Complete Collection. 2012. (ENG.). 2016p. (J). (gr. 3-7). pap. 38.99 *(978-0-316-21981-5(9))* Little, Brown Bks. for Young Readers.

—Write This Book: A Do-It-Yourself Mystery. (Secret Ser.). (ENG., Illus.). (J). (gr. 3-7). 2014. 304p. pap. 8.99 *(978-0-316-20780-5(2))* 2013. 288p. 16.99 *(978-0-316-20781-2(0))* Little, Brown Bks. for Young Readers.

Bosco, Don. Sherlock Hong: The Immortal Nightingale. 2016. (Sherlock Hong Adventures Ser.: Volume 1). (ENG.). 80p. pap. 6.99 *(978-981-4721-19-6(0))* Marshall Cavendish International (Asia) Private Ltd. SGP. Dist: National Bk. Network.

—Sherlock Hong: The Legend of Lady Yue. 2016. (Sherlock Hong Adventures Ser.: Volume 4). (ENG.). 80p. pap. 6.99 *(978-981-4721-22-6(0))* Marshall Cavendish International (Asia) Private Ltd. SGP. Dist: National Bk. Network.

—Sherlock Hong: The Peranakan Princess. 2016. (Sherlock Hong Adventures Ser.: Volume 2). (ENG.). 80p. pap. 6.99 *(978-981-4721-20-2(4))* Marshall Cavendish International (Asia) Private Ltd. SGP. Dist: National Bk. Network.

—Sherlock Hong: The Scroll of Greatness. 2016. (Sherlock Hong Adventures Ser.: Volume 3). (ENG.). 80p. pap. 6.99 *(978-981-4721-21-9(2))* Marshall Cavendish International (Asia) Private Ltd. SGP. Dist: National Bk. Network.

Bossley, Michele Martin. Bio-Pirate, 1 vol. 2008. (Orca Currents Ser.). (ENG.). (J). (gr. 5-9). 112p. 16.95 *(978-1-55143-895-5(X));* 128p. pap. 9.95 *(978-1-55143-893-1(3))* Orca Bk. Pubs. USA.

—Cracked, 1 vol. 2007. (Orca Currents Ser.). (ENG.). (J). (gr. 5-9). 112p. lib. bdg. 14.95 *(978-1-55143-702-6(3));* 128p. per. 9.95 *(978-1-55143-700-2(7))* Orca Bk. Pubs. USA.

—Swiped, 1 vol. 2006. (Orca Currents Ser.). (ENG.). 136p. (J). (gr. 5-9). per. 9.95 *(978-1-55143-646-3(9))* Orca Bk. Pubs. USA.

—Tampered, 1 vol. 2013. (Orca Currents Ser.). (ENG.). 136p. (J). (gr. 5-9). pap. 9.95 *(978-1-4598-0356-5(6));* lib. bdg. 16.95 *(978-1-4598-0357-2(4))* Orca Bk. Pubs. USA.

Bourgeois, Paulette & Clark, Brenda. Franklin the Detective. 2004. (Kids Can Read Ser.). (ENG., Illus.). 32p. (J). (gr. 1-2). 14.95 *(978-1-55337-497-8(5))* Kids Can Pr., Ltd. CAN. Dist: Hachette Bk. Group.

Bow, James. The Unwritten Girl. 2006. (Unwritten Bks.: 1). (ENG.). 180p. (YA). (gr. 7). pap. 12.99 *(978-1-55002-604-7(6),* Boardwalk Bks.) Dundurn CAN. Dist: Ingram Publisher Services.

Bow, Patricia. The Spiral Maze, 1 vol. 2006. (ENG.). 192p. pap. 11.00 *(978-1-895449-68-6(5))* Thistledown Pr., Ltd. CAN. Dist: Univ. of Toronto Pr.

Bowditch, Eden Unger. The Atomic Weight of Secrets or the Arrival of the Mysterious Men in Black. 2011. (Young

Inventors Guild Ser.: 1). (ENG.). 320p. (YA). 19.95 (978-1-61088-002-2(1), 33471904-45bf-4a52-9f65-44ef10fff3b6) Bancroft Pr.

Bowen, Carl & Poe, Edgar Allen. The Murders in the Rue Morgue, 1 vol. Dimaya, Emerson & Calero, Dennis, illus. 2013. (Edgar Allan Poe Graphic Novels Ser.). (ENG.). 72p. (gr. 2-3). 27.99 (978-1-4342-3033-1(3)); pap. 6.10 (978-1-4342-4259-4(5)) Stone Arch Bks.

Bowler, Tim. Frozen Fire. 2010. (ENG.). 352p. (YA). (gr. 7-18). 8.99 (978-0-14-241465-1(4), Speak) Penguin Young Readers Group.

Boyce, Frank Cottrell. Framed, 1. Lenton, Steven, illus. 2nd ed. 2008. (ENG.). 336p. 17.95 (978-0-330-45292-2(4), Macmillan) Pan Macmillan GBR. Dist: Trans-Atlantic Pubns., Inc.

Boyd, David. Beware the Vikings. Rooth, Mike, illus. 2007. 48p. (J). lib. bdg. 23.08 (978-1-4242-1624-6(9)) Fitzgerald Bks.

Bracegirdle, P. J. Fiendish Deeds. 2009. (Joy of Spooking Ser.: 1). (ENG.). 224p. (J). (gr. 3-7). pap. 5.99 (978-1-4169-3417-2(0), McElderry, Margaret K. Bks.) McElderry, Margaret K. Bks.

Bracken, Beth & Fraser, Kay. Faerieground. Sawyer, Odessa, illus. 2013. (Faerieground Ser.). (ENG.). 96p. (gr. 1-3). 95.96 (978-1-4342-6050-5(X)); 191.92 (978-1-4342-6049-9(6)) Stone Arch Bks. (Faerieground).

Bradford, Quebe Merritt. In the Absence of My Father: Grief. Grit. Gangs. Guts. Grace. 2011. 188p. 24.79 (978-1-4567-4026-9(1)); pap. 14.99 (978-1-4567-3968-3(9)) AuthorHouse.

Brafman, Bonnie. Treasure in Marci's House. 2007. (J). pap. 8.00 (978-0-8059-7418-8(0)) Dorrance Publishing Co., Inc.

Bramlett, Timothy A. Sharkey Explores the Unknown. 2007. pap. 14.95 (978-0-9796444-0-5(2)) Azuria Bks.

Brannigan's Folly. 64p. (YA). (gr. 6-12). pap. (978-0-8224-2360-7(X)) Globe Fearon Educational Publishing.

Branning, Debe. The Adventures of Chickolet Pigolet: The Bribe of Frankenbeans. Knold, Nijlon, illus. 2008. 48p. pap. 7.95 (978-1-935137-40-5(9)) Guardian Angel Publishing, Inc.

Brasch, Nicolas & Webb, Melissa. The Mystery of the Missing Bike. 2008. (Rigby Focus Forward: Level F Ser.). (Illus.). 24p. (J). (gr. 4-7). pap. (978-1-4190-3688-0(2), Rigby) Pearson Education Australia.

Brauning, Kate. How We Fall. 2014. (ENG.). 304p. (YA). 17.99 (978-1-4405-8179-3(7), Simon Pulse) Simon Pulse.

Bray, Libba. The Diviners. 2012. 578p. (YA). 9.99 (978-0-316-23242-5(4)) Little Brown & Co.

—The Diviners. (Diviners Ser.: 1). (ENG.). (YA). (gr. 10-17). 2013. 496p. pap. 12.99 (978-0-316-12610-6(1)) 2012. 800p. 42.99 (978-0-316-22426-0(X)) Little, Brown Bks. for Young Readers.

—The Diviners. 2013. (Diviners Ser.: 1). (YA). lib. bdg. 24.50 (978-0-606-32284-3(1), Turtleback) Turtleback Bks.

—Lair of Dreams. 2015. (Diviners Ser.: 2). (ENG.). 624p. (YA). (gr. 10-17). 19.00 (978-0-316-12604-5(7)); (gr. 7-17). E-Book (978-0-316-36488-1(6)) Little, Brown Bks. for Young Readers.

Brewer, Zac. The Blood Between Us. (YA). (gr. 8). 2017. 304p. pap. 9.99 **(978-0-06-230792-7(4))** 2016. 288p. 17.99 (978-0-06-230791-0(6)) HarperCollins Pubs. (HarperTeen).

Brezenoff, Steve. Ballgame with No One at Bat. 2013. (Field Trip Mysteries Ser.). (ENG.). 88p. (gr. 2-3). pap. 35.70 (978-1-4342-6230-1(8)) Stone Arch Bks.

—The Ballgame with No One at Bat. Calo, Marcos, illus. 2013. (Field Trip Mysteries Ser.). (ENG.). 88p. (gr. 2-3). pap. 6.10 (978-1-4342-6211-0(1)); lib. bdg. 25.32 (978-1-4342-5978-3(1)) Stone Arch Bks.

—Bowling Lane Without Any Strikes. 2013. (Field Trip Mysteries Ser.). (ENG.). 88p. (gr. 2-3). pap. 35.70 (978-1-4342-6231-8(6)) Stone Arch Bks.

—The Burglar Who Bit the Big Apple, 1 vol. Canga, C. B., illus. 2010. (Field Trip Mysteries Ser.). (ENG.). 88p. (gr. 2-3). 25.32 (978-1-4342-2139-1(3)); pap. 6.10 (978-1-4342-2771-3(5)) Stone Arch Bks.

—The Carnival Caper: An Interactive Mystery Adventure. Calo, Marcos, illus. 2017. (You Choose Stories: Field Trip Mysteries Ser.). (ENG.). 112p. (gr. 3-7). lib. bdg. 32.65 (978-1-4965-2645-8(7)) Stone Arch Bks.

—The Case of the Counterfeit Painting. Weber, Lisa K., illus. 2016. (Museum Mysteries Ser.). (ENG.). 128p. (gr. 2-3). lib. bdg. 26.65 (978-1-4965-2518-5(3), Museum Mysteries) Stone Arch Bks.

—The Case of the Soldier's Ghost. Weber, Lisa K., illus. 2016. (Museum Mysteries Ser.). (ENG.). 128p. (gr. 2-3). pap. 6.95 (978-1-4965-2523-9(X)); lib. bdg. 26.65 (978-1-4965-2519-2(1)) Stone Arch Bks. (Museum Mysteries).

—The Cave That Shouldn't Collapse, 1 vol. Calo, Marcos, illus. 2011. (Field Trip Mysteries Ser.). (ENG.). 88p. (gr. 2-3). pap. 6.10 (978-1-4342-3430-8(4)); lib. bdg. 25.32 (978-1-4342-3227-4(1)) Stone Arch Bks.

—The Crook That Made Kids Cry, 1 vol. Calo, Marcos, illus. 2013. (Field Trip Mysteries Ser.). (ENG.). 88p. (gr. 2-3). pap. 6.10 (978-1-4342-6210-3(3)); lib. bdg. 25.32 (978-1-4342-5977-6(3)) Stone Arch Bks.

—Crook That Made Kids Cry. 2013. (Field Trip Mysteries Ser.). (ENG.). 88p. (gr. 2-3). pap. 35.70 (978-1-4342-6232-5(4)) Stone Arch Bks.

—The Crook Who Crossed the Golden Gate Bridge, 1 vol. Canga, C. B., illus. 2010. (Field Trip Mysteries Ser.). (ENG.). 88p. (gr. 2-3). 25.32 (978-1-4342-2138-4(5)); pap. 6.10 (978-1-4342-2770-6(7)) Stone Arch Bks.

—Dinosaur That Disappeared. 2013. (Field Trip Mysteries Ser.). (ENG.). 88p. (gr. 2-3). pap. 35.70 (978-1-4342-6233-2(2)) Stone Arch Bks.

—The Dinosaur That Disappeared, 1 vol. Calo, Marcos, illus. 2013. (Field Trip Mysteries Ser.). (ENG.). 88p. (gr. 2-3). pap. 6.10 (978-1-4342-6213-4(8)); lib. bdg. 25.32 (978-1-4342-5980-6(3)) Stone Arch Bks.

—The Disappearing Fruit: An Interactive Mystery Adventure. Calo, Marcos, illus. 2017. (You Choose Stories: Field Trip Mysteries Ser.). (ENG.). 112p. (gr. 3-7). lib. bdg. 32.65 (978-1-4965-2643-4(0)) Stone Arch Bks.

—The Everglades Poacher Who Pretended, 1 vol. Calo, Marcos, illus. 2012. (Field Trip Mysteries Ser.). (ENG.). 88p. (gr. 2-3). pap. 6.10 (978-1-4342-4197-9(1)); lib. bdg. 25.32 (978-1-4342-3790-3(7)) Stone Arch Bks.

—Field Trip Mysteries. 2013. (Field Trip Mysteries Ser.). (ENG.). 88p. (gr. 2-3). lib. bdg. 506.40 (978-1-4342-6048-2(8)) Stone Arch Bks.

—The Ghost Who Haunted the Capitol, 1 vol. Canga, C. B., illus. 2010. (Field Trip Mysteries Ser.). (ENG.). 88p. (gr. 2-3). 25.32 (978-1-4342-2140-7(7)); pap. 6.10 (978-1-4342-2772-0(3)) Stone Arch Bks.

—The Grand Canyon Burros That Broke, 1 vol. Calo, Marcos, illus. 2012. (Field Trip Mysteries Ser.). (ENG.). 88p. (gr. 2-3). pap. 6.10 (978-1-4342-4198-6(X)); lib. bdg. 25.32 (978-1-4342-3788-0(5)) Stone Arch Bks.

—I Dare You! Hilliker, Phillip, illus. 2008. (Vortex Bks.). (ENG.). 112p. (gr. 2-3). 26.65 (978-1-4342-0798-2(6), Vortex Bks.) Stone Arch Bks.

—The Mount Rushmore Face That Couldn't See, 1 vol. Calo, Marcos, illus. 2012. (Field Trip Mysteries Ser.). (ENG.). 88p. (gr. 2-3). pap. 6.10 (978-1-4342-4199-3(8)) Stone Arch Bks.

—Museum Mysteries. Weber, Lisa K., illus. 2015. (Museum Mysteries Ser.). (ENG.). 128p. (gr. 2-3). 106.60 (978-1-4965-0262-9(0), Museum Mysteries) Stone Arch Bks.

—On the Bus, on the Case, 1 vol. Canga, C. B., illus. 2010. (Field Trip Mysteries Ser.). (ENG.). 240p. (gr. 3-6). 12.95 (978-1-4342-2531-3(3)) Stone Arch Bks.

—The Outlaw from Outer Space: An Interactive Mystery Adventure. Calo, Marcos, illus. 2017. (You Choose Stories: Field Trip Mysteries Ser.). (ENG.). 112p. (gr. 3-7). lib. bdg. 32.65 (978-1-4965-2644-1(9)) Stone Arch Bks.

—The Painting That Wasn't There, 1 vol. Canga, C. B., illus. 2009. (Field Trip Mysteries Ser.). (ENG.). 88p. (gr. 2-3). lib. bdg. 25.32 (978-1-4342-1608-3(X)) Stone Arch Bks.

—The Ride That Was Really Haunted, 1 vol. Calo, Marcos, illus. 2011. (Field Trip Mysteries Ser.). (ENG.). 88p. (gr. 2-3). pap. 6.10 (978-1-4342-3427-8(4)); lib. bdg. 25.32 (978-1-4342-3224-3(7)) Stone Arch Bks.

—The Seals That Wouldn't Swim, 1 vol. Calo, Marcos, illus. 2011. (Field Trip Mysteries Ser.). (ENG.). 88p. (gr. 2-3). pap. 6.10 (978-1-4342-3428-5(2)); lib. bdg. 25.32 (978-1-4342-3225-0(5)) Stone Arch Bks.

—The Symphony That Was Silent, 1 vol. Calo, Marcos, illus. 2011. (Field Trip Mysteries Ser.). (ENG.). 88p. (gr. 2-3). pap. 6.10 (978-1-4342-3429-2(0)); lib. bdg. 25.32 (978-1-4342-3226-7(3)) Stone Arch Bks.

—The Teacher Who Forgot Too Much, 1 vol. Canga, C. B., illus. 2009. (Field Trip Mysteries Ser.). (ENG.). 88p. (gr. 2-3). lib. bdg. 25.32 (978-1-4342-1609-0(8)) Stone Arch Bks.

—The Village That Almost Vanished, 1 vol. Canga, C. B., illus. 2009. (Field Trip Mysteries Ser.). (ENG.). 88p. (gr. 2-3). lib. bdg. 25.32 (978-1-4342-1611-3(X)) Stone Arch Bks.

—The Yellowstone Kidnapping That Wasn't, 1 vol. Calo, Marcos, illus. 2012. (Field Trip Mysteries Ser.). (ENG.). 88p. (gr. 2-3). pap. 6.10 (978-1-4342-4200-6(5)); lib. bdg. 25.32 (978-1-4342-3789-7(3)) Stone Arch Bks.

—You Choose Stories Field Trip Mysteries. 2017. (You Choose Stories: Field Trip Mysteries Ser.). (ENG.). 112p. (gr. 3-7). 130.60 (978-1-4965-2658-8(9)) Stone Arch Bks.

—The Zombie Who Visited New Orleans, 1 vol. Canga, C. B., illus. 2010. (Field Trip Mysteries Ser.). (ENG.). 88p. (gr. 2-3). 25.32 (978-1-4342-2141-4(5)); pap. 6.10 (978-1-4342-2773-7(1)) Stone Arch Bks.

—The Zoo with the Empty Cage, 1 vol. Canga, C. B., illus. 2009. (Field Trip Mysteries Ser.). (ENG.). 88p. (gr. 2-3). lib. bdg. 25.32 (978-1-4342-1610-6(1)) Stone Arch Bks.

Brezenoff, Steve & Calo, Marcos. Field Trip Mysteries. 2013. (Field Trip Mysteries Ser.). (ENG.). 88p. (gr. 2-3). pap. 571.20 (978-1-4342-6318-6(5)); pap. 95.20 (978-1-4342-6223-3(5)); pap. 23.80 (978-1-4342-6222-6(7)); lib. bdg. 101.28 (978-1-4342-6047-5(X)) Stone Arch Bks.

Brezenoff, Steven. Case of the Counterfeit Painting. Weber, Lisa K., illus. 2017. 118p. (J). pap. (978-1-4965-2530-7(2)) Stone Arch Bks.

—The Case of the Haunted History Museum. Weber, Lisa K., illus. 2015. (Museum Mysteries Ser.). (ENG.). 128p. (gr. 2-3). lib. bdg. 26.65 (978-1-4342-9687-0(3)) Stone Arch Bks.

—The Case of the Missing Mom. Weber, Lisa K., illus. 2016. (Museum Mysteries Ser.). (ENG.). 128p. (gr. 2-3). 26.65 (978-1-4965-2517-8(5)) Stone Arch Bks.

—The Case of the Missing Museum Archives. Weber, Lisa K., illus. 2015. (Museum Mysteries Ser.). (ENG.). 128p. (gr. 2-3). lib. bdg. 26.65 (978-1-4342-9688-7(1)) Stone Arch Bks.

—The Case of the Portrait Vandal. Weber, Lisa K., illus. 2015. (Museum Mysteries Ser.). (ENG.). 128p. (gr. 2-3). lib. bdg. 26.65 (978-1-4342-9685-6(7)) Stone Arch Bks.

—The Case of the Soldier's Ghost. Weber, Lisa K., illus. 2017. 120p. (J). pap. (978-1-4965-2531-4(0)) Stone Arch Bks.

—The Case of the Stolen Sculpture. Weber, Lisa K., illus. 2015. (Museum Mysteries Ser.). (ENG.). 128p. (gr. 2-3). lib. bdg. 26.65 (978-1-4342-9686-3(5)) Stone Arch Bks.

—The Case of the Stolen Space Suit. Weber, Lisa K., illus. 2016. (Museum Mysteries Ser.). (ENG.). 128p. (gr. 2-3). 26.65 (978-1-4965-2516-1(7)) Stone Arch Bks.

—The Missing Bully: An Interactive Mystery Adventure. Calo, Marcos, illus. 2017. (You Choose Stories: Field Trip Mysteries Ser.). (ENG.). 112p. (gr. 3-7). lib. bdg. 32.65 (978-1-4965-2642-7(2)) Stone Arch Bks.

Brian, Kate, pseud. Inner Circle. 2007. (Private Ser.: No. 5). (ENG.). 224p. (YA). (gr. 9-12). pap. 9.99 (978-1-4169-5041-7(9), Simon & Schuster Bks. For Young Readers) Simon & Schuster Bks. For Young Readers.

—Revelation. 2008. (Private Ser.: No. 8). (ENG.). 288p. (YA). (gr. 9-18). pap. 11.99 (978-1-4169-5883-3(5), Simon & Schuster Bks. For Young Readers) Simon & Schuster Bks. For Young Readers.

Bright, J. E. The Case of the Cheese Thief, 1 vol. Neely, Scott, illus. 2014. (You Choose Stories: Scooby-Doo Ser.). (ENG.). 112p. (gr. 2-3). pap. 6.95 (978-1-4342-7927-9(8), You Choose Bks.) Capstone Press of Coughlan Cos.

Bright, J. E., et al. You Choose Stories: Scooby-Doo. 2016. (You Choose Stories: Scooby-Doo Ser.). (ENG.). 112p. (gr. 2-3). 391.80 (978-1-4965-2669-4(4), You Choose Bks.) Capstone Press of Coughlan Cos.

Brignole, Giancarla, tr. El Misterio del Condor. Polastri, Rosa Elena, illus. (Fabulas De Familia Ser.). (SPA.). 32p. (978-970-20-0270-3(2)) Castillo, Ediciones, S. A. de C. V.

Briner, Karen. Snowize & Snitch: Highly Effective Defective Detectives. Rivas, Victor, illus. 2016. (ENG.). 272p. (J). 16.95 (978-0-8234-3567-8(9)) Holiday Hse., Inc.

Brisland, Toni. DemiChat & the Lost Mummy. de los reyes Cruz, Cheryl, illus. 2013. 142p. (J). pap. 14.95 (978-1-60131-173-3(7)) Big Tent Bks.

Broach, Elise. Masterpiece. 2010. 18.00 (978-1-60686-888-1(8)) Perfection Learning Corp.

—Masterpiece. Murphy, Kelly, illus. 2010. (ENG.). 320p. (J). (gr. 4-7). pap. 7.99 (978-0-312-60870-5(5), 9780312608705) Square Fish.

—Masterpiece. 2010. (J). lib. bdg. 18.40 (978-0-606-14604-3(0), Turtleback) Turtleback Bks.

—Missing on Superstition Mountain. Caparó, Antonio Javier, illus. 2011. (Superstition Mountain Mysteries Ser.: 1). (ENG.). 272p. (J). (gr. 3-7). 15.99 (978-0-8050-9047-5(9), 9780805090475, Holt, Henry & Co. Bks. For Young Readers) Holt, Henry & Co.

—Revenge of Superstition Mountain. Ivanov, Aleksey & Ivanov, Olga, illus. 2014. (Superstition Mountain Mysteries Ser.: 3). (ENG.). 304p. (J). (gr. 3-7). 16.99 (978-0-8050-8909-7(8), 9780805089097, Holt, Henry & Co. Bks. For Young Readers) Holt, Henry & Co.

—Revenge of Superstition Mountain. Ivanov, Olga & Ivanov, Aleksey, illus. 2015. (Superstition Mountain Mysteries Ser.: 3). (ENG.). 320p. (J). (gr. 3-7). pap. 8.99 (978-1-250-05686-3(1), 9781250056863) Square Fish.

—Shakespeare's Secret. 2007. (Illus.). 258p. (gr. 4-9). 17.00 (978-0-7569-8204-1(9)) Perfection Learning Corp.

—Shakespeare's Secret. 2007. (ENG.). 272p. (YA). (gr. 5-10). per. 7.99 (978-0-312-37132-6(2), 9780312371326) Square Fish.

—Shakespeare's Secret. l.t. ed. 2006. (Thorndike Literacy Bridge Ser.). (Illus.). 263p. (J). (gr. 5-10). 22.95 (978-0-7862-8735-2(7)) Thorndike Pr.

—Treasure on Superstition Mountain. Caparó, Antonio Javier, illus. 2013. (Superstition Mountain Mysteries Ser.: 2). (ENG.). 288p. (J). (gr. 3-7). 15.99 (978-0-8050-7763-6(4), 9780805077636, Holt, Henry & Co. Bks. For Young Readers) Holt, Henry & Co.

—Treasure on Superstition Mountain. Caparo, Antonio Javier, illus. 2014. (Superstition Mountain Mysteries Ser.: 2). (ENG.). 304p. (J). (gr. 3-7). pap. 9.99 (978-1-250-03990-3(8), 9781250039903) Square Fish.

—The Wolf Keepers. Ratterree, Alice, illus. 2016. (ENG.). 352p. (J). 16.99 (978-0-8050-9899-0(2), 9780805098990, Holt, Henry & Co. Bks. For Young Readers) Holt, Henry & Co.

Broberg, Penelope Northrop. Sleuthy Gumshoe: The Remarkable Detective. 2011. 32p. (gr. -1). pap. 14.39 (978-1-4567-6404-3(7)) AuthorHouse.

Brody, Jessica. Disney Descendants School of Secrets, Bk. 3. No New Art Needed & Disney Storybook Art Team, illus. 2017. (School of Secrets Ser.: 3). (ENG.). 192p. (J). (gr. 3-7). bds. 9.99 (978-1-4847-7866-1(9)) Disney Pr.

Bronstein, S. N. Private Eye Cats: Book One: the Case of the Neighborhood Burglars. 2012. 108p. (gr. 4-6). 23.99 (978-1-4685-4557-9(4)); pap. 14.95 (978-1-4685-4558-6(2)) AuthorHouse.

—Private Eye Cats Book Two: The Case of the Kidnapped Dog. 2013. 116p. (gr. 4-6). 23.99 (978-1-4817-2421-0(5)); pap. 14.95 (978-1-4817-2422-7(3)) AuthorHouse.

Brooks, Dawn Marie. Cat-Ice. 2004. 175p. pap. 13.95 (978-0-7414-2240-8(9)) Infinity Publishing.

Brooks, Kevin. The Danger Game: A Travis Delaney Mystery. unabr. ed. 2016. (Travis Delaney Investigates Ser.: 2). (ENG.). 368p. (J). (gr. 5-9). pap. 11.99 (978-1-4472-3897-3(4)) Pan Macmillan GBR. Dist: Independent Pubs. Group.

—The Snake Trap: Travis Delaney Investigates. unabr. ed. 2016. (Travis Delaney Investigates Ser.: 3). (ENG.). 320p. (J). (gr. 5-9). pap. 11.99 (978-1-4472-3898-0(2)) Pan Macmillan GBR. Dist: Independent Pubs. Group.

—The Ultimate Truth. unabr. ed. 2016. (Travis Delaney Investigates Ser.: 1). (ENG.). 320p. (J). (gr. 5-9). pap. 11.99 (978-1-4472-3896-6(6)) Pan Macmillan GBR. Dist: Independent Pubs. Group.

Brooks, Martha. Traveling on into the Light: And Other Stories. 160p. (J). reprint ed. 7.95 (978-0-88899-237-6(8)) Groundwood Bks. CAN. Dist: Publishers Group West (PGW).

Brooks, Walter R. The Clockwork Twin: A Freddy the Pig Book on Everything. Wiese, Kurt, illus. 2013. (ENG.). 256p. (gr. 4-13). pap. 10.99 (978-1-4683-0349-0(X), 460349) Overlook Pr., The.

—Freddy & the Flying Saucer Plans. Wiese, Kurt, illus. 2013. (ENG.). 256p. (gr. 4-13). pap. 10.99 (978-1-4683-0319-3(8), 460319) Overlook Pr., The.

—Freddy & the Ignormus. Wiese, Kurt, illus. 2011. (ENG.). 288p. (gr. 4-13). pap. 10.99 (978-1-59020-467-2(0), 902467) Overlook Pr., The.

—Freddy & the Men from Mars. Wiese, Kurt, illus. 2011. (ENG.). 256p. 10.99 (978-1-59020-695-9(9), 902695) Overlook Pr., The.

—Freddy Plays Football. Wiese, Kurt, illus. 2013. (ENG.). 288p. (gr. 4-13). pap. 10.99 (978-1-4683-0667-5(7), 460667) Overlook Pr., The.

—Freddy the Detective. Wiese, Kurt, illus. 2010. (ENG.). 272p. (gr. 4-13). 11.99 (978-1-59020-418-4(2), 902418) Overlook Pr., The.

Brouwer, Sigmund. Absolute Pressure, 1 vol. 2009. (Orca Sports Ser.). (ENG.). 176p. (YA). (gr. 6-10). pap. 9.95 (978-1-55469-130-2(3)) Orca Bk. Pubs. USA.

—All-Star Pride, 1 vol. 2006. (Orca Sports Ser.). (ENG.). 176p. (YA). (gr. 6-10). per. 9.95 (978-1-55143-635-7(3)) Orca Bk. Pubs. USA.

—Cobra Strike, 1 vol. 2007. (Orca Sports Ser.). (ENG.). 176p. (YA). (gr. 6-10). per. 9.95 (978-1-55143-725-5(2)) Orca Bk. Pubs. USA.

—Hurricane Power, 1 vol. 2007. (Orca Sports Ser.). (ENG.). 176p. (YA). (gr. 6-10). per. 9.95 (978-1-55143-865-8(8)) Orca Bk. Pubs. USA.

—Maverick Mania, 1 vol. 2008. (Orca Sports Ser.). (ENG.). 176p. (YA). (gr. 6-10). pap. 9.95 (978-1-55469-047-3(1)) Orca Bk. Pubs. USA.

Brown, Anne Greenwood & Anastasiu, Heather. Girl Last Seen. 2016. (ENG.). 272p. (YA). (gr. 8-12). 16.99 (978-0-8075-8140-7(2)) Whitman, Albert & Co.

Brown, Gary. Sam's Mission Call. Tanner, Stephanie, illus. 24p. (J). 12.95 (978-0-910523-13-4(4)) Grandin Bk. Co.

Brown, Jeff. Flat Stanley & the Missing Pumpkins. Pamintuan, Macky, illus. 2017. (I Can Read Level 2 Ser.). 32p. (J). (gr. -1-3). 16.99 **(978-0-06-236598-9(3))**; pap. 3.99 **(978-0-06-236594-1(0))** HarperCollins Pubs.

Brown, Jeff. Framed in France. Pamintuan, Macky, illus. 2014. (Flat Stanley's Worldwide Adventures Ser.: 11). (ENG.). 128p. (J). (gr. 1-5). 15.99 (978-0-06-218985-1(9)); pap. 4.99 (978-0-06-218984-4(0)) HarperCollins Pubs.

—Framed in France. 2014. (Flat Stanley's Worldwide Adventures Ser.: 11). (J). lib. bdg. 14.75 (978-0-606-35480-6(8)) Turtleback Bks.

Brown, Jennifer. Dare You. 2017. (Shade Me Ser.: 2). 480p. (YA). (gr. 9). 17.99 (978-0-06-232446-7(2), Tegen, Katherine Bks) HarperCollins Pubs.

—Pennybaker School Is Headed for Disaster. Kissi, Marta, illus. 2017. (ENG.). 320p. (J). 16.99 (978-1-68119-174-4(1), 9781681191744, Bloomsbury USA Childrens) Bloomsbury Publishing USA.

—Shade Me. (Shade Me Ser.: 1). (YA). (gr. 9). 2017. 464p. pap. 9.99 (978-0-06-232444-3(6)) 2016. 448p. 17.99 (978-0-06-232443-6(8)) HarperCollins Pubs. (Tegen, Katherine Bks).

Brown, Jim. The Foster Twins in the Mystery at Moore's Lake. 2005. 164p. 22.95 (978-0-595-67087-1(3)) iUniverse, Inc.

Brown, Liz. Misty's Revenge. (Illus.). 65p. (978-1-897039-21-2(2)) High Interest Publishing (HIP).

Brown, Marc. Arthur's Mystery Babysitter. Brown, Marc, illus. 2004. (ENG., Illus.). 24p. (J). (gr. -1-1). pap. 3.99 (978-0-316-73394-6(6), Tingley, Megan Bks.) Little, Brown Bks. for Young Readers.

Brown, Ruth. A Dark, Dark Tale. 2004. (Illus.). 27p. (J). (978-1-85269-457-9(2)) Mantra Lingua.

Brown, Shannon L. The Feather Chase. 2016. (ENG.). 24.95 (978-0-9898438-9-8(0)) 2014. pap. 12.95 (978-0-9898438-0-5(7)) Sienna Bay Pr.

—The Treasure Key: (the Crime-Solving Cousins Mysteries Book 2), vol. 2. 2016. (Crime-Solving Cousins Mysteries Ser.: Vol. 2). (ENG., Illus.). 216p. (J). (gr. 3-6). 24.95 (978-0-9898438-7-4(4)) Sienna Bay Pr.

Bruchac, Joseph. Skeleton Man. Comport, Sally Wern, illus. 2003. (Skeleton Man Ser.: 1). (ENG.). 128p. (J). (gr. 5-18). pap. 5.99 (978-0-06-440888-2(4)) HarperCollins Pubs.

—Skeleton Man. Comport, Sally Wern, illus. 2003. 114p. (J). (gr. 5). 12.65 (978-0-7569-3399-9(4)) Perfection Learning Corp.

Bruzon, Louise A. The Grimstone Galleries. 2010. 192p. pap. (978-1-907652-17-2(5)) Grosvenor Hse. Publishing Ltd.

Bryant, Annie. Ghost Town. 2007. (Beacon Street Girls Ser.: No. 11). (Illus.). 217p. (J). (gr. 4-7). per. 7.10 (978-1-933566-09-2(4)) B*tween Productions, Inc.

Bryant, Clive, ed. Sweeney Todd: The Demon Barber of Fleet Street. Shalvey, Declan et al, illus. 2012. (ENG.). 176p. pap. 16.95 (978-1-907127-10-6(0), Classical Comics, Ltd.); pap. 16.95 (978-1-907127-09-0(7), Classical Comics, Ltd.); (gr. 9). lib. bdg. 24.95 (978-1-907127-82-3(8)) Classical Comics GBR. Dist: Publishers Group West (PGW).

Bryant, Jen. Kaleidoscope Eyes. 2010. (ENG.). 272p. (J). (gr. 3-7). 7.99 (978-0-440-42190-0(X), Yearling) Random Hse. Children's Bks.

Buckeridge, Anthony. Jennings Follows a Clue. 2008. (Jennings Ser.: 2). (ENG.). 226p. (J). (gr. -1-12). pap. 12.95 (978-0-7551-1366-8(7)) House of Stratus, Inc. GBR. Dist: Gardners Bks. Ltd.

—Just Like Jennings. 2008. (Jennings Ser.: 12). (ENG.). 184p. (J). (gr. -1-12). pap. 12.95 (978-0-7551-0170-2(7)) House of Stratus, Inc. GBR. Dist: Gardners Bks. Ltd.

Buckey, Sarah Masters. Clue in the Castle Tower: A Samantha Mystery. Ross, Peg, ed. Giovine, Sergio, illus. 2011. (ENG.). 184p. (YA). (gr. 4-18). pap. 6.95 (978-1-59369-752-5(X)) American Girl Publishing, Inc.

—The Curse of Ravenscourt: A Samantha Mystery. 2005. (ENG., Illus.). 192p. (YA). pap. 6.95 (978-1-58485-987-1(3), American Girl) American Girl Publishing, Inc.

—The Light in the Cellar: A Molly Mystery. 2003. (American Girl Mysteries Ser.). (ENG., Illus.). 176p. (gr. 4-7). 10.95 (978-1-59369-159-2(9)) American Girl Publishing, Inc.

—The Stolen Sapphire. 2007. (American Girl Mysteries Ser.). (Illus.). 181p. (gr. 4-7). 17.45 (978-0-7569-8278-2(2)) Perfection Learning Corp.

—The Stolen Sapphire: A Samantha Mystery. Tibbles, JeanPaul, illus. 2006. (ENG.). 192p. (J). (gr. 4-7). pap. 6.95 (978-1-59369-099-1(1), American Girl) American Girl Publishing, Inc.

Buckley, Michael. The Council of Mirrors. Ferguson, Peter, illus. (Sisters Grimm Ser.). (ENG.). 352p. (gr. 3-7). 2013. (YA). pap. 7.95 (978-1-4197-0538-0(5)) 2012. (J). 16.95 (978-1-4197-0186-3(X)) Abrams, Inc. (Amulet Bks.).

—The Council of Mirrors. 2013. (Sisters Grimm Ser.: 9). (J). lib. bdg. 18.40 (978-0-606-31650-7(7), Turtleback) Turtleback Bks.

—The Everafter War. Ferguson, Peter, illus. (Sisters Grimm Ser.: Bk. 7). (ENG.). (J). (gr. 3-7). 2010. 336p. pap. 8.95 (978-0-8109-8429-5(6))Bk. 7. 2009. 320p. 16.95 (978-0-8109-8355-7(9)) Abrams, Inc. (Amulet Bks.).

—The Everafter War. 2010. (Sisters Grimm Ser.: 7). (J). lib. bdg. 19.60 (978-0-606-12500-0(0), Turtleback) Turtleback Bks.

—The Fairy-Tale Detectives. Ferguson, Peter, illus. 2005. (ENG.). 288p. (J). (gr. 3-7). 16.95 (978-0-8109-5925-5(9), Abrams Bks. for Young Readers) Abrams, Inc.

—The Fairy-Tale Detectives. (Sisters Grimm Ser.: 1). (J). 2008. 81.45 (978-1-4361-0398-5(3)) 2007. 214.75 (978-1-4193-6197-5(X)) 2007. 1.25 (978-1-4193-6193-7(7)) 2006. 74.75 (978-1-4193-6196-8(1)) 2006. 86.75 (978-1-4193-8749-4(9)) 2006. 71.75 (978-1-4193-6198-2(8)) 2006. 89.75 (978-1-4193-8747-0(2)) Recorded Bks., Inc.

—The Fairy-Tale Detectives. 2017. (Sisters Grimm Ser.: 1). (J). lib. bdg. 19.60 **(978-0-606-39685-1(3))** Turtleback Bks.

—The Inside Story. Ferguson, Peter, illus. 2011. (Sisters Grimm Ser.: 8). (ENG.). 288p. (J). (gr. 3-7). pap. 7.95 (978-0-8109-9726-4(6), Amulet Bks.) Abrams, Inc.

—The Inside Story, 6 vols. 2010. (Sisters Grimm Ser.: 8). (J). 89.75 *(978-1-4498-1969-9(9))*; 72.75 *(978-1-4498-1967-5(2))*; 87.75 *(978-1-4498-1971-2(0))*; 219.75 *(978-1-4498-1966-8(4))*; 1.25 *(978-1-4498-1973-6(7))* Recorded Bks., Inc.

—The Inside Story. 2011. (Sisters Grimm Ser.: 8). (J). lib. bdg. 18.40 *(978-0-606-23818-2(2)*, Turtleback) Turtleback Bks.

—The Inside Story Bk. 8, Bk. 8. Ferguson, Peter, illus. 2010. (Sisters Grimm Ser.: Bk. 8). (ENG.). 288p. (J). (gr. 3-7). 16.95 *(978-0-8109-8430-1(X)*, Amulet Bks.) Abrams, Inc.

—Magic & Other Misdemeanors. Ferguson, Peter, illus. (Sisters Grimm Ser.). (ENG.). 304p. (gr. 3-7). 2008. (J). pap. 7.95 *(978-0-8109-7263-6(8))* 2007. (YA). 16.95 *(978-0-8109-9358-7(9))* Abrams, Inc. (Amulet Bks.).

—Once upon a Crime. Ferguson, Peter, illus. 2007. (ENG.). 288p. (J). (gr. 2-8). 16.95 *(978-0-8109-1610-4(X)*, Amulet Bks.) Abrams, Inc.

—The Problem Child: The Sisters Grimm. 2007. (Sisters Grimm Ser.: 3). (YA). lib. bdg. 18.40 *(978-1-4178-0733-8(4)*, Turtleback) Turtleback Bks.

—The Sisters Grimm: The Unusual Suspects. Ferguson, Peter, illus. 10th ed. 2017. (Sisters Grimm Ser.). (ENG.). 288p. (J). (gr. 3-7). pap. 8.95 *(978-1-4197-2008-6(2)*, Amulet Bks.) Abrams, Inc.

—Tales from the Hood. Ferguson, Peter, illus. 2008. (Sisters Grimm Ser.). (ENG.). 288p. (J). (gr. 3-7). 16.95 *(978-0-8109-9478-2(X)*, Amulet Bks.) Abrams, Inc.

—The Unusual Suspects. 2006. (Sisters Grimm Ser.: Bk. 2). 1.00 *(978-1-4237-8623-8(8))* Recorded Bks., Inc.

—The Unusual Suspects. 2017. (Sisters Grimm Ser.: 2). (J). lib. bdg. 19.60 **(978-0-606-39686-8(1))** Turtleback Bks.

—The Unusual Suspects. 2007. (Sisters Grimm Ser.: 2). (J). lib. bdg. 18.40 *(978-1-4178-0732-1(6)*, Turtleback) Turtleback Bks.

—A Very Grimm Guide. Ferguson, Peter, illus. 2012. (Sisters Grimm Ser.). (ENG.). 128p. (J). (gr. 3-7). 16.95 *(978-1-4197-0201-3(7)*, Amulet Bks.) Abrams, Inc.

Buckmaster, Heath L. The Venus Diary, 3 bks., Bk. 2. ltd. ed. 2008. 132p. (YA). lib. bdg. 19.95 *(978-0-9771802-6-4(3))* Transaltar Publishing.

Bullard, Lisa. Turn Left at the Cow. 2013. (ENG.). 304p. (J). (gr. 5-7). 16.99 *(978-0-544-02900-2(3))* Houghton Mifflin Harcourt Publishing Co.

Bunce, Elizabeth C. Liar's Moon. 2011. (YA). pap. *(978-0-545-13607-5(5))*; (ENG.). 368p. (J). (gr. 7-7). 17.99 *(978-0-545-13608-2(3))* Scholastic, Inc. (Levine, Arthur A. Bks.).

Bundy, E. A. Phillip Marrow, Jr. 2013. (ENG.). 206p. (YA). pap. 10.99 *(978-1-61955-008-7(3))* Singing Winds Pr.

Bunting, Eve. The Man with the Red Bag. 2007. 230p. (J). (gr. 5-9). 15.99 *(978-0-06-081828-9(X)*, Cotler, Joanna Books) HarperCollins Pubs.

Bunting, Eve & Giblin, James Cross. The Ghost Children. 2005. (ENG.). 176p. (J). (gr. 5-7). pap. 12.95 *(978-0-618-60477-7(4))* Houghton Mifflin Harcourt Publishing Co.

The Buried Eye, 6 vols. (Woodland Mysteriestm Ser.). 133p. (gr. 3-7). 42.50 *(978-0-7802-7932-2(8))* Wright Group/McGraw-Hill.

Burke, Anjalena Anita. Ghost: The Dead End Series Book 1, 1 vol. 2009. 73p. pap. 16.95 *(978-1-61582-686-5(6))* PublishAmerica, Inc.

Burke, Bob. The Third Pig Detective Agency: The Complete Casebook. 2015. (ENG.). 432p. 8.99 *(978-0-00-747940-5(9)*, Friday Project) HarperCollins Pubs. Ltd. GBR. Dist: HarperCollins Pubs.

Burke, Morgan. Get It Started. 2010. (Party Room Ser.: 1). (ENG.). 272p. (J). (gr. 11). pap. 12.99 *(978-1-4424-1420-4(0)*, Simon Pulse) Simon Pulse.

Burket, Shelia. Detective Morris Norris & the Case of the Missing Socks. 2011. 20p. pap. 24.95 *(978-1-4626-2822-3(2))* America Star Bks.

Burns, Emily. Manitou Art Caper. 2003. (Rocky Mountain Mysteries Ser.: 2). 128p. (J). per. 4.95 *(978-0-9723259-1-2(3)*, RMM2) Covered Wagon Publishing LLC.

—Marked Evidence. 2003. (Rocky Mountain Mysteries Ser.: 3). (J). per. 4.95 *(978-0-9723259-2-9(1)*, RMM3) Covered Wagon Publishing LLC.

Burns, Laura & Metz, Melinda. Sanctuary Bay. 2016. (ENG.). 320p. (YA). 18.99 *(978-1-250-05136-3(3)*, 9781250051363, St. Martin's Griffin) St. Martin's Pr.

Burroughs, Scott, illus. Balloon Blow-Up. 2013. (Hardy Boys: the Secret Files Ser.: 13). (ENG.). 112p. (J). (gr. 1-4). pap. 5.99 *(978-1-4424-5371-5(0)*, Aladdin) Simon & Schuster Children's Publishing.

—The Great Coaster Caper. 2012. (Hardy Boys: the Secret Files Ser.: 9). (ENG.). 112p. (J). (gr. 1-4). pap. 4.99 *(978-1-4424-1669-7(6)*, Aladdin) Simon & Schuster Children's Publishing.

—The Hardy Boys Secret Files Collection: Trouble at the Arcade - The Missing Mitt - Mystery Map - Hopping Mad - A Monster of a Mystery. 2014. (Hardy Boys: the Secret Files Ser.). (ENG.). 496p. (J). (gr. 1-4). pap. 29.99 *(978-1-4814-1473-9(9)*, Aladdin) Simon & Schuster Children's Publishing.

—Lights, Camera ... Zombies! 2013. (Hardy Boys: the Secret Files Ser.: 12). (ENG.). 96p. (J). (gr. 1-4). pap. 4.99 *(978-1-4424-5369-2(9)*, Aladdin) Simon & Schuster Children's Publishing.

—The Missing Mitt. 2010. (Hardy Boys: the Secret Files Ser.: 2). (ENG.). 112p. (J). (gr. 1-4). pap. 5.99 *(978-1-4169-9394-0(0)*, Aladdin) Simon & Schuster Children's Publishing.

—A Monster of a Mystery. 2011. (Hardy Boys: the Secret Files Ser.: 5). (ENG.). 96p. (J). (gr. 1-4). pap. 4.99 *(978-1-4169-9166-3(2)*, Aladdin) Simon & Schuster Children's Publishing.

—Mystery Map. 2010. (Hardy Boys: the Secret Files Ser.: 3). (ENG.). 96p. (J). (gr. 1-4). pap. 5.99 *(978-1-4169-9165-6(4)*, Aladdin) Simon & Schuster Children's Publishing.

—Robot Rumble. 2013. (Hardy Boys: the Secret Files Ser.: 11). (ENG.). 96p. (J). (gr. 1-4). pap. 5.99 *(978-1-4424-5367-8(2)*, Aladdin) Simon & Schuster Children's Publishing.

—A Rockin' Mystery. 2012. (Hardy Boys: the Secret Files Ser.: 10). (ENG.). 96p. (J). (gr. 1-4). pap. 5.99 *(978-1-4424-1671-0(8)*, Aladdin) Simon & Schuster Children's Publishing.

—Trouble at the Arcade. 2010. (Hardy Boys: the Secret Files Ser.: 1). (ENG.). 96p. (J). (gr. 1-4). pap. 5.99 *(978-1-4169-9164-9(6)*, Aladdin) Simon & Schuster Children's Publishing.

Burt, Steve. Oddest Yet: Even More Stories to Chill the Heart. Hagerman, Jessica, illus. 2004. 144p. (gr. 5-18). pap. 14.95 *(978-0-9741407-1-1(6))* Burt, Steven E.

Bustani, Juma. Adventure in Nairobi. 2005. 72p. pap. *(978-9966-46-842-0(0))* Heinemann Kenya, Limited (East African Educational Publishers Ltd E.A.E.P.) KEN. Dist: Michigan State Univ. Pr.

Butcher, A. J. The Serpent Scenario. 2004. (ENG.). 224p. (J). (gr. 5-8). pap. 18.99 *(978-0-316-73766-1(6))* Little, Brown Bks. for Young Readers.

Butcher, Kristin. Alibi, 1 vol. 2014. (Orca Currents Ser.). (ENG.). 120p. (J). (gr. 5-9). pap. 9.95 *(978-1-4598-0767-9(7))* Orca Bk. Pubs. USA.

—Cheat, 1 vol. 2010. (Orca Currents Ser.). (ENG.). 128p. (J). (gr. 5-9). pap. 9.95 *(978-1-55469-274-3(1))* Orca Bk. Pubs. USA.

—Return to Bone Tree Hill. 2009. (ENG.). 176p. (J). pap. 12.95 *(978-1-897235-58-4(5))* Thistledown Pr., Ltd. CAN. Dist: Univ. of Toronto Pr.

—Zach & Zoe: Bully & the Beagle, 1 vol. 2009. (Lorimer Streetlights Ser.). (ENG.). 120p. (J). (gr. 2-4). 8.95 *(978-1-55277-427-4(9)*, 9781552774274) Lorimer, James & Co., Ltd., Pubs. CAN. Dist: Casemate Pubs. & Bk. Distributors, LLC.

—Zach & Zoe & the Bank Robber, 1 vol. 2008. (Lorimer Streetlights Ser.). (ENG.). 112p. (J). (gr. 2-4). 8.95 *(978-1-55277-015-3(X)*, 9781552770153) Lorimer, James & Co., Ltd., Pubs. CAN. Dist: Casemate Pubs. & Bk. Distributors, LLC.

Butler, Darren J. The Masterpiece: An Abbie Girl Spy Mystery. Casteel, Kay, illus. 2004. (Abbie, Girl Spy Ser.: 4). (ENG.). 278p. (J). mass mkt. 8.50 *(978-0-9753367-3-1(8))* Onstage Publishing, LLC.

—The Secret of Crybaby Hollow. 2004. (YA). mass mkt. 6.99 *(978-0-9753367-5-5(4))* Onstage Publishing, LLC.

Butler, Dori. Detective Cluck & the Missing Hens. 2005. (J). pap. *(978-1-4108-4192-6(8))* Benchmark Education Co.

Butler, Dori H. Campus Attack, Sabotage! 2011. (Readers' & Writers' Genre Workshop Ser.). (YA). pap. *(978-1-4509-3018-5(2))* Benchmark Education Co.

—The Hide-And-Seek Ghost. 2016. (Haunted Library: 8). lib. bdg. 14.75 *(978-0-606-38838-2(9))* Turtleback Bks.

Butler, Dori Hillestad. The Buddy Files Bk. 3: The Case of the Missing Family. Tugeau, Jeremy, illus. 2010. (Buddy Files Ser.: 3). (ENG.). 128p. (J). (gr. 1-5). 14.99 *(978-0-8075-0912-8(4))* Whitman, Albert & Co.

—The Buddy Files Bk. 4: The Case of the Fire Alarm. Tugeau, Jeremy, illus. 2011. (Buddy Files Ser.: 4). (ENG.). 144p. (J). (gr. 1-5). pap. 5.99 *(978-0-8075-0935-7(3))* Whitman, Albert & Co.

—The Case of the Library Monster. Tugeau, Jeremy, illus. 2012. (Buddy Files Ser.: 5). (J). lib. bdg. 16.00 *(978-0-606-23839-7(5)*, Turtleback) Turtleback Bks.

—The Case of the Library Monster. Tugeau, Jeremy & Crisp, Dan, illus. 2012. (Buddy Files Ser.: 5). (ENG.). 128p. (J). (gr. 1-5). pap. 5.99 *(978-0-8075-0936-4(1))* Whitman, Albert & Co.

—The Case of the Lost Boy. Tugeau, Jeremy, illus. 2010. (Buddy Files Ser.: 1). (ENG.). 128p. (J). (gr. 1-5). 14.99 *(978-0-8075-0910-4(8))*;Bk. 1. pap. 5.99 *(978-0-8075-0932-6(9))* Whitman, Albert & Co.

—The Case of the Missing Family, 1 vol., Bk. 3. Tugeau, Jeremy, illus. 2010. (Buddy Files Ser.: 3). (ENG.). 144p. (J). (gr. 1-5). pap. 5.99 *(978-0-8075-0934-0(5))* Whitman, Albert & Co.

—The Case of the Mixed-Up Mutts, Bk. 2. Tugeau, Jeremy, illus. 2010. (Buddy Files Ser.: 2). (ENG.). 128p. (J). (gr. 1-5). 14.99 *(978-0-8075-0911-1(6))* Whitman, Albert & Co.

—The Case of the Mixed-Up Mutts Bk. 2, 1 vol., Bk. 2. Tugeau, Jeremy, illus. 2010. (Buddy Files Ser.: 2). (ENG.). 128p. (J). (gr. 1-5). pap. 5.99 *(978-0-8075-0933-3(7))* Whitman, Albert & Co.

—The Case of the School Ghost. 2013. (Buddy Files Ser.: 6). lib. bdg. 16.00 *(978-0-606-31843-3(7)*, Turtleback) Turtleback Bks.

—The Case of the School Ghost. Tugeau, Jeremy, illus. (Buddy Files Ser.: 6). (ENG.). (J). (gr. 1-5). 2012. 128p. 14.99 *(978-0-8075-0915-9(9))*Bk. 6. 2013. 144p. pap. 5.99 *(978-0-8075-0937-1(X))* Whitman, Albert & Co.

—The Ghost Backstage. Damant, Aurore, illus. 2014. (Haunted Library: 3). (ENG.). 128p. (J). (gr. 1-3). 5.99 *(978-0-448-46246-2(X)*, Grosset & Dunlap) Penguin Young Readers Group.

—The Ghost in the Attic, No. 2. Damant, Aurore, illus. 2014. (Haunted Library: 2). (ENG.). 128p. (J). (gr. 1-3). 5.99 *(978-0-448-46244-8(3)*, Grosset & Dunlap) Penguin Young Readers Group.

—The Ghosts at the Movie Theater. 2017. (Haunted Library: 9). lib. bdg. 16.00 **(978-0-606-39772-8(8))** Turtleback Bks.

—The Haunted Library #1. Damant, Aurore, illus. 2014. (Haunted Library: 1). (ENG.). 128p. (J). (gr. 1-3). 5.99 *(978-0-448-46242-4(7)*, Grosset & Dunlap) Penguin Young Readers Group.

—King & Kayla & the Case of the Mysterious Mouse, 1 vol. Meyers, Nancy, illus. 2017. (King & Kayla Ser.). (ENG.). 48p. (J). (gr. 2-4). 14.95 **(978-1-56145-879-0(1))** Peachtree Pubs.

Butler, Dori Hillestad. King & Kayla & the Case of the Secret Code, 1 vol. Meyers, Nancy, illus. 2017. (King & Kayla Ser.). (ENG.). 48p. (J). (gr. 2-4). 14.95 *(978-1-56145-878-3(3))* Peachtree Pubs.

Butler, Dori Hillestad & dePaola, Tomie. The Five O'Clock Ghost, No. 4. Damant, Aurore, illus. 2015. (Haunted Library: 4). (ENG.). 144p. (J). (gr. 1-3). bds. 5.99 *(978-0-448-46248-6(6)*, Grosset & Dunlap) Penguin Young Readers Group.

—The Ghost at the Fire Station, No. 6. Damant, Aurore, illus. 2015. (Haunted Library: 6). (ENG.). 128p. (J). (gr. 1-3). bds. 5.99 *(978-0-448-48334-4(3)*, Grosset & Dunlap) Penguin Young Readers Group.

Butler, Heather. The Milkshake Detectives. 2017. (ENG.). 208p. (J). (gr. 4-6). pap. 7.99 *(978-0-349-12410-0(8))* Little, Brown Bks. for Young Readers.

Butler, William S. Scraper Jones: Treasure Hunter. 2007. 320p. pap. 19.95 *(978-1-59663-770-2(6)*, Castle Keep Pr.) Rock, James A. & Co. Pubs.

Byars, Betsy. The Black Tower. 2007. (Herculeah Jones Mystery Ser.). (ENG.). 144p. (J). (gr. 3-7). 6.99 *(978-0-14-240937-4(5)*, Puffin Books) Penguin Young Readers Group.

—The Blossoms & the Green Phantom. (Blossom Family Ser.: Bk. 3). 146p. (J). (gr. 4-6). pap. 3.99 *(978-0-8072-1443-5(4)*, Listening Library) Random Hse. Audio Publishing Group.

—The Dark Stairs. 2006. (Herculeah Jones Mystery Ser.). (ENG.). 160p. (J). (gr. 3-7). pap. 5.99 *(978-0-14-240592-5(2)*, Puffin Books) Penguin Young Readers Group.

—The Dark Stairs. 2006. (Herculeah Jones Mystery Ser.). 130p. (gr. 3-7). 16.00 *(978-0-7569-6736-9(8))* Perfection Learning Corp.

—The Dark Stairs. (Herculeah Jones Mystery Ser.). 160p. (J). (gr. 3-5). pap. 4.99 *(978-0-8072-1478-7(7)*, Listening Library) Random Hse. Audio Publishing Group.

—Dead Letter. 2006. (Herculeah Jones Mystery Ser.). (ENG.). 160p. (J). (gr. 3-7). 5.99 *(978-0-14-240564-2(7)*, Puffin Books) Penguin Young Readers Group.

—Death's Door. 2006. (Herculeah Jones Mystery Ser.). (ENG.). 144p. (J). (gr. 3-7). 6.99 *(978-0-14-240565-9(5)*, Puffin Books) Penguin Young Readers Group.

—Disappearing Acts. 2006. (Herculeah Jones Mystery Ser.). (ENG.). 144p. (J). (gr. 3-7). 6.99 *(978-0-14-240566-6(3)*, Puffin Books) Penguin Young Readers Group.

—King of Murder. 2007. (Herculeah Jones Mystery Ser.). (ENG.). 144p. (J). (gr. 3-7). 5.99 *(978-0-14-240759-2(3)*, Puffin Books) Penguin Young Readers Group.

—Tarot Says Beware, No. 2. 2006. (Herculeah Jones Mystery Ser.). (ENG.). 160p. (J). (gr. 3-7). 5.99 *(978-0-14-240593-2(0)*, Puffin Books) Penguin Young Readers Group.

—Tarot Says Beware. 2006. (Herculeah Jones Mystery Ser.). 151p. (gr. 3-7). 16.00 *(978-0-7569-6737-6(6))* Perfection Learning Corp.

Byrne, Marlene F. Treasure Hunt. Graber, Jesse, illus. 2009. 36p. (J). 14.99 *(978-0-9777135-0-9(4))* Celtic Marketing Inc.

Cabot, Meg. Safe House - Sanctuary. 2011. (Vanished Ser.: Bks. 3 & 4). (ENG.). 512p. (YA). (gr. 7). pap. 12.99 *(978-1-4424-0631-5(3)*, Simon Pulse) Simon Pulse.

—Shadowland & Ninth Key. 2010. (Mediator Ser.). (ENG.). 544p. (YA). (gr. 8). pap. 9.99 *(978-0-06-204020-6(0)*, HarperTeen) HarperCollins Pubs.

—When Lightning Strikes; Code Name Cassandra. 2010. (Vanished Ser.: Bks. 1 & 2). (ENG., Illus.). 560p. (YA). (gr. 7). pap. 12.99 *(978-1-4424-0629-2(1)*, Simon Pulse) Simon Pulse.

Cadose, Linda A. The Hidden Chamber in the Great Sphinx. 2012. 110p. (gr. 4-6). 23.99 *(978-1-4685-0806-2(7))*; pap. 14.95 *(978-1-4685-0807-9(5))* AuthorHouse.

Caine, Paul. Jake's Journey. 2010. 68p. pap. 10.49 *(978-1-4520-0508-9(7))* AuthorHouse.

Calandrelli, Emily. Ada Lace, on the Case: An ADA Lace Adventure. Kurilla, Renée, illus. 2017. (Ada Lace Adventure Ser.: 1). (ENG.). 128p. (J). (gr. 1-5). pap. 6.99 **(978-1-4814-8598-2(9)**, Simon & Schuster Bks. For Young Readers) Simon & Schuster Bks. For Young Readers.

—Ada Lace Sees Red. Kurilla, Renée, illus. 2017. (Ada Lace Adventure Ser.: 2). (ENG.). 144p. (J). (gr. 1-5). 16.99 **(978-1-4814-8602-6(0))**; pap. 6.99 **(978-1-4814-8601-9(2))** Simon & Schuster Bks. For Young Readers. (Simon & Schuster Bks. For Young Readers).

Calderon, Eduardo Caballero. Bolívar: Una Historia que Parece un Cuento. 2011. (SPA.). 64p. (gr. 5-8). pap. 11.99 *(978-958-04-7161-5(4))* Norma S.A. COL. Dist: Lectorum Pubns., Inc.

Call of the Selkie: Individual Title Six-Packs. (Action Packs Ser.). 104p. (gr. 3-5). 44.00 *(978-0-7635-2991-8(5))* Rigby Education.

Callaghan, Cindy. Sydney Mackenzie Knocks 'Em Dead. 2017. (ENG., Illus.). 256p. (J). (gr. 4-8). 17.99 *(978-1-4814-6569-4(4)*, Simon & Schuster/Paula Wiseman Bks.) Simon & Schuster/Paula Wiseman Bks.

Cameron, Bill. Accelerant. 2016. (ENG.). 276p. (YA). (gr. 9-13). pap. 10.95 *(978-1-929345-22-9(4))* Poisoned Pen Pr.

Cameron, Erica. Island of Exiles. 2017. (Ryogan Chronicles Ser.). (ENG.). 400p. (YA). pap. 9.99 *(978-1-63375-592-5(4)*, 9781633755925) Entangled Publishing, LLC.

Cameron, Sam. The Missing Juliet: a Fisher Key Adventure. 2013. (ENG.). 264p. (gr. 7). pap. 11.95 *(978-1-60282-959-6(4))* Bold Strokes Bks.

Cameron, Sharon. A Spark Unseen. 2013. (ENG.). 352p. (J). (gr. 7). 17.99 *(978-0-545-32813-5(6)*, Scholastic Pr.) Scholastic, Inc.

Campbell, Julie. The Secret of the Mansion. Stevens, Mary, illus. 2003. (Trixie Belden Ser.: No. 1). (ENG.). 272p. (J). (gr. 3-7). 6.99 *(978-0-375-82412-8(X)*, Random Hse. Bks. for Young Readers) Random Hse. Children's Bks.

—The Secret of the Mansion: Trixie Belden. 2004. 236p. (J). (gr. 3-7). pap. 29.00 incl. audio *(978-1-4000-9000-6(8)*, Listening Library) Random Hse. Audio Publishing Group.

Campbell, Morgan. Shots, Lies, & That Party. 2013. 178p. pap. 19.95 *(978-1-4489-4324-1(8))* America Star Bks.

Campbell, R. W. Merrick Tumbledorf: The Last Talcomite Dragon. 2013. (ENG.). 250p. (YA). pap. 15.95 *(978-1-4787-1312-8(7))* Outskirts Pr., Inc.

Capeci, Anne. Danger! Dynamite!, 1 vol. Casale, Paul, illus. 2003. (Cascade Moutain Railroad Mystery Ser.: No. 1). (ENG.). 144p. (J). (gr. 2-5). 12.95 *(978-1-56145-288-0(2))* Peachtree Pubs.

—Ghost Train, 1 vol., Vol. 3. Casale, Paul, illus. 2004. (Cascade Moutain Railroad Mystery Ser.: 3). (ENG.). 144p. (J). (gr. 2-5). 12.95 *(978-1-56145-324-5(2))* Peachtree Pubs.

—Missing!, 1 vol. Casale, Paul, illus. 2005. (Cascade Mountain Railroad Mysteries Ser.). (ENG.). 144p. (J). (gr. 2-5). 12.95 *(978-1-56145-334-4(X))* Peachtree Pubs.

Carey, Anna. Blackbird. 2014. (Blackbird Ser.: 1). (ENG.). 256p. (YA). (gr. 9). 17.99 *(978-0-06-229973-4(5)*, HarperTeen) HarperCollins Pubs.

—Blackbird. 2015. (SPA.). 240p. (YA). (gr. 9-12). pap. 17.99 *(978-987-612-909-1(0))* Lectorum Pubns., Inc.

—Deadfall. 2015. 256p. (J). pap. *(978-0-06-242788-5(1))* HarperCollins Pubs.

Carey, Benedict. Poison Most Vial: A Mystery. 2012. (ENG.). 240p. (J). (gr. 3-7). 17.95 *(978-1-4197-0031-6(6)*, Amulet Bks.) Abrams, Inc.

—The Unknowns: A Mystery. 2009. (ENG., Illus.). 272p. (YA). (gr. 3-7). 17.95 *(978-0-8109-7991-8(8)*, Amulet Bks.) Abrams, Inc.

Carlson, Caroline. The World's Greatest Detective. 2017. 368p. (J). (gr. 3-7). 16.99 *(978-0-06-236827-0(3))* HarperCollins Pubs.

Carman, Patrick. The Black Circle. 2009. (Playaway Children Ser.: Bk. 5). (J). 49.99 *(978-1-61545-995-7(2))* Findaway World, LLC.

—The Black Circle. 2009. (J). (39 Clues Ser.: 5). (ENG.). 176p. (gr. 3-7). 12.99 *(978-0-545-06045-5(1)*, Scholastic Pr.); 160p. *(978-0-545-15291-4(7))* Scholastic, Inc.

—Shantorian, Bk. 2. 2011. (Trackers Ser.: 2). (ENG.). 176p. (J). (gr. 3-7). 14.99 *(978-0-545-16501-3(6)*, Scholastic Pr.) Scholastic, Inc.

Carman, Patrick & Scholastic, Inc. Staff. The Black Circle. 2009. (39 Clues Ser.: 5). (ENG., Illus.). 176p. (J). (gr. 3-7). 12.99 *(978-0-545-09063-6(6)*, Scholastic Pr.) Scholastic, Inc.

Carman, Patrick & Studios, P. c. The Crossbones. 2010. (Skeleton Creek Ser.: 3). (ENG.). 224p. (J). (gr. 3-7). 14.99 *(978-0-545-24994-2(5))* Scholastic, Inc.

Caroll, Robin. Samantha Sanderson at the Movies, 1 vol. 2014. (FaithGirlz / Samantha Sanderson Ser.). (ENG.). 272p. (J). pap. 8.99 *(978-0-310-74245-6(5))* Zonderkidz.

—Samantha Sanderson on the Scene, 1 vol. 2014. (FaithGirlz / Samantha Sanderson Ser.). (ENG.). 256p. (J). pap. 8.99 *(978-0-310-74247-0(1))* Zonderkidz.

Caron, Eleonore. Gizmo & Ellen Mysteries: The Case of the Missing Boy. 2012. 24p. pap. 24.95 *(978-1-4626-6747-5(3))* America Star Bks.

Carr, Annie Roe. Nan Sherwood at Pine Camp or the Old Lum. 2007. pap. *(978-1-4065-1294-6(X))* Dodo Pr.

—Nan Sherwood at Rose Ranch. 2007. 124p. per. *(978-1-4068-4396-5(2))* Echo Library.

—Nan Sherwood at Rose Ranch or the Old Me. 2007. pap. *(978-1-4065-1295-3(8))* Dodo Pr.

—Nan Sherwoods Winter Holidays or Rescuin. 2007. pap. *(978-1-4065-1296-0(6))* Dodo Pr.

Carr, Debra. The Curry Comb Caper. Carr, Stephen, illus. 2006. 48p. per. 8.95 *(978-1-933912-59-2(6))* Westview Publishing Co., Inc.

—The Feed Trough Thriller. Carr, Stephen, illus. 2007. 56p. per. 8.95 *(978-1-933912-66-0(9))* Westview Publishing Co., Inc.

—Misty Is Missing. Carr, Stephen, illus. 2008. 52p. pap. 8.95 *(978-0-9816172-7-5(1))* Westview Publishing Co., Inc.

Carr, Patrick W. The Legend's Granddaughter: Not Quite Super, Book 1. Dabbs, Douglas, illus. 2007. 281p. (J). pap. *(978-0-9793168-0-7(4))* NQSBks.

Carroll, Jenny, pseud. Safe House. 2011. (1-800-Where-R-You Ser.: 3). (ENG.). 272p. (YA). (gr. 9). pap. 12.99 *(978-1-4424-3084-6(2)*, Simon Pulse) Simon Pulse.

Carroll, Jenny, pseud & Cabot, Meg. Darkest Hour. 2004. (Mediator Ser.: 4). (ENG.). 336p. (YA). (gr. 8-18). pap. 7.99 *(978-0-06-072514-3(1)*, HarperTeen) HarperCollins Pubs.

—Reunion. 2004. (Mediator Ser.: 3). (ENG.). 304p. (YA). (gr. 8-18). pap. 7.99 *(978-0-06-072513-6(3)*, HarperTeen) HarperCollins Pubs.

—Sanctuary. 2007. (1-800-Where-R-You Ser.: No. 4). (ENG., Illus.). 240p. (YA). (gr. 9-12). mass mkt. 6.99 *(978-1-4169-2707-5(7)*, Simon Pulse) Simon Pulse.

Carson, Donna Wren. The Mystery of Grimly Manor. 2012. 114p. 29.99 *(978-1-4771-5508-0(2))*; pap. 19.99 *(978-1-4771-5507-3(4))* Xlibris Corp.

Carter, Ally. Don't Judge a Girl by Her Cover (10th Anniversary Edition) 2016. (Gallagher Girls Ser.). (ENG.). 288p. (J). (gr. 5-9). pap. 9.99 *(978-1-4847-8504-1(5))* Hyperion Bks. for Children.

—Perfect Scoundrels. 2014. (Heist Society Novel Ser.). (ENG.). 336p. (YA). (gr. 7-12). pap. 9.99 *(978-1-4231-6681-8(7))* Hyperion Bks. for Children.

Carter, Keisha. Maloni's Shoes. 2013. 28p. pap. 9.95 *(978-1-4327-9958-8(4))* Outskirts Pr., Inc.

Carthew, Natasha. The Light That Gets Lost. 2017. (ENG.). 320p. (YA). pap. 13.99 *(978-1-4088-3587-6(8)*, 9781408835876, Bloomsbury USA Childrens) Bloomsbury Publishing USA.

Cartwright, Stephen, illus. Find the Duck. 2007. (Find-its Board Bks). 12p. (J). (gr. -1-k). bds. 6.99 *(978-0-7945-1804-2(4)*, Usborne) EDC Publishing.

—Find the Kitten. 2007. (Find-its Board Bks). 12p. (J). (gr. -1-k). bds. 6.99 *(978-0-7945-1803-5(6)*, Usborne) EDC Publishing.

—Find the Puppy. 2007. (Find-its Board Bks). 12p. (J). (gr. -1-k). bds. 6.99 *(978-0-7945-1802-8(8)*, Usborne) EDC Publishing.

Casanova, Mary. The Turtle-Hatching Mystery. Rayyan, Omar, illus. 2008. (Dog Watch Ser.: 6). (ENG.). 144p. (J). (gr. 3-7). pap. 8.99 *(978-1-4169-4783-7(3)*, Simon & Schuster/Paula Wiseman Bks.) Simon & Schuster/Paula Wiseman Bks.

Case, Linda. Brigits Day of Fun. 2006. 28p. pap. 9.95 *(978-1-4327-0001-0(4))* Outskirts Pr., Inc.

The Case of the Myface Kidnapper (W. T.) 2012. (Hardy Boys (All New) Undercover Brothers Ser.: 40). (ENG.). 160p. (J). pap. 5.99 *(978-1-4424-2235-3(1)*, Simon & Schuster/Paula Wiseman Bks.) Simon & Schuster/Paula Wiseman Bks.

The Case of the Secret Box. 2007. 56p. pap. 7.75 *(978-0-8341-2288-8(X)*, 083-412-288X) Beacon Hill Pr. of Kansas City.

The Case of the Vanishing Emerald. 2015. (Mysteries of Maisie Hitchins Ser.: 2). (ENG., Illus.). 176p. (J). (gr. 2-5). 14.99 *(978-0-544-33927-9(4)*, HMH Books For Young Readers) Houghton Mifflin Harcourt Publishing Co.

Casey, Barbara. The Cadence of Gypsies. 2011. (ENG.). 272p. (J). (gr. 7-12). 16.95 *(978-0-9822812-8-0(6))*, Hungry Goat Pr.) Gauthier Pubns. Inc.

Casey, Jane. Bet Your Life. 2015. (Jess Tennant Mysteries Ser.: 2). (ENG.). 336p. (YA). (gr. 8-12). 18.99 *(978-1-250-04066-4(3)*, 9781250040664, St. Martin's Griffin) St. Martin's Pr.

Cashore, Kristin. Jane, Unlimited. 2017. (ENG.). 464p. (YA). (gr. 9). 18.99 **(978-0-8037-4149-2(9)**, Kathy Dawson Books) Penguin Young Readers Group.

Cassidy, Anne. Butterfly Grave. 2014. (ENG.). 304p. (YA). (gr. 7). pap. 13.99 *(978-1-4088-1552-6(4)*, 9781408815526, Bloomsbury USA Childrens) Bloomsbury Publishing USA.

A Castle Mystery. 2013. (Illus.). (J). *(978-1-4351-4945-8(9))* Disney Pr.

Castle, Regina F. Henry Hopper. 2011. 20p. pap. 24.95 *(978-1-4560-6563-8(7))* America Star Bks.

Castleberry, Stephen B., Sr. & Castleberry, Susie. The History Mystery. 2005. (Farm Mystery Ser.). per. 8.50 *(978-1-891907-16-6(6))* Castleberry Farms Pr.

—Where There's Smoke. 2004. (Farm Mystery Ser.). (J). per. 8.50 *(978-1-891907-14-2(X))* Castleberry Farms Pr.

Castor, Daniel & Castor, Harriet. Jam Sponge & Sneakers. (Illus.). 60p. (J). pap. 7.99 *(978-0-340-63441-7(3))* Hodder & Stoughton GBR. Dist: Trafalgar Square Publishing.

Castro, Adam-Troy. Gustav Gloom & the Four Terrors #3. Margiotta, Kristen, illus. 2014. (Gustav Gloom Ser.: 3). (ENG.). 248p. (J). (gr. 3-7). 7.99 *(978-0-448-48330-6(0)*, Grosset & Dunlap) Penguin Young Readers Group.

Caswell, Brian. Double Exposure. 2005. 240p. (YA). pap. *(978-0-7022-3533-7(4))* Univ. of Queensland Pr.

Caton, Peter. Josh: Hero. 2012. 114p. pap. *(978-1-908128-40-9(2))* Spiderwize.

Caulfield, Annie. Solves Crimes: And So On... 2006. (Katie Milk Ser.). (ENG.). 208p. (J). (gr. 4-7). pap. 9.95 *(978-0-440-86686-2(3))* Transworld Publishers Ltd. GBR. Dist: Independent Pubs. Group.

Cavallaro, Brittany. The Last of August. (Charlotte Holmes Novel Ser.: 2). (YA). (gr. 8). 2018. 352p. pap. 9.99 **(978-0-06-239895-6(4))** 2017. (Illus.). 336p. 17.99 *(978-0-06-239894-9(6))* HarperCollins Pubs. (Tegen, Katherine Bks).

Cavallaro, Brittany. A Study in Charlotte. (Charlotte Holmes Novel Ser.: 1). (YA). (gr. 8). 2017. 352p. pap. 9.99 *(978-0-06-239891-8(1))* 2016. 336p. 17.99 *(978-0-06-239890-1(3))* HarperCollins Pubs. (Tegen, Katherine Bks).

Cavendish, Grace. The Grace Mysteries: Assassin & Betrayal. 2011. (Grace Mysteries Ser.). (ENG.). 384p. (J). (gr. 3-7). pap. 6.99 *(978-0-385-74005-0(0)*, Delacorte Bks. for Young Readers) Random Hse. Children's Bks.

Chadda, Sarwat. Mission Atomic. 2016. (39 Clues: Doublecross Ser.: 4). (ENG.). 256p. (J). (gr. 3-7). 12.99 *(978-0-545-76751-4(2))* Scholastic, Inc.

Chaisson, Samuel Jam. Larry & Joe's Detective Agency. 2005. pap. 26.50 *(978-1-4184-6878-1(9))* AuthorHouse.

Chambliss Bertman, Jennifer. Book Scavenger. 2015. (Book Scavenger Ser.). (ENG., Illus.). 368p. (J). (gr. 4-9). 16.99 *(978-1-62779-115-1(9)*, 9781627791151, Holt, Henry & Co. Bks. For Young Readers) Holt, Henry & Co.

—Book Scavenger. 2016. (Book Scavenger Ser.). (ENG.). 368p. (J). pap. 7.99 *(978-1-250-07980-0(2)*, 9781250079800) Square Fish.

—The Unbreakable Code. 2017. (Book Scavenger Ser.). (ENG., Illus.). 368p. (J). 16.99 *(978-1-62779-116-8(7)*, 9781627791168, Holt, Henry & Co. Bks. For Young Readers) Holt, Henry & Co.

Chan, Marty. The Mystery of the Frozen Brains, 1 vol. MacIntyre, R. P., ed. 2004. (ENG.). 112p. (J). pap. 10.95 *(978-1-894345-71-2(1))* Thistledown Pr., Ltd. CAN. Dist: Univ. of Toronto Pr.

—The Mystery of the Mad Science Teacher. 2008. (ENG.). 127p. (J). (gr. 2-7). pap. 10.95 *(978-1-897235-38-6(0))* Thistledown Pr., Ltd. CAN. Dist: Univ. of Toronto Pr.

Chancey, Loren. Blue Sneaker Breakdown. 2010. 146p. (J). pap. 6.99 *(978-0-9844649-1-3(3))* DIASOT Pubns.

Chand, Emlyn. Davey the Detective: A Bird Brain Book. Shaw, Sarah, illus. l.t. ed. 2012. (ENG.). 42p. (gr. k-1). pap. 10.95 *(978-1-62253-119-6(1))*; 21.95 *(978-1-62253-107-3(8))* Evolved Publishing.

Chandler, Elizabeth. The Back Door of Midnight. 2004. (Dark Secrets Ser.: 5). (ENG.). 224p. (YA). mass mkt. 5.99 *(978-0-689-86642-5(9)*, Simon Pulse) Simon Pulse.

—Legacy of Lies - Don't Tell. 2009. (Dark Secrets Ser.: 1). (ENG., Illus.). 496p. (YA). (gr. 7-18). pap. 9.99 *(978-1-4169-9461-9(0)*, Simon Pulse) Simon Pulse.

—No Time to Die - The Deep End of Fear No. 2. 2010. (Dark Secrets Ser.: 2). (ENG.). 624p. (YA). (gr. 7). pap. 9.99 *(978-1-4169-9462-6(9)*, Simon Pulse) Simon Pulse.

Chapman, Brenda. Hiding in Hawk's Creek. 2006. (Jennifer Bannon Mystery Ser.: 2). (ENG.). 144p. (YA). per. 9.95 *(978-1-894917-24-7(3)*, Napoleon & Co.) Dundum CAN. Dist: Ingram Publisher Services.

—Trail of Secrets. 2009. (Jennifer Bannon Mystery Ser.: 4). (ENG.). 144p. (YA). (gr. 7-18). pap. 9.95 *(978-1-894917-76-6(6)*, Napoleon & Co.) Dundum CAN. Dist: Ingram Publisher Services.

Chari, Sheela. Finding Mighty. 2017. (ENG., Illus.). 320p. (J). (gr. 5-9). 16.95 *(978-1-4197-2296-7(4)*, Amulet Bks.) Abrams, Inc.

Chase, L. P. Elliot Stone & the Mystery of the Summer Vacation Sea Monster. DiRocco, Carl, illus. 2011. (ENG.). 165p. (J). pap. 8.99 *(978-0-9792918-7-6(9))* Blue Marlin Pubns.

—Elliott Stone & the Mystery of the Backyard Treasure. 2008. 122p. (J). pap. 11.95 *(978-0-7414-4804-0(1))* Infinity Publishing.

Chatterton, Martin. The Brain Finds a Leg. 2007. 207p. *(978-1-921049-79-8(0))* Little Hare Bks. AUS. Dist: HarperCollins Pubs. Australia.

—The Brain Finds a Leg, 1 vol. 2009. (ENG.). 224p. (YA). (gr. 5-9). 16.95 *(978-1-56145-503-4(2))* Peachtree Pubs.

—The Brain Full of Holes, 1 vol. 2010. (ENG.). 256p. (J). (gr. 5-9). 16.95 *(978-1-56145-527-0(X))* Peachtree Pubs.

Cheaney, J. B. Somebody on This Bus Is Going to Be Famous. 2014. (ENG.). 304p. (J). (gr. 4-7). 16.99 *(978-1-4022-9297-2(X)*, 9781402292972, Sourcebooks Jabberwocky) Sourcebooks, Inc.

Cherub: The Recruit; the Dealer; Maximum Security. 2013. (Cherub Ser.). (ENG.). 1008p. (YA). (gr. 7). pap. 29.99 *(978-1-4424-8376-7(8)*, Simon Pulse) Simon Pulse.

Cheshire, Simon. The Treasure of Dead Man's Lane & Other Case Files: Saxby Smart, Private Detective: Book 2. Alley, R. W., illus. 2011. (Saxby Smart, Private Detective Ser.: 2). (ENG.). 224p. (J). (gr. 3-7). pap. 8.99 *(978-0-312-67434-2(1)*, 9780312674342) Square Fish.

Chick, Bryan. Secrets & Shadows. 2011. (Secret Zoo Ser.: 2). (ENG.). 272p. (J). (gr. 3-7). pap. 6.99 *(978-0-06-198926-1(6))*; 16.99 *(978-0-06-198925-4(8))* HarperCollins Pubs. (Greenwillow Bks.).

Child, Lauren. Don't Look Now. Child, Lauren, illus. 2008. (Clarice Bean Ser.). (ENG., Illus.). 256p. (J). (gr. 3-7). pap. 5.99 *(978-0-7636-3935-8(4))* Candlewick Pr.

—Ruby Redfort Catch Your Death (Book #3) Child, Lauren, illus. 2015. (Ruby Redfort Ser.: 3). (ENG., Illus.). 432p. (J). (gr. 5-9). 17.99 *(978-0-7636-5469-6(8))* Candlewick Pr.

—Ruby Redfort Feel the Fear. Child, Lauren, illus. 2016. (Ruby Redfort Ser.). (ENG., Illus.). 528p. (J). (gr. 5-9). 16.99 *(978-0-7636-5470-2(1))* Candlewick Pr.

—Ruby Redfort Look into My Eyes. Child, Lauren, illus. 2013. (Ruby Redfort Ser.: 1). (ENG., Illus.). 400p. (J). (gr. 5-9). pap. 7.99 *(978-0-7636-6257-8(7))* Candlewick Pr.

—Ruby Redfort Pick Your Poison. Child, Lauren, illus. 2017. (Ruby Redfort Ser.: 5). (ENG., Illus.). 528p. (J). (gr. 5-9). 16.99 *(978-0-7636-5471-9(X))* Candlewick Pr.

—Ruby Redfort Take Your Last Breath. Child, Lauren, illus. 2013. (Ruby Redfort Ser.: 2). (ENG., Illus.). 432p. (J). (gr. 5-9). 16.99 *(978-0-7636-5468-9(X))* Candlewick Pr.

—Utterly Me, Clarice Bean. Child, Lauren, illus. 2005. (Clarice Bean Ser.). (ENG., Illus.). 208p. (J). (gr. 3-7). reprint ed. pap. 5.99 *(978-0-7636-2788-1(7))* Candlewick Pr.

—Utterly Me, Clarice Bean. Child, Lauren, illus. 2006. (Clarice Bean Ser.). (Illus.). 16.00 *(978-0-7569-6567-9(5))* Perfection Learning Corp.

The Children of the Lost, Bk. 1. 2010. (Hardy Boys (All New) Undercover Brothers Ser.: 34). (ENG.). 192p. (J). (gr. 3-7). pap. 5.99 *(978-1-4424-0262-1(8)*, Aladdin) Simon & Schuster Children's Publishing.

Childress, David Hatcher & Shaver, Richard. Lost Continents & the Hollow Earth: I Remember Lemuria & the Shaver Mystery. 2015. (ENG., Illus.). 100p. pap. 16.95 *(978-0-932813-63-3(1))* Adventures Unlimited Pr.

Christian, Anna. The Newcomer. 2013. 56p. pap. 6.99 *(978-0-9799273-5-5(8))* Dadlelte Production.

Christie, Agatha. Asesinato en el Orient Expreso.Tr. of Murder on the Orient Express. (SPA.). 240p. (J). 7.95 *(978-84-272-0005-0(6))* Molino, Editorial ESP. Dist: AIMS International Bks., Inc.

Christopher, Lucy. The Killing Woods. 2014. (ENG.). 384p. (J). (gr. 9). pap. 10.99 *(978-0-545-46101-6(4))*; 17.99 *(978-0-545-46100-9(6))* Scholastic, Inc. (Chicken Hse., The).

Christopher, Matt. The Hockey Machine. 2008. (New Matt Christopher Sports Library). 128p. (J). (gr. 4-6). lib. bdg. 26.60 *(978-1-59953-214-1(X))* Norwood Hse. Pr.

—Skateboard Tough. 2007. (New Matt Christopher Sports Library). 167p. (J). (gr. 4-6). lib. bdg. 26.60 *(978-1-59953-115-1(1))* Norwood Hse. Pr.

Ciminera, Siobhan & Faulkner, Keith. A Yummy Mystery: A Scratch-and-Sniff Story. 2007. (Puppy Scooby-Doo Ser.). 16p. (J). pap. 5.99 *(978-0-448-44406-2(2)*, Grosset & Dunlap) Penguin Publishing Group.

The Circus Mystery, 6 vols., Vol. 2. (Woodland Mysteriestm Ser.). 133p. (gr. 3-7). 42.50 *(978-0-7802-7942-1(5))* Wright Group/McGraw-Hill.

Cirrone, Dorian. The Big Scoop, 1 vol. Woodruff, Liza, illus. 2006. (Marshall Cavendish Chapter Book Ser.). (ENG.). 74p. (J). (gr. 2-5). 14.99 *(978-0-7614-5323-9(7))* Marshall Cavendish Corp.

Cirrone, Dorian & Cirrone. The Missing Silver Dollar, 1 vol. Woodruff, Liza, illus. 2006. (Lindy Blues Ser.). (ENG.). 32p. (J). (gr. -1-3). 14.95 *(978-0-7614-5284-3(2))* Marshall Cavendish Corp.

Citra, Becky. Missing, 1 vol. 2011. (ENG.). 184p. (J). (gr. 4-7). pap. 9.95 *(978-1-55469-345-0(4))* Orca Bk. Pubs. USA.

Clark, Hannah L. Uncovering Cobbogoth. 2014. pap. 17.99 *(978-1-4621-1426-9(1))* Cedar Fort, Inc./CFI Distribution.

Clark, Joan. Penny Nichols & the Black Imp. 2012. 136p. pap. *(978-1-78139-156-3(4))* Benediction Classics.

—Penny Nichols & the Knob Hill Mystery. 2012. 124p. pap. *(978-1-78139-157-0(2))* Benediction Classics.

—Penny Nichols & the Mystery of the Lost Key. 2012. 124p. pap. *(978-1-78139-155-6(6))* Benediction Classics.

—Penny Nichols Finds a Clue. 2012. 128p. pap. *(978-1-78139-154-9(8))* Benediction Classics.

—Penny Nichols Omnibus - Finds a Clue, Mystery of the Lost Key, Black Imp, & Knob Hill Mystery. 2012. 484p. *(978-1-78139-158-7(0))* Benediction Classics.

Clark, Kristin Elizabeth. Freakboy. 2013. (ENG.). 448p. (YA). (gr. 7). 18.99 *(978-0-374-32472-8(7)*, 9780374324728, Farrar, Straus & Giroux (BYR)) Farrar, Straus & Giroux.

Clark, Lisa M. The Messengers: Concealed. 2017. (ENG.). (YA). (gr. 7-12). pap. 12.99 **(978-0-7586-5657-5(2))** Concordia Publishing Hse.

Clark, Terri A. Sleepless. 2008. (ENG.). 288p. (YA). (gr. 9-18). pap. 5.99 *(978-0-06-137596-5(9)*, HarperTeen) HarperCollins Pubs.

Clasicos de Misterio. (Clasicos Juveniles Coleccion).Tr. of Classic Mystery Stories II. (SPA.). (YA). (gr. 5-8). pap. *(978-950-11-1279-5(9)*, SG4720) Sigmar ARG. Dist: Lectorum Pubns., Inc.

Class 1-208. Pizza Place Ghost, 1 vol. 2013. (Scooby-Doo! Picture Clue Bks.). (ENG.). 24p. (J). (gr. -1-1). lib. bdg. 24.21 *(978-1-61479-038-9(8)*, Essential Library) ABDO Publishing Co.

Clement-Moore, Rosemary. Spirit & Dust. 2014. (ENG.). 400p. (YA). (gr. 7). pap. 9.99 *(978-0-385-74081-4(6)*, Ember) Random Hse. Children's Bks.

Clements, Andrew. Fear Itself. Stower, Adam, illus. 2011. (Benjamin Pratt & the Keepers of the School Ser.: 2). (ENG.). 240p. (J). (gr. 2-5). pap. 7.99 *(978-1-4169-3908-5(3)*, Atheneum Bks. for Young Readers) Simon & Schuster Children's Publishing.

—In Harm's Way. Stower, Adam, illus. (Benjamin Pratt & the Keepers of the School Ser.: 4). (ENG.). (J). (gr. 2-5). 2014. 240p. pap. 7.99 *(978-1-4169-3910-8(5))* 2013. 224p. 14.99 *(978-1-4169-3889-7(3))* Simon & Schuster Children's Publishing. (Atheneum Bks. for Young Readers).

—The Map Trap. Andreasen, Dan, illus. 2016. (ENG.). 160p. (J). (gr. 3-7). pap. 7.99 *(978-1-4169-9728-3(8))* Simon & Schuster Children's Publishing.

—The Map Trap. LaMarche, Jim & Andreasen, Dan, illus. 2014. (ENG.). 144p. (J). (gr. 3-7). 17.99 *(978-1-4169-9727-6(X)*, Atheneum Bks. for Young Readers) Simon & Schuster Children's Publishing.

—The Map Trap. 2016. lib. bdg. 18.40 *(978-0-606-38977-8(6))* Turtleback Bks.

—Room One: A Mystery or Two. Elliott, Mark, illus. 2008. (ENG.). 192p. (J). (gr. 3-7). pap. 7.99 *(978-0-689-86687-6(9)*, Atheneum Bks. for Young Readers) Simon & Schuster Children's Publishing.

—Room One: A Mystery or Two. Blair, Chris & Elliott, Mark, illus. 2006. (ENG.). 176p. (J). (gr. 3-7). 17.99 *(978-0-689-86686-9(0)*, Atheneum Bks. for Young Readers) Simon & Schuster Children's Publishing.

—Things That Are. 2008. (ENG.). 176p. (YA). (gr. 7-18). 16.99 *(978-0-399-24691-3(6)*, Philomel Bks.) Penguin Young Readers Group.

—We Hold These Truths. Stower, Adam, illus. 2013. (Benjamin Pratt & the Keepers of the School Ser.: 5). (ENG.). 272p. (J). (gr. 2-5). 14.99 *(978-1-4169-3890-3(7)*, Atheneum Bks. for Young Readers) Simon & Schuster Children's Publishing.

—We the Children. 2011. (Benjamin Pratt & the Keepers of the School Ser.: 1). (ENG.). 176p. (J). (gr. 2-5). pap. 7.99 *(978-1-4169-3907-8(5)*, Atheneum Bks. for Young Readers) Simon & Schuster Children's Publishing.

—The Whites of Their Eyes. Stower, Adam, illus. (Benjamin Pratt & the Keepers of the School Ser.: 3). (ENG.). (J). (gr. 2-5). 2013. 240p. pap. 6.99 *(978-1-4169-3909-2(1))* 2012. 224p. 14.99 *(978-1-4169-3888-0(5))* Simon & Schuster Children's Publishing. (Atheneum Bks. for Young Readers).

Cleverly, Sophie. The Lost Twin. 2016. (Scarlet & Ivy Ser.: 1). (ENG.). 304p. (J). (gr. 5-8). 16.99 *(978-1-4926-3339-6(9)*, 9781492633396, Sourcebooks Jabberwocky) Sourcebooks, Inc.

Clewarth, John. Firestorm Rising. 2012. (Illus.). 200p. pap. *(978-1-4710-3681-1(2))* Lulu.com.

The Clue in the Castle, 6 vols., Vol. 2. (Woodland Mysteriestm Ser.). 133p. (gr. 3-7). 42.50 *(978-0-7802-7935-3(2))* Wright Group/McGraw-Hill.

Coben, Harlan. Found. 2014. (Mickey Bolitar Novel Ser.: 3). (ENG.). 336p. (YA). (gr. 7). 18.99 *(978-0-399-25652-3(0)*, G.P. Putnam's Sons Books for Young Readers) Penguin Young Readers Group.

—Seconds Away. (Mickey Bolitar Novel Ser.: 2). (ENG.). (YA). (gr. 7). 2012. 352p. 18.99 *(978-0-399-25651-6(2)*, G.P. Putnam's Sons Books for Young Readers)Bk. 2. 2013. 368p. pap. 9.99 *(978-0-14-242635-7(0)*, Speak) Penguin Young Readers Group.

—Seconds Away. l.t. ed. 2012. (Mickey Bolitar Ser.: 2). (ENG.). 396p. 23.99 *(978-1-4104-5348-8(0))* Thorndike Pr.

—Seconds Away. 2013. (Mickey Bolitar Ser.: 2). lib. bdg. 20.85 *(978-0-606-32141-9(1)*, Turtleback) Turtleback Bks.

—Shelter. (Mickey Bolitar Novel Ser.: 1). (ENG.). (YA). (gr. 7-18). 2011. 288p. 18.99 *(978-0-399-25650-9(4)*, G.P. Putnam's Sons Books for Young Readers)Bk. 1. 2012. 336p. pap. 9.99 *(978-0-14-242203-8(7)*, Speak) Penguin Young Readers Group.

—Shelter. l.t. ed. 2011. (Mickey Bolitar Ser.: Bk. 1). (ENG.). 354p. (J). (gr. 9-12). 23.99 *(978-1-4104-4365-6(5))* Thorndike Pr.

—Shelter. 2012. (Mickey Bolitar Ser.: 1). lib. bdg. 20.85 *(978-0-606-26669-7(0)*, Turtleback) Turtleback Bks.

Cody, Matthew. Powerless. 2011. (Supers of Noble's Green Ser.). (ENG.). 288p. (J). (gr. 3-7). 7.99 *(978-0-375-84489-8(9)*, Yearling) Random Hse. Children's Bks.

—Villainous. 2015. (Supers of Noble's Green Ser.). (ENG.). 320p. (J). (gr. 3-7). 6.99 *(978-0-385-75492-7(2)*, Yearling) Random Hse. Children's Bks.

Cofer, Amadeus. Mystery of the Golden Pearls: A Halloween Adventure in Clarkesville, 1. l.t. ed. 2004. (Illus.). 36p. (J). 14.00 *(978-1-932957-02-0(2))* Legacy Pubs.

Coffey, M. Carol. Zoe Lucky: And the Green Gables' Mystery. 2008. 156p. pap. 12.95 *(978-1-4327-3190-8(4))* Outskirts Pr., Inc.

—Zoe Lucky & the Mystery of the Pink Pearl Necklace. 2013. 176p. pap. 12.95 *(978-1-4327-9789-8(1))* Outskirts Pr., Inc.

Cohn, Edith. Spirit's Key. 2014. (ENG.). 320p. (J). (gr. 4-7). 16.99 *(978-0-374-30011-1(9)*, 9780374300111, Farrar, Straus & Giroux (BYR)) Farrar, Straus & Giroux.

Coleman, Evelyn. Mystery of the Dark Tower. 2009. (Mysteries Through Time Ser.). 160p. (YA). (gr. 4-8). 31.95 *(978-1-60754-188-2(2))*; pap. 15.25 *(978-1-60754-189-9(0))* Windmill Bks.

—Shadows on Society Hill. 2007. (American Girl Mysteries Ser.). (ENG., Illus.). 192p. (J). (gr. 4-7). 10.95 *(978-1-59369-163-9(7)*, American Girl) American Girl Publishing, Inc.

Coleman, Tamala J. Donovan's Shoes. 2010. 28p. pap. 9.95 *(978-1-4327-5801-1(2))* Outskirts Pr., Inc.

Coles, William E., Jr. Compass in the Blood: A Reissue of the Simon & Schuster Original Novel. 2004. (YA). per. 9.95 *(978-1-59571-034-5(5))* Word Association Pubs.

Colfer, Eoin. Half-Moon Investigations. 2006. 290p. (J). *(978-1-4156-7354-6(3))* Hyperion Bks. for Children.

Collard, Sneed B., III. Dog 4491. 2013. (Illus.). 256p. (J). 13.99 *(978-0-9844460-4-9(4))* Bucking Horse Bks.

Collard, Sneed B., 3rd. Dog 4491. 2013. (ENG., Illus.). 256p. (J). pap. 8.00 *(978-0-9844460-5-6(2))* Mountain Pr. Publishing Co., Inc.

Collard, Sneed B., III. The Governor's Dog Is Missing. 2011. (Slate Stephens Mysteries Ser.). 176p. (J). (gr. 4-6). 16.00 *(978-0-9844460-1-8(X))* Bucking Horse Bks.

Collicutt, Paul. Murder on the Robot City Express. Collicutt, Paul, illus. 2010. (Robot City Ser.: 4). (ENG., Illus.). 48p. (J). (gr. 3-7). pap. 8.99 *(978-0-7636-5015-5(3)*, Templar) Candlewick Pr.

Collier, Christine. Twelve Months of Mystery. 2003. 72p. pap. 8.95 *(978-0-595-29943-0(1)*, Mystery & Suspense Pr.) iUniverse, Inc.

Collier, Kathy Lynn. Walter S. (Spy) Pigeon, 1 vol. Pace, Brittany Lee Ann, illus. 2009. 20p. pap. 24.95 *(978-1-60813-543-1(8))* America Star Bks.

Collins, Amberly & Collins, Brandilyn. Final Touch, 1 vol. 2010. (Rayne Tour Ser.). (ENG.). 224p. (YA). (gr. 8-11). pap. 9.99 *(978-0-310-71933-5(X))* Zondervan.

Colvin, S. R. R. The Krybosian Stairpath: Magnetic Reversal. 2009. 200p. pap. 14.95 *(978-1-4401-5927-5(0))* iUniverse, Inc.

Comeau, Ceara. Adventures of the Young & Curious. 2008. 136p. pap. 10.94 *(978-0-557-00914-5(6))* Lulu Pr., Inc.

Conford, Ellen. A Case for Jenny Archer. Palmisciano, Diane & Brooks, Erik, illus. 2nd ed. 2006. (ENG.). 64p. (J). (gr. 1-4). per. 13.99 *(978-0-316-01486-1(9))* Little, Brown Bks. for Young Readers.

Conn, Bruce. The Curse of Durgan's Reef. 2004. 142p. (YA). 21.95 *(978-0-595-66223-4(4))*; pap. 11.95 *(978-0-595-30935-1(6))* iUniverse, Inc.

Conrad, Joseph & Snyder, John K., III. The Secret Agent. (Classics Illustrated Ser.). (Illus.). 52p. (YA). pap. 4.95 *(978-1-57209-017-0(0))* Classics International Entertainment, Inc.

Conrique, Samantha. The Pod-Poppers. 2007. (J). pap. 8.00 *(978-0-8059-7200-9(5))* Dorrance Publishing Co., Inc.

Constable, Cathryn. The Wolf Princess. (ENG.). 320p. (J). (gr. 5-9). 2014. pap. 6.99 *(978-0-545-52841-2(0))* 2013. 16.99 *(978-0-545-52839-9(9))* Scholastic, Inc. (Chicken Hse., The).

The Contagious Colors of Mumpley Middle School. 2014. (ENG., Illus.). 288p. (J). (gr. 2-5). pap. 8.99 *(978-1-4424-7830-5(6)*, Atheneum Bks. for Young Readers) Simon & Schuster Children's Publishing.

Conway, Gerry. Break-Up! 2011. (Hardy Boys the New Case Files Ser.). (ENG., Illus.). 64p. (J). (gr. 3-7). pap. 6.99 *(978-1-59707-242-7(7)*, 9781597072427) Papercutz.

—Break-Up! Henrique, Paulo, illus. 2011. (Hardy Boys the New Case Files Ser.: 2). (ENG.). 64p. (J). (gr. 3-7). 10.99 *(978-1-59707-243-4(5)*, 9781597072434) Papercutz.

—Nancy Drew: Together with the Hardy Boys. 2011. (Nancy Drew the New Case Files Ser.). (ENG., Illus.). 64p. (J). (gr. 3-7). pap. 7.99 *(978-1-59707-262-5(1)*, 9781597072625) Papercutz.

Cook, Eileen. The Hanging Girl. 2017. (ENG.). 320p. (YA). (gr. 9). 17.99 **(978-0-544-82982-4(4)**, HMH Books For Young Readers) Houghton Mifflin Harcourt Publishing Co.

Cook, Eileen. With Malice. 2016. (ENG.). 320p. (YA). (gr. 9). 17.99 *(978-0-544-80509-5(7)*, HMH Books For Young Readers) Houghton Mifflin Harcourt Publishing Co.

Cook, Gerri. Where the Buffalo Jump. Yu, Chao & Wang, Jue, illus. 2003. (Dinosaur Soup Ser.). 120p. (YA). (gr. 3-5). pap. 9.95 *(978-1-895836-95-0(6))* River Bks. CAN. Dist: Fitzhenry & Whiteside, Ltd.

Cooke, Tobias. The Secret of the Lost Soul: A Ben Street Mystery. 2011. 272p. pap. *(978-1-907499-80-7(6))* Pen Pr. Pubs., Ltd.

Cool by the Pool: Coloring/Activity Book. 2005. (Illus.). (J). 2.99 *(978-0-9770455-2-5(8))* Mighty Kids Media.

Cool by the Pool: Picture Book (English) 2005. (Illus.). 47p. (J). 5.99 *(978-0-9770455-3-2(6))* Mighty Kids Media.

Cooley Peterson, Megan. Scooby-Doo Solves It with S. T. E. M. Brizuela, Dario & Comia, Christian, illus. 2016. (Scooby-Doo Solves It with S. T. E. M. Ser.). (ENG.). 32p. (gr. 3-4). 111.96 *(978-1-5157-2663-0(0))* Capstone Press of Coughlan Cos.

Coombs, Charles. Detective Stories: Young Readers. Geer, Charles H., illus. 2011. 194p. 42.95 *(978-1-258-10586-0(1))* Literary Licensing, LLC.

—Ranch Mystery: Young Readers. Priscilla, Louis, illus. 2011. 188p. 42.95 *(978-1-258-09854-4(7))* Literary Licensing, LLC.

Cooney, Caroline B. Emergency Room. 2016. (ENG.). 184p. (gr. 7-12). pap. 11.99 *(978-1-5040-3554-5(2))* Open Road Integrated Media, Inc.

—Fatality. 2016. (ENG.). 184p. (J). (gr. 7-12). pap. 11.99 *(978-1-5040-3558-3(5))* Open Road Integrated Media, Inc.

—Hush Little Baby. 2016. (ENG.). 198p. (J). (gr. 7-12). pap. 11.99 *(978-1-5040-3556-9(9))* Open Road Integrated Media, Inc.

—No Such Person. (ENG.). 256p. (YA). (gr. 7). 2016. pap. 9.99 *(978-0-385-74292-4(4)*, Ember) 2015. 17.99 *(978-0-385-74291-7(6)*, Delacorte Pr.) 2015. lib. bdg. 20.99 *(978-0-375-99084-7(4)*, Delacorte Pr.) Random Hse. Children's Bks.

—The Terrorist. 2012. (ENG.). 144p. (YA). pap. 6.99 *(978-1-4532-7467-5(7))* Open Road Integrated Media, Inc.

Coons, Mary. The Piglys & the Hundred-Year Mystery. 2013. 216p. (gr. 4-6). 33.99 *(978-1-4808-0141-7(0))*; pap. 15.99 *(978-1-4808-0139-4(9))* Archway Publishing.

Cooper, Dolores Thome. The Story of the Knus. 2005. (Illus.). 64p. (J). pap. 9.95 *(978-1-881539-38-4(5)*, Strathmoor) Tabby Hse. Bks.

Cooper, E. E. Avenged. 2016. (Vanished Ser.: 2). 352p. (YA). (gr. 9). 17.99 *(978-0-06-229392-3(3)*, Tegen, Katherine Bks) HarperCollins Pubs.

—Vanished. 2015. (Vanished Ser.: 1). (ENG.). 320p. (YA). (gr. 9). 17.99 *(978-0-06-229390-9(7)*, Tegen, Katherine Bks) HarperCollins Pubs.

Coren, Alan. Railroad Arthur. 2004. (Illus.). 64p. *(978-0-903895-92-7(7)*, Robson Bks. Ltd.) Pavilion Bks.

Corrossi, Steven A. Angus & the Hidden Fort. 2003. 162p. pap. 9.95 *(978-0-595-27540-3(0)*, Writer's Showcase Pr.) iUniverse, Inc.

Corley, Sandra Y. The Crochet Detective Case #101: The Case of the Missing African Treasure. 2011. 36p. (gr. 4-6). pap. 16.86 *(978-1-4567-4678-0(2))* AuthorHouse.

Cormier, Robert. I Am the Cheese. l.t. ed. 2005. 255p. pap. 10.95 *(978-0-7862-7336-2(4)*, Large Print Pr.) Thorndike Pr.

—The Rag & Bone Shop. 2003. (ENG.). 176p. (YA). (gr. 7). mass mkt. 6.99 *(978-0-440-22971-1(5)*, Laurel Leaf) Random Hse. Children's Bks.

Corona, Sarah. El Misterio del Tiempo Robado. (Barril Sin Fondo Ser.). (SPA.). (J). (gr. 3-5). pap. *(978-968-6465-16-7(2))* Casa de Estudios de Literatura y Talleres Artisticos Amaquemecan A.C. MEX. Dist: Lectorum Pubns., Inc.

Corrigan, Eireann. The Believing Game. 2012. (ENG.). 384p. (J). (gr. 7). 17.99 *(978-0-545-29983-1(7)*, Scholastic Pr.) Scholastic, Inc.

Corriveau, Art. How I Got a Life & a Dog. 2012. (ENG.). 288p. (J). (gr. 3-7). pap. 7.95 *(978-1-4197-0015-6(4)*, Amulet Bks.) Abrams, Inc.

—How I, Nicky Flynn, Finally Got a Life (And a Dog) 2010. (ENG.). 272p. (YA). (gr. 3-7). 16.95 *(978-0-8109-8298-7(6)*, Amulet Bks.) Abrams, Inc.

—13 Hangmen. 2012. (ENG.). 352p. (J). (gr. 3-7). 17.95 (978-1-4197-0159-7(2), Amulet Bks.) Abrams, Inc.

Cortez, Sarah, ed. You Don't Have a Clue: Latino Mystery Stories for Teens. 2011. 320p. (YA). (gr. 6-18). pap. (978-1-55885-692-9(7)) Arte Publico Pr.

Cosimano, Elle & Carey, Janet Lee. Nearly Found. 2015. (Nearly Boswell Mysteries Ser.). (ENG.). 384p. (YA). (gr. 7-12). 17.99 (978-0-8037-3927-7(3), Kathy Dawson Books) Penguin Young Readers Group.

Cosson, M. J. The Mystery of the Old Car. 2005. (Cover-to-Cover Kooties Club Mysteries Ser.). (Illus.). 56p. (J). (gr. k-3). lib. bdg. 14.95 (978-0-7569-4606-7(9)) Perfection Learning Corp.

—Sherlock Holmes & A Scandal in Bohemia. rev. ed. 2010. pap. 39.62 (978-0-7613-6954-7(6)) Lerner Publishing Group.

—Sherlock Holmes & the Adventure at the Abbey Grange. 2nd rev. ed. 2010. pap. 39.62 (978-0-7613-6957-8(0)) Lerner Publishing Group.

—Sherlock Holmes & the Adventure of the Blue Gem. 3rd rev. ed. 2010. pap. 39.62 (978-0-7613-6959-2(7)) Lerner Publishing Group.

—Sherlock Holmes & the Adventure of the Dancing Men. 4th rev. ed. 2010. pap. 39.62 (978-0-7613-6961-5(9)) Lerner Publishing Group.

—Sherlock Holmes & the Adventure of the Speckled Band. 5th rev. ed. 2010. pap. 39.62 (978-0-7613-6962-2(7)) Lerner Publishing Group.

—Sherlock Holmes & the Adventure of the Sussex Vampire. 6th rev. ed. 2010. pap. 39.62 (978-0-7613-6963-9(5)) Lerner Publishing Group.

Côté, Denis. La Machination du Scorpion Noir. 2004. (Mon Roman Ser.). (FRE.). 160p. (J). (gr. 2). pap. (978-2-89021-667-9(5)) Diffusion du livre Mirabel (DLM).

Cote, Denis. Un Parfum de Mystere. 2003. (Premier Roman Ser.). (Illus.). 64p. (J). (gr. 2-5). pap. (978-2-89021-352-4(8)) Diffusion du livre Mirabel (DLM).

Cousineau-Peiffer, Trisha. Have You Ever Heard of a Rainbow Farm. Everett-Hawkes, Bonnie, illus. 2006. 32p. (J). 12.95 (978-0-9792084-1-6(6)) Dream Ridge Pr.

—Have You Ever Heard of a Rainbow Farm: The Missing Color Kittens. Everett-Hawkes, Bonnie, illus. 2007. 48p. (J). per. 15.95 (978-0-9792084-2-3(4)) Dream Ridge Pr.

Covington, Nichole. Melinda the Miserable: Eeriness in the Attic. 2011. 116p. pap. 19.95 (978-1-4560-7250-6(1)) America Star Bks.

Cowan, C. C. Amanda's Amazing Adventures: The Case of the Missing Pooch, 6 vols., Vol. 1. Rashid, Abdul, illus. 2009. 100p. pap. 14.95 (978-0-9677385-1-2(2)); 40p. pap. 14.95 (978-0-9677385-0-5(4)) CCP Publishing & Entertainment.

Cox, James. Earth Dogs Don't Speak. 2009. (Illus.). 112p. pap. 31.99 (978-1-4389-3990-2(6)) AuthorHouse.

Cox, Judy. The Case of the Purloined Professor, 0 vols. Rayyan, Omar, illus. 2009. (Tails of Frederick & Ishbu Ser.: 0). (ENG.). 256p. (J). (gr. 5-7). 16.99 (978-0-7614-5544-8(2), 9780761455448, Amazon Children's Publishing) Amazon Publishing.

—The Mystery of the Burmese Bandicoot, 1 vol. Rayyan, Omar, illus. 2007. (Tails of frederick & Ishbu Ser.). (ENG.). 224p. (J). (gr. 5-9). lib. bdg. 16.99 (978-0-7614-5376-5(8)) Marshall Cavendish Corp.

—The Mystery of the Burmese Bandicoot. 2012. 254p. (gr. 4-6). pap. 15.95 (978-1-4759-3838-8(1)) iUniverse, Inc.

Cox, Katherine. The Missing Fox. 2015. (Scholastic Reader Level 2 Ser.). lib. bdg. 13.55 (978-0-606-37748-5(4)) Turtleback Bks.

Cox, M. M. Accidental Mobster. 2012. 252p. pap. (978-1-927134-89-4(7)) Bluewood Publishing, Ltd.

Cox, Suzy. The Dead Girls Detective Agency. 2012. (ENG.). 368p. (YA). (gr. 9). pap. 9.99 (978-0-06-202064-2(1), HarperTeen) HarperCollins Pubs.

Crain, Kira. SEK Statton. 2009. (GER.). 136p. 29.95 (978-1-4092-6127-8(1)) Lulu Pr., Inc.

Crawford, Clint. The Rag Tag Gang, 1 vol. 2009. 83p. pap. 19.95 (978-1-4489-9697-1(X)) America Star Bks.

Crawford, K. Michael. The Mystery of Journeys Crowne-an Adventure Drawing Game. Crawford, K. Michael, illus. 2008. (Illus.). 52p. pap. 14.95 (978-0-9817940-0-6(9)) Virtualbookworm.com Publishing, Inc.

Crawford, Ruth. Squirrel Boy & Brad: Solve a Mystery. 2010. 24p. pap. 12.99 (978-1-4490-1612-8(X)) AuthorHouse.

Cray, Jordan. Dead Man's Hand. 2009. (Danger. com Ser.: 8). (ENG.). 224p. (YA). (gr. 7). pap. 10.99 (978-1-4169-9852-5(7), Simon Pulse) Simon Pulse.

—Most Wanted. 2009. (Danger. com Ser.: 7). (ENG.). 240p. (YA). (gr. 7). pap. 11.99 (978-1-4169-9851-8(9), Simon Pulse) Simon Pulse.

—Shadow Man. 2009. (Danger. com Ser.: 3). (ENG.). 192p. (YA). (gr. 7). pap. 9.99 (978-1-4169-9848-8(9), Simon Pulse) Simon Pulse.

—Shiver. 2009. (Danger. com Ser.: 9). (ENG.). 224p. (YA). (gr. 7). pap. 10.99 (978-1-4169-9853-2(5), Simon Pulse) Simon Pulse.

—Stalker. 2009. (Danger. com Ser.: 5). (ENG.). 224p. (YA). (gr. 7). pap. 10.99 (978-1-4169-9850-1(0), Simon Pulse) Simon Pulse.

Crilley, Paul. The Osiris Curse: A Tweed & Nightingale Adventure. 2013. (ENG.). 287p. (J). (gr. 7). 17.99 (978-1-61614-857-7(8)) Prometheus Bks., Pubs.

Cronin, Doreen. The Case of the Weird Blue Chicken: The Next Misadventure. 2015. (Chicken Squad Ser.: 2). 35.75 (978-1-4906-4049-5(5)) Recorded Bks., Inc.

—The Chicken Squad. Cornell, Kevin, illus. 2014. 92p. (J). **(978-0-605-90609-9(2))** Simon & Schuster Children's Publishing.

—The Chicken Squad: The First Misadventure. 2014. (Chicken Squad Ser.: 1). 33.75 (978-1-4906-2064-0(8)); 1.25 (978-1-4906-2066-4(4)); 35.75 (978-1-4906-2065-7(6)) Recorded Bks., Inc.

—The Chicken Squad: The First Misadventure. Cornell, Kevin, illus. (Chicken Squad Ser.: 1). (ENG.). 112p. (J). (gr. 2-5). 2015. pap. 6.99 (978-1-4424-9677-4(0)) 2014. 12.99 (978-1-4424-9676-7(2)) Simon & Schuster Children's Publishing. (Atheneum Bks. for Young Readers).

—Into the Wild: Yet Another Misadventure. Warrick, Jessica & Gilpin, Stephen, illus. 2017. (Chicken Squad Ser.: 3). (ENG.). 112p. (J). (gr. 2-5). pap. 6.99 (978-1-4814-5047-8(6)) Simon & Schuster Children's Publishing.

—Into the Wild: Yet Another Misdventure. Gilpin, Stephen, illus. 2016. (Chicken Squad Ser.: 3). (ENG.). 112p. (J). (gr. 2-5). 12.99 (978-1-4814-5046-1(8), Atheneum/Caitlyn Dlouhy Books) Simon & Schuster Children's Publishing.

—The Legend of Diamond Lil. Cornell, Kevin, illus. 144p. (J). (gr. 1-5). 2013. (ENG.). pap. 5.99 (978-0-06-177997-8(0)) 2012. (ENG.). 14.99 (978-0-06-177996-1(2)) 2012. lib. bdg. 15.89 (978-0-06-198578-2(3)) HarperCollins Pubs.

—The Trouble with Chickens. Cornell, Kevin, illus. (J). (gr. 1-5). 2012. (ENG.). 144p. pap. 5.99 (978-0-06-121534-6(1)) 2011. (ENG.). 128p. 14.99 (978-0-06-121532-2(5)) 2011. 128p. lib. bdg. 15.89 (978-0-06-121533-9(3)) HarperCollins Pubs.

Cross, P. C. Summer Job: A Virgil & Cy Mystery. 2008. 260p. pap. 16.95 (978-0-595-50921-8(5)) iUniverse, Inc.

Crossman, D. A. The Legend of Burial Island: A Bean & Ab Mystery. 2009. (J). pap. (978-0-89272-812-1(4)) Down East Bks.

Crossman, David. The Legend of Burial Island: A Bean & Ab Mystery. 2009. (ENG.). 201p. (J). (gr. 3-7). pap. 11.95 (978-0-89272-797-1(7)) Down East Bks.

Crowley, Ashley. Officer Panda - Fingerprint Detective. Crowley, Ashley, illus. 2015. (Officer Panda Ser.: 1). (ENG., Illus.). 32p. (J). (gr. -1-3). 17.99 (978-0-06-236626-9(2)) HarperCollins Pubs.

—Officer Panda: Sky Detective. Crowley, Ashley, illus. 2016. (Officer Panda Ser.: 2). (Illus.). 32p. (J). (gr. -1-3). 17.99 (978-0-06-236627-6(0)) HarperCollins Pubs.

Crowley, Kieran Mark. Colm & the Ghost's Revenge. 2012. (ENG.). 320p. (J). pap. 13.95 (978-1-85635-997-9(2)) Mercier Pr., Ltd., The IRL. Dist: Dufour Editions, Inc.

—Colm & the Lazarus Key. 2009. (ENG., Illus.). 224p. (J). pap. 14.95 (978-1-85635-646-6(9)) Mercier Pr., Ltd., The IRL. Dist: Dufour Editions, Inc.

Croy, Anita. Titanic: The Search for the Lost Fugitives. Posen, Mick, illus. 2012. (ENG.). 48p. (J). (gr. 3-7). 16.99 (978-0-7534-6672-8(4), 9780753466728, Kingfisher) Roaring Brook Pr.

Crutcher, Chris. Period 8. 2013. 288p. (YA). (gr. 9). (ENG.). 17.99 (978-0-06-191480-5(0)); lib. bdg. 18.89 (978-0-06-191481-2(9)) HarperCollins Pubs. (Greenwillow Bks.).

Cullen-Skowronski, Fiona. The Smugglers' Caves. 2009. 284p. pap. (978-1-84923-435-1(3)) YouWriteOn.

Cunliffe, John. Postman Pat & the Mystery Tour. (Postman Pat Ser.: Bk. 13). (Illus.). 32p. (J). pap. 8.99 (978-0-340-71333-4(X)) Hodder & Stoughton GBR. Dist: Trafalgar Square Publishing.

Cunning, Concord. Scripture Sleuth 3. 2004. pap. 8.95 (978-1-885904-39-3(8)) Focus Publishing.

Curtis, Christopher Paul. Mr. Chickee's Funny Money. 2007. (ENG.). 160p. (J). (gr. 3-7). 6.99 (978-0-440-22919-3(7), Yearling) Random Hse. Children's Bks.

—Mr. Chickee's Messy Mission. 2008. (ENG., Illus.). 240p. (J). (gr. 3-7). 6.99 (978-0-440-22922-3(7), Yearling) Random Hse. Children's Bks.

Curtiss, A. B. & Curtiss, A. B. Hanner & the Bullies. Brown, Jason, illus. 2012. 140p. pap. 9.99 (978-0-932529-63-3(1)) Oldcastle Publishing.

Cushman, Doug. Dirk Bones & the Mystery of the Haunted House. Cushman, Doug, illus. 2009. (I Can Read Level 1 Ser.). (ENG., Illus.). 32p. (J). (gr. k-3). pap. 3.99 (978-0-06-073767-2(0)) HarperCollins Pubs.

—Dirk Bones & the Mystery of the Haunted House. 2009. (I Can Read! Level 1 Ser.). (J). lib. bdg. 13.55 (978-0-606-04778-4(6), Turtleback) Turtleback Bks.

Cushman, Doug, illus. Dirk Bones & the Mystery of the Missing Books. 2009. (I Can Read Level 1 Ser.). (ENG.). 32p. (J). (gr. -1-3). 16.99 (978-0-06-073768-9(9)) HarperCollins Pubs.

Cusick, Richie Tankersley. Starstruck. 2013. (ENG., Illus.). 240p. (YA). (gr. 7). pap. 15.99 (978-1-4814-0161-6(0), Simon Pulse) Simon Pulse.

—Summer of Secrets. 2013. (ENG., Illus.). 224p. (YA). (gr. 7). pap. 15.99 (978-1-4814-0160-9(2), Simon Pulse) Simon Pulse.

—Walk of the Spirits. 2008. (ENG.). 336p. (YA). (gr. 7-18). 9.99 (978-0-14-241050-9(0), Speak) Penguin Young Readers Group.

Czernecki, Stefan. Mystery at Midnight Museum. Date not set. 32p. (J). 14.99 (978-0-06-026199-3(4)) HarperCollins Pubs.

Dahl, Michael. The Assistant Vanishes!, 1 vol. Weber, Lisa K., illus. 2013. (Hocus Pocus Hotel Ser.). (ENG.). 112p. (gr. 2-3). lib. bdg. 25.32 (978-1-4342-4101-6(7)) Stone Arch Bks.

—Curtains! A High School Musical Mystery. Prothero, Tiffany, illus. 2008. (Vortex Bks.). (ENG.). 112p. (gr. 2-3). 26.65 (978-1-4342-0801-9(X), Vortex Bks.) Stone Arch Bks.

—Hocus Pocus Hotel, 1 vol. Weber, Lisa K., illus. 2014. (Hocus Pocus Hotel Ser.). (ENG.). 128p. (gr. 2-3). 50.64 (978-1-4342-8937-7(0)) Stone Arch Bks.

—Hocus Pocus Hotel. 2013. (Hocus Pocus Hotel Ser.). (ENG.). 112p. (gr. 2-3). 101.28 (978-1-4342-4821-3(6)); 50.64 (978-1-4342-4820-6(8)) Stone Arch Bks.

—Hocus Pocus Hotel, 1 vol. Weber, Lisa K., illus. 2012. (Hocus Pocus Hotel Ser.). (ENG.). 216p. (gr. 2-3). 10.95 (978-1-4342-4253-2(6)) Stone Arch Bks.

—The Horizontal Man: Finnegan Zwake #1. 2008. (Finnegan Zwake Ser.: 1). (ENG.). 192p. (YA). (gr. 7). (978-1-4169-8668-3(5), Simon Pulse) Simon Pulse.

—Out the Rear Window, 1 vol. Weber, Lisa K., illus. 2012. (Hocus Pocus Hotel Ser.). (ENG.). 112p. (gr. 2-3). lib. bdg. 25.32 (978-1-4342-4038-5(X)) Stone Arch Bks.

—The Prisoners of the Thirteenth Floor, 1 vol. Weber, Lisa K., illus. 2014. (Hocus Pocus Hotel Ser.). (ENG.). 128p. (gr. 2-3). 25.32 (978-1-4342-6508-1(0)) Stone Arch Bks.

—The Return of Abracadabra. Weber, Lisa K., illus. (Hocus Pocus Hotel Ser.). (ENG.). 208p. (gr. 2-3). 2015. pap. 7.95 (978-1-4965-2486-7(1)) 2013. 10.95 (978-1-4342-4721-6(X)) Stone Arch Bks.

—The Ruby Raven. 2008. (Finnegan Zwake Ser.: 3). (ENG.). 192p. (YA). (gr. 7). pap. 9.99 (978-1-4169-8666-9(9), Simon Pulse) Simon Pulse.

—The Thirteenth Mystery. Weber, Lisa K., illus. (Hocus Pocus Hotel Ser.). (ENG.). 224p. (gr. 2-3). 2016. pap. 7.95 (978-1-4965-0755-6(X)) 2014. 10.95 (978-1-4342-6509-8(9)) Stone Arch Bks.

—To Catch a Ghost, 1 vol. Weber, Lisa K., illus. 2012. (Hocus Pocus Hotel Ser.). (ENG.). 112p. (gr. 2-3). lib. bdg. 25.32 (978-1-4342-4100-9(9)) Stone Arch Bks.

—The Trouble with Abracadabra, 1 vol. Weber, Lisa K., illus. 2013. (Hocus Pocus Hotel Ser.). (ENG.). 112p. (gr. 2-3). lib. bdg. 25.32 (978-1-4342-4102-3(5)) Stone Arch Bks.

—The Viking Claw. 2011. (Finnegan Zwake Ser.: 4). (ENG.). 192p. (YA). (gr. 7). pap. 9.99 (978-1-4424-3101-0(6), Simon Pulse) Simon Pulse.

—The Wizard & the Wormhole, 1 vol. Weber, Lisa K., illus. 2014. (Hocus Pocus Hotel Ser.). (ENG.). 128p. (gr. 2-3). 25.32 (978-1-4342-6507-4(2)) Stone Arch Bks.

—The Worm Tunnel: Finnegan Zwake #2. 2008. (Finnegan Zwake Ser.: 2). (ENG.). 176p. (YA). (gr. 7). pap. 9.99 (978-1-4169-8667-6(7), Simon Pulse) Simon Pulse.

Dairman, Tara. The Great Hibernation. 2017. (ENG.). 272p. (J). (gr. 3-7). 16.99 **(978-1-5247-1785-8(1))**; lib. bdg. 19.99 **(978-1-5247-1786-5(X))** Random Hse. Children's Bks. (Lamb, Wendy Bks.).

Dalton, Andrew & Boatfield, Jonny. The Lost People of Malplaquet. 2007. (ENG., Illus.). 144p. (C). (gr. 4-7). 34.00 (978-0-7188-3049-6(0)); per. 17.00 (978-0-7188-3050-2(4)) Lutherworth Pr., The GBR. Dist: Casemate Academic.

Daly, Joseph M. Strange Town Volume One: The Woods Behind Trevor Malone's House. 2007. 265p. (YA). pap. 9.99 net. (978-0-9779921-0-2(1)) Wolfs Corner Publishing.

Damian, Jeremy. Darius & Chums & the Missing Sapphire. 2015. (ENG.). 260p. (J). (gr. 2-3). 11.95 (978-1-84963-924-8(8), 02ca5635-cf45-4b43-9dde-b1ce4eb19de3) Austin, Stan AUS. Dist: Bookmasters Distribution.

Damico, Gina. Wax. (ENG.). (gr. 7). 2017. 384p. (YA). pap. 9.99 (978-0-544-93718-5(X)) 2016. 368p. (J). 17.99 (978-0-544-63315-5(6)) Houghton Mifflin Harcourt Publishing Co. (HMH Books For Young Readers).

Dandridge, Gwen. The Stone Lions. 2013. 230p. pap. 10.99 (978-0-9893157-8-4(9)) Hickory Tree Publishing.

Daneshvari, Gitty. Class Is Not Dismissed! 2011. (School of Fear Ser.: 2). (ENG.). 336p. (J). (gr. 3-7). pap. 8.99 (978-0-316-03329-9(4)) Little, Brown Bks. for Young Readers.

—Who's That Ghoulfriend? 2013. Bk. 3. (ENG., Illus.). 272p. (J). (gr. 3-7). 13.00 (978-0-316-22254-9(2)) Little, Brown Bks. for Young Readers.

Daniels, W. J. The Empress Academy: The Secret of Glittershine. 2009. 144p. pap. 16.95 (978-1-4327-2335-4(9)) Outskirts Pr., Inc.

David, Erica. The Great Ice Engine. RH Disney Staff et al, illus. 2015. (Stepping Stone Book(TM) Ser.: 4). (ENG.). 128p. (J). (gr. 1-4). 9.99 (978-0-7364-3431-7(3), RH/Disney) Random Hse. Children's Bks.

Davidson, Michele R. Stowaways to Smith Island: Hayden & Chloe's Enchanted Journey with the Nurses to Maryland's Mysterious Smith Island. Watjen, Laureen, illus. 2004. 128p. (J). pap. 8.95 (978-0-9754170-1-0(0)) Smith Island Foundation.

Davies, Jacqueline. The Bell Bandit. (Lemonade War Ser.). (ENG., Illus.). 192p. (J). (gr. 2-5). 2013. pap. 7.99 (978-0-544-02274-4(2)) 2012. 16.99 (978-0-547-56737-2(5)) Houghton Mifflin Harcourt Publishing Co.

—The Bell Bandit. 2013. (Lemonade War Ser.: 3). lib. bdg. 18.40 (978-0-606-31669-9(8), Turtleback) Turtleback Bks.

Davies, Katie. The Great Cat Conspiracy. Shaw, Hannah, illus. 2012. (Great Critter Capers Ser.). (ENG.). 224p. (J). (gr. 3-7). 12.99 (978-1-4424-4513-0(0), Beach Lane Bks.) Beach Lane Bks.

—The Great Hamster Massacre. Shaw, Hannah, illus. 2011. (Great Critter Capers Ser.). (ENG.). 208p. (J). (gr. 3-7). 12.99 (978-1-4424-2062-5(6), Beach Lane Bks.) Beach Lane Bks.

Davies, Nicola. Escape from Silver Street Farm. McEwen, Katharine, illus. 2013. (Silver Street Farm Ser.). (ENG.). 80p. (J). (gr. 2-5). 12.99 (978-0-7636-6133-5(3)) Candlewick Pr.

Davis, Christy. Newshounds. 2010. 156p. pap. 12.50 (978-1-4389-7869-7(3)) AuthorHouse.

Davis, Tim, illus. The Case of the Purple Diamonds. 2011. 88p. pap. 9.95 (978-1-934606-07-0(3)) TAG Publishing, LLC.

De Campi, Alex. Kat & Mouse Vol. 1: Teacher Torture, 1 vol. Manfredi, Federica, illus. 2009. (Tokyopop Ser.). (ENG.). 96p. (gr. 2-6). 25.65 (978-1-59961-564-6(9)) Spotlight.

—Kat & Mouse Vol. 2: Tripped, 1 vol. Manfredi, Federica, illus. 2009. (Tokyopop Ser.). (ENG.). 96p. (gr. 2-6). 25.65 (978-1-59961-565-3(7)) Spotlight.

De felice, Cynthia. Devil's Bridge. 2008. (ENG.). 96p. (YA). (gr. 7). pap. 9.99 (978-1-4169-8307-1(4), Atheneum Bks. for Young Readers) Simon & Schuster Children's Publishing.

—The Light on Hogback Hill. 2008. (ENG.). 128p. (J). (gr. 4-6). pap. 7.99 (978-1-4169-8691-1(X), Simon & Schuster/Paula Wiseman Bks.) Simon & Schuster/Paula Wiseman Bks.

de Groot, Bob. Clifton Vol. 6: Kidnapping. 2009. (Clifton Ser.: 6). (ENG., Illus.). 48p. (J). (gr. 3-17). pap. 11.95 (978-1-905460-87-8(2)) CineBook GBR. Dist: National Bk. Network.

de los Santos, Marisa & Teague, David. Connect the Stars. 2015. (ENG.). 352p. (J). (gr. 3-7). 16.99 (978-0-06-227465-6(1)) HarperCollins Pubs.

—Saving Lucas Biggs. (ENG.). (J). (gr. 3-7). 2015. 320p. pap. 6.99 (978-0-06-227463-2(5)) 2014. 288p. 16.99 (978-0-06-227462-5(7)) HarperCollins Pubs.

DeAnda, Diane. The Monster in the Mattress & Other Stories: El Monstruo en el Colchón y Otros Cuentos. 2011. (SPA & ENG., Illus.). 90p. (J). (gr. 3-7). pap. 9.95 (978-1-55885-693-6(5), Piñata Books) Arte Publico Pr.

DeArville, J. It's Kambri Time! 2007. 28p. per. 9.95 (978-1-4327-0812-2(0)) Outskirts Pr., Inc.

Death at the Border. 64p. (YA). (gr. 6-12). pap. (978-0-8224-2361-4(8)) Globe Fearon Educational Publishing.

Deathman Don't Follow Me. 2003. (J). pap. 2.95 (978-0-590-44006-6(3)) Scholastic, Inc.

Deborah Strandberg, Rebecca Reynolds and. Trammler Triplet Tales #2 - HIDDEN in TIME. 2007. 116p. pap. 8.94 (978-1-4303-2097-5(4)) Lulu Pr., Inc.

—Trammler Triplet Tales Advente #4 MYSTERIOUS ABBY. 2007. 113p. pap. 8.90 (978-1-4357-0651-4(X)) Lulu Pr., Inc.

DeFelice, Cynthia. The Ghost & Mrs. Hobbs. 2010. (Ghost Mysteries Ser.: 2). (ENG.). 208p. (J). (gr. 3-7). pap. 8.99 (978-0-312-62909-0(5), 9780312629090) Square Fish.

—The Ghost of Cutler Creek. 2011. (Ghost Mysteries Ser.: 3). (ENG.). 208p. (J). (gr. 3-7). pap. 9.99 (978-0-312-62967-0(2), 9780312629670) Square Fish.

DeFelice, Cynthia C. The Ghost of Cutler Creek. 2006. (Ghost Mysteries Ser.). 181p. (J). (gr. 3-7). 13.60 (978-0-7569-8185-3(9)) Perfection Learning Corp.

—The Missing Manatee. 2008. (ENG.). 192p. (J). (gr. 3-7). pap. 8.99 (978-0-374-40020-0(2), 9780374400200) Square Fish.

Defreitas, Henrietta. Henratty Mortimer: The Meerville Myth. 2011. (Illus.). 88p. pap. 28.14 (978-1-4520-8237-0(5)) AuthorHouse.

Degrado, Louis Paul. The Questors' Adventures: The Round House & the Moaning Walls. 2012. 326p. 29.95 (978-1-4759-4469-3(1)); pap. 19.95 (978-1-4759-4470-9(5)) iUniverse, Inc.

Deiss, A. The Sullivan Girls & the Mystery of Moonhouse. 2003. 104p. (Orig.). pap. 9.95 (978-0-595-29580-7(0)) iUniverse, Inc.

Dekker, James. Scum, 1 vol. 2008. (Orca Soundings Ser.). (ENG.). 112p. (YA). (gr. 8-12). pap. 9.95 (978-1-55143-924-2(7)) Orca Bk. Pubs. USA.

Dekker, James C. Scum, 1 vol. 2008. (Orca Soundings Ser.). (ENG.). 112p. (YA). (gr. 8-12). 16.95 (978-1-55143-926-6(3)) Orca Bk. Pubs. USA.

Delashmit, Margaret V. Thief! 2012. 148p. (gr. 4-6). pap. 12.99 (978-1-4624-0348-6(4), Inspiring Voices) Author Solutions, Inc.

De'Leon, Lunden. Oops Loops. 2006. 28p. pap. 9.95 (978-1-4327-0114-7(2)) Outskirts Pr., Inc.

DeMeulemeester, Linda. The Forgotten Secret. 2016. (ENG.). 208p. (J). pap. **(978-1-77203-100-3(3)**, Wandering Fox) Heritage Hse.

Deming, Lynette. Day in Matthews Shoes. 2006. 28p. pap. 9.95 (978-1-4327-0100-0(2)) Outskirts Pr., Inc.

DeMitchell, Terri A. You Will Come Back - the First in the Olde Locke Beach Mysteries. 2004. (ENG., Illus.). 176p. 14.95 (978-1-932278-02-6(8)) Mayhaven Publishing, Inc.

Denton, Shannon Eric & Warner, Gertrude Chandler. The Boxcar Children, 1 vol. Dubisch, Michael, illus. 2009. (Boxcar Children Graphic Novels Ser.). (ENG.). 32p. (J). (gr. 2-5). lib. bdg. 28.50 (978-1-60270-586-9(0)) ABDO Publishing Co.

Derting, Kimberly. The Last Echo. 2013. (Body Finder Ser.: 3). (ENG.). 384p. (YA). (gr. 9). pap. 9.99 (978-0-06-208220-6(5)) HarperCollins Pubs.

DeSio, Delores . Up a Tree with Mary Mcphee: A Mystery for Children. 2006. 86p. pap. 16.95 (978-1-4241-4309-2(8)) PublishAmerica, Inc.

DeStefano, Lauren. A Curious Tale of the In-Between. 2016. (ENG.). 256p. (J). pap. 7.99 (978-1-61963-602-6(6), 9781619636026, Bloomsbury USA Childrens) Bloomsbury Publishing USA.

Destefano, Merrie. Lost Girls. 2017. (ENG.). 360p. (YA). pap. 9.99 (978-1-63375-605-2(X), 9781633756052) Entangled Publishing, LLC.

Devine, Eric. Look Past. 2016. (ENG.). 288p. (YA). (gr. 2-17). 16.95 (978-0-7624-5921-6(2), Running Pr. Kids) Running Pr. Bk. Pubs.

Devine, Ginger. The Missing Goose Egg: A Sam the Lamb Mystery. 2009. 32p. pap. 14.95 (978-1-4389-8839-9(7)) AuthorHouse.

Devlin Affair. 64p. (YA). (gr. 6-12). pap. (978-0-8224-2362-1(6)) Globe Fearon Educational Publishing.

Devlin, Wende. Cranberry Halloween. Devlin, Harry, illus. 2013. (Cranberryport Ser.). (ENG.). (J). (gr. -1-3). 18.95 (978-1-930900-69-1(4)) Purple Hse. Pr.

Diamond, Jill. Lou Lou & Pea & the Mural Mystery. Vamos, Lesley, illus. 2016. (ENG.). 272p. (J). 16.99 (978-0-374-30295-5(2), 9780374302955, Farrar, Straus & Giroux (BYR)) Farrar, Straus & Giroux.

The Diamond of Doom, 6 vols. (Woodland Mysteriestm Ser.). 133p. (gr. 3-7). 42.50 (978-0-7802-7927-8(1)) Wright Group/McGraw-Hill.

Diaz, Enrique Perez. Los Pelusos, Cuentos Policiacos. Martinez, Enrique, illus. 2003. (SPA.). 95p. (J). (gr. 3-5). pap. 8.95 (978-968-19-1018-1(4)) Santillana USA Publishing Co., Inc.

Dickens, Charles. Great Expectations: And Related Readings. 2006. (McDougal Littell Literature Connections Ser.). (ENG., Illus.). 704p. (gr. 10-10). lib. bdg. 18.50 (978-0-395-87484-4(X), 2-70843) Great Source Education Group, Inc.

Dickey, Janet. Anyone's Guess Jr: Who's a Fraidy Kat? 2003. 39.95 (978-1-57950-093-1(5), Upstart Bks.) Highsmith Inc.

Dickson, Diane. 3 Things That Might Have Happened. 2010. 100p. pap. 15.50 (978-1-4452-3414-4(9)) Lulu Pr., Inc.

Dickson, Robert. Sam Ferret Mysteries. 2010. 88p. pap. 14.95 (978-1-4259-2741-7(6)) AuthorHouse.

Dillon, Eilis. The Island of Horses. 2004. (New York Review Children's Collection). (ENG.). 224p. (J). (gr. 4-7). 17.95 (978-1-59017-102-8(0), NYR Children's Collection) New York Review of Bks., Inc., The.

Dillon, Kimberly M. The Ghosts of Wolf Creek. 2008. 73p. pap. 19.95 (978-1-60563-996-3(6)) America Star Bks.

Dionne, Erin. Moxie & the Art of Rule Breaking: A 14-Day Mystery. (ENG.). (J). (gr. 5). 2014. 288p. pap. 6.99 (978-0-14-242614-2(8), Puffin Books) 2013. 256p. 16.99 (978-0-8037-3871-3(4), Dial Bks) Penguin Young Readers Group.

DiOrio, Ariel, illus. The Mystery of the Missing Menorahs: A Hanukkah Humdinger! 2007. 52p. (J). pap. 9.95 (978-0-9659546-4-8(1)) Oak Leaf Systems.

Disney Book Group Staff & Richards, Kitty. The Lost Tiara. Disney Storybook Art Team & Studio Iboix Staff, illus. 2012. (Jewel Story Ser.). (ENG.). 96p. (J). (gr. 1-3). pap. 4.99 (978-1-4231-5197-5(6)) Disney Pr.

DiTocco, Robyn & DiTocco, Tony. Atlas' Revenge: Another Mad Myth Mystery. 2005. 234p. 19.95 (978-0-9723429-2-6(3)); pap. 11.95 (978-0-9723429-3-3(1)) Brainstorm Pubns., Inc.

Dittman, Jeffery. Jungle Heroes. 2013. 36p. pap. 15.95 (978-1-4327-9935-9(5)) Outskirts Pr., Inc.

Dixon, Franklin W. Bayport Buccaneers. 16th ed. 2007. (Hardy Boys (All New) Undercover Brothers Ser.: 16). (ENG., Illus.). 176p. (J). (gr. 3-7). pap. 5.99 (978-1-4169-3403-5(0), Aladdin) Simon & Schuster Children's Publishing.

—The Best of the Hardy Boys(r) Classic Collection: The House on the Cliff - The Ghost on Skeleton Rock - The Sting of the Scorpion, 2 vols. 2004. (Hardy Boys Ser.: 2). (ENG.). 546p.

(J). (gr. 3-7). 14.99 *(978-0-448-43628-9(0)*, Grosset & Dunlap) Penguin Young Readers Group.
—The Bicycle Thief. Burroughs, Scott, illus. 2011. (Hardy Boys: the Secret Files Ser.: 6). (ENG.). 96p. (J). (gr. 1-4). pap. 5.99 *(978-1-4169-9396-4(7)*, Aladdin) Simon & Schuster Children's Publishing.
—Blown Away. 10th ed. 2006. (Hardy Boys (All New) Undercover Brothers Ser.: 10). (ENG., Illus.). 160p. (J). (gr. 3-7). pap. 5.99 *(978-1-4169-1173-9(1)*, Aladdin) Simon & Schuster Children's Publishing.
—Boardwalk Bust, Vol. 3. 3rd ed. 2005. (Hardy Boys (All New) Undercover Brothers Ser.: 3). (ENG.). 176p. (J). (gr. 3-7). pap. 6.99 *(978-1-4169-0004-7(7)*, Aladdin) Simon & Schuster Children's Publishing.
—Bound for Danger. 2016. (Hardy Boys Adventures Ser.: 13). (ENG., Illus.). 144p. (J). (gr. 3-7). pap. 6.99 *(978-1-4814-6831-2(6)*, Aladdin) Simon & Schuster Children's Publishing.
—Burned. 2005. 154p. (J). lib. bdg. 16.92 *(978-1-4242-0391-8(0))* Fitzgerald Bks.
—Burned. 6th ed. 2005. (Hardy Boys (All New) Undercover Brothers Ser.: 6). (ENG., Illus.). 160p. (J). (gr. 3-7). pap. 5.99 *(978-1-4169-0008-5(X)*, Aladdin) Simon & Schuster Children's Publishing.
—Camping Chaos. 2014. (Hardy Boys: Secret Files Ser.: 16). lib. bdg. 16.00 *(978-0-606-36100-2(6))* Turtleback Bks.
—Comic con Artist. 21st ed. 2008. (Hardy Boys (All New) Undercover Brothers Ser.: 21). (ADY & ENG., Illus.). 192p. (J). (gr. 3-7). pap. 5.99 *(978-1-4169-5498-9(8)*, Aladdin) Simon & Schuster Children's Publishing.
—The Curse of the Ancient Emerald. 2015. (Hardy Boys Adventures Ser.: 9). (ENG., Illus.). 128p. (J). (gr. 3-7). pap. 6.99 *(978-1-4814-2475-2(0)*, Aladdin) Simon & Schuster Children's Publishing.
—The Dangerous Transmission. 2005. (Hardy Boys II Ser.: No. 184). 147p. (J). lib. bdg. 15.00 *(978-1-59054-850-9(7))* Fitzgerald Bks.
—Death & Diamonds. 15th ed. 2007. (Hardy Boys (All New) Undercover Brothers Ser.: 15). (ENG., Illus.). 176p. (J). (gr. 3-7). pap. 5.99 *(978-1-4169-3402-8(2)*, Aladdin) Simon & Schuster Children's Publishing.
—Deception on the Set. 2015. (Hardy Boys Adventures Ser.: 8). (ENG., Illus.). 128p. (J). (gr. 3-7). pap. 6.99 *(978-1-4814-1406-7(2)*, Aladdin) Simon & Schuster Children's Publishing.
—Double Down. 26th ed. 2008. (Hardy Boys (All New) Undercover Brothers Ser.: 26). (ENG.). 172p. (J). (gr. 3-7). pap. 5.99 *(978-1-4169-7446-8(6)*, Aladdin) Simon & Schuster Children's Publishing.
—Extreme Danger. 2005. (Hardy Boys (All New) Undercover Brothers Ser.: 1). (ENG.). 176p. (J). (gr. 3-7). pap. 5.99 *(978-1-4169-0002-3(0)*, Aladdin) Simon & Schuster Children's Publishing.
—Farming Fear. 2005. (Hardy Boys II Ser.: No. 188). 154p. (J). lib. bdg. 15.00 *(978-1-59054-839-4(6))* Fitzgerald Bks.
—Feeding Frenzy. 20th ed. 2008. (Hardy Boys (All New) Undercover Brothers Ser.: 20). (ENG., Illus.). 160p. (J). (gr. 3-7). pap. 7.99 *(978-1-4169-5499-6(6)*, Aladdin) Simon & Schuster Children's Publishing.
—Fossil Frenzy. 2014. (Hardy Boys: Secret Files Ser.: 14). lib. bdg. 16.00 *(978-0-606-35434-9(4))* Turtleback Bks.
—Foul Play. 19th ed. 2007. (Hardy Boys (All New) Undercover Brothers Ser.: 19). (ENG., Illus.). 192p. (J). (gr. 3-7). pap. 5.99 *(978-1-4169-4977-0(1)*, Aladdin) Simon & Schuster Children's Publishing.
—The Great Escape. Burroughs, Scott, illus. 2015. (Hardy Boys: the Secret Files Ser.: 17). (ENG.). 112p. (J). (gr. 1-4). pap. 4.99 *(978-1-4814-2267-3(7)*, Aladdin) Simon & Schuster Children's Publishing.
—Hardy Boys Collector's Boxed Set. 2010. (Hardy Boys Ser.). (ENG., Illus.). 1250p. (gr. 3). 75.00 *(978-1-55709-153-6(6))* Applewood Bks.
—Haunted. 2008. (Hardy Boys Undercover Brothers: Super Mystery Ser.). (ENG., Illus.). 192p. (J). (gr. 3-7). pap. 5.99 *(978-1-4169-6169-7(0)*, Aladdin) Simon & Schuster Children's Publishing.
—Hazed. 14th ed. 2007. (Hardy Boys (All New) Undercover Brothers Ser.: 14). (ENG., Illus.). 160p. (J). (gr. 3-7). pap. 6.99 *(978-1-4169-1803-5(5)*, Aladdin) Simon & Schuster Children's Publishing.
—The Hidden Harbor Mystery, No. 14. Gretter, J. Clemens, illus. 2003. (Hardy Boys Ser.). (ENG.). 228p. (J). (gr. 4-7). 14.95 *(978-1-55709-272-4(9))* Applewood Bks.
—House Arrest. 23rd ed. 2008. (Hardy Boys (All New) Undercover Brothers Ser.: 23). (ENG., Illus.). 176p. (J). (gr. 3-7). pap. 5.99 *(978-1-4169-6171-0(2)*, Aladdin) Simon & Schuster Children's Publishing.
—Hurricane Joe. 11th ed. 2006. (Hardy Boys (All New) Undercover Brothers Ser.: 11). (ENG., Illus.). 160p. (J). (gr. 3-7). pap. 5.99 *(978-1-4169-1174-6(X)*, Aladdin) Simon & Schuster Children's Publishing.
—In Plane Sight. 2005. (Hardy Boys I Ser.: No. 176). 148p. (J). lib. bdg. 15.00 *(978-1-59054-842-4(6))* Fitzgerald Bks.
—Kickoff to Danger. 2005. (Hardy Boys I Ser.: No. 170). 149p. (J). lib. bdg. 15.00 *(978-1-59054-843-1(4))* Fitzgerald Bks.
—Kidnapped at the Casino. 2007. (Hardy Boys Undercover Brothers: Super Mystery Ser.: 2). (ENG., Illus.). 240p. (J). (gr. 3-7). pap. 5.99 *(978-1-4169-3923-8(7)*, Aladdin) Simon & Schuster Children's Publishing.
—Line of Fire. (Illus.). (J). mass mkt. 2.95 *(978-0-671-70492-6(3)*, Simon Pulse) Simon Pulse.
—The Madman of Black Bear Mountain. 2016. (Hardy Boys Adventures Ser.: 12). (ENG., Illus.). 144p. (J). (gr. 3-7). pap. 6.99 *(978-1-4814-3880-3(8)*, Aladdin) Simon & Schuster Children's Publishing.
—The Missing Playbook. David, Matt, illus. 2016. (Hardy Boys Clue Book Ser.: 2). (ENG.). 96p. (J). (gr. 1-4). pap. 5.99 *(978-1-4814-5177-2(4)*, Aladdin) Simon & Schuster Children's Publishing.
—Motocross Madness. 2005. (Hardy Boys II Ser.: No. 190). 154p. (J). lib. bdg. 15.00 *(978-1-59054-844-8(2))* Fitzgerald Bks.
—The Mummy's Curse. 13th ed. 2006. (Hardy Boys (All New) Undercover Brothers Ser.: 13). (ENG., Illus.). 176p. (J). (gr. 3-7). pap. 5.99 *(978-1-4169-1507-2(9)*, Aladdin) Simon & Schuster Children's Publishing.
—Murder at the Mall. 17th ed. 2007. (Hardy Boys (All New) Undercover Brothers Ser.: 17). (ENG., Illus.). 176p. (J). (gr. 3-7). pap. 5.99 *(978-1-4169-3930-6(X)*, Aladdin) Simon & Schuster Children's Publishing.
—Murder House, Bk. 3. 24th ed. 2008. (Hardy Boys (All New) Undercover Brothers Ser.: 24). (ENG.). 160p. (J). (gr. 3-7). pap. 6.99 *(978-1-4169-6409-4(6)*, Aladdin) Simon & Schuster Children's Publishing.
—The Mystery of the Black Rhino. 2005. (Hardy Boys I Ser.: No. 178). 151p. (J). lib. bdg. 15.00 *(978-1-59054-851-6(5))* Fitzgerald Bks.
—No Way Out. 2005. (Hardy Boys II Ser.: No. 187). 149p. (J). lib. bdg. 15.00 *(978-1-59054-845-5(0))* Fitzgerald Bks.
—One False Step. 2005. (Hardy Boys II Ser.: No. 189). 150p. (J). lib. bdg. 15.00 *(978-1-59054-846-2(9))* Fitzgerald Bks.
—Passport to Danger. 2005. (Hardy Boys I Ser.: No. 179). 147p. (J). lib. bdg. 15.00 *(978-1-59054-847-9(7))* Fitzgerald Bks.
—Pushed. 18th ed. 2007. (Hardy Boys (All New) Undercover Brothers Ser.: 18). (ENG., Illus.). 160p. (J). (gr. 3-7). pap. 5.99 *(978-1-4169-4802-5(3)*, Aladdin) Simon & Schuster Children's Publishing.
—The Race Is On. Burroughs, Scott, illus. 2015. (Hardy Boys: the Secret Files Ser.: 19). (ENG.). 96p. (J). (gr. 1-4). pap. 5.99 *(978-1-4814-2271-0(5)*, Aladdin) Simon & Schuster Children's Publishing.
—The Race Is On. 2015. (Hardy Boys: Secret Files Ser.: 19). lib. bdg. 16.00 *(978-0-606-37840-6(5))* Turtleback Bks.
—Running on Fumes. 2005. 150p. (J). lib. bdg. 16.92 *(978-1-4242-0384-0(8))* Fitzgerald Bks.
—Running on Fumes, Vol. 2. 2nd ed. 2005. (Hardy Boys (All New) Undercover Brothers Ser.: 2). (ENG.). 160p. (J). (gr. 3-7). pap. 6.99 *(978-1-4169-0003-0(9)*, Aladdin) Simon & Schuster Children's Publishing.
—The Secret of the Soldier's Gold. 2005. (Hardy Boys II Ser.: No. 182). 147p. (J). lib. bdg. 15.00 *(978-1-59054-852-3(3))* Fitzgerald Bks.
—Ship of Secrets. 2014. (Hardy Boys: Secret Files Ser.: 15). lib. bdg. 14.75 *(978-0-606-35781-4(5))* Turtleback Bks.
—Showdown at Widow Creek. 2016. (Hardy Boys Adventures Ser.: 11). (ENG., Illus.). 128p. (J). (gr. 3-7). 17.99 *(978-1-4814-3878-0(6)*, Aladdin) Simon & Schuster Children's Publishing.
—The Sinister Sign Post, No. 15. 2004. (Hardy Boys Ser.). (ENG.). 228p. (J). (gr. 4-7). 17.95 *(978-1-55709-273-1(7))* Applewood Bks.
—Skin & Bones. 2005. (Hardy Boys I Ser.: No. 164). 148p. (J). lib. bdg. 15.00 *(978-1-59054-848-6(5))* Fitzgerald Bks.
—Speed Times Five. 2005. (Hardy Boys I Ser.: No. 173). 150p. (J). lib. bdg. 15.00 *(978-1-59054-849-3(3))* Fitzgerald Bks.
—Talent Show Tricks. David, Matt, illus. 2016. (Hardy Boys Clue Book Ser.: 4). (ENG.). 96p. (J). (gr. 1-4). pap. 5.99 *(978-1-4814-5180-2(4)*, Aladdin) Simon & Schuster Children's Publishing.
—Top Ten Ways to Die. 2006. 169p. (J). lib. bdg. 16.92 *(978-1-4242-0390-1(2))* Fitzgerald Bks.
—Training for Trouble. 2005. (Hardy Boys I Ser.: No. 161). 147p. (J). lib. bdg. 15.00 *(978-1-59054-853-0(1))* Fitzgerald Bks.
—Trick-or-Trouble. 2005. (Hardy Boys I Ser.: No. 175). 154p. (J). lib. bdg. 15.00 *(978-1-59054-854-7(X))* Fitzgerald Bks.
—Trouble in Paradise. 12th ed. 2006. (Hardy Boys (All New) Undercover Brothers Ser.: 12). (ENG., Illus.). 176p. (J). (gr. 3-7). pap. 5.99 *(978-1-4169-1178-4(2)*, Aladdin) Simon & Schuster Children's Publishing.
—Trouble in Warp Space. 2005. (Hardy Boys I Ser.: No. 172). 154p. (J). lib. bdg. 15.00 *(978-1-59054-855-4(8))* Fitzgerald Bks.
—Tunnel of Secrets. 2015. (Hardy Boys Adventures Ser.: 10). (ENG., Illus.). 144p. (J). (gr. 3-7). pap. 6.99 *(978-1-4814-3874-2(3)*, Aladdin) Simon & Schuster Children's Publishing.
—The Video Game Bandit. David, Matt, illus. 2016. (Hardy Boys Clue Book Ser.: 1). (ENG.). 96p. (J). (gr. 1-4). 16.99 *(978-1-4814-5053-9(0))*; pap. 5.99 *(978-1-4814-5052-2(2))* Simon & Schuster Children's Publishing. (Aladdin).
—Wanted. 2006. (Hardy Boys Undercover Brothers: Super Mystery Ser.: 1). (ENG., Illus.). 192p. (J). (gr. 3-7). pap. 5.99 *(978-1-4169-1258-3(4)*, Aladdin) Simon & Schuster Children's Publishing.
—Warehouse Rumble. 2005. (Hardy Boys II Ser.: No. 183). 152p. (J). lib. bdg. 15.00 *(978-1-59054-858-5(2))* Fitzgerald Bks.
—Water-Ski Wipeout. David, Matt, illus. 2016. (Hardy Boys Clue Book Ser.: 3). (ENG.). 96p. (J). (gr. 1-4). pap. 5.99 *(978-1-4814-5055-3(7)*, Aladdin) Simon & Schuster Children's Publishing.
—Wreck & Roll. 2005. (Hardy Boys II Ser.: No. 185). 153p. (J). lib. bdg. 15.00 *(978-1-59054-859-2(0))* Fitzgerald Bks.
Dixon, Franklin W. & Frost, Michael. Double Trouble. 25th ed. 2008. (Hardy Boys (All New) Undercover Brothers Ser.: 25). (ENG.). 176p. (J). (gr. 3-7). pap. 5.99 *(978-1-4169-6765-1(6)*, Aladdin) Simon & Schuster Children's Publishing.
Dixon, Franklin W. & Keele, Kevin. A con Artist in Paris. 2017. (Hardy Boys Adventures Ser.: 15). (ENG.). 128p. (J). (gr. 3-7). 17.99 ***(978-1-4814-9007-8(9))***; pap. 6.99 ***(978-1-4814-9006-1(0))*** Simon & Schuster Children's Publishing. (Aladdin).
Dixon, Franklin W. & Keene, Carolyn. Bonfire Masquerade. 2011. (Nancy Drew/Hardy Boys Ser.: 5). (ENG.). 176p. (J). (gr. 3-7). pap. 6.99 *(978-1-4424-0328-4(4)*, Aladdin) Simon & Schuster Children's Publishing.
Dixon, Franklin W. & Walker, Jeff. The Mystery of the Black Rhino. 178th ed. 2003. (Hardy Boys Ser.: 178). (ENG., Illus.). 160p. (J). (gr. 3-7). pap. 6.99 *(978-0-689-85598-6(2)*, Aladdin) Simon & Schuster Children's Publishing.
—Passport to Danger, Vol. 179. 179th ed. 2003. (Hardy Boys Ser.: 179). (ENG., Illus.). 160p. (J). (gr. 3-7). pap. 5.99 *(978-0-689-85779-9(9)*, Aladdin) Simon & Schuster Children's Publishing.
—Typhoon Island, Vol. 180. 2003. (Hardy Boys Ser.: 180). (ENG., Illus.). 160p. (J). (gr. 3-7). pap. 5.99 *(978-0-689-85884-0(1)*, Aladdin) Simon & Schuster Children's Publishing.
d'Lacey, Chris. A Dark Inheritance. 2014. (UFiles Ser.). (ENG.). 304p. (J). (gr. 3-7). 16.99 *(978-0-545-60876-3(7)*, Scholastic Pr.) Scholastic, Inc.
—The Fire Eternal. 2010. (Last Dragon Chronicles Ser.: 4). (ENG.). 512p. (J). (gr. 3-7). 8.99 *(978-0-545-05164-4(9)*, Orchard Bks.) Scholastic, Inc.
—UFiles #1: a Dark Inheritance. 2014. (UFiles Ser.: 1). (ENG.). 304p. (J). (gr. 3-7). pap. 7.99 *(978-0-545-60878-7(3)*, Scholastic Paperbacks) Scholastic, Inc.
Dobinson, Tony. The Crossing. 2006. 158p. (YA). (gr. 8-12). per. 10.00 *(978-1-84427-003-3(3))* Send The Light Distribution LLC.
Doering Tourville, Amanda. Community Helper Mysteries. 2011. (Community Helper Mysteries Ser.). (ENG.). 24p. (gr. k-1). lib. bdg. 79.95 *(978-1-4296-6084-6(8)*, Pebble Plus) Capstone Press of Coughlan Cos.
Doerr, Bonnie J. Kenzie's Key. Aberle, Xylena Apotheloz, illus. 2003. 211p. (J). 16.95 *(978-0-9619155-6-8(0))* Laurel & Herbert, Inc.
Dominguez, Elaudy. The Mountain Mystery. 2006. (Neighborhood Readers Ser.). (ENG.). 16p. (gr. 1-3). pap. 6.50 *(978-1-4042-7124-1(4)*, Rosen Classroom) Rosen Publishing Group, Inc., The.
Donbavand, Tommy. Cyber Shock. Gibbons, Alan, ed. 2014. (Read On Ser.). (ENG., Illus.). 640p. (YA). (gr. 7). 9.99 *(978-0-00-746473-9(8))* HarperCollins Pubs. Ltd. GBR. Dist: Independent Pubs. Group.
Donnell, Annie Hamilton. Four Girls & a Compact. 2005. 76p. pap. 10.95 *(978-1-59540-606-4(9)*, 1st World Library - Literary Society) 1st World Publishing, Inc.
—Four Girls & A Compact. 2005. 26.95 *(978-1-4218-0906-9(0)*, 1st World Library - Literary Society) 1st World Publishing, Inc.
—Four Girls & A Compact. 2004. reprint ed. pap. 15.95 *(978-1-4191-2048-0(4))*; pap. 1.99 *(978-1-4192-2048-7(9))* Kessinger Publishing, LLC.
Dorato, A. P. Arthur, Donna, & the Magic Crown of Tiabora. 2006. pap. 24.95 *(978-1-4137-8898-3(X))* PublishAmerica, Inc.
Doro, Ann. The Missing Canary. l.t. ed. 2005. 93p. 12.95 *(978-0-9745052-2-0(6)*, Peeper & Friends) Tree Of Life Publishing.
Dorpinghaus, Penny. Fear Balls & Button Wads. 2006. 52p. pap. 16.95 *(978-1-4241-2281-3(3))* PublishAmerica, Inc.
Double Deception, Bk. 3. 2009. (Hardy Boys (All New) Undercover Brothers Ser.: 27). (ENG.). 176p. (J). (gr. 3-7). pap. 5.99 *(978-1-4169-6766-8(4)*, Aladdin) Simon & Schuster Children's Publishing.
Dowd, Siobhan. The London Eye Mystery. 2009. (ENG.). 336p. (J). (gr. 3-7). 7.99 *(978-0-385-75184-1(2)*, Yearling) Random Hse. Children's Bks.
—The London Eye Mystery. 2009. lib. bdg. 18.40 *(978-0-606-14413-1(7)*, Turtleback) Turtleback Bks.
Dower, Laura. On the Case. 2004. 170p. (J). lib. bdg. 16.92 *(978-1-4242-0648-3(0))* Fitzgerald Bks.
Doyle, Arthur Conan. The Adventures of Sherlock Holmes: With a Discussion of Curiosity. Butterfield, Ned, tr. Butterfield, Ned, illus. 2003. (Values in Action Illustrated Classics Ser.). (J). *(978-1-59203-045-3(9))* Learning Challenge, Inc.
—The Boys' Sherlock Holmes. Haycraft, Howard, ed. 2011. 366p. 51.95 *(978-1-258-00844-4(0))* Literary Licensing, LLC.
—The Extraordinary Cases of Sherlock Holmes. 2010. (Puffin Classics Ser.). (ENG.). 304p. (J). (gr. 5-7). pap. 5.99 *(978-0-14-133004-4(X)*, Puffin Books) Penguin Young Readers Group.
—The Hound of the Baskervilles. 2004. (Fast Track Classics Ser.). (Illus.). 48p. (J). pap. *(978-0-237-52402-9(3))* Evans Brothers, Ltd.
—The Hound of the Baskervilles. 2008. (Bring the Classics to Life Ser.). (Illus.). 72p. (gr. 5-12). pap., act. bk. ed. 10.95 *(978-0-931334-67-2(5)*, EDCTR-502B) EDCON Publishing Group.
—The Hound of the Baskervilles. 2012. (Puffin Classics Ser.). (ENG.). 256p. (J). (gr. 5). pap. 5.99 *(978-0-14-132939-0(4)*, Puffin Books) Penguin Young Readers Group.
—The Man with the Twisted Lip - Lego - the Adventures of Sherlock Holmes. Macaluso, James, illus. 2014. (ENG.). pap. *(978-1-78092-698-8(7))* MX Publishing, Ltd.
—El Sabueso de Los Baskerville, 1 vol. Ferran, Adriana & Ferran, Daniel, illus. 2010. (Classic Fiction Ser.). (SPA.). 72p. (gr. 2-3). 27.99 *(978-1-4342-2325-8(6)*, Graphic Revolve en Español) Stone Arch Bks.
—Sherlock Holmes. 2003. (Retold Ser.). (Illus.). 282p. (J). (gr. 7-18). 15.99 *(978-0-7569-1196-6(6))* Perfection Learning Corp.
—Sherlock Holmes & a Scandal in Bohemia. Rohrbach, Sophie, illus. 2010. (On the Case with Holmes & Watson Ser.: 1). (ENG.). 48p. (J). (gr. 4-6). lib. bdg. 27.93 *(978-0-7613-6185-5(5))* Lerner Publishing Group.
—Sherlock Holmes & the Adventure at the Abbey Grange. Rohrbach, Sophie, illus. 2010. (On the Case with Holmes & Watson Ser.: 2). (ENG.). 48p. (J). (gr. 4-6). lib. bdg. 27.93 *(978-0-7613-6189-3(8))* Lerner Publishing Group.
—Sherlock Holmes & the Adventure of Black Peter. Rohrbach, Sophie & Morrow, J. T., illus. 2012. (On the Case with Holmes & Watson Ser.: 11). (ENG.). 48p. (J). (gr. 4-6). lib. bdg. 27.93 *(978-0-7613-7092-5(7))* Lerner Publishing Group.
—Sherlock Holmes & the Adventure of Black Peter. Rohrbach, Sophie & Morrow, J. T., illus. 2012. (On the Case with Holmes & Watson Ser.). 48p. (J). (gr. 4-6). pap. 39.62 *(978-0-7613-9274-3(2))*; (ENG.). pap. 6.95 *(978-0-7613-7100-7(1))* Lerner Publishing Group. (Graphic Universe™).
—Sherlock Holmes & the Adventure of the Blue Gem. Rohrbach, Sophie, illus. 2010. (On the Case with Holmes & Watson Ser.: 3). (ENG.). 48p. (J). (gr. 4-6). lib. bdg. 27.93 *(978-0-7613-6190-9(1))* Lerner Publishing Group.
—Sherlock Holmes & the Adventure of the Cardboard Box. Rohrbach, Sophie & Morrow, J. T., illus. 2012. (On the Case with Holmes & Watson Ser.: 12). (ENG.). 48p. (J). (gr. 4-6). lib. bdg. 27.93 *(978-0-7613-7090-1(0))* Lerner Publishing Group.
—Sherlock Holmes & the Adventure of the Cardboard Box. Rohrbach, Sophie & Morrow, J. T., illus. 2012. (On the Case with Holmes & Watson Ser.). 48p. (J). (gr. 4-6). pap. 39.62 *(978-0-7613-9275-0(0))*; (ENG.). pap. 6.95 *(978-0-7613-7098-7(6))* Lerner Publishing Group. (Graphic Universe™).
—Sherlock Holmes & the Adventure of the Dancing Men. Rohrbach, Sophie, illus. 2010. (On the Case with Holmes & Watson Ser.: 4). (ENG.). 48p. (J). (gr. 4-6). lib. bdg. 27.93 *(978-0-7613-6188-6(X))* Lerner Publishing Group.
—Sherlock Holmes & the Adventure of the Sussex Vampire. Rohrbach, Sophie, illus. 2010. (On the Case with Holmes & Watson Ser.: 6). (ENG.). 48p. (J). (gr. 4-6). lib. bdg. 27.93 *(978-0-7613-6187-9(1))* Lerner Publishing Group.
—Sherlock Holmes & the Adventure of the Three Garridebs. Rohrbach, Sophie & Morrow, J. T., illus. 2012. (On the Case with Holmes & Watson Ser.). 48p. (J). (gr. 4-6). pap. 39.62 *(978-0-7613-9276-7(9))*; (ENG.). pap. 6.95 *(978-0-7613-7099-4(4))* Lerner Publishing Group. (Graphic Universe™).
—Sherlock Holmes & the Boscombe Valley Mystery. Rohrbach, Sophie & Morrow, J. T., illus. 2011. (On the Case with Holmes & Watson Ser.: 10). (ENG.). 48p. (J). (gr. 4-6). 27.93 *(978-0-7613-7089-5(7))*; pap. 6.95 *(978-0-7613-7097-0(8))* Lerner Publishing Group. (Graphic Universe™).
—Sherlock Holmes & the Case of the Hound of the Baskervilles. Vogel, Malvina G., ed. Marcos, Pablo, illus. 2006. 237p. (YA). (gr. 4-8). 10.00 *(978-0-7567-9834-5(5))* DIANE Publishing Co.
—Sherlock Holmes & the Gloria Scott. Rohrbach, Sophie & Morrow, J. T., illus. 2012. (On the Case with Holmes & Watson Ser.: 14). (ENG.). 48p. (J). (gr. 4-6). lib. bdg. 27.93 *(978-0-7613-7093-2(5))* Lerner Publishing Group.
—Sherlock Holmes & the Gloria Scott. Rohrbach, Sophie & Morrow, J. T., illus. 2012. (On the Case with Holmes & Watson Ser.). 48p. (J). (gr. 4-6). pap. 39.62 *(978-0-7613-9277-4(7))*; (ENG.). pap. 6.95 *(978-0-7613-7101-4(X))* Lerner Publishing Group. (Graphic Universe™).
—Sherlock Holmes & the Three Garridebs. Rohrbach, Sophie & Morrow, J. T., illus. 2012. (On the Case with Holmes & Watson Ser.: 13). (ENG.). 48p. (J). (gr. 4-6). lib. bdg. 27.93 *(978-0-7613-7091-8(9))* Lerner Publishing Group.
—A Study in Scarlet & Other Sherlock Holmes Adventures. 2011. (Oxford Children's Classics Ser.). (ENG.). 320p. (YA). 9.95 *(978-0-19-273283-5(8))* Oxford Univ. Pr., Inc.
—#07 Sherlock Holmes & the Redheaded League. Rohrbach, Sophie & Morrow, Jt, illus. 2011. (On the Case with Holmes & Watson Set II Ser.). pap. 39.62 *(978-0-7613-7609-5(7)*, Graphic Universe™) Lerner Publishing Group.
—#08 Sherlock Holmes & the Adventure at the Copper Beeches. Rohrbach, Sophie & Morrow, Jt, illus. 2011. (On the Case with Holmes & Watson Set II Ser.). (J). pap. 39.62 *(978-0-7613-7610-1(0)*, Graphic Universe™) Lerner Publishing Group.
—#09 Sherlock Holmes & the Adventure of the Six Napoleons. Rohrbach, Sophie & Morrow, Jt, illus. 2011. (On the Case with Holmes & Watson Set II Ser.). pap. 39.62 *(978-0-7613-7611-8(9)*, Graphic Universe™) Lerner Publishing Group.
—#10 Sherlock Holmes & the Boscombe Valley Mystery. Rohrbach, Sophie & Morrow, Jt, illus. 2011. (On the Case with Holmes & Watson Set II Ser.). pap. 39.62 *(978-0-7613-7612-5(7)*, Graphic Universe™) Lerner Publishing Group.
Doyle, Bill. Trapped! The 2031 Journal of Otis Fitzmorgan. 6th ed. 2006. (ENG., Illus.). 144p. (J). (gr. 3-7). per. 16.99 *(978-0-316-05754-7(1))* Little, Brown Bks. for Young Readers.
Doyle, Bill H. Betrayed! The 1977 Journal of Zeke Moorie. 4th ed. 2006. (ENG., Illus.). 144p. (J). (gr. 3-7). per. 16.99 *(978-0-316-05741-7(X))* Little, Brown Bks. for Young Readers.
Doyle, Patrick H. T. Edgar Font's Hunt for a House to Haunt: Adventure Three: the Flint Island Treehouse. 2008. (Illus.). 300p. (J). per. 7.99 *(978-0-9786132-2-8(8))* Armadillo Bks.
—Edgar Font's Hunt for a House to Haunt: Adventure Two: the Fakersville Power Station. Doyle, Patrick H. T., illus. 2007. (Edgar Font's Hunt for a House to Haunt Ser.). (Illus.). 303p. (J). (gr. 4-7). per. 7.99 *(978-0-9786132-1-1(X))* Armadillo Bks.
Draper, Sharon M. The Buried Bones Mystery. Watson, Jesse Joshua, illus. 2011. (Clubhouse Mysteries Ser.: 1). (ENG.). 112p. (J). (gr. 3-7). pap. 5.99 *(978-1-4424-2709-9(4)*, Aladdin) Simon & Schuster Children's Publishing.
—The Buried Bones Mystery. Watson, Jesse Joshua, illus. 2011. (Clubhouse Mysteries Ser.: 1). (ENG.). 112p. (J). (gr. 3-7). lib. bdg. 15.99 *(978-1-4424-2710-5(8)*, Simon & Schuster/Paula Wiseman Bks.) Simon & Schuster/Paula Wiseman Bks.
—Shadows of Caesar's Creek. Watson, Jesse Joshua, illus. 2011. (Clubhouse Mysteries Ser.: 3). (ENG.). 128p. (J). (gr. 3-7). 15.99 *(978-1-4424-2712-9(4))*; pap. 5.99 *(978-1-4424-2711-2(6))* Simon & Schuster Children's Publishing. (Aladdin).
Dubisch, Mike, illus. The Haunted Cabin Mystery. 2009. (Boxcar Children Graphic Novels Ser.: 9). (ENG.). 32p. (J). (gr. 1-5). pap. 6.99 *(978-0-8075-3180-8(4))* Whitman, Albert & Co.
—Mike's Mystery, No. 5. 2009. (Boxcar Children Graphic Novels Ser.). (ENG.). 32p. (J). (gr. 2-5). 6.99 *(978-0-8075-2871-6(4))* Whitman, Albert & Co.
—Mystery Ranch. 2009. (Boxcar Children Graphic Novels Ser.: 4). (ENG.). 32p. (J). (gr. 1-5). 6.99 *(978-0-8075-2870-9(6))* Whitman, Albert & Co.
—The Pizza Mystery. 2010. (Boxcar Children Graphic Novels Ser.: 11). (ENG.). 32p. (J). (gr. 1-5). pap. 6.99 *(978-0-8075-6537-7(7))* Whitman, Albert & Co.
—Tree House Mystery. 2009. (Boxcar Children Graphic Novels Ser.: 8). (ENG.). 32p. (J). (gr. 1-5). pap. 6.99 *(978-0-8075-8088-2(0))* Whitman, Albert & Co.
Ducharme, Huguette. Enquete Tres Speciale. Caron, Romi, illus. 2004. (Collection des 6 Ans: Vol. 32). (FRE.). 68p. (YA). 7.95 *(978-2-922565-94-2(7))* Editions de la Paix CAN. Dist: World of Reading, Ltd.
Duckett, Brenda. Casey's Shadow. 2008. pap. 10.96 *(978-0-615-17289-7(X))* Duckett, Brenda.
Dudley, Sean. Who's Afraid of the Pumpkin Man??? 2009. 47p. pap. 10.01 *(978-0-557-12616-3(9))* Lulu Pr., Inc.

Duey, Kathleen. Arthur. Epstein, Eugene, illus. Gould, Robert, photos by. 2005. (Time Soldiers Ser.: Vol. 4). (ENG.). 96p. (J). (gr. k-2). per. 5.95 *(978-1-929945-56-6(6))* Big Guy Bks., Inc.

—Leonardo. Epstein, Eugene, illus. 2009. (Time Soldiers Ser.). (ENG.). (J). (gr. k-2). 95p. 9.95 *(978-1-929945-89-4(2))*;Bk. 8. 48p. 15.95 *(978-1-929945-88-7(4))* Big Guy Bks., Inc.

—Time Soldiers - Patch. Epstein, Eugene, illus. Gould, Robert, photos by. 2005. (Time Soldiers Ser.: Bk. 3). (ENG.). 96p. (J). (gr. k-2). per. 5.95 *(978-1-929945-55-9(8))* Big Guy Bks., Inc.

Duff, Hilary. Devoted: An Elixir Novel. 2012. (Elixir Ser.). (ENG.). 368p. (YA). (gr. 9). pap. 9.99 *(978-1-4424-0856-2(1)*, Simon & Schuster Bks. For Young Readers) Simon & Schuster Bks. For Young Readers.

—Elixir. 2011. (Playaway Young Adult Ser.). (YA). 59.99 *(978-1-4417-7416-3(5))* Findaway World, LLC.

—Elixir. 2011. (Elixir Ser.). (ENG.). 336p. (YA). (gr. 9). pap. 9.99 *(978-1-4424-0854-8(5)*, Simon & Schuster Bks. For Young Readers) Simon & Schuster Bks. For Young Readers.

—True: An Elixir Novel. (Elixir Ser.). (ENG., 304p. (YA). (gr. 7). 2014. Illus.). pap. 9.99 *(978-1-4424-0858-6(8))* 2013. 17.99 *(978-1-4424-0857-9(X))* Simon & Schuster Bks. For Young Readers. (Simon & Schuster Bks. For Young Readers).

Duff, Hilary & Allen, Elise. Elixir. 2010. (Elixir Ser.). (ENG.). 336p. (YA). (gr. 9-18). 17.99 *(978-1-4424-0853-1(7)*, Simon & Schuster Bks. For Young Readers) Simon & Schuster Bks. For Young Readers.

Duffy, James. Desaparecida. (SPA.). 142p. (YA). (gr. 5-8). *(978-84-279-3200-5(6)*, NG4451) Noguer y Caralt Editores, S. A. ESP. Dist: Lectorum Pubns., Inc.

Duffris, William, reader. The Case of the Climbing Cat. 2004. (High-Rise Private Eyes Ser.: No. 2). (Illus.). (J). (gr. -1-2). pap. 31.95 incl. audio compact disk *(978-1-59112-612-6(6))* Live Oak Media.

Dumas Lachtman, Ofelia. Looking for la Unica. 2004. (ENG & SPA., Illus.). 190p. (J). pap. 9.95 *(978-1-55885-412-3(6)*, Piñata Books) Arte Publico Pr.

Duncan, Lois. Don't Look Behind You. 2010. (ENG.). 240p. (YA). (gr. 7-17). pap. 10.99 *(978-0-316-12658-8(6))* Little, Brown Bks. for Young Readers.

—Don't Look Behind You, 6 vols. 2004. (J). 82.75 *(978-1-4025-5005-8(7))*; 1.25 *(978-1-4025-6754-4(5))* Recorded Bks., Inc.

—Don't Look Behind You. 2010. (YA). lib. bdg. 19.65 *(978-0-606-15155-9(9)*, Turtleback) Turtleback Bks.

—I Know What You Did Last Summer. 2011. (ENG.). 200p. (gr. 6-10). 19.00 *(978-1-60686-921-5(3))* Perfection Learning Corp.

—Killing Mr. Griffin. 2010. (ENG.). 272p. (YA). (gr. 7-17). pap. 10.99 *(978-0-316-09900-4(7))* Little, Brown Bks. for Young Readers.

—Killing Mr. Griffin. 2009. 7.61 *(978-0-7848-3597-5(7)*, Everbind) Marco Bk. Co.

—Killing Mr. Griffin. 223p. (YA). (gr. 7-18). pap. 4.50 *(978-0-8072-1373-5(X)*, Listening Library) Random Hse. Audio Publishing Group.

—Locked in Time. 2011. (ENG.). 272p. (YA). (gr. 7-17). pap. 10.99 *(978-0-316-09902-8(3))* Little, Brown Bks. for Young Readers.

—Stranger with My Face. 235p. (YA). (gr. 7-18). pap. 4.99 *(978-0-8072-1371-1(3)*, Listening Library) Random Hse. Audio Publishing Group.

—The Third Eye. 2012. (ENG.). 288p. (YA). (gr. 7-17). pap. 10.99 *(978-0-316-09908-0(2))* Little, Brown Bks. for Young Readers.

Dunkleberger, Amy. Write a Mystery in 5 Simple Steps. 2012. (Creative Writing in 5 Simple Steps Ser.). (Illus.). 48p. (J). (gr. 5-9). 25.27 *(978-0-7660-3835-6(1))* Enslow Pubs., Inc.

Dunlap, Susanne. The Musician's Daughter. (ENG.). (YA). (gr. 7). 2010. 352p. pap. 8.99 *(978-1-59990-452-8(7)*, 9781599904528) 2009. 336p. 16.99 *(978-1-59990-332-3(6)*, 9781599903323) Bloomsbury Publishing USA. (Bloomsbury USA Childrens).

Dunlop, Ed. Sherlock Jones: The Assassination Plot. 2004. 116p. (J). 8.99 *(978-1-59166-315-7(6))* BJU Pr.

—Sherlock Jones: The Missing Diamond. 2005. (Sherlock Jones Ser.). 109p. (J). (gr. 3-7). per. 8.99 *(978-1-59166-316-4(4))* BJU Pr.

—Sherlock Jones: The Willoughby Bank Robbery. 2004. 96p. (J). 8.99 *(978-1-59166-314-0(8))* BJU Pr.

Dunn, Joeming. The Lighthouse Mystery. Dunn, Ben, illus. 2010. (Boxcar Children Graphic Novels Ser.: 14). (ENG.). 32p. (J). (gr. 2-5). pap. 6.99 *(978-0-8075-4547-8(3))* Whitman, Albert & Co.

—Mountain Top Mystery, No. 15. Dunn, Ben, illus. 2010. (Boxcar Children Graphic Novels Ser.: 15). (ENG.). 32p. (J). (gr. 1-5). pap. 6.99 *(978-0-8075-5294-0(1))* Whitman, Albert & Co.

—The Woodshed Mystery. Dunn, Ben, illus. 2010. (Boxcar Children Graphic Novels Ser.: 13). (ENG.). 32p. (J). (gr. 1-5). pap. 6.99 *(978-0-8075-9208-3(0))* Whitman, Albert & Co.

Dunn, Joeming & Dunn, Ben, illus. Houseboat Mystery. 2011. (Boxcar Children Graphic Novels Ser.: 16). (ENG.). 32p. (J). (gr. 1-5). pap. 6.99 *(978-0-8075-3395-6(5))* Whitman, Albert & Co.

Dunn, Joeming & Warner, Gertrude Chandler. The Lighthouse Mystery, 1 vol., Bk. 14. Dunn, Ben, illus. 2011. (Boxcar Children Graphic Novels Ser.). (ENG.). 32p. (J). (gr. 2-5). 28.50 *(978-1-61641-122-0(8))* ABDO Publishing Co.

—The Woodshed Mystery, 1 vol., Bk. 13. Dunn, Ben, illus. 2011. (Boxcar Children Graphic Novels Ser.). (ENG.). 32p. (J). (gr. 2-5). 28.50 *(978-1-61641-121-3(X))* ABDO Publishing Co.

Durant, Alan. Humpty Dumpty's Great Fall. Heming, Leah-Ellen, illus. 2012. (ENG.). 32p. (J). *(978-0-7787-8028-1(7))*; pap. *(978-0-7787-8039-7(2))* Crabtree Publishing Co.

—Little Bo-Peep's Missing Sheep. Heming, Leah-Ellen, illus. 2012. (ENG.). 32p. (J). *(978-0-7787-8029-8(5))*; pap. *(978-0-7787-8040-3(6))* Crabtree Publishing Co.

—Little Miss Muffet's Big Scare. Heming, Leah-Ellen, illus. 2012. (ENG.). 32p. (J). *(978-0-7787-8030-4(9))*; pap. *(978-0-7787-8041-0(4))* Crabtree Publishing Co.

—Old Mother Hubbard's Stolen Bone. Heming, Leah-Ellen, illus. 2012. (ENG.). 32p. (J). *(978-0-7787-8031-1(7))*; pap. *(978-0-7787-8042-7(2))* Crabtree Publishing Co.

Durst, Sarah Beth. Chasing Power. 2014. (ENG.). 376p. (YA). (gr. 9). 17.99 *(978-0-8027-3755-7(2)*, 9780802737557, Bloomsbury USA Childrens) Walker & Co.

Dyan, Penelope. Tammy's Left Shoe — -As Opposed to Her Right. Dyan, Penelope, illus. 2008. (Illus.). 44p. pap. 11.95 *(978-1-935118-41-1(2))* Bellissima Publishing, LLC.

Earhart, Kristin. Buttercup Mystery. Geddes, Serena, illus. 2015. (Marguerite Henry's Misty Inn Ser.: 2). (ENG.). 128p. (J). (gr. 2-5). pap. 5.99 *(978-1-4814-1416-6(X)*, Aladdin) Simon & Schuster Children's Publishing.

—Buttercup Mystery. 2015. (Marguerite Henry's Misty Inn Ser.: 2). lib. bdg. 16.00 *(978-0-606-37127-8(3))* Turtleback Bks.

East, Bob. Tommy Cat & the Haunted Well, 1 vol. 2009. 42p. pap. 24.95 *(978-1-60703-754-5(8))* America Star Bks.

Ecton, Emily. Night of the Living Lawn Ornaments. 2009. (ENG.). 240p. (J). (gr. 3-7). pap. 5.99 *(978-1-4169-6451-3(7)*, Aladdin) Simon & Schuster Children's Publishing.

Eden, Alexandra. The Duchess to the Rescue: A Bones & the Duchess Mystery. 2006. (Bones & the Duchess Mysteries Ser.). 120p. (J). (gr. 3-7). 16.00 *(978-1-888310-55-9(3))* Knoll, Allen A. Pubs.

—Holy Smoke: A Bones & the Duchess Mystery. 2004. (ENG., Illus.). 117p. (J). 16.00 *(978-1-888310-46-7(4))*; 128p. (YA). pap. 8.00 *(978-1-888310-47-4(2))* Knoll, Allen A. Pubs.

Edge, Christopher. The Black Crow Conspiracy. 2015. (Penelope Tredwell Mysteries Ser.: 3). (ENG.). 272p. (J). (gr. 3-7). 16.99 *(978-0-8075-0780-3(6))* Whitman, Albert & Co.

—Shadows of the Silver Screen. 2014. (Penelope Tredwell Mysteries Ser.: 2). (ENG.). 256p. (J). (gr. 3-7). 16.99 *(978-0-8075-7319-8(1))* Whitman, Albert & Co.

—Twelve Minutes to Midnight. 2014. (Penelope Tredwell Mysteries Ser.: Book 1). (ENG.). 256p. (J). (gr. 3-7). 16.99 *(978-0-8075-8133-9(X))* Whitman, Albert & Co.

Edwards, Jason. Will Allen & the Great Monster Detective: Chronicles of the Monster Detective Agency Volume 1. Friedman, Jeffrey, illus. l.t. ed. 2007. (Chronicles of the Monster Detective Agency Ser.: 1). (ENG.). 96p. (J). (gr. 2-6). per. 5.95 *(978-0-9789512-0-7(4))* Rogue Bear Pr.

Edwards, Julie Andrews & Hamilton, Emma Walton. Dragon: Hound of Honor. 2005. (ENG.). 208p. (J). (gr. 4-18). pap. 6.99 *(978-0-06-057121-4(7))* HarperCollins Pubs.

Edwards, Leo. Jerry Todd & the Rose-Colored Cat. 2007. 264p. 29.95 *(978-1-4344-9192-3(7))*; per. 19.95 *(978-1-4344-9098-8(X))* Wildside Pr., LLC.

—Poppy Ott Hits the Trail. Salg, Bert, illus. 2011. 218p. 44.95 *(978-1-258-10146-6(7))* Literary Licensing, LLC.

Eggleton, Jill. The Mystery of Missing Big Wig. (Sails Literacy Ser.). 24p. (gr. 3-18). 27.00 *(978-0-7578-6982-2(3))* Rigby Education.

Ehrenhaft, Daniel. Friend Is Not a Verb. 2010. (ENG.). 256p. (YA). (gr. 8-18). 16.99 *(978-0-06-113106-6(7)*, HarperTeen) HarperCollins Pubs.

Eisenstein, Ann. Fallen Prey, a Sean Gray Junior Special Agent Mystery. Waugh, Leslie, ed. 2013. 190p. pap. 9.99 *(978-1-935711-31-5(8))* Peak City Publishing, LLC.

Eisenstein, Ann E. Hiding Carly, a Sean Gray Junior Special Agent Mystery. 2013. 162p. pap. 9.99 *(978-1-935711-27-8(X))* Peak City Publishing, LLC.

Eldridge, Courtney. Ghost Time, 0 vols. unabr. ed. 2013. (ENG.). 416p. (YA). (gr. 9-12). 17.99 *(978-1-4778-1657-8(7)*, 9781477816578, Amazon Children's Publishing) Amazon Publishing.

Ellen, Raskin. The Westing Game. 2014. (Puffin Modern Classics Ser.). (ENG.). 192p. (J). (gr. 5-12). 12.24 *(978-1-63245-142-2(5))* Lectorum Pubns., Inc.

Elliott, Julia. Where Did God Come From? Elliott, Julia, illus. 2005. (Illus.). (J). 15.95 *(978-0-9764129-0-8(X))* Rain Tree Bks.

Ellis, Kat. Breaker. 2016. (ENG.). 336p. (YA). (gr. 2-17). pap. 9.95 *(978-0-7624-5908-7(5)*, Running Pr. Kids) Running Pr. Bk. Pubs.

Ellis, Sarah. Odd Man Out, 1 vol. 2008. (ENG.). 168p. (J). (gr. 3-7). pap. 8.95 *(978-0-88899-703-6(5))* Groundwood Bks. CAN. Dist: Publishers Group West (PGW).

Ellwand, Ruth & Ellwand, David. The Mystery of the Fool & the Vanisher. Ellwand, David, illus. 2008. (ENG., Illus.). 104p. (J). (gr. 5). 18.99 *(978-0-7636-2096-7(3))* Candlewick Pr.

Elston, Ashley. The Rules for Disappearing. 2014. (Rules Ser.). (ENG.). 336p. (YA). (gr. 7-12). pap. 8.99 *(978-1-4231-6926-0(3))* Hyperion Bks. for Children.

—This Is Our Story. 2016. (ENG.). 320p. (YA). (gr. 7-12). 17.99 *(978-1-4847-3089-8(5))* Hyperion Bks. for Children.

Elys Dayton, Arwen. Seeker. 2015. (Seeker Ser.). (ENG.). 480p. (YA). (gr. 9). pap. 9.99 *(978-0-385-74408-9(0)*, Ember) Random Hse. Children's Bks.

Emerson, Scott. The Case of the Cat with the Missing Ear: From the Notebooks of Edward R. Smithfield, D. V. M. Mullett, Viv, illus. 2011. (Adventures of Samuel Blackthorne Ser.: 1). (ENG.). 240p. (J). (gr. 3-7). pap. 11.99 *(978-0-689-87615-8(7)*, Simon & Schuster Bks. For Young Readers) Simon & Schuster Bks. For Young Readers.

Encyclopedia Brown & the Case of the Exploding Plumbing & Other Stories. 2003. (J). pap. 2.95 *(978-0-590-44093-6(4))* Scholastic, Inc.

Enright, Elizabeth. The Four-Story Mistake. Enright, Elizabeth, illus. 3rd ed. 2008. (Melendy Quartet Ser.: 2). (ENG., Illus.). 208p. (J). (gr. 3-7). per. 8.99 *(978-0-312-37599-7(9)*, 9780312375997) Square Fish.

—Spiderweb for Two: A Melendy Maze. Enright, Elizabeth, illus. 3rd ed. 2008. (Melendy Quartet Ser.: 4). (ENG., Illus.). 224p. (J). (gr. 3-7). per. 8.99 *(978-0-312-37601-7(4)*, 9780312376017) Square Fish.

Ensor, Rod. Getting It. 2007. 216p. per. 14.95 *(978-0-595-44800-5(3))* iUniverse, Inc.

Erickson, John R. The Big Question. Holmes, Gerald L., illus. 2012. 128p. (J). pap. *(978-1-59188-160-5(9))* Maverick Bks.

—The Big Question. Holmes, Gerald L., illus. 2012. (Hank the Cowdog Ser.: Vol. 60). (ENG.). 128p. (J). (gr. 3-6). 15.99 *(978-1-59188-260-2(5))* Maverick Bks., Inc.

—The Case of the Black-Hooded Hangmans. Holmes, Gerald L., illus. 2011. (Hank the Cowdog Ser.). (ENG.). 113p. (J). (gr. 3-6). pap. 5.99 *(978-1-59188-124-7(2))* Maverick Bks., Inc.

—The Case of the Burrowing Robot. Holmes, Gerald L., illus. 2011. (Hank the Cowdog Ser.). (ENG.). 125p. (J). (gr. 3-6). pap. 5.99 *(978-1-59188-142-1(0))* Maverick Bks., Inc.

—The Case of the Deadly Ha-Ha Game. Holmes, Gerald L., illus. 2011. (Hank the Cowdog Ser.). (ENG.). 128p. (J). (gr. 3-6). pap. 5.99 *(978-1-59188-137-7(4))* Maverick Bks., Inc.

—The Case of the Falling Sky. Holmes, Gerald L., illus. 2011. (Hank the Cowdog Ser.: No. 45). (ENG.). 129p. (J). (gr. 3-6). pap. 5.99 *(978-1-59188-145-2(5))* Maverick Bks., Inc.

—The Case of the Fiddle-Playing Fox. Holmes, Gerald L., illus. 2011. (Hank the Cowdog Ser.: No. 12). (ENG.). 118p. (J). (gr. 3-6). pap. 5.99 *(978-1-59188-112-4(9))* Maverick Bks., Inc.

—The Case of the Halloween Ghost. Holmes, Gerald L., illus. 2011. (Hank the Cowdog Ser.). (ENG.). 123p. (J). (gr. 3-6). pap. 5.99 *(978-1-59188-109-4(9))* Maverick Bks., Inc.

—The Case of the Kidnapped Collie. Holmes, Gerald L., illus. 2011. (Hank the Cowdog Ser.). (ENG.). 113p. (J). (gr. 3-6). pap. 5.99 *(978-1-59188-126-1(9))* Maverick Bks., Inc.

—The Case of the Midnight Rustler. Holmes, Gerald L., illus. 2011. (Hank the Cowdog Ser.: No. 19). (ENG.). 113p. (J). (gr. 3-6). pap. 5.99 *(978-1-59188-119-3(6))* Maverick Bks., Inc.

—The Case of the Most Ancient Bone. Holmes, Gerald L., illus. 2011. (Hank the Cowdog Ser.). (ENG.). 239p. (J). (gr. 3-6). pap. 5.99 *(978-1-59188-150-6(1))* Maverick Bks., Inc.

—The Case of the One-Eyed Killer Stud Horse. Holmes, Gerald L., illus. 2011. (Hank the Cowdog Ser.: No. 8). (ENG.). 120p. (J). (gr. 3-6). pap. 5.99 *(978-1-59188-108-7(0))* Maverick Bks., Inc.

—The Case of the Perfect Dog. Holmes, Gerald L., illus. 2012. 127p. (J). *(978-1-59188-259-6(1))* Maverick Bks.

—The Case of the Perfect Dog. Holmes, Gerald L., illus. 2012. (Hank the Cowdog (Quality) Ser.). (ENG.). 127p. (J). (gr. 3-6). pap. 5.99 *(978-1-59188-159-9(5))* Maverick Bks., Inc.

—The Case of the Secret Weapon. Holmes, Gerald L., illus. 2011. (Hank the Cowdog Ser.). (ENG.). 125p. (J). (gr. 3-6). pap. 5.99 *(978-1-59188-155-1(2))* Maverick Bks., Inc.

—The Case of the Tender Cheeping Chickies. Holmes, Gerald L., illus. 2011. (Hank the Cowdog Ser.). (ENG.). 129p. (J). (gr. 3-6). pap. 5.99 *(978-1-59188-147-6(1))* Maverick Bks., Inc.

—The Case of the Tricky Trap. Holmes, Gerald L., illus. 2011. (Hank the Cowdog Ser.). (ENG.). 126p. (J). (gr. 3-6). pap. 5.99 *(978-1-59188-146-9(3))* Maverick Bks., Inc.

—The Case of the Vampire Cat. Holmes, Gerald L., illus. 2011. (Hank the Cowdog Ser.). (ENG.). 115p. (J). (gr. 3-6). pap. 5.99 *(978-1-59188-121-6(8))* Maverick Bks., Inc.

—The Curse of the Incredible Priceless Corncob. Holmes, Gerald L., illus. 2011. (Hank the Cowdog Ser.: No. 7). (ENG.). 127p. (J). (gr. 3-6). pap. 5.99 *(978-1-59188-107-0(2))* Maverick Bks., Inc.

—The Disappearance of Drover. Holmes, Gerald L., illus. 2011. (Hank the Cowdog Ser.). (ENG.). 122p. (J). (gr. 3-6). pap. 5.99 *(978-1-59188-157-5(9))* Maverick Bks., Inc.

—The Garbage Monster from Outer Space. Holmes, Gerald L., illus. 2011. (Hank the Cowdog Ser.). (ENG.). 126p. (J). (gr. 3-6). pap. 5.99 *(978-1-59188-132-2(3))* Maverick Bks., Inc.

—It's a Dog's Life. Holmes, Gerald L., illus. (Hank the Cowdog Ser.: No. 3). 100p. (J). (gr. 2-5). 9.95 *(978-0-916941-04-8(3))* Maverick Bks., Inc.

—Murder in the Middle Pasture. Holmes, Gerald L., illus. 2011. (Hank the Cowdog Ser.). (ENG.). 120p. (J). (gr. 3-6). pap. 5.99 *(978-1-59188-104-9(8))* Maverick Bks., Inc.

—The Original Adventures of Hank the Cowdog. Holmes, Gerald L., illus. (ENG.). 127p. (J). (gr. 3-6). 2012. (Hank the Cowdog Ser.: Vol. 1). 15.99 *(978-1-59188-201-5(X))* 2011. (Hank the Cowdog Ser.: No. 1). pap. 5.99 *(978-1-59188-101-8(3))* Maverick Bks., Inc.

—The Phantom in the Mirror. Holmes, Gerald L., illus. 2011. (Hank the Cowdog Ser.: No. 20). (ENG.). 114p. (J). (gr. 3-6). pap. 5.99 *(978-1-59188-120-9(X))* Maverick Bks., Inc.

—The Quest for the Great White Quail. Holmes, Gerald L., illus. 2011. (Hank the Cowdog Ser.). (ENG.). 123p. (J). (gr. 3-6). pap. 5.99 *(978-1-59188-152-0(8))* Maverick Bks., Inc.

—The Return of the Charlie Monsters. Holmes, Gerald L., illus. 2014. 128p. (J). pap. *(978-1-59188-163-6(3))* Maverick Bks., Inc.

Erickson, John R. & Holmes, Gerald L., illus. The Case of the Prowling Bear. 2013. 126p. (J). *(978-1-59188-261-9(3))*; pap. *(978-1-59188-161-2(7))* Maverick Bks.

Erickson, Mary Ellen. What Happened to the Deer? Peanut Butter Club Mysteries. 2007. 182p. (J). 23.95 *(978-0-595-68396-3(7))*; per. 13.95 *(978-0-595-42799-4(5))* iUniverse, Inc.

—Who Jinxed the CG Ranch? 2009. 196p. 24.95 *(978-1-4401-4218-5(1))*; pap. 14.95 *(978-1-4401-4216-1(5))* iUniverse, Inc.

Ernst, Kathleen. Midnight in Lonesome Hollow: A Kit Mystery. 2007. (American Girl Mysteries Ser.). (ENG., Illus.). 192p. (gr. 4-7). 10.95 *(978-1-59369-161-5(0)*, American Girl) American Girl Publishing, Inc.

—Midnight in Lonesome Hollow: A Kit Mystery. Tibbles, Jean-Paul, illus. 2007. (ENG.). 192p. (gr. 4-7). pap. 6.95 *(978-1-59369-160-8(2)*, American Girl) American Girl Publishing, Inc.

—The Runaway Friend. Tibbles, Jean-Paul, illus. 2008. (ENG.). 192p. (gr. 3-7). pap. 6.95 *(978-1-59369-298-8(6))* American Girl Publishing, Inc.

—Whistler in the Dark. 2009. (Mysteries Through Time Ser.). 144 - 176p. (YA). (gr. 4-8). 31.95 *(978-1-60754-429-6(6))*; pap. 15.25 *(978-1-60754-432-6(6))* Windmill Bks.

Ervin, Randy. Maycroft From 232nd. 2010. 150p. (YA). pap. 10.00 *(978-0-578-05732-3(8))* Ervin, Randy.

Erwin, Vicki Berger. Elizabeth Bryan Mysteries Set, 6 vols. (Elizabeth Bryan Mysteries Ser.). (J). 29.99 *(978-0-7586-0008-0(9))* Concordia Publishing Hse.

Eschler, Linda. The Strawberry Fairies & the Secret of Mystery Island. 2008. 57p. pap. 16.95 *(978-1-60610-960-1(X))* America Star Bks.

—The Strawberry Fairies Save Sandcastle Island. 2007. 52p. per. 16.95 *(978-1-4241-9175-8(0))* America Star Bks.

Escott, John & Pearson Education Staff. Ghost of Genny Castle. 2nd ed. 2008. (ENG., Illus.). 48p. pap. 11.99 *(978-1-4058-6953-9(4))* Pearson Education.

Eskeland, N. L. Menace in the Walls: A Summer Project Turns Treacherous. 2004. (Joshua Keegan Mysteries Ser.). 142p. (J). per. 10.95 *(978-0-9673811-6-9(9))* Science2Discover, Inc.

Estes, Eleanor. The Alley. Ardizzone, Edward, illus. 2003. (ENG.). 288p. (J). (gr. 2-5). pap. 18.95 *(978-0-15-204918-8(5))* Houghton Mifflin Harcourt Publishing Co.

—The Alley. Ardizzone, Edward, illus. 2004. (Odyssey/Harcourt Young Classic Ser.). 283p. 15.95 *(978-0-7569-3475-0(3))* Perfection Learning Corp.

Etherly, L. D. Winter Arrives This Summer. 2012. 34p. pap. 12.95 *(978-0-9833877-1-8(0))* Inkspil Publishing.

Etienne, Doris. Jewels of Sofia Tate. 2009. (ENG.). 272p. (J). (gr. 6). pap. 12.99 *(978-1-55488-230-4(3)*, Dundurn Pr.) Dundurn CAN. Dist: Ingram Publisher Services.

Eulberg, Elizabeth. The Great Shelby Holmes. 2017. (ENG., Illus.). 272p. (J). pap. 7.99 ***(978-1-68119-053-2(2)***, 9781681190532, Bloomsbury USA Childrens) Bloomsbury Publishing USA.

Eulberg, Elizabeth. The Great Shelby Holmes: Girl Detective. 2016. (ENG., Illus.). 256p. (J). 16.99 *(978-1-68119-051-8(6)*, 9781681190518, Bloomsbury USA Childrens) Bloomsbury Publishing USA.

Eustace, Robert & Meade, L. T. A Master of Mysteries. Walton, J. Ambrose, illus. 2013. 106p. pap. 8.00 *(978-1-927558-41-6(7))* Birch Tree Publishing.

Evanovich, Alex & Evanovich, Janet. Troublemaker. Jackson, Dan, illus. 2011. (Alex Barnaby Ser.: Bk. 3). (ENG.). 112p. pap. 16.99 *(978-1-59582-722-7(6))* Dark Horse Comics.

Evatt, Harriet. The Mystery of the Alpine Castle. 2011. 242p. 46.95 *(978-1-258-08839-2(8))* Literary Licensing, LLC.

Everett, George W. G. W. Frog & the Haunted House in Misty Meadows. 2010. 44p. 16.95 *(978-1-4497-0752-1(1)*, WestBow Pr.) Author Solutions, Inc.

Everheart, Chris. Concrete Gallery. 2014. (ENG.). 96p. (J). *(978-1-63235-053-4(X))* Pr. Room Editions LLC.

Extreme Danger. 2007. 15.00 *(978-0-7569-7603-3(0))* Perfection Learning Corp.

Fairchild, Simone. The Plight of the Queen Bee. Key, Pamela, illus. 2006. 34p. (J). per. 17.95 *(978-0-9767732-3-8(6))* Black Jackal Bks. Ltd.

—Queen Bee's Midnight Caper, 3 vols. Key, Pamela Marie, illus. 2006. 33p. (J). (gr. -1-3). per. 17.95 *(978-0-9771971-4-9(X))* Brass Frog Bookworks.

Fairlie, Emily. The Lost Treasure of Tuckernuck. Caparo, Antonio Javier, illus. 2012. (Tuckernuck Mysteries Ser.). (ENG.). 304p. (J). (gr. 3-7). 16.99 *(978-0-06-211890-5(0)*, Tegen, Katherine Bks) HarperCollins Pubs.

—The Magician's Bird. Caparo, Antonio Javier, illus. 2014. (Tuckernuck Mysteries Ser.: 2). (ENG.). 288p. (J). (gr. 3-7). pap. 6.99 *(978-0-06-211894-3(3)*, Tegen, Katherine Bks) HarperCollins Pubs.

—The Magician's Bird. 2013. (Tuckernuck Mysteries Ser.: 2). (ENG.). 288p. (J). (gr. 3-7). 16.99 *(978-0-06-211893-6(5)*, Tegen, Katherine Bks) HarperCollins Pubs.

Fairstein, Linda. Into the Lion's Den. 2016. (Devlin Quick Mysteries Ser.). (ENG.). 320p. (J). (gr. 3-7). 16.99 *(978-0-399-18643-1(3)*, Dial Bks) Penguin Young Readers Group.

Falcone, L. M. The Ghost & Max Monroe, Case #1: The Magic Box. Smith, Kim, illus. 2014. (Ghost & Max Monroe Ser.). (ENG.). 88p. (J). (gr. 1-4). pap. 6.95 *(978-1-77138-017-1(9))* Kids Can Pr., Ltd. CAN. Dist: Hachette Bk. Group.

Falconer, Ian. Olivia y el Juguete Desaparecido. Mlawer, Teresa, tr. from ENG. Falconer, Ian, illus. 2004. (Olivia Ser.).Tr. of Olivia & the Missing Toy. (SPA., Illus.). 30p. (J). 16.95 *(978-1-930332-71-3(8))* Lectorum Pubns., Inc.

Falksen, G. D. The Transatlantic Conspiracy. Iwata, Nat, illus. 2016. (ENG.). 240p. (YA). (gr. 7). 18.99 *(978-1-61695-417-8(5)*, Soho Teen) Soho Pr., Inc.

Fangs for the Memories. 2008. (Looney Tunes 8*8 Ser.). 24p. pap. *(978-1-4075-2630-0(8))*; pap. *(978-1-4075-2640-9(5))* Parragon, Inc.

Fanning, Kieran. Code Crackers: Trapdoor to Treachery. 2010. (Dover Children's Classics Ser.). (ENG.). 128p. (J). (gr. 3-5). pap. 5.99 *(978-0-486-47880-7(7))* Dover Pubns., Inc.

—Code Crackers: Voyage to Victory. 2010. (Dover Children's Classics Ser.). (ENG., Illus.). 128p. (J). (gr. 3-5). pap. 5.99 *(978-0-486-47881-4(5))* Dover Pubns., Inc.

Fantaskey, Beth. Buzz Kill. 2015. (ENG.). 384p. (YA). (gr. 7). pap. 8.99 *(978-0-544-43943-6(0)*, HMH Books For Young Readers) Houghton Mifflin Harcourt Publishing Co.

—Isabel Feeney, Star Reporter. 2017. (ENG.). 352p. (J). (gr. 5-7). pap. 7.99 *(978-0-544-93696-6(5)*, HMH Books For Young Readers) Houghton Mifflin Harcourt Publishing Co.

—Isabel Feeney, Star Reporter. 2017. (ENG.). (J). (gr. 5-7). lib. bdg. 18.40 ***(978-0-606-39809-1(0))*** Turtleback Bks.

Farber, E. S. Fish Finelli (Book 1) Seagulls Don't Eat Pickles. Beene, Jason, illus. 2014. (Fish Finelli Ser.). (ENG.). 168p. (J). (gr. 3-7). pap. 6.99 *(978-1-4521-2853-5(7))* Chronicle Bks. LLC.

—Fish Finelli (Book 2) Operation Fireball. Beene, Jason, illus. 2015. (Fish Finelli Ser.). (ENG.). 184p. (J). (gr. 3-7). pap. 6.99 *(978-1-4521-2875-7(8))* Chronicle Bks. LLC.

Farrell-Whelan, Max. Something Fishy Aboard the Red Herring: Can You Catch the Killer? 2013. 130p. pap. 11.95 *(978-1-61204-239-8(2)*, Strategic Bk. Publishing) Strategic Book Publishing & Rights Agency (SBPRA).

Faulkner, Michael H. The Pearl Necklace: Miss Kitty Mysteries. 2006. (Illus.). 43p. (J). per. 21.95 *(978-1-59858-150-8(3))* Dog Ear Publishing, LLC.

Feagins, Sistah L. E. T. M. E. TELL'YA Bernadine. Hakim & Terrance Shadow Mystery ! 2009. 68p. pap. 15.72 *(978-0-557-09041-9(5))* Lulu Pr., Inc.

Feehan-Vileria, Elaine. The Legend of Old Mr. Clarke. 2004. 58p. per. 17.95 *(978-1-4116-1523-6(9))* Lulu Pr., Inc.

Feiffer, Kate. Signed by Zelda. (ENG.). 240p. (J). (gr. 3-7). 2013. pap. 6.99 *(978-1-4424-3332-8(9))* 2012. (Illus.). 16.99 *(978-1-4424-3331-1(0))* Simon & Schuster/Paula Wiseman Bks. (Simon & Schuster/Paula Wiseman Bks.).

Fein, Eric. Mystery at Manzanar: A WWII Internment Camp Story, 1 vol. Hartman, Kurt, illus. 2008. (Historical Fiction Ser.). (ENG.). 56p. (gr. 2-3). pap. 6.25 *(978-1-4342-0847-7(8)*, Graphic Flash) Stone Arch Bks.

Feinstein, John. Change-Up. 2010. (Sports Beat Ser.). (ENG.). 336p. (J). (gr. 5). 8.99 *(978-0-375-84759-2(6)*, Yearling) Random Hse. Children's Bks.

—Cover-Up: Mystery at the Super Bowl. 2008. (Sports Beat Ser.). (ENG.). 320p. (J). (gr. 5). 7.99 *(978-0-440-42205-1(1)*, Yearling) Random Hse. Children's Bks.

—Last Shot - Mystery at the Final Four. 2006. (Sports Beat Ser.). (ENG.). 272p. (J). (gr. 7-9). reprint ed. per. 8.99 (978-0-553-49460-0(0), Yearling) Random Hse. Children's Bks.

—Rush for the Gold: Mystery at the Olympics. 2013. (Sports Beat Ser.). (ENG.). 336p. (J). (gr. 5). pap. 7.99 (978-0-375-87168-9(3), Yearling) Random Hse. Children's Bks.

—Vanishing Act: Mystery at the U. S. Open. 2008. (Sports Beat Ser.). (ENG.). 304p. (J). (gr. 3-7). 7.99 (978-0-440-42125-2(X), Yearling) Random Hse. Children's Bks.

Feld, Ellen F. Annie: The Mysterious Morgan Horse. Mellin, Jeanne, illus. 2007. 206p. (J). per. 9.95 (978-0-9709002-9-6(5)) Willow Bend Publishing.

Ferguson, Alane. The Angel of Death. 2008. (Forensic Mystery Ser.). 258p. 17.00 (978-0-7569-8929-3(9)) Perfection Learning Corp.

—The Christopher Killer. 2008. (Forensic Mystery Ser.). (ENG.). 288p. (YA). (gr. 7-18). 7.99 (978-0-14-240811-7(5), Puffin Books) Penguin Young Readers Group.

—The Christopher Killer. 2008. (Forensic Mystery Ser.). 274p. (gr. 7-12). 17.00 (978-0-7569-8930-9(2)) Perfection Learning Corp.

Ferguson, Alane & Skurzynski, Gloria. Deadly Waters. 2007. (Mysteries in Our National Park Ser.). (ENG., Illus.). 160p. (J). (gr. 3-7). 4.99 (978-1-4263-0093-6(X), National Geographic Children's Bks.) National Geographic Society.

—Escape from Fear: A Mystery in Virgin Islands National Park. 2008. (Mysteries in Our National Park Ser.). (ENG., Illus.). 160p. (J). (gr. 3-7). mass mkt. 4.99 (978-1-4263-0181-0(2), National Geographic Children's Bks.) National Geographic Society.

—Running Scared. 2008. (Mysteries in Our National Park Ser.). (ENG., Illus.). 160p. (J). (gr. 3-7). mass mkt. 4.99 (978-1-4263-0182-7(0), National Geographic Children's Bks.) National Geographic Society.

Ferguson, Donald. Chums of Scranton High on the Cinder Pat. 2006. 25.95 (978-1-4218-2937-1(1)); pap. 10.95 (978-1-4218-3037-7(X)) 1st World Publishing, Inc.

—The Chums of Scranton High on the Cinder Path. 2007. 124p. per. (978-1-4065-2363-8(1)) Dodo Pr.

Ferguson, Dwayne. Ghost Ranch: The Legend of Mad Jake, 2004. (Kid Caramel: Bk. 4). (J). pap. 4.50 (978-0-940975-17-0(3), Sankofa Bks.) Just Us Bks., Inc.

Ferraiolo, Jack D. The Big Splash. 2008. (ENG.). 288p. (YA). (gr. 5-9). 16.95 (978-0-8109-7067-0(8), Amulet Bks.) Abrams, Inc.

—The Quick Fix. 2012. (ENG.). 304p. (J). (gr. 3-7). 16.95 (978-0-8109-9725-7(8), Amulet Bks.) Abrams, Inc.

Ferraro, Maureen. Sugar & Els: The Mystery. 2011. 28p. pap. 15.99 (978-1-4628-5347-2(1)) Xlibris Corp.

Ferrell, Deen. Cryptic Spaces: Book One. 2013. 396p. pap. 16.95 (978-1-60047-864-2(6)) Wasteland Pr.

Fertig, Michael P. Musical Mystery Scooby Doo! McKee, Darren, illus. 2007. (Scooby Doo Ser.). (J). (gr. -1-3). 12.98 (978-1-4127-7429-1(2)) Publications International, Ltd.

Fickey, Brenda. Whispering Darkness. 2007. (ENG.). 136p. per. 24.95 (978-1-4241-6932-0(1)) America Star Bks.

Fiedler, Lisa. The Green-Eyed Monster. 2012. 168p. (J). (978-0-545-48424-4(3)) Scholastic, Inc.

Fields, Jan. Ghost Light Burning: An Up2U Mystery Adventure, 1 vol. Fabbretti, Valerio, illus. 2015. (ENG.). 80p. (J). (978-1-62402-092-6(5)) Magic Wagon.

—Meet the Mothman, 1 vol. Brundage, Scott, illus. 2016. (ENG.). 80p. (J). lib. bdg. (978-1-62402-153-4(0)) Magic Wagon.

—Track the Turtle Lake Monster, 1 vol. Brundage, Scott, illus. 2016. (ENG.). 80p. (J). lib. bdg. (978-1-62402-155-8(7)) Magic Wagon.

The Fiji Flood, 6 vols. (Woodland Mysteriestm Ser.). 133p. (gr. 3-7). 42.50 (978-0-7802-7925-4(5)) Wright Group/McGraw-Hill.

Finding Conway: Seek the Truth. 2006. (YA). (978-0-9771114-1-1(5)) LIP Publishing LLC.

Finley, Leah. Ms T. 2007. 108p. (J). per. 8.95 (978-0-9794815-1-2(1)) Bellissima Publishing, LLC.

—The One & Only Mr C. 2009. 82p. pap. 8.95 (978-1-935118-75-6(7)) Bellissima Publishing, LLC.

Fisch, Sholly. Scooby-Doo in Fangs, but No Fangs!, 1 vol. 2013. (Scooby-Doo Graphic Novels Set 3 Ser.). (ENG.). 24p. (J). (gr. 2-6). lib. bdg. 24.21 (978-1-61479-051-8(5), Essential Library) ABDO Publishing Co.

The Fishy, Flashy Fourth, 6 vols., Vol. 3. (Woodland Mysteriestm Ser.). 133p. (gr. 3-7). 42.50 (978-0-322-02373-4(4)) Wright Group/McGraw-Hill.

Fitzgerald, John D. More Adventures of the Great Brain. Mayer, Mercer, illus. 2004. (Great Brain Ser.). (ENG.). 176p. (J). (gr. 3-7). pap. 6.99 (978-0-14-240065-4(3), Puffin Books) Penguin Young Readers Group.

—More Adventures of the Great Brain. 2004. (Great Brain Ser.). 142p. (J). (gr. 3-7). pap., tchr.'s training gde. ed. 36.00 incl. audio (978-0-8072-0860-1(4), Listening Library) Random Hse. Audio Publishing Group.

Fitzgerald, Laura Marx. The Gallery. 2016. (ENG.). 336p. (J). (gr. 5-7). 16.99 (978-0-525-42865-7(8), Dial Bks) Penguin Young Readers Group.

—The Gallery. 2017. lib. bdg. 18.40 **(978-0-606-40088-6(5))** Turtleback Bks.

Fitzgerald, Laura Marx. Under the Egg. (ENG.). 256p. (J). (gr. 3-7). 2015. 7.99 (978-0-14-242765-1(9), Puffin Books) 2014. 16.99 (978-0-8037-4001-3(8), Dial Bks) Penguin Young Readers Group.

Fitzhugh, Louise. The Long Secret. unabr. ed. 2004. 224p. (J). (gr. 3-7). pap. 38.00 incl. audio (978-0-8072-0666-9(0), LYA 303 SP, Listening Library) Random Hse. Audio Publishing Group.

Fiz. George & the Treasure Box Mysteries. 2012. (Illus.). 105p. pap. 8.49 (978-1-78035-223-7(9), Fastprint Publishing) Upfront Publishing Ltd. GBR. Dist: Printondemand-worldwide.com.

Flake, Sharon. Unstoppable Octobia May. 2014. (ENG.). 288p. (J). (gr. 3-7). 16.99 (978-0-545-60960-9(7), Scholastic Pr.) Scholastic, Inc.

Fleischman, Paul. The Dunderheads. 2012. lib. bdg. 17.20 (978-0-606-23804-5(2), Turtleback) Turtleback Bks.

—The Dunderheads Behind Bars. Roberts, David, illus. 2012. (ENG.). 48p. (J). (gr. 1-4). 16.99 (978-0-7636-4543-4(5)) Candlewick Pr.

Fleischman, Sid. Jim Ugly. Smith, Jos. A., illus. 2003. (ENG.). 144p. (J). (gr. 3-7). pap. 6.99 (978-0-06-052121-9(X), Greenwillow Bks.) HarperCollins Pubs.

Fletcher, J. S. Scarhaven Keep. 2011. (YA). (978-1-60682-173-2(3)) BJU Pr.

Flint, Garrison. The Butler Did It! A Raymond Masrters Mystery. 2003. (Raymond Masters Mystery: 10). 206p. per. 13.99 (978-1-885631-72-5(3)) Hutchison, G.F. Pr.

—Sanity in Search of Peter Alexander. 2003. 198p. (YA). per. 13.95 (978-1-885631-73-2(1)) Hutchison, G.F. Pr.

Floreen, Tim. Tattoo Atlas. 2016. (ENG., Illus.). 384p. (YA). (gr. 9). 17.99 (978-1-4814-3280-1(X), Simon Pulse) Simon Pulse.

Florence, Debbi Michiko. Jasmine Toguchi, Super Sleuth. Vukovic, Elizabet, illus. 2017. (Jasmine Toguchi Ser.: 2). (ENG.). 128p. (J). pap. 5.99 **(978-0-374-30835-3(7)**, 9780374308353, Farrar, Straus & Giroux (BYR)) Farrar, Straus & Giroux.

Flower, Amanda. Andi under Pressure, 1 vol. 2014. (Andi Boggs Novel Ser.). (ENG.). 176p. (J). 10.99 (978-0-310-73702-5(8)) Zonderkidz.

—Andi under Pressure: An Andi Boggs Novel. 2014. 176p. (J). pap. (978-0-310-74022-3(3)) Zondervan.

—Andi Unstoppable, 1 vol. 2015. (Andi Boggs Novel Ser.). (ENG.). 176p. (J). 10.99 (978-0-310-73766-7(4)) Zonderkidz.

Floyd, Brandi. Alex's Choice. 2012. 38p. 24.95 (978-1-4626-6028-5(2)) America Star Bks.

Fodi, Lee Edward. Kendra Kandlestar & the Crack in Kazah. Fodi, Lee Edward, illus. 2011. (ENG., Illus.). 282p. (J). (gr. 4-7). 16.95 (978-1-61254-018-4(X)) Brown Books Publishing Group.

Fogelin, Adrian. Some Kind of Magic, 1 vol. 2015. (Neighborhood Novels Ser.). (ENG.). 232p. (J). (gr. 3-6). 15.95 (978-1-56145-820-2(1)) Peachtree Pubs.

Foley, Lizzie K. Remarkable. 2013. (ENG.). 336p. (J). (gr. 3-7). pap. 7.99 (978-0-14-242410-0(2), Puffin Books) Penguin Young Readers Group.

Fontes, Justine & Fontes, Ron. Casebook: Atlantis. 2009. (Top Secret Graphica Mysteries Ser.). (Illus.). 48p. (YA). (gr. 2-6). 29.25 (978-1-60754-588-0(8)); pap. 11.75 (978-1-60754-590-3(X)) Windmill Bks.

Ford, John C. The Cipher. 2016. (ENG.). 400p. (YA). (gr. 7). pap. 10.99 (978-0-14-750942-0(4), Speak) Penguin Young Readers Group.

Forever Lost. 2011. (Hardy Boys (All New) Undercover Brothers Ser.: 36). (ENG.). 160p. (J). (gr. 3-7). pap. 6.99 (978-1-4424-0264-5(4), Aladdin) Simon & Schuster Children's Publishing.

The Forgotten Hiding Place, 6 vols., Vol. 3. (Woodland Mysteriestm Ser.). 133p. (gr. 3-7). 42.50 (978-0-322-02376-5(9)) Wright Group/McGraw-Hill.

Forman, Gayle. I Was Here. l.t. ed. 2015. (ENG.). 420p. 24.99 (978-1-4104-8255-6(3)) Cengage Gale.

—I Was Here. 2015. (ENG.). 288p. (J). (gr. 9). 18.99 (978-0-451-47147-5(4), Viking Books for Young Readers) Penguin Publishing Group.

—I Was Here. 2016. (ENG.). 304p. (YA). (gr. 9). pap. 10.99 (978-0-14-751403-5(7), Speak) Penguin Young Readers Group.

—I Was Here. 2016. lib. bdg. 22.10 (978-0-606-38404-9(9)) Turtleback Bks.

Forrest. Sign of Blood. (Thumbprint Mysteries Ser.). 32.86 (978-0-8092-0408-3(8)) McGraw-Hill/Contemporary.

Foster, Martha S. Ginger Box. Geer, Charles, illus. 2011. 126p. 40.95 (978-1-258-06588-1(6)) Literary Licensing, LLC.

Fox, Janet. The Charmed Children of Rookskill Castle. (ENG.). 400p. (J). (gr. 5). 2017. 8.99 (978-0-14-751713-5(3), Puffin Books) 2016. (Illus.). 16.99 (978-0-451-47633-3(6), Viking Books for Young Readers) Penguin Young Readers Group.

Fox, R. J. Stuart & His Incredibly Obnoxious Magical Book: Soccer, 1 vol. 2009. 86p. pap. 19.95 (978-1-4489-9833-3(6)) America Star Bks.

Fox, Valerie P. Deefa: Seek the Vixen. 2008. 92p. pap. 10.49 (978-1-4389-0723-9(0)) AuthorHouse.

Fraustino, Lisa Rowe. The Hole in the Wall. 2010. (ENG.). 280p. (J). (gr. 2-7). 16.95 (978-1-57131-696-7(5)) Milkweed Editions.

Frazier, Angie. The Mastermind Plot. 2012. (ENG.). 240p. (J). (gr. 3-7). 16.99 (978-0-545-20864-2(5), Scholastic Pr.) Scholastic, Inc.

—The Midnight Tunnel: A Suzanna Snow Mystery. 2011. (ENG.). 288p. (J). (gr. 3-7). 17.99 (978-0-545-20862-8(9), Scholastic Pr.) Scholastic, Inc.

Frazier, Janet. The Case of the Theme Park Cry. l.t. ed. 2004. 90p. (J). per. (978-1-59196-737-8(6)) Instant Pub.

Frazier, Janet L. The Mysterious Mall Disapperance: P. K. Mystery Series # 2. 2004. 100p. (J). per. (978-1-59196-811-5(9)) Instant Pub.

Frederick, Heather Vogel. Absolutely Truly. 2015. (Pumpkin Falls Mystery Ser.). (ENG., Illus.). 368p. (J). (gr. 3-7). pap. 7.99 (978-1-4424-2973-4(9), Simon & Schuster Bks. For Young Readers) Simon & Schuster Bks. For Young Readers.

Fredericks, Mariah. The Girl in the Park. 2013. (ENG.). 224p. (YA). (gr. 9). pap. 8.99 (978-0-449-81591-5(9), Ember) Random Hse. Children's Bks.

Fredo, Sophia E. The Girls of Oak Court: Death at Whitford Pond. 2012. 172p. (gr. 10-12). pap. 13.95 (978-1-4759-4057-2(2)) iUniverse, Inc.

Freedom's Whisper. 2007. (J). (978-1-933343-52-5(4), PONY) Stabenfeldt Inc.

Freeman, J. Miller. Creak in the Night - Mystery of the Crypts. Lavender, Todd, illus. 2012. 74p. pap. 9.99 (978-0-9850410-1-4(3)) Akmaeon Publishing, LLC.

Freeman, Martha. The Case of the Bug on the Run. 2014. (First Kids Mystery Ser.: 6). (ENG.). 144p. (J). (gr. 2-7). pap. 6.99 (978-0-8234-3188-5(6)) Holiday Hse., Inc.

—The Case of the Bug on the Run: First Kids Mystery #6. 2013. (First Kids Mystery Ser.: 6). (ENG.). 144p. (J). (gr. 2-7). 16.95 (978-0-8234-2872-4(9)) Holiday Hse., Inc.

—The Case of the Diamond Dog Collar. 2nd ed. (First Kids Mystery Ser.: 2). (ENG., 144p. (J). 2012. Illus.). (gr. 3-5). pap. 6.99 (978-0-8234-2642-3(4)) 2011. 16.95 (978-0-8234-2337-8(9)) Holiday Hse., Inc.

—The Case of the Missing Dinosaur Egg. Dibley, Glin, illus. 2014. (First Kids Mystery Ser.: 5). (ENG.). 115p. (J). (gr. 3-7). pap. 6.99 (978-0-8234-3061-1(8)) Holiday Hse., Inc.

—The Case of the Missing Dinosaur Egg. 2013. (First Kids Mystery Ser.: 5). (ENG.). 144p. (J). (gr. 3-7). 16.95 (978-0-8234-2523-5(1)) Holiday Hse., Inc.

—The Case of the Piggy Bank Thief. 2012. (First Kids Mystery Ser.: 4). (ENG.). 144p. (J). (gr. 1-5). 16.95 (978-0-8234-2517-4(7)) Holiday Hse., Inc.

—The Case of the Rock 'N' Roll Dog. 2010. (First Kids Mystery Ser.: 1). (ENG., Illus.). 128p. (J). (gr. 1-5). 16.95 (978-0-8234-2267-8(4)) Holiday Hse., Inc.

—The Case of the Ruby Slippers. (First Kids Mystery Ser.: 3). (ENG.). 128p. (J). 2013. pap. 6.99 (978-0-8234-2764-2(1)) 2012. 16.95 (978-0-8234-2409-2(X)) Holiday Hse., Inc.

—Effie Starr Zook Has One More Question. 2017. (ENG., Illus.). 224p. (J). (gr. 3-7). 16.99 (978-1-4814-7264-7(X), Simon & Schuster/Paula Wiseman Bks.) Simon & Schuster/Paula Wiseman Bks.

—Who Is Stealing the 12 Days of Christmas? 2008. (ENG., Illus.). 200p. (J). (gr. 3-7). pap. 7.95 (978-0-8234-2167-1(8)) Holiday Hse., Inc.

—Who Stole Grandma's Million-Dollar Pumpkin Pie? 2009. (Chickadee Court Mystery Ser.). (ENG.). 256p. (J). (gr. 3-7). 16.95 (978-0-8234-2215-9(1)) Holiday Hse., Inc.

—Who Stole Halloween? 2005. (Chickadee Court Mystery Ser.). (ENG.). 224p. (J). (gr. 3-7). 16.95 (978-0-8234-1962-3(2)) Holiday Hse., Inc.

—Who Stole New Year's Eve? 2013. (Chickadee Court Mystery Ser.). (ENG.). 224p. (J). (gr. 2-7). 16.95 (978-0-8234-2750-5(1)) Holiday Hse., Inc.

—Who Stole Uncle Sam? 2008. (Chickadee Court Mystery Ser.). (ENG., Illus.). 128p. (J). (gr. 3-7). 16.95 (978-0-8234-2091-9(4)) Holiday Hse., Inc.

Freese, Thomas, reader. Fog Swirler & 11 Other Ghost Stories. 2006. (J). Pt. 1. cd-rom 13.95 (978-0-9789511-0-8(7))Pt. 2. cd-rom 13.95 (978-0-9789511-1-5(5))Pt. 3. cd-rom 13.95 (978-0-9789511-2-2(3)) Illumination Pubns.

Frey, Hildegard G. The Camp Fire Girls Go Motoring. 2004. reprint ed. pap. 1.99 (978-1-4192-5583-0(5)); pap. 20.95 (978-1-4191-5583-3(0)) Kessinger Publishing, LLC.

Freyburger, Nancy. The Case of the Hiccuping Clown. 2008. 108p. pap. 10.99 (978-1-4389-2699-5(5)) AuthorHouse.

Friedman, Kinky. Curse of the Missing Puppet Head. 2003. lib. bdg. 29.95 (978-0-9702383-6-8(3), CMPH01) Vandam Pr., Inc.

Friedman, Mel. The Mystery of the Backlot Banshee: A ClueFinders Mystery Adventure. 2004. (Illus.). 96p. (J). pap. (978-0-7630-7620-7(1)) Magma.

Friedmann, Patty. Taken Away. 2010. (ENG.). 427p. (J). (gr. 6). pap. 18.95 (978-0-9845318-2-0(3)) Tiny Stachel Pr.

Froley, Margaux. Hero Complex. 2015. (ENG., Illus.). 216p. (YA). (gr. 9). pap. 10.99 (978-1-61695-573-1(2), Soho Teen) Soho Pr., Inc.

Fromental, Jean-Luc. Bonesville. Jolivet, Joëlle, illus. 2016. (ENG.). 48p. (J). (gr. k-2). 18.95 (978-1-4197-2277-6(8), Abrams Bks. for Young Readers) Abrams, Inc.

Frost, Michael. Killer Mission. 2009. (Hardy Boys (All New) Undercover Brothers Ser.: 31). (ENG.). 192p. (J). (gr. 3-7). pap. 6.99 (978-1-4169-8695-9(2), Aladdin) Simon & Schuster Children's Publishing.

Frost, Michael, photos by. Private Killer, Bk. 2. 2010. (Hardy Boys (All New) Undercover Brothers Ser.: 32). (ENG., Illus.). 160p. (J). (gr. 3-7). pap. 5.99 (978-1-4169-8697-3(9), Aladdin) Simon & Schuster Children's Publishing.

Fryer, Mary Beacock. Escape: Adventures of a Loyalist Family. 2006. (ENG., Illus.). 188p. (J). pap. 7.99 (978-1-895681-17-8(0), Boardwalk Bks.) Dundurn CAN. Dist: Ingram Publisher Services.

Fultz, Steven D. The Adventures of the Barnyard Detectives: Where's Mr. Peacock, 1 vol. 2009. 79p. pap. 19.95 (978-1-60749-965-7(7)) America Star Bks.

Funke, Cornelia. Thief Lord. Birmingham, Christian, illus. 2010. (ENG.). 376p. (J). (gr. 3-7). 7.99 (978-0-545-22770-4(4), Chicken Hse., The) Scholastic, Inc.

Fuqua, J. Scott. Secrets of the Greaser Hotel. 2014. (ENG., Illus.). 280p. 25.00 (978-1-61088-130-2(3)) Bancroft Pr.

Fuss, Kevin. The Brothers Geek. 2010. 180p. 24.99 (978-1-4490-7366-4(2)); pap. 14.49 (978-1-4490-7365-7(4)) AuthorHouse.

Gaetz, Dayle Campbell. Alberta Alibi, 1 vol. 2005. (ENG.). 208p. (J). (gr. 3-7). per. 6.95 (978-1-55143-404-9(0)) Orca Bk. Pubs. USA.

—Crossbow, 1 vol. 2007. (Orca Currents Ser.). (ENG.). 112p. (J). (gr. 5-9). pap. 9.95 (978-1-55143-841-2(0)); lib. bdg. 14.95 (978-1-55143-843-6(7)) Orca Bk. Pubs. USA.

—Something Suspicious in Saskatchewan, 1 vol. 2006. (ENG.). 208p. (J). (gr. 4-7). per. 7.95 (978-1-55143-565-7(9)) Orca Bk. Pubs. USA.

Gagnon, Michelle. Don't Let Go. 2015. (Don't Turn Around Ser.: 3). (ENG.). 368p. (YA). (gr. 8). pap. 9.99 (978-0-06-210297-3(4)) HarperCollins Pubs.

Gallagher, Mary. The Legend of Lisnashee. 2006. (ENG., Illus.). 100p. (J). pap. 10.95 (978-1-903464-71-7(4)) Collins Pr., The IRL. Dist: Dufour Editions, Inc.

Galvin, Larry J. The Pythagoras Solution. 2008. 102p. pap. 19.95 (978-1-60441-990-0(3)) America Star Bks.

Ganeri, Anita. Mystery Stories: Writing Stories, 1 vol. 2013. (Writing Stories Ser.). (ENG.). 32p. (gr. 1-3). 27.32 (978-1-4329-7532-6(3)); pap. 8.95 (978-1-4329-7539-5(0)) Heinemann-Raintree. (Heinemann First Library).

Gant, Gene. Always Leaving. 2016. (ENG., Illus.). (YA). (gr. 8-12). 24.99 **(978-1-63477-934-0(7)**, Harmony Ink Pr.) Dreamspinner Pr.

Gantos, Jack. From Norvelt to Nowhere. 2013. (Norvelt Ser.: 2). (ENG.). 288p. (J). (gr. 5-9). 16.99 (978-0-374-37994-0(7), 9780374379940, Farrar, Straus & Giroux (BYR)) Farrar, Straus & Giroux.

—From Norvelt to Nowhere. 2015. (J). lib. bdg. 18.40 (978-0-606-37280-0(6)) Turtleback Bks.

Gardner, Sally. The Door That Led to Where. 2016. (ENG.). 288p. (YA). (gr. 7). 17.99 (978-0-399-54997-7(8), Delacorte Pr.) Random Hse. Children's Bks.

—Operation Bunny. Roberts, David, illus. 2014. (Wings & Co Ser.: 1). (ENG.). 192p. (J). (gr. 2-5). 12.99 (978-0-8050-9892-1(5), 9780805098921, Holt, Henry & Co. Bks. For Young Readers) Holt, Henry & Co.

—Operation Bunny. Roberts, David, illus. 2014. (Wings & Co Ser.: 1). (ENG.). 208p. (J). (gr. 2-5). pap. 6.99 (978-1-250-05053-3(7), 9781250050533) Square Fish.

—The Vanishing of Billy Buckle. Roberts, David, illus. 2015. (Wings & Co Ser.: 3). (ENG.). 240p. (J). (gr. 2-5). 13.99 (978-0-8050-9915-7(8), 9780805099157, Holt, Henry & Co. Bks. For Young Readers) Holt, Henry & Co.

Garis, Howard R. The Curlytops & Their Playmates. 2009. 120p. 22.95 (978-1-60664-610-6(9)); pap. 10.95 (978-1-60664-342-6(8)) Rodgers, Alan Bks.

Garmon, Larry Mike. The Calamari Code: an Agatha Pixie Mystery. 2007. 244p. pap. 15.49 (978-0-615-15267-7(8)) Zu Bks.

Garrett, Kelly. The Last to Die. 2017. (ENG.). (YA). pap. 10.95 (978-1-929345-30-4(5)) Poisoned Pen Pr.

Garthwaite, Lynn D. Dirkle Smat Inside Mount Flatbottom. Howarth, Craig, illus. 2006. 48p. (J). pap. 9.95 (978-1-59663-512-8(6), Castle Keep Pr.) Rock, James A. & Co. Pubs.

Garton, Kevan. The Cockleton Mystery. 2006. 68p. pap. (978-1-84401-788-1(5)) Athena Pr.

Gary R Kirby. Stories of Sunshine & Funtime of Wonder & Thunder of Mystery & Magic for the Young to Grow On. 2009. 404p. pap. 22.95 (978-1-4401-8640-0(5)) iUniverse, Inc.

Gauthier, Gail. Happy Kid! 2006. 230p. (J). (978-1-4156-6311-0(4), Putnam Juvenile) Penguin Publishing Group.

Gavin, Rohan. K-9. 2016. (Knightley & Son Ser.: 2). (ENG.). 320p. (J). pap. 7.99 (978-1-61963-687-3(5), 9781619636873, Bloomsbury USA Childrens) Bloomsbury Publishing USA.

—Knightley & Son - K-9. 2015. (Knightley & Son Ser.: 2). (ENG., Illus.). 304p. (YA). (gr. 4-6). 16.99 (978-1-61963-494-7(5), 9781619634947, Bloomsbury USA Childrens) Bloomsbury Publishing USA.

Gayle, Juliet V. Emily & Beautiful & the Great Strawberry Whipped Cream Pie Mystery. 2011. 24p. pap. 13.95 (978-1-4520-9744-2(5)) AuthorHouse.

Gee, Maurice. The Fire Raiser. 2007. (ENG.). 176p. (J). (gr. 5-7). pap. 11.95 (978-0-618-75041-2(X)) Houghton Mifflin Harcourt Publishing Co.

Geesey, Kathleen. Black Fog. 2011. 200p. pap. 24.95 (978-1-4560-7000-7(2)) America Star Bks.

Gegner, Rose G. Detective Rooster Rue. 2014. 32p. pap. 22.54 (978-1-4828-9517-9(X)) Partridge Pub.

Geiger, A. V. Follow Me Back. 2017. (Follow Me Back Ser.: 1). (ENG.). 368p. (YA). (gr. 8-12). pap. 10.99 (978-1-4926-4523-8(0)) Sourcebooks, Inc.

Gelsey, James. The Baseball Boogeyman. 2004. (Illus.). 44p. (J). (978-0-439-55713-9(5)) Scholastic, Inc.

—Scooby-Doo! & the Carnival Creeper, 1 vol. 2013. (Scooby-Doo Mysteries Set 2 Ser.). (ENG.). 64p. (J). (gr. 3-6). lib. bdg. 24.21 (978-1-61479-042-6(6)) ABDO Publishing Co.

—Scooby-Doo! & the Frankenstein Monster, 1 vol. 2013. (Scooby-Doo Mysteries Set 2 Ser.). (ENG.). 64p. (J). (gr. 3-6). lib. bdg. 24.21 (978-1-61479-043-3(4)) ABDO Publishing Co.

—Scooby-Doo! & the Gruesome Goblin, 1 vol. 2013. (Scooby-Doo Mysteries Set 2 Ser.). (ENG.). 64p. (J). (gr. 3-6). lib. bdg. 24.21 (978-1-61479-045-7(0)) ABDO Publishing Co.

—Scooby-Doo! & the Howling Wolfman, 1 vol. 2013. (Scooby-Doo Mysteries Set 2 Ser.). (ENG.). 64p. (J). (gr. 3-6). lib. bdg. 24.21 (978-1-61479-046-4(9)) ABDO Publishing Co.

—Scooby-Doo! & the Spooky Strikeout, 1 vol. 2013. (Scooby-Doo Mysteries Set 2 Ser.). (ENG.). 64p. (J). (gr. 3-6). lib. bdg. 24.21 (978-1-61479-047-1(7)) ABDO Publishing Co.

Gelsey, James & Duendes Del Sur Staff. Scooby-Doo & the Karate Caper, 1 vol. 2011. (Scooby-Doo Mysteries Ser.). (ENG., Illus.). 64p. (J). (gr. 3-6). 24.21 (978-1-59961-891-3(5)) Spotlight.

—Scooby-Doo & the Runaway Robot, 1 vol. 2011. (Scooby-Doo Mysteries Ser.). (ENG., Illus.). 64p. (J). (gr. 3-6). 24.21 (978-1-59961-892-0(3)) Spotlight.

—Scooby-Doo & the Sunken Ship, 1 vol. 2011. (Scooby-Doo Mysteries Ser.). (ENG., Illus.). 64p. (J). (gr. 3-6). 24.21 (978-1-59961-893-7(1)) Spotlight.

—Scooby-Doo & the Vampire's Revenge, 1 vol. 2011. (Scooby-Doo Mysteries Ser.). (ENG., Illus.). 64p. (J). (gr. 3-6). 24.21 (978-1-59961-894-4(X)) Spotlight.

—Scooby-Doo & the Witch Doctor, 1 vol. 2011. (Scooby-Doo Mysteries Ser.). (ENG., Illus.). 64p. (J). (gr. 3-6). 24.21 (978-1-59961-895-1(8)) Spotlight.

—Scooby-Doo & the Zombie's Treasure, 1 vol. 2011. (Scooby-Doo Mysteries Ser.). (ENG., Illus.). 64p. (J). (gr. 3-6). 24.21 (978-1-59961-896-8(6)) Spotlight.

Gemmell, N. J. The Luna Laboratorium. 2016. (Kensington Reptilarium Ser.: 3). (ENG.). 304p. (J). (gr. 4-7). pap. 12.99 (978-0-85798-569-9(8)) Random Hse. Australia AUS. Dist: Independent Pubs. Group.

Gentile, Joe. Mysterious Traveler. 2003. (ENG., Illus.). 48p. (gr. 12-18). pap. 5.50 (978-0-9721668-5-0(8), 9780972166850) Moonstone.

George, Elizabeth. The Edge of the Light. 2016. (Edge of Nowhere Ser.). (ENG.). 400p. (YA). (gr. 7). 18.99 (978-0-670-01299-2(8), Viking Books for Young Readers) Penguin Young Readers Group.

George, Elizabeth. The Edge of the Light. 2017. (Edge of Nowhere Ser.). (ENG.). 416p. (YA). (gr. 7). pap. 10.99 **(978-0-14-751396-0(0)**, Speak) Penguin Young Readers Group.

George, J. A. Camp Aconyte. 2008. 65p. pap. 19.95 (978-1-60610-631-0(7)) America Star Bks.

Gerber, Linda. Death by Denim. 2009. (Death by ... Mysteries Ser.). (ENG.). 272p. (YA). (gr. 7-18). pap. 7.99 (978-0-14-241119-3(1), Puffin Books) Penguin Young Readers Group.

Gerwitz, Felice & Gerwitz, Christina. Dinosaur Quest at Diamond Peak, 3, Vol. 2. 2nd rev. ed. 2007. (Truth Seeker's Mystery Ser.). 208p. (YA). per. 8.99 (978-1-931941-11-2(4)) Media Angels, Inc.

—The Missing Link: Found, 3, Vol. 1. 2nd rev. ed. 2004. (Truth Seeker's Mystery Ser.). 208p. (YA). per. 8.99 (978-1-931941-08-2(4)) Media Angels, Inc.

Gibbons, Alan. End Game. 2016. (ENG.). 304p. (YA). pap. 7.99 (978-1-78062-181-4(7), Orion Children's Bks.) Hachette Children's Group GBR. Dist: Hachette Bk. Group.

Gibbs, Anna. The Mystery of the Healing Waters. 2005. 55p. pap. 10.00 (978-1-4134-4533-6(0)) Xlibris Corp.

Gibbs, Gretchen. The Book of Maggie Bradstreet. 2012. (Bradstreet Chronicles). (ENG.). 183p. (YA). pap. 9.99 (978-0-9852948-0-9(9)) Glenmere Pr.

Gibbs, Stuart. Belly Up. (FunJungle Ser.). (ENG.). (J). (gr. 3-7). 2011. 320p. pap. 7.99 (978-1-4169-8732-1(0)) 2010. (Illus.). 304p. 17.99 (978-1-4169-8731-4(2)) Simon & Schuster Bks. For Young Readers. (Simon & Schuster Bks. For Young Readers).

—Big Game. 2015. (FunJungle Ser.). (ENG.). 352p. (J). (gr. 3-7). 17.99 (978-1-4814-2333-5(9), Simon & Schuster Bks. For Young Readers) Simon & Schuster Bks. For Young Readers.

—Panda-Monium. 2017. (FunJungle Ser.). (ENG., Illus.). 352p. (J). (gr. 3-7). 16.99 (978-1-4814-4567-2(7), Simon & Schuster Bks. For Young Readers) Simon & Schuster Bks. For Young Readers.

—Poached. 2014. (FunJungle Ser.). (ENG., Illus.). 352p. (J). (gr. 3-7). 17.99 (978-1-4424-6777-4(0), Simon & Schuster Bks. For Young Readers) Simon & Schuster Bks. For Young Readers.

—Space Case. 2015. (Moon Base Alpha Ser.). (ENG., Illus.). 368p. (J). (gr. 3-7). pap. 7.99 (978-1-4424-9487-9(5), Simon & Schuster Bks. For Young Readers) Simon & Schuster Bks. For Young Readers.

—Space Case. 2015. (Moon Base Alpha Ser.: 1). lib. bdg. 18.40 (978-0-606-37883-3(9)) Turtleback Bks.

—Spaced Out. (Moon Base Alpha Ser.). (ENG.). (J). (gr. 3-7). 2017. 368p. pap. 7.99 (978-1-4814-2337-3(1)) 2016. (Illus.). 352p. 17.99 (978-1-4814-2336-6(3)) Simon & Schuster Bks. For Young Readers. (Simon & Schuster Bks. For Young Readers).

—Spaced Out. 2017. (Moon Base Alpha Ser.: 2). lib. bdg. 18.40 **(978-0-606-39762-9(0))** Turtleback Bks.

Gibson, Jo. Twisted. 2014. (ENG.). 560p. (YA). (gr. 13). pap. 9.95 (978-1-61773-240-9(0), K-Teen) Kensington Publishing Corp.

Giff, Patricia Reilly. Hunter Moran Hangs Out. (ENG.). 144p. (J). (gr. 3-7). 2014. pap. 6.99 (978-0-8234-3189-2(4)) 2013. (Illus.). 16.95 (978-0-8234-2859-5(1)) Holiday Hse., Inc.

—Hunter Moran Saves the Universe. (ENG.). 128p. (J). (gr. 2-7). 2013. pap. 6.99 (978-0-8234-2917-2(2)) 2012. 16.95 (978-0-8234-1949-4(5)) Holiday Hse., Inc.

—The Mystery of the Blue Ring. 73p. (J). (gr. 1-2). pap. 3.99 (978-0-8072-1272-1(5), Listening Library) Random Hse. Audio Publishing Group.

—The Powder Puff Puzzle. 75p. (J). pap. 3.99 (978-0-8072-1275-2(X), Listening Library) Random Hse. Audio Publishing Group.

—The Riddle of the Red Purse. 68p. (J). pap. 3.99 (978-0-8072-1273-8(3), Listening Library) Random Hse. Audio Publishing Group.

Giffen, Keith. Scooby Apocalypse Vol. 1. 2017. lib. bdg. 29.40 **(978-0-606-39806-0(6))** Turtleback Bks.

Gilbert, D. Hide & Seek: A Mystery Novel for Children. 2005. 187p. pap. 24.95 (978-1-4137-9748-0(2)) PublishAmerica, Inc.

Gilbert, Kelly Loy. Conviction. 2017. (YA). lib. bdg. 20.85 **(978-0-606-39170-2(3))** Turtleback Bks.

Giles, Lamar. Endangered. (YA). (gr. 9). 2016. 304p. pap. 9.99 (978-0-06-229757-0(0)) 2015. (ENG.). 288p. 17.99 (978-0-06-229756-3(2), HarperTeen) HarperCollins Pubs.

—Fake ID. 2014. (ENG.). 320p. (YA). (gr. 8). 17.99 (978-0-06-212184-4(7), Amistad) HarperCollins Pubs.

Gilligan, Shannon. The Case of the Silk King. Pornkerd, Vorrarit et al, illus. 2006. (Choose Your Own Adventure Ser.). 144p. (J). (gr. 4-8). per. 6.99 (978-1-933390-14-7(X), CHCL14) Chooseco LLC.

—The Case of the Silk King. 2005. 116p. (J). pap. (978-0-7608-9702-7(6)) Sundance/Newbridge Educational Publishing.

—Choose Your Own Adventure: The Case of the Silk King. 2007. 144p. (J). pap. (978-1-74169-069-9(2)) Chooseco LLC.

—The Mystery of Ura Senke. 2005. (Illus.). 120p. (Orig.). (J). (978-0-7608-9701-0(8)) Sundance/Newbridge Educational Publishing.

Gilman, David. Blood Sun. 2012. (Danger Zone Ser.). (ENG.). 432p. (YA). (gr. 7). pap. 10.99 (978-0-440-42241-9(8), Ember) Random Hse. Children's Bks.

Giovannoli, Renato. Misterio en Villa Jamaica. 2005. (SPA.). 122p. (J). (gr. 4-5). 7.95 (978-84-348-6713-0(3)) SM Ediciones ESP. Dist: Iaconi, Mariuccia Bk. Imports.

Gipson, Morrell, ed. Stories of Mystery, Adventure & Fun from Calling All Girls. Dawson, Isabel, illus. 2011. 252p. 46.95 (978-1-258-10497-9(0)) Literary Licensing, LLC.

Girard, Geoffrey. Truthers. 2017. (ENG.). 360p. (YA). (gr. 7-12). 17.99 (978-1-5124-2779-0(9)) Lerner Publishing Group.

Girdner, Randall P. Mr. Ping's Almanac of the Twisted & Weird presents Boyd Mccloyd & the Perpetual Motion Machine. 2009. 473p. pap. 25.00 (978-0-615-25755-6(0)) Acclimated Spooks, Light, & Power.

Glaze, Dave. The Light-Fingered Gang, 1 vol. 2005. (1912: the Mackenzie Davis Files Ser.). (ENG.). 168p. (J). (gr. 3-7). per. 7.95 (978-1-55050-326-5(X)) Coteau Bks. CAN. Dist: Orca Bk. Pubs. USA.

Gleason, Colleen. The Chess Queen Enigma: A Stoker & Holmes Novel. (ENG.). 360p. (YA). (gr. 7-12). 2016. pap. 9.99 (978-1-4521-5649-1(2)) 2015. (Stoker & Holmes Ser.: 3). 17.99 (978-1-4521-4317-0(X)) Chronicle Bks. LLC.

—The Clockwork Scarab. 2013. (Stoker & Holmes Ser.: 1). (ENG.). 356p. (YA). (gr. 7-12). 17.99 (978-1-4521-1070-7(0)) Chronicle Bks. LLC.

Godfrey. Murder in the Shadows. (Thumbprint Mysteries Ser.). 32.86 (978-0-8092-0418-2(5)) McGraw-Hill/Contemporary.

Goeglein, T. M. Cold Fury. 2013. (Cold Fury Novel Ser.: 1). (ENG.). 336p. (YA). (gr. 7). pap. 9.99 (978-0-14-242631-9(8), Speak) Penguin Young Readers Group.

—Flicker & Burn. 2014. (Cold Fury Novel Ser.: 2). (ENG.). 368p. (YA). (gr. 7). pap. 9.99 (978-0-14-751141-6(0), Speak) Penguin Young Readers Group.

Goguen, Martha M. Andromed: Dream Believe Achieve Series. Walker, Patricia M., illus. 2011. 36p. pap. (978-1-897435-35-9(5)) Agio Publishing Hse.

Goldish, Meish. Mystery at the Mall. Andrae, Tom, illus. 2017. (Hound Town Chronicles Ser.). (ENG.). 32p. (J). (gr. 2-6). 19.95 **(978-1-62724-870-9(6))** Bearport Publishing Co., Inc.

Gonzalez, Christina Diaz. Moving Target. 2015. (ENG.). 256p. (J). (gr. 3-7). 17.99 (978-0-545-77318-8(0), Scholastic Pr.) Scholastic, Inc.

—Return Fire. (Moving Target Ser.: 2). (ENG.). (J). (gr. 3-7). 2017. 224p. pap. 6.99 **(978-0-545-77323-2(7))** 2016. 352p. 17.99 (978-0-545-77322-5(9)) Scholastic, Inc. (Scholastic Pr.).

Goodhart, Pippa. Nature Detectives, 1 vol. Mason, Sue, illus. 2013. (Start Reading Ser.). (ENG.). 24p. (gr. k-1). pap. 7.95 (978-1-4765-4121-1(3)) Capstone Press of Coughlan Cos.

Goodwin, Vincent. The Adventure of the Blue Carbuncle, 1 vol. Dunn, Ben, illus. 2012. (Graphic Novel Adventures of Sherlock Holmes Set 2 Ser.). (ENG.). 48p. (J). (gr. 3-8). lib. bdg. 29.93 (978-1-61641-891-5(5), Graphic Planet) Magic Wagon.

—The Adventure of the Cardboard Box, 1 vol. Dunn, Ben, illus. 2013. (Graphic Novel Adventures of Sherlock Holmes Set 3 Ser.). (ENG.). 48p. (J). (gr. 3-8). lib. bdg. 29.93 (978-1-61641-971-4(7), Graphic Planet) Magic Wagon.

—The Adventure of the Copper Beeches, 1 vol. Dunn, Ben, illus. 2012. (Graphic Novel Adventures of Sherlock Holmes Set 2 Ser.). (ENG.). 48p. (J). (gr. 3-8). lib. bdg. 29.93 (978-1-61641-892-2(3), Graphic Planet) Magic Wagon.

—The Adventure of the Dying Detective, 1 vol. Dunn, Ben, illus. 2013. (Graphic Novel Adventures of Sherlock Holmes Set 3 Ser.). (ENG.). 48p. (J). (gr. 3-8). lib. bdg. 29.93 (978-1-61641-972-1(5), Graphic Planet) Magic Wagon.

—The Adventure of the Engineer's Thumb, 1 vol. Dunn, Ben, illus. 2012. (Graphic Novel Adventures of Sherlock Holmes Set 2 Ser.). (ENG.). 48p. (J). (gr. 3-8). lib. bdg. 29.93 (978-1-61641-893-9(1), Graphic Planet) Magic Wagon.

—The Adventure of the Priory School, 1 vol. Dunn, Ben, illus. 2013. (Graphic Novel Adventures of Sherlock Holmes Set 3 Ser.). (ENG.). 48p. (J). (gr. 3-8). lib. bdg. 29.93 (978-1-61641-973-8(3), Graphic Planet) Magic Wagon.

—The Adventure of the Red Circle, 1 vol. Dunn, Ben, illus. 2013. (Graphic Novel Adventures of Sherlock Holmes Set 3 Ser.). (ENG.). 48p. (J). (gr. 3-8). lib. bdg. 29.93 (978-1-61641-974-5(1), Graphic Planet) Magic Wagon.

—The Adventure of the Second Stain, 1 vol. Dunn, Ben, illus. 2013. (Graphic Novel Adventures of Sherlock Holmes Set 3 Ser.). (ENG.). 48p. (J). (gr. 3-8). lib. bdg. 29.93 (978-1-61641-975-2(X), Graphic Planet) Magic Wagon.

—The Adventure of the Six Napoleons, 1 vol. Dunn, Ben, illus. 2013. (Graphic Novel Adventures of Sherlock Holmes Set 3 Ser.). (ENG.). 48p. (J). (gr. 3-8). lib. bdg. 29.93 (978-1-61641-976-9(8), Graphic Planet) Magic Wagon.

—The Adventure of the Solitary Cyclist, 1 vol. Dunn, Ben, illus. 2012. (Graphic Novel Adventures of Sherlock Holmes Set 2 Ser.). (ENG.). 48p. (J). (gr. 3-8). lib. bdg. 29.93 (978-1-61641-894-6(X), Graphic Planet) Magic Wagon.

—The Adventure of the Three Students, 1 vol. Dunn, Ben, illus. 2012. (Graphic Novel Adventures of Sherlock Holmes Set 2 Ser.). (ENG.). 48p. (J). (gr. 3-8). lib. bdg. 29.93 (978-1-61641-895-3(8), Graphic Planet) Magic Wagon.

—The Adventure of Wisteria Lodge, 1 vol. Dunn, Ben, illus. 2012. (Graphic Novel Adventures of Sherlock Holmes Set 2 Ser.). (ENG.). 48p. (J). (gr. 3-8). lib. bdg. 29.93 (978-1-61641-896-0(6), Graphic Planet) Magic Wagon.

Gordon, Fran & Tischler, Faye. Dutch Double. 2007. (Illus.). 88p. pap. 15.95 (978-1-59299-242-3(0)) Inkwater Pr.

Gordon, Lynn, et al. Circus Fantastico. 2010. (ENG., Illus.). 38p. (J). (gr. k-3). 16.99 (978-0-7407-9199-4(0)) Andrews McMeel Publishing.

Gore, E. J. Taya Bayliss - Treasure Hunter. 2012. 86p. (J). pap. (978-0-9873708-0-8(4)) Coppertop Pr.

Gorman, Karyn. Betty Q Investigates. 2015. (Race Further with Reading Ser.). (ENG., Illus.). 48p. (J). (978-0-7787-2029-4(2)) Crabtree Publishing Co.

Gosling, Sharon. The Diamond Thief. 2014. (Diamond Thief Ser.). (ENG.). 336p. (gr. 9-12). 16.95 (978-1-63079-002-8(8)) Switch Pr.

—The Ruby Airship. 2015. (Diamond Thief Ser.). (ENG.). 496p. (gr. 9-12). 16.95 (978-1-63079-004-2(4)) Switch Pr.

—The Sapphire Cutlass. 2016. (Diamond Thief Ser.). (ENG.). 336p. (gr. 9-12). 16.95 (978-1-63079-041-7(9)) Switch Pr.

Grabenstein, Chris. Escape from Mr. Lemoncello's Library. (ENG.). (J). (gr. 3-7). 2014. 336p. 7.99 (978-0-307-93147-4(1), Yearling) 2013. 304p. 17.99 (978-0-375-87089-7(X), Random Hse. Bks. for Young Readers) 2013. 304p. lib. bdg. 19.99 (978-0-375-97089-4(4), Random Hse. Bks. for Young Readers) 2017. 336p. 7.99 **(978-0-525-58037-9(9)**, Yearling) Random Hse. Children's Bks.

—Escape from Mr. Lemoncello's Library. 2014. lib. bdg. 18.40 (978-0-606-37114-8(1)) Turtleback Bks.

—Home Sweet Motel. Allen, Brooke, illus. 2016. (Welcome to Wonderland Ser.: 1). (ENG.). 304p. (J). (gr. 3-7). 13.99 (978-0-553-53602-7(8), Random Hse. Bks. for Young Readers) Random Hse. Children's Bks.

—Riley Mack & the Other Known Troublemakers. 2012. (Riley Mack Ser.: 1). (ENG.). 272p. (J). (gr. 3-7). 16.99 (978-0-06-202620-0(8)) HarperCollins Pubs.

—Riley Mack Stirs up More Trouble. 2013. (Riley Mack Ser.: 2). (ENG.). 336p. (J). (gr. 3-7). 16.99 (978-0-06-202622-4(4)) HarperCollins Pubs.

Graham, Cheryl. Stephanie's Shoes. 2010. 28p. pap. 9.95 (978-1-4327-5944-5(2)) Outskirts Pr., Inc.

Graham, Deborah. The Magic Comes Back: A Max & Sam Adventure. 2012. 66p. (gr. 2-4). pap. 8.95 (978-1-4759-4758-8(5)) iUniverse, Inc.

Granny's Favorite Tales. 2006. (Illus.). 156p. (J). per. 39.95 (978-1-60002-098-8(4), 3915) Mountain Valley Publishing, LLC.

Grant, Michael & Applegate, Katherine. Eve & Adam. 2012. (ENG.). 304p. (YA). (gr. 8-12). 17.99 (978-0-312-58351-4(6), 9780312583514) Feiwel & Friends.

Grant, Natalie. The Miracle in Music City, 1 vol. 2016. (Faithgirlz / Glimmer Girls Ser.). (ENG.). 208p. (J). pap. 8.99 (978-0-310-75250-9(7)) Zonderkidz.

Grant, Vicki. Cochonnet: (Pigboy), 1 vol. 2011. (FRE.). 112p. (J). (gr. 5-9). pap. 9.95 (978-1-4598-0006-9(0)) Orca Bk. Pubs. USA.

—Hold the Pickles, 1 vol. 2012. (Orca Currents Ser.). (ENG.). 112p. (J). (gr. 5-9). 16.95 (978-1-55469-921-6(5)); pap. 9.95 (978-1-55469-920-9(7)) Orca Bk. Pubs. USA.

—Pigboy, 1 vol. 2006. (Orca Currents Ser.). (ENG.). 128p. (J). (gr. 5-9). per. 9.95 (978-1-55143-643-2(4)) Orca Bk. Pubs. USA.

—Res Judicata, 1 vol. 2008. (ENG.). 184p. (YA). (gr. 7-12). pap. 9.95 (978-1-55143-940-2(9)) Orca Bk. Pubs. USA.

—Triggered, 1 vol. 2013. (Orca Soundings Ser.). (ENG.). 128p. (YA). (gr. 8-12). pap. 9.95 (978-1-4598-0526-2(7)); lib. bdg. 16.95 (978-1-4598-0529-3(1)) Orca Bk. Pubs. USA.

Grau, Sheila. Dr. Critchlore's School for Minions. Sutphin, Joe, illus. 2015. (Dr. Critchlore's School for Minions Ser.). (ENG.). 288p. (J). (gr. 3-7). 14.95 (978-1-4197-1370-5(1), Amulet Bks.) Abrams, Inc.

Grau, Sheila & Sutphin, Joe. Dr. Critchlore's School for Minions: Gorilla Tactics. 2016. (Dr. Critchlore's School for Minions Ser.). (ENG., Illus.). 304p. (J). (gr. 3-7). 14.95 (978-1-4197-1371-2(X), Amulet Bks.) Abrams, Inc.

Gray, C. M. Infected. 2nd ed. 2016. (Zombiefied Ser.: 02). 192p. pap. 5.99 (978-0-7333-3422-1(9)) ABC Bks. AUS. Dist: HarperCollins Pubs.

Gray, Jennifer. Atticus Claw Breaks the Law. Ecob, Mark, illus. 2016. (Atticus Claw Ser.). (ENG.). 224p. (gr. 1-4). pap. 7.95 (978-0-571-28449-8(3)) Faber & Faber, Inc.

The Great Paua Mystery: Kyss Series. 2003. (J). mass mkt. (978-1-932233-69-8(5)) Aurora Libris Corp.

Green, Jacqueline. Kiss & Tell. 2015. (Truth or Dare Ser.: 3). (ENG.). 288p. (YA). (gr. 10-17). 18.00 (978-0-316-22033-0(7), Poppy) Little, Brown Bks. for Young Readers.

—Secrets & Lies. 2014. (Truth or Dare Ser.: 2). (ENG.). 336p. (YA). (gr. 10-17). pap. 21.99 (978-0-316-22030-9(2), Poppy) Little, Brown Bks. for Young Readers.

Green, Jim. Shadows of the Moon... Dancing. 2007. (YA). pap. 14.95 (978-1-59705-872-8(6)) Wings ePress, Inc.

Green, John. Paper Towns. 2011. 11.04 (978-0-7848-3497-8(0), Everbind) Marco Bk. Co.

—Paper Towns. movie tie-in ed. 2015. (ENG.). 336p. (YA). (gr. 9). pap. 10.99 (978-0-14-751765-4(6), Penguin Books) Penguin Publishing Group.

—Paper Towns. (ENG.). (YA). (gr. 9-18). 2009. 336p. 10.99 (978-0-14-241493-4(X), Speak) 2008. 320p. 18.99 (978-0-525-47818-8(3), Dutton Books for Young Readers) Penguin Young Readers Group.

—Paper Towns. 2010. (ENG., Illus.). 305p. (gr. 9-12). 20.00 (978-1-60686-913-0(2)) Perfection Learning Corp.

—Paper Towns. 2009. lib. bdg. 20.85 (978-0-606-10658-0(8), Turtleback) Turtleback Bks.

Green, Ken. Not a Chance. (Thumbprint Mysteries Ser.). 32.86 (978-0-8092-0422-9(3)) McGraw-Hill/Contemporary.

Green, Risa. Projection. 2014. (ENG., Illus.). 286p. (YA). (gr. 9). pap. 9.99 (978-1-61695-454-3(X), Soho Teen) Soho Pr., Inc.

Green, Terry. Moonstone. 2010. 188p. pap. 14.49 (978-1-4520-4634-1(4)) AuthorHouse.

Green, Timothy. Mystery of Coyote Canyon, 1 vol. Green, Timothy, illus. 2008. (ENG., Illus.). 137p. (gr. 8-12). pap. 12.95 (978-0-941270-83-0(1)) Gibbs Smith, Publisher.

Greenburg, Dan. The Shluffmuffin Boy Is History, Bk. 5. Fischer, Scott M., illus. 2006. (Secrets of Dripping Fang Ser.: Bk. 5). (ENG.). 176p. (J). (gr. 2-5). 12.99 (978-0-15-206035-0(9)) Houghton Mifflin Harcourt Publishing Co.

Greene, Jacqueline. Secrets at Camp Nokomis: A Rebecca Mystery. Hirsch, Jennifer, ed. Tibbles, JeanPaul, illus. 2010. (ENG.). 192p. (J). (gr. 4-8). pap. 6.95 (978-1-59369-657-3(4)) American Girl Publishing, Inc.

Greene, Janice. The Girl Who Had Everything (Suspense), 1 vol. 2017. (Pageturners Ser.). (ENG.). 80p. (YA). (gr. 9-12). 8.95 **(978-1-68021-407-9(1))** Saddleback Educational Publishing, Inc.

Greene, Janice. The White Room, 1 vol. unabr. ed. 2010. (Q Reads Ser.). (ENG.). 32p. (YA). (gr. 9-12). pap. 6.95 (978-1-61651-197-5(4)) Saddleback Educational Publishing, Inc.

Greenwald, Owen B. Big Bet. 2016. (Big Bet Ser.: 6). (ENG.). 200p. (YA). (gr. 6-12). lib. bdg. 162.78 (978-1-68076-182-5(X), Epic Pr.) ABDO Publishing Co.

Greenwood, Anna. The Children at St Bartholomew's Hospital. 2008. 172p. pap. 13.95 (978-1-4401-0558-6(8)) iUniverse, Inc.

Gregory, Nan. How Smudge Came, 1 vol. Lightburn, Ron, illus. (ENG.). 32p. (J). pap. 15.95 (978-0-88995-161-7(6)) Red Deer Pr. CAN. Dist: Ingram Publisher Services.

Grey, Allan. Alienology. Steer, Dugald A., ed. Carrell, Douglas, illus. 2010. (Ologies Ser.: 10). (ENG.). 32p. (J). (gr. 3-7). 21.99 (978-0-7636-4565-6(6)) Candlewick Pr.

Griffin, Adele. The Unfinished Life of Addison Stone: A Novel. 2016. (ENG., Illus.). 256p. (YA). (gr. 9). pap. 11.99 (978-1-61695-596-0(1), Soho Teen) Soho Pr., Inc.

Griffin, N. Smashie Mcperter & the Mystery of Room 11. Hindley, Kate, illus. 2015. (ENG.). 256p. (J). (gr. 2-5). 15.99 (978-0-7636-6145-8(7)) Candlewick Pr.

Griffin, N. Smashie Mcperter & the Mystery of the Missing Goop. Hindley, Kate, illus. (Smashie Mcperter Investigates Ser.). (ENG.). 304p. (J). (gr. 2-5). 2017. pap. 5.99 **(978-0-7636-9795-2(8))** 2016. 15.99 (978-0-7636-8535-5(6)) Candlewick Pr.

Griffiths, Andy. The 52-Story Treehouse. Denton, Terry, illus. 2016. (Treehouse Bks.: 4). (ENG.). 336p. (J). (gr. 2-5). 13.99 (978-1-250-02693-4(8), 9781250026934) Feiwel & Friends.

—The 52-Story Treehouse. Denton, Terry, illus. 2017. (Treehouse Bks.). (ENG.). 352p. (J). pap. 6.99 (978-1-250-10379-6(7), 9781250103796) Square Fish.

—The 52-Story Treehouse. 2017. (Treehouse Adventures Ser.: 4). (J). lib. bdg. 17.20 **(978-0-606-40350-4(7))** Turtleback Bks.

Griffo, Michael. Starfall. 2014. (Darkborn Legacy Ser.). (ENG.). 384p. (YA). (gr. 13). pap. 20.00 (978-0-7582-8076-3(9), K-Teen) Kensington Publishing Corp.

Griggs, Joyce. Imanis Good Deed. 2006. pap. 9.95 (978-1-4327-0071-3(5)) Outskirts Pr., Inc.

Grigsby, Cynthia. Hollow Creek: A Haunted Beginning, 01. 2006. 163p. (J). 14.95 (978-0-9786840-0-6(1)) Grigsby, Cynthia.

Grisham, John. The Abduction. 2009. (Theodore Boone Ser.: Bk. 2). 9.68 (978-0-7848-3783-2(X), Everbind) Marco Bk. Co.

—The Abduction, 2 vols. (Theodore Boone Ser.: 2). (ENG.). 256p. (J). (gr. 3-7). 2012. pap. 8.99 (978-0-14-242137-6(5), Puffin Books) 2011. 16.99 (978-0-525-42557-1(8), Dutton Books for Young Readers) Penguin Young Readers Group.

—The Abduction. 2012. (Theodore Boone Ser.: 2). lib. bdg. 19.65 (978-0-606-26079-4(X), Turtleback) Turtleback Bks.

—The Accused. (Theodore Boone Ser.: 3). (ENG.). (J). (gr. 3-7). 2013. 304p. pap. 8.99 (978-0-14-242613-5(X), Puffin Books) 2012. 288p. 16.99 (978-0-525-42576-2(4), Dutton Books for Young Readers) Penguin Young Readers Group.

—The Accused. 2013. (Theodore Boone Ser.: 3). lib. bdg. 18.40 (978-0-606-31696-5(5), Turtleback) Turtleback Bks.

—The Activist. 2013. (Theodore Boone Ser.: Bk. 4). (ENG.). 272p. (J). (gr. 3-7). 16.99 (978-0-525-42577-9(2), Dutton Books for Young Readers) Penguin Young Readers Group.

—The Fugitive. 2015. (Theodore Boone Ser.: 5). (ENG.). 256p. (J). (gr. 3-7). 17.99 (978-0-525-42638-7(8), Dutton Books for Young Readers) Penguin Young Readers Group.

—The Fugitive. 2016. (Theodore Boone Ser.: 5). 272p. lib. bdg. 18.40 (978-0-606-38847-4(8)) Turtleback Bks.

—Kid Lawyer. (Theodore Boone Ser.: 1). (ENG.). (J). (gr. 3-7). 2011. 288p. 8.99 (978-0-14-241722-5(X), Puffin Books) 2010. 272p. 16.99 (978-0-525-42384-3(2), Dutton Books for Young Readers) Penguin Young Readers Group.

—Kid Lawyer. l.t. ed. 2010. (Theodore Boone Ser.: Bk. 1). (ENG.). 278p. (J). 24.99 (978-1-4104-3050-2(2)) Thorndike Pr.

—Kid Lawyer. 2011. (Theodore Boone Ser.: 1). lib. bdg. 19.65 (978-0-606-23071-1(8), Turtleback) Turtleback Bks.

—The Scandal. 2016. (Theodore Boone Ser.: 6). (ENG.). 224p. (J). (gr. 3-7). 17.99 (978-0-525-42639-4(6), Dutton Books for Young Readers) Penguin Young Readers Group.

—Theodore Boone Box Set, 5 vols. 2013. (Theodore Boone Ser.). (ENG.). 816p. (J). (gr. 3-7). 50.97 (978-0-525-42637-0(X), Dutton Books for Young Readers) Penguin Young Readers Group.

Groot, Bob de. Jade Vol. 5. Rodrigue, illus. 2008. (Clifton Ser.: 5). (ENG.). 48p. pap. 11.95 (978-1-905460-52-6(X)) CineBook GBR. Dist: National Bk. Network.

Groot, De. Black Moon. Spear, Luke, tr. from FRE. Rodrigue, illus. 2007. (Clifton Ser.: 4). (ENG.). 48p. (J). (gr. 4-7). pap. 9.99 (978-1-905460-30-4(9)) CineBook GBR. Dist: National Bk. Network.

Gross, Scott. Scooby-Doo & the Aliens of Area 49, 1 vol. 2013. (Scooby-Doo Graphic Novels Set 3 Ser.). (ENG.). 24p. (J). (gr. 2-6). lib. bdg. 24.21 (978-1-61479-049-5(3), Essential Library) ABDO Publishing Co.

Guest, Jacqueline. At Risk, 1 vol. 2004. (Lorimer SideStreets Ser.). (ENG.). 192p. (YA). (gr. 9-12). 9.95 (978-1-55028-846-9(6), 9781550288469); 16.95 (978-1-55028-847-6(4), 9781550288476) Lorimer, James & Co., Ltd., Pubs. CAN. Dist: Casemate Pubs. & Bk. Distributors, LLC.

Gunderson, Jessica A. How to Keep a Secret for Detectives. 2008. 206p. pap. 15.50 (978-0-557-01369-2(0)) Lulu Pr., Inc.

Gustafson, Scott. Eddie: The Lost Youth of Edgar Allan Poe. Gustafson, Scott, illus. (ENG., Illus.). 208p. (J). (gr. 3-7). 2012. pap. 6.99 (978-1-4169-9765-8(2)) 2011. 15.99 (978-1-4169-9764-1(4)) Simon & Schuster Bks. For Young Readers. (Simon & Schuster Bks. For Young Readers).

Gutman, Dan. The Million Dollar Strike. 2004. 176p. (J). lib. bdg. 18.46 (978-1-4242-2107-3(2)) Fitzgerald Bks.

—The Million Dollar Strike. 2006. 176p. (J). (gr. 3-7). 13.65 (978-0-7569-7023-9(7)) Perfection Learning Corp.

Guzaldo, Jessica. Murder & Betrayal DeFalco, Julie & Cowhey, Dennis R., eds. Cowhey, Dennis E., illus. 2003. 72p. (YA). (gr. 7-8). pap. 9.95 (978-0-9642823-2-2(1)) Key Answer Products, Inc.

Haas, Abigail. Dangerous Girls. (ENG., Illus.). 400p. (YA). (gr. 9). 2014. pap. 10.99 (978-1-4424-8660-7(0)) 2013. 16.99 (978-1-4424-8659-1(7)) Simon Pulse. (Simon Pulse).

Hadcroft, Will. Anne Droyd & the Ghosts of Winter Hill. 2013. 210p. pap. (978-0-9560537-2-5(6)) Nordic.

Haddix, Margaret Peterson. The House on the Gulf. (ENG., Illus.). 208p. (J). (gr. 3-7). 2006. pap. 7.99 (978-1-4169-1406-8(4)) 2004. 17.99 (978-0-689-85422-4(6)) Simon & Schuster Bks. For Young Readers. (Simon & Schuster Bks. For Young Readers).

—Into the Gauntlet. 2010. (39 Clues Ser.: 10). (ENG.). 336p. (J). (gr. 3-7). 12.99 (978-0-545-06050-9(8)) Scholastic, Inc.

Hadnot, Victor. The Wheels of God. 2003. 140p. (YA). pap. 11.95 (978-0-595-27507-6(9), Writers Club Pr.) iUniverse, Inc.

Haesche, Richard, Sr. The Mystery of Monster Manor. 2007. (ENG.). 306p. (YA). 11.99 (978-0-9798536-6-1(4)) Kreative X-Pressions Pubns.

Haesche, Richard Paul, Sr. The Mystery of Dismal Swamp. 2007. 402p. (YA). 10.99 (978-0-9798536-8-5(0)) Kreative X-Pressions Pubns.

—The Treasure of Pirates Cave. 2007. (ENG.). 378p. (YA). 11.99 (978-0-9798536-7-8(2)) Kreative X-Pressions Pubns.

Hahn, Mary Downing. Closed for the Season. 2010. (ENG.). 192p. (J). (gr. 5-7). pap. 6.99 (978-0-547-39853-2(0)) Houghton Mifflin Harcourt Publishing Co.

—The Dead Man in Indian Creek. 2009. (gr. 3-6). 17.20 (978-0-8335-6693-5(8), Turtleback) Turtleback Bks.

Haight, Jessica & Robinson, Stephanie. The Secret Files of Fairday Morrow. Muradov, Roman, illus. 2015. (ENG.). 272p. (J). (gr. 4-7). 18.99 (978-0-375-99182-0(4), Delacorte Bks. for Young Readers) Random Hse. Children's Bks.

Hainsworth, Emily. Take the Fall. 2016. 368p. (YA). (gr. 9). 17.99 (978-0-06-209422-3(X)) HarperCollins Pubs.

Hale, Bruce. The Big Nap. unabr. ed. 2004. (Chet Gecko Mystery Ser.: No. 4). 128p. (J). (gr. 3-6). pap. 17.00 incl. audio (978-0-8072-1707-8(7), S FTR 272 SP, Listening Library) Random Hse. Audio Publishing Group.

—The Big Nap. Hale, Bruce, illus. 2008. (Chet Gecko Mystery Ser.: No. 4). (ENG., Illus.). 128p. (gr. 1-5). 24.21 (978-1-59961-461-8(8)) Spotlight.

—Curse of the Were-Hyena: A Monstertown Mystery. Hale, Bruce, illus. 2016. (Monstertown Mysteries Ser.). (ENG., Illus.). 220p. (J). (gr. 3-7). 14.99 *(978-1-4847-1325-9(7))* Disney Pr.
—Dial M for Mongoose: A Chet Gecko Mystery. 2010. (Chet Gecko Ser.: 15). (ENG., Illus.). 128p. (J). (gr. 2-5). pap. 5.99 *(978-0-547-48079-4(2))* Houghton Mifflin Harcourt Publishing Co.
—Farewell, My Lunchbag. 2009. (Chet Gecko Ser.: 3). (ENG., Illus.). 128p. (J). (gr. 2-5). pap. 6.99 *(978-0-15-202629-5(0))* Houghton Mifflin Harcourt Publishing Co.
—Farewell, My Lunchbag. unabr. ed. 2004. (Chet Gecko Mystery Ser.: No. 3). 128p. (J). (gr. 3-6). pap. 17.00 incl. audio *(978-0-8072-1708-5(5)*, S FTR 273 SP, Listening Library) Random Hse. Audio Publishing Group.
—From Russia with Lunch: A Chet Gecko Mystery. 2010. (Chet Gecko Ser.: 14). (ENG., Illus.). 128p. (J). (gr. 2-5). pap. 6.99 *(978-0-547-32882-9(6))* Houghton Mifflin Harcourt Publishing Co.
—Give My Regrets to Broadway. 2005. (Chet Gecko Ser.: 9). (ENG., Illus.). 144p. (J). (gr. 2-5). pap. 5.99 *(978-0-15-216730-1(7))* Houghton Mifflin Harcourt Publishing Co.
—Give My Regrets to Broadway. 2005. (Chet Gecko Mystery Ser.). (Illus.). 115p. (gr. 3-7). 16.00 *(978-0-7569-5247-1(6))* Perfection Learning Corp.
—The Hamster of the Baskervilles. 2003. (Chet Gecko Ser.: 5). (ENG., Illus.). 144p. (J). (gr. 2-5). pap. 6.99 *(978-0-15-202509-0(X))* Houghton Mifflin Harcourt Publishing Co.
—Hiss Me Deadly. Hale, Bruce, illus. 2009. (Chet Gecko Ser.: 13). (ENG., Illus.). 128p. (J). (gr. 2-5). pap. 5.99 *(978-0-15-206424-2(9))* Houghton Mifflin Harcourt Publishing Co.
—Key Lardo: A Chet Gecko Mystery. Hale, Bruce, illus. 2007. (Chet Gecko Ser.: 12). (ENG., Illus.). 128p. (J). (gr. 2-5). pap. 5.99 *(978-0-15-205235-5(6))* Houghton Mifflin Harcourt Publishing Co.
—The Malted Falcon. 2007. (Chet Gecko Mystery Ser.). (Illus.). 107p. (J). (gr. 4-7). pap. 6.60 *(978-1-4189-5239-6(7))* Harcourt Trade Pubs.
—The Malted Falcon. 2008. (Chet Gecko Ser.: 7). (ENG., Illus.). 128p. (J). (gr. 2-5). pap. 5.99 *(978-0-15-216712-7(9))* Houghton Mifflin Harcourt Publishing Co.
—The Malted Falcon. Hale, Bruce, illus. 2008. (Chet Gecko Mystery Ser.: No. 7). (ENG., Illus.). 128p. (gr. 1-5). 24.21 *(978-1-59961-467-0(7))* Spotlight.
—Monsters on the Loose! A Seek & Solve Mystery! Garbot, Dave, illus. 2013. (ENG.). 32p. (J). (gr. -1-3). 7.99 *(978-0-06-223706-4(3))* HarperCollins Pubs.
—Murder, My Tweet. 2005. (Chet Gecko Ser.: 10). (ENG., Illus.). 144p. (J). (gr. 2-5). pap. 5.99 *(978-0-15-205219-5(4))* Houghton Mifflin Harcourt Publishing Co.
—Murder, My Tweet. 2005. (Chet Gecko Mystery Ser.). (Illus.). 117p. (gr. 3-7). 16.00 *(978-0-7569-5248-8(4))* Perfection Learning Corp.
—Murder, My Tweet. Hale, Bruce, illus. 2008. (Chet Gecko Mystery Ser.: No. 10). (ENG., Illus.). 136p. (gr. 1-5). 24.21 *(978-1-59961-468-7(5))* Spotlight.
—Mutant Mantis Lunch Ladies! 2017. (Monstertown Mysteries Ser.). (ENG.). 208p. (J). (gr. 3-7). 14.99 *(978-1-4847-1324-2(9))* Disney Pr.
—The Mystery of Mr. Nice. Hale, Bruce, illus. 2008. (Chet Gecko Ser.: 2). (ENG., Illus.). 128p. (J). (gr. 2-5). pap. 6.99 *(978-0-15-202515-1(4))* Houghton Mifflin Harcourt Publishing Co.
—The Mystery of Mr. Nice. unabr. ed. 2004. (Chet Gecko Mystery Ser.: No. 2). 112p. (J). (gr. 3-6). pap. 17.00 incl. audio *(978-0-8072-0343-9(2)*, Listening Library) Random Hse. Audio Publishing Group.
—The Mystery of Mr. Nice. Hale, Bruce, illus. 2008. (Chet Gecko Mystery Ser.: No. 2). (ENG., Illus.). 112p. (gr. 1-5). 24.21 *(978-1-59961-469-4(3))* Spotlight.
—The Possum Always Rings Twice. Hale, Bruce, illus. 2007. (Chet Gecko Ser.: 11). (ENG., Illus.). 128p. (J). (gr. 2-5). pap. 5.99 *(978-0-15-205233-1(X))* Houghton Mifflin Harcourt Publishing Co.
—This Gum for Hire. 2003. (Chet Gecko Ser.: 6). (ENG., Illus.). 144p. (J). (gr. 2-5). pap. 5.99 *(978-0-15-202497-0(2))* Houghton Mifflin Harcourt Publishing Co.
—This Gum for Hire. 2007. (Chet Gecko Mystery Ser.). (Illus.). 115p. (J). (gr. 4-7). pap. 6.60 *(978-1-4189-5216-7(8))* Houghton Mifflin Harcourt Supplemental Pubs.
—This Gum for Hire. Hale, Bruce, illus. 2008. (Chet Gecko Mystery Ser.: No. 6). (ENG., Illus.). 128p. (gr. 1-5). 24.21 *(978-1-59961-471-7(5))* Spotlight.
—Trouble Is My Beeswax. 2004. (Chet Gecko Mystery Ser.). (Illus.). 111p. (gr. 3-7). 16.00 *(978-0-7569-3488-0(5))* Perfection Learning Corp.
—Trouble Is My Beeswax. Hale, Bruce, illus. 2008. (Chet Gecko Mystery Ser.: No. 8). (ENG., Illus.). 128p. (gr. 1-5). 24.21 *(978-1-59961-472-4(3))* Spotlight.
—Trouble Is My Beeswax: A Chet Gecko Mystery. 2004. (Chet Gecko Ser.: 8). (ENG., Illus.). 144p. (J). (gr. 2-5). pap. 6.99 *(978-0-15-216724-0(2))* Houghton Mifflin Harcourt Publishing Co.
Hale, Kathleen. No One Else Can Have You. 2014. (Kippy Bushman Ser.). (ENG.). 384p. (YA). (gr. 9). 17.99 *(978-0-06-221119-4(6))* HarperCollins Pubs.
—Nothing Bad Is Going to Happen. (Kippy Bushman Ser.). 272p. (YA). (gr. 9). 2017. pap. 9.99 *(978-0-06-221123-1(4))* 2016. 17.99 *(978-0-06-221121-7(8))* HarperCollins Pubs. (HarperTeen).
Hale, Shannon. The Forgotten Sisters. 2015. (Princess Academy Ser.: 3). (ENG.). 336p. (YA). (gr. 5-8). 17.99 *(978-1-61963-485-5(6)*, 9781619634855, Bloomsbury USA Childrens) Bloomsbury Publishing USA.
—The Forgotten Sisters. 2016. (Princess Academy Ser.: 3). (J). lib. bdg. 18.40 *(978-0-606-38441-4(3))* Turtleback Bks.
Hall, Duncan. Brambleholme Summer. 2010. 125p. pap. 12.95 *(978-1-4461-4462-6(3))* Lulu Pr., Inc.
Hall, Jacque. Tommy Turns Dtective. 2009. pap. 10.95 *(978-1-61584-268-1(3))* Independent Pub.
Hall, Leanne. Iris & the Tiger. 2016. (ENG., Illus.). 240p. (J). (gr. 3-7). 8.99 *(978-1-925240-79-5(7))* Text Publishing Co. AUS. Dist: Consortium Bk. Sales & Distribution.
Hall, Maggie. The Conspiracy of Us. 2015. (Conspiracy of Us Ser.). (ENG.). (YA). 336p. (gr. 7). 17.99 *(978-0-399-16650-1(5))*;Pack. 161.91 *(978-0-399-17404-9(4))* Penguin Young Readers Group. (G.P. Putnam's Sons Books for Young Readers).
—Map of Fates. 2016. (Conspiracy of Us Ser.). (ENG.). 320p. (YA). (gr. 7). 17.99 *(978-0-399-16651-8(3)*, G.P. Putnam's Sons Books for Young Readers) Penguin Young Readers Group.
Halley, Jane E. The Unidentified Flight-Less Object. 2008. 52p. pap. 22.49 *(978-1-4343-6491-3(7))* AuthorHouse.
Halliday, Gemma. Deadly Cool. 2011. (Deadly Cool Ser.: 1). (ENG.). 320p. (YA). (gr. 8). pap. 8.99 *(978-0-06-200331-7(3)*, HarperTeen) HarperCollins Pubs.
—Social Suicide. 2012. (Deadly Cool Ser.: 2). (ENG.). 288p. (YA). (gr. 8). pap. 8.99 *(978-0-06-200332-4(1)*, HarperTeen) HarperCollins Pubs.
Halverson, Mathew. Concord Cunningham Pursues the Clues: The Scripture Sleuth 5. 2008. (Mystery Ser.). (Illus.). 98p. (J). (gr. 4-7). pap. 8.95 *(978-1-885904-55-3(X))* Focus Publishing.
Hamilton, Elizabeth L. Mystery at Lake Cachuma. 2003. (Character Mystery Ser.: No. 1). (Illus.). 114p. (J). (gr. 3-6). per. 9.95 *(978-0-9713749-4-2(5)*, Character-in-Action) Quiet Impact, Inc.
—Surprise at Pearl Harbor. 2004. (Character Mystery Ser.: No. 2). (Illus.). 144p. (J). per. 9.95 *(978-0-9754629-2-8(X)*, Character-in-Action) Quiet Impact, Inc.
Hamilton, Virginia. The House of Dies Drear. 8.97 *(978-0-13-437491-8(6))* Prentice Hall PTR.
—The House of Dies Drear. 2006. (ENG.). 256p. (J). (gr. 6-9). pap. 7.99 *(978-1-4169-1405-1(6)*, Aladdin) Simon & Schuster Children's Publishing.
Hamley, Dennis. Oxford Anthology of Mystery Stories. 2014. (ENG.). 224p. (J). 11.95 *(978-0-19-275404-2(1))* Oxford Univ. Pr., Inc.
—Very Far from Here. 2007. 208p. per. *(978-1-904529-33-0(X)*, Back to Front) Solidus.
Hammel, Sara. The Underdogs. 2016. (ENG.). 320p. (J). 16.99 *(978-0-374-30161-3(1)*, 9780374301613, Farrar, Straus & Giroux (BYR)) Farrar, Straus & Giroux.
Handwerk, Marina. Hey Cool, I've Never Seen a Teacher with His Head Cut off Before! 2007. 284p. per. 11.95 *(978-1-4327-0332-5(3))* Outskirts Pr., Inc.
Hannah, Vickie. There's A Schnoozle in My Closet. 2004. (J). lib. bdg. 19.95 *(978-0-9754728-4-2(4))* Big Ransom Studio.
Hannibal, James R. The Lost Property Office. 2016. (Section 13 Ser.: 1). (ENG., Illus.). 400p. (J). (gr. 3-7). 16.99 *(978-1-4814-6709-4(3)*, Simon & Schuster Bks. For Young Readers) Simon & Schuster Bks. For Young Readers.
Hannigan, Kate. The Detective's Assistant. 2015. (ENG.). 368p. (J). (gr. 3-7). 17.00 *(978-0-316-40351-1(2))* Little Brown & Co.
—The Detective's Assistant. 2016. (ENG.). 368p. (J). (gr. 3-7). pap. 6.99 *(978-0-316-40349-8(0))* Little, Brown Bks. for Young Readers.
Hansen, Ace. Julius Caesar Brown & the Green Gas Mystery. 2013. 114p. pap. *(978-1-77127-424-1(7))* MuseItUp Publishing.
Hansen, Lynne & Bosco, Sally. AltDeath.com. 2004. 152p. (YA). pap. 9.00 *(978-0-7599-4572-2(1))* Hard Shell Word Factory.
Hanson, Ed. Mystery at Bear Lake. 2005. (Barclay Family Adventures 2 Ser.). 64p. (J). per. 3.95 *(978-1-56254-807-0(7)*, SP8077) Saddleback Educational Publishing, Inc.
Hapka, Catherine, pseud. Forever Free. 5th ed. 2009. (ENG.). 288p. pap. 7.99 *(978-1-4231-1668-4(2))* Disney Pr.
Harbourt, Kathi. The Adventures of Kat VanDrat. 2013. (ENG.). 111p. (YA). pap. 11.95 *(978-1-4787-1010-3(1))* Outskirts Pr., Inc.
Hardie, Richard. Leap of Faith. 2013. (Illus.). 272p. pap. *(978-1-909841-26-0(9))* Crooked Cat Publishing.
Hardinge, Frances. The Lie Tree. 2016. (ENG.). 384p. (YA). (gr. 8-17). 17.95 *(978-1-4197-1895-3(9)*, Amulet Bks.) Abrams, Inc.
Harel, Moshe. Elf Prince. 2012. (ENG.). 258p. pap. *(978-965-550-089-9(6))* Contento De Semrik.
Harkrader, Lisa. A Fishy Mystery: Venn Diagrams. Pillo, Cary, illus. 2017. (Math Matters (r) Ser.). (ENG.). 32p. (gr. k-3). (J). 5.95 *(978-1-57565-866-7(6))*; 23.99 ***(978-1-57565-869-8(0))*** Kane Press, Inc.
—The Mystery of the Whispering Fountain. 2016. (Spring Forward Ser.). (J). (gr. 1). *(978-1-4900-9400-7(8))* Benchmark Education Co.
Harrington, K. A. Forget Me. (ENG.). 288p. (YA). (gr. 7). 2015. pap. 9.99 *(978-0-14-750941-3(6)*, Speak) 2014. 17.99 *(978-0-399-16529-0(0)*, G.P. Putnam's Sons Books for Young Readers) Penguin Young Readers Group.
Harrington, Kim. Clarity. (ENG.). 256p. (J). (gr. 9-9). 2012. pap. 8.99 *(978-0-545-23051-3(9))* 2011. 16.99 *(978-0-545-23050-6(0))* Scholastic, Inc.
—The Dead & Buried. 2013. (ENG.). 304p. (J). (gr. 7). 17.99 *(978-0-545-33302-3(4))* Scholastic, Inc.
—Perception. 2012. (ENG.). 288p. (J). (gr. 9). 16.99 *(978-0-545-23053-7(5))* Scholastic, Inc.
Harris, Donna. Ruff Life. 2011. 240p. pap. 17.99 *(978-1-4567-5081-7(X))* AuthorHouse.
Harris, Loretta. A Gangsta's Life. 2007. 26p. (YA). 1.99 *(978-0-9786681-4-3(6))* Triumphant Living Enterprises, Inc.
—The Rise of Death Valley. 2007. 41p. (YA). 1.99 *(978-0-9786681-0-5(3))* Triumphant Living Enterprises, Inc.
Harris, Patricia. Rosalina & Jethro Solve a Mystery. 2017. (Rosalina's Flower Garden Ser.). 24p. (gr. 4-6). pap. 8.25 ***(978-1-5383-2105-8(X)***, PowerKids Pr.) Rosen Publishing Group, Inc., The.
Harrison, Margot. The Killer in Me. 2016. (ENG., Illus.). 364p. (YA). (gr. 9-17). 17.99 *(978-1-4847-2799-7(1))* Hyperion Bks. for Children.
Harrison, Michelle. The Thirteen Curses. 2014. (ENG., Illus.). 464p. (YA). pap. 8.99 *(978-1-4711-2168-5(2)*, Simon & Schuster Children's) Simon & Schuster, Ltd. GBR. Dist: Simon & Schuster, Inc.
—The Thirteen Secrets. 2014. (ENG.). 400p. (YA). pap. 8.99 *(978-1-4711-2169-2(0)*, Simon & Schuster Children's) Simon & Schuster, Ltd. GBR. Dist: Simon & Schuster, Inc.
—The Thirteen Treasures. 2014. (ENG., Illus.). 352p. pap. 8.99 *(978-1-4711-2167-8(4)*, Simon & Schuster Children's) Simon & Schuster, Ltd. GBR. Dist: Simon & Schuster, Inc.
—13 Treasures. 2011. (13 Treasures Trilogy Ser.: 1). (ENG.). 384p. (J). (gr. 3-7). pap. 8.99 *(978-0-316-04147-8(5))* Little, Brown Bks. for Young Readers.
Hart, Alison. Fires of Jubilee. 2003. (ENG., Illus.). 192p. (J). (gr. 3-7). pap. 9.99 *(978-0-689-85528-3(1)*, Simon & Schuster/Paula Wiseman Bks.) Simon & Schuster/Paula Wiseman Bks.
—Whirlwind. 2010. (ENG.). 272p. (YA). (gr. 7-8). pap. 8.99 *(978-0-375-86005-8(3)*, Laurel Leaf) Random Hse. Children's Bks.
Hart, Anne. Roman Justice: Too Roman to Handle. 2003. 186p. (YA). pap. 13.95 *(978-0-595-27282-2(7)*, Writers Advantage Pr.) iUniverse, Inc.
Hartinger, Brent. Three Truths & a Lie. 2016. (ENG., Illus.). 272p. (YA). (gr. 9). 17.99 *(978-1-4814-4960-1(5)*, Simon Pulse) Simon Pulse.
Hartley, A. J. Steeplejack. 2016. (Steeplejack Ser.: 1). (ENG.). 336p. (YA). 17.99 *(978-0-7653-8342-6(X)*, 9780765383426, Tor Teen) Doherty, Tom Assocs., LLC.
Hartley, Susan. Stephanie Investigates. 2004. (Shared Connections Ser.). (J). instr.'s gde. ed. 27.00 *(978-1-4108-1618-4(4))* Benchmark Education Co.
—Stephanie Investigates: Small Book. 2004. (Shared Connections Ser.). (J). pap. *(978-1-4108-1642-9(7))* Benchmark Education Co.
Hartnett, Sonya. What the Birds See. 2007. (ENG., Illus.). 208p. (YA). (gr. 9). pap. 7.99 *(978-0-7636-3680-7(0))* Candlewick Pr.
Hartt-Snowbell, Sarah. Vivian Untangled. 2006. (ENG., Illus.). 136p. (J). per. 8.95 *(978-1-894917-25-4(1)*, Napoleon & Co.) Dundurn CAN. Dist: Ingram Publisher Services.
Harvey, Jacqueline. Alice-Miranda at School. 2012. (ENG.). 272p. (J). (gr. 2-5). 7.99 *(978-0-385-73994-8(X)*, Yearling) Random Hse. Children's Bks.
—Alice-Miranda to the Rescue. 2016. (Alice-Miranda Ser.: 13). (ENG.). 336p. (J). (gr. 3-7). pap. 9.99 *(978-0-85798-522-4(1))* Random Hse. Australia AUS. Dist: Independent Pubs. Group.
Harvey, M. A. Attack of the Jaguar: Dare to Take the Test. 2004. (Illus.). 128p. (J). pap. *(978-1-84458-051-4(2)*, Pavilion Children's Books) Pavilion Bks.
—The Scorpion Secret: Dare to Take the Test. 2004. (Illus.). 128p. (J). pap. *(978-1-84458-050-7(4)*, Pavilion Children's Books) Pavilion Bks.
Harvey, Pam & Panckridge, Michael. Ghost of a Chance. 2007. 208p. *(978-0-207-20063-2(7))* HarperCollins Pubs. Australia.
—Into the Fire. 2008. 192p. (J). *(978-0-207-20061-8(0))* HarperCollins Pubs. Australia.
Hauf, Kyle. Annabelle Discovers the Missing Lunch Money. PA Illustrator, illus. 2011. 36p. pap. 24.95 *(978-1-4560-3656-0(4))* America Star Bks.
Hautman, Pete. The Forgetting Machine. 2016. (Flinkwater Chronicles Ser.: 2). (ENG., Illus.). 224p. (J). (gr. 4-8). 16.99 *(978-1-4814-6438-3(8)*, Simon & Schuster Bks. For Young Readers) Simon & Schuster Bks. For Young Readers.
Hautman, Pete & Logue, Mary. Skullduggery. 2007. (Bloodwater Mysteries Ser.). (ENG.). 192p. (J). (gr. 5-18). 16.99 *(978-0-399-24378-3(X)*, G.P. Putnam's Sons Books for Young Readers) Penguin Young Readers Group.
—Snatched. 2007. (Bloodwater Mysteries Ser.). (ENG.). 224p. (J). (gr. 5-7). 7.99 *(978-0-14-240795-0(X)*, Puffin Books) Penguin Young Readers Group.
Hawke, Rosanne. Sailmaker. (Illus.). 160p. pap. *(978-0-7344-0318-6(6)*, Lothian Children's Bks.) Hachette Australia.
Hawking, Stephen W. & Hawking, Lucy. George's Secret Key to the Universe. Parsons, Garry, illus. 2009. (George's Secret Key Ser.). (ENG.). 336p. (J). (gr. 3-7). pap. 12.99 *(978-1-4169-8584-6(0)*, Simon & Schuster Bks. For Young Readers) Simon & Schuster Bks. For Young Readers.
Hawkins, Rachel. Hex Hall, Bk. 1. 2010. (ENG.). 336p. (J). (gr. 7-17). 16.99 *(978-1-4231-2130-5(9))* Hyperion Pr.
Hay, Sam. Goldfish from Beyond the Grave #4. Cooper, Simon, illus. 2015. (Undead Pets Ser.: 4). (ENG.). 112p. (J). (gr. 1-3). 5.99 *(978-0-448-47798-5(X)*, Grosset & Dunlap) Penguin Young Readers Group.
Hayes, Celeste. The Puzzle Box of Nefertiti: A Sphinx & Trevi Adventure. Bishop, Christina, illus. 2011. 42p. (J). pap. 19.95 *(978-0-9785695-3-2(9))* Adam's Creations Publishing, LLC.
Hayes, Geoffrey. Benny & Penny in the Big No-No! Hayes, Geoffrey, illus. 2014. (Benny & Penny Ser.). (ENG., Illus.). 32p. (J). (gr. -1-3). pap. 6.99 *(978-1-935179-35-1(7))* TOON Books / RAW Junior, LLC.
—The Mystery of the Riverboat Robber. 2016. (Step into Reading Ser.). (ENG., Illus.). 48p. (J). (gr. k-3). lib. bdg. 12.99 *(978-0-375-97470-0(9)*, Random Hse. Bks. for Young Readers) Random Hse. Children's Bks.
Hays, Anna Jane. The Secret of the Circle-K Cave. Smath, Jerry, illus. 2006. (Science Solves It! Ser.). 32p. (J). (gr. -1-3). pap. 5.95 *(978-1-57565-189-7(0))* Kane Press, Inc.
Hays, Phillip. Porka-Bella-Snu & the Mystery of the Letters. Spencer, Chip, illus. 2013. 54p. pap. 6.95 *(978-1-938679-05-6(9))* Written World Communications.
Headrick, Tammy Hill. That Famous Bird, Sir Thornton the Third. 2009. 24p. pap. 12.00 *(978-1-4269-0550-6(5))* Trafford Publishing.
Healey, Karen. The Shattering. 2013. (ENG.). 336p. (YA). (gr. 7-17). pap. 8.99 *(978-0-316-12573-4(3))* Little, Brown Bks. for Young Readers.
Hechtman, Betty Jacobson. Blue Schwartz & Nefertiti's Necklace: A Mystery with Recipes. 2006. 152p. (J). (gr. 5-9). per. 8.95 *(978-0-9768126-3-0(0))* Brown Barn Bks.
Hees, Miriam. The Adventures of Jilly & Brad: Noises in the Attic. Kinneman, D. Michael, illus. 2003. 128p. (J). pap. 5.95 *(978-0-9718348-4-2(9))* Blooming Tree Pr.
Helou, Sandra & Chown, Xanna Eve. Grover on the Case: Follow the Reader Level 1. 2008. (Sesame Street Ser.). (ENG.). 24p. (J). 24.99 *(978-1-4169-5852-9(5)*, Simon Scribbles) Simon Scribbles.
Heltzel, Anne. Charlie, Presumed Dead. (ENG.). 272p. (YA). (gr. 9). 2016. pap. 8.99 *(978-0-544-66869-0(3))* 2015. 17.99 *(978-0-544-38849-9(6))* Houghton Mifflin Harcourt Publishing Co. (HMH Books For Young Readers).
Henderson, Dianne. The Frightening Old Mansion. 2006. 116p. pap. 19.95 *(978-1-4241-2486-2(7))* PublishAmerica, Inc.
Henderson, Lauren. Kiss Me Kill Me. 2009. (ENG.). 272p. (YA). (gr. 9). pap. 8.99 *(978-0-385-73488-2(3)*, Delacorte Pr.) Random Hse. Children's Bks.
—Kiss of Death. 2012. (ENG.). 318p. (YA). (gr. 9). pap. 9.99 *(978-0-385-73780-7(7)*, Ember) Random Hse. Children's Bks.
Heneghan, James. The Grave, 1 vol. (ENG.). 240p. pap. 8.95 *(978-0-88899-499-8(0))* Groundwood Bks. CAN. Dist: Publishers Group West (PGW).
Henry, April. Blood Will Tell. 2015. (Point Last Seen Ser.: 2). (ENG.). 272p. (YA). (gr. 7). 17.99 *(978-0-8050-9853-2(4)*, 9780805098532, Holt, Henry & Co. Bks. For Young Readers) Holt, Henry & Co.
—The Body in the Woods. 2014. (Point Last Seen Ser.: 1). (ENG.). 272p. (YA). (gr. 7). 17.99 *(978-0-8050-9852-5(6)*, 9780805098525, Holt, Henry & Co. Bks. For Young Readers) Holt, Henry & Co.
—The Girl I Used to Be. 2016. (ENG., Illus.). 240p. (YA). 17.99 *(978-1-62779-332-2(1)*, 9781627793322, Holt, Henry & Co. Bks. For Young Readers) Holt, Henry & Co.
—The Girl I Used to Be. 2017. (YA). lib. bdg. 20.85 ***(978-0-606-39999-9(2))*** Turtleback Bks.
—The Girl Who Was Supposed to Die. 2014. (ENG.). 240p. (YA). (gr. 9-12). pap. 10.99 *(978-1-250-04437-2(5)*, 9781250044372) Square Fish.
—The Night She Disappeared. 2013. (ENG.). 256p. (YA). (gr. 7-12). pap. 10.99 *(978-1-250-01674-4(6)*, 9781250016744) Square Fish.
Henry, Regene. The Barefoot Boys of Fayette. Stich, Carolyn R., illus. 2005. 180p. (J). (gr. 4-7). pap. 9.95 *(978-0-9749412-3-3(9))* EDCO Publishing, Inc.
Henson, Heather, et al. The Vampire Bunny. Mack, Jeff, tr. Mack, Jeff, illus. 2004. (Bunnicula & Friends Ser.: 1). (ENG.). 48p. (J). (gr. 1-3). 16.99 *(978-0-689-85724-9(1)*, Simon Spotlight) Simon Spotlight.
Herman, Gail. Fall Fright. Duendes Del Sur Staff, illus. 2005. (Hello Reader! Ser.). 32p. (J). pap. *(978-0-439-78358-3(5))* Scholastic, Inc.
—Scooby-Doo: A Scooby-Rific Reader. 2012. (Illus.). (J). *(978-1-4351-3986-2(0))* Scholastic, Inc.
—Scooby-Doo in the Lighthouse Mystery, 1 vol. 2016. (Scooby-Doo! Set 3 Ser.). (ENG., Illus.). 32p. (J). (gr. k-4). lib. bdg. 24.21 *(978-1-61479-410-3(3))* Spotlight.
Herndon, Lee G. The Land of Always & Forever: The Trilogy, 1 vol. 2009. 77p. pap. 19.95 *(978-1-60836-898-3(X))* America Star Bks.
Herren, Greg. Lake Thirteen. 2013. (ENG.). 264p. (gr. 7). pap. 11.95 *(978-1-60282-894-0(6))* Bold Strokes Bks.
—Sleeping Angel. 2011. (ENG.). 288p. (J). (gr. 7). pap. 13.95 *(978-1-60282-214-6(X))* Bold Strokes Bks.
Herrick, Steven. Cold Skin. 2009. (ENG.). 279p. (YA). (gr. 9-18). 18.95 *(978-1-59078-572-0(X)*, Front Street) Boyds Mills Pr.
Hesse, Monica. Girl in the Blue Coat. (ENG.). 320p. (gr. 7-17). 2017. (YA). pap. 9.99 *(978-0-316-26063-3(0))* 2016. 17.99 *(978-0-316-26060-2(6))* 2016. (YA). E-Book *(978-0-316-26064-0(9))* Little, Brown Bks. for Young Readers.
—Girl in the Blue Coat. 2017. (YA). lib. bdg. 20.85 ***(978-0-606-39918-0(6))*** Turtleback Bks.
Hiaasen, Carl. Hoot. 2005. (ENG.). 304p. (J). (gr. 5-7). 6.99 *(978-0-440-41939-6(5)*, Yearling) Random Hse. Children's Bks.
—Skink - No Surrender. (ENG.). 288p. (gr. 7). 2015. (YA). pap. 9.99 *(978-0-307-93059-0(9)*, Ember) 2014. (J). 18.99 *(978-0-375-87051-4(2)*, Knopf Bks. for Young Readers) Random Hse. Children's Bks.
Hickey, Tony. Where's Jacko? Myler, Terry, illus. 2006. (ENG.). 64p. (J). pap. 10.95 *(978-1-901737-47-9(0))* Anvil Bks., Ltd. IRL. Dist: Dufour Editions, Inc.
Hicks, Clifford B. Alvin Fernald, Mayor for a Day. Sokol, Bill, illus. 2015. 138p. (J). pap. 9.99 *(978-1-930900-86-8(4))* Purple Hse. Pr.
—Alvin Fernald, Mayor for a Day. Schluenderfritz, Theodore, illus. 2007. (Secret Panel Mysteries Ser.). 142p. (J). (gr. 8-12). pap. 11.95 *(978-1-883937-98-0(1))* Bethlehem Bks.
—Alvin Fernald's Incredible Buried Treasure. Bradfield, Roger, illus. 2009. (J). 17.95 *(978-1-930900-43-1(0))* Purple Hse. Pr.
—Alvin's Secret Code. Sokol, Bill, illus. 2015. (J). pap. 9.99 *(978-1-930900-85-1(6))* Purple Hse. Pr.
—The Marvelous Inventions of Alvin Fernald. Geer, Charles, illus. 2006. 119p. (J). (gr. 3-7). 16.95 *(978-1-930900-21-9(X))* Purple Hse. Pr.
Hicks, Deron R. Secrets of Shakespeare's Grave. Geyer, Mark Edward, illus. (Shakespeare Mysteries Ser.: 1). (ENG.). (J). (gr. 2-5). 2012. 304p. 16.99 *(978-0-547-84074-1(9))*Bk. 1. 2013. 320p. pap. 7.99 *(978-0-544-10504-1(4))* Houghton Mifflin Harcourt Publishing Co.
—Tower of the Five Orders. Geyer, Mark Edward, illus. 2013. (Shakespeare Mysteries Ser.: 2). (ENG.). 320p. (J). (gr. 5-7). 16.99 *(978-0-547-83953-0(7))* Houghton Mifflin Harcourt Publishing Co.
—Tower of the Five Orders: The Shakespeare Mysteries, Book 2. Geyer, Mark Edward, illus. 2014. (Shakespeare Mysteries Ser.). (ENG.). 320p. (J). (gr. 5-7). pap. 7.99 *(978-0-544-33630-8(5)*, HMH Books For Young Readers) Houghton Mifflin Harcourt Publishing Co.
—The Van Gogh Deception. 2017. (ENG.). 320p. (J). (gr. 5-7). 16.99 *(978-0-544-75927-5(3)*, HMH Books For Young Readers) Houghton Mifflin Harcourt Publishing Co.
The Hidden Hand, 6 vols., Vol. 2. (Woodland Mysteriestm Ser.). 133p. (gr. 3-7). 42.50 *(978-0-7802-7939-1(5))* Wright Group/McGraw-Hill.
Higgins, F. E. The Bone Magician. 2011. (ENG.). 304p. (J). (gr. 5-9). pap. 10.99 *(978-0-312-65944-8(X)*, 9780312659448) Square Fish.
—The Eyeball Collector. 2011. (ENG.). 272p. (J). (gr. 5-9). pap. 9.99 *(978-0-312-66097-0(9)*, 9780312660970) Square Fish.
—A Game of Ghouls. unabr. ed. 2011. (Phenomenals Ser.: 2). (ENG.). 240p. (J). (gr. 4-6). pap. 8.99 *(978-0-330-50756-1(7))* Pan Macmillan GBR. Dist: Independent Pubs. Group.

M N O

Higman, Anita. The Living Darkness: Texas Caves. 2nd ed. 2003. (Illus.). xiii, 93p. (J). (978-1-57168-783-8(1), Eakin Pr.) Eakin Pr.

Hill, Janet Muirhead. The Horse & the Crow: A Miranda & Starlight Story. 2015. (ENG.). 268p. (J). pap. 13.00 (978-1-937849-27-6(9)) Raven Publishing Inc. of Montana.

Hillan, Pam & Dyan, Penelope. Dem Bones, Dem Bones! 2013. 110p. pap. 8.95 (978-1-61477-122-7(7)) Bellissima Publishing, LLC.

Hillan, Pamela & Dyan, Penelope. The Hidden Treasure at Dragon Lake. 2013. 112p. pap. 8.95 (978-1-61477-101-2(4)) Bellissima Publishing, LLC.

—The Mystery on Burgundy Street. 2013. 134p. pap. 8.95 (978-1-61477-086-2(7)) Bellissima Publishing, LLC.

—The Secret at Fort Huachuca. 2013. 130p. pap. 8.95 (978-1-61477-093-0(X)) Bellissima Publishing, LLC.

Hilmo, Tess. With a Name Like Love. 2013. (ENG.). 272p. (J). (gr. 5-9). pap. 10.99 (978-1-250-02733-7(0), 9781250027337) Square Fish.

Hilton, Nette. A Grave Catastrophe. 2005. (Illus.). 160p. (J). (gr. -1-7). pap. (978-0-7344-0494-7(8), Lothian Children's Bks.) Hachette Australia.

Hirsch, Jennifer. Minute Mysteries: Brainteasers, Puzzlers, & Stories to Solve. 2008. (American Girls Collection Sidelines Ser.). (ENG., Illus.). 64p. (gr. 4-7). pap. 5.95 (978-1-59369-030-4(4), American Girl) American Girl Publishing, Inc.

Hirschmann, Kris. A Serious Case of the Sillies. Jennings, C. S., illus. 2013. 32p. (J). pap. (978-0-545-56765-7(3)) Scholastic, Inc.

Hitchcock, Alfred. Misterio de la Arana de Plata. (Alfred Hitchcock y los Tres Investigadores Ser.). (SPA.). (YA). 8.95 (978-84-272-4908-0(X), MO60) Molino, Editorial ESP. Dist: Continental Bk. Co., Inc.

—Misterio de la Calavera Parlante. (Alfred Hitchcock y los Tres Investigadores Ser.). (SPA.). (YA). 8.95 (978-84-272-4911-0(X), MO63) Molino, Editorial ESP. Dist: Continental Bk. Co., Inc.

—Misterio de la Cueva de los Lamentos. (Alfred Hitchcock y los Tres Investigadores Ser.). (SPA.). 160p. (YA). 8.95 (978-84-272-4910-3(1), MO62) Molino, Editorial ESP. Dist: Continental Bk. Co., Inc.

—Misterio de la Montana del Monstruo. (Alfred Hitchcock y los Tres Investigadores Ser.). (SPA.). (YA). 8.95 (978-84-272-4920-2(9), MO72) Molino, Editorial ESP. Dist: Continental Bk. Co., Inc.

—Misterio de la Serpiente Susurrante. (Alfred Hitchcock y los Tres Investigadores Ser.). (SPA.). (YA). 8.95 (978-84-272-4917-2(9), MO69) Molino, Editorial ESP. Dist: Continental Bk. Co., Inc.

—Misterio de Leon Mervioso. (Alfred Hitchcock y los Tres Investigadores Ser.). (SPA.). 192p. (YA). 8.95 (978-84-272-4916-5(0), MO68) Molino, Editorial ESP. Dist: Continental Bk. Co., Inc.

—Misterio del Dragon. (Alfred Hitchcock y los Tres Investigadores Ser.). (SPA.). 176p. (YA). 8.95 (978-84-272-4914-1(4), MO66) Molino, Editorial ESP. Dist: Continental Bk. Co., Inc.

—Misterio del Gato de Trapo. (Alfred Hitchcock y los Tres Investigadores Ser.). (SPA.). 152p. (YA). 8.95 (978-84-272-4913-4(6), MO65) Molino, Editorial ESP. Dist: Continental Bk. Co., Inc.

—Misterio del Lago Fantasma. (Alfred Hitchcock y los Tres Investigadores Ser.). (SPA.). 173p. (YA). 8.95 (978-84-272-4919-6(5), MO71) Molino, Editorial ESP. Dist: Continental Bk. Co., Inc.

—Misterio del Testamento Sorprendiente. (Alfred Hitchcock y los Tres Investigadores Ser.). (SPA.). (YA). 8.95 (978-84-272-4922-6(5), MO74) Molino, Editorial ESP. Dist: Continental Bk. Co., Inc.

Hobbs, Constance. Dreamers. 2008. 436p. 50.50 (978-0-9556783-6-3(6)) Hobbs, Constance GBR. Dist: Lulu Pr., Inc.

Hobbs, Valerie. Sweetie McGinnis Solves Them All. Date not set. (J). (978-0-374-37352-8(3), Farrar, Straus & Giroux (BYR)) Farrar, Straus & Giroux.

Hock, Dan. The Birthday Bash 2 vols. An Iggy & Igor Mystery (#2) Hock, Dan, illus. l.t. ed. 2004. (Illus.). 51p. (J). per. 4.99 (978-0-9754046-1-4(X)) Anticipation Pr.

Hodder, Beth. Stealing the Wild. 2010. 166p. (J). pap. 11.95 (978-0-9793963-1-1(X)) Grizzly Ridge Publishing.

Hodges, Meredith. Jasper: A Christmas Caper. Shields, Bonnie, illus. 2004. 85p. (J). 24.95 (978-1-928624-20-2(0)) Lucky 3 Ranch, Inc.

Hoena, Blake. Museum Mystery. Regan, Dana, illus. 2014. (Jess & Jaylen Ser.). (ENG.). 48p. (J). (gr. 1-4). 27.07 (978-1-63143-439-6(X), 208263) Child's World, Inc., The.

Hoeye, Michael. Una Cuestion de Tiempo. (SPA.). 304p. (J). (gr. 6-8). 17.56 (978-84-8441-167-3(2), MO1007) Grijalbo Mondadori, S.A.-Montena ESP. Dist: Lectorum Pubns., Inc.

—The Sands of Time. 2007. (ENG.). 288p. (J). (gr. 3-7). pap. 8.99 (978-0-14-240983-1(9), Puffin Books) Penguin Young Readers Group.

—The Sands of Time: A Hermux Tantamoq AdventureTM. 2004. 288p. (J). (gr. 5-9). pap. 40.00 incl. audio (978-1-4000-9016-7(4), Listening Library) Random Hse. Audio Publishing Group.

—Time Stops for No Mouse. 2007. (ENG.). 272p. (J). (gr. 3-7). 7.99 (978-0-14-240984-8(7), Puffin Books) Penguin Young Readers Group.

—Time Stops for No Mouse. 2003. (Hermux Tantamoq Adventure Ser.). (Illus.). 250p. (J). (gr. 4-7). 18.40 (978-0-613-62122-9(0), Turtleback) Turtleback Bks.

—Time Stops for No Mouse: A Hermux Tantamoq AdventureTM. 2004. 272p. (J). (gr. 5-9). pap. 40.00 incl. audio (978-0-8072-2280-5(1), Listening Library) Random Hse. Audio Publishing Group.

Hoffman, Mary. The Falconer's Knot: A Story of Friars, Flirtation & Foul Play. (ENG., Illus.). 304p. (YA). (gr. 7). 2008. pap. 7.99 (978-1-59990-229-6(X), 9781599902296) 2007. 16.95 (978-1-59990-056-8(4), 9781599900568) Bloomsbury Publishing USA. (Bloomsbury USA Childrens).

Hoffman, Mary Ann. The Maple Tree Mystery. (Neighborhood Readers Ser.). (ENG.). 16p. 2007. 37.95 (978-1-4042-7342-9(5)) 2006. (gr. 1-3). pap. 6.50 (978-1-4042-7220-0(8)) Rosen Publishing Group, Inc., The. (Rosen Classroom).

—El misterio en el árbol (the Maple Tree Mystery) 2007. (Lecturas del barrio (Neighborhood Readers) Ser.). (SPA.). 16p. 37.95 (978-1-4042-7343-6(3), Rosen Classroom) Rosen Publishing Group, Inc., The.

The Hole in the Hill: Individual Title Six-Packs. (Action Packs Ser.). 104p. (gr. 3-5). 44.00 (978-0-7635-2993-2(1)) Rigby Education.

Holland, Robert. The Black Queen. 2003. (Books Boys Want to Read). 220p. (J). pap. 12.00 (978-0-9720922-1-0(8)) Frost Hollow Pubs., LLC.

—Spooks: A Charles Oliver Jones, P.I. 2005. 219p. (J). (978-0-9720922-5-8(0)) Frost Hollow Pubs., LLC.

Holm, Jennifer L. & Hamel, Jonathan. The Postman Always Brings Mice. Weinman, Brad, illus. 2005. (Stink Files Ser.: No. 1). 129p. (J). 12.65 (978-0-7569-6529-7(2)) Perfection Learning Corp.

—To Scratch a Thief. Weinman, Brad, illus. (Stink Files Ser.: No. 2). 144p. 2005. pap. 4.99 (978-0-06-052984-0(9), Harper Trophy) 2004. (J). 14.99 (978-0-06-052982-6(2)) 2004. (J). lib. bdg. 15.89 (978-0-06-052983-3(0)) HarperCollins Pubs.

Holsather, Kent. Henry of York: The Secret of Juan de Vega. Holsather, Bill, illus. 2003. 176p. (YA). (gr. 5-18). 22.95 (978-0-9729101-0-1(7)); 2nd ed. per. 12.95 (978-0-9729101-1-8(5)) Lonejack Mountain Pr.

Holt, Martha. The Adventures of Jillian & Sam: Tiger in Our Town. 2009. 28p. pap. 12.49 (978-1-4389-6773-8(X)) AuthorHouse.

Hoobler, Dorothy & Hoobler, Thomas. The Demon in the Teahouse. 2005. 181p. (J). (gr. 4-7). 13.65 (978-0-7569-6725-3(2)) Perfection Learning Corp.

—The Ghost in the Tokaido Inn. 2005. (ENG.). 240p. (J). (gr. 3-7). 6.99 (978-0-14-240541-3(8), Puffin Books) Penguin Young Readers Group.

—The Ghost in the Tokaido Inn. 2005. 214p. (J). (gr. 4-7). 14.65 (978-0-7569-6403-0(2)) Perfection Learning Corp.

—In Darkness, Death. 2005. (Puffin Sleuth Novels Ser.). 195p. (J). (gr. 5-9). 14.65 (978-0-7569-5457-4(6)) Perfection Learning Corp.

—Seven Paths to Death. 2009. (ENG.). 208p. (YA). (gr. 7-7). 7.99 (978-0-14-241466-8(2), Puffin Books) Penguin Young Readers Group.

—The Sword That Cut the Burning Grass. 2006. 211p. (gr. 5-9). 17.00 (978-0-7569-6907-3(7)) Perfection Learning Corp.

Hood, Karen Jean Matsko. Lost Medal, Bk.1. Whispering Pine Press International, Inc. Staff, ed. Artistic Design Service, illus. 2014. (Hood Horse Story Ser.). 160p. (J). (gr. 4-8). 25.95 (978-1-930948-94-5(8)) Whispering Pine Pr. International, Inc.

—Lost Medal, Vol. 1. Whispering Pine Press International, ed. Artistic Design Service, illus. 2014. (Hood Horse Story Ser.). (ENG.). 160p. (J). (gr. 4-8). per. 9.95 (978-1-930948-95-2(6)) Whispering Pine Pr. International, Inc.

—Lost Medal, Christian Edition: With Bible Verses & Christian Themes. Whispering Pine Press International, ed. Artistic Design Services Staff, illus. 2014. (Hood Christian Horse Story Ser.). 160p. (J). Bk.1. pap. 19.95 (978-1-59808-618-8(9)) Vol. 1. 29.95 (978-1-59808-617-1(0)) Whispering Pine Pr. International, Inc.

—Spokane Falls. Whispering Pine Press International, ed. Artistic Design Service, illus. l.t. ed. 2015. (Banacek & Flannigan Mystery Ser.). 224p. pap. 22.95 (978-1-59434-223-3(7)); Vol. 1. 29.95 (978-1-59434-228-8(8)); Vol. 1. per. 19.95 (978-1-59434-226-4(1)) Whispering Pine Pr. International, Inc.

Hood, Susan. Pup & Hound Catch a Thief. Hendry, Linda, illus. 2007. (Kids Can Read Ser.). (ENG.). 32p. (J). (gr. k-1). 3.95 (978-1-55337-973-7(X)) Kids Can Pr., Ltd. CAN. Dist: Hachette Bk. Group.

Hooks, Gwendolyn. The Cat Food Mystery: A Pet Club Story, 1 vol. Byrne, Mike, illus. 2011. (Pet Club Ser.). (ENG.). 32p. (gr. 1-2). pap. 6.25 (978-1-4342-3051-5(1)); lib. bdg. 22.65 (978-1-4342-2511-5(9)) Stone Arch Bks.

Hoopmann, Kathy. Blue Bottle Mystery - the Graphic Novel: An Asperger Adventure. 2015. (Asperger Adventures Ser.). (ENG., Illus.). 64p. (J). 18.95 (978-1-84905-650-2(1), 7952) Kingsley, Jessica Pubs. GBR. Dist: Macmillan Distribution Ltd.

Hope, Kathleen. Isiah Thomas & the Mysterious Castle Mcscary. 2012. (Illus.). 44p. pap. 24.40 (978-1-4685-0496-5(7)) AuthorHouse.

—Jack Eagle the Pirate & Other Mysterious Tales. 2012. (Illus.). 48p. pap. 24.40 (978-1-4678-9611-5(X)) AuthorHouse.

Hope, Laura. The Bobbsey Twins on Blueberry Island. 2007. 112p. (gr. 3-9). per. 11.95 (978-1-4344-0033-8(6)) Wildside Pr., LLC.

—Bobbsey Twins or Merry Days Indoors and. 2006. 18.99 (978-1-4219-7001-1(5)) IndyPublish.com.

Hope, Laura Lee. The Bobbsey Twins: The First Fifteen Stories, Including Merry Days Indoors & Out, in the Country, at the Seashore, at School, at Snow Lodge, on A. 2013. 1080p. (978-1-78139-372-7(9)) Benediction Classics.

—The Bobbsey Twins at Meadow Brook. 2004. 200p. pap. 12.95 (978-1-59540-103-8(2), 1st World Library - Literary Society) 1st World Publishing, Inc.

—The Bobbsey Twins at School. 2004. per. 11.95 (978-1-59540-104-5(0)) 1st World Publishing, Inc.

—The Bobbsey Twins in the Country. 2004. 208p. pap. 12.95 (978-1-59540-105-2(9), 1st World Library - Literary Society) 1st World Publishing, Inc.

—The Bobbsey Twins on a House Boat. 2005. 204p. pap. 12.95 (978-1-4218-1167-3(7), 1st World Library - Literary Society) 1st World Publishing, Inc.

—The Bobbsey Twins on A House Boat. 2005. 27.95 (978-1-4218-1067-6(0), 1st World Library - Literary Society) 1st World Publishing, Inc.

Hope, Lee Laura. Six Little Bunkers at Aunt Jo's. 2007. (ENG.). 144p. pap. 18.99 (978-1-4346-3234-0(2)); 156p. pap. 21.99 (978-1-4346-3235-7(0)) Creative Media Partners, LLC.

—Six Little Bunkers at Cowboy Jack's. 2007. (ENG.). 138p. pap. 18.99 (978-1-4346-3242-5(3)); 156p. pap. 21.99 (978-1-4346-3243-2(1)) Creative Media Partners, LLC.

Horowitz, Anthony. Public Enemy Number Two. 2004. (Diamond Brothers Ser.). (ENG.). 208p. (J). (gr. 3-7). 16.99 (978-0-399-24154-3(X), Philomel Bks.); pap. 6.99 (978-0-14-240218-4(4), Puffin Books) Penguin Young Readers Group.

—South by Southeast. 2005. (Diamond Brothers Ser.). (ENG.). 160p. (J). (gr. 3-7). 6.99 (978-0-14-240374-7(1), Puffin Books) Penguin Young Readers Group.

—Three of Diamonds. 2005. (Diamond Brothers Ser.). (ENG.). 240p. (J). (gr. 3-7). 6.99 (978-0-14-240298-6(2), Puffin Books) Penguin Young Readers Group.

Horseshoe Canyon. 2005. (J). 30.00 (978-1-884270-38-3(7)) Hall, Nancy Inc.

Horvath, Polly. Mr. & Mrs. Bunny: Detectives Extraordinaire! Blackall, Sophie, illus. 2012. (ENG.). 256p. (J). (gr. 3-7). 16.99 (978-0-375-86755-2(4), Schwartz & Wade Bks.) Random Hse. Children's Bks.

Hosch, Amanda. Mabel Opal Pear & the Rules for Spying. Sluyterman van Langeweyde, Ira, illus. 2017. (Middle-Grade Novels Ser.). (ENG.). 272p. (gr. 4-7). lib. bdg. 26.65 **(978-1-4965-4051-5(4))** Stone Arch Bks.

Houghton, Jackolyn. Detective Billy Pears & the Missing Hat. 2008. 36p. pap. 24.95 (978-1-60474-543-6(6)) America Star Bks.

Hounam, Donald. A Dangerous Magic. 2017. (ENG.). 352p. (YA). (gr. 5-12). 17.99 **(978-1-5124-3232-9(6))** Lerner Publishing Group.

Howard, Ann. The Mystery of Dragon Bridge: A Peach Blossom Village Story. 2014. (ENG & CHI., Illus.). 40p. (J). (gr. 2-5). pap. 16.95 (978-1-58394-813-2(9)) North Atlantic Bks.

Howard, Jeremy. The Countdown: The Adventures of Starforce. 2005. 114p. 23.45 (978-1-4208-2398-1(1)); pap. 11.95 (978-1-4208-2397-4(3)) AuthorHouse.

Howard, Lee. Scooby-Doo & the High Tech House of the Future, 1 vol. 2016. (Scooby-Doo Comic Readers Ser.). (ENG.). 32p. (J). (gr. k-3). lib. bdg. 24.21 (978-1-61479-452-3(9), Graphic Planet) Magic Wagon.

—Scooby-Doo in Mummy Scares Best, 1 vol. 2016. (Scooby-Doo Comic Readers Ser.). (ENG.). 32p. (J). (gr. k-3). lib. bdg. 24.21 (978-1-61479-455-4(3), Graphic Planet) Magic Wagon.

Howe, Deborah & Howe, James. Bunnicula. Daniel, Alan, illus. 2006. (Bunnicula & Friends Ser.). (ENG.). 128p. (J). (gr. 3-7). pap. 7.99 (978-1-4169-2817-1(0), Atheneum Bks. for Young Readers) Simon & Schuster Children's Publishing.

Howe, James. Bud Barkin, Private Eye. Helquist, Brett, illus. (Tales from the House of Bunnicula Ser.: 5). (ENG.). (J). (gr. 2-5). 2004. 112p. pap. 5.99 (978-0-689-86989-1(4)) 2003. 96p. 13.99 (978-0-689-85632-7(6)) 2003. 96p. 13.99 (978-0-689-85632-7(6)) Simon & Schuster Children's Publishing. (Atheneum Bks. for Young Readers).

—Howliday Inn. Munsinger, Lynn, illus. 2006. 195p. (gr. 3-7). 16.00 (978-0-7569-6807-6(0)) Perfection Learning Corp.

—Howliday Inn. unabr. ed. 2004. (Bunnicula Ser.). 195p. (J). (gr. 3-7). pap. 29.00 incl. audio (978-0-8072-8382-0(7), YA179SP, Listening Library) Random Hse. Audio Publishing Group.

—Howliday Inn. Munsinger, Lynn, illus. 2nd ed. 2006. (Bunnicula & Friends Ser.). (ENG.). 224p. (J). (gr. 3-7). pap. 7.99 (978-1-4169-2815-7(4), Atheneum Bks. for Young Readers) Simon & Schuster Children's Publishing.

—Nighty-Nightmare. Morrill, Leslie, illus. 2007. (Bunnicula & Friends Ser.). (ENG.). 144p. (J). (gr. 3-7). pap. 6.99 (978-1-4169-3966-5(0), Atheneum Bks. for Young Readers) Simon & Schuster Children's Publishing.

—Return to Howliday Inn. Daniel, Alan, illus. 2007. (Bunnicula & Friends Ser.). (ENG.). 192p. (J). (gr. 3-7). pap. 6.99 (978-1-4169-3967-2(9), Atheneum Bks. for Young Readers) Simon & Schuster Children's Publishing.

—Return to Howliday Inn. Daniel, Alan, illus. 2007. (Bunnicula Ser.: 5). (gr. 4-7). lib. bdg. 17.20 (978-1-4177-9044-9(X), Turtleback) Turtleback Bks.

—The Vampire Bunny. Mack, Jeff, illus. 2005. (Bunnicula & Friends Ser.). 41p. (J). (gr. 1-3). 11.65 (978-0-7569-6832-8(1)) Perfection Learning Corp.

Howell, Kathy. Skoob. Linton, Vera, illus. 2004. (J). per. 6.95 (978-1-59571-026-0(4)) Word Association Pubs.

—Skoob: The Kingdom Awaits. 2005. (J). per. 7.95 (978-1-59571-072-7(8)) Word Association Pubs.

Howland, Ashley. Ghostnapped. 2009. 64p. pap. 9.99 (978-1-60860-145-5(5), Strategic Bk. Publishing) Strategic Book Publishing & Rights Agency (SBPRA).

Hubbard, L. Ron, contrib. by. The Carnival of Death: Literature Guide for Teachers & Librarians Based on Common Core ELA Standards for Classrooms 6-9. 2013. (Stories from the Golden Age Ser.). (ENG.). 35p. (gr. 6-9). pap., tchr. ed. 14.95 (978-1-59212-809-9(2)) Galaxy Pr., LLC.

—Common Core Literature Guide: Dead Men Kill: Literature Guide for Teachers & Librarians Based on Common Core ELA Standards for Classrooms 6-9. 2013. (Stories from the Golden Age Ser.). (ENG.). 35p. (gr. 6-9). pap., tchr. ed. 14.95 (978-1-61986-218-0(2)) Galaxy Pr., LLC.

Hubner, Carol Korb. The Devora Doresh Mysteries. 2006. (Illus.). 288p. (J). 16.95 (978-1-932443-59-2(2)) Judaica Pr., Inc., The.

—The Devora Doresh Mysteries 2. 2007. (Illus.). 280p. (J). 16.95 (978-1-932443-68-4(1)) Judaica Pr., Inc., The.

Hughes, Dean. Missing in Action. 2010. (ENG.). 240p. (J). (gr. 5-9). 16.99 (978-1-4169-1502-7(8), Atheneum Bks. for Young Readers) Simon & Schuster Children's Publishing.

Hughes, Holly. Hoofbeats of Danger. 2009. (Mysteries Through Time Ser.). 144p. (YA). (gr. 4-8). 31.95 (978-1-60754-176-9(9)); pap. 15.25 (978-1-60754-177-6(7)) Windmill Bks.

Hughes, Jenny. Dark Horse. 2014. (ENG.). 224p. (J). (gr. 3-7). pap. 9.95 (978-1-62124-010-5(X)) Breakaway Bks.

—A Horse by Any Other Name. 2014. (ENG.). 224p. (J). (gr. 3-7). pap. 9.95 (978-1-62124-009-9(6)) Breakaway Bks.

—Horse in the Diary. 2014. (ENG.). 128p. (J). (gr. 3-7). pap. 9.95 (978-1-62124-014-3(2)) Breakaway Bks.

—Mystery at Black Horse Farm. 2013. (ENG.). 144p. (J). (gr. 3-7). pap. 9.95 (978-1-62124-003-7(7)) Breakaway Bks.

Hughes, Shirley. Digby o'Day & the Great Diamond Robbery. Vulliamy, Clara, illus. 2015. (ENG.). 136p. (J). (gr. k-3). 12.99 (978-0-7636-7445-8(1)) Candlewick Pr.

Hughes, Vi. The Graveyard Hounds, 1 vol. Liest, Christina, illus. 2009. (ENG.). 168p. (J). (gr. 3-5). pap. 12.95 (978-1-896580-49-4(1)) Tradewind Bks. CAN. Dist: Orca Bk. Pubs. USA.

Hummel, Jim. A Bubble C. 2009. 32p. pap. 14.95 (978-1-4269-0034-1(1)) Trafford Publishing.

Hunt, Elizabeth Singer. The Caper of the Crown Jewels, Bk. 4. 2008. (Secret Agent Jack Stalwart Ser.: 4). (ENG., Illus.). 144p. (J). (gr. 1-4). per. 5.99 (978-1-60286-013-1(0), Weinstein Bks.) Perseus Bks. Group.

—The Escape of the Deadly Dinosaur - USA. Williamson, Brian, illus. 2007. (Secret Agent Jack Stalwart Ser.: 1). (ENG.). 128p. (J). (gr. 1-4). per. 5.99 (978-1-60286-004-9(1), Weinstein Bks.) Perseus Bks. Group.

—The Fight for the Frozen Land, Bk.12. Williamson, Brian, illus. 2009. (Secret Agent Jack Stalwart Ser.: 12). (ENG.). 128p. (J). (gr. 1-4). pap. 5.99 (978-1-60286-099-5(8), Weinstein Bks.) Perseus Bks. Group.

—The Mystery of the Mona Lisa, Bk. 3. Williamson, Brian, illus. 2007. (Secret Agent Jack Stalwart Ser.: 3). (ENG.). 128p. (J). (gr. 1-4). per. 5.99 (978-1-60286-001-8(7), Weinstein Bks.) Perseus Bks. Group.

—The Search for the Sunken Treasure. Williamson, Brian, illus. 2007. (Secret Agent Jack Stalwart Ser.: 2). (ENG.). 128p. (J). (gr. 1-4). per. 5.99 (978-1-60286-002-5(5), Weinstein Bks.) Perseus Bks. Group.

—The Search for the Sunken Treasure Bk. 2: Australia. 2007. (Illus.). 110p. (J). (978-1-4242-4190-3(1), Weinstein Bks.) Perseus Bks. Group.

Hunt, Elizabeth Singer. Secret Agents Jack & Max Stalwart: Book 1: the Battle for the Emerald Buddha: Thailand. Williamson, Brian, illus. 2017. (Secret Agents Jack & Max Stalwart Ser.: 1). (ENG.). 144p. (gr. 1-4). pap. 5.99 **(978-1-60286-359-0(8)**, Weinstein Bks.) Perseus Bks. Group.

Hurd, Thacher & Hurd. Art Dog. Hurd, Thacher, illus. 2004. (ENG., Illus.). 32p. (J). (gr. -1-3). 18.99 (978-0-06-024424-8(0)) HarperCollins Pubs.

Hurd, Thacher & Hurd, Thacher. Mystery on the Docks. Hurd, Thacher, illus. 25th anniv. ed. 2008. (Trophy Picture Bks.). (ENG., Illus.). 32p. (J). (gr. -1-3). pap. 8.99 (978-0-06-443058-6(8)) HarperCollins Pubs.

Hurst, Melissa E. The Edge of Forever. 2015. (ENG.). 272p. (J). (gr. 6). pap. 14.99 (978-1-63220-424-0(X), Sky Pony Pr.) Skyhorse Publishing Co., Inc.

Huston, Harriette "Ree". The Rescue of Buster Bus: A True Adventure Mystery with Sparkling Intrigue for All Ages. 2012. 36p. pap. 21.99 (978-1-4771-1658-6(3)) Xlibris Corp.

Hutton, Sam. Countdown. 2011. (Special Agents Ser.: 3). (ENG.). 224p. (J). pap. 9.99 (978-0-00-714843-1(7), HarperCollins Children's Bks.) HarperCollins Pubs. Ltd. GBR. Dist: HarperCollins Pubs.

—Deep End. 2010. (Special Agents Ser.). (ENG.). 240p. (J). (gr. 5-7). pap. 9.99 (978-0-00-714842-4(9)) HarperCollins Pubs. Ltd. GBR. Dist: HarperCollins Pubs.

—Final Shot. 2010. (Special Agents Ser.: 2). (ENG.). 224p. (J). (gr. 5-7). pap. 9.99 (978-0-00-714844-8(5)) HarperCollins Pubs. Ltd. GBR. Dist: HarperCollins Pubs.

—Kiss & Kill. 2004. (Special Agents Ser.: 4). (ENG.). 240p. (J). (gr. 4-7). pap. 9.99 (978-0-00-714845-5(3)) HarperCollins Pubs. Ltd. GBR. Dist: HarperCollins Pubs.

—Meltdown. 2005. (Special Agents Ser.: 6). (ENG., Illus.). 224p. (J). pap. 9.99 (978-0-00-714847-9(X), HarperCollins Children's Bks.) HarperCollins Pubs. Ltd. GBR. Dist: HarperCollins Pubs.

Hyde, Natalie. I Owe You One, 1 vol. 2011. (Orca Young Readers Ser.). (ENG.). 136p. (J). (gr. 3-6). pap. 7.95 (978-1-55469-414-3(0)) Orca Bk. Pubs. USA.

Hymas, Allison K. Under Locker & Key. 2017. (Max Ser.). (ENG., Illus.). 256p. (J). (gr. 4-8). pap. 7.99 (978-1-4814-6342-3(X), Simon & Schuster/Paula Wiseman Bks.) Simon & Schuster/Paula Wiseman Bks.

Ibbotson, Eva. The Star of Kazan. Hawkes, Kevin, illus. 2006. (ENG.). 416p. (J). (gr. 3-7). reprint ed. 8.99 (978-0-14-240582-6(5), Puffin Books) Penguin Young Readers Group.

Ice Water Press Staff. Secrets of the Deep. 2010. (J). pap. (978-1-921639-95-1(4)) Ripley Entertainment, Inc.

Ikaris, Despoina. The Little Red Jacket: A True Almost Christmas Almost Mystery Almost Ghost Story for Children And Certain Grown-Ups. 2008. 48p. pap. 10.99 (978-1-60647-898-1(2)) Salem Author Services.

Imfeld, Robert. Baylor's Guide to the Other Side. 2016. (Beyond Baylor Ser.: 1). (ENG., Illus.). 320p. (J). (gr. 5-9). 16.99 (978-1-4814-6636-3(4), Aladdin) Simon & Schuster Children's Publishing.

Ingold, Jeanette. Paper Daughter. 2013. (ENG.). 224p. (YA). (gr. 7). pap. 7.99 (978-0-544-10484-6(6)) Houghton Mifflin Harcourt Publishing Co.

Inspector Grub & the Fizzer-X Spy: Individual Title Six-Packs. (Bookweb Ser.). 32p. (gr. 5-18). 34.00 (978-0-7635-3786-9(1)) Rigby Education.

Inspector Grub & the Gourmet Mystery: Individual Title Six-Packs. (Bookweb Ser.). 32p. (gr. 4-18). 34.00 (978-0-7635-3726-5(8)) Rigby Education.

Into Thin Air. 2013. (Hardy Boys Adventures Ser.: 4). (ENG., Illus.). 128p. (J). (gr. 3-7). 15.99 (978-1-4424-7345-4(2)); pap. 6.99 (978-1-4424-5983-0(2)) Simon & Schuster Children's Publishing. (Aladdin).

Ip, Ivy S. Clues at the Carnival, 1 vol. 2013. (Scooby-Doo! Picture Clue Bks.). (ENG.). 24p. (J). (gr. -1-1). lib. bdg. 24.21 (978-1-61479-036-5(1), Essential Library) ABDO Publishing Co.

Ironside, Meredith. Spoon Creek Mystery. 2009. 244p. pap. 16.95 (978-0-595-53490-6(2)) iUniverse, Inc.

Jackson, Melanie. High Wire, 1 vol. 2012. (Orca Currents Ser.). (ENG.). 128p. (J). (gr. 5-9). pap. 9.95 (978-1-4598-0236-0(5)); lib. bdg. 16.95 (978-1-4598-0237-7(3)) Orca Bk. Pubs. USA.

—The Mask on the Cruise Ship, 1 vol. 2004. (Dinah Galloway Ser.). (ENG.). 192p. (J). (gr. 3-7). pap. 6.95 (978-1-55143-305-9(2)) Orca Bk. Pubs. USA.

—Queen of Disguises, 1 vol. 2009. (Dinah Galloway Ser.). (ENG.). 176p. (J). (gr. 4-8). pap. 9.95 (978-1-55469-037-4(4)) Orca Bk. Pubs. USA.

Jacobs, Brian C. The Case of the Old Man in the Mailbox. 2010. (Enigma Squad Ser.). (ENG.). 192p. (J). pap. 10.95

(978-0-9841658-8-9(6), Excite Kids Pr.) Publishing Services @ Thomson-Shore.

Jacobs, Edgar P. Atlantis Mystery. 2012. (Blake & Mortimer Ser.: 12). (ENG., Illus.). 72p. (J). (gr. 5-12). pap. 15.95 (978-1-84918-107-5(1)) CineBook GBR. Dist: National Bk. Network.

—Blake & Mortimer Vol. 15: The Secret of the Swordfish Part 1. 2013. (Blake & Mortimer Ser.: 15). (ENG., Illus.). 64p. pap. 15.95 (978-1-84918-148-8(9)) CineBook GBR. Dist: National Bk. Network.

—Blake & Mortimer Vol. 17: the Secret of the Swordfish Part 3. 2014. (Blake & Mortimer Ser.: 17). (ENG., Illus.). 64p. pap. 15.95 (978-1-84918-174-7(8)) CineBook GBR. Dist: National Bk. Network.

—The Mystery of the Great Pyramid. (Blake & Mortimer Ser.: 2). (ENG., Illus.). Pt. 1. 2007. 72p. pap. 15.95 (978-1-905460-37-3(6))Pt. 2. 2008. 56p. pap. 15.95 (978-1-905460-38-0(4)) CineBook GBR. Dist: National Bk. Network.

—S. O. S. Meteors. 2009. (Blake & Mortimer Ser.: 6). (ENG., Illus.). 64p. pap. 15.95 (978-1-905460-97-7(X)) CineBook GBR. Dist: National Bk. Network.

—The Secret of the Swordfish. 2013. (Blake & Mortimer Ser.: 16). (ENG., Illus.). 64p. pap. 15.95 (978-1-84918-161-7(6)) CineBook GBR. Dist: National Bk. Network.

—The Yellow "M" 2007. (Blake & Mortimer Ser.: 1). (ENG., Illus.). 72p. per. 15.95 (978-1-905460-21-2(X)) CineBook GBR. Dist: National Bk. Network.

Jacobs, Jordan. Samantha Sutton & the Labyrinth of Lies. 2012. (Samantha Sutton Ser.: 0). (ENG., Illus.). 368p. (J). (gr. 4-7). pap. 6.99 (978-1-4022-7560-9(9), 1350497, Sourcebooks Jabberwocky) Sourcebooks, Inc.

Jacobson, Jennifer Richard. Andy Shane & the Barn Sale Mystery. Carter, Abby, illus. (Andy Shane Ser.: 5). (ENG.). 64p. (J). (gr. k-3). 2010. 4.99 (978-0-7636-4827-5(2)) 2009. 14.99 (978-0-7636-3599-2(5)) Candlewick Pr.

Jaffe, Michele. Bad Kitty. 2006. (Bad Kitty Ser.: Bk. 1). (ENG., Illus.). 288p. (YA). (gr. 7-12). 16.99 (978-0-06-078108-8(4)) HarperCollins Pubs.

—Kitty Kitty. 2008. (Bad Kitty Ser.: Bk. 2). 320p. (YA). (gr. 7-18). lib. bdg. 17.89 (978-0-06-078114-9(9), HarperTeen) HarperCollins Pubs.

Jager, Hartmut. The Secret of the Green Paint: Annette Vetter Adventure #2. 2007. (Illus.). 196p. (YA). pap. 9.95 (978-0-944851-28-9(2)) Earth Star Pubns.

Jaimet, Kate. Break Point, 1 vol. 2013. (Orca Sports Ser.). (ENG.). 176p. (YA). (gr. 6-10). pap. 9.95 (978-1-4598-0352-7(3)) Orca Bk. Pubs. USA.

Jakubowski, Michele. The Professor's Discovery. Pinelli, Amerigo, illus. 2016. (Sleuths of Somerville Ser.). (ENG.). 144p. (gr. 4-6). lib. bdg. 25.99 (978-1-4965-3177-3(9)) Stone Arch Bks.

—The Professor's Discovery. Pinelli, Amerigo, illus. 2017. (Sleuths of Somerville Ser.). (ENG.). 144p. (gr. 4-6). pap. 6.95 (978-1-4965-3181-0(7)) Stone Arch Bks.

—Tour of Trouble. Pinelli, Amerigo, illus. 2016. (Sleuths of Somerville Ser.). (ENG.). 144p. (gr. 4-6). lib. bdg. 25.99 (978-1-4965-3176-6(0)) Stone Arch Bks.

—Tour of Trouble. Pinelli, Amerigo, illus. 2017. (Sleuths of Somerville Ser.). (ENG.). 144p. (gr. 4-6). pap. 6.95 (978-1-4965-3180-3(9)) Stone Arch Bks.

James, David. Sherlock Holmes & the Midnight Bell. Wilkes, Ian, ed. unabr. ed. 2003. 164p. (YA). (gr. 4-12). 30.00 (978-0-86025-292-4(2)) Henry, Ian Pubns. GBR. Dist: Empire Publishing Service.

James, Kristopher. Lyrian. 2009. (Illus.). 171p. pap. 16.95 (978-1-4092-8986-9(9)) Lulu Pr., Inc.

James, Richard E., III. Adventures of the Elements Vol. 3: Dangerous Games. Lyle, Maryann, ed. Welch, Chad, illus. 2004. 169p. (YA). (gr. 3-12). pap. 5.95 (978-0-9675901-2-7(4)) Alchemy Creative, Inc.

Jan Baer: And the Mystery of the Silent Circus. 2005. (J). per. 10.00 (978-1-930052-29-1(4)) Cherokee Bks.

Jane, Rebecca. Hamster Heroes to the Rescue: The Mystery of the Shadow in the Yard & Retirement. 2012. 84p. 19.95 (978-1-4626-6862-5(3)) America Star Bks.

Janeway, Paul. Dragon Eye Connection. 2011. 202p. pap. 14.95 (978-1-60976-854-6(X), Strategic Bk. Publishing) Strategic Book Publishing & Rights Agency (SBPRA).

Jannazo, Michelle A. Isabella's Shoes. 2012. 28p. pap. 11.95 (978-1-4327-9019-6(6)) Outskirts Pr., Inc.

Jasnoch, Dorothy. Frankie the Bunny: Mystery in the Forest. Korzeniowski, Samson O., ed. Jasnoch, Dorothy, illus. 2013. (Illus.). 32p. 17.99 (978-1-937752-16-3(X)) Owl About Bks. Pub., Inc.

Jayne, Hannah. The Escape. 2015. (ENG., Illus.). 256p. (YA). (gr. 8-12). pap. 9.99 (978-1-4926-1654-2(0), 9781492616542) Sourcebooks, Inc.

—The Revenge. 2017. (ENG.). 288p. (YA). (gr. 8-12). pap. 10.99 (978-1-4926-4736-2(5)) Sourcebooks, Inc.

Jeffrey, Leonard J. Journeys of the Mind-Book. 2011. 116p. (J). pap. (978-1-4269-9333-6(1)) Trafford Publishing (UK) Ltd.

Jenkins, Amanda. The Strong & the Weak Hammurabi's Code, Tomb Robbers! A Story of Ancient Egypt. 2011. (Readers' & Writers' Genre Workshop Ser.). (YA). pap. (978-1-4509-3020-8(4)) Benchmark Education Co.

Jenkins, Carla LaVern. The Disappearance of Mrs. Brown: A Jenkins Girl Mystery. 2010. 72p. 23.55 (978-1-4269-4537-3(X)); pap. 13.55 (978-1-4251-6659-5(8)) Trafford Publishing.

Jenkins, Jerry B. & Fabry, Chris. Canyon Echoes. 2005. (Red Rock Mysteries Ser.: 8). (ENG.). 234p. (YA). pap. 6.99 (978-1-4143-0147-1(2), Tyndale Kids) Tyndale Hse. Pubs.

—Dead End. 2006. (Red Rock Mysteries Ser.: 15). (ENG.). 248p. (YA). (gr. 3-7). per. 6.99 (978-1-4143-0154-9(5), Tyndale Kids) Tyndale Hse. Pubs.

—Double Fault. 2005. (Red Rock Mysteries Ser.: 7). (ENG.). 272p. (YA). pap. 6.99 (978-1-4143-0146-4(4), Tyndale Kids) Tyndale Hse. Pubs.

—Escaping Darkness. 2006. (Red Rock Mysteries Ser.: 10). (ENG.). 240p. (YA). (gr. 8-12). per. 6.99 (978-1-4143-0149-5(9), Tyndale Kids) Tyndale Hse. Pubs.

—Hidden Riches. 2006. (Red Rock Mysteries Ser.: 13). (ENG.). 262p. (YA). (gr. 3-7). per. 6.99 (978-1-4143-0152-5(9), Tyndale Kids) Tyndale Hse. Pubs.

—Hollywood Holdup. 2006. (Red Rock Mysteries Ser.: 12). (ENG.). 224p. (YA). (gr. 8-12). per. 6.99 (978-1-4143-0151-8(0), Tyndale Kids) Tyndale Hse. Pubs.

—Instant Menace. 2006. (Red Rock Mysteries Ser.: 9). (ENG.). 256p. (YA). (gr. 3-7). per. 6.99 (978-1-4143-0148-8(0), Tyndale Kids) Tyndale Hse. Pubs.

—Phantom Writer. 2005. (Red Rock Mysteries Ser.: 6). (ENG.). 256p. (YA). pap. 5.99 (978-1-4143-0145-7(6), Tyndale Kids) Tyndale Hse. Pubs.

—Stolen Secrets. 2005. (Red Rock Mysteries Ser.: 2). (ENG., Illus.). 224p. (YA). (gr. -1-7). pap. 6.99 (978-1-4143-0141-9(3), Tyndale Kids) Tyndale Hse. Pubs.

—Wind Chill. 2006. (Red Rock Mysteries Ser.: 14). (ENG.). 240p. (YA). (gr. 3-7). per. 6.99 (978-1-4143-0153-2(7), Tyndale Kids) Tyndale Hse. Pubs.

—Windy City Danger. 2006. (Red Rock Mysteries Ser.: 11). (ENG.). 246p. (YA). (gr. 8-12). per. 6.99 (978-1-4143-0150-1(2), Tyndale Kids) Tyndale Hse. Pubs.

Jennings, Sharon. Bats in the Graveyard. 69p. (978-1-897039-18-2(2)) High Interest Publishing (HIP).

—Bats on Horseback. (978-1-897039-13-7(1)) High Interest Publishing (HIP).

—Jingle Bats. Malloy, Kalle, illus. 72p. pap. (978-1-897039-22-9(0)) High Interest Publishing (HIP).

Jennings, Sharon, et al. Franklin the Detective. Gagnon, Céleste, illus. 2004. 32p. (J). pap. (978-0-439-41822-5(4)) Scholastic, Inc.

Jessell, Tim. The Boardwalk Mystery. Dunn, Robert, illus. 2013. (Boxcar Children Mysteries Ser.: 131). (ENG.). 144p. (J). (gr. 1-5). 15.99 (978-0-8075-0802-2(0)); pap. 5.99 (978-0-8075-0803-9(9)) Whitman, Albert & Co.

—The Mystery of the Stolen Snowboard. 2014. (Boxcar Children Mysteries Ser.: 134). (ENG.). 128p. (J). (gr. 1-5). 15.99 (978-0-8075-8728-7(1)) Whitman, Albert & Co.

—The Mystery of the Wild West Bandit. 2014. (Boxcar Children Mysteries Ser.: 135). (ENG.). 128p. (J). (gr. 1-5). 15.99 (978-0-8075-8725-6(7)) Whitman, Albert & Co.

Jessell, Tim, illus. The Boxcar Children, Set. 2013. (Boxcar Children Mysteries Ser.). (ENG.). 538p. (J). (gr. 1-5). 45.00 (978-0-8075-0864-0(0)) Whitman, Albert & Co.

—Mystery of the Fallen Treasure. 2013. (Boxcar Children Mysteries Ser.: 132). (ENG.). 128p. (J). (gr. 1-5). 15.99 (978-0-8075-5508-8(8)); 5.99 (978-0-8075-5506-4(1)) Whitman, Albert & Co.

—The Return of the Graveyard Ghost. 2013. (Boxcar Children Mysteries Ser.: 133). (ENG.). 128p. (J). (gr. 1-5). 15.99 (978-0-8075-6935-1(6)); 5.99 (978-0-8075-6936-8(4)) Whitman, Albert & Co.

Jinks, Catherine. The Reformed Vampire Support Group. 2010. (ENG.). 384p. (YA). (gr. 7). pap. 8.99 (978-0-547-41166-8(9)) Houghton Mifflin Harcourt Publishing Co.

Johansen, K. V. The Black Box. 2010. (Illus.). 212p. (J). pap. 13.00 (978-0-9864974-0-7(1)) Sybertooth, Inc. CAN. Dist: Lightning Source, Inc.

Johansen, Zdenka. When You Give of Yourself. 2006. 28p. pap. 9.95 (978-1-4327-0059-1(6)) Outskirts Pr., Inc.

Johansson, J. R. Cut Me Free. 2015. (ENG.). 304p. (YA). (gr. 9-16). 17.99 (978-0-374-30023-4(2), 9780374300234, Farrar, Straus & Giroux (BYR)) Farrar, Straus & Giroux.

—The Row. O'Malley, Janine, ed. 2016. (ENG.). 352p. (YA). 17.99 (978-0-374-30025-8(9), 9780374300258, Farrar, Straus & Giroux (BYR)) Farrar, Straus & Giroux.

John, Antony. Imposter. 2015. (ENG.). 320p. (YA). (gr. 7). 17.99 (978-0-8037-4124-9(3), Dial Bks) Penguin Young Readers Group.

Johns, Linda & National Geographic Learning Staff. Hannah West in Deep Water. 2010. (Rise & Shine Ser.). (ENG., Illus.). 160p. (C). (gr. 5-18). 9.95 (978-0-14-240700-4(3)) National Geographic School Publishing, Inc.

Johnson, Alaya Dawn. Detective Frankenstein. Ota, Yuko, illus. 2011. (Twisted Journeys (r) Ser.: 17). (ENG.). 112p. (J). (gr. 4-7). pap. 7.95 (978-0-8225-8943-3(5)); pap. 45.32 (978-0-7613-7613-2(5)); lib. bdg. 27.93 (978-0-8225-8942-6(7)) Lerner Publishing Group. (Graphic Universe™).

Johnson, Allen, Jr. The Dead House. McMorris, Kelley, illus. 2014. (Blackwater Novels Ser.: Vol. 2). (ENG.). 212p. (J). (gr. 4-7). 14.99 (978-1-933725-34-5(6)) Premium Pr. America.

Johnson, Carol V. Somerset Dreams. 2011. (Illus.). 112p. pap. 32.12 (978-1-4567-9012-7(9)) AuthorHouse.

Johnson, Denise Donna. The Veridical Circle. 2011. 78p. pap. 19.95 (978-1-4626-0472-2(2)) America Star Bks.

Johnson, Lois Walfrid. The Creeping Shadows. 2009. (Orig.). (J). 8.99 (978-0-88062-277-6(6)) Mott Media.

—The Disappearing Stranger. 2009. (Orig.). (J). 8.99 (978-0-88062-275-2(X)) Mott Media.

—Disaster on Windy Hill. 2009. (J). 8.99 (978-0-88062-284-4(9)) Mott Media.

—Grandpa's Stolen Treasure. 2009. (Orig.). (J). 8.99 (978-0-88062-281-3(4)) Mott Media.

—The Hidden Message. 2009. (Orig.). (J). 8.99 (978-0-88062-276-9(8)) Mott Media.

—Mystery of the Missing Map. 2009. (J). 8.99 (978-0-88062-283-7(0)) Mott Media.

—The Runaway Clown. 2009. (Orig.). (J). 8.99 (978-0-88062-282-0(2)) Mott Media.

—Trouble at Wild River. 2009. (J). 8.99 (978-0-88062-279-0(2)) Mott Media.

—The Vanishing Footprints. 2009. (J). 8.99 (978-0-88062-278-3(4)) Mott Media.

Johnson, Maureen. The Madness Underneath. 2013. (Shades of London Ser.: 2). (ENG.). 304p. (YA). (gr. 7). pap. 9.99 (978-0-14-242754-5(3), Speak) Penguin Young Readers Group.

Johnston, Jeffry W. The Truth. 2016. (ENG., Illus.). 256p. (YA). (gr. 8-12). pap. 10.99 (978-1-4926-2320-5(2), 9781492623205) Sourcebooks, Inc.

Johnston, K. E. M. The Witness Tree & the Shadow of the Noose: Mystery, Lies, & Spies in Manassas. 2009. 111p. (J). (gr. 5-7). pap. 8.95 (978-1-57249-397-1(6), White Mane Kids) White Mane Publishing Co., Inc.

Johnston, Mark & Spizman, Robyn Freedman. The Secret Agents Strike Back. 2008. (ENG., Illus.). 160p. (J). (gr. 4-7). 16.99 (978-1-4169-0086-3(1), Atheneum Bks. for Young Readers) Simon & Schuster Children's Publishing.

Jones, C. B. The Cats' Meow. Green, Chris, illus. 2017. (Bog Hollow Boys Ser.). (ENG.). 72p. (gr. 4-5). lib. bdg. 25.32 (978-1-4965-4057-7(3)) Stone Arch Bks.

—Gone to the Buzzards. Green, Chris, illus. 2017. (Bog Hollow Boys Ser.). (ENG.). 72p. (gr. 4-5). lib. bdg. 25.32 (978-1-4965-4058-4(1)) Stone Arch Bks.

—Kiss of the Snake. Green, Chris, illus. 2017. (Bog Hollow Boys Ser.). (ENG.). 72p. (gr. 4-5). lib. bdg. 25.32 (978-1-4965-4056-0(5)) Stone Arch Bks.

—Sleeping with the Fishes. Green, Chris, illus. 2017. (Bog Hollow Boys Ser.). (ENG.). 72p. (gr. 4-5). lib. bdg. 25.32 (978-1-4965-4055-3(7)) Stone Arch Bks.

Jones, Darynda. Death & the Girl He Loves. 2013. (Darklight Ser.: 3). (ENG.). 272p. (YA). (gr. 8-12). pap. 9.99 (978-0-312-62522-1(7), 9780312625221, St. Martin's Griffin) St. Martin's Pr.

Jones, Elizabeth McDavid. Peril at King's Creek: A Felicity Mystery. Tibbles, JeanPaul, illus. 2006. (ENG.). 176p. (gr. 4-7). pap. 6.95 (978-1-59369-101-1(7), American Girl) American Girl Publishing, Inc.

Jones, Kim P. Maggie & the Halloween Bandit. 2007. 124p. per. 19.95 (978-1-60441-158-4(9)) America Star Bks.

Jones, Lee. Whimper. 2011. 142p. pap. 12.00 (978-0-557-57961-7(9)) Lulu Pr., Inc.

Jones, Rob Lloyd. Wild Boy: The Real Life of the Savage of Aveyron. (ENG.). 304p. (J). (gr. 5). 2015. pap. 8.99 (978-0-7636-7157-0(6)) 2013. 16.99 (978-0-7636-6252-3(6)) Candlewick Pr.

—Wild Boy & the Black Terror. 2015. (ENG.). 336p. (J). (gr. 5). 16.99 (978-0-7636-6253-0(4)) Candlewick Pr.

Jones, Ruth Fosdick. Boy of the Pyramids: A Mystery of Ancient Egypt. Morse, Dorothy Bayley, illus. 2011. 150p. 40.95 (978-1-258-06798-4(6)) Literary Licensing, LLC.

Jonsberg, Barry. Reckoning. 2016. (Pandora Jones Ser.). (ENG.). 336p. (YA). (gr. 8). pap. 12.99 (978-1-74331-813-3(8)) Allen & Unwin AUS. Dist: Independent Pubs. Group.

Josephs, Rudy & Barba, Rick. The Gemini Agent. 2011. (ENG.). 224p. (YA). (gr. 7). 14.99 (978-1-4424-1961-2(X)); pap. 7.99 (978-1-4424-1342-9(5)) Simon Spotlight. (Simon Spotlight).

Joy, Linda. Little Wave & the Mystery of the Lost Whale. 2011. 28p. pap. 15.99 (978-1-4628-9711-7(8)) Xlibris Corp.

Juby, Susan. Getting the Girl: A Guide to Private Investigation, Surveillance, & Cookery. 2010. (ENG.). 352p. (YA). (gr. 8). pap. 8.99 (978-0-06-076528-6(3), HarperTeen) HarperCollins Pubs.

Jude, Sarah. The May Queen Murders. 2016. (ENG.). 304p. (YA). (gr. 9). 17.99 (978-0-544-64041-2(1), HMH Books For Young Readers) Houghton Mifflin Harcourt Publishing Co.

Judge, Malcolm. Jonny Jakes Investigates the Hamburgers of Doom. Brown, Alan, illus. 2016. (Middle-Grade Novels Ser.). (ENG.). 240p. (gr. 4-7). lib. bdg. 26.65 (978-1-4965-2678-6(3)) Stone Arch Bks.

Kang, Lydia. Control. 2015. (Control Duology Ser.). (ENG.). 416p. (YA). (gr. 7). pap. 9.99 (978-0-14-242361-5(0), Speak) Penguin Young Readers Group.

Kantor, Melissa. The Amanda Project. 2011. 287p. (J). 8.99 (978-0-06-202706-1(9), HarperTeen) HarperCollins Pubs.

Kanzaka, Hajime & Yoshinaka, Shoko. Super-Explosive Demon Story: City of Lost Souls, 7 vols., Vol. 5. 2004. (Slayers Ser.). (Illus.). 192p. 9.99 (978-1-58664-915-9(9), CMX 64605G, CPM Manga) Central Park Media Corp.

Karas, G. Brian, illus. The Case of the Missing Monkey. 2004. (High-Rise Private Eyes Ser.: No. 1). (J). (gr. -1-2). pap. 31.95 incl. audio compact disk (978-1-59112-616-4(9)) Live Oak Media.

—The Case of the Puzzling Possum. 2004. (High-Rise Private Eyes Ser.: No. 3). (J). (gr. -1-2). pap. 31.95 incl. audio compact disk (978-1-59112-620-1(7)) Live Oak Media.

Karkevandian, Parisa. No Way Out. 2004. 108p. (YA). 20.95 (978-0-595-66242-5(0)); pap. 10.95 (978-0-595-31011-1(7)) iUniverse, Inc.

Karr, Kathleen. The Seventh Knot, 1 vol. 2003. (ENG., Illus.). 300p. (J). 15.95 (978-0-7614-5135-8(8)) Marshall Cavendish Corp.

—The 7th Knot, 1 vol. 2007. (ENG., Illus.). 192p. (J). (gr. 5-9). pap. 5.99 (978-0-7614-5368-0(7)) Marshall Cavendish Corp.

Kassel, Roger de. Mr P & the Silver Red Bag. 2013. (Illus.). 12p. pap. 7.00 (978-1-78035-536-8(X), Fastprint Publishing) Upfront Publishing Ltd. GBR. Dist: Printondemand-worldwide.com.

Kästner, Erich. Emil & the Detectives. Stahl, J. D., tr. Trier, Walter, illus. 2014. (ENG.). 224p. (gr. 4-13). pap. 13.99 (978-1-4683-0829-7(7), 460829) Overlook Pr., The.

—Emil & the Detectives. Martin, W. & Stahl, J. D., trs. Trier, Walter, illus. 2007. (ENG.). 220p. (gr. 4-13). 19.95 (978-1-58567-586-9(5), 856586) Overlook Pr., The.

Katherine's Story 1848. 2014. (Secrets of the Manor Ser.: 4). (ENG., Illus.). 160p. (J). (gr. 3-7). pap. 6.99 (978-1-4814-1843-0(2), Simon Spotlight) Simon Spotlight.

Keene, Carolyn. Action! 2005. (Nancy Drew Ser.: 6). 138p. (J). lib. bdg. 15.00 (978-1-59054-809-7(4)) Fitzgerald Bks.

—Action!, No. 6. 6th ed. 2004. (Nancy Drew (All New) Girl Detective Ser.: 6). (ENG.). 144p. (J). (gr. 3-7). pap. 6.99 (978-0-689-86571-8(6), Aladdin) Simon & Schuster Children's Publishing.

—The Apple Bandit. Jones, Jan Naimo, illus. 2005. (Nancy Drew Notebooks). 74p. (J). (gr. 1-4). 11.65 (978-0-7569-6505-1(5)) Perfection Learning Corp.

—The Apple Bandit. Jones, Jan Naimo, illus. Frost, Michael, photos by. 68th ed. 2005. (Nancy Drew Notebooks Ser.: 68). (ENG.). 80p. (J). (gr. 1-4). pap. 4.99 (978-1-4169-0829-6(3), Aladdin) Simon & Schuster Children's Publishing.

—April Fool's Day. Pamintuan, Macky, illus. 2009. (Nancy Drew & the Clue Crew Ser.: 19). (ENG.). 96p. (J). (gr. 1-4). pap. 5.99 (978-1-4169-7518-2(7), Aladdin) Simon & Schuster Children's Publishing.

—Babysitting Bandit. Pamintuan, Macky, illus. 2009. (Nancy Drew & the Clue Crew Ser.: 23). (ENG.). 96p. (J). (gr. 1-4). pap. 5.99 (978-1-4169-7813-8(5), Aladdin) Simon & Schuster Children's Publishing.

—Bad Times, Big Crimes. 14th ed. 2005. (Nancy Drew (All New) Girl Detective Ser.: 14). (ENG.). 160p. (J). (gr. 3-7). pap. 6.99 (978-0-689-87883-1(4), Aladdin) Simon & Schuster Children's Publishing.

—The Best of Nancy Drew Classic Collection Vol. 1. 2004. (Nancy Drew Ser.: 1). (ENG.). 546p. (J). (gr. 3-7). 15.99 (978-0-448-44079-8(2), Grosset & Dunlap) Penguin Young Readers Group.

—Big Top Flop. Francis, Peter, illus. 2016. (Nancy Drew Clue Book Ser.: 4). (ENG.). 96p. (J). (gr. 1-4). pap. 5.99 (978-1-4814-3752-3(6), Aladdin) Simon & Schuster Children's Publishing.

—The Bungalow Mystery, No. 3. 2014. (Nancy Drew Ser.: 3). (ENG.). 192p. (J). (gr. 3-7). 7.99 (978-0-448-47971-2(0), Grosset & Dunlap) Penguin Young Readers Group.

—The Bunny-Hop Hoax. Jones, Jan Naimo, illus. Frost, Michael, photos by. 64th ed. 2005. (Nancy Drew Notebooks Ser.: 64). (ENG.). 80p. (J). (gr. 1-4). pap. 3.99 (978-0-689-87754-4(4), Simon & Schuster/Paula Wiseman Bks.) Simon & Schuster/Paula Wiseman Bks.

—Butterfly Blues. Francis, Peter, illus. 2015. (Nancy Drew & the Clue Crew Ser.: 40). (ENG.). 96p. (J). (gr. 1-4). pap. 5.99 (978-1-4814-1470-8(4), Aladdin) Simon & Schuster Children's Publishing.

—California Schemin' 2011. (Nancy Drew (All New) Girl Detective Ser.: 45). (ENG.). 160p. (J). (gr. 3-7). pap. 5.99 (978-1-4424-2295-7(5), Aladdin) Simon & Schuster Children's Publishing.

—Camp Creepy. Pamintuan, Macky, illus. 2010. (Nancy Drew & the Clue Crew Ser.: 26). (ENG.). 96p. (J). (gr. 1-4). pap. 4.99 (978-1-4169-9438-1(6), Aladdin) Simon & Schuster Children's Publishing.

—Candy Is Dandy. Jones, Jan Naimo, illus. 2004. (Nancy Drew Notebooks). 74p. (gr. 2-4). 17.00 (978-0-7569-3437-8(0)) Perfection Learning Corp.

—Candy Kingdom Chaos. Francis, Peter, illus. 2017. (Nancy Drew Clue Book Ser.: 7). (ENG.). 96p. (J). (gr. 1-4). pap. 5.99 (978-1-4814-5826-9(4), Simon & Schuster/Paula Wiseman Bks.) Simon & Schuster/Paula Wiseman Bks.

—Cape Mermaid Mystery. Pamintuan, Macky, illus. 2012. (Nancy Drew & the Clue Crew Ser.: 32). (ENG.). 96p. (J). (gr. 1-4). pap. 5.99 (978-1-4424-4625-0(0), Aladdin) Simon & Schuster Children's Publishing.

—Case of the Sneaky Snowman. Pamintuan, Macky, illus. 5th ed. 2006. (Nancy Drew & the Clue Crew Ser.: 5). (ENG.). 96p. (J). (gr. 1-4). pap. 4.99 (978-1-4169-1254-5(1), Aladdin) Simon & Schuster Children's Publishing.

—Chick-Napped! Pamintuan, Macky, illus. 13th ed. 2008. (Nancy Drew & the Clue Crew Ser.: 13). (ENG.). 96p. (J). (gr. 1-4). pap. 5.99 (978-1-4169-5522-1(4), Aladdin) Simon & Schuster Children's Publishing.

—The Cinderella Ballet Mystery. Pamintuan, Macky, illus. 4th ed. 2006. (Nancy Drew & the Clue Crew Ser.: 4). (ENG.). 96p. (J). (gr. 1-4). pap. 5.99 (978-1-4169-1256-9(8), Aladdin) Simon & Schuster Children's Publishing.

—The Cinderella Ballet Mystery, 1 vol. Pamintuan, Macky, illus. 2007. (Nancy Drew & the Clue Crew Ser.). (ENG.). 83p. (gr. 1-4). 24.21 (978-1-59961-345-1(X)) Spotlight.

—The Circus Scare, 1 vol. Pamintuan, Macky, illus. 2009. (Nancy Drew & the Clue Crew Set II Ser.). (ENG.). 96p. (gr. 2-4). 24.21 (978-1-59961-642-1(4)) Spotlight.

—Close Encounters. 21st ed. 2006. (Nancy Drew (All New) Girl Detective Ser.: 21). (ENG.). 176p. (J). (gr. 3-7). pap. 5.99 (978-1-4169-1245-3(2), Aladdin) Simon & Schuster Children's Publishing.

—Club Dread. 2009. (Nancy Drew/Hardy Boys Ser.: 3). (ENG.). 192p. (J). (gr. 3-7). pap. 5.99 (978-1-4169-7871-8(2), Aladdin) Simon & Schuster Children's Publishing.

—The Clue in the Diary. 2015. (Nancy Drew Ser.: 7). (ENG.). 192p. (J). (gr. 3-7). 8.99 (978-0-448-48907-0(4), Grosset & Dunlap) Penguin Young Readers Group.

—The Clue in the Jewel Box, No. 20. Tandy, Russell H., illus. 2005. (Nancy Drew Mystery Stories Ser.). (ENG.). 228p. (J). (gr. 5-9). 17.95 (978-1-55709-277-9(X)) Applewood Bks.

—Cooking Camp Disaster. Pamintuan, Macky, illus. 2013. (Nancy Drew & the Clue Crew Ser.: 35). (ENG.). 96p. (J). (gr. 1-4). pap. 4.99 (978-1-4169-9466-4(1), Aladdin) Simon & Schuster Children's Publishing.

—Cupcake Chaos. Pamintuan, Macky, illus. 2013. (Nancy Drew & the Clue Crew Ser.: 34). (ENG.). 96p. (J). (gr. 1-4). pap. 5.99 (978-1-4424-5351-7(6), Aladdin) Simon & Schuster Children's Publishing.

—Curse of the Arctic Star. 2013. (Nancy Drew Diaries: 1). (ENG.). 208p. (J). (gr. 3-7). 15.99 (978-1-4424-6610-4(3)); pap. 6.99 (978-1-4169-9072-7(0)) Simon & Schuster Children's Publishing. (Aladdin).

—Dangerous Plays. 16th ed. 2006. (Nancy Drew (All New) Girl Detective Ser.: 16). (ENG.). 160p. (J). (gr. 3-7). pap. 6.99 (978-1-4169-0605-6(3), Aladdin) Simon & Schuster Children's Publishing.

—Designed for Disaster. Pamintuan, Macky, illus. 2011. (Nancy Drew & the Clue Crew Ser.: 29). (ENG.). 96p. (J). (gr. 1-4). pap. 5.99 (978-1-4169-9439-8(4), Aladdin) Simon & Schuster Children's Publishing.

—The Dollhouse Mystery. Jones, Jan Naimo, illus. 2004. (Nancy Drew Notebooks). 68p. (J). (gr. 1-4). 12.65 (978-0-7569-5524-3(6)) Perfection Learning Corp.

—The Dollhouse Mystery. Jones, Jan Naimo, illus. 58th ed. 2004. (Nancy Drew Notebooks Ser.: 58). (ENG.). 80p. (J). (gr. 1-4). pap. 6.99 (978-0-689-86534-3(1), Aladdin) Simon & Schuster Children's Publishing.

—Double Take. Pamintuan, Macky, illus. 2009. (Nancy Drew & the Clue Crew Ser.: 21). (ENG.). 112p. (J). (gr. 1-4). pap. 5.99 (978-1-4169-7812-1(7), Aladdin) Simon & Schuster Children's Publishing.

—Dressed to Steal. 22nd ed. 2007. (Nancy Drew (All New) Girl Detective Ser.: 22). (ENG.). 160p. (J). (gr. 3-7). pap. 5.99 (978-1-4169-3385-4(9), Aladdin) Simon & Schuster Children's Publishing.

—Earth Day Escapade. Pamintuan, Macky, illus. 2009. (Nancy Drew & the Clue Crew Ser.: 18). (ENG.). 96p. (J). (gr. 1-4). pap. 5.99 (978-1-4169-7218-1(8), Aladdin) Simon & Schuster Children's Publishing.

—En Garde. 17th ed. 2006. (Nancy Drew (All New) Girl Detective Ser.: 17). (ENG.). 160p. (J). (gr. 3-7). pap. 4.99 (978-1-4169-0603-2(7), Aladdin) Simon & Schuster Children's Publishing.

—False Notes. 3rd ed. 2004. (Nancy Drew (All New) Girl Detective Ser.: 3). (ENG.). 160p. (J). (gr. 3-7). pap. 5.99

(978-0-689-86568-8(6), Aladdin) Simon & Schuster Children's Publishing.

—The Fashion Disaster. Pamintuan, Macky, illus. 6th ed. 2007. (Nancy Drew & the Clue Crew Ser.: 6). (ENG.). 96p. (J). (gr. 1-4). pap. 5.99 *(978-1-4169-3485-1(5)*, Aladdin) Simon & Schuster Children's Publishing.

—Fishing for Clues. 26th ed. 2007. (Nancy Drew (All New) Girl Detective Ser.: 26). (ENG.). 144p. (J). (gr. 3-7). pap. 5.99 *(978-1-4169-3525-4(8)*, Aladdin) Simon & Schuster Children's Publishing.

—The Flower Show Fiasco. Pamintuan, Macky, illus. 2014. (Nancy Drew & the Clue Crew Ser.: 37). (ENG.). 96p. (J). (gr. 1-4). pap. 5.99 *(978-1-4424-8668-3(6)*, Aladdin) Simon & Schuster Children's Publishing.

—Framed. 15th ed. 2006. (Nancy Drew (All New) Girl Detective Ser.: 15). (ENG.). 160p. (J). (gr. 3-7). pap. 5.99 *(978-0-689-87863-3(X)*, Aladdin) Simon & Schuster Children's Publishing.

—Getting Burned. 20th ed. 2006. (Nancy Drew (All New) Girl Detective Ser.: 20). (ENG.). 160p. (J). (gr. 3-7). pap. 5.99 *(978-0-689-87703-2(X)*, Aladdin) Simon & Schuster Children's Publishing.

—The Ghost of Grey Fox Inn. 2016. (Nancy Drew Diaries: 13). (ENG., Illus.). 192p. (J). (gr. 3-7). 17.99 *(978-1-4814-6596-0(1)*, Simon & Schuster/Paula Wiseman Bks.) Simon & Schuster/Paula Wiseman Bks.

—Ghost Stories. 2008. (Nancy Drew (All New) Girl Detective Ser.). (ENG.). 240p. (J). (gr. 3-7). pap. 5.99 *(978-1-4169-5909-0(2)*, Aladdin) Simon & Schuster Children's Publishing.

—Green-Eyed Monster: Book One in the Eco Mystery Trilogy. 2009. (Nancy Drew (All New) Girl Detective Ser.: 39). (ENG.). 176p. (J). (gr. 3-7). pap. 5.99 *(978-1-4169-7844-2(5)*, Aladdin) Simon & Schuster Children's Publishing.

—Green with Envy: Book Two in the Eco Mystery Trilogy. 2010. (Nancy Drew (All New) Girl Detective Ser.: 40). (ENG.). 160p. (J). (gr. 3-7). pap. 6.99 *(978-1-4169-7842-8(9)*, Aladdin) Simon & Schuster Children's Publishing.

—The Hidden Staircase, No. 2. 2014. (Nancy Drew Ser.: 2). (ENG.). 192p. (J). (gr. 3-7). 7.99 *(978-0-448-47970-5(2)*, Grosset & Dunlap) Penguin Young Readers Group.

—High Risk. 4th ed. 2004. (Nancy Drew (All New) Girl Detective Ser.: 4). (ENG.). 160p. (J). (gr. 3-7). mass mkt. 5.99 *(978-0-689-86569-5(4)*, Aladdin) Simon & Schuster Children's Publishing.

—Identity Revealed. 2009. (Nancy Drew (All New) Girl Detective Ser.: 35). (ENG.). 208p. (J). (gr. 3-7). pap. 5.99 *(978-1-4169-6828-3(8)*, Aladdin) Simon & Schuster Children's Publishing.

—Identity Theft. 34th ed. 2009. (Nancy Drew (All New) Girl Detective Ser.: 34). (ENG.). 176p. (J). (gr. 3-7). pap. 5.99 *(978-1-4169-6831-3(8)*, Aladdin) Simon & Schuster Children's Publishing.

—Intruder. 27th ed. 2007. (Nancy Drew (All New) Girl Detective Ser.: 27). (ENG.). 160p. (J). (gr. 3-7). pap. 5.99 *(978-1-4169-3526-1(6)*, Aladdin) Simon & Schuster Children's Publishing.

—The Kitten Caper. Jones, Jan Naimo, illus. Frost, Michael, photos by. 69th ed. 2005. (Nancy Drew Notebooks Ser.: 69). (ENG.). 80p. (J). (gr. 1-4). pap. 5.99 *(978-1-4169-0830-2(7)*, Simon & Schuster/Paula Wiseman Bks.) Simon & Schuster/Paula Wiseman Bks.

—Last Lemonade Standing. Francis, Peter, illus. 2015. (Nancy Drew Clue Book Ser.: 2). (ENG.). 96p. (J). (gr. 1-4). pap. 5.99 *(978-1-4814-3748-6(8)*, Aladdin) Simon & Schuster Children's Publishing.

—The Magician's Secret. 2015. (Nancy Drew Diaries: 8). (ENG., Illus.). 176p. (J). (gr. 3-7). pap. 6.99 *(978-1-4814-1700-6(2)*, Aladdin) Simon & Schuster Children's Publishing.

—The Make-a-Pet Mystery. Pamintuan, Macky, illus. 2012. (Nancy Drew & the Clue Crew Ser.: 31). (ENG.). 96p. (J). (gr. 1-4). pap. 5.99 *(978-1-4169-9464-0(5)*, Aladdin) Simon & Schuster Children's Publishing.

—Mall Madness. Pamintuan, Macky, illus. 15th ed. 2008. (Nancy Drew & the Clue Crew Ser.: 15). (ENG.). 96p. (J). (gr. 1-4). pap. 5.99 *(978-1-4169-5900-7(9)*, Aladdin) Simon & Schuster Children's Publishing.

—Mardi Gras Masquerade. 28th ed. 2008. (Nancy Drew (All New) Girl Detective Ser.: 28). (ENG.). 144p. (J). (gr. 3-7). pap. 5.99 *(978-1-4169-5103-2(2)*, Aladdin) Simon & Schuster Children's Publishing.

—Model Menace: Book Two in the Model Mystery Trilogy. 2009. (Nancy Drew (All New) Girl Detective Ser.: 37). (ENG.). 176p. (J). (gr. 3-7). pap. 5.99 *(978-1-4169-7843-5(7)*, Aladdin) Simon & Schuster Children's Publishing.

—Model Suspect: Book Three in the Model Mystery Trilogy. 2009. (Nancy Drew (All New) Girl Detective Ser.: 38). (ENG.). 160p. (J). (gr. 3-7). pap. 5.99 *(978-1-4169-7841-1(0)*, Aladdin) Simon & Schuster Children's Publishing.

—Movie Madness. Francis, Peter, illus. 2016. (Nancy Drew Clue Book Ser.: 5). (ENG.). 96p. (J). (gr. 1-4). pap. 5.99 *(978-1-4814-5820-7(5)*, Aladdin) Simon & Schuster Children's Publishing.

—Movie Madness. Francis, Peter, illus. 2016. (Nancy Drew Clue Book Ser.: 5). (ENG.). 96p. (J). (gr. 1-4). 16.99 *(978-1-4814-5821-4(3)*, Simon & Schuster/Paula Wiseman Bks.) Simon & Schuster/Paula Wiseman Bks.

—Murder on the Set. 24th ed. 2007. (Nancy Drew (All New) Girl Detective Ser.: 24). (ENG.). 176p. (J). (gr. 3-7). pap. 4.99 *(978-1-4169-3397-7(2)*, Aladdin) Simon & Schuster Children's Publishing.

—The Mystery at Lilac Inn. 2014. (Nancy Drew Ser.: 4). (ENG.). 192p. (J). (gr. 3-7). 7.99 *(978-0-448-47972-9(9)*, Grosset & Dunlap) Penguin Young Readers Group.

—Mystery at Malachite Mansion. 2011. (Nancy Drew (All New) Girl Detective Ser.: 46). (ENG.). 144p. (J). (gr. 3-7). pap. 5.99 *(978-1-4424-2297-1(1)*, Aladdin) Simon & Schuster Children's Publishing.

—Mystery of the Midnight Rider. 2013. (Nancy Drew Diaries: 3). (ENG.). 208p. (J). (gr. 1-7). 15.99 *(978-1-4424-7861-9(6))*; pap. 6.99 *(978-1-4424-7860-2(8))* Simon & Schuster Children's Publishing. (Aladdin).

—Nancy Drew Diaries: Curse of the Arctic Star; Strangers on a Train; Mystery of the Midnight Rider; Once upon a Thriller. 2013. (Nancy Drew Diaries). (ENG., Illus.). 768p. (J). (gr. 3-7). pap. 27.99 *(978-1-4424-8896-0(4)*, Aladdin) Simon & Schuster Children's Publishing.

—Nancy Drew Diaries 3-Books-In-1! Curse of the Arctic Star; Strangers on a Train; Mystery of the Midnight Rider. 2016. (Nancy Drew Diaries). (ENG., Illus.). 592p. (J). (gr. 3-7). pap. 8.99 *(978-1-4814-8554-8(7)*, Aladdin) Simon & Schuster Children's Publishing.

—Nancy's Mysterious Letter, Bk. 8. 2015. (Nancy Drew Ser.: 8). (ENG.). 192p. (J). (gr. 3-7). 8.99 *(978-0-448-48908-7(2)*, Grosset & Dunlap) Penguin Young Readers Group.

—Once upon a Crime. 2nd ed. 2006. (Nancy Drew: Girl Detective Super Mystery Ser.: 2). (ENG.). 192p. (J). (gr. 3-7). pap. 6.99 *(978-1-4169-1248-4(7)*, Aladdin) Simon & Schuster Children's Publishing.

—Once upon a Thriller. 2013. (Nancy Drew Diaries: 4). (ENG., Illus.). 144p. (J). (gr. 3-7). 15.99 *(978-1-4424-6612-8(X))*; pap. 6.99 *(978-1-4169-9074-1(7))* Simon & Schuster Children's Publishing. (Aladdin).

—The Orchid Thief. 19th ed. 2006. (Nancy Drew (All New) Girl Detective Ser.: 19). (ENG.). 144p. (J). (gr. 3-7). pap. 5.99 *(978-1-4169-0980-4(X)*, Aladdin) Simon & Schuster Children's Publishing.

—Pageant Perfect Crime: Book One in the Perfect Mystery Trilogy. 30th ed. 2008. (Nancy Drew (All New) Girl Detective Ser.: 30). (ENG.). 160p. (J). (gr. 3-7). pap. 5.99 *(978-1-4169-5528-3(3)*, Aladdin) Simon & Schuster Children's Publishing.

—Perfect Cover. 31st ed. 2008. (Nancy Drew (All New) Girl Detective Ser.: 31). (ENG.). 160p. (J). (gr. 3-7). pap. 5.99 *(978-1-4169-5530-6(5)*, Aladdin) Simon & Schuster Children's Publishing.

—Pets on Parade. Francis, Peter, illus. 2016. (Nancy Drew Clue Book Ser.: 6). (ENG.). 96p. (J). (gr. 1-4). pap. 5.99 *(978-1-4814-5823-8(X)*, Aladdin) Simon & Schuster Children's Publishing.

—Pit of Vipers. 18th ed. 2006. (Nancy Drew (All New) Girl Detective Ser.: 18). (ENG.). 160p. (J). (gr. 3-7). pap. 5.99 *(978-1-4169-1180-7(4)*, Aladdin) Simon & Schuster Children's Publishing.

—Pony Problems. Pamintuan, Macky, illus. 3rd ed. 2006. (Nancy Drew & the Clue Crew Ser.: 3). (ENG.). 96p. (J). (gr. 1-4). pap. 5.99 *(978-1-4169-1815-8(9)*, Aladdin) Simon & Schuster Children's Publishing.

—Pony Problems, 1 vol. Pamintuan, Macky, illus. 2007. (Nancy Drew & the Clue Crew Ser.). (ENG.). 80p. (gr. 1-4). 24.21 *(978-1-59961-346-8(8))* Spotlight.

—Pool Party Puzzler. Francis, Peter, illus. 2015. (Nancy Drew Clue Book Ser.: 1). (ENG.). 96p. (J). (gr. 1-4). 16.99 *(978-1-4814-3896-4(4)*, Aladdin) Simon & Schuster Children's Publishing.

—Princess Mix-Up Mystery, No. 24. Pamintuan, Macky, illus. 2009. (Nancy Drew & the Clue Crew Ser.: 24). (ENG.). 96p. (J). (gr. 1-4). pap. 5.99 *(978-1-4169-7811-4(9)*, Aladdin) Simon & Schuster Children's Publishing.

—The Pumpkin Patch Puzzle. Pamintuan, Macky, illus. 2012. (Nancy Drew & the Clue Crew Ser.: 33). (ENG.). 112p. (J). (gr. 1-4). pap. 5.99 *(978-1-4169-9465-7(3)*, Aladdin) Simon & Schuster Children's Publishing.

—Real Fake. 3rd ed. 2007. (Nancy Drew: Girl Detective Super Mystery Ser.: 3). (ENG.). 224p. (J). (gr. 3-7). pap. 5.99 *(978-1-4169-3881-1(8)*, Aladdin) Simon & Schuster Children's Publishing.

—The Red Slippers. 2015. (Nancy Drew Diaries: 11). (ENG., Illus.). 192p. (J). (gr. 3-7). pap. 6.99 *(978-1-4814-3813-1(1)*, Aladdin) Simon & Schuster Children's Publishing.

—Sabotage at Willow Woods. 2014. (Nancy Drew Diaries: 5). (ENG., Illus.). 176p. (J). (gr. 3-7). pap. 6.99 *(978-1-4424-9392-6(5)*, Aladdin) Simon & Schuster Children's Publishing.

—Sabotage Surrender: Book Three in the Sabotage Mystery Trilogy. 2011. (Nancy Drew (All New) Girl Detective Ser.: 44). (ENG.). 128p. (J). (gr. 3-7). pap. 6.99 *(978-1-4169-9071-0(2)*, Aladdin) Simon & Schuster Children's Publishing.

—The Scarlet Macaw Scandal. Frost, Michael, illus. 8th ed. 2004. (Nancy Drew (All New) Girl Detective Ser.: 8). (ENG.). 160p. (J). (gr. 3-7). pap. 5.99 *(978-0-689-86844-3(8)*, Aladdin) Simon & Schuster Children's Publishing.

—Scream for Ice Cream. Pamintuan, Macky, illus. 2nd ed. 2006. (Nancy Drew & the Clue Crew Ser.: 2). (ENG.). 96p. (J). (gr. 1-4). pap. 5.99 *(978-1-4169-1253-8(3)*, Aladdin) Simon & Schuster Children's Publishing.

—Scream for Ice Cream, 1 vol. Pamintuan, Macky, illus. 2007. (Nancy Drew & the Clue Crew Ser.). (ENG.). 89p. (gr. 1-4). 24.21 *(978-1-59961-347-5(6))* Spotlight.

—Secret at Mystic Lake. 2014. (Nancy Drew Diaries: 6). (ENG., Illus.). 160p. (J). (gr. 3-7). pap. 6.99 *(978-1-4814-0012-1(6)*, Aladdin) Simon & Schuster Children's Publishing.

—Secret Identity, Bk. 1. 33rd ed. 2008. (Nancy Drew (All New) Girl Detective Ser.: 33). (ENG.). 176p. (J). (gr. 3-7). pap. 5.99 *(978-1-4169-6827-6(X)*, Aladdin) Simon & Schuster Children's Publishing.

—The Secret of Red Gate Farm. 2015. (Nancy Drew Ser.: 6). (ENG.). 192p. (J). (gr. 3-7). 8.99 *(978-0-448-48906-3(6)*, Grosset & Dunlap) Penguin Young Readers Group.

—Secret of Shadow Ranch. 2015. (Nancy Drew Ser.: 5). (ENG.). 192p. (J). (gr. 3-7). 8.99 *(978-0-448-48905-6(8)*, Grosset & Dunlap) Penguin Young Readers Group.

—The Secret of the Old Clock, Bk. 1. 2014. (Nancy Drew Ser.: 1). (ENG.). 192p. (J). (gr. 3-7). 7.99 *(978-0-448-47969-9(9)*, Grosset & Dunlap) Penguin Young Readers Group.

—Secret of the Spa, Vol. 9. 9th ed. 2005. (Nancy Drew (All New) Girl Detective Ser.: 9). (ENG.). 160p. (J). (gr. 3-7). pap. 5.99 *(978-0-689-86858-0(8)*, Aladdin) Simon & Schuster Children's Publishing.

—Secret Sabotage, Bk. 1. 2010. (Nancy Drew (All New) Girl Detective Ser.: 42). (ENG.). 144p. (J). (gr. 3-7). pap. 5.99 *(978-1-4169-9069-7(0)*, Aladdin) Simon & Schuster Children's Publishing.

—Seeing Green: Book Three in the Eco Mystery Trilogy. 2010. (Nancy Drew (All New) Girl Detective Ser.: 41). (ENG.). 160p. (J). (gr. 3-7). pap. 6.99 *(978-1-4169-7845-9(3)*, Aladdin) Simon & Schuster Children's Publishing.

—Serial Sabotage: Book Two in the Sabotage Mystery Trilogy. 2010. (Nancy Drew (All New) Girl Detective Ser.: 43). (ENG.). 144p. (J). (gr. 3-7). pap. 5.99 *(978-1-4169-9070-3(4)*, Aladdin) Simon & Schuster Children's Publishing.

—The Singing Suspects. Jones, Jan Naimo, illus. 2005. (Nancy Drew Notebooks). 69p. (J). (gr. 1-4). 11.65 *(978-0-7569-5952-4(7))* Perfection Learning Corp.

—Ski School Sneak. Pamintuan, Macky, illus. 11th ed. 2007. (Nancy Drew & the Clue Crew Ser.: 11). (ENG.). 96p. (J). (gr. 1-4). pap. 5.99 *(978-1-4169-4936-7(4)*, Aladdin) Simon & Schuster Children's Publishing.

—Sleepover Sleuths. Pamintuan, Macky, illus. 2006. (Nancy Drew & the Clue Crew Ser.: 1). (ENG.). 96p. (J). (gr. 1-4). pap. 5.99 *(978-1-4169-1255-2(X)*, Aladdin) Simon & Schuster Children's Publishing.

—Sleepover Sleuths, 1 vol. Pamintuan, Macky, illus. 2007. (Nancy Drew & the Clue Crew Ser.). (ENG.). 81p. (gr. 1-4). 24.21 *(978-1-59961-348-2(4))* Spotlight.

—Snowman Surprise. Casale, Paul, illus. Frost, Michael, photos by. 63rd ed. 2004. (Nancy Drew Notebooks Ser.: 63). (ENG.). 80p. (J). (gr. 1-4). pap. 4.99 *(978-0-689-87411-6(1)*, Aladdin) Simon & Schuster Children's Publishing.

—Stage Fright. 2012. (Nancy Drew/Hardy Boys Ser.: 6). (ENG.). 176p. (J). (gr. 3-7). pap. 6.99 *(978-1-4424-5681-5(7)*, Aladdin) Simon & Schuster Children's Publishing.

—Stalk, Don't Run. 2012. (Nancy Drew (All New) Girl Detective Ser.: 47). (ENG.). 160p. (J). (gr. 3-7). pap. 5.99 *(978-1-4424-2299-5(8)*, Aladdin) Simon & Schuster Children's Publishing.

—The Stolen Bones. 29th ed. 2008. (Nancy Drew (All New) Girl Detective Ser.: 29). (ENG.). 160p. (J). (gr. 3-7). pap. 5.99 *(978-1-4169-3614-5(9)*, Aladdin) Simon & Schuster Children's Publishing.

—The Stolen Relic. 7th ed. 2004. (Nancy Drew (All New) Girl Detective Ser.: 7). (ENG.). 160p. (J). (gr. 3-7). mass mkt. 6.99 *(978-0-689-86843-6(X)*, Aladdin) Simon & Schuster Children's Publishing.

—Strangers on a Train. 2013. (Nancy Drew Diaries: 2). (ENG.). 208p. (J). (gr. 3-7). 15.99 *(978-1-4424-6611-1(1)*, Simon & Schuster/Paula Wiseman Bks.) Simon & Schuster/Paula Wiseman Bks.

—Thanksgiving Thief. Pamintuan, Macky, illus. 2008. (Nancy Drew & the Clue Crew Ser.: 16). (ENG.). 96p. (J). (gr. 1-4). pap. 5.99 *(978-1-4169-6777-4(X)*, Aladdin) Simon & Schuster Children's Publishing.

—Ticket Trouble. Pamintuan, Macky, illus. 10th ed. 2007. (Nancy Drew & the Clue Crew Ser.: 10). (ENG.). 96p. (J). (gr. 1-4). pap. 5.99 *(978-1-4169-4733-2(7)*, Aladdin) Simon & Schuster Children's Publishing.

—Time Thief. Pamintuan, Macky, illus. 2011. (Nancy Drew & the Clue Crew Ser.: 28). (ENG.). 96p. (J). (gr. 1-4). pap. 5.99 *(978-1-4169-9458-9(0)*, Aladdin) Simon & Schuster Children's Publishing.

—Trails of Treachery. 25th ed. 2007. (Nancy Drew (All New) Girl Detective Ser.: 25). (ENG.). 144p. (J). (gr. 3-7). pap. 5.99 *(978-1-4169-3524-7(X)*, Aladdin) Simon & Schuster Children's Publishing.

—Treasure Trouble. Pamintuan, Macky, illus. 2009. (Nancy Drew & the Clue Crew Ser.: 20). (ENG.). 112p. (J). (gr. 1-4). pap. 4.99 *(978-1-4169-7809-1(7)*, Aladdin) Simon & Schuster Children's Publishing.

—Troubled Waters. 23rd ed. 2007. (Nancy Drew (All New) Girl Detective Ser.: 23). (ENG.). 160p. (J). (gr. 3-7). pap. 5.99 *(978-1-4169-2513-2(9)*, Aladdin) Simon & Schuster Children's Publishing.

—Uncivil Acts. 10th ed. 2005. (Nancy Drew (All New) Girl Detective Ser.: 10). (ENG.). 160p. (J). (gr. 3-7). pap. 5.99 *(978-0-689-86937-2(1)*, Aladdin) Simon & Schuster Children's Publishing.

—Unicorn Uproar. Pamintuan, Macky, illus. 2009. (Nancy Drew & the Clue Crew Ser.: 22). (ENG.). 96p. (J). (gr. 1-4). pap. 4.99 *(978-1-4169-7810-7(0)*, Aladdin) Simon & Schuster Children's Publishing.

—Valentine's Day Secret. Pamintuan, Macky, illus. 12th ed. 2007. (Nancy Drew & the Clue Crew Ser.: 12). (ENG.). 96p. (J). (gr. 1-4). pap. 5.99 *(978-1-4169-4944-2(5)*, Aladdin) Simon & Schuster Children's Publishing.

—Where's Nancy? 2005. (Nancy Drew: Girl Detective Super Mystery Ser.: 1). (ENG.). 176p. (J). (gr. 3-7). pap. 5.99 *(978-1-4169-0034-4(9)*, Aladdin) Simon & Schuster Children's Publishing.

—Without a Trace. 2005. (Nancy Drew Ser.: 1). (Illus.). 154p. (J). lib. bdg. 15.00 *(978-1-59054-819-6(1))* Fitzgerald Bks.

—Without a Trace. 2004. (Nancy Drew (All New) Girl Detective Ser.: 1). (ENG.). 160p. (J). (gr. 3-7). pap. 5.99 *(978-0-689-86566-4(X)*, Aladdin) Simon & Schuster Children's Publishing.

—Without a Trace Set: A Race Against Time - False Notes - High Risk. 2004. (Nancy Drew (All New) Girl Detective Ser.). (ENG., Illus.). 640p. (J). (gr. 3-7). pap. 23.99 *(978-0-689-03691-0(4)*, Aladdin) Simon & Schuster Children's Publishing.

—The Zoo Crew. Pamintuan, Macky, illus. 14th ed. 2008. (Nancy Drew & the Clue Crew Ser.: 14). (ENG.). 96p. (J). (gr. 1-4). pap. 4.99 *(978-1-4169-5899-4(1)*, Aladdin) Simon & Schuster Children's Publishing.

Keene, Carolyn & Dixon, Franklin W. Danger Overseas. 2008. (Nancy Drew/Hardy Boys Ser.: 2). (ENG., Illus.). 224p. (J). (gr. 3-7). pap. 5.99 *(978-1-4169-5777-5(4)*, Aladdin) Simon & Schuster Children's Publishing.

—Terror on Tour. 2007. (Nancy Drew/Hardy Boys Ser.: 1). (ENG., Illus.). 224p. (J). (gr. 3-7). pap. 5.99 *(978-1-4169-2726-6(3)*, Aladdin) Simon & Schuster Children's Publishing.

Keene, Carolyn & Drew, Nancy. Lights, Camera... 5th ed. 2004. (Nancy Drew (All New) Girl Detective Ser.: 5). (ENG., Illus.). 160p. (J). (gr. 3-7). pap. 5.99 *(978-0-689-86570-1(8)*, Aladdin) Simon & Schuster Children's Publishing.

Keene, Carolyn & Whelan, Patrick. Danger on the Great Lakes. 173rd ed. 2003. (Nancy Drew Ser.: 173). (ENG., Illus.). 160p. (J). (gr. 3-7). pap. 5.99 *(978-0-689-86146-8(X)*, 53545777, Simon & Schuster/Paula Wiseman Bks.) Simon & Schuster/Paula Wiseman Bks.

Kehret, Peg. Backstage Fright. 2008. (ENG.). 128p. (J). (gr. 3-7). pap. 7.99 *(978-1-4169-9107-6(7)*, Simon & Schuster/Paula Wiseman Bks.) Simon & Schuster/Paula Wiseman Bks.

—Race to Disaster. 2008. (ENG.). 128p. (J). (gr. 3-7). pap. 7.99 *(978-1-4169-9108-3(5)*, Simon & Schuster/Paula Wiseman Bks.) Simon & Schuster/Paula Wiseman Bks.

—Screaming Eagles. 2008. (ENG.). 128p. (J). (gr. 3-7). pap. 7.99 *(978-1-4169-9106-9(9)*, Simon & Schuster/Paula Wiseman Bks.) Simon & Schuster/Paula Wiseman Bks.

Keller, Laurie. Bowling Alley Bandit. Keller, Laurie, illus. 2013. (Adventures of Arnie the Doughnut Ser.: 1). (ENG., Illus.). 128p. (J). (gr. 2-5). 13.99 *(978-0-8050-9076-5(2)*, 9780805090765, Holt, Henry & Co. Bks. For Young Readers) Holt, Henry & Co.

—The Spinny Icky Showdown. Keller, Laurie, illus. 2015. (Adventures of Arnie the Doughnut Ser.: 3). (ENG., Illus.). 128p. (J). (gr. 2-5). 12.99 *(978-0-8050-9074-1(6)*, 9780805090741, Holt, Henry & Co. Bks. For Young Readers) Holt, Henry & Co.

Keller, William B. Olivia & the Mystery. 2011. 88p. pap. 14.95 *(978-1-4327-7636-7(3))* Outskirts Pr., Inc.

Kelly, David A. The All-Star Joker. Meyers, Mark, illus. 2012. (Ballpark Mysteries Ser.: 5). (ENG.). 112p. (J). (gr. 1-4). 4.99 *(978-0-375-86884-9(4)*, Random Hse. Bks. for Young Readers) Random Hse. Children's Bks.

—The All-Star Joker. Meyers, Mark, illus. 2012. (Ballpark Mysteries Ser.: Bk. 5). lib. bdg. 14.75 *(978-0-606-26401-3(9)*, Turtleback) Turtleback Bks.

—The Astro Outlaw. Meyers, Mark, illus. 2012. (Ballpark Mysteries Ser.: Bk. 4). (ENG.). 112p. (J). (gr. 1-4). pap. 4.99 *(978-0-375-86883-2(6)*, Random Hse. Bks. for Young Readers) Random Hse. Children's Bks.

—The Astro Outlaw. 2012. (Ballpark Mysteries Ser.: Bk. 4). lib. bdg. 14.75 *(978-0-606-23861-8(1)*, Turtleback) Turtleback Bks.

—The Capital Catch. Meyers, Mark, illus. 2017. (Ballpark Mysteries Ser.: Bk. 13). (ENG.). 112p. (J). (gr. 1-4). 4.99 *(978-0-399-55189-5(1)*, Random Hse. Bks. for Young Readers) Random Hse. Children's Bks.

—The Capital Catch. 2017. (Ballpark Mysteries Ser.: Bk. 13). lib. bdg. 14.75 ***(978-0-606-39869-5(4))*** Turtleback Bks.

—The Fenway Foul-Up. Meyers, Mark, illus. 2011. (Ballpark Mysteries Ser.: Bk. 1). (ENG.). 112p. (J). (gr. 1-4). pap. 4.99 *(978-0-375-86703-3(1)*, Random Hse. Bks. for Young Readers) Random Hse. Children's Bks.

—The Gold Medal Mess. Brundage, Scott, illus. 2016. (Most Valuable Players Ser.: 1). (ENG.). 128p. (J). (gr. 1-4). 4.99 *(978-0-553-51319-6(2)*, Random Hse. Bks. for Young Readers) Random Hse. Children's Bks.

—The L. A. Dodger. Meyers, Mark, illus. 2011. (Ballpark Mysteries Ser.: Bk. 3). (ENG.). 112p. (J). (gr. 1-4). 4.99 *(978-0-375-86885-6(2)*, Random Hse. Bks. for Young Readers) Random Hse. Children's Bks.

—The Missing Marlin. Meyers, Mark, illus. 2014. (Ballpark Mysteries Ser.: Bk. 8). (ENG.). 112p. (J). (gr. 1-4). 4.99 *(978-0-307-97782-3(X)*, Random Hse. Bks. for Young Readers) Random Hse. Children's Bks.

—The Missing Marlin. 2014. (Ballpark Mysteries Ser.: Bk. 8). lib. bdg. 14.75 *(978-0-606-35565-0(0))* Turtleback Bks.

—The Philly Fake. Meyers, Mark, illus. 2014. (Ballpark Mysteries Ser.: Bk. 9). (ENG.). 112p. (J). (gr. 1-4). 4.99 *(978-0-307-97785-4(4)*, Random Hse. Bks. for Young Readers) Random Hse. Children's Bks.

—The Pinstripe Ghost. Meyers, Mark, illus. 2011. (Ballpark Mysteries Ser.: 2). (ENG.). 112p. (J). (gr. 1-4). 4.99 *(978-0-375-86704-0(X)*, Random Hse. Bks. for Young Readers) Random Hse. Children's Bks.

—The Rangers Rustlers. Meyers, Mark, illus. 2016. (Ballpark Mysteries Ser.: Bk. 12). (ENG.). 112p. (J). (gr. 1-4). pap. 4.99 *(978-0-385-37881-9(5)*, Random Hse. Bks. for Young Readers) Random Hse. Children's Bks.

—The Rookie Blue Jay. Meyers, Mark, illus. 2015. (Ballpark Mysteries Ser.: 10). (ENG.). 112p. (J). (gr. 1-4). 4.99 *(978-0-385-37875-8(0)*, Random Hse. Bks. for Young Readers) Random Hse. Children's Bks.

—The San Francisco Splash. Meyers, Mark, illus. 2013. (Ballpark Mysteries Ser.: Bk. 7). (ENG.). 112p. (J). (gr. 1-4). pap. 4.99 *(978-0-307-97779-3(X)*, Random Hse. Bks. for Young Readers) Random Hse. Children's Bks.

—The San Francisco Splash. 2013. (Ballpark Mysteries Ser.: Bk. 7). lib. bdg. 14.75 *(978-0-606-31940-9(9)*, Turtleback) Turtleback Bks.

—The Tiger Troubles. Meyers, Mark, illus. 2015. (Ballpark Mysteries Ser.: 11). (ENG.). 112p. (J). (gr. 1-4). pap. 4.99 *(978-0-385-37878-9(5)*, Random Hse. Bks. for Young Readers) Random Hse. Children's Bks.

—The Tiger Troubles. 2015. (Ballpark Mysteries Ser.: Bk. 11). lib. bdg. 14.75 *(978-0-606-36414-0(5))* Turtleback Bks.

—The World Series Curse. Meyers, Mark, illus. 2016. (Ballpark Mysteries Ser.: 13). (ENG.). 144p. (J). (gr. 1-4). 5.99 *(978-0-385-37884-0(X)*, Random Hse. Bks. for Young Readers) Random Hse. Children's Bks.

—The Wrigley Riddle. Meyers, Mark, illus. 2013. (Ballpark Mysteries Ser.: Bk. 6). (ENG.). 112p. (J). (gr. 1-4). pap. 4.99 *(978-0-307-97776-2(5)*, Random Hse. Bks. for Young Readers) Random Hse. Children's Bks.

—The Wrigley Riddle. 2013. (Ballpark Mysteries Ser.: Bk. 6). lib. bdg. 14.75 *(978-0-606-26998-8(3)*, Turtleback) Turtleback Bks.

Kelly, Erin. The Mystery at the Eiffel Tower: Paris, France. 2005. (Carole Marsh Mysteries Ser.). (Illus.). 144p. (J). (gr. 3-5). pap. 7.99 *(978-0-635-03468-7(9))* Gallopade International.

Kelly, Margo. Who R U Really? 2015. (ENG.). 240p. (YA). pap. 9.99 *(978-1-4405-9226-3(8)*, Simon Pulse) Simon Pulse.

Kelsey, Marybeth. A Recipe for Robbery. 2009. (ENG.). 288p. (J). (gr. 3-7). 16.99 *(978-0-06-128843-2(8)*, Greenwillow Bks.) HarperCollins Pubs.

Kemmerer, Brigid. Secret. 2014. (Elemental Ser.). (ENG.). 336p. (YA). (gr. 13). pap. 9.95 *(978-0-7582-9437-1(9)*, K-Teen) Kensington Publishing Corp.

Kennedy, Emma. The Case of the Fatal Phantom, 3 vols. Marc, Sylvain, illus. 2012. (Wilma Tenderfoot Ser.: 3). (ENG.). 368p. (J). (gr. 3-7). 16.99 *(978-0-8037-3542-2(1)*, Dial Bks) Penguin Young Readers Group.

—The Case of the Frozen Hearts. 2012. (Wilma Tenderfoot Ser.: 1). (ENG.). 368p. (J). (gr. 3-7). 7.99

(978-0-14-242140-6(5), Puffin Books) Penguin Young Readers Group.
—The Case of the Putrid Poison, 2 vols. Marc, Sylvain & Dorman, Brandon, illus. 2011. (Wilma Tenderfoot Ser.: 2). (ENG.). 336p. (J). (gr. 3-7). 16.99 (978-0-8037-3541-5(3), Dial Bks) Penguin Young Readers Group.
—Wilma Tenderfoot - The Case of the Frozen Hearts. Marc, Sylvain et al, illus. 2011. (Wilma Tenderfoot Ser.: 1). (ENG.). 352p. (J). (gr. 3-7). 16.99 (978-0-8037-3540-8(5), Dial Bks) Penguin Young Readers Group.
—Wilma Tenderfoot: the Case of the Fatal Phantom. Marc, Sylvain, illus. 2013. (Wilma Tenderfoot Ser.: 3). (ENG.). 384p. (J). (gr. 3-7). pap. 7.99 (978-0-14-242609-8(1), Puffin Books) Penguin Young Readers Group.
Kennedy, Kim. Misty Gordon & the Mystery of the Ghost Pirates. 2010. (ENG., Illus.). 240p. (YA). (gr. 3-7). 15.95 (978-0-8109-9357-0(0), Amulet Bks.) Abrams, Inc.
Kerbel, Deborah. Lure. 2010. (ENG.). 200p. (YA). (gr. 9). pap. 12.99 (978-1-55488-754-5(2)) Dundurn CAN. Dist: Ingram Publisher Services.
Kerr, Esme. The Girl with the Glass Bird. 2015. (ENG.). 272p. (J). (gr. 3-7). 16.99 (978-0-545-69984-6(3)) Scholastic, Inc.
—Mischief at Midnight. 2016. (ENG.). 272p. (J). (gr. 3-7). 16.99 (978-0-545-90403-2(X), Chicken Hse., The) Scholastic, Inc.
Kerrin, Jessica Scott. The Spotted Dog Last Seen, 1 vol. 2013. (ENG.). 196p. (J). 14.95 (978-1-55498-387-2(8)) Groundwood Bks. CAN. Dist: Publishers Group West (PGW).
Kessler, Liz. Emily Windsnap & the Land of the Midnight Sun. 2014. (Emily Windsnap Ser.: 5). lib. bdg. 16.00 (978-0-606-35165-2(5)) Turtleback Bks.
—North of Nowhere. 2013. (ENG., Illus.). 272p. (J). (gr. 4-7). 15.99 (978-0-7636-6727-6(7)) Candlewick Pr.
Key, Watt. Hideout. 2017. (ENG.). 320p. (J). 16.99 (978-0-374-30482-9(3), 9780374304829, Farrar, Straus & Giroux (BYR)) Farrar, Straus & Giroux.
Khan, Farheen. Ibrahim Khan & the Mystery of the Haunted Lake. 2011. (Ibrahim Khan Ser.). (ENG., Illus.). 64p. (J). (gr. k-5). pap. 7.50 (978-0-86037-423-7(8)) Kube Publishing Ltd. GBR. Dist: Consortium Bk. Sales & Distribution.
—Ibrahim Khan & the Mystery of the Roaring Lion. 2010. (Ibrahim Khan Ser.). (ENG., Illus.). 56p. (J). (gr. 2-6). pap. 6.50 (978-0-86037-467-1(X)) Kube Publishing Ltd. GBR. Dist: Consortium Bk. Sales & Distribution.
Kiarie, Vivian W. The Waltz, the Weasel & the Lair. 2008. 50p. pap. 16.95 (978-1-60474-265-7(8)) America Star Bks.
Kidd, Ronald. Undercover Kid: The Comic Book King. Sklar, Andy, illus. 2007. (All Aboard Mystery Reader Ser.). (ENG.). 48p. (J). pap. 3.99 (978-0-448-44438-3(0), Grosset & Dunlap) Penguin Publishing Group.
Kiem, Elizabeth. Hider, Seeker, Secret Keeper. 2014. (Bolshoi Saga Ser.). (ENG., Illus.). 264p. (YA). (gr. 9). 17.99 (978-1-61695-412-3(4), Soho Teen) Soho Pr., Inc.
Kilman, Nancy. The Lockgate Mystery: Level O, 6 vols. (Raging Rivers Ser.). 128p. (gr. 3-6). 36.95 (978-0-322-05895-8(3)) Wright Group/McGraw-Hill.
Kimmel, Elizabeth Cody. Legend of the Ghost Dog. (J). 2014. (ENG.). 208p. (gr. 3-7). pap. 6.99 (978-0-545-39128-3(8)) 2012. 200p. pap. (978-0-545-50705-9(7)) Scholastic, Inc. (Scholastic Pr.).
Kimpton, Diana. Princess Ellie Solves a Mystery. Finlay, Lizzie, illus. 8th rev. ed. 2007. (ENG.). 96p. (gr. 1-4). pap. 3.99 (978-1-4231-0901-3(5)) Hyperion Pr.
—Princess Ellie's Moonlight Mystery. 2015. (Pony-Crazed Princess Ser.). (ENG.). 96p. (J). (gr. k-5). pap. 4.99 (978-0-7945-3431-8(7), Usborne) EDC Publishing.
Kindl, Patrice. Lost in the Labyrinth. 2005. (ENG.). 208p. (J). (gr. 5-7). pap. 13.95 (978-0-618-39402-9(8)) Houghton Mifflin Harcourt Publishing Co.
Kindl, Patrice & Wells, Rosemary. A School for Brides. 2015. (ENG.). 272p. (J). (gr. 7). bds. 17.99 (978-0-670-78608-4(X), Viking Books for Young Readers) Penguin Young Readers Group.
King George the Thirty Third. Come Go with Me. 2017. (ENG.). 185p. pap. 13.95 (**978-1-78612-438-8(6)**, 9781786124388) Austin, Stan AUS. Dist: Bookmasters Distribution.
King, Glynda T. Skippy the Flea Is off to see the President. 2010. 52p. pap. 22.49 (978-1-4520-0860-8(4)) AuthorHouse.
King, J. Eric & Graham, Greg. Byron Carmichael Book One: The Human Corpse Trade. Mizer, Lindsay, ed. Warner, Michael, illus. 2008. (ENG.). 408p. (gr. 8-12). 18.95 (978-0-615-15770-2(X)) G & K Publishing.
King, Jane. Welcome to Chillsville Elementary. 2013. (Ghoul School Ser.: 1). (ENG.). 80p. (J). (gr. 1-4). pap. 13.99 (978-1-4814-2162-1(X), Simon & Schuster/Paula Wiseman Bks.) Simon & Schuster/Paula Wiseman Bks.
King, Jeremy Jordan. Dark Rites. 2015. (ENG.). 264p. (J). (gr. 7). pap. 11.95 (978-1-62639-245-8(5)) Bold Strokes Bks.
King, Peter. Changels: The Crucible. 2nd ed. 2013. 298p. pap. (978-1-927264-16-4(2)) King, Peter Publishing.
King, Trey. Mystery on the Lego Express. Wang, Sean, illus. 2014. (Lego City Ser.). (ENG.). 24p. (J). (gr. -1-3). 3.99 (978-0-545-60366-9(8)) Scholastic, Inc.
—Mystery on the LEGO Express. Wang, Sean, illus. 2014. 24p. (J). (978-1-4242-6168-0(6)) Scholastic, Inc.
—Mystery on the Lego Express. 2014. (LEGO City 8X8 Ser.). (Illus.). 24p. (J). lib. bdg. 13.55 (978-0-606-36068-5(9)) Turtleback Bks.
King, Trey. Wrecking Valentine's Day! Wang, Sean, illus. 2015. 24p. (J). (**978-1-4806-9662-4(5)**) Scholastic, Inc.
King, Zelda. The Class Surprise. 2006. (Neighborhood Readers Ser.). (ENG.). 16p. (gr. 1-3). pap. 6.50 (978-1-4042-6994-1(0), Rosen Classroom) Rosen Publishing Group, Inc., The.
Kinney, Sarah. Enter the Dragon Mystery. 2013. (Nancy Drew & the Clue Crew Ser.). (ENG., Illus.). 64p. (J). (gr. k-3). pap. 7.99 (978-1-59707-437-7(3), 9781597074377) Papercutz.
—Nancy Drew & the Clue Crew #3: Enter the Dragon Mystery. 2013. (Nancy Drew & the Clue Crew Ser.). (ENG., Illus.). 64p. (J). (gr. k-3). 11.99 (978-1-59707-438-4(1), 9781597074384) Papercutz.
Kinney, Sarah & Petrucha, Stefan. Secret Sand Sleuths. 2013. (Nancy Drew & the Clue Crew Ser.). (ENG., Illus.). 64p. (J). (gr. k-3). pap. 7.99 (978-1-59707-376-9(8), 9781597073769) Papercutz.
Kirby, Matthew J. The Rogue World. 2017. (Dark Gravity Sequence Ser.: 3). 400p. (J). (gr. 3-7). 16.99 (978-0-06-222493-4(X)) HarperCollins Pubs.
Kittscher, Kristen. The Tiara on the Terrace. 2016. 400p. (J). (gr. 3-7). 16.99 (978-0-06-222798-0(X)) HarperCollins Pubs.
—The Wig in the Window. 2013. (ENG.). 368p. (J). (gr. 3-7). 16.99 (978-0-06-211050-3(0)) HarperCollins Pubs.
Klavan, Andrew. Hostage Run, 1 vol. 2015. (MindWar Trilogy Ser.: 2). (ENG.). 352p. (YA). 15.99 (978-1-4016-8895-0(0)) Nelson, Thomas Inc.
Klein, Jen. Jillian Cade: (Fake) Paranormal Investigator. 2016. (ENG.). 288p. (YA). (gr. 9). pap. 10.99 (978-1-61695-690-5(9), Soho Teen) Soho Pr., Inc.
Kleyla, Mary Pat. Identity Unknown. 2003. 154p. (YA). 22.95 (978-0-595-65812-1(1)); pap. 12.95 (978-0-595-28473-3(6)) iUniverse, Inc.
Klim, Christopher. Firecracker Jones Is on the Case. 2005. (Illus.). 111p. (J). per. 9.95 (978-0-9726906-7-6(0)) Hopewell Pubns., LLC.
Kline, Suzy. Horrible Harry & the Locked Closet. Remkiewicz, Frank, illus. 2005. (Horrible Harry Ser.). (ENG.). 80p. (J). (gr. 2-4). 4.99 (978-0-14-240451-5(9), Puffin Books) Penguin Young Readers Group.
—Horrible Harry & the Locked Closet. Remkiewicz, Frank, illus. 2005. (Horrible Harry Ser.). 68p. (gr. 2-5). 14.00 (978-0-7569-5825-1(3)) Perfection Learning Corp.
—Horrible Harry & the Secret Treasure. Wummer, Amy, illus. (Horrible Harry Ser.). (ENG.). 80p. (J). (gr. 2-4). 2012. 4.99 (978-0-14-242021-8(2), Puffin Books) 2011. 14.99 (978-0-670-01181-0(9), Viking Books for Young Readers) Penguin Young Readers Group.
—Horrible Harry Cracks the Code. Remkiewicz, Frank, illus. 2008. (Horrible Harry Ser.). (ENG.). 80p. (J). (gr. 2-4). 4.99 (978-0-14-241247-3(3), Puffin Books) Penguin Young Readers Group.
Klise, Kate. Regarding the Bathrooms: A Privy to the Past. Klise, Kate & Klise, M. Sarah, illus. 2008. (Regarding The ... Ser.: Bk. 4). (ENG.). 160p. (J). (gr. 2-5). pap. 6.99 (978-0-15-206261-3(0)) Houghton Mifflin Harcourt Publishing Co.
—Till Death Do Us Bark. Klise, M. Sarah, illus. 2012. (43 Old Cemetery Road Ser.: 3). (ENG.). 144p. (J). (gr. 2-5). pap. 6.99 (978-0-547-85081-8(6)) Houghton Mifflin Harcourt Publishing Co.
Knight, Andrew. Dead Beckoning. (Thumbprint Mysteries Ser.). 32.86 (978-0-8092-0421-2(5)) McGraw-Hill/Contemporary.
—The Monster in the Loch. (Thumbprint Mysteries Ser.). 32.86 (978-0-8092-0411-3(8)) McGraw-Hill/Contemporary.
Knighton, Kate, retold by. Phantom of the Opera. 2008. (Young Reading Series 2 Gift Bks). 64p. (J). 8.99 (978-0-7945-2082-3(0), Usborne) EDC Publishing.
Knox, Regina. The Clintonville Abduction. 2007. 108p. per. 19.95 (978-1-4241-2996-6(6)) PublishAmerica, Inc.
Konigsburg, E. L. My Father's Daughter. 2nd ed. 2008. (ENG.). 144p. (J). (gr. 3-7). pap. 7.99 (978-1-4169-5500-9(3), Atheneum Bks. for Young Readers) Simon & Schuster Children's Publishing.
Korman, Gordon. Criminal Destiny. 2016. (Masterminds Ser.: 2). 320p. (J). (gr. 3-7). 16.99 (978-0-06-230002-7(4)) HarperCollins Pubs.
—Criminal Destiny. 2017. (Masterminds Ser.: 2). (J). lib. bdg. 18.40 (**978-0-606-39612-7(8)**) Turtleback Bks.
—Jingle (Swindle #8) 2016. (Swindle Ser.: 8). (ENG.). 208p. (J). (gr. 3-7). 16.99 (978-0-545-86142-7(X), Scholastic Pr.) Scholastic, Inc.
—Masterminds. (Masterminds Ser.: 2). (J). (gr. 3-7). 2017. 336p. 7.99 (978-0-06-230003-4(2)) 2016. 352p. pap. 7.99 (978-0-06-229999-4(9)) 2015. 336p. 16.99 (978-0-06-229996-3(4)) HarperCollins Pubs.
—Masterminds. 2016. (Masterminds Ser.: 1). (J). lib. bdg. 18.40 (978-0-606-38138-3(4)) Turtleback Bks.
—One False Note. 2009. (39 Clues Ser.: 2). (ENG.). 160p. (J). (gr. 3-7). 12.99 (978-0-545-06042-4(7)); (Illus.). 12.99 (978-0-545-09060-5(1)) Scholastic, Inc.
—Titanic. 2011. (Titanic Ser.: 3). (ENG.). 176p. (J). (gr. 3-7). pap. 6.99 (978-0-545-12333-4(X), Scholastic Paperbacks) Scholastic, Inc.
Kostro, Ed. Mystery of Madera Canyon. 2004. 108p. (gr. -1-7). per. 11.95 (978-1-59113-622-4(9)) Booklocker.com, Inc.
Kotzwinkle, William. Trouble in Bugland: A Collection of Inspector Mantis Mysteries. Servello, Joe, illus. 2012. (Godine Storyteller Ser.). (ENG.). 190p. (gr. 4-7). reprint ed. pap. 14.95 (978-1-56792-070-3(5)) Godine, David R. Pub.
Krailing, Tessa. La Mano Verde. (SPA.). 96p. (J). (gr. 3-5). 7.95 (978-84-88061-84-3(6)) Serres, Ediciones, S. L. ESP. Dist: Lectorum Pubns., Inc.
Kreilein, Debra. The Tombstone Treasure Mystery. 2013. 142p. pap. 12.99 (978-1-62509-458-2(2)) Salem Author Services.
Krensky, Stephen. Case of the Missing Mice: A Simon Mystery. 2003. (Illus.). 14.95 (978-1-59319-022-4(0)) LeapFrog Enterprises, Inc.
—Case of the Missing Pail. 2003. (Illus.). (J). 14.95 (978-1-59319-018-7(2)) LeapFrog Enterprises, Inc.
Kristie Smith-Armand M.Ed Ctvi. Adventures of Abby Diamond: Out of Sight. 2009. 300p. pap. 18.95 (978-1-4401-7013-3(4)) iUniverse, Inc.
Kristie Smith-Armand M.Ed Tvi. Adventures of Abby Diamond: Abby Diamond in Teenage Wizard & Secrets in the Attic. 2009. 276p. pap. 17.95 (978-1-4401-6626-6(9)) iUniverse, Inc.
Kristina Takes the Stage. 2008. (Illus.). 56p. (J). mass mkt. 10.95 (978-0-9792361-3-6(4)) Inspire U., LLC.
Kropp, Paul. The Countess & Me. 2003. 144p. (J). pap. (978-1-55041-689-3(8)) Fitzhenry & Whiteside, Ltd.
Krosoczka, Jarrett J. The Frog Who Croaked. Krosoczka, Jarrett J., illus. 2013. (Platypus Police Squad Ser.: 1). (ENG., Illus.). 240p. (J). (gr. 3-7). 12.99 (978-0-06-207164-4(5), Waldon Pond Pr.) HarperCollins Pubs.
—Lunch Lady & the Field Trip Fiasco. 2011. (Lunch Lady Ser.). (ENG.). 96p. (J). (gr. 3-7). pap. 6.99 (978-0-375-86730-9(9), Knopf Bks. for Young Readers) Random Hse. Children's Bks.
—Lunch Lady & the Mutant Mathletes. 2012. (Lunch Lady Ser.). (ENG., Illus.). 96p. (J). (gr. 2-5). pap. 6.99 (978-0-375-87028-6(8)); lib. bdg. 12.99 (978-0-375-97028-3(2)) Random Hse. Children's Bks. (Knopf Bks. for Young Readers).
—Lunch Lady & the Mutant Mathletes. 2012. (Lunch Lady Ser.: 7). lib. bdg. 17.20 (978-0-606-23871-7(9), Turtleback) Turtleback Bks.
—Lunch Lady & the Picture Day Peril. 2012. (Lunch Lady Ser.). (ENG., Illus.). 96p. (J). (gr. 2-5). pap. 6.99 (978-0-375-87035-4(0)); lib. bdg. 12.99 (978-0-375-97035-1(5)) Random Hse. Children's Bks. (Knopf Bks. for Young Readers).
—Lunch Lady & the Picture Day Peril. 2012. (Lunch Lady Ser.: 8). lib. bdg. 17.20 (978-0-606-26811-0(1), Turtleback) Turtleback Bks.
—Lunch Lady & the Schoolwide Scuffle. 2014. (Lunch Lady Ser.). (ENG., Illus.). 96p. (J). (gr. 2-5). pap. 6.99 (978-0-385-75279-4(2)); lib. bdg. 12.99 (978-0-385-75280-0(6)) Random Hse. Children's Bks. (Knopf Bks. for Young Readers).
—Lunch Lady & the Schoolwide Scuffle. 2014. (Lunch Lady Ser.: 10). lib. bdg. 17.20 (978-0-606-32235-5(3), Turtleback) Turtleback Bks.
—Lunch Lady & the Summer Camp Shakedown. 2010. (Lunch Lady Ser.). (ENG.). 96p. (J). (gr. 3-7). pap. 6.99 (978-0-375-86095-9(9)); lib. bdg. 12.99 (978-0-375-96095-6(3)) Random Hse. Children's Bks. (Knopf Bks. for Young Readers).
—Lunch Lady & the Video Game Villain. 2013. (Lunch Lady Ser.: 9). lib. bdg. 17.20 (978-0-606-27003-8(5), Turtleback) Turtleback Bks.
—Platypus Police Squad: Last Panda Standing. Krosoczka, Jarrett J., illus. 2015. (Platypus Police Squad Ser.: 3). (ENG., Illus.). 256p. (J). (gr. 3-7). 12.99 (978-0-06-207168-2(8), Waldon Pond Pr.) HarperCollins Pubs.
—Platypus Police Squad: The Ostrich Conspiracy. Krosoczka, Jarrett J., illus. 2014. (Platypus Police Squad Ser.: 2). (ENG., Illus.). 240p. (J). (gr. 3-7). 12.99 (978-0-06-207166-8(1), Waldon Pond Pr.) HarperCollins Pubs.
Kruse, Donald W. Jasper Has Left the Building! Crank, Donny, illus. 2013. 50p. pap. 12.95 (978-1-59663-863-1(X), Castle Keep Pr.) Rock, James A. & Co. Pubs.
Krys, Michelle. Dead Girls Society. 2016. (ENG.). 304p. (YA). (gr. 7). 17.99 (978-0-553-50802-4(4), Delacorte Pr.) Random Hse. Children's Bks.
Kubica, Jeremy. The CS Detective: An Algorithmic Tale of Crime, Conspiracy, & Computation. 2016. (ENG., Illus.). 256p. (YA). pap. 17.95 (978-1-59327-749-9(0)) No Starch Pr., Inc.
Kudina Steinberg, Ganna V. The Princess Conspiracy: an Inspector Poopchyk Mystery. 2009. 143p. 30.00 (978-0-557-08936-9(0)) Lulu Pr., Inc.
Kumar, Naresh, illus. The Dusk Society. 2011. (Campfire Graphic Novels Ser.). (ENG.). 88p. (YA). (gr. 3-7). pap. 11.99 (978-93-80028-63-7(6), Campfire) Steerforth Pr.
Kunze, Nansi. Kill the Music. l.t. ed. 2013. 330p. pap. (978-1-4596-6983-3(5)) ReadHowYouWant.com, Ltd.
Kupperberg, Paul. Scooby-Doo & the Night of the Undead!, 1 vol. 2013. (Scooby-Doo Graphic Novels Set 3 Ser.). (ENG.). 24p. (J). (gr. 2-6). lib. bdg. 24.21 (978-1-61479-050-1(7), Essential Library) ABDO Publishing Co.
—Scooby-Doo in over the Boardwalk, 1 vol. 2013. (Scooby-Doo Graphic Novels Set 3 Ser.). (ENG., Illus.). 24p. (J). (gr. 2-6). lib. bdg. 24.21 (978-1-61479-052-5(3), Essential Library) ABDO Publishing Co.
—Scooby-Doo in Read All about It!, 1 vol. 2013. (Scooby-Doo Graphic Novels Set 3 Ser.). (ENG.). 24p. (J). (gr. 2-6). lib. bdg. 24.21 (978-1-61479-053-2(1), Essential Library) ABDO Publishing Co.
Kvasnosky, Laura McGee. Zelda & Ivy - The Big Picture. Kvasnosky, Laura McGee, illus. 2013. (Candlewick Sparks Ser.). (ENG., Illus.). 48p. (J). (gr. k-4). pap. 3.99 (978-0-7636-6637-8(8)) Candlewick Pr.
Labeda, Patricia R. Miko & the Mystery Friend. Labeda, Patricia R., illus. 2007. (Illus.). 73p. (J). (gr. 4-7). per. 10.99 (978-1-59879-415-1(9), Lifevest) Lifevest Publishing, Inc.
LaBree Stute, Lela. Wonder Pugs. 2010. 36p. pap. 19.99 (978-0-557-42611-9(1)) Lulu Pr., Inc.
LaBrot, Matthew & Daniel, Hale. Green Streak. 2004. (Zeke Armstrong Mysteries Ser.: 2). 236p. (J). per. 8.95 (978-1-929976-28-7(3)) Top Pubns., Ltd.
Lacey, Josh. Island of Thieves. 2013. (ENG.). 240p. (J). (gr. 5-7). pap. 7.99 (978-0-544-10485-3(4)) Houghton Mifflin Harcourt Publishing Co.
Lacey, Josh & Pakenham, Sarah. Island of Thieves. 2012. (ENG.). 240p. (J). (gr. 5-7). 15.99 (978-0-547-76327-9(1)) Houghton Mifflin Harcourt Publishing Co.
Lachtman, Ofelia Dumas. The Truth about las Mariposas. 2007. 144p. (J). (gr. 6-18). pap. 9.95 (978-1-55885-494-9(0), Piñata Books) Arte Publico Pr.
Lackey, Mercedes & Edghill, Rosemary. Legacies, No. 1. 2010. (Shadow Grail Ser.: 1). (ENG.). 320p. (YA). (gr. 8-12). pap. 11.99 (978-0-7653-1761-2(3), Tor Teen) Doherty, Tom Assocs., LLC.
Ladd, Debbie. Ethan the Ending Eater. Nakasone, Shaun, illus. 2008. 64p. (J). 17.95 (978-0-9727615-2-9(7)) Deb on Air Bks.
LaFevers, R. L. The Basilisk's Lair. Murphy, Kelly, illus. 2nd ed. 2010. (Nathaniel Fludd, Beastologist Ser.: 2). (ENG.). 160p. (J). (gr. 1-4). 15.00 (978-0-547-23867-8(3)) Houghton Mifflin Harcourt Publishing Co.
Lagonegro, Melissa. Cars - The Spooky Sound. 2010. (Cars Step into Reading Ser.). lib. bdg. 13.55 (978-0-606-14562-6(1), Turtleback) Turtleback Bks.
Laidlaw, S. J. The Voice Inside My Head. 2014. (ENG., Illus.). 252p. (YA). (gr. 9). 17.99 (978-1-77049-565-4(7), Tundra Bks.) Tundra Bks. CAN. Dist: Penguin Random Hse. LLC.
Laird, Chynna. Dark Water. 2012. 166p. pap. (978-1-926997-76-6(X)) Imajin Bks.
Lalicki, Tom. Danger in the Dark: A Houdini & Nate Mystery. 2010. (Houdini & Nate Mysteries Ser.: 1). (ENG.). 208p. (J). (gr. 3-7). pap. 14.99 (978-0-312-60214-7(6), 9780312602147) Square Fish.
—Shots at Sea: A Houdini & Nate Mystery. 2011. (Houdini & Nate Mysteries Ser.). 224p. (J). pap. 6.99 (978-0-312-65920-2(2)) Square Fish.
Lamotte, Kathleen. The Horsetrailer Mystery. 2008. 49p. pap. 16.95 (978-1-60474-449-1(9)) America Star Bks.
Lamplighter Staff. What Is Her Name. 2004. 16.00 (978-1-58474-036-0(1)) Cornerstone Family Ministries/Lamplighter Publishing.
Lancett, Peter. Playing the Dark Game, 1 vol. unabr. ed. 2011. (Dark Man Ser.). (ENG.). 47p. (YA). (gr. 9-12). 7.95 (978-1-61651-296-5(2)) Saddleback Educational Publishing, Inc.
Land, Linda C. The Mysterious Traveling Trunk. 2011. 156p. 23.50 (978-1-4269-6160-1(X)); pap. 13.50 (978-1-4269-6161-8(8)) Trafford Publishing.
Landon, Lucinda. Meg Mackintosh & the Mystery at Red Herring Beach: A Solve-It-Yourself Mystery. 2013. (Meg Mackintosh Mystery Ser.). (ENG.). 48p. (J). (gr. 2-4). pap. 6.95 (978-1-888695-14-4(5)) Secret Passage Pr.
—Meg Mackintosh & the Stage Fright Secret: A Solve-It-Yourself Mystery. 2004. (Meg Mackintosh Mystery Ser.: 8). (ENG., Illus.). 48p. (J). (gr. 2-4). pap. 6.95 (978-1-888695-07-6(2)) Secret Passage Pr.
—Meg Mackintosh Solves Seven American History Mysteries: A Solve-It-Yourself Mystery. 2008. (Meg Mackintosh Mystery Ser.: 9). (ENG.). 96p. (J). (gr. 2-4). pap. 8.95 (978-1-888695-12-0(9)) Secret Passage Pr.
Lane, Andrew. Black Ice. 2013. (Sherlock Holmes: the Legend Begins Ser.: 3). (ENG.). 288p. (YA). (gr. 7-12). 17.99 (978-0-374-38769-3(9), 9780374387693, Farrar, Straus & Giroux (BYR)) Farrar, Straus & Giroux.
—Black Ice. 2013. (Sherlock Holmes: the Legend Begins Ser.: 3). (ENG.). 304p. (YA). (gr. 7-12). pap. 11.99 (978-1-250-03654-4(2), 9781250036544) Square Fish.
—Death Cloud. 2012. (ENG.). (YA). (gr. 7-12). 64.99 (978-1-4272-2800-0(0)) Findaway World, LLC.
—Death Cloud. 2011. (Sherlock Holmes: the Legend Begins Ser.: 1). (ENG.). 336p. (YA). (gr. 7-12). pap. 10.99 (978-0-312-56371-4(X), 9780312563714) Square Fish.
—Death Cloud. l.t. ed. 2011. (Young Sherlock Holmes Ser.). 367p. 23.99 (978-1-4104-3971-0(2)) Thorndike Pr.
—Death Cloud. 2011. (Sherlock Holmes: the Legend Begins Ser.: 1). (YA). lib. bdg. 22.10 (978-0-606-23781-9(X), Turtleback) Turtleback Bks.
—Fire Storm. 2013. (Sherlock Holmes: the Legend Begins Ser.: 4). (ENG.). 352p. (YA). (gr. 7-12). 17.99 (978-0-374-32311-0(9), 9780374323110, Farrar, Straus & Giroux (BYR)) Farrar, Straus & Giroux.
—Fire Storm. 2014. (Sherlock Holmes: the Legend Begins Ser.: 4). (ENG.). 368p. (YA). (gr. 7-12). pap. 12.99 (978-1-250-05072-4(3), 9781250050724) Square Fish.
—Knife Edge. 2015. (Sherlock Holmes: the Legend Begins Ser.: 6). (ENG.). 320p. (YA). (gr. 7). 18.99 (978-0-374-38011-3(2), 9780374380113, Farrar, Straus & Giroux (BYR)) Farrar, Straus & Giroux.
—Rebel Fire. 2012. (Sherlock Holmes: the Legend Begins Ser.: 2). (ENG.). 352p. (YA). (gr. 7-12). 16.99 (978-0-374-38768-6(0), 9780374387686, Farrar, Straus & Giroux (BYR)) Farrar, Straus & Giroux.
Lariviere, Sarah. The Bad Kid. 2016. (ENG., Illus.). 304p. (J). (gr. 3-7). 16.99 (978-1-4814-3581-9(7), Simon & Schuster Bks. For Young Readers) Simon & Schuster Bks. For Young Readers.
Larry, H. I. Deep Waters. Oswald, Ash, illus. 2008. (Zac Power Ser.: 2). (ENG.). 96p. (J). (gr. 3-6). pap. 5.99 (978-0-312-34655-3(7), 9780312346553) Square Fish.
—Poison Island. Oswald, Ash, illus. 2008. (Zac Power Ser.: 1). (ENG.). 96p. (J). (gr. 3-6). pap. 5.99 (978-0-312-34659-1(X), 9780312346591) Square Fish.
Larry Sweitzer. The Ghost, the Eggheads, & Babe Ruth's Piano: A Novel. 2009. 180p. 23.95 (978-1-4401-7103-1(3)); pap. 13.95 (978-1-4401-7104-8(1)) iUniverse, Inc.
Larson, Mark. The Adventures of Pinky, the Pink Flamingo. 2008. 24p. pap. 24.95 (978-1-60610-046-2(7)) America Star Bks.
Larson, Rachel. Jesse Strong & Courageous Runaway: There Comes A Time When the Roads of Destiny Will No Longer Wait... 2011. 192p. (J). (gr. -1). pap. 14.03 (978-1-4520-0421-1(8)) AuthorHouse.
Larwood, Kieran. Freaks. 2013. (J). (ENG.). 256p. (gr. 5-9). 16.99 (978-0-545-47424-5(8)); (978-0-545-47425-2(6)) Scholastic, Inc. (Chicken Hse., The).
Lashawn Graves, M. Ed. Listen & Embrace When Children Care. 2012. 28p. pap. 9.95 (978-1-4327-8895-7(7)) Outskirts Pr., Inc.
Lasky, Kathryn. Double Trouble Squared. 2008. (ENG., Illus.). 240p. (J). (gr. 2-5). pap. 14.99 (978-0-15-205878-4(8)) Houghton Mifflin Harcourt Publishing Co.
—The Rescue. 2004. (Guardians of Ga'Hoole Ser.: 3). (gr. 3-6). lib. bdg. 17.20 (978-0-613-72136-3(5), Turtleback) Turtleback Bks.
—Shadows in the Water. 2008. (ENG., Illus.). 224p. (J). (gr. 2-5). pap. 14.95 (978-0-15-205874-6(5)) Houghton Mifflin Harcourt Publishing Co.
—A Voice in the Wind. 2008. (ENG., Illus.). 272p. (J). (gr. 2-5). pap. 15.95 (978-0-15-205875-3(3)) Houghton Mifflin Harcourt Publishing Co.
Latham, Jennifer. Dreamland Burning. 2017.Tr. of s. (ENG.). 384p. (YA). (gr. 9-17). 18.99 (978-0-316-38493-3(3)) Little, Brown Bks. for Young Readers.
—Scarlett Undercover. 2016. (ENG.). 336p. (YA). (gr. 7-17). pap. 9.99 (978-0-316-28394-6(0)) Little, Brown Bks. for Young Readers.
Latimer, Alex. Never Follow a Dinosaur, 1 vol. Latimer, Alex, illus. 2016. (ENG., Illus.). 32p. (J). (gr. -1-3). 16.95 (978-1-56145-704-5(3)) Peachtree Pubs.
Latta, Ruth. The Revenant & Other Stories for Hallowe'en. 2004. 54p. (978-0-9683382-8-5(3)) Latta, Roger K.
Lattimore, Deborah Nourse. Mystery at Midnight Museum. Date not set. 32p. (J). 15.89 (978-0-06-026202-0(8)) HarperCollins Pubs.
Laura Lee Hope. Six Little Bunkers at Grandma Bell's. l.t. ed. 2007. (ENG.). 162p. pap. 21.99 (978-1-4264-8193-2(4)) Creative Media Partners, LLC.
Lauren, Whitney. Vanessa & Johnny: The Cabinets. 2011. 84p. pap. 9.99 (978-1-4269-5827-4(7)) Trafford Publishing.
Laurentine, Florianne Daphne. The Mystery Chronicles: The Amazing Chocolate Mystery & the Case of the Phantom Cat. 2008. 100p. pap. 8.99 (978-1-934360-61-3(9)) Raider Publishing International.
—The Mystery Chronicles: The Unknown Masterpiece & the Case of the Practical Joker. 2012. 98p. pap. 7.99 (978-1-61667-427-4(X)) Raider Publishing International.

MNO

Laurie, Victoria. Forever, Again. 2016. (ENG.). 368p. (YA). (gr. 7-12). 17.99 (978-1-4847-0009-9(0)) Hyperion Bks. for Children.

—When. 2016. (ENG.). 336p. (YA). (gr. 7-12). pap. 9.99 (978-1-4847-0149-2(6)) Hyperion Bks. for Children.

—When. 2015. (ENG.). 336p. (YA). (gr. 7-12). 17.99 (978-1-4847-0008-2(2)) Hyperion Pr.

Lavoie, Jennifer. Tristant & Elijah. 2014. (ENG.). 264p. (J). (gr. 7). pap. 11.95 (978-1-62639-075-1(4)) Bold Strokes Bks.

Law, Felicia & Way, Steve. Castaway Code: Sequencing in Action. Law, Felicia et al, illus. 2010. (Mandrill Mountain Math Mysteries Ser.). 32p. (J). (gr. 2-6). 22.60 (978-1-60754-817-1(8)); pap. 10.55 (978-1-60754-822-5(4)) Windmill Bks.

—Crocodile Teeth: Geometric Shapes in Action. Spoor, Mike & Mostyn, David, illus. 2010. (Mandrill Mountain Math Mysteries Ser.). 32p. (J). (gr. 2-6). 22.60 (978-1-60754-816-4(X)); pap. 10.55 (978-1-60754-821-8(6)) Windmill Bks.

—Mirage in the Mist: Measurement in Action. Spoor, Mike & Mostyn, David, illus. 2010. (Mandrill Mountain Math Mysteries Ser.). 32p. (J). (gr. 2-6). pap. 10.55 (978-1-60754-823-2(2)) Windmill Bks.

—Mirage in the Mist: Measurements in Action. Spoor, Mike & Mostyn, David, illus. 2010. (Mandrill Mountain Math Mysteries Ser.). 32p. (J). (gr. 2-6). 22.60 (978-1-60754-818-8(6)) Windmill Bks.

—The Mystery of Nine: Number Place & Value in Action. Spoor, Mike & Mostyn, David, illus. 2010. (Mandrill Mountain Math Mysteries Ser.). 32p. (J). (gr. 2-6). 22.60 (978-1-60754-819-5(4)); pap. 10.55 (978-1-60754-824-9(0)) Windmill Bks.

—A Storm at Sea: Sorting, Mapping, & Grids in Action. Spoor, Mike & Mostyn, David, illus. 2010. (Mandrill Mountain Math Mysteries Ser.). 32p. (J). (gr. 2-6). 22.60 (978-1-60754-815-7(1)); pap. 10.55 (978-1-60754-820-1(8)) Windmill Bks.

Lawrence, Caroline. The Assassins of Rome. 2003. (ENG., Illus.). 224p. (gr. 2-4). pap. 10.99 (978-1-84255-023-6(3), Orion Children's Bks.) Hachette Children's Group GBR. Dist: Hachette Bk. Group.

—The Assassins of Rome. 2005. (Roman Mysteries Ser.). (Illus.). 161p. (J). (gr. 3-7). 14.65 (978-0-7569-5879-4(2)) Perfection Learning Corp.

—The Charioteer of Delphi. 2007. (ENG., Illus.). 256p. (gr. 4-6). pap. 10.99 (978-1-84255-544-6(8), Orion Children's Bks.) Hachette Children's Group GBR. Dist: Hachette Bk. Group.

—The Dolphins of Laurentum. 2003. (ENG., Illus.). 224p. (gr. 4-6). pap. 10.99 (978-1-84255-024-3(1), Orion Children's Bks.) Hachette Children's Group GBR. Dist: Hachette Bk. Group.

—The Dolphins of Laurentum. 2005. (Roman Mysteries Ser.). (Illus.). 161p. (J). (gr. 6-9). 13.65 (978-0-7569-6538-9(1)) Perfection Learning Corp.

—The Enemies of Jupiter. 2004. (ENG., Illus.). 224p. (gr. 4-6). pap. 10.99 (978-1-84255-164-6(7), Orion Children's Bks.) Hachette Children's Group GBR. Dist: Hachette Bk. Group.

—The Fugitive from Corinth. 2006. (ENG., Illus.). 240p. (gr. 7-9). pap. 10.99 (978-1-84255-515-6(4), Orion Children's Bks.) Hachette Children's Group GBR. Dist: Hachette Bk. Group.

—The Gladiators from Capua. 2005. (ENG., Illus.). 224p. (gr. 4-6). pap. 10.99 (978-1-84255-123-3(X), Orion Children's Bks.) Hachette Children's Group GBR. Dist: Hachette Bk. Group.

—The Legionary from Londinium. 2013. (ENG., Illus.). 192p. (J). (gr. 7-17). 10.99 (978-1-84255-192-9(2), Orion Children's Bks.) Hachette Children's Group GBR. Dist: Hachette Bk. Group.

—The Man from Pomegranate Street, Bk. 17. 2010. (ENG., Illus.). 272p. (YA). (gr. 7-17). 10.99 (978-1-84255-608-5(8), Orion Children's Bks.) Hachette Children's Group GBR. Dist: Hachette Bk. Group.

—P. K. Pinkerton & the Deadly Desperados. 2013. (P. K. Pinkerton Ser.: 1). (ENG.). 304p. (J). (gr. 3-7). pap. 7.99 (978-0-14-242381-3(5), Puffin Books) Penguin Young Readers Group.

—P. K. Pinkerton & the Pistol-Packing Widows. 2015. (P. K. Pinkerton Ser.: 3). (ENG.). 320p. (J). (gr. 3-7). 7.99 (978-0-14-751130-0(5), Puffin Books) Penguin Young Readers Group.

—Los Piratas de Pompeya. 2003. (SPA.). 192p. (978-84-7888-798-9(9), 1952) Emece Editores.

—The Pirates of Pompeii. 2004. (Roman Mysteries Ser.). (Illus.). 159p. (J). (gr. 3-7). 13.65 (978-0-7569-5938-8(1)) Perfection Learning Corp.

—The Prophet from Ephesus. 2009. (ENG., Illus.). 224p. (YA). (gr. 7-17). pap. 10.99 (978-1-84255-606-1(1), Orion Children's Bks.) Hachette Children's Group GBR. Dist: Hachette Bk. Group.

—The Secrets of Vesuvius. 2004. (Roman Mysteries Ser.). (Illus.). 173p. (J). (gr. 3-7). 13.65 (978-0-7569-5947-0(0)) Perfection Learning Corp.

—The Sirens of Surrentum. 2006. (ENG., Illus.). 272p. (gr. 7-9). pap. 10.99 (978-1-84255-506-4(5), Orion Children's Bks.) Hachette Children's Group GBR. Dist: Hachette Bk. Group.

—The Sirens of Surrentum. 2007. (Roman Mysteries Ser.: Bk. 11). (ENG., Illus.). 224p. (J). (gr. 6-9). 16.95 (978-1-59643-084-6(2)) Roaring Brook Pr.

—The Slave-Girl from Jerusalem. 2007. (ENG., Illus.). 240p. (gr. 4-6). pap. 10.99 (978-1-84255-572-9(3), Orion Children's Bks.) Hachette Children's Group GBR. Dist: Hachette Bk. Group.

—Trimalchio's Feast: And Other Mini-Mysteries. 2013. (ENG., Illus.). 144p. (J). (gr. 4-6). pap. 10.99 (978-1-84255-593-4(6), Orion Children's Bks.) Hachette Children's Group GBR. Dist: Hachette Bk. Group.

—The Twelve Tasks of Flavia Gemina. 2003. (ENG., Illus.). 224p. (gr. 2-4). pap. 10.99 (978-1-84255-025-0(X), Orion Children's Bks.) Hachette Children's Group GBR. Dist: Hachette Bk. Group.

Lawrence, Casey. Order in the Court. 2016. (ENG., Illus.). (YA). 24.99 **(978-1-63533-059-5(9)**, Harmony Ink Pr.) Dreamspinner Pr.

Lawrence, Treat. You're the Detective! 23 Solve-Them-Yourself Mysteries. Borowick, Kathleen, illus. 2010. (ENG.). 80p. pap. 8.95 (978-1-56792-397-1(6)) Godine, David R. Pub.

Laws, Jamie Lynn. Cameron & the Mysterious Shack. 2008. pap. 16.95 (978-1-60563-434-0(4)) America Star Bks.

Lawson, Jessica. Nooks & Crannies. Andrewson, Natalie, illus. 2015. (ENG.). 336p. (J). (gr. 3-7). 16.99 (978-1-4814-1921-5(8), Simon & Schuster Bks. For Young Readers) Simon & Schuster Bks. For Young Readers.

Lawson, Shandy. The Loop. 2014. (ENG.). 208p. (YA). (gr. 7-12). pap. 8.99 (978-1-4231-6948-2(4)) Hyperion Bks. for Children.

Lay, Eddie. Mystery of the Hats. 2006. 61p. pap. 16.95 (978-1-4241-2649-1(5)) PublishAmerica, Inc.

Layos, Alexandra. Timeless: Blue Ribbon Days #2, 2, 2. 2005. (Illus.). 128p. (YA). pap. 10.95 (978-0-9655501-4-7(1)) Saddle & Bridle, Inc.

Lazar, Tara. 7 Ate 9. MacDonald, Ross, illus. 2017. (ENG.). 32p. (J). (gr. -1-k). 17.99 **(978-1-4847-1779-0(1))** Hyperion Bks. for Children.

Le Gall, Frank. Rooftop Cat. Balthazar, Flore, illus. 2012. (Miss Annie Ser.: 2). (ENG.). 48p. (J). (gr. 2-4). pap. 6.95 (978-0-7613-8547-9(9), Graphic Universe™) Lerner Publishing Group.

Le Queux, William. The House of Whispers. 2007. (ENG.). 260p. pap. 21.99 (978-1-4264-4356-5(0)); 284p. pap. 23.99 (978-1-4264-4394-7(3)) Creative Media Partners, LLC.

Leblanc, Margaret Ann. Ms Maddy & the Lake Adventure. 2008. 89p. pap. 19.95 (978-1-60474-003-5(5)) America Star Bks.

Lee Hope, Laura. The Bobbsey Twins in the Great West. 2005. 200p. pap. 12.95 (978-1-4218-0465-1(4), 1st World Library - Literary Society) 1st World Publishing, Inc.

—The Bobbsey Twins in the Great West. 2004. reprint ed. pap. 1.99 (978-1-4192-5444-4(8)); pap. 20.95 (978-1-4191-5444-7(3)) Kessinger Publishing, LLC.

Lee, Kathy. The Runaway Train. 2011. 144p. pap. (978-1-84427-505-2(1)) Scripture Union.

Lee, Y. S. The Agency: A Spy in the House. 2016. (Agency Ser.). (ENG.). 352p. (YA). (gr. 7). pap. 7.99 (978-0-7636-8748-9(0)) Candlewick Pr.

—The Agency: the Body at the Tower. 2016. (Agency Ser.). (ENG.). 352p. (YA). (gr. 7). pap. 7.99 (978-0-7636-8750-2(2)) Candlewick Pr.

—The Agency: the Traitor in the Tunnel. 2016. (Agency Ser.). (ENG.). 384p. (YA). (gr. 7). pap. 7.99 (978-0-7636-8751-9(0)) Candlewick Pr.

—The Body at the Tower. 2010. (Agency Ser.: 2). (ENG., Illus.). 352p. (YA). (gr. 7-18). 16.99 (978-0-7636-4968-5(6)) Candlewick Pr.

—Rivals in the City. 2015. (Agency Ser.). (ENG.). 304p. (YA). (gr. 7). 16.99 (978-0-7636-5914-1(2)) Candlewick Pr.

—The Traitor in the Tunnel. 2012. (Agency Ser.: 3). (ENG., Illus.). 384p. (YA). (gr. 7). 16.99 (978-0-7636-5316-3(0)) Candlewick Pr.

Leighton, Noreen. Mr Tilly & the Halloween Mystery. Wilson, Lorna, illus. 2013. 42p. pap. (978-0-9573315-6-3(8)) Tatterdemalion Blue.

Lenard, Steve. The Mysterious Maze #1: The Search for the Skeleton Key. 2009. 60p. pap. 21.99 (978-1-4389-5029-7(2)) AuthorHouse.

L'Engle, Madeleine. Dragons in the Waters. 2011. (ENG.). 320p. (YA). (gr. 6-10). pap. 11.99 (978-0-312-67442-7(2), 9780312674427) Square Fish.

—Troubling a Star. 2008. (Austin Family Ser.: 5). (ENG.). 336p. (J). (gr. 6-12). pap. 10.99 (978-0-312-37934-6(X), 9780312379346) Square Fish.

Lenihan, Eddie. Eddie Lenihan's Irish Tales of Mystery. Clarke, Alan, illus. 2006. (ENG.). 224p. (J). 33.95 (978-1-85635-519-3(5)) Mercier Pr., Ltd., The IRL. Dist: Dufour Editions, Inc.

Lennon, Stella, et al. The Amanda Project, Bk. 1. 2010. (Amanda Project Ser.: 1). (ENG.). 320p. (YA). (gr. 8). pap. 8.99 (978-0-06-174213-2(9), HarperTeen) HarperCollins Pubs.

—Revealed, Bk. 2. 2011. (Amanda Project Ser.: 2). (ENG.). 240p. (YA). (gr. 8-18). pap. 8.99 (978-0-06-174215-6(5), HarperTeen) HarperCollins Pubs.

Leonard, Julia Platt. Cold Case. 2012. (ENG.). 288p. (J). (gr. 3-7). pap. 5.99 (978-1-4424-2010-6(3), Simon & Schuster/Paula Wiseman Bks.) Simon & Schuster/Paula Wiseman Bks.

—Cold Case. Mauro, Tony, illus. 2011. (ENG.). 288p. (J). (gr. 3-7). 15.99 (978-1-4424-2009-0(X), Simon & Schuster/Paula Wiseman Bks.) Simon & Schuster/Paula Wiseman Bks.

Leonard, M. G. Beetle Boy. (ENG.). (J). (gr. 3-7). 2017. 304p. pap. 6.99 **(978-0-545-85347-7(8))** 2016. 288p. 16.99 (978-0-545-85346-0(X)) Scholastic, Inc. (Chicken Hse., The).

Leonard, Niall. Crusher. 2013. (ENG.). 368p. (YA). (gr. 9). pap. 9.99 (978-0-385-74362-4(9), Ember) Random Hse. Children's Bks.

Leonhardt, Alice & Hart, Alison. Return of the Gypsy Witch. Burleson, Joe, illus. 2003. (ENG.). 176p. (J). (gr. 3-7). pap. 9.99 (978-0-689-85527-6(3), Simon & Schuster/Paula Wiseman Bks.) Simon & Schuster/Paula Wiseman Bks.

Leppard, Lois Gladys. The Mandie Collection. (ENG.). (J). 2011. 368p. (gr. 3-8). pap. 12.99 (978-0-7642-0932-1(9)) 2011. 384p. (gr. 3-8). pap. 13.00 (978-0-7642-0878-2(0)) 2011. 368p. (gr. 3-8). pap. 10.99 (978-0-7642-0689-4(3)) 2011. 368p. (gr. 3-8). pap. 12.99 (978-0-7642-0877-5(2))Bks. 16-20, Vol. 4. 2009. 608p. pap. 16.99 (978-0-7642-0663-4(X)) Vol. 1. 2007. 544p. (gr. 3-8). pap. 15.99 (978-0-7642-0446-3(7)) Vol. 2. 2008. (Illus.). 576p. (gr. 3-8). pap. 15.99 (978-0-7642-0538-5(2)) Bethany Hse. Pubs.

—Mandie Collection, Vol. 3. 2008. (ENG.). 608p. (J). pap. 15.99 (978-0-7642-0593-4(5)) Bethany Hse. Pubs.

Lerangis, Peter. The Code. 2004. (Spy X Ser.: No. 1). 139p. (Orig.). (J). (978-0-439-70242-3(9)) Scholastic, Inc.

—The Dead of Night. 2012. (39 Clues: Cahills vs. Vespers Ser.: 3). (ENG., Illus.). 192p. (J). (gr. 3-7). 12.99 (978-0-545-29841-4(5)); lib. bdg. 12.99 (978-0-545-32412-0(2)) Scholastic, Inc.

—Wow! Blast from the Past! Talbot, Jim, illus. 2003. (Abracadabra Ser.: No. 8). (ENG.). 112p. (J). pap. 3.99 (978-0-439-38939-6(9), Scholastic Paperbacks) Scholastic, Inc.

—Wtf. 2013. (ENG., Illus.). 288p. (YA). (gr. 9). 17.99 (978-1-4424-9369-8(0)); pap. 9.99 (978-1-4424-9368-1(2)) Simon Pulse. (Simon Pulse).

Leung, Julie. Mice of the Round Table #1: a Tail of Camelot. Carr, Lindsey, illus. 2017. (Mice of the Round Table Ser.: 1). 320p. (J). (gr. 3-7). pap. 6.99 **(978-0-06-240400-8(8))** HarperCollins Pubs.

—Mice of the Round Table #2: Voyage to Avalon. Carr, Lindsey, illus. 2017. (Mice of the Round Table Ser.: 2). 336p. (J). (gr. 3-7). 16.99 **(978-0-06-240402-2(4))** HarperCollins Pubs.

Leveen, Tom. Shackled: The Truth Doesn't Always Set You Free. 2015. (ENG., Illus.). 224p. (YA). (gr. 9). 17.99 (978-1-4814-2249-9(9), Simon Pulse) Simon Pulse.

Levine, Gail Carson. Stolen Magic. 2015. (ENG., Illus.). 336p. (J). (gr. 3-7). 16.99 (978-0-06-170637-0(X)) HarperCollins Pubs.

—A Tale of Two Castles. Call, Greg, illus. (ENG.). (J). (gr. 3-7). 2012. 352p. pap. 6.99 (978-0-06-122967-1(9)) 2011. 336p. 16.99 (978-0-06-122965-7(2)) HarperCollins Pubs.

Levy, Elizabeth. A Hare-Raising Tale. Gerstein, Mordicai, illus. unabr. ed. 2006. (First Chapter Bks.). (J). (gr. 2-4). pap. 20.95 incl. audio compact disk (978-1-59519-705-4(2)); pap. 17.95 incl. audio (978-1-59519-704-7(4)) Live Oak Media.

—The Mixed-Up Mask Mystery: A Fletcher Mystery. Gorstein, Mordicai, illus. unabr. ed. 2006. (First Chapter Bks.). (J). (gr. 2-4). pap. 20.95 incl. audio compact disk (978-1-59519-711-5(7)); pap. 17.95 incl. audio (978-1-59519-710-8(9)) Live Oak Media.

Levy, Elizabeth & Brunkus, Denise. The Mystery of the Missing Dog. (Hello Reader! Ser.). (FRE., Illus.). (J). pap. 5.99 (978-0-590-16010-0(9)) Scholastic, Inc.

Levy, Elizabeth & Coville, Bruce. The Dragon of Doom. Gerstein, Mordicai & Coville, Katherine, illus. 2005. 71p. (J). lib. bdg. 15.00 (978-1-59054-903-2(1)) Fitzgerald Bks.

Levy, Viv. The Mysterious Disappearance at Bird Bridge: A Dog Detective Story. 2013. (ENG., Illus.). 156p. 24.00 (978-0-906362-75-4(X)) Gothic Image Pubns. GBR. Dist: SCB Distributors.

Lewis, Gill. Scout & the Sausage Thief. Horne, Sarah, illus. 2016. (Puppy Academy Ser.). (ENG.). 128p. (J). 16.99 (978-1-62779-794-8(7), 9781627797948, Holt, Henry & Co. Bks. For Young Readers) Holt, Henry & Co.

Lewis, J. Patrick & Innocenti, Roberto. El último Refugio. 2003. (Los Especiales de A la Orilla del Viento Ser.). (SPA., Illus.). 48p. (J). (gr. -1-7). 16.99 (978-968-16-6860-0(X)) Fondo de Cultura Economica USA.

Lewman, David. The Case of the Missing Moola. 2012. (Club CSI Ser.: 2). (ENG.). 160p. (J). (gr. 3-7). pap. 7.99 (978-1-4424-3395-3(7));No. 2. 15.99 (978-1-4424-4670-0(6)) Simon Spotlight. (Simon Spotlight).

—The Case of the Mystery Meat Loaf. 2012. (Club CSI Ser.: 1). (ENG.). 160p. (J). (gr. 3-7). 15.99 (978-1-4424-4646-5(3)); pap. 7.99 (978-1-4424-3394-6(9)) Simon Spotlight. (Simon Spotlight).

—The Case of the Plagued Play. 2013. (Club CSI Ser.: 6). (ENG., Illus.). 160p. (J). (gr. 3-7). 15.99 (978-1-4424-7261-7(8)); pap. 6.99 (978-1-4424-7260-0(X)) Simon Spotlight. (Simon Spotlight).

—The Case of the Ruined Ram. 2012. (Club CSI Ser.: 4). (ENG.). 160p. (J). (gr. 3-7). 15.99 (978-1-4424-4672-4(2)); pap. 5.99 (978-1-4424-3397-7(3)) Simon Spotlight. (Simon Spotlight).

—Double Trouble: The Case of the Missing Spatula - The Case of the Vanished Squirrel. Moore, Harry, Jr., illus. 2010. (SpongeBob SquarePants Ser.). (ENG.). 36p. (J). bds. 10.99 (978-1-4424-1337-5(9), Simon Spotlight/Nickelodeon) Simon Spotlight/Nickelodeon.

Liess, Claudia Schmidt. Henry the Magical, Mythical Dragon. 2008. 74p. pap. 19.95 (978-1-60672-956-4(X)) America Star Bks.

Lilly, Suzanne. Untellable. 2013. 158p. pap. 9.99 (978-1-62237-218-8(2)) Turquoise Morning Pr.

Lin, Alex. The Little Detective. 2012. 24p. (-18). pap. 15.99 (978-1-4797-0286-2(2)) Xlibris Corp.

Lindsey, Julie Anne. Reinventing Chloe. 2013. 278p. pap. 13.99 (978-1-62237-152-5(6)) Turquoise Morning Pr.

Liphardt, Linda. Secret in the Old Barn. 2008. 116p. pap. 19.95 (978-1-60703-615-9(0)) America Star Bks.

Llama, Gram. The Bunny Fuzz Mystery. 2007. 32p. per. 24.95 (978-1-4241-8371-5(5)) America Star Bks.

Llewellyn, Tom. The Shadow of Seth: A Seth Anomundy Murder Mystery. 2015. (Seth Anomundy Murder Mysteries Ser.). (ENG.). viii, 174p. (YA). pap. 10.95 (978-1-929345-18-2(6)) Poisoned Pen Pr.

Lloyd, Hugh. Held for Ransom: A Skippy Dare Mystery Story. Fogel, Seymour, illus. 2011. 228p. 46.95 (978-1-258-07879-9(1)) Literary Licensing, LLC.

—The Lonesome Swamp Mystery: A Hal Keen Mystery Story. Salg, Bert, illus. 2011. 278p. 47.95 (978-1-258-10174-9(2)) Literary Licensing, LLC.

—The Lost Mine of the Amazon. Salg, Bert, illus. 2011. 232p. 46.95 (978-1-258-10175-6(0)) Literary Licensing, LLC.

Lloyd, Jennifer. Murilla Gorilla & the Hammock Problem. Lee, Jacqui, illus. 2014. (Murilla Gorilla Ser.: 3). (ENG.). 42p. (J). (gr. -1-3). 9.95 (978-1-927018-47-7(1)) Simply Read Bks. CAN. Dist: Ingram Publisher Services.

—Murilla Gorilla & the Lost Parasol. Lee, Jacqui, illus. 2013. (Murilla Gorilla Ser.: 2). (ENG.). 42p. (J). (gr. -1-3). 9.95 (978-1-927018-23-1(4)) Simply Read Bks. CAN. Dist: Ingram Publisher Services.

Lobdell, Scott. Identity Theft. Rendon, Daniel, illus. 2005. (Hardy Boys Undercover Brothers Ser.). 88p. (gr. 3-8). 24.21 (978-1-59961-062-7(0)) Spotlight.

—Mad House. Rendon, Daniel, illus. 2005. (Hardy Boys Undercover Brothers Ser.). 88p. (gr. 3-7). 24.21 (978-1-59961-063-4(9)) Spotlight.

—The Ocean of Osyria. Rendon, Daniel, illus. 2005. (Hardy Boys Undercover Brothers Ser.). 88p. (gr. 3-7). 24.21 (978-1-59961-061-0(2)) Spotlight.

Lockhart, E. Genuine Fraud. 2017. (YA). **(978-1-5247-7067-9(1)**, Delacorte Pr) Random House Publishing Group.

—Genuine Fraud, 9 vols. 2017. (ENG.). (YA). 170.91 **(978-0-525-50205-0(X))**; 75.96 **(978-0-525-50207-4(6))**; 170.91 **(978-0-525-50206-7(8))**; 288p. (gr. 7). 18.99 **(978-0-385-74477-5(3))**; 288p. (gr. 7). lib. bdg. 21.99 **(978-0-375-99184-4(0))** Random Hse. Children's Bks. (Delacorte Pr.).

Lockwood, Cara. Moby Clique. 2008. (Bard Academy Ser.: No. 3). (ENG.). 304p. (gr. 7-12). pap. 19.99 (978-1-4165-5050-1(X), MTV Bks.) MTV Books.

Lockwood, Vicki. The Magnificent Lizzie Brown, 1 vol. 2014. (Magnificent Lizzie Brown Ser.). (ENG.). 200p. (gr. 5-9). 53.30 (978-1-4342-9515-6(X)) Stone Arch Bks.

—The Magnificent Lizzie Brown & the Devil's Hound, 1 vol. 2014. (Magnificent Lizzie Brown Ser.). (ENG., Illus.). 200p. (gr. 5-9). lib. bdg. 26.65 (978-1-4342-7941-5(3)) Stone Arch Bks.

—The Magnificent Lizzie Brown & the Fairy Child. Hans, Stephanie, illus. 2015. (Magnificent Lizzie Brown Ser.). (ENG.). 200p. (gr. 5-9). 10.95 (978-1-62370-210-6(0)) Stone Arch Bks.

—The Magnificent Lizzie Brown & the Mysterious Phantom, 1 vol. 2014. (Magnificent Lizzie Brown Ser.). (ENG., Illus.). 200p. (gr. 5-9). 10.95 (978-1-62370-069-0(8)); lib. bdg. 26.65 (978-1-4342-7940-8(5)) Stone Arch Bks.

—The Magnificent Lizzie Brown & the Mysterious Phantom, 1 vol. Hans, Stephanie, illus. 2014. (ENG.). 200p. (J). pap. (978-1-4342-7942-2(1)) Stone Arch Bks.

Long, Angela Pullam. Salvador the Spy in the Case of the Missing Cats. 2008. 32p. pap. 24.95 (978-1-60672-724-9(9)) America Star Bks.

Long, Loren & Bildner, Phil. Horsin' Around. Long, Loren, illus. 2009. (Sluggers Ser.: 2). (ENG., Illus.). 224p. (J). (gr. 3-7). pap. 8.99 (978-1-4169-1888-2(4), Simon & Schuster Bks. For Young Readers) Simon & Schuster Bks. For Young Readers.

The Long-Lost Friends, 6 vols., Vol. 3. (Woodland Mysteriestm Ser.). 133p. (gr. 3-7). 42.50 (978-0-322-02377-2(7)) Wright Group/McGraw-Hill.

Longley, Joshua. Barnaby's Buccaneers. 2011. 240p. (gr. 4-6). 25.95 (978-1-4620-6112-9(5)); pap. 15.95 (978-1-4620-6110-5(9)) iUniverse, Inc.

Lopez, Joe. Solemates. 2013. 28p. pap. 9.95 (978-1-4787-2494-0(3)) Outskirts Pr., Inc.

Lord, Gabrielle. Malice. 2013. (Illus.). 175p. (J). (978-1-61067-167-5(8)) Kane Miller.

Lord, Kenniston. The Pirates of Peary Village. 2004. 182p. (J). pap. 9.18 (978-1-4116-7893-4(1)) Lulu Pr., Inc.

Lorimer, Janet. The Tiger Lily Code, 1 vol. unabr. ed. 2010. (Q Reads Ser.). (ENG.). 32p. (YA). (gr. 9-12). pap. 6.95 (978-1-61651-195-1(8)) Saddleback Educational Publishing, Inc.

—Tug-of-War, 1 vol. unabr. ed. 2010. (Q Reads Ser.). (ENG.). 32p. (YA). (gr. 9-12). pap. 6.95 (978-1-61651-196-8(6)) Saddleback Educational Publishing, Inc.

Lost Brother: Book Two in the Lost Mystery Trilogy. 2010. (Hardy Boys (All New) Undercover Brothers Ser.: 35). (ENG.). 160p. (J). (gr. 3-7). pap. 5.99 (978-1-4424-0256-0(3), Aladdin) Simon & Schuster Children's Publishing.

Loughead, Deb. Time & Again, 1 vol. 2005. (ENG.). 192p. (YA). (gr. 7-12). pap. (978-1-894549-39-4(2), Sumach Pr.) Canadian Scholars.

Lovegrove, James. Kill Swap. 2012. (Stoke Books Titles Ser.). (ENG.). 64p. (YA). (gr. 8-12). pap. 6.95 (978-1-78112-112-2(5)); lib. bdg. 22.60 (978-1-78112-113-9(3)) Lerner Publishing Group.

Low, A. J. Sherlock Sam & the Ghostly Moans in Fort Canning: Book Two. 2016. (Sherlock Sam Ser.: 2). (ENG.). 120p. (J). pap. 7.99 (978-1-4494-7788-2(7)) Andrews McMeel Publishing.

—Sherlock Sam & the Sinister Letters in Bras Basah. 2017. (Sherlock Sam Ser.: 3). (ENG.). 144p. (J). pap. 7.99 (978-1-4494-7975-6(8)) Andrews McMeel Publishing.

Loye, Scott. Moon Ring. 2011. 160p. (gr. 10-12). 22.95 (978-1-4502-9682-3(3)); pap. 12.95 (978-1-4502-9680-9(7)) iUniverse, Inc.

Lu, Tina. The Mystery of the Starry Night. Liu, Jenny, ed. 2004. (ENG & CHI., Illus.). 64p. (J). pap. 12.00 net. (978-0-9759126-0-7(7)) Global Alliances.

Lubar, David. Dog Days. (Exceptional Reading & Language Arts Titles for Intermediate Grades Ser.). 80p. (J). (gr. 4-8). 2011. (ENG.). per. 6.95 (978-1-58196-025-9(5)) 2004. 15.95 (978-1-58196-013-6(1)) Lerner Publishing Group. (Darby Creek).

Lucky, A. E. Kyle the Detective, 1 vol. 2010. 70p. pap. 19.95 (978-1-4512-2042-1(1)) America Star Bks.

Ludwig, Elisa. Pretty Wanted. 2015. (Pretty Crooked Trilogy Ser.: 3). (ENG.). 336p. (YA). (gr. 8). 17.99 (978-0-06-206612-1(9), Tegen, Katherine Bks) HarperCollins Pubs.

Luna, Rachel Nickerson. The Haunting of Captain Snow. 2005. (Eel Grass Girls Mystery Ser.: No. 2). (Illus.). 332p. pap. 11.95 (978-1-886551-08-4(1)) Howard, Emma Bks.

—The Strange Disappearance of Agatha Buck. 2005. (Eel Grass Girls Mystery Ser.: Book 3). (Illus.). 284p. pap. 11.95 (978-1-886551-09-1(X)) Howard, Emma Bks.

Lunsford, Judy. Sally & the Buccaneers. 2009. 77p. pap. 12.98 (978-0-557-10064-4(X)) Lulu Pr., Inc.

Luper, Eric. The Mysterious Moonstone. 2016. (Key Hunters Ser.: 1). (ENG., Illus.). 128p. (J). (gr. 2-5). pap. 4.99 (978-0-545-82204-6(1)) Scholastic, Inc.

—The Wizard's War (Key Hunters #4) 2017. (Key Hunters Ser.: 4). (ENG.). 128p. (J). (gr. 2-5). pap. 4.99 (978-0-545-82213-8(0), Scholastic Paperbacks) Scholastic, Inc.

Luxa, Sue. One Golden Summer. 2004. (Illus.). 80p. (J). pap. 8.95 (978-1-890437-99-2(9), 1234248) Western Reflections Publishing Co.

Lyall, Casey. Howard Wallace, P. I. (Howard Wallace, P. I. Ser.). (ENG.). (J). (gr. 3-7). 2017. 288p. pap. 6.95 **(978-1-4549-2604-7(X))** 2016. 272p. 14.95 (978-1-4549-1949-0(3)) Sterling Publishing Co., Inc.

Lyga, Barry. Blood of My Blood. 2014. (ENG.). 480p. (YA). (gr. 10-17). 18.00 (978-0-316-19870-7(6)) Little, Brown Bks. for Young Readers.

—I Hunt Killers. (ENG.). (YA). (gr. 10-17). 2014. 464p. mass mkt. 8.00 (978-0-316-28363-2(0)) 2013. 384p. pap. 10.00 (978-0-316-12583-3(0)) Little, Brown Bks. for Young Readers.

Lynch, Chris. Freewill. 2006. 148p. (YA). (gr. 7-10). reprint ed. 16.00 *(978-0-7567-9869-7(8))* DIANE Publishing Co.
Lysaght, Richard. The Black Bag Mystery. Wolfhound Publishing Editors, ed. (ENG., Illus.). 240p. pap. 6.95 *(978-0-86327-886-0(8))* Wolfhound Pr. IRL. Dist: Interlink Publishing Group, Inc.
Lysiak, Hilde & Lysiak, Matthew. Hero Dog! Lew-Vriethoff, Joanne, illus. 2017. (Hilde Cracks the Case Ser.: 1). (ENG.). 96p. (J). (gr. 1-3). pap. 4.99 ***(978-1-338-14155-9(4))*** Scholastic, Inc.
Mac & MAC. Anna Smudge: Professional Shrink. 2008. (Professionals Ser.: 1). (Illus.). 256p. (J). (gr. 14-18). pap. 9.99 *(978-1-934906-00-2(X))* Toasted Coconut Media LLC.
MacAndrew, Richard. A Little Trouble in the Yorkshire Dales Level 3 Lower-Intermediate. 2009. (ENG.). 80p. pap. 12.75 *(978-84-8323-584-3(6))* Cambridge Univ. Pr.
Macauley, Jo. Plague, 1 vol. 2014. (Secrets & Spies Ser.). (ENG.). 224p. (gr. 4-7). 26.65 *(978-1-4342-7947-7(2))* Stone Arch Bks.
—Treason, 1 vol. 2014. (Secrets & Spies Ser.). (ENG.). 224p. (gr. 4-7). 26.65 *(978-1-4342-7946-0(4))* Stone Arch Bks.
MacColl, Michaela. Always Emily. (ENG.). (YA). (gr. 7-12). 2015. 304p. pap. 9.99 *(978-1-4521-4130-5(4))* 2014. 282p. 16.99 *(978-1-4521-1174-2(X))* Chronicle Bks. LLC.
—Nobody's Secret. (ENG.). (gr. 7-17). 2014. 256p. (YA). pap. 9.99 *(978-1-4521-2854-2(5))* 2013. 241p. (J). 16.99 *(978-1-4521-0860-5(9))* Chronicle Bks. LLC.
—Secrets in the Snow: A Novel of Intrigue & Romance. 2016. (ENG., Illus.). 288p. (YA). (gr. 7-12). 16.99 *(978-1-4521-3358-4(1))* Chronicle Bks. LLC.
MacDonald, Bailey. The Secret of the Sealed Room: A Mystery of Young Benjamin Franklin. 2010. (ENG.). 224p. (J). (gr. 3-7). 17.99 *(978-1-4169-9760-3(1)*, Simon & Schuster/Paula Wiseman Bks.) Simon & Schuster/Paula Wiseman Bks.
—Wicked Will: A Mystery of Young William Shakespeare. 2010. (ENG.). 224p. (J). (gr. 4-7). pap. 5.99 *(978-1-4169-8661-4(8)*, Aladdin) Simon & Schuster Children's Publishing.
—Wicked Will: A Mystery of Young William Shakespeare. 2009. (ENG.). 208p. (J). (gr. 4-7). 16.99 *(978-1-4169-8660-7(X)*, Simon & Schuster/Paula Wiseman Bks.) Simon & Schuster/Paula Wiseman Bks.
MacGregor, Roy. The Ghost of the Stanley Cup. 2013. (Screech Owls Ser.). (ENG.). 176p. (J). (gr. 4-7). pap. 8.99 *(978-1-77049-416-9(2)*, Tundra Bks.) Tundra Bks. CAN. Dist: Penguin Random Hse. LLC.
—The Kindergarten Caper: The Screech Owls Prequel. 2008. (ENG.). 144p. (YA). (gr. 3-7). mass mkt. 6.99 *(978-0-7710-5608-6(7)*, Screech Owls) McClelland & Stewart CAN. Dist: Penguin Random Hse. LLC.
—Mystery at Lake Placid. 2013. (Screech Owls Ser.). (ENG.). 272p. (J). (gr. 4-7). pap. 8.95 *(978-1-77049-413-8(8)*, Tundra Bks.) Tundra Bks. CAN. Dist: Penguin Random Hse. LLC.
—The Night They Stole the Stanley Cup. 2013. (Screech Owls Ser.). (ENG.). 176p. (J). (gr. 4-7). pap. 8.99 *(978-1-77049-414-5(6)*, Tundra Bks.) Tundra Bks. CAN. Dist: Penguin Random Hse. LLC.
—Peril at the World's Biggest Hockey Tournament. 2013. (Screech Owls Ser.). (ENG.). 208p. (J). (gr. 4-7). pap. 8.99 *(978-1-77049-417-6(0)*, Tundra Bks.) Tundra Bks. CAN. Dist: Penguin Random Hse. LLC.
—Sudden Death in New York City. 2013. (Screech Owls Ser.). (ENG.). 176p. (J). (gr. 4-7). pap. 8.95 *(978-1-77049-415-2(4)*, Tundra Bks.) Tundra Bks. CAN. Dist: Penguin Random Hse. LLC.
MacHale, D.J. Black Moon Rising. 2017. (J). pap. ***(978-1-101-93260-5(0))*** Random Hse., Inc.
Machale, D.j. The Library: Mysterious Messenger (Book 1) 2016. (Library: 1). (ENG.). 256p. (J). (gr. 3-7). 16.99 *(978-1-101-93253-7(8)*, Random Hse. Bks. for Young Readers) Random Hse. Children's Bks.
Mack, Karen. The Magical Adventures of Sun Beams. 2009. 42p. 31.99 *(978-1-4415-3636-5(1))* Xlibris Corp.
Mack, Tracy & Citrin, Michael. The Fall of the Amazing Zalindas. 2006. (Illus.). 259p. (J). *(978-1-4287-0951-5(7)*, Orchard Bks.) Scholastic, Inc.
—Fall of the Amazing Zalindas. 2009. (Sherlock Holmes & the Baker St. Irregulars Ser.: 1). (ENG.). 272p. (J). (gr. 3-7). 6.99 *(978-0-545-06939-7(4)*, Scholastic Paperbacks) Scholastic, Inc.
Mackall, Dandi Daley. Cinnamon Lake Mysteries Set, 6 vols. (Cinnamon Lake Mysteries Ser.). (J). 33.74 *(978-0-7586-0006-6(2))* Concordia Publishing Hse.
—The Silence of Murder. (ENG.). 336p. (YA). (gr. 9). 2012. pap. 9.99 *(978-0-375-87293-8(0)*, Ember) 2011. 16.99 *(978-0-375-86896-2(8)*, Knopf Bks. for Young Readers) Random Hse. Children's Bks.
MacKenzie, Buckley. PAW Patrol: Movie Theater Storybook & Movie Projector. 2016. (ENG.). 32p. (J). (gr. -1-1). 19.99 *(978-0-7944-3325-3(1)*, Reader's Digest Children's Bks.) Studio Fun International.
Mackey, R. Scott. The Bugfish Experiment. 2003. 208p. *(978-1-930093-12-6(8))* Brookfield Reader, Inc., The.
MacLean, Sarah. The Season. (ENG.). 352p. (J). (gr. 7). 2010. 8.99 *(978-0-545-04887-3(7))* 2009. 17.99 *(978-0-545-04886-6(9))* Scholastic, Inc. (Orchard Bks.).
Maddock, Lisa. The Bridezilla Who Stole Christmas: A Teddy & Pip Story. 2009. 108p. pap. 9.95 *(978-1-60844-258-4(6))* Dog Ear Publishing, LLC.
Madormo, John V. The Homemade Stuffing Caper, Bk. 1. 2013. (Charlie Collier, Snoop for Hire Ser.: 1). (ENG.). 272p. (J). (gr. 5). pap. 7.99 *(978-0-14-242380-6(7)*, Puffin Books) Penguin Young Readers Group.
Madsen, Cindi. All the Broken Pieces. 2016. (ENG., Illus.). (YA). (gr. 9). pap. 15.99 ***(978-1-68281-305-8(3))*** Entangled Publishing, LLC.
Madsen, W. J. Arkeepers: Episode One. 2012. 142p. pap. 7.95 *(978-0-9830487-0-1(3))* little m Bks.
—Arkeepers: Episode Two. 2012. 206p. pap. 9.30 *(978-0-9830487-1-8(1))* little m Bks.
Maetani, Valynne E. Ink & Ashes. 2015. (ENG.). 368p. (YA). 19.95 *(978-1-62014-211-0(2)*, Tu Bks.) Lee & Low Bks., Inc.
Magic Wagon Staff. Ghost Detectors Set 2, 1 vol. 2012. (Ghost Detectors Ser.: 6). (ENG., Illus.). 80p. 162.42 *(978-1-61641-622-5(X)*, Calico Chapter Bks) Magic Wagon.
Magill, Sharon L. Chloe Madison & the Beach Heists. 2009. 60p. pap. 10.49 *(978-1-4389-4191-2(9))* AuthorHouse.
Mahle, Melissa & Dennis, Kathryn. Lost in Petra. 2012. (Anatolia Steppe Mysteries: 1). (ENG., Illus.). 246p. (J). pap. 10.99 *(978-0-9852273-0-2(3))* SpyGirls Pr.
The Mall Mystery, 6 vols., Vol. 3. (Woodland Mysteriestm Ser.). 133p. (gr. 3-7). 42.50 *(978-0-322-02370-3(X))* Wright Group/McGraw-Hill.
Maloney, Peter. The Big Apple Mystery. 2004. 32p. *(978-0-439-67638-0(X))* Scholastic, Inc.
Malton, H. Mel. Pioneer Poltergeist. 2007. (Alan Nearing Mystery Ser.: 2). (ENG.). 208p. (J). pap. 9.95 *(978-1-894917-60-5(X)*, Napoleon & Co.) Dundurn CAN. Dist: Ingram Publisher Services.
Malton, Mel. The Drowned Violin. 2006. (Alan Nearing Mystery Ser.: 1). (ENG.). 168p. (J). (gr. 3-7). pap. 8.95 *(978-1-894917-23-0(5)*, Napoleon & Co.) Dundurn CAN. Dist: Ingram Publisher Services.
Maniscalco, Kerri. Hunting Prince Dracula. 2017. (Stalking Jack the Ripper Ser.: 2). (ENG., Illus.). (YA). (gr. 10-17). 448p. 18.99 ***(978-0-316-55166-3(X))***; 608p. 20.99 ***(978-0-316-43986-2(X))*** Little Brown & Co. (Jimmy Patterson).
Maniscalco, Kerri. Stalking Jack the Ripper. (ENG., Illus.). (YA). (gr. 10-17). 2017. 352p. pap. 10.99 ***(978-0-316-27351-0(1))*** 2016. 336p. 18.99 *(978-0-316-27349-7(X))* 2016. 464p. 20.99 *(978-0-316-46428-4(7))* Little Brown & Co. (Jimmy Patterson).
Manning, Dennis & Crisalli, Joseph. The Emeritus Peabody Mysteries. 2008. 212p. pap. 13.98 *(978-1-4303-2186-6(5))* Lulu Pr., Inc.
Manning, Matthew K. The Mystery of the Mayhem Mansion. Neely, Scott, illus. 2016. (You Choose Stories: Scooby-Doo Ser.). (ENG.). 112p. (gr. 2-3). lib. bdg. 32.65 *(978-1-4965-2661-8(9)*, You Choose Bks.) Capstone Press of Coughlan Cos.
—Secret of the Haunted Cave. Neely, Scott, illus. 2016. (Scooby-Doo Comic Chapter Bks.). (ENG.). 88p. (gr. 3-7). pap. 5.95 *(978-1-4965-3589-4(8))* Capstone Press of Coughlan Cos.
Manning, Matthew K. & Steele, Michael Anthony. You Choose Stories: Scooby-Doo. 2016. (You Choose Stories: Scooby-Doo Ser.). (ENG.). 112p. (gr. 2-3). pap. 13.90 *(978-1-4965-2670-0(8)*, You Choose Bks.) Capstone Press of Coughlan Cos.
Manushkin, Fran. Pedro's Mystery Club. Lyon, Tammie, illus. 2016. (Pedro Ser.). (ENG.). 32p. (gr. k-2). lib. bdg. 21.32 *(978-1-5158-0084-2(9))* Pedro Pubns. GBR. Dist: Capstone Pub.
Marathon, creator. Trouble in the Tropics. 2005. (Totally Spies! Ser.: Vol. 3). (Illus.). pap. 14.99 *(978-1-59532-817-5(3)*, Tokyopop Kids) TOKYOPOP, Inc.
Marchi, Sergio. The Emerald Table. 2008. 192p. pap. 19.95 *(978-1-84799-226-0(9))* Lulu Pr., Inc.
Marcus, Mary J. The Digger. 2013. 180p. pap. 12.99 *(978-1-60820-872-2(9))* MLR Pr., LLC.
Margolin, Phillip & Rome, Ami Margolin. Vanishing Acts. (ENG.). 176p. (J). (gr. 3-7). 2012. pap. 8.99 *(978-0-06-188558-7(4))* 2011. 16.99 *(978-0-06-188556-3(8))* HarperCollins Pubs.
Margolis, Leslie. Girl's Best Friend. (Maggie Brooklyn Mystery Ser.). (ENG.). (YA). (gr. 3-12). 2011. 288p. pap. 7.99 *(978-1-59990-690-4(2)*, 9781599906904) 2010. 272p. 14.99 *(978-1-59990-525-9(6)*, 9781599905259) Bloomsbury Publishing USA. (Bloomsbury USA Childrens).
—The Secrets at the Chocolate Mansion. 2013. (Maggie Brooklyn Mystery Ser.). (ENG.). 256p. (YA). (gr. 3-6). 16.99 *(978-1-61963-036-9(2)*, 9781619630369, Bloomsbury USA Childrens) Bloomsbury Publishing USA.
—Secrets at the Chocolate Mansion. 2014. (Maggie Brooklyn Mystery Ser.). (ENG.). 272p. (YA). (gr. 3-6). pap. 7.99 *(978-1-61963-493-0(7)*, 9781619634930, Bloomsbury USA Childrens) Bloomsbury Publishing USA.
—Vanishing Acts. (Maggie Brooklyn Mystery Ser.). (ENG.). (YA). (gr. 3-6). 2013. 256p. pap. 6.99 *(978-1-59990-981-3(2)*, 9781599909813) 2012. 240p. 15.99 *(978-1-59990-536-5(1)*, 9781599905365) Bloomsbury Publishing USA. (Bloomsbury USA Childrens).
Mariotti, Celine Rose. Olivia Macallister, Who Are You? A Ghost Mystery Set in Maine. Tango-Schurmann, Ann, illus. 2004. 85p. (YA). (gr. 3-6). pap. 12.95 *(978-0-9721389-6-3(X))* Rock Village Publishing.
Marks, Burton. Tanya Tinker & the Gizmo Gang. Smath, Jerry, illus. 2003. 20p. (J). (gr. -1-3). reprint ed. 22.00 *(978-0-7567-6760-0(1))* DIANE Publishing Co.
Marlow, Herb. The Classroom Vandal. 2003. (J). 19.95 *(978-1-893595-36-1(6))* Four Seasons Bks., Inc.
Marmon, Jim. Alexander Barnaby Meadowlark. 2007. 132p. per. 19.95 *(978-1-4241-7662-5(X))* America Star Bks.
Marois, Andre. The Sandwich Thief. Doyon, Patrick, illus. 2016. (ENG.). 160p. (J). (gr. 1-4). 14.99 *(978-1-4521-4659-1(4))* Chronicle Bks. LLC.
Marois, André & Norman, Taylor. The Poisoned Cake. Doyon, Patrick, illus. 2017. (J). ***(978-1-4521-4660-7(8))*** Chronicle Bks. LLC.
Marquis, Michelle. Mikey & the Mysterious Door. 2008. 32p. pap. 14.99 *(978-1-4343-4823-4(7))* AuthorHouse.
Marsh, Carole. Adventure to the Eight Wonders of the World. 2007. (Field Trips (Gallopade International) Ser.). (Illus.). 118p. (J). (gr. 2-9). 14.95 *(978-0-635-06391-5(3))* Gallopade International.
—The Awesome Aquarium Mystery. 2006. (Awesome Mystery Ser.). (Illus.). 104p. (J). (gr. 7-14). 14.95 *(978-0-635-06227-7(5))* Gallopade International.
—The Awesome Aquarium Mystery! 2006. (Awesome Mystery Ser.). (Illus.). 104p. (J). per. 5.99 *(978-0-635-06225-3(9)*, Marsh, Carole Bks.) Gallopade International.
—The Baseball Bully. 2006. 64p. (gr. 2-4). 14.95 *(978-0-635-06221-5(6))*; pap. 3.99 *(978-0-635-06215-4(1))* Gallopade International.
—The Baskerville Basketball. 2006. 64p. (gr. 2-4). 14.95 *(978-0-635-06222-2(4))*; pap. 3.99 *(978-0-635-06216-1(X))* Gallopade International.
—The Behemoth Blizzard Mystery. (Masters of Disasters Ser.). (Illus.). 118p. (J). (gr. 3-5). 2008. per. 5.99 *(978-0-635-06464-6(2))* 2007. 14.95 *(978-0-635-06467-7(7))* Gallopade International.
—The Breathtaking Mystery on Mt. Everest. 2009. (Around the World in 80 Mysteries Ser.). 144p. (J). 18.99 *(978-0-635-06836-1(2)*, Marsh, Carole Bks.) Gallopade International.
—The Case of the Crybaby Cowboy. 2006. (Carole Marsh Mysteries Ser.). (Illus.). 54p. (J). (gr. 4-7). per. 4.99 *(978-0-635-06166-9(X)*, Marsh, Carole Bks.); 14.95 *(978-0-635-06199-7(6))* Gallopade International.
—The Case of the Hunchback Hairdresser. 2006. (Criss Cross Applesauce Ser.). (Illus.). 54p. (J). (gr. 4-7). 14.95 *(978-0-635-06202-4(X))*; per. 4.99 *(978-0-635-06169-0(4)*, Marsh, Carole Bks.) Gallopade International.
—The Castaway Cheerleaders. 2006. 64p. (gr. 2-4). 14.95 *(978-0-635-06224-6(0))*; pap. 3.99 *(978-0-635-06218-5(6))* Gallopade International.
—The Colonial Caper Mystery at Williamsburg. 2009. (Real Kids, Real Places Ser.). (J). (gr. 2-9). lib. bdg. 18.99 *(978-0-635-06832-3(X))*; (Illus.). 143p. (gr. 4-7). pap. 7.99 *(978-0-635-06826-2(5)*, Marsh, Carole Bks.) Gallopade International.
—The Cookie Thief Girl Scout Mystery. 2016. (Girl Scouts Ser.). (ENG.). (J). (gr. 3-7). pap. 7.99 *(978-0-635-12170-7(0))* Gallopade International.
—The Counterfeit Constitution Mystery. (Real Kids, Real Places Ser.). (Illus.). 144p. (J). 2009. lib. bdg. 18.99 *(978-0-635-07043-2(X)*, Marsh, Carole Mysteries) 2008. (gr. 3-5). 14.95 *(978-0-635-06517-9(7))* 2008. (gr. 3-5). per. 5.95 *(978-0-635-06512-4(6))* Gallopade International.
—The Curse of the Ancient Acropolis: Athens, Greece. 2008. (Carole Marsh Mysteries Ser.). 133p. (J). (gr. 3-5). per. 7.99 *(978-0-635-06470-7(7)*, Marsh, Carole Bks.) Gallopade International.
—Dear Alien: The Little Green Man Mystery. 2007. (Postcard Mysteries Ser.). (Illus.). 115p. (J). (gr. 2-9). 14.95 *(978-0-635-06397-7(2))*; per. 5.99 *(978-0-635-06341-0(7))* Gallopade International. (Marsh, Carole Family CD-Rom).
—Dear Bats: The Creepy Cave Caper Mystery. 2007. (Postcard Mysteries Ser.). (Illus.). 115p. (J). (gr. 2-9). per. 5.99 *(978-0-635-06342-7(5))* Gallopade International.
—Dear Granny: The Spooky State Fair Fiasco. 2007. (Postcard Mysteries Ser.). 128p. (J). (gr. 2-9). 14.95 *(978-0-635-06399-1(9)*, Marsh, Carole Family CD-Rom) Gallopade International.
—Dear Pirate, the Buried Treasure Mystery. 2007. (Postcard Mysteries Ser.). (Illus.). 114p. (J). (gr. 2-9). per. 5.99 *(978-0-635-06343-4(3)*, Marsh, Carole Family CD-Rom) Gallopade International.
—The Earthshaking Earthquake Mystery! 2007. (Masters of Disasters Ser.). (Illus.). 118p. (J). (gr. 2-9). per. 5.99 *(978-0-635-06339-7(5))* Gallopade International.
—The Football Phantom. 2006. 64p. (gr. 2-4). 14.95 *(978-0-635-06223-9(2))*; pap. 3.99 *(978-0-635-06217-8(8))* Gallopade International.
—The Gargoyle Golf Course. 2006. 64p. (gr. 2-4). 14.95 *(978-0-635-06220-8(8))*; pap. 3.99 *(978-0-635-06214-7(3))* Gallopade International.
—The Ghost of Pickpocket Plantation. 2006. (Pretty Darn Scary Mysteries Ser.). (Illus.). 109p. (YA). (gr. 7-14). 14.95 *(978-0-635-06237-6(2))*; (J). (gr. 3-5). per. 7.99 *(978-0-635-06233-8(X))* Gallopade International.
—The Ghost of the Golden Gate Bridge. 2009. (Real Kids, Real Places Ser.). (Illus.). 146p. (J). lib. bdg. 18.99 *(978-0-635-07047-0(2)*, Marsh, Carole Mysteries) Gallopade International.
—The Giggling Ghost Girl Scout Mystery. 2012. (ENG., Illus.). 158p. (J). pap. 7.99 *(978-0-635-10230-0(7)*, Marsh, Carole Mysteries) Gallopade International.
—The Gosh Awful! Gold Rush Mystery. (Real Kids, Real Places Ser.). (Illus.). 146p. (J). 2009. lib. bdg. 18.99 *(978-0-635-07026-5(X)*, Marsh, Carole Mysteries) 2007. (gr. 2-8). per. 5.95 *(978-0-635-06334-2(4))* Gallopade International.
—The Horrendous Hurricane Mystery. 2007. (Carole Marsh Mysteries Ser.). (Illus.). 118p. (J). (gr. 2-9). per. 7.99 *(978-0-635-06340-3(9))* Gallopade International.
—The Madcap Mystery of the Missing Liberty Bell. 2009. 160p. (J). (gr. 4-7). 18.99 *(978-0-635-06834-7(6)*, Marsh, Carole Bks.) Gallopade International.
—The Mission Possible Mystery at Space Center Houston. 2009. 160p. (J). 18.99 *(978-0-635-06833-0(8)*, Marsh, Carole Bks.) Gallopade International.
—The Mystery at Big Ben. 2005. (Carole Marsh Mysteries Ser.). (Illus.). 129p. (J). (gr. 4-7). per. 7.99 *(978-0-635-03469-4(7))* Gallopade International.
—The Mystery at Cape Cod. 2010. (Real Kids, Real Places Ser.). (Illus.). 158p. (J). pap. 18.99 *(978-0-635-07594-9(6)*, Marsh, Carole Mysteries) Gallopade International.
—The Mystery at Cape Cod. Friedlander, Randolyn, illus. 2010. (Real Kids, Real Places Teacher Guides). 32p. (J). pap. 7.99 *(978-0-635-07600-7(4))* Gallopade International.
—The Mystery at Death Valley. 2010. (Real Kids, Real Places Ser.). (Illus.). 158p. (J). 24.99 *(978-0-635-07608-3(X))*; pap. 7.99 *(978-0-635-07596-3(2))* Gallopade International. (Marsh, Carole Mysteries).
—The Mystery at Disney World. (Real Kids, Real Places Ser.). (Illus.). 146p. (J). 2009. lib. bdg. 18.99 *(978-0-635-06990-0(3)*, Marsh, Carole Mysteries) 2003. (gr. 2-8). lib. bdg. 14.95 *(978-0-635-02105-2(6))* Gallopade International.
—The Mystery at Dracula's Castle: Transylvania, Romania. 2009. (Around the World in 80 Mysteries Ser.). 133p. (J). 18.99 *(978-0-635-07039-5(1)*, Marsh, Carole Mysteries) Gallopade International.
—The Mystery at Fort Sumter. Friedlander, Randolyn, illus. 2010. (Real Kids, Real Places Ser.). 32p. (J). pap. 7.99 *(978-0-635-07432-4(X)*, Marsh, Carole Mysteries) Gallopade International.
—The Mystery at Fort Thunderbolt. 2007. (Pretty Darn Scary Mysteries Ser.). (Illus.). 113p. (J). (gr. 3-5). per. 5.99 *(978-0-635-06235-2(6))*; (YA). lib. bdg. 18.99 *(978-0-635-07021-0(9)*, Marsh, Carole Mysteries); (YA). (gr. 7-14). 14.95 *(978-0-635-06239-0(9))* Gallopade International.
—The Mystery at Hollywood. 2011. (Carole Marsh Mysteries Ser.). (J). pap. 7.99 *(978-0-635-07959-6(3)*, Marsh, Carole Mysteries) Gallopade International.
—The Mystery at Jamestown: First Permanent English Colony in America! 2009. (Real Kids, Real Places Ser.). (Illus.). 137p. (J). lib. bdg. 18.99 *(978-0-635-07023-4(5)*, Marsh, Carole Mysteries) Gallopade International.
—The Mystery at Kill Devil Hills. 2009. (Real Kids, Real Places Ser.). (Illus.). 145p. (J). lib. bdg. 18.99 *(978-0-635-06999-3(7)*, Marsh, Carole Mysteries) Gallopade International.
—The Mystery at Motown. Friedlander, Randolyn, illus. 2011. (Carole Marsh Mysteries Ser.). 32p. pap. 7.99 *(978-0-635-07962-6(3)*, Marsh, Carole Mysteries) Gallopade International.
—The Mystery at Mount Fuji: Tokyo, Japan. 2007. (Around the World in 80 Mysteries Ser.). (Illus.). 131p. (J). (gr. 3-5). per. 7.99 *(978-0-635-06207-9(0))* Gallopade International.
—The Mystery at Mount Vernon. Friedlander, Randolyn, illus. 2010. (Real Kids, Real Places Ser.). 32p. pap. 7.99 *(978-0-635-07444-7(3)*, Marsh, Carole Mysteries) Gallopade International.
—The Mystery at Mount Vernon: Home of America's First President George Washington. 2010. (Real Kids, Real Places Ser.). (Illus.). 158p. (J). 18.99 *(978-0-635-07443-0(5)*, Marsh, Carole Mysteries) Gallopade International.
—The Mystery at Mt. Fuji: Tokyo, Japan. (Around the World in 80 Mysteries Ser.). 131p. (J). 2009. 18.99 *(978-0-635-07016-6(2)*, Marsh, Carole Mysteries) 2007. (Illus.). (gr. 3-5). 14.95 *(978-0-635-06211-6(9))* Gallopade International.
—The Mystery at the Boston Marathon. 2003. 160p. (gr. 2-8). 14.95 *(978-0-635-01642-3(7)*, Marsh, Carole Bks.) Gallopade International.
—The Mystery at the Eiffel Tower. 2009. (Around the World in 80 Mysteries Ser.). (Illus.). 132p. (J). 18.99 *(978-0-635-07004-3(9)*, Marsh, Carole Mysteries) Gallopade International.
—The Mystery at the Kentucky Derby. 2009. (Real Kids, Real Places Ser.). (Illus.). 146p. (J). lib. bdg. 18.99 *(978-0-635-07002-9(2)*, Marsh, Carole Mysteries) Gallopade International.
—The Mystery at the Mayan Ruins: Mexico. 2014. (Around the World in 80 Mysteries Ser.: Vol. 16). (ENG., Illus.). 133p. (J). (gr. 3-5). pap. 7.99 *(978-0-635-11163-0(2)*, Marsh, Carole Bks.) Gallopade International.
—The Mystery at the Roman Coloseum. 2006. (Around the World in 80 Mysteries Ser.). (Illus.). 132p. (J). (gr. 4-7). per. 7.99 *(978-0-635-06156-0(2)*, Marsh, Carole Bks.) Gallopade International.
—The Mystery at the Roman Colosseum. 2006. (Around the World in 80 Mysteries Ser.). (Illus.). 132p. (J). (gr. 4-7). 14.95 *(978-0-635-06157-7(0))* Gallopade International.
—Mystery at the Space Needle. 2016. (Real Kids, Real Places Ser.). (ENG.). (J). (gr. 3-7). pap. 7.99 *(978-0-635-12432-6(7)*, Marsh, Carole Mysteries) Gallopade International.
—The Mystery at Yellowstone National Park. 2010. (Real Kids, Real Places Ser.). (Illus.). 158p. (J). 18.99 *(978-0-635-07437-9(0)*, Marsh, Carole Mysteries) Gallopade International.
—The Mystery in Chocolate Town: Hershey, Pennsylvania. (Real Kids, Real Places Ser.). (Illus.). (J). 2009. 143p. lib. bdg. 18.99 *(978-0-635-07025-8(1)*, Marsh, Carole Mysteries) 2007. 145p. (gr. 2-8). 14.95 *(978-0-635-06389-2(1))* Gallopade International.
—The Mystery in Chocolate Town Hershey, Pennsylvania. 2007. (Real Kids, Real Places Ser.). (Illus.). 145p. (J). (gr. 2-8). per. 7.99 *(978-0-635-06333-5(6))* Gallopade International.
—The Mystery in Hawaii. Friedlander, Randolyn, illus. 2010. (Real Kids, Real Places Ser.). 32p. pap. 7.99 *(978-0-635-07447-8(8)*, Marsh, Carole Mysteries) Gallopade International.
—The Mystery in Hawaii: The 50th State. 2010. (Real Kids, Real Places Ser.). (Illus.). 157p. (J). 18.99 *(978-0-635-07446-1(X)*, Marsh, Carole Mysteries) Gallopade International.
—The Mystery in Las Vegas. 2009. (Real Kids, Real Places Ser.). (Illus.). 145p. (J). lib. bdg. 18.99 *(978-0-635-07045-6(6)*, Marsh, Carole Mysteries) Gallopade International.
—The Mystery in New York City. (Real Kids, Real Places Ser.). (J). 2009. (Illus.). 146p. lib. bdg. 18.99 *(978-0-635-06998-6(9)*, Marsh, Carole Mysteries) 2003. 160p. (gr. 2-8). pap. 5.95 *(978-0-635-02099-4(8))* Gallopade International.
—The Mystery in the Amazon Rainforest: South America. (Around the World in 80 Mysteries Ser.). (Illus.). 131p. (J). 2009. lib. bdg. 18.99 *(978-0-635-07017-3(0)*, Marsh, Carole Mysteries) 2007. (gr. 3-5). 14.95 *(978-0-635-06212-3(7))* 2007. (gr. 3-5). per. 7.99 *(978-0-635-06208-6(9))* Gallopade International.
—The Mystery in the Rocky Mountains. 2009. (Real Kids, Real Places Ser.). (Illus.). 145p. (J). lib. bdg. 18.99 *(978-0-635-07000-5(6)*, Marsh, Carole Mysteries) Gallopade International.
—The Mystery in the Twin Cities. Baker, Janice, ed. 2011. (Carole Marsh Mysteries Ser.). (Illus.). (J). pap. 7.99 *(978-0-635-07960-2(7)*, Marsh, Carole Mysteries) Gallopade International.
—The Mystery of Blackbeard the Pirate. Marsh, Carole, photos by. 2009. (Real Kids, Real Places Ser.). (Illus.). 150p. (J). 18.99 *(978-0-635-06992-4(X)*, Marsh, Carole Mysteries) Gallopade International.
—The Mystery of Blackbeard the Pirate. 2003. (Carole Marsh Mysteries Ser.). 160p. (J). (gr. 2-8). 14.95 *(978-0-635-01650-8(8))*; pap. 7.99 *(978-0-635-01648-5(6))* Gallopade International.
—The Mystery of Kill Devil Hills. 2003. (Carole Marsh Mysteries Ser.). 160p. (J). (gr. 2-8). 14.95 *(978-0-635-02095-6(5))*; pap. 5.95 *(978-0-635-02094-9(7))* Gallopade International.
—The Mystery of the Alamo Ghost. (Real Kids, Real Places Ser.). (J). 2009. (Illus.). 146p. lib. bdg. 18.99 *(978-0-635-06993-1(8)*, Marsh, Carole Mysteries) 2003. 160p. (gr. 2-8). 14.95 *(978-0-635-01654-6(0))* 2003. 160p. (gr. 2-8). pap. 7.99 *(978-0-635-01652-2(4))* Gallopade International.
—The Mystery of the Ancient Pyramid: Cairo, Egypt. 2006. (Around the World in 80 Mysteries Ser.). (Illus.). 128p. (J). lib. bdg. 18.99 *(978-0-635-07006-7(5)*, Marsh, Carole Mysteries); (gr. 4-7). 14.95 *(978-0-635-03473-1(5))*; (gr. 4-7).

M
N
O

per. 5.95 *(978-0-635-03470-0(0)*, Marsh, Carole Bks.) Gallopade International.

—The Mystery of the Biltmore House. 25th ed. 2009. (Real Kids, Real Places Ser.). 148p. (J). 18.99 *(978-0-635-06989-4(X)*, Marsh, Carole Mysteries) Gallopade International.

—The Mystery of the Crystal Castle: Bavaria, Germany. 2009. (Around the World in 80 Mysteries Ser.). 133p. (J). 18.99 *(978-0-635-07041-8(3)*, Marsh, Carole Mysteries) Gallopade International.

—The Mystery of the Graveyard of the Atlantic. 2009. (Real Kids, Real Places Ser.). (Illus.). 144p. (J). lib. bdg. 18.99 *(978-0-635-07046-3(4)*, Marsh, Carole Mysteries) Gallopade International.

—The Mystery of the Haunted Ghost Town. 2009. (Real Kids, Real Places Ser.). 144p. (J). 18.99 *(978-0-635-07044-9(8)*, Marsh, Carole Mysteries) Gallopade International.

—The Mystery of the Lost Colony. 2010. (Real Kids, Real Places Ser.). (Illus.). 158p. (J). 24.99 *(978-0-635-07607-6(1))*; 158p. (J). pap. 18.99 *(978-0-635-07595-6(4))*; pap. 7.99 *(978-0-635-07601-4(2))* Gallopade International. (Marsh, Carole Mysteries).

—The Mystery of the Missing Dinosaurs. 2009. (Real Kids, Real Places Ser.). 146p. (J). 18.99 *(978-0-635-06995-5(4)*, Marsh, Carole Mysteries) Gallopade International.

—The Mystery on Alaska's Iditarod Trail. 2009. (Real Kids, Real Places Ser.). 145p. (J). 18.99 *(978-0-635-06997-9(0)*, Marsh, Carole Mysteries) Gallopade International.

—Mystery on California Mission Trail. 2003. 160p. (J). (gr. 2-8). pap. 7.99 *(978-0-635-01656-0(7))* Gallopade International.

—The Mystery on the California Mission Trail. 2009. (Real Kids, Real Places Ser.). (Illus.). 147p. (J). lib. bdg. 18.99 *(978-0-635-06994-8(6)*, Marsh, Carole Mysteries) Gallopade International.

—The Mystery on the California Mission Trail (Hardcover) 2003. 160p. (gr. 2-8). 14.95 *(978-0-635-01658-4(3))* Gallopade International.

—The Mystery on the Freedom Trail. (Real Kids, Real Places Ser.). (J). 2009. 148p. 18.99 *(978-0-635-06988-7(1)*, Marsh, Carole Mysteries) 2003. 160p. (gr. 2-8). pap. 5.95 *(978-0-635-01640-9(0))* Gallopade International.

—The Mystery on the Great Barrier Reef. 2006. (Around the World in 80 Mysteries Ser.). (Illus.). 132p. (J). (gr. 3-5). per. 5.95 *(978-0-635-06206-2(2))* Gallopade International.

—The Mystery on the Great Barrier Reef: Sydney, Austrailia. 2009. (Around the World in 80 Mysteries Ser.). 132p. (J). 18.99 *(978-0-635-07015-9(4)*, Marsh, Carole Mysteries) Gallopade International.

—The Mystery on the Great Barrier Reef: Sydney, Australia. 2006. (Around the World in 80 Mysteries Ser.). (Illus.). 132p. (J). (gr. 3-5). 14.95 *(978-0-635-06210-9(0))* Gallopade International.

—The Mystery on the Great Lakes. 2010. (Real Kids, Real Places Ser.). (Illus.). 158p. (J). 18.99 *(978-0-635-07449-2(4)*, Marsh, Carole Mysteries) Gallopade International.

—The Mystery on the Great Wall of China. 2006. (Around the World in 80 Mysteries Ser.). (Illus.). 132p. (J). (gr. 3-5). per. 7.99 *(978-0-635-06205-5(4))* Gallopade International.

—The Mystery on the Great Wall of China: Beijing, China. (Around the World in 80 Mysteries Ser.). (Illus.). 132p. (J). 2009. lib. bdg. 18.99 *(978-0-635-07014-2(6)*, Marsh, Carole Mysteries) 2006. (gr. 3-5). 14.95 *(978-0-635-06209-3(7))* Gallopade International.

—The Mystery on the Mighty Mississippi. 2009. (Real Kids, Real Places Ser.). (Illus.). 146p. (J). lib. bdg. 18.99 *(978-0-635-07001-2(4)*, Marsh, Carole Mysteries) Gallopade International.

—The Mystery on the Oregon Trail. 2010. (Real Kids, Real Places Ser.). (Illus.). 158p. (J). 18.99 *(978-0-635-07440-9(0)*, Marsh, Carole Mysteries) Gallopade International.

—The Mystery on the Oregon Trail. Friedlander, Randolyn, illus. 2010. (Real Kids, Real Places Ser.). 32p. pap. 7.99 *(978-0-635-07441-6(9)*, Marsh, Carole Mysteries) Gallopade International.

—The Mystery on the Underground Railroad. 2009. (Real Kids, Real Places Ser.). (Illus.). 146p. (J). lib. bdg. 18.99 *(978-0-635-06991-7(1)*, Marsh, Carole Mysteries) Gallopade International.

—The Puzzle of the Indian Arrowhead. 2006. (Three Amigos Ser.). (Illus.). 54p. (J). (gr. 1-3). 14.95 *(978-0-635-06201-7(1))*; (gr. 4-7). per. 3.99 *(978-0-635-06168-3(6)*, Marsh, Carole Bks.) Gallopade International.

—The Puzzle of the Shark Surfer Girl. 2006. (Criss Cross Applesauce Ser.). (Illus.). 54p. (J). (gr. 1-3). 14.95 *(978-0-635-06204-8(6))*; (gr. 4-7). per. 3.99 *(978-0-635-06171-3(6)*, Marsh, Carole Bks.) Gallopade International.

—The Riddle of the Missing Puppies. 2006. (Criss Cross Applesauce Ser.). (Illus.). 54p. (J). (gr. 4-7). 14.95 *(978-0-635-06203-1(8))*; per. 4.99 *(978-0-635-06170-6(8)*, Marsh, Carole Bks.) Gallopade International.

—The Riddle of the Oogli Boogli. 2006. (Illus.). 54p. (J). (gr. 4-7). 14.95 *(978-0-635-06200-0(3))* Gallopade International.

—The Riddle of the Ooglie Booglie. 2006. (Three Amigos Ser.). (Illus.). 54p. (J). (gr. 4-7). per. 3.99 *(978-0-635-06167-6(8)*, Marsh, Carole Bks.) Gallopade International.

—The Secret of Eyesocket Island. (Pretty Darn Scary Mysteries Ser.). (Illus.). 113p. 2009. (J). lib. bdg. 18.99 *(978-0-635-07022-7(7)*, Marsh, Carole Mysteries) 2007. (J). (gr. 3-5). per. 5.99 *(978-0-635-06236-9(4))* 2007. (YA). (gr. 7-14). 14.95 *(978-0-635-06240-6(2))* Gallopade International.

—The Secret of Skullcracker Swamp. (Pretty Darn Scary Mysteries Ser.). (Illus.). 113p. 2009. (YA). lib. bdg. 18.99 *(978-0-635-07020-3(0)*, Marsh, Carole Mysteries) 2006. (YA). (gr. 7-14). 14.95 *(978-0-635-06238-3(0))* 2006. (J). (gr. 3-5). per. 7.99 *(978-0-635-06234-5(8))* Gallopade International.

—The Secret Soccer Ball. 2006. 64p. (gr. 2-4). 14.95 *(978-0-635-06219-2(4))*; pap. 3.99 *(978-0-635-06213-0(5))* Gallopade International.

—The Treacherous Tornado Mystery. 2007. (Carole Marsh Mysteries Ser.). (Illus.). 118p. (J). (gr. 2-9). per. 5.99 *(978-0-635-06338-0(7))* Gallopade International.

—The White House Christmas Mystery. (Real Kids, Real Places Ser.). (J). 2009. 146p. 18.99 *(978-0-635-06996-2(2)*, Marsh, Carole Mysteries) 2003. 160p. (gr. 2-8). 14.95 *(978-0-635-01666-9(4))* 2003. 160p. (gr. 2-8). pap. 5.95 *(978-0-635-01664-5(8))* Gallopade International.

—The Zany Zoo Mystery. 2007. 128p. (J). pap. 5.99 *(978-0-635-06332-8(8))* Gallopade International.

Martin, Andreu & Ribero, J. No Pidas Sardinas Fuera de Temporada. 35th ed. 2003. (SPA., Illus.). 178p. (J). (gr. 8-12). pap. 11.95 *(978-84-204-4796-4(X))* Santillana USA Publishing Co., Inc.

Martin, Ann M. Claudia & the Phantom Phone Calls. 2010. (Baby-Sitters Club Ser.: 2). (ENG.). 176p. (J). (gr. 3-7). 6.99 *(978-0-545-17476-3(7)*, Scholastic Paperbacks) Scholastic, Inc.

—Mallory y el Gato Fantasma. Peraire del Molino, Conchita, tr. (Club de las Canguro Misterios Ser.: Vol. 3).Tr. of Mallory & the Ghost Cat. (SPA.). 159p. (J). 9.95 *(978-84-272-2603-6(9))* Molino, Editorial ESP. Dist: AIMS International Bks., Inc.

—Stacey y el Anillo Perdido. (Club de las Canguro Misterios Ser.: Vol. 1).Tr. of Stacy & the Missing Ring. (SPA.). 134p. (J). 9.95 *(978-84-272-2601-2(2))* Molino, Editorial ESP. Dist: AIMS International Bks., Inc.

Martin, Justin McCory. The Mystery of the Missing Socks. Kennedy, Kelly, illus. 2004. (Grammar Tales Ser.). (ENG.). 16p. (J). (gr. 3-7). pap. 3.25 *(978-0-439-45823-8(4))* Scholastic, Inc.

Martin, W. D. Dragonfly Valley: When Best Plans Go Awry. 2012. (ENG.). 176p. (J). pap. 11.95 *(978-1-4787-1832-1(3))* Outskirts Pr., Inc.

Marvel Book Group, et al. Doctor Strange: Mystery of the Dark Magic. Pham, Khoi & Sotomayor, Chris, illus. 2016. (Mighty Marvel Chapter Book Ser.). (ENG.). 128p. (J). (gr. 3-7). pap. 5.99 *(978-1-4847-3127-7(1)*, Marvel Pr.) Disney Publishing Worldwide.

Marzollo, Jean. Four Picture Riddle Books. Wick, Walter, illus. 2005. (Scholastic Reader Level 1 Ser.). (ENG.). 128p. (J). (gr. -1-3). 6.99 *(978-0-439-76309-7(6)*, Cartwheel Bks.) Scholastic, Inc.

Maselli, Christopher P. N. The Runaway Mission. 2004. 104p. 5.99 *(978-1-57562-805-9(8))* Copeland, Kenneth Pubns.

Maselli, Christopher P. N. & Hoose, Bob. Jones & Parker Case Files. 2015. (Adventures in Odyssey Bks.). (ENG., Illus.). 128p. (J). pap. 9.99 *(978-1-58997-806-5(4))* Focus on the Family Publishing.

Mason, Adrienne. Secret Spies. Cupples, Patricia & Cupples, Pat, illus. 2008. (Kids Can Read Ser.). (ENG.). 32p. (J). (gr. 1-2). 14.95 *(978-1-55453-276-6(0))*; pap. 3.95 *(978-1-55453-277-3(9))* Kids Can Pr., Ltd. CAN. Dist: Hachette Bk. Group.

Mason, Jane B. & Hines-Stephens, Sarah. Let Sleeping Dogs Spy. Phillips, Craig, illus. 2012. 91p. (J). pap. *(978-0-545-37470-5(7))* Scholastic, Inc.

Mason, Jane B. & Stephens, Sarah Hines. Bella Baxter & the Lighthouse Mystery. Shelley, John, illus. 2006. (Bella Baxter Ser.: 3). (ENG.). 80p. (J). (gr. 1-4). pap. 6.99 *(978-0-689-86282-3(2)*, Simon & Schuster/Paula Wiseman Bks.) Simon & Schuster/Paula Wiseman Bks.

—A Dog & His Girl Mysteries #3: Cry Woof. 2013. (ENG.). 208p. (J). (gr. 3-7). pap. 5.99 *(978-0-545-43626-7(5)*, Scholastic Paperbacks) Scholastic, Inc.

Mason, Simon. Running Girl. 2016. (ENG.). 432p. (J). (gr. 9). 18.99 *(978-1-338-03642-8(4))* Scholastic, Inc.

Massey, Eithne. Where the Stones Sing: Who Are the Mysterious Voices in Christ Church? 2012. (ENG., Illus.). 208p. (J). pap. 12.95 *(978-1-84717-277-8(6))* O'Brien Pr., Ltd., The IRL. Dist: Dufour Editions, Inc.

Masters, M. The Case of the Chocolate Snatcher: Can You Solve the Mystery #2. 2013. (Can You Solve the Mystery? Ser.: 2). (ENG.). 112p. (J). (gr. 1-7). pap. 4.99 *(978-1-4424-6900-6(5))* Meadowbrook Pr.

—The Case of the Mysterious Dognapper: Can You Solve the Mystery #4. 2013. (Can You Solve the Mystery? Ser.: 4). (ENG.). 112p. (J). (gr. 1-7). pap. 4.99 *(978-1-4424-6902-0(1))* Meadowbrook Pr.

—The Case of the Video Game Smugglers: Can You Solve the Mystery #3. 2013. (Can You Solve the Mystery? Ser.: 3). (ENG.). 112p. (J). (gr. 1-7). pap. 4.99 *(978-1-4424-6901-3(3))* Meadowbrook Pr.

—The Secret of the Long-Lost Cousin: Can You Solve the Mystery #1. 2013. (Can You Solve the Mystery? Ser.: 1). (ENG.). 112p. (J). (gr. 1-7). pap. 4.99 *(978-1-4424-6899-3(8))* Meadowbrook Pr.

Matas, Carol. Visions. 2nd rev. ed. 2008. (Freak Ser.). (ENG.). 128p. (J). (gr. 7-18). pap. *(978-1-55263-932-0(0))* Me to We.

Matas, Carol & Nodelman, Perry. The Proof That Ghosts Exist. 2008. (Ghosthunters Ser.: Bk. 1). (ENG.). 216p. (J). (gr. 4-7). *(978-1-55470-014-1(0))* Me to We.

Matheson, Dan. Before: The Smith & Miya Collection. 2016. (ENG., Illus.). (J). (gr. 3-6). pap. ***(978-1-925590-11-1(9))*** Vivid Publishing.

Matthews. Death in the Desert. (Thumbprint Mysteries Ser.). 32.86 *(978-0-8092-0416-8(9))* McGraw-Hill/Contemporary.

Matthies, Don-Oliver. Detective Mazes. 2004. (ENG., Illus.). 40p. (J). pap. 3.95 *(978-1-4027-1293-7(6))* Sterling Publishing Co., Inc.

Maxwell, Susan. Good Red Herring. Simpson, Steve, illus. 2016. (ENG.). 304p. (YA). (gr. 7). pap. 12.99 *(978-1-908195-93-7(2))* Little Island IRL. Dist: Independent Pubs. Group.

Mayer, Jeni. The Mystery of the Missing Will. 2007. (ENG.). 160p. (J). mass mkt. 6.95 *(978-0-920633-90-8(0))* Thistledown Pr., Ltd. CAN. Dist: Univ. of Toronto Pr.

Mazer, Anne. Now You See It, Now You Don't. 2005. (Amazing Days of Abby Hayes Ser.: Bk. 15). (Illus.). 126p. (J). (gr. 4-7). 12.65 *(978-0-7569-5932-6(2))* Perfection Learning Corp.

Mazzio, Joann. The One Who Came Back. 2015. (ENG.). 192p. (YA). (gr. 7). pap. 8.99 *(978-0-544-33612-4(7)*, HMH Books For Young Readers) Houghton Mifflin Harcourt Publishing Co.

McArthur, Nancy. The Mystery of the Plant That Ate Dirty Socks. 2004. 162p. pap. 11.95 *(978-0-595-33693-7(0)*, Backinprint.com) iUniverse, Inc.

McArthur, Shallee. The Unhappening of Genesis Lee. 2014. (ENG.). 352p. (J). (gr. 6). 16.95 *(978-1-62914-647-8(1)*, Sky Pony Pr.) Skyhorse Publishing Co., Inc.

McBride, Susan. Very Bad Things. 2014. (ENG.). 240p. (YA). (gr. 7). lib. bdg. 20.99 *(978-0-385-90704-0(4)*, Delacorte Pr.) Random Hse. Children's Bks.

McCall Smith, Alexander. The Great Cake Mystery: Precious Ramotswe's Very First Case. 2012. (Precious Ramotswe Mysteries for Young Readers Ser.: 1). (ENG.). 96p. (J). (gr. 2-5). 12.99 *(978-0-307-94944-8(3))*; (Illus.). pap. 6.99 *(978-0-307-74389-3(6))* Knopf Doubleday Publishing Group. (Anchor).

—Harriet Bean & the League of Cheats. 2006. (Harriet Bean Ser.: 2). (J). 106.75 *(978-1-4281-0376-4(7))* Recorded Bks., Inc.

—The Mystery of Meerkat Hill. McIntosh, Iain, illus. 2013. (Precious Ramotswe Mysteries for Young Readers Ser.: 2). (ENG.). 112p. (J). (gr. 2-5). pap. 6.99 *(978-0-345-80446-4(5)*, Anchor) Knopf Doubleday Publishing Group.

—The Mystery of Meerkat Hill: A Precious Ramotswe Mystery for Young Readers. McIntosh, Iain, illus. 2013. (Precious Ramotswe Mysteries for Young Readers Ser.: 2). (ENG.). 112p. (J). (gr. 2-5). 12.99 *(978-0-345-80458-7(9))*; lib. bdg. 13.99 *(978-0-345-80616-1(6))* Knopf Doubleday Publishing Group. (Anchor).

—The Mystery of the Missing Lion: A Precious Ramotswe Mystery for Young Readers. 2014. (Precious Ramotswe Mysteries for Young Readers Ser.: 3). (ENG., Illus.). 112p. (J). (gr. 2-5). pap. 6.99 *(978-0-8041-7327-8(3)*, Anchor) Knopf Doubleday Publishing Group.

—Precious & the Puggies: Precious Ramotswe's Very First Case. Robertson, James, tr. from ENG. 2011. (ENG., Illus.). 96p. pap. 10.95 *(978-1-84502-332-4(3))* Black and White Publishing Ltd. GBR. Dist: Interlink Publishing Group, Inc.

—The Sands of Shark Island. 2017. (School Ship Tobermory Ser.: 2). (ENG.). 256p. (J). (gr. 3-7). 15.99 ***(978-0-399-55401-8(7)***, Delacorte Bks. for Young Readers) Random Hse. Children's Bks.

McCall Smith, Alexander. School Ship Tobermory. 2016. (School Ship Tobermory Ser.). (ENG., Illus.). 224p. (J). (gr. 3-7). 15.99 *(978-0-399-55261-8(8)*, Delacorte Bks. for Young Readers) Random Hse. Children's Bks.

McCann, Jesse Leon. Scooby-Doo & Museum Madness, 1 vol. Duendes Del Sur Staff, illus. 2012. (Scooby-Doo! Set 2 Ser.: No. 2). (ENG.). 24p. (J). (gr. k-3). lib. bdg. 24.21 *(978-1-59961-867-8(2))* Spotlight.

—Scooby-Doo & the Fishy Phantom, 1 vol. Duendes Del Sur Staff, illus. 2012. (Scooby-Doo! Set 2 Ser.: No. 2). (ENG.). 24p. (J). (gr. k-3). lib. bdg. 24.21 *(978-1-59961-866-1(4))* Spotlight.

McCann, M. L. The Search for Black January: Third Mystery in the Longjohners' Series. 2004. 100p. per. 15.95 *(978-0-9754823-2-2(7))* Pumpkin Patch Publishing.

McCaughan, Timothy. Crimson Soul. 2005. 200p. per. 12.95 *(978-1-58961-438-3(0))* PageFree Publishing, Inc.

McCaughren, Tom. Children of the Forge. (Illus.). 128p. 3.95 *(978-0-900068-98-0(1))* Penguin Publishing Group.

—Legend of the Corrib King. 2nd rev. ed. 2012. (McCaughren's Legends Trilogy Ser.). (ENG., Illus.). 128p. (J). pap. 14.95 *(978-1-85635-801-9(1))* Mercier Pr., Ltd., The IRL. Dist: Dufour Editions, Inc.

—Legend of the Corrib King. (Illus.). 96p. 2.25 *(978-0-900068-86-7(8))* Penguin Publishing Group.

—Legend of the Golden Key. 2nd rev. ed. 2012. (McCaughren's Legends Trilogy Ser.). (ENG., Illus.). 190p. (J). pap. 14.95 *(978-1-85635-803-3(8))* Mercier Pr., Ltd., The IRL. Dist: Dufour Editions, Inc.

—Legend of the Golden Key. (Illus.). 96p. 3.95 *(978-0-900068-73-7(6))* Penguin Publishing Group.

—Legend of the Phantom Highwayman. 2nd rev. ed. 2012. (McCaughren's Legends Trilogy Ser.). (ENG., Illus.). 128p. (J). pap. 14.95 *(978-1-85635-802-6(X))* Mercier Pr., Ltd., The IRL. Dist: Dufour Editions, Inc.

Mccauley, Plum. It All Started with A Bicycle. 2011. (ENG.). 220p. pap. 11.95 *(978-1-4327-7412-7(3))* Outskirts Pr., Inc.

McCaw, Neil. My Dad the Crab. 2008. 160p. pap. 10.95 *(978-1-4092-0156-4(2))* Lulu Pr., Inc.

McClafferty, Lisa. Is the Sky Really Falling? A Matilda Private Eye Book. 2012. 26p. 24.95 *(978-1-4626-8093-1(3))* America Star Bks.

—Matilda Private Eye: The Case of the Missing Socks. Aines, Diane, illus. 2012. 34p. 29.95 *(978-1-4489-5049-2(X))* America Star Bks.

McClintock, Norah. About That Night, 1 vol. 2014. (ENG.). 248p. (YA). (gr. 8-12). pap. 12.95 *(978-1-4598-0594-1(1))* Orca Bk. Pubs. USA.

—At the Edge. 2013. (Robyn Hunter Mysteries Ser.: 9). (ENG.). 200p. (gr. 6-12). (J). lib. bdg. 27.93 *(978-0-7613-8319-2(0))*; (YA). pap. 8.95 *(978-1-4677-0703-9(1))* Lerner Publishing Group.

—Change of Heart. 2013. (Robyn Hunter Mysteries Ser.: 7). (ENG.). 224p. (YA). (gr. 6-12). pap. 8.95 *(978-1-4677-0701-5(5))*; lib. bdg. 27.93 *(978-0-7613-8317-8(4))* Lerner Publishing Group.

—Dead & Gone. 2014. (Mike & Riel Mysteries Ser.: No. 3). 224p. (YA). (gr. 6-12). lib. bdg. 27.93 *(978-1-4677-2607-8(9))*; (ENG.). pap. 8.95 *(978-1-4677-2615-3(X))* Lerner Publishing Group. (Darby Creek).

—Dead Silence. 2014. (Mike & Riel Mysteries Ser.: No. 5). 240p. (YA). (gr. 6-12). lib. bdg. 27.93 *(978-1-4677-2609-2(5))*; (ENG.). pap. 8.95 *(978-1-4677-2619-1(2))* Lerner Publishing Group. (Darby Creek).

—Guilty, 1 vol. 2012. (ENG.). 224p. (YA). (gr. 8-12). pap. 12.95 *(978-1-55469-989-6(4))* Orca Bk. Pubs. USA.

—Hit & Run. 2014. (Mike & Riel Mysteries Ser.: 1). (ENG.). 240p. (YA). (gr. 6-12). pap. 8.95 *(978-1-4677-2611-5(7)*, Darby Creek) Lerner Publishing Group.

—I, Witness, 1 vol. Deas, Mike, illus. 2012. (ENG.). 144p. (YA). (gr. 8-12). pap. 16.95 *(978-1-55469-789-2(1))* Orca Bk. Pubs. USA.

—In Too Deep. 2013. (Robyn Hunter Mysteries Ser.: 8). (ENG.). 224p. (YA). (gr. 6-12). pap. 8.95 *(978-1-4677-0702-2(3))*; lib. bdg. 27.93 *(978-0-7613-8318-5(2))* Lerner Publishing Group.

—Last Chance. 2012. (Robyn Hunter Mysteries Ser.: 1). (ENG.). 232p. (YA). (gr. 6-12). pap. 8.95 *(978-0-7613-8529-5(0)*, Darby Creek); lib. bdg. 27.93 *(978-0-7613-8311-6(5))* Lerner Publishing Group.

—Marked, 1 vol. 2008. (Orca Currents Ser.). (ENG.). (J). (gr. 5-9). 128p. pap. 9.95 *(978-1-55143-992-1(1))*; 112p. lib. bdg. 16.95 *(978-1-55143-994-5(8))* Orca Bk. Pubs. USA.

—Marqué, 1 vol. 2011.Tr. of Marked. (FRE.). 128p. (J). (gr. 5-9). pap. 9.95 *(978-1-55469-855-4(3))* Orca Bk. Pubs. USA.

—Nothing to Lose. 2012. (Robyn Hunter Mysteries Ser.: 3). (ENG.). 200p. (YA). (gr. 6-12). pap. 8.95 *(978-0-7613-8531-8(2)*, Darby Creek); lib. bdg. 27.93 *(978-0-7613-8313-0(1))* Lerner Publishing Group.

—Nowhere to Turn. 2012. (Robyn Hunter Mysteries Ser.: 6). (ENG.). 240p. (YA). (gr. 6-12). pap. 8.95 *(978-0-7613-9398-6(6)*, Darby Creek); lib. bdg. 27.93 *(978-0-7613-8316-1(6))* Lerner Publishing Group.

—Out of the Cold. 2012. (Robyn Hunter Mysteries Ser.: 4). (ENG.). 232p. (YA). (gr. 6-12). pap. 8.95 *(978-0-7613-9396-2(X)*, Darby Creek); lib. bdg. 27.93 *(978-0-7613-8314-7(X))* Lerner Publishing Group.

—Seeing & Believing. 2014. (Mike & Riel Mysteries Ser.: No. 4). 240p. (YA). (gr. 6-12). lib. bdg. 27.93 *(978-1-4677-2608-5(7)*, Darby Creek) Lerner Publishing Group.

—Shadow of Doubt. 2012. (Robyn Hunter Mysteries Ser.: 5). (ENG.). 232p. (YA). (gr. 6-12). pap. 8.95 *(978-0-7613-9397-9(8)*, Darby Creek); lib. bdg. 27.93 *(978-0-7613-8315-4(8))* Lerner Publishing Group.

—Tell, 1 vol. 2006. (Orca Soundings Ser.). (ENG.). 128p. (YA). (gr. 8-12). per. 9.95 *(978-1-55143-511-4(X))* Orca Bk. Pubs. USA.

—Trial by Fire, 1 vol. 2016. (Riley Donovan Ser.). (ENG.). 240p. (YA). (gr. 8-12). pap. 10.95 *(978-1-4598-0936-9(X))* Orca Bk. Pubs. USA.

—Truth & Lies. 2014. (Mike & Riel Mysteries Ser.: No. 2). 216p. (YA). (gr. 6-12). lib. bdg. 27.93 *(978-1-4677-2606-1(0))*; (ENG.). pap. 8.95 *(978-1-4677-2613-9(3))* Lerner Publishing Group. (Darby Creek).

—You Can Run. 2012. (Robyn Hunter Mysteries Ser.: 2). (ENG.). 216p. (YA). (gr. 6-12). pap. 8.95 *(978-0-7613-8530-1(4)*, Darby Creek); lib. bdg. 27.93 *(978-0-7613-8312-3(3))* Lerner Publishing Group.

McCollum, Lynn Tragesser. The Green School Caper: The Adventures of the Five Amigos. 2008. 164p. pap. 9.95 *(978-1-4327-2564-8(5))* Outskirts Pr., Inc.

McCormack, Devon. When Ryan Came Back. 2016. (ENG., Illus.). (J). 24.99 ***(978-1-63477-994-4(0)***, Harmony Ink Pr.) Dreamspinner Pr.

McCoy, Mary. Dead to Me. 2015. (ENG.). 304p. (YA). (gr. 7-12). 17.99 *(978-1-4231-8712-7(1))* Hyperion Bks. for Children.

McCullough, Victoria. Charlotte's Hummock: a Young Adult Woman's Mystery Detective Novel. 2007. 124p. per. 19.95 *(978-1-4241-6703-6(5))* America Star Bks.

McCusker, Paul & Elmer, Robert. Ripple Effect, 1 vol., Bk. 1. 2008. (Time Thriller Trilogy Ser.: Bk. 1). (ENG., Illus.). 224p. (YA). (gr. 8-11). pap. 9.99 *(978-0-310-71436-1(2))* Zondervan.

McDavid-Jones, Elizabeth. Ghost Light on Graveyard Shoal. 2009. (Mysteries Through Time Ser.). 144 - 176p. (YA). (gr. 4-8). 31.95 *(978-1-60754-443-2(1))*; pap. 15.25 *(978-1-60754-444-9(X))* Windmill Bks.

—Watcher in the Piney Woods. 2009. (Mysteries Through Time Ser.). 160p. (YA). (gr. 4-8). 31.95 *(978-1-60754-304-6(4))*; pap. 15.25 *(978-1-60754-305-3(2))* Windmill Bks.

McDonald, Ellie. Danger after Dark. 4th ed. 2005. (Creative Girls Club Mystery Book Ser.). (Illus.). 118p. (J). pap. *(978-1-59635-127-1(6)*, Annie's) Annie's Publishing, LLC.

McDonald, Megan. Girl Detective. Reynolds, Peter H., illus. (Judy Moody Ser.: 9). (ENG.). 192p. (J). (gr. 1-4). 2011. pap. 5.99 *(978-0-7636-4349-2(1))*Bk. 9. 2010. 15.99 *(978-0-7636-3450-6(6))* Candlewick Pr.

—Judy Moody's Mini-Mysteries & Other Sneaky Stuff for Super-Sleuths. Reynolds, Peter H., illus. 2012. (Judy Moody Ser.). (ENG.). 96p. (J). (gr. 1-4). pap. 4.99 *(978-0-7636-5941-7(X))* Candlewick Pr.

McDonnell, Vincent. Chill Factor. 2004. (ENG.). 224p. (J). pap. 12.95 *(978-0-86278-888-9(9))* O'Brien Pr., Ltd., The IRL. Dist: Dufour Editions, Inc.

McDoogle, Farrah. A Mystery in Gabba Land. Scanlon, Michael, illus. 2010. (Yo Gabba Gabba! Ser.). (ENG.). 24p. (J). (gr. -1-k). pap. 3.99 *(978-1-4424-0652-0(6)*, Simon Spotlight) Simon Spotlight.

McFall, Claire. Bomb Maker. 2014. (ENG.). 368p. (YA). (gr. 8). pap. 11.99 *(978-1-84877-767-5(1))* Bonnier Publishing GBR. Dist: Independent Pubs. Group.

McFall, Jessica & McFall, Ernest. Unselfish Love. l.t. ed. 2006. (ENG., Illus.). 28p. per. 9.95 *(978-1-4327-0076-8(6))* Outskirts Pr., Inc.

McFarlane, Susannah. Drama Queen: EJ12 Girl Hero. 2017. (Illus.). 128p. (J). pap. 5.99 *(978-1-61067-509-3(6))* Kane Miller.

—On the Ball: EJ12 Girl Hero. 2017. (Illus.). 128p. (J). pap. 5.99 *(978-1-61067-507-9(X))* Kane Miller.

—Rocky Road. 2015. 121p. (J). *(978-1-61067-384-6(0))* Kane Miller.

McGee, Pamela M. Keri. Miller, Dawn Ellen, illus. 2012. 20p. pap. 24.95 *(978-1-4626-8593-6(5))* America Star Bks.

—Keri: Dandelions. Miller, Dawn Ellen, illus. 2012. 24p. pap. 24.95 *(978-1-4626-9977-3(4))* America Star Bks.

McGinnis, Mindy. The Female of the Species. (YA). (gr. 9). 2017. 368p. pap. 9.99 ***(978-0-06-232090-2(4))*** 2016. 352p. 17.99 *(978-0-06-232089-6(0))* HarperCollins Pubs. (Tegen, Katherine Bks).

McGregor, Kristen. Danny & Jacob Case #081548 Savanco Inc, 1 vol. 2010. 76p. pap. 19.95 *(978-1-4489-5931-0(4))* America Star Bks.

McIntosh, Kenneth. Close-Up: Forensic Photography. 2009. (J). pap. 24.95 *(978-1-4222-1455-8(9))* Mason Crest.

—Close-Up: Forensic Photography, 5 vols. Sanborn, Casey, illus. 2007. (Crime Scene Club Ser.: Bk. 5). 144p. (YA). (gr. 9-12). lib. bdg. 24.95 *(978-1-4222-0251-7(8))* Mason Crest.

—Devil's Canyon: Forensic Geography. 2009. (J). 24.95 *(978-1-4222-1450-3(8))* Mason Crest.

—Devil's Canyon: Forensic Geography. Miller, Justin, illus. 2007. (Crime Scene Club Ser.: Bk. 1). 144p. (YA). (gr. 9-12). 24.95 *(978-1-4222-0247-0(X))* Mason Crest.

—The Earth Cries Out: Forensic Chemistry & Environmental Science. 2009. (J). pap. 24.95 *(978-1-4222-1457-2(5))* Mason Crest.

—The Earth Cries Out: Forensic Chemistry & Environmental Science, 8 vols. Miller, Justin, illus. 2007. (Crime Scene Club Ser.: Bk. 9). 144p. (YA). (gr. 9-12). lib. bdg. 24.95 *(978-1-4222-0254-8(2))* Mason Crest.

—Face from the Past: Skull Reconstruction. 2009. (J). pap. 24.95 *(978-1-4222-1454-1(0))* Mason Crest.

—If the Shoe Fits: Footwear Analysis. 2009. (J). pap. 24.95 *(978-1-4222-1456-5(7))* 2007. (Illus.). 144p. (YA). (gr. 8-12). pap. 9.95 *(978-1-4222-0877-9(X))* Mason Crest.

—If the Shoe Fits: Footwear Analysis, 7 vols. Miller, Justin, illus. 2007. (Crime Scene Club Ser.). 144p. (YA). (gr. 9-12). lib. bdg. 24.95 *(978-1-4222-0253-1(4))* Mason Crest.

—Monsoon Murder: Forensic Meteorology. 2009. (J). pap. 24.95 *(978-1-4222-1461-9(3))* Mason Crest.

—Monsoon Murder: Forensic Meteorology, 12 vols. Holland, Joe, illus. 2007. (Crime Scene Club Ser.). 144p. (YA). (gr. 9-12). lib. bdg. 24.95 *(978-1-4222-0258-6(5))* Mason Crest.

—Numbering the Crime: Forensic Mathematics, 11 vols. Golden, John Ashton, illus. 2007. (Crime Scene Club Ser.). 144p. (YA). (gr. 9-12). lib. bdg. 24.95 *(978-1-4222-0257-9(7))* Mason Crest.

—Over the Edge: Forensic Accident Reconstruction. 2009. (J). pap. 24.95 *(978-1-4222-1451-0(6))* Mason Crest.

—Over the Edge: Forensic Accident Reconstruction, 2 vols. Sanborn, Casey, illus. 2007. (Crime Scene Club Ser.: Bk. 2). 144p. (YA). (gr. 9-12). lib. bdg. 24.95 *(978-1-4222-0248-7(8))* Mason Crest.

—Poison & Peril: Forensic Toxicology. 2009. (J). pap. 24.95 *(978-1-4222-1453-4(2))* Mason Crest.

—Poison & Peril: Forensic Toxicology, 4 vols. Miller, Justin, illus. 2007. (Crime Scene Club Ser.). 144p. (YA). (gr. 9-12). lib. bdg. 24.95 *(978-1-4222-0250-0(X))* Mason Crest.

—A Stranger's Voice: Forensic Speech. 2007. (Crime Scene Club: Fact & Fiction Ser.). (Illus.). 144p. (YA). (gr. 8-12). pap. 9.95 *(978-1-4222-0879-3(6))* Mason Crest.

—A Stranger's Voice: Forensic Speech Identification, 9 vols. Golden, John Ashton, illus. 2007. (Crime Scene Club Ser.). 144p. (YA). (gr. 9-12). lib. bdg. 24.95 *(978-1-4222-0255-5(0))* Mason Crest.

—Things Fall Apart: Forensic Engineering. 2009. (J). pap. 24.95 *(978-1-4222-1459-6(1))* 2007. (Illus.). 144p. (YA). (gr. 8-12). pap. 9.95 *(978-1-4222-0880-9(X))* Mason Crest.

—Things Fall Apart: Forensic Engineering, 10 vols. Golden, John Ashton, illus. 2007. (Crime Scene Club Ser.). 144p. (YA). (gr. 9-12). lib. bdg. 24.95 *(978-1-4222-0256-2(9))* Mason Crest.

—The Trickster's Image: Forensic Art. 2009. (J). pap. 24.95 *(978-1-4222-1452-7(4))* 2007. (Illus.). 144p. (YA). (gr. 8-12). pap. 9.95 *(978-1-4222-0873-1(7))* Mason Crest.

—The Trickster's Image: Forensic Art, 3 vols. Miller, Justin, illus. 2007. (Crime Scene Club Ser.). 144p. (YA). (gr. 9-12). lib. bdg. 24.95 *(978-1-4222-0249-4(6))* Mason Crest.

Mcintyre, Mel. Flutter Bunnies. Grady, Kit, illus. 2008. 24p. pap. 10.95 *(978-1-933090-68-9(5))* Guardian Angel Publishing, Inc.

McKain, W. J. Morris Hollett - & St Vernon's Ward for Strange & Unusual Diseases. 2013. 140p. pap. *(978-1-78148-193-6(8))* Grosvenor Hse. Publishing Ltd.

McKay, Lise Y. The Mysterious Well. 2012. 130p. pap. 14.95 *(978-1-59663-865-5(6)*, Mount Helicon Pr.) Rock, James A. & Co. Pubs.

McLaren, Meg. Pigeon P. I. 2017. (ENG., Illus.). 40p. (J). (gr. -1-3). 16.99 ***(978-1-328-71561-6(2)***, Clarion Bks.) Houghton Mifflin Harcourt Trade & Reference Pubs.

McLaughlin, Lauren. Mitzi Tulane, Preschool Detective in the Secret Ingredient. Ohi, Debbie Ridpath, illus. 2017. (ENG.). (J). (-k). 32p. 17.99 ***(978-0-449-81916-6(7))***; 40p. lib. bdg. 20.99 ***(978-0-375-97177-8(7))*** Random Hse. Children's Bks. (Random Hse. Bks. for Young Readers).

McLaughlin, Lauren. Mitzi Tulane, Preschool Detective, in What's That Smell? Ohi, Debbie Ridpath, illus. 2016. (ENG.). 32p. (J). (-k). 19.99 *(978-0-375-97176-1(9)*, Random Hse. Bks. for Young Readers) Random Hse. Children's Bks.

McLean, Allan Campbell. The Hill of the Red Fox. 2nd ed. 2006. (Kelpies Ser.). (ENG.). 272p. (J). 11.95 *(978-0-86315-556-7(1))* Floris Bks. GBR. Dist: SteinerBooks, Inc.

McLean, Hope. Battle of the Brightest. 2013. 140p. (J). *(978-0-545-48292-9(5))* Scholastic, Inc.

—Jewel Society #3: Keep Friends Close, Emeralds Closer. 2013. (Jewel Thieves Ser.: 3). (ENG.). 144p. (J). (gr. 3-7). pap. 5.99 *(978-0-545-60764-3(7))* Scholastic, Inc.

—Jewel Society #4: Battle of the Brightest. 2013. (Jewel Society Ser.: 4). (ENG.). 144p. (J). (gr. 3-7). pap. 5.99 *(978-0-545-60765-0(5)*, Scholastic Paperbacks) Scholastic, Inc.

McLeod MacKnight, Wendy. It's a Mystery, Pig Face! 2017. (ENG.). 352p. (J). (gr. 2-7). 15.99 *(978-1-5107-0621-7(6)*, Sky Pony Pr.) Skyhorse Publishing Co., Inc.

McMahon, P. J. Case of the Psychic Hamster. Manders, John, illus. 2005. 153p. (J). lib. bdg. 15.38 *(978-1-4242-0404-5(6))* Fitzgerald Bks.

—The Case of the Psychic Hamster. Manders, John, illus. 4th ed. 2005. (Freaky Joe Club Ser.: 4). (ENG.). 160p. (J). (gr. 2-5). pap. 8.99 *(978-0-689-86263-2(6)*, Simon & Schuster/Paula Wiseman Bks.) Simon & Schuster/Paula Wiseman Bks.

—Case of the Singing Sea Dragons. Manders, John, illus. 2005. 153p. (J). lib. bdg. 15.38 *(978-1-4242-0406-9(2))* Fitzgerald Bks.

—The Case of the Singing Sea Dragons. Manders, John, illus. 6th ed. 2005. (Freaky Joe Club Ser.: 6). (ENG.). 160p. (J). (gr. 2-5). pap. 8.99 *(978-1-4169-0050-4(0)*, Aladdin) Simon & Schuster Children's Publishing.

—The Case of the Smiling Shark. Manders, John, illus. 2004. (Freaky Joe Club Ser.: 2). (ENG.). 128p. (J). (gr. 2-5). pap. 7.99 *(978-0-689-86261-8(X)*, Aladdin) Simon & Schuster Children's Publishing.

—Case of the Smiling Shark. Manders, John, illus. 2004. 116p. (J). lib. bdg. 15.38 *(978-1-4242-0402-1(X))* Fitzgerald Bks.

—The Mystery of the Morphing Hockey Stick. Manders, John, illus. 3rd ed. 2004. (Freaky Joe Club Ser.: 3). (ENG.). 144p. (J). (gr. 2-5). pap. 8.99 *(978-0-689-86262-5(8)*, Aladdin) Simon & Schuster Children's Publishing.

—The Mystery of the Swimming Gorilla. Manders, John, illus. 2004. (Freaky Joe Club Ser.: 1). (ENG.). 112p. (J). (gr. 2-5). pap. 6.99 *(978-0-689-86260-1(1)*, Aladdin) Simon & Schuster Children's Publishing.

—Mystery of the Swimming Gorilla. Manders, John, illus. 2004. 106p. (J). lib. bdg. 15.38 *(978-1-4242-0401-4(1))* Fitzgerald Bks.

McMann, Lisa. Cryer's Cross. 2011. (ENG.). (YA). (gr. 9). 256p. pap. 9.99 *(978-1-4169-9482-4(3))*; (Illus.). 240p. 16.99 *(978-1-4169-9481-7(5))* Simon Pulse. (Simon Pulse).

—Don't Close Your Eyes: Wake; Fade; Gone. 2013. (ENG., Illus.). 720p. (YA). (gr. 9). pap. 12.99 *(978-1-4424-9913-3(3)*, Simon Pulse) Simon Pulse.

McManus, Karen M. One of Us Is Lying. 2017. (ENG.). 368p. (YA). (gr. 9). 17.99 ***(978-1-5247-1468-0(2))***; lib. bdg. 20.99 ***(978-1-5247-1469-7(0))*** Random Hse. Children's Bks. (Delacorte Pr.).

McMillan, Melody DeFields. Addison Addley & the Trick of the Eye, 1 vol. 2009. (Orca Young Readers Ser.). (ENG.). 96p. (J). (gr. 3-6). pap. 7.95 *(978-1-55469-189-0(3))* Orca Bk. Pubs. USA.

McMurtrie, Kevin. The Prince That Always Wore His Top Hat. 2013. 40p. pap. 16.26 *(978-1-4669-9602-1(1))* Trafford Publishing.

McNally, Amber. Henry & the World of the Missing Socks. 2008. 60p. pap. 16.95 *(978-1-60563-288-9(0))* America Star Bks.

McNamee, Graham. Acceleration. 2012. (ENG.). 240p. (YA). (gr. 7). pap. 9.99 *(978-0-307-97595-9(9)*, Ember) Random Hse. Children's Bks.

—Defender. 2016. (ENG.). 240p. (YA). (gr. 9). 17.99 *(978-0-553-49895-0(9)*, Lamb, Wendy Bks.) Random Hse. Children's Bks.

McNeal, Laura. The Incident on the Bridge. 2016. (ENG.). 336p. (YA). (gr. 7). 17.99 *(978-0-375-87079-8(2)*, Knopf Bks. for Young Readers) Random Hse. Children's Bks.

McNeil, Gretchen. Get Dirty. 2015. (Don't Get Mad Ser.). (ENG.). 384p. (YA). (gr. 8). pap. 9.99 *(978-0-06-226087-1(1))* HarperCollins Pubs.

McNicoll, Sylvia. Artsy Mistake Mystery. 2017. (Great Mistake Mysteries Ser.: 2). (ENG.). 208p. (J). pap. 8.99 ***(978-1-4597-3880-5(2))*** Dundurn CAN. Dist: Ingram Publisher Services.

McOmber, Rachel B., ed. McOmber Phonics Storybooks: The Cove of Gloom. rev. ed. (Illus.). (J). *(978-0-944991-83-1(1))* Swift Learning Resources.

McQuestion, Karen. Favorite, 0 vols. unabr. ed. 2011. (ENG.). 172p. (gr. 7-9). pap. 9.95 *(978-1-935597-25-4(6)*, 9781935597254, Skyscape) Amazon Publishing.

McShane, Pol. The Button That Should Never, Ever, Ever Be Pushed! 2008. 140p. pap. 11.95 *(978-0-595-53194-3(6)*, iUniverse, Inc.) iUniverse, Inc.

McSkimming, Geoffrey. Phyllis Wong & the Waking of the Wizard. 2016. (Phyllis Wong Ser.). (ENG.). 400p. (J). (gr. 3-7). pap. 12.99 *(978-1-76011-338-4(7))* Allen & Unwin AUS. Dist: Independent Pubs. Group.

Meacham, Margaret. The Secret of Heron Creek, 1 vol. Lockhart, Lynne N., illus. 2009. (ENG.). 136p. (Orig.). (J). (gr. 2-18). pap. 7.95 *(978-0-87033-414-6(X)*, 9780870334146, Cornell Maritime Pr./Tidewater Pubs.) Schiffer Publishing, Ltd.

Mead, Richelle. Shadow Kiss. Vieceli, Emma, illus. 2013. (Vampire Academy Ser.: 3). (ENG.). 160p. (YA). (gr. 7). pap. 12.99 *(978-1-59514-431-7(5)*, Razorbill) Penguin Young Readers Group.

Meddaugh, Susan. Detective Dog. 2013. (Martha Speaks Ser.). (ENG., Illus.). 96p. (J). (gr. 1-4). pap. 5.99 *(978-0-547-77512-8(1))* Houghton Mifflin Harcourt Publishing Co.

—Haunted House. 2010. (Martha Speaks Ser.). (ENG., Illus.). 24p. (J). (gr. -1-3). pap. 3.99 *(978-0-547-21073-5(6))* Houghton Mifflin Harcourt Publishing Co.

—Martha on the Case. 2010. (Martha Speaks Ser.). (ENG., Illus.). 112p. (J). (gr. 1-4). pap. 5.99 *(978-0-547-21055-1(8))* Houghton Mifflin Harcourt Publishing Co.

—Martha Speaks: Detective Dog (Chapter Book) 2013. (Martha Speaks Ser.). (ENG., Illus.). 96p. (J). (gr. 1-4). 14.99 *(978-0-547-86021-3(8))* Houghton Mifflin Harcourt Publishing Co.

—Martha Speaks: Haunted House (Reader) 2010. (Martha Speaks Ser.). (ENG., Illus.). 24p. (J). (gr. -1-3). 12.99 *(978-0-547-39353-7(9))* Houghton Mifflin Harcourt Publishing Co.

—Martha Speaks: Secret Agent Dog (Chapter Book) 2012. (Martha Speaks Ser.). (ENG., Illus.). 96p. (J). (gr. 1-4). pap. 5.99 *(978-0-547-57660-2(9))* Houghton Mifflin Harcourt Publishing Co.

Meddour, Wendy. The Black Cat Detectives. 2012. (Cinnamon Grove Ser.). (Illus.). 176p. (J). pap. *(978-1-84780-226-2(5)*, Frances Lincoln) Quarto Publishing Group UK.

Meigs, Cornelia. The Windy Hill. 2017. (ENG.). 144p. (J). pap. 5.99 ***(978-0-486-81741-5(5))*** Dover Pubns., Inc.

Meisels, Dovid. Bar Mitzvah & Tefillin Secrets: The Mysteries Revealed. 2004. 245p. 24.95 *(978-1-931681-56-8(2))* Israel Bookshop Pubns.

Mele, Leo. Closet Creeps: A Bedtime Mystery. Demmers, Justina, illus. 2011. 20p. pap. 24.95 *(978-1-4560-9002-9(X))* America Star Bks.

Melissa Strangway. Abigail's Mirror. 2010. 316p. pap. 18.95 *(978-1-4401-6176-6(3))* iUniverse, Inc.

Mellor, Jodie. Missing! Dann, Penny, illus. 2010. (Mystery Pups Ser.). (ENG.). 112p. (J). (gr. k-2). pap. 6.99 *(978-1-84738-226-9(6))* Simon & Schuster, Ltd. GBR. Dist: Independent Pubs. Group.

Melvin, Treva. Mr. Samuel's Penny. 2014. (Elizabeth Parrot Landers Mysteries Ser.: 1). (ENG.). 264p. (YA). pap. 10.95 *(978-1-929345-04-5(6))* Poisoned Pen Pr.

Metcalf, Dan. The Catacombs of Chaos: A Lottie Lipton Adventure. Panagarry, Rachelle, illus. 2017. (Adventures of Lottie Lipton Ser.). (ENG.). (J). (gr. 2-5). 80p. pap. 6.99 ***(978-1-5124-8185-3(8))***; lib. bdg. 25.32 ***(978-1-5124-8183-9(1))*** Lerner Publishing Group. (Darby Creek).

—The Curse of the Cairo Cat: A Lottie Lipton Adventure. Panagarry, Rachelle, illus. 2017. (Adventures of Lottie Lipton Ser.). (ENG.). (J). (gr. 2-5). 80p. pap. 6.99 ***(978-1-5124-8186-0(6))***; lib. bdg. 25.32 ***(978-1-5124-8179-2(3))*** Lerner Publishing Group. (Darby Creek).

—The Eagle of Rome: A Lottie Lipton Adventure. Panagarry, Rachelle, illus. 2017. (Adventures of Lottie Lipton Ser.). (ENG.). (J). (gr. 2-5). 80p. pap. 6.99 ***(978-1-5124-8187-7(4))***; lib. bdg. 25.32 ***(978-1-5124-8184-6(X))*** Lerner Publishing Group. (Darby Creek).

—The Egyptian Enchantment: A Lottie Lipton Adventure. Panagarry, Rachelle, illus. 2017. (Adventures of Lottie Lipton Ser.). (ENG.). (J). (gr. 2-5). 96p. pap. 6.99 ***(978-1-5124-8188-4(2))***; lib. bdg. 25.32 ***(978-1-5124-8182-2(3))*** Lerner Publishing Group. (Darby Creek).

—The Scroll of Alexandria: A Lottie Lipton Adventure. Panagarry, Rachelle, illus. 2017. (Adventures of Lottie Lipton Ser.). (ENG.). 80p. (J). (gr. 2-5). 25.32 ***(978-1-5124-8181-5(5))***; pap. 6.99 ***(978-1-5124-8189-1(0))*** Lerner Publishing Group. (Darby Creek).

—The Secrets of the Stone: A Lottie Lipton Adventure. Panagarry, Rachelle, illus. 2017. (Adventures of Lottie Lipton Ser.). (ENG.). 80p. (J). (gr. 2-5). 25.32 ***(978-1-5124-8180-8(7))***; pap. 6.99 ***(978-1-5124-8190-7(4))*** Lerner Publishing Group. (Darby Creek).

Metz, Melinda. The Droid of Doom. McKenzie, Heath, illus. 2016. (S. M. A. R. T. S. Ser.). (ENG.). 128p. (gr. 3-6). pap. 9.95 *(978-1-4965-3017-2(9))* Stone Arch Bks.

—The Mars Mission Mayhem. McKenzie, Heath, illus. 2016. (S. M. A. R. T. S. Ser.). (ENG.). 128p. (gr. 3-6). pap. 9.95 *(978-1-4965-3018-9(7))* Stone Arch Bks.

—S. M. A. R. T. S. & the Droid of Doom. McKenzie, Heath, illus. 2016. (S. M. A. R. T. S. Ser.). (ENG.). 128p. (gr. 3-6). lib. bdg. 22.65 *(978-1-4965-3015-8(2))* S.M.A.R.T.S. Learning System.

—S. M. A. R. T. S. & the Invisible Robot. McKenzie, Heath, illus. 2015. (S. M. A. R. T. S. Ser.). (ENG.). 128p. (gr. 3-6). 22.65 *(978-1-4965-0463-0(1))* S.M.A.R.T.S. Learning System.

—S. M. A. R. T. S. & the Mars Mission Mayhem. McKenzie, Heath, illus. 2016. (S. M. A. R. T. S. Ser.). (ENG.). 128p. (gr. 3-6). lib. bdg. 22.65 *(978-1-4965-3016-5(0))* S.M.A.R.T.S. Learning System.

—S. M. A. R. T. S. & the Poison Plates. McKenzie, Heath, illus. 2015. (S. M. A. R. T. S. Ser.). (ENG.). 128p. (gr. 3-6). 22.65 *(978-1-4965-0464-7(X))* S.M.A.R.T.S. Learning System.

Midnight at the August Tree House. 2004. (Illus.). 100p. (J). per. 15.95 *(978-0-9754823-1-5(9))* Pumpkin Patch Publishing.

Miley, Berry. Christmas Village Chronicles & Other Short Stories. 2005. 63p. pap. 8.95 *(978-1-4116-2617-1(6))* Lulu Pr., Inc.

Milford, Kate. Ghosts of Greenglass House. 2017. (ENG., Illus.). 464p. (J). (gr. 5-7). 17.99 ***(978-0-544-99146-0(X)***, Clarion Bks.) Houghton Mifflin Harcourt Trade & Reference Pubs.

Milford, Kate. Greenglass House. 2015. (CHI.). 352p. (J). (gr. 5-7). pap. *(978-986-320-886-0(8))* Commonwealth Publishing Co., Ltd.

—Greenglass House. Zollars, Jaime, illus. (ENG.). (J). (gr. 5-7). 2016. 400p. pap. 7.99 *(978-0-544-54028-6(X)*, HMH Books For Young Readers) 2014. 384p. 17.99 *(978-0-544-05270-3(6))* Houghton Mifflin Harcourt Publishing Co.

—Greenglass House. 2016. lib. bdg. 18.40 *(978-0-606-38908-2(3))* Turtleback Bks.

Miller, Ashley Edward & Stentz, Zack. Colin Fischer. 2012. (Colin Fischer Ser.: 1). (ENG.). 256p. (YA). (gr. 7). 17.99 *(978-1-59514-578-9(8)*, Razorbill) Penguin Young Readers Group.

Miller, D. C. Hurricane Hunters: A Craig Hancock Adventure. 2005. (YA). pap. 12.95 *(978-1-59088-646-5(1))* Wings ePress, Inc.

Miller, Daniel, et al. A Miller Cousin Mystery. 2010. 120p. pap. 17.80 *(978-0-557-57118-5(9))*; pap. 49.00 *(978-0-557-57235-9(5))* Lulu Pr., Inc.

Miller, Marvin. You Be the Jury: Courtroom Collection. Roper, Bob, illus. 2005. 361p. pap. *(978-0-439-77480-2(2))* Scholastic, Inc.

Miller, Nathan. The Official Librarian: Bessy's Back! 2009. 124p. pap. 12.49 *(978-1-4490-2391-1(6))* AuthorHouse.

Millman, Calanitte. The Adventures of the Gimmel Gang III: The Cave. 2005. (J). pap. 8.95 *(978-1-931681-84-1(8))* Israel Bookshop Pubns.

Mills, Charles. The Bandit of Benson Park. 2003. (Honors Club Story Ser.: Vol. 1). 127p. (J). *(978-0-8163-1977-0(4))* Pacific Pr. Pubns.

—The Secret of Scarlett Cove. 2004. (Honors Club Story Ser.: Bk. 3). 127p. (J). 7.99 *(978-0-8163-1999-2(5))* Pacific Pr. Publishing Assn.

Mills, Patricia Anne. Oswald Daydreams. 2010. (Illus.). 32p. pap. 12.99 *(978-1-4520-2209-3(7))* AuthorHouse.

Mills, Rob. Charlie's Key, 1 vol. 2011. (ENG.). 264p. (J). (gr. 6-12). pap. 9.95 *(978-1-55469-872-1(3))* Orca Bk. Pubs. USA.

Mills, Timothy. The Mystery Kids: the Mystery of Ghost Lake. 2009. 87p. pap. 14.96 *(978-0-557-01282-4(1))* Lulu Pr., Inc.

Minden, Cecilia & Roth, Kate. How to Write a Mystery. 2012. (Explorer Junior Library: Language Arts Explorer Junior Ser.). (ENG.). 24p. (gr. 1-4). 25.64 *(978-1-61080-488-2(0)*, 202098); pap. 12.79 *(978-1-61080-662-6(X)*, 202272) Cherry Lake Publishing.

Miner, Sharon. Octavia's Quest. 2005. 113p. pap. 11.95 *(978-0-7414-2647-5(1))* Infinity Publishing.

The Missing Will, 6 vols., Vol. 3. (Woodland Mysteriestm Ser.). 133p. (gr. 3-7). 42.50 *(978-0-322-02369-7(6))* Wright Group/McGraw-Hill.

Mitchard, Jacquelyn. What We Lost in the Dark. 2014. (ENG., Illus.). 266p. (YA). (gr. 9). pap. 9.99 *(978-1-61695-471-0(X)*, Soho Teen) Soho Pr., Inc.

Mitchelhill, Barbara. Supersleuth: Megaquiz. Ross, Tony, illus. 2015. (ENG.). 64p. (J). pap. 11.99 *(978-1-78344-258-4(1))* Andersen Pr. GBR. Dist: Independent Pubs. Group.

Mitchell, Briar Lee & Keely, Jack. The Whistlebrass Storm Watcher. 2016. (Whistlebrass Mysteries Ser.: 2). (ENG.). 272p. (YA). pap. 12.95 *(978-1-68261-268-2(6))* Simon & Schuster.

Mitchell, Jack. The Ancient Ocean Blues. 2008. (ENG.). 200p. (YA). (gr. 5-8). pap. 9.95 *(978-0-88776-832-3(6)*, Tundra Bks.) Tundra Bks. CAN. Dist: Penguin Random Hse. LLC.

Mitchell, Laurence. The Mean Root of Crowteal Pond: Inside a Hollow Oak Tree, Book #4. 2009. 28p. pap. 12.49 *(978-1-4389-5406-6(9))* AuthorHouse.

Mitchell, Marie & Smith, Mason. Squatch Watch & Other Stories. 2013. 130p. pap. 9.95 *(978-0-692-02010-4(1))* Smith, Mason.

Mockford, Caroline. What's This? (Illus.). 32p. (J). pap. 6.99 *(978-1-84148-166-1(1))* Barefoot Bks., Inc.

Mogford, Thomas. Sleeping Dogs: A Spike Sanguinetti Novel. 2015. (Spike Sanguinetti Novel Ser.). (ENG.). 256p. 26.00 *(978-1-63286-088-0(0)*, 9781632860880) Bloomsbury Publishing USA.

Moiser, Liam. Moore Field School & the Mystery. 2013. 118p. pap. 10.95 *(978-1-62516-787-3(3)*, Strategic Bk. Publishing) Strategic Book Publishing & Rights Agency (SBPRA).

Molnar, Gwen. Hate Cell: A Casey Templeton Mystery. 2009. (Casey Templeton Mystery Ser.: 1). (ENG.). 184p. (YA). (gr. 5). pap. 11.99 *(978-1-55002-850-8(2))* Dundurn CAN. Dist: Ingram Publisher Services.

—Old Bones: A Casey Templeton Mystery. 2014. (Casey Templeton Mystery Ser.: 2). (ENG.). 136p. (YA). pap. 12.99 *(978-1-4597-1404-5(0)*, 9781459714045) Dundurn CAN. Dist: Ingram Publisher Services.

Moloney, James. Black Taxi. 2005. 272p. (J). (gr. 7-18). 15.99 *(978-0-06-055937-3(3))* HarperCollins Pubs.

—Black Taxi. 2003. 288p. *(978-0-207-19989-9(2))* HarperCollins Pubs. Australia.

Monir, Alexandra. The Girl in the Picture. 2016. (ENG.). 272p. (YA). (gr. 7). 17.99 *(978-0-385-74390-7(4)*, Delacorte Pr.) Random Hse. Children's Bks.

Monroe, Ayshia. Kiki: Doin' It, 1 vol. unabr. ed. 2012. (Juicy Central Ser.). (ENG.). 128p. (YA). (gr. 9-12). pap. 9.95 *(978-1-61651-669-7(0))* Saddleback Educational Publishing, Inc.

Monroe, Chris. Monkey with a Tool Belt & the School Mystery. Monroe, Chris, illus. 2017. (ENG., Illus.). 32p. (gr. -1-2). 17.99 ***(978-1-5124-3010-3(2)***, Carolrhoda Bks.) Lerner Publishing Group.

Monroe, Mary A. Tagger: Graffiti Was His Life - & Soul. 2011. 176p. 29.99 *(978-1-4567-5028-2(3))*; pap. 19.99 *(978-1-4567-5029-9(1))* AuthorHouse.

Monsell, Mary Elise. A Fish Named Yum Vol. IV: MR. PIN. 2007. 72p. (gr. 1-4). per. 8.95 *(978-0-595-47246-8(X)*, Backinprint.com) iUniverse, Inc.

—The Mysterious Cases of Mr. Pin, Vol. I. 2007. 68p. (gr. -1-3). per. 8.95 *(978-0-595-47247-5(8)*, Backinprint.com) iUniverse, Inc.

—The Spy Who Came North from the Pole. 2007. 68p. (gr. -1-3). per. 8.95 *(978-0-595-47248-2(6)*, Backinprint.com) iUniverse, Inc.

Montgomery, E. j. Hailey Walker & the Mystery of the Absent Professor. 2013. 180p. pap. 13.95 *(978-1-4575-2068-6(0))* Dog Ear Publishing, LLC.

Montgomery, Lewis B. The Case of the Amazing Zelda. Wummer, Amy, illus. 2009. (Milo & Jazz Mysteries Ser.). 96p. (J). (ENG.). (gr. -1-2). pap. 6.95 *(978-1-57565-296-2(X))*; Vol. 4. (gr. k-3). 22.60 *(978-1-57565-298-6(6))* Kane Press, Inc.

—The Case of the Amazing Zelda. Wummer, Amy, illus. 2012. (Milo & Jazz Mysteries Ser.: Vol. 4). (ENG.). (J). (gr. 2-4). pap. 20.95 incl. audio compact disk *(978-1-4301-1209-9(3))* Live Oak Media.

—The Case of the Buried Bones. Wummer, Amy, illus. 2014. (Milo & Jazz Mysteries (r) Ser.: 12). 112p. (J). (gr. 2-5). lib. bdg. 22.60 *(978-1-57565-640-3(X))* Kane Press, Inc.

—The Case of the Crooked Campaign. Wummer, Amy, illus. 2012. (Milo & Jazz Mysteries (r) Ser.: 9). (ENG.). 112p. (J). (gr. 2-5). pap. 6.95 *(978-1-57565-436-2(9))*; lib. bdg. 22.60 *(978-1-57565-435-5(0))* Kane Press, Inc.

—The Case of the Diamonds in the Desk. Wummer, Amy, illus. 2012. (Milo & Jazz Mysteries Ser.). 96p. (J). (gr. 2-5). pap. 39.62 *(978-0-7613-9207-1(6))*; (ENG.). pap. 6.95 *(978-1-57565-391-4(5))*; lib. bdg. 22.60 *(978-1-57565-392-1(3))* Kane Press, Inc.

—The Case of the Haunted Haunted House, Vol. 3. Wummer, Amy, illus. 2009. (Milo & Jazz Mysteries Ser.). 96p. (J). (gr. k-3). 22.60 *(978-1-57565-297-9(8))*; (ENG.). (gr. 3-7). pap. 6.95 *(978-1-57565-295-5(1))* Kane Press, Inc.

—The Case of the Haunted Haunted House. Wummer, Amy, illus. 2012. (Milo & Jazz Mysteries Ser.: Vol. 3). (ENG.). (J). (gr. 2-4). pap. 20.95 incl. audio compact disk *(978-1-4301-1206-8(9))* Live Oak Media.

—The Case of the July 4th Jinx. Wummer, Amy, illus. 2010. (Milo & Jazz Mysteries Ser.). 96p. (J). (gr. 2-6). (ENG.). pap. 6.95 *(978-1-57565-308-2(7))*; lib. bdg. 22.60 *(978-1-57565-315-0(X))* Kane Press, Inc.

—The Case of the Locked Box. Wummer, Amy, illus. 2013. (ENG.). (J). (gr. 2-4). (Milo & Jazz Mysteries (r) Ser.: 11). 112p. pap. 6.95 *(978-1-57565-626-7(4))*; (Milo & Jazz Mysteries Ser.: Vol. 11). 106p. lib. bdg. 22.60 *(978-1-57565-625-0(6))* Kane Press, Inc.

—The Case of the Missing Moose. Wummer, Amy, illus. 2011. (Milo & Jazz Mysteries Ser.). 96p. (J). 22.60 *(978-1-57565-331-0(1))*; pap. 39.62 *(978-0-7613-7607-1(0))*; (ENG.). (gr. 2-6). pap. 6.95 *(978-1-57565-322-8(2))* Kane Press, Inc.

—The Case of the Poisoned Pig. Montgomery, Lewis B., illus. 2009. (Milo & Jazz Mysteries Ser.). 96p. (J). (gr. 2-5). 22.60 *(978-1-57565-289-4(7))* Kane Press, Inc.

—The Case of the Poisoned Pig. Wummer, Amy, illus. 2009. (Milo & Jazz Mysteries Ser.). (ENG.). 96p. (J). (gr. 2-6). pap. 6.95 *(978-1-57565-286-3(2))* Kane Press, Inc.

—The Case of the Purple Pool. Wummer, Amy, illus. 2011. (Milo & Jazz Mysteries Ser.). (ENG.). 96p. (J). pap. 6.95 *(978-1-57565-342-6(7))*; pap. 39.62 *(978-0-7613-8358-1(1))*; No. 7. 96p. (J). lib. bdg. 22.60 *(978-1-57565-343-3(5))* Kane Press, Inc.

—The Case of the Stinky Socks. Wummer, Amy, illus. 2009. (Milo & Jazz Mysteries Ser.). 96p. (J). (gr. 2-5). 22.60 *(978-1-57565-288-7(9))*; (ENG.). pap. 6.95 *(978-1-57565-285-6(4))* Kane Press, Inc.

—The Case of the Superstar Scam. Wummer, Amy, illus. 2013. (Milo & Jazz Mysteries (r) Ser.). 112p. (J). (gr. 2-5). 22.60 *(978-1-57565-518-5(7))*; (ENG.). pap. 6.95 *(978-1-57565-519-2(5))* Kane Press, Inc.

M
N
O

Montgomery, R. A. Dragonlark Bind Up-#02. 2009. 0192p. pap. 6.99 *(978-1-933390-89-5(1))* Chooseco LLC.
—Fire! 2015. (ENG.). 80p. (Orig.). (J). pap. 7.99 *(978-1-937133-49-8(4))* Chooseco LLC.
—Lost on the Amazon. Millet, Jason, illus. 2006. (Choose Your Own Adventure Ser.: No. 9). 144p. (J). (gr. 4-8). per. 6.99 *(978-1-933390-09-3(3)*, CHCL09) Chooseco LLC.
Moore, Jordan. The Mystery of the Grand Bazaar, 1 vol. rev. ed. 2013. (Fiction Readers Ser.). (ENG., Illus.). 32p. (J). (gr. 3-3). pap. 8.99 *(978-1-4333-5645-2(7))* Shell Educational Publishing.
Moore, Kelly, et al. Amber House. 2013. (Amber House Ser.: 1). (ENG.). 384p. (J). (gr. 7). pap. 9.99 *(978-0-545-43417-1(3)*, Levine, Arthur A. Bks.) Scholastic, Inc.
Moore, Nathan. The Little Princess & the Backyard Mystery: A Children's Story. 2008. 27p. pap. 24.95 *(978-1-60610-805-5(0))* America Star Bks.
Moracho, Cristina. A Good Idea. 2017. (ENG.). 368p. (YA). (gr. 9). 18.99 *(978-0-451-47624-1(7)*, Viking Books for Young Readers) Penguin Young Readers Group.
Morgan, Gloria. The Ducking Stool. 2013. (Illus.). 298p. pap. 24.99 *(978-1-78035-684-6(6)*, Fastprint Publishing) Upfront Publishing Ltd. GBR. Dist: Printondemand-worldwide.com.
Moriarty, Chris. The Inquisitor's Apprentice. Geyer, Mark Edward, illus. (ENG.). 352p. (J). (gr. 5-7). 2013. pap. 7.99 *(978-0-547-85084-9(0))* 2011. 16.99 *(978-0-547-58135-4(1))* Houghton Mifflin Harcourt Publishing Co.
—The Watcher in the Shadows. Geyer, Mark Edward, illus. (ENG.). 336p. (J). (gr. 5-7). 2014. pap. 7.99 *(978-0-544-22776-7(X)*, HMH Books For Young Readers) 2013. 16.99 *(978-0-547-46632-3(3))* Houghton Mifflin Harcourt Publishing Co.
Morin, Al. Brandon Abroad: The Mystery of the Ruins. 2017. (ENG., Illus.). (J). pap. 7.99 ***(978-1-911079-61-3(1)**, Acorn)* Heinemann-Raintree.
Morris, Paula. The Eternal City. 2015. (ENG.). 304p. (J). (gr. 7). 17.99 *(978-0-545-25133-4(8))* Scholastic, Inc.
—The Eternal City. 2015. 291p. (YA). ***(978-0-545-91986-9(X))*** Scholastic, Inc.
Morris, Paula. Unbroken. (ENG.). 304p. (J). (gr. 7). 2014. pap. 9.99 *(978-0-545-41642-9(6))* 2013. 17.99 *(978-0-545-41641-2(8))* Scholastic, Inc.
Morton-Shaw, Christine. The Hunt for the Seventh. 2009. (ENG.). 288p. (J). (gr. 5). pap. 7.99 *(978-0-06-072824-3(8)*, Tegen, Katherine Bks) HarperCollins Pubs.
Moss, Marissa. The Pharaoh's Secret. 2009. (ENG., Illus.). 320p. (J). (gr. 3-7). 16.95 *(978-0-8109-8378-6(8)*, Amulet Bks.) Abrams, Inc.
Mosso, Tyfanny. The Mud Puddle Gang. 2006. pap. 17.00 *(978-0-8059-9067-6(4))* Dorrance Publishing Co., Inc.
Movie Mayhem. 2012. (Hardy Boys (All New) Undercover Brothers Ser.: 39). (ENG.). 176p. (J). (gr. 3-7). pap. 5.99 *(978-1-4424-0260-7(1)*, Aladdin) Simon & Schuster Children's Publishing.
Movie Menace. 2011. (Hardy Boys (All New) Undercover Brothers Ser.: 37). (ENG.). 176p. (J). (gr. 3-7). pap. 5.99 *(978-1-4424-0258-4(X)*, Aladdin) Simon & Schuster Children's Publishing.
Muldoon, Kathleen M. The Runaway Skeleton. Hilliker, Phillip, illus. 2008. (Vortex Bks.). (ENG.). 112p. (gr. 2-3). 26.65 *(978-1-4342-0800-2(1)*, Vortex Bks.) Stone Arch Bks.
Mullarkey, Lisa. Battle of the Bunks, 1 vol. Franco, Paula, illus. 2016. (ENG.). 112p. (J). lib. bdg. *(978-1-62402-162-6(X))* Magic Wagon.
—The Campfire Capers, 1 vol. 2014. (Storm Cliff Stables Ser.). (ENG., Illus.). 112p. (J). (gr. 7-11). 27.07 *(978-1-62402-049-0(6))* Magic Wagon.
—A Feast of Fun, 1 vol. Franco, Paula, illus. 2016. (ENG.). 112p. (J). lib. bdg. *(978-1-62402-163-3(8))* Magic Wagon.
—A Filming Fiasco, 1 vol. Franco, Paula, illus. 2016. (ENG.). 112p. (J). lib. bdg. *(978-1-62402-164-0(6))* Magic Wagon.
—Gold Medal Glitch, 1 vol. 2014. (Storm Cliff Stables Ser.). (ENG., Illus.). 112p. (J). (gr. 7-11). 27.07 *(978-1-62402-050-6(X))* Magic Wagon.
—Hopes in Hiding, 1 vol. Franco, Paula, illus. 2016. (ENG.). 112p. (J). lib. bdg. *(978-1-62402-165-7(4))* Magic Wagon.
—Horsenapped!, 1 vol. 2014. (Storm Cliff Stables Ser.). (ENG., Illus.). 112p. (J). (gr. 7-11). 27.07 *(978-1-62402-051-3(8))* Magic Wagon.
—Trail Ride Troubles, 1 vol. 2014. (Storm Cliff Stables Ser.). (ENG.). 112p. (J). (gr. 7-11). lib. bdg. 27.07 *(978-1-62402-052-0(6)*, Calico Chapter Bks) Magic Wagon.
Muller, Rachel. When the Curtain Rises, 1 vol. 2007. (ENG.). 144p. (J). (gr. 3-7). per. 7.95 *(978-1-55143-615-9(9))* Orca Bk. Pubs. USA.
Mulligan, Andy. Return to Ribblestrop. 2016. (Ribblestrop Ser.). (ENG., Illus.). 352p. (J). (gr. 3-7). 17.99 *(978-1-4424-9907-2(9)*, Beach Lane Bks.) Beach Lane Bks.
—Ribblestrop. (Ribblestrop Ser.). (ENG., Illus.). (J). (gr. 3-7). 2016. 400p. pap. 7.99 *(978-1-4424-9905-8(2))* 2014. 384p. 16.99 *(978-1-4424-9904-1(4))* Beach Lane Bks. (Beach Lane Bks.).
—Ribblestrop Forever! 2016. (Ribblestrop Ser.). (ENG., Illus.). 320p. (J). (gr. 3-7). 16.99 *(978-1-4424-9910-2(9)*, Beach Lane Bks.) Beach Lane Bks.
—Trash. 2011. (ENG., Illus.). 240p. (YA). (gr. 7). pap. 9.99 *(978-0-385-75216-9(4)*, Ember) Random Hse. Children's Bks.
Mulligan, Richard. Marvin's Mysteries. 2009. 120p. pap. 11.30 *(978-0-557-06550-9(X))* Lulu Pr., Inc.
Munday, Evan. The Dead Kid Detective Agency. 2011. (Dead Kid Detective Agency Ser.). (ENG., Illus.). 320p. (J). (gr. 4-7). pap. *(978-1-55022-971-4(0))* Me to We.
—Dial M for Morna. 2013. (Dead Kid Detective Agency Ser.). (ENG., Illus.). 320p. (J). (gr. 3-8). pap. 11.95 *(978-1-77041-073-2(2))* Purple Bear Bks., Inc.
—Loyalist to a Fault: The Dead Kid Detective Agency #3. 2015. (Dead Kid Detective Agency Ser.: 3). (ENG., Illus.). 320p. (J). (gr. 2-7). pap. 11.95 *(978-1-77041-074-9(0))* Purple Bear Bks., Inc.
Mundy, Charlene & Chapline, Jo. David's Donkey Tales. 2007. 73p. pap. 12.50 *(978-0-615-16825-8(6))* Knee-High Adventures.
Munro, Ken. The Cross Keys Caper. 2006. (Sammy & Brian Mystery Ser.: 18). 154p. pap. 5.95 *(978-1-932864-94-6(6))* Masthof Pr.
—Fireball. 2003. (Sammy & Brian Mystery Ser.: No. 15). (J). pap. 6.95 *(978-1-930353-84-8(7))* Masthof Pr.
—Grandfather's Secret: Sammy & Brian Mystery Series #16. 2004. (Sammy & Brian Mystery Ser.: 16). (J). pap. 6.95 *(978-1-932864-04-5(0))* Masthof Pr.
—The Mysterious Baseball Scorecard: Sammy & Brian Mystery Series #17. 2005. (Sammy & Brian Mystery Ser.: 17). pap. 6.95 *(978-1-932864-31-1(8))* Masthof Pr.
Murphy, Antoinette S. Does It Hurt When You Die? 2004. 30p. (J). pap. 24.95 *(978-1-4137-3520-8(7))* PublishAmerica, Inc.
Murphy, Emily Bain. The Disappearances. 2017. (ENG.). 400p. (YA). (gr. 7). 17.99 *(978-0-544-87936-2(8)*, HMH Books For Young Readers) Houghton Mifflin Harcourt Publishing Co.
Murray Prisant, Guillermo. Mas Que Oscuro. rev. ed. 2005. (Castillo del Terror Ser.). (SPA & ENG.). 136p. (J). (gr. -1-7). pap. 6.95 *(978-970-20-0217-8(6))* Castillo, Ediciones, S. A. de C. V. MEX. Dist: Macmillan.
Museum Mayhem. 2014. (Nancy Drew & the Clue Crew Ser.: 39). (ENG., Illus.). 96p. (J). (gr. 1-4). pap. 5.99 *(978-1-4424-9967-6(2)*, Aladdin) Simon & Schuster Children's Publishing.
Myers, Suzanne. Stone Cove Island. (ENG., Illus.). (YA). (gr. 9). 2015. 256p. pap. 10.99 *(978-1-61695-575-5(9))* 2014. 236p. 17.99 *(978-1-61695-437-6(X))* Soho Pr., Inc. (Soho Teen).
Myers, Walter Dean. Somewhere in the Darkness. 2003. (ENG.). 176p. (J). (gr. 3-7). mass mkt. 5.99 *(978-0-439-52356-1(7)*, Scholastic Paperbacks) Scholastic, Inc.
The Mysteries of Shapeville. l.t. ed. 2005. (Illus.). 48p. (J). 18.95 *(978-0-9747509-1-0(3))* Del Gatto, Maria.
Mysterious Chills & Thrills: 10 creepy, strange, adventurous short stories for kids to tickle the imagination. 2004. (J). per. 6.95 *(978-0-9749013-0-5(X))* LH Pubns. & Productions.
The Mysterious IOU, 6 vols., Vol. 3. (Woodland Mysteriestm Ser.). 133p. (gr. 3-7). 42.50 *(978-0-322-02375-8(0))* Wright Group/McGraw-Hill.
The Mysterious Mansion. (Get a Clue Mystery Puzzles Ser.). 16p. (J). (gr. 5). 12.99 *(978-0-7847-0734-0(0))* Standard Publishing.
Mystery Bay: Individual Title Six-Packs. (Action Packs Ser.). 128p. (gr. 3-5). 44.00 *(978-0-7635-3310-6(6))* Rigby Education.
Mystery Mountain: Individual Title Six-Packs. (Bookweb Ser.). 32p. (gr. 6-18). 34.00 *(978-0-7578-0897-5(2))* Rigby Education.
The Mystery of Moody Manor, 6 vols. (Ragged Island Mysteriestm Ser.). 161p. (gr. 5-7). 42.50 *(978-0-322-01655-2(X))* Wright Group/McGraw-Hill.
The Mystery of October Island. 2003. (Illus.). 50p. (J). per. 12.95 *(978-0-9754823-0-8(0))* Pumpkin Patch Publishing.
The Mystery of the Dark Old House, 6 vols., Vol. 2. (Woodland Mysteriestm Ser.). 133p. (gr. 3-7). 42.50 *(978-0-7802-7940-7(9))* Wright Group/McGraw-Hill.
Mystery of the Desert Giant: Hardy Boys Mystery Stories. 2011. 190p. (gr. 5-9). 42.95 *(978-1-258-10226-5(9))* Literary Licensing, LLC.
The Mystery of the Lion's Tail. 2014. (Greetings from Somewhere Ser.: 5). (ENG., Illus.). 128p. (J). (gr. -1-4). pap. 5.99 *(978-1-4814-1464-7(X)*, Little Simon) Little Simon.
The Mystery of the Missing Lion: A Precious Ramotswe Mystery for Young Readers. 2014. (Precious Ramotswe Mysteries for Young Readers Ser.: 3). (ENG., Illus.). 112p. (J). (gr. 2-5). 12.99 *(978-1-101-87202-4(0)*, Anchor) Knopf Doubleday Publishing Group.
Mystery of the Phantom Heist. 2013. (Hardy Boys Adventures Ser.: 2). (ENG.). 160p. (J). (gr. 3-7). 15.99 *(978-1-4424-6586-2(7))*; pap. 6.99 *(978-1-4424-2237-7(8))* Simon & Schuster Children's Publishing. (Aladdin).
The Mystery of the Three Keys, 6 vols., Vol. 3. (Woodland Mysteriestm Ser.). 133p. (gr. 3-7). 42.50 *(978-0-322-02371-0(8))* Wright Group/McGraw-Hill.
The Mystery of the Tiny Key. 2008. 32p. pap. 4.99 *(978-0-8341-2351-9(7)*, 083-412-3517) Beacon Hill Pr. of Kansas City.
Mystery on Church Hill. 2013. 196p. (J). pap. 8.99 *(978-0-9893414-3-1(7))* MyBoys3 Pr.
Mystery Valley: Individual Title Six-Packs. (Bookweb Ser.). 32p. (gr. 4-18). 34.00 *(978-0-7635-3730-2(6))* Rigby Education.
Nagle, Jeanne, ed. Great Authors of Mystery, Horror & Thrillers. 2013. (Essential Authors for Children & Teens Ser.). (Illus.). 182p. (YA). (gr. 7-12). 45.00 *(978-1-62275-094-8(2))* Rosen Publishing Group, Inc., The.
Nalbantsky, Danail. Bludnia Sin (the Prodigal Son) Guetov, Dimitar, ed. 2nd unabr. ed. 2004. (BUL.). 228p. per. 9.99 *(978-0-9753970-3-9(6))* Capricorn Publishing.
Nash, Scott. Tuff Fluff: The Case of Duckie's Missing Brain. Nash, Scott, illus. 2004. (Illus.). (J). 101.94 *(978-0-7636-2503-0(5))*; (ENG.). 40p. (gr. 1-4). 16.99 *(978-0-7636-1882-7(9))* Candlewick Pr.
Nass, Marcia & Campisi, Stephanie. Mini Mysteries & Kooky Spookies. Innes, Calvin, illus. 2007. 176p. per. 6.99 *(978-0-9795364-2-7(1))* Chowder Bay Bks.
Nayeri, Daniel. Straw House, Wood House, Brick House, Blow: Four Novellas by Daniel Nayeri. Weinberg, James, illus. 2011. (ENG.). 432p. (YA). (gr. 9). 19.99 *(978-0-7636-5526-6(0))* Candlewick Pr.
Nayeri, Daniel and Dina. Another Faust. 2010. (ENG., Illus.). 400p. (YA). (gr. 9). pap. 8.99 *(978-0-7636-4834-3(5))* Candlewick Pr.
Neal, Bethany. My Last Kiss. 2014. (ENG.). 368p. (YA). (gr. 7). 17.99 *(978-0-374-35128-1(7)*, Farrar, Straus & Giroux (BYR)) Farrar, Straus & Giroux.
Neenan, Colin. Thick. 2006. 126p. (YA). (gr. 7-16). per. 6.95 *(978-0-9746481-9-4(7))* Brown Barn Bks.
Nelson, Suzanne. The Ghoul Next Door. 2012. 186p. (J). *(978-0-545-48421-3(9))* Scholastic, Inc.
Neri, G. Tru & Nelle. 2016. (ENG., Illus.). 336p. (J). (gr. 3-5). 16.99 *(978-0-544-69960-1(2)*, HMH Books For Young Readers) Houghton Mifflin Harcourt Publishing Co.
Nesbit, E. The Seven Dragons & Other Stories. 2006. 140p. 24.95 *(978-1-59818-171-5(8))* Aegypan.
Nesbit, Troy. Diamond Cave Mystery. 2013. (Wilderness Mystery Ser.). (ENG., Illus.). 280p. (J). (gr. 3-7). pap. 12.95 *(978-1-58979-809-0(0))* Taylor Trade Publishing.
—Forest Fire Mystery. 2014. (Wilderness Mystery Ser.). (ENG., Illus.). 284p. (J). (gr. 3-7). pap. 12.95 *(978-1-58979-869-4(4))* Taylor Trade Publishing.
—Jinx of Payrock Canyon. 2014. (Wilderness Mystery Ser.). (ENG., Illus.). 282p. (J). (gr. 3-7). pap. 12.95 *(978-1-58979-865-6(1))* Taylor Trade Publishing.
—Mystery at Rustlers Fort. 2014. (Wilderness Mystery Ser.). (ENG., Illus.). 282p. (J). (gr. 3-7). pap. 12.95 *(978-1-58979-867-0(8))* Taylor Trade Publishing.
Nettrour, Nelani. The Dragon Lands Bk. 1: The Ripple. Nettrour, Heather, illus. 2003. 100p. pap. 11.95 *(978-1-929381-46-3(8)*, Third Millennium Publishing) Sci Fi-Arizona, Inc.
Newcomb, Ambrose. Eagles of the Sky or with Jack Ralston along the Air Lanes. 2005. reprint ed. pap. 26.95 *(978-1-4179-8865-5(7))* Kessinger Publishing, LLC.
Newman, Robin. The Case of the Poached Egg. Zemke, Deborah, illus. 2017. (Wilcox & Griswold Mystery Ser.). (ENG.). 48p. (J). (gr. -1-3). 15.95 *(978-1-939547-30-9(X))* Creston Bks.
—A Wilcox & Griswold Mystery: the Case of the Missing Carrot Cake. Zemke, Deborah, illus. 2015. (Wilcox & Griswold Mystery Ser.). (ENG.). 40p. (J). (gr. -1-3). 15.95 *(978-1-939547-17-0(2))* Creston Bks.
Newman, Terry. A Dead Elf. 2015. (ENG.). 312p. 11.99 ***(978-0-00-812066-5(8)**, Harper Voyager)* HarperCollins Pubs.
Newsome, Richard. The Billionaire's Curse. Duddle, Jonny, illus. 2011. (Archer Legacy Ser.). 384p. (J). (gr. 3-7). pap. 7.99 *(978-0-06-194491-8(2)*, Waldon Pond Pr.) HarperCollins Pubs.
—The Emerald Casket. Duddle, Jonny, illus. (Archer Legacy Ser.). (J). (gr. 3-7). 2012. 384p. pap. 6.99 *(978-0-06-194493-2(9))* 2011. 368p. 16.99 *(978-0-06-194492-5(0))* HarperCollins Pubs. (Waldon Pond Pr.).
—The Mask of Destiny. Duddle, Jonny, illus. 2013. 384p. (J). (gr. 3-7). pap. 6.99 *(978-0-06-194495-6(5)*, Waldon Pond Pr.) HarperCollins Pubs.
Nichols, Travis. Fowl Play. 2015. (ENG., Illus.). 40p. (J). (gr. k-3). 14.99 *(978-1-4521-3182-5(1))* Chronicle Bks. LLC.
Nickel, Scott. Monster Trouble. Fentz, Mike, illus. 2004. (Scholastic Reader Ser.). 22p. (J). pap. *(978-0-439-66977-1(4))* Scholastic, Inc.
Nickerson, Jane. Strands of Bronze & Gold. 2014. (ENG.). 368p. (YA). (gr. 9). pap. 9.99 *(978-0-307-97599-7(1)*, Ember) Random Hse. Children's Bks.
Nickerson, Sara. How to Disappear Completely & Never Be Found. Comport, Sally Wern, illus. 2003. (ENG.). 288p. (J). (gr. 5-18). pap. 5.99 *(978-0-06-441027-4(7))* HarperCollins Pubs.
Nienstedt, L. a. Phineas T Pudgepot & the Mysterious Flying Fish. 2009. 32p. pap. 14.49 *(978-1-4343-5123-4(8))* AuthorHouse.
Night, P. J. The House Next Door. 2013. (You're Invited to a Creepover Ser.: 16). (ENG., Illus.). 160p. (J). (gr. 3-7). pap. 6.99 *(978-1-4424-8233-3(8)*, Simon Spotlight) Simon Spotlight.
—You're Invited to a Creepover Collection: Truth or Dare...; You Can't Come in Here!; Ready for a Scare?; the Show Must Go On! 2012. (You're Invited to a Creepover Ser.). (ENG.). 640p. (J). (gr. 3-7). pap. 23.99 *(978-1-4424-8444-3(6)*, Simon Spotlight) Simon Spotlight.
Nilsson, Ulf. A Case in Any Case. Spee, Gitte, illus. 2017. (Detective Gordon Ser.). (ENG.). 108p. (gr. k-5). 16.99 *(978-1-77657-108-6(8))* Gecko Pr. NZL. Dist: Lerner Publishing Group.
—Detective Gordon: A Case in Any Case. Spee, Gitte, illus. 2017. (Detective Gordon Ser.). (ENG.). 108p. (gr. k-5). 9.99 ***(978-1-77657-110-9(X))*** Gecko Pr. NZL. Dist: Lerner Publishing Group.
Nilsson, Ulf. Detective Gordon - The First Case. Spee, Gitte, illus. 2015. (Detective Gordon Ser.). (ENG.). 96p. (J). (gr. k-5). 16.99 *(978-1-927271-49-0(5))* Gecko Pr. NZL. Dist: Lerner Publishing Group.
Nitz, Kristin Wolden. Suspect, 1 vol. 2010. (ENG.). 224p. (YA). (gr. 7-11). 16.95 *(978-1-56145-543-0(1))* Peachtree Pubs.
Nix, Garth & Williams, Sean. The Mystery. 2013. (Troubletwisters Ser.: 3). (ENG.). 304p. (J). (gr. 3-7). 16.99 *(978-0-545-25899-9(5))* Scholastic, Inc.
Nixon & Brush. Champagne with a Corpse. (Thumbprint Mysteries Ser.). 32.86 *(978-0-8092-0420-5(7))* McGraw-Hill/Contemporary.
Nixon, Joan Lowery. A Deadly Game of Magic. 2004. 228p. (YA). (gr. 7). 13.60 *(978-0-7569-7230-1(2))* Perfection Learning Corp.
—The Kidnapping of Christina Lattimore. 2004. (ENG.). 320p. (YA). (gr. 7-12). pap. 8.99 *(978-0-15-205031-3(0))* Houghton Mifflin Harcourt Publishing Co.
—Nightmare. 2005. 166p. (gr. 5-7). 17.00 *(978-0-7569-5239-6(5))* Perfection Learning Corp.
Nobel, Zack. The Twisted Teenage Mysteries. 2009. 48p. pap. 17.49 *(978-1-4389-1127-4(0))* AuthorHouse.
Noble, Sarah. Hannah & Horatio Pea. 2006. (Illus.). 336p. pap. *(978-1-84401-673-0(0))* Athena Pr.
Nobleman, Marc Tyler, et al. Rescue in the Bermuda Triangle: An Isabel Soto Investigation. 2010. (Graphic Expeditions Ser.). (ENG., Illus.). 32p. (gr. 3-4). pap. 47.70 *(978-1-4296-5713-6(8)*, Graphic Library) Capstone Press of Coughlan Cos.
Noël, Alyson. Blacklist. 2017. (Beautiful Idols Ser.: 2). 448p. (YA). (gr. 9). 17.99 *(978-0-06-232455-9(1)*, Tegen, Katherine Bks) HarperCollins Pubs.
—Shadowland. 2009. (Immortals Ser.: 3). (ENG.). 368p. (YA). (gr. 8-12). 17.99 *(978-0-312-59044-4(X)*, 9780312590444, St. Martin's Griffin) St. Martin's Pr.
—Unrivaled. (Beautiful Idols Ser.: 1). (YA). (gr. 9). 2017. 448p. pap. 9.99 *(978-0-06-232453-5(5))* 2016. 432p. 17.99 *(978-0-06-232452-8(7))* HarperCollins Pubs. (Tegen, Katherine Bks).
—Unrivaled. 2017. (Beautiful Idols Ser.: 1). (YA). lib. bdg. 20.85 *(978-0-606-39609-7(8))* Turtleback Bks.
—Unrivaled: A Beautiful Idols Novel. 2016. 420p. (YA). *(978-0-06-245840-7(X))* HarperCollins Pubs.
Nolan, Alan. Destination: Homicide! 2012. (ENG., Illus.). 80p. (J). pap. 12.95 *(978-1-84717-256-3(3))* O'Brien Pr., Ltd., The IRL. Dist: Dufour Editions, Inc.
Nomura, Mizuki. Book Girl & the Captive Fool. 2011. (Book Girl Ser.: 3). (ENG., Illus.). 240p. (YA). (gr. 8-17). pap. 13.00 *(978-0-316-07693-7(7)*, Yen Pr.) Orbit.
—Book Girl & the Corrupted Angel. 2012. (Book Girl Ser.: 4). (ENG., Illus.). 240p. (YA). (gr. 8-17). pap. 13.00 *(978-0-316-07694-4(5)*, Yen Pr.) Orbit.
—Book Girl & the Suicidal Mime. 2010. (Book Girl Ser.: 1). (ENG., Illus.). 192p. (YA). (gr. 8-17). pap. 13.00 *(978-0-316-07690-6(2)*, Yen Pr.) Orbit.
—Book Girl & the Undine Who Bore a Moonflower. 2013. (Book Girl Ser.: 6). (ENG., Illus.). 240p. (YA). (gr. 8-17). pap. 11.99 *(978-0-316-07696-8(1)*, Yen Pr.) Orbit.
—Book Girl & the Wayfarer's Lamentation, Vol. 5. 2012. (Book Girl Ser.: 5). (ENG., Illus.). 272p. (YA). (gr. 8-17). pap. 11.99 *(978-0-316-07695-1(3)*, Yen Pr.) Orbit.
Nordin, Ruth Ann. Witness to a Murder. 2007. 140p. per. 11.95 *(978-0-595-45089-3(X))* iUniverse, Inc.
Norman, C. S. The Lockview Logans: Fire One. 2012. 316p. (gr. 4-6). pap. 18.95 *(978-1-4697-9840-0(9))* iUniverse, Inc.
Norris, Elizabeth. Unbreakable. 2013. (Unraveling Ser.: 2). (ENG.). 496p. (YA). (gr. 9). 17.99 *(978-0-06-210376-5(8))* HarperCollins Pubs.
—Unraveling. (Unraveling Ser.: 1). (ENG.). (YA). (gr. 8). 2013. 480p. pap. 9.99 *(978-0-06-210374-1(1))* 2012. 464p. 17.99 *(978-0-06-210373-4(3))* HarperCollins Pubs.
Norris, Zack. The Secret of Skull Island. 2012. (Double Detectives Ser.). (ENG.). 144p. (J). (gr. 3-7). pap. 4.95 *(978-1-4027-7912-1(7))* Sterling Publishing Co., Inc.
—Tunnel of Bones. 2012. (Double Detectives Ser.). (ENG.). 144p. (J). (gr. 3-7). pap. 4.95 *(978-1-4027-9147-5(X))* Sterling Publishing Co., Inc.
Norton, Andre. Ralestone Luck. 2006. pap. *(978-1-4068-3557-1(9))* Echo Library.
Norville, Rod. Moonshine Express: Revised Edition with a History of Moonshine Today & Yesterday. 2003. 178p. (YA). per. 13.95 *(978-1-891929-99-1(2))* Four Seasons Pubs.
Nye, Julie & Nye, Julie. Scout: The Secret at les Cheneaux. 2007. (Illus.). 160p. (YA). per. *(978-0-9767762-1-5(9))* Fieldstone Hill Pr.
Oakes, Stephanie. The Arsonist. 2017. (ENG.). 496p. (YA). (gr. 7). 17.99 ***(978-0-8037-4071-6(9)**, Dial Bks)* Penguin Young Readers Group.
O'Brien, Carola. Bobby Dazzler & the Three Rubies of Ishmalan. 2010. 236p. 28.99 *(978-1-60911-285-1(7)*, Eloquent Bks.) Strategic Book Publishing & Rights Agency (SBPRA).
O'Brien, Robert C. Z for Zachariah. 2007. 249p. (gr. 7-12). 20.00 *(978-0-7569-8098-6(4))* Perfection Learning Corp.
Obrist, Jurg. Case Closed?! 40 Mini-Mysteries for You to Solve. 2003. (Single Titles Ser.). 96p. (J). pap. 6.95 *(978-0-7613-1999-3(9))* Lerner Publishing Group.
Obrist, Jürg. Case Closed?! 40 Mini-Mysteries for You to Solve. 2003. (Mini-Mysteries for You to Solve Ser.). (ENG.). 96p. (gr. 4-6). 23.93 *(978-0-7613-2739-4(8)*, Millbrook Pr.) Lerner Publishing Group.
—Complex Cases: Three Major Mysteries for You to Solve. Obrist, Jürg, illus. 2006. (Mini-Mysteries for You to Solve Ser.). (ENG., Illus.). 96p. (gr. 4-6). 23.93 *(978-0-7613-3419-4(X)*, Millbrook Pr.) Lerner Publishing Group.
Obrist, Jurg. Complex Cases: Three Major Mysteries for You to Solve. 2006. (Illus.). (J). pap. 6.95 *(978-0-8225-5975-7(7)*, First Avenue Editions) Lerner Publishing Group.
Obrist, Jürg. Open & Shut Cases: 40 More Mini - Mysteries for You to Solve. 2005. (Mini-Mysteries for You to Solve Ser.). (ENG.). 96p. (gr. 4-6). lib. bdg. 23.93 *(978-0-7613-2740-0(1)*, Millbrook Pr.) Lerner Publishing Group.
Obrist, Jurg. Open & Shut Cases: 40 More Mini-Mysteries for You to Solve. 2005. (Illus.). 96p. (J). (gr. 4-7). pap. 6.95 *(978-0-7613-2344-0(9)*, First Avenue Editions) Lerner Publishing Group.
Ocker, Christa Holder. A Crow Named Robin. 2006. (J). per. *(978-1-59872-712-8(5))* Instant Pub.
O'Connor, Finbar. Wolfgran Returns. Fagan, Martin, illus. 2004. (ENG.). 96p. (J). pap. 10.95 *(978-0-86278-884-1(6))* O'Brien Pr., Ltd., The IRL. Dist: Dufour Editions, Inc.
O'Connor, Jane. Fancy Nancy: Nancy Clancy, Super Sleuth. 2013. (Nancy Clancy Ser.: 1). (J). lib. bdg. 14.75 *(978-0-606-31795-5(3)*, Turtleback) Turtleback Bks.
—Nancy Clancy - Super Sleuth. Glasser, Robin Preiss, illus. 2013. (Nancy Clancy Ser.: 1). (ENG.). 144p. (J). (gr. 1-5). pap. 5.99 *(978-0-06-208419-4(4))* HarperCollins Pubs.
—Nancy Clancy, Secret of the Silver Key. 2015. (Nancy Clancy Ser.: 4). (J). lib. bdg. 14.75 *(978-0-606-36956-5(2))* Turtleback Bks.
—Nancy Clancy, Super Sleuth, 3 vols. Glasser, Robin Preiss, illus. 2012. (Nancy Clancy Ser.: 1). (ENG.). 128p. (J). (gr. 1-5). 9.99 *(978-0-06-208293-0(0))* HarperCollins Pubs.
—Nancy Clancy's Tres Charming, 3 vols., Set. Glasser, Robin Preiss, illus. 2013. (Fancy Nancy Ser.). (ENG.). 384p. (J). (gr. 1-5). 24.99 *(978-0-06-227793-0(6))* HarperCollins Pubs.
—The Secret of the Silver Key. Glasser, Robin Preiss, illus. 2014. (Fancy Nancy Ser.). (ENG.). 128p. (J). (gr. 1-5). 9.99 *(978-0-06-208299-2(X))* HarperCollins Pubs.
—Super Sleuth. Glasser, Robin Preiss, illus. 2015. (Fancy Nancy Ser.). (ENG.). 256p. (J). (gr. 1-5). 12.99 *(978-0-06-240364-3(8))* HarperCollins Pubs.
Odgers, Darrel & Odgers, Sally. The Awful Pawful. Dawson, Janine, illus. 2007. (Jack Russell: Dog Detective Ser.: 5). 96p. (J). (gr. 1-6). pap. 4.99 *(978-1-933605-53-1(7))* Kane Miller.
—The Awful Pawful. 2006. (Illus.). 78p. (J). *(978-0-439-88021-3(1))* Scholastic, Inc.
—The Kitnapped Creature. Dawson, Janine, illus. 2008. (Jack Russell: Dog Detective Ser.: 8). 96p. (J). (gr. 2-6). pap. 4.99 *(978-1-933605-82-1(0))* Kane Miller.
—The Kitnapped Creature. 2008. (Illus.). 76p. (J). pap. *(978-0-545-03338-1(1))* Scholastic, Inc.
—The Lying Postman. 2005. (Illus.). 78p. (J). pap. *(978-0-439-88020-6(3))* Scholastic, Inc.
—The Sausage Situation. Dawson, Janine, illus. 2007. (Jack Russell: Dog Detective Ser.: 6). 96p. (J). (gr. 1-6). pap. 4.99 *(978-1-933605-54-8(5))* Kane Miller.
—The Sausage Situation. 2006. (Jack Russell, Dog Detective Ser.: Bk. 6). (Illus.). 78p. (J). pap. *(978-0-439-92197-8(X))* Scholastic, Inc.

Odgers, Sally & Odgers, Darrel. The Buried Biscuits. Dawson, Janine, illus. 2008. (Jack Russell: Dog Detective Ser.: 7). 96p. (J). (gr. 1-6). pap. 4.99 *(978-1-933605-77-7(4))* Kane Miller.
—Dog Den Mystery. Dawson, Janine, illus. 2006. (Jack Russell: Dog Detective Ser.: 1). 96p. (J). (gr. 1-5). pap. 4.99 *(978-1-933605-18-0(9))* Kane Miller.
O'Donnell, Liam. Ganked: Geeked Out Mysteries #1. 2013. 214p. pap. *(978-0-9919281-3-2(X))* Feeding Change Media.
—Max Finder Mystery, Vol. 2. Cho, Michael & Owlkids Books Inc. Staff, illus. 2007. (Max Finder Mystery Collected Casebook Ser.: 2). (ENG.). 96p. (J). (gr. 3-6). 9.95 *(978-2-89579-121-8(X))* Owlkids Bks. Inc. CAN. Dist: Publishers Group West (PGW).
—Max Finder Mystery Collected Casebook, Vol. 1. Cho, Michael & Owlkids Books Inc. Staff, illus. 2006. (Max Finder Mystery Collected Casebook Ser.: 1). (ENG.). 96p. (J). (gr. 3-6). pap. 9.95 *(978-2-89579-116-4(3),* Owlkids) Owlkids Bks. Inc. CAN. Dist: Publishers Group West (PGW).
—Max Finder Mystery Collected Casebook Vol. 3, Vol. 3. Cho, Michael & Owlkids Books Inc. Staff, illus. 2007. (Max Finder Mystery Collected Casebook Ser.: 3). (ENG.). 96p. (J). (gr. 3-6). pap. 9.95 *(978-2-89579-149-2(X),* Owlkids) Owlkids Bks. Inc. CAN. Dist: Publishers Group West (PGW).
—Tank & Fizz: the Case of the Battling Bots, 1 vol. Deas, Mike, illus. 2016. (Tank & Fizz Ser.: 2). (ENG.). 176p. (J). (gr. 3-6). pap. 9.95 *(978-1-4598-0813-3(4))* Orca Bk. Pubs. USA.
O'Donnell, Liam & Battle, Craig. Max Finder Mystery Collected Casebook, Vol. 4. Pérez, Ramón & Owlkids Books Inc. Staff, illus. 2010. (Max Finder Mystery Collected Casebook Ser.: 4). (ENG.). 96p. (J). (gr. 3-6). pap. 9.95 *(978-1-897349-80-9(7))* Owlkids Bks. Inc. CAN. Dist: Publishers Group West (PGW).
Oelschlager, Vanita. Ariel Bradley, Spy for General Washington. 2013. (ENG., Illus.). 56p. (J). (gr. 1-5). pap. 6.99 *(978-0-9832904-8-3(2))* VanitaBooks.
Ogden, Charles. Hot Air. Carton, Rick, illus. 2008. (Edgar & Ellen Nodyssey Ser.: 1). (ENG.). 192p. (J). (gr. 3-7). 9.99 *(978-1-4169-5465-1(1),* Aladdin) Simon & Schuster Children's Publishing.
Ogilvie, Elizabeth. Masquerade at Sea House. 2007. (J). reprint ed. lib. bdg. 28.95 *(978-0-88411-333-1(7))* Amereon Ltd.
O'Hara, Diarmuid H. The Pool. 2004. 184p. pap. 24.95 *(978-1-4137-2116-4(8))* America Star Bks.
Oldman, James. Superhighway. Ingram, Chris, illus. 2012. 184p. pap. *(978-1-78176-206-6(6))* FeedARead.com.
Olds, Barbara Anne. Haven House. Amatrula, Michele, illus. 2007. (ENG.). 141p. (J). pap. 8.95 *(978-0-9744446-0-4(X))* All About Kids Publishing.
O'Leary, Edward J. Murder in the I. R. S. 2003. (YA). per. 18.95 *(978-0-9708590-9-9(0))* First Word Publishing, The.
Olien, Jessica. Shark Detective! Olien, Jessica, illus. 2015. (ENG., Illus.). 32p. (J). (gr. -1-3). 17.99 *(978-0-06-235714-4(X))* HarperCollins Pubs.
Olin, Sean. Wicked Games. 2014. (Wicked Games Ser.: 1). (ENG.). 352p. (YA). (gr. 9). 17.99 *(978-0-06-219237-0(X),* Tegen, Katherine Bks) HarperCollins Pubs.
Oliver, Andrew. Haunted Hill. 2006. (Sam & Stephanie Mystery Ser.). 268p. (J). (gr. 5-9). per. 12.95 *(978-0-9661009-7-6(2))* Adams-Pomeroy Pr.
—If Photos Could Talk. 2005. (Sam & Stephanie Mystery Ser.). 264p. (J). per. 12.95 *(978-0-9661009-6-9(4))* Adams-Pomeroy Pr.
—Scrambled. 2007. 288p. (J). per. 12.95 *(978-0-9661009-8-3(0))* Adams-Pomeroy Pr.
Oliver, Lauren. Panic. 2015. (ENG.). 432p. (YA). (gr. 9). pap. 9.99 *(978-0-06-201456-6(0))* 2014. (J). 137.91 *(978-0-06-230092-8(X))* 2014. (ENG.). 400p. (J). (gr. 9). 17.99 *(978-0-06-201455-9(2))* HarperCollins Pubs.
—Panic. 2015. (YA). lib. bdg. 20.85 *(978-0-606-36509-3(5))* Turtleback Bks.
Oliver, Lauren & Chester, H. C. The Fearsome Firebird. 2017. (Curiosity House Ser.: 3). 336p. (J). (gr. 3-7). 16.99 *(978-0-06-227087-0(7))* HarperCollins Pubs.
—The Screaming Statue. 2017. (Curiosity House Ser.: 2). 384p. (J). (gr. 3-7). pap. 6.99 *(978-0-06-227085-6(0))* HarperCollins Pubs.
—The Shrunken Head. Lacombe, Benjamin, illus. 2015. (Curiosity House Ser.: 1). (ENG.). 368p. (J). (gr. 3-7). 16.99 *(978-0-06-227081-8(8))* HarperCollins Pubs.
Olney, Ross R. Time Dial, 1 vol. 2010. 134p. pap. 24.95 *(978-1-4489-4371-5(X))* America Star Bks.
O'Malley, Kevin. Captain Raptor & the Moon Mystery. O'Brien, Patrick, illus. 2005. (Captain Raptor Ser.). (ENG.). 32p. (J). (gr. k-5). 17.99 *(978-0-8027-8935-8(8),* 9780802789358, Bloomsbury USA Childrens) Bloomsbury Publishing USA.
O'Neil-Andrews, Milly. Bandolines & Bubbles. 2011. 88p. pap. 11.25 *(978-1-4269-3089-8(5))* Trafford Publishing.
Orczy, Emmuska. The Old Man in the Corner. 2008. (J). 8.99 *(978-1-59166-952-4(9))* BJU Pr.
—The Old Man in the Corner. 2008. 188p. pap. 13.95 *(978-1-60664-231-3(6))* Rodgers, Alan Bks.
—The Scarlet Pimpernel. 2008. 208p. 27.95 *(978-1-60664-862-9(4));* pap. 14.95 *(978-1-60664-109-5(3))* Aegypan.
Orlando, Martha Jane. A Trip, a Tryst & a Terror. 2012. 134p. pap. 10.95 *(978-1-939289-03-2(3),* Little Creek Bks.) Jan-Carol Publishing, INC.
Orloff, Karen Kaufman. Nightlight Detective: Big Top Circus Mystery. Smith, Jamie, illus. 2013. 42p. spiral bd. 12.99 *(978-1-4413-1227-3(7))* Peter Pauper Pr. Inc.
—Nightlight Detective: Mystery at the Museum. Smith, Jamie, illus. 2013. 42p. spiral bd. 12.99 *(978-1-4413-1228-0(5))* Peter Pauper Pr. Inc.
Oroge, Sabinah. Oluwatofarati & Friends. 2013. 28p. pap. 9.95 *(978-1-4787-0520-8(5))* Outskirts Pr., Inc.
O'Rourke, Tim. Flashes. 2015. (ENG.). 320p. (J). (gr. 9). 16.99 *(978-0-545-82959-5(3))* Scholastic, Inc.
Orris, Cornelius F. The Curious Adventures of Nigel & Viol. 2010. 94p. 19.99 *(978-1-4500-4463-9(8))* Xlibris Corp.
Orshoski, Paul. We Read Phonics-Who Took the Cookbook? Light, Kelly, illus. 2012. 32p. (J). 9.95 *(978-1-60115-347-0(3));* pap. 4.99 *(978-1-60115-348-7(1))* Treasure Bay, Inc.
O'Ryan, Ellie. The Case of the Digital Deception. 2013. (Club CSI Ser.: 5). (ENG.). 160p. (J). (gr. 3-7). 15.99 *(978-1-4424-7258-7(8));* pap. 6.99 *(978-1-4424-7257-0(X))* Simon Spotlight. (Simon Spotlight).
O'Ryan, Ellie & Lewman, David. The Case of the Disappearing Dogs. 2012. (Club CSI Ser.: 3). (ENG.). 160p. (J). (gr. 3-7). 15.99 *(978-1-4424-4671-7(4));* pap. 7.99 *(978-1-4424-3396-0(5))* Simon Spotlight. (Simon Spotlight).
Osorio, Rick. The Great Adventure of Sally Rock & el Lobo. 2007. (ENG.). 96p. per. 19.95 *(978-1-4241-5869-0(9))* America Star Bks.
Ostow, Micol. GoldenGirl. 2009. (Bradford Ser.). (ENG.). 224p. (YA). (gr. 9-18). pap. 9.99 *(978-1-4169-6118-5(6),* Simon Pulse) Simon Pulse.
Ostow, Micol & Ostow, David. The Devil & Winnie Flynn. 2016. (ENG., Illus.). 336p. (YA). (gr. 9). pap. 10.99 *(978-1-61695-703-2(4),* Soho Teen) Soho Pr., Inc.
Packard, Edward. The Forbidden Castle. Willis, Drew, illus. 2013. (U-Ventures Ser.). (ENG.). 192p. (J). (gr. 3-7). pap. 5.99 *(978-1-4424-3428-8(7),* Simon & Schuster Bks. For Young Readers) Simon & Schuster Bks. For Young Readers.
Packham, Simon. Only We Know. 2016. (ENG.). 240p. (YA). (gr. 7). pap. 9.99 *(978-1-84812-427-1(9))* Bonnier Publishing GBR. Dist: Independent Pubs. Group.
PaleoJoe. The Disappearance of Dinosaur Sue. Casztt-Allen, Wendy, illus. 2006. (PaleoJoe's Dinosaur Detective Club Ser.: 1). (ENG.). 144p. (J). (gr. 2-5). pap. 8.95 *(978-1-934133-03-3(5),* Mackinac Island Press, Inc.) Charlesbridge Publishing, Inc.
PaleoJoe & Casztt-Allen, Wendy. Mysterious Mammoths. 2008. (ENG., Illus.). 200p. (J). (gr. 2-5). pap. 7.95 *(978-1-934133-43-9(4),* Mackinac Island Press, Inc.) Charlesbridge Publishing, Inc.
—Raptor's Revenge. 2007. (ENG.). 184p. (J). (gr. 2-5). pap. 8.95 *(978-1-934133-37-8(X),* Mackinac Island Press, Inc.) Charlesbridge Publishing, Inc.
—Secret Sabertooth. 2007. (PaleoJoe's Dinosaur Detective Club Ser.: 3). (ENG., Illus.). 168p. (J). (gr. 2-5). pap. 8.95 *(978-1-934133-10-1(8),* Mackinac Island Press, Inc.) Charlesbridge Publishing, Inc.
Palund, Linda. The Little Black Dress. 2016. (ENG., Illus.). (J). 24.99 ***(978-1-63477-970-8(3),*** Harmony Ink Pr.) Dreamspinner Pr.
Panda, Jake G. The Case of the Cursed Dodo. 2014. (Illus.). 173p. (J). pap. 8.99 *(978-0-9909391-1-5(1))* Woolley Family Studios.
Pandanas, Ms L. A. The Slinky Luminescence: Two Plus Who? 2013. 84p. pap. *(978-0-9870702-9-6(0))* Reed, Laura.
Pankhurst, Kate. Mariella Mystery Investigates a Cupcake Conundrum. 2014. (Mariella Mysteries Ser.). (ENG., Illus.). 176p. (J). (gr. 2-6). pap. 5.99 *(978-1-4380-0459-4(1))* Barron's Educational Series, Inc.
—Mariella Mystery Investigates a Kitty Calamity. 2015. (Mariella Mysteries Ser.). (ENG., Illus.). 176p. (J). (gr. 2-6). pap. 5.99 *(978-1-4380-0704-5(3))* Barron's Educational Series, Inc.
—Mariella Mystery Investigates the Disappearing Dinner Lady. 2015. (Mariella Mysteries Ser.). (ENG., Illus.). 176p. (J). (gr. 2-6). pap. 5.99 *(978-1-4380-0720-5(5))* Barron's Educational Series, Inc.
—Mariella Mystery Investigates the Ghostly Guinea Pig. 2014. (Mariella Mysteries Ser.). (ENG., Illus.). 176p. (J). (gr. 2-6). pap. 5.99 *(978-1-4380-0460-0(5))* Barron's Educational Series, Inc.
—Mariella Mystery Investigates the Huge Hair Scare. 2014. (Mariella Mysteries Ser.). (ENG., Illus.). 176p. (J). (gr. 2-6). pap. 5.99 *(978-1-4380-0461-7(3))* Barron's Educational Series, Inc.
—Mariella Mystery Investigates the Mystery of the Cursed Poodle. 2014. (Mariella Mysteries Ser.). (ENG., Illus.). 176p. (J). (gr. 2-6). pap. 5.99 *(978-1-4380-0462-4(1))* Barron's Educational Series, Inc.
—Mariella Mystery Investigates the Mystic Mustache. 2016. (Mariella Mysteries Ser.). (ENG., Illus.). 176p. (J). (gr. 2-6). pap. 5.99 *(978-1-4380-0721-2(3))* Barron's Educational Series, Inc.
—Mariella Mystery Investigates the Spaghetti Yeti. 2015. (Mariella Mysteries Ser.). (ENG., Illus.). 176p. (J). (gr. 2-6). pap. 5.99 *(978-1-4380-0705-2(1))* Barron's Educational Series, Inc.
Papp, Robert, illus. The Amazing Mystery Show. 2010. (Boxcar Children Mysteries Ser.: 123). (ENG.). 128p. (J). (gr. 1-5). pap. 6.99 *(978-0-8075-0315-7(0));*No. 123. 14.99 *(978-0-8075-0314-0(2))* Whitman, Albert & Co.
—The Box That Watch Found. 2007. (Boxcar Children Mysteries Ser.: 113). (ENG.). 128p. (J). (gr. 1-5). lib. bdg. 14.99 *(978-0-8075-5568-2(1));* per. 5.99 *(978-0-8075-5569-9(X))* Whitman, Albert & Co.
—The Clue in the Recycling Bin. 2011. (Boxcar Children Mysteries Ser.: 126). (ENG.). 128p. (J). (gr. 1-5). pap. 6.99 *(978-0-8075-1209-8(5))* Whitman, Albert & Co.
—The Clue in the Recycling Bin. 2011. (Boxcar Children Mysteries Ser.: 126). (ENG.). 128p. (J). (gr. 1-5). lib. bdg. 14.99 *(978-0-8075-1208-1(7))* Whitman, Albert & Co.
—The Creature in Ogopogo Lake. 2006. (Boxcar Children Mysteries Ser.: 108). (ENG.). 128p. (J). (gr. 1-5). per. 6.99 *(978-0-8075-1337-8(7))* Whitman, Albert & Co.
—The Cupcake Caper. 2010. (Boxcar Children Mysteries Ser.: 125). (ENG.). 128p. (J). (gr. 1-5). 14.99 *(978-0-8075-1373-6(3));*No. 125. pap. 5.99 *(978-0-8075-1374-3(1))* Whitman, Albert & Co.
—The Game Store Mystery. 2005. (Boxcar Children Mysteries Ser.: 104). (ENG.). (J). (gr. 1-5). 128p. 14.99 *(978-0-8075-2738-2(6));* 144p. per. 6.99 *(978-0-8075-2739-9(4))* Whitman, Albert & Co.
—The Ghost in the First Row, Vol. 112. 2007. (Boxcar Children Mysteries Ser.: 112). (ENG.). 128p. (J). (gr. 1-5). per. 5.99 *(978-0-8075-5567-5(3))* Whitman, Albert & Co.
—The Ghost of the Chattering Bones. 2007. (Boxcar Children Ser.). 120p. 15.00 *(978-0-7569-7611-8(1))* Perfection Learning Corp.
—The Ghost of the Chattering Bones. 2005. (Boxcar Children Mysteries Ser.: 102). (ENG.). 128p. (J). (gr. 1-5). pap. 5.99 *(978-0-8075-0874-9(8))* Whitman, Albert & Co.
—The Giant Yo-Yo Mystery. 2006. (Boxcar Children Mysteries Ser.: 107). (ENG.). 128p. (J). (gr. 1-5). per. 5.99 *(978-0-8075-0879-4(9))* Whitman, Albert & Co.
—The Great Turkey Heist. 2011. (Boxcar Children Mysteries Ser.: 129). (ENG.). (J). (gr. 1-5). 144p. 6.99 *(978-0-8075-3051-1(4));* 128p. lib. bdg. 14.99 *(978-0-8075-3050-4(6))* Whitman, Albert & Co.
—A Horse Named Dragon. 2008. (Boxcar Children Mysteries Ser.: 114). (ENG.). 128p. (J). (gr. 1-5). lib. bdg. 14.99 *(978-0-8075-5571-2(1));* per. 5.99 *(978-0-8075-5572-9(X))* Whitman, Albert & Co.
—Monkey Trouble. 2011. (Boxcar Children Mysteries Ser.: 127). (ENG.). 128p. (J). (gr. 1-5). pap. 5.99 *(978-0-8075-5240-7(2))* Whitman, Albert & Co.
—Monkey Trouble. 2011. (Boxcar Children Mysteries Ser.: 127). (ENG.). 128p. (J). (gr. 1-5). lib. bdg. 14.99 *(978-0-8075-5239-1(9))* Whitman, Albert & Co.
—The Mystery of the Orphan Train. 2005. (Boxcar Children Mysteries Ser.: 105). (ENG.). 128p. (J). (gr. 1-5). lib. bdg. 14.99 *(978-0-8075-5558-3(4));* per. 6.99 *(978-0-8075-5559-0(2))* Whitman, Albert & Co.
—The Pumpkin Head Mystery, No. 124. 2010. (Boxcar Children Mysteries Ser.: 124). (ENG.). 128p. (J). (gr. 1-5). pap. 5.99 *(978-0-8075-6669-5(1))* Whitman, Albert & Co.
—The Rock 'n' Roll Mystery. 2006. (Boxcar Children Mysteries Ser.: 109). (ENG.). 128p. (J). (gr. 1-5). lib. bdg. 14.99 *(978-0-8075-7089-0(3));* per. 5.99 *(978-0-8075-7090-6(7))* Whitman, Albert & Co.
—The Seattle Puzzle. 2007. (Boxcar Children Mysteries Ser.: 111). (ENG.). 128p. (J). (gr. 1-5). lib. bdg. 14.99 *(978-0-8075-5560-6(6));* per. 5.99 *(978-0-8075-5561-3(4))* Whitman, Albert & Co.
—The Secret of the Mask. 2007. (Boxcar Children Mysteries Ser.: 110). (ENG.). 128p. (J). (gr. 1-5). lib. bdg. 14.99 *(978-0-8075-5564-4(9));* per. 5.99 *(978-0-8075-5565-1(7))* Whitman, Albert & Co.
—Spooktacular Special. 2013. (Boxcar Children Mysteries Ser.). (ENG.). 400p. (J). (gr. 1-5). 9.99 *(978-0-8075-7605-2(0))* Whitman, Albert & Co.
—The Spy Game. 2009. (Boxcar Children Mysteries Ser.: 118). (ENG.). 128p. (J). (gr. 1-5). pap. 5.99 *(978-0-8075-7604-5(2))* Whitman, Albert & Co.
—The Spy in the Bleachers. 2010. (Boxcar Children Mysteries Ser.: 122). (ENG.). 128p. (J). (gr. 1-5). 14.99 *(978-0-8075-7606-9(9))* Whitman, Albert & Co.
—The Sword of the Silver Knight. 2005. (Boxcar Children Mysteries Ser.: 103). (ENG.). 128p. (J). (gr. 1-5). per. 6.99 *(978-0-8075-0876-3(4))* Whitman, Albert & Co.
—The Vanishing Passenger. 2006. (Boxcar Children Mysteries Ser.: 106). (ENG.). 128p. (J). (gr. 1-5). 14.99 *(978-0-8075-1066-7(1))* Whitman, Albert & Co.
—The Zombie Project. 2011. (Boxcar Children Mysteries Ser.: 128). (ENG.). 128p. (J). (gr. 1-5). 6.99 *(978-0-8075-9493-3(8));* lib. bdg. 14.99 *(978-0-8075-9492-6(X))* Whitman, Albert & Co.
Papp, Robert & Papp, Kathy, illus. The Pumpkin Head Mystery. 2010. (Boxcar Children Mysteries Ser.: 124). (ENG.). 128p. (J). (gr. 1-5). 14.99 *(978-0-8075-6668-8(3))* Whitman, Albert & Co.
Papp, Robert L., illus. The Dog-Gone Mystery. 2009. (Boxcar Children Mysteries Ser.: 119). (ENG.). 128p. (J). (gr. 1-5). pap. 5.99 *(978-0-8075-1657-7(0));* lib. bdg. 14.99 *(978-0-8075-1658-4(9))* Whitman, Albert & Co.
—The Spy Game. 2009. (Boxcar Children Mysteries Ser.: 118). (ENG.). 128p. (J). (gr. 1-5). 14.99 *(978-0-8075-7603-8(4))* Whitman, Albert & Co.
—Superstar Watch. 2009. (Boxcar Children Mysteries Ser.: 121). (ENG.). 128p. (J). (gr. 1-5). pap. 5.99 *(978-0-8075-7668-7(9));* lib. bdg. 14.99 *(978-0-8075-7667-0(0))* Whitman, Albert & Co.
—The Vampire Mystery. 2009. (Boxcar Children Mysteries Ser.: 120). (ENG.). 128p. (J). (gr. 1-5). pap. 5.99 *(978-0-8075-8461-3(4));* lib. bdg. 14.99 *(978-0-8075-8460-6(6))* Whitman, Albert & Co.
Paris, Harper. The Mystery Across the Secret Bridge. Calo, Marcos, illus. 2015. (Greetings from Somewhere Ser.: 7). (ENG.). 128p. (J). (gr. k-4). pap. 5.99 *(978-1-4814-2367-0(3),* Little Simon) Little Simon.
—The Mystery at the Coral Reef. Calo, Marcos, illus. 2015. (Greetings from Somewhere Ser.: 8). (ENG.). 128p. (J). (gr. k-4). pap. 5.99 *(978-1-4814-2370-0(3),* Little Simon) Little Simon.
—The Mystery in the Forbidden City. Calo, Marcos, illus. 2014. (Greetings from Somewhere Ser.: 4). (ENG.). 128p. (J). (gr. k-2). pap. 5.99 *(978-1-4814-0299-6(4),* Little Simon) Little Simon.
—The Mystery of the Gold Coin. Calo, Marcos, illus. 2014. (Greetings from Somewhere Ser.: 1). (ENG.). 128p. (J). (gr. k-4). pap. 5.99 *(978-1-4424-9718-4(1),* Little Simon) Little Simon.
—The Mystery of the Icy Paw Prints. Calo, Marcos, illus. 2015. (Greetings from Somewhere Ser.: 9). (ENG.). 128p. (J). (gr. k-4). pap. 5.99 *(978-1-4814-2373-1(8),* Little Simon) Little Simon.
—The Mystery of the Mosaic. Calo, Marcos, illus. 2014. (Greetings from Somewhere Ser.: 2). (ENG.). 128p. (J). (gr. k-2). pap. 5.99 *(978-1-4424-9721-4(1),* Little Simon) Little Simon.
—The Mystery of the Secret Society. Calo, Marcos, illus. 2016. (Greetings from Somewhere Ser.: 10). (ENG.). 128p. (J). (gr. k-4). pap. 5.99 *(978-1-4814-5171-0(5),* Little Simon) Little Simon.
—The Mystery of the Stolen Painting. Calo, Marcos, illus. 2014. (Greetings from Somewhere Ser.: 3). (ENG.). 128p. (J). (gr. k-2). pap. 5.99 *(978-1-4814-0296-5(X),* Little Simon) Little Simon.
—The Mystery of the Suspicious Spices. Calo, Marcos, illus. 2014. (Greetings from Somewhere Ser.: 6). (ENG.). 128p. (J). (gr. k-4). pap. 5.99 *(978-1-4814-1467-8(4),* Little Simon) Little Simon.
Park, Alexander. The Thunderbolts & the Circle of Power. 2012. 316p. pap. 25.86 *(978-1-60746-939-1(1))* FastPrncil, Inc.
Parker, Amy Christine. Astray (Gated Sequel) 2015. (ENG.). 352p. (YA). (gr. 9). pap. 9.99 *(978-0-449-81605-9(2),* Ember) Random Hse. Children's Bks.
Parker, Robert B. The Boxer & the Spy. 2009. (ENG.). 240p. (YA). (gr. 9-18). pap. 8.99 *(978-0-14-241439-2(5),* Puffin Books) Penguin Young Readers Group.
Parkhurst, Johanna. Every Inferno. 2016. (ENG., Illus.). (J). 24.99 ***(978-1-63533-009-0(2),*** Harmony Ink Pr.) Dreamspinner Pr.
Parkin, Lance & Jones, Mark. Dark Matters: An Unofficial & Unauthorised Guide to Philip Pullman's Dark Materials Trilogy. 2005. (ENG.). 272p. (YA). mass mkt. *(978-0-7535-1025-4(1),* Virgin Books Limited) Ebury Publishing GBR. Dist: Independent Pubs. Group.
Parkinson, Curtis. Death in Kingsport. 2007. (ENG.). 224p. (YA). (gr. 5-9). per. 11.95 *(978-0-88776-827-9(X),* Tundra Bks.) Tundra Bks. CAN. Dist: Penguin Random Hse. LLC.
Parsons, Carol. Mystery at Eagle Harbor Lighthouse. 2006. (J). pap. 11.95 *(978-1-59705-985-5(4))* Wings ePress, Inc.
Parsons, Caroline Renee. The Coffins in the Basement. 2008. 134p. pap. 24.95 *(978-1-60563-140-0(X))* America Star Bks.
Parsons, Tom. Pinky the Rat at the Brussels Sprout Museum. 2007. 194p. 27.76 *(978-1-4303-1538-4(5))* Lulu Pr., Inc.
Parus, M. V. The Adventures of Mamma Simone, Jodie & Zed: The Mystery of the Pirate's Lost Treasure. 2006. 115p. (YA). per. 12.95 *(978-1-58374-148-1(8))* Chicago Spectrum Pr.
Pasha, Georgia. Jelly Bean & Key Mystery. 2005. 17.00 *(978-0-8059-9909-9(4),* RoseDog Bks.) Dorrance Publishing Co., Inc.
Pastis, Stephan. Mistakes Were Made. Pastis, Stephan, illus. 2013. (Timmy Failure Ser.: No. 1). (ENG., Illus.). 304p. (J). (gr. 3-7). 14.99 *(978-0-7636-6050-5(7));* 100.00 *(978-0-7636-6689-7(0))* Candlewick Pr.
—Now Look What You've Done. Pastis, Stephan, illus. 2014. (Timmy Failure Ser.: No. 2). (ENG., Illus.). 288p. (J). (gr. 3-7). 14.99 *(978-0-7636-6051-2(5))* Candlewick Pr.
—Now Look What You've Done. 2016. (Timmy Failure Ser.: 2). lib. bdg. 18.40 *(978-0-606-37947-2(9))* Turtleback Bks.
—Timmy Failure: Mistakes Were Made. Pastis, Stephan, illus. 2015. (Timmy Failure Ser.). (ENG., Illus.). 320p. (J). (gr. 3-7). pap. 7.99 *(978-0-7636-6927-0(X))* Candlewick Pr.
—Timmy Failure: Now Look What You've Done. Pastis, Stephan, illus. 2016. (Timmy Failure Ser.: 2). (ENG., Illus.). 304p. (J). (gr. 3-7). pap. 7.99 *(978-0-7636-8014-5(1))* Candlewick Pr.
—Timmy Failure: the Book You're Not Supposed to Have. Pastis, Stephan, illus. 2016. (Timmy Failure Ser.). (ENG., Illus.). 304p. (J). (gr. 3-7). 14.99 *(978-0-7636-9004-5(X))* Candlewick Pr.
—Timmy Failure: the Cat Stole My Pants. Pastis, Stephan, illus. 2017. (Timmy Failure Ser.: 6). (ENG., Illus.). 288p. (J). (gr. 3-7). 14.99 *(978-0-7636-9733-4(8))* Candlewick Pr.
Pastor, Norma. The Young Alchemists & the Vatican's Legion of Evil. 2013. 472p. pap. 30.95 *(978-1-4633-6179-2(3))* Palibrio.
Patchin, Frank Gee. The Pony Rider Boys in the Grand Canyon: The Mystery of Bright Angel Gulch. 2007. (ENG.). 158p. pap. 19.99 *(978-1-4264-7084-4(3));* 176p. pap. 21.99 *(978-1-4264-7160-5(2))* Creative Media Partners, LLC.
Paterson, Katherine. La Busqueda de Park. 2003. (Katherine Patterson Ser.).Tr. of Park's Quest. (SPA., Illus.). 208p. (J). (gr. 4-7). 9.95 *(978-84-239-2816-3(0),* EC3399) Espasa Calpe, S.A. ESP. Dist: Planeta Publishing Corp.
Patron, Susan. Behind the Masks: The Diary of Angeline Reddy - Bodie, California 1880. 2012. (Dear America Ser.). (ENG.). 304p. (J). (gr. 3-7). 12.99 *(978-0-545-30437-5(7))* Scholastic, Inc.
Patterson, Eric. Something Lurking in the Bell Tower. Christopher, Wright, illus. 2007. 99p. (J). pap. 6.95 *(978-0-9797106-1-2(8))* Avid Readers Publishing Group.
Patterson, James & Paetro, Maxine. Confessions: The Paris Mysteries. 2014. (Confessions Ser.). (ENG.). 320p. (YA). (gr. 7-17). 18.00 *(978-0-316-37084-4(3),* Jimmy Patterson) Little Brown & Co.
—Confessions: The Private School Murders. 2013. 422p. (YA). *(978-0-316-24263-9(2))* Little Brown & Co.
—Confessions of a Murder Suspect. 2014. (Confessions Ser.: 1). (ENG.). 352p. (gr. 7-17). mass mkt. 8.00 *(978-1-4555-4774-6(3),* Jimmy Patterson) 2013. (ENG.). 400p. (J). (gr. 7-17). pap. 10.00 *(978-0-316-20700-3(4),* Jimmy Patterson) 2012. (Confessions Ser.: 1). (ENG.). 384p. (YA). (gr. 7-17). 19.99 *(978-0-316-20698-3(9),* Jimmy Patterson) 2012. 372p. (J). 11.99 *(978-0-316-22641-7(6))* 2012. (Confessions Ser.: 1). (ENG.). 400p. (YA). (gr. 7-17). 31.99 *(978-0-316-22418-5(9),* Jimmy Patterson) Little Brown & Co.
—Confessions of a Murder Suspect. 2013. (Confessions Ser.: 1). lib. bdg. 20.85 *(978-0-606-32278-2(7),* Turtleback) Turtleback Bks.
—Confessions: the Murder of an Angel. 2015. (Confessions Ser.: 4). (ENG.). 304p. (YA). (gr. 7-12). 18.00 *(978-0-316-30102-2(7),* Jimmy Patterson) Little Brown & Co.
—The Paris Mysteries. l.t. ed. 2014. (Confessions Ser.: 3). (ENG.). 352p. (YA). (gr. 7-17). 30.99 *(978-0-316-40963-6(4),* Jimmy Patterson) Little Brown & Co.
—The Paris Mysteries. 2015. (Confessions Ser.: 3). (YA). lib. bdg. 20.85 *(978-0-606-37526-9(0))* Turtleback Bks.
—The Private School Murders. 2015. (Confessions Ser.: 2). (ENG.). 400p. mass mkt. 8.00 *(978-1-4555-5946-6(6),* Jimmy Patterson) Grand Central Publishing.
—The Private School Murders. (Confessions Ser.: 2). (ENG.). (YA). (gr. 7-17). 2014. 448p. pap. 10.00 *(978-0-316-20764-5(0))* 2013. 448p. 18.00 *(978-0-316-20765-2(9))* 2013. 480p. 22.00 *(978-0-316-23992-9(5))* Little Brown & Co. (Jimmy Patterson).
—The Private School Murders. 2014. (Confessions Ser.: 2). (YA). lib. bdg. 20.85 *(978-0-606-35945-0(1))* Turtleback Bks.
Pattison, Caroline Rennie. The Whole, Entire, Complete Truth. 2006. (ENG.). 180p. (YA). pap. 12.99 *(978-1-55002-583-5(X),* Dundurn Pr.) Dundurn CAN. Dist: Ingram Publisher Services.
Patton, Donna Alice. The Gift of Summer Snow: A Tale from the Garden of Mysteries. 2010. (Illus.). ix, 133p. (J). *(978-0-9826867-3-7(0))* Philothea Pr.
Paul, Naomi. Code Name Komiko. 2014. 285p. 19.95 *(978-1-62324-023-3(9))* Enslow Pubs., Inc.
Pauley, Kimberly. Cat Girl's Day Off, 1 vol. 2012. (ENG.). 336p. (YA). 17.95 *(978-1-60060-883-4(3),* Tu Bks.) Lee & Low Bks., Inc.
Paulits, John. Philip & the Case of the Mistaken Identity & Philip & the Baby. 2007. (ENG.). 150p. (YA). pap. 10.95 *(978-1-59705-897-1(1))* Wings ePress, Inc.

MNO

Paulson, Michael W. The Baker Street Bunch & the Missing Pig Mystery. l.t. ed. 2004. (Illus.). 90p. (J). per. 3.95 (978-0-9754241-1-7(4)) MiMar Publishing.

Paulson, Michael William. The Baker Street Bunch & the Hidden Map Mystery. 2005. (Illus.). (J). per. (978-0-9754241-4-8(9)) MiMar Publishing.

—The Baker Street Bunch & the Missing Bracelet Mystery. 2005. (Illus.). (J). per. (978-0-9754241-2-4(2)) MiMar Publishing.

—The Baker Street Bunch & the Missing Pie Mystery. 2005. (J). per. (978-0-9754241-9-3(X)) MiMar Publishing.

Pavanello, Roberto. The Dancing Vampire. Zeni, Marco, tr. from ITA. Pisapia, Blasco & Brughera, Pamela, illus. 2012. (Echo & the Bat Pack Ser.). (ENG.). 128p. (gr. 2-3). 25.32 (978-1-4342-3837-5(7), Echo & the Bat Pack) Stone Arch Bks.

—The Ghost of Dr. Mold. Zeni, Marco, tr. from ITA. Pisapia, Blasco & Brughera, Pamela, illus. 2012. (Echo & the Bat Pack Ser.). (ENG.). 128p. (gr. 2-3). 25.32 (978-1-4342-3834-4(2), Echo & the Bat Pack) Stone Arch Bks.

—King Tut's Grandmother, 1 vol. Zeni, Marco, tr. from ITA. Pisapia, Blasco & Brughera, Pamela, illus. 2012. (Echo & the Bat Pack Ser.). (ENG.). 128p. (gr. 2-3). lib. bdg. 25.32 (978-1-4342-3823-8(7), Echo & the Bat Pack) Stone Arch Bks.

—The Midnight Witches, 1 vol. Zeni, Marco, tr. from ITA. Pisapia, Blasco & Brughera, Pamela, illus. 2012. (Echo & the Bat Pack Ser.). (ENG.). 128p. (gr. 2-3). 9.95 (978-1-4342-4246-4(3)); lib. bdg. 25.32 (978-1-4342-3822-1(9), Echo & the Bat Pack) Stone Arch Bks.

—The Thing in the Sewers, 1 vol. Zeni, Marco, tr. from ITA. Pisapia, Blasco & Brughera, Pamela, illus. 2012. (Echo & the Bat Pack Ser.). (ENG.). 128p. (gr. 2-3). 9.95 (978-1-4342-4247-1(1)); 25.32 (978-1-4342-3824-5(5), Echo & the Bat Pack) Stone Arch Bks.

—Treasure in the Graveyard, 1 vol. Zeni, Marco, tr. from ITA. Pisapia, Blasco & Brughera, Pamela, illus. 2012. (Echo & the Bat Pack Ser.). (ENG.). 128p. (gr. 2-3). 9.95 (978-1-4342-4248-8(X)) Stone Arch Bks.

Payjack, Amy J. The Valorean. 2012. 426p. 34.99 (978-1-4771-5239-3(3)); pap. 23.99 (978-1-4771-5238-6(5)) Xlibris Corp.

Payson, Howard. Boy Scouts' Mountain Camp. 2005. (Illus.). pap. 28.95 (978-1-885529-54-1(6)) Stevens Publishing.

Peacock, Kathleen. Hemlock. (Hemlock Trilogy Ser.: 1). (ENG.). (YA). (gr. 9). 2013. 432p. pap. 9.99 (978-0-06-204866-0(X)) 2012. 416p. 17.99 (978-0-06-204865-3(1)) HarperCollins Pubs. (Tegen, Katherine Bks).

—Thornhill. (Hemlock Trilogy Ser.: 2). (ENG.). (YA). (gr. 9). 2015. 368p. pap. 9.99 (978-0-06-204869-1(4)) 2013. 352p. 17.99 (978-0-06-204868-4(6)) HarperCollins Pubs. (Tegen, Katherine Bks).

—Willowgrove. 2015. (Hemlock Trilogy Ser.: 3). (ENG.). 384p. (YA). (gr. 9). 17.99 (978-0-06-204871-4(6), Tegen, Katherine Bks) HarperCollins Pubs.

Peacock, Shane. Eye of the Crow: The Boy Sherlock Holmes, His 1st Case. 2007. (Boy Sherlock Holmes Ser.). (ENG.). 264p. (YA). (gr. 5-9). 19.95 (978-0-88776-850-7(4), Tundra Bks.) Tundra Bks. CAN. Dist: Penguin Random Hse. LLC.

—The Secret Fiend: The Boy Sherlock Holmes, His Fourth Case. 2012. (Boy Sherlock Holmes Ser.). (ENG., Illus.). 262p. (YA). (gr. 5-9). pap. 9.95 (978-1-77049-385-8(9), Tundra Bks.) Tundra Bks. CAN. Dist: Penguin Random Hse. LLC.

—Vanishing Girl: The Boy Sherlock Holmes, His 3rd Case. 2010. (Boy Sherlock Holmes Ser.). (ENG., Illus.). 326p. (YA). (gr. 5-9). pap. 11.99 (978-1-77049-234-9(8), Tundra Bks.) Tundra Bks. CAN. Dist: Penguin Random Hse. LLC.

Pearce, Bryony. The Weight of Souls. 2013. (ENG.). 288p. (YA). 17.99 (978-1-908844-64-4(7), Strange Chemistry) Watkins Media Limited GBR. Dist: Penguin Random Hse. LLC.

Pearl, Beverly. Poison Ivy. 2008. 98p. pap. 9.99 (978-1-4357-1386-4(9)) Lulu Pr., Inc.

Pearson, Ridley. Lock & Key: the Downward Spiral. 2017. (Lock & Key Ser.: 2). 432p. (J). (gr. 3-7). 17.99 **(978-0-06-239904-5(7))** HarperCollins Pubs.

—Lock & Key: the Initiation. 2017. (Lock & Key Ser.: 1). 384p. (J). (gr. 3-7). pap. 9.99 **(978-0-06-239902-1(0))** HarperCollins Pubs.

Pease, Elaine. Tallie's Christmas Lights Surprise!, 1 vol. Crum, Anna-Maria, illus. 2012. (ENG.). 32p. (J). (gr. k-3). 16.99 (978-1-4556-1586-5(2)) Pelican Publishing Co., Inc.

Peckham, Lori, ed. Guide's Greatest Mystery Stories. 2007. 155p. per. 11.99 (978-0-8280-2038-1(8)) Review & Herald Publishing Assn.

Penn, Audrey. Mystery at Blackbeard's Cove. Howard, Philip & Miller, Joshua, illus. 2004. (ENG.). 263p. (J). (gr. 2-7). per. 7.95 (978-1-933718-09-5(9)) Tanglewood Pr.

—Mystery at Blackbeard's Cove. Howard, Philip & Miller, Josh, illus. 2004. (ENG.). 200p. (J). (gr. 3-7). 14.95 (978-0-9749303-1-2(8)) Tanglewood Pr.

Penn, Audrey & Miller, Joshua. Blackbeard & the Gift of Silence. 2009. (ENG.). 350p. (J). (gr. 2-7). pap. 8.95 (978-1-933718-32-3(3)) Tanglewood Pr.

—Blackbeard & the Sandstone Pillar: When Lightning Strikes. 2009. (ENG.). 350p. (J). (gr. 2-7). pap. 8.95 (978-1-933718-31-6(5)) Tanglewood Pr.

Pennell, Kathleen. The Phantom Stallion. Pennell, Lauren, illus. 2003. (Pony Investigators Ser.: Vol. 4). 118p. (J). (gr. 3-7). pap. 5.95 (978-1-930353-73-2(1)) Masthof Pr.

—The Secret Passage: Pony Investigators Series #5. 2005. (Pony Investigators Ser.: 5). (Illus.). 108p. (J). pap. 5.95 (978-1-932864-42-7(3)) Masthof Pr.

Penner, Stephen. Professor Barrister's Dinosaur Mysteries #1: The Case of the Truncated Troodon. Penner, Stephen, illus. 2010. (Illus.). 44p. pap. 19.25 (978-1-60888-005-8(2)) Nimble Bks. LLC.

—Professor Barrister's Dinosaur Mysteries #2: The Case of the Armored Allosaurus. 2010. 54p. pap. 19.60 (978-1-60888-018-8(4)) Nimble Bks. LLC.

Penney, Shannon. Decodes a Mystery. 2005. 22p. (978-0-439-67841-4(2)) Scholastic, Inc.

Peralta, Joaquin. An Almost Private Eye: Mystery of the Starfighter. 2008. 260p. (YA). (gr. 8-18). per. 17.00 (978-1-934376-17-1(5)) Balona Bks.

Perelman, Helen. Marshmallow Mystery. Waters, Erica-Jane, illus. 2014. (Candy Fairies Ser.: 12). (ENG.). 128p. (J). (gr. 2-5). 15.99 (978-1-4424-6500-8(X)); pap. 5.99 (978-1-4424-5301-2(X)) Simon & Schuster Children's Publishing. (Aladdin).

Peretti, Frank E. Hangman's Curse. 2008. 352p. (YA). mass mkt. 7.99 (978-1-4003-1016-6(4)) Nelson, Thomas Inc.

—Nightmare Academy. 2008. 352p. (YA). mass mkt. 7.99 (978-1-4003-1017-3(2)) Nelson, Thomas Inc.

Peril at Granite Peak. 2014. (Hardy Boys Adventures Ser.: 5). (ENG., Illus.). 160p. (J). (gr. 3-7). pap. 6.99 (978-1-4424-9395-7(X), Aladdin) Simon & Schuster Children's Publishing.

Perkins, T. J. Image in the Tapestry: A Kim & Kelly Mystery. 2005. (Illus.). 155p. (YA). 10.99 (978-0-9777538-3-3(2)) GumShoe Press.

—In the Grand Scheme of Things: A Kim & Kelly Mystery. 2007. (Illus.). 151p. (YA). 10.99 (978-0-9777538-4-0(0)) GumShoe Press.

—Mystery of the Attic. 2006. (Illus.). 113p. (YA). 10.99 (978-0-9777538-6-4(7)) GumShoe Press.

—The Secret in Phantom Forest: A Kim & Kelly Mystery. 2004. (Illus.). 130p. (YA). 10.99 (978-0-9777538-1-9(6)) GumShoe Press.

—Wound Too Tight. 2006. (Illus.). 141p. (YA). 10.99 (978-0-9777538-5-7(9)) GumShoe Press.

Perkins, TJ. Fantasies Are Murder: A Kim & Kelly Mystery. novel ed. 2005. (Illus.). 148p. (YA). 10.99 (978-0-9777538-0-2(8)) GumShoe Press.

—Trade Secret: A Kim & Kelly Mystery. 2004. (Illus.). 175p. (YA). 10.99 (978-0-9777538-2-6(4)) GumShoe Press.

Perry, Phyllis J. The Secret of the Silver Key. Lipking, Ron, illus. 2003. (Fribble Mouse Library Mystery Ser.). 90p. (J). pap. 16.95 (978-1-932146-03-5(2)) Highsmith Inc.

—The Secrets of the Rock. Lipking, Ron, illus. 2004. (Fribble Mouse Library Mystery Ser.). 96p. (J). 16.95 (978-1-932146-22-6(9), 1237661) Highsmith Inc.

Perry, R. W. Kelly Mccabe in Slow Boat to Terror. 2003. 160p. (J). (gr. 3-6). pap. 11.95 (978-0-9745522-0-0(8), Greenleaf Book Group Pr.) Greenleaf Book Group.

Peters, Tony. Kids on a Case: The Case of the Ten Grand Kidnapping. 2008. 84p. pap. 9.95 (978-1-60693-173-8(3), Eloquent Bks.) Strategic Book Publishing & Rights Agency (SBPRA).

Peterson Haddix, Margaret. EL DESAFÍO FINAL: THE 39 CLUES 10. 2013. (SPA.). 304p. (J). pap. 14.99 (978-84-08-10876-4(X)) Noguer y Caralt Editores, S. A. ESP. Dist: Lectorum Pubns., Inc.

Peterson, Paige. Logic Lotty: The Fortune Teller's Spoon. Sabater, Gaspar, illus. 2015. (ENG.). 82p. (J). pap. 6.99 (978-0-9907895-0-5(0)) Hollingale Bks. LLC.

Peterson, Shelley. Stagestruck: The Saddle Creek Series. 2017. (Saddle Creek Ser.: 1). (ENG.). 344p. (YA). pap. 12.99 **(978-1-4597-3945-1(0))** Dundurn CAN. Dist: Ingram Publisher Services.

Pettit, Karen. The Mystery of the Screecher Creature: A Shandon's Ivy League Mystery. 2006. (J). per. 14.95 (978-1-59872-666-4(8)) Instant Pub.

Petrucha, Stefan. The Demon of River Heights. Murase, Sho, illus. 2005. (Nancy Drew: Girl Detective Ser.). 88p. (gr. 3-8). 24.21 (978-1-59961-057-3(4)) Spotlight.

—The Haunted Dollhouse. Murase, Sho, illus. 2005. (Nancy Drew: Girl Detective Ser.). 88p. (gr. 3-7). 24.21 (978-1-59961-059-7(0)) Spotlight.

—Mr. Cheeters Is Missing. 6th rev. ed. 2006. (Nancy Drew Graphic Novels: Girl Detective Ser.: 6). (ENG., Illus.). 96p. (J). (gr. 3-7). pap. 7.95 (978-1-59707-030-0(0), 9781597070300) Papercutz.

—The Nancy Drew Diaries. 2014. (Nancy Drew Diaries). (ENG., Illus.). 176p. (J). (gr. 3-7). pap. 9.99 (978-1-59707-501-5(9), 9781597075015) Papercutz.

—Ripper. 2013. (ENG.). 432p. (YA). (gr. 7). pap. 9.99 (978-0-14-242418-6(8), Speak) Penguin Young Readers Group.

—Writ in Stone. Murase, Sho, illus. 2005. (Nancy Drew: Girl Detective Ser.). 88p. (gr. 3-9). 24.21 (978-1-59961-058-0(2)) Spotlight.

Petrucha, Stefan & Kinney, Sarah. City under the Basement. Murase, Sho, illus. 2009. (Nancy Drew Graphic Novels: Girl Detective Ser.: 18). (ENG.). 96p. (J). (gr. 3-7). pap. 7.95 (978-1-59707-154-3(4), 9781597071543); 18th ed. 12.95 (978-1-59707-155-0(2), 9781597071550) Papercutz.

—High School Musical Mystery. 2010. (Nancy Drew Graphic Novels: Girl Detective Ser.). (ENG., Illus.). 96p. (J). (gr. 3-7). pap. 8.99 (978-1-59707-178-9(1), 9781597071789) Papercutz.

—Nancy Drew: High School Musical Mystery II - "The Lost Verse" 2010. (Nancy Drew Graphic Novels: Girl Detective Ser.). (ENG., Illus.). 96p. (J). (gr. 3-7). pap. 8.99 (978-1-59707-195-6(1), 9781597071956) Papercutz.

—Night of the Living Chatchke. 2009. (Nancy Drew Graphic Novels: Girl Detective Ser.). (ENG., Illus.). 96p. (J). (gr. 3-7). pap. 7.95 (978-1-59707-143-7(9), 9781597071437) Papercutz.

—Night of the Living Chatchke. Murase, Sho, illus. 17th ed. 2009. (Nancy Drew Graphic Novels: Girl Detective Ser.: 17). (ENG.). 96p. (J). (gr. 3-7). 12.95 (978-1-59707-144-4(7), 9781597071444) Papercutz.

—Sleight of Dan. 14th ed. 2008. (Nancy Drew Graphic Novels: Girl Detective Ser.: 14). (ENG., Illus.). 112p. (J). (gr. 3-7). pap. 7.95 (978-1-59707-107-9(2), 9781597071079) Papercutz.

—Vampire Slayer, No. 2. 2010. (Nancy Drew the New Case Files Ser.). (ENG., Illus.). 64p. (J). (gr. 3-7). pap. 6.99 (978-1-59707-233-5(8), 9781597072335) Papercutz.

—What Goes Up... 2009. (Nancy Drew Graphic Novels: Girl Detective Ser.: 16). (ENG., Illus.). 96p. (J). (gr. 3-7). 12.95 (978-1-59707-135-2(8), 9781597071352) Papercutz.

Petrucha, Stefan & Pendleton, Thomas. Wicked Dead: Skin. (Wicked Dead Ser.). 224p. (J). pap. 7.99 (978-0-06-113854-6(1), HarperTeen) HarperCollins Pubs.

Petrucha, Stefan, et al. The Fake Heir. Ross, Daniel Vaughn, illus. 2006. (J). (978-1-59707-060-7(2)) Papercutz.

Petty, Heather. Final Fall. 2017. (YA). pap. **(978-1-4814-2310-6(X)**, Simon & Schuster Bks. For Young Readers) Simon & Schuster Bks. For Young Readers.

Petty, Heather. Lock & Mori. 2016. (Lock & Mori Ser.). (ENG.). 272p. (YA). (gr. 9). pap. 10.99 (978-1-4814-2304-5(5)) Simon & Schuster, Inc.

Petty, Heather W. Mind Games. 2016. (Lock & Mori Ser.). (ENG., Illus.). 304p. (YA). (gr. 9). 17.99 (978-1-4814-2306-9(1), Simon & Schuster Bks. For Young Readers) Simon & Schuster Bks. For Young Readers.

Pfeffer, Susan Beth. Revenge of the Aztecs. 2004. 118p. (J). lib. bdg. 16.92 (978-1-4242-0763-3(0)) Fitzgerald Bks.

Pfitsch, Patricia Curtis. Riding the Flume. 2004. (ENG., Illus.). 240p. (J). (gr. 5-9). pap. 11.99 (978-0-689-86692-0(5), Simon & Schuster/Paula Wiseman Bks.) Simon & Schuster/Paula Wiseman Bks.

Pflugfelder, Bob & Hockensmith, Steve. Nick & Tesla's Solar-Powered Showdown: A Mystery with Sun-Powered Gadgets You Can Build Yourself. 2016. (Nick & Tesla Ser.). (ENG., Illus.). 264p. (J). (gr. 4-7). 12.95 (978-1-59474-866-0(7)) Quirk Bks.

—Nick & Tesla's Special Effects Spectacular: A Mystery with Animatronics, Alien Makeup, Camera Gear, & Other Movie Magic You Can Make Yourself! 2015. (Nick & Tesla Ser.: 5). (ENG.). 256p. (J). (gr. 4-7). 12.95 (978-1-59474-760-1(1)) Quirk Bks.

Pfoutz, Sally. Missing Person. 2009. 192p. (gr. 7-18). pap. 12.95 (978-1-4401-5108-8(3)) iUniverse, Inc.

The Phantom of Nantucket. 2014. (Nancy Drew Diaries: 7). (ENG., Illus.). 192p. (J). (gr. 3-7). pap. 6.99 (978-1-4814-0015-2(0), Aladdin) Simon & Schuster Children's Publishing.

Phillips, Gin. A Little Bit of Spectacular. 2015. (ENG.). 176p. (J). (gr. 5). 16.99 (978-0-8037-3837-9(4), Dial Bks) Penguin Young Readers Group.

Phillips, Grant R. Jay Walker & the Case of the Missing Action Figure. 2004. (J). pap. 10.95 (978-0-9749608-4-5(5)) Quiet Storm Publishing Group.

Pierson, Jan. The Haunted Horse of Gold Hill. 2005. (Ghostowners Ser.: Vol. 4). (Illus.). 109p. (J). per. 9.95 (978-0-9721800-3-0(6)) WildWest Publishing.

Pike, Aprilynne. Sleep No More. 2014. (ENG.). 352p. (YA). (gr. 8). 17.99 (978-0-06-199903-1(2), HarperTeen) HarperCollins Pubs.

Pike, Christopher, pseud. Chain Letter: Chain Letter; the Ancient Evil. 2013. (ENG., Illus.). 496p. (J). (gr. 9). pap. 12.99 (978-1-4424-7215-0(4), Simon Pulse) Simon Pulse.

—Remember Me: Her Death Will Not Go Unpunished... 2010. (Remember Me Ser.: Vols. 1-3). (ENG., Illus.). 848p. (YA). (gr. 9). pap. 9.99 (978-1-4424-0596-7(1), Simon Pulse) Simon Pulse.

—To Die For. 2010. (ENG.). 416p. (J). (gr. 9-9). pap. 9.99 (978-0-545-26434-1(0)) Scholastic, Inc.

Pitcher, Chelsea. The S-Word. 2013. (ENG.). 320p. pap. 19.99 (978-1-4516-9516-8(0), Gallery Bks.) Gallery Bks.

Pitt, Darrell. The Broken Sun. 2015. (Jack Mason Adventure Ser.). (ENG., Illus.). 304p. (J). (gr. 2-7). 7.99 (978-1-922182-16-6(8)) Text Publishing Co. AUS. Dist: Consortium Bk. Sales & Distribution.

—The Monster Within. 2015. (Jack Mason Adventure Ser.). (ENG., Illus.). 264p. (J). (gr. 2-7). 7.99 (978-1-922182-87-6(7)) Text Publishing Co. AUS. Dist: Consortium Bk. Sales & Distribution.

Platt, Kin. Big Max & the Mystery of the Missing Giraffe. Cravath, Lynne Avril, illus. (I Can Read Level 2 Ser.). 64p. (J). 2006. (ENG.). (gr. k-3). pap. 3.99 (978-0-06-009920-6(8)) 2005. (gr. -1). 15.99 (978-0-06-009918-3(6)) 2005. (gr. -1 — 1). lib. bdg. 17.89 (978-0-06-009919-0(4)) HarperCollins Pubs.

Podos, Rebecca. The Mystery of Hollow Places. 2016. 304p. (YA). (gr. 9). 17.99 (978-0-06-237334-2(X)) HarperCollins Pubs.

Poe, Edgar Allen. Edgar Allan Poe's Tales of Death & Dementia. Grimly, Gris, illus. 2009. (ENG.). 144p. (J). (gr. 6-9). 19.99 (978-1-4169-5025-7(7), Atheneum Bks. for Young Readers) Simon & Schuster Children's Publishing.

Pohl-Weary, Emily. Not Your Ordinary Wolf Girl, 0 vols. 2013. (ENG.). 224p. (YA). (gr. 9-12). pap. 9.99 (978-1-4778-1688-2(7), 9781477816882, Amazon Children's Publishing) Amazon Publishing.

Polak, Monique. All In, 1 vol. 2006. (Lorimer SideStreets Ser.). (ENG.). 168p. (YA). (gr. 9-12). 9.95 (978-1-55028-912-1(8), 9781550289121) Lorimer, James & Co., Ltd., Pubs. CAN. Dist: Casemate Pubs. & Bk. Distributors, LLC.

Polan, Alex. Catching the Jigglypuff Thief. 2016. (Unofficial Adventures for Pokemon GO Players Ser.: 1). lib. bdg. 18.40 **(978-0-606-39657-8(8))** Turtleback Bks.

Polan, Alex. Catching the Jigglypuff Thief: PokéStop Stories, Book One. 2016. (ENG.). 112p. (J). (gr. 1-7). pap. 7.99 (978-1-5107-2157-9(6), Sky Pony Pr.) Skyhorse Publishing Co., Inc.

Pollock, J. A. Titus & Otis & the Arctic Adventure. 2009. 151p. pap. 12.00 (978-0-557-03427-7(2)) Lulu Pr., Inc.

Ponti, James. Framed! 2016. (Framed! Ser.: 1). (ENG., Illus.). 304p. (J). (gr. 3-7). 17.99 (978-1-4814-3630-4(9), Aladdin) Simon & Schuster Children's Publishing.

Ponti, James. Vanished! 2017. (Framed! Ser.: 2). (ENG., Illus.). 384p. (J). (gr. 3-7). 16.99 **(978-1-4814-3633-5(3)**, Aladdin) Simon & Schuster Children's Publishing.

Poole, Gabriella. Secret Lives. 2010. (ENG.). 288p. (YA). (gr. 7-17). pap. 9.99 (978-0-340-98924-1(6)) Hodder & Stoughton GBR. Dist: Hachette Bk. Group.

Poon, Janice. Claire & the Bakery Thief. Poon, Janice, illus. 2008. (ENG., Illus.). 104p. (J). (gr. 2-5). 15.95 (978-1-55453-286-5(8)); pap. 7.95 (978-1-55453-245-2(0)) Kids Can Pr., Ltd. CAN. Dist: Hachette Bk. Group.

Pope, Paul, et al. The Fall of the House of West. 2015. (J). lib. bdg. 20.85 (978-0-606-37806-2(5)) Turtleback Bks.

Portes, Andrea & Silverman, Joel. Liberty: The Spy Who (Kind of) Liked Me. 2017. 400p. (YA). (gr. 8). 17.99 (978-0-06-242199-9(9), HarperTeen) HarperCollins Pubs.

Portman, Frank. King Dork. 2007. 344p. 19.00 (978-0-7569-7950-8(1)) Perfection Learning Corp.

—King Dork. 2008. (ENG.). 368p. (YA). (gr. 9-12). pap. 9.99 (978-0-385-73450-9(6), Delacorte Bks. for Young Readers) Random Hse. Children's Bks.

Poth, Karen. Listen up, Larry, 1 vol. 2013. (I Can Read! / Big Idea Books / VeggieTales Ser.). (ENG.). 32p. (J). pap. 3.99 (978-0-310-73215-0(8)) Zonderkidz.

—The Mess Detectives & the Case of the Lost Temper, 1 vol. 2014. (I Can Read! / Big Idea Books / VeggieTales Ser.). (ENG.). 32p. (J). pap. 3.99 (978-0-310-74170-1(X)) Zonderkidz.

Potter, Ellen. Pish Posh. 2011. (ENG.). 176p. (J). (gr. 3-7). 6.99 (978-0-14-241906-9(0), Puffin Books) Penguin Young Readers Group.

Potter-Kotecki, Kerry. I'm a Doggie Detective. 2008. (J). pap. 10.00 (978-0-9792371-7-1(3), Moo Pr.) Keene Publishing.

Poulsen, David A. The Book of Vampire. 4th rev. ed. 2007. (Salt & Pepper Chronicles). (ENG., Illus.). 160p. (J). (gr. 4-7). 6.95 (978-1-55263-805-7(7)) Leaf Storm Pr.

—No Time Like the Past. 3rd rev. ed. 2007. (Salt & Pepper Chronicles). (ENG., Illus.). 160p. (J). (gr. 4-7). 6.95 (978-1-55263-807-1(3)) Leaf Storm Pr.

Povey, Jeff. Delete. 2017. (ENG.). 352p. (J). pap. 9.99 **(978-1-4711-1870-8(3)**, Simon & Schuster Children's) Simon & Schuster, Ltd. GBR. Dist: Simon & Schuster, Inc.

Preble, Joy. Finding Paris. 2015. (ENG.). 272p. (YA). (gr. 9). 17.99 (978-0-06-232130-5(7)) HarperCollins Pubs.

—The Sweet Dead Life. 2014. (ENG., Illus.). 278p. (YA). (gr. 9). pap. 10.99 (978-1-61695-368-3(3), Soho Teen) Soho Pr., Inc.

Preller, James. The Case of the Groaning Ghost. Smith, Jamie & Alley, R. W., illus. 2008. (Jigsaw Jones Mysteries Ser.: Bk. 32). 89p. (gr. 1-5). 15.00 (978-0-7569-8302-4(9)) Perfection Learning Corp.

—Jigsaw Jones: The Case of the Glow in the Dark Ghost. 2017. (Jigsaw Jones Mysteries Ser.). (ENG., Illus.). 96p. (J). pap. 4.99 (978-1-250-11020-6(3), 9781250110206) Feiwel & Friends.

—Jigsaw Jones: The Case of the Smelly Sneaker. 2017. (Jigsaw Jones Mysteries Ser.). (ENG.). 96p. (J). pap. 4.99 (978-1-250-11080-0(7), 9781250110800) Feiwel & Friends.

—Jigsaw Jones: the Case from Outer Space. 2017. (Jigsaw Jones Mysteries Ser.). (ENG., Illus.). 96p. (J). pap. 4.99 (978-1-250-11017-6(3), 9781250110176) Feiwel & Friends.

—Jigsaw Jones: the Case of the Bicycle Bandit. 2017. (Jigsaw Jones Mysteries Ser.). (ENG., Illus.). 96p. (J). pap. 4.99 (978-1-250-11084-8(X), 9781250110848) Feiwel & Friends.

—Jigsaw Jones: the Case of the Mummy Mystery. 2017. (Jigsaw Jones Mysteries Ser.). (ENG., Illus.). 96p. (J). pap. 4.99 (978-1-250-11082-4(3), 9781250110824) Feiwel & Friends.

Press, Julian. Operation Yellow Dragon, No. 3. 2008. (Get a Clue Ser.: 3). (ENG.). 128p. (J). (gr. 2-5). 7.99 (978-0-448-44875-6(0), Grosset & Dunlap) Penguin Young Readers Group.

Preston, Natasha. The Cabin. 2016. (ENG.). 336p. (YA). (gr. 8-12). pap. 10.99 (978-1-4926-1855-3(1), 9781492618553) Sourcebooks, Inc.

—The Cellar. 2014. (ENG.). 368p. (YA). (gr. 10-12). pap. 9.99 (978-1-4926-0097-8(0), 9781492600978) Sourcebooks, Inc.

Preus, Margi. Enchantment Lake: A Northwoods Mystery. 2015. (ENG.). 200p. (YA). 16.95 (978-0-8166-8302-4(6)) Univ. of Minnesota Pr.

Price, Kevin, ed. The Mystery of Love: A Born Storyteller Collection of Mystery Adventure & Science Fiction Stories. 2013. (Illus.). 308p. pap. (978-0-9872559-6-9(7), Crotchet Quaver) Logorythm.

Priestley, Chris. Death & the Arrow: A Gripping Tale of Murder & Revenge. 2007. (Tom Marlowe Ser.). (ENG., Illus.). 240p. (YA). (gr. 7). per. 12.95 (978-0-552-55475-6(8)) Transworld Publishers Ltd. GBR. Dist: Independent Pubs. Group.

Princess Protection Program Staff. The Palace of Mystery, No. 4. 2010. (Princess Protection Program Ser.). 144p. pap. 4.99 (978-1-4231-2727-7(7)) Disney Pr.

Prins, Piet. The Flying Phantom. 2006. (Illus.). 142p. (J). pap. (978-1-894666-45-9(3)) Inheritance Pubns.

—The Haunted Castle. 2006. (Illus.). 139p. (J). pap. (978-1-894666-44-2(5)) Inheritance Pubns.

—The Mystery of the Abandoned Mill. Kramer, Jaap, illus. 2006. 127p. (J). pap. (978-1-894666-48-0(8)) Inheritance Pubns.

—The Sailing Sleuths. Kramer, Jaap, illus. 2006. 137p. (J). pap. (978-1-894666-46-6(1)) Inheritance Pubns.

—Scout's Distant Journey. 2006. (Illus.). 141p. (J). pap. (978-1-894666-49-7(6)) Inheritance Pubns.

—The Treasure of Rodensteyn Castle. Kramer, Jaap, illus. 2006. 132p. (J). pap. (978-1-894666-47-3(X)) Inheritance Pubns.

Prinz, Yvonne. If You're Lucky. (ENG.). 288p. (YA). (gr. 9-12). 2016. pap. 9.95 (978-1-61620-639-0(X)) 2015. 17.95 (978-1-61620-463-1(X)) Algonquin Bks. of Chapel Hill.

Prisant, Guillermo Murray & Murray, Guillermo. Escalofrio. rev. ed. 2007. (Ediciones Castillo Castillo Del Terror Ser.). (SPA & ENG.). 140p. (J). (gr. 6-9). pap. 6.95 (978-970-20-0293-2(1)) Castillo, Ediciones, S. A. de C. V. MEX. Dist: Macmillan.

—La Gente de Las Sombras. rev. ed. 2007. (Ediciones Castillo Castillo Del Terror Ser.). (ENG.). 104p. (J). (gr. 6-9). pap. 6.95 (978-970-20-0336-6(9)) Castillo, Ediciones, S. A. de C. V. MEX. Dist: Macmillan.

Promitzer, Rebecca. The Pickle King. 2010. (ENG.). 416p. (J). (gr. 3-7). 17.99 (978-0-545-17087-1(7), Chicken Hse., The) Scholastic, Inc.

The Prophesied. 2013. 152p. (978-1-4602-3111-1(2)) FriesenPress.

Prophet, John. Mystery at the Salt Marsh Winery: A Casey Miller Mystery. 2003. 240p. (YA). pap. 16.95 (978-0-595-26598-5(7), Mystery & Suspense Pr.) iUniverse, Inc.

Prophet, John M. Body in the Salt Marsh Boatyard: A Casey Miller Mystery. 2004. 162p. (YA). pap. 13.95 (978-0-595-30991-7(7), Mystery & Suspense Pr.) iUniverse, Inc.

Pullman, Philip. El Reloj Mecanico. Netzel, Carmen, tr. 2005. (Escritura desatada Ser.). (SPA.). 112p. (J). 15.95 (978-84-406-8065-5(1)) Ediciones B ESP. Dist: Independent Pubs. Group.

—The Ruby in the Smoke. 2009. 9.84 (978-0-7848-2919-6(5), Everbind) Marco Bk. Co.

—The Ruby in the Smoke. (Sally Lockhart Ser.: Bk. 1). (YA). 2008. (ENG.). 256p. (gr. 7). pap. 9.99 (978-0-375-84516-1(X), Ember) 2003. (Illus.). pap. 9.95

(978-0-375-82545-3(2), Knopf Bks. for Young Readers) Random Hse. Children's Bks.

—The Shadow in the North. (Sally Lockhart Ser.: Bk. 2). (J). 2008. (ENG.). 384p. (gr. 7). pap. 10.99 (978-0-375-84515-4(1), Ember) 2003. (Illus.). pap. 9.95 (978-0-375-82546-0(0), Knopf Bks. for Young Readers) Random Hse. Children's Bks.

—The Shadow in the North. 2006. (Sally Lockhart Ser.: Bk. 2). 23.75 (978-0-8446-7289-2(0)) Smith, Peter Pub., Inc.

—The Tiger in the Well. (Sally Lockhart Ser.: Bk. 3). 2008. (ENG.). 432p. (YA). (gr. 7). pap. 9.99 (978-0-375-84517-8(8), Ember) 2003. (Illus.). (J). pap. 9.95 (978-0-375-82547-7(9)) Random Hse. Children's Bks.

—The Tin Princess. 2008. (Sally Lockhart Ser.). (ENG.). 304p. (YA). (gr. 7). pap. 7.99 (978-0-375-84514-7(3), Knopf Bks. for Young Readers) Random Hse. Children's Bks.

—Two Crafty Criminals! And How They Were Captured by the Daring Detectives of the New Cut Gang. (ENG.). 288p. (J). (gr. 3-7). 2013. 7.99 (978-0-307-93035-4(1), Yearling) 2012. (Illus.). 16.99 (978-0-375-87029-3(6), Knopf Bks. for Young Readers) Random Hse. Children's Bks.

Quackenbush, Robert. Detective Mole. 2010. 68p. (J). (gr. k-4). pap. 8.95 (978-1-4502-1529-9(7)) iUniverse, Inc.

—Piet Potter Returns: A Piet Potter Mystery. 2010. 52p. (J). (gr. k-4). pap. 8.95 (978-1-4502-1352-3(9)) iUniverse, Inc.

—Piet Potter Strikes Again: A Piet Potter Mystery. 2010. 52p. (J). (gr. k-4). pap. 8.95 (978-1-4502-1530-5(0)) iUniverse, Inc.

Quinn, Spencer, pseud. ARF - A Bowser & Birdie Novel. 2016. (ENG.). 304p. (J). (gr. 3-7). 16.99 (978-0-545-64334-4(1), Scholastic Pr.) Scholastic, Inc.

—Bow Wow: a Bowser & Birdie Novel. 2017. (ENG.). 304p. (J). (gr. 3-7). 16.99 **(978-1-338-09134-2(4)**, Scholastic Pr.) Scholastic, Inc.

—Paw & Order: A Chet & Bernie Mystery. 2015. (Chet & Bernie Mystery Ser.: 7). (ENG.). 336p. pap. 16.00 (978-1-4767-0340-4(X)) Simon & Schuster, Inc.

—Woof. (Bowser & Birdie Mystery Ser.). (ENG.). 304p. (J). (gr. 3-7). 2016. pap. 7.99 (978-0-545-64332-0(5)) 2015. 16.99 (978-0-545-64331-3(7), Scholastic Pr.) Scholastic, Inc.

Raab, Ralph. The Dewey Deception: The First Adventure from the Biblio Files. 2009. (ENG.). 248p. 26.95 (978-1-4401-4687-9(X)); pap. 16.95 (978-1-4401-4685-5(3)) iUniverse, Inc.

Rabley, Stephen. Marcel & the Mona Lisa. 2nd ed. 2009. (ENG., Illus.). 20p. pap. 11.99 (978-1-4058-6955-3(0)) Pearson Education.

Rader, Josh. Detective Stephy Wephy Holmes in the Missing Cake. Meyer, Sarah, illus. 2007. 36p. (J). (gr. -1-3). per. 14.99 (978-1-59879-399-4(3)) Lifevest Publishing, Inc.

Radwan, Hassan. Rashid & the Missing Body. 2010. (ENG., Illus.). 80p. (J). (gr. 2-6). pap. 5.95 (978-0-86037-395-7(9)) Kube Publishing Ltd. GBR. Dist: Consortium Bk. Sales & Distribution.

Ragged Island Mysteries: Classroom Library Set. (Ragged Island Mysteriestm Ser.). (gr. 5-7). 150.95 (978-0-322-02634-6(2)) Wright Group/McGraw-Hill.

Raglin, Tim. The Curse of Catunkhamun. 2007. (Illus.). (J). (978-0-9788969-0-4(4), Exhibit A) TR Bks.

Rahim, Rahimah. The Trunk. 2012. 64p. pap. (978-1-78176-715-3(7)) FeedARead.com.

Rainbird, Becky. Taking Notes. 2010. (Lucky Six Ser.: 3). (ENG., Illus.). 160p. (J). (gr. 4-7). pap. 6.99 (978-1-4052-3944-8(1)) Egmont Bks., Ltd. GBR. Dist: Independent Pubs. Group.

Rainfield, Cheryl. Stained. 2015. (ENG.). 304p. (YA). (gr. 9). pap. 8.99 (978-0-544-43947-4(3), HMH Books For Young Readers) Houghton Mifflin Harcourt Publishing Co.

Ralph, Grampa. How Santa Knows. 2007. 56p. pap. 16.95 (978-1-4241-2284-4(8)) America Star Bks.

Rameaka, T. Mystery of Wolf Den Cave. 2005. 74p. pap. 19.95 (978-1-4137-5551-0(8)) America Star Bks.

Ramirez, D. a. & Ramirez, D. A. Kingdom of Glass. 2012. 336p. pap. 12.99 (978-0-9834198-8-4(4)) Vinspire Publishing LLC.

Rand, Johnathan. American Chillers #29 Oregon Oceanauts. 2010. 208p. (J). pap. 5.99 (978-1-893699-24-3(2)) AudioCraft Publishing, Inc.

Random House. The Great Train Mystery. 2013. (Spongebob Squarepants Step into Reading Ser.). lib. bdg. 13.55 (978-0-606-35116-4(7)) Turtleback Bks.

Random House Disney Staff. Big Trouble in Little Rodentia. Random House Disney Staff, illus. 2016. (Pictureback(R) Ser.). (ENG., Illus.). 24p. (J). (gr. -1-2). 4.99 (978-0-7364-3531-4(X), RH/Disney) Random Hse. Children's Bks.

—Zootopia Big Golden Book (Disney Zootopia) Random House Disney Staff, illus. 2016. (Big Golden Book Ser.). (ENG., Illus.). 64p. (J). (gr. -1-2). 9.99 (978-0-7364-3384-6(8), Golden/Disney) Random Hse. Children's Bks.

Ranjalkar, Shreyans. My Sunny British Days - Stories for Children by a Child. 2013. (Illus.). 70p. pap. (978-1-78148-596-5(8)) Grosvenor Hse. Publishing Ltd.

Ransom, Jeanie Franz. The Crown Affair. Axelsen, Stephen, illus. 2015. (Nursery-Rhyme Mysteries Ser.). (ENG.). 40p. (J). (gr. 1-4). lib. bdg. 16.95 (978-1-58089-552-1(2)) Charlesbridge Publishing, Inc.

Raskin, Ellen. The Mysterious Disappearance of Leon. Raskin, Ellen, illus. 2011. (ENG., Illus.). 176p. (J). (gr. 3-7). 6.99 (978-0-14-241700-3(9), Puffin Books) Penguin Young Readers Group.

—The Tattooed Potato & Other Clues. Raskin, Ellen, illus. 2011. (ENG., Illus.). 176p. (J). (gr. 5-18). 6.99 (978-0-14-241699-0(1), Puffin Books) Penguin Young Readers Group.

—The Westing Game. 2003. 182p. (J). lib. bdg. 15.00 (978-1-4242-2271-1(0)) Fitzgerald Bks.

—The Westing Game. (Puffin Modern Classics Ser.). (ENG., 192p. (J). (gr. 3-7). 2004. Illus.). 7.99 (978-0-14-240120-0(X), Puffin Books) 25th anniv. ed. 2003. 16.99 (978-0-525-47137-0(5), Dutton Books for Young Readers) Penguin Young Readers Group.

Rautenberg, Karen Rita. Ballerina Detective & the Missing Jeweled Tiara. 2009. (ENG.). 198p. (J). (gr. 5-8). pap. (978-1-933255-47-7(1)) DNA Pr.

Ravishankar, Anushka. Captain Coconut: And the Case of the Missing Bananas. Sundram, Priya, illus. 2015. (ENG.). 96p. (gr. 2). 16.95 (978-93-83145-22-5(6)) Tara Books Agency IND. Dist: Publishers Group West (PGW).

Ray, Delia. Finding Fortune. 2015. (ENG.). 288p. (J). (gr. 5-7). 16.99 (978-0-374-30065-4(8), 9780374300654, Farrar, Straus & Giroux (BYR)) Farrar, Straus & Giroux.

Ray, Gracie. Falling Slowly. 2012. 270p. (978-1-105-59084-9(4)) Lulu.com.

Rayes, Michael. Bank Robbery! 2007. (J). per. 13.95 (978-0-9779628-0-8(6)) Rafka Pr. LLC.

Raymond, Roger & Savoy, Darryl. Ralph Filmore: Paranormal Investigator. O'Reilly, Sean Patrick, ed. 2012. (Illus.). 78p. (J). pap. 14.95 (978-1-926914-31-2(7)) Arcana Studio, Inc.

Razzi, Jim. The Sherluck Bones Mystery Detective. 2003. 62p. Bk. 1. pap. 9.95 (978-0-595-29088-8(4))Bk. 2. pap. 9.95 (978-0-595-29089-5(2)) iUniverse, Inc. (Mystery Writers of America Presents).

Read, Miss. The Howards of Caxley. (J). 17.95 (978-0-8488-1454-0(1)) Amereon Ltd.

Redbank, Tennant. The Secret Sea Monster. 2016. (Barbie Chapters Ser.). (ENG., Illus.). 64p. (J). (gr. 1-4). 5.99 (978-1-101-93844-7(7), Random Hse. Bks. for Young Readers) Random Hse. Children's Bks.

Reece, P. J. Roxy. 1 vol. 2010. (ENG., Illus.). 192p. (YA). (gr. 9-12). pap. 12.95 (978-1-896580-01-2(7)) Tradewind Bks. CAN. Dist: Orca Bk. Pubs. USA.

Reese Martin, Faith. Ghost Train to Freedom: An Adventure on the Underground Railroad. Sachs, Barry, illus. 2012. (JMP Mystery Ser.: Bk. 3). (ENG.). 416p. (YA). pap. 14.99 (978-1-60800-014-2(1), American Literary Publishing) LifeReloaded Specialty Publishing LLC.

Reichs, Kathy. Virals. 2014. lthr. 79.00 (978-1-62715-582-3(1)) Leatherbound Bestsellers.

—Virals. (Virals Ser.: 1). (ENG.). (J). (gr. 5-18). 2011. 480p. 10.99 (978-1-59514-426-3(9), Puffin Books) 2010. 464p. 17.99 (978-1-59514-342-6(4), Razorbill) Penguin Young Readers Group.

—Virals. 2011. 20.00 (978-1-61383-226-4(5)) Perfection Learning Corp.

Reichs, Kathy & Reichs, Brendan. Code. 2013. (Virals Ser.: 3). lib. bdg. 19.65 (978-0-606-32140-2(3), Turtleback) Turtleback Bks.

—Seizure. 2013. (Virals Ser.: 2). (ENG.). 512p. (J). (gr. 5). pap. 9.99 (978-1-59514-486-7(2), Puffin Books) Penguin Young Readers Group.

—Seizure. 2013. (Virals Ser.: 2). lib. bdg. 20.85 (978-0-606-30050-6(3), Turtleback) Turtleback Bks.

—Trace Evidence. 2016. (Virals Ser.). lib. bdg. 20.85 (978-0-606-38400-1(6)) Turtleback Bks.

—Virals. 2011. (Virals Ser.: 1). lib. bdg. 20.85 (978-0-606-23069-8(6), Turtleback) Turtleback Bks.

—Virals Short Stories Omnibus. 2016. (Virals Ser.). (ENG.). 304p. (J). (gr. 5). 9.99 (978-0-14-751920-7(9), Puffin Books) Penguin Young Readers Group.

Reid, F. J. The Midwinter Child. 2009. 224p. pap. (978-1-84923-496-2(5)) YouWriteOn.

Reid, Isabelle. Serafina Moon. 2009. 48p. pap. (978-1-84923-771-0(9)) YouWriteOn.

Reid, Kimberly. Sweet 16 to Life. 2013. (ENG., Illus.). 256p. (YA). (gr. 9). pap. 9.95 (978-0-7582-6742-9(8), K-Teen/Dafina) Kensington Publishing Corp.

—Sweet 16 to Life. 2013. 233p. (J). lib. bdg. 20.80 (978-0-606-27166-0(X), Turtleback) Turtleback Bks.

Reid, Roger. Space. 2008. (ENG.). 160p. (J). 19.95 (978-1-58838-230-6(3), NewSouth Bks.) NewSouth, Inc.

Reide, MacKenzie. The Adventurers the Mask of the Troll. 2013. 326p. pap. (978-0-9869647-2-5(7)) MR Bks.

Reiner, Carl. Tell Me Another Scary Story... but Not Too Scary! Bennett, James & Bennett, Carl A., illus. 2009. (ENG.). 32p. (J). (gr. 4-7). 16.95 (978-1-59777-630-1(0)) Phoenix Bks., Inc.

Reiss, Kathryn. A Bundle of Trouble: A Rebecca Mystery. Giovine, Sergio, illus. 2011. (ENG.). 192p. (YA). (gr. 4-18). pap. 6.95 (978-1-59369-754-9(6)) American Girl Publishing, Inc.

—Riddle of the Prairie Bride. 2009. (Mysteries Through Time Ser.). 144 - 176p. (YA). (gr. 4-8). 31.95 (978-1-60754-421-0(0)); pap. 15.25 (978-1-60754-420-3(2)) Windmill Bks.

—The Silver Guitar: A Julie Mystery. Ansfield, Elizabeth, ed. Giovine, Sergio, illus. 2011. (ENG.). 192p. (YA). (gr. 4-18). pap. 6.95 (978-1-59369-756-3(2)) American Girl Publishing, Inc.

—The Tangled Web: A Julie Mystery. Tibbles, Jean-Paul, illus. 2009. (ENG.). 168p. (J). (gr. 4-18). 10.95 (978-1-59369-475-3(X)); pap. 6.95 (978-1-59369-476-0(8)) American Girl Publishing, Inc.

Renn, Diana. Blue Voyage. 2015. (ENG.). 464p. (YA). (gr. 7). 18.99 (978-0-670-01559-7(8), Viking Books for Young Readers) Penguin Young Readers Group.

—Tokyo Heist. 2013. (ENG.). 384p. (YA). (gr. 7). pap. 8.99 (978-0-14-242654-8(7), Speak) Penguin Young Readers Group.

Rennie-Pattison, Caroline. The Law of Three. 2007. (ENG.). 232p. (YA). (gr. 6). pap. 10.99 (978-1-55002-733-4(6), Boardwalk Bks.) Dundurn CAN. Dist: Ingram Publisher Services.

Rey, H. A. Curious George Museum Mystery (CGTV 8x8) 2017. (Curious George Ser.). (ENG., Illus.). 24p. (J). (gr. -1-3). 12.99 (978-0-544-85992-0(8), HMH Books For Young Readers) Houghton Mifflin Harcourt Publishing Co.

RH Disney Staff & Trine, Greg. The Stinky Cheese Caper. RH Disney Staff & Loftis, Cory, illus. 2016. (Disney Chapters Ser.). (ENG.). 80p. (J). (gr. 1-4). 4.99 (978-0-7364-3610-6(3), RH/Disney) Random Hse. Children's Bks.

Rhodes, O. K. The Rock Holler Gang: Jr. Detectives Mystery of the Cornerstone. 2003. 11.99 (978-0-9740799-0-5(1)) Maple Bend Farms Pr.

Rhodes, O. K. & Spencer, Octavia. The Case of the Time-Capsule Bandit. To, Vivienne, illus. 2013. (Randi Rhodes, Ninja Detective Ser.: 1). (ENG.). 224p. (J). (gr. 3-7). 16.99 (978-1-4424-7681-3(8), Simon & Schuster Bks. For Young Readers) Simon & Schuster Bks. For Young Readers.

Ricchi, Brenda. The Grandchildren's Bible Journeys - the Creation Story. 2010. 35p. pap. 17.00 (978-0-557-14903-2(7)) Lulu Pr., Inc.

Ricchiuti, Paul B. Treasure on Spyglass Hill. 2015. 143p. (J). pap. (978-0-8163-5771-0(4)) Pacific Pr. Publishing Assn.

Richards, Justin. The Chaos Code. 2007. (ENG.). 400p. (YA). (gr. 7-12). 17.95 (978-1-59990-124-4(2), 9781599901244, Bloomsbury USA Childrens) Bloomsbury Publishing USA.

Richards, Kitty & Studio IBOIX. Belle: The Mysterious Message, 1 vol. 2012. (Disney Princess Ser.). (ENG., Illus.). 96p. (J). (gr. 2-5). 24.21 (978-1-59961-878-4(8)) Spotlight.

Richards, Linda L. Death Was in the Blood. 2013. (ENG.). 332p. 25.95 (978-1-4328-2716-8(2), Five Star Trade) Cengage Gale.

Richards, Natalie D. One Was Lost. (ENG., (YA). (gr. 7-12). 2017. Illus.). 23.99 **(978-1-4926-6232-7(1))** 2016. 320p. pap. 10.99 (978-1-4926-1574-3(9), 9781492615743) Sourcebooks, Inc.

Richardson, D. L. Feedback. 2013. 254p. pap. 11.99 (978-1-939194-83-1(0)) Etopia Pr.

Richardson, Travis. Lost in Clover. 2012. 198p. pap. 9.99 (978-1-61187-466-2(1)) Untreed Reads Publishing, LLC.

Richter, Virginia Rose. Taken (a Willow Lane Mystery, #4) 2015. (ENG., Illus.). 114p. (J). pap. 10.00 (978-1-61187-795-3(4)) Untreed Reads Publishing, LLC.

Ridell, Chris. Ottoline y la gata amarilla/ Ottolina & the Yellow Cat. 2008. (SPA.). 172p. (J). 13.95 (978-84-263-6832-4(8)) Vives, Luis Editorial (Edelvives) ESP. Dist: Baker & Taylor Bks.

Riehecky, Janet. The Red Door Detective Club Mysteries, 4 bks., Set. Halverson, Lydia, illus. (J). (gr. 3-6). lib. bdg. 51.80 (978-1-56674-900-8(X)) Forest Hse. Publishing Co., Inc.

Rifkin, L. (Lauren). The Nine Lives of Romeo Crumb: Life Three. 2010. 276p. (J). pap. 8.95 (978-0-9743221-5-5(6)) Sunrise Publishing Co.

Rigby Education Staff. The Robbers. (Sails Literacy Ser.). (Illus.). 16p. (gr. 1-2). 27.00 (978-0-7635-9913-3(1), 699131C99) Rigby Education.

Riker, Richard K. Scary Days Daze. l.t. ed. 2005. (Illus.). 224p. (J). 15.95 (978-0-9760416-1-0(8), 3,000) Safe Harbor Pubns.

Riley, D. H. The Mysterians, 1 vol. 2009. 54p. pap. 16.95 (978-1-60836-374-2(0)) America Star Bks.

Rinehart, Mary Roberts. Bab: A Sub-Deb. 2005. (ENG., Illus.). 300p. pap. 15.95 (978-0-9740636-8-3(1)) ARose Books Publishing, LLC.

Ring, Susan. Pete's Surprise. 2009. (ENG.). 24p. (J). pap. 3.99 (978-1-4231-1827-5(8)) Disney Pr.

Riordan, Rick. The Maze of Bones. 2008. (39 Clues Ser.: 1). (ENG.). 224p. (J). (gr. 3-7). 12.99 (978-0-545-06039-4(7), Scholastic Pr.); (Illus.). 12.99 (978-0-545-09054-4(7)) Scholastic, Inc.

Ripken, Cal, Jr. & Cowherd, Kevin. Super Slugger. 2013. (ENG.). 200p. (YA). (gr. 3-7). pap. 6.99 (978-1-4231-4004-7(4)) Hyperion Pr.

Ripley's Believe It or Not Editors. Danger Underground. 2011. (Ripley RBI Ser.). 128p. (J). pap. 4.99 (978-1-893951-64-8(2)) Ripley Entertainment, Inc.

—Haunted Hotel. 2011. (Ripley RBI Ser.). 128p. (J). pap. 4.99 (978-1-893951-65-5(0)) Ripley Entertainment, Inc.

Ripley's Believe It Or Not! Staff. Shock Horror. 2010. (Rbi Ser.: 7). (ENG.). 128p. (J). pap. 4.99 (978-1-893951-58-7(8)) Ripley Entertainment, Inc.

Rippin, Sally. Code Breakers. Fukuoka, Aki, illus. 2015. (ENG.). 96p. (J). pap. 4.99 (978-1-61067-312-9(3)) Kane Miller.

—Spooky House. Fukuoka, Aki, illus. 2015. (ENG.). 96p. (J). pap. 4.99 (978-1-61067-311-2(5)) Kane Miller.

Rippl, Terry. Tippy, Dog Gone Detective: From the Files of the World's Shortest Private Eye. 2012. 36p. pap. 12.99 (978-1-4575-1599-6(7)) Dog Ear Publishing, LLC.

Ritchie, Brendan. Carousel. 2015. (ENG.). 352p. (YA). (gr. 7). 13.95 (978-1-925162-14-1(1)) Fremantle Pr. AUS. Dist: Independent Pubs. Group.

Ritter, William. Beastly Bones. (Jackaby Ser.: 2). (ENG.). (YA). (gr. 8-12). 2016. 320p. pap. 9.95 (978-1-61620-636-9(5)) 2015. 304p. 17.95 (978-1-61620-354-2(4)) Algonquin Bks. of Chapel Hill.

—Beastly Bones. 2016. (Jackaby Ser.: 2). lib. bdg. 20.80 (978-0-606-39017-0(0)) Turtleback Bks.

—Ghostly Echoes: A Jackaby Novel. 2016. (Jackaby Ser.: 3). (ENG.). 352p. (YA). (gr. 8-12). 17.95 (978-1-61620-579-9(2)) Algonquin Bks. of Chapel Hill.

—Jackaby. (Jackaby Ser.: 1). (ENG.). 304p. (YA). (gr. 9-12). 2015. pap. 9.95 (978-1-61620-546-1(6)) 2014. 16.95 (978-1-61620-353-5(6), 73353) Algonquin Bks. of Chapel Hill.

Rivas, Spelile. The Cucuy Stole My Cascarones / el Coco Me Robó Los Cascarones. Baeza Ventura, Gabriela, tr. Cervantes, Valeria, illus. 2013. (SPA & ENG.). 32p. (J). 17.95 (978-1-55885-771-1(0), Piñata Books) Arte Publico Pr.

Robbins, Trina. The Bark in Space. Page, Tyler, illus. 2013. (Chicagoland Detective Agency Ser.: 5). (ENG.). 64p. (gr. 4-8). (J). lib. bdg. 29.27 (978-0-7613-8166-2(X)); pap. 6.95 (978-1-4677-0725-1(2)) Lerner Publishing Group. (Graphic Universe™).

—The Maltese Mummy. Page, Tyler, illus. 2011. (Chicagoland Detective Agency Ser.: 2). (ENG.). 64p. (gr. 4-8). 29.27 (978-0-7613-4615-9(5)); pap. 6.95 (978-0-7613-5636-3(3), Graphic Universe™) Lerner Publishing Group.

—A Midterm Night's Scheme. Page, Tyler, illus. 2014. (Chicagoland Detective Agency Ser.: 6). (ENG.). 64p. (gr. 4-8). lib. bdg. 29.27 (978-0-7613-8167-9(8), Graphic Universe™) Lerner Publishing Group.

Roberts, D. W. Pep Squad Mysteries Book 1: Cavern in the Hills. 2009. 71p. pap. 8.99 (978-0-557-05513-5(X)) Lulu Pr., Inc.

—Pep Squad Mysteries Book 2:the Haunting of Townsand Hall. 2009. 77p. pap. 8.95 (978-0-557-05289-9(0)) Lulu Pr., Inc.

—Pep Squad Mysteries Book 4: Prediction of Danger. 2010. 90p. pap. 8.99 (978-0-557-46495-1(1)) Lulu Pr., Inc.

Roberts, Daniel. Young Pep Squad Mysteries. 2011. 36p. pap. 16.99 (978-1-4567-9640-2(2)) AuthorHouse.

Roberts, Dw. Pep Squad Mysteries Book: Cavern in the Hills. 2008. (Illus.). 68p. pap. 9.96 (978-0-557-02446-9(3)) Lulu Pr., Inc.

—Pep Squad Mysteries Book: Mystery in the Lions' Maze. 2012. 102p. pap. 9.95 (978-1-257-92360-1(9)) Lulu Pr., Inc.

—Pep Squad Mysteries Book: Trouble on Avalance Mountain. 2010. (Illus.). 86p. pap. 8.99 (978-0-557-16575-9(X)) Lulu Pr., Inc.

—Pep Squad Mysteries Book 7: The Deadly Doll. 2012. 120p. pap. 9.95 (978-1-105-49215-0(X)) Lulu Pr., Inc.

—Pep Squad Mysteries Book 8: Shock of the Scarecrow. 2012. (Illus.). 124p. pap. 9.95 (978-1-105-83468-4(9)) Lulu Pr., Inc.

Roberts, Ken. Thumb & the Bad Guys, 1 vol. Franson, Leanne, illus. 2011. (ENG.). 120p. (J). (gr. 1-5). pap. 7.95 (978-0-88899-917-7(8)) Groundwood Bks. CAN. Dist: Publishers Group West (PGW).

—Thumb & the Bad Guys. 2013. 104p. pap. (978-1-4596-6491-3(4)) ReadHowYouWant.com, Ltd.

Roberts, P. J. I Lost My Sock! A Matching Mystery. Eliopolous, Chris, illus. 2017. (ENG.). 24p. (J). (gr. -1-k). 12.95 (978-1-4197-2301-8(4), Abrams Appleseed) Abrams, Inc.

Roberts, Willo Davis. Baby-Sitting Is a Dangerous Job. 2016. (ENG., Illus.). 224p. (J). (gr. 3-7). pap. 6.99 (978-1-4814-3704-2(6), Aladdin) Simon & Schuster Children's Publishing.

—Megan's Island. 2016. (ENG., Illus.). 288p. (J). (gr. 3-7). 17.99 (978-1-4814-4908-3(7)); pap. 6.99 (978-1-4814-4907-6(9)) Simon & Schuster Children's Publishing. (Aladdin).

—Nightmare. 2012. (ENG.). 224p. (J). (gr. 5-9). pap. 10.99 (978-1-4424-7229-7(4), Atheneum Bks. for Young Readers) Simon & Schuster Children's Publishing.

—The Old House. 2016. (ENG., Illus.). 272p. (J). (gr. 3-7). pap. 6.99 (978-1-4814-5785-9(3), Aladdin) Simon & Schuster Children's Publishing.

—Pawns. Pohl, David, illus. 2012. (ENG.). 160p. (J). (gr. 5-9). pap. 8.99 (978-0-689-83320-5(2), Simon & Schuster/Paula Wiseman Bks.) Simon & Schuster/Paula Wiseman Bks.

—The Pet-Sitting Peril. 2016. (ENG., Illus.). 256p. (J). (gr. 3-7). pap. 7.99 (978-1-4814-7492-4(8), Aladdin) Simon & Schuster Children's Publishing.

—The Pet-Sitting Peril. 2nd ed. 2012. (ENG., Illus.). 192p. (J). (gr. 3-7). reprint ed. pap. 9.99 (978-0-689-71427-6(0), Simon & Schuster/Paula Wiseman Bks.) Simon & Schuster/Paula Wiseman Bks.

—Rebel. 2005. 153p. (J). (gr. 3-7). 13.65 (978-0-7569-5076-7(7)) Perfection Learning Corp.

—Rebel. 2012. (ENG., Illus.). 160p. (J). (gr. 3-7). pap. 8.99 (978-0-689-85081-3(6), Aladdin) Simon & Schuster Children's Publishing.

—Scared Stiff. 2016. (ENG., Illus.). 256p. (J). (gr. 3-7). pap. 7.99 (978-1-4814-4910-6(9), Aladdin) Simon & Schuster Children's Publishing.

—Surviving Summer Vacation. 2015. (ENG., Illus.). 208p. (J). (gr. 3-7). pap. 6.99 (978-1-4814-3718-9(6), Aladdin) Simon & Schuster Children's Publishing.

—The View from the Cherry Tree. 2015. (ENG., Illus.). 256p. (J). (gr. 3-7). pap. 6.99 (978-1-4814-3994-7(4), Aladdin) Simon & Schuster Children's Publishing.

—What Could Go Wrong? 2016. (ENG., Illus.). 240p. (J). (gr. 3-7). pap. 7.99 (978-1-4814-7489-4(8), Aladdin) Simon & Schuster Children's Publishing.

—What Could Go Wrong? 2012. (ENG., Illus.). 176p. (J). (gr. 3-7). reprint ed. pap. 9.99 (978-0-689-71690-4(7), Simon & Schuster/Paula Wiseman Bks.) Simon & Schuster/Paula Wiseman Bks.

Roberts, Willo Davis & Davis, Wayne R. Secrets at Hidden Valley. 2012. (ENG., Illus.). 160p. (J). (gr. 5-9). pap. 8.99 (978-0-689-81167-8(5), Simon & Schuster/Paula Wiseman Bks.) Simon & Schuster/Paula Wiseman Bks.

Robins, Eleanor. Art Show Mystery, 1 vol. unabr. ed. 2011. (Carter High Mysteries Ser.). (ENG.). 46p. (YA). (gr. 9-12). 7.95 (978-1-61651-560-7(0)) Saddleback Educational Publishing, Inc.

—The Aztec Ring Mystery. 2006. (Walker High Mysteries Ser.). (Illus.). 48p. (J). per. (978-1-59905-028-7(5)) Saddleback Educational Publishing, Inc.

—Aztec Ring Mystery, 1 vol. unabr. ed. 2011. (Carter High Mysteries Ser.). (ENG.). 46p. (YA). (gr. 9-12). 7.95 (978-1-61651-561-4(9)) Saddleback Educational Publishing, Inc.

—Drama Club Mystery, 1 vol. unabr. ed. 2011. (Carter High Mysteries Ser.). (ENG.). 47p. (YA). (gr. 9-12). 7.95 (978-1-61651-562-1(7)) Saddleback Educational Publishing, Inc.

—The Field Trip Mystery. (Walker High Mysteries Ser.). 48p. 2006. (Illus.). (J). per. (978-1-59905-031-7(5)) 2011. (ENG.). (YA). (gr. 9-12). 7.95 (978-1-61651-563-8(5)) Saddleback Educational Publishing, Inc.

—The Last Time. 2005. (Carter High Chronicles Senior Year Ser.). (Illus.). 48p. (J). per. 3.95 (978-1-56254-786-8(0), SP7860) Saddleback Educational Publishing, Inc.

—Library Book Mystery, 1 vol. unabr. ed. 2011. (Carter High Mysteries Ser.). (ENG.). 48p. (YA). (gr. 9-12). 7.95 (978-1-61651-564-5(3)) Saddleback Educational Publishing, Inc.

—Lucky Falcon Mystery, 1 vol. unabr. ed. 2011. (Carter High Mysteries Ser.). (ENG.). 47p. (YA). (gr. 9-12). 7.95 (978-1-61651-565-2(1)) Saddleback Educational Publishing, Inc.

—The Missing Test Mystery. (Walker High Mysteries Ser.). 2006. (Illus.). 48p. (J). per. (978-1-59905-033-1(1)) 2011. (ENG.). 47p. (YA). (gr. 9-12). 7.95 (978-1-61651-566-9(X)) Saddleback Educational Publishing, Inc.

—The Secret Admirer Mystery. (Walker High Mysteries Ser.). 48p. 2006. (Illus.). (J). per. (978-1-59905-036-2(6)) 2011. (ENG.). (YA). (gr. 9-12). 7.95 (978-1-61651-567-6(8)) Saddleback Educational Publishing, Inc.

—Where Is Mr. Zane?, 1 vol. unabr. ed. 2011. (Carter High Mysteries Ser.). (ENG.). 48p. (YA). (gr. 9-12). 7.95 (978-1-61651-569-0(4)) Saddleback Educational Publishing, Inc.

Robinson, Fiona. The 3-2-3 Detective Agency: The Disappearance of Dave Warthog. 2009. (ENG., Illus.). 80p. (J). (gr. 1-4). 18.95 (978-0-8109-8489-9(X), Amulet Bks.) Abrams, Inc.

Robles, Eduardo. La Computadora Maldita. rev. ed. 2007. (Ediciones Castillo Castillo Del Terror Ser.). (SPA & ENG.).

108p. (J). (gr. 4-7). pap. 6.95 (978-970-20-0315-1(6)) Castillo, Ediciones, S. A. de C. V. MEX. Dist: Macmillan.

Rocheleau, Nicole. Ryan, Me, & the Mysterious Book. 2006. (ENG.). 204p. per. 24.95 (978-1-4241-3422-9(6)) PublishAmerica, Inc.

Rochester, B. The Joey Jenkins Mysteries: Something Is Missing at Redding Lake. 2005. 67p. pap. 16.95 (978-1-4241-0065-1(8)) PublishAmerica, Inc.

Rock, Brian. The Deductive Detective, 1 vol. Rogers, Sherry, illus. 2013. (SPA.). 32p. (J). (gr. -1-2). pap. 9.95 (978-1-62855-347-5(2)) Arbordale Publishing.

Rock, Brian & Rogers, Sherry. El Detective Deductivo, 1 vol. Rogers, Sherry, illus. 2013. (SPA., Illus.). 32p. (J). (gr. -1-2). 17.95 (978-1-60718-708-0(6)) Arbordale Publishing.

Rock, Peter. Klickitat. 2016. (ENG.). 240p. (YA). (gr. 8-17). 17.95 (978-1-4197-1894-6(0), Amulet Bks.) Abrams, Inc.

Rockley, Frank. Tinderbox Cottage. 2010. 136p. pap. 10.99 (978-1-4490-3120-6(X)) AuthorHouse.

Rodda, Emily. The Ghost of Raven Hill. 2005. (Illus.). 112p. (J). (978-0-439-79770-2(5)) Scholastic, Inc.

Roddy, Lee. Case of the Dangerous Cruise. 2007. (Ladd Family Adventure Ser.: Vol. 11). (Illus.). 145p. (J). (gr. 3-7). per. 7.99 (978-0-88062-260-8(1)) Mott Media.

—The Mystery of the Wild Surfer. 2006. (Ladd Family Adventure Ser.: Vol. 6). (Illus.). 135p. (J). (gr. 4-7). per. 7.99 (978-0-88062-255-4(5)) Mott Media.

—Panic in the Wild Waters. 2007. (Ladd Family Adventure Ser.: Vol. 12). (Illus.). 136p. (J). (gr. 3-7). per. 7.99 (978-0-88062-261-5(X)) Mott Media.

—Terror at Forbidden Falls. 2006. (Ladd Family Adventure Ser.: Vol. 8). (Illus.). 157p. (J). (gr. 3-7). per. 7.99 (978-0-88062-257-8(1)) Mott Media.

Rodrigue, Nancy Temple. Hidden Mickey Adventures 3: The Mermaid's Tale, vol. 3. 2014. (Hidden Mickey Adventures Ser.: 3). (ENG.). 272p. (YA). (gr. 4-17). pap. 14.99 (978-1-938319-05-1(2), DOUBLE-R BKS.) Rodrigue & Sons Co./Double R Books Publishing.

Rodrigues, Naomi. Molly Mouse & the Christmas Mystery. 2013. 24p. pap. 15.99 (978-1-4797-6511-9(2)) Xlibris Corp.

Roe, D. J. The Impossible Dream. 2008. 59p. pap. 16.95 (978-1-60610-173-5(0)) America Star Bks.

Roecker, Lisa & Roecker, Laura. The Liar Society. 2011. (Liar Society Ser.: 1). (ENG.). 368p. (YA). (gr. 7-12). pap. 9.99 (978-1-4022-5633-2(7)) Sourcebooks, Inc.

Roehrig, Caleb. Last Seen Leaving. 2016. (ENG.). 336p. (YA). 17.99 (978-1-250-08563-4(2), 9781250085634) Feiwel & Friends.

Roemermann, Jennifer. The Long Grass Tunnel. 2012. 50p. pap. 18.68 (978-1-4797-0300-5(1)) Xlibris Corp.

Rogers, Derek G. Monstrous Myths & Fabulous Fables. 2012. 184p. pap. (978-1-78176-741-2(6)) FeedARead.com.

Rohmer, Sax, pseud. The Quest of the Sacred Slipper. 2007. 136p. per. 11.95 (978-1-60312-363-1(6)); 24.95 (978-1-60312-701-1(1)) Aegypan.

—The Sins of Severac Bablon. 2008. 200p. per. 14.95 (978-1-60312-545-1(0)) Aegypan.

Rollason, Jane. Killer Bees. 2009. (ENG.). 64p. pap. 12.00 (978-84-8323-503-4(X)) Cambridge Univ. Pr.

Rollins, James. Jake Ransom & the Howling Sphinx. 2011. (Jake Ransom Ser.: 2). (ENG.). 384p. (J). (gr. 5-18). 16.99 (978-0-06-147382-1(0)) HarperCollins Pubs.

—Jake Ransom & the Skull King's Shadow. 2010. (Jake Ransom Ser.: 1). (ENG.). 432p. (J). (gr. 5). pap. 7.99 (978-0-06-147381-4(2)) HarperCollins Pubs.

Romeu, Emma. Gregorio Vuelve a Mexico. 2003. (SPA., Illus.). 148p. (J). (gr. 5-8). pap. 9.95 (978-968-19-0367-1(6)) Santillana USA Publishing Co., Inc.

Ronco, Dan. PeaceMaker. Pidlubny, Donna, illus. 2004. (YA). per. 15.49 (978-0-9752711-4-8(8)) Winterwolf Publishing.

Rooney, Anne. Wallace & Gromit's World of Mysteries. 2004. (Illus.). 30p. (gr. 5-9). reprint ed. 30.00 (978-0-7567-7410-3(1)) DIANE Publishing Co.

Ropal, Monica. When You Leave. 2015. (ENG.). 336p. (YA). (gr. 7). pap. 9.95 (978-0-7624-5455-6(5), Running Pr. Kids) Running Pr. Bk. Pubs.

Rosas, Beverly. The Hand That Scared Jenny. Davis, Jeff, illus. 2008. 47p. pap. 24.95 (978-1-4241-9138-3(6)) PublishAmerica, Inc.

Rose, Simon. The Sphere of Septimus, 1 vol. 2015. (ENG., Illus.). 96p. (J). (gr. 6-9). pap. 9.95 (978-1-896580-75-3(0)) Tradewind Bks. CAN. Dist: Orca Bk. Pubs. USA.

Rosellini, Eleanor. Mystery of the Ancient Coins. 2003. (Illus.). 116p. 18.95 (978-1-57860-122-6(3)) Clerisy Pr.

Rosen, Devora. Mystery in Spain. 2009. 250p. 19.99 (978-1-59826-327-5(7)) Feldheim Pubs.

Rosenberg, Aaron. Case of the Secret Sauce, Vol. 1. Harrington, David, illus. 2011. (Pete & Penny's Pizza Puzzles Ser.: 1). (ENG.). 64p. (J). (gr. 1-3). pap. 3.99 (978-0-8431-9928-4(8), Price Stern Sloan) Penguin Young Readers Group.

—Case of the Topsy-Turvy Toy. Harrington, David, illus. 2011. (Pete & Penny's Pizza Puzzles Ser.: 2). (ENG.). 64p. (J). (gr. 1-3). pap. 3.99 (978-0-8431-9929-1(6), Price Stern Sloan) Penguin Young Readers Group.

Rosenberg, Madelyn. Nanny X. 2015. (ENG., Illus.). 128p. (J). (gr. 2-5). 16.95 (978-0-8234-3533-3(4)) Holiday Hse., Inc.

Rosenberg, Meira. Indiana Bamboo: A Novel. 2017. (J). pap. **(978-1-60454-245-5(4)**, Iris Pr.) Iris Publishing Group, Inc., The.

Rosenfield, Kat. Amelia Anne Is Dead & Gone. 2013. (ENG.). 288p. (YA). (gr. 9). pap. 8.99 (978-0-14-242610-4(5), Speak) Penguin Young Readers Group.

Rosoff, Meg. Picture Me Gone. 2013. (ENG.). 256p. (J). (gr. 7). 17.99 (978-0-399-25765-0(9), G.P. Putnam's Sons Books for Young Readers) Penguin Young Readers Group.

Ross, Jeff. Coming Clean, 1 vol. 2012. (Orca Soundings Ser.). (ENG.). 128p. (YA). (gr. 8-12). pap. 9.95 (978-1-4598-0331-2(0)) Orca Bk. Pubs. USA.

Ross, Jill. The Real Nitty-Gritty. Pruitt, Gwendolyn, illus. 2010. (ENG.). 60p. (J). (gr. 3-7). pap. 9.95 (978-1-59825-949-0(0)) Shenanigans Series.

Rossell, Judith. Inspector Stilton & the Missing Jewels. Rossell, Judith, illus. 2005. (Illus.). 32p. pap. (978-1-921049-09-5(X)) Little Hare Bks. AUS. Dist: HarperCollins Pubs. Australia.

—Withering-By-Sea. Rossell, Judith, illus. 2017. (ENG., Illus.). 288p. (J). (gr. 3-7). pap. 7.99 (978-1-4814-4368-5(2)) Simon & Schuster Children's Publishing.

Rossell, Judith. Wormwood Mire. Rossell, Judith, illus. 2017. (ENG., Illus.). 288p. (J). (gr. 3-7). 16.99 **(978-1-4814-4370-8(4)**, Atheneum Bks. for Young Readers) Simon & Schuster Children's Publishing.

Roth, Silke. Creak, Thump, Bonk! 2007. (ENG.). 40p. (J). (gr. -1-3). 11.99 (978-1-4169-6159-8(3), Simon & Schuster/Paula Wiseman Bks.) Simon & Schuster/Paula Wiseman Bks.

Rouncville, Bibi. Sea Bugs & Moose Eggs. 2009. 52p. pap. 9.50 (978-1-4357-4004-4(1)) Lulu Pr., Inc.

Roux, Madeleine. Asylum. (ENG.). (gr. 9). 2014. 336p. (J). pap. 9.99 (978-0-06-222097-4(7)) 2013. (Illus.). 320p. (YA). 17.99 (978-0-06-222096-7(9)) HarperCollins Pubs.

—Asylum. 2015. (SPA.). 320p. (YA). (gr. 9-12). pap. 20.99 (978-987-612-778-3(0)) V&R Editoras.

—The Asylum Novellas: The Scarlets, the Bone Artists, & the Warden. 2016. (Asylum Novella Ser.). (Illus.). 352p. (YA). (gr. 9). pap. 9.99 (978-0-06-242446-4(7)) HarperCollins Pubs.

—Sanctum. 2014. (Illus.). 343p. (YA). (978-0-06-235182-1(6)) Harper & Row Ltd.

—Sanctum. 2014. (Asylum Ser.: 2). (ENG., Illus.). 352p. (YA). (gr. 9). 17.99 (978-0-06-222099-8(3)) HarperCollins Pubs.

Rouzer, Walter. Rebel Stone & the Ghost Whisperers. 2009. 304p. 28.95 (978-0-595-51192-1(9)); pap. 18.95 (978-0-595-52313-9(7)) iUniverse, Inc.

Rowe, John. Little Stories for Little People. 2013. 92p. pap. 25.95 (978-1-62516-542-8(0), Strategic Bk. Publishing) Strategic Book Publishing & Rights Agency (SBPRA).

Rowe, W. W. Jerry's Mystery. 2016. (ENG., Illus.). 96p. (J). (gr. 6-9). pap. 8.95 (978-1-936012-70-1(7)) Larson Pubns.

Roy, James. Ichabod Hart & the Lighthouse Mystery. 2003. (Steampunk Ser.). (Illus.). 392p. pap. (978-0-7022-3364-7(1)) Univ. of Queensland Pr.

Roy, Ron. A to Z Mysteries Collection, No. 1. Gurney, John Steven, illus. 2010. (to Z Mysteries Ser.: Nos. 1-4). (ENG.). 384p. (J). (gr. 1-4). 9.99 (978-0-375-85946-5(2), Random Hse. Bks. for Young Readers) Random Hse. Children's Bks.

—The Absent Author. Gurney, John Steven, illus. unabr. ed. 2004. (A to Z Mysteries Ser.: No. 1). 86p. (J). (gr. k-3). pap. 17.00 incl. audio (978-0-8072-1703-0(4), S FTR 269 SP, Listening Library) Random Hse. Audio Publishing Group.

—April Adventure. Gurney, John Steven, illus. 2010. (Calendar Mysteries Ser.: 4). (ENG.). 80p. (J). (gr. 1-4). 4.99 (978-0-375-86116-1(5), Random Hse. Bks. for Young Readers) Random Hse. Children's Bks.

—April Adventure. 2010. (Calendar Mysteries Ser.: 4). lib. bdg. 14.75 (978-0-606-12465-2(9), Turtleback) Turtleback Bks.

—August Acrobat. Gurney, John Steven, illus. 2012. (Calendar Mysteries Ser.: 8). (ENG.). 80p. (J). (gr. 1-4). 4.99 (978-0-375-86886-3(0)); lib. bdg. 12.99 (978-0-375-96886-0(5)) Random Hse. Children's Bks. (Random Hse. Bks. for Young Readers).

—August Acrobat. 2012. (Calendar Mysteries Ser.: 8). lib. bdg. 14.75 (978-0-606-26403-7(5), Turtleback) Turtleback Bks.

—The Bald Bandit. Gurney, John Steven, illus. unabr. ed. 2004. (A to Z Mysteries Ser.: No. 2). 80p. (J). (gr. k-3). pap. 17.00 incl. audio (978-0-8072-1704-7(2), S FTR 270 SP, Listening Library) Random Hse. Audio Publishing Group.

—The Canary Caper. Gurney, John Steven, illus. unabr. ed. 2004. (A to Z Mysteries Ser.: No. 3). 80p. (J). (gr. k-3). pap. 17.00 incl. audio (978-0-8072-1705-4(0), S FTR 271 SP, Listening Library) Random Hse. Audio Publishing Group.

—Capital Mysteries #13: Trapped on the D. C. Train! Bush, Timothy, illus. 2011. (Capital Mysteries Ser.). (ENG.). 96p. (J). (gr. 1-4). 4.99 (978-0-375-85926-7(8), Random Hse. Bks. for Young Readers) Random Hse. Children's Bks.

—The Castle Crime. 2014. (to Z Mysteries Ser.: 32). lib. bdg. 16.00 (978-0-606-35190-4(6)) Turtleback Bks.

—Detective Camp. Gurney, John Steven, illus. 2006. (to Z Mysteries Ser.: No. 1). (ENG.). 144p. (J). (gr. 1-4). per. 5.99 (978-0-375-83534-6(2), Random Hse. Bks. for Young Readers) Random Hse. Children's Bks.

—The Election-Day Disaster. Bush, Timothy, illus. 2008. (Capital Mysteries Ser.: No. 10). 87p. (gr. 1-4). 15.00 (978-0-7569-8802-9(0)) Perfection Learning Corp.

—The Election-Day Disaster. Bush, Timothy, illus. 2008. (Capital Mysteries Ser.: No. 10). (ENG.). 96p. (J). (gr. 1-4). 4.99 (978-0-375-84805-6(3), Random Hse. Bks. for Young Readers) Random Hse. Children's Bks.

—February Friend. Gurney, John Steven, illus. 2009. (Calendar Mysteries Ser.: 2). (ENG.). 80p. (J). (gr. 1-4). 4.99 (978-0-375-85662-4(5), Random Hse. Bks. for Young Readers) Random Hse. Children's Bks.

—The Ghost at Camp David. Bush, Timothy, illus. 2010. (Capital Mysteries Ser.: 12). (ENG.). 96p. (J). (gr. 1-4). pap. 4.99 (978-0-375-85925-0(X), Random Hse. Bks. for Young Readers) Random Hse. Children's Bks.

—The Ghost at Camp David. 2010. (Capital Mysteries Ser.: 12). lib. bdg. 14.75 (978-0-606-14010-2(7), Turtleback) Turtleback Bks.

—January Joker. Gurney, John Steven, illus. 2009. (Calendar Mysteries Ser.: 1). (ENG.). 96p. (J). (gr. 1-4). 4.99 (978-0-375-85661-7(7), Random Hse. Bks. for Young Readers) Random Hse. Children's Bks.

—July Jitters. Gurney, John Steven, illus. 2012. (Calendar Mysteries Ser.: 7). (ENG.). 80p. (J). (gr. 1-4). 4.99 (978-0-375-86882-5(8), Random Hse. Bks. for Young Readers) Random Hse. Children's Bks.

—July Jitters. 2012. (Calendar Mysteries Ser.: 7). lib. bdg. 14.75 (978-0-606-26402-0(7), Turtleback) Turtleback Bks.

—June Jam. Gurney, John Steven, illus. 2011. (Calendar Mysteries Ser.: 6). (ENG.). 80p. (J). (gr. 1-4). 4.99 (978-0-375-86112-3(2), Random Hse. Bks. for Young Readers) Random Hse. Children's Bks.

—March Mischief. Gurney, John Steven, illus. 2010. (Calendar Mysteries Ser.: 3). (ENG.). 80p. (J). (gr. 1-4). 4.99 (978-0-375-85663-1(3), Random Hse. Bks. for Young Readers) Random Hse. Children's Bks.

—March Mischief. 2010. (Calendar Mysteries Ser.: 3). lib. bdg. 14.75 (978-0-606-12460-7(8), Turtleback) Turtleback Bks.

—May Magic. Gurney, John Steven, illus. 2011. (Calendar Mysteries Ser.: 5). (ENG.). 80p. (J). (gr. 1-4). 4.99 (978-0-375-86111-6(4), Random Hse. Bks. for Young Readers) Random Hse. Children's Bks.

—Mayflower Treasure Hunt. Gurney, John Steven, illus. 2nd ed. 2007. (to Z Mysteries Ser.: 2). (ENG.). 128p. (J). (gr. 1-4). per. 5.99 (978-0-375-83937-5(2), Random Hse. Bks. for Young Readers) Random Hse. Children's Bks.

—Mayflower Treasure Hunt. Gurney, John Steven, illus. 2007. (to Z Mysteries Ser.: 28). 114p. (gr. 4-7). lib. bdg. 16.00 (978-1-4177-9141-5(1), Turtleback) Turtleback Bks.

—The Missing Mummy. (A to Z Mystery Ser.: Vol. 13). (J). 11.32 (978-0-7383-3465-3(0)) Booksource, The.

—Mystery at the Washington Monument. Bush, Timothy, illus. 2007. (Capital Mysteries Ser.: No. 8). 87p. (gr. 1-4). 15.00 (978-0-7569-7845-7(9)) Perfection Learning Corp.

—Mystery at the Washington Monument. Bush, Timothy, illus. 2007. (Capital Mysteries Ser.: No. 8). (ENG.). 96p. (J). (gr. 1-4). per. 4.99 (978-0-375-83970-2(4), Random Hse. Bks. for Young Readers) Random Hse. Children's Bks.

—The New Year Dragon Dilemma. Gurney, John Steven, illus. 2011. (to Z Mysteries Ser.). (ENG.). 144p. (J). (gr. 1-4). 5.99 (978-0-375-86880-1(1), Random Hse. Bks. for Young Readers) Random Hse. Children's Bks.

—October Ogre. Gurney, John Steven, illus. 2013. (Calendar Mysteries Ser.: 10). (ENG.). 80p. (J). (gr. 1-4). lib. bdg. 12.99 (978-0-375-96888-4(1), Random Hse. Bks. for Young Readers) Random Hse. Children's Bks.

—October Ogre. 2013. (Calendar Mysteries Ser.: 10). lib. bdg. 14.75 (978-0-606-32232-4(9), Turtleback) Turtleback Bks.

—Operation Orca. Gurney, John Steven, illus. 2015. (to Z Mysteries Ser.). (ENG.). 144p. (J). (gr. 1-4). 12.99 (978-0-553-52397-3(X), Random Hse. Bks. for Young Readers) Random Hse. Children's Bks.

—The School Skeleton. Gurney, John Steven, illus. 2003. (to Z Mysteries Ser.: 19). (ENG.). 96p. (J). (gr. 1-4). pap. 4.99 (978-0-375-81368-9(3), Random Hse. Bks. for Young Readers) Random Hse. Children's Bks.

—The School Skeleton. Gurney, John Steven, illus. 2003. (to Z Mysteries Ser.: 19). (gr. k-3). lib. bdg. 14.75 (978-0-613-62405-3(X), Turtleback) Turtleback Bks.

—Secret Admirer. Gurney, John Steven, illus. 2015. (to Z Mysteries Ser.: No. 8). (ENG.). 144p. (J). (gr. 1-4). 5.99 (978-0-553-52399-7(6), Random Hse. Bks. for Young Readers) Random Hse. Children's Bks.

—The Secret at Jefferson's Mansion. Bush, Timothy, illus. 2009. (Capital Mysteries Ser.: 11). (ENG.). 96p. (J). (gr. 1-4). 4.99 (978-0-375-84533-8(X), Random Hse. Bks. for Young Readers) Random Hse. Children's Bks.

—September Sneakers. Gurney, John Steven, illus. 2013. (Calendar Mysteries Ser.: 9). (ENG.). 80p. (J). (gr. 1-4). 4.99 (978-0-375-86887-0(9), Random Hse. Bks. for Young Readers) Random Hse. Children's Bks.

—September Sneakers. 2013. (Calendar Mysteries Ser.: 9). lib. bdg. 14.75 (978-0-606-32231-7(0), Turtleback) Turtleback Bks.

—Sleepy Hollow Sleepover. Gurney, John Steven, illus. 4th ed. 2010. (to Z Mysteries Ser.: 4). (ENG.). 144p. (J). (gr. 1-4). pap. 5.99 (978-0-375-86669-2(8), Random Hse. Bks. for Young Readers) Random Hse. Children's Bks.

—Sleepy Hollow Sleepover. 4th ed. 2010. (to Z Mysteries Ser.: 30). lib. bdg. 16.00 (978-0-606-14007-2(7), Turtleback) Turtleback Bks.

—A Spy in the White House. Bush, Timothy, tr. Bush, Timothy, illus. 2004. (Capital Mysteries Ser.: No. 4). (ENG.). 96p. (J). (gr. 1-4). 4.99 (978-0-375-82557-6(6), Random Hse. Bks. for Young Readers) Random Hse. Children's Bks.

—The Talking T. Rex. Gurney, John Steven, illus. 2003. (to Z Mysteries Ser.: 20). (ENG.). 96p. (J). (gr. 1-4). pap. 4.99 (978-0-375-81369-6(1), Random Hse. Bks. for Young Readers) Random Hse. Children's Bks.

—A Thief at the National Zoo. Bush, Timothy, illus. 2008. (Capital Mysteries Ser.: No. 9). 87p. (gr. k-3). 15.00 (978-0-7569-8329-1(0)) Perfection Learning Corp.

—A Thief at the National Zoo. Bush, Timothy, illus. 2007. (Capital Mysteries Ser.: No. 9). (ENG.). 96p. (J). (gr. 1-4). per. 4.99 (978-0-375-84804-9(5), Random Hse. Bks. for Young Readers) Random Hse. Children's Bks.

—Trouble at the Treasury. Bush, Timothy, illus. 2006. (Capital Mysteries Ser.: No. 7). (ENG.). 96p. (J). (gr. 1-4). per. 4.99 (978-0-375-83969-6(0), Random Hse. Bks. for Young Readers) Random Hse. Children's Bks.

—The Unwilling Umpire. Gurney, John Steven, illus. 2004. (to Z Mysteries Ser.: 21). (ENG.). 96p. (J). (gr. 1-4). 4.99 (978-0-375-81370-2(5), Random Hse. Bks. for Young Readers) Random Hse. Children's Bks.

—The Unwilling Umpire. Gurney, John Steven, illus. 2004. (to Z Mysteries Ser.: 21). (gr. k-3). lib. bdg. 14.75 (978-0-613-82496-5(2), Turtleback) Turtleback Bks.

—The Vampire's Vacation. Gurney, John Steven, illus. 2004. (to Z Mysteries Ser.: 22). (ENG.). 96p. (J). (gr. 1-4). pap. 4.99 (978-0-375-82479-1(0), Random Hse. Bks. for Young Readers) Random Hse. Children's Bks.

—White House White-Out. Gurney, John Steven, illus. 2008. (A to Z Mysteries Ser.: No. 3). 124p. (gr. 1-4). 15.00 (978-0-7569-8799-2(7)) Perfection Learning Corp.

—White House White-Out. Gurney, John Steven, illus. 2008. (to Z Mysteries Ser.: 3). (ENG.). 144p. (J). (gr. 1-4). 5.99 (978-0-375-84721-9(9), Random Hse. Bks. for Young Readers) Random Hse. Children's Bks.

—The White Wolf. Gurney, John Steven, tr. Gurney, John Steven, illus. 2004. (to Z Mysteries Ser.: No. 23). (ENG.). 96p. (J). (gr. 1-4). pap. 4.99 (978-0-375-82480-7(4), Random Hse. Bks. for Young Readers) Random Hse. Children's Bks.

—Who Broke Lincoln's Thumb? Bush, Timothy, illus. 2005. (Capital Mysteries Ser.: No. 5). (ENG.). 96p. (J). (gr. 1-4). per. 4.99 (978-0-375-82558-3(4), Random Hse. Bks. for Young Readers) Random Hse. Children's Bks.

—The X'ed-Out X-Ray. Gurney, John Steven, illus. 2005. (to Z Mysteries Ser.: No. 24). (ENG.). 96p. (J). (gr. 1-4). 4.99 (978-0-375-82481-4(2), Random Hse. Bks. for Young Readers) Random Hse. Children's Bks.

—The Yellow Yacht. Gurney, John Steven, illus. 2005. (to Z Mysteries Ser.: 25). (ENG.). 96p. (J). (gr. 1-4). pap. 4.99 (978-0-375-82482-1(0), Random Hse. Bks. for Young Readers) Random Hse. Children's Bks.

—The Zombie Zone. Gurney, John Steven, illus. 2005. (to Z Mysteries Ser.: 26). (ENG.). 96p. (J). (gr. 1-4). pap. 4.99 (978-0-375-82483-8(9), Random Hse. Bks. for Young Readers) Random Hse. Children's Bks.

Roy, Ronald. April Fools' Fiasco. Gurney, John Steven, illus. 2017. (to Z Mysteries Ser.: 9). (ENG.). 144p. (J). (gr. 1-4). 5.99 (978-0-399-55195-6(6), Random Hse. Bks. for Young Readers) Random Hse. Children's Bks.

—Calendar Mysteries #12: December Dog. Gurney, John Steven, illus. 2014. (Calendar Mysteries Ser.: 12). (ENG.). 80p. (J). (gr. 1-4). 4.99 (978-0-385-37168-1(3), Random Hse. Bks. for Young Readers) Random Hse. Children's Bks.

—Calendar Mysteries #13: New Year's Eve Thieves. Gurney, John Steven, illus. 2014. (Calendar Mysteries Ser.: 13). (ENG.). 80p. (J). (gr. 1-4). 4.99 (978-0-385-37171-1(3), Random Hse. Bks. for Young Readers) Random Hse. Children's Bks.

—The Castle Crime. Gurney, John Steven, illus. 2014. (to Z Mysteries Ser.: No. 6). (ENG.). 144p. (J). (gr. 1-4). 5.99 (978-0-385-37159-9(4), Random Hse. Bks. for Young Readers) Random Hse. Children's Bks.

—December Dog. 2014. (Calendar Mysteries Ser.: 12). lib. bdg. 14.75 (978-0-606-36019-7(0)) Turtleback Bks.

—New Year's Eve Thieves. 2014. (Calendar Mysteries Ser.: 13). lib. bdg. 14.75 (978-0-606-36020-3(4)) Turtleback Bks.

—November Night. Gurney, John Steven, illus. 2014. (Calendar Mysteries Ser.: 11). (ENG.). 80p. (J). (gr. 1-4). 4.99 (978-0-385-37165-0(9), Random Hse. Bks. for Young Readers) Random Hse. Children's Bks.

—November Night. 2014. (Calendar Mysteries Ser.: 11). lib. bdg. 14.75 (978-0-606-36018-0(2)) Turtleback Bks.

—Turkey Trouble on the National Mall. Bush, Timothy, illus. 2012. (Capital Mysteries Ser.: 14). (ENG.). 96p. (J). (gr. 1-4). 4.99 (978-0-307-93220-4(6), Random Hse. Bks. for Young Readers) Random Hse. Children's Bks.

Rozum, John. Scooby-Doo in Yankee Doodle Danger, 1 vol. 2013. (Scooby-Doo Graphic Novels Set 3 Ser.). (ENG.). 24p. (J). (gr. 2-6). lib. bdg. 24.21 (978-1-61479-054-9(X), Essential Library) ABDO Publishing Co.

Rubin, Sarah. The Impossible Clue. 2017. (J). pap. **(978-0-545-94272-0(1)**, Chicken Hse., The) Scholastic, Inc.

Ruby, Laura. York: The Shadow Cipher. 2017. (York Ser.: 1). (ENG.). 496p. (J). (gr. 3-7). E-Book (978-0-06-230695-1(2), Waldon Pond Pr.) HarperCollins Pubs.

—York: The Shadow Cipher. Stevenson, Dave, illus. 2017. (York Ser.: 1). 496p. (J). (gr. 3-7). 17.99 (978-0-06-230693-7(6), Waldon Pond Pr.) HarperCollins Pubs.

Ruby, Lois. Rebel Spirits. 2013. (ENG.). 304p. (J). (gr. 7). 17.99 (978-0-545-42623-7(5)); 292p. (YA). (978-0-545-55282-0(6)) Scholastic, Inc.

Rucker, Noah. Mystery of the Shadows. 2005. 27p. (J). 5.00 (978-1-882695-21-8(6)) Patagonia Pr.

Ruiz Zafón, Carlos. Marina. 2009. (Best Seller (Edebe) Ser.). (SPA.). 286p. pap. (978-84-236-8726-8(0)) Edebé.

Runholt, Susan. The Mystery of the Third Lucretia. 2009. (Kari & Lucas Mystery Ser.). (ENG.). 304p. (J). (gr. 5-18). pap. 6.99 (978-0-14-241338-8(0), Puffin Books) Penguin Young Readers Group.

—Rescuing Seneca Crane. 2009. (Kari & Lucas Mystery Ser.). (ENG.). 288p. (J). (gr. 5-18). 16.99 (978-0-670-06291-1(X), Viking Books for Young Readers) Penguin Young Readers Group.

Rusch, Elizabeth. Muddy Max: The Mystery of Marsh Creek. Lawrence, Mike, illus. 2014. (ENG.). 224p. (J). pap. 9.99 (978-1-4494-3561-5(0)) Andrews McMeel Publishing.

Rusch, Elizabeth & Lawrence, Mike. Muddy Max: The Mystery of Marsh Creek. 2016. (ENG., Illus.). (J). (gr. 2-6). 37.99 **(978-1-4494-7388-4(1))** Andrews McMeel Publishing.

Rush, Barbara & Stratton, Jane. The Boat in the Attic. 2012. (ENG.). 30p. pap. 15.00 (978-1-938002-02-1(4), Hummingbird World Media) Double Edge Pr.

Rush, Jennifer. Erased. 2014. (Altered Ser.: 2). (ENG.). 352p. (YA). (gr. 7-17). pap. 10.99 (978-0-316-19714-4(9)) Little, Brown Bks. for Young Readers.

—Reborn. 2016. (Altered Ser.: 3). (ENG.). 384p. (YA). (gr. 7-17). pap. 10.00 (978-0-316-19707-6(6)) Little, Brown Bks. for Young Readers.

Rushford, Patricia H. Secrets of Ghost Island. 2007. (J). (978-88-02-46255-4(0)) Moody Pubs.

Russel, Mary. Flickertail & Paint, Barnyard Sleuths, 1 vol. 2010. 96p. pap. 19.95 (978-1-4489-7248-7(5)) America Star Bks.

Russell, Elaine. Martin Mcmillan & the Lost Inca City. Cornell du Houx, Emily M. D., illus. 2005. 128p. (gr. 5-18). pap. 10.00 (978-1-882190-86-7(6)) Polar Bear & Co.

Russell, Sharman Apt. Teresa of the New World. 2015. (ENG.). 192p. (gr. 6). 14.99 (978-1-63158-042-0(6), Yucca Publishing) Skyhorse Publishing Co., Inc.

Ruth, Greg. The Lost Boy. 2013. (ENG.). 192p. (J). (gr. 3-7). pap. 12.99 (978-0-439-82332-6(3), Graphix) Scholastic, Inc.

Ryan, Jessica. The Mystery of Arroyo Seco. Stone, David, illus. 2011. 186p. 42.95 (978-1-258-08470-7(8)) Literary Licensing, LLC.

Ryan, John, illus. Pugwash the Smuggler. fac. ed. 2009. (ENG.). 32p. (J). (gr. -1-2). (978-1-84507-889-8(6)) Rough Guides, Ltd.

Rylander, Chris. Countdown Zero. 2016. (Codename Conspiracy Ser.: 2). 384p. (J). (gr. 3-7). pap. 6.99 (978-0-06-212012-0(3), Waldon Pond Pr.) HarperCollins Pubs.

Rylant, Cynthia. The Case of the Climbing Cat. Karas, G. Brian, illus. 2003. (High-Rise Private Eyes Ser.: No. 2). (J). (gr. k-3). 28.95 incl. audio compact disk (978-1-59112-611-9(8)) Live Oak Media.

—The Case of the Desperate Duck. Karas, G. Brian, illus. (I Can Read Level 2 Ser.: No. 8). 48p. (J). (gr. k-3). 2006. (ENG.). pap. 3.99 (978-0-06-053453-0(2), Greenwillow Bks.) 2005. 14.99 (978-0-06-053451-6(6)) 2005. lib. bdg. 15.89 (978-0-06-053452-3(4)) HarperCollins Pubs.

—The Case of the Desperate Duck, 4 bks., Set. 2007. (High-Rise Private Eyes Ser.: Bk. 8). (J). (gr. k-2). pap. 31.95 incl. audio compact disk (978-1-4301-0067-6(2)); pap. 29.95 incl. audio (978-1-4301-0065-2(6)) Live Oak Media.

—The Case of the Desperate Duck. Karas, G. Brian, illus. 2006. (High-Rise Private Eyes Ser.). 48p. (gr. -1-3). 14.00 (978-0-7569-6958-5(1)) Perfection Learning Corp.

—The Case of the Fidgety Fox. Karas, G. Brian, illus. unabr. ed. 2005. (High-Rise Private Eyes Ser.: No. 6). (J). (gr. k-4). 25.95 incl. audio (978-1-59519-405-3(3));Set. pap. 31.95 incl. audio compact disk (978-1-59519-410-7(X));Set. pap. 29.95 incl. audio (978-1-59519-406-0(1)) Live Oak Media.

—The Case of the Fidgety Fox. Karas, G. Brian, illus. 2004. (High-Rise Private Eyes Ser.). 58p. (J). (gr. 1-3). 11.65 (978-0-7569-3210-7(6)) Perfection Learning Corp.

—The Case of the Missing Monkey. Karas, G. Brian, illus. 2003. (I Can Read Level 2 Ser.: No. 1). (ENG.). 48p. (J). (gr. k-3). pap. 3.99 *(978-0-06-444306-7(X),* Greenwillow Bks.) HarperCollins Pubs.
—The Case of the Missing Monkey. Karas, G. Brian, illus. 2003. (High-Rise Private Eyes Ser.: No. 1). 28.95 incl. audio compact disk *(978-1-59112-615-7(0))* Live Oak Media.
—The Case of the Puzzling Possum. Karas, G. Brian, illus. 2003. (High-Rise Private Eyes Ser.: No. 3). (J). (gr. k-3). 28.95 incl. audio compact disk *(978-1-59112-619-5(3))* Live Oak Media.
—The Case of the Sleepy Sloth. Karas, G. Brian, illus. unabr. ed. 2005. (High-Rise Private Eyes Ser.: No. 5). (J). (gr. k-4). 29.95 incl. audio *(978-1-59519-413-8(4))*; 28.95 incl. audio compact disk *(978-1-59519-417-6(7))*;Set. pap. 31.95 incl. audio compact disk *(978-1-59519-418-3(5))*;Set. pap. 29.95 incl. audio *(978-1-59519-414-5(2))* Live Oak Media.
—The High-Rise Private Eye: The\Case of the Troublesome Turtle. Karas, G. Brian, illus. 2003. (High-Rise Private Eyes Ser.: No. 4). (J). (gr. k-3). 25.95 incl. audio *(978-1-59112-202-9(3))*; 28.95 incl. audio compact disk *(978-1-59112-623-2(1))*; pap. 31.95 incl. audio compact disk *(978-1-59112-624-9(X))*; pap. 29.95 incl. audio *(978-1-59112-203-6(1))* Live Oak Media.
—The High-Rise Private Eyes Series. Karas, G. Brian, illus. 2003. pap. 61.95 incl. audio *(978-1-59112-430-6(1))*; pap. 68.95 incl. audio compact disk *(978-1-59112-858-8(7))* Live Oak Media.
Sadar, Albin. Hamster Holmes: A Mystery Comes Knocking. Fabbretti, Valerio, illus. 2015. (Hamster Holmes Ser.: 1). (ENG.). 32p. (J). (gr. k-2). 16.99 *(978-1-4814-2037-2(2),* Simon Spotlight) Simon Spotlight.
—Hamster Holmes: A Mystery Comes Knocking. 2015. (Simon & Schuster Ready-To-Read Level 2 Ser.). lib. bdg. 13.55 *(978-0-606-37142-1(7))* Turtleback Bks.
—Hamster Holmes, Combing for Clues. Fabbretti, Valerio, illus. 2015. (Hamster Holmes Ser.: 2). (ENG.). 32p. (J). (gr. k-2). pap. 3.99 *(978-1-4814-2039-6(9),* Simon Spotlight) Simon Spotlight.
—Hamster Holmes, on the Right Track. Fabbretti, Valerio, illus. 2016. (Hamster Holmes Ser.). (ENG.). 32p. (J). (gr. k-2). pap. 3.99 *(978-1-4814-2042-6(9),* Simon Spotlight) Simon Spotlight.
—Hamster Holmes, on the Right Track. 2016. (Simon & Schuster Ready-To-Read Level 2 Ser.). lib. bdg. 13.55 *(978-0-606-38245-8(3))* Turtleback Bks.
—A Mystery Comes Knocking. Fabbretti, Valerio, illus. 2015. (Hamster Holmes Ser.: 1). (ENG.). 32p. (J). (gr. k-2). pap. 3.99 *(978-1-4814-2036-5(4),* Simon Spotlight) Simon Spotlight.
Saddleback Educational Publishing Staff, creator. Saddleback's Dark Man Full Set. 2010. (Illus.). (YA). pap. *(978-1-61651-257-6(1))* Saddleback Educational Publishing, Inc.
Sadler, Marilyn & Comstock, Eric. Charlie Piechart & the Case of the Missing Hat. Comstock, Eric, illus. 2016. (Charlie Piechart Ser.). (Illus.). 40p. (J). (gr. -1-3). 17.99 *(978-0-06-237056-3(1),* Tegen, Katherine Bks) HarperCollins Pubs.
Sage, Angie. Frognapped. Pickering, Jimmy, illus. 2008. (Araminta Spookie Ser.: 3). (ENG.). 224p. (J). (gr. 2-5). pap. 6.99 *(978-0-06-077489-9(4),* Tegen, Katherine Bks) HarperCollins Pubs.
—Gargoyle Hall: An Araminta Spookie Adventure. 2015. (Araminta Spookie Adventure Ser.: 1). (ENG., Illus.). 224p. (YA). (gr. 3-6). 16.99 *(978-1-61963-626-2(3),* 9781619636262, Bloomsbury USA Childrens) Bloomsbury Publishing USA.
—Skeleton Island. 2016. (Araminta Spookie Adventure Ser.: 2). (ENG.). 176p. (J). 16.99 *(978-1-61963-945-4(9),* 9781619639454, Bloomsbury USA Childrens) Bloomsbury Publishing USA.
Said, S. F. Varjak Paw. McKean, Dave, illus. 2005. (ENG.). 256p. (J). (gr. 3-7). reprint ed. pap. 7.99 *(978-0-440-42076-7(8),* Yearling) Random Hse. Children's Bks.
Saldana, Rene. Case of Pen Gone Missing/El Caso de la Pluma Perdida. Villarroel, Carolina, tr. from ENG. Mora, Giovanni, illus. 2009. (SPA & ENG.). 80p. (J). (gr. 3-7). pap. 9.95 *(978-1-55885-555-7(6),* Piñata Books) Arte Publico Pr.
Saldaña, René. The Lemon Tree Caper: A Mickey Rangel Mystery / la Intriga del limonero: Colección Mickey Rangel, detective Privado. Rosales-Yeomans, Natalia, tr. from ENG. 2011. (SPA & ENG.). (J). pap. 9.95 *(978-1-55885-709-4(5),* Piñata Books) Arte Publico Pr.
Saldana, Rene, Jr. A Mystery Bigger Than Big / un Misterio Mas Grande Que Grandisimo: A Mickey Rangel Mystery / Colección Mickey Rangel, Detective Privado. 2016. (Mickey Rangel Mystery / Coleccion Mickey Rangel, Detective P Ser.). (MUL, ENG & SPA., Illus.). 64p. (J). (gr. 3-6). pap. 9.95 *(978-1-55885-824-4(5),* Piñata Books) Arte Publico Pr.
Saldaña, René. The Mystery of the Mischievous Marker / el Misterio Del Malvado Marcador: A Mickey Rangel Mystery / Colección Mickey Rangel, Detective Privado. Villarroel, Carolina, tr. from ENG. 2013. (Mickey Rangel Mystery / Colección Mickey Rangel, Detective Privado Ser.). (SPA.). 64p. (J). pap. 9.95 *(978-1-55885-776-6(1),* Piñata Books) Arte Publico Pr.
Salisbury, Linda G. The Mysterious Jamestown Suitcase: A Bailey Fish Adventure. Grotke, Christopher A., illus. 2006. (Bailey Fish Adventures Ser.). 191p. (J). (gr. 3-7). per. 8.95 *(978-1-881539-43-8(1))* Tabby Hse. Bks.
—The Thief at Keswick Inn: A Bailey Fish Adventure. Grotke, Christopher A., illus. 2006. (Bailey Fish Adventures Ser.). 191p. (J). (gr. 3-7). per. 8.95 *(978-1-881539-41-4(5))* Tabby Hse. Bks.
Salmon, Charles Ray, afterword by. The Adventures of Pittypat & Tippytoe, 1vol., 1vol. 2004. (ENG.). 232p. (YA). per. 12.99 *(978-0-9760045-0-9(X),* Reluctant Reader Bks.) Cronus College.
Salomon, Peter Adam. All Those Broken Angels. 2014. (ENG.). 240p. (YA). pap. 11.99 *(978-0-7387-4079-9(9),* Flux) North Star Editions.
Salote, Ana. Oy Yew. 2013. 276p. pap. *(978-1-78299-659-0(1))* FeedARead.com.
Sam, Kagan, illus. Mr. Duz Solves a Mystery. 2007. 24p. (J). 5.95 *(978-0-9796226-0-1(3))* MrDuz.com.
Sampson, Brent. Aidan's Shoes. Switzer, Bobbi, illus. 2006. (ENG.). 28p. per. 12.95 *(978-1-59800-684-1(3))* Outskirts Pr., Inc.
Sam's Last Summer. 2006. (J). per. 5.95 *(978-0-9790796-3-4(2))* PJR Assocs., Ltd.
Sander, Sonia. Scooby-Doo & the Chocolate Phantom, 1 vol. 2016. (Scooby-Doo Comic Readers Ser.). (ENG.). 32p. (J). (gr. k-3). lib. bdg. 24.21 *(978-1-61479-451-6(0),* Graphic Planet) Magic Wagon.
—Scooby-Doo & the International Express. 2009. (Illus.). 32p. (J). pap. *(978-0-545-16283-8(1))* Scholastic, Inc.
—Scooby-Doo in Food Fight!, 1 vol. 2016. (Scooby-Doo Comic Readers Ser.). (ENG.). 32p. (J). (gr. k-3). lib. bdg. 24.21 *(978-1-61479-454-7(5),* Graphic Planet) Magic Wagon.
—Scooby-Doo in Shiver Me Timbers, 1 vol. 2016. (Scooby-Doo! Set 3 Ser.). (ENG., Illus.). 32p. (J). (gr. k-4). lib. bdg. 24.21 *(978-1-61479-408-0(1),* 1401184) Spotlight.
—Witching Hour. 2009. (Scooby Reader 25 Ser.). (ENG., Illus.). 32p. (J). (gr. -1-3). pap. 3.99 *(978-0-545-16106-0(1))* Scholastic, Inc.
Sanders, Gaye Lynn. Chameleon Girl. 2008. 60p. pap. 16.95 *(978-1-60703-643-2(6))* America Star Bks.
Sanders, Russell J. Special Effect. 2016. (ENG., Illus.). (J). 24.99 ***(978-1-63533-074-8(2),*** Harmony Ink Pr.) Dreamspinner Pr.
Sanderson, Nancy. Summer of the Painted Horse. 2009. 188p. pap. 14.49 *(978-1-4490-2312-6(6))* AuthorHouse.
Sands, Kevin. The Blackthorn Key. 2016. lib. bdg. 18.40 *(978-0-606-38966-2(0))* Turtleback Bks.
Santomenna, Joan E. & Santomenna, Marco D. Caribbean Capers. 2003. (Illus.). 144p. (YA). (gr. 3-9). pap. 9.95 *(978-0-9643407-2-5(0))* WindSpirit Publishing.
Sarfati, Sonia. La Comédienne Disparue. 2003. (Roman Jeunesse Ser.). (FRE.). 96p. (YA). (gr. 4-7). pap. *(978-2-89021-211-4(4))* Diffusion du livre Mirabel (DLM).
Sargeant, Glen. Finders Keepers, 1 vol. 2009. 142p. pap. 24.95 *(978-1-61582-202-7(X))* America Star Bks.
—Ghost Ship: A y-Files Mystery. 2012. 128p. pap. 19.95 *(978-1-4626-8020-7(8))* America Star Bks.
Savage, J. Scott. Making the Team. Holgate, Doug, illus. 2015. (Case File 13 Ser.: 2). (ENG.). 288p. (J). (gr. 3-7). pap. 6.99 *(978-0-06-213335-9(7))* HarperCollins Pubs.
Savage, Kim. Beautiful Broken Girls. 2017. (ENG.). 336p. (YA). 17.99 *(978-0-374-30059-3(3),* 9780374300593, Farrar, Straus & Giroux (BYR)) Farrar, Straus & Giroux.
Savageau, Tony. The Mud House Mystery: A Wild Bunch Adventure. Raditz, JoAnne, illus. 2004. (J). pap. 9.95 *(978-0-9759737-0-7(3))* Blue Mustang Pr.
Saxon, Victoria. Big Trouble in Little Rodentia. 2016. (Illus.). (J). ***(978-1-5182-0883-6(5))*** Random House Children's Books.
Saxon, Victoria. Message in a Bottle. 2016. (Barbie Chapters Ser.). (ENG., Illus.). 64p. (J). (gr. 1-4). 5.99 *(978-0-399-54962-5(5),* Random Hse. Bks. for Young Readers) Random Hse. Children's Bks.
Sazaklis, John. The Mystery of the Maze Monster, 1 vol. Neely, Scott, illus. 2014. (You Choose Stories: Scooby-Doo Ser.). (ENG.). 112p. (gr. 2-3). pap. 6.95 *(978-1-4342-7928-6(6),* You Choose Bks.) Capstone Press of Coughlan Cos.
Scanes, Amy. The Chosen: Book Two of the Abon Trilogy. 2007. 304p. per. 18.95 *(978-0-595-45990-2(0))* iUniverse, Inc.
Scarry, Richard. Richard Scarry's the Great Pie Robbery & Other Mysteries. 2008. (ENG., Illus.). 104p. (J). (gr. 1-3). 12.95 *(978-1-4027-5823-2(5))* Sterling Publishing Co., Inc.
Scattergood, Augusta. The Way to Stay in Destiny. 2015. (ENG.). 192p. (J). (gr. 3-7). 16.99 *(978-0-545-53824-4(6),* Scholastic Pr.) Scholastic, Inc.
Schaedler, Peggy. Dagger & Dash: The Scrimshaw Medallion. 2012. 156p. (gr. 4-6). 30.95 *(978-1-4582-0279-6(8))*; (J). pap. 12.99 *(978-1-4582-0277-2(1))* Author Solutions, Inc. (Abbott Pr.).
Scheier, Leah. Secret Letters. 2013. (ENG., Illus.). 320p. (J). (gr. 5-17). pap. 8.99 *(978-1-4231-2758-1(7))* Hyperion Pr.
Scheunemann, Pam. Cat Tails, 1 vol. Chawla, Neena, illus. 2006. (Animal Tales Ser.). 24p. (J). (gr. k-3). (ENG.). lib. bdg. 24.21 *(978-1-59679-927-1(7),* SandCastle); pap. 48.42 *(978-1-59679-928-8(5))* ABDO Publishing Co.
Schindler, Holly. Feral. 2014. (ENG.). 432p. (YA). (gr. 8). 17.99 *(978-0-06-222020-2(9),* HarperTeen) HarperCollins Pubs.
Schlegl, Stacey Lynn & Schlegl, Abigail. MerMountain. 2012. 84p. (J). pap. 11.95 *(978-0-9850272-2-3(3))* Jan-Carol Publishing, INC.
Schmitt, Gary. R. O. Dents in the School. 2009. 73p. pap. 19.95 *(978-1-60813-737-4(6))* America Star Bks.
Scholastic, Inc. Staff. Cahills vs Vespers, Pack. 2011. (39 Clues: Cahills vs. Vespers Ser.). (ENG.). 16p. (J). (gr. 3-7). 6.99 *(978-0-545-31640-8(5))* Scholastic, Inc.
Scholastic, Inc. Staff & Duendes Del Sur Staff, contrib. by. Scooby-Doo! & the Mummy's Curse. 2005. (Illus.). 24p. (J). *(978-1-4156-3913-9(2))* Scholastic, Inc.
Scholastic, Inc. Staff & King, Trey. Detective Chase McCain - Stop That Heist! Kiernan, Kenny, illus. 2013. (Lego City Ser.). (ENG.). 32p. (J). (gr. -1-3). pap. 3.99 *(978-0-545-49596-7(2))* Scholastic, Inc.
Schorr, Titus. The Matzo Mystery, 01 vols., 1. 2016. (Rosen REAL Readers: Social Studies Nonfiction / Fiction: Family, Community, & the World Ser.). (ENG.). 12p. (J). pap. 6.33 *(978-1-5081-1985-2(6),* Rosen Classroom) Rosen Publishing Group, Inc., The.
Schraff, Anne. The Case of the Bad Seed (Detective), 1 vol. 2017. (Pageturners Ser.). (ENG.). 76p. (YA). (gr. 9-12). 8.95 ***(978-1-68021-383-6(0))*** Saddleback Educational Publishing, Inc.
—The Case of the Cursed Chalet (Detective), 1 vol. 2017. (Pageturners Ser.). (ENG.). 76p. (YA). (gr. 9-12). 8.95 ***(978-1-68021-384-3(9))*** Saddleback Educational Publishing, Inc.
—The Case of the Dead Duck (Detective), 1 vol. 2017. (Pageturners Ser.). (ENG.). 76p. (YA). (gr. 9-12). 8.95 ***(978-1-68021-385-0(7))*** Saddleback Educational Publishing, Inc.
—The Case of the Wanted Man (Detective), 1 vol. 2017. (Pageturners Ser.). (ENG.). 76p. (YA). (gr. 9-12). 8.95 ***(978-1-68021-386-7(5))*** Saddleback Educational Publishing, Inc.
—The Case of the Watery Grave (Detective), 1 vol. 2017. (Pageturners Ser.). (ENG.). 76p. (YA). (gr. 9-12). 8.95 ***(978-1-68021-387-4(3))*** Saddleback Educational Publishing, Inc.
—The Cold, Cold Shoulder (Suspense), 1 vol. 2017. (Pageturners Ser.). (ENG.). 76p. (YA). (gr. 9-12). 8.95 ***(978-1-68021-406-2(3))*** Saddleback Educational Publishing, Inc.
—The Darkest Secret. 2008. (Passages Ser.). 114p. (YA). (gr. 7-9). lib. bdg. 13.95 *(978-0-7569-8376-5(2))* Perfection Learning Corp.
—The Howling House. Miller, Fujiko, illus. rev. ed. 2004. (Standing Tall Mysteries Ser.). 51p. (J). (gr. 4-12). pap. 4.95 *(978-1-58659-083-3(9))* Artesian Pr.
—The Hunter (Mystery), 1 vol. 2017. (Pageturners Ser.). (ENG.). 76p. (YA). (gr. 9-12). 8.95 ***(978-1-68021-389-8(X))*** Saddleback Educational Publishing, Inc.
—Once upon a Crime (Mystery), 1 vol. 2017. (Pageturners Ser.). (ENG.). 76p. (YA). (gr. 9-12). 8.95 ***(978-1-68021-388-1(1))*** Saddleback Educational Publishing, Inc.
—The Power of the Rose. 2008. (Passages Ser.). 94p. (YA). (gr. 7-12). pap. 8.50 *(978-0-7891-7541-0(X))*; (J). lib. bdg. 13.95 *(978-0-7569-8381-9(9))* Perfection Learning Corp.
—The Shadow Man. 2008. (Passages Ser.). 134p. (YA). (gr. 7-9). lib. bdg. 13.95 *(978-0-7569-8382-6(7))* Perfection Learning Corp.
—The Shining Mark. 2008. (Passages Ser.). 109p. (J). lib. bdg. 13.95 *(978-0-7569-8383-3(5))* Perfection Learning Corp.
—Sounds of Terror, 1 vol. unabr. ed. 2010. (Q Reads Ser.). (ENG.). 32p. (YA). (gr. 9-12). pap. 6.95 *(978-1-61651-206-4(7))* Saddleback Educational Publishing, Inc.
—Unbroken, 1 vol. unabr. ed. 2012. (Urban Underground Ser.). (ENG.). 204p. (YA). (gr. 9-12). pap. 9.95 *(978-1-61651-960-5(6))* Saddleback Educational Publishing, Inc.
—Whatever Happened to Megan Marie? (Mystery), 1 vol. 2017. (Pageturners Ser.). (ENG.). 80p. (YA). (gr. 9-12). 8.95 ***(978-1-68021-390-4(3))*** Saddleback Educational Publishing, Inc.
—When Sleeping Dogs Awaken (Mystery), 1 vol. 2017. (Pageturners Ser.). (ENG.). 76p. (YA). (gr. 9-12). 8.95 ***(978-1-68021-391-1(1))*** Saddleback Educational Publishing, Inc.
—Where's Dudley? (Mystery), 1 vol. 2017. (Pageturners Ser.). (ENG.). 76p. (YA). (gr. 9-12). 8.95 ***(978-1-68021-392-8(X))*** Saddleback Educational Publishing, Inc.
Schraff, Anne E. Unbroken. 2012. (Urban Underground—Cesar Chavez High School Ser.: 28). (YA). lib. bdg. 20.80 *(978-0-606-26598-0(8),* Turtleback) Turtleback Bks.
Schroeder, Doris. Annie Oakley in the Ghost Town Secret. Sgroi, Tony, illus. 2011. 280p. 47.95 *(978-1-258-06482-2(0))* Literary Licensing, LLC.
Schulkers, Robert. The Gray Ghost: A Seckatary Hawkins Mystery. 2016. (ENG., Illus.). 352p. 24.95 *(978-0-8131-6794-7(9))* Univ. Pr. of Kentucky.
—Stoner's Boy: A Seckatary Hawkins Mystery. 2016. (ENG., Illus.). 380p. 24.95 *(978-0-8131-6791-6(4))* Univ. Pr. of Kentucky.
Schurch, Maylan Henry. The Meatless Mayhem Mystery. 2003. (Justin Case Adventures Ser.: 5). 121p. (J). pap. 7.99 *(978-0-8280-1615-5(1),* 133-650) Review & Herald Publishing Assn.
Schwartz, Ellen. The Case of the Missing Deed. 2011. (Teaspoon Detectives Ser.). (ENG., Illus.). 154p. (J). (gr. 4-7). 15.95 *(978-0-88776-959-7(4),* Tundra Bks.) Tundra Bks. CAN. Dist: Penguin Random Hse. LLC.
Schwarzkopf, Tom. Danger at Mason's Island, 1 vol. 2007. (ENG.). 128p. (J). (gr. 4-7). pap. 10.95 *(978-1-55109-562-2(9))* Nimbus Publishing, Ltd. CAN. Dist: Orca Bk. Pubs. USA.
Schweizer, Chris. The Creeps: Book 1: Night of the Frankenfrogs. 2015. (ENG., Illus.). 128p. (J). (gr. 3-7). 17.95 *(978-1-4197-1379-8(5),* Amulet Bks.) Abrams, Inc.
—The Creeps: Curse of the Attack-O-Lanterns. 2016. (Creeps Ser.: 3). (ENG., Illus.). 128p. (J). (gr. 3-7). 17.95 *(978-1-4197-2190-8(9),* Amulet Bks.) Abrams, Inc.
—Curse of the Attack-O-Lanterns. 2016. (Creeps Ser.: 3). (J). lib. bdg. 20.80 *(978-0-606-39018-7(9))* Turtleback Bks.
Scieszka, Jon. Thriller. Helquist, Brett, illus. 2011. (Guys Read Ser.: 2). (ENG.). 288p. (J). (gr. 3-7). 16.99 *(978-0-06-196376-6(3))*; pap. 6.99 *(978-0-06-196375-9(5))* HarperCollins Pubs. (Walden Pond Pr.).
Scollon, William & Disney Book Group Staff. The Case of the Missing Sparkle-Izer, Level Pre-1. Disney Storybook Art Team, illus. 2013. (World of Reading Ser.). (ENG.). 32p. (J). (gr. -1-k). pap. 3.99 *(978-1-4231-8482-9(3))* Disney Pr.
Scott, Christina. All in A Night's Work. 2006. (J). lib. bdg. 19.95 *(978-1-933732-19-0(9))* Big Ransom Studio.
—The Chimney. 2006. (J). lib. bdg. 19.95 *(978-1-933732-18-3(0))* Big Ransom Studio.
Scott, Dan. The Secret of Fort Pioneer: A Bret King Mystery. Beeler, Joe, illus. 2011. 190p. 42.95 *(978-1-258-09951-0(9))* Literary Licensing, LLC.
Scott, Jeff. The Discovery of Monkey Island. 2008. 64p. pap. 19.95 *(978-1-60610-921-2(9))* America Star Bks.
Scott, Michele. Perfect Harmony: A Vivienne Taylor Horse Lover's Mystery, 0 vols. 2014. (Fairmont Riding Academy Ser.). (ENG.). 274p. (YA). (gr. 7-9). pap. 9.99 *(978-1-4778-4779-4(0),* 9781477847794, Skyscape) Amazon Publishing.
Scott, Terrence. Bryce Coris Blessing. 2006. 28p. pap. 9.95 *(978-1-4327-0000-3(6))* Outskirts Pr., Inc.
Scotton, Rob. Secret Agent Splat! Scotton, Rob, illus. 2012. (Splat the Cat Ser.). (Illus.). 40p. (J). (gr. -1-2). (ENG.). 16.99 *(978-0-06-197871-5(X))*; lib. bdg. 17.89 *(978-0-06-197872-2(8))* HarperCollins Pubs.
Scroggs, Kirk. Snoop Troop - Sloppy Joe Stink-O-Rama. 2015. (Snoop Troop Ser.: 3). (ENG., Illus.). 192p. (J). (gr. 3-7). 13.99 *(978-0-316-24278-3(0))* Little, Brown Bks. for Young Readers.
—Snoop Troop: Attack of the Ninja Potato Clones. 2015. (Snoop Troop Ser.: 2). (ENG., Illus.). 192p. (J). (gr. 1-4). 13.99 *(978-0-316-24277-6(2))* Little, Brown Bks. for Young Readers.
Seaman, Augusta Huiell. The Boarded-Up House. 2014. (ENG.). 250p. (J). (gr. 6-8). pap. 9.99 *(978-0-486-78188-4(7))* Dover Pubns., Inc.
The Search for the Lost Cave, 6 vols. (Woodland Mysteriestm Ser.). 133p. (gr. 3-7). 42.50 *(978-0-7802-7943-8(3))* Wright Group/McGraw-Hill.
Searcy, Amanda. I'll Find You. 2017. (YA). ***(978-1-5247-0090-4(8),*** Delacorte Pr) Random House Publishing Group.
Secret Agent Cat Purse: The Case of the Dog with Golden Wings. 2006. (J). *(978-0-9743359-3-3(2))* Murdock Publishing Co.
The Secret of the Monster Book, 6 vols., Vol. 2. (Woodland Mysteriestm Ser.). 133p. (gr. 3-7). 42.50 *(978-0-7802-7933-9(6))* Wright Group/McGraw-Hill.
The Secret of the Old Oak Trunk, 6 vols. (Woodland Mysteriestm Ser.). 133p. (gr. 3-7). 42.50 *(978-0-7802-7926-1(3))* Wright Group/McGraw-Hill.
Secret of the Red Arrow. 2013. (Hardy Boys Adventures Ser.: 1). (ENG.). 176p. (J). (gr. 3-7). 15.99 *(978-1-4424-6585-5(9))*; pap. 6.99 *(978-1-4424-4615-1(3))* Simon & Schuster Children's Publishing. (Aladdin).
The Secret of the Song, 6 vols., Vol. 2. (Woodland Mysteriestm Ser.). 133p. (gr. 3-7). 42.50 *(978-0-7802-7937-7(9))* Wright Group/McGraw-Hill.
A Secret Silver Lining, 6 vols. (Ragged Island Mysteriestm Ser.). 161p. (gr. 5-7). 42.50 *(978-0-322-01647-7(9))* Wright Group/McGraw-Hill.
Sedgwick, Julian. The Palace of Memory. Moffett, Patricia, illus. 2017. (Mysterium Ser.: 2). (ENG.). 352p. (gr. 4-8). (J). 18.99 *(978-1-4677-7568-7(1))*; 38.65 ***(978-1-5124-2690-8(3))*** Lerner Publishing Group. (Carolrhoda Bks.).
Sedgwick, Marcus. She Is Not Invisible. 2014. (ENG.). 224p. (YA). (gr. 7). 16.99 *(978-1-59643-801-9(0),* 9781596438019) Roaring Brook Pr.
—She Is Not Invisible. 2015. (ENG.). 240p. (YA). (gr. 7). pap. 9.99 *(978-1-250-05698-6(5),* 9781250056986) Square Fish.
Sedoti, Chelsea. The Hundred Lies of Lizzie Lovett. 2017. (ENG.). 400p. (YA). (gr. 8-12). 17.99 *(978-1-4926-3608-3(8),* 9781492636083) Sourcebooks, Inc.
Selfors, Suzanne. Smells Like Treasure. 2012. (Smells Like Dog Ser.: 2). (ENG.). 432p. (J). (gr. 3-7). pap. 8.99 *(978-0-316-04402-8(4))* Little, Brown Bks. for Young Readers.
Sente, Yves. The Sarcophagi of the Sixth Coninent, Pt. 1, Vol. 9. Juillard, André, illus. 2011. (Blake & Mortimer Ser.: 9). (ENG.). 64p. (gr. 5-17). pap. 15.95 *(978-1-84918-067-2(9))* CineBook GBR. Dist: National Bk. Network.
Sente, Yves & Juillard, Andre. The Gondwana Shrine. 2012. (Blake & Mortimer Ser.: 11). (ENG., Illus.). 64p. pap. 15.95 *(978-1-84918-094-8(6))* CineBook GBR. Dist: National Bk. Network.
—The Oath of the Five Swords, Vol. 18. 2014. (Blake & Mortimer Ser.: 18). (ENG., Illus.). 72p. pap. 15.95 *(978-1-84918-191-4(8))* CineBook GBR. Dist: National Bk. Network.
—The Sarcophagi of the Sixth Continent, Pt. 2. 2011. (Blake & Mortimer Ser.: 10). (ENG., Illus.). 64p. pap. 15.95 *(978-1-84918-077-1(6))* CineBook GBR. Dist: National Bk. Network.
Senzai, N. H. Saving Kabul Corner. 2014. (Kabul Chronicles Ser.). (ENG., Illus.). 288p. (J). (gr. 3-7). 16.99 *(978-1-4424-8494-8(2),* Simon & Schuster/Paula Wiseman Bks.) Simon & Schuster/Paula Wiseman Bks.
Sepetys, Ruta. Out of the Easy. 2013. (ENG.). 352p. (YA). (gr. 9). 17.99 *(978-0-399-25692-9(X),* Philomel Bks.) Penguin Young Readers Group.
Serrano, Tina. Urban Scavenger Hunt, 1 vol. 2010. 50p. pap. 16.95 *(978-1-4489-4451-4(1))* America Star Bks.
Seykora, Teresa. The Case of the Missing Peanut Butter: The Adventures of Peanut Butter Bob. Drewes, Dan, illus. 2010. 32p. 12.99 *(978-1-4520-2678-7(5))* AuthorHouse.
Shadows at Predator Reef. 2014. (Hardy Boys Adventures Ser.: 7). (ENG., Illus.). 128p. (J). (gr. 3-7). 17.99 *(978-1-4814-0010-7(X))*; pap. 6.99 *(978-1-4814-0009-1(6))* Simon & Schuster Children's Publishing. (Aladdin).
Shankman, Adam & Sullivan, Laura L. Murder among the Stars. 2017. (YA). pap. ***(978-1-4814-4791-1(2))***; (ENG., Illus.). 320p. (gr. 9). 17.99 ***(978-1-4814-4790-4(4))*** Simon & Schuster Children's Publishing. (Atheneum Bks. for Young Readers).
Sharmat, Andrew & Sharmat, Marjorie Weinman. Nate the Great & the Missing Birthday Snake. Wheeler, Jody, illus. 2017. (Nate the Great Ser.). (ENG.). 64p. (J). (gr. 1-4). 12.99 ***(978-1-101-93467-8(0))***; lib. bdg. 15.99 ***(978-1-101-93469-2(7))*** Random Hse. Children's Bks. (Delacorte Bks. for Young Readers).
Sharmat, Marjorie Weinman. Nate the Great. Simont, Marc, illus. (Nate the Great Ser.: No. 1). 48p. (J). (gr. 1-4). pap. 4.50 *(978-0-8072-1351-3(9),* Listening Library) Random Hse. Audio Publishing Group.
—Nate the Great & the Halloween Hunt. Simont, Marc, illus. (Nate the Great Ser.: No. 12). 48p. (J). (gr. 1-4). pap. 4.50 *(978-0-8072-1283-7(0),* Listening Library) Random Hse. Audio Publishing Group.
—Nate the Great & the Missing Key. Simont, Marc, illus. (Nate the Great Ser.: No. 6). 48p. (J). (gr. 1-4). pap. 4.50 *(978-0-8072-1335-3(7),* Listening Library) Random Hse. Audio Publishing Group.
—Nate the Great Goes Undercover. Simont, Marc, illus. (Nate the Great Ser.: No. 2). 48p. (J). (gr. 1-4). pap. 4.50 *(978-0-8072-1284-4(9),* Listening Library) Random Hse. Audio Publishing Group.
—Nate the Great on the Owl Express. Sharmat, Mitchell & Weston, Martha, illus. 2004. (Nate the Great Ser.: No. 24). (ENG.). 80p. (J). (gr. 1-4). 5.99 *(978-0-440-41927-3(1),* Yearling) Random Hse. Children's Bks.
—Yo, el Gran Fercho y el Ladron. (Torre de Papel Ser.).Tr. of Nate the Great Goes Undercover. (SPA., Illus.). (J). 7.95 *(978-958-04-2540-3(X))* Norma S.A. COL. Dist: Distribuidora Norma, Inc.
Sharmat, Marjorie Weinman & Sharmat, Mitchell. The Green Toenails Gang. Brunkus, Denise, illus. 2nd ed. 2005. (Olivia Sharp: Agent for Secrets Ser.). (ENG.). 80p. (J). (gr. 3-7). per. 5.99 *(978-0-440-42063-7(6),* Yearling) Random Hse. Children's Bks.

M N O

—Nate the Great & the Big Sniff. Weston, Martha, illus. 2003. (Nate the Great Ser.: No. 23). (ENG.). 80p. (J). (gr. 1-4). pap. 5.99 (978-0-440-41502-2(0), Yearling) Random Hse. Children's Bks.

—Nate the Great & the Big Sniff. Weston, Martha, illus. 2003. (Nate the Great Ser.). 47p. (gr. -1-3). lib. bdg. 16.00 (978-0-613-63966-8(9), Turtleback) Turtleback Bks.

—Nate the Great & the Hungry Book Club. Wheeler, Jody, illus. 2011. (Nate the Great Ser.: No. 26). (ENG.). 80p. (J). (gr. 1-4). 5.99 (978-0-375-84548-2(8), Yearling) Random Hse. Children's Bks.

—Nate the Great Talks Turkey. Wheeler, Jody, illus. 2007. (Nate the Great Ser.: No. 25). (ENG.). 96p. (J). (gr. 1-4). per. 5.99 (978-0-440-42126-9(8), Yearling) Random Hse. Children's Bks.

—Nate the Great Talks Turkey: With Help from Olivia Sharp. Wheeler, Jody, illus. 2007. (Nate the Great Ser.). (gr. -1-3). lib. bdg. 16.00 (978-1-4177-9248-1(5), Turtleback) Turtleback Bks.

—Nate the Great, Where Are You? Wheeler, Jody, illus. 2015. (Nate the Great Ser.). (ENG.). 80p. (J). (gr. 1-4). 5.99 (978-0-449-81078-1(X), Yearling) Random Hse. Children's Bks.

—The Pizza Monster. Brunkus, Denise, illus. 2nd ed. 2005. (Olivia Sharp: Agent for Secrets Ser.). (ENG.). 80p. (J). (gr. 3-7). reprint ed. 5.99 (978-0-440-42059-0(8), Yearling) Random Hse. Children's Bks.

Sharpe, Tess. Far from You. 2014. (ENG.). 352p. (YA). (gr. 9-17). 17.99 (978-1-4231-8462-1(9)) Hyperion Bks. for Children.

Shaskan, Trisha Speed. The Case of the Missing Mola Lisa! Shaskan, Stephen, illus. 2017. (Q & Ray Ser.: 1). (ENG.). 48p. (gr. 2-5). 26.65 (978-1-5124-1147-8(7), Graphic Universe™) Lerner Publishing Group.

Shaw, J. D. Leave No Footprints. 2011. (ENG.). 276p. (J). (gr. 7). pap. 14.95 (978-0-9845318-6-8(6)) Tiny Stachel Pr.

—The Secrets of Loon Lake. 2010. (ENG.). 338p. (J). (gr. 5). pap. 16.95 (978-0-9845318-0-6(7)) Tiny Stachel Pr.

Shaw, Murray & Cosson, M. J. Sherlock Holmes & a Scandal in Bohemia. Rohrbach, Sophie, illus. 2010. (On the Case with Holmes & Watson Ser.: 1). (ENG.). 48p. (J). (gr. 4-6). pap. 6.95 (978-0-7613-6197-8(9), Graphic Universe™) Lerner Publishing Group.

—Sherlock Holmes & the Adventure at the Abbey Grange. Rohrbach, Sophie, illus. 2010. (On the Case with Holmes & Watson Ser.: 2). (ENG.). 48p. (J). (gr. 4-6). pap. 6.95 (978-0-7613-6200-5(2), Graphic Universe™) Lerner Publishing Group.

—Sherlock Holmes & the Adventure of the Blue Gem. Rohrbach, Sophie, illus. 2010. (On the Case with Holmes & Watson Ser.: 3). (ENG.). 48p. (J). (gr. 4-6). pap. 6.95 (978-0-7613-6202-9(9), Graphic Universe™) Lerner Publishing Group.

—Sherlock Holmes & the Adventure of the Dancing Men. Rohrbach, Sophie, illus. 2010. (On the Case with Holmes & Watson Ser.: 4). (ENG.). 48p. (J). (gr. 4-6). pap. 6.95 (978-0-7613-6199-2(5), Graphic Universe™) Lerner Publishing Group.

—Sherlock Holmes & the Adventure of the Speckled Band. Rohrbach, Sophie, illus. 2010. (On the Case with Holmes & Watson Ser.: 5). (ENG.). 48p. (J). (gr. 4-6). 27.93 (978-0-7613-6186-2(3)); pap. 6.95 (978-0-7613-6198-5(7), Graphic Universe™) Lerner Publishing Group.

—Sherlock Holmes & the Adventure of the Sussex Vampire. Rohrbach, Sophie, illus. 2010. (On the Case with Holmes & Watson Ser.: 6). (ENG.). 48p. (J). (gr. 4-6). pap. 6.95 (978-0-7613-6201-2(0), Graphic Universe™) Lerner Publishing Group.

Shaw, Sandy. Do You Know Where the Bus Driver Will Go? 2012. 24p. pap. 15.99 (978-1-4771-2107-8(2)) Xlibris Corp.

Shaw Wolf, Jennifer. Dead Girls Don't Lie. 2013. 336p. pap. 17.99 (978-0-8027-3450-1(2)) Walker & Co.

Shea, Therese. The School Bus Mystery. 2006. (Neighborhood Readers Ser.). (ENG.). 16p. (gr. 1-3). pap. 6.50 (978-1-4042-6982-8(7), Rosen Classroom) Rosen Publishing Group, Inc., The.

Shearer, Alex. Canned. 2008. (J). (978-0-439-90310-3(6), Scholastic Pr.) Scholastic, Inc.

Sheehan, Judy. I Woke up Dead at the Mall. 2016. (ENG.). 288p. (YA). (gr. 7). 17.99 (978-0-553-51246-5(3), Delacorte Pr.) Random Hse. Children's Bks.

Shepard, Sara. The Amateurs. 2016. (Amateurs Ser.). (ENG.). 320p. (YA). (gr. 9-17). 17.99 (978-1-4847-4227-3(3)) Hyperion Bks. for Children.

—Cross My Heart, Hope to Die. 2013. (Lying Game Ser.: 5). (ENG.). 336p. (YA). (gr. 9). 17.99 (978-0-06-212819-5(1), HarperTeen) HarperCollins Pubs.

—Crushed. 2013. (Pretty Little Liars Ser.: No. 13). (ENG.). 336p. (J). (gr. 9). 17.99 (978-0-06-219971-3(4), HarperTeen) HarperCollins Pubs.

—Deadly. 2014. (Pretty Little Liars Ser.: 14). (ENG.). 336p. (YA). (gr. 9). pap. 10.99 (978-0-06-219975-1(7)) HarperCollins Pubs.

—Deadly. 2014. (Pretty Little Liars Ser.: 14). (YA). lib. bdg. 20.85 (978-0-606-35972-6(9)) Turtleback Bks.

—Flawless. (Pretty Little Liars Ser.: 2). (ENG.). (YA). (gr. 9-12). 2008. 352p. pap. 10.99 (978-0-06-088735-3(4)) 2007. 352p. 16.99 (978-0-06-088733-9(8)) 2010. 368p. pap. 8.99 (978-0-06-205987-1(4)) HarperCollins Pubs. (HarperTeen).

—Flawless. 2008. (Pretty Little Liars Ser.: 2). (YA). lib. bdg. 20.85 (978-0-606-12267-2(2), Turtleback) Turtleback Bks.

—The Good Girls. 2015. (Perfectionists Ser.: 2). (ENG.). 368p. (YA). (gr. 9). 17.99 (978-0-06-207452-2(0), HarperTeen); 341p. (J). (978-0-06-239115-5(1)) HarperCollins Pubs.

—Heartless. 2010. (Pretty Little Liars Ser.: 7). (ENG.). (YA). (gr. 9-18). 304p. pap. 10.99 (978-0-06-156616-5(0)); 288p. 16.99 (978-0-06-156614-1(4)) HarperCollins Pubs. (HarperTeen).

—Hide & Seek. 2012. (YA). (Lying Game Ser.: 4). (ENG.). 304p. (gr. 9). 17.99 (978-0-06-186976-1(7)); (Lying Game Ser.: Bk. 4). 289p. 9.99 (978-0-06-219369-8(4)) HarperCollins Pubs. (HarperTeen).

—Killer. (Pretty Little Liars Ser.: 6). (ENG.). (YA). (gr. 9). 2010. 352p. pap. 9.99 (978-0-06-156613-4(6))No. 6. 2009. 336p. 16.99 (978-0-06-156611-0(X)) HarperCollins Pubs. (HarperTeen).

—Killer. 2010. (Pretty Little Liars Ser.: 6). (YA). lib. bdg. 20.85 (978-0-606-12278-8(8), Turtleback) Turtleback Bks.

—The Lying Game. (Lying Game Ser.: 1). (ENG.). (YA). (gr. 9-18). 2011. 336p. pap. 10.99 (978-0-06-186971-6(6)) 2010. 320p. 16.99 (978-0-06-186970-9(8)) 2011. 336p. 16.99 (978-0-06-211416-7(6)) HarperCollins Pubs. (HarperTeen).

—The Lying Game. 2011. (Lying Game (Quality) Ser.: Vol. 1). (ENG.). (YA). (gr. 9). lib. bdg. 20.60 **(978-1-61383-667-5(8))** Perfection Learning Corp.

—Never Have I Ever. (Lying Game Ser.: 2). (ENG.). (YA). (gr. 9). 2012. 336p. pap. 9.99 (978-0-06-186973-0(2)) 2011. 320p. 16.99 (978-0-06-186972-3(4)) HarperCollins Pubs. (HarperTeen).

—Perfect. (Pretty Little Liars Ser.: No. 3). (ENG.). (YA). (gr. 9-12). 2007. 320p. 16.99 (978-0-06-088736-0(2))No. 3. 2008. 336p. pap. 9.99 (978-0-06-088738-4(9)) HarperCollins Pubs. (HarperTeen).

—The Perfectionists. 2014. (Perfectionists Ser.: 1). (ENG.). 336p. (YA). (gr. 9). 17.99 (978-0-06-207469-0(5)) HarperCollins Pubs.

—Pretty Little Liars. (Pretty Little Liars Ser.: 1). (YA). (gr. 9-12). 2007. (ENG.). 304p. pap. 9.99 (978-0-06-088732-2(X)) 2010. (ENG.). 304p. pap. 9.99 (978-0-06-200954-8(0))Set, Bks. 1-4. 2009. pap. 29.99 (978-0-06-180131-0(3)) HarperCollins Pubs. (HarperTeen).

—Pretty Little Liars #16: Vicious. 2016. (Pretty Little Liars Ser.: 16). 368p. (YA). (gr. 9). pap. 10.99 (978-0-06-228705-2(2), HarperTeen) HarperCollins Pubs.

—Pretty Little Liars Bind-Up #2: Perfect & Unbelievable. 2014. (Pretty Little Liars Ser.). (ENG.). 672p. (YA). (gr. 9). pap. 10.99 (978-0-06-232293-7(1), HarperTeen) HarperCollins Pubs.

—Ruthless. 2011. (Pretty Little Liars Ser.: 10). (ENG.). 352p. (YA). (gr. 9). 17.99 (978-0-06-208186-5(1), HarperTeen) HarperCollins Pubs.

—Seven Minutes in Heaven. (ENG.). (YA). (gr. 9). 2014. (Lying Game Ser.: 6). 400p. pap. 10.99 (978-0-06-212823-2(X)) 2013. (Lying Game Ser.: Bk. 6). 384p. 17.99 (978-0-06-212822-5(1)) HarperCollins Pubs. (HarperTeen).

—Stunning. 2013. (Pretty Little Liars Ser.: 11). (ENG.). 336p. (YA). (gr. 9). pap. 10.99 (978-0-06-208190-2(X), HarperTeen) HarperCollins Pubs.

—Stunning. 2013. (Pretty Little Liars Ser.: 11). (YA). lib. bdg. 20.85 (978-0-606-31813-6(5), Turtleback) Turtleback Bks.

—Toxic. 2014. (Pretty Little Liars Ser.: 15). (ENG.). 352p. (J). (gr. 9). 17.99 (978-0-06-228701-4(X), HarperTeen) HarperCollins Pubs.

—Twisted. (Pretty Little Liars Ser.: 9). (ENG.). (YA). (gr. 9). 2012. 336p. pap. 10.99 (978-0-06-208102-5(0)) 2011. 320p. 16.99 (978-0-06-208101-8(2)) HarperCollins Pubs. (HarperTeen).

—Twisted. 2012. (Pretty Little Liars Ser.: 9). (YA). lib. bdg. 20.85 (978-0-606-26288-0(1), Turtleback) Turtleback Bks.

—Two Truths & a Lie. (Lying Game Ser.: 3). (ENG.). (YA). (gr. 9). 2013. 320p. pap. 9.99 (978-0-06-186975-4(9)) 2012. 304p. 17.99 (978-0-06-186974-7(0)) HarperCollins Pubs. (HarperTeen).

—Unbelievable. 2008. (Pretty Little Liars Ser.: 4). (ENG.). (gr. 9). 368p. (YA). pap. 9.99 (978-0-06-088741-4(9)); 352p. (J). 16.99 (978-0-06-088739-1(7)) HarperCollins Pubs. (HarperTeen).

—Vicious. 2014. (Pretty Little Liars Ser.: 16). (ENG.). 352p. (YA). (gr. 9). 17.99 (978-0-06-228704-5(4)) HarperCollins Pubs.

—Wanted. (Pretty Little Liars Ser.: 8). (ENG.). (YA). (gr. 9). 2011. 288p. pap. 9.99 (978-0-06-156619-6(5)) 2010. 272p. 16.99 (978-0-06-156617-2(9)) HarperCollins Pubs. (HarperTeen).

Sherman, Harold M. Ding Palmer, Air Detective. 2011. 264p. 47.95 (978-1-258-07222-3(X)) Literary Licensing, LLC.

Sherman, M. Zachary. Unchained, Vol. 4. Majado, Caio & Emery, Thomas J., illus. 2011. (Tony Hawk's 900 Revolution Ser.). (ENG.). 128p. (gr. 3-4). pap. 7.19 (978-1-4342-3454-4(1)); lib. bdg. 26.65 (978-1-4342-3215-1(8)) Stone Arch Bks. (Tony Hawk's 900 Revolution).

Sherrard, Valerie. Chasing Shadows. 2004. (ENG.). 216p. (YA). pap. 9.99 (978-1-55002-502-6(3)) Dundum CAN. Dist: Ingram Publisher Services.

—Eyes of a Stalker. 2006. (ENG.). 180p. (YA). (gr. 6). pap. 12.99 (978-1-55002-643-6(7), Boardwalk Bks.) Dundum CAN. Dist: Ingram Publisher Services.

—Hiding in Plain Sight: A Shelby Belgarden Mystery. 2005. (ENG.). 236p. (YA). (gr. 6). pap. 12.99 (978-1-55002-546-0(5)) Dundum CAN. Dist: Ingram Publisher Services.

—In Too Deep: A Shelby Belgarden Mystery. 2003. (ENG.). 200p. (YA). pap. 8.99 (978-1-55002-443-2(4)) Dundum CAN. Dist: Ingram Publisher Services.

—Searching for Yesterday: A Shelby Belgarden Mystery. 2008. (ENG.). 224p. (YA). (gr. 6-10). pap. 12.99 (978-1-55002-788-4(3), Boardwalk Bks.) Dundum CAN. Dist: Ingram Publisher Services.

Sherry, Kevin. Attack of the Kraken (the Yeti Files #3) 2016. (Yeti Files Ser.: 3). (ENG.). 128p. (J). (gr. 2-5). 8.99 (978-0-545-85781-9(3), Scholastic Pr.) Scholastic, Inc.

Sherry, Maureen. Walls Within Walls. Stower, Adam, illus. (ENG.). 368p. (J). (gr. 3-7). 2012. pap. 6.99 (978-0-06-176703-6(4)) 2010. 16.99 (978-0-06-176700-5(X)) HarperCollins Pubs. (Tegen, Katherine Bks).

The Ship in a Bottle, 6 vols. (Ragged Island Mysteriestm Ser.). 161p. (gr. 5-7). 42.50 (978-0-322-01648-4(7)) Wright Group/McGraw-Hill.

Shoemaker, Tim. Below the Surface, 1 vol. 2015. (Code of Silence Novel Ser.). (ENG.). 416p. (J). pap. 9.99 (978-0-310-73765-0(6)) Zonderkidz.

Shotz, Jennifer Li. Hero - Rescue Mission. 2017. (Hero Ser.: 3). 192p. (J). (gr. 3-7). pap. 7.99 **(978-0-06-256045-2(X))** HarperCollins Pubs.

Siegal, Ida. Undercover! (Emma Is on the Air #4) 2016. (Emma Is on the Air Ser.: 4). (ENG.). 128p. (J). (gr. 2-5). pap. 4.99 (978-0-545-68710-2(1), Scholastic Paperbacks) Scholastic, Inc.

Silver, Ruth. Aberrant. 2013. 250p. pap. 14.99 (978-0-9917897-8-8(4)) Patchwork Pr.

Silverthorne, Judith. The Secret of Sentinel Rock, 1 vol. 2006. (From Many Peoples Ser.). (ENG.). 168p. (J). (gr. 3-6). pap. 7.95 (978-1-55050-103-2(8)) Coteau Bks. CAN. Dist: Orca Bk. Pubs. USA.

Silvey, Craig. Jasper Jones. 2012. 20.00 (978-1-61383-806-8(9)) Perfection Learning Corp.

—Jasper Jones. 2012. (ENG.). 320p. (YA). (gr. 7). pap. 9.99 (978-0-375-86627-2(2), Ember) Random Hse. Children's Bks.

Simmons, H. Two Tales from Our Corner Lot. 2004. 68p. pap. 19.95 (978-1-4137-5251-9(9)) America Star Bks.

Simmons, Lynn. Bo & the Christmas Bandit, 1 vol. Lyne, Alison, illus. 2009. (Bo Ser.). (ENG.). 128p. (J). (gr. 3-6). pap. 8.95 (978-1-58980-723-5(5)) Pelican Publishing Co., Inc.

Simmons, Lynn Sheffield. Bo & the Missing Dogs, 1 vol. Hampton, Lin, illus. 2003. (Bo Ser.). (ENG.). 128p. (J). (gr. 3-6). 8.95 (978-1-58980-219-3(5)) Pelican Publishing Co., Inc.

—Bo & the Roaring Pines, 1 vol. Lyne, Alison Davis, illus. 2008. (Bo Ser.). (ENG.). 120p. (J). (gr. 3-6). pap. 8.95 (978-1-58980-522-4(4)) Pelican Publishing Co., Inc.

Simner, Janni Lee. Secret of the Three Treasures. 2006. (ENG.). 160p. (YA). (gr. 8-12). 16.95 (978-0-8234-1914-2(2)) Holiday Hse., Inc.

Simons Låda. 2013. 26p. pap. (978-91-981097-3-3(1)) Woldekidan Songs.

Simpson, Pat. A Compilation of Tales to Thrill & Chill. 2008. 103p. pap. 15.95 (978-1-4357-2976-6(5)) Lulu Pr., Inc.

Singleton, Linda Joy. The Curious Cat Spy Club. 2015. (Curious Cat Spy Club Ser.: 1). (ENG.). 256p. (J). (gr. 3-7). 14.99 (978-0-8075-1376-7(8)) Whitman, Albert & Co.

—Kelsey the Spy. 2016. (Curious Cat Spy Club Ser.: 3). (ENG.). (J). (gr. 3-7). 304p. pap. 9.99 (978-0-8075-1384-2(9)); 288p. 14.99 (978-0-8075-1380-4(6)) Whitman, Albert & Co.

—Melissa's Mission Impossible. 2003. pap. 4.99 (978-1-58608-609-1(X)) New Concepts Publishing.

—The Mystery of the Zorse's Mask. (Curious Cat Spy Club Ser.: 2). (ENG.). (J). (gr. 3-7). 2016. 272p. pap. 9.99 (978-0-8075-1383-5(0)) 2015. 256p. 14.99 (978-0-8075-1378-1(4)) Whitman, Albert & Co.

—The Secret of the Shadow Bandit. (Curious Cat Spy Club Ser.). (ENG.). (J). (gr. 3-7). 2017. 296p. pap. 9.99 **(978-0-8075-1387-3(3))** 2016. 288p. 14.99 (978-0-8075-1385-9(7)) Whitman, Albert & Co.

Singleton, Linda Joy. Witch Ball. 2006. (Seer Ser.: 3). (ENG.). 216p. (YA). (gr. 3-7). pap. 9.95 (978-0-7387-0821-8(6), Flux) North Star Editions.

Siobhan, Dowd. The London Eye Mystery. 2014. (ENG.). 336p. (J). (gr. 3-7). 12.24 (978-1-63245-320-4(7)) Lectorum Pubns., Inc.

Sirowy, Alexandra. The Creeping: If You Hunt for Monsters, You'll Find Them. 2015. (ENG., Illus.). 400p. (YA). (gr. 7). 17.99 (978-1-4814-1886-7(6)) Simon & Schuster Children's Publishing.

Sirowy, Alexandra. First We Were IV. 2017. (ENG., Illus.). 448p. (YA). (gr. 7). 18.99 **(978-1-4814-7842-7(7)**, Simon & Schuster Bks. For Young Readers) Simon & Schuster Bks. For Young Readers.

Skae, Hilda T. The Adventure League. 2013. 138p. pap. 9.00 (978-1-927558-40-9(9)) Birch Tree Publishing.

Skelton, Matthew. Endymion Spring. 2008. (ENG.). 416p. (YA). (gr. 7). pap. 9.99 (978-0-385-73456-1(5), Delacorte Bks. for Young Readers) Random Hse. Children's Bks.

Skelton, Vonda Skinner. Bitsy & the Mystery at Amelia Island. 2005. (Bitsy Burroughs Mysteries Ser.). (ENG.). 183p. (J). 15.95 (978-1-57072-306-3(0), Silver Dagger Mysteries) Overmountain Pr.

—Bitsy & the Mystery at Hilton Head Island. 2008. 192p. (J). (gr. 4-7). pap. 8.95 (978-1-57072-325-4(7)) Overmountain Pr.

—Bitsy & the Mystery at Tybee Island. 2003. (Bitsy Burroughs Mysteries Ser.). 120p. (J). (ENG.). 23.95 (978-1-57072-253-0(6)); pap. 13.95 (978-1-57072-254-7(4)) Overmountain Pr. (Silver Dagger Mysteries).

Skillchecks for Mystery. 2005. (Double Fastback Ser.). (J). (gr. 6-12). 64p. pap. 5.95 (978-0-13-024473-4(2)); 32p. pap. 5.95 (978-0-13-024455-0(4)) Globe Fearon Educational Publishing.

Skilton, Sarah. High & Dry. 2014. (ENG.). 272p. (YA). (gr. 9-17). 16.95 (978-1-4197-0929-6(1), Amulet Bks.) Abrams, Inc.

Skofield, James. Detective Dinosaur Undercover. Alley, R. W., illus. 2010. (I Can Read Level 2 Ser.). (ENG.). 48p. (J). (gr. -1-3). 16.99 (978-0-06-623878-4(1)); pap. 3.99 (978-0-06-444319-7(1)) HarperCollins Pubs.

Skurzynski, Gloria & Ferguson, Alane. Buried Alive. 2003. (Mysteries in Our National Park Ser.: No. 12). (ENG.). 160p. (J). (gr. 3-7). 15.95 (978-0-7922-6966-3(7), National Geographic Children's Bks.) National Geographic Society.

—Buried Alive! 2008. (Mysteries in Our National Park Ser.). (ENG., Illus.). 160p. (J). (gr. 3-7). pap. 4.99 (978-1-4263-0252-7(5), National Geographic Children's Bks.) National Geographic Society.

—Cliff-Hanger: A Mystery in Mesa Verde National Park. 2007. (Mysteries in Our National Park Ser.). (ENG., Illus.). 160p. (J). (gr. 3-7). per. 4.99 (978-1-4263-0092-9(1), National Geographic Children's Bks.) National Geographic Society.

—Ghost Horses. 2007. (Mysteries in Our National Park Ser.). (ENG., Illus.). 160p. (J). (gr. 3-7). per. 4.99 (978-1-4263-0108-7(1), National Geographic Children's Bks.) National Geographic Society.

—Night of the Black Bear: A Mystery in Great Smoky Mountains National Park. 2007. (Mysteries in Our National Park Ser.). (ENG., Illus.). 160p. (J). (gr. 3-7). 4.99 (978-1-4263-0094-3(8)); 18.90 (978-1-4263-0105-6(7)) National Geographic Society. (National Geographic Children's Bks.).

—Out of the Deep. 2008. (Mysteries in Our National Park Ser.). (ENG., Illus.). 160p. (J). (gr. 3-7). pap. 4.99 (978-1-4263-0251-0(7), National Geographic Children's Bks.) National Geographic Society.

—Over the Edge. 2008. (Mysteries in Our National Park Ser.). (ENG., Illus.). 160p. (J). (gr. 3-7). per. 4.99 (978-1-4263-0177-3(4), National Geographic Children's Bks.) National Geographic Society.

—Valley of Death: A Mystery in Death Valley National Park. 2008. (Mysteries in Our National Park Ser.). (ENG., Illus.). 160p. (J). (gr. 3-7). per. 4.99 (978-1-4263-0178-0(2), National Geographic Children's Bks.) National Geographic Society.

—Wolf Stalker: A Mystery in Yellowstone National Park. 2007. (Mysteries in Our National Park Ser.). (ENG., Illus.). 160p. (J). (gr. 3-7). per. 4.99 (978-1-4263-0096-7(4), National Geographic Children's Bks.) National Geographic Society.

Sleator, William & Monticone, Ann. The Phantom Limb. 2011. (ENG.). 224p. (YA). (gr. 9-17). 16.95 (978-0-8109-8428-8(8), Amulet Bks.) Abrams, Inc.

Sleep, Betty. Purrlock Holmes, & the Case of the Vanishing Valuables. 2004. (J). mass mkt. 8.95 (978-1-58961-330-0(9)) PageFree Publishing, Inc.

Sleepers. 64p. (YA). (gr. 6-12). pap. (978-0-8224-2366-9(9)) Globe Fearon Educational Publishing.

Sloane, Roxy. Missing: The Heather Harding Mysteries. 2011. 100p. pap. 15.99 (978-1-4628-9061-3(X)) Xlibris Corp.

Smi. Screams in the Night. 2004. 92p. pap. (978-0-14-333575-7(8), Puffin) Penguin Publishing Group.

Smith-Armand, Kristie. Diamond in the Rough: More Fun Adventures with Abby Diamond. 2010. 256p. pap. 16.95 (978-1-4502-4618-7(4)) iUniverse, Inc.

Smith, Elise & Smith, Kimanne, illus. The Missing Trumpet Blues. 2003. (ENG.). 56p. (J). (gr. 6-8). pap. 7.97 net. (978-0-7652-3276-2(6), Celebration Pr.) Pearson Schl.

Smith, Jeff. Old Man's Cave. Smith, Jeff & Hamaker, Steve, illus. 2007. (Bone Ser.: 6). (ENG.). 128p. (J). (gr. 4-7). 26.99 (978-0-439-70628-5(9)); pap. 12.99 (978-0-439-70635-3(1)) Scholastic, Inc.

Smith, Jim. Barry Loser & the Case of the Crumpled Carton. 2015. (Barry Loser Ser.: 6). (ENG., Illus.). 240p. (J). (gr. 2-4). pap. 10.99 (978-1-4052-6803-5(4)) Egmont Bks., Ltd. GBR. Dist: Independent Pubs. Group.

Smith, Lauren E. Ashley Enright & the Darnell Diamonds, 1 vol. 2009. 90p. pap. 19.95 (978-1-60836-332-2(5)) America Star Bks.

Smith, Roger. The Adventures of Xavier Winfield & His Pal Oggie, the Great Camping Adventure. 2013. 184p. pap. 7.99 (978-0-9854439-0-0(1)) Backpack Pubs.

Smith, Roland. Cryptid Hunters. 2006. (ENG.). 352p. (J). (gr. 5-17). pap. 6.99 (978-0-7868-5162-1(7)) Hyperion Pr.

—Independence Hall. (I, Q Ser.: Bk. 1). (ENG., 312p. (gr. 5-9). 2009. Illus.). (J). 15.95 (978-1-58536-468-8(1)) 2008. (YA). pap. 8.95 (978-1-58536-325-4(1)) Sleeping Bear Pr.

—Kitty Hawk. 2012. (I, Q Ser.: Bk. 3). (ENG., Illus.). 240p. (J). (gr. 5). pap. 8.95 (978-1-58536-604-0(8)); lib. bdg. 15.95 (978-1-58536-605-7(6)) Sleeping Bear Pr.

—Tentacles. 2011. (ENG.). 336p. (J). (gr. 3-7). pap. 7.99 (978-0-545-17816-7(9), Scholastic Paperbacks) Scholastic, Inc.

Smith, Roland & Spradlin, Michael P. The Windy City, Bk.5. 2014. (I, Q Ser.). (ENG.). 240p. (YA). (gr. 5-7). 9.99 (978-1-58536-823-5(7), 202902) Sleeping Bear Pr.

Smith, Sherri L. Pasadena. 2016. (ENG.). 240p. (YA). (gr. 9). 17.99 (978-1-101-99625-6(0), G.P. Putnam's Sons Books for Young Readers) Penguin Young Readers Group.

Smith, Sherry Weaver. Search for the Hidden Garden: A Discovery with Saint Thérèse. Thornburgh, Rebecca McKillip, illus. 2016. 128p. (J). pap. 9.95 (978-0-8198-9050-4(2)) Pauline Bks. & Media.

Smith, Steven K. Summer of the Woods. 2013. 158p. pap. 7.99 (978-0-9893414-1-7(0)) MyBoys3 Pr.

Smith, Timothy R. The Owls Don't Give a Hoot. 2007. (Buck Wilder's Adventure Ser.: 4). (Illus.). 80p. (J). (gr. -1-3). per. 5.95 (978-1-934133-11-8(6), Mackinac Island Press, Inc.) Charlesbridge Publishing, Inc.

—The Salmon Stop Running. 2008. (ENG., Illus.). 80p. (J). pap. 5.95 (978-1-934133-34-7(5), Mackinac Island Press, Inc.) Charlesbridge Publishing, Inc.

Snell, Roy J. Curlie Carson Listens In. 2009. 108p. 22.95 (978-1-60664-674-8(5)); 100p. pap. 8.95 (978-1-60664-303-7(7)) Rodgers, Alan Bks.

Snicket, Lemony, pseud. File Under - 13 Suspicious Incidents. Seth, illus. 2014. (ENG.). 272p. (J). (gr. 3-17). 12.00 (978-0-316-28403-5(3)) Little, Brown Bks. for Young Readers.

—File under: 13 Suspicious Incidents. Seth, illus. 2016. (ENG.). 288p. (J). (gr. 3-17). pap. 7.99 (978-0-316-39306-5(1)) Little, Brown Bks. for Young Readers.

—Shouldn't You Be in School? Seth, illus. (All the Wrong Questions Ser.: 3). (ENG.). (J). (gr. 3-17). 2015. 352p. pap. 7.99 (978-0-316-38060-7(1)) 2014. 336p. 16.00 (978-0-316-12306-8(4)) 2014. 352p. 18.00 (978-0-316-40968-1(5)) Little, Brown Bks. for Young Readers.

—When Did You See Her Last? Seth, illus. (All the Wrong Questions Ser.: 2). (ENG.). (J). (gr. 3-17). 2014. 304p. pap. 7.99 (978-0-316-33684-0(X)) 2013. 288p. 16.00 (978-0-316-12305-1(6)) 2013. 304p. 29.99 (978-0-316-23993-6(3)) Little, Brown Bks. for Young Readers.

—Who Could That Be at This Hour? Seth, illus. (All the Wrong Questions Ser.: 1). (ENG.). (J). (gr. 3-17). 2014. 288p. pap. 7.99 (978-0-316-33547-8(9)) 2012. 272p. 15.99 (978-0-316-12308-2(0)) Little, Brown Bks. for Young Readers.

Snicket, Lemony, pseud & Seth. Who Could That Be at This Hour? 2012. (978-0-316-24771-9(5)) Little Brown & Co.

Snider, Jesse Blaze. Muppet Snow White. Paroline, Shelli, illus. 2010. (Muppet Show Ser.). 112p. (J). (gr. 3-6). pap. 9.99 (978-1-60886-574-1(6)) Boom! Studios.

Snyder, Lavinia Branca. The Treasure of Lodian: The Kyss Family Mysteries. 2003. (Illus.). (J). mass mkt. (978-1-932233-68-1(7)) Aurora Libris Corp.

Snyder, Zilpha Keatley. The Egypt Game. 2014. (ENG.). 240p. (J). (gr. 3-7). 11.24 (978-1-63245-327-3(4)) Lectorum Pubns., Inc.

—The Egypt Game. Raible, Alton, illus. 2009. (ENG.). 240p. (J). (gr. 3-7). pap. 8.99 (978-1-4169-9051-2(8), Atheneum Bks. for Young Readers) Simon & Schuster Children's Publishing.

—The Egypt Game. Raible, Alton, illus. 2009. 215p. (gr. 5-9). 19.65 (978-0-8085-5303-8(8), Turtleback) Turtleback Bks.

Sobol, Donald J. Encyclopedia Brown, 1 vol. 2015. (Encyclopedia Brown Ser.: Vol. 13). (ENG.). 96p. (J). (gr. 4-7). 314.73 (978-1-61479-307-6(7), Spotlight) ABDO Publishing Co.

—Encyclopedia Brown, 4 vols., Set. Shortall, Leonard W., illus. 2007. (Encyclopedia Brown Ser.). (ENG.). 384p. (J). (gr. 2-18). 19.96 *(978-0-14-240985-5(5),* Puffin Books) Penguin Young Readers Group.

—Encyclopedia Brown & His Best Cases Ever. 2013. (Encyclopedia Brown Ser.). (ENG.). 160p. (J). (gr. 3-7). pap. 6.99 *(978-0-14-750871-3(1),* Puffin Books) Penguin Young Readers Group.

—Encyclopedia Brown & the Case of the Dead Eagles, 1 vol. Shortall, Leonard, illus. 2015. (ENG.). 96p. (J). *(978-1-61479-308-3(5))* ABDO Publishing Co.

—Encyclopedia Brown & the Case of the Dead Eagles. Shortall, Leonard W., illus. 2008. (Encyclopedia Brown Ser.: 12). (ENG.). 96p. (J). (gr. 3-7). 4.99 *(978-0-14-241135-3(3),* Puffin Books) Penguin Young Readers Group.

—Encyclopedia Brown & the Case of the Jumping Frogs. Papp, Robert, illus. 2005. (Encyclopedia Brown Ser.). 69p. (J). (gr. 3-7). 13.15 *(978-0-7569-5100-9(3))* Perfection Learning Corp.

—Encyclopedia Brown & the Case of the Jumping Frogs. 2005. (Encyclopedia Brown Ser.: No. 23). (ENG., Illus.). 80p. (J). (gr. 3-7). 5.99 *(978-0-553-48758-9(2),* Yearling) Random Hse. Children's Bks.

—Encyclopedia Brown & the Case of the Midnight Visitor, 1 vol. Brandi, Lillian, illus. 2015. (ENG.). 96p. (J). *(978-1-61479-309-0(3))* ABDO Publishing Co.

—Encyclopedia Brown & the Case of the Midnight Visitor. Brandi, Lillian, illus. 2008. (Encyclopedia Brown Ser.: 13). (ENG.). 96p. (J). (gr. 3-7). 4.99 *(978-0-14-241106-3(X),* Puffin Books) Penguin Young Readers Group.

—Encyclopedia Brown & the Case of the Secret Pitch, 1 vol. Shortall, Leonard, illus. 2015. (ENG.). 96p. (J). *(978-1-61479-310-6(7))* ABDO Publishing Co.

—Encyclopedia Brown & the Case of the Secret Pitch. Shortall, Leonard W., illus. 2007. (Encyclopedia Brown Ser.: 2). (ENG.). 96p. (J). (gr. 3-7). 4.99 *(978-0-14-240889-6(1),* Puffin Books) Penguin Young Readers Group.

—Encyclopedia Brown & the Case of the Secret Pitch. 2004. (Encyclopedia Brown Ser.: No. 2). 112p. (J). (gr. 3-7). pap. 17.00 incl. audio *(978-0-8072-1985-0(1),* Listening Library) Random Hse. Audio Publishing Group.

—Encyclopedia Brown & the Case of the Secret Pitch. 2007. (Encyclopedia Brown Ser.: 2). 14.75 *(978-1-4177-8623-7(X),* Turtleback) Turtleback Bks.

—Encyclopedia Brown & the Case of the Secret UFOs. 2011. (Encyclopedia Brown Ser.). (ENG.). 96p. (J). (gr. 3-7). 4.99 *(978-0-14-241933-5(8),* Puffin Books) Penguin Young Readers Group.

—Encyclopedia Brown & the Case of the Slippery Salamander. Chang, Warren, illus. 2003. (Encyclopedia Brown Ser.). 87p. (gr. 3-7). 16.00 *(978-0-7569-1619-0(4))* Perfection Learning Corp.

—Encyclopedia Brown & the Case of the Soccer Scheme. Bernadin, James, illus. (Encyclopedia Brown Ser.). (ENG.). 96p. (J). (gr. 3-7). 2013. pap. 4.99 *(978-0-14-242288-5(6),* Puffin Books) 2012. 16.99 *(978-0-525-42582-3(9),* Dutton Books for Young Readers) Penguin Young Readers Group.

—Encyclopedia Brown, Boy Detective, 1 vol. Shortall, Leonard, illus. 2015. (ENG.). 96p. (J). *(978-1-61479-320-5(4))* ABDO Publishing Co.

—Encyclopedia Brown, Boy Detective. Shortall, Leonard W., illus. 2007. (Encyclopedia Brown Ser.: 1). (ENG.). 96p. (J). (gr. 3-7). 4.99 *(978-0-14-240888-9(3),* Puffin Books) Penguin Young Readers Group.

—Encyclopedia Brown, Boy Detective. Shortall, Leonard W., illus. 2009. (Encyclopedia Brown Ser.). 88p. lib. bdg. 15.00 *(978-1-60686-386-2(X))* Perfection Learning Corp.

—Encyclopedia Brown, Boy Detective. 2004. (Encyclopedia Brown Ser.: No. 1). 128p. (J). (gr. 3-7). pap. 17.00 incl. audio *(978-0-8072-1984-3(3),* Listening Library) Random Hse. Audio Publishing Group.

—Encyclopedia Brown, Boy Detective. Shortall, Leonard W., illus. 2007. (Encyclopedia Brown Ser.: 1). 88p. (J). (gr. 4-7). 14.75 *(978-1-4177-8622-0(1),* Turtleback) Turtleback Bks.

—Encyclopedia Brown Cracks the Case. 2008. (Encyclopedia Brown Ser.). (ENG.). 96p. (J). (gr. 3-7). 4.99 *(978-0-14-241167-4(1),* Puffin Books) Penguin Young Readers Group.

—Encyclopedia Brown Finds the Clues, 1 vol. Shortall, Leonard, illus. 2015. (ENG.). 96p. (J). *(978-1-61479-311-3(5))* ABDO Publishing Co.

—Encyclopedia Brown Finds the Clues. Shortall, Leonard W., illus. 2007. (Encyclopedia Brown Ser.: 3). (ENG.). 96p. (J). (gr. 3-7). 4.99 *(978-0-14-240890-2(5),* Puffin Books) Penguin Young Readers Group.

—Encyclopedia Brown Finds the Clues. Shortall, Leonard W., illus. 2008. (Encyclopedia Brown Ser.). 96p. (gr. 4-7). 15.00 *(978-0-7569-8846-3(2))* Perfection Learning Corp.

—Encyclopedia Brown Finds the Clues. 2007. (Encyclopedia Brown Ser.: 3). 14.75 *(978-1-4177-8624-4(8),* Turtleback) Turtleback Bks.

—Encyclopedia Brown Gets His Man, 1 vol. Shortall, Leonard, illus. 2015. (ENG.). 96p. (J). *(978-1-61479-312-0(3))* ABDO Publishing Co.

—Encyclopedia Brown Gets His Man. Shortall, Leonard W., illus. 2007. (Encyclopedia Brown Ser.: 4). (ENG.). 96p. (J). (gr. 3-7). 4.99 *(978-0-14-240891-9(3),* Puffin Books) Penguin Young Readers Group.

—Encyclopedia Brown Gets His Man. Shortall, Leonard W., illus. 2009. (Encyclopedia Brown Ser.). 96p. lib. bdg. 15.00 *(978-1-60686-464-7(5))* Perfection Learning Corp.

—Encyclopedia Brown Gets His Man. 2007. (Encyclopedia Brown Ser.: 4). 14.75 *(978-1-4177-8626-8(4),* Turtleback) Turtleback Bks.

—Encyclopedia Brown Keeps the Peace, 1 vol. Shortall, Leonard, illus. 2015. (ENG.). 96p. (J). *(978-1-61479-313-7(1))* ABDO Publishing Co.

—Encyclopedia Brown Keeps the Peace. Shortall, Leonard W., illus. 2008. (Encyclopedia Brown Ser.: 6). (ENG.). 96p. (J). (gr. 3-7). 4.99 *(978-0-14-240950-3(2),* Puffin Books) Penguin Young Readers Group.

—Encyclopedia Brown Lends a Hand, 1 vol. Shortall, Leonard, illus. 2015. (ENG.). 96p. (J). *(978-1-61479-314-4(X))* ABDO Publishing Co.

—Encyclopedia Brown Lends a Hand. Shortall, Leonard W., illus. 2008. (Encyclopedia Brown Ser.: 11). (ENG.). 96p. (J). (gr. 3-7). 4.99 *(978-0-14-241105-6(1),* Puffin Books) Penguin Young Readers Group.

—Encyclopedia Brown Saves the Day, 1 vol. Shortall, Leonard, illus. 2015. (ENG.). 96p. (J). *(978-1-61479-315-1(8))* ABDO Publishing Co.

—Encyclopedia Brown Saves the Day. Shortall, Leonard W., illus. 2008. (Encyclopedia Brown Ser.: 7). (ENG.). 96p. (J). (gr. 3-7). 4.99 *(978-0-14-240921-3(9),* Puffin Books) Penguin Young Readers Group.

—Encyclopedia Brown Shows the Way, 1 vol. Shortall, Leonard, illus. 2015. (ENG.). 96p. (J). *(978-1-61479-316-8(6))* ABDO Publishing Co.

—Encyclopedia Brown Shows the Way. Shortall, Leonard W., illus. 2008. (Encyclopedia Brown Ser.: 9). (ENG.). 96p. (J). (gr. 3-7). 4.99 *(978-0-14-241086-8(1),* Puffin Books) Penguin Young Readers Group.

—Encyclopedia Brown Shows the Way. Shortall, Leonard W., illus. 2008. (Encyclopedia Brown Ser.). 96p. (J). (gr. 2-5). 12.65 *(978-0-7569-8937-8(X))* Perfection Learning Corp.

—Encyclopedia Brown Solves Them All, 1 vol. Shortall, Leonard, illus. 2015. (ENG.). 96p. (J). *(978-1-61479-317-5(4))* ABDO Publishing Co.

—Encyclopedia Brown Solves Them All. Shortall, Leonard W., illus. 2008. (Encyclopedia Brown Ser.: 5). (ENG.). 96p. (J). (gr. 3-7). 4.99 *(978-0-14-240920-6(0),* Puffin Books) Penguin Young Readers Group.

—Encyclopedia Brown, Super Sleuth. 2010. (Encyclopedia Brown Ser.). (ENG.). 96p. (J). (gr. 3-7). 4.99 *(978-0-14-241688-4(6),* Puffin Books) Penguin Young Readers Group.

—Encyclopedia Brown Takes the Case, 1 vol. Shortall, Leonard, illus. 2015. (ENG.). 96p. (J). *(978-1-61479-318-2(2))* ABDO Publishing Co.

—Encyclopedia Brown Takes the Case. Shortall, Leonard W., illus. 2008. (Encyclopedia Brown Ser.: 10). (ENG.). 96p. (J). (gr. 3-7). 4.99 *(978-0-14-241085-1(3),* Puffin Books) Penguin Young Readers Group.

—Encyclopedia Brown Takes the Case. Shortall, Leonard W., illus. 2008. (Encyclopedia Brown Ser.). 96p. (J). (gr. 3-7). 12.65 *(978-0-7569-9078-7(5))* Perfection Learning Corp.

—Encyclopedia Brown Tracks Them Down, 1 vol. Shortall, Leonard, illus. 2015. (ENG.). 96p. (J). *(978-1-61479-319-9(0),* 1383123) ABDO Publishing Co.

—Encyclopedia Brown Tracks Them Down. Shortall, Leonard W., illus. 2008. (Encyclopedia Brown Ser.: No. 8). (ENG.). 96p. (J). (gr. 3-7). 4.99 *(978-0-14-240951-0(0),* Puffin Books) Penguin Young Readers Group.

Soderberg, Erin. Dinosaur Dig, 1 vol. 2013. (Scooby-Doo! Picture Clue Bks.). (ENG.). 24p. (J). (gr. -1-1). lib. bdg. 24.21 *(978-1-61479-037-2(X),* Essential Library) ABDO Publishing Co.

Soileau, Hodges, illus. The Black Widow Spider Mystery. 2004. (Boxcar Children Special Ser.). 130p. (gr. 2-7). 15.50 *(978-0-7569-3266-4(1))* Perfection Learning Corp.

—The Comic Book Mystery. 2003. (Boxcar Children Ser.). 106p. (gr. 4-7). 15.00 *(978-0-7569-1611-4(9))* Perfection Learning Corp.

—The Great Shark Mystery. 2003. (Boxcar Children Mystery & Activities Specials Ser.: 20). (ENG.). 160p. (J). (gr. 1-5). pap. 6.99 *(978-0-8075-5532-3(0))* Whitman, Albert & Co.

—The Great Shark Mystery. 2003. (Boxcar Children Special Ser.). 130p. (gr. 4-7). 15.50 *(978-0-7569-1616-9(X))* Perfection Learning Corp.

—The Mystery at Skeleton Point. 2003. (Boxcar Children Ser.). 120p. (gr. 4-7). 15.00 *(978-0-7569-1609-1(7))* Perfection Learning Corp.

—The Mystery in the Fortune Cookie. 2003. (Boxcar Children Mysteries Ser.: 96). (ENG.). 144p. (J). (gr. 2-5). pap. 6.99 *(978-0-8075-5540-8(1))* Whitman, Albert & Co.

—The Radio Mystery. 2003. (Boxcar Children Mysteries Ser.: 97). (ENG.). 128p. (J). (gr. 1-5). mass mkt. 6.99 *(978-0-8075-5547-7(9))* Whitman, Albert & Co.

Somoskey, Rebecca. Summer of the Buckeye Whistle. 2004. (J). 5.00 *(978-0-9768514-0-0(7))* Bearwallow Blessings Ministries.

Sonik, Madeline. Belinda & the Dustbunnys. Bridal, Grania, tr. 2004. (Illus.). 80p. (J). (gr. 4-7). 12.95 *(978-0-9730831-4-9(X))* Hodgepog Bks. CAN. Dist: Fitzhenry & Whiteside, Ltd.

Sonneborn, Scott. The Computer Meltdown. Lozano, Omar, illus. 2015. (North Police Ser.). (ENG.). 32p. (gr. k-2). lib. bdg. 21.32 *(978-1-4795-6485-9(0))* Picture Window Bks.

—The Mystery of Santa's Sleigh. Lozano, Omar, illus. 32p. 2016. (J). *(978-1-4747-0031-3(4))* 2015. (ENG.). lib. bdg. 21.32 *(978-1-4795-6484-2(2))* Picture Window Bks.

—The North Police. Lozano, Omar, illus. 2015. (North Police Ser.). (ENG.). 32p. (gr. k-2). 85.28 *(978-1-4795-7929-7(7))* Picture Window Bks.

Sonneborn, Scott. The Reindeer Games. Lozano, Omar, illus. 32p. 2016. (J). ***(978-1-4747-0034-4(9))*** 2015. (ENG.). lib. bdg. 21.32 *(978-1-4795-6487-3(7))* Picture Window Bks.

Sorrells, W. A. Nairobi Nightmare. Bancroft, Tom & Corley, Rob, illus. 2007. 144p. (J). *(978-0-9792912-1-0(6))* KidsGive, LLC.

Sorrells, Walter. Club Dread. 2007. (Hunted Ser.). (ENG.). 272p. (YA). (gr. 7-18). 8.99 *(978-0-14-240904-6(9),* Puffin Books) Penguin Young Readers Group.

—Fake ID. 2007. (Hunted Ser.). (ENG.). 336p. (YA). (gr. 7-18). 9.99 *(978-0-14-240762-2(3),* Puffin Books) Penguin Young Readers Group.

Space Case. 2014. (Moon Base Alpha Ser.). (ENG., Illus.). 352p. (J). (gr. 3-7). 17.99 *(978-1-4424-9486-2(7),* Simon & Schuster Bks. For Young Readers) Simon & Schuster Bks. For Young Readers.

Spalding, Andrea. Heart of the Hill, 1 vol. 2005. (Summer of Magic Quartet Ser.: 3). (ENG., Illus.). 192p. (J). (gr. 3-7). per. 7.95 *(978-1-55143-486-5(5))* Orca Bk. Pubs. USA.

Spalding, Andrea & Spalding, David. The Silver Boulder. (Adventure Net Ser.). 8p. tchr. ed. 3.95 *(978-1-55285-160-9(5),* Walrus Bks.) Whitecap Bks., Ltd. CAN. Dist: Graphic Arts Ctr. Publishing Co.

Spangler, Brie, illus. We Both Read-the Mystery of Pirate's Point. 2007. (We Both Read Ser.). 40p. (J). (gr. 1-5). 7.99 *(978-1-60115-009-7(1))* Treasure Bay, Inc.

—We Both Read-The Mystery of Pirate's Point: Level 3. 2008. (We Both Read Ser.). 40p. (J). (gr. 1-5). per. 4.99 *(978-1-60115-010-3(5))* Treasure Bay, Inc.

Specter, Baron. All in a Night's Work, 1 vol. Kneupper, Setch, illus. 2012. (Graveyard Diaries Ser.). (ENG.). 128p. (J). (gr. 3-8). 27.07 *(978-1-61641-903-5(2))* Magic Wagon.

—To Werewolf or Not to Werewolf, 1 vol. Kneupper, Setch, illus. 2012. (Graveyard Diaries Ser.). (ENG.). 128p. (J). (gr. 3-8). 27.07 *(978-1-61641-901-1(6))* Magic Wagon.

—Vampires Are Not Your Friends, 1 vol. Kneupper, Setch, illus. 2012. (Graveyard Diaries Ser.). (ENG.). 128p. (J). (gr. 3-8). 27.07 *(978-1-61641-902-8(4))* Magic Wagon.

Spector, Baron. Approaching the Undead, 1 vol. Kneupper, Setch, illus. 2012. (Graveyard Diaries Ser.). (ENG.). 128p. (J). (gr. 3-8). lib. bdg. 27.07 *(978-1-61641-899-1(0),* Calico Chapter Bks) Magic Wagon.

Spoor, Mike, illus. Desperate Measures: Units of Measurement in Action. 2010. (Mandrill Mountain Math Mysteries Ser.). (ENG.). 32p. (J). (gr. 2-6). pap. 10.55 *(978-1-60754-925-3(5))* Windmill Bks.

—Desperate Measures: Units of Measurement in Action. 2010. (Mandrill Mountain Math Mysteries Ser.). (ENG.). 32p. (J). (gr. 2-6). lib. bdg. 22.60 *(978-1-60754-920-8(4))* Windmill Bks.

—The Emperor's Guards: Concepts of Time. 2010. (Mandrill Mountain Math Mysteries Ser.). (ENG.). 32p. (J). (gr. 2-6). pap. 10.55 *(978-1-60754-927-7(1));* lib. bdg. 22.60 *(978-1-60754-922-2(0))* Windmill Bks.

—The Emperor's Last Command: Problem-solving in Action. 2010. (Mandrill Mountain Math Mysteries Ser.). (ENG.). 32p. (J). (gr. 2-6). pap. 10.55 *(978-1-60754-928-4(X))* Windmill Bks.

—The Emperor's Last Command: Problem-Solving in Action. 2010. (Mandrill Mountain Math Mysteries Ser.). (ENG.). 32p. (J). (gr. 2-6). lib. bdg. 22.60 *(978-1-60754-923-9(9))* Windmill Bks.

—The Hidden Valley: Reasoning in Action. 2010. (Mandrill Mountain Math Mysteries Ser.). (ENG.). 32p. (J). (gr. 2-6). pap. 10.55 *(978-1-60754-924-6(7));* lib. bdg. 22.60 *(978-1-60754-919-2(0))* Windmill Bks.

—Lightning Flash: Probability in Action. 2010. (Mandrill Mountain Math Mysteries Ser.). (ENG.). 32p. (J). (gr. 2-6). pap. 10.55 *(978-1-60754-926-0(3));* lib. bdg. 22.60 *(978-1-60754-921-5(2))* Windmill Bks.

Spradlin, Michael P. & Smith, Roland. Alcatraz. 2014. (I, Q Ser.). (ENG.). 272p. (J). (gr. 5-7). 16.99 *(978-1-58536-826-6(1),* 203667); pap. 9.99 *(978-1-58536-825-9(3),* 203727) Sleeping Bear Pr.

Spratt, R. A. Friday Barnes, Girl Detective. Gosier, Phil, illus. 2016. (Friday Barnes Mysteries Ser.: Bk. 1). (ENG.). 272p. (J). 13.99 *(978-1-62672-297-2(8),* 9781626722972) Roaring Brook Pr.

—Friday Barnes, Girl Detective. 2017. (Friday Barnes Ser.: 1). (J). lib. bdg. 18.40 ***(978-0-606-39603-5(9))*** Turtleback Bks.

—Friday Barnes, No Rules. Gosier, Phil, illus. 2017. (Friday Barnes Mysteries Ser.). (ENG.). 272p. (J). 13.99 *(978-1-62672-639-0(6),* 9781626726390) Roaring Brook Pr.

—Under Suspicion. Gosier, Phil, illus. 2016. (Friday Barnes Mysteries Ser.). (ENG.). 288p. (J). 13.99 *(978-1-62672-299-6(4),* 9781626722996) Roaring Brook Pr.

Springer, Nancy. Blood Trail. 2006. (ENG.). 164p. (YA). (gr. 8-12). pap. 6.95 *(978-0-8234-2063-6(9))* Holiday Hse., Inc.

—The Case of the Bizarre Bouquets. 2009. (Enola Holmes Mystery Ser.: 3). (ENG.). 176p. (J). (gr. 3-7). pap. 6.99 *(978-0-14-241390-6(9),* Puffin Books) Penguin Young Readers Group.

—The Case of the Cryptic Crinoline. 2011. (Enola Holmes Mystery Ser.: 5). (ENG.). 176p. (J). (gr. 5-7). 6.99 *(978-0-14-241690-7(8),* Puffin Books) Penguin Young Readers Group.

—The Case of the Gypsy Goodbye. 2011. (Enola Holmes Mystery Ser.: 6). (ENG.). 192p. (J). (gr. 3-7). 6.99 *(978-0-14-241888-8(9),* Puffin Books) Penguin Young Readers Group.

—The Case of the Left-Handed Lady. 2008. (Enola Holmes Mystery Ser.: 2). (ENG.). 256p. (J). (gr. 5-7). 7.99 *(978-0-14-241190-2(6),* Puffin Books) Penguin Young Readers Group.

—The Case of the Missing Marquess. 2007. (Enola Holmes Mystery Ser.: 1). (ENG.). 240p. (J). (gr. 3-7). 7.99 *(978-0-14-240933-6(2),* Puffin Books) Penguin Young Readers Group.

—The Case of the Peculiar Pink Fan: An Enola Holmes Mystery. 2010. (Enola Holmes Mystery Ser.: 4). (ENG.). 192p. (J). (gr. 5-7). 6.99 *(978-0-14-241517-7(0),* Puffin Books) Penguin Young Readers Group.

Springstubb, Tricia. Cody & the Mysteries of the Universe. Wheeler, Eliza, illus. 2016. (ENG.). 144p. (J). (gr. 2-5). 14.99 *(978-0-7636-5858-8(8))* Candlewick Pr.

The Spy down the Street, 6 vols., Vol. 2. (Woodland Mysteriestm Ser.). 133p. (gr. 3-7). 42.50 *(978-0-7802-7938-4(7))* Wright Group/McGraw-Hill.

St. Antoine, Sarah. Three Bird Summer. 2014. (ENG.). 256p. (J). (gr. 5). 16.99 *(978-0-7636-6564-7(9))* Candlewick Pr.

St. George, Victoria. Barnyard Bandits. 2011. 28p. pap. 12.99 *(978-1-4567-3040-6(1))* AuthorHouse.

St. John, Lauren. Kentucky Thriller. Dean, David, illus. 2014. (Jóvenes Lectores. Los Misterios de Laura Ser.). (SPA.). 248p. (J). (gr. 4-7). pap. 8.95 *(978-84-8343-271-6(4),* Bambu, Editorial) Combel Editorial, S.A. ESP. Dist: Independent Pubs. Group.

Stamper, Judith Bauer. Rocky Road Trip. Gangloff, Hope, illus. 2004. (Magic School Bus Science Chapter Bks.). 89p. (gr. 2-5). lib. bdg. 15.00 *(978-0-7569-3093-6(6))* Perfection Learning Corp.

Stampler, Ann Redisch. How to Disappear. 2016. (ENG., Illus.). 416p. (YA). (gr. 9). 18.99 *(978-1-4814-4393-7(3),* Simon Pulse) Simon Pulse.

Stancic, Giselle M. The Paganini Curse. 2013. 166p. 22.95 *(978-1-4759-6161-4(8));* pap. 12.95 *(978-1-4759-6159-1(6))* iUniverse, Inc.

Standiford, Natalie. The Secret Tree. (J). 2014. (ENG.). 256p. (gr. 3-7). pap. 6.99 *(978-0-545-33480-8(2),* Scholastic Paperbacks) 2012. 245p. pap. *(978-0-545-48976-8(8),* Scholastic Pr.) Scholastic, Inc.

Stanek, Mary Beth. The Fire Keepers: Mystery at Manitou Beach. Stanek, Mary Beth, illus. Stanek, Linda, photos by. 2003. (Illus.). (J). pap. 20.00 *(978-0-9747556-0-1(5))* Stanek, Mary Beth.

Stanford, K. B. Sixteen Wishes (paperback) 2008. 188p. pap. 15.47 *(978-1-4357-1773-2(2))* Lulu Pr., Inc.

Stangherlin, Tonia. T-Bird & the Island of Lost Cats. 2006. 116p. pap. 14.99 *(978-1-4116-6697-9(6))* Lulu Pr., Inc.

Stanley, George E. The Case of the Bank-Robbing Bandit. Murdocca, Sal, illus. 2004. (Third-Grade Detectives Ser.: 9). (ENG.). 80p. (J). (gr. 1-4). pap. 5.99 *(978-0-689-86489-6(2),* Aladdin) Simon & Schuster Children's Publishing.

—The Case of the Dirty Clue. Murdocca, Sal, illus. 2003. (Third-Grade Detectives Ser.: 7). (ENG.). 80p. (J). (gr. 1-4). pap. 5.99 *(978-0-689-86357-8(8),* Simon & Schuster/Paula Wiseman Bks.) Simon & Schuster/Paula Wiseman Bks.

—The Clue of the Left-Handed Envelope. Murdocca, Sal, illus. 2004. (Third-Grade Detectives Ser.: Bk. 1). (ENG.). 144p. (J). (gr. 1-4). pap. 6.99 *(978-0-689-87106-1(6),* Aladdin) Simon & Schuster Children's Publishing.

—The Mystery of the Stolen Statue. Murdocca, Sal, illus. 2004. (Third-Grade Detectives Ser.: 10). (ENG.). 80p. (J). (gr. 1-4). pap. 5.99 *(978-0-689-86491-9(4),* Simon & Schuster/Paula Wiseman Bks.) Simon & Schuster/Paula Wiseman Bks.

—The Riddle of the Stolen Sand. Murdocca, Sal, illus. 2003. (Third-Grade Detectives Ser.: 5). (ENG.). 64p. (J). (gr. 1-4). pap. 5.99 *(978-0-689-85376-0(9),* Aladdin) Simon & Schuster Children's Publishing.

—The Secret of the Wooden Witness. Murdocca, Sal, illus. 2004. (Third-Grade Detectives Ser.: 8). (ENG.). 80p. (J). (gr. 1-4). pap. 4.99 *(978-0-689-86487-2(6),* Aladdin) Simon & Schuster Children's Publishing.

Stanley, George Edward. The Case of the Dirty Clue. Murdocca, Sal, illus. 2005. (Ready-for-Chapters Ser.). (J). lib. bdg. 15.00 *(978-1-59054-898-1(1))* Fitzgerald Bks.

—The Secret of the Green Skin. Murdocca, Sal, illus. 2005. (Third-Grade Detectives Ser.: Bk. 6). 62p. (J). lib. bdg. 15.00 *(978-1-59054-916-2(3))* Fitzgerald Bks.

Stanley, Phillip Orin, 2nd. The Castle Rock Critter. Stanley, Christopher Heath & Parsons, Arielle, illus. l.t. ed. 2004. 16p. (J). 8.00 *(978-0-9761355-0-0(7))* Floodgate Publishing.

Stanton, Andy. Mr. Gum & the Goblins. Tazzyman, David, illus. 3rd ed. 2015. (Mr Gum Ser.: 3). (ENG.). 208p. (J). (gr. 2-4). pap. 8.99 *(978-1-4052-7494-4(8))* Egmont Bks., Ltd. GBR. Dist: Independent Pubs. Group.

Stanton, Nicholas Sheridan. KK Undercover Mystery: The Cookie Caper. 2011. 80p. (gr. 4-6). pap. 26.01 *(978-1-4567-6597-2(3))* AuthorHouse.

Star, Nancy. The Case of the April Fool's Frogs. 2006. 77p. *(978-0-439-67266-5(X))* Scholastic, Inc.

—The Case of the Sneaky Strangers. 2006. 77p. pap. *(978-0-439-67267-2(8))* Scholastic, Inc.

—The Case of the Thanksgiving Thief. Bernardin, James, illus. 2004. 79p. (J). *(978-0-439-67261-0(9))* Scholastic, Inc.

—Mystery of the Snow Day Bigfoot. Bernardin, James, illus. 2005. (Calendar Club Mysteries Ser.: Vol. 3). 77p. (J). pap. 3.95 *(978-0-439-67262-7(7))* Scholastic, Inc.

Steele, Michael Anthony. The Case of the Fright Flight. Neely, Scott, illus. 2016. (You Choose Stories: Scooby-Doo Ser.). (ENG.). 112p. (gr. 2-3). lib. bdg. 32.65 *(978-1-4965-2662-5(7),* You Choose Bks.) Capstone Press of Coughlan Cos.

—Creepy Cowboy Caper. Jeralds, Scott, illus. 2017. (Scooby-Doo! Beginner Mysteries Ser.). (ENG.). 112p. (gr. 2-3). lib. bdg. 22.65 ***(978-1-4965-4768-2(3))*** Capstone Press of Coughlan Cos.

—Monster Mutt Madness. Jeralds, Scott, illus. 2017. (Scooby-Doo! Beginner Mysteries Ser.). (ENG.). 112p. (gr. 2-3). lib. bdg. 22.65 ***(978-1-4965-4767-5(5))*** Capstone Press of Coughlan Cos.

—Skeleton Crew Showdown. Jeralds, Scott, illus. 2017. (Scooby-Doo! Beginner Mysteries Ser.). (ENG.). 112p. (gr. 2-3). lib. bdg. 22.65 ***(978-1-4965-4769-9(1))*** Capstone Press of Coughlan Cos.

—Vampire Zoo Hullabaloo. Jeralds, Scott, illus. 2017. (Scooby-Doo! Beginner Mysteries Ser.). (ENG.). 112p. (gr. 2-3). lib. bdg. 22.65 ***(978-1-4965-4770-5(5))*** Capstone Press of Coughlan Cos.

Steensland, Mark. Behind the Bookcase. Murphy, Kelly, illus. 2013. (ENG.). 288p. (J). (gr. 3-7). 6.99 *(978-0-385-74072-2(7),* Yearling) Random Hse. Children's Bks.

Steiner. Murder Takes a Fast Track. (Thumbprint Mysteries Ser.). 32.86 *(978-0-8092-0417-5(7))* McGraw-Hill/Contemporary.

Steiner, Barbara. The Cry of the Loon: A Samantha Mystery. Tibbles, Jean-Paul, illus. (ENG.). 192p. (gr. 4-18). 2009. (YA). pap. 6.95 *(978-1-59369-480-7(6))* 2006. 10.95 *(978-1-59369-479-1(2))* American Girl Publishing, Inc.

—23 Shadow Street: Deadly Dreams. 2007. (ENG.). 304p. (J). (gr. -1-12). per. 8.95 *(978-1-59687-329-2(9))* IBks., Inc.

Steinhöfel, Andreas & Wright, Chantal. The Spaghetti Detectives. 2011. (ENG.). 176p. (J). (gr. 3-7). 16.99 *(978-0-545-28975-7(0),* Chicken Hse., The) Scholastic, Inc.

Steinkraus, Kyla. Case of the Uncrackable Code. 2015. (ENG.). 64p. (gr. 3-6). 29.95 *(978-1-63430-388-0(1))* Rourke Educational Media.

—Curious Case of the Ransom Riddler. 2015. (ENG.). 64p. (gr. 3-6). 29.95 *(978-1-63430-382-8(2))* Rourke Educational Media.

—Gumshoe Gang Cracks the Case. 2015. (ENG.). 64p. (gr. 3-6). 29.95 *(978-1-63430-381-1(4))* Rourke Educational Media.

—Mystery of the Turtle Snatcher. 2015. (ENG.). 64p. (gr. 3-6). 29.95 *(978-1-63430-380-4(6))* Rourke Educational Media.

Stern, Jacqueline. The Ghosts of Goliad. 2003. iii, 165p. (J). 17.95 *(978-1-57168-785-2(8),* Eakin Pr.) Eakin Pr.

—Mystery of the Whispering Walls. 2004. (J). 148p. pap. *(978-1-57168-844-6(7));* (Hollow Tree Mystery Ser.: Bk. 6). (Illus.). v, 142p. *(978-1-57168-850-7(1),* Eakin Pr.) Eakin Pr.

Stern, Jacqueline C. The Secret of the Dragonfly Pin. 2006. (Hollow Tree Mystery Ser.: 7). 115p. (J). (gr. 3-7). per. 12.95 *(978-1-57168-264-2(3),* Eakin Pr.) Eakin Pr.

Steps To Literacy Staff, compiled by. Capitol Mysteries: Gen014. 2005. (ENG., Illus.). (J). *(978-1-59564-732-0(5))* Steps To Literacy, LLC.

—Tales for the House of Bunnicula: Lib710. 2005. (ENG., Illus.). (J). pap. *(978-1-59564-678-1(7))* Steps To Literacy, LLC.

Stern, D. G. Disappearing Diamonds: An Upton Charles Adventure. Bartlett, Rebecca, illus. 2008. (ENG.). 126p. (J). pap. 9.99 *(978-0-9754676-9-5(7))* Yeoman Hse.
Sternberg, Libby. Finding the Forger. 2004. 192p. (YA). 19.95 *(978-1-890862-32-9(0))*; (ENG.). pap. 14.95 *(978-1-890862-37-4(1))* Bancroft Pr.
—Uncovering Sadie's Secrets. 2003. (ENG.). 196p. pap. 14.95 *(978-1-890862-28-2(2))*; 183p. (YA). (gr. 5-9). 16.95 *(978-1-890862-23-7(1))* Bancroft Pr.
Steuerwald, Shannon B. From Scrawny to Brawny. 2006. (J). per. 9.95 *(978-1-931787-19-2(0))* Fundamental Christian Endeavors.
Stevens, Bonnie. Fighting Chance. 2015. (ENG.). 326p. (YA). pap. 10.95 *(978-1-929345-14-4(3))* Poisoned Pen Pr.
Stevens, Robin. Murder Is Bad Manners. 2015. (Wells & Wong Mystery Ser.). (ENG., Illus.). 320p. (J). (gr. 5). 17.99 *(978-1-4814-2212-3(X))*, Simon & Schuster Bks. For Young Readers) Simon & Schuster Bks. For Young Readers.
—Poison Is Not Polite. 2016. (Wells & Wong Mystery Ser.). (ENG., Illus.). 336p. (J). (gr. 5). 17.99 *(978-1-4814-2215-4(4))*, Simon & Schuster Bks. For Young Readers) Simon & Schuster Bks. For Young Readers.
Stevenson-Ringo, Angela. Keith's Shoes. 2009. 28p. pap. 9.95 *(978-1-4327-2344-6(8))* Outskirts Pr., Inc.
Stevenson, S. Roy. The Magic Act: A Mystery by S. Roy Stevenson. 2008. 108p. 20.95 *(978-0-595-51841-8(9))*; pap. 10.95 *(978-0-595-53062-5(1))* iUniverse, Inc.
Stevenson, Sarah Jamila. The Truth Against the World. 2014. (ENG.). 360p. (YA). pap. 9.99 *(978-0-7387-4058-4(6))*, Flux) North Star Editions.
Stevenson, Steve. The Crime on the Norwegian Sea. 2016. (Agatha Girl of Mystery Ser.: 10). lib. bdg. 16.00 *(978-0-606-38415-5(4))* Turtleback Bks.
—The Crown of Venice, No. 7. Turconi, Stefano, illus. 2014. (Agatha: Girl of Mystery Ser.: 7). (ENG.). 144p. (J). (gr. 2-5). 5.99 *(978-0-448-46225-7(7))*, Grosset & Dunlap) Penguin Young Readers Group.
—The Crown of Venice. 2014. (Agatha Girl of Mystery Ser.: 7). lib. bdg. 16.00 *(978-0-606-36164-4(2))* Turtleback Bks.
—The Curse of the Pharaoh. Turconi, Stefano, illus. 2013. (Agatha: Girl of Mystery Ser.: 1). (ENG.). 144p. (J). (gr. 2-5). pap. 6.99 *(978-0-448-46217-2(6))*, Grosset & Dunlap) Penguin Young Readers Group.
—The Curse of the Pharaoh. 2013. (Agatha Girl of Mystery Ser.: 1). lib. bdg. 17.20 *(978-0-606-29986-2(6))*, Turtleback) Turtleback Bks.
—The Eiffel Tower Incident. 2014. (Agatha Girl of Mystery Ser.: 5). lib. bdg. 16.00 *(978-0-606-34153-0(6))*, Turtleback) Turtleback Bks.
—The Eiffel Tower Incident #5. Turconi, Stefano, illus. 2014. (Agatha: Girl of Mystery Ser.: 5). (ENG.). 144p. (J). (gr. 2-5). 6.99 *(978-0-448-46223-3(0))*, Grosset & Dunlap) Penguin Young Readers Group.
—The Heist at Niagara Falls. Turconi, Stefano, illus. 2013. (Agatha: Girl of Mystery Ser.: 4). (ENG.). 144p. (J). (gr. 2-5). 6.99 *(978-0-448-46221-9(4))*, Grosset & Dunlap) Penguin Young Readers Group.
—The Heist at Niagara Falls. 2013. (Agatha Girl of Mystery Ser.: 4). lib. bdg. 16.00 *(978-0-606-32128-0(4))*, Turtleback) Turtleback Bks.
—The Kenyan Expedition. 2015. (Agatha Girl of Mystery Ser.: 8). lib. bdg. 16.00 *(978-0-606-36763-9(2))* Turtleback Bks.
—The Kenyan Expedition #8. Turconi, Stefano, illus. 2015. (Agatha: Girl of Mystery Ser.: 8). (ENG.). 144p. (J). (gr. 3-7). 5.99 *(978-0-448-48679-6(2))*, Grosset & Dunlap) Penguin Young Readers Group.
—The King of Scotland's Sword. Turconi, Stefano, illus. 2013. (Agatha: Girl of Mystery Ser.: 3). (ENG.). 144p. (J). (gr. 2-5). pap. 5.99 *(978-0-448-46220-2(6))*, Grosset & Dunlap) Penguin Young Readers Group.
—The Pearl of Bengal. Turconi, Stefano, illus. 2013. (Agatha: Girl of Mystery Ser.: 2). (ENG.). 144p. (J). (gr. 2-5). pap. 6.99 *(978-0-448-46219-6(2))*, Grosset & Dunlap) Penguin Young Readers Group.
—The Pearl of Bengal. 2013. (Agatha Girl of Mystery Ser.: 2). lib. bdg. 17.20 *(978-0-606-30016-2(3))*, Turtleback) Turtleback Bks.
Stewart, Barbara. What We Knew. 2015. (ENG.). 256p. (YA). (gr. 9). 18.99 *(978-1-250-05139-4(8))*, 9781250051394, St. Martin's Griffin) St. Martin's Pr.
Stewart, Dianne C. Season of the Cold Moon. 2011. (ENG.). 108p. (J). (gr. 2). pap. 8.95 *(978-0-9831032-0-2(8))*, BeanPole Bks.) Harren Communications, LLC.
Stewart, Jane. The Island Escapade. 2003. 102p. (YA). pap. 9.95 *(978-0-595-27734-6(9))* iUniverse, Inc.
Stewart, Linda. The Great Catsby: A Sam the Cat Mystery. 2013. 4. (ENG.). 152p. (J). pap. 10.95 *(978-0-9675073-6-1(7))* Cheshire House Bks.
Stewart, Paul & Riddell, Chris. Barnaby Grimes: Curse of the Night Wolf. 2012. (Barnaby Grimes Ser.). (ENG.). 224p. (J). (gr. 3-7). 6.99 *(978-0-385-73697-8(5))*, Yearling) Random Hse. Children's Bks.
—Barnaby Grimes: Phantom of Blood Alley. 2013. (Barnaby Grimes Ser.). (ENG.). 208p. (J). (gr. 3-7). 6.99 *(978-0-385-73700-5(9))*, Yearling) Random Hse. Children's Bks.
Stewart, Trenton Lee. The Extraordinary Education of Nicholas Benedict. Sudyka, Diana, illus. (Mysterious Benedict Society Ser.). (ENG.). (J). (gr. 3-7). 2013. 496p. pap. 9.99 *(978-0-316-17620-0(6))* 2012. 480p. 18.99 *(978-0-316-17619-4(2))* Little, Brown Bks. for Young Readers.
—The Extraordinary Education of Nicholas Benedict. 2013. (Mysterious Benedict Society Ser.: 0). (J). lib. bdg. 19.65 *(978-0-606-31743-6(0))*, Turtleback) Turtleback Bks.
Stiberth, Elizabeth. Halloween Mystery. 2008. 32p. pap. 14.49 *(978-1-4389-1112-0(2))* AuthorHouse.
Stilton, Geronimo. Geronimo & the Gold Medal Mystery. 2008. (Geronimo Stilton Ser.). (Illus.). 87p. (J). (gr. 2-5). lib. bdg. 14.65 *(978-0-7569-8803-6(9))* Perfection Learning Corp.
—Geronimo & the Gold Medal Mystery. 2008. (Geronimo Stilton Ser.: 33). (ENG., Illus.). 128p. (J). (gr. 2-5). pap. 7.99 *(978-0-545-02133-3(2))*, Scholastic Paperbacks) Scholastic, Inc.
—Geronimo's Valentine. 2009. (Geronimo Stilton Ser.: 36). (Illus.). 103p. (J). 18.40 *(978-1-4364-5051-5(9))*, Turtleback) Turtleback Bks.
—The Haunted Castle. 2011. (ENG.). 128p. (J). (gr. 2-5). pap. 7.99 *(978-0-545-10374-9(6))*, Scholastic Paperbacks) Scholastic, Inc.
—The Karate Mouse. 2010. (Geronimo Stilton Ser.: 40). lib. bdg. 18.40 *(978-0-606-06847-5(3))*, Turtleback) Turtleback Bks.
—Meet Me in Horrorwood. 2011. (Geronimo Stilton — Creepella Von Cacklefur Ser.: 2). (Illus.). 112p. (J). lib. bdg. 18.40 *(978-0-606-22947-0(7))*, Turtleback) Turtleback Bks.
—The Mona Mousa Code. Wolf, Matt, illus. 2005. (Geronimo Stilton Ser.: No. 15). 113p. (J). lib. bdg. 10.00 *(978-1-4242-0284-3(1))* Fitzgerald Bks.
—The Mysterious Cheese Thief. 2007. (Geronimo Stilton Ser.). (Illus.). 111p. (J). (gr. 2-5). 14.65 *(978-0-7569-8303-1(7))* Perfection Learning Corp.
—The Mysterious Cheese Thief. 2007. (Geronimo Stilton Ser.: 31). (ENG., Illus.). 128p. (J). (gr. 2-5). pap. 7.99 *(978-0-439-02312-2(2))* Scholastic, Inc.
—The Mysterious Cheese Thief. 2007. (Geronimo Stilton Ser.: 31). (Illus.). 111p. (gr. 4-7). 18.40 *(978-1-4177-9646-5(4))*, Turtleback) Turtleback Bks.
—The Mystery in Venice. 2012. (Geronimo Stilton Ser.: Bk. 48). (ENG.). 128p. (J). (gr. 2-5). pap. 7.99 *(978-0-545-34097-7(7))*, Scholastic Paperbacks) Scholastic, Inc.
—The Mystery in Venice. 2012. (Geronimo Stilton Ser.: 48). lib. bdg. 18.40 *(978-0-606-23729-1(1))*, Turtleback) Turtleback Bks.
—Paws Off, Cheddarface! Wolf, Matt & Keys, Larry, illus. 2004. (Geronimo Stilton Ser.: 6). (ENG.). 128p. (J). (gr. 2-5). pap. 7.99 *(978-0-439-55968-3(5))* Scholastic, Inc.
—The Peculiar Pumpkin Thief. 2010. (Geronimo Stilton Ser.: 42). (ENG.). 128p. (J). (gr. 2-5). 7.99 *(978-0-545-10372-5(X))*, Scholastic Paperbacks) Scholastic, Inc.
—The Phantom of the Subway. Wolf, Matt, illus. 2004. (Geronimo Stilton Ser.: No. 13). 112p. (J). lib. bdg. 10.00 *(978-1-4242-0282-9(5))* Fitzgerald Bks.
—The Phantom of the Subway. 2004. (Geronimo Stilton Ser.: No. 13). (ENG., Illus.). 128p. (J). (gr. 2-5). pap. 7.99 *(978-0-439-66162-1(5))*, Scholastic Paperbacks) Scholastic, Inc.
—Singing Sensation. 2009. (Geronimo Stilton Ser.: 39). (ENG.). 128p. (J). (gr. 2-5). pap. 7.99 *(978-0-545-10368-8(1))*, Scholastic Paperbacks) Scholastic, Inc.
—The Golden Statue Plot. 2013. (ENG.). 128p. (J). (gr. 2-5). pap. 7.99 *(978-0-545-55629-3(5))*, Scholastic Paperbacks) Scholastic, Inc.
—Thea Stilton & the Dragon's Code. 2009. (Geronimo Stilton Special Edition Ser.: No. 1). (Illus.). 158p. 18.00 *(978-1-60686-420-3(3))* Perfection Learning Corp.
—Thea Stilton & the Dragon's Code. 2009. (Thea Stilton Ser.: 1). lib. bdg. 19.65 *(978-0-606-00231-8(6))*, Turtleback) Turtleback Bks.
—This Hotel Is Haunted! 2012. (Geronimo Stilton Ser.: Bk. 50). (ENG., Illus.). 128p. (J). (gr. 2-5). pap. 7.99 *(978-0-545-34102-8(7))*, Scholastic Paperbacks) Scholastic, Inc.
Stilton, Geronimo & Stilton, Thea. Thea Stilton & the Dragon's Code. 2009. (Thea Stilton Ser.: 1). (ENG.). 176p. (J). (gr. 2-5). pap. 8.99 *(978-0-545-10367-1(3))*, Scholastic Paperbacks) Scholastic, Inc.
—Thea Stilton & the Ghost of the Shipwreck. 2010. (Thea Stilton Ser.: 3). lib. bdg. 19.65 *(978-0-606-06843-7(0))*, Turtleback) Turtleback Bks.
—Thea Stilton & the Mountain of Fire. 2009. (Thea Stilton Ser.: 2). (ENG.). 176p. (J). (gr. 2-5). pap. 8.99 *(978-0-545-15060-6(4))*, Scholastic Paperbacks) Scholastic, Inc.
—Thea Stilton & the Mystery in Paris. 2010. (Thea Stilton Ser.: 5). (ENG.). 176p. (J). (gr. 2-5). pap. 8.99 *(978-0-545-22773-5(9))*, Scholastic Paperbacks) Scholastic, Inc.
—Thea Stilton & the Mystery on the Orient Express. 2012. (Thea Stilton Ser.: 13). (ENG.). 176p. (J). (gr. 2-5). pap. 8.99 *(978-0-545-34105-9(1))*, Scholastic Paperbacks) Scholastic, Inc.
—Thea Stilton & the Prince's Emerald. 2012. (Thea Stilton Ser.: 12). (ENG.). 176p. (J). (gr. 2-5). pap. 8.99 *(978-0-545-34108-0(6))*, Scholastic Paperbacks) Scholastic, Inc.
—Thea Stilton & the Secret of the Old Castle. 2012. (Thea Stilton Ser.: 10). (ENG., Illus.). 176p. (J). (gr. 2-5). pap. 8.99 *(978-0-545-34107-3(8))*, Scholastic Paperbacks) Scholastic, Inc.
Stilton, Thea. The Spanish Dance Mission. 2013. (Thea Stilton Ser.: 16). (ENG., Illus.). 176p. (J). (gr. 2-5). pap. 8.99 *(978-0-545-55626-2(0))*, Scholastic Paperbacks) Scholastic, Inc.
—Thea Stilton & the Hollywood Hoax. 2016. (Thea Stilton Ser.: 23). lib. bdg. 18.40 *(978-0-606-38799-6(4))* Turtleback Bks.
—Thea Stilton & the Journey to the Lion's Den. 2013. (Thea Stilton Ser.: 17). lib. bdg. 19.65 *(978-0-606-32382-6(1))*, Turtleback) Turtleback Bks.
—Thea Stilton & the Legend of the Fire Flowers. 2013. (Thea Stilton Ser.: 15). lib. bdg. 19.65 *(978-0-606-32000-9(8))*, Turtleback) Turtleback Bks.
—Thea Stilton & the Lost Letters. 2015. (Thea Stilton Ser.: 21). (Illus.). 159p. (J). lib. bdg. 18.40 *(978-0-606-37061-5(7))* Turtleback Bks.
—Thea Stilton & the Missing Myth. 2014. (Thea Stilton Ser.: 20). (ENG.). 176p. (J). (gr. 2-5). pap. 8.99 *(978-0-545-65601-6(X))*, Scholastic Paperbacks) Scholastic, Inc.
—Thea Stilton & the Missing Myth. 2014. (Thea Stilton Ser.: 20). lib. bdg. 19.65 *(978-0-606-36058-6(1))* Turtleback Bks.
—Thea Stilton & the Mystery on the Orient Express. 2012. (Thea Stilton Ser.: 13). lib. bdg. 19.65 *(978-0-606-26757-1(3))*, Turtleback) Turtleback Bks.
—Thea Stilton & the Secret City. 2010. (Thea Stilton Ser.: 4). (ENG.). 176p. (J). (gr. 2-5). 8.99 *(978-0-545-15061-3(2))*, Scholastic Paperbacks) Scholastic, Inc.
—Thea Stilton & the Secret of the Old Castle. 2012. (Thea Stilton Ser.: 10). lib. bdg. 19.65 *(978-0-606-23930-1(8))*, Turtleback) Turtleback Bks.
—Thea Stilton & the Spanish Dance Mission. 2013. (Thea Stilton Ser.: 16). lib. bdg. 19.65 *(978-0-606-32381-9(3))*, Turtleback) Turtleback Bks.
Stine, R. L. Espanto Marino. 2009. (Goosebumps Horrorland Ser.: 2). (SPA.). 160p. (J). (gr. 3-7). pap. 6.99 *(978-0-545-15408-6(1))*, Scholastic en Espanol) Scholastic, Inc.
—Frankenstein's Dog. 2013. (Goosebumps Most Wanted Ser.: 4). (ENG.). 160p. (J). (gr. 3-7). pap. 6.99 *(978-0-545-41801-0(1))*, Scholastic Paperbacks) Scholastic, Inc.
—Frankenstein's Dog. 2013. (Goosebumps Most Wanted Ser.: 4). 136p. (J). lib. bdg. 17.20 *(978-0-606-32006-1(7))*, Turtleback) Turtleback Bks.
—Give Me a K-I-L-L: A Fear Street Novel. 2017. (Fear Street Ser.). (ENG.). 288p. (YA). 18.99 *(978-1-250-05896-6(1))*, 9781250058966) St. Martin's Pr.
—Heads, You Lose. 2010. (Goosebumps Horrorland Ser.: 15). (ENG.). 160p. (J). (gr. 3-7). 6.99 *(978-0-545-16196-1(7))*, Scholastic Paperbacks) Scholastic, Inc.
—The Perfect Date. 2005. (Fear Street Ser.). (ENG.). 160p. (YA). (gr. 7). pap. 7.99 *(978-1-4169-0323-9(2))*, Simon Pulse) Simon Pulse.
—Who's Your Mummy? 2009. (Goosebumps Horrorland Ser.: 6). (ENG.). 160p. (J). (gr. 3-7). 6.99 *(978-0-439-91874-9(X))*, Scholastic Paperbacks) Scholastic, Inc.
Stinson, Kathy. One More Clue, 1 vol. 2005. (Lorimer Streetlights Ser.). (ENG.). 104p. (J). (gr. 2-5). 7.95 *(978-1-55028-888-9(1))*, 9781550288889) Lorimer, James & Co., Ltd., Pubs. CAN. Dist: Casemate Pubs. & Bk. Distributors, LLC.
—Seven Clues, 1 vol. 2005. (Lorimer Streetlights Ser.). (ENG.). 104p. (J). (gr. 2-5). 7.95 *(978-1-55028-889-6(X))*, 9781550288896) Lorimer, James & Co., Ltd., Pubs. CAN. Dist: Casemate Pubs. & Bk. Distributors, LLC.
Stohl, Margaret. Royce Rolls. 2017. (ENG.). 400p. (YA). (gr. 9-17). 18.99 *(978-1-4847-3233-5(2))* Disney Publishing Worldwide.
Stokes, Jonathan W. Addison Cooke & the Treasure of the Incas. 2016. (Addison Cooke Ser.). (ENG., Illus.). 336p. (J). (gr. 3-7). 16.99 *(978-0-399-17377-6(3))*, Philomel Bks.) Penguin Young Readers Group.
Stokes, N. L. Mystery of the Missing Teacup. l.t. ed. 2003. (Illus.). 48p. per. 19.95 *(978-0-9729411-1-2(8))* Stylewriter Pubns.
Stokes, Paula. Liars, Inc. 2015. (ENG.). 368p. (YA). (gr. 8). 17.99 *(978-0-06-232328-6(8))*, HarperTeen) HarperCollins Pubs.
Stokes, Roy Eliot. Andy at Yale: Or the Great Quadrangle Mystery. 2007. (ENG.). 202p. pap. 20.99 *(978-1-4264-9506-9(4))*; 222p. pap. 22.99 *(978-1-4264-9887-9(X))* Creative Media Partners, LLC.
Storck, Patrick. Muppet Sherlock Holmes. Mebberson, Amy, illus. 2011. (Muppet Show Ser.). 128p. pap. 9.99 *(978-1-60886-613-7(0))* Boom! Studios.
Storer, Megan. Cowbelle - Snow Day. 2005. (Illus.). 54p. (J). per. 6.99 *(978-0-9769856-0-0(8))*, 0-9769856-0-8) Little River Bookshelf.
Storey, Margaret & Storey, Mags. If Only You Knew, 1 vol. 2009. 272p. pap. 14.99 *(978-0-8254-3895-0(0))* Kregel Pubns.
Storm, Michael. Pulp7: A Sweet Deal, a Killer Calling, & a Man Inside. 2nd enl. ed. 2005. (YA). 23.95 *(978-0-9744929-6-4(5))* Leeway Pubs.
Strange, Spencer. Operation Billion Gazillion. 2005. (Spy Five Ser.). 93p. *(978-0-439-70352-9(2))* Scholastic, Inc.
Strangway, Melissa. 56 Water Street. 2008. 156p. pap. 8.95 *(978-1-60528-031-8(3))*, iUniverse Star) iUniverse, Inc.
Stratemeyer, Edward. The Mystery at Putnam Hall: Or the School Chums' Strange Discovery. 2007. (ENG.). 186p. pap. 19.99 *(978-1-4346-1186-4(8))*; 204p. pap. 22.99 *(978-1-4346-1257-1(0))* Creative Media Partners, LLC.
Stratford, Jordan. The Case of the Girl in Grey (the Wollstonecraft Detective Agency, Book 2) Murphy, Kelly, illus. 2016. (Wollstonecraft Detective Agency Ser.). (ENG.). 224p. (J). (gr. 3-7). 16.99 *(978-0-385-75444-6(2))*, Knopf Bks. for Young Readers) Random Hse. Children's Bks.
—The Case of the Missing Moonstone. Murphy, Kelly, illus. 2015. (Wollstonecraft Detective Agency Ser.). (ENG.). 240p. (J). (gr. 3-7). 16.99 *(978-0-385-75440-8(X))*, Knopf Bks. for Young Readers) Random Hse. Children's Bks.
Strohmeyer, Sarah. The Secrets of Lily Graves. 2014. (ENG.). 304p. (YA). (gr. 8). pap. 9.99 *(978-0-06-225960-8(1))* HarperCollins Pubs.
Stromberg, Ronica. A Shadow in the Dark. 2009. (J). pap. *(978-0-88092-751-2(8))*; lib. bdg. *(978-0-88092-750-5(X))* Royal Fireworks Publishing Co.
Stroud, Jonathan. The Creeping Shadow. 2016. (Lockwood & Co Ser.). (ENG., Illus.). 464p. (J). (gr. 3-7). 16.99 *(978-1-4847-0967-2(5))* Hyperion Bks. for Children.
—The Hollow Boy. 2015. (Lockwood & Co Ser.). (ENG.). 400p. (J). (gr. 3-7). 16.99 *(978-1-4847-0968-9(3))* Hyperion Bks. for Children.
—Lockwood & Co. Book Three the Hollow Boy. 2016. (Lockwood & Co Ser.). (ENG.). 416p. (J). (gr. 3-7). pap. 7.99 *(978-1-4847-1189-7(0))* Hyperion Bks. for Children.
—The Whispering Skull. (ENG.). (J). (gr. 3-7). 2015. (Lockwood & Co Ser.). 464p. pap. 7.99 *(978-1-4231-9462-0(4))* 2014. (Lockwood & Co. Ser.: 2). 448p. 17.99 *(978-1-4231-6492-0(X))* Hyperion Bks. for Children.
Strutz, Amuel U. Santa's New Reindeer Team. 2009. (Illus.). 60p. pap. 24.99 *(978-1-4389-6455-3(2))* AuthorHouse.
Stuchner, Joan Betty. Bagels on Board, 1 vol. Whamond, Dave, illus. 2015. (Orca Echoes Ser.). (ENG.). 80p. (J). (gr. 2-3). pap. 6.95 *(978-1-4598-0695-5(6))* Orca Bk. Pubs. USA.
Sturk, Karl. Movie Star Mystery. 2010. (Scooby Doo Reader Ser.: 24). lib. bdg. 13.55 *(978-0-606-07085-0(0))*, Turtleback) Turtleback Bks.
Sturman, Jennifer. And Then Everything Unraveled. 2010. (ENG.). 256p. (J). (gr. 7). 8.99 *(978-0-545-08723-0(6))* Scholastic, Inc.
—And Then I Found Out the Truth. 2010. (ENG.). 272p. (J). (gr. 7-18). 16.99 *(978-0-545-08724-7(4))* Scholastic, Inc.
Stute, Lela LaBree. When Pugs Fly! 2011. 36p. pap. 24.95 *(978-1-4489-5484-1(3))* America Star Bks.
Styles, Walker. The Big Bad Woof. Whitehouse, Ben, illus. 2017. (Rider Woofson Ser.: 8). (ENG.). 128p. (J). (gr. k-4). pap. 5.99 ***(978-1-4814-9188-4(1))***, Little Simon) Little Simon.
—The Case of the Missing Tiger's Eye. Whitehouse, Ben, illus. 2016. (Rider Woofson Ser.: 1). (ENG.). 128p. (J). (gr. k-4). 16.99 *(978-1-4814-5738-5(1))*, Little Simon) Little Simon.
—Ghosts & Goblins & Ninja, Oh My! Whitehouse, Ben, illus. 2016. (Rider Woofson Ser.: 4). (ENG.). 128p. (J). (gr. k-4). pap. 5.99 *(978-1-4814-6306-5(3))*, Little Simon) Little Simon.
—Labra-Cadabra-dor's Revenge. Whitehouse, Ben, illus. 2017. (Rider Woofson Ser.: 7). (ENG.). 128p. (J). (gr. k-4). 16.99 *(978-1-4814-8593-7(8))*, Little Simon) Little Simon.
—Labra-Cadabra-Dor's Revenge. Whitehouse, Ben, illus. 2017. (Rider Woofson Ser.: 7). (ENG.). 128p. (J). (gr. k-4). pap. 5.99 *(978-1-4814-8592-0(X))*, Little Simon) Little Simon.
—The Rival Detective. Whitehouse, Ben, illus. 2016. (Rider Woofson Ser.: 5). (ENG.). 128p. (J). (gr. k-4). pap. 5.99 *(978-1-4814-7107-7(4))*, Little Simon) Little Simon.
—The Soccer Ball Monster Mystery. Whitehouse, Ben, illus. 2016. (Rider Woofson Ser.: 6). (ENG.). 128p. (J). (gr. k-4). pap. 5.99 *(978-1-4814-7110-7(4))*, Little Simon) Little Simon.
—Something Smells Fishy. Whitehouse, Ben, illus. 2016. (Rider Woofson Ser.: 2). (ENG.). 128p. (J). (gr. k-4). 16.99 *(978-1-4814-5742-2(X))*, Little Simon) Little Simon.
—Undercover in the Bow-Wow Club. Whitehouse, Ben, illus. 2016. (Rider Woofson Ser.: 3). (ENG.). 128p. (J). (gr. k-4). pap. 5.99 *(978-1-4814-6303-4(9))*, Little Simon) Little Simon.
Suma, Nova Ren. Dani Noir. 2009. (ENG.). 272p. (J). (gr. 4-9). 15.99 *(978-1-4169-7564-9(0))*, Simon & Schuster/Paula Wiseman Bks.) Simon & Schuster/Paula Wiseman Bks.
—Fade Out. 2012. (ENG.). 288p. (YA). (gr. 7). pap. 9.99 *(978-1-4169-7565-6(9))*, Simon Pulse) Simon Pulse.
Summer of the Secret Squadron. 2005. Orig. Title: Return of the Secret Squadron. (YA). kivar 14.95 *(978-0-9765750-0-9(0))* Ball, Michael.
Summers, Courtney. Fall for Anything. 2010. (ENG.). 240p. (YA). (gr. 7-18). pap. 15.99 *(978-0-312-65673-7(4))*, 9780312656737, St. Martin's Griffin) St. Martin's Pr.
Summy, Barrie. The Disappearance of Emily H. 2015. (ENG.). 256p. (J). (gr. 5). 16.99 *(978-0-385-73943-6(5))*, Delacorte Bks. for Young Readers) Random Hse. Children's Bks.
—I So Don't Do Famous. 2012. (ENG.). 304p. (J). (gr. 5). 7.99 *(978-0-385-73791-3(2))*, Yearling) Random Hse. Children's Bks.
—I So Don't Do Makeup. 2011. (ENG.). 288p. (J). (gr. 3-7). 7.99 *(978-0-385-73789-0(0))*, Yearling) Random Hse. Children's Bks.
—I So Don't Do Mysteries. 2009. (ENG.). 288p. (J). (gr. 3-7). 6.99 *(978-0-385-73603-9(7))*, Yearling) Random Hse. Children's Bks.
—I So Don't Do Spooky. 2010. (ENG.). 304p. (J). (gr. 3-7). 7.99 *(978-0-385-73605-3(3))*, Yearling) Random Hse. Children's Bks.
Sumner, M. C. Inhuman Fury. 2013. (Extreme Zone Ser.: 6). (ENG., Illus.). 192p. (YA). (gr. 11). pap. 13.99 *(978-1-4814-2116-4(6))*, Simon Pulse) Simon Pulse.
—Night Terrors. 2013. (Extreme Zone Ser.: 1). (ENG., Illus.). 208p. (YA). (gr. 11). pap. 14.99 *(978-1-4814-2126-3(3))*, Simon Pulse) Simon Pulse.
Surrisi, C. M. The Maypop Kidnapping. 2016. (Quinnie Boyd Mysteries Ser.: 1). (ENG.). 304p. (gr. 4-8). 35.99 *(978-1-4677-9560-9(7))*; (Illus.). (J). 17.99 *(978-1-4677-5789-8(6))* Lerner Publishing Group. (Carolrhoda Bks.).
Surrisi, C. M. Vampires on the Run: A Quinnie Boyd Mystery. 2017. (Quinnie Boyd Mysteries Ser.: 2). (ENG.). 296p. (gr. 4-8). 33.32 ***(978-1-5124-2692-2(X))***, Carolrhoda Bks.) Lerner Publishing Group.
Surrisi, Cynthia & Surrisi, C. M. Vampires on the Run: A Quinnie Boyd Mystery. 2017. (Quinnie Boyd Mysteries Ser.: 2). (ENG.). 296p. (J). (gr. 4-8). 16.99 *(978-1-5124-1150-8(7))*, Carolrhoda Bks.) Lerner Publishing Group.
Sutherland, Tui T. & Sutherland, Kari H. The Menagerie. (Menagerie Ser.: 3). (J). (gr. 3-7). 2016. 368p. pap. 6.99 *(978-0-06-078069-2(X))* 2015. (ENG.). 368p. 16.99 *(978-0-06-078067-8(3))* 2013. (ENG., Illus.). 288p. 16.99 *(978-0-06-078064-7(9))* HarperCollins Pubs.
Sutton, Kelsey. Some Quiet Place. 2013. (ENG.). 336p. (YA). pap. 9.99 *(978-0-7387-3643-3(0))*, Flux) North Star Editions.
Sutton, Laurie S. The Curse of Atlantis. Neely, Scott, illus. 2015. (You Choose Stories: Scooby-Doo Ser.). (ENG.). 112p. (gr. 2-3). lib. bdg. 32.65 *(978-1-4965-0477-7(1))* Stone Arch Bks.
—The Fright at Zombie Farm. Neely, Scott, illus. 2015. (You Choose Stories: Scooby-Doo Ser.). (ENG.). 112p. (gr. 2-3). lib. bdg. 32.65 *(978-1-4342-9713-6(6))*, You Choose Bks.) Capstone Press of Coughlan Cos.
—The Ghost of the Bermuda Triangle, 1 vol. Neely, Scott, illus. 2014. (You Choose Stories: Scooby-Doo Ser.). (ENG.). 112p. (gr. 2-3). 32.65 *(978-1-4342-9126-4(X))*, You Choose Bks.) Capstone Press of Coughlan Cos.
—The House on Spooky Street. Neely, Scott, illus. 2015. (You Choose Stories: Scooby-Doo Ser.). (ENG.). 112p. (gr. 2-3). lib. bdg. 32.65 *(978-1-4342-9714-3(4))*, You Choose Bks.) Capstone Press of Coughlan Cos.
—Legend of the Gator Man. Neely, Scott, illus. 2016. (Scooby-Doo Comic Chapter Bks.). (ENG.). 88p. (gr. 3-7). lib. bdg. 27.32 *(978-1-4965-3584-9(7))* Capstone Press of Coughlan Cos.
—The Mystery of the Aztec Tomb, 1 vol. Neely, Scott, illus. 2014. (You Choose Stories: Scooby-Doo Ser.). (ENG.). 112p. (gr. 2-3). 32.65 *(978-1-4342-9127-1(8))*, You Choose Bks.) Capstone Press of Coughlan Cos.
—The Secret of the Flying Saucer. Neely, Scott, illus. 2015. (You Choose Stories: Scooby-Doo Ser.). (ENG.). 112p. (gr. 2-3). lib. bdg. 32.65 *(978-1-4965-0478-4(X))* Stone Arch Bks.
—The Secret of the Sea Creature, 1 vol. Neely, Scott, illus. 2014. (You Choose Stories: Scooby-Doo Ser.). (ENG.). 112p. (gr. 2-3). pap. 6.95 *(978-1-4342-7925-5(1))*, You Choose Bks.) Capstone Press of Coughlan Cos.
—The Terror of the Bigfoot Beast, 1 vol. Neely, Scott, illus. 2014. (You Choose Stories: Scooby-Doo Ser.). (ENG.). 112p. (gr. 2-3). pap. 6.95 *(978-1-4342-7926-2(X))*, You Choose Bks.) Capstone Press of Coughlan Cos.
—You Choose: Scooby-Doo. 2013. (You Choose Stories: Scooby Doo Ser.). (ENG.). 112p. pap. 166.80 *(978-1-4342-9604-7(0))* Stone Arch Bks.

Sutton, Margaret. The Black Cat's Clue, No. 23. Doane, Pelagie, illus. 2008. (Judy Bolton Mysteries Ser.). (ENG.). 224p. (J). (gr. 4-7). pap. 14.95 *(978-1-4290-9043-8(X))* Applewood Bks.

—The Clue in the Patchwork Quilt, No. 14. Doane, Pelagie, illus. 2008. (Judy Bolton Mysteries Ser.). (ENG.). 228p. (J). (gr. 4-7). pap. 14.95 *(978-1-4290-9034-6(0))* Applewood Bks.

—The Clue in the Ruined Castle, No. 26. Doane, Pelagie, illus. 2008. (Judy Bolton Mysteries Ser.). 192p. (J). (gr. 4-7). pap. 14.95 *(978-1-4290-9046-9(4))* Applewood Bks.

—The Clue of the Stone Lantern, No. 21. Doane, Pelagie, illus. 2008. (Judy Bolton Mysteries Ser.). (ENG.). 224p. (J). (gr. 4-7). pap. 14.95 *(978-1-4290-9041-4(3))* Applewood Bks.

—The Discovery at Dragon's Mouth, No. 31. Doane, Pelagie, illus. 2008. (Judy Bolton Mysteries Ser.). (ENG.). 196p. (J). (gr. 4-7). pap. 14.95 *(978-1-4290-9051-3(0))* Applewood Bks.

—The Discovery at the Dragon's Mouth: A Judy Bolton Mystery. 2011. 192p. 42.95 *(978-1-258-10071-1(1))* Literary Licensing, LLC.

—The Haunted Attic, No. 2. Doane, Pelagie, illus. 2008. (Judy Bolton Mysteries Ser.). (ENG.). 240p. (J). (gr. 4-7). pap. 14.95 *(978-1-4290-9022-3(7))* Applewood Bks.

—The Haunted Fountain, No. 28. Doane, Pelagie, illus. 2008. (Judy Bolton Mysteries Ser.). (ENG.). 196p. (J). (gr. 4-7). pap. 14.95 *(978-1-4290-9048-3(0))* Applewood Bks.

—The Haunted Fountain: A Judy Bolton Mystery. 2011. 192p. 42.95 *(978-1-258-10127-5(0))* Literary Licensing, LLC.

—The Hidden Clue, No. 35. Doane, Pelagie, illus. 2008. (Judy Bolton Mysteries Ser.). (ENG.). 184p. (J). (gr. 4-7). pap. 14.95 *(978-1-4290-9055-1(3))* Applewood Bks.

—The Invisible Chimes, No. 3. Doane, Pelagie, illus. 2008. (Judy Bolton Mysteries Ser.). (ENG.). 236p. (J). (gr. 4-7). pap. 14.95 *(978-1-4290-9023-0(5))* Applewood Bks.

—The Midnight Visitor, No. 12. 2008. (Judy Bolton Mysteries Ser.). (ENG.). 264p. (J). (gr. 4-7). pap. 14.95 *(978-1-4290-9032-2(4))* Applewood Bks.

—The Mystic Ball, No. 7. Doane, Pelagie, illus. 2008. (Judy Bolton Mysteries Ser.). (ENG.). 236p. (J). (gr. 4-7). pap. 14.95 *(978-1-4290-9027-8(8))* Applewood Bks.

—The Phantom Friend, No. 30. Doane, Pelagie, illus. 2008. (Judy Bolton Mysteries Ser.). (ENG.). 188p. (J). (gr. 4-7). pap. 14.95 *(978-1-4290-9050-6(2))* Applewood Bks.

—The Secret Quest: Judy Bolton. 2011. 182p. 42.95 *(978-1-258-10241-8(2))* Literary Licensing, LLC.

—Seven Strange Clues, No. 4. Doane, Pelagie, illus. Sutton, Margaret, photos by. 2008. (Judy Bolton Mysteries Ser.). (ENG.). 236p. (J). (gr. 4-7). pap. 14.95 *(978-1-4290-9024-7(3))* Applewood Bks.

—The Trail of the Green Doll, No. 27. Doane, Pelagie, illus. 2008. (Judy Bolton Mysteries Ser.). (ENG.). 196p. (J). (gr. 4-7). pap. 14.95 *(978-1-4290-9047-6(2))* Applewood Bks.

—The Trail of the Green Doll: A Judy Bolton Mystery. 2011. 192p. 42.95 *(978-1-258-09886-5(5))* Literary Licensing, LLC.

—The Unfinished House, No. 11. Doane, Pelagie, illus. 2008. (Judy Bolton Mysteries Ser.). (ENG.). 264p. (gr. 4-7). pap. 14.95 *(978-1-4290-9031-5(6))* Applewood Bks.

—The Vanishing Shadow, No. 1. 2008. (Judy Bolton Mysteries Ser.). (ENG.). 240p. (J). (gr. 4-7). pap. 14.95 *(978-1-4290-9021-6(9))* Applewood Bks.

—The Whispered Watchword, No. 32. Doane, Pelagie, illus. 2008. (Judy Bolton Mysteries Ser.). (ENG.). 196p. (J). (gr. 4-7). pap. 14.95 *(978-1-4290-9052-0(9))* Applewood Bks.

—The Yellow Phantom: A Judy Bolton Mystery. Doane, Pelagie, illus. 2011. 222p. 44.95 *(978-1-258-10044-5(4))* Literary Licensing, LLC.

Swann, Stephen. The Blooter Boys. 2009. 42p. pap. 21.50 *(978-1-4452-2665-1(0))* Lulu Pr., Inc.

Swanson, Matthew. The Real McCoys. Behr, Robbi, illus. 2017. (J). pap. ***(978-1-250-09853-5(X))*** ETT Imprint.

Swartz, Michael. Bikes & Bullies: A Neil Everheart Mystery. 2003. 163p. pap. 11.95 *(978-0-595-26550-3(2),* Writers Club Pr.) iUniverse, Inc.

The Sweetest Heist in History. 2015. (Randi Rhodes, Ninja Detective Ser.: 2). (ENG., Illus.). 224p. (J). (gr. 3-7). 16.99 *(978-1-4424-7684-4(2),* Simon & Schuster Bks. For Young Readers) Simon & Schuster Bks. For Young Readers.

Swift, John. Tea with a Vampire. 2007. pap. 9.00 *(978-0-8059-8963-2(3))* Dorrance Publishing Co., Inc.

Swindells, Robert. The Ghosts of Givenham Keep. 2015. (ENG., Illus.). 108p. (J). pap. 9.99 *(978-1-78270-056-2(0))* Award Pubns. Ltd. GBR. Dist: Parkwest Pubns., Inc.

—Kidnap at Denton Farm. 2015. (ENG., Illus.). 106p. (J). pap. 9.99 *(978-1-78270-055-5(2))* Award Pubns. Ltd. GBR. Dist: Parkwest Pubns., Inc.

—The Secret of Weeping Wood. 2015. (ENG., Illus.). 117p. (J). pap. 9.99 *(978-1-78270-053-1(6))* Award Pubns. Ltd. GBR. Dist: Parkwest Pubns., Inc.

—The Strange Tale of Ragger Bill. 2015. (ENG., Illus.). 103p. (J). pap. 9.99 *(978-1-78270-058-6(7))* Award Pubns. Ltd. GBR. Dist: Parkwest Pubns., Inc.

—We Didn't Mean to, Honest! 2015. (ENG., Illus.). 107p. (J). pap. 9.99 *(978-1-78270-054-8(4))* Award Pubns. Ltd. GBR. Dist: Parkwest Pubns., Inc.

Swinford, Betty. Cry of the Wild. 2003. (Flamingo Fiction 9-13s Ser.). (ENG.). 192p. (J). mass mkt. 6.99 *(978-1-85792-853-2(9),* 57f373c8-3223-4d9d-9e0d-40a9937df740) Christian Focus Pubns. GBR. Dist: Bookmasters Distribution.

Syers, Rita Hsu. Mystery of the Crying Ghost. 2007. 155p. 9.95 *(978-0-9779267-1-8(0))* Bronwen Publishing.

Sylvester, Kevin. Neil Flambé & the Aztec Abduction. Sylvester, Kevin, illus. (Neil Flambe Capers Ser.: 2). (ENG., Illus.). (J). (gr. 3-7). 2014. 336p. pap. 7.99 *(978-1-4424-4608-3(0))* 2012. 320p. 14.99 *(978-1-4424-4607-6(2))* Simon & Schuster Bks. For Young Readers. (Simon & Schuster Bks. For Young Readers).

—Neil Flambé & the Bard's Banquet. Sylvester, Kevin, illus. 2015. (Neil Flambe Capers Ser.: 5). (ENG., Illus.). 320p. (J). (gr. 3-7). 12.99 *(978-1-4814-1038-0(5),* Simon & Schuster Bks. For Young Readers) Simon & Schuster Bks. For Young Readers.

—Neil Flambé & the Crusader's Curse. Sylvester, Kevin, illus. (Neil Flambe Capers Ser.: 3). (ENG., Illus.). (J). (gr. 3-7). 2014. 320p. pap. 7.99 *(978-1-4424-4287-0(5))* 2012. 304p. 13.99 *(978-1-4424-4286-3(7))* Simon & Schuster Bks. For Young Readers. (Simon & Schuster Bks. For Young Readers).

—Neil Flambé & the Duel in the Desert. Sylvester, Kevin, illus. (Neil Flambe Capers Ser.: 6). (ENG., Illus.). 304p. (J). (gr. 3-7). 2017. pap. 7.99 *(978-1-4814-1042-7(3))* 2016. 13.99 *(978-1-4814-1041-0(5))* Simon & Schuster Bks. For Young Readers. (Simon & Schuster Bks. For Young Readers).

—Neil Flambé & the Marco Polo Murders. 2010. (Neil Flambé Capers Ser.: No. 1). (Illus.). 304p. (YA). (gr. 5-9). *(978-1-55470-266-4(6))* Me to We.

—Neil Flambé & the Marco Polo Murders. Sylvester, Kevin, illus. (Neil Flambe Capers Ser.: 1). (ENG., Illus.). (J). (gr. 3-7). 2014. 320p. pap. 7.99 *(978-1-4424-4605-2(6))* 2012. 304p. 14.99 *(978-1-4424-4604-5(8))* Simon & Schuster Bks. For Young Readers. (Simon & Schuster Bks. For Young Readers).

—Neil Flambé & the Tokyo Treasure. Sylvester, Kevin, illus. (Neil Flambe Capers Ser.: 4). (ENG., Illus.). (J). (gr. 3-7). 2014. 368p. pap. 7.99 *(978-1-4424-4289-4(1))* 2012. 352p. 13.99 *(978-1-4424-4288-7(3))* Simon & Schuster Bks. For Young Readers. (Simon & Schuster Bks. For Young Readers).

—The Neil Flambé Capers Collection: Neil Flambé & the Marco Polo Murders; Neil Flambé & the Aztec Abduction; Neil Flambé & the Crusader's Curse; Neil Flambé & the Tokyo Treasure. Sylvester, Kevin, illus. 2014. (Neil Flambe Capers Ser.). (ENG., Illus.). 1344p. (J). (gr. 3-7). pap. 31.99 *(978-1-4814-3238-2(9),* Simon & Schuster Bks. For Young Readers) Simon & Schuster Bks. For Young Readers.

Sylvester, Kevin, illus. Neil Flambé & the Aztec Abduction. 2010. (Neil Flambé Capers Ser.: No. 2). 304p. (J). (gr. 4-7). *(978-1-55470-329-6(8))* Me to We.

Taft, Christopher C. The Witch of Green Spring. 2013. 120p. pap. 11.00 *(978-1-61204-198-8(1),* Strategic Bk. Publishing) Strategic Book Publishing & Rights Agency (SBPRA).

Tait, Elena. The Day My Peanut Butter Lost Its Stick. Lee, Joe, illus. 2008. 24p. pap. 12.99 *(978-1-4389-1936-2(0))* AuthorHouse.

Tama. Black Cow. 2012. 116p. pap. 14.95 *(978-1-4685-6680-2(6))* AuthorHouse.

Tamura, Mitsuhisa & Fujita, Kazuhiro. BakéGyamon, Vol. 1. 2009. (ENG.). 200p. (J). pap. 7.99 *(978-1-4215-1793-3(0))* Viz Media.

—BakéGyamon, Vol. 2. 2009. (ENG.). 200p. (J). pap. 7.99 *(978-1-4215-1794-0(9))* Viz Media.

Tashjian, Janet. Marty Frye, Private Eye Bk. 2: The Case of the Missing Action Figure. Keller, Laurie, illus. 2017. (Marty Frye, Private Eye Ser.). (ENG.). 96p. (J). 15.99 *(978-1-250-11661-1(9),* 9781250116611, Holt, Henry & Co. Bks. For Young Readers) Holt, Henry & Co.

—Marty Frye, Private Eye Bk. 2: The Case of the Missing Poodle. Keller, Laurie, illus. 2017. (Marty Frye, Private Eye Ser.). (ENG.). 96p. (J). 15.99 *(978-1-62779-460-2(3),* 9781627794602, Holt, Henry & Co. Bks. For Young Readers) Holt, Henry & Co.

Taylor, G. P. The First Escape. 2008. (Dopple Ganger Chronicles Ser.: 1). (ENG., Illus.). 288p. (J). (gr. 3-7). 19.99 *(978-1-4143-1947-6(9),* SaltRiver) Tyndale Hse. Pubs.

—The Great Mogul Diamond. 2011. (Dopple Ganger Chronicles Ser.: 3). (ENG.). 304p. (J). (gr. 3-7). 19.99 *(978-1-4143-1949-0(5),* SaltRiver) Tyndale Hse. Pubs.

—The Secret of Indigo Moon. 2009. (Dopple Ganger Chronicles Ser.: 2). (ENG., Illus.). 304p. (J). (gr. 3-7). 19.99 *(978-1-4143-1948-3(7),* SaltRiver) Tyndale Hse. Pubs.

Taylor, Jo-Ann. The Alchemist's Secret. 2011. 268p. pap. *(978-1-907652-87-5(6))* Grosvenor Hse. Publishing Ltd.

Taylor, Joseph. Allison Investigates. 2009. 202p. pap. 12.95 *(978-0-9815894-1-1(3))* Four Star Publishing.

Taylor, Kara. Prep School Confidential. 2013. (Prep School Confidential Novel Ser.: 1). (ENG.). 336p. (YA). (gr. 7). pap. 9.99 *(978-1-250-01759-8(9),* 9781250017598, St. Martin's Griffin) St. Martin's Pr.

—Wicked Little Secrets. 2014. (Prep School Confidential Novel Ser.: 2). (ENG.). 320p. (YA). (gr. 7). pap. 9.99 *(978-1-250-03360-4(8),* 9781250033604, St. Martin's Griffin) St. Martin's Pr.

Taylor, L. D. Motive Games. 2012. (ENG.). 192p. pap. *(978-1-921632-25-9(9))* Wombat Bks.

Taylor, Mary Ann. Spies: A Gander's Cove Mystery. Casteel, Kay, illus. 2006. (J). mass mkt. 5.99 *(978-0-9753367-7-9(0))* Onstage Publishing, LLC.

—Traitors: A Gander's Cove Mystery. Casteel, Kay, illus. 2006. (J). mass mkt. 5.99 *(978-0-9753367-9-3(7))* Onstage Publishing, LLC.

Taylor, Phillip J. Brian, His Granddad & the Cup of Ages. 2012. 310p. pap. *(978-1-78003-422-5(9))* Pen Pr. Pubs., Ltd.

Taylor, Theodore. Teetoncey. 2004. (ENG., Illus.). 228p. (J). (gr. 2-5). pap. 13.95 *(978-0-15-205294-2(1))* Houghton Mifflin Harcourt Publishing Co.

Tell Me No Lies, 6 vols. (Ragged Island Mysteriestm Ser.). 161p. (gr. 5-7). 42.50 *(978-0-322-01654-5(1))* Wright Group/McGraw-Hill.

Temple, Bob. The Ghost of J. Stokely. Nitzsche, Shane, illus. 2008. (Shade Bks.). (ENG.). 80p. (gr. 2-3). 25.32 *(978-1-4342-0796-8(X),* Shade Bks.) Stone Arch Bks.

—A Nose for Danger. Harpster, Steve, illus. 2006. (Graphic Sparks Ser.). (ENG.). 40p. (gr. 1-3). per. 5.95 *(978-1-59889-171-3(5),* Graphic Sparks) Stone Arch Bks.

Tenbeth, Kate. Burly & Grum & the Birthday Surprise. Jones, Rob, illus. 2012. 108p. pap. *(978-0-9572119-9-5(6))* Magic Toy Bks.

Terrell, Brandon. The Cursed Stage. Epelbaum, Mariano, illus. 2017. (Snoops, Inc Ser.). (ENG.). 112p. (gr. 4-6). lib. bdg. 26.65 *(978-1-4965-4346-2(7))* Stone Arch Bks.

—Phantom of the Library. Epelbaum, Mariano, illus. 2017. (Snoops, Inc Ser.). (ENG.). 112p. (gr. 4-6). lib. bdg. 26.65 ***(978-1-4965-5060-6(9))*** Stone Arch Bks.

—Science Fair Sabotage. Epelbaum, Mariano, illus. 2017. (Snoops, Inc Ser.). (ENG.). 112p. (gr. 4-6). lib. bdg. 26.65 *(978-1-4965-4347-9(5))* Stone Arch Bks.

—Snoops, Inc. 2017. (Snoops, Inc Ser.). (ENG.). 112p. (gr. 4-6). 106.60 *(978-1-4965-4369-1(6))* Stone Arch Bks.

—Tracking Champ. Epelbaum, Mariano, illus. 2017. (Snoops, Inc Ser.). (ENG.). 112p. (gr. 4-6). lib. bdg. 26.65 *(978-1-4965-4348-6(3))* Stone Arch Bks.

—The Undercover Cheerleader. Epelbaum, Mariano, illus. 2017. (Snoops, Inc Ser.). (ENG.). 112p. (gr. 4-6). lib. bdg. 26.65 ***(978-1-4965-5061-3(7))*** Stone Arch Bks.

Terrell, Brandon. The Vanishing Treasure. Epelbaum, Mariano, illus. 2017. (Snoops, Inc Ser.). (ENG.). 112p. (gr. 4-6). lib. bdg. 26.65 *(978-1-4965-4345-5(9))* Stone Arch Bks.

Tharp, Tim. Mojo. 2014. (ENG.). 288p. (YA). (gr. 7). pap. 8.99 *(978-0-375-86402-5(4),* Ember) Random Hse. Children's Bks.

Theer, Justine M. The Backwards Town, 1 vol. 2010. 82p. pap. 19.95 *(978-1-4489-5361-5(8))* America Star Bks.

Thielbar, Melinda. The Ancient Formula: A Mystery with Fractions. Pantoja, Tintin, illus. 2011. (Manga Math Mysteries Ser.: 5). (ENG.). 46p. (gr. 3-5). pap. 6.95 *(978-0-7613-8134-1(1),* Graphic Universe™) Lerner Publishing Group.

—The Ancient Formula No. 5: A Mystery with Fractions. Pantoja, Tintin, illus. 2010. (Manga Math Mysteries Ser.: 5). (ENG.). 48p. (gr. 3-5). 29.27 *(978-0-7613-4907-5(3))* Lerner Publishing Group.

—The Book Bandit: A Mystery with Geometry. Grandt, Eve et al, illus. 2010. (Manga Math Mysteries Ser.: 7). (ENG.). 48p. (gr. 3-5). 29.27 *(978-0-7613-4909-9(X))* Lerner Publishing Group.

—The Book Bandit No. 7: A Mystery with Geometry. Lee, Jenn Manley & Chow, Candice, illus. 2011. (Manga Math Mysteries Ser.: 7). (ENG.). 48p. (gr. 3-5). pap. 6.95 *(978-0-7613-8136-5(8),* Graphic Universe™) Lerner Publishing Group.

—The Fishy Fountain. Lin, Yali, illus. 2010. (Manga Math Mysteries Ser.: 6). (ENG.). 48p. (gr. 3-5). 29.27 *(978-0-7613-4908-2(1))* Lerner Publishing Group.

—The Fishy Fountain: A Mystery with Multiplication & Division. Lin, Yali, illus. 2011. (Manga Math Mysteries Ser.: 6). (ENG.). 48p. (gr. 3-5). pap. 6.95 *(978-0-7613-8135-8(X),* Graphic Universe™) Lerner Publishing Group.

—The Hundred-Dollar Robber. Pantoja, Tintin, illus. 2010. (Manga Math Mysteries Ser.: 2). (ENG.). 48p. (gr. 3-5). pap. 6.95 *(978-0-7613-5243-3(0),* Graphic Universe™) Lerner Publishing Group.

—The Hundred-Dollar Robber: A Mystery with Money. Pantoja, Maria Kristina, illus. 2009. (Manga Math Mysteries Ser.: 2). (ENG.). 48p. (gr. 3-5). 29.27 *(978-0-7613-3854-3(3))* Lerner Publishing Group.

—The Kung Fu Puzzle: A Mystery with Time & Temperature. Helmer, Der-Shing, illus. 2010. (Manga Math Mysteries Ser.: 4). (ENG.). 46p. (gr. 3-5). pap. 6.95 *(978-0-7613-5246-4(5),* Graphic Universe™) Lerner Publishing Group.

—The Kung Fu Puzzle: A Mystery with Time & Temperature. Ota, Yuko & Helmer, Der-Shing, illus. 2009. (Manga Math Mysteries Ser.: No. 4). 48p. (J). (gr. 2-5). 29.27 *(978-0-7613-3856-7(X))* Lerner Publishing Group.

—The Lost Key. Pantoja, Tintin, illus. 2010. (Manga Math Mysteries Ser.: 1). (ENG.). 45p. (gr. 3-5). pap. 6.95 *(978-0-7613-5244-0(9),* Graphic Universe™) Lerner Publishing Group.

—The Lost Key. rev. ed. 2010. pap. 39.62 *(978-0-7613-6942-4(2))* Lerner Publishing Group.

—The Secret Ghost. 3rd rev. ed. 2010. pap. 39.62 *(978-0-7613-6944-8(9))* Lerner Publishing Group.

—The Secret Ghost: A Mystery with Distance & Measurement. Ota, Yuko, illus. 2010. (Manga Math Mysteries Ser.: 3). (ENG.). 46p. (gr. 3-5). pap. 6.95 *(978-0-7613-5245-7(7),* Graphic Universe™) Lerner Publishing Group.

—#5 the Ancient Formula: A Mystery with Fractions. Pantoja, Tintin, illus. 2011. (Manga Math Mysteries Set II Ser.). pap. 39.62 *(978-0-7613-8362-8(X),* Graphic Universe™) Lerner Publishing Group.

—#6 the Fishy Fountain: A Mystery with Multiplication & Division. Lin, Yali, illus. 2011. (Manga Math Mysteries Set II Ser.). pap. 39.62 *(978-0-7613-8363-5(8),* Graphic Universe™) Lerner Publishing Group.

—#7 the Book Bandit: A Mystery with Geometry. Lee, Jenn Manley & Chow, Candice, illus. 2011. (Manga Math Mysteries Set II Ser.). pap. 39.62 *(978-0-7613-8364-2(6),* Graphic Universe™) Lerner Publishing Group.

Thomas, Kara. The Darkest Corners. (ENG.). (YA). (gr. 9). 2017. 352p. pap. 9.99 ***(978-0-553-52148-1(9),*** Ember) 2016. 336p. 17.99 *(978-0-553-52145-0(4),* Delacorte Pr.) Random Hse. Children's Bks.

—Little Monsters. 2017. (ENG.). 336p. (YA). (gr. 9). 17.99 ***(978-0-553-52149-8(7),*** Delacorte Pr.) Random Hse. Children's Bks.

Thompson, J. E. Disappearance at Hangman's Bluff. (Felony Bay Mysteries Ser.: 2). (ENG.). 336p. (J). (gr. 3-7). 2015. pap. 6.99 *(978-0-06-210450-2(0))* 2014. (Illus.). 16.99 *(978-0-06-210449-6(7))* HarperCollins Pubs. (Walden Pond Pr.).

—The Girl from Felony Bay. 2013. (Felony Bay Mysteries Ser.: 1). (ENG.). 384p. (J). (gr. 3-7). 16.99 *(978-0-06-210446-5(2),* Waldon Pond Pr.) HarperCollins Pubs.

Thompson, Kate. La Musica del Tiempo. Delgado, Diana, tr. 2nd ed. 2007. (SPA., Illus.). 317p. (J). (gr. 4-7). 18.95 *(978-84-96544-97-0(4))* Roca Editorial ESP. Dist: Spanish Pubs., LLC.

Thompson, Lisa. The Goldfish Boy. 2017. (ENG.). 320p. (J). (gr. 3-7). 16.99 *(978-1-338-05392-0(2),* Scholastic Pr.) Scholastic, Inc.

Thomson, Elizabeth & Albert, Sarah. Andros: the Last Villager. 2008. 226p. pap. 17.04 *(978-1-4357-3557-6(9))* Lulu Pr., Inc.

Thomson, Kerr. Washed Ashore. 2017. (ENG.). 320p. (J). (gr. 7). 17.99 ***(978-0-545-90420-9(X),*** Chicken Hse., The) Scholastic, Inc.

Thomson, Sarah L. The Eureka Key. 2016. (Secrets of the Seven Ser.). (ENG.). 240p. (J). 16.99 *(978-1-61963-731-3(6),* 9781619637313, Bloomsbury USA Childrens) Bloomsbury Publishing USA.

Thornburg, Michael. The Monster Kids' Adventures: The Retur. 2005. pap. 19.95 *(978-1-4137-8556-2(5))* PublishAmerica, Inc.

Thornton, M. H. Kylee & Lexie: Mystery of the Gholdees. 2010. 64p. pap. 10.99 *(978-1-4269-3713-2(X))* Trafford Publishing.

Thorpe, Kiki. On the Trail. Christy, Jana, illus. 2015. (Never Girls Ser.: No. 10). (ENG.). 128p. (J). (gr. 1-4). 5.99 *(978-0-7364-3306-8(6),* RH/Disney) Random Hse. Children's Bks.

Thrash, Maggie. We Know It Was You. 2016. (Strange Ser.). (ENG., Illus.). 352p. (YA). (gr. 9). 17.99 *(978-1-4814-6200-6(8),* Simon Pulse) Simon Pulse.

Tims, Laura. Please Don't Tell. 2016. 336p. (YA). (gr. 8). 17.99 *(978-0-06-231732-2(6),* HarperTeen) HarperCollins Pubs.

Titus, Eve. Basil & the Cave of Cats. Galdone, Paul, illus. 2016. (Great Mouse Detective Ser.: 2). (ENG.). 112p. (J). (gr. 1-4). pap. 5.99 *(978-1-4814-6404-8(3),* Aladdin) Simon & Schuster Children's Publishing.

—Basil & the Lost Colony. Galdone, Paul, illus. 2017. (Great Mouse Detective Ser.: 5). (ENG.). 96p. (J). (gr. 1-4). pap. 5.99 ***(978-1-4814-6413-0(2),*** Aladdin) Simon & Schuster Children's Publishing.

—Basil in Mexico. Galdone, Paul, illus. 2016. (Great Mouse Detective Ser.: 3). (ENG.). 112p. (J). (gr. 1-4). pap. 5.99 *(978-1-4814-6407-9(8),* Aladdin) Simon & Schuster Children's Publishing.

—Basil of Baker Street. Galdone, Paul, illus. 2016. (Great Mouse Detective Ser.: 1). (ENG.). 112p. (J). (gr. 1-4). 16.99 *(978-1-4814-6402-4(7));* pap. 5.99 *(978-1-4814-6401-7(9))* Simon & Schuster Children's Publishing. (Aladdin).

Titus, Eve. The Great Mouse Detective Crumbs & Clues Collection: Basil of Baker Street; Basil & the Cave of Cats; Basil in Mexico; Basil in the Wild West; Basil & the Lost Colony. Galdone, Paul, illus. 2017. (Great Mouse Detective Ser.). (ENG.). 544p. (J). (gr. 1-4). pap. 29.99 ***(978-1-4814-7717-8(X),*** Aladdin) Simon & Schuster Children's Publishing.

Todesco, Angelique. The Way of the Pendant. 2007. 196p. pap. 19.95 *(978-1-84753-846-8(0))* Lulu Pr., Inc.

Tolbert-Klein, Wa-Landa. Paladin: A Different Type of Werewolf Story. 2011. 156p. pap. 11.95 *(978-1-4327-6185-1(4))* Outskirts Pr., Inc.

Tomblin, Marian Strong. The Mystery at Hotel Ormond 2004. (Illus.). 142p. (J). per. 9.95 *(978-0-9766620-0-6(0))* Avery Goode-Reid Pubs.

—Where's Capone's Cash? 2005. (Illus.). 232p. (J). per. 9.95 *(978-0-9766620-1-3(9))* Avery Goode-Reid Pubs.

Tooley, S. D. The Skull. 2006. (YA). 178p. 23.00 *(978-0-9785402-1-0(2));* per. 12.95 *(978-0-9785402-0-3(4))* Full Moon Publishing LLC.

Toombs, Tom. The Mysterious Money Tree: Little Tommy Learns a Lesson in Giving. Smith, Abby, illus. 2012. 28p. (J). pap. 12.95 *(978-1-61314-033-8(9),* Innovo Pr.) Innovo Publishing, LLC.

Top Ten Clues You're Clueless. 2014. (ENG.). 304p. (YA). (gr. 8). pap. 9.99 *(978-0-06-227242-3(X))* HarperCollins Pubs.

Torres, Jennifer. The Battle. 2014. (Briny Deep Mysteries Ser.: Bk. 3). (Illus.). 96p. (J). (gr. 4-9). 17.95 *(978-1-62285-186-7(2));* pap. 10.95 *(978-1-62285-187-4(0))* Enslow Pubs., Inc.

—The Disappearing. 2014. (Briny Deep Mysteries Ser.). (Illus.). 96p. (J). (gr. 4-9). 17.95 *(978-1-62285-172-0(2));* pap. 10.95 *(978-1-62285-173-7(0))* Enslow Pubs., Inc.

—The Return. 2014. (Briny Deep Mysteries Ser.: Bk. 2). (Illus.). 96p. (J). (gr. 4-9). 17.95 *(978-1-62285-181-2(1));* pap. 10.95 *(978-1-62285-182-9(X))* Enslow Pubs., Inc.

Torrey, Michele. The Case of the Barfy Birthday. Newman, Barbara Johansen, illus. 2009. (Doyle & Fossey, Science Detectives Ser.: 4). (ENG.). 96p. (J). pap. 6.95 *(978-1-4027-4964-3(3))* Sterling Publishing Co., Inc.

—The Case of the Crooked Carnival. Newman, Barbara Johansen, illus. 2010. (Doyle & Fossey, Science Detectives Ser.). (ENG.). 96p. (J). (gr. 4-7). pap. 6.95 *(978-1-4027-4965-0(1))* Sterling Publishing Co., Inc.

—The Case of the Gasping Garbage. Torrey, Michele & Newman, Barbara Johansen, illus. 2009. (Doyle & Fossey, Science Detectives Ser.: 1). (ENG.). 96p. (J). (gr. 4-7). pap. 6.95 *(978-1-4027-4960-5(0))* Sterling Publishing Co., Inc.

—The Case of the Graveyard Ghost. Newman, Barbara Johansen, illus. 2009. (Doyle & Fossey, Science Detectives Ser.: 3). (ENG.). 96p. (J). pap. 6.95 *(978-1-4027-4963-6(5))* Sterling Publishing Co., Inc.

—The Case of the Mossy Lake Monster. Torrey, Michele & Newman, Barbara Johansen, illus. 2009. (Doyle & Fossey, Science Detectives Ser.: 2). (ENG.). 96p. (J). (gr. 4-7). pap. 6.95 *(978-1-4027-4962-9(7))* Sterling Publishing Co., Inc.

—The Case of the Terrible T. Rex. Newman, Barbara Johansen, illus. 2010. (Doyle & Fossey, Science Detectives Ser.). (ENG.). 96p. (J). (gr. 3-5). pap. 6.95 *(978-1-4027-4966-7(X))* Sterling Publishing Co., Inc.

Toussaint, Simone. Sharing My Shoes. 2010. 28p. pap. 9.95 *(978-1-4327-5701-4(6))* Outskirts Pr., Inc.

Town, Vicky. Mayhem in the Museum. 2013. 74p. pap. 9.99 *(978-1-61720-974-1(0))* Wilder Pubns., Corp.

Townley, Roderick. A Bitter Magic. 2015. (ENG.). 304p. (J). (gr. 4-7). 16.99 *(978-0-449-81649-3(4),* Knopf Bks. for Young Readers) Random Hse. Children's Bks.

—The Red Thread: A Novel in Three Incarnations. 2012. (ENG.). 304p. (YA). (gr. 7). pap. 14.99 *(978-1-4169-0895-1(1),* Atheneum Bks. for Young Readers) Simon & Schuster Children's Publishing.

Townsend, John. The Messenger. 2004. (Shades Ser.). 64p. (J). pap. *(978-0-237-52809-6(6))* Evans Brothers, Ltd.

Trabert, John. Gnome Chronicles. 2007. 172p. pap. 4.99 *(978-1-4343-1950-0(4))* AuthorHouse.

Treacy, Ann. The Search for the Homestead Treasure: A Mystery. 2016. (ENG., Illus.). 160p. 16.95 *(978-0-8166-9956-8(9))* Univ. of Minnesota Pr.

Trees, Annie Mae. The Last Days of Summer: A Mystery of Two Children & Their Grandma Set Out on an Adventure. 2012. 40p. pap. 24.95 *(978-1-4626-6103-9(3))* America Star Bks.

Trembath, Don. Emville Confidential, 1 vol. 2007. (ENG.). 198p. (J). (gr. 4-8). per. 7.95 *(978-1-55143-671-5(X))* Orca Bk. Pubs. USA.

Trenowden, Mark. The Miracle of Bean's Bullion. 2012. 192p. pap. *(978-1-84667-041-1(1))* Derwent Pr., The.

Trigg, Michael J. Greanwold & the Mystery Cave: Greanwold & the Minosaurs Story Books. 2013. 148p. pap. 12.97 *(978-1-61897-466-2(1),* Strategic Bk. Publishing) Strategic Book Publishing & Rights Agency (SBPRA).

Trine, Greg. The Stinky Cheese Caper. 2016. lib. bdg. 14.75 *(978-0-606-38490-2(1))* Turtleback Bks.

Trionfo, Nikki. Shatter. 2017. (YA). pap. 18.99 ***(978-1-4621-2013-0(X),*** Horizon Pubs.) Cedar Fort, Inc./CFI Distribution.

Trivas, Tracy. The Wish Stealers. 2010. (ENG.). 288p. (J). (gr. 3-7). 17.99 *(978-1-4169-8725-3(8),* Simon & Schuster/Paula Wiseman Bks.) Simon & Schuster/Paula Wiseman Bks.

Tromly, Stephanie. Trouble Is a Friend of Mine. 2015. (ENG.). 336p. (YA). (gr. 7-12). 17.99 *(978-0-525-42840-4(2),* Kathy Dawson Books) Penguin Young Readers Group.

Tromly, Stephanie. Trouble Makes a Comeback. (ENG.). (YA). (gr. 7). 2017. 320p. pap. 10.99 ***(978-0-14-751544-5(0),*** Speak) 2016. 304p. 17.99 *(978-0-525-42841-1(0),* Kathy Dawson Books) Penguin Young Readers Group.

Troupe, Thomas Kingsley. Darling Doll. Faber, Rudy, illus. 2016. (Hauntiques Ser.). (ENG.). 128p. (gr. 4-6). lib. bdg. 25.32 *(978-1-4965-3548-1(0))* Stone Arch Bks.

—Phantom's Favorite. Faber, Rudy, illus. 2016. (Hauntiques Ser.). (ENG.). 128p. (gr. 4-6). lib. bdg. 25.32 *(978-1-4965-3546-7(4))* Stone Arch Bks.

—Wandering Wagon. Faber, Rudy, illus. 2016. (Hauntiques Ser.). (ENG.). 128p. (gr. 4-6). lib. bdg. 25.32 *(978-1-4965-3547-4(2))* Stone Arch Bks.

Truckey, Don. The Adventures of Caraway Kim... Southpaw. Macintyre, R P, ed. 2006. (ENG.). 192p. pap. 10.95 *(978-1-894345-90-3(8))* Thistledown Pr., Ltd. CAN. Dist: Univ. of Toronto Pr.

Trumbauer, Lisa. Mountain Manor Mystery. Hawkes, Kevin, illus. 2006. 96p. (J). pap. *(978-1-59034-810-9(9))* Mondo Publishing.

Tucholke, April Genevieve. Wink Poppy Midnight. 2016. (ENG.). 256p. (YA). (gr. 9). 17.99 *(978-0-8037-4048-8(4),* Dial Bks) Penguin Young Readers Group.

Tulip, Jenny, illus. Who's Hiding in the Garden? 2008. 10p. (gr. -1-k). bds. 6.99 *(978-1-57755-785-2(9))* Gardner Pubns.

Turk, Judy Vanslyke, et al. Laughing Thief. 2007. (Clifton Ser.: 2). (ENG., Illus.). 48p. (J). (gr. 4-7). per. 9.99 *(978-1-905460-07-6(4))* CineBook GBR. Dist: National Bk. Network.

—My Dear Wilkinson. 2007. (Clifton Ser.: 1). (ENG., Illus.). 48p. (J). (gr. 4-7). per. 11.95 *(978-1-905460-06-9(6))* CineBook GBR. Dist: National Bk. Network.

Turnage, Sheila. The Ghosts of Tupelo Landing. 2015. (ENG.). 368p. (J). (gr. 5). 7.99 *(978-0-14-242571-8(0),* Puffin Books) Penguin Young Readers Group.

—The Odds of Getting Even. 2015. (ENG., Illus.). 352p. (J). (gr. 5). 16.99 *(978-0-8037-3961-1(3),* Kathy Dawson Books) Penguin Young Readers Group.

—The Odds of Getting Even. 2017. (Mo & Dale Mystery Ser.: 3). lib. bdg. 19.65 ***(978-0-606-39791-9(4))*** Turtleback Bks.

Turnage, Sheila. Three Times Lucky. (ENG.). (J). (gr. 5). 2013. 336p. pap. 7.99 *(978-0-14-242605-0(9),* Puffin Books) 2012. 314p. 16.99 *(978-0-8037-3670-2(3),* Dial Bks) Penguin Young Readers Group.

—Three Times Lucky. 2013. lib. bdg. 18.40 *(978-0-606-34168-4(4),* Turtleback) Turtleback Bks.

Turner, Henry. Ask the Dark. (ENG.). 256p. (YA). (gr. 9). 2016. pap. 9.99 *(978-0-544-81353-3(7),* HMH Books For Young Readers) 2015. 17.99 *(978-0-544-30827-5(1),* Clarion Bks.) Houghton Mifflin Harcourt Publishing Co.

Turner, Suzy. The Temporal Stone: A Morgan Sisters Novel. 2013. 288p. pap. *(978-989-98351-0-8(2))* Turner, Suzanne.

Twain, Mark, pseud. No. 44, the Mysterious Stranger. 2004. 160p. pap. 11.95 *(978-1-59540-326-1(4),* 1st World Library - Literary Society) 1st World Publishing, Inc.

—Tom Sawyer, Detective. (SPA., Illus.). 160p. (YA). 11.95 *(978-84-7281-062-4(3),* AF0623) Auriga, Ediciones S.A. ESP. Dist: Continental Bk. Co., Inc.

Tysinger, Dona. The Cheyenne Dragon & the Dragonfly. 2011. 52p. (gr. 4-6). pap. 10.99 *(978-1-4634-3032-0(9))* AuthorHouse.

U. S. National Geographic Society Staff. The Mystery of the Disappearing Swing. 2008. (Toot & Puddle Ser.). (ENG., Illus.). 24p. (J). (gr. -1-2). pap. 3.99 *(978-1-4263-0224-4(X));* lib. bdg. 11.90 *(978-1-4263-0372-2(6))* National Geographic Society. (National Geographic Children's Bks.).

Ulrich, Ann Carol. The Mystery at Hickory Hill: Annette Vetter Adventure #1. 2006. (Illus.). 196p. (YA). per. 9.95 *(978-0-944851-25-8(8))* Earth Star Pubns.

Unexpected Treasure, 6 vols. (Ragged Island Mysteriestm Ser.). 161p. (gr. 5-7). 42.50 *(978-0-322-01650-7(9))* Wright Group/McGraw-Hill.

Updale, Eleanor. Johnny Swanson. 2012. (ENG.). 384p. (J). (gr. 3-7). 8.99 *(978-0-385-75228-2(8),* Yearling) Random Hse. Children's Bks.

Urrea, Lourdes, et al. Tenebroso. 2005. (Ediciones Castillo Castillo Del Terror Ser.).Tr. of Sinister. (SPA.). (J). (gr. 2-6). pap. 7.95 *(978-970-20-0332-8(6))* Castillo, Ediciones, S. A. de C. V. MEX. Dist: Iaconi, Mariuccia Bk. Imports.

Vaid, Raj. A Case of Cold Feet: The Super Sleuth - Mystery #2. 2011. 68p. pap. 9.99 *(978-1-4520-6981-4(6))* AuthorHouse.

—The Case of the Holi Chocolate: The Super Sleuth - Mystery #1. 2011. 56p. pap. 9.99 *(978-1-4520-6903-6(4))* AuthorHouse.

Vail, Emily Blake. Carla & the Con Men. 2006. (J). per. 8.90 *(978-0-935087-28-4(1))* Wright Publishing, Inc.

Valencia, O. R. Savior in the Blue Mermaid. 2008. 180p. pap. 14.35 *(978-1-4251-2824-1(6))* Trafford Publishing.

Valentino, Amanda & Bell, Cathleen Davitt. Unraveled, Bk. 4. 2012. (Amanda Project Ser.: 4). (ENG.). 352p. (YA). (gr. 8). pap. 8.99 *(978-0-06-174219-4(8),* HarperTeen) HarperCollins Pubs.

Valentino, Amanda & Stolarz, Laurie Faria. Shattered, Bk. 3. 2011. (Amanda Project Ser.: 3). (ENG.). 272p. (YA). (gr. 8). pap. 8.99 *(978-0-06-174217-0(1),* HarperTeen) HarperCollins Pubs.

Van Draanen, Wendelin. Sammy Keyes & the Art of Deception. 2008. (Sammy Keyes Ser.: Bk. 8). (J). 64.99 *(978-1-60640-640-3(X))* Findaway World, LLC.

—Sammy Keyes & the Art of Deception. Van Draanen, Wendelin, illus. 2004. (Sammy Keyes Ser.: Bk. 8). (Illus.). pap. 54.95 incl. audio compact disk *(978-1-59519-003-1(1));* pap. 36.95 incl. audio *(978-1-59519-001-7(5))* Live Oak Media.

—Sammy Keyes & the Art of Deception. 2005. (Sammy Keyes Ser.). (Illus.). 272p. (J). (gr. 4-7). 14.15 *(978-0-7569-5069-9(4))* Perfection Learning Corp.

—Sammy Keyes & the Art of Deception. 2005. (Sammy Keyes Ser.: 8). (ENG.). 304p. (J). (gr. 5-7). 7.99 *(978-0-440-41992-1(1),* Yearling) Random Hse. Children's Bks.

—Sammy Keyes & the Cold Hard Cash. 2010. (Sammy Keyes Ser.: Bk. 12). (ENG.). 320p. (J). (gr. 5-7). 8.99 *(978-0-440-42113-9(6),* Yearling) Random Hse. Children's Bks.

—Sammy Keyes & the Curse of Moustache Mary. 2008. (Sammy Keyes Ser.: Bk. 5). (J). 59.99 *(978-1-60640-638-0(8))* Findaway World, LLC.

—Sammy Keyes & the Dead Giveaway. 2008. (Sammy Keyes Ser.: Bk. 10). (J). 64.99 *(978-1-60640-639-7(6))* Findaway World, LLC.

—Sammy Keyes & the Dead Giveaway. unabr. ed. 2006. (Sammy Keyes Ser.: Bk. 10). (J). (gr. 5-7). pap. 54.95 incl. audio compact disk *(978-1-59519-771-9(0));* pap. 36.95 incl. audio *(978-1-59519-770-2(2))* Live Oak Media.

—Sammy Keyes & the Dead Giveaway. 2007. (Sammy Keyes Ser.: Bk. 10). (ENG., Illus.). 304p. (J). (gr. 5-7). per. 7.99 *(978-0-440-41911-2(5),* Yearling) Random Hse. Children's Bks.

—Sammy Keyes & the Hollywood Mummy. 2008. (Sammy Keyes Ser.: Bk. 6). (J). 64.99 *(978-1-60640-641-0(8))* Findaway World, LLC.

—Sammy Keyes & the Hotel Thief. 2008. (Sammy Keyes Ser.: Bk. 1). (J). 54.99 *(978-1-60640-642-7(6))* Findaway World, LLC.

—Sammy Keyes & the Killer Cruise. (Sammy Keyes Ser.). (ENG.). (J). (gr. 5). 2014. 352p. 7.99 *(978-0-307-93062-0(9),* Yearling) 2013. 336p. 16.99 *(978-0-375-87054-5(7),* Knopf Bks. for Young Readers) Random Hse. Children's Bks.

—Sammy Keyes & the Kiss Goodbye. 2014. 236p. (J). pap. *(978-0-307-93063-7(7))* Knopf, Alfred A. Inc.

—Sammy Keyes & the Kiss Goodbye. 2014. (Sammy Keyes Ser.). (ENG.). 240p. (J). (gr. 5). 16.99 *(978-0-375-87055-2(5),* Knopf Bks. for Young Readers) Random Hse. Children's Bks.

—Sammy Keyes & the Night of Skulls. 2012. (Sammy Keyes Ser.: 14). (ENG.). 336p. (J). (gr. 5-7). 8.99 *(978-0-375-85457-6(6),* Yearling) Random Hse. Children's Bks.

—Sammy Keyes & the Power of Justice Jack. 2012. (Sammy Keyes Ser.: Bk. 15). (ENG.). 320p. (J). (gr. 5-7). 7.99 *(978-0-307-93060-6(2),* Yearling) Random Hse. Children's Bks.

—Sammy Keyes & the Psycho Kitty Queen. 2008. (Sammy Keyes Ser.: Bk. 9). (J). 64.99 *(978-1-60640-643-4(4))* Findaway World, LLC.

—Sammy Keyes & the Psycho Kitty Queen. 2006. (Sammy Keyes Ser.: Bk. 9). (J). pap. 36.95 incl. audio *(978-1-59519-774-0(5));* pap. 54.95 incl. audio compact disk *(978-1-59519-775-7(3))* Live Oak Media.

—Sammy Keyes & the Psycho Kitty Queen. 2006. (Sammy Keyes Ser.: 9). (ENG., Illus.). 320p. (J). (gr. 5-7). 7.99 *(978-0-440-41910-5(7),* Yearling) Random Hse. Children's Bks.

—Sammy Keyes & the Runaway Elf. 2008. (Sammy Keyes Ser.: Bk. 4). (J). 54.99 *(978-1-60640-644-1(2))* Findaway World, LLC.

—Sammy Keyes & the Search for Snake Eyes. 2008. (Sammy Keyes Ser.: Bk. 7). (J). 64.99 *(978-1-60640-645-8(0))* Findaway World, LLC.

—Sammy Keyes & the Search for Snake Eyes. Van Draanen, Wendelin, illus. 2003. (Sammy Keyes Ser.: Bk. 7). (Illus.). pap. 36.95 incl. audio *(978-1-59112-273-9(2));* pap. 54.95 incl. audio compact disk *(978-1-59112-281-4(3))* Live Oak Media.

—Sammy Keyes & the Search for Snake Eyes. 2003. (Sammy Keyes Ser.: Bk. 7). (Illus.). 277p. (gr. 5-9). 17.00 *(978-0-7569-1445-5(0))* Perfection Learning Corp.

—Sammy Keyes & the Search for Snake Eyes. 2003. (Sammy Keyes Ser.: 7). (ENG.). 320p. (J). (gr. 5-7). 7.99 *(978-0-440-41900-6(X),* Yearling) Random Hse. Children's Bks.

—Sammy Keyes & the Showdown in Sin City. 2013. (Sammy Keyes Ser.: Bk. 16). (ENG.). 304p. (J). (gr. 5). pap. 7.99 *(978-0-307-93061-3(0),* Yearling) Random Hse. Children's Bks.

—Sammy Keyes & the Sisters of Mercy. 2008. (Sammy Keyes Ser.: Bk. 3). (J). 59.99 *(978-1-60640-646-5(9))* Findaway World, LLC.

—Sammy Keyes & the Wedding Crasher. 2011. (Sammy Keyes Ser.: Bk. 13). (ENG.). 320p. (J). (gr. 5). 7.99 *(978-0-375-85456-9(8),* Yearling) Random Hse. Children's Bks.

—Sammy Keyes & the Wild Things. Biggs, Brian, illus. 2008. (Sammy Keyes Ser.: 11). (ENG.). 320p. (J). (gr. 5-7). 7.99 *(978-0-440-42112-2(8),* Yearling) Random Hse. Children's Bks.

Van Dyke, Edith. Mary Louise. l.t. ed. 2005. 280p. pap. *(978-1-84637-096-0(5))* Echo Library.

Van Dyne, Edith. Aunt Jane's Nieces. l.t. ed. 2007. (ENG.). 170p. pap. 19.99 *(978-1-4264-3951-3(2));* 462p. pap. 30.99 *(978-1-4264-4009-0(X))* Creative Media Partners, LLC.

—Aunt Jane's Nieces & Uncle John. 2005. 26.95 *(978-1-4218-1024-9(7));* 176p. pap. 11.95 *(978-1-4218-1124-6(3))* 1st World Publishing, Inc. (1st World Library - Literary Society).

—Aunt Jane's Nieces at Millville. 2005. 27.95 *(978-1-4218-1026-3(3));* 204p. pap. 12.95 *(978-1-4218-1126-0(X))* 1st World Publishing, Inc. (1st World Library - Literary Society).

—Aunt Jane's Nieces at Millville. l.t. ed. 2006. 158p. pap. 19.99 *(978-1-4264-4058-8(8));* 172p. pap. 22.99 *(978-1-4264-4117-2(7))* Creative Media Partners, LLC.

—Aunt Jane's Nieces at Millville. 2004. reprint ed. pap. 1.99 *(978-1-4192-0823-2(3));* pap. 21.95 *(978-1-4191-0823-5(9))* Kessinger Publishing, LLC.

—Aunt Jane's Nieces at Work. 2005. 204p. pap. 12.95 *(978-1-4218-1523-7(0),* 1st World Library - Literary Society) 1st World Publishing, Inc.

—Aunt Jane's Nieces in Society. 2005. 28.95 *(978-1-4218-1424-7(2));* 276p. pap. 13.95 *(978-1-4218-1524-4(9))* 1st World Publishing, Inc. (1st World Library - Literary Society).

—Aunt Jane's Nieces in Society. 2007. (ENG.). 144p. pap. 18.99 *(978-1-4264-4161-5(4));* 156p. pap. 21.99 *(978-1-4264-4202-5(5))* Creative Media Partners, LLC.

—Aunt Jane's Nieces in Society. 2004. reprint ed. pap. 20.95 *(978-1-4191-0824-2(7));* pap. 1.99 *(978-1-4192-0824-9(1))* Kessinger Publishing, LLC.

—Aunt Jane's Nieces on Vacation. 2005. 27.95 *(978-1-4218-1027-0(1));* 200p. pap. 12.95 *(978-1-4218-1127-7(8))* 1st World Publishing, Inc. (1st World Library - Literary Society).

—Aunt Jane's Nieces on Vacation. 2004. reprint ed. pap. 1.99 *(978-1-4192-0825-6(X));* pap. 21.95 *(978-1-4191-0825-9(5))* Kessinger Publishing, LLC.

—Aunt Jane's Nieces out West. 2005. 27.95 *(978-1-4218-1425-4(0));* 212p. pap. 12.95 *(978-1-4218-1525-1(7))* 1st World Publishing, Inc. (1st World Library - Literary Society).

—Aunt Jane's Nieces Out West. 2004. reprint ed. pap. 21.95 *(978-1-4191-0826-6(3));* pap. 1.99 *(978-1-4192-0826-3(8))* Kessinger Publishing, LLC.

—Mary Louise. 2007. (ENG.). 148p. pap. 18.99 *(978-1-4264-1952-2(X));* 144p. pap. 19.99 *(978-1-4264-2063-4(3))* Creative Media Partners, LLC.

Van Hamme, Jean. The Curse of the 30 Pieces of Silver, Vol. 14, Pt. 2. Shreder, Etienne & Aubin, Antoine, illus. 2012. (Blake & Mortimer Ser.: 14). (ENG.). 64p. (J). (gr. 5-12). pap. 15.95 *(978-1-84918-130-3(6))* CineBook GBR. Dist: National Bk. Network.

—The Strange Encounter, Vol. 5. 2009. (Blake & Mortimer Ser.: 5). (ENG., Illus.). 66p. pap. 15.95 *(978-1-905460-75-5(9))* CineBook GBR. Dist: National Bk. Network.

Van Tol, Alex. Redline, 1 vol. 2011. (Orca Soundings Ser.). (ENG.). (YA). (gr. 8-12). 136p. pap. 9.95 *(978-1-55469-893-6(6));* 128p. lib. bdg. 16.95 *(978-1-55469-894-3(4))* Orca Bk. Pubs. USA.

—Shallow Grave, 1 vol. 2012. (Orca Soundings Ser.). (ENG.). 136p. (YA). (gr. 8-12). pap. 9.95 *(978-1-4598-0202-5(0));* lib. bdg. 16.95 *(978-1-4598-0203-2(9))* Orca Bk. Pubs. USA.

VanArsdale, Anthony, illus. The Sleepy Hollow Mystery. 2015. 111p. (J). ***(978-1-4806-9407-1(X))*** Whitman, Albert & Co.

Vande Velde, Vivian. Magic Can Be Murder. 2009. (ENG.). 208p. (YA). (gr. 7). pap. 12.99 *(978-0-547-25872-0(0))* Houghton Mifflin Harcourt Publishing Co.

—Never Trust a Dead Man. 2008. (ENG., Illus.). 208p. (YA). (gr. 7). pap. 13.95 *(978-0-15-206448-8(6))* Houghton Mifflin Harcourt Publishing Co.

—Witch Dreams, 0 vols. 2008. (ENG.). 128p. (YA). (gr. 5-9). pap. 7.99 *(978-0-7614-5460-1(8),* 9780761454601, Amazon Children's Publishing) Amazon Publishing.

VanDycke, Lilian Claudine. The Mystery Fire. 2012. 56p. pap. *(978-1-77097-382-4(6))* FriesenPress.

Vanished. 64p. (YA). (gr. 6-12). pap. *(978-0-8224-2367-6(7))* Globe Fearon Educational Publishing.

The Vanishing Game. 2013. (Hardy Boys Adventures Ser.: 3). (ENG.). 144p. (J). (gr. 3-7). 15.99 *(978-1-4424-7344-7(4));* (Illus.). pap. 6.99 *(978-1-4424-5981-6(6))* Simon & Schuster Children's Publishing. (Aladdin).

Vanneman, Alan. Sherlock Holmes & the Giant Rat of Sumatra. 2003. (Otto Penzler Bks.). (ENG.). 304p. pap. 15.00 *(978-0-7867-1125-3(6))* Westview Pr.

Varley, Dax. The Crow. Proctor, Jon, illus. 2016. (ENG.). 48p. (J). lib. bdg. *(978-1-62402-160-2(3))* Magic Wagon.

—Graveyard Dirt. Proctor, Jon, illus. 2016. (ENG.). 48p. (J). lib. bdg. *(978-1-62402-158-9(1))* Magic Wagon.

—The Locket. Proctor, Jon, illus. 2016. (ENG.). 48p. (J). lib. bdg. *(978-1-62402-159-6(X))* Magic Wagon.

Vaught, Susan. Footer Davis Probably Is Crazy. Reinhardt, Jennifer Black, illus. 2015. (ENG.). 240p. (J). (gr. 5-9). 16.99 *(978-1-4814-2276-5(6),* Simon & Schuster Bks. For Young Readers) Simon & Schuster Bks. For Young Readers.

—Freaks Like Us. 2014. (ENG.). 256p. (YA). (gr. 7). pap. 9.99 *(978-1-61963-163-2(6),* 9781619631632, Bloomsbury USA Childrens) Bloomsbury Publishing USA.

Vaught, Susan. Super Max & the Mystery of Thornwood's Revenge. 2017. (ENG., Illus.). 352p. (J). (gr. 3-7). 16.99 ***(978-1-4814-8683-5(7),*** Simon & Schuster/Paula Wiseman Bks.) Simon & Schuster/Paula Wiseman Bks.

Vegas, Peter. The Iron Tomb. 2016. (Pyramid Hunters Ser.: 1). (ENG., Illus.). 304p. (J). (gr. 5-9). 16.99 *(978-1-4814-4578-8(2),* Aladdin) Simon & Schuster Children's Publishing.

Venable, Colleen A. F. And Then There Were Gnomes. Yue, Stephanie, illus. 2010. (Guinea Pig, Pet Shop Private Eye Ser.: 2). (ENG.). 48p. (J). (gr. 2-5). pap. 6.95 *(978-0-7613-5480-2(8));* lib. bdg. 27.93 *(978-0-7613-4599-2(X))* Lerner Publishing Group.

—The Ferret's a Foot, 3 vols. Yue, Stephanie, illus. 2011. (Guinea Pig, Pet Shop Private Eye Ser.: 3). (ENG.). 48p. (J). (gr. 2-5). 27.93 *(978-0-7613-5223-5(6));* pap. 6.95 *(978-0-7613-5629-5(0))* Lerner Publishing Group.

—Fish You Were Here, No. 4. Yue, Stephanie, illus. 2011. (Guinea Pig, Pet Shop Private Eye Ser.: 4). (ENG.). 48p. (J). (gr. 2-5). pap. 6.95 *(978-0-7613-5630-1(4));* lib. bdg. 27.93 *(978-0-7613-5224-2(4))* Lerner Publishing Group.

—Going, Going, Dragon! 2013. 48p. pap. 14.95 *(978-1-4677-0973-6(5))* Lerner Publishing Group.

—Going, Going, Dragon! Yue, Stephanie, illus. 2013. (Guinea Pig, Pet Shop Private Eye Ser.: 6). (ENG.). 48p. (J). (gr. 2-5). pap. 6.95 *(978-1-4677-0726-8(0));* lib. bdg. 27.93 *(978-0-7613-6009-4(3))* Lerner Publishing Group.

—Hamster & Cheese. Yue, Stephanie, illus. 2010. (Guinea Pig, Pet Shop Private Eye Ser.: 1). (ENG.). 48p. (J). (gr. 2-5). pap. 6.95 *(978-0-7613-5479-6(4));* lib. bdg. 27.93 *(978-0-7613-4598-5(1))* Lerner Publishing Group.

—Raining Cats & Detectives. Yue, Stephanie, illus. 2012. (Guinea Pig, Pet Shop Private Eye Ser.: 5). (ENG.). 48p. (J). (gr. 2-5). lib. bdg. 27.93 *(978-0-7613-6008-7(5))* Lerner Publishing Group.

—Raining Cats & Detectives. Yue, Stephanie, illus. 2012. (Guinea Pig, Pet Shop Private Eye Ser.: 5). lib. bdg. 17.15 *(978-0-606-26631-4(3),* Turtleback) Turtleback Bks.

Ventresca, Yvonne. Black Flowers, White Lies. 2016. (ENG.). 272p. (YA). (gr. 6). 16.99 *(978-1-5107-0988-1(6),* Sky Pony Pr.) Skyhorse Publishing Co., Inc.

—Pandemic. 2016. (ENG.). 368p. (J). (gr. 6). pap. 9.99 *(978-1-5107-0390-2(X),* Sky Pony Pr.) Skyhorse Publishing Co., Inc.

Verano, M. Diary of a Haunting. (Diary of a Haunting Ser.). (ENG., Illus.). (YA). (gr. 9). 2016. 336p. pap. 10.99 *(978-1-4814-3068-5(8))* 2015. 320p. 17.99 *(978-1-4814-3069-2(6))* Simon Pulse. (Simon Pulse).

Vernon, Ursula. The Case of the Toxic Mutants. 2013. (Dragonbreath Ser.: 9). (ENG., Illus.). 208p. (J). (gr. 3-7). 12.99 *(978-0-8037-3847-8(1),* Dial Bks) Penguin Young Readers Group.

Via, Jennifer Welsh. The Foggy Meadow Discovery. 2007. 216p. per. 14.95 *(978-0-595-44680-3(9))* iUniverse, Inc.

Vicary, Tim. The Hitchhiker, 5. 2014. (Garnet Oracle Readers Ser.). (Illus.). 40p. pap., stu. ed. 4.50 *(978-1-907575-18-1(9))* Garnet Education GBR. Dist: Garnet Publishing, Ltd.

Vicente, Alidis. The Case of the Three Kings / el Caso de Los Reyes Magos: The Flaca Files / Los Expedientes de Flaca. 2016. (Flaca Files / Los Expedientes de Flaca Ser.). (MUL, ENG & SPA., Illus.). 96p. (J). (gr. 3-6). pap. 9.95 *(978-1-55885-822-0(9),* Piñata Books) Arte Publico Pr.

—The Missing Chancleta & Other Top-Secret Cases / la Chancleta Perdida y Otros Casos Secretos. 2013. (SPA & ENG., Illus.). 64p. (J). pap. 9.95 *(978-1-55885-779-7(6),* Piñata Books) Arte Publico Pr.

Villar Liébana, Luisa. El Ladron de Salchichon. 2005. (Investigator Big Ears Ser.). (SPA., Illus.). 62p. (J). (gr. 2-3). 8.95 *(978-84-348-9384-9(3))* SM Ediciones ESP. Dist: Iaconi, Mariuccia Bk. Imports.

Villareal, Ray. Who's Buried in the Garden? 2009. 160p. (YA). (gr. 6-18). pap. 10.95 *(978-1-55885-546-5(7),* Piñata Books) Arte Publico Pr.

Vincent, Cindy. Mystery of the Missing Ming: A Daisy Diamond Detective Novel. 2004. 172p. (YA). 9.97 *(978-1-932169-37-9(7))* Mysteries by Vincent, LLC.

Viney, Peter. The Case of the Dead Batsman, 7. 2013. (Garnet Oracle Readers Ser.). (Illus.). 40p. pap., stu. ed. 4.50 *(978-1-907575-21-1(9))* Garnet Education GBR. Dist: Garnet Publishing, Ltd.

Vize, Bonnie. The Mystery of the Park Pavilion. 2009. pap. 14.22 *(978-1-61584-491-3(0))* Independent Pub.

Voices in the Night. 64p. (YA). (gr. 6-12). pap. *(978-0-8224-2368-3(5))* Globe Fearon Educational Publishing.

Voigt, Cynthia. The Book of Secrets. 2015. (Mister Max Ser.: 2). lib. bdg. 17.20 *(978-0-606-37702-7(6))* Turtleback Bks.

—Mister Max: the Book of Secrets. Bruno, Iacopo, illus. 2014. (Mister Max Ser.). (ENG.). 384p. (J). (gr. 3-7). 16.99 *(978-0-307-97684-0(X),* Knopf Bks. for Young Readers) Random Hse. Children's Bks.

Voskuil, Hannah. Horus & the Curse of Everlasting Regret. 2016. (ENG.). 224p. (J). (gr. 3-7). 16.99 *(978-1-101-93333-6(X),* Knopf Bks. for Young Readers) Random Hse. Children's Bks.

Wachtel, Shirley Russak. Brad Sureshot — Coach-Detective: The Baffling Case of the Disappearing Dribbler. 2007. 76p. per. 8.95 *(978-0-595-47266-6(4))* iUniverse, Inc.

Wade, Mary Dodson. Joan Lowery Nixon: Masterful Mystery Writer. 2004. (Authors Teens Love Ser.). (Illus.). 128p. (J). lib. bdg. 27.94 *(978-0-7660-2194-5(7))* Enslow Pubs., Inc.

Wade, Rebecca. The Whispering House. 2012. (ENG.). 272p. (J). (gr. 3-7). 16.99 *(978-0-06-077497-4(5),* Tegen, Katherine Bks) HarperCollins Pubs.

Walker, Landry. Secrets & Lies. Takara, Marcio, illus. 2010. (Incredibles Ser.). 112p. (J). (gr. 3-8). pap. 9.99 *(978-1-60886-583-3(5))* Boom! Studios.

Walker Styles Staff. Something Smells Fishy. Whitehouse, Ben, illus. 2016. (Rider Woofson Ser.: 2). (ENG.). 128p. (J). (gr. k-4). pap. 5.99 *(978-1-4814-5741-5(1),* Little Simon) Little Simon.

Wall, Billy James. The Mystery of Marcy & the Stony Squirrel. 2009. 40.00 *(978-1-61584-580-4(1))* Independent Pub.

Wallace, James. Tsunami: Ghost Eagle 1. 2003. 149p. (YA). pap. 11.95 *(978-0-595-27372-0(6))* iUniverse, Inc.

Wallace, Karen. The Case of the Howling Armor. 2004. (Illus.). 47p. *(978-0-439-66552-0(3))* Scholastic, Inc.

—Diamond Takers. 2007. (Lady Violet Mysteries Ser.: 3). (ENG.). 240p. (J). (gr. 4-7). pap. 9.95 *(978-1-4169-0100-6(0),* Simon & Schuster Children's) Simon & Schuster, Ltd. GBR. Dist: Simon & Schuster, Inc.

—Flash Harriet & the Loch Ness Monster. Nayler, Sarah, illus. 2007. (Collins Big Cat Ser.). (ENG.). 160p. (J). (gr. 2-4). pap. 8.99 *(978-0-00-723082-2(6))* HarperCollins Pubs. Ltd. GBR. Dist: Independent Pubs. Group.

—Footprints in the Snow, 1 vol. Harland, Jackie, illus. 2013. (Start Reading Ser.). (ENG.). 24p. (gr. k-1). pap. 7.95 *(978-1-4765-4099-3(3))* Capstone Press of Coughlan Cos.

—Lost Kittens. Harland, Jackie, illus. 2013. (Start Reading Ser.). (ENG.). 24p. (gr. k-1). pap. 7.95 *(978-1-4765-4115-0(9))* Capstone Press of Coughlan Cos.

—Treasure Trail, 1 vol. Harland, Jackie, illus. 2013. (Start Reading Ser.). (ENG.). 24p. (gr. k-1). pap. 7.95 *(978-1-4765-4143-3(4))* Capstone Press of Coughlan Cos.

Wallace, Nancy K. The Haunted Sleepover, 1 vol. Chronister, Amanda, illus. 2013. (Abby & the Book Bunch Ser.). (ENG.). 80p. (J). (gr. 2-5). 27.07 *(978-1-61641-913-4(X))* Magic Wagon.

—The Mystery of the Golden Key, 1 vol. Chronister, Amanda, illus. 2013. (Abby & the Book Bunch Ser.). (ENG.). 80p. (J). (gr. 2-5). 27.07 *(978-1-61641-915-8(6))* Magic Wagon.

—Presumed Missing, 1 vol. Chronister, Amanda, illus. 2013. (Abby & the Book Bunch Ser.). (ENG.). 80p. (J). (gr. 2-5). 27.07 *(978-1-61641-917-2(2))* Magic Wagon.

Wallace, Sheila Ryan. Diving for the Gold. 2004. 142p. (YA). pap. 15.95 *(978-0-7414-2269-9(7))* Infinity Publishing.

—Miss Abigail's Antique Treasures. 2007. (ENG.). 152p. per. 15.95 *(978-0-7414-3942-0(5))* Infinity Publishing.

Waller, Stephen & Pearson Education Staff. Run for Your Life, Level 1. 2nd ed. 2009. (ENG., Illus.). 32p. pap. 11.99 *(978-1-4058-6970-6(4))* Pearson Education.

Walsh, Alice. Buried Truth, 1 vol. 2013. (ENG.). 100p. (J). (gr. 4-8). pap. 11.95 *(978-1-77103-009-0(7),* Tuckamore Bks) Creative Bk. Publishing CAN. Dist: Orca Bk. Pubs. USA.

Walsh, Ann. Moses, Me, & Murder: A Barkerville Mystery. 2nd ed. 2013. (Barkerville Mystery Ser.: 1). (ENG., Illus.). 112p. (J). pap. 10.99 *(978-1-4597-0967-6(5))* Dundurn CAN. Dist: Ingram Publisher Services.

Walsh, Brendan & Benchmark Education Co., LLC. Hats off to the President: A White House Mystery. McEvenue, Tim, illus. 2014. (Text Connections Ser.). (J). (gr. 3). *(978-1-4509-9660-0(4))* Benchmark Education Co.

Walsh, Ellen Stoll. Dot & Jabber & the Big Bug Mystery. 2017. (Green Light Readers — Level 2 Ser.: Vol. 3). (ENG.). (J). (gr. -1-3). lib. bdg. 13.55 **(978-0-606-39827-5(9))** Turtleback Bks.

Walsh, Laurence & Walsh, Suella. In the Middle of the Night. 2006. (J). pap. *(978-0-88092-473-3(X))* Royal Fireworks Publishing Co.

Walters, Eric & Spreekmeester, Kevin. Death by Exposure. 2nd ed. 2006. (ENG., Illus.). 88p. (J). (gr. 4-8). pap. 9.99 *(978-1-55002-632-0(1),* Dundurn Pr.) Dundurn CAN. Dist: Ingram Publisher Services.

Walton, Rick. Mini Mysteries 2: 20 More Tricky Tales to Untangle. Scheuer, Lauren, illus. 2006. 87p. (J). *(978-1-4156-6869-6(8),* American Girl) American Girl Publishing, Inc.

—Mini Mysteries 3: 20 More Tricky Tales to Untangle. Scheuer, Lauren, illus. 2007. (ENG.). 80p. (gr. 4-7). pap. 7.95 *(978-1-59369-281-0(1))* American Girl Publishing, Inc.

Waltz, Dan. Kornstalkers: Corn Maze Massacre. Waltz, Dan, illus. l.t. ed. 2005. (Chilled to the Bone! Ser.: No. 1). (Illus.). 120p. (J). per. 6.99 *(978-0-9741774-3-4(1))* D. W. Publishing.

Ward, Ian. Bobby Blah Blah & the Mystery of the U F O in Sniggery Woods. 2009. (Illus.). 84p. pap. 10.49 *(978-1-4389-7963-2(0))* AuthorHouse.

Ward, Matthew. War of the World Records. 2nd ed. 2015. (Fantastic Family Whipple Ser.: 2). (ENG.). 384p. (J). (gr. 3-7). pap. 8.99 *(978-1-59514-692-2(X),* Razorbill) Penguin Young Readers Group.

Ward-Showers, Latanya. Could It Be a Monster in the Attic? 2013. 24p. pap. 17.99 *(978-1-4817-0542-4(3))* AuthorHouse.

Ware, Fletcher K. The Empress Conspiracy. 2004. 285p. (YA). per. 14.95 *(978-1-932496-17-8(3))* Penman Publishing, Inc.

Warman, Jessica. Beautiful Lies. 2014. (ENG.). 432p. (YA). (gr. 9). pap. 9.99 *(978-0-8027-3543-0(6),* 9780802735430, Bloomsbury USA Childrens) Bloomsbury Publishing USA.

Warner, Gertrude Chandler. Blue Bay Mystery, 1 vol. Dubisch, Michael, illus. 2009. (Boxcar Children Graphic Novels Ser.). (ENG.). 32p. (J). (gr. 2-5). 28.50 *(978-1-60270-591-3(7))* ABDO Publishing Co.

—The Boxcar Children. Date not set. (Boxcar Children Ser.: No. 1). (J). (gr. 2-5). lib. bdg. 18.95 *(978-0-8488-1712-1(5))* Amereon Ltd.

—The Boxcar Children. (Boxcar Children Ser.: No. 1). 154p. (J). (gr. 2-5). pap. 3.95 *(978-0-8072-1447-3(7),* Listening Library) Random Hse. Audio Publishing Group.

—Boxcar Children Graphic Novels, 6 vols., Set 2. Incl. Amusement Park Mystery. Denton, Shannon Eric. Dubisch, Mike, illus. 28.50 *(978-1-60270-718-4(9));* Castle Mystery. Denton, Shannon Eric. Dubisch, Mike, illus. 28.50 *(978-1-60270-720-7(0));* Haunted Cabin Mystery. Bloodworth, Mark, illus. 28.50 *(978-1-60270-717-7(0));* Pizza Mystery. Worley, Rob M. Dubisch, Mike, illus. 28.50 *(978-1-60270-719-1(7));* Snowbound Mystery. Dubisch, Mike, illus. 28.50 *(978-1-60270-715-3(4));* Tree House Mystery. Long, Christopher E. Bloodworth, Mark, illus. 28.50 *(978-1-60270-716-0(2));* (J). (gr. 2-5). (Boxcar Children Graphic Novels Ser.). 32p. 2010. 171.00 *(978-1-60270-714-6(6),* Graphic Planet- Fiction) ABDO Publishing Co.

—Boxcar Children Graphic Novels, 6 vols., Set 3. Dunn, Ben, illus. Incl. Bk. 13. Woodshed Mystery. Dunn, Joeming. 28.50 *(978-1-61641-121-3(X));* Bk. 14. Lighthouse Mystery. Dunn, Joeming. 28.50 *(978-1-61641-122-0(8));* Bk. 15. Mountain Top Mystery. Dunn, Joeming. 28.50 *(978-1-61641-123-7(6));* Bk. 16. Houseboat Mystery. Dunn, Joeming W., illus. & adapted by. 28.50 *(978-1-61641-124-4(4));* Bk. 17. Bicycle Mystery. Dunn, Joeming W., illus. & adapted by. 28.50 *(978-1-61641-125-1(2));* Bk. 18. Mystery in the Sand. Dunn, Joeming. 28.50 *(978-1-61641-126-8(0));* (J). (gr. 2-5). (Boxcar Children Graphic Novels Ser.). (Illus.). 32p. 2011. 171.00 *(978-1-61641-120-6(1),* Graphic Planet- Fiction) ABDO Publishing Co.

—The Boxcar Children Guide to Adventure: A How-To for Mystery Solving, Make-It-Yourself Projects, & More. 2014. (Boxcar Children Mysteries Ser.). (ENG.). 144p. (J). (gr. 1-5). 12.99 *(978-0-8075-0905-0(1))* Whitman, Albert & Co.

—The Dog-Gone Mystery. 2009. (First Read-Alone Mysteries Ser.). (Illus.). (J). (gr. 1-3). lib. bdg. 14.99 *(978-0-8075-1656-0(2))* Whitman, Albert & Co.

—The Lighthouse Mystery. (Boxcar Children Ser.: No. 8). 147p. (J). (gr. 2-5). pap. 3.95 *(978-0-8072-1474-9(4),* Listening Library) Random Hse. Audio Publishing Group.

—Mike's Mystery. (Boxcar Children Ser.: No. 5). 128p. (J). (gr. 2-5). pap. 3.95 *(978-0-8072-1462-6(0),* Listening Library) Random Hse. Audio Publishing Group.

—Mike's Mystery, 1 vol. Dubisch, Michael, illus. 2009. (Boxcar Children Graphic Novels Ser.). (ENG.). 32p. (J). (gr. 2-5). 28.50 *(978-1-60270-590-6(9))* ABDO Publishing Co.

—The Mystery of the Grinning Gargoyle. VanArsdale, Anthony, illus. 2014. (Boxcar Children Mysteries Ser.: 137). (ENG.). 128p. (J). (gr. 1-5). pap. 5.99 *(978-0-8075-0893-0(4))* Whitman, Albert & Co.

—The Mystery of the Runaway Ghost. Soileau, Hodges, illus. 2004. (Boxcar Children Ser.). 135p. (J). 12.65 *(978-0-7569-3264-0(5))* Perfection Learning Corp.

—The Mystery of the Soccer Snitch. VanArsdale, Anthony, illus. 2014. (Boxcar Children Mysteries Ser.: 136). (ENG.). 128p. (J). (gr. 1-5). pap. 5.99 *(978-0-8075-0896-1(9))* Whitman, Albert & Co.

—Mystery Ranch. (Boxcar Children Ser.: No. 4). 128p. (J). (gr. 2-5). pap. 3.95 *(978-0-8072-1450-3(7),* Listening Library) Random Hse. Audio Publishing Group.

—Mystery Ranch, 1 vol. Dubisch, Michael, illus. 2009. (Boxcar Children Graphic Novels Ser.). (ENG.). 32p. (J). (gr. 2-5). 28.50 *(978-1-60270-589-0(5))* ABDO Publishing Co.

—Snowbound Mystery. Dubisch, Mike, illus. 2009. (Boxcar Children Graphic Novels Ser.: 7). (ENG.). 32p. (J). (gr. 1-5). pap. 6.99 *(978-0-8075-7515-4(1))* Whitman, Albert & Co.

—The Yellow House Mystery. (Boxcar Children Ser.: No. 3). 191p. (J). (gr. 2-5). pap. 3.95 *(978-0-8072-1449-7(3),* Listening Library) Random Hse. Audio Publishing Group.

—The Yellow House Mystery, 1 vol. Dubisch, Michael, illus. 2009. (Boxcar Children Graphic Novels Ser.). (ENG.). 32p. (J). (gr. 2-5). 28.50 *(978-1-60270-588-3(7))* ABDO Publishing Co.

—The Yellow House Mystery, No. 3. Dubisch, Mike, illus. 2009. (Boxcar Children Graphic Novels Ser.). (ENG.). 32p. (J). (gr. 2-5). 6.99 *(978-0-8075-2869-3(2))* Whitman, Albert & Co.

Warner, Gertrude Chandler, creator. The Black Widow Spider Mystery. 2003. (Boxcar Children Mystery & Activities Specials Ser.: 21). (ENG.). 128p. (J). (gr. 1-5). pap. 5.99 *(978-0-8075-5544-6(4))* Whitman, Albert & Co.

—The Boxcar Children, 12 bks. 2010. (Boxcar Children Mysteries Ser.: 1). (ENG.). 1p. (J). (gr. 1-5). pap. 59.99 *(978-0-8075-0855-8(1))* Whitman, Albert & Co.

—The Celebrity Cat Caper. 2016. (Boxcar Children Mysteries Ser.: 143). (ENG., Illus.). 128p. (J). (gr. 1-5). 15.99 *(978-0-8075-0711-7(3))* Whitman, Albert & Co.

—The Comic Book Mystery. 2003. (Boxcar Children Mysteries Ser.: 93). (ENG., Illus.). 112p. (J). (gr. 1-5). 5.99 *(978-0-8075-5529-3(0))* Whitman, Albert & Co.

—The Creature in Ogopogo Lake. 2006. (Boxcar Children Mysteries Ser.: 108). (ENG., Illus.). 128p. (J). (gr. 1-5). lib. bdg. 14.99 *(978-0-8075-1336-1(9))* Whitman, Albert & Co.

—The Garden Thief. 2012. (Boxcar Children Mysteries Ser.: 130). (ENG., Illus.). 128p. (J). (gr. 1-5). 5.99 *(978-0-8075-2752-8(1))* Whitman, Albert & Co.

—The Garden Thief. 2012. (Boxcar Children Mysteries Ser.: 130). (ENG., Illus.). 128p. (J). (gr. 1-5). 15.99 *(978-0-8075-2751-1(3))* Whitman, Albert & Co.

—The Ghost at the Drive-In Movie. 2008. (Boxcar Children Mysteries Ser.: 116). (ENG.). 128p. (J). (gr. 1-5). 14.99 *(978-0-8075-5577-4(0))* Whitman, Albert & Co.

—Hidden in the Haunted School. 2016. (Boxcar Children Mysteries Ser.: 144). (ENG.). 128p. (J). (gr. 1-5). 15.99 *(978-0-8075-0718-6(0))* Whitman, Albert & Co.

—The Ice Cream Mystery. 2003. (Boxcar Children Mysteries Ser.: 94). (ENG., Illus.). 128p. (J). (gr. 1-5). pap. 5.99 *(978-0-8075-5535-4(5))* Whitman, Albert & Co.

—The Legend of the Irish Castle. 2016. (Boxcar Children Mysteries Ser.: 142). (ENG., Illus.). 128p. (J). (gr. 1-5). 15.99 *(978-0-8075-0705-6(9))* Whitman, Albert & Co.

—The Midnight Mystery. 2003. (Boxcar Children Mysteries Ser.: 95). (ENG., Illus.). 128p. (J). (gr. 1-5). pap. 5.99 *(978-0-8075-5538-5(X))* Whitman, Albert & Co.

—The Mystery of the Missing Pop Idol. 2015. (Boxcar Children Mysteries Ser.: 138). (ENG., Illus.). 128p. (J). (gr. 1-5). 15.99 *(978-0-8075-5605-4(X))* Whitman, Albert & Co.

—The Mystery of the Stolen Dinosaur Bones. 2015. (Boxcar Children Mysteries Ser.: 139). (ENG., Illus.). 128p. (J). (gr. 1-5). 15.99 *(978-0-8075-5608-5(4))* Whitman, Albert & Co.

—The Mystery of the Traveling Tomatoes. 2008. (Boxcar Children Mysteries Ser.: 117). (ENG.). 128p. (J). (gr. 1-5). pap. 6.99 *(978-0-8075-5580-4(0))* Whitman, Albert & Co.

—The Radio Mystery. 2003. (Boxcar Children Mysteries Ser.: 97). (ENG., Illus.). 128p. (J). (gr. 1-5). lib. bdg. 14.99 *(978-0-8075-5546-0(0))* Whitman, Albert & Co.

—The Sleepy Hollow Mystery. 2015. (Boxcar Children Mysteries Ser.: 141). (ENG., Illus.). 128p. (J). (gr. 1-5). 15.99 *(978-0-8075-2843-3(9))* Whitman, Albert & Co.

—The Tattletale Mystery. 2003. (Boxcar Children Mysteries Ser.: 92). (ENG., Illus.). 128p. (J). (gr. 1-5). pap. 5.99 *(978-0-8075-5526-2(6))* Whitman, Albert & Co.

—The Vanishing Passenger. 2006. (Boxcar Children Mysteries Ser.: 106). (ENG., Illus.). 112p. (J). (gr. 1-5). per. 6.99 *(978-0-8075-1067-4(X))* Whitman, Albert & Co.

Warner, Penny. The Code Busters Club, Case #2: the Haunted Lighthouse. 2013. (Code Busters Club Ser.). (ENG.). 208p. (J). (gr. 4-7). pap. 6.99 *(978-1-60684-455-7(5),* Darby Creek) Lerner Publishing Group.

—The Code Busters Club, Case #4: the Mummy's Curse. 2014. (ENG., Illus.). 224p. (J). (gr. 3-7). 16.99 *(978-1-60684-459-5(8),* Darby Creek) Lerner Publishing Group.

—The Hunt for the Missing Spy. 2016. (Code Busters Club Ser.: 5). (ENG.). 168p. (gr. 3-6). (J). 16.99 *(978-1-5124-0304-6(0));* 33.32 *(978-1-5124-0305-3(9))* Lerner Publishing Group.

—The Mystery of the Missing Mustangs. 2012. 107p. (J). *(978-0-88166-411-9(1))* Meadowbrook Pr.

—Mystery of the Pirate's Treasure. 2013. (Code Busters Club Ser.). (ENG.). 192p. (J). (gr. 4-7). 16.99 *(978-1-60684-457-1(1),* Darby Creek) Lerner Publishing Group.

—The Secret of the Puzzle Box. 2016. (Code Busters Club Ser.: 6). (ENG.). 192p. (gr. 3-6). 16.99 *(978-1-5124-0307-7(5),* Darby Creek) Lerner Publishing Group.

—The Secret of the Skeleton Key. (Code Busters Club Ser.). (ENG.). 224p. (J). (gr. 4-7). 2012. pap. 6.99 *(978-1-60684-390-1(7))* 2011. (Illus.). 15.99 *(978-1-60684-162-4(9))* Lerner Publishing Group. (Darby Creek).

Warren George A. Staff. The Banner Boy Scouts. rev. ed. 2006. 248p. 27.95 *(978-1-4218-1729-3(2));* pap. 12.95 *(978-1-4218-1829-0(9))* 1st World Publishing, Inc. (1st World Library - Literary Society).

Warrington, Dean Grey. Perfiction. 2007. 188p. per. 13.95 *(978-0-595-43758-0(3))* iUniverse, Inc.

Wasserman, Robin. The Book of Blood & Shadow. 2012. (ENG.). 448p. (YA). (gr. 7). 17.99 *(978-0-375-86876-4(3));* lib. bdg. 20.99 *(978-0-375-96876-1(8))* Random Hse. Children's Bks. (Knopf Bks. for Young Readers).

—Search for Scooby Snacks, 1 vol. 2013. (Scooby-Doo! Picture Clue Bks.). (ENG.). 24p. (J). (gr. -1-1). lib. bdg. 24.21 *(978-1-61479-039-6(6),* Essential Library) ABDO Publishing Co.

Wassner, Gary. The Mystery of the Jubilee Emerald. 2006. (J). pap. *(978-1-59336-712-1(0))* Mondo Publishing.

Watching Josh, 6 vols. (Ragged Island Mysteriestm Ser.). 161p. (gr. 5-7). 42.50 *(978-0-322-01651-4(7))* Wright Group/McGraw-Hill.

Watkins, Christopher. Exposure. 2012. 212p. pap. 19.99 *(978-1-4797-1599-2(9))* Xlibris Corp.

Watkins, Elaine. Billy Bobbin at Mystery Farm. 2014. (ENG.). 56p. (J). (gr. 3-4). pap. 8.95 *(978-1-84963-823-4(3),* f1c1638b-abbd-4463-9b5b-9133593e7447) Austin, Stan AUS. Dist: Bookmasters Distribution.

Watkins, Steve. Awol in North Africa. 2016. (Ghosts of War Ser.: 3). (ENG.). 208p. (J). (gr. 3-7). pap. 5.99 *(978-0-545-83706-4(5))* Scholastic, Inc.

Watkins, T. a. Joey & the Ancient Horn: A Mystery Revealed. Davis, Marcus, illus. 2007. 333p. (J). (gr. -1). per. 12.95 *(978-0-9762788-0-1(4))* Great I-AM Publishing Co., The.

Watson, Jude. In Too Deep. 2009. (39 Clues Ser.: 6). (ENG.). 208p. (J). (gr. 3-7). 12.99 *(978-0-545-09064-3(4));* 12.99 *(978-0-545-06046-2(X))* Scholastic, Inc.

—A King's Ransom. 2011. (39 Clues: Cahills vs. Vespers Ser.: 2). (ENG.). 192p. (J). (gr. 3-7). 12.99 *(978-0-545-29840-7(7),* Scholastic Pr.);Bk. 2. 12.99 *(978-0-545-32410-6(6))* Scholastic, Inc.

—Mission Titanic. 2015. (39 Clues: Doublecross Ser.: 1). (ENG.). 224p. (J). (gr. 3-7). 12.99 *(978-0-545-74781-3(3))* Scholastic, Inc.

—Nowhere to Run. 2013. (39 Clues Ser.: Bk. 1). (ENG., Illus.). 272p. (J). (gr. 3-7). 12.99 *(978-0-545-52137-6(8))* Scholastic, Inc.

—The 39 Clues # 6: En Las Profundidades. 2012. (SPA.). 208p. (J). (gr. 5-8). pap. 14.99 *(978-84-08-10768-2(2))* Noguer y Caralt Editores, S. A. ESP. Dist: Lectorum Pubns., Inc.

Watson, Jude & Scholastic, Inc. Staff. Beyond the Grave. 2009. (39 Clues Ser.: 4). (ENG., Illus.). 192p. (J). (gr. 3-7). 12.99 *(978-0-545-09061-2(X))* Scholastic, Inc.

Watson, Lena. Noise in My Room: The Adventure of Jane Barnette, the Problem Solver. 2012. 32p. pap. 19.99 *(978-1-4685-8780-7(3))* AuthorHouse.

Watson, Stephanie Elaine. Elvis & Olive: Super Detectives. 2010. (ENG.). 288p. (J). (gr. 3-7). 15.99 *(978-0-545-15148-1(1),* Scholastic Pr.) Scholastic, Inc.

Watts, Julia. Free Spirits. 2009. (ENG.). 176p. (J). (gr. 1). pap. 8.95 *(978-0-9667359-2-5(7),* BeanPole Bks.) Harren Communications, LLC.

—Kindred Spirits. 2008. (ENG.). 147p. (gr. 3-18). pap. 8.95 *(978-0-9667359-9-4(4))* Harren Communications, LLC.

Waysman, Dvora. Jewish Detective Stories for Kids. 2005. (Jewish Stories for Kids Ser.). (Illus.). 184p. (J). (gr. 5-9). 16.95 *(978-1-930143-14-2(1));* pap. 12.95 *(978-1-930143-15-9(X))* Simcha Media Group. (Devora Publishing).

We Hold These Truths. 2014. (Benjamin Pratt & the Keepers of the School Ser.: 5). (ENG., Illus.). 288p. (J). (gr. 2-5). pap. 7.99 *(978-1-4169-3911-5(3),* Atheneum Bks. for Young Readers) Simon & Schuster Children's Publishing.

Webb, Holly. The Case of the Feathered Mask. Lindsay, Marion, illus. 2016. (Mysteries of Maisie Hitchins Ser.: 4). (ENG.). 176p. (J). (gr. 2-5). 15.99 *(978-0-544-61993-7(5),* HMH Books For Young Readers) Houghton Mifflin Harcourt Publishing Co.

—The Case of the Phantom Cat. Lindsay, Marion, illus. (Mysteries of Maisie Hitchins Ser.: 3). (ENG.). 176p. (J). (gr. 2-5). 2016. pap. 5.99 *(978-0-544-81084-6(8))* 2015. 15.99 *(978-0-544-58243-9(8))* Houghton Mifflin Harcourt Publishing Co. (HMH Books For Young Readers).

—The Case of the Secret Tunnel. Lindsay, Marion, illus. 2016. (Mysteries of Maisie Hitchins Ser.: 5). (ENG.). 176p. (J). (gr. 2-5). 15.99 *(978-0-544-81554-4(8),* HMH Books For Young Readers) Houghton Mifflin Harcourt Publishing Co.

—The Case of the Vanishing Emerald. Lindsay, Marion, illus. 2016. (Mysteries of Maisie Hitchins Ser.: 2). (ENG.). 176p. (J). (gr. 2-5). pap. 5.99 *(978-0-544-66851-5(0),* HMH Books For Young Readers) Houghton Mifflin Harcourt Publishing Co.

Webb, Holly & Lindsay, Marion. The Case of the Stolen Sixpence. Lindsay, Marion, illus. (Mysteries of Maisie Hitchins Ser.: 1). (ENG., Illus.). 176p. (J). (gr. 2-5). 2014. 14.99 *(978-0-544-33928-6(2))* 2015. pap. 5.99 *(978-0-544-58234-7(9))* Houghton Mifflin Harcourt Publishing Co. (HMH Books For Young Readers).

Weeks, Sarah. Pie. 2013. (ENG.). 192p. (J). (gr. 3-7). pap. 6.99 *(978-0-545-27012-0(X),* Scholastic Paperbacks) Scholastic, Inc.

Wegelius, Jakob. The Murderer's Ape. 2017. (ENG.). 624p. (YA). (gr. 7). 17.99 *(978-1-101-93175-2(2),* Delacorte Pr.) Random Hse. Children's Bks.

Wegelius, Jakob & Graves, Peter. The Murderer's Ape. 2017. (YA). lib. bdg. *(978-1-101-93176-9(0),* Delacorte Pr) Random House Publishing Group.

Wegman, William. The Hardy Boys. Date not set. (J). *(978-0-7868-0195-4(6))* Hyperion Pr.

Weil, Cynthia. I'm Glad I Did. 2015. (ENG., Illus.). 272p. (YA). (gr. 9). 18.99 *(978-1-61695-356-0(X),* Soho Teen) Soho Pr., Inc.

Weil, Zoe. Claude & Medea: The Hellburn Dogs. 2007. (ENG., Illus.). 103p. (J). (gr. 2-7). per. 12.00 *(978-1-59056-105-8(8))* Lantern Bks.

Wein, Elizabeth. The Pearl Thief. 2017. (ENG.). 336p. (YA). (gr. 7-12). 18.99 *(978-1-4847-1716-5(3))* Hyperion Bks. for Children.

Weisman, Greg. Rain of the Ghosts. 2013. (Rain of the Ghosts Ser.: 1). (ENG., Illus.). 240p. (YA). (gr. 6-13). pap. 9.99 *(978-1-250-02979-9(1),* 9781250029799, St. Martin's Griffin) St. Martin's Pr.

Weiss, Ellen. The Mystery of Microsneezia: A ClueFinders Mystery Adventure. 2004. (Illus.). 96p. (J). pap. *(978-0-7630-7619-1(8))* Magma.

Welch, Jim. Steven Stevens' Killer App. 2012. 232p. pap. 16.50 *(978-1-105-06310-7(0))* Lulu Pr., Inc.

Wells, Charity. The Trouble with the Supernatural, 1 vol. 2010. 84p. pap. 19.95 *(978-1-4489-2117-1(1))* America Star Bks.

Wells, Dan. Ones & Zeroes. 2017. (Mirador Ser.: 2). 416p. (YA). (gr. 8). 17.99 *(978-0-06-234790-9(X))* HarperCollins Pubs.

Wells, Helen. Cherry Ames, Boarding School Nurse. 10th ed. 2007. (Cherry Ames Nurse Stories Ser.). 224p. (YA). (gr. 7-12). 14.95 *(978-0-8261-0413-7(4))* Springer Publishing Co., Inc.

—Cherry Ames Boxed Set: Volumes 17-20. 2007. 896p. (J). 39.95 *(978-0-8261-0439-7(8))* Springer Publishing Co., Inc.

—Cherry Ames, Camp Nurse. 2007. (Cherry Ames Nurse Stories Ser.). 224p. (YA). (gr. 7-12). 14.95 *(978-0-8261-0417-5(7))* Springer Publishing Co., Inc.

—Cherry Ames, Companion Nurse. 2007. (Cherry Ames Nurse Stories Ser.). 224p. (J). (gr. 3-7). 14.95 *(978-0-8261-0431-1(2))* Springer Publishing Co., Inc.

—Cherry Ames, Cruise Nurse. 2007. (Cherry Ames Nurse Stories Ser.). 232p. (YA). (gr. 7-12). 14.95 *(978-0-8261-0411-3(8))* Springer Publishing Co., Inc.

—Cherry Ames, Department Store Nurse. 2007. (Cherry Ames Nurse Stories Ser.). 224p. (YA). (gr. 8-12). 14.95 *(978-0-8261-0415-1(0))* Springer Publishing Co., Inc.

—Cherry Ames, Island Nurse. 2007. (Cherry Ames Nurse Stories Ser.). 224p. (J). (gr. 3-7). 14.95 *(978-0-8261-0423-6(1))* Springer Publishing Co., Inc.

—Cherry Ames Jungle Nurse. 2007. (Cherry Ames Nurse Stories Ser.). 224p. (J). (gr. 3-7). 14.95 *(978-0-8261-0433-5(9))* Springer Publishing Co., Inc.

—Cherry Ames, Ski Nurse Mystery. 2007. (Cherry Ames Nurse Stories Ser.). 224p. (J). (gr. 3-7). 14.95 *(978-0-8261-0437-3(1))* Springer Publishing Co., Inc.

—Cherry Ames, the Mystery in the Doctor's Office. 2007. (Cherry Ames Nurse Stories Ser.). 224p. (J). (gr. 3-7). 14.95 *(978-0-8261-0435-9(5))* Springer Publishing Co., Inc.

—The Silver Ring Mystery: The Vicki Barr Flight Stewardess Series. 2011. 190p. 42.95 *(978-1-258-10005-6(3))* Literary Licensing, LLC.

Wells, Marcia. Doom at Grant's Tomb. Calo, Marcos, illus. 2017. (Eddie Red Undercover Ser.: 3). (ENG.). (J). (gr. 5-7). lib. bdg. 17.20 **(978-0-606-39813-8(9))** Turtleback Bks.

—Mystery in Mayan Mexico. Calo, Marcos, illus. 2016. (Eddie Red Undercover Ser.: 2). (ENG.). 224p. (J). (gr. 5-7). pap. 7.99 *(978-0-544-66850-8(2),* HMH Books For Young Readers) Houghton Mifflin Harcourt Publishing Co.

—Mystery on Museum Mile. Calo, Marcos, illus. (Eddie Red Undercover Ser.). (ENG.). 256p. (J). (gr. 5-7). 2015. pap. 7.99 *(978-0-544-43940-5(6))* 2014. 16.99 *(978-0-544-23833-6(8))* Houghton Mifflin Harcourt Publishing Co. (HMH Books For Young Readers).

Wenger, Shaunda. The Farm Stand Mystery. 2006. (Early Explorers Ser.). (J). pap. *(978-1-4108-6121-4(X))* Benchmark Education Co.

West, Tracey. The Audio Files. Harrington, Rich, illus. 2006. 96p. (J). pap. *(978-0-439-90719-4(5))* Scholastic, Inc.

—The Clothing Capers. Harrington, Rich, illus. 2007. 96p. (J). pap. *(978-0-439-91452-9(3))* Scholastic, Inc.

—The Fingerprint Files. Harrington, Rich, illus. 2007. 96p. (J). *(978-0-439-91451-2(5))* Scholastic, Inc.

—The Secret Cipher Cases. Harrington, Rich, illus. 2006. 96p. (J). *(978-0-439-91448-2(5))* Scholastic, Inc.

—The Teeny Tiny Cases. Harrington, Rich, illus. 2007. 96p. (J). *(978-0-439-91450-5(7))* Scholastic, Inc.

Westerfeld, Scott. So Yesterday. (ENG.). (YA). (gr. 7-12). 2004. 240p. 16.99 *(978-1-59514-000-5(X))* 2005. 256p. reprint ed. 8.99 *(978-1-59514-032-6(8))* Penguin Young Readers Group. (Razorbill).

Weston, Elise. The Coastwatcher, 1 vol. 2009. (ENG.). 160p. (J). (gr. 3-7). pap. 7.95 *(978-1-56145-484-6(2))* Peachtree Pubs.

Weyn, Suzanne. Dr. Frankenstein's Daughters. 2013. (ENG.). 256p. (J). (gr. 7). 17.99 *(978-0-545-42533-9(6),* Scholastic Pr.) Scholastic, Inc.

—The Titanic Locket. 2014. (Hauntings: the Haunted Museum Ser.: 1). lib. bdg. 17.20 *(978-0-606-35809-5(9))* Turtleback Bks.

Whalen, Diane. Tales of the Christmas Store. 2011. 92p. pap. 9.99 *(978-1-4567-1783-4(9))* AuthorHouse.

What's in the Suitcase, Grandma? My Solar-Powered History, Book 3. 2013. (Illus.). 116p. pap. 12.99 *(978-1-937848-08-8(6))* Do Life Right, Inc.

Wheeler, Elizabeth. Asher's Shot. 2014. (Supreme Constellations Ser.). (ENG.). 264p. (J). (gr. 7). pap. 11.95 *(978-1-62639-229-8(3))* Bold Strokes Bks.

Wheeler, Esther. The Loner. 2003. (J). pap. 4.99 *(978-1-58608-614-5(6))* New Concepts Publishing.

Wheeler, Janet D. Billie Bradley & Her Inheritance or the Queer Homestead at Cherry Corners. 2004. reprint ed. pap. 20.95 *(978-1-4191-0995-9(2))* Kessinger Publishing, LLC.

Whelan, Gloria. After the Train. 2009. 160p. (J). lib. bdg. 16.89 *(978-0-06-029597-4(X));* (ENG.). (gr. 3-7). 15.99 *(978-0-06-029596-7(1))* HarperCollins Pubs.

Whild, Katharine. Marlowe the Great Detective. Whild, Katharine, illus. l.t. ed. 2005. (Illus.). 36p. (J). 16.95 *(978-0-9712488-4-7(2))* Deerbrook Editions.

Whitby, Adele. Beth's Story 1914. 2014. (Secrets of the Manor Ser.: 1). (ENG., Illus.). 160p. (J). (gr. 3-7). 16.99 *(978-1-4814-0632-1(9),* Simon Spotlight) Simon Spotlight.

White, J. Scratch & Sniff: The Case of the Stuck Seagull. 2013. 32p. pap. *(978-1-4602-0552-5(9))* FriesenPress.

White, Jan. Mystery of Mingus Mountain. 2012. (ENG., Illus.). 138p. (YA). (gr. 7-13). pap. 9.99 *(978-0-89824-370-3(X))* Royal Fireworks Publishing Co.

White, K. B. Adrianna Angelica Andrea Mystery Stories: The Case of the Missing Bath Towel. 2012. 24p. pap. 17.99 *(978-1-4772-7058-5(2))* AuthorHouse.

White, Ruth. Belle Prater's Boy. unabr. ed. 2004. 196p. (J). (gr. 5-9). pap. 38.00 incl. audio *(978-0-8072-8682-1(6),* YA234SP, Listening Library) Random Hse. Audio Publishing Group.

Whiting, Sue. Portraits of Celina. 2015. (ENG.). 352p. 16.95 *(978-1-63079-024-0(9))* Switch Pr.

Whybrow, Ian. Little Wolf, Forest Detective. Ross, Tony, illus. 2005. (Middle Grade Fiction Ser.). 112p. (J). (gr. 3-6). 14.95 *(978-1-57505-413-1(2));* pap. 6.95 *(978-1-57505-829-0(4))* Lerner Publishing Group.

—Little Wolf, Pack Leader. Ross, Tony, illus. 2005. (Little Wolf Adventures Ser.). 126p. (gr. 3-6). 14.95 *(978-1-57505-400-1(0))* Lerner Publishing Group.

Whyman, Matt. The Savages. 2014. (ENG.). 288p. (gr. 8-14). 16.99 *(978-1-4683-0856-3(4),* 460856) Overlook Pr., The.

Whyte, June. Murder Sucks. 2008. (ENG., Illus.). 192p. (J). pap. 12.99 *(978-1-934841-12-9(9),* Zumaya Thresholds) Zumaya Pubns. LLC.

Wickstrom, Lois June & Darling, Lucrecia. The Orange Forest Rabbit Mysteries: Book One. 2003. (J). per. 13.95 *(978-0-916176-23-5(1))* Gripper Products.

Widmark, Martin. The Cafe Mystery. Willis, Helena, illus. 2015. (Whodunit Detective Agency Ser.: 4). (ENG.). 80p. (J). (gr. 2-4). 13.99 *(978-0-448-48073-2(5),* Grosset & Dunlap) Penguin Young Readers Group.

—The Diamond Mystery, No. 1. Willis, Helena, illus. 2014. (Whodunit Detective Agency Ser.: 1). (ENG.). 80p. (J). (gr. 2-4). 5.99 *(978-0-448-48066-4(2),* Grosset & Dunlap) Penguin Young Readers Group.

—The Mummy Mystery #5. Willis, Helena, illus. 2015. (Whodunit Detective Agency Ser.: 5). (ENG.). 80p. (J). (gr.

2-4). 13.99 *(978-0-448-48075-6(1)*, Grosset & Dunlap) Penguin Young Readers Group.

Wight, Tamra. Mystery of the Mystery Fox, 1 vol. 2016. (Cooper & Packrat Ser.: 3). (ENG.). 200p. (J). pap. 16.95 *(978-1-939017-89-5(0)*, 9781939017895) Islandport Pr., Inc.

—Mystery on Pine Lake: A Cooper & Packrat Mystery, 1 vol. DiRocco, Carl, illus. 2015. (ENG.). 152p. (J). pap. 12.95 *(978-1-939017-02-4(5)*, ff36fa6a-bd2a-4739-8ca6-7fd795cee511) Islandport Pr., Inc.

Wilcox. The Hidden Men. (Thumbprint Mysteries Ser.). 32.86 *(978-0-8092-0415-1(0))* McGraw-Hill/Contemporary.

Wiles, Patricia. Early-Morning Cemetery: A Novel. 2006. 243p. (YA). pap. *(978-1-59811-077-7(2))* Covenant Communications.

Wilkes, Nita. Stalking Bailey. 2010. 185p. pap. 10.95 *(978-1-4327-4862-3(9))* Outskirts Pr., Inc.

Wilkey, David. Through the Black Hole: The Incredible Adventures of Justin Hart. 2003. 154p. pap. 12.95 *(978-0-595-29497-8(9))* iUniverse, Inc.

William H. Sadlier Staff. The Yellow Yarn Mystery. 2005. (Emergent Library: Vol. 2). (gr. -1-1). 24.00 net. *(978-0-8215-8938-0(5))* Sadlier, William H. Inc.

Williams, Anthony, illus. The Hound of the Baskervilles. 2014. (ENG.). 32p. pap. 8.95 *(978-1-78404-357-5(5))* Arcturus Publishing GBR. Dist: Bookmasters Distribution.

Williams, Brenda May. The Shop of Magical Things. 2013. (Illus.). 44p. pap. 13.50 *(978-1-78035-526-9(2)*, Fastprint Publishing) Upfront Publishing Ltd. GBR. Dist: Printondemand-worldwide.com.

Williams, Carol Lynch. The Chosen One. 2010. (ENG.). 240p. (YA). (gr. 7). pap. 10.99 *(978-0-312-62775-1(0)*, 9780312627751, St. Martin's Griffin) St. Martin's Pr.

—Messenger. 2016. (ENG., Illus.). 288p. (YA). (gr. 7). 17.99 *(978-1-4814-5776-7(4)*, Simon & Schuster/Paula Wiseman Bks.) Simon & Schuster/Paula Wiseman Bks.

Williams, Hays. The Tangled Web: A Mother's Secret - a Jenny & Pete Mystery. 2013. 94p. pap. 12.95 *(978-1-62646-673-9(4))* Booklocker.com, Inc.

Williams, Vanessa A. The Missing Penny. 2013. 28p. pap. 9.95 *(978-1-4787-2429-2(3))* Outskirts Pr., Inc.

Willoughby, Holly & Willoughby, Kelly. The Missing Ballerina Mystery. 2016. (School for Stars Ser.). (ENG., Illus.). 192p. (J). (gr. 4-7). pap. 7.99 *(978-1-4440-1457-0(9)*, Orion Children's Bks.) Hachette Children's Group GBR. Dist: Hachette Bk. Group.

Wilson, F. Paul. Jack: Secret Histories. 2009. (Repairman Jack Ser.). (ENG.). 320p. (YA). (gr. 7). pap. 6.99 *(978-0-7653-5811-0(5)*, 9780765358110, Tor Teen) Doherty, Tom Assocs., LLC.

Wilson, Heather Gemmen. Lydia Barnes & the Escape from Shark Bay. 2008. 160p. (J). 9.99 *(978-0-89827-352-6(8))* Wesleyan Publishing Hse.

—Lydia Barnes & the Mystery of the Broken Cross. 2007. (Global Warning Ser.). 157p. (J). (gr. 3-7). per. 7.99 *(978-0-89827-351-9(X))* Wesleyan Publishing Hse.

Wilson, Jacqui. Little Johnny's Faith Adventures: Creation Curiosity! 2012. 30p. pap. 15.95 *(978-1-4497-5994-0(7)*, WestBow Pr.) Author Solutions, Inc.

Wilson, John. Bones, 1 vol. 2014. (Orca Currents Ser.). (ENG.). 128p. (J). (gr. 5-9). pap. 9.95 *(978-1-4598-0698-6(0))* Orca Bk. Pubs. USA.

—Lost. 2016. (Orca Currents Ser.). lib. bdg. 20.80 *(978-0-606-38694-4(7))* Turtleback Bks.

Wilson, W. Shane. War for Ice. 2010. 158p. pap. 13.99 *(978-0-557-23572-8(3))* Lulu Pr., Inc.

Winfield, Arthur M. Putnam Hall Champions or Bound to Win Ou. 2006. pap. 28.95 *(978-1-4286-2346-0(9))* Kessinger Publishing, LLC.

—The Rover Boys on the Plains or the Mystery of Red Rock Ranch. 2004. reprint ed. pap. 27.95 *(978-1-4179-2626-8(0))* Kessinger Publishing, LLC.

—The Rover Boys on the River. 2007. 248p. 26.95 *(978-1-4218-4139-7(8))*; per. 11.95 *(978-1-4218-4237-0(8))* 1st World Publishing, Inc. (1st World Library - Literary Society).

Wingo, W. Bruce. There Grows a Crooked Tree. 2003. 188p. 23.95 *(978-0-595-75271-3(3))*; pap. 13.95 *(978-0-595-28903-5(7))* iUniverse, Inc.

Winter, Barbara. The Golden Scarab. 2007. (Illus.). 48p. (J). lib. bdg. 15.00 *(978-1-4242-1617-8(6))* Dingles & Co.

Winters, Ben H. The Mystery of the Missing Everything. (ENG.). 272p. (J). (gr. 3-7). 2012. pap. 6.99 *(978-0-06-196546-3(4))* 2011. 16.99 *(978-0-06-196544-9(8))* HarperCollins Pubs.

Wirt, Mildred A. Guilt of the Brass Thieves. 2011. 178p. pap. 9.99 *(978-1-935774-80-8(8)*, Resurrected Pr.) Intrepid Ink, LLC.

—Saboteurs on the River. 2011. 174p. pap. 12.99 *(978-1-935774-86-0(7)*, Resurrected Pr.) Intrepid Ink, LLC.

—Signal in the Dark. 2011. 170p. pap. 9.99 *(978-1-935774-82-2(4)*, Resurrected Pr.) Intrepid Ink, LLC.

—Swamp Island. 2011. 176p. pap. 12.99 *(978-1-935774-85-3(9)*, Resurrected Pr.) Intrepid Ink, LLC.

—Voice from the Cave. 2011. 168p. pap. 9.99 *(978-1-935774-81-5(6)*, Resurrected Pr.) Intrepid Ink, LLC.

—Whispering Walls. 2011. 174p. pap. 9.99 *(978-1-935774-83-9(2)*, Resurrected Pr.) Intrepid Ink, LLC.

Witrago, Jost. The Wooden Dove. 2007. 16p. per. 24.95 *(978-1-4241-9011-9(8))* America Star Bks.

Wofford, Delaney. For Courage. 2010. 229p. pap. 17.98 *(978-0-557-17045-6(1))* Lulu Pr., Inc.

Wolf, Jennifer Shaw. Breaking Beautiful. 2014. (ENG.). 384p. (YA). (gr. 9). pap. 9.99 *(978-0-8027-3440-2(5)*, 9780802734402, Bloomsbury USA Childrens) Bloomsbury Publishing USA.

—Dead Girls Don't Lie. 2014. (ENG.). 368p. (YA). (gr. 9). pap. 9.99 *(978-0-8027-3753-3(6)*, 9780802737533, Bloomsbury USA Childrens) Bloomsbury Publishing USA.

Wolper, Joanna. The Man Who Could Be Santa. 2008. (Illus.). 78p. (J). pap. *(978-0-88092-765-9(8))*; lib. bdg. *(978-0-88092-764-2(X))* Royal Fireworks Publishing Co.

Wood, Audrey. Alphabet Mystery. Wood, Bruce, illus. 2003. (ENG.). 40p. (J). (gr. -1 — 1). 17.99 *(978-0-439-44337-1(7)*, Blue Sky Pr., The) Scholastic, Inc.

Wood, Maryrose. The Incorrigible Children of Ashton Place Bk. IV: The Interrupted Tale. Wheeler, Eliza, illus. 2013. (Incorrigible Children of Ashton Place Ser.: 4). (ENG.). 400p. (J). (gr. 3-7). 16.99 *(978-0-06-179122-2(9))* HarperCollins Pubs.

—The Unmapped Sea Bk. 5. Wheeler, Eliza, illus. 2015. (Incorrigible Children of Ashton Place Ser.: 5). (ENG.). 416p. (J). (gr. 3-7). 15.99 *(978-0-06-211041-1(1))* HarperCollins Pubs.

Woodbury, Mary. The Innocent Polly McDoodle. 2005. (Polly McDoodle Mystery Ser.: Vol. 3). (ENG.). 192p. (J). (gr. 4-7). pap. 6.95 *(978-1-55050-168-1(2))* Coteau Bks. CAN. Dist: Fitzhenry & Whiteside, Ltd.

Woodland Mysteries. (gr. 3-7). Set 1. 424.95 *(978-0-7802-7245-3(5))*Set 2. 424.95 *(978-0-7802-8002-1(4))* Wright Group/McGraw-Hill.

Woodland Mysteries: Classroom Library Set. (gr. 3-7). 313.95 *(978-0-322-02628-5(8))* Wright Group/McGraw-Hill.

Woodland Mysteries: Complete Boxed Set. (gr. 3-7). 1238.95 *(978-0-322-02625-4(3))* Wright Group/McGraw-Hill.

Worley, Rob M. & Warner, Gertrude Chandler. Surprise Island, 1 vol. Dubisch, Michael, illus. 2009. (Boxcar Children Graphic Novels Ser.). (ENG.). 32p. (J). (gr. 2-5). 28.50 *(978-1-60270-587-6(9))* ABDO Publishing Co.

Wortman, Barbara. Key in the Candle. (Young Hawk Mystery Ser.). 189p. (YA). (gr. 7-18). 9.99 *(978-0-88092-379-8(2))* Royal Fireworks Publishing Co.

Wright, Betty Ren. Christina's Ghost. 2008. (ENG.). 149p. (J). (gr. 3-7). pap. 7.99 *(978-0-8234-2171-8(6))* Holiday Hse., Inc.

—The Dollhouse Murders. 2008. (ENG.). 149p. (J). (gr. 4-7). pap. 7.99 *(978-0-8234-2172-5(4))* Holiday Hse., Inc.

—Princess for a Week. Rogers, Jacqueline, illus. (ENG.). 160p. (J). (gr. 4-7). 2007. pap. 6.95 *(978-0-8234-2111-4(2))* 2006. 16.95 *(978-0-8234-1945-6(2))* Holiday Hse., Inc.

Wright, Deana. The Playground. 2009. 48p. pap. 9.95 *(978-1-60693-680-1(8)*, Eloquent Bks.) Strategic Book Publishing & Rights Agency (SBPRA).

Wright, Dee. The Peanut Butter Finger Mystery. 2013. (Little Ruth Ser.). (ENG., Illus.). 38p. (J). pap. *(978-1-59684-606-7(2))* Penman Publishers.

Wright, Elsie. Patty & Jo, Detectives. 2005. reprint ed. pap. 24.95 *(978-1-4179-9752-7(4))* Kessinger Publishing, LLC.

Wright Johnson, Shelli. Falcon in the Nest: A Story of Bes Adventure. 2004. 273p. pap. 27.95 *(978-1-4137-5263-2(2))* America Star Bks.

Wynne-Jones, Tim. The Boy in the Burning House. braille ed. 2003. (J). (gr. 2). spiral bd. *(978-0-616-15275-1(2))* Canadian National Institute for the Blind/Institut National Canadien pour les Aveugles.

—The Boy in the Burning House. 2003. (ENG.). 224p. (J). (gr. 5-9). pap. 12.99 *(978-0-374-40887-9(4)*, 9780374408879, Farrar, Straus & Giroux (BYR)) Farrar, Straus & Giroux.

—The Boy in the Burning House, 1 vol. (ENG.). 232p. pap. 8.95 *(978-0-88899-500-1(8))* Groundwood Bks. CAN. Dist: Publishers Group West (PGW).

—The Uninvited. (ENG., Illus.). 368p. (YA). (gr. 9). 2010. pap. 8.99 *(978-0-7636-4826-8(4))* 2009. 16.99 *(978-0-7636-3984-6(2))* Candlewick Pr.

The X-Factor. 2009. (Hardy Boys (All New) Undercover Brothers Ser.: 30). (ENG.). 176p. (J). (gr. 3-7). pap. 5.99 *(978-1-4169-7802-2(X)*, Aladdin) Simon & Schuster Children's Publishing.

X-Plosion. 2009. (Hardy Boys (All New) Undercover Brothers Ser.: 29). (ENG.). 160p. (J). (gr. 3-7). pap. 6.99 *(978-1-4169-7870-1(4)*, Aladdin) Simon & Schuster Children's Publishing.

Yang, Gene Luen. Secret Coders. Holmes, Mike, illus. 2015. (Secret Coders Ser.: 1). (ENG.). 96p. (J). (gr. 3-7). 17.99 *(978-1-62672-276-7(5)*, 9781626722767); pap. 9.99 *(978-1-62672-075-6(4)*, 9781626720756) Roaring Brook Pr. (First Second Bks.).

Yardley, Liz. The Firefly Legacy - Book Vii. Yardley, Liz, illus. 2013. (Illus.). 314p. pap. *(978-0-9872013-2-4(8))* BlueFlower Bks.

Yasuda, Anita. The Beach Bandit, 1 vol. Harpster, Steve, illus. 2013. (Dino Detectives Ser.). (ENG.). 32p. (gr. 1-2). pap. 5.95 *(978-1-4342-4830-5(5))*; lib. bdg. 22.65 *(978-1-4342-4154-2(8))* Stone Arch Bks.

—The Crazy Clues, 1 vol. Harpster, Steve, illus. 2013. (Dino Detectives Ser.). (ENG.). 32p. (gr. 1-2). lib. bdg. 22.65 *(978-1-4342-5971-4(4))* Stone Arch Bks.

—Crazy Clues. Harpster, Steve, illus. 2013. (Dino Detectives Ser.). (ENG.). 32p. (gr. 1-2). pap. 5.95 *(978-1-4342-6200-4(6))* Stone Arch Bks.

—Dino Detectives. Harpster, Steve, illus. 2013. (Dino Detectives Ser.). (ENG.). 32p. (gr. 1-2). pap. 23.80 *(978-1-4342-3937-2(3))* Stone Arch Bks.

—Ghost Sounds, 1 vol. Harpster, Steve, illus. 2013. (Dino Detectives Ser.). (ENG.). 32p. (gr. 1-2). pap. 5.95 *(978-1-4342-4831-2(3))*; lib. bdg. 22.65 *(978-1-4342-4152-8(1))* Stone Arch Bks.

—The Haunted House, 1 vol. Harpster, Steve, illus. 2013. (Dino Detectives Ser.). (ENG.). 32p. (gr. 1-2). lib. bdg. 22.65 *(978-1-4342-5970-7(6))* Stone Arch Bks.

—Haunted House. Harpster, Steve, illus. 2013. (Dino Detectives Ser.). (ENG.). 32p. (gr. 1-2). pap. 5.95 *(978-1-4342-6199-1(9))* Stone Arch Bks.

—The Missing Trumpet, 1 vol. Harpster, Steve, illus. 2013. (Dino Detectives Ser.). (ENG.). 32p. (gr. 1-2). pap. 5.95 *(978-1-4342-4832-9(1))*; lib. bdg. 22.65 *(978-1-4342-4155-9(6))* Stone Arch Bks.

—The Mystery Coins, 1 vol. Harpster, Steve, illus. 2013. (Dino Detectives Ser.). (ENG.). 32p. (gr. 1-2). lib. bdg. 22.65 *(978-1-4342-5972-1(2))* Stone Arch Bks.

—Mystery Coins. Harpster, Steve, illus. 2013. (Dino Detectives Ser.). (ENG.). 32p. (gr. 1-2). pap. 5.95 *(978-1-4342-6201-1(4))* Stone Arch Bks.

—The Slime Attack, 1 vol. Harpster, Steve, illus. 2013. (Dino Detectives Ser.). (ENG.). 32p. (gr. 1-2). pap. 5.95 *(978-1-4342-4833-6(X))*; lib. bdg. 22.65 *(978-1-4342-4153-5(X))* Stone Arch Bks.

—The Surprise Prize, 1 vol. Harpster, Steve, illus. 2013. (Dino Detectives Ser.). (ENG.). 32p. (gr. 1-2). lib. bdg. 22.65 *(978-1-4342-5969-1(2))* Stone Arch Bks.

—Surprise Prize. Harpster, Steve, illus. 2013. (Dino Detectives Ser.). (ENG.). 32p. (gr. 1-2). pap. 5.95 *(978-1-4342-6198-4(0))* Stone Arch Bks.

Yasuda, Anita & Harpster, Steve. The Crazy Clues. 2013. (Dino Detectives Ser.). (ENG.). 32p. (gr. 1-2). pap. 29.70 *(978-1-4342-6226-4(X))* Stone Arch Bks.

—The Haunted House. 2013. (Dino Detectives Ser.). (ENG.). 32p. (gr. 1-2). pap. 29.70 *(978-1-4342-6227-1(8))* Stone Arch Bks.

—The Mystery Coins. 2013. (Dino Detectives Ser.). (ENG.). 32p. (gr. 1-2). pap. 29.70 *(978-1-4342-6228-8(6))* Stone Arch Bks.

—The Surprise Prize. 2013. (Dino Detectives Ser.). (ENG.). 32p. (gr. 1-2). pap. 29.70 *(978-1-4342-6229-5(4))* Stone Arch Bks.

The Yellow Yarn Mystery: Take-Home Book. 2005. (Emergent Library: Vol. 2). (YA). (gr. -1-1). 12.60 *(978-0-8215-7268-9(7))* Sadlier, William H. Inc.

Ylvisaker, Anne. Button Down. 2013. (ENG.). 192p. (J). (gr. 3-7). pap. 6.99 *(978-0-7636-6463-3(4))* Candlewick Pr.

—The Luck of the Buttons. 2012. (ENG., Illus.). 240p. (J). (gr. 3-7). pap. 6.99 *(978-0-7636-6061-1(2))* Candlewick Pr.

Yoder, Eric & Yoder, Natalie. One Minute Mysteries: 65 Short Mysteries You Solve with Math! 2010. (One Minute Mysteries Ser.). (ENG., Illus.). 192p. (J). (gr. 5-9). pap. 12.95 *(978-0-9678020-0-8(8))* Platypus Media, L.L.C.

Yolen, Jane & Stemple, Adam. Stone Cold. Zangara, Orion, illus. 2016. (Stone Man Mysteries Ser.: 1). (ENG.). 80p. (J). (gr. 7-12). lib. bdg. 29.32 *(978-1-4677-4196-5(5)*, Graphic Universe™) Lerner Publishing Group.

Yolen, Jane & Stemple, Heidi E. Y. The Salem Witch Trials: An Unsolved Mystery from History. Roth, Roger, Sr., illus. 2004. (Unsolved Mystery from History Ser.). (ENG.). 32p. (J). (gr. 1-5). 17.99 *(978-0-689-84620-5(7)*, Simon & Schuster Bks. For Young Readers) Simon & Schuster Bks. For Young Readers.

Yorke, Malcolm. La Casa de los Sustez. (Raton de Biblioteca Coleccion). (SPA., Illus.). 128p. (J). (gr. 3). 7.95 *(978-84-88061-71-3(4))* Serres, Ediciones, S. L. ESP. Dist: Lectorum Pubns., Inc.

Young, Judy. The Missing Grizzly Cubs. 2016. (Wild World of Buck Bray Ser.). (ENG.). 240p. (J). (gr. 3-6). 16.99 *(978-1-58536-970-6(5)*, 204107) Sleeping Bear Pr.

Young, Ruth. Aunty Marmalade. 2009. 218p. pap. 13.78 *(978-1-60693-893-5(2)*, Eloquent Bks.) Strategic Book Publishing & Rights Agency (SBPRA).

Youree, Barbara. Senegal Sleuths. 2006. 56p. 7.75 *(978-0-8341-2226-0(X))* Beacon Hill Pr. of Kansas City.

Yuricich, Jillian Grace, illus. What did Grandma See? 2006. (J). lib. bdg. 15.99 *(978-0-9774696-0-4(3))* Gilboy Publishing.

Zafón, Carlos Ruiz. Marina. 2014. (ENG.). 336p. (YA). (gr. 7-17). 19.00 *(978-0-316-04471-4(7))* Little, Brown Bks. for Young Readers.

Zalonis, C. B. Strangers in the Forest. 2006. (J). pap. 8.00 *(978-0-8059-6820-0(2))* Dorrance Publishing Co., Inc.

Zaugg, Sandra L. Secret of the Desert Lights: A Story about Following God's Laws. 2009. (J). pap. 9.99 *(978-0-8163-2294-7(5))* Pacific Pr. Publishing Assn.

Zaugg, Sandy. Murdock Mystery #2: The Cats of Rome. 2010. 88p. pap. 10.95 *(978-1-4327-5062-6(3))* Outskirts Pr., Inc.

Zindel, Paul. Egyptian Mystery. Date not set. 192p. (YA). (gr. 6-18). lib. bdg. 16.89 *(978-0-06-028509-8(5))* HarperCollins Pubs.

Zusak, Markus. I Am the Messenger. 2009. 10.52 *(978-0-7848-2491-7(6)*, Everbind) Marco Bk. Co.

—I Am the Messenger. 2006. 21.00 *(978-0-7569-7034-5(2))* Perfection Learning Corp.

—I Am the Messenger. (ENG.). 368p. (YA). (gr. 7). 2005. 16.95 *(978-0-375-83099-0(5))* 2006. (Illus.). reprint ed. pap. 10.99 *(978-0-375-83667-1(5))* Random Hse. Children's Bks. (Knopf Bks. for Young Readers).

—I Am the Messenger. (J). 2007. 1.25 *(978-1-4281-2308-3(3))* 2007. 77.75 *(978-1-4281-2309-0(1))* 2006. 74.75 *(978-1-4281-2311-3(3))* Recorded Bks., Inc.

4RV Publishing LLC Staff. Case of the Missing Coach. 2007. (Illus.). 144p. (J). per. 18.99 *(978-0-9797513-1-8(4))* 4RV Publishing, LLC.

MYTHICAL ANIMALS

see Animals, Mythical

MYTHOLOGY

see also Animals, Mythical; Art and Mythology; Folklore; Heroes; Indians of North America—Religion; Totems and Totemism

ABDO Publishing Company Staff. Short Tales Chinese Myths. 2014. (Short Tales Chinese Myths Ser.: 6). 32p. (J). (gr. 3-6). lib. bdg. 145.26 *(978-1-62402-029-2(1)*, Short Tales) Magic Wagon.

ABDO Publishing Company Staff, ed. World of Mythology Set 2, 1 vol. 2011. (World of Mythology Set 2 Ser.). (ENG., Illus.). 32p. 162.42 *(978-1-61714-986-3(1)*, Abdo & Daughters) ABDO Publishing Co.

African. 2nd rev. ed. 2010. (Mythology A to Z Ser.). (Illus.). 176p. (gr. 5-8). 45.00 *(978-1-60413-415-5(1)*, Chelsea Hse.) Facts On File, Inc.

Alexander, David E. The Myths of the Lechuza. Smith, Duriel, illus. Date not set. 78p. (Orig.). (J). pap. 12.95 *(978-0-9623078-5-0(8))* Alexander Pubns.

Alexander, Heather. A Child's Introduction to Greek Mythology: The Stories of the Gods, Goddesses, Heroes, Monsters, & Other Mythical Creatures. Hamilton, Meredith, illus. 2011. (ENG.). 96p. (J). (gr. 3-7). 19.99 *(978-1-57912-867-8(X)*, 81867, Black Dog & Leventhal Pubs. Inc.) Hachette Bks.

Allan, Tony. Exploring the Life, Myth, & Art of Ancient Rome. 2011. (Civilizations of the World Ser.). (YA). (gr. 7-12). lib. bdg. 42.60 *(978-1-4488-4831-7(8))* Rosen Publishing Group, Inc., The.

Allan, Tony, et al. Exploring the Life, Myth, & Art of the Medieval World. 2016. (Civilizations of the World Ser.). (ENG.). 144p. (J). (gr. 8-8). lib. bdg. 45.10 *(978-1-4994-6395-8(2))* Rosen Publishing Group, Inc., The.

Altman, Linda Jacobs. African Mythology. Bock, William Sauts, illus. 2003. (Mythology Ser.). 112p. (J). lib. bdg. 26.60 *(978-0-7660-2125-9(4))* Enslow Pubs., Inc.

—African Mythology Rocks! Bock, William Sauts, illus. 2011. (Mythology Rocks! Ser.). 112p. (J). (gr. 6-18). pap. 10.95 *(978-1-59845-328-7(9))* Enslow Pubs., Inc.

Amery, H. Mini Greek Myths. rev. ed. 2013. (Mini Editions Ser.). 128p. (J). ring bd. 7.99 *(978-0-7945-3366-3(3)*, Usborne) EDC Publishing.

Apel, Melanie Ann. Art & Religion in Ancient Greece. 2004. (Primary Sources of Ancient Civilizations Ser.). (ENG., Illus.). 24p. (gr. 4-8). pap. 8.25 *(978-0-8239-8938-6(0)*, PowerKids Pr.) Rosen Publishing Group, Inc., The.

Armitage, Kimo. Akua Hawaii: Hawaiian Gods & Their Stories. Enos, Solomon, illus. 2005. 72p. (J). 16.95 *(978-1-58178-042-0(7))* Bishop Museum Pr.

Aronson, Marc. The Griffin & the Dinosaur: How Adrienne Mayor Discovered a Fascinating Link Between Myth & Science. Müller, Chris, illus. 2014. (ENG.). 48p. (J). (gr. 5). 18.99 *(978-1-4263-1108-6(7)*, National Geographic Children's Bks.) National Geographic Society.

Arrington, Joseph & Parker, Mike. The World's Most Unusual Humans. 2016. (Making Headlines Ser.). 160p. (J). lib. bdg. 39.93 *(978-0-7660-8380-6(2))* Enslow Pubs., Inc.

Baldwin, James. Old Greek Storie. 2006. (Illus.). pap. *(978-1-4065-0511-5(0))* Dodo Pr.

—Old Greek Stories. 2005. 192p. pap. 11.95 *(978-1-4218-0155-1(8)*, 1st World Library - Literary Society) 1st World Publishing, Inc.

—Old Greek Stories. 2007. (ENG.). 134p. pap. 18.99 *(978-1-4346-2275-4(4))*; pap. 19.99 *(978-1-4346-2333-1(5))* Creative Media Partners, LLC.

—Old Greek Stories. 2004. reprint ed. pap. 1.99 *(978-1-4192-3803-1(5))*; pap. 19.95 *(978-1-4191-3803-4(0))* Kessinger Publishing, LLC.

—Old Greek Stories. 2008. (Illus.). 192p. pap. 9.95 *(978-1-59915-296-7(7))* Yesterday's Classics.

Barker, Geoff. What Is a Myth?, 1 vol., 1. 2014. (Britannica Common Core Library). (ENG.). 32p. (gr. 2-5). 23.45 *(978-1-62275-195-2(7))* Rosen Publishing Group, Inc., The.

Basher, Simon & Budzik, Mary. Mythology: Oh My! Gods & Godesses. 2014. (Basher History Ser.). (ENG., Illus.). 128p. (J). (gr. 5-9). 14.99 *(978-0-7534-7171-5(X)*, 9780753471715); pap. 8.99 *(978-0-7534-7172-2(8)*, 9780753471722) Roaring Brook Pr. (Kingfisher).

Baxter, Nicola. Celtic Tales & Legends. Shuttleworth, Cathie, illus. 2012. (ENG.). 80p. (J). (gr. 2-7). pap. 9.99 *(978-1-84322-950-6(1))* Anness Publishing GBR. Dist: National Bk. Network.

Benjamin, Cynthia, adapted by. Hare Rescues the Sun: And Other Sky Myths. 2003. (ENG., Illus.). 56p. (J). (gr. 6-8). pap. 7.97 net. *(978-0-7652-3278-6(2)*, Celebration Pr.) Pearson Schl.

Bernard, Catherine. Celtic Mythology. Bock, William Sauts, illus. 2003. (Mythology Ser.). 104p. (J). lib. bdg. 27.94 *(978-0-7660-2204-1(8))* Enslow Pubs., Inc.

—Celtic Mythology Rocks! Bock, William Sauts, illus. 2011. (Mythology Rocks! Ser.). 104p. (J). (gr. 6-18). pap. 10.95 *(978-1-59845-326-3(2))* Enslow Pubs., Inc.

Bernard, Evslin. Heroes, Gods & Monsters of the Greek Myths. 2014. (ENG.). 224p. (YA). (gr. 12-12). 11.24 *(978-1-63245-079-1(8))* Lectorum Pubns., Inc.

Besant, Annie W. Legends & Tales Lotus Leaves for the Y. 2006. pap. 19.95 *(978-1-4286-2494-8(5))* Kessinger Publishing, LLC.

Bingham, Jane & Sansom, Fiona. Chinese Myths. Kennedy, Graham, illus. 2009. (Myths from Many Lands Ser.). 48p. (YA). (gr. 2-6). pap. 12.85 *(978-1-60754-219-3(6))*; (gr. 4-7). 29.25 *(978-1-60754-218-6(8))* Windmill Bks.

Black Ships Before Troy. 2011. 8.80 *(978-0-7848-3649-1(3)*, Everbind) Marco Bk. Co.

Blackwood, Gary L. & Siburt, Ruth. Legends or Lies? 2009. (Benchmark Rockets: History's Mysteries Ser.). 32p. (gr. 3). 28.50 *(978-0-7614-4359-9(2))* Marshall Cavendish GBR. Dist: Marshall Cavendish Corp.

Bowen, Carl. Loki & Thor. Smith, Tod & Lokus, Rex, illus. 2016. (Norse Myths: a Viking Graphic Novel Ser.). (ENG.). 56p. (gr. 3-4). pap. 5.95 *(978-1-4965-3494-1(8))* Stone Arch Bks.

Brezina, Corona. Celtic Mythology. 2009. (Mythology Around the World Ser.). 64p. (gr. 5-5). 58.50 *(978-1-61514-748-9(9)*, Rosen Reference) Rosen Publishing Group, Inc., The.

Bryant, Megan E. Oh My Gods! A Look-It-Up Guide to the Gods of Mythology. 2009. (Mythlopedia Ser.). (ENG.). 128p. (J). (gr. 5-9). pap. 13.95 *(978-1-60631-058-8(5)*, Watts, Franklin) Scholastic Library Publishing.

—She's All That! A Look-It-Up Guide to the Goddesses of Mythology. 2009. (Mythlopedia Ser.). (ENG.). 128p. (J). (gr. 5-9). pap. 13.95 *(978-1-60631-059-5(3)*, Watts, Franklin) Scholastic Library Publishing.

Byrd, Robert. Jason & the Argonauts. 2016. (ENG., Illus.). 48p. (J). (gr. 1-4). 17.99 *(978-0-8037-4118-8(9)*, Dial Bks) Penguin Young Readers Group.

Campbell, Trenton, ed. Gods & Goddesses of Ancient China. 2014. (Gods & Goddesses of Mythology Ser.). 160p. (J). (gr. 9-12). 32.90 *(978-1-62275-393-2(3))* Rosen Publishing Group, Inc., The.

Capstone Press Editors. The Story of Orion: A Roman Constellation Myth, 1 vol. Guerlais, Gérald, illus. 2012. (Night Sky Stories Ser.). (ENG.). 24p. (gr. 2-3). lib. bdg. 26.65 *(978-1-4048-7377-3(5))* Picture Window Bks.

Capstone Press Staff. The Story of Cassiopeia: A Roman Constellation Myth, 1 vol. Squier, Robert, illus. 2012. (Night Sky Stories Ser.). (ENG.). 24p. (gr. 2-3). lib. bdg. 26.65 *(978-1-4048-7376-6(7))* Picture Window Bks.

—The Story of Ursa Major & Ursa Minor: A Roman Constellation Myth, 1 vol. Guerlais, Gérald, illus. 2012. (Night Sky Stories Ser.). (ENG.). 24p. (gr. 2-3). lib. bdg. 26.65 *(978-1-4048-7374-2(0))* Picture Window Bks.

Ceceri, Kathy. World Myths & Legends: 25 Projects You Can Build Yourself. Braley, Shawn, illus. 2010. (Build It Yourself Ser.). (ENG.). 128p. (J). (gr. 3-7). 21.95 *(978-1-934670-44-6(8))* Octavio Publishing.

Celtic. 2nd rev. ed. 2010. (Mythology A to Z Ser.). (Illus.). 152p. (J). (gr. 5-8). 45.00 *(978-1-60413-413-1(5)*, Chelsea Hse.) Facts On File, Inc.

Chambers, Catherine. Autobiographies You Never Thought You'd Read! 2015. (Autobiographies You Never Thought You'd Read! Ser.). (ENG.). 32p. (gr. 1-3). lib. bdg. 119.96 *(978-1-4109-7965-0(2)*, Read Me!) Heinemann-Raintree.

Chambers, Catherine, et al. All about Myths. 2013. (All about Myths Ser.). (ENG.). 48p. (gr. 5-8). pap. 71.92 *(978-1-4109-5477-0(3))*; pap. 35.96 *(978-1-4109-5476-3(5))*; lib. bdg. 228.55 *(978-1-4109-5471-8(4))*; lib. bdg. 97.95 *(978-1-4109-5470-1(6))*; pap. 35.96 *(978-1-4109-4980-6(X))*; lib. bdg. 130.60 *(978-1-4109-4975-2(3))* Heinemann-Raintree.

Child's Book of Myths & Enchantments. (J). (gr. 4-7). 12.95 *(978-1-56288-395-9(X))* Checkerboard Pr., Inc.

Christopher, Neil. Those That Cause Fear, 1 vol. Amaktauyok, Germaine, illus. 2016. (ENG.). 40p. (J). (gr. 2-4). 16.95 *(978-1-77227-085-3(7))* Inhabit Media Inc. CAN. Dist: Independent Pubs. Group.

Claybourne, Anna. Greek Myths. Sansom, Fiona, illus. 2009. (Myths from Many Lands Ser.). 48p. (YA). (gr. 2-6). pap. 12.85 *(978-1-60754-225-4(0))*; (gr. 4-7). 29.25 *(978-1-60754-224-7(2))* Windmill Bks.

Collier, Irene Dea. Chinese Mythology Rocks! Bock, William Sauts, illus. 2011. (Mythology Rocks! Ser.). 128p. (J). (gr. 6-18). pap. 10.95 *(978-1-59845-330-0(0))*; lib. bdg. 33.27 *(978-0-7660-3898-1(X))* Enslow Pubs., Inc.

Colum, Padraic. The Golden Fleece: And the Heroes Who Lived Before Achilles. Pogány, Willy, illus. 2004. 316p. (J). (gr. 5). 17.60 *(978-0-7569-4048-5(6))* Perfection Learning Corp.

—The Golden Fleece & the Heroes Who Lived Before Achilles. Pogány, Willy, illus. 2010. (Looking Glass Library). (ENG.). 368p. (J). (gr. 3-7). 10.99 *(978-0-375-86709-5(0)*, Random Hse. Bks. for Young Readers) Random Hse. Children's Bks.

Coolidge, Olivia E. Hercules & Other Tales from Greek Myths. Lockhart, David, illus. 2011. 120p. 39.95 *(978-1-258-02308-9(3))* Literary Licensing, LLC.

Cooper, Gilly Cameron. How the World Began: Creation in Myths & Legends. Ludlow, Patricia, illus. 2006. (ENG.). 48p. (J). (gr. 3-7). pap. 11.99 *(978-1-84476-246-0(7))* Anness Publishing GBR. Dist: National Bk. Network.

Cope, Beatrice. Mythical Monsters. 2014. (ENG., Illus.). 32p. (J). lib. bdg. 25.70 *(978-1-62469-003-7(3))* Purple Toad Publishing, Inc.

Cox, Barbara & Forbes, Scott. Beyond the Grave, Vol. 1. 2014. (Creepy Chronicles Ser.). (ENG., Illus.). 32p. (J). (gr. 5-6). 26.60 *(978-1-4824-0226-1(2))* Stevens, Gareth Publishing LLLP.

Crabtree Staff & Hynson, Colin. Understanding Indian Myths. 2012. (ENG., Illus.). 48p. (J). pap. *(978-0-7787-4529-7(5))* Crabtree Publishing Co.

Croft, Malcolm. Cool Mythology. Weighill, Damien, illus. 2016. (ENG.). 112p. (J). (gr. 5). 14.99 *(978-1-910232-84-2(X)*, Pavilion) Pavilion Bks. GBR. Dist: Independent Pubs. Group.

Croy, Anita. Myths & Legends of Ancient Rome. 2015. (Illus.). 64p. (J). *(978-0-7166-2635-0(7))* World Bk., Inc.

—Myths & Legends of Australia, New Zealand, & Pacific Islands. 2015. (Illus.). 64p. (J). *(978-0-7166-2629-9(2))* World Bk., Inc.

Dalal, Anita. Mesoamerican Myths. 2010. (Myths from Around the World Ser.). 48p. (gr. 6-8). (YA). lib. bdg. 31.00 *(978-1-4339-3539-8(2))*; (Illus.). (J). pap. 14.05 *(978-1-4339-3540-4(6))* Stevens, Gareth Publishing LLLP. (Gareth Stevens Secondary Library).

Daning, Tom. Chinese Mythology: The Four Dragons. 2009. (Jr. Graphic Mythologies Ser.). (ENG.). 24p. (J). (gr. 2-3). 47.90 *(978-1-61513-858-6(7)*, PowerKids Pr.) Rosen Publishing Group, Inc., The.

—The Four Dragons: A Chinese Myth. 2007. (Graphic Myths (New York, N.Y.) Ser.). (ENG., Illus.). 24p. (J). (gr. 3-8). pap. 10.60 *(978-1-4042-2153-6(0)*, PowerKids Pr.) Rosen Publishing Group, Inc., The.

—Mitología China: Los Cuatro Dragones. 2009. (Historietas Juveniles: Mitologías (Jr. Graphic Mythologies) Ser.). (SPA., Illus.). 24p. (gr. 3-8). pap. 10.60 *(978-1-4358-3326-5(0))* Rosen Publishing Group, Inc., The.

Demarco, Stacey. Goddesses & Sirens. Manton, Jimmy, illus. 2013. 165p. (J). pap. *(978-1-58270-381-7(7))* Beyond Words Publishing, Inc.

—Gods & Titans. Manton, Jimmy, illus. 2013. 160p. (J). *(978-1-58270-380-0(9))* Beyond Words Publishing, Inc.

Dorling Kindersley Publishing Staff. DK Adventures: Myths & Legends. 2015. (DK Adventures Ser.). (ENG., Illus.). 128p. (J). (gr. 3-7). pap. 5.99 *(978-1-4654-3906-2(4)*, DK Children) Dorling Kindersley Publishing, Inc.

—DK Eyewitness Books: Mythology. 2017. (DK Eyewitness Bks.). (ENG., Illus.). 72p. (J). (gr. 3-7). pap. 9.99 ***(978-1-4654-6246-6(5)**,* DK Children) Dorling Kindersley Publishing, Inc.

—Mythology. 2017. (DK Eyewitness Bks.). (ENG., Illus.). 72p. (J). (gr. 3-7). lib. bdg. 19.99 ***(978-1-4654-6254-1(6)**,* DK Children) Dorling Kindersley Publishing, Inc.

D'Ottavi, Francesca, illus. Isis & Osiris, 1 vol. 2012. (Egyptian Myths Ser.). (ENG.). 32p. (gr. 3-4). pap. 7.95 *(978-1-4048-7240-0(X))*; lib. bdg. 28.65 *(978-1-4048-7148-9(9))* Picture Window Bks.

Elgin, Kathy. Roman Myths. Sansom, Fiona, illus. 2009. (Myths from Many Lands Ser.). 48p. (YA). (gr. 2-6). pap. 12.85 *(978-1-60754-231-5(5))*; (J). (gr. 4-7). 29.25 *(978-1-60754-230-8(7))* Windmill Bks.

Encyclopaedia Britannica, Inc. Staff, compiled by. Legends, Myths & Folktales. 2003. (Illus.). 64p. 14.95 *(978-1-59339-037-2(8))* Encyclopaedia Britannica, Inc.

Fajardo, Anika, et al. You Choose: Ancient Greek Myths. Nathan, James et al, illus. 2016. (You Choose: Ancient Greek Myths Ser.). (ENG.). 112p. (gr. 3-4). 127.96 *(978-1-4914-8151-6(X)*, You Choose Bks.) Capstone Press of Coughlan Cos.

Field, Jon Eben & Hoena, Blake. Mythology: Begin Your Quest for Facts, Photos, & Fun Fit for Gods & Goddesses. 2014. (National Geographic Kids Everything Ser.). (ENG., Illus.). 64p. (J). (gr. 3-7). pap. 12.99 *(978-1-4263-1498-8(1)*, National Geographic Children's Bks.) National Geographic Society.

Fisher, Leonard Everett. The Gods & Goddesses of Ancient China. 2003. (ENG., Illus.). 36p. (J). (gr. 4-6). tchr. ed. 16.95 *(978-0-8234-1694-3(1))* Holiday Hse., Inc.

Frankfeldt, Gwen & Fleischman, Paul. Dateline - Troy. Frankfeldt, Gwen & Morrow, Glenn, illus. 2006. (ENG.). 80p. (J). (gr. 7-10). pap. 8.99 *(978-0-7636-3084-3(5))* Candlewick Pr.

Ganeri, Anita. Chinese Myths & Legends, 1 vol. 2013. (All about Myths Ser.). (ENG.). 48p. (gr. 5-8). 32.65 *(978-1-4109-5467-1(6))*; pap. 9.25 *(978-1-4109-5473-2(0))* Heinemann-Raintree.

—Mesoamerican Myth: A Treasury of Legends, Art, & History. 2007. (ENG., Illus.). 96p. (C). (gr. 6-18). lib. bdg. 158.00 *(978-0-7656-8106-5(4)*, Y182745) Routledge.

Garcia, Emmett Shkeme & Garcia, Emmett. Coyote & the Sky: How the Sun, Moon, & Stars Began. Pringle, Victoria, illus. 2006. (ENG.). 32p. (J). (gr. 6-18). 19.95 *(978-0-8263-3730-6(9))* Univ. of New Mexico Pr.

Gavin, Jamila. Tales from India. Hall, Amanda, illus. 2011. (ENG.). 96p. (J). (gr. 4-7). 19.99 *(978-0-7636-5564-8(3)*, Templar) Candlewick Pr.

Giles, Bridget. West African Myths. 2010. (Myths from Around the World Ser.). 48p. (gr. 6-8). (YA). lib. bdg. 31.00 *(978-1-4339-3536-7(8))*; (Illus.). (J). pap. 14.05 *(978-1-4339-3537-4(6))* Stevens, Gareth Publishing LLLP. (Gareth Stevens Secondary Library).

Gill, Shelley. Up on Denali: Alaska's Wild Mountain. Cartwright, Shannon, illus. 2006. (Paws IV Ser.). (ENG.). 32p. (J). (gr. -1-2). pap. 10.99 *(978-1-57061-365-4(6)*, Little Bigfoot) Sasquatch Bks.

Girls' Guides to Everything Unexplained. 2010. (Girls' Guides to Everything Unexplained Ser.). (ENG.). 32p. (gr. 3-4). lib. bdg. 111.96 *(978-1-4296-5456-2(2)*, Snap Bks.) Capstone Press of Coughlan Cos.

Gods & Goddesses of Mythology: Set 2. 2014. (Gods & Goddesses of Mythology Ser.). 160p. (YA). (gr. 9-12). 263.20 *(978-1-62275-762-6(9))*; 131.60 *(978-1-62275-402-1(6))* Rosen Publishing Group, Inc., The.

Gods & Goddesses of Mythology: Sets 1-2. 2014. (Gods & Goddesses of Mythology Ser.). 160p. (YA). (gr. 9-12). 263.20 *(978-1-62275-537-0(5))* Rosen Publishing Group, Inc., The.

Got, Yves & Zero to Ten Publication Staff. Greek Myths & Legends. 2007. (ENG., Illus.). 192p. (gr. k). *(978-1-84089-514-8(4))* Zero to Ten, Ltd.

Green, Jen. Ancient Greek Myths. 2010. (Myths from Around the World Ser.). 48p. (gr. 6-8). (YA). lib. bdg. 31.00 *(978-1-4339-3524-4(4))*; (Illus.). (J). pap. 14.05 *(978-1-4339-3525-1(2))* Stevens, Gareth Publishing LLLP. (Gareth Stevens Secondary Library).

—Chinese & Japanese Myths. 2010. (Myths from Around the World Ser.). 48p. (gr. 6-8). (YA). lib. bdg. 31.00 *(978-1-4339-3533-6(3))*; (Illus.). (J). pap. 14.05 *(978-1-4339-3534-3(1))* Stevens, Gareth Publishing LLLP. (Gareth Stevens Secondary Library).

Green, Roger Lancelyn. Tales of the Greek Heroes. (Puffin Pixels Ser.). (ENG., Illus.). 304p. (J). 2015. 11.99 *(978-0-14-751715-9(X))* 2009. (gr. 5-7). pap. 5.99 *(978-0-14-132528-6(3))* Penguin Young Readers Group. (Puffin Books).

Griffin, Ingrid. The Story of the Great Bear. 2015. (Stories in the Stars Ser.). (ENG., Illus.). 24p. (J). (gr. 1-2). pap. 8.15 *(978-1-4824-2665-6(X))* Stevens, Gareth Publishing LLLP.

Guerlais, Gérald, illus. The Story of Orion: A Roman Constellation Myth, 1 vol. 2012. (Night Sky Stories Ser.). (ENG.). 24p. (gr. 2-3). pap. 8.95 *(978-1-4048-7718-4(5))* Picture Window Bks.

—The Story of Ursa Major & Ursa Minor: A Roman Constellation Myth, 1 vol. 2012. (Night Sky Stories Ser.). (ENG.). 24p. (gr. 2-3). pap. 8.95 *(978-1-4048-7720-7(7))* Picture Window Bks.

Guillain, Charlotte. Writing & Staging Myths & Legends. 2016. (Writing & Staging Plays Ser.). (ENG., Illus.). 48p. (gr. 4-6). lib. bdg. 33.32 *(978-1-4846-2772-3(5)*, Heinemann InfoSearch) Heinemann-Raintree.

Gunderson, Jessica. Olympians vs. Titans: An Interactive Mythological Adventure. Arcabascio, Carolyn, illus. 2017. (You Choose: Ancient Greek Myths Ser.). (ENG.). 112p. (gr. 3-4). pap. 6.95 *(978-1-5157-4825-0(1)*, You Choose Bks.) Capstone Press of Coughlan Cos.

Haaren, John. Famous Men of Greece. 2008. 112p. pap. 12.95 *(978-1-60459-523-9(X))* Wilder Pubns., Corp.

—Famous Men of Rome. 2008. 120p. pap. 12.95 *(978-1-60459-524-6(8))* Wilder Pubns., Corp.

Hale, Vincent, ed. Mesopotamian Gods & Goddesses, 1 vol., 1. 2014. (Gods & Goddesses of Mythology Ser.). (ENG.). 112p. (YA). (gr. 7-12). 32.90 *(978-1-62275-161-7(2))* Rosen Publishing Group, Inc., The.

Hamilton, John. Magic Rings & Other Magical Things, 1 vol. 2006. (Fantasy & Folklore Ser.). (ENG., Illus.). 32p. (gr. 5-8). 27.07 *(978-1-59679-337-8(6)*, Abdo & Daughters) ABDO Publishing Co.

Hamilton, Sue. Lost Cities, 1 vol. 2007. (Unsolved Mysteries Ser.). (ENG.). 32p. (gr. 4-7). 27.07 *(978-1-59928-832-1(X)*, Abdo & Daughters) ABDO Publishing Co.

Haus, Estudio, illus. Ancient Myths. 2015. (Ancient Myths Ser.). (ENG.). 32p. (gr. 3-4). lib. bdg. 183.90 *(978-1-4914-2522-0(9)*, Graphic Library) Capstone Press of Coughlan Cos.

Hawthorne, Nathaniel. Tanglewood Tales for Girls & Boys. 2013. (Notable American Authors Ser.). 425p. reprint ed. lthr. 79.00 *(978-0-7812-3046-9(2))* Reprint Services Corp.

—A Wonder Book for Girls & Boys. 2013. (Notable American Authors Ser.). 425p. reprint ed. lthr. 79.00 *(978-0-7812-3045-2(4))* Reprint Services Corp.

Hayes, Amy. Medusa & Pegasus. 2015. (Creatures of Fantasy Ser.). (ENG.). 64p. (J). (gr. 5-5). 34.21 *(978-1-5026-0506-1(6))* Cavendish Square Publishing.

Herdling, Glenn. African Mythology: Anansi. 2009. (Jr. Graphic Mythologies Ser.). (ENG.). 24p. (J). (gr. 2-3). 47.90 *(978-1-61513-855-5(2)*, PowerKids Pr.) Rosen Publishing Group, Inc., The.

Herdling, Glenn & Obregón, José María. Mitología Griega: Jasón y el Vellocino de Oro. 2009. (Historietas Juveniles: Mitologías (Jr. Graphic Mythologies) Ser.). (SPA., Illus.). 24p. (J). (gr. 3-6). lib. bdg. 25.25 *(978-1-4358-8568-4(6))*; pap. 10.60 *(978-1-4358-3330-2(9))* Rosen Publishing Group, Inc., The.

Hibbert, Clare. Terrible Tales of Africa, Vol. 1. 2014. (Monstrous Myths Ser.). (ENG., Illus.). 32p. (J). (gr. 4-5). 26.60 *(978-1-4824-0194-3(0))* Stevens, Gareth Publishing LLLP.

—Terrible Tales of Ancient Greece, Vol. 1. 2014. (Monstrous Myths Ser.). 32p. (J). (gr. 4-6). 26.60 *(978-1-4824-0181-3(9))* Stevens, Gareth Publishing LLLP.

Higgins, Nadia. Perseus the Hero: An Interactive Mythological Adventure. 2016. (You Choose: Ancient Greek Myths Ser.). (ENG., Illus.). 112p. (gr. 3-4). lib. bdg. 31.99 *(978-1-4914-8112-7(9))* Capstone Press of Coughlan Cos.

Hinds, Kathryn. Sphinxes & Centaurs. 2013. 64p. (J). (gr. 4-8). 34.21 *(978-0-7614-4927-0(2))* Cavendish Square Publishing.

Hoena, B. A. Jason & the Argonauts: A Graphic Retelling. 2015. (Ancient Myths Ser.). (ENG., Illus.). 32p. (gr. 3-4). lib. bdg. 30.65 *(978-1-4914-2072-0(3)*, Graphic Library) Capstone Press of Coughlan Cos.

—Theseus & the Minotaur: A Graphic Retelling. 2015. (Ancient Myths Ser.). (ENG., Illus.). 32p. (gr. 3-4). lib. bdg. 30.65 *(978-1-4914-2075-1(8)*, Graphic Library) Capstone Press of Coughlan Cos.

Hoena, Blake. Jason, the Argonauts, & the Golden Fleece: An Interactive Mythological Adventure. Nathan, James, illus. 2016. (You Choose: Ancient Greek Myths Ser.). (ENG.). 112p. (gr. 3-4). lib. bdg. 31.99 *(978-1-4914-8113-4(7)*, You Choose Bks.) Capstone Press of Coughlan Cos.

Hoena, Blake, retold by. The Voyages of Odysseus: A Graphic Retelling. 2015. (Ancient Myths Ser.). (ENG., Illus.). 32p. (gr. 3-4). lib. bdg. 30.65 *(978-1-4914-2076-8(6)*, Graphic Library) Capstone Press of Coughlan Cos.

Homer. Classic Starts - The Iliad. Freeberg, Eric, illus. 2014. (Classic Starts(tm) Ser.). (ENG.). 160p. (J). (gr. 2-4). 6.95 *(978-1-4549-0612-4(X))* Sterling Publishing Co., Inc.

Houle, Michelle M. Gods & Goddesses in Greek Mythology Rock! Bock, William Sauts, illus. 2011. (Mythology Rocks! Ser.). 128p. (J). (gr. 6-18). pap. 10.95 *(978-1-59845-329-4(7))* Enslow Pubs., Inc.

Hunt, Jilly. Roman Myths & Legends, 1 vol. 2013. (All about Myths Ser.). (ENG., Illus.). 48p. (gr. 5-8). 32.65 *(978-1-4109-4974-5(5))*; pap. 9.25 *(978-1-4109-4979-0(6))* Heinemann-Raintree.

Husain, Shahrukh. Indian Myths. Willey, Bee, illus. 2007. (Stories from Ancient Civilisations Ser.). (ENG.). 32p. (J). pap. 10.99 *(978-0-237-53376-2(6))* Evans Brothers, Ltd. GBR. Dist: Independent Pubs. Group.

Hyde, Natalie. Understanding Greek Myths. 2012. (ENG.). 48p. (J). *(978-0-7787-4509-9(0))*; pap. *(978-0-7787-4514-3(7))* Crabtree Publishing Co.

Hynson, Colin. Understanding Indian Myths. 2012. (ENG.). 48p. (J). *(978-0-7787-4524-2(4))* Crabtree Publishing Co.

Ingri, D'Aulaire & Parin, D'Aulaire Edgar. D'Aulaires Book of Greek Myths. 2014. (Yearling Special Ser.). (ENG.). 192p. (gr. 8-12). 24.20 *(978-1-63245-092-0(5))* Lectorum Pubns., Inc.

Innes, Brian. Ancient Roman Myths. 2010. (Myths from Around the World Ser.). 48p. (gr. 6-8). (YA). lib. bdg. 31.00 *(978-1-4339-3527-5(9))*; (Illus.). (J). pap. 14.05 *(978-1-4339-3528-2(7))* Stevens, Gareth Publishing LLLP. (Gareth Stevens Secondary Library).

James Baldwin. Fifty Famous Stories Retold. 2009. (Illus.). 132p. pap. 5.95 *(978-1-60386-206-6(4)*, Merchant Bks.) Rough Draft Printing.

Jarvie, Gordon, ed. Irish Folk & Fairy Tales. 2nd rev. ed. 2009. (ENG.). 224p. pap. 16.95 *(978-0-85640-836-6(0))* Blackstaff Pr., Ltd. GBR. Dist: Dufour Editions, Inc.

Jeffrey, Gary. Achilles & the Trojan War. 2012. (Graphic Mythical Heroes Ser.). (Illus.). 24p. (J). (gr. 3-5). pap. 8.15 *(978-1-4339-7508-0(4))*; lib. bdg. 23.95 *(978-1-4339-7507-3(6))* Stevens, Gareth Publishing LLLP.

—African Myths. 2009. (Graphic Mythology Ser.). (ENG.). 48p. (YA). (gr. 4-5). 58.50 *(978-1-61512-976-8(6)*, Rosen Reference) Rosen Publishing Group, Inc., The.

—Jason & the Argonauts. 2012. (Graphic Mythical Heroes Ser.). (Illus.). 24p. (J). (gr. 3-5). pap. 8.15 *(978-1-4339-7516-5(5))*; lib. bdg. 23.95 *(978-1-4339-7515-8(7))* Stevens, Gareth Publishing LLLP.

Jennings, Ken. Greek Mythology. Lowery, Mike, illus. 2014. (Ken Jennings' Junior Genius Guides). (ENG.). 160p. (J). (gr. 3-5). 18.99 *(978-1-4424-9849-5(8))*; pap. 7.99 *(978-1-4424-7330-0(4))* Little Simon. (Little Simon).

Johnson, Robin. Understanding Roman Myths. 2012. (ENG.). 48p. (J). *(978-0-7787-4510-5(4))*; pap. *(978-0-7787-4515-0(5))* Crabtree Publishing Co.

Jr. Graphic American Legends: Sets 1-2. 2014. (Jr. Graphic American Legends Ser.). 24p. (J). (gr. 3-6). pap. 763.20 *(978-1-4777-7263-8(4)*, PowerKids Pr.) Rosen Publishing Group, Inc., The.

Kallen, Stuart A. African Mythology. Greenhaven Press Editors, ed. 2015. (Mythology & Culture Worldwide Ser.). (ENG., Illus.). 128p. (gr. 7-10). lib. bdg. 39.40 *(978-1-4205-1145-1(9)*, Lucent Bks.) Cengage Gale.

Kampman, Marcella. Inanna, Goddess of Love: Great Myths & Legends from Sumer. 2008. (ENG., Illus.). 220p. (J). 10.95 *(978-1-897411-03-2(0))* Bayeux Arts, Inc. CAN. Dist: Chicago Distribution Ctr.

Kelkar, Gauri. Little Monk's Durga. 2011. (ENG., Illus.). 60p. 14.95 *(978-81-8328-190-4(7))* Wisdom Tree IND. Dist: SCB Distributors.

—Little Monk's Lakshmi. 2011. (ENG., Illus.). 60p. 14.95 *(978-81-8328-191-1(5))* Wisdom Tree IND. Dist: SCB Distributors.

—Little Monk's Parvati. 2011. (ENG.). 60p. 14.95 *(978-81-8328-192-8(3))* Wisdom Tree IND. Dist: SCB Distributors.

—Little Monk's Saraswati. 2011. (ENG.). 60p. 14.95 *(978-81-8328-189-8(3))* Wisdom Tree IND. Dist: SCB Distributors.

Kelly, Sophia. What a Beast! A Look-It-Up Guide to the Monsters & Mutants of Mythology. 2009. (Mythlopedia Ser.). (ENG.). 128p. (J). (gr. 5-9). pap. 13.95 *(978-1-60631-060-1(7)*, Watts, Franklin) Scholastic Library Publishing.

Kerrigan, Michael, et al. Exploring the Life, Myth, & Art of the Ancient near East. 2016. (Civilizations of the World Ser.). (ENG.). 144p. (J). (gr. 8-8). lib. bdg. 45.10 *(978-1-4994-6397-2(9))* Rosen Publishing Group, Inc., The.

Kingsley, Charles. The Heroes. Robinson, T. H., illus. 2009. 240p. pap. 10.95 *(978-1-59915-291-2(6))* Yesterday's Classics.

—The Heroes: Or Greek Fairy Tales for My Children. 2012. 314p. pap. *(978-1-290-05368-6(5))* HardPr.

—Heroes of Greek Mythology. Squire, M H & Mars, E., illus. 2006. (Dover Children's Classics Ser.). (ENG.). 240p. (YA). (gr. 3-12). per. 9.95 *(978-0-486-44854-1(1))* Dover Pubns., Inc.

Kopp, Megan. Understanding Chinese Myths. 2012. (ENG.). 48p. (J). *(978-0-7787-4507-5(4))*; pap. *(978-0-7787-4512-9(0))* Crabtree Publishing Co.

Krieg, Katherine. What We Get from Greek Mythology. 2015. (21st Century Skills Library: Mythology & Culture Ser.). (ENG., Illus.). 32p. (J). (gr. 3-6). 29.93 *(978-1-63188-913-4(3)*, 205976) Cherry Lake Publishing.

Kuhtz, Cleo & Martell, Hazel. Ancient Greek Civilization. D'Ottavi, Francesca, illus. 2009. (Ancient Civilizations & Their Myths & Legends Ser.). (YA). (gr. 5-9). lib. bdg. 29.25 *(978-1-4042-8033-5(2))* Rosen Publishing Group, Inc., The.

Kutner, Richard, tr. from FRE. Oedipus: Trapped by Destiny: A TOON Graphic. Pommaux, Yvan, illus. 2016. (TOON Graphic Mythology Ser.). (ENG.). 48p. (J). (gr. 2-7). 16.95 *(978-1-935179-95-5(0))* TOON Books / RAW Junior, LLC.

Laflamme, Sonia K. & Delezenne, Christine. Les Hommes de Mais. (FRE., Illus.). 71p. (J). pap. 9.95 *(978-2-923234-58-8(8))* Editions de l'Isatis CAN. Dist: Crabtree Publishing Co.

Lang, Andrew. Tales of Troy: Ulysses the Sacker of Cities. 2004. reprint ed. pap. 1.99 *(978-1-4192-5072-9(8))* Kessinger Publishing, LLC.

—Tales of Troy & Greece. Ford, H. J., illus. 2006. (Dover Children's Classics Ser.). (ENG.). 336p. (gr. 9-12). per. 9.95 *(978-0-486-44917-3(3))* Dover Pubns., Inc.

LaRoche, Amy. Chimaera. 2010. (Monsters in Myth Ser.). (Illus.). 48p. (J). (gr. 4-7). lib. bdg. 29.95 *(978-1-58415-925-4(1))* Mitchell Lane Pubs., Inc.

Leavy, Una. Magical Celtic Tales. O'Connor, Fergal, illus. 2017. (ENG.). 96p. (J). 21.00 ***(978-1-84717-546-5(5))*** O'Brien Pr., Ltd., The IRL. Dist: Dufour Editions, Inc.

Leonard, Scott A. Myths & Legends of Ancient Britain & Ireland. 2015. (Illus.). 64p. (J). *(978-0-7166-2637-4(3))* World Bk., Inc.

—Myths & Legends of China. 2015. (Illus.). 64p. (J). *(978-0-7166-2632-9(2))* World Bk., Inc.

—Myths & Legends of South Asia & Southeast Asia. 2015. (Illus.). 64p. (J). *(978-0-7166-2630-5(6))* World Bk., Inc.

Lindgren, Astrid. The Brothers Lionheart. Morgan, Jill, tr. from SWE. Wikland, Ilon, illus. 2004. 231p. (J). 17.95 *(978-1-930900-24-0(4))* Purple Hse. Pr.

Loewen, Nancy. Cyclops Tells All: The Way Eye See It. Pentney, Ryan, illus. 2014. (Other Side of the Myth Ser.). (ENG.). 32p. (gr. 2-3). pap. 6.95 *(978-1-4795-2937-7(0))* Picture Window Bks.

—Helen of Troy Tells All: Blame the Boys, 1 vol. Gilpin, Stephen, illus. 2014. (Other Side of the Myth Ser.). (ENG.). 32p. (gr. 2-3). 27.32 *(978-1-4795-2182-1(5))* Picture Window Bks.

Loh-Hagan, Virginia. Artemis. 2017. (Gods & Goddesses of the Ancient World Ser.). (ENG., Illus.). 32p. (J). (gr. 4-8). 29.93 *(978-1-63472-136-3(5)*, 209116, 45th Parallel Press) Cherry Lake Publishing.

—Athena. 2017. (Gods & Goddesses of the Ancient World Ser.). (ENG.). 32p. (J). (gr. 4-8). 29.93 *(978-1-63472-135-6(7)*, 209112, 45th Parallel Press) Cherry Lake Publishing.

—Demeter. 2017. (Gods & Goddesses of the Ancient World Ser.). (ENG.). 32p. (J). (gr. 4-8). 29.93 *(978-1-63472-138-7(1)*, 209124, 45th Parallel Press) Cherry Lake Publishing.

—Hades. 2017. (Gods & Goddesses of the Ancient World Ser.). (ENG., Illus.). 32p. (J). (gr. 4-8). 29.93 *(978-1-63472-132-5(2)*, 209100, 45th Parallel Press) Cherry Lake Publishing.

—Hera. 2017. (Gods & Goddesses of the Ancient World Ser.). (ENG., Illus.). 32p. (J). (gr. 4-8). 29.93 *(978-1-63472-137-0(3)*, 209120, 45th Parallel Press) Cherry Lake Publishing.

—Hydra. 2016. (Magic, Myth, & Mystery Ser.). (ENG.). 32p. (J). (gr. 4-8). 29.93 *(978-1-63471-114-2(9)*, 208567, 45th Parallel Press) Cherry Lake Publishing.

—Poseidon. 2017. (Gods & Goddesses of the Ancient World Ser.). (ENG., Illus.). 32p. (J). (gr. 4-8). 29.93 *(978-1-63472-133-2(0)*, 209104, 45th Parallel Press) Cherry Lake Publishing.

Looney, Bill, illus. The Flood of Noah: Legends & Lore of Survival. 2014. 24p. (J). 18.99 *(978-0-89051-801-4(7))* Master Bks.

Lunge-Larsen, Lise. Gifts from the Gods: Ancient Words & Wisdom from Greek & Roman Mythology. Hinds, Gareth, illus. 2011. (ENG.). 96p. (J). (gr. 5-7). 18.99 *(978-0-547-15229-5(9))* Houghton Mifflin Harcourt Publishing Co.

Mabie, Hamilton Wright. Myths That Every Child Should Know. 2007. (ENG.). 270p. pap. 21.99 *(978-1-4346-0177-3(3))*; 306p. pap. 24.99 *(978-1-4346-0251-0(6))* Creative Media Partners, LLC.

Macdonald, Fiona. Celtic Myths & Legends, 1 vol. 2013. (All about Myths Ser.). (ENG.). 48p. (gr. 5-8). pap. 9.25 *(978-1-4109-5472-5(2))* Heinemann-Raintree.

Mackay, Jenny. Hindu Mythology. Lucent Books Staff, ed. 2014. (Mythology & Culture Worldwide Ser.). (ENG., Illus.). 128p. (J). (gr. 7-10). lib. bdg. 39.40 *(978-1-4205-1147-5(5)*, Lucent Bks.) Cengage Gale.

Mandala Publishing Staff. Gopal the Infallible. Dasi, Padmavati D., illus. 2009. (ENG.). 38p. (J). (gr. k-4). 9.95 *(978-1-886069-17-6(4)*, 1212) Mandala Publishing.

Marshall, James Vance. Stories from the Billabong. Firebrace, Francis, illus. 2010. (ENG.). 64p. (J). (gr. k-3). pap. 12.99 *(978-1-84780-124-1(2)*, Frances Lincoln) Quarto Publishing Group UK GBR. Dist: Hachette Bk. Group.

Marsico, Katie. What We Get from Celtic Mythology. 2015. (21st Century Skills Library: Mythology & Culture Ser.). (ENG.). 32p. (J). (gr. 3-6). 29.93 *(978-1-63188-910-3(9)*, 205964) Cherry Lake Publishing.

Mason, Paul. The Fact or Fiction Behind Urban Myths. 2016. (Fact or Phony? Ser.). (ENG.). 96p. (J). (gr. 5-6). lib. bdg. 33.25 *(978-1-4824-4274-8(4))* Stevens, Gareth Publishing LLLP.

Matthews, Rupert & Van Pelt, Todd. Ancient Chinese Civilization. D'Ottavi, Francesca, illus. 2009. (Ancient Civilizations & Their Myths & Legends Ser.). 48p. (J). (gr. 5-9). lib. bdg. 29.25 *(978-1-4042-8035-9(9))* Rosen Publishing Group, Inc., The.

McCaughrean, Geraldine. Jason y el Vellocino de Oro: Aracne, la Tejedora. Barroso, Paz, tr. Ross, Tony, illus. 2005. (Mythology Series Collection Mitos Ser.).Tr. of Jason & the Golden Fleece. (SPA.). 48p. (J). (gr. 2-3). 9.95 *(978-84-348-6425-2(8))* SM Ediciones ESP. Dist: Iaconi, Mariuccia Bk. Imports.

M N O

—Perseo y la Gorgona Medisa. Barroso, Paz, tr. Ross, Tony, illus. 2005. (Mythology Series Collection Mitos Ser.).Tr. of Perseus & the Gorgon Medusa. (SPA.). 48p. (J). (gr. 2-3). 9.95 *(978-84-348-6430-6(4))* SM Ediciones ESP. Dist: Iaconi, Mariuccia Bk. Imports.

McKinley, Herald P. Myths of the Aztecs. 2016. (World Mythologies Ser.). (ENG., Illus.). 96p. (J). (gr. 6-6). lib. bdg. 42.79 *(978-1-5026-0996-0(7))* Cavendish Square Publishing.

McMullan, Kate. Get to Work, Hercules! 2003. (Myth-o-Mania Ser.: No. 7). (ENG., Illus.). (J). 9.99 *(978-0-7868-0863-2(2))* Hyperion Bks. for Children.

McNeely, Tom, illus. Isis & the Seven Scorpions, 1 vol. 2012. (Egyptian Myths Ser.). (ENG.). 32p. (gr. 3-4). lib. bdg. 28.65 *(978-1-4048-7150-2(0))* Picture Window Bks.

Mellado, Carisa. Mythic Oracle: Wisdom of the Ancient Greek Pantheon. Phelan, Michele-lee, illus. 2012. (ENG.). 160p. (YA). (gr. 7). pap. 17.99 *(978-1-58270-325-1(6))* Simon Pulse/Beyond Words.

Meschini, Leonardo, illus. The Prince & the Sphinx, 1 vol. 2012. (Egyptian Myths Ser.). (ENG.). 32p. (gr. 3-4). pap. 8.95 *(978-1-4048-7242-4(6))*; lib. bdg. 28.65 *(978-1-4048-7149-6(7))* Picture Window Bks.

Mhlophe, Gcina. African Tales: A Barefoot Collection. 2017. (ENG., Illus.). 96p. (J). (gr. 1-4). 16.99 ***(978-1-78285-359-6(6))*** Barefoot Bks., Inc.

—African Tales: A Barefoot Collection. Griffin, Rachel, illus. 2015. 96p. (J). (gr. 3-6). 14.99 *(978-1-84686-590-9(5))* Barefoot Bks., Inc.

Milbourne, Anna & Stowell, Louie. The Usborne Book of Greek Myths. Brocklehurst, Ruth, ed. Bursi, Simona et al, illus. 2014. (ENG.). 301p. (J). (gr. 4-7). pap. 22.99 *(978-0-7945-2130-1(4)*, Usborne) EDC Publishing.

Miller, Reagan & Walker, Robert. How to Tell a Myth. Crabtree Publishing Staff, ed. 2011. (Text Styles Ser.: No. 4). (ENG.). 32p. (J). (gr. 3-6). pap. *(978-0-7787-1638-9(4))* Crabtree Publishing Co.

Mincks, Margaret. What We Get from Roman Mythology. 2015. (21st Century Skills Library: Mythology & Culture Ser.). (ENG., Illus.). 32p. (J). (gr. 3-6). pap. 14.21 *(978-1-63188-931-8(1)*, 205985) Cherry Lake Publishing.

Mitchell, Chris. How Many Greeks Can You Fit Inside a Horse? Pinder, Andrew, illus. 2016. (Dr Dino's Learnatorium Ser.). (ENG.). 192p. (J). (gr. 4-7). pap. 8.99 *(978-1-78418-654-8(6))* Blake, John Publishing, Ltd. GBR. Dist: Independent Pubs. Group.

Mitton, Jacqueline. Once upon a Starry Night: A Book of Constellations. Balit, Christina, illus. 2009. (ENG.). 32p. (J). (gr. 1-4). pap. 8.95 *(978-1-4263-0391-3(2)*, National Geographic Children's Bks.) National Geographic Society.

Monsters in Myth, 8 vols., Set. Incl. Cerberus. Tracy, Kathleen. lib. bdg. 29.95 *(978-1-58415-924-7(3))*; Chimaera. LaRoche, Amy. lib. bdg. 29.95 *(978-1-58415-925-4(1))*; Cyclopes. Roberts, Russell. lib. bdg. 29.95 *(978-1-58415-926-1(X))*; Medusa. Tracy, Kathleen. lib. bdg. 29.95 *(978-1-58415-928-5(6))*; Minotaur. Roberts, Russell. lib. bdg. 29.95 *(978-1-58415-929-2(4))*; Monsters of Hercules. Orr, Tamra. lib. bdg. 29.95 *(978-1-58415-927-8(8))*; Sirens. Orr, Tamra. lib. bdg. 29.95 *(978-1-58415-930-8(8))*; Sphinx. DiPrimio, Pete. lib. bdg. 29.95 *(978-1-58415-931-5(6))*; (Illus.). 48p. (J). (gr. 4-7). 2010. 239.60 *(978-1-58415-932-2(4))* Mitchell Lane Pubs., Inc.

Mora, Pat. The Night the Moon Fell: A Maya Myth, 1 vol. Domi, Carlos, illus. 2009. (ENG.). 32p. (J). (gr. k-k). pap. 6.95 *(978-0-88899-938-2(0))* Groundwood Bks. CAN. Dist: Publishers Group West (PGW).

—La Noche Que Se Cayó la Luna. Domi, illus. 2009. (SPA.). 32p. (J). (gr. k-k). pap. 6.95 *(978-0-88899-963-4(1))* Groundwood Bks. CAN. Dist: Publishers Group West (PGW).

Morley, Jacqueline & Salariya, David. World of Myths & Legends. Franklin, Carolyn, illus. 2013. (Mythology Ser.). 64p. (gr. 3-6). 41.35 ***(978-1-908973-93-1(5))*** Book Hse. GBR. Dist: Black Rabbit Bks.

Morris, Neil. African Myths. Kennedy, Graham, illus. 2009. (Myths from Many Lands Ser.). 48p. (YA). (gr. 2-6). pap. 12.85 *(978-1-60754-216-2(1))* Windmill Bks.

Murphy, John, ed. Gods & Goddesses of the Inca, Maya, & Aztec Civilizations. 2014. (Gods & Goddesses of Mythology Ser.). 160p. (J). (gr. 9-12). 32.90 *(978-1-62275-396-3(8))* Rosen Publishing Group, Inc., The.

Muten, Burleigh. Goddesses: A World of Myth & Magic. Guay, Rebecca, illus. 2003. (ENG.). 80p. (J). 19.99 *(978-1-84148-075-6(4))* Barefoot Bks., Inc.

Mythology A to Z, 9 vols., Set. 2010. (Mythology A to Z Ser.). (gr. 5-8). 405.00 *(978-1-60413-956-3(0)*, Chelsea Hse.) Facts On File, Inc.

Mythology Around the World, 6 vols., Set 2. Incl. Celtic Mythology. Brezina, Corona. (YA). lib. bdg. 31.95 *(978-1-4042-0737-0(6))*; Scandinavian Mythology. Porterfield, Jason. (J). lib. bdg. 31.95 *(978-1-4042-0740-0(6))*; (Illus.). 64p. (gr. 5-8). 2007. 2008. Set lib. bdg. 175.50 *(978-1-4042-1096-7(2))* Rosen Publishing Group, Inc., The.

Myths & Legends. pap. *(978-1-84458-374-4(0)*, Pavilion Children's Books) Pavilion Bks.

Nagle, Frances. Medusa. 2016. (Monsters! Ser.). (Illus.). 32p. (J). (gr. 2-1). pap. 10.50 *(978-1-4824-4867-2(X))* Stevens, Gareth Publishing LLLP.

Namm, Diane. Roman Myths. Freeberg, Eric, illus. 2014. (Classic Starts(tm) Ser.). (ENG.). 160p. (J). (gr. 2-4). 6.95 *(978-1-4549-0611-7(1))* Sterling Publishing Co., Inc.

Napoli, Donna Jo. Treasury of Greek Mythology: Classic Stories of Gods, Goddesses, Heroes & Monsters. Balit, Christina, illus. 2011. (ENG.). 192p. (J). (gr. 3-7). 24.95 *(978-1-4263-0844-4(2))*; lib. bdg. 33.90 *(978-1-4263-0845-1(0))* National Geographic Society. (National Geographic Children's Bks.).

Nardo, Don. Aztec Mythology. Currie, Stephen, ed. 2014. (Mythology & Culture Worldwide Ser.). (ENG., Illus.). 128p. (gr. 7-10). lib. bdg. 39.40 *(978-1-4205-0922-9(5)*, Lucent Bks.) Cengage Gale.

Nardo, Don, ed. Greek Mythology. 2012. (Mythology & Culture Worldwide Ser.). (ENG., Illus.). 128p. (gr. 7-10). lib. bdg. 34.45 *(978-1-4205-0633-4(1)*, Lucent Bks.) Cengage Gale.

—Persian Mythology. 2012. (Mythology & Culture Worldwide Ser.). (ENG., Illus.). 128p. (J). (gr. 7-10). lib. bdg. 34.45 *(978-1-4205-0794-2(X)*, Lucent Bks.) Cengage Gale.

—Roman Mythology. 2012. (Mythology & Culture Worldwide Ser.). (ENG., Illus.). 128p. (J). (gr. 7-10). lib. bdg. 34.45 *(978-1-4205-0746-1(X)*, Lucent Bks.) Cengage Gale.

National Geographic Kids. My Mythology Adventure. 2015. (NG Kids Funny Fill In Ser.). (ENG.). 48p. (J). (gr. 3-7). pap. 4.99 *(978-1-4263-2198-6(8)*, National Geographic Children's Bks.) National Geographic Society.

Nordenstrom, Michael, illus. & adapted by. Hina & the Sea of Stars. Nordenstrom, Michael, adapted by. 2003. 32p. 10.95 *(978-1-57306-167-4(0))* Bess Pr., Inc.

O'Brian, Pliny. Myths of the Ancient Romans. 2016. (World Mythologies Ser.). (ENG., Illus.). 96p. (J). (gr. 6-6). lib. bdg. 42.79 *(978-1-5026-0994-6(0))* Cavendish Square Publishing.

O'Connor, George. Apollo: The Brilliant One. 2016. (Olympians Ser.: 8). (ENG., Illus.). 80p. (J). pap. 10.99 *(978-1-62672-015-2(0)*, 9781626720152, First Second Bks.) Roaring Brook Pr.

—Ares. O'Connor, George, illus. 2015. (Olympians Ser.: 7). (ENG., Illus.). 80p. (J). (gr. 4-9). pap. 10.99 *(978-1-62672-013-8(4)*, 9781626720138, First Second Bks.) Roaring Brook Pr.

Ollhoff, Jim. African Mythology, 1 vol. 2011. (World of Mythology Ser.). (ENG., Illus.). 32p. (gr. 5-9). 27.07 *(978-1-61714-716-6(8)*, Abdo & Daughters) ABDO Publishing Co.

—Chinese Mythology, 1 vol. 2011. (World of Mythology Ser.). (ENG., Illus.). 32p. (gr. 5-9). 27.07 *(978-1-61714-718-0(4)*, Abdo & Daughters) ABDO Publishing Co.

—European Mythology, 1 vol. 2011. (World of Mythology Ser.). (ENG., Illus.). 32p. (gr. 5-9). 27.07 *(978-1-61714-720-3(6)*, Abdo & Daughters) ABDO Publishing Co.

—Greek Mythology, 1 vol. 2011. (World of Mythology Ser.). (ENG., Illus.). 32p. (gr. 5-9). 27.07 *(978-1-61714-721-0(4)*, Abdo & Daughters) ABDO Publishing Co.

—Japanese Mythology, 1 vol. 2011. (World of Mythology Ser.). (ENG., Illus.). 32p. 27.07 *(978-1-61714-723-4(0)*, Abdo & Daughters) ABDO Publishing Co.

—Mayan & Aztec Mythology, 1 vol. 2011. (World of Mythology Ser.). (ENG., Illus.). 32p. 27.07 *(978-1-61714-724-1(9)*, Abdo & Daughters) ABDO Publishing Co.

—Middle Eastern Mythology, 1 vol. 2011. (World of Mythology Ser.). (ENG., Illus.). 32p. (YA). (gr. 5-9). 27.07 *(978-1-61714-725-8(7))* ABDO Publishing Co.

—World of Mythology, 6 vols., Set. Incl. African Mythology. 27.07 *(978-1-61714-716-6(8))*; Chinese Mythology. 27.07 *(978-1-61714-718-0(4))*; Egyptian Mythology. (J). 27.07 *(978-1-61714-719-7(2))*; European Mythology. 27.07 *(978-1-61714-720-3(6))*; Greek Mythology. 27.07 *(978-1-61714-721-0(4))*; Norse Mythology. 27.07 *(978-1-61714-726-5(5))*; (gr. 5-9). (World of Mythology Ser.). (Illus.). 32p. 2011. 162.42 *(978-1-61714-715-9(X)*, Abdo & Daughters) ABDO Publishing Co.

Olmstead, Kathleen. King Midas. Quarello, Maurizio A. C., illus. 2014. (Silver Penny Stories Ser.). (ENG.). 48p. (J). (gr. -1-1). 4.95 *(978-1-4027-8346-3(9))* Sterling Publishing Co., Inc.

Orr, Tamra. The Sirens. 2010. (Monsters in Myth Ser.). (Illus.). 48p. (J). (gr. 4-7). lib. bdg. 29.95 *(978-1-58415-930-8(8))* Mitchell Lane Pubs., Inc.

O'Shei, Tim. Bone-Chilling Myths, 1 vol. 2010. (Scary Stories Ser.). (ENG.). 32p. (gr. 3-4). lib. bdg. 27.99 *(978-1-4296-4573-7(3)*, Edge Bks.) Capstone Press of Coughlan Cos.

Pearce, Q. L. Celtic Mythology. Lucent Books, ed. 2014. (Mythology & Culture Worldwide Ser.). (ENG., Illus.). 128p. (gr. 7-10). lib. bdg. 39.40 *(978-1-4205-0923-6(3)*, Lucent Bks.) Cengage Gale.

Peebles, Alice. Demons & Dragons. Chilvers, Nigel, illus. 2015. (Mythical Beasts Ser.). (ENG.). 32p. (J). (gr. 3-6). pap. 7.99 *(978-1-4677-7651-6(3)*, Lerner Pubns.) Lerner Publishing Group.

Philipps, Francis, illus. Jason & the Golden Fleece: A Greek Legend. 2004. (ENG.). 24p. (J). (gr. 3-3). pap. 6.47 net. *(978-0-7685-2126-9(2)*, Dominie Elementary) Pearson Schl.

Pommaux, Yvan. Orpheus in the Underworld. Kutner, Richard, tr. from FRE. 2015. (TOON Graphic Mythology Ser.). (ENG., Illus.). 56p. (J). (gr. 2-7). 16.95 *(978-1-935179-84-9(5))* TOON Books / RAW Junior, LLC.

Posner, Pat. Gods & Goddesses from Greek Myths. 2010. (ENG.). 45p. (J). 19.00 *(978-1-4379-7397-6(3))* DIANE Publishing Co.

Ram-Prasad, Chakravarthi. Exploring the Life, Myth, & Art of India. 2009. (Civilizations of the World Ser.). (YA). (gr. 7-12). lib. bdg. 42.60 *(978-1-4358-5615-8(5))* Rosen Publishing Group, Inc., The.

Randall, Ron. Psyche & Eros: The Lady & the Monster: A Greek Myth. 2008. (Illus.). 48p. (J). (gr. 4-8). 27.93 *(978-0-8225-7177-3(3)*, Graphic Universe™) Lerner Publishing Group.

Randall, Ronne. The Children's Book of Myths & Legends. Howells, Graham, illus. 2012. (ENG.). 128p. (J). (gr. 2-7). pap. 11.99 *(978-1-84322-819-6(X))* Anness Publishing GBR. Dist: National Bk. Network.

Randall, Ronne. Children's Stories from Myths & Legends: Classic Tales from Around the World. Howells, Graham, illus. 2017. (ENG.). 128p. (J). (gr. 3-12). 16.99 ***(978-1-86147-852-8(6)****, Armadillo)* Anness Publishing GBR. Dist: National Bk. Network.

Redmond, Shirley Raye. Cerberus. 2008. (Monsters Ser.). (ENG., Illus.). 48p. (gr. 4-7). lib. bdg. 35.20 *(978-0-7377-4274-9(7)*, LML02109-244485) Cengage Gale.

Reed, Natasha. Mythical Creatures: Sticker Book. Kincaid, Angela, illus. 2005. (Stickertastic Ser.). 24p. (J). (gr. -1-7). pap. *(978-1-84510-119-0(7))* Top That! Publishing PLC.

Reinhart, Matthew & Sabuda, Robert. Dragons & Monsters. Reinhart, Matthew & Sabuda, Robert, illus. 2011. (Encyclopedia Mythologica Ser.). (ENG., Illus.). 12p. (J). (gr. k-4). 250.00 *(978-0-7636-3476-6(X))* Candlewick Pr.

—Gods & Heroes. Reinhart, Matthew & Sabuda, Robert, illus. 2010. (Encyclopedia Mythologica Ser.: 2). (ENG., Illus.). 12p. (J). (gr. k-4). 29.99 *(978-0-7636-3171-0(X))*; 250.00 *(978-0-7636-3486-5(7))* Candlewick Pr.

Riordan, Rick. Percy Jackson's Greek Heroes. Rocco, John, illus. (ENG.). (J). (gr. 3-7). 2017. 528p. pap. 12.99 *(978-1-4847-7643-8(7))* 2015. 416p. 24.99 *(978-1-4231-8365-5(7))* Hyperion Bks. for Children.

—Percy Jackson's Greek Heroes. 2017. (Percy Jackson & the Olympians Ser.). (J). lib. bdg. 24.50 *(978-0-606-39498-7(2))* Turtleback Bks.

Roberts, Jeremy. Chinese Mythology A to Z, Second Edition. 2nd rev. ed. 2009. (Mythology A to Z Ser.). (Illus.). 176p. (gr. 5-8). 45.00 *(978-1-60413-436-0(4)*, Chelsea Hse.) Facts On File, Inc.

—Japanese Mythology A to Z, Second Edition. 2nd rev. ed. 2009. (Mythology A to Z Ser.). (Illus.). 168p. (gr. 5-8). 45.00 *(978-1-60413-435-3(6)*, Chelsea Hse.) Facts On File, Inc.

Roesser, Blanche. The Story of Pegasus. 2015. (Stories in the Stars Ser.). (ENG., Illus.). 24p. (J). (gr. 1-2). pap. 8.15 *(978-1-4824-2677-9(3))* Stevens, Gareth Publishing LLLP.

—The Story of Perseus. 2015. (Stories in the Stars Ser.). (ENG., Illus.). 24p. (J). (gr. 1-2). 22.60 *(978-1-4824-2683-0(8))* Stevens, Gareth Publishing LLLP.

Román, Pedro Josél. PANDORA -la portadora de todos los Dones- 2005. (SPA.). 32p. *(978-958-30-1924-1(0))* Panamericana Editorial.

Rose, Simon. Orion: The Myth & Science. 2015. (Illus.). 24p. (J). *(978-1-5105-0018-1(9))* SmartBook Media, Inc.

Rosemary, Sutcliff. Black Ships Before Troy: The Story of the Iliad. 2014. (ENG.). 160p. (YA). 11.24 *(978-1-63245-187-3(5))* Lectorum Pubns., Inc.

Rosenberg, Donna & McGraw-Hill Staff. World Mythology. 2005. (Ntc: World Mythology Ser.). (ENG., Illus.). 752p. (gr. 9-12). stu. ed. 82.40 *(978-0-07-872909-6(2)*, 0078729092) McGraw-Hill Higher Education.

Rylant, Cynthia. The Beautiful Stories of Life: Six Greek Myths, Retold. Ellis, Carson, illus. 2009. (ENG.). 88p. (J). (gr. 5-7). 17.99 *(978-0-15-206184-5(3))* Houghton Mifflin Harcourt Publishing Co.

Schomp, Virginia. The Ancient Chinese. 2009. (Myths of the World 3 Ser.). 96p. (gr. 6). 34.21 *(978-0-7614-4216-5(2))* Marshall Cavendish GBR. Dist: Marshall Cavendish Corp.

—The Ancient Maya. 2009. (Myths of the World 3 Ser.). 96p. (gr. 6). 34.21 *(978-0-7614-4217-2(0))* Marshall Cavendish Corp.

—The Ancient Mesopotamians. 2008. (Myths of the World Ser.). 96p. (gr. 6-18). lib. bdg. 34.21 *(978-0-7614-3095-7(4)*, Benchmark Bks.) Marshall Cavendish Corp.

—Myths of the World - Group 2, 4 bks., Set. Incl. Ancient Africans. lib. bdg. 34.21 *(978-0-7614-3099-5(7))*; Ancient Mesopotamians. lib. bdg. 34.21 *(978-0-7614-3095-7(4))*; Ancient Romans. (Illus.). (J). lib. bdg. 34.21 *(978-0-7614-3094-0(6))*; Aztecs. lib. bdg. 34.21 *(978-0-7614-3096-4(2))*; 96p. (gr. 6-18). (Myths of the World 2 Ser.). 2008. Set lib. bdg. 136.84 *(978-0-7614-3093-3(8)*, Benchmark Bks.) Marshall Cavendish Corp.

Schomp, Virginia & Hinds, Kathryn. Mermaids. 2013. (Illus.). 64p. (J). (gr. 4-8). 34.21 *(978-0-7614-4924-9(8))* Cavendish Square Publishing.

Schulte, Mary. The Minotaur. 2008. (Monsters Ser.). (ENG., Illus.). 48p. (gr. 4-7). lib. bdg. 35.20 *(978-0-7377-3590-1(2))* Cengage Gale.

Schuman, Michael A. Maya & Aztec Mythology Rocks! Bock, William Sauts, illus. 2011. (Mythology Rocks! Ser.). 128p. (J). (gr. 6-18). pap. 10.95 *(978-1-59845-327-0(0))*; lib. bdg. 33.27 *(978-0-7660-3899-8(8))* Enslow Pubs., Inc.

Scurman, Ike & Malam, John. Ancient Roman Civilization. D'Ottavi, Francesca, illus. 2009. (Ancient Civilizations & Their Myths & Legends Ser.). 48p. (YA). (gr. 5-9). lib. bdg. 29.25 *(978-1-4042-8038-0(3))* Rosen Publishing Group, Inc., The.

Shahrukh Husain. Greece. 2004. (Stories from Ancient Civilizations Ser.). (J). lib. bdg. 27.10 *(978-1-58340-619-9(0))* Black Rabbit Bks.

Shaughnessy, Edward L. Exploring the Life, Myth, & Art of Ancient China. 2009. (Civilizations of the World Ser.). (Illus.). 144p. (J). (gr. 7-12). lib. bdg. 42.60 *(978-1-4358-5617-2(1))* Rosen Publishing Group, Inc., The.

Sheppard, Si. Heroes of the Trojan War. 2015. (Heroes & Legends Ser.). (ENG., Illus.). 80p. (J). (gr. 7-8). 35.60 *(978-1-4994-6172-5(0)*, Rosen Young Adult) Rosen Publishing Group, Inc., The.

Shone, Rob. Greek Myths. 2006. (Graphic Mythology Ser.). (ENG., Illus.). 48p. (J). (gr. 4-7). lib. bdg. 31.95 *(978-1-4042-0801-8(1))*; (gr. 5-8). pap. 14.05 *(978-1-4042-0813-1(5))* Rosen Publishing Group, Inc., The.

Silva, Gabriel, adapted by. HERACLES -Doce años tras la Inmortalidad. 2006. (SPA.). 32p. *(978-958-30-2002-5(8))* Panamericana Editorial.

—POSIDÓN -el dios del Mar- 2005. (SPA.). 32p. *(978-958-30-2003-2(6))* Panamericana Editorial.

—ZEUS -el padre de los Dioses. 2006. (SPA.). 32p. *(978-958-30-2000-1(1))* Panamericana Editorial.

Simonson, Louise. The Death of Balder. Garcia, Eduardo, illus. 2016. (Norse Myths: a Viking Graphic Novel Ser.). (ENG.). 56p. (gr. 3-4). lib. bdg. 27.99 *(978-1-4965-3488-0(3))* Stone Arch Bks.

Smith, Neil. Jason & the Argonauts, 1 vol. 2015. (ENG., Illus.). 80p. (J). 35.60 *(978-1-4777-8138-8(2)*, Rosen Young Adult) Rosen Publishing Group, Inc., The.

Sperling, Vatsala. Ganga: The River That Flows from Heaven to Earth. Johari, Harish & Weltevrede, Pieter, illus. 2008. (ENG.). 32p. (J). (gr. -1-6). 15.95 *(978-1-59143-089-6(5))* Bear & Co.

—Kama: The Greatest Archer in the World. Johari, Sandeep, illus. 2007. (ENG.). 32p. (J). (gr. -1-6). 15.95 *(978-1-59143-073-5(9)*, Bear Cub Bks.) Bear & Co.

Spies, Karen Bornemann. Heroes in Greek Mythology Rock! Bock, William Sauts, illus. 2011. (Mythology Rocks! Ser.). 128p. (J). (gr. 6-18). pap. 10.95 *(978-1-59845-331-7(9))* Enslow Pubs., Inc.

Squier, Robert, illus. The Story of Cassiopeia: A Roman Constellation Myth, 1 vol. 2012. (Night Sky Stories Ser.). (ENG.). 24p. (gr. 2-3). pap. 8.95 *(978-1-4048-7716-0(9))* Picture Window Bks.

Steele, Philip. Incredible Quests: Epic Journeys in Myth & Legend. Climpson, Sue, illus. 2006. (ENG.). 48p. (J). (gr. 3-7). pap. 11.99 *(978-1-84476-247-7(5))* Anness Publishing GBR. Dist: National Bk. Network.

Storrie, Paul D. Amaterasu. 2008. pap. 52.95 *(978-0-8225-9459-8(5))* Lerner Publishing Group.

—Amaterasu: Return of the Sun. Randall, Ron, illus. 2007. (Graphic Myths & Legends Ser.). (ENG.). 48p. (J). (gr. 4-8). lib. bdg. 27.93 *(978-0-8225-5968-9(4))* Lerner Publishing Group.

—Amaterasu: Return of the Sun - A Japanese Myth. Randall, Ron, illus. 2010. (Rise & Shine Ser.). (ENG.). 48p. (C). (gr. 4-8). per. 14.95 *(978-0-8225-6573-4(0))* National Geographic School Publishing, Inc.

Sutcliff, Rosemary. Black Ships Before Troy: The Story of the Iliad. 2005. (ENG.). 176p. (YA). (gr. 7). mass mkt. 7.99 *(978-0-553-49483-9(X)*, Laurel Leaf) Random Hse. Children's Bks.

Swain, Cynthia & Benchmark Education Co., LLC. Opinions about Odysseus: A Greek Hero. Ramos, Jose, illus. 2014. (Text Connections Ser.). (J). (gr. 3). *(978-1-4509-9669-3(8))* Benchmark Education Co.

Szac, Murielle. The Adventures of Hermes, God of Thieves: 100 Journeys Through Greek Mythology. Provata-Carlone, Mika, tr. from FRE. 2015. (ENG.). 380p. (J). (gr. 3-7). 24.95 *(978-1-78269-030-6(1)*, Pushkin Children's Bks.) Steerforth Pr.

Takvorian, Nadine, illus. Jason & the Argonauts, 1 vol. 2011. (Greek Myths Ser.). (ENG.). 32p. (gr. 4-5). lib. bdg. 28.65 *(978-1-4048-6669-0(8)*, 1329957) Picture Window Bks.

Temple, Teri. Aphrodite. 2016. (J). *(978-1-4896-4631-6(0))* Weigl Pubs., Inc.

—Aphrodite: Goddess of Love & Beauty. Squier, Robert, illus. 2012. (Greek Mythology Ser.). (ENG.). 32p. (J). (gr. 2-5). 29.93 *(978-1-61473-253-2(1)*, 204926) Child's World, Inc., The.

—Apollo. 2016. (J). *(978-1-4896-4633-0(7))* Weigl Pubs., Inc.

—Ares. 2016. (J). *(978-1-4896-4635-4(3))* Weigl Pubs., Inc.

—Ares: God of War. Squier, Robert, illus. 2012. (Greek Mythology Ser.). (ENG.). 32p. (J). (gr. 2-5). 29.93 *(978-1-61473-255-6(8)*, 204928) Child's World, Inc., The.

—Artemis. 2016. (J). *(978-1-4896-4637-8(X))* Weigl Pubs., Inc.

—Athena. 2016. (J). *(978-1-4896-4639-2(6))* Weigl Pubs., Inc.

—Athena: Goddess of Wisdom, War, & Crafts. Squier, Robert, illus. 2012. (Greek Mythology Ser.). (ENG.). 32p. (J). (gr. 2-5). 29.93 *(978-1-61473-257-0(4)*, 204930) Child's World, Inc., The.

—Eros. 2016. (J). *(978-1-4896-4641-5(8))* Weigl Pubs., Inc.

—Eros: God of Love. Squier, Robert, illus. 2012. (Greek Mythology Ser.). (ENG.). 32p. (J). (gr. 2-5). 29.93 *(978-1-61473-258-7(2)*, 204931) Child's World, Inc., The.

—Hades. 2016. (J). *(978-1-4896-4643-9(4))* Weigl Pubs., Inc.

—Hephaestus. 2016. (J). *(978-1-4896-4645-3(0))* Weigl Pubs., Inc.

—Hera. 2016. (J). *(978-1-4896-4647-7(7))* Weigl Pubs., Inc.

—Hermes. 2016. (J). *(978-1-4896-4649-1(3))* Weigl Pubs., Inc.

—Poseidon. 2016. (J). *(978-1-4896-4651-4(5))* Weigl Pubs., Inc.

—Zeus. 2016. (J). *(978-1-4896-4653-8(1))* Weigl Pubs., Inc.

Temple, Teri & Temple, Emily. Diana: Goddess of Hunting & Protector of Animals. Young, Eric, illus. 2015. (Roman Mythology Ser.). (ENG.). 32p. (J). (gr. 2-5). 29.93 *(978-1-63143-716-8(X)*, 208559) Child's World, Inc., The.

—Juno: Queen of the Gods, Goddess of Marriage. Young, Eric, illus. 2015. (Roman Mythology Ser.). (ENG.). 32p. (J). (gr. 2-5). 29.93 *(978-1-63143-717-5(8)*, 208560) Child's World, Inc., The.

—Jupiter: King of the Gods, God of Sky & Storms. Young, Eric, illus. 2015. (Roman Mythology Ser.). (ENG.). 32p. (J). (gr. 2-5). 29.93 *(978-1-63143-718-2(6)*, 208561) Child's World, Inc., The.

—Mars: God of War. Young, Eric, illus. 2015. (Roman Mythology Ser.). (ENG.). 32p. (J). (gr. 2-5). 29.93 *(978-1-63143-719-9(4)*, 208562) Child's World, Inc., The.

—Mercury: God of Travels & Trade. Young, Eric, illus. 2015. (Roman Mythology Ser.). (ENG.). 32p. (J). (gr. 2-5). 29.93 *(978-1-63143-720-5(8)*, 208563) Child's World, Inc., The.

—Minerva: Goddess of Wisdom, War, & Crafts. Young, Eric, illus. 2015. (Roman Mythology Ser.). (ENG.). 32p. (J). (gr. 2-5). 29.93 *(978-1-63143-721-2(6)*, 208564) Child's World, Inc., The.

—Neptune: God of the Sea & Earthquakes. Young, Eric, illus. 2015. (Roman Mythology Ser.). (ENG.). 32p. (J). (gr. 2-5). 29.93 *(978-1-63143-722-9(4)*, 208565) Child's World, Inc., The.

—Pluto: God of the Underworld. Young, Eric, illus. 2015. (Roman Mythology Ser.). (ENG.). 32p. (J). (gr. 2-5). 29.93 *(978-1-63143-723-6(2)*, 208566) Child's World, Inc., The.

—Saturn: God of Sowing & Seeds. Young, Eric, illus. 2015. (Roman Mythology Ser.). (ENG.). 32p. (J). (gr. 2-5). 29.93 *(978-1-63143-724-3(0)*, 208567) Child's World, Inc., The.

—Venus: Goddess of Love & Beauty. Young, Eric, illus. 2015. (Roman Mythology Ser.). (ENG.). 32p. (J). (gr. 2-5). 29.93 *(978-1-63143-725-0(9)*, 208568) Child's World, Inc., The.

Tracy, Kathleen. The Life & Times of Homer. 2004. (Biography from Ancient Civilizations Ser.). (Illus.). 48p. (J). (gr. 4-8). lib. bdg. 29.95 *(978-1-58415-260-6(5))* Mitchell Lane Pubs., Inc.

—Medusa. 2010. (Monsters in Myth Ser.). (Illus.). 48p. (J). (gr. 4-7). lib. bdg. 29.95 *(978-1-58415-928-5(6))* Mitchell Lane Pubs., Inc.

Turnbull, Ann. Greek Myths. Young, Sarah, illus. 2010. (ENG.). 168p. (J). (gr. 5). 18.99 *(978-0-7636-5111-4(7))* Candlewick Pr.

Turner, Tracey. Hard As Nails in Myths & Legends. 2015. (Hard As Nails in History Ser.). (ENG., Illus.). 64p. (J). (gr. 3-7). lib. bdg. *(978-0-7787-1520-7(5))* Crabtree Publishing Co.

Turner, Tracey & Kindberg, Sally. The Comic Strip Big Fat Book of Knowledge. 2012. (ENG., Illus.). 288p. (J). (gr. 6-9). pap. 18.99 *(978-1-4088-0824-5(2)*, 9781408808245, Bloomsbury USA Childrens) Bloomsbury Publishing USA.

Uschan, Michael V. Chinese Mythology. 2014. (Mythology & Culture Worldwide Ser.). (ENG., Illus.). 128p. (gr. 7-10). lib. bdg. 39.40 *(978-1-4205-1146-8(7)*, Lucent Bks.) Cengage Gale.

Van Lente, Fred. Hercules, 1 vol. 2015. (ENG., Illus.). 80p. (J). 35.60 *(978-1-4777-8137-1(4)*, Rosen Young Adult) Rosen Publishing Group, Inc., The.

Wargin, Kathy-jo. The Legend of the Petoskey Stone. van Frankenhuyzen, Gijsbert, illus. 2004. (Great Lakes Legend Ser.). (ENG.). 40p. (J). 17.95 *(978-1-58536-217-2(4))* Sleeping Bear Pr.

Wildwood, Gretchen. Ancient Mesopotamian Civilization. Cantucci, Alessandro & Morandi, Andrea, illus. 2009. (Ancient Civilizations & Their Myths & Legends Ser.). (YA).

(gr. 5-9). lib. bdg. 29.25 *(978-1-4042-8037-3(5))* Rosen Publishing Group, Inc., The.

Wilkinson, Philip. Chinese Myth: A Treasury of Legends, Art, & History. 2007. (Myth Ser.). (Illus.). 96p. (J). (gr. 4-7). pap. 7.99 *(978-0-7858-2348-3(4)*, Chartwell) Book Sales, Inc.

—Chinese Myth: A Treasury of Legends, Art, & History. 2007. (ENG., Illus.). 96p. (C). (gr. 6-18). lib. bdg. 158.00 *(978-0-7656-8103-4(X)*, Y181705) Routledge.

Williams, Marcia. Greek Myths. Williams, Marcia, illus. 2011. (ENG., Illus.). 40p. (J). (gr. k-4). pap. 8.99 *(978-0-7636-5384-2(5))* Candlewick Pr.

Wolfson, Evelyn. Mythology of the Romans. 2014. (Mythology, Myths, & Legends Ser.). 96p. (J). (gr. 6-12). 27.94 *(978-0-7660-6187-3(6))* Enslow Pubs., Inc.

World Book, Inc Staff, contrib. by. Myths & Legends of Africa. 2015. (Illus.). 64p. (J). *(978-0-7166-2631-2(4))* World Bk., Inc.

—Tales Through Time: A Supplement to Childcraft-The How & Why Library. 2009. (Illus.). 204p. (J). *(978-0-7166-0622-2(4))* World Bk., Inc.

World Mythology. 2003. 320p. 5.98 *(978-1-4054-0326-9(8))* Parragon, Inc.

The World of Mythology, 5 bks., Set. Incl. Celtic Myth: A Treasury of Legends, Art, & History. Harpur, James. lib. bdg. 158.00 *(978-0-7656-8102-7(1)*, Y181569); Chinese Myth: A Treasury of Legends, Art, & History. Wilkinson, Philip. lib. bdg. 158.00 *(978-0-7656-8103-4(X)*, Y181705); Classical Myth: A Treasury of Greek & Roman Legends, Art, & History. Bingham, Jane. lib. bdg. 140.00 *(978-0-7656-8104-1(8)*, Y181755); Egyptian Myth: A Treasury of Legends, Art, & History. Kramer, Ann. lib. bdg. 158.00 *(978-0-7656-8105-8(6)*, Y182128); Mesoamerican Myth: A Treasury of Legends, Art, & History. Ganeri, Anita. lib. bdg. 158.00 *(978-0-7656-8106-5(4)*, Y182745); (C). (gr. 6-18). (ENG., Illus.). 96p. 2007. Set lib. bdg. 158.00 *(978-0-7656-8101-0(3)*, Y184677) Routledge.

Yasuda, Anita. Dragon, the Phoenix, & the Beautiful Pearl: A Chinese Dragon Spirit Myth. 2014. (Short Tales Chinese Myths Ser.). 32p. (J). (gr. 3-6). lib. bdg. 24.21 *(978-1-62402-030-8(5)*, Short Tales) Magic Wagon.

—Jade Emperor: A Chinese Zodiac Myth. 2014. (Short Tales Chinese Myths Ser.). 32p. (J). (gr. 3-6). lib. bdg. 24.21 *(978-1-62402-031-5(3)*, Short Tales) Magic Wagon.

—Monkey King: A Chinese Monkey Spirit Myth. 2014. (Short Tales Chinese Myths Ser.). 32p. (J). (gr. 3-6). lib. bdg. 24.21 *(978-1-62402-032-2(1)*, Short Tales) Magic Wagon.

—N Gua Mends the Sky: A Chinese Flood Myth. 2014. (Short Tales Chinese Myths Ser.). 32p. (J). (gr. 3-6). lib. bdg. 24.21 *(978-1-62402-033-9(X)*, Short Tales) Magic Wagon.

—Pangu Separates the Sky from the Earth: A Chinese Creation Myth. 2014. (Short Tales Chinese Myths Ser.). (Illus.). 32p. (J). (gr. 3-6). lib. bdg. 24.21 *(978-1-62402-034-6(8)*, Short Tales) Magic Wagon.

—Yu the Great Conquers the Flood: A Chinese Nature Myth. 2014. (Short Tales Chinese Myths Ser.). 32p. (J). (gr. 3-6). lib. bdg. 24.21 *(978-1-62402-035-3(6)*, Short Tales) Magic Wagon.

—The 12 Most Amazing American Myths & Legends. 2014. (ENG., Illus.). 32p. (J). *(978-1-63235-010-7(6))* Pr. Room Editions LLC.

—The 12 Most Amazing American Myths & Legends. 2015. (ENG., Illus.). 32p. (J). pap. 9.95 *(978-1-63235-070-1(X))* RiverStream Publishing.

MYTHOLOGY, CLASSICAL

Amery, Heather. Greek Myths. 2015. (Stories for Young Children Ser.). (ENG.). 128p. (J). (gr. k-5). 18.99 *(978-0-7945-3466-0(X)*, Usborne) EDC Publishing.

—Greek Myths for Young Children. Edwards, Linda, illus. 2004. (Greek Myths for Young Children Ser.). 128p. (J). (gr. -1-3). lib. bdg. 26.95 *(978-1-58086-261-5(6))*; 7.99 *(978-0-7945-0141-9(9)*, Usborne) EDC Publishing.

Antoniades, Basil. Having Fun with the Gods & Goddesses of the Ancient Greeks. 2008. 108p. pap. 9.94 *(978-0-615-24661-1(3))* Antoniades, Basil.

Bailey, Carolyn Sherwin. Wonder Stories the Best Myths for Boys & Girls. 2004. reprint ed. pap. 31.95 *(978-1-4179-3481-2(6))* Kessinger Publishing, LLC.

Barkow, Henriette. Pandora's Box: English Only. Mayo, Diana, illus. 2004. (ENG.). 32p. (J). pap. *(978-1-84444-380-2(9))* Mantra Lingua.

Bingham, Jane. Classical Myth: A Treasury of Greek & Roman Legends, Art, & History. 2007. (Myth Ser.). (Illus.). 96p. (J). (gr. 4-7). pap. 7.99 *(978-0-7858-2350-6(6))* Book Sales, Inc.

—Classical Myth: A Treasury of Greek & Roman Legends, Art, & History. 2007. (ENG., Illus.). 96p. (C). (gr. 6-18). lib. bdg. 140.00 *(978-0-7656-8104-1(8)*, Y181755) Routledge.

Bloom, Harold, ed. Sophocles' Oedipus Rex. 2007. (Bloom's Guides). 118p. (YA). (gr. 9-12). 30.00 *(978-0-7910-9360-3(3))* Facts On File, Inc.

Calcium Staff, contrib. by. The Epics of Greek Mythology, 1 vol. 2011. (Ancient Greek Mythology Ser.). (ENG.). 64p. (gr. 5-7). lib. bdg. 33.99 *(978-0-7565-4482-9(3)*, CPB Grades 4-8) Compass Point Bks.

—The Heroes & Mortals of Greek Mythology, 1 vol. 2011. (Ancient Greek Mythology Ser.). (ENG.). 64p. (gr. 5-7). lib. bdg. 33.99 *(978-0-7565-4480-5(7)*, CPB Grades 4-8) Compass Point Bks.

—The Monsters & Creatures of Greek Mythology, 1 vol. 2011. (Ancient Greek Mythology Ser.). (ENG.). 64p. (gr. 5-7). lib. bdg. 33.99 *(978-0-7565-4481-2(5)*, CPB Grades 4-8) Compass Point Bks.

Catherine, Mary. Classic Myths. 2004. reprint ed. pap. 1.99 *(978-1-4192-1334-2(2))*; pap. 15.95 *(978-1-4191-1334-5(8))* Kessinger Publishing, LLC.

Church, Alfred John. Stories of the Iliad & the Aeneid. 2006. pap. 24.95 *(978-1-4286-0468-1(5))* Kessinger Publishing, LLC.

—The Story of the Iliad. 2005. reprint ed. pap. 31.95 *(978-1-4191-5466-9(4))* Kessinger Publishing, LLC.

Clarke, M. The Story of Troy. 2007. (Illus.). 184p. per. *(978-1-4065-1381-3(4))* Dodo Pr.

Clarke, Michael. The Story of Troy. Lt. ed. 2007. (ENG.). 202p. pap. 22.99 *(978-1-4346-0682-2(1))* Creative Media Partners, LLC.

—The Story of Troy: The Story of Troy. 2007. (ENG.). 178p. pap. 19.99 *(978-1-4346-0607-5(4))* Creative Media Partners, LLC.

Clayton, Sally Pomme. Persephone. Lee, Virginia, illus. 2009. (ENG.). 28p. (J). (gr. 2-5). 18.00 *(978-0-8028-5349-3(8)*, Eerdmans Bks For Young Readers) Eerdmans, William B. Publishing Co.

Colum, Padraic. The Golden Fleece & the Heroes Who Lived Before Achilles. Pogány, Willy, illus. 2007. 144p. per. 8.99 *(978-1-4209-3040-5(0))* Digireads.com Publishing.

Craft, Charlotte. King Midas & the Golden Touch. Craft, Kinuko Y., illus. 2003. (ENG.). 32p. (J). (gr. -1-3). pap. 6.99 *(978-0-06-054063-0(X))* HarperCollins Pubs.

Curlee, Lynn. Mythological Creatures: A Classical Bestiary. Curlee, Lynn, illus. 2008. (ENG., Illus.). 40p. (J). (gr. 3-7). 19.99 *(978-1-4169-1453-2(6)*, Atheneum Bks. for Young Readers) Simon & Schuster Children's Publishing.

Daly, Kathleen N. Greek & Roman Mythology A to Z. 3rd rev. ed. 2009. (Mythology A to Z Ser.). (Illus.). 176p. (gr. 5-8). 45.00 *(978-1-60413-412-4(7)*, Chelsea Hse.) Facts On File, Inc.

DiPrimio, Pete. The Sphinx. 2010. (Monsters in Myth Ser.). (Illus.). 48p. (J). (gr. 4-7). lib. bdg. 29.95 *(978-1-58415-931-5(6))* Mitchell Lane Pubs., Inc.

Evans, C & Millard, A. Greek Myths & Legends. 2004. (Myths & Legends Ser.). 64p. (J). pap. 10.95 *(978-0-7945-0455-7(8))* EDC Publishing.

Evans, Cheryl & Millard, Anne. Greek Myths & Legends. Matthews, Rodney, illus. 2006. (Myths & Legends Ser.). 64p. (J). (gr. 6). lib. bdg. 18.95 *(978-1-58086-553-1(4))* EDC Publishing.

Evans, Hestia. Mythology. Steer, Dugald A., ed. Harris, Nick et al, illus. 2007. (Ologies Ser.). (ENG.). 32p. (J). (gr. 3-7). 24.99 *(978-0-7636-3403-2(4))* Candlewick Pr.

—The Mythology Handbook: An Introduction to the Greek Myths. Steer, Dugald A., ed. 2009. (Ologies Ser.). (ENG., Illus.). 80p. (J). (gr. 4-7). 12.99 *(978-0-7636-4291-4(6))* Candlewick Pr.

Fontes, Justine & Fontes, Ron. Atalanta: The Race Against Destiny. Yeates, Thomas, illus. (Graphic Myths & Legends Ser.). (ENG.). 48p. (gr. 4-8). 2008. per. 8.95 *(978-0-8225-6569-7(2))* 2007. (J). lib. bdg. 27.93 *(978-0-8225-5965-8(X))* Lerner Publishing Group.

Fontes, Ron & Fontes, Justine. Demeter & Persephone. 2008. pap. 52.95 *(978-0-8225-9461-1(7))* Lerner Publishing Group.

Francillon, R. E. Gods & Heroes: An Introduction to Greek Mythology (Yesterday's Classics) 2007. 276p. per. 11.95 *(978-1-59915-085-7(9))* Yesterday's Classics.

Freeman, Philip. Heroes of Olympus. Willis, Drew, illus. 2012. (ENG.). 352p. (J). (gr. 3-7). 17.99 *(978-1-4424-1729-8(3)*, Simon & Schuster Bks. For Young Readers) Simon & Schuster Bks. For Young Readers.

—Heroes of Olympus. Willis, Drew, illus. 2013. (ENG.). 352p. (J). (gr. 3-7). pap. 10.99 *(978-1-4424-1730-4(7)*, Simon & Schuster Bks. For Young Readers) Simon & Schuster Bks. For Young Readers.

Geras, Adèle. Troy. 2004. 368p. (J). (gr. 8-18). pap. 48.00 incl. audio *(978-0-8072-2288-1(7)*, Listening Library) Random Hse. Audio Publishing Group.

Gerstein, Mordicai. I Am Pan. 2016. (ENG., Illus.). 80p. (J). 18.99 *(978-1-62672-035-0(5)*, 9781626720350) Roaring Brook Pr.

Gifford, Clive. Think Again! False Facts Attacked & Myths Busted. 2013. (Think Again! Ser.). (ENG., Illus.). 160p. (J). (gr. 3-7). 18.99 *(978-0-7534-7069-5(1)*, 9780753470695, Kingfisher) Roaring Brook Pr.

Gunderson, Jessica. Olympians vs. Titans: An Interactive Mythological Adventure. Arcabascio, Carolyn, illus. 2017. (You Choose: Ancient Greek Myths Ser.). (ENG.). 112p. (gr. 3-4). lib. bdg. 31.99 *(978-1-5157-4820-5(0)*, You Choose Bks.) Capstone Press of Coughlan Cos.

—Olympians vs. Titans: An Interactive Mytholoical Adventure. 2017. (Illus.). 112p. (J). *(978-1-4747-3767-8(6))* Capstone Press of Coughlan Cos.

Harris, Nick, illus. The Wooden Horse of Troy, 1 vol. 2011. (Greek Myths Ser.). (ENG.). 32p. (gr. 4-5). lib. bdg. 28.65 *(978-1-4048-6670-6(1))* Picture Window Bks.

Hawthorne, Nathaniel. Tanglewood Tales. Sterrett, Virginia, illus. 2012. (Calla Editions Ser.). (ENG.). 304p. (gr. 4). 40.00 *(978-1-60660-026-9(5))* Dover Pubns., Inc.

—Tanglewood Tales. Pogány, Willy, illus. 2009. 272p. pap. 11.95 *(978-1-59915-091-8(3))* Yesterday's Classics.

—A Wonder Book: Heroes & Monsters of Greek Mythology. 2003. (Dover Children's Evergreen Classics Ser.). (ENG.). 176p. (J). (gr. 3-8). pap. 5.99 *(978-0-486-43209-0(2))* Dover Pubns., Inc.

—A Wonder Book & Tanglewood Tales. Lt. ed. 2004. (Large Print Ser.). 563p. 26.00 *(978-1-58287-673-3(8))* North Bks.

Herdling, Glenn. Greek Mythology: Jason & the Golden Fleece. (Jr. Graphic Mythologies Ser.). (ENG.). 24p. (J). (gr. 2-3). 2009. 47.90 *(978-1-61513-864-7(1)*, PowerKids Pr.) 2007. (Illus.). lib. bdg. 25.25 *(978-1-4042-3396-6(2))* Rosen Publishing Group, Inc., The.

—Jason & the Golden Fleece: A Greek Myth. 2007. (Jr. Graphic Mythologies Ser.). (ENG., Illus.). 24p. (J). (gr. 3-8). pap. 10.60 *(978-1-4042-2149-9(2)*, PowerKids Pr.) Rosen Publishing Group, Inc., The.

Hibbert, Clare. Terrible Tales of Ancient Greece, Vol. 1. 2014. (Monstrous Myths Ser.). (ENG.). 32p. (J). (gr. 4-5). pap. 10.50 *(978-1-4824-0184-4(3))* Stevens, Gareth Publishing LLLP.

Hoena, Blake. Hades & the Underworld: An Interactive Mythological Adventure. Takvorian, Nadine, illus. 2017. (You Choose: Ancient Greek Myths Ser.). (ENG.). 112p. (gr. 3-4). lib. bdg. 31.99 *(978-1-5157-4823-6(5)*, You Choose Bks.) Capstone Press of Coughlan Cos.

—The Trojan War: An Interactive Mythological Adventure. Takvorian, Nadine, illus. 2017. (You Choose: Ancient Greek Myths Ser.). (ENG.). 112p. (gr. 3-4). lib. bdg. 31.99 *(978-1-5157-4822-9(7)*, You Choose Bks.) Capstone Press of Coughlan Cos.

Hoena, Blake, retold by. The 12 Labors of Hercules: A Graphic Retelling. 2015. (Ancient Myths Ser.). (ENG.). 32p. (gr. 3-4). lib. bdg. 30.65 *(978-1-4914-2071-3(5)*, Graphic Library) Capstone Press of Coughlan Cos.

Hoena, Blake & Gunderson, Jessica. You Choose: Ancient Greek Myths. 2017. (You Choose: Ancient Greek Myths Ser.). (ENG.). 112p. (gr. 3-4). 255.92 *(978-1-5157-4824-3(3)*, You Choose Bks.) Capstone Press of Coughlan Cos.

Houle, Michelle M. Gods & Goddesses in Greek Mythology Rock! Bock, William Sauts, illus. 2011. (Mythology Rocks! Ser.). 128p. (J). (gr. 6-18). lib. bdg. 33.27 *(978-0-7660-3897-4(1))* Enslow Pubs., Inc.

Jeffrey, Gary. Centaurs. Poluzzi, Alessandro, illus. 2012. (Graphic Mythical Creatures Ser.). (ENG.). 24p. (J). (gr. 3-5). pap. 8.15 *(978-1-4339-6753-5(7))*; lib. bdg. 23.95 *(978-1-4339-6751-1(0))* Stevens, Gareth Publishing LLLP. (Gareth Stevens Learning Library).

Jennings, Ken. Greek Mythology. Lowery, Mike, illus. 2014. (Ken Jennings' Junior Genius Guides). (ENG.). 160p. (J). (gr. 3-5). 12.99 *(978-1-4814-2615-2(X)*, Little Simon) Little Simon.

Judd, Mary Catherine. Classic Myths. 2007. 148p. pap. 18.99 *(978-1-4346-2099-6(9))*; 156p. pap. 21.99 *(978-1-4346-2127-6(8))* Creative Media Partners, LLC.

—Classic Myths. MacDonall, Angus, illus. 2007. 172p. per. *(978-1-4065-4675-0(5))* Dodo Pr.

Katz, Leon. The Greek Myths: Puppet Plays for Children from Ovid's Metamorphoses. 2004. (ENG.). 160p. pap. 12.95 *(978-1-55783-502-4(0)*, 1557835020, Applause Theatre & Cinema) Leonard, Hal Corp.

Kendree, McLean, illus. Pandora's Vase, 1 vol. 2011. (Greek Myths Ser.). (ENG.). 32p. (gr. 4-5). lib. bdg. 28.65 *(978-1-4048-6668-3(X))* Picture Window Bks.

Kimmel, Eric A. The Mcelderry Book of Greek Myths. Montserrat, Pep, illus. 2008. (ENG.). 112p. (J). (gr. 1-5). 21.99 *(978-1-4169-1534-8(6)*, McElderry, Margaret K. Bks.) McElderry, Margaret K. Bks.

Korba, Joanna. Demeter & Persephone: A Myth from Ancient Greece. 2006. (J). pap. *(978-1-4108-7166-4(5))* Benchmark Education Co.

Kovacs, Charles. Ancient Greece, 1 vol. 2004. (ENG.). 176p. (J). pap. 20.00 *(978-0-86315-429-4(8))* Floris Bks. GBR. Dist: SteinerBooks, Inc.

Leonard, Scott A. Myths & Legends of Ancient Greece. 2015. (Illus.). 64p. (J). *(978-0-7166-2634-3(9))* World Bk., Inc.

Limke, Jeff. Jason. 2008. pap. 52.95 *(978-0-8225-9462-8(5))* Lerner Publishing Group.

Loewen, Nancy. Cyclops Tells All: The Way EYE See It, 1 vol. Pentney, Ryan, illus. 2014. (Other Side of the Myth Ser.). (ENG.). 32p. (gr. 2-3). lib. bdg. 27.32 *(978-1-4795-2180-7(9))* Picture Window Bks.

Loewen, Nancy, et al. The Other Side of the Myth, 1 vol. Gilpin, Stephen & Pentney, Ryan, illus. 2014. (Other Side of the Myth Ser.). (ENG.). 32p. (gr. 2-3). lib. bdg. 109.28 *(978-1-4795-3336-7(X))* Picture Window Bks.

Loria, Laura. What Is a Constellation? 2014. (Let's Find Out! Ser.). 32p. (J). (gr. 3-6). 23.45 *(978-1-62275-476-2(X))* Rosen Publishing Group, Inc., The.

Lupton, Hugh, et al. The Adventures of Achilles. Henaff, Carole, illus. 2012. (Advanced Readers: Classics Ser.). (ENG.). (J). 128p. (gr. 3-6). pap. 12.99 *(978-1-84686-800-9(9))*; 96p. (gr. 6-9). 23.99 *(978-1-84686-420-9(8))* Barefoot Bks., Inc.

McCaughrean, Geraldine. Los Doce Trabajos de Hércules: Eco y Narciso. Barroso, Paz, tr. Ross, Tony, illus. 2005. (Mythology Series Collection Mitos Ser.).Tr. of Twelve Labours of Heracles. (SPA.). 48p. (J). (gr. 2-3). 9.95 *(978-84-348-6429-0(0))* SM Ediciones ESP. Dist: Iaconi, Mariuccia Bk. Imports.

McCaughrean, Geraldine, retold by. Odysseus. 2004. (Heroes Ser.). (ENG., Illus.). 128p. (J). 17.95 *(978-0-8126-2721-3(0))* Cricket Bks.

Mckerley, Jennifer Guess. Hydra. 2008. (Monsters Ser.). (ENG., Illus.). 48p. (gr. 4-7). lib. bdg. 35.20 *(978-0-7377-4081-3(7)*, LML02109-242876) Cengage Gale.

Mitchell Lane Publishers Inc. Staff. Profiles in Greek & Roman Mythology, 15 vols., Set. 2010. (J). (gr. 4-8). lib. bdg. 449.25 *(978-1-58415-751-9(8))* Mitchell Lane Pubs., Inc.

Oberman, Sheldon. Island of the Minotaur: The Greek Myths of Ancient Crete. Drawson, Blair, illus. 2003. 96p. (J). 19.95 *(978-1-56656-531-8(6)*, Crocodile Bks.) Interlink Publishing Group, Inc.

O'Connor, George. Poseidon: Earth Shaker. O'Connor, George, illus. 2013. (Olympians Ser.: 5). (ENG., Illus.). 80p. (J). (gr. 4-9). 18.99 *(978-1-59643-828-6(2)*, 9781596438286); pap. 9.99 *(978-1-59643-738-8(3)*, 9781596437388) Roaring Brook Pr. (First Second Bks.).

Orr, Tamra. Achilles. 2008. (Profiles in Greek & Roman Mythology Ser.). (Illus.). 48p. (YA). (gr. 4-7). lib. bdg. 29.95 *(978-1-58415-706-9(2))* Mitchell Lane Pubs., Inc.

—Apollo. 2008. (Profiles in Greek & Roman Mythology Ser.). (Illus.). 48p. (YA). (gr. 4-7). lib. bdg. 29.95 *(978-1-58415-704-5(6))* Mitchell Lane Pubs., Inc.

Osborne, Mary Pope. Mitos Griegos. (Torre de Papel Ser.). (SPA.). (YA). (gr. 6-18). 8.95 *(978-958-04-2863-3(8))* Norma S.A. COL. Dist: Distribuidora Norma, Inc.

Pandora's Box. 2004. (J). cd-rom *(978-1-84444-465-6(1))* Mantra Lingua.

The Parthenon Code. 2006. (ENG., Illus.). 29.95 *(978-0-9705438-3-7(2))* Solving Light Bks.

Payment, Simone. Greek Mythology. 2009. (Mythology Around the World Ser.). 64p. (gr. 5-5). 58.50 *(978-1-61514-750-2(0)*, Rosen Reference) Rosen Publishing Group, Inc., The.

Pearce, Q. L. The Furies. 2010. (Monsters Ser.). (ENG., Illus.). 48p. (J). 30.45 *(978-0-7377-5035-5(9)*, Kidhaven) Cengage Gale.

Peebles, Alice. Monsters of the Gods. Chilvers, Nigel, illus. 2015. (Mythical Beasts Ser.). (ENG.). 32p. (J). (gr. 3-6). 26.65 *(978-1-4677-6342-4(X)*, Lerner Pubns.) Lerner Publishing Group.

Pommaux, Yvan. Theseus & the Minotaur. Kutner, Richard, tr. from FRE. Pommaux, Yvan, illus. 2013. (TOON Graphic Mythology Ser.). (ENG., Illus.). 56p. (J). (gr. 2-7). 16.95 *(978-1-935179-61-0(6))* TOON Books / RAW Junior, LLC.

Profiles in Greek & Roman Mythology, 12 vols., Set. Incl. Achilles. Orr, Tamra. (YA). 2008. lib. bdg. 29.95 *(978-1-58415-706-9(2))*; Apollo. Orr, Tamra. (YA). 2008. lib. bdg. 29.95 *(978-1-58415-704-5(6))*; Artemis. O'Neal, Claire. (YA). 2007. lib. bdg. 29.95 *(978-1-58415-555-3(8))*; Athena. Roberts, Russell. (J). 2007. lib. bdg. 29.95 *(978-1-58415-556-0(6))*; Dionysus. Roberts, Russell. (YA). 2007. lib. bdg. 29.95 *(978-1-58415-557-7(4))*; Hercules. Whiting, Jim. (YA). 2007. lib. bdg. 29.95 *(978-1-58415-553-9(1))*; Jason. Whiting, Jim. (J). 2007. lib. bdg. 29.95 *(978-1-58415-552-2(3))*; Odysseus. Tracy, Kathleen. (J). 2008. lib. bdg. 29.95 *(978-1-58415-705-2(4))*; Perseus. Harkins, Susan Sales & Harkins, William H. (YA). 2007. lib. bdg. 29.95 *(978-1-58415-558-4(2))*; Poseidon. Roberts, Russell. (J). 2008. lib. bdg. 29.95 *(978-1-58415-707-6(0))*; Theseus. Tracy, Kathleen. (YA). 2007. lib. bdg. 29.95 *(978-1-58415-554-6(X))*; Zeus. Roberts, Russell. (YA). 2007. lib. bdg. 29.95 *(978-1-58415-559-1(0))*; (Illus.). 48p. (gr. 4-7). 2009. Set lib. bdg. 359.40 *(978-1-58415-708-3(9))* Mitchell Lane Pubs., Inc.

Redmond, Diane & Mould, Chris. Hercules - Superhero. 2005. (Collins Big Cat Ser.). (ENG.). 288p. (J). (gr. 1-3). pap. 7.99 *(978-0-00-718638-9(X))* HarperCollins Pubs. Ltd. GBR. Dist: Independent Pubs. Group.

Riordan, James. Jason & the Golden Fleece. Cockcroft, Jason, illus. 2004. 64p. (YA). *(978-1-84507-271-1(5))* ReiseArt Buchhandlung GmbH.

—Jason & the Golden Fleece. Cockcroft, Jason, tr. Cockcroft, Jason, illus. 2003. 64p. (J). *(978-0-7112-2081-2(6))* ReiseArt Buchhandlung GmbH.

Roberts, Russell. Athena. 2007. (Profiles in Greek & Roman Mythology Ser.). (Illus.). 48p. (J). (gr. 4-7). lib. bdg. 29.95 *(978-1-58415-556-0(6))* Mitchell Lane Pubs., Inc.

—The Cyclopes. 2010. (Monsters in Myth Ser.). (Illus.). 48p. (J). (gr. 4-7). lib. bdg. 29.95 *(978-1-58415-926-1(X))* Mitchell Lane Pubs., Inc.

—Dionysus. 2007. (Profiles in Greek & Roman Mythology Ser.). (Illus.). 48p. (YA). (gr. 4-7). lib. bdg. 29.95 *(978-1-58415-557-7(4))* Mitchell Lane Pubs., Inc.

—The Minotaur. 2010. (Monsters in Myth Ser.). (Illus.). 48p. (J). (gr. 4-7). lib. bdg. 29.95 *(978-1-58415-929-2(4))* Mitchell Lane Pubs., Inc.

—Poseidon. 2008. (Profiles in Greek & Roman Mythology Ser.). (Illus.). 48p. (J). (gr. 4-7). lib. bdg. 29.95 *(978-1-58415-707-6(0))* Mitchell Lane Pubs., Inc.

—Zeus. 2007. (Profiles in Greek & Roman Mythology Ser.). (Illus.). 48p. (YA). (gr. 4-7). lib. bdg. 29.95 *(978-1-58415-559-1(0))* Mitchell Lane Pubs., Inc.

Rose, Simon. Orion: The Myth & Science. 2015. (Illus.). 24p. (J). pap. *(978-1-5105-0268-0(8))* SmartBook Media, Inc.

Salariya, David. Ancient Greek Myths. 2013. (Illus.). 168p. (J). *(978-1-4351-5066-9(X))* Barnes & Noble, Inc.

Schomp, Virginia. The Ancient Greeks. 2007. (Myths of the World Ser.). (Illus.). 96p. (gr. 6-7). lib. bdg. 34.21 *(978-0-7614-2547-2(0)*, Benchmark Bks.) Marshall Cavendish Corp.

—The Ancient Romans. 2008. (Myths of the World Ser.). (Illus.). 96p. (J). (gr. 6-18). lib. bdg. 34.21 *(978-0-7614-3094-0(6)*, Benchmark Bks.) Marshall Cavendish Corp.

Seeley, Tim & Schulz, Barbara, illus. Jason: Quest for the Golden Fleece. 2006. (Graphic Myths & Legends Ser.). 48p. (J). (gr. 4-7). lib. bdg. 26.60 *(978-0-8225-5967-2(6))* Lerner Publishing Group.

Shanower, Eric. Betrayal, Pt. 1, Vol. 3. 2007. (ENG., Illus.). 176p. (YA). (gr. 10-18). 27.99 *(978-1-58240-845-3(9)*, 9781582408453) Image Comics.

Sherman, Patrice. Legendary Creatures. 2015. (Illus.). 64p. *(978-1-61900-067-4(9))* Eldorado Ink.

Shone, Rob. Greek Myths. 2009. (Graphic Mythology Ser.). (ENG.). 48p. (YA). (gr. 4-5). 58.50 *(978-1-61512-985-0(5)*, Rosen Reference) Rosen Publishing Group, Inc., The.

Spies, Karen Bornemann. Heroes in Greek Mythology Rock! Bock, William Sauts, illus. 2011. (Mythology Rocks! Ser.). 128p. (J). (gr. 6-18). lib. bdg. 33.27 *(978-0-7660-3900-1(5))* Enslow Pubs., Inc.

Spinner, Stephanie. Atlanta, la Cazadora. Holguin, Magdalena, tr. 2003. (Zona Libre Ser.). (SPA.). 174p. 7.50 *(978-958-04-7080-9(4))* Norma S.A. COL. Dist: Lectorum Pubns., Inc.

Spires, Elizabeth. I Am Arachne: Fifteen Greek & Roman Myths. Gerstein, Mordicai, illus. 2009. (ENG.). 112p. (J). (gr. 3-7). pap. 8.99 *(978-0-312-56125-3(3)*, 9780312561253) Square Fish.

Temple, Teri. Zeus: King of the Gods, God of Sky & Storms. Squier, Robert, illus. 2012. (Greek Mythology Ser.). (ENG.). 32p. (J). (gr. 2-5). 29.93 *(978-1-61473-264-8(7)*, 204937) Child's World, Inc., The.

Tracy, Kathleen. Cerberus. 2010. (Monsters in Myth Ser.). (Illus.). 48p. (J). (gr. 4-7). lib. bdg. 29.95 *(978-1-58415-924-7(3))* Mitchell Lane Pubs., Inc.

Ware, Kay & Sutherland, Lucille. Greek & Roman Myths. Kottmeyer, William, ed. 2011. 146p. 40.95 *(978-1-258-02410-9(1))* Literary Licensing, LLC.

West, David. Roman Myths. Watton, Ross, illus. 2006. (Graphic Mythology Ser.). (ENG.). 48p. (J). (gr. 4-7). lib. bdg. 31.95 *(978-1-4042-0803-2(8))* Rosen Publishing Group, Inc., The.

Whiting, Jim. Jason. 2007. (Profiles in Greek & Roman Mythology Ser.). (Illus.). 48p. (J). (gr. 4-7). lib. bdg. 29.95 *(978-1-58415-552-2(3))* Mitchell Lane Pubs., Inc.

Wilbur, Helen L. Z Is for Zeus: A Greek Mythology Alphabet. Juhasz, Victor, illus. rev. ed. 2008. (Art & Culture Ser.). (ENG.). 40p. (J). (gr. 1-7). 17.95 *(978-1-58536-341-4(3))* Sleeping Bear Pr.

Williams, Rose. The Labors of Aeneas: What a Pain It Was to Found the Roman Race. 2003. (Illus.). (YA). 18.00 *(978-0-86516-556-4(4))* Bolchazy-Carducci Pubs.

Woff, Richard. Pocket Dictionary of Greek & Roman Gods & Goddesses. 2003. (ENG., Illus.). 48p. (gr. 3-7). 9.95 *(978-0-89236-706-1(7))* Oxford Univ. Pr., Inc.

MYTHOLOGY, EGYPTIAN

Asselin, Kristine Carlson. Ancient Egyptian Myths. 2012. (Ancient Egyptian Civilization Ser.). (ENG.). 32p. (gr. 3-4). pap. 47.70 *(978-1-4296-8402-6(X))*; pap. 8.10 *(978-1-4296-7977-0(8))*; lib. bdg. 27.32 *(978-1-4296-7630-4(2))* Capstone Press of Coughlan Cos. (Fact Finders).

Bell, Michael & Quie, Sarah. Ancient Egyptian Civilization. D'Ottavi, Francesca, illus. 2009. (Ancient Civilizations & Their Myths & Legends Ser.). 48p. (YA). (gr. 5-9). lib. bdg. 29.25 *(978-1-4042-8034-2(0))* Rosen Publishing Group, Inc., The.

Broyles, Janell. Egyptian Mythology. 2005. (Mythology Around the World Ser.). (Illus.). 64p. (YA). (gr. 5-9). lib. bdg. 31.95 *(978-1-4042-0770-7(8))* Rosen Publishing Group, Inc., The.

Casey, Dawn. Isis & Osiris. Mayo, Diana & Mistry, Nilesh, illus. 2004. (ENG & HIN.). 32p. (J). pap. *(978-1-84444-433-5(3))*;

M
N
O

pap. *(978-1-84444-315-4(9))*; pap. *(978-1-84444-330-7(2))*; pap. *(978-1-84444-323-9(X))*; pap. *(978-1-84444-435-9(X))*; pap. *(978-1-84444-434-2(1))* Mantra Lingua.

Daning, Tom. Egyptian Mythology: Osiris & Isis. (Jr. Graphic Mythologies Ser.). (ENG.). 24p. 2009. (J). (gr. 2-3). 47.90 *(978-1-61513-861-6(7)*, PowerKids Pr.) 2007. (Illus.). (J). (gr. 2-5). lib. bdg. 25.25 *(978-1-4042-3399-7(7))* 2007. (Illus.). (gr. 3-8). pap. 10.60 *(978-1-4042-2152-9(2)*, PowerKids Pr.) Rosen Publishing Group, Inc., The.

—Mitología Egipcia: Isis y Osiris. 2009. (Historietas Juveniles: Mitologías (Jr. Graphic Mythologies) Ser.). (SPA., Illus.). 24p. (gr. 3-8). pap. 10.60 *(978-1-4358-3328-9(7)*, Editorial Buenas Letras) Rosen Publishing Group, Inc., The.

Doyle, Sheri. Understanding Egyptian Myths. 2012. (ENG.). 48p. (J). *(978-0-7787-4508-2(2))*; pap. *(978-0-7787-4513-6(9))* Crabtree Publishing Co.

Egyptian. 3rd rev. ed. 2010. (Mythology A to Z Ser.). (Illus.). 232p. (gr. 5-8). 45.00 *(978-1-60413-926-6(9)*, Chelsea Hse.) Facts On File, Inc.

Elgin, Kathy. Egyptian Myths. Sansom, Fiona, illus. 2009. (Myths from Many Lands Ser.). 48p. (YA). (gr. 2-6). pap. 12.85 *(978-1-60754-222-3(6))*; (gr. 4-7). 29.25 *(978-1-60754-221-6(8))* Windmill Bks.

Forest, Christopher. Ancient Egyptian Gods & Goddesses, 1 vol. 2012. (Ancient Egyptian Civilization Ser.). (ENG.). 32p. (gr. 3-4). pap. 8.10 *(978-1-4296-7970-1(0))*; pap. 47.70 *(978-1-4296-8400-2(3))*; lib. bdg. 27.32 *(978-1-4296-7628-1(0))* Capstone Press of Coughlan Cos. (Fact Finders).

Green, Roger Lancelyn. Tales of Ancient Egypt. 2016. (Puffin Pixels Ser.). (ENG., Illus.). 256p. (J). 11.99 *(978-0-14-751917-7(9)*, Puffin Books) Penguin Young Readers Group.

—Tales of Ancient Egypt. 2011. (Puffin Classics Ser.). (ENG., Illus.). 256p. (J). (gr. 5-7). 4.99 *(978-0-14-133259-8(X)*, Puffin Books) Penguin Young Readers Group.

Greenhaven Press Editors. Egyptian Mythology. Mckerley, Jennifer Guess, ed. 2012. (Mythology & Culture Worldwide Ser.). (ENG., Illus.). 128p. (gr. 7-10). lib. bdg. 34.45 *(978-1-4205-0745-4(1)*, Lucent Bks.) Cengage Gale.

Hibbert, Clare. Terrible Tales of Ancient Egypt, Vol. 1. 2014. (Monstrous Myths Ser.). (ENG.). 32p. (J). (gr. 4-5). 26.60 *(978-1-4824-0177-6(0))* Stevens, Gareth Publishing LLLP.

Hunt, Jilly. Greek Myths & Legends, 1 vol. 2013. (All about Myths Ser.). (ENG., Illus.). 48p. (gr. 5-8). 32.65 *(978-1-4109-5468-8(4))*; pap. 9.25 *(978-1-4109-5474-9(9))* Heinemann-Raintree.

Isis & Osiris. 2004. (J). cd-rom *(978-1-84444-461-8(9))* Mantra Lingua.

Jacq, Christian. Cuentos y Leyendas de la Época de Las Pirámides. Corral, Mercedes, tr. from FRE. 6th ed. 2003. (Fables & Legends Ser.). (SPA., Illus.). 144p. (J). 9.95 *(978-84-239-8893-8(7))* Espasa Calpe, S.A. ESP. Dist: Planeta Publishing Corp.

Jeffrey, Gary. Egyptian Myths. 2009. (Graphic Mythology Ser.). (ENG.). 48p. (YA). (gr. 4-5). 58.50 *(978-1-61512-982-9(0)*, Rosen Reference) Rosen Publishing Group, Inc., The.

—Egyptian Myths. Felmang, Romano, illus. 2006. (Graphic Mythology Ser.). (ENG.). 48p. (J). (gr. 4-7). lib. bdg. 31.95 *(978-1-4042-0800-1(3))*; (gr. 5-8). pap. 14.05 *(978-1-4042-0812-4(7))* Rosen Publishing Group, Inc., The.

Kramer, Ann. Egyptian Myth: A Treasury of Legends, Art, & History. 2007. (Myth Ser.). (Illus.). 96p. (J). (gr. 4-7). pap. 7.99 *(978-0-7858-2347-6(6)*, Chartwell) Book Sales, Inc.

—Egyptian Myth: A Treasury of Legends, Art, & History. 2007. (ENG., Illus.). 96p. (C). (gr. 6-18). lib. bdg. 158.00 *(978-0-7656-8105-8(6)*, Y182128) Routledge.

Mayo, Diana, illus. Isis & Osiris. 2004. (J). *(978-1-84444-326-0(4))*; *(978-1-84444-325-3(6))*; *(978-1-84444-324-6(8))*; *(978-1-84444-322-2(1))*; *(978-1-84444-321-5(3))*; (GER.). 30p. *(978-1-84444-320-8(5))*; *(978-1-84444-318-5(3))*; *(978-1-84444-316-1(7))*; *(978-1-84444-331-4(0))*; *(978-1-84444-329-1(9))*; *(978-1-84444-314-7(0))*; (SPA.). 30p. *(978-1-84444-327-7(2))*; *(978-1-84444-328-4(0))*; *(978-1-84444-313-0(2))*; (ENG & FRE.). 32p. pap. *(978-1-84444-319-2(1))* Mantra Lingua.

McNeely, Tom, illus. Isis & the Seven Scorpions, 1 vol. 2012. (Egyptian Myths Ser.). (ENG.). 32p. (gr. 3-4). pap. 8.95 *(978-1-4048-7241-7(8))* Picture Window Bks.

Napoli, Donna Jo. Treasury of Egyptian Mythology: Classic Stories of Gods, Goddesses, Monsters & Mortals. Balit, Christina, illus. 2013. (ENG.). 192p. (J). (gr. 3-7). 24.95 *(978-1-4263-1380-6(2))*; lib. bdg. 33.90 *(978-1-4263-1381-3(0))* National Geographic Society. (National Geographic Children's Bks.).

Nardo, Don. Mythology of the Egyptians. 2014. (Mythology, Myths, & Legends Ser.). 96p. (J). (gr. 6-12). 27.94 *(978-0-7660-6167-5(1))* Enslow Pubs., Inc.

Ollhoff, Jim. Egyptian Mythology, 1 vol. 2011. (World of Mythology Ser.). (ENG., Illus.). 32p. (J). (gr. 5-9). 27.07 *(978-1-61714-719-7(2)*, Abdo & Daughters) ABDO Publishing Co.

Orme, David. Ancient Mysteries. 2010. (Fact to Fiction Grafx Ser.). (Illus.). 36p. (J). lib. bdg. 16.95 *(978-1-60686-470-8(X))* Perfection Learning Corp.

Owings, Lisa. What We Get from Egyptian Mythology. 2015. (21st Century Skills Library: Mythology & Culture Ser.). (ENG., Illus.). 32p. (J). (gr. 3-6). pap. 14.21 *(978-1-63188-928-8(1)*, 205973) Cherry Lake Publishing.

Shahrukh Husain & Willey, Bee. Egypt. 2004. (Stories from Ancient Civilizations Ser.). (J). lib. bdg. 27.10 *(978-1-58340-618-2(2))* Black Rabbit Bks.

Viegas, Jennifer, ed. Critical Perspectives on Natural Disasters. 2006. (Scientific American Critical Anthologies on Environment & Climate Ser.). (Illus.). 247p. (J). (gr. 3-7). 37.95 *(978-1-4042-0824-7(0))* Rosen Publishing Group, Inc., The.

World Book, Inc Staff, contrib. by. Myths & Legends of Ancient Egypt. 2015. (Illus.). 64p. (J). *(978-0-7166-2633-6(0))* World Bk., Inc.

MYTHOLOGY, INDIAN

see Indian Mythology

MYTHOLOGY, NORSE

Allan, Tony. Exploring the Life, Myth, & Art of the Vikings. 2011. (Civilizations of the World Ser.). (YA). (gr. 7-12). lib. bdg. 42.60 *(978-1-4488-4833-1(4))* Rosen Publishing Group, Inc., The.

Bowen, Carl, et al. Gods & Thunder: A Graphic Novel of Old Norse Myths. Garcia, Eduardo et al, illus. 2017. (ENG.). 208p. (gr. 3-4). pap. 14.95 *(978-1-62370-848-1(6))* Capstone Young Readers of Coughlan Cos.

Colum, Padraic. The Children of Odin: The Book of Northern Myths. Pogány, Willy, illus. 2008. 216p. (gr. 5-9). pap. *(978-1-4065-9868-1(2))* Dodo Pr.

—The Children of Odin: The Book of Northern Myths. Pogány, Willy, illus. 2004. (ENG.). 288p. (J). (gr. 5-9). pap. 9.99 *(978-0-689-86885-6(5)*, Aladdin) Simon & Schuster Children's Publishing.

Colum, Padraic & Pogány, Willy. The Children of Odin the Book of Northern Myths. 2011. (Illus.). 224p. *(978-1-84902-498-3(7))* Benediction Classics.

Crabtree Staff & Williams, Brian. Understanding Norse Myths. 2012. (ENG., Illus.). 48p. (J). pap. *(978-0-7787-4532-7(5))* Crabtree Publishing Co.

Daly, Kathleen N. Norse Mythology A to Z, Third Edition. 3rd rev. ed. 2009. (Mythology A to Z Ser.). (Illus.). 144p. (gr. 5-8). 45.00 *(978-1-60413-411-7(9)*, Chelsea Hse.) Facts On File, Inc.

Dawson, Patricia A. Myths of the Norsemen. 2016. (World Mythologies Ser.). (ENG., Illus.). 96p. (J). (gr. 6-6). lib. bdg. 42.79 *(978-1-5026-0992-2(4))* Cavendish Square Publishing.

Ganeri, Anita. Norse Myths & Legends, 1 vol. 2013. (All about Myths Ser.). (ENG., Illus.). 48p. (gr. 5-8). 32.65 *(978-1-4109-4973-8(7))*; pap. 9.25 *(978-1-4109-4978-3(8))* Heinemann-Raintree.

Hopkins, Andrea. Viking Gods & Legends. 2009. (Viking Library). 24p. (gr. 3-3). 42.50 *(978-1-60854-258-1(0)*, PowerKids Pr.) Rosen Publishing Group, Inc., The.

Husain, Shahrukh. The Vikings. 2005. (Stories from Ancient Civilizations Ser.). (Illus.). 32p. (J). (gr. 4-18). lib. bdg. 27.10 *(978-1-58340-621-2(2)*, 1236428) Black Rabbit Bks.

Krieg, Katherine. What We Get from Norse Mythology. 2015. (21st Century Skills Library: Mythology & Culture Ser.). (ENG., Illus.). 32p. (J). (gr. 3-6). 29.93 *(978-1-63188-914-1(1)*, 205980) Cherry Lake Publishing.

Leonard, Scott A. Myths & Legends of Scandinavia. 2015. (Illus.). 63p. (J). *(978-0-7166-2636-7(5))* World Bk., Inc.

Limke, Jeff. Thor & Loki. 2008. pap. 52.95 *(978-0-8225-9458-1(7))* Lerner Publishing Group.

—Thor & Loki: In the Land of Giants - A Norse Myth. Randall, Ron, illus. 2006. (Graphic Myths & Legends Ser.). (ENG.). 48p. (J). (gr. 4-8). 27.93 *(978-0-8225-3087-9(2))* Lerner Publishing Group.

—Thor Y Loki: En la Tierra de Los Gigantes; Thor & Loki: in the Land of Giants. 2008. pap. 52.95 *(978-0-8225-9675-2(X))* Lerner Publishing Group.

Mabie, Hamilton Wright. Norse Stories Retold from the Eddas. 2006. (Illus.). pap. 30.95 *(978-1-4254-9336-3(X))* Kessinger Publishing, LLC.

Menges, Jeff A. Norse Gods & Goddesses. 2004. (Dover Classic Stories Coloring Book Ser.). (ENG., Illus.). 32p. (J). (gr. 3-8). pap., spiral bd. 3.99 *(978-0-486-43337-0(4))* Dover Pubns., Inc.

Napoli, Donna Jo. Treasury of Norse Mythology: Stories of Intrigue, Trickery, Love, & Revenge. Balit, Christina, illus. 2015. (ENG.). 192p. (J). (gr. 3-7). 24.99 *(978-1-4263-2098-9(1)*, National Geographic Children's Bks.) National Geographic Society.

Ollhoff, Jim. Norse Mythology, 1 vol. 2011. (World of Mythology Ser.). (ENG., Illus.). 32p. (gr. 5-9). 27.07 *(978-1-61714-726-5(5)*, Abdo & Daughters) ABDO Publishing Co.

Padraic & Colum, Padraic. The Children of Odin: Nordic Gods & Heroes. 2006. (Barnes & Noble Library of Essential Reading Ser.). (ENG.). 224p. pap. 9.95 *(978-0-7607-8331-3(4))* Barnes & Noble, Inc.

Rayner, Olivia, illus. World Book Myths & Legends Series, 8 vols., Vol. 8. 2007. (World Book Myths & Legends Ser.). 64p. (gr. 4-8). 239.00 *(978-0-7166-2613-8(6)*, 31020) World Bk., Inc.

Redmond, Shirley Raye, ed. Norse Mythology. 2012. (Mythology & Culture Worldwide Ser.). (ENG., Illus.). 128p. (J). (gr. 7-10). lib. bdg. 34.45 *(978-1-4205-0717-1(6)*, Lucent Bks.) Cengage Gale.

Rydberg, Viktor & Reaves, William P. Our Fathers' Godsaga: Retold for the Young. 2003. 223p. pap. 15.95 *(978-0-595-29978-2(4))* iUniverse, Inc.

Rydberg, Viktor & Reeves, William P. Our Fathers' Godsaga: Retold for the Young. Rydberg, Viktor, tr. 2003. (Illus.). 223p. 25.95 *(978-0-595-66097-1(5))* iUniverse, Inc.

Schomp, Virginia. The Norsemen. 2007. (Myths of the World Ser.). (Illus.). 96p. (gr. 6-7). lib. bdg. 34.21 *(978-0-7614-2548-9(9)*, Benchmark Bks.) Marshall Cavendish Corp.

Williams, Brian. Understanding Norse Myths. 2012. (ENG.). 48p. (J). *(978-0-7787-4527-3(9))* Crabtree Publishing Co.

Wilmot-Buxton, E. M. Viking Gods & Heroes. 2004. (Dover Children's Classics Ser.). (ENG.). 160p. (gr. 6-12). pap. 7.95 *(978-0-486-43704-0(3))* Dover Pubns., Inc.

Worley, Rob M. Heimdall. Moll, Shawn, illus. 2011. (Short Tales Norse Myths Ser.). 32p. (J). (gr. 3-6). 24.21 *(978-1-60270-566-1(6)*, 1315659) Magic Wagon.

Yasuda, Anita. Explore Norse Myths! With 25 Great Projects. Stone, Bryan, illus. 2015. (Explore Your World Ser.). (ENG.). 96p. (J). (gr. 1-5). 19.95 *(978-1-61930-316-4(7)*, 1398135) Open City Bks.

MYTHOLOGY, POLYNESIAN

Croy, Anita. Myths & Legends of Australia, New Zealand, & Pacific Islands. 2015. (Illus.). 64p. (J). *(978-0-7166-2629-9(2))* World Bk., Inc.

MYTHOLOGY IN ART

see Art and Mythology

MYTHS

see Mythology

N

NAGASAKI-SHI (JAPAN)

Bodden, Valerie. The Bombing of Hiroshima & Nagasaki. 2007. (Days of Change Ser.). (Illus.). 48p. (J). (gr. 4-7). lib. bdg. 31.35 *(978-1-58341-545-0(9)*, Creative Education) Creative Co., The.

—The Bombing of Hiroshima & Nagasaki: Odysseys in History. 2016. (Odysseys in History Ser.). (ENG., Illus.). 80p. (J). (gr. 7-10). pap. 14.99 *(978-1-62832-126-5(1)*, Creative Paperbacks) Creative Co., The.

Kaelberer, Angie Peterson & Langley, Andrew. Hiroshima & Nagasaki. 2017. (Eyewitness to World War II Ser.). (ENG.). 112p. (gr. 5-7). lib. bdg. 35.99 ***(978-0-7565-5584-9(1)***, CPB Grades 4-8) Compass Point Bks.

Orr, Tamra. The Atom Bomb: Creating & Exploding the First Nuclear Weapon. 2004. (Library of Weapons of Mass Destruction Ser.). (Illus.). 64p. (J). lib. bdg. 31.95 *(978-1-4042-0292-4(7))* Rosen Publishing Group, Inc., The.

Peppas, Lynn. Hiroshima & Nagasaki. 2013. (ENG., Illus.). 48p. (J). *(978-0-7787-1171-1(4))*; pap. *(978-0-7787-1179-7(X))* Crabtree Publishing Co.

Poolos, J. The Atomic Bombings of Hiroshima & Nagasaki. 2008. (Great Historic Disasters Ser.). (Illus.). 128p. (gr. 5-8). 35.00 *(978-0-7910-9738-0(2)*, Chelsea Hse.) Facts On File, Inc.

Stelson, Caren. Sachiko: A Nagasaki Bomb Survivor's Story. 2016. (ENG., Illus.). (gr. 5-12). 120p. 19.99 *(978-1-4677-8903-5(8))*; 144p. 38.65 *(978-1-5124-0893-5(X))*; 144p. 38.65 *(978-1-5124-1885-9(4))*; (YA). 9.99 *(978-1-5124-1884-2(6))* Lerner Publishing Group. (Carolrhoda Bks.).

NAMES—FICTION

August, Rachel. Adventures of Libby Nickel: What's your Mommy's First Name? 2011. 25p. (J). pap. 17.95 *(978-1-4327-6513-2(2))* Outskirts Pr., Inc.

Belonie, Shannon. Oliver Andrew Ostrich: My Full Name. 2008. 12p. pap. 8.74 *(978-1-4343-5849-3(6))* AuthorHouse.

Blackstone, Stella. Who Are You, Baby Kangaroo? Beaton, Clare, illus. 2004. 32p. (J). 14.99 *(978-1-84148-217-0(X))* Barefoot Bks., Inc.

Choi, Yangsook. The Name Jar. 2003. (gr. k-3). lib. bdg. 18.40 *(978-0-613-82979-3(4)*, Turtleback) Turtleback Bks.

Farnsley, Kathleen. This Little Piggy Named Pony. 2008. 24p. pap. 12.99 *(978-1-4389-2659-9(6))* AuthorHouse.

Gunderson, Jessica. Frankly, I'd Rather Spin Myself a New Name! The Story of Rumpelstiltskin As Told by Rumpelstiltskin. Bock, Janna, illus. 2016. (Other Side of the Story Ser.). (ENG.). 24p. (gr. 2-3). lib. bdg. 27.32 *(978-1-4795-8624-0(2))* Picture Window Bks.

Hartman, Colleen Kelley. My Grandma Calls Me Lovey. Hammons, Mark, illus. 2011. pap. 19.95 *(978-1-934333-26-6(3))* Eagle Bk. Bindery.

Ivey, Douglas G. The Three Cows. 2010. 28p. pap. 13.99 *(978-1-4520-4272-5(1))* AuthorHouse.

Kappler, Kathleen. Whitney's School Morning. 2004. 38p. pap. 24.95 *(978-1-4137-3711-0(0))* PublishAmerica, Inc.

Katz, Karen. Princess Baby. Katz, Karen, illus. 2008. (Princess Baby Ser.). (ENG., Illus.). 32p. (J). (gr. k-k). 14.99 *(978-0-375-84119-4(9)*, Schwartz & Wade Bks.) Random Hse. Children's Bks.

Kay, Cassandra. A Week in the Life of Mertyle. 2009. 96p. pap. 10.49 *(978-1-4389-4049-6(1))* AuthorHouse.

Little Bear, Shena. How the lone wolf got her Name. 2008. 80p. pap. 9.95 *(978-0-578-00171-5(3))* Stone Castle Publishing.

Mawhinney, Art & Johnson, Shane L., illus. OLIVIA Meets Olivia. 2011. (Olivia TV Tie-In Ser.). (ENG.). 24p. (J). (gr. -1-2). pap. 3.99 *(978-1-4424-4707-3(9)*, Simon Spotlight) Simon Spotlight.

Mervine, M. A. How Katie Got a Voice: (and a Cool New Nickname) 2012. 40p. pap. 19.57 *(978-1-4269-6649-1(0))* Trafford Publishing.

Neelon, Caleb. Lilman Makes a Name for Himself. 2004. (J). lib. bdg. *(978-0-9745150-0-7(0))* Cantab Publishing.

Raschka, Chris. New York Is English, Chattanooga Is Creek. Raschka, Chris, illus. 2005. (ENG., Illus.). 40p. (J). (gr. -1-2). 17.99 *(978-0-689-84600-7(2)*, Atheneum/Richard Jackson Bks.) Simon & Schuster Children's Publishing.

Recorvits, Helen. Me Llamo Yoon. Swiatkowska, Gabi, illus. 2003.Tr. of My Name is Yoon. (SPA.). 32p. (gr. k-2). 18.99 *(978-84-261-3335-9(5))* Juventud, Editorial ESP. Dist: Lectorum Pubns., Inc.

Renard Roach, Marietta. Come, Bless the Baby. 2006. 28p. pap. 21.95 incl. audio compact disk *(978-0-9768626-0-4(3))* Aaduna.

Roddy-Worsham, Clara. Bear Baby & New Baby Forever. 2012. 24p. 24.95 *(978-1-4626-4672-2(7))* America Star Bks.

Russo, Angela B. Beautiful. 2013. 28p. pap. 24.95 *(978-1-62709-040-7(1))* America Star Bks.

Siegel, Rv. A Bee Called Kangaroo. 2005. 81p. pap. 9.16 *(978-1-4116-2890-8(X))* Lulu Pr., Inc.

Walters, Eric. Laggan Lard Butts, 1 vol. 2006. (Orca Currents Ser.). (ENG.). 112p. (J). (gr. 5-9). per. 9.95 *(978-1-55143-518-3(7))* Orca Bk. Pubs. USA.

Yolen, Jane. My Father Knows the Names of Things. Jorisch, Stéphane, illus. 2010. (ENG.). 32p. (J). (gr. -1-3). 17.99 *(978-1-4169-4895-7(3)*, Simon & Schuster Bks. For Young Readers) Simon & Schuster Bks. For Young Readers.

NAMES, GEOGRAPHICAL

Herman, Debbie. From Pie Town to Yum Yum: Weird & Wacky Place Names Across the United States. Goldman, Linda Sarah, illus. 2011. (ENG.). 120p. (J). pap. 10.99 *(978-1-935279-79-2(3))* Kane Miller.

MacKinnon, Christopher. Canadian Sports Sites for Kids: Places Named for Speedsters, Scorers, & Other Sportsworld Citizens (Large Print 16pt) 2013. 208p. pap. *(978-1-4596-6305-3(5))* ReadHowYouWant.com, Ltd.

Places in Time: A Kid's Historic Guide to the Changing Names & Places of the World, 6 vols., Set. Incl. Brief Political & Geographic History of Africa: Where Are... Belgian Congo, Rhodesia, & Kush. Davenport, John. lib. bdg. 37.10 *(978-1-58415-624-6(4))*; Brief Political & Geographic History of Asia: Where Are... Saigon, Kampuchea, & Burma. Dillon, Doug. lib. bdg. 37.10 *(978-1-58415-623-9(6))*; Brief Political & Geographic History of Europe: Where Are... Prussia, Gaul, & the Holy Roman Empire. Davey, Frances. lib. bdg. 37.10 *(978-1-58415-625-3(2))*; Brief Political & Geographic History of Latin America: Where Are... Gran Colombia, la Plata, & Dutch Guiana. Rice, Earle, Jr. lib. bdg. 37.10 *(978-1-58415-626-0(0))*; Brief Political & Geographic History of North America: Where Are... New France, New Netherland, & New Sweden. Johnston, Lissa. lib. bdg. 37.10 *(978-1-58415-627-7(9))*; Brief Political & Geographic History of the Middle East: Where Are... Persia, Babylon, & the Ottoman Empire. Davenport, John. lib. bdg. 37.10 *(978-1-58415-622-2(8))*; 112p. (YA). (gr. 5-9). 2007. (Places in Time Ser.). (Illus.). 2007. Set lib. bdg. 222.60 *(978-1-58415-628-4(7))* Mitchell Lane Pubs., Inc.

NAMES, PERSONAL

EchoHawk, Terry. Call Me Little Echo Hawk. 2005. (Illus.). 22p. (J). 15.99 *(978-1-55517-804-8(9))* Cedar Fort, Inc./CFI Distribution.

Haas, Kristin. The Shape Family Babies, 1 vol. Bersani, Shennen, illus. 2014. (ENG.). 32p. (J). (gr. -1-3). 17.95 *(978-1-62855-211-9(5))* Arbordale Publishing.

Haas, Kristin, et al. Los Bebés de la Familia Geométrica, 1 vol. Bersani, Shennen, illus. 2014.Tr. of Shape Family Babies. (SPA.). 32p. (J). (gr. -1-3). pap. 9.95 *(978-1-62855-229-4(8))* Arbordale Publishing.

Hayes, Larry E. My Name Starts with J. Anderson, Airlie, illus. 2004. (My Name Starts With Ser.). 31p. (J). spiral bd. 12.95 *(978-0-9725292-2-8(5))* Inspire Pubns.

—My Name Starts with M. Anderson, Airlie, illus. Hayes, Larry E., photos by. 2004. (My Name Starts With Ser.). 31p. (J). spiral bd. 12.95 *(978-0-9725292-3-5(3)*, 1) Inspire Pubns.

—My Name Starts with S. Anderson, Airlie, illus. Hayes, Larry E., photos by. 2003. (My Name Starts With Ser.). 31p. spiral bd. 10.95 *(978-0-9725292-1-1(7))* Inspire Pubns.

Onuoha-Ezemma, Glory. Don't Make Fun of My Name: My Name Is Special to My Parents & Me. unabr. ed. 2003. (Illus.). 47p. (J). (gr. k-6). pap. 9.95 *(978-0-9661598-6-8(1))* Ekwike Bks. & Publishing.

Onyefulu, Ifeoma. Your Name Is Dede: An African Baby's Naming Ceremony. 2003. (Illus.). 32p. (J). *(978-0-7112-1938-0(9))* ReiseArt Buchhandlung GmbH.

Phillips, Karen. The Truth about My Name: And What It Reveals about Me! 2010. (ENG.). 50p. (J). (gr. 3-18). 16.99 *(978-1-59174-855-7(0))* Klutz.

Schultz, Sam. Ivan to Make You Laugh: Jokes about Novel, Nifty, & Notorious Names. Gable, Brian, illus. 2005. (Make Me Laugh! Ser.). 32p. (J). (gr. k-3). lib. bdg. 19.93 *(978-1-57505-659-3(3))* Lerner Publishing Group.

Wolfsgruber, Linda. A Daisy Is a Daisy Is a Daisy (Except When It's Girl's Name), 1 vol. 2011. (ENG., Illus.). 32p. (J). (gr. -1). 16.95 *(978-1-55498-099-4(2))* Groundwood Bks. CAN. Dist: Publishers Group West (PGW).

Wood, Vanessa, ed. Antique Names: Tried & True & Truly Rare Historical Names. 2003. 92p. per. 11.00 *(978-0-9744281-1-6(6))* Bisham Hill Bks.

NAMES, PERSONAL—FICTION

Alderton, Sylvia. A Real Name for Puppy. McCartney, Michael David, illus. 2006. (J). *(978-1-930566-58-3(1)*, WestWind Pr.) Scott, D.& F. Publishing, Inc.

Alexie, Sherman. Thunder Boy Jr. Morales, Yuyi, illus. 2016. (ENG.). 40p. (J). (gr. -1-3). 17.99 *(978-0-316-01372-7(2))* Little, Brown Bks. for Young Readers.

Anderson, Robert Gordon. Seven O'Clock Stories. l.t. ed. 2007. (ENG.). 122p. pap. 19.99 *(978-1-4264-2903-3(7))* Creative Media Partners, LLC.

Angelou, Maya. Cedric of Jamaica. Rockwell, Lizzy, illus. 2005. (Random House Pictureback Book Ser.). (J). *(978-0-375-83269-7(6))* Random Hse., Inc.

Answer Why for Mee Mee: Work & Play Book. 2006. (J). *(978-0-9748715-3-0(2))* Vision Harmony Publishing.

Bailey, Jennifer P. I Call Mine Mimi. What Do You Call Your Grandmother?, 1 vol. 2010. 24p. pap. 24.95 *(978-1-4489-7141-1(1))* PublishAmerica, Inc.

Benton, Jim. The Fran That Time Forgot. Benton, Jim, illus. 4th ed. 2005. (Franny K. Stein, Mad Scientist Ser.: 4). (ENG., Illus.). 112p. (J). (gr. 2-5). mass mkt. 5.99 *(978-0-689-86298-4(9))*; 16.99 *(978-0-689-86294-6(6))* Simon & Schuster Bks. For Young Readers. (Simon & Schuster Bks. For Young Readers).

—The Fran That Time Forgot, 1 vol. Benton, Jim, illus. 2011. (Franny K. Stein, Mad Scientist Ser.). (ENG., Illus.). 112p. (gr. 3-6). 24.21 *(978-1-59961-820-3(6))* Spotlight.

Blasi, Kathleen McAlpin. A Name of Honor. Bowman, Leslie W., illus. 2006. (J). *(978-1-59336-692-6(2))* Mondo Publishing.

Brimmer, Debi & Coleson, Julie. How Six Little Ipu Got Their Names. Coleson, Julie, illus. 2005. (Illus.). 30p. (J). 9.95 incl. audio compact disk *(978-1-57306-186-5(7))* Bess Pr., Inc.

Choi, Yangsook. The Name Jar. Choi, Yangsook, illus. 2003. (ENG., Illus.). 40p. (J). (gr. -1-2). pap. 7.99 *(978-0-440-41799-6(6)*, Dragonfly Bks.) Random Hse. Children's Bks.

Dunklee, Annika. My Name Is Elizabeth! Forsythe, Matthew, illus. 2011. (ENG.). 24p. (J). (gr. -1-2). 14.95 *(978-1-55453-560-6(3))* Kids Can Pr., Ltd. CAN. Dist: Hachette Bk. Group.

Flood, Pansie Hart. Tiger's Trouble with Donut Head. Wummer, Amy, illus. 2005. 71p. (J). lib. bdg. 19.93 *(978-1-57505-814-6(6)*, Carolrhoda Bks.) Lerner Publishing Group.

Friedman, Laurie. Merry Christmas, Mary Christmas! Durst, Kathryn, illus. 2017. (ENG.). 32p. (J). (gr. -1-3). lib. bdg. 17.99 ***(978-1-4677-9261-5(6)***, Carolrhoda Bks.) Lerner Publishing Group.

Gadot, A. S. The First Gift. Lafrance, Marie, illus. 2006. (ENG.). 24p. (J). (gr. -1-3). lib. bdg. 15.95 *(978-1-58013-146-9(8)*, Kar-Ben Publishing) Lerner Publishing Group.

Glassman, Miriam. Call Me Oklahoma! 2013. (ENG.). 128p. (J). (gr. 2-7). 16.95 *(978-0-8234-2742-0(0))* Holiday Hse., Inc.

Green, John. Will Grayson, Will Grayson. 2011. lib. bdg. 22.10 *(978-0-606-15358-4(6)*, Turtleback) Turtleback Bks.

Green, John & Levithan, David. Will Grayson, Will Grayson. 2015. (SPA.). 336p. (YA). (gr. 7). pap. 12.95 *(978-1-101-91070-2(4)*, Vintage Espanol) Knopf Doubleday Publishing Group.

—Will Grayson, Will Grayson. (ENG., (YA). (gr. 9-18). 2011. Illus.). 352p. 10.99 *(978-0-14-241847-5(1)*, Speak) 2010. 320p. 17.99 *(978-0-525-42158-0(0)*, Dutton Books for Young Readers) Penguin Young Readers Group.

Greenspan, Shari Dash. Shemot Muzarim. Katz, Avi, illus. 2005.Tr. of Strange Names. (HEB.). 32p. 14.00 *(978-965-7108-58-1(6))* Urim Pubns. ISR. Dist: Coronet Bks.

Harris, Carol Gahara. My Name is Leona. Fujiwara, Kim, illus. 2013. 24p. (J). 19.95 *(978-0-9860324-0-0(9))* Snowy Night Pub.

Henkes, Kevin. Chrysanthemum. 2004. (Illus.). (J). (gr. k-3). spiral bd. *(978-0-616-14575-3(6))* Canadian National Institute for the Blind/Institut National Canadien pour les Aveugles.

—Chrysanthemum. Henkes, Kevin, illus. (ENG., Illus.). 32p. (J). (gr. -1-3). 2008. pap. 7.99 *(978-0-688-14732-7(1))* 2007. pap. 24.99 *(978-0-06-111974-3(1))* HarperCollins Pubs. (Greenwillow Bks.).

—Chrysanthemum. 2008. (J). (gr. -1-2). lib. bdg. 17.20 *(978-0-613-00459-6(0)*, Turtleback) Turtleback Bks.

—Crisantemo. 2017.Tr. of Chrysanthemum. (SPA.). (J). pap. ***(978-1-63245-664-9(8))*** Lectorum Pubns., Inc.

—Crisantemo. Mlawer, Teresa, tr. from ENG. 2006.Tr. of Chrysanthemum. (Illus.). 31p. (gr. 4-7). 19.00 *(978-0-7569-7316-2(3))* Perfection Learning Corp.

—Penny & Her Doll. Henkes, Kevin, illus. 2012. (Illus.). 32p. (J). (gr. -1-3). (ENG.). 12.99 *(978-0-06-208199-5(3))*; lib. bdg. 14.89 *(978-0-06-208200-8(0))* HarperCollins Pubs. (Greenwillow Bks.).

—Penny & Her Doll. 2013. (I Can Read! Level 1 Ser.). (J). lib. bdg. 13.55 *(978-0-606-27147-9(3)*, Turtleback) Turtleback Bks.

Jules, Jacqueline. Picnic at Camp Shalom. Melmon, Deborah, illus. 2011. (ENG.). 32p. (J). (gr. k-3). pap. 7.95 *(978-0-7613-6662-1(8)*, Kar-Ben Publishing) Lerner Publishing Group.

Jules, Jacqueline & Hechtkopf, Jacqueline. Picnic at Camp Shalom. Melmon, Deborah, illus. 2011. (Kar-Ben Favorites Ser.). (ENG.). 32p. (J). (gr. k-3). 17.95 *(978-0-7613-6661-4(X)*, Kar-Ben Publishing) Lerner Publishing Group.

Katz, Karen. Princess Baby. Katz, Karen, illus. 2012. (Princess Baby Ser.). (ENG., Illus.). 30p. (J). (gr. k-k). bds. 7.99 *(978-0-307-93146-7(3)*, Schwartz & Wade Bks.) Random Hse. Children's Bks.

Kevin, Henkes. Chrysanthemum. 2014. (ENG.). 32p. (J). (gr. k-3). 11.24 *(978-1-63245-281-8(2))* Lectorum Pubns., Inc.

Korngold, Jamie S. Mazel Tov! It's a Boy: Mazel Tov! It's a Girl. Finkelstein, Jeff, illus. Finkelstein, Jeff, photos by. 2015. (J). (ENG.). 32p. (gr. -1-1). lib. bdg. 17.95 *(978-1-4677-1957-5(9))*; 6.99 *(978-1-4677-6206-9(7))* Lerner Publishing Group. (Kar-Ben Publishing).

Lafrance, Marie, illus. The First Gift. 2006. 24p. (J). (gr. 2). per. 6.95 *(978-1-58013-149-0(2)*, Kar-Ben Publishing) Lerner Publishing Group.

Laínez, René Colato. I Am Rene, the Boy. Graullera, Fabiola, illus. 2005.Tr. of Yo Soy Rene, el Nino. (ENG & SPA.). 32p. (J). (gr. -1-2). 16.95 *(978-1-55885-378-2(2)*, Piñata Books) Arte Publico Pr.

—René Has Two Last Names/René Tiene Dos Apellidos. Laínez, René Colato & Graullera Ramírez, Fabiola, illus. 2009. (SPA & ENG.). 32p. (J). (gr. -1-3). 16.95 *(978-1-55885-530-4(0))* Arte Publico Pr.

Lester, Helen. A Porcupine Named Fluffy. Munsinger, Lynn, illus. 2013. (Laugh-Along Lessons Ser.). (ENG.). 32p. (J). (gr. -1-3). 8.99 *(978-0-544-00319-4(5))* Houghton Mifflin Harcourt Publishing Co.

Meyers, Tim. Let's Call Him Lau-Wiliwili-Humuhumu-Nukunuku-Nukunuku-Apua'a-Oi'oi. 2005. (Illus.). 24p. (J). 16.95 incl. audio compact disk *(978-1-57306-252-7(9))* Bess Pr., Inc.

Michiko Florence, Debbi. What's Your Name? Roe, Monika, illus. 2016. (Dorothy & Toto Ser.). (ENG.). 40p. (gr. k-2). lib. bdg. 21.32 *(978-1-4795-8702-5(8))* Capstone Press of Coughlan Cos.

Mohammed, Khadra & Williams, Karen Lynn. My Name Is Sangoel. Stock, Catherine, illus. 2009. (ENG.). 36p. (J). (gr. 1-5). 17.00 *(978-0-8028-5307-3(2)*, Eerdmans Bks For Young Readers) Eerdmans, William B. Publishing Co.

Monk, Isabell. Hope. Porter, Janice Lee, illus. 2004. (Carolrhoda Picture Books Ser.). 32p. (J). (gr. -1-3). 6.95 *(978-1-57505-792-7(1))* Lerner Publishing Group.

Moss, Marissa. The Name Game! Moss, Marissa, illus. 2011. (Daphne's Diary of Daily Disasters Ser.). (ENG., Illus.). 80p. (J). (gr. 2-5). pap. 5.99 *(978-1-4424-1738-0(2))*; lib. bdg. 9.99 *(978-1-4424-2676-4(4))* Simon & Schuster/Paula Wiseman Bks. (Simon & Schuster/Paula Wiseman Bks.).

Murphy, Stuart J. Write on, Carlos! Jones, Tim, illus. 2011. (I See I Learn Ser.). (ENG.). 32p. (J). (-k). 14.95 *(978-1-58089-464-7(X))*; pap. 6.95 *(978-1-58089-465-4(8))* Charlesbridge Publishing, Inc.

Murphy, Stuart J. & Mlawer, Teresa. Carlos Escribe Su Nombre! Jones, Tim, illus. 2014. (I See I Learn Ser.). (SPA.). 32p. (J). (-k). 14.95 *(978-1-58089-496-8(8))*; pap. 6.95 *(978-1-58089-497-5(6))* Charlesbridge Publishing, Inc.

Newman, Lesléa. My Name Is Aviva. Jatkowska, Ag, illus. 2015. (ENG.). 32p. (J). (gr. -1-2). pap. 7.99 *(978-1-4677-2656-6(7))*; lib. bdg. 17.99 *(978-1-4677-2654-2(0))* Lerner Publishing Group. (Kar-Ben Publishing).

Nöstlinger, Christine. Piruleta. Kaufman, Angelika, illus. 2003. (SPA.). 132p. (gr. 3-5). pap. 9.95 *(978-968-19-0983-3(6))* Santillana USA Publishing Co., Inc.

Philip, Simon. I Don't Know What to Call My Cat. Bailey, Ella, illus. 2017. (ENG.). 32p. (J). (gr. -1-3). 16.99 *(978-0-544-97143-1(4)*, HMH Books For Young Readers) Houghton Mifflin Harcourt Publishing Co.

Recorvits, Helen. My Name Is Yoon. Swiatkowska, Gabi, illus. 2003. (ENG.). 32p. (J). (gr. -1-3). 17.99 *(978-0-374-35114-4(7)*, 9780374351144, Farrar, Straus & Giroux (BYR)) Farrar, Straus & Giroux.

—My Name Is Yoon. Swiatkowska, Gabi, illus. 2014. (ENG.). 32p. (J). (gr. -1-3). 6.99 *(978-1-250-05711-2(6)*, 9781250057112) Square Fish.

Sadu, Itah & Condy, Roy. Christopher Changes His Name. (Illus.). 32p. (J). pap. 4.99 *(978-0-590-24624-8(0))* Scholastic, Inc.

Sandburg, Carl. Rootabaga Stories. 2009. 128p. (gr. 3-18). pap. 10.95 *(978-1-60664-425-6(4))* Rodgers, Alan Bks.

Schatz, Letta. So Many Henrys, 1 vol. rev. ed. 2013. (Fiction Readers Ser.). (ENG., Illus.). 28p. (J). (gr. 3-3). pap. 8.99 *(978-1-4333-5602-5(3))* Shell Educational Publishing.

—So Many Henrys. rev. ed. 2013. (Fiction Readers Ser.). (ENG., Illus.). 28p. (gr. 3-3). pap. 19.96 *(978-1-4807-1724-4(X))* Teacher Created Materials, Inc.

Sharp, Rhonda Winchell. The Nine Most Famous Reindeer of All. Vandewater, Rena, illus. 2004. 40p. (J). pap. 15.99 *(978-0-9748047-8-1(9))* Hickory Bark Productions.

Sheinmel, Courtney & Bell, Jennifer A. Stella Batts: Needs a New Name. 2012. (Stella Batts Ser.). (ENG., Illus.). 160p. (J). (gr. 1-3). pap. 5.99 *(978-1-58536-183-0(6)*, 202266); lib. bdg. 9.99 *(978-1-58536-185-4(2)*, 202267) Sleeping Bear Pr.

Shurtliff, Liesl. Rump: The True Story of Rumpelstiltskin. (ENG.). 272p. (J). (gr. 3-7). 2014. pap. 7.99 *(978-0-307-97796-0(X)*, Yearling) 2013. 16.99 *(978-0-307-97793-9(5)*, Knopf Bks. for Young Readers) 2013. lib. bdg. 19.99 *(978-0-307-97794-6(3)*, Knopf Bks. for Young Readers) Random Hse. Children's Bks.

Springer, Nancy. Somebody. 2009. (ENG.). 128p. (YA). (gr. 7-18). 16.95 *(978-0-8234-2099-5(X))* Holiday Hse., Inc.

Stein, Gertrude. To Do: A Book of Alphabets & Birthdays. 2011. (ENG., Illus.). 128p. 30.00 *(978-0-300-17097-9(1))* Yale Univ. Pr.

Wells, Rosemary. Use Your Words, Sophie! 2015. (ENG., Illus.). 24p. (J). (gr. -1 — 1). 16.99 *(978-0-670-01663-1(2)*, Viking Books for Young Readers) Penguin Young Readers Group.

Yangsook, Choi. The Name Jar. 2014. (ENG.). 40p. (J). (gr. k-2). 11.24 *(978-1-63245-313-6(4))* Lectorum Pubns., Inc.

NAMIBIA

Streissguth, Thomas. Namibia in Pictures. 2008. (Visual Geography Ser.). (YA). (gr. 7-12). lib. bdg. 31.93 *(978-0-8225-8574-9(X))* Twenty First Century Bks.

NANTUCKET ISLAND (MASS.)

Herold, Vickey. Discover A Whaling Community: Nantucket. 2006. (J). pap. *(978-1-4108-6429-1(4))* Benchmark Education Co.

Thompson, Gare. A Whaling Community: New Bedford, Mass: Text Pairs. 2008. (Bridges/Navigators Ser.). (J). (gr. 3). 89.00 *(978-1-4108-8377-3(9))* Benchmark Education Co.

Zschock, Martha Day. Journey Around Nantucket from A to Z. Zschock, Martha Day, illus. 2008. (Journeys Ser.). (Illus.). 32p. (J). (gr. 1-6). 17.95 *(978-1-933212-82-1(9)*, Commonwealth Editions) Applewood Bks.

NANTUCKET ISLAND (MASS.)—FICTION

Alderson, Sarah. The Sound Where Secrets Are Buried. 2014. (ENG.). 320p. (J). pap. *(978-1-4711-1573-8(9)*, Simon Pulse) Simon Pulse.

Angelini, Josephine. Dreamless. 2013. (Starcrossed Trilogy Ser.: 2). (ENG.). 512p. (YA). (gr. 8). pap. 9.99 *(978-0-06-201202-9(9)*, HarperTeen) HarperCollins Pubs.

—Starcrossed. 2012. (Starcrossed Trilogy Ser.: 1). (ENG.). 512p. (YA). (gr. 8). pap. 9.99 *(978-0-06-201200-5(2)*, HarperTeen) HarperCollins Pubs.

Bagley, Conor. Ziggy McFinster's Nantucket Adventure. Bernard Westcott, Nadine, illus. 2008. (ENG.). 40p. (J). (gr. -1-3). 16.95 *(978-1-56625-315-4(2))* Bonus Bks., Inc.

Bouton, Warren Hussey. The Captain's Return: A Spooky Tale from Nantucket. Locke, Barbara Kauffmann, illus. 2004. (J). per. 5.95 *(978-0-9700555-4-5(4))* Hither Creek Pr.

Gamble, Adam. Good Night Nantucket. Rosen, Anne, illus. 2007. (Good Night Our World Ser.). (ENG.). 20p. (J). (gr. k — 1). bds. 9.95 *(978-1-60219-013-9(5))* Good Night Bks.

Howland, Leila. Nantucket Blue. 2014. (Nantucket Blue Ser.). (ENG.). 320p. (YA). (gr. 9-17). pap. 8.99 *(978-1-4231-6139-4(4))* Hyperion Bks. for Children.

—Nantucket Red. 2014. (Nantucket Blue Ser.). (ENG.). 288p. (YA). (gr. 9-17). 16.99 *(978-1-4231-6095-3(9))* Hyperion Bks. for Children.

Manley, Molly. A Nantucket Nanny. Marshall, Janet, illus. 2005. (Little Limericks Ser.). (ENG.). 24p. (J). (gr. k-3). 12.95 *(978-1-889833-96-5(7)*, Commonwealth Editions) Applewood Bks.

My Time on Nantucket. 2005. (J). cd-rom 11.95 *(978-0-9755078-2-7(6))* Sweet Punkin Pr.

The Phantom of Nantucket. 2014. (Nancy Drew Diaries: 7). (ENG., Illus.). 192p. (J). (gr. 3-7). pap. 6.99 *(978-1-4814-0015-2(0)*, Aladdin) Simon & Schuster Children's Publishing.

Snedeker, Caroline. Downright Dencey. Barney, Maginel Wright, illus. 2003. (Young Adult Library). 268p. (YA). pap. 12.95 *(978-1-883937-79-9(5))* Bethlehem Bks.

Stewart, Whitney. Marshall: A Nantucket Sea Rescue. Lyall, Dennis, illus. 2008. (ENG.). 32p. (J). (gr. -1-2). 6.95 *(978-1-59249-855-0(8))*; 2.95 *(978-1-59249-856-7(6))*; 10.95 *(978-1-59249-857-4(4))* Soundprints.

Thorpe, Rochelle O'Neal. Gabe's Nantucket Adventure: Daffodils, Dogs, & Cars. Nakell, Eugenie, ed. Margolis, Al, illus. I.t. ed. 2010. 28p. (YA). pap. 7.95 *(978-1-935706-02-1(0))* Wiggles Pr.

Turkle, Brinton. Obadiah the Bold. 2004. 36p. pap. 7.95 *(978-1-893103-19-1(6))* Beautiful Feet Bks.

—Rachel & Obadiah. 2004. 30p. pap. 7.95 *(978-1-893103-18-4(8))* Beautiful Feet Bks.

NAPOLEON I, EMPEROR OF THE FRENCH, 1769-1821

Baicker, Karen. Napoleon Complex: A Young General Takes France by Storm. 2011. (J). pap. *(978-0-545-32938-5(8))* Scholastic, Inc.

Boyd, David. Napoleon's Last Stand. Okum, David, illus. 2007. 48p. (J). lib. bdg. 23.08 *(978-1-4242-1639-0(7))* Fitzgerald Bks.

Doyle, William. Napoleon Bonaparte: Emperor. 2016. (History Makers Ser.). 144p. (J). 45.64 *(978-1-5026-2447-5(8))* Cavendish Square Publishing.

Foa, Eugenie. The Boy Life of Napoleon: Afterwards Emperor of the French. I.t. ed. 2007. (ENG.). 298p. pap. 23.99 *(978-1-4264-3615-4(7))* Creative Media Partners, LLC.

—Boy Life of Napoleon Afterwards Emperor of the French. 2004. reprint ed. pap. 19.95 *(978-1-4191-5499-7(0))*; pap. 1.99 *(978-1-4192-5499-4(5))* Kessinger Publishing, LLC.

Freedman, Jeri. Strategic Inventions of the Napoleonic Wars. 2016. (Tech in the Trenches Ser.). 112p. (J). 42.79 *(978-1-5026-2351-5(X))* Cavendish Square Publishing.

Goldberg, Jan. Napoleon Bonaparte. 2004. (ZB Reads Trio Books). 87p. (gr. 5-7). pap. 5.00 *(978-0-7367-1799-1(4))* Zaner-Bloser, Inc.

Greenblatt, Miriam. Napoleon Bonaparte & Imperial France. 2005. (Rulers & Their Times Ser.). (Illus.). 96p. (J). (gr. 3-7). lib. bdg. *(978-0-7614-1837-5(7)*, Benchmark Bks.) Marshall Cavendish Corp.

Heuston, Kimberley. Napoleon I: Emperor & Conqueror. 2010. (Wicked History Ser.). (ENG.). 128p. (J). (gr. 6-12). pap. 5.95 *(978-0-531-22823-4(1)*, Watts, Franklin) Scholastic Library Publishing.

Heuston, Kimberley & Heuston, Kimberley Burton. Napoleon I: Emperor & Conqueror. 2009. (Wicked History Ser.). (ENG., Illus.). 128p. (J). (gr. 5-9). 31.00 *(978-0-531-21277-6(7))* Scholastic Library Publishing.

Hoffman, Megan Mills. Napoleon Bonaparte. 2017. (J). ***(978-1-5026-2782-7(5))*** Cavendish Square Publishing.

Ladybird Books Staff & Peach, L. Du Garde. The a Ladybird Adventure from History Book Story of Nelson. 2016. (Adventure from History Ser.). (ENG., Illus.). 56p. (J). (gr. 3-7). 9.99 *(978-0-7232-9799-4(1))* Penguin Bks., Ltd. GBR. Dist: Independent Pubs. Group.

Landau, Elaine. Jefferson's Louisiana Purchase: Would You Make the Deal of the Century? 2015. (What Would You Do? Ser.). 48p. (J). (gr. 3-4). 25.27 *(978-0-7660-6305-1(4))*; pap. 8.95 *(978-0-7660-6306-8(2)*, Enslow Elementary) Enslow Pubs., Inc.

—The Louisiana Purchase: Would You Close the Deal? (What Would You Do? Ser.). (Illus.). 48p. (J). 2010. pap. 8.95 *(978-1-59845-196-2(0))* 2008. (gr. 3-7). lib. bdg. 25.27 *(978-0-7660-2902-6(6))* Enslow Pubs., Inc. (Enslow Elementary).

—Napoleon Bonaparte. 2006. (Illus.). 112p. (J). 27.93 *(978-0-8225-3420-4(7)*, Twenty-First Century Bks.) Lerner Publishing Group.

Lethbridge, Lucy. Napoleon. 2005. (Illus.). 64p. (J). 8.95 *(978-0-7945-1050-3(7)*, Usborne) EDC Publishing.

Lynette, Rachel. The Louisiana Purchase. 2013. (Pioneer Spirit: the Westward Expansion Ser.). (Illus.). 24p. (J). (gr. 3-6). pap. 8.25 *(978-1-4777-0895-8(2))*; pap. 49.50 *(978-1-4777-0896-5(0))*; lib. bdg. 22.60 *(978-1-4777-0781-4(6))* Rosen Publishing Group, Inc., The. (PowerKids Pr.).

O'Donoghue, Sean. Thomas Jefferson & the Louisiana Purchase. 2016. (Spotlight on American History Ser.). (Illus.). 24p. (J). (gr. 6-4). 26.25 *(978-1-5081-4948-4(8)*, PowerKids Pr.) Rosen Publishing Group, Inc., The.

Roberts, Russell. Battle of Waterloo. 2011. (Technologies & Strategies in Battle Ser.). (Illus.). 48p. (J). (gr. 4-7). lib. bdg. 29.95 *(978-1-61228-076-9(5))* Mitchell Lane Pubs., Inc.

Schaffer, David. The Louisiana Purchase: The Deal of the Century That Doubled the Nation. 2006. (Wild History of the American West Ser.). (Illus.). 128p. (J). (gr. 5-9). lib. bdg. 34.60 *(978-1-59845-018-7(2)*, MyReportLinks.com Bks.) Enslow Pubs., Inc.

Streissguth, Thomas. The Napoleonic Wars: Defeat of the Grand Army. 2003. (History's Great Defeats Ser.). (ENG., Illus.). 112p. (J). 32.10 *(978-1-59018-065-5(8)*, Lucent Bks.) Cengage Gale.

Yasuda, Anita. 12 Incredible Facts about the Louisiana Purchase. 2015. (Turning Points in US History Ser.). (ENG., Illus.). 32p. (J). (gr. 3-5). *(978-1-63235-131-9(5)*, 12-Story Library) Pr. Room Editions LLC.

Zurn, Jon. The Louisiana Purchase, 1 vol. 2007. (Essential Events Set 1 Ser.). (ENG., Illus.). 112p. (J). (gr. 6-12). lib. bdg. 35.64 *(978-1-59928-853-6(2))* ABDO Publishing Co.

NAPOLEON I, EMPEROR OF THE FRENCH, 1769-1821—FICTION

Brighton, Catherine. My Napoleon. Brighton, Catherine, illus. 2005. (Illus.). 26p. (J). (gr. k-4). reprint ed. 17.00 *(978-0-7567-8931-2(1))* DIANE Publishing Co.

Dunlap, Susanne. The Academie. 2012. (ENG.). 368p. (YA). 16.99 *(978-1-59990-586-0(8)*, 9781599905860, Bloomsbury USA Childrens) Bloomsbury Publishing USA.

Hausman, Gerald & Hausman, Loretta. Farewell, Josephine: The Romance of Josephine & Napoleon. 2013. 248p. pap. 13.95 *(978-1-61720-381-7(5))* Wilder Pubns., Corp.

Henty, George Alfred. At Aboukir & Acre: A Story of Napoleon's Invasion of Egypt (Henty Homeschool History Series) 2010. 344p. pap. 19.95 *(978-1-935585-23-7(1))* Fireship Pr.

Rabin, Staton. Betsy & the Emperor. 2006. (ENG., Illus.). 304p. (YA). (gr. 7). reprint ed. mass mkt. 7.99 *(978-1-4169-1336-8(X)*, Simon Pulse) Simon Pulse.

NAPOLEONIC WARS, 1800-1815

Allport, Alan. The Congress of Vienna. 2011. (Milestones in Modern World History Ser.). (Illus.). 126p. (J). (gr. 9). 35.00 *(978-1-60413-497-1(6)*, Chelsea Hse.) Facts On File, Inc.

Freedman, Jeri. Strategic Inventions of the Napoleonic Wars. 2016. (Tech in the Trenches Ser.). 112p. (J). 42.79 *(978-1-5026-2351-5(X))* Cavendish Square Publishing.

Roberts, Russell. Battle of Waterloo. 2011. (Technologies & Strategies in Battle Ser.). (Illus.). 48p. (J). (gr. 4-7). lib. bdg. 29.95 *(978-1-61228-076-9(5))* Mitchell Lane Pubs., Inc.

Streissguth, Thomas. The Napoleonic Wars: Defeat of the Grand Army. 2003. (History's Great Defeats Ser.). (ENG., Illus.). 112p. (J). 32.10 *(978-1-59018-065-5(8)*, Lucent Bks.) Cengage Gale.

NARCOTIC HABIT

see Drug Addiction

NARCOTICS

Bankston, John. Ecstasy = Busted! 2005. (Busted! Ser.). (Illus.). 104p. (J). (gr. 6-13). lib. bdg. 33.27 *(978-0-7660-2387-1(7))* Enslow Pubs., Inc.

Cashin, John. The Heroin Crisis. 2017. (Opioids & Opiates: the Silent Epidemic* Ser.: Vol. 5). (ENG.). (YA). (gr. 7-12). 23.95 ***(978-1-4222-3825-7(3))*** Mason Crest.

Ferguson, Grace. Chronic Pain & Prescription Painkillers. 2017. (Opioids & Opiates: the Silent Epidemic* Ser.: Vol. 5). (ENG.). (YA). (gr. 7-12). 23.95 ***(978-1-4222-3823-3(7))*** Mason Crest.

Glass, George. Narcotics: Dangerous Painkiller. rev. ed. 2005. (Drug Abuse Prevention Library). (Illus.). 64p. (YA). (gr. 7-12). lib. bdg. 31.95 *(978-0-8239-3300-6(8))* Rosen Publishing Group, Inc., The.

Gleason, Carrie. The Biography of Tobacco. 2006. (How Did That Get Here? Ser.). (ENG., Illus.). 32p. (J). (gr. 4-7). pap. *(978-0-7787-2525-1(1)*, 1259497) Crabtree Publishing Co.

Goldsmith, Connie. Addiction & Overdose: Confronting an American Crisis. 2017. (ENG.). 128p. (YA). (gr. 8-12). 37.32 ***(978-1-5124-0953-6(7)****, Twenty-First Century Bks.) Lerner Publishing Group.

Grinapol, Corinne. Racial Profiling & Discrimination: Your Legal Rights. 2015. (Know Your Rights Ser.). (ENG., Illus.). 64p. (J). (gr. 6-6). 33.25 *(978-1-4777-8020-6(3)*, Rosen Young Adult) Rosen Publishing Group, Inc., The.

Illicit & Misused Drugs, 16 vols., Set. Incl. Addiction in America: Society, Psychology, & Heredity. Walker, Ida. (Illus.). (YA). lib. bdg. 24.95 *(978-1-4222-0151-0(1))*; Addiction Treatment: Escaping the Trap. Walker, Ida. (Illus.). (YA). lib. bdg. 24.95 *(978-1-4222-0152-7(X))*; Alcohol Addiction: Not Worth the Buzz. Walker, Ida J. (YA). lib. bdg. 24.95 *(978-1-4222-0153-4(8))*; Hallucinogens: Unreal Visions. Nelson, Sheila. (Illus.). (YA). lib. bdg. 24.95 *(978-1-4222-0155-8(4))*; Inhalants & Solvents: Sniffing Disaster. Flynn, Noa. (Illus.). (YA). lib. bdg. 24.95 *(978-1-4222-0157-2(0))*; Marijuana: Mind-Altering Weed. Sanna, E. J. (Illus.). (YA). lib. bdg. 24.95 *(978-1-4222-0158-9(9))*; Methamphetamines: Unsafe Speed. Etingoff, Kim. (Illus.). (YA). lib. bdg. 24.95 *(978-1-4222-0159-6(7))*; Sedatives & Hypnotics: Deadly Downers. Walker, Ida J. (Illus.). (J). lib. bdg. 24.95 *(978-1-4222-0163-3(5))*; Tobacco: Through the Smokescreen. Chastain, Zachary. (YA). lib. bdg. 24.95 *(978-1-4222-0165-7(1))*; (gr. 7-18). 2009. (Illus.). 128p. 2007. Set lib. bdg. 399.20 *(978-1-4222-0149-7(X))* Mason Crest.

Kerrigan, Michael. The War Against Drugs. 2004. (Crime & Detection Ser.). (Illus.). 96p. (J). (gr. 7-18). lib. bdg. 22.95 *(978-1-59084-368-0(1))* Mason Crest.

Lew, Kristi. The Truth about Oxycodone & Other Narcotics. 2013. (Drugs & Consequences Ser.). (Illus.). 64p. (J). (gr. 7-12). 31.95 *(978-1-4777-1894-0(X))* Rosen Publishing Group, Inc., The.

Mirman, Heather Moehn. Issues in Drug Abuse. 2003. (Contemporary Issues Ser.). (ENG., Illus.). 112p. (YA). (gr. 7-10). 30.85 *(978-1-59018-035-8(6)*, Lucent Bks.) Cengage Gale.

Olive, M. Foster. Morphine. 2011. (Understanding Drugs Ser.). (Illus.). 112p. (J). (gr. 9-12). 34.95 *(978-1-60413-544-2(1))* Facts On File, Inc.

Paris, Stephanie. Drugs & Alcohol, 1 vol. 2nd rev. ed. 2012. (Nonfiction Readers Ser.). (ENG., Illus.). 48p. (J). (gr. 4-4). pap. 9.99 *(978-1-4333-4859-4(4))* Teacher Created Materials, Inc.

Petersen, Christine. Vicodin & Oxycontin. 2013. 64p. (J). (gr. 6-9). 34.21 *(978-1-60870-827-7(6))* Cavendish Square Publishing.

—Vicodin & OxyContin. 2013. (Dangerous Drugs Ser.). 64p. (J). (gr. 6-9). pap. 15.28 *(978-1-62712-063-0(7))* Cavendish Square Publishing.

Sanna, E. J. Heroin & Other Opioids: Poppies' Perilous Children. Henningfield, Jack E., ed. 2012. (Illicit & Misused Drugs Ser.). 128p. (J). (gr. 7). 24.95 *(978-1-4222-2433-5(3))*; pap. 14.95 *(978-1-4222-2452-6(X))* Mason Crest.

Somerville, Clive. The Drug Enforcement Administration. 2004. (Rescue & Prevention Ser.). (Illus.). 96p. (YA). (gr. 7-18). lib. bdg. 22.95 *(978-1-59084-413-7(0))* Mason Crest.

NARNIA (IMAGINARY PLACE)—FICTION

Baynes, Pauline & Lewis, C. S. Prince Caspian, Bk. 7. Baynes, Pauline, illus. 2008. (Chronicles of Narnia Ser.). (Illus.). 768p. (J). (gr. 3). pap. 99.99 *(978-0-06-076552-1(6))* HarperCollins Pubs.

Beahm, George. Passport to Narnia: A Newcomer's Guide. Kirk, Tim, illus. 2005. (ENG.). 200p. (YA). (gr. 8-12). per. 12.95 *(978-1-57174-465-4(7))* Hampton Roads Publishing Co., Inc.

—Passport to Narnia: The Unofficial Giude. Kirk, Tim, illus. 2005. (J). lib. bdg. 15.95 *(978-1-57174-481-4(9))* Hampton Roads Publishing Co., Inc.

Bloom, Harold, ed. The Chronicles of Narnia. 2006. (Bloom's Modern Critical Interpretations Ser.). 248p. (C). (gr. 9). lib. bdg. 45.00 *(978-0-7910-9310-8(7)*, Chelsea Hse.) Facts On File, Inc.

Frantz, Jennifer, adapted by. Narnia: Welcome to Narnia. 2005. (Illus.). 32p. (J). lib. bdg. 13.85 *(978-1-4242-0617-9(0))* Fitzgerald Bks.

Lewis, C. S. L' Armoire Magique. Orig. Title: The Lion, the Witch & the Wardrobe. (FRE.). pap. 12.95 *(978-2-08-161994-4(6))* Flammarion et Cie FRA. Dist: Distribooks, Inc.

—The Chronicles of Narnia. Baynes, Pauline, illus. (Chronicles of Narnia Ser.). (J). 2004. (ENG.). 784p. (gr. 5). 32.99 *(978-0-06-059824-2(7))*Set. 2007. (gr. 3-18). 120.00 *(978-0-06-024488-0(7))* HarperCollins Pubs.

—Las Cronicas de Narnia, 1 vol. Baynes, Pauline, illus. 2006. (Cronicas de Narnia Ser.). (SPA.). 816p. (gr. 4-7). pap. 19.99 *(978-0-06-119900-4(1))* HarperCollins Pubs.

—The Horse & His Boy. Baynes, Pauline, illus. (Chronicles of Narnia Ser.: 3). (ENG.). 240p. (J). (gr. 3-18). 2008. pap. 8.99 *(978-0-06-440501-0(X))* 2007. 17.99 *(978-0-06-023488-1(1))* HarperCollins Pubs.

—The Last Battle. Baynes, Pauline, illus. (Chronicles of Narnia Ser.: 7). (ENG.). 224p. (J). (gr. 3-18). 2008. pap. 7.99 *(978-0-06-440503-4(6))* 2007. 17.99 *(978-0-06-023493-5(8))* HarperCollins Pubs.

—El Leon, la Bruja y el Ropero, 1 vol. 2005. (Cronicas de Narnia Ser.). (ESP, SPA & ENG.). 208p. pap. 9.99 *(978-0-06-084253-6(9))* HarperCollins Pubs.

—The Lion, the Witch & the Wardrobe. Humphries, Tudor, illus. 2004. (Chronicles of Narnia Ser.). 48p. (J). (gr. -1-2). lib. bdg. 17.89 *(978-0-06-055651-8(X))* HarperCollins Pubs.

—The Lion, the Witch & the Wardrobe. Baynes, Pauline, illus. abr. ed. (Chronicles of Narnia Ser.: 2). 208p. (J). (gr. 3-18). 2008. (ENG.). pap. 7.99 *(978-0-06-440499-0(4))* 2007. (ENG.). 17.99 *(978-0-06-023481-2(4))* 2007. lib. bdg. 18.89 *(978-0-06-023482-9(2))* HarperCollins Pubs.

—The Lion, the Witch & the Wardrobe. 2008. (Chronicles of Narnia Ser.: 2). (J). 18.40 *(978-0-613-94066-5(0)*, Turtleback) Turtleback Bks.

—The Magician's Nephew. Baynes, Pauline, illus. 2008. (Chronicles of Narnia Ser.: 1). (ENG.). 208p. (J). (gr. 3-18). pap. 7.99 *(978-0-06-440505-8(2))* HarperCollins Pubs.

M
N
O

—The Magician's Nephew. Baynes, Pauline & Van Allsburg, Chris, illus. 2007. (Chronicles of Narnia Ser.: 1). (ENG.). 208p. (J). (gr. 3-18). 17.99 *(978-0-06-023497-3(0))* HarperCollins Pubs.

—Prince Caspian. Baynes, Pauline, illus. 2007. (Chronicles of Narnia Ser.: 4). (ENG.). 240p. (J). (gr. 3-18). 17.99 *(978-0-06-023483-6(0))* HarperCollins Pubs.

—Prince Caspian: The Return to Narnia. Baynes, Pauline, illus. 2008. (Chronicles of Narnia Ser.: 4). (ENG.). 240p. (J). (gr. 3-18). pap. 8.99 *(978-0-06-440500-3(1))* HarperCollins Pubs.

—The Silver Chair. Baynes, Pauline, illus. (Chronicles of Narnia Ser.: 6). (ENG.). 256p. (J). (gr. 3-18). 2008. pap. 8.99 *(978-0-06-440504-1(4))* 2007. 17.99 *(978-0-06-023495-9(4))* HarperCollins Pubs.

—The Voyage of the Dawn Treader. Baynes, Pauline, illus. (Chronicles of Narnia Ser.: 5). (ENG.). 256p. (J). (gr. 3-18). 2008. pap. 8.99 *(978-0-06-440502-7(8))* 2007. 17.99 *(978-0-06-023486-7(5))* HarperCollins Pubs.

Lewis, C. S. & Orem, Hiawyn. The Lion, the Witch & the Wardrobe. Humphries, Tudor, illus. 2004. (Chronicles of Narnia Ser.). (ENG.). 48p. (J). (gr. -1-2). 16.99 *(978-0-06-055650-1(1))* HarperCollins Pubs.

Peacock, Ann & Lewis, C. S. The Chronicles of Narnia. Barbera, Tony et al, illus. Barbera, Tony et al, photos by. 2005. (Chronicles of Narnia Ser.). 64p. (J). *(978-1-4156-3678-7(8))* HarperCollins Pubs.

Prince Caspian Chapter Book #1. 2008. (Chronicles of Narnia Ser.). 96p. (J). pap. 3.99 *(978-0-06-147260-2(3),* Harper Trophy) HarperCollins Pubs.

Prince Caspian Chapter Book #2. 2008. (Chronicles of Narnia Ser.). 96p. (J). pap. 3.99 *(978-0-06-147261-9(1),* Harper Trophy) HarperCollins Pubs.

Prince Caspian Chapter Book #3. 2008. (Chronicles of Narnia Ser.). 96p. (J). pap. 3.99 *(978-0-06-147262-6(X),* Harper Trophy) HarperCollins Pubs.

Prince Caspian Chapter Book #4. 2008. (Chronicles of Narnia Ser.). 96p. (J). pap. 3.99 *(978-0-06-147263-3(8),* Harper Trophy) HarperCollins Pubs.

Wilson, Douglas, reader. What I Learned in Narnia. 2004. cd-rom 35.00 *(978-1-59128-438-3(4))* Canon Pr.

NASCIMENTO, EDSON ARANTES DO, 1940-

see Pele, 1940-

NATE THE GREAT (FICTITIOUS CHARACTER)—FICTION

Sharmat, Marjorie Weinman. Nate the Great. Simont, Marc, illus. (Nate the Great Ser.: No. 1). 48p. (J). (gr. 1-4). pap. 4.50 *(978-0-8072-1351-3(9),* Listening Library) Random Hse. Audio Publishing Group.

—Nate the Great & the Halloween Hunt. Simont, Marc, illus. (Nate the Great Ser.: No. 12). 48p. (J). (gr. 1-4). pap. 4.50 *(978-0-8072-1283-7(0),* Listening Library) Random Hse. Audio Publishing Group.

—Nate the Great & the Missing Key. Simont, Marc, illus. (Nate the Great Ser.: No. 6). 48p. (J). (gr. 1-4). pap. 4.50 *(978-0-8072-1335-3(7),* Listening Library) Random Hse. Audio Publishing Group.

—Nate the Great Goes Undercover. Simont, Marc, illus. (Nate the Great Ser.: No. 2). 48p. (J). (gr. 1-4). pap. 4.50 *(978-0-8072-1284-4(9));* 2004. pap. 17.00 incl. audio *(978-0-8072-0201-2(0),* FTR172SP) Random Hse. Audio Publishing Group. (Listening Library).

Sharmat, Marjorie Weinman & Sharmat, Mitchell. Nate the Great & the Big Sniff. Weston, Martha, illus. 2003. (Nate the Great Ser.: No. 23). (ENG.). 80p. (J). (gr. 1-4). pap. 5.99 *(978-0-440-41502-2(0),* Yearling) Random Hse. Children's Bks.

—Nate the Great & the Big Sniff. Weston, Martha, illus. 2003. (Nate the Great Ser.). 47p. (gr. -1-3). lib. bdg. 16.00 *(978-0-613-63966-8(9),* Turtleback) Turtleback Bks.

—Nate the Great, Where Are You? Wheeler, Jody, illus. 2015. (Nate the Great Ser.). (ENG.). 80p. (J). (gr. 1-4). 5.99 *(978-0-449-81078-1(X),* Yearling) Random Hse. Children's Bks.

NATION OF ISLAM (MOVEMENT)

see Black Muslims

NATIONAL ANTHEMS

see National Songs

NATIONAL BASEBALL HALL OF FAME AND MUSEUM

Kellogg, David. True Stories of Baseball's Hall of Famers. 2015. (ENG., Illus.). 100p. (J). pap. 8.95 *(978-0-912517-41-4(7))* Bluewood Bks.

Nicholson, Lois P. From Maryland to Cooperstown: Seven Maryland Natives in Baseball's Hall of Fame, 1 vol. 2010. (ENG., Illus.). 144p. (J). (gr. 4-8). 19.95 *(978-0-87033-494-8(8),* 9780870334948, Cornell Maritime Pr./Tidewater Pubs.) Schiffer Publishing, Ltd.

NATIONAL BASKETBALL ASSOCIATION

ABDO Publishing Company Staff. Inside the NBA. 2011. (Inside the NBA Ser.). (ENG., Illus.). 48p. lib. bdg. 983.70 *(978-1-61783-148-5(4),* SportsZone) ABDO Publishing Co.

De Medeiros, Michael. The NBA. 2007. (Sporting Championships Ser.). (Illus.). 32p. (J). (gr. 4-6). lib. bdg. 26.00 *(978-1-59036-691-2(3));* per. 9.95 *(978-1-59036-692-9(1))* Weigl Pubs., Inc.

—NBA. 2012. (J). *(978-1-61913-060-9(2));* pap. 28.55 *(978-1-61913-622-9(8))* Weigl Pubs., Inc.

Donnelly, Patrick. Best NBA Centers of All Time, 1 vol. 2014. (NBA's Best Ever Ser.). (ENG., Illus.). 64p. (J). (gr. 8-12). lib. bdg. 32.79 *(978-1-62403-409-1(8),* SportsZone) ABDO Publishing Co.

—Best NBA Forwards of All Time, 1 vol. 2014. (NBA's Best Ever Ser.). (ENG.). 64p. (gr. 8-12). lib. bdg. 32.79 *(978-1-62403-411-4(X),* SportsZone) ABDO Publishing Co.

Graves, Will. Best NBA Guards of All Time, 1 vol. 2014. (NBA's Best Ever Ser.). (ENG.). 64p. (gr. 8-12). lib. bdg. 32.79 *(978-1-62403-412-1(8),* SportsZone) ABDO Publishing Co.

—Best NBA Teams of All Time, 1 vol. 2014. (NBA's Best Ever Ser.). (ENG.). 64p. (gr. 8-12). lib. bdg. 32.79 *(978-1-62403-414-5(4),* SportsZone) ABDO Publishing Co.

Hareas, John. NBA Slam Dunk 3-D. 2006. (J). pap. *(978-0-439-78814-4(5))* Scholastic, Inc.

Hoffman, Mary Ann. Dwayne Wade: Basketball Star. 2009. (Sports Superstars Ser.). 24p. (gr. 1-1). 42.50 *(978-1-60853-176-9(7),* PowerKids Pr.) Rosen Publishing Group, Inc., The.

—Dwayne Wade: Basketball Star/Estrella del Baloncesto. 2009. (Amazing Athletes/Atletas increíbles Ser.). (ENG & SPA.). 24p. (gr. 1-2). 42.50 *(978-1-61511-305-7(3),* Editorial Buenas Letras) Rosen Publishing Group, Inc., The.

LeBoutillier, Nate. The Best of Everything Basketball Book, 1 vol. (All-Time Best of Sports Ser.). (ENG.). 64p. (gr. 3-4). 2011. pap. 8.95 *(978-1-4296-6327-4(8))* 2011. pap. 53.70 *(978-1-4296-6453-0(3))* 2010. lib. bdg. 34.65 *(978-1-4296-5468-5(6))* Capstone Press of Coughlan Cos.

—The Ultimate Guide to Pro Basketball Teams. 2010. (Ultimate Pro Team Guides (Sports Illustrated for Kids) Ser.). (ENG.). 72p. (gr. 3-4). pap. 8.95 *(978-1-4296-5641-2(7));* pap. 53.70 *(978-1-4296-5734-1(0))* Capstone Press of Coughlan Cos.

Silverman, Drew. Nba Finals, 1 vol. 2013. (Sports' Great Championships Ser.). (ENG., Illus.). 64p. (J). (gr. 4-6). lib. bdg. 32.79 *(978-1-61783-671-8(0),* SportsZone) ABDO Publishing Co.

Wilner, Barry. Best NBA Dunkers of All Time, 1 vol. 2014. (NBA's Best Ever Ser.). (ENG.). 64p. (gr. 8-12). lib. bdg. 32.79 *(978-1-62403-410-7(1),* SportsZone) ABDO Publishing Co.

—Best NBA Shooters of All Time, 1 vol. 2014. (NBA's Best Ever Ser.). (ENG., Illus.). 64p. (J). (gr. 8-12). lib. bdg. 32.79 *(978-1-62403-413-8(6),* SportsZone) ABDO Publishing Co.

NATIONAL DANCES

see Folk Dancing

NATIONAL FOOTBALL LEAGUE

ABDO Publishing Company Staff. NFL's Best Ever. 2013. (NFL's Best Ever Ser.: 6). 64p. (gr. 3-6). lib. bdg. 196.74 *(978-1-61783-906-1(X),* SportsZone) ABDO Publishing Co.

Brock, Ted. Running Pro Football: Commissioner, Owners, Front Office, & More, Vol. 10. 2016. (All about Professional Football Ser.: Vol. 10). (ENG., Illus.). 64p. (J). (gr. 7-12). 23.95 *(978-1-4222-3585-0(8))* Mason Crest.

Bryant, Howard & Mack, Jeff. Legends: The Best Players, Games, & Teams in Football. 2015. (ENG., Illus.). 336p. (J). (gr. 3-7). bds. 17.99 *(978-0-399-16904-5(0),* Philomel Bks.) Penguin Young Readers Group.

Frederick, Shane. The Best of Everything Football Book, 1 vol. (All-Time Best of Sports Ser.). (ENG.). 64p. (gr. 3-4). 2011. pap. 8.95 *(978-1-4296-6326-7(X))* 2011. pap. 53.70 *(978-1-4296-6454-7(1))* 2010. lib. bdg. 34.65 *(978-1-4296-5466-1(X))* Capstone Press of Coughlan Cos.

—The Ultimate Guide to Pro Football Teams. 2010. (Ultimate Pro Team Guides (Sports Illustrated for Kids) Ser.). (ENG.). 72p. (gr. 3-4). pap. 53.70 *(978-1-4296-5735-8(9))* Capstone Press of Coughlan Cos.

Gigliotti, Jim. The Intense World of a Pro Football Coach, Vol. 10. 2016. (All about Professional Football Ser.). (Illus.). 64p. (J). (gr. 7). 23.95 *(978-1-4222-3582-9(3))* Mason Crest.

—The Pro Football Draft, Vol. 10. 2016. (All about Professional Football Ser.: Vol. 10). (ENG., Illus.). 64p. (J). (gr. 7-12). 23.95 *(978-1-4222-3583-6(1))* Mason Crest.

Gilbert, Sara. The Story of the NFL. (Built for Success Ser.). (J). 2012. (ENG.). 48p. (gr. 4-7). pap. 12.00 *(978-0-89812-661-7(4),* Creative Paperbacks) 2011. (Illus.). (gr. 5-9). 34.25 *(978-1-60818-063-9(8))* Creative Co., The.

Graves, Will. Best NFL Defenses of All Time, 1 vol. 2013. (NFL's Best Ever Ser.). (ENG., Illus.). 64p. (J). (gr. 3-6). lib. bdg. 32.79 *(978-1-61783-907-8(8),* SportsZone) ABDO Publishing Co.

—Best NFL Offenses of All Time, 1 vol. 2013. (NFL's Best Ever Ser.). (ENG., Illus.). 64p. (J). (gr. 3-6). lib. bdg. 32.79 *(978-1-61783-909-2(4),* SportsZone) ABDO Publishing Co.

Howell, Brian. Denver Broncos. 2015. (Insider's Guide to Pro Football Ser.). (ENG.). 32p. (J). (gr. k-3). 28.50 *(978-1-63143-999-5(5),* 208834) Child's World, Inc., The.

Kelley, K. C. Quarterback Superstars 2015. 2015. (Illus.). 32p. (J). *(978-0-545-88736-6(4))* Scholastic, Inc.

Kortemeier, Todd. Pro Football by the Numbers. 2016. (Illus.). (J). pap. *(978-1-4914-9070-9(5))* Capstone Press of Coughlan Cos.

Kortemeier, Tom. Pro Football by the Numbers. 2016. (Pro Sports by the Numbers Ser.). (ENG., Illus.). 32p. (gr. 3-4). lib. bdg. 27.99 *(978-1-4914-9060-0(8),* Edge Bks.) Capstone Press of Coughlan Cos.

Latimer, Clay. VIP Pass to a Pro Football Game Day: From the Locker Room to the Press Box (and Everything in Between) 2011. (Game Day (Sports Illustrated for Kids) Ser.). (ENG.). 32p. (gr. 3-4). pap. 47.70 *(978-1-4296-6449-3(5))* Capstone Press of Coughlan Cos.

Layden, Joseph. Rising Stars, NFL. 2005. (Illus.). 32p. (J). pap. *(978-0-439-80247-5(4))* Scholastic, Inc.

Monnig, Alex. Arizona Cardinals. 2015. (Insider's Guide to Pro Football Ser.). (ENG.). 32p. (J). (gr. k-3). 28.50 *(978-1-63407-015-7(1),* 208850) Child's World, Inc., The.

—Atlanta Falcons. 2015. (Insider's Guide to Pro Football Ser.). (ENG.). 32p. (J). (gr. k-3). 28.50 *(978-1-63407-011-9(9),* 208846) Child's World, Inc., The.

Norman, J. T. Houston Texans. 2017. (Illus.). 32p. (J). ***(978-1-68079-894-4(4),*** SportsZone) ABDO Publishing Co.

Patrick, James. Football Madness: The Road to Super Bowl XXXVII. 2003. (Illus.). 24p. (J). *(978-0-439-48650-7(5))* Scholastic, Inc.

Rausch, David. National Football League. 2014. (Major League Sports Ser.). (ENG.). 24p. (J). (gr. 3-7). 25.95 *(978-1-62617-136-7(X),* Epic Bks.) Bellwether Media.

Robinson, Tom. Today's 12 Hottest NFL Superstars. 2015. (ENG., Illus.). 32p. (J). *(978-1-63235-022-0(X))* Pr. Room Editions LLC.

Ryan, Mike. Amazing Football: Stars, Stats & Facts. 2016. (ENG., Illus.). 64p. (J). (gr. 5-10). pap. 9.95 *(978-1-77085-777-3(X),* 9781770857773) Firefly Bks., Ltd.

Scheff, Matt. Amazing NFL Stories: 12 Highlights from NFL History. 2015. (NFL at a Glance Ser.). (ENG., Illus.). 32p. (gr. 3-5). *(978-1-63235-151-7(X),* 12-Story Library) Pr. Room Editions LLC.

—Best NFL Quarterbacks of All Time, 1 vol. 2013. (NFL's Best Ever Ser.). (ENG., Illus.). 64p. (J). (gr. 3-6). lib. bdg. 32.79 *(978-1-61783-910-8(8),* SportsZone) ABDO Publishing Co.

—Best NFL Running Backs of All Time, 1 vol. 2013. (NFL's Best Ever Ser.). (ENG., Illus.). 64p. (J). (gr. 3-6). lib. bdg. 32.79 *(978-1-61783-912-2(4),* SportsZone) ABDO Publishing Co.

—Classic NFL Games: 12 Thrillers from NFL History. 2015. (NFL at a Glance Ser.). (ENG., Illus.). 32p. (gr. 3-5). *(978-1-63235-154-8(4),* 12-Story Library) Pr. Room Editions LLC.

Silverman, Drew. The Super Bowl: 12 Reasons to Love the NFL's Big Game. 2015. (NFL at a Glance Ser.). (ENG., Illus.). 32p. (J). (gr. 3-5). *(978-1-63235-157-9(9),* 12-Story Library) Pr. Room Editions LLC.

—Today's NFL: 12 Reasons Fans Follow the Game. 2015. (NFL at a Glance Ser.). (ENG., Illus.). 32p. (J). (gr. 3-5). *(978-1-63235-158-6(7),* 12-Story Library) Pr. Room Editions LLC.

Tustison, Matt. Awesome NFL Records: 12 Hard-to-Reach Marks. 2015. (NFL at a Glance Ser.). (ENG., Illus.). 32p. (J). (gr. 3-5). *(978-1-63235-156-2(0),* 12-Story Library) Pr. Room Editions LLC.

Wilner, Barry. Best NFL Defensive Players of All Time, 1 vol. 2013. (NFL's Best Ever Ser.). (ENG., Illus.). 64p. (J). (gr. 3-6). lib. bdg. 32.79 *(978-1-61783-908-5(6),* SportsZone) ABDO Publishing Co.

—Best NFL Receivers of All Time, 1 vol. 2013. (NFL's Best Ever Ser.). (ENG., Illus.). 64p. (J). (gr. 3-6). lib. bdg. 32.79 *(978-1-61783-911-5(6),* SportsZone) ABDO Publishing Co.

—Dallas Cowboys. 2015. (Insider's Guide to Pro Football Ser.). (ENG.). 32p. (J). (gr. k-3). 28.50 *(978-1-63407-003-4(8),* 208838) Child's World, Inc., The.

Wyner, Zach. Atlanta Falcons. 2014. (Inside the NFL Ser.). (ENG., Illus.). 32p. (J). (gr. 4-7). lib. bdg. 28.55 *(978-1-4896-0786-7(2),* AV2 by Weigl) Weigl Pubs., Inc.

—Dallas Cowboys. 2014. (Inside the NFL Ser.). (ENG., Illus.). 32p. (J). (gr. 4-7). lib. bdg. 28.55 *(978-1-4896-0814-7(1),* AV2 by Weigl) Weigl Pubs., Inc.

—Denver Broncos. 2014. (Inside the NFL Ser.). (ENG., Illus.). 32p. (J). (gr. 4-7). lib. bdg. 28.55 *(978-1-4896-0818-5(4),* AV2 by Weigl) Weigl Pubs., Inc.

—Philadelphia Eagles. 2014. (Inside the NFL Ser.). (ENG., Illus.). 32p. (J). (gr. 4-7). lib. bdg. 28.55 *(978-1-4896-0874-1(5),* AV2 by Weigl) Weigl Pubs., Inc.

Zappa, Marcia. NFL's Greatest Teams Set 2, 1 vol. 2014. (NFL's Greatest Teams Set 2 Ser.: 8). (ENG.). 32p. (gr. 2-5). lib. bdg. 228.00 *(978-1-62403-584-5(1),* Big Buddy Bks.) ABDO Publishing Co.

NATIONAL GUARD (UNITED STATES)

see United States—National Guard

NATIONAL HOLIDAYS

see Holidays

NATIONAL HYMNS

see National Songs

NATIONAL MONUMENTS

see Monuments; National Parks and Reserves; Natural Monuments

NATIONAL PARKS AND RESERVES

see also Natural Monuments

also names of national parks, e.g. Yellowstone National park

ABDO Publishing Company Staff. National Parks Set 1. 2005. (National Parks Ser.). (gr. 3-8). 162.42 *(978-1-59197-422-2(4),* Abdo & Daughters) ABDO Publishing Co.

Adams, Presley. Let's Go to Acadia National Park: Solve Problems Involving the Four Operations, 1 vol. 2015. (InfoMax Common Core Math Readers Ser.). (ENG.). 24p. (J). pap. 8.25 *(978-1-4777-4687-5(0),* Rosen Classroom) Rosen Publishing Group, Inc., The.

Augustin, Byron & Kubena, Jake. Yellowstone National Park. 2009. (Nature's Wonders 2 Ser.). (Illus.). 96p. (gr. 6). 35.64 *(978-0-7614-3936-3(6))* Marshall Cavendish Corp.

Burnham, Brad. Mammoth Cave: The World's Longest Cave System. (Famous Caves of the World Ser.). 24p. 2009. (gr. 3-4). 42.50 *(978-1-61512-498-5(5))* 2003. (Illus.). (J). lib. bdg. 22.60 *(978-0-8239-6258-7(X))* Rosen Publishing Group, Inc., The. (PowerKids Pr.).

Buzzeo, Toni. A Passion for Elephants: The Real Life Adventure of Field Scientist Cynthia Moss. Berry, Holly, illus. 2015. (ENG.). 32p. (J). (gr. k-3). E-Book *(978-0-399-18600-4(X),* Dial Bks) Penguin Young Readers Group.

Chapman, Helen. Landmarks of the World. 2015. (Collins Big Cat Ser.). (ENG., Illus.). 24p. (J). (gr. 2-2). pap. 6.95 *(978-0-00-759112-1(8))* HarperCollins Pubs. Ltd. GBR. Dist: Independent Pubs. Group.

Connors, Kathleen. Acadia National Park. 2015. (Road Trip Ser.). (ENG., Illus.). 24p. (J). (gr. 2-3). lib. bdg. 22.60 *(978-1-4824-1674-9(3))* Stevens, Gareth Publishing LLLP.

DeFries, Cheryl L. What Are the 7 Natural Wonders of the United States? 2013. (What Are the Seven Wonders of the World? Ser.). 48p. (J). (gr. 4-18). 25.27 *(978-0-7660-4154-7(9))* Enslow Pubs., Inc.

Doeden, Matt. Gettysburg Battlefield: A Chilling Interactive Adventure. 2017. (You Choose: Haunted Places Ser.). (ENG., Illus.). 112p. (gr. 3-4). lib. bdg. 31.99 *(978-1-5157-3649-3(0),* You Choose Bks.) Capstone Press of Coughlan Cos.

Domeniconi, David. M Is for Majestic: A National Parks Alphabet. Carroll, Pam, illus. (ENG.). (J). (gr. k-6). 2007. 48p. per. 7.95 *(978-1-58536-333-9(2))* 2003. 40p. 17.95 *(978-1-58536-138-0(0))* Sleeping Bear Pr.

Dunton, Blair. Where the Animals Are King: Ranthambore National Park. Dunton, Blair, illus. 2016. (ENG., Illus.). (J). 12.95 *(978-1-934159-29-3(8))* ThingsAsian Pr.

Establishment of Mount McKinley Park. (Shorey Historical Ser.). (Illus.). 32p. (J). reprint ed. pap. 10.00 *(978-0-8466-0015-2(3),* S15) Shorey's Bookstore.

Fodor's Travel Publications, Inc. Staff. National Parks Guide USA. 2016. (ENG., Illus.). 176p. (J). (gr. 3-7). pap. 14.99 *(978-1-4263-2314-0(X),* National Geographic Children's Bks.) National Geographic Society.

Frisch, Nate. Badlands National Park: Preserving America. 2016. (Preserving America Ser.). (ENG.). 48p. (J). (gr. 5-9). pap. 12.00 *(978-1-62832-179-1(2),* Creative Paperbacks) Creative Co., The.

—Big Bend National Park: Preserving America. 2016. (Preserving America Ser.). (ENG.). 48p. (J). (gr. 5-9). pap. 12.00 *(978-1-62832-180-7(6),* Creative Paperbacks) Creative Co., The.

—Death Valley National Park. 2013. (Illus.). 48p. (J). 35.65 *(978-1-60818-194-0(4),* Creative Education) Creative Co., The.

—Everglades National Park. 2013. (Illus.). 48p. (J). 35.65 *(978-1-60818-195-7(2),* Creative Education) Creative Co., The.

—Grand Canyon National Park. 2013. (Illus.). 48p. (J). 35.65 *(978-1-60818-196-4(0),* Creative Education) Creative Co., The.

—Grand Teton National Park: Preserving America. 2016. (Preserving America Ser.). (ENG.). 48p. (J). (gr. 5-9). pap. 12.00 *(978-1-62832-181-4(4),* Creative Paperbacks) Creative Co., The.

—Great Smoky Mountains National Park. 2013. (Illus.). 48p. (J). 35.65 *(978-1-60818-197-1(9),* Creative Education) Creative Co., The.

Graf, Mike. Grand Teton National Park: to the Top of the Grand. 2013. (Adventures with the Parkers Ser.: 12). (ENG., Illus.). 96p. pap. 12.95 *(978-0-7627-8274-1(9),* Falcon Guides) Globe Pequot Pr., The.

Herrington, Lisa M. Rocky Mountain. 2017. (Rookie National Parks Ser.). (ENG.). 32p. (J). pap. 5.95 ***(978-0-531-23905-6(5),*** Children's Pr.) Scholastic Library Publishing.

Hodge, Deborah. West Coast Wild: A Nature Alphabet, 1 vol. Reczuch, Karen, illus. 2015. (ENG.). 48p. (J). (gr. -1-2). 18.95 *(978-1-55498-440-4(8))* Groundwood Bks. CAN. Dist: Publishers Group West (PGW).

Holtz, Monica Stauber. Behind the Zoo: Find Out What the Animals Eat & Do at Irvine Park Zoo, Chippewa Falls, Wisconsin. Opatz, Shane, illus. Opatz, Shane, photos by. 2011. (J). *(978-0-9837617-1-6(X))* Holtz Creative Enterprises.

Hurtig, Jennifer. Uluru: Sacred Rock of the Australian Desert. 2006. (Natural Wonders Ser.). (Illus.). 32p. (J). (gr. 3-7). pap. 9.95 *(978-1-59036-454-3(6));* lib. bdg. 26.00 *(978-1-59036-448-2(1))* Weigl Pubs., Inc.

Leavitt, Amie Jane. National Parks Volunteer. 2016. (J). ***(978-1-4896-5854-8(8))*** Weigl Pubs., Inc.

Lewin, Ted & Lewin, Betsy. Balarama: A Royal Elephant. Lewin, Ted & Lewin, Betsy, illus. 2009. (Adventures Around the World Ser.). (ENG., Illus.). 56p. (J). (gr. 1-6). 19.95 *(978-1-60060-265-8(7))* Lee & Low Bks., Inc.

McReynolds, Stacy. San Antonio Zoo. 2009. (Great Zoos of the United States Ser.). 24p. (gr. 3-4). 42.50 *(978-1-61513-223-2(6),* PowerKids Pr.) Rosen Publishing Group, Inc., The.

National Geographic Kids Staff. My National Parks Adventure. 2016. (NG Kids Funny Fill In Ser.). (ENG.). 48p. (J). (gr. 3-7). pap. 4.99 *(978-1-4263-2303-4(4),* National Geographic Children's Bks.) National Geographic Society.

—National Parks Guide USA. 2016. (ENG., Illus.). 176p. (J). (gr. 3-7). lib. bdg. 24.90 *(978-1-4263-2315-7(8),* National Geographic Children's Bks.) National Geographic Society.

O'Reilly, Wenda. Amazing places natl Parks. 2007. n/ap. pap. 119.40 *(978-1-59960-014-7(5))* Birdcage Pr.

Orme, David. Weird Places. 2009. (Fact to Fiction Ser.). (Illus.). 36p. (J). pap. 6.95 *(978-0-7891-7897-8(4))* Perfection Learning Corp.

Peabody, Erin. A Weird & Wild Beauty: The Story of Yellowstone, the World's First National Park. 2016. (ENG., Illus.). 192p. (J). (gr. 6). 14.99 *(978-1-63450-204-7(3),* Sky Pony Pr.) Skyhorse Publishing Co., Inc.

Pecorella, Jane. Yellowstone: Our First National Park. 2009. (Reading Room Collection 2 Ser.). 24p. (gr. 3-4). 42.50 *(978-1-60852-004-6(8),* PowerKids Pr.) Rosen Publishing Group, Inc., The.

Pero, Denis & Auzou Publishing Staff. My Book of Animals: A Walk Through the National Parks. 2013. (ENG., Illus.). 96p. (J). (gr. 2). 16.95 *(978-2-7338-2315-6(9))* Auzou, Philippe Editions FRA. Dist: Consortium Bk. Sales & Distribution.

Rath, Robert. Go Wild for Puzzles Glacier National Park. Rath, Robert, illus. 2008. (Illus.). 32p. (J). (gr. k-3). pap. 5.95 *(978-1-56037-428-2(4))* Farcountry Pr.

Raum, Elizabeth. Star Spangled Banner in Translation: What It Really Means. 2016. (Kids' Translations Ser.). (ENG.). 32p. (gr. 3-4). pap. 8.10 *(978-1-5157-6274-4(2),* Fact Finders) Capstone Press of Coughlan Cos.

Road Trip: National Parks. 2015. (Road Trip Ser.). (ENG.). 24p. (J). (gr. 2-3). pap., pap., pap. 293.40 *(978-1-4824-3487-3(3))* Stevens, Gareth Publishing LLLP.

Shepherd, Jodie. Zion. 2017. (Rookie National Parks Ser.). (ENG.). 32p. (J). pap. 5.95 ***(978-0-531-23908-7(X))*** Scholastic Library Publishing.

Steck-Vaughn Staff. National Parks. 2003. pap. 4.10 *(978-0-7398-7651-0(1))* Steck-Vaughn.

Thompson, Gare. Serengeti Journey: On Safari in Africa. 2006. (Science Chapters Ser.). (ENG., Illus.). 48p. (J). (gr. 1-4). 17.90 *(978-0-7922-5952-7(1),* National Geographic Children's Bks.) National Geographic Society.

Tomio, Stacy & Keffer, Ken. The National Parks! 2016. (Ranger Rick's Travels Ser.). (ENG., Illus.). 144p. (J). (gr. 2-6). pap. 14.95 *(978-1-63076-230-8(X))* Muddy Boots Pr.

Trumbauer, Lisa. National Parks. 2005. (Yellow Umbrella Fluent Level Ser.). (ENG., Illus.). 16p. (gr. k-1). pap. 35.70 *(978-0-7368-5314-9(6),* Yellow Umbrella Bks.) Capstone Press of Coughlan Cos.

Van Valkenburgh, Norman J. America's First Wilderness: New York State's Forest Preserves. 2008. (Illus.). 44p. (J). 6.50 *(978-1-930098-88-6(X))* Purple Mountain Pr., Ltd.

Weil, Ann. The World's Most Amazing National Parks, 1 vol. 2011. (Landmark Top Tens Ser.). (ENG., Illus.). 32p. (gr. 3-5). pap. 8.29 *(978-1-4109-4254-8(6));* 30.65 *(978-1-4109-4243-2(0))* Heinemann-Raintree. (Raintree Perspectives).

Williams, Colleen Madonna Flood. My Adventure at the Safari Park. 2007. 44p. (J). 8.99 *(978-1-59092-577-5(7))* Blue Forge Pr.

Winterberg, Jenna. Parks for All: U. S. National Parks (Level 4) 2017. (Exploring Reading Ser.). (Illus.). 32p. (gr. 4-4). 9.99 ***(978-1-4258-4979-5(2))*** Teacher Created Materials, Inc.

Woods, Michael & Woods, Mary B. Seven Natural Wonders of North America. 2009. (Seven Wonders Ser.). (ENG., Illus.). 80p. (gr. 5-8). lib. bdg. 33.26 *(978-0-8225-9069-9(7))* Lerner Publishing Group.

World Book, Inc Staff, contrib. by. Enchanted Landscapes. 2017. (J). ***(978-0-7166-3366-2(3))*** World Bk., Inc.

NATIONAL PARKS AND RESERVES—FICTION

Allred, Sylvester & Iverson, Diane. Rascal, the Tassel-Eared Squirrel. 2007. (ENG., Illus.). 64p. pap. 9.95 *(978-0-938216-44-5(9))* Grand Canyon Assn.

Beall, Linda R. We , Four Paws & Me at Yellowstone National Park. 2012. 40p. pap. 24.95 *(978-1-4626-8305-5(3))* America Star Bks.

Beaty, Janice C. Jarod & the Mystery of the Joshua Trees: A National Park Adventure Series Book. 2015. (Illus.). 108p. (J). pap. *(978-1-63293-037-8(4))* Sunstone Pr.

Beaty, Janice J. & Beaty, Lillian C., illus. Jarod & the Mystery of the Utah Arches: A National Park Adventure Series Book. 2016. 118p. (J). pap. *(978-1-63293-122-1(2))* Sunstone Pr.

Bowen, Carl. Back Burn. Lee, Marc, illus. 2016. (Firestormers Ser.). (ENG.). 112p. (gr. 4-8). lib. bdg. 26.65 *(978-1-4965-3305-0(4))* Stone Arch Bks.

—Bone Yard. Lee, Marc, illus. 2016. (Firestormers Ser.). (ENG.). 112p. (gr. 4-8). lib. bdg. 26.65 *(978-1-4965-3306-7(2))* Stone Arch Bks.

—Fire Front. Lee, Marc, illus. 2016. (Firestormers Ser.). (ENG.). 112p. (gr. 4-8). lib. bdg. 26.65 *(978-1-4965-3308-1(9))* Stone Arch Bks.

Bush, Laura & Hager, Jenna Bush. Our Great Big Backyard. Rogers, Jacqueline, illus. 40p. (J). (gr. -1-3). 2018. pap. 7.99 ***(978-0-06-246841-3(3))*** 2016. (ENG.). 18.99 *(978-0-06-246835-2(9))* 2016. lib. bdg. 19.89 *(978-0-06-246836-9(7))* HarperCollins Pubs.

Chandler, Mitzi. I See Something Grand. 2003. (Illus.). 32p. (J). (gr. -1-1). pap. 8.95 *(978-0-938216-50-6(3))* Grand Canyon Assn.

Coyle, Carmela Lavigna. Do Princesses & Super Heroes Hit the Trails? A National Park Adventure, Vol. 2016. (ENG., Illus.). 32p. (J). (gr. -1-12). 15.95 *(978-1-63076-244-5(X))* Muddy Boots Pr.

de Gramont, Nina. Every Little Thing in the World. 2010. (ENG., Illus.). 288p. (YA). (gr. 9-18). 16.99 *(978-1-4169-8013-1(X),* Atheneum Bks. for Young Readers) Simon & Schuster Children's Publishing.

Dunbar, Paula J. Ruby's Rainbow: A Story of Acadia National Park. l.t. ed. 2005. (Illus.). 32p. (J). *(978-1-931207-59-1(3))* Dilligaf Publishing.

Farnsworth, Frances. Cubby in Wonderland. 2005. pap. 20.95 *(978-1-4179-8778-8(2))* Kessinger Publishing, LLC.

Farnsworth, Frances Joyce. Tike & Tiny in the Tetons. 2007. (Illus.). 172p. (J). pap. 14.95 *(978-0-943972-79-4(5))* Homestead Publishing.

Ferguson, Alane & Skurzynski, Gloria. Deadly Waters. 2007. (Mysteries in Our National Park Ser.). (ENG., Illus.). 160p. (J). (gr. 3-7). 4.99 *(978-1-4263-0093-6(X),* National Geographic Children's Bks.) National Geographic Society.

—Escape from Fear: A Mystery in Virgin Islands National Park. 2008. (Mysteries in Our National Park Ser.). (ENG., Illus.). 160p. (J). (gr. 3-7). mass mkt. 4.99 *(978-1-4263-0181-0(2),* National Geographic Children's Bks.) National Geographic Society.

—Running Scared. 2008. (Mysteries in Our National Park Ser.). (ENG., Illus.). 160p. (J). (gr. 3-7). mass mkt. 4.99 *(978-1-4263-0182-7(0),* National Geographic Children's Bks.) National Geographic Society.

Gallicano, Todd Calgi. Guardians of the Gryphon's Claw. 2017. (Sam London Adventure Ser.: 1). (ENG.). 384p. (J). (gr. 5). 16.99 ***(978-1-5247-1365-2(1))***; lib. bdg. 19.99 ***(978-1-5247-1366-9(X))*** Random Hse. Children's Bks. (Delacorte Bks. for Young Readers).

Hill, Carolyn Swan. A Summer to Remember. 2013. 256p. (YA). (gr. 10-12). pap. 17.99 *(978-1-4624-0543-5(6),* Inspiring Voices) Author Solutions, Inc.

Hoena, Blake. Can You Survive a Supervolcano Eruption? An Interactive Doomsday Adventure. Vanzo, Filippo, illus. 2016. (You Choose: Doomsday Ser.). (ENG.). 112p. (gr. 3-4). lib. bdg. 31.99 *(978-1-4914-8108-0(0),* You Choose Bks.) Capstone Press of Coughlan Cos.

Iverson, Diane. Rascal, the Tassel Eared Squirrel. 2007. 64p. pap. 9.95 *(978-0-932821-64-5(2))* Grand Canyon Assn.

Kittredge, James M. The Three Little Explorers, 1 vol. Reyes, Glendalys, illus. 2010. 16p. pap. 24.95 *(978-1-4489-8973-7(6))* PublishAmerica, Inc.

Lamond, Peter. The Rainforest Family & Those Terrible Toads. Purnell, Teresa, illus. 2011. 92p. pap. 27.25 *(978-1-60976-297-1(5),* Eloquent Bks.) Strategic Book Publishing & Rights Agency (SBPRA).

Marsh, Carole. The Mystery at Cape Cod. 2010. (Real Kids, Real Places Ser.). (Illus.). 158p. (J). pap. 18.99 *(978-0-635-07594-9(6),* Marsh, Carole Mysteries) Gallopade International.

—The Mystery at Cape Cod. Friedlander, Randolyn, illus. 2010. (Real Kids, Real Places Teacher Guides). 32p. (J). pap. 7.99 *(978-0-635-07600-7(4))* Gallopade International.

—The Mystery at Death Valley. 2010. (Real Kids, Real Places Ser.). (Illus.). 158p. (J). pap. 7.99 *(978-0-635-07596-3(2),* Marsh, Carole Mysteries) Gallopade International.

—The Mystery at Grizzly Graveyard. 2014. (Real Kids, Real Places Ser.: Vol. 3). (ENG., Illus.). 158p. (J). (gr. 3-5). pap. 7.99 *(978-0-635-11187-6(X),* Marsh, Carole Mysteries) Gallopade International.

—The Mystery at Yellowstone National Park. 2010. (Real Kids, Real Places Ser.). (Illus.). 158p. (J). 18.99 *(978-0-635-07437-9(0),* Marsh, Carole Mysteries) Gallopade International.

—The Rip-Roaring Mystery on the African Safari. 2009. (Around the World in 80 Mysteries Ser.). (J). (gr. 2-9). lib. bdg. 18.99 *(978-0-635-06835-4(4))* Gallopade International.

Parks, M. Elizabeth. The Sea Cow. 2013. (Illus.). 44p. pap. 16.95 *(978-0-9824565-2-1(2))* Sibyl Merritt.

Redmon, Jaylyle. Gracie the Lop-Eared Burro. 2008. 17p. pap. 24.95 *(978-1-60672-626-6(9))* America Star Bks.

Schuette, Leslie Elaine. Little Autumn's Adventure in the Smoky Mountains. 2013. 32p. pap. 24.95 *(978-1-4626-9924-7(3))* America Star Bks.

Service, Pamela F. Alien Contact. Gorman, Mike, illus. (Alien Agent Ser.: 5). (ENG.). 144p. (J). (gr. 4-6). 2010. lib. bdg. 16.95 *(978-0-7613-5363-8(1),* Carolrhoda Bks.)No. 5. 2011. pap. 5.95 *(978-0-7613-7297-4(0),* Darby Creek) Lerner Publishing Group.

—#5 Alien Contact. Gorman, Mike, illus. 2011. (Alien Agent Ser.). pap. 33.92 *(978-0-7613-8347-5(6),* Darby Creek) Lerner Publishing Group.

Skurzynski, Gloria & Ferguson, Alane. Buried Alive. 2003. (Mysteries in Our National Park Ser.: No. 12). (ENG.). 160p. (J). (gr. 3-7). 15.95 *(978-0-7922-6966-3(7),* National Geographic Children's Bks.) National Geographic Society.

—Buried Alive! 2008. (Mysteries in Our National Park Ser.). (ENG., Illus.). 160p. (J). (gr. 3-7). pap. 4.99 *(978-1-4263-0252-7(5),* National Geographic Children's Bks.) National Geographic Society.

—Cliff-Hanger: A Mystery in Mesa Verde National Park. 2007. (Mysteries in Our National Park Ser.). (ENG., Illus.). 160p. (J). (gr. 3-7). per. 4.99 *(978-1-4263-0092-9(1),* National Geographic Children's Bks.) National Geographic Society.

—Ghost Horses. 2007. (Mysteries in Our National Park Ser.). (ENG., Illus.). 160p. (J). (gr. 3-7). per. 4.99 *(978-1-4263-0108-7(1),* National Geographic Children's Bks.) National Geographic Society.

—The Hunted. 2007. (Mysteries in Our National Park Ser.). (ENG., Illus.). 160p. (J). (gr. 3-7). per. 4.99 *(978-1-4263-0095-0(6),* National Geographic Children's Bks.) National Geographic Society.

—Night of the Black Bear: A Mystery in Great Smoky Mountains National Park. 2007. (Mysteries in Our National Park Ser.). (ENG., Illus.). 160p. (J). (gr. 3-7). 4.99 *(978-1-4263-0094-3(8))*; 18.90 *(978-1-4263-0105-6(7))* National Geographic Society. (National Geographic Children's Bks.).

—Out of the Deep. 2008. (Mysteries in Our National Park Ser.). (ENG., Illus.). 160p. (J). (gr. 3-7). pap. 4.99 *(978-1-4263-0251-0(7),* National Geographic Children's Bks.) National Geographic Society.

—Over the Edge. 2008. (Mysteries in Our National Park Ser.). (ENG., Illus.). 160p. (J). (gr. 3-7). per. 4.99 *(978-1-4263-0177-3(4),* National Geographic Children's Bks.) National Geographic Society.

—Valley of Death: A Mystery in Death Valley National Park. 2008. (Mysteries in Our National Park Ser.). (ENG., Illus.). 160p. (J). (gr. 3-7). per. 4.99 *(978-1-4263-0178-0(2),* National Geographic Children's Bks.) National Geographic Society.

—Wolf Stalker: A Mystery in Yellowstone National Park. 2007. (Mysteries in Our National Park Ser.). (ENG., Illus.). 160p. (J). (gr. 3-7). per. 4.99 *(978-1-4263-0096-7(4),* National Geographic Children's Bks.) National Geographic Society.

Wood, Audrey. Bunyans. 2014. 17.00 *(978-1-63419-650-5(3))* Perfection Learning Corp.

Young, Judy. The Missing Grizzly Cubs. 2016. (Wild World of Buck Bray Ser.). (ENG.). 240p. (J). (gr. 3-6). 16.99 *(978-1-58536-970-6(5),* 204107) Sleeping Bear Pr.

NATIONAL PARKS AND RESERVES—UNITED STATES

Acadia National Park Park Pal Booklet: 7 Years or Younger. 2004. (Illus.). 16p. (J). 1.95 *(978-1-59091-031-3(1))* Eastern National.

Adams, Colleen. Exploring the Grand Canyon. 2009. (Reading Room Collection 2 Ser.). 24p. (gr. 3-4). 42.50 *(978-1-60851-963-7(5),* PowerKids Pr.) Rosen Publishing Group, Inc., The.

Aretha, David. Denali National Park & Preserve: Adventure, Explore, Discover. 2009. (America's National Parks Ser.). (Illus.). 128p. (J). (gr. 5-9). lib. bdg. 34.60 *(978-1-59845-089-7(1))* Enslow Pubs., Inc.

Beckman, Wendy Hart. National Parks in Crisis: Debating the Issues. 2004. (Issues in Focus Ser.). (Illus.). 128p. (J). lib. bdg. 27.94 *(978-0-7660-1947-8(0))* Enslow Pubs., Inc.

Bottone, Ann. My National Parks & Monuments Photo Journal. 2007. (Illus.). (J). (gr. -1-10). spiral bd. 9.95 *(978-1-58071-065-7(4))* Sierra Pr.

Burnham, Brad. Carlsbad Caverns: America's Largest Underground Chamber. 2009. (Famous Caves of the World Ser.). 24p. (gr. 3-4). 42.50 *(978-1-61512-494-7(2),* PowerKids Pr.) Rosen Publishing Group, Inc., The.

DeFries, Cheryl L. What Are the 7 Natural Wonders of the United States? 2013. (What Are the Seven Wonders of the World? Ser.). 48p. (J). (gr. 4-10). pap. 8.95 *(978-1-4644-0233-3(7))* Enslow Pubs., Inc.

Dyan, Penelope. The Comeback Kids, Book 12, the Redwood Forest. Weigand, John D., photos by. 2013. (Illus.). 34p. pap. 14.95 *(978-1-61477-081-7(6))* Bellissima Publishing, LLC.

Feinstein, Stephen. Hawai'i Volcanoes National Park: Adventure, Explore, Discover. 2009. (America's National Parks Ser.). (Illus.). 128p. (J). (gr. 5-9). lib. bdg. 34.60 *(978-1-59845-094-1(8))* Enslow Pubs., Inc.

—Yosemite National Park: Adventure, Explore, Discover. 2009. (America's National Parks Ser.). (Illus.). 128p. (J). (gr. 5-9). lib. bdg. 34.60 *(978-1-59845-095-8(6))* Enslow Pubs., Inc.

Friedman, Mel. The Oregon Trail. 2010. (True Book Ser.). (ENG., Illus.). 48p. (J). (gr. 2-5). 29.00 *(978-0-531-20584-6(3))* Scholastic Library Publishing.

Frisch, Nate. Badlands National Park. 2015. (Illus.). 48p. (J). *(978-1-60818-604-4(0),* Creative Education) Creative Co., The.

—Big Bend National Park. 2015. (Illus.). 48p. (J). *(978-1-60818-605-1(9),* Creative Education) Creative Co., The.

—Grand Teton National Park. 2015. (Illus.). 48p. (J). *(978-1-60818-606-8(7),* Creative Education) Creative Co., The.

—Preserving America: Death Valley National Park. 2014. (Preserving America Ser.). (ENG.). 48p. (J). (gr. 4-7). pap. 12.00 *(978-0-89812-877-2(3),* Creative Paperbacks) Creative Co., The.

—Preserving America: Grand Canyon National Park. 2014. (Preserving America Ser.). (ENG.). 48p. (J). (gr. 4-7). pap. 12.00 *(978-0-89812-879-6(X),* Creative Paperbacks) Creative Co., The.

—Rocky Mountain National Park. 2015. (Illus.). 48p. (J). *(978-1-60818-607-5(5),* Creative Education) Creative Co., The.

Gonzales, Doreen. Rocky Mountain National Park: Adventure, Explore, Discover. 2009. (America's National Parks Ser.). (Illus.). 128p. (J). (gr. 5-9). lib. bdg. 34.60 *(978-1-59845-096-5(4))* Enslow Pubs., Inc.

Graf, Mike. Acadia National Park: Eye of the Whale. 2013. (Adventures with the Parkers Ser.: 11). (ENG., Illus.). 96p. pap. 12.95 *(978-0-7627-8262-8(5),* Falcon Guides) Globe Pequot Pr., The.

—Arches & Canyonlands National Parks - In the Land of Standing Rocks. Leggitt, Marjorie, illus. 2012. (Adventures with the Parkers Ser.: 10). (ENG.). 112p. pap. 12.95 *(978-0-7627-7962-8(4),* Falcon Guides) Globe Pequot Pr., The.

—Glacier National Park: Going to the Sun. Leggitt, Marjorie, illus. 2012. (Adventures with the Parkers Ser.: 7). (ENG.). 96p. pap. 12.95 *(978-0-7627-7964-2(0),* Falcon Guides) Globe Pequot Pr., The.

—Grand Canyon National Park: Tail of the Scorpion. Leggitt, Marjorie, illus. 2012. (Adventures with the Parkers Ser.: 2). (ENG.). 96p. pap. 14.95 *(978-0-7627-7965-9(9),* Falcon Guides) Globe Pequot Pr., The.

—Great Smokies National Park: Ridge Runner Rescue. Leggitt, Marjorie, illus. 2012. (Adventures with the Parkers Ser.: 6). (ENG.). 96p. pap. 12.95 *(978-0-7627-7966-6(7),* Falcon Guides) Globe Pequot Pr., The.

—Olympic National Park: Touch of the Tide Pool, Crack of the Glacier. Marjorie, Leggitt, illus. 2012. (Adventures with the Parkers Ser.: 5). (ENG.). 96p. pap. 12.95 *(978-0-7627-7969-7(1),* Falcon Guides) Globe Pequot Pr., The.

—Rocky Mountain National Park: Peril on Long's Peak. Marjorie, Leggitt, illus. 2012. (Adventures with the Parkers Ser.: 8). (ENG.). 96p. pap. 12.95 *(978-0-7627-7970-3(5),* Falcon Guides) Globe Pequot Pr., The.

—Yellowstone National Park: Eye of the Grizzly. Leggitt, Marjorie, illus. 2012. (Adventures with the Parkers Ser.: 4). (ENG.). 96p. pap. 12.95 *(978-0-7627-7972-7(1),* Falcon Guides) Globe Pequot Pr., The.

—Yosemite National Park: Harrowing Ascent of Half Dome. Leggitt, Marjorie, illus. 2012. (Adventures with the Parkers Ser.: 3). (ENG.). 96p. pap. 12.95 *(978-0-7627-7973-4(X),* Falcon Guides) Globe Pequot Pr., The.

Graham, Amy. Acadia National Park: Adventure, Explore, Discover. 2008. (America's National Parks Ser.). (Illus.). 128p. (J). (gr. 5-9). lib. bdg. 34.60 *(978-1-59845-090-3(5))* Enslow Pubs., Inc.

Gregory, Josh. Grand Canyon National Park. 2017. (True Book — National Parks Ser.). (ENG.). 48p. (J). lib. bdg. 31.00 ***(978-0-531-23393-1(6),*** Children's Pr.) Scholastic Library Publishing.

Hamilton, John. Grand Teton National Park. 2008. (National Parks Set II Ser.). 32p. (gr. 4-9). 27.07 *(978-1-60453-092-6(8),* Abdo & Daughters) ABDO Publishing Co.

—Olympic National Park. 2008. (National Parks Set II Ser.). 32p. (gr. 4-9). 27.07 *(978-1-60453-093-3(6),* Abdo & Daughters) ABDO Publishing Co.

—Rocky Mountain National Park. 2008. (National Parks Set II Ser.). 32p. (gr. 4-9). 27.07 *(978-1-60453-094-0(4),* Abdo & Daughters) ABDO Publishing Co.

—Theodore Roosevelt National Park. 2008. (National Parks Set II Ser.). 32p. (gr. 4-9). 27.07 *(978-1-60453-095-7(2),* Abdo & Daughters) ABDO Publishing Co.

Hansen, Doug, illus. The Sierra Adventure Coloring Book: Featuring Yosemite National Park. 2013. (ENG.). 24p. (J). (gr. -1-2). pap. 4.95 *(978-1-930238-39-8(8))* Yosemite Assn.

Heacox, Kim. The National Parks: An Illustrated History. 2015. (ENG., Illus.). 384p. 50.00 *(978-1-4262-1559-9(2))* National Geographic Society.

Hunt, Santana. Grand Canyon National Park. 2015. (Road Trip Ser.). (ENG., Illus.). 24p. (J). (gr. 2-3). lib. bdg. 22.60 *(978-1-4824-1682-4(4))* Stevens, Gareth Publishing LLLP.

Jango-Cohen, Judith. Mount Rushmore. 2010. (Lightning Bolt Books (tm) — Famous Places Ser.). (ENG.). 32p. (gr. k-2). pap. 7.95 *(978-0-7613-6049-0(2))* Lerner Publishing Group.

Jankowski, Susan. Olympic National Park: Adventure, Explore, Discover. 2008. (America's National Parks Ser.). (Illus.). 128p. (J). (gr. 5-9). lib. bdg. 34.60 *(978-1-59845-092-7(1))* Enslow Pubs., Inc.

Lerner Classroom & Zuehlke, Jeffrey. The Grand Canyon. 2010. (Lightning Bolt Books (tm) — Famous Places Ser.). (ENG.). 32p. (gr. k-2). pap. 7.95 *(978-0-7613-5573-1(1))* Lerner Publishing Group.

Lindeen, Mary. Natural States. 2011. (Wonder Readers Fluent Level Ser.). (ENG.). 16p. (gr. -1-2). pap. 35.94 *(978-1-4296-8131-5(4),* Wonder Readers) Capstone Press of Coughlan Cos.

—Parks of the U. S. A. 2011. (Wonder Readers Fluent Level Ser.). (ENG.). 32p. (gr. -1-2). pap. 5.99 *(978-1-4296-7949-7(2),* Wonder Readers) Capstone Press of Coughlan Cos.

Marsico, Katie. The Everglades. 2013. (Explorer Library: Social Studies Explorer Ser.). (ENG.). 32p. (gr. 4-8). pap. 14.21 *(978-1-62431-041-6(9),* 202521); lib. bdg. 28.50 *(978-1-62431-017-1(6),* 202519) Cherry Lake Publishing.

McHugh, Erin. National Parks: A Kid's Guide to America's Parks, Monuments & Landmarks. Aspinall, Neal, illus. 2012. (ENG.). 128p. (gr. 1-8). 19.99 *(978-1-57912-884-5(X),* Black Dog & Leventhal Pubs. Inc.) Hachette Bks.

National Geographic Kids Staff. National Parks Guide U. S. A. The Most Amazing Sights, Scenes, & Cool Activities from Coast to Coast! 2012. (ENG., Illus.). 160p. (J). (gr. 2-4). pap. 14.95 *(978-1-4263-0931-1(7),* National Geographic Children's Bks.) National Geographic Society.

National Geographic Society (U.S.) Staff, contrib. by. National Parks Guide U. S. A: The Most Amazing Sights, Scenes, & Cool Activities from Coast to Coast! 2012. (ENG., Illus.). 160p. (J). (gr. 2-4). lib. bdg. 21.90 *(978-1-4263-0932-8(5),* National Geographic Children's Bks.) National Geographic Society.

O'Donnell, Kerri. Denali National Park: An Alaskan Ecosystem: Creating Graphical Representations of Data. 2009. (PowerMath: Advanced Proficiency Plus Ser.). 32p. (gr. 5-5). 47.90 *(978-1-60851-353-6(X),* PowerKids Pr.) Rosen Publishing Group, Inc., The.

—Denali National Park, an Alaskan Ecosystem: Creating Graphical Representations of Data. (Math for the Real World Ser.). (Illus.). 32p. 2009. (ENG.). (gr. 6-7). pap. 10.00 *(978-1-4042-6083-2(8))* 2006. (J). lib. bdg. 23.95 *(978-1-4042-3365-2(2))* Rosen Publishing Group, Inc., The.

—Denali State Park - An Alaskan Ecosystem: Creating Graphical Representation of Data. 2006. (Math Bog Bookstm Ser.). 32p. (gr. 6-7). 47.50 *(978-1-4042-6368-0(3))* Rosen Publishing Group, Inc., The.

Pearce, Claudia. San Diego Zoo. 2009. (Great Zoos of the United States Ser.). 24p. (gr. 3-4). 42.50 *(978-1-61513-224-9(4),* PowerKids Pr.) Rosen Publishing Group, Inc., The.

Prior, Jennifer. America's Natural Landmarks. rev. ed. 2014. (Primary Source Readers Content & Literacy Ser.). (ENG., Illus.). 32p. (gr. 3-3). pap. 8.99 *(978-1-4333-7371-8(8))* Teacher Created Materials, Inc.

Purslow, Neil. Redwood National Park: Forest of Giants. 2006. (Natural Wonders Ser.). 32p. (J). (gr. 3-7). pap. 9.95 *(978-1-59036-457-4(0))*; (Illus.). lib. bdg. 26.00 *(978-1-59036-451-2(1))* Weigl Pubs., Inc.

Richter, Bernd & Richter, Susan. Discover Alaskas Denali Park. 2008. (Illus.). 48p. (J). pap. 9.95 *(978-1-931353-37-3(9))* Saddle Pal Creations, Inc.

Road Trip: National Parks. 2015. (Road Trip Ser.). (ENG.). 24p. (J). (gr. 2-3). pap., pap., pap. 48.90 *(978-1-4824-3488-0(1))* Stevens, Gareth Publishing LLLP.

Robson, Gary D. Who Pooped in Park: Grand Teton. 2004. (Illus.). 48p. (J). pap. 11.95 *(978-1-56037-280-6(X))* Farcountry Pr.

—Who Pooped in the Park? Clark, Elijah Brady, illus. 2006. 48p. (J). pap. 9.95 *(978-1-56037-388-9(1))* Farcountry Pr.

—Who Pooped in the Park? Sequoia & Kings Canyon National Parks: Scats & Tracks for Kids. 2006. (Who Pooped in the Park? Ser.). (Illus.). 48p. (J). (gr. -1-3). pap. 9.95 *(978-1-56037-327-8(X))* Farcountry Pr.

Rosenstock, Barb. The Camping Trip That Changed America: Theodore Roosevelt, John Muir, & Our National Parks. Gerstein, Mordecai, illus. 2012. (ENG.). 32p. (J). (gr. 1-3). 17.99 *(978-0-8037-3710-5(6),* Dial Bks) Penguin Young Readers Group.

Rowell, Rebecca. The 12 Most Amazing American Natural Wonders. 2014. (ENG.). 32p. (J). *(978-1-63235-011-4(4))* Pr. Room Editions LLC.

Selda, Toby. Simply Father: Life with Theodore Roosevelt As Seen through the Eyes of His Children. Roosevelt, Theodore, illus. 2007. 28p. (J). 7.95 *(978-1-59091-030-6(3))* Eastern National.

Travelers Guide to National Parks 2005: Your Digital Gateway to 467 Vacation Destinations Across America. 2nd ed. 2004. cd-rom 15.00 *(978-0-9747471-5-6(7))* Belknap Digital Archives.

Wadsworth, Ginger. Camping with the President. Dugan, Karen, illus. 2009. (ENG.). 32p. (J). (gr. 4-18). 16.95 *(978-1-59078-497-6(9),* Calkins Creek) Boyds Mills Pr.

Weintraub, Aileen. Secrets of the National Parks: Weird & Wonderful Facts about America's Natural Wonders. 2016. (ENG., Illus.). 160p. (J). (gr. 1-3). 8.95 *(978-1-4549-2004-5(1))* Sterling Publishing Co., Inc.

Windsor, Wesley. American Wilderness: Alaska & the National Parks, 1865-1890. 2013. (Illus.). 48p. (J). pap. *(978-1-4222-2419-9(8))* Mason Crest.

—American Wilderness: Alaska & the National Parks (1865-1890) Rakove, Jack N., ed. 2012. (How America Became America Ser.). (Illus.). 48p. (J). (gr. 3-4). 19.95 *(978-1-4222-2405-2(8))* Mason Crest.

Yanuchi, Lori & Yanuchi, Jeff. Ranger Trails: Jobs of Adventure in America's Parks. Morris, James R., illus. 2005. 64p. (J). per. 12.95 *(978-0-9670177-2-3(6))* Ridge Rock Pr.

NATIONAL PLANNING

see Social Policy

see names of countries with the subdivision Economic Policy; Social Policy; e.g. United States—Economic Policy; United States—Social Policy

NATIONAL RESOURCES

see Natural Resources

see names of countries with the subdivision Economic Conditions, e.g. United States.—Economic Conditions

NATIONAL SECURITY

see also United States—Defenses

Beyer, Mark. Homeland Security & Weapons of Mass Destruction: How Prepared Are We? 2009. (Library of Weapons of Mass Destruction Ser.). 64p. (gr. 5-5). 58.50 *(978-1-60853-952-9(0))* Rosen Publishing Group, Inc., The.

Campbell, Geoffrey A. A Vulnerable America: An Overview of National Security. 2007. (Lucent Library of Homeland Security). (ENG., Illus.). 112p. (J). 30.85 *(978-1-59018-383-0(5),* Lucent Bks.) Cengage Gale.

Coddington, Andrew. Mass Government Surveillance: Spying on Citizens. 2017. (J). ***(978-1-5026-2672-1(1))*** Cavendish Square Publishing.

Doak, Robin S. Homeland Security. 2011. (Cornerstones of Freedom, Third Ser.). (Illus.). 64p. (J). (ENG.). pap. 8.95 *(978-0-531-26561-1(7))*; lib. bdg. 30.00 *(978-0-531-25036-5(9))* Scholastic Library Publishing. (Children's Pr.).

Freedman, Jeri. America Debates Privacy Versus Security. 2007. (America Debates Ser.). (Illus.). 64p. (YA). (gr. 5-9). lib. bdg. 31.95 *(978-1-4042-1929-8(3))* Rosen Publishing Group, Inc., The.

Gaines, Ann Graham. Border Patrol Agent & Careers in Border Protection. 2006. (Homeland Security & Counterterrorism Careers Ser.). (Illus.). 128p. (J). (gr. 5-9). 33.27 *(978-0-7660-2646-9(9))* Enslow Pubs., Inc.

Gerdes, Louise, ed. How Safe Is America's Infrastructure? 2009. (At Issue Ser.). (ENG., Illus.). 128p. (gr. 10-12). 39.40 *(978-0-7377-4104-9(X),* Greenhaven Pr., Inc.) Cengage Gale.

Gerdes, Louise I. How Safe Is America's Infrastructure? 2009. (At Issue Ser.). (ENG., Illus.). 128p. (gr. 10-12). pap. 27.80 *(978-0-7377-4105-6(8),* Greenhaven Pr., Inc.) Cengage Gale.

Gonzalez, Lissette. The U. S. Military: Defending the Nation. (Dangerous Jobs Ser.). 24p. 2009. (gr. 2-3). 42.50 *(978-1-61512-137-3(4),* PowerKids Pr.) 2007. (Illus.). (J). (gr. 3-7). lib. bdg. 22.60 *(978-1-4042-3777-3(1))* Rosen Publishing Group, Inc., The.

Grant, R. G. Why Did Hiroshima Happen? 2010. (Moments in History Ser.). (Illus.). 48p. (YA). (gr. 5-9). lib. bdg. 31.95 *(978-1-4339-4163-4(5))*; (gr. 6-8). pap. 14.05 *(978-1-4339-4164-1(3),* Gareth Stevens Secondary Library) Stevens, Gareth Publishing LLLP.

Grayson, Robert. The FBI & National Security. 2009. (FBI Story Ser.). 64p. (J). (gr. 4-7). lib. bdg. 22.95 *(978-1-4222-0564-8(9))* Mason Crest.

Haugen, David M. National Security. 2008. (At Issue Ser.). (ENG., Illus.). 128p. (gr. 10-12). 39.40 (978-0-7377-3924-4(X)); pap. 27.80 (978-0-7377-3925-1(8), Greenhaven Pr., Inc.) Cengage Gale.

Haulley, Fletcher. The Deparment of Homeland Security. 2005. (This Is Your Government Ser.). (Illus.). 64p. (J). (gr. k-3). lib. bdg. 31.95 (978-1-4042-0209-2(9)) Rosen Publishing Group, Inc., The.

—The Department of Homeland Security. (This Is Your Government Ser.). 64p. 2009. (gr. 5-6). 58.50 (978-1-60854-371-7(4), Rosen Reference) 2006. (ENG., Illus.). (gr. 4-8). per. 12.95 (978-1-4042-0662-5(0)) Rosen Publishing Group, Inc., The.

Immell, Myra. Homeland Security. 2009. (At Issue Ser.). (ENG., Illus.). 128p. (gr. 10-12). pap. 27.80 (978-0-7377-4421-7(9)) Cengage Gale.

Immell, Myra, ed. Homeland Security. 2009. (At Issue Ser.). (ENG., Illus.). 128p. (gr. 10-12). 39.40 (978-0-7377-4420-0(0)) Cengage Gale.

Katz, Samuel M. U. S. Counterstrike: American Counterterrorism. 2005. (Terrorist Dossiers Ser.). (Illus.). 72p. (J). (gr. 6-12). 26.60 (978-0-8225-1569-2(5)) Lerner Publishing Group.

Keeter, Hunter. The U. S. Homeland Security Forces. 2004. (America's Armed Forces Ser.). (Illus.). 48p. (gr. 5-12). lib. bdg. 31.00 (978-0-8368-5682-8(1), Gareth Stevens Secondary Library) Stevens, Gareth Publishing LLLP.

Kerrigan, Michael. The Department of Homeland Security. 2004. (Rescue & Prevention Ser.). (Illus.). 96p. (J). (gr. 7-18). lib. bdg. 22.95 (978-1-59084-409-0(2)) Mason Crest.

Kerrigan, Michael. Homeland Security. 2017. (J). **(978-1-4222-3767-0(2))** Mason Crest.

Koestler-Grack, Rachel A. The Department of Homeland Security. 2007. (U. S. Government Ser.). (Illus.). 104p. (J). (gr. 5-9). lib. bdg. 30.00 (978-0-7910-9286-6(0)) Facts On File, Inc.

Kowalski, Kathiann M. A Pro/con Look at Homeland Security: Safety vs. Liberty After 9/11. 2008. (Issues in Focus Today Ser.). (Illus.). 112p. (J). (gr. 3-7). lib. bdg. 33.27 (978-0-7660-2914-9(X)) Enslow Pubs., Inc.

Labov, Steven L., ed. Rescue & Prevention: Defending Our Nation, 15 vols., Set. (Illus.). 96p. (YA). (gr. 7-18). lib. bdg. (978-1-59084-401-4(7)) Mason Crest.

Mara, Wil. Homeland Security. 2016. (21st Century Skills Library: a Citizen's Guide Ser.). (ENG., Illus.). 32p. (J). (gr. 4-7). 29.93 (978-1-63471-068-8(1), 208351) Cherry Lake Publishing.

Miller, Debra A. Homeland Security. 2008. (Current Controversies Ser.). (ENG., Illus.). (gr. 10-12). 176-240p. pap. 40.95 (978-0-7377-4138-4(4)); 224p. pap. 32.00 (978-0-7377-4139-1(2)) Cengage Gale. (Greenhaven Pr., Inc.).

—The Patriot Act. 2007. (Hot Topics Ser.). (ENG., Illus.). 112p. (YA). (gr. 7-12). lib. bdg. 33.95 (978-1-59018-981-8(7), LML02109-229790) Cengage Gale.

Mullins, Matt. Homeland Security. 2010. (21st Century Skills Library: Citizens & Their Governments Ser.). (ENG.). 32p. (gr. 4-8). lib. bdg. 28.50 (978-1-60279-633-1(5), 200338) Cherry Lake Publishing.

parks, peggy j. Cyberterrorism. 2012. (Illus.). 96p. (J). lib. bdg. (978-1-60152-264-1(9)) ReferencePoint Pr., Inc.

Pavlovic, Zoran. Terrorism & Security. 2009. (Global Connections Ser.). (Illus.). 120p. (gr. 5-8). 35.00 (978-1-60413-282-3(5), Chelsea Hse.) Facts On File, Inc.

Perritano, John. Border Security, Vol. 12. 2015. (On a Mission Ser.). (Illus.). 48p. (J). (gr. 5). 20.95 (978-1-4222-3393-1(6)) Mason Crest.

Ruffin, David C. The Duties & Responsibilities of the Secretary of Homeland Security. (Your Government in Action Ser.). 32p. (gr. 3-3). 2009. 43.90 (978-1-60854-918-4(6)) 2005. (Illus.). (J). lib. bdg. 23.95 (978-1-4042-2693-7(1)) Rosen Publishing Group, Inc., The. (PowerKids Pr.).

Ruschmann, Paul. Mandatory Military Service. 2003. (Point/Counterpoint Ser.). (Illus.). 112p. (C). (gr. 9-13). 35.00 (978-0-7910-7919-5(8), Chelsea Hse.) Facts On File, Inc.

Scherer, Lauri S. Privacy. Gale Editors, ed. 2014. (Introducing Issues with Opposing Viewpoints Ser.). (ENG., Illus.). 144p. (gr. 10-12). lib. bdg. 42.00 (978-0-7377-6927-2(0), Greenhaven Pr., Inc.) Cengage Gale.

Souter, Janet. Air Marshal: And Careers in Transportation Security. 2006. (Homeland Security & Counterterrorism Careers Ser.). (Illus.). 128p. (J). (gr. 6). lib. bdg. 33.27 (978-0-7660-2647-6(7)) Enslow Pubs., Inc.

Stefoff, Rebecca. Security V. Privacy. 2007. (Open for Debate Ser.). (Illus.). 128p. (gr. 7-7). lib. bdg. 42.79 (978-0-7614-2578-6(0), Benchmark Bks.) Marshall Cavendish Corp.

Stinson, Doug. Protecting the Nation's Borders. 2005. (At Issue Ser.). (ENG.). 80-128p. (gr. 10-12). pap. 24.45 (978-0-7377-2740-1(3), Greenhaven Pr., Inc.) Cengage Gale.

Stinson, Douglass, ed. Protecting America's Borders. 2005. (At Issue Ser.). 94p. (YA). (gr. 10-13). lib. bdg. 29.95 (978-0-7377-2739-5(X), Greenhaven Pr., Inc.) Cengage Gale.

Streissguth, Tom. America's Security Agencies: The Department of Homeland Security, FBI, NSA, & CIA. 2008. (Federal Government Ser.). (Illus.). 128p. (J). (gr. 3-7). lib. bdg. 34.60 (978-1-59845-058-3(1), MyReportLinks.com Bks.) Enslow Pubs., Inc.

—The Security Agencies of the United States: How the CIA, FBI, NSA, & Homeland Security Keep Us Safe. 2012. (Constitution & the United States Government Ser.). (Illus.). 104p. (J). (gr. 5-18). 33.27 (978-0-7660-4064-9(X)) Enslow Pubs., Inc.

Wade, Mary Dodson. Condoleezza Rice: Being the Best. 2003. (Gateway Biography Ser.: 4). 48p. lib. bdg. 23.90 (978-0-7613-2619-9(7)); (Illus.). (gr. 2-4). pap. 8.95 (978-0-7613-1927-6(1)) Lerner Publishing Group. (Millbrook Pr.).

NATIONAL SOCIALISM

see also Socialism

Adolf Hitler & Nazi Germany. 2006. (World Leaders Ser.). (Illus.). 176p. (gr. 3-7). lib. bdg. 28.95 (978-1-931798-78-5(8)) Reynolds, Morgan Inc.

Altman, Linda Jacobs. Adolf Hitler & the Rise of the Third Reich. 2016. (People & Events That Changed the World Ser.). (ENG., Illus.). 112p. (J). (gr. 7-8). 37.27 (978-0-7660-7175-9(8)) Enslow Pubs., Inc.

Dolan, Sean. Adolf Eichmann: Engineer of Death. 2005. (Holocaust Biographies Ser.). (Illus.). 112p. (YA). (gr. 7-12). lib. bdg. 34.60 (978-0-8239-3308-2(3), HBEICH) Rosen Publishing Group, Inc., The.

Dufner, Annette. The Rise of Adolf Hitler. 2003. (At Issue in History Ser.). (ENG., Illus.). 144p. (YA). 26.70 (978-0-7377-1519-4(7)); pap. 35.75 (978-0-7377-1518-7(9)) Cengage Gale. (Greenhaven Pr., Inc.).

Freeman, Charles. The Rise of the Nazis. 2005. (How Did It Happen? Ser.). (ENG., Illus.). 48p. (gr. 7-10). lib. bdg. 36.70 (978-1-59018-608-4(7), Lucent Bks.) Cengage Gale.

—Why Did the Rise of the Nazis Happen? 2010. (Moments in History Ser.). (Illus.). 48p. (YA). (gr. 5-9). lib. bdg. 31.95 (978-1-4339-4175-7(9)); (ENG., (J). (gr. 6-8). pap. 14.05 (978-1-4339-4176-4(7), Gareth Stevens Secondary Library) Stevens, Gareth Publishing LLLP.

Giblin, James Cross. The Life & Death of Adolf Hitler. 2015. (ENG., Illus.). 256p. (J). (gr. 5-7). pap. 9.99 (978-0-544-45591-7(6), HMH Books For Young Readers) Houghton Mifflin Harcourt Publishing Co.

—The Life & Death of Adolf Hitler. 2015. lib. bdg. 20.85 (978-0-606-36830-8(2)) Turtleback Bks.

Gottfried, Ted. Nazi Germany: The Face of Tyranny. Alcorn, Stephen, illus. (Holocaust History Ser.). 112p. (YA). (gr. 7-12). 22.95 (978-1-58013-203-9(0), Kar-Ben Publishing) Lerner Publishing Group.

Hitler's Treasure: Nazi Gold. 2004. (YA). cd-rom 1500.00 (978-0-934269-58-2(0)) UFO Photo Archives.

Knight, Patricia. Mussolini & Fascism. 2003. (Questions & Analysis in History Ser.). (ENG., Illus.). 144p. (C). 115.00 (978-0-415-27921-5(6), 0415279216); per. 30.95 (978-0-415-27922-2(4)) Routledge.

Lowery, Zoe & Norton, James R. The Nazi Regime & the Holocaust. 2016. (Bearing Witness: Genocide & Ethnic Cleansing in the Modern World Ser.). 64p. (J). (gr. 6-6). 34.45 (978-1-5081-7163-8(7)) Rosen Publishing Group, Inc., The.

Marcovitz, Hal. Life in Nazi Germany. 2015. (ENG., Illus.). 96p. (J). lib. bdg. (978-1-60152-776-9(4)) ReferencePoint Pr., Inc.

—The Rise of the Nazis. 2014. (Understanding World History Ser.). (ENG., Illus.). 96p. (J). lib. bdg. (978-1-60152-654-0(7)) ReferencePoint Pr., Inc.

McIlroy, Michelle. Sophie Scholl: Student Resister & Anti-Nazi Political Activist. 2017. (J). **(978-1-5383-8108-3(7))** Rosen Publishing Group, Inc., The.

McKay, Jenny. Children of the Holocaust. 2015. (ENG., Illus.). 80p. (J). (gr. 5-12). lib. bdg. (978-1-60152-838-4(8)) ReferencePoint Pr., Inc.

Oshiro, Beverly & Sachs, Ruth. Adolf Eichmann, 01 vols., 1. 2016. (Holocaust Ser.). (ENG., Illus.). 112p. (J). 35.60 (978-1-4994-6246-3(8), Rosen Young Adult) Rosen Publishing Group, Inc., The.

Price, Sean Stewart. Adolf Hitler. 2010. (Wicked History Ser.). (ENG.). 128p. (J). (gr. 6-12). pap. 5.95 (978-0-531-22357-4(4)); (Illus.). 31.00 (978-0-531-20757-4(9)) Scholastic Library Publishing. (Watts, Franklin).

Ramen, Fred. Albert Speer: Hitler's Architect. 2005. (Holocaust Biographies Ser.). (Illus.). 112p. (YA). (gr. 7-12). lib. bdg. 34.60 (978-0-8239-3372-3(5)) Rosen Publishing Group, Inc., The.

—Hermann Goering: Hitler's Second in Command. 2005. (Holocaust Biographies Ser.). (Illus.). 112p. (YA). (gr. 7-12). lib. bdg. 34.60 (978-0-8239-3307-5(5), HBGORI) Rosen Publishing Group, Inc., The.

Saxena, Shalini, ed. Dictatorship, Fascism, & Totalitarianism. 2014. (Political & Economic Systems Ser.). 312p. (YA). (gr. 9-12). 45.00 (978-1-62275-350-5(X)) Rosen Publishing Group, Inc., The.

Vander Hook, Sue. Adolf Hitler: German Dictator, 1 vol. 2011. (Essential Lives Set 6 Ser.). (ENG., Illus.). 112p. (J). (gr. 6-12). lib. bdg. 35.64 (978-1-61714-781-4(8), Essential Library) ABDO Publishing Co.

Woolf, Alex. The Rise of Nazi Germany. 2004. (Questioning History Ser.). (J). lib. bdg. 28.50 (978-1-58340-442-3(2)) Black Rabbit Bks.

NATIONAL SOCIALISM—FICTION

Stasse, Lisa M. The Forsaken. 2012. (ENG.). 384p. (YA). (gr. 7). 16.99 (978-1-4424-3265-9(9), Simon & Schuster Bks. For Young Readers) Simon & Schuster Bks. For Young Readers.

Van Ryk, Laverne. A Garland of Emeralds. 2006. (Illus.). 305p. 31.50 (978-1-4122-0156-8(X)) Trafford Publishing.

NATIONAL SONGS

see also Folk Songs

Brannon, Cecelia H. Zoom in on the National Anthem. 2016. (Zoom in on American Symbols Ser.). (Illus.). 24p. (J). pap. 9.35 (978-0-7660-8446-9(9)) Enslow Pubs., Inc.

Damanda, Lori. The Story of the "Star-Spangled Banner" 2009. (Real Life Readers Ser.). 32p. (J). (ENG., Illus.). (gr. 5-6). pap. 10.00 (978-1-4358-0205-6(5)); (gr. 4-6). lib. bdg. 25.25 (978-1-4358-3015-8(6)) Rosen Publishing Group, Inc., The. (PowerKids Pr.).

—The Story of the Star-Spangled Banner. 2009. (American History Milestones Ser.). 32p. (gr. 5-5). 47.90 (978-1-61511-375-0(4), PowerKids Pr.) Rosen Publishing Group, Inc., The.

Dell, Pamela. The Star-Spangled Banner. 2016. (Spring Forward Ser.). (J). (gr. 1). (978-1-4900-9383-3(4)) Benchmark Education Co.

Gershenson, Harold P. America the Musical 1776-1899: A Nation's History Through Music. Chesworth, Michael, illus. 2005. 21p. (J). (978-1-58987-116-8(2)) Kindermusik International.

Harrison, Ted. O Canada. 2004. (J). (gr. k-3). spiral bd. (978-0-616-03038-7(X)) Canadian National Institute for the Blind/Institut National Canadien pour les Aveugles.

Healy, Nick. The Star-Spangled Banner. 2003. (J). (978-1-58417-055-6(7)); pap. (978-1-58417-118-8(9)) Lake Street Pubs.

Hess, Deborah. The Star-Spangled Banner. 2007. (J). pap. 6.99 (978-0-7614-3392-7(9)) Marshall Cavendish Corp.

Kallio, Jamie. 12 Questions about "The Star-Spangled Banner" 2017. (Examining Primary Sources Ser.). (ENG., Illus.). 32p. (J). (gr. 3-6). 21.95 (978-1-63235-288-0(5)) Pr. Room Editions LLC.

Key, Francis Scott. The Star Spangled Banner. 2005. (Illus.). 32p. pap. 7.95 (978-1-894997-12-6(3), Fox Music Bks.) Quarry Pr. CAN. Dist: SCB Distributors.

Landau, Elaine. The National Anthem. 2008. (True Bks.). (ENG., Illus.). 48p. (J). (gr. 3-5). pap. 6.95 (978-0-531-14783-2(5), Children's Pr.) Scholastic Library Publishing.

McKinney, Devon. I Sing the Star-Spangled Banner. 2016. (Symbols of Our Country Ser.). 00024p. (J). (gr. 1-1). 23.60 (978-1-4994-2730-1(1)); pap. 8.25 (978-1-4994-2729-5(8)) Rosen Publishing Group, Inc., The. (PowerKids Pr.).

Mills, Nathan & Wesolowski, Harriet. The Songs We Sing: Honoring Our Country. 2012. (Rosen Readers Ser.). (ENG., Illus.). 24p. (J). (gr. 1-2). pap. 8.25 (978-1-4488-8821-4(2), Rosen Classroom) Rosen Publishing Group, Inc., The.

Monroe, Tyler. Star-Spangled Banner. 2013. (U. S. Symbols Ser.). (ENG.). 24p. (gr. k-1). 26.65 (978-1-4765-3087-1(4)); pap. 7.95 (978-1-4765-3536-4(1)) Capstone Press of Coughlan Cos. (Pebble Plus).

Ouren, Todd, illus. Patriotic Songs, 5 vols. Incl. Star-Spangled Banner: America's National Anthem & Its History. (ENG., Illus.). 24p. (gr. -1-4). 2003. 26.65 (978-1-4048-0175-2(8)); (Patriotic Songs Ser.). (ENG.). Illus.). 24p. 2003. 26.65 o.p. (978-1-4048-0170-7(7)) Picture Window Bks.

—The Star-Spangled Banner: America's National Anthem & Its History, 1 vol. 2003. (Patriotic Songs Ser.). (ENG.). 24p. (gr. -1-4). 26.65 (978-1-4048-0175-2(8)) Picture Window Bks.

Pingry, Patricia A. O Little Town of Bethlehem. 2008. (ENG., Illus.). 16p. (J). bds. 12.99 (978-0-8249-6566-2(3), Ideal Pubns.) Worthy Publishing.

Reed, Cristie. The Star Spangled Banner. 2014. (ENG.). 32p. (gr. 3-6). 32.79 (978-1-62717-737-5(X)) Rourke Educational Media.

Sonneborn, Liz. America the Beautiful: The Story Behind Our National Hymn. 2003. (America in Words & Song Ser.). (Illus.). 32p. (gr. 4-6). 23.00 (978-0-7910-7332-2(7), Chelsea Hse.) Facts On File, Inc.

—The Star-Spangled Banner: The Story Behind Our National Anthem. 2003. (America in Words & Song Ser.). (Illus.). 32p. (gr. 4-6). 23.00 (978-0-7910-7337-7(8), Chelsea Hse.) Facts On File, Inc.

Spier, Peter. The Star-Spangled Banner. 2014. (ENG., Illus.). 56p. (J). (gr. k-4). 17.99 (978-0-385-37618-1(9), Doubleday Bks. for Young Readers) Random Hse. Children's Bks.

Vilsaint, Fequiere. Children Songs from Haiti: Chante Timoun Ayiti. Date not set. 28p. (J). (gr. 1-5). wbk. ed. 25.00 (978-1-881839-55-2(9)) Educa Vision Inc.

Wesolowski, Harriet. The Songs We Sing: Honoring Our Country. 2012. (I'm an American Citizen Ser.). (ENG., Illus.). 24p. (J). (gr. 1-3). 22.60 (978-1-4488-8581-7(7), PowerKids Pr.) Rosen Publishing Group, Inc., The.

NATIONALITY (CITIZENSHIP)

see Citizenship

NATIONS, LAW OF

see International Law

NATIVE PEOPLES

see Indigenous Peoples

NATIVE RACES

see Indigenous Peoples

NATIVITY OF CHRIST

see Jesus Christ—Nativity

NATO

see North Atlantic Treaty Organization

NATURAL CALAMITIES

see Natural Disasters

NATURAL DISASTERS

see also Earthquakes; Floods; Forest Fires; Storms; Volcanoes

ABDO Publishing Company Staff. Natural Disasters, 1 vol. 2011. (Natural Disasters Ser.). (ENG., Illus.). 32p. 171.00 (978-1-61783-030-3(5), Big Buddy Bks.) ABDO Publishing Co.

Aboff, Marcie & Gray-Wilburn, Renée. First Graphics: Wild Earth. Sotirovski, Aleksandar, illus. 2012. (First Graphics: Wild Earth Ser.). (ENG.). 24p. (gr. 1-2). pap. 142.80 (978-1-4296-8375-3(9)); pap. 25.16 (978-1-4296-8374-6(0)); lib. bdg. 71.97 (978-1-4296-8146-9(2)) Capstone Press of Coughlan Cos.

Aguilar, David A. Cosmic Catastrophes. 2016. (Smithsonian Ser.). (ENG., Illus.). 80p. (J). (gr. 3-7). 18.99 (978-0-451-47684-5(0), Viking Books for Young Readers) Penguin Young Readers Group.

Anaxos Inc. Staff, contrib. by. UXL Encyclopedia of Weather & Natural Disasters. 2007. (J). (978-1-4144-1883-4(3)); (978-1-4144-1882-7(5)); (978-1-4144-1881-0(7)); (978-1-4144-1880-3(9)); (978-1-4144-1884-1(1)) Cengage Gale.

Aronin, Miriam. Slammed by a Tsunami! 2010. (Disaster Survivors Ser.). (Illus.). 32p. (YA). (gr. 4-7). lib. bdg. 25.27 (978-1-936087-48-8(0)) Bearport Publishing Co., Inc.

Augsburger, A. Don. The World Is a Beautiful Place. Ressler-Horst, Lara, illus. 2007. 48p. per. 14.95 (978-1-934246-44-3(1)) Peppertree Pr., The.

Bailey, Gerry. Fragile Planet. 2011. (Planet SOS Ser.). (Illus.). 48p. (J). (gr. 3-6). pap. 14.05 (978-1-4339-4975-3(X)); lib. bdg. 31.95 (978-1-4339-4974-6(1)) Stevens, Gareth Publishing LLLP. (Gareth Stevens Learning Library).

Baker, John R. The World's Worst Natural Disasters. 2016. (World's Worst Natural Disasters Ser.). (ENG.). 32p. (gr. 1-2). 106.60 (978-1-5157-1810-9(7), Blazers) Capstone Press of Coughlan Cos.

Baltzer, Rochelle. Landslides, 1 vol. 2011. (Natural Disasters Ser.). (ENG., Illus.). 32p. (J). (gr. 2-5). 28.50 (978-1-61783-033-4(X)) ABDO Publishing Co.

—Tsunamis, 1 vol. 2011. (Natural Disasters Ser.). (ENG., Illus.). 32p. (J). (gr. 2-5). 28.50 (978-1-61783-034-1(8)) ABDO Publishing Co.

Bankoff, Greg. Cultures of Disaster: Society & Natural Hazard in the Philippines. 2015. (ENG.). 256p. (C). pap. 49.95 (978-1-138-87926-3(6), Y179793) Routledge.

Barker, Geoff. Hunger. 2010. (Voices Ser.). (YA). (gr. 5-9). 34.25 (978-1-59920-281-5(6)) Black Rabbit Bks.

Bearce, Stephanie. Twisted True Tales from Science: Disaster Discoveries. 2017. (Twisted True Tales from Science Ser.: 0). (ENG.). 125p. (J). (gr. 4-7). pap. 8.95 (978-1-61821-574-1(4)) Prufrock Pr.

Bell, Samantha S. Detecting Hurricanes. 2017. (Detecting Disasters (hardcover) Ser.). (ENG., Illus.). 32p. (J). (gr. 4-7). lib. bdg. 28.50 **(978-1-63517-003-0(6)**, Focus Readers) North Star Editions.

Blackwell, Amy Hackney, ed. U-X-L Encyclopedia of Weather & Natural Disasters, 5 vols. 2nd ed. 2016. (U-X-L Encyclopedia of Weather & Natural Disasters Ser.). (ENG., Illus.). 1200p. (J). (gr. 6-8). 458.00 (978-1-4103-3290-5(X), UXL) Cengage Gale.

Blohm, Craig E. Catastrophic Events of The 2000s. 2013. (YA). lib. bdg. (978-1-60152-522-2(2)) ReferencePoint Pr., Inc.

Brezina, Corona. Disappearing Forests: Deforestation, Desertification, & Drought. 2009. (Extreme Environmental Threats Ser.). 64p. (gr. 6-6). 58.50 (978-1-61512-426-8(8)) Rosen Publishing Group, Inc., The.

Bullard, Lisa. Tsunamis. 2009. pap. 40.95 (978-0-7613-4770-5(4)) 2008. (ENG.). 32p. 22.60 (978-0-8225-8829-0(3), Lerner Pubns.) Lerner Publishing Group.

Burnie, David. Disasters. 2013. (Illus.). 112p. (J). pap. (978-1-4071-3653-0(4)) Scholastic, Inc.

Burton, Margie, et al. The Power of Nature. 2011. (Early Connections Ser.). (J). (978-1-61672-507-5(9)) Benchmark Education Co.

Capaccio, George. Tsunamis: Set Of 6. 2011. (Navigators Ser.). (J). pap. 48.00 net. (978-1-4108-5081-2(1)) Benchmark Education Co.

—Tsunamis: Text Pairs. 2008. (Bridges/Navigators Ser.). (J). (gr. 5). 89.00 (978-1-4108-8424-4(4)) Benchmark Education Co.

Ceban, Bonnie J. Hurricanes, Typhoons, & Cyclones: Disaster & Survival. 2005. (Deadly Disasters Ser.). (Illus.). 48p. (J). (gr. 4-10). lib. bdg. 23.93 (978-0-7660-2388-8(5)) Enslow Pubs., Inc.

Challen, Paul C. Environmental Disaster Alert! 2004. (Disaster Alert! Ser.). (ENG., Illus.). 32p. (J). lib. bdg. (978-0-7787-1581-8(7)) Crabtree Publishing Co.

Challen, Paul C. & Challen, Paul. Environmental Disaster Alert! 2004. (Disaster Alert! Ser.). (ENG., Illus.). 32p. (J). pap. (978-0-7787-1613-6(9)) Crabtree Publishing Co.

Challoner, Jack. DK Eyewitness Books: Hurricane & Tornado: Hurricane & Tornado. 2014. (DK Eyewitness Bks.). (ENG., Illus.). 72p. (J). (gr. 3-7). pap. 9.99 (978-1-4654-2053-4(3), DK Children) Dorling Kindersley Publishing, Inc.

Chambers, Catherine. Can We Protect People from Natural Disasters? 2015. (Earth Debates Ser.). (ENG., Illus.). 48p. (gr. 4-6). 33.32 (978-1-4846-0995-8(6), Heinemann InfoSearch) Heinemann-Raintree.

Cheney, Glenn. Trapped, 1 vol. unabr. ed. 2012. (Astonishing Headlines Ser.). (ENG.). 92p. (YA). (gr. 9-12). 8.95 (978-1-61651-927-8(4)) Saddleback Educational Publishing, Inc.

Claybourne, Anna. 100 Deadliest Things on the Planet. 2012. (100 Most Ser.). lib. bdg. 18.40 (978-0-606-26744-1(1), Turtleback) Turtleback Bks.

—100 Most Destructive Natural Disasters Ever. 2014. (ENG.). 112p. (J). (gr. 3-7). pap. 7.99 (978-0-545-80859-0(6), Scholastic Paperbacks) Scholastic, Inc.

—100 Most Destructive Natural Disasters Ever. 2014. (100 Most... Ser.). lib. bdg. 18.40 (978-0-606-36336-5(X)) Turtleback Bks.

Close, Edward. Extreme Weather, 1 vol., 1. 2014. (Discovery Education: Earth & Space Science Ser.). (ENG.). 32p. (gr. 3-6). 26.25 (978-1-4777-6194-6(2), PowerKids Pr.) Rosen Publishing Group, Inc., The.

Collins, Andrew. Violent Weather: Thunderstorms, Tornadoes, & Hurricanes. 2006. (Science Chapters Ser.). (ENG., Illus.). 48p. (J). (gr. 1-4). lib. bdg. 17.90 (978-0-7922-5947-3(5), National Geographic Children's Bks.) National Geographic Society.

Connell, Kate & National Geographic Learning Staff. Dust Bowl Days. 2007. (Reading Expeditions Ser.). (ENG., Illus.). 40p. (J). pap. 19.95 (978-0-7922-4557-5(1)) CENGAGE Learning.

Corbett, Sean. Heat Waves. 2015. (Illus.). 32p. (J). (978-1-5105-0078-5(2)) SmartBook Media, Inc.

—Heat Waves. 2014. (J). (978-1-4896-3272-2(7)) Weigl Pubs., Inc.

Creative Media Applications. Environmental Disasters Set. 2005. (Environmental Disasters Ser.). 112p. (gr. 6-12). 210.00 (978-0-8160-5753-5(2)) Facts On File, Inc.

Cunningham, Kevin. Surviving Tsunamis, 1 vol. 2011. (Children's True Stories: Natural Disasters Ser.). (ENG.). 32p. (gr. 3-3). pap. 8.29 (978-1-4109-4102-2(7)); 30.65 (978-1-4109-4095-7(0)) Heinemann-Raintree. (Raintree Perspectives).

Currie, Stephen. Escapes from Natural Disasters. 2004. (Great Escapes Ser.). (ENG., Illus.). 112p. (J). 30.85 (978-1-59018-278-9(2), Lucent Bks.) Cengage Gale.

Disaster Plan: Individual Title Six-Packs. (Bookweb Ser.). 32p. (gr. 5-18). 34.00 (978-0-7635-3794-4(2)) Rigby Education.

Doudna, Kelly & Craig, Diane. Tidal Wave or Tsunami?, 1 vol. 2016. (This or That? Weather Ser.). (ENG., Illus.). 24p. (J). (gr. k-4). 25.65 (978-1-62403-956-0(1)) ABDO Publishing Co.

Dougherty, Terri. The Worst Tsunamis of All Time, 1 vol. 2012. (Epic Disasters Ser.). (ENG.). 32p. (gr. 3-4). lib. bdg. 27.99 (978-1-4296-8416-3(X)) Capstone Press of Coughlan Cos.

Draper, Allison Stark. Coping with Natural Disasters. (Coping Ser.). 192p. (gr. 7-12). 2009. 63.90 (978-1-61512-006-2(8)) 2005. (Illus.). (YA). lib. bdg. 34.60 (978-0-8239-2071-6(2), CONADI) Rosen Publishing Group, Inc., The.

Dunn, Karen Lewit. Technology & Natural Disasters. 2008. (Discovering & Exploring Science Ser.). (Illus.). 16p. (J). (gr. -1-3). lib. bdg. 12.95 (978-0-7569-8435-9(1)) Perfection Learning Corp.

Dwyer, Helen. Tsunamis! 2010. (Eyewitness Disaster Ser.). 32p. (J). (gr. 2-5). 28.50 (978-1-60870-005-9(4)) Marshall Cavendish GBR. Dist: Marshall Cavendish Corp.

Earth's Natural Disasters. 2015. (Earth's Natural Disasters Ser.). (ENG.). 32p. (J). (gr. 3-4). 151.62 (978-0-7660-6680-9(0)); pap., pap., pap. 378.72

(978-0-7660-6681-6(9)); pap., pap., pap. 63.12 (978-0-7660-7055-4(7)) Enslow Pubs., Inc.
Eaton, Gale & Hoose, Phillip. A History of Civilization in 50 Disasters, 1 vol. 2015. (History In 50 Ser.: 0). (ENG., Illus.). 240p. (gr. 6-12). 24.95 (978-0-88448-383-0(5), 884383) Tilbury Hse. Pubs.
Elkins, Elizabeth. Investigating Earthquakes. 2017. (Investigating Natural Disasters Ser.). (ENG., Illus.). 32p. (gr. 3-4). lib. bdg. 27.99 (978-1-5157-4038-4(2), Edge Bks.) Capstone Press of Coughlan Cos.
—Investigating Floods. 2017. (Investigating Natural Disasters Ser.). (ENG., Illus.). 32p. (gr. 3-4). lib. bdg. 27.99 (978-1-5157-4040-7(4), Edge Bks.) Capstone Press of Coughlan Cos.
—Investigating Natural Disasters. 2017. (Investigating Natural Disasters Ser.). (ENG.). 32p. (gr. 3-4). 111.96 (978-1-5157-4130-5(3), Edge Bks.) Capstone Press of Coughlan Cos.
—Investigating Tornadoes. 2017. (Investigating Natural Disasters Ser.). (ENG., Illus.). 32p. (gr. 3-4). lib. bdg. 27.99 (978-1-5157-4037-7(4), Edge Bks.) Capstone Press of Coughlan Cos.
Englar, Mary, et al. Epic Disasters. 2012. (Epic Disasters Ser.). (ENG.). 32p. (gr. 3-4). pap. 31.80 (978-1-4296-8511-5(5)); pap. 190.80 (978-1-4296-8512-2(3)); lib. bdg. 55.98 (978-1-4296-8187-2(X)) Capstone Press of Coughlan Cos. (Edge Bks.).
Espejo, Roman. Are Natural Disasters Increasing? 2014. (At Issue Ser.). (ENG.). 128p. (gr. 10-12). lib. bdg. 39.40 (978-0-7377-6822-0(3), Greenhaven Pr., Inc.) Cengage Gale.
Estigarribia, Diana. Learning about the Effects of Natural Events with Graphic Organizers. (Graphic Organizers in Science Ser.). 24p. 2009. (gr. 3-4). 42.50 (978-1-61513-050-4(0)) 2006. (ENG., Illus.). (gr. 4-6). pap. 8.25 (978-1-4042-5038-3(7)) 2005. (Illus.). (J). (gr. -1-3). lib. bdg. 22.60 (978-1-4042-2804-7(7)) Rosen Publishing Group, Inc., The. (PowerKids Pr.).
Farndon, John. Extreme Volcanoes. 2017. (When Nature Attacks Ser.). (ENG., Illus.). 32p. (J). (gr. 3-6). 26.65 **(978-1-5124-3220-6(2)**, Hungry Tomato (r)) Lerner Publishing Group.
Faust, Daniel R. Collision Course: Asteroids & Earth. 2008. (Jr. Graphic Environmental Dangers Ser.). (ENG., Illus.). 24p. (J). (gr. 3-6). lib. bdg. 25.25 (978-1-4042-4228-9(7)) Rosen Publishing Group, Inc., The.
Fecher, Sarah & Oliver, Clare. Freaky Facts about Natural Disasters. Anderson, Jill, ed. Bines, Gary & Boller, Gary, illus. 2006. (Freaky Facts Ser.). (ENG.). 32p. (J). (gr. 2-5). pap. 8.95 (978-1-58728-542-4(8)) Cooper Square Publishing Llc.
Feldman, Sarah. Twisters: Set Of 6. 2010. (Early Connections Ser.). (J). pap. 39.00 net. (978-1-4108-1544-6(7)) Benchmark Education Co.
Flows & Quakes & Spinning Winds: Individual Title Six-Packs. (gr. k-1). 23.00 (978-0-7635-9043-7(6)) Rigby Education.
Fradin, Dennis Brindell & Fradin, Judy. Tsunamis. 2008. (Witness to Disaster Ser.). (ENG., Illus.). 48p. (J). (gr. 4-7). 16.95 (978-0-7922-5380-8(9), National Geographic Children's Bks.) National Geographic Society.
Fradin, Judy & Fradin, Dennis Brindell. Droughts. 2008. (Witness to Disaster Ser.). (ENG., Illus.). 48p. (J). (gr. 4-7). 16.95 (978-1-4263-0339-5(4)); lib. bdg. 26.90 (978-1-4263-0340-1(8)) National Geographic Society. (National Geographic Children's Bks.).
—Tsunamis. 2008. (Witness to Disaster Ser.). (ENG., Illus.). 48p. (J). (gr. 4-7). lib. bdg. 26.90 (978-0-7922-5381-5(7), National Geographic Children's Bks.) National Geographic Society.
Fry, Erin. Earth: Fast Changes: Text Pairs. 2008. (Bridges/Navigators Ser.). (J). (gr. 4). 81.00 (978-1-4108-8382-7(5)) Benchmark Education Co.
Gale Editors & Immell, Myra. Japan's 2011 Natural Distaster & Nucular Meltdown. 2014. (Perspectives on Modern World History Ser.). (ENG., Illus.). 224p. (gr. 10-12). lib. bdg. 47.80 (978-0-7377-6973-9(4), Greenhaven Pr., Inc.) Cengage Gale.
Garbe, Suzanne. Threatening Skies: History's Most Dangerous Weather, 1 vol. 2013. (Dangerous History Ser.). (ENG.). 32p. (gr. 3-4). 27.99 (978-1-4765-0128-4(9), Edge Bks.) Capstone Press of Coughlan Cos.
Garbe, Suzanne, et al. Epic Disasters. 2012. (Epic Disasters Ser.). (ENG.). 32p. (gr. 3-4). lib. bdg. 111.96 (978-1-4296-9140-6(9), Edge Bks.) Capstone Press of Coughlan Cos.
Gardiner, Lisa. Catastrophic Colorado! The History & Science of Our Natural Disasters. 2006. (Illus.). 48p. (J). (gr. 1-8). 14.95 (978-1-56579-549-5(0), Westcliffe Pubs.) Bower Hse.
Gelletly, LeeAnne. Ecological Issues. Ojakorotu, Victor & Rotberg, Robert I., eds. 2013. (Africa: Progress & Problems Ser.: 13). (Illus.). 112p. (J). (gr. 7-18). 24.95 (978-1-4222-2937-8(8)) Mason Crest.
Gibson, Karen Bush. Mudslide in la Conchita, California 2005. 2005. (Natural Disasters Ser.). (Illus.). 32p. (J). (gr. 1-4). lib. bdg. 25.70 (978-1-58415-418-1(7)) Mitchell Lane Pubs., Inc.
Goldstein, Natalie. Droughts & Heat Waves: A Practical Survival Guide. 2005. (Library of Emergency Preparedness Ser.). (Illus.). 64p. (YA). (gr. 5-9). lib. bdg. 31.95 (978-1-4042-0536-9(5)) Rosen Publishing Group, Inc., The.
Goyal, Anuj, ed. Higher Ground. 2006. (Illus.). 160p. (gr. 7-9). per. 8.99 (978-1-84458-581-6(6), Pavilion Children's Books) Pavilion Bks. GBR. Dist: Trafalgar Square Publishing.
Graham, Ian. Tsunami: Perspectives on Tsunami Disasters, 1 vol. 2014. (Disaster Dossiers Ser.). (ENG., Illus.). 56p. (gr. 7-8). 34.65 (978-1-4846-0184-6(X)) Heinemann-Raintree.
—The Ultimate Interactive Guide to Natural Disasters. Quigley, Sebastian & Forder, Nicholas, illus. 2016. (ENG.). 48p. (J). (gr. 1). spiral bd. 19.95 (978-1-62686-567-9(1), Silver Dolphin Bks.) Readerlink Distribution Services, LLC.
Greve, Tom. Plate Tectonics & Disasters. 2012. (ENG.). 48p. (gr. 4-6). pap. 10.95 (978-1-61810-255-3(9)) Rourke Educational Media.
Griffey, Harriet. Earthquakes & Other Natural Disasters, Level 4. 2010. (DK Readers Ser.). (ENG.). 48p. (J). (gr. 2-5). 3.99 (978-0-7566-5932-5(9), DK Children) Dorling Kindersley Publishing, Inc.
Gullo, Arthur. Tsunamis. 2015. (J). lib. bdg. (978-1-62713-515-3(4)) Cavendish Square Publishing.
Hackney Blackwell, Amy & Manar, Elizabeth P. U-X-L Encyclopedia of Weather & Natural Disasters. 2016. (Illus.). (J). (978-1-4103-3291-2(8)); (978-1-4103-3292-9(6)) Cengage Gale. (Blackbirch Pr., Inc.).
Hamilton, John. Droughts, 1 vol. 2006. (Nature's Fury Ser.). (ENG., Illus.). 32p. (gr. 3-8). 27.07 (978-1-59679-329-3(5), Abdo & Daughters) ABDO Publishing Co.
—Nature's Fury Set 2. 2006. (Nature's Fury Set 2 Ser.). (gr. 3-8). 162.42 (978-1-59679-327-9(9), Abdo & Daughters) ABDO Publishing Co.
—Tsunamis, 1 vol. 2006. (Nature's Fury Ser.). (ENG., Illus.). 32p. (gr. 4-8). 27.07 (978-1-59679-333-0(3), Abdo & Daughters) ABDO Publishing Co.
Hamilton, S. L. Tsunamis. 2012. 32p. 27.07 (978-1-61783-263-5(4), Abdo & Daughters) ABDO Publishing Co.
Hawkins, John. Tsunami Disasters. 2011. (Catastrophe! Ser.). (ENG., Illus.). 48p. (J). (gr. 5-9). lib. bdg. 29.25 (978-1-4488-6005-0(9)) Rosen Publishing Group, Inc., The.
—Volcano Disasters. 2011. (Catastrophe! Ser.). (ENG., Illus.). 48p. (J). (gr. 5-9). lib. bdg. 29.25 (978-1-4488-6008-1(3)) Rosen Publishing Group, Inc., The.
Heitzmann, Connie & Koch, Janie. Gulf Coast Memory Scrapbook: A Pictorial Journey of Hope & Healing. 2007. (Illus.). 32p. (J). 16.95 (978-1-883651-30-5(1)) Winters Publishing.
Henry, Claire. The World's Deadliest Man-Made Disasters, 1 vol., 1. 2014. (World's Deadliest Ser.). (ENG.). 32p. (J). (gr. 3-6). pap. 10.00 (978-1-4777-6141-0(1), PowerKids Pr.) Rosen Publishing Group, Inc., The.
—The World's Deadliest Natural Disasters, 1 vol., 1. 2014. (World's Deadliest Ser.). (ENG.). 32p. (J). (gr. 3-6). lib. bdg. 26.25 (978-1-4777-6142-7(X), PowerKids Pr.) Rosen Publishing Group, Inc., The.
Higgins, Nadia. Natural Disasters Through Infographics. Sciuto, Alex, illus. 2013. (Super Science Infographics Ser.). (ENG.). 32p. (gr. 3-5). pap. 8.95 (978-1-4677-1593-5(X)); lib. bdg. 26.60 (978-1-4677-1287-3(6), Lerner Pubns.) Lerner Publishing Group.
Hile, Lori. Animal Survival. 2011. (Extreme Survival Ser.). (ENG.). 56p. (gr. 5-5). pap. 9.49 (978-1-4109-3980-7(4), Raintree Freestyle) Heinemann-Raintree.
Hillstrom, Kevin. Natural Disaster Response. Lucent Books Staff, ed. 2015. (Hot Topics Ser.). (ENG., Illus.). 128p. (gr. 7-10). lib. bdg. 39.40 (978-1-4205-0873-4(3), Lucent Bks.) Cengage Gale.
Hoffman, Mary Ann. Hurricane Katrina. (Nature in the News Ser.). 32p. 2009. (gr. 3-4). 42.50 (978-1-61514-821-9(3), PowerKids Pr.) 2007. (Illus.). (YA). (gr. 2-5). lib. bdg. 21.25 (978-1-4042-3537-3(X)) Rosen Publishing Group, Inc., The.
Hollingsworth, Tamara. Desastres Naturales Que Marcaron la Historia. 2016. (TIME for Kids en Español - Level 5 Ser.). (SPA.). 64p. (gr. 5-5). lib. bdg. 31.99 (978-1-5157-2929-7(X)) Time for Kids Inc AUS. Dist: Capstone Pub.
—Unforgettable Natural Disasters, 1 vol. 2nd rev. ed. 2013. (Nonfiction Readers Ser.). (ENG.). 64p. (J). (gr. 5-5). pap. 10.99 (978-1-4333-4944-7(2)); (Illus.). pap. 31.96 (978-1-4333-7443-2(9)) Teacher Created Materials, Inc.
Hoose, Phillip & Eaton, Gale. A History in Civilization in 50 Disasters. 2015. (History In 50 Ser.: 0). (ENG., Illus.). 240p. (gr. 6-12). pap. 16.95 (978-0-88448-489-9(0), 884489) Tilbury Hse. Pubs.
Isaacs, April. Tornadoes, Hurricanes, & Tsunamis: A Practical Survival Guide. (Library of Emergency Preparedness Ser.). 64p. 2009. (gr. 6-6). 58.50 (978-1-60853-598-9(3), Rosen Reference) 2005. (Illus.). (YA). (gr. 5-9). 31.95 (978-1-4042-0533-8(0)) Rosen Publishing Group, Inc., The.
Jacobs, Elaina & Benchmark Education Co. Staff. The Dust Bowl. 2014. (Text Connections Ser.). (J). (gr. 6). (978-1-4900-1527-9(2)) Benchmark Education Co.
Jeffrey, Gary. Tsunamis & Floods. 2009. (Graphic Natural Disasters Ser.). (ENG.). 48p. (YA). (gr. 5-5). 58.50 (978-1-61513-005-4(5), Rosen Reference) Rosen Publishing Group, Inc., The.
Jennings, Terry J. Earthquakes & Tsunamis. 2009. (Amazing Planet Earth Ser.). 32p. (gr. 4-7). 31.35 (978-1-59920-372-0(3)) Black Rabbit Bks.
Joanne, O'Sullivan. Bizarre Weather: Howling winds, pouring rain, blazing heat, freezing cold, huge hurricanes, violent earthquakes, tsunami's, tornadoes & more of nature's Fury. 2013. (ENG., Illus.). 160p. (J). pap. 7.95 (978-1-936140-72-5(1), Imagine Publishing) Charlesbridge Publishing, Inc.
Jordan, Shirley. America's Greatest Natural Disaster. 2003. (Cover-to-Cover Informational Ser.). (Illus.). 72p. (J). (gr. 4-7). lib. bdg. 17.95 (978-0-7569-1184-3(2)) Perfection Learning Corp.
—America's Greatest Natural Disasters. 2003. (Cover-To-Cover Books). (Illus.). 72p. pap. 9.00 (978-0-7891-5916-8(3)) Perfection Learning Corp.
Karwoski, Gail Langer. Tsunami: The True Story of an April Fools' Day Disaster. MacDonald, John, illus. 2006. (ENG.). 64p. (J). (gr. 5-12). lib. bdg. 17.95 (978-1-58196-044-0(1), Darby Creek) Lerner Publishing Group.
Katirgis, Jane & Drohan, Michele Ingber. Scary Tsunamis. 2015. (Earth's Natural Disasters Ser.). (ENG., Illus.). 32p. (J). (gr. 3-4). 25.27 (978-0-7660-6807-0(2)) Enslow Pubs., Inc.
Katirgis, Jane & Ingber Drohan, Michele. Scary Tsunamis. 2015. (Earth's Natural Disasters Ser.). (ENG.). 32p. (J). (gr. 3-4). pap. 10.52 (978-0-7660-6805-6(6)) Enslow Pubs., Inc.
Kopp, Megan. Avalanches. 2015. (Illus.). 32p. (J). (978-1-5105-0074-7(X)) SmartBook Media, Inc.
—Avalanches. 2014. (J). (978-1-4896-3264-7(6)) Weigl Pubs., Inc.
Kopp, Megan. Tsunamis. 2016. (J). **(978-1-5105-2079-0(1))** SmartBook Media, Inc.
Kusky, Timothy. Landslides: Mass Wasting, Soil, & Mineral Hazards. 2008. (Hazardous Earth Ser.). (Illus.). 128p. (gr. 6-12). 39.50 (978-0-8160-6465-6(2)) Facts On File, Inc.
—Tsunamis: Giant Waves from the Sea. 2008. (Hazardous Earth Ser.). (Illus.). 134p. (gr. 6-12). 39.50 (978-0-8160-6464-9(4)) Facts On File, Inc.
La Bella, Laura. Not Enough to Drink: Pollution, Drought, & Tainted Water Supplies. 2009. (Extreme Environmental Threats Ser.). (ENG., Illus.). 64p. (J). (gr. 7-12). pap. 12.95 (978-1-4358-5376-8(8)); (YA). (gr. 5-9). lib. bdg. 31.95 (978-1-4358-5020-0(3)) Rosen Publishing Group, Inc., The.
Lace, William W. The Indian Ocean Tsunami Of 2004. 2008. (Great Historic Disasters Ser.). (Illus.). 127p. (gr. 5-8). lib. bdg. 35.00 (978-0-7910-9642-0(4), Chelsea Hse.) Facts On File, Inc.
Lanier, Wendy. Avalanches, 1 vol. 2013. (Earth in Action Ser.). (ENG., Illus.). 48p. (J). (gr. 3-6). lib. bdg. 32.79 (978-1-61783-936-8(1)) ABDO Publishing Co.
Larson, Kirsten. Tsunamis. 2015. (ENG.). 48p. (gr. 3-6). 35.64 (978-1-63430-429-0(2)) Rourke Educational Media.
Lerner, K. Lee, et al. U-X-L Doomed: The Science Behind Disasters. 2015. (J). (978-1-4103-1777-3(3)) Cengage Gale.
Levete, Sarah. Destroying the Oceans. 2010. (Protecting Our Planet Ser.). (ENG., Illus.). 32p. (J). (gr. 3-6). (978-0-7787-5211-0(9)); pap. (978-0-7787-5228-8(3)) Crabtree Publishing Co.
Levy, Janey. World's Worst Tsunamis. 2009. (Deadly Disasters Ser.). 24p. (gr. 2-6). pap. 9.40 (978-1-4042-4538-9(3), Rosen Classroom); (gr. 2-3). 42.50 (978-1-61512-142-7(0), PowerKids Pr.); (Illus.). (J). lib. bdg. 22.60 (978-1-4042-4514-3(6), PowerKids Pr.) Rosen Publishing Group, Inc., The.
Life Nature's Fury. 2008. (Time Inc. Home Entertainment Library-Bound Titles Ser.). (ENG.). 144p. (gr. 5-12). lib. bdg. 39.93 (978-0-7613-4051-5(3), Twenty-First Century Bks.) Lerner Publishing Group.
Linde, Barbara M. Ecological Disasters: Set Of 6. 2011. (Navigators Ser.). (J). pap. 50.00 net. (978-1-4108-5091-1(9)) Benchmark Education Co.
—Ecological Disasters: Text Pairs. 2008. (Bridges/Navigators Ser.). (J). (gr. 6). 81.00 (978-1-4108-8433-6(3)) Benchmark Education Co.
Loeschnig, L. V. Experimentos Sencillos de Quimica. (Juego de la Ciencia Ser.). (SPA.). 124p. (gr. 5-8). (978-84-95456-49-6(4), 87802) Ediciones Oniro S.A.
Lusted, Marcia Amidon. Surviving Natural Disasters. 2014. (Shockzone: True Survival Stories Ser.). (ENG., Illus.). 32p. (gr. 5-8). lib. bdg. 26.60 (978-1-4677-1438-9(0), Lerner Pubns.) Lerner Publishing Group.
—The 2004 Indian Ocean Tsunami, 1 vol. 2008. (Essential Events Set 2 Ser.). (ENG., Illus.). 112p. (J). (gr. 6-12). lib. bdg. 35.64 (978-1-60453-047-6(2)) ABDO Publishing Co.
Lusted, Marcia Amidon & Elkins, Elizabeth. Investigating Hurricanes. 2017. (Investigating Natural Disasters Ser.). (ENG., Illus.). 32p. (gr. 3-4). lib. bdg. 27.99 (978-1-5157-4039-1(0), Edge Bks.) Capstone Press of Coughlan Cos.
Malaspina, Ann. Tsunamis. (In the News Ser.). 64p. 2009. (gr. 6-6). 58.50 (978-1-61513-491-5(3)) 2006. (Illus.). (YA). (gr. 7-12). lib. bdg. 31.95 (978-1-4042-0978-7(6)) Rosen Publishing Group, Inc., The.
Marrin, Albert. Years of Dust: The Story of the Dust Bowl. 2012. (ENG.). 144p. (J). (gr. 5). mass mkt. 9.99 (978-0-14-242579-4(6), Puffin Books) Penguin Young Readers Group.
McCollum, Sean. Volcanic Eruptions, Earthquakes, & Tsunamis. 2007. (Scientific American Ser.). (Illus.). 80p. (YA). (gr. 5-9). lib. bdg. 30.00 (978-0-7910-9047-3(7)) Facts On File, Inc.
McDowell, Pamela. Landslides. 2015. (J). (978-1-5105-0082-2(0)) SmartBook Media, Inc.
—Landslides. 2014. (J). (978-1-4896-3260-9(3)) Weigl Pubs., Inc.
McFadzean, Lesley. Earth in Peril. 2012. (Discovery Education: the Environment Ser.). (ENG., Illus.). 32p. (J). (gr. 3-6). pap. 10.00 (978-1-4488-7977-9(9)); lib. bdg. 25.25 (978-1-4488-7889-5(6)) Rosen Publishing Group, Inc., The. (PowerKids Pr.).
McNab, Chris. World's Worst Historical Disasters. 2009. (World's Worst: from Innovation to Disaster Ser.). 80p. (gr. 8-8). 61.20 (978-1-60854-859-0(7)) Rosen Publishing Group, Inc., The.
Meister, Cari. Tsunamis. 2015. (Illus.). 24p. (J). lib. bdg. 25.65 (978-1-62031-226-1(3)) Jump! Inc.
Michele, Tracey. When Can A Flood Happen? 2014. (Little Books of Answers: Level d Ser.). (Illus.). 16p. (gr. k-2). pap. 7.95 (978-1-927136-35-5(0)) Three Crows Media NZL. Dist: RiverStream Publishing.
Miller, Connie Colwell. The Deadliest Places on Earth. 2010. (World's Deadliest Ser.). (ENG.). 32p. (gr. 1-2). lib. bdg. 26.65 (978-1-4296-3932-3(6), Blazers) Capstone Press of Coughlan Cos.
Mitchell Lane Publishers Inc. Staff. Natural Disasters, 15 vols., Set. 2007. (Natural Disasters Ser.). (J). (gr. 1-5). lib. bdg. 385.50 (978-1-58415-572-0(8)) Mitchell Lane Pubs., Inc.
Morris, Janel. Disaster Planning. 2008. (At Issue Ser.). (ENG., Illus.). 128p. (gr. 10-12). 39.40 (978-0-7377-4090-5(6)); pap. 27.80 (978-0-7377-4091-2(4)) Cengage Gale. (Greenhaven Pr., Inc.).
Natural Disasters. (Eyes on Adventure Ser.). 32p. (J). (gr. 1). pap. (978-1-882210-64-0(6)) Action Publishing, Inc.
Natural Disasters, 3 cass.; set. 2004. (NOVA Ser.). (gr. 7-18). 49.95 incl. VHS (978-1-57807-041-1(4), WG165) WGBH Boston Video.
Natural Disasters, 11 bks., Set. Incl. Ancient Mystery of Easter Island. Torres, John A. (gr. 1-4). 2006. lib. bdg. 25.70 (978-1-58415-495-2(0)); Bermuda Triangle. Whiting, Jim. (gr. 1-4). 2006. lib. bdg. 25.70 (978-1-58415-497-6(7)); Bubonic Plague. Whiting, Jim. (gr. 1-4). 2006. lib. bdg. 25.70 (978-1-58415-494-5(2)); Earthquake in Loma Prieta, California 1989. Harkins, William & Harkins, Susan. (gr. 1-4). 2005. lib. bdg. 25.70 (978-1-58415-417-4(9)); Fury of Hurricane Andrew 1992. Gibson, Karen Bush. (gr. 1-4). 2005. lib. bdg. 25.70 (978-1-58415-416-7(0)); Hurricane Katrina 2005. Torres, John. (gr. 1-4). 2006. lib. bdg. 25.70 (978-1-58415-498-3(5)); Lost Continent of Atlantis. Roberts, Russell. (gr. 3-7). 2006. lib. bdg. 25.70 (978-1-58415-496-9(9)); Mt. Vesuvius & the Destruction of Pompei, A. D. 79. Roberts, Russell. (gr. 1-4). 2005. lib. bdg. 25.70 (978-1-58415-419-8(5)); Mudslide in la Conchita, California 2005. Gibson, Karen Bush. (gr. 1-4). 2005. lib. bdg. 25.70 (978-1-58415-418-1(7)); Tsunami Disaster in Indonesia 2004. Torres, John Albert. (gr. 1-4). 2005. lib. bdg. 25.70 (978-1-58415-415-0(2)); Where Did All the Dinosaurs Go? Roberts, Russell. (gr. 1-4). 2005. lib. bdg. 25.70 (978-1-58415-420-4(9)); (Illus.). 32p. (J). 2007. 186.45 (978-1-58415-499-0(3)) Mitchell Lane Pubs., Inc.
Nelson, John. Collision Course: Asteroids & Earth. 2009. (Jr. Graphic Environmental Dangers Ser.). (ENG., Illus.). 24p. (gr. 3-8). pap. 10.60 (978-1-4042-4595-2(2), PowerKids Pr.) Rosen Publishing Group, Inc., The.
Oliver, Clare. Natural Disasters: Atlas in the Round. 2005. (Illus.). 32p. (J). (gr. k-4). 16.00 (978-0-7567-9190-2(1)) DIANE Publishing Co.
Orme, David. Great Disasters. 2009. (Fact to Fiction Ser.). (Illus.). 36p. (J). pap. 6.95 (978-0-7891-7903-6(2)) Perfection Learning Corp.
Orme, David & Orme, David. Great Disasters. 2008. (ENG., Illus.). 36p. pap. (978-1-84167-694-4(2)) Ransom Publishing Ltd.
Orr, Tamra B. Tsunamis. 2012. (21st Century Skills Library: Real World Math Ser.). (ENG.). 32p. (J). (gr. 4-8). pap. 14.21 (978-1-61080-410-3(4), 201342); lib. bdg. 28.50 (978-1-61080-327-4(2), 201306) Cherry Lake Publishing.
Osborne, Mary Pope & Boyce, Natalie Pope. Tsunamis & Other Natural Disasters: A Nonfiction Companion to High Tide in Hawaii. Murdocca, Sal, illus. 2007. (Magic Tree House - Fact Tracker Ser.: 15). (ENG.). 128p. (J). (gr. 2-5). 6.99 (978-0-375-83221-5(1), Random Hse. Bks. for Young Readers) Random Hse. Children's Bks.
Otfinoski, Steven. Major Disasters in U.S. History. 2005. (Illus.). 48p. (J). (978-0-669-51416-2(0)) Great Source Education Group, Inc.
Owings, Lisa. Craco: The Medieval Ghost Town. 2017. (Abandoned Places Ser.). (ENG., Illus.). 24p. (J). (gr. 3-7). lib. bdg. 25.95 **(978-1-62617-695-9(7)**, Torque Bks.) Bellwether Media.
Owings, Lisa. What Protects Us During Natural Disasters? 2015. (ENG., Illus.). 32p. (gr. 4-6). (J). 26.65 (978-1-4677-7914-2(8)); 26.65 (978-1-4677-8649-2(7)) Lerner Publishing Group. (Lerner Pubns.).
Peacock, L. A. The Truth (and Myths) about Disasters. Davis, Jon, illus. 2014. 96p. (J). pap. (978-0-545-70565-3(7)) Scholastic, Inc.
Probst, Jeff. Extreme Weather. 2017. (Challenge Yourself Ser.: 4). (ENG., Illus.). 176p. (J). (gr. 3-7). 8.99 (978-0-14-751810-1(5), Puffin Books) Penguin Young Readers Group.
Rea, Amy C. Perspectives on the Dust Bowl. 2018. (ENG.). 32p. (gr. 3-6). **(978-1-63235-399-3(7)**, 12-Story Library) Pr. Room Editions LLC.
Reilly, Kathleen M. Natural Disasters: Investigate Earth's Most Destructive Forces with 25 Projects. Casteel, Tom, illus. 2012. (Build It Yourself Ser.). (ENG.). 128p. (J). (gr. 3-7). pap. 15.95 (978-1-61930-146-7(6)); 21.95 (978-1-61930-147-4(4)) Open City Bks.
The Remarkable World, 16 bks., Set. Incl. Birds of Prey. Penny, Malcolm. (Illus.). 1996. lib. bdg. 18.98 (978-1-56847-414-8(8)); Fossils & Bones. Pirotta, Saviour. (Illus.). 1997. lib. bdg. 18.98 (978-0-8172-4542-9(1)); Great Journeys. Chrisp, Peter. 1996. lib. bdg. 18.98 (978-0-8172-4537-5(5)); Hidden Past. Hicks, Peter. (Illus.). 1997. lib. bdg. 18.98 (978-0-8172-4541-2(3)); Land Predators. Stidworthy, John. (Illus.). 1996. lib. bdg. 18.98 (978-1-56847-416-8(4)); Mapping the Unknown. Chrisp, Peter. (Illus.). 1996. lib. bdg. 18.98 (978-0-8172-4535-1(9)); Monsters of the Deep. Pirotta, Saviour. (Illus.). 1995. lib. bdg. 18.98 (978-1-56847-367-3(2)); Night Creatures. Penny, Malcolm. (Illus.). 1996. lib. bdg. 18.98 (978-1-56847-371-0(0)); Pirates & Treasure. Pirotta, Saviour. (Illus.). 1997. lib. bdg. 18.98 (978-0-8172-4820-8(X)); Search for Riches. Langley, Andrew. (Illus.). 1997. lib. bdg. 18.98 (978-0-8172-4544-3(8)); Volcano, Earthquake & Hurricane. Arnold, Nick. (Illus.). 1997. lib. bdg. 18.98 (978-0-8172-4540-5(5)); Voyages of Exploration. Arnold, Nick. (Illus.). 1995. lib. bdg. 18.98 (978-1-56847-368-0(0)); Whalers. Chrisp, Peter. (Illus.). 1995. lib. bdg. 18.98 (978-1-56847-421-2(0)); When Dinosaurs Ruled the Earth. Theodorou, Rod. (Illus.). 1996. lib. bdg. 18.98 (978-1-56847-415-1(6)); Wild, Wild West. Pirotta, Saviour. (Illus.). 1997. lib. bdg. 18.98 (978-0-8172-4536-8(7)); World's Wild Places. Morgan, Sally. (Illus.). 1997. lib. bdg. 18.98 (978-0-8172-4538-2(3)); 48p. (J). (gr. 4-7). (Illus.). Set lib. bdg. 303.68 (978-0-8172-5397-4(1)) Heinemann-Raintree.
Remson, Billie. Mississippi Autumn on Bluebird Hill: A True Story about our Little Farm in the Hills of Southern Mississippi. 2006. (J). per. 14.95 (978-1-59571-121-2(X)) Word Association Pubs.
—A Mississippi Autumn on Bluebird Hill: A true story about our little farm in the hills of Southern Mississippi. 2006. (J). 21.95 (978-1-59571-158-8(9)) Word Association Pubs.
Rissman, Rebecca. Swept Away: The Story of the 2011 Japanese Tsunami. 2017. (Tangled History Ser.). (ENG., Illus.). 112p. (gr. 3-4). lib. bdg. 31.99 (978-1-5157-3605-9(9)) Capstone Press of Coughlan Cos.
Roza, Greg. The Indian Ocean Tsunami. (Nature in the News Ser.). 32p. 2009. (gr. 3-4). 42.50 (978-1-61514-822-6(1), PowerKids Pr.) 2007. (Illus.). (YA). (gr. 2-5). lib. bdg. 23.95 (978-1-4042-3538-0(8)) Rosen Publishing Group, Inc., The.
Rusch, Elizabeth. Eruption! Volcanoes & the Science of Saving Lives. Uhlman, Tom, illus. 2013. (Scientists in the Field Ser.). (ENG.). 80p. (J). (gr. 5-7). 18.99 (978-0-547-50350-9(4)) Houghton Mifflin Harcourt Publishing Co.
Sanna, Ellyn. Nature's Wrath: Surviving Natural Disasters. (Survivors Ser.). 2010. 128p. (YA). (gr. 7-12). 24.95 (978-1-4222-0454-2(5)) 2009. (J). pap. 24.95 (978-1-4222-1467-1(2)) Mason Crest.
Searl, Duncan. Trapped! 2005. (Illus.). 48p. (J). (978-0-669-51413-1(6)) Great Source Education Group, Inc.
Sepahban, Lois. Floods. 2013. (Illus.). 48p. (J). pap. 15.64 (978-1-62403-003-1(3)); (ENG., (gr. 3-6). lib. bdg. 32.79 (978-1-61783-938-2(8)) ABDO Publishing Co.
Shea, Therese. Freaky Weather Stories. 2015. (Freaky True Science Ser.). (ENG.). 32p. (J). (gr. 4-5). pap. 10.50 (978-1-4824-2968-8(3)) Stevens, Gareth Publishing LLLP.
Shofner, Melissa Raé. Weather & Natural Disasters. 2016. (Spotlight on Earth Science Ser.). 00024p. (J). (gr. 4-6). pap. 10.00 (978-1-4994-2547-5(3), PowerKids Pr.) Rosen Publishing Group, Inc., The.
Shone, Rob. Avalanches & Landslides. 2009. (Graphic Natural Disasters Ser.). (ENG.). 48p. (YA). (gr. 5-5). 58.50 (978-1-61512-994-2(4), Rosen Reference) Rosen Publishing Group, Inc., The.

M
N
O

Shulman, Mark. Super Storms That Rocked the World: Hurricanes, Tsunamis, & Other Disasters. 2007. (Illus.). 40p. (J). (978-0-696-23702-7(4)) Meredith Bks.
Somervill, Barbara A. Graphing Natural Disasters, 1 vol. 2010. (Real World Data Ser.). (ENG., Illus.). 32p. (gr. 3-5). pap. 8.95 (978-1-4329-2631-1(4)); lib. bdg. 29.99 (978-1-4329-2622-9(5)) Heinemann-Raintree. (NA-h).
Sommers, Michael. Tsunami: True Stories of Survival. 2009. (Survivor Stories Ser.). 48p. (gr. 5-5). 53.00 (978-1-60853-258-2(5), Rosen Reference) Rosen Publishing Group, Inc., The.
Spilsbury, Louise. The Science of Avalanches. 2013. (Nature's Wrath: the Science Behind Natural Disasters Ser.). (Illus.). 48p. (J). (gr. 4-6). 31.95 (978-1-4339-8651-2(5)); pap. 14.05 (978-1-4339-8652-9(3)) Stevens, Gareth Publishing LLLP. (Gareth Stevens Learning Library).
—What Are Natural Disasters?, 1 vol., 1. 2014. (Let's Find Out! Ser.). (ENG.). 32p. (gr. 3-6). 23.45 (978-1-62275-271-3(6)) Rosen Publishing Group, Inc., The.
Spilsbury, Louise & Spilsbury, Richard. Awesome Forces of Nature, 1 vol., Set. 2nd ed. Incl. Howling Hurricanes. pap. 8.29 (978-1-4329-3788-1(X)); Raging Floods. pap. 8.29 (978-1-4329-3789-8(8)); Shattering Earthquakes. pap. 8.29 (978-1-4329-3791-1(X)); Sweeping Tsunamis. pap. 8.29 (978-1-4329-3792-8(8)); Terrifying Tornadoes. pap. 8.29 (978-1-4329-3793-5(6)); Violent Volcanoes. pap. 8.29 (978-1-4329-3790-4(1)); (Illus.). (gr. 3-6). (Awesome Forces of Nature Ser.). (ENG.). 32p. 2010. Set pap. 47.94 (978-1-4329-3794-2(4), Heinemann InfoSearch) Heinemann-Raintree.
—Sweeping Tsunamis, 1 vol. 2nd ed. 2010. (Awesome Forces of Nature Ser.). (ENG., Illus.). 32p. (gr. 3-6). 33.32 (978-1-4329-3785-0(5)); pap. 8.29 (978-1-4329-3792-8(8)) Heinemann-Raintree. (Heinemann InfoSearch).
—Top 10 Worst Tsunamis. 2016. (Nature's Ultimate Disasters Ser.). 00032p. (J). (gr. 3-4). pap. 10.00 (978-1-4994-3081-3(7), PowerKids Pr.) Rosen Publishing Group, Inc., The.
—Top 10 Worst Volcanic Eruptions. 2016. (Nature's Ultimate Disasters Ser.). 00032p. (J). (gr. 3-4). pap. 10.00 (978-1-4994-3085-1(X), PowerKids Pr.) Rosen Publishing Group, Inc., The.
—Tsunamis in Action. 2009. (Natural Disasters in Action Ser.). (Illus.). 48p. (gr. 5-8). pap. 11.75 (978-1-4358-5136-8(6), Rosen Classroom) Rosen Publishing Group, Inc., The.
Spilsbury, Richard & Spilsbury, Louise. Tsunamis in Action. 2008. (Natural Disasters in Action Ser.). (Illus.). 48p. (J). lib. bdg. 29.25 (978-1-4042-1866-6(1)) Rosen Publishing Group, Inc., The.
Stiefel, Chana. Tsunamis. 2009. (True Book(tm), a — Earth Science Ser.). (ENG., 48p. (J). Illus.). (gr. 2-5). 31.00 (978-0-531-16885-1(9)); pap. 6.95 (978-0-531-21353-7(6), Children's Pr.) Scholastic Library Publishing.
Swanson, Jennifer. Tsunamis. 2013. (Illus.). 48p. (J). pap. 15.64 (978-1-62403-006-2(8)); (ENG., (gr. 3-6). lib. bdg. 32.79 (978-1-61783-941-2(8)) ABDO Publishing Co.
Tarshis, Lauren. I Survived: True Stories, Five Epic Disasters. 2014. (I Survived Ser.). (ENG.). 176p. (J). (gr. 2-5). 12.99 (978-0-545-78224-1(4)) Scholastic, Inc.
Thoron, Joe. Kaleidoscope Natural Disasters Group 1, 4 bks., Set. Incl. Earthquakes. lib. bdg. 20.95 (978-0-7614-2102-3(5)); Hurricanes. lib. bdg. 20.95 (978-0-7614-2103-0(3)); Tornadoes. lib. bdg. 20.95 (978-0-7614-2104-7(1)); Volcanoes. lib. bdg. 20.95 (978-0-7614-2105-4(X)); (Illus.). 48p. (gr. 3-7). 2006. 2007. Set lib. bdg. 119.71 (978-0-7614-2101-6(7), Benchmark Bks.) Marshall Cavendish Corp.
Torres, John Albert. Disaster in the Indian Ocean, Tsunami 2004. 2005. (Monumental Milestones Ser.). (Illus.). 48p. (YA). (gr. 4-7). lib. bdg. 29.95 (978-1-58415-344-3(X)) Mitchell Lane Pubs., Inc.
—Threat to Haiti. 2008. (On the Verge of Extinction Ser.). (Illus.). 32p. (YA). (gr. 2-5). lib. bdg. 25.70 (978-1-58415-686-4(4)) Mitchell Lane Pubs., Inc.
—Tsunami Disaster in Indonesia 2004. 2005. (Natural Disasters Ser.). (Illus.). 32p. (J). (gr. 1-4). lib. bdg. 25.70 (978-1-58415-415-0(2)) Mitchell Lane Pubs., Inc.
Tsunamis & Seiches. 2nd ed. 2009. (Illus.). 47p. (J). (978-0-7166-9830-2(7)) World Bk., Inc.
U X L, ed. UXL Man-Made Disasters, 3 vols. 2015. (ENG.). (J). 286.00 (978-1-4103-1774-2(9), UXL) Cengage Gale.
Veigas, Jennifer, ed. Critical Perspectives on Natural Disasters. 2009. (Scientific American Critical Anthologies on Environment & Climate Ser.). 208p. (gr. 9-9). 63.90 (978-1-60853-067-0(1)) Rosen Publishing Group, Inc., The.
Ventura, Marne. Detecting Tsunamis. 2017. (Detecting Disasters (hardcover) Ser.). (ENG., Illus.). 32p. (J). (gr. 4-7). lib. bdg. 28.50 **(978-1-63517-005-4(2)**, Focus Readers) North Star Editions.
Ventura, Marne. How to Survive a Tsunami. 2015. (Survival Guides). (ENG.). 24p. (J). (gr. 2-5). 27.07 (978-1-60973-164-9(6), 208793) Child's World, Inc., The.
Wade, Mary Dodson. Deadly Waves: Tsunamis. 2012. (Disasters — People in Peril Ser.). (Illus.). 48p. (J). (gr. 5-18). 25.27 (978-0-7660-4018-2(6)) Enslow Pubs., Inc.
Walker, Niki. Tsunami Alert! 2005. (Disaster Alert! Ser.). (ENG., Illus.). 32p. (J). (gr. 4-7). pap. (978-0-7787-1614-3(7)); lib. bdg. (978-0-7787-1582-5(5)) Crabtree Publishing Co.
Watts, Claire & Day, Trevor. DK Eyewitness Books: Natural Disasters. 2015. (DK Eyewitness Bks.). (ENG., Illus.). 72p. (J). (gr. 3-7). pap. 9.99 (978-1-4654-3808-9(4), DK Children) Dorling Kindersley Publishing, Inc.
—Natural Disasters. 2015. (DK Eyewitness Bks.). (ENG., Illus.). 72p. (J). (gr. 3-7). lib. bdg. 19.99 (978-1-4654-3809-6(2), DK Children) Dorling Kindersley Publishing, Inc.
Wendorff, Anne. Droughts. 2008. (Extreme Weather Ser.). (ENG., Illus.). 24p. (J). (gr. 2-5). lib. bdg. 25.95 (978-1-60014-184-3(6)) Bellwether Media.
—Tsunamis. 2008. (Extreme Weather Ser.). (ENG., Illus.). 24p. (J). (gr. 2-5). lib. bdg. 25.95 (978-1-60014-188-1(9)) Bellwether Media.
West, David & Parker, Steve. Natural Disasters. 2011. (ENG., Illus.). 32p. (J). pap. (978-0-7787-7579-9(8)); pap. (978-0-7787-7581-2(X)); lib. bdg. (978-0-7787-7576-8(3)) Crabtree Publishing Co.
When Disaster Strikes! 2005. (Illus.). 48p. (gr. 5-8). lib. bdg. 143.70 (978-0-8239-3892-6(1)) Rosen Publishing Group, Inc., The.
Whitmore, Andrew. How to Survive Asteroids & Other Disasters. 2007. 96p. (J). (978-1-4207-0733-5(7)) Sundance/Newbridge Educational Publishing.
Wilson, Patrick. Surviving Natural Disasters. Carney, John, ed. 2014. (Extreme Survival in the Military Ser.: 12). 64p. (J). (gr. 7-18). lib. bdg. 23.95 (978-1-4222-3091-6(0)) Mason Crest.
Winchester, Simon. The Day the World Exploded: The Earthshaking Catastrophe at Krakatoa. Chin, Jason, illus. 2008. 96p. (J). (gr. 5-9). lib. bdg. 23.89 (978-0-06-123983-0(6)) HarperCollins Pubs.
—When the Sky Breaks: Hurricanes, Tornadoes, & the Worst Weather in the World. 2017. (Smithsonian Ser.). (ENG., Illus.). 96p. (J). (gr. 5). 22.99 (978-0-451-47635-7(2), Viking Books for Young Readers) Penguin Young Readers Group.
Wiseman, Blaine. Blizzards. 2015. (J). (978-1-5105-0076-1(6)) SmartBook Media, Inc.
—Blizzards. 2014. (J). (978-1-4896-3268-5(9)) Weigl Pubs., Inc.
—Volcanoes. 2014. (J). (978-1-4896-3276-0(X)) Weigl Pubs., Inc.
Wood, Alix. Disasters on the Map. 2014. (Fun with Map Skills Ser.). (Illus.). 32p. (J). (gr. 3-6). lib. bdg. 26.25 (978-1-4777-6976-8(5), PowerKids Pr.) Rosen Publishing Group, Inc., The.
Woods, Michael. Mudflows & Landslides. 2009. pap. 8.95 (978-0-8225-6861-2(6)) Lerner Publishing Group.
Woods, Michael & Woods, Mary B. Droughts. 2007. (Disasters up Close Ser.). (Illus.). 64p. (J). (gr. 3-7). lib. bdg. 27.93 (978-0-8225-6576-5(5), Lerner Pubns.) Lerner Publishing Group.
—Tsunamis. 2006. (Disasters up Close Ser.). (Illus.). 64p. (J). (gr. 3-7). lib. bdg. 27.93 (978-0-8225-6054-8(2), Lerner Pubns.) Lerner Publishing Group.
Woolf, Alex, et al. A World After. 2013. (World After Ser.). (ENG.). 56p. (gr. 7-8). pap. 37.96 (978-1-4329-7627-9(3)); lib. bdg. 103.95 (978-1-4329-7622-4(2)) Heinemann-Raintree.
World Book, Inc Staff, contrib. by. Droughts. 2007. (J). (978-0-7166-9803-6(X)) World Bk., Inc.
—Heat Waves. (J). 2007. (978-0-7166-9807-4(2)) 2nd ed. 2009. (Illus.). 47p. (978-0-7166-9823-4(4)) World Bk., Inc.
—Ice Storms. (J). 2007. (978-0-7166-9809-8(9)) 2nd ed. 2009. (Illus.). 47p. (978-0-7166-9825-8(0)) World Bk., Inc.
—Tornadoes. 2nd ed. 2009. (Illus.). 47p. (J). (978-0-7166-9829-6(3)) World Bk., Inc.
—Tsunamis & Seiches. 2007. (Illus.). 47p. (J). (978-0-7166-9814-2(5)) World Bk., Inc.
Zuehlke, Jeffrey. Landslides. 2009. pap. 40.95 (978-0-7613-4769-9(0)) 2008. (ENG.). 32p. 22.60 (978-0-8225-8831-3(5), Lerner Pubns.) Lerner Publishing Group.
Zullo, Allan. Heroes of Hurricane Katrina. 2015. (Ten True Tales Ser.). (ENG.). 192p. (J). (gr. 3-7). pap. 5.99 (978-0-545-83123-9(7)) Scholastic, Inc.

NATURAL DISASTERS—FICTION

Bauer, Marion Dane. A Mama for Owen. Butler, John, illus. 2007. (ENG.). 32p. (J). (gr. -1-3). 17.99 (978-0-689-85787-4(X), Simon & Schuster Bks. For Young Readers) Simon & Schuster Bks. For Young Readers.
Bywaters, Mayer. Tempest. (J). 16.95 (978-1-58717-206-9(2), SeaStar Bks.) Chronicle Bks. LLC.
Conway, David. Lila & the Secret of Rain. Daly, Jude, illus. 2008. (ENG.). 32p. (J). (gr. k-4). (978-1-84507-407-4(6)) Rough Guides, Ltd.
Cummings, Lindsay. The Pillars of Ponderay. 2015. (Balance Keepers Ser.: 2). (ENG.). 384p. (J). (gr. 3-7). 16.99 (978-0-06-227521-9(6), Tegen, Katherine Bks) HarperCollins Pubs.
Dashner, James. The Fever Code. 2016. (Maze Runner Ser.). (ENG.). 384p. (YA). (gr. 7). 18.99 (978-0-553-51309-7(5)); lib. bdg. 21.99 (978-0-553-51310-3(9)) Random Hse. Children's Bks. (Delacorte Pr.).
—The Kill Order. 2014. (Maze Runner Ser.: 4). (ENG.). 384p. (YA). (gr. 7). pap. 9.99 (978-0-385-74289-4(4), Delacorte Pr.) Random Hse. Children's Bks.
—The Kill Order. 2014. (Maze Runner Ser.: 0). lib. bdg. 20.85 (978-0-606-35572-8(3)) Turtleback Bks.
—The Maze Runner: Virus Letal. 2013. 362p. (YA). pap. 15.99 (978-987-612-565-9(6)) V&R Editoras.
De la Peña, Matt. The Hunted. 2015. (ENG.). 384p. (YA). (gr. 9). lib. bdg. 20.99 (978-0-375-98992-6(7), Delacorte Pr.) Random Hse. Children's Bks.
—The Living. (ENG.). (YA). (gr. 9). 2015. 336p. pap. 9.99 (978-0-385-74121-7(9), Ember) 2013. 320p. lib. bdg. 20.99 (978-0-375-98991-9(9), Delacorte Pr.) Random Hse. Children's Bks.
Diggle, David Mark. Annie: A Small Ant with Some Big Questions. Preuss, Sarah Louise, illus. 2011. 24p. (J). pap. (978-0-9871658-2-4(8)) Diggle de Doo Productions Pty, Ltd.
Donald, Margaret. Eli the Elephant: A Tsunami Story. Grant, Sophia & Noble, Stuart, illus. 2007. (ENG.). 25p. (gr. 3-7). (978-81-8386-024-6(9)) India Research Pr. IND. Dist: Independent Pubs. Group.
Easton, Tom. Seven Second Delay. 2015. (ENG.). 240p. (J). (gr. 7-12). 16.95 (978-0-8234-3209-7(2)) Holiday Hse., Inc.
Ebwelleson, Nelson. The Helpless King. 2012. 24p. pap. 17.99 (978-1-4772-8262-5(9)) AuthorHouse.
Farmer, Nancy. The Lord of Opium. 2013. (ENG., Illus.). 432p. (YA). (gr. 7). 17.99 (978-1-4424-8254-8(0)) Simon & Schuster Children's Publishing.
Fournier, Kevin Mark. Sandbag Shuffle. 2007. (ENG.). 240p. (gr. 8-13). per. 12.95 (978-1-897235-22-5(4)) Thistledown Pr., Ltd. CAN. Dist: Univ. of Toronto Pr.
Groth-fleming, Professor Fergus Fahrenheit & His Wonderful Weat. 2009. (ENG.). 36p. (J). (gr. -1-3). pap. 10.99 (978-1-4424-0220-1(2), Simon & Schuster Bks. For Young Readers) Simon & Schuster Bks. For Young Readers.
Hall, Barbara. Dixie Storms. 2006. (ENG., Illus.). 224p. (YA). (gr. 7-12). pap. 12.95 (978-0-15-205756-5(0)) Houghton Mifflin Harcourt Publishing Co.
Hanson, Ed. Mountain Blizzard. 2003. (Barclay Family Adventure Ser.: Bk. 7). (Illus.). 64p. (J). (gr. k-6). per. 3.95 (978-1-56254-556-7(6), SP 5566) Saddleback Educational Publishing, Inc.
Hobbie, Holly. I'll Be Home for Christmas. 2008. (Toot & Puddle Ser.: 5). (ENG.). 32p. (gr. -1-3). pap. 6.99 (978-0-316-03383-1(9)) Little, Brown Bks. for Young Readers.
Kajikawa, Kimiko. Tsunami! Young, Ed, illus. 2010. (Rise & Shine Ser.). (ENG.). 32p. (C). (gr. -1-k). 27.95 (978-0-399-25006-4(9)) National Geographic School Publishing, Inc.
Kroll, Virginia. Selvakumar Knew Better. Li, Xiaojun, illus. 2009. (Selvakumar Knew Better Ser.). 32p. (J). (gr. -1-3). pap. 8.95 (978-1-885008-36-7(8), Shen's Bks.) Lee & Low Bks., Inc.
Kropp, Paul. Avalanche. (Illus.). 91p. (978-1-897039-07-6(7)) High Interest Publishing (HIP).
Laiz, Jana. Elephants of the Tsunami. Cafiero, Tara, illus. 2005. (J). 10.00 (978-0-9771818-3-4(9)) EarthBound Bks.
Lawrence, Kelsey. Rune. 2006. (Illus.). 92p. pap. 13.50 (978-1-84426-399-8(1)) Upfront Publishing Ltd. GBR. Dist: Printondemand-worldwide.com.
Lawrence, Margaret. Earthshakers, Top Blowers & High Rollers. 2012. 170p. pap. 36.95 (978-1-937600-74-7(2)) Salem Author Services.
Laybourne, Emmy. Monument 14. 2013. (Monument 14 Ser.: 1). (ENG.). 352p. (YA). (gr. 8-13). pap. 10.99 (978-1-250-02738-2(1), 9781250027382) Square Fish.
—Savage Drift. 2014. (Monument 14 Ser.: 3). (ENG.). 320p. (YA). (gr. 8). 17.99 (978-1-250-03642-1(9), 9781250036421) Feiwel & Friends.
—Sky on Fire. 2013. (Monument 14 Ser.: 2). (YA). (ENG.). 224p. (gr. 8-13). 18.99 (978-0-312-56904-4(1), 9780312569044); vi, 217p. (978-1-4449-1765-9(X)) Feiwel & Friends.
—Sky on Fire. 2014. (Monument 14 Ser.: 2). (ENG.). 272p. (YA). (gr. 8-13). pap. 9.99 (978-1-250-04432-7(4), 9781250044327) Square Fish.
Lewis, Richard. The Killing Sea. 2008. (ENG., Illus.). 256p. (YA). (gr. 7-12). mass mkt. 7.99 (978-1-4169-5372-2(8), Simon Pulse) Simon Pulse.
MacHale, D. J. The Rivers of Zadaa. 2006. (Pendragon Ser.: Bk. 6). 405p. (gr. 5-9). 19.00 (978-0-7569-7040-6(7)) Perfection Learning Corp.
Padula, Stacy A. The Aftermath. 2013. 176p. pap. 13.00 (978-1-62857-057-1(1), Strategic Bk. Publishing) Strategic Book Publishing & Rights Agency (SBPRA).
Parker, John. Chaos Mountain. 2007. 96p. (YA). pap. (978-1-4207-0734-2(5)) Sundance/Newbridge Educational Publishing.
Pfeffer, Susan Beth. The Dead & the Gone. 2010. (Life As We Knew It Ser.: 2). (ENG.). 336p. (YA). (gr. 7-12). pap. 8.99 (978-0-547-25855-3(0)) Houghton Mifflin Harcourt Publishing Co.
—The Dead & the Gone. 2010. (Last Survivors Ser.: 2). 321p. lib. bdg. 19.65 (978-0-606-14464-3(1), Turtleback) Turtleback Bks.
—Life As We Knew It. 2008. (Life As We Knew It Ser.: 1). (ENG., Illus.). 352p. (YA). (gr. 7-18). pap. 9.99 (978-0-15-206154-8(1)) Houghton Mifflin Harcourt Publishing Co.
—Life As We Knew It. Howard, Arthur, illus. 2006. (Life As We Knew It Ser.: 1). (ENG.). 352p. (YA). (gr. 7-12). 17.99 (978-0-15-205826-5(5)) Houghton Mifflin Harcourt Publishing Co.
—Life As We Knew It. 2008. (Last Survivors Ser.: 1). 347p. (gr. 7-12). lib. bdg. 19.65 (978-1-4178-1541-8(8), Turtleback) Turtleback Bks.
—The Life As We Knew It Collection. 2015. (Life As We Knew It Ser.). (ENG.). 1252p. (YA). (gr. 7). 29.99 (978-0-544-54263-1(0), HMH Books For Young Readers) Houghton Mifflin Harcourt Publishing Co.
—The Shade of the Moon. (Life As We Knew It Ser.: 4). (ENG.). 304p. (YA). (gr. 7). 2014. pap. 8.99 (978-0-544-33615-5(1), HMH Books For Young Readers) 2013. 17.99 (978-0-547-81337-0(6)) Houghton Mifflin Harcourt Publishing Co.
Pratchett, Terry. Nation. 2009. 384p. (YA). (gr. 8-18). pap. 9.99 (978-0-06-143303-0(9)) 2008. 504p. (J). pap. 16.99 (978-0-06-170913-5(1)) 2008. 384p. (YA). (gr. 8-18). 17.99 (978-0-06-143301-6(2)) HarperCollins Pubs.
Prentiss, Timothy. A Good Pick. 2006. (Early Explorers Ser.). (J). pap. (978-1-4108-6111-5(2)) Benchmark Education Co.
Robbins, Sandra. The Earth & Me. 2004. (J). (978-1-882601-48-6(3)); 23.95 incl. audio compact disk (978-1-882601-49-3(1)); pap. 9.95 (978-1-882601-47-9(5)); pap. 16.95 incl. audio (978-1-882601-52-3(1)) See-More's Workshop.
—The Earth & Me (Hard Cover Book & Tape Set) 2004. (J). mass mkt. 21.95 incl. audio (978-1-882601-50-9(5)) See-More's Workshop.
Robbins, Sandra, told to. The Earth & Me (Soft Cover Book & CD Set) 2004. (J). pap. 18.95 incl. audio compact disk (978-1-882601-51-6(3)) See-More's Workshop.
Robison, Dan. Death Chant: Kimo's Battle with the Shamanic Forces. 2006. 194p. (J). pap. (978-0-922993-52-9(1)) Marquette Bks., LLC.
Salkey, Andrew. Drought. 2011. (Caribbean Modern Classics Ser.). (ENG., Illus.). 128p. (J). (gr. 7). pap. 13.95 (978-1-84523-183-5(X)) Peepal Tree Pr., Ltd. GBR. Dist: Independent Pubs. Group.
Sugg, Nan. Erin & Katrina. Huber, Becca & Pope, Lauren, illus. 2007. 32p. (J). 19.90 (978-0-9788889-0-9(1)) Acorn Hill Pr.
Tarshis, Lauren. I Survived the Japanese Tsunami 2011. 2013. (I Survived Ser.: No. 8). (ENG., Illus.). 112p. (J). (gr. 2-5). pap. 4.99 (978-0-545-45937-2(0)) Scholastic, Inc.
—I Survived the Japanese Tsunami 2011. 2013. (I Survived, Ser.: No. 8). lib. bdg. 14.75 (978-0-606-32390-1(2), Turtleback) Turtleback Bks.

NATURAL HISTORY

Here are entered popular works describing animals, plants, minerals and nature in general. Handbooks on the detailed study of birds, flowers, etc. are entered under Nature Study.

see also Aquariums; Biology; Botany; Fossils; Freshwater Biology; Geology; Marine Biology; Mineralogy; Zoology

Alexander, Heather. A Child's Introduction to Natural History: The Story of Our Living Earth-From Amazing Animals & Plants to Fascinating Fossils & Gems. Hamilton, Meredith, illus. 2016. (ENG.). 96p. (J). (gr. 3-7). 19.99 (978-0-316-31136-6(7), Black Dog & Leventhal Pubs. Inc.) Hachette Bks.
Aloian, Molly. The Andes. 2011. (ENG., Illus.). 48p. (J). pap. (978-0-7787-7567-6(4)); (gr. 4-7). lib. bdg. (978-0-7787-7560-7(7)) Crabtree Publishing Co.
Andrews, Jane. The Stories Mother Nature Told Her Child. 2004. reprint ed. pap. 15.95 (978-1-4191-8357-7(5)) Kessinger Publishing, LLC.
—The Stories Mother Nature Told Her Children. 2004. reprint ed. pap. 1.99 (978-1-4192-8357-4(X)) Kessinger Publishing, LLC.
Arnold, Jude. The Lipizzan Reunion: A True Story. 2009. 48p. pap. 19.49 (978-1-4389-7060-8(9)) AuthorHouse.
Atwood, Frederick D. Rocks & Minerals - Pb: A Portrait of the Natural World. 2013. (Portrait of the Natural World Ser.). (Illus.). 72p. pap. 9.95 (978-1-59764-332-0(7)) New Line Bks.
Augustin, Byron & Kubena, Jake. Yellowstone National Park. 2009. (Nature's Wonders 2 Ser.). (Illus.). 96p. (gr. 6). 35.64 (978-0-7614-3936-3(6)) Marshall Cavendish Corp.
Banes, Graham L. Kingfisher Encyclopedia of Life. 2014. (ENG., Illus.). 160p. (J). (gr. 4-9). pap. 12.99 (978-0-7534-7193-7(0), 9780753471937, Kingfisher) Roaring Brook Pr.
Banting, Erinn. The Galapagos Islands. 2006. (Natural Wonders Ser.). (Illus.). 32p. (gr. 3-7). 17.95 (978-0-7569-6994-3(8)) Perfection Learning Corp.
Barlowe, Dot. Rocky Mountains Plants & Animals. 2004. (Dover Nature Coloring Book Ser.). (ENG., Illus.). 32p. (gr. 3-8). pap. 3.99 (978-0-486-43045-4(6)) Dover Pubns., Inc.
Beebe, Katherine & Kingsley, Nellie F. The First Year Nature Reader. 2004. reprint ed. pap. 21.95 (978-1-4191-3072-4(2)) Kessinger Publishing, LLC.
Benjamin, Tina. Let's Walk in the Woods. 2015. (Let's Go Outdoors! Ser.). (ENG.). 24p. (J). (gr. k-k). lib. bdg. 22.60 (978-1-4824-2635-9(8)) Stevens, Gareth Publishing LLLP.
Berenstain, Stan, et al. The Berenstain Bears' Big Book of Science & Nature. 2013. (Dover Children's Science Bks.). (ENG.). 192p. (J). (gr. k-3). pap. 14.99 (978-0-486-49834-8(4)) Dover Pubns., Inc.
Blythe, Philip. Nature Hunt! Bewildering Puzzles of the Animal Kingdom. Blythe, Philip, illus. 2005. (Illus.). 32p. pap., act. bk. ed. (978-1-877003-82-0(4)) Little Hare Bks. AUS. Dist: HarperCollins Pubs. Australia.
Brooks, Sheldon. Life in the Arctic. (Life in Extreme Environments Ser.). 64p. (gr. 5-8). 2009. 53.00 (978-1-61514-270-5(3)) 2004. (Illus.). lib. bdg. 31.95 (978-0-8239-3984-8(7)) Rosen Publishing Group, Inc., The. (Rosen Reference).
Brown, Jordan D. Micro Mania: A Really Close-up Look at Bacteria, Bedbugs & the Zillions of Other Gross Little Creatures That Live in, on & All Around You! 2009. (ENG., Illus.). 80p. (J). (gr. 4-7). 19.95 (978-0-9823064-2-0(3)) Charlesbridge Publishing, Inc.
Brynie, Faith Hickman. Six-Minute Nature Experiments. Whittingham, Kim, illus. 2006. 80p. (J). (gr. 4-8). reprint ed. pap. 11.00 (978-1-4223-5105-5(X)) DIANE Publishing Co.
Burns, Judy & Richards, Wayne. Nature's Notes: Bite-sized Learning & Projects for All Ages. 2012. (ENG., Illus.). 232p. spiral bd. (978-1-60755-477-6(1)) Willow Creek Pr., Inc.
Burton, Virginia Lee. Life Story. 2009. (ENG., Illus.). 80p. (J). (gr. 2-5). pap. 8.99 (978-0-547-20359-1(4)) Houghton Mifflin Harcourt Publishing Co.
Calhoun, Yael. Plant & Animal Science Fair Projects: Using Beetles, Weeds, Seeds, & More. 2005. (Biology! Best Science Projects Ser.). (Illus.). 128p. (J). (gr. 6-13). lib. bdg. 27.94 (978-0-7660-2368-0(0)) Enslow Pubs., Inc.
Castella, Krystina & Boyl, Brian. Discovering Nature's Hidden Alphabet. 2017. (J). **(978-1-59714-358-5(8))** Heyday.
Chapman, S. I. mon. In the Desert. 2006. (Illus.). 111p. (J). lib. bdg. 20.00 (978-1-4242-0628-5(6)) Fitzgerald Bks.
Chin, Jason. Island: A Story of the Galápagos. Chin, Jason, illus. 2012. (ENG., Illus.). 40p. (J). (gr. k-3). 17.99 (978-1-59643-716-6(2), 9781596437166) Roaring Brook Pr.
Clarke, Nadine. Get Bushwise: on Safari Desert, River, Bushveld: A Young Explorer's Guide. 2013. 192p. pap. 23.00 (978-1-4317-0206-0(4)) Penguin Random House Grupo Editorial ESP. Dist: Casemate Pubs. & Bk. Distributors, LLC.
Cohen, Fiona. Curious Kids Nature Guide: Explore the Amazing Outdoors of the Pacific Northwest. Fylling, Marni, illus. 2017. (ENG.). 96p. (J). (gr. k-4). 19.99 (978-1-63217-083-5(3), Little Bigfoot) Sasquatch Bks.
Connors, Kathleen. Plants & Animals of the Chesapeake Bay. 2013. 32p. (J). (gr. 3-6). 26.60 (978-1-4339-9780-8(0)); pap. 10.50 (978-1-4339-9781-5(9)); pap. 63.00 (978-1-4339-9782-2(7)) Stevens, Gareth Publishing LLLP.
Craats, Rennay. Natural Landmarks. 2004. (American Symbols Ser.). (Illus.). 24p. (J). (gr. 4-7). per. 8.95 (978-1-59036-177-1(6)); (gr. 1-3). lib. bdg. 24.45 (978-1-59036-133-7(4)) Weigl Pubs., Inc.
Crewe, Sabrina. In the Backyard. 2010. (Under the Microscope Ser.). 32p. (gr. 2-4). 30.00 (978-1-60413-822-1(X), Chelsea Clubhouse) Facts On File, Inc.
Cuthbert, Megan. Europe. 2014. (J). (978-1-4896-0950-2(4)) Weigl Pubs., Inc.
Davies, Valeries & Engelman, Lucy. Field Guide: Creatures Great & Small. 2015. (ENG.). 72p. (J). (gr. 2-5). pap. 19.99 (978-1-84780-697-0(X), Wide Eyed Editions) Quarto Publishing Group UK GBR. Dist: Hachette Bk. Group.
Day, Nancy Raines. What in the World? Sets in Nature. Cyrus, Kurt, illus. 2015. (ENG.). 32p. (J). (gr. -1-3). 17.99 (978-1-4814-0060-2(6), Beach Lane Bks.) Beach Lane Bks.
Dorling Kindersley Publishing Staff. The Amazon. 2015. (DK Eyewitness Bks.). (ENG., Illus.). 72p. (J). (gr. 3-7). 19.99 (978-1-4654-3567-5(0), DK Children) Dorling Kindersley Publishing, Inc.
—Eyewitness Explorer: Nature Ranger: Nature Ranger. 2015. (ENG., Illus.). 72p. (J). (gr. 3-7). pap. 9.99 (978-1-4654-3500-2(X), DK Children) Dorling Kindersley Publishing, Inc.
Drake, Nadia. Little Book of Wonders: Celebrating the Gifts of the Natural World. 2016. (ENG., Illus.). 128p. (J). 12.95 (978-1-4262-1689-3(0)) National Geographic Society.
Dyan, Penelope. The Comeback Kids — Book 9 — the Barbary Macaques of Gibraltar. Weigand, John D., photos

by. 2012. (Illus.). 36p. pap. 14.95 *(978-1-61477-036-7(0))* Bellissima Publishing, LLC.

Esbaum, Jill & National Geographic Kids Staff. Everything Spring. 2010. (ENG., Illus.). 16p. (J). (gr. -1-3). pap. 5.95 *(978-1-4263-0607-5(5),* National Geographic Children's Bks.) National Geographic Society.

Fabiny, Sarah. Where Is the Amazon? Colón, Daniel & Groff, David, illus. 2016. (Where Is? Ser.). (ENG.). 112p. (J). (gr. 3-7). lib. bdg. 15.99 *(978-0-399-54233-6(7),* Grosset & Dunlap) Penguin Young Readers Group.

Fabre, J. Henri. Animal Life in Field & Garden. 2005. pap. 34.95 *(978-1-4179-0762-5(2))* Kessinger Publishing, LLC.

Facts on File, Inc. Staff. Nature. 2010. (New Discovering Careers for Your Future Ser.). (Illus.). 128p. (gr. 4-9). 24.95 *(978-0-8160-8046-5(1),* Ferguson Publishing Co.) Facts On File, Inc.

Farndon, John. Questions & Answers Science & Nature. 2012. (Illus.). 224p. (J). *(978-1-4351-4352-4(3))* Barnes & Noble, Inc.

Forte, Imogene. Nature Crafts. 2004. (Fun Things to Make & Do Ser.). (Illus.). 80p. (J). per. 9.95 *(978-0-86530-617-2(6))* Incentive Pubns., Inc.

Ganeri, Anita. Protecting Polar Regions. 2005. (Protecting Habitats Ser.). 32p. (gr. 4-7). lib. bdg. 26.00 *(978-0-8368-4993-6(0),* Gareth Stevens Learning Library) Stevens, Gareth Publishing LLLP.

—Record-Breaking Earth. 2010. (ENG.). 32p. (J). *(978-0-7787-9908-5(5));* pap. *(978-0-7787-9929-0(8))* Crabtree Publishing Co.

Gatty. Parables from Nature. 2006. 320p. per. *(978-1-4067-9365-9(5),* Pomona Pr.) Read Bks.

Gatty, Alfred. Parables from Nature. 2009. 248p. (gr. 4-7). pap. 10.35 *(978-1-60459-621-2(X))* Wilder Pubns., Corp.

Gladstone, James. When Planet Earth Was New. Diemert, Katherine, illus. 2017. (ENG.). 40p. (J). (gr. -1-5). 18.95 ***(978-1-77147-203-6(0))*** Owlkids Bks. Inc. CAN. Dist: Publishers Group West (PGW).

Goldsworthy, Steve. Antarctica. 2014. (J). *(978-1-4896-0938-0(5))* Weigl Pubs., Inc.

Granström, Brita. What Mr Darwin Saw. Manning, Mick, illus. 2014. (ENG.). 48p. (J). (gr. 1-4). pap. 9.95 *(978-1-84780-107-4(2),* Frances Lincoln) Quarto Publishing Group UK GBR. Dist: Hachette Bk. Group.

Grice, Gordon. Cabinet of Curiosities: A Kid's Guide to Collecting & Understanding the Wonders of the Natural World. 2015. (ENG., Illus.). 200p. (J). (gr. 3-12). 24.95 *(978-0-7611-6927-7(X))* Workman Publishing Co., Inc.

Guin, Valerie. In the Country. 2005. (One World (Smart Apple Media) Ser.). (Illus.). 30p. (J). (gr. 3-6). lib. bdg. 27.10 *(978-1-58340-695-3(6))* Black Rabbit Bks.

Haegele, Katie. Cool Careers Without College for Nature Lovers. 2009. (Cool Careers Without College Ser.). 144p. (gr. 6-6). 66.50 *(978-1-61511-961-5(2));* (Illus.). (J). 35.95 *(978-1-4358-5245-7(1))* Rosen Publishing Group, Inc., The.

Helbrough, Emma. Great Planet Earth Search. Jackson, Ian, illus. 2006. 32p. (J). *(978-0-439-83402-5(3))* Scholastic, Inc.

Hengel, Katherine. Cool Parks & Trails: Great Things to Do in the Great Outdoors, 1 vol. 2016. (ENG., Illus.). 32p. (J). *(978-1-62403-698-9(8))* ABDO Publishing Co.

Holland, Gini. I Live in the Country. 2004. (Where I Live Ser.). (Illus.). 24p. (gr. k-3). lib. bdg. 22.00 *(978-0-8368-4079-7(8),* Weekly Reader Leveled Readers) Stevens, Gareth Publishing LLLP.

—I Live in the Country/Vivo en el Campo. Coffey, Colleen & Carrillo, Consuelo, trs. 2004. (Weekly Reader Early Learning Library). (SPA & ENG., Illus.). 24p. (gr. k-3). lib. bdg. 22.00 *(978-0-8368-4127-5(1),* Weekly Reader Leveled Readers) Stevens, Gareth Publishing LLLP.

Holt, Jane E. In Madera Canyon. 2009. pap. 15.95 *(978-1-60494-002-2(6))* Wheatmark, Inc.

Hooper, Meredith. Pebble in My Pocket: A History of Our Earth. Coady, Chris, illus. rev. ed. 2015. (ENG.). 40p. (J). (gr. 2-5). pap. 9.99 *(978-1-84780-768-7(2),* Frances Lincoln Children's Bks.) Quarto Publishing Group UK GBR. Dist: Hachette Bk. Group.

Jacobs, Pat. I Wonder Why Penguins Can't Fly. 2014. 32p. pap. 7.00 *(978-1-61003-350-3(7))* Center for the Collaborative Classroom.

—I Wonder Why Penguins Can't Fly: And Other Questions about Polar Lands. 2011. (I Wonder Why Ser.). (ENG., Illus.). 32p. (J). (gr. k-3). pap. 6.99 *(978-0-7534-6530-1(2),* 9780753465301, Kingfisher) Roaring Brook Pr.

Johnson, Robin. The Urals. 2011. (ENG., Illus.). 48p. (J). pap. *(978-0-7787-7571-3(2));* (gr. 4-7). lib. bdg. *(978-0-7787-7564-5(X))* Crabtree Publishing Co.

Kalman, Bobbie. What Is Super Nature? 2010. (Big Science Ideas Ser.). (ENG.). 32p. (J). (gr. k-3). pap. *(978-0-7787-3307-2(6));* lib. bdg. *(978-0-7787-3287-7(8))* Crabtree Publishing Co.

—Yellowstone National Park. 2009. (Introducing Habitats Ser.). (ENG., Illus.). 32p. (J). (gr. k-3). pap. *(978-0-7787-2989-1(3))* Crabtree Publishing Co.

Kenison, Misti, illus. The Tiny Traveler: Japan: A Book of Nature. 2016. (ENG.). 24p. (J). (— 1). bds. 5.99 *(978-1-5107-0472-5(8),* Sky Pony Pr.) Skyhorse Publishing Co., Inc.

Latham, Irene. When the Sun Shines on Antarctica: And Other Poems about the Frozen Continent. Wadham, Anna, illus. 2016. (ENG.). 32p. (gr. 3-6). (J). 19.99 *(978-1-4677-5216-9(9));* 30.65 *(978-1-4677-9729-0(4),* Millbrook Pr.) Lerner Publishing Group.

Lazor, Stephanie. Life on the Equator. 2009. (Life in Extreme Environments Ser.). 64p. (gr. 5-8). 53.00 *(978-1-61514-275-0(4),* Rosen Reference) Rosen Publishing Group, Inc., The.

Lerner Publishing Group Staff, ed. Time Nature's Wonders: The Science & Splendor of Earth's Most Fascinating Places. 2008. (Time Inc. Home Entertainment Library-Bound Titles Ser.). (ENG.). 128p. (gr. 5-12). lib. bdg. 39.93 *(978-0-7613-4228-1(1),* Twenty-First Century Bks.) Lerner Publishing Group.

LernerClassroom Editors, ed. Teaching Guide for Fsn / Discovering Nature's Cycles. 2010. pap. 5.95 *(978-0-7613-6683-6(0))* Lerner Publishing Group.

Leslie, Clare Walker. The Curious Nature Guide: Explore the Natural Wonders All Around You. 2015. (ENG., Illus.). 144p. pap. 14.95 *(978-1-61212-509-1(3))* Storey Publishing, LLC.

Lord, Michelle. La Naturaleza Recicla¿lo Haces Tú?, 1 vol. Morrison, Cathy, illus. 2013. (ENG & SPA.). 32p. (J). (gr. -1-4). 17.95 *(978-1-60718-711-0(6))* Arbordale Publishing.

—Nature Recycles: How about You?, 1 vol. Morrison, Cathy, illus. 2013. (ENG.). 32p. (J). (gr. -1-4). 17.95 *(978-1-60718-615-1(2));* pap. 9.95 *(978-1-60718-627-4(6))* Arbordale Publishing.

Lowrie, Paul. Hooray for Minnesota Lakes. 2008. 19.95 *(978-0-9755801-8-9(3))* Questmarc Publishing.

Mahaney, Ian F. Energy in Action, 6 bks., Set. Incl. Electricity. (YA). (gr. 4-7). lib. bdg. 22.60 *(978-1-4042-3478-9(0));* Heat. (YA). (gr. 4-7). lib. bdg. 22.60 *(978-1-4042-3477-2(2));* Light. (YA). (gr. 4-7). lib. bdg. 22.60 *(978-1-4042-3476-5(4));* Sound Waves. (J). (gr. 3-7). lib. bdg. 21.25 *(978-1-4042-3480-2(2),* PowerKids Pr.); (Illus.). 24p. 2007. 2007. Set lib. bdg. 127.50 *(978-1-4042-3504-5(3))* Rosen Publishing Group, Inc., The.

Manning, Mick & Granström, Brita, illus. Nature School. 2009. (ENG.). 48p. (J). (gr. 1-5). *(978-1-84507-843-0(8))* Rough Guides, Ltd.

Marciniak, Kristin. Incredible Nature. 2018. (ENG.). 32p. (gr. 3-6). 31.35 ***(978-1-63235-421-1(7),*** 12-Story Library) Pr. Room Editions LLC.

Martineau, Susan. Bugs in the Garden. Noyes, Leighton, illus. 2011. (Everyday Science Experiments Ser.). (ENG.). 24p. (J). (gr. 3-6). pap. 10.60 *(978-1-61533-408-7(4));* lib. bdg. 25.25 *(978-1-61533-370-7(3))* Windmill Bks.

Miché, Mary. Nature's Patchwork Quilt: Understanding Habitats. Powell, Consie, illus. 2012. 32p. (J). (gr. k-6). 16.95 *(978-1-58469-169-3(7));* (ENG.). pap. 8.95 *(978-1-58469-170-9(0))* Dawn Pubns.

Miles, Liz. Linnaeus: Organising Nature. 2017. (ENG., Illus.). 80p. (J). pap. 9.99 ***(978-0-00-820897-4(2))*** HarperCollins Pubs. Ltd. GBR. Dist: Independent Pubs. Group.

Montgomery, Heather L. Unsolved Mysteries of Nature. 2015. (Unsolved Mystery Files Ser.). (ENG., Illus.). 32p. (gr. 3-4). pap. 7.95 *(978-1-4914-4341-5(3))* Capstone Press of Coughlan Cos.

Morgan, Sally. The Incredible Life of David Attenborough, Bd. 16. 2017. (ENG.). 56p. (J). pap. 8.99 ***(978-0-00-820889-9(1))*** HarperCollins Pubs. Ltd. GBR. Dist: Independent Pubs. Group.

Morley, Margaret W. Little Wanderers. 2009. (Illus.). 116p. pap. 8.95 *(978-1-59915-317-9(3))* Yesterday's Classics.

Morley, Margaret Warner. A Song of Life 1922. Forsyth, Robert, illus. 2004. reprint ed. pap. 21.95 *(978-1-4179-7842-7(2))* Kessinger Publishing, LLC.

Morris, Sandra. Welcome to New Zealand: a Nature Journal. Morris, Sandra, illus. 2015. (ENG., Illus.). 48p. (J). (gr. 3-7). 16.99 *(978-0-7636-7477-9(X))* Candlewick Pr.

National Geographic Learning Staff. Saguaro Moon: A Desert Journal. Pratt-Serafini, Kristin Joy, illus. 2010. (Rise & Shine Ser.). (ENG.). 32p. (C). pap. 14.95 *(978-1-58469-036-8(4))* National Geographic School Publishing, Inc.

Natural History. (Illus.). (J). (gr. -1-6). pap., act. bk. ed. 2.95 *(978-0-565-00857-4(9))* Natural History Museum Pubns. GBR. Dist: Parkwest Pubns., Inc.

O'Connell, Caitlin & Jackson, Donna M. The Elephant Scientist. Rodwell, Timothy, illus. 2016. (Scientists in the Field Ser.). (ENG.). 80p. (J). (gr. 5-7). 9.99 *(978-0-544-66830-0(8),* HMH Books For Young Readers) Houghton Mifflin Harcourt Publishing Co.

Oxlade, Chris. Hands-on Science Projects: Nature. 2008. (ENG., Illus.). 64p. (J). (gr. 4-7). pap. 7.99 *(978-1-84476-532-4(6))* Anness Publishing GBR. Dist: National Bk. Network.

Paquette, Ammi-Joan & Thompson, Laurie Ann. Two Truths & a Lie: It's Alive! Weber, Lisa K., illus. 2017. 176p. (J). (gr. 3-7). 17.99 ***(978-0-06-241879-1(3),*** Walden Pond Pr.) HarperCollins Pubs.

Parker, Francis W. Uncle Robert's Geography (Uncle Robert's Visit, V. 3) 2006. 84p. pap. *(978-1-84702-205-9(7))* Echo Library.

Parker, Steve & Parker, Jane. Show Me How: Nature Projects. 2015. (ENG., Illus.). 48p. (J). (gr. -1-12). 7.99 *(978-1-86147-298-4(6),* Armadillo) Anness Publishing GBR. Dist: National Bk. Network.

Pecorella, Jane. Yellowstone: Our First National Park. 2009. (Reading Room Collection 2 Ser.). 24p. (gr. 3-4). 42.50 *(978-1-60852-004-6(8),* PowerKids Pr.) Rosen Publishing Group, Inc., The.

—Yellowstone, Our First National Park. 2003. (Reading Room Collection 2 Ser.). (Illus.). 24p. (J). lib. bdg. 22.60 *(978-0-8239-3712-7(7))* Rosen Publishing Group, Inc., The.

Peixe Dias, Maria Ana & Teixeira do Rosari, Ines. Outside: A Complete Guide to Discovering Nature. Carvalho, Bernardo P., illus. 2016. (ENG.). 368p. (J). (gr. 3-6). 27.99 *(978-1-84780-769-4(0),* Frances Lincoln Children's Bks.) Quarto Publishing Group UK GBR. Dist: Hachette Bk. Group.

Peppas, Lynn. The Alps. 2011. (ENG., Illus.). 48p. (J). pap. *(978-0-7787-7566-9(6));* (gr. 4-7). lib. bdg. *(978-0-7787-7559-1(3))* Crabtree Publishing Co.

Percy, J.P. Nature. 2013. (Can You Guess What I Am? Ser.). 24p. (gr. k-3). 28.50 *(978-1-59920-895-4(4))* Black Rabbit Bks.

Pipe, Jim. Wonderful World. 2009. (ENG.). 112p. (J). (gr. 4-7). pap. 12.95 *(978-1-84696-204-2(8),* TickTock Books) Octopus Publishing Group GBR. Dist: Independent Pubs. Group.

Pomeroy, Sarah B. & Kathirithamby, Jeyaraney. Maria Sibylla Merian: Artist, Scientist, Adventurer. 2017. (J). ***(978-1-60606-555-6(6),*** J. Paul Getty Museum) Getty Pubns.

Pratt-Serafini, Kristin Joy, illus. Saguaro Moon: A Desert Journal. 2004. (Sharing Nature with Children Book Ser.). 32p. (YA). 16.95 *(978-1-58469-037-5(2))* Dawn Pubns.

Pyers, Greg. Biodiversity of Polar Regions. 2010. (Biodiversity Ser.). 32p. (gr. 4-18). 28.50 *(978-1-60870-072-1(0))* Marshall Cavendish Corp.

Questions & Answers of the Natural World. 2003. (Illus.). 256p. (J). 12.98 *(978-1-4054-1682-5(3))* Parragon, Inc.

Reeves, Diane Lindsey. Food & Natural Resources. 2017. (Bright Futures Press: World of Work Ser.). (ENG., Illus.). 32p. (J). (gr. 4-7). lib. bdg. 29.93 *(978-1-63472-622-1(7),* 209522) Cherry Lake Publishing.

Rice, David L. Lifetimes. Maydak, Michael S., illus. 2015. 32p. pap. 9.00 *(978-1-61003-549-1(6))* Center for the Collaborative Classroom.

Rice, Dona. Environment: A World of Change, 1 vol. rev. ed. 2014. (Science Readers: Content & Literacy Ser.). (ENG.). 32p. (gr. 2-2). pap. 8.99 *(978-1-4807-4602-2(9))* Teacher Created Materials, Inc.

Rice, William. El Desierto Del Valle de la Muerte. 2017. (TIME for Kids en Español - Level 3 Ser.). (SPA.). 32p. (gr. 3-3). lib. bdg. 31.99 ***(978-1-5157-5179-3(1))*** Time for Kids Inc AUS. Dist: Capstone Pub.

Richards, Jon & Simkins, Ed. The Natural World. 2016. 32p. (J). *(978-0-7787-2658-6(4))* Crabtree Publishing Co.

Richardson, Donna. Yellowstone: A Blast from the Past. 2007. (Illus.). 14p. pap. 4.75 *(978-0-15-377369-3(3))* Harcourt Schl. Pubs.

A Ride Around Presque Isle: Natural History along the Roadsides. 2004. (Illus.). spiral bd. 15.00 *(978-0-9747001-1-3(8))* Edinboro Bk. Arts Collective.

Rissman, Rebecca. Living & Nonliving in the Polar Regions, 1 vol. 2013. (Is It Living or Nonliving? Ser.). (ENG.). 24p. (gr. k-2). 23.32 *(978-1-4109-5383-4(1));* pap. 6.95 *(978-1-4109-5390-2(4))* Heinemann-Raintree.

Rossouw, Andre J. & Bitline S. A. 1010. Natural Sciences Matters Grade 8 Learner's Book Afrikaans Translation. 2006. 160p. pap. 14.00 *(978-0-521-67894-0(3))* Cambridge Univ. Pr.

Roth, Susan L. & Trumbore, Cindy. Parrots over Puerto Rico, 1 vol. Roth, Susan L., illus. 2013. (ENG., Illus.). 48p. (J). 19.95 *(978-1-62014-004-8(7))* Lee & Low Bks., Inc.

Rustad, Martha E. H. Do Trees Get Hungry? Noticing Plant & Animal Traits. Moran, Mike, illus. 2015. (ENG.). 24p. (gr. k-2). lib. bdg. 25.32 *(978-1-4677-8559-4(8),* Millbrook Pr.) Lerner Publishing Group.

Sanchez, Anita & Stock, Catherine. Karl, Get Out of the Garden! Carolus Linnaeus & the Naming of Everything. 2017. (ENG., Illus.). 48p. (J). (gr. 2-5). lib. bdg. 17.99 *(978-1-58089-606-1(5))* Charlesbridge Publishing, Inc.

Sayre, April Pulley. Greeting, Asia! The Ultimate Guide to America's 4 Regional Styles of 'Cue. 2003. (Illus.). 32p. lib. bdg. 21.90 *(978-0-7613-2124-8(1),* Millbrook Pr.) Lerner Publishing Group.

Seiple, Samantha. Death on the River of Doubt: Theodore Roosevelt's Amazon Adventure. 2017. (ENG.). 240p. (J). (gr. 7). 17.99 *(978-0-545-70916-3(4),* Scholastic Pr.) Scholastic, Inc.

Seton, Ernest Thompson. Woodmyth & Fable. 2005. pap. 22.95 *(978-1-885529-83-1(X))* Stevens Publishing.

Silva Lee, Alfonso. Mi Isla y Yo: La Naturaleza de Puerto Rico. Hayskar, Bonnie J., ed. Lago, Alexis, illus. 2007. (SPA.). 32p. (J). pap. 8.95 *(978-1-929165-19-3(6))* PANGAEA.

—Mi isla y yo/My Island & I: La naturaleza de Puerto Rico/The Nature of Puerto Rico. Hayskar, Bonnie J., ed. Lago, Alexis, illus. 2003. (SPA & ENG.). 32p. (J). pap. 9.95 *(978-1-929165-12-4(9))* PANGAEA.

Smith, David J. If: A Mind-Bending New Way of Looking at Big Ideas & Numbers. Adams, Steve, illus. 2014. (ENG.). 40p. (J). (gr. 3-7). 18.95 *(978-1-894786-34-8(3))* Kids Can Pr., Ltd. CAN. Dist: Hachette Bk. Group.

Smith, Lynn & Faust Kalscheur, Jann. ABC's Naturally: A Child's Guide to the Alphabet Through Nature. Faust Kalscheur, Jann, photos by. 2003. (Illus.). (J). 16.95 *(978-1-931599-27-6(0),* Trails Bks.) Bower Hse.

Sollinger, Emily. This Is Our World: A Story about Taking Care of the Earth. Brown, Jo, illus. 2010. (Little Green Bks.). (ENG.). 12p. (J). (gr. -1-1). bds. 7.99 *(978-1-4169-7821-3(6),* Little Simon) Little Simon.

St. Antoine, Sara, ed. The North Atlantic Coast: A Literary Field Guide. Mirocha, Paul & Nicholson, Trudy, illus. 2004. (Stories from Where We Live Ser.). (ENG.). 288p. (J). pap., instr.'s gde. ed. 10.95 *(978-1-57131-643-1(4))* Milkweed Editions.

Stienecker, David. Blast Zone: The Eruption & Recovery of Mount St. Helens. 2003. (ENG., Illus.). 32p. (J). (gr. 6-8). pap. 7.97 net. *(978-0-7652-3265-6(0),* Celebration Pr.) Pearson Schl.

Suzuki, David. There's a Barnyard in My Bedroom. Fernandes, Eugenie, illus. 2010. (ENG.). 64p. (gr. -1-3). pap. 10.95 *(978-1-55365-532-9(X))* Greystone Books Ltd. CAN. Dist: Publishers Group West (PGW).

Suzuki, David & Vanderlinden, Kathy. You Are the Earth: Know Your World So You Can Help Make It Better. Edwards, Wallace, illus. 2nd rev. ed. 2010. (ENG.). 160p. (gr. k-7). pap. 18.95 *(978-1-55365-476-6(5))* Greystone Books Ltd. CAN. Dist: Publishers Group West (PGW).

Swinburne, Stephen R. Lots & Lots of Zebra Stripes. 2014. 21.45 *(978-1-63419-671-0(6))* Perfection Learning Corp.

Ticktock Media, Ltd. Staff. Living Planet: Uncovering the Wonders of the Natural World. 2008. (ENG.). 128p. (J). (gr. 4-7). pap. 12.95 *(978-1-84696-816-7(X),* TickTock Books) Octopus Publishing Group GBR. Dist: Independent Pubs. Group.

Troupe, Thomas Kingsley. Diggin' Dirt: Science Adventures with Kitanai the Origami Dog, 1 vol. Christoph, Jamey, illus. 2013. (Origami Science Adventures Ser.). (ENG.). 24p. (gr. 3-4). pap. 6.95 *(978-1-4048-8066-5(6));* lib. bdg. 27.32 *(978-1-4048-7969-0(2))* Picture Window Bks.

Trumbauer, Lisa. A Year in the Desert, 6 vols., Set. 2005. (Yellow Umbrella Fluent Level Ser.). (ENG., Illus.). 16p. (gr. k-1). pap. 35.70 *(978-0-7368-5302-6(2),* Yellow Umbrella Bks.) Capstone Press of Coughlan Cos.

U. S. National Geographic Society Staff, ed. Books for Young Explorers, 4 vols., Set 6. (J). lib. bdg. 16.95 *(978-0-87044-250-6(3))* National Geographic Society.

Usborne Books Staff, creator. The Young Naturalist Kid Kit. 2007. (Kid Kits Ser.). (Illus.). 32p. (J). pap. 14.99 *(978-1-60130-037-9(9),* Usborne) EDC Publishing.

Viano, Hannah. B Is for Bear: A Natural Alphabet. Viano, Hannah, illus. 2015. (ENG., Illus.). 32p. (J). (-k). 16.99 *(978-1-63217-039-2(6),* Little Bigfoot) Sasquatch Bks.

Vierow, Wendy. Australia. 2004. (Atlas of the Seven Continents Ser.). (Illus.). 24p. (YA). (gr. 3-6). lib. bdg. 22.60 *(978-0-8239-6690-5(9))* Rosen Publishing Group, Inc., The.

—Europe. (Atlas of the Seven Continents Ser.). 24p. 2009. (gr. 3-3). 42.50 *(978-1-61511-480-1(7))* 2004. (Illus.). (J). lib. bdg. 22.60 *(978-0-8239-6691-2(7))* Rosen Publishing Group, Inc., The. (PowerKids Pr.).

Wadsworth, Pamela. Gwahanol Blanhigion AC Anifeiliaid. Owen, Ken & Owen, Siân, illus. 2005. (WEL.). 24p. pap. *(978-1-85596-223-1(3))* Dref Wen.

—Rhagor Am Wahanol Blanhigion Ac Anifeiliaid. 2005. (WEL., Illus.). 24p. pap. *(978-1-85596-224-8(1))* Dref Wen.

Watson, Jane Werner. Wonders of Nature. Wilkin, Eloise, illus. 2010. (Little Golden Book Ser.). (ENG.). 24p. (J). (gr. -1-2). 4.99 *(978-0-375-85486-6(X),* Golden Bks.) Random Hse. Children's Bks.

Williams, Brian. The Natural World. 2010. (What About... Ser.). (Illus.). 40p. (J). (gr. 6-8). lib. bdg. 19.95 *(978-1-4222-1562-3(8))* Mason Crest.

Williams, Zella. Experiments about the Natural World. (Do-It-Yourself Science Ser.). 24p. (gr. 2-3). 2009. 47.90 *(978-1-61512-186-1(2),* PowerKids Pr.) 2007. (Illus.). (J). lib. bdg. 25.25 *(978-1-4042-3661-5(9))* Rosen Publishing Group, Inc., The.

Wiseman, Blaine. The Midwest. 2014. (Illus.). 32p. (J). *(978-1-4896-1226-7(2))* Weigl Pubs., Inc.

Wood, A. J. & Jolley, Mike. Natural World: A Visual Compendium of Wonders from Nature. Davey, Owen, illus. 2016. (Curiositree Ser.). (ENG.). 112p. (J). (gr. 3-6). 27.99 *(978-1-84780-782-3(8),* Wide Eyed Editions) Quarto Publishing Group UK GBR. Dist: Hachette Bk. Group.

Woods, Michael & Woods, Mary B. Seven Natural Wonders of the Arctic, Antarctica, & the Oceans. 2009. (Seven Wonders Ser.). (ENG., Illus.). 80p. (gr. 5-8). 33.26 *(978-0-8225-9075-0(1))* Lerner Publishing Group.

Woodward, John & Gray, Leon. Backyard. 2007. (Close-up Ser.). (Illus.). 32p. (J). (gr. 4-7). lib. bdg. *(978-1-933834-13-9(7))* Brown Bear Books.

World Book, Inc Staff, contrib. by. Explore & Learn — The Natural World. 2008. (J). *(978-0-7166-3019-7(2))* World Bk., Inc.

—Icy Worlds. 2011. (J). *(978-0-7166-1788-4(9))* World Bk., Inc.

Young, Caroline & Needham, Kate. Great Wildlife Search: Big Bug Search, Great Animal Search & Great Undersea Search. Jackson, Ian, illus. 2004. (Great Searches Ser.). 112p. (J). pap. 15.99 *(978-0-7945-0892-0(8),* Usborne) EDC Publishing.

NATURAL HISTORY—AFRICA

Aloian, Molly. The Kalahari Desert. 2012. (ENG.). 32p. (J). lib. bdg. *(978-0-7787-0712-7(1));* (Illus.). pap. *(978-0-7787-0720-2(2))* Crabtree Publishing Co.

Cuthbert, Megan. Africa. 2014. (J). *(978-1-4896-0934-2(2))* Weigl Pubs., Inc.

Galvin, Laura Gates. Alphabet of African Animals. Leeper, Christopher J. et al, illus. 2011. (Alphabet Bks.). (ENG.). 40p. (J). (gr. -1-3). 17.95 *(978-1-60727-574-9(0))* Soundprints.

—Alphabet of African Animals. Denman, Michael et al, illus. 2008. (ENG.). 40p. (J). (gr. -1-2). 17.95 *(978-1-59249-854-3(X))* Soundprints.

Rebus, Anna. Victoria Falls: One of the World's Most Spectacular Waterfalls. 2006. (Natural Wonders Ser.). (Illus.). 32p. (J). (gr. 3-7). lib. bdg. 26.00 *(978-1-59036-453-6(8));* per. 9.95 *(978-1-59036-459-8(7))* Weigl Pubs., Inc.

Wojahn, Rebecca Hogue & Wojahn, Donald. A Cloud Forest Food Chain: A Who-Eats-What Adventure in Africa. 2009. (Follow That Food Chain Ser.). (ENG.). 64p. (gr. 3-5). 30.60 *(978-0-8225-7612-9(0))* Lerner Publishing Group.

Woods, Michael & Woods, Mary B. Seven Natural Wonders of Africa. 2009. (Seven Wonders Ser.). (ENG., Illus.). 80p. (gr. 5-8). lib. bdg. 33.26 *(978-0-8225-9071-2(9))* Lerner Publishing Group.

NATURAL HISTORY—ASIA

Aloian, Molly. The Himalayas. 2011. (ENG., Illus.). 48p. (J). pap. *(978-0-7787-7569-0(0));* (gr. 4-7). lib. bdg. *(978-0-7787-7562-1(3))* Crabtree Publishing Co.

Yasuda, Anita. Asia. 2014. (J). *(978-1-4896-0942-7(3))* Weigl Pubs., Inc.

NATURAL HISTORY—AUSTRALIA

Barwood, Lee. Klassic Koalas: Ancient Aboriginal Tales in New Retellings, BW Edition. 2007. (ENG., Illus.). 24p. (J). pap. 14.99 *(978-0-9764698-6-5(3))* Koala Jo Publishing.

Collard, Sneed B., III. One Night in the Coral Sea. Brickman, Robin, illus. 2006. 32p. (gr. 3-7). 17.95 *(978-0-7569-6969-1(7))* Perfection Learning Corp.

Lewin, Betsy & Lewin, Ted, illus. Top to Bottom down under Top to Bottom down Under, 1 vol. 2014. (Adventures Around the World Ser.). (ENG.). 48p. (J). pap. 11.95 *(978-1-62014-184-7(1))* Lee & Low Bks., Inc.

Myers, Jenna. Australia. 2014. (J). *(978-1-4896-0946-5(6))* Weigl Pubs., Inc.

Tieck, Sarah. Bindi Irwin: Star of Bindi the Jungle Girl, 1 vol. 2008. (Big Buddy Biographies Ser.). (ENG.). 32p. (J). (gr. 2-5). 28.50 *(978-1-60453-122-0(3))* ABDO Publishing Co.

Vierow, Wendy. Australia. 2004. (Atlas of the Seven Continents Ser.). (Illus.). 24p. (YA). (gr. 3-6). lib. bdg. 22.60 *(978-0-8239-6690-5(9))* Rosen Publishing Group, Inc., The.

Woods, Michael & Woods, Mary B. Seven Natural Wonders of Australia & Oceania. 2009. (Seven Wonders Ser.). (ENG., Illus.). 80p. (gr. 5-8). 33.26 *(978-0-8225-9074-3(3))* Lerner Publishing Group.

NATURAL HISTORY, BIBLICAL

see Bible—Natural History

NATURAL HISTORY—CANADA

Kitts, Wendy. Sable Island: The Wandering Sandbar, 1 vol. 2012. (ENG., Illus.). 96p. (J). (gr. 2-4). pap. 15.95 *(978-1-55109-865-4(2))* Nimbus Publishing, Ltd. CAN. Dist: Orca Bk. Pubs. USA.

Matthews, Sheelagh. Canadian Shield. 2010. (Illus.). 32p. *(978-1-55388-628-0(3));* pap. *(978-1-55388-629-7(1))* Weigl Educational Pubs. Ltd.

Morrison, Jessica. Maritimes. 2010. (Illus.). 32p. *(978-1-55388-637-2(2));* pap. *(978-1-55388-638-9(0))* Weigl Educational Pubs. Ltd.

Pratt, Laura. Arctic. 2010. (Illus.). 32p. *(978-1-55388-631-0(3));* pap. *(978-1-55388-632-7(1))* Weigl Educational Pubs. Ltd.

—Plains. 2010. (Illus.). 32p. *(978-1-55388-625-9(9));* pap. *(978-1-55388-626-6(7))* Weigl Educational Pubs. Ltd.

NATURAL HISTORY—DICTIONARIES

Brooks, F. First Encyclopedia of Our World. 2004. (First Encyclopedia Ser.). (ENG., Illus.). 1p. (J). (gr. 3-18). pap. 9.99 *(978-0-7945-0216-4(4),* Usborne) EDC Publishing.

M
N
O

NATURAL HISTORY—FICTION

Andrews, Jane. Stories Mother Nature Told Her Children. 2006. pap. *(978-1-4065-0875-8(6))* Dodo Pr.

—Young Reader's Series: The stories mother nature told her Children. 2009. 156p. pap. 16.95 *(978-1-60444-036-2(8))* IndoEuropeanPublishing.com.

Ballantyne, R. M. Blown to Bits; or, the Lonely Man of Rak. 2006. pap. *(978-1-4065-0515-3(3))* Dodo Pr.

—Red Rooney: Or, the Last of the Crew. 2007. (R. M. Ballantyne Collection). (Illus.). 408p. 22.00 *(978-1-934554-08-1(1))* Vision Forum, Inc., The.

Ballantyne, Robert Michael. Red Rooney: The Last of the Crew. 2007. (ENG.). 270p. pap. 21.99 *(978-1-4346-3693-5(3))*; 302p. pap. 24.99 *(978-1-4346-3741-3(7))* Creative Media Partners, LLC.

—The Rover of the Andes: A Tale of Adventure in South America. 2007. (ENG.). 266p. pap. 21.99 *(978-1-4346-3753-6(0))*; 296p. pap. 23.99 *(978-1-4346-3767-3(0))* Creative Media Partners, LLC.

Barnum, P. T. Dick Broadhead: A Story of Perilous Adve. 2006. pap. 30.95 *(978-1-4286-1959-3(3))* Kessinger Publishing, LLC.

Belaney, Archibald Stansfeld. On the Trail: Pages from the Writings of Grey Owl. Reynolds, E. E., ed. 2011. (ENG.). 130p. pap. 21.99 *(978-1-107-60015-7(4))* Cambridge Univ. Pr.

Delacre, Lulu. Rafi & Rosi. Delacre, Lulu, illus. 2005. (I Can Read Bks.). (Illus.). 64p. (J). (gr. k-3). pap. 3.99 *(978-0-06-009897-1(X),* Rayo) HarperCollins Pubs.

—Rafi & Rosi. Delacre, Lulu, illus. 2016. (Rafi & Rosi Ser.). (ENG., Illus.). 63p. (J). (gr. k-3). pap. 8.95 *(978-0-89239-377-0(7))* Lee & Low Bks., Inc.

—Rafi y Rosi. Delacre, Lulu, illus. 2016. (Rafi & Rosi Ser.).Tr. of Rafi & Rosi. (SPA., Illus.). (J). pap. 8.95 *(978-0-89239-378-7(5))* Lee & Low Bks., Inc.

Ganeri, Anita. My Pop-Up World Atlas. Waterhouse, Stephen, illus. 2012. (ENG.). 16p. (J). (gr. k-3). 19.99 *(978-0-7636-6094-9(9),* Templar) Candlewick Pr.

Grant, Robert. Jack in the Bush or A Summer on a Salmon River. 2005. pap. 33.95 *(978-1-4179-5573-2(2))* Kessinger Publishing, LLC.

Hadley, Caroline. Woodside; or, Look, Listen & Learn. 2007. (ENG., Illus.). 80p. per. *(978-1-4065-1557-2(4))* Dodo Pr.

McCabe, James Dabney, Jr. Planting the Wilderness or, the Pioneer Boys: a Story of Frontier Life. 2007. pap. 27.95 *(978-1-4304-8187-4(0))* Kessinger Publishing, LLC.

Meyer, Carolyn. The True Adventures of Charley Darwin. 2011. (ENG., Illus.). 336p. (YA). (gr. 7). pap. 9.99 *(978-0-547-41564-2(8))* Houghton Mifflin Harcourt Publishing Co.

Miranda, Edward. The Truth about Dragons & Dinosaurs. Cassetta, Andrea, illus. 2007. 32p. per. 10.95 *(978-1-934246-22-1(0))* Peppertree Pr., The.

Shapiro, David R. Blunderbuss Wanderlust: Being an Account of the Temporal Travels of Colonel Victor Von Vector & the Eras of His Ways. Herndon, Christopher, illus. 2nd ed. 2016. (ENG.). 44p. (J). (gr. 4-7). 14.99 *(978-1-940052-13-7(0))* Craigmore Creations.

—Terra Tempo Vol. 3: The Academy of Planetary Evolution. Herndon, Christopher, illus. 2014. (Terra Tempo Ser.). (ENG.). 182p. (J). (gr. 2-4). pap. 17.99 *(978-1-940052-09-0(2))* Craigmore Creations.

Stauffer, Sharon. Cornfield Baby: And Other Nature Surprises. 2003. (Illus.). 179p. 8.40 *(978-0-7399-2314-6(5),* 2344) Rod & Staff Pubs., Inc.

Stockton, Frank Richard. Round-about Rambles in Lands of Fact & Fancy. 2006. pap. *(978-1-4068-3083-5(6))* Echo Library.

Thomes, William Henry. The Bushrangers a Yankee's Adventures During His Second Visit to Australia by William H Thomes. 2006. 420p. per. 26.99 *(978-1-4255-4567-3(X))* Michigan Publishing.

Verne, Jules. The English at the North Pole. 2009. 160p. 24.95 *(978-1-60664-684-7(2))*; pap. 13.95 *(978-1-60664-313-6(4))* Rodgers, Alan Bks.

Weaver, Anne H. The Voyage of the Beetle: A Journey Around the World with Charles Darwin & the Search for the Solution to the Mystery of Mysteries, As Narrated by Rosie, an Articulate Beetle. Lawrence, George, tr. Lawrence, George, illus. 2004. (Roman Mysteries Ser.). 80p. (J). (gr. 5-8). lib. bdg. 26.90 *(978-0-7613-2923-7(4),* Millbrook Pr.) Lerner Publishing Group.

NATURAL HISTORY—HAWAII

Looye, Juliette, text. I Live on an Island. 2004. (Illus.). 16p. (J). pap. *(978-0-7367-1936-0(9))* Zaner-Bloser, Inc.

NATURAL HISTORY—MIDDLE EAST

Vogel, Carole Garbuny & Leshem, Yossi. The Man Who Flies with Birds. 2009. (Israel Ser.). (ENG., Illus.). 64p. (J). (gr. 5-12). 18.95 *(978-0-8225-7643-3(0),* Kar-Ben Publishing) Lerner Publishing Group.

NATURAL HISTORY—NORTH AMERICA

Aloian, Molly. The Appalachians. 2011. (ENG., Illus.). 48p. (J). pap. *(978-0-7787-7568-3(2))*; (gr. 4-7). lib. bdg. *(978-0-7787-7561-4(5))* Crabtree Publishing Co.

—The Rocky Mountains. 2011. (ENG., Illus.). 48p. (J). pap. *(978-0-7787-7570-6(4))*; (gr. 4-7). lib. bdg. *(978-0-7787-7563-8(1))* Crabtree Publishing Co.

Ashcroft, Minnie & National Geographic Learning Staff. North America - People & Places. 2007. (Reading Expeditions Ser.). (ENG., Illus.). 64p. (J). pap. 25.95 *(978-0-7922-4381-6(1))* CENGAGE Learning.

Bauer, Marion Dane. The Rocky Mountains. Wallace, John, illus. 2006. (Wonders of America Ser.). (ENG.). 32p. (J). (gr. -1-1). pap. 3.99 *(978-0-689-86948-8(7),* Simon Spotlight) Simon Spotlight.

Berkes, Marianne. Over in a River: Flowing Out to the Sea, 1 vol. Dubin, Jill, illus. 2013. (ENG.). 32p. (J). (gr. -1-3). 16.95 *(978-1-58469-329-1(0))*; pap. 8.95 *(978-1-58469-330-7(4))* Dawn Pubns.

Daly, Ruth. North America. 2014. (J). *(978-1-4896-0954-0(7))* Weigl Pubs., Inc.

Loughran, Donna. Living in the Tundra. 2004. (Rookie Read-About Geography Ser.). (ENG., Illus.). 32p. (J). (gr. 1-2). pap. 5.95 *(978-0-516-27331-0(0),* Children's Pr.) Scholastic Library Publishing.

Morrison, Jessica. Cordillera. 2010. (Illus.). 32p. *(978-1-55388-634-1(8))*; pap. *(978-1-55388-635-8(6))* Weigl Educational Pubs. Ltd.

Munro, Roxie. Desert Days, Desert Nights. 2010. (ENG.). 32p. (J). 17.95 *(978-1-933979-77-9(1),* 7eb1e541-2180-4d1b-847f-abe71cd7cdcd) Bright Sky Pr.

Sheinkin, Steve & National Geographic Learning Staff. North America - Geography & Environments. 2007. (Reading Expeditions Ser.). (ENG., Illus.). 64p. (J). pap. 25.95 *(978-0-7922-4380-9(3))* CENGAGE Learning.

NATURAL HISTORY—OUTDOOR BOOKS

see Nature Study

NATURAL HISTORY—POETRY

Canetti, Yanitzia. El mundo es una Semilla: Un mundo Mejor. 2010. (SPA.). 32p. (J). 9.99 *(978-1-59835-287-0(3),* BrickHouse Education) Cambridge BrickHouse, Inc.

—Our Great Big World. 2010. 32p. pap. 9.99 *(978-1-59835-288-7(1),* BrickHouse Education) Cambridge BrickHouse, Inc.

Ewing, Susan. Lucky Hares & Itchy Bears: And Other Alaskan Animals. Blessing, Marlene, ed. Zerbetz, Evon, illus. 2012. (ENG.). 32p. (J). 16.95 *(978-0-9858506-0-9(4))* Octopoda Pr.

NATURAL HISTORY—SOUTH AMERICA

Banting, Erinn. The Galapagos Islands. 2006. (Natural Wonders Ser.). (Illus.). 32p. (J). (gr. 3-7). per. 9.95 *(978-1-59036-455-0(4))* Weigl Pubs., Inc.

—The Galapagos Islands: A Unique Ecosystem. 2006. (Natural Wonders Ser.). (Illus.). 32p. (J). (gr. 3-7). lib. bdg. 26.00 *(978-1-59036-449-9(X))* Weigl Pubs., Inc.

Roza, Greg. The Galapagos Islands. 2009. (Reading Room Collection 2 Ser.). 24p. (gr. 3-4). 42.50 *(978-1-60851-993-4(7),* PowerKids Pr.) Rosen Publishing Group, Inc., The.

Sirota, Lyn A. South America. 2014. (J). *(978-1-4896-0958-8(X))* Weigl Pubs., Inc.

NATURAL HISTORY—UNITED STATES

Ake, Anne. Everglades: An Ecosystem Facing Choices & Challenges. 2008. (ENG., Illus.). 110p. (J). (gr. 6-9). 19.95 *(978-1-56164-410-0(2))* Pineapple Pr., Inc.

America's Great Outdoors. (YA). (gr. 7-12). 39.00 *(978-0-87827-250-1(X))* Encyclopaedia Britannica, Inc.

Augustin, Byron & Kubena, Jake. The Grand Canyon. 2009. (Nature's Wonders 2 Ser.). 96p. (gr. 6). 35.64 *(978-0-7614-3935-6(8))* Marshall Cavendish Corp.

Bakshi, Kelly. The First Americans. Bakshi, Kelly, illus. 2012. (Illus.). 16p. pap. 9.95 *(978-1-61633-278-5(6))* Guardian Angel Publishing, Inc.

Barlowe, Dot. Grand Canyon Plants & Animals. 2010. (Dover Nature Coloring Book Ser.). (ENG., Illus.). 32p. (gr. 3-8). pap. 3.99 *(978-0-486-47294-2(9))* Dover Pubns., Inc.

Burnham, Brad. Mammoth Cave: The World's Longest Cave System. (Famous Caves of the World Ser.). 24p. 2009. (gr. 3-4). 42.50 *(978-1-61512-498-5(5))* 2003. (Illus.). (J). lib. bdg. 22.60 *(978-0-8239-6258-7(X))* Rosen Publishing Group, Inc., The. (PowerKids Pr.).

Chin, Jason. Grand Canyon. 2017. (ENG., Illus.). 56p. (J). 19.99 *(978-1-59643-950-4(5),* 9781596439504) Roaring Brook Pr.

Clickard, Carrie. Thomas Jefferson & the Mammoth Hunt. Carpenter, Nancy, illus. 2017. (J). *(978-1-4814-4268-8(6),* Beach Lane Bks.) Beach Lane Bks.

Cunningham, Laura. The Bay Area Through Time. 2015. (Illus.). (J). *(978-1-59714-301-1(4))* Heyday.

Dunphy, Madeleine. Here Is the Southwestern Desert. Coe, Anne, illus. 2006. (Web of Life Ser.). (ENG.). 32p. (J). (gr. -1-3). 16.95 *(978-0-9773795-7-6(4))*; pap. 9.95 *(978-0-9773795-6-9(6))* Web of Life Children's Bks.

Furstinger, Nancy. The Everglades. 2013. (J). *(978-1-62127-473-5(X))*; pap. *(978-1-62127-479-7(9))* Weigl Pubs., Inc.

Hale, Wendy & Lantz, Peggy. The Young Naturalist's Guide to Florida. 2nd ed. 2006. (ENG., Illus.). 195p. (J). (gr. 10-14). per. 21.95 *(978-1-56164-377-6(7))* Pineapple Pr., Inc.

Hawley, Linda Gallo. Nature Adventures: A Guidebook of Nature Facts, Songs, & Hikes in San Diego County. 2017. (ENG., Illus.). (J). (gr. 3-7). pap. 12.95 ***(978-1-941384-28-2(5))*** Sunbelt Pubns., Inc.

Helman, Andrea. O Is for Orca: An Alphabet Book. Wolfe, Art, photos by. 2003. (ENG., Illus.). 32p. (J). (gr. -1-2). pap. 10.99 *(978-1-57061-392-0(3),* Little Bigfoot) Sasquatch Bks.

—Southwest Colors. Jecan, Gavriel, photos by. 2011. (Illus.). 24p. (J). 12.95 *(978-1-933855-64-6(9))* Rio Nuevo Pubs.

HELMAN, Wolfe Jecan. C Is for Coyote: A Southwest Alphabet Book, Vol. 2017. (ENG., Illus.). 32p. (J). (gr. k-3). 7.95 *(978-1-63076-300-8(4))* Muddy Boots Pr.

Hubbs, Brian. Mountain Kings: A Collective Natural History of California, Sonoran, Durango & Queretaro Mountain Kingsnakes 2004. (Illus.). 356p. per. 45.00 *(978-0-9754641-0-6(8))* Tricolor Bks.

Jankowski, Susan. Everglades National Park: Adventure, Explore, Discover. 2008. (America's National Parks Ser.). (Illus.). 128p. (J). (gr. 5-9). lib. bdg. 34.60 *(978-1-59845-091-0(3))* Enslow Pubs., Inc.

Kalman, Bobbie. Everglades National Park. 2009. (Introducing Habitats Ser.). (ENG., Illus.). 32p. (J). (gr. k-3). pap. *(978-0-7787-2988-4(5))*; (gr. 1-3). lib. bdg. *(978-0-7787-2960-0(5))* Crabtree Publishing Co.

Lantz, Peggy Sias & Hale, Wendy A. The Coastlines of Florida. 2014. (Florida Water Story Ser.). (ENG., Illus.). 34p. (J). (gr. 4). pap. 6.95 *(978-1-56164-702-6(0))* Pineapple Pr., Inc.

—The Coral Reefs of Florida. 2014. (Florida Water Story Ser.). (ENG., Illus.). 34p. (J). (gr. 4). pap. 6.95 *(978-1-56164-703-3(9),* 9781561647033) Pineapple Pr., Inc.

—The Oceans of Florida. 2014. (Florida Water Story Ser.). (ENG., Illus.). 34p. (J). (gr. 4). pap. 6.95 *(978-1-56164-704-0(7))* Pineapple Pr., Inc.

—The Wetlands of Florida. 2014. (Florida Water Story Ser.). (ENG., Illus.). 34p. (J). (gr. 4). pap. 6.95 *(978-1-56164-705-7(5))* Pineapple Pr., Inc.

Larsen, Laurel. One Night in the Everglades. Turley, Joyce Mihran, illus. 2012. (Long Term Ecological Research Ser.). (ENG.). 32p. (J). (gr. 3-7). 15.95 *(978-0-9817700-4-8(5))* Taylor Trade Publishing.

Leotti-Bachem, Janice. The Everglades. 2005. (Rookie Read-About Geography Ser.). (ENG., Illus.). 32p. (J). (gr. 1-2). 20.50 *(978-0-516-22750-4(5),* Children's Pr.) Scholastic Library Publishing.

Lindeen, Mary. Natural States. 2011. (Wonder Readers Fluent Level Ser.). (ENG.). 16p. (gr. -1-2). pap. 35.94 *(978-1-4296-8131-5(4),* Wonder Readers) Capstone Press of Coughlan Cos.

—Parks of the U. S. A. 2011. (Wonder Readers Fluent Level Ser.). (ENG.). 32p. (gr. -1-2). pap. 5.99 *(978-1-4296-7949-7(2),* Wonder Readers) Capstone Press of Coughlan Cos.

Lynch, Wayne. Sonoran Desert. 2009. (ENG.). 64p. (J). (gr. 3-7). 16.95 *(978-1-58979-389-7(7))* Taylor Trade Publishing.

Matthews, Sheelagh. Canadian Shield. 2010. (Illus.). 32p. *(978-1-55388-628-0(3))*; pap. *(978-1-55388-629-7(1))* Weigl Educational Pubs. Ltd.

McCurdy, Michael. Walden Then & Now: An Alphabetical Tour of Henry Thoreau's Pond. McCurdy, Michael, illus. 2010. (ENG., Illus.). 32p. (J). (gr. k-12). 16.95 *(978-1-58089-253-7(1))* Charlesbridge Publishing, Inc.

Milkweed Editions Staff. The California Coast: A Literary Field Guide. St. Antoine, Sara, ed. 2005. (Stories from Where We Live Ser.). (ENG., Illus.). 248p. (J). pap. 10.95 *(978-1-57131-653-0(1))* Milkweed Editions.

—The South Atlantic Coast & Piedmont: A Literary Field Guide. St. Antoine, Sara, ed. Nicholson, Trudy & Mirocha, Paul, illus. 2006. (Stories from Where We Live Ser.). (ENG.). 256p. (J). (gr. 4-7). per. 10.95 *(978-1-57131-664-6(7))* Milkweed Editions.

Mullen, Amy. Colors of New England. 2017. (Naturally Local Ser.). (ENG., Illus.). 20p. (J). (gr. -1-k). bds. 8.95 ***(978-1-938093-99-9(2))*** Duo Pr. LLC.

Putnam, Jeff. National Monuments: Nature. 2004. (ZB Reads Trio Books). (Illus.). iii, 92p. (gr. 4-6). pap. 5.00 *(978-0-7367-1788-5(9))* Zaner-Bloser, Inc.

Rossi, Joe, photos by. Minnesota's Hidden Alphabet. 2010. (ENG., Illus.). 48p. (J). (gr. -1-1). 16.95 *(978-0-87351-808-6(X))* Minnesota Historical Society Pr.

Rowell, Rebecca. The 12 Most Amazing American Natural Wonders. 2014. (ENG.). 32p. (J). *(978-1-63235-011-4(4))* Pr. Room Editions LLC.

Smith, J. Batty about Texas, 1 vol. Coates, Kathy, illus. 2008. (ENG.). 32p. (J). (gr. k-3). 16.99 *(978-1-58980-582-8(8))* Pelican Publishing Co., Inc.

St. Antoine, Sara & Milkweed Editions Staff. The Great Lakes: A Literary Field Guide. 2005. (Stories from Where We Live Ser.). (ENG., Illus.). 264p. (J). pap., instr.'s gde. ed. 10.95 *(978-1-57131-654-7(X))* Milkweed Editions.

Viano, Hannah. S Is for Salmon: A Pacific Northwest Alphabet. Viano, Hannah, illus. 2014. (ENG., Illus.). 32p. (J). (-k). 16.99 *(978-1-57061-873-4(9),* Little Bigfoot) Sasquatch Bks.

Wade, Mary Dodson. Texas Plants & Animals. 2003. (Heinemann State Studies). (Illus.). 48p. (J). lib. bdg. 27.07 *(978-1-4034-0690-3(1))* Heinemann-Raintree.

Walch, Michelle E. & Maddin, John. Letters of the West. Maddin, John, illus. 2014. (Little Naturalist Ser.). (ENG., Illus.). 32p. (J). (gr. -1-k). 17.99 *(978-1-940052-10-6(6))* Craigmore Creations.

Weintraub, Aileen. The Grand Canyon: The Widest Canyon. 2009. (Great Record Breakers in Nature Ser.). 24p. (gr. 3-4). 42.50 *(978-1-61513-183-9(3),* PowerKids Pr.) Rosen Publishing Group, Inc., The.

Wiseman, Blaine. The Northeast. 2014. (Illus.). 32p. (J). *(978-1-4896-1230-4(0))* Weigl Pubs., Inc.

—The Southeast. 2014. (Illus.). 32p. (J). *(978-1-4896-1234-2(3))* Weigl Pubs., Inc.

—The Southwest. 2014. (Illus.). 32p. (J). *(978-1-4896-1238-0(6))* Weigl Pubs., Inc.

—The West. 2014. (Illus.). 32p. (J). *(978-1-4896-1242-7(4))* Weigl Pubs., Inc.

NATURAL HISTORY MUSEUMS

Lee, Sally. The National Museum of Natural History. 2017. (Smithsonian Field Trips Ser.). (ENG.). 32p. (gr. 3-4). lib. bdg. 27.99 ***(978-1-5157-7978-0(5))*** Capstone Press of Coughlan Cos.

NATURAL LAW

see Civil Rights; Ethics; International Law; Liberty

NATURAL MONUMENTS

Bateman, Teresa. Red, White, Blue & Uncle Who? The Story Behind Some of America's Patriotic Symbols. 2003. (ENG., Illus.). 64p. (J). (gr. 4-6). pap. 7.95 *(978-0-8234-1784-1(0))* Holiday Hse., Inc.

Diemer, Lauren. Natural Landmarks. 2009. (U. S. Sites & Symbols Ser.). (Illus.). 48p. (J). (gr. 3-5). lib. bdg. 29.05 *(978-1-60596-146-0(9))* Weigl Pubs., Inc.

Freund, Lisa. The Seven Natural Wonders & Las siete maravillas naturales del Mundo: 6 English, 6 Spanish Adaptations. 2011. (ENG & SPA.). (J). 89.00 net. *(978-1-4108-5671-5(2))* Benchmark Education Co.

Gonzales, Doreen & Graham, Amy. What Are the 7 Wonders of the Natural World? 2013. (What Are the Seven Wonders of the World? Ser.). 48p. (J). (gr. 4-18). 25.27 *(978-0-7660-4153-0(0))* Enslow Pubs., Inc.

Graham, Amy. What Are the 7 Wonders of the Natural World? 2013. (What Are the Seven Wonders of the World? Ser.). 48p. (J). (gr. 4-10). pap. 8.95 *(978-1-4644-0232-6(9))* Enslow Pubs., Inc.

Lawrence, Ellen. Famous Rocks. 2015. (Illus.). 24p. (J). lib. bdg. *(978-1-62724-297-4(X))* Bearport Publishing Co., Inc.

Lewison, Wendy Cheyette. L Is for Liberty. Hines, Laura Freeman, illus. 2003. (Reading Railroad Ser.). (ENG.). 24p. (J). (gr. -1-3). mass mkt. 3.99 *(978-0-448-43228-1(5),* Grosset & Dunlap) Penguin Young Readers Group.

Moore, David. Expl on Your Own the Old Man of the Mtn. 2009. (Explore on Your Own Ser.). (ENG., Illus.). 12p. (J). pap. 7.95 *(978-0-7362-5581-3(8))* National Geographic School Publishing, Inc.

O'Donnell, Kerri. Natural Wonders of the World: Converting Distance Measurements to Metric Units. 2009. (PowerMath: Proficiency Plus Ser.). 32p. (gr. 4-5). 47.90 *(978-1-60851-414-4(5),* PowerKids Pr.) Rosen Publishing Group, Inc., The.

—Natural Wonders of the World: Converting Measurements to Metric Units. 2005. (PowerMath: Proficiency Plus Ser.). (Illus.). 32p. (J). (gr. 3-6). lib. bdg. 25.25 *(978-1-4042-2928-0(0),* PowerKids Pr.) Rosen Publishing Group, Inc., The.

—Natural Wonders of the World: Understanding & Representing Numbers in the Billions. 2009. (Math for the REAL World Ser.). (Illus.). 32p. (gr. 5-6). pap. 10.00 *(978-1-4042-5119-9(7))* Rosen Publishing Group, Inc., The.

Woods, Michael & Woods, Mary B. Seven Natural Wonders of North America. 2009. (Seven Wonders Ser.). (ENG., Illus.). 80p. (gr. 5-8). lib. bdg. 33.26 *(978-0-8225-9069-9(7))* Lerner Publishing Group.

NATURAL MONUMENTS—UNITED STATES

Bauman, Amy & Durman, Laura. Personalities & Places. 2010. (CC: Native North Americans Ser.). 112p. (gr. 6-12). 42.80 *(978-1-933834-81-8(1))* Brown Bear Bks.

Craats, Rennay. Natural Landmarks. 2004. (American Symbols Ser.). (Illus.). 24p. (J). (gr. 4-7). per. 8.95 *(978-1-59036-177-1(6))*; (gr. 1-3). lib. bdg. 24.45 *(978-1-59036-133-7(4))* Weigl Pubs., Inc.

DeFries, Cheryl L. Seven Natural Wonders of the United States & Canada: A MyReportLinks. com Book. 2005. (Seven Wonders of the World Ser.). (Illus.). 48p. (J). lib. bdg. 26.60 *(978-0-7660-5291-8(5),* MyReportLinks.com Bks.) Enslow Pubs., Inc.

—What Are the 7 Natural Wonders of the United States? 2013. (What Are the Seven Wonders of the World? Ser.). 48p. (J). (gr. 4-10). pap. 8.95 *(978-1-4644-0233-3(7))*; 25.27 *(978-0-7660-4154-7(9))* Enslow Pubs., Inc.

Firestone, Mary, et al. Celebrate America: A Guide to America's Greatest Symbols. Skeens, Matthew, illus. 2010. (American Symbols Ser.). (ENG.). 208p. (gr. 1-2). pap. 15.95 *(978-1-4048-6170-1(X))* Picture Window Bks.

Hurtig, Jennifer. Natural Landmarks. 2009. (U. S. Sites & Symbols Ser.). (Illus.). 48p. (J). (gr. 3-5). 10.95 *(978-1-60596-147-7(7))* Weigl Pubs., Inc.

Keppeler, Jill. Betsy Ross Didn't Create the American Flag: Exposing Myths about US Symbols. 2016. (Exposed! Myths about Early American History Ser.). 00032p. (J). pap. 10.50 *(978-1-4824-5717-9(2))* Stevens, Gareth Publishing LLLP.

Shava, Ryder. Famous American Landmarks, 01 vols., 1. 2016. (Rosen REAL Readers: Social Studies Nonfiction / Fiction: Family, Community, & the World Ser.). (ENG.). 12p. (J). pap. 6.33 *(978-1-5081-1800-8(0),* Rosen Classroom) Rosen Publishing Group, Inc., The.

NATURAL RESOURCES

see also Conservation of Natural Resources; Fisheries; Forests and Forestry; Marine Resources; Mines and Mineral Resources; Power Resources; Reclamation of Land; Soil Conservation; Water Power; Water Resources Development; Water-Supply

Aboff, Marcie. The Giving Earth Natural Resources. 2016. (Spring Forward Ser.). (J). (gr. 2). *(978-1-4900-9427-4(X))* Benchmark Education Co.

Anniss, Matt. Planet under Pressure: Too Many People on Earth? 2013. (Ask the Experts Ser.). (Illus.). 48p. (gr. 6-8). 31.95 *(978-1-4339-8643-7(4))*; pap. 14.04 *(978-1-4339-8644-4(2))* Stevens, Gareth Publishing LLLP. (Gareth Stevens Secondary Library).

Apel, Melanie Ann. Land & Resources of Ancient Greece. 2004. (Primary Sources of Ancient Civilizations Ser.). (ENG., Illus.). 24p. (J). (gr. 4-8). pap. 8.25 *(978-0-8239-8937-9(2),* PowerKids Pr.) Rosen Publishing Group, Inc., The.

Bailey, Gerry. Out of Energy. 2011. (Planet SOS Ser.). (Illus.). 48p. (J). (gr. 3-6). pap. 14.05 *(978-1-4339-4979-1(2))*; lib. bdg. 31.95 *(978-1-4339-4978-4(4))* Stevens, Gareth Publishing LLLP. (Gareth Stevens Learning Library).

Bensinger, Henry. Ancient Greek Geography. 2013. (Spotlight on Ancient Civilizations: Greece Ser.). (ENG., Illus.). 24p. (J). (gr. 3-4). pap. 10.00 *(978-1-4777-0879-8(0))*; lib. bdg. 23.60 *(978-1-4777-0773-9(5))* Rosen Publishing Group, Inc., The. (PowerKids Pr.).

Besel, Jennifer M. The Hottest Places on Earth. 2010. (Extreme Planet Ser.). (ENG.). 24p. (gr. 1-2). lib. bdg. 25.32 *(978-1-4296-3964-4(4),* First Facts) Capstone Press of Coughlan Cos.

Bethune, Helen. Why Do Diamonds Sparkle? All about Earth's Resources. 2010. (Illus.). 24p. (J). 49.50 *(978-1-61531-920-6(4),* PowerKids Pr.) Rosen Publishing Group, Inc., The.

Blankenship, LeeAnn. What Are Community Resources? 2017. (Let's Find Out! Communities Ser.). 32p. (J). (gr. 6-8). 24.45 ***(978-1-68048-719-0(1))***; pap. 12.90 ***(978-1-68048-717-6(5))*** Rosen Publishing Group, Inc., The. (Britannica Educational Publishing).

Bouler, Olivia. Olivia's Birds: Saving the Gulf. 2011. (ENG., Illus.). 32p. (J). (gr. -1-4). 14.95 *(978-1-4027-8665-5(4))* Sterling Publishing Co., Inc.

Burgan, Michael. Polar Politics: Earth's Next Battlegrounds? 2017. (Exploring the Polar Regions Today Ser.: Vol. 8). (ENG.). (YA). (gr. 7-12). 23.95 ***(978-1-4222-3871-4(7))*** Mason Crest.

Burton, Margie, et al. Riches from Nature. 2011. (Early Connections Ser.). (J). *(978-1-61672-504-4(4))* Benchmark Education Co.

Cardenas, Ernesto & Saavedra, Patricia. Recursos Naturales. 1.t. ed. 2006. (SPA., Illus.). 16p. pap. 4.95 *(978-1-933668-34-5(2))* Milo Educational Bks. & Resources.

Cardenas, Ernesto A. Natural Resources. 2009. pap. 4.95 *(978-1-60698-084-2(X))* Milo Educational Bks. & Resources.

Carr, Aaron. Natural o Hecho Por el Hombre. 2013. (SPA., Illus.). 24p. (J). *(978-1-62127-607-4(4))* Weigl Pubs., Inc.

Casper, Julie Kerr. Natural Resources Set, 8-Volumes. 2007. (Natural Resources Ser.). (gr. 6-12). 316.00 *(978-0-8160-7220-0(5),* Chelsea Hse.) Facts On File, Inc.

Cohn, Jessica. What Is Scarcity of Resources? 2008. (Economics in Action Ser.). (ENG., Illus.). 32p. (J). (gr. 3-7). pap. *(978-0-7787-4261-6(X))* Crabtree Publishing Co.

Davis, Deneena. The 10 Most Essential Natural Resources. 2008. 14.99 *(978-1-55448-549-9(5))* Scholastic Library Publishing.

Des Chenes, Elizabeth, ed. Natural Gas. 2006. (Fueling the Future Ser.). (ENG., Illus.). 124p. (YA). (gr. 8-12). lib. bdg. 39.35 *(978-0-7377-3598-7(8),* Greenhaven Pr., Inc.) Cengage Gale.

Doeden, Matt. Finding Out about Geothermal Energy. 2014. (Searchlight Books — What Are Energy Sources? Ser.). (Illus.). 40p. (gr. 3-4). pap. 8.95 *(978-1-4677-4554-3(5))*;

(ENG., (J). lib. bdg. 27.93 *(978-1-4677-3658-9(9)*, Lerner Pubns.) Lerner Publishing Group.

Downing, David. Geography & Resources of the Middle East. 2006. (World Almanac Library of the Middle East). (Illus.). 48p. (gr. 5-12). pap. 14.05 *(978-0-8368-7341-2(6))*; lib. bdg. 31.00 *(978-0-8368-7334-4(3))* Stevens, Gareth Publishing LLLP. (Gareth Stevens Secondary Library).

Environment & Natural Resources. 2010. (Global Connections Ser.). (Illus.). 112p. (gr. 5-8). 35.00 *(978-1-60413-289-2(2)*, Chelsea Hse.) Facts On File, Inc.

Explore Natural Resources! With 25 Great Projects. 2014. (Explore Your World Ser.). (ENG., Illus.). 96p. (J). (gr. k-4). pap. 13.95 *(978-1-61930-223-5(3))* Open City Bks.

From the Earth: How Resources Are Made. 2016. (From the Earth: How Resources Are Made Ser.). 32p. (gr. 4-3). pap. 63.00 *(978-1-4824-5321-8(5))*; lib. bdg. 159.60 *(978-1-4824-4605-0(7))* Stevens, Gareth Publishing LLLP.

Gedacht, Daniel C. Land & Resources in Ancient Rome. 2004. (Primary Sources of Ancient Civilizations Ser.). (Illus.). 24p. (J). lib. bdg. 22.60 *(978-0-8239-6775-9(1)*, PowerKids Pr.) Rosen Publishing Group, Inc., The.

—Land & Resources of Ancient Rome. 2004. (Primary Sources of Ancient Civilizations Ser.). (ENG., Illus.). 24p. (gr. 4-8). pap. 8.25 *(978-0-8239-8943-0(7)*, PowerKids Pr.) Rosen Publishing Group, Inc., The.

Gillett, Jack & Gillett, Meg. Natural-Resource Maps. 2012. (Maps of the Environmental World Ser.). (ENG., Illus.). 32p. (J). (gr. 4-6). pap. 10.60 *(978-1-4488-8616-6(3)*, PowerKids Pr.) Rosen Publishing Group, Inc., The.

—Natural Resource Maps. 2013. (Illus.). 32p. (J). lib. bdg. *(978-1-4488-8612-8(0)*, PowerKids Pr.) Rosen Publishing Group, Inc., The.

Gleason, Carrie. Geothermal Energy: Using Earth's Furnace. 2008. (Energy Revolution Ser.). (ENG.). 32p. (J). (gr. 3-8). pap. *(978-0-7787-2931-0(1))* Crabtree Publishing Co.

Grady, Colin. Fossil Fuels. 2016. (Saving the Planet Through Green Energy Ser.). 24p. (J). pap. 9.35 *(978-0-7660-8276-2(8))* Enslow Pubs., Inc.

—Hydropower. 2016. (Saving the Planet Through Green Energy Ser.). (Illus.). 24p. (J). pap. 9.35 *(978-0-7660-8284-7(9))* Enslow Pubs., Inc.

—Solar Energy. 2016. (Saving the Planet Through Green Energy Ser.). 24p. (J). pap. 9.35 *(978-0-7660-8292-2(X))* Enslow Pubs., Inc.

—Wind Energy. 2016. (Saving the Planet Through Green Energy Ser.). 24p. (J). pap. 9.35 *(978-0-7660-8296-0(2))* Enslow Pubs., Inc.

Hansen, Amy. Geothermal Energy: Hot Stuff! 2010. (Powering Our World Ser.). (ENG.). 24p. (J). pap. 8.25 *(978-1-4358-9748-9(X)*, PowerKids Pr.) Rosen Publishing Group, Inc., The.

Hansen, Amy S. Geothermal Energy: Hot Stuff! 2010. (Powering Our World Ser.). 24p. (J). (gr. 2-5). E-Book 42.50 *(978-1-4488-0205-0(9))*; (Illus.). lib. bdg. 22.60 *(978-1-4358-9330-6(1)*, PowerKids Pr.) Rosen Publishing Group, Inc., The.

Haugen, David M. Coal. 2006. (Fueling the Future Ser.). (ENG., Illus.). 120p. (gr. 10-12). lib. bdg. 44.60 *(978-0-7377-3591-8(0)*, Greenhaven Pr., Inc.) Cengage Gale.

Holt, Rinehart and Winston Staff. Environmental Science Chptr. 18: Renewable Energy. 4th ed. Date not set. pap. 11.20 *(978-0-03-068079-3(4))* Holt McDougal.

—Holt Science Spectrum Chptr. 23: Using Natural Resources. 4th ed. Date not set. pap. 11.20 *(978-0-03-068062-5(X))* Holt McDougal.

Horn, Geoffrey M., et al. Coal, Oil, & Natural Gas. 2010. (Energy Today Ser.). 48p. (J). (gr. 3-6). 30.00 *(978-1-60413-785-9(1))* Facts On File, Inc.

Johanson, Paula. Making Good Choices about Nonrenewable Resources. 2009. 64p. (YA). pap. 12.95 *(978-1-4358-5604-2(X))*; (Illus.). (gr. 5-9). 31.95 *(978-1-4358-5311-9(3))* Rosen Publishing Group, Inc., The.

Kaplan, Leslie C. Land & Resources in Ancient Egypt. 2004. (Primary Sources of Ancient Civilizations Ser.). (Illus.). 24p. (J). lib. bdg. 22.60 *(978-0-8239-6781-0(6)*, PowerKids Pr.) Rosen Publishing Group, Inc., The.

—Land & Resources of Ancient Egypt. (Primary Sources of Ancient Civilizations Ser.). 24p. 2009. (gr. 3-3). 42.50 *(978-1-60851-560-8(5))* 2004. (ENG., Illus.). (gr. 4-8). pap. 8.25 *(978-0-8239-8931-7(3))* Rosen Publishing Group, Inc., The. (PowerKids Pr.).

Kerrod, Robin. New Materials. 2003. (21st Century Science Ser.). 48p. (J). lib. bdg. 27.10 *(978-1-58340-353-2(1))* Black Rabbit Bks.

Killian, Maryellen. Energy for Earth. 2013. (InfoMax Readers Ser.). (ENG.). 24p. (J). (gr. 2-3). pap. 49.50 *(978-1-4777-2435-4(4))*; (Illus.). pap. 8.25 *(978-1-4777-2434-7(6))* Rosen Publishing Group, Inc., The. (Rosen Classroom).

Loria, Laura. What Are Resources? 2016. (Let's Find Out! Ser.). (ENG.). 32p. (J). (gr. 3-2). lib. bdg. 24.45 *(978-1-68048-404-5(4))* Rosen Publishing Group, Inc., The.

MacAulay, Kelley. Why Do We Need Soil? 2014. (ENG., Illus.). 24p. (J). lib. bdg. *(978-0-7787-0493-5(9))* Crabtree Publishing Co.

Maurer, Tracy Nelson. Using Economic & Resource Maps. 2016. (Searchlight Books (tm) — What Do You Know about Maps? Ser.). (ENG., Illus.). 40p. (J). (gr. 3-5). 30.65 *(978-1-5124-0951-2(0))* Lerner Publishing Group.

McPherson, Stephanie Sammartino. Arctic Thaw: Climate Change & the Global Race for Energy Resources. 2014. (Illus.). 64p. (J). (gr. 6-12). lib. bdg. 34.60 *(978-1-4677-2043-4(7)*, Twenty-First Century Bks.) Lerner Publishing Group.

Michele, Tracey. What Is A Natural Resource? 2014. (Little Books of Answers: Level B Ser.). (Illus.). 16p. (gr. k-2). pap. 7.95 *(978-1-927136-15-7(6))* Three Crows Media NZL. Dist: RiverStream Publishing.

Montgomery, Anne. Nature Made, 1 vol. (Science Readers: Content & Literacy Ser.). (ENG., Illus.). 24p. (gr. k-k). 2015. pap. 22.96 *(978-1-4938-1138-0(X))* 2014. pap. 8.99 *(978-1-4807-4528-5(6))* Teacher Created Materials, Inc.

Morgan, Sally. Natural Resources. 2009. (Illus.). 46p. (J). 32.80 *(978-1-59920-102-3(X)*, 1283677) Black Rabbit Bks.

Morrill, Amos. Augusta & Elliott. 2007. (ENG., Illus.). (J). 15.95 *(978-1-892738-36-3(8))* Island Nation Pr., LLC.

Morris, Neil. Geothermal Power: Now & in the Future. 2010. (J). 34.25 *(978-1-59920-340-9(5))* Black Rabbit Bks.

Nagle, Jeanne. Making Good Choices about Renewable Resources. 2009. (J). 77.70 *(978-1-4358-5603-5(1))*; (ENG.). 64p. (YA). pap. 12.95 *(978-1-4358-5602-8(3))*; (Illus.). 64p. (YA). (gr. 5-9). lib. bdg. 31.95 *(978-1-4358-5310-2(5))* Rosen Publishing Group, Inc., The.

New Careers for the 21st Century: Finding Your Role in the Global Renewal, 15 vols., Set. Incl. Environmental Science & Protection: Keeping Our Planet Green. Strange, Cordelia. pap. 9.95 *(978-1-4222-2034-4(6))*; Freelance & Technical Writers: Words for Sale. Flath, Camden. pap. 9.95 *(978-1-4222-2035-1(4))*; Green Construction: Creating Energy-Efficient, Low-Impact Buildings. Miller, Malinda. pap. 9.95 *(978-1-4222-2036-8(2))*; Medical Technicians: Health-Care Support for the 21st Century. Strange, Cordelia. pap. 9.95 *(978-1-4222-2038-2(9))*; Modern Mechanics: Maintaining Tomorrow's Green Vehicles. Miller, Malinda. pap. 9.95 *(978-1-4222-2039-9(7))*; Pharmaceutical Industry: Better Medicine for the 21st Century. Miller, Malinda. pap. 9.95 *(978-1-4222-2040-5(0))*; Physicians Assistants & Nurses: New Opportunities in the 21st-Century Health System. Strange, Cordelia. pap. 9.95 *(978-1-4222-2041-2(9))*; Social Workers: Finding Solutions for Tomorrow's Society. Flath, Camden. (Illus.). pap. 9.95 *(978-1-4222-2042-9(7))*; Therapy Jobs in Educational Settings: Speech, Physical, Occupational & Audiology. Flath, Camden. (Illus.). pap. 9.95 *(978-1-4222-2047-4(8))*; Tomorrow's Enterprising Scientists: Computer Software Designers & Specialists. Flath, Camden. pap. 9.95 *(978-1-4222-2043-6(5))*; Tomorrow's Teachers: Urban Leadership, Empowering Students & Improving Lives. Miller, Malinda. pap. 9.95 *(978-1-4222-2044-3(3))*; Tomorrow's Transportation: Green Solutions for Air, Land, & Sea. Miller, Malinda. pap. 9.95 *(978-1-4222-2045-0(1))*; 21st-Century Counselors: New Approaches to Mental Health & Substance Abuse. Flath, Camden. pap. 9.95 *(978-1-4222-2046-7(X))*; 64p. (YA). (gr. 7-18). 2010. 2011. Set pap. 149.25 *(978-1-4222-2032-0(X))* Mason Crest.

Otfinoski, Steven. Wind, Solar, & Geothermal Power: From Concept to Consumer. 2015. (ENG.). 64p. (J). lib. bdg. *(978-0-531-21897-6(X)*, Orchard Bks.) Scholastic, Inc.

Paderewski, Elliot. The Natural Resources of My Community. 2016. (Rosen REAL Readers: Social Studies Nonfiction / Fiction: Family, Community, & the World Ser.). 12p. (gr. 1-k). pap. 6.33 *(978-1-5081-2362-0(4)*, Rosen Classroom) Rosen Publishing Group, Inc., The.

Peacock, Kathy Wilson. Natural Resources & Sustainable Development. 2008. (Global Issues Ser.). 400p. (C). (gr. 9). 45.00 *(978-0-8160-7215-6(9))* Facts On File, Inc.

Prior, Jennifer. Our Natural Resources. rev. ed. 2014. (Primary Source Readers Content & Literacy Ser.). (ENG., Illus.). 32p. (gr. 3-3). pap. 8.99 *(978-1-4333-7373-2(4))* Teacher Created Materials, Inc.

Ravilious, Kate. Power: Ethical Debates about Resources & the Environment. 2009. (Dilemmas in Modern Science Ser.). (YA). (gr. 7-12). 34.25 *(978-1-59920-096-5(1))* Black Rabbit Bks.

—Power - Ethical Debates about Resources & the Environment. 2008. (Dilemmas in Modern Science Ser.). (ENG., Illus.). 48p. (J). 23.99 *(978-0-237-53369-4(3))* Evans Brothers, Ltd. GBR. Dist: Independent Pubs. Group.

Resources: Nature's Riches. (Earthworks Ser.). (J). 29.93 *(978-0-7614-1369-1(3)*, Benchmark Bks.) Marshall Cavendish Corp.

Reynoldson, Fiona. Geothermal Energy & Bioenergy. 2010. (World of Energy Ser.). (ENG.). 48p. (J). (gr. 6-8). lib. bdg. 31.95 *(978-1-4339-4121-4(X)*, Gareth Stevens Learning Library) Stevens, Gareth Publishing LLLP.

Rice, William B. Our Resources. 2015. (Science Readers: Content & Literacy Ser.). (ENG., Illus.). 32p. (gr. 4-4). pap. 8.99 *(978-1-4807-4689-3(4))* Teacher Created Materials, Inc.

—The Story of Fossil Fuels. 2015. (Science Readers: Content & Literacy Ser.). (ENG., Illus.). 32p. (gr. 4-4). pap. 8.99 *(978-1-4807-4690-9(8))* Teacher Created Materials, Inc.

Robert, Nolan. What Are Natural Resources? 2009. (Real Life Readers Ser.). 12p. (gr. 2-3). pap. 5.90 *(978-1-4042-7953-7(9)*, Rosen Classroom) Rosen Publishing Group, Inc., The.

Smith, David J. If: A Mind-Bending New Way of Looking at Big Ideas & Numbers. Adams, Steve, illus. 2014. (ENG.). 40p. (J). (gr. 3-7). 18.95 *(978-1-894786-34-8(3))* Kids Can Pr., Ltd. CAN. Dist: Hachette Bk. Group.

Smuskiewicz, Alfred J. Earth's Resources. 2007. (Gareth Stevens Vital Science: Earth Science Ser.). (Illus.). 48p. (gr. 5-12). pap. 14.05 *(978-0-8368-7874-5(4)*, Gareth Stevens Secondary Library) Stevens, Gareth Publishing LLLP.

Stewart, Audrey. Our Natural Resources. 2013. (InfoMax Readers Ser.). (ENG.). 24p. (J). (gr. 2-3). pap. 49.50 *(978-1-4777-2357-9(9))*; pap. 8.25 *(978-1-4777-2356-2(0))* Rosen Publishing Group, Inc., The. (Rosen Classroom).

Sundance/Newbridge LLC Staff. Our Natural Resources. 2004. (Reading PowerWorks Ser.). (gr. 1-3). 37.50 *(978-0-7608-9221-3(0))*; pap. 6.10 *(978-0-7608-9222-0(9))* Sundance/Newbridge Educational Publishing.

White, Nancy. Using Earth's Underground Heat. 2009. (Going Green Ser.). (Illus.). 32p. (YA). (gr. 3-6). lib. bdg. 25.27 *(978-1-59716-963-9(3))* Bearport Publishing Co., Inc.

Winters, Adam. Destruction of Earth's Resources: The Need for Sustainable Development. (Extreme Environmental Threats Ser.). 64p. 2009. (gr. 6-6). 58.50 *(978-1-61512-425-1(X))* 2006. (Illus.). (YA). (gr. 5-9). lib. bdg. 31.95 *(978-1-4042-0746-2(5))* Rosen Publishing Group, Inc., The.

Zuchora-Walske, Christine. Energy in the Real World. 2013. (Science in the Real World EBook Ser.). (ENG.). 48p. (J). pap. 15.64 *(978-1-61783-789-0(X)*, Core Library) ABDO Publishing Co.

NATURAL RESOURCES—UNITED STATES

Conklin, Wendy. Georgia's Location & Resources. 2016. (Primary Source Readers Ser.). (Illus.). 32p. (gr. 2-2). 8.99 *(978-1-4938-2549-3(6))* Teacher Created Materials, Inc.

Fourment, Tiffany. My Water Comes from the Rocky Mountains. Emerling, Dorothy, illus. 2009. (Long Term Ecological Research Ser.). (ENG.). 32p. (J). (gr. 1-5). 16.95 *(978-0-9817700-0-0(2))*; pap. 9.95 *(978-0-9817700-1-7(0))* Taylor Trade Publishing.

—My Water Comes from the San Juan Mountains. 2009. (ENG.). 32p. (J). (gr. 4-7). 16.95 *(978-0-9817700-2-4(9))* Taylor Trade Publishing.

Fourment, Tiffany & Gianniny, Gary. My Water Comes from the San Juan Mountains. Emerling, Dorothy, illus. 2009. (ENG.). 32p. (J). (gr. 4-7). pap. 9.95 *(978-0-9817700-3-1(7))* Taylor Trade Publishing.

Marfa, Isabelle. The Land & Resources of Texas: Shaping the Growth of the State. 2010. (Spotlight on Texas Ser.). (ENG., Illus.). 32p. (J). (gr. 3-4). pap. 11.75 *(978-1-61532-478-1(X))*; lib. bdg. 26.25 *(978-1-61532-480-4(1))* Rosen Publishing Group, Inc., The.

McAneney, Robert. America's Natural Resources. 2013. (Rosen Readers Ser.). (ENG.). 24p. (J). (gr. 2-3). pap. 8.25 *(978-1-4777-2361-6(7))*; pap. 49.50 *(978-1-4777-2363-0(3))* Rosen Publishing Group, Inc., The. (Rosen Classroom).

Schimel, Kate & Roza, Greg. The Land & Resources of New York. 2012. (Illus.). 24p. (J). 60.00 *(978-1-4488-5754-8(6))*; pap. 10.00 *(978-1-4488-5753-1(8))*; lib. bdg. 22.60 *(978-1-4488-5740-1(6))* Rosen Publishing Group, Inc., The. (PowerKids Pr.).

NATURAL SELECTION

see also Evolution

Bortz, Fred. Charles Darwin & the Theory of Evolution by Natural Selection. 2013. (Revolutionary Discoveries of Scientific Pioneers Ser.). (Illus.). 80p. (J). (gr. 7-12). 33.25 *(978-1-4777-1802-5(8))* Rosen Publishing Group, Inc., The.

Byrne, Eugene. Darwin: A Graphic Biography. Gurr, Simon, illus. 2013. (ENG.). 100p. (J). (gr. 7). pap. 9.95 *(978-1-58834-352-9(9)*, Smithsonian Bks.) Smithsonian Institution Scholarly Pr.

Claybourne, Anna. Who Discovered Natural Selection? 2010. (Breakthroughs in Science & Technology Ser.). 48p. lib. bdg. 32.80 *(978-1-84837-682-3(0))* Arcturus Publishing GBR. Dist: Black Rabbit Bks.

Gray, Susan H. Australian Spotted Jellyfish. 2010. (21st Century Skills Library: Animal Invaders Ser.). (ENG.). 32p. (gr. 4-8). lib. bdg. 28.50 *(978-1-60279-628-7(9)*, 200333) Cherry Lake Publishing.

Highet, Alistair. Lucas. Delessert, Etienne, illus. 2011. (ENG.). 40p. (J). (gr. 4-17). pap. 8.95 *(978-0-89812-014-1(4)*, Creative Paperbacks) Creative Co., The.

Jackson, Cari. Alien Invasion: Invasive Species Become Major Menaces. 2009. (Current Science Ser.). (ENG.). 48p. (J). (gr. 4-6). pap. 8.95 *(978-1-4339-2128-5(6)*, Gareth Stevens Learning Library) Stevens, Gareth Publishing LLLP.

Latta, Sara L. Keep Out! Invasive Species, 1 vol. 2013. (Nature's Invaders Ser.). (ENG.). 32p. (gr. 3-4). lib. bdg. 27.99 *(978-1-4765-0140-6(8))* Capstone Press of Coughlan Cos.

Luongo, Charlotte. Evolution. 2009. (Big Ideas in Science Ser.). (Illus.). 48p. (gr. 5-8). 31.36 *(978-0-7614-4393-3(2))* Marshall Cavendish Corp.

McCormick, Joyce. Natural Selection. 2016. (Spotlight on Ecology & Life Science Ser.). 00024p. (J). (gr. 4-6). pap. 10.00 *(978-1-4994-2583-3(X)*, PowerKids Pr.) Rosen Publishing Group, Inc., The.

Murphy, Glenn. Evolution: The Whole Life on Earth Story. unabr. ed. 2014. (Science Sorted Ser.). (ENG., Illus.). 176p. (J). (gr. 4-6). pap. 7.99 *(978-1-4472-5460-7(0))* Pan Macmillan GBR. Dist: Independent Pubs. Group.

O'Connor, Karen. The Threat of Invasive Species. 2013. (Animal 911: Environmental Threats Ser.). 48p. (J). (gr. 3-5). pap. 84.30 *(978-1-4339-9724-2(X))*; pap. 14.05 *(978-1-4339-9723-5(1))*; (ENG., Illus.). lib. bdg. 31.95 *(978-1-4339-9722-8(3))* Stevens, Gareth Publishing LLLP.

Tweet, Jonathan. Grandmother Fish: A Child's First Book of Evolution. Lewis, Karen, illus. 2016. (ENG.). 40p. (J). 17.99 *(978-1-250-11323-8(7)*, 9781250113238) Feiwel & Friends.

NATURALISTS

Adamson, Heather. Charles Darwin & the Theory of Evolution, 1 vol. Purcell, Gordon & Milgrom, Al, illus. 2007. (Inventions & Discovery Ser.). (ENG.). 32p. (gr. 3-4). 30.65 *(978-1-4296-0145-0(0)*, Graphic Library) Capstone Press of Coughlan Cos.

Anastasio, Dina. Who Was Steve Irwin? 2015. (Who Was... ? Ser.). lib. bdg. 16.00 *(978-0-606-36749-3(7))* Turtleback Bks.

Anderson, Margaret J. Carl Linnaeus: Genius of Classification. 2015. (Genius Scientists & Their Genius Ideas Ser.). 96p. (J). (gr. 5-12). 27.94 *(978-0-7660-6540-6(5))*; pap. 10.95 *(978-0-7660-6541-3(3))* Enslow Pubs., Inc.

—Charles Darwin: Genius of a Revolutionary Theory. 2015. (Genius Scientists & Their Genius Ideas Ser.). 96p. (J). (gr. 5-12). 27.94 *(978-0-7660-6545-1(6))*; pap. 10.95 *(978-0-7660-6546-8(4))* Enslow Pubs., Inc.

Anderson, Margaret Jean. Carl Linnaeus: Father of Classification. 2009. (Great Minds of Science Ser.). (Illus.). 128p. (J). (gr. 5). lib. bdg. 33.27 *(978-0-7660-3009-1(1))* Enslow Pubs., Inc.

Ashby, Ruth. Young Charles Darwin & the Voyage of the Beagle, 1 vol. Duranceau, Suzanne, illus. 2009. (ENG.). 128p. (J). (gr. 2-5). 12.95 *(978-1-56145-478-5(8)*, Peachtree Junior) Peachtree Pubs.

Barnham, Kay. Charles Darwin: Father of Evolution. 2016. (History VIPs Ser.). (ENG., Illus.). 32p. (J). (gr. 4-6). 17.99 *(978-0-7502-8849-1(3)*, Wayland) Hachette Children's Group GBR. Dist: Hachette Bk. Group.

Bortz, Fred. Charles Darwin & the Theory of Evolution by Natural Selection. 2013. (Revolutionary Discoveries of Scientific Pioneers Ser.). (Illus.). 80p. (J). (gr. 7-12). 33.25 *(978-1-4777-1802-5(8))* Rosen Publishing Group, Inc., The.

Bowler, Peter J. An Interview with Charles Darwin. 2014. (Meet the Masters Ser.). 112p. (YA). (gr. 9-12). lib. bdg. 42.79 *(978-1-62712-909-1(X))* Cavendish Square Publishing.

Burleigh, Robert. Into the Woods: John James Audubon Lives His Dream. Minor, Wendell, illus. 2011. (ENG.). 40p. (J). (gr. 1-4). pap. 19.99 *(978-1-4424-5337-1(0)*, Atheneum Bks. for Young Readers) Simon & Schuster Children's Publishing.

Burns, Monique. Cool Careers Without College for People Who Love to Make Things Grow. 2009. (Cool Careers Without College Ser.). 144p. (gr. 6-6). 66.50 *(978-1-61511-975-2(2))* Rosen Publishing Group, Inc., The.

Colson, Mary. Charles Darwin & Alfred Russel Wallace. 2014. (Dynamic Duos of Science Ser.). 48p. (YA). (gr. 5-8). pap. 84.30 *(978-1-4824-1280-2(2))* Stevens, Gareth Publishing LLLP.

Cook, Diane. Charles Darwin: British Naturalist. 2013. (People of Importance Ser.: 21). (Illus.). 32p. (J). (gr. 4-18). 19.95 *(978-1-4222-2844-9(4))* Mason Crest.

Crum, Anna-Maria. Animal Behaviorists & Conductistas de Animales: 6 English, 6 Spanish Adaptations. 2011. (ENG & SPA.). (J). 89.00 net. *(978-1-4108-5679-1(8))* Benchmark Education Co.

—Trackers of Dynamic Earth & Rastreadores de nuestra dinámica Tierra: 6 English, 6 Spanish Adaptations. 2011. (ENG & SPA.). (J). 97.00 net. *(978-1-4108-5718-7(2))* Benchmark Education Co.

Danneberg, Julie. John Muir Wrestles a Waterfall. Hogan, Jamie, illus. 2015. (ENG.). 32p. (J). (gr. -1-3). lib. bdg. 16.95 *(978-1-58089-586-6(7))* Charlesbridge Publishing, Inc.

Doeden, Matt. Mohandas Gandhi. 2011. (J). lib. bdg. *(978-0-7613-5483-3(2))* Twenty First Century Bks.

Edwards, Roberta. Who Is Jane Goodall? 2012. (Who Is... ? Ser.). lib. bdg. 16.00 *(978-0-606-26651-2(8)*, Turtleback) Turtleback Bks.

Eggerling, Kristin J. Breath of Wilderness: The Life of Sigurd Olson. 2014. (ENG., Illus.). 112p. (J). (gr. 4-7). pap. 12.95 *(978-1-938486-10-4(2))* Fulcrum Publishing.

Elliot, Henry. John Muir: Protecting & Preserving the Environment. 2009. (Voices for Green Choices Ser.). (ENG., Illus.). 48p. (J). (gr. 5-9). pap. *(978-0-7787-4681-2(X))*; lib. bdg. *(978-0-7787-4668-3(2))* Crabtree Publishing Co.

Ferguson. Animal Care. 4th rev. ed. 2011. (Careers in Focus Ser.). 236p. (gr. 6-12). 32.95 *(978-0-8160-8037-3(2)*, Ferguson Publishing Co.) Facts On File, Inc.

Ferrara, Cos. Anna Comstock: A Love Affair with Nature. 2004. (Girls Explore, Reach for the Stars Ser.). (Illus.). 112p. (J). 20.00 *(978-0-9749456-1-3(7)*, Girls Explore) Girls Explore LLC.

Gibbons, Alan. Charles Darwin. 2008. (Illus.). 64p. (J). *(978-0-7534-1729-4(4)*, Kingfisher) Roaring Brook Pr.

Gillam, Scott. Rachel Carson: Pioneer of Environmentalism, 1 vol. 2010. (Essential Lives Set 5 Ser.). (ENG.). 112p. (J). (gr. 6-12). lib. bdg. 35.64 *(978-1-61613-511-9(5))* ABDO Publishing Co.

Goldstein, Natalie. John Muir. 2011. (Conservation Heroes Ser.). (Illus.). 144p. (YA). (gr. 6-12). 35.00 *(978-1-60413-945-7(5)*, Chelsea Hse.) Facts On File, Inc.

Goodridge, Catherine. Jane Goodall & Jane Goodall (Spanish) 6 English, 6 Spanish Adaptations. 2011. (ENG & SPA.). (J). 79.00 net. *(978-1-4108-5658-6(5))* Benchmark Education Co.

Green, John. Charles Darwin. 2009. (Dover History Coloring Book Ser.). (ENG.). 32p. (J). (gr. 3-8). pap. 3.99 *(978-0-486-47282-9(5))* Dover Pubns., Inc.

Hand, Carol. Cool Careers Without College for People Who Love Animals. 2013. (New Cool Careers Without College Ser.). 144p. (YA). (gr. 7-12). 35.95 *(978-1-4777-1822-3(2))* Rosen Publishing Group, Inc., The.

Hanson-Harding, Alexandra. Charles Darwin, Naturalist. 2017. (J). pap. ***(978-1-68048-800-5(7))*** Rosen Publishing Group, Inc., The.

Hayhurst, Chris. Cool Careers Without College for Animal Lovers. 2009. (Cool Careers Without College Ser.). 144p. (gr. 6-6). 66.50 *(978-1-61511-955-4(8))* Rosen Publishing Group, Inc., The.

Heiligman, Deborah. Charles & Emma: The Darwins' Leap of Faith. 2011. (ENG., Illus.). 296p. (YA). (gr. 8-12). pap. 10.99 *(978-0-312-66104-5(5)*, 9780312661045) Square Fish.

Hile, Lori. Rachel Carson: Environmental Pioneer, 1 vol. 2014. (Women in Conservation Ser.). (ENG., Illus.). 48p. (gr. 3-6). 33.32 *(978-1-4846-0471-7(7))*; pap. 8.99 *(978-1-4846-0476-2(8))* Heinemann-Raintree. (Heinemann InfoSearch).

Hopkinson, Deborah. Who Was Charles Darwin? Harrison, Nancy, illus. 2005. (Who Was? Ser.). (ENG.). 112p. (J). (gr. 3-7). pap. 5.99 *(978-0-448-43764-4(3)*, Grosset & Dunlap) Penguin Young Readers Group.

Hunt, Nancy Nye & Bradley, Nina Leopold. Aldo Leopold's Shack: Nina's Story. 2011. (Center for American Places - Center Books on American Places Ser.). (ENG., Illus.). 88p. 29.95 *(978-1-935195-17-7(4))* Ctr. for American Places, Inc.

Hunter, Nick. Charles Darwin, 1 vol. 2014. (Science Biographies Ser.). (ENG.). 32p. (gr. 2-4). pap. 8.95 *(978-1-4109-6602-5(X)*, Raintree Perspectives) Heinemann-Raintree.

Hurwitz, Jane. Choosing a Career in Animal Care. 2009. (World of Work Ser.). 64p. (gr. 5-5). 58.50 *(978-1-60854-329-8(3))* Rosen Publishing Group, Inc., The.

Hustad, Douglas. Environmentalist Rachel Carson. 2016. (STEM Trailblazer Bios Ser.). (ENG., Illus.). 32p. (J). (gr. 2-5). lib. bdg. 26.65 *(978-1-5124-0787-7(9))* Lerner Publishing Group.

Knowlton, Laurie Lazzaro. Cowgirl Alphabet, 1 vol. Knowlton, Charlotte & Coates, Kathy, illus. 2011. (ENG.). 32p. (J). (gr. k-3). 16.99 *(978-1-58980-669-6(7))* Pelican Publishing Co., Inc.

Krohn, Katherine. Jane Goodall: Animal Scientist, 1 vol. Martin, Cynthia & Timmons, Anne, illus. 2006. (Graphic Biographies Ser.). (ENG.). 32p. (gr. 3-4). 30.65 *(978-0-7368-5485-6(1)*, Graphic Library) Capstone Press of Coughlan Cos.

Krull, Kathleen. Charles Darwin. Kulikov, Boris, illus. (Giants of Science Ser.). (ENG.). 144p. (J). (gr. 3-7). 2015. 7.99 *(978-0-14-751463-9(0)*, Puffin Books) 2010. 15.99 *(978-0-670-06335-2(5)*, Viking Books for Young Readers) Penguin Young Readers Group.

Kuligowski, Stephanie. Wild Work! Animal Trainers, 1 vol. 2nd rev. ed. 2013. (Nonfiction Readers Ser.). (ENG., Illus.). 64p. (J). (gr. 5-5). pap. 31.96 *(978-1-4333-7441-8(2))* Teacher Created Materials, Inc.

Lantier, Patricia. Rachel Carson: Fighting Pesticides & Other Chemical Pollutants. 2009. (Voices for Green Choices Ser.). (ENG., Illus.). 48p. (J). (gr. 5-9). pap. *(978-0-7787-4676-8(3))* Crabtree Publishing Co.

Lasky, Kathryn. One Beetle Too Many: The Extraordinary Adventures of Charles Darwin. Trueman, Matthew, illus. 2014. (Candlewick Biographies Ser.). (ENG.). 48p. (J). (gr. 2-5). 14.99 *(978-0-7636-6842-6(7))* Candlewick Pr.

Lawson, Kristan. Darwin & Evolution for Kids: His Life & Ideas with 21 Activities. 2003. (For Kids Ser.). (ENG., Illus.). 160p. (J). (gr. 4). pap. 16.95 *(978-1-55652-502-5(8))* Chicago Review Pr., Inc.

Lin, Yoming S. Charles Darwin & Evolution. 2012. (Eureka! Ser.). (Illus.). 24p. (YA). (gr. 3-6). lib. bdg. 22.60 *(978-1-4488-5031-0(2))* Rosen Publishing Group, Inc., The.

Locker, Thomas. John Muir: America's Naturalist. 2010. (ENG.). 32p. (J). (gr. -1-3). pap. 12.95 *(978-1-55591-705-0(4))* Fulcrum Publishing.

Lorbiecki, Marybeth. Things Natural, Wild, & Free: The Life of Aldo Leopold. 2011. (ENG., Illus.). 112p. (J). (gr. 4-7). pap. 12.95 *(978-1-55591-474-5(8))* Fulcrum Publishing.

Malnor, Carol L. & Malnor, Bruce. Earth Heroes, Champions of Wild Animals, 1 vol. Hovemann, Anisa Claire, illus. 2010. (ENG.). 144p. (J). pap. 11.95 *(978-1-58469-123-5(9))* Dawn Pubns.

Mara, Wil & National Geographic Learning Staff. John Muir. 2010. (Rise & Shine Ser.). (ENG., Illus.). 32p. (C). (gr. 1-2). pap. 8.95 *(978-0-516-27342-6(6))* National Geographic School Publishing, Inc.

Matthews, Sheelagh. Steve Irwin. 2007. (Remarkable People Ser.). (Illus.). 24p. (J). (gr. 3-7). pap. 8.95 *(978-1-59036-650-9(6))*; lib. bdg. 24.45 *(978-1-59036-649-3(2))* Weigl Pubs., Inc.

Matthewson, Sarah. On the Lookout: Lives of Naturalists. 2007. (Shockwave: Life Stories Ser.). (ENG., Illus.). 36p. (J). (gr. 4-6). lib. bdg. 25.00 *(978-0-531-17772-3(6)*, Children's Pr.) Scholastic Library Publishing.

Maynard, Charles W. John Muir: Naturalist & Explorer. 2009. (Famous Explorers of the American West Ser.). 24p. (gr. 3-4). 42.50 *(978-1-61512-504-3(3)*, PowerKids Pr.) Rosen Publishing Group, Inc., The.

McCarthy, Pat. Henry David Thoreau: Writer, Thinker, Naturalist. 2003. (Historical American Biographies Ser.). (Illus.). 128p. (J). (gr. 6-12). lib. bdg. 26.60 *(978-0-7660-1978-2(0))* Enslow Pubs., Inc.

McDonnell, Patrick. Me... Jane. 2011. (ENG., Illus.). 40p. (J). (gr. -1-3). 17.99 *(978-0-316-04546-9(2))* Little, Brown Bks. for Young Readers.

—Me... Jane. 2011. (J). *(978-1-4618-4349-8(9))* Recorded Bks., Inc.

McVey, James. Martha Maxwell: Natural History Pioneer. 2005. (Now You Know Bio Ser.: 4). (Illus.). 84p. (J). pap. *(978-0-86541-075-6(5))* Filter Pr., LLC.

Meltzer, Milton. Henry David Thoreau: A Biography. 2007. (Literary Greats Ser.). (ENG., Illus.). 160p. (gr. 7-12). lib. bdg. 33.26 *(978-0-8225-5893-4(9)*, Twenty-First Century Bks.) Lerner Publishing Group.

Miles, Liz. Linnaeus: Organising Nature. 2017. (ENG., Illus.). 80p. (J). pap. 9.99 ***(978-0-00-820897-4(2))*** HarperCollins Pubs. Ltd. GBR. Dist: Independent Pubs. Group.

Miller, Barbara Kiely. John Muir. 2007. (Grandes Personajes (Great Americans) Ser.). 24p. (gr. 1-4). (SPA.). pap. 8.15 *(978-0-8368-8339-8(X))*; (SPA.). lib. bdg. 22.00 *(978-0-8368-8332-9(2))*; lib. bdg. 22.00 *(978-0-8368-8318-3(7))* Stevens, Gareth Publishing LLLP. (Weekly Reader Leveled Readers).

Morgan, Sally. The Incredible Life of David Attenborough, Bd. 16. 2017. (ENG.). 56p. (J). pap. 8.99 ***(978-0-00-820889-9(1))*** HarperCollins Pubs. Ltd. GBR. Dist: Independent Pubs. Group.

Muir, John & Cornell, Joseph Bharat. John Muir: My Life with Nature, 1 vol. 2004. (Sharing Nature with Children Book Ser.). (ENG., Illus.). 80p. (YA). (gr. 4-7). pap. 8.95 *(978-1-58469-009-2(7))* Dawn Pubns.

Newland, Sonya. David Attenborough: Naturalist Visionary. 2016. (Inspirational Lives Ser.). (ENG., Illus.). 32p. (J). (gr. 4-6). 17.99 *(978-0-7502-8569-8(9)*, Wayland) Hachette Children's Group GBR. Dist: Hachette Bk. Group.

Niver, Heather Moore. Henry David Thoreau: Author of Civil Disobedience. 2017. (J). ***(978-1-5383-8113-7(3))***; pap. ***(978-1-5383-8112-0(5))*** Rosen Publishing Group, Inc., The. (Rosen Young Adult).

Ollhoff, Jim. The Germ Detectives, 1 vol. 2009. (History of Germs Ser.). (ENG., Illus.). 32p. (YA). (gr. 5-9). 27.07 *(978-1-60453-499-3(0))* ABDO Publishing Co.

Pomeroy, Sarah B. & Kathirithamby, Jeyaraney. Maria Sibylla Merian: Artist, Scientist, Adventurer. 2017. (J). ***(978-1-60606-555-6(6)***, J. Paul Getty Museum) Getty Pubns.

Rice, William B. Jane Goodall, 1 vol. 2nd rev. ed. 2014. (TIME for KIDS(r) Nonfiction Readers Ser.). (ENG., Illus.). 32p. (J). (gr. 3-3). pap. 25.96 *(978-1-4807-1093-1(8))* Shell Educational Publishing.

Ridley, Sarah. Charles Darwin. 2017. (Super Scientists Ser.). (ENG., Illus.). 24p. (J). (gr. 1-3). pap. 9.99 ***(978-1-4451-5355-1(6)***, Franklin Watts) Hachette Children's Group GBR. Dist: Hachette Bk. Group.

—David Attenborough. 2017. (Super Scientists Ser.). (ENG., Illus.). 24p. (J). (gr. 1-3). pap. 9.99 ***(978-1-4451-5357-5(2)***, Franklin Watts) Hachette Children's Group GBR. Dist: Hachette Bk. Group.

Ritchey, Richard I. True Adventures of the Reptileman. 2007. 60p. per. 10.95 *(978-0-595-45020-6(2))* iUniverse, Inc.

Rose, Simon. Animal Caretaker. 2014. (J). *(978-1-4896-2982-1(3))* Weigl Pubs., Inc.

Sanchez, Anita & Stock, Catherine. Karl, Get Out of the Garden! Carolus Linnaeus & the Naming of Everything. 2017. (ENG., Illus.). 48p. (J). (gr. 2-5). lib. bdg. 17.99 *(978-1-58089-606-1(5))* Charlesbridge Publishing, Inc.

Schanzer, Rosalyn & Darwin, Charles. What Darwin Saw: The Journey That Changed the World. 2009. (ENG., Illus.). 48p. (J). (gr. 5). lib. bdg. 26.90 *(978-1-4263-0397-5(1))*; 17.95 *(978-1-4263-0396-8(3))* National Geographic Society. (National Geographic Children's Bks.).

Schier, Helga. George Washington Carver: Agricultural Innovator, 1 vol. 2008. (Essential Lives Set 2 Ser.). (ENG., Illus.). 112p. (J). (gr. 6-12). lib. bdg. 35.64 *(978-1-60453-035-3(9))* ABDO Publishing Co.

Silvey, Anita. The Plant Hunters: True Stories of Their Daring Adventures to the Far Corners of the Earth, 1 vol. 2012. (ENG., Illus.). 96p. (J). (gr. 3-7). 21.99 *(978-0-374-30908-4(6)*, 9780374309084, Farrar, Straus & Giroux (BYR)) Farrar, Straus & Giroux.

Sís, Peter. The Tree of Life: Charles Darwin. Sís, Peter, illus. 2003. (ENG., Illus.). 44p. (J). (gr. k-3). 21.99 *(978-0-374-45628-3(3)*, 9780374456283, Farrar, Straus & Giroux (BYR)) Farrar, Straus & Giroux.

—The Tree of Life: Charles Darwin. (Illus.). 22.95 *(978-0-88899-564-3(4))* Groundwood Bks. CAN. Dist: Publishers Group West (PGW).

Stanley, Phyllis M. Elizabeth Terwilliger - Someone Special: A Biography of the Celebrated Naturalist. 2003. (ENG., Illus.). 110p. (J). (gr. 4-10). pap. 17.95 *(978-1-878044-54-9(0))* Mayhaven Publishing, Inc.

Stansfield, John. Enos Mills: Rocky Mountain Naturalist. 2005. (Now You Know Bio Ser.). (Illus.). 103p. (J). pap. 8.95 *(978-0-86541-072-5(0))* Filter Pr., LLC.

Thermes, Jennifer. Charles Darwin's Around-The-World Adventure. 2016. (ENG., Illus.). 48p. (J). (gr. k-2). 18.95 *(978-1-4197-2120-5(8)*, Abrams Bks. for Young Readers) Abrams, Inc.

Tieck, Sarah. Zookeepers, 1 vol. 2011. (Extreme Jobs Ser.). (ENG., Illus.). 32p. (J). (gr. 2-5). 28.50 *(978-1-61783-029-7(1))* ABDO Publishing Co.

Trueit, Trudi Strain. Animal Trainer. 2013. (J). *(978-0-7614-8075-4(7))* Marshall Cavendish Corp.

Walsh, Steve. Enos Mills: Rocky Mountain Conservationist. 2011. (ENG & SPA., Illus.). 64p. (J). pap. 8.95 *(978-0-86541-122-7(0))* Filter Pr., LLC.

Waxman, Laura Hamilton. Jane Goodall. Butler, Tad, illus. 2007. (History Maker Biographies Ser.). (ENG.). 48p. (J). (gr. 3-6). lib. bdg. 27.93 *(978-0-8225-7610-5(4)*, Lerner Pubns.) Lerner Publishing Group.

Weaver, Anne H. The Voyage of the Beetle: A Journey Around the World with Charles Darwin & the Search for the Solution to the Mystery of Mysteries, as Narrated by Rosie, an Articulate Beetle. Lawrence, George, illus. 2007. (ENG.). 80p. (J). (gr. 5-8). 19.95 *(978-0-8263-4304-8(X))* Univ. of New Mexico Pr.

Webster, Stephen. Charles Darwin. 2016. (History Makers Ser.). (ENG., Illus.). 144p. (J). (gr. 9-9). 45.64 *(978-1-5026-1916-7(4))* Cavendish Square Publishing.

Whiting, Jim. Charles Darwin & the Origin of the Species. 2005. (Uncharted, Unexplored, & Unexplained Ser.). (Illus.). 48p. (J). (gr. 3-8). lib. bdg. 29.95 *(978-1-58415-364-1(4))* Mitchell Lane Pubs., Inc.

Yount, Lisa. Craig Venter. 2011. (Trailblazers in Science & Technology Ser.). 160p. (gr. 6-12). 35.00 *(978-1-60413-662-3(6)*, Chelsea Hse.) Facts On File, Inc.

NATURE

Adamson, Heather. Blue in Nature. 2013. (ENG., Illus.). 24p. (J). lib. bdg. 25.65 *(978-1-62031-040-3(6))* Jump! Inc.

Alexander, Cecil Frances & Hudson, Katy, illus. All Things Bright & Beautiful. 2016. (J). *(978-0-8249-5676-9(1)*, Ideal Pubns.) Worthy Publishing.

All Things Bright & Beautiful. 2006. 16p. (J). pap. 1.99 *(978-0-7847-1588-8(2)*, 22135) Standard Publishing.

Amazing Magnets: Level E. 8p. 20.95 *(978-0-322-00353-8(9))* Wright Group/McGraw-Hill.

Anderson, Debby. Let's Explore God's World. Anderson, Debby, illus. 2009. (Illus.). 32p. (J). (gr. -1-1). 10.99 *(978-1-4335-0708-3(0))* Crossway.

Animals Hide & Seek: Level E. 8p. 20.95 *(978-0-322-00354-5(7))* Wright Group/McGraw-Hill.

Arnosky, Jim. Crinkleroot's Guide to Giving Back to Nature. Arnosky, Jim, illus. 2012. (ENG., Illus.). 32p. (J). (gr. k-3). 17.99 *(978-0-399-25520-5(6)*, G.P. Putnam's Sons Books for Young Readers) Penguin Young Readers Group.

AZ Books Staff. Discovering the Savanna. Gorojan, Elena, ed. 2012. (Wild Theater Ser.). (ENG.). 8p. (J). (gr. -1-3). bds. 17.95 *(978-1-61889-017-7(4))* AZ Bks. LLC.

Azadi, Azita. Thank You Sun. 2009. 32p. pap. 16.50 *(978-1-4269-2197-1(7))* Trafford Publishing.

Barradas, Michele. Rainbow of Shapes: Learn shapes & Colors. 2008. 20p. pap. 15.95 *(978-1-4389-0177-0(1))* AuthorHouse.

Baxter, Nicola. My First Words: Nature. Lacome, Susie, illus. 2016. (ENG.). 24p. (J). (gr. -1-12). pap. 7.99 *(978-1-86147-770-5(8)*, Armadillo) Anness Publishing GBR. Dist: National Bk. Network.

Benchmark Education Company, LLC Staff, compiled by. Cactus & Canyons & Ecosystems. 2005. spiral bd. 225.00 *(978-1-4108-5806-1(5))* Benchmark Education Co.

—Cactus & Canyons & Regions. 2005. spiral bd. 225.00 *(978-1-4108-5805-4(7))* Benchmark Education Co.

Bernath, Stefen. Trees of the Northeast. 2013. (Dover Nature Coloring Book Ser.). (ENG., Illus.). 48p. (J). (gr. 6-12). pap. 4.99 *(978-0-486-23734-3(6))* Dover Pubns., Inc.

Blocksma, Mary. What's in the Woods? A Michigan Treasure Hunt. 2012. (ENG., Illus.). 200p. (gr. 3-8). pap. 12.50 *(978-0-9708575-3-8(5))* Beaver Island Arts.

Bockol, Leslie & Ikids Staff. One Tree. Phillips, Jillian, illus. 2009. (ENG.). 20p. (J). (gr. -1-1). 6.99 *(978-1-58476-811-1(8))* Innovative Kids.

Bodden, Valerie. Wildlife in Danger. 2010. (Earth Issues Ser.). (Illus.). 48p. (J). (gr. 5-18). 23.95 *(978-1-58341-987-8(X)*, Creative Education) Creative Co., The.

Bowers, Jenny. Animal Art. 2016. (Little Collectors Ser.). (ENG.). 24p. (J). (gr. k-3). 18.99 *(978-1-84780-773-1(9)*, Frances Lincoln Children's Bks.) Quarto Publishing Group UK GBR. Dist: Hachette Bk. Group.

Bowman, Debbie. The Happy Tree. 2013. 20p. pap. 8.99 *(978-1-62509-760-6(3))* Salem Author Services.

Brady, Irene. Illustrating Nature: Right-brain Art in a Left-Brain World. Brady, Irene, illus. 2004. (Illus.). spiral bd. 25.95 *(978-0-915965-09-0(7))* Nature Works Press.

Britannica, Learning Library. Science & Nature. 2003. (Illus.). 64p. 14.95 *(978-1-59339-033-4(5))* Encyclopaedia Britannica, Inc.

Brookes, Olivia. Uncover Nature. Inklink Staff, illus. 2009. (Hide-and-Seek Visual Adventures Ser.). 24p. (J). (gr. 2-5). lib. bdg. 22.60 *(978-1-60754-655-9(8))* Windmill Bks.

Brunelle, Lynn. Camp Out! The Ultimate Kids' Guide. Biggs, Brian & Tanguy, Elara, illus. 2007. (ENG.). 256p. (J). (gr. 2-7). pap. 13.95 *(978-0-7611-4122-8(7)*, 14122) Workman Publishing Co., Inc.

Burrill, Richard L. Somewhere Behind the Eyes: Surprise Images in Nature Aha! Date not set. (Somewhere Behind the Eyes Ser.). (Illus.). 96p. (J). (gr. 4-12). pap. 12.95 *(978-1-878464-19-4(1))* Anthro Co., The.

—Somewhere Behind the Eyes Vol. 3: Surprise Images in Nature Aha! Date not set. (Illus.). 96p. (J). (gr. 4-12). 10.95 *(978-1-878464-18-7(3))* Anthro Co., The.

Canetti, Yanitzia. Colorful Sights Paisajes de Colores: A World of Color. 2010. (SPA & ENG.). 24p. (J). pap. 6.99 *(978-1-59835-280-1(6)*, BrickHouse Education) Cambridge BrickHouse, Inc.

Capstone Press. Natural Wonders, 1 vol. 2010. (Natural Wonders Ser.). (ENG.). 32p. lib. bdg. 143.94 *(978-1-4296-5920-8(3)*, Pebble Plus) Capstone Press of Coughlan Cos.

Carr, Aaron. Nature Patterns. 2011. (J). *(978-1-61690-592-7(1))* Weigl Pubs., Inc.

Changing Habitats. 2015. (Illus.). 44p. (J). *(978-0-7166-2708-1(6))* World Bk., Inc.

Chinery, Michael & Michael, Chinery. Las Costas.Tr. of Seashores. (SPA.). 40p. (J). (gr. 3-5). 12.76 *(978-84-241-2053-5(1))* Everest Editora ESP. Dist: Lectorum Pubns., Inc.

—Los Desiertos.Tr. of Desert Animals. (SPA.). 40p. (J). (gr. 3-5). 12.76 *(978-84-241-2051-1(5))* Everest Editora ESP. Dist: Lectorum Pubns., Inc.

—Los Lagos y los Rios.Tr. of Lakes & Rivers. (SPA.). 40p. (J). (gr. 3-5). 12.76 *(978-84-241-2058-0(2))* Everest Editora ESP. Dist: Lectorum Pubns., Inc.

—Los Oceanos.Tr. of Oceans. (SPA.). 40p. (J). (gr. 3-5). 12.76 *(978-84-241-2055-9(8))* Everest Editora ESP. Dist: Lectorum Pubns., Inc.

—Los Polos.Tr. of Polar Lands. (SPA.). 40p. (J). (gr. 3-5). 12.76 *(978-84-241-2056-6(6))* Everest Editora ESP. Dist: Lectorum Pubns., Inc.

—Las Sabanas y las Praderas.Tr. of Grassland Animals. (SPA.). (J). (gr. 3-5). 12.76 *(978-84-241-2054-2(X))* Everest Editora ESP. Dist: Lectorum Pubns., Inc.

Colvin, L. Living World Encyclopedia. 2009. pap. 14.99 *(978-0-7945-2784-6(1))* EDC Publishing.

Colvin, L. & Speare, E. Living World Encyclopedia. 2004. (Encyclopedias Ser.). (Illus.). 128p. (J). 7.95 *(978-0-7945-0005-4(6))* EDC Publishing.

Confluence 2004. 2004. (YA). per. *(978-0-9745192-4-1(3))* Little Bay Pr.

Connolly, Randy, et al. Poison Ivy, Pets & People: Scratching the Poison Ivy, Oak & Sumac Itch. 2005. (10thingstoknow about ... Ser.). (Illus.). 104p. pap. 9.95 *(978-0-9722400-1-7(2))* 2Lakes Publishing.

Conroy, Jim & Alexander, Basia. Messages from Trees Set 1: A Coloring Book for the Young & Young-At-Heart. 2013. (ENG., Illus.). 32p. (J). pap. 8.00 *(978-0-9834114-5-1(X))* Plant Kingdom Communications.

Corcorane, Ann. Patterns Everywhere! 2011. (Wonder Readers Emergent Level Ser.). (ENG.). 32p. (gr. -1-1). pap. 5.99 *(978-1-4296-7869-8(0)*, Wonder Readers) Capstone Press of Coughlan Cos.

Cork, Barbara. Pocket Nature. 2004. (First Nature Ser.). (Illus.). 170p. (J). 8.95 *(978-0-7945-0346-8(2)*, Usborne) EDC Publishing.

Cousteau, Philippe & Hopkinson, Deborah. Follow the Moon Home. So, Meilo, illus. 2016. (ENG.). 48p. (J). (gr. k-3). 16.99 *(978-1-4521-1241-1(X))* Chronicle Bks. LLC.

Cowcher, Helen. Rainforest. (Illus.). 40p. (CHI, ENG, URD, TUR & VIE.). 16.95 *(978-1-84059-017-3(3))*; (VIE, ENG, URD, TUR & CHI., 16.95 *(978-1-84059-022-7(X))* Milet Publishing.

—Whistling Thorn. (CHI, ENG, URD, TUR & VIE., Illus.). 40p. (J). 16.95 *(978-1-84059-033-3(5))* Milet Publishing.

Cromarty, Jim. Great Barrier Reef Adventures. 2005. (Adventure Ser.). (ENG., Illus.). 96p. (J). (gr. 3-7). per. 8.99 *(978-1-84550-068-9(7)*, 3ec344eb-b5a7-45bd-8d58-a6ba056815cc) Christian Focus Pubns. GBR. Dist: Bookmasters Distribution.

Curious Nature. 2017. (Curious Nature Ser.). 32p. (gr. 8-8). 157.50 ***(978-1-4994-3399-9(9))***; pap. 60.00 ***(978-1-5081-5368-9(X))*** Rosen Publishing Group, Inc., The. (PowerKids Pr.).

Cycles in Nature. 2015. (Cycles in Nature Ser.). (ENG.). 24p. (J). (gr. 1-2). pap., pap., pap. 293.40 *(978-1-4824-3446-0(6))*; pap., pap., pap. 48.90 *(978-1-4824-3447-7(4))* Stevens, Gareth Publishing LLLP.

Dalby, Elizabeth. Mysteries & Marvels of Nature. Tatchell, Judy, ed. Whatmore, Candice & Barrance, Reuben, illus. 2008. (Nature Encyclopedias Ser.). 128p. (J). (gr. 4-7). pap. 16.99 *(978-0-7945-1738-0(2)*, Usborne) EDC Publishing.

Dalby, L. Mysteries & Marvels of Nature. 2004. (First Stories Ser.). 128p. (J). 19.95 *(978-0-7945-0597-4(X))*; lib. bdg. 27.95 *(978-1-58086-610-1(7)*, Usborne) EDC Publishing.

Davidson, Annie. Colour Together: Nature. 2016. (ENG., Illus.). 64p. (J). (gr. k-2). pap. 16.99 ***(978-1-78344-517-2(3))*** Andersen Pr. GBR. Dist: Independent Pubs. Group.

Davies, Gill & Morris, Neil. 365 Awesome Facts & Records about Nature. 2008. (365 Awesome Facts & Records Ser.). (ENG., Illus.). 176p. (J). (gr. 1-18). 19.95 *(978-88-6098-112-7(3))* McRae Bks. Srl ITA. Dist: Independent Pubs. Group.

Day, Trevor. Taiga. Garratt, Richard, illus. 2006. (Biomes of the Earth Ser.). 240p. (gr. 6-12). 39.50 *(978-0-8160-5329-2(4))* Facts On File, Inc.

De Koning, Lezanne. The Magic of Nature. 2011. (Illus.). 44p. pap. 19.48 *(978-1-4520-9231-7(1))* AuthorHouse.

Debacque, Pascal. Create Your Own Mandalas — Nature. 2013. (ENG.). 32p. (J). (gr. -1-12). pap. 6.99 *(978-0-486-49375-6(X))* Dover Pubns., Inc.

Delano, Marfe Ferguson. Cielo. 2008. (Descubre la Naturaleza Ser.). (Illus.). 60p. (J). 12.95 *(978-1-58087-127-3(5))* Stampley, C. D. Enterprises, Inc.

Dempski, Seth. Natalie's Nature Walk: Represent & Interpret Data. 2014. (Math Masters: Measurement & Data Ser.). 24p. (J). (gr. 2-3). 23.60 *(978-1-4777-6440-4(2))*; (ENG.). pap. 8.25 *(978-1-4777-4828-2(8))* Rosen Publishing Group, Inc., The. (Rosen Classroom).

Desonie, Dana. Our Fragile Planet Set, 8-Volumes. 2008. (Our Fragile Planet Ser.). (gr. 6-12). 280.00 *(978-0-8160-7424-2(0)*, Chelsea Hse.) Facts On File, Inc.

Discover Series: Science, Nature, Wildlife, 11 bks. (Illus.). (J). (gr. 3-6). lib. bdg. 175.45 *(978-1-56674-935-0(2))* Forest Hse. Publishing Co., Inc.

Donnelly, Karen. Biomes of the Past & the Future. 2009. (Earth's Changing Weather & Climate Ser.). 24p. (gr. 4-4). 42.50 *(978-1-61512-243-1(5)*, PowerKids Pr.) Rosen Publishing Group, Inc., The.

Dorling Kindersley Publishing Staff. First Nature Encyclopedia. 2006. (ENG., Illus.). 160p. (J). (gr. 3-7). 16.99 *(978-0-7566-1415-7(5)*, DK Children) Dorling Kindersley Publishing, Inc.

—Nature Trail. 2016. (Skills for Starting School Ser.). (ENG.). 18p. (J). (-k). 13.99 *(978-1-4654-5133-0(1)*, DK Children) Dorling Kindersley Publishing, Inc.

Dowdy, Penny. Nature Math. 2008. (Math Alive! Ser.). 32p. (gr. 4-18). lib. bdg. 28.50 *(978-0-7614-3214-2(0)*, Benchmark Bks.) Marshall Cavendish Corp.

Durber, Matt & Jones, Stephanie, illus. First Picture Nature. MMStudios, photos by. 2007. (First Picture Board Bks). 16p. (J). (gr. -1-k). bds. 11.99 *(978-0-7945-1751-9(X)*, Usborne) EDC Publishing.

Earth's Treasures. (Eyes on Adventure Ser.). 32p. (J). (gr. 1). pap. *(978-1-882210-63-3(8))* Action Publishing, Inc.

Earthworks Series, 6 bks., Set. 179.57 *(978-0-7614-1364-6(2)*, Benchmark Bks.) Marshall Cavendish Corp.

Education.com. Fun with Nature: A Workbook of Natural Science Topics. 2015. (ENG.). 128p. (J). (gr. 2-2). pap. 7.99 *(978-0-486-80265-7(5))* Dover Pubns., Inc.

—Let's Go Outside! A Workbook of Plants, Animals, & the Outdoors. 2015. (ENG.). 128p. (J). (gr. 1-1). pap. 7.99 *(978-0-486-80259-6(0))* Dover Pubns., Inc.

Elmore, Amber. Betsy Beansprout Camping Guide. Hickey, Josh, illus. 2013. 50p. pap. 13.99 *(978-1-937331-37-5(7))* ShadeTree Publishing, LLC.

Enciclopedia Ilustrada de Ciencia Naturaleza (Understanding Science & Nature), 16 bks. Incl. Comportamiento de los Animales (Animal Behavior) 17.95 *(978-0-7835-3358-2(6))*; Cuerpo Humano (Human Body) 17.95 *(978-0-7835-3350-6(0))*; Era de la Computadora. 17.95 *(978-0-7835-3375-9(6))*; Espacio y Planetas. 17.95 *(978-0-7835-3370-4(5))*; Estructura de la Materia (Structure of Matter) 17.95 *(978-0-7835-3383-4(7))*; Evolucion de la Vida. 17.95 *(978-0-7835-3354-4(3))*; Fuerzas Fisicas (Physical Forces) 17.95 *(978-0-7835-3395-7(0))*; Geografia. 17.95 *(978-0-7835-3387-2(X))*; Insectos y Aranas. 17.95 *(978-0-7835-3398-8(5))*; Maquinas e Inventos (Machines & Inventions) 17.95 *(978-0-7835-3400-8(0))*; Mundo Submarino (Underwater World) 17.95 *(978-0-7835-3397-1(7))*; Planeta Tierra (Planet Earth) 17.95 *(978-0-7835-3396-4(9))*; Plantas (Plant Life) 17.95 *(978-0-7835-3399-5(3))*; Tiempo y Clima (Weather & Climate) 17.95 *(978-0-7835-3366-7(7))*; Transporte y la Navegacion (Transportation) 17.95 *(978-0-7835-3379-7(9))*; 152p. (YA). (gr. 6-18). 1996. (Illus.). Set lib. bdg. 319.20 *(978-0-7835-3391-9(8))* Time-Life, Inc.

Encyclopaedia Britannica, Inc. Staff, compiled by. Science & Nature. 2003. (Britannica Learning Library). (Illus.). (gr. 2-5). 14.95 *(978-1-59339-002-0(5)*, 049903-EN-REF) Encyclopaedia Britannica, Inc.

Evans, Bill. It's Raining Fish & Spiders. 2012. (ENG., Illus.). 240p. (J). (gr. 5). pap. 18.99 *(978-0-7653-2132-9(7)*, 9780765321329, Forge Bks.) Doherty, Tom Assocs., LLC.

Everett, Jason M. U-X-L Sustainable Living. 2015. (Illus.). (J). *(978-1-4103-1784-1(6)*, UXL) Cengage Gale.

Explora la Naturaleza, Set. 2004. (SPA.). 170.50 *(978-1-4042-7552-2(5))* Rosen Publishing Group, Inc., The.

Eyre, Jane. Creatures of the New Jersey Pine Barrens Coloring Book, 1 vol. Eyre, Jane, illus. 2004. (Illus.). 36p. spiral bd. 6.00 *(978-0-9762483-0-9(1))* Fun Fitness Publishing.

Facts on File, Inc. Staff, ed. Nature Walk, 7 Vols., Set. 2006. (Nature Walk Ser.). 80p. (gr. 4-6). 196.00 *(978-0-7910-9445-7(6)*, Chelsea Clubhouse) Facts On File, Inc.

Falchetta, Drew. Is This Living or Non-Living? 2016. (1-3Y Science Ser.). (ENG., Illus.). 24p. (J). pap. 5.99 ***(978-1-63437-605-1(6))*** American Reading Co.

Ferris, Diane J. Weather Watcher. 2009. (Illus.). 20p. pap. 13.00 *(978-1-4490-1218-2(3))* AuthorHouse.

First Graphics: Nature Cycles. 2011. (First Graphics: Nature Cycles Ser.). (ENG.). 24p. (gr. 1-2). pap. 142.80 *(978-1-4296-6401-1(0))* Capstone Press of Coughlan Cos.

First Graphics: Nature Cycles. 2010. (First Graphics: Nature Cycles Ser.). (ENG.). 24p. (gr. 1-2). pap. 25.16 *(978-1-4296-6232-1(8))* Capstone Press of Coughlan Cos.

Fitzsimons, Cecilia. 50 Nature Projects for Kids: Fun-Packed Outdoor & Indoor Things to Do & Make. 2013. (ENG., Illus.). 96p. (J). (gr. 2-9). 13.99 *(978-1-84322-852-3(1)*, Armadillo) Anness Publishing GBR. Dist: National Bk. Network.

Flatt, Lizann. Counting on Fall. Barron, Ashley, illus. 2017. (Math in Nature Ser.: 1). (ENG.). 32p. (J). (gr. k-2). pap. 7.95 ***(978-1-77147-310-1(X))*** Owlkids Bks. Inc. CAN. Dist: Publishers Group West (PGW).

—Counting on Fall. Barron, Ashley & Owlkids Books Inc. Staff, illus. 2012. (Math in Nature Ser.: 1). (ENG.). 32p. (J). (gr. k-2). 15.95 *(978-1-926973-36-4(4)*, Owlkids) Owlkids Bks. Inc. CAN. Dist: Publishers Group West (PGW).

—Sorting Through Spring. Barron, Ashley, illus. 2013. (Math in Nature Ser.: 2). (ENG.). 32p. (J). (gr. 1-4). 15.95 *(978-1-926973-59-3(3)*, Owlkids) Owlkids Bks. Inc. CAN. Dist: Publishers Group West (PGW).

French, Felicity. Colour & Frame - Nature. 2016. (ENG.). 64p. pap. 12.95 *(978-1-78243-584-6(0))* O'Mara, Michael Bks., Ltd. GBR. Dist: Independent Pubs. Group.

Furgang, Kathy. Nature in Focus: Set Of 6. 2011. (Navigators Ser.). (J). pap. 48.00 net. *(978-1-4108-0420-4(8))* Benchmark Education Co.

—Nature in Focus & Enfoque en la Naturaleza: 6 English, 6 Spanish Adaptations. 2011. (ENG & SPA.). (J). 97.00 net. *(978-1-4108-5690-6(9))* Benchmark Education Co.

La Furia de la Naturaleza: El Poder del Clima. (Colección Ventana Transparente). (SPA., Illus.). (J). (gr. 3-5). *(978-950-11-1361-7(2)*, SG0561) Sigmar ARG. Dist: Lectorum Pubns., Inc.

Galvin, Laura Gates. Peep's Nature. 2006. (ENG., Illus.). 24p. (J). (gr. -1-k). 15.99 *(978-1-59249-519-1(2)*, 1C301) Soundprints.

Ganeri, Anita. Fearsome Forces of Nature, 1 vol. 2012. (Extreme Nature Ser.). (ENG.). 32p. (gr. 1-3). pap. 8.29 *(978-1-4109-4701-7(7))*; lib. bdg. 29.99 *(978-1-4109-4696-6(7))* Heinemann-Raintree. (Read Me!).

—Tell Me Where Is the Top of the World? And More about Planet Earth. 2004. (Illus.). 32p. (J). pap.

(978-1-84458-060-6(1), Pavilion Children's Books) Pavilion Bks.

Gatty, Alfred. Parables from Nature (Yesterday's Classics) 2006. (Illus.). 456p. (J). per. 14.95 (978-1-59915-005-5(0)) Yesterday's Classics.

Gerbracht, Edie. Especially Me! Stoner, Alexis, illus. 2012. 34p. pap. 11.77 (978-0-9843855-5-3(X)) aBASK Publishing.

Getting into Nature. (Illus.). (J). (gr. k-5). 170.00 (978-0-8239-7668-3(8)) Rosen Publishing Group, Inc., The.

Gibson, J. Phil & Gibson, Terri R. Natural Selection. 2009. (Science Foundations Ser.). (Illus.). 112p. (YA). (gr. 7-12). lib. bdg. 35.00 (978-0-7910-9784-7(6)) Facts On File, Inc.

Gifford, Peggy. The Great Big Green. Desimini, Lisa, illus. 2014. (ENG.). 32p. (J). (gr. -1-2). 15.95 (978-1-62091-629-2(0)) Boyds Mills Pr.

Glaser, Rebecca. Red in Nature. 2013. (ENG.). 24p. (J). lib. bdg. 25.65 (978-1-62031-036-6(8)) Jump! Inc.

God's Wonders. 3.50 (978-0-8054-5877-0(8)) B&H Publishing Group.

Goodings, Christina. Growing Green: A Young Person's Guide to Taking Care of the Planet. Furukawa, Masumi, illus. 2008. (ENG.). 32p. (J). (gr. k-2). 12.95 (978-0-7459-6171-2(1)) Lion Hudson PLC GBR. Dist: Independent Pubs. Group.

Hanneman, Monika, et al. Gardening with Children. Tomasello, Sam, illus. 2011. (BBG Guides for a Greener Planet Ser.). (ENG.). 120p. pap. 12.95 (978-1-889538-78-5(7)) Brooklyn Botanic Garden.

Hansen, Amy S. & Olien, Rebecca. First Graphics: Science Mysteries. Scott, Korey & McDee, Katie, illus. 2011. (First Graphics: Science Mysteries Ser.). (ENG.). 24p. (gr. 1-2). lib. bdg. 47.98 (978-1-4296-6099-0(6)) Capstone Press of Coughlan Cos.

—First Graphics: Science Mysteries: A Science Mystery. Scott, Korey & McDee, Katie, illus. 2011. (First Graphics: Science Mysteries Ser.). (ENG.). 24p. (gr. 1-2). pap. 25.16 (978-1-4296-7181-1(5)); pap. 142.80 (978-1-4296-7182-8(3)) Capstone Press of Coughlan Cos.

Hays, Susan. Nature Friends Creativity Book. 2003. (Illus.). 52p. (J). 11.95 (978-0-9729192-0-3(1)) Art & Soul Expressions.

Hegbrook, Thomas. Story Worlds: Nature. Hegbrook, Thomas, illus. 2016. (360 Degrees Ser.). (ENG., Illus.). 64p. (J). (gr. 3-12). 24.99 (978-1-944530-01-3(0), 360 Degrees) Tiger Tales.

Hilton, Samantha. Nature's Neighborhoods. Holmes, Steve, illus. 2004. (Interfact Ladders Ser.). (ENG.). 48p. (J). (gr. -1-2). 14.95 incl. cd-rom (978-1-58728-420-5(0)) Cooper Square Publishing Llc.

Hooker, Worthington. The Child's Book of Nature. 2005. reprint ed. pap. 37.95 (978-1-4179-3598-7(7)) Kessinger Publishing, LLC.

Houbre, Gilbert. Light. Houbre, Gilbert, illus. 2012. (ENG., Illus.). 36p. (J). (gr. -1-k). 12.99 (978-1-85103-405-5(6)) Moonlight Publishing, Ltd. GBR. Dist: Independent Pubs. Group.

Hunter, William. Nature & Nurture: The Causes of Obesity. Garcia, Victor, ed. 2014. (Understanding Obesity Ser.: 10). 104p. (J). (gr. 7-18). lib. bdg. 24.95 (978-1-4222-3064-0(3)) Mason Crest.

Hvass & Hannibal. Pattern-Tastic Treasure Hunt: Spot the Odd One Out with Nature. 2016. (ENG.). 14p. (J). (gr. -1-k). bds. 12.99 (978-1-84780-779-3(8), Wide Eyed Editions) Quarto Publishing Group UK GBR. Dist: Hachette Bk. Group.

—Technicolor Treasure Hunt: Learn to Count with Nature. 2016. (ENG.). 14p. (J). (gr. -1-k). bds. 12.99 (978-1-84780-780-9(1), Wide Eyed Editions) Quarto Publishing Group UK GBR. Dist: Hachette Bk. Group.

Hvass, Nan Na & Hannibal, Sofie, illus. Technicolour Treasure Hunt: Learn to Count with Nature. 2016. (ENG.). 14p. (J). bds. 12.99 (978-1-84780-744-1(5), Wide Eyed Editions) Quarto Publishing Group UK GBR. Dist: Littlehampton Bk Services, Ltd.

I See You: Level E. 8p. 20.95 (978-0-322-00342-2(3)) Wright Group/McGraw-Hill.

Ikids Staff. The Five Senses. 2009. (ENG., Illus.). 20p. (J). (gr. -1-1). 6.99 (978-1-58476-812-8(6)) Innovative Kids.

In the Rain Forest: Level F. 16p. 31.50 (978-0-322-00376-7(8)) Wright Group/McGraw-Hill.

Ireland, Karin. Wonderful Nature, Wonderful You, 1 vol. Canyon, Christopher, illus. 2017. (ENG.). 32p. (J). (gr. k-3). 16.95 (978-1-58469-582-0(X)) Dawn Pubns.

Jenkins, Steve. Just a Second: A Different Way to Look at Time. 2011. (ENG., Illus.). 40p. (J). (gr. -1-3). 17.99 (978-0-618-70896-3(0)) Houghton Mifflin Harcourt Publishing Co.

Johnson, Kathy. Let's Take a Walk in the Rain. Peer, Kate, illus. 2012. 28p. pap. 13.54 (978-1-4669-3252-4(X)) Trafford Publishing.

Johnson, Rebecca L. A Walk in the Tundra. Saroff, Phyllis V., illus. Braasch, Gary, photos by. 2005. (Biomes of North America Ser.). 48p. (gr. 3-6). lib. bdg. 23.93 (978-1-57505-157-4(5)) Lerner Publishing Group.

Joyce, Susan. ABC Nature Riddles. DuBosque, Doug, illus. 2004. (ABC Riddles Ser.). 32p. (J). (gr. -1-k). 13.95 (978-0-939217-53-3(8)) Peel Productions, Inc.

Der Jugend Brockhaus: Natur und Technik. (GER., Illus.). 640p. (YA). (gr. 5-11). (978-3-7653-1851-1(5)) Brockhaus, F. A., GmbH DEU. Dist: International Bk. Import Service, Inc.

Kalman, Bobbie. ¿Cómo se siente al tocarlo? 2008. (SPA.). 24p. (J). lib. bdg. (978-0-7787-8722-8(2)) Crabtree Publishing Co.

—¿Como Se Siente Al Tocarlo? 2008.Tr. of How Does It Feel? (SPA.). 24p. (J). pap. (978-0-7787-8731-0(1)) Crabtree Publishing Co.

—My Backyard Community. 2010. (My World Ser.). (ENG., Illus.). 24p. (J). (gr. k-2). (978-0-7787-9448-6(2)); pap. (978-0-7787-9492-9(X)) Crabtree Publishing Co.

—What Are Opposites in Nature? 2010. (Looking at Nature Ser.). (ENG.). 24p. (J). (gr. -1-2). pap. (978-0-7787-3346-1(7)); lib. bdg. (978-0-7787-3326-3(2)) Crabtree Publishing Co.

—What Is Super Nature? 2010. (Big Science Ideas Ser.). (ENG.). 32p. (J). (gr. k-3). pap. (978-0-7787-3307-2(6)); lib. bdg. (978-0-7787-3287-7(8)) Crabtree Publishing Co.

—Where Is It? 2007. (Looking at Nature Ser.). (ENG., Illus.). 24p. (J). (gr. -1-2). pap. (978-0-7787-3341-6(6)); lib. bdg. (978-0-7787-3321-8(1)) Crabtree Publishing Co.

Kalman, Bobbie & Smithyman, Kathryn. El Ciclo de Vida del Arbol. Bedell, Barbara, illus. 2005. (Serie Ciclos de Vida Ser.). (SPA.). 32p. (J). (gr. 1-4). pap. (978-0-7787-8711-2(7)) Crabtree Publishing Co.

Kaplan, Osman. Animal Wonders of the Sky. Kalender, Oznur, illus. 2009. (Amazing Animals Ser.). (ENG.). 56p. (J). (gr. 2-4). 9.95 (978-1-59784-201-3(X)) Tughra Bks.

Kauffman, Judy. The Lord God Made Them All. 2003. (Illus.). 40p. 1.90 (978-0-7399-2347-4(1), 2927) Rod & Staff Pubs., Inc.

Kavanagh, James. In God's Kitchen. Belisle, John, illus. 2004. (ENG.). 32p. (J). 15.95 (978-1-58355-241-4(3)) Western National Parks Assn.

—My First Forests Nature. Leung, Raymond, illus. 2011. (Nature Activity Book Ser.). (ENG.). 32p. (J). (gr. 2-4). act. bk. ed. 6.95 (978-1-58355-588-0(9)) Western National Parks Assn.

Kids Can Press Staff. This Is Daniel Cook on a Hike. Li, Karen, ed. 2006. (This Is Daniel Cook Ser.). (ENG., Illus.). 24p. (J). (gr. -1-1). 4.95 (978-1-55453-080-9(6)) Kids Can Pr., Ltd. CAN. Dist: Hachette Bk. Group.

Knight, M. J. Why Should I Care about Nature? 2009. (One Small Step Ser.). (YA). (gr. 2-5). 27.10 (978-1-59920-266-2(2)) Black Rabbit Bks.

Koniver, Laura. From the Ground Up. Koniver, Laura, illus. 2012. (Illus.). 44p. (J). pap. 16.99 (978-1-937848-03-3(5)) Do Life Right, Inc.

Kowalski, Gary A. Earth Day: An Alphabet Book. Baviera, Rocco, illus. 2009. (ENG.). 32p. (J). (gr. -1-4). 12.00 (978-1-55896-542-3(4), 1297770, Skinner Hse. Bks.) Unitarian Universalist Assn.

Kranz, Linda. My Nature Book: A Journal And. 2nd ed. 2013. (ENG., Illus.). 128p. (gr. 1-5). pap., act. bk. ed. 12.95 (978-1-58979-822-9(8)) Taylor Trade Publishing.

Krusinski, Anna. Farm Friends: A Visit to the Local Farm. 2016. (Kubu Ser.). (ENG., Illus.). 34p. (J). (gr. -1-2). pap. 5.99 (978-1-57826-475-9(8), Hatherleigh Pr.) Hatherleigh Co., Ltd., The.

Laber-Warren, Emily. A Walk in the Woods: Into the Field Guide. 2013. (ENG.). 112p. (J). (gr. k). 19.99 (978-1-935703-23-5(4)) Downtown Bookworks.

Lambert, Mark John. The 10 Most Incredible Landforms. 2008. (J). 14.99 (978-1-55448-529-1(0)) Scholastic Library Publishing.

Laval, Thierry. Look & Find Nature. 2016. (Look & Find Ser.). (ENG., Illus.). 14p. (J). 18.99 (978-0-531-22238-6(1), Children's Pr.) Scholastic Library Publishing.

Lehman-Wilzig, Tami. Green Bible Stories for Children. Bernhard, Durga Yael, illus. 2011. (Bible Ser.). (ENG.). 48p. (J). (gr. 3-5). pap. 7.95 (978-0-7613-5136-8(1), Kar-Ben Publishing) Lerner Publishing Group.

—Green Bible Stories for Children. Bernhard, Durga, illus. 2011. (Bible Ser.). (ENG.). 48p. (J). (gr. 3-5). lib. bdg. 17.95 (978-0-7613-5135-1(3), Kar-Ben Publishing) Lerner Publishing Group.

Leslie, Clare Walker. The Curious Nature Guide: Explore the Natural Wonders All Around You. 2015. (ENG., Illus.). 144p. pap. 14.95 (978-1-61212-509-1(3)) Storey Publishing, LLC.

Lewis, J. Patrick. Earth & You - A Closer View: Nature's Features. Canyon, Christopher, illus. 2004. (Sharing Nature with Children Book Ser.). 36p. (J). (gr. -1-3). 16.95 (978-1-58469-016-0(X)); (gr. 4-7). pap. 7.95 (978-1-58469-015-3(1)) Dawn Pubns.

Lewis, Kelly. From Egg to Butterfly. 2016. (Spring Forward Ser.). (J). (gr. 1). (978-1-4900-6020-0(0)) Benchmark Education Co.

Llanas, Sheila Griffin. Nature Poetry: Make Me a Picture of the Sun. 2014. (Pure Poetry Ser.). 128p. (J). lib. bdg. 33.27 (978-0-7660-4244-5(8)) Enslow Pubs., Inc.

Locker, Thomas. Walking with Henry: The Life & Works of Henry David Thoreau. 2011. (ENG., Illus.). 32p. (J). (gr. -1-5). pap. 9.95 (978-1-55591-016-7(5)) Fulcrum Publishing.

Londt, Claire, et al. English Matters for Zambia Basic Education Grade 3 Pupil's Book. 2nd ed. 2007. pap., stu. ed. 5.75 (978-0-521-68755-3(1)) Cambridge Univ. Pr.

Lowcountry A to Z. 2004. (J). 24.95 (978-0-9744035-0-2(4)) Makai Concepts, LLC.

Lunchbox Lessons Staff, creator. The Neighborhood Naturalist. 2009. (Backyard Pioneers Ser.). (ENG., Illus.). 80p. (gr. 1-10). pap., wbk. ed. (978-1-60507-047-6(5)) Lunchbox Lessons.

MacCoon, Nancy. Backyard Wonders. Watkins, Courtney, illus. l.t. ed. 2003. 38p. (J). pap. 14.95 (978-0-9742495-0-6(5)) Vibatorium LLC.

MacKenzie, Catherine. Scottish Highland. 2007. (Adventure Ser.). (ENG., Illus.). 96p. (J). per. 8.99 (978-1-84550-281-2(7), beeaf3cf-4408-4d2c-89dc-81ff3e31e46b) Christian Focus Pubns. GBR. Dist: Bookmasters Distribution.

Maguire, Kay. Nature's Day. Kroll, Danielle, illus. 2016. (Nature's Day Ser.). (ENG.). 80p. (J). (gr. k-3). 24.99 (978-1-84780-707-6(0), Wide Eyed Editions) Quarto Publishing Group UK GBR. Dist: Hachette Bk. Group.

—Nature's Day: Discover the World of Wonder on Your Doorstep. Kroll, Danielle, illus. 2015. (Nature's Day Ser.). (ENG.). 80p. (J). 24.99 (978-1-84780-608-6(2), Wide Eyed Editions) Quarto Publishing Group UK GBR. Dist: Littlehampton Bk Services, Ltd.

Mangieri, Catherine C. & National Geographic Learning Staff. What Is a Rainbow? 2012. (ENG., Illus.). 12p. (C). (gr. 1-2). pap. 9.95 (978-0-8239-8135-9(5)) National Geographic School Publishing, Inc.

Marciniak, Kristin. Incredible Nature. 2018. (ENG.). 32p. (gr. 3-6). 31.35 **(978-1-63235-421-1(7)**, 12-Story Library) Pr. Room Editions LLC.

Marsico, Katie. The Nature Conservancy. 2016. (Community Connections: How Do They Help? Ser.). (ENG., Illus.). 24p. (J). (gr. 2-5). 27.07 (978-1-63471-051-0(7), 208284) Cherry Lake Publishing.

—World Wildlife Fund. 2016. (Community Connections: How Do They Help? Ser.). (ENG., Illus.). 24p. (J). (gr. 2-5). 27.07 (978-1-63471-055-8(X), 208300) Cherry Lake Publishing.

Martin, Bill, Jr. & Sampson, Michael. I Love Our Earth / Amo Nuestra Tierra. Lipow, Dan, photos by. 2013. (ENG., Illus.). 32p. (J). (gr. -1-2). pap. 7.95 (978-1-58089-557-6(3)) Charlesbridge Publishing, Inc.

Mattern, Joanne. Angel Falls: World's Highest Waterfall. 2009. (Nature's Greatest Hits Ser.). 24p. (gr. 2-2). 42.50 (978-1-61514-837-0(X), PowerKids Pr.) Rosen Publishing Group, Inc., The.

Mattern, Joanne & Herndon, Ryan, compiled by. Guinness World Records. 2005. (Illus.). 47p. pap. (978-0-439-71568-3(7)) Scholastic, Inc.

McCarroll, Tolbert. A Winter Walk. Beebee, Dorothy, illus. 2006. (ENG.). 160p. 14.95 (978-0-8245-2416-6(0)) Crossroad Publishing Co., The.

McConnell, Lynn. Grandma's Tree. 2009. 24p. pap. 11.49 (978-1-4389-8069-0(8)) AuthorHouse.

Meachen Rau, Dana. El Arco Iris. 2007. (Maravillas de la Naturaleza Ser.). (SPA & ENG., Illus.). 32p. (gr. 1-2). lib. bdg. 15.95 (978-0-7614-2807-7(0), Benchmark Bks.) Marshall Cavendish Corp.

—Las Cataratas. 2007. (Maravillas de la Naturaleza Ser.). (SPA & ENG., Illus.). 32p. (gr. 1-2). lib. bdg. 15.95 (978-0-7614-2810-7(0), Benchmark Bks.) Marshall Cavendish Corp.

—Rainbows. 2007. (Wonders of Nature Ser.). (SPA & ENG.). 32p. (J). (gr. k-2). lib. bdg. 22.79 (978-0-7614-2669-1(8), Benchmark Bks.) Marshall Cavendish Corp.

—Rainbows/el Arco Iris. 2007. (Wonders of Nature/Maravillas de la Naturaleza Ser.). (SPA & ENG., Illus.). 32p. (gr. 1-2). lib. bdg. 15.95 (978-0-7614-2831-2(3), Benchmark Bks.) Marshall Cavendish Corp.

—Waterfalls. 2007. (Wonders of Nature Ser.). (SPA & ENG.). 32p. (gr. 1-2). lib. bdg. 15.95 (978-0-7614-2671-4(X), Benchmark Bks.) Marshall Cavendish Corp.

Meredith, Susan & Cullis, Megan. Nature to Color. Cooper, Jenny, illus. 2013. (ENG.). 96p. (J). 9.99 (978-0-7945-1913-1(X), Usborne) EDC Publishing.

Miché, Mary. Nature's Patchwork Quilt: Understanding Habitats. Powell, Consie, illus. 2012. 32p. (J). (gr. k-6). 16.95 (978-1-58469-169-3(7)); (ENG.). pap. 8.95 (978-1-58469-170-9(0)) Dawn Pubns.

Miles Kelly Staff. Nature. 2003. (Ask Me a Question Ser.). (Illus.). 20p. spiral bd. 7.95 (978-1-84236-125-2(2)) Miles Kelly Publishing, Ltd. GBR. Dist: Independent Pubs. Group.

Molina, M. Isabel. Arco Iris (The Rainbow) (SPA.). (J). 7.95 (978-84-86563-03-5(8)) Nuevas Estructuras Gondomar ESP. Dist: AIMS International Bks., Inc.

Monroe, Colleen. The Wonders of Nature Sketchbook: Learn about Nature & How to Draw It. Monroe, Michael Glenn, illus. 2006. 40p. (J). (gr. 4-7). lib. bdg. 15.00 (978-0-9754942-1-9(X)) Storytime Pr., Inc.

Montgomery, Anne. Nature Made, 1 vol. (Science Readers: Content & Literacy Ser.). (ENG., Illus.). 24p. (gr. k-k). 2015. pap. 22.96 (978-1-4938-1138-0(X)) 2014. pap. 8.99 (978-1-4807-4528-5(6)) Teacher Created Materials, Inc.

Morris, Neil. Our Wonderful World: Fun Finding Out. 2003. (Fun Finding Out Ser.). (Illus.). 48p. (J). pap. 7.95 (978-1-902947-36-5(3)) Miles Kelly Publishing, Ltd. GBR. Dist: Independent Pubs. Group.

El Mundo de la Naturaleza. (Coleccion Lo Sabias?). (SPA., Illus.). 44p. (J). 12.95 (978-950-11-0938-2(0), SGM9380) Sigmar ARG. Dist: Continental Bk. Co., Inc.

Murphy, Julie & Amstutz, Lisa J. Nature Starts. 2012. (Nature Starts Ser.). (ENG.). 32p. (gr. 1-2). pap. 24.30 (978-1-4296-8301-2(5)); pap. 190.80 (978-1-4296-8302-9(3)); lib. bdg. 81.96 (978-1-4296-8104-9(7)) Capstone Press of Coughlan Cos. (Aplus Bks.).

Muse, Elizabeth St. Cloud. A Child's Garden: Introducing Your Child to the Joys of the Garden. Saull, Eve, illus. 2007. 45p. reprint ed. 15.00 (978-1-4223-6638-7(3)) DIANE Publishing Co.

My First Nature Books, 11 bks., Set. Incl. Air. Benedict, Kitty & Soutter-Perrot, Andrienne. Delessert, Etienne, illus. lib. bdg. 14.60 (978-0-88682-547-8(4)); Ant. Benedict, Kitty. Felix, Monique, illus. lib. bdg. 14.60 (978-0-88682-564-5(4)); Cow. Benedict, Kitty. Wuest, Gerard, illus. lib. bdg. 14.60 (978-0-88682-567-6(9)); Earth. Soutter-Perrot, Andrienne. Delessert, Etienne, illus. lib. bdg. 14.60 (978-0-88682-548-5(2)); Earthworm. Soutter-Perrot, Andrienne. Delessert, Etienne, illus. lib. bdg. 14.60 (978-0-88682-566-9(0)); Fire. Soutter-Perrot, Andrienne. Gaudard, Patrick, illus. lib. bdg. 14.60 (978-0-88682-553-9(9)); Oak. Soutter-Perrot, Andrienne. Schmid, Eleonore, illus. lib. bdg. 14.60 (978-0-88682-550-8(4)); Toad. Felix, Monique, illus. lib. bdg. 14.60 (978-0-88682-568-3(7)); 32p. (J). (gr. 1-5). 1993. o.p. (978-0-88682-570-6(9), Creative Education) Creative Co., The.

My First Reference Book about Nature IR. 2017. (Reference Bks.). (ENG.). (J). 9.99 **(978-0-7945-3774-6(X)**, Usborne) EDC Publishing.

Nadeau, Isaac. Canyons. 2006. (Library of Landforms Ser.). (Illus.). 24p. (J). (gr. 3-7). lib. bdg. 22.60 (978-1-4042-3123-8(4), PowerKids Pr.) Rosen Publishing Group, Inc., The.

Natural Wonders, 1 vol. 2010. (Natural Wonders Ser.). (ENG.). 24p. (gr. k-1). pap. 13.90 (978-1-4296-6221-5(2)); lib. bdg. 106.60 (978-1-4296-5324-4(8)); pap. 29.16 (978-1-4296-5598-9(4)); lib. bdg. 79.95 (978-1-4296-5007-6(9)) Capstone Press of Coughlan Cos. (Pebble Plus).

Natural Wonders Classroom Collection. 2010. (Natural Wonders Ser.). (ENG.). 24p. (gr. k-1). pap. 250.20 (978-1-4296-5596-5(8), Pebble Plus) Capstone Press of Coughlan Cos.

Natural Wonders Collection. 2010. (Natural Wonders Ser.). (ENG.). 24p. (gr. k-1). pap. 29.16 (978-1-4296-5597-2(6), Pebble Plus) Capstone Press of Coughlan Cos.

Naturaleza. 2005. (Coleccion Primeras Imagenes).Tr. of Wind & Weather. (SPA., Illus.). 86p. (J). (gr. -1-18). pap. 7.95 (978-950-11-0989-4(5), SGM9895) Sigmar ARG. Dist: Continental Bk. Co., Inc.

Nature (Gr. PreK-5) 2003. (J). (978-1-58232-023-6(3)) ECS Learning Systems, Inc.

Nature Hike: Big Book: Level D. 8p. 20.95 (978-0-322-00366-8(0)) Wright Group/McGraw-Hill.

Nature Riddles [Capstone Sole Source]. 2010. (Nature Riddles Ser.). 32p. lib. bdg. 103.96 (978-1-4296-5873-7(8), Aplus Bks.) Capstone Press of Coughlan Cos.

Nature Watch. 2004. (Illus.). lib. bdg. 7.95 (978-0-8225-4365-7(6)) 2004. (Illus.). lib. bdg. 7.95 (978-0-8225-4353-4(2))Set. 2007. (J). (gr. 4-8). lib. bdg. 771.40 (978-0-8225-8465-0(4)) Lerner Publishing Group.

Nature's Got Talent. 2014. (Nature's Got Talent Ser.). 32p. (J). (gr. k-5). 157.50 (978-1-4777-7076-4(3)); pap. 60.00 (978-1-4777-7236-2(7)) Rosen Publishing Group, Inc., The. (PowerKids Pr.).

Nature's Mysteries. 2016. (Nature's Mysteries Ser.). 32p. (gr. 3-2). 195.60 (978-1-5081-0218-2(X)); pap. 103.20 (978-1-68048-600-1(4)) Rosen Publishing Group, Inc., The. (Britannica Educational Publishing).

Nature's Wonders, 5 bks., Set. Incl. Galapagos Islands. Kras, Sara Louise. lib. bdg. 35.64 (978-0-7614-2856-5(9)); Great Barrier Reef. Kummer, Patricia K. lib. bdg. 35.64 (978-0-7614-2852-7(6)); Great Lakes. Kummer, Patricia K. lib. bdg. 35.64 (978-0-7614-2853-4(4)); Nile River. Heinrichs, Ann. lib. bdg. 35.64 (978-0-7614-2854-1(2)); Sahara Desert. Heinrichs, Ann. lib. bdg. 35.64 (978-0-7614-2855-8(0)); 96p. (gr. 6-18). (Nature's Wonders Ser.). 2008. Set lib. bdg. 178.20 (978-0-7614-2851-0(8), Benchmark Bks.) Marshall Cavendish Corp.

Nosy Crow Staff. The Coloring Book of Cards & Envelopes: Nature. Jones, Rebecca, illus. 2016. (ENG.). 74p. (J). (gr. k-12). pap. 10.99 (978-0-7636-9245-2(X), Nosy Crow) Candlewick Pr.

Nuevo Investiguemos 8: Ciencias Naturales y de la Salud. (SPA.). (YA). (gr. 8). (978-958-02-1536-3(7)) Editorial Voluntad S.A. COL. Dist: Distribuidora Norma, Inc.

Nuevo Investiguemos 9: Ciencias Naturales y de la Salud. (SPA.). (YA). (gr. 9). (978-958-02-1537-0(5)) Editorial Voluntad S.A. COL. Dist: Distribuidora Norma, Inc.

Nunn, Daniel. ABCs in Nature, 1 vol. 2012. (Everyday Alphabet Ser.). (ENG.). 32p. (J). (gr. -1-k). pap. 9.95 (978-1-4109-4737-6(8)) Heinemann-Raintree.

Paderewski, Elliot. Animals Help Plants Pollinate. 2016. (Rosen REAL Readers: STEM & STEAM Collection). 12p. (gr. 1-k). pap. 6.33 (978-1-5081-2455-9(8), Rosen Classroom) Rosen Publishing Group, Inc., The.

Parker, Vic. Saving the Environment, 1 vol. 2012. (Kids Making a Difference Ser.). (ENG.). 48p. (gr. 3-5). pap. 9.95 (978-1-4329-6509-9(3)); lib. bdg. 32.65 (978-1-4329-6504-4(2)) Heinemann-Raintree. (NA-h).

Parramón, José María. Mi Calle. Borday, Irene, illus. (Coleccion Estoy En...).Tr. of My Street. (SPA.). 32p. (J). (gr. k-3). 6.36 (978-84-342-1003-5(7)) Parramon Ediciones S.A. ESP. Dist: Lectorum Pubns., Inc.

—Mi Casa. Borday, Irene, illus. (Coleccion Estoy En...).Tr. of My House. (SPA.). 32p. (J). (gr. k-3). 6.36 (978-84-342-1002-8(9)) Parramon Ediciones S.A. ESP. Dist: Lectorum Pubns., Inc.

—Mi Jardin. Borday, Irene, illus. (Coleccion Estoy En...).Tr. of My Garden. (SPA.). 32p. (J). (gr. k-3). 6.36 (978-84-342-1005-9(3)) Parramon Ediciones S.A. ESP. Dist: Lectorum Pubns., Inc.

Parramón, José María & Bordoy, Irene. Mi Calle.Tr. of My Street. (SPA., Illus.). (J). (gr. -1-1). 6.95 (978-958-04-1277-9(4)) Norma S.A. COL. Dist: Distribuidora Norma, Inc.

Peixe Dias, Maria Ana & Teixeira do Rosari, Ines. Outside: A Complete Guide to Discovering Nature. Carvalho, Bernardo P., illus. 2016. (ENG.). 368p. (J). (gr. 3-6). 27.99 (978-1-84780-769-4(0), Frances Lincoln Children's Bks.) Quarto Publishing Group UK GBR. Dist: Hachette Bk. Group.

Percy, J.P. Nature. 2013. (Can You Guess What I Am? Ser.). 24p. (gr. k-3). 28.50 (978-1-59920-895-4(4)) Black Rabbit Bks.

Pérols, Sylvaine. La Tierra y el Cielo. (Coleccion Mundo Maravilloso). (SPA., Illus.). 24p. (J). (gr. 2-4). (978-84-348-6322-4(7), SM30014) SM Ediciones.

Peters, Scott. What We Like. 2011. (Early Connections Ser.). (J). (978-1-61672-339-2(4)) Benchmark Education Co.

Playhouse Disney Encyclopedia. 2009. (ENG.). 196p. (gr. -1-k). 19.99 (978-1-4231-1921-0(5)) Disney Pr.

Plomer, William. The Butterfly Ball & the Grasshopper's Feast. Aldridge, Alan, illus. 2009. (ENG.). 96p. (J). (gr. k-12). 22.99 (978-0-7636-4422-2(6), Templar) Candlewick Pr.

Podojil, Catherine. Saving Endangered Species. 2005. (ENG., Illus.). 24p. (J). (gr. 5-5). pap. 5.97 net. (978-0-328-13528-8(3), Scott Foresman) Pearson Schl.

Polito, James A. My First Book of Critters. 2004. (Illus.). 24p. (J). spiral bd. 12.95 (978-0-9752842-0-9(7)) Kind Critter Junction.

Potter, Jean. La Naturaleza Explicada A Los Ninos En Pocas Palabras: Mas De 100 Actividades Realizables En 10 Minutos O Menos. 2003. (SPA.). 264p. (978-84-493-0278-7(1)) Ediciones Paidos Iberica, S.A.

Priest, Saira, photos by & des. If We Were... Priest, Saira, des. l.t. ed. 2003. (Illus.). 20p. 12.95 (978-0-9726628-7-1(1)) Niche Publishing & Marketing.

Prokos, Anna. Blades of Green: Adventures in Backyard Habitats. Blake, Mike, illus. 2017. (Imagine That! Ser.). (ENG.). 32p. (J). (gr. 2-4). lib. bdg. 26.65 (978-1-63440-147-0(6)); 39.99 **(978-1-63440-159-3(X))** Red Chair Pr.

Racanelli, Marie. Crazy Nature, 6 vols., Set. Incl. Albino Animals. (J). 2010. lib. bdg. 22.60 (978-1-4358-9381-8(6)); Animal Mimics. (YA). 2010. lib. bdg. 22.60 (978-1-4358-9382-5(4)); Animals with Armor. (J). 2010. lib. bdg. 22.60 (978-1-4358-9386-3(7)); Animals with Pockets. (J). 2010. lib. bdg. 22.60 (978-1-4358-9385-6(9)); Camouflaged Creatures. (YA). 2010. lib. bdg. 22.60 (978-1-4358-9383-2(2)); Underground Animals. (J). 2011. lib. bdg. 22.60 (978-1-4358-9384-9(0)); (gr. 1-4). (Illus.). 24p. 2010. Set lib. bdg. 127.50 (978-1-4358-9411-2(1), PowerKids Pr.) Rosen Publishing Group, Inc., The.

Randolph, Joanne. All about a Day. 2007. (It's about Time Ser.). (Illus.). 24p. (J). (gr. k-2). lib. bdg. 22.60 (978-1-4042-3767-4(4)) Rosen Publishing Group, Inc., The.

Ranger Rick's Naturescope. 2005. (Ranger Rick's Naturescope Ser.). (gr. 5-8). 279.50 (978-0-7910-9168-5(6), Chelsea Hse.) Facts On File, Inc.

Ransone, Rob & Ransone Associates Inc Staff. Lit'L Drip: The Life Story of a Drop of Water. 2010. 24p. pap. 14.99 (978-1-4490-8512-4(1)) AuthorHouse.

Rappoport, Bernice. Outside My Window. Johnson, Pamela G., illus. 2004. (Treasure Tree Ser.). 32p. (J). (978-0-7166-1622-1(X)) World Bk., Inc.

Rau, Dana Meachen. Bookworms: Nature's Cycles, 6 vols., Set. Incl. Animals. 15.95 (978-0-7614-4093-2(3)); Day & Night. 15.95 (978-0-7614-4094-9(1)); Food Chains. 15.95 (978-0-7614-4095-6(X)); Plants. 15.95 (978-0-7614-4097-0(6)); Seasons. 15.95 (978-0-7614-4098-7(4)); Water. 15.95 (978-0-7614-4099-4(2)); 32p. (gr. 1-2). (Bookworms: Nature's Cycles Ser.). 2009. Set lib. bdg. 95.70 o.p. (978-0-7614-4092-5(5)) Marshall Cavendish Corp.

—Day & Night. 2009. (Bookworms Ser.). 32p. (gr. 1-2). 15.95 (978-0-7614-4094-9(1)) Marshall Cavendish Corp.

Reda, Sheryl A. A Forest Tree House. Barrett, Peter, illus. 2004. (Treasure Tree Ser.). 32p. (J). (978-0-7166-1606-1(8)) World Bk., Inc.

Reeve, Penny. Himalayan Adventures. 2005. (Adventure Ser.). (ENG., Illus.). 96p. (J). (gr. 3-7). per. 8.99 (978-1-84550-080-1(6), 9781845500801, CF4Kids) Christian Focus Pubns. GBR. Dist: Bookmasters Distribution.

Richards, Jon. The Natural World. Simkins, Ed, illus. 2013. (World in Infographics Ser.). (ENG.). 32p. (J). (gr. 3-7). 15.95 (978-1-926973-74-6(7)) Owlkids Bks. Inc. CAN. Dist: Publishers Group West (PGW).

Richards, Jon & Simkins, Ed. The Natural World. 2016. 32p. (J). (978-0-7787-2658-6(4)) Crabtree Publishing Co.

Robbins, Eliza. Vegetables & How They Grow. 2008. (Rosen Real Readers: Upper Emergent Ser.). (ENG., Illus.). 12p. (gr. 1-2). pap. 5.90 (978-0-8239-8128-1(2)) Rosen Publishing Group, Inc., The.

Rockett, Paul. The Big Countdown. Ruffle, Mark, illus. 2015. (Big Countdown Ser.). (ENG.). 32p. (gr. 3-5). 179.94 (978-1-4109-6881-4(2), Raintree Perspectives) Heinemann-Raintree.

Ross, Michael Elsohn. Nature Art with Chiura Obata. Smith, Wendy, illus. 2005. (Naturalist's Apprentice Biographies Ser.). 48p. (gr. 3-6). lib. bdg. 19.93 (978-1-57505-378-3(0)) Lerner Publishing Group.

—Rolypolyology. 2003. (Backyard Buddies Ser.). 48p. (YA). (gr. 3-5). 6.95 (978-0-87614-901-0(8), Carolrhoda Bks.) Lerner Publishing Group.

Rotner, Shelley & Kreisler, Ken. Nature Spy. Rotner, Shelley, illus. 2014. (ENG., Illus.). 32p. (J). (gr. -1-1). pap. 13.99 (978-1-4814-5042-3(5), Atheneum Bks. for Young Readers) Simon & Schuster Children's Publishing.

Salzmann, Mary Elizabeth. Know Your Numbers: Nature, 1 vol. 2014. (Numbers 1-20 Ser.). (ENG.). 24p. (J). (gr. k-3). lib. bdg. 24.21 (978-1-62403-266-0(4), SandCastle) ABDO Publishing Co.

San Antonio 2004. 2003. (YA). 11.99 (978-0-9721368-0-8(0)) Apollo Pubs.

Scholastic Library Publishing. Nature's Children. 2012. (J). 280.00 (978-0-531-24499-9(7)); 560.00 (978-0-531-25950-4(1)) Scholastic Library Publishing. (Children's Pr.).

Schuh, Mari C. Compost Basics. 2011. (Science Builders Ser.). (ENG.). 24p. (gr. k-1). pap. 41.70 (978-1-4296-7112-5(2), Pebble Plus) Capstone Press of Coughlan Cos.

Shand, Jennifer. Why Do Rainbows Have So Many Colors? 2015. (Why Do... ? Ser.). lib. bdg. 19.65 (978-1-4867-0625-9(8)) Turtleback Bks.

Shand, Jennifer & Fabbri, Daniele. Why Do Rainbows Have So Many Colors? Paiva, Johannah Gilman, ed. 2014. (ENG., Illus.). 20p. (J). (gr. k-4). 8.99 (978-1-4867-0383-8(6)) Flowerpot Children's Pr. Inc. CAN. Dist: Cardinal Pubs. Group.

Silva Lee, Alfonso. Mi Isla y Yo: La Naturaleza de Republica Dominicana. Hayskar, Bonnie, ed. Lago, Alexis, illus. 2010. (SPA.). 32p. (J). pap. 9.95 (978-1-929165-25-4(0)) PANGAEA.

—Mon Ile et Moi: La Nature d'Haiti: Lanati an Ayti: Peym Avem. Hayskar, Bonnie, ed. Hilaire, Jean Vilmond, tr. Lago, Alexis, illus. 2010. (FRE & CRP.). 32p. (J). pap. 9.95 (978-1-929165-28-5(5)) PANGAEA.

Singley, Judith M. A B C Trees. 2012. 32p. pap. 17.25 (978-1-4669-4640-8(7)) Trafford Publishing.

Smith, Alastair. Nighttime. 2004. (Lift-the-Flap Learners Ser.). (Illus.). 16p. (J). (gr. 1-18). pap. 8.95 (978-0-7945-0366-6(7), Usborne) EDC Publishing.

Smith, Alastair & Howell, Laura. On the Beach. 2004. (Lift-the-Flap Learners Ser.). (Illus.). 16p. (J). (gr. 1-18). pap. 8.95 (978-0-7945-0213-3(X), Usborne) EDC Publishing.

Smith, Corinne Hosfeld. Henry David Thoreau for Kids: His Life & Ideas, with 21 Activities. 2016. (For Kids Ser.). (ENG., Illus.). 128p. (J). (gr. 4). pap. 16.95 (978-1-61373-146-8(9)) Chicago Review Pr., Inc.

Smith, Laurie Chance. Snapshots: Nature Stories in the Bible. 2012. 128p. (J). pap. 19.99 (978-0-8280-2689-5(0)) Review & Herald Publishing Assn.

Spilsbury, Louise & Spilsbury, Richard. Nature Walks, 1 vol. 2014. (Nature Walks Ser.). (ENG.). 24p. (gr. k-2). 93.28 (978-1-4846-0404-5(0), Heinemann Read & Learn) Heinemann-Raintree.

Spilsbury, Richard & Spilsbury, Louise. Look Inside. 2013. (Look Inside Ser.). (ENG.). 32p. (gr. 1-3). pap. 47.94 (978-1-4329-7206-6(5)); lib. bdg. 163.92 (978-1-4329-7199-1(9)) Heinemann-Raintree. (Heinemann First Library).

Start to Finish, Second Series - Nature's Cycles: Spring 2012 New Releases. 2012. (Start to Finish, Second Series: Nature's Cycles Ser.). (ENG.). 24p. (gr. k-3). lib. bdg. 143.58 (978-0-7613-6559-4(1), Lerner Pubns.) Lerner Publishing Group.

Start to Finish, Second Series, Nature's Cycles. 2012. (Start to Finish, Second Series: Nature's Cycles Ser.). (ENG.). 24p. (gr. k-3). pap. 39.62 (978-0-7613-9297-2(1));Set, Pack. pap. 237.69 (978-0-7613-9298-9(X)) Lerner Publishing Group.

Stewart, Henry. He Created Me. 2007. (Illus.). (J). 28.99 (978-1-59879-345-1(4)); per. 20.99 (978-1-59879-269-0(5)) Lifevest Publishing, Inc.

Stoop, Naoko, illus. All Creatures Great & Small. 2012. (ENG.). 22p. (J). (gr. k — 1). bds. 6.95 (978-1-4027-8581-8(X)) Sterling Publishing Co., Inc.

Story, Dan. Where Wild Things Live: Wildlife Watching Techniques & Adventures. 2009. (J). (978-0-87961-276-4(2)) Naturegraph Pubs., Inc.

Street, Sharon & National Geographic Learning Staff. Living Things Need Water. 2007. (Windows on Literacy Ser.). (ENG., Illus.). 16p. (J). (gr. k-2). pap. 11.95 (978-0-7922-9211-1(1)) CENGAGE Learning.

Sundance/Newbridge LLC Staff. The Four Seasons. 2007. (Early Science Ser.). (gr. k-3). 18.95 (978-1-4007-6143-2(3)); pap. 6.10 (978-1-4007-6139-5(5)) Sundance/Newbridge Educational Publishing.

Tallarico, Tony. Nature Trivia Mazes. 2007. (Dover Children's Activity Bks.). (ENG., Illus.). 48p. (J). (gr. 3-3). per. 4.99 (978-0-486-45364-4(2)) Dover Pubns., Inc.

Teckentrup, Britta, illus. Big & Small. 2013. (ENG.). 14p. (J). (gr. -1-k). bds. 6.99 (978-1-84686-951-8(X)) Barefoot Bks., Inc.

—Grande y Pequeno. 2013. (ENG & SPA.). 14p. (J). (gr. -1-k). bds. 6.99 (978-1-78285-034-2(1)) Barefoot Bks., Inc.

Tell Me Why, Tell Me How, 6 vols., Group 3. Incl. How Do Caterpillars Become Butterflies? Bailer, Darice. 29.93 (978-0-7614-3987-5(0)); How Do Mountains Form? Hicks, Terry Allan. 29.93 (978-0-7614-3992-9(7)); Why Do Bears Hibernate? Bailer, Darice. 29.93 (978-0-7614-3990-5(0)); Why Do Volcanoes Erupt? Mara, Wil. 29.93 (978-0-7614-3989-9(7)); Why Does It Rain? Mara, Wil. 29.93 (978-0-7614-3991-2(9)); Why Does the Sun Set? Hicks, Terry Allan. 29.93 (978-0-7614-3993-6(5)); 32p. (gr. 3-18). (Tell Me Why, Tell Me How 3 Ser.). 2009. Set lib. bdg. 179.58 o.p. (978-0-7614-3986-8(2)) Marshall Cavendish Corp.

Tell Me Why, Tell Me How, 6 bks., Set. Incl. How Do Birds Fly? Stewart, Melissa. (J). (gr. 3-7). lib. bdg. 29.93 (978-0-7614-2110-8(6)); How Do Fish Breathe Underwater? Stewart, Melissa. (J). lib. bdg. 29.93 (978-0-7614-2109-2(2)); How Do Plants Grow? Stewart, Melissa. (gr. 3-7). lib. bdg. 29.93 (978-0-7614-2111-5(4)); How Does the Wind Blow? Murphy, Patricia J. (J). (gr. 3-7). lib. bdg. 29.93 (978-0-7614-2107-8(6)); Why Do the Seasons Change? Stewart, Melissa. (gr. 3-7). lib. bdg. 29.93 (978-0-7614-2112-2(2)); Why Is the Sky Blue? Mara, Wil. (J). (gr. 3-7). lib. bdg. 28.50 (978-0-7614-2108-5(4)); (Illus.). 32p. 2006. 2007. Set lib. bdg. 171.00 (978-0-7614-2106-1(8), Benchmark Bks.) Marshall Cavendish Corp.

Thoreau, Henry. Walking. Clifton Johnson, illus. 2010. 100p. pap. 3.49 (978-1-60386-305-6(2), Watchmaker Publishing) Wexford College Pr.

Tief im Meer. (GER.). 19.95 (978-3-411-09271-0(8)) Bibliographisches Institut & F. A. Brockhaus AG DEU. Dist: Distribooks, Inc.

Tiere unter der Erde. (GER.). (978-3-411-09251-2(3)) Bibliographisches Institut & F. A. Brockhaus AG DEU. Dist: i. b. d., Ltd.

Tilmont, Amy. Man vs. Animal: Species at Risk. 2011. (Second Nature Ser.). 48p. (J). (gr. 5-8). lib. bdg. 26.60 (978-1-59953-460-2(6)) Norwood Hse. Pr.

Tomio, Stacy & Keffer, Ken. The Kids' Outdoor Adventure Book: 448 Great Things to Do in Nature Before You Grow Up. 2013. (ENG., Illus.). 224p. pap. 18.95 (978-0-7627-8352-6(4), Falcon Guides) Globe Pequot Pr., The.

—The Truth about Nature: A Family's Guide to 144 Common Myths about the Great Outdoors. 2014. (ENG., Illus.). 232p. pap. 18.95 (978-0-7627-9628-1(6), Falcon Guides) Globe Pequot Pr., The.

Tullet, Hervé. The Countryside Game. 2013. (ENG., Illus.). 14p. 12.95 (978-0-7148-6074-9(3)) Phaidon Pr., Inc.

Tuxworth, Nicola. Nature. 2015. (ENG., Illus.). 20p. bds. 6.99 (978-1-86147-411-7(3), Armadillo) Anness Publishing GBR. Dist: National Bk. Network.

Unpredictable Nature: Changing Man's Daily Life, 15 vols., Set. Incl. Archeology. Farndon, John. (Illus.). lib. bdg. 19.95 (978-1-4222-1994-2(1)); Coral Reef. De la Bédoyère, Camilla. (Illus.). lib. bdg. 19.95 (978-1-4222-1995-9(X)); Deadly Creatures. De la Bédoyère, Camilla. (Illus.). lib. bdg. 19.95 (978-1-4222-1996-6(8)); Deep Ocean. De la Bédoyère, Camilla. (Illus.). lib. bdg. 19.95 (978-1-4222-1997-3(6)); Extinction. Parker, Steve. (Illus.). lib. bdg. 19.95 (978-1-4222-1998-0(4)); Extreme Survival. Green, Jen. (Illus.). lib. bdg. 19.95 (978-1-4222-1999-7(2)); Fossils. Parker, Steve. (Illus.). lib. bdg. 19.95 (978-1-4222-2000-9(1)); Magic & Mystery. Scott, Carey. (Illus.). lib. bdg. 19.95 (978-1-4222-2001-6(X)); Prehistoric Life. Matthews, Rupert. (Illus.). lib. bdg. 19.95 (978-1-4222-2003-0(6)); Rainforests. De la Bédoyère, Camilla. (Illus.). lib. bdg. 19.95 (978-1-4222-2004-7(4)); Rocks & Minerals. Callery, Sean. (Illus.). lib. bdg. 19.95 (978-1-4222-2005-4(2)); Seashore. Parker, Steve. (Illus.). lib. bdg. 19.95 (978-1-4222-2006-1(0)); Volcanoes. Oxlade, Chris. (Illus.). lib. bdg. 19.95 (978-1-4222-2007-8(9)); World Wonders. Hibbert, Adam. lib. bdg. 19.95 (978-1-4222-2008-5(7)); 48p. (J). (gr. 3-18). 2010. 2011. Set lib. bdg. 299.25 (978-1-4222-1993-5(3)) Mason Crest.

Usborne Books Staff, creator. 100 Things to Spot in the Night Sky. 2008. (Spotter's Cards Ser.). (Illus.). 52p. (J). 9.99 (978-0-7945-1966-7(0), Usborne) EDC Publishing.

Vann, Donna. Wild West Adventures. 2006. (Adventure Ser.). (ENG., Illus.). 96p. (J). per. 8.99 (978-1-84550-065-8(2), 9f994332-def5-4d9f-abc1-2f97eaba348d) Christian Focus Pubns. GBR. Dist: Bookmasters Distribution.

Wadkovsky, Alex. Forces of Mother Nature. 2010. 20p. 13.99 (978-1-4520-5370-7(7)) AuthorHouse.

Walton, Rick. The Sky's the Limit: Naturally Funny Jokes. Gable, Brian, illus. 2005. (Make Me Laugh! Ser.). 32p. (J). (gr. k-3). lib. bdg. 19.93 (978-1-57505-663-0(1)) Lerner Publishing Group.

Wargin, Kathy-jo. K Is for Kite: God's Springtime Alphabet, 1 vol. Gatto, Kim, illus. 2010. (ENG.). 40p. (J). (gr. -1-2). 15.99 (978-0-310-71662-4(4)) Zonderkidz.

Water Goes Round, 4 vols. Incl. Eggs, Legs, Wings: A Butterfly Life Cycle. Knudsen, Shannon. Smith, Simon, illus. lib. bdg. 23.99 (978-1-4296-5367-1(1)); Hide & Seek Moon: The Moon Phases. Koontz, Robin Michal. Davidson, Chris, illus. 23.99 (978-1-4296-5365-7(5)); Water Goes Round: The Water Cycle. Koontz, Robin Michal. Davidson, Chris, illus. lib. bdg. 23.99 (978-1-4296-5364-0(7)); (gr. 1-2). (First Graphics: Nature Cycles Ser.). (ENG.). 24p. 2010. Set lib. bdg. 71.97 (978-1-4296-5368-8(X)) Capstone Press of Coughlan Cos.

Watson, Lori Ann. Beginnings. Bersani, Shennen, illus. 2009. 32p. (J). (gr. -1-1). 12.95 (978-0-8198-1172-1(6)) Pauline Bks. & Media.

We Can Read about Nature! - Group 3, 6 bks., Set. 128.14 (978-0-7614-1429-2(0), Benchmark Bks.) Marshall Cavendish Corp.

West, Edith. A World Just for Me. 2009. 32p. pap. 13.99 (978-1-4389-7083-7(8)) AuthorHouse.

Weston Woods Staff, creator. Giving Thanks. 2011. 38.75 (978-0-439-72676-4(X)); 18.95 (978-0-439-72673-3(5)); 29.95 (978-0-439-73469-1(X)) Weston Woods Studios, Inc.

World Book, Inc Staff, contrib. by. Nature's Patterns. 2010. (J). (978-0-7166-7740-6(7)) World Bk., Inc.

—Wildlife & Climate Change. 2015. (Illus.). 44p. (J). (978-0-7166-2709-8(4)) World Bk., Inc.

Wright, Holly. Sky. 2004. (Illus.). (J). (978-0-9743690-9-9(8)) Britt Allcroft Productions.

Zondervan Bibles Staff. Big Bugs, Little Bugs, 1 vol. 2011. (I Can Read! / Made by God Ser.). (ENG., Illus.). 32p. (J). (gr. -1-2). pap. 3.99 (978-0-310-72186-4(5)) Zonderkidz.

Zoobooks, 56 bks., Set. Incl. Animal Champions. Wexo, John Bonnett. 32p. (gr. 1-4). lib. bdg. 19.95 (978-0-88682-409-9(5)); Animal Champions 2. Shaw, Marjorie B. & Elwood, Ann. 24p. (gr. 1-4). lib. bdg. 19.95 (978-0-88682-774-8(4)); Animal Wonders. Wexo, John Bonnett. 32p. (gr. 1-4). lib. bdg. 14.95 (978-0-88682-407-5(9)); Apes. Wexo, John Bonnett. 24p. (gr. 2-12). lib. bdg. 19.95 (978-0-88682-265-1(3)); Baby Animals. Wexo, John Bonnett. 24p. (gr. 1-4). lib. bdg. 19.95 (978-0-88682-270-5(X)); Bats. Wood, Linda C. & Rink, Deane. 24p. (gr. 2-12). lib. bdg. 19.95 (978-0-88682-337-5(4)); Bears. Wexo, John Bonnett. 24p. (gr. 3-12). lib. bdg. 19.95 (978-0-88682-221-7(1)); Birds of Prey. Wexo, John Bonnett. 24p. (gr. 2-12). lib. bdg. 19.95 (978-0-88682-332-0(3)); Butterflies. Brust, Beth Wagner. 32p. (gr. 3-12). lib. bdg. 19.95 (978-0-88682-421-1(4)); Camels. Wexo, John Bonnett. 32p. (gr. 2-12). lib. bdg. 19.95 (978-0-88682-222-4(X)); Cheetahs. Wood, Linda C. & Jenson, Cynthia L. 32p. (gr. 2-12). lib. bdg. 19.95 (978-0-88682-417-4(6)); Chimpanzees & Bonobos. Elwood, Ann. 24p. (gr. 2-12). lib. bdg. 19.95 (978-0-88682-340-5(4)); Deer Family. Biel, Timothy Levi. 24p. (gr. 2-12). lib. bdg. 19.95 (978-0-88682-775-5(2)); Dinosaurs. Wexo, John Bonnett. 24p. (gr. 2-12). lib. bdg. 19.95 (978-0-88682-223-1(8)); Dolphins & Porpoises. Brust, Beth Wagner. 24p. (gr. 2-12). lib. bdg. 19.95 (978-0-88682-339-9(0)); Ducks, Geese & Swans. Wexo, John Bonnett. 24p. (gr. 3-12). lib. bdg. 19.95 (978-0-88682-224-8(6)); Eagles. Richardson, Adele D. 24p. (gr. 2-12). lib. bdg. 19.95 (978-0-88682-225-5(4)); Elephants. Wexo, John Bonnett. 24p. (gr. 2-12). lib. bdg. 19.95 (978-0-88682-226-2(2)); Endangered Animals. Wexo, John Bonnett. 24p. (gr. 2-12). lib. bdg. 19.95 (978-0-88682-269-9(6)); Giant Pandas. Wexo, John Bonnett. 24p. (gr. 2-12). lib. bdg. 19.95 (978-0-88682-228-6(9)); Giraffes. Wexo, John Bonnett. 24p. (gr. 2-12). lib. bdg. 19.95 (978-0-88682-334-4(X)); Gorillas. Wexo, John Bonnett. 32p. (gr. 2-12). lib. bdg. 19.95 (978-0-88682-423-5(0)); Hippos. Brust, Beth Wagner. 32p. (gr. 2-12). lib. bdg. 19.95 (978-0-88682-424-2(9)); Hummingbirds. Biel, Timothy Levi. 24p. (gr. 2-12). lib. bdg. 19.95 (978-0-88682-336-8(6)); Insects. Wexo, John Bonnett. 24p. (gr. 2-12). lib. bdg. 19.95 (978-0-88682-335-1(8)); Insects 2. Wexo, John Bonnett. 24p. (gr. 2-12). lib. bdg. 19.95 (978-0-88682-776-2(0)); Kangaroos. Brust, Beth Wagner. 32p. (gr. 2-12). lib. bdg. 19.95 (978-0-88682-425-9(7)); Koalas. Wexo, John Bonnett. 24p. (gr. 2-12). lib. bdg. 19.95 (978-0-88682-227-9(0)); Lions. Elwood, Ann & Estrada, Jackie. 32p. (gr. 2-12). lib. bdg. 19.95 (978-0-88682-422-8(2)); Little Cats. Wexo, John Bonnett. 32p. (gr. 2-12). lib. bdg. 19.95 (978-0-88682-413-6(3)); Night Animals. Wexo, John Bonnett. 24p. (gr. 2-12). lib. bdg. 19.95 (978-0-88682-777-9(9)); Old World Monkeys. Elwood, Ann. 32p. (gr. 3-12). lib. bdg. 19.95 (978-0-88682-419-8(2)); Orangutans. Wexo, John Bonnett. 32p. (gr. 2-12). lib. bdg. 19.95 (978-0-88682-412-9(5)); Ostriches, Emus, Rheas, Kiwis & Cassowaries. Elwood, Ann. 24p. (gr. 2-12). lib. bdg. 19.95 (978-0-88682-338-2(2)); Owls. Biel, Timothy Levi. 24p. (gr. 3-12). lib. bdg. 19.95 (978-0-88682-268-2(8)); Parrots. Wexo, John Bonnett. 32p. (gr. 2-12). lib. bdg. 19.95 (978-0-88682-408-2(7)); Penguins. Wexo, John Bonnett. 24p. (gr. 2-12). lib. bdg. 19.95 (978-0-88682-263-7(7)); Polar Bears. Biel, Timothy Levi. 32p. (gr. 2-12). lib. bdg. 19.95 (978-0-88682-414-3(1)); Rattlesnakes. Brust, Beth Wagner & Dorn, Bob. 32p. (gr. 2-12). lib. bdg. 19.95 (978-0-88682-426-6(5)); Rhinos. Wexo, John Bonnett. 24p. (gr. 2-12). lib. bdg. 19.95 (978-0-88682-333-7(1)); Sea Birds. Brust, Beth Wagner. 32p. (gr. 2-12). lib. bdg. 19.95 (978-0-88682-416-7(8)); Sea Otters. Brust, Beth Wagner. 32p. (gr. 2-12). lib. bdg. 19.95 (978-0-88682-415-0(X)); Seals, Sea Lions & Walruses. Wexo, John Bonnett. 24p. (gr. 2-12). lib. bdg. 19.95 (978-0-88682-271-2(8)); Sharing the World with Animals. Shaw, Marjorie B. & Elwood, Ann. 24p. (gr. 1-4). lib. bdg. 19.95 (978-0-88682-778-6(7)); Sharks. Wexo, John Bonnett. 24p. (gr. 2-12). lib. bdg. 19.95 (978-0-88682-229-3(7)); Skunks & Their Relatives. Biel, Timothy Levi. 24p. (gr. 2-12). lib. bdg. 19.95 (978-0-88682-779-3(5)); Snakes. Wexo, John Bonnett. 24p. (gr. 2-12). lib. bdg. 19.95 (978-0-88682-331-3(5)); Spiders. Biel, Timothy Levi. 32p. (gr. 2-12). lib. bdg. 19.95 (978-0-88682-410-5(9)); Tigers. Biel, Timothy Levi. 24p. (gr. 2-12). lib. bdg. 19.95 (978-0-88682-266-8(1)); Turtles. Biel, Timothy Levi. 32p. (gr. 2-12). lib. bdg. 19.95 (978-0-88682-411-2(7)); Whales. Wexo, John Bonnett. 24p. (gr. 2-12). lib. bdg. 19.95 (978-0-88682-272-9(6)); Wolves. Wexo, John Bonnett. 24p. (gr. 2-12). lib. bdg. 19.95 (978-0-88682-267-5(X)); Zebras. Wood, Linda C. 32p. (gr. 2-12). lib. bdg. 19.95 (978-0-88682-420-4(6)); (J). 1995. (Illus.). 1157.10 (978-0-88682-238-5(6), Creative Education) Creative Co., The.

NATURE (AESTHETICS)

Baumbusch, Brigitte. Nature in Art. 2005. (What Makes a Masterpiece? Ser.). (Illus.). 32p. (gr. 1-4). lib. bdg. 23.00 (978-0-8368-4448-1(3), Gareth Stevens Learning Library) Stevens, Gareth Publishing LLLP.

Luxbacher, Irene. The Jumbo Book of Outdoor Art. Luxbacher, Irene, illus. 2006. (Jumbo Bks.). (ENG., Illus.). 144p. (J). (gr. 3-7). 16.95 (978-1-55337-680-4(3)) Kids Can Pr., Ltd. CAN. Dist: Hachette Bk. Group.

Noble, Marty, et al. Nature Mandalas. 2012. (Adult Coloring Ser.). (ENG., Illus.). 64p. (gr. 3). pap. 5.99 (978-0-486-49137-0(4)) Dover Pubns., Inc.

NATURE CRAFT

Bolte, Mari. Amazing Outdoor Art: You Can Make & Share. 2015. (Sleepover Girls Crafts Ser.). (ENG., Illus.). 64p. (gr. 3-4). pap. 9.95 (978-1-62370-423-0(5)) Capstone Press of Coughlan Cos.

—Amazing Outdoor Art You Can Make & Share. 2015. (Sleepover Girls Crafts Ser.). (ENG., Illus.). 32p. (gr. 3-4). lib. bdg. 27.99 (978-1-4765-0229-8(3), Snap Bks.) Capstone Press of Coughlan Cos.

Chapman, Gillian & Robson, Pam. Making Art with Sand & Earth. 2007. (Everyday Art Ser.). (Illus.). 32p. (YA). (gr. 4-7). lib. bdg. 26.50 (978-1-4042-3723-0(2)) Rosen Publishing Group, Inc., The.

—Making Art with Wood. 2007. (Everyday Art Ser.). (Illus.). 32p. (YA). (gr. 4-7). lib. bdg. 26.50 (978-1-4042-3726-1(7)) Rosen Publishing Group, Inc., The.

Crexells, Cristina, et al. Plants & Seeds. 2003. (Let's Create! Ser.). (Illus.). 32p. (gr. 1-4). lib. bdg. 26.00 (978-0-8368-3748-3(7), Gareth Stevens Learning Library) Stevens, Gareth Publishing LLLP.

Forte, Imogene. Nature Crafts. 2004. (Fun Things to Make & Do Ser.). (Illus.). 80p. (J). per. 9.95 (978-0-86530-617-2(6)) Incentive Pubns., Inc.

Henry, Sally & Cook, Trevor. Eco Crafts. 2010. (Make Your Own Art Ser.). (Illus.). 32p. (J). pap. 11.75 (978-1-4488-1611-8(4)); (gr. 3-6). lib. bdg. 26.50 (978-1-4488-1582-1(7)) Rosen Publishing Group, Inc., The. (PowerKids Pr.).

Jones, Jen. Cool Crafts with Flowers, Leaves, & Twigs: Green Projects for Resourceful Kids, 1 vol. 2010. (Green Crafts Ser.). (ENG.). 32p. (gr. 3-4). lib. bdg. 27.99 (978-1-4296-4766-3(3), Snap Bks.) Capstone Press of Coughlan Cos.

—Cool Crafts with Seeds, Beans, & Cones: Green Projects for Resourceful Kids, 1 vol. 2010. (Green Crafts Ser.). (ENG.). 32p. (gr. 3-4). lib. bdg. 27.99 (978-1-4296-4767-0(1), Snap Bks.) Capstone Press of Coughlan Cos.

Levete, Sarah. Maker Projects for Kids Who Love Exploring the Outdoors. 2016. (Be a Maker! Ser.). (ENG., Illus.). 32p. (J). (gr. 5-8). (978-0-7787-2576-3(6)) Crabtree Publishing Co.

Lim, Annalees. Nature Crafts, Vol. 1. 2014. (Craft Attack! Ser.). 32p. (J). (gr. 3-3). (ENG.). pap. 10.50 (978-1-4824-0205-6(X)); 26.60 (978-1-4824-0203-2(3)) Stevens, Gareth Publishing LLLP.

Llimós, Anna. Earth-Friendly Crafts with Nuts & Veggies in 5 Easy Steps. 2013. (Earth-Friendly Crafts in 5 Easy Steps Ser.). 32p. (J). (gr. 3-4). pap. 7.95 (978-1-4644-0313-2(9), Enslow Elementary) Enslow Pubs., Inc.

Llimós Plomer, Anna. Earth-Friendly Crafts with Nuts & Veggies in 5 Easy Steps. 2013. (Earth-Friendly Crafts in 5 Easy Steps Ser.). (Illus.). 32p. (J). lib. bdg. 23.94 (978-0-7660-4191-2(3)) Enslow Pubs., Inc.

Martin, Laura C. & Cain, David. Nature's Art Box: From T-Shirts to Twig Baskets, 65 Cool Projects for Crafty Kids to Make with Natural Materials You Can Find Anywhere. Cain, David, illus. 2003. (ENG., Illus.). 192p. (J). (gr. 3-8). pap. 16.95 (978-1-58017-490-9(6), 67490) Storey Publishing, LLC.

Parramon's Editorial Team Staff. Stones & "Stuff" Parramon's Editorial Team Staff, photos by. 2004. (Let's Create! Ser.). (Illus.). 32p. (gr. 1-4). lib. bdg. 26.00 (978-0-8368-4019-3(4), Gareth Stevens Learning Library) Stevens, Gareth Publishing LLLP.

Ryall, Jeanette. Nature Art. 2012. (Awesome Art Ser.). (ENG., Illus.). 32p. (J). (gr. 3-6). 26.50 (978-1-4488-8088-1(2)); pap. 11.75 (978-1-4488-8141-3(2)) Windmill Bks.

—Sand Art. 2012. (Awesome Art Ser.). (ENG., Illus.). 32p. (J). (gr. 3-6). 26.50 (978-1-4488-8090-4(4)); pap. 11.75 (978-1-4488-8143-7(9)) Windmill Bks.

Senisi, Ellen B. Berry Smudges & Leaf Prints: Finding & Making Colors from Nature. Senisi, Ellen B., photos by. 2005. (Illus.). 40p. (J). (gr. 4-8). reprint ed. 17.00 (978-0-7567-9707-2(1)) DIANE Publishing Co.

NATURE—EFFECT OF HUMAN BEINGS ON

Blake, Kevin. Feral Pigs: Chomp, Chomp! 2015. (They Don't Belong: Tracking Invasive Species Ser.). (ENG., Illus.). 32p. (J). (gr. 2-7). lib. bdg. 26.60 (978-1-62724-829-7(3)) Bearport Publishing Co., Inc.

—Guam's Brown Tree Snakes: Hanging Out. 2015. (They Don't Belong: Tracking Invasive Species Ser.). (ENG., Illus.). 32p. (J). (gr. 2-7). lib. bdg. 26.60 (978-1-62724-830-3(7)) Bearport Publishing Co., Inc.

Bodden, Valerie. Wildlife in Danger. 2010. (Earth Issues Ser.). (Illus.). 48p. (J). (gr. 5-18). 23.95 (978-1-58341-987-8(X), Creative Education) Creative Co., The.

Booth, Edison. Animals & Their Environments. 2016. (Spotlight on Ecology & Life Science Ser.). 00024p. (J). (gr. 4-6). 26.25 (978-1-4994-2558-1(9)); pap. 10.00 (978-1-4994-2556-7(2)) Rosen Publishing Group, Inc., The. (PowerKids Pr.).

Buchanan, Shelly. Shaping Our Environment. rev. ed. 2014. (Primary Source Readers Content & Literacy Ser.). (ENG., Illus.). 32p. (gr. 3-3). pap. 8.99 (978-1-4333-7368-8(8)) Teacher Created Materials, Inc.

Callery, Sean. I Wonder Why There's a Hole in the Sky. 2012. (I Wonder Why Ser.). (ENG., Illus.). 32p. (J). (gr. k-3). 6.99 (978-0-7534-6799-2(2), 9780753467992, Kingfisher) Roaring Brook Pr.

Changing Climates. 2010. (Global Connections Ser.). (Illus.). 120p. (gr. 5-8). 35.00 (978-1-60413-291-5(4), Chelsea Hse.) Facts On File, Inc.

Cherry, Lynne. A River Ran Wild. 2015. 40p. pap. 7.00 (978-1-61003-490-6(2)) Center for the Collaborative Classroom.

—A River Ran Wild. 2005. 17.00 (978-0-7569-5231-0(X)) Perfection Learning Corp.

Collard, Sneed B. & Collard, Sneed B., III. Australia's Cane Toads: Overrun! 2015. (They Don't Belong: Tracking Invasive Species Ser.). (ENG., Illus.). 32p. (J). (gr. 2-7). lib.

bdg. 26.60 (978-1-62724-828-0(5)) Bearport Publishing Co., Inc.

Dal Fuoco, Gina. Spaceship Earth, 1 vol. 2007. (Science Readers Ser.). (ENG., Illus.). 32p. (J). (gr. 4-4). pap. 8.99 (978-0-7439-0565-7(2)) Shell Educational Publishing.

Diamond, Jared. The Third Chimpanzee for Young People: On the Evolution & Future of the Human Animal. 2015. (For Young People Ser.). (ENG., Illus.). 368p. (J). (gr. 7). pap. 17.95 (978-1-60980-611-8(5), Triangle Square) Seven Stories Pr.

Donnelly, Karen. Biomes of the Past & Future. 2003. (Earth's Changing Weather & Climate Ser.). (Illus.). 24p. (J). lib. bdg. 22.60 (978-0-8239-6215-0(6), PowerKids Pr.) Rosen Publishing Group, Inc., The.

—Rising Temperatures of the Past & Future. 2009. (Earth's Changing Weather & Climate Ser.). 24p. (gr. 4-4). 42.50 (978-1-61512-249-3(4), PowerKids Pr.) Rosen Publishing Group, Inc., The.

—Rising Temperatures of the Past & the Future. 2003. (Earth's Changing Weather & Climate Ser.). (Illus.). 24p. (J). lib. bdg. 22.60 (978-0-8239-6214-3(8), PowerKids Pr.) Rosen Publishing Group, Inc., The.

Downer, Ann. Wild Animal Neighbors: Sharing Our Urban World. 2013. 64p. pap. 24.95 (978-1-4677-1663-5(4)); (ENG., Illus.). (gr. 5-12). 33.27 (978-0-7613-9021-3(9), Twenty-First Century Bks.) Lerner Publishing Group.

Doyle, James. A Young Scientist's Guide to Faulty Freaks of Nature, 1 vol. Brozyna, Andrew, illus. 2013. (ENG.). 160p. (J). (gr. 5-6). 14.99 (978-1-4236-2455-4(6)) Gibbs Smith, Publisher.

—A Young Scientist's Guide to Faulty Freaks of Nature: Including 20 Experiments for the Sink, Bathtub & Backyard (Large Print 16pt) 2013. 200p. pap. (978-1-4596-5848-6(5)) ReadHowYouWant.com, Ltd.

Green, Mary. Rivers in Action. 2004. (Earth's Changing Landscape Ser.). (Illus.). 46p. (YA). (gr. 7-12). lib. bdg. 28.50 (978-1-58340-477-5(5)) Black Rabbit Bks.

Hawley, Ella. Exploring Our Impact on the Environment. 2012. (Let's Explore Life Science Ser.). (ENG., Illus.). 24p. (J). (gr. 3-6). pap. 8.25 (978-1-4488-6308-2(2)); lib. bdg. 22.60 (978-1-4488-6177-4(2)) Rosen Publishing Group, Inc., The. (PowerKids Pr.).

Hunter, Nick. Offshore Oil Drilling, 1 vol. 2011. (Hot Topics Ser.). (ENG., Illus.). 56p. (gr. 7-8). 34.65 (978-1-4329-5176-4(9), NA-h) Heinemann-Raintree.

Iyengar, Godha. The Stinkiest Day in May: The Story of a Stink. 2010. (Illus.). 22p. (J). pap. 16.95 (978-1-4327-4825-8(4)) Outskirts Pr., Inc.

Jakab, Cheryl. Ecological Footprints. 2010. (Environment in Focus Ser.). 32p. (gr. 4). 28.50 (978-1-60870-088-2(7)) Marshall Cavendish Corp.

Jerome, Kate Boehm & National Geographic Learning Staff. Protecting the Planet. 2007. (Reading Expeditions Ser.). (ENG., Illus.). 32p. (J). pap. 17.95 (978-0-7922-8864-0(5)) CENGAGE Learning.

Kinsner, Kathy. Relationships in Nature & Relaciones en la Naturaleza: 6 English, 6 Spanish Adaptations. 2011. (ENG & SPA.). (J). 101.00 net. (978-1-4108-5729-3(8)) Benchmark Education Co.

Kirk, Ellen. Human Footprint: Everything You Will Eat, Use, Wear, Buy, & Throw Out in Your Lifetime. 2011. (ENG., Illus.). 32p. (J). (gr. 3-7). pap. 6.95 (978-1-4263-0767-6(5), National Geographic Children's Bks.) National Geographic Society.

Leathers, Dan. The Snows of Kilimanjaro. 2007. (On the Verge of Extinction Ser.). (Illus.). 32p. (YA). (gr. 2-5). lib. bdg. 25.70 (978-1-58415-584-3(1)) Mitchell Lane Pubs., Inc.

Lepetit, Angie. Three Cheers for Trees! A Book about Our Carbon Footprint, 1 vol. 2013. (Earth Matters Ser.). (ENG.). 32p. (gr. 1-2). pap. 8.10 (978-1-62065-741-6(4)); pap. 47.70 (978-1-62065-742-3(2)); lib. bdg. 27.32 (978-1-62065-048-6(7)) Capstone Press of Coughlan Cos. (Aplus Bks.).

Lundgren, Julie K. How Do Humans Depend on Earth? 2012. (ENG., Illus.). 24p. (J). (gr. 4-5). pap. 8.95 (978-1-61810-238-6(9)) Rourke Educational Media.

Maloof, Torrey. People & the Planet, 1 vol. 2015. (Science Readers: Content & Literacy Ser.). (ENG., Illus.). 32p. (gr. 3-3). pap. 8.99 (978-1-4807-4650-3(9)) Teacher Created Materials, Inc.

Mason, Adrienne. Planet Ark: Preserving Earth's Biodiversity. Thompson, Margot, illus. 2013. (CitizenKid Ser.). (ENG.). 32p. (J). (gr. 3-7). 18.95 (978-1-55453-753-2(3)) Kids Can Pr., Ltd. CAN. Dist: Hachette Bk. Group.

Morgan, Anne. The Smallest Carbon Footprint in the Land & Other Eco-Tales. McKinnon, Gay, illus. 2012. 80p. pap. (978-1-922120-23-6(5), IP Kidz) Interactive Pubns. Pty, Ltd.

Morrison, Yvonne. Earth Partners: Saving the Planet. 2007. (Shockwave: History & Politics Ser.). (Illus.). 36p. (J). (gr. 4-6). (ENG.). lib. bdg. 25.00 (978-0-531-17753-2(X)); pap. 6.95 (978-0-531-15489-2(0)) Scholastic Library Publishing. (Children's Pr.).

Nelson, John. Collision Course: Asteroids & Earth. 2009. (Jr. Graphic Environmental Dangers Ser.). (ENG., Illus.). 24p. (gr. 3-8). pap. 10.60 (978-1-4042-4595-2(2), PowerKids Pr.) Rosen Publishing Group, Inc., The.

Orme, Helen. Habitat Destruction. 2008. (Earth in Danger Ser.). (Illus.). 32p. (YA). (gr. 3-6). lib. bdg. 25.27 (978-1-59716-725-3(8), 1284353) Bearport Publishing Co., Inc.

The Power of Nature. 2015. (Power of Nature Ser.). (ENG.). 48p. (J). (gr. 4-4). 188.16 (978-1-5026-0306-7(3)) Cavendish Square Publishing.

Redlin, Janice L. Saving the Natural World. 2006. (Understanding Global Issues Ser.). (Illus.). 56p. per. 11.95 (978-1-59036-510-6(0), 1266440) Weigl Pubs., Inc.

Riley, Joelle. Erosion. 2006. (Early Bird Earth Science Ser.). (Illus.). 48p. (J). (gr. 3-7). lib. bdg. 25.26 (978-0-8225-5949-8(8), Lerner Pubns.) Lerner Publishing Group.

Rooney, Anne. Reducing the Carbon Footprint. 2010. (World at Risk Ser.). (YA). (gr. 5-9). 34.25 (978-1-59920-375-1(8)) Black Rabbit Bks.

Rose, Elizabeth. Human Impact on the Environment. (Life Science Library). 24p. (gr. 3-4). 2009. 42.50 (978-1-60854-006-8(5), PowerKids Pr.) 2006. (Illus.). (YA). lib. bdg. 22.60 (978-1-4042-2822-1(5)) Rosen Publishing Group, Inc., The.

Royston, Angela. The Race to Survive Climate Change. 2014. (World in Crisis Ser.). 48p. (YA). (gr. 5-8). 30.25 (978-1-4777-7848-7(9), Rosen Reference) Rosen Publishing Group, Inc., The.

Sawyer, Ava. Human Environmental Impact: How We Affect Earth. 2017. (Humans & Our Planet Ser.). (ENG.). 32p. (gr. 3-4). lib. bdg. 27.32 **(978-1-5157-7196-8(2)**, Fact Finders) Capstone Press of Coughlan Cos.

—Humans & Earth's Atmosphere: What's in the Air? 2017. (Humans & Our Planet Ser.). (ENG.). 32p. (gr. 3-4). lib. bdg. 27.32 **(978-1-5157-7199-9(7)**, Fact Finders) Capstone Press of Coughlan Cos.

—Humans & Other Life on Earth: Sharing the Planet. 2017. (Humans & Our Planet Ser.). (ENG.). 32p. (gr. 3-4). lib. bdg. 27.32 **(978-1-5157-7197-5(0)**, Fact Finders) Capstone Press of Coughlan Cos.

—Humans & the Hydrosphere: Protecting Earth's Water Sources. 2017. (Humans & Our Planet Ser.). (ENG.). 32p. (gr. 3-4). lib. bdg. 27.32 **(978-1-5157-7198-2(9)**, Fact Finders) Capstone Press of Coughlan Cos.

Schafer, Susan. Invasive Mammals. 2016. (Invasive Species Ser.). (ENG.). 48p. (J). (gr. 4-4). 31.36 (978-1-5026-1832-0(X)) Cavendish Square Publishing.

—Invasive Reptiles & Amphibians. 2016. (Invasive Species Ser.). 48p. (J). (gr. 4-4). 31.36 (978-1-5026-1830-6(3)) Cavendish Square Publishing.

Shone, Rob. Avalanches & Landslides. (Graphic Natural Disasters Ser.). (ENG.). 48p. (gr. 5-5). 2009. (YA). 58.50 (978-1-61512-994-2(4), Rosen Reference) 2007. (Illus.). (J). lib. bdg. 31.95 (978-1-4042-1992-2(7)) Rosen Publishing Group, Inc., The.

—Avalanches & Mudslides. 2007. (Graphic Natural Disasters Ser.). (ENG., Illus.). 48p. (gr. 5-8). pap. 14.05 (978-1-4042-1983-0(8)) Rosen Publishing Group, Inc., The.

Sirota, Lyn. People & the Planet. 2016. (Let's Explore Science Ser.). (ENG., Illus.). 48p. (gr. 5-8). 35.64 (978-1-68191-396-4(8)) Rourke Educational Media.

Smith, Andrea Claire Harte. The Effects of Farming. 2004. (Earth's Changing Landscape Ser.). (Illus.). 45p. (J). lib. bdg. 28.50 (978-1-58340-475-1(9)) Black Rabbit Bks.

Smith, Paula. Be the Change for the Environment. 2014. (ENG., Illus.). 24p. (J). (978-0-7787-0620-5(6)) Crabtree Publishing Co.

Snedden, Robert. The Growth of Cities. 2004. (Earth's Changing Landscape Ser.). (J). lib. bdg. 28.50 (978-1-58340-474-4(0)) Black Rabbit Bks.

Steele, Phillip W. Changing Coastlines. 2004. (Earth's Changing Landscape Ser.). (Illus.). 46p. (J). lib. bdg. 28.50 (978-1-58340-476-8(7)) Black Rabbit Bks.

Stefoff, Rebecca, adapted by. The Third Chimpanzee for Young People: On the Evolution & Future of the Human Animal. 2014. (For Young People Ser.). (ENG., Illus.). 352p. (J). (gr. 7). 22.95 (978-1-60980-522-7(4), Triangle Square) Seven Stories Pr.

Stein, Paul. Floods of the Future. 2009. (Library of Future Weather & Climate Ser.). 64p. (gr. 5-5). 58.50 (978-1-60853-645-0(9)) Rosen Publishing Group, Inc., The.

—Ice Ages of the Future. 2009. (Library of Future Weather & Climate Ser.). 64p. (gr. 5-5). 58.50 (978-1-60853-647-4(5)) Rosen Publishing Group, Inc., The.

Stewart, Melissa. A Place for Frogs, 1 vol. Bond, Higgins, illus. 2010. (ENG.). 32p. (J). (gr. 1-5). 16.95 (978-1-56145-521-8(0)) Peachtree Pubs.

—Place for Frogs, 1 vol. Bond, Higgins, illus. rev. ed. 2016. (Place For... Ser.). (ENG.). 32p. (J). (gr. 1-5). 16.95 (978-1-56145-901-8(1)) Peachtree Pubs.

Sturm, Jeanne. Nuestra Huella en la Tierra. 2012. (SPA & ENG.). 48p. (gr. 4-8). pap. 10.95 (978-1-61810-473-1(X)) Rourke Educational Media.

—Our Footprint on Earth. 2009. (ENG., Illus.). 48p. (gr. 4-8). pap. 10.95 (978-1-60694-526-1(2)) Rourke Educational Media.

Vogel, Carole G. Human Impact. 2003. (Restless Sea Ser.). (ENG., Illus.). 96p. (J). (gr. 5-8). 30.50 (978-0-531-12323-2(5), Watts, Franklin) Scholastic Library Publishing.

Webb, Barb. Endangered! 2011. (ENG., Illus.). 24p. (gr. k-2). pap. 8.95 (978-1-61741-974-4(5)) Rourke Educational Media.

West, David & Parker, Steve. Ecological Disasters. 2011. (ENG., Illus.). 32p. (J). pap. (978-0-7787-7578-2(X)); lib. bdg. (978-0-7787-7573-7(9)) Crabtree Publishing Co.

—Human-Made Disasters. 2011. (ENG., Illus.). 32p. (J). pap. (978-0-7787-7580-5(1)); lib. bdg. (978-0-7787-7575-1(5)) Crabtree Publishing Co.

Wild Earth. 2007. (Illus.). 32p. (J). (978-0-696-24002-7(5)) Meredith Bks.

World Book, Inc Staff, contrib. by. Understanding Climate Change. 2015. (Illus.). 48p. (J). (978-0-7166-2706-7(X)) World Bk., Inc.

—Weather & Climate Change. 2015. (Illus.). 47p. (J). (978-0-7166-2707-4(8)) World Bk., Inc.

—Wildlife & Climate Change. 2016. (Illus.). 44p. (J). (978-0-7166-2719-7(1)) World Bk., Inc.

NATURE—EFFECT OF HUMAN BEINGS ON—FICTION

Barkley, Callie. Amy on Park Patrol. Bishop, Tracy, illus. 2017. (Critter Club Ser.: 17). (ENG.). 128p. (J). (gr. k-3). pap. 5.99 **(978-1-4814-9432-8(5)**, Little Simon) Little Simon.

Cooper, Susan. Green Boy. 2003. (ENG., Illus.). 208p. (J). (gr. 4-7). pap. 7.99 (978-0-689-84760-8(2), McElderry, Margaret K. Bks.) McElderry, Margaret K. Bks.

Gleitzman, Morris. Second Childhood. 2016. (ENG.). 128p. (Orig.). (J). (gr. 4-6). 14.99 **(978-0-14-330877-5(7))** Random Hse. Australia AUS. Dist: Independent Pubs. Group.

Hale, Shannon. Enna Burning. 2004. (Books of Bayern Ser.: No. 2). (ENG., Illus.). 300p. (YA). 18.99 (978-1-58234-889-6(8), 9781582348896, Bloomsbury USA Childrens) Bloomsbury Publishing USA.

—River Secrets. 2006. (Books of Bayern Ser.). (ENG., Illus.). 304p. (YA). (gr. 7-12). 18.99 (978-1-58234-901-5(0), 9781582349015, Bloomsbury USA Childrens) Bloomsbury Publishing USA.

Handy, Femida & Carpenter, Carole H. Sandy's Incredible Shrinking Footprint, 1 vol. Steele-Card, Adrianna & Second Story Press Staff, illus. 2010. (ENG.). 24p. (J). (gr. 3 — 1). 15.95 (978-1-897187-69-2(6)) Second Story Pr. CAN. Dist: Orca Bk. Pubs. USA.

Liberto, Lorenzo. Save the Planet / Salva el Planeta. Gomez, Rocio, tr. Torres, Irving, illus. 2005. (Matt the Rat Ser. / La Serie de Ratón Mateo). (ENG & SPA.). 32p. (J). lib. bdg. 20.00 (978-0-9743668-5-2(4)) Harvest Sun Pr., LLC.

Mon, S. Aka - the Wonder Girl. 2011. (Illus.). 40p. pap. 18.79 (978-1-4567-8047-0(6)) AuthorHouse.

Oe, Patricia Daly. Where Are My Stripes? Oe, Patricia Daly, illus. 2007. (R. I. C. Story Chest Ser.). (Illus.). 20p. (J). (gr. -1-k). 11.95 incl. audio compact disk (978-1-74126-438-8(3)) R.I.C. Pubns. AUS. Dist: SCB Distributors.

Patricia Diane Craine, Ma-Lmft. Our Miracle Our Earth. 2009. 56p. pap. 24.49 (978-1-4389-5918-4(4)) AuthorHouse.

Samos (Amos Amir). Nemo the Mole Rat: Stories from the Woodland. 2011. (Illus.). 52p. pap. 23.51 (978-1-4567-8187-3(1)) AuthorHouse.

Thomas, Rosemary. The Kiwi Kingdom. 2010. 154p. pap. 18.00 (978-1-4349-0857-5(7)) Dorrance Publishing Co., Inc.

von Olfers, Sibylle. Mother Earth & Her Children Coloring Book: Color the Wonderful World of Nature As You See It! 24 Magical, Mythical Coloring Scenes. Zipes, Jack, tr. Schoen-Smith, Sieglinde, illus. 2015. (ENG.). 24p. (J). (gr. 2-4). pap. 6.95 (978-1-933308-54-8(0)) Breckling Pr.

Wood, Douglas. Old Turtle: Questions of the Heart. Ruth, Greg, illus. 2017. (ENG.). 56p. (J). (gr. -1-3). 19.99 (978-0-439-32111-2(5), Scholastic Pr.) Scholastic, Inc.

—Old Turtle & the Broken Truth. Muth, Jon J., illus. 2003. (ENG.). 64p. (J). (gr. -1-3). 17.99 (978-0-439-32109-9(3)) Scholastic, Inc.

NATURE—FICTION

Addy, Sharon. In Grandpa's Woods. Akins, Tamlyn, illus. 2004. (J). (978-1-931599-42-9(4), Trails Bks.) Bower Hse.

Alexander, John. The Adventures of Thunder & Avalanche: Laws of Nature. Alexander, John, illus. 2013. (Illus.). 46p. 18.99 (978-0-9887625-0-3(1)) Mountain Thunder Publishing.

Allamand, Maite. Alamito el Largo. (SPA.). (J). (gr. 2-3). pap. (978-956-13-1428-3(2), AB3840) Bello, Andres CHL. Dist: Lectorum Pubns., Inc.

Allen, Elaine Ann. Olly Explores 7 Wonders of the Chesapeake Bay, 1 vol. Nash, Kelli, illus. 2015. (ENG.). 32p. (J). 16.99 (978-0-7643-4938-6(4), 9780764349386) Schiffer Publishing, Ltd.

Allen, Elise & Stanford, Halle. Autumn's Secret Gift. Pooler, Paige, illus. 2014. (Enchanted Sisters Ser.). (ENG.). 128p. (J). (gr. 2-4). pap. 5.99 (978-1-61963-254-7(3), 9781619632547, Bloomsbury USA Childrens) Bloomsbury Publishing USA.

—Spring's Sparkle Sleepover. Pooler, Paige, illus. 2015. (Enchanted Sisters Ser.). (ENG.). 128p. (J). (gr. 2-4). 15.99 (978-1-61963-296-7(9), 9781619632967); pap. 5.99 (978-1-61963-269-1(1), 9781619632691) Bloomsbury Publishing USA. (Bloomsbury USA Childrens).

—Summer's Friendship Games. Pooler, Paige, illus. 2015. (Enchanted Sisters Ser.). (ENG.). 128p. (J). (gr. 2-4). 15.99 (978-1-61963-271-4(3), 9781619632714, Bloomsbury USA Childrens) Bloomsbury Publishing USA.

—Winter's Flurry Adventure. Pooler, Paige, illus. 2014. (Enchanted Sisters Ser.). (ENG.). 128p. (YA). (gr. 2-4). pap. 5.99 (978-1-61963-267-7(5), 9781619632677, Bloomsbury USA Childrens) Bloomsbury Publishing USA.

—Winter's Flurry Adventure. Pooler, Paige, illus. 2014. (Enchanted Sisters Ser.: 2). (YA). lib. bdg. 16.00 (978-0-606-36217-7(7)) Turtleback Bks.

Allen, Page. Madison's Descent: A Child's Journey. (Illus.). (J). 2006. pap. 25.00 (978-0-9752516-2-1(7)) 2004. lib. bdg. 60.00 (978-0-9752516-1-4(9)) Otis & Randolph Pr.

—The Way to Davis: On the River of Stars. collector's ed. 2007. (Illus.). (J). 75.00 (978-0-9752516-3-8(5)) Otis & Randolph Pr.

Anderson, Henry Morgan. Timmy the Goat: Spelunking Adventure. Falk, Wendy & Makepeace, Jonathan, eds. Funnell, Sonja, illus. 2011. (Adventures of Henry Ser.). 48p. 14.99 (978-1-936813-00-1(9)) Adventures of Henry, LLC.

Andrews, Jane. Young Reader's Series: The stories mother nature told her Children. 2011. 150p. pap. 11.89 (978-1-61279-069-5(0)) Publishing in Motion.

Archer, Micha. Daniel Finds a Poem. Archer, Micha, illus. 2016. (ENG., Illus.). 32p. (J). (gr. k-3). 16.99 (978-0-399-16913-7(X), Nancy Paulsen Books) Penguin Young Readers Group.

Arden, Carolyn. Goose Moon. Postier, Jim, illus. 2004. (ENG.). 32p. (J). (gr. k-7). 15.95 (978-1-59078-040-4(X)) Boyds Mills Pr.

Arrington, Linda. Purple Time. 2012. 36p. pap. 24.95 (978-1-4626-9613-0(9)) America Star Bks.

—Ugly Trees. Arrington, Linda, photos by. 2012. (Illus.). 24p. pap. 24.95 (978-1-4626-8925-5(6)) America Star Bks.

Atteberry, Kevan. Bunnies!!! Atteberry, Kevan, illus. 2015. (ENG., Illus.). 32p. (J). (gr. -1-3). 12.99 (978-0-06-230783-5(5)) HarperCollins Pubs.

Austin, Sarah & Boyle, Eleanor Vere. The Story Without an End. 2015. (ENG., Illus.). 64p. (J). (gr. 2-5). pap. 5.99 (978-0-486-79495-2(4)) Dover Pubns., Inc.

Avalos, Francisco. Amazon Tale. 2013. 124p. 29.99 (978-1-4797-6689-5(5)); pap. 19.99 (978-1-4797-6688-8(7)) Xlibris Corp.

Avignone, June. A Peek into the Secret Little Ones of Turtle Back Island. My Wolf Dog, illus. 2004. 40p. (J). pap. (978-0-9654628-2-2(X)) Mill Street Forward, The.

Azman, Hacer. God Loves Us All. 2011. (ENG.). 103p. 14.95 (978-1-59784-233-4(8)) Tughra Bks.

Baby Bear Sees Blue. 2014. (Baby Bear Ser.). (ENG., Illus.). 42p. (J). (gr. -1 — 1). bds. 7.99 (978-1-4814-1503-3(4), Little Simon) Little Simon.

Baby Lauren & Theodore, Paperback. 2007. (J). pap. 9.95 (978-0-9779643-0-7(2)) Healing Tree Arts.

Bailey, Dawn Wentz. Joey & the Mighty Oak. 2008. 20p. pap. 24.95 (978-1-60813-377-2(X)) PublishAmerica, Inc.

Bailey, S. D. All While Holding My Ladybug Lunch Pail. 2008. 24p. pap. 11.49 (978-1-4389-0617-1(X)) AuthorHouse.

Barkley, Callie. Liz at Marigold Lake. Riti, Marsha, illus. 2014. (Critter Club Ser.: 7). (ENG.). 128p. (J). (gr. k-4). pap. 5.99 (978-1-4424-9525-8(1), Little Simon) Little Simon.

—Liz at Marigold Lake. 2014. (Critter Club Ser.: 7). lib. bdg. 16.00 (978-0-606-35445-5(X)) Turtleback Bks.

Base, Graeme. Uno's Garden. 2006. (ENG., Illus.). 44p. (J). (gr. -1-3). 19.95 (978-0-8109-5473-1(7)) Abrams, Inc.

Baum, L. Frank. Twinkle & Chubbins. 2011. 106p. pap. 9.95 (978-1-60664-470-6(X)) Rodgers, Alan Bks.

Baum, L. Frank & Bancroft, Laura. Policeman Bluejay. 2009. 116p. pap. 9.95 (978-1-60664-382-2(7)) Rodgers, Alan Bks.

Bekis, Joanne. Bubble & Butterfly. 2009. 20p. pap. 10.50 (978-1-60693-696-2(4), Strategic Bk. Publishing) Strategic Book Publishing & Rights Agency (SBPRA).

Bentley, Dawn. Saber-Tooth Trap. (Smithsonian's Prehistoric Pals Ser.). (ENG., Illus.). 36p. (J). (gr. -1-2). 9.95 (978-1-59249-457-6(9), PS2456) Soundprints.

—Saber-Tooth Trap. Reavely, Trever, illus. (Smithsonian's Prehistoric Pals Ser.). (ENG.). 36p. (J). (gr. -1-2). 2.95 (978-1-59249-456-9(0), S2456) Soundprints.

—Saber-Tooth Trap. Reavely, Trevor, illus. 2005. (Smithsonian's Prehistoric Pals Ser.). (ENG.). 36p. (J). (gr. k-2). 14.95 (978-1-59249-453-8(6), H2406); pap. 6.95 (978-1-59249-454-5(4), S2406) Soundprints.

Berenstain, Jan & Berenstain, Mike. All Things Bright & Beautiful, 1 vol. 2012. (Berenstain Bears/Living Lights Ser.). (ENG., Illus.). 32p. (J). pap. 4.99 (978-0-310-72088-1(5)) Zonderkidz.

Berenstain, Stan, et al. The Berenstain Bears Discover God's Creation, 1 vol. 2010. (Berenstain Bears/Living Lights Ser.). (ENG.). 40p. (J). (gr. -1-2). 6.99 (978-0-310-71936-6(4)) Zonderkidz.

Berry, Ron. Look for the Rainbow! Sharp, Chris, illus. 2009. (ENG.). 18p. bds. 10.99 (978-0-8249-1428-8(7), Ideal Pubns.) Worthy Publishing.

Bird, Jodi Stiriz. Going on a Tree Hunt: A Tree Identification Book for Young Children. 2011. 28p. (gr. 1-2). pap. 14.99 (978-1-4490-8308-3(0)) AuthorHouse.

Bissonette, Aimee M. North Woods Girl. McGehee, Claudia, illus. 2015. (ENG.). 32p. (J). 16.95 (978-0-87351-966-3(3)) Minnesota Historical Society Pr.

Blume, Rebecca. When the World Was Green! Blume, Rebecca, illus. 2007. (Illus.). 32p. (J). per. 14.00 (978-0-9785427-1-9(1)) Liberty Artists Management.

Bogart, Jo Ellen. The Big Tree Gang. Griffiths, Dean, illus. 2005. 60p. (J). lib. bdg. 20.00 (978-1-4242-1251-4(0)) Fitzgerald Bks.

Bond, A. Russell. Scientific American Boy: Or the Camp at Willow Clump Island. 2006. (ENG., Illus.). 320p. (J). (gr. 4-7). per. 19.95 (978-1-55709-185-7(4)) Applewood Bks.

Bonnell, Kris. Look Up! 2007. (J). pap. 5.95 (978-1-933727-48-6(9)) Reading Reading Bks., LLC.

Brodland, Rita, ed. All Dried Out. Freeman, Troy, illus. l.t. ed. 2006. (WeWrite Kids! Ser.: 50). 68p. (J). pap. 11.95 (978-1-57635-063-8(0)) WeWrite LLC.

Budbill, David. Snowshoe Trek to Otter River. 2005. (J). pap. (978-0-9657144-9-5(7)) Onion River Pr.

Bunce, Margaret. Adventures with Nature: A Story about Olivia & Her Little Dog, Jake. 2011. 24p. pap. 12.95 (978-1-4567-2497-9(5)) AuthorHouse.

Bunting, Eve. Anna's Table. Morley, Taia, illus. 2003. (ENG.). 32p. (J). (gr. 3-6). 16.95 (978-1-55971-841-7(2)) Cooper Square Publishing Llc.

Burke, Gloreen. Mother Nature Dear. 2008. 16p. pap. 24.95 (978-1-60672-235-0(2)) America Star Bks.

Caglaroglu, Nurefsan. My Sweet Grandparents. 2011. (ENG.). 120p. 14.95 (978-1-59784-230-3(3)) Tughra Bks.

Carlstrom, Nancy White. This Is the Day!, 1 vol. Cowdrey, Richard, illus. 2009. (ENG.). 32p. (J). (gr. -1-2). 15.99 (978-0-310-71428-6(1)) Zonderkidz.

Carrie C Yakola. Lucy's Shooting Star. 2009. 32p. pap. 15.99 (978-1-4343-5276-7(5)) AuthorHouse.

Carson, Penny & Hess, Amy. Simon Goes Camping. 2008. 19p. 10.95 (978-1-4357-1560-8(8)) Lulu Pr., Inc.

Casanova, Mary. Wake up, Island. Wroblewski, Nick, illus. 2016. (J). (ENG.). 40p. 14.95 (978-0-8166-8935-4(0)); pap. (978-0-8166-8936-1(9)) Univ. of Minnesota Pr.

Chapman, Joan. A Cloud Called Cleo. 2006. (Neighborhood Readers Ser.). (ENG.). 12p. (gr. 1-3). pap. 5.90 (978-1-4042-7050-3(7), Rosen Classroom) Rosen Publishing Group, Inc., The.

Charters, Janet. The General. Foreman, Michael, illus. 2010. (ENG.). 48p. (J). (gr. k-12). 16.99 (978-0-7636-4875-6(2), Templar) Candlewick Pr.

Chatel, Kim. A Talent for Quiet. Chatel, Kim, photos by. 2009. (Illus.). 32p. pap. 10.95 (978-1-935137-56-6(5)) Guardian Angel Publishing, Inc.

Chen, Julia. On the Way Home. Stewart, Fion, illus. 2009. (J). (978-0-9787550-6-5(5)) Heryin Publishing Corp.

Chur, R. G. Penny the Pink Cloud. 2012. pap. 9.95 (978-0-7414-7028-7(4)) Infinity Publishing.

Churchill, Ginger. Wild Rose's Weaving. Wong, Nicole, illus. 2011. (ENG.). 32p. (J). (gr. -1-3). 15.95 (978-1-933718-56-9(0)) Tanglewood Pr.

Cole, Henry. On Meadowview Street. Cole, Henry, illus. 2007. (ENG., Illus.). 32p. (J). (gr. -1-3). 17.99 (978-0-06-056481-0(4), Greenwillow Bks.) HarperCollins Pubs.

Collard, Sneed B., III. Flash Point, 1 vol. (ENG.). 256p. (YA). 2011. (gr. 5-9). pap. 7.95 (978-1-56145-577-5(6)) 2006. (Illus.). (gr. 7-18). 16.95 (978-1-56145-385-6(4)) Peachtree Pubs.

Collins, Pat Lowery. The Deer Watch. Slonim, David, illus. 2013. (ENG.). 32p. (J). (gr. -1-2). 15.99 (978-0-7636-4890-9(6)) Candlewick Pr.

Cook, Sherry & Johnson, Terri. Watery William, 26. Kuhn, Jesse, illus. l.t. ed. 2006. (Quirkles — Exploring Phonics through Science Ser.: 23). 32p. (J). 7.99 (978-1-933815-22-0(1), Quirkles, The) Creative 3, LLC.

Cooke, Flora J. Nature Myths & Stories for Little Chil. 2006. pap. 19.95 (978-1-4254-9629-6(6)) Kessinger Publishing, LLC.

Cordery-Maring, Jeanee. Climbing over Rainbows. 2008. 76p. pap. 19.95 (978-1-4241-6243-7(2)) America Star Bks.

Corso, Joseph. Mother Earth Four. 2012. (ENG.). 39p. (J). pap. 15.95 (978-1-4327-8041-8(7)) Outskirts Pr., Inc.

Corwin, Jeff. The Wild, Wild Southwest!, 3 vols. 2010. (Jeff Corwin Ser.: 3). (ENG.). 112p. (J). (gr. 1-3). 4.99 (978-0-14-241440-8(9), Puffin Books) Penguin Young Readers Group.

Coste, Marion. Wild Beach. Gray, Cissy, illus. 2005. 32p. (J). pap. 8.25 (978-0-89317-062-2(3), WW-623); lib. bdg. 17.95

(978-0-89317-061-5(5), WW-0615) Finney Co., Inc. (Windward Publishing).

Covey, Richard D. & Pappas, Diane H. What Is Global Warming? 2009. (Planet Earth Patrol Ser.). (Illus.). (J). (978-0-545-06104-9(0)) Scholastic, Inc.

Cox Gray, Marjorie. Bucky's Adventures. Griffin, Marlin, illus. 2008. 100p. pap. 28.99 (978-1-4389-2645-2(6)) AuthorHouse.

Crawford, Laura. In Arctic Waters, 1 vol. Hodson, Ben, illus. 2007. (ENG.). 32p. (J). (gr. -1-2). 15.95 (978-0-9768823-4-3(5)) Arbordale Publishing.

Cruz De Jesus, Marta. Chosen: By Nature. 2010. 116p. 21.49 (978-1-4520-3479-9(6)); pap. 10.99 (978-1-4520-3480-5(X)) AuthorHouse.

D. Good Morning World. 2013. 46p. pap. 21.99 (978-1-4575-2154-6(7)) Dog Ear Publishing, LLC.

Da Puzzo, Allegra & Da Puzzo, Jackson. A Cloudy Day. Gauvin, Matthew, illus. 2012. 24p. pap. (978-0-9843477-5-9(5)) Roxby Media Ltd.

Dal Santo, Sandy. I See a Zoo up in the Sky. 2009. 28p. pap. 12.89 (978-1-4389-4871-3(9)) AuthorHouse.

Dane, Dichira A. Pathway of Pebbles. 2008. 20p. pap. 24.95 (978-1-60703-801-6(3)) America Star Bks.

Dann, Colin. The Animals of Farthing Wood. 2016. (Egmont Modern Classics Ser.). (ENG., Illus.). 400p. (J). (gr. 2-6). pap. 10.99 (978-1-4052-8180-5(4)) Egmont Bks., Ltd. GBR. Dist: Independent Pubs. Group.

—The Animals of Farthing Wood: The Adventure Begins. 2017. (Puffin Book Ser.). (ENG., Illus.). 272p. (J). (gr. 2-4). pap. 11.99 (978-0-14-136874-0(8)) Penguin Bks., Ltd. GBR. Dist: Independent Pubs. Group.

Danyi, Barb. The Maker of Heaven & Earth. 2011. 28p. (gr. -1). pap. 11.99 (978-1-4634-1300-2(9)) AuthorHouse.

Darlison, Aleesah & Hart, James. Awesome Animal Stories for Kids. 2016. (ENG., Illus.). 208p. (J). (gr. 1-4). pap. 9.99 (978-0-85798-968-0(5)) Random Hse. Australia AUS. Dist: Independent Pubs. Group.

Dee, Carolyn. The Tree Who Couldn't Choose. 2008. 36p. pap. 15.49 (978-1-4389-2950-7(1)) AuthorHouse.

Delacre, Lulu. How Far Do You Love Me? Delacre, Lulu, illus. 2014. (ENG., Illus.). (J). pap. 8.95 (978-1-62014-208-0(2)) Lee & Low Bks., Inc.

Denver, John. John Denver's Sunshine on My Shoulders, 1 vol. Canyon, Christopher, illus. 2004. (ENG.). 32p. pap. 8.95 (978-1-58469-050-4(X)) Dawn Pubns.

dePaola, Tomie. Michael Bird-Boy. dePaola, Tomie, illus. 2015. (ENG., Illus.). 32p. (J). (gr. -1-3). 16.99 (978-1-4814-4333-3(X), Simon & Schuster Bks. For Young Readers) Simon & Schuster Bks. For Young Readers.

Dundon, Adamarie. Niklas Rogers: The Adventure Begins. 2004. 60p. pap. 13.95 (978-1-4184-4361-0(1)) AuthorHouse.

Durand, Delphine. Bob & Co. 2007. (ENG., Illus.). 64p. (J). (gr. -1-3). pap. 9.95 (978-1-85437-723-4(X)) Tate Publishing, Ltd. GBR. Dist: Hachette Bk. Group.

Dussling, Jennifer. El Misterio Del Arco Iris (the Rainbow Mystery) Gott, Barry, illus. 2009. (Science Solves It! (r) en Espanol Ser.). (SPA.). (gr. 1-3). pap. 33.92 (978-0-7613-4798-9(4)) Lerner Publishing Group.

Duvall, Sheila Marie. I See Fun. 2009. 16p. pap. 8.75 (978-1-4389-4963-5(4)) AuthorHouse.

Earth Coffee Table Book. 2009. 128p. 24.95 (978-1-4231-2205-0(4), Disney Editions) Disney Pr.

Earth Picture Book. 2009. 64p. 8.99 (978-1-4231-2204-3(6)) Disney Pr.

Edwards, Glenna S. Rainbow Bed: A child's perspective on coping with Grief. 2009. 20p. pap. 17.95 (978-1-4327-2422-1(3)) Outskirts Pr., Inc.

Edwards, Pamela Duncan. Clara Caterpillar. Cole, Henry, illus. 2004. (ENG.). 40p. (J). (gr. -1-1). reprint ed. pap. 6.99 (978-0-06-443691-5(8)) HarperCollins Pubs.

Ehlert, Lois. In My World. 2006. (ENG., Illus.). 36p. (J). (gr. -1-3). reprint ed. pap. 7.99 (978-0-15-205429-8(4)) Houghton Mifflin Harcourt Publishing Co.

Ekholm, Jan. The Little Red Rascal. 2011. 88p. pap. 30.28 (978-1-4567-9501-6(5)) AuthorHouse.

Eleanor, Coalson. Simon Says Run. 2006. (Illus.). (J). 8.95 (978-1-56167-944-7(5)) American Literary Pr.

Elmore, Amber. Betsy Beansprout Adventure Guide. Short, Kasey, illus. 2011. (J). pap. 15.99 (978-0-9822632-8-0(7)) ShadeTree Publishing, LLC.

Ergün, Erol. The Generous Bestower. 2011. (ENG., Illus.). 176p. pap. 9.95 (978-1-59784-258-7(3)) Tughra Bks.

—The Supreme Ruler. 2011. (ENG., Illus.). 192p. pap. 9.95 (978-1-59784-259-4(1)) Tughra Bks.

Evers, Alf. Treasure of Watchdog Mountain: The Story of a Mountain in the Catskills. Yanow-Schwartz, Jo & Schwartz, Arthur, eds. 2006. 76p. (J). 16.95 (978-1-879504-19-6(7)) Woodstocker Books/Arthur Schwartz & Company.

Ewing, Juliana Horatia. Mary's Meadow: And Other Tales of Fields & Flowers. 2007. (ENG.). 154p. pap. 19.99 (978-1-4346-3334-7(9)); 168p. pap. 21.99 (978-1-4346-3335-4(7)) Creative Media Partners, LLC.

Fazio, Nicole. Journey of the Sea Glass, 1 vol. 2012. (ENG., Illus.). 32p. (J). (gr. -1-3). 16.95 (978-1-60893-177-4(3)) Down East Bks.

Flatley, Paula Chorman. Olivia's Tree, 1 vol. Palmer, Kimmy, illus. 2010. 16p. pap. 24.95 (978-1-4489-5870-2(9)) America Star Bks.

Fletcher, Ralph. Hello, Harvest Moon. Kiesler, Kate, illus. 2017. (ENG.). 32p. (J). (gr. -1-3). pap. 7.99 **(978-1-328-74049-6(8)**, HMH Books For Young Readers) Houghton Mifflin Harcourt Publishing Co.

Fletcher, Ralph J. & Fletcher, Ralph. Hello, Harvest Moon. Kiesler, Kate, illus. 2003. (ENG.). 32p. (J). (gr. -1-3). 17.99 (978-0-618-16451-6(0)) Houghton Mifflin Harcourt Publishing Co.

The Flower Pot Bunnies Return. 2006. (J). (978-0-9755390-2-6(7)) Fifth Ave Pr.

Fontes, Justine. El Dia Que Jordan Se Enfermo: Jordan's Silly Sick Day. Lee, Jared, illus. 2005. (Rookie Reader Español Ser.). 32p. (gr. k-2). 19.50 (978-0-516-24445-7(0), Children's Pr.) Scholastic Library Publishing.

Forbes, J. L. Under the Faithful Watch of the River Hawk. Forbes, Justin, illus. 2013. 20p. pap. 24.95 (978-1-62709-899-1(2)) America Star Bks.

Forte, Lauren. Olivia Helps Mother Nature. 2014. (Olivia Ready-To-Read Level 1 Ser.). lib. bdg. 13.55 (978-0-606-35452-3(2)) Turtleback Bks.

Fox, Paula. Traces. Kuskin, Karla, illus. 2011. (ENG.). 32p. (J). (gr. 2-4). pap. 9.95 (978-1-59078-870-7(2)) Boyds Mills Pr.

Frederick Edward Pitts. Tale of the Hummingopotomus: The Flight for Life. 2009. 40p. pap. 18.49 (978-1-4389-6453-9(6)) AuthorHouse.

Freedman, Deborah. This House, Once. Freedman, Deborah, illus. 2017. (ENG., Illus.). 40p. (J). (gr. -1-3). 17.99 (978-1-4814-4284-8(8)) Simon & Schuster Children's Publishing.

Frisch, Aaron. The Lonely Pine. Delessert, Etienne, illus. 2011. (ENG.). 32p. (J). (gr. 1-3). 17.99 (978-1-56846-214-1(X), Creative Editions) Creative Co., The.

Frontiera, Deborah. Eric & the Enchanted Leaf: A Night with Echo. Scott, Korey, illus. 2007.Tr. of Eric y la hojita encantada: una noche con Eco. (SPA.). 32p. (J). (978-0-9795474-2-3(3)) KAM Publishing.

Frye, Karen. Flake, 1 vol. 2010. 16p. 24.95 (978-1-4489-4935-9(1)) PublishAmerica, Inc.

Fuhr, Ute & Sautai, Raoul. The Earth's Surface. 2012. (ENG., Illus.). 32p. (J). (gr. k-3). pap. 11.99 (978-1-85103-362-1(9)) Moonlight Publishing, Ltd. GBR. Dist: Independent Pubs. Group.

Gamble, Adam. Good Night World. Kelly, Cooper, illus. 2009. (Good Night Our World Ser.). (ENG.). 28p. (J). (gr. k — 1). bds. 9.95 (978-1-60219-030-6(5)) Good Night Bks.

Gates, Mysti. Noises in the Night. 2009. 52p. pap. 22.99 (978-1-4389-4359-6(8)) AuthorHouse.

Gentner, Norma L. & Young, Steve. Save a Tree for Me. (Song Box Ser.). (Illus.). 16p. (gr. 1-2). 31.50 (978-0-7802-2264-9(4)) Wright Group/McGraw-Hill.

Gershator, Phillis. Listen, Listen. Jay, Alison, illus. 2007. (ENG.). 32p. (J). (gr. -1-3). 16.99 (978-1-84686-084-3(9)) Barefoot Bks., Inc.

Getz, Jeanine Behr. Think Green! Nightingale, Jenny, illus. 2008. (ENG.). 32p. (J). 15.50 (978-0-9797362-0-9(X)) Kids Think Big LLC.

Gingold, Janet. Finch Goes Wild. 2007. 280p. (YA). pap. 14.99 (978-1-59092-385-6(5)) Blue Forge Pr.

Gisbert, Joan Manuel. El Palacio de los Tres Ojos. Lucini, Chata, illus. 2006. (SPA.). 127p. (J). (gr. 4-7). pap. 10.99 (978-84-263-4614-8(6)) Vives, Luis Editorial (Edelvives) ESP. Dist: Lectorum Pubns., Inc.

Goddard, Mary Beth. How Would It Feel? Mycek-Wodecki, Anna, illus. 2005. (ENG.). 32p. (J). (gr. -1-6). 15.95 (978-1-59143-050-6(X), Bear Cub Bks.) Bear & Co.

Golden Books Staff. Eloise Wilkin Stories. Wilkin, Eloise, illus. 2005. (Little Golden Book Treasury Ser.). (ENG.). 224p. (J). (gr. -1-2). 10.95 (978-0-375-82928-4(8), Golden Bks.) Random Hse. Children's Bks.

Golden Eagle Productions Staff. Grandmother Moon & Sammy the Loon, 36 vols. l.t. ed. 2003. (Illus.). 24p. per. 12.99 (978-1-932338-24-9(1)) Lifevest Publishing, Inc.

Golden, Robert Charles. Pee Wee: The Blackcapped Chickadee. 2013. 36p. pap. 24.95 (978-1-62709-101-5(7)) America Star Bks.

Goodhart, Pippa. Slow Magic. Kelly, John, illus. (Flying Foxes Ser.). (J). 2015. (ENG.). 32p. (978-0-7787-1535-1(3)) 2003. (978-0-7787-1489-7(6)) Crabtree Publishing Co.

Goodhart, Pippa & Goodheart, Pippa. Slow Magic. Kelly, John, illus. 2003. (Flying Foxes Ser.). (ENG.). 48p. (J). (978-0-7787-1528-3(0)); lib. bdg. (978-0-7787-1482-8(9)) Crabtree Publishing Co.

Grahame, Kenneth. The Wind in the Willows. Freeman, Tor, illus. 2017. (ENG.). 192p. (J). pap. 9.99 **(978-1-84749-638-6(5)**, 9781847496386, Alma Classics) Bloomsbury Publishing USA.

—The Wind in the Willows. 3rd ed. 2008. (ENG., Illus.). 80p. 10.00 (978-0-19-479137-3(8)) Oxford Univ. Pr., Inc.

Grahame, Kenneth & Williams, Nicholas. An Gwyns I'n Helyk. Shepard, Ernest H., illus. 2013. (COR.). 202p. pap. (978-1-78201-029-6(7)) Evertype.

Griggs, Rosemarie. The Adventures of Donkey Tom Volume 2: Crystal Forest. 2012. 40p. pap. 32.70 (978-1-4797-0553-5(5)) Xlibris Corp.

Grindley, Sally & Foreman, Michael. La Playa de Pedro. 2003.Tr. of Peter's Place. (SPA., Illus.). 32p. (J). (gr. 1-3). 19.99 (978-84-261-3314-4(2)) Juventud, Editorial ESP. Dist: Lectorum Pubns., Inc.

Hale, Shannon. River Secrets. 2008. (Books of Bayern Ser.). (ENG., Illus.). 320p. (YA). (gr. 7). 9.99 (978-1-59990-293-7(1), 9781599902937, Bloomsbury USA Childrens) Bloomsbury Publishing USA.

Hallinan, P. K. The Looking Book. Barton, Patrice, illus. (J). 2015. pap. (978-0-8249-5670-7(2)) 2009. (ENG.). 32p. (gr. -1-2). 16.99 (978-0-8249-5607-3(9)) Worthy Publishing. (Ideal Pubns.).

Hamilton, L. Los Ninos y la Naturaleza. (SPA.). 198p. 12.00 (978-84-89920-62-0(1), 87106) Ediciones Oniro S.A. ESP. Dist: Lectorum Pubns., Inc.

Hannigan, Katherine. Ida B: ... And Her Plans to Maximize Fun, Avoid Disaster, & (Possibly) Save the World. 2004. 256p. (gr. 4-18). lib. bdg. 16.89 (978-0-06-073025-3(0)); (ENG.). (J). 17.99 (978-0-06-073024-6(2), Greenwillow Bks.) HarperCollins Pubs.

—Ida B: And Her Plans to Maximize Fun Avoid Disaster, & (Possibly) Save the World. 2011. (ENG.). 272p. (J). (gr. 5-9). reprint ed. pap. 6.99 (978-0-06-073026-0(9), Greenwillow Bks.) HarperCollins Pubs.

Harris, Annaka. I Wonder. Rowe, John, illus. 2013. (ENG.). 32p. (J). 16.95 (978-1-940051-04-8(5)) Four Elephants Pr.

Hatton, Laura. The Fairy's Garden. 2012. 64p. pap. 26.52 (978-1-4669-3961-5(3)) Trafford Publishing.

Healy, Reneé. You Are Safe in the Universe. 2011. 28p. pap. 25.00 (978-1-936688-07-4(7)) AKA:yoLa.

Heather Rose Brabant. The Moon Princess. 2009. 20p. pap. 11.95 (978-1-4389-2980-4(3)) AuthorHouse.

Heathfield, Lisa. Seed. 2015. (ENG.). 336p. (YA). (gr. 7). 16.95 (978-0-7624-5634-5(5), Running Pr. Kids) Running Pr. Bk. Pubs.

Heinz, Brian. The Great North Woods. Rothman, Michael, illus. 2016. (ENG.). 32p. (J). (gr. 1-3). 18.99 (978-1-56846-275-2(1), Creative Editions) Creative Co., The.

Heinz, Brian J. A Coming of Winter in the Adirondacks. Healy, Maggie, illus. 2011. 32p. (J). 19.95 (978-1-59531-038-5(X)) North Country Bks., Inc.

Hemery, Kathleen Maresh. Sunflower Promise. Bordelois, Augusto, illus. 2005. (J). (978-1-56123-188-1(6)) Centering Corp.

Hensley, Sarah M. Water Fun. Crowell, Knox, illus. l.t. ed. 2005. (J). (gr. -1-k). pap. 10.95 (978-1-57332-343-7(8)); pap. 10.95 (978-1-57332-342-0(X)) Carson-Dellosa Publishing, LLC. (HighReach Learning, Incorporated).

Herbauts, Anne, creator. What Color Is the Wind? 2016. (ENG., Illus.). 48p. (J). (gr. k). pap. 19.95 (978-1-59270-221-3(X)) Enchanted Lion Bks., LLC.

Herndon, Susen A. Janie's World: Walk with Me Through Nature's Door. 2013. 36p. pap. 16.46 (978-1-4669-8057-0(5)) Trafford Publishing.

Hildreth, Ruth Erixon. Fun Lovin' Delanie Jo. Aughe, Roger, illus. 2012. 36p. pap. 24.95 (978-1-4626-7851-8(3)) America Star Bks.

Hillert, Margaret. ¿Qué Hay en el Estanque, Querido Dragón? Fernandez, Queta, tr. from ENG. Schimmell, David, illus. 2014. (BeginningtoRead Ser.).Tr. of What's in the Pond, Dear Dragon? (ENG & SPA.). 32p. (J). (-2). lib. bdg. 22.60 (978-1-59953-608-8(0)) Norwood Hse. Pr.

—What's in the Pond, Dear Dragon? Schimmell, David, illus. 2014. (BeginningtoRead Ser.). (ENG.). 32p. (J). (-2). pap. 11.94 (978-1-60357-601-7(0)); lib. bdg. 22.60 (978-1-59953-607-1(2)) Norwood Hse. Pr.

—What's in the Woods, Dear Dragon? Schimmell, David, illus. 2014. (BeginningtoRead Ser.). (ENG.). 32p. (J). (-2). pap. 11.94 (978-1-60357-599-7(5)); lib. bdg. 22.60 (978-1-59953-606-4(4)) Norwood Hse. Pr.

Hillert, Margaret & Fernández, Queta. ¿Que Hay en el Bosque, Querido Dragon? Schimmell, David, illus. 2014. (BeginningtoRead Ser.).Tr. of What's in the Woods, Dear Dragon? (ENG & SPA.). 32p. (J). (-2). lib. bdg. 22.60 (978-1-59953-609-5(9)) Norwood Hse. Pr.

Hix, Melvin. The Magic Speech Flower: Or Little Luke & His Animal Friends. 2007. (ENG.). 110p. pap. 18.99 (978-1-4346-0790-4(9)); 114p. pap. 19.99 (978-1-4346-0797-3(6)) Creative Media Partners, LLC.

Hochman, Marisa. A Walk in Pirate's Cove. Woodland, Bette, illus. 2012. (ENG.). 32p. (J). (978-0-9865679-0-2(6)) Fitzhenry & Whiteside, Ltd.

Hoffelt, Jane. We Share One World. Husted, Marty, illus. 2004. 32p. (J). per. 15.95 (978-0-9701907-8-9(6)) Illumination Arts Publishing Co., Inc.

Holbrook, Florence. Why the Crocodile Has a Wide Mouth: And Other Nature Myths. 2004. (Dover Children's Classics Ser.). (ENG., Illus.). 128p. (gr. 3-5). pap. 5.95 (978-0-486-43649-4(7)) Dover Pubns., Inc.

Hougasian, Amy. The Big Foot Sun. 2008. 36p. pap. 16.99 (978-1-4343-3920-1(3)) AuthorHouse.

Houston, Rebecca. My Butterfly. 2013. 20p. pap. 24.95 (978-1-62709-079-7(7)) America Star Bks.

Howard, Jim & Welsh-Howard, Paula. Tell Me Tell Me If You Can. 2006. (J). per. 14.95 (978-1-60002-291-3(X)) Mountain Valley Publishing, LLC.

Howerton-Willis, Deborah. Amos the Aardvark. 2012. 48p. pap. 24.99 (978-1-62419-623-2(3)) Salem Author Services.

Hughes, Fox Carlton. Rainbow Rhino. Hughes, Fox Carlton, illus. 2007. (ENG., Illus.). 36p. (J). (gr. -1-3). 16.95 (978-0-9790275-3-6(5)) Ovation Bks.

Hughes-Odgers, Kyle. One Thousand Trees. 2017. (ENG.). 32p. (J). (gr. -1-3). 14.99 **(978-1-925164-72-5(1))** Fremantle Pr. AUS. Dist: Independent Pubs. Group.

Hunter, Erin. The Rise of Scourge. Kurkoski, Bettina M., illus. 2008. (Warriors Manga Ser.: No. 3). (ENG.). 112p. (J). (gr. 3-7). pap. 6.99 (978-0-06-147867-3(9)) HarperCollins Pubs.

Hutton, John. Yard: Baby Unplugged. Kang, Andrea, illus. 2011. (Baby Unplugged Ser.). (ENG.). 14p. (J). (— 1). bds. 7.99 (978-1-936669-01-1(3)) Blue Manatee Press.

James, Ian. Why the Sky Is Far Away: A Tale from Nigeria. 2006. (J). pap. (978-1-4108-6172-6(4)) Benchmark Education Co.

Jameson, Catherine. Zoe & the Fawn. Flett, Julie, illus. 2006. (ENG.). 32p. pap. 11.95 (978-1-894778-43-5(X)) Theytus Bks., Ltd. CAN. Dist: Univ. of Toronto Pr.

Jay, Alison & Gershator, Phillis. Listen, Listen. 2008. (ENG., Illus.). 32p. (J). (gr. -1-k). 14.99 (978-1-84686-201-4(9)) Barefoot Bks., Inc.

Jean Emily Myers, Emily Myers & Jean Emily Myers. Mickey's Mini Farm. Tanner Voyles, illus. 2009. 32p. pap. 21.99 (978-1-4389-5544-5(8)) AuthorHouse.

Jeanmarie, Michele. Curiosity, Curiosity: Lost in an Array. 2008. 74p. pap. 19.95 (978-1-60610-169-8(2)) America Star Bks.

Jennings, Arleen Naish. God Is in the Rain. 2012. 64p. (gr. 1-2). pap. 8.95 (978-1-4759-3292-8(8)) iUniverse, Inc.

Johnson, Christine. Deep in Alaska. Johnson, Gary R., illus. 2013. 42p. pap. 12.95 (978-1-60223-215-0(6)) Univ. of Alaska Pr.

Johnson, D. B. Henry Hikes to Fitchburg. 2006. (ENG., Illus.). 32p. (J). (gr. -1-3). reprint ed. 7.99 (978-0-618-73749-9(9)) Houghton Mifflin Harcourt Publishing Co.

—Henry Hikes to Fitchburg. Johnson, D. B., illus. 2006. (Illus.). (gr. -1-3). 16.95 (978-0-7569-6798-7(8)) Perfection Learning Corp.

Johnston, Julie. A Very Fine Line. 2006. (ENG.). 208p. (J). (gr. 5). 18.95 (978-0-88776-746-3(X), Tundra Bks.) Tundra Bks. CAN. Dist: Penguin Random Hse. LLC.

Jon Scieszkas Trucktown, et al. Take a Trip with Trucktown! Gordon, David et al, illus. 2011. (Jon Scieszka's Trucktown Ser.). (ENG.). 24p. (J). (gr. -1-3). pap. 3.99 (978-1-4169-4181-1(9), Simon & Schuster Bks. For Young Readers) Simon & Schuster Bks. For Young Readers.

Jones, Andrea Koehle. The Wish Trees. 2008. (Illus.). 24p. pap. 12.99 (978-1-4343-9205-3(8)) AuthorHouse.

Jones, Angela. The Bird Lady. Newell, Brian, illus. 2009. 16p. pap. 7.31 (978-1-4251-8612-8(2)) Trafford Publishing.

Jue, Thea. Remember the Love. Lenz, Mary, illus. 2013. 36p. pap. 13.95 (978-0-9827753-3-2(4)) Interdimensional Pr.

Kaplan, Madeline. Planet Earth Gets Well. 2008. (ENG.). 24p. pap. 9.99 (978-1-4196-8986-4(X)) CreateSpace Independent Publishing Platform.

Kaplan, Osman. Animal Wonders of the Water. Kalender, Oznur, illus. 2009. (Amazing Animals Ser.). (ENG.). 56p. (J). (gr. 2-4). 9.95 (978-1-59784-200-6(1)) Tughra Bks.

Kato, Yukiko. In the Meadow. Sakai, Komako, illus. 2011. (Being in the World Ser.). (ENG.). 32p. (J). (gr. k-k). 14.95 (978-1-59270-108-7(6)) Enchanted Lion Bks., LLC.

Katz, Susan B. My Mama Earth. Launay, Melissa, illus. 2012. (ENG.). 24p. (J). 16.99 (978-1-84686-418-6(6)) Barefoot Bks., Inc.

Kelly, Jacqueline. La Evolución de Calpurnia Tate. 2010.Tr. of Evolution of Calpurnia Tate. (SPA.). 272p. (YA). pap. 20.95 (978-84-9918-103-5(1)) Roca Editorial ESP. Dist: Spanish Pubs., LLC.

—La Evolucion de Calpurnia Tate, Vol. 2. 2011.Tr. of Evolution of Calpurnia Tate. (SPA.). 272p. pap. 12.95 (978-84-92833-15-3(7)) Roca Editorial ESP. Dist: Spanish Pubs., LLC.

—The Evolution of Calpurnia Tate. 2009. (Calpurnia Tate Ser.: 1). (ENG.). 352p. (J). (gr. 4-7). 17.99 (978-0-8050-8841-0(5), 9780805088410, Holt, Henry & Co. Bks. For Young Readers) Holt, Henry & Co.

—The Evolution of Calpurnia Tate. 2010. 340p. 18.00 (978-1-60686-849-2(7)) Perfection Learning Corp.

—The Evolution of Calpurnia Tate. 2011. (Calpurnia Tate Ser.: 1). (ENG.). 368p. (J). (gr. 4-7). pap. 7.99 (978-0-312-65930-1(X), 9780312659301) Square Fish.

—The Evolution of Calpurnia Tate. 2011. (Calpurnia Tate Ser.: 1). (J). lib. bdg. 18.40 (978-0-606-20974-8(3), Turtleback) Turtleback Bks.

Khan, Nafeesa. Pompom's Rainbow Day. 2012. 24p. pap. 28.03 (978-1-4771-2918-0(9)) Xlibris Corp.

Kimmelman, Leslie. Sam & Charlie (and Sam Too) at Camp! Owl, William, illus. 2015. (ENG.). 48p. (J). (gr. k-3). 13.99 (978-0-8075-7217-7(9)) Whitman, Albert & Co.

Kirk B. Gradin. Jadhu Ram & the Thirsty Forest. 2012. 36p. 17.95 (978-1-105-04735-0(0)); pap. 10.95 (978-0-9855683-0-6(5)) Banyan Bks.

Kitzmiller, Brenda. Muddy Mud — an Easy to Read Beginning Reader Book. 2005. 24p. 7.85 (978-1-4116-2937-0(X)) Lulu Pr., Inc.

Kleczka, John A. Flick the Butterfly: Flick & Mom Go to Grandma's. 2008. 48p. per. 24.95 (978-1-60441-290-1(9)) America Star Bks.

Knight, Hilary. A Firefly in a Fir Tree: A Carol for Mice. Knight, Hilary, illus. 2004. (Illus.). 32p. (J). (gr. -1-3). lib. bdg. 15.89 (978-0-06-000992-2(6), Tegen, Katherine Bks) HarperCollins Pubs.

Krishnaswami, Uma. Out of the Way! Out of the Way!, 1 vol. Krishnaswamy, Uma, illus. 2012. (ENG.). 28p. (J). (gr. -1-2). 17.95 (978-1-55498-130-4(1)) Groundwood Bks. CAN. Dist: Publishers Group West (PGW).

Krohn, Kathryn T. Sarah's Most Perfect Day. Sage, Trina, illus. 2007. 24p. (J). 13.99 (978-1-59879-325-3(X), Lifevest) Lifevest Publishing, Inc.

Krovatin, Christopher. Mountain of Bones. (Gravediggers Ser.: 1). (ENG.). (J). (gr. 3-7). 2013. 352p. pap. 6.99 (978-0-06-207741-7(4)) 2012. 336p. 16.99 (978-0-06-207740-0(6)) HarperCollins Pubs. (Tegen, Katherine Bks).

Kurtz, Jane. Lanie's Real Adventures. Papp, Robert, illus. 2010. (American Girl Today Ser.). (ENG.). 112p. (YA). (gr. 3-18). 12.95 (978-1-59369-685-6(X)) American Girl Publishing, Inc.

Lacamara, Laura. Dalia's Wondrous Hair / el Maravilloso Cabello de Dalia. Baeza Ventura, Gabriela, tr. from SPA. Lacamara, Laura, illus. 2014. (ENG & SPA., Illus.). (J). 17.95 (978-1-55885-789-6(3), Piñata Books) Arte Publico Pr.

LaMarche, Jim. Pond. LaMarche, Jim, illus. 2016. (ENG., Illus.). 40p. (J). (gr. -1-3). 17.99 (978-1-4814-4735-5(1), Simon & Schuster/Paula Wiseman Bks.) Simon & Schuster/Paula Wiseman Bks.

Lampert, Diane Charlotte. Suite for Human Nature. Puybaret, Eric, illus. 2016. (ENG.). 48p. (J). 17.99 (978-1-4169-5373-9(6), Atheneum Bks. for Young Readers) Simon & Schuster Children's Publishing.

Langdale, Mark Roland. Professor Doppelganger & the Fantastical Cloud Factory. 2012. 106p. pap. (978-1-78003-267-2(6)) Pen Pr. Pubs., Ltd.

Lavin, Christine. Amoeba Hop. Feeney, Betsy Franco, illus. 2003. 36p. (J). (gr. 2-3). 19.95 incl. audio compact disk (978-0-9726487-4-5(7)) Puddle Jump Pr., Ltd.

Lawrence, Kelsey. Rune. 2006. (Illus.). 92p. pap. 13.50 (978-1-84426-399-8(1)) Upfront Publishing Ltd. GBR. Dist: Printondemand-worldwide.com.

Leadbetter, Lesley. Harold the Owl Who Couldn't Sleep. Leszek, Cedryll, illus. 2012. 30p. (J). pap. (978-1-921869-89-1(5), Digital Publishing Centre) Interactive Pubns. Pty, Ltd.

Léger, Diane Carmel. Who's in Maxine's Tree?, 1 vol. Gait, Darlene, illus. 2006. (ENG.). 32p. (J). (gr. -1-3). 17.95 (978-1-55143-346-2(X)) Orca Bk. Pubs. USA.

Lehner, Montserrat. The Legend of the Açaí: Retold & Illustrated by Montserrat Lehner. 2010. 30p. pap. 14.00 (978-1-60911-364-3(0), Eloquent Bks.) Strategic Book Publishing & Rights Agency (SBPRA).

Lenart, Claudia, illus. Seasons of Joy: Every Day Is for Outdoor Play. 2017. (J). pap. **(978-1-61599-317-8(7))** Loving Healing Pr., Inc.

Lewis, Rose A. Sweet Dreams. Corace, Jen, illus. 2012. (ENG.). 32p. (J). (gr. -1-k). 16.95 (978-1-4197-0189-4(4), Abrams Bks. for Young Readers) Abrams, Inc.

Linenthal, Peter. Look Look Outside! 2012. (ENG.). 16p. (J). (gr. -1 — 1). bds. 6.99 (978-0-8037-3729-7(7), Dial Bks) Penguin Young Readers Group.

Linke, Uwe. In the Meadow. Boldt, Fabienne & Wensell, Ulises, illus. 2007. (Moving Book Ser.). (ENG.). 20p. (J). bds. 11.95 (978-0-7358-2126-2(7)) North-South Bks., Inc.

Little Green Giants. 2008. (Illus.). 28p. (J). 14.95 (978-0-615-21480-1(0)) Allocca, Christine A.

Livingston, Mary A. & Shufelberger, Amanda. Buddy & the Magic Chicken Tree, 2 bks. Livingston, Tim, illus. 2014th ed. 2014. (ENG.). 34p. (J). 19.99 (978-0-9635757-3-9(2)) Red Tail Publishing.

Lloyd, Megan Wagner. Finding Wild. Halpin, Abigail, illus. 2016. (ENG.). 32p. (J). (gr. -1-2). 16.99 (978-1-101-93281-0(3), Knopf Bks. for Young Readers) Random Hse. Children's Bks.

Locker, Thomas. Cloud Dance. 2003. (ENG., Illus.). 32p. (J). (gr. -1-3). pap. 7.99 (978-0-15-204596-8(1)) Houghton Mifflin Harcourt Publishing Co.

LoDestro, Christine. The Littlest Cloud. 2005. 15p. (J). 12.01 (978-1-4116-6377-0(2)) Lulu Pr., Inc.

London, Jack. White Fang. 2005. 28.95 (978-1-4218-1472-8(2)); 276p. pap. 13.95 (978-1-4218-1572-5(9)) 1st World Publishing, Inc. (1st World Library - Literary Society).

—White Fang. 2005. (ENG.). 176p. (gr. 3-7). per. 14.95 (978-1-59818-531-7(4)) Aegypan.

—White Fang. 2005. 120p. per. 5.95 (978-1-4209-2246-2(7)) Digireads.com Publishing.

—White Fang. 2004. reprint ed. pap. 1.99 (978-1-4192-9386-3(9)); pap. 22.95 (978-1-4191-9386-6(4)) Kessinger Publishing, LLC.

—White Fang. 2006. (Aladdin Classics Ser.). (ENG., Illus.). 368p. (J). (gr. 4-7). pap. 7.99 (978-1-4169-1414-3(5), Aladdin) Simon & Schuster Children's Publishing.

London, Jonathan. Giving Thanks. Manchess, Gregory, illus. 2011. (ENG.). 32p. (J). (gr. -1-2). pap. 6.99 (978-0-7636-5594-5(5)) Candlewick Pr.

—Grizzly Peak. London, Sean, illus. 2017. (Aaron's Wilderness Ser.). (ENG.). 174p. (YA). pap. 12.99 (978-1-943328-77-2(3), West Winds Pr.) Graphic Arts Ctr. Publishing Co.

Lonsdale, Cathy. Bill the Brush Turkey. 2008. 24p. 13.95 (978-1-4092-0414-5(6)) Lulu Pr., Inc.

Lukkarinen, Ritva. Amy. Vainio, Pirkko, illus. 2009. (ENG.). 30p. (J). (gr. -1-k). 16.95 (978-1-60537-058-3(4)) Cobblestone Publishing Co.

Madison's Descent: A Child's Journey. collector's ed. 2004. (J). 75.00 (978-0-9752516-0-7(0)) Otis & Randolph Pr.

Mahoney, Liana. Forest Green: A Walk Through the Adirondack Seasons. Henry, Maggie, illus. 2014. (J). (978-1-59531-047-7(9)) North Country Bks., Inc.

Mair, J. Samia. Amira's Totally Chocolate World. 2010. (ENG., Illus.). 29p. (J). (gr. k-3). 8.95 (978-0-86037-408-4(4)) Kube Publishing Ltd. GBR. Dist: Consortium Bk. Sales & Distribution.

Mallory, Alex. Wild. 2014. (ENG.). 448p. (YA). (gr. 8). 17.99 (978-0-06-221874-2(3), HarperTeen) HarperCollins Pubs.

Mallory, Carolyn. Painted Skies, 1 vol. Zhao, Amei, illus. 2015. (ENG.). 36p. (J). (gr. k-2). 16.95 (978-1-77227-004-4(0)) Inhabit Media Inc. CAN. Dist: Independent Pubs. Group.

Manning, Lisa C. Falcons in the City. Manning, Lisa C., illus. 2013. (ENG., Illus.). 40p. (J). pap. 14.95 (978-1-59299-886-9(0)) Inkwater Pr.

Margulies, Paul. What Julianna Could See. Zonneveld, Famke, illus. 2004. 32p. (J). pap. 11.95 (978-0-88010-515-6(1)) SteinerBooks, Inc.

Marino Walters, Jennifer. Amazing Autumn. Nez, John, illus. 2016. (Seasons Ser.). (ENG.). 24p. (J). (gr. -1-1). lib. bdg. 25.32 (978-1-63440-045-9(3)) Red Chair Pr.

—Surprising Spring. Nez, John, illus. 2016. (Seasons Ser.). (ENG.). 24p. (J). (gr. -1-1). lib. bdg. 25.32 (978-1-63440-047-3(X)) Red Chair Pr.

—Sweet Summer. Nez, John, illus. 2016. (Seasons Ser.). (ENG.). 24p. (J). (gr. -1-1). lib. bdg. 25.32 (978-1-63440-048-0(8)) Red Chair Pr.

—Wonderful Winter. Nez, John, illus. 2016. (Seasons Ser.). (ENG.). 24p. (J). (gr. -1-1). lib. bdg. 25.32 (978-1-63440-046-6(1)) Red Chair Pr.

Marsh, Carole. The Voracious Volcano Mystery. 2008. (Masters of Disasters Ser.). (Illus.). 118p. (J). (gr. 3-5). 14.95 (978-0-635-06466-0(9)); per. 5.99 (978-0-635-06463-9(4)) Gallopade International.

Marston, Hope Irvin. My Little Book of Manatees. Mirocha, Stephanie, illus. 2007. 32p. (J). (gr. k-5). pap. 7.95 (978-0-89317-065-3(8), Windward Publishing) Finney Co., Inc.

Mason, David. Davey McGravy. Silverstein, Grant, illus. 2015. (ENG.). 120p. (J). (gr. k). pap. 14.95 (978-1-58988-099-3(4)) Dry, Paul Bks., Inc.

Mayer, Mercer. It's Earth Day!, No. 5. Mayer, Mercer, illus. 2008. (Little Critter Ser.: No. 5). (ENG., Illus.). 24p. (J). (gr. -1-2). pap. 3.99 (978-0-06-053959-7(3), HarperFestival) HarperCollins Pubs.

McCarthy, Mary. A Closer Look. McCarthy, Mary, illus. 2007. (ENG., Illus.). 40p. (J). (gr. -1-k). 17.99 (978-0-06-124073-7(7), Greenwillow Bks.) HarperCollins Pubs.

McFadden, Patricia. Oh No, Woolly Bear!, 1 vol. Coxon, Michele, illus. 2008. (ENG.). 32p. (J). (gr. -1-3). 6.50 (978-1-59572-149-5(5)) Star Bright Bks., Inc.

McKelvey, Lonnie. Benny the Brave. Wooten, Neal, illus. 2008. 28p. (J). pap. 7.99 (978-0-9817521-3-6(6)) Mirror Publishing.

McNish, Cliff. Savannah Grey. (ENG.). 272p. (YA). (gr. 7-12). 2013. pap. 9.95 (978-1-4677-0913-2(1)) 2011. 17.95 (978-0-7613-7025-3(0)) Lerner Publishing Group. (Carolrhoda Lab™).

Meachen Rau, Dana. Floating. 2006. (On the Move Ser.). (SPA., Illus.). 24p. (gr. k-1). lib. bdg. 15.95 (978-0-7614-2315-7(X), Benchmark Bks.) Marshall Cavendish Corp.

—A Flotar. 2006. (En Movimiento Ser.). (SPA., Illus.). 24p. (gr. k-1). lib. bdg. 15.95 (978-0-7614-2420-8(2), Benchmark Bks.) Marshall Cavendish Corp.

Meadows, Daisy. Shannon the Ocean Fairy. 2009. (Rainbow Magic Ser.). (ENG.). 176p. (J). (gr. 2-5). 6.99 (978-0-545-10576-7(5), Scholastic Paperbacks) Scholastic, Inc.

Meil, Gabriel & Rylander, Emily. Goodbye Earth Hello Moon. 2008. (ENG.). 32p. (J). (gr. k-2). 16.95 (978-1-934866-02-3(4)) Warren Machine Co.

Las Mil y una Noches. (Coleccion Estrella). (SPA., Illus.). 64p. (J). 14.95 (978-950-11-0001-3(4), SGM001) Sigmar ARG. Dist: Continental Bk. Co., Inc.

Milbourne, Anna. Sunny Day (Picture Book) 2008. (Picture Bks). 24p. (J). 9.99 (978-0-7945-2117-2(7), Usborne) EDC Publishing.

Mills, Wynette. The Backyard Explorer: The Nana & Me Series. 2010. 36p. pap. 15.49 (978-1-4520-2483-7(9)) AuthorHouse.

Mjolhus, Joy. Squirrel Babies & Friends. 2008. 16p. pap. 24.95 (978-1-4241-8562-7(9)) America Star Bks.

Montijo, Rhode. Cloud Boy/Nino Nube. Mlawer, Teresa, tr. from ENG. 2006. (SPA & ENG., Illus.). 24p. (J). (gr. -1-3). 12.99 (978-1-933032-06-1(5)) Lectorum Pubns., Inc.

Mooney, Ginger. Spirit Elk. 2009. 16p. pap. 9.99 (978-1-4490-0447-7(4)) AuthorHouse.

Morel, Alicia. Cuentos Araucanos: La Gente de la Tierra. (SPA.). (J). (gr. 4-6). pap. (978-956-13-1152-7(6), AB1252) Bello, Andres CHL. Dist: Lectorum Pubns., Inc.

Morningforest, Chris & Raymond, Rebecca. The Adventures of Nate & Naomi. 2006. 36p. (J). pap. 15.43 (978-1-4116-9244-2(6)) Lulu Pr., Inc.

Moulton, Erin E. Flutter: The Story of Four Sisters & an Incredible Journey. 2012. (ENG.). 224p. (J). (gr. 3-7). pap. 6.99 (978-0-14-242133-8(2), Puffin Books) Penguin Young Readers Group.

Mundy, Dawn. The Gift: A Woodsong Story. Tigue, Terry & Turner, Diane, illus. 2003. (J). lib. bdg. (978-1-932139-16-7(8)) DEMDACO.

Murphy & Pimlott. Certain Island. 2014. (ENG.). 240p. (J). (gr. 5-8). pap. 14.95 (978-1-59077-324-6(1)) Evans, M. & Co., Inc.

Mwangi, Nyaruai. Argwings & the Lamplighters. 2008. 96p. (YA). pap. 13.95 (978-0-9796476-8-0(1)) HM Bks.

Nesbit, E. In Homespun. 2007. 108p. per. (978-1-4065-3079-7(4)) Dodo Pr.

Neubert, Oliver. Chantel's Quest for the Enchanted Medallion. 2009. (Cozy Classics Ser.). (ENG., Illus.). 224p. (J). (gr. 3-6). 16.95 (978-1-897476-15-4(9)) Simply Read Bks. CAN. Dist: Ingram Publisher Services.

Nevins, Mary. The Adventures of Molly. 2009. 20p. pap. 14.50 (978-1-60693-919-2(X), Eloquent Bks.) Strategic Book Publishing & Rights Agency (SBPRA).

Nichols, Lori. Maple & Willow Together. Nichols, Lori, illus. 2014. (ENG., Illus.). 32p. (J). (gr. -1-k). 16.99 (978-0-399-16283-1(6), Nancy Paulsen Books) Penguin Young Readers Group.

Nigro Heroux, Regina. Grandma's Butterfly Garden. 2009. 28p. pap. 13.99 (978-1-4490-3054-4(8)) AuthorHouse.

Nolan, Allia Zobel. God's Rainbow. Chung, Chi, illus. 2007. 16p. (J). 12.99 (978-0-8254-5537-7(5)) Kregel Pubns.

Obed, Ellen Bryan. Who Would Like a Christmas Tree? A Tree for All Seasons. Hunter, Anne, illus. 2009. (ENG.). 32p. (J). (gr. -1-3). 16.00 (978-0-547-04625-9(1)) Houghton Mifflin Harcourt Publishing Co.

O'Brien, Anne Sibley. Abracadabra, It's Spring! Gal, Susan, illus. 2016. (Seasonal Magic Ser.). (ENG.). 24p. (J). (gr. -1-k). 14.95 (978-1-4197-1891-5(6), Abrams Appleseed) Abrams, Inc.

O'Donnel, Liam. Scout Hits the Trail. Huerta, Catherine, illus. (Pet Tales Ser.). (ENG.). 32p. (J). (gr. -1-3). 2008. 4.95 (978-1-59249-740-9(3)) 2007. 9.95 (978-1-59249-742-3(X)) Soundprints.

O'Donnell, Candy. Where Is God, Grandfather. Gillen, Rosemarie, illus. 2008. 28p. pap. 12.95 (978-0-9814532-1-7(X)) Living Waters Publishing Co.

O'Donnell, Liam. Scout Hits the Trail. Huerta, Catherine, illus. 2007. (ENG.). 32p. (J). 2.95 (978-1-59249-741-6(1)) Soundprints.

O'Garden, Irene. Forest, What Would You Like? Schories, Pat, illus. 2013. (ENG.). 32p. (J). (gr. -1-3). 16.95 (978-0-8234-2322-4(0)) Holiday Hse., Inc.

Olivia's Sensational Stories: Olivia Helps Mother Nature; Olivia Goes to the Library; Olivia Plays Soccer; Olivia Measures Up; Olivia Builds a House; Olivia Becomes a Vet. 2014. (Olivia TV Tie-In Ser.). (ENG., Illus.). 144p. (J). (gr. -1-1). pap. 15.99 (978-1-4814-2148-5(4), Simon Spotlight) Simon Spotlight.

Oppenheim, Shulamith. Where Do I End & You Begin? Felix, Monique, illus. 2015. (ENG.). 32p. (J). (gr. 1-3). 17.99 (978-1-56846-274-5(3), Creative Editions) Creative Co., The.

Pages, Christina. The Mountain Boy. Caruth, Jeannette, illus. 2007. (Nature Children Ser.). 39p. (J). (gr. -1-3). 12.95 (978-0-9794863-9-5(4)) Summerland Publishing.

Pak, Kenard. Goodbye Autumn, Hello Winter. Pak, Kenard, illus. 2017. (ENG., Illus.). 32p. (J). 17.99 (**978-1-62779-416-9(6)**, 9781627794169, Holt, Henry & Co. Bks. For Young Readers) Holt, Henry & Co.

Pak, Kenard. Goodbye Summer, Hello Autumn. Pak, Kenard, illus. 2016. (ENG., Illus.). 32p. (J). 17.99 (978-1-62779-415-2(8), 9781627794152, Holt, Henry & Co. Bks. For Young Readers) Holt, Henry & Co.

Pandell, Karen. Te Amo, Sol - Te Amo, Luna. dePaola, Tomie, illus. 2003.Tr. of I Love You, Sun - I Love You, Moon. (SPA & ENG.). 12p. (J). (gr. -1 — 1). bds. 7.99 (978-0-399-24165-9(5), G.P. Putnam's Sons Books for Young Readers) Penguin Young Readers Group.

Paquette, Ammi-Joan. The Tiptoe Guide to Tracking Fairies. Unzner, Christa, illus. 2009. (ENG.). 32p. (J). (gr. -1-3). 15.95 (978-1-933718-20-0(X)) Tanglewood Pr.

Paquette, Ammi-Joan & Unzner, Christa. The Tiptoe Guide to Tracking Fairies. 2010. (ENG., Illus.). 32p. (J). (gr. -1-3). pap. 8.95 (978-1-933718-50-7(1)) Tanglewood Pr.

Paterson, John B., Jr. & Paterson, John B., Sr. Roberto's Trip to the Top. Alarcao, Renato, illus. 2009. (ENG.). 40p. (J). (gr. -1-3). 16.99 (978-0-7636-2708-9(9)) Candlewick Pr.

Paterson, Katherine. Brother Sun, Sister Moon. Dalton, Pamela, illus. 2011. (ENG.). 36p. (J). (gr. -1-1). 17.99 (978-0-8118-7734-3(5)) Chronicle Bks. LLC.

Patten, William. Animal & Nature Stories Vol. 8: The Junior Classics. 2004. reprint ed. pap. 1.99 (978-1-4192-6805-2(8)) Kessinger Publishing, LLC.

Patterson, Eric. Nature Boy Nature Strikes Back. Wright, Chris, illus. 2008. 108p. pap. 6.95 (978-1-935105-15-2(9)) Avid Readers Publishing Group.

Paulsen, Gary. Fishbone's Song. 2016. (ENG., Illus.). 160p. (J). (gr. 5). 16.99 (978-1-4814-5226-7(6), Simon & Schuster Bks. For Young Readers) Simon & Schuster Bks. For Young Readers.

—The Island. 2006. (Point Ser.). 202p. (gr. 7-12). 16.00 (978-0-7569-6382-8(6)) Perfection Learning Corp.

Penick Phillips-Cermak, Mosetta. The Wishing Flower. 2007. 24p. 16.50 (978-0-615-15573-9(1)) PM Moon Pubs., Ltd.

Perry, Rex. All Things Bright & Beautiful. 2004. 24p. (J). lib. bdg. 8.00 (978-1-4242-0638-4(3)) Fitzgerald Bks.

Pfister, Marcus. Questions, Questions. 2011. (ENG & GER., Illus.). 32p. (J). (gr. -1-2). 16.95 (978-0-7358-4000-3(8)) North-South Bks., Inc.

Pirnot, Karen Hutchins. Rainbows Are the Best. Allen, Sandra Hutchins, illus. 2009. 24p. pap. 12.95 (978-1-936051-01-4(X)) Peppertree Pr., The.

Plourde, Lynn. The First Feud: Between the Mountain & the Sea. Sollers, Jim, illus. 2003. (ENG.). 30p. (J). (gr. k-17). 15.95 (978-0-89272-611-0(3)) Down East Bks.

Plum, Amy. Until the Beginning. 2015. (After the End Ser.: 2). (ENG.). 336p. (YA). (gr. 8). 17.99 (978-0-06-222563-4(4), HarperTeen) HarperCollins Pubs.

Polinski, Jo. Minnesota Moon. Webber, Carol, illus. 2007. 20p. per. 12.95 (978-1-933482-60-6(5)) White Turtle Bks.

Price, Ellen Ann. Gladly's Magic. 2011. 160p. 27.50 (978-0-557-71561-9(X)); pap. 18.00 (978-1-257-10561-8(2)) Lulu Pr., Inc.

Ramsey, Ann Louise. Me, the Tree. Ramsey, Ann Louise, illus. 2006. (ENG., Illus.). 56p. (J). 19.95 (978-0-9645663-4-7(6)) Crown Peak Publishing.

Rawlinson, Julia. Fletcher & the Falling Leaves. 2011. (J). (gr. -1-2). 18.95 (978-0-545-19705-2(8)); 29.95 (978-0-545-19699-4(X)) Weston Woods Studios, Inc.

Rebello, Kevin. Julia & Mckinley's Day at the Beach. 2009. 32p. pap. 12.99 (978-1-4389-7330-2(6)) AuthorHouse.

Reed-Jones, C, et al. El Arbol Del Viejo Bosque. 2005. (SPA.). 32p. 18.95 (978-84-7720-789-4(5)) Ediciones Obelisco ESP. Dist: Spanish Pubs., LLC.

Rehm, Carolyn. The Flower Pot Bunnies: Not A Good Place For A Nest. Schanck, Agnes, illus. 2004. 48p. (J). bds. 12.99 (978-0-9755390-1-9(9)) Fifth Ave Pr.

Richards, Brenda. A Woodland Tale. 2011. 32p. pap. 21.99 (978-1-4568-5708-0(8)) Xlibris Corp.

Riggs, Kate. Colors of Nature. Domeniconi, Paolo, illus. 2017. (ENG.). 14p. (J). (gr. -1 — 1). bds. 8.99 (978-1-56846-299-8(9), Creative Education) Creative Co., The.

Rockwell, Anne. My Spring Robin. Rockwell, Harlow, illus. 2015. (ENG.). 24p. (J). (gr. -1-3). 16.99 (978-1-4814-1137-0(3), Aladdin) Simon & Schuster Children's Publishing.

Rodricks, Marie. Razzle the Sunbeam. 2008. 68p. pap. 10.49 (978-1-4343-9651-8(7)) AuthorHouse.

Rogers, Suzanne J. Cody Meets A Butterfly. 2008. 72p. pap. 19.95 (978-1-4327-2069-8(4)) Outskirts Pr., Inc.

Ross, Patrick. Joseph & Snowy Joe Blue, 1 vol. Burcham, David, illus. 2009. 25p. pap. 24.95 (978-1-61582-314-7(X)) PublishAmerica, Inc.

Ross, Thea. Molly Mole Takes a Nature Walk. 2004. (Lift-the-Flap Surprise on Every Spread! Ser.). 12p. (J). 5.99 (978-1-59384-045-7(4)) Parklane Publishing.

Rossiter, Nan Parson. The Fo'c'sle: Henry Beston's Outermost House. 2012. (Illus.). 32p. (J). (gr. 5-18). 17.95 (978-1-56792-433-6(6)) Godine, David R. Pub.

Ruley, Garrett. Hollin. 2011. 226p. pap. 15.00 (978-0-557-55873-5(5)) Lulu Pr., Inc.

Russell-Gilmer, Phyllis A. Where Do Crickets Go When Winter Comes? Jones, Chamira, illus. 2009. 32p. (J). 16.95 (978-1-934363-10-2(3)) Zoe Life Publishing.

Russell, Lyndsay & Hanson, Tippi. Rainbow Weaver. Russell, Lyndsay & Hanson, Tippi, illus. 2007. (ENG., Illus.). 48p. (J). (gr. k-2). 13.99 (978-1-84243-229-7(X)) Oldcastle Bks., Ltd. GBR. Dist: Independent Pubs. Group.

Ruth, Nick. The Breezes of Inspire. Concannon, Sue, illus. 2005. (Remin Chronicles: 2). (ENG.). 264p. (J). (gr. 3-7). 16.95 (978-0-9745603-3-5(2)) Imaginator Pr.

Ryder, Joanne. The Waterfall's Gift, 1 vol. Watson, Richard Jesse, illus. 2004. (ENG.). 40p. pap. 7.95 (978-1-57805-113-7(4)) Gibbs Smith, Publisher.

Rylant, Cynthia. Life. Wenzel, Brendan, illus. 2017. (ENG.). 48p. (J). (gr. -1). 17.99 (**978-1-4814-5162-8(6)**, Beach Lane Bks.) Beach Lane Bks.

Sage, Cathryn. Destiny's Secret. 2012. 44p. (-18). pap. 21.99 (978-1-4389-1530-2(6)) AuthorHouse.

Salwey, Kenny. Muskrat for Supper: Exploring the Natural World with the Last River Rat. 2012. (ENG., Illus.). 260p. (J). (gr. 4-9). pap. 12.95 (978-1-55591-567-4(1)) Fulcrum Publishing.

Sams II, Carl R. & Stoick, Jean, photos by. When Snowflakes Fall. 2009. (ENG., Illus.). 14p. bds. 7.95 (978-0-9770108-9-9(9)) Sams, II, Carl R. Photography, Inc.

Santos de las Heras, José María. Cachicos. 2007. 176p. pap. 20.95 (978-1-84799-885-9(2)) Lulu Pr., Inc.

Santos, Penelope. Paula's Pinecone. 2015. (Rosen REAL Readers: STEM & STEAM Collection). (ENG.). 8p. pap. 5.46 (978-1-4994-9545-4(5), Rosen Classroom) Rosen Publishing Group, Inc., The.

Scanlon, Liz Garton. In the Canyon. Wolff, Ashley, illus. 2015. (ENG.). 40p. (J). (gr. -1-3). 17.99 (978-1-4814-0348-1(6), Beach Lane Bks.) Beach Lane Bks.

Scelsa, Greg. Rainbow of Colors. Faulkner, Stacey, ed. Sexton, Brenda, illus. 2006. (J). pap. 2.99 (978-1-59198-351-4(7)) Creative Teaching Pr., Inc.

—The World Is a Rainbow. Faulkner, Stacey, ed. Schneider, Christine, illus. 2006. (J). pap. 2.99 (978-1-59198-319-4(3)) Creative Teaching Pr., Inc.

Schkolnik, Saul. Cuentos Ecologicos. Cardemil, Carmen, illus. 2nd ed. 2003. (la Orilla del Viento Ser.).Tr. of Ecological Tales. (SPA.). 56p. (J). (gr. 3-7). per. (978-968-16-4757-5(2), FC6400) Fondo de Cultura Economica MEX. Dist: Lectorum Pubns., Inc.

Schmidt, Hans-Christian & Bieber, Hartmut. The Wondrous Day. 2004. (Illus.). 18p. (J). 10.99 (978-1-59384-047-1(0)) Parklane Publishing.

Schwartz, Betty Ann. One to Ten... & Back Again. Shakir, Susie, illus. 2009. 24p. bds. 12.99 (978-0-8249-1436-3(8), Ideal Pubns.) Worthy Publishing.

Schwartz, Tom. How Mother Nature Flowered the Fields. 2006. (Illus.). 120p. (J). per. 14.95 (978-1-57545-102-2(6), Reagent Pr. Echo) RP Media.

Segarra, Angelo M. Coca Finds a Shell. Segarra, Kirstie, ed. Segarra, Angelo M., illus. 2004. (Illus.). 24p. (J). 14.95 (978-0-9752664-0-3(3)) Segarra, Angelo.

Senir, Mirik & Shubow, Mary Jane. When I First Held You: A Lullaby from Israel. 2009. (J). lib. bdg. 17.95 (978-0-7613-5096-5(9), Kar-Ben Publishing) Lerner Publishing Group.

Seton, Ernest Thompson. The Biography of a Silver Fox. 2005. pap. 24.95 (978-1-885529-39-8(2)) Stevens Publishing.

Seven, John. Gorilla Gardener: How to Help Nature Take over the World. Christy, Jana, illus. 2017. (Wee Rebel Ser.). (ENG.). 44p. (J). (gr. -1). 16.95 (978-1-945665-00-4(9)) Manic D Pr.

Shearer, Tony. The Praying Flute: Song of the Earth Mother. rev. ed. 2006. (Illus.). 96p. pap. 16.95 (978-0-87961-268-9(1)) Naturegraph Pubs., Inc.

Sherrell, Deborah. Baby Lauren & Theodore,hardcover. 2007. (Illus.). (J). bds. 17.95 (978-0-9779643-5-2(3)) Healing Tree Arts.

Shields, Kathleen J. Hamilton Troll Meets Elwood Woodpecker. Klug, Leigh A. & Bryant, Carol W., illus. 5th ed. 2013. 36p. 14.00 (978-0-9882745-4-9(X)) Erin Go Bragh Publishing.

Simler, Isabelle, illus. The Blue Hour. 2017. (J). 19.00 (**978-0-8028-5488-9(5)**, Eerdmans Bks For Young Readers) Eerdmans, William B. Publishing Co.

Skipper, Cecil. The Deer Lick. 2004. 166p. (YA). pap. 12.95 (978-0-595-30949-8(6)) iUniverse, Inc.

Smith, David. Nature's Garden. 2009. 132p. 22.50 (978-1-60693-169-1(5), Eloquent Bks.) Strategic Book Publishing & Rights Agency (SBPRA).

Snyder, Betsy E. Sweet Dreams Lullaby. 2012. (ENG., Illus.). 32p. (J). (— 1). bds. 6.99 (978-0-307-98060-1(X), Random Hse. Bks. for Young Readers) Random Hse. Children's Bks.

Sparks, Shanti. Honey & the Sunset. 2008. (Illus.). 38p. (J). pap. 9.00 (978-0-8059-7553-6(5)) Dorrance Publishing Co., Inc.

Stack, Kevin W. The Great Oak Tree. 2008. (Illus.). 32p. pap. 12.99 (978-1-4389-1856-3(9)) AuthorHouse.

Stauffer, Sharon. Cornfield Baby: And Other Nature Surprises. 2003. (Illus.). 179p. 8.40 (978-0-7399-2314-6(5), 2344) Rod & Staff Pubs., Inc.

Steinberg, Laya. All Around Me, I See. Arbo, Cris, illus. 2005. (Sharing Nature with Children Book Ser.). 32p. (J). 16.95 (978-1-58469-068-9(2)); pap. 8.95 (978-1-58469-069-6(0)) Dawn Pubns.

Stiverson, Charlotte L. Nellie's Walk. Aitken, Kati, illus. 2016. (J). (978-1-935864-62-2(9)) Oncology Nursing Society.

Stone, Jodi. I Want to Catch a Dragonfly. 2008. 28p. per. 24.95 (978-1-4241-8770-6(2)) America Star Bks.

Stuart, Tara. Trees: A Tara's Tale about Being Yourself. 2006. (Illus.). (J). bds. 15.00 (978-0-9765060-3-4(3)) TouchSmart Publishing, LLC.

Sudo, Kumiko. Coco-Chan's Kimono. Sudo, Kumiko, illus. 2010. (ENG., Illus.). 32p. (J). (gr. k-2). 16.95 (978-1-933308-26-5(5)) Breckling Pr.

Sullivan, Silvia. Hip Hip Hurray We Found Teddy: A Book Series to Teach Children Practical Life Skills & Eco-Friendly Skills. 2008. 32p. pap. 15.48 (978-1-4343-5897-4(6)) AuthorHouse.

Tarter, Mildred. Alexis Uses the Elements of Nature. 2011. 24p. pap. 16.49 (978-1-4389-6879-7(5)) AuthorHouse.

Tate, Suzanne. Skippy Scallop: A Tale of Bright Blue Eyes. Melvin, James, illus. 2003. (Suzanne Tate's Nature Ser.: No. 26). 28p. (J). pap. 4.95 (978-1-878405-43-2(8)) Nags Head Art, Inc.

Thompson, Lauren. Mouse's First Fall. Erdogan, Buket, illus. 2010. (Classic Board Bks.). (ENG.). 34p. (J). (gr. -1 — 1). bds. 7.99 (978-1-4169-9477-0(7), Little Simon) Little Simon.

—Mouse's First Fall. Erdogan, Buket, illus. 2006. (ENG.). 32p. (J). (gr. -1-1). 15.99 (978-0-689-85837-6(X), Simon & Schuster Bks. For Young Readers) Simon & Schuster Bks. For Young Readers.

—Mouse's First Spring. Erdogan, Buket, illus. 2012. (Classic Board Bks.). (ENG.). 34p. (J). (gr. -1-3). bds. 7.99 (978-1-4424-3431-8(7), Little Simon) Little Simon.

—Mouse's First Spring. Erdogan, Buket, illus. 2005. (ENG.). 32p. (J). (gr. -1-3). 17.99 (978-0-689-85838-3(8), Simon & Schuster Bks. For Young Readers) Simon & Schuster Bks. For Young Readers.

Thorpe, Rochelle O'Neal. Gabe's Nantucket Adventure: Daffodils, Dogs, & Cars. Nakell, Eugenie, ed. Margolis, Al, illus. l.t. ed. 2010. 28p. (YA). pap. 7.95 (978-1-935706-02-1(0)) Wiggles Pr.

Ticktock Media, Ltd. Staff. Zoom into Space with the Shiny Red Rocket. 2009. (Touch & Feel Fun Ser.). (ENG.). 10p. (J). (gr. k — 1). bds. 5.95 (978-1-84696-812-9(7), TickTock Books) Octopus Publishing Group GBR. Dist: Independent Pubs. Group.

Tietz, Heather. Yes, Jesus Loves You. Miller, Nancy, illus. 2009. 20p. (J). (gr. k-4). 14.95 (978-0-8091-6743-2(3), Ambassador Bks.) Paulist Pr.

Tillman, Nancy. On the Night You Were Born. 2010. (ENG., Illus.). 32p. (J). (— 1). bds. 7.99 (978-0-312-60155-3(7), 9780312601553) Feiwel & Friends.

—On the Night You Were Born, 1 vol., Set. unabr. ed. 2012. (ENG., Illus.). 32p. (J). (— 1). 12.99 (978-1-4272-2646-4(6), 9781427226464) Macmillan Audio.

Todd, Pamela. The Blind Faith Hotel. (ENG.). 320p. (YA). (gr. 7). 2010. pap. 8.99 (978-1-4169-9509-8(9)) 2008. 16.99 (978-1-4169-5494-1(5)) McElderry, Margaret K. Bks. (McElderry, Margaret K. Bks.).

Townsend, Wendy. The Sundown Rule. 2011. (J). (gr. 5-9). 18.95 (978-1-60898-099-4(5)) namelos llc.

Turnbull, Victoria. Pandora. 2017. (ENG., Illus.). 32p. (J). (gr. -1-3). 16.99 (978-0-544-94733-7(9), Clarion Bks.) Houghton Mifflin Harcourt Trade & Reference Pubs.

Twigger, J. Nicci & Her Amazing Adventure. 2008. (Illus.). 40p. pap. 18.49 (978-1-4389-1295-0(1)) AuthorHouse.

U. S. National Geographic Society Staff. How Does Your Garden Grow? 2009. (Toot & Puddle Ser.). (ENG., Illus.). 24p. (J). (gr. -1-2). lib. bdg. 11.90 (978-1-4263-0483-5(8), National Geographic Children's Bks.) National Geographic Society.

Updike, John. A Child's Calendar. Updike, John & Hyman, Trina Schart, illus. 2004. (J). (gr. k-4). 28.95 incl. audio compact disk (978-1-59112-932-5(X)) Live Oak Media.

—A Child's Calendar. Hyman, Trina Schart, illus. unabr. ed. 2004. (J). (gr. k-4). 25.95 incl. audio (978-1-59112-472-6(7)) Live Oak Media.

Valverde, Mikel. Paula en Nueva York. 2006. (SPA., Illus.). 32p. (J). (gr. 6-8). 14.99 (978-1-933032-15-3(4)) Lectorum Pubns., Inc.

Van Pelt, Jason. The Color Wheel. 2013. 28p. pap. 24.95 (978-1-4626-9697-0(X)) America Star Bks.

Vanalstine, Carrie. Frizzy Izzy Yelp! 2012. 32p. pap. 11.95 (978-1-4685-4609-5(0)) AuthorHouse.

MNO

Voake, Charlotte. Tweedle Dee Dee. Voake, Charlotte, illus. 2008. (ENG., Illus.). 32p. (J). (gr. -1-2). 16.99 *(978-0-7636-3797-2(1))* Candlewick Pr.

Vrba, Christina. Good Night Connecticut. Rosen, Anne, illus. 2009. (Good Night Our World Ser.). (ENG.). 20p. (J). (gr. k — 1). bds. 9.95 *(978-1-60219-035-1(6))* Good Night Bks.

Walker, Johnny. The Planet Blue: The Adventures of Harry Lee & Bingo. 2011. 24p. pap. 11.32 *(978-1-4567-4879-1(3))* AuthorHouse.

Walters, Jennifer Marino. Amazing Autumn. Nez, John, illus. 2016. (Seasons Ser.). (ENG.). 24p. (J). (gr. -1-1). pap. 6.99 *(978-1-63440-120-3(4))* Red Chair Pr.

Ward, Kaitlin. Bleeding Earth. 2016. (ENG.). 256p. (YA). 17.99 *(978-0-9864484-8-5(6))* Adaptive Studios.

Ward, Terri & Ward, Tom. Aunt Tami's Strawberry Farm. Kindt, Rita, illus. 2010. 38p. pap. 14.50 *(978-1-60693-935-2(1),* Eloquent Bks.) Strategic Book Publishing & Rights Agency (SBPRA).

Welles, Lee. Enter the Earth. Hameister, Ann, illus. 2007. (Gaia Girls Ser.: 1). (ENG.). 336p. (YA). (gr. 4-7). pap. 24.95 *(978-1-933609-01-0(X))* Chelsea Green Publishing.

—Gaia Girls: Way of Water. Coogan, Carol, illus. 2007. (Gaia Girls Ser.). (ENG.). 336p. (J). (gr. 4-7). 18.95 *(978-1-933609-02-7(8))* Chelsea Green Publishing.

—Way of Water. Coogan, Carol, illus. 2007. (Gaia Girls Ser.: 2). (ENG.). 336p. (YA). (gr. 4-7). pap. 19.95 *(978-1-933609-03-4(6))* Chelsea Green Publishing.

Weston Woods Staff, creator. Fletcher & the Falling Leaves. 2011. 38.75 *(978-0-545-19710-6(4))* Weston Woods Studios, Inc.

—Henry Hikes to Fitchburg. 2011. 38.75 *(978-0-439-90698-2(9));* 18.95 *(978-0-439-90696-8(2))* Weston Woods Studios, Inc.

Whincup, Sara. The St John's Cross Spider. Yapsangco, Kenn, illus. 2015. (ENG.). 28p. (J). pap. 28.22 *(978-1-5035-0985-6(0))* Xlibris Corp.

Williams, Mavis E. A Cricket. 2009. 24p. pap. 11.99 *(978-1-4389-7714-0(X))* AuthorHouse.

Williams, S. L. Polka-Dot Maddy's Birthday Fun: Colors of the Rainbow. 2008. 36p. pap. 24.95 *(978-1-60672-908-3(X))* America Star Bks.

Wilshire, Florence. All from the Skies. 2005. 82p. pap. 18.08 *(978-1-4116-3114-4(5))* Lulu Pr., Inc.

Wilson, Jacqui. Little Johnny's Faith Adventures: Creation Curiosity! 2012. 30p. pap. 15.95 *(978-1-4497-5994-0(7),* WestBow Pr.) Author Solutions, Inc.

The Wind in the Willows. 2016. (Ladybird Classics Ser.). (ENG., Illus.). 72p. (J). (gr. 3-7). 10.99 *(978-1-4093-1356-4(5))* Penguin Bks., Ltd. GBR. Dist: Independent Pubs. Group.

Winnie the Pooh. The Close-up Day. 2010. 16p. 5.99 *(978-1-4231-3096-3(0))* Disney Pr.

Wisdom, Eileen Mary. Harry Meets Mathilda, 5 bks., Bk.1. Saunders, M. D., illus. 2007. 36p. (J). pap. 20.00 *(978-0-9771102-2-3(2))* Pelican Pr.

Wissinger, Tamera Will. Gone Camping: A Novel in Verse. Cordell, Matthew, illus. 2017. (ENG.). 112p. (J). (gr. 1-4). 15.99 *(978-0-544-63873-0(5),* HMH Books For Young Readers) Houghton Mifflin Harcourt Publishing Co.

Wolff, Ashley. Baby Bear Sees Blue. Wolff, Ashley, illus. 2012. (Baby Bear Ser.). (ENG., Illus.). 40p. (J). (gr. -1-1). 17.99 *(978-1-4424-1306-1(9),* Beach Lane Bks.) Beach Lane Bks.

Wood, Douglas. Grandad's Prayers of the Earth. Lynch, P. J., illus. 2009. 32p. pap. 6.99 *(978-0-7636-1865-0(9));* (ENG.). (J). (gr. 1-4). pap. 7.99 *(978-0-7636-4675-2(X))* Candlewick Pr.

—Making the World. Yoshi, illus. 2008. (ENG.). 44p. (J). (gr. -1-2). 13.99 *(978-1-4169-8596-9(4),* Simon & Schuster Bks. For Young Readers) Simon & Schuster Bks. For Young Readers.

—No One but You. Lynch, P. J., illus. 2011. (ENG.). 32p. (J). (gr. 1-4). 17.99 *(978-0-7636-3848-1(X))* Candlewick Pr.

—Where the Sunrise Begins. Popp, K. Wendy, illus. 2010. (ENG.). 32p. (J). (gr. -1-3). 17.99 *(978-0-689-86172-7(9),* Simon & Schuster Bks. For Young Readers) Simon & Schuster Bks. For Young Readers.

Wuehr, Tina L. Field Dance. Brown, Mari, illus. 2005. 18p. (J). (gr. -1-3). *(978-0-9739962-0-3(X))* Wuehr, Tina.

Yang, Angela. Out of the Dark. 2012. 166p. pap. 12.85 *(978-0-578-09356-7(1))* Yang, Jennifer.

Yee, Wong Herbert. Abracadabra! Magic with Mouse & Mole. 2010. (Mouse & Mole Story Ser.). (ENG., Illus.). 48p. (J). (gr. -1-3). pap. 3.99 *(978-0-547-40621-3(5))* Houghton Mifflin Harcourt Publishing Co.

Yerushalmi, Miriam. Let's Go Camping & Discover Our Nature. Perez, Esther Ido, illus. 2007. 28p. (J). (gr. 2-4). 16.50 *(978-0-911643-38-1(9))* Aura Printing, Inc.

Yost, B. L. Have You Ever Seen a Wild Bird Dance? Perkins, Chelsea, illus. 2008. 16p. pap. 24.95 *(978-1-60703-127-7(2))* America Star Bks.

Young, Sunshine. Mother Earth's ABC. 2007. (J). spiral bd. 14.95 *(978-0-9796180-2-4(9))* Williams, Benjamin Publishing.

Zaidi, Nadeem, illus. Baby Mozart: Musica Por Todas Partes. 2005. (Baby Einstein: Libros de Carton Ser.). (SPA.). 16p. (J). (gr. -1). bds. *(978-970-718-309-4(8),* Silver Dolphin en Español) Advanced Marketing, S. de R. L. de C. V.

NATURE IN LITERATURE

see also Nature—Poetry

Collins, Carolyn Strom & Eriksson, Christina Wyss. Inside the Secret Garden: A Treasury of Crafts, Recipes, & Activities. Tudor, Tasha, illus. 2004. 130p. (J). (gr. 2-8). reprint ed. 25.00 *(978-0-7567-7630-5(9))* DIANE Publishing Co.

Llanas, Sheila Griffin. Nature Poetry: Make Me a Picture of the Sun. 2014. (Pure Poetry Ser.). 128p. (J). lib. bdg. 33.27 *(978-0-7660-4244-5(8))* Enslow Pubs., Inc.

NATURE IN ORNAMENT

see Design, Decorative

NATURE PHOTOGRAPHY

see also Photography of Animals

Fielder, John, photos by. Do You See What I See? 2006. (Illus.). (J). 14.99 *(978-1-56579-554-9(7))* Fielder, John Publishing.

Martin, Jacqueline Briggs. Snowflake Bentley. Azarian, Mary, illus. 2009. (ENG.). 32p. (J). (gr. -1-3). pap. 7.99 *(978-0-547-24829-5(6))* Houghton Mifflin Harcourt Publishing Co.

—Snowflake Bentley. 2004. (Illus.). (J). (gr. -1-3). spiral bd. *(978-0-616-01714-2(6))* Canadian National Institute for the Blind/Institut National Canadien pour les Aveugles.

McAdam, Claudia Cangilla. Do You See What I See? Texas. 2007. (Illus.). (J). (gr. 3-7). 14.95 *(978-1-56579-589-1(X),* Westcliffe Pubs.) Bower Hse.

Swimow, Linda. Take on Alaska! a Photophonics Reader. 2009. 28p. pap. 12.99 *(978-1-4389-1394-0(X))* AuthorHouse.

Weston Woods Staff, creator. Snowflake Bentley. 2011. 38.75 *(978-0-545-31415-2(1));* 18.95 *(978-0-545-31414-5(3))* Weston Woods Studios, Inc.

NATURE—POETRY

Alexander, Cecil F. All Things Bright & Beautiful. Bryan, Ashley, illus. 2010. (ENG.). 40p. (J). (gr. -1-3). 17.99 *(978-1-4169-8939-4(0),* Atheneum Bks. for Young Readers) Simon & Schuster Children's Publishing.

Brown, Margaret Wise. Nibble Nibble. Minor, Wendell, illus. 2007. (ENG.). 32p. (J). (gr. -1-3). 17.99 *(978-0-06-059208-0(7))* HarperCollins Pubs.

Camden, Marian Louise. An Earth Child's Book of Verse. Wright, Diane Beem, illus. 2011. 32p. pap. *(978-1-77067-695-4(3))* FriesenPress.

Canetti, Yanitzia. Imagine a Better World. 2010. (Illus.). 32p. (J). pap. 9.99 *(978-1-59835-284-9(9),* BrickHouse Education) Cambridge BrickHouse, Inc.

Cooling, Wendy. All the Wild Wonders. Grobler, Piet, illus. 2017. (ENG.). 48p. (J). (gr. 2-5). pap. 17.99 ***(978-1-84780-994-0(4),*** Frances Lincoln) Quarto Publishing Group UK GBR. Dist: Littlehampton Bk Services, Ltd.

Davies, Nicola. Outside Your Window: A First Book of Nature. Hearld, Mark, illus. 2012. (ENG.). 108p. (J). (gr. -1-2). 19.99 *(978-0-7636-5549-5(X))* Candlewick Pr.

Freese, Susan M. Bees to Trees: Reading, Writing, & Reciting Poems about Nature, 1 vol. Westberg, Jan, illus. 2008. (Poetry Power Ser.). (ENG.). 32p. (J). (gr. 1-4). 27.07 *(978-1-60453-001-8(4))* ABDO Publishing Co.

Frost, Helen. Step Gently Out. Lieder, Rick, photos by. 2012. (ENG., Illus.). 32p. (J). (gr. k-k). 15.99 *(978-0-7636-5601-0(1))* Candlewick Pr.

—Sweep up the Sun. Lieder, Rick, illus. 2015. (ENG.). 32p. (J). (-k). 15.99 *(978-0-7636-6904-1(0))* Candlewick Pr.

Giovanni, Nikki. The Sun Is So Quiet. Bryan, Ashley, illus. 2014. (ENG.). 32p. (J). (gr. -1-3). 8.99 *(978-1-250-04669-7(6),* 9781250046697) Square Fish.

Lewis, J. Patrick. Book of Nature Poetry: More Than 200 Poems with Photographs That Float, Zoom, & Bloom! 2015. (ENG., Illus.). 192p. (J). (gr. -1-3). 24.99 *(978-1-4263-2094-1(9),* National Geographic Children's Bks.) National Geographic Society.

Nash, Myrna Lee. Spinman, Katydid & Bump: A Spider Vane Collection. Johnson, Sharon, illus. 2003. 48p. (YA). (gr. 4-10). 11.95 *(978-0-9724549-0-2(X))* Chapter & Verse Pr.

Paolilli, Paul & Brewer, Dan. Silver Seeds. 2014. 32p. pap. 7.00 *(978-1-61003-311-4(6))* Center for the Collaborative Classroom.

—Silver Seeds. Fancher, Lou & Johnson, Steve, illus. 2003. (ENG.). 32p. (J). (gr. k-4). pap. 6.99 *(978-0-14-250010-1(0),* Puffin Books) Penguin Young Readers Group.

Robbins, Karen. Care for Our World. Ball, Alexandra, illus. 2012. (ENG.). 36p. (J). (gr. -1-3). 16.95 *(978-1-935414-61-2(5))* Compendium, Inc., Publishing & Communications.

Scanlon, Liz Garton. All the World. Frazee, Marla, illus. 2009. (ENG.). 40p. (J). (gr. -1-3). 17.99 *(978-1-4169-8580-8(8),* Beach Lane Bks.) Beach Lane Bks.

—All the World. Frazee, Marla, illus. 2015. (Classic Board Bks.). (ENG.). 44p. (J). (gr. -1-k). bds. 7.99 *(978-1-4814-3121-7(8),* Little Simon) Little Simon.

—All the World. Frazee, Marla, illus. 2011. (J). (gr. -1-2). 29.95 *(978-0-545-32716-9(4))* Weston Woods Studios, Inc.

Sidman, Joyce. Ubiquitous: Celebrating Nature's Survivors. Prange, Beckie, illus. 2010. (ENG.). 40p. (J). (gr. 1-4). 17.99 *(978-0-618-71719-4(6))* Houghton Mifflin Harcourt Publishing Co.

White, Mandy. Imagine with Me. 2012. 24p. pap. 12.45 *(978-1-4525-0714-9(7))* Balboa Pr.

Yolen, Jane & Stemple, Jason. Shape Me a Rhyme: Nature's Forms in Poetry. 2015. (ENG., Illus.). 32p. (J). (gr. k-5). 6.95 *(978-1-62091-791-6(2),* Wordsong) Boyds Mills Pr.

NATURE POETRY

see Nature—Poetry

NATURE STUDY

see also Animals—Habits and Behavior; Botany; Nature Photography; Zoology

Baggott, Stella, illus. Baby's Very First Outdoors Book. 2009. (Baby Board Bks). 10p. (J). bds. 6.99 *(978-0-7945-2468-5(0),* Usborne) EDC Publishing.

Bauer, Cheryl. Our Visit to the Nature Center: Nuestra Visita Al Centro Ecologico. 2003. (SPA.). (J). lib. bdg. 22.00 *(978-1-59298-013-0(9))* Beaver's Pond Pr., Inc.

Buckley, Arabella. Plant Life in Field & Garden. 2008. 88p. pap. 11.95 *(978-1-59915-273-8(8))* Yesterday's Classics.

Buckley, Arabella B. By Pond & River. 2008. (Illus.). 60p. pap. 9.95 *(978-1-59915-272-1(X))* Yesterday's Classics.

—Insect Life. 2008. (Illus.). 88p. pap. 11.95 *(978-1-59915-276-9(2))* Yesterday's Classics.

—Wild Life in Woods & Fields (Yesterday's Classics) 2008. (Illus.). 60p. pap. 9.95 *(978-1-59915-271-4(1))* Yesterday's Classics.

Burnie, David. Bug Hunter. 2015. (ENG., Illus.). 72p. (J). (gr. 3-7). pap. 9.99 *(978-1-4654-3016-8(4),* DK Children) Dorling Kindersley Publishing, Inc.

Burris, Judy & Richards, Wayne. Nature's Notes: Bite-sized Learning & Projects for All Ages. 2012. (ENG., Illus.). 232p. spiral bd. *(978-1-60755-477-6(1))* Willow Creek Pr., Inc.

Burroughs, John. Fresh Fields. Fuert, L. A. & Woodbury et al, Charles H., illus. 2008. 196p. pap. *(978-1-4099-2065-6(8))* Dodo Pr.

—Fresh Fields. 2008. 348p. 32.95 *(978-1-4344-9784-0(4));* per. 19.95 *(978-1-4344-9783-3(6))* Wildside Pr., LLC.

Clark, Rosalyn. A Visit to the Nature Center. 2017. (Bumba Books (tm) — Places We Go Ser.). (ENG.). 24p. (J). (gr. -1-1). pap. 6.99 ***(978-1-5124-5564-9(4));*** (Illus.). 25.32 ***(978-1-5124-3376-0(4),*** Lerner Pubns.) Lerner Publishing Group.

Cornell, Kari. Nature up Close. 2016. (Illus.). 24p. (J). pap. *(978-0-87659-703-3(7))* Gryphon Hse., Inc.

Cycles in Nature. 2015. (Cycles in Nature Ser.). (ENG.). 24p. (J). (gr. 1-2). 135.60 *(978-1-4824-1636-7(0))* Stevens, Gareth Publishing LLLP.

Dael, Do Van. An Earthly Walk: A Season-Ing Story. 2012. (Illus.). 20p. pap. 19.82 *(978-1-4685-8629-9(7))* AuthorHouse.

Dorling Kindersley Publishing Staff. Eyewitness Explorer: Nature Ranger: Nature Ranger. 2015. (ENG., Illus.). 72p. (J). (gr. 3-7). pap. 9.99 *(978-1-4654-3500-2(X),* DK Children) Dorling Kindersley Publishing, Inc.

Ferrara, Cos. Anna Comstock: A Love Affair with Nature. 2004. (Girls Explore, Reach for the Stars Ser.). (Illus.). 112p. (J). 20.00 *(978-0-9749456-1-3(7),* Girls Explore) Girls Explore LLC.

Fitzsimmons, Kakie. Anna Goes Hiking: Discover Hiking & Explore Nature. l.t. ed. 2007. (Bur Bur & Friends Ser.). (Illus.). 40p. (J). (gr. 3-7). lib. bdg. 14.95 *(978-0-9777121-7-5(6))* IGI Pr.

Fleischman, Paul. Eyes Wide Open: Going Behind the Environmental Headlines. 2014. (ENG., Illus.). 208p. (YA). (gr. 9). 17.99 *(978-0-7636-7102-0(9));* pap. 9.99 *(978-0-7636-7545-5(8))* Candlewick Pr.

Fredericks, Anthony D. Simple Nature Experiments with Everyday Materials. Zweifel, Frances, illus. 2004. 128p. (J). (gr. 4-8). reprint ed. pap. 6.00 *(978-0-7567-7727-2(5))* DIANE Publishing Co.

Ganeri, Anita. Hunt for Food. (Illus.). 32p. (YA). (gr. 4-18). lib. bdg. 27.10 *(978-1-931983-88-4(7))* Chrysalis Education.

Glassman, Michael & Ely, Lisa. Kinder Gardens: Games & Adventures, 1 vol. 2011. (ENG., Illus.). 64p. (J). pap. 12.99 *(978-0-7643-3811-3(0),* 9780764338113, Schiffer Publishing Ltd) Schiffer Publishing, Ltd.

Great Things to Do Outside. 2014. (ENG.). 192p. (J). (gr. k-4). pap. 12.99 *(978-1-4654-1685-8(4),* DK Children) Dorling Kindersley Publishing, Inc.

Hands-On Nature. 2004. (Illus.). 96p. (J). (gr. -1-k). 11.95 *(978-1-885358-65-3(2));* (gr. 1-2). 11.95 *(978-1-885358-66-0(0));* (gr. 3-4). 11.95 *(978-1-885358-67-7(9))* Rainbow Pubs. & Legacy Pr.

Harris, Nicholas & Joanna, Turner. El Porque de las Cosas: Naturaleza y Ciencia. (Coleccion Enciclopedia Ilustrada del Conocimiento).Tr. of Why Things Occur: Nature & Science. (SPA., Illus.). 64p. (J). (gr. 3-5). 7.96 *(978-84-7630-749-6(7))* Editorial Libsa, S.A. ESP. Dist: Lectorum Pubns., Inc.

Hickman, Pamela & Federation of Ontario Naturalists. Naturaleza Divertida. Shore, Judie, illus. (SPA.). 92p. *(978-84-9754-095-7(6),* 87821) Ediciones Oniro S.A.

—La Naturaleza y Tú. Shore, Judie, illus. (SPA.). 63p. *(978-84-9754-106-0(5),* 87822) Ediciones Oniro S.A.

Hoena, Blake A. If You Plant a Seed... & Other Nature Predictions, 1 vol. 2012. (If Bks.). (ENG., Illus.). 32p. (gr. 1-2). lib. bdg. 27.32 *(978-1-4296-8721-8(5))* Capstone Press of Coughlan Cos.

—If You Plant a Seed... & Other Nature Predictions. 2012. (If Bks.). (ENG.). 32p. (gr. 1-2). pap. 47.70 *(978-1-4296-9252-6(9),* Aplus Bks.); (Illus.). pap. 8.10 *(978-1-4296-9251-9(0))* Capstone Press of Coughlan Cos.

Holt, Rinehart and Winston Staff. Holt Science & Technology Chapter 19: Life Science: Cycles in Nature. 5th ed. 2004. (Illus.). pap. 12.86 *(978-0-03-030229-9(3))* Holt McDougal.

Isaacs, Kathleen T. Bugs, Bogs, Bats, & Books: Sharing Nature with Children Through Reading. 2014. (ENG.). 272p. (J). pap. 19.95 *(978-1-937589-58-5(7),* Huron Street Pr.) American Library Assn.

Kochanoff, Peggy. You Can Be a Nature Detective, 1 vol. 2009. (ENG.). 64p. (J). pap. 14.00 *(978-0-87842-556-3(X))* Mountain Pr. Publishing Co., Inc.

Larsen, Laurel. One Night in the Everglades. Turley, Joyce Mihran, illus. 2012. (Long Term Ecological Research Ser.). (ENG.). 32p. (J). (gr. 3-7). 15.95 *(978-0-9817700-4-8(5))* Taylor Trade Publishing.

LernerClassroom Editors, ed. Teaching Guide for Fsn / Discovering Nature's Cycles. 2010. pap. 5.95 *(978-0-7613-6683-6(0))* Lerner Publishing Group.

Levy, Duncan. Happy about Animals: An 8-Year-Old's View (Now 11) on Sharing the Earth. 2010. 48p. pap. 14.95 *(978-1-60005-177-7(4))* Happy About.

Maguire, Kay. Out & About. Kroll, Danielle, illus. 2016. (Nature's Day Ser.). (ENG.). 56p. (J). pap. 10.99 *(978-1-84780-800-4(X),* Wide Eyed Editions) Quarto Publishing Group UK GBR. Dist: Littlehampton Bk Services, Ltd.

Maguire, Kay & Kroll, Danielle. Nature's Day: Out & About: Spotting, Making & Collecting Activities. 2016. (ENG.). 56p. (J). (gr. k-3). pap. 9.99 *(978-1-84780-836-3(0),* Wide Eyed Editions) Quarto Publishing Group UK GBR. Dist: Hachette Bk. Group.

Maynard, Christopher. Why Do Sunflowers Face the Sun? Questions Children Ask about Nature. (Why Bks.). (Illus.). 24p. (J). pap. 10.99 *(978-0-590-24954-6(1))* Scholastic, Inc.

Miché, Mary. Nature's Patchwork Quilt: Understanding Habitats. Powell, Consie, illus. 2012. 32p. (J). (gr. k-6). 16.95 *(978-1-58469-169-3(7));* (ENG.). pap. 8.95 *(978-1-58469-170-9(0))* Dawn Pubns.

Mitchell, Andrew. The Young Naturalist. Jacquemier, Sue & Bramwell, Martyn, eds. Jackson, Ian, illus. 2008. (Hobby Guides Ser.). 32p. (J). (gr. 5-9). pap. 6.99 *(978-0-7945-2219-3(X),* Usborne) EDC Publishing.

Nadeau, Isaac. Learning about Earth's Cycles with Graphic Organizers. (Graphic Organizers in Science Ser.). 24p. 2009. (gr. 3-4). 42.50 *(978-1-61513-029-0(2))* 2006. (ENG., Illus.). (gr. 4-6). pap. 8.25 *(978-1-4042-5044-4(1))* 2005. (Illus.). (J). (gr. 3-7). lib. bdg. 22.60 *(978-1-4042-2807-8(1))* Rosen Publishing Group, Inc., The. (PowerKids Pr.).

Orr, Richard. Richard Orr's Nature Cross-Sections. (Illus.). 30p. (J). pap. 22.99 *(978-0-590-24633-0(X))* Scholastic, Inc.

Owen, Ruth. Science & Craft Projects with Insects, Spiders, & Other Minibeasts. 2013. (Get Crafty Outdoors Ser.). (ENG., Illus.). 32p. (J). (gr. k-3). 26.50 *(978-1-4777-0245-1(8));* pap. 11.75 *(978-1-4777-0253-6(9))* Rosen Publishing Group, Inc., The. (PowerKids Pr.).

—Science & Craft Projects with Plants & Seeds. 2013. (Get Crafty Outdoors Ser.). (ENG., Illus.). 32p. (J). (gr. k-3). 26.50 *(978-1-4777-0247-5(4));* pap. 11.75 *(978-1-4777-0257-4(1))* Rosen Publishing Group, Inc., The. (PowerKids Pr.).

—Science & Craft Projects with Rocks & Soil. 2013. (Get Crafty Outdoors Ser.). (ENG., Illus.). 32p. (J). (gr. k-3). 26.50 *(978-1-4777-0246-8(6));* pap. 11.75 *(978-1-4777-0255-0(5))* Rosen Publishing Group, Inc., The. (PowerKids Pr.).

—Science & Craft Projects with Trees & Leaves. 2013. (Get Crafty Outdoors Ser.). (ENG., Illus.). 32p. (J). (gr. k-3). 26.50 *(978-1-4777-0248-2(2));* pap. 11.75 *(978-1-4777-0259-8(8))* Rosen Publishing Group, Inc., The. (PowerKids Pr.).

—Science & Craft Projects with Weather. 2013. (Get Crafty Outdoors Ser.). (ENG., Illus.). 32p. (J). (gr. k-3). 26.50 *(978-1-4777-0244-4(X));* pap. 11.75 *(978-1-4777-0251-2(2))* Rosen Publishing Group, Inc., The. (PowerKids Pr.).

—Science & Craft Projects with Wildlife. 2013. (Get Crafty Outdoors Ser.). (ENG., Illus.). 32p. (J). (gr. k-3). 26.50 *(978-1-4777-0243-7(1),* PowerKids Pr.) Rosen Publishing Group, Inc., The.

Schwartz, David M. Animal Noses. Kuhn, Dwight, photos by. (Plants & Animals Ser.). (Illus.). 16p. (J). (gr. 1-3). pap. 2.99 *(978-1-57471-321-3(3),* 3030) Creative Teaching Pr., Inc.

Spilsbury, Louise & Spilsbury, Richard. A Nature Walk in the City, 1 vol. 2014. (Nature Walks Ser.). (ENG., Illus.). 24p. (gr. k-2). 23.32 *(978-1-4846-0401-4(6),* Heinemann Read & Learn) Heinemann-Raintree.

—A Nature Walk in the Woods, 1 vol. 2014. (Nature Walks Ser.). (ENG., Illus.). 24p. (gr. k-2). 23.32 *(978-1-4846-0403-8(2),* Heinemann Read & Learn) Heinemann-Raintree.

—A Nature Walk on the Beach, 1 vol. 2014. (Nature Walks Ser.). (ENG., Illus.). 24p. (gr. k-2). 23.32 *(978-1-4846-0400-7(8),* Heinemann Read & Learn) Heinemann-Raintree.

—A Nature Walk on the Farm, 1 vol. 2014. (Nature Walks Ser.). (ENG., Illus.). 24p. (gr. k-2). 23.32 *(978-1-4846-0402-1(4),* Heinemann Read & Learn) Heinemann-Raintree.

Stevens, Sky. Looking Close: Teaching Kids to Love the Earth. 2012. 32p. pap. 24.95 *(978-1-4772-8446-9(X))* AuthorHouse.

Usborne Books Staff, creator. The Young Naturalist Kid Kit. 2007. (Kid Kits Ser.). (Illus.). 32p. (J). pap. 14.99 *(978-1-60130-037-9(9),* Usborne) EDC Publishing.

White, Nancy. Why Polar Bears Like Snow... & Flamingos Don't & Por qué hay osos polares en la nieve ... y no hay Flamencos: 6 English, 6 Spanish Adaptations, 122 vols., Vol. 2. 2011. (SPA.). (J). instr.'s gde. ed. 89.00 net. *(978-1-4108-2222-2(2),* 2222-2) Benchmark Education Co.

Williams, Brian. What about the Natural World. 2008. 40p. pap. *(978-1-84810-071-8(X))* Miles Kelly Publishing, Ltd.

Woodward, John & Gray, Leon. Backyard. 2007. (Close-up Ser.). (Illus.). 32p. (J). (gr. 4-7). lib. bdg. *(978-1-933834-13-9(7))* Brown Bear Books.

World Book, Inc. Staff, contrib. by. World Book's Science & Nature Guides, 12 vols. 2004. (World Book's Science & Nature Guides Ser.). (Illus.). 80p. (gr. 5-9). 319.00 *(978-0-7166-4208-4(5),* SKU 30119) World Bk., Inc.

NATURE STUDY—DICTIONARIES

Enciclopedia Juvenil de la Naturaleza. rev. ed. (SPA., Illus.). 256p. (J). 39.95 *(978-84-272-5930-0(1),* MO500) Molino, Editorial ESP. Dist: Continental Bk. Co., Inc.

NATURE STUDY—FICTION

Baskwill, Jane & National Geographic Learning Staff. Touch the Earth. Fiore, Peter M., illus. 2010. (Rise & Shine Ser.). (ENG.). 32p. (C). (gr. 1-5). pap. 10.95 *(978-1-57255-428-3(2))* National Geographic School Publishing, Inc.

Blunt, Michele. A Walk Through Time. 2011. 36p. pap. 21.99 *(978-1-4653-6182-0(0))* Xlibris Corp.

Burgess, Thornton W. Old Mother West Wind. (J). 16.95 *(978-0-8488-0385-8(X))* Amereon Ltd.

Corwin, Jeff. The Great Alaska Adventure!, 2 vols., Bk. 2. 2010. (Jeff Corwin Ser.: 2). (ENG.). 112p. (J). (gr. 1-3). 4.99 *(978-0-14-241409-5(3),* Puffin Books) Penguin Young Readers Group.

—Your Backyard Is Wild. 2009. (Jeff Corwin Ser.: 1). (ENG.). 96p. (J). (gr. 1-3). 4.99 *(978-0-14-241404-0(2),* Puffin Books) Penguin Young Readers Group.

Donaldson, Julia. The Wrong Kind of Bark. Parsons, Garry, illus. 2005. (Red Bananas Ser.). (ENG.). 48p. (J). lib. bdg. *(978-0-7787-1073-8(4));* (gr. 1-3). *(978-0-7787-1089-9(0))* Crabtree Publishing Co.

Klein, Adria F. Max Goes to the Nature Center, 1 vol. Gallagher-Cole, Memie, illus. 2009. (Read-It! Readers: the Life of Max Ser.). (ENG.). 24p. (J). (gr. -1-2). 21.32 *(978-1-4048-5269-3(7),* Easy Readers) Picture Window Bks.

Lewis, J. Patrick. Earth & Me, Our Family Tree: Nature's Creatures. Canyon, Christopher, illus. 2004. (Sharing Nature with Children Book Ser.). 36p. (J). (gr. -1-5). 16.95 *(978-1-58469-031-3(3));* pap. 7.95 *(978-1-58469-030-6(5))* Dawn Pubns.

Li, Judith L. Ellie's Log: Exploring the Forest Where the Great Tree Fell. Herring, M. L., illus. 2013. (ENG.). 112p. (J). (gr. 3-6). pap. 17.95 *(978-0-87071-696-6(4))* Oregon State Univ. Pr.

Li, Judith L. & Herring, M. L. Ricky's Atlas: Mapping a Land on Fire. 2016. (ENG., Illus.). 128p. (J). (gr. 3-6). pap. 17.95 *(978-0-87071-842-7(8))* Oregon State Univ. Pr.

Mohler, Marie. Hearts of Trees. 2008. 32p. pap. 18.95 *(978-1-4357-4614-5(7))* Lulu Pr., Inc.

—Little Bird's Earth Nest. 2008. 32p. 18.95 *(978-1-4357-1711-4(2))* Lulu Pr., Inc.

Parish, Herman. Amelia Bedelia Hits the Trail. Avril, Lynne, illus. 2013. (I Can Read Level 1 Ser.). (ENG.). 32p. (J). (gr. -1-3). 16.99 *(978-0-06-209527-5(7),* Greenwillow Bks.) HarperCollins Pubs.

—Amelia Bedelia Hits the Trail. 2013. (Amelia Bedelia: I Can Read! Ser.). (J). lib. bdg. 13.55 *(978-0-606-27135-6(X),* Turtleback) Turtleback Bks.

Reader's Digest Staff. Let's Help the Earth. Brannon, Tom, illus. 2008. (Sesame Street Ser.). (ENG.). 12p. (J). (gr. -1-k). bds. 12.99 *(978-0-7944-1696-6(9))* Reader's Digest Assn., Inc., The.

Wasson, Dawn K. T. Kuu Tutu. 2008. (ENG & HAW., Illus.). (J). lib. bdg. *(978-0-9773495-8-6(6))* Na Kamalei Koolauloa Early Education Program.

Weber, Jen Funk. Alguien Ha Estado Aquí, Alguien lo Ha Hecho: Descifrando Las Señales de Los Animales, 1 vol. Gabriel, Andrea, illus. 2016. (SPA.). 32p. (J). (gr. k-3). pap. 9.95 *(978-1-62855-741-1(9))* Arbordale Publishing.
—Been There, Done That: Reading Animal Signs, 1 vol. Gabriel, Andrea, illus. 2016. (ENG & SPA.). 32p. (J). (gr. k-3). 17.95 *(978-1-62855-727-5(3))* Arbordale Publishing.
Yee, Wong Herbert. My Autumn Book. Yee, Wong Herbert, illus. 2015. (ENG., Illus.). 32p. (J). (gr. -1-1). 14.99 *(978-0-8050-9922-5(0)*, 9780805099225, Holt, Henry & Co. Bks. For Young Readers) Holt, Henry & Co.
Yep, Laurence. Sweetwater. Noonan, Julia, illus. 2004. 191p. (J). pap. 5.99 *(978-0-06-056029-4(0))* HarperCollins Pubs.

NAVAL ADMINISTRATION

see Naval Art and Science
see names of countries with the subhead Navy, e.g. United States—Navy

NAVAL AERONAUTICS

see Aeronautics, Military

NAVAL AIR BASES

see Air Bases

NAVAL AIRPLANES

see Airplanes, Military

NAVAL ART AND SCIENCE

see also Military Art and Science; Navigation; Sea Power; Shipbuilding; Signals and Signaling; Submarine Warfare; Submarines (Ships); Warships

Bolitho, Mark. Fold Your Own Origami Navy. 2013. 32p. (J). (gr. 3-6). 26.50 *(978-1-4777-1318-1(2))*; pap. 11.75 *(978-1-4777-1467-6(7))* Rosen Publishing Group, Inc., The. (PowerKids Pr.).
Dougherty, Martin J. Sea Warfare. 2010. (Modern Warfare Ser.). (Illus.). 32p. (J). (gr. 2-5). lib. bdg. 26.00 *(978-1-4339-2734-8(9))* Stevens, Gareth Publishing LLLP.
Fold Your Own Origami Navy. 2013. (Origami Army Ser.). 32p. (J). (gr. 3-6). pap. 70.50 *(978-1-4777-1468-3(5)*, PowerKids Pr.) Rosen Publishing Group, Inc., The.
Hobbs, Richard R. Naval Science 2 2: Maritime History, Leadership, & Nautical Sciences for the NJROTC Student. 2nd ed. 2006. (ENG., Illus.). 360p. 34.95 *(978-1-59114-366-6(7))* Naval Institute Pr.
—Naval Science 3: Naval Knowledge & Skills for the NJROTC Student. 2003. (Illus.). 252p. 27.95 *(978-1-55750-319-0(2))* Naval Institute Pr.
Press, Cider Mill & Entin, Cindy. Navy. 2013. (ENG.). 10p. (J). bds. 5.99 *(978-1-60433-323-7(5)*, Applesauce Pr.) Cider Mill Pr. Bk. Pubs., LLC.

NAVAL BATTLES

see also Battles; Naval History
also names of countries with the subdivision History, Naval, e.g. U. S.—History, Naval, etc.; and names of battles

Califf, David J. Battle of Actium. 2003. (Great Battles Through the Ages Ser.). (Illus.). 112p. (gr. 6-12). 30.00 *(978-0-7910-7440-4(4)*, Chelsea Hse.) Facts On File, Inc.
Williams, Brian. Sailors under Fire, 1 vol. 2011. (War Stories Ser.). (ENG.). 32p. (gr. 3-6). pap. 8.29 *(978-1-4329-4840-5(7))*; 30.65 *(978-1-4329-4832-0(6))* Heinemann-Raintree. (NA-h).

NAVAL BIOGRAPHY

see also Admirals; Sailors
also names of navies with the subdivision Biography, e.g. United States—Navy—Biography

Cawthorne, Nigel. Military Commanders: The 100 Greatest Throughout History. 2004. (Illus.). 208p. 18.95 *(978-1-59270-029-5(2))* Enchanted Lion Bks., LLC.
—Victory: 100 Great Military Commanders. 2012. (Illus.). 208p. (J). *(978-1-4351-4242-8(X))* Metro Bks.

NAVAL HISTORY

see also Military History; Naval Biography; Pirates
also names of countries with the subhead Navy or the subdivision History, Naval, e.g. United States—Navy; United States—History, Naval

Barrington, Richard. The History of Navies Around the World, 1 vol., 1. Saxena, Shalini, ed. 2014. (World's Armed Forces Ser.). (ENG.). 136p. (YA). (gr. 7-12). 35.25 *(978-1-62275-142-6(6))* Rosen Publishing Group, Inc., The.
Cawthorne, Nigel. Military Commanders: The 100 Greatest Throughout History. 2004. (Illus.). 208p. 18.95 *(978-1-59270-029-5(2))* Enchanted Lion Bks., LLC.
—Victory: 100 Great Military Commanders. 2012. (Illus.). 208p. (J). *(978-1-4351-4242-8(X))* Metro Bks.
Hobbs, Richard R. Naval Science 2 2: Maritime History, Leadership, & Nautical Sciences for the NJROTC Student. 2nd ed. 2006. (ENG., Illus.). 360p. 34.95 *(978-1-59114-366-6(7))* Naval Institute Pr.
Hull, Robert. Trade & Warfare. 2007. (World of Ancient Greece Ser.). (Illus.). 32p. (YA). (gr. 3-6). lib. bdg. 27.10 *(978-1-59771-062-6(8))* Sea-To-Sea Pubns.
Marsico, Katie. Warships. 2016. (True Book(tm) — Engineering Wonders Ser.). (ENG., Illus.). 48p. (J). pap. 6.95 *(978-0-531-22274-4(8)*, Children's Pr.) Scholastic Library Publishing.
Thornton, Jeremy. The Birth of the American Navy. 2003. (Building America's Democracy Ser.). (Illus.). 24p. (J). lib. bdg. 22.60 *(978-0-8239-6274-7(1)*, PowerKids Pr.) Rosen Publishing Group, Inc., The.
Williams, Brian. Sailors under Fire, 1 vol. 2011. (War Stories Ser.). (ENG.). 32p. (gr. 3-6). pap. 8.29 *(978-1-4329-4840-5(7))*; 30.65 *(978-1-4329-4832-0(6))* Heinemann-Raintree. (NA-h).

NAVAL SCIENCE

see Naval Art and Science

NAVAL SIGNALING

see Signals and Signaling

NAVAL UNIFORMS

see Military Uniforms

NAVAL WARFARE

see Naval Art and Science; Naval Battles; Submarine Warfare

NAVIGATION

see also Harbors; Knots and Splices; Lighthouses; Naval Art and Science; Pilots and Pilotage; Radar; Shipwrecks; Signals and Signaling; Tides; Winds

Champion, Neil. Orienteering. 2009. (Get Outdoors Ser.). (Illus.). 32p. (ENG.). (J). pap. 10.00 *(978-1-4358-3052-3(0)*, PowerKids Pr.); (YA). (gr. 4-7). lib. bdg. 25.25 *(978-1-4358-3044-8(X))* Rosen Publishing Group, Inc., The.
Faulkner, Nicholas. A Visual History of Ships & Navigation. 2016. (Visual History of the World Ser.). 00096p. (J). (gr. 8-8). 37.10 *(978-1-4994-6594-5(7))* Rosen Publishing Group, Inc., The.
Gray, Leon. How Does GPS Work?, Vol. 1. 2014. (High-Tech Science Ser.). (ENG., Illus.). 48p. (J). (gr. 4-5). 31.95 *(978-1-4824-0393-0(5))* Stevens, Gareth Publishing LLLP.
Green, Cathy, et al. Great Ships on the Great Lakes: A Maritime History. 2013. (ENG., Illus.). 144p. (J). pap. 18.95 *(978-0-87020-582-8(X))* Wisconsin Historical Society.
—Great Ships on the Great Lakes Teacher's Guide: A Maritime History. 2013. (ENG., Illus.). cd-rom 49.95 *(978-0-87020-583-5(8))* Wisconsin Historical Society.
Krebs, Laurie. A Day in the Life of a Colonial Lighthouse Keeper. 2004. (Library of Living & Working in Colonial Times Ser.). (Illus.). 24p. (J). lib. bdg. 22.60 *(978-0-8239-6226-6(1)*, PowerKids Pr.) Rosen Publishing Group, Inc., The.
Macdonald, Fiona. You Wouldn't Want to Sail with Christopher Columbus! (Revised Edition) 2014. (You Wouldn't Want to... Ser.). (ENG.). 32p. (J). lib. bdg. 29.00 *(978-0-531-21177-9(0)*, Watts, Franklin) Scholastic Library Publishing.
McNab, Chris. Survival in the Wilderness. 2015. (Illus.). 64p. (J). *(978-1-4222-3081-7(3))* Mason Crest.
Nagelhout, Ryan, ed. The Problem with Early Navigation Tools. 2015. (Bloopers of Invention Ser.). (ENG., Illus.). 24p. (J). (gr. 2-3). pap. 8.15 *(978-1-4824-2776-9(1))* Stevens, Gareth Publishing LLLP.
Pritchard, Herman S. The Nautical Road: A Straight Forward Approach to Learning the Navigation Rules. Helwig, Teresa L., ed. Sink, Cynthia, illus. 2nd rev. l.t. ed. 2004. 176p. (YA). 29.95 *(978-0-9716479-3-0(3))* Selby Dean Ventures, Inc.
Quinlan, Julia J. GPS & Computer Maps. 2012. (How to Use Maps Ser.). (ENG.). 24p. (J). (gr. 3-6). pap. 8.25 *(978-1-4488-6276-4(0)*, PowerKids Pr.); lib. bdg. 22.60 *(978-1-4488-6159-0(4))* Rosen Publishing Group, Inc., The.
Richardson, Gillian. 10 Ships That Rocked the World. Rosen, Kim, illus. 2015. (World of Tens Ser.). (ENG.). 176p. (J). (gr. 4-7). pap. 14.95 *(978-1-55451-781-7(8)*, 9781554517817) Annick Pr., Ltd. CAN. Dist: Publishers Group West (PGW).
Williams, Linda D. Navigational Aids. 2007. (Great Inventions Ser.). (Illus.). 128p. (gr. 8-18). lib. bdg. 29.95 *(978-0-7614-2599-1(3)*, Benchmark Bks.) Marshall Cavendish Corp.
Wilson, Patrick. Surviving with Navigation & Signaling. Carney, John, ed. 2014. (Extreme Survival in the Military Ser.: 12). 64p. (J). (gr. 7-18). lib. bdg. 23.95 *(978-1-4222-3093-0(7))* Mason Crest.
Wood, Alix. Pirates on the Map. 2014. (Fun with Map Skills Ser.). 32p. (J). (gr. 3-6). lib. bdg. 26.25 *(978-1-4777-6964-5(1)*, PowerKids Pr.) Rosen Publishing Group, Inc., The.

NAVIGATORS

see Explorers

NAVY

see Naval Art and Science; Sea Power
see names of countries with the subhead Navy, e.g. United States—Navy

NAZI MOVEMENT

see National Socialism

NEAR EAST

see Asia; Middle East

NEBRASKA

Brown, Jonatha A. Nebraska. 2006. (Portraits of the States Ser.). 32p. (gr. 2-6). pap. 10.50 *(978-0-8368-4720-8(2))*; (Illus.). lib. bdg. 26.00 *(978-0-8368-4703-1(2))* Stevens, Gareth Publishing LLLP. (Gareth Stevens Learning Library).
Galiano, Dean. Nebraska. Brusca, Maria Cristina, tr. 2006. (Bilingual Library of the United States of America Ser.: Set 2). (ENG & SPA., Illus.). 32p. (J). (gr. 3-6). lib. bdg. 25.25 *(978-1-4042-3092-7(0))* Rosen Publishing Group, Inc., The.
Haack, Kelly J. Nebraska: A MyReportLinks. Com Book. 2003. (States Ser.). (Illus.). 48p. (J). lib. bdg. 25.26 *(978-0-7660-5145-4(5)*, MyReportLinks.com Bks.) Enslow Pubs., Inc.
Heinrichs, Ann. Nebraska. rev. ed. 2014. (America the Beautiful Ser.: 3). (ENG.). 144p. (J). lib. bdg. 40.00 *(978-0-531-24892-8(5))* Scholastic Library Publishing.
Luebs Shepherd, Rajean. C Is for Cornhusker: A Nebraska Alphabet. Appleoff, Sandy, illus. 2004. (State Ser.). (ENG.). 40p. (J). 17.95 *(978-1-58536-147-2(X))* Sleeping Bear Pr.
Marsh, Carole. Nebraska Current Events Projects: 30 Cool, Activities, Crafts, Experiments & More for Kids to Do to Learn about Your State! 2003. (Nebraska Experience Ser.). 32p. (gr. k-8). pap. 5.95 *(978-0-635-02046-8(7)*, Marsh, Carole Bks.) Gallopade International.
—Nebraska Government Projects: 30 Cool, Activities, Crafts, Experiments & More for Kids to Do to Learn about Your State! 2003. (Nebraska Experience Ser.). 32p. (gr. k-5). pap. 5.95 *(978-0-635-01946-2(9)*, Marsh, Carole Bks.) Gallopade International.
—Nebraska People Projects: 30 Cool, Activities, Crafts, Experiments & More for Kids to Do to Learn about Your State! 2003. (Nebraska Experience Ser.). 32p. (gr. k-5). pap. 5.95 *(978-0-635-01996-7(5)*, Marsh, Carole Bks.) Gallopade International.
—Nebraska Symbols & Facts Projects: 30 Cool, Activities, Crafts, Experiments & More for Kids to Do to Learn about Your State! 2003. (Nebraska Experience Ser.). 32p. (gr. k-5). pap. 5.95 *(978-0-635-01896-0(9)*, Marsh, Carole Bks.) Gallopade International.
McNamara, Connie. My First Nebraska Words. 2004. (J). 0.00 *(978-0-9759703-0-0(5))* Shamrock Publishing, Inc.
Murray, Julie. Nebraska, 1 vol. 2006. (Buddy Book Ser.). (ENG., Illus.). 32p. (gr. 2-4). 27.07 *(978-1-59197-686-8(3)*, Buddy Bks.) ABDO Publishing Co.
Porter, A. P. Nebraska. (J). 2012. lib. bdg. 25.26 *(978-0-7613-4543-5(4))* 2nd exp. rev. ed. 2003. (Illus.). 84p. (gr. 3-6). 25.26 *(978-0-8225-4093-9(2))* Lerner Publishing Group. (Lerner Pubns.).
Sanders, Doug. Nebraska. 2006. (It's My State! Ser.). (Illus.). 80p. (J). (gr. 4-7). lib. bdg. 21.95 *(978-0-7614-1911-2(X)*, Benchmark Bks.) Marshall Cavendish Corp.
Weatherly, Myra S. Nebraska. 2003. (From Sea to Shining Sea Ser.: 2). (ENG., Illus.). 80p. (J). 30.50 *(978-0-516-22396-4(8)*, Children's Pr.) Scholastic Library Publishing.
Weintraub, A. How to Draw Nebraska's Sights & Symbols. 2009. (Kid's Guide to Drawing America Ser.). 32p. (gr. k-k). 50.50 *(978-1-61511-076-6(3)*, PowerKids Pr.) Rosen Publishing Group, Inc., The.
Zollman, Pam. Nebraska. 2007. (Rookie Read-About Geography Ser.). (Illus.). 31p. (J). (gr. 1-2). 20.50 *(978-0-516-25466-1(9)*, Children's Pr.) Scholastic Library Publishing.

NEBRASKA—FICTION

Clements, Andrew. Room One: A Mystery or Two. Elliott, Mark, illus. 2008. (ENG.). 192p. (J). (gr. 3-7). pap. 7.99 *(978-0-689-86687-6(9)*, Atheneum Bks. for Young Readers) Simon & Schuster Children's Publishing.
—Room One: A Mystery or Two. Blair, Chris & Elliott, Mark, illus. 2006. (ENG.). 176p. (J). (gr. 3-7). 17.99 *(978-0-689-86686-9(0)*, Atheneum Bks. for Young Readers) Simon & Schuster Children's Publishing.
Connor, Leslie. All Rise for the Honorable Perry T. Cook. 2016. 400p. (J). (gr. 3-7). 16.99 *(978-0-06-233346-9(1)*, Tegen, Katherine Bks) HarperCollins Pubs.
Figley, Marty Rhodes. The Schoolchildren's Blizzard. Haas, Shelly O., illus. 2004. (On My Own History Ser.). (ENG.). 48p. (gr. 2-4). lib. bdg. 25.26 *(978-1-57505-586-2(4)*, Carolrhoda Bks.) Lerner Publishing Group.
Gray, Dianne & Gray, Dianne E. Holding up the Earth. 2006. (ENG.). 210p. (J). (gr. 5-7). pap. 12.95 *(978-0-618-73747-5(2))* Houghton Mifflin Harcourt Publishing Co.
Griffo, Michael. Starfall. 2014. (Darkborn Legacy Ser.). (ENG.). 384p. (YA). (gr. 13). pap. 20.00 *(978-0-7582-8076-3(9)*, K-Teen) Kensington Publishing Corp.
Jacobs, Lily. The Littlest Bunny in Nebraska: An Easter Adventure. Dunn, Robert, illus. 2015. (ENG.). 32p. (J). (-3). 9.99 *(978-1-4926-1132-5(8)*, Sourcebooks Jabberwocky) Sourcebooks, Inc.
—The Littlest Bunny in Omaha: An Easter Adventure. Dunn, Robert, illus. 2015. (ENG.). 32p. (J). (-3). 9.99 *(978-1-4926-1168-4(9)*, Sourcebooks Jabberwocky) Sourcebooks, Inc.
Jacoby, Sue. The Sneakies in Las Vegas: A Coby Jay Adventure. 2012. 128p. (gr. 4-6). 22.60 *(978-1-4669-6672-7(6))*; pap. 12.60 *(978-1-4669-6670-3(X))* Trafford Publishing.
James, Eric. A Halloween Scare in Nebraska. Le Ray, Marina, illus. 2015. (ENG.). 32p. (J). (-5). 9.99 *(978-1-4926-2385-4(7)*, 9781492623854, Sourcebooks Jabberwocky) Sourcebooks, Inc.
—A Halloween Scare in Omaha. Le Ray, Marina, illus. 2015. (ENG.). 32p. (J). (-5). 9.99 *(978-1-4926-2392-2(X)*, 9781492623922, Sourcebooks Jabberwocky) Sourcebooks, Inc.
—Santa's Sleigh Is on Its Way to Nebraska: A Christmas Adventure. Dunn, Robert, illus. 2016. (ENG.). 32p. (J). (-2). 12.99 *(978-1-4926-4339-5(4)*, 9781492643395, Sourcebooks Jabberwocky) Sourcebooks, Inc.
—Santa's Sleigh Is on Its Way to Omaha: A Christmas Adventure. Dunn, Robert, illus. 2016. (ENG.). 32p. (J). (-2). 12.99 *(978-1-4926-4347-0(5)*, 9781492643470, Sourcebooks Jabberwocky) Sourcebooks, Inc.
LaFaye, A. Worth. unabr. ed. 2006. (Live Oak Histories Ser.). (J). (gr. 3-6). pap. 24.95 incl. audio *(978-1-59519-766-5(4))* Live Oak Media.
—Worth. 2006. (ENG.). 160p. (J). (gr. 4-7). reprint ed. pap. 7.99 *(978-1-4169-1624-6(5)*, Simon & Schuster Bks. For Young Readers) Simon & Schuster Bks. For Young Readers.
Lieb, Josh. I Am a Genius of Unspeakable Evil & I Want to Be Your Class President. 2010. (ENG.). 304p. (J). (gr. 5-7). 8.99 *(978-1-59514-354-9(8)*, Razorbill) Penguin Young Readers Group.
Liess, Claudia Schmidt. But Where Is Dad? 2007. 96p. per. 19.95 *(978-1-4241-6912-2(7))* America Star Bks.
McGaa, Ed. Spirit Horse: An Adventure in Crazy Horse Country. 2007. 80p. (YA). pap. *(978-1-57579-360-3(1))* Pine Hill Pr.
Merrill, Karen Grill. Oh, What a State I'm In: The USA in Rhyme & Riddle, 1 vol. Grill, Gerald, illus. 2010. 48p. pap. 24.95 *(978-1-4489-7979-0(X))* PublishAmerica, Inc.
Miller, Scott E. Prairie Sunsets. 2008. 103p. pap. 19.95 *(978-1-60441-763-0(3))* America Star Bks.
Moskowitz, Hannah. Not Otherwise Specified: A Novel. 2015. (ENG., Illus.). 304p. (YA). (gr. 9). pap. 11.99 *(978-1-4814-0595-9(0)*, Simon Pulse) Simon Pulse.
Myers, Jason. Dead End. 2011. (ENG.). 384p. (YA). (gr. 10-18). pap. 9.99 *(978-1-4424-1430-3(8)*, Simon Pulse) Simon Pulse.
Polk, Douglas. Marie's Home, 1 vol. 2009. 48p. pap. 16.95 *(978-1-60749-454-6(X))* America Star Bks.
Pyrtle Second Graders & Writers' Circle. Poetry & a Fifth Grade Cinderell: An Anthology from Nebraska. 2009. 60p. pap. 8.95 *(978-0-595-53233-9(0))* iUniverse, Inc.
Reed, Amy. Over You. (ENG., Illus.). (YA). (gr. 9). 2014. 336p. pap. 9.99 *(978-1-4424-5697-6(3))* 2013. 320p. 16.99 *(978-1-4424-5696-9(5))* Simon Pulse. (Simon Pulse).
Richardson, Arleta. Whistle Stop West. 2003. (Orphans' Journey Ser.: Vol. 2). 144p. (J). (gr. 3-7). pap., pap. 5.99 *(978-0-7814-3537-6(4)*, 0781435374) Cook, David C.
—Whistle-Stop West. 2016. (Beyond the Orphan Train Ser.: 2). (ENG.). 192p. (J). pap. 7.99 *(978-1-4347-0956-1(6))* Cook, David C.
Sandburg, Carl. The Huckabuck Family: And How They Raised Popcorn in Nebraska & Quit & Came Back. Small, David, illus. 2006. 30p. (J). (gr. k-4). reprint ed. 16.00 *(978-1-4223-5854-2(2))* DIANE Publishing Co.
Silvano, Wendi. Love Is All Around Nebraska. Czernichowska, Joanna, illus. 2016. (ENG.). 32p. (J). (-6). 12.99 *(978-1-4926-2939-9(1)*, Sourcebooks Jabberwocky) Sourcebooks, Inc.
—Love Is All Around Omaha. Czernichowska, Joanna, illus. 2016. (ENG.). 32p. (J). (-6). 12.99 *(978-1-4926-2951-1(0)*, Sourcebooks Jabberwocky) Sourcebooks, Inc.
Smallman, Steve. Santa Is Coming to Nebraska. Dunn, Robert, illus. 2013. (ENG.). 32p. (J). (-3). 9.99 *(978-1-4022-9072-5(1)*, Sourcebooks Jabberwocky) Sourcebooks, Inc.
—Santa Is Coming to Omaha. Dunn, Robert, illus. 2013. (ENG.). 32p. (J). (-3). 9.99 *(978-1-4022-9006-0(3)*, Sourcebooks Jabberwocky) Sourcebooks, Inc.
Sourcebooks & Silverman, Laura. Girl Out of Water. 2017. (ENG.). 368p. (YA). (gr. 8-12). pap. 10.99 *(978-1-4926-4686-0(5)*, 9781492646860) Sourcebooks, Inc.
Valente, Catherynne M. The Girl Who Circumnavigated Fairyland in a Ship of Her Own Making. Juan, Ana, illus. 2011. (Fairyland Ser.: 1). (ENG.). 256p. (YA). (gr. 5-9). 16.99 *(978-0-312-64961-6(4)*, 9780312649616) Feiwel & Friends.
—The Girl Who Circumnavigated Fairyland in a Ship of Her Own Making. 2012. (CHI & ENG., Illus.). 304p. (J). (gr. 5-8). pap. *(978-986-6026-24-9(8))* Muses Publishing Hse.
—The Girl Who Circumnavigated Fairyland in a Ship of Her Own Making. Juan, Ana, illus. 2012. (Fairyland Ser.: 1). (ENG.). 288p. (YA). (gr. 5-9). pap. 7.99 *(978-1-250-01019-3(5)*, 9781250010193) Square Fish.
Walker, Lane. The Hunt for Scarface. 2014. (ENG.). 161p. (YA). (gr. 7-13). pap. 9.99 *(978-1-58169-518-2(7)*, Evergreen Pr.) Genesis Communications, Inc.
Wilson, John. Ghost Moon, 1 vol. 2011. (Desert Legend Trilogy Ser.: 2). (ENG.). 192p. (YA). (gr. 8-12). pap. 12.95 *(978-1-55469-879-0(0))* Orca Bk. Pubs. USA.

NEBRASKA—HISTORY

Abraham Lincoln's Shining Star: The Inspiring Story of Abraham Lincoln & Nebraska. 2010. (Illus.). 64p. 18.95 *(978-0-615-34265-8(5))* America's Great Stories.
Bailer, Darice. What's Great about Nebraska? 2015. (Our Great States Ser.). (ENG., Illus.). 32p. (J). (gr. 2-5). pap. 7.95 *(978-1-4677-6094-2(3))*; lib. bdg. 26.60 *(978-1-4677-3870-5(0))* Lerner Publishing Group. (Lerner Pubns.).
Bjorklund, Ruth, et al. Nebraska. 2nd rev. ed. 2009. (Celebrate the States 11 Ser.). 144p. (gr. 6). 42.79 *(978-0-7614-4732-0(6))* Marshall Cavendish GBR. Dist: Marshall Cavendish Corp.
Bringle, Jennifer. Nebraska: Past & Present. 2010. (United States: Past & Present Ser.). (ENG.). 48p. (YA). pap. 11.75 *(978-1-4358-9514-0(2))*; lib. bdg. 29.25 *(978-1-4358-9487-7(1))* Rosen Publishing Group, Inc., The. (Rosen Reference).
Coleman, Miriam. Nebraska: The Cornhusker State. 2010. (Our Amazing States Ser.). (ENG.). 24p. (J). pap. 8.25 *(978-1-4488-0744-4(1))*; lib. bdg. 22.60 *(978-1-4488-0656-0(9))* Rosen Publishing Group, Inc., The. (PowerKids Pr.).
Foran, Jill. Nebraska. 2011. (Guide to American States Ser.). (Illus.). 48p. (YA). (gr. 3-6). 29.99 *(978-1-61690-799-0(1))*; (J). *(978-1-61690-475-3(5))* Weigl Pubs., Inc.
—Nebraska: The Cornhusker State. 2016. (J). *(978-1-4896-4896-9(8))* Weigl Pubs., Inc.
Gamble, Adam & Jasper, Mark. Good Night Nebraska. 2015. (Good Night Our World Ser.). (ENG., Illus.). 20p. (J). (— 1). bds. 9.95 *(978-1-60219-087-0(9))* Good Night Bks.
Hanel, Rachael. Nebraska. 2009. (This Land Called America Ser.). (Illus.). 32p. (YA). (gr. 3-6). 19.95 *(978-1-58341-780-5(X))* Creative Co., The.
Herschbach, Elisabeth. Lower Plains: Kansas, Nebraska, Vol. 19. 2015. (Let's Explore the States Ser.). (Illus.). 64p. (J). (gr. 5). 23.95 *(978-1-4222-3326-9(X))* Mason Crest.
Kopp, Megan. Nebraska: The Cornhusker State. 2012. (J). *(978-1-61913-373-0(3))*; pap. *(978-1-61913-374-7(1))* Weigl Pubs., Inc.
Lukesh, Jean A. Sky Rider: Story of Evelyn Sharp, World War II WASP. 2011. (Noteworthy Americans Young Readers Biography Book Ser.). (ENG., Illus.). 161p. (J). pap. 14.95 *(978-0-9647586-3-6(6))* Field Mouse Productions.
Marsh, Carole. Exploring Nebraska Through Project-Based Learning: Geography, History, Government, Economics & More. 2016. (Nebraska Experience Ser.). (ENG.). (J). pap. 9.99 *(978-0-635-12351-0(7))* Gallopade International.
—I'm Reading about Nebraska. 2014. (Nebraska Experience Ser.). (ENG., Illus.). (J). pap., pap. 8.99 *(978-0-635-11302-3(3))* Gallopade International.
—Nebraska History Projects: 30 Cool, Activities, Crafts, Experiments & More for Kids to Do to Learn about Your State! 2003. (Nebraska Experience Ser.). 32p. (gr. k-5). pap. 5.95 *(978-0-635-01796-3(2)*, Marsh, Carole Bks.) Gallopade International.
Mills, Jordan. Nebraska. 2016. (States Ser.). (ENG., Illus.). 32p. (gr. 3-4). lib. bdg. 27.32 *(978-1-5157-0414-0(9))* Next Page Pr., The.
Murray, Julie. Nebraska, 1 vol. 2012. (Explore the United States Ser.). (ENG., Illus.). 32p. (J). (gr. 2-5). lib. bdg. 28.50 *(978-1-61783-365-6(7)*, Big Buddy Bks.) ABDO Publishing Co.
The Nebraska Adventure Program Kit: All program components for the Nebraska Adventure, 1 vol. 2009. 99.95 *(978-1-4236-0722-9(8))* Gibbs Smith, Publisher.
Ollhoff, Jim. Nebraska, 1 vol. 2009. (United States Ser.). (ENG., Illus.). 48p. (YA). (gr. 2-5). 27.07 *(978-1-60453-662-1(4))* ABDO Publishing Co.
Plain, Nancy. Light on the Prairie: Solomon D. Butcher, Photographer of Nebraska's Pioneer Days. 2012. (ENG., Illus.). 128p. (YA). pap. 16.95 *(978-0-8032-3520-5(8)*, Bison Bks.) Univ. of Nebraska Pr.
Sanders, Doug. Nebraska. 2014. (J). pap. *(978-1-62712-498-0(5))*; (Illus.). 80p. *(978-1-62712-241-2(9))* Cavendish Square Publishing.
Sanders, Doug & Schauer, Pete. Nebraska. 2016. (It's My State! (r) Ser.). (Illus.). 80p. (J). (gr. 4-4). 34.21 *(978-1-62713-247-3(3))* Cavendish Square Publishing.
Warren, Andrea. Pioneer Girl: A True Story of Growing up on the Prairie. 2009. (ENG., Illus.). 104p. pap. 14.95 *(978-0-8032-2526-8(1)*, Bison Bks.) Univ. of Nebraska Pr.
Weatherly, Myra. Nebraska. 2009. (From Sea to Shining Sea, Second Ser.). (ENG.). 80p. (J). pap. 7.95 *(978-0-531-21136-6(3)*, Children's Pr.) Scholastic Library Publishing.

M N O

NEBRASKA—HISTORY—FICTION

Blanc, Esther Silverstein & Eagle, Godeane. Long Johns for a Small Chicken. Dixon, Tennessee, illus. 2003. (J). 16.95 (978-1-884244-23-0(8)) volcano pr.

Figley, Marty Rhodes. The Prairie Adventure of Sarah & Annie, Blizzard Survivors. Hammond, Ted & Carbajal, Richard Pimentel, illus. 2011. (History's Kid Heroes Set III Ser.). pap. 51.02 (978-0-7613-8621-6(1)); (ENG.). 32p. (gr. 3-5). pap. 8.95 (978-0-7613-7808-2(1)) Lerner Publishing Group. (Graphic Universe™).

—The Prairie Adventure of Sarah & Annie, Blizzard Survivors. Hammond, Ted & Carbajal, Richard, illus. 2011. (History's Kid Heroes Ser.). (ENG.). 32p. (gr. 3-5). lib. bdg. 26.60 (978-0-7613-7805-1(7)) Lerner Publishing Group.

Hart, Alison. Anna's Blizzard, 1 vol. Bachem, Paul, illus. 2017. (ENG.). 160p. (J). (gr. 2-4). pap. 7.95 **(978-1-68263-002-0(1))** Peachtree Pubs.

Hoffman, Emily Allen. A Friend of the Enemy. 2003. 108p. (J). pap. 7.95 (978-1-57249-312-4(7), White Mane Kids) White Mane Publishing Co., Inc.

LaFaye, A. Worth. unabr. ed. 2006. (Live Oak Histories Ser.). (J). (gr. 3-6). pap. 28.95 incl. audio compact disk (978-1-59519-767-2(2)) Live Oak Media.

—Worth. 2006. 144p. (J). (gr. 4-7). 13.65 (978-0-7569-6614-0(0)) Perfection Learning Corp.

—Worth. 2004. (ENG., Illus.). 160p. (J). (gr. 3-7). 17.99 (978-0-689-85730-0(6), Simon & Schuster Bks. For Young Readers) Simon & Schuster Bks. For Young Readers.

Levinson, Nancy Smiler. Prairie Friends. Schuett, Stacey, illus. 2003. (I Can Read Bks.). 64p. (J). (gr. k-3). 15.99 (978-0-06-028001-7(8)) HarperCollins Pubs.

McGaa Tonemah, Paula & McGaa, Ed. The Animals Talk. 2009. 72p. (J). pap. (978-1-57579-373-3(3)) Pine Hill Pr.

Riege, Cheryl. Tracks Rivers Roads: Across Nebraska on the Meridian Highway. 2012. (ENG.). 184p. pap. 12.95 (978-1-4327-8573-4(7)) Outskirts Pr., Inc.

Yolen, Jane. Elsie's Bird. Small, David, illus. 2010. (ENG.). 40p. (J). (gr. k-3). 17.99 (978-0-399-25292-1(4), Philomel Bks.) Penguin Young Readers Group.

NECROMANCY

see Divination; Witchcraft

NEEDLEWORK

see also names of needlework; e.g. Dressmaking; Embroidery; Sewing; Tapestry

Akass, Susan. My First Sewing Book. 2011. (ENG., Illus.). 128p. (J). (gr. 7-11). pap. 14.95 (978-1-907563-71-3(7), CICO Books) Ryland Peters & Small GBR. Dist: WIPRO.

Falconer, Ian, illus. Olivia Lacing Cards. 2013. (ENG.). 10p. (J). (gr. -1-1). 14.99 (978-1-4521-1177-3(4)) Chronicle Bks. LLC.

Kuskowski, Alex. Cool Needle Felting for Kids: A Fun & Creative Introduction to Fiber Art, 1 vol. 2014. (Cool Fiber Art Ser.). (ENG.). 32p. (gr. 8-12). lib. bdg. 28.50 (978-1-62403-309-4(1), Checkerboard Library) ABDO Publishing Co.

—Cool Punch Needle for Kids: A Fun & Creative Introduction to Fiber Art, 1 vol. 2014. (Cool Fiber Art Ser.). (ENG.). 32p. (gr. 8-12). lib. bdg. 28.50 (978-1-62403-310-0(5), Checkerboard Library) ABDO Publishing Co.

NEFERTITI, QUEEN OF EGYPT, ACTIVE 14TH CENTURY B.C.

Lange, Brenda. Nefertiti. 2008. (Ancient World Leaders Ser.). (Illus.). 112p. (gr. 6-12). 30.00 (978-0-7910-9581-2(9), Chelsea Hse.) Facts On File, Inc.

Spirn, Michele Sobel. Mysterious People. 2006. (True Tales: A Chapter Book Ser.). (ENG., Illus.). 48p. (J). (gr. 2-4). per. 4.95 (978-0-516-25454-8(5), Children's Pr.) Scholastic Library Publishing.

NEFERTITI, QUEEN OF EGYPT, ACTIVE 14TH CENTURY B.C.—FICTION

Friesner, Esther M. Sphinx's Princess. 2010. (Princesses of Myth Ser.). (ENG.). 400p. (YA). (gr. 7). pap. 9.99 (978-0-375-85655-6(2), Random Hse. Bks. for Young Readers) Random Hse. Children's Bks.

—Sphinx's Queen. 2011. (Princesses of Myth Ser.). (ENG., Illus.). 368p. (YA). (gr. 7). pap. 9.99 (978-0-375-85658-7(7), Ember) Random Hse. Children's Bks.

Hofmeyr, Dianne. Eye of the Sun. 2011. (ENG.). 336p. (J). (gr. 3-7). pap. 6.99 (978-1-4424-1186-9(4), Aladdin) Simon & Schuster Children's Publishing.

NEGROES

see African Americans; Blacks

NEGRO RACE

see Blacks

NEIGHBORHOOD

see Community Life

NEIGHBORHOOD CENTERS

see Social Settlements

NEIGHBORHOOD SCHOOLS

see Schools

NEIGHBORS

Bullard, Lisa. This Is My Neighborhood. Conger, Holli, illus. 2016. (Cloverleaf Books (tm) — Where I Live Ser.). (ENG.). 24p. (J). (gr. k-2). 25.32 (978-1-4677-9521-0(6), Millbrook Pr.) Lerner Publishing Group.

Donner, Candie. Apologia Worldview: Assembled: 'Who Is My Neighbor? Lapbook. Kinney, Cyndi, ed. 2013. (J). pap. 35.99 (978-1-61625-531-2(5)) Knowledge Box Central.

—Apologia Worldview: 'Who Is My Neighbor? Lapbook. Kinney, Cyndi, ed. 2013. (J). pap. 25.99 (978-1-61625-529-9(3)); cd-rom 19.99 (978-1-61625-528-2(5)) Knowledge Box Central.

Holko, Suzanne L. Grampy & Me. 2012. 34p. pap. 13.95 (978-1-4624-0080-5(9), Inspiring Voices) Author Solutions, Inc.

Holland, Trish. Neighborhood Song. 2010. (J). (978-1-60617-143-1(7)) Teaching Strategies, LLC.

Lyons, Shelly. People in My Neighborhood. 2013. (My Neighborhood Ser.). (ENG.). 24p. (gr. k-1). pap. 41.70 (978-1-62065-884-0(4)); (Illus.). pap. 7.29 (978-1-62065-883-3(6)); (Illus.). lib. bdg. 26.65 (978-1-62065-099-8(1)) Capstone Press of Coughlan Cos. (Pebble Plus).

—Places in My Neighborhood. 2013. (My Neighborhood Ser.). (ENG.). 24p. (gr. k-1). pap. 41.70 (978-1-62065-886-4(0), Pebble Plus) Capstone Press of Coughlan Cos.

Summers, Portia. My Neighborhood. 2016. (Zoom in on Communities Ser.). 24p. (J). (gr. 2-2). pap. 9.35 (978-0-7660-7800-0(0)) Enslow Pubs., Inc.

NEIGHBORS—FICTION

Abrahams, Peter. Outlaws of Sherwood Street: Stealing from the Rich. 2013. (ENG.). 320p. (J). (gr. 5). 7.99 (978-0-14-242438-4(2), Puffin Books) Penguin Young Readers Group.

Adderson, Caroline. Middle of Nowhere. 2013. 212p. pap. (978-1-4596-6452-4(3)) ReadHowYouWant.com, Ltd.

Adler, David A. Not Wanted by the Police. Franson, Leanne, illus. 2005. (Andy Russell Ser.: Bk. 5). (ENG.). 128p. (J). (gr. 1-4). pap. 5.99 (978-0-15-216719-6(6)) Houghton Mifflin Harcourt Publishing Co.

Alter, Anna. Sprout Street Neighbors: Bon Voyage. 2017. (Sprout Street Neighbors Ser.: 3). (ENG., Illus.). 96p. (J). (gr. 1-4). pap. 6.99 **(978-1-5247-0053-9(3)**, Yearling) Random Hse. Children's Bks.

Anderson, Alice. Danny Be Good! 2012. 24p. pap. 17.99 (978-1-4685-6433-4(1)) AuthorHouse.

Ashman, Linda. Rain! Robinson, Christian, illus. (ENG.). (J). 2017. 30p. (— 1). bds. 7.99 (978-0-544-88037-5(4), HMH Books For Young Readers) 2013. 32p. (gr. -1-3). 16.99 (978-0-547-73395-1(X)) Houghton Mifflin Harcourt Publishing Co.

Atchison, David C. The Adventures of Black Bart: an Encounter with Regret. 2008. 84p. pap. 7.94 (978-0-615-23723-7(1)) Black Bart Bks.

Atkinson, Elizabeth. From Alice to Zen & Everyone in Between. (gr. 4-7). 2013. (ENG.). 248p. (J). pap. 9.95 (978-1-4677-0861-6(5), Carolrhoda Bks.) 2008. 247p. (YA). 16.95 (978-0-8225-7271-8(0)) Lerner Publishing Group.

Atwell, A. Erika Laura. 2008. 157p. pap. 24.95 (978-1-60703-006-5(3)) PublishAmerica, Inc.

Auerbach, Annie. Naughty Nautical Neighbors, Vol. 2. 2004. 64p. (J). (gr. 2-5). pap. 17.00 incl. audio (978-0-8072-1987-4(8), Listening Library) Random Hse. Audio Publishing Group.

Axelrod, Amy. Your Friend in Fashion, Abby Shapiro. 2011. (ENG.). 288p. (J). (gr. 3-7). 17.95 (978-0-8234-2340-8(9)) Holiday Hse., Inc.

Babineaux, Jim. Cody Cottontail Makes a Wise Choice! Babineaux, Jim, illus. l.t. ed. 2005. (Illus.). 18p. (J). (978-0-9769769-0-5(0)) ALCAPS, LLC.

Baicker-McKee, Carol, illus. An Apple Pie for Dinner, 0 vols. 2009. (ENG.). 32p. (J). (gr. k-3). 17.99 (978-0-7614-5452-6(7), 9780761454526, Amazon Children's Publishing) Amazon Publishing.

Baker, Jeannie. Home. Baker, Jeannie, illus. 2004. (ENG., Illus.). 32p. (J). (gr. k-5). 16.99 (978-0-06-623935-4(4), Greenwillow Bks.) HarperCollins Pubs.

Banks, Robin Washington. Big Boy. Morgan, Vincent, illus. 2011. 20p. pap. 24.95 (978-1-4560-7068-7(1)) PublishAmerica, Inc.

Banks, Steven. The Song That Never Ends. DePorter, Vince, illus. 2004. (Spongebob Squarepants Ser.). 32p. (J). (gr. k-2). 11.65 (978-0-7569-5374-4(X)) Perfection Learning Corp.

Baraou, Anne & Sardon, Vincent. The Skeleton Family: The Neighbors from Elsewhere. 2005. (Illus.). 64p. (978-1-59687-825-9(8), ipicturebooks) ibooks, Inc.

Barbo, Maria S. & Preller, James. The Case of the Four-Leaf Clover. Smith, Jamie, illus. 2008. 104p. (J). pap. (978-0-545-03837-9(5)) Scholastic, Inc.

Barkow, Henriette. Don't Cry, Sly! Johnson, Richard, illus. 2004. 32p. (J). (ENG & TUR.). pap. (978-1-85269-670-2(2)); (ENG & TAM.). pap. (978-1-85269-663-4(X)); (ENG & SOM.). pap. (978-1-85269-661-0(3)); (ENG.). pap. (978-1-85269-660-3(5)); (ENG & PAN.). pap. (978-1-85269-658-0(3)); (ENG & ITA.). pap. (978-1-85269-657-3(5)); (ENG & GUJ.). pap. (978-1-85269-656-6(7)); (GER & ENG.). pap. (978-1-85269-655-9(9)); (ENG & CZE.). pap. (978-1-85269-652-8(4)); (ENG & CHI.). pap. (978-1-85269-651-1(6)); (ENG & BEN.). pap. (978-1-85269-650-4(8)); (ENG & POL.). pap. (978-1-85269-813-3(6)); (ENG & URD.). pap. (978-1-85269-671-9(0)) Mantra Lingua.

Barnes, Ben. Don't Eat My Garden. Barnes, Page, illus. 2007. 28p. per. 24.95 (978-1-4241-8964-9(0)) America Star Bks.

Barrett, Ms S. Moe. Mangoe & Marlie: Mangoe Takes Care of Marlie. 2013. 56p. pap. 11.93 (978-0-9701289-5-9(9)) Moselle Productions, Inc.

Barrows, Annie. Bound to Be Bad. 2009. (Ivy & Bean Ser.: 5). (J). lib. bdg. 16.00 (978-0-606-14473-5(0), Turtleback) Turtleback Bks.

—Ivy + Bean. Blackall, Sophie, illus. (Ivy & Bean Ser.: IVYB). (ENG.). 120p. (J). (gr. 1-5). 2007. pap. 5.99 (978-0-8118-4909-8(0))Bk. 1. 2006. 14.99 (978-0-8118-4903-6(1)) Chronicle Bks. LLC.

—Ivy + Bean. Blackall, Sophie, illus. 2007. (Ivy & Bean Ser.: Bk. 1). 120p. (gr. 1-5). 16.00 (978-0-7569-8142-6(5)) Perfection Learning Corp.

—Ivy + Bean. Blackall, Sophie, illus. 2007. (Ivy & Bean Ser.: 1). (J). lib. bdg. 16.00 (978-1-4177-7972-7(1), Turtleback) Turtleback Bks.

—Ivy + Bean: No News Is Good News. Blackall, Sophie, illus. 2012. (Ivy & Bean Ser.). (ENG.). 144p. (J). (gr. 1-5). pap. 5.99 (978-1-4521-0781-3(5)) Chronicle Bks. LLC.

—Ivy + Bean Bound to Be Bad. Blackall, Sophie, illus. (Ivy & Bean Ser.: IVYB). (ENG.). (J). (gr. 1-5). 2009. 128p. pap. 5.99 (978-0-8118-6857-0(5)) 2008. 124p. 14.99 (978-0-8118-6265-3(8)) Chronicle Bks. LLC.

—Ivy + Bean Boxed Set: Books 7-9. Blackall, Sophie, illus. 2013. (Ivy & Bean Ser.). (ENG.). 428p. (J). (gr. 1-5). 19.99 (978-1-4521-1732-4(2)) Chronicle Bks. LLC.

—Ivy + Bean Break the Fossil Record. Blackall, Sophie, illus. 2007. (Ivy & Bean Ser.: IVYB). (ENG.). 132p. (J). (gr. 1-5). 14.99 (978-0-8118-5683-6(6)) Chronicle Bks. LLC.

—Ivy + Bean Doomed to Dance. Blackall, Sophie, illus. 2009. (Ivy & Bean Ser.: IVYB). (ENG.). 136p. (J). (gr. 1-5). 14.99 (978-0-8118-6266-0(6)) Chronicle Bks. LLC.

—Ivy + Bean No News Is Good News. Blackall, Sophie, illus. 2011. (Ivy & Bean Ser.: IVYB). (ENG.). 128p. (J). (gr. 1-5). 14.99 (978-0-8118-6693-4(9)) Chronicle Bks. LLC.

—No News Is Good News. Blackall, Sophie, illus. 2012. (Ivy & Bean Ser.: 8). (J). lib. bdg. 16.00 (978-0-606-26950-6(9), Turtleback) Turtleback Bks.

Barrows, Annie & Blackall, Sophie. Ivy + Bean, 1 vol. 2011. (Ivy & Bean Ser.). (ENG., Illus.). 128p. (J). (gr. 1-4). 24.21 (978-1-59961-928-6(8)) Spotlight.

—Ivy + Bean Bound to Be Bad, 1 vol. 2011. (Ivy & Bean Ser.). (ENG., Illus.). 128p. (J). (gr. 1-4). 24.21 (978-1-59961-932-3(6)) Spotlight.

Behar, Ruth. Lucky Broken Girl. 2017. (ENG.). 256p. (J). (gr. 5). 16.99 (978-0-399-54644-0(8), Nancy Paulsen Books) Penguin Young Readers Group.

Belmore, Vickie J. Paul the Pack Rat: Helping Children Learn to Share. Ciaravino, Paul, illus. 2009. (Let's Talk Ser.). (ENG.). 48p. (J). (gr. -1-4). pap. 8.95 (978-0-88282-307-2(8)) New Horizon Pr. Pubs., Inc.

Benchmark Education Co., LLC. Guess Who Lives on My Street Big Book. 2014. (Shared Reading Foundations Ser.). (J). (gr. -1). (978-1-4509-9428-6(8)) Benchmark Education Co.

Berenda, M. J. Helping with Pocket Change. 2011. 24p. pap. 12.95 (978-1-4567-5836-3(5)) AuthorHouse.

Bessler, edward. A Smile for Billy. 2008. 175p. pap. 13.95 (978-1-4357-4439-4(X)) Lulu Pr., Inc.

Birdsall, Jeanne. Lucky & Squash. Dyer, Jane, illus. 2012. (ENG.). 32p. (J). (gr. -1-2). 16.99 (978-0-06-083150-9(2)) HarperCollins Pubs.

Birney, Betty G. The Seven Wonders of Sassafras Springs. Phelan, Matt, illus. 2007. 210p. 17.00 (978-0-7569-8075-7(5)) Perfection Learning Corp.

—The Seven Wonders of Sassafras Springs. Phelan, Matt, illus. (ENG.). 224p. (J). (gr. 3-7). 2007. pap. 7.99 (978-1-4169-3489-9(8)) 2005. 16.95 (978-0-689-87136-8(8)) Simon & Schuster Children's Publishing. (Atheneum Bks. for Young Readers).

Black, Holly. Kind. Naifeh, Ted, illus. 2011. (Good Neighbors Ser.: 3). (ENG.). 128p. (J). (gr. 7-7). pap. 12.99 (978-0-439-85567-9(5), Graphix) Scholastic, Inc.

Blackford, Andy. The Three Little Pigs & the New Neighbor. 2014. (ENG., Illus.). 32p. (J). (978-0-7787-0447-8(5)); pap. (978-0-7787-0482-9(3)) Crabtree Publishing Co.

Blackwood, Gary L. The Just-So Woman. Manning, Jane K., illus. 2006. (I Can Read Bks.). 48p. (J). (gr. -1-3). lib. bdg. 16.89 (978-0-06-057728-5(2)) HarperCollins Pubs.

Bluemle, Elizabeth. How Do You Wokka-Wokka? Cecil, Randy, illus. 2012. (ENG.). 32p. (J). (gr. -1-2). pap. 6.99 (978-0-7636-6085-7(X)) Candlewick Pr.

Blume, Lesley M. M. Cornelia & the Audacious Escapades of the Somerset Sisters. (ENG.). 272p. (J). (gr. 3-7). 2008. 7.99 (978-0-440-42110-8(1), Yearling) 2006. 15.95 (978-0-375-83523-0(7), Knopf Bks. for Young Readers) Random Hse. Children's Bks.

Blyton, Enid. Those Dreadful Children: Family Adventure. 2013. (ENG.). 224p. (J). pap. 9.99 (978-1-84135-646-4(8)) Award Pubns. Ltd. GBR. Dist: Parkwest Pubns., Inc.

Borsky, Mary. Benny Bensky & the Parrot-Napper. Hendry, Linda, illus. 2008. (ENG.). 128p. (J). (gr. 4-7). pap. 9.95 (978-0-88776-840-8(7), Tundra Bks.) Tundra Bks. CAN. Dist: Penguin Random Hse. LLC.

Bourgeois, Paulette. Neighborhood. 2004. (Illus.). (J). (gr. k-3). spiral bd. (978-0-616-01588-9(7)); spiral bd. (978-0-616-01589-6(5)) Canadian National Institute for the Blind/Institut National Canadien pour les Aveugles.

Bradley, Jess, illus. I Know Sasquatch. 2015. (Fiction Picture Bks.). (ENG.). 32p. (gr. -1-2). lib. bdg. 22.60 (978-1-4795-6481-1(8), Fiction Picture Bks.) Picture Window Bks.

Brennan-Nelson, Denise. Willow & the Snow Day Dance. Moore, Cyd, illus. 2010. (ENG.). 32p. (J). (gr. k-6). lib. bdg. 16.95 (978-1-58536-522-7(X)) Sleeping Bear Pr.

Broach, Elise. Shakespeare's Secret. 2007. (Illus.). 258p. (gr. 4-9). 17.00 (978-0-7569-8204-1(9)) Perfection Learning Corp.

—Shakespeare's Secret. 2007. (ENG.). 272p. (YA). (gr. 5-10). per. 7.99 (978-0-312-37132-6(2), 9780312371326) Square Fish.

—Shakespeare's Secret. l.t. ed. 2006. (Thorndike Literacy Bridge Ser.). (Illus.). 263p. (J). (gr. 5-10). 22.95 (978-0-7862-8735-2(7)) Thorndike Pr.

Brookins, Cara. Doris Free. Barrow, Ann, illus. 2006. 127p. (J). pap. (978-1-59336-333-8(8)) Mondo Publishing.

Bullman, Carol & Madsen, James. The Christmas House. Madsen, James, illus. 2009. (Illus.). 32p. (J). (gr. -1-3). 16.99 (978-0-8249-5598-4(6), Ideal Pubns.) Worthy Publishing.

Burket, Shelia. Silver & Gold: Sissy Stringbean Meets Morris Norris. 2012. 28p. 24.95 (978-1-4626-3591-7(1)) America Star Bks.

Byrd, Lee Merrill. El Ttesoro en la Calle Oro: A Neighborhood Story in English & Spanish. Franco, Sharon, tr. Castro L., Antonio, illus. 2007.Tr. of Treasure on Gold Street. (SPA & ENG.). 40p. (J). (gr. 4-6). pap. 8.95 (978-1-933693-11-8(8)) Cinco Puntos Pr.

Capucilli, Alyssa Satin. Katy Duck Makes a Friend. Cole, Henry, illus. 2012. (Katy Duck Ser.). (ENG.). 24p. (J). (gr. -1-1). 16.99 (978-1-4424-1977-3(6)); pap. 3.99 (978-1-4424-1976-6(8)) Simon Spotlight. (Simon Spotlight).

Carey, Benedict. Poison Most Vial: A Mystery. 2012. (ENG.). 240p. (J). (gr. 3-7). 17.95 (978-1-4197-0031-6(6), Amulet Bks.) Abrams, Inc.

Carney, Larry, adapted by. Silly Neighborhood. 2010. (ENG., Illus.). 24p. (J). pap. 6.95 (978-1-60072-157-1(5)) PC Treasures, Inc.

Cartaya, Pablo. The Epic Fail of Arturo Zamora. 2017. (ENG.). 256p. (J). (gr. 5). 16.99 (978-1-101-99723-9(0), Viking Books for Young Readers) Penguin Young Readers Group.

Cecil, Lauren. Harmony Takes the Stage. 2013. (Lalaloopsy Ser.). (ENG.). 24p. (J). (gr. -1-3). pap. 3.99 (978-0-545-53180-1(2)) Math Solutions.

Cepeda, Joe. The Swing. 2006. (Illus.). (J). 15.99 (978-0-439-14261-8(X), Levine, Arthur A. Bks.) Scholastic, Inc.

Cheaney, J. B. My Friend the Enemy. 2007. 266p. (gr. 4-7). 16.50 (978-0-7569-7946-1(3)) Perfection Learning Corp.

Clark, Chris Elliott. Hazel's Secret. 2008. 64p. pap. 19.95 (978-1-60474-500-9(2)) America Star Bks.

Clary, Julian. The Bolds. Roberts, David, illus. (Bolds Ser.). (ENG.). 272p. (J). (gr. 3-6). 2017. pap. 7.99 **(978-1-5124-8174-7(2))** 2016. 16.99 (978-1-5124-0440-1(3)) Lerner Publishing Group. (Carolrhoda Bks.).

Colin, Beatrice & Pinto, Sara. My Invisible Sister. Pinto, Sara, illus. 2011. (ENG., Illus.). 128p. (YA). (gr. 3-6). pap. 6.99 (978-1-59990-678-2(3), 9781599906782, Bloomsbury USA Childrens) Bloomsbury Publishing USA.

Cormier, Robert. Frenchtown Summer. unabr. ed. 2004. 128p. (J). (gr. 7-18). pap. 29.00 incl. audio (978-0-8072-0663-8(6), Listening Library) Random Hse. Audio Publishing Group.

Couloumbis, Audrey. Jake. 2011. (ENG.). 176p. (J). (gr. 3-7). pap. 6.99 (978-0-375-85631-0(5), Yearling) Random Hse. Children's Bks.

Crimi, Carolyn. The Louds Move In!, 1 vol. Dunnick, Regan, illus. 2006. (ENG.). 32p. (J). (gr. -1-3). 14.95 (978-0-7614-5221-8(4)) Marshall Cavendish Corp.

Cumpiano, Ina. Quinito's Neighborhood (El Vecindario de Quinito) Ramirez, José, illus. 2009. (ENG & SPA.). 32p. (J). (gr. -1-3). pap. 9.95 (978-0-89239-229-2(0)) Lee & Low Bks., Inc.

—Quinito's Neighborhood (El Vecindario de Quinito) Ramirez, Jose, illus. 2005. (ENG & SPA.). 24p. (J). (gr. -1-1). 16.95 (978-0-89239-209-4(6)) Lee & Low Bks., Inc.

De Marco, Clare. The Mad Scientist Next Door. 2014. (ENG., Illus.). 32p. (J). (978-0-7787-1305-0(9)) Crabtree Publishing Co.

Demas, Corinne. Two Christmas Mice. Roth, Stephanie, illus. 2005. (ENG.). 32p. (J). (gr. -1-3). 16.95 (978-0-8234-1785-8(9)) Holiday Hse., Inc.

Denton, P. J. Girls Against Boys. Denos, Julia, illus. 2013. (Sleepover Squad Ser.: 7). (ENG.). 96p. (J). (gr. 1-4). pap. 4.99 (978-1-4169-5933-5(5), Simon & Schuster/Paula Wiseman Bks.) Simon & Schuster/Paula Wiseman Bks.

Deveze, Winky. Hewitch. Neate, Andy, illus. 2006. (J). (978-0-9787174-0-7(6)) Love Bug Bks.

DiCamillo, Kate. Mercy Watson to the Rescue. DiCamillo, Kate & Van Dusen, Chris, illus. 2009. (Mercy Watson Ser.: 1). (ENG.). 80p. (J). (gr. 1-4). pap. 5.99 (978-0-7636-4504-5(4)) Candlewick Pr.

—Mercy Watson to the Rescue. Van Dusen, Chris, illus. 2005. (Mercy Watson Ser.: 1). (ENG.). 80p. (J). (gr. k-4). 14.99 (978-0-7636-2270-1(2)) Candlewick Pr.

—Mercy Watson to the Rescue. 2009. (Mercy Watson Ser.: Bk. 1). lib. bdg. 16.00 (978-0-606-06704-1(3), Turtleback) Turtleback Bks.

Donnelly, Rebecca. How to Stage a Catastrophe. 2017. (ENG.). 256p. (gr. 4-7). 12.95 (978-1-62370-807-8(9)) Capstone Young Readers of Coughlan Cos.

Dooley, Norah. Everybody Brings Noodles. Thornton, Peter J., illus. 40p. (J). 2005. (ENG.). (gr. k-3). pap. 6.95 (978-1-57505-916-7(9)) 2003. (gr. -1-3). 15.95 (978-0-87614-455-8(5), Carolrhoda Bks.) Lerner Publishing Group.

Duddle, Jonny. The Pirates Next Door. 2012. (ENG., Illus.). 44p. (J). (gr. -1-2). 15.99 (978-0-7636-5842-7(1), Templar) Candlewick Pr.

Durango, Julia. The One-Day House. Diaz, Blanca, illus. 2017. (ENG.). 32p. (J). (gr. -1-2). lib. bdg. 16.99 (978-1-58089-709-6(6)) Charlesbridge Publishing, Inc.

Ecton, Emily. Project Jackalope. 2012. (ENG., Illus.). 256p. (J). (gr. 3-7). 15.99 (978-1-4521-0155-2(8)) Chronicle Bks. LLC.

Edwards, Michelle. A Hat for Mrs. Goldman: A Story about Knitting & Love. Karas, G. Brian, illus. 2016. (ENG.). 40p. (J). (gr. -1-3). 17.99 (978-0-553-49710-6(3), Schwartz & Wade Bks.) Random Hse. Children's Bks.

Ellis, Julie. The New Neighbors. Lewis, Naomi C., illus. 2009. (Rigby PM Stars Bridge Bks.). (ENG.). 16p. (gr. 2-3). pap. 8.70 (978-1-4190-5507-2(0)) Rigby Education.

English, Karen. The Newsy News Newsletter. Freeman, Laura, illus. 2011. (ENG.). 96p. (J). (gr. 1-4). pap. 5.99 (978-0-547-40626-8(6)) Houghton Mifflin Harcourt Publishing Co.

Felix, Monique. The Rumor. Felix, Monique, illus. 2011. (ENG., Illus.). 24p. (J). (gr. 1-3). 19.99 (978-1-56846-219-6(0), Creative Editions) Creative Co., The.

Fields, Terri. One Good Deed. Melmon, Deborah, illus. 2015. (ENG.). 24p. (J). (gr. -1-3). pap. 7.99 (978-1-4677-3479-0(9), Kar-Ben Publishing) Lerner Publishing Group.

—One Good Deed. Melmon, Deborah, illus. 2015. (ENG.). 24p. (J). (gr. -1-3). 17.99 (978-1-4677-3478-3(0)) Lerner Publishing Group.

Fontaine, Catherine Silliman. Have a Not for Christmas ... & Always. 2006. (Illus.). 44p. (J). 11.95 (978-0-9776958-0-5(8)) CyPress Pubns.

Foston, Desirae. The Hawaiian Hiatus of Herkimer Street. Foston, Desirae, illus. 2013. (Illus.). 24p. 24.00 (978-1-940021-00-3(6)) Bliss Group.

Frank, Lucy. Just Ask Iris. 2003. (ENG., Illus.). 224p. (J). (gr. 5-9). pap. 10.99 (978-0-689-84454-6(9), Atheneum Bks. for Young Readers) Simon & Schuster Children's Publishing.

Friedman, Becky. Nighttime in the Neighborhood. 2015. (Daniel Tiger's Neighborhood 8X8 Ser.). lib. bdg. 13.55 (978-0-606-37876-5(6)) Turtleback Bks.

—Welcome to the Neighborhood! Style Guide Staff & Garwood, Gord, illus. 2014. (Daniel Tiger's Neighborhood Ser.). (ENG.). 24p. (J). (gr. -1-1). pap. 3.99 (978-1-4424-9741-2(6), Simon Spotlight) Simon Spotlight.

—Welcome to the Neighborhood! 2014. (Daniel Tiger's Neighborhood 8X8 Ser.). lib. bdg. 13.55 (978-0-606-35458-5(1)) Turtleback Bks.

Fruchter, Jason, illus. Daniel's New Friend. 2015. (Daniel Tiger's Neighborhood Ser.). (ENG.). 24p. (J). (gr. -1-2). pap. 3.99 (978-1-4814-3543-7(4), Simon Spotlight) Simon Spotlight.

—Friends Help Each Other. 2014. (Daniel Tiger's Neighborhood Ser.). (ENG.). 32p. (J). (gr. -1-k). pap. 3.99 (978-1-4814-0366-5(4), Simon Spotlight) Simon Spotlight.

Garland, Sarah, illus. Eddie's Toolbox: And How to Make & Mend Things. 2011. (ENG.). 40p. (J). (gr. -1-2). (978-1-84780-053-4(X)) Rough Guides, Ltd.

Gellock, Ed. The Top Dog Lives Indoors & My Neighbors Live Outside. 2013. 32p. pap. 24.95 (978-1-63000-511-5(8)) America Star Bks.

Gilbert, Michael T., et al. Walt Disney's Comics & Stories #693. Clark, John, ed. 2008. (ENG., Illus.). 64p. pap. 7.99 (978-1-60360-038-5(8), 9781603600385) Gemstone Publishing, Inc.

Gilmore, Rachna. Roses for Gita. Priestley, Alice, illus. 2004. 24p. (J). *(978-1-85269-367-1(3)); (978-1-85269-369-5(X))* Mantra Lingua.

Glines, Abbi. Bad for You. 2015. (Sea Breeze Ser.). (ENG., Illus.). 320p. (YA). (gr. 11). pap. 11.99 *(978-1-4814-2074-7(7)*, Simon Pulse) Simon Pulse.

Gray, Shelly. A Cat Called Spot. 2011. 24p. pap. 24.95 *(978-1-4626-0346-6(7))* America Star Bks.

Green, Ruth. Noisy Neighbors. 2011. (ENG., Illus.). 32p. (J). (gr. -1-3). 14.95 *(978-1-85437-994-8(1))* Tate Publishing, Ltd. GBR. Dist: Abrams, Inc.

Greenwald, Lisa. Sweet Treats & Secret Crushes. 2010. (ENG.). 304p. (YA). (gr. 3-7). 16.95 *(978-0-8109-8990-0(5)*, Amulet Bks.) Abrams, Inc.

Grey, Mini. Hermelin the Detective Mouse. 2014. (ENG.). 32p. (J). (gr. k-3). 17.99 *(978-0-385-75433-0(7)*, Knopf Bks. for Young Readers) Random Hse. Children's Bks.

Gunderson, Jessica. Olivia Bitter, Spooked-Out Sitter! 2016. (Babysitter Chronicles Ser.). (ENG.). 160p. (gr. 4-7). pap. 6.95 *(978-1-4914-8862-1(X))* Stone Arch Bks.

Hahn, Mary Downing. Closed for the Season. 2010. (ENG.). 192p. (J). (gr. 5-7). pap. 6.99 *(978-0-547-39853-2(0))* Houghton Mifflin Harcourt Publishing Co.

Hamilton, Martha & Weiss, Mitch. The Stolen Smell. Wrenn, Tom, illus. 2007. (Story Cove Ser.). (ENG.). 32p. (J). (gr. -1-3). 3.95 *(978-0-87483-838-1(X))* August Hse. Pubs., Inc.

Hamilton, Pat. Peaches the Private Eye Poodle: The Missing Muffin Caper. 2008. 32p. pap. 13.50 *(978-1-60693-277-3(2)*, Eloquent Bks.) Strategic Book Publishing & Rights Agency (SBPRA).

Handelsman, Valerie. A Coral Reef Neighborhood. Handelsman, Valerie, illus. 2004. (Illus.). 16p. (J). 7.95 *(978-0-9748884-1-5(9))* Little Thoughts For Little Ones Publishing, Inc.

Harnett, Katie, illus. Archie Snufflekins Oliver Valentine Cupcake Tiberius Cat. 2016. (ENG.). 32p. (J). (gr. -1-k). 16.95 *(978-1-909263-37-6(0))* Flying Eye Bks. GBR. Dist: Consortium Bk. Sales & Distribution.

Harper, Charise Mericle. Just Grace. 2008. (Just Grace Ser.: 1). (ENG., Illus.). 144p. (J). (gr. 1-4). pap. 5.99 *(978-0-547-01440-1(6))* Houghton Mifflin Harcourt Publishing Co.

Havill, Juanita. Grow, 1 vol. Kodman, Stansislawa, illus. 2011. (ENG.). 160p. (J). (gr. 3-7). pap. 7.95 *(978-1-56145-575-1(X))* Peachtree Pubs.

—Grow, 1 vol. Kodman, Stanislawa, illus. 2008. (ENG.). 144p. (J). (gr. 3-7). 14.95 *(978-1-56145-441-9(9))* Peachtree Pubs.

Hayes, Geoffrey. Benny & Penny in Just Pretend. 2013. (Toon Books Level 2 Ser.). lib. bdg. 14.75 *(978-0-606-31597-5(7)*, Turtleback) Turtleback Bks.

—Benny & Penny in the Big No-No! Mouly, Francoise, ed. Hayes, Geoffrey, illus. 2009. (Benny & Penny Ser.). (ENG., Illus.). 32p. (J). (gr. -1-3). 12.95 *(978-0-9799238-9-0(1))* TOON Books / RAW Junior, LLC.

—Benny & Penny in the Big No-No! 2014. (Toon Books Level 1 Ser.). lib. bdg. 14.75 *(978-0-606-32102-0(0)*, Turtleback) Turtleback Bks.

Hayes, Geoffrey & Rosenstiehl, Agnes. Toon Books. 2013. (Toon Bks: 10). 36p. (J). (gr. k-3). lib. bdg. 270.70 *(978-1-61479-147-8(3))* Spotlight.

Herman, Gail. New Dog in Town. Nez, John, illus. 2006. (Social Studies Connects). 32p. (J). (gr. -1-3). pap. 5.95 *(978-1-57565-165-1(3))* Kane Press, Inc.

Herman, Gail & Bridwell, Norman. Halloween Howl. Goldberg, Barry, illus. 2004. (Clifford's Puppy Days Ser.). (ENG.). 24p. (J). (gr. -1-k). 3.99 *(978-0-439-58353-4(5)*, Cartwheel Bks.) Scholastic, Inc.

Herman, Michael. The Cholent Brigade. Harmer, Sharon, illus. 2017. (ENG.). 24p. (gr. -1-2). 17.99 ***(978-1-5124-0844-7(1)***, Kar-Ben Publishing) Lerner Publishing Group.

Hicks, Benjamin. Byron's Tie. Hicks, Benjamin & Hicks, Rosetta, eds. 2013. 35p. pap. 8.95 *(978-1-929883-08-0(0))* Ingleside Pr.

Higgins, Nadia. The Zombie Next Door: Zombie Zappers Book 3. (Zombie Zappers Ser.). 64p. (J). 2014. (gr. 5-9). pap. 9.95 *(978-1-62285-011-2(4))* 2013. 15.95 *(978-1-62285-010-5(6))* Enslow Pubs., Inc.

Higginson, Hadley. Keeker & the Crazy, Upside-Down Birthday. Perrett, Lisa, illus. 2008. (ENG.). 56p. (J). (gr. k-3). pap. 4.99 *(978-0-8118-6256-1(9))* Chronicle Bks. LLC.

Horowitz, Ruth. Are We Still Friends? Gomez, Blanca, illus. 2017. (ENG.). 40p. (J). (gr. -1-3). 16.99 *(978-0-545-64521-8(2)*, Scholastic Pr.) Scholastic, Inc.

Horvath, Polly. The Pepins & Their Problems, 1 vol. Hafner, Marylin, illus. (ENG.). 192p. pap. 13.95 *(978-0-88899-633-6(0))* Groundwood Bks. CAN. Dist: Publishers Group West (PGW).

—The Pepins & Their Problems. Hafner, Marylin, illus. 2008. (ENG.). 208p. (J). (gr. 3-7). per. 9.99 *(978-0-312-37751-9(7)*, 9780312377519) Square Fish.

Hughes, Melissa. Myles & Otis: A Story of Friendship. 2009. (Illus.). 30p. (J). pap. 14.95 *(978-1-4327-5182-1(4))* Outskirts Pr., Inc.

Hulst, W. G. van de & Hulst, Willem G. van de. illus. Kittens, Kittens Everywhere. 2014. (J). *(978-1-928136-20-0(6))* Inheritance Pubns.

—The Rockity Rowboat. 2014. (J). *(978-1-928136-18-7(4))* Inheritance Pubns.

Hurwitz, Michele Weber. The Summer I Saved the World ... in 65 Days. 2015. (ENG.). 272p. (J). (gr. 5). pap. 9.99 *(978-0-385-37109-4(8)*, Ember) Random Hse. Children's Bks.

Isadora, Rachel. Say Hello! Isadora, Rachel, illus. (ENG & MUL., Illus.). (J). 2017. 30p. (-k). bds. 7.99 *(978-0-399-25632-5(6)*, Nancy Paulsen Books) 2010. 32p. (gr. -1-k). 16.99 *(978-0-399-25230-3(4)*, G.P. Putnam's Sons Books for Young Readers) Penguin Young Readers Group.

Jakubowski, Michele. Sidney & Sydney. 2013. (Sidney & Sydney Ser.). (ENG.). 128p. (gr. 1-3). 50.64 *(978-1-4795-1696-4(1))* Picture Window Bks.

—Third Grade Mix-Up, 1 vol. Montalto, Luisa, illus. 2013. (Sidney & Sydney Ser.). (ENG.). 128p. (gr. 1-3). 8.95 *(978-1-4048-8104-4(2))*; lib. bdg. 25.32 *(978-1-4048-8001-6(1))* Picture Window Bks.

James, Kristopher. Lyrian. 2009. (Illus.). 171p. pap. 16.95 *(978-1-4092-8986-9(9))* Lulu Pr., Inc.

Jenkins, Emily. The Little Bit Scary People. Boiger, Alexandra, illus. 2008. (ENG.). 32p. (gr. -1-1). 16.99 *(978-1-4231-0075-1(1))* Hyperion Pr.

John, Jory. Goodnight Already! Davies, Benji, illus. 2014. (ENG.). 32p. (J). (gr. -1-3). 17.99 *(978-0-06-228620-8(X))* HarperCollins Pubs.

Johnson, Deanna. Blarron Creek Chronicles. 2009. 108p. 23.49 *(978-1-4389-5580-3(4))* AuthorHouse.

Johnson, Peter. The Amazing Adventures of John Smith, Jr. Aka Houdini. 2012. (ENG.). 176p. (J). (gr. 3-7). 16.99 *(978-0-06-198890-5(1))* HarperCollins Pubs.

Johnson, Regan. Little Bunny Kung Fu. Johnson, Regan, illus. 2005. (ENG., Illus.). 32p. (J). (gr. -1 — 1). 14.95 *(978-0-9769417-8-1(3))* Blooming Tree Pr.

Johnson, Richard, illus. Don't Cry, Sly! 2004. 32p. (J). (SPA & ENG.). pap. *(978-1-85269-662-7(1))*; (ENG & POR.). pap. *(978-1-85269-659-7(1))*; (ENG, ARA & BEN.). pap. *(978-1-85269-649-8(4))*; (ENG & PER.). pap. *(978-1-85269-653-5(2))* Mantra Lingua.

Kaiser, Lori. Florence Flamingo Gets the Flu. Kaiser, Lori, illus. 2012. (Illus.). 30p. pap. *(978-0-9836651-5-1(X))* Roxby Media Ltd.

Karsten, Margo & Karsten, Steven. The Story of Sugar Cookie. 2010. 36p. 18.99 *(978-1-4520-8177-9(8))* AuthorHouse.

Keller, Laurie. Do unto Otters: A Book about Manners. Keller, Laurie, illus. 2007. (ENG., Illus.). 40p. (J). (gr. k-3). 18.99 *(978-0-8050-7996-8(3)*, 9780805079968, Holt, Henry & Co. Bks. For Young Readers) Holt, Henry & Co.

—Do unto Otters: A Book about Manners. Keller, Laurie, illus. 2009. (ENG., Illus.). 40p. (J). (gr. k-3). pap. 7.99 *(978-0-312-58140-4(8)*, 9780312581404) Square Fish.

Kittinger, Jo S. The House on Dirty-Third Street, 1 vol. González, Thomas, illus. 2012. (ENG.). 32p. (J). 16.95 *(978-1-56145-619-2(5))* Peachtree Pubs.

Konigsburg, E. L. The Mysterious Edge of the Heroic World. 2007. (ENG., Illus.). 256p. (J). (gr. 4-8). 16.99 *(978-1-4169-4972-5(0)*, Atheneum Bks. for Young Readers) Simon & Schuster Children's Publishing.

Kroll, Steven. Stuff! Reduce, Reuse, Recycle, 0 vols. Cox, Steve, illus. 2012. (ENG.). 32p. (J). (gr. -1-3). pap. 7.99 *(978-0-7614-6237-8(6)*, 9780761462378, Amazon Children's Publishing) Amazon Publishing.

Kroll, Virginia. Good Neighbor Nicholas: A Concept Book. Cote, Nancy, illus. 2006. (Way I Act Bks.: Vol. 5). (ENG.). 24p. (J). (gr. 1-3). lib. bdg. 15.99 *(978-0-8075-2998-0(2))* Whitman, Albert & Co.

—Makayla Cares about Others. Cote, Nancy, illus. 2007. (Way I Act Bks.). (ENG.). 24p. (J). (gr. k-3). lib. bdg. 15.99 *(978-0-8075-4945-2(2))* Whitman, Albert & Co.

Krulik, Nancy. Doggone It! John and Wendy Staff, illus. 8th ed. 2006. (Katie Kazoo, Switcheroo Ser.: 8). (ENG.). 80p. (J). (gr. 2-4). pap. 4.99 *(978-0-448-43172-7(6)*, Grosset & Dunlap) Penguin Young Readers Group.

Kvasnosky, Laura McGee. Zelda & Ivy One Christmas. Kvasnosky, Laura McGee, illus. 2013. (Candlewick Sparks Ser.). (ENG., Illus.). 40p. (J). (gr. k-4). pap. 3.99 *(978-0-7636-6865-5(6))* Candlewick Pr.

Lachtman, Ofelia Dumas. Pepita on Pepper Street/Pepita en la Calle Pepper. Monsivais, Maria Estela, tr. from ENG. Delange, Alex Pardo, illus. 2008. (SPA & ENG.). 32p. (J). (gr. -1-3). 16.95 *(978-1-55885-443-7(6)*, Piñata Books) Arte Publico Pr.

—Pepita Packs Up: Pepita Empaca. Ventura, Gabriela Baeza, tr. from ENG. Delange, Alex Pardo, illus. 2005. 48p. (J). (gr. -1-k). lib. bdg. 16.95 *(978-1-55885-431-4(2)*, Piñata Books) Arte Publico Pr.

—The Trouble with Tessa. 2005. 122p. (J). (gr. 3-7). per. 9.95 *(978-1-55885-448-2(7)*, Piñata Books) Arte Publico Pr.

Lange, Willem. Favor Johnson: A Christmas Story. Dodson, Bert, illus. 2009. (ENG.). 32p. (J). (gr. 1-3). 16.95 *(978-1-59373-082-6(9))* Bunker Hill Publishing, Inc.

Lasky, Kathryn. Chasing Orion. 2010. (ENG., Illus.). 368p. (J). (gr. 5-18). 17.99 *(978-0-7636-3982-2(6))* Candlewick Pr.

Lehman-Wilzig, Tami & Katzman, Nicole. Nathan Blows Out the Hanukkah Candles. Tugeau, Jeremy, illus. 2011. (Hanukkah Ser.). (ENG.). 32p. (J). (gr. k-3). pap. 7.95 *(978-0-7613-6658-4(X)*, Kar-Ben Publishing) Lerner Publishing Group.

Leoni, Gail. Chalk Dust. 2008. 36p. pap. 24.95 *(978-1-60474-881-9(8))* America Star Bks.

Levin, Betty. The Unmaking of Duncan Veerick. 2007. (ENG.). 212p. (J). (gr. 9-12). 16.95 *(978-1-932425-96-3(9)*, Front Street) Boyds Mills Pr.

Levy, Dana Alison. The Family Fletcher Takes Rock Island. (ENG.). 272p. (J). (gr. 4-7). 2017. 6.99 ***(978-0-553-52133-7(0)***, Yearling) 2016. 16.99 *(978-0-553-52130-6(6)*, Delacorte Bks. for Young Readers) Random Hse. Children's Bks.

Liphardt, Linda. Secret in the Old Barn. 2008. 116p. pap. 19.95 *(978-1-60703-615-9(0))* America Star Bks.

Lisle, Janet Taylor. Afternoon of the Elves. 2017. (ENG., Illus.). 128p. (J). (gr. 3-7). 16.99 ***(978-1-4814-9908-8(4)***, Atheneum Bks. for Young Readers) Simon & Schuster Children's Publishing.

Littman, Sarah Darer. Backlash. 2015. (ENG.). 336p. (J). (gr. 7). 17.99 *(978-0-545-65126-4(3)*, Scholastic Pr.) Scholastic, Inc.

Lloyd, Sam R. Yummy Yummy! Food for My Tummy. Tickle, Jack, illus. 2004. 32p. (J). tchr. ed. 15.95 *(978-1-58925-035-2(4))* Tiger Tales.

Look, Lenore. Ruby Lu, Brave & True. 2004. (Illus.). 104p. (J). lib. bdg. 15.00 *(978-1-4242-0914-9(5))* Fitzgerald Bks.

—Ruby Lu, Brave & True. Wilsdorf, Anne, illus. 2006. (ENG.). 112p. (J). (gr. 1-5). pap. 6.99 *(978-1-4169-1389-4(0)*, Atheneum Bks. for Young Readers) Simon & Schuster Children's Publishing.

Louie, Therese On & Wang, Suling. Raymond's Perfect Present, 1 vol. 2015. (ENG.). 32p. (J). pap. 9.95 *(978-1-62014-229-5(5))* Lee & Low Bks., Inc.

Lozano, José. Once Around the Block (Una Vuelta a la Manzana) Crosthwaite, Luis Humberto, tr. 2009. (SPA & ENG., Illus.). 32p. (J). (gr. -1-4). 16.95 *(978-1-933693-57-6(6))* Cinco Puntos Pr.

Lundebrek, Amy & Rich, Anna. Under the Night Sky, 1 vol. 2008. (ENG., Illus.). 32p. (gr. 3-6). 16.95 *(978-0-88448-297-0(9)*, 884297) Tilbury Hse. Pubs.

Macomber, Debbie & Carney, Mary Lou. The Yippy, Yappy Yorkie in the Green Doggy Sweater. Lambert, Sally Anne, illus. 2011. (ENG.). 32p. (J). (gr. -1-2). 16.99 *(978-0-06-165096-3(X))* HarperCollins Pubs.

Maithya, Susan M. Struffel Cares: Struffel's New Pet. 2012. 40p. pap. 20.99 *(978-1-4772-3323-8(7))* AuthorHouse.

Manning, Maurie J. Laundry Day. 2012. (ENG., Illus.). 40p. (J). (gr. -1-3). 16.99 *(978-0-547-24196-8(8))* Houghton Mifflin Harcourt Publishing Co.

Mannone, Christine. Flowers for Pudding Street. Carolan, Christine, illus. 2009. (ENG.). 32p. (J). 15.95 *(978-1-934860-02-1(6))* Shenanigan Bks.

Mansfield, Creina. My Nutty Neighbours. 2006. (ENG., Illus.). 192p. (J). pap. 12.95 *(978-0-86278-788-2(2))* O'Brien Pr., Ltd., The IRL. Dist: Dufour Editions, Inc.

Manushkin, Fran. Katie Saves Thanksgiving, 1 vol. Lyon, Tammie, illus. 2010. (Katie Woo Ser.). (ENG.). 32p. (gr. k-2). lib. bdg. 21.32 *(978-1-4048-5988-3(8))*; pap. 5.95 *(978-1-4048-6367-5(2))* Picture Window Bks.

Manzano, Sonia. Miracle on 133rd Street. Priceman, Marjorie, illus. 2015. (ENG.). 48p. (J). (gr. -1-3). 17.99 *(978-0-689-87887-9(7))* Simon & Schuster Children's Publishing.

Marino, Nan. Neil Armstrong Is My Uncle & Other Lies Muscle Man McGinty Told Me. 2012. (ENG.). 176p. (J). (gr. 3-7). pap. 6.99 *(978-0-312-66548-7(2)*, 9780312665487) Square Fish.

Marsh, Carole. The Puzzle of the Shark Surfer Girl. 2006. (Criss Cross Applesauce Ser.). (Illus.). 54p. (J). (gr. 1-3). 14.95 *(978-0-635-06204-8(6))* Gallopade International.

Marston, Elsa. The Olive Tree. Ewart, Claire, illus. 2014. (ENG.). 32p. (J). (gr. -1-2). 16.95 *(978-1-937786-29-8(3)*, Wisdom Tales) World Wisdom, Inc.

Martin, Ann M. Here Today. 2005. (ENG.). 336p. (J). (gr. 3-7). pap. 7.99 *(978-0-439-57945-2(7)*, Scholastic Paperbacks) Scholastic, Inc.

Martinez, Claudia Guadalupe. Pig Park. 2014. (ENG.). 248p. (J). 15.95 *(978-1-935955-76-4(4))* Cinco Puntos Pr.

Martins, Isabel Minhós. My Neighbor Is a Dog. Herring, John, tr. from POR. Matoso, Madalena, illus. 2013. (ENG.). 32p. (J). (gr. -1-4). 16.95 *(978-1-926973-68-5(2))* Owlkids Bks. Inc. CAN. Dist: Publishers Group West (PGW).

Massie, Elizabeth. Ameri-Scares: Virginia. 2013. 150p. pap. 12.99 *(978-1-937530-52-5(3))* Crossroad Pr.

May, Kyla. Coco: My Delicious Life. 2013. (Lotus Lane Ser.: 2). (ENG., Illus.). 96p. (J). (gr. 1-3). 15.99 *(978-0-545-49615-5(2))*; pap. 4.99 *(978-0-545-44514-6(0))* Scholastic, Inc.

—Coco: My Delicious Life. 2013. (Lotus Lane Ser.: 2). lib. bdg. 14.75 *(978-0-606-31978-2(6)*, Turtleback) Turtleback Bks.

—Lulu: My Glamorous Life. 2013. (Lotus Lane Ser.: 3). (ENG.). 96p. (J). (gr. 1-3). 15.99 *(978-0-545-49618-6(7))*; pap. 4.99 *(978-0-545-44516-0(7))*; E-Book *(978-0-545-49682-7(9))* Scholastic, Inc.

—My Glamorous Life. 2013. (Lotus Lane Ser.: 3). lib. bdg. 14.75 *(978-0-606-32364-2(3)*, Turtleback) Turtleback Bks.

McBay, Bruce. Angels Inc., 1 vol. LaFave, Kim, illus. 2008. (ENG.). 71p. (J). (gr. 1-3). pap. 7.95 *(978-1-896580-30-2(0))* Tradewind Bks. CAN. Dist: Orca Bk. Pubs. USA.

Mcghee, Alison. Julia Gillian - And the Art of Knowing. Kozjan, Drazen, illus. 2009. (Julia Gillian Ser.). (ENG.). 304p. (J). (gr. 3-7). 6.99 *(978-0-545-03349-7(7)*, Scholastic Paperbacks) Scholastic, Inc.

McKay, Hilary. Lulu & the Rabbit Next Door. Lamont, Priscilla, illus. 2014. (Lulu Ser.: Book 4). (ENG.). 112p. (J). (gr. 1-5). 13.99 *(978-0-8075-4816-5(2))* Whitman, Albert & Co.

Meister, Cari & Ritchey, Kate. Happy Doodling! 2014. (Mr. Men & Little Miss Ser.). (ENG., Illus.). 128p. (J). (gr. -1-2). 12.99 *(978-0-8431-8043-5(9)*, Price Stern Sloan) Penguin Young Readers Group.

Meltzer, Amy. A Mezuzah on the Door. Fried, Janice, illus. 2007. (Jewish Identity Ser.). 32p. (J). (gr. -1-3). 17.95 *(978-1-58013-249-7(9))*; (ENG.). 7.95 *(978-1-58013-251-0(0))* Lerner Publishing Group. (Kar-Ben Publishing).

Miller, Tiwana Mutch. Praying Time. 2008. (YA). per. 10.00 *(978-0-9788937-8-1(6))* Amani Publishing, LLC.

Mills, Claudia. Basketball Disasters. Francis, Guy, illus. 2013. (Mason Dixon Ser.). (ENG.). 176p. (J). (gr. 2-5). pap. 6.99 *(978-0-375-87276-1(0)*, Yearling) Random Hse. Children's Bks.

Mills, Nathan & Nolan, Mary. Mike's Busy Neighborhood. 2012. (Rosen Readers Ser.). (ENG., Illus.). 16p. (J). (gr. k-1). pap. 7.00 *(978-1-4488-8758-3(5)*, Rosen Classroom) Rosen Publishing Group, Inc., The.

Miyares, Daniel. That Neighbor Kid. Miyares, Daniel, illus. 2017. (ENG., Illus.). 32p. (J). (gr. -1-3). 17.99 ***(978-1-4814-4979-3(6)***, Simon & Schuster Bks. For Young Readers) Simon & Schuster Bks. For Young Readers.

Monninger, Joseph. Whippoorwill. 2015. (ENG.). 288p. (YA). (gr. 7). 17.99 *(978-0-544-53123-9(X)*, HMH Books For Young Readers) Houghton Mifflin Harcourt Publishing Co.

Mora, Oge, illus. Thank You, Omu! 2017. (J). ***(978-0-316-43124-8(9))*** Little Brown & Co.

Muir, Leslie. C. R. Mudgeon. Hector, Julian, illus. 2012. (ENG.). 32p. (J). (gr. -1-3). 15.99 *(978-1-4169-7906-7(9)*, Atheneum Bks. for Young Readers) Simon & Schuster Children's Publishing.

Mullican, Judy. Someone New in the Neighborhood. Storch, Ellen N. & Gillen, Lisa P., illus. 1st. ed. 2005. 20p. (J). (gr. -1-k). pap. 10.95 *(978-1-57332-356-7(X)*, HighReach Learning, Incorporated) Carson-Dellosa Publishing, LLC.

Munsell, Jill. What a Day for a Parade. 2010. 48p. pap. 19.95 *(978-1-4389-9080-4(4))* AuthorHouse.

Murphy, Stuart J. Emma's Friendwich. 2010. (I See I Learn Ser.). (ENG., Illus.). 32p. (J). (gr. -1-k). pap. 6.95 *(978-1-58089-451-7(8))* Charlesbridge Publishing, Inc.

Muth, Jon J. Zen Ties. Muth, Jon J., illus. 2008. (ENG., Illus.). 40p. (J). (gr. -1-3). 17.99 *(978-0-439-63425-0(3)*, Scholastic Pr.) Scholastic, Inc.

My Super-Spy Diary. 2014. (Eliza Boom Ser.: 2). (ENG., Illus.). 128p. (J). (gr. 1-4). pap. 5.99 *(978-1-4814-0652-9(3)*, Aladdin) Simon & Schuster Children's Publishing.

Naylor, Phyllis Reynolds. Boys Rock! 2007. (Boy/Girl Battle Ser.). (ENG.). 144p. (J). (gr. 3-7). 5.99 *(978-0-440-41990-7(5)*, Yearling) Random Hse. Children's Bks.

—Cuckoo Feathers, 0 vols. Ramsey, Marcy, illus. 2009. (Simply Sarah Ser.: 0). (ENG.). 96p. (J). (gr. 2-5). pap. 6.99 *(978-0-7614-5541-7(8)*, 9780761455417, Amazon Children's Publishing) Amazon Publishing.

—The Girls Take Over. 2004. (Boys Against Girls Ser.: No. 8). 146p. (J). (gr. 4-7). 13.65 *(978-0-7569-2804-9(4))* Perfection Learning Corp.

—The Girls Take Over. 2004. (Boy/Girl Battle Ser.: No. 8). (ENG.). 160p. (J). (gr. 3-7). 6.99 *(978-0-440-41678-4(7)*, Yearling) Random Hse. Children's Bks.

—Patches & Scratches, 0 vols. Ramsey, Marcy, illus. 2010. (Simply Sarah Ser.: 0). (ENG.). 80p. (J). (gr. 2-6). pap. 6.99 *(978-0-7614-5731-2(3)*, 9780761457312, Amazon Children's Publishing) Amazon Publishing.

—Who Won the War? 2008. (Boy/Girl Battle Ser.). (ENG.). 160p. (J). (gr. 3-7). 5.99 *(978-0-440-41991-4(3)*, Yearling) Random Hse. Children's Bks.

Norfleet, Mary Crockett. Hand Me down House. Mallory, Edgar, illus. 2011. 98p. 38.95 *(978-1-258-07946-8(1))* Literary Licensing, LLC.

O'Coyne, James. Gravelle's Land of Horror. Whispering Pine Press International, Inc. Staff, ed. Baer, Brian, illus. 2007. (ENG.). 120p. (J). per. 9.95 *(978-1-59649-604-0(5))* Whispering Pine Pr. International, Inc.

Oldcome, Michelle. Landy Saves the Day. 2009. (Illus.). 32p. pap. 12.49 *(978-1-4490-0574-0(8))* AuthorHouse.

Oliver, Lin. Beware! Shadows in the Night. Kallis, Samantha, illus. 2016. (Fantastic Frame Ser.: 3). (ENG.). 128p. (J). (gr. 2-4). 11.99 *(978-0-448-48091-6(3)*, Grosset & Dunlap) Penguin Young Readers Group.

—Danger! Tiger Crossing. 2016. (Illus.). 115p. (J). pap. *(978-0-448-48086-2(7)*, Grosset & Dunlap) Penguin Young Readers Group.

—Splat! Another Messy Sunday 2. 2016. (Fantastic Frame Ser.: 2). (ENG., Illus.). 128p. (J). (gr. 2-4). 11.99 *(978-0-448-48089-3(1))*, Grosset & Dunlap) Penguin Young Readers Group.

Olson, Norah. Twisted Fate. (YA). (gr. 8). 2016. 288p. pap. 9.99 *(978-0-06-227206-5(3)*, Tegen, Katherine Bks) 2015. (ENG.). 272p. 17.99 *(978-0-06-227204-1(7))* HarperCollins Pubs.

Packer, Rachel Ornstein. Sky-High Sukkah. Zemke, Deborah, illus. 2016. (J). *(978-1-68115-513-5(3))* Behrman Hse., Inc.

Parish, Herman. Amelia Bedelia Makes a Friend. Avril, Lynne, illus. 2011. (I Can Read Level 1 Ser.). (ENG.). 32p. (J). (gr. k-3). 16.99 *(978-0-06-207516-1(0))*; pap. 3.99 *(978-0-06-207515-4(2))* HarperCollins Pubs. (Greenwillow Bks.).

Parker, Deborah. In the Garden (Cj) 2008. 24p. 7.95 *(978-1-60231-000-1(9)*, Cub Bks.) Global Business Information Strategies, Inc.

Patch, Lisa. Tales of the Lush Green Woods. Patch, Michael, illus. 2012. 42p. 16.50 *(978-0-9852501-5-7(1))* Inkwell Books LLC.

Paulsen, Gary. Notes from the Dog. 2011. (ENG.). 144p. (YA). (gr. 7). pap. 6.99 *(978-0-375-85542-9(4)*, Ember) Random Hse. Children's Bks.

Payne, C. C. Something to Sing About. 2008. (ENG.). 167p. (J). (gr. 4-7). pap. 8.50 *(978-0-8028-5344-8(7))* Eerdmans, William B. Publishing Co.

Peck, Richard. A Season of Gifts. 2010. (ENG.). 208p. (J). (gr. 5-18). 7.99 *(978-0-14-241729-4(7)*, Puffin Books) Penguin Young Readers Group.

Perkins, Stephanie. Lola & the Boy Next Door. (ENG.). (YA). (gr. 9). 2013. 368p. pap. 10.99 *(978-0-14-242201-4(0)*, Speak) 2011. 352p. 16.99 *(978-0-525-42328-7(1)*, Dutton Books for Young Readers) Penguin Young Readers Group.

Peterson, Esther Allen. The House That Cared. 2010. (J). pap. *(978-0-88092-505-1(1))* Royal Fireworks Publishing Co.

—Will Spring Come? 2009. (Illus.). 157p. (J). *(978-0-88092-768-0(2))* Royal Fireworks Publishing Co.

Pierro, Rita. No Veggies for Me. Iukel, Onur, illus. 2011. 32p. pap. 24.95 *(978-1-4626-4554-1(2))* America Star Bks.

Pitchford, Dean. Nickel Bay Nick. 2014. (ENG.). 272p. (J). (gr. 3-7). pap. 7.99 *(978-0-14-751227-7(1)*, Puffin Books) Penguin Young Readers Group.

Polak, Monique. Home Invasion, 1 vol. 2005. (Orca Soundings Ser.). (ENG.). 128p. (YA). (gr. 8-12). per. 9.95 *(978-1-55143-482-7(2))* Orca Bk. Pubs. USA.

Politi, Leo. Emmet. 2009. (ENG., Illus.). 32p. 16.95 *(978-0-89236-992-8(2))* Oxford Univ. Pr., Inc.

Polk, James. Mr. & Mrs. Love & the Neighborhood Children. 2003. pap. 11.00 *(978-0-8059-9232-8(4)*, RoseDog Bks.) Dorrance Publishing Co., Inc.

Powell, Alma. America's Promise. Winborn, Marsha, illus. 2003. 32p. (J). (gr. -1-2). 16.89 *(978-0-06-052173-8(2))* HarperCollins Pubs.

Powell, Lenora Y. Ardo: The Mysterious New House. 2008. 105p. pap. 19.95 *(978-1-60672-133-9(X))* America Star Bks.

Publications International Ltd. Staff, ed. Elmo's Neighborhood Lights & Music Treasury. 2009. 160p. (J). bds. 17.98 *(978-1-4127-2388-6(4)*, PIL Kids) Publications International, Ltd.

Ran, Gila. The Lemonheads, the Crown of Wisdom. 2011. 24p. pap. 11.00 *(978-1-257-12995-9(3))* Lulu Pr., Inc.

Reich, Dale. Noah's Neighbor. 2015. (ENG., Illus.). 34p. (J). pap. 9.95 *(978-1-55571-799-5(3)*, Grid Pr.) L & R Publishing, LLC.

Reiner, Carl. Tell Me A Scary Story... but Not Too Scary. 2009. (ENG.). (J). (gr. 1-3). 18.95 incl. lp *(978-1-59687-926-3(2))* IBks., Inc.

Reynolds, Alison. A New Friend for Marmalade. McKenzie, Heath, illus. 2014. (ENG.). 40p. (J). (gr. -1-1). 15.99 *(978-1-4814-2046-4(1)*, Little Simon) Little Simon.

Richler, Mordecai. Jacob Two-Two's First Spy Case. Petricic, Dusan, illus. 2009. (Jacob Two-Two Ser.). (ENG.). 168p. (J). (gr. 4-7). 10.95 *(978-0-88776-927-6(6))* Tundra Bks. CAN. Dist: Random Hse., Inc.

Rigby Education Staff. Jacko of Baker Street. (Sails Literacy Ser.). (Illus.). 16p. (gr. 1-2). 27.00 *(978-0-7635-9931-7(X)*, 699319C99) Rigby Education.

Roberts, Emma Perry. Mrs. Murphy's Marvelous Mansion. Rogalski, Robert, illus. 2006. 32p. (J). (gr. -1-3). 15.95 *(978-0-9740190-4-8(6)*, 888-210-8216) Illumination Arts Publishing Co., Inc.

Roberts, Willo Davis. Hostage. 2016. (ENG., Illus.). 176p. (J). (gr. 3-7). pap. 6.99 *(978-1-4814-5788-0(8),* Aladdin) Simon & Schuster Children's Publishing.
—Hostage. 2016. (ENG., Illus.). 176p. (J). (gr. 3-7). 17.99 *(978-1-4814-5789-7(6),* Simon & Schuster/Paula Wiseman Bks.) Simon & Schuster/Paula Wiseman Bks.
Robey, Katharine Crawford. Hare & the Big Green Lawn. MacDougall, Larry, illus. 2006. (ENG.). 32p. (J). (gr. -1-3). 15.95 *(978-0-87358-889-8(4))* Cooper Square Publishing Llc.
Rockliff, Mara. Chik Chak Shabbat. Brooker, Kyrsten, illus. (ENG.). 32p. (J). (gr. -1-2). 2016. 7.99 *(978-0-7636-8895-0(9))* 2014. 15.99 *(978-0-7636-5528-0(7))* Candlewick Pr.
Rocklin, Joanne. One Day & One Amazing Morning on Orange Street. 2012. (ENG., Illus.). 240p. (J). (gr. 3-7). pap. 8.95 *(978-1-4197-0181-8(9),* Amulet Bks.) Abrams, Inc.
Rowe, Vicki J. Yellow Roses. 2012. 64p. pap. 15.99 *(978-1-4771-2636-3(8))* Xlibris Corp.
Roy, Ronald. November Night. Gurney, John Steven, illus. 2014. (Calendar Mysteries Ser.: 11). (ENG.). 80p. (J). (gr. 1-4). 4.99 *(978-0-385-37165-0(9),* Random Hse. Bks. for Young Readers) Random Hse. Children's Bks.
Rubin, Adam. Those Darn Squirrels! Salmieri, Daniel, illus. 2011. (ENG.). 32p. (J). (gr. -1-3). pap. 7.99 *(978-0-547-57681-7(1))* Houghton Mifflin Harcourt Publishing Co.
—Those Darn Squirrels & the Cat Next Door. Salmieri, Daniel, illus. 2011. (ENG.). 32p. (J). (gr. -1-3). 17.99 *(978-0-547-42922-9(3))* Houghton Mifflin Harcourt Publishing Co.
Rykken, John. Bloodwood: The Chronicles of Max Mayhem. 2011. 264p. (gr. 10-12). 26.95 *(978-1-4620-0656-4(6));* pap. 16.95 *(978-1-4620-0657-1(4))* iUniverse, Inc.
Rylant, Cynthia. Annie & Snowball & the Thankful Friends. Stevenson, Sucie, illus. 2011. (Annie & Snowball Ser.: 10). (ENG.). 40p. (J). (gr. k-2). 15.99 *(978-1-4169-7200-6(5),* Simon Spotlight) Simon Spotlight.
—Mr. Putter & Tabby Clear the Decks. Howard, Arthur, illus. alt. ed. 2011. (Mr. Putter & Tabby Ser.). (ENG.). 44p. (J). (gr. 1-4). pap. 5.99 *(978-0-547-57695-4(1))* Houghton Mifflin Harcourt Publishing Co.
—Mr. Putter & Tabby Dance the Dance. Howard, Arthur, illus. 2012. (Mr. Putter & Tabby Ser.: 21). (ENG.). 40p. (J). (gr. 1-4). 14.99 *(978-0-15-206415-0(X))* Houghton Mifflin Harcourt Publishing Co.
—Mr. Putter & Tabby Dance the Dance. 2013. (Mr. Putter & Tabby Ser.). lib. bdg. 16.00 *(978-0-606-32338-3(4),* Turtleback) Turtleback Bks.
—Mr. Putter & Tabby Drop the Ball. Howard, Arthur, illus. 2013. (Mr. Putter & Tabby Ser.: 22). (ENG.). 44p. (J). (gr. 1-4). 14.99 *(978-0-15-205072-6(8))* Houghton Mifflin Harcourt Publishing Co.
—Mr. Putter & Tabby Hit the Slope. Howard, Arthur, illus. 2016. (Mr. Putter & Tabby Ser.). (ENG.). 40p. (J). (gr. 1-4). 14.99 *(978-0-15-206427-3(3),* HMH Books For Young Readers) Houghton Mifflin Harcourt Publishing Co.
—Mr. Putter & Tabby Make a Wish. Howard, Arthur, illus. 2006. (Mr. Putter & Tabby Ser.). (ENG.). 44p. (J). (gr. -1-3). pap. 5.99 *(978-0-15-205443-4(X))* Houghton Mifflin Harcourt Publishing Co.
—Mr. Putter & Tabby Make a Wish. Howard, Arthur, illus. 2006. (Mr. Putter & Tabby Ser.). (gr. 1-4). 16.00 *(978-0-7569-6892-2(5))* Perfection Learning Corp.
—Mr. Putter & Tabby Ring the Bell. Howard, Arthur, illus. (Mr. Putter & Tabby Ser.). (ENG.). 44p. (J). (gr. 1-4). 2012. pap. 5.99 *(978-0-547-85075-7(1))* 2011. 14.99 *(978-0-15-205071-9(X))* Houghton Mifflin Harcourt Publishing Co.
—Mr. Putter & Tabby Ring the Bell. Howard, Arthur, illus. 2012. (Mr. Putter & Tabby Ser.). lib. bdg. 16.00 *(978-0-606-26614-7(3),* Turtleback) Turtleback Bks.
—Mr. Putter & Tabby See the Stars. Howard, Arthur, illus. 2008. (Mr. Putter & Tabby Ser.). (ENG.). 44p. (J). (gr. 1-4). pap. 5.99 *(978-0-15-206366-5(8))* Houghton Mifflin Harcourt Publishing Co.
—Mr. Putter & Tabby Spill the Beans. Howard, Arthur, illus. 2010. (Mr. Putter & Tabby Ser.). (ENG.). 44p. (J). (gr. 1-4). pap. 5.99 *(978-0-547-41433-1(1))* Houghton Mifflin Harcourt Publishing Co.
—Mr. Putter & Tabby Spin the Yarn. Howard, Arthur, illus. 2007. (Mr. Putter & Tabby Ser.). (ENG.). 44p. (J). (gr. 1-4). pap. 5.99 *(978-0-15-206095-4(2))* Houghton Mifflin Harcourt Publishing Co.
—Mr. Putter & Tabby Spin the Yarn. Howard, Arthur, illus. 2007. (Mr. Putter & Tabby Ser.). (gr. 1-4). lib. bdg. 16.00 *(978-0-7569-8062-7(3))* Perfection Learning Corp.
—Mr. Putter & Tabby Stir the Soup. Howard, Arthur, illus. 2004. (Mr. Putter & Tabby Ser.). (ENG.). 44p. (J). (gr. 1-4). pap. 5.99 *(978-0-15-205058-0(2))* Houghton Mifflin Harcourt Publishing Co.
—Mr. Putter & Tabby Stir the Soup. Howard, Arthur, illus. 2004. (Mr. Putter & Tabby Ser.). (gr. 1-4). 16.00 *(978-0-7569-3915-1(1))* Perfection Learning Corp.
Rylant, Cynthia & Howard, Arthur. Mr. Putter & Tabby Dance the Dance. Howard, Arthur, illus. 2013. (Mr. Putter & Tabby Ser.). (ENG., Illus.). 40p. (J). (gr. 1-4). pap. 5.99 *(978-0-544-10496-9(X))* Houghton Mifflin Harcourt Publishing Co.
Scarry, Richard. Richard Scarry's Postman Pig & His Busy Neighbors. 2015. lib. bdg. 14.75 *(978-0-606-36401-0(3))* Turtleback Bks.
Schaefer, Laura. Littler Women: A Modern Retelling. 2017. (ENG., Illus.). 224p. (J). (gr. 3-7). 16.99 ***(978-1-4814-8761-0(2),*** Simon & Schuster/Paula Wiseman Bks.) Simon & Schuster/Paula Wiseman Bks.
Schanen, Adriana Brad. Quinny & Hopper. Swearingen, Greg, illus. 2014. (ENG.). 240p. (J). (gr. 3-7). 15.99 *(978-1-4231-7829-3(7))* Hyperion Bks. for Children.
Schneider, Antonie & Maccarone, Grace. Mr. Happy & Miss Grimm. Strasser, Susanne, illus. 2015. (ENG.). 32p. (J). (gr. -1-3). 16.95 *(978-0-8234-3198-4(3))* Holiday Hse., Inc.
Schulman, Janet. 10 Trim-the-Tree'ers. Davick, Linda, illus. 2011. (ENG.). 32p. (J). (gr. -1 — 1). bds. 6.99 *(978-0-375-87302-7(3),* Knopf Bks. for Young Readers) Random Hse. Children's Bks.
Schwartz, Amy. A Glorious Day. Schwartz, Amy, illus. 2010. (ENG., Illus.). 32p. (J). (gr. -1-k). 16.99 *(978-1-4424-2190-5(8),* Atheneum Bks. for Young Readers) Simon & Schuster Children's Publishing.
Sharp, N. L. Effie's Image. 2008. (ENG., Illus.). 29p. pap. 8.95 *(978-0-9759829-2-1(3))* Prairieland Pr.
Smalley, Ruth Ann. Sheila Says We're Weird, 1 vol. Emery, Jennifer, illus. 2011. (ENG.). 32p. (J). 16.95 *(978-0-88448-326-7(6))* Tilbury Hse. Pubs.
Smallman, Jeff. Stump's in the Cellar. 2008. 100p. pap. 13.95 *(978-0-557-03091-0(9))* Lulu Pr., Inc.
Smith, Craig. Remarkably Rexy. 2016. (ENG., Illus.). 32p. (J). (gr. -1-2). 17.99 *(978-1-76011-394-0(8))* Allen & Unwin AUS. Dist: Independent Pubs. Group.
Snyder, Laurel. The Forever Garden. Cotterill, Samantha, illus. 2017. (ENG.). 40p. (J). (gr. -1-3). 17.99 ***(978-0-553-51273-1(0));*** lib. bdg. 20.99 ***(978-0-553-51274-8(9))*** Random Hse. Children's Bks. (Schwartz & Wade Bks.).
Soileau, Hodges, illus. The Black Widow Spider Mystery. 2004. (Boxcar Children Special Ser.). 130p. (gr. 2-7). 15.50 *(978-0-7569-3266-4(1))* Perfection Learning Corp.
Soman, David. The Monster Next Door. 2016. (ENG., Illus.). 40p. (J). (-k). 17.99 *(978-0-525-42783-4(X),* Dial Bks) Penguin Young Readers Group.
Springfield, Pepper. Meet the Bobs & Tweets. Caldwell, Kristy, illus. 2016. (Bobs & Tweets Ser.: No. 1). (ENG.). 80p. (J). (gr. -1-3). 9.99 *(978-0-545-87072-6(0))* Scholastic, Inc.
Springfield, Pepper. Perfecto Pet Show. Caldwell, Kristy, illus. 2017. (Bobs & Tweets Ser.: 2). (ENG.). 80p. (J). (gr. -1-3). 9.99 ***(978-0-545-87073-3(9))*** Scholastic, Inc.
Springstubb, Tricia. Mo Wren, Lost & Found. Ross, Heather, illus. 2011. (Fox Street Ser.: 2). (ENG.). 256p. (J). (gr. 3-7). 15.99 *(978-0-06-199039-7(6))* HarperCollins Pubs.
—What Happened on Fox Street. Ross, Heather, illus. 2011. (Fox Street Ser.: 1). (ENG.). 240p. (J). (gr. 3-7). pap. 6.99 *(978-0-06-198636-9(4))* HarperCollins Pubs.
Sprout Street Neighbors: Five Stories. 2015. (Sprout Street Neighbors Ser.). (ENG., Illus.). 112p. (J). (gr. 1-4). 12.99 *(978-0-385-75558-0(9),* Knopf Bks. for Young Readers) Random Hse. Children's Bks.
Stampler, Ann Redisch. The Cats on Ben Yehuda Street. Carabelli, Francesca, illus. 2013. (Israel Ser.). (ENG.). 32p. (J). (gr. -1-2). 7.95 *(978-0-7613-8124-2(4));* lib. bdg. 16.95 *(978-0-7613-8123-5(6))* Lerner Publishing Group. (Kar-Ben Publishing).
Stead, Philip C. Ideas Are All Around. 2016. (ENG., Illus.). 48p. (J). 18.99 *(978-1-62672-181-4(5),* 9781626721814) Roaring Brook Pr.
Stine, R. L. Zombie Halloween. 2014. (Goosebumps Most Wanted Ser.). lib. bdg. 18.40 *(978-0-606-35855-2(2))* Turtleback Bks.
Stinson, Kathy. One More Clue, 1 vol. 2005. (Lorimer Streetlights Ser.). (ENG.). 104p. (J). (gr. 2-5). 7.95 *(978-1-55028-888-9(1),* 9781550288889) Lorimer, James & Co., Ltd., Pubs. CAN. Dist: Casemate Pubs. & Bk. Distributors, LLC.
Stroud, Scott. Baby Kong. Hunt, Jim, illus. 2006. (J). 8.95 *(978-1-60131-001-9(3),* Castlebridge Bks.) Big Tent Bks.
—Grumpy Mr. Grady. Hunt, Jim, illus. 2007. 24p. (J). 8.95 *(978-1-60131-008-8(0),* Castlebridge Bks.) Big Tent Bks.
Sullivan, Kate. On Linden Square. Sullivan, Kate, illus. 2013. (ENG., Illus.). 40p. 15.99 *(978-1-58536-832-7(6))* Sleeping Bear Pr.
Summers, Natalie. The Noweos: Neighbors One with Each Other. 2009. 20p. pap. 12.99 *(978-1-4490-3710-9(0))* AuthorHouse.
Sutton, Katisha Barner. Caring & Sharing. 2011. 26p. pap. 12.50 *(978-1-60976-177-6(4),* Strategic Bk. Publishing) Strategic Book Publishing & Rights Agency (SBPRA).
Taylor, Marilyn. 17 Martin Street. 2012. (ENG.). 208p. (J). pap. 12.95 *(978-1-84717-286-0(5))* O'Brien Pr., Ltd., The IRL. Dist: Dufour Editions, Inc.
Teague, David. The Red Hat. Portis, Antoinette, illus. 2015. (ENG.). 36p. (J). (gr. -1-k). 16.99 *(978-1-4231-3411-4(7))* Hyperion Bks. for Children.
Thayer, Jane. Part-Time Dog. Barasch, Lynne & McCue, Lisa, illus. 2004. (ENG.). 32p. (J). (gr. -1-3). 14.99 *(978-0-06-029693-3(3))* HarperCollins Pubs.
Thiel, Annie. Danny Is Moving. Edwards, William M., illus. 2006. (Playdate Kids Ser.). 32p. (J). (gr. -1-3). 14.95 *(978-1-933721-02-6(2))* Playdate Kids Publishing.
Thomas, Mary Ann. The New Neighbors. 2006. (Neighborhood Readers Ser.). (ENG.). 8p. (gr. -1-3). pap. 5.15 *(978-1-4042-6694-0(1),* Rosen Classroom) Rosen Publishing Group, Inc., The.
Thompson, Colin. Good Neighbors. Scrambly, Crab, illus. 2008. (Floods Ser.: No. 1). 214p. (J). (gr. 3-7). 15.99 *(978-0-06-113196-7(2))* HarperCollins Pubs.
Thompson, Lisa. The Goldfish Boy. 2017. (ENG.). 320p. (J). (gr. 3-7). 16.99 *(978-1-338-05392-0(2),* Scholastic Pr.) Scholastic, Inc.
Thong, Roseanne Greenfield. Round Is a Mooncake: A Book of Shapes. Lin, Grace, illus. 2014. (ENG.). 40p. (J). (gr. -1-k). 7.99 *(978-1-4521-3644-8(0))* Chronicle Bks. LLC.
Trowbridge, Terri. Tulowly the Possum. McConkey, Barbara, illus. I.t. ed. 2005. 24p. (J). 9.95 *(978-0-9766418-0-3(1))* Sidewalk Publishing.
Tyler-Vaughn, Savanna. Flour Sack Wear. 2006. (ENG.). 48p. per. 16.95 *(978-1-4241-2501-2(4))* America Star Bks.
Upperman, Katy. Kissing Max Holden. Brzozowski, Kat, ed. 2017. (ENG.). 304p. (YA). 17.99 *(978-1-250-11116-6(1),* 9781250111166) Feiwel & Friends.
USCCB Department of Justice, Peace, and Human Development. Green Street Park. 2015. (ENG., Illus.). 32p. (J). (gr. k-3). pap. 7.95 *(978-0-8294-4099-7(2))* Loyola Pr.
Vickery-Bharadwaj, Janice. Valentino & His Friends: It's Magic! 2012. 28p. pap. 12.99 *(978-1-4691-7709-0(9))* Xlibris Corp.
Wahl, Jan. Candy Shop. Wong, Nicole, illus. 2005. (ENG.). 32p. (J). (gr. -1-3). pap. 7.95 *(978-1-57091-668-7(3))* Charlesbridge Publishing, Inc.
Walsh, Ann. Flower Power, 1 vol. 2005. (Orca Currents Ser.). (ENG.). 128p. (J). (gr. 5-9). per. 9.95 *(978-1-55143-386-8(9))* Orca Bk. Pubs. USA.
Walsh, Sheila. Meet My Best Friend. 2015. (Bible Is My Best Friend Ser.). (ENG.). 32p. (J). (gr. -1-3). 14.99 *(978-1-4336-8805-8(0),* B&H Kids) B&H Publishing Group.
Walters, Eric. Fight for Power. 2015. (Rule of Three Ser.: 2). (ENG.). 352p. (YA). (gr. 7). 17.99 *(978-0-374-30179-8(4),* 9780374301798, Farrar, Straus & Giroux (BYR)) Farrar, Straus & Giroux.
Weeks, Sarah. Oggie Cooder - Party Animal! 2011. (Oggie Cooder Ser.). (ENG.). 176p. (J). (gr. 2-5). pap. 6.99 *(978-0-439-92796-3(X),* Scholastic Paperbacks) Scholastic, Inc.
Weitzman, Jacqueline Preiss. Superhero Joe & the Creature Next Door. Barrett, Ron, illus. 2013. (ENG.). 32p. (J). (gr. -1-3). 16.99 *(978-1-4424-1268-2(2),* Simon & Schuster Bks. For Young Readers) Simon & Schuster Bks. For Young Readers.
Weller, Frances Ward. The Day the Animals Came: A Story of Saint Francis Day. Long, Loren, illus. 2006. 35p. (J). (gr. k-4). reprint ed. 17.00 *(978-1-4223-5396-7(6))* DIANE Publishing Co.
Wildsmith, Brian. The Owl & the Woodpecker, 1 vol. Wildsmith, Brian, illus. 2006. (ENG., Illus.). 32p. (J). (gr. -1-3). 16.95 *(978-1-59572-043-6(X))* Star Bright Bks., Inc.
Wood, Deanna Plummer. Whenever Monkeys Move Next Door, 1 volume. 2005. (Illus.). 24p. (J). pap. 8.50 *(978-0-9762935-1-4(X))* Perkins Crawford.
Wright, Lynda. Flowers for Addison. 2012. 24p. pap. 24.95 *(978-1-4626-5787-2(7))* America Star Bks.
Wuest, Marcia. Twelve Things to Do at Age 12. 2009. (ENG.). 26p. pap. 7.25 *(978-0-521-73733-3(8))* Cambridge Univ. Pr.
Yee, Wong Herbert. Upstairs Mouse, Downstairs Mole. 12th ed. 2007. (Mouse & Mole Story Ser.). (ENG., Illus.). 48p. (J). (gr. -1-3). 3.99 *(978-0-618-91586-6(9))* Houghton Mifflin Harcourt Publishing Co.
Yim, Natasha. Goldy Luck & the Three Pandas. Zong, Grace, illus. (ENG.). 32p. (J). (gr. -1-3). 2015. pap. 7.95 *(978-1-58089-653-5(7))* 2014. lib. bdg. 16.95 *(978-1-58089-652-8(9))* Charlesbridge Publishing, Inc.
Yost, B. L. Have You Ever Seen a Wild Bird Dance? Perkins, Chelsea, illus. 2008. 16p. pap. 24.95 *(978-1-60703-127-7(2))* America Star Bks.

NELSON, HORATIO NELSON, VISCOUNT, 1758-1805

Lacey, Minna. Nelson. Cuzik, David, illus. 2006. (Usborne Famous Lives Gift Bks.). 64p. (J). 8.95 *(978-0-7945-1121-0(X),* Usborne) EDC Publishing.

NELSON, HORATIO NELSON, VISCOUNT, 1758-1805—FICTION

Bell, Ted. Nick of Time. 2009. (Nick McIver Adventures Through Time Ser.: 1). (ENG., Illus.). 464p. (J). (gr. 5-9). pap. 8.99 *(978-0-312-58143-5(2),* 9780312581435) Square Fish.
Henty, George Alfred. By Conduct & Courage: A Story of the Days of Nelson. 2011. 364p. pap. 19.95 *(978-1-61179-089-4(1))* Fireship Pr.

NEO-IMPRESSIONISM (ART)

see Impressionism (Art)

NEOLITHIC PERIOD

see Stone Age

NEPAL

Adhikary, Anita. N Is for Nepal. Mundy, Jen, illus. 2011. (J). 14.95 *(978-1-936319-52-7(7))* Mascot Bks., Inc.
Athans, Sandra K. Secrets of the Sky Caves: Danger & Discovery on Nepal's Mustang Cliffs. 2014. (ENG., Illus.). 64p. (gr. 4-8). lib. bdg. 33.27 *(978-1-4677-0016-0(9),* Millbrook Pr.) Lerner Publishing Group.
Bailey, Diane & Chhetri, Purneema. My Teenage Life in Nepal. 2017. (Illus.). 128p. (J). ***(978-1-4222-3909-4(8))*** Mason Crest.
Burleigh, Robert. Tiger of the Snows: Tenzing Norgay: the Boy Whose Dream Was Everest. Young, Ed, illus. 2010. (ENG.). 40p. (J). (gr. 2-5). 16.99 *(978-1-4424-2192-9(4),* Atheneum Bks. for Young Readers) Simon & Schuster Children's Publishing.
Mattern, Joanne. Nepal. 2017. (J). pap. 19.95 ***(978-1-5026-2500-7(8))*** Cavendish Square Publishing.
Owings, Lisa. Nepal. 2014. (Exploring Countries Ser.). (ENG., Illus.). 32p. (J). (gr. 3-7). lib. bdg. 26.95 *(978-1-62617-069-8(X),* Blastoff! Readers) Bellwether Media.
Trussell-Cullen, Alan. Edmund Hillary. 2009. pap. 13.25 *(978-1-60559-058-5(4))* Hameray Publishing Group, Inc.
Zuchora-Walske, Christine. Nepal in Pictures. 2008. (Visual Geography Ser.). (YA). (gr. 7-12). lib. bdg. 31.93 *(978-0-8225-8578-7(2))* Twenty First Century Bks.

NEPAL—FICTION

Asnong, Jocey, illus. Nuptse & Lohtse Go to the Rockies, 1 vol. 2014. (ENG.). 40p. (J). (gr. k). pap. 12.00 *(978-1-77160-019-4(5))* Road West Publishing Co.
Cohn, Diana. Namaste! Cordova, Amy, illus. 2012. (ENG.). 32p. (J). pap. 9.95 *(978-1-62148-005-1(4))* SteinerBooks, Inc.
Dinerstein, Eric. What Elephants Know. 2016. (ENG.). 288p. (J). (gr. 3-7). 16.99 *(978-1-4847-2854-3(8))* Disney Publishing Worldwide.
Doan, Lisa. Jack at the Helm. Stevanovic, Ivica, illus. 2015. (J). 9.99 *(978-1-4677-7787-2(0));* (Berenson Schemes Ser.: 3). (ENG.). 152p. (gr. 4-6). 17.95 *(978-1-4677-1078-7(4))* Lerner Publishing Group.
Heine, Theresa & Barefoot Books Staff. Chandra's Magic Light. Gueyfier, Judith, illus. 2013. (J). 16.99 *(978-1-84686-493-3(3))* Barefoot Bks., Inc.
Hobbie, Holly. Top of the World. 2008. (Toot & Puddle Ser.: 6). (ENG.). 32p. (gr. -1-3). pap. 7.99 *(978-0-316-03384-8(7))* Little, Brown Bks. for Young Readers.
Hunt, Elizabeth Singer. Secret Agent Jack Stalwart: Book 13: the Hunt for the Yeti Skull: Nepal. 2011. (Secret Agent Jack Stalwart Ser.: 13). (ENG.). 128p. (J). (gr. 1-4). pap. 5.99 *(978-1-60286-151-0(X),* Weinstein Bks.) Perseus Bks. Group.
Jeffrey, Rosemary. Allio, Are you Free. 2010. 176p. pap. 12.00 *(978-0-557-75342-0(2))* Lulu Pr., Inc.
Korman, Gordon. The Summit. 2012. (Everest Ser.: 3). lib. bdg. 17.20 *(978-0-606-23935-6(9),* Turtleback) Turtleback Bks.
Lumry, Amanda & Hurwitz, Laura. Tigers in Terai. McIntyre, Sarah, illus. 2003. (Adventures of Riley Ser.). 36p. 15.95 *(978-0-9662257-7-8(5))* Eaglemont Pr.
McCormick, Patricia. Sold. 2008. (ENG.). 272p. (J). (gr. 7-17). pap. 8.99 *(978-0-7868-5172-0(4))* Hyperion Pr.
—Sold. 2011. 10.36 *(978-0-7848-3420-6(2),* Everbind) Marco Bk. Co.
—Sold. 2008. 263p. (J). (gr. 7-12). 19.65 *(978-1-4178-1810-5(7),* Turtleback) Turtleback Bks.
Michaelis, Antonia. The Dragons of Darkness. Bell, Anthea, tr. from GER. 2010. (ENG.). 566p. (YA). (gr. 7-11). 18.95 *(978-0-8109-4074-1(4),* Amulet Bks.) Abrams, Inc.
—Dragons of Darkness. Bell, Anthea, tr. 2011. (ENG.). 576p. (YA). (gr. 7-17). pap. 8.95 *(978-1-4197-0085-9(5),* Amulet Bks.) Abrams, Inc.
Pelletier, Cynthia L. & Rabin, Shri. She Who Walks with Tigers, 1 vol. 2010. 80p. pap. 19.95 *(978-1-4512-8767-7(4))* America Star Bks.
Stewart, Jennifer J. Close Encounters of a Third World Kind. 2004. (ENG.). 128p. (J). (gr. 4-6). tchr. ed. 16.95 *(978-0-8234-1850-3(2))* Holiday Hse., Inc.
—Close Encounters of a Third-World Kind. 2008. (ENG., Illus.). 181p. (J). (gr. 3-7). 6.95 *(978-0-8234-2161-9(9))* Holiday Hse., Inc.

NEPTUNE (PLANET)

Adamson, Thomas K. Neptune [Scholastic]: Revised Edition. 2010. (Exploring the Galaxy Ser.). (ENG.). 24p. pap. 0.49 *(978-1-4296-5813-3(4),* Pebble Plus) Capstone Press of Coughlan Cos.
—The Secrets of Neptune. 2015. (Planets Ser.). (ENG., Illus.). 32p. (gr. 2-4). lib. bdg. 31.99 *(978-1-4914-5867-9(4))* Capstone Press of Coughlan Cos.
Asimov, Isaac & Hantula, Richard. Neptuno. Porras, Carlos & D'Andrea, Patricia, trs. 2003. (Isaac Asimov's Biblioteca del Universo del Siglo XXI).Tr. of Neptune: The Farthest Giant. (SPA & ENG., Illus.). 32p. (gr. 2-6). lib. bdg. 26.00 *(978-0-8368-3858-9(0),* Gareth Stevens Learning Library) Stevens, Gareth Publishing LLLP.
Bloom, J. P. Neptune, 1 vol. 2014. (Planets Ser.). (ENG., Illus.). 24p. (J). (gr. 2-4). lib. bdg. 28.50 *(978-1-62970-719-8(8))* ABDO Publishing Co.
Brockman, Noah. Journey to Neptune, 1 vol. 2014. (Spotlight on Space Science Ser.). (ENG.). 32p. (J). (gr. 5-5). pap. 11.75 *(978-1-4994-0374-9(7),* PowerKids Pr.) Rosen Publishing Group, Inc., The.
Carlson, Sally Kephart. Your Mission to Neptune, 1 vol. 2011. (Planets Ser.). (ENG., Illus.). 32p. (J). (gr. k-3). 28.50 *(978-1-61641-681-2(5))* Magic Wagon.
Carson, Mary Kay. Far-Out Guide to Neptune. 2010. (Far-Out Guide to the Solar System Ser.). (Illus.). 48p. (J). pap. 8.95 *(978-1-59845-189-4(8),* Enslow Elementary); (gr. 2-5). 25.27 *(978-0-7660-3186-9(1))* Enslow Pubs., Inc.
Chrismer, Melanie. Neptune. (Scholastic News Nonfiction Readers Ser.). (ENG., Illus.). 24p. (J). (gr. 1-2). 2008. pap. 6.95 *(978-0-531-14765-8(7))* 2007. 22.00 *(978-0-531-14750-4(9))* Scholastic Library Publishing.
Elkins-Tanton, Linda T. Uranus, Neptune, Pluto, & the Outer Solar System. 2nd rev. ed. 2010. (Solar System Ser.). (Illus.). 272p. (C). (gr. 9). 39.50 *(978-0-8160-7701-4(0))* Facts On File, Inc.
Fleisher, Paul. Neptune. 2009. (Early Bird Astronomy Ser.). (ENG.). 48p. (gr. 2-5). lib. bdg. 26.60 *(978-0-7613-4155-0(2));* (Illus.). pap. 8.95 *(978-0-7613-4984-6(7),* Lerner Pubns.) Lerner Publishing Group.
Hayhurst, Chris. Neptune. (Library of Planets Ser.). 2009. 48p. (gr. 5-8). 55.90 *(978-1-60853-819-5(2),* Rosen Reference) 2006. 29.25 *(978-1-4042-1966-3(8))* Rosen Publishing Group, Inc., The.
Howard, Fran. Neptune, 1 vol. 2007. (Planets Ser.). (ENG.). 32p. (J). (gr. 3-7). lib. bdg. 27.07 *(978-1-59928-830-7(3),* Buddy Bks.) ABDO Publishing Co.
Jefferis, David. Gas Giants: Huge Far off Worlds. 2008. (ENG., Illus.). 32p. (J). (gr. 3-7). pap. *(978-0-7787-3750-6(0))* Crabtree Publishing Co.
Jones, Emma. Exploring Neptune. 2017. (J). ***(978-1-5345-2257-2(3),*** KidHaven Publishing) Greenhaven Publishing LLC.
Kazunas, Ariel. Neptune. 2011. (21st Century Junior Library: Solar System Ser.). (ENG.). 24p. (gr. 2-5). lib. bdg. 25.64 *(978-1-61080-083-9(4),* 201076) Cherry Lake Publishing.
Lawrence, Ellen. Neptune: The Stormiest Planet. 2013. (Zoom into Space Ser.). 24p. (J). (gr. -1-3). lib. bdg. 23.93 *(978-1-909673-18-2(8))* Ruby Tuesday Books Limited GBR. Dist: Bearport Publishing Co., Inc.
Loewen, Nancy. Farthest from the Sun: The Planet Neptune, 1 vol. Yesh, Jeff, illus. 2008. (Amazing Science: Planets Ser.). (ENG.). 24p. (gr. k-4). lib. bdg. 26.65 *(978-1-4048-3955-7(0),* 1278900) Picture Window Bks.
Markovics, Joyce. Neptuno: Muy, Muy Lejos. 2015. (Fuera de Este Mundo Ser.). (SPA., Illus.). 24p. (J). (gr. -1-3). lib. bdg. 23.93 *(978-1-62724-593-7(6))* Bearport Publishing Co., Inc.
Markovics, Joyce L. Neptune: Far, Far Away. 2015. (Out of This World Ser.). (ENG.). 24p. (J). (gr. -1-3). lib. bdg. 23.93 *(978-1-62724-568-5(5))* Bearport Publishing Co., Inc.
Neptune. 2nd rev. ed. 2008. (New Solar System Ser.). 32p. (YA). (gr. 3-6). 23.00 *(978-1-60413-215-1(9))* Facts On File, Inc.
Orme, Helen & Orme, David. Let's Explore Neptune. 2007. (Space Launch! Ser.). 24p. (gr. 1-4). pap. 8.15 *(978-0-8368-8129-5(X));* (Illus.). lib. bdg. 23.00 *(978-0-8368-7944-5(9))* Stevens, Gareth Publishing LLLP. (Gareth Stevens Learning Library).
Owen, Ruth. Neptune. 2013. (Explore Outer Space Ser.). 32p. (J). (gr. 3-6). 25.25 *(978-1-61533-729-3(6));* pap. 60.00 *(978-1-61533-776-7(8));* pap. 10.00 *(978-1-61533-775-0(X))* Windmill Bks.
Ring, Susan. Neptune. (J). 2013. 27.13 *(978-1-62127-267-0(2))* 2013. pap. 12.95 *(978-1-62127-276-2(1))* 2004. pap. 8.95 *(978-1-59036-229-7(2))* 2004. (Illus.). 24p. (gr. 4-7). lib. bdg. 24.45 *(978-1-59036-102-3(4))* Weigl Pubs., Inc.
Ring, Susan & Roumanis, Alexis. Neptune. 2016. (Illus.). 24p. (J). *(978-1-5105-0986-3(0))* SmartBook Media, Inc.
Roumanis, Alexis. Neptune. 2016. (J). ***(978-1-5105-2053-0(8))*** SmartBook Media, Inc.
—Neptune. 2015. (Illus.). 24p. (J). *(978-1-4896-3296-8(4))* Weigl Pubs., Inc.
Roza, Greg. Neptune: The Stormy Planet. 2010. (Our Solar System Ser.). 24p. (J). (gr. k-3). (ENG.). pap. 8.15 *(978-1-4339-3834-4(0));* (Illus.). lib. bdg. 22.60 *(978-1-4339-3833-7(2))* Stevens, Gareth Publishing LLLP.

Scherer, Glenn & Fletcher, Marty. Neptune: A MyReportLinks.com Book. 2005. (Solar System Ser.). (Illus.). 48p. (J). lib. bdg. 26.60 *(978-0-7660-5211-6(7),* MyReportLinks.com Bks.) Enslow Pubs., Inc.

Sherman, Josepha. Neptune. 2009. (Space!). 64p. (gr. 5-18). lib. bdg. 32.79 *(978-0-7614-4246-2(4))* Marshall Cavendish Corp.

Slade, Suzanne. A Look at Neptune. (Astronomy Now! Ser.). 24p. (gr. 2-3). 2009. 42.50 *(978-1-61511-471-9(8),* PowerKids Pr.) 2007. (Illus.). (YA). lib. bdg. 22.60 *(978-1-4042-3832-9(8))* Rosen Publishing Group, Inc., The.

Sparrow, Giles. Destination Uranus, Neptune, & Pluto. 2009. (Destination Solar System Ser.). (Illus.). 32p. (J). 25.25 *(978-1-4358-3446-0(1));* pap. 10.00 *(978-1-4358-3463-7(1))* Rosen Publishing Group, Inc., The. (PowerKids Pr.).

Squire, Ann O. Planet Neptune. 2014. (True Book — Space (Revised Edition) Ser.). (ENG.). 48p. (J). lib. bdg. 29.00 *(978-0-531-21155-7(X))* Scholastic Library Publishing.

Steinkraus, Kyla. Giant Gas Planets: Jupiter, Saturn, Uranus, & Neptune. 2014. (ENG.). 24p. (gr. k-3). 28.50 *(978-1-62717-728-3(0))* Rourke Educational Media.

Thompson, Luke. Neptune. 2009. (Library of the Planets Ser.). 24p. (gr. 3-3). 42.50 *(978-1-60853-919-2(9),* PowerKids Pr.) Rosen Publishing Group, Inc., The.

Waxman, Laura Hamilton. Neptune. 2005. (Pull Ahead Bks.). (Illus.). 32p. (gr. 2-4). lib. bdg. 22.60 *(978-0-8225-4655-9(8))* Lerner Publishing Group.

Wimmer, Teresa. Neptune. 2007. (My First Look at: Planets Ser.). (Illus.). 24p. (J). (gr. -1-3). lib. bdg. 24.25 *(978-1-58341-520-7(3),* Creative Education) Creative Co., The.

World Book, contrib. by. Neptune & the Distant Dwarf Planets. 2nd ed. 2006. (World Book's Solar System & Space Exploration Library). (Illus.). 64p. (J). *(978-0-7166-9518-9(9))* World Bk., Inc.

World Book, Inc Staff, contrib. by. Neptune & Pluto. 2006. (World Book's Solar System & Space Exploration Library). (Illus.). 63p. (J). *(978-0-7166-9507-3(3))* World Bk., Inc.

—Neptune, Comets, & Dwarf Planets. 2010. (J). *(978-0-7166-9538-7(3))* World Bk., Inc.

Zobel, Derek. Neptune. 2010. (Exploring Space Ser.). (ENG., Illus.). 24p. (J). (gr. k-3). lib. bdg. 25.95 *(978-1-60014-409-7(8),* Blastoff! Readers) Bellwether Media.

NERO, EMPEROR OF ROME, 37-68

Abbott, Jacob. Nero. 2009. 202p. (J). pap. 12.00 *(978-1-59128-057-6(5))* Canon Pr.

Lowery, Zoe & Morgan, Julian. Nero. 2016. (Leaders of the Ancient World Ser.). 00112p. (J). (gr. 6-6). 37.10 *(978-1-5081-7256-7(0))* Rosen Publishing Group, Inc., The.

Morgan, Julian. Nero: Destroyer of Rome. (Ancient Leaders Ser.). 112p. (gr. 5-8). 2009. 66.50 *(978-1-61511-426-9(2))* 2003. (Illus.). (YA). lib. bdg. 34.60 *(978-0-8239-3596-3(5))* Rosen Publishing Group, Inc., The. (Rosen Reference).

Saxena, Shalini. Nero: Ruthless Roman Emperor. 2016. (History's Most Murderous Villains Ser.). (Illus.). 32p. (J). (gr. 5-4). pap. 10.50 *(978-1-4824-4799-6(1))* Stevens, Gareth Publishing LLLP.

Whiting, Jim. The Life & Times of Nero. 2005. (Biography from Ancient Civilizations Ser.). (Illus.). 48p. (J). (gr. 5-8). lib. bdg. 29.95 *(978-1-58415-349-8(0))* Mitchell Lane Pubs., Inc.

NERO, EMPEROR OF ROME, 37-68—FICTION

Weerstand, R. Quintus: A Story about the Persecution of Christians at the Time of Emperor Nero. 2006. (Illus.). 135p. (J). *(978-1-894666-70-1(4))* Inheritance Pubns.

NERVOUS SYSTEM

see also Brain; Psychology, Pathological

Andrews, Barbara. Discover the Nervous & Digestive Systems. 2006. (J). pap. *(978-1-4108-6515-1(0))* Benchmark Education Co.

—The Nervous & Digestive Systems. 2006. (J). pap. *(978-1-4108-6512-0(6))* Benchmark Education Co.

Becker, Jack & Hayhurst, Chris. The Brain & Spinal Cord in 3D. 2015. (Human Body In 3D Ser.). (ENG., Illus.). 64p. (J). (gr. 5-6). 32.95 *(978-1-4994-3581-8(9),* Rosen Central) Rosen Publishing Group, Inc., The.

Birmingham, Maria. Tastes Like Music: 17 Quirks of the Brain & Body. Melnychuk, Monika, illus. 2014. (ENG.). 40p. (J). (gr. 3-7). 17.95 *(978-1-77147-010-0(0),* Owlkids) Owlkids Bks. Inc. CAN. Dist: Publishers Group West (PGW).

Boothroyd, Jennifer. Vision: Nearsightedness, Farsightedness, & More. 2012. (Lightning Bolt Books (tm) — What Traits Are in Your Genes? Ser.). (ENG., Illus.). 32p. (gr. k-2). lib. bdg. 26.60 *(978-0-7613-8940-8(7),* Lerner Pubns.) Lerner Publishing Group.

Brett, Flora. Your Nervous System Works! 2015. (Your Body Systems Ser.). (ENG.). 24p. (gr. 1-2). lib. bdg. 25.32 *(978-1-4914-2066-9(9))* Capstone Press of Coughlan Cos.

Brinkerhoff, Shirley. Attention — Deficit/Hyperactivity Disorder. 2014. (Illus.). 128p. (J). *(978-1-4222-3027-5(9))* Mason Crest.

Burstein, John. The Astounding Nervous System: How Does My Brain Work? 2009. (Slim Goodbody's Body Buddies Ser.). (ENG., Illus.). 32p. (J). (gr. 3-5). pap. *(978-0-7787-4428-3(0));* lib. bdg. *(978-0-7787-4414-6(0))* Crabtree Publishing Co.

Canavan, Thomas. Sensing the World: The Nervous System. 2015. (How Your Body Works). (ENG.). 32p. (J). (gr. 4-4). pap. 10.00 *(978-1-4994-1232-1(0),* PowerKids Pr.) Rosen Publishing Group, Inc., The.

Canetti, Yanitzia. La Adaptación, ¡qué Sensación! 2010. (SPA.). (J). *(978-1-59835-170-5(2))* Cambridge BrickHouse, Inc.

Chudler, Eric H., ed. Gray Matter, 19 vols., Set. 2007. (Gray Matter Ser.). (C). (gr. 9). 665.00 *(978-0-7910-9659-8(9),* Chelsea Hse.) Facts On File, Inc.

DeSalle, Rob. Brain: A 21st Century Look at a 400 Million Year Old Organ. Wynne, Patricia, illus. 2010. (Wallace & Darwin Ser.: 2). (ENG.). 40p. (gr. 3-7). 18.95 *(978-1-59373-085-7(3))* Bunker Hill Publishing, Inc.

Duke, Shirley. The Nervous System. 2012. (ENG.). 48p. (gr. 4-6). pap. 10.95 *(978-1-61810-254-6(0))* Rourke Educational Media.

Einspruch, Andrew. Brain Works, 1 vol., 1. 2014. (Discovery Education: How It Works). (ENG.). 32p. (gr. 3-6). 26.25 *(978-1-4777-6305-6(8),* PowerKids Pr.) Rosen Publishing Group, Inc., The.

Engdahl, Sylvia. Meningitis. 2010. (Perspectives on Diseases & Disorders Ser.). (Illus.). 144p. (YA). 38.95 *(978-0-7377-4790-4(0),* Greenhaven Pr., Inc.) Cengage Gale.

—Neurodegenerative Disorders. Greenhaven Press Editors, ed. 2013. (Perspectives on Diseases & Disorders Ser.). (ENG., Illus.). 144p. (gr. 10-12). lib. bdg. 44.30 *(978-0-7377-6357-7(4),* Greenhaven Pr., Inc.) Cengage Gale.

Evans-Martin, F. Fay. The Nervous System. 2009. (Human Body: How It Works Ser.). (Illus.). 128p. (C). (gr. 9-18). 35.00 *(978-1-60413-374-5(0),* Chelsea Hse.) Facts On File, Inc.

Farndon, John. Stickmen's Guide to Your Brilliant Brain. Dean, Venitia, illus. 2017. (Stickmen's Guides to Your Awesome Body Ser.). (ENG.). 32p. (J). (gr. 3-6). 26.65 ***(978-1-5124-3213-8(X))*** Lerner Publishing Group.

Faulk, Michelle. The Case of the Rusty Nail: Annie Biotica Solves Nervous System Disease Crimes. 2013. (Body System Disease Investigations Ser.). 48p. (J). (gr. 5-12). pap. 8.95 *(978-1-4644-0227-2(2));* lib. bdg. 25.27 *(978-0-7660-3949-0(8))* Enslow Pubs., Inc.

Freedman, Jeri. Tay-Sachs Disease. 2009. (Genes & Disease Ser.). (Illus.). 128p. (YA). (gr. 7-12). 35.00 *(978-0-7910-9634-5(3))* Facts On File, Inc.

French, Kathy. Your Nervous System: Set Of 6. 2010. (Early Connections Ser.). (J). pap. 39.00 net. *(978-1-4108-1538-5(2))* Benchmark Education Co.

Gay, Michelle. Brain Breaks for the Classroom: Quick & Easy Breathing & Movement Activities That Help Students Reenergize, Refocus, & Boost Brain Power-Anytime of the Day! 2009. (ENG.). 48p. (gr. k-5): pap. 13.99 *(978-0-545-07474-2(6),* Teaching Resources) Scholastic, Inc.

Gold, Martha V. Learning about the Nervous System. 2013. (Learning about the Human Body Systems Ser.). 48p. (J). (gr. 5-12). pap. 8.95 *(978-1-4644-0241-8(8));* 25.27 *(978-0-7660-4160-8(3))* Enslow Pubs., Inc.

—The Nervous System. 2004. (Human Body Library Ser.). (Illus.). 48p. (J). lib. bdg. 23.93 *(978-0-7660-2018-4(5))* Enslow Pubs., Inc.

Goldsmith, Connie. Meningitis. 2007. (Twenty-First Century Medical Library). (Illus.). 128p. (YA). (gr. 7-12). lib. bdg. 30.60 *(978-0-8225-7034-9(3))* Twenty First Century Bks.

—Traumatic Brain Injury: From Concussion to Coma. 2014. (Illus.). 88p. (gr. 6-12). lib. bdg. 34.60 *(978-1-4677-1348-1(1),* Twenty-First Century Bks.) Lerner Publishing Group.

Gordon, Sharon. My Brain. 2004. (Bookworms Ser.). (ENG & SPA., Illus.). 31p. (J). 22.79 *(978-0-7614-1781-1(8),* Benchmark Bks.) Marshall Cavendish Corp.

Gray, Susan H. The Nervous System. 2014. (Human Body Ser.). (ENG.). 24p. (J). (gr. 2-5). 28.50 *(978-1-62687-337-7(2),* 207177) Child's World, Inc., The.

Gray-Wilburn, Renée. What You Need to Know about Meningitis. 2015. (Focus on Health Ser.). (ENG., Illus.). 32p. (gr. 3-4). pap. 7.95 *(978-1-4914-4900-4(4))* Capstone Press of Coughlan Cos.

Green, Emily & Manolis, Kay. The Nervous System. 2009. (Body Systems Ser.). (ENG., Illus.). 24p. (J). (gr. 2-5). lib. bdg. 25.95 *(978-1-60014-245-1(1))* Bellwether Media.

Harrold, Kimberly. Sometimes, MS Is Yucky. Whitfield, Eric, illus. 2005. (ENG.). 40p. (J). pap. 12.95 *(978-1-59630-006-4(X),* 1-59630-006-X) Science & Humanities Pr.

Holt, Rinehart and Winston Staff. Holt Science & Technology Chapter 25: Life Science: Communication & Control. 5th ed. 2004. (Illus.). pap. 12.86 *(978-0-03-030246-6(3))* Holt McDougal.

Houghton, Gillian. The Nervous System. 2007. (Body Works Ser.). (ENG., Illus.). 24p. (gr. 3-5). pap. 7.05 *(978-1-4042-2183-3(2),* PowerKids Pr.) Rosen Publishing Group, Inc., The.

Jerome, Kate Boehm & National Geographic Learning Staff. Understanding the Brain. 2007. (Nonfiction Reading & Writing Workshops Ser.). (ENG., Illus.). 32p. (J). pap. 17.95 *(978-0-7922-8859-6(9))* CENGAGE Learning.

Klosterman, Lorrie. The Nervous System. 2009. (Amazing Human Body 2 Ser.). 80p. (gr. 5). 34.21 *(978-0-7614-4039-0(9))* Marshall Cavendish GBR. Dist: Marshall Cavendish Corp.

Kneib, Martha. Meningitis. 2009. (Epidemics Ser.). 64p. (gr. 5-5). 58.50 *(978-1-61512-297-4(4))* Rosen Publishing Group, Inc., The.

Knowles, Johanna. Huntington's Disease. 2009. (Genetic Diseases & Disorders Ser.). 64p. (gr. 6-6). 58.50 *(978-1-61512-668-2(6))* Rosen Publishing Group, Inc., The.

Kolpin, Molly. A Tour of Your Nervous System. Jones, Chris B., illus. 2012. (First Graphics: Body Systems Ser.). (ENG.). 24p. (gr. 1-2). pap. 35.70 *(978-1-4296-9329-5(0));* lib. bdg. 23.99 *(978-1-4296-8739-3(8))* Capstone Press of Coughlan Cos.

Laird, Chynna T. I'm Not Weird, I Have Sensory Processing Disorder (SPD) Alexandra's Journey. 2nd ed. 2012. (J). 24p. 29.95 *(978-1-61599-159-4(X));* (Illus.). 22p. pap. *(978-1-61599-158-7(1))* Loving Healing Pr., Inc.

Libra, Anna. Why Does My Head Hurt? An Inside Look at the Nervous System. 2003. (J). pap. *(978-1-58417-065-5(4));* lib. bdg. *(978-1-58417-002-0(6))* Lake Street Pubs.

Manolis, Kay. The Nervous System. 2009. (Blastoff! Readers Ser.). (ENG., Illus.). 24p. (J). (gr. k-3). 20.00 *(978-0-531-21704-7(3),* Children's Pr.) Scholastic Library Publishing.

Mason, Paul. Your Mind-Bending Brain & Networking Nervous System. 2015. (Your Brilliant Body! Ser.). (ENG., Illus.). 32p. (J). *(978-0-7787-2199-4(X))* Crabtree Publishing Co.

Meachen Rau, Dana. El Cerebro: Que Hay Dentro de Mi? 2006. (Bookworms Ser.). (SPA & ENG., Illus.). 32p. (gr. 1-2). lib. bdg. 15.95 *(978-0-7614-2402-4(4))* Marshall Cavendish Corp.

—My Brain/el Cerebro. 2006. (Bookworms Ser.). (SPA & ENG., Illus.). 32p. (gr. 1-2). lib. bdg. 15.95 *(978-0-7614-2480-2(6))* Marshall Cavendish Corp.

Moe, Barbara. Coping with Tourette's Syndrome & Other Tic Disorders. 2009. (Coping Ser.). 192p. (gr. 7-12). 63.90 *(978-1-61512-016-1(5))* Rosen Publishing Group, Inc., The.

Morgan, Philip. Sending Messages. 2010. (How Your Body Works). 32p. (YA). (gr. 4-7). 28.50 *(978-1-60753-055-8(4))* Amicus Publishing.

—Sending Messages. 2012. (Illus.). 32p. (gr. 4-7). pap. 8.95 *(978-1-926722-65-8(5))* Saunders Bk. Co. CAN. Dist: RiverStream Publishing.

Morgan, Philip & Turnbull, Stephanie. Sending Messages. 2011. (Secrets of Magic Ser.). 32p. (gr. 4-7). lib. bdg. 31.35 *(978-1-59920-496-3(7))* Black Rabbit Bks.

Naff, Clayton Farris, ed. Huntington's Disease. 2012. (Perspectives on Diseases & Disorders Ser.). (ENG., Illus.). 144p. (gr. 10-12). lib. bdg. 38.95 *(978-0-7377-5775-0(2),* Greenhaven Pr., Inc.) Cengage Gale.

Nervensystem und Sinnesorgane: Fachliche Inhalte und Uebungsaufgaben. 2nd ed. (Duden Abiturhilfen Ser.). (GER.). 112p. (YA). (gr. 12-13). *(978-3-411-04152-7(8))* Bibliographisches Institut & F. A. Brockhaus AG DEU. Dist: International Bk. Import Service, Inc.

The Nervous System/The Senses/The Skin. 2006. (World Book's Human Body Works). (Illus.). 48p. (J). *(978-0-7166-4430-9(4))* World Bk., Inc.

Niver, Heather Moore. The Nervous System. 2012. (Human Body Ser.). (ENG., Illus.). 32p. (J). (gr. 4-6). pap. 10.50 *(978-1-4339-6590-6(9),* Gareth Stevens Learning Library); lib. bdg. 26.60 *(978-1-4339-6588-3(7))* Stevens, Gareth Publishing LLLP.

Petrie, Kristin. The Nervous System, 1 vol. 2007. (Human Body Ser.). (ENG., Illus.). 32p. (gr. 4-7). 27.07 *(978-1-59679-712-3(6),* Checkerboard Library) ABDO Publishing Co.

Porterfield, Jason. Downers: Depressant Abuse. (Incredibly Disgusting Drugs Ser.). 48p. (gr. 5-8). 2009. 53.00 *(978-1-61513-496-0(4),* Rosen Reference) 2007. (Illus.). (YA). lib. bdg. 29.25 *(978-1-4042-1957-1(9))* Rosen Publishing Group, Inc., The.

Rau, Dana Meachen. My Brain. 2013. (Bookworms Fluent — My Body Ser.). 24p. (gr. 1-3). pap. 8.22 *(978-1-62712-033-3(5))* Cavendish Square Publishing.

Riley, Joelle. The Nervous System. (Early Bird Body Systems Ser.). (Illus.). 48p. (J). 2005. (gr. 2-4). lib. bdg. 25.26 *(978-0-8225-1249-3(1))* 2004. pap. 8.95 *(978-0-8225-2521-9(6))* Lerner Publishing Group.

—El Sistema Nervioso. Translations.com Staff, tr. 2006. (Libros Sobre el Cuerpo Humano para Madrugadores Ser.). (ENG & SPA., Illus.). 48p. (gr. 2-4). lib. bdg. 26.60 *(978-0-8225-6255-9(3))* Lerner Publishing Group.

—El sistema nervioso (the Nervous System) 2006. (Libros Sobre el Cuerpo Humano para Madrugadores Ser.). (Illus.). 48p. (J). (gr. -1-3). per. 8.95 *(978-0-8225-6651-9(6),* Ediciones Lerner) Lerner Publishing Group.

—Your Nervous System. 2012. (Searchlight Books — How Does Your Body Work? Ser.). (ENG., Illus.). 40p. (gr. 3-5). pap. 8.95 *(978-1-58013-962-5(0));* lib. bdg. 27.93 *(978-0-7613-7450-3(7),* Lerner Pubns.) Lerner Publishing Group.

Rose, Simon. Nervous System. 2014. (J). *(978-1-4896-1174-1(6))* Weigl Pubs., Inc.

Simon, Seymour. The Brain: Our Nervous System. 2006. (ENG., Illus.). 32p. (J). (gr. k-4). pap. 6.99 *(978-0-06-087719-4(7),* Collins) HarperCollins Pubs.

—The Brain: Our Nervous System. 2006. (Illus.). 30p. (gr. k-4). 17.00 *(978-0-7569-6740-6(6))* Perfection Learning Corp.

El Sistema Nervioso, Nuestro Proceso de Datos. (Coleccion Mundo Invisible).Tr. of Nervous System & the Brain. (SPA.). (YA). (gr. 5-8). pap. 8.00 *(978-958-04-3226-5(0))* Norma S.A. COL. Dist: Distribuidora Norma, Inc.

El Sistema Nervioso Nuestro Proceso de Datos. (SPA.). (J). 10.00 *(978-84-342-1907-6(7))* Parramon Ediciones S.A. ESP. Dist: Distribuidora Norma, Inc.

Snedden, Robert. Understanding the Brain & the Nervous System. 2010. (Understanding the Human Body Ser.). (Illus.). 48p. (YA). pap. 11.75 *(978-1-4358-9691-8(2));* (gr. 5-8). lib. bdg. 29.25 *(978-1-4358-9685-7(8))* Rosen Publishing Group, Inc., The. (Rosen Reference).

Stewart, Melissa. You've Got Nerve! The Secrets of the Brain & Nerves. 2010. (Gross & Goofy Body 2 Ser.). 48p. (gr. 3). 29.93 *(978-0-7614-4157-1(3))* Marshall Cavendish GBR. Dist: Marshall Cavendish Corp.

Taylor-Butler, Christine. The Nervous System. 2008. (True Book(tm), a — Health & the Human Body Ser.). (ENG.). 48p. (J). (gr. 3-7). 31.00 *(978-0-531-16861-5(1));* pap. 6.95 *(978-0-531-20735-2(8))* Scholastic Library Publishing. (Children's Pr.).

Tieck, Sarah. Nervous System, 1 vol. 2011. (Body Systems Ser.). (ENG., Illus.). 32p. (J). (gr. 2-5). lib. bdg. 27.07 *(978-1-61613-500-3(X))* ABDO Publishing Co.

Viegas, Jennifer. The Revolution in Healing the Brain. (Library of Future Medicine Ser.). 64p. 2009. (gr. 5-5). 58.50 *(978-1-60853-633-7(5))* 2005. (Illus.). (YA). (gr. 7-12). lib. bdg. 31.95 *(978-0-8239-3668-7(6))* Rosen Publishing Group, Inc., The.

West, Krista. Biofeedback. 2007. (Gray Matter Ser.). (Illus.). 98p. (YA). (gr. 9-12). lib. bdg. 35.00 *(978-0-7910-9436-5(7))* Facts On File, Inc.

Williams, Mary E. Tourette Syndrome. 2012. (Perspectives on Diseases & Disorders Ser.). (ENG., Illus.). 144p. (gr. 10-12). lib. bdg. 44.30 *(978-0-7377-6360-7(4),* Greenhaven Pr., Inc.) Cengage Gale.

World Book, Inc Staff, contrib. by. The Nervous System. 2013. (J). *(978-0-7166-1846-1(X))* World Bk., Inc.

NESS, LOCH (SCOTLAND)

Brassey, Richard. Nessie the Loch Ness Monster. 2010. (ENG., Illus.). 24p. (gr. k-2). pap. 9.99 *(978-1-4440-0056-6(X),* Orion Children's Bks.) Hachette Children's Group GBR. Dist: Hachette Bk. Group.

DeMolay, Jack. The Loch Ness Monster: Scotland's Mystery Beast. 2009. (Jr. Graphic Mysteries Ser.). (ENG.). 24p. (J). (gr. 2-3). 47.90 *(978-1-61513-849-4(8),* PowerKids Pr.) Rosen Publishing Group, Inc., The.

NETHERLANDS

Abramson, Ann. Who Was Anne Frank? Harrison, Nancy, illus. 2007. (Who Was... ? Ser.). 103p. (J). (gr. 4-7). 16.00 *(978-1-4177-6854-7(1),* Turtleback) Turtleback Bks.

Bowen, Richard. Vincent Van Gogh: Modern Artist. 2013. (People of Importance Ser.: 21). (Illus.). 32p. (J). (gr. 4-18). 19.95 *(978-1-4222-2858-6(4))* Mason Crest.

Dematons, Charlotte, illus. Holland & a Thousand Things about Holland. 2013. (ENG.). 176p. (J). (gr. 3). 29.95 *(978-1-935954-33-0(4),* 9781935954330) Lemniscaat USA.

Docalavich, Heather & Indovino, Shaina C. The Netherlands. Bruton, John, ed. 2012. (Major European Union Nations Ser.). 64p. (J). (gr. 7). 22.95 *(978-1-4222-2253-9(5))* Mason Crest.

Dunn, Joe. Anne Frank, 1 vol. 2007. (Bio-Graphics Ser.). (ENG., Illus.). 32p. (gr. 3-6). 28.50 *(978-1-60270-065-9(6),* Graphic Planet- Nonfiction) ABDO Publishing Co.

Kaltenhauser, Bettina & van Swol-Ulbrich, Hilly. When Abroad - Do As the Local Children Do: Ori's Guide for Young Expats. 2004. (ENG., Illus.). 112p. (J). pap. *(978-90-5594-262-6(6))* Cyan Communications GBR. Dist: Independent Pubs. Group.

Lossani, Chiara & van Gogh, Vincent. Vincent Van Gogh & the Colors of the Wind. Monaco, Octavia, illus. 2011. (ENG.). 36p. (YA). (gr. 2). 19.00 *(978-0-8028-5390-5(0),* Eerdmans Bks For Young Readers) Eerdmans, William B. Publishing Co.

Marran, James F. The Netherlands. 2003. (Modern World Nations Ser.). (Illus.). 150p. (gr. 6-12). 35.00 *(978-0-7910-7476-3(5),* Chelsea Hse.) Facts On File, Inc.

Raczka, Bob & Vermeer, Johannes. The Vermeer Interviews: Conversations with Seven Works of Art. 2009. (Bob Raczka's Art Adventures Ser.). (ENG.). 32p. (gr. 3-12). 25.26 *(978-0-8225-9402-4(1),* Millbrook Pr.) Lerner Publishing Group.

Seward, Pat & Lal, Sunandini Arora. Netherlands. 2nd rev. ed. 2005. (Cultures of the World Ser.). (Illus.). 144p. (gr. 6-10). lib. bdg. 42.79 *(978-0-7614-2052-1(5),* Benchmark Bks.) Marshall Cavendish Corp.

Van Maarsen, Jacqueline. A Friend Called Anne: One Girl's Story of War, Peace, & a Unique Friendship with Anne Frank. 2007. (Illus.). 163p. (J). (gr. 5-9). 14.65 *(978-0-7569-8146-4(8))* Perfection Learning Corp.

Yount, Lisa. Antoni Van Leeuwenhoek: Genius Discoverer of Microscopic Life. 2015. (Genius Scientists & Their Genius Ideas Ser.). 96p. (J). (gr. 5-12). pap. 10.95 *(978-0-7660-6526-0(X))* Enslow Pubs., Inc.

NETHERLANDS—FICTION

Abbott, Jacob. Rollo in Holland. 2008. 108p. 23.95 *(978-1-60664-820-9(9));* pap. 9.95 *(978-1-60664-065-4(8))* Aegypan.

Borden, Louise & Daly, Niki. The Greatest Skating Race: A World War II Story from the Netherlands. Daly, Niki, illus. 2004. (ENG., Illus.). 48p. (J). (gr. 4-7). 19.99 *(978-0-689-84502-4(2),* McElderry, Margaret K. Bks.) McElderry, Margaret K. Bks.

Brandeis, Madeline. The Little Dutch Tulip Girl. 2011. 194p. 42.95 *(978-1-258-09813-1(X))* Literary Licensing, LLC.

Brust, Beth Wagner. The Great Tulip Trade. Mattheson, Jenny, illus. 2005. (Step into Reading Ser.). 48p. (J). (gr. 1-3). 11.65 *(978-0-7569-5160-3(7))* Perfection Learning Corp.

Chambers, Aidan. Postcards from No Man's Land. (ENG.). 320p. (YA). (gr. 9-18). 2007. 10.00 *(978-0-14-240788-2(7))* 2004. reprint ed. 8.99 *(978-0-14-240145-3(5))* Penguin Young Readers Group. (Speak).

Cinema, Bobby. Princess School. 2012. 68p. 18.66 *(978-1-4669-3968-4(0));* 18p. pap. 8.66 *(978-1-4669-3967-7(2))* Trafford Publishing.

Comora, Madeleine. Rembrandt & Titus: Artist & Son. Locker, Thomas, illus. 2005. (ENG.). 32p. (J). (gr. 3-5). 17.95 *(978-1-55591-490-5(X))* Fulcrum Publishing.

Crain, Kira. SEK Statton. 2009. (GER.). 136p. 29.95 *(978-1-4092-6127-8(1))* Lulu Pr., Inc.

Cullen, Lyn. I Am Rembrandt's Daughter. 2011. 8.88 *(978-0-7848-3491-6(1),* Everbind) Marco Bk. Co.

Dematons, Charlotte. Holland. 2013. (ENG., Illus.). 56p. (J). (gr. -1). 19.95 *(978-1-935954-28-6(8),* 9781935954286) Lemniscaat USA.

Devries, Maggie. Hunger Journeys. 2012. (ENG.). 288p. (J). mass mkt. 7.99 *(978-1-55468-580-6(X),* Harper Trophy) HarperCollins Pubs.

di Vries, Maggie. Hunger Journeys. 2014. 240p. (YA). (gr. 8). pap. 8.99 *(978-0-06-231351-5(7))* HarperCollins Pubs.

Dodge, Mary Mapes. Hans Brinker, or the Silver Skates. 2007. 308p. (gr. 3-7). 32.95 *(978-1-4344-9309-5(1));* per. 19.95 *(978-1-4344-9308-8(3))* Wildside Pr., LLC.

—Hans Brinker or the Silver Skates A Story of Life in Holland. Doggett, Allen B., illus. 2004. reprint ed. pap. 34.95 *(978-1-4179-4127-8(8))* Kessinger Publishing, LLC.

—Hans Brinker; or, the Silver Skates (Dod. 2006. pap. *(978-1-4065-0961-8(2))* Dodo Pr.

Duble, Kathleen Benner. Quest. 2008. (ENG.). 256p. (J). (gr. 5-9). 17.99 *(978-1-4169-3386-1(7),* McElderry, Margaret K. Bks.) McElderry, Margaret K. Bks.

Flegg, Aubrey. Wings over Delft, Vol. 1. 2nd rev. ed. 2004. (Louise Trilogy Ser.: 01). (ENG.). 208p. (J). pap. 12.95 *(978-0-86278-886-5(2))* O'Brien Pr., Ltd., The IRL. Dist: Dufour Editions, Inc.

Fleming, Candace. Boxes for Katje. Dressen-McQueen, Stacey, illus. 2003. (ENG.). 40p. (J). (gr. -1-3). 18.99 *(978-0-374-30922-0(1),* 9780374309220, Farrar, Straus & Giroux (BYR)) Farrar, Straus & Giroux.

—Boxes for Katje. Dressen-McQueen, Stacey, illus. 2004. (YA). 27.95 incl. audio *(978-0-8045-6930-9(4),* SAC6930) Spoken Arts, Inc.

Garlick, Nicholas. Storm Horse. 2017. (J). pap. ***(978-0-545-90415-5(3))*** Scholastic, Inc.

Gottesfeld, Jeff. The Tree in the Courtyard: Looking Through Anne Frank's Window. McCarty, Peter, illus. 2016. (ENG.). 40p. (J). (gr. k-3). 17.99 *(978-0-385-75397-5(7));* lib. bdg. 20.99 *(978-0-385-75398-2(5))* Random Hse. Children's Bks. (Knopf Bks. for Young Readers).

Griffis, William. Dutch Fairy Tales for Young Folks. 2005. pap. 15.95 *(978-1-59605-348-9(8),* Cosimo Classics) Cosimo, Inc.

Griffis, William Elliot. Dutch Fairy Tales for Young Folks. 2004. reprint ed. pap. 1.99 *(978-1-4192-1705-0(4))* Kessinger Publishing, LLC.

Hapka, Catherine, pseud. Horse Diaries #12: Luna. Sanderson, Ruth, illus. 2015. (Horse Diaries). (ENG.). 160p. (J). (gr. 3-7). lib. bdg. 12.99 *(978-0-553-53371-2(1),* Random Hse. Bks. for Young Readers) Random Hse. Children's Bks.

—Luna. 2015. (Horse Diaries: 12). lib. bdg. 18.40 *(978-0-606-37711-9(5))* Turtleback Bks.

Hering, Marianne & Younger, Marshal. Escape to the Hiding Place. 2012. (AIO Imagination Station Bks.: 9). (ENG., Illus.).

MNO

128p. (J). pap. 4.99 *(978-1-58997-693-1(2))* Tyndale Hse. Pubs.

Hesse, Monica. Girl in the Blue Coat. (ENG.). 320p. (gr. 7-17). 2017. (YA). pap. 9.99 *(978-0-316-26063-3(0))* 2016. 17.99 *(978-0-316-26060-2(6))* 2016. (YA). E-Book *(978-0-316-26064-0(9))* Little, Brown Bks. for Young Readers.

—Girl in the Blue Coat. 2017. (YA). lib. bdg. 20.85 ***(978-0-606-39918-0(6))*** Turtleback Bks.

Heuvel, Eric & Miller, Lorraine T. A Family Secret. Miller, Lorraine T., tr. from DUT. Heuvel, Eric, illus. 2009. (ENG., Illus.). 64p. (J). (gr. 5-9). pap. 11.99 *(978-0-374-42265-3(6)*, 9780374422653) Square Fish.

Kuijer, Guus & Nieuwenhuizen, John. The Book of Everything. 2006. ix, 101p. (J). 16.99 *(978-0-439-74919-0(0)*, Levine, Arthur A. Bks.) Scholastic, Inc.

Lindelauf, Benny. Nine Open Arms. 2014. (ENG., Illus.). 264p. (J). (gr. 3). 16.95 *(978-1-59270-146-9(9))* Enchanted Lion Bks., LLC.

Lucy Fitch Perkins. The Dutch Twins. 2005. pap. *(978-1-905432-05-9(4))* Dodo Pr.

Miller, Jennifer. Run, Rasputin, Run! Trials & Friendships (Book 2) 2006. (ENG., Illus.). 172p. per. 14.85 *(978-1-4120-8494-9(6))* Trafford Publishing.

Osborne, William. Winter's Bullet. 2016. (ENG.). 240p. (J). (gr. 7). 18.99 *(978-0-545-85344-6(3)*, Chicken Hse., The) Scholastic, Inc.

Peet, Mal. Tamar: A Novel of Espionage, Passion, & Betrayal. (ENG., Illus.). 432p. (YA). (gr. 9). 2008. pap. 8.99 *(978-0-7636-4063-7(8))* 2007. 17.99 *(978-0-7636-3488-9(3))* Candlewick Pr.

Perkins, Lucy Fitch. The Dutch Twins. 2004. reprint ed. pap. 1.99 *(978-1-4192-6040-7(5))* Kessinger Publishing, LLC.

Polak, Monique. What World Is Left. 1 vol. 2008. (ENG.). 232p. (YA). (gr. 7-12). pap. 12.95 *(978-1-55143-847-4(X))* Orca Bk. Pubs. USA.

Priestley, Chris. Through Dead Eyes. 2014. (ENG.). 240p. (YA). (gr. 7). pap. 13.99 *(978-1-4088-1107-8(3)*, 9781408811078, Bloomsbury USA Childrens) Bloomsbury Publishing USA.

Prins, Piet. The Flying Phantom. 2006. (Illus.). 142p. (J). pap. *(978-1-894666-45-9(3))* Inheritance Pubns.

—The Grim Reaper. 2006. (Illus.). 130p. (J). pap. *(978-1-894666-74-9(7))* Inheritance Pubns.

—The Haunted Castle. 2006. (Illus.). 139p. (J). pap. *(978-1-894666-44-2(5))* Inheritance Pubns.

—Hideout in the Swamp. 2006. (Illus.). 136p. (J). pap. *(978-1-894666-73-2(9))* Inheritance Pubns.

—The Lonely Sentinel. 2006. (Illus.). 140p. (J). pap. *(978-1-894666-72-5(0))* Inheritance Pubns.

—The Mystery of the Abandoned Mill. Kramer, Jaap, illus. 2006. 127p. (J). pap. *(978-1-894666-48-0(8))* Inheritance Pubns.

—The Sailing Sleuths. Kramer, Jaap, illus. 2006. 137p. (J). pap. *(978-1-894666-46-6(1))* Inheritance Pubns.

—Scout's Distant Journey. 2006. (Illus.). 141p. (J). pap. *(978-1-894666-49-7(6))* Inheritance Pubns.

—The Search for Sheltie. Kramer, Jaap, illus. 2006. 137p. (J). pap. *(978-1-894666-43-5(7))* Inheritance Pubns.

—Stefan Derksen's Polar Adventure. 2004. (Illus.). 237p. (J). pap. *(978-1-894666-67-1(4))* Inheritance Pubns.

—The Treasure of Rodensteyn Castle. Kramer, Jaap, illus. 2006. 132p. (J). pap. *(978-1-894666-47-3(X))* Inheritance Pubns.

Prins, Piet & McAdam, Fraser. The Beggars Victory: The Sequel to Dispelling the Tyranny. 2006. (Illus.). 173p. (J). pap. *(978-0-921100-53-9(1))* Inheritance Pubns.

—For the Heart of Holland. 2008. (J). *(978-1-894666-20-6(8))* Inheritance Pubns.

Propp, Vera W. When the Soldiers Were Gone: A Novel. 2006. 101p. (J). (gr. 4-8). reprint ed. 15.00 *(978-1-4223-5310-3(9))* DIANE Publishing Co.

Robb, Jackie & Stringle, Berny. The Story of Pea Brain. Duncan, Karen & Stringle, Sam, illus. 2004. (Bang on the Door Ser.). 32p. (YA). pap. *(978-1-85602-383-2(4)*, Pavilion Children's Books) Pavilion Bks.

Rogers, Gregory. The Hero of Little Street. Rogers, Gregory, illus. 2012. (ENG., Illus.). 32p. (J). (gr. k-3). 17.99 *(978-1-59643-729-6(4)*, 9781596437296) Roaring Brook Pr.

Smet, Margaret. Exploring Amsterdam from A to Z. 2009. 32p. 18.50 *(978-1-4092-0577-7(0))* Lulu Pr., Inc.

Spring, Debbie. The Righteous Smuggler, 1 vol. 2006. (Holocaust Remembrance Ser.). (ENG., Illus.). 160p. (J). (gr. 4-7). pap. 9.95 *(978-1-896764-97-5(5))* Second Story Pr. CAN. Dist: Orca Bk. Pubs. USA.

Stilton, Thea. Thea Stilton & the Great Tulip Heist. 2014. (Thea Stilton Ser.: 18). (ENG.). 176p. (J). (gr. 2-5). pap. 8.99 *(978-0-545-55628-6(7)*, Scholastic Paperbacks) Scholastic, Inc.

—Thea Stilton & the Great Tulip Heist. 2014. (Thea Stilton Ser.: 18). lib. bdg. 19.65 *(978-0-606-35386-1(0))* Turtleback Bks.

Van Ryk, Laverne. A Garland of Emeralds. 2006. (Illus.). 305p. 31.50 *(978-1-4122-0156-8(X))* Trafford Publishing.

Van Stockum, Hilda. The Borrowed House. 2016. 203p. (J). pap. *(978-1-930900-89-9(9))* Purple Hse. Pr.

—A Day on Skates: The Story of a Dutch Picnic. Van Stockum, Hilda, illus. 2007. (Illus.). 40p. (J). (gr. 1). 19.95 *(978-1-932350-18-0(7))* Bethlehem Bks.

William Elliot, Griffis. Dutch Fairy Tales for Young Folks. 2007. (ENG.). 140p. pap. 18.99 *(978-1-4264-3924-7(5))* Creative Media Partners, LLC.

Wilson, Martha. Latin Primer II - Student. 3rd ed. 2003. (ENG & LAT.). 138p. (gr. 3-6). spiral bd. 17.00 *(978-1-885767-52-3(8))* Canon Pr.

NETHERLANDS—HISTORY

Brown, Jonatha A. Anne Frank. Acosta, Tatiana & Gutierrez, Guillermo, trs. 2004. (Gente Que Hay Que Conocer Ser.). (SPA., Illus.). 24p. (gr. 1-4). lib. bdg. 22.00 *(978-0-8368-4351-4(7)*, Weekly Reader Leveled Readers) Stevens, Gareth Publishing LLLP.

Docalavich, Heather. The Netherlands. 2007. (European Union Ser.). (Illus.). 88p. (YA). (gr. 4-7). lib. bdg. 21.95 *(978-1-4222-0057-5(4))* Mason Crest.

Docalavich, Heather & Indovino, Shaina Carmel. The Netherlands. 2012. (J). pap. *(978-1-4222-2284-3(5))* Mason Crest.

Gibson, Karen Bush. New Netherland: The Dutch Settle the Hudson Valley. 2006. (Building America Ser.). (Illus.). 48p. (J). (gr. 3-7). lib. bdg. 29.95 *(978-1-58415-461-7(6))* Mitchell Lane Pubs., Inc.

Hintz, Martin. The Netherlands. 2015. (ENG., Illus.). 144p. (J). lib. bdg. *(978-0-531-21697-2(7)*, Orchard Bks.) Scholastic, Inc.

Huey, Lois Miner. American Archeology Uncovers the Dutch Colonies. 2009. (American Archaeology Ser.). 64p. (gr. 5-6). 31.36 *(978-0-7614-4263-9(4))* Marshall Cavendish Corp.

Landau, Jennifer. Vincent Van Gogh: Master of Post-Impressionist Painting. 2015. (Britannica Beginner Bios Ser.). (ENG., Illus.). 32p. (J). 23.45 *(978-1-62275-946-0(X)*, Britannica Educational Publishing) Rosen Publishing Group, Inc., The.

McDowell, Pamela. Anne Frank. 2014. (J). *(978-1-4896-2456-7(2))* Weigl Pubs., Inc.

Owings, Lisa. The Netherlands. 2012. (Exploring Countries Ser.). (ENG., Illus.). 32p. (J). (gr. 3-7). lib. bdg. 26.95 *(978-1-60014-766-1(6)*, Blastoff! Readers) Bellwether Media.

Parker, Lewis K. Dutch Colonies in the Americas. (European Colonies in the Americas Ser.). 24p. 2009. (gr. 2-2). 42.50 *(978-1-61512-316-2(4))* 2003. (Illus.). (J). lib. bdg. 22.60 *(978-0-8239-6472-7(8))* Rosen Publishing Group, Inc., The. (PowerKids Pr.).

Seward, Pat, et al. Netherlands. 2016. (Cultures of the World (r) Ser.). (Illus.). 144p. (J). (gr. 5-5). 47.07 *(978-1-5026-1695-1(5))* Cavendish Square Publishing.

Slier, Deborah & Shine, Ian, eds. Hidden Letters, 1 vol. Van Binsbergen-Pritchard, Marion, tr. from DUT. 2008. (ENG., Illus.). 32p. (YA). (gr. 7-18). 35.00 *(978-1-887734-88-2(0))* Star Bright Bks., Inc.

Spence, Kelly. Cultural Traditions in the Netherlands. 2016. (ENG., Illus.). 32p. (J). *(978-0-7787-8089-2(9))* Crabtree Publishing Co.

Thomson, Ruth. Vincent Van Gogh, 01 vols., 1. 2016. (Inspiring Artists Ser.). (ENG.). 48p. (J). 30.25 *(978-1-5081-7056-3(8)*, Rosen Young Adult) Rosen Publishing Group, Inc., The.

Waxman, Laura Hamilton. Anne Frank. 2009. (History Maker Biographies Ser.). (ENG.). 48p. (gr. 3-6). 27.93 *(978-0-7613-4221-2(4)*, Lerner Pubns.) Lerner Publishing Group.

Whitehurst, Susan. The Pilgrims Before the Mayflower. 2009. (Library of the Pilgrims Ser.). 24p. (gr. 3-4). 42.50 *(978-1-60853-915-4(6)*, PowerKids Pr.) Rosen Publishing Group, Inc., The.

Wood, Alix. Johannes Vermeer. 2013. (Artists Through the Ages Ser.). (ENG., Illus.). 32p. (J). (gr. 3-6). pap. 10.00 *(978-1-61533-633-3(8))*; lib. bdg. 25.25 *(978-1-61533-623-4(0))* Windmill Bks.

—Vincent Van Gogh. 2013. (Artists Through the Ages Ser.). (ENG., Illus.). 32p. (gr. 3-6). 25.25 *(978-1-61533-622-7(2))*; pap. 10.00 *(978-1-61533-631-9(1))* Windmill Bks.

Yount, Lisa. Antoni Van Leeuwenhoek: Genius Discoverer of Microscopic Life. 2015. (Genius Scientists & Their Genius Ideas Ser.). 96p. (J). (gr. 5-12). 27.94 *(978-0-7660-6525-3(1))* Enslow Pubs., Inc.

Zaczek, Iain. Vincent Van Gogh. 2014. (Great Artists Ser.). 32p. (J). (gr. 3-6). pap. 63.00 *(978-1-4824-1249-9(7))* Stevens, Gareth Publishing LLLP.

NETHERLANDS—HISTORY—GERMAN OCCUPATION, 1940-1945

Alma, Ann. Brave Deeds: How One Family Saved Many from the Nazis. 2008. (ENG., Illus.). 96p. (J). (gr. 3-7). 17.95 *(978-0-88899-791-3(4))* Groundwood Bks. CAN. Dist: Publishers Group West (PGW).

NEUMANN, JOHN, SAINT, 1811-1860

Brown, Laura Rhoderica. Saint John Neumann: Missionary to Immigrants. Esquinaldo, Virginia, illus. 2016. (J). pap. *(978-0-8198-9066-5(9))* Pauline Bks. & Media.

NEUMANN, JOHN NEPOMUCENE, SAINT, 1811-1860

see Neumann, John, Saint, 1811-1860

NEUROLOGY

see Nervous System

NEUTRINOS

Bortz, Alfred B. The Neutrino. 2004. (Library of Subatomic Particles Ser.). (Illus.). 64p. (gr. 7-12). lib. bdg. 31.95 *(978-0-8239-4529-0(4))* Rosen Publishing Group, Inc., The.

Bortz, Fred. The Neutrino. 2009. (Library of Subatomic Particles Ser.). 64p. (gr. 6-6). 58.50 *(978-1-60853-879-9(6))* Rosen Publishing Group, Inc., The.

NEUTRON, JIMMY (FICTITIOUS CHARACTER)—FICTION

Banks, Steven. Thanks a Lot, Robo-Turkey! LaPadula, Tom, illus. 2005. (Adventures of Jimmy Neutron Ser.: 10). 24p. (J). lib. bdg. 15.00 *(978-1-59054-787-8(X))* Fitzgerald Bks.

Mattern, Joanne. Dino Disaster! Spaziante, Patrick & Giles, Mike, illus. 2005. (Adventures of Jimmy Neutron Ser.: 9). 24p. (J). lib. bdg. 15.00 *(978-1-59054-782-3(9))* Fitzgerald Bks.

McCann, Jesse Leon. The Science Project. Fruchter, Jason, illus. 2003. 61p. (J). *(978-0-439-56271-3(6))* Scholastic, Inc.

NEVADA

Brown, Jonatha A. Nevada. 2006. (Portraits of the States Ser.). (Illus.). 32p. (gr. 2-6). pap. 10.50 *(978-0-8368-4690-4(7))*; lib. bdg. 26.00 *(978-0-8368-4671-3(0))* Stevens, Gareth Publishing LLLP. (Gareth Stevens Learning Library).

Coerr, Eleanor. S Is for Silver: A Nevada Alphabet. Park, Darcie, illus. 2004. (State Ser.). (ENG.). 40p. (J). 17.95 *(978-1-58536-117-5(8))* Sleeping Bear Pr.

Deford, Debra & Craig, Janet. Nevada: The Silver State. 2003. (World Almanac Library of the States). (Illus.). 48p. (gr. 4-9). pap. 14.05 *(978-0-8368-5325-4(3))*; lib. bdg. 31.00 *(978-0-8368-5154-0(4))* Stevens, Gareth Publishing LLLP. (Gareth Stevens Learning Library).

Fein, E. How to Draw Nevada's Sights & Symbols. 2009. (Kid's Guide to Drawing America Ser.). 32p. (gr. k-k). 50.50 *(978-1-61511-077-3(1)*, PowerKids Pr.) Rosen Publishing Group, Inc., The.

Heinrichs, Ann. Nevada. 2014. (America the Beautiful Ser.: 3). (ENG.). 144p. (J). lib. bdg. 40.00 *(978-0-531-24893-5(3))* Scholastic Library Publishing.

Hicks, Terry Allan. Nevada. 2013. (It's My State 2nd Ed 5 Ser.). 80p. (J). (gr. 4-8). pap. 17.64 *(978-1-62712-101-9(3))* Cavendish Square Publishing.

—Nevada. 2005. (It's My State! Ser.). (Illus.). 80p. (J). (gr. 4-7). lib. bdg. 27.07 *(978-0-7614-1860-3(1)*, Benchmark Bks.) Marshall Cavendish Corp.

Labella, Susan. Nevada. 2007. (Rookie Read-About Geography Ser.). (Illus.). 31p. (J). (gr. 1-2). 20.50 *(978-0-516-25467-8(7)*, Children's Pr.) Scholastic Library Publishing.

Lynette, Rachel. Area 51. 2009. (Mysterious Encounters Ser.). (ENG., Illus.). 48p. (J). (gr. 4-8). lib. bdg. 29.00 *(978-0-7377-4410-1(3)*, LML02109-245411, Kidhaven) Cengage Gale.

Marsh, Carole. Nevada Current Events Projects: 30 Cool, Activities, Crafts, Experiments & More for Kids to Do to Learn about Your State! 2003. (Nevada Experience Ser.). 32p. (gr. k-5). pap. 5.95 *(978-0-635-02047-5(5)*, Marsh, Carole Bks.) Gallopade International.

—Nevada Geography Projects: 30 Cool, Activities, Crafts, Experiments & More for Kids to Do to Learn about Your State! 2003. (Nevada Experience Ser.). 32p. (gr. k-5). pap. 5.95 *(978-0-635-01847-2(0)*, Marsh, Carole Bks.) Gallopade International.

—Nevada Government Projects: 30 Cool, Activities, Crafts, Experiments & More for Kids to Do to Learn about Your State! 2003. (Nevada Experience Ser.). 32p. (gr. k-5). pap. 5.95 *(978-0-635-01947-9(7)*, Marsh, Carole Bks.) Gallopade International.

—Nevada People Projects: 30 Cool, Activities, Crafts, Experiments & More for Kids to Do to Learn about Your State! 2003. (Nevada Experience Ser.). 32p. (gr. k-5). pap. 5.95 *(978-0-635-01997-4(3)*, Marsh, Carole Bks.) Gallopade International.

—Nevada Symbols & Facts Projects: 30 Cool, Activities, Crafts, Experiments & More for Kids to Do to Learn about Your State! 2003. (Nevada Experience Ser.). 32p. (gr. k-5). pap. 5.95 *(978-0-635-01897-7(7)*, Marsh, Carole Bks.) Gallopade International.

Mills, Jordan. Nevada. 2016. (States Ser.). (ENG., Illus.). 32p. (gr. 3-4). lib. bdg. 27.32 *(978-1-5157-0415-7(7))* Next Page Pr., The.

Murray, Julie. Nevada, 1 vol. 2006. (United States Ser.). (ENG., Illus.). 32p. (gr. 2-4). 27.07 *(978-1-59197-687-5(1)*, Buddy Bks.) ABDO Publishing Co.

Obregon, Jose Maria. Nevada. Brusca, Maria Cristina, tr. from ENG. 2006. (Bilingual Library of the United States of America Ser.: Set 2). (ENG & SPA., Illus.). 32p. (J). (gr. 3-6). lib. bdg. 25.25 *(978-1-4042-3093-4(9))* Rosen Publishing Group, Inc., The.

Obregón, José María. Nevada. 2009. (Bilingual Library of the United States of America Ser.). (ENG & SPA.). 32p. (gr. 2-2). 47.90 *(978-1-60853-372-5(7)*, Editorial Buenas Letras) Rosen Publishing Group, Inc., The.

Sirvaitis, Karen. Nevada. 2012. (J). lib. bdg. 25.26 *(978-0-7613-4544-2(2)*, Lerner Pubns.) Lerner Publishing Group.

Voz, Samuel. Exploring the Great Basin. 2013. (InfoMax Readers Ser.). (ENG.). 24p. (J). (gr. 3-4). pap. 49.50 *(978-1-4777-2492-7(3))*; pap. 8.25 *(978-1-4777-2491-0(5))* Rosen Publishing Group, Inc., The. (Rosen Classroom).

NEVADA—FICTION

Acton, Vanessa. Backfire. 2017. (Day of Disaster Ser.). (ENG.). 112p. (gr. 6-12). (J). 26.65 *(978-1-5124-2775-2(6))*; (YA). 12.99 ***(978-1-5124-3504-7(X)***, Darby Creek); (YA). 39.99 ***(978-1-5124-2782-0(9)***, Darby Creek); (YA). 39.99 ***(978-1-5124-3503-0(1)***, Darby Creek) Lerner Publishing Group.

Ayarbe, Heidi. Wanted. 2012. (ENG.). 400p. (YA). (gr. 9). 17.99 *(978-0-06-199388-6(3))* HarperCollins Pubs.

Bond, Gwenda. Girl in the Shadows, 0 vols. 2016. (Cirque American Ser.: 2). (ENG.). 380p. (YA). (gr. 9-13). pap. 9.99 *(978-1-5039-5393-2(9)*, 9781503953932, Skyscape) Amazon Publishing.

Brand, Mary. Aspen Cat: Adventurer Extraordinaire. Roberts, Tempie, illus. 2009. 44p. pap. 24.95 *(978-1-60749-165-1(6))* America Star Bks.

Carlson, Melody. Lost in Las Vegas, 1 vol. 2014. (Carter House Girls Ser.). (ENG.). 208p. (YA). pap. 9.99 *(978-0-310-74716-1(3))* Zondervan.

Farley, Terri. Heartbreak Bronco. 2004. 227p. (J). lib. bdg. 16.92 *(978-1-4242-0830-2(0))* Fitzgerald Bks.

—Rain Forest Rose Bk. 3. 2007. (Phantom Stallion: Wild Horse Island Ser.: 3). (ENG.). 224p. (J). (gr. 5-18). pap. 4.99 *(978-0-06-088616-5(1))* HarperCollins Pubs.

Fields, Jan. Tame Tahoe Tessie, 1 vol. Brundage, Scott, illus. 2014. (Monster Hunters Ser.). (ENG.). 80p. (J). (gr. 8-12). 27.07 *(978-1-62402-047-6(X))* Magic Wagon.

Gamble, Adam & Jasper, Mark. Good Night Nevada. Rosen, Anne & Veno, Joe, illus. 2012. (Good Night Our World Ser.). (ENG.). 20p. (J). (gr. k — 1). bds. 9.95 *(978-1-60219-060-3(7))* Good Night Bks.

Giles, Lamar. Overturned. 2017. (ENG.). 352p. (J). (gr. 7). 17.99 *(978-0-545-81250-4(X)*, Scholastic Pr.) Scholastic, Inc.

Hancock, H. Irving. The Young Engineers in Nevada. rev. ed. 2006. 220p. 27.95 *(978-1-4218-1754-5(3))*; pap. 12.95 *(978-1-4218-1854-2(X))* 1st World Publishing, Inc. (1st World Library - Literary Society).

—The Young Engineers in Nevada. 2007. 188p. per. *(978-1-4065-1995-2(2))* Dodo Pr.

Hautman, Pete. All-In. 2012. (ENG.). 208p. (YA). (gr. 7). pap. 8.99 *(978-1-4424-3335-9(3)*, Simon & Schuster Bks. For Young Readers) Simon & Schuster Bks. For Young Readers.

—All-In. 2008. (ENG., Illus.). 208p. (YA). (gr. 7). mass mkt. 5.99 *(978-1-4169-1326-9(2)*, Simon Pulse) Simon Pulse.

Hemphill, Helen. Long Gone Daddy. (ENG.). 176p. 2014. (YA). (gr. 6). pap. 8.95 *(978-1-62091-737-4(8))* 2006. (J). (gr. 8-12). 16.95 *(978-1-932425-38-3(1)*, Lemniscaat) Boyds Mills Pr.

Hendershot, Eric. A Horse for Christmas. 2012. pap. 8.99 *(978-1-4621-1078-0(9))* Cedar Fort, Inc./CFI Distribution.

Hermes, Patricia. Black Cloud, No. 8. Sheckels, Astrid, illus. 2012. (Horse Diaries). (ENG.). 176p. (J). (gr. 3-7). pap. 7.99 *(978-0-375-86881-8(X)*, Random Hse. Bks. for Young Readers) Random Hse. Children's Bks.

—Black Cloud. 2012. (Horse Diaries: 8). lib. bdg. 18.40 *(978-0-606-26553-9(8)*, Turtleback) Turtleback Bks.

Hopkins, Ellen. Burned. 2013. (ENG., Illus.). 560p. (YA). (gr. 9). pap. 12.99 *(978-1-4424-9461-9(1)*, McElderry, Margaret K. Bks.) McElderry, Margaret K. Bks.

—Perfect. (ENG., (YA). (gr. 9). 2013. Illus.). 656p. pap. 12.99 *(978-1-4169-8325-5(2))* 2011. 640p. 18.99 *(978-1-4169-8324-8(4))* McElderry, Margaret K. Bks. (McElderry, Margaret K. Bks.).

—Tilt. (ENG., (YA). (gr. 9). 2014. Illus.). 624p. pap. 12.99 *(978-1-4169-8331-6(7))* 2012. 608p. 18.99 *(978-1-4169-8330-9(9))* McElderry, Margaret K. Bks. (McElderry, Margaret K. Bks.).

Horowitz, Anthony. Nightrise. 2008. (Gatekeepers Ser.: 3). (ENG.). 368p. (J). (gr. 3-7). pap. 8.99 *(978-0-439-68007-3(7)*, Scholastic Paperbacks) Scholastic, Inc.

Horvath, Polly. Northward to the Moon. 2012. (ENG.). 256p. (J). (gr. 5-8). 7.99 *(978-0-307-92980-8(9)*, Yearling) Random Hse. Children's Bks.

Howe, Norma. Angel in Vegas: The Chronicles of Noah Sark. 2009. (ENG., Illus.). 256p. (YA). (gr. 7-18). 16.99 *(978-0-7636-3985-3(0))* Candlewick Pr.

Inagaki, Riichiro. Eyeshield 21, Vol. 12. Murata, Yusuke, illus. 2007. (ENG.). 208p. pap. 9.99 *(978-1-4215-1061-3(8))* Viz Media.

—Eyeshield 21, Vol. 13. Murata, Yusuke, illus. 2007. (ENG.). 216p. pap. 7.99 *(978-1-4215-1062-0(6))* Viz Media.

Ius, Dawn. Overdrive. 2016. (ENG., Illus.). 352p. (YA). (gr. 9). 17.99 *(978-1-4814-3944-2(8)*, Simon Pulse) Simon Pulse.

Jacobs, Lily. The Littlest Bunny in Las Vegas: An Easter Adventure. 2015. (ENG.). 32p. (J). (-3). 9.99 *(978-1-4926-1099-1(2)*, Sourcebooks Jabberwocky) Sourcebooks, Inc.

—The Littlest Bunny in Nevada: An Easter Adventure. Dunn, Robert, illus. 2015. (ENG.). 32p. (J). (-3). 9.99 *(978-1-4926-1135-6(2)*, Sourcebooks Jabberwocky) Sourcebooks, Inc.

Jaffe, Michele. Bad Kitty. 2006. (Bad Kitty Ser.: Bk. 1). (ENG., Illus.). 288p. (YA). (gr. 7-12). 16.99 *(978-0-06-078108-8(4))* HarperCollins Pubs.

—Kitty Kitty. 2008. (Bad Kitty Ser.: Bk. 2). 320p. (YA). (gr. 7-18). lib. bdg. 17.89 *(978-0-06-078114-9(9)*, HarperTeen) HarperCollins Pubs.

James, Eric. A Halloween Scare in Las Vegas. Le Ray, Marina, illus. 2015. (ENG.). 32p. (J). (-5). 9.99 *(978-1-4926-2378-6(4)*, 9781492623786, Sourcebooks Jabberwocky) Sourcebooks, Inc.

—A Halloween Scare in Nevada. Le Ray, Marina, illus. 2015. (ENG.). 32p. (J). (-5). 9.99 *(978-1-4926-2386-1(5)*, 9781492623861, Sourcebooks Jabberwocky) Sourcebooks, Inc.

—Santa's Sleigh Is on Its Way to Las Vegas: A Christmas Adventure. Dunn, Robert, illus. 2016. (ENG.). 32p. (J). (-2). 12.99 *(978-1-4926-4332-6(7)*, 9781492643326, Sourcebooks Jabberwocky) Sourcebooks, Inc.

—Santa's Sleigh Is on Its Way to Nevada: A Christmas Adventure. Dunn, Robert, illus. 2016. (ENG.). 32p. (J). (-2). 12.99 *(978-1-4926-4340-1(8)*, 9781492643401, Sourcebooks Jabberwocky) Sourcebooks, Inc.

Jan, Young. Starting the Colt. 2014. (ENG.). 174p. (J). pap. 12.00 *(978-1-937849-10-8(4))* Raven Publishing Inc. of Montana.

Kelso, Mary Jean. Andy & Spirit in the Big Rescue. Snider, K. C., illus. 2009. 24p. pap. 10.95 *(978-1-935137-67-2(0))* Guardian Angel Publishing, Inc.

—Andy & Spirit Meet the Rodeo Queen. Snider, K. C., illus. 2010. 24p. pap. 10.95 *(978-1-61633-031-6(7))* Guardian Angel Publishing, Inc.

Kirov, Erica. The Chalice of Immortality. 2011. (ENG.). 208p. (J). (gr. 4-7). pap. 7.99 *(978-1-4022-1503-2(7)*, Sourcebooks Jabberwocky) Sourcebooks, Inc.

—Magickeepers: The Eternal Hourglass. Fortune, Eric, illus. 2010. (ENG.). 256p. (J). (gr. 4-7). pap. 10.99 *(978-1-4022-3855-0(X)*, Sourcebooks Jabberwocky) Sourcebooks, Inc.

Kristina Simmons. Winter Beauty. 2010. 192p. pap. 13.95 *(978-1-4401-4449-3(4))* iUniverse, Inc.

Lawrence, Caroline. P. K. Pinkerton & the Deadly Desperados. 2013. (P. K. Pinkerton Ser.: 1). (ENG.). 304p. (J). (gr. 3-7). pap. 7.99 *(978-0-14-242381-3(5)*, Puffin Books) Penguin Young Readers Group.

—P. K. Pinkerton & the Pistol-Packing Widows. 2015. (P. K. Pinkerton Ser.: 3). (ENG.). 320p. (J). (gr. 3-7). 7.99 *(978-0-14-751130-0(5)*, Puffin Books) Penguin Young Readers Group.

Leavitt, Lindsey. The Chapel Wars. 2014. (ENG.). 304p. (YA). (gr. 7). 17.99 *(978-1-59990-788-8(7)*, 9781599907888, Bloomsbury USA Childrens) Bloomsbury Publishing USA.

Lee, Sharon Alberta. Mickey of Las Vegas. 2009. 32p. (J). 31.99 *(978-1-4363-4642-9(8))* Xlibris Corp.

Love, Jessica. In Real Life: A Novel. 2016. (ENG.). 240p. (YA). 18.99 *(978-1-250-06471-4(6)*, 9781250064714, St. Martin's Griffin) St. Martin's Pr.

Lu, Marie. Prodigy: The Graphic Novel. 2016. (Legend Graphic Novels Ser.: 2). lib. bdg. 26.95 *(978-0-606-38425-4(1))* Turtleback Bks.

Magoon, Kekla. Camo Girl. 2012. (ENG.). 224p. (J). (gr. 3-9). pap. 7.99 *(978-1-4169-7805-3(4)*, Aladdin) Simon & Schuster Children's Publishing.

—Camo Girl. 2011. (ENG., Illus.). 224p. (J). (gr. 3-9). 16.99 *(978-1-4169-7804-6(6)*, Simon & Schuster/Paula Wiseman Bks.) Simon & Schuster/Paula Wiseman Bks.

Mariotte, Jeff. Fall. 2011. (Witch Season Ser.). (ENG.). 320p. (YA). (gr. 9). pap. 14.99 *(978-1-4424-3099-0(0)*, Simon Pulse) Simon Pulse.

Marsh, Carole. The Mystery at Area 51. Friedlander, Randolyn, illus. 2011. (Carole Marsh Mysteries Ser.). 32p. pap. 7.99 *(978-0-635-07961-9(5)*, Marsh, Carole Mysteries) Gallopade International.

—The Mystery in Las Vegas. 2009. (Real Kids, Real Places Ser.). (Illus.). 145p. (J). lib. bdg. 18.99 *(978-0-635-07045-6(6)*, Marsh, Carole Mysteries) Gallopade International.

Michael Batdorf. Pair of Jacks: A Novel. 2009. 332p. 29.95 *(978-1-4401-4482-0(6))*; pap. 19.95 *(978-1-4401-4479-0(6))* iUniverse, Inc.

O'Neill, Elizabeth. Alfred Visits Nevada. 2007. (ENG., Illus.). 24p. (J). pap. 12.00 *(978-0-9799121-1-5(3))* Global Business Information Strategies, Inc.
Ostow, Micol. Gettin' Lucky. 2012. (Romantic Comedies Ser.). (ENG.). 256p. (YA). (gr. 9). pap. 12.99 *(978-1-4424-8568-6(X)*, Simon Pulse) Simon Pulse.
Otis, James. Dick in the Desert. 2005. reprint ed. pap. 15.95 *(978-1-4179-0335-1(X))* Kessinger Publishing, LLC.
Painchaud, Michelle. Pretending to Be Erica. 2015. (ENG.). 272p. (YA). (gr. 7). 17.99 *(978-0-670-01497-2(4)*, Viking Books for Young Readers) Penguin Young Readers Group.
Pierson, Jan. The Haunted Horse of Gold Hill. 2005. (Ghostowners Ser.: Vol. 4). (Illus.). 109p. (J). per. 9.95 *(978-0-9721800-3-0(6))* WildWest Publishing.
Platt, Chris. Moon Shadow. 2006. (ENG.). 176p. (J). (gr. 3-7). 14.95 *(978-1-56145-382-5(X))* Peachtree Pubs.
Ralphson, G. Harvey. Boy Scouts in Death Valley. 2005. pap. 27.95 *(978-1-885529-51-0(1))* Stevens Publishing.
Reichart, George. A Bag of Lucky Rice. Mitchell, Mark, illus. 2004. (ENG.). 160p. pap. 10.95 *(978-1-56792-278-3(3))* Godine, David R. Pub.
Salter, Sydney. My Big Nose & Other Natural Disasters. 2009. (ENG., Illus.). 352p. (J). (gr. 7-18). pap. 19.95 *(978-0-15-206643-7(8))* Houghton Mifflin Harcourt Publishing Co.
Sargent, Dave & Sargent, Pat. Gus: (Slate Grullo) Be Thankful, 30 vols., Vol. 32. Lenoir, Jane, illus. 2003. (Saddle up Ser.: Vol. 32). 42p. (J). lib. bdg. 23.60 *(978-1-56763-693-2(4))*; pap. 10.95 *(978-1-56763-694-9(2))* Ozark Publishing.
Silvano, Wendi. Love Is All Around Las Vegas. Czernichowska, Joanna, illus. 2016. (ENG.). 32p. (J). (-6). 12.99 *(978-1-4926-2928-3(6)*, Sourcebooks Jabberwocky) Sourcebooks, Inc.
—Love Is All Around Nevada. Czernichowska, Joanna, illus. 2016. (ENG.). 32p. (J). (-6). 12.99 *(978-1-4926-2940-5(5)*, Sourcebooks Jabberwocky) Sourcebooks, Inc.
Skurzynski, Gloria & Ferguson, Alane. Valley of Death: A Mystery in Death Valley National Park. 2008. (Mysteries in Our National Park Ser.). (ENG., Illus.). 160p. (J). (gr. 3-7). per. 4.99 *(978-1-4263-0178-0(2)*, National Geographic Children's Bks.) National Geographic Society.
Smallman, Steve. Santa Is Coming to Las Vegas. Dunn, Robert, illus. 2013. (ENG.). 32p. (J). (-3). 9.99 *(978-1-4022-8836-4(0)*, Sourcebooks Jabberwocky) Sourcebooks, Inc.
—Santa Is Coming to Nevada. Dunn, Robert, illus. 2013. (ENG.). 32p. (J). (-3). 9.99 *(978-1-4022-9523-2(5)*, Sourcebooks Jabberwocky) Sourcebooks, Inc.
Smith, Roland. Zach's Lie. 2003. (ENG.). 224p. (J). (gr. 5-9). pap. 6.99 *(978-0-7868-1440-4(3))* Hyperion Pr.
—Zach's Lie. 2003. (J). (gr. 5-8). lib. bdg. 17.20 *(978-0-613-63491-5(8)*, Turtleback) Turtleback Bks.
Van Draanen, Wendelin. Sammy Keyes & the Showdown in Sin City. 2013. (Sammy Keyes Ser.: Bk. 16). (ENG.). 304p. (J). (gr. 5). pap. 7.99 *(978-0-307-93061-3(0)*, Yearling) Random Hse. Children's Bks.
Walsh, Stephen & O'Donovan, Marita. Vinnie Goes to Vegas. Le Feyer, Diane, illus. 2017. (ENG.). 32p. (J). pap. 13.00 ***(978-1-84717-724-7(7))*** O'Brien Pr., Ltd., The IRL. Dist: Dufour Editions, Inc.
Warner, Penny. The Mystery of the Missing Mustangs. 2012. 107p. (J). *(978-0-88166-411-9(1))* Meadowbrook Pr.
Weiss, Sonya. Rising. 2017. (ENG., Illus.). (YA). pap. 15.00 ***(978-1-5161-0028-6(X))*** Kensington Publishing Corp.
Wells, Rosemary. Ivy Takes Care. LaMarche, Jim, illus. (ENG.). 208p. (J). (gr. 3-7). 2015. pap. 6.99 *(978-0-7636-7660-5(8))* 2013. 15.99 *(978-0-7636-5352-1(7))* Candlewick Pr.
Young, Jan. Starting the Colt. 2014. 173p. (J). *(978-1-937849-11-5(2))* Raven Publishing Inc. of Montana.

NEVADA—HISTORY

Felix, Rebecca. What's Great about Nevada? 2015. (ENG., Illus.). 32p. (J). (gr. 2-5). 26.65 *(978-1-4677-3880-4(8))* Lerner Publishing Group.
Hanel, Rachael. Nevada. 2009. (This Land Called America Ser.). (Illus.). 32p. (YA). (gr. 3-6). 19.95 *(978-1-58341-781-2(8))* Creative Co., The.
Haney, Jill. Area 51. 2015. (Red Rhino Nonfiction Ser.). (J). lib. bdg. 20.80 *(978-0-606-37198-8(2))* Turtleback Bks.
Hicks, Terry Allan. Nevada. 2nd ed. 2013. 80p. (J). (gr. 4-8). 31.36 *(978-0-7614-8000-6(5))* Cavendish Square Publishing.
Hicks, Terry Allan, et al. Nevada. 2016. (ENG., Illus.). 80p. (J). 34.21 *(978-1-62713-207-7(4))* Cavendish Square Publishing.
Higgins, Nadia. Area 51. 2014. (Unexplained Mysteries Ser.). (ENG., Illus.). 24p. (J). (gr. 3-7). lib. bdg. 25.95 *(978-1-62617-101-5(7)*, Epic Bks.) Bellwether Media.
Jerome, Kate B. Lucky to Live in Nevada. 2017. (Arcadia Kids Ser.). (ENG., Illus.). 32p. (J). 16.99 ***(978-0-7385-2802-1(1))*** Arcadia Publishing.
—The Wise Animal Handbook Nevada. 2017. (Arcadia Kids Ser.). (ENG., Illus.). 32p. (J). 16.99 ***(978-0-7385-2831-1(5))*** Arcadia Publishing.
Karst, Ken. Enduring Mysteries: Area 51. 2015. (Enduring Mysteries Ser.). (ENG.). 48p. (J). (gr. 5-8). pap. 12.00 *(978-1-62832-070-1(2)*, Creative Paperbacks) Creative Co., The.
Kopp, Megan. Nevada: The Silver State. 2012. (J). *(978-1-61913-375-4(X))*; pap. *(978-1-61913-376-1(8))* Weigl Pubs., Inc.
Larson, Kirsten W. The West: Arizona, California, Nevada. 2015. (Let's Explore the States Ser.). (Illus.). 64p. (J). (gr. 5). 23.95 *(978-1-4222-3337-5(5))* Mason Crest.
Linde, Barbara M. What Happened at Area 51? 2015. (History's Mysteries Ser.). (ENG., Illus.). 32p. (J). (gr. 4-5). pap. 10.50 *(978-1-4824-2102-6(X))* Stevens, Gareth Publishing LLLP.
Lusted, Marcia Amidon. Nevada: The Silver State. 2010. (Our Amazing States Ser.). (ENG.). 24p. (J). pap. 8.25 *(978-1-4488-0750-5(6))*; lib. bdg. 22.60 *(978-1-4488-0659-1(3))* Rosen Publishing Group, Inc., The. (PowerKids Pr.).
Marsh, Carole. Exploring Nevada Through Project-Based Learning: Geography, History, Government, Economics & More. 2016. (Nevada Experience Ser.). (ENG.). (J). pap. 9.99 *(978-0-635-12352-7(5))* Gallopade International.
—I'm Reading about Nevada. 2014. (Nevada Experience Ser.). (ENG., Illus.). (J). pap., pap. 8.99 *(978-0-635-11303-0(1))* Gallopade International.
—Nevada History Projects: 30 Cool, Activities, Crafts, Experiments & More for Kids to Do to Learn about Your State! 2003. (Nevada Experience Ser.). 32p. (gr. k-5). pap. 5.95 *(978-0-635-01797-0(0)*, Marsh, Carole Bks.) Gallopade International.
Martin, Ted. Area 51. 2011. (Unexplained Ser.). (ENG., Illus.). 24p. (YA). (gr. 3-7). lib. bdg. 25.95 *(978-1-60014-642-8(2)*, Torque Bks.) Bellwether Media.
McLuskey, Krista. Nevada. 2011. (Guide to American States Ser.). (Illus.). 48p. (YA). (gr. 3-6). 29.99 *(978-1-61690-800-3(9))* Weigl Pubs., Inc.
—Nevada: The Silver State. 2016. (J). *(978-1-4896-4899-0(2))* Weigl Pubs., Inc.
Murray, Julie. Nevada, 1 vol. 2012. (Explore the United States Ser.). (ENG., Illus.). 32p. (J). (gr. 2-5). lib. bdg. 28.50 *(978-1-61783-366-3(5)*, Big Buddy Bks.) ABDO Publishing Co.
Nevada, Our Home Program Kit: All program components for Nevada, Our Home, 1 vol. 2009. 99.95 *(978-1-4236-0723-6(6))* Gibbs Smith, Publisher.
Ollhoff, Jim. Nevada, 1 vol. 2009. (United States Ser.). (ENG., Illus.). 48p. (YA). (gr. 2-5). 27.07 *(978-1-60453-663-8(2))* ABDO Publishing Co.
Roza, Greg. Nevada: Past & Present. 2010. (United States: Past & Present Ser.). (ENG.). 48p. (YA). pap. 11.75 *(978-1-4358-9515-7(0))*; lib. bdg. 29.25 *(978-1-4358-9488-4(X))* Rosen Publishing Group, Inc., The. (Rosen Reference).
Stefoff, Rebecca. Nevada. 2nd rev. ed. 2009. (Celebrate the States 10 Ser.). 144p. (gr. 6). 42.79 *(978-0-7614-4728-3(8))* Marshall Cavendish Corp.
Williams, Suzanne. Nevada. 2009. (From Sea to Shining Sea, Second Ser.). (ENG.). 80p. (J). pap. 7.95 *(978-0-531-21137-3(1)*, Children's Pr.) Scholastic Library Publishing.

NEVER-NEVER LAND (IMAGINARY PLACE)—FICTION

Barrie, J. M. Peter Pan. 2008. 124p. (gr. 5-18). 23.95 *(978-1-60664-889-6(6))*; pap. 10.95 *(978-1-60664-007-4(0))* Aegypan.
—Peter Pan. Press, Jenny, illus. 2013. (Storyteller Book Ser.). (ENG.). 48p. (J). (gr. k-5). pap. 7.99 *(978-1-84322-884-4(X)*, Armadillo) Anness Publishing GBR. Dist: National Bk. Network.
—Peter Pan. 2005. 112p. per. 6.95 *(978-1-933652-07-8(1))* Bed Bks.
—Peter Pan. Date not set. (C). pap. *(978-0-7593-9877-1(1)*, Cengage Learning) CENGAGE Learning.
—Peter Pan. Cowley, Joy, ed. Jang, Yeong-seon, illus. 2015. (World Classics Ser.). (ENG.). 32p. (gr. k-4). 26.65 *(978-1-925246-19-3(1))*; 7.99 *(978-1-925246-71-1(X))*; 26.65 *(978-1-925246-45-2(0))* ChoiceMaker Pty. Ltd., The AUS. (Big and SMALL). Dist: Lerner Publishing Group.
—Peter Pan. 2005. 96p. per. 4.95 *(978-1-4209-2538-8(5))* Digireads.com Publishing.
—Peter Pan. 2006. pap. *(978-1-4065-0949-6(3))* Dodo Pr.
—Peter Pan. 2009. 276p. (gr. 3-7). pap. *(978-1-4068-9291-8(2))* Echo Library.
—Peter Pan. Bustelo, Gabriela, tr. Vicente, Fernando, illus. 2006. (Alfaguara Infantil y Juvenil Ser.). 229p. (J). (gr. 4-7). pap. *(978-970-770-677-4(5))* Ediciones Alfaguara.
—Peter Pan. pap. 16.95 *(978-2-07-051627-8(X))* Gallimard, Editions FRA. Dist: Distribooks, Inc.
—Peter Pan. Minalima Staff, illus. 2015. (ENG.). 256p. 27.99 *(978-0-06-236222-3(4)*, Collins Design) HarperCollins Pubs.
—Peter Pan. Cowley, Joy, ed. Jang, Yeong-seon, illus. 2015. (World Classics Ser.). (ENG.). 32p. (J). (gr. k-4). 26.65 *(978-1-925186-71-0(7))*; pap. 7.99 *(978-1-925186-65-9(2))* Lerner Publishing Group.
—Peter Pan, 1 vol. Mullarkey, Lisa, illus. 2010. (Calico Illustrated Classics Ser.: No. 1). (ENG.). 112p. (J). (gr. 3-6). 27.07 *(978-1-60270-710-8(3))* Magic Wagon.
—Peter Pan. 160p. pap. *(978-1-85471-231-8(4))* Penguin Bks., Ltd.
—Peter Pan. (Puffin Chalk Ser.). (ENG.). (J). 2013. 224p. (gr. 3-7). pap. 7.99 *(978-0-14-750865-2(7))* 2009. (Illus.). 240p. (gr. 5-7). 5.99 *(978-0-14-132257-5(8))* Penguin Young Readers Group. (Puffin Books).
—Peter Pan. 2013. (ENG., Illus.). 256p. (J). (gr. 4-7). pap. 10.99 *(978-0-09-957304-3(0))* Random Hse. GBR. Dist: Independent Pubs. Group.
—Peter Pan. McKowen, Scott, illus. 2008. (Sterling Unabridged Classics Ser.). (ENG.). 160p. (J). 9.95 *(978-1-4027-5426-5(4))* Sterling Publishing Co., Inc.
—Peter Pan: The Original Tale of Neverland. Jaramillo, Raquel, illus. Jaramillo, Raquel, photos by. unabr. ed. 2003. 135p. (YA). (gr. 5-8). reprint ed. 25.00 *(978-0-7567-6883-6(7))* DIANE Publishing Co.
—Peter Pan - the Original Classic Edition. 2011. pap. *(978-1-74244-781-0(3)*, Tebbo) Emereo Pty Ltd.
—Peter Pan & Wendy. 2013. (ENG.). 172p. (YA). 14.95 *(978-1-940849-05-8(5))* Ancient Wisdom Pubns.
—Peter Pan & Wendy. Foreman, Michael, illus. 2003. (Chrysalis Childrens Classics Ser.). 176p. (YA). pap. *(978-1-84365-039-3(8)*, Pavilion Children's Books) Pavilion Bks.
—Peter Pan & Wendy. Foreman, Michael, illus. 2010. (ENG.). 160p. (J). (gr. 2-7). 19.99 *(978-1-84365-136-9(X)*, Pavilion Children's Books) Pavilion Bks. GBR. Dist: Independent Pubs. Group.
—Peter Pan & Wendy: Centenary Edition. Ingpen, Robert R., illus. 2004. (ENG.). 216p. (J). *(978-1-897035-12-2(8)*, Blue Heron Bks.) Raincoast Bk. Distribution.
—Peter Pan, by J. M. Barrie - the Original Classic Edition. 2011. mass mkt. *(978-1-74244-961-6(1)*, Tebbo) Emereo Pty Ltd.
—Peter Pan in Kensington Gardens. (J). 18.95 *(978-0-8488-0427-5(9))* Amereon Ltd.
—Peter Pan in Kensington Gardens. 2013. 123p. reprint ed. lthr. 69.00 *(978-0-7426-2518-1(4))* Classic Bks.
—Peter Pan in Kensington Gardens. unabr. ed. 2012. (Illus.). 147p. 39.99 *(978-1-4622-8152-7(4))* Repressed Publishing LLC.
—Peter Pan in Kensington Gardens. 2009. 108p. (gr. -1-18). pap. 9.95 *(978-1-60664-381-5(9))* Rodgers, Alan Bks.
—Peter Pan in Kensington Gardens & Peter & Wendy. 2009. 120p. pap. 7.99 *(978-1-4209-3191-4(1))* Digireads.com Publishing.
Barrie, J. M. & Lindner, Brooke. Peter Pan. Bedford, Francis Donkin & Rackham, Arthur, illus. 2015. (Word Cloud Classics Ser.). (ENG.). 272p. pap. 14.99 *(978-1-62686-392-7(X)*, Thunder Bay Pr.) Readerlink Distribution Services, LLC.
Barrie, J. M. & Sterne, Laurence. The Life & Opinions of Tristram Shandy, Gentleman. 2015. (Vintage Classics Ser.). (ENG.). 762p. pap. 13.95 *(978-0-09-951915-7(1))* Random Hse. GBR. Dist: Independent Pubs. Group.
Disney Book Group Staff. Captain Jake & the Never Land Pirates the Great Never Sea Conquest. Disney Storybook Art Team, illus. 2015. (ENG.). 24p. (J). (gr. -1-k). pap. 4.99 *(978-1-4847-1150-7(5))* Disney Pr.
Hoena, B. A. & Barrie, J. M. Peter Pan. Cano, Fernando, illus. 2015. (Graphic Revolve: Common Core Editions Ser.). (ENG.). 72p. (gr. 2-3). lib. bdg. 27.99 *(978-1-4965-0372-5(4))* Stone Arch Bks.
Impey, Rose. Peter Pan. Beck, Ian, illus. 2015. (ENG.). 96p. (J). (gr. k-2). pap. 11.99 *(978-1-4083-3822-3(X))* Hodder & Stoughton GBR. Dist: Hachette Bk. Group.
Jenny Press Staff. Peter Pan. 2016. (ENG., Illus.). 24p. pap. 7.99 *(978-1-86147-815-3(1)*, Armadillo) Anness Publishing GBR. Dist: National Bk. Network.
LaRose, Melinda & Disney Book Group Staff. The Croc Takes the Cake. Disney Storybook Artists Staff, illus. 2012. (World of Reading Ser.). (ENG.). 32p. (J). (gr. -1-k). pap. 3.99 *(978-1-4231-5543-0(2))* Disney Pr.
—Jake Hatches a Plan, Pre-Level 1. Disney Storybook Art Team, illus. 2012. (World of Reading Ser.). (ENG.). 32p. (J). (gr. -1-k). pap. 3.99 *(978-1-4231-5542-3(4))* Disney Pr.
Levine, Gail Carson. Fairy Haven & the Quest for the Wand. Christiana, David, illus. 2007. 191p. (J). *(978-1-4287-6391-3(0))* Disney Pr.
Posner-Sanchez, Andrea. Jake & the Never Land Pirates LGB Favorites (Jake & the Never Land Pirates) Random House Disney Staff, illus. 2015. (Little Golden Book Favorites Ser.). (ENG.). 80p. (J). (-k). 7.99 *(978-0-7364-3404-1(6)*, Golden/Disney) Random Hse. Children's Bks.
Publications International Ltd. Staff, ed. Jake & the Neverland Pirates: Playful Pirates: Play-A-Sound Book. 2013. 10p. (J). (gr. k-3). bds. 7.99 *(978-1-4508-6772-6(3)*, 922eff8e-f9be-4736-a025-2bb18924e404) Phoenix International Publications, Inc.
Random House Disney Staff. Peter Pan Step into Reading (Disney Peter Pan) Random House Disney Staff, illus. 2013. (Step into Reading Ser.). (ENG., Illus.). 32p. (J). (gr. -1-1). 3.99 *(978-0-7364-3114-9(4)*, RH/Disney) Random Hse. Children's Bks.
Random House Editors. Disney Peter Pan. 2013. (Step into Reading Level 1 Ser.). lib. bdg. 13.55 *(978-0-606-26973-5(8)*, Turtleback) Turtleback Bks.
RH Disney Staff. Never Girls - In a Blink, 2 bks. in 1. Christy, Jana, illus. 2015. (Never Girls Ser.). (ENG.). 256p. (J). (gr. 1-4). 9.99 *(978-0-7364-3432-4(1)*, RH/Disney) Random Hse. Children's Bks.
Sabuda, Robert, illus. Peter Pan: A Pop-Up Adaptation of J. M. Barrie's Original Tale. 2008. (ENG.). 16p. (J). 39.99 *(978-0-689-85364-7(5)*, Little Simon) Little Simon.
Scollon, Bill. The Pirate Pup. 2013. (Picture Viewer Ser.: 1). (ENG.). 24p. (J). (gr. -1-2). 12.99 *(978-0-7944-2592-0(5))* Reader's Digest Assn., Inc., The.
Thorpe, Kiki. A Dandelion Wish. Christy, Jana, illus. 2013. (Stepping Stone Book Series: No. 3). (ENG.). 128p. (J). (gr. 1-4). 5.99 *(978-0-7364-2796-8(1)*, RH/Disney) Random Hse. Children's Bks.
—A Dandelion Wish. Christy, Jana, illus. 2013. (Never Girls Ser.: 3). lib. bdg. 16.00 *(978-0-606-32199-0(3)*, Turtleback) Turtleback Bks.
—A Pinch of Magic. Christy, Jana, illus. 2014. (Never Girls Ser.: No. 7). (ENG.). 128p. (J). (gr. 1-4). 5.99 *(978-0-7364-3097-5(0)*, RH/Disney) Random Hse. Children's Bks.
—A Pinch of Magic. 2014. (Never Girls Ser.: 7). lib. bdg. 16.00 *(978-0-606-36008-1(5))* Turtleback Bks.
—The Space Between. Christy, Jana & Random House Disney Staff, illus. 2013. (Never Girls Ser.: 2). (ENG.). 128p. (J). (gr. 1-4). 5.99 *(978-0-7364-2795-1(3)*, RH/Disney) Random Hse. Children's Bks.
—The Space Between. Christy, Jana, illus. 2013. (Never Girls Ser.: 2). lib. bdg. 16.00 *(978-0-606-26974-2(6)*, Turtleback) Turtleback Bks.

NEW ENGLAND

Connery-Boyd, Peg. New England. 2016. (Hawk's Nest Activity Bks.: 0). (ENG.). 64p. (J). pap. 8.99 *(978-1-4926-3379-2(8)*, 9781492633792, Sourcebooks Jabberwocky) Sourcebooks, Inc.
Koestler-Grack, Rachel A. Northern Colonial Town: Plymouth. 2003. (J). pap. *(978-1-58417-079-2(4))* Lake Street Pubs.

NEW ENGLAND—FICTION

Adams, James D. Creepy Campfire Tales: Halloween Campout, Vol. 1. 2008. 132p. (J). per. 12.95 *(978-1-60404-103-3(X))* Owl Creek Media Ltd.
—Creepy Campfire Tales Vol. 1: Halloween Campout. 2008. 132p. (YA). 26.95 *(978-1-60404-104-0(8))* Owl Creek Media Ltd.
Alcott, Louisa May. The Annotated Little Women. Matteson, John, ed. 2015. (Annotated Bks.: 0). (ENG., Illus.). 736p. (gr. 11-17). 39.95 *(978-0-393-07219-8(3)*, 7219) Norton, W. W. & Co., Inc.
—Jack & Jill. Date not set. 352p. (YA). 25.95 *(978-0-8488-2671-0(X))* Amereon Ltd.
—Jack & Jill. 2013. (Works of Louisa May Alcott). 425p. reprint ed. lthr. 79.00 *(978-0-7812-1638-8(9))* Reprint Services Corp.
—Jo's Boys. l.t. ed. 2007. (ENG.). 288p. pap. 23.99 *(978-1-4346-0451-4(9))* Creative Media Partners, LLC.
—Jo's Boys. 2005. pap. *(978-1-4065-0107-0(7))* Dodo Pr.
—Jo's Boys. abr. ed. 2011. (Dover Children's Thrift Classics Ser.). (ENG., Illus.). 112p. (J). (gr. 3-8). pap. 4.00 *(978-0-486-40789-0(6))* Dover Pubns., Inc.
—Jo's Boys. l.t. ed. 2005. 424p. pap. *(978-1-84637-067-0(1))* Echo Library.
—Jo's Boys. 2013. (Works of Louisa May Alcott). 366p. reprint ed. lthr. 79.00 *(978-0-7812-1642-5(7))* Reprint Services Corp.
—Little Men. Andreasen, Dan, illus. 2009. (Classic Starts(tm) Ser.). (ENG.). 160p. (J). (gr. 2-4). 6.95 *(978-1-4027-5423-4(X))* Sterling Publishing Co., Inc.
—Little Men. rev. ed. 2006. 352p. 31.95 *(978-1-4218-1800-9(0))*; pap. 15.95 *(978-1-4218-1900-6(7))* 1st World Publishing, Inc. (1st World Library - Literary Society).
—Little Men. l.t. ed. 2005. 564p. pap. *(978-1-84637-068-7(X))* Echo Library.
—Little Men: Life at Plumfield with Jo's Boys. 2013. (Early Best Sellers Ser.). 425p. reprint ed. lthr. 69.00 *(978-0-7426-1004-0(7))* Classic Bks.
—Little Men: Life at Plumfield with Jo's Boys. 2013. (Works of Louisa May Alcott). 292p. reprint ed. lthr. 79.00 *(978-0-7812-1629-6(X))* Reprint Services Corp.
—Little Women. Corvino, Lucy, illus. 2005. (Classic Starts(tm) Ser.). (ENG.). 160p. (J). (gr. 2-4). 6.95 *(978-1-4027-1236-4(7))* Sterling Publishing Co., Inc.
—Little Women. Dunn, Robert, illus. 2013. 46p. (J). *(978-1-4351-4813-0(4))* Barnes & Noble, Inc.
—Little Women. 2007. 264p. (YA). 11.95 *(978-1-933486-01-7(5))* Core Knowledge Foundation.
—Little Women. unabr. ed. 2004. (Chrysalis Childrens Classics Ser.). (Illus.). 190p. (YA). pap. *(978-1-84365-049-2(5)*, Pavilion Children's Books) Pavilion Bks.
—Little Women. 2013. (ENG., Illus.). 426p. (J). (gr. 4-7). pap. 10.99 *(978-0-09-957296-1(6))* Random Hse. GBR. Dist: Independent Pubs. Group.
—Little Women. 2013. (Works of Louisa May Alcott). 451p. reprint ed. lthr. 79.00 *(978-0-7812-1627-2(3))* Reprint Services Corp.
—Little Women. 2008. (Puffin Classics Ser.). (gr. k-3). lib. bdg. 19.65 *(978-0-613-86261-5(9)*, Turtleback) Turtleback Bks.
—Little Women: Bring the Classics to Life. 2008. (Bring the Classics to Life Ser.). (Illus.). 72p. (gr. 1-12). pap., act. bk. ed. 10.95 *(978-1-55576-047-2(3)*, EDCTR-103B) EDCON Publishing Group.
—Little Women: With a Discussion of Family. Lauter, Richard, illus. 2003. (Values in Action Illustrated Classics Ser.). 191p. (J). *(978-1-59203-032-3(7))* Learning Challenge, Inc.
—Mujercitas.Tr. of Little Women. (SPA., Illus.). 192p. (YA). 11.95 *(978-84-7281-101-0(8)*, AF1101) Auriga, Ediciones S.A. ESP. Dist: Continental Bk. Co., Inc.
—Mujercitas. 2004.Tr. of Little Women. (SPA.). lib. bdg. *(978-1-4135-2067-5(7))* El Cid Editor Incorporated.
—Mujercitas. (Coleccion Estrella).Tr. of Little Women. (SPA., Illus.). 64p. (J). 14.95 *(978-950-11-0010-5(3)*, SGM010) Sigmar ARG. Dist: Continental Bk. Co., Inc.
—An Old-Fashioned Girl. 2013. (Works of Louisa May Alcott). 409p. reprint ed. lthr. 79.00 *(978-0-7812-1628-9(1))* Reprint Services Corp.
—An Old-Fashioned Thanksgiving. Wheeler, Jody, illus. 2010. 40p. (J). (gr. -1-3). 14.99 *(978-0-8249-5620-2(6)*, Ideal Pubns.) Worthy Publishing.
Alcott, Louisa May & Barbarese, J. T. Little Men. 2012. (ENG.). 368p. (gr. 12). mass mkt. 5.95 *(978-0-451-53223-7(6)*, Signet) Penguin Publishing Group.
Alcott, Louisa May & Lacey, Mike. Little Women, 1 vol. 2012. (Calico Illustrated Classics Ser.: No. 4). (ENG., Illus.). 112p. (J). (gr. 3-6). 27.07 *(978-1-61641-617-1(3))* Magic Wagon.
Alcott, Louisa May, et al. Little Women. 2003. (Norton Critical Editions Ser.: 0). (ENG., Illus.). 665p. (C). pap. 13.00 *(978-0-393-97614-4(9)*, 97614) Norton, W. W. & Co., Inc.
Aldrich, Thomas Bailey. The Story of a Bad Boy. 2006. pap. *(978-1-4065-0613-6(3))* Dodo Pr.
—The Story of a Bad Boy. 2005. pap. 26.95 *(978-1-885529-78-7(3))* Stevens Publishing.
Alger, Horatio. Struggling Upward: Or, Luke Larkin's Luck. 2006. pap. *(978-1-4065-0723-2(7))* Dodo Pr.
—Struggling Upward; or, Luck Larkin's Luck. 2008. 104p. pap. 7.99 *(978-1-4209-3044-3(3))* Digireads.com Publishing.
Allbritton, Stacy Demoran. The Diary of Marie Landry, Acadian Exile, 1 vol. Haynes, Joyce, illus. 2012. (ENG.). 160p. (J). (gr. 3-7). pap. 14.95 *(978-1-58980-865-2(7))* Pelican Publishing Co., Inc.
Atwood, Megan. Ice Cream Summer. Andrewson, Natalie, illus. 2017. (Orchard Novel Ser.: 1). (ENG.). 272p. (J). (gr. 2-6). 12.99 ***(978-1-4814-9047-4(8)**, Aladdin)* Simon & Schuster Children's Publishing.
Bardsley-Sirois, Lois. Katherine's Winter Garden. 2012. 24p. pap. 12.99 *(978-1-4525-6269-8(5))* Balboa Pr.
Barker, M. P. Mending Horses. 2014. (ENG.). 320p. (J). (gr. 5). 17.95 *(978-0-8234-2948-6(2))* Holiday Hse., Inc.
Bass, Ruth. Sarah's Daughter. 2007. 389p. (YA). (gr. 8-12). per. 14.95 *(978-0-9774053-4-3(6))* North River Pr. Publishing Corp., The.
Buzzeo, Toni. The Twelve Days of Christmas in New England. Woodruff, Liza, illus. 2015. (Twelve Days of Christmas in America Ser.). (ENG.). 40p. (J). (gr. k). 12.95 *(978-1-4549-1492-1(0))* Sterling Publishing Co., Inc.
Cathie & Jessie's Noisy New England Adventure. 2006. (Illus.). 32p. (J). cd-rom 12.99 *(978-0-9773526-1-6(7))* Diversified A+ Pubns.
Coatsworth, Elizabeth. Away Goes Sally. Sewell, Helen, illus. 2004. 118p. (J). pap. 10.95 *(978-1-883937-83-6(3))* Bethlehem Bks.
Cooper, Blayne. Blind Side of the Moon. 2016. (ENG.). 240p. (J). (gr. 7). pap. 16.95 *(978-1-59493-531-2(9))* Bella Bks., Inc.
Cornelia Meigs. Master Simon's Garden. 2010. (Illus.). 244p. pap. 6.95 *(978-1-60386-299-8(4)*, Watchmaker Publishing) Wexford College Pr.
Courtenay, Christina. New England Rocks. 2013. (ENG.). 192p. pap. 6.95 *(978-1-78189-030-1(7))* Choc Lit Limited GBR. Dist: Casemate Pubs. & Bk. Distributors, LLC.
Cronin, Carol Newman. Oliver's Surprise: A Boy, a Schooner, & the Great Hurricane of 1938. Cronin, Laurie, illus. rev. ed. 2009. (ENG.). 150p. (J). (gr. 4-7). pap. 9.95 *(978-1-934848-62-3(X))* GemmaMedia.
Dalton, Linda J. The Mystery of the Broomstick Horse. 2012. 116p. 29.99 *(978-1-4797-4781-8(5))*; pap. 19.99 *(978-1-4797-4780-1(7))* Xlibris Corp.
Daly, Mariah. James Has Diabetes. 2009. 56p. pap. 21.99 *(978-1-4389-3188-3(3))* AuthorHouse.

MNO

DeMitchell, Terri A. You Will Come Back - the First in the Olde Locke Beach Mysteries. 2004. (ENG., Illus.). 176p. 14.95 (978-1-932278-02-6(8)) Mayhaven Publishing, Inc.

Devlin, Wende. Old Black Witch! Devlin, Harry, illus. 2012. (ENG.). 32p. (J). (gr. -1-3). 18.95 (978-1-930900-62-2(7)) Purple Hse. Pr.

Digby Tracks a Catamount. 2008. (Illus.). 36p. (J). per. (978-0-9745931-1-1(7)) Vermont Bookworks.

Dunn, Joeming. The Woodshed Mystery. Dunn, Ben, illus. 2010. (Boxcar Children Graphic Novels Ser.: 13). (ENG.). 32p. (J). (gr. 1-5). pap. 6.99 (978-0-8075-9208-3(0)) Whitman, Albert & Co.

Dzidrums, Christine. Fair Youth: Emylee of Forest Springs. Lopez, Lyle & Dzidrums, Joseph, illus. 2012. 120p. pap. 9.99 (978-1-938438-05-9(1)) Creative Media Publishing.

Edwards, Nicholas. The Adventures of Santa Paws. 2010. (Santa Paws Ser.). (ENG.). 336p. (J). (gr. 3-7). pap. 7.99 (978-0-545-22551-9(5), Scholastic Paperbacks) Scholastic, Inc.

Ehrenhaft, Daniel. Drawing a Blank: Or How I Tried to Solve a Mystery, End a Feud, & Land the Girl of My Dreams. Ristow, Trevor, illus. 2009. (ENG.). 352p. (J). pap. 8.99 (978-0-06-075254-5(8), HarperTeen) HarperCollins Pubs.

Frederick, Heather Vogel. A Little Women Christmas. Ibatoulline, Bagram, illus. 2014. (ENG.). 32p. (J). (gr. -1-3). 17.99 (978-1-4424-1359-7(X), Simon & Schuster Bks. For Young Readers) Simon & Schuster Bks. For Young Readers.

Freeberg, Jane. The Scallop Christmas. Sheckels, Astrid, illus. 2011. (ENG.). 36p. (J). 16.95 (978-1-934031-25-4(9), 9781934031254) Islandport Pr., Inc.

Hathaway, Lucinda Churchman. 'Round the World: Takashi Sails Home. 2008. (Illus.). 135p. (J). 12.95 (978-1-59322-034-1(0)) Down The Shore Publishing Corp.

Hawthorne, Nathaniel. The House of the Seven Gables, 1 vol. Fisher, Scott, illus. 2011. (Calico Illustrated Classics Ser.). (ENG.). 112p. (J). (gr. 3-6). 27.07 (978-1-60270-746-7(4)) Magic Wagon.

Hemphill, Stephanie. Wicked Girls: A Novel of the Salem Witch Trials. 2010. (YA). 336p. (gr. 7-18). lib. bdg. 17.89 (978-0-06-185329-6(1)); (ENG.). 416p. (gr. 8-18). 17.99 (978-0-06-185328-9(3)) HarperCollins Pubs.

Holdman, Shirley Terrill. The Adventures of Giggles & Owen: A True Story. Riecks Goss, Carol, illus. 2010. 26p. pap. 14.95 (978-1-60844-490-8(2)) Dog Ear Publishing, LLC.

Hunter, Sara Hoagland. The Lighthouse Santa. Miner, Julia, illus. 2011. 36p. (J). (gr. -1-3). 17.95 (978-1-61168-006-5(9)) Univ. Pr. of New England.

Huntington, Geoffrey. Blood Moon. 2013. (Ravenscliff Ser.: 3). (ENG.). 260p. pap. 17.99 (978-1-62681-169-0(5)) Diversion Publishing Corp.

Hyatt, Patricia Rusch. The Quite Contrary Man: A True American Tale. Brown, Kathryn, illus. 2011. (ENG.). 32p. (J). (gr. 1-4). 16.95 (978-0-8109-4065-9(5), Abrams Bks. for Young Readers) Abrams, Inc.

Irving, Washington. The Devil & Tom Walker. 2007. (Tale Blazers: American Literature Ser.). 37p. (J). (gr. 4-7). pap. 3.30 (978-0-89598-665-8(5)) Perfection Learning Corp.

Isenhoff, Michelle. The Quill Pen. 2011. (ENG.). 168p. pap. 9.98 (978-1-4664-9691-0(6)) CreateSpace Independent Publishing Platform.

Jacobs, Lily. The Littlest Bunny in New England: An Easter Adventure. Dunn, Robert, illus. 2015. (ENG.). 32p. (J). (-3). 9.99 (978-1-4926-1138-7(7), Sourcebooks Jabberwocky) Sourcebooks, Inc.

Jacobson, Jennifer Richard. Small as an Elephant. 2011. (ENG., Illus.). 288p. (J). (gr. 4-7). 15.99 (978-0-7636-4155-9(3)) Candlewick Pr.

James, Eric. A Halloween Scare in New England. Le Ray, Marina, illus. 2014. (ENG.). 32p. (J). (-5). 9.99 (978-1-4926-0615-4(4), 9781492606154, Sourcebooks Jabberwocky) Sourcebooks, Inc.

—Santa's Sleigh Is on Its Way to New England: A Christmas Adventure. Dunn, Robert, illus. 2016. (ENG.). 32p. (J). (-2). 12.99 (978-1-4926-4341-8(6), 9781492643418, Sourcebooks Jabberwocky) Sourcebooks, Inc.

Jewett, Sarah Orne. A White Heron. Alvord, Douglas, illus. 2005. (ENG.). 32p. (J). pap. 10.95 (978-1-56792-287-5(2)) Godine, David R. Pub.

Kennedy, Kim. Misty Gordon & the Mystery of the Ghost Pirates. 2010. (ENG., Illus.). 240p. (YA). (gr. 3-7). 15.95 (978-0-8109-9357-0(0), Amulet Bks.) Abrams, Inc.

Killer Connections. 2010. (Hardy Boys (All New) Undercover Brothers Ser.: 33). (ENG.). 176p. (J). (gr. 3-7). pap. 6.99 (978-1-4169-8696-6(0), Aladdin) Simon & Schuster Children's Publishing.

Kimmel, Elizabeth Cody. ParaNormaN. 2012. (ENG.). (J). (gr. 4-7). 64.99 (978-1-61969-450-7(6)) Findaway World, LLC.

—ParaNorman: A Novel. 2013. (ENG., Illus.). 256p. (J). (gr. 3-7). pap. 6.99 (978-0-316-20987-8(2)) Little, Brown Bks. for Young Readers.

Kinkade, Thomas. Katherine's Story. 2004. (Girls of Lighthouse Lane Ser.). 176p. (J). (gr. 5-18). 13.89 (978-0-06-054342-6(6)) HarperCollins Pubs.

Kinkade, Thomas & Tamar, Erika. Rose's Story. 2004. (Girls of Lighthouse Lane Ser.: No. 2). (Illus.). 192p. (J). (gr. 5-18). 12.99 (978-0-06-054344-0(2)) HarperCollins Pubs.

Lauter, Richard, illus. Little Women. (Young Collector's Illustrated Classics Ser.). 192p. (J). 9.95 (978-1-56156-371-5(4)) Kidsbooks, LLC.

Levin, Betty. Shoddy Cove. 2003. 208p. (J). (gr. 5-18). 15.99 (978-0-06-052271-1(2)) HarperCollins Pubs.

Lindskoog, Kathryn, ed. Little Women. Chitouras, Barbara, illus. 2003. (Classics for Young Readers Ser.). 432p. (J). per. 12.99 (978-0-87552-734-5(5)) P & R Publishing.

Litrel, Suzanne M. Jackie Tempo & the Emperor's Seal. 2007. 172p. (YA). per. 13.95 (978-0-595-46822-5(5)) iUniverse, Inc.

MacLachlan, Patricia. Your Moon, My Moon: A Grandmother's Words to a Faraway Child. Collier, Bryan, illus. 2011. (ENG.). 32p. (J). (gr. -1-3). 16.99 (978-1-4169-7950-0(6), Simon & Schuster Bks. For Young Readers) Simon & Schuster Bks. For Young Readers.

Martin, Ann M. Needle & Thread. 2007. (Main Street Ser.). (Illus.). 205p. (J). (gr. 4-7). 14.65 (978-0-7569-8328-4(2)) Perfection Learning Corp.

—Needle & Thread. Andreasen, Dan, illus. 2007. 205p. (J). pap. (978-0-545-03660-3(7)) Scholastic, Inc.

—The Secret Book Club. 2008. (Main Street Ser.). (Illus.). 212p. (J). (gr. 4-7). 14.65 (978-0-7569-8823-4(3)) Perfection Learning Corp.

—Tis the Season. 2007. (Main Street Ser.). (Illus.). 195p. (J). (gr. 4-7). 14.65 (978-0-7569-8327-7(4)) Perfection Learning Corp.

Mckenzie, Riford. The Witches of Dredmoore Hollow, 0 vols. unabr. ed. 2013. (ENG.). 274p. (J). (gr. 5-7). pap. 9.99 (978-1-4778-1702-5(6), 9781477817025, Amazon Children's Publishing) Amazon Publishing.

Myers, Suzanne. Stone Cove Island. (ENG., Illus.). (YA). (gr. 9). 2015. 256p. pap. 10.99 (978-1-61695-575-5(9)) 2014. 236p. 17.99 (978-1-61695-437-6(X)) Soho Pr., Inc. (Soho Teen).

Ohlin, Nancy. Always, Forever. 2014. (ENG., Illus.). 320p. (YA). (gr. 9). pap. 9.99 (978-1-4424-6487-2(9), Simon Pulse) Simon Pulse.

—Thorn Abbey. 2013. (ENG.). 304p. (YA). (gr. 9). 16.99 (978-1-4424-6486-5(0), Simon Pulse) Simon Pulse.

Ostow, Micol. Amity. 2014. (ENG.). 362p. (J). (gr. 9). 18.99 (978-1-60684-156-3(4), Carolrhoda Lab™) Lerner Publishing Group.

Papp, Robert, illus. The Pumpkin Head Mystery, No. 124. 2010. (Boxcar Children Mysteries Ser.: 124). (ENG.). 128p. (J). (gr. 1-5). pap. 5.99 (978-0-8075-6669-5(1)) Whitman, Albert & Co.

Papp, Robert & Papp, Kathy, illus. The Pumpkin Head Mystery. 2010. (Boxcar Children Mysteries Ser.: 124). (ENG.). 128p. (J). (gr. 1-5). 14.99 (978-0-8075-6668-8(3)) Whitman, Albert & Co.

Parker, John. Chaos Mountain. 2007. 96p. (YA). pap. (978-1-4207-0734-2(5)) Sundance/Newbridge Educational Publishing.

Parramore, Helen. The Fragments of Fern Valley. 2009. 112p. pap. 10.95 (978-1-4401-2943-8(6)) iUniverse, Inc.

Penrose, Margaret. The Motor Girls Through New England: Or Held by the Gypsies. 2007. (ENG.). 154p. pap. 19.99 (978-1-4346-5805-0(8)); 172p. pap. 21.99 (978-1-4346-5806-7(6)) Creative Media Partners, LLC.

Ritter, William. Beastly Bones. (Jackaby Ser.: 2). (ENG.). (YA). (gr. 8-12). 2016. 320p. pap. 9.95 (978-1-61620-636-9(5)) 2015. 304p. 17.95 (978-1-61620-354-2(4)) Algonquin Bks. of Chapel Hill.

—Beastly Bones. 2016. (Jackaby Ser.: 2). lib. bdg. 20.80 (978-0-606-39017-0(0)) Turtleback Bks.

—Ghostly Echoes: A Jackaby Novel. (Jackaby Ser.: 3). (ENG.). 352p. (YA). (gr. 8-12). 2017. pap. 9.95 (978-1-61620-744-1(2)) 2016. 17.95 (978-1-61620-579-9(2)) Algonquin Bks. of Chapel Hill.

Ritter, William. Jackaby. (Jackaby Ser.: 1). (ENG.). 304p. (YA). (gr. 9-12). 2015. pap. 9.95 (978-1-61620-546-1(6)) 2014. 16.95 (978-1-61620-353-5(6), 73353) Algonquin Bks. of Chapel Hill.

Rodriguez, Jason, ed. Colonial Comics: New England, 1620 ¿ 1750. 2014. (Colonial Comics Ser.). (ENG., Illus.). 208p. (gr. 4). pap. 29.95 (978-1-938486-30-2(7)) Fulcrum Publishing.

Sales, Leila. Past Perfect. 2012. (ENG.). 336p. (YA). (gr. 9). pap. 10.99 (978-1-4424-0683-4(6), Simon Pulse) Simon Pulse.

Santaniello, Shelly W. Tommy's Needham Rocket. 2011. 53p. pap. 10.95 (978-1-4327-7000-6(4)) Outskirts Pr., Inc.

Schaefer, Laura. Littler Women: A Modern Retelling. 2017. (ENG., Illus.). 224p. (J). (gr. 3-7). 16.99 (978-1-4814-8761-0(2), Simon & Schuster/Paula Wiseman Bks.) Simon & Schuster/Paula Wiseman Bks.

Schmidt, Gary D. Trouble. 2010. (ENG.). 304p. (YA). (gr. 7). pap. 8.99 (978-0-547-33133-1(9)) Houghton Mifflin Harcourt Publishing Co.

Seidler, Tor. The Dulcimer Boy. Selznick, Brian, illus. 2003. 160p. (J). (gr. 3-7). lib. bdg. 16.89 (978-0-06-623610-0(X)) HarperCollins Pubs.

—The Dulcimer Boy. Selznick, Brian, illus. 2004. 153p. (gr. 5-7). 17.00 (978-0-7569-3520-7(2)) Perfection Learning Corp.

Sewell, Anna. Black Beauty. 2006. (My First Classics Ser.). 112p. (J). (gr. k-3). pap. 4.99 (978-0-06-079148-3(9), HarperFestival) HarperCollins Pubs.

Shasha, Mark. Night of the Moonjellies: 15th Anniversary Edition. 2007. (Illus.). 32p. (J). (gr. -1-2). 12.95 (978-1-930900-34-9(1)) Purple Hse. Pr.

Sheckels, Astrid, illus. Nic & Nellie, 1 vol. 2013. (ENG.). 32p. (J). (gr. 1-4). 17.95 (978-1-934031-52-0(6), 9781934031520) Islandport Pr., Inc.

Shute, Henry. Sequil or Things Whitch Aint Finished in The. 2007. 108p. per. 14.99 (978-0-9773040-3-5(5)) Wilder Pubns., Corp.

Sidney, Margaret. Five Little Peppers & How They Grew. 2006. (Dover Children's Classics Ser.). (ENG., Illus.). 224p. (J). (gr. 3-5). per. 6.95 (978-0-486-45267-8(0)) Dover Pubns., Inc.

—Five Little Peppers & How They Grew. Andreasen, Dan, illus. 2009. (Classic Starts(tm) Ser.). (ENG.). 160p. (J). (gr. 2-4). 6.95 (978-1-4027-5420-3(5)) Sterling Publishing Co., Inc.

Silvano, Wendi. Love Is All Around New England. Czernichowska, Joanna, illus. 2016. (ENG.). 32p. (J). (-6). 12.99 (978-1-4926-2941-2(3), Sourcebooks Jabberwocky) Sourcebooks, Inc.

Smallman, Steve. Santa Is Coming to New England. Dunn, Robert, illus. 2012. (ENG.). 32p. (J). (-3). 9.99 (978-1-4022-7551-7(X), Sourcebooks Jabberwocky) Sourcebooks, Inc.

Smith, Cynthia Leitich. Diabolical. 2012. (Tantalize Ser.). (ENG., Illus.). 368p. (YA). (gr. 9). 17.99 (978-0-7636-5118-3(4)) Candlewick Pr.

Solod, Margo. Coyote Summer: A Summerhood Island Book. 2014. 1. (Illus.). 118p. (J). pap. 15.00 (978-1-939930-18-7(9)) Brandylane Pubs., Inc.

Spotswood, Jessica. Born Wicked. 2013. (Cahill Witch Chronicles Ser.: 1). (ENG.). 352p. (YA). (gr. 7). pap. 10.99 (978-0-14-242187-1(1), Speak) Penguin Young Readers Group.

—Born Wicked. 2013. lib. bdg. 22.10 (978-0-606-26729-8(8), Turtleback) Turtleback Bks.

Stowe, Harriet Beecher. Betty's Bright Idea. 2006. pap. (978-1-4068-3093-4(3)) Echo Library.

Swegles, Maryanne. Digging for Bottles. 2005. (Illus.). 28p. (J). 15.00 (978-0-9768418-0-7(0)) Hydrangea Pr.

Terrill Holdman, Shirley. The Adventures of Giggles & Owen: Adventure Three - Unlimited Pawsibilities. Leeds, Marjorie M., illus. 2013. 50p. pap. 17.95 (978-1-4575-2175-1(X)) Dog Ear Publishing, LLC.

Thorson, Robert & Thorson, Kristine. Stone Wall Secrets. Moore, Gustav, illus. 2010. 40p. (J). (gr. 3-7). 16.95 (978-0-88448-195-9(6)) Tilbury Hse. Pubs.

Tuthill, Louisa C. Hurrah for New England! or the Virginia Boy's Vacation. 2004. reprint ed. pap. 1.99 (978-1-4192-2504-8(9)); pap. 15.95 (978-1-4191-2504-1(4)) Kessinger Publishing, LLC.

Wall, Patricia Q. Child Out of Place: A Story for New England. Ronnquist, Debby, illus. 2003. 116p. (J). (gr. 6-9). pap. 12.00 (978-0-9742185-0-2(2)) Fall Rose Bks.

Wallace, Carey. The Ghost in the Glass House. 2014. (ENG.). 240p. (YA). (gr. 7). pap. 13.99 (978-0-544-33618-6(6), HMH Books For Young Readers) Houghton Mifflin Harcourt Publishing Co.

Wiggin, Kate Douglas. Rebecca of Sunnybrook Farm. (J). 23.95 (978-0-8488-0854-9(1)) Amereon Ltd.

—Rebecca of Sunnybrook Farm. 2003. (Dover Children's Evergreen Classics Ser.). (ENG.). 240p. (J). (gr. 3-8). pap. 4.50 (978-0-486-42845-1(1)) Dover Pubns., Inc.

—Rebecca of Sunnybrook Farm. 2005. pap. 30.95 (978-1-4179-1457-9(2)) Kessinger Publishing, LLC.

—Rebecca of Sunnybrook Farm. 2003. (Aladdin Classics Ser.). (ENG.). 368p. (J). pap. 7.99 (978-0-689-86001-0(3), Aladdin) Simon & Schuster Children's Publishing.

—Rebecca of Sunnybrook Farm. Akib, Jamel, illus. 2007. (Classic Starts(tm) Ser.). (ENG.). 160p. (J). (gr. 2-4). 6.95 (978-1-4027-3693-3(2)) Sterling Publishing Co., Inc.

—Rebecca of Sunnybrook Farm. l.t. ed. 2007. (ENG.). 236p. pap. 22.99 (978-1-4264-9986-9(8)) Creative Media Partners, LLC.

—Rebecca of Sunnybrook Farm. Warren, Eliza Gatewood, ed. Tadiello, Ed, illus. 2006. 240p. (YA). (gr. 4-8). reprint ed. 10.00 (978-0-7567-9830-7(2)) DIANE Publishing Co.

—Rebecca of Sunnybrook Farm. 2004. reprint ed. pap. 19.95 (978-1-4179-9996-5(9)); pap. 1.99 (978-1-4179-9946-0(2)) Kessinger Publishing, LLC.

Wiggin, Kate Douglas & Fisher, Eric Scott. Rebecca of Sunnybrook Farms, 1 vol. 2012. (Calico Illustrated Classics Ser.: No. 4). (ENG., Illus.). 112p. (J). (gr. 3-6). 27.07 (978-1-61641-620-1(3)) Magic Wagon.

Winfield, Arthur M. The Rover Boys down East or the Struggle for the Stanhope Fortune. 2006. (ENG.). 316p. per. 30.95 (978-1-4286-4113-6(0)) Kessinger Publishing, LLC.

Yancey, Rick. The Monstrumologist. (Monstrumologist Ser.: 1). (ENG.). (YA). (gr. 9). 2010. 464p. pap. 11.99 (978-1-4169-8449-8(6)) 2009. 448p. 21.99 (978-1-4169-8448-1(8)) Simon & Schuster Bks. For Young Readers. (Simon & Schuster Bks. For Young Readers).

NEW ENGLAND—HISTORY

Arenstam, Peter, et al. MayFlower 1620: A New Look at a Pilgrim Voyage. 2004. (Illus.). 47p. (J). (gr. k-4). 18.00 (978-0-7567-7967-2(7)) DIANE Publishing Co.

Baker, Alison. New England a to Z. Coffey, Kevin, illus. 2012. 38p. (J). 14.95 (978-1-62086-065-6(1)) Mascot Bks., Inc.

Bartley, Niccole. New England. 2014. (Land That I Love: Regions of the United States Ser.). (Illus.). 32p. (J). (gr. 3-6). 26.25 (978-1-4777-6849-5(1), PowerKids Pr.) Rosen Publishing Group, Inc., The.

Carole Marsh. New England Coloring. 2004. (City Bks.). 24p. (gr. k-5). pap., act. bk. ed. 3.95 (978-0-635-02233-2(8)) Gallopade International.

Cowan, Mary Morton. Timberrr! A History of Logging in New England. 2003. (Women at War Ser.). (Illus.). 128p. (gr. 5-18). lib. bdg. 25.90 (978-0-7613-1866-8(6), Twenty-First Century Bks.) Lerner Publishing Group.

Ferguson, Isabel, et al. A World More Bright: The Life of Mary Baker Eddy. 2013. (Illus.). vi, 279p. (J). (978-0-87510-494-2(0)) Christian Science Publishing Society.

Jameson, W. C. Buried Treasures of New England. 2005. (Buried Treasure Ser.). (ENG.). 192p. (J). (gr. 4-17). pap. 11.95 (978-0-87483-485-7(6)) August Hse. Pubs., Inc.

Koestler-Grack, Rachel A. Northern Colonial Town: Plymouth. 2003. (J). (978-0-58417-016-7(6)) Lake Street Pubs.

Rajczak, Kristen. The Mayflower Compact. 2013. (Documents That Shaped America Ser.). (Illus.). 32p. (J). (gr. 4-6). pap. 10.50 (978-1-4339-9006-9(7)); (ENG.). lib. bdg. 26.60 (978-1-4339-9005-2(9)) Stevens, Gareth Publishing LLLP.

Rajczak Nelson, Kristen. The Mayflower Compact. 2013. (Documents That Shaped America Ser.). (Illus.). 32p. (J). (gr. 4-6). pap. 63.00 (978-1-4339-9007-6(5)) Stevens, Gareth Publishing LLLP.

Seguin, Marilyn. No Ordinary Lives: Four 19th Century Teenage Diaries. 2009. (J). pap. (978-0-8283-2158-7(2)) Branden Bks.

NEW ENGLAND PATRIOTS (FOOTBALL TEAM)

Barrington, Richard. Tom Brady: Super Bowl Champion. 2015. (Living Legends of Sports Ser.). (ENG., Illus.). 48p. (J). (gr. 5-6). 25.85 (978-1-68048-119-8(3), Britannica Educational Publishing) Rosen Publishing Group, Inc., The.

Bell, Lonnie. The History of the New England Patriots. 2004. (NFL Today Ser.). (Illus.). 32p. (YA). (gr. 5-9). 18.95 (978-1-58341-304-3(9)) Creative Co., The.

Buckley, James & Buckley, James, Jr. Tom Brady & the New England Patriots: Super Bowl XLIX. 2015. (Super Bowl Superstars Ser.). (ENG., Illus.). 24p. (J). (gr. 1-3). lib. bdg. 22.61 (978-1-62724-869-3(2)) Bearport Publishing Co., Inc.

Burgess, Zack. Meet the New England Patriots. 2016. (Big Picture Sports Ser.). (ENG., Illus.). 24p. (J). (gr. k-3). lib. bdg. 22.60 (978-1-59953-742-9(7)) Norwood Hse. Pr.

Epstein, Brad M. New England Patriots 101. 2010. (Illus.). 24p. (J). bds. (978-1-60730-118-9(0), 101 Bk.) Michaelson Entertainment.

Frisch, Aaron. New England Patriots. 2014. (Illus.). 24p. (J). (978-1-60818-380-7(7), Creative Education) Creative Co., The.

Leboutillier, Nate. New England Patriots. 2005. (Super Bowl Champions Ser.). (Illus.). 24p. (J). (gr. 1-4). lib. bdg. 16.95 (978-1-58341-386-9(3), Creative Education) Creative Co., The.

MacRae, Sloan. The New England Patriots. 2011. (America's Greatest Teams Ser.). (Illus.). 24p. (J). pap. 8.25 (978-1-4488-2739-8(6)); lib. bdg. 22.60 (978-1-4488-2575-2(X)) Rosen Publishing Group, Inc., The. (PowerKids Pr.).

Motzko, Mary. New England Patriots, 1 vol. 2010. (Inside the NFL Ser.). (ENG.). 48p. (YA). (gr. 3-6). lib. bdg. 32.79 (978-1-61714-019-8(8)) ABDO Publishing Co.

O'Hearn, Michael. The Story of the New England Patriots. 2009. (NFL Today Ser.). (Illus.). 48p. (YA). (gr. 5-9). 22.95 (978-1-58341-763-8(X)) Creative Co., The.

Publications International Ltd. Staff. Yesterday & Today Nfl New England Patriots. 2009. 160p. 24.98 (978-1-4127-9828-0(0)) Publications International, Ltd.

Whiting, Jim. NFL Today: New England Patriots. 2013. (NFL Today Ser.). (ENG.). 48p. (J). (gr. 4-7). pap. 12.00 (978-0-89812-863-5(3), Creative Paperbacks) Creative Co., The.

—The Story of the New England Patriots. 2013. (J). 35.65 (978-1-60818-310-4(6), Creative Education) Creative Co., The.

Wilner, Barry. New England Patriots. 2015. (Insider's Guide to Pro Football Ser.). (ENG.). 32p. (J). (gr. k-3). 28.50 (978-1-63143-989-6(8), 208824) Child's World, Inc., The.

Wyner, Zach. New England Patriots. (Illus.). 32p. (J). 2015. pap. (978-1-4896-0855-0(9)) 2014. (ENG., (gr. 4-7). lib. bdg. 28.55 (978-1-4896-0854-3(0), AV2 by Weigl) Weigl Pubs., Inc.

Zappa, Marcia. New England Patriots, 1 vol. 2014. (NFL's Greatest Teams Ser.). (ENG.). 32p. (gr. 7-11). lib. bdg. 28.50 (978-1-62403-363-6(6), Big Buddy Bks.) ABDO Publishing Co.

NEW FRANCE—HISTORY

see *Canada—History—To 1763 (New France); Mississippi River Valley—History*

NEW GUINEA—FICTION

Crabbe, Kay. The Pearl-Shell Diver: A Story of Adventure from the Torres Strait. 2016. (ENG.). 192p. (J). (gr. 4-8). 11.99 (978-1-76029-047-4(5)) Allen & Unwin AUS. Dist: Independent Pubs. Group.

Nighthawk, Tori. Don't Judge a Bird by Its Feathers. Nighthawk, Tori, illus. 2013. (ENG., Illus.). 60p. (J). (gr. -1-3). 17.99 (978-0-9858811-9-1(4)) Stone, Anne Publishing.

NEW HAMPSHIRE

Brown, Dottie. New Hampshire. 2012. (J). lib. bdg. 25.26 (978-0-7613-4545-9(0), Lerner Pubns.) Lerner Publishing Group.

Graham, Amy. New Hampshire: A MyReportLinks.com Book. 2003. (States Ser.). (Illus.). 48p. (J). (gr. 4-10). lib. bdg. 25.26 (978-0-7660-5108-9(0), MyReportLinks.com Bks.) Enslow Pubs., Inc.

Harris, Marie. Primary Numbers: A New Hampshire Numbers Book. Holman, Karen Busch, illus. 2004. (Count Your Way Across the U. S. A. Ser.). (ENG.). 40p. (J). 16.95 (978-1-58536-192-2(5)) Sleeping Bear Pr.

Hicks, Terry Allan. New Hampshire. 2004. (It's My State! Ser.). (Illus.). 78p. (J). (gr. 3-7). lib. bdg. 27.07 (978-0-7614-1825-2(3), Benchmark Bks.) Marshall Cavendish Corp.

Marsh, Carole. New Hampshire Geography Projects: 30 Cool, Activities, Crafts, Experiments & More for Kids to Do to Learn about Your State! 2003. (New Hampshire Experience Ser.). 32p. (gr. k-5). pap. 5.95 (978-0-635-01848-9(9), Marsh, Carole Bks.) Gallopade International.

—New Hampshire Government Projects: 30 Cool, Activities, Crafts, Experiments & More for Kids to Do to Learn about Your State! 2003. (New Hampshire Experience Ser.). 32p. (gr. k-5). pap. 5.95 (978-0-635-01948-6(5), Marsh, Carole Bks.) Gallopade International.

—New Hampshire People Projects: 30 Cool, Activities, Crafts, Experiments & More for Kids to Do to Learn about Your State! 2003. (New Hampshire Experience Ser.). 32p. (gr. k-5). pap. 5.95 (978-0-635-01998-1(1), Marsh, Carole Bks.) Gallopade International.

—New Hampshire Symbols & Facts Projects: 30 Cool, Activities, Crafts, Experiments & More for Kids to Do to Learn about Your State! 2003. (New Hampshire Experience Ser.). 32p. (gr. k-8). pap. 5.95 (978-0-635-01898-4(5), Marsh, Carole Bks.) Gallopade International.

Mattern, Joanne. New Hampshire: The Granite State. 2003. (World Almanac Library of the States). (Illus.). 48p. (gr. 4-9). pap. 14.05 (978-0-8368-5326-1(1)); lib. bdg. 31.00 (978-0-8368-5155-7(2)) Stevens, Gareth Publishing LLLP. (Gareth Stevens Learning Library).

Mills, Jordan. New Hampshire. 2016. (States Ser.). (ENG., Illus.). 32p. (gr. 3-4). lib. bdg. 27.32 (978-1-5157-0416-4(5)) Next Page Pr., The.

Murray, Julie. New Hampshire, 1 vol. 2006. (United States Ser.). (ENG., Illus.). 32p. (gr. 2-4). 27.07 (978-1-59197-688-2(X), Buddy Bks.) ABDO Publishing Co.

Otfinoski, Steven. New Hampshire. 2nd rev. ed. 2007. (Celebrate the States Ser.). 144p. (gr. 6). lib. bdg. 42.79 (978-0-7614-2718-6(X), Benchmark Bks.) Marshall Cavendish Corp.

Peters, S. True. How to Draw New Hampshire's Sights & Symbols. 2009. (Kid's Guide to Drawing America Ser.). 32p. (gr. k-k). 50.50 (978-1-61511-078-0(X), PowerKids Pr.) Rosen Publishing Group, Inc., The.

Thomas, William David. New Hampshire. 2006. (Portraits of the States Ser.). (gr. 2-6). pap. 10.50 (978-0-8368-4721-5(0), Gareth Stevens Learning Library) Stevens, Gareth Publishing LLLP.

—New Hampshire. 2006. (Portraits of the States Ser.). (Illus.). 32p. (gr. 2-6). lib. bdg. 26.00 (978-0-8368-4704-8(0), Gareth Stevens Learning Library) Stevens, Gareth Publishing LLLP.

Way, Jennifer. New Hampshire. 2009. (Bilingual Library of the United States of America Ser.). (ENG & SPA.). 32p. (gr. 2-2). 47.90 (978-1-60853-373-2(5), Editorial Buenas Letras) Rosen Publishing Group, Inc., The.

—New Hampshire/Nuevo Hampshire. Brusca, Maria Cristina, tr. from ENG. 2006. (Bilingual Library of the United States of America Ser.: Set 2). (ENG & SPA., Illus.). 32p. (J). (gr. 3-6). lib. bdg. 25.25 (978-1-4042-3094-1(7)) Rosen Publishing Group, Inc., The.

NEW HAMPSHIRE—FICTION

Absolutely Truly: A Pumpkin Falls Mystery. 2014. (Pumpkin Falls Mystery Ser.). (ENG., Illus.). 368p. (J). (gr. 3-7). 17.99 *(978-1-4424-2972-7(0)*, Simon & Schuster Bks. For Young Readers) Simon & Schuster Bks. For Young Readers.

Aldridge, Janet. The Meadow-Brook Girls in the Hills: Or the Missing Pilot of the White Mountains. 2006. pap. *(978-1-4065-0694-5(X))* Dodo Pr.

Alger, Horatio. Bound to Rise: Or: up the Ladder. 2007. (ENG.). 172p. per. 19.99 *(978-1-4346-5059-7(6))*; 188p. per. 21.99 *(978-1-4346-5060-3(X))* Creative Media Partners, LLC.

—Risen from the Ranks: Or, Harry Walton's Success. 2006. (ENG.). 194p. pap. 19.99 *(978-1-4264-6391-4(X))*; 216p. pap. 22.99 *(978-1-4264-6465-2(7))* Creative Media Partners, LLC.

—Risen from the Ranks: Or, Harry Walton's Success. 2006. pap. *(978-1-4065-0721-8(0))* Dodo Pr.

Arenstam, Peter. Nicholas: A New Hampshire Tale. Holman, Karen Busch, illus. 2009. (Nicholas Northeastern Ser.: 3). (ENG.). 144p. (J). (gr. k-7). 14.95 *(978-1-58726-521-1(4)*, Mitten Pr.) Ann Arbor Editions LLC.

Banks, Kate. Dillon Dillon. 2005. 149p. (gr. 3-7). 18.00 *(978-0-7569-5767-4(2))* Perfection Learning Corp.

Bruchac, Joseph. The Heart of a Chief. 2007. 153p. (gr. 4-7). 17.00 *(978-0-7569-7805-1(X))* Perfection Learning Corp.

—Night Wings. Comport, Sally Wern, illus. 2009. (ENG.). 208p. (J). (gr. 3-7). 15.99 *(978-0-06-112318-4(8))* HarperCollins Pubs.

Cornwell, Betsy. Tides. 2014. (ENG.). 304p. (YA). (gr. 7). pap. 8.99 *(978-0-544-30296-9(6)*, HMH Books For Young Readers) Houghton Mifflin Harcourt Publishing Co.

DeMitchell, Terri A. The Portsmouth Alarm. 2013. 161p. pap. 16.95 *(978-1-932278-92-7(3))* Mayhaven Publishing, Inc.

Douglass, E. The Squirrel Friends Adventures: The Monster & the Great Storm. 2013. 100p. 19.95 *(978-1-4759-6640-4(7))*; pap. 9.95 *(978-1-4759-6638-1(5))* iUniverse, Inc.

Eaton, Walter Prichard. Boy Scouts in the White Mountains: the Story of a Long Hike. Merrill, Frank T., illus. 2006. (ENG.). 316p. per. 30.95 *(978-1-4286-4117-4(3))* Kessinger Publishing, LLC.

Emerson, Kevin. Carlos Is Gonna Get It. 2008. (J). pap. *(978-0-439-93526-5(1)*, Levine, Arthur A. Bks.) Scholastic, Inc.

Farish, Terry. Either the Beginning or the End of the World. 2015. (ENG.). 200p. (YA). (gr. 8-12). 18.99 *(978-1-4677-8813-7(9)*, Carolrhoda Lab™); 18.99 *(978-1-4677-7483-3(9))* Lerner Publishing Group.

Frederick, Heather Vogel. Absolutely Truly. 2015. (Pumpkin Falls Mystery Ser.). (ENG., Illus.). 368p. (J). (gr. 3-7). pap. 7.99 *(978-1-4424-2973-4(9)*, Simon & Schuster Bks. For Young Readers) Simon & Schuster Bks. For Young Readers.

—Mother-Daughter Book Camp. 2016. (Mother-Daughter Book Club Ser.). (ENG., Illus.). 336p. (J). (gr. 5-9). 16.99 *(978-1-4424-7183-2(2)*, Simon & Schuster Bks. For Young Readers) Simon & Schuster Bks. For Young Readers.

Frizzell, Sally Parker. The Adventures in the Secret Valley. 2007. 40p. pap. 9.00 *(978-0-8059-7615-1(9))* Dorrance Publishing Co., Inc.

Gamble, Adam. Good Night New Hampshire. Rosen, Anne, illus. 2009. (Good Night Our World Ser.). (ENG.). 20p. (J). (gr. k — 1). bds. 9.95 *(978-1-60219-037-5(2))* Good Night Bks.

Hall, Donald. Lucy's Summer. McCurdy, Michael, illus. 2008. (ENG.). 40p. (J). (gr. 1-18). pap. 10.95 *(978-1-56792-348-3(8))* Godine, David R. Pub.

Harrar, George. The Trouble with Jeremy Chance. Thayer, Elizabeth, illus. 2007. (Historical Fiction for Young Readers Ser.). (ENG.). 168p. (J). (gr. 2-8). per. 6.95 *(978-1-57131-669-1(8))* Milkweed Editions.

Hendrickson, David H. Cracking the Ice. 2011. (YA). 365p. (gr. 9-18). 16.95 *(978-1-934813-55-3(9))*; 366p. *(978-1-934813-56-0(7))* Westside Bks.

Hilton, Marilyn. Found Things. (ENG.). 240p. (J). (gr. 4-7). 2015. pap. 7.99 *(978-1-4424-6088-1(1))* 2014. 16.99 *(978-1-4424-6087-4(3))* Simon & Schuster Children's Publishing.

Jacobs, Lily. The Littlest Bunny in New Hampshire: An Easter Adventure. Dunn, Robert, illus. 2015. (ENG.). 32p. (J). (-3). 9.99 *(978-1-4926-1141-7(7)*, Sourcebooks Jabberwocky) Sourcebooks, Inc.

Jacobson, Jennifer Richard. Stained. (ENG.). 208p. (YA). (gr. 8). 2012. pap. 10.99 *(978-1-4424-8565-5(5)*, Atheneum Bks. for Young Readers) 2005. (Illus.). 16.95 *(978-0-689-86745-3(X)*, Atheneum/Richard Jackson Bks.) Simon & Schuster Children's Publishing.

James, Eric. A Halloween Scare in New Hampshire. Le Ray, Marina, illus. 2015. (ENG.). 32p. (J). (-5). 9.99 *(978-1-4926-2387-8(3)*, 9781492623878, Sourcebooks Jabberwocky) Sourcebooks, Inc.

—Santa's Sleigh Is on Its Way to New Hampshire: A Christmas Adventure. Dunn, Robert, illus. 2016. (ENG.). 32p. (J). (-2). 12.99 *(978-1-4926-4342-5(4)*, 9781492643425, Sourcebooks Jabberwocky) Sourcebooks, Inc.

Janelle, Dick. Salmon Falls 1956. 2012. (ENG.). (YA). pap. 15.00 *(978-0-9856073-7-1(8))* RIVERRUN BOOKSTORE INC.

Jensen, Dorothea. A Buss from Lafayette. 2016. (ENG.). 266p. (J). (gr. 5-9). pap. 16.95 *(978-1-939371-90-4(2))* Boutique of Quality Books Publishing Co., Inc.

Koncerak, Veronica. The Bubble That Never Popped. 2010. 24p. 11.49 *(978-1-4520-3935-0(6))* AuthorHouse.

Logue, C. Robert & Logue, Michael. From the Top of the Mountain. 2013. (ENG.). 50p. (J). pap. 12.99 *(978-1-936172-74-0(7))* Eifrig Publishing.

Lord, Cynthia. Half a Chance. 2014. (ENG.). 224p. (J). (gr. 3-7). 16.99 *(978-0-545-03533-0(3)*, Scholastic Pr.) Scholastic, Inc.

Monninger, Joseph. Game Change. 2017. (ENG.). 240p. (YA). (gr. 9). 17.99 ***(978-0-544-53122-2(1)***, HMH Books For Young Readers) Houghton Mifflin Harcourt Publishing Co.

Monninger, Joseph. Whippoorwill. 2016. (ENG.). 288p. (YA). (gr. 7). pap. 9.99 *(978-0-544-81356-4(1)*, HMH Books For Young Readers) Houghton Mifflin Harcourt Publishing Co.

Philbrick, Rodman. The Big Dark. (ENG.). 192p. (J). (gr. 3-7). 2017. pap. 6.99 ***(978-0-545-78976-9(1))*** 2016. 17.99 *(978-0-545-78975-2(3))* Scholastic, Inc. (Blue Sky Pr., The).

Rand, Johnathan. American Chillers #24 Haunting in New Hampshire. 2008. 208p. (J). pap. 5.99 *(978-1-893699-96-0(X))* AudioCraft Publishing, Inc.

Rowland, Wickie. Good Morning, Strawbery Banke. 2010. (ENG.). 40p. (J). (gr. -1-5). pap. 12.95 *(978-1-935557-62-3(9))* PublishingWorks.

Schmidt, Gary D. First Boy. 2007. (ENG.). 224p. (YA). (gr. 5-9). per. 10.99 *(978-0-312-37149-4(7)*, 9780312371494) Square Fish.

Schoen, Robin. Grandmother's Guest: The Blue Lady of Wilton. Hoar, Gail, illus. 2013. 32p. 16.95 *(978-0-615-89154-5(3))* Hobby Horse Publishing, LLC.

Silvano, Wendi. Love Is All Around New Hampshire. Czernichowska, Joanna, illus. 2016. (ENG.). 32p. (J). (-6). 12.99 *(978-1-4926-2942-9(1)*, Sourcebooks Jabberwocky) Sourcebooks, Inc.

Smallman, Steve. Santa Is Coming to New Hampshire. Dunn, Robert, illus. 2014. (ENG.). 32p. (J). (-3). 9.99 *(978-1-4926-0676-5(6)*, Sourcebooks Jabberwocky) Sourcebooks, Inc.

Specter, Baron. The Star Island Spirits: #5, 1 vol. Evans, Dustin, illus. 2010. (Ghostly Graphic Adventures Ser.). (ENG.). 32p. (J). (gr. 3-6). 28.50 *(978-1-60270-774-0(X))* ABDO Publishing Co.

Tomaszewski, Suzanne Lyon. Samuel's Exeter Walkabout. Dionne, Nina, illus. 2003. 37p. (J). *(978-0-9744855-0-8(0))* Gold Charm Publishing, LLC.

Townley, Roderick. The Red Thread: A Novel in Three Incarnations. 2012. (ENG.). 304p. (YA). (gr. 7). pap. 14.99 *(978-1-4169-0895-1(1)*, Atheneum Bks. for Young Readers) Simon & Schuster Children's Publishing.

Tregay, Sarah. Love & Leftovers. (ENG.). (YA). (gr. 8). 2014. 464p. pap. 9.99 *(978-0-06-202360-5(8))* 2011. 448p. 17.99 *(978-0-06-202358-2(6))* HarperCollins Pubs. (Tegen, Katherine Bks).

Urban, Linda. The Center of Everything. (ENG.). 208p. (J). (gr. 5-7). 2015. pap. 7.99 *(978-0-544-34069-5(8)*, HMH Books For Young Readers) 2013. 15.99 *(978-0-547-76348-4(4))* Houghton Mifflin Harcourt Publishing Co.

Wallace, Rich. Wicked Cruel. 2015. (ENG.). 208p. (J). (gr. 5). pap. 6.99 *(978-0-375-86514-5(4)*, Yearling) Random Hse. Children's Bks.

NEW HAMPSHIRE—HISTORY

Auden, Scott. New Hampshire 1603-1776. 2007. (National Geographic Voices from ColonialAmerica Ser.). (ENG., Illus.). 112p. (J). (gr. 5-9). 21.95 *(978-1-4263-0034-9(4))*; lib. bdg. 32.90 *(978-1-4263-0035-6(2))* National Geographic Society. (National Geographic Children's Bks.).

Cherry, Lynne. A River Ran Wild. 2005. 17.00 *(978-0-7569-5231-0(X))* Perfection Learning Corp.

Ciarleglio, Lauren. New Hampshire: Past & Present. 2010. (United States: Past & Present Ser.). (ENG.). 48p. (YA). pap. 11.75 *(978-1-4358-9516-4(9))*; lib. bdg. 29.25 *(978-1-4358-9489-1(8))* Rosen Publishing Group, Inc., The. (Rosen Reference).

Craats, Rennay. New Hampshire. 2011. (Guide to American States Ser.). (Illus.). 48p. (YA). (gr. 3-6). 29.99 *(978-1-61690-801-0(7))* Weigl Pubs., Inc.

—New Hampshire: The Granite State. 2016. (J). *(978-1-4896-4902-7(6))* Weigl Pubs., Inc.

Cunningham, Kevin. The New Hampshire Colony. 2011. (True Bk Ser.). (ENG., Illus.). 48p. (J). pap. 6.95 *(978-0-531-26605-2(2))*; lib. bdg. 29.00 *(978-0-531-25392-2(9))* Scholastic Library Publishing. (Children's Pr.).

Doherty, Craig A. & Doherty, Katherine M. New Hampshire. 2005. (Thirteen Colonies Ser.). (Illus.). 144p. (gr. 5-8). 35.00 *(978-0-8160-5411-4(8))* Facts On File, Inc.

Gagnon, Lauren. An Exeter Alphabet: Learning about Exeter from A to Z. 2005. (Illus.). 44p. (J). (gr. 3-7). per. *(978-1-933002-05-7(0))* PublishingWorks.

Haulley, Fletcher. A Primary Source History of the Colony of New Hampshire. (Primary Sources of the Thirteen Colonies & the Lost Colony Ser.). 64p. 2009. (gr. 5-8). 58.50 *(978-1-60851-881-4(7))* 2006. (Illus.). (YA). (gr. 4-7). lib. bdg. 31.95 *(978-1-4042-0429-4(6))* 2006. (ENG., Illus.). (gr. 4-8). per. 12.95 *(978-1-4042-0676-2(0))* Rosen Publishing Group, Inc., The.

Jensen, Niels R. New Hampshire, 1 vol. 2009. (United States Ser.). (ENG., Illus.). 48p. (YA). (gr. 2-5). 27.07 *(978-1-60453-664-5(0))* ABDO Publishing Co.

Kent, Deborah. New Hampshire (Revised Edition) 2014. (America the Beautiful, Third Ser. (Revised Edition) Ser.). (ENG., Illus.). 144p. (J). lib. bdg. 40.00 *(978-0-531-28284-7(8))* Scholastic Library Publishing.

Koontz, Robin Michal. New Hampshire: The Granite State. 2010. (Our Amazing States Ser.). (ENG.). 24p. (J). pap. 8.25 *(978-1-4488-0728-4(X))*; lib. bdg. 22.60 *(978-1-4488-0648-5(8))* Rosen Publishing Group, Inc., The. (PowerKids Pr.).

Kopp, Megan. New Hampshire: The Granite State. 2012. (J). *(978-1-61913-377-8(6))*; pap. *(978-1-61913-378-5(4))* Weigl Pubs., Inc.

Marsh, Carole. Exploring New Hampshire Through Project-Based Learning: Geography, History, Government, Economics & More. 2016. (New Hampshire Experience Ser.). (ENG.). (J). pap. 9.99 *(978-0-635-12353-4(3))* Gallopade International.

—I'm Reading about New Hampshire. 2014. (New Hampshire Experience Ser.). (ENG., Illus.). (J). pap., pap. 8.99 *(978-0-635-11304-7(X))* Gallopade International.

—New Hampshire History Projects: 30 Cool, Activities, Crafts, Experiments & More for Kids to Do to Learn about Your State! 2003. (New Hampshire Experience Ser.). 32p. (gr. k-5). pap. 5.95 *(978-0-635-01798-7(9)*, Marsh, Carole Bks.) Gallopade International.

Mis, Melody S. The Colony of New Hampshire: A Primary Source History. (Primary Source Library of the Thirteen Colonies & the Lost Colony Ser.). 24p. (gr. 3-4). 2009. 42.50 *(978-1-60854-143-0(6))* 2006. (Illus.). (J). lib. bdg. 22.60 *(978-1-4042-3435-2(7))* Rosen Publishing Group, Inc., The. (PowerKids Pr.).

Moore, David. Expl on Your Own the Old Man of the Mtn. 2009. (Explore on Your Own Ser.). (ENG., Illus.). 12p. (J). pap. 7.95 *(978-0-7362-5581-3(8))* National Geographic School Publishing, Inc.

Murray, Julie. New Hampshire, 1 vol. 2012. (Explore the United States Ser.). (ENG., Illus.). 32p. (J). (gr. 2-5). lib. bdg. 28.50 *(978-1-61783-367-0(3)*, Big Buddy Bks.) ABDO Publishing Co.

Raum, Elizabeth. Exploring the New Hampshire Colony. 2016. (Exploring the 13 Colonies Ser.). (ENG., Illus.). 48p. (gr. 3-4). lib. bdg. 31.99 *(978-1-5157-2236-6(8))* Capstone Press of Coughlan Cos.

Rissman, Rebecca. What's Great about New Hampshire? 2015. (Our Great States Ser.). (ENG., Illus.). 32p. (J). (gr. 2-5). lib. bdg. 26.60 *(978-1-4677-3858-3(1)*, Lerner Pubns.) Lerner Publishing Group.

Shannon, Terry Miller. New Hampshire. 2009. (From Sea to Shining Sea, Second Ser.). (ENG.). 80p. (J). pap. 7.95 *(978-0-531-21138-0(X)*, Children's Pr.) Scholastic Library Publishing.

Waring, Kerry Jones, et al. New Hampshire. 2015. (It's My State! (r) Ser.). (ENG., Illus.). 80p. (J). (gr. 4-4). 34.21 *(978-1-62713-166-7(3))* Cavendish Square Publishing.

Wimmer, Teresa. New Hampshire. 2009. (This Land Called America Ser.). (Illus.). 32p. (YA). (gr. 3-6). 19.95 *(978-1-58341-782-9(6))* Creative Co., The.

Wyborny, Sheila. New Hampshire. 2003. (Seeds of a Nation Ser.). (Illus.). 48p. (J). (gr. 3-5). 23.70 *(978-0-7377-1448-7(4)*, Kidhaven) Cengage Gale.

Ziff, John. Northern New England: Maine, New Hampshire, Vermont, Vol. 19. 2015. (Let's Explore the States Ser.). (Illus.). 64p. (J). (gr. 5). 23.95 *(978-1-4222-3330-6(8))* Mason Crest.

NEW JERSEY

Brown, Vanessa. New Jersey. 2009. (Bilingual Library of the United States of America Ser.). (ENG & SPA.). 32p. (gr. 2-2). 47.90 *(978-1-60853-374-9(3)*, Editorial Buenas Letras) Rosen Publishing Group, Inc., The.

—New Jersey/Nueva Jersey. Brusca, Maria Cristina, tr. from ENG. 2006. (Bilingual Library of the United States of America Ser.: Set 2). (ENG & SPA., Illus.). 32p. (J). (gr. 3-6). lib. bdg. 25.25 *(978-1-4042-3095-8(5))* Rosen Publishing Group, Inc., The.

Cameron, Eileen. G Is for Garden State: A New Jersey Alphabet. Ettlinger, Doris, illus. 2004. (Discover America State by State Ser.). (ENG.). 40p. (J). 17.95 *(978-1-58536-152-6(6))* Sleeping Bear Pr.

Evento, Susan. Nueva Jersey. Hamilton, Harriet, tr. from ENG. 2005. (Rookie Español Geografía Ser.). (ENG & SPA., Illus.). 32p. (J). (gr. k-2). lib. bdg. 19.50 *(978-0-516-25246-9(1)*, Children's Pr.) Scholastic Library Publishing.

Evento, Susan & Vargus, Nanci Reginelli. New Jersey. 2004. (Rookie Read-About Geography Ser.). (J). 20.50 *(978-0-516-22754-2(8)*, Children's Pr.) Scholastic Library Publishing.

Fredeen, Charles. New Jersey. (J). 2012. lib. bdg. 25.26 *(978-0-7613-4546-6(9)*, Lerner Pubns.) 2nd exp. rev. ed. 2003. (Illus.). 84p. (gr. 3-6). pap. 6.95 *(978-0-8225-4148-6(3))* Lerner Publishing Group.

Gamble, Adam & Clark, Dennis. Good Night New Jersey. Veno, Joe, illus. 2008. (Good Night Our World Ser.). (ENG.). 20p. (J). (gr. k — 1). bds. 9.95 *(978-1-60219-025-2(9))* Good Night Bks.

Herman, Gail & dePaola, Tomie. Who Is Derek Jeter? Thomson, Andrew, illus. 2015. (Who Was? Ser.). (ENG.). 112p. (J). (gr. 3-7). 5.99 *(978-0-448-48697-0(0)*, Grosset & Dunlap) Penguin Young Readers Group.

Holden, Henry M. New Jersey: A MyReportLinks. Com Book. 2003. (States Ser.). (Illus.). 48p. (J). lib. bdg. 25.26 *(978-0-7660-5124-9(2)*, MyReportLinks.com Bks.) Enslow Pubs., Inc.

Holtz, Eric Siegfried. Nueva Jersey. Porras, Carlos & D'Andrea, Patricia, trs. from ENG. 2003. (World Almanac Biblioteca de los Estados). (SPA., Illus.). 48p. (gr. 4-9). lib. bdg. 31.00 *(978-0-8368-5545-6(0)*, Gareth Stevens Learning Library) Stevens, Gareth Publishing LLLP.

Kent, Deborah. New Jersey. 144p. (J). 2011. (America the Beautiful, Third Ser.). pap. 12.95 *(978-0-531-22921-7(1)*, Children's Pr.) 2014. (America the Beautiful Ser.: 3). (ENG.). lib. bdg. 40.00 *(978-0-531-24894-2(1))* Scholastic Library Publishing.

Lohnes, Marilyn. F Is for Fiddlehead: A New Brunswick Alphabet. Tooke, Susan, illus. rev. ed. 2007. (Discover Canada Province by Province Ser.). (ENG.). 40p. (J). (gr. 1-7). 17.95 *(978-1-58536-318-6(9))* Sleeping Bear Pr.

Malaspina, Ann. New Jersey. 2005. (Portraits of the States Ser.). (Illus.). 32p. (gr. 2-6). pap. 10.50 *(978-0-8368-4648-5(6))*; lib. bdg. 26.00 *(978-0-8368-4629-4(X))* Stevens, Gareth Publishing LLLP. (Gareth Stevens Learning Library).

Marsh, Carole. My First Book about New Jersey. 2004. (New Jersey Experience! Ser.). (Illus.). 32p. (J). (gr. k-4). pap. 7.95 *(978-0-7933-9521-7(6))* Gallopade International.

—My First Pocket Guide New Jersey. 2004. (New Jersey Experience! Ser.). (Illus.). 96p. (J). (gr. 3-8). pap. 6.95 *(978-0-7933-9453-1(8))* Gallopade International.

—New Jersey Current Events Projects: 30 Cool, Activities, Crafts, Experiments & More for Kids to Do to Learn about Your State! 2003. (New Jersey Experience Ser.). 32p. (gr. k-8). pap. 5.95 *(978-0-635-02049-9(1)*, Marsh, Carole Bks.) Gallopade International.

—New Jersey Geography Projects: 30 Cool, Activities, Crafts, Experiments & More for Kids to Do to Learn about Your State! 2003. (New Jersey Experience Ser.). 32p. (gr. k-5). pap. 5.95 *(978-0-635-01849-6(7)*, Marsh, Carole Bks.) Gallopade International.

—New Jersey Government Projects: 30 Cool, Activities, Crafts, Experiments & More for Kids to Do to Learn about Your State! 2003. (New Jersey Experience Ser.). 32p. (gr. k-5). pap. 5.95 *(978-0-635-01949-3(3)*, Marsh, Carole Bks.) Gallopade International.

—New Jersey Jeopardy! Answers & Questions about Our State! 2004. (New Jersey Experience! Ser.). (Illus.). 32p. (J). (gr. 3-8). pap. 7.95 *(978-0-7933-9522-4(4))* Gallopade International.

—New Jersey "Jography" A Fun Run Thru Our State! 2004. (New Jersey Experience! Ser.). (Illus.). 32p. (J). (gr. 3-8). pap. 7.95 *(978-0-7933-9523-1(2))* Gallopade International.

—New Jersey People Projects: 30 Cool, Activities, Crafts, Experiments & More for Kids to Do to Learn about Your State! 2003. (New Jersey Experience Ser.). 32p. (gr. k-5). pap. 5.95 *(978-0-635-01999-8(X)*, Marsh, Carole Bks.) Gallopade International.

—New Jersey Symbols & Facts Projects: 30 Cool, Activities, Crafts, Experiments & More for Kids to Do to Learn about Your State! 2003. (New Jersey Experience Ser.). 32p. (gr. k-5). pap. 5.95 *(978-0-635-01899-1(3)*, Marsh, Carole Bks.) Gallopade International.

—The Nifty New Jersey Coloring Book. 2004. (New Jersey Experience! Ser.). (Illus.). 32p. (J). (gr. k-2). pap. 3.95 *(978-0-7933-9473-9(2))* Gallopade International.

Mills, Jordan. New Jersey. 2016. (States Ser.). (ENG., Illus.). 32p. (gr. 3-4). lib. bdg. 27.32 *(978-1-5157-0417-1(3))* Next Page Pr., The.

Mis, M. S. How to Draw New Jersey's Sights & Symbols. 2009. (Kid's Guide to Drawing America Ser.). 32p. (gr. k-k). 50.50 *(978-1-61511-079-7(8)*, PowerKids Pr.) Rosen Publishing Group, Inc., The.

Murray, Julie. New Jersey, 1 vol. 2006. (Buddy Book Ser.). (ENG., Illus.). 32p. (gr. 2-4). 27.07 *(978-1-59197-689-9(8)*, Buddy Bks.) ABDO Publishing Co.

Nagelhout, Ryan. The Hindenburg Disaster. 2015. (Doomed! Ser.). (ENG., Illus.). 32p. (J). (gr. 4-5). 26.60 *(978-1-4824-2938-1(1))* Stevens, Gareth Publishing LLLP.

New Jersey. 2003. (Switched on Schoolhouse Ser.). cd-rom 24.95 *(978-0-7403-0654-9(5))* Alpha Omega Pubns., Inc.

Otfinoski, Steven. The Hindenburg Explosion: Core Events of a Disaster in the Air, 1 vol. 2014. (What Went Wrong? Ser.). (ENG.). 32p. (gr. 3-4). lib. bdg. 27.32 *(978-1-4765-4184-6(1))* Capstone Press of Coughlan Cos.

Scholl, Elizabeth J. New Jersey. 2008. (From Sea to Shining Sea, Second Ser.). (ENG., Illus.). 80p. (J). (gr. 3-5). pap. 7.95 *(978-0-531-18806-4(X)*, Children's Pr.) Scholastic Library Publishing.

Webber, Diane. Celebrity's Son Snatched: Can Handwriting Help Nab the Perp? 2011. (J). pap. *(978-0-545-32810-4(1))* Scholastic, Inc.

Yomtov, Nelson. New Jersey. 2017. (True Book — My United States Ser.). (ENG.). 48p. (J). pap. 7.95 ***(978-0-531-23291-0(3)***, Children's Pr.) Scholastic Library Publishing.

You, New jersey & the World. 2004. lib. bdg. *(978-0-89359-121-2(1))* Afton Publishing.

NEW JERSEY—FICTION

Amato, Anne McCoy. Moving Shelly: A Novel. 2010. 148p. (gr. 4-6). pap. 12.95 *(978-1-4502-2584-7(5))* iUniverse, Inc.

Arnold, David. Kids of Appetite. (ENG.). (YA). (gr. 9). 2017. 368p. pap. 10.99 ***(978-0-14-751366-3(9)***, Speak) 2016. 352p. 18.99 *(978-0-451-47078-2(8)*, Viking Books for Young Readers) Penguin Young Readers Group.

—Kids of Appetite. 2017. lib. bdg. 22.10 ***(978-0-606-40491-4(0))*** Turtleback Bks.

Bauman, Beth Ann. Rosie & Skate. 2011. (ENG.). 224p. (YA). (gr. 9). pap. 8.99 *(978-0-385-73736-4(X)*, Ember) Random Hse. Children's Bks.

Blake-Garrett, Andrea. Las Aventuras de Izzy y Juju: Gemelos Detectives Investigadores (G. D. I.) 2012. 28p. pap. 19.99 *(978-1-4772-2523-3(4))* AuthorHouse.

Blume, Judy. Superfudge. 2007. (Fudge Bks.: 3).Tr. of Superfudge. lib. bdg. 18.40 *(978-1-4177-8843-9(7)*, Turtleback) Turtleback Bks.

—Then Again, Maybe I Won't. (J). 125p. pap. 3.99 *(978-0-8072-1445-9(0))*; 2004. 164p. (gr. 5-9). pap. 29.00 incl. audio *(978-0-8072-0796-3(9)*, LYA 354 SP) Random Hse. Audio Publishing Group. (Listening Library).

Brendler, Carol. Radio Girl. 2013. (ENG.). 224p. (J). (gr. 5-9). 16.95 *(978-0-8234-2861-8(3))* Holiday Hse., Inc.

Bryant, Jen. Kaleidoscope Eyes. 2010. (ENG.). 272p. (J). (gr. 3-7). 7.99 *(978-0-440-42190-0(X)*, Yearling) Random Hse. Children's Bks.

Bryant, Jennifer. The Trial. 2005. (ENG., Illus.). 176p. (J). (gr. 3-7). 5.99 *(978-0-440-41986-0(7)*, Yearling) Random Hse. Children's Bks.

Budhos, Marina. Tell Us We're Home. 2011. (ENG.). 320p. (YA). (gr. 7). pap. 9.99 *(978-1-4424-2128-8(2)*, Atheneum Bks. for Young Readers) Simon & Schuster Children's Publishing.

Campbell, Angella. Angel & Turkish. 2011. 32p. pap. 14.99 *(978-1-4634-0372-0(0))* AuthorHouse.

Carbone, Elisa. Heroes of the Surf. Carpenter, Nancy, illus. 2012. (ENG.). 40p. (J). (gr. -1-3). 16.99 *(978-0-670-06312-3(6)*, Viking Books for Young Readers) Penguin Young Readers Group.

Carestio, Michael A. Black Jack Jetty: A Boy's Journey Through Grief. 2010. (Illus.). 64p. (J). (gr. 3-8). 14.95 *(978-1-4338-0784-8(X))*; pap. 9.95 *(978-1-4338-0786-2(6))* American Psychological Assn. (Magination Pr.).

Carlos the Sailor Visits Atlantic City. 2005. (J). pap. 12.95 *(978-0-9766889-0-7(5))* ComteQ Publishing.

Cofer, Judith Ortiz. An Island Like You: Stories of the Barrio. 2009. 243p. 17.00 *(978-1-60686-446-3(7))* Perfection Learning Corp.

Constantine, Robin. The Promise of Amazing. (ENG.). (YA). (gr. 9). 2015. 400p. pap. 9.99 *(978-0-06-227949-1(1))* 2013. 384p. 17.99 *(978-0-06-227948-4(3))* HarperCollins Pubs.

—The Secrets of Attraction. 2015. (ENG.). 384p. (YA). (gr. 9). 17.99 *(978-0-06-227951-4(3))* HarperCollins Pubs.

Corrigan, Eireann. Accomplice. 2010. (ENG.). 304p. (J). (gr. 7-7). 17.99 *(978-0-545-05236-8(X)*, Scholastic Pr.) Scholastic, Inc.

Danziger, Paula. Amber Brown Is Green with Envy. 2014. (Amber Brown Ser.: 9). (ENG., Illus.). 176p. (J). (gr. 2-5). pap. 5.99 *(978-0-14-242699-9(7)*, Puffin Books) Penguin Young Readers Group.

Díaz, Junot. Drown. 2014. (ENG.). 1p. (gr. 1-4). 20.25 *(978-1-63245-053-1(4))* Lectorum Pubns., Inc.

—Drown. 2011. 14.45 *(978-0-7848-3380-3(X))*; 14.45 *(978-0-7848-3428-2(8))* Marco Bk. Co. (Everbind).

Doktorski, Jennifer Salvato. The Summer after You & Me. 2015. (ENG.). 304p. (YA). (gr. 8-12). pap. 10.99 *(978-1-4926-1903-1(5))* Sourcebooks, Inc.

Dorisann. Blasting Ogres. 2012. 108p. (gr. 4-6). 20.95 *(978-1-4759-2900-3(5))*; pap. 10.95 *(978-1-4759-2899-0(8))* iUniverse, Inc.

M
N
O

Durst, Sarah Beth. Enchanted Ivy. (ENG.). (YA). (gr. 7). 2011. 336p. pap. 9.99 *(978-1-4169-8646-1(4))* 2010. 320p. 16.99 *(978-1-4169-8645-4(6))* McElderry, Margaret K. Bks. (McElderry, Margaret K. Bks.).

Funari Willever, Lisa. Nicky Fifth on 32 Dandelion Court. 2003. 160p. pap. 5.95 *(978-0-9679227-7-5(1)*, 329-008) Franklin Mason Pr.

Goodman, Carol. Blythewood. 2014. (Blythewood Novel Ser.). (ENG.). 512p. (YA). (gr. 7). pap. 9.99 *(978-0-14-242251-9(7)*, Speak) Penguin Young Readers Group.

Grandpa Dennis, as told by. George Washington's Smallest Army: The Miracle Before Trenton. 2009. 216p. (J). pap. 17.49 *(978-1-4389-3147-0(6))* AuthorHouse.

Green, Tim. Football Hero. (Football Genius Ser.: 2). (ENG.). (J). (gr. 3-7). 2009. 320p. pap. 6.99 *(978-0-06-112276-7(9))* 2008. (Illus.). 304p. 16.99 *(978-0-06-112274-3(2))* HarperCollins Pubs.

—Football Hero. l.t. ed. 2008. (YA). 23.95 *(978-1-4104-1116-7(8))* Thorndike Pr.

Grosso, Alissa. Ferocity Summer. 2012. (ENG., Illus.). 288p. (YA). pap. 9.95 *(978-0-7387-3070-7(X)*, Flux) North Star Editions.

Holm, Jennifer L. Penny from Heaven. 2007. 265p. (gr. 3-7). 17.00 *(978-0-7569-8206-5(5))* Perfection Learning Corp.

—Penny from Heaven. 2007. (ENG., Illus.). 304p. (J). (gr. 3-7). 7.99 *(978-0-375-83689-3(6)*, Yearling) Random Hse. Children's Bks.

—Penny from Heaven. l.t. ed. 2007. (Literacy Bridge Middle Reader Ser.). (Illus.). 285p. (J). (gr. 5-7). 23.95 *(978-0-7862-9698-9(4))* Thorndike Pr.

Hull, Norman. Robin's Big Brother. 2011. 56p. (gr. 4-6). pap. 9.99 *(978-1-4634-3691-9(2))* AuthorHouse.

Jacobs, Lily. The Littlest Bunny in New Jersey: An Easter Adventure. Dunn, Robert, illus. 2015. (ENG.). 32p. (J). (-3). 9.99 *(978-1-4926-1144-8(1)*, Sourcebooks Jabberwocky) Sourcebooks, Inc.

James, Eric. A Halloween Scare in New Jersey. Le Ray, Marina, illus. 2014. (ENG.). 32p. (J). (-5). 9.99 *(978-1-4926-0618-5(9)*, 9781492606185, Sourcebooks Jabberwocky) Sourcebooks, Inc.

—Santa's Sleigh Is on Its Way to New Jersey. Dunn, Robert, illus. 2015. (ENG.). 32p. (J). (-2). 12.99 *(978-1-4926-2758-6(5)*, Sourcebooks Jabberwocky) Sourcebooks, Inc.

Jessell, Tim. The Boardwalk Mystery. Dunn, Robert, illus. 2013. (Boxcar Children Mysteries Ser.: 131). (ENG.). 144p. (J). (gr. 1-5). 15.99 *(978-0-8075-0802-2(0))*; pap. 5.99 *(978-0-8075-0803-9(9))* Whitman, Albert & Co.

Jonas. Three's a Crowd. 6th ed. 2010. 128p. pap. 4.99 *(978-1-4231-2282-1(8))* Disney Pr.

Kantor, Melissa. Maybe One Day. 2014. (ENG.). 400p. (YA). (gr. 8). 17.99 *(978-0-06-227920-0(3)*, HarperTeen) HarperCollins Pubs.

Kephart, Beth. This Is the Story of You. 2016. (ENG., Illus.). 264p. (YA). (gr. 7-12). 17.99 *(978-1-4521-4284-5(X))* Chronicle Bks. LLC.

Knights, David. Stumpy the Tree. 2013. 28p. pap. 24.95 *(978-1-62709-375-0(3))* America Star Bks.

Kramer, Stacy & Thomas, Valerie. Karma Bites. 2010. (ENG.). 348p. (J). (gr. 5-7). pap. 18.99 *(978-0-547-36301-1(X))* Houghton Mifflin Harcourt Publishing Co.

Larsen, Elizabeth. Buster Hardings: Buster Makes New Friends. 2008. 104p. pap. 19.95 *(978-1-60563-951-2(6))* America Star Bks.

Lascurain, Anna. Apollo in the Moon House. 2006. Orig. Title: The Moonboy. (J). per. 7.99 *(978-0-9769612-3-9(7))* Darker Intentions Pr.

Lewis, Anne Margaret. What Am I? New Jersey. DeWidt, Jim, illus. 2007. 32p. (J). 9.95 *(978-1-934133-19-4(1)*, Mackinac Island Press, Inc.) Charlesbridge Publishing, Inc.

Lipsyte, Robert. Center Field. 2010. (ENG.). 288p. (YA). (gr. 8-18). 17.99 *(978-0-06-055704-1(4)*, HarperTeen) HarperCollins Pubs.

Litzenberg, Corinne M. The Sand Lady: A Cape May Tale, 1 vol. 2006. (ENG., Illus.). 32p. (J). 14.95 *(978-0-7643-2479-6(9)*, 9780764324796) Schiffer Publishing, Ltd.

Lowthert, Carrie. Minkie & Emily. 2007. 66p. pap. 11.95 *(978-1-4303-2576-5(3))* Lulu Pr., Inc.

Lubar, David. Dunk. 2004. (ENG.). 272p. (YA). (gr. 7-18). reprint ed. pap. 7.99 *(978-0-618-43909-6(9))* Houghton Mifflin Harcourt Publishing Co.

Many Ways to Be a Soldier. 2009. (On My Own History Ser.). (gr. 2-4). pap. 6.95 *(978-0-8225-9021-7(2)*, First Avenue Editions) Lerner Publishing Group.

Marino, Nan. Hiding Out at the Pancake Palace. 2014. (ENG.). 272p. (J). (gr. 3-7). pap. 7.99 *(978-1-250-04000-8(0)*, 9781250040008) Square Fish.

Martin, Ann M. Family Tree Book Three: Best Kept Secret. 2014. (ENG.). 224p. (J). (gr. 3-7). 16.99 *(978-0-545-35944-3(9)*, Scholastic Pr.) Scholastic, Inc.

—Welcome to Camden Falls. 2007. (Main Street Ser.: 1). (ENG., Illus.). 192p. (J). (gr. 3-7). 6.99 *(978-0-439-86879-2(3)*, Scholastic Paperbacks) Scholastic, Inc.

Martino, Alfred C. Pinned: There Can Be Only One Winner... 2006. (ENG., Illus.). 320p. (YA). (gr. 7-12). reprint ed. pap. 8.99 *(978-0-15-205631-5(9))* Houghton Mifflin Harcourt Publishing Co.

Maxwell, Ruth H. Eighteen Roses Red: A Young Girl's Heroic Mission in the Revolutionary War. 2006. (American Revolution Adventures Ser.). 126p. (J). (gr. 3-7). per. 8.95 *(978-1-57249-380-3(1)*, White Mane Kids) White Mane Publishing Co., Inc.

McDonald, Joyce. Shades of Simon Gray. 2003. (Readers Circle Ser.). 245p. (YA). 14.15 *(978-0-7569-1880-4(4))* Perfection Learning Corp.

Moses, Jennifer Anne. Tales from My Closet. 2014. (J). 298p. pap. *(978-0-545-66811-8(5))*; (ENG.). 304p. (gr. 7-9). 17.99 *(978-0-545-51608-2(0))* Scholastic, Inc. (Scholastic Pr.).

Myers, Walter Dean & Workman, Ross. Kick. (ENG.). (YA). (gr. 9). 2012. 224p. pap. 9.99 *(978-0-06-200491-8(3))* 2011. 208p. 16.99 *(978-0-06-200489-5(1))* HarperCollins Pubs. (HarperTeen).

O'Neill, Elizabeth. Alfred Visits New Jersey. 2007. 24p. (J). pap. 12.00 *(978-0-9790240-7-8(2))* Global Business Information Strategies, Inc.

Patterson, Nancy. May the Magnificent Lighthouse. Patterson, Nancy, illus. 2012. (Illus.). 24p. 18.95 *(978-0-615-61021-4(8))* Bayberry Cottage Gallery.

Pearce, Arline June. Sunrise the Barnegat Pony. 2011. 28p. pap. 15.99 *(978-1-4628-8601-2(9))* Xlibris Corp.

Pinkwater, Daniel M. Four Hoboken Stories. 2017. (ENG.). 224p. (J). pap. 16.95 ***(978-0-486-81571-8(4))*** Dover Pubns., Inc.

Plum-Ucci, Carol. Fire Will Fall. 2011. (ENG.). 492p. (YA). (gr. 9). pap. 25.99 *(978-0-547-55007-7(3))* Houghton Mifflin Harcourt Publishing Co.

Prose, Francine. Bullyville. 2007. 260p. (YA). (gr. 7-12). 16.99 *(978-0-06-057497-0(6))*; lib. bdg. 17.89 *(978-0-06-057498-7(4))* HarperCollins Pubs. (HarperTeen).

—Bullyville. 2011. 10.36 *(978-0-7848-3625-5(6)*, Everbind) Marco Bk. Co.

Rand, Johnathan. American Chillers #22 Nuclear Jelly Fish of New Jersey. 2007. 208p. (J). pap. 5.99 *(978-1-893699-93-9(5))* AudioCraft Publishing, Inc.

Raskin, Joyce. My Misadventures As a Teenage Rock Star. Chu, Carol, illus. 2011. (ENG.). 112p. (YA). (gr. 7-18). pap. 8.99 *(978-0-547-39311-7(3))* Houghton Mifflin Harcourt Publishing Co.

Rinaldi, Ann. Keep Smiling Through. 2005. (ENG.). 208p. (J). (gr. 2-5). pap. 13.95 *(978-0-15-205399-4(9))* Houghton Mifflin Harcourt Publishing Co.

Rivers, Phoebe. Ghost Town. 2012. (Saranormal Ser.: 1). (ENG.). 160p. (J). (gr. 3-7). pap. 5.99 *(978-1-4424-4038-8(4)*, Simon Spotlight) Simon Spotlight.

—Haunted Memories. 2012. (Saranormal Ser.: 2). (ENG.). 176p. (J). (gr. 3-7). 15.99 *(978-1-4424-5381-4(8))*; pap. 5.99 *(978-1-4424-4040-1(6))* Simon Spotlight. (Simon Spotlight).

—A Perfect Storm. 2013. (Saranormal Ser.: 10). (ENG., Illus.). 160p. (J). (gr. 3-7). 15.99 *(978-1-4424-8959-2(6))*; pap. 5.99 *(978-1-4424-8958-5(8))* Simon Spotlight. (Simon Spotlight).

—The Secrets Within. 2013. (Saranormal Ser.: 7). (ENG.). 160p. (J). (gr. 3-7). 15.99 *(978-1-4424-6850-4(5))*; pap. 5.99 *(978-1-4424-6849-8(1))* Simon Spotlight. (Simon Spotlight).

Robertson, Keith. Henry Reed, Inc. abr. ed. (J). (gr. 4-7). pap. 15.95 incl. audio *(978-0-670-36801-3(0))* Live Oak Media.

—Henry Reed, Inc., Set. McCloskey, Robert, illus. abr. ed. (J). (gr. 4-7). 24.95 incl. audio *(978-0-670-36800-6(8))* Live Oak Media.

Ruby, Laura. Lily's Ghosts. 2005. (Illus.). 258p. (J). (gr. 5-9). 13.65 *(978-0-7569-5115-3(1))* Perfection Learning Corp.

Schumacher, Julie. The Book of One Hundred Truths. 2008. (Yearling Bks.). (ENG.). 192p. (J). (gr. 3-7). 6.99 *(978-0-440-42085-9(7)*, Yearling) Random Hse. Children's Bks.

Scott, Kieran. He's So Not Worth It. (He's So/She's So Trilogy Ser.). (ENG.). (YA). (gr. 7). 2012. 384p. pap. 9.99 *(978-1-4169-9954-6(X))* 2011. 368p. 17.99 *(978-1-4169-9953-9(1))* Simon & Schuster Bks. For Young Readers. (Simon & Schuster Bks. For Young Readers).

—She's So Dead to Us. (He's So/She's So Trilogy Ser.). (ENG.). (YA). (gr. 7). 2011. 304p. pap. 9.99 *(978-1-4169-9952-2(3))* 2010. 288p. 16.99 *(978-1-4169-9951-5(5))* Simon & Schuster Bks. For Young Readers. (Simon & Schuster Bks. For Young Readers).

—This Is So Not Happening. (He's So/She's So Trilogy Ser.). (ENG., 320p. (YA). (gr. 7). 2013. Illus.). pap. 9.99 *(978-1-4169-9956-0(6))* 2012. 16.99 *(978-1-4169-9955-3(8))* Simon & Schuster Bks. For Young Readers. (Simon & Schuster Bks. For Young Readers).

Seuling, Barbara. Robert Finds a Way. Brewer, Paul, illus. 2005. (Robert Bks.). (ENG.). 150p. (J). 15.95 *(978-0-8126-2734-3(2))* Cricket Bks.

Sharenow, Robert. The Girl in the Torch. 2015. (ENG.). 304p. (J). (gr. 3-7). 16.99 *(978-0-06-222795-9(5))* HarperCollins Pubs.

Silvano, Wendi. Love Is All Around New Jersey. Czernichowska, Joanna, illus. 2016. (ENG.). 32p. (J). (-6). 12.99 *(978-1-4926-2943-6(X)*, Sourcebooks Jabberwocky) Sourcebooks, Inc.

Skinner, Tina. The Story of Story Book Land, 1 vol. 2008. (ENG., Illus.). 96p. pap. 19.95 *(978-0-7643-2957-9(X)*, 9780764329579) Schiffer Publishing, Ltd.

Smallman, Steve. Santa Is Coming to New Brunswick. Dunn, Robert, illus. 2014. (ENG.). 32p. (J). (-3). 11.99 *(978-1-4926-0712-0(6)*, Sourcebooks Jabberwocky) Sourcebooks, Inc.

—Santa Is Coming to New Jersey. Dunn, Robert, illus. 2013. (ENG.). 32p. (J). (-3). 9.99 *(978-1-4022-8797-8(6)*, Sourcebooks Jabberwocky) Sourcebooks, Inc.

—Santa Is Coming to the Jersey Shore. Dunn, Robert, illus. 2014. (ENG.). 32p. (J). (-3). 9.99 *(978-1-4926-0691-8(X)*, Sourcebooks Jabberwocky) Sourcebooks, Inc.

Smallman, Steve, et al. My First Santa's Coming to New Jersey. Dunn, Robert, illus. 2015. (ENG.). 18p. (J). bds. 9.99 *(978-1-4926-2882-8(4)*, Sourcebooks Jabberwocky) Sourcebooks, Inc.

Sonnenblick, Jordan. After Ever After. (ENG.). 272p. (J). 2014. pap. 9.99 *(978-0-545-72287-2(X))* 2010. (gr. 7-12). 17.99 *(978-0-439-83706-4(5)*, Scholastic Pr.) Scholastic, Inc.

Sparling, Eric. Tantramar. 2012. (ENG.). 144p. pap. *(978-1-55081-257-2(2))* Breakwater Bks., Ltd.

Starmer, Aaron. Spontaneous. 2016. (ENG.). 368p. (YA). (gr. 9). 17.99 *(978-0-525-42974-6(3)*, Dutton Books for Young Readers) Penguin Young Readers Group.

Strasser, Todd & Thacker, Nola. The Shore: Shirt & Shoes Not Required; LB (Laguna Beach) 2011. (ENG.). 480p. (YA). (gr. 9). pap. 9.99 *(978-1-4424-1970-4(9)*, Simon Pulse) Simon Pulse.

Strohmeyer, Sarah. How Zoe Made Her Dreams (Mostly) Come True. 2013. (ENG.). 320p. (YA). (gr. 8). pap. 9.99 *(978-0-06-218745-1(7))* HarperCollins Pubs.

Sully, Katherine. Night-Night New Jersey. Kolanovic, Dubravka & Poole, Helen, illus. 2016. (ENG.). 20p. (J). (-1). bds. 9.99 *(978-1-4926-3933-6(8)*, 9781492639336, Sourcebooks Jabberwocky) Sourcebooks, Inc.

Suma, Nova Ren. Imaginary Girls. 2012. (ENG.). 352p. (YA). (gr. 9-18). pap. 8.99 *(978-0-14-242143-7(X)*, Speak) Penguin Young Readers Group.

Tarshis, Lauren. I Survived the Shark Attacks of 1916. 2010. (I Survived Ser.: 2). (ENG.). 112p. (J). (gr. 3-7). pap. 4.99 *(978-0-545-20695-2(2)*, Scholastic Paperbacks) Scholastic, Inc.

—I Survived the Shark Attacks of 1916. 2010. (I Survived Ser.: No. 2). lib. bdg. 14.75 *(978-0-606-23742-0(9)*, Turtleback) Turtleback Bks.

Telmosse, Gerard. The Curse of the Sourlands. 2008. 132p. pap. 14.51 *(978-1-4357-0169-4(0))* Lulu Pr., Inc.

Vivian, Siobhan. Same Difference. 2014. (ENG.). 304p. (J). pap. 9.99 *(978-0-545-75802-4(5))* Scholastic, Inc.

Voltaire, Aurelio. Call of the Jersey Devil. 2013. (ENG.). 352p. pap. 7.95 *(978-1-939392-00-8(4)*, Spence City) Spencer Hill Pr.

Wallace, Rich. The Roar of the Crowd. 2005. (Winning Season Ser.). (ENG.). 128p. (J). (gr. 3-7). pap. 5.99 *(978-0-14-240443-0(8)*, Puffin Books) Penguin Young Readers Group.

—Roar of the Crowd. 2004. 101p. (J). lib. bdg. 15.38 *(978-1-4242-2165-3(X))* Fitzgerald Bks.

—Takedown, No. 8. 2007. (Winning Season Ser.: Bk. 8). (ENG.). 128p. (J). (gr. 3-7). 5.99 *(978-0-14-240919-0(7)*, Puffin Books) Penguin Young Readers Group.

—Technical Foul. 2nd ed. 2005. (Winning Season Ser.). (ENG.). 128p. (J). (gr. 3-7). pap. 5.99 *(978-0-14-240444-7(6)*, Puffin Books) Penguin Young Readers Group.

—War & Watermelon. 2012. (ENG.). 192p. (J). (gr. 5-18). pap. 6.99 *(978-0-14-242138-3(3)*, Puffin Books) Penguin Young Readers Group.

Warstler, Mary Lu. Michael's Angel, 1 vol. 2009. 227p. pap. 24.95 *(978-1-61546-723-5(8))* PublishAmerica, Inc.

Wasserman, Sand. The Sun's Special Blessing: Happens Only Once in 28 Years - French Flap. Koffsky, Ann, illus. 2009. 36p. 12.95 *(978-1-934440-76-6(0)*, Pitspopany Pr.) Simcha Media Group.

—The Sun's Special Blessing: Happens Only Once in 28 Years - HC. Koffsky, Ann, illus. 2009. 36p. 17.95 *(978-1-934440-92-6(2)*, Pitspopany Pr.) Simcha Media Group.

Wilson, F. Paul. Jack: Secret Histories. 2009. (Repairman Jack Ser.). (ENG.). 320p. (YA). (gr. 7). pap. 6.99 *(978-0-7653-5811-0(5)*, 9780765358110, Tor Teen) Doherty, Tom Assocs., LLC.

Woollatt, Margaret. The Twelve Days of Christmas in New Jersey. Rossi, Richard, illus. 2008. (Twelve Days of Christmas in America Ser.). (ENG.). 40p. (J). (gr. k). 12.95 *(978-1-4027-3816-6(1))* Sterling Publishing Co., Inc.

NEW JERSEY—HISTORY

ABC Atlantic City: An Alphabet Book, Travel Guide & Souvenir for Kids! 2006. (J). 8.95 *(978-0-9760047-1-4(2))* Rosenberger, Matthew.

Barnham, Kay. Thomas Edison, 1 vol. 2014. (Science Biographies Ser.). (ENG.). 32p. (gr. 2-4). lib. bdg. 30.65 *(978-1-4109-6239-3(3)*, Raintree Perspectives) Heinemann-Raintree.

Barth, Linda J. Hidden New Jersey. Mitchell, Hazel, illus. 2012. (Search & Seek Bks.). (ENG.). 32p. (J). (gr. 1-4). 17.95 *(978-1-934133-21-7(X))*; pap. 8.95 *(978-1-934133-40-8(X))* Charlesbridge Publishing, Inc. (Mackinac Island Press, Inc.).

Benoit, Peter. The Hindenburg Disaster. 2011. (Illus.). 48p. (J). pap. *(978-0-531-29025-5(5))* Children's Pr., Ltd.

—The Hindenburg Disaster. 2011. (True Book(tm), A — Disasters Ser.). (ENG.). 48p. (J). (gr. 3-5). lib. bdg. 31.00 *(978-0-531-20626-3(2))*; pap. 6.95 *(978-0-531-28995-2(8))* Scholastic Library Publishing. (Children's Pr.).

The Colors of the Lighthouse: A Children's History of Absecon Lighthouse. 2006. (J). 8.95 *(978-0-9779988-0-7(0))* Absecon Lighthouse.

Cunningham, Kevin. The New Jersey Colony. 2011. (True Bk Ser.). (ENG., Illus.). 48p. (J). pap. 6.95 *(978-0-531-26606-9(0))*; lib. bdg. 29.00 *(978-0-531-25393-9(7))* Scholastic Library Publishing. (Children's Pr.).

Davis, Lynn. Thomas Edison, 1 vol. 2016. (ENG., Illus.). 24p. (J). 25.65 *(978-1-62403-723-8(2))* ABDO Publishing Co.

Doak, Robin S. New Jersey, 1609-1776. 2005. (National Geographic Voices from ColonialAmerica Ser.). (ENG., Illus.). 112p. (J). (gr. 5-9). 32.90 *(978-0-7922-6680-8(3)*, National Geographic Children's Bks.) National Geographic Society.

Doak, Robin S. & McConville, Brendan. New Jersey, 1609-1776. 2005. (National Geographic Voices from ColonialAmerica Ser.). (ENG., Illus.). 112p. (J). (gr. 5-9). 21.95 *(978-0-7922-6385-2(5)*, National Geographic Children's Bks.) National Geographic Society.

Doherty, Craig A. & Doherty, Katherine M. New Jersey, 13 vols. 2005. (Thirteen Colonies Ser.). (Illus.). 144p. (gr. 5-8). 35.00 *(978-0-8160-5408-4(8))* Facts On File, Inc.

Downey, Tika. New Jersey: The Garden State. 2010. (Our Amazing States Ser.). (Illus.). 24p. (J). pap. 8.25 *(978-1-4358-9806-6(0))*; lib. bdg. 22.60 *(978-1-4358-9355-9(7))* Rosen Publishing Group, Inc., The. (PowerKids Pr.).

Dzidrums, Christine. Mike Trout: Baseball Sensation. Dzidrums, Joseph, photos by. 2013. (Illus.). 64p. pap. 9.99 *(978-1-938438-28-8(0))* Creative Media Publishing.

Jerome, Kate B. The Wise Animal Handbook New Jersey. 2017. (Arcadia Kids Ser.). (ENG., Illus.). 32p. (J). 16.99 ***(978-0-7385-2832-8(3))*** Arcadia Publishing.

Jordan, Joe. Cape May Point: The Illustrated History From 1875-Present, 1 vol. 2003. (ENG., Illus.). 144p. (gr. 10-13). 24.95 *(978-0-7643-1830-6(6)*, 9780764318306) Schiffer Publishing, Ltd.

King, David C. & McGeveran, William. New Jersey. 2nd rev. ed. 2010. (It's My State! Ser.). 80p. (gr. 3-18). lib. bdg. 31.36 *(978-1-60870-055-4(0))* Marshall Cavendish Corp.

King, David C., et al. New Jersey. 2015. (J). lib. bdg. *(978-1-62712-505-5(1))*; (ENG., Illus.). 80p. (gr. 4-4). 34.21 *(978-1-5026-0013-4(7))* Cavendish Square Publishing.

Kopp, Megan. New Jersey: The Garden State. 2012. (J). *(978-1-61913-379-2(2))*; pap. *(978-1-61913-380-8(6))* Weigl Pubs., Inc.

Krasner, Barbara. Exploring the New Jersey Colony. 2016. (Exploring the 13 Colonies Ser.). (ENG., Illus.). 48p. (gr. 3-4). lib. bdg. 31.99 *(978-1-5157-2235-9(X))* Capstone Press of Coughlan Cos.

Landau, Elaine. General Washington Crosses the Delaware: Would You Join the American Revolution? 2015. (What Would You Do? Ser.). 48p. (J). (gr. 3-4). 25.27 *(978-0-7660-6315-0(1))* Enslow Pubs., Inc.

—George Washington Crosses the Delaware: Would You Risk the Revolution? 2008. (What Would You Do? Ser.). (Illus.). 48p. (J). (gr. 3-4). lib. bdg. 25.27 *(978-0-7660-2904-0(2)*, Enslow Elementary) Enslow Pubs., Inc.

Marsh, Carole. Exploring New Jersey Through Project-Based Learning: Geography, History, Government, Economics & More. 2016. (New Jersey Experience Ser.). (ENG.). (J). pap. 9.99 *(978-0-635-12354-1(1))* Gallopade International.

—I'm Reading about New Jersey. 2014. (New Jersey Experience Ser.). (ENG., Illus.). (J). pap., pap. 8.99 *(978-0-635-11305-4(8))* Gallopade International.

—New Jersey History Projects: 30 Cool, Activities, Crafts, Experiments & More for Kids to Do to Learn about Your State! 2003. (New Jersey Experience Ser.). 32p. (gr. k-5). pap. 5.95 *(978-0-635-01799-4(7)*, Marsh, Carole Bks.) Gallopade International.

McCloy, James F., et al. The Jersey Devil. 2005. (Illus.). 121p. (J). (gr. 5). per. *(978-0-912608-11-2(0))* Middle Atlantic Pr.

McGrath, Brian. Aaron Burr: More Than a Villain (Alexander Hamilton) 2017. (Primary Source Readers Focus On Ser.). (Illus.). 32p. (J). (gr. 4-8). pap. 8.99 ***(978-1-4258-6355-5(8))*** Teacher Created Materials, Inc.

McHugh, Erin. New Jersey. Schrier, Alfred, illus. 2010. (ENG.). 52p. (J). (gr. -1-17). 9.95 *(978-1-57912-820-3(3)*, 81820, Black Dog & Leventhal Pubs. Inc.) Hachette Bks.

McMahon, William. Pine Barrens Legends & Lore. 2005. (Illus.). 149p. (J). (gr. 6). per. *(978-0-912608-19-8(6))* Middle Atlantic Pr.

Meinking, Mary. What's Great about New Jersey? 2015. (ENG., Illus.). 32p. (J). (gr. 2-5). 26.65 *(978-1-4677-3873-6(5))* Lerner Publishing Group.

Micklos, John. Washington's Crossing the Delaware & the Winter at Valley Forge—Through Primary Sources. 2013. (American Revolution Through Primary Sources Ser.). 48p. (J). (gr. 4-10). pap. 8.95 *(978-1-4644-0190-9(X))* Enslow Pubs., Inc.

Miller, Jake. The Colony of New Jersey: A Primary Source History. (Primary Source Library of the Thirteen Colonies & the Lost Colony Ser.). 24p. (gr. 3-4). 2009. 42.50 *(978-1-60854-146-1(0))* 2006. (Illus.). (J). lib. bdg. 22.60 *(978-1-4042-3031-6(9))* Rosen Publishing Group, Inc., The. (PowerKids Pr.).

Moragne, Wendy & Orr, Tamra. New Jersey. 2nd rev. ed. 2008. (Celebrate the States Ser.). 144p. (gr. 6-18). lib. bdg. 42.79 *(978-0-7614-3006-3(7)*, Benchmark Bks.) Marshall Cavendish Corp.

Mortensen, Lori. Ellis Island, 1 vol. Skeens, Matthew, illus. 2008. (American Symbols Ser.). (ENG.). 24p. (gr. 1-2). 26.65 *(978-1-4048-4705-7(7))* Picture Window Bks.

Murray, Julie. New Jersey, 1 vol. 2012. (Explore the United States Ser.). (ENG.). 32p. (J). (gr. 2-5). lib. bdg. 28.50 *(978-1-61783-368-7(1)*, Big Buddy Bks.) ABDO Publishing Co.

Nault, Jennifer. New Jersey. 2011. (Guide to American States Ser.). (Illus.). 48p. (YA). (gr. 3-6). 29.99 *(978-1-61690-802-7(5))* Weigl Pubs., Inc.

—New Jersey: The Garden State. 2016. (J). *(978-1-4896-4905-8(0))* Weigl Pubs., Inc.

The New Jersey Adventure Program Kit: All program components for the New Jersey Adventure, 1 vol. 2009. 99.95 *(978-1-4236-0725-0(2))* Gibbs Smith, Publisher.

Noble, Trinka Hakes. Little New Jersey. Brett, Jeannie, illus. 2012. (My Little State Ser.). (ENG.). 20p. (J). bds. 9.95 *(978-1-58536-786-3(9))* Sleeping Bear Pr.

Orr, Tamra. A Primary Source History of the Colony of New Jersey. 2009. (Primary Sources of the Thirteen Colonies & the Lost Colony Ser.). 64p. (gr. 5-8). 58.50 *(978-1-60851-882-1(5))* Rosen Publishing Group, Inc., The.

Orr, Tamra B. A Primary Source History of the Colony of New Jersey. 2006. (Primary Sources of the Thirteen Colonies & the Lost Colony Ser.). (Illus.). 64p. (gr. 4-7). (YA). lib. bdg. 31.95 *(978-1-4042-0430-0(X))*; (ENG., per. 12.95 *(978-1-4042-0668-7(X))* Rosen Publishing Group, Inc., The.

Otfinoski, Steven. The Hindenburg Explosion: Core Events of a Disaster in the Air, 1 vol. 2014. (What Went Wrong? Ser.). (ENG.). 32p. (gr. 3-4). pap. 7.95 *(978-1-4765-5133-3(2))* Capstone Press of Coughlan Cos.

Pfeffer, Wendy. Many Ways to Be a Soldier. Verstraete, Elaine, illus. 2008. (On My Own History Ser.). (ENG.). 48p. (gr. 2-4). lib. bdg. 25.26 *(978-0-8225-7279-4(6)*, Millbrook Pr.) Lerner Publishing Group.

—Many Ways to Be A Soldier. 2009. pap. 40.95 *(978-0-7613-4795-8(X))* Lerner Publishing Group.

Rameck, Hunt, et al. We Beat the Street: How a Friendship Pact Led to Success. 2014. (ENG.). 208p. (J). 12.24 *(978-1-63245-093-7(3))* Lectorum Pubns., Inc.

Wheeler, Jill C. New Jersey, 1 vol. 2009. (United States Ser.). (ENG., Illus.). 48p. (YA). (gr. 2-5). 27.07 *(978-1-60453-665-2(9))* ABDO Publishing Co.

Wimmer, Teresa. New Jersey. 2009. (This Land Called America Ser.). (Illus.). 32p. (YA). (gr. 3-6). 19.95 *(978-1-58341-783-6(4))* Creative Co., The.

Words for All Time: Students Letters to Holocaust Survivors. 2008. (YA). mass mkt. 19.95 *(978-0-9793771-6-7(1))* ComteQ Publishing.

Ziff, John. Northeast: New Jersey, New York, Pennsylvania, Vol. 19. 2015. (Let's Explore the States Ser.). (Illus.). 64p. (J). (gr. 5). 23.95 *(978-1-4222-3329-0(4))* Mason Crest.

NEW MEXICO

Barco, Kathy. READiscover New Mexico: A Tri-Lingual Adventure in Literacy. 2007. (ENG, SPA & NAV.). 192p. (J). per. 24.95 *(978-0-86534-544-7(9))* Sunstone Pr.

Baxter, Roberta. Battles for Gold & Glory: Civil War Skirmishes in New Mexico Territory. 2012. (ENG.). 81p. pap. 11.95 *(978-1-4327-8643-4(1))* Outskirts Pr., Inc.

Bjorklund, Ruth. New Mexico. 2013. (It's My State 2nd Ed 4 Ser.). 80p. (J). (gr. 4-8). pap. 17.64 *(978-1-62712-095-1(5))* Cavendish Square Publishing.

Burgan, Michael. New Mexico: Land of Enchantment. 2003. (World Almanac Library of the States). (Illus.). 48p. (gr. 4-9). pap. 14.05 *(978-0-8368-5327-8(X))*; lib. bdg. 31.00 *(978-0-8368-5156-4(0))* Stevens, Gareth Publishing LLLP. (Gareth Stevens Learning Library).

—Nuevo Mexico. 2004. (World Almanac Ser.).Tr. of New Mexico. (SPA.). 48p. (gr. 4-9). lib. bdg. 31.00 *(978-0-8368-5725-2(9)*, GHS32692, Gareth Stevens Learning Library) Stevens, Gareth Publishing LLLP.

Cash, Marie Romero. Santos: A Coloring Book of New Mexican Saints. 2008. 80p. (J). pap. 10.95 (978-0-86534-701-4(8)) Sunstone Pr.

Early, Theresa S. New Mexico. 2012. (J). lib. bdg. 25.26 (978-0-7613-4547-3(7), Lerner Pubns.) Lerner Publishing Group.

Finley, Toiya Kristen. Russell Simmons. 2007. (Sharing the American Dream Ser.). 64p. (YA). (gr. 7-18). pap. 9.95 (978-1-4222-0762-8(5)) Mason Crest.

Grace, N. B. UFO Lands in USA! Was a Spacecraft Crash Covered Up? 2011. (J). pap. (978-0-545-32947-7(7)) Scholastic, Inc.

Hernández, Roger E. 1898 to World War II. 2009. (Hispanic America 2 Ser.). 80p. (gr. 5). 34.21 (978-0-7614-4176-2(X)) Marshall Cavendish Corp.

James, Helen Foster. E Is for Enchantment: A New Mexico Alphabet. Twinem, Neecy, illus. 2004. (State Ser.). (ENG.). 40p. (J). 17.95 (978-1-58536-153-3(4), 1235984) Sleeping Bear Pr.

Lavash, Donald R. A Journey Through New Mexico History: The Land of Enchantment. 3rd rev. ed. 2006. (Illus.). 208p. (YA). (gr. 8-12). pap. 26.95 (978-0-86534-194-4(X)) Sunstone Pr.

Maine, Tyler. New Mexico. 2016. (States Ser.). (ENG., Illus.). 32p. (gr. 3-4). lib. bdg. 27.32 (978-1-5157-0418-8(1)) Next Page Pr., The.

Marsh, Carole. New Mexico Current Events Projects: 30 Cool, Activities, Crafts, Experiments & More for Kids to Do to Learn about Your State! 2003. (New Mexico Experience Ser.). 32p. (gr. k-8). pap. 5.95 (978-0-635-02050-5(5), Marsh, Carole Bks.) Gallopade International.

—New Mexico Geography Projects: 30 Cool, Activities, Crafts, Experiments & More for Kids to Do to Learn about Your State! 2003. (New Mexico Experience Ser.). 32p. (gr. k-5). pap. 5.95 (978-0-635-01850-2(0), Marsh, Carole Bks.) Gallopade International.

—New Mexico Government Projects: 30 Cool, Activities, Crafts, Experiments & More for Kids to Do to Learn about Your State! 2003. (New Mexico Experience Ser.). 32p. (gr. k-5). pap. 5.95 (978-0-635-01950-9(7), Marsh, Carole Bks.) Gallopade International.

—New Mexico People Projects: 30 Cool, Activities, Crafts, Experiments & More for Kids to Do to Learn about Your State! 2003. (New Mexico Experience Ser.). 32p. (gr. k-5). pap. 5.95 (978-0-635-02000-0(9), Marsh, Carole Bks.) Gallopade International.

—New Mexico Symbols & Facts Projects: 30 Cool, Activities, Crafts, Experiments & More for Kids to Do to Learn about Your State! 2003. (New Mexico Experience Ser.). 32p. (gr. k-5). pap. 5.95 (978-0-635-01900-4(0), Marsh, Carole Bks.) Gallopade International.

McDaniel, Melissa, et al. New Mexico. 2nd rev. ed. 2007. (Celebrate the States Ser.). 144p. (gr. 6). lib. bdg. 42.79 (978-0-7614-2719-3(8), Benchmark Bks.) Marshall Cavendish Corp.

Moskal, Greg. An Apache Indian Community. 2009. (Reading Room Collection 2 Ser.). 24p. (gr. 3-4). 42.50 (978-1-60851-956-9(2), PowerKids Pr.) Rosen Publishing Group, Inc., The.

Murray, Julie. New Mexico, 1 vol. 2006. (Buddy Book Ser.). (ENG., Illus.). 32p. (gr. 2-4). 27.07 (978-1-59197-690-5(1), Buddy Bks.) ABDO Publishing Co.

Obregón, José María. New Mexico. 2009. (Bilingual Library of the United States of America Ser.). (ENG & SPA.). 32p. (gr. 2-2). 47.90 (978-1-60853-375-6(1), Editorial Buenas Letras) Rosen Publishing Group, Inc., The.

Obregon, Jose Maria. New Mexico/Nuevo Mexico. Brusca, Maria Cristina, tr. 2006. (Bilingual Library of the United States of America Ser.: Set 2). (ENG & SPA., Illus.). 32p. (J). (gr. 3-6). lib. bdg. 25.25 (978-1-4042-3096-5(3)) Rosen Publishing Group, Inc., The.

Phillips, Larissa. Cochise: Apache Chief / Cochise: Jefe Apache. 2009. (Famous People in American History/Grandes personajes en la historia de los Estados Unidos Ser.). (ENG & SPA.). 32p. (gr. 2-3). 47.90 (978-1-61512-540-1(X), Editorial Buenas Letras) Rosen Publishing Group, Inc., The.

Rice, Liz. Bill Richardson. 2009. (Sharing the American Dream Ser.). 64p. (YA). (gr. 7-12). 22.95 (978-1-4222-0589-1(4)) Mason Crest.

VanVoorst, Jenny Fretland. What's Great about New Mexico? 2014. (Our Great States Ser.). (ENG.). 32p. (gr. 2-5). lib. bdg. 26.60 (978-1-4677-3347-2(4), Lerner Pubns.) Lerner Publishing Group.

Walker, Cynthia. Nuevo Mexico. 2005. (Rookie Español Geografía Ser.). (ENG & SPA., Illus.). 32p. (J). (gr. k-2). lib. bdg. 19.50 (978-0-516-25247-6(X), Children's Pr.) Scholastic Library Publishing.

Walker, Cynthia & Vargus, Nanci Reginelli. New Mexico. 2004. (Rookie Read-About Geography Ser.). (Illus.). 31p. (J). 20.50 (978-0-516-22755-9(6), Children's Pr.) Scholastic Library Publishing.

Weintraub, A. How to Draw New Mexico's Sights & Symbols. 2009. (Kid's Guide to Drawing America Ser.). 32p. (gr. k-k). 50.50 (978-1-61511-080-3(1), PowerKids Pr.) Rosen Publishing Group, Inc., The.

Weiss-Malik, Linda S. New Mexico. 2006. (Portraits of the States Ser.). 32p. (gr. 2-6). pap. 10.50 (978-0-8368-4722-2(9)); (Illus.). lib. bdg. 26.00 (978-0-8368-4705-5(9)) Stevens, Gareth Publishing LLLP. (Gareth Stevens Learning Library).

NEW MEXICO—FICTION

Abraham, Susan Gonzales & Abraham, Denise Gonzales. Cecilia's Year. 2007. (Latino Fiction for Young Adults Ser.). (ENG., Illus.). 210p. (J). (gr. 4-6). pap. 11.95 (978-1-933693-02-6(9)) Cinco Puntos Pr.

—Surprising Cecilia. 2005. (Latino Fiction for Young Adults Ser.). (ENG., Illus.). 216p. (J). (gr. -1-7). 16.95 (978-0-938317-96-8(2)) Cinco Puntos Pr.

Abruzzo, Nancy. Pop Flop's Great Balloon Ride. Chilton, Noel, illus. 2005. (ENG.). 32p. (J). (gr. k-17). bds. 12.95 (978-0-89013-475-7(8)) Museum of New Mexico Pr.

Alarid, Carilyn & Markel, Marilyn. Talks All Day Has the Courage to Speak: Mimbres Children Learn Citizenship. Alarid, Carilyn & Markel, Marilyn, illus. 2006. (Illus.). 125p. (J). pap. 16.95 (978-0-86534-470-9(1)) Sunstone Pr.

Alarid, Carilyn & Markel, Marilyn, illus. Runs Like the Wind Stops in Her Tracks: Mimbres Children Learn about Trustworthiness. 2016. (J). pap. (978-1-63293-099-6(4)) Sunstone Pr.

Amato, Carol J. The Lost Treasure of the Golden Sun. 2005. 172p. (J). (978-0-9713756-3-5(1)) Stargazer Publishing Co.

Anaya, Rudolfo. ChupaCabra & the Roswell UFO. 2008. (ENG.). 144p. (YA). (gr. 9-18). 9.95 (978-0-8263-4469-4(0)) Univ. of New Mexico Pr.

—How Hollyhocks Came to New Mexico. Garcia, Nasario, tr. Otero, Nicolas, illus. 2012. 48p. 24.95 (978-1-936744-12-1(0), Rio Grande Bks.) LPD Pr.

Anaya, Rudolfo A. The Santero's Miracle: A Bilingual Story. Lamadrid, Enrique R., tr. Córdova, Amy, illus. 2004. (ENG & SPA.). 32p. (J). 19.95 (978-0-8263-2847-2(4)) Univ. of New Mexico Pr.

Aragón, Carla, et al. Dance of the Eggshells: Baile de los Cascarones. Saville, Kathy Dee, illus. 2010. (SPA & ENG.). 32p. (J). (gr. 1). 18.95 (978-0-8263-4770-1(3)) Univ. of New Mexico Pr.

Beaty, Janice J. Jarod & the Mystery of the Petroglyphs: A National Park Adventure Series Book. Beaty, Lillian C., illus. 2015. 118p. (J). pap. (978-1-63293-071-2(4)) Sunstone Pr.

Bell, Juliet. Kepler's Dream. 2013. (ENG.). 256p. (J). (gr. 5). pap. 6.99 (978-0-14-242648-7(2), Puffin Books) Penguin Young Readers Group.

Blume, Judy. Tiger Eyes. 2014. (ENG., Illus.). 256p. (YA). (gr. 7). pap. 10.99 (978-1-4814-1387-9(2), Atheneum Bks. for Young Readers) Simon & Schuster Children's Publishing.

Bostick, B. k. Huber Hill & the Golden Staff of Cibola. 2013. (J). pap. 14.99 (978-1-4621-1098-8(3), Horizon Pubs.) Cedar Fort, Inc./CFI Distribution.

Bradley, Timothy J. Infestation. Bradley, Timothy J., illus. 2013. (ENG., Illus.). 192p. (J). (gr. 3-7). pap. 5.99 (978-0-545-45904-4(4), Scholastic Paperbacks) Scholastic, Inc.

Bronson, Wilfrid S. Pinto's Journey. 2007. (ENG.). 64p. (J). per. 14.95 (978-0-86534-557-7(0)) Sunstone Pr.

Caban, Connie. Don't Be Afraid of the Storm. Page, illus. 2011. 32p. pap. 12.95 (978-1-936343-97-3(5)) Peppertree Pr., The.

Cervantes, Jennifer. Tortilla Sun. 2014. (ENG.). 224p. (J). (gr. 3-7). pap. 6.99 (978-1-4521-3150-4(3)) Chronicle Bks. LLC.

Cervantes, Jennifer & Chronicle Books Staff. Tortilla Sun. 2010. (ENG.). 224p. (J). (gr. 4-7). 16.99 (978-0-8118-7015-3(4)) Chronicle Bks. LLC.

Church, Peggy Pond. The Burro of Angelitos. 2013. 52p. pap. 18.95 (978-0-86534-965-0(7)) Sunstone Pr.

—Shoes for the Santo Niño. Carrillo, Charles M., illus. 2013. 64p. 25.95 (978-1-936744-23-7(6), Rio Grande Bks.) LPD Pr.

—Shoes for the Santo Niño: Zapatillos para el Santo Niño: A Bilingual Tale. Carrillo, Charles M., illus. 2009. (SPA & ENG.). 61p. (J). pap. (978-1-890689-64-3(5), Rio Grande Bks.) LPD Pr.

Cole, Steve. Z. Rex. (ENG.). 256p. (J). (gr. 5-18). 2010. 8.99 (978-0-14-241712-6(2), Puffin Books) 2009. 16.99 (978-0-399-25253-2(3), Philomel Bks.) Penguin Young Readers Group.

Crane, Phyllis F. Anything but the Most Boring Place on Earth. 2011. 174p. pap. 24.95 (978-1-4560-6802-8(4)) America Star Bks.

Creel, Ann Howard. Under a Stand Still Moon. 2005. 183p. (YA). (gr. 7-12). per. 8.95 (978-0-9746481-8-7(3)) Brown Barn Bks.

Dahlstrom, S. J. The Elk Hunt: The Adventure Begins. 2013. (Adventures of Wilder Good Ser.). (ENG., Illus.). 110p. (J). (gr. 3). pap. 8.95 (978-1-58988-087-0(0)) Dry, Paul Bks., Inc.

Deal, Paul. Lighting Candles. 2003. 122p. (YA). 20.95 (978-0-595-65804-6(0)); pap. 10.95 (978-0-595-28457-3(4)) iUniverse, Inc.

Dix, Catherine R. Rosetta Stones. 2009. (ENG.). 213p. pap. 14.95 (978-0-9798452-2-2(X)) Central Ave. Pr.

Duncan, Lois. Summer of Fear. 2011. (ENG.). 256p. (YA). (gr. 7-17). pap., pap. 9.99 (978-0-316-09907-3(4)) Little, Brown Bks. for Young Readers.

Eagar, Lindsay. Hour of the Bees. (ENG.). 368p. (J). (gr. 5-9). 2017. pap. 8.99 **(978-0-7636-9120-2(8))** 2016. 16.99 (978-0-7636-7922-4(4)) Candlewick Pr.

Eschberger, Beverly. The Elephants in the Land of Enchantment: An Elephant Family Adventure. Gower, Jim, illus. 2009. 96p. (J). pap. 3.99 (978-1-932926-02-6(X), Kinkajou Pr.) Artemesia Publishing, LLC.

Ferguson, Alane & Skurzynski, Gloria. Running Scared. 2008. (Mysteries in Our National Park Ser.). (ENG., Illus.). 160p. (J). (gr. 3-7). mass mkt. 4.99 (978-1-4263-0182-7(0), National Geographic Children's Bks.) National Geographic Society.

A First Clay Gathering (Review Multiple Meanings), Level C. 2003. ("Plaid" Phonics & Stories Libraries). 43.50 (978-0-8136-9234-0(2)) Modern Curriculum Pr.

Foard, Sheila Wood. Harvey Girl. 2006. (ENG., Illus.). 176p. (YA). (gr. 7-12). per. 18.95 (978-0-89672-570-6(7)) Texas Tech Univ. Pr.

Garcia, Nasario. Grandpa Lolo & Trampa: A Story of Surprise & Mystery = Abuelito Lolo y Trampa: Un Cuento de Sorpresa y Misterio. Montoya, Jeremy, illus. 2014. (SPA & ENG.). (J). 9.99 (978-1-936744-30-5(9)) LPD Pr.

—Grandpa Lolo's Navajo Saddle Blanket: La Tilma de Abuelito Lolo. Moeller, Richard, illus. Moeller, Richard, photos by. 2012. (J). (978-0-8263-5078-7(X)); (SPA.). 72p. pap. (978-0-8263-5079-4(8)); 61p. pap. (978-0-8263-5080-0(1)) Univ. of New Mexico Pr.

—Rattling Chains & Other Stories for Children/Ruido de Cadenas y Otros Cuentos para Ninos. Mora, Giovanni, illus. 2009. (SPA & ENG.). 160p. (J). (gr. 3-7). pap. 9.95 (978-1-55885-544-1(0), Piñata Books) Arte Publico Pr.

García, Nasario & Aragon, Dolores, illus. Grandpa Lolo's Matanza: A New Mexican Tradition = la Matanza de Abuelito Lolo: Una Tradición Nuevo Mexicana. 2015. (SPA & ENG.). 70p. (J). (978-1-936744-47-3(3), Rio Grande Bks.) LPD Pr.

Gonzales, Felipe C. Little Folk Stories & Tales by Don Pablo: Bilingual Stories in Spanish & English = Chistes y Cuentos de Don Pablo: Cuentos Bilingües en Español e Inglés. 2010. (SPA & ENG.). (J). pap. 24.95 (978-0-86534-772-4(7)) Sunstone Pr.

Grill, William, illus. The Wolves of Currumpaw. 2016. (ENG.). 80p. (J). (gr. 1-9). 24.00 (978-1-909263-83-3(4)) Flying Eye Bks. GBR. Dist: Consortium Bk. Sales & Distribution.

Haas, Jessie. Saige. Davis, Sarah, illus. 2012. (American Girl Today Ser.: Bk. 1). lib. bdg. 17.15 (978-0-606-31568-5(3), Turtleback) Turtleback Bks.

—Saige Paints the Sky. Davis, Sarah, illus. 2012. (American Girl Today Ser.: Bk. 2). lib. bdg. 17.15 (978-0-606-31569-2(1), Turtleback) Turtleback Bks.

Haston, Meg. Paperweight. 2015. (ENG.). 304p. (YA). (gr. 9). 17.99 (978-0-06-233574-6(X), HarperTeen) HarperCollins Pubs.

Hawkins, Aaron. The Year Money Grew on Trees. 2011. (ENG.). 304p. (J). (gr. 5-7). pap. 6.99 (978-0-547-57716-6(8)) Houghton Mifflin Harcourt Publishing Co.

Hayes, Joe. The Coyote under the Table (El Coyote Debajo de la Mesa) Castro L., Antonio, illus. 2011. (ENG & SPA.). 144p. (J). (gr. 1-7). pap. 12.95 (978-1-935955-06-1(3)) Cinco Puntos Pr.

—El Día que Nevaron Tortillas. Hayes, Joe, tr. Lopez, Antonio Castro & Castro L., Antonio, illus. 2003.Tr. of Day It Snowed Tortillas. (SPA & ENG.). 160p. (J). (gr. 4-6). pap. 12.95 (978-0-938317-76-0(8)) Cinco Puntos Pr.

Hays, Anna Jane. The Secret of the Circle-K Cave. Smath, Jerry, illus. 2006. (Science Solves It! Ser.). 32p. (J). (gr. -1-3). pap. 5.95 (978-1-57565-189-7(0)) Kane Press, Inc.

Heller, Marcy. Loco Dog & the Dust Devil in the Railyard. Poes, Nancy, illus. 2007. 30p. (J). (gr. -1-7). 19.95 (978-1-929115-17-4(2)) Azro Pr., Inc.

—Loco Dog in the Santa Fe Rail Yard, 1 vol. 2nd rev. ed. 2015. (Historical New Mexico for Children Ser.: Volume 1). (ENG., Illus.). 48p. pap. 16.95 (978-0-9912516-1-2(X)) SCB Distributors.

Hiscock, Bruce. Coyote & Badger: Desert Hunters of the Southwest. 2003. (ENG., Illus.). 32p. (J). (gr. 2-4). 15.95 (978-1-56397-848-7(2)) Boyds Mills Pr.

Hobbs, Will. Kokopelli's Flute. 2005. 148p. (gr. 5-9). 17.00 (978-0-7569-5503-8(3)) Perfection Learning Corp.

—Kokopelli's Flute. 2005. (ENG.). 160p. (J). (gr. 5-9). pap. 7.99 (978-1-4169-0250-8(3), Simon & Schuster/Paula Wiseman Bks.) Simon & Schuster/Paula Wiseman Bks.

Hodder, Beth. The Ghost of Schafer Meadows. 2007. (J). per. 7.99 (978-0-9793963-0-4(1)) Grizzly Ridge Publishing.

Hulme, Joy N. Climbing the Rainbow. 2004. 224p. (J). 15.99 (978-0-380-81572-2(9)) HarperCollins Pubs.

Hyde, Heidi Smith. Elan, Son of Two Peoples. Prevost, Mikela, illus. 2014. (Life Cycle Ser.). (ENG.). 32p. (J). (gr. k-3). 17.95 (978-0-7613-9051-0(0), Kar-Ben Publishing) Lerner Publishing Group.

Jacobs, Lily. The Littlest Bunny in Albuquerque: An Easter Adventure. Dunn, Robert, illus. 2015. (ENG.). 32p. (J). (-3). 9.99 (978-1-4926-1021-2(6), Sourcebooks Jabberwocky) Sourcebooks, Inc.

—The Littlest Bunny in New Mexico: An Easter Adventure. Dunn, Robert, illus. 2015. (ENG.). 32p. (J). (-3). 9.99 (978-1-4926-1147-9(6), Sourcebooks Jabberwocky) Sourcebooks, Inc.

James, Eric. A Halloween Scare in New Mexico. Le Ray, Marina, illus. 2015. (ENG.). 32p. (J). (-5). 9.99 (978-1-4926-2388-5(1), 9781492623885, Sourcebooks Jabberwocky) Sourcebooks, Inc.

—Santa's Sleigh Is on Its Way to Albuquerque: A Christmas Adventure. Dunn, Robert, illus. 2016. (ENG.). 32p. (J). (-2). 12.99 (978-1-4926-4315-9(7), 9781492643159, Sourcebooks Jabberwocky) Sourcebooks, Inc.

—Santa's Sleigh Is on Its Way to New Mexico: A Christmas Adventure. Dunn, Robert, illus. 2016. (ENG.). 32p. (J). (-2). 12.99 (978-1-4926-4343-2(2), 9781492643432, Sourcebooks Jabberwocky) Sourcebooks, Inc.

James, Jenni. Pride & Popularity. 2011. (Jane Austen Diaries). (ENG.). 238p. (YA). (gr. 8-12). pap. 11.99 (978-0-9836293-0-0(6)) Inkberry Pr.

Johnson, LouAnne. Muchacho. 2011. (ENG.). 208p. (YA). (gr. 7). pap. 9.99 (978-0-375-85903-8(9), Ember) Random Hse. Children's Bks.

Jolley, Dan. My Boyfriend Bites, 3 vols., No. 3. Martinez, Alitha E., illus. 2011. (My Boyfriend Is a Monster Ser.: 3). (ENG.). 128p. (YA). (gr. 7-12). 29.27 (978-0-7613-5599-1(5)) Lerner Publishing Group.

—My Boyfriend Is a Monster - My Boyfriend Bites. Martinez, Alitha E., illus. 2011. (My Boyfriend Is a Monster Ser.: 3). (ENG.). 128p. (YA). (gr. 7-12). pap. 9.95 (978-0-7613-7078-9(1), Graphic Universe™) Lerner Publishing Group.

Kellerman, Faye & Kellerman, Aliza. Prism. 2009. 272p. (YA). (gr. 7-18). lib. bdg. 17.89 (978-0-06-168722-8(7), HarperTeen) HarperCollins Pubs.

Klages, Ellen. White Sands, Red Menace. 2010. (ENG.). 352p. (J). (gr. 5-18). 8.99 (978-0-14-241518-4(9), Puffin Books) Penguin Young Readers Group.

Lamadrid, Enrique R. & Arellano, Juan Estevan. Juan the Bear & the Water of Life: La Acequia de Juan del Oso. Córdova, Amy, illus. 2008. (Paso Por Aqui Ser. in the Nuevomexicano Literary Heritage Ser.). (SPA & ENG.). 48p. (J). (gr. 5-18). 17.95 (978-0-8263-4543-1(3)) Univ. of New Mexico Pr.

Lasky, Kathryn. A Voice in the Wind. 2008. (ENG., Illus.). 272p. (J). (gr. 2-5). pap. 15.95 (978-0-15-205875-3(3)) Houghton Mifflin Harcourt Publishing Co.

Leonard, Julia Platt. Cold Case. 2012. (ENG.). 288p. (J). (gr. 3-7). pap. 5.99 (978-1-4424-2010-6(3), Simon & Schuster/Paula Wiseman Bks.) Simon & Schuster/Paula Wiseman Bks.

—Cold Case. Mauro, Tony, illus. 2011. (ENG.). 288p. (J). (gr. 3-7). 15.99 (978-1-4424-2009-0(X), Simon & Schuster/Paula Wiseman Bks.) Simon & Schuster/Paula Wiseman Bks.

Little, Kimberley Griffiths. The Last Snake Runner. 2006. 201p. (YA). (gr. 7-10). reprint ed. 16.00 (978-1-4223-5838-2(0)) DIANE Publishing Co.

Martinez, Mario X. Abran & Isabella's Hidden Faith. 2015. 103p. (J). pap. (978-1-935604-73-0(2)) Gaon Bks.

Mazzio, Joann. Leaving Eldorado. 2014. (ENG.). 176p. (YA). (gr. 7). pap. 10.99 (978-0-544-33613-1(5), HMH Books For Young Readers) Houghton Mifflin Harcourt Publishing Co.

McCormick, Wilfred. Eagle Scout: A Bronc Burnett Story. 2011. 192p. 42.95 (978-1-258-07309-1(9)) Literary Licensing, LLC.

—Quick Kick: A Bronc Burnett Story. 2011. 192p. 42.95 (978-1-258-10149-7(1)) Literary Licensing, LLC.

McKann, Anna. Chavos: The Kids of Distrito Federal. 2006. (Illus.). 261p. (J). per. (978-0-9554438-0-0(6)) Sharon Hse. Publishing, Ltd.

Meyer, Carolyn. Diary of a Waitress: The Not-So-Glamorous Life of a Harvey Girl. 2015. (ENG., Illus.). 288p. (J). (gr. 4). 17.95 (978-1-62091-652-0(5), Calkins Creek) Boyds Mills Pr.

—Rio Grande Stories. 2007. (ENG., Illus.). 272p. (J). (gr. 5-7). pap. 7.99 (978-0-15-200066-0(6)) Houghton Mifflin Harcourt Publishing Co.

Mora, Pat & Carling, Amelia Lau. Abuelos, 1 vol. 2011. (ENG., Illus.). 32p. (J). (gr. -1-2). pap. 9.95 (978-1-55498-101-4(8)) Groundwood Bks. CAN. Dist: Publishers Group West (PGW).

Murphy, Barbara Beasley. Ace Flies Like an Eagle. 2003. (Can't Stop Ace Ser.: No. 3). 180p. (J). pap. 16.95 (978-0-86534-409-9(4)) Sunstone Pr.

Nesbit, Troy. Diamond Cave Mystery. 2013. (Wilderness Mystery Ser.). (ENG., Illus.). 280p. (J). (gr. 3-7). pap. 12.95 (978-1-58979-809-0(0)) Taylor Trade Publishing.

New Mexico Night Before Christmas. 2006. (YA). per. 19.99 (978-0-9710675-5-4(4)) 2020 Vision Pr.

Nickell, Judy. A New Mexico Dictionary for Young People. 2012. (J). pap. (978-1-890689-93-3(9), Rio Grande Bks.) LPD Pr.

Noël, Alyson. Echo. (Soul Seekers Ser.: 2). (ENG.). 352p. (YA). (gr. 7). 2013. mass mkt. 9.99 (978-1-250-04689-5(0), 9781250046895, St. Martin's Paperbacks) 2012. pap. 10.99 (978-0-312-57566-3(1), 9780312575663, St. Martin's Griffin) St. Martin's Pr.

—Fated. 2012. (Soul Seekers Ser.: 1). (ENG.). 368p. (YA). (gr. 7). pap. 10.99 (978-0-312-57565-6(3), 9780312575656); 18.99 (978-0-312-66485-5(0), 9780312664855) St. Martin's Pr. (St. Martin's Griffin).

—Mystic. 2013. (Soul Seekers Ser.: 3). (ENG.). 320p. (YA). (gr. 7). mass mkt. 9.99 (978-1-250-04818-9(4), 9781250048189, St. Martin's Paperbacks); 18.99 (978-0-312-66488-6(5), 9780312664886, St. Martin's Griffin); pap. 9.99 (978-0-312-57567-0(X), 9780312575670, St. Martin's Griffin) St. Martin's Pr.

Oppenlander, Annette. Escape from the Past: The Kid (book 2) 2016. (ENG.). 304p. (YA). (gr. 8-17). pap. 12.95 (978-1-78535-213-3(X), Lodestone Bks.) Hunt, John Publishing Ltd. GBR. Dist: National Bk. Network.

Orona-Ramirez, Kristy. Kiki's Journey. Warm Day, Jonathan, illus. (ENG.). 32p. (J). 2017. pap. 9.95 **(978-0-89239-410-4(2)**, Children's Book Press) 2013. 16.95 (978-0-89239-214-8(2)) Lee & Low Bks., Inc.

Ortega, Cristina. The Eyes of the Weaver: Los Ojos Del Tejedor. Garcia, Patricio E., illus. 2006. (ENG.). 64p. (J). 19.95 (978-0-8263-3990-4(5)) Univ. of New Mexico Pr.

Palma, B. El Dorado: A Palo Alto Adventure. 2012. 136p. (gr. -1). 23.99 (978-1-4634-3110-5(4)); pap. 13.99 (978-1-4634-3111-2(2)) AuthorHouse.

Patchin, Frank Gee. The Pony Rider Boys in New Mexico. 2005. 28.95 (978-1-4218-1429-2(3)); 252p. pap. 13.95 (978-1-4218-1529-9(X)) 1st World Publishing, Inc. (1st World Library - Literary Society).

Plum, Amy. Until the Beginning. 2016. (After the End Ser.: 2). 352p. (YA). (gr. 8). pap. 9.99 (978-0-06-222564-1(2), HarperTeen) HarperCollins Pubs.

Poulsen, David A. No Time Like the Past. 3rd rev. ed. 2007. (Salt & Pepper Chronicles). (ENG., Illus.). 160p. (J). (gr. 4-7). 6.95 (978-1-55263-807-1(3)) Leaf Storm Pr.

Random House Staff. The Great Train Mystery (SpongeBob SquarePants) Random House Staff, illus. 2013. (Step into Reading Ser.). (ENG., Illus.). 32p. (J). (gr. -1-1). pap. 3.99 (978-0-449-81441-3(6), Random Hse. Bks. for Young Readers) Random Hse. Children's Bks.

Reeder, Carolyn. The Secret Project Notebook. 2005. 247p. (J). 15.00 (978-0-941232-33-3(6)) Bathtub Row Pr.

Robinson, Gary. Danny Blackgoat, Rugged Road to Freedom. 2014. (ENG.). (YA). pap. 9.95 (978-1-939053-05-3(6), 7th Generation) Book Publishing Co.

Rowe, Anne Burgess, illus. The Newest Angel. 2015. 47p. (J). pap. (978-1-63293-039-2(0)) Sunstone Pr.

Ruiz, Joseph J. Angel on Daniel's Shoulder. 2004. (SPA & ENG., Illus.). 108p. (J). pap. 12.95 (978-0-86534-402-0(7)) Sunstone Pr.

—Manuel & the Magic Ring. 2003. (SPA & ENG., Illus.). 108p. (J). pap. 12.95 (978-0-86534-399-3(3)) Sunstone Pr.

Sáenz, Benjamin Alire. Sammy & Juliana in Hollywood. 2004. (ENG.). 240p. (J). (gr. 10-12). 19.95 (978-0-938317-81-4(4)) Cinco Puntos Pr.

Sandoval, John. The Witches of Ruidoso. 2013. (ENG.). 120p. (YA). pap. 12.95 (978-1-55885-766-7(4), Piñata Books) Arte Publico Pr.

Service, Pamela F. Alien Encounter. Gorman, Mike, illus. (Alien Agent Ser.: 4). (ENG.). 152p. (J). (gr. 4-6). 2011. pap. 5.95 (978-0-7613-5248-8(1)) 2010. 16.95 (978-0-8225-8873-3(0), Carolrhoda Bks.) Lerner Publishing Group.

—#4 Alien Encounter. Gorman, Mike, illus. 2011. (Alien Agent Ser.). 152p. (J). pap. 33.92 (978-0-7613-7608-8(9), Darby Creek) Lerner Publishing Group.

Silvano, Wendi. Love Is All Around Albuquerque. Czernichowska, Joanna, illus. 2016. (ENG.). 32p. (J). (-6). 12.99 (978-1-4926-2902-3(2), Sourcebooks Jabberwocky) Sourcebooks, Inc.

—Love Is All Around New Mexico. Czernichowska, Joanna, illus. 2016. (ENG.). 32p. (J). (-6). 12.99 (978-1-4926-2944-3(8), Sourcebooks Jabberwocky) Sourcebooks, Inc.

Slate, Joseph & Slate. The Secret Stars, 1 vol. Dávalos, Felipe, illus. 2005. (ENG.). 32p. (J). pap. 5.95 (978-0-7614-5152-5(8)) Marshall Cavendish Corp.

Smallman, Steve. Santa Is Coming to Albuquerque. Dunn, Robert, illus. 2013. (ENG.). 32p. (J). (-3). 9.99 (978-1-4022-9042-8(X), Sourcebooks Jabberwocky) Sourcebooks, Inc.

—Santa Is Coming to New Mexico. Dunn, Robert, illus. 2013. (ENG.). 32p. (J). (-3). 9.99 (978-1-4022-9520-1(0), Sourcebooks Jabberwocky) Sourcebooks, Inc.

—Santa Is Coming to Santa Fe. Dunn, Robert, illus. 2013. (ENG.). 32p. (J). (-3). 9.99 (978-1-4022-9124-1(8), Sourcebooks Jabberwocky) Sourcebooks, Inc.

Smith, Lane. Return to Augie Hobble. 2015. (ENG., Illus.). 288p. (J). (gr. 3-7). 16.99 (978-1-62672-054-1(1), 9781626720541) Roaring Brook Pr.
—Return to Augie Hobble. 2017. (J). lib. bdg. 18.40 (978-0-606-38550-3(9)) Turtleback Bks.
Stanley, Diane. Saving Sky. 2012. (ENG.). 208p. (J). (gr. 3-7). pap. 6.99 (978-0-06-123907-6(0)) HarperCollins Pubs.
Steinlage, Ben. Bird Boy. 2011. 290p. pap. 17.95 (978-1-4327-6667-2(8)) Outskirts Pr., Inc.
Steinsiek, Sabra Brown. The Tale of the Pronghorned Cantaloupe. Chilton, Noel Dora, illus. 2013. 48p. 24.95 (978-1-936744-11-4(2), Rio Grande Bks.) LPD Pr.
—The Tale of the Pronghorned Cantaloupe. Chilton, Noel, illus. 2009. (SPA & ENG.). 48p. (J). (gr. -1-3). pap. 17.95 (978-1-890689-85-8(8), Rio Grande Bks.) LPD Pr.
Stern, Jacqueline. Mystery of the Whispering Walls. 2004. (J). 148p. pap. (978-1-57168-844-6(7)); (Hollow Tree Mystery Ser.: Bk. 6). (Illus.). v, 142p. (978-1-57168-850-7(1), Eakin Pr.) Eakin Pr.
Stork, Francisco X. The Last Summer of the Death Warriors. 2010. (ENG.). 352p. (J). (gr. 9-7). 18.99 (978-0-545-15133-7(3), Levine, Arthur A. Bks.) Scholastic, Inc.
Strickland, Deborah. Mary Reeder, Prairie Girl. 2007. 68p. per. 8.95 (978-0-595-44514-1(4)) iUniverse, Inc.
Taschek, Karen. Horse of Seven Moons. 2005. (ENG., Illus.). 192p. (YA). pap. 14.95 (978-0-8263-3215-8(3)) Univ. of New Mexico Pr.
—The Risen Horse. 2010. (ENG.). 248p. (YA). (gr. 7-18). pap. 15.95 (978-0-8263-4837-1(8)) Univ. of New Mexico Pr.
Tripp, Valerie. Josefina Story Collection. Tibbles, Jean-Paul, illus. 2008. 420p. pap. 29.95 (978-1-59369-453-1(9)) American Girl Publishing, Inc.
Valdes, Alisa. Perdition: A Kindred Novel. 2013. (YA). pap. (978-0-06-202421-3(3), HarperTeen) HarperCollins Pubs.
—The Temptation. 2012. (ENG.). 320p. (YA). (gr. 9). pap. 8.99 (978-0-06-202420-6(5), HarperTeen) HarperCollins Pubs.
Williams Hall, Kathy. Kay Kay's Adventures on Ojo Caliente: The Old Aspen Tree & the Posi Ouinge. 2012. 32p. pap. 19.99 (978-1-4772-7667-9(X)) AuthorHouse.
Yeager, Graham. Diablo: The Third Millersburg Novel. 2006. 145p. (YA). per. 7.99 (978-0-9765478-4-6(8)) Stone Acres Publishing Co.
Zindel, Paul & Zindel, Paul. The Gadget. 2003. (ENG., Illus.). 192p. (YA). (gr. 7). mass mkt. 6.99 (978-0-440-22951-3(0), Laurel Leaf) Random Hse. Children's Bks.

NEW MEXICO—HISTORY

The Art Illustrations & Brief History of Padre Antonio Jose Martinez de Taos: New Mexico 1793-1867. 2003. pap. 10.00 (978-0-9748002-0-2(1)) Martinez, Leroy F.
Art Illustrations & Brief History of Padre Antonio Jose Martinez de Taos: New Mexico 1793-1867 Version: Color. 2003. pap. (978-0-9748002-1-9(X)) Martinez, Leroy F.
Bodden, Valerie. New Mexico. 2009. (This Land Called America Ser.). 32p. (YA). (gr. 3-6). 19.95 (978-1-58341-784-3(2)) Creative Co., The.
Boehme, Gerry, et al. New Mexico. 2015. (It's My State! (r) Ser.). (ENG., Illus.). 80p. (J). (gr. 4-4). 34.21 (978-1-62713-210-7(4)) Cavendish Square Publishing.
Brezina, Corona. New Mexico: Past & Present. 2010. (United States: Past & Present Ser.). (ENG.). 48p. (YA). pap. 11.75 (978-1-4358-9517-1(7)); lib. bdg. 29.25 (978-1-4358-9490-7(1)) Rosen Publishing Group, Inc., The. (Rosen Reference).
Brown, Rachel K. Santa Fe: Daily Life in a Western Trading Center. 2003. (J). pap. (978-1-58417-074-7(3)) Lake Street Pubs.
Burgan, Michael. New Mexico (Revised Edition) 2014. (America the Beautiful, Third Ser. (Revised Edition) Ser.). (ENG.). 144p. (J). lib. bdg. 40.00 (978-0-531-28285-4(6)) Scholastic Library Publishing.
Coleman, Miriam. New Mexico: Land of Enchantment. 2010. (Our Amazing States Ser.). (ENG.). 24p. (J). pap. 8.25 (978-1-4488-0748-2(4)); lib. bdg. 22.60 (978-1-4488-0658-4(5)) Rosen Publishing Group, Inc., The. (PowerKids Pr.).
Craats, Rennay. New Mexico. 2011. (Guide to American States Ser.). (Illus.). 48p. (YA). (gr. 3-6). 29.99 (978-1-61690-803-4(3)) Weigl Pubs., Inc.
—New Mexico: The Land of Enchantment. 2016. (J). (978-1-4896-4908-9(5)) Weigl Pubs., Inc.
Daugherty, Sharleen, ed. Young Voices of Silver City. 2013. 40p. pap. 10.99 (978-1-936744-16-9(3), Rio Grande Bks.) LPD Pr.
De Angelis, Therese. New Mexico. 2009. (From Sea to Shining Sea, Second Ser.). (ENG.). 80p. (J). pap. 7.95 (978-0-531-21139-7(8), Children's Pr.) Scholastic Library Publishing.
DeMolay, Jack. Ovnis: El Caso Roswell. Obregón, José María, tr. from ENG. 2008. (Historietas Juveniles: Misterios (Jr. Graphic Mysteries) Ser.). (SPA., Illus.). 24p. (J). (gr. 2-5). lib. bdg. 25.25 (978-1-4358-2539-0(X)) Rosen Publishing Group, Inc., The.
Eboch, Chris. Chaco Canyon, 1 vol. 2014. (Digging up the Past Ser.). (ENG.). 112p. (J). (gr. 6-12). lib. bdg. 35.64 (978-1-62403-231-8(1), Essential Library) ABDO Publishing Co.
Gamble, Adam & Jasper, Mark. Good Night New Mexico. Palmer, Ruth, illus. 2014. (Good Night Our World Ser.). (ENG.). 20p. (J). (— 1). bds. 9.95 (978-1-60219-088-7(7)) Good Night Bks.
Jerome, Kate B. Lucky to Live in New Mexico. 2017. (Arcadia Kids Ser.). (ENG., Illus.). 32p. (J). 16.99 **(978-0-7385-2804-5(8))** Arcadia Publishing.
—The Wise Animal Handbook New Mexico. 2017. (Arcadia Kids Ser.). (ENG., Illus.). 32p. (J). 16.99 **(978-0-7385-2833-5(1))** Arcadia Publishing.
Laird, Johnna M. Southwest: New Mexico, Oklahoma, Texas, Vol. 19. 2015. (Let's Explore the States Ser.). (Illus.). 64p. (J). (gr. 5). 23.95 (978-1-4222-3334-4(0)) Mason Crest.
Lavash, Donald. Journey Through New Mexico History Hardc. 2006. 300p. 34.95 (978-0-86534-541-6(4)) Sunstone Pr.
Lyon, Robin. Spanish Missions of New Mexico. 2010. (True Book(tm), a — Spanish Missions Ser.). (ENG.). 48p. (J). (gr. 2-5). 31.00 (978-0-531-20579-2(7)) Scholastic Library Publishing.
—The Spanish Missions of New Mexico. 2010. (True Book Ser.). (ENG.). 48p. (J). pap. 6.95 (978-0-531-21242-4(4), Children's Pr.) Scholastic Library Publishing.
Marsh, Carole. Exploring New Mexico Through Project-Based Learning: Geography, History, Government, Economics & More. 2016. (New Mexico Experience Ser.). (ENG.). (J). pap. 9.99 (978-0-635-12355-8(X)) Gallopade International.
—I'm Reading about New Mexico. 2014. (New Mexico Experience Ser.). (ENG., Illus.). (J). pap., pap. 8.99 (978-0-635-11306-1(6)) Gallopade International.
—New Mexico History Projects: 30 Cool, Activities, Crafts, Experiments & More for Kids to Do to Learn about Your State! 2003. (New Mexico Experience Ser.). 32p. (gr. k-5). pap. 5.95 (978-0-635-01800-7(4), Marsh, Carole Bks.) Gallopade International.
McNeese, Tim. Santa Fe. 2007. (Colonial Settlements in America Ser.). (Illus.). 116p. (YA). (gr. 5-9). lib. bdg. 30.00 (978-0-7910-9332-0(8)) Facts On File, Inc.
Murray, Julie. New Mexico, 1 vol. 2012. (Explore the United States Ser.). (ENG.). 32p. (J). (gr. 2-5). lib. bdg. 28.50 (978-1-61783-369-4(X), Big Buddy Bks.) ABDO Publishing Co.
O'Neill, Elizabeth. Alfred Visits New Mexico. 2009. (ENG.). 24p. (J). pap. 12.00 (978-0-9822288-7-6(2)) Global Business Information Strategies, Inc.
Pacheco, Robert, illus. Trade on the Taos Mountain Trail. 2010. (ENG.). 48p. (J). pap. 16.99 (978-0-9823445-0-7(3)) Vanishing Horizons.
Rodriguez, Cindy. New Mexico: The Land of Enchantment. 2012. (J). (978-1-61913-381-5(4)); pap. (978-1-61913-382-2(2)) Weigl Pubs., Inc.
Todras, Ellen & Bjorklund, Ruth. New Mexico. 2nd ed. 2013. 80p. (J). (gr. 4-8). 31.36 (978-1-60870-882-6(9)) Cavendish Square Publishing.
VanVoorst, Jenny. What's Great about New Mexico? 2014. (Our Great States Ser.). (ENG., Illus.). 32p. (gr. 2-5). pap. 7.95 (978-1-4677-4533-8(2)) Lerner Publishing Group.
Wheeler, Jill C. New Mexico, 1 vol. 2009. (United States Ser.). (ENG., Illus.). 48p. (YA). (gr. 2-5). 27.07 (978-1-60453-666-9(7)) ABDO Publishing Co.
Winter, Jonah. The Secret Project. Winter, Jeanette, illus. 2017. (ENG.). 40p. (J). (gr. k-3). 17.99 (978-1-4814-6913-5(4), Beach Lane Bks.) Beach Lane Bks.

NEW ORLEANS (LA.)

Benoit, Peter. Hurricane Katrina. 2011. (True Bk Ser.). (ENG., Illus.). 48p. (J). pap. 6.95 (978-0-531-26626-7(5)); (gr. 3-5). lib. bdg. 29.00 (978-0-531-25421-9(6)) Scholastic Library Publishing. (Children's Pr.).
Bridges, Ruby. Ruby Bridges Goes to School: My True Story. 2009. (Scholastic Reader Level 2 Ser.). (ENG.). 32p. (J). (gr. -1-3). pap. 3.99 (978-0-545-10855-3(1)) Scholastic, Inc.
Bridges, Ruby & Maccarone, Grace. Let's Read About — Ruby Bridges. Van Wright, Cornelius & Hu, Ying-Hwa, illus. 2003. (Scholastic First Biographies Ser.). (J). (978-0-439-51362-3(6)) Scholastic, Inc.
Fradin, Dennis Brindell & Fradin, Judith Bloom. Hurricane Katrina. 2009. (Turning Points in U. S. History Ser.). 48p. (gr. 3-6). 31.36 (978-0-7614-4261-5(8)) Marshall Cavendish Corp.
Goodman, Steve. The Train They Call the City of New Orleans. McCurdy, Michael, illus. 2003. 16.99 (978-3-00-100280-8(8), Putnam Juvenile) Penguin Publishing Group.
Hedlund, Stephanie F. New Orleans, 1 vol. 2007. (Cities Set 2 Ser.). (ENG., Illus.). 32p. (gr. -1-3). 27.07 (978-1-59679-721-5(5), Checkerboard Library) ABDO Publishing Co.
Koontz, Robin & dePaola, Tomie. What Was Hurricane Katrina? Hinderliter, John & McVeigh, Kevin, illus. 2015. (What Was? Ser.). (ENG.). 112p. (J). (gr. 3-7). 5.99 (978-0-448-48662-8(8), Penguin Workshop) Penguin Young Readers Group.
Looye, Juliette. Ruby Bridges. (Voices Reading Ser.). (Illus.). 16p. (J). pap. (978-0-7367-2913-0(5)) Zaner-Bloser, Inc.
Lundy, Kathleen Gould. In a Class of Her Own. Alward, Jeff, illus. 2007. 48p. (J). lib. bdg. 23.08 (978-1-4242-1629-1(X)) Fitzgerald Bks.
Zullo, Allan. Heroes of Hurricane Katrina. 2015. xii, 180p. (J). (978-1-4806-8729-5(4)) Scholastic, Inc.

NEW ORLEANS (LA.)—FICTION

Agresti, Aimee. Illuminate: A Gilded Wings Novel, Book One. 2013. (ENG.). 544p. (YA). (gr. 7). pap. 9.99 (978-0-544-02222-5(X)) Houghton Mifflin Harcourt Publishing Co.
—Infatuate: A Gilded Wings Novel, Book Two. (ENG.). 416p. (YA). (gr. 7). 2014. pap. 9.99 (978-0-544-23291-4(7), HMH Books For Young Readers) 2013. 17.99 (978-0-547-62615-4(0)) Houghton Mifflin Harcourt Publishing Co.
Amoss, Berthe. Secret Lives. 2014. (ENG., Illus.). 200p. (gr. 4). pap. 12.95 (978-1-939601-05-6(3)) Ig Publishing, Inc.
Bildner, Phil. Marvelous Cornelius: Hurricane Katrina & the Spirit of New Orleans. Parra, John, illus. 2015. (ENG.). 44p. (J). (gr. k-3). 16.99 (978-1-4521-2578-7(3)) Chronicle Bks. LLC.
Blume, Lesley M. M. Tennyson. 2009. (ENG.). 240p. (J). (gr. 3-7). 7.99 (978-0-440-24061-7(1), Yearling) Random Hse. Children's Bks.
Brezenoff, Steve. The Zombie Who Visited New Orleans, 1 vol. Canga, C. B., illus. 2010. (Field Trip Mysteries Ser.). (ENG.). 88p. (gr. 2-3). 25.32 (978-1-4342-2141-4(5)); pap. 6.10 (978-1-4342-2773-7(1)) Stone Arch Bks.
Burk, Rachelle. Tree House in a Storm. Schneider, Rex, illus. 2009. 42p. (J). (gr. k-4). 16.95 (978-0-916144-23-4(2)) Stemmer Hse. Pubs.
Chopin, Kate. The Awakening: An Icelandic Classic. Davis, Stephen, illus. 2014. (American Classics Ser.). (ENG.). 64p. pap. 6.95 (978-1-906230-78-4(1)) Real Reads Ltd. GBR. Dist: Casemate Pubs. & Bk. Distributors, LLC.
Cole, Henry. A Nest for Celeste: A Story about Art, Inspiration, & the Meaning of Home. Cole, Henry, illus. (Nest for Celeste Ser.: 1). (ENG., Illus.). 352p. (J). (gr. 3-7). 2012. pap. 6.99 (978-0-06-170412-3(1)) 2010. 16.99 (978-0-06-170410-9(5)) HarperCollins Pubs. (Tegen, Katherine Bks).
Curtis, Alice. A Little Maid of New Orleans. 2011. (Little Maid Ser.). (ENG.). 236p. pap. 12.95 (978-1-4290-9746-8(9)) Applewood Bks.
Dawson, Keila. The King Cake Baby, 1 vol. Smith, Vernon, illus. 2015. (ENG.). 32p. (J). (gr. k-3). 8.99 (978-1-4556-2013-5(0)) Pelican Publishing Co., Inc.
de Las Casas, Dianne. Dinosaur Mardi Gras, 1 vol. Gentry, Marita, illus. 2011. (ENG.). 32p. (J). (gr. k-3). 16.99 (978-1-58980-966-6(1)) Pelican Publishing Co., Inc.
Decker, Jeni. Far from Happy. 2014. 200p. pap. 14.99 (978-1-62798-407-2(0)) Dreamspinner Pr.
Dixon, Franklin W. & Keene, Carolyn. Bonfire Masquerade. 2011. (Nancy Drew/Hardy Boys Ser.: 5). (ENG.). 176p. (J). (gr. 3-7). pap. 6.99 (978-1-4424-0328-4(4), Aladdin) Simon & Schuster Children's Publishing.
Dragon, Laura. Hurricane Boy, 1 vol. 2014. (ENG., Illus.). 160p. (J). (gr. 3-7). pap. 8.95 (978-1-4556-1916-0(7)) Pelican Publishing Co., Inc.
Falter, Laury. Residue. 2013. 306p. pap. 12.99 (978-0-9855110-0-5(1)) Falter, Laury.
Friedmann, Patty. Taken Away. 2010. (ENG.). 427p. (J). (gr. 6). pap. 18.95 (978-0-9845318-2-0(3)) Tiny Stachel Pr.
Gamble, Adam, et al. Good Night New Orleans. Kelly, Cooper, illus. 2012. (Good Night Our World Ser.). (ENG.). 20p. (J). (gr. k — 1). bds. 9.95 (978-1-60219-061-0(5)) Good Night Bks.
Gerowin, Sean. Catte au Lait & the Big Hurricane. 2005. 36p. (J). 8.99 (978-1-4116-5157-9(X)) Lulu Pr., Inc.
Gumbo Goes Downtown - Evaluation Guide: Evaluation Guide. 2006. (J). (978-1-55942-407-3(9)) Witcher Productions.
Guzman, Lila & Guzman, Rick. Lorenzo & the Turncoat. 2006. 183p. (J). (gr. 5). per. 9.95 (978-1-55885-471-0(1), Piñata Books) Arte Publico Pr.
HarperCollins Publishers Ltd. Staff, et al. Origins No. 5. 2010. (Vampire Diaries: Stefan's Diaries: 1). (ENG.). 256p. (YA). (gr. 9-18). pap. 9.99 (978-0-06-200393-5(3), HarperTeen) HarperCollins Pubs.
Hawthorne, Rachel. Labor of Love. 2008. (ENG.). 320p. (YA). (gr. 9-18). pap. 5.99 (978-0-06-136384-9(7), HarperTeen) HarperCollins Pubs.
—One Perfect Summer: Labor of Love & Thrill Ride. 2015. (ENG.). 544p. (YA). (gr. 9). pap. 9.99 (978-0-06-232134-3(X), HarperTeen) HarperCollins Pubs.
Herlong, M. H. Buddy. 2013. (ENG.). 320p. (J). (gr. 5). pap. 7.99 (978-0-14-242544-2(3), Puffin Books) Penguin Young Readers Group.
Jackson, Nellie O. The Worst Day of My Life. 2008. 24p. pap. 24.95 (978-1-60474-524-5(X)) America Star Bks.
Jacobs, Lily. The Littlest Bunny in New Orleans. Dunn, Robert, illus. 2016. (ENG.). 32p. (J). (-7). 9.99 (978-1-4926-3350-1(X), 9781492633501, Sourcebooks Jabberwocky) Sourcebooks, Inc.
Jennings, Carol E. Marshall & Satchmo. 2008. 40p. pap. 21.32 (978-1-4363-7117-9(1)) Xlibris Corp.
Karwoski, Gail Langer. When Hurricane Katrina Hit Home. Marshall, Julia, illus. 2013. Orig. Title: When Hurricane Katrina Hit Home. (ENG.). 192p. (gr. 4-7). 15.99 (978-1-62619-083-2(6), History Pr., The) Arcadia Publishing.
Keaton, Kelly. A Beautiful Evil. (ENG.). (YA). (gr. 9). 2013. 320p. pap. 11.99 (978-1-4424-0928-6(2)) 2012. 304p. 17.99 (978-1-4424-0927-9(4)) Simon Pulse. (Simon Pulse).
—Darkness Becomes Her. (ENG.). (YA). (gr. 9). 2012. 320p. pap. 9.99 (978-1-4424-0925-5(8)) 2011. 288p. 16.99 (978-1-4424-0924-8(X)) Simon Pulse. (Simon Pulse).
—The Wicked Within. (ENG., Illus.). 288p. (YA). (gr. 9). 2014. pap. 9.99 (978-1-4424-9316-2(X)) 2013. 17.99 (978-1-4424-9315-5(1)) Simon Pulse. (Simon Pulse).
Kenyon, Sherrilyn. Inferno. 2014. (Chronicles of Nick Ser.: 4). (ENG.). 464p. (YA). (gr. 7). pap. 11.99 (978-1-250-00286-0(9), 9781250002860, St. Martin's Griffin) St. Martin's Pr.
—Infinity, Vol. 1. Ahn, JiYoung, illus. 2013. (Dark-Hunters Ser.: 1). (ENG.). 240p. (gr. 11-17). 13.00 (978-0-316-19053-4(5), Yen Pr.) Orbit.
—Infinity. (Chronicles of Nick Ser.: 1). (ENG.). 480p. (YA). (gr. 7-18). 2011. pap. 11.99 (978-0-312-60304-5(5), 9780312603045) 2010. 19.99 (978-0-312-59907-2(2), 9780312599072) St. Martin's Pr. (St. Martin's Griffin).
—Invincible. (Chronicles of Nick Ser.: 2). (ENG.). 432p. (YA). (gr. 7). 2012. pap. 11.99 (978-0-312-60327-4(4), 9780312603274) 2011. 27.99 (978-0-312-59906-5(4), 9780312599065) St. Martin's Pr. (St. Martin's Griffin).
Lamana, Julie T. Upside down in the Middle of Nowhere. (ENG.). (J). 2015. 328p. (gr. 4-7). pap. 7.99 (978-1-4521-2880-1(4)) 2014. 320p. (gr. 3-7). 16.99 (978-1-4521-2456-8(6)) Chronicle Bks. LLC.
Larson, Hope. Compass South. 2017. (Four Points Ser.: 1). (J). lib. bdg. 24.50 **(978-0-606-39953-1(4))** Turtleback Bks.
Lawson, Shandy. The Loop. 2014. (ENG.). 208p. (YA). (gr. 7-12). pap. 8.99 (978-1-4231-6948-2(4)) Hyperion Bks. for Children.
Lee, Chris. Becoming a Sant: A Guidebook for Parents & Santa's Helpers. 2008. 48p. pap. 16.95 (978-1-60563-449-4(2)) America Star Bks.
Littell, William Adams. Guillaume. 2008. 74p. pap. 10.00 (978-0-8059-7757-8(0)) Dorrance Publishing Co., Inc.
Long, Loren & Bildner, Phil. Blastin' the Blues. Long, Loren, illus. 2011. (Sluggers Ser.: 5). (ENG., Illus.). 448p. (J). (gr. 3-7). pap. 8.99 (978-1-4169-1891-2(4), Simon & Schuster Bks. For Young Readers) Simon & Schuster Bks. For Young Readers.
Mack, Iris Marie. Mama Says, Money Doesn't Grow on Trees! 2004. (World of Dr. Mackamatix Mathematics Edutainment Book Ser.). (Illus.). 48p. (J). per. 18.99 (978-1-4134-0891-1(5)) Xlibris Corp.
Maria, Miss Yvonne. Beautiful Black Mermaids of the Bayou, 1 vol. 2009. 48p. pap. 16.95 (978-1-60836-236-3(1)) America Star Bks.
Marsh, Carole. The Mystery on the Mighty Mississippi. 2009. (Real Kids, Real Places Ser.). (Illus.). 146p. (J). lib. bdg. 18.99 (978-0-635-07001-2(4), Marsh, Carole Mysteries) Gallopade International.
Maxwell, Lisa. Sweet Unrest. 2014. (ENG.). 336p. (YA). pap. 11.99 (978-0-7387-4081-2(0), Flux) North Star Editions.
McAlpine, Gordon. Once upon a Midnight Eerie. Zuppardi, Sam, illus. 2015. (Misadventures of Edgar & Allan Poe Ser.: 2). (ENG.). 208p. (J). (gr. 3-7). 6.99 (978-0-14-242349-3(1), Puffin Books) Penguin Young Readers Group.
—Once upon a Midnight Eerie: Book #2. Zuppardi, Sam, illus. 2014. (Misadventures of Edgar & Allan Poe Ser.: 2). (ENG.). 192p. (J). (gr. 3-7). 16.99 (978-0-670-78493-6(1), Viking Books for Young Readers) Penguin Young Readers Group.
McConduit, Alexander Brian. Snoballs for All, 1 vol. Ganucheau, Paulina, illus. 2015. (ENG.). 32p. (J). (gr. k-3). pap. 8.99 (978-1-4556-2002-9(5)) Pelican Publishing Co., Inc.
Miller, William. Rent Party Jazz. Riley-Webb, Charlotte, illus. (ENG.). 32p. (J). 2013. (gr. 1-5). 16.95 (978-1-58430-025-0(6)) 2011. pap. 9.95 (978-1-60060-344-0(0)) Lee & Low Bks., Inc.
Morris, Paula. Unbroken. 2013. (ENG.). 304p. (J). (gr. 7). 17.99 (978-0-545-41641-2(8)) Scholastic, Inc.
Nicholson, Simon. The Demon Curse. 2015. (Young Houdini Ser.: 2). (ENG.). 240p. (J). (gr. 5-8). 15.99 (978-1-4926-0335-1(X), 9781492603351, Sourcebooks Jabberwocky) Sourcebooks, Inc.
Osborne, Mary Pope. A Good Night for Ghosts. 2010. (Magic Tree House Merlin Missions Ser.: No. 14). (Illus.). 157p. (J). pap. (978-4-8401-3411-8(1)) Fukuinkan Shoten.
—A Good Night for Ghosts. Murdocca, Sal, illus. (Magic Tree House Merlin Mission Ser.: 14). (ENG.). (J). (gr. 2-5). 2011. 144p. 5.99 (978-0-375-85649-5(8)) 2009. 128p. 12.99 (978-0-375-85648-8(X)) Random Hse. Children's Bks. (Random Hse. Bks. for Young Readers).
Owen, Rob. Spy Boy, Cheyenne, & Ninety-Six Crayons: A "Mardi Gras" Indian's Story, 1 vol. Owen, Rob, illus. 2013. (ENG., Illus.). 32p. (J). (gr. k-3). 16.99 (978-1-4556-1799-9(7)) Pelican Publishing Co., Inc.
Patrick, Denise Lewis. Finding Someplace. 2015. (ENG.). 224p. (J). (gr. 3-7). 16.99 (978-0-8050-4716-5(6), 9780805047165, Holt, Henry & Co. Bks. For Young Readers) Holt, Henry & Co.
—Finding Someplace. 2016. (ENG.). 224p. (J). pap. 7.99 (978-1-250-07982-4(9), 9781250079824) Square Fish.
—Finding Someplace. 2016. (J). lib. bdg. 17.20 (978-0-606-38560-2(6)) Turtleback Bks.
Perelman, Helen & Studio IBOIX. Tiana: The Grand Opening, 1 vol. 2012. (Disney Princess Ser.). (ENG., Illus.). 96p. (J). (gr. 2-5). 24.21 (978-1-59961-880-7(X)) Spotlight.
Philbrick, Rodman. Zane & the Hurricane: A Story of Katrina. (ENG.). 192p. (J). (gr. 5-9). 2015. pap. 6.99 (978-0-545-34239-1(2)) 2014. (Illus.). 16.99 (978-0-545-34238-4(4)) Scholastic, Inc. (Blue Sky Pr., The).
Pogo the Clown. A Taste of Shrimp: Harley's Great Adventures. Miller, Richard D., illus. 2005. (J). 12.95 (978-0-9755253-4-0(4)) Chiliric Pubns.
Preble, Laura. Lica's Angel. 2003. 142p. (YA). 21.95 (978-0-595-74914-0(3)); pap. 11.95 (978-0-595-28253-1(9)) iUniverse, Inc.
Prieto, Anita C. Timothy Hubble & the King Cake Party, 1 vol. Howard, Virginia, illus. 2008. (ENG.). 32p. (J). (gr. k-3). 16.99 (978-1-58980-584-2(4)) Pelican Publishing Co., Inc.
RH Disney Staff. The Princess & the Frog. RH Disney Staff, illus. 2009. (Little Golden Book Ser.). (ENG., Illus.). 24p. (J). (gr. -1-2). 4.99 (978-0-7364-2628-2(0), Golden/Disney) Random Hse. Children's Bks.
Rhodes, Jewell Parker. Ninth Ward. 2010. (ENG.). 224p. (J). (gr. 5-17). 15.99 (978-0-316-04307-6(9)) Little, Brown Bks. for Young Readers.
—Ninth Ward. 2012. (J). lib. bdg. 18.40 (978-0-606-26158-6(3), Turtleback) Turtleback Bks.
Rowley, Julie P. The Little Purple Mardi Gras Bead, 1 vol. Paquette, John R., illus. 2016. (ENG.). 32p. (J). pap. 8.99 **(978-1-4556-2344-0(X))** Pelican Publishing Co., Inc.
Roy, Ron. The Zombie Zone. Gurney, John Steven, illus. 2005. (to Z Mysteries Ser.: 26). (ENG.). 96p. (J). (gr. 1-4). pap. 4.99 (978-0-375-82483-8(9), Random Hse. Bks. for Young Readers) Random Hse. Children's Bks.
Scheffler, Stephanie. Elizabeth & the War of 1812. 2010. 292p. (YA). 28.95 (978-1-4502-3539-6(5)); (ENG.). pap. 18.95 (978-1-4502-3540-2(9)) iUniverse, Inc.
Sepetys, Ruta. Out of the Easy. 2013. (ENG.). 352p. (YA). (gr. 9). 17.99 (978-0-399-25692-9(X), Philomel Bks.) Penguin Young Readers Group.
Shankman, Ed. The Bourbon Street Band Is Back. O'Neill, Dave, illus. 2011. (Shankman & O'Neill Ser.). (ENG.). 32p. (gr. -1-3). 14.95 (978-1-933212-79-1(9), Commonwealth Editions) Applewood Bks.
Sharenow, Robert. My Mother the Cheerleader. 2009. (ENG.). 320p. (YA). (gr. 8). pap. 9.99 (978-0-06-114898-9(9), HarperTeen) 2007. 304p. (J). (gr. 7-18). 16.99 (978-0-06-114896-5(2), Geringer, Laura Book) 2007. 304p. (J). (gr. 7-18). lib. bdg. 17.89 (978-0-06-114897-2(0), Geringer, Laura Book) HarperCollins Pubs.
Sickler, Jonas, illus. Hey Diddle Diddle: Hey Baby Look at the Cat & His Fiddle - in New Orleans! 2010. (Indestructibles Ser.). (ENG.). 12p. (J). (gr. k — 1). pap. 5.95 (978-0-7611-5862-2(6), 15862) Workman Publishing Co., Inc.
Smallman, Steve. Santa Is Coming to New Orleans. Dunn, Robert, illus. 2014. (ENG.). 32p. (J). (-3). 9.99 (978-1-4926-0694-9(4), Sourcebooks Jabberwocky) Sourcebooks, Inc.
Smith, Sherri L. Orleans. 2013. (ENG.). 336p. (YA). (gr. 7). 17.99 (978-0-399-25294-5(0), G.P. Putnam's Sons Books for Young Readers) Penguin Young Readers Group.
Sobel, Sheila. Color Blind. 2016. (ENG.). 253p. (YA). 17.99 (978-1-4405-9746-6(4), Simon Pulse) Simon Pulse.
Stanley, Shalanda. Drowning Is Inevitable. 2015. (ENG.). 288p. (YA). (gr. 9). 17.99 (978-0-553-50828-4(8), Knopf Bks. for Young Readers) Random Hse. Children's Bks.
Stewart, Emma. The Adventures of Fillmore the Gerbil. 2008. 24p. pap. 13.50 (978-1-60693-033-5(8), Eloquent Bks.) Strategic Book Publishing & Rights Agency (SBPRA).
Sutton, Laurie S. The House on Spooky Street. Neely, Scott, illus. 2015. (You Choose Stories: Scooby-Doo Ser.). (ENG.). 112p. (gr. 2-3). lib. bdg. 32.65 (978-1-4342-9714-3(4), You Choose Bks.) Capstone Press of Coughlan Cos.
Tangerine, Tracey. Buddy Zooka: In the French Quarter & Beyond. 2010. (ENG.). 201p. (J). (gr. 7-12). pap. 16.00 (978-0-9741995-8-0(3)) Chin Music Pr.
Tarshis, Lauren. I Survived Hurricane Katrina 2005. 2011. (I Survived Ser.: 3). (ENG.). 112p. (J). (gr. 3-7). pap. 4.99 (978-0-545-20696-9(0), Scholastic Paperbacks) Scholastic, Inc.

—I Survived Hurricane Katrina 2005. 2011. (I Survived ... Ser.: No. 3). lib. bdg. 14.75 *(978-0-606-23743-7(7),* Turtleback) Turtleback Bks.

Thomas, Deborah Kadiar. Cemetery Jamboree, 1 vol. Thomas, Deborah Kadiar, illus. 2016. (ENG., Illus.). 32p. (J). (gr. k-5). pap. 9.95 *(978-1-4556-2239-9(7))* Pelican Publishing Co., Inc.

Tubb, Kristin O'Donnell. The 13th Sign. 2013. (ENG.). 272p. (J). (gr. 5-9). 16.99 *(978-0-312-58352-1(4),* 9780312583521) Feiwel & Friends.

—The 13th Sign. 2014. (ENG.). 288p. (J). (gr. 5-9). pap. 9.99 *(978-1-250-05059-5(6),* 9781250050595) Square Fish.

Uhlberg, Myron. A Storm Called Katrina, 1 vol. Bootman, Colin, illus. 2015. (ENG.). 40p. (J). (gr. 2-4). pap. 8.95 *(978-1-56145-887-5(2))* Peachtree Pubs.

—A Storm Called Katrina. 2015. lib. bdg. 19.60 *(978-0-606-37467-5(1))* Turtleback Bks.

Watson, Renée. A Place Where Hurricanes Happen. Stickland, Shadra, illus. 2014. (ENG.). 40p. (J). (gr. k-4). 7.99 *(978-0-385-37668-6(5),* Dragonfly Bks.) Random Hse. Children's Bks.

—A Place Where Hurricanes Happen. Strickland, Shadra, illus. 2010. (ENG.). 40p. (J). (gr. k-4). 17.99 *(978-0-375-85609-9(9),* Random Hse. Bks. for Young Readers) Random Hse. Children's Bks.

Weatherford, Carole Boston. Freedom in Congo Square. Christie, R. Gregory, illus. 2016. (ENG.). 40p. (J). (gr. -1-3). 17.99 *(978-1-4998-0103-3(3))* Little Bee Books Inc.

Webber, Jake. Lafitte's Black Box: Boit Noir. 2009. 228p. 32.95 *(978-1-60594-361-9(4));* pap. 14.95 *(978-1-60594-360-2(6))* Aeon Publishing Inc. (Llumina Pr.).

Whiteside, S. K. Inheritance. 2013. 320p. (YA). pap. 12.99 *(978-1-939769-27-5(2))* Crushing Hearts and Black Butterfly Publishing.

Woods, Brenda. Saint Louis Armstrong Beach. 2012. (ENG.). 160p. (J). (gr. 5). pap. 5.99 *(978-0-14-242186-4(3),* Puffin Books) Penguin Young Readers Group.

—Saint Louis Armstrong Beach. 2012. lib. bdg. 16.00 *(978-0-606-26661-1(5),* Turtleback) Turtleback Bks.

Zschock, Martha Day. Hello, New Orleans! 2011. (Hello! Ser.). (ENG., Illus.). 16p. (J). (gr. -1-k). bds. 9.95 *(978-1-933212-63-0(2),* Commonwealth Editions) Applewood Bks.

NEW ORLEANS (LA.)—HISTORY

Allberti, Frances C. Finding Rover. Gremillion, Barry, illus. 2006. (J). per. *(978-0-9785937-1-1(5))* Open Pages Publishing.

Brown, Don. Drowned City: Hurricane Katrina & New Orleans. 2015. (ENG., Illus.). 96p. (YA). (gr. 7). 18.99 *(978-0-544-15777-4(X),* HMH Books For Young Readers) Houghton Mifflin Harcourt Publishing Co.

—Drowned City: Hurricane Katrina & New Orleans. 2017. (ENG.). (YA). (gr. 7). lib. bdg. 20.85 ***(978-0-606-39819-0(8))*** Turtleback Bks.

Canasi, Brittany. Dropping in on New Orleans. 2017. (Dropping in On Ser.). (ENG.). (J). (gr. 3-5). 32.80 ***(978-1-68342-174-0(4))*** Rourke Educational Media.

Coles, Robert. The Story of Ruby Bridges. 2009. 8.44 *(978-0-7848-3016-1(9),* Everbind) Marco Bk. Co.

—The Story of Ruby Bridges. 2011. 17.00 *(978-1-61383-173-1(0))* Perfection Learning Corp.

—The Story of Ruby Bridges. Ford, George, illus. 50th anniv. ed. 2010. (ENG.). 32p. (J). (gr. -1-3). pap. 6.99 *(978-0-439-47226-5(1),* Scholastic Paperbacks) Scholastic, Inc.

—The Story of Ruby Bridges. 2010. lib. bdg. 17.20 *(978-0-606-23189-3(7),* Turtleback) Turtleback Bks.

Epstein, Brad M. New Orleans Saints 101. 2010. (Illus.). 24p. (J). bds. *(978-1-60730-119-6(9),* 101 Bk.) Michaelson Entertainment.

Ferut, Michael. St. Louis Cemetery No. 1. 2014. (Scariest Places on Earth Ser.). (ENG., Illus.). 24p. (J). (gr. 3-7). lib. bdg. 25.95 *(978-1-60014-997-9(9),* Torque Bks.) Bellwether Media.

Foran, Jill. Mardi Gras. 2003. (Celebrating Cultures Ser.). (Illus.). 24p. (J). lib. bdg. 24.45 *(978-1-59036-093-4(1))* Weigl Pubs., Inc.

Hoffman, Mary Ann. Hurricane Katrina. 2009. (Nature in the News Ser.). 32p. (gr. 3-4). 42.50 *(978-1-61514-821-9(3),* PowerKids Pr.) Rosen Publishing Group, Inc., The.

McGee, Randel. Paper Crafts for Mardi Gras. 2011. (Paper Craft Fun for Holidays Ser.). (Illus.). 48p. (J). (gr. 3-18). pap. 8.95 *(978-1-59845-334-8(3),* Enslow Elementary) Enslow Pubs., Inc.

Person, Stephen. Voodoo in New Orleans. 2010. (HorrorScapes Ser.). 32p. (YA). (gr. 4-7). lib. bdg. 25.27 *(978-1-936087-99-0(5))* Bearport Publishing Co., Inc.

Strom, Laura Layton. Built below Sea Level: New Orleans. 2007. (Shockwave: People & Communities Ser.). (ENG., Illus.). 36p. (J). (gr. 3-5). 25.00 *(978-0-531-17746-4(7),* Children's Pr.) Scholastic Library Publishing.

Vierow, Wendy. The Capture of New Orleans: Union Fleet Takes Control of the Lower Mississippi River. 2004. (Headlines from History Ser.). (Illus.). 24p. (YA). (gr. 2-5). lib. bdg. 22.60 *(978-0-8239-6222-8(9))* Rosen Publishing Group, Inc., The.

Zullo, Allan. Heroes of Hurricane Katrina. 2015. (Ten True Tales Ser.). (ENG.). 192p. (J). (gr. 3-7). pap. 5.99 *(978-0-545-83123-9(7))* Scholastic, Inc.

NEW ORLEANS, BATTLE OF, NEW ORLEANS, LA., 1815

Weintraub, Aileen. Jean Lafitte: Pirate Hero of the War Of 1812. 2009. (Library of Pirates Ser.). 24p. (gr. 3-3). 42.50 *(978-1-60853-813-3(3),* PowerKids Pr.) Rosen Publishing Group, Inc., The.

NEW ORLEANS, BATTLE OF, NEW ORLEANS, LA., 1815—FICTION

Lane, Frederick A. A Flag for Lafitte: Story of the Battle of New Orleans. Vosburgh, Leonard, illus. 2011. 192p. 42.95 *(978-1-258-06624-6(6))* Literary Licensing, LLC.

Williams Evans, Freddi & Evans, Freddi Williams. The Battle of New Orleans: The Drummer's Story, 1 vol. Henriquez, Emile, illus. 2005. (ENG.). 32p. (J). (gr. k-3). 16.99 *(978-1-58980-300-8(0))* Pelican Publishing Co., Inc.

NEW TESTAMENT

see Bible—New Testament

NEW YEAR

Amstutz, Lisa J. Chinese New Year. 2017. (Holidays Around the World Ser.). (ENG., Illus.). 24p. (gr. k-1). lib. bdg. 21.99 *(978-1-5157-4851-9(0),* Pebble Bks.) Capstone Press of Coughlan Cos.

Appleby, Alex. Happy New Year!, Vol. 1. 2014. (Happy Holidays! Ser.). (ENG.). 24p. (J). (gr. k-k). 22.60 *(978-1-4339-9943-7(9))* Stevens, Gareth Publishing LLLP.

Bledsoe, Karen E. Chinese New Year Crafts. 2005. (Fun Holiday Crafts Kids Can Do! Ser.). (Illus.). 32p. (J). lib. bdg. 23.94 *(978-0-7660-2347-5(8),* Enslow Elementary) Enslow Pubs., Inc.

—Fun Chinese New Year Crafts. 2015. (Kid Fun Holiday Crafts! Ser.). 32p. (J). (gr. 3-4). 23.94 *(978-0-7660-6240-5(6))* Enslow Pubs., Inc.

Bullard, Lisa. Chelsea's Chinese New Year. Saunders, Katie, illus. 2012. (Holidays & Special Days Ser.). 24p. (gr. k-2). (J). pap. 39.62 *(978-0-7613-9247-7(5),* Millbrook Pr.); (ENG.). pap. 6.95 *(978-0-7613-8579-0(7),* Millbrook Pr.); (ENG.). lib. bdg. 23.93 *(978-0-7613-5078-1(0))* Lerner Publishing Group.

Chapman, Helen. Happy New Year. 2015. (Collins Big Cat Ser.). (ENG.). 24p. (J). (gr. 1-1). pap. 6.95 *(978-0-00-759104-6(7))* HarperCollins Pubs. Ltd. GBR. Dist: Independent Pubs. Group.

Chinese New Year's Dragon. (J). 48.95 *(978-0-8136-2242-2(5))* Modern Curriculum Pr.

Coleman, Clara O. Happy New Year! 2016. (Celebrations Ser.). 00024p. (J). (gr. 1-1). pap. 8.25 *(978-1-4994-2671-7(2),* PowerKids Pr.) Rosen Publishing Group, Inc., The.

Compestine, Ying Chang. D Is for Dragon Dance. Xuan, YongSheng, illus. (ENG.). 32p. (J). (gr. -1-3). 2006. pap. 6.95 *(978-0-8234-2058-2(2))* 2005. 17.95 *(978-0-8234-1887-9(1))* Holiday Hse., Inc.

Dice, Elizabeth A. & Matters, Print. Western & Chinese New Year's Celebrations. 2009. (Holidays & Celebration Ser.). (Illus.). 120p. (gr. 5-8). 40.00 *(978-1-60413-093-5(8),* Chelsea Hse.) Facts On File, Inc.

Gleason, Carrie. Chinese New Year. 2008. (Celebrations in My World Ser.). (ENG., Illus.). 32p. (J). (gr. k-3). pap. *(978-0-7787-4298-2(9));* lib. bdg. *(978-0-7787-4280-7(6))* Crabtree Publishing Co.

Grack, Rachel. Chinese New Year. 2017. (Chinese New Year Ser.). 24p. (J). (gr. k-3). pap. 6.99 ***(978-1-61891-270-1(4),*** Blastoff! Readers) Bellwether Media.

Heinrichs, Ann. Chinese New Year. Huang, Benrei, illus. 2013. (Holidays & Celebrations Ser.). (ENG.). 32p. (J). (gr. k-3). 27.07 *(978-1-62323-504-8(9),* 206275) Child's World, Inc., The.

Jalali, Yassaman. Celebrating Norouz (Persian New Year) Zamanian, Marjan, illus. 2003. 28p. (J). (gr. -1-6). pap. 12.99 *(978-0-9728020-0-0(2))* Saman Publishing.

Jeffrey, Laura S. Celebrate Tet. 2007. (Celebrate Holidays Ser.). (Illus.). 104p. (J). (gr. 3-7). lib. bdg. 33.27 *(978-0-7660-2775-6(9))* Enslow Pubs., Inc.

Kaplan, Leslie C. Chinese New Year. 2009. (Library of Holidays Ser.). 24p. (gr. 2-3). 42.50 *(978-1-60853-707-5(2),* PowerKids Pr.) Rosen Publishing Group, Inc., The.

Kule, Elaine A. Celebrate Chinese New Year. 2006. (Celebrate Holidays Ser.). (Illus.). 112p. (J). (gr. 5-6). lib. bdg. 33.27 *(978-0-7660-2577-6(2))* Enslow Pubs., Inc.

Lee, Jen. Chinese New Year: A Celebration for Everyone, 1 vol. 2017. (Orca Origins Ser.). (ENG., Illus.). 88p. (J). (gr. 3-7). 24.95 ***(978-1-4598-1126-3(7))*** Orca Bk. Pubs. USA.

Lee, Michelle. Chinese New Year. 2016. (World's Greatest Celebrations Ser.). (ENG., Illus.). 32p. (gr. 3-8). 27.99 *(978-1-62920-566-3(4))* Scobre Pr. Corp.

MacMillan, Dianne M. Chinese New Year. rev. ed. 2008. (Best Holiday Bks.). (Illus.). 48p. (J). (gr. 3-4). lib. bdg. 25.27 *(978-0-7660-3038-1(5))* Enslow Pubs., Inc.

McGee, Randel. Celebrate Chinese New Year with Paper Crafts. 2015. (Celebrate Holidays with Paper Crafts Ser.). 48p. (J). (gr. 3-4). 25.27 *(978-0-7660-6350-1(X))* Enslow Pubs., Inc.

McNeil, Niki, et al. HOCPP1022 New Years. 2004. spiral bd. 17.50 *(978-1-60308-022-4(8))* In the Hands of a Child.

Mercer, Abbie. Happy New Year. (Holiday Fun Ser.). 24p. 2009. (gr. 2-3). 42.50 *(978-1-61513-376-5(3),* PowerKids Pr.) 2007. (Illus.). (J). (gr. 3-7). lib. bdg. 22.60 *(978-1-4042-3808-4(5))* Rosen Publishing Group, Inc., The.

MoonRattles. Heritage Holiday Activity Guide: Chinese New Year 2007, 1 vol. 2006. (Illus.). 52p. (J). spiral bd. *(978-0-9790920-0-8(0))* MoonRattles.

Morrill, Ann & Matters, Print. Religious New Year's Celebrations. 2009. (Holidays & Celebration Ser.). (Illus.). 112p. (gr. 5-8). 40.00 *(978-1-60413-094-2(6),* Chelsea Hse.) Facts On File, Inc.

Morrissey, Tricia. Hiss! Pop! Boom! Celebrating Chinese New Year. Lee, Kong, illus. 2006. (ENG.). 32p. (J). (gr. -1-3). 12.95 *(978-0-9715940-7-4(4))* ThingsAsian Pr.

Peppas, Lynn. New Year's Day. 2010. (ENG., Illus.). 32p. (J). *(978-0-7787-4762-8(X));* pap. *(978-0-7787-4780-2(8))* Crabtree Publishing Co.

Peter, Val J., creator. Reflections for a Happy New Year: From the Kids at Boys Town. 2004. 121p. pap. 5.95 *(978-1-889322-40-7(7),* 19-016) Boys Town Pr.

Pettiford, Rebecca. Chinese New Year. 2015. (Illus.). 24p. (J). (gr. k-3). lib. bdg. *(978-1-62031-184-4(4),* Bullfrog Bks.) Jump! Inc.

Pirotta, Saviour. Chinese New Year. 2007. (We Love Holidays Ser.). (Illus.). 24p. (J). (gr. 3-7). lib. bdg. 21.25 *(978-1-4042-3709-4(7),* PowerKids Pr.) Rosen Publishing Group, Inc., The.

Sebra, Richard. It's Chinese New Year! 2016. (Bumba Books (tm) — It's a Holiday! Ser.). (ENG., Illus.). 24p. (J). (gr. -1-1). 25.32 *(978-1-5124-1425-7(5))* Lerner Publishing Group.

Sebra, Richard. It's New Year's Day! 2017. (Bumba Books (tm) — It's a Holiday! Ser.). (ENG.). 24p. (J). (gr. -1-1). 12.99 ***(978-1-5124-3702-7(6),*** Lerner Pubns.); 38.65 ***(978-1-5124-2744-8(6),*** Lerner Pubns.); 38.65 ***(978-1-5124-3701-0(8),*** Lerner Pubns.); (Illus.). lib. bdg. 25.32 *(978-1-5124-2565-9(6))* Lerner Publishing Group.

Tang, Sanmu. Celebrating the Chinese New Year. Ying, Wu, tr. from CHI. 2010. (Chinese Festivals Ser.). (ENG., Illus.). 32p. (J). (gr. -1-3). pap. 4.95 *(978-1-60220-958-9(8))* BetterLink Pr., Inc.

Trumbore, Cindy. New Year's Around the World. 2012. (ENG., Illus.). 48p. (J). (gr. 2-3). pap. 9.50 *(978-0-7652-0885-9(7),* Modern Curriculum Pr.) Pearson Schl.

Walker, Sylvia. Happy New Year Around the World. 2012. (Dover Holiday Coloring Book Ser.). (ENG., Illus.). 32p. (J). (gr. -1-3). pap. 3.99 *(978-0-486-48988-9(4))* Dover Pubns., Inc.

Williams, Colleen Madonna Flood. My Adventure on New Year's Day. 2006. 44p. (J). 8.99 *(978-1-59092-554-6(8))* Blue Forge Pr.

World Book, Inc Staff, contrib. by. New Year's Celebrations. 2009. (Illus.). 46p. (J). *(978-0-7166-5040-9(1))* World Bk., Inc.

Yasuda, Anita. Chinese New Year. 2011. (J). (gr. 3-5). pap. 12.95 *(978-1-61690-683-2(9),* AV2 by Weigl); (Illus.). 24p. (YA). (gr. 2-5). 27.13 *(978-1-61690-677-1(4))* Weigl Pubs., Inc.

Zocchi, Judy. Number 1 What Grows in the Sun? Wallis, Rebecca, illus. 2005. (Holiday Happenings Ser.). 32p. (J). per. 10.95 *(978-1-59646-273-1(6))* Dingles & Co.

—On Chinese New Year. Wallis, Rebecca, illus. 2005. (Holiday Happenings Ser.). 32p. (J). per. 10.95 *(978-1-59646-189-5(6))* Dingles & Co.

—On Chinese New Year/el Año Nuevo Chino. Wallis, Rebecca, illus. 2005. (Holiday Happenings Ser.).Tr. of Año Nuevo Chino. (ENG & SPA.). 32p. (J). per. 10.95 *(978-1-59646-191-8(8))* Dingles & Co.

—On New Year's Eve. Wallis, Rebecca, illus. 2005. (Holiday Happenings Ser.). 32p. (J). pap. 10.95 *(978-1-59646-216-8(7));* lib. bdg. 21.65 *(978-1-891997-51-8(3));* per. 10.95 *(978-1-59646-217-5(5))* Dingles & Co.

—On New Year's Eve/la Nochevieja. Wallis, Rebecca, illus. 2005. (Holiday Happenings Ser.).Tr. of Nochevieja. (ENG & SPA.). 32p. (J). pap. 10.95 *(978-1-59646-218-2(3));* lib. bdg. 21.65 *(978-1-891997-52-5(1));* per. 10.95 *(978-1-59646-219-9(1))* Dingles & Co.

NEW YEAR—FICTION

Ackelsberg, Amy. Happy New Year! 2014. (Strawberry Shortcake Ser.). (ENG., Illus.). 24p. (J). (gr. -1-k). 4.99 *(978-0-448-48248-4(7),* Grosset & Dunlap) Penguin Young Readers Group.

Bunting, Eve. Frog & Friends Celebrate Thanksgiving, Christmas, & New Year's Eve. Masse, Josée, illus. 2015. (I AM a READER!: Frog & Friends Ser.). (ENG.). 40p. (J). (gr. 1-2). 9.99 *(978-1-58536-897-6(0),* 203949) Sleeping Bear Pr.

Cabot, Meg. Runaway. 2010. (Airhead Ser.: 3). (ENG.). 320p. (J). (gr. 7-18). 16.99 *(978-0-545-04060-0(4))* Scholastic, Inc.

Chen, Yong. A Gift. 2011. (ENG.). 32p. (J). (gr. k-2). pap. 6.95 *(978-1-59078-898-1(2))* Boyds Mills Pr.

Compestine, Ying Chang. The Runaway Wok: A Chinese New Year Tale. Serra, Sebastia, illus. 2011. (ENG.). 32p. (J). (gr. 1-3). 16.99 *(978-0-525-42068-2(1),* Dutton Books for Young Readers) Penguin Young Readers Group.

Crompton, Lee. 12 Months. 2006. 230p. pap. 9.14 *(978-1-4116-2196-1(4))* Lulu Pr., Inc.

Di Luzio-Poitras, Linda & Poitras, Bruno. Kitchi's New Year's Resolution. 2011. 44p. (gr. -1). pap. 16.59 *(978-1-4520-2152-2(X))* AuthorHouse.

England, Nora. The Witches of Dorkdom. 2013. 180p. pap. 9.95 *(978-0-9676344-4-9(X))* Penury Pr.

Erickson, John R. The Case of the Three Rings. Holmes, Gerald L., illus. 2014. 124p. (J). pap. *(978-1-59188-164-3(1))* Maverick Bks., Inc.

Flor Ada, Alma. Celebra el Ano Nuevo Chino con la Familia Fong. 2006. (Cuentos para Celebrar / Stories to Celebrate Ser.). (Illus.). 30p. (gr. k-6). per. 11.95 *(978-1-59820-114-7(X),* Alfaguara) Santillana USA Publishing Co., Inc.

—Celebrate Chinese New Year with the Fong Family. Castro, Mima, illus. 2006. (Cuentos para Celebrar / Stories to Celebrate Ser.). 30p. (gr. k-6). per. 11.95 *(978-1-59820-126-0(3))* Santillana USA Publishing Co., Inc.

Friedman, Laurie. Happy New Year, Mallory! Kalis, Jennifer, illus. (Mallory Ser.: 12). (ENG.). 176p. (J). (gr. 2-5). 2010. pap. 5.95 *(978-0-7613-3947-2(7))* 2009. 15.95 *(978-0-8225-8883-2(8))* Lerner Publishing Group. (Carolrhoda Bks.).

Glaser, Karina. The Vanderbeekers of 141st Street. 2017. (Vanderbeekers Ser.: 1). (ENG., Illus.). 304p. (J). (gr. 2-5). 16.99 ***(978-0-544-87639-2(3),*** HMH Books For Young Readers) Houghton Mifflin Harcourt Publishing Co.

Haugaard, Kay. The Day the Dragon Danced. Barritt, Carolyn Reed, illus. 2004. (Day the Dragon Danced Ser.). 32p. (J). (gr. -1-3). 16.95 *(978-1-885008-30-5(9),* Shen's Bks.) Lee & Low Bks., Inc.

Katz, Karen. My First Chinese New Year. Katz, Karen, illus. 2012. (My First Holiday Ser.). (ENG., Illus.). 32p. (J). (gr. -1-k). 6.99 *(978-1-250-01868-7(4),* 9781250018687) Square Fish.

Klein, Adria F. Max Celebra el Ano Nuevo Chino, 1 vol. Robledo, Sol, tr. from ENG. Gallagher-Cole, Mernie, illus. 2007. (Read-It! Readers en Español: la Vida de Max Ser.). (SPA.). 24p. (gr. -1-3). lib. bdg. 21.32 *(978-1-4048-3794-2(9),* Easy Readers) Picture Window Bks.

Li-Qiong, Yu. A New Year's Reunion: A Chinese Story. Cheng-Liang, Zhu, illus. 2013. (ENG.). 40p. (J). (gr. -1-2). 6.99 *(978-0-7636-6748-1(X))* Candlewick Pr.

Lin, Grace. Bringing in the New Year. (ENG., (J). 2013. Illus.). 28p. (— 1). bds. 6.99 *(978-0-385-75365-4(9),* Knopf Bks. for Young Readers) 2010. 34p. (gr. -1-2). pap. 7.99 *(978-0-375-86605-0(1),* Dragonfly Bks.) 2008. (Illus.). 34p. (gr. -1-2). 15.99 *(978-0-375-83745-6(0),* Knopf Bks. for Young Readers) Random Hse. Children's Bks.

—The Year of the Dog. 2007. (Pacy Lin Novel Ser.). (ENG., Illus.). 160p. (J). (gr. 3-7). per. 6.99 *(978-0-316-06002-8(X))* Little, Brown Bks. for Young Readers.

Lo, Rich. New Year. 2016. (ENG., Illus.). 40p. (J). (gr. -1-k). 16.99 *(978-1-5107-0723-8(9),* Sky Pony Pr.) Skyhorse Publishing Co., Inc.

McDonald, Megan. Happy New Year, Julie, Bk. 3. McAliley, Susan & Hunt, Robert, illus. 2007. (American Girl Ser.). (ENG.). 88p. (J). (gr. 3-7). 12.95 *(978-1-59369-292-6(7))* American Girl Publishing, Inc.

Miller, Pat. Squirrel's New Year's Resolution. Ember, Kathi, illus. 2012. (J). 34.28 *(978-1-61913-135-4(8))* Weigl Pubs., Inc.

—Squirrel's New Year's Resolution. Ember, Kathi, illus. (ENG.). 32p. (J). (gr. k-2). 2017. pap. 7.99 ***(978-0-8075-7592-5(5))*** 2010. 16.99 *(978-0-8075-7591-8(7))* Whitman, Albert & Co.

Mitsui Brown, Janet, illus. Oshogatsu with Obaachan. 2005. (J). *(978-1-879965-24-9(0))* Polychrome Publishing Corp.

Neely, Kirk H. Santa Almost Got Caught: Stories for Thanksgiving, Christmas, & the New Year. Cash, Emory, illus. 2011. 152p. pap. 14.99 *(978-1-4575-0477-8(4))* Dog Ear Publishing, LLC.

Night, P. J. The House Next Door. 2013. (Creepover Ser.: 16). lib. bdg. 17.20 *(978-0-606-32323-9(6),* Turtleback) Turtleback Bks.

—Your Worst Nightmare. 2013. (Creepover Ser.: 17). lib. bdg. 17.20 *(978-0-606-32324-6(4),* Turtleback) Turtleback Bks.

Piernas-Davenport, Gail. Shante Keys & the New Year's Peas. Eldridge, Marion, illus. (ENG.). 32p. (J). (gr. k-2). 2017. pap. 7.99 ***(978-0-8075-7331-0(0))*** 2007. lib. bdg. 16.99 *(978-0-8075-7330-3(2))* Whitman, Albert & Co.

Rolleston-Cummins, Toni. The Seven Stars of Matariki. Slade-Robinson, Nikki, illus. 28p. pap. 12.00 *(978-1-86969-327-5(2))* Huia Pubs. NZL. Dist: Univ. of Hawaii Pr.

Roy, Ronald. Calendar Mysteries #13: New Year's Eve Thieves. Gurney, John Steven, illus. 2014. (Calendar Mysteries Ser.: 13). (ENG.). 80p. (J). (gr. 1-4). 4.99 *(978-0-385-37171-1(3),* Random Hse. Bks. for Young Readers) Random Hse. Children's Bks.

—New Year's Eve Thieves. 2014. (Calendar Mysteries Ser.: 13). lib. bdg. 14.75 *(978-0-606-36020-3(4))* Turtleback Bks.

Roza, Greg. Happy New Year! 2006. (Neighborhood Readers Ser.). (ENG., Illus.). 16p. (gr. 1-3). pap. 6.50 *(978-1-4042-7026-8(4),* Rosen Classroom) Rosen Publishing Group, Inc., The.

Ruelle, Karen Gray. Just in Time for New Year's! 2004. (ENG., Illus.). 32p. (J). tchr. ed. 14.95 *(978-0-8234-1841-1(3))* Holiday Hse., Inc.

Shields, Carrie. Sweet Dreams. 2012. 32p. pap. 19.99 *(978-1-4772-9321-8(3))* AuthorHouse.

Stine, R. L. Slappy New Year! 2010. (Goosebumps Horrorland Ser.: 18). (ENG.). 160p. (J). (gr. 3-7). pap. 6.99 *(978-0-545-16199-2(1),* Scholastic Paperbacks) Scholastic, Inc.

Stuart, Carrie. Chinese New Year. 2006. (Neighborhood Readers Ser.). (ENG.). 12p. (gr. -1-3). pap. 5.90 *(978-1-4042-6461-8(2),* Rosen Classroom) Rosen Publishing Group, Inc., The.

Thong, Roseanne Greenfield. The Wishing Tree. McLennan, Connie, illus. 2004. (Wishing Tree Ser.). 32p. (J). (gr. -1-3). 16.95 *(978-1-885008-26-8(0),* Shen's Bks.) Lee & Low Bks., Inc.

Tran, Quoc. The Tet Pole/Su Tich Cay Neu Ngay Tet: The Story of Tet Festival. Smith, William, tr. from VIE. Nguyen, Bich, illus. 2006. (ENG & VIE.). 32p. (J). (gr. 1-4). 16.95 *(978-0-9701654-5-9(5))* East West Discovery Pr.

Van Draanen, Wendelin. Sammy Keyes & the Curse of Moustache Mary. 2008. (Sammy Keyes Ser.: Bk. 5). (J). 59.99 *(978-1-60640-638-0(8))* Findaway World, LLC.

Wang, Gabrielle. The Race for the Chinese Zodiac. Rippin, Sally & Abos, Regine, illus. 2013. (ENG.). 32p. (J). (gr. k-4). 14.99 *(978-0-7636-6778-8(1))* Candlewick Pr.

Wayland, April Halprin. New Year at the Pier: A Rosh Hashanah Story. Jorisch, Stéphane, illus. 2009. 352p. (J). *(978-0-8037-3110-3(8),* Dial) Penguin Publishing Group.

Yep, Laurence. When the Circus Came to Town. Wang, Suling, illus. 2004. 112p. (J). (gr. 3-5). 13.65 *(978-0-7569-2969-5(5))* Perfection Learning Corp.

Yim, Natasha. Goldy Luck & the Three Pandas. Zong, Grace, illus. (ENG.). 32p. (J). (gr. -1-3). 2015. pap. 7.95 *(978-1-58089-653-5(7))* 2014. lib. bdg. 16.95 *(978-1-58089-652-8(9))* Charlesbridge Publishing, Inc.

NEW YORK (N.Y.)

Ball, Jacqueline A. Blizzard! The 1888 Whiteout. 2005. (X-Treme Disasters That Changed America Ser.). (Illus.). 32p. (J). (gr. 2-5). lib. bdg. 25.27 *(978-1-59716-006-3(7))* Bearport Publishing Co., Inc.

De Capua, Sarah. Nueva York. 2004. (Rookie Readers Spanish Ser.). 19.50 *(978-0-516-25109-7(0),* Watts, Franklin) Scholastic Library Publishing.

—Nueva York: New York. 2005. (Rookie Espanol: Geografia Ser.). (SPA., Illus.). 32p. (J). (gr. k-2). pap. 5.95 *(978-0-516-25515-6(0),* Children's Pr.) Scholastic Library Publishing.

Dugan, Joanne. 123 Nyc: A Counting Book of New York City. 2007. (ENG., Illus.). 52p. (J). (gr. -1-1). 17.95 *(978-0-8109-1381-3(X),* Abrams Bks. for Young Readers) Abrams, Inc.

Eldridge, Alison & Eldridge, Stephen. The Statue of Liberty: An American Symbol. 2012. (All about American Symbols Ser.). 24p. (J). (gr. -1-16). 22.60 *(978-0-7660-4061-8(5),* Enslow Elementary) Enslow Pubs., Inc.

Evans, Colin. New York Police Department. 2011. (Law Enforcement Agencies Ser.). (Illus.). 120p. (gr. 6-12). 35.00 *(978-1-60413-614-2(6),* Chelsea Hse.) Facts On File, Inc.

Feeley, Kathleen, et al. Nueva York. 2003. (World Almanac Biblioteca de los Estados). (SPA., Illus.). 48p. (gr. 4-9). pap. 14.05 *(978-0-8368-5553-1(1),* Gareth Stevens Learning Library) Stevens, Gareth Publishing LLLP.

Garrington, Sally. New York. Fairclough, Chris, photos by. 2006. (Global Cities Ser.). (Illus.). 61p. (gr. 5-8). lib. bdg. 30.00 *(978-0-7910-8853-1(7))* Facts On File, Inc.

Gerstein, Mordicai. The Man Who Walked Between the Towers. 2007. (J). 18.40 *(978-1-4177-7491-3(6),* Turtleback) Turtleback Bks.

Grabowski, John F. Bobby Flay. 2012. (J). *(978-1-61900-010-0(5));* pap. *(978-1-61900-011-7(3))* Eldorado Ink.

Gutman, Anne. Lisa a New York. (FRE.). pap. 17.95 *(978-2-01-224058-2(5))* Hachette Groupe Livre FRA. Dist: Distribooks, Inc.

Halpern, Monica. Three Immigrant Communities: New York City In 1900: Text Pairs. 2008. (Bridges/Navigators Ser.). (J). (gr. 3). 89.00 *(978-1-4108-8376-6(0))* Benchmark Education Co.

Hicer, Nancy. Maps & New York City. 2011. (My Community Ser.). 12p. (gr. 2-2). pap. 6.95 *(978-1-4488-5732-6(5))* Rosen Publishing Group, Inc., The.
—New York City's Five Boroughs. 2011. (My Community Ser.). 12p. (gr. 2-2). pap. 6.95 *(978-1-4488-5730-2(9))* Rosen Publishing Group, Inc., The.
Jakobsen, Kathy. My New York. Jakobsen, Kathy, illus. anniv. rev. ed. 2005. (Illus.). 54p. (J). (gr. k-4). 19.00 *(978-0-7567-8588-8(X))* DIANE Publishing Co.
—My New York. Jakobsen, Kathy, illus. anniv. ed. 2003. (ENG., Illus.). 48p. (J). (gr. -1-3). 20.00 *(978-0-316-92711-6(2))* Little, Brown Bks. for Young Readers.
Johnson, Stephen T. & Johnson, Stephen. City by Numbers. 2003. (gr. k-3). lib. bdg. 18.40 *(978-0-613-67534-5(7),* Turtleback) Turtleback Bks.
Kenney, Karen Latchana. David Karp: The Mastermind Behind Tumblr. 2015. (Gateway Biographies Ser.). (ENG., Illus.). 48p. (gr. 4-8). 34.65 *(978-1-4677-5975-5(9),* Lerner Digital) Lerner Publishing Group.
Ketchum, Ron, illus. Rochestrivia: 2,000 Amazing questions & answers all about Rochester NY, it's people & surrounding Towns. lt. ed. 2005. 250p. per. 19.95 *(978-0-930249-01-4(1))* Big Kids Productions (Publishing).
Kirkpatrick, Robert. Bob Cousy. 2009. (Basketball Hall of Famers Ser.). 112p. (gr. 5-8). 63.90 *(978-1-61511-531-0(5),* Rosen Reference) Rosen Publishing Group, Inc., The.
Markovics, Joyce L. New York City. 2017. (Citified! Ser.). (ENG.). 24p. (J). (gr. k-3). 17.95 ***(978-1-68402-230-4(4))*** Bearport Publishing Co., Inc.
Mattern, Joanne. New York City, 1 vol. 2007. (Cities Set 2 Ser.). (ENG., Illus.). 32p. (gr. -1-3). 27.07 *(978-1-59679-719-2(3),* Checkerboard Library) ABDO Publishing Co.
Melmed, Laura Krauss. New York, New York! The Big Apple from A to Z. Lessac, Frané, illus. 2008. (ENG.). 48p. (J). (gr. 1-6). pap. 6.99 *(978-0-06-054877-3(0),* Collins) HarperCollins Pubs.
Mills, Clifford W. Isaac Mizrahi. 2011. (Famous Fashion Designers Ser.). (Illus.). 112p. (gr. 6-12). 35.00 *(978-1-60413-984-6(6),* Chelsea Hse.) Facts On File, Inc.
Munro, Roxie. The Inside-Outside Book of New York City. Munro, Roxie, illus. 2005. (Illus.). 44p. (J). (gr. 4-8). reprint ed. 16.00 *(978-0-7567-9455-2(2))* DIANE Publishing Co.
Neumann, Dietrich. Joe & the Skyscraper: The Empire State Building in New York City. Heritage, Anne, tr. 2005. (GER., Illus.). 28p. (J). (gr. 4-8). 17.00 *(978-0-7567-9380-7(7))* DIANE Publishing Co.
NY Boys and Girls Clubs Rochester Staff & Boys & Girls Clubs Rochester, Ny. N Is for New York. 2011. (See My State Ser.). (ENG., Illus.). 32p. (J). (gr. -1-3). 13.95 *(978-0-88240-777-7(5),* West Winds Pr.) Graphic Arts Ctr. Publishing Co.
Obregón, José María. New York / Nueva York. 2009. (Bilingual Library of the United States of America Ser.). (ENG & SPA.). 32p. (gr. 2-2). 47.90 *(978-1-60853-376-3(X),* Editorial Buenas Letras) Rosen Publishing Group, Inc., The.
O'Dell, Kathryn. Bright Lights on Broadway. 2014. (ENG., Illus.). 28p. (J). pap. 9.50 *(978-1-107-65022-0(4))* Cambridge Univ. Pr.
Paradis, Anne. New York Monsters: A Search-And-Find Book. Danis Drouot, Lucile, illus. 2017. (ENG.). 22p. (J). bds. 9.99 ***(978-2-924734-02-5(9))*** City Monsters Bks. CAN. Dist: Publishers Group West (PGW).
Puck. New York Baby. Lemay, Violet, illus. 2012. (Local Baby Bks.). (ENG.). 22p. (J). (gr. k — 1). bds. 8.95 *(978-0-9838121-4-2(4))* Duo Pr. LLC.
Randall, Marisa. The Geographic Features of New York City. 2011. (My Community Ser.). 12p. (gr. 2-2). pap. 6.95 *(978-1-4488-5733-3(3))* Rosen Publishing Group, Inc., The.
Rauf, Don. Bobby Flay. 2016. (Celebrity Chefs Ser.). (ENG., Illus.). 128p. (J). (gr. 7-8). 37.27 *(978-0-7660-7172-8(3))* Enslow Pubs., Inc.
Romanek, Trudee. Life in a Commercial City. 2010. (Learn about Urban Life Ser.). (ENG., Illus.). 32p. (J). (gr. 4-9). pap. *(978-0-7787-7401-3(5));* lib. bdg. *(978-0-7787-7391-7(4))* Crabtree Publishing Co.
Rubbino, Salvatore. A Walk in New York. Rubbino, Salvatore, illus. (ENG., Illus.). 40p. (J). (gr. -1-3). 2017. 8.99 ***(978-0-7636-9510-1(6))*** 2009. 16.99 *(978-0-7636-3855-9(2))* Candlewick Pr.
Sasek, Miroslav. This Is New York. 2003. (This Is ... Ser.). (ENG., Illus.). 64p. (J). (gr. 2-12). 17.95 *(978-0-7893-0884-9(3))* Universe Publishing.
Somers, Kevin & Puck. 1 2 3 New York. Somers, Kevin, illus. 2008. (Cool Counting Bks.). (ENG., Illus.). 22p. (J). (gr. k — 1). bds. 7.95 *(978-0-9796213-0-7(5))* Duo Pr. LLC.
Tan, Richard. The Bridges & Tunnels of New York City. 2011. (My Community Ser.). (ENG., Illus.). 12p. (gr. 2-2). pap. 6.95 *(978-1-4488-5717-3(1),* Rosen Classroom) Rosen Publishing Group, Inc., The.
Thompson, Gare. We Came Through Ellis Island: The Immigrant Adventures of Emma Markowitz. 2003. (I Am American Ser.). (ENG., Illus.). 40p. (J). (gr. 3-7). pap. 6.99 *(978-0-7922-5682-3(4))* CENGAGE Learning.
van der Meulen, Majel, illus. My New York: Color, Draw, Explore. 2017. (ENG.). 40p. (J). (gr. 1-4). pap. 12.99 *(978-1-78067-962-4(9))* King, Laurence Publishing GBR. Dist: Hachette Bk. Group.
Von La Valette, Desiree, ed. Cool Shops New York. 2005. (ENG, SPA, FRE, ITA & GER., Illus.). 135p. pap.; pap. 16.95 *(978-3-8327-9021-9(7))* teNeues Publishing Co.
Wade, Angela. New York City. 2006. (Illus.). 8p. (J). pap. *(978-0-439-74035-7(5))* Scholastic, Inc.
Walsh, Frank. New York City. 2003. (Great Cities of the World Ser.). (Illus.). 48p. (gr. 5-12). lib. bdg. 31.00 *(978-0-8368-5025-3(4),* Gareth Stevens Secondary Library) Stevens, Gareth Publishing LLLP.

NEW YORK (N.Y.)—ANTIQUITIES

Goodman, Susan E. & Goodman, Susan. On This Spot: An Expedition Back Through Time. Christiansen, Lee, illus. 2004. (ENG.). 32p. (J). (gr. k-5). 17.99 *(978-0-688-16913-8(9),* Greenwillow Bks.) HarperCollins Pubs.
Murphy, Jim. The Giant & How He Humbugged America. 2012. (ENG.). 112p. (J). (gr. 4-7). 19.99 *(978-0-439-69184-0(2),* Scholastic Pr.) Scholastic, Inc.
Reis, Ronald A. The Empire State Building. 2009. (Building America Ser.). (Illus.). 144p. (gr. 5-8). 35.00 *(978-1-60413-045-4(8),* Chelsea Hse.) Facts On File, Inc.
Shea, Therese. The African Burial Ground. 2016. (Hidden History Ser.). 00032p. (J). pap. 10.50 *(978-1-4824-5787-2(3))* Stevens, Gareth Publishing LLLP.

NEW YORK (N.Y.)—BRIDGES

Stine, Megan. Where Is the Brooklyn Bridge? 2016. (Where Is... ? Ser.). lib. bdg. 16.00 *(978-0-606-38411-7(1))* Turtleback Bks.

NEW YORK (N.Y.)—DESCRIPTION AND TRAVEL

Adams, Jennifer. My Little Cities: New York. Pizzoli, Greg, illus. 2017. (ENG.). 22p. (J). (gr. -1-k). bds. 9.99 *(978-1-4521-5388-9(4))* Chronicle Bks. LLC.
Banting, Erinn. Empire State Building. 2007. (Structural Wonders Ser.). (Illus.). 32p. (J). (gr. 4-7). lib. bdg. 26.00 *(978-1-59036-721-6(9));* per. 9.95 *(978-1-59036-722-3(7))* Weigl Pubs., Inc.
Boehm Jerome, Kate. Buffalo, Ny: Cool Stuff Every Kid Should Know. 2010. (Arcadia Kids Ser.). (ENG., Illus.). 48p. (J). (gr. 3-6). pap. 9.99 *(978-1-4396-0069-6(4))* Arcadia Publishing.
Braithwaite, Jill. The Statue of Liberty. 2010. (Lightning Bolt Books (tm) — Famous Places Ser.). (ENG.). 32p. (gr. k-2). pap. 7.95 *(978-0-7613-6052-0(2))* Lerner Publishing Group.
Bullard, Lisa. The Empire State Building. 2009. (Lightning Bolt Books (tm) — Famous Places Ser.). (ENG.). 32p. (gr. k-2). 26.60 *(978-0-8225-9404-8(8),* Lerner Pubns.) Lerner Publishing Group.
Cochran, Josh. Inside & Out: New York. Cochran, Josh, illus. 2014. (ENG., Illus.). 16p. (J). (gr. 2-5). 17.99 *(978-0-7636-7520-2(2),* Big Picture Press) Candlewick Pr.
Cordier, Claire. Candy Apple. 2009. (JPN & ENG.). 32p. pap. 19.50 *(978-0-557-08498-2(9))* Lulu Pr., Inc.
—Candy Apple; Dolce Mela. 2009. 32p. pap. 19.50 *(978-0-557-08531-6(4))* Lulu Pr., Inc.
—Candy Apple; Maçã do Amor. 2009. 32p. pap. 19.50 *(978-0-557-08439-5(3))* Lulu Pr., Inc.
—Candy Apple; Manzana de Dulce. 2009. 32p. pap. 19.50 *(978-0-557-08530-9(6))* Lulu Pr., Inc.
—Candy Apple; Pomme d'Amour. 2009. 32p. pap. 19.50 *(978-0-557-08454-8(7))* Lulu Pr., Inc.
—Candy Apple; Ponm-madousiwo. 2009. 32p. pap. 19.50 *(978-0-557-08539-2(X))* Lulu Pr., Inc.
D'Angelo, Gus. New York ABCs. 2013. (ENG.). 30p. (J). (-k). bds. 9.95 *(978-0-615-70443-2(3))* DAngelo, Gus.
Dugan, Joanne. ABC Nyc: A Book about Seeing New York City. 2005. (ENG., Illus.). 56p. (J). (gr. -1-1). 17.95 *(978-0-8109-5854-8(6))* Abrams, Inc.
Dyan, Penelope. New York! New York! a Kid's Guide to New York City. Weigand, John D., photos by. 2009. (Illus.). 44p. pap. 11.95 *(978-1-935118-79-4(X))* Bellissima Publishing, LLC.
Epstein, Brad M. New York 101. lt. ed. 2009. (My First City Ser.). (Illus.). 24p. (J). (gr. -1-k). bds. *(978-1-60730-003-8(6),* 101 Bk.) Michaelson Entertainment.
Evanson, Ashley. New York: A Book of Colors. Evanson, Ashley, illus. 2015. (Hello, World Ser.). (ENG., Illus.). 14p. (J). (— 1). bds. 6.99 *(978-0-448-48913-1(9),* Grosset & Dunlap) Penguin Young Readers Group.
Fowler, Gloria. New York Board Book. 2015. (ENG., Illus.). 56p. 16.95 *(978-1-62326-050-7(7))* AMMO Bks., LLC.
Gamble, Adam. Good Night New York City. Veno, Joe, illus. 2006. (Good Night Our World Ser.). (ENG.). 24p. (J). (gr. k — 1). bds. 9.95 *(978-0-9777979-3-6(7))* Good Night Bks.
Gamble, Adam & Jasper, Mark. Good Night Brooklyn. 2013. (Good Night Our World Ser.). (ENG., Illus.). 20p. (J). (— 1). bds. 9.95 *(978-1-60219-094-8(1))* Good Night Bks.
Gloor, Elizabeth. The Cultural Institutions of New York City. 2011. (My Community Ser.). (ENG., Illus.). 12p. (gr. 2-2). pap. 6.95 *(978-1-4488-5716-6(3),* Rosen Classroom) Rosen Publishing Group, Inc., The.
—New York City: An Urban Community. 2011. (My Community Ser.). (ENG., Illus.). 12p. (gr. 2-2). pap. 6.95 *(978-1-4488-5720-3(1),* Rosen Classroom) Rosen Publishing Group, Inc., The.
Goode, Teresa. Wildcat Adventures: A Vacation in the Big Apple. Kotrous, Chad, illus. 2006. 31p. (J). pap. 5.95 *(978-1-890622-13-8(3))* Leathers Publishing.
Gregory, Joy. The Metropolitan Museum of Art. 2014. (Illus.). 24p. (J). *(978-1-4896-1194-9(0))* Weigl Pubs., Inc.
Hayn, Carter. New York City: Old & New. 2011. (My Community Ser.). (ENG., Illus.). 12p. (gr. 2-2). pap. 6.95 *(978-1-4488-5723-4(6),* Rosen Classroom) Rosen Publishing Group, Inc., The.
Herrington, Lisa M. The Statue of Liberty. 2014. (Rookie Read-About(r) American Symbols Ser.). (ENG., Illus.). 32p. (J). pap. 5.95 *(978-0-531-21838-9(4))* Scholastic Library Publishing.
Holub, Joan. What Is the Statue of Liberty? Mantha, John et al, illus. 2014. (What Was? Ser.). (ENG.). 112p. (J). (gr. 3-7). 5.99 *(978-0-448-47917-0(6),* Grosset & Dunlap) Penguin Young Readers Group.
Hurtig, Jennifer & Kissock, Heather. The Statue of Liberty. 2014. (J). *(978-1-4896-1966-2(6))* Weigl Pubs., Inc.
Kallen, Stuart A. A Travel Guide to Harlem Renaissance. 2003. (Travel Guide To Ser.). (ENG.). (J). 30.85 *(978-1-59018-358-8(4),* Lucent Bks.) Cengage Gale.
Kent, Deborah. The Statue of Liberty. 2012. (Cornerstones of Freedom, Third Ser.). (ENG.). 64p. (J). pap. 8.95 *(978-0-531-28166-6(3));* (gr. 4-6). lib. bdg. 30.00 *(978-0-531-23066-4(X))* Scholastic Library Publishing. (Children's Pr.).
Mahler, Zdenek. New York: A Mod Portrait of the City. Fuka, Vladimir, illus. 2014. (ENG.). 128p. 24.95 *(978-0-7893-2727-7(9))* Universe Publishing.
Maizels, Jennie. Pop-Up New York. Maizels, Jennie, illus. 2014. (ENG., Illus.). 12p. (J). (gr. k-4). 19.99 *(978-0-7636-7162-4(2))* Candlewick Pr.
Marcovitz, Hal. Statue of Liberty: A Beacon of Welcome & Hope. Moreno, Barry, ed. 2014. (Patriotic Symbols of America Ser.: 20). 48p. (J). (gr. 4-18). 20.95 *(978-1-4222-3130-2(5))* Mason Crest.
Markovics, Joyce L. Haunted Gotham. 2017. (Scary Places Ser.). (ENG., Illus.). 32p. (J). (gr. 4-8). 19.95 *(978-1-68402-020-1(4))* Bearport Publishing Co., Inc.
Mason Crest. New York, Vol. 8. 2016. (Major World Cities Ser.: Vol. 8). (ENG., Illus.). 48p. (J). (gr. 5-8). 20.95 *(978-1-4222-3543-0(2))* Mason Crest.
McMenemy, Sarah. New York - A 3D Keepsake Cityscape. 2011. (Panorama Pops Ser.). (ENG., Illus.). 20p. (J). (gr. k-12). 8.99 *(978-0-7636-5483-2(3))* Candlewick Pr.
Melmed, Laura Krauss. New York, New York City: The Big Apple from A to Z. Lessac, Frané, illus. 2005. (ENG.). 48p. (J). (gr. 1-6). 16.99 *(978-0-06-054874-2(6))* HarperCollins Pubs.
Metropolitan Museum of Art Staff. Nyc ABC. 2011. (ENG., Illus.). 60p. (J). (gr. -1-3). 15.95 *(978-0-8478-3701-4(7),* Skira) Rizzoli International Pubns., Inc.
Meyers, Haily & Meyers, Kevin. All Aboard! New York, 1 vol. Meyers, Haily, illus. 2015. (ENG., Illus.). 22p. (J). bds. 9.99 *(978-1-4236-4074-5(8))* Gibbs Smith, Publisher.
Moore, Andrew. Traveling in New York City. 2011. (My Community Ser.). (ENG., Illus.). 12p. (gr. 2-2). pap. 6.95 *(978-1-4488-5719-7(8),* Rosen Classroom) Rosen Publishing Group, Inc., The.
New York Russian Language Restaurant Guide. 2005. (RUS.). per. *(978-0-9764633-0-6(X))* Press Release Group Corp.
Plenty: The Ultimate Guide to Life & Leisure in Clinton Hill/Fort Greene. 2003. (Illus.). (YA). pap. 20.00 *(978-0-9721708-0-2(4),* PCHFG01) RedMEDIA.
RJF Publishing Staff & Staton, Hilarie. The Statue of Liberty. 2009. (Symbols of American Freedom Ser.). 48p. (gr. 4-6). 30.00 *(978-1-60413-516-9(6),* Chelsea Clubhouse) Facts On File, Inc.
Rudd, Brandon Kyle. Cooper's Pack — New York City: New York City, Vol. 1. McCann, Martin, illus. 2007. 72p. (J). per. 14.95 *(978-0-9794882-0-7(6))* Cooper's Pack.
Sarg, Tony. Up & down New York. 2007. (New York Bound Bks.). (ENG., Illus.). 64p. (J). (gr. 1-4). 19.95 *(978-0-7893-1548-9(3))* Universe Publishing.
Scholl, Elizabeth. New York City. 2009. (Class Trip Ser.). (Illus.). 48p. (J). (gr. 2-5). lib. bdg. 29.95 *(978-1-58415-808-0(5))* Mitchell Lane Pubs., Inc.
Skewes, John. Larry Loves New York City! Skewes, John, illus. 2014. (Larry Gets Lost Ser.). (ENG., Illus.). 20p. (J). (— 1). bds. 9.99 *(978-1-57061-936-6(0),* Little Bigfoot) Sasquatch Bks.
Skewes, John & Mullin, Michael. Larry Gets Lost in New York City. Skewes, John, illus. 2010. (Larry Gets Lost Ser.). (ENG., Illus.). 32p. (J). (gr. -1-2). 17.99 *(978-1-57061-620-4(5),* Little Bigfoot) Sasquatch Bks.
Staton, Hilarie. New York City. 2016. (Dropping in On Ser.). (ENG., Illus.). 32p. (gr. 2-4). 32.79 *(978-1-68191-403-9(4))* Rourke Educational Media.
Tieck, Sarah. Brooklyn Bridge, 1 vol. 2008. (All Aboard America Ser.). (ENG.). 24p. (J). (gr. 1-4). 25.65 *(978-1-59928-934-2(2))* ABDO Publishing Co.
—Empire State Building, 1 vol. 2008. (All Aboard America Ser.). (ENG.). 24p. (YA). (gr. 1-4). 25.65 *(978-1-59928-935-9(0))* ABDO Publishing Co.
Wishinsky, Frieda. What's up, Bear? A Book about Opposites. Moore, Sean L., illus. 2012. (ENG.). 32p. (J). (gr. -1-2). 16.95 *(978-1-926973-41-8(0),* Owlkids) Owlkids Bks. Inc. CAN. Dist: Publishers Group West (PGW).
Zimmerman, Bill. City Doodles New York, 1 vol. 2013. (ENG., Illus.). 240p. (J). pap., pap. 9.99 *(978-1-4236-3227-6(3))* Gibbs Smith, Publisher.

NEW YORK (N.Y.)—FICTION

Abbott, E. F. Mary Jemison: Native American Captive. 2016. (Based on a True Story Ser.). (ENG., Illus.). 224p. (J). 15.99 *(978-1-250-06838-5(X),* 9781250068385) Feiwel & Friends.
—Nettie & Nellie Crook: Orphan Train Sisters. 2016. (Based on a True Story Ser.). (ENG., Illus.). 176p. (J). 15.99 *(978-1-250-06835-4(5),* 9781250068354) Feiwel & Friends.
Abrams, Amir. Diva Rules. 2015. (Mcpherson High Ser.). (ENG., Illus.). 300p. (YA). (gr. 9). pap. 9.95 *(978-0-7582-9480-7(8),* Dafina) Kensington Publishing Corp.
Acheson, A. S. Fighting Words. 2014. (Bareknuckle Ser.). 96p. (YA). (gr. 6-12). lib. bdg. 27.93 *(978-1-4677-1461-7(5),* Darby Creek) Lerner Publishing Group.
Ackerman, Peter. The Lonely Phone Booth. Dalton, Max, illus. 2010. (ENG.). 32p. (J). (gr. k-2). 16.95 *(978-1-56792-414-5(X))* Godine, David R. Pub.
Adams, Jennifer. My Little New York City Skyline. Pizzoli, Greg, illus. 2017. (ENG.). 8p. (J). (gr. -1-k). 14.99 *(978-1-4521-5389-6(2))* Chronicle Bks. LLC.
Adams, Lisa. The Twelve Days of Christmas in New York City. Adams, Lisa, illus. 2009. (Twelve Days of Christmas in America Ser.). (ENG., Illus.). 40p. (J). (gr. k-3). 12.95 *(978-1-4027-6440-0(5))* Sterling Publishing Co., Inc.
Adler, David A. Don't Talk to Me about the War. 2009. (ENG.). 224p. (J). (gr. 3-7). 7.99 *(978-0-14-241372-2(0),* Puffin Books) Penguin Young Readers Group.
Ain, Beth. Starring Jules (in Drama-Rama) Higgins, Anne Keenan, illus. 2013. (Starring Jules Ser.: 2). (ENG.). 176p. (J). (gr. 2-5). 14.99 *(978-0-545-44354-8(7),* Scholastic Pr.) Scholastic, Inc.
—Starring Jules (Third Grade Debut) (Starring Jules Ser.: 4). (ENG.). 176p. (J). (gr. 2-5). 2015. pap. 5.99 *(978-0-545-44359-3(8))* 2014. 14.99 *(978-0-545-44358-6(X))* Scholastic, Inc. (Scholastic Pr.).
Airgood, Ellen. Prairie Evers. (ENG.). 224p. (J). (gr. 3-7). 2014. pap. 7.99 *(978-0-14-242668-5(7),* Puffin Books) 2012. 15.99 *(978-0-399-25691-2(1),* Nancy Paulsen Books) Penguin Young Readers Group.
Alderson, Sarah. Out of Control. 2015. (ENG., Illus.). 320p. (J). (gr. 9). 17.99 *(978-1-4814-2716-6(4),* Simon Pulse) Simon Pulse.
Alger, Horatio. Jack's Ward. 2005. 28.95 *(978-1-4218-1454-4(4),* 1st World Library - Literary Society) 1st World Publishing, Inc.
Alger Jr. Horatio Staff. Struggling Upward. rev. ed. 2006. 284p. 28.95 *(978-1-4218-1760-6(8));* pap. 13.95 *(978-1-4218-1860-3(4))* 1st World Publishing, Inc. (1st World Library - Literary Society).
Alice B. Emerson. Ruth Fielding of the Red Mill: Or Jasper Parloe's Secret. 2007. (ENG.). 134p. per. 18.99 *(978-1-4346-3930-1(4));* 146p. per. 19.99 *(978-1-4346-3931-8(2))* Creative Media Partners, LLC.
Allen, Eleanor. Mouse Monk in a Christmas Adventure. 2009. 36p. pap. 15.49 *(978-1-4490-2197-9(2))* AuthorHouse.
Altreche, Jeanine. Talula Goes to New York. 2007. 32p. per. 12.95 *(978-1-4327-0538-1(5))* Outskirts Pr., Inc.
Anastos, Ernie. Ernie & the Big Newz. 2007. 32p. pap. 15.95 *(978-0-9705100-5-1(5))* NK Pubns.
Andrews, Julie & Hamilton, Emma Walton. The Great American Mousical. Walton, Tony, illus. 2006. (Julie Andrews Collection). (J). (gr. k-4). 160p. 15.99 *(978-0-06-057918-0(8),* Julie Andrews Collection); 147p. lib. bdg. 16.89 *(978-0-06-057919-7(6))* HarperCollins Pubs.
Angel, Ido. Vipo in New York: Uncle Florence. 2015. (AV2 Animated Storytime Ser.). (ENG.). (J). lib. bdg. 29.99 *(978-1-4896-3917-2(9),* AV2 by Weigl) Weigl Pubs., Inc.
Archibald, Laura. The Cats of Grand Central. Beckett, Garner, illus. 2004. 30p. 16.95 *(978-0-9730951-0-4(5))* Solomon's Signature CAN. Dist: Hushion Hse. Publishing, Ltd.
Arena, Jen. Lady Liberty's Holiday. Hunt, Matt, illus. 2016. (ENG.). 40p. (J). (gr. k-3). 17.99 *(978-0-553-52067-5(9),* Knopf Bks. for Young Readers) Random Hse. Children's Bks.
Armistead, Cal. Being Henry David. (ENG.). 312p. (YA). (gr. 8-12). 2014. pap. 9.99 *(978-0-8075-0616-5(8))* 2013. 16.99 *(978-0-8075-0615-8(X))* Whitman, Albert & Co.
Armstrong, Kim. Petunia in Manhattan. 2009. 50p. pap. 12.99 *(978-1-935436-97-3(X))* Rodaian Pr.
Arnold, George "Speedy". What's an Elephant Doing in the Ausable River?!! Arnold, George "Speedy", illus. 2012. (ENG., Illus.). 64p. (J). 20.00 *(978-0-9836925-5-3(6))* Bloated Toe Publishing.
Aronskind, Ofer. Escape from Sunday School. 2009. 152p. pap. 12.95 *(978-1-4401-3217-9(8))* iUniverse, Inc.
Aronson, Marc & Smith, Charles R., Jr., eds. Pick-Up Game: A Full Day of Full Court. Smith, Charles R., Jr., illus. (ENG., Illus.). 176p. (YA). (gr. 9). 2012. pap. 7.99 *(978-0-7636-6068-0(X))* 2011. 15.99 *(978-0-7636-4562-5(1))* Candlewick Pr.
Arruzza, Rick. El Paseo de Sparky. Newton, Pilar, illus. 2003. (SPA.). 24p. mass mkt. 7.95 *(978-0-9744509-1-9(X))* Three Spots Productions.
—Sparky's Walk. Newton, Pilar, illus. 2003. 24p. (J). mass mkt. 7.95 *(978-0-9744509-0-2(1))* Three Spots Productions.
Ashton, Victoria. Confessions of a Teen Nanny. (Confessions of a Teen Nanny Ser.). (ENG.). 208p. 2005. (J). (gr. 8-18). 15.99 *(978-0-06-073173-1(7))* 2006. (YA). (gr. 9-12). reprint ed. pap. 8.99 *(978-0-06-073178-6(8),* HarperTeen) HarperCollins Pubs.
At Your Service. 2014. (Mix Ser.). (ENG., Illus.). 272p. (J). (gr. 4-8). pap. 7.99 *(978-1-4814-0283-5(8),* Aladdin) Simon & Schuster Children's Publishing.
Atwood, Megan. Molly Discovers Magic (Then Wants to Un-Discover It) Fleming, Lucy, illus. 2017. (Dear Molly, Dear Olive Ser.). (ENG.). 96p. (gr. 1-3). pap. 5.95 *(978-1-62370-616-6(5))* Picture Window Bks.
—Molly Meets Trouble (Whose Real Name Is Jenna) Fleming, Lucy, illus. 2016. (Dear Molly, Dear Olive Ser.). (ENG.). 96p. (gr. 1-3). lib. bdg. 21.99 *(978-1-4795-8696-7(X))* Picture Window Bks.
—Olive Finds Treasure (of the Most Precious Kind) Fleming, Lucy, illus. (Dear Molly, Dear Olive Ser.). (ENG.). 96p. (gr. 1-3). 2017. pap. 5.95 *(978-1-62370-615-9(7))* 2016. lib. bdg. 21.99 *(978-1-4795-8693-6(5))* Picture Window Bks.
—Olive Spins a Tale (and It's a Doozy!) Fleming, Lucy, illus. 2016. (Dear Molly, Dear Olive Ser.). (ENG.). 96p. (gr. 1-3). lib. bdg. 21.99 *(978-1-4795-8695-0(1))* Picture Window Bks.
Auch, Mary Jane. Ashes of Roses. 2004. 250p. (YA). (gr. 8-12). 14.15 *(978-0-7569-4069-0(9))* Perfection Learning Corp.
Augenstein, Marianne R. The Quest for Kair, 1 vol. 2009. 152p. pap. 24.95 *(978-1-60813-899-9(2))* America Star Bks.
Aureliani, Franco. Dino-Mike & the Museum Mayhem. Aureliani, Franco, illus. 2015. (Dino-Mike! Ser.). (ENG., Illus.). 128p. (gr. 1-3). lib. bdg. 25.32 *(978-1-4342-9628-3(8),* Dino-Mike!) Stone Arch Bks.
Aureliani, Franco, illus. Dino-Mike & the Museum Mayhem. 2015. (J). lib. bdg. *(978-1-4062-9391-3(1))* Stone Arch Bks.
Averill, Esther. Jenny's Birthday Book. Averill, Esther, illus. 2005. (New York Review Children's Collection). (ENG., Illus.). 44p. (J). (gr. -1-2). reprint ed. 15.95 *(978-1-59017-154-7(3),* NYR Children's Collection) New York Review of Bks., Inc., The.
Avi. Don't You Know There's a War On? 2003. (ENG.). 208p. (J). (gr. 3-7). pap. 7.99 *(978-0-380-81544-9(3))* HarperCollins Pubs.
—Silent Movie. Mordan, C. B., illus. 2003. (ENG.). 48p. (J). (gr. -1-3). 19.99 *(978-0-689-84145-3(0),* Atheneum Bks. for Young Readers) Simon & Schuster Children's Publishing.
Avi & Vail, Rachel. Never Mind! 2005. (Twin Novels Ser.). 200p. (gr. 5-9). 16.00 *(978-0-7569-5667-7(6))* Perfection Learning Corp.
Axelsson, Carina. Model Undercover: New York. 2015. (Model Undercover Ser.: 2). (ENG.). 320p. (J). (gr. 4-8). pap. 6.99 *(978-1-4926-0785-4(1),* Sourcebooks Jabberwocky) Sourcebooks, Inc.
Baccalario, Pierdomenico. Star of Stone. Janeczko, Leah D., tr. 2011. (Century Ser.). (ENG.). 320p. (J). (gr. 3-7). 7.99 *(978-0-375-85796-6(6),* Yearling) Random Hse. Children's Bks.
Bailey's Birthday - Evaluation Guide: Evaluation Guide. 2006. (J). *(978-1-55942-399-1(4))* Witcher Productions.
Banash, Jennifer. The Elite. 2008. (ENG.). 256p. (YA). (gr. 9-18). 9.99 *(978-0-425-22157-0(1),* Berkley) Penguin Publishing Group.
—In Too Deep. 2009. (ENG.). 256p. (YA). (gr. 9-18). 9.99 *(978-0-425-22353-6(1),* Berkley) Penguin Publishing Group.
—Simply Irresistible. 2009. (ENG.). 256p. (YA). (gr. 9-18). 9.99 *(978-0-425-22783-1(9),* Berkley) Penguin Publishing Group.
Bancks, Tristan. Mac Slater vs. the City. (Mac Slater Hunts the Cool Ser.). (ENG.). 192p. (J). (gr. 3-7). 2012. pap. 6.99 *(978-1-4169-8577-8(8))* 2011. 15.99 *(978-1-4169-8576-1(X))* Simon & Schuster Bks. For Young Readers. (Simon & Schuster Bks. For Young Readers).
Barbour, Ralph Henry. The Half-Back. 2007. 132p. per. *(978-1-4068-3665-3(6))* Echo Library.
Bartone, Elisa. Peppe the Lamplighter. Lewin, Ted, illus. 2015. 32p. pap. 7.00 *(978-1-61003-612-2(3))* Center for the Collaborative Classroom.

Behar, Ruth. Lucky Broken Girl. 2017. (ENG.). 256p. (J). (gr. 5). 16.99 *(978-0-399-54644-0(8)*, Nancy Paulsen Books) Penguin Young Readers Group.

Beil, Michael D. Agents of the Glass: a New Recruit. 2016. (ENG.). 400p. (J). (gr. 4-7). 16.99 *(978-0-385-75321-0(7)*, Knopf Bks. for Young Readers) Random Hse. Children's Bks.

Benincasa, Sara. Great. 2014. (ENG.). 272p. (YA). (gr. 9). 17.99 *(978-0-06-222269-5(4)*, HarperTeen) HarperCollins Pubs.

Bennardo, Charlotte & Zaman, Natalie. Sirenz. 2011. 270p. pap. 9.95 *(978-0-7387-2968-8(X))* Flux: Image Theory Group.

—Sirenz. 2011. (ENG.). 288p. (YA). (gr. 7-18). pap. 9.95 *(978-0-7387-2319-8(3)*, Flux) North Star Editions.

—Sirenz Back in Fashion. 2012. (ENG.). 288p. (YA). pap. 9.95 *(978-0-7387-3187-2(0)*, Flux) North Star Editions.

Berk, Sheryl & Berk, Carrie. Designer Drama. 2016. (Fashion Academy Ser.: 3). (ENG.). 192p. (J). (gr. 5-8). pap. 7.99 *(978-1-4926-1353-4(3)*, 9781492613534, Sourcebooks Jabberwocky) Sourcebooks, Inc.

—Fashion Academy. 2015. (Fashion Academy Ser.: 1). (ENG.). 160p. (J). (gr. 5-8). pap. 6.99 *(978-1-4926-0162-3(4)*, Sourcebooks Jabberwocky) Sourcebooks, Inc.

—Model Madness. 2017. (Fashion Academy Ser.: 4). (ENG.). 192p. (J). (gr. 5-8). pap. 7.99 *(978-1-4926-4496-5(X)*, 9781492644965, Sourcebooks Jabberwocky) Sourcebooks, Inc.

Berman, Valerie & Berman, Neil. Bubba Goes to New York: Bubba Travel Series. 2009. 44p. pap. 16.99 *(978-1-4389-6860-5(4))* AuthorHouse.

Berry, Andrea. Goalie: The Dynamite Diaries. 2003. 144p. (YA). pap. 11.95 *(978-0-595-27678-3(4))* iUniverse, Inc.

Bhakta, Sanjini. My Life as a Dollar Bill. 2010. 28p. pap. 12.95 *(978-1-4520-6152-8(1))* AuthorHouse.

Bildner, Phil. Derek Jeter Presents Night at the Stadium. Booth, Tom, illus. 2016. (Jeter Publishing Ser.). (ENG.). 32p. (J). (gr. -1-3). 17.99 *(978-1-4814-2655-8(9)*, Aladdin) Simon & Schuster Children's Publishing.

Black, Holly. Valiant: A Modern Faerie Tale. 2006. (ENG.). 320p. (YA). (gr. 8-12). pap. 10.99 *(978-0-689-86823-8(5)*, McElderry, Margaret K. Bks.) McElderry, Margaret K. Bks.

Black, Yelena. Dance of Shadows. (Dance of Shadows Ser.). (ENG., Illus.). 384p. (YA). (gr. 7). 2014. pap. 9.99 *(978-1-61963-185-4(7)*, 9781619631854) 2013. 17.99 *(978-1-59990-940-0(5)*, 9781599909400) Bloomsbury Publishing USA. (Bloomsbury USA Childrens).

Bliss, Harry. Luke on the Loose. Bliss, Harry, illus. 2009. (ENG., Illus.). 32p. (J). (gr. -1-3). 12.95 *(978-1-935179-00-9(4))* TOON Books / RAW Junior, LLC.

—Luke on the Loose. 2014. (Toon Books Level 2 Ser.). lib. bdg. 14.75 *(978-0-606-32101-3(2)*, Turtleback) Turtleback Bks.

Blue Moon. 2014. (Dead City Ser.: 2). (ENG., Illus.). 336p. (J). (gr. 4-8). pap. 7.99 *(978-1-4424-4132-3(1)*, Aladdin) Simon & Schuster Children's Publishing.

Bluemle, Elizabeth. Tap Tap Boom Boom. Karas, G. Brian, illus. 2014. (ENG.). 32p. (J). (gr. -1-2). 16.99 *(978-0-7636-5696-6(8))* Candlewick Pr.

Blume-D'Ausilio, Carole Ed. D. The Bronx Bully. 2011. 28p. pap. 15.99 *(978-1-4628-5235-2(1))* Xlibris Corp.

Blume, Judy. Otherwise Known as Sheila the Great. 2007. (ENG.). 176p. (J). (gr. 3-7). 7.99 *(978-0-14-240879-7(4)*, Puffin Books) Penguin Young Readers Group.

—Otherwise Known as Sheila the Great. 2007. 154p. (gr. 4-7). 16.00 *(978-0-7569-7915-7(3))* Perfection Learning Corp.

—Otherwise Known as Sheila the Great. 2007. (Fudge Bks.: 2). 138p. (gr. 4-7). lib. bdg. 18.40 *(978-1-4177-8370-0(2)*, Turtleback) Turtleback Bks.

Blume, Lesley M. M. Modern Fairies, Dwarves, Goblins, & Other Nasties: A Practical Guide by Miss Edythe McFate. Foote, David, illus. 2010. (ENG.). 256p. (J). (gr. 3-7). 16.99 *(978-0-375-86203-8(X)*, Knopf Bks. for Young Readers) Random Hse. Children's Bks.

Blundell, Judy. Strings Attached. 2012. (ENG.). 320p. (J). (gr. 7). pap. 9.99 *(978-0-545-22127-6(7)*, Scholastic Paperbacks) Scholastic, Inc.

Bond, Gwenda & Rowe, Chistopher. The Lost Legacy. Thomas, Glenn, illus. 2017. (Supernormal Sleuthing Service Ser.: 1). 416p. (J). (gr. 3-7). 16.99 *(978-0-06-245994-7(5)*, Greenwillow Bks.) HarperCollins Pubs.

Booth, Coe. Bronxwood. 2013. (ENG.). 336p. (J). (gr. 9). pap. 10.99 *(978-0-439-92535-8(5)*, PUSH) Scholastic, Inc.

—Tyrell. 2011. 9.04 *(978-0-7848-3385-8(0)*, Everbind) Marco Bk. Co.

Bowden, Roger. Tales from Wild Westernville. 2007. 52p. per. 16.95 *(978-1-4241-6923-8(2))* America Star Bks.

Brashares, Ann. The Here & Now. 2014. 242p. (YA). *(978-0-385-39008-8(4)*, Delacorte Pr) Random House Publishing Group.

—The Here & Now. (ENG.). 256p. (YA). (gr. 7). 2015. pap. 10.99 *(978-0-385-73683-1(5)*, Ember) 2014. 18.99 *(978-0-385-73680-0(0)*, Delacorte Pr.) Random Hse. Children's Bks.

Brege, K. B. Champ... A Wave of Terror! Five Ways to Finish. 2006. (Mick Morris Myth Solver Ser.: No. 3). (J). mass mkt. 6.99 *(978-0-9774119-2-4(3))* Team B Creative LLC.

Brennan, Sarah Rees. Tell the Wind & Fire. 2017. (ENG.). 368p. (YA). (gr. 7). pap. 9.99 *(978-0-544-93887-8(9)*, HMH Books For Young Readers) Houghton Mifflin Harcourt Publishing Co.

Brezenoff, Steve. The Burglar Who Bit the Big Apple, 1 vol. Canga, C. B., illus. 2010. (Field Trip Mysteries Ser.). (ENG.). 88p. (gr. 2-3). 25.32 *(978-1-4342-2139-1(3))*; pap. 6.10 *(978-1-4342-2771-3(5))* Stone Arch Bks.

Broach, Elise. Masterpiece. 2010. 18.00 *(978-1-60686-888-1(8))* Perfection Learning Corp.

—Masterpiece. Murphy, Kelly, illus. 2010. (ENG.). 320p. (J). (gr. 4-7). pap. 7.99 *(978-0-312-60870-5(5)*, 9780312608705) Square Fish.

—Masterpiece. 2010. (J). lib. bdg. 18.40 *(978-0-606-14604-3(0)*, Turtleback) Turtleback Bks.

Brown, Anne. The Dumari Chronicles: Year One: Year One. 2007. 376p. (YA). per. 20.95 *(978-0-595-45725-0(8))* iUniverse, Inc.

Brown, Ian L. Clement & Oscar's American Adventure. Launos, Nina, illus. 2017. (ENG.). 84p. (J). pap. 16.95 ***(978-1-78629-995-6(X)***, 80b9564b-3043-4c5f-b05c-8b40dac9ad8a) Austin, Stan AUS. Dist: Bookmasters Distribution.

Brown, Marc. Arthur in New York. 2008. (Step into Reading Ser.). (ENG., Illus.). 24p. (J). (gr. k-3). pap. 3.99 *(978-0-375-82976-5(8)*, Random Hse. Bks. for Young Readers) Random Hse. Children's Bks.

Brown, Teri. Born of Illusion. 2013. (Born of Illusion Ser.: 1). (ENG.). 384p. (YA). (gr. 8). 17.99 *(978-0-06-218754-3(6))* HarperCollins Pubs.

Brumbach, Andrew. The Eye of Midnight. 2016. (ENG.). 256p. (J). (gr. 4-7). 16.99 *(978-0-385-74461-4(7)*, Delacorte Bks. for Young Readers) Random Hse. Children's Bks.

Bryant, Annie. Fashion Frenzy. 2006. (Beacon Street Girls Ser.: No. 9). (Illus.). 203p. (J). (gr. 4-8). per. 7.99 *(978-1-933566-02-3(7)*, Beacon Street Girls); *(978-1-4156-9393-3(5))* B*tween Productions, Inc.

—Fashion Frenzy. 2009. (Beacon Street Girls Ser.: 9). (ENG.). 256p. (J). (gr. 4-8). pap. 7.99 *(978-1-4169-6439-1(8)*, Aladdin) Simon & Schuster Children's Publishing.

Buckley, Michael. Once upon a Crime. Ferguson, Peter, illus. 2007. (ENG.). 288p. (J). (gr. 2-8). 16.95 *(978-0-8109-1610-4(X)*, Amulet Bks.) Abrams, Inc.

—Raging Sea. 2016. (Undertow Trilogy Ser.: 2). (ENG.). 368p. (YA). (gr. 7). 18.99 *(978-0-544-34844-8(3)*, HMH Books For Young Readers) Houghton Mifflin Harcourt Publishing Co.

—Tales from the Hood. Ferguson, Peter, illus. 2008. (Sisters Grimm Ser.). (ENG.). 288p. (J). (gr. 3-7). 16.95 *(978-0-8109-9478-2(X)*, Amulet Bks.) Abrams, Inc.

—Undertow. (Undertow Trilogy Ser.). (ENG.). (gr. 7). 2016. 400p. (YA). pap. 10.99 *(978-0-544-81319-9(7))* 2015. 384p. (J). 18.99 *(978-0-544-34825-7(7))* Houghton Mifflin Harcourt Publishing Co. (HMH Books For Young Readers).

Budhos, Marina. Ask Me No Questions. 2007. 159p. (gr. 7-12). 20.00 *(978-0-7569-8114-3(X))* Perfection Learning Corp.

—Ask Me No Questions. 2007. (ENG.). 192p. (YA). (gr. 7-12). pap. 10.99 *(978-1-4169-4920-6(8)*, Atheneum Bks. for Young Readers) Simon & Schuster Children's Publishing.

—Watched. 2016. (ENG.). 272p. (YA). (gr. 7). 17.99 *(978-0-553-53418-4(1)*, Lamb, Wendy Bks.) Random Hse. Children's Bks.

Bukiet, Melvin Jules. Undertown. 2013. (ENG.). 304p. (J). (gr. 3-7). 17.95 *(978-1-4197-0589-2(X)*, Amulet Bks.) Abrams, Inc.

Burkhart, Jessica. Jealousy. 2013. (Canterwood Crest Ser.: 17). (ENG.). 208p. (J). (gr. 4-7). pap. 7.99 *(978-1-4424-3657-2(3)*, Aladdin) Simon & Schuster Children's Publishing.

—Jealousy. 2013. (Canterwood Crest Ser.: 17). lib. bdg. 17.20 *(978-0-606-27032-8(9)*, Turtleback) Turtleback Bks.

Burleigh, Robert. Zoom! Zoom! Sounds of Things That Go in the City. Carpenter, Tad, illus. 2014. (ENG.). 32p. (J). (gr. -1-3). 17.99 *(978-1-4424-8315-6(6)*, Simon & Schuster Bks. For Young Readers) Simon & Schuster Bks. For Young Readers.

Burns, Catherine Lloyd. The Good, the Bad & the Beagle. 2014. (ENG.). 336p. (J). (gr. 5-7). 16.99 *(978-0-374-30039-5(9)*, 9780374300395, Farrar, Straus & Giroux (BYR)) Farrar, Straus & Giroux.

—The Half-True Lies of Cricket Cohen. 2017. (ENG.). 256p. (J). 16.99 *(978-0-374-30041-8(0)*, 9780374300418, Farrar, Straus & Giroux (BYR)) Farrar, Straus & Giroux.

Bushnell, Candace. Summer & the City. (Carrie Diaries: 2). (ENG.). 416p. (YA). (gr. 9). 2012. pap. 9.99 *(978-0-06-172900-3(0))* 2013. pap. 10.99 *(978-0-06-223686-9(5))* HarperCollins Pubs.

Busiek, Kurt. Marvels: The Platinum Edition Slipcase. 2014. (ENG., Illus.). 512p. (J). (gr. 4-17). 200.00 *(978-0-7851-5471-6(X))* Marvel Worldwide, Inc.

Byng, Georgia. Molly Moon y el Increíble Libro. 2003. (SPA.). 349p. (J). 18.99 *(978-84-348-9076-3(3))* SM Ediciones ESP. Dist: Lectorum Pubns., Inc.

—Molly Moon's Incredible Book of Hypnotism. 2003. 135.92 *(978-0-06-057217-4(5))* 2003. (Molly Moon Ser.: 1). (Illus.). 384p. (J). (gr. 3-7). 17.99 *(978-0-06-051406-8(X))* 2004. (Molly Moon Ser.: 1). (ENG., Illus.). 384p. (J). (gr. 3-7). reprint ed. pap. 7.99 *(978-0-06-051409-9(4))* HarperCollins Pubs.

—Molly Moon's Incredible Book of Hypnotism. 2004. (Molly Moon Ser.). 371p. (gr. 3-7). 18.00 *(978-0-7569-3484-2(2))* Perfection Learning Corp.

Cabot, Meg. Airhead. (Airhead Ser.: 1). (ENG.). 352p. (J). (gr. 7). 2009. pap. 9.99 *(978-0-545-04054-9(X))* 2008. 16.99 *(978-0-545-04052-5(3))* Scholastic, Inc.

—Being Nikki. (Airhead Ser.: 2). (ENG.). 352p. (J). 2010. (gr. 3-7). pap. 9.99 *(978-0-545-04058-7(2))* 2009. (gr. 7-18). 16.99 *(978-0-545-04056-3(6))* Scholastic, Inc.

—In Waiting. 2008. (Princess Diaries: 4). (ENG.). 256p. (YA). (gr. 8). pap. 9.99 *(978-0-06-154364-7(0)*, HarperTeen) HarperCollins Pubs.

—Jinx. 2009. (ENG.). 288p. (YA). (gr. 8). pap. 8.99 *(978-0-06-083766-2(7))* 2007. 262p. (YA). (gr. 7-12). lib. bdg. 17.89 *(978-0-06-083765-5(9))* 2007. (ENG.). 272p. (J). (gr. 7-18). 16.99 *(978-0-06-083764-8(0))* HarperCollins Pubs. (HarperTeen).

—Journal d'une Princesse.Tr. of Princess Diaries. pap. 13.95 *(978-2-01-321853-5(2))* Hachette Groupe Livre FRA. Dist: Distribooks, Inc.

—The Princess Diaries. 2008. (Princess Diaries: 1). (ENG.). 256p. (YA). (gr. 8). pap. 9.99 *(978-0-06-147993-9(4))*Vols. 1-3, Set. 2006. (Princess Diaries: Vol. I). (J). pap., pap. 19.99 *(978-0-06-115389-1(3))* HarperCollins Pubs. (HarperTeen).

—The Princess Diaries. 2008. 20.00 *(978-0-7569-8793-0(8))* Perfection Learning Corp.

—The Princess Diaries. unabr. ed. 2004. (Princess Diaries: Vol. I). 240p. (J). (gr. 7-18). pap. 38.00 incl. audio *(978-0-8072-0669-0(5)*, Listening Library) Random Hse. Audio Publishing Group.

—The Princess Diaries. 2008. (Princess Diaries: 1). (YA). lib. bdg. 20.85 *(978-1-4178-2328-4(3)*, Turtleback) Turtleback Bks.

—The Princess Diaries Box Set: The Princess Diaries; Princess in the Spotlight; Princess in Love. 2003. (Princess Diaries). 304p. (gr. 7-18). pap. 19.99 *(978-0-06-058745-1(8))* HarperCollins Pubs.

—Princess in Love, Vol. 3. 2008. (Princess Diaries: 3). (ENG.). 256p. (YA). (gr. 8-12). pap. 9.99 *(978-0-06-147995-3(0)*, HarperTeen) HarperCollins Pubs.

—Princess in Love. 2004. (Princess Diaries: Vol. 3). 288p. (J). (gr. 7-18). pap. 38.00 incl. audio *(978-0-8072-2284-3(4)*, Listening Library) Random Hse. Audio Publishing Group.

—Princess in Pink. (ENG.). 2008. (Princess Diaries: 5). 288p. (YA). (gr. 8). pap. 9.99 *(978-0-06-154363-0(2)*, HarperTeen) 2004. (Princess Diaries: Vol. 5). (Illus.). 272p. (J). (gr. 7-18). 15.99 *(978-0-06-009610-6(1))* HarperCollins Pubs.

—Princess in the Spotlight. 2008. (Princess Diaries). 222p. (gr. 7-12). 19.00 *(978-0-7569-8794-7(6))* Perfection Learning Corp.

—Princess in the Spotlight, unabr. ed. 2004. (Princess Diaries: Vol. 2). 272p. (J). (gr. 7-18). pap. 38.00 incl. audio *(978-0-8072-1197-7(4)*, S YA 332 SP, Listening Library) Random Hse. Audio Publishing Group.

—Princess in the Spotlight Vol. 2. 2008. (Princess Diaries: 2). (ENG.). 256p. (YA). (gr. 8-12). pap. 9.99 *(978-0-06-147994-6(2)*, HarperTeen) HarperCollins Pubs.

—Princess in Training. (ENG., 2005. (Princess Diaries: Vol. 6). Illus.). 288p. (J). (gr. 7-18). 16.99 *(978-0-06-009613-7(6))* Vol. VI. 2008. (Princess Diaries: 6). 304p. (YA). (gr. 8). pap. 9.99 *(978-0-06-154365-4(9)*, HarperTeen) HarperCollins Pubs.

—Princess Mia. (ENG.). 2008. (Princess Diaries: Vol. 9). 256p. (J). (gr. 7-18). 16.99 *(978-0-06-072461-0(7))* Vol. 9. 2009. (Princess Diaries: 9). 304p. (YA). (gr. 8). pap. 9.99 *(978-0-06-072463-4(3)*, HarperTeen) HarperCollins Pubs.

—Princess Mia. 2009. (Princess Diaries: 9). (YA). lib. bdg. 20.85 *(978-0-606-02178-4(7)*, Turtleback) Turtleback Bks.

—Princess on the Brink. 2007. (ENG.). (Princess Diaries: 8). 272p. (YA). (gr. 8). pap. 9.99 *(978-0-06-072460-3(9)*, HarperTeen); (Princess Diaries: Vol. 8). 256p. (J). 16.99 *(978-0-06-072456-6(0))* HarperCollins Pubs.

—Valentine Princess. 2006. (Princess Diaries: 7.75). (ENG.). 96p. (YA). (gr. 8-12). 12.99 *(978-0-06-084718-0(2)*, HarperTeen) HarperCollins Pubs.

Calonita, Jen. Summer State of Mind. 2014. (ENG.). 256p. (YA). (gr. 7-17). pap. 10.00 *(978-0-316-09115-2(4)*, Poppy) Little, Brown Bks. for Young Readers.

Cameron, Peter. Someday This Pain Will Be Useful to You. 2009. (ENG.). 240p. (YA). (gr. 9-13). pap. 16.00 *(978-0-312-42816-7(2)*, 9780312428167) Picador.

Caraballo, Samuel & Torrecilla, Pablo. Estrellita in the Big City/Estrellita en la Ciudad Grande. Caraballo, Samuel & Torrecilla, Pablo, illus. 2008. (SPA & ENG., Illus.). 32p. (J). (gr. -1-4). 16.95 *(978-1-55885-498-7(3)*, Piñata Books) Arte Publico Pr.

Carbone, Courtney. Lights Out! (Marvel: Mighty Avengers) Spaziante, Patrick, illus. 2016. (Little Golden Book Ser.). (ENG.). 24p. (J). (-k). 4.99 *(978-0-307-97658-1(0)*, Golden Bks.) Random Hse. Children's Bks.

Carey, Anna. Deadfall: The Sequel to Blackbird. 2015. (Blackbird Ser.: 2). (ENG.). 256p. (YA). (gr. 9). 17.99 *(978-0-06-229976-5(X)*, HarperTeen) HarperCollins Pubs.

Carlson, Melody. Catwalk, 1 vol. 2014. (On the Runway Ser.). (ENG.). 224p. (YA). pap. 9.99 *(978-0-310-74810-6(0))* Zondervan.

—Ciao, 1 vol. 2014. (On the Runway Ser.). (ENG.). 208p. (YA). pap. 9.99 *(978-0-310-74843-4(7))* Zondervan.

—Rendezvous, 1 vol. 2014. (On the Runway Ser.). (ENG.). 224p. (YA). pap. 9.99 *(978-0-310-74861-8(5))* Zondervan.

Carter, Aimée. Simon Thorn & the Wolf's Den. 2016. (Simon Thorn Ser.). (ENG.). 320p. (YA). (gr. 3-6). 16.99 *(978-1-61963-704-7(9)*, 9781619637047, Bloomsbury USA Childrens) Bloomsbury Publishing USA.

—Simon Thorn & the Wolf's Den. 2017. (Simon Thorn Ser.). (ENG.). 336p. (J). pap. 7.99 *(978-1-61963-706-1(5)*, 9781619637061, Bloomsbury USA Childrens) Bloomsbury Publishing USA.

Casciano, Christie & Moziak, Rose Mary Casciano, illus. Haunted Hockey in Lake Placid. 2012. 72p. (J). pap. *(978-1-59531-040-8(1))* North Country Bks., Inc.

Cassidy, Yvonne. How Many Letters Are in Goodbye? 2016. (ENG.). 432p. (YA). pap. 11.99 *(978-0-7387-4745-3(9)*, Flux) North Star Editions.

Castillo, Lauren. Nana in the City. 2014. (ENG., Illus.). 40p. (J). (gr. -1-3). 16.99 *(978-0-544-10443-3(9))* Houghton Mifflin Harcourt Publishing Co.

Cataneo, D. M. Eggplant Alley. 2013. (ENG.). 352p. (YA). (gr. 7-9). 17.95 *(978-1-59373-146-5(9))* Bunker Hill Publishing, Inc.

Chace, Rebecca. June Sparrow & the Million-Dollar Penny. Schwartz, Kacey, illus. 2017. 352p. (J). (gr. 3-7). 16.99 *(978-0-06-246498-9(1))* HarperCollins Pubs.

Chambers, Veronica. Plus. 2010. (ENG.). 272p. (YA). (gr. 7-18). 8.99 *(978-1-59514-165-1(0)*, Razorbill) Penguin Young Readers Group.

Chance, Megan. The Veil, 0 vols. 2015. (Fianna Trilogy Ser.: 3). (ENG.). 366p. (YA). (gr. 7-12). 16.99 *(978-1-5039-4571-5(5)*, 9781503945715, Skyscape) Amazon Publishing.

—The Web, 0 vols. 2015. (Fianna Trilogy Ser.: 2). (ENG.). 384p. (YA). pap. 9.99 *(978-1-4778-2708-6(0)*, 9781477827086, Skyscape) Amazon Publishing.

Chang, Ifay, as told by. Outopians. 2007. (Illus.). 27p. (YA). pap. *(978-0-9771594-1-3(8))* TLC Information Services.

Chari, Sheela. Finding Mighty. 2017. (ENG., Illus.). 320p. (J). (gr. 5-9). 16.95 *(978-1-4197-2296-7(4)*, Amulet Bks.) Abrams, Inc.

Chibbaro, Julie. Deadly. Sovak, Jean-Marc Superville, illus. 2012. (ENG.). 304p. (YA). (gr. 7). pap. 10.99 *(978-0-689-85739-3(X)*, Atheneum Bks. for Young Readers) Simon & Schuster Children's Publishing.

Christopher, Matt. Fairway Phenom. 2003. (ENG.). 144p. (J). (gr. 5-8). pap. 16.99 *(978-0-316-07551-0(5))* Little, Brown Bks. for Young Readers.

Chronicle Books Staff. New York, Baby! Jenkins, Ward, illus. 2012. (ENG.). 24p. (J). (gr. -1 — 1). 12.99 *(978-1-4521-0619-9(3))* Chronicle Bks. LLC.

Clare, Cassandra. City of Ashes. 2008. (Mortal Instruments Ser.: 2). (YA). (gr. 9). 64.99 *(978-1-60640-964-0(6))* Findaway World, LLC.

—City of Ashes. 2008. (Mortal Instruments Ser.: 2). (ENG.). 464p. (YA). (gr. 9-12). 24.99 *(978-1-4169-1429-7(3)*, McElderry, Margaret K. Bks.) McElderry, Margaret K. Bks.

—City of Bones. (Mortal Instruments Ser.: Bk. 1). (ENG., Illus.). (YA). (gr. 9). 2015. 544p. pap. 13.99 *(978-1-4814-5592-3(3))* 2007. 496p. 21.99 *(978-1-4169-1428-0(5))* 2015. 544p. pap. 13.99 *(978-1-4814-7030-8(2))* McElderry, Margaret K. Bks. (McElderry, Margaret K. Bks.).

—City of Bones. 2008. (Mortal Instruments Ser.: Bk. 1). 485p. (gr. 9-12). 23.00 *(978-1-60686-361-9(4))* Perfection Learning Corp.

—City of Bones, 12 vols. 2007. (Mortal Instruments Ser.: 1). (YA). 131.75 *(978-1-4281-5454-4(X))*; 133.75 *(978-1-4281-5452-0(3))*; 286.75 *(978-1-4281-5449-0(3))*; 1.25 *(978-1-4281-5445-2(0))*; 120.75 *(978-1-4281-5450-6(7))*; 122.75 *(978-1-4281-5448-3(5))* Recorded Bks., Inc.

—City of Bones. 2013. (The Mortal Instruments Ser.: Bk. 1). pap. *(978-1-4424-9306-3(2))* Simon & Schuster, Inc.

—City of Bones. l.t. ed. 2008. (Mortal Instruments Ser.: 1). 629p. (YA). 31.95 *(978-1-4104-0958-4(9))* Thorndike Pr.

—City of Bones. 2015. (Mortal Instruments Ser.: Bk. 1). 544p. (YA). lib. bdg. 25.75 *(978-0-606-37731-7(X))* Turtleback Bks.

—City of Fallen Angels. 2011. (Mortal Instruments Ser.: 4). (ENG.). 432p. (YA). (gr. 9-18). 24.99 *(978-1-4424-0354-3(3)*, McElderry, Margaret K. Bks.) McElderry, Margaret K. Bks.

—City of Fallen Angels, 11 vols. (Mortal Instruments Ser.: 4). (YA). 2012. 133.75 *(978-1-4618-0638-7(0))* 2011. 135.75 *(978-1-4618-0637-0(2))* 2011. 317.75 *(978-1-4618-0642-4(9))* 2011. 1.25 *(978-1-4640-2483-2(9))* 2011. 133.75 *(978-1-4618-0641-7(0))* Recorded Bks., Inc.

—City of Glass. (Mortal Instruments Ser.: Bk. 3). (ENG., (YA). (gr. 9). 2015. Illus.). 592p. pap. 13.99 *(978-1-4814-5598-5(2))* 2009. 560p. 24.99 *(978-1-4169-1430-3(7))* McElderry, Margaret K. Bks. (McElderry, Margaret K. Bks.).

—City of Glass. 2010. 23.00 *(978-1-60686-827-0(6))* Perfection Learning Corp.

—City of Glass. 2009. pap. *(978-1-4424-9308-7(9))* Simon & Schuster.

—City of Glass. 2015. (Mortal Instruments Ser.: Bk. 3). 592p. (YA). lib. bdg. 25.75 *(978-0-606-37733-1(6))* Turtleback Bks.

—City of Heavenly Fire. 2014. (Mortal Instruments Ser.: No. 6). (ENG., Illus.). 752p. (YA). (gr. 9). 24.99 *(978-1-4424-1689-5(0)*, McElderry, Margaret K. Bks.) McElderry, Margaret K. Bks.

—City of Lost Souls. (Mortal Instruments Ser.: Bk. 5). (ENG., (YA). (gr. 9). 2015. Illus.). 592p. pap. 13.99 *(978-1-4814-5600-5(8))* 2012. 544p. 21.99 *(978-1-4424-1686-4(6))* McElderry, Margaret K. Bks. (McElderry, Margaret K. Bks.).

—City of Lost Souls, 16 vols. 2012. (Mortal Instruments Ser.: Bk. 5). (YA). 135.75 *(978-1-4640-3948-5(8))*; 317.75 *(978-1-4640-3949-2(6))*; 133.75 *(978-1-4640-3951-5(8))*; 133.75 *(978-1-4640-3952-2(6))* Recorded Bks., Inc.

—City of Lost Souls. 2015. (Mortal Instruments Ser.: Bk. 5). 592p. (YA). lib. bdg. 25.75 *(978-0-606-37736-2(0))* Turtleback Bks.

—City of Lost Souls. 2012. 512p. pap. *(978-1-4063-3760-0(9))* Walker Bks., Ltd.

Clements, Andrew. Things Hoped For. 2008. (ENG.). 176p. (J). (gr. 5-18). 7.99 *(978-0-14-241073-8(X)*, Puffin Books) Penguin Young Readers Group.

—Things Hoped For. 2008. 167p. (gr. 5-9). 17.00 *(978-0-7569-8933-0(7))* Perfection Learning Corp.

—Things Hoped For. l.t. ed. 2008. (Thorndike Literacy Bridge Ser.). 207p. 23.95 *(978-1-4104-0500-5(1))* Thorndike Pr.

Coburn, Jake. Prep. 2005. (ENG.). 192p. (YA). (gr. 7-7). 6.99 *(978-0-14-240307-5(5)*, Speak) Penguin Young Readers Group.

Cochrane, Mick. The Girl Who Threw Butterflies. 2010. (ENG.). 192p. (J). (gr. 3-7). 6.99 *(978-0-375-84610-6(7)*, Yearling) Random Hse. Children's Bks.

Cody, Matthew. The Dead Gentleman. 2012. (ENG.). 288p. (J). (gr. 5). 6.99 *(978-0-375-84490-4(2)*, Yearling) Random Hse. Children's Bks.

Cofer, Judith Ortiz. Call Me Maria. 2006. (First Person Fiction Ser.). (ENG.). 176p. (J). (gr. 3-7). per. 6.99 *(978-0-439-38578-7(4)*, Scholastic Paperbacks) Scholastic, Inc.

Cohen, Miriam. Down in the Subway, 1 vol. Greenberg, Melanie Hope, illus. 2003. (ENG.). 32p. (J). (gr. k-3). pap. 6.95 *(978-1-932065-24-4(5))*; 15.95 *(978-1-932065-08-4(3))* Star Bright Bks., Inc.

Cohn, Rachel & Levithan, David. Dash & Lily's Book of Dares. 2011. (ENG.). 288p. (YA). (gr. 7). pap. 9.99 *(978-0-375-85955-7(1)*, Ember) Random Hse. Children's Bks.

—Naomi & Ely's No Kiss List. 2008. (ENG.). 256p. (YA). (gr. 9). pap. 9.99 *(978-0-375-84441-6(4)*, Ember) Random Hse. Children's Bks.

—Nick & Norah's Infinite Playlist. 2009. 10.54 *(978-0-7848-2769-7(9)*, Everbind) Marco Bk. Co.

—Nick & Norah's Infinite Playlist. 2007. 183p. (gr. 9-12). 19.00 *(978-0-7569-7949-2(8))* Perfection Learning Corp.

—Nick & Norah's Infinite Playlist. (ENG.). 208p. (YA). (gr. 9-12). 2007. pap. 9.99 *(978-0-375-83533-9(4))* 2008. (Illus.). pap. 9.99 *(978-0-375-84614-4(X))* Random Hse. Children's Bks. (Ember).

—The Twelve Days of Dash & Lily. 2016. (ENG.). 224p. (YA). (gr. 7). 17.99 *(978-0-399-55380-6(0)*, Knopf Bks. for Young Readers) Random Hse. Children's Bks.

Colasanti, Susane. City Love. 2015. (City Love Ser.: 1). (ENG.). 336p. (YA). (gr. 9). 17.99 *(978-0-06-230768-2(1)*, Tegen, Katherine Bks) HarperCollins Pubs.

—Forever in Love. 2017. (City Love Ser.: 3). 320p. (YA). (gr. 9). 17.99 *(978-0-06-230776-7(2)*, Tegen, Katherine Bks) HarperCollins Pubs.

—Lost in Love. 2016. (City Love Ser.: 2). 352p. (YA). (gr. 9). 17.99 *(978-0-06-230773-6(8)*, Tegen, Katherine Bks) HarperCollins Pubs.

—So Much Closer. 2012. (ENG.). 272p. (YA). (gr. 7-18). pap. 8.99 *(978-0-14-242114-7(6)*, Speak) Penguin Young Readers Group.

—Take Me There. 2009. (ENG.). 320p. (YA). (gr. 7-18). 9.99 *(978-0-14-241435-4(2)*, Speak) Penguin Young Readers Group.

Cold Moon. 2nd ed. 2014. 180p. pap. 14.99 *(978-1-62798-459-1(3)*, Harmony Ink Pr.) Dreamspinner Pr.

M
N
O

Cole, Brock. The Money We'll Save. Cole, Brock, illus. 2011. (ENG., Illus.). 40p. (J). (gr. -1-3). 16.99 *(978-0-374-35011-6(6)*, 9780374350116, Farrar, Straus & Giroux (BYR)) Farrar, Straus & Giroux.

Collins, Nancy A. After Dark. 3rd ed. 2009. (Vamps Ser.: 3). (ENG.). 192p. (YA). (gr. 9-18). pap. 8.99 *(978-0-06-134919-5(4)*, HarperTeen) HarperCollins Pubs.

—Night Life. 2009. (Vamps Ser.: 2). (ENG.). 256p. (YA). (gr. 9-18). pap. 8.99 *(978-0-06-134918-8(6)*, HarperTeen) HarperCollins Pubs.

—Vamps. 2008. (Vamps Ser.: 1). (ENG.). 256p. (YA). (gr. 9-18). pap. 8.99 *(978-0-06-134917-1(8)*, HarperTeen) HarperCollins Pubs.

Colon, Edie. Good-Bye, Havana! Hola, New York! Colón, Raúl, illus. 2011. (ENG.). 32p. (J). (gr. -1-3). 17.99 *(978-1-4424-0674-2(7)*, Simon & Schuster/Paula Wiseman Bks.) Simon & Schuster/Paula Wiseman Bks.

Conklin, Melanie. Counting Thyme. 2016. (ENG.). 320p. (J). (gr. 5). 16.99 *(978-0-399-17330-1(7)*, G.P. Putnam's Sons Books for Young Readers) Penguin Young Readers Group.

Connor, Leslie. Waiting for Normal. 2008. (ENG.). 304p. (J). (gr. 5-18). 16.99 *(978-0-06-089088-9(6)*, Tegen, Katherine Bks) HarperCollins Pubs.

Cooke, Majorie Benton. Bambi. 2007. (ENG.). 226p. pap. 20.99 *(978-1-4264-4618-4(7))* Creative Media Partners, LLC.

Cooney, Caroline B. Code Orange. 2007. 200p. (gr. 7-12). 17.00 *(978-0-7569-8210-2(3))* Perfection Learning Corp.

—Code Orange. 2007. (ENG.). 224p. (YA). (gr. 7-12). mass mkt. 6.99 *(978-0-385-73260-4(0)*, Laurel Leaf) Random Hse. Children's Bks.

—Code Orange. 2007. lib. bdg. 17.20 *(978-1-4177-7788-4(5)*, Turtleback) Turtleback Bks.

—Janie Face to Face. 2013. (ENG.). 352p. (YA). (gr. 7). 17.99 *(978-0-385-74206-1(1)*, Delacorte Bks. for Young Readers) Random Hse. Children's Bks.

Cordier, Claire. The POLAR BEAR in CENTRAL PARK. 2010. 32p. pap. 23.50 *(978-0-557-08167-7(X))* Lulu Pr., Inc.

Corey, Shana. Milly & the Macy's Parade. Helquist, Brett, illus. 2006. 38p. (J). (gr. 4-8). reprint ed. 17.00 *(978-1-4223-5174-1(2))* DIANE Publishing Co.

Corris, Charles R. Donald Ditz & the Red Tiger, 1 vol. 2010. 64p. pap. 19.95 *(978-1-4512-2193-0(2))* America Star Bks.

Corwin, Jeff. Your Backyard Is Wild. 2009. (Jeff Corwin Ser.: 1). (ENG.). 96p. (J). (gr. 1-3). 4.99 *(978-0-14-241404-0(2)*, Puffin Books) Penguin Young Readers Group.

Cosson, Kip. Ned Visits New York. 2006. (ENG., Illus.). 40p. (J). 16.95 *(978-0-9789384-0-6(2))* Kip Kids of New York.

Cotten, Cynthia. The Book Boat's In. Lessac, Frané, illus. 2013. (ENG.). 32p. (J). (gr. 1-5). 16.95 *(978-0-8234-2521-1(5))* Holiday Hse., Inc.

Cotter, Natasha. Pj Is Special. 2011. 20p. pap. 24.95 *(978-1-4560-6564-5(5))* America Star Bks.

Cox, Suzy. The Dead Girls Detective Agency. 2012. (ENG.). 368p. (YA). (gr. 9). pap. 9.99 *(978-0-06-202064-2(1)*, HarperTeen) HarperCollins Pubs.

Crawford, Laura. Postcards from New York City/Postales Desde New York City. de La Vega, Eida, tr. Adamson, Bonnie, illus. 2008. (Traveling with Anna Ser.). (ENG.). 32p. (J). (gr. 4-7). 16.95 *(978-0-9795477-2-0(5))*; per. 7.95 *(978-0-9795477-3-7(3))* Continental Sales, Inc. (Raven Tree Pr.,Csi).

Creek, Silent. All the Ice of Afric. 2009. 160p. 22.95 *(978-1-4401-2118-0(4))* iUniverse, Inc.

Cross, Julie & Perini, Mark. You Before Anyone Else. 2016. (ENG.). 400p. (YA). (gr. 8-12). pap. 10.99 *(978-1-4926-0492-1(5)*, 9781492604921) Sourcebooks, Inc.

Crowl, M. Tara. Eden's Escape. (Eden of the Lamp Ser.). (ENG.). 320p. (J). (gr. 3-7). 2017. pap. 7.99 ***(978-1-4847-4917-3(0))*** 2016. 16.99 *(978-1-4847-1186-6(6))* Hyperion Bks. for Children.

Curry, Don, ed. The Crate Escape No. 2. 2008. (I Can Find It Ser.). 22p. (J). 7.99 *(978-0-696-23490-3(4))* Meredith Bks.

—Esape Africa. 2008. 22p. (J). 15.95 *(978-0-696-23488-0(2))* Meredith Bks.

Curtis, Alice Turner. A Frontier Girl of New York. Snyder, Harold E., illus. 2011. 282p. 48.95 *(978-1-258-01096-6(8))* Literary Licensing, LLC.

Czerw, Nancy Carpenter. Itty & Bitty - On the Road. Berlin, Rose Mary, illus. 2008. (Itty & Bitty Ser.: 3). (ENG.). 32p. (J). (gr. -1-3). 16.95 *(978-0-9755618-4-3(7))* McWitty Pr., Inc.

The Daisy Bug Kids Say Hello New York. 2004. (J). *(978-0-9712349-2-5(2))* Univ. At Buffalo, Child Care Ctr.

La Dama de Cobre (the Copper Lady) 2006. (J). pap. 6.95 *(978-0-8225-6616-8(8)*, Ediciones Lerner) Lerner Publishing Group.

Danziger, Paula. Amber Brown Wants Extra Credit. Ross, Tony, illus. 2008. (Amber Brown Ser.: 4). (ENG.). 144p. (J). (gr. 2-5). 5.99 *(978-0-14-241049-3(7)*, Puffin Books) Penguin Young Readers Group.

—Remember Me to Harold Square. (Remember Me to Harold Square Ser.: No. 1). 139p. (YA). (gr. 6-18). pap. 3.99 *(978-0-8072-1472-5(8)*, Listening Library) Random Hse. Audio Publishing Group.

Davies, Jocelyn. The Odds of Lightning. 2016. (ENG., Illus.). 384p. (YA). (gr. 9). 17.99 *(978-1-4814-4053-0(5)*, Simon Pulse) Simon Pulse.

Davis, Cynthia. Drink the Rain. 2007. (Illus.). 256p. (YA). per. 12.95 *(978-0-9712163-1-0(2))* Greenroom Bks.

De la Cruz, Melissa. Beach Lane. 2013. (Beach Lane Ser.: 1). (ENG., Illus.). 320p. (YA). (gr. 9). pap. 9.99 *(978-1-4424-7409-3(2)*, Simon & Schuster Bks. For Young Readers) Simon & Schuster Bks. For Young Readers.

—Blue Bloods. (Blue Bloods Ser.). (ENG.). (J). (gr. 5-9). 2007. 336p. pap. 9.99 *(978-1-4231-0126-0(X))*Set. 2009. 944p. pap. 24.99 *(978-1-4231-2595-2(9))* Hyperion Pr.

—Blue Bloods. 2007. (Blue Bloods Ser.: 1). (J). lib. bdg. 20.85 *(978-1-4178-2375-8(5)*, Turtleback) Turtleback Bks.

—Double Eclipse. 2016. (Summer on East End Ser.). (ENG.). 336p. (YA). (gr. 7). 17.99 *(978-0-399-17356-1(0)*, G.P. Putnam's Sons Books for Young Readers) Penguin Young Readers Group.

—Gates of Paradise. 2013. (ENG.). 368p. (Blue Bloods Ser.: Bk. 7). (J). (gr. 5-9). pap. 9.99 *(978-1-4231-6110-3(6))*; (YA). (gr. 7-17). 16.99 *(978-1-4231-5741-0(9))* Hyperion Pr.

—Lost in Time. 2012. (Blue Bloods Ser.). (ENG.). 368p. (J). (gr. 5-9). pap. 8.99 *(978-1-4231-3413-8(3))* Hyperion Pr.

—Masquerade. 2008. (Blue Bloods Ser.). (ENG.). 336p. (J). (gr. 5-9). pap. 9.99 *(978-1-4231-0127-7(8))* Hyperion Pr.

—Skinny-Dipping. 2006. (Au Pairs Ser.: 2). (ENG.). 304p. (YA). (gr. 9-18). reprint ed. pap. 8.99 *(978-1-4169-0383-3(6)*, Simon & Schuster Bks. For Young Readers) Simon & Schuster Bks. For Young Readers.

—Sun-Kissed. (Au Pairs Ser.: 3). (ENG.). 320p. (YA). (gr. 9-12). 2007. pap. 8.99 *(978-1-4169-1747-2(0))* 2006. 15.95 *(978-1-4169-1746-5(2))* Simon & Schuster Bks. For Young Readers. (Simon & Schuster Bks. For Young Readers).

De Los Heros, Luis & Wilson, Elizabeth. Chifa Chi's Little Adventure in New York City. 2011. 44p. pap. 21.99 *(978-0-557-91842-3(1))* Lulu Pr., Inc.

Dean, Myers Walter. Fast Sam, Cool Clyde, & Stuff. 2014. (ENG.). 192p. (J). (gr. 12-12). 11.24 *(978-1-63245-241-2(3))* Lectorum Pubns., Inc.

Decker, Jeni. Far from Happy. 2014. 200p. pap. 14.99 *(978-1-62798-407-2(0))* Dreamspinner Pr.

Dee, Carolyn. The Tree Who Couldn't Choose. 2008. 36p. pap. 15.49 *(978-1-4389-2950-7(1))* AuthorHouse.

Defelice, Cynthia & DeFelice, Cynthia C. Under the Same Sky. 2005. (ENG.). 224p. (J). (gr. 5-9). pap. 9.99 *(978-0-374-48065-3(6)*, 9780374480653) Square Fish.

DEKELB-RITTENHOUSE, Diane. Immortal Longings. 2012. (ENG.). 340p. (J). (gr. 7). pap. 14.95 *(978-0-9845318-4-4(X))* Tiny Stachel Pr.

DeKeyser, Stacy. Jump the Cracks. 2008. (ENG.). 216p. (YA). (gr. 7-18). per. 9.95 *(978-0-7387-1274-1(4)*, Flux) North Star Editions.

Dempsey, Kristy. A Dance Like Starlight: One Ballerina's Dream. Cooper, Floyd, illus. 2014. (ENG.). 32p. (J). (gr. k-3). 16.99 *(978-0-399-25284-6(3)*, Philomel Bks.) Penguin Young Readers Group.

DeVillers, Julia & Roy, Jennifer. Double Feature. 2012. (Mix Ser.). (ENG.). 288p. (J). (gr. 4-8). pap. 7.99 *(978-1-4424-3403-5(1)*, Aladdin) Simon & Schuster Children's Publishing.

DeVillers, Julia & Roy, Jennifer Rozines. Times Squared. 2011. (Mix Ser.). (ENG.). (J). (gr. 4-8). 272p. pap. 7.99 *(978-1-4169-6732-3(X))*; 240p. 16.99 *(978-1-4169-7532-8(2))* Simon & Schuster Children's Publishing. (Aladdin).

Diallo, Elishia Shelene. Boogalou: A Boogie down Bronx Tale. 2015. (ENG.). 272p. (YA). pap. 14.99 *(978-1-4951-7655-5(X))* Independent Pub.

DiCerto, Joseph J. The Wall People: In Search of a Home. 2014. (Illus.). 128p. (J). pap. 14.00 *(978-0-87842-633-1(7))* Mountain Pr. Publishing Co., Inc.

Disney Press Staff. School's Out. 2010. 128p. pap. 4.99 *(978-1-4231-2677-5(7))* Disney Pr.

Dixon, Amy. Marathon Mouse. Denlinger, Sam, illus. 2012. (ENG.). 32p. (J). (gr. -1-k). 16.95 *(978-1-61608-966-5(0)*, 608966, Sky Pony Pr.) Skyhorse Publishing Co., Inc.

Dolby, Tom. Secret Society. 2011. (ENG.). 368p. (YA). (gr. 8). pap. 8.99 *(978-0-06-172163-2(8)*, Tegen, Katherine Bks) HarperCollins Pubs.

—The Trust. 2011. (ENG.). 368p. (YA). (gr. 8-18). 16.99 *(978-0-06-172164-9(6)*, Tegen, Katherine Bks) HarperCollins Pubs.

Dorismond, Joanne R. A Day in New York with Beatrice & Duke. 2010. 37p. pap. 17.95 *(978-0-557-23850-7(1))* Lulu Pr., Inc.

Dreyer, Ellen. Speechless in New York. Huerta, Catherine, illus. 2nd rev. ed. 2003. (Going to Ser.). (ENG.). 129p. (J). (gr. 4-8). pap. 6.95 *(978-1-893577-09-1(0))* Fruitbearer Publishing, LLC.

Driftin' Aarong. Claude Henry, the Iditarod Mouse ~3: The Great Castaway Adventure. 2009. 92p. pap. 9.95 *(978-1-4401-1949-1(X))* iUniverse, Inc.

D'shindia, Albert. The Fable Musical. 2012. 56p. (gr. -1). pap. 10.95 *(978-1-4567-9978-6(9))* AuthorHouse.

Dubrule, Jackie. Kelli, God & New York. Baker, David, illus. 2013. 28p. pap. 24.95 *(978-1-4560-0969-4(9))* America Star Bks.

Dunshee, Gloria. Will & the Red Ball. 2010. 32p. pap. 11.95 *(978-0-9828231-0-1(X))* WillGo Pr.

Egan, Tim. Dodsworth in New York. 2009. (Dodsworth Book Ser.). (ENG., Illus.). 48p. (J). (gr. 2-5). pap. 3.99 *(978-0-547-24831-8(8))* Houghton Mifflin Harcourt Publishing Co.

Ehrenhaft, Daniel. 10 Things to Do Before I Die. 2006. (ENG.). 224p. (YA). (gr. 7). per. 7.95 *(978-0-385-73406-6(9)*, Delacorte Bks. for Young Readers) Random Hse. Children's Bks.

Eldridge, Courtney. Ghost Time. (ENG.). (YA). 2016. 418p. pap. 9.99 *(978-1-4778-1697-4(6)*, 9781477816974) 2013. 416p. (gr. 9-12). 17.99 *(978-1-4778-1657-8(7)*, 9781477816578, Amazon Children's Publishing) Amazon Publishing.

Elish, Dan. The Attack of the Frozen Woodchucks. Call, Greg, illus. 2008. (ENG.). 256p. (J). (gr. 3-7). 16.99 *(978-0-06-113870-6(3)*, Geringer, Laura Book) HarperCollins Pubs.

Elliot, Rachel. Who Is New York's Prettiest Princess? Spenceley, Annabel, illus. 2012. (ENG.). 32p. (J). (-3). 9.99 *(978-1-4022-8221-8(4)*, Sourcebooks Jabberwocky) Sourcebooks, Inc.

Enright, Elizabeth. The Saturdays. Enright, Elizabeth, illus. 3rd ed. 2008. (Melendy Quartet Ser.: 1). (ENG., Illus.). 192p. (J). (gr. 3-7). per. 7.99 *(978-0-312-37598-0(0)*, 9780312375980) Square Fish.

Fairstein, Linda. Into the Lion's Den. 2016. (Devlin Quick Mysteries Ser.). (ENG.). 320p. (J). (gr. 3-7). 16.99 *(978-0-399-18643-1(3)*, Dial Bks) Penguin Young Readers Group.

Falk, Barbara Bustetter & Hyman, Helen Kandel. Don't Park on the Roof. 2007. 36p. per. 21.32 *(978-1-4257-7096-9(7))* Xlibris Corp.

Famularo, Joe. Chiara's Bite of the Big Apple: A Happy Book. 2013. 28p. pap. 16.09 *(978-1-4669-5274-4(1))* Trafford Publishing.

Farnol, Jeffery. Money Moon. 2006. pap. 13.95 *(978-1-4218-3066-7(3))* 1st World Publishing, Inc.

Federle, Tim. Better Nate Than Ever. (ENG., Illus.). (J). (gr. 4-8). 2014. 296p. pap. 7.99 *(978-1-4424-4691-5(9))* 2013. 288p. 17.99 *(978-1-4424-4689-2(7))* Simon & Schuster Bks. For Young Readers. (Simon & Schuster Bks. For Young Readers).

—Five, Six, Seven, Nate! (ENG., Illus.). (J). (gr. 5-9). 2015. 320p. pap. 7.99 *(978-1-4424-4695-3(1))* 2014. 304p. 16.99 *(978-1-4424-4693-9(5))* Simon & Schuster Bks. For Young Readers. (Simon & Schuster Bks. For Young Readers).

Ferrari, Vincent. Blogosfear. 2005. 143p. (YA). pap. 15.00 *(978-1-4116-6814-0(6))* Lulu Pr., Inc.

Fiedler, Lisa. Mouseheart. To, Vivienne, illus. 2014. (Mouseheart Ser.: 1). (ENG.). 320p. (J). (gr. 3-7). 16.99 *(978-1-4424-8781-9(X)*, McElderry, Margaret K. Bks.) McElderry, Margaret K. Bks.

Fields, Jan. Hunt for Sewer Gators, 1 vol. Brundage, Scott, illus. 2014. (Monster Hunters Ser.). (ENG.). 80p. (J). (gr. 8-12). 27.07 *(978-1-62402-045-2(3))* Magic Wagon.

Finley, Leah. The One & Only Mr C. 2009. 82p. pap. 8.95 *(978-1-935118-75-6(7))* Bellissima Publishing, LLC.

Firestone, Carrie. The Unlikelies. 2017. (ENG.). 336p. (YA). (gr. 9-17). 17.99 ***(978-0-316-38286-1(8))*** Little, Brown Bks. for Young Readers.

Fitzgerald, Laura Marx. The Gallery. 2016. (ENG.). 336p. (J). (gr. 5-7). 16.99 *(978-0-525-42865-7(8)*, Dial Bks) Penguin Young Readers Group.

—Under the Egg. (ENG.). 256p. (J). (gr. 3-7). 2015. 7.99 *(978-0-14-242765-1(9)*, Puffin Books) 2014. 16.99 *(978-0-8037-4001-3(8)*, Dial Bks) Penguin Young Readers Group.

Fitzgerald, Scott. The Great Gatsby. Kalda, Sam, illus. adapted ed. 2014. (American Classics Ser.). (ENG.). 64p. pap. 6.95 *(978-1-906230-74-6(9))* Real Reads Ltd. GBR. Dist: Casemate Pubs. & Bk. Distributors, LLC.

Fitzhugh, Louise. Harriet the Spy. 298p. (J). (gr. 3-5). pap. 5.95 *(978-0-8072-1535-7(X)*, Listening Library) Random Hse. Audio Publishing Group.

—Harriet the Spy. 50th anniv. ed. 2014. (ENG.). 336p. (J). (gr. 3-7). 17.99 *(978-0-385-37610-5(3)*, Delacorte Bks. for Young Readers) Random Hse. Children's Bks.

Fitzhugh, Percy K. Pee-Wee Harris. 2004. reprint ed. pap. 1.99 *(978-1-4192-4057-7(9))*; pap. 15.95 *(978-1-4191-4057-0(4))* Kessinger Publishing, LLC.

Flack, Sophie. Bunheads. 2012. (ENG.). 320p. (YA). (gr. 7-17). pap. 10.99 *(978-0-316-12654-0(3)*, Poppy) Little, Brown Bks. for Young Readers.

Flinn, Alex. Beastly. (Kendra Chronicles Ser.: 1). (ENG.). (YA). (gr. 9). 2009. 336p. pap. 9.99 *(978-0-06-199866-9(4))* 2007. 320p. 17.99 *(978-0-06-087416-2(3))* 2012. 512p. pap. 9.99 *(978-0-06-211391-7(7))* 2011. 336p. pap. 9.99 *(978-0-06-196328-5(3))* HarperCollins Pubs. (HarperTeen).

Forman, Gayle. Where She Went. l.t. ed. 2015. (If I Stay Ser.: BK.2). (ENG.). 288p. (YA). 23.99 *(978-1-4104-7562-6(X))* Cengage Gale.

—Where She Went. (If I Stay Ser.: BK.2). (ENG.). (YA). (gr. 9-18). 2012. 304p. 10.99 *(978-0-14-242089-8(1)*, Speak) 2011. 272p. 17.99 *(978-0-525-42294-5(3)*, Dutton Books for Young Readers) Penguin Young Readers Group.

—Where She Went. 2012. (If I Stay Ser.: BK.2). (YA). 21.00 *(978-1-61383-394-0(6))* Perfection Learning Corp.

—Where She Went. l.t. ed. 2015. (If I Stay Ser.: BK.2). (ENG.). 286p. (YA). pap. 12.99 *(978-1-59413-855-3(9)*, Large Print Pr.) Thorndike Pr.

—Where She Went. 2012. (If I Stay Ser.: BK.2). (YA). lib. bdg. 22.10 *(978-0-606-23644-7(9)*, Turtleback) Turtleback Bks.

Forsberg, Victoria. Little Irma Shirley & the Wand of Better: City Adventures. 2013. (ENG.). 23p. (J). pap. 10.95 *(978-1-4327-9671-6(2))* Outskirts Pr., Inc.

Fox, Erin. A Butterfly's Dream. 2012. 16p. pap. 12.68 *(978-1-4669-2066-8(1))* Trafford Publishing.

Fox, Janet. Sirens. 2012. (ENG.). 384p. (YA). (gr. 7). pap. 9.99 *(978-0-14-242430-8(7)*, Speak) Penguin Young Readers Group.

Frank, Lucy. Just Ask Iris. 2003. (ENG., Illus.). 224p. (J). (gr. 5-9). pap. 10.99 *(978-0-689-84454-6(9)*, Atheneum Bks. for Young Readers) Simon & Schuster Children's Publishing.

—Lucky Stars. 2014. (ENG.). 304p. (J). (gr. 5-9). pap. 14.99 *(978-1-4814-2901-6(9)*, Atheneum Bks. for Young Readers) Simon & Schuster Children's Publishing.

Fredericks, Mariah. Life. Watkins, Liselotte, illus. 2009. (In the Cards Ser.: No. 3). (ENG.). 272p. (J). pap. 5.99 *(978-0-689-87659-2(9)*, Simon & Schuster/Paula Wiseman Bks.) Simon & Schuster/Paula Wiseman Bks.

Freedman, Paula J. My Basmati Bat Mitzvah. 2013. (ENG., Illus.). 256p. (YA). (gr. 3-7). 17.95 *(978-1-4197-0806-0(6)*, Amulet Bks.) Abrams, Inc.

Frenette, Liza. Dead End. Gillis, Jane, illus. 2005. x, 65p. (J). *(978-1-59531-001-9(0))* North Country Bks., Inc.

Freymann-Weyr, Garret. Stay with Me. 2007. (ENG.). 320p. (YA). (gr. 9-12). pap. 8.99 *(978-0-618-88404-9(1))* Houghton Mifflin Harcourt Publishing Co.

Friedman, Aimee. Two Summers. 2016. (ENG.). 368p. (J). (gr. 7). 17.99 *(978-0-545-51807-9(5))* Scholastic, Inc.

Friedman, Laurie. Mallory & Mary Ann Take New York. Kalis, Jennifer, illus. (Mallory Ser.: 19). (ENG.). 160p. (J). (gr. 2-5). 2014. pap. 5.95 *(978-1-4677-0935-4(2)*, Darby Creek) 2013. 15.95 *(978-0-7613-6074-2(3))* Lerner Publishing Group.

Frossard, Claire, illus. Emma's Journey. Frossard, Etienne, photos by. 2010. (ENG.). 56p. (J). (gr. -1-3). 17.95 *(978-1-59270-099-8(3))* Enchanted Lion Bks., LLC.

Fyne, Olga M. Be Satisfied with Who You Are. Mathis, Leslie, illus. 2013. 24p. pap. 9.99 *(978-1-61286-142-5(3))* Avid Readers Publishing Group.

Gallo, Tina. Behold the Power of Gargamel! Riley, Kellee, illus. 2011. (Smurfs Movie Ser.). (ENG.). 24p. (J). (gr. -1-3). pap. 6.99 *(978-1-4424-2395-4(1)*, Simon Spotlight) Simon Spotlight.

Galvin, Larry J. The Pythagoras Solution. 2008. 102p. pap. 19.95 *(978-1-60441-990-0(3))* America Star Bks.

Gamble, Adam. Buenas Noches, Nueva York. Veno, Joe & Jasper, Mark, illus. 2013. (Buenas Noches Ser.). (SPA & ENG.). 24p. (J). (— 1). bds. 9.95 *(978-1-60219-091-7(7))* Good Night Bks.

Ganeshram, Ramin. Stir It Up! 2011. (J). *(978-0-545-16583-9(0))*; (ENG.). 176p. (gr. 5-9). 16.99 *(978-0-545-16582-2(2)*, Scholastic Pr.) Scholastic, Inc.

George, Jean Craighead. Frightful's Mountain. 2014. (ENG.). 272p. (J). (gr. 4-8). 11.24 *(978-1-63245-351-8(7))* Lectorum Pubns., Inc.

Giuliani, Al. New Nanny. 2013. (Jessie Junior Novel Ser.). (ENG.). 128p. (J). (gr. 3-7). pap. 5.99 *(978-1-4231-8369-3(X))* Disney Pr.

Glasthal, Jacqueline B. Liberty on 23rd Street. Reingold, Alan, illus. 2006. (Adventures in America Ser.). (gr. 4). 14.95 net. *(978-1-893110-45-8(1))* Silver Moon Pr.

Godbersen, Anna. The Lucky Ones. 2013. (Bright Young Things Ser.: 3). (ENG.). 400p. (YA). (gr. 9). pap. 9.99 *(978-0-06-196271-4(6))* HarperCollins Pubs.

—The Luxe, Rumors, & Envy, Set, Bks. 1-3. 2009. (Luxe Ser.). (YA). (gr. 9). pap. 24.99 *(978-0-06-192116-6(1))* HarperCollins Pubs.

Goerzen, Christy. The Big Apple Effect, 1 vol. 2014. (Orca Currents Ser.). (ENG.). 136p. (J). (gr. 5-9). pap. 9.95 *(978-1-4598-0738-9(3))* Orca Bk. Pubs. USA.

Going, K. L. Fat Kid Rules the World. 2004. (ENG.). 224p. (YA). (gr. 7-18). reprint ed. pap. 9.99 *(978-0-14-240208-5(7)*, Speak) Penguin Young Readers Group.

Gold, Maya & Fitzhugh, Louise. Harriet the Spy, Double Agent. 2007. (Harriet the Spy Adventures Ser.). (ENG.). 160p. (J). (gr. 3-7). 6.99 *(978-0-440-41691-3(4)*, Yearling) Random Hse. Children's Bks.

Goldberg, Whoopi. Sugar Plum to the Rescue! Roos, Maryn, illus. 2011. (ENG.). 160p. (J). (gr. 1-5). pap. 4.99 *(978-0-7868-5264-2(X)*, Jump at the Sun) Hyperion Bks. for Children.

Goldblatt, Mark. Twerp. 2013. (ENG.). 288p. (J). (gr. 4-7). 16.99 *(978-0-375-97142-6(4)*, Random Hse. Bks. for Young Readers) Random Hse. Children's Bks.

Goldman, Leslie & Trenc, Milan. Night at the Museum. 2006. (ENG., Illus.). 144p. (J). (gr. 3-7). per. 4.99 *(978-0-7641-3576-7(7))* Barron's Educational Series, Inc.

González, Lucía. The Storyteller's Candle: La Velita de Los Cuentos. Delacre, Lulu, illus. 2013. (ENG & SPA.). 32p. (J). pap. 9.95 *(978-0-89239-237-7(1)*, Children's Book Press) Lee & Low Bks., Inc.

Gonzalez, Lucia M. & Delacre, Lulu. The Storyteller's Candle. 2008.Tr. of La Velita de los Cuentos. (SPA & ENG., Illus.). 32p. (J). (gr. k-4). 16.95 *(978-0-89239-222-3(3))* Lee & Low Bks., Inc.

Goodman, Carol. Blythewood. 2014. (Blythewood Novel Ser.). (ENG.). 512p. (YA). (gr. 7). pap. 9.99 *(978-0-14-242251-9(7)*, Speak) Penguin Young Readers Group.

Gordon, Fran & Tischler, Faye. Dutch Double. 2007. (Illus.). 88p. pap. 15.95 *(978-1-59299-242-3(0))* Inkwater Pr.

Gordon, Gus. Herman & Rosie. Gordon, Gus, illus. 2013. (ENG., Illus.). 32p. (J). (gr. 2-5). 17.99 *(978-1-59643-856-9(8)*, 9781596438569) Roaring Brook Pr.

Gownley, Jimmy. Amelia in Joy & Wonder, 1 vol. 2013. (Amelia Rules! Set 2 Ser.). (ENG.). 36p. (J). (gr. 3-6). 24.21 *(978-1-61479-072-3(8))* Spotlight.

Grace, N. B. Rev It Up! 9th ed. 2010. (Wizards of Waverly Place Ser.: No. 9). 128p. (J). (gr. 3-7). pap. 4.99 *(978-1-4231-2676-8(9))* Disney Pr.

Graff, Lisa. Absolutely Almost. 2014. (ENG.). 304p. (J). (gr. 3-7). 16.99 *(978-0-399-16405-7(7)*, Philomel Bks.) Penguin Young Readers Group.

—A Tangle of Knots. 2013. (ENG.). 240p. (J). (gr. 3-7). 16.99 *(978-0-399-25517-5(6)*, Philomel Bks.) Penguin Young Readers Group.

Grambling, Lois G. Can I Bring Saber to New York, Ms. Mayor? Love, Judy, illus. 2014. (Prehistoric Pets Ser.). (ENG.). 32p. (J). (gr. k-3). 17.95 *(978-1-58089-570-5(0))* Charlesbridge Publishing, Inc.

Grant, Natalie. Light up New York, 1 vol. 2017. (Faithgirlz / Glimmer Girls Ser.). (ENG.). 208p. (J). pap. 8.99 *(978-0-310-75274-5(4))* Zonderkidz.

Green, Tim. Football Hero. (Football Genius Ser.: 2). (ENG.). (J). (gr. 3-7). 2009. 320p. pap. 6.99 *(978-0-06-112276-7(9))* 2008. (Illus.). 304p. 16.99 *(978-0-06-112274-3(2))* HarperCollins Pubs.

—Football Hero. l.t. ed. 2008. (YA). 23.95 *(978-1-4104-1116-7(8))* Thorndike Pr.

—Rivals: A Baseball Great Novel. (Baseball Great Ser.: 2). (ENG.). (J). (gr. 3-7). 2011. 288p. pap. 6.99 *(978-0-06-162694-4(5))* 2010. 272p. 16.99 *(978-0-06-162692-0(9))* HarperCollins Pubs.

Greenburg, Dan. How I Went from Bad to Verse. Davis, Jack E., illus. 2004. (Zack Files Ser.). 59p. lib. bdg. 15.00 *(978-0-7569-2235-1(6))* Perfection Learning Corp.

Griffin, Adele. The Knaveheart's Curse. 2009. (Vampire Island Ser.). (ENG.). 160p. (J). (gr. 3-7). 6.99 *(978-0-14-241407-1(7)*, Puffin Books) Penguin Young Readers Group.

—The Unfinished Life of Addison Stone: A Novel. 2016. (ENG., Illus.). 256p. (YA). (gr. 9). pap. 11.99 *(978-1-61695-596-0(1)*, Soho Teen) Soho Pr., Inc.

Griffin, Paul. The Orange Houses. 2011. (ENG.). 176p. (YA). (gr. 9-18). 8.99 *(978-0-14-241982-3(6)*, Speak) Penguin Young Readers Group.

—Ten Mile River. 2011. (ENG.). 208p. (YA). (gr. 7-18). 7.99 *(978-0-14-241983-0(4)*, Speak) Penguin Young Readers Group.

Grimes, Nikki. Bronx Masquerade. (ENG.). (YA). (gr. 7). 2017. 192p. pap. 8.99 ***(978-0-425-28976-1(1))*** 2003. 176p. 6.99 *(978-0-14-250189-4(1))* Penguin Young Readers Group. (Speak).

—Bronx Masquerade. 2003. (gr. 7-12). lib. bdg. 17.20 *(978-0-613-81701-1(X)*, Turtleback) Turtleback Bks.

Gromosiak, Paul. Owahonton: Maid of the Mist. 2012. (ENG.). (J). pap. 12.95 *(978-1-4675-4107-7(9))* Independent Pub.

Grossinger, Tania. Jackie & Me: A Very Special Friendship. Esperanza, Charles George, illus. 2013. (ENG.). 32p. (J). (gr. -1-3). 16.95 *(978-1-62087-683-1(3)*, 620683, Sky Pony Pr.) Skyhorse Publishing Co., Inc.

Gulledge, Laura Lee. Page by Paige. 2011. (ENG., Illus.). 192p. (YA). (gr. 7-17). 18.95 *(978-0-8109-9721-9(5))*; pap. 9.95 *(978-0-8109-9722-6(3))* Abrams, Inc. (Amulet Bks.).

Gunther, Joseph. The Bluff, 1. Sabiston, Susan, illus. l.t. ed. 2006. 28p. (J). 14.95 *(978-0-9789525-0-1(2))* Young Readers Publications.

Gurevich, Margaret. Balancing ACT. Hagel, Brooke, illus. 2015. (Chloe by Design Ser.). (ENG.). 384p. (gr. 4-8). 14.95 *(978-1-62370-258-8(5))* Capstone Young Readers of Coughlan Cos.

—Design Destiny, 1 vol. Hagel, Brooke, illus. 2014. (Chloe by Design Ser.). (ENG.). 96p. (gr. 5-8). 25.32 *(978-1-4342-9180-6(4))* Stone Arch Bks.

—Design Disaster. Hagel, Brooke, illus. 2015. (Chloe by Design Ser.). (ENG.). 96p. (gr. 5-8). 25.32 *(978-1-4965-0505-7(0))* Stone Arch Bks.

—Fashion Week Finale. Hagel, Brooke, illus. 2015. (Chloe by Design Ser.). (ENG.). 96p. (gr. 5-8). 25.32 *(978-1-4965-0507-1(7))* Stone Arch Bks.

—Intern Ambition. Hagel, Brooke, illus. 2015. (Chloe by Design Ser.). (ENG.). 96p. (gr. 5-8). 25.32 *(978-1-4965-0504-0(2))* Stone Arch Bks.

—Runway Rundown. Hagel, Brooke, illus. 2015. (Chloe by Design Ser.). (ENG.). 96p. (gr. 5-8). 25.32 *(978-1-4965-0506-4(9))* Stone Arch Bks.

—Unraveling, 1 vol. Hagel, Brooke, illus. 2014. (Chloe by Design Ser.). (ENG.). 96p. (gr. 5-8). 25.32 *(978-1-4342-9179-0(0))* Stone Arch Bks.

Gutman, Dan. Willie & Me. 2015. (Baseball Card Adventures Ser.: 12). (ENG.). 176p. (J). (gr. 3-7). 16.99 *(978-0-06-170404-8(0))* HarperCollins Pubs.

Hall, Bruce Edward & Hall, Bruce. Henry & the Kite Dragon. Low, William, tr. Low, William, illus. 2004. (ENG.). 40p. (J). (gr. 1-4). 17.99 *(978-0-399-23727-0(5)*, Philomel Bks.) Penguin Young Readers Group.

Hamilton, Rachel. Louie Lets Loose! (Unicorn in New York #1) 2017. (Unicorn in New York Ser.: 1). (ENG.). 128p. (J). (gr. 2-5). pap. 4.99 ***(978-1-338-05508-5(9)***, Scholastic Paperbacks) Scholastic, Inc.

—Louie Takes the Stage! (Unicorn in New York #2) 2017. (Unicorn in New York Ser.: 2). (ENG.). 128p. (J). (gr. 2-5). pap. 4.99 ***(978-1-338-05512-2(7)***, Scholastic Paperbacks) Scholastic, Inc.

Hansen, Joyce. One True Friend. Giblin, James Cross, ed. 2005. (ENG.). 160p. (J). (gr. 5-7). pap. 11.95 *(978-0-618-60991-8(1))* Houghton Mifflin Harcourt Publishing Co.

Hapka, Catherine, pseud & Bloomberg, Georgina. My Favorite Mistake: An a Circuit Novel. 2012. (a Circuit Ser.). (ENG.). 256p. (YA). pap. 9.99 *(978-1-59990-642-3(2)*, 9781599906423, Bloomsbury USA Childrens) Bloomsbury Publishing USA.

Harden, Perry Lee. The Percy Hargrove Stories: It's All Elementary. 2012. 160p. pap. 14.95 *(978-1-4772-2438-0(6))* AuthorHouse.

Harkins, Philip. Knockout. 2011. 250p. 46.95 *(978-1-258-08794-4(4))* Literary Licensing, LLC.

Harper, Suzanne. The Secret Life of Sparrow Delaney. (YA). 2008. (ENG.). 368p. (gr. 8-12). pap. 8.99 *(978-0-06-113160-8(1)*, Greenwillow Bks.) 2007. 224p. (gr. 7-12). 16.99 *(978-0-06-113158-5(X))* 2007. 362p. (gr. 7-12). lib. bdg. 17.89 *(978-0-06-113159-2(8))* HarperCollins Pubs.

Harris, Isobel. Little Boy Brown. François, André, illus. 2013. (ENG.). 48p. (J). (gr. -1-3). 15.95 *(978-1-59270-135-3(3))* Enchanted Lion Bks., LLC.

Harrison, Lisi. Bratfest at Tiffany's, No. 9. 2008. (Clique Ser.: 9). (ENG., Illus.). 256p. (YA). (gr. 7-17). per. 9.99 *(978-0-316-00680-4(7)*, Poppy) Little, Brown Bks. for Young Readers.

—Charmed & Dangerous: The Clique Prequel. 2012. (Clique Ser.). (ENG.). 208p. (YA). (gr. 7-17). pap. 8.99 *(978-0-316-05536-9(0)*, Poppy) Little, Brown Bks. for Young Readers.

—Dial L for Loser. 2006. (Clique Ser.: 6). (ENG.). 272p. (J). (gr. 7-17). per. 9.99 *(978-0-316-11504-9(5)*, Poppy) Little, Brown Bks. for Young Readers.

—Dial L for Loser. 2008. (Clique Novels Ser.). 268p. 20.00 *(978-1-60686-291-9(X))* Perfection Learning Corp.

—It's Not Easy Being Mean, No. 7. rev. ed. 2007. (Clique Ser.: 7). (ENG.). 224p. (J). (gr. 7-17). per. 9.99 *(978-0-316-11505-6(3)*, Poppy) Little, Brown Bks. for Young Readers.

—It's Not Easy Being Mean. 2008. (Clique Ser.). 193p. 20.00 *(978-1-60686-330-5(4))* Perfection Learning Corp.

—The Pretty Committee Strikes Back, No. 5. 2006. (Clique Ser.: 5). (ENG.). 272p. (J). (gr. 7-17). per. 9.99 *(978-0-316-11500-1(2)*, Poppy) Little, Brown Bks. for Young Readers.

—Sealed with a Diss. 2007. (Clique Ser.: 8). (ENG.). 272p. (YA). (gr. 7-17). pap. 9.99 *(978-0-316-11506-3(1)*, Poppy) Little, Brown Bks. for Young Readers.

—Sealed with a Diss. 2008. (Clique Novels Ser.). 248p. 20.00 *(978-1-60686-345-9(2))* Perfection Learning Corp.

—A Tale of Two Pretties. 2011. (Clique Ser.: 14). (ENG.). 224p. (YA). (gr. 7-17). pap. 9.99 *(978-0-316-08442-0(5)*, Poppy) Little, Brown Bks. for Young Readers.

—These Boots Are Made for Stalking. 12th ed. 2010. (Clique Ser.: 12). (ENG.). 256p. (YA). (gr. 7-17). pap. 9.99 *(978-0-316-00683-5(1)*, Poppy) Little, Brown Bks. for Young Readers.

Haseley, Dennis. The Invisible Moose. Kellogg, Steven, illus. 2008. (ENG.). 40p. (J). (gr. -1-3). pap. 6.99 *(978-0-14-241066-0(7)*, Puffin Books) Penguin Young Readers Group.

Hawkes, Kevin. The Wicked Big Toddlah Goes to New York. 2011. (ENG., Illus.). 40p. (J). (gr. -1-2). 16.99 *(978-0-375-86188-8(2)*, Knopf Bks. for Young Readers) Random Hse. Children's Bks.

Haydu, Corey Ann. The Careful Undressing of Love. 2017. (ENG.). 288p. (YA). (gr. 9). 17.99 *(978-0-399-18673-8(5)*, Dutton Books for Young Readers) Penguin Young Readers Group.

—Making Pretty. 2015. (ENG.). 368p. (YA). (gr. 9). 17.99 *(978-0-06-229408-1(3)*, Tegen, Katherine Bks) HarperCollins Pubs.

Hazen, Lynn E. The Amazing Trail of Seymour Snail. Cushman, Doug, illus. 2009. (ENG.). 64p. (J). (gr. 1-4). 16.99 *(978-0-8050-8698-0(6)*, 9780805086980, Holt, Henry & Co. Bks. For Young Readers) Holt, Henry & Co.

Heasley, Gwendolyn. A Long Way from You. 2012. (Where I Belong Ser.: 2). (ENG.). 336p. (YA). (gr. 8). pap. 8.99 *(978-0-06-197885-2(X)*, HarperTeen) HarperCollins Pubs.

Helfand, Lewis. Photo Booth. Nagar, Sachin, illus. 2011. (Campfire Graphic Novels Ser.). (ENG.). 80p. (YA). (gr. 3-7). pap. 9.99 *(978-93-80028-65-1(2)*, Campfire) Steerforth Pr.

Henry, O. One Thousand Dollars & Other Plays, Level 2. Oxford University Press Staff & West, Clare, eds. 2nd ed. 2008. (ENG., Illus.). 64p. 9.38 *(978-0-19-423520-4(3))* Oxford Univ. Pr., Inc.

Herren, Greg. Lake Thirteen. 2013. (ENG.). 264p. (gr. 7). pap. 11.95 *(978-1-60282-894-0(6))* Bold Strokes Bks.

Herrera, Juan Felipe. Cinnamon Girl: Letters Found Inside a Cereal Box. 2016. 176p. (YA). (gr. 8). pap. 9.99 *(978-0-06-244759-3(9)*, HarperTeen) HarperCollins Pubs.

Hesse, Karen. Brooklyn Bridge. Sheban, Chris, illus. 2011. (ENG.). 256p. (J). (gr. 5-9). pap. 9.99 *(978-0-312-67428-1(7)*, 9780312674281) Square Fish.

Hest, Amy. Remembering Mrs. Rossi. Maione, Heather, illus. 2007. (ENG.). 192p. (J). (gr. 3-7). 14.99 *(978-0-7636-2163-6(3))* Candlewick Pr.

—Remembering Mrs. Rossi. Maione, Heather, illus. 2010. (ENG.). 192p. (J). (gr. 3-7). 6.99 *(978-0-7636-4089-7(1))* Candlewick Pr.

Hieber, Leanna Renee. Darker Still. 2011. (Magic Most Foul Ser.: 1). (ENG.). 336p. (YA). (gr. 7-12). pap. 8.99 *(978-1-4022-6052-0(0))* Sourcebooks, Inc.

Holm, M. S. How Mohammed Saved Miss Liberty: The Story of a Good Muslim Boy. 2008. (ENG., Illus.). 270p. (YA). (gr. 7-12). pap. 12.00 *(978-0-9796199-0-8(4)*, Sentry Bks.) Great West Publishing.

Hope, Laura Lee. The Bobbsey Twins in a Great City. 2005. 27.95 *(978-1-4218-1482-7(X))*; 204p. pap. 12.95 *(978-1-4218-1582-4(6))* 1st World Publishing, Inc. (1st World Library - Literary Society).

—The Outdoor Girls of Deepdale. 2005. 180p. pap. 11.95 *(978-1-4218-1164-2(2)*, 1st World Library - Literary Society) 1st World Publishing, Inc.

Hopkinson, Deborah. Sky Boys: How They Built the Empire State Building. Ransome, James E., illus. 2012. (ENG.). 48p. (J). (gr. -1-3). pap. 7.99 *(978-0-375-86541-1(1)*, Dragonfly Bks.) Random Hse. Children's Bks.

Horender, Philip M. A Brave New Mouse: Ellis Island Approved Immigrant, 1 vol. Wolek, Guy, illus. 2013. (Maximilian P. Mouse, Time Traveler Ser.). (ENG.). 112p. (J). (gr. 3-6). lib. bdg. 27.07 *(978-1-61641-961-5(X)*, Calico Chapter Bks) Magic Wagon.

Howard, J. J. That Time I Joined the Circus. 2013. (ENG.). 272p. (J). (gr. 7). 17.99 *(978-0-545-43381-5(9))* Scholastic, Inc.

Howe, Katherine. The Appearance of Annie Van Sinderen. 2015. (ENG.). 400p. (YA). (gr. 7). 18.99 *(978-0-399-16778-2(1)*, G.P. Putnam's Sons Books for Young Readers) Penguin Young Readers Group.

Howe, Peter. Waggit Forever. Rayyan, Omar, illus. (Waggit Ser.: 3). (ENG.). (J). (gr. 5). 2011. 288p. pap. 6.99 *(978-0-06-176516-2(3))* 2010. 272p. 16.99 *(978-0-06-176517-9(1))* HarperCollins Pubs.

Howells, Amanda. The Summer of Skinny Dipping. 2010. (ENG.). 304p. (YA). (gr. 7-12). pap. 9.99 *(978-1-4022-3862-8(2)*, Sourcebooks Jabberwocky) Sourcebooks, Inc.

Hughes, Cheryl. Jackson, the Pigeon Who Was Afraid of Heights. 2008. 44p. pap. 16.99 *(978-1-4389-2143-3(8))* AuthorHouse.

Hull, Norman. Robin's Big Brother. 2011. 56p. (gr. 4-6). pap. 9.99 *(978-1-4634-3691-9(2))* AuthorHouse.

Hyde, Catherine Ryan. Becoming Chloe. 2008. (ENG.). 224p. (YA). (gr. 9). pap. 8.99 *(978-0-375-83260-4(2)*, Knopf Bks. for Young Readers) Random Hse. Children's Bks.

Hyde, Heidi Smith. Feivel's Flying Horses. van der Sterre, Johanna, illus. 2010. (ENG.). 32p. (J). (gr. k-4). lib. bdg. 17.95 *(978-0-7613-3957-1(4))*; pap. 7.95 *(978-0-7613-3959-5(0))* Lerner Publishing Group. (Kar-Ben Publishing).

Iacovone, Lauren Marie. Here Lies Thomas Crawford, 1 vol. 2010. 252p. pap. 27.95 *(978-1-61582-690-2(4))* America Star Bks.

Jablonski, Carla. Thicker Than Water. 2007. (ENG.). 272p. (YA). (gr. 9-12). 8.99 *(978-1-59514-123-1(5)*, Razorbill) Penguin Young Readers Group.

—The Travelers, Bk. 1. 2009. (Pendragon: Before the War Ser.: 1). (ENG.). 256p. (J). (gr. 5-9). pap. 7.99 *(978-1-4169-6522-0(X)*, Aladdin) Simon & Schuster Children's Publishing.

Jacobs, Lily. The Littlest Bunny in Buffalo. Dunn, Robert, illus. 2016. (ENG.). 32p. (J). (-7). 9.99 *(978-1-4926-3346-4(1)*, 9781492633464, Sourcebooks Jabberwocky) Sourcebooks, Inc.

—The Littlest Bunny in New York: An Easter Adventure. Dunn, Robert, illus. 2015. (ENG.). 32p. (J). (-3). 9.99 *(978-1-4926-1150-9(6)*, Sourcebooks Jabberwocky) Sourcebooks, Inc.

—The Littlest Bunny in New York City: An Easter Adventure. Dunn, Robert, illus. 2015. (ENG.). 32p. (J). (-3). 9.99 *(978-1-4926-1153-0(0)*, Sourcebooks Jabberwocky) Sourcebooks, Inc.

Jacobs, Paul DuBois & Swender, Jennifer. Count on the Subway. Yaccarino, Dan, illus. 2014. (ENG.). 32p. (J). (-k). 14.99 *(978-0-307-97923-0(7))*; lib. bdg. 17.99 *(978-0-307-97924-7(5))* Random Hse. Children's Bks. (Knopf Bks. for Young Readers).

—My Subway Ride, 1 vol. Alko, Selina, illus. 2004. (ENG.). 32p. (J). (gr. 2-3). 15.99 *(978-1-58685-357-0(0))* Gibbs Smith, Publisher.

Jahn-Clough, Lisa. Country Girl, City Girl. 2009. (ENG.). 192p. (YA). (gr. 7). pap. 12.95 *(978-0-547-22322-3(6))* Houghton Mifflin Harcourt Publishing Co.

James, Eric. A Halloween Scare in New York. Le Ray, Marina, illus. 2014. (ENG.). 32p. (J). (-5). 9.99 *(978-1-4926-0621-5(9)*, 9781492606215, Sourcebooks Jabberwocky) Sourcebooks, Inc.

—A Halloween Scare in New York City. Le Ray, Marina, illus. 2015. (ENG.). 32p. (J). (-5). 9.99 *(978-1-4926-2389-2(X)*, 9781492623892, Sourcebooks Jabberwocky) Sourcebooks, Inc.

—Santa's Sleigh Is on Its Way to New York. Dunn, Robert, illus. 2015. (ENG.). 32p. (J). (-2). 12.99 *(978-1-4926-2751-7(8)*, Sourcebooks Jabberwocky) Sourcebooks, Inc.

—Santa's Sleigh Is on Its Way to New York City: A Christmas Adventure. Dunn, Robert, illus. 2016. (ENG.). 32p. (J). (-2). 12.99 *(978-1-4926-4344-9(0)*, 9781492643449, Sourcebooks Jabberwocky) Sourcebooks, Inc.

James, Henry. Washington Square. 2004. (gr. 7-12). reprint ed. pap. *(978-0-87720-743-6(7)*, N387ALS) AMSCO Schl. Pubns., Inc.

Jane, Pamela. Winky Blue Goes Wild! Tilley, Debbie, illus. 2003. 64p. (J). 13.95 *(978-1-59034-588-7(6))*; pap. *(978-1-59034-589-4(4))* Mondo Publishing.

Jean, April. A Little Dachshund's Tale. Cross, Kevin, illus. 2012. 36p. pap. 9.95 *(978-1-61897-367-2(3)*, Strategic Bk. Publishing) Strategic Book Publishing & Rights Agency (SBPRA).

Jeremiah, Omari. Paper Boy Four: L. O. E. P. S. Worst Nightmare. Rollins, Berni, illus. 2007. 96p. (YA). (gr. 7-12). pap. 12.99 *(978-1-929188-15-4(3))* Morton Bks.

Johnson, Harvell. What about Johnson? Howard, Vanetta, ed. Clark, Donna Osborn, illus. 2013. 132p. pap. 11.95 *(978-0-9885056-0-5(6))* Word on Da Street Publishing.

Johnson, Maureen. Scarlett Fever. (ENG.). 352p. (J). (gr. 7-7). 2011. pap. 9.99 *(978-0-545-09633-1(2))* 2010. 16.99 *(978-0-439-89928-4(1))* Scholastic, Inc.

—Suite Scarlett. 2009. (ENG.). 368p. (J). (gr. 3-7). 8.99 *(978-0-545-09632-4(4))* Scholastic, Inc.

Jones, Patrick. The Gamble. 2014. (Bareknuckle Ser.). 104p. (YA). (gr. 6-12). lib. bdg. 27.93 *(978-1-4677-1462-4(3)*, Darby Creek) Lerner Publishing Group.

Joseph, Lynn. Flowers in the Sky. 2013. (ENG.). 240p. (YA). (gr. 8). 17.99 *(978-0-06-029794-7(8)*, HarperTeen) HarperCollins Pubs.

Jules, Jacqueline. Freddie Ramos Rules New York. Benítez, Miguel, illus. 2016. (Zapato Power Ser.: 6). (ENG.). 96p. (J). (gr. 1-5). 14.99 *(978-0-8075-9497-1(0))* Whitman, Albert & Co.

Kaldor, Connie. A Duck in New York City. Fil and Julie Staff, illus. 2005. (ENG.). 36p. (J). (gr. -1-2). 16.95 *(978-2-923163-02-4(8))* La Montagne Secrete CAN. Dist: Independent Pubs. Group.

Kalman, Maira. Max Makes a Million. 2017. (ENG., Illus.). 48p. (J). (gr. k-3). 18.95 ***(978-1-68137-170-2(7)***, NYR Children's Collection) New York Review of Bks., Inc., The.

Kantor, Melissa. If I Have a Wicked Stepmother, Where's My Prince? 2005. 283p. (YA). *(978-1-4156-2763-1(0))* Hyperion Pr.

Karasyov, Carrie & Kargman, Jill. Summer Intern. 2007. 184p. (YA). (gr. 7-18). lib. bdg. 17.89 *(978-0-06-115376-1(1)*, HarperTeen) HarperCollins Pubs.

Kargman, Jill & Karasyov, Carrie. Bittersweet Sixteen. 2006. (YA). (gr. 7-12). (ENG.). 240p. 15.99 *(978-0-06-077844-6(X))*; 230p. lib. bdg. 16.89 *(978-0-06-077845-3(8))* HarperCollins Pubs.

Kaye, Marilyn. Gloss. unabr. ed. 2015. (Gloss Ser.: 1). (ENG.). 400p. (YA). (gr. 7). pap. 9.99 *(978-1-4472-2397-9(7))* Pan Macmillan GBR. Dist: Independent Pubs. Group.

—Gloss - Summer Scandal, No. 2. 2015. (Gloss Ser.: 2). (ENG.). 336p. (YA). (gr. 7). pap. 9.99 *(978-1-4472-2399-3(3))* Pan Macmillan GBR. Dist: Independent Pubs. Group.

Kearney, Meg. When You Never Said Goodbye: An Adoptee's Search for Her Birth Mother. 2017. (ENG.). 224p. (YA). (gr. 9-17). 17.95 *(978-0-89255-479-9(7)*, 255479) Persea Bks., Inc.

Kebbi, Yann. Americanine: A Haute Dog in New York. 2015. (ENG., Illus.). 72p. (J). 19.95 *(978-1-59270-172-8(8))* Enchanted Lion Bks., LLC.

Kelley, Jane. The Book of Dares for Lost Friends. 2015. (ENG.). 304p. (J). (gr. 3-7). 16.99 *(978-1-250-05087-8(1)*, 9781250050878) Feiwel & Friends.

Kelman, Jennifer. Mrs Pinkelmeyer & Moopus Mcglinden Prance into New York City. 2011. 44p. pap. 15.99 *(978-1-4575-0497-6(9))* Dog Ear Publishing, LLC.

Kennedy, C. Omorphi. Girault, Bénédicte, tr. 2016. (ENG., Illus.). (J). 34.99 ***(978-1-63533-055-7(6)***, Harmony Ink Pr.) Dreamspinner Pr.

Kent, Rose. Rocky Road. 2012. (ENG.). 304p. (J). (gr. 3-7). 7.99 *(978-0-375-86345-5(1)*, Yearling) Random Hse. Children's Bks.

Kern, Peggy. Little Peach. 2015. (ENG.). 208p. (YA). (gr. 9). 17.99 *(978-0-06-226695-8(0))* HarperCollins Pubs.

Keyes, Joseph W. The Sparrows of Saint Thomas. 2007. 92p. pap. 14.95 *(978-1-4303-1410-3(9))* Lulu Pr., Inc.

Kiem, Elizabeth. Hider, Seeker, Secret Keeper. 2017. (Bolshoi Saga Ser.: 2). (ENG., Illus.). 272p. (YA). (gr. 9). pap. 10.99 *(978-1-61695-569-4(4)*, Soho Teen) Soho Pr., Inc.

Kiernan, Patrick. Good Morning, City. Campion, Pascal, illus. 2016. (ENG.). 32p. (J). 16.99 *(978-0-374-30346-4(0)*, 9780374303464, Farrar, Straus & Giroux (BYR)) Farrar, Straus & Giroux.

Kimmel, Elizabeth Cody. Secret of the Mountain Dog. 2014. (ENG.). 208p. (J). (gr. 3-7). 16.99 *(978-0-545-60369-0(2)*, Scholastic Pr.) Scholastic, Inc.

—Stories from New York, No. 3. Mingus, Cathi, illus. 2012. (Forever Four Ser.: 3). (ENG.). 208p. (J). (gr. 3-7). pap. 6.99 *(978-0-448-45550-1(1)*, Grosset & Dunlap) Penguin Young Readers Group.

Kingsley, Kate. Pretty on the Outside. 2010. (Young, Loaded, & Fabulous Ser.: 1). (ENG.). 320p. (YA). (gr. 9-18). pap. 9.99 *(978-1-4169-9399-5(1)*, Simon Pulse) Simon Pulse.

Kirby, Matthew J. Last Descendants. 2016. (Last Descendants Ser.: 1). (ENG.). 320p. (J). (gr. 7). pap. 9.99 *(978-0-545-85551-8(9))* Scholastic, Inc.

Kirk, Connie Ann. Sky Dancers, 1 vol. Hale, Christy, illus. 2013. (ENG.). 32p. (J). (gr. 2-4). pap. 8.95 *(978-1-62014-147-2(7))* Lee & Low Bks., Inc.

Klass, David. Grandmaster. 2014. (ENG.). 240p. (YA). (gr. 7). 16.99 *(978-0-374-32771-2(8)*, 9780374327712, Farrar, Straus & Giroux (BYR)) Farrar, Straus & Giroux.

Klepeis, Alicia. Cairo, Camels, & Chaos. 2015. (ENG.). 96p. (gr. 3-6). 31.36 *(978-1-63430-397-2(0))* Rourke Educational Media.

Kloepfer, John. Empire State of Slime. DeGrand, Ned & DeGrand, David, illus. 2013. (Zombie Chasers Ser.: 4). (ENG.). 208p. (J). (gr. 3-7). 16.99 *(978-0-06-223095-9(6))* HarperCollins Pubs.

—Nothing Left to Ooze. DeGrand, David, illus. 2014. (Zombie Chasers Ser.: 5). (ENG.). 240p. (J). (gr. 3-7). pap. 6.99 *(978-0-06-223099-7(9))* HarperCollins Pubs.

Konigsburg, E. L. From the Mixed-up Files of Mrs. Basil E. Frankweiler. 2007. (Illus.). 74p. (J). pap. *(978-0-545-04173-7(2))* Scholastic, Inc.

—From the Mixed-up Files of Mrs. Basil E. Frankweiler. l.t. ed. 2005. 186p. pap. 10.95 *(978-0-7862-7358-4(5)*, Large Print Pr.) Thorndike Pr.

Korman, Gordon. The Hypnotists. (ENG.). 240p. (J). (gr. 3-7). 2013. (Hypnotists Ser.: 1). 16.99 *(978-0-545-50322-8(1)*, Scholastic Pr.)Bk. 1. 2014. pap. 6.99 *(978-0-545-50325-9(6)*, Scholastic Paperbacks) Scholastic, Inc.

—The Hypnotists. 2014. (Hypnotists Ser.: 1). lib. bdg. 17.20 *(978-0-606-35808-8(0))* Turtleback Bks.

Kraulis, Julie. An Armadillo in New York. 2016. (ENG., Illus.). 32p. (J). (gr. k-4). 16.99 *(978-1-77049-891-4(5)*, Tundra Bks.) Tundra Bks. CAN. Dist: Penguin Random Hse. LLC.

Kredensor, Diane. Ollie & Moon in New York City. Meskin, Mike, photos by. 2017. (Pictureback(R) Ser.). (ENG., Illus.). 32p. (J). (gr. -1-2). pap. 5.99 ***(978-1-5247-1574-8(3)***, Random Hse. Bks. for Young Readers) Random Hse. Children's Bks.

Kroll, Steven. Pooch on the Loose: A Christmas Adventure, 0 vols. Garland, Michael, illus. 2013. (ENG.). 40p. (J). (gr. -1-3). pap. 9.99 *(978-0-7614-5443-4(8)*, 9780761454434, Two Lions) Amazon Publishing.

—When I Dream of Heaven: Angelina's Story. 2004. 156p. (J). lib. bdg. 16.92 *(978-1-4242-0770-1(3))* Fitzgerald Bks.

Kroll, Steven & Droll. Pooch on the Loose: A Christmas Adventure, 1 vol. Garland, Michael, illus. 2005. (ENG.). 32p. (J). (gr. -1-3). 14.95 *(978-0-7614-5239-3(7))* Marshall Cavendish Corp.

Krosoczka, Jarrett J. Ollie the Purple Elephant. 2011. (ENG.). 40p. (J). (gr. -1-2). 16.99 *(978-0-375-86654-8(X)*, Knopf Bks. for Young Readers) Random Hse. Children's Bks.

Krovatin, Christopher. Venomous. Yates, Kelly, illus. 2011. (ENG.). 336p. (YA). (gr. 8). pap. 8.99 *(978-1-4424-1298-9(4)*, Atheneum Bks. for Young Readers) Simon & Schuster Children's Publishing.

Krulik, Nancy. Ripped at the Seams. 2004. (Romantic Comedies Ser.). (ENG.). 336p. (YA). (gr. 9). mass mkt. 6.99 *(978-0-689-86771-2(9)*, Simon Pulse) Simon Pulse.

Krulik, Nancy E. Broadway Doggie. 2016. (Magic Bone Ser.: 10). lib. bdg. 14.75 *(978-0-606-38416-2(2))* Turtleback Bks.

Kuhlman, Evan. Brother from a Box. Bruno, Iacopo, illus. (ENG.). 288p. (J). (gr. 4-7). 2013. pap. 6.99 *(978-1-4424-2659-7(4))* 2012. 16.99 *(978-1-4424-2658-0(6))* Simon & Schuster Children's Publishing. (Atheneum Bks. for Young Readers).

Laberje, Reji. Max Explores New York. Fenech, Liza, illus. 2014. (Max Explores Ser.). (ENG.). 20p. (J). (— 1). bds. 9.95 *(978-1-62937-004-0(5))* Triumph Bks.

LaBrot, Matthew & Daniel, Hale. Green Streak. 2004. (Zeke Armstrong Mysteries Ser.: 2). 236p. (J). per. 8.95 *(978-1-929976-28-7(3))* Top Pubns., Ltd.

Lane, Dakota. The Orpheus Obsession. 2008. (ENG., Illus.). 288p. (YA). (gr. 9). pap. 8.99 *(978-0-06-074175-4(9)*, HarperTeen) HarperCollins Pubs.

Lane, Nathan & Elliott, Devlin. Naughty Mabel Sees It All. Krall, Dan, illus. 2016. (Naughty Mabel Ser.). (ENG.). 48p. (J). (gr. -1-3). 17.99 *(978-1-4814-3024-1(6)*, Simon & Schuster Bks. For Young Readers) Simon & Schuster Bks. For Young Readers.

Larbalestier, Justine. Magic's Child. 2007. (Magic or Madness Trilogy). 291p. (YA). *(978-1-4287-3603-0(4)*, Razorbill) Penguin Publishing Group.

Larkin, Jillian. Ingenue. 2012. (Flappers Ser.). (ENG.). 368p. (YA). (gr. 7). pap. 9.99 *(978-0-385-74037-1(9)*, Ember) Random Hse. Children's Bks.

Lavoie, Jennifer. Andy Squared. 2012. (ENG.). 264p. (J). (gr. 7). pap. 11.95 *(978-1-60282-743-1(5))* Bold Strokes Bks.

Law, Jerel. Spirit Fighter, 1 vol. 2012. (Son of Angels, Jonah Stone Ser.). (ENG.). 256p. (J). pap. 9.99 *(978-1-4003-1843-8(2))* Nelson, Thomas Inc.

Lawrence, Theo. Mystic City. (Mystic City Trilogy Ser.). (ENG.). 416p. (YA). (gr. 7). 2014. pap. 9.99 *(978-0-385-74161-3(8)*, Ember) 2012. 17.99 *(978-0-385-74160-6(X)*, Delacorte Pr.) Random Hse. Children's Bks.

—Toxic Heart: a Mystic City Novel. 2015. (Mystic City Trilogy Ser.). (ENG.). 368p. (YA). (gr. 7). pap. 9.99 *(978-0-385-74163-7(4)*, Ember) Random Hse. Children's Bks.

Lawson, Brandi. The Soap Bubble Frog. Kinra, Richa, illus. 2012. 32p. pap. 14.50 *(978-1-61897-784-7(9)*, Strategic Bk. Publishing) Strategic Book Publishing & Rights Agency (SBPRA).

Leblond, Michaël. New York in Pajamarama. Bertrand, Frederique, illus. 2013. (ENG.). 32p. (J). (gr. -1-2). 15.99 *(978-1-907912-23-8(1))* Phoenix Yard Bks. GBR. Dist: Independent Pubs. Group.

Lee, Mary Ellen. Danny & Life on Bluff Point: Blizzard of '95 revised Edition. 2009. 160p. (gr. 4-7). 22.95 *(978-1-4401-1383-3(1))*; pap. 12.95 *(978-0-595-53308-4(6))* iUniverse, Inc.

—Danny & Life on Bluff Point: Lost in the Dark. 2009. 160p. (gr. 4-7). 22.95 *(978-1-4401-4607-7(1))*; pap. 12.95 *(978-1-4401-4608-4(X))* iUniverse, Inc.

Lee, Thomas. The Battle at Otter Lake. 2007. 167p. pap. 24.95 *(978-1-60441-488-2(X))* America Star Bks.

L'Engle, Madeleine. Camilla. 2009. (ENG.). 272p. (YA). (gr. 7-12). pap. 18.99 *(978-0-312-56132-1(6)*, 9780312561321) Square Fish.

—The Young Unicorns. 2008. (Austin Family Ser.: 3). (ENG.). 304p. (J). (gr. 7-12). pap. 11.99 *(978-0-312-37933-9(1)*, 9780312379339) Square Fish.

Lenzi, Danielle E. My Search for Prince Charming's Normal Brother. 2011. 136p. pap. 25.70 *(978-1-4634-0446-8(8))*; (gr. 10-12). 33.70 *(978-1-4634-0445-1(X))* AuthorHouse.

Lerangis, Peter. Wtf. (ENG., (YA). (gr. 9). 2013. Illus.). 288p. 17.99 *(978-1-4424-9369-8(0))* 2013. (Illus.). 288p. pap. 9.99 *(978-1-4424-9368-1(2))* 2009. 272p. pap. 8.99 *(978-1-4169-1360-3(2))* Simon Pulse. (Simon Pulse).

Levine, Rhoda. Arthur. Aison, Everett, illus. 2015. (ENG.). 48p. (J). (gr. -1-2). 15.95 *(978-1-59017-935-2(8)*, NYR Children's Collection) New York Review of Bks., Inc., The.

Levis, Caron. Ida, Always. Santoso, Charles, illus. 2016. (ENG.). 40p. (J). (gr. -1-3). 17.99 *(978-1-4814-2640-4(0))* Simon & Schuster Children's Publishing.

Levithan, David. Love Is the Higher Law. 2010. (ENG.). 176p. (YA). (gr. 7). pap. 9.99 *(978-0-375-83469-1(9)*, Knopf Bks. for Young Readers) Random Hse. Children's Bks.

Levoy, Myron. Alan & Naomi. 2011. 14.12 (978-0-7848-3566-1(7), Everbind) Marco Bk. Co.

Lewis, Linda. All for the Love of That Boy. 2007. (ENG.). 224p. (YA). (gr. 7). pap. 12.95 (978-1-4169-6142-0(9), Simon Pulse) Simon Pulse.

Lewis, Stewart. You Have Seven Messages. 2012. (ENG.). 304p. (YA). (gr. 7). pap. 9.99 (978-0-385-74029-6(8), Ember) Random Hse. Children's Bks.

Lewman, David. Out of the Shadows Junior Novelization. 2016. lib. bdg. 17.20 (978-0-606-38886-3(9)) Turtleback Bks.

—Secret Life of Pets. Random House, illus. 2016. (Deluxe Junior Novel Ser.). (ENG.). 144p. (J). (gr. 2-5). 9.99 (978-0-399-55490-2(4), Random Hse. Bks. for Young Readers) Random Hse. Children's Bks.

Light, Steve. Have You Seen My Dragon? Light, Steve, illus. 2014. (ENG., Illus.). 48p. (J). (-k). 16.99 (978-0-7636-6648-4(3)) Candlewick Pr.

Lindner, April. Catherine. 2014. (ENG.). 336p. (YA). (gr. 10-17). pap. 10.00 (978-0-316-19693-2(2), Poppy) Little, Brown Bks. for Young Readers.

Lipsyte, Robert. The Brave. 2003. (Charlotte Zolotow Bk.). (ENG.). 240p. (J). (gr. 8-18). pap. 6.99 (978-0-06-447079-7(2)) HarperCollins Pubs.

Littlefield, Holly. The Rooftop Adventure of Minnie & Tessa, Factory Fire Survivors. Hammond, Ted & Carbajal, Richard, illus. 2011. (History's Kid Heroes Ser.). 32p. pap. 51.02 (978-0-7613-7639-2(9)); (ENG.). (gr. 3-5). pap. 8.95 (978-0-7613-7071-0(4)) Lerner Publishing Group. (Graphic Universe™).

Littman, Sarah Darer. Life, After. 2010. (ENG.). 288p. (J). (gr. 7-18). 17.99 (978-0-545-15144-3(9), Scholastic Pr.) Scholastic, Inc.

Livingston, Lesley. Starling. 2075. (ENG.). 368p. (J). (gr. 8). 9.99 (978-0-06-206308-3(1), HarperTeen) HarperCollins Pubs.

—Transcendent. 2014. (Starling Trilogy Ser.: 3). (ENG.). 352p. (YA). (gr. 8). 17.99 (978-0-06-206313-7(8), HarperTeen) HarperCollins Pubs.

Lockhart, E. Fly on the Wall: How One Girl Saw Everything. 2007. (ENG., Illus.). 192p. (YA). (gr. 7-12). pap. 8.99 (978-0-385-73282-6(1), Delacorte Pr) Random House Publishing Group.

Lombard, Jenny. Drita, My Homegirl. 2008. (ENG.). 144p. (J). (gr. 3-7). 5.99 (978-0-14-240905-3(7), Puffin Books) Penguin Young Readers Group.

—Drita, My Homegirl. 2008. 135p. (J). (gr. 4-6). 13.65 (978-0-7569-8919-4(1)) Perfection Learning Corp.

Lovascio, Jane. Casey & Bella Go to New York. Jasuna, Aija, illus. 2008. 24p. (J). 14.95 (978-1-60131-007-1(2)) Big Tent Bks.

Low, William. Chinatown. 2014. 32p. pap. 9.00 (978-1-61003-224-7(1)) Center for the Collaborative Classroom.

Luciano, Sonia. Mr. I Forgot. 2009. 48p. pap. 16.95 (978-1-61582-765-7(X)) America Star Bks.

Lupica, Mike. Hero. (ENG.). 304p. (J). (gr. 5-18). 2011. 7.99 (978-0-14-241960-1(5), Puffin Books) 2010. 17.99 (978-0-399-25283-9(5), Philomel Bks.) Penguin Young Readers Group.

—Hero. 2011. lib. bdg. 18.40 (978-0-606-23142-8(0), Turtleback) Turtleback Bks.

Lyga, Barry. Blood of My Blood. 2014. (ENG.). 480p. (YA). (gr. 10-17). 18.00 (978-0-316-19870-7(6)) Little, Brown Bks. for Young Readers.

Lyttleton, Kay. Jean Craig in New York. 2005. pap. 24.95 (978-1-4179-9293-5(X)) Kessinger Publishing, LLC.

Mac & MAC. Anna Smudge: Professional Shrink. 2008. (Professionals Ser.: 1). (Illus.). 256p. (J). (gr. 14-18). pap. 9.99 (978-1-934906-00-2(X)) Toasted Coconut Media LLC.

Macaraeg, Diane. Last Meal. 2008. 132p. pap. (978-3-639-03548-3(8)) AV Akademikerverlag GmbH & Co. KG.

MacColl, Michaela & Nichols, Rosemary. Rory's Promise. 2014. (Hidden Histories Ser.). (ENG.). 288p. (J). (gr. 4-7). 16.95 (978-1-62091-623-0(1), Calkins Creek) Boyds Mills Pr.

MacCullough, Carolyn. Once a Witch. 2010. (ENG.). 320p. (YA). (gr. 7). pap. 8.99 (978-0-547-41730-1(6)) Houghton Mifflin Harcourt Publishing Co.

MacGregor, Roy. Sudden Death in New York City. 2013. (Screech Owls Ser.). (ENG.). 176p. (J). (gr. 4-7). pap. 8.95 (978-1-77049-415-2(4), Tundra Bks.) Tundra Bks. CAN. Dist: Penguin Random Hse. LLC.

Mak, Kam. My Chinatown. Mak, Kam, illus. 2016. (Illus.). 32p. (J). (gr. -1-3). pap. 6.99 (978-0-06-443732-5(9)) HarperCollins Pubs.

Malloy, Brian. Twelve Long Months. 2010. (ENG.). 320p. (J). (gr. 7). 9.99 (978-0-439-87763-3(6), Scholastic Paperbacks) Scholastic, Inc.

Manning, Dennis & Crisalli, Joseph. The Emeritus Peabody Mysteries. 2008. 212p. pap. 13.98 (978-1-4303-2186-6(5)) Lulu Pr., Inc.

Manning, Matthew K. & Majado, Caio. Lockdown, Vol. 8. Ito, Leonardo, illus. 2012. (Tony Hawk's 900 Revolution Ser.). (ENG.). 128p. (gr. 3-4). pap. 7.19 (978-1-4342-3890-0(3)); lib. bdg. 26.65 (978-1-4342-3314-1(6)) Stone Arch Bks. (Tony Hawk's 900 Revolution).

Manzano, Sonia. No Dogs Allowed! Muth, Jon J., illus. 2005. (J). 29.95 incl. audio compact disk (978-0-8045-4101-5(9), SACD4101); 27.95 incl. audio (978-0-8045-6927-9(4), SAC6927) Spoken Arts, Inc.

—The Revolution of Evelyn Serrano. 2014. (ENG.). 224p. (J). (gr. 9). pap. 9.99 (978-0-545-32506-6(4)) Scholastic, Inc.

Manzo, Christopher. Oliver Brightside: You Don't Want That Penny. Adams, Lisa, illus. 2016. (ENG.). 36p. (J). 16.95 (978-0-9963756-4-1(3)) All About Kids Publishing.

Marina, Budhos. Ask Me No Questions. 2014. (ENG.). 176p. (YA). (gr. 7-12). 14.24 (978-1-63245-300-6(2)) Lectorum Pubns., Inc.

Marsh, Carole. The Behemoth Blizzard Mystery. (Masters of Disasters Ser.). (Illus.). 118p. (J). (gr. 3-5). 2008. per. 5.99 (978-0-635-06464-6(2)) 2007. 14.95 (978-0-635-06467-7(7)) Gallopade International.

—The Mystery in New York City. (Real Kids, Real Places Ser.). (J). 2009. (Illus.). 146p. lib. bdg. 18.99 (978-0-635-06998-6(9), Marsh, Carole Mysteries) 2003. 160p. (gr. 2-8). pap. 5.95 (978-0-635-02099-4(8)) Gallopade International.

Marsh, Laura F. Steps to Liberty. Wright, John R., illus. 2007. 32p. (J). 17.95 (978-0-615-16563-9(X)) Junior League of Central Westchester.

Marsh, Scott. Hannah & the Golden Swan. 2011. 216p. pap. 24.95 (978-1-4626-1084-6(6)) America Star Bks.

Martin, Ann M. The Long Way Home. 2013. (Family Tree Ser.: 2). (ENG.). 224p. (J). (gr. 3-7). 16.99 (978-0-545-35943-6(0), Scholastic Pr.) Scholastic, Inc.

—Ten Good & Bad Things about My Life (So Far) 2013. (ENG.). 288p. (J). (gr. 4-7). pap. 7.99 (978-1-250-03413-7(2), 9781250034137) Square Fish.

—Ten Rules for Living with My Sister. 2011. (ENG.). 240p. (J). (gr. 4-7). 16.99 (978-0-312-36766-4(X), 9780312367664) Feiwel & Friends.

—Ten Rules for Living with My Sister. 2012. (ENG.). 256p. (J). (gr. 4-7). pap. 7.99 (978-1-250-01021-6(7), 9781250010216) Square Fish.

Marz, Ron. Witchblade Redemption, Vol. 4. 2012. (ENG., Illus.). 160p. pap. 19.99 (978-1-60706-424-4(3), 9781607064244) Image Comics.

Maskame, Estelle. Did I Mention I Need You? 2016. (Did I Mention I Love You (DIMILY) Ser.: 2). (ENG.). 384p. (YA). (gr. 8-12). pap. 10.99 (978-1-4926-3218-4(X), 9781492632184) Sourcebooks, Inc.

Massie, Elizabeth. Ameri-Scares: New York. 2013. 148p. pap. 12.99 (978-1-937530-55-6(8)) Crossroad Pr.

Mata, Julie. Kate Walden Directs: Bride of Slug Man. 2016. (Kate Walden Directs Ser.). (ENG.). 288p. (J). (gr. 3-7). pap. 6.99 (978-1-4847-4746-9(1)) Hyperion Bks. for Children.

Matas, Carol. Rosie in New York City: Gotcha! 2003. (ENG., Illus.). 128p. (J). (gr. 4-7). pap. 9.95 (978-0-689-85714-0(4), Simon & Schuster/Paula Wiseman Bks.) Simon & Schuster/Paula Wiseman Bks.

Matti, Truus. Mister Orange. 2013. (ENG., Illus.). 156p. (J). (gr. 3). 16.95 (978-1-59270-123-0(X)) Enchanted Lion Bks., LLC.

McClatchy, Lisa. Eloise & the Snowman, 1 vol. Lyon, Tammie, illus. 2016. (ENG.). 32p. (J). **(978-1-61479-402-8(2))** Spotlight.

McClatchy, Lisa & Thompson, Kay. Eloise & the Dinosaurs. Lyon, Tammie Speer & Lyon, Tammie, illus. 2007. (Eloise Ser.). (ENG.). 32p. (J). (gr. -1-1). pap. 3.99 (978-0-689-87453-6(7), Simon Spotlight) Simon Spotlight.

—Eloise & the Snowman. Lyon, Tammie Speer, illus. 2006. (Eloise Ser.). (ENG.). 32p. (J). (gr. -1-1). pap. 3.99 (978-0-689-87451-2(0), Simon Spotlight) Simon Spotlight.

—Eloise's New Bonnet. Lyon, Tammie Speer & Lyon, Tammie, illus. 2007. (Eloise Ser.). (ENG.). 32p. (J). (gr. -1-1). pap. 3.99 (978-0-689-87452-9(9), Simon Spotlight) Simon Spotlight.

McDavid-Jones, Elizabeth. Secrets on 26th Street. 2009. (Mysteries Through Time Ser.). 144 - 176p. (YA). (gr. 4-8). 31.95 (978-1-60754-200-1(5)); pap. 15.25 (978-1-60754-201-8(3)) Windmill Bks.

McGee, Katharine. The Dazzling Heights. 2017. (Thousandth Floor Ser.: 2). 432p. (YA). (gr. 8). 18.99 **(978-0-06-241862-3(9))** HarperCollins Pubs.

McGee, Katharine. The Thousandth Floor. (Thousandth Floor Ser.: 1). (YA). (gr. 8). 2017. 496p. pap. 9.99 **(978-0-06-241860-9(2))** 2016. (ENG.). 448p. 18.99 (978-0-06-241859-3(9)) HarperCollins Pubs.

McGee, Ron. Ryan Quinn & the Rebel's Escape. Samnee, Chris, illus. 2016. (Ryan Quinn Ser.: 1). 368p. (J). (gr. 3-7). 16.99 (978-0-06-242164-7(6)) HarperCollins Pubs.

McGhee, Patti Gray. Ducky Bill's Great Race. Vermillion, Danny, illus. 2013. 46p. 24.95 (978-1-63000-424-8(3)); 48p. pap. 24.95 (978-1-62709-522-8(5)) America Star Bks.

McGuigan, Mary Ann. Crossing into Brooklyn. 2015. (ENG.). 224p. (YA). 17.99 (978-1-4405-8463-3(X), Simon Pulse) Simon Pulse.

McIntyre, Will. Burning Midnight. 2016. (ENG.). 320p. (YA). (gr. 7). 17.99 (978-0-553-53410-8(6), Delacorte Pr.) Random Hse. Children's Bks.

McMorrow, T. E. & Hoffmann, E. T. A. Nutcracker in Harlem. Ransome, James, illus. 2017. 32p. (J). (gr. -1-3). 17.99 (978-0-06-117598-5(6)) HarperCollins Pubs.

McNally, Janet. Girls in the Moon. 2016. 352p. (YA). (gr. 8). 17.99 (978-0-06-243624-5(4), HarperTeen) HarperCollins Pubs.

Mebus, Scott. Spirits in the Park. 2009. (Gods of Manhattan Ser.: No. 2). (J). (978-0-525-47963-5(5), Dutton Juvenile) Penguin Publishing Group.

—Spirits in the Park, Vol. 2. 2010. (ENG.). 400p. (J). (gr. 3-7). 8.99 (978-0-14-241645-7(2), Puffin Books) Penguin Young Readers Group.

Mechling, Lauren & Moser, Laura. All Q, No A: More Tales of a 10th-Grade Social Climber. 2006. (ENG.). 288p. (YA). (gr. 7-12). pap. 15.95 (978-0-618-66378-1(9)) Houghton Mifflin Harcourt Publishing Co.

Medina, Meg. Burn Baby Burn. 2016. (ENG.). 320p. (YA). (gr. 9). 17.99 (978-0-7636-7467-0(2)) Candlewick Pr.

Mendle, Jane. My Ultimate Sister Disaster: A Novel. 2010. (ENG.). 208p. (YA). (gr. 7-18). pap. 18.99 (978-0-312-36904-0(2), 9780312369040, St. Martin's Griffin) St. Martin's Pr.

Mermelstein, Yael. The Face in the Mirror: A Fantasy. 2012. 285p. (J). pap. (978-1-4226-1292-7(9), Shaar Pr.) Mesorah Pubns., Ltd.

Merrill, Jean. The Pushcart War. 2006. (J). 1.25 (978-1-4193-8348-9(5)) Recorded Bks., Inc.

—The Pushcart War. Solbert, Ronni, illus. 50th ed. 2015. (ENG.). 232p. (J). (gr. 3-7). pap. 11.99 (978-1-59017-936-9(6), NYRB Kids) New York Review of Bks., Inc., The.

—The Pushcart War. Solbert, Ronni, illus. 50th anniv. ed. 2014. (ENG.). 232p. (J). (gr. 3-7). 15.95 (978-1-59017-819-5(X), NYR Children's Collection) New York Review of Bks., Inc., The.

Messner, Kate. Spitfire. 2007. (J). (978-1-59531-018-7(5)) North Country Bks., Inc.

Metaxas, Eric. Mose the Fireman, 1 vol. Peck, Everett, illus. 2004. (Rabbit Ears-A Classic Tale Ser.). (ENG.). 40p. (gr. k-5). 25.65 (978-1-59197-766-7(5)) Spotlight.

Metzger, Steve. Dancing Clock. Nez, John Abbott, illus. 2011. (ENG.). 32p. 12.95 (978-1-58925-100-7(8)); (J). pap. 7.95 (978-1-58925-429-9(5)) Tiger Tales.

Mihaley, James. You Can't Have My Planet: But Take My Brother, Please. 2013. (ENG.). 272p. (J). (gr. 4-7). pap. 8.99 (978-1-250-01667-6(3), 9781250016676) Square Fish.

Milanes, Janelle. The Victoria in My Head. 2017. (ENG., Illus.). 400p. (YA). (gr. 7). 17.99 **(978-1-4814-8089-5(8)**, Simon Pulse) Simon Pulse.

Miller, Kirsten. The Darkness Dwellers. 2013. (Kiki Strike Ser.). (ENG., Illus.). 416p. (YA). (gr. 7-12). 17.99 (978-1-59990-736-9(4), 9781599907369, Bloomsbury USA Childrens) Bloomsbury Publishing USA.

—The Empress's Tomb. 2013. (Kiki Strike Ser.). (ENG.). 384p. (YA). (gr. 7-12). pap. 9.99 (978-1-59990-921-9(9), 9781599909219, Bloomsbury USA Childrens) Bloomsbury Publishing USA.

—The Eternal Ones: What If Love Refused to Die? 2011. (ENG.). 432p. (YA). (gr. 7-18). 9.99 (978-1-59514-375-4(0), Razorbill) Penguin Young Readers Group.

—Inside the Shadow City. (Kiki Strike Ser.). (ENG.). 400p. (YA). 2013. (gr. 7-12). pap. 9.99 (978-1-59990-920-2(0), 9781599909202) 2006. (gr. 4-8). 16.95 (978-1-58234-960-2(6), 9781582349602) Bloomsbury Publishing USA. (Bloomsbury USA Childrens).

Miller-Stehr, Felicia. Are You Chanukah or Christmas? 2008. 32p. pap. 17.99 (978-1-4343-9517-7(0)) AuthorHouse.

Millner, Denene. Miss You, Mina. 2010. 163p. (J). pap. (978-0-545-25106-8(0)) Scholastic, Inc.

Milner, Robert W. The Chicken Coop Gang. 2011. 130p. 29.99 (978-1-4568-5517-8(4)); pap. 19.99 (978-1-4568-5516-1(6)) Xlibris Corp.

Minter, J. The Insiders. 2004. (Insiders Ser.). (ENG.). 288p. (YA). (gr. 9-18). pap. 8.95 (978-1-58234-895-7(2), 9781582348957, Bloomsbury USA Childrens) Bloomsbury Publishing USA.

Mitchell, Dennis. First Day of School: A Day in the Life of Noah. 2009. 36p. pap. 16.99 (978-1-4389-9198-6(3)) AuthorHouse.

Mlynowski, Sarah. Don't Even Think about It. 2014. (ENG.). 336p. (YA). (gr. 7). 17.99 (978-0-385-73738-8(6), Delacorte Pr.) Random Hse. Children's Bks.

—Frogs & French Kisses. 2007. (Magic in Manhattan Ser.: No. 2). (ENG.). 304p. (YA). (gr. 7). pap. 8.99 (978-0-385-73185-0(X), Delacorte Pr.) Random Hse. Children's Bks.

—Magic in Manhattan: Bras & Broomsticks Frogs; French Kisses. 2012. (Magic in Manhattan Ser.). (ENG.). 608p. (YA). (gr. 7). pap. 10.99 (978-0-385-74232-0(0), Ember) Random Hse. Children's Bks.

—Parties & Potions. 2010. (Magic in Manhattan Ser.: No. 4). (ENG., Illus.). 368p. (YA). (gr. 7). pap. 10.99 (978-0-385-73646-6(0), Ember) Random Hse. Children's Bks.

Moldavsky, Goldy. Kill the Boy Band. (ENG.). 320p. (J). (gr. 9). 2017. pap. 9.99 (978-0-545-86750-4(9)) 2016. 17.99 (978-0-545-86747-4(9)) Scholastic, Inc.

—Kill the Boy Band. 2017. lib. bdg. 20.85 **(978-0-606-39701-8(9))** Turtleback Bks.

Moore, Ted. Eagle Eye & the Fall of Creek Canyon. 2007. 112p. per. 10.95 (978-0-595-43133-5(X)) iUniverse, Inc.

Morgan, Melissa J. RSVP. 2005. (Camp Confidential Ser.: 6). (ENG., Illus.). 160p. (J). (gr. 3-7). pap. 4.99 (978-0-448-43962-4(X), Grosset & Dunlap) Penguin Young Readers Group.

Morgan, Melissa J. & Morgan, Melissa. Super Special No. 21. 2009. (Camp Confidential Ser.: 21). (ENG.). 256p. (J). (gr. 4-7). pap. 5.99 (978-0-448-45187-9(5), Grosset & Dunlap) Penguin Young Readers Group.

Mullarkey, Lisa & Mullarkey, John. Get Ella to the Apollo, 1 vol. Bernard, Courtney, illus. 2015. (ENG.). 128p. (J). (978-1-62402-087-2(9)) Magic Wagon.

Murphy, Barbara Beasley & Wolkoff, Judie. Ace Hits Rock Bottom. 2003. (Can't Stop Ace Ser.: No. 2). 204p. (J). pap. 16.95 (978-0-86534-408-2(6)) Sunstone Pr.

—Ace Hits the Big Time. 2003. (Can't Stop Ace Ser.: No. 1). 184p. (J). pap. 16.95 (978-0-86534-407-5(8)) Sunstone Pr.

Musselwhite, Harry. Martin - The Guitar. 2012. (ENG.). 32p. 19.99 incl. audio compact disk (978-1-57424-280-5(6), 1574242806) Centerstream Publishing.

Muszynski, Julie. Henley on Safari. 2012. (ENG., Illus.). 48p. (J). (gr. -1-12). 20.00 (978-0-9832702-3-2(6)) Glitterati, Inc.

My Day in New York City. 2004. (J). ring bd. 4.50 (978-0-9762740-1-8(9), Flat Kids) Smart Smiles Co., The.

Myers, Walter Dean. All the Right Stuff. 2013. (ENG.). 240p. (YA). (gr. 8). pap. 9.99 (978-0-06-196089-5(6), Amistad) HarperCollins Pubs.

—Darius & Twig. 2013. 208p. (YA). (gr. 8). (ENG.). 17.99 (978-0-06-172823-5(3)); lib. bdg. 18.89 (978-0-06-172824-2(1)) HarperCollins Pubs. (Amistad).

—Juba! 2015. (ENG., Illus.). 208p. (YA). (gr. 8-12). 17.99 (978-0-06-211271-2(6), HarperTeen) HarperCollins Pubs.

—145th Street: Short Stories. 2012. (ENG.). 192p. (YA). (gr. 7). pap. 9.99 (978-0-307-97610-9(6), Ember) Random Hse. Children's Bks.

Nastro, Caroline. The Bear Who Couldn't Sleep. Nastanlieva, Vanya, illus. 2016. (ENG.). 32p. 17.95 (978-0-7358-4268-7(X)) North-South Bks., Inc.

Nayeri, Daniel and Dina. Another Faust. 2010. (ENG., Illus.). 400p. (YA). (gr. 9). pap. 8.99 (978-0-7636-4834-3(5)) Candlewick Pr.

Nelson, Vaunda Micheaux. The Book Itch: Freedom, Truth & Harlem's Greatest Bookstore. Christie, R. Gregory, illus. 2015. (ENG.). 32p. (J). (gr. 2-4). 17.99 (978-1-4677-4618-2(5), Carolrhoda Bks.) Lerner Publishing Group.

Neville, Emily. It's Like This, Cat. Weiss, Emil, illus. 2017. (ENG.). 192p. (J). (gr. 2-6). pap. 5.95 (978-0-486-81478-0(5)) Dover Pubns., Inc.

Nicholasa, Mohr. El Bronx Remembered. 2014. (Trophy Keypoint Bks). (ENG.). 272p. (J). (gr. 8-12). 13.24 (978-1-63245-280-1(4)) Lectorum Pubns., Inc.

Nicholson, Simon. The Magician's Fire. (Young Houdini Ser.: 1). (ENG.). (J). 2015. 272p. (gr. 4-7). pap. 7.99 (978-1-4926-0949-0(8)) 2014. (Illus.). 240p. (gr. 5-8). 15.99 (978-1-4926-0332-0(5), 9781492603320, Sourcebooks Jabberwocky) Sourcebooks, Inc.

Niemann, Christoph. Subway. Niemann, Christoph, illus. 2010. (Illus.). 40p. (J). (gr. -1-k). lib. bdg. 17.89 (978-0-06-157780-2(4), Greenwillow Bks.) HarperCollins Pubs.

Nikki, Grimes. Bronx Masquerade. 2014. (ENG.). 176p. (YA). 11.24 (978-1-63245-077-7(1)) Lectorum Pubns., Inc.

Nolan, Han. When We Were Saints. 2005. (ENG.). 312p. (YA). (gr. 7-12). pap. 15.95 (978-0-15-205322-2(0)) Houghton Mifflin Harcourt Publishing Co.

Northrop, Michael. Book of the Dead. 2015. (TombQuest Ser.: Bk. 1). (J). 197p. (978-1-76015-315-1(X)); 208p. pap. (978-1-74362-924-6(9)) Scholastic, Inc.

O'Hearn, Kate. Olympus at War. 2013. (Pegasus Ser.: 2). (ENG.). 400p. (J). (gr. 3-7). 16.99 (978-1-4424-4412-6(6), Simon & Schuster/Paula Wiseman Bks.) Simon & Schuster/Paula Wiseman Bks.

Older, Daniel José. Shadowhouse Fall. 2017. (Shadowshaper Cypher Ser.). (ENG.). 368p. (J). (gr. 7-7). 18.99 **(978-0-545-95282-8(4)**, Levine, Arthur A. Bks.) Scholastic, Inc.

Older, Daniel José. Shadowshaper. (ENG.). (J). 2016. 320p. (gr. 7). pap. 9.99 (978-1-338-03247-5(X)) 2015. 304p. (gr. 9). 17.99 (978-0-545-59161-4(9)) Scholastic, Inc.

Oliver, Lin. Beware! Shadows in the Night. Kallis, Samantha, illus. 2016. (Fantastic Frame Ser.: 3). (ENG.). 128p. (J). (gr. 2-4). 11.99 (978-0-448-48091-6(3), Grosset & Dunlap) Penguin Young Readers Group.

Olsen, Nora. Swans & Klons. 2013. (ENG.). 192p. (gr. 7). pap. 11.95 (978-1-60282-874-2(1)) Bold Strokes Bks.

Olswanger, Anna. Greenhorn. Nerlove, Miriam, illus. 2012. (ENG.). (J). E-Book 9.99 (978-1-60306-159-9(2)); 48p. 17.95 (978-1-58838-235-1(4)) NewSouth, Inc. (NewSouth Bks.).

O'Neill, Elizabeth & McPherson, Missie. Alfred Visits New York City. 2003. (Illus.). 24p. (J). pap. 12.00 (978-1-4120-1338-3(0)) Funny Bone Bks.

Osborne, Mary Pope & National Geographic Learning Staff. New York's Bravest. Johnson, Steve & Fancher, Lou, illus. 2006. (ENG.). 32p. (J). (gr. -1-2). 7.99 (978-0-375-83841-5(4), Dragonfly Bks.) Random Hse. Children's Bks.

O'Shea, M.J. Cold Moon. 2nd ed. 2016. (ENG., Illus.). (J). 24.99 **(978-1-63477-954-8(1)**, Harmony Ink Pr.) Dreamspinner Pr.

—Hunter's Moon. 3rd ed. 2016. (ENG., Illus.). (J). 27.99 **(978-1-63533-032-8(7)**, Harmony Ink Pr.) Dreamspinner Pr.

Otis, James. Peter of New Amsterdam: A story of Old New York. 2007. 136p. per. 9.95 (978-0-9790876-2-2(7)) Living Bks. Pr.

Paley, Jane. Hooper Finds a Family: A Hurricane Katrina Dog's Survival Tale. 2011. (ENG.). 144p. (J). (gr. 3-7). 16.99 (978-0-06-201103-9(0)) HarperCollins Pubs.

Palmer, Robin. Sealed with a Kiss, 2 vols., No. 2. 2010. (Yours Truly, Lucy B. Parker Ser.: 2). (ENG.). 224p. (J). (gr. 5-18). 6.99 (978-0-14-241501-6(4), Puffin Books) Penguin Young Readers Group.

Papademetriou, Lisa. Apartment 1986. 2017. 272p. (J). (gr. 3-7). 16.99 (978-0-06-237108-9(8)) HarperCollins Pubs.

Paratore, Coleen Murtagh. Roar Like a Girl. 2016. (Always Willa Ser.). (ENG., Illus.). 190p. (J). (gr. 3-8). pap. 9.95 (978-1-939775-07-8(8)) March 4th, Inc.

Pascucci, Adele. Duck on a Dock. 2012. 20p. pap. 13.95 (978-1-105-40403-0(X)) Lulu Pr., Inc.

Patterson, James & Grabenstein, Chris. I Totally Funniest: A Middle School Story. Park, Laura, illus. 2015. 320p. (J). (978-0-316-26161-6(0)) Little Brown & Co.

—Treasure Hunters. Neufeld, Juliana, illus. (Treasure Hunters Ser.: 1). (ENG.). 480p. (J). (gr. 3-7). 2015. pap. 8.00 (978-0-316-20757-7(8)) 2013. 14.99 (978-0-316-20756-0(X)) Little Brown & Co. (Jimmy Patterson).

—Treasure Hunters. 2015. (Treasure Hunters Ser.: 1). (J). lib. bdg. 18.45 (978-0-606-37305-0(5)) Turtleback Bks.

Patterson, James & Paetro, Maxine. Confessions: The Private School Murders. 2013. 422p. (YA). (978-0-316-24263-9(2)) Little Brown & Co.

—Confessions of a Murder Suspect. 2014. (Confessions Ser.: 1). (ENG.). 352p. (gr. 7-17). mass mkt. 8.00 (978-1-4555-4774-6(3), Jimmy Patterson) 2013. (ENG.). 400p. (J). (gr. 7-17). pap. 10.00 (978-0-316-20700-3(4), Jimmy Patterson) 2012. (Confessions Ser.: 1). (ENG.). 384p. (YA). (gr. 7-17). 19.99 (978-0-316-20698-3(9), Jimmy Patterson) 2012. 372p. (J). 11.99 (978-0-316-22641-7(6)) 2012. (Confessions Ser.: 1). (ENG.). 400p. (YA). (gr. 7-17). 31.99 (978-0-316-22418-5(9), Jimmy Patterson) Little Brown & Co.

—Confessions of a Murder Suspect. 2013. (Confessions Ser.: 1). lib. bdg. 20.85 (978-0-606-32278-2(7), Turtleback) Turtleback Bks.

—Confessions: the Murder of an Angel. 2016. (Confessions Ser.: 4). (ENG.). 304p. (YA). (gr. 7-17). pap. 9.99 (978-0-316-39218-1(9), Jimmy Patterson) Little Brown & Co.

—The Private School Murders. 2015. (Confessions Ser.: 2). (ENG.). 400p. mass mkt. 8.00 (978-1-4555-5946-6(6), Jimmy Patterson) Grand Central Publishing.

—The Private School Murders. (Confessions Ser.: 2). (ENG.). (YA). (gr. 7-17). 2014. 448p. pap. 10.00 (978-0-316-20764-5(0)) 2013. 448p. 18.00 (978-0-316-20765-2(9)) 2013. 480p. 22.00 (978-0-316-23992-9(5)) Little Brown & Co. (Jimmy Patterson).

—The Private School Murders. 2014. (Confessions Ser.: 2). (YA). lib. bdg. 20.85 (978-0-606-35945-0(1)) Turtleback Bks.

Patterson, James, et al. Treasure Hunters. Neufeld, Juliana, illus. 2013. 451p. (J). (978-0-316-24262-2(4)) Little Brown & Co.

Paul, John. Copters. Young, Bill, illus. 2012. 36p. 24.95 (978-1-4626-9458-7(6)) America Star Bks.

Pavlicin, Karen. Perch, Mrs. Sackets, & Crow's Nest. 2007. (J). (ENG.). 160p. 16.95 (978-1-934617-00-7(8)); pap. (978-1-934617-01-4(6)) Elva Resa Publishing, LLC. (Alma Little).

—Summer of Courage. 2014. (ENG.). 160p. (J). pap. 12.95 (978-1-934617-24-3(5), Alma Little) Elva Resa Publishing, LLC.

Penn, Astor. All the Devils Here. 2016. (ENG., Illus.). (YA). (gr. 8-12). 24.99 **(978-1-63477-933-3(9)**, Harmony Ink Pr.) Dreamspinner Pr.

Perelman, Helen. Heart to Heart. 2007. (High School Musical Stories from East High Ser.). 125p. (J). (gr. 3-7). 12.65 (978-0-7569-8340-6(1)) Perfection Learning Corp.

Perkins, Mitali. You Bring the Distant Near. 2017. (ENG.). 320p. (YA). 17.99 **(978-0-374-30490-4(4)**, 9780374304904, Farrar, Straus & Giroux (BYR)) Farrar, Straus & Giroux.

Perl, Lila. Isabel's War. 2014. (ENG.). 224p. (J). (gr. 2-7). pap. 12.95 (978-1-939601-27-8(4)) Ig Publishing, Inc.

Peschke, M. Vacation Queen. Mourning, Tuesday, illus. 2016. (Kylie Jean Ser.). (ENG.). 112p. (gr. 2-3). 8.95 (978-1-5158-0059-0(8)) Picture Window Bks.

Peschke, Marci. Vacation Queen. Mourning, Tuesday, illus. 2016. (Kylie Jean Ser.). (ENG.). 112p. (gr. 2-3). lib. bdg. 22.65 (978-1-5158-0058-3(X)) Picture Window Bks.

Peterson, Kathryn. Reilly's Leap of Faith, 1 vol. 2010. 48p. pap. 16.95 (978-1-4512-0154-3(0)) America Star Bks.

Philbin, Joanna. The Daughters Break the Rules. 2011. (Daughters Ser.: 2). (ENG.). 304p. (J). (gr. 7-17). pap., pap. 10.00 (978-0-316-04905-4(0), Poppy) Little, Brown Bks. for Young Readers.

—The Daughters Take the Stage. 2011. (Daughters Ser.: 3). (ENG.). 304p. (J). (gr. 7-17). pap. 8.99 (978-0-316-04908-5(5), Poppy) Little, Brown Bks. for Young Readers.

—Rules of Summer. 2014. (Rules of Summer Ser.: 1). (ENG.). 368p. (YA). (gr. 10-17). pap. 10.99 (978-0-316-21204-5(0), Poppy) Little, Brown Bks. for Young Readers.

Phillips, Ruby Ann. Dream Birthday, 1 vol. Isik, Semur, illus. 2014. (Krystal Ball Ser.). (ENG.). 112p. (gr. 2-3). 25.32 (978-1-4795-2178-4(7)) Picture Window Bks.

—Pet Psychic. Isik, Semur, illus. 2015. (Krystal Ball Ser.). (ENG.). 112p. (gr. 2-3). lib. bdg. 25.32 (978-1-4795-5875-9(3)) Picture Window Bks.

Pirzada, Nefes & Simeone, Angelique. Young Equestrian: Something in Common. 2012. 386p. (gr. 4-18). pap. 21.14 (978-1-4669-5242-3(3)) Trafford Publishing.

Platt, Kin. The Blue Man. 3rd collector's ed. 2005. (YA). 125.00 (978-1-59885-000-0(8)); 192p. 24.95 (978-1-59885-001-7(6)) Two Lakes Pr., Inc.

Polisner, Gae. The Pull of Gravity. 2013. (ENG.). 224p. (YA). (gr. 7). pap. 10.99 (978-1-250-01933-2(8), 9781250019332) Square Fish.

Ponti, James. Blue Moon. 2013. (Dead City Ser.: 2). (ENG., Illus.). 336p. (J). (gr. 4-8). 17.99 (978-1-4424-4131-6(3), Aladdin) Simon & Schuster Children's Publishing.

—Dark Days. 2015. (Dead City Ser.: 3). (ENG., Illus.). 304p. (J). (gr. 3-7). 17.99 (978-1-4814-3636-6(8), Aladdin) Simon & Schuster Children's Publishing.

—Dead City. 2013. (Dead City Ser.: 1). (ENG., Illus.). 304p. (J). (gr. 4-8). pap. 7.99 (978-1-4424-4130-9(5), Aladdin) Simon & Schuster Children's Publishing.

Potter, Ellen. Olivia Kidney & the Secret Beneath the City. 2009. (ENG.). 336p. (J). (gr. 3-7). 9.99 (978-0-14-241263-3(5), Puffin Books) Penguin Young Readers Group.

—Otis Dooda: Strange but True. Heatley, David, illus. 2013. (Otis Dooda Ser.: 1). (ENG.). 240p. (J). (gr. 2-5). 13.99 (978-1-250-01176-3(0), 9781250011763) Feiwel & Friends.

—Otis Dooda: Downright Dangerous. Heatley, David, illus. 2014. (Otis Dooda Ser.: 2). (ENG.). 240p. (J). (gr. 2-5). 13.99 (978-1-250-01177-0(9), 9781250011770) Feiwel & Friends.

—Pish Posh. 2011. (ENG.). 176p. (J). (gr. 3-7). 6.99 (978-0-14-241906-9(0), Puffin Books) Penguin Young Readers Group.

—Slob. 2009. (ENG.). 208p. (J). (gr. 3-7). 16.99 (978-0-399-24705-7(X), Philomel Bks.) Penguin Young Readers Group.

Power, Michael. The Zoo. 2009. 201p. pap. 13.75 (978-1-60695-075-3(4)) EchoRoad, Inc.

Primavera, Elise. Auntie Claus: Home for the Holidays. Primavera, Elise, illus. 2009. (ENG., Illus.). 40p. (J). (gr. -1-3). 17.99 (978-1-4169-5485-9(6), Simon & Schuster/Paula Wiseman Bks.) Simon & Schuster/Paula Wiseman Bks.

Publications International Ltd. Staff, ed. The Smurfs Large Play a Sound. 2011. 24p. (J). 14.98 (978-1-60553-403-9(X)) Phoenix International Publications, Inc.

Quintero, Sofia. Efrain's Secret. 2011. (ENG.). 276p. (YA). (gr. 9). pap. 8.99 (978-0-440-24062-4(X), Ember) Random Hse. Children's Bks.

—Show & Prove. 2015. (ENG.). 352p. (YA). (gr. 7). 17.99 (978-0-375-84707-3(3), Knopf Bks. for Young Readers) Random Hse. Children's Bks.

Raab, Ralph. The Dewey Deception: The First Adventure from the Biblio Files. 2009. (ENG.). 248p. 26.95 (978-1-4401-4687-9(X)); pap. 16.95 (978-1-4401-4685-5(3)) iUniverse, Inc.

Rabley, Stephen & Pearson Education Staff. Flying Home. 2nd ed. 2008. (ENG.). 20p. pap. 11.99 (978-1-4058-6946-1(1)) Pearson Education.

Ramsey, Charmaine J. Frollica & Frenzi: New York City Friends. Steinlage, Kelly, illus. 2009. 36p. pap. 15.49 (978-1-4490-0487-3(3)) AuthorHouse.

Random House. Pizza Party! (Teenage Mutant Ninja Turtles) Random House, illus. 2017. (Step into Reading Ser.). (ENG., Illus.). 24p. (J). (gr. -1-1). pap. 4.99 **(978-1-5247-6982-6(7))**; lib. bdg. 12.99 **(978-1-5247-6983-3(5))** Random Hse. Children's Bks. (Random Hse. Bks. for Young Readers).

Random House Editors. Out of the Shadows. 2016. (Step into Reading Level 2 Ser.). lib. bdg. 14.75 (978-0-606-38896-2(6)) Turtleback Bks.

Ray, Anna Chapin. Half a Dozen Girls. 2007. 148p. (gr. 4-7). per. (978-1-4068-3752-0(0)) Echo Library.

Redding, LaTisha. Calling the Water Drum, 1 vol. Boyd, Aaron, illus. 2016. (ENG.). 32p. (J). (gr. 1-4). 17.95 (978-1-62014-194-6(9)) Lee & Low Bks., Inc.

Reisenauer, Cynthia Mauro. Emerita. Reisenauer, Cynthia Mauro, illus. 2007. (Illus.). 48p. (J). 18.95 (978-0-9726487-5-2(5)) Puddle Jump Pr., Ltd.

Reiss, Mike & Reiss, Mike. Late for School, 1 vol. Austin, Michael, illus. 2003. (ENG.). 32p. (J). (gr. k-3). 16.95 (978-1-56145-286-6(6), Q35957) Peachtree Pubs.

Resnicoff, Stan. The BIG Parade: New York. 2012. (ENG.). (J). pap. (978-1-4675-1538-2(8)) Independent Pub.

Reyes, Nikki. An Unexpected Guest: It Started with a fish. It ended with a Friend. 2009. 48p. pap. 17.49 (978-1-4363-9133-7(4)) Xlibris Corp.

Reynolds, Jason. When I Was the Greatest. Frost, Michael, photos by. 2014. (ENG., Illus.). 240p. (YA). (gr. 7). 17.99 (978-1-4424-5947-2(6), Atheneum Bks. for Young Readers) Simon & Schuster Children's Publishing.

Ringgold, Faith, et al. Cassie's Word Quilt. Ringgold, Faith, illus. 2004. (Avenues Ser.). (ENG., Illus.). 32p. (J). (gr. -1-2). pap. 6.99 (978-0-553-11233-7(3), Dragonfly Bks.) Random Hse. Children's Bks.

Rivera, Lilliam. The Education of Margot Sanchez. 2017. (ENG., Illus.). 304p. (YA). (gr. 9). 17.99 (978-1-4814-7211-1(9), Simon & Schuster Bks. For Young Readers) Simon & Schuster Bks. For Young Readers.

Roberts, Willo Davis. The Kidnappers. 2016. (ENG., Illus.). 208p. (J). (gr. 3-7). pap. 6.99 (978-1-4814-4904-5(4), Aladdin) Simon & Schuster Children's Publishing.

Robertson, Jacob Ryan. Far Away. 2012. 50p. (-18). pap. 15.99 (978-1-4797-4679-8(7)) Xlibris Corp.

Robinson, Gwen. The Renshaw Diversion. 2007. (Illus.). 204p. per. (978-0-7552-0275-1(9)) Authors OnLine, Ltd.

Robinson, Sharon. The Hero Two Doors Down: A Story of Friendship Between a Boy & a Baseball Legend. 2016. (ENG.). 208p. (J). (gr. 3-7). 16.99 (978-0-545-80451-6(5), Scholastic Pr.) Scholastic, Inc.

Rockliff, Mara. Around America to Win the Vote: Two Suffragists, a Kitten, & 10,000 Miles. Hooper, Hadley, illus. 2016. (ENG.). 40p. (J). (gr. k-3). 16.99 (978-0-7636-7893-7(7)) Candlewick Pr.

—Me & Momma & Big John. Low, William, illus. 2012. (ENG.). 32p. (J). (gr. -1-2). 16.99 (978-0-7636-4359-1(9)) Candlewick Pr.

Rodkey, Geoff. The Tapper Twins Go to War (with Each Other) 2015. (Tapper Twins Ser.: 1). (ENG., Illus.). 240p. (J). (gr. 3-7). 13.99 (978-0-316-29779-0(8)) Little Brown & Co.

—The Tapper Twins Go to War (with Each Other) 2016. (Tapper Twins Ser.: 1). (ENG., Illus.). 240p. (J). (gr. 3-7). pap. 5.99 (978-0-316-31597-5(4)) Little, Brown Bks. for Young Readers.

—The Tapper Twins Go Viral. 2017. (Tapper Twins Ser.: 4). (ENG., Illus.). 256p. (J). (gr. 3-7). 13.99 (978-0-316-29784-4(4)) Little Brown & Co.

—The Tapper Twins Run for President. 2016. (Tapper Twins Ser.: 3). (ENG., Illus.). 304p. (J). (gr. 3-7). 13.99 (978-0-316-29785-1(2)) Little, Brown Bks. for Young Readers.

—The Tapper Twins Tear up New York. 2015. (Tapper Twins Ser.: 2). (ENG., Illus.). 288p. (J). (gr. 3-7). 13.99 (978-0-316-29783-7(6)) Little Brown & Co.

—The Tapper Twins Tear up New York. 2016. (Tapper Twins Ser.: 2). (ENG., Illus.). 288p. (J). (gr. 3-7). pap. 5.99 (978-0-316-31601-9(6)) Little, Brown Bks. for Young Readers.

Rodriguez, Cindy L. Heroes Were Made On 9/11, 1 vol. Elliott, Joyce L., illus. 2010. 26p. 24.95 (978-1-4489-6070-5(3)) PublishAmerica, Inc.

Ross, Alice & Ross, Kent. La Dama de Cobre. Bowman, Leslie, illus. 2006. (Yo Solo - Historia (on My Own - History) Ser.). (SPA.). 48p. (gr. 2-4). lib. bdg. 25.26 (978-0-8225-6262-7(6)) Lerner Publishing Group.

Rothenberger, Suzanne. Mattie: Life at Paddock Mansion. 2013. 136p. pap. 9.95 (978-0-9890509-4-4(7)) Garland City Bks. of Watertown.

Roy, Lillian Elizabeth. Polly in New York. Barbour, H. S., illus. 2004. reprint ed. pap. 28.95 (978-1-4179-0068-8(7)) Kessinger Publishing, LLC.

Roy, Ron. Sleepy Hollow Sleepover. Gurney, John Steven, illus. 4th ed. 2010. (to Z Mysteries Ser.: 4). (ENG.). 144p. (J). (gr. 1-4). pap. 5.99 (978-0-375-86669-2(8), Random Hse. Bks. for Young Readers) Random Hse. Children's Bks.

—Sleepy Hollow Sleepover. 4th ed. 2010. (to Z Mysteries Ser.: 30). lib. bdg. 16.00 (978-0-606-14007-2(7), Turtleback) Turtleback Bks.

Rubel, David. The Carpenter's Gift: A Christmas Tale about the Rockefeller Center Tree. LaMarche, Jim, illus. 2011. (ENG.). 48p. (J). (gr. k-4). 17.99 (978-0-375-86922-8(0), Random Hse. Bks. for Young Readers) Random Hse. Children's Bks.

Rubin, Sarah. Someday Dancer. 2012. (J). (978-0-545-39379-9(5)); (ENG.). 256p. (gr. 7-7). 16.99 (978-0-545-39378-2(7), Chicken Hse., The) Scholastic, Inc.

Rudetsky, Seth. The Rise & Fall of a Theater Geek. 2015. (ENG.). 288p. (YA). (gr. 7). pap. 9.99 (978-0-449-81672-1(9), Random Hse. Bks. for Young Readers) Random Hse. Children's Bks.

Russell, David. Who'z Who at the Zoo. 2012. (Illus.). 26p. pap. 12.95 (978-1-4575-1395-4(1)) Dog Ear Publishing, LLC.

Russell, Paul. Immaculate Blue: A Novel. 2015. (ENG., Illus.). 340p. pap. 16.95 (978-1-62778-095-7(5)) Cleis Pr.

Rutledge, Eddie. Amani's World: Amani & Friends Go to New York City. 2012. 24p. pap. 17.99 (978-1-4772-9554-0(2)) AuthorHouse.

Salamon, Julie. Cat in the City. Weber, Jill, illus. 2014. (ENG.). 208p. (J). (gr. 3-7). 16.99 (978-0-8037-4056-3(5), Dial Bks) Penguin Young Readers Group.

Saldana, Theresa. The Almost Murder & Other Stories. 2008. (ENG.). 144p. (YA). (gr. 6-18). pap. 10.95 (978-1-55885-507-6(6), Piñata Books) Arte Publico Pr.

Sanrio Company, Ltd. Staff. Hello Kitty, Hello New York! Hirashima, Jean, illus. 2014. (ENG.). 16p. (J). (gr. -1 — 1). bds. 7.95 (978-1-4197-1096-4(6), Abrams Appleseed) Abrams, Inc.

Sarcone-Roach, Julia. Subway Story. 2011. (ENG.). 40p. (J). (gr. k-3). 16.99 (978-0-375-85859-8(8), Knopf Bks. for Young Readers) Random Hse. Children's Bks.

Schmidt, Gary D. Okay for Now. 2011. (Playaway Children Ser.). (J). (gr. 5-9). 54.99 (978-1-61707-313-7(X)) Random Hse., Inc.

Schmidt, Tiffany. Hold Me Like a Breath. (ENG.). (YA). 2016. 416p. pap. 9.99 (978-1-61963-870-9(3), 9781619638709) 2015. (Once upon a Crime Family Ser.: Bk. 1). 400p. 17.99 (978-0-8027-3782-3(X), 9780802737823) Bloomsbury Publishing USA. (Bloomsbury USA Childrens).

Scholastic, Inc. Staff & Northrop, Michael. Book of the Dead. 2015. (TombQuest Ser.: 1). (ENG.). 208p. (J). (gr. 3-7). 12.99 (978-0-545-72338-1(8)) Scholastic, Inc.

Scholastic, Inc. Staff & Ryals, Lexi. Annie. movie tie-in ed. 2014. (ENG., Illus.). 144p. (J). (gr. 2-5). pap. 5.99 (978-0-545-79751-1(9)) Scholastic, Inc.

Schroeder, Lisa. Keys to the City. 2017. (ENG.). 240p. (J). (gr. 3-7). 16.99 **(978-0-545-90738-5(1)**, Scholastic Pr.) Scholastic, Inc.

Scieszka, Jon. Hey Kid, Want to Buy a Bridge? McCauley, Adam, illus. 2004. (Time Warp Trio Ser.: 11). (ENG.). 80p. (J). (gr. 2-4). pap. 5.99 (978-0-14-240089-0(0), Puffin Books) Penguin Young Readers Group.

—Hey Kid, Want to Buy a Bridge? McCauley, Adam, illus. 2005. (Time Warp Trio Ser.: No. 11). 74p. (gr. 4-7). 15.00 (978-0-7569-5988-3(8)) Perfection Learning Corp.

—Spaceheadz. Prigmore, Shane, illus. 2010. (Spaceheadz Ser.: 1). (ENG.). 176p. (J). (gr. 2-5). 14.99 (978-1-4169-7951-7(4), Simon & Schuster Bks. For Young Readers) Simon & Schuster Bks. For Young Readers.

—2095. Smith, Lane, illus. 2004. (Time Warp Trio Ser.: 5). (ENG.). 80p. (J). (gr. 2-4). pap. 5.99 (978-0-14-240044-9(0), Puffin Books) Penguin Young Readers Group.

—2095. Smith, Lane, illus. 2005. (Time Warp Trio Ser.: No. 5). 72p. (gr. 4-7). 15.00 (978-0-7569-5989-0(6)) Perfection Learning Corp.

Scott, D. P. The Christmas Elf. Hayward, Roy, illus. 2013. 86p. pap. (978-0-9880635-2-5(2)) Scott, Daren.

Scott, Kieran. What Waits in the Woods. 2017. (ENG.). 288p. (J). (gr. 7). pap. 9.99 **(978-0-545-83763-7(4))** Scholastic, Inc.

Selden, George. The Cricket in Times Square. Williams, Garth, illus. (Chester Cricket Ser.). 151p. (J). (gr. 3-6). pap. 5.50 (978-0-8072-8311-0(8), Listening Library) Random Hse. Audio Publishing Group.

—The Cricket in Times Square. unabr. ed. 2004. (Chester Cricket Ser.). 151p. (J). (gr. 3-7). pap. 29.00 incl. audio (978-0-8072-8310-3(X), S YA 158 SP, Listening Library) Random Hse. Audio Publishing Group.

—The Cricket in Times Square. Williams, Garth, illus. 2008. (Chester Cricket & His Friends Ser.: 1). (ENG.). 144p. (J). (gr. 1-4). pap. 6.99 (978-0-312-38003-8(8), 9780312380038) Square Fish.

—Harry Kitten & Tucker Mouse. Williams, Garth, illus. 2009. (Chester Cricket & His Friends Ser.). (ENG.). 144p. (J). (gr. 1-4). pap. 8.99 (978-0-312-58248-7(X), 9780312582487) Square Fish.

Serle, Rebecca. The Edge of Falling. 2014. (ENG., Illus.). 304p. (YA). (gr. 9). 17.99 (978-1-4424-3316-8(7), Simon Pulse) Simon Pulse.

Sharenow, Robert. The Girl in the Torch. 2015. (ENG.). 304p. (J). (gr. 3-7). 16.99 (978-0-06-222795-9(5)) HarperCollins Pubs.

Sharon, Callen. This Is the Tower That Frank Built, 1 vol. 2013. (Fiction Readers Ser.). (ENG., Illus.). 24p. (J). (gr. 2-2). pap. 6.99 (978-1-4333-5535-6(3)) Shell Educational Publishing.

Shaw, Tucker. Oh Yeah, Audrey! 2014. (ENG., Illus.). 256p. (YA). (gr. 8-17). 16.95 (978-1-4197-1223-4(3), Amulet Bks.) Abrams, Inc.

Sheinmel, Courtney. All the Things You Are. (ENG.). 256p. (J). (gr. 4-8). 2012. pap. 6.99 (978-1-4169-9718-4(0)) 2011. 15.99 (978-1-4169-9717-7(2)) Simon & Schuster Bks. For Young Readers. (Simon & Schuster Bks. For Young Readers).

—My So-Called Family. 2009. (ENG.). 208p. (J). (gr. 4-7). pap. 6.99 (978-1-4169-7942-5(5), Simon & Schuster Bks. For Young Readers) Simon & Schuster Bks. For Young Readers.

—Sincerely: Sincerely, Sophie; Sincerely, Katie. 2010. (ENG.). 400p. (J). (gr. 3-7). 15.99 (978-1-4169-4010-4(3), Simon & Schuster Bks. For Young Readers) Simon & Schuster Bks. For Young Readers.

—Sincerely: Sincerely, Sophie, Sincerely, Katie. 2011. (ENG.). 416p. (J). (gr. 3-7). pap. 7.99 (978-1-4169-4022-7(7), Simon & Schuster Bks. For Young Readers) Simon & Schuster Bks. For Young Readers.

Sherman, M. Zachary. Impulse, Vol. 2. Majado, Caio et al, illus. 2011. (Tony Hawk's 900 Revolution Ser.). (ENG.). 128p. (gr. 3-4). pap. 7.19 (978-1-4342-3452-0(5)); lib. bdg. 26.65 (978-1-4342-3203-8(4)) Stone Arch Bks. (Tony Hawk's 900 Revolution).

Sherry, Maureen. Walls Within Walls. Stower, Adam, illus. (ENG.). 368p. (J). (gr. 3-7). 2012. pap. 6.99 (978-0-06-176703-6(4)) 2010. 16.99 (978-0-06-176700-5(X)) HarperCollins Pubs. (Tegen, Katherine Bks).

Shortt, Yvonne. A New York City Public School Goes Green. 2009. 44p. pap. 19.95 (978-0-557-07182-1(8)) Lulu Pr., Inc.

Shrum, Brianna. How to Make Out. 2016. (ENG.). 284p. (J). (gr. 6). 16.99 (978-1-5107-0167-0(2), Sky Pony Pr.) Skyhorse Publishing Co., Inc.

Shulman, Polly. The Grimm Legacy. (ENG.). (J). (gr. 5-18). 2011. 352p. 8.99 (978-0-14-241904-5(4), Puffin Books) 2010. (Illus.). 336p. 16.99 (978-0-399-25096-5(4), G.P. Putnam's Sons Books for Young Readers) Penguin Young Readers Group.

Shusterman, Neal. Downsiders. 2009. (ENG.). 272p. (YA). (gr. 7). pap. 10.99 (978-1-4169-9747-4(4), Simon & Schuster Bks. For Young Readers) Simon & Schuster Bks. For Young Readers.

—The Schwa Was Here. 2006. (ENG.). 240p. (YA). (gr. 7-18). reprint ed. 6.99 (978-0-14-240577-2(9), Puffin Books) Penguin Young Readers Group.

Silvano, Wendi. Love Is All Around New York. Czernichowska, Joanna, illus. 2016. (ENG.). 32p. (J). (-6). 12.99 (978-1-4926-2945-0(6), Sourcebooks Jabberwocky) Sourcebooks, Inc.

—Love Is All Around New York City. Czernichowska, Joanna, illus. 2016. (ENG.). 32p. (J). (-6). 12.99 (978-1-4926-2946-7(4), Sourcebooks Jabberwocky) Sourcebooks, Inc.

Silvera, Adam. More Happy Than Not. (ENG.). (YA). (gr. 9). 2016. 336p. pap. 10.99 (978-1-61695-677-6(1)) 2015. 304p. 18.99 (978-1-61695-560-1(0)) Soho Pr., Inc. (Soho Teen).

Silvera, Adam. They Both Die at the End. 2017. 384p. (YA). (gr. 9). 17.99 **(978-0-06-245779-0(9))** HarperCollins Pubs.

Smale, Holly. Geek Girl: Picture Perfect. 2016. (Geek Girl Ser.: 3). 416p. (YA). (gr. 8). 17.99 (978-0-06-233363-6(1), HarperTeen) HarperCollins Pubs.

Smallman, Steve. Santa Is Coming to Buffalo. Dunn, Robert, illus. 2013. (ENG.). 32p. (J). (-3). 9.99 (978-1-4022-8858-6(1), Sourcebooks Jabberwocky) Sourcebooks, Inc.

—Santa Is Coming to New York. Dunn, Robert, illus. 2012. (ENG.). 32p. (J). (-3). 9.99 (978-1-4022-7503-6(X), Sourcebooks Jabberwocky) Sourcebooks, Inc.

—Santa Is Coming to New York City. Dunn, Robert, illus. 2015. (ENG.). 32p. (J). (-3). 9.99 (978-1-4926-2662-6(7), Sourcebooks Jabberwocky) Sourcebooks, Inc.

Smith, Alexander Gordon. Hellraisers. 2015. (Devil's Engine Ser.: 1). (ENG.). 352p. (YA). (gr. 7). 17.99 (978-0-374-30169-9(7), 9780374301699, Farrar, Straus & Giroux (BYR)) Farrar, Straus & Giroux.

—Hellraisers. 2016. (Devil's Engine Ser.: 1). (ENG.). 368p. (YA). (gr. 7). 22.10 (978-0-606-39284-6(X)) Turtleback Bks.

Smith, Roland. Beneath. 2015. (ENG., Illus.). 272p. (J). (gr. 4-7). 16.99 (978-0-545-56486-1(7), Scholastic Pr.) Scholastic, Inc.

Snow, Susie. The Old Cookie Jar. Motz, Mike, illus. 2012. 34p. pap. 19.99 (978-1-61996-595-9(X)) Salem Author Services.

Snyder, Marilyn. A Second Chance for Tina. Shiffman, Lena, illus. 2003. (Hello Reader! Ser.). (J). (978-0-439-44154-4(4)) Scholastic, Inc.

Sobel, Deane. Philip the Sea Lion. 2012. (ENG.). (J). pap. (978-1-4675-2347-9(X)) Independent Pub.

Sollano, Carolyn. Tree Top Angels. 2010. 56p. (gr. 4-6). pap. 8.95 (978-1-4502-2276-1(5)) iUniverse, Inc.

Sonneborn, Scott. A Pain in the Butt. Banks, Timothy, illus. 2015. (Frankenstein Journals). (ENG.). 80p. (gr. 2-3). 22.65 (978-1-4965-0222-3(1)) Stone Arch Bks.

Sorrells, Walter. The Travelers, Bk. 2. 2009. (Pendragon: 2). (ENG.). 240p. (J). (gr. 5-9). pap. 6.99 (978-1-4169-6523-7(8), Aladdin) Simon & Schuster Children's Publishing.

Spiegelman, Nadja. Lost in NYC: A Subway Adventure. Sánchez, Sergio García, illus. 2015. (ENG.). 52p. (J). (gr. 2-7). 16.95 (978-1-935179-81-8(0)) TOON Books / RAW Junior, LLC.

Spizman, Robyn Freedman & Johnston, Mark. Secret Agent. 2006. (ENG.). 240p. (J). (gr. 4-7). pap. 11.99 (978-1-4169-1862-2(0), Atheneum Bks. for Young Readers) Simon & Schuster Children's Publishing.

—The Secret Agents Strike Back. 2012. (ENG.). 160p. (YA). (gr. 4-7). pap. 8.99 (978-1-4424-8189-3(7), Atheneum Bks. for Young Readers) Simon & Schuster Children's Publishing.

St Jean, Catherine Avery. A Staten Island Ferry Tale. Frahm, Paul, illus. 2006. 32p. (J). per. 26.99 (978-1-4134-0262-9(3)) Xlibris Corp.

Staake, Bob. Bluebird. Staake, Bob, illus. 2013. (ENG., Illus.). 40p. (J). (gr. -1-3). 17.99 (978-0-375-87037-8(7), Schwartz & Wade Bks.) Random Hse. Children's Bks.

Stampler, Laura. Little Black Dresses, Little White Lies. 2016. (ENG., Illus.). 352p. (YA). (gr. 9). 17.99 (978-1-4814-5989-1(9), Simon Pulse) Simon Pulse.

Stancic, Giselle M. The Paganini Curse. 2013. 166p. 22.95 (978-1-4759-6161-4(8)); pap. 12.95 (978-1-4759-6159-1(6)) iUniverse, Inc.

Staub, Rusty. Hello, Mr. Met. Moore, Danny, illus. 2006. 24p. (J). lib. bdg. 17.95 (978-1-932888-82-9(9)) Mascot Bks., Inc.

Stead, Rebecca. Goodbye Stranger. (ENG.). (J). (gr. 5). 2017. 320p. 7.99 (978-0-307-98086-1(3), Yearling) 2015. 304p. 16.99 (978-0-385-74317-4(3), Lamb, Wendy Bks.) 2015. 304p. lib. bdg. 19.99 (978-0-375-99098-4(4), Lamb, Wendy Bks.) Random Hse. Children's Bks.

Sternin, Joshua & Ventimilia, Jeffrey. Teenage Mutant Ninja Turtles: Pizza Party! 2014. (Step into Reading Level 2 Ser.). lib. bdg. 13.55 (978-0-606-36282-5(7)) Turtleback Bks.

Stevens, Carla & National Geographic Learning Staff. Lily & Miss Liberty. Ray, Deborah Kogan, illus. 2010. (Rise & Shine Ser.). (ENG.). 80p. (C). (gr. 2-5). pap. 6.95 (978-0-590-44920-5(6)) National Geographic School Publishing, Inc.

Stevenson, James. Runaway Horse! Date not set. (J). 15.99 (978-0-06-051978-0(9)); 16.89 (978-0-06-051979-7(7)) HarperCollins Pubs.

Stevenson, Steve. The Heist at Niagara Falls. 2013. (Agatha Girl of Mystery Ser.: 4). lib. bdg. 16.00 (978-0-606-32128-0(4), Turtleback) Turtleback Bks.

Stilton, Geronimo. A Very Merry Christmas. 2008. (Geronimo Stilton Ser.: 35). (ENG.). 128p. (J). (gr. 2-5). pap. 7.99 (978-0-545-02135-7(9), Scholastic Paperbacks) Scholastic, Inc.

Stilton, Thea. Big Trouble in the Big Apple. 2011. (Thea Stilton Ser.: 8). (ENG., Illus.). 176p. (J). (gr. 2-5). pap. 8.99 (978-0-545-22775-9(5), Scholastic Paperbacks) Scholastic, Inc.

Stock, Catherine. A Porc in New York. 2007. (ENG., Illus.). 32p. (J). (gr. -1-3). 16.95 (978-0-8234-1994-4(0)) Holiday Hse., Inc.

Stoddard, William O. Dab Kinzer A Story of A Growing Boy. 2004. reprint ed. pap. 1.99 (978-1-4192-1488-2(8)); pap. 24.95 (978-1-4191-1488-5(3)) Kessinger Publishing, LLC.

Stone, Heather Duffy. Fighter's Alley. 2014. (Bareknuckle Ser.). 104p. (YA). (gr. 6-12). lib. bdg. 27.93 (978-1-4677-1460-0(7), Darby Creek) Lerner Publishing Group.

Strasser, Todd. Can't Get There from Here. (ENG.). (YA). (gr. 7). 2012. 224p. pap. 8.99 (978-1-4424-3357-1(4)) 2004. 208p. 17.99 (978-0-689-84169-9(8)) Simon & Schuster Bks. For Young Readers. (Simon & Schuster Bks. For Young Readers).

—Can't Get There from Here. 2005. (ENG.). 208p. (YA). (gr. 7-12). mass mkt. 7.99 (978-0-689-84170-5(1), Simon Pulse) Simon Pulse.

Sturman, Jennifer. And Then Everything Unraveled. 2010. (ENG.). 256p. (J). (gr. 7). 8.99 (978-0-545-08723-0(6)) Scholastic, Inc.

Sullivan, Maureen. Cabbages & Queens. Ferrando, Carol, illus. 2010. 57p. (J). pap. (978-0-9820381-3-0(5)) MoJo InkWorks.

Sullivan, Maureen & Josephs, Alison. Ankle Soup: A Thanksgiving Story. Josephs, Alison, illus. 2008. (Illus.). 32p. 17.95 (978-0-9820381-0-9(0)) MoJo InkWorks.

Sully, Katherine. Night-Night New York City. Kolanovic, Dubravka & Poole, Helen, illus. 2016. (ENG.). 20p. (J). (-1). bds. 9.99 (978-1-4926-3932-9(X), 9781492639329, Sourcebooks Jabberwocky) Sourcebooks, Inc.

Suma, Nova Ren. Imaginary Girls. 2012. (ENG.). 352p. (YA). (gr. 9-18). pap. 8.99 (978-0-14-242143-7(X), Speak) Penguin Young Readers Group.

Sutherland, Tui T. Shadow Falling. 2007. (Avatars Ser.: Bk.2). 356p. (YA). (gr. 7-12). lib. bdg. 17.89 (978-0-06-085147-7(3), Eos) HarperCollins Pubs.

Swendson, Shanna. Rebel Mechanics. 2015. (ENG.). 320p. (YA). (gr. 7). 18.99 (978-0-374-30009-8(7), 9780374300098, Farrar, Straus & Giroux (BYR)) Farrar, Straus & Giroux.

Swift, Hildegarde H. The Little Red Lighthouse & the Great Gray Bridge: Restored Edition. Ward, Lynd, illus. 2003. (ENG.). 64p. (J). (gr. -1-3). pap. 8.99 *(978-0-15-204573-9(2))* Houghton Mifflin Harcourt Publishing Co.
Takabayashi, Mari. I Live in Brooklyn. 2004. (ENG., Illus.). 32p. (J). (gr. -1-3). tchr. ed. 17.99 *(978-0-618-30899-6(7))* Houghton Mifflin Harcourt Publishing Co.
Tarshis, Lauren. I Survived the Attacks of September 11, 2001. 2012. (I Survived Ser.: 6). (ENG.). 112p. (J). (gr. 2-5). pap. 4.99 *(978-0-545-20700-3(2),* Scholastic Paperbacks) Scholastic, Inc.
—I Survived the Attacks of September 11, 2001. 2012. (I Survived . Ser.: No. 6). lib. bdg. 14.75 *(978-0-606-26205-7(9),* Turtleback) Turtleback Bks.
Tash, Sarvenaz. Three Day Summer. 2016. (ENG.). 320p. (YA). (gr. 7). pap. 10.99 *(978-1-4814-3932-9(4))* Simon & Schuster Children's Publishing.
Taylor, Janet B. Sparks of Light. 2017. (ENG.). 448p. (YA). (gr. 9). 16.99 *(978-0-544-60957-0(3),* HMH Books For Young Readers) Houghton Mifflin Harcourt Publishing Co.
Taylor, Kara. Deadly Little Sins. 2014. (Prep School Confidential Novel Ser.: 3). (ENG.). 288p. (YA). (gr. 7). pap. 19.99 *(978-1-250-03363-5(2),* 9781250033635, St. Martin's Griffin) St. Martin's Pr.
Taylor, Sydney. All-Of-a-Kind Family Uptown. 2014. (ENG.). 200p. (J). (gr. 3). pap. 12.95 *(978-1-939601-17-9(7))* Ig Publishing, Inc.
Tesler, Ellen. Zeke in Central Park. 2010. 32p. pap. 12.99 *(978-1-4490-7211-7(9))* AuthorHouse.
Testa, Maria. Becoming Joe Dimaggio. Hunt, Scott, illus. 2005. (ENG.). 64p. (J). (gr. 5-9). reprint ed. pap. 6.99 *(978-0-7636-2444-6(6))* Candlewick Pr.
Thomas, Rich. The Amazing Spider-Man: An Origin Story, 1 vol. Clark, Jeff, illus. 2012. (Marvel Origins Ser.). (ENG.). 48p. (J). (gr. -1-4). lib. bdg. 24.21 *(978-1-61479-007-5(8))* Spotlight.
Thompson II, Roger E. A Sister's Love: A Novel. 2007. 80p. per. 8.95 *(978-0-595-44549-3(7))* iUniverse, Inc.
Thompson, Kay. Eloise at the Wedding. Lyon, Tammie Speer, illus. 2006. (Eloise Ser.). (ENG.). 32p. (J). (gr. -1-1). pap. 3.99 *(978-0-689-87449-9(9),* Simon Spotlight) Simon Spotlight.
Tiernan, Cate. The Calling, Bk. 7. 2008. (Sweep Ser.: 7). (ENG.). 192p. (YA). (gr. 7-18). 7.99 *(978-0-14-241022-6(5),* Speak) Penguin Young Readers Group.
Tome. Spirou & Fantasio in New York. Janry, illus. 2011. (Spirou & Fantasio Ser.: 2). (ENG.). 48p. (J). (gr. 3-17). pap. 11.95 *(978-1-84918-054-2(7))* CineBook GBR. Dist: National Bk. Network.
Tonatiuh, Duncan. Dear Primo: A Letter to My Cousin. 2010. (ENG., Illus.). 32p. (J). (gr. k-2). 16.95 *(978-0-8109-3872-4(3),* Abrams Bks. for Young Readers) Abrams, Inc.
Topol, Carolyn LeVine. Run for It All. 2016. (ENG., Illus.). (YA). pap. 14.99 ***(978-1-63477-065-1(X),*** Harmony Ink Pr.) Dreamspinner Pr.
Townsend, Wendy. Lizard Love. 2013. 198p. 18.95 *(978-1-60898-151-9(7))* namelos llc.
Treggiari, Jo. Ashes, Ashes. (ENG.). 352p. (J). (gr. 7). 2013. pap. 9.99 *(978-0-545-25564-6(3),* Scholastic Paperbacks) 2011. 17.99 *(978-0-545-25563-9(5),* Scholastic Pr.) Scholastic, Inc.
Trooboff, Rhoda. Ben, the Bells & the Peacocks. Bucher, Cecile, illus. 2006. (ENG.). 36p. (J). per. 15.00 *(978-0-9773536-0-6(5))* Univ. of Toledo Pr.
Uhlberg, Myron & Papoulas, Ted. The Sound of All Things, 1 vol. 2016. (ENG.). 36p. (J). (gr. 1-5). 17.95 *(978-1-56145-833-2(3))* Peachtree Pubs.
Vail, Rachel. Well, That Was Awkward. 2017. (ENG.). 320p. (J). (gr. 5). 16.99 *(978-0-670-01308-1(0),* Viking Books for Young Readers) Penguin Young Readers Group.
Vail, Rachel & Avi. Never Mind! 2005. (ENG.). 208p. (J). (gr. 5-18). reprint ed. pap. 6.99 *(978-0-06-054316-7(7))* HarperCollins Pubs.
Valentine, Sally. The Ghost of the Charlotte Lighthouse. 2006. (J). *(978-1-59531-013-2(4))* North Country Bks., Inc.
van Diepen, Allison. Raven. 2010. (ENG.). 304p. (YA). (gr. 9). pap. 8.99 *(978-1-4169-7468-0(7),* Simon Pulse) Simon Pulse.
Van Dyne, Edith. Aunt Jane's Nieces & Uncle John. 2005. 26.95 *(978-1-4218-1024-9(7),* 1st World Library - Literary Society) 1st World Publishing, Inc.
—Aunt Jane's Nieces in Society. 2005. 28.95 *(978-1-4218-1424-7(2));* 276p. pap. 13.95 *(978-1-4218-1524-4(9))* 1st World Publishing, Inc. (1st World Library - Literary Society).
—Aunt Jane's Nieces in Society. 2007. (ENG.). 144p. pap. 18.99 *(978-1-4264-4161-5(4));* 156p. pap. 21.99 *(978-1-4264-4202-5(5))* Creative Media Partners, LLC.
—Aunt Jane's Nieces in Society. 2004. reprint ed. pap. 1.99 *(978-1-4192-0824-9(1));* pap. 20.95 *(978-1-4191-0824-2(7))* Kessinger Publishing, LLC.
—Aunt Jane's Nieces out West. 2005. 27.95 *(978-1-4218-1425-4(0));* 212p. pap. 12.95 *(978-1-4218-1525-1(7))* 1st World Publishing, Inc. (1st World Library - Literary Society).
Vanasse, Patricia. Resilient. Shalaby, Asharaf, illus. 2013. (ENG.). 328p. (YA). pap. 13.99 *(978-0-9860373-2-0(X))* Pants On Fire Pr.
Vardamaskos, Angela. Everlasting Truth. Boumakis, Maria, illus. 2008. 48p. pap. 24.95 *(978-1-60610-950-2(2))* America Star Bks.
Velasquez, Eric. Grandma's Gift. Velasquez, Eric, illus. 2013. (ENG., Illus.). 32p. (J). (gr. k-1). pap. 9.99 *(978-0-8027-3536-2(3),* 9780802735362, Bloomsbury USA Childrens) Bloomsbury Publishing USA.
Verday, Jessica. The Hidden. (ENG.). 400p. (YA). (gr. 9). 2012. pap. 12.99 *(978-1-4169-7898-5(4))* 2011. 17.99 *(978-1-4169-7897-8(6))* Simon Pulse. (Simon Pulse).
—The Hollow. (ENG.). (YA). (gr. 7). 2010. 528p. pap. 11.99 *(978-1-4169-7894-7(1))*No. 1. 2009. 544p. 17.99 *(978-1-4169-7893-0(3))* Simon Pulse. (Simon Pulse).
Vestry, Annabelle. The Carlyles, Vol. 1. 2008. (Gossip Girl: the Carlyles Ser.: 1). (ENG.). 256p. (YA). (gr. 10-17). pap. 10.99 *(978-0-316-02064-0(8),* Poppy) Little, Brown Bks. for Young Readers.
Viva, Frank. Outstanding in the Rain. 2015. (ENG., Illus.). 32p. (J). (gr. -1-3). 18.00 *(978-0-316-36627-4(7))* Little, Brown Bks. for Young Readers.
Vizzini, Ned. It's Kind of a Funny Story. 2007. (ENG.). 464p. (YA). (gr. 7-12). per. 9.99 *(978-0-7868-5197-3(X))* Disney Publishing Worldwide.
—It's Kind of a Funny Story. 2011. 11.04 *(978-0-7848-3383-4(4),* Everbind) Marco Bk. Co.
—It's Kind of a Funny Story. 2007. (YA). lib. bdg. 20.85 *(978-1-4178-1818-1(2),* Turtleback) Turtleback Bks.
Volponi, Paul. Rikers High. 2010. (ENG.). 256p. (YA). (gr. 7-18). 16.99 *(978-0-670-01107-0(X),* Viking Books for Young Readers) Penguin Young Readers Group.
—Rooftop. 2007. 199p. 17.00 *(978-0-7569-7958-4(7))* Perfection Learning Corp.
Vrettos, Adrienne Maria. Burnout. (ENG.). 208p. (YA). (gr. 7). 2012. Illus.). pap. 8.99 *(978-1-4169-9470-1(X))* 2011. 16.99 *(978-1-4169-9469-5(6))* McElderry, Margaret K. Bks. (McElderry, Margaret K. Bks.).
Walters, Eric. I've Got an Idea. 2004. 166p. (J). pap. *(978-0-00-639196-8(6),* HarperTrophy) HarperCollins Canada, Ltd.
Ward, Lindsay. When Blue Met Egg. 2012. (ENG.). 32p. (J). (gr. -1-k). 16.99 *(978-0-8037-3718-1(1),* Dial Bks) Penguin Young Readers Group.
Warnes, Tim. Chalk & Cheese. Warnes, Tim, illus. 2008. (ENG., Illus.). 32p. (J). (gr. -1-3). 18.99 *(978-1-4169-1378-8(5),* Simon & Schuster Bks. For Young Readers) Simon & Schuster Bks. For Young Readers.
Warwick, J. M. An Open Vein. 2007. (YA). per. 12.95 *(978-1-933963-96-9(4))* Grove Creek Publishing, LLC.
Waters, Kate. Lion Dancer: Ernie Wan's Chinese New Year. Cooper, Martha & Slovenz-Low, Madeline, illus. 2010. (Rise & Shine Ser.). (ENG.). 40p. (C). (gr. -1-3). pap. 9.95 *(978-0-590-43047-0(5))* National Geographic School Publishing, Inc.
Weil, Zoe. Claude & Medea: The Hellburn Dogs. 2007. (ENG., Illus.). 103p. (J). (gr. 2-7). per. 12.00 *(978-1-59056-105-8(8))* Lantern Bks.
Weiss, Ellen. Eloise & the Very Secret Room. Lyon, Tammie Speer & Lyon, Tammie, illus. 2006. (Eloise Ser.). (ENG.). 32p. (J). (gr. -1-1). pap. 3.99 *(978-0-689-87450-5(2),* Simon Spotlight) Simon Spotlight.
—Eloise & the Very Secret Room, 1 vol. Lyon, Tammie, illus. 2016. (ENG.). 32p. (J). ***(978-1-61479-403-5(0))*** Spotlight.
Weitz, Chris. The New Order. 2015. (Young World Ser.: 2). (ENG.). 320p. (YA). (gr. 10-17). 19.00 *(978-0-316-22630-1(0))* Little, Brown Bks. for Young Readers.
—The Revival. 2016. (Young World Ser.: 3). (ENG.). 272p. (YA). (gr. 10-17). 18.99 *(978-0-316-22634-9(3))* Little, Brown Bks. for Young Readers.
—The Young World. (Young World Ser.: 1). (ENG.). (YA). (gr. 10-17). 2015. 400p. pap. 10.99 *(978-0-316-22628-8(9))* 2014. 384p. 19.00 *(978-0-316-22629-5(7))* Little, Brown Bks. for Young Readers.
Weller, Frances Ward. The Day the Animals Came: A Story of Saint Francis Day. Long, Loren, illus. 2006. 35p. (J). (gr. k-4). reprint ed. 17.00 *(978-1-4223-5396-7(6))* DIANE Publishing Co.
Wells, Carolyn & E. C. CASWELL. Two Little Women on a Holiday. l.t. ed. 2006. 178p. pap. 21.99 *(978-1-4264-2807-4(3))* Creative Media Partners, LLC.
Wells, Helen. Cherry Ames, the Mystery in the Doctor's Office. 2007. (Cherry Ames Nurse Stories Ser.). 224p. (J). (gr. 3-7). 14.95 *(978-0-8261-0435-9(5))* Springer Publishing Co., Inc.
Wells, Marcia. Doom at Grant's Tomb. Calo, Marcos, illus. 2017. (Eddie Red Undercover Ser.: 3). (ENG.). (J). (gr. 5-7). lib. bdg. 17.20 ***(978-0-606-39813-8(9))*** Turtleback Bks.
Wells, Marcia. Mystery on Museum Mile. Calo, Marcos, illus. (Eddie Red Undercover Ser.). (ENG.). 256p. (J). (gr. 5-7). 2015. pap. 7.99 *(978-0-544-43940-5(6))* 2014. 16.99 *(978-0-544-23833-6(8))* Houghton Mifflin Harcourt Publishing Co. (HMH Books For Young Readers).
Westerfeld, Scott. Afterworlds. 2014. (ENG., Illus.). 608p. (YA). (gr. 9). 19.99 *(978-1-4814-2234-5(0),* Simon Pulse) Simon Pulse.
—So Yesterday. (ENG.). (YA). (gr. 7-12). 2004. 240p. 16.99 *(978-1-59514-000-5(X))* 2005. 256p. reprint ed. 8.99 *(978-1-59514-032-6(8))* Penguin Young Readers Group. (Razorbill).
Weston, Carol. Speed of Life. 2017. (ENG.). 352p. (J). (gr. 6-8). 16.99 ***(978-1-4926-5449-0(3),*** Sourcebooks Jabberwocky) Sourcebooks, Inc.
Wetterer, Margaret K. & Wetterer, Charles M. The Snowshoeing Adventure of Milton Daub, Blizzard Trekker. 2010. pap. 51.02 *(978-0-7613-6921-9(X))* Lerner Publishing Group.
—The Snowshoeing Adventure of Milton Daub, Blizzard Trekker. Trover, Zachary, illus. 2010. (History's Kid Heroes Ser.). (ENG.). 32p. (gr. 3-5). lib. bdg. 26.60 *(978-0-7613-6175-6(8))* Lerner Publishing Group.
Wheeler-Cribb, Peggy. Madeline Becomes a Star. Bensch, April, illus. 2013. 50p. 29.95 *(978-0-9886194-1-8(5))* ProsePress.
White, Ramy Allison. Sunny Boy & His Playmates. 2007. 104p. pap. 18.99 *(978-1-4346-1569-5(3));* (ENG.). 112p. pap. 19.99 *(978-1-4346-1782-8(3))* Creative Media Partners, LLC.
Wilbur, Helen L. Finnegan & Fox: The Ten-Foot Cop. Manders, John, illus. 2013. (ENG.). 32p. (J). (gr. 1-4). 16.95 *(978-1-58536-784-9(2),* 202354) Sleeping Bear Pr.
Wilcox, Brian & David, Lawrence. Full Moon. Wilcox, Brian, illus. 2004. (Illus.). 30p. (J). (gr. k-4). reprint ed. 16.00 *(978-0-7567-7762-3(3))* DIANE Publishing Co.
Wilsdon, Christina. A New York Sailing Adventure. Hockerman, Dennis, illus. 2006. 26p. (J). 7.99 *(978-1-59939-014-7(0))* Cornerstone Pr.
Winfield, Arthur M. The Rover Boys in Business or the Search for the Missing Bonds. 2006. (ENG.). 316p. per. 30.95 *(978-1-4286-4098-6(3))* Kessinger Publishing, LLC.
—The Rover Boys in New York. 2007. 268p. 26.95 *(978-1-4218-4133-5(9));* per. 11.95 *(978-1-4218-4231-8(9))* 1st World Publishing, Inc. (1st World Library - Literary Society).
—The Rover Boys in New York or Saving the. 2004. reprint ed. pap. 22.95 *(978-1-4191-8117-7(3))* Kessinger Publishing, LLC.
Winfield, Arthur M. The Rover Boys in New York or Saving Their Father's Honor. 2004. reprint ed. pap. 1.99 *(978-1-4192-8117-4(8))* Kessinger Publishing, LLC.
Witherow, Wendy. Bridget's Blog. Pulley, Kelly, illus. 2007. 95p. (J). pap. *(978-1-934306-09-3(6))* Mission City Pr., Inc.
Woltz, Anna. A Hundred Hours of Night. Watkinson, Laura, tr. from DUT. 2016. (ENG.). 256p. (YA). (gr. 9). 17.99 *(978-0-545-84828-2(8),* Levine, Arthur A. Bks.) Scholastic, Inc.
Woodruff, Stephen B. Among Friends: A Quaker Boy at the Battle of Plattsburgh. 2013. x, 155p. (J). pap. ***(978-1-59531-044-6(4))*** North Country Bks., Inc.
Woodson, Jacqueline. After Tupac & D Foster. 2008. (ENG.). 160p. (J). (gr. 5-18). 17.99 *(978-0-399-24654-8(1),* G.P. Putnam's Sons Books for Young Readers) Penguin Young Readers Group.
—After Tupac & D Foster. 2010. lib. bdg. 18.40 *(978-0-606-10720-4(7),* Turtleback) Turtleback Bks.
—Behind You. 2010. (ENG.). 176p. (YA). (gr. 7-18). 7.99 *(978-0-14-241554-2(5),* Puffin Books) Penguin Young Readers Group.
—If You Come Softly & Behind You. 2010. (ENG.). 352p. (YA). (gr. 7-18). 8.99 *(978-0-14-241918-2(4),* Puffin Books) Penguin Young Readers Group.
Woodward, J. Howland. A Moment in Time. 2006. 55p. pap. 16.95 *(978-1-4241-1334-7(2))* America Star Bks.
Wright, Bil. Putting Makeup on the Fat Boy. (ENG.). 240p. (YA). (gr. 7). 2012. Illus.). pap. 9.99 *(978-1-4169-4004-3(9))* 2011. 16.99 *(978-1-4169-3996-2(2))* Simon & Schuster Bks. For Young Readers. (Simon & Schuster Bks. For Young Readers).
Wurge, B. B. Billy & the Birdfrogs. 2008. (ENG.). 178p. (J). (gr. 3-8). pap. 9.95 *(978-0-9815148-2-6(0))* Leapfrog Pr.
—Squiggle. 2009. (LeapKids Ser.). (ENG., Illus.). 152p. (J). (gr. 2-7). pap. 9.95 *(978-0-9815148-9-5(8))* Leapfrog Pr.
Yolen, Jane. Foiled. Cavallaro, Mike, illus. 2010. (ENG.). 160p. (J). (gr. 6-9). pap. 17.99 *(978-1-59643-279-6(9),* 9781596432796, First Second Bks.) Roaring Brook Pr.
Yoo, Paula. Lily's New Home. Ng-Benitez, Shirley, illus. 2016. (Confetti Kids Ser.). (ENG.). 32p. (J). (gr. -1-3). 14.95 *(978-1-62014-249-3(X))* Lee & Low Bks., Inc.
Zadoff, Allen. I Am the Weapon. 2014. (Unknown Assassin Ser.: 1). (ENG.). 368p. (YA). (gr. 10-17). pap. 10.99 *(978-0-316-19967-4(2))* Little, Brown Bks. for Young Readers.
Zalben, Jane Breskin. A Moon for Moe & Mo. Quraishi, Mariam, illus. 2017. (J). lib. bdg. *(978-1-58089-727-3(4))* Charlesbridge Publishing, Inc.
Zarin, Cynthia. Albert, the Dog Who Liked to Ride in Taxis. Pratt, Pierre, illus. 2004. (ENG.). 32p. (J). (gr. -1-3). 18.99 *(978-0-689-84762-2(9),* Atheneum/Richard Jackson Bks.) Simon & Schuster Children's Publishing.
Zevin, Gabrielle. Because It Is My Blood, 1 vol. 2012. (Birthright Ser.: 2). (ENG.). 368p. (YA). (gr. 7). 17.99 *(978-0-374-38074-8(0),* 9780374380748, Farrar, Straus & Giroux (BYR)) Farrar, Straus & Giroux.
—Because It Is My Blood. 2013. (Birthright Ser.: 2). (ENG.). 384p. (YA). (gr. 7). pap. 9.99 *(978-1-250-03422-9(1),* 9781250034229) Square Fish.
—In the Age of Love & Chocolate. 2014. (Birthright Ser.: 3). (ENG.). 320p. (YA). (gr. 7). pap. 10.99 *(978-1-250-05071-7(5),* 9781250050717) Square Fish.
Ziegesar, Cecily von. I Like It Like That. 2004. (Gossip Girl Ser.: 5). (ENG.). 224p. (YA). (gr. 10-17). pap. 10.99 *(978-0-316-73518-6(3),* Poppy) Little, Brown Bks. for Young Readers.
—I Will Always Love You. 2010. (Gossip Girl Ser.: 12). (ENG.). 400p. (YA). (gr. 10-17). pap. 10.99 *(978-0-316-04359-5(1),* Poppy) Little, Brown Bks. for Young Readers.
—It Had to Be You. 2009. (Gossip Girl Ser.). (ENG.). 432p. (YA). (gr. 10-17). pap. 10.99 *(978-0-316-01769-5(8),* Poppy) Little, Brown Bks. for Young Readers.
—Nobody Does It Better. 7th ed. 2005. (Gossip Girl Ser.: 7). (ENG.). 256p. (YA). (gr. 10-17). pap. 10.99 *(978-0-316-73512-4(4),* Poppy) Little, Brown Bks. for Young Readers.
—Only in Your Dreams. 2006. (Gossip Girl Ser.: 9). (ENG.). 256p. (YA). (gr. 10-17). per. 10.99 *(978-0-316-01182-2(7),* Poppy) Little, Brown Bks. for Young Readers.
—Would I Lie to You. 2006. (Gossip Girl Ser.: 10). (ENG.). 224p. (YA). (gr. 10-17). per. 10.99 *(978-0-316-01183-9(5),* Poppy) Little, Brown Bks. for Young Readers.
—You're the One That I Want. 2004. (Gossip Girl Ser.: 6). (ENG.). 256p. (YA). (gr. 10-17). pap. 11.99 *(978-0-316-73516-2(7),* Poppy) Little, Brown Bks. for Young Readers.
Ziegesar, Cecily von, creator. Don't You Forget about Me. 2007. (Gossip Girl Ser.: 11). (ENG.). 304p. (YA). (gr. 10-17). per. 10.99 *(978-0-316-01184-6(3),* Poppy) Little, Brown Bks. for Young Readers.

NEW YORK (N.Y.)—FIRES AND FIRE PREVENTION

Broyles, Janell. The Triangle Shirtwaist Factory Fire of 1911. 2004. (Tragic Fires Throughout History Ser.). (Illus.). 48p. (gr. 5-8). lib. bdg. 29.25 *(978-0-8239-4489-7(1),* Rosen Reference) Rosen Publishing Group, Inc., The.

NEW YORK (N.Y.)—HISTORY

Adams, Alison. The Geography of New York City. 2017. (Text Connections Guided Close Reading Ser.). (J). (gr. 1). *(978-1-4900-1823-2(9))* Benchmark Education Co.
Alko, Selina. B Is for Brooklyn. Alko, Selina, illus. 2012. (ENG., Illus.). 40p. (J). (gr. -1-1). 17.99 *(978-0-8050-9213-4(7),* 9780805092134, Holt, Henry & Co. Bks. For Young Readers) Holt, Henry & Co.
Bailey, Rachel A. The Triangle Shirtwaist Factory Fire. 2014. (Perspectives Library). (ENG., Illus.). 32p. (J). (gr. 4-8). 28.50 *(978-1-63137-620-7(9),* 205263) Cherry Lake Publishing.
Barter, James. Colonial New York. 2003. (Travel Guide To Ser.). (ENG., Illus.). 112p. (J). 30.85 *(978-1-59018-250-5(2),* Lucent Bks.) Cengage Gale.
Bartoletti, Susan Campbell. Terrible Typhoid Mary: A True Story of the Deadliest Cook in America. 2015. (ENG., Illus.). 240p. (YA). (gr. 5-7). 18.99 *(978-0-544-31367-5(4),* HMH Books For Young Readers) Houghton Mifflin Harcourt Publishing Co.
Beckman, Wendy Hart. Harlem Renaissance Artists & Writers. 2013. (Inspiring Collective Biographies Ser.). 112p. (J). (gr. 5-12). pap. 10.95 *(978-1-4644-0269-2(8))* Enslow Pubs., Inc.
Belovitch, Jeanne & Bonnevie, Bonnie. New York City Firsts: A Coloring Book for Families about New York History & America's. Belovitch, Jeanne, ed. 2004. 19p. (J). (gr. -1-6). pap. 3.00 *(978-0-9722969-1-5(3))* CMB Publishing Co.
Birle, Pete. New York Knicks. 2013. (On the Hardwood Ser.). (ENG., Illus.). 48p. (gr. 3-8). pap. 8.95 *(978-1-61570-834-5(0))* Scobre Pr. Corp.
Boehm Jerome, Kate. Buffalo, Ny: Cool Stuff Every Kid Should Know. 2010. (Arcadia Kids Ser.). (ENG., Illus.). 48p. (J). (gr. 3-6). pap. 9.99 *(978-1-4396-0069-6(4))* Arcadia Publishing.
Bolden, Tonya. Maritcha: A Nineteenth-Century American Girl. 2015. (ENG., Illus.). 56p. (J). (gr. k-4). 9.95 *(978-1-4197-1626-3(3),* Abrams Bks. for Young Readers) Abrams, Inc.
Braithwaite, Jill. The Statue of Liberty. 2010. (Lightning Bolt Books (tm) — Famous Places Ser.). (ENG., Illus.). 32p. (gr. k-2). lib. bdg. 26.60 *(978-0-7613-6020-9(4),* Lerner Pubns.) Lerner Publishing Group.
Branscomb, Leslie Wolf. Marc Jacobs. 2011. (Profiles in Fashion Ser.). (Illus.). 112p. 28.95 *(978-1-59935-153-7(6),* 1320457) Reynolds, Morgan Inc.
Brezina, Corona. America's Political Scandals in the Late 1800s: Boss Tweed & Tammany Hall. 2009. (America's Industrial Society in the 19th Century Ser.). 32p. (gr. 4-4). 47.90 *(978-1-61511-336-1(3))* Rosen Publishing Group, Inc., The.
Brown, Marc. In New York. 2014. (ENG.). 40p. (J). (gr. k-12). 17.99 *(978-0-375-86454-4(7));* lib. bdg. 20.99 *(978-0-375-96454-1(1))* Random Hse. Children's Bks. (Knopf Bks. for Young Readers).
Broyles, Janell. The Triangle Shirtwaist Factory Fire of 1911. 2004. (Tragic Fires Throughout History Ser.). (Illus.). 48p. (gr. 5-8). lib. bdg. 29.25 *(978-0-8239-4489-7(1),* Rosen Reference) Rosen Publishing Group, Inc., The.
—The Triangle Shirtwaist Factory Fire Of 1911. 2009. (Tragic Fires Throughout History Ser.). 48p. (gr. 5-8). 53.00 *(978-1-60854-584-1(9),* Rosen Reference) Rosen Publishing Group, Inc., The.
Burgan, Michael. New York, 1609-1776. 2006. (National Geographic Voices from ColonialAmerica Ser.). (ENG., Illus.). 112p. (J). (gr. k-3). 21.95 *(978-0-7922-6390-6(1));* lib. bdg. 32.90 *(978-0-7922-6860-4(1))* National Geographic Society. (National Geographic Children's Bks.).
Carole Marsh. New York City Coloring & Activity Book. 2004. (City Bks.). 24p. (gr. k-5). pap. 3.95 *(978-0-635-02226-4(5))* Gallopade International.
Catal, Patrick. Exploring the New York Colony. 2016. (Exploring the 13 Colonies Ser.). (ENG., Illus.). 48p. (gr. 3-4). lib. bdg. 31.99 *(978-1-5157-2234-2(1))* Capstone Press of Coughlan Cos.
Copeland, Peter F. Scenes of Olde New York Coloring Book. 2009. (Dover History Coloring Book Ser.). (ENG.). 48p. (gr. 3-8). pap. 4.99 *(978-0-486-47494-6(1))* Dover Pubns., Inc.
Crewe, Sabrina & Schaefer, Adam. The Triangle Shirtwaist Factory Fire. 2004. (Events That Shaped America Ser.). (Illus.). 32p. (gr. 3-6). lib. bdg. 26.00 *(978-0-8368-3402-4(X),* Gareth Stevens Learning Library) Stevens, Gareth Publishing LLLP.
Cunningham, Kevin. The New York Colony. 2011. (True Bk Ser.). (ENG., Illus.). 48p. (J). (gr. 3-5). pap. 6.95 *(978-0-531-26607-6(9));* lib. bdg. 29.00 *(978-0-531-25394-6(5))* Scholastic Library Publishing. (Children's Pr.).
Curtiss, A. B. The Little Chapel That Stood Golino, Mirto, illus. l.t. ed. 2005. (ENG.). 36p. (J). (gr. -1-3). 18.95 *(978-0-932529-77-0(1))* Oldcastle Publishing.
Derezinski, Amelia. Star Turns: Dancing on Broadway. 2009. (Curtain Call Library of Dance Ser.). 48p. (gr. 5-8). 53.00 *(978-1-60853-422-7(7),* Rosen Reference) Rosen Publishing Group, Inc., The.
Doman, Mary Kate. Tragedy at the Triangle: Friendship in the Tenements & the Shirtwaist Factory Fire. 2015. (ENG., Illus.). 96p. (J). 14.99 *(978-1-62619-645-2(1),* History Pr., The) Arcadia Publishing.
Edge, Laura Bufano. We Stand As One: The International Ladies Garment Workers' Strike, New York, 1909. 2010. (Civil Rights Struggles around the World Ser.). (ENG., Illus.). 160p. (gr. 9-12). lib. bdg. 38.60 *(978-0-7613-4609-8(0))* Lerner Publishing Group.
Francis, Isabelle. New York City: Yesterday & Today: Understand Properties of Multiplication, 1 vol. 2015. (InfoMax Common Core Math Readers Ser.). (ENG.). 24p. (J). pap. 8.25 *(978-1-4777-4699-8(4),* Rosen Classroom) Rosen Publishing Group, Inc., The.
Furgang, Kathy. The Declaration of Independence & Robert Livingston of New York. 2009. (Framers of the Declaration of Independence Ser.). 24p. (gr. 3-3). 42.50 *(978-1-61512-631-6(7),* PowerKids Pr.) Rosen Publishing Group, Inc., The.
George, Lynn & Schimel, Kate. New York's Early Explorers. 2012. (Spotlight on New York Ser.). (Illus.). 24p. (J). lib. bdg. 22.60 *(978-1-4488-5749-4(X),* PowerKids Pr.) Rosen Publishing Group, Inc., The.
Gloor, Elizabeth. New York City: An Urban Community. 2011. (My Community Ser.). (ENG., Illus.). 12p. (gr. 2-2). pap. 6.95 *(978-1-4488-5720-3(1),* Rosen Classroom) Rosen Publishing Group, Inc., The.
Goldish, Meish. The Empire State Building. 2016. (American Places: from Vision to Reality Ser.). (ENG.). 32p. (J). (gr. 2-7). lib. bdg. 19.95 *(978-1-944102-43-2(4))* Bearport Publishing Co., Inc.
—Ground Zero Dogs. 2012. (Dog Heroes Ser.). 32p. (J). (gr. 2-7). lib. bdg. 25.27 *(978-1-61772-576-0(5))* Bearport Publishing Co., Inc.
Goldsworthy, Steve. Estatua de la Libertad. 2013. (SPA.). (J). *(978-1-62127-623-4(6))* Weigl Pubs., Inc.
—Statue of Liberty with Code. 2012. (AV2 American Icons Ser.). (ENG., Illus.). 24p. (J). (gr. -1-3). pap. 12.95 *(978-1-61913-303-7(2),* AV2 by Weigl) Weigl Pubs., Inc.
Goodman, Susan E. & Goodman, Susan. On This Spot: An Expedition Back Through Time. Christiansen, Lee, illus. 2004. (ENG.). 32p. (J). (gr. k-5). 17.99 *(978-0-688-16913-8(9),* Greenwillow Bks.) HarperCollins Pubs.

Greene, Jacqueline Dembar. The Triangle Shirtwaist Factory Fire. 2007. (Code Red Ser.). (Illus.). 32p. (YA). (gr. 2-5). lib. bdg. 25.27 *(978-1-59716-359-0(7))* Bearport Publishing Co., Inc.
Gregory, Joy. St. Patrick's Cathedral. 2014. (J). *(978-1-4896-2610-3(7))* Weigl Pubs., Inc.
Gunderson, Jessica. The Triangle Shirtwaist Factory Fire. Miller, Phil & Barnett III, Charles, illus. 2006. (Disasters in History Ser.). (ENG.). 32p. (gr. 3-4). pap. 47.70 *(978-0-7368-6999-7(9)*, Graphic Library) Capstone Press of Coughlan Cos.
Gunderson, Jessica Sarah. The Triangle Shirtwaist Factory Fire. Miller, Phil & Barnett, Charles, III, illus. 2006. (Disasters in History Ser.). (ENG.). 32p. (gr. 3-4). per. 8.10 *(978-0-7368-6878-5(X)*, Graphic Library) Capstone Press of Coughlan Cos.
Hannigan, Paula. New York City. Chandler, Shannon, illus. 2012. (ENG.). 12p. (J). bds. 12.99 *(978-1-4494-1876-2(7))* Andrews McMeel Publishing.
Hayn, Carter. New York City: Old & New. 2011. (My Community Ser.). (ENG., Illus.). 12p. (gr. 2-2). pap. 6.95 *(978-1-4488-5723-4(6)*, Rosen Classroom) Rosen Publishing Group, Inc., The.
—New York City's Historical Heritage. 2011. (My Community Ser.). (ENG., Illus.). 12p. (gr. 2-2). pap. 6.95 *(978-1-4488-5722-7(8)*, Rosen Classroom) Rosen Publishing Group, Inc., The.
Herringshaw, DeAnn. The Harlem Renaissance, 1 vol. 2011. (Essential Events Set 7 Ser.). (ENG., Illus.). 112p. (J). (gr. 6-12). lib. bdg. 35.64 *(978-1-61783-101-0(8))* ABDO Publishing Co.
Hintz, Martin. The New York Colony. 2016. (American Colonies Ser.). (ENG.). 32p. (gr. 3-4). pap. 8.10 *(978-1-5157-4220-3(2)*, Fact Finders) Capstone Press of Coughlan Cos.
The History of New York City: Understand Properties of Multiplication. 2014. (Rosen Common Core Math Readers Ser.). (ENG., Illus.). 24p. (J). (gr. 3-4). pap. 8.25 *(978-1-4777-4958-6(6)*, PowerKids Pr.) Rosen Publishing Group, Inc., The.
Hopkinson, Deborah. Shutting Out the Sky: Life in the Tenements of New York, 1880-1924. 2003. (ENG., Illus.). 144p. (J). (gr. 3-7). 19.99 *(978-0-439-37590-0(8)*, Orchard Bks.) Scholastic, Inc.
Humphrey, Jeff & O'Donnell, Kerri. The American Revolution in New York. 2012. (Illus.). 24p. (J). 60.00 *(978-1-4488-5756-2(2))*; pap. 10.00 *(978-1-4488-5755-5(4))*; lib. bdg. 22.60 *(978-1-4488-5741-8(4))* Rosen Publishing Group, Inc., The. (PowerKids Pr.).
Jerome, Kate B. Lucky to Live in New York. 2017. (Arcadia Kids Ser.). (ENG., Illus.). 32p. (J). 16.99 ***(978-0-7385-2778-9(5))*** Arcadia Publishing.
Kallen, Stuart A. The Harlem Renaissance. 2009. (American History Ser.). (ENG.). 128p. (J). (gr. 7-10). 34.80 *(978-1-4205-0104-9(6)*, Lucent Bks.) Cengage Gale.
Katz, Jon. Lenore Finds a Friend: A True Story from Bedlam Farm. Katz, Jon, photos by. 2012. (My Readers Ser.). (ENG., Illus.). 32p. (J). (gr. -1-3). 15.99 *(978-0-8050-9220-2(X)*, 9780805092202, Holt, Henry & Co. Bks. For Young Readers) Holt, Henry & Co.
Kaur, Ramandeep. One World Trade Center. 2015. (How Did They Build That? Ser.). (ENG., Illus.). 32p. (gr. 3-8). 27.99 *(978-1-62920-554-0(0))* Scobre Pr. Corp.
Kent, Deborah. The Great Civil War Draft Riots. 2005. (Cornerstones of Freedom Ser.). (ENG., Illus.). 48p. (YA). (gr. 4-7). lib. bdg. 26.00 *(978-0-516-23632-2(6))* Scholastic Library Publishing.
Lamprell, Klay. Mi Primera Lonely Planet Nueva York, 1 vol. 2013.Tr. of New York Not for Parents. (SPA & ENG.). 96p. (J). pap. 14.99 *(978-84-08-10916-7(2)*, 103549) Lonely Planet Pubns.
Landau, Elaine. The Triangle Shirtwaist Factory Fire. 2005. (Cornerstones of Freedom Ser.). (ENG., Illus.). 48p. (YA). (gr. 4-7). 26.00 *(978-0-516-23626-1(1))* Scholastic Library Publishing.
Lange, Brenda. The Triangle Shirtwaist Factory Fire. 2008. (Great Historic Disasters Ser.). (Illus.). 112p. (gr. 5-8). lib. bdg. 35.00 *(978-0-7910-9641-3(6)*, Chelsea Hse.) Facts On File, Inc.
LaPlante, Walter. The Erie Canal. 2016. (Road Trip Ser.). (Illus.). 24p. (J). (gr. 3-2). pap. 8.15 *(978-1-4824-4674-6(X))* Stevens, Gareth Publishing LLLP.
Lassieur, Allison. Building the Empire State Building: An Interactive Engineering Adventure, 1 vol. 2014. (You Choose: Engineering Marvels Ser.). (ENG.). 112p. (gr. 3-4). 31.99 *(978-1-4914-0400-3(0)*, You Choose Bks.) Capstone Press of Coughlan Cos.
Leoni, Cristiana. New York in the 1930s with La Guardia. 2008. (Come See My City Ser.). 48p. (gr. 4). 28.50 *(978-0-7614-4336-0(3))* Marshall Cavendish Corp.
Libretto, Ellen V. The General Slocum Steamboat Fire Of 1904. 2009. (Tragic Fires Throughout History Ser.). 48p. (gr. 5-8). 53.00 *(978-1-60854-581-0(4)*, Rosen Reference) Rosen Publishing Group, Inc., The.
Lieurance, Suzanne. The Triangle Shirtwaist Fire & Sweatshop Reform in American History. 2003. (In American History Ser.). (Illus.). 128p. (J). (gr. 5-12). lib. bdg. 27.94 *(978-0-7660-1839-6(3))* Enslow Pubs., Inc.
Loewen, Nancy. Scarlett the Cat to the Rescue: Fire Hero, 1 vol. Sorra, Kristin, illus. 2014. (Animal Heroes Ser.). (ENG.). 32p. (gr. k-2). 28.65 *(978-1-4795-5464-5(2))* Picture Window Bks.
Lonely Planet & Mansfield, Andy. POP-UP NEW YORK, 1 vol. 2016. (Lonely Planet Kids Ser.). (ENG., Illus.). 16p. (J). 9.99 *(978-1-76034-337-8(4)*, 5337) Lonely Planet Pubns.
Malaspina, Ann. What's Great about New York? 2014. (Our Great States Ser.). (ENG., Illus.). 32p. (gr. 2-5). pap. 7.95 *(978-1-4677-4527-7(8))* Lerner Publishing Group.
Markel, Michelle. Brave Girl: Clara & the Shirtwaist Makers' Strike of 1909. Sweet, Melissa, illus. 2013. (ENG.). 32p. (J). (gr. -1-3). 17.99 *(978-0-06-180442-7(8))* HarperCollins Pubs.
Marsh, Carole. Exploring New York Through Project-Based Learning: Geography, History, Government, Economics & More. 2016. (New York Experience Ser.). (ENG.). (J). pap. 9.99 *(978-0-635-12356-5(8))* Gallopade International.
—I'm Reading about New York. 2014. (New York Experience Ser.). (ENG., Illus.). (J). pap., pap. 8.99 *(978-0-635-11307-8(4))* Gallopade International.
—The NYC-5 Boroughs: Activity Book. Baker, Janice, ed. 2005. (Illus.). 24p. (gr. k-8). pap. 8.95 *(978-0-635-03080-1(2))* Gallopade International.
Marsico, Katie. The Triangle Shirtwaist Factory Fire: Its Legacy of Labor Rights. 2009. (Perspectives Ser.). 112p. (gr. 7-18). 39.93 *(978-0-7614-4027-7(5))* Marshall Cavendish Corp.
Maynard, Charles W. Fort Ticonderoga. 2009. (Famous Forts Throughout American History Ser.). 24p. (gr. 3-4). 42.50 *(978-1-61512-521-0(3)*, PowerKids Pr.) Rosen Publishing Group, Inc., The.
McCartney, Tania. A New York Year: Twelve Months in the Life of New York's Kids. Snerling, Tina, illus. 2016. (Kids' Year Ser.). (ENG.). 32p. (J). (gr. -1-3). 17.99 *(978-1-925335-07-1(0)*, EK Bks.) Exisle Publishing Pty Ltd. AUS. Dist: Hachette Bk. Group.
McKendry, Joe. One Times Square: A Century of Change at the Crossroads of the World. McKendry, Joe, illus. 2012. (ENG., Illus.). 64p. (J). 19.95 *(978-1-56792-364-3(X))* Godine, David R. Pub.
Morley, Jacqueline. You Wouldn't Want to Meet Typhoid Mary! A Deadly Cook You'd Rather Not Know. Antram, David, illus. 2013. (You Wouldn't Want to... Ser.). (ENG.). 32p. (J). 29.00 *(978-0-531-25944-3(7))*; pap. 9.95 *(978-0-531-23041-1(4))* Scholastic Library Publishing. (Watts, Franklin).
Mortensen, Lori. Ellis Island, 1 vol. Skeens, Matthew, illus. 2008. (American Symbols Ser.). (ENG.). 24p. (gr. 1-2). 26.65 *(978-1-4048-4705-7(7))* Picture Window Bks.
Munro, Roxie. Christmastime in New York City. 2014. (ENG., Illus.). 32p. (J). (gr. -1-3). 14.95 *(978-0-7893-2740-6(6))* Rizzoli International Pubns., Inc.
Murray, Julie. New York, 1 vol. 2012. (Explore the United States Ser.). (ENG., Illus.). 32p. (J). (gr. 2-5). lib. bdg. 28.50 *(978-1-61783-370-0(3)*, Big Buddy Bks.) ABDO Publishing Co.
Nelson, Vaunda Micheaux. The Book Itch: Freedom, Truth & Harlem's Greatest Bookstore. Christie, R. Gregory, illus. 2015. (ENG.). 32p. (J). (gr. 2-4). lib. bdg. 17.99 *(978-0-7613-3943-4(4)*, Carolrhoda Bks.) Lerner Publishing Group.
Otfinoski, Steven. The Triangle Shirtwaist Factory Fire: Core Events of an Industrial Disaster, 1 vol. 2014. (What Went Wrong? Ser.). (ENG.). 32p. (gr. 3-4). lib. bdg. 27.32 *(978-1-4765-4183-9(3)*, Fact Finders) Capstone Press of Coughlan Cos.
Panchyk, Richard. New York City History for Kids: From New Amsterdam to the Big Apple with 21 Activities. 2012. (For Kids Ser.). (ENG., Illus.). 144p. (J). (gr. 4). pap. 17.99 *(978-1-883052-93-5(9))* Chicago Review Pr., Inc.
Pascal, Janet. Where Is the Empire State Building? 2015. (Where Is... ? Ser.). lib. bdg. 16.00 *(978-0-606-36758-5(6))* Turtleback Bks.
Pascal, Janet & dePaola, Tomie. Where Is the Empire State Building? Groff, David, illus. 2015. (Where Is? Ser.). (ENG.). 112p. (J). (gr. 3-7). 5.99 *(978-0-448-48426-6(9)*, Grosset & Dunlap) Penguin Young Readers Group.
Peterson, Sheryl. Empire State Building. 2006. (Modern Wonders of the World Ser.). (Illus.). 32p. (J). 18.95 *(978-1-58341-439-2(8)*, Creative Education) Creative Co., The.
Publications International Ltd. Staff. Yesterday & Today New York. 2009. 192p. 24.95 *(978-1-4127-4294-8(3))* Publications International, Ltd.
Regan, Lisa. Broadway Star. 2012. (Stage School Ser.). (ENG., Illus.). 32p. (J). (gr. 3-6). 25.25 *(978-1-4488-8092-8(0))*; pap. 10.00 *(978-1-4488-8151-2(X))* Windmill Bks.
Riggs, Kate. Empire State Building. 2009. (Now That's Big Ser.). 24p. (J). (gr. 1-5). lib. bdg. 24.25 *(978-1-58341-703-4(6)*, Creative Education) Creative Co., The.
Ringgold, Faith. My Grandmother's Story Quilt. 2016. (ENG., Illus.). 32p. (J). (gr. k-3). lib. bdg. 20.99 *(978-0-517-70948-1(1)*, Knopf Bks. for Young Readers) Random Hse. Children's Bks.
—We Came to America. 2016. (ENG., Illus.). 32p. (J). (gr. k-3). 17.99 *(978-0-517-70947-4(3)*, Knopf Bks. for Young Readers) Random Hse. Children's Bks.
Rubinstein, Robert. Zishe the Strongman. Miller, Woody, illus. 2010. (Kar-Ben Favorites Ser.). (ENG.). 32p. (J). (gr. k-3). pap. 7.95 *(978-0-7613-3960-1(4)*, Kar-Ben Publishing) Lerner Publishing Group.
Rubinstein, Robert E. Zishe the Strongman. Miller, Woody, illus. 2010. (Kar-Ben Favorites Ser.). (ENG.). 32p. (J). (gr. k-3). lib. bdg. 17.95 *(978-0-7613-3958-8(2)*, Kar-Ben Publishing) Lerner Publishing Group.
Rudd, Brandon Kyle. Cooper's Pack Travel Guide to New York City. McCann, Martin, illus. rev. ed. 2012. (ENG.). 72p. (J). (gr. 1-6). pap. 12.95 *(978-0-9794882-5-2(7))* Cooper's Pack.
Sanderson, Jeanette. A Visit to the New Amsterdam. 2005. (J). pap. *(978-1-4108-4229-9(0))* Benchmark Education Co.
Shipton, Vicky & Lerner, Alan J. New York. 2nd ed. 2016. (ENG.). (C). pap. 14.65 incl. cd-rom ***(978-1-4479-2569-9(6))*** Pearson Education.
Spotlight on New York. 2014. (Spotlight on New York Ser.). (ENG.). 24p. (J). (gr. 4-4). 330.40 *(978-1-4777-7345-1(2))*; pap. 140.00 *(978-1-4777-7346-8(0))* Rosen Publishing Group, Inc., The. (Rosen Classroom).
Stanley, Ed. Grand Central Terminal: Gateway to New York City. 2003. (Illus.). 48p. (J). 16.95 *(978-1-59034-491-0(X))*; pap. *(978-1-59034-492-7(8))* Mondo Publishing.
Sweet, Melissa. Balloons over Broadway: The True Story of the Puppeteer of Macy's Parade. 2011. (ENG., Illus.). 40p. (J). (gr. -1-3). 17.99 *(978-0-547-19945-0(7))* Houghton Mifflin Harcourt Publishing Co.
Tan, Richard. Dutch New Amsterdam & English New York. 2011. (My Community Ser.). (ENG., Illus.). 12p. (gr. 2-2). pap. 6.95 *(978-1-4488-5726-5(0)*, Rosen Classroom) Rosen Publishing Group, Inc., The.
—The Famous Explorers of New York City. 2011. (My Community Ser.). (ENG., Illus.). 12p. (gr. 2-2). pap. 6.95 *(978-1-4488-5725-8(2)*, Rosen Classroom) Rosen Publishing Group, Inc., The.
—The Native American Peoples of New York City. 2011. (My Community Ser.). (ENG., Illus.). 12p. (gr. 2-2). pap. 6.95 *(978-1-4488-5724-1(4)*, Rosen Classroom) Rosen Publishing Group, Inc., The.
Tani, Branca. New York in The 1700s. 2011. (My Community Ser.). (ENG., Illus.). 12p. (gr. 2-2). pap. 6.95 *(978-1-4488-5727-2(9)*, Rosen Classroom) Rosen Publishing Group, Inc., The.
—New York in The 1800s. 2011. (My Community Ser.). (ENG., Illus.). 12p. (gr. 2-2). pap. 6.95 *(978-1-4488-5728-9(7)*, Rosen Classroom) Rosen Publishing Group, Inc., The.
—New York in The 1900s. 2011. (My Community Ser.). (ENG., Illus.). 12p. (gr. 2-2). pap. 6.95 *(978-1-4488-5729-6(5)*, Rosen Classroom) Rosen Publishing Group, Inc., The.
Thornton, Jeremy. The History of Early New York. (Building America's Democracy Ser.). 24p. 2009. (gr. 3-3). 42.50 *(978-1-61511-767-3(9))* 2003. (Illus.). (J). lib. bdg. 22.60 *(978-0-8239-6278-5(4))* Rosen Publishing Group, Inc., The. (PowerKids Pr.).
Van Valkenburgh, Norman J. America's First Wilderness: New York State's Forest Preserves. 2008. (Illus.). 44p. (J). 6.50 *(978-1-930098-88-6(X))* Purple Mountain Pr., Ltd.
Vila, Laura. Building Manhattan. 2008. (ENG., Illus.). 40p. (J). (gr. 1-3). 18.99 *(978-0-670-06284-3(7)*, Viking Books for Young Readers) Penguin Young Readers Group.
Watson, Renée. Harlem's Little Blackbird. Robinson, Christian, illus. 2012. (ENG.). 40p. (J). (gr. -1-2). 17.99 *(978-0-375-86973-0(5)*, Random Hse. Bks. for Young Readers) Random Hse. Children's Bks.
Weston Woods Staff, creator. Man Who Walked Between the Towers. 2011. 38.75 *(978-0-545-14931-0(2))*; 18.95 *(978-0-545-14930-3(4))* Weston Woods Studios, Inc.
—The Man Who Walked Between the Towers. 2011. 29.95 *(978-0-439-76703-3(2))* Weston Woods Studios, Inc.
Wetterer, Margaret K. & Wetterer, Charles M. Caminando Bajo la Nieve. Young, Mary O'Keefe, illus. 2007. (Yo Solo Historia Ser.). 48p. (J). (gr. 4-7). per. 6.95 *(978-0-8225-7789-8(5))* Lerner Publishing Group.
—Caminando Bajo la Nieve. Young, Mary, illus. 2007. (Yo Solo - Historia (on My Own - History) Ser.). (SPA.). 48p. (gr. 2-4). lib. bdg. 25.26 *(978-0-8225-7786-7(0))* Lerner Publishing Group.
—Caminando Bajo la Nieve; the Snow Walker. 2008. pap. 40.95 *(978-0-8225-9699-8(7))* Lerner Publishing Group.
—The Snow Walker. Young, Mary, illus. 2010. (ENG.). 48p. (C). (gr. 2-4). pap. 10.95 *(978-0-87614-959-1(X))* National Geographic School Publishing, Inc.
Wilson, Jon. The Statue of Liberty. 2014. (United States Landmarks Ser.). (ENG.). 24p. (J). (gr. 1-4). 27.07 *(978-1-62323-958-9(3)*, 206733) Child's World, Inc., The.
Ziff, John. Northeast: New Jersey, New York, Pennsylvania, Vol. 19. 2015. (Let's Explore the States Ser.). (Illus.). 64p. (J). (gr. 5). 23.95 *(978-1-4222-3329-0(4))* Mason Crest.

NEW YORK (N.Y.)—HISTORY—FICTION

Adler, David A. The Babe & I. Widener, Terry, illus. 2006. 28p. (gr. 1-4). 18.00 *(978-0-7569-6560-0(8))* Perfection Learning Corp.
—The Babe & I. Widener, Terry, illus. 2004. (ENG.). 32p. (J). (gr. -1-3). reprint ed. pap. 7.99 *(978-0-15-205026-9(4))* Houghton Mifflin Harcourt Publishing Co.
Alger, Horatio. Fame & Fortune: Or the Progress of Richard Hunter. 2007. (ENG.). 160p. per. 19.99 *(978-1-4346-5061-0(8))*; 176p. per. 21.99 *(978-1-4346-5062-7(6))* Creative Media Partners, LLC.
—Helping Himself. 2006. 180p. pap. 19.99 *(978-1-4264-0881-6(1))*; (ENG.). 168p. pap. 21.99 *(978-1-4264-0862-5(5))* Creative Media Partners, LLC.
—Helping Himself. 2006. pap. *(978-1-4065-0709-6(1))* Dodo Pr.
—Jack's Ward. 2005. 260p. pap. 13.95 *(978-1-4218-1554-1(0)*, 1st World Library - Literary Society) 1st World Publishing, Inc.
—Jack's Ward. 2006. pap. *(978-1-4065-0711-9(3))* Dodo Pr.
—Jack's Ward: Or, The Boy Guardian. 2006. 176p. pap. 19.99 *(978-1-4264-0882-3(X))*; (ENG.). 168p. pap. 21.99 *(978-1-4264-0863-2(3))* Creative Media Partners, LLC.
—Phil the Fiddler. 2006. pap. *(978-1-4068-0667-0(6))* Echo Library.
—The Store Boy. 2005. 256p. 28.95 *(978-1-4218-0954-0(0)*, 1st World Library - Literary Society) 1st World Publishing, Inc.
—The Store Boy. 2007. (ENG.). 170p. pap. 19.99 *(978-1-4264-4359-6(5))*; 182p. pap. 21.99 *(978-1-4264-4397-8(8))* Creative Media Partners, LLC.
—The Store Boy. 2006. pap. *(978-1-4065-0722-5(9))* Dodo Pr.
—The Store Boy. 2007. 116p. per. *(978-1-4068-1617-4(5))* Echo Library.
—Timothy Crump's Ward. 2005. 27.95 *(978-1-4218-1451-3(X))*; 220p. pap. 12.95 *(978-1-4218-1551-0(6))* 1st World Publishing, Inc. (1st World Library - Literary Society).
—Tom Temple's Career. reprint ed. pap. 79.00 *(978-1-4047-3611-5(5))* Classic Textbooks.
—The Young Outlaw: Or, Adrift in the Streets. 2004. (Illus.). 15.90 *(978-1-4145-0294-6(X))* Pavilion Pr., Inc.
Anderson, Laurie Halse. Chains. l.t. ed. 2017. (Seeds of America Ser.). (ENG.). 442p. 22.99 ***(978-1-4104-9917-2(0))*** Cengage Gale.
—Chains. 2014. (Seeds of America Trilogy). (ENG.). 336p. (J). 12.24 *(978-1-63245-094-4(1))* Lectorum Pubns., Inc.
—Chains. 2009. 9.00 *(978-0-7848-3678-1(7)*, Everbind) Marco Bk. Co.
—Chains. (Seeds of America Trilogy Ser.). (ENG., Illus.). (J). (gr. 5-9). 2010. 336p. pap. 8.99 *(978-1-4169-0586-8(3))* 2008. 320p. 18.99 *(978-1-4169-0585-1(5))* Simon & Schuster Children's Publishing. (Atheneum Bks. for Young Readers).
—Chains. l.t. ed. 2009. (ENG.). 390p. (YA). 23.95 *(978-1-4104-1425-0(6))* Thorndike Pr.
—Chains. 2010. (Seeds of America Trilogy Ser.: 1). lib. bdg. 19.65 *(978-0-606-14520-6(6))*, Turtleback) Turtleback Bks.
Arato, Rona. Mrs. Kaputnik's Pool Hall & Matzo Ball Emporium. 2010. (ENG., Illus.). 192p. (J). (gr. 4-7). pap. 9.95 *(978-0-88776-967-2(5)*, Tundra Bks.) Tundra Bks. CAN. Dist: Penguin Random Hse. LLC.
Auch, Mary Jane. One-Handed Catch. 2009. 272p. (J). (gr. 5-9). pap. 6.99 *(978-0-312-58002-5(9))* Square Fish.
Avi. Catch You Later, Traitor. 2015. (ENG.). 304p. (J). (gr. 3-7). 16.95 *(978-1-61620-359-7(5))* Algonquin Bks. of Chapel Hill.
—City of Orphans. Ruth, Greg, illus. (ENG.). 368p. (J). (gr. 5-9). 2012. pap. 8.99 *(978-1-4169-7108-5(4)*, Atheneum Bks. for Young Readers) 2011. 17.99 *(978-1-4169-7102-3(5)*, Atheneum/Richard Jackson Bks.) Simon & Schuster Children's Publishing.
—The Mayor of Central Park. Floca, Brian, illus. 2003. (ENG.). 208p. (J). (gr. 3-6). 15.99 *(978-0-06-000682-2(X))* HarperCollins Pubs.
—The Mayor of Central Park. Floca, Brian, illus. 2005. 193p. (J). (gr. 3-7). 13.65 *(978-0-7569-5125-2(9))* Perfection Learning Corp.
—The Seer of Shadows. 2009. (ENG.). 224p. (J). (gr. 4-7). pap. 6.99 *(978-0-06-000017-2(1))* HarperCollins Pubs.
—Sophia's War: A Tale of the Revolution. 2012. (ENG., Illus.). 320p. (J). (gr. 3-7). 17.99 *(978-1-4424-1441-9(3)*, Beach Lane Bks.) Beach Lane Bks.
—Sophia's War: A Tale of the Revolution. 2013. (ENG., Illus.). 336p. (J). (gr. 3-7). pap. 7.99 *(978-1-4424-1442-6(1))* Simon & Schuster Children's Publishing.
Axelrod, Amy & Axelrod, David. The Bullet Catch. 2015. (ENG.). 320p. (J). (gr. 5-9). 17.95 *(978-0-8234-2858-8(3))* Holiday Hse., Inc.
Bennett, Carolyn Hart. Seven Sisters: The Voyage. 2008. 232p. 25.95 *(978-0-595-51213-3(5))*; pap. 15.95 *(978-0-595-52242-2(4))* iUniverse, Inc.
Bildner, Phil. Twenty-One Elephants. Pham, LeUyen, illus. 2004. (ENG.). 40p. (J). (gr. -1-3). 17.99 *(978-0-689-87011-8(6)*, Simon & Schuster Bks. For Young Readers) Simon & Schuster Bks. For Young Readers.
Blundell, Judy. Strings Attached. 2011. (ENG.). 320p. (J). (gr. 7-8). 17.99 *(978-0-545-22126-9(9)*, Scholastic Pr.) Scholastic, Inc.
Bray, Libba. The Diviners. 2012. 578p. (YA). 9.99 *(978-0-316-23242-5(4))* Little Brown & Co.
—The Diviners. (Diviners Ser.: 1). (ENG.). (YA). (gr. 10-17). 2013. 496p. pap. 12.99 *(978-0-316-12610-6(1))* 2012. 800p. 42.99 *(978-0-316-22426-0(X))* Little, Brown Bks. for Young Readers.
—The Diviners. 2013. (Diviners Ser.: 1). (YA). lib. bdg. 24.50 *(978-0-606-32284-3(1)*, Turtleback) Turtleback Bks.
—Lair of Dreams. 2015. (Diviners Ser.: 2). (ENG.). 624p. (YA). (gr. 10-17). 19.00 *(978-0-316-12604-5(7))*; (gr. 7-17). E-Book *(978-0-316-36488-1(6))* Little, Brown Bks. for Young Readers.
Brown, Teri. Born of Illusion. 2013. (ENG.). 384p. (YA). pap. 9.99 *(978-0-06-227720-6(0))* HarperCollins Pubs.
Brumbach, Andrew. The Eye of Midnight. 2016. (ENG.). 256p. (J). (gr. 4-7). lib. bdg. 19.99 *(978-0-375-99176-9(X)*, Delacorte Bks. for Young Readers) Random Hse. Children's Bks.
Burack, Emilie Christie. The Runaway's Gold. 2015. (ENG., Illus.). 320p. (YA). (gr. 3-9). 16.95 *(978-1-4197-1369-9(8)*, Amulet Bks.) Abrams, Inc.
Carter, Rachel. Find Me Where the Water Ends. 2014. (ENG.). 352p. (YA). (gr. 9). 17.99 *(978-0-06-208111-7(X)*, HarperTeen) HarperCollins Pubs.
—This Strange & Familiar Place. 2013. (ENG.). 272p. (YA). (gr. 9). 17.99 *(978-0-06-208108-7(X)*, HarperTeen) HarperCollins Pubs.
Chibbaro, Julie. Deadly. Sovak, Jean-Marc Superville, illus. 2011. (ENG.). 304p. (YA). (gr. 7-18). 17.99 *(978-0-689-85738-6(1)*, Atheneum Bks. for Young Readers) Simon & Schuster Children's Publishing.
Clark, Clara Gillow. Hattie on Her Way. Thompson, John, illus. 2005. (ENG.). 208p. (J). (gr. 5-18). 15.99 *(978-0-7636-2286-2(9))* Candlewick Pr.
Donnelly, Jennifer. These Shallow Graves. (ENG.). (YA). (gr. 7). 2016. 512p. pap. 10.99 *(978-0-385-73766-1(1)*, Ember) 2015. 496p. lib. bdg. 22.99 *(978-0-385-90679-1(X)*, Delacorte Pr.) 2015. (Illus.). 496p. 19.99 *(978-0-385-73765-4(3)*, Delacorte Pr.) Random Hse. Children's Bks.
—These Shallow Graves. 2016. (ENG.). 496p. (YA). (gr. 7). 22.10 *(978-0-606-39341-6(2))* Turtleback Bks.
Godbersen, Anna. Beautiful Days. 2012. (Bright Young Things Ser.: 2). (ENG.). 368p. (YA). (gr. 9). pap. 9.99 *(978-0-06-196269-1(4))* HarperCollins Pubs.
—The Luxe. (ENG.). (YA). (gr. 9). 2008. (Luxe Ser.: 1). 464p. pap. 9.99 *(978-0-06-134568-5(7))* 2007. (Luxe Ser.: No. 1). 448p. 17.99 *(978-0-06-134566-1(0)*, HarperTeen) HarperCollins Pubs.
—Rumors. 2009. (Luxe Ser.: 2). (ENG.). 448p. (YA). (gr. 9). pap. 9.99 *(978-0-06-134571-5(7))* 2008. (Luxe Ser.: No. 2). 456p. (J). pap. 17.99 *(978-0-06-170950-0(6))* HarperCollins Pubs.
—Splendor. 2010. (Luxe Ser.: 4). (ENG.). 416p. (YA). (gr. 9). pap. 9.99 *(978-0-06-162633-3(3))* HarperCollins Pubs.
Goodman, Carol. Ravencliffe. 2015. (Blythewood Novel Ser.). (ENG.). 432p. (YA). (gr. 7). pap. 10.99 *(978-0-14-242252-6(5)*, Speak) Penguin Young Readers Group.
Goodman, Gabriel. Lightning's Run. 2014. (Bareknuckle Ser.). (ENG.). 104p. (YA). (gr. 6-12). pap. 7.95 *(978-1-4677-2162-2(X)*, Darby Creek) Lerner Publishing Group.
Greene, Jacqueline. Rebecca Story Collection. Hirsch, Jennifer, ed. Hunt, Robert, illus. 2009. (ENG.). 456p. (YA). (gr. 3-18). 29.95 *(978-1-59369-626-9(4))* American Girl Publishing, Inc.
Haddix, Margaret Peterson. Uprising: Three Young Women Caught in the Fire That Changed America. (ENG.). 352p. (YA). (gr. 7). 2011. pap. 11.99 *(978-1-4169-1172-2(3))* 2007. 16.99 *(978-1-4169-1171-5(5))* Simon & Schuster Bks. For Young Readers. (Simon & Schuster Bks. For Young Readers).
Haines, Kathryn Miller. The Girl Is Trouble. 2012. (ENG.). 336p. (YA). (gr. 7-12). 17.99 *(978-1-59643-610-7(7))* Roaring Brook Pr.
High, Linda Oatman. Tenth Avenue Cowboy. Farnsworth, Bill, illus. 2008. 32p. (J). (gr. 4-7). 17.00 *(978-0-8028-5330-1(7)*, Eerdmans Bks For Young Readers) Eerdmans, William B. Publishing Co.
Hood, Ann & Altmann, Scott. Alexander Hamilton: Little Lion. Kwasney, Karl & Zilber, Denis, illus. 2012. (Treasure Chest Ser.: 2). (ENG.). 224p. (J). (gr. 3-7). pap. 6.99 *(978-0-448-45468-9(8)*, Grosset & Dunlap) Penguin Young Readers Group.

M
N
O

Hopkinson, Deborah. A Bandit's Tale: The Muddled Misadventures of a Pickpocket. 2016. (ENG.). 304p. (J). (gr. 3-7). lib. bdg. 19.99 *(978-0-385-75500-9(7),* Knopf Bks. for Young Readers) Random Hse. Children's Bks.

—Knit Your Bit. Guarnaccia, Steven, illus. 2013. (ENG.). 32p. (J). (gr. k-3). 16.99 *(978-0-399-25241-9(X),* G.P. Putnam's Sons Books for Young Readers) Penguin Young Readers Group.

—Sky Boys: How They Built the Empire State Building. Ransome, James E., illus. 2012. lib. bdg. 18.40 *(978-0-606-23847-2(6),* Turtleback) Turtleback Bks.

Horatio Alger Jr. Cast upon the Breakers. l.t. ed. 2007. 226p. pap. 22.99 *(978-1-4264-8224-3(8))* Creative Media Partners, LLC.

Kerr, M. E., pseud. If I Love You, Am I Trapped Forever?, 0 vols. 2011. (ENG.). 192p. (J). (gr. 7-9). pap. 9.99 *(978-0-7614-5839-5(5),* 9780761458395, Amazon Children's Publishing) Amazon Publishing.

Kirkpatrick, Katherine. Escape Across the Wide Sea. 2004. (ENG., Illus.). 224p. (J). (gr. 4-6). tchr. ed. 17.95 *(978-0-8234-1854-1(5))* Holiday Hse., Inc.

Krensky, Stephen. The Great Moon Hoax. Bisaillon, Josée, illus. 2011. (Carolrhoda Picture Bks.). (ENG.). 32p. (J). (gr. 2-5). lib. bdg. 16.95 *(978-0-7613-5110-8(8))* Lerner Publishing Group.

Kroll, Steven. Sweet America: An Immigrant's Story. 2004. 172p. (J). lib. bdg. 16.92 *(978-1-4242-0773-2(8))* Fitzgerald Bks.

Larkin, Jillian. Diva. 2013. (Flappers Ser.). (ENG.). 320p. (YA). (gr. 7). pap. 9.99 *(978-0-385-74042-5(5),* Ember) Random Hse. Children's Bks.

Larson, Kirby. Audacity Jones Steals the Show (Audacity Jones #2) 2017. (Audacity Jones Ser.: 2). (ENG.). 192p. (J). (gr. 3-7). 16.99 *(978-0-545-84065-1(1),* Scholastic Pr.) Scholastic, Inc.

Lieurance, Suzanne. The Locket: Surviving the Triangle Shirtwaist Fire. 2008. (Historical Fiction Adventures (HFA) Ser.). (Illus.). 160p. (J). (gr. 3-7). lib. bdg. 29.27 *(978-0-7660-2928-6(X))* Enslow Pubs., Inc.

Littlefield, Holly. The Rooftop Adventure of Minnie & Tessa, Factory Fire Survivors. Trover, Zachary et al, illus. 2011. (History's Kid Heroes Ser.). (ENG.). 32p. (gr. 3-5). 26.60 *(978-0-7613-6179-4(0))* Lerner Publishing Group.

Loughrey, Eithne. Annie Moore: First in Line for America. l.t. ed. 2006. (Dales Ser.). 224p. (J). (gr. 4-7). 23.99 *(978-1-84262-446-3(6))* Magna Large Print Bks. GBR. Dist: Ulverscroft Large Print Bks., Ltd.

—Annie Moore: New York City Girl. l.t. ed. 2006. (Dales Ser.). 208p. 23.99 *(978-1-84262-448-7(2))* Dales Large Print Bks. GBR. Dist: Ulverscroft Large Print Bks., Ltd.

—Annie Moore: The Golden Dollar Girl. l.t. ed. 2006. (Dales Ser.). 208p. (J). 23.99 *(978-1-84262-447-0(4))* Magna Large Print Bks. GBR. Dist: Ulverscroft Large Print Bks., Ltd.

Lunievicz, Joe. Open Wounds. 2011. 352p. (YA). (gr. 9-18). 16.95 *(978-1-934813-51-5(6))* Westside Bks.

Maltbie, P. I. Bambino & Mr. Twain. Miyares, Daniel, illus. 2012. (ENG.). 40p. (J). (gr. k-3). 15.95 *(978-1-58089-272-8(8))* Charlesbridge Publishing, Inc.

Manning, Maurie J. Laundry Day. 2012. (ENG., Illus.). 40p. (J). (gr. -1-3). 16.99 *(978-0-547-24196-8(8))* Houghton Mifflin Harcourt Publishing Co.

Manzano, Sonia. The Revolution of Evelyn Serrano. 2012. (ENG.). 224p. (J). (gr. 7-9). 17.99 *(978-0-545-32505-9(6),* Scholastic Pr.) Scholastic, Inc.

Martin, Ann M. Here Today. 2005. (ENG.). 336p. (J). (gr. 3-7). pap. 7.99 *(978-0-439-57945-2(7),* Scholastic Paperbacks) Scholastic, Inc.

Mary-Todd, Jonathan. The Giant. 2014. (Bareknuckle Ser.). 104p. (YA). (gr. 6-12). lib. bdg. 27.93 *(978-1-4677-1457-0(7),* Darby Creek) Lerner Publishing Group.

McDonough, Yona Zeldis. The Cats in the Doll Shop. Maione, Heather, illus. 2012. (ENG.). 160p. (J). (gr. 3-7). pap. 5.99 *(978-0-14-242198-7(7),* Puffin Books) Penguin Young Readers Group.

McGuigan, Mary Ann. Morning in a Different Place. 2009. (ENG.). 195p. (YA). (gr. 7-18). 17.95 *(978-1-59078-551-5(7),* Front Street) Boyds Mills Pr.

Mebus, Scott. Gods of Manhattan, 1 vol. 2009. (ENG.). 368p. (J). (gr. 3-7). 8.99 *(978-0-14-241307-4(0),* Puffin Books) Penguin Young Readers Group.

—The Sorcerer's Secret, Bk. 3. 2011. (ENG.). 384p. (J). (gr. 5-18). 8.99 *(978-0-14-241878-9(1),* Puffin Books) Penguin Young Readers Group.

—Spirits in the Park. 2009. (Gods of Manhattan Ser.: No. 2). (J). *(978-0-525-47963-5(5),* Dutton Juvenile) Penguin Publishing Group.

mendelsohn, martha. Bromley Girls. 2015. (ENG.). 192p. (YA). pap. 14.95 *(978-0-89672-922-3(2))* Texas Tech Univ. Pr.

Meyer, Susan Lynn. Skating with the Statue of Liberty. 2016. (ENG.). 320p. (J). (gr. 3-7). 19.99 *(978-0-375-99010-6(0),* Delacorte Bks. for Young Readers) Random Hse. Children's Bks.

Milford, Kate. The Broken Lands. Offermann, Andrea, illus. (ENG.). 464p. 2015. (J). (gr. 5-7). pap. 8.99 *(978-0-544-43942-9(2),* HMH Books For Young Readers) 2012. (YA). (gr. 7). 16.99 *(978-0-547-73966-3(4))* Houghton Mifflin Harcourt Publishing Co.

Monir, Alexandra. Timekeeper. (ENG.). (YA). (gr. 7). 2014. 304p. pap. 8.99 *(978-0-385-73841-5(2),* Ember) 2013. 288p. 16.99 *(978-0-385-73840-8(4),* Delacorte Bks. for Young Readers) Random Hse. Children's Bks.

—Timeless. 2012. (ENG.). 300p. (YA). (gr. 7). pap. 8.99 *(978-0-385-73839-2(0),* Ember) Random Hse. Children's Bks.

Moriarty, Chris. The Inquisitor's Apprentice. Geyer, Mark Edward, illus. 2011. (ENG.). 352p. (J). (gr. 5-7). 16.99 *(978-0-547-58135-4(1))* Houghton Mifflin Harcourt Publishing Co.

Morpurgo, Michael. Kaspar the Titanic Cat. Foreman, Michael, illus. 2012. 208p. (J). (gr. 3-7). 16.99 *(978-0-06-200618-9(5))* HarperCollins Pubs.

Myers, Walter Dean. Juba! 2016. (Illus.). 208p. (YA). (gr. 8). pap. 9.99 *(978-0-06-211273-6(2))* HarperCollins Pubs.

Napoli, Donna Jo. The King of Mulberry Street. 2007. (ENG.). 256p. (J). (gr. 3-7). 6.99 *(978-0-553-49416-7(3),* Yearling) Random Hse. Children's Bks.

Nelson, Suzanne. Serendipity's Footsteps. 2015. (ENG.). 368p. (YA). (gr. 7). 17.99 *(978-0-385-39212-9(5),* Knopf Bks. for Young Readers) Random Hse. Children's Bks.

Nolan, Han. A Summer of Kings. 2006. 334p. (J). *(978-1-4156-7340-9(3))* Harcourt Trade Pubs.

Osborne, Mary Pope. Blizzard of the Blue Moon. Murdocca, Sal, illus. 2007. (Magic Tree House Merlin Mission Ser.: 8). (ENG.). 144p. (J). (gr. 2-5). 5.99 *(978-0-375-83038-9(3),* Random Hse. Bks. for Young Readers) Random Hse. Children's Bks.

—Hurry up, Houdini! Murdocca, Sal, illus. 2013. (Magic Tree House Merlin Missions Ser.: No. 22). (ENG.). 128p. (J). (gr. 2-5). 12.99 *(978-0-307-98045-8(6),* Random Hse. Bks. for Young Readers) Random Hse. Children's Bks.

Osborne, Mary Pope, et al. A Time to Dance: Virginia's Civil War Diary. 2003. (My America Ser.). (ENG.). 112p. (J). 12.95 *(978-0-439-44341-8(5))* Scholastic, Inc.

Osborne, Mary Pope, et al. Tormenta de Nieve en Luna Azul. Murdocca, Sal, illus. 2016. (SPA.). (J). (gr. 2-4). pap. 5.99 ***(978-1-63245-646-5(X))*** Lectorum Pubns., Inc.

Petrucha, Stefan. Ripper. 2013. (ENG.). 432p. (YA). (gr. 7). pap. 9.99 *(978-0-14-242418-6(8),* Speak) Penguin Young Readers Group.

Plehal, Christopher J. Yes, Virginia: There Is a Santa Claus. Bernardin, James, illus. 2010. (ENG.). 32p. (J). (gr. -1-2). 16.99 *(978-0-06-200173-3(6))* HarperCollins Pubs.

Pollack, Jenny. Klepto. 2008. (ENG.). 288p. (YA). (gr. 7-18). 8.99 *(978-0-14-241072-1(1),* Speak) Penguin Young Readers Group.

Prince, April Jones. Twenty-One Elephants & Still Standing. Roca, François, illus. 2005. (ENG.). 32p. (J). (gr. -1-3). 17.99 *(978-0-618-44887-6(X))* Houghton Mifflin Harcourt Publishing Co.

Rebecca, Stead. When You Reach Me. 2014. (ENG.). 208p. (J). (gr. 12-12). 11.24 *(978-1-63245-235-1(9))* Lectorum Pubns., Inc.

Reiss, Kathryn. A Bundle of Trouble: A Rebecca Mystery. Giovine, Sergio, illus. 2011. (ENG.). 192p. (YA). (gr. 4-18). pap. 6.95 *(978-1-59369-754-9(6))* American Girl Publishing, Inc.

Sacks, Nathan. The Big Fix. 2014. (Bareknuckle Ser.). 112p. (YA). (gr. 6-12). lib. bdg. 27.93 *(978-1-4677-1459-4(3),* Darby Creek) Lerner Publishing Group.

Saxena, Shalini. The Legend of Sleepy Hollow. 2015. (Famous Legends Ser.). (ENG., Illus.). 32p. (J). (gr. 2-3). pap. 10.50 *(978-1-4824-2752-3(4))* Stevens, Gareth Publishing LLLP.

Selznick, Brian. Wonderstruck. Selznick, Brian, illus. 2011. (ENG., Illus.). 640p. (J). (gr. 4-7). 29.99 *(978-0-545-02789-2(6),* Scholastic Pr.); 300.00 *(978-0-545-38985-3(2))* Scholastic, Inc.

Stead, Rebecca. Cuando Me Alcances. 2011.Tr. of When You Reach Me. (SPA.). 294p. pap. *(978-958-45-3215-2(4))* Norma S.A.

—When You Reach Me. (ENG.). (J). (gr. 3-7). 2010. 224p. 7.99 *(978-0-375-85086-8(4),* Yearling) 2009. 208p. 16.99 *(978-0-385-73742-5(4),* Lamb, Wendy Bks.) Random Hse. Children's Bks.

—When You Reach Me. 2010. lib. bdg. 18.40 *(978-0-606-15179-5(6),* Turtleback) Turtleback Bks.

Stephens, John. The Fire Chronicle. 2012. (Illus.). 437p. (J). *(978-0-449-81015-6(1))* Knopf, Alfred A. Inc.

—The Fire Chronicle. (Books of Beginning Ser.). (ENG.). 448p. (J). (gr. 3-7). 2013. 7.99 *(978-0-375-87272-3(8),* Yearling) 2012. (Illus.). 17.99 *(978-0-375-86871-9(2),* Knopf Bks. for Young Readers) Random Hse. Children's Bks.

Townley, Roderick. Sky. 2010. (ENG.). 272p. (YA). (gr. 7). pap. 12.99 *(978-1-4423-3973-6(X),* Atheneum Bks. for Young Readers) Simon & Schuster Children's Publishing.

Waldman, Neil. Say-Hey & the Babe: Two Mostly True Baseball Stories. Waldman, Neil, illus. 2006. (ENG., Illus.). 40p. (J). (gr. 4-7). 16.95 *(978-0-8234-1857-2(X))* Holiday Hse., Inc.

Weatherford, Carole Boston. Sugar Hill: Harlem's Historic Neighborhood. Christie, R. Gregory, illus. 2014. (ENG.). 32p. (J). (gr. k-3). 16.99 *(978-0-8075-7650-2(6))* Whitman, Albert & Co.

Wells, Helen. Cherry Ames, Visiting Nurse. 2006. (Cherry Ames Nurse Stories Ser.). 224p. (J). (gr. 3-7). 14.95 *(978-0-8261-0399-4(5))* Springer Publishing Co., Inc.

Wetterer, Margaret K. & Wetterer, Charles M. The Snowshoeing Adventure of Milton Daub, Blizzard Trekker. Trover, Zachary, illus. 2010. (History's Kid Heroes Ser.). (ENG.). 32p. (gr. 3-5). pap. 8.95 *(978-0-7613-6194-7(4),* Graphic Universe™) Lerner Publishing Group.

NEW YORK (N.Y.)—POETRY

Myers, Walter Dean. Here in Harlem: Poems in Many Voices. 2004. (ENG., Illus.). 96p. (J). (gr. 7-18). tchr. ed. 18.95 *(978-0-8234-1853-4(7))* Holiday Hse., Inc.

NEW YORK (N.Y.)—POLITICS AND GOVERNMENT

Bankston, John. Rudy Giuliani. l.t. ed. 2003. (Blue Banner Biography Ser.). (Illus.). 32p. (J). (gr. 3-8). lib. bdg. 25.70 *(978-1-58415-194-4(3))* Mitchell Lane Pubs., Inc.

Brezina, Corona. America's Political Scandals in the Late 1800s: Boss Tweed & Tammany Hall. 2009. (America's Industrial Society in the 19th Century Ser.). 32p. (gr. 4-4). 47.90 *(978-1-61511-336-1(3))* Rosen Publishing Group, Inc., The.

Shichtman, Sandra H. Michael Bloomberg. 2010. (Political Profiles Ser.). 112p. (J). 28.95 *(978-1-59935-135-3(8))* Reynolds, Morgan Inc.

NEW YORK (N.Y.)—SOCIAL CONDITIONS

Arora, Sabina G. The Great Migration & the Harlem Renaissance. 2015. (African American Experience: from Slavery to the Presidency Ser.). (ENG., Illus.). 80p. (J). (gr. 7-8). 32.90 *(978-1-68048-045-0(6),* Britannica Educational Publishing) Rosen Publishing Group, Inc., The.

Bolden, Tonya. Maritcha: A Nineteenth-Century American Girl. 2005. (ENG., Illus.). 48p. (J). (gr. k-4). 19.95 *(978-0-8109-5045-0(6))* Abrams, Inc.

Greve, Tom. World Trade Center. 2015. (ENG.). 32p. (gr. 3-6). 32.79 *(978-1-63430-042-1(4))* Rourke Educational Media.

Halpern, Monica. Three Immigrant Communities New York City In 1900: Set Of 6. 2011. (Navigators Ser.). (J). pap. 44.00 net. *(978-1-4108-6249-5(6))* Benchmark Education Co.

Hopkinson, Deborah. Shutting Out the Sky: Life in the Tenements of New York, 1880-1924. 2003. (ENG., Illus.). 144p. (J). (gr. 3-7). 19.99 *(978-0-439-37590-0(8),* Orchard Bks.) Scholastic, Inc.

Johnson, Linda Carlson & Johnson, Keri. 9.11 Helping the Heroes: A Salvation Army Story. 2011. (Illus.). (J). *(978-0-89216-130-0(2))* Salvation Army.

Moore, Andrew. New York City's Industries: Jobs for People. 2011. (My Community Ser.). (ENG., Illus.). 12p. (gr. 2-2). pap. 6.95 *(978-1-4488-5721-0(X),* Rosen Classroom) Rosen Publishing Group, Inc., The.

Puck. One to Ten NYC. Pettingill, Charla, illus. 2013. (ENG.). 22p. (J). (— 1). bds. 9.95 *(978-1-938093-19-7(4))* Duo Pr. LLC.

Schimel, Kate & Levy, Janey. New York: The Dutch Colony of New Amsterdam. 2012. (Illus.). 24p. (J). 60.00 *(978-1-4488-5758-6(9));* pap. 10.00 *(978-1-4488-5757-9(0));* lib. bdg. 22.60 *(978-1-4488-5742-5(2))* Rosen Publishing Group, Inc., The. (PowerKids Pr.).

Tan, Richard. New York City's Neighborhoods. 2011. (My Community Ser.). (ENG., Illus.). 12p. (gr. 2-2). pap. 6.95 *(978-1-4488-5718-0(X),* Rosen Classroom) Rosen Publishing Group, Inc., The.

Thomas, Zachary & Wilson, Natashya. The Melting Pot: The People & Cultures of New York. 2012. (Illus.). 24p. (J). 60.00 *(978-1-4488-5768-5(6));* pap. 10.00 *(978-1-4488-5767-8(8));* lib. bdg. 22.60 *(978-1-4488-5747-0(3))* Rosen Publishing Group, Inc., The. (PowerKids Pr.).

NEW YORK (STATE)

Bodden, Valerie. New York. 2010. (Let's Explore America Ser.). 24p. (J). (gr. k-2). 19.95 *(978-1-58341-835-2(0))* Creative Co., The.

Burg, Ann. E Is for Empire: A New York State Alphabet. Brookfield, Maureen, illus. 2003. (Discover America State by State Ser.). (ENG.). 40p. (J). 17.95 *(978-1-58536-113-7(5))* Sleeping Bear Pr.

Burg, Ann E. The New York Reader. Darnell, K. L., illus. 2008. (Readers Ser.). (ENG.). 96p. (J). pap. 5.95 *(978-1-58536-349-0(9))* Sleeping Bear Pr.

—Times Square: A New York State Number Book. Brookfield, Maureen K., illus. 2005. (Count Your Way Across the USA Ser.). (ENG.). 40p. (J). (gr. k-6). 16.95 *(978-1-58536-195-3(X))* Sleeping Bear Pr.

Crane, Cody. New York. 2017. (True Book — My United States Ser.). (ENG.). 48p. (J). pap. 7.95 ***(978-0-531-23292-7(1),*** Children's Pr.) Scholastic Library Publishing.

DeMolay, Jack. Amityville: La casa encantada (Ghosts in Amityville:the Haunted House) 2009. (Historietas Juveniles: Misterios (Jr. Graphic Mysteries) Ser.). (SPA.). 24p. (gr. 2-3). 47.90 *(978-1-61513-344-4(5),* Editorial Buenas Letras) Rosen Publishing Group, Inc., The.

Dunn, Mary. My Adventure in a Mohawk Village. 2006. 44p. (J). 8.99 *(978-1-59092-419-8(3))* Blue Forge Pr.

Dunn, Mary R. I Want to Be in Musicals. 2009. (Dream Jobs Ser.). 24p. (gr. 2-3). 42.50 *(978-1-61512-215-8(X),* PowerKids Pr.) Rosen Publishing Group, Inc., The.

Fein, E. How to Draw New York's Sights & Symbols. 2009. (Kid's Guide to Drawing America Ser.). 32p. (gr. k-k). 50.50 *(978-1-61511-081-0(X),* PowerKids Pr.) Rosen Publishing Group, Inc., The.

Gelman, Amy. New York. (J). 2012. lib. bdg. 25.26 *(978-0-7613-4548-0(5),* Lerner Pubns.) 2nd rev. exp. ed. 2003. (Illus.). 84p. (gr. 3-6). pap. 6.95 *(978-0-8225-4151-6(3))* Lerner Publishing Group.

Glaser, Linda. Emma's Poem: The Voice of the Statue of Liberty. Nivola, Claire A., illus. 2010. (ENG.). 32p. (J). (gr. -1-3). 17.99 *(978-0-547-17184-5(6))* Houghton Mifflin Harcourt Publishing Co.

Lawton, Val. New York: The Empire State. 2016. (J). ***(978-1-5105-2089-9(9))*** SmartBook Media, Inc.

Maine, Tyler. New York. 2016. (States Ser.). (ENG., Illus.). 32p. (gr. 3-4). lib. bdg. 27.32 *(978-1-5157-0419-5(X))* Next Page Pr., The.

Malaspina, Ann. Heart on Fire: Susan B. Anthony Votes for President. James, Steven, illus. 2012. (ENG.). 32p. (J). (gr. 1-3). 16.99 *(978-0-8075-3188-4(X))* Whitman, Albert & Co.

Marsh, Carole. The Big New York Activity Book! 2004. (New York Experience! Ser.). (Illus.). 96p. (gr. 2-6). per. 9.95 *(978-0-635-00165-8(9))* Gallopade International.

—Jography. 2004. (New York Experience! Ser.). 32p. (J). (gr. 3-8). pap. 7.95 *(978-0-635-00162-7(4))* Gallopade International.

—New York Current Events Projects: 30 Cool, Activities, Crafts, Experiments & More for Kids to Do to Learn about Your State! 2003. (New York Experience Ser.). 32p. (gr. k-8). pap. 5.95 *(978-0-635-02051-2(3),* Marsh, Carole Bks.) Gallopade International.

—New York Geography Projects: 30 Cool, Activities, Crafts, Experiments & More for Kids to Do to Learn about Your State! 2003. (New York Experience Ser.). 32p. (gr. k-5). pap. 5.95 *(978-0-635-01851-9(9),* Marsh, Carole Bks.) Gallopade International.

—New York People Projects: 30 Cool, Activities, Crafts, Experiments & More for Kids to Do to Learn about Your State! 2003. (New York Experience Ser.). 32p. (gr. k-5). pap. 5.95 *(978-0-635-02001-7(7),* Marsh, Carole Bks.) Gallopade International.

—New York Pocket Guide. 2004. (New York Experience! Ser.). 96p. (J). (gr. 3-8). pap. 6.95 *(978-0-635-00163-4(2))* Gallopade International.

—New York Symbols & Facts Projects: 30 Cool, Activities, Crafts, Experiments & More for Kids to Do to Learn about Your State! 2003. (New York Experience Ser.). 32p. (gr. k-5). pap. 5.95 *(978-0-635-01901-1(9),* Marsh, Carole Bks.) Gallopade International.

Mezzanotte, Jim & Orr, Tamra B. New York. 2005. (Portraits of the States Ser.). (Illus.). 32p. (gr. 2-6). lib. bdg. 26.00 *(978-0-8368-4630-0(3),* Gareth Stevens Learning Library) Stevens, Gareth Publishing LLLP.

Mills, J. Elizabeth. New York: Past & Present. 2009. (Illus.). 48p. (J). 70.50 *(978-1-4358-5569-4(8));* pap. 11.75 *(978-1-4358-5568-7(X));* (ENG., lib. bdg. 29.25 *(978-1-4358-5285-3(0))* Rosen Publishing Group, Inc., The. (Rosen Reference).

Murray, Julie. New York, 1 vol. 2006. (Buddy Book Ser.). (ENG., Illus.). 32p. (gr. 2-4). 27.07 *(978-1-59197-691-2(X),* Buddy Bks.) ABDO Publishing Co.

Obregon, Jose Maria. Nueva York/New York. Brusca, Maria Cristina, tr. 2006. (Bilingual Library of the United States of America Ser.: Set 1). (ENG & SPA., Illus.). 32p. (J). (gr. 3-6). lib. bdg. 25.25 *(978-1-4042-3097-2(1))* Rosen Publishing Group, Inc., The.

Oestreicher, David M. The Algonquian of New York. 2009. (Library of Native Americans Ser.). 64p. (gr. 4-4). 58.50 *(978-1-60853-742-6(0),* PowerKids Pr.) Rosen Publishing Group, Inc., The.

Schomp, Virginia. New York. 2nd rev. ed. 2005. (Celebrate the States Ser.). (Illus.). 144p. (gr. 6-7). lib. bdg. 42.79 *(978-0-7614-1738-5(9),* Benchmark Bks.) Marshall Cavendish Corp.

Somervill, Barbara A. New York. 144p. (J). 2014. (America the Beautiful Ser.: 3). (ENG.). lib. bdg. 40.00 *(978-0-531-24895-9(X))* 2011. (America the Beautiful, Third Ser.). pap. 12.95 *(978-0-531-22919-4(X),* Children's Pr.) Scholastic Library Publishing.

Von La Valette, Desiree, ed. Cool Shops New York. 2005. (ENG, SPA, FRE, ITA & GER., Illus.). 135p. pap., pap. 16.95 *(978-3-8327-9021-9(7))* teNeues Publishing Co.

NEW YORK (STATE)—FICTION

Airgood, Ellen. The Education of Ivy Blake. 2015. (ENG.). 240p. (J). (gr. 5). 16.99 *(978-0-399-16278-7(X),* Nancy Paulsen Books) Penguin Young Readers Group.

Altebrando, Tara. My Life in Dioramas. 2015. (ENG., Illus.). 256p. (J). (gr. 2-7). 14.95 *(978-0-7624-5681-9(7),* Running Pr. Kids) Running Pr. Bk. Pubs.

Altsheler, Joseph A. The French & Indian War Novels: The Lords of the Wild & The Sun of Quebec, Vol. 3. 2008. (J). reprint ed. 428p. *(978-1-84677-590-1(6));* 424p. pap. *(978-1-84677-589-5(2))* Leonaur Ltd.

—The French & Indian War Novels: The Rulers of the Lakes & The Masters of the Peaks, Vol. 2. 2008. 416p. (J). reprint ed. *(978-1-84677-588-8(4));* pap. *(978-1-84677-587-1(6))* Leonaur Ltd.

—The Hunters of the Hills: A Story of the Great French & Indian War. l.t. ed. 2007. (French & Indian War Ser.). (ENG.). 282p. (J). pap. 23.99 *(978-1-4264-8308-0(2))* Creative Media Partners, LLC.

—The Lords of the Wild: A Story of the Old New York Border. rev. ed. 2006. (French & Indian War Ser.). 264p. (J). 28.95 *(978-1-4218-2335-5(7));* pap. 13.95 *(978-1-4218-2435-2(3))* 1st World Publishing, Inc. (1st World Library - Literary Society).

—The Lords of the Wild: A Story of the Old New York Border. (French & Indian War Ser.: Vol. 1). (J). reprint ed. 24.95 *(978-0-8488-0905-8(X))* Amereon Ltd.

—The Lords of the Wild: A Story of the Old New York Border. (French & Indian War Ser.). (J). 2007. (ENG.). 212p. pap. 20.99 *(978-1-4264-5696-1(4))* 2007. (ENG.). 234p. pap. 22.99 *(978-1-4264-5741-8(3))* 2008. 236p. reprint ed. 27.99 *(978-0-554-24080-0(7))* 2008. 236p. reprint ed. 24.99 *(978-0-554-33383-0(X))* Creative Media Partners, LLC.

—The Lords of the Wild: A Story of the Old New York Border. 2006. (French & Indian War Ser.). (J). pap. *(978-1-4065-0816-1(0))* Dodo Pr.

—The Lords of the Wild: A Story of the Old New York Border. 2007. (French & Indian War Ser.). 156p. (J). per. *(978-1-4068-1681-5(7))* Echo Library.

—The Lords of the Wild: A Story of the Old New York Border. 2010. (French & Indian War Ser.: Vol. 5). (Illus.). 138p. (J). (gr. 4-7). reprint ed. pap. 19.99 *(978-1-153-71020-6(X))* General Bks. LLC.

—The Lords of the Wild: A Story of the Old New York Border. (French & Indian War Ser.: Vol. 5). (J). reprint ed. 2010. 208p. (gr. 4-7). 31.96 *(978-1-169-28834-8(0))* 2010. 208p. (gr. 4-7). pap. 19.96 *(978-1-162-70072-4(6))* 2010. 39.95 *(978-1-161-46937-0(0))* 2004. pap. 24.95 *(978-1-4191-7070-6(8))* 2004. pap. 1.99 *(978-1-4192-7070-3(2))* Kessinger Publishing, LLC.

—The Lords of the Wild: A Story of the Old New York Border. 2011. (French & Indian War Ser.: Vol. 5). 236p. (J). reprint ed. pap. *(978-3-8424-4395-2(1))* Tredition GmbH.

—The Scouts of the Valley: A Story of Wyoming & the Chemung. 2010. (Young Trailers Ser.: Vol. 7). (Illus.). 184p. (J). (gr. 4-7). reprint ed. pap. 19.99 *(978-1-153-72010-6(8))* General Bks. LLC.

—The Scouts of the Valley: A Story of Wyoming & the Chemung. 2010. (Young Trailers Ser.: Vol. 7). 250p. (J). pap. *(978-1-4076-0985-0(8))* HardPr.

—The Scouts of the Valley: A Story of Wyoming & the Chemung. 2010. (Young Trailers Ser.: Vol. 7). (J). reprint ed. 268p. (gr. 4-7). 34.36 *(978-1-169-30757-5(4));* 42.95 *(978-1-161-47633-0(4))* Kessinger Publishing, LLC.

—The Shadow of the North: A Story of Old New York & a Lost Campaign. 2006. (French & Indian War Ser.: Vol. 2). (J). reprint ed. pap. *(978-1-4065-0823-9(3))* Dodo Pr.

Auch, M. J. Guitar Boy. 2012. (ENG.). 288p. (J). (gr. 5-9). pap. 14.99 *(978-0-312-64124-5(9),* 9780312641245) Square Fish.

—One-Handed Catch. 2009. (ENG.). 272p. (J). (gr. 5-9). pap. 6.99 *(978-0-312-53575-9(9),* 9780312535759) Square Fish.

Auch, Mary Jane. Journey to Nowhere. 2004. (Illus.). 202p. (gr. 5-9). 16.00 *(978-0-7569-4144-4(X))* Perfection Learning Corp.

Bauer, Joan. Backwater. rev. ed. 2005. (ENG.). 192p. (YA). (gr. 7-12). pap. 7.99 *(978-0-14-240434-8(9),* Speak) Penguin Young Readers Group.

—Peeled. 2009. (ENG.). 256p. (YA). (gr. 7-18). 8.99 *(978-0-14-241430-9(1),* Speak) Penguin Young Readers Group.

Beck, Nina. This Book Isn't Fat, It's Fabulous. 2009. (ENG.). 256p. (J). (gr. 9). pap. 8.99 *(978-0-545-01704-6(1))* Scholastic, Inc.

Bennese, Ray & Bennese, Kristian. Till the Train Runs Out of Track. 2007. 76p. per. 19.95 *(978-1-4241-7567-3(4))* America Star Bks.

Bruchac, Joseph. The Return of Skeleton Man. Comport, Sally Wern, illus. 144p. (J). (gr. 5). 2008. (Skeleton Man Ser.: 2). (ENG.). pap. 7.99 *(978-0-06-058092-6(5))* 2006. lib. bdg. 16.89 *(978-0-06-058091-9(7))* HarperCollins Pubs.

—Walking Two Worlds. 2015. (ENG.). 152p. (YA). pap. *(978-1-939053-10-7(2))* Book Publishing Co.

Carter, Ally. Heist Society. 2011. (Heist Society Novel Ser.). (ENG.). 304p. (J). (gr. 5-9). pap. 9.99 *(978-1-4231-1661-5(5))* Hyperion Pr.

—Uncommon Criminals. 2011. (Playaway Children Ser.). (YA). (gr. 7-12). 69.99 *(978-1-4558-2483-0(6))* Findaway World, LLC.
—Uncommon Criminals. 2012. (Heist Society Novel Ser.). (ENG.). 304p. (J). (gr. 5-9). pap. 9.99 *(978-1-4231-4807-4(X))* Hyperion Pr.
Coleman, Alice Scovell. The Spirit of Chatsworth Mansion. 2006. 176p. (J). (gr. 4-7). pap. 6.99 *(978-0-9729846-1-4(5))* Tiara Bks. LLC.
Connor, Leslie. Waiting for Normal. 2010. (ENG.). 320p. (J). (gr. 5). pap. 6.99 *(978-0-06-089090-2(8)*, Tegen, Katherine Bks) HarperCollins Pubs.
Cook, Kristi. Haven. (ENG.). (YA). (gr. 9). 2012. 448p. pap. 9.99 *(978-1-4424-0761-9(1))* 2011. 416p. 16.99 *(978-1-4424-0760-2(3))* Simon Pulse. (Simon Pulse).
—Mirage. (ENG., (YA). (gr. 9). 2013. Illus.). 416p. pap. 9.99 *(978-1-4424-4300-6(6))* 2012. 384p. 16.99 *(978-1-4424-4299-3(9))* Simon Pulse. (Simon Pulse).
Cremer, Andrea. The Inventor's Secret. 2014. (Inventor's Secret Ser.: 1). (ENG.). 336p. (YA). (gr. 7). 18.99 *(978-0-399-15962-6(2)*, Philomel Bks.) Penguin Young Readers Group.
Dairman, Tara. All Four Stars. 2014. (All Four Stars Ser.: Bk. 1). (ENG.). 288p. (J). (gr. 3-7). 16.99 *(978-0-399-16252-7(6)*, G.P. Putnam's Sons Books for Young Readers) Penguin Young Readers Group.
De Baun, Hillary Hall. The Last Stop Before Heaven. Cooper, Floyd, illus. 2012. (ENG.). 236p. (J). pap. 9.00 *(978-0-8028-5398-1(6)*, Eerdmans Bks For Young Readers) Eerdmans, William B. Publishing Co.
De la Cruz, Melissa. Crazy Hot. (Beach Lane Ser.: 4). (ENG., (YA). (gr. 9). 2013. Illus.). 288p. pap. 9.99 *(978-1-4424-7412-3(2))* 2008. 320p. pap. 9.99 *(978-1-4169-4808-7(2))* Simon & Schuster Bks. For Young Readers. (Simon & Schuster Bks. For Young Readers).
—Skinny-Dipping. 2013. (Beach Lane Ser.: 2). (ENG., Illus.). 320p. (YA). (gr. 9). pap. 9.99 *(978-1-4424-7410-9(6)*, Simon & Schuster Bks. For Young Readers) Simon & Schuster Bks. For Young Readers.
—Sun-Kissed. 2013. (Beach Lane Ser.: 3). (ENG., Illus.). 336p. (YA). (gr. 9). pap. 9.99 *(978-1-4424-7411-6(4)*, Simon & Schuster Bks. For Young Readers) Simon & Schuster Bks. For Young Readers.
Demas, Corinne. Everything I Was. (Carolrhoda YA Ser.). (ENG.). 216p. (YA). (gr. 6-10). 2012. pap. 9.95 *(978-0-7613-9011-4(1))* 2011. 17.95 *(978-0-7613-7303-2(9))* Lerner Publishing Group. (Carolrhoda Lab™).
Dreyer, Ellen. The Glow Stone. 1 vol. 2006. (ENG.). 224p. (YA). (gr. 7-18). 15.95 *(978-1-56145-370-2(6))* Peachtree Pubs.
Emery, Joanna. Brothers of the Falls. Erickson, David, illus. 2004. (Adventures in America Ser.). (gr. 4). 14.95 *(978-1-893110-37-3(0))* Silver Moon Pr.
Felin, M. Sindy. Touching Snow. (ENG., Illus.). 240p. (YA). (gr. 7). 2011. pap. 11.99 *(978-1-4424-1735-9(8))* 2007. 16.99 *(978-1-4169-1795-3(0))* Simon & Schuster Children's Publishing. (Atheneum Bks. for Young Readers).
Foehner, Ashley & Irving, Washington. Washington Irving's Rip Van Winkle. Locker, Thomas, illus. 2008. (ENG.). 32p. (J). (gr. -1-3). 12.95 *(978-1-55591-713-5(5))* Fulcrum Publishing.
George, Jean Craighead. My Side of the Mountain. l.t. ed. 2005. (ENG.). 211p. pap. 10.95 *(978-0-7862-7359-1(3)*, Large Print Pr.) Thorndike Pr.
Giff, Patricia Reilly. Eleven. 2009. (ENG.). 176p. (J). (gr. 3-7). 7.99 *(978-0-440-23802-7(1)*, Yearling) Random Hse. Children's Bks.
—Pictures of Hollis Woods. 2014. (ENG.). 176p. (J). (gr. 3-7). 11.24 *(978-1-63245-318-1(5))* Lectorum Pubns., Inc.
—Pictures of Hollis Woods. 2004. (ENG.). 176p. (J). (gr. 3-7). 7.99 *(978-0-440-41578-7(0)*, Yearling) Random Hse. Children's Bks.
—Wild Girl. 2011. (ENG.). 160p. (J). (gr. 3-7). pap. 6.99 *(978-0-440-42177-1(2)*, Yearling) Random Hse. Children's Bks.
Going, K. L. The Garden of Eve. 2009. (ENG., Illus.). 240p. (J). (gr. 2-5). pap. 14.95 *(978-0-15-206614-7(4))* Houghton Mifflin Harcourt Publishing Co.
Grab, Daphne. Alive & Well in Prague, New York. 2008. (Laura Geringer Bks.). 247p. (YA). (gr. 7-18). lib. bdg. 17.89 *(978-0-06-125671-4(4)*, Geringer, Laura Book) HarperCollins Pubs.
Hagar, Erin. Doing Her Bit: A Story about the Women's Land Army of America. Hill, Jen, illus. 2016. (ENG.). 32p. (J). (gr. 1-4). lib. bdg. 16.95 *(978-1-58089-646-7(4))* Charlesbridge Publishing, Inc.
Harrison, Lisi. Best Friends for Never. 2004. (Clique Ser.: 2). (ENG.). 208p. (YA). (gr. 7-17). pap. 9.99 *(978-0-316-70131-0(9)*, Poppy) Little, Brown Bks. for Young Readers.
—Revenge of the Wannabes. 2005. (Clique Ser.: 3). (ENG.). 304p. (YA). (gr. 7-17). pap. 9.99 *(978-0-316-70133-4(5)*, Poppy) Little, Brown Bks. for Young Readers.
Hepler, Heather. The Cupcake Queen. 2010. (ENG.). 256p. (YA). (gr. 7-18). 7.99 *(978-0-14-241668-6(1)*, Speak) Penguin Young Readers Group.
Holden, Anthony. Massie. 2008. (ENG.). 144p. (YA). (gr. 7-17). pap. 6.99 *(978-0-316-02751-9(0)*, Poppy) Little, Brown Bks. for Young Readers.
Holmes, Elizabeth. The Normal Kid. 2012. (Exceptional Reading & Language Arts Titles for Intermediate Grades Ser.). (ENG.). 248p. (J). (gr. 4-9). 17.95 *(978-0-7613-8085-6(X)*, Carolrhoda Bks.) Lerner Publishing Group.
Hope, Laura Lee. Bunny Brown & His Sister Sue at Aunt Lu's City Home. 2007. 184p. 25.96 *(978-1-4218-3886-1(9)*, 1st World Library - Literary Society) 1st World Publishing, Inc.
Irving, Washington. The Legend of Sleepy Hollow. 2008. 48p. (gr. -1-4). pap. 6.45 *(978-1-60597-509-2(5)*, Book Jungle) Standard Pubns., Inc.
—The Legend of Sleepy Hollow. Van Nutt, Robert, illus. 2005. (Rabbit Ears Ser.). 36p. (J). (gr. k-5). 25.65 *(978-1-59679-225-8(6))* Spotlight.
—Rip Van Winkle. 2010. (Illus.). 40p. (J). 19.95 *(978-1-58341-923-6(3)*, Creative Education) Creative Co., The.
—Rip Van Winkle: The Mountaintop Edition. Wyeth, N. C., illus. 2016. 96p. pap. 13.95 *(978-1-883789-85-5(0))* Black Dome Pr. Corp.
Irving, Washington & Busch, Jeffrey. Rip Van Winkle. (Classics Illustrated Ser.). (Illus.). 52p. (YA). pap. 4.95 *(978-1-57209-009-5(X))* Classics International Entertainment, Inc.
Irving, Washington & Gutierrez, Dave. La Leyenda Del Jinete Sin Cabeza, 1 vol. Tobon, Sara, tr. from ENG. Smith, Tod G., illus. 2009. (Classic Fiction Ser.). (SPA.). 72p. (gr. 2-3). lib. bdg. 27.99 *(978-1-4342-1688-5(8)*, Graphic Revolve en Español) Stone Arch Bks.
Kerr, M. E., pseud. Your Eyes in Stars. 2006. (YA). (gr. 7-12). (ENG.). 240p. 16.99 *(978-0-06-075682-6(9))*; 229p. lib. bdg. 17.89 *(978-0-06-075683-3(7))* HarperCollins Pubs.
LaCour, Nina. We Are Okay. 2017. (ENG.). 240p. (YA). (gr. 9). 17.99 *(978-0-525-42589-2(6)*, Dutton Books for Young Readers) Penguin Young Readers Group.
Laura Lee Hope. Bunny Brown & His Sister Sue at Aunt Lu's City Home. 2007. 184p. per. 11.95 *(978-1-4218-3986-8(5)*, 1st World Library - Literary Society) 1st World Publishing, Inc.
Lesczynski, Jim. The Walton Street Tycoons. 2007. 269p. (YA). pap. 9.95 *(978-0-9791283-0-1(7))* East River Pr.
Lin, Grace. The Year of the Dog. 2007. (Illus.). 134p. (gr. 3-7). 16.00 *(978-0-7569-8143-3(3))* Perfection Learning Corp.
Lincoln, Dallas Ford. The Sawmill Sant. 2011. 36p. pap. 16.95 *(978-1-4626-4335-6(3))* America Star Bks.
Mackler, Carolyn. Tangled. (ENG.). (YA). (gr. 9). 2011. 336p. pap. 9.99 *(978-0-06-173106-8(4))* 2009. 320p. 16.99 *(978-0-06-173104-4(8))* HarperCollins Pubs. (HarperTeen).
Martin, Ann M. Here Today. 2005. 308p. (gr. 5-9). 18.00 *(978-0-7569-5104-7(6))* Perfection Learning Corp.
Maurer, Shari. Change of Heart. 2010. 290p. (YA). 16.95 *(978-1-934813-36-2(2))* Westside Bks.
Mazer, Norma Fox. The Missing Girl. 2010. (ENG.). 304p. (YA). (gr. 8). pap. 8.99 *(978-0-06-447365-1(1)*, HarperTeen) HarperCollins Pubs.
—Ten Ways to Make My Sister Disappear. 2007. (ENG.). 128p. (J). (gr. 4-7). 16.99 *(978-0-439-83983-9(1)*, Levine, Arthur A. Bks.) Scholastic, Inc.
—Ten Ways to Make My Sister Disappear. l.t. ed. 2008. (Thorndike Literacy Bridge Ser.). 207p. (J). (gr. 4-7). 22.95 *(978-1-4104-0510-4(9))* Thorndike Pr.
McDonough, Yona Zeldis. The Doll Shop Downstairs. Malone, Heather, illus. 2011. (ENG.). 128p. (J). (gr. 2-5). 5.99 *(978-0-14-241691-4(6)*, Puffin Books) Penguin Young Readers Group.
Moldavsky, Goldy. No Good Deed. 2017. (ENG.). 352p. (J). (gr. 9). 17.99 ***(978-0-545-86751-1(7))*** Scholastic, Inc.
Ockler, Sarah. Bittersweet. 2012. (ENG.). (YA). (gr. 9). 400p. pap. 9.99 *(978-1-4424-3036-5(2))*; 384p. 16.99 *(978-1-4424-3035-8(4))* Simon Pulse. (Simon Pulse).
Oliver, Lauren. Panic. 2015. (ENG.). 432p. (YA). (gr. 9). pap. 9.99 *(978-0-06-201456-6(0))* 2014. (J). 137.91 *(978-0-06-230092-8(X))* 2014. (ENG.). 400p. (J). (gr. 9). 17.99 *(978-0-06-201455-9(2))* HarperCollins Pubs.
—Panic. 2015. (YA). lib. bdg. 20.85 *(978-0-606-36509-3(5))* Turtleback Bks.
Osborne, Mary Pope. My Secret War: The World War II Diary of Madeline Beck, Long Island, New York 1941. 2008. (Dear America Ser.). (J). (gr. 3-7). 39.95 incl. audio compact disk *(978-1-4301-0359-2(0))* Live Oak Media.
Paratore, Coleen Murtagh. Dreamsleeves. 2012. (ENG.). 288p. (J). (gr. 5-9). 16.99 *(978-0-545-31020-8(2)*, Scholastic Pr.) Scholastic, Inc.
Russo, Richard. Bridge of Sighs. 2007. *(978-0-7393-2751-7(8))* Random Hse. Large Print.
Rycroft, Frederick. Young World: Book Two - Friends 'Til the End. 2012. 568p. pap. 23.99 *(978-1-4797-1311-0(2))* Xlibris Corp.
Schneeberger, Thomas M. Catch the Wind & Spin, Spin, Spin, 1 vol. 2008. (ENG.). 23p. 24.95 *(978-1-4241-8874-1(1))* America Star Bks.
Sheinmel, Courtney. My So-Called Family. 2008. (ENG.). 208p. (J). (gr. 4-7). 15.99 *(978-1-4169-5785-0(5)*, Simon & Schuster Bks. For Young Readers) Simon & Schuster Bks. For Young Readers.
Small, Cathleen. The Legend of Sleepy Hollow: The Headless Horseman. Antal, Lara, illus. 2016. (American Legends & Folktales Ser.). 32p. (J). pap. 10.58 *(978-1-5026-2206-8(8))* Cavendish Square Publishing.
Sonnenblick, Jordan. Are You Experienced? 2013. (ENG.). 304p. (YA). (gr. 7). 17.99 *(978-1-250-02564-7(8))* Feiwel & Friends.
Starmer, Aaron. The Riverman. 2015. (Riverman Trilogy Ser.: 1). (ENG.). 336p. (YA). (gr. 5-9). pap. 8.99 *(978-1-250-05685-6(3)*, 9781250056856) Square Fish.
Stern, A. J. Fashion Frenzy. Marts, Doreen Mulryan, illus. 2011. (Frankly, Frannie Ser.: 6). (ENG.). 128p. (J). (gr. 1-3). pap. 5.99 *(978-0-448-45544-0(7)*, Grosset & Dunlap) Penguin Young Readers Group.
Stilton, Geronimo. Field Trip to Niagara Falls. Keys, Larry et al, illus. 2005. (Geronimo Stilton Ser.: No. 24). 121p. (J). lib. bdg. 18.46 *(978-1-4242-0293-5(0))* Fitzgerald Bks.
—Field Trip to Niagara Falls. 2006. (Geronimo Stilton Ser.: 24). (ENG., Illus.). 128p. (J). (gr. 2-5). pap. 7.99 *(978-0-439-69146-8(X)*, Scholastic Paperbacks) Scholastic, Inc.
Strasser, Todd. Wish You Were Dead. (ENG.). 240p. (gr. 9). 2010. (J). pap. 8.99 *(978-1-60684-138-9(6))* 2009. 16.99 *(978-1-60684-007-8(X))* Lerner Publishing Group. (Carolrhoda Lab™).
Stratemeyer, Edward. Richard Dare's Venture. 2007. 232p. 26.95 *(978-1-4218-4146-5(0))*; per. 11.95 *(978-1-4218-4244-8(0))* 1st World Publishing, Inc. (1st World Library - Literary Society).
Taylor, Gaylia. George Crum & the Saratoga Chip, 1 vol. Morrison, Frank, illus. 2006. (ENG.). 32p. (J). (gr. 1-5). 16.95 *(978-1-58430-255-1(0))* Lee & Low Bks., Inc.
Taylor, Gaylia & Morrison, Frank. George Crum & the Saratoga Chip. 2006. (ENG., Illus.). 32p. (J). pap. 9.95 *(978-1-60060-656-4(3))* Lee & Low Bks., Inc.
Tocher, Timothy. Bill Pennant, Babe Ruth, & Me. 2009. (ENG.). 184p. (J). (gr. 3-7). 17.95 *(978-0-8126-2755-8(5))* Cricket Bks.
Tooke, Wes. Lucky: Maris, Mantle, & My Best Summer Ever. 2011. (ENG.). 192p. (J). (gr. 3-7). pap. 6.99 *(978-1-4169-8664-5(2)*, Simon & Schuster Bks. For Young Readers) Simon & Schuster Bks. For Young Readers.
Vail, Rachel. Gorgeous. (Avery Sisters Trilogy Ser.: 2). (ENG.). (YA). (gr. 8). 2010. 304p. pap. 9.99 *(978-0-06-089048-3(7))* 2009. 288p. 16.99 *(978-0-06-089046-9(0))* HarperCollins Pubs.
Van Dyne, Edith. Aunt Jane's Nieces & Uncle John. 2005. 176p. pap. 11.95 *(978-1-4218-1124-6(3)*, 1st World Library - Literary Society) 1st World Publishing, Inc.
—Aunt Jane's Nieces at Millville. 2005. 27.95 *(978-1-4218-1026-3(3))*; 204p. pap. 12.95 *(978-1-4218-1126-0(X))* 1st World Publishing, Inc. (1st World Library - Literary Society).
—Aunt Jane's Nieces at Work. 2005. 204p. pap. 12.95 *(978-1-4218-1523-7(0)*, 1st World Library - Literary Society) 1st World Publishing, Inc.
Vande Velde, Vivian. There's a Dead Person Following My Sister Around. 2008. (ENG., Illus.). 160p. (J). (gr. 5-7). pap. 11.95 *(978-0-15-206467-9(2))* Houghton Mifflin Harcourt Publishing Co.
Verday, Jessica. The Haunted. (ENG.). (YA). (gr. 9). 2011. 496p. pap. 11.99 *(978-1-4169-7896-1(8))* 2010. 480p. 17.99 *(978-1-4169-7895-4(X))* Simon Pulse. (Simon Pulse).
Vlahos, Len. The Scar Boys. 2014. (ENG.). 256p. (J). (gr. 9). 17.99 *(978-1-60684-439-7(3))* Lerner Publishing Group.
Volponi, Paul. Rikers High. 2011. (ENG.). 272p. (YA). (gr. 7-18). 7.99 *(978-0-14-241778-2(5)*, Speak) Penguin Young Readers Group.
Weeks, Sarah. As Simple as It Seems. 2010. (ENG.). 192p. (J). (gr. 3-7). 15.99 *(978-0-06-084663-3(1))* HarperCollins Pubs.
Wilder, Laura Ingalls. Farmer Boy. Williams, Garth, illus. (Little House Ser.: 2). (ENG.). 384p. (J). (gr. 3-7). 2008. pap. 7.99 *(978-0-06-440003-9(4))* 2004. pap. 8.99 *(978-0-06-058182-4(4))* HarperCollins Pubs.
Winfield, Arthur M. Putnam Hall Champions or Bound to Win Ou. 2006. pap. 28.95 *(978-1-4286-2346-0(9))* Kessinger Publishing, LLC.
—The Rover Boys on the Ocean. 2007. 232p. 26.95 *(978-1-4218-4138-0(X))*; per. 11.95 *(978-1-4218-4236-3(X))* 1st World Publishing, Inc. (1st World Library - Literary Society).
Zevin, Gabrielle. Because It Is My Blood, 1 vol. 2012. (Birthright Ser.: 2). (ENG.). 368p. (YA). (gr. 7). 17.99 *(978-0-374-38074-8(0)*, 9780374380748, Farrar, Straus & Giroux (BYR)) Farrar, Straus & Giroux.
Ziegesar, Cecily von. Adored. 2009. (It Girl Ser.: 8). (ENG.). 240p. (YA). (gr. 10-17). pap. 9.99 *(978-0-316-02509-6(7)*, Tingley, Megan Bks.) Little, Brown Bks. for Young Readers.
Ziegesar, Cecily von, creator. Notorious. 2006. (It Girl Ser.: 2). (ENG.). 288p. (YA). (gr. 10-17). per. 9.99 *(978-0-316-01186-0(X)*, Poppy) Little, Brown Bks. for Young Readers.

NEW YORK (STATE)—HISTORY

Ball, Jacqueline A. & Behrens, Kristen. Nueva York. Porras, Carlos & D'Andrea, Patricia, trs. from ENG. 2003. (World Almanac Biblioteca de los Estados). (SPA., Illus.). 48p. (gr. 4-9). lib. bdg. 31.00 *(978-0-8368-5546-3(9)*, Gareth Stevens Learning Library) Stevens, Gareth Publishing LLLP.
Bauer, Marion Dane. Celebrating New York: 50 States to Celebrate. Canga, C. B., illus. 2013. (Green Light Readers Level 3 Ser.). (ENG.). 40p. (J). (gr. 1-4). 12.99 *(978-0-547-89782-0(0))*; pap. 3.99 *(978-0-547-89781-3(2))* Houghton Mifflin Harcourt Publishing Co.
Boehm Jerome, Kate. Rochester & the State of New York: Cool Stuff Every Kid Should Know. 2011. (Arcadia Kids Ser.). (ENG., Illus.). 48p. (J). (gr. 3-6). pap. 9.99 *(978-1-4396-0093-1(7))* Arcadia Publishing.
Bolden, Tonya. Maritcha: A Nineteenth-Century American Girl. 2005. (ENG., Illus.). 48p. (J). (gr. k-4). 19.95 *(978-0-8109-5045-0(6))* Abrams, Inc.
Brill, Marlene Targ. Annie Shapiro & the Clothing Workers' Strike. 2010. pap. 56.72 *(978-0-7613-6924-0(4))* Lerner Publishing Group.
—Annie Shapiro & the Clothing Workers' Strike. Akib, Jamel, illus. 2010. (History Speaks: Picture Books Plus Reader's Theater Ser.). (ENG.). 48p. (gr. 2-4). lib. bdg. 27.93 *(978-1-58013-672-3(9)*, Millbrook Pr.) Lerner Publishing Group.
Catal, Patrick. Exploring the New York Colony. 2016. (Exploring the 13 Colonies Ser.). (ENG., Illus.). 48p. (gr. 3-4). lib. bdg. 31.99 *(978-1-5157-2234-2(1))* Capstone Press of Coughlan Cos.
Cunningham, Kevin. The New York Colony. 2011. (True Bk Ser.). (ENG., Illus.). 48p. (J). (gr. 3-5). pap. 6.95 *(978-0-531-26607-6(9))*; lib. bdg. 29.00 *(978-0-531-25394-6(5))* Scholastic Library Publishing. (Children's Pr.).
Doherty, Craig A. & Doherty, Katherine M. New York, 13 vols. 2005. (Thirteen Colonies Ser.). (Illus.). 144p. (gr. 5-8). 35.00 *(978-0-8160-5410-7(X))* Facts On File, Inc.
Downey, Tika. New York: The Empire State. (Illus.). 24p. (J). 2010. pap. 8.25 *(978-1-4358-3336-4(8)*, 1300530) 2009. lib. bdg. 22.60 *(978-1-4042-8108-0(8)*, 1300530) Rosen Publishing Group, Inc., The. (PowerKids Pr.).
Dunn, Mary R. & Alamán, Eduardo. Quiero Trabajar en Los Musicales. 2009. (Trabajos de Ensueño (Dream Jobs) Ser.). (SPA., Illus.). 24p. (J). (gr. 2-4). lib. bdg. 22.60 *(978-1-4042-8153-0(3)*, PowerKids Pr.) Rosen Publishing Group, Inc., The.
Elish, Dan & Fitzgerald, Stephanie. New York. 2014. (It's My State! (r) Ser.). (Illus.). 80p. (J). (gr. 4-8). lib. bdg. 34.21 *(978-1-62712-752-3(6))* Cavendish Square Publishing.
—New York. 2nd rev. ed. 2010. (It's My State! Ser.). 80p. (gr. 3-18). lib. bdg. 31.36 *(978-1-60870-056-1(9))* Marshall Cavendish Corp.
Flynn, Andy. New York State's Mountain Heritage: Adirondack Attic 2. 2005. (Illus.). 240p. per. 18.00 *(978-0-9754007-1-5(1))* Hungry Bear Publishing.
—New York State's Mountain Heritage Vol. 1: Adirondack Attic 1. 2004. (Illus.). 184p. per. 16.95 *(978-0-9754007-0-8(3))* Hungry Bear Publishing.
Gamble, Jasper, et al. Good Night New York State. Jasper, Mark, illus. 2012. (Good Night Our World Ser.). (ENG.). 20p. (J). (gr. k — 1). bds. 9.95 *(978-1-60219-063-4(1))* Good Night Bks.
George, Lynn & Schimel, Kate. New York's Early Explorers. 2012. (Illus.). 24p. (J). 60.00 *(978-1-4488-5772-2(4))*; pap. 10.00 *(978-1-4488-5771-5(6))* Rosen Publishing Group, Inc., The. (PowerKids Pr.).
Goodman, Michael E. The Story of the New York Knicks. 2010. (NBA — A History of Hoops Ser.). 48p. (YA). (gr. 5-18). 23.95 *(978-1-58341-955-7(1)*, Creative Education) Creative Co., The.
Holub, Joan. What Was Woodstock? Copeland, Gregory & McVeigh, Kevin, illus. 2016. (What Was? Ser.). (ENG.). 112p. (J). (gr. 3-7). 5.99 *(978-0-448-48696-3(2)*, Grosset & Dunlap) Penguin Young Readers Group.
—What Was Woodstock? 2016. (What Was... ? Ser.). lib. bdg. 16.00 *(978-0-606-38414-8(6))* Turtleback Bks.
Houghton, Gillian. The Oneida of Wisconsin. 2009. (Library of Native Americans Ser.). 64p. (gr. 4-4). 58.50 *(978-1-60853-759-4(5)*, PowerKids Pr.) Rosen Publishing Group, Inc., The.
Ingram, Scott. The Battle of Valcour Bay. 2003. (Triangle Histories of the American Revolution Ser.). (Illus.). 32p. (J). 22.45 *(978-1-56711-778-3(3)*, Blackbirch Pr., Inc.) Cengage Gale.
Jensen, Niels R. New York, 1 vol. 2009. (United States Ser.). (ENG., Illus.). 48p. (YA). (gr. 2-5). 27.07 *(978-1-60453-667-6(5))* ABDO Publishing Co.
Katz, Jon. Meet the Dogs of Bedlam Farm. Katz, Jon, photos by. 2011. (ENG., Illus.). 32p. (J). (gr. -1-3). 17.99 *(978-0-8050-9219-6(6)*, 9780805092196, Holt, Henry & Co. Bks. For Young Readers) Holt, Henry & Co.
Kenney, Karen Latchana. Bea on Broadway: A Story about New York, 1 vol. 2008. (Fact & Fable: State Stories Ser.). (ENG., Illus.). 24p. (J). (gr. -1-2). 25.65 *(978-1-60453-182-4(7))* ABDO Publishing Co.
Krizner, L. J. Peter Stuyvesant: New Amsterdam, & the Origins of New York. 2009. (Library of American Lives & Times Ser.). 112p. (gr. 5-5). 69.20 *(978-1-60853-498-2(7))* Rosen Publishing Group, Inc., The.
Krizner, L. J. & Sita, Lisa. Peter Stuyvesant: New Amsterdam & the Origins of New York. 2005. (Library of American Lives & Times). (Illus.). 112p. (J). (gr. 4-8). lib. bdg. 34.60 *(978-0-8239-5732-3(2))* Rosen Publishing Group, Inc., The.
Kupperberg, Paul. A Primary Source History of the Colony of New York. 2006. (Primary Sources of the Thirteen Colonies & the Lost Colony Ser.). (ENG., Illus.). 64p. (gr. 4-8). per. 12.95 *(978-1-4042-0677-9(9))* Rosen Publishing Group, Inc., The.
Lawton, Val. New York. 2011. (Guide to American States Ser.). (Illus.). 48p. (YA). (gr. 3-6). 29.99 *(978-1-61690-804-1(1))*; (J). 29.99 *(978-1-61690-480-7(1))* Weigl Pubs., Inc.
—New York: The Empire State. 2016. (J). *(978-1-4896-4911-9(5))* Weigl Pubs., Inc.
Malaspina, Ann. What's Great about New York? 2014. (Our Great States Ser.). (ENG.). 32p. (gr. 2-5). lib. bdg. 26.60 *(978-1-4677-3335-9(0)*, Lerner Pubns.) Lerner Publishing Group.
Marsh, Carole. My First Book. 2004. (New York Experience! Ser.). 32p. (J). (gr. k-4). pap. 7.95 *(978-0-635-00160-3(8))* Gallopade International.
—New York History Projects: 30 Cool, Activities, Crafts, Experiments & More for Kids to Do to Learn about Your State! 2003. (New York Experience Ser.). 32p. (gr. k-5). pap. 5.95 *(978-0-635-01801-4(2)*, Marsh, Carole Bks.) Gallopade International.
McNeese, Tim. New Amsterdam. 2007. (Colonial Settlements in America Ser.). (Illus.). 109p. (YA). (gr. 5-9). lib. bdg. 30.00 *(978-0-7910-9334-4(4))* Facts On File, Inc.
Mezzanotte, Jim & Orr, Tamra B. New York. 2005. (Portraits of the States Ser.). (Illus.). 32p. (gr. 2-6). pap. 10.50 *(978-0-8368-4649-2(4)*, Gareth Stevens Learning Library) Stevens, Gareth Publishing LLLP.
Mis, Melody S. The Colony of New York: A Primary Source History. (Primary Source Library of the Thirteen Colonies & the Lost Colony Ser.). 24p. (gr. 3-4). 2009. 42.50 *(978-1-60854-147-8(9))* 2006. (Illus.). (J). lib. bdg. 22.60 *(978-1-4042-3432-1(2))* Rosen Publishing Group, Inc., The. (PowerKids Pr.).
Reis, Ronald A. The New York City Subway System. 2009. (Building America Ser.). (Illus.). 144p. (J). (gr. 5-8). 35.00 *(978-1-60413-046-1(6)*, Chelsea Hse.) Facts On File, Inc.
Rodriguez, Cindy. New York: The Empire State. 2012. (J). *(978-1-61913-383-9(0))*; pap. *(978-1-61913-384-6(9))* Weigl Pubs., Inc.
Schimel, Kate & Adams, Colleen. Colonial Leaders in New York. 2012. 24p. (J). 60.00 *(978-1-4488-5762-3(7))*; pap. 10.00 *(978-1-4488-5761-6(9))* Rosen Publishing Group, Inc., The. (PowerKids Pr.).
Schimel, Kate & Cefrey, Holly. New York's Industrial Growth. 2012. (Illus.). 24p. (J). 60.00 *(978-1-4488-5774-6(0))*; pap. 10.00 *(978-1-4488-5773-9(2))*; lib. bdg. 22.60 *(978-1-4488-5750-0(3))* Rosen Publishing Group, Inc., The. (PowerKids Pr.).
Schimel, Kate & Khu, Jannell. The British Colony of New York. 2012. (Illus.). 24p. (J). 60.00 *(978-1-4488-5760-9(0))*; pap. 10.00 *(978-1-4488-5759-3(7))*; lib. bdg. 22.60 *(978-1-4488-5743-2(0))* Rosen Publishing Group, Inc., The. (PowerKids Pr.).
Schimel, Kate & Levy, Janey. New York: The Dutch Colony of New Amsterdam. 2012. (Illus.). 24p. (J). 60.00 *(978-1-4488-5758-6(9))*; pap. 10.00 *(978-1-4488-5757-9(0))*; lib. bdg. 22.60 *(978-1-4488-5742-5(2))* Rosen Publishing Group, Inc., The. (PowerKids Pr.).
Schimel, Kate & Zuravicky, Orli. New York's Role in the New Nation. 2012. (Illus.). 24p. (J). 60.00 *(978-1-4488-5770-8(8))*; pap. 10.00 *(978-1-4488-5769-2(4))*; lib. bdg. 22.60 *(978-1-4488-5748-7(1))* Rosen Publishing Group, Inc., The. (PowerKids Pr.).
Schnobrich, Emily. New York. 2013. (Exploring the States Ser.). (ENG., Illus.). 32p. (J). (gr. 3-7). lib. bdg. 26.95 *(978-1-62617-031-5(2)*, Blastoff! Readers) Bellwether Media.
Thompson, Gare. A Suburban Community of the 1950s. 2007. (Reading Expeditions Ser.). (ENG., Illus.). 24p. (J). pap. 14.95 *(978-0-7922-8691-2(X))* CENGAGE Learning.
Tougas, Joe. New York. 2009. (This Land Called America Ser.). (Illus.). 32p. (YA). (gr. 3-6). 19.95 *(978-1-58341-785-0(0))* Creative Co., The.

M
N
O

Wilbur, Helen. Little New York. Brett, Jeannie, illus. 2010. (My Little State Ser.). (ENG.). 22p. (J). 9.95 (978-1-58536-491-6(6)) Sleeping Bear Pr.

Worth, Richard. The Harlem Renaissance: An Explosion of African-American Culture. 2008. (America's Living History Ser.). (Illus.). 128p. (J). (gr. 5-9). lib. bdg. 33.27 (978-0-7660-2907-1(7)) Enslow Pubs., Inc.

Wyner, Zach. Brooklyn Nets. 2013. (On the Hardwood Ser.). (ENG., Illus.). 48p. (gr. 3-8). pap. 8.95 (978-1-61570-835-2(9)) Scobre Pr. Corp.

NEW YORK (STATE)—HISTORY—FICTION

Alger, Horatio. Hector's Inheritance: Or, The Boys of Smith Institute. 2006. pap. (978-1-4065-0708-9(3)) Dodo Pr.

—Hector's Inheritance: Or: the Boys of Smith Institute. 2007. (ENG.). 186p. pap. 19.99 (978-1-4346-5065-8(0)); 192p. pap. 21.99 (978-1-4346-5066-5(9)) Creative Media Partners, LLC.

—Herbert Carter's Legacy. 2006. pap. (978-1-4065-0710-2(5)) Dodo Pr.

—Herbert Carter's Legacy: Or: the Inventor's Son. 2007. 174p. pap. 19.99 (978-1-4346-5067-2(7)); (ENG.). 188p. pap. 21.99 (978-1-4346-5068-9(5)) Creative Media Partners, LLC.

Alger Jr. Horatio Staff. Hector's Inheritance. rev. ed. 2006. 276p. 28.95 (978-1-4218-1758-3(6)); pap. 13.95 (978-1-4218-1858-0(2)) 1st World Publishing, Inc. (1st World Library - Literary Society).

Altsheler, Joseph A. The Hunters of the Hills: A Story of the Great French & Indian War. rev. ed. 2006. (French & Indian War Ser.). 316p. (J). 29.95 (978-1-4218-2334-8(9)); pap. 14.95 (978-1-4218-2434-5(5)) 1st World Publishing, Inc. (1st World Library - Literary Society).

—The Hunters of the Hills: A Story of the Great French & Indian War. (French & Indian War Ser.: Vol. 1). (J). reprint ed. 26.95 (978-0-8488-0904-1(1)) Amereon Ltd.

—The Hunters of the Hills: A Story of the Great French & Indian War. 2009. (French & Indian War Ser.: Vol. 1). 200p. (J). reprint ed. pap. (978-0-217-62835-8(4)) Books LLC.

—The Hunters of the Hills: A Story of the Great French & Indian War. 2012. 392p. reprint ed. pap. 33.75 (978-1-277-16849-5(0)) 2008. (French & Indian War Ser.: Vol. 2). 284p. (J). reprint ed. 25.99 (978-0-554-34450-8(5)) 2008. (French & Indian War Ser.: Vol. 2). 284p. (J). reprint ed. 28.99 (978-0-554-25147-9(7)) 2007. (French & Indian War Ser.). (ENG.). 256p. (J). pap. 21.99 (978-1-4264-8271-7(X)) Creative Media Partners, LLC.

—The Hunters of the Hills: A Story of the Great French & Indian War. 2006. (French & Indian War Ser.). (J). pap. (978-1-4065-0815-4(2)) Dodo Pr.

—The Hunters of the Hills: A Story of the Great French & Indian War. 2007. (French & Indian War Ser.). 188p. (J). per. (978-1-4068-1680-8(9)) Echo Library.

—The Hunters of the Hills: A Story of the Great French & Indian War. 2010. (French & Indian War Ser.: Vol. 1). (Illus.). 168p. (J). (gr. 4-7). reprint ed. pap. 19.99 (978-1-153-70670-4(9)) General Bks. LLC.

—The Hunters of the Hills: A Story of the Great French & Indian War. (French & Indian War Ser.: Vol. 1). (J). reprint ed. 2011. 372p. (gr. 4-7). 48.95 (978-1-169-83864-2(2)) 2010. 372p. (gr. 4-7). 39.16 (978-1-163-20015-5(8)) 2010. 372p. (gr. 4-7). pap. 27.16 (978-1-162-64218-5(1)) 2004. pap. 33.95 (978-1-4179-1500-2(5)) Kessinger Publishing, LLC.

—The Hunters of the Hills: A Story of the Great French & Indian War. 2011. (French & Indian War Ser.: Vol. 1). 284p. (J). (gr. 4-7). reprint ed. pap. (978-3-8424-7700-1(7)) Tredition GmbH.

—The Shadow of the North: A Story of Old New York & a Lost Campaign. l.t. ed. (French & Indian War Ser.: Vol. 2). (J). reprint ed. 2007. (ENG.). 290p. pap. 23.99 (978-1-4264-5705-0(7)) 2010. (ENG.). 378p. (gr. 4-7). pap. 33.75 (978-1-176-98060-0(2)) 2008. 292p. 25.99 (978-0-554-33349-6(X)) 2008. 292p. 28.99 (978-0-554-24046-6(7)) 2007. (ENG.). 260p. pap. 21.99 (978-1-4264-5660-2(3)) Creative Media Partners, LLC.

—The Shadow of the North: A Story of Old New York & a Lost Campaign. 2007. (French & Indian War Ser.: Vol. 2). 188p. (J). reprint ed. per. (978-1-4068-1687-7(6)) Echo Library.

—The Shadow of the North: A Story of Old New York & a Lost Campaign. 2010. (French & Indian War Ser.: Vol. 2). (Illus.). 170p. (J). (gr. 4-7). reprint ed. pap. 19.99 (978-1-153-72063-2(9)) General Bks. LLC.

—The Shadow of the North: A Story of Old New York & a Lost Campaign. (French & Indian War Ser.: Vol. 2). (J). reprint ed. 2010. 256p. (gr. 4-7). 34.36 (978-1-169-30396-6(X)) 2010. 256p. (gr. 4-7). pap. 22.36 (978-1-162-70813-3(1)) 2010. 42.95 (978-1-161-47677-4(6)) 2004. pap. 1.99 (978-1-4192-8225-6(5)) 2004. pap. 27.95 (978-1-4191-8225-9(0)) Kessinger Publishing, LLC.

—The Shadow of the North: A Story of Old New York & a Lost Campaign. 2011. (French & Indian War Ser.: Vol. 2). 286p. (J). reprint ed. pap. (978-3-8424-4397-6(8)) Tredition GmbH.

Believarexic, 1 vol. 2015. (ENG.). 464p. (YA). (gr. 8-11). 18.95 (978-1-56145-771-7(X)) Peachtree Pubs.

Clark, Clara Gillow. Secrets of Greymoor. 2009. (ENG., Illus.). 176p. (J). (gr. 5). 15.99 (978-0-7636-3249-6(X)) Candlewick Pr.

Cremer, Andrea. The Inventor's Secret. 2015. (Inventor's Secret Ser.). (ENG.). 416p. (YA). (gr. 7). pap. 10.99 (978-0-14-751438-7(X), Speak) Penguin Young Readers Group.

Donnelly, Jennifer. A Northern Light. 2004. (ENG.). 416p. (YA). (gr. 9-12). reprint ed. pap. 9.99 (978-0-15-205310-9(7)) Houghton Mifflin Harcourt Publishing Co.

—A Northern Light. 2004. 396p. (gr. 9-12). 20.00 (978-0-7569-3614-3(4)) Perfection Learning Corp.

Falk, Elizabeth Sullivan. Lettie's North Star. Wolf, Elizabeth, illus. 2006. (J). (978-1-59336-694-0(9)) Mondo Publishing.

Gansworth, Eric L. If I Ever Get Out of Here. (ENG.). 368p. (J). (gr. 7). 2015. pap. 10.99 (978-0-545-41731-0(7)) 2013. 17.99 (978-0-545-41730-3(9)) Scholastic, Inc. (Levine, Arthur A. Bks.).

Giff, Patricia Reilly. Gingersnap. 2014. (ENG.). 160p. (J). (gr. 3-7). 6.99 (978-0-440-42178-8(0), Yearling) Random Hse. Children's Bks.

Greene, Jacqueline. Secrets at Camp Nokomis: A Rebecca Mystery. Hirsch, Jennifer, ed. Tibbles, JeanPaul, illus. 2010. (ENG.). 192p. (J). (gr. 4-8). pap. 6.95 (978-1-59369-657-3(4)) American Girl Publishing, Inc.

Griffith, A. J. America's Child. 2008. (J). pap. 9.99 (978-0-88092-493-1(4)) Royal Fireworks Publishing Co.

Irving, Washington. The Legend of Sleepy Hollow & Rip Van Winkle, 1 vol. McWilliam, Howard, illus. 2011. (Calico Illustrated Classics Ser.). (ENG.). 112p. (YA). (gr. 3-6). 27.07 (978-1-60270-747-4(2)) Magic Wagon.

Johnson, J. J. Believarexic, 1 vol. 2017. (ENG.). 464p. (YA). (gr. 8-11). pap. 9.95 **(978-1-68263-007-5(2))** Peachtree Pubs.

Levine, Ellen. In Trouble. 2011. (Carolrhoda YA Ser.). (ENG.). 208p. (YA). (gr. 9-12). 17.95 (978-0-7613-6558-7(3), Carolrhoda Lab™) Lerner Publishing Group.

Napoli, Donna Jo. The King of Mulberry Street. 2007. 245p. (gr. 3-7). 17.00 (978-0-7569-7945-4(5)) Perfection Learning Corp.

Neale, Cynthia. Hope in New York City: The Continuing Story of the Irish Dresser. 2008. (ENG.). 176p. (J). pap. 7.95 (978-1-57249-387-2(9), White Mane Kids) White Mane Publishing Co., Inc.

Peterson, Mike. Freehand: A Young Boy's Adventures in the War Of 1812. Baldwin, Christopher, illus. 2012. (ENG.). 44p. (J). pap. 6.95 (978-1-938384-03-5(2)) Baldwin, Christopher John.

Pinkney, Andrea Davis. Bird in a Box. Qualls, Sean, illus. 2012. (J). lib. bdg. 18.45 (978-0-606-26157-9(5), Turtleback) Turtleback Bks.

Stafford, Gerry. Young Canaller. Wanecski, Erica Joan, illus. 2012. 60p. (J). pap. (978-0-9667989-7-5(X)) Carlisle Pr.-Walnut Creek.

Thomas, Peggy. Joshua the Giant Frog, 1 vol. Smith, Cat Bowman, illus. 2005. (ENG.). 32p. (J). (gr. k-3). 16.99 (978-1-58980-267-4(5)) Pelican Publishing Co., Inc.

Tooke, Wes. Lucky: Maris, Mantle, & My Best Summer Ever. 2010. (ENG.). 192p. (J). (gr. 3-7). 15.99 (978-1-4169-8663-8(4), Simon & Schuster Bks. For Young Readers) Simon & Schuster Bks. For Young Readers.

Vernick, Shirley Reva. The Blood Lie. 2011. (ENG.). 144p. (J). (gr. 7). 15.95 (978-1-933693-84-2(3)) Cinco Puntos Pr.

Villani, Donna. The Capture of Art. 2008. 244p. pap. 14.95 (978-1-60693-104-2(0), Eloquent Bks.) Strategic Book Publishing & Rights Agency (SBPRA).

Walvoord, Linda & Walvoord. Rosetta, Rosetta, Sit by Me!, 0 vols. Velasquez, Eric, illus. 2004. (ENG.). 80p. (J). (gr. 3-6). 14.95 (978-0-7614-5171-6(4), 9780761451716, Amazon Children's Publishing) Amazon Publishing.

Zink, Michelle. Prophecy of the Sisters. 2010. (Prophecy of the Sisters Trilogy Ser.: 1). (ENG.). 368p. (YA). (gr. 7-17). pap. 8.99 (978-0-316-02741-0(3)) Little, Brown Bks. for Young Readers.

NEW YORK (STATE)—POLITICS AND GOVERNMENT

Schimel, Kate & Alagna, Magdalena. New York's Government. 2012. (Illus.). 24p. (J). 60.00 (978-1-4488-5764-7(3)); pap. 10.00 (978-1-4488-5763-0(5)); lib. bdg. 22.60 (978-1-4488-5745-6(7)) Rosen Publishing Group, Inc., The. (PowerKids Pr.).

White, Casey. John Jay: Diplomat of the American Experiment. (Library of American Thinkers Ser.). 112p. 2009. (gr. 6-6). 66.50 (978-1-60853-515-6(0), Rosen Reference) 2005. (Illus.). (YA). (gr. 5-9). lib. bdg. 34.60 (978-1-4042-0507-9(1)) Rosen Publishing Group, Inc., The.

NEW YORK GIANTS (FOOTBALL TEAM)

Burgess, Zack. Meet the New York Giants. 2016. (Big Picture Sports Ser.). (ENG., Illus.). 24p. (J). (gr. k-3). lib. bdg. 22.60 (978-1-59953-736-8(2)) Norwood Hse. Pr.

Epstein, Brad. New York Giants 101. 2010. (Illus.). 24p. (J). bds. (978-1-60730-120-2(2), 101 Bk.) Michaelson Entertainment.

Frisch, Aaron. New York Giants. 2011. (Super Bowl Champions Ser.). (J). (gr. 1-3). 24.25 (978-1-60818-023-3(9)) Creative Co., The.

—New York Giants. 2014. (Illus.). 24p. (J). (978-1-60818-382-1(3), Creative Education) Creative Co., The.

Goodman, Michael E. The History of the New York Giants. 2004. (NFL Today Ser.). (Illus.). 32p. (YA). (gr. 5-9). 18.95 (978-1-58341-306-7(5)) Creative Co., The.

—The Story of the New York Giants. 2009. (NFL Today Ser.). 48p. (YA). (gr. 5-9). 22.95 (978-1-58341-804-8(0)) Creative Co., The.

Grayson, Robert. Plaxico Burress. 2009. (Superstars of Pro Football Ser.). (Illus.). 64p. (YA). (gr. 7-12). lib. bdg. 22.95 (978-1-4222-0552-5(5)) Mason Crest.

Leboutillier, Nate. New York Giants. 2005. (Super Bowl Champions Ser.). (Illus.). 24p. (J). (gr. 1-4). lib. bdg. 16.95 (978-1-58341-387-6(1), Creative Education) Creative Co., The.

Mack, Larry. The New York Giants Story. 2016. (NFL Teams Ser.). (ENG., Illus.). 32p. (J). (gr. 3-7). lib. bdg. 26.95 (978-1-62617-375-0(3), Torque Bks.) Bellwether Media.

MacRae, Sloan. The New York Giants. 2011. (America's Greatest Teams Ser.). (Illus.). 24p. (J). pap. 8.25 (978-1-4488-2741-1(8)); lib. bdg. 22.60 (978-1-4488-2576-9(8)) Rosen Publishing Group, Inc., The. (PowerKids Pr.).

New York Giants, 1 vol. 2014. (NFL's Greatest Teams Ser.). (ENG.). 32p. (gr. 7-11). 28.50 (978-1-62403-364-3(4)) ABDO Publishing Co.

Publications International Ltd. Staff. Yesterday & Today Nfl New York Giants. 2010. 160p. 24.95 (978-1-4127-9829-7(9)) Publications International, Ltd.

Sandler, Michael. Eli Manning & the New York Giants: Super Bowl Xlvi. 2012. (Super Bowl Superstars Ser.). (Illus.). 24p. (J). (gr. 1-6). lib. bdg. 22.61 (978-1-61772-578-4(1)) Bearport Publishing Co., Inc.

Whiting, Jim. NFL Today: New York Giants. 2013. (NFL Today Ser.). (ENG.). 48p. (J). (gr. 4-7). pap. 12.00 (978-0-89812-865-9(X), Creative Paperbacks) Creative Co., The.

—The Story of the New York Giants. 2013. (J). 35.65 (978-1-60818-312-8(2), Creative Education) Creative Co., The.

Wilner, Barry. New York Giants. 2015. (Insider's Guide to Pro Football Ser.). (ENG.). 32p. (J). (gr. k-3). 28.50 (978-1-63407-004-1(6), 208839) Child's World, Inc., The.

Wyner, Zach. New York Giants. 2014. (Inside the NFL Ser.). (ENG., Illus.). 32p. (J). (gr. 4-7). lib. bdg. 28.55 (978-1-4896-0862-8(1), AV2 by Weigl) Weigl Pubs., Inc.

NEW YORK JETS (FOOTBALL TEAM)

Burgess, Zack. Meet the New York Jets. 2016. (Big Picture Sports Ser.). (ENG., Illus.). 24p. (J). (gr. k-3). lib. bdg. 22.60 (978-1-59953-738-2(9)) Norwood Hse. Pr.

Epstein, Brad. New York Jets 101. 2010. (ENG., Illus.). 24p. (J). bds. (978-1-60730-121-9(0), 101 Bk.) Michaelson Entertainment.

Frisch, Aaron. New York Jets. 2011. (Super Bowl Champions Ser.). (J). (gr. 1-3). 24.25 (978-1-60818-024-0(7)) Creative Co., The.

—New York Jets. 2014. (Illus.). 24p. (J). (978-1-60818-383-8(1), Creative Education) Creative Co., The.

Goodman, Michael E. The History of the New York Jets. 2004. (NFL Today Ser.). (Illus.). 32p. (YA). (gr. 5-9). 18.95 (978-1-58341-307-4(3)) Creative Co., The.

—The Story of the New York Jets. 2009. (NFL Today Ser.). 48p. (YA). (gr. 5-9). 22.95 (978-1-58341-805-5(9)) Creative Co., The.

Robinson, Tom. New York Jets, 1 vol. 2010. (Inside the NFL Ser.). (ENG.). 48p. (YA). (gr. 3-6). lib. bdg. 32.79 (978-1-61714-022-8(8)) ABDO Publishing Co.

Temple, Ramey. New York Jets. 2014. (Inside the NFL Ser.). (ENG., Illus.). 32p. (J). (gr. 4-7). lib. bdg. 28.55 (978-1-4896-0866-6(4), AV2 by Weigl) Weigl Pubs., Inc.

Whiting, Jim. NFL Today: New York Jets. 2013. (NFL Today Ser.). (ENG.). 48p. (J). (gr. 4-7). pap. 12.00 (978-0-89812-866-6(8), Creative Paperbacks) Creative Co., The.

—The Story of the New York Jets. 2013. (J). 35.65 (978-1-60818-313-5(0), Creative Education) Creative Co., The.

Wilner, Barry. New York Jets. 2015. (Insider's Guide to Pro Football Ser.). (ENG.). 32p. (J). (gr. k-3). 28.50 (978-1-63143-990-2(1), 208825) Child's World, Inc., The.

Wyner, Zach. New York Jets. 2015. (Illus.). 32p. (J). pap. (978-1-4896-0867-3(2)) Weigl Pubs., Inc.

Zappa, Marcia. New York Jets, 1 vol. 2014. (NFL's Greatest Teams Set 2 Ser.). (ENG., Illus.). 32p. (J). (gr. 2-5). 28.50 (978-1-62403-589-0(2)) ABDO Publishing Co.

NEW YORK METS (BASEBALL TEAM)

Boone, Mary. David Wright. 2010. (Blue Banner Biography Ser.). (Illus.). 32p. (YA). (gr. 4-7). lib. bdg. 25.70 (978-1-58415-910-0(3)) Mitchell Lane Pubs., Inc.

Epstein, Brad. New York Mets 101. 2013. (My First Team-Board-Book Ser.). (ENG., Illus.). 24p. (J). bds. (978-1-60730-285-8(3), 101 Bk.) Michaelson Entertainment.

—New York Mets ABC. 2013. (My First Alphabet Books (Michaelson Entertainment) Ser.). (ENG., Illus.). 28p. (J). bds. (978-1-60730-208-7(X), ABC Bk.) Michaelson Entertainment.

Gilbert, Sara. New York Mets. 2013. (Illus.). 24p. (J). 25.65 (978-1-60818-268-8(1), Creative Education) Creative Co., The.

—World Series Champs: New York Mets. 2013. (World Series Champions Ser.). (ENG.). 24p. (J). (gr. 1-3). pap. 7.99 (978-0-89812-819-2(6), Creative Paperbacks) Creative Co., The.

Goodman, Michael E. The Story of the New York Mets. 2011. (J). 35.65 (978-1-60818-048-6(4), Creative Education) 2007. (Illus.). 48p. (YA). (gr. 4-7). lib. bdg. 32.80 (978-1-58341-494-1(0)) Creative Co., The.

Knobel, Andy. New York Mets, 1 vol. (Inside MLB Ser.). (ENG., Illus.). 48p. (gr. 3-6). 2011. (YA). lib. bdg. 32.79 (978-1-61714-051-8(1)) 2014. (J). lib. bdg. 32.79 (978-1-62403-477-0(2), SportsZone) ABDO Publishing Co.

MacRae, Sloan. The New York Mets. 2012. (Illus.). 24p. (J). 49.50 (978-1-4488-5154-6(8), 1329148); pap. 8.25 (978-1-4488-5153-9(X), 1329148); lib. bdg. 22.60 (978-1-4488-5010-5(X), 1329148) Rosen Publishing Group, Inc., The. (PowerKids Pr.).

Noble, Marty. Mike Piazza: Mike & the Mets. Rains, Rob, ed. 2003. (Superstar Ser.). (Illus.). 96p. (J). (gr. 4-7). pap. 4.95 (978-1-58261-051-1(7)) Sports Publishing, LLC.

Snyder, John. Mets Journal: Year by Year & Day by Day with the New York Mets Since 1962. 2011. (ENG., Illus.). 448p. pap. 24.95 (978-1-57860-473-9(7)) Clerisy Pr.

Stewart, Mark. Los Mets de Nueva York. Kalmanovitz, Manuel, tr. from ENG. 2007. (Espíritu de Equipo Ser.). (SPA., Illus.). 48p. (J). (gr. 3-6). lib. bdg. 26.60 (978-1-59953-103-8(8)) Norwood Hse. Pr.

—The New York Mets. 2012. (Team Spirit Ser.). 48p. (J). (gr. 3-6). lib. bdg. 29.27 (978-1-59953-489-3(4)) Norwood Hse. Pr.

NEW YORK STOCK EXCHANGE

Ingram, Scott. The Stock Market Crash of 1929. 2004. (Landmark Events in American History Ser.). (Illus.). 48p. (gr. 5-12). pap. 14.05 (978-0-8368-5425-1(X), Gareth Stevens Secondary Library) Stevens, Gareth Publishing LLLP.

NEW YORK TIMES

Herda, D. J. New York Times V. United States: National Security & Censorship. rev. ed. 2010. (Landmark Supreme Court Cases, Gold Edition Ser.). (Illus.). 112p. (J). (gr. 6-18). 33.27 (978-0-7660-3429-7(1)) Enslow Pubs., Inc.

NEW YORK YANKEES (BASEBALL TEAM)

Appel, Marty. Pinstripe Pride: The Inside Story of the New York Yankees. (ENG.). (J). (gr. 3-7). 2016. 352p. pap. 12.99 (978-1-4814-1603-0(0)) 2015. (Illus.). 288p. 19.99 (978-1-4814-1602-3(2)) Simon & Schuster Bks. For Young Readers. (Simon & Schuster Bks. For Young Readers).

Aretha, David. Power in Pinstripes: The New York Yankees. 2007. (Sensational Sports Teams Ser.). (Illus.). 128p. (J). (gr. 5-9). lib. bdg. 34.60 (978-1-59845-044-6(1), MyReportLinks.com Bks.) Enslow Pubs., Inc.

Boothroyd, Jennifer. Lou Gehrig. 2008. pap. 40.95 (978-0-8225-9473-4(0)) Lerner Publishing Group.

—Lou Gehrig: A Life of Dedication. 2008. (Pull Ahead Bks.). (Illus.). 32p. (J). (gr. -1-3). lib. bdg. 22.60 (978-0-8225-8587-9(1), Lerner Pubns.) Lerner Publishing Group.

Christopher, Matt. The New York Yankees: The Most Successful Team in Major League History. 2008. (ENG., Illus.). 128p. (J). (gr. 3-7). per. 4.99 (978-0-316-01115-0(0)) Little, Brown Bks. for Young Readers.

Connery-Boyd, Peg. New York Yankees. 2016. (Hawk's Nest Activity Bks.: 0). (ENG.). 64p. (J). (gr. k-3). pap., act. bk. ed. 8.99 (978-1-4926-3373-0(9)) Sourcebooks, Inc.

Frisch, Aaron. New York Yankees. 2009. (World Series Champions Ser.). (Illus.). 23p. (J). (gr. 2-3). 24.25 (978-1-58341-697-6(8), Creative Education) Creative Co., The.

Gilbert, Sara. New York Yankees. 2013. (Illus.). 24p. (J). 25.65 (978-1-60818-269-5(X), Creative Education) Creative Co., The.

—World Series Champs: New York Yankees. 2013. (World Series Champions Ser.). (ENG.). 24p. (J). (gr. 1-3). pap. 7.99 (978-0-89812-820-8(X), Creative Paperbacks) Creative Co., The.

Goodman, Michael E. The Story of the New York Yankees. 2011. (J). 35.65 (978-1-60818-049-3(2), Creative Education) 2007. (Illus.). 48p. (YA). (gr. 4-7). lib. bdg. 32.80 (978-1-58341-495-8(9)) Creative Co., The.

Greenberg, Keith Elliot. Derek Jeter. 2005. (Sports Heroes & Legends Ser.). (Illus.). 106p. (J). (gr. 3-7). lib. bdg. 27.93 (978-0-8225-3068-8(6), Lerner Pubns.) Lerner Publishing Group.

Herman, Gail. Who Is Derek Jeter? 2015. (Who Is... ? Ser.). lib. bdg. 16.00 (978-0-606-37552-8(X)) Turtleback Bks.

Herman, Gail & dePaola, Tomie. Who Is Derek Jeter? Thomson, Andrew, illus. 2015. (Who Was? Ser.). (ENG.). 112p. (J). (gr. 3-7). 5.99 (978-0-448-48697-0(0), Grosset & Dunlap) Penguin Young Readers Group.

Howell, Brian. Derek Jeter: Yankee Great, 1 vol. 2011. (Playmakers Ser.). (ENG., Illus.). 32p. (J). (gr. 3-6). 27.07 (978-1-61714-747-0(8)) ABDO Publishing Co.

—New York Yankees, 1 vol. (Inside MLB Ser.). (ENG., 48p. (gr. 3-6). 2011. Illus.). (YA). lib. bdg. 32.79 (978-1-61714-052-5(X)) 2014. lib. bdg. 32.79 (978-1-62403-478-7(0), SportsZone) ABDO Publishing Co.

Kelley, K. C. New York Yankees. 2016. (J). **(978-1-4896-5941-5(2)**, AV2 by Weigl) Weigl Pubs., Inc.

Kelly, David A. Babe Ruth & the Baseball Curse. Jessell, Tim, illus. 2009. (Totally True Adventures Ser.). (ENG.). 112p. (J). (gr. 2-5). 4.99 (978-0-375-85603-7(X), Random Hse. Bks. for Young Readers) Random Hse. Children's Bks.

Kennedy, Mike & Stewart, Mark. Meet the Yankees. 2010. (Smart about Sports Ser.). (Illus.). 24p. (J). (gr. k-3). lib. bdg. 22.60 (978-1-59953-372-8(3), 1309057) Norwood Hse. Pr.

Klein, Fredrick C. For the Love of the Yankees: An A-to-Z Primer for Yankees Fans of All Ages. Anderson, Mark, illus. 2003. 48p. (J). 19.95 (978-1-57243-579-7(8)) Triumph Bks.

MacRae, Sloan. The New York Yankees. (Illus.). 24p. (J). 2010. pap. 8.25 (978-1-4358-3390-6(2)) 2009. lib. bdg. 22.60 (978-1-4042-8129-5(0)) Rosen Publishing Group, Inc., The. (PowerKids Pr.).

Marlin, John. Mickey Mantle. 2004. (Sports Heroes & Legends Ser.). (ENG., Illus.). 112p. (gr. 5-12). lib. bdg. 30.60 (978-0-8225-1796-2(5)) Lerner Publishing Group.

O'Connell, Jack. Derek Jeter: The Yankee Kid. Rains, Rob, ed. 2003. (Super Star Ser.). 96p. (J). pap. 4.95 (978-1-58261-043-6(6)) Sports Publishing, LLC.

Rappoport, Ken. Super Sports Star Derek Jeter. 2004. (Super Sports Star Ser.). (Illus.). 48p. (J). lib. bdg. 25.27 (978-0-7660-2139-6(4)) Enslow Pubs., Inc.

Reis, Ronald A. Lou Gehrig. 2007. (Baseball Superstars Ser.). (Illus.). 130p. (YA). (gr. 7-12). lib. bdg. 30.00 (978-0-7910-9423-5(5)) Facts On File, Inc.

Rivera, Mariano. The Closer: Young Readers Edition. l.t. ed. 2014. (ENG.). 432p. (J). (gr. 3-7). 19.00 (978-0-316-40962-9(6)) Little, Brown Bks. for Young Readers.

Robinson, Tom. Derek Jeter: Captain on & off the Field. 2006. (Sports Stars with Heart Ser.). (Illus.). 128p. (J). (gr. 5-9). lib. bdg. 33.27 (978-0-7660-2819-7(4)) Enslow Pubs., Inc.

Sandler, Michael. Derek Jeter & the New York Yankees: 2000 World Series. 2008. (World Series Superstars). (Illus.). 24p. (J). (gr. 1-4). lib. bdg. 22.61 (978-1-59716-641-6(3)) Bearport Publishing Co., Inc.

Shaughnessy, Dan. The Legend of the Curse of the Bambino. Payne, C. F., illus. 2005. (ENG.). 32p. (J). (gr. k-3). 16.95 (978-0-689-87235-8(6), Simon & Schuster/Paula Wiseman Bks.) Simon & Schuster/Paula Wiseman Bks.

Stewart, Mark. The New York Yankees. 2012. (Team Spirit Ser.). 48p. (J). (gr. 3-6). lib. bdg. 29.27 (978-1-59953-490-9(8)) Norwood Hse. Pr.

Tieck, Sarah. Derek Jeter: Baseball Superstar, 1 vol. 2010. (Big Buddy Bks.). (ENG.). 32p. (J). (gr. 2-5). 28.50 (978-1-61613-975-9(7)) ABDO Publishing Co.

Tometich, Annabelle. Superstars of the New York Yankees. 2014. (Pro Sports Superstars Ser.). 24p. (J). 27.10 (978-1-60753-594-2(7)) Amicus Publishing.

Viola, Kevin. Lou Gehrig. (Sports Heroes & Legends Ser.). (J). 2005. (Illus.). 112p. (gr. 6-12). lib. bdg. 27.93 (978-0-8225-1794-8(9)) 2004. pap. 9.95 (978-0-8225-5311-3(2)) Lerner Publishing Group.

Weinstein, Howard. Mickey Mantle. (Baseball Hall of Famers Ser.). 112p. (gr. 5-8). 2009. 63.90 (978-1-61511-513-6(7)) 2004. (Illus.). lib. bdg. 34.60 (978-0-8239-3782-0(8)) Rosen Publishing Group, Inc., The. (Rosen Reference).

Winter, Jonah. You Never Heard of Casey Stengel?! Blitt, Barry, illus. 2016. (ENG.). 40p. (J). (gr. -1-3). 20.99 (978-0-375-97013-9(4)); 17.99 (978-0-375-87013-2(X)) Random Hse. Children's Bks. (Schwartz & Wade Bks.).

NEW ZEALAND

Beech, Terry. Design, Graphics & Visual Communication for New Zealand Years 9 & 10. 2013. (ENG.). pap., stu. ed. (978-1-107-61205-1(5)) Cambridge Univ. Pr.

Boom, Rosie. Where Lions Roar at Night. 2nd ed. 2013. (Illus.). 240p. (978-1-921161-18-6(3)) Boom Tree Publishing.

Calman, Ross. The Treaty of Waitangi. 2014. (Illus.). 32p. pap. 20.00 (978-1-877514-34-0(9)) Oratia Media NZL. Dist: Casemate Pubs. & Bk. Distributors, LLC.

Colson, Mary. New Zealand, 1 vol. 2012. (Countries Around the World Ser.). (ENG., Illus.). 48p. (gr. 3-6). pap. 9.95 (978-1-4329-6132-9(2), NA-h) Heinemann-Raintree.

Comire, S. Joshua & Porter, Malcolm. Atlas of Australia & the Pacific. 2009. (Atlases of the World Ser.). (Illus.). 48p. (YA). (gr. 5-8). 29.25 (978-1-4358-8456-4(6), Rosen Reference) Rosen Publishing Group, Inc., The.

Cox, Lynne. Elizabeth, Queen of the Seas. Floca, Brian, illus. 2014. (ENG.). 48p. (J). (gr. -1-3). 17.99 *(978-0-375-85888-8(1))*; 20.99 *(978-0-375-95888-5(6))* Random Hse. Children's Bks. (Schwartz & Wade Bks.).

DiPiazza, Francesca Davis. New Zealand in Pictures. 2nd ed. 2005. (Visual Geography Series, Second Ser.). (ENG., Illus.). 80p. (gr. 5-12). lib. bdg. 31.93 *(978-0-8225-2550-9(X))* Lerner Publishing Group.

Encyclopaedia Britannica, Inc. Staff, compiled by. My First Britannica: Asia, Australia, & New Zealand. 2008. (gr. 7-12). *(978-1-59339-407-3(1))* Encyclopaedia Britannica, Inc.

Frazel, Ellen. New Zealand. 2013. (Exploring Countries Ser.). (ENG., Illus.). 32p. (J). (gr. 3-7). lib. bdg. 26.95 *(978-1-60014-862-0(X))* Bellwether Media.

Gillespie, Carol Ann. New Zealand. Gritzner, Charles F., ed. rev. ed. 2005. (Modern World Nations Ser.). (Illus.). 150p. (gr. 6-12). 35.00 *(978-0-7910-8708-4(5))* Facts On File, Inc.

Hill, Bartha. Kiwi Adventures. 2007. (Adventure Ser.). (ENG., Illus.). 96p. (J). per. 8.99 *(978-1-84550-282-9(5)*, bc2e1b1f-fc91-4f29-9bc6-4fd6af488a81) Christian Focus Pubns. GBR. Dist: Bookmasters Distribution.

Hill, Valerie. New Zealand. 2004. (Ask about Asia Ser.). (Illus.). 48p. (J). (gr. 4-18). lib. bdg. 19.95 *(978-1-59084-207-2(3))* Mason Crest.

Hirsch, Rebecca. New Zealand, 1 vol. 2013. (Countries of the World Set 2 Ser.). (ENG.). 144p. (J). (gr. 6-12). lib. bdg. 37.07 *(978-1-61783-631-2(1)*, Essential Library) ABDO Publishing Co.

Jackson, Barbara & National Geographic Kids Staff. New Zealand. 2008. (Countries of the World Ser.). (ENG., Illus.). 64p. (J). (gr. 5). lib. bdg. 27.90 *(978-1-4263-0301-2(7)*, National Geographic Children's Bks.) National Geographic Society.

Kopp, Megan. New Zealand. 2016. (J). ***(978-1-4896-5421-2(6))*** Weigl Pubs., Inc.

Krumenauer, Heidi. Lorde. 2015. (ENG., Illus.). 32p. (J). 26.50 *(978-1-62469-122-5(6))* Purple Toad Publishing, Inc.

Larson, Lyn. New Zealand. 2011. (Country Explorers Ser.). 48p. pap. 51.02 *(978-0-7613-7626-2(7))*; (ENG.). (gr. 2-4). lib. bdg. 29.27 *(978-0-7613-6413-9(7))*; (ENG., Illus.). (gr. 2-4). pap. 9.95 *(978-0-7613-7083-3(8))* Lerner Publishing Group.

Mara, Wil. Peter Jackson. 2014. (Great Filmmakers Ser.). (Illus.). 80p. (YA). (gr. 8-11). lib. bdg. 35.64 *(978-1-62712-942-8(1))* Cavendish Square Publishing.

Murray, Julie. New Zealand, 1 vol. 2014. (Explore the Countries Set 2 Ser.). (ENG.). 40p. (gr. 7-11). lib. bdg. 29.93 *(978-1-62403-344-5(X)*, Big Buddy Bks.) ABDO Publishing Co.

O'Brien, Gregory. Back & Beyond: New Zealand in Painting for the Young & Curious. 2008. (ENG., Illus.). 104p. 24.95 *(978-1-86940-404-8(1))* Auckland Univ. Pr. NZL. Dist: Independent Pubs. Group.

Oxford University Press Staff & Lindop, Christine, eds. Australia & New Zealand, Level 3. 3rd ed. 2008. (ENG., Illus.). 80p. 10.00 *(978-0-19-423390-3(1))* Oxford Univ. Pr., Inc.

Schroeder, Holly. New Zealand ABCs: A Book about the People & Places of New Zealand. Wolf, Claudia, illus. 2004. (Country ABCs Ser.). (ENG.). 32p. (gr. k-5). 27.99 *(978-1-4048-0178-3(2)*, 1229507) Picture Window Bks.

Schwartz, Heather E. Lorde: Songstress with Style. 2015. (Pop Culture Bios Ser.). (ENG., Illus.). 32p. (J). (gr. 3-6). pap. 7.95 *(978-1-4677-6100-0(1)*, Lerner Pubns.) Lerner Publishing Group.

Smelt, Roselynn. New Zealand. 2nd rev. ed. 2008. (Cultures of the World Ser.). 144p. (gr. 6-18). lib. bdg. 42.79 *(978-0-7614-3415-3(1)*, Benchmark Bks.) Marshall Cavendish Corp.

Tieck, Sarah. Lorde: Singing Sensation, 1 vol. 2014. (Big Buddy Biographies Set 12 Ser.). (ENG.). 32p. (gr. 2-5). 28.50 *(978-1-62403-569-2(8))* ABDO Publishing Co.

Trussell-Cullen, Alan. Edmund Hillary. 2009. pap. 13.25 *(978-1-60559-058-5(4))* Hameray Publishing Group, Inc.

Walsh Shepherd, Donna. New Zealand. 2016. (Enchantment of the World Ser.). (ENG., Illus.). 144p. (J). lib. bdg. 40.00 *(978-0-531-23296-5(4)*, Children's Pr.) Scholastic Library Publishing.

Weil, Ann. Meet Our New Student from New Zealand. 2008. (Meet Our New Student Ser.). (Illus.). 48p. (J). (gr. 2-5). lib. bdg. 29.95 *(978-1-58415-657-4(0))* Mitchell Lane Pubs., Inc.

World Book, Inc Staff, contrib. by. Endangered Animals of Australia, New Zealand, & Pacific Islands. 2014. *(978-0-7166-5623-4(X))* World Bk., Inc.

NEW ZEALAND—FICTION

Bassett, Jennifer, ed. Long White Cloud: Stories from New Zealand. 3rd ed. 2008. (ENG., Illus.). 80p. 10.00 *(978-0-19-479139-7(4))* Oxford Univ. Pr., Inc.

Brammer, Deb. Two Sides to Everything. 2003. (Illus.). 151p. (J). *(978-1-59166-166-5(8))* BJU Pr.

Brocker, Susan. Restless Spirit. 2007. 176p. *(978-1-86950-623-0(5))* HarperCollins Pubs. Australia.

Catran, Ken. Dawn Hawk. 96p. pap. *(978-0-7344-0468-8(9)*, Lothian Children's Bks.) Hachette Australia.

Cowley, Joy. The Hungry Giant's Shoe Big Book. 2010. 48.25 *(978-1-60559-250-3(1))* Hameray Publishing Group, Inc.

—Meanies in the House Big Book. 2010. 48.25 *(978-1-60559-251-0(X))* Hameray Publishing Group, Inc.

—Mrs. WishyWashy & the Big Wash Big Book. 2010. 48.25 *(978-1-60559-247-3(1))* Hameray Publishing Group, Inc.

—Smarty Pants at the Circus Big Book. 2010. 48.25 *(978-1-60559-249-7(8))* Hameray Publishing Group, Inc.

Dauphin, Vaya. The Greenstone Garden: The Elementals of Aotearoa, Vol. 2. 2013. viii, 297p. pap. *(978-1-74284-346-9(8))* ReadOnTime.

De Goldi, Kate. The 10 PM Question. 2010. (ENG., Illus.). 256p. (YA). (gr. 7-18). 15.99 *(978-0-7636-4939-5(2))* Candlewick Pr.

Dixon, Pamela. A Windy Day Walk. Homer, Maree, illus. 2016. (ENG.). 32p. (J). (gr. 1-4). *(978-0-473-34486-3(6))* Lizzy Web Bks.

Falkner, Brian. The Tomorrow Code. 2009. (ENG.). 368p. (YA). (gr. 7). pap. 9.99 *(978-0-375-84365-5(5)*, Ember) Random Hse. Children's Bks.

Friedman, J. S. In the Beginning. Beatrice, Chris, illus. 2013. (Maurice's Valises: Moral Tails in an Immoral World Ser.: Vol. 1). (ENG.). 45p. (J). (gr. k-4). *(978-94-91613-03-6(0))* Mouse Prints Pr.

Gee, Maurice. The Fire Raiser. 2007. (ENG.). 176p. (J). (gr. 5-7). pap. 11.95 *(978-0-618-75041-2(X))* Houghton Mifflin Harcourt Publishing Co.

Gibbs, Jephson. Rata & the Waka: A Tale from New Zealand. Williamson, Fraser, illus. 2016. 24p. (J). pap. *(978-1-927244-55-5(2))* Flying Start Bks.

—Rata & the Waka (Big Book Edition) A Tale from New Zealand. Williamson, Fraser, illus. 2016. 24p. (J). pap. *(978-1-927244-65-4(X))* Flying Start Bks.

Hall, Barbara. That Is Choice! 2009. 192p. pap. *(978-1-84748-314-0(3))* Athena Pr.

Healey, Karen. The Shattering. 2013. (ENG.). 336p. (YA). (gr. 7-17). pap. 8.99 *(978-0-316-12573-4(3))* Little, Brown Bks. for Young Readers.

Hollyer, Belinda. River Song. 2008. (ENG.). 198p. (J). (gr. 3-7). 16.95 *(978-0-8234-2149-7(X))* Holiday Hse., Inc.

Ireland, Kenneth. Noises in the Night. 2004. 126p. (J). 5.00 *(978-1-84161-031-3(3))* Ravette Publishing, Ltd. GBR. Dist: Parkwest Pubns., Inc.

Knox, Elizabeth. Dreamquake. 2007. (Dreamhunter Duet Ser.: No. 2). 528p. *(978-0-7322-8194-6(6)*, Fourth Estate) HarperCollins Pubs. Australia.

Locke, Elsie. A Canoe in the Mist. 2005. 224p. *(978-1-86950-568-4(9))* HarperCollins Pubs. Australia.

MacAndrew, Richard. The Black Pearls Starter/Beginner. 2008. (Cambridge English Readers Ser.). (ENG.). 32p. pap. 8.50 *(978-0-521-73289-5(1))* Cambridge Univ. Pr.

Mahy, Margaret. The Great Piratical Rumbustification & the Librarian & the Robbers. Blake, Quentin, illus. 2012. (ENG.). 64p. (J). pap. 6.95 *(978-1-56792-169-4(8))* Godine, David R. Pub.

McConchie, Lyn. Autumn of the Wild Poney. 2012. (ENG.). 126p. (YA). pap. 12.00 *(978-1-936021-40-6(4)*, Banana Oil Bks.) Cyberwizard Productions.

—Winter of Waiting. 2015. (YA). (gr. 5-18). pap. 15.00 *(978-1-936021-55-0(2)*, Banana Oil Bks.) Cyberwizard Productions.

Milton, Jane. Moo & Moo & the Little Calf Too. Hinde, Deborah, illus. 2017. (ENG.). 32p. (J). (-3). pap. 14.99 ***(978-1-877505-92-8(7))*** Allen & Unwin AUS. Dist: Independent Pubs. Group.

Morgan, Clay. The Boy Who Returned from the Sea. 2009. (ENG.). 256p. (J). (gr. 3-7). pap. 7.99 *(978-0-14-241395-1(X)*, Puffin Books) Penguin Young Readers Group.

Nooks, Nanny. Nina in the Forest of Faces. 2011. 46p. pap. 16.00 *(978-1-61204-606-8(1)*, Strategic Bk. Publishing) Strategic Book Publishing & Rights Agency (SBPRA).

Owen, Sarah. The Enchanted Tales. 2009. 39p. pap. 26.50 *(978-1-4452-5948-2(6))* Lulu Pr., Inc.

Russell, Ann. Little Truff & the Siamese Cat. Morris, Adrienne, ed. 2nd ed. 2013. 144p. pap. *(978-0-473-26077-4(8))* Bellbird Pubns.

Summer of Dreaming. 2010. (Illus.). 157p. (YA). pap. *(978-1-936021-22-2(6)*, Banana Oil Bks.) Cyberwizard Productions.

Sutcliffe, Kathy. When Romeo Kissed Mercutio. 2012. (ENG.). 240p. pap. *(978-1-922120-28-1(6)*, IP Digital) Interactive Pubns. Pty, Ltd.

Thomas, Rosemary. The Kiwi Kingdom. 2010. 154p. pap. 18.00 *(978-1-4349-0857-5(7))* Dorrance Publishing Co., Inc.

Tulloch, Scott. Willy's Mum. 2008. (Illus.). 32p. pap. *(978-1-86950-682-7(0))* HarperCollins Pubs. Australia.

Vaughn, Richard. Rowena & the Magic Hawk, the First Adventure. 2009. 224p. pap. 14.95 *(978-1-60860-157-8(9)*, Eloquent Bks.) Strategic Book Publishing & Rights Agency (SBPRA).

Vyvyan, Taylor. A Dragon's Odyssey. 2012. 120p. pap. *(978-1-78281-021-6(8))* Athena Pr.

West, Joyce. The Drovers Road Collection: Three New Zealand Adventures, 3 vols. West, Joyce, illus. 2003. (Bethlehem Budget Bks.). (Illus.). 416p. (YA). pap. 16.95 *(978-1-883937-69-0(8))* Bethlehem Bks.

NEWBERY, JOHN, 1713-1767

Granahan, Shirley. John Newbery: Father of Children's Literature, 1 vol. 2009. (Publishing Pioneers Ser.). (ENG., Illus.). 112p. (J). (gr. 6-12). lib. bdg. 35.64 *(978-1-60453-764-2(7)*, Essential Library) ABDO Publishing Co.

Markel, Michelle. Balderdash! John Newbery & the Boisterous Birth of Children's Books. Carpenter, Nancy, illus. 2017. (ENG.). 44p. (J). 17.99 *(978-0-8118-7922-4(4))* Chronicle Bks. LLC.

Roberts, Russell. John Newbery & the Story of the Newbery Medal. 2003. (Great Achiever Awards Ser.). (Illus.). 48p. (J). (gr. 4-8). lib. bdg. 29.95 *(978-1-58415-201-9(X))* Mitchell Lane Pubs., Inc.

NEWBERY MEDAL BOOKS

Roberts, Russell. John Newbery & the Story of the Newbery Medal. 2003. (Great Achiever Awards Ser.). (Illus.). 48p. (J). (gr. 4-8). lib. bdg. 29.95 *(978-1-58415-201-9(X))* Mitchell Lane Pubs., Inc.

NEWFOUNDLAND

see Newfoundland and Labrador

NEWFOUNDLAND AND LABRADOR

Beckett, Harry. Newfoundland & Labrador. 2003. (Eye on Canada Ser.). (Illus.). 32p. (J). pap. 9.95 *(978-1-894705-03-5(3))* Weigl Pubs., Inc.

Huey, Lois Miner. American Archaeology Uncovers the Vikings. 2009. (American Archaeology Ser.). 64p. (gr. 5-6). 31.36 *(978-0-7614-4270-7(7))* Marshall Cavendish Corp.

Keating, Laurel. Find Scruncheon & Touton 2: All Around Newfoundland, 1 vol. Keating, Nancy, illus. 2012. (ENG.). 32p. (J). (gr. k-3). pap. 10.95 *(978-1-897174-89-0(6)*, Tuckamore Bks) Creative Bk. Publishing CAN. Dist: Orca Bk. Pubs. USA.

—Search for Scruncheon & Touton, 1 vol. Keating, Nancy, illus. 2012. (ENG.). 32p. (J). (gr. -1-3). 10.95 *(978-1-897174-69-2(1)*, Tuckamore Bks) Creative Bk. Publishing CAN. Dist: Orca Bk. Pubs. USA.

Skirving, Janet. P Is for Puffin: A Newfoundland & Labrador Alphabet. Archibald, Odell, illus. rev. ed. 2006. (Discover Canada Province by Province Ser.). (ENG.). 40p. (J). (gr. 1-3). 17.95 *(978-1-58536-287-5(5)*, 202098) Sleeping Bear Pr.

Walsh, Alice. Change of Heart, 1 vol. Banks, Erin, illus. 2016. (ENG.). 32p. (J). (gr. -1-4). 19.95 *(978-1-77108-371-3(9))* Nimbus Publishing, Ltd. CAN. Dist: Orca Bk. Pubs. USA.

NEWFOUNDLAND AND LABRADOR—FICTION

Alberts, Nancy Markham. Just One More? Butler, John, illus. 2007. (ENG.). 24p. (J). (gr. -1-7). 14.95 *(978-1-59354-195-8(3)*, Handprint Bks.) Chronicle Bks. LLC.

Ballantyne, R. M. The Crew of the Water Wagtail. 2011. 146p. 24.95 *(978-1-4638-9596-9(8))* Rodgers, Alan Bks.

Browne, Susan Chalker. The Land of a Thousand Whales, 1 vol. Keating, Nancy, illus. 2007. (ENG.). 32p. (J). (gr. 3-7). pap. 8.95 *(978-1-897174-08-1(X))* Creative Bk. Publishing CAN. Dist: Orca Bk. Pubs. USA.

Choyce, Lesley. Refuge Cove. 2004. (Orca Soundings Ser.). 89p. 19.95 *(978-0-7569-4325-7(6))* Perfection Learning Corp.

Davidge, Bud. The Mummer's Song, 1 vol. Wallace, Ian, illus. 2009. (ENG.). 32p. (J). (gr. k). 14.95 *(978-0-88899-960-3(7))* Groundwood Bks. CAN. Dist: Publishers Group West (PGW).

Eubank, Patricia Reeder. Seaman's Journal. 2010. 40p. (J). pap. 9.99 *(978-0-8249-5619-6(2)*, Ideal Pubns.) Worthy Publishing.

Harlow, Joan Hiatt. Secret of the Night Ponies. 2009. (ENG.). 336p. (J). (gr. 3-7). 16.99 *(978-1-4169-0783-1(1)*, McElderry, Margaret K. Bks.) McElderry, Margaret K. Bks.

—Thunder from the Sea. 2004. (ENG., Illus.). 208p. (J). (gr. 3-7). 17.99 *(978-0-689-86403-2(5)*, McElderry, Margaret K. Bks.) McElderry, Margaret K. Bks.

Jacobs, Lily. The Littlest Bunny in Newfoundland. Dunn, Robert, illus. 2016. (ENG.). 32p. (J). (-7). 11.99 *(978-1-4926-3352-5(6)*, 9781492633525, Sourcebooks Jabberwocky) Sourcebooks, Inc.

James, Eric. Santa's Sleigh Is on It's Way to Newfoundland: A Christmas Adventure. Dunn, Robert, illus. 2016. (ENG.). 32p. (J). (-2). 12.99 *(978-1-4926-4505-4(2)*, 9781492645054, Sourcebooks Jabberwocky) Sourcebooks, Inc.

Lane, Lori & Winsor, Kathy. Nana's Quilt: Stitched in St. John'S, Newfoundland & Labrador, 1 vol. Costello, Jim, illus. 2007. (ENG.). 32p. (J). (gr. -1-4). per. 8.95 *(978-1-894294-82-9(3)*, Tuckamore Bks) Creative Bk. Publishing CAN. Dist: Orca Bk. Pubs. USA.

—Poppy & Allie: Hooked on St. John's, Newfoundland, 1 vol. Costello, Jim, photos by. 2009. (ENG., Illus.). 32p. (J). (gr. 1-8). pap. 10.95 *(978-1-897174-22-7(5))* Creative Bk. Publishing CAN. Dist: Orca Bk. Pubs. USA.

Mahoney, Jan. Moose Tales. 2010. 12p. 9.99 *(978-1-4520-6950-0(6))* AuthorHouse.

Malone, Beni & White, Marian Frances. The Sights Before Christmas, 1 vol. Erdelji, Darka, illus. 2007. (ENG.). 32p. (J). (gr. -1-2). per. 8.95 *(978-1-894294-94-2(7)*, Tuckamore Bks) Creative Bk. Publishing CAN. Dist: Orca Bk. Pubs. USA.

McGrath, Robin. Livyers World. 2007. (ENG.). 150p. (J). (gr. 4-7). per. *(978-1-897174-15-9(2))* Creative Bk. Publishing.

McMurchy-Barber, Gina. A Bone to Pick: A Peggy Henderson Adventure. 2015. (Peggy Henderson Adventure Ser.: 4). (ENG.). 152p. (J). pap. 12.99 *(978-1-4597-3072-4(0))* Dundurn CAN. Dist: Ingram Publisher Services.

Mowat, Farley. The Black Joke. 2009. (ENG.). 192p. pap. 9.95 *(978-0-7710-6469-2(1)*, Emblem Editions) McClelland & Stewart CAN. Dist: Random Hse., Inc.

Pryse-Phillips, William. Free Flight. 2013. 24p. pap. *(978-1-4602-0671-3(1))* FriesenPress.

Simons, Alan L. The Incredible Adventures of Captain Cameron MacDuddyfunk in Cuggermuggerland. Boggelen-Heutink, Ellen van, illus. 2013. 98p. pap. *(978-0-9877503-8-9(0))* Baronel Bks.

Smallman, Steve. Santa Is Coming to Newfoundland. Dunn, Robert, illus. 2014. (ENG.). 32p. (J). (-3). 11.99 *(978-1-4926-0715-1(0)*, Sourcebooks Jabberwocky) Sourcebooks, Inc.

Smith, Heather. Baygirl, 1 vol. 2013. (ENG.). 288p. (YA). (gr. 8-12). pap. 12.95 *(978-1-4598-0274-2(8))* Orca Bk. Pubs. USA.

Sullivan-Fraser, Deannie. Johnny & the Gypsy Moth, 1 vol. Rose, Hilda, illus. 2009. (ENG.). 32p. (J). (gr. k-5). 10.95 *(978-1-897174-40-1(3)*, Tuckamore Bks) Creative Bk. Publishing CAN. Dist: Orca Bk. Pubs. USA.

Wallace, Dillon. Ungava Bob. 2007. (ENG.). 196p. pap. 19.99 *(978-1-4346-0196-4(X))*; 216p. pap. 22.99 *(978-1-4346-0270-1(2))* Creative Media Partners, LLC.

Walsh, Alice. Buried Truth, 1 vol. 2013. (ENG.). 100p. (J). (gr. 4-8). pap. 11.95 *(978-1-77103-009-0(7)*, Tuckamore Bks) Creative Bk. Publishing CAN. Dist: Orca Bk. Pubs. USA.

—Heroes of Isle aux Morts. 2004. (J). (gr. k-3). spiral bd. *(978-0-616-11138-3(X))*; spiral bd. *(978-0-616-11139-0(8))* Canadian National Institute for the Blind/Institut National Canadien pour les Aveugles.

Wells, Helen. Cherry Ames, Island Nurse. 2007. (Cherry Ames Nurse Stories Ser.). 224p. (J). (gr. 3-7). 14.95 *(978-0-8261-0423-6(1))* Springer Publishing Co., Inc.

NEWMAN, JOHN HENRY, 1801-1890

Schmid, Evan. Cardinal from Oxford: A Story of John Henry Newman. 2011. 142p. 40.95 *(978-1-258-06803-5(5))* Literary Licensing, LLC.

NEWS BROADCASTS

see Radio Broadcasting; Television Broadcasting

NEWS PHOTOGRAPHY

see Photojournalism

NEWSPAPER WORK

see Journalism; Reporters and Reporting

NEWSPAPERS

see also Periodicals; Reporters and Reporting

Emmer, Rae. School Newspaper. 2009. (School Activities Ser.). 24p. (gr. 1-1). 42.50 *(978-1-60852-999-5(1)*, PowerKids Pr.) Rosen Publishing Group, Inc., The.

—School Newspaper: Periodico Escolar. 2004. (School Activities / Actividades Escolares Ser.). (SPA & ENG., Illus.). 24p. (J). lib. bdg. 22.60 *(978-0-8239-6901-2(0)*, Editorial Buenas Letras) Rosen Publishing Group, Inc., The.

—School Newspaper / Periódico Escolar. 2009. (School Activities / Actividades escolares Ser.). (ENG & SPA.). 24p. (gr. 1-2). 42.50 *(978-1-60853-005-2(1)*, Editorial Buenas Letras) Rosen Publishing Group, Inc., The.

Engdahl, Sylvia. Free Press. 2011. (Teen Rights & Freedoms Ser.). (ENG., Illus.). 176p. (gr. 10-12). 42.00 *(978-0-7377-5827-6(9))* Cengage Gale.

Fandel, Jennifer. You Can Write a Terrific Opinion Piece. 2012. (You Can Write Ser.). (ENG.). 24p. (gr. 1-2). pap. 41.70 *(978-1-4296-9317-2(7)*, First Facts) Capstone Press of Coughlan Cos.

—You Can Write a Terrific Opinion Piece, 1 vol. 2012. (You Can Write Ser.). (ENG., Illus.). 24p. (gr. 1-2). pap. 7.29 *(978-1-4296-9316-5(9))*; lib. bdg. 25.32 *(978-1-4296-8409-5(7))* Picture Window Bks.

Fromowitz, Lori. 12 Great Moments That Changed Newspaper History. 2015. (ENG., Illus.). 32p. (J). *(978-1-63235-025-1(4))* Pr. Room Editions LLC.

—12 Great Moments that Changed Newspaper History. 2015. (ENG., Illus.). 32p. (J). pap. 9.95 *(978-1-63235-085-5(8))* RiverStream Publishing.

Gish, Melissa. A Newspaper Publisher. 2003. 24p. (J). lib. bdg. 21.35 *(978-1-58340-324-2(8))* Black Rabbit Bks.

Hamilton, John. Newspapers, 1 vol. 2005. (Straight to the Source Ser.). (ENG., Illus.). 32p. (gr. k-6). 27.07 *(978-1-59197-547-2(6)*, Checkerboard Library) ABDO Publishing Co.

Hunt, Jilly. Beyond the Headlines! 2017. (Beyond the Headlines! Ser.). (ENG.). 48p. (gr. 4-6). 133.28 ***(978-1-4846-4160-6(4)***, Heinemann InfoSearch) Heinemann-Raintree.

Levin, Mark. Kids in Print: Publishing A School Newspaper. 2nd ed. 2004. 80p. (J). (gr. 3-9). pap. 15.00 *(978-0-9676409-2-1(X))* Mind - Stretch.

Mattern, Joanne. Katharine Graham & 20th Century American Journalism. 2003. (Women Who Shaped History Ser.). (Illus.). 24p. (J). lib. bdg. 22.60 *(978-0-8239-6500-7(7)*, PowerKids Pr.) Rosen Publishing Group, Inc., The.

Pascual Marquina, Cira. Newspapers: A Project by Siemon Allen. 2000th ed. 2004. (Illus.). 60p. per. 20.00 *(978-0-9749296-1-3(1))* Drake Univ., Anderson Gallery.

Pelleschi, Andrea. Olivia & Oscar Build an Opinion Piece. Hu, Caroline, illus. 2014. (Writing Builders Ser.). (ENG.). 32p. (J). (gr. 2-4). pap. 11.94 *(978-1-60357-556-0(1))*; lib. bdg. 25.27 *(978-1-59953-582-1(3))* Norwood Hse. Pr.

Pelusey, Michael & Pelusey, Jane. Newspapers. 2005. (Media Ser.). (Illus.). 32p. (gr. 5-8). lib. bdg. 21.95 *(978-0-7910-8800-5(6)*, Chelsea Hse.) Facts On File, Inc.

Petley, Julian. Newspapers & Magazines. 2003. (Media Wise Ser.). (Illus.). 64p. (J). lib. bdg. 28.50 *(978-1-58340-258-0(6))* Black Rabbit Bks.

Shea, Kitty. Out & about at the Newspaper. Trover, Zachary, illus. 2005. (Field Trips Ser.). (ENG.). 24p. (gr. -1-3). lib. bdg. 27.32 *(978-1-4048-1149-2(4))* Picture Window Bks.

Spilsbury, Richard & Spilsbury, Louise. The Printing Press, 1 vol. 2011. (Tales of Invention Ser.). (ENG.). 32p. (gr. 3-5). pap. 8.95 *(978-1-4329-4885-6(7)*, NA-h) Heinemann-Raintree.

USA Today's Debate Set: Voices & Perspectives, 8 vols. Incl. Legalized Gambling: Revenue Boom or Social Bust? Doeden, Matt. (Illus.). lib. bdg. 35.93 *(978-0-7613-5114-6(0))*; Legalizing Drugs: Crime Stopper or Social Risk? Goldstein, Margaret J. lib. bdg. 35.93 *(978-0-7613-5116-0(7))*; 160p. (gr. 9-12). (USA TODAY's Debate: Voices & Perspectives Ser.). (ENG., Illus.). 2010. Set lib. bdg. 431.16 *(978-0-7613-4078-2(5)*, Twenty-First Century Bks.) Lerner Publishing Group.

Whitelaw, Nancy. Joseph Pulitzer: And the New York World. 2004. (Makers of the Media Ser.). (Illus.). 112p. (YA). (gr. 6-12). 21.95 *(978-1-883846-44-2(7)*, First Biographies) Reynolds, Morgan Inc.

—William Randolph Hearst & the American Century. rev. exp. ed. 2004. (Makers of the Media Ser.). (Illus.). 128p. (gr. 6-12). 28.95 *(978-1-931798-35-8(4))* Reynolds, Morgan Inc.

NEWSPAPERS—FICTION

Alger Jr. Horatio Staff. Herbert Carter's Legacy. rev. ed. 2006. 264p. 28.95 *(978-1-4218-1756-9(X))*; pap. 13.95 *(978-1-4218-1856-6(6))* 1st World Publishing, Inc. (1st World Library - Literary Society).

Banks, Steven. Stop the Presses! DePorter, Vince, illus. 2005. 22p. (J). lib. bdg. 15.00 *(978-1-4242-0973-6(0))* Fitzgerald Bks.

Barrows, Annie. Ivy + Bean: No News Is Good News. Blackall, Sophie, illus. 2012. (Ivy & Bean Ser.). (ENG.). 144p. (J). (gr. 1-5). pap. 5.99 *(978-1-4521-0781-3(5))* Chronicle Bks. LLC.

—Ivy + Bean No News Is Good News. Blackall, Sophie, illus. 2011. (Ivy & Bean Ser.: IVYB). (ENG.). 128p. (J). (gr. 1-5). 14.99 *(978-0-8118-6693-4(9))* Chronicle Bks. LLC.

—No News Is Good News. Blackall, Sophie, illus. 2012. (Ivy & Bean Ser.: 8). (J). lib. bdg. 16.00 *(978-0-606-26950-6(9)*, Turtleback) Turtleback Bks.

Barrows, Annie & Blackall, Sophie. Ivy + Bean, 1 vol. 2011. (Ivy & Bean Ser.). (ENG., Illus.). 128p. (J). (gr. 1-4). 24.21 *(978-1-59961-928-6(8))* Spotlight.

Breault, Christie Merriman. Logan West, Printer's Devil. Archambault, Matthew, illus. 2006. 142p. (J). pap. *(978-1-59336-762-6(7))* Mondo Publishing.

Butler, Dori Hillestad. The Truth about Truman School, 1 vol. (ENG.). (J). (gr. 3-7). 2009. 192p. pap. 7.99 *(978-0-8075-8096-7(1))* 2008. (Illus.). 176p. lib. bdg. 15.99 *(978-0-8075-8095-0(3))* Whitman, Albert & Co.

Clements, Andrew. Head of the Class: Frindle - The Landry News - The Janitor's Boy. Selznick, Brian, illus. 2007. (ENG.). 416p. (J). (gr. 3-7). pap. 20.99 *(978-1-4169-4974-9(7)*, Atheneum Bks. for Young Readers) Simon & Schuster Children's Publishing.

—El Periodico Landry. Selznick, Brian, illus. 2004.Tr. of Landry News. (SPA.). (YA). pap. 9.99 *(978-84-241-7886-4(6))* Everest Editora ESP. Dist: Lectorum Pubns., Inc.

Corbett, Sue. The Last Newspaper Boy in America. 2010. (ENG.). 208p. (J). (gr. 5-18). 6.99 *(978-0-14-241696-9(7)*, Puffin Books) Penguin Young Readers Group.

Devlin, Calla. Right Where You Left Me. 2017. (ENG., Illus.). 256p. (YA). (gr. 9). 17.99 ***(978-1-4814-8699-6(3)***, Atheneum Bks. for Young Readers) Simon & Schuster Children's Publishing.

El diario de mis Abejas: Individual Title, 6 packs. (Literatura 2000 Ser.). (SPA.). (gr. 2-3). 33.00 *(978-0-7635-1647-5(3))* Rigby Education.

M
N
O

Doktorski, Jennifer Salvato. Famous Last Words. 2013. (ENG.). 288p. (YA). (gr. 7). 17.99 (978-0-8050-9367-4(2), 9780805093674, Holt, Henry & Co. Bks. For Young Readers) Holt, Henry & Co.

Elmore, Barbara. Saviors of the Bugle. 2003. 208p. (YA). per. 6.99 (978-0-9714941-0-7(X)) Mud Pie Pr.

English, Karen. The Newsy News Newsletter. Freeman, Laura, illus. 2011. (ENG.). 96p. (J). (gr. 1-4). pap. 5.99 (978-0-547-40626-8(6)) Houghton Mifflin Harcourt Publishing Co.

Fantaskey, Beth. Isabel Feeney, Star Reporter. 2017. (ENG.). 352p. (J). (gr. 5-7). pap. 7.99 (978-0-544-93696-6(5), HMH Books For Young Readers) Houghton Mifflin Harcourt Publishing Co.

—Isabel Feeney, Star Reporter. 2017. (ENG.). (J). (gr. 5-7). lib. bdg. 18.40 **(978-0-606-39809-1(0))** Turtleback Bks.

Frampton, David. Beastie ABC. Frampton, David, illus. Date not set. (Illus.). 32p. (J). (gr. -1-1). pap. 5.99 (978-0-06-443653-3(5)) HarperCollins Pubs.

Goo, Maurene. Since You Asked... 2013. (YA). pap. (978-0-545-44822-2(0)); (ENG.). 272p. (J). (gr. 7). 17.99 (978-0-545-44821-5(2)) Scholastic, Inc. (Scholastic Pr.).

Hoena, Blake A. Swamp Sting!, 1 vol. Facio, Sebastian, illus. 2011. (Graphic Sparks Ser.). (ENG.). 40p. (gr. 1-3). pap. 5.95 (978-1-4342-3065-2(1)); lib. bdg. 23.99 (978-1-4342-2960-1(2)) Stone Arch Bks. (Graphic Sparks).

Kerr, M. E., pseud. If I Love You, Am I Trapped Forever?, 0 vols. 2011. (ENG.). 192p. (J). (gr. 7-9). pap. 9.99 (978-0-7614-5839-5(5), 9780761458395, Amazon Children's Publishing) Amazon Publishing.

Krensky, Stephen. The Great Moon Hoax. Bisaillon, Josée, illus. 2011. (Carolrhoda Picture Bks.). (ENG.). 32p. (J). (gr. 2-5). lib. bdg. 16.95 (978-0-7613-5110-8(8)) Lerner Publishing Group.

Levine, Kristin. The Paper Cowboy. 2014. (ENG.). 352p. (J). (gr. 5). 16.99 (978-0-399-16328-9(X), G.P. Putnam's Sons Books for Young Readers) Penguin Young Readers Group.

May, Kyla. Mika: My New Life. 2013. (Lotus Lane Ser.: 4). (ENG.). 96p. (J). (gr. 1-3). pap. 4.99 (978-0-545-44519-1(1)) Scholastic, Inc.

McMahen, Chris. Tabloidology, 1 vol. 2009. (ENG.). 176p. (J). (gr. 4-7). pap. 9.95 (978-1-55469-009-1(9)) Orca Bk. Pubs. USA.

Meddaugh, Susan. Martha Speaks: Martha's Nose for News (chapter Book) 2013. (Martha Speaks Ser.). (ENG., Illus.). 96p. (J). (gr. 1-4). 14.99 (978-0-544-13567-3(9)) Houghton Mifflin Harcourt Publishing Co.

—Nose for News. 2013. (Martha Speaks Ser.). (ENG., Illus.). 96p. (J). (gr. 1-4). pap. 5.99 (978-0-544-08572-5(8)) Houghton Mifflin Harcourt Publishing Co.

Mercer, Sienna. Fangtastic! 2007. (My Sister the Vampire Ser.: 2). (ENG.). 208p. (J). (gr. 3-7). per. 6.99 (978-0-06-087115-4(6)) HarperCollins Pubs.

Meyers, Dolores. Herbie's New Home. 2011. 20p. pap. 24.95 (978-1-60749-665-6(8)) America Star Bks.

Montgomery, L. M. The Golden Road. l.t. ed. 2007. (ENG.). 254p. pap. 23.99 (978-1-4264-7144-5(0)) Creative Media Partners, LLC.

Myers, Walter Dean. Checkmate. 2015. (News Crew Ser.). (ENG.). 144p. (J). (gr. 5-9). pap. 6.99 (978-0-545-82875-8(9), Scholastic Pr.) Scholastic, Inc.

—The Cruisers. (ENG.). 144p. (J). (gr. 5-9). 2015. (News Crew Ser.). pap. 6.99 (978-0-545-82874-1(0)) 2011. (Cruisers Ser.: 1). pap. 5.99 (978-0-439-91633-2(X)) 2010. (Cruisers Ser.: 1). 15.99 (978-0-439-91626-4(7)) Scholastic, Inc. (Scholastic Pr.).

—Oh, Snap! 2013. (Cruisers Ser.: Bk. 4). (ENG.). 128p. (J). (gr. 5-9). 17.99 (978-0-439-91629-5(1), Scholastic Pr.) Scholastic, Inc.

Naylor, Phyllis Reynolds. Boys Rock! 2007. (Boy/Girl Battle Ser.). (ENG.). 144p. (J). (gr. 3-7). 5.99 (978-0-440-41990-7(5), Yearling) Random Hse. Children's Bks.

Nelson, Blake. The New Rules of High School. 2004. (ENG.). 240p. (YA). (gr. 7-18). reprint ed. 7.99 (978-0-14-240242-9(7), Speak) Penguin Young Readers Group.

Nixon, Joan Lowery. Maria's Story, 1773. 2004. (J). (978-0-87935-227-1(2)) Colonial Williamsburg Foundation.

Pratchett, Terry. The Truth. 2014. (Discworld Ser.: 25). (gr. 5-8). 20.85 (978-0-613-57290-3(4), Turtleback) Turtleback Bks.

Robinson, A. M. Vampire Crush. 2010. (ENG.). 416p. (YA). (gr. 8-18). pap. 8.99 (978-0-06-198971-1(1), HarperTeen) HarperCollins Pubs.

Spalding, Amy. Ink Is Thicker Than Water. 2013. (Entangled Teen Ser.). (ENG.). 320p. (YA). (gr. 7-12). pap. 9.99 (978-1-62266-040-7(4), 9781622660407) Entangled Publishing, LLC.

Stewart, Paul. Far-Flung Adventures: Hugo Pepper. 2012. (Far-Flung Adventures Ser.). (ENG.). 272p. (J). (gr. 3-7). 7.99 (978-0-385-75223-7(7), Yearling) Random Hse. Children's Bks.

Stilton, Geronimo. The Stone of Fire. 2013. (Geronimo Stilton Cavemice Ser.: 1). lib. bdg. 18.40 (978-0-606-31526-5(8), Turtleback) Turtleback Bks.

Winerip, Michael. Adam Canfield: The Last Reporter. 2009. (Adam Canfield of the Slash Ser.: 3). (ENG., Illus.). 384p. (J). (gr. 3-7). 16.99 (978-0-7636-2342-5(3)) Candlewick Pr.

—Adam Canfield of the Slash. (Adam Canfield of the Slash Ser.: 1). (ENG., Illus.). 336p. (J). (gr. 3-7). 2007. per. 7.99 (978-0-7636-2794-2(1)) 2005. 15.99 (978-0-7636-2340-1(7)) Candlewick Pr.

—Adam Canfield the Last Reporter. 2010. (Adam Canfield of the Slash Ser.: 3). (ENG., Illus.). 384p. (J). (gr. 3-7). 7.99 (978-0-7636-4838-1(8)) Candlewick Pr.

—Adam Canfield Watch Your Back! 2009. (Adam Canfield of the Slash Ser.: 2). (ENG., Illus.). 352p. (J). (gr. 3-7). 7.99 (978-0-7636-4412-3(9)) Candlewick Pr.

Wise, Rachel. Black & White & Gray All Over. 2013. (Dear Know-It-All Ser.: 7). (ENG.). 160p. (J). (gr. 3-7). 15.99 (978-1-4424-7517-5(X)); (Illus.). pap. 5.99 (978-1-4424-7515-1(3)) Simon Spotlight. (Simon Spotlight).

—Digital Disaster! 2013. (Dear Know-It-All Ser.: 6). (ENG.). 160p. (J). (gr. 3-7). 15.99 (978-1-4424-7218-1(9)); pap. 5.99 (978-1-4424-7217-4(0)) Simon Spotlight. (Simon Spotlight).

—Stop the Presses! 2014. (Dear Know-It-All Ser.: 12). (ENG., Illus.). 160p. (J). (gr. 3-7). pap. 5.99 (978-1-4424-9797-9(1), Simon Spotlight) Simon Spotlight.

Yeh, Kat. The Way to Bea. 2017. (ENG.). 352p. (J). (gr. 3-7). 16.99 **(978-0-316-23667-6(5))** Little, Brown Bks. for Young Readers.

NEWTON, ISAAC, SIR, 1642-1727

Anderson, Margaret J. Isaac Newton: Greatest Genius of Science. 2015. (Genius Scientists & Their Genius Ideas Ser.). 96p. (J). (gr. 5-12). 27.94 (978-0-7660-6570-3(7)); pap. 10.95 (978-0-7660-6571-0(5)) Enslow Pubs., Inc.

Anderson, Margaret Jean. Isaac Newton: The Greatest Scientist of All Time. 2008. (Great Minds of Science Ser.). (Illus.). 128p. (J). (gr. 3-7). lib. bdg. 33.27 (978-0-7660-2793-0(7)) Enslow Pubs., Inc.

Barnham, Kay. Isaac Newton, 1 vol. 2014. (Science Biographies Ser.). (ENG.). 32p. (gr. 2-4). lib. bdg. 30.65 (978-1-4109-6235-5(0), Raintree Perspectives) Heinemann-Raintree.

Benchmark Education Company. Newton & His Laws (Teacher Guide) 2005. (978-1-4108-4670-9(9)) Benchmark Education Co.

Bortz, Fred. Laws of Motion & Isaac Newton. 2013. (Revolutionary Discoveries of Scientific Pioneers Ser.). (Illus.). 80p. (J). (gr. 7-12). 33.25 (978-1-4777-1808-7(7)) Rosen Publishing Group, Inc., The.

Brannon, Barbara. Discover Sir Isaac Newton. 2005. (J). pap. (978-1-4108-5127-7(3)) Benchmark Education Co.

Chiang, Mona. Isaac Newton & His Laws of Motion: Set Of 6. 2011. (Navigators Ser.). (J). pap. 50.00 net. (978-1-4108-5089-8(7)) Benchmark Education Co.

—Isaac Newton & His Laws of Motion: Text Pairs. 2008. (Bridges/Navigators Ser.). (J). (gr. 6). 94.00 (978-1-4108-8442-8(2)) Benchmark Education Co.

Ferrie, Chris. Newtonian Physics for Babies. 2017. (Baby University Ser.: 0). (ENG., Illus.). 24p. (J). bds. 9.99 **(978-1-4926-5620-3(8)**, Sourcebooks Jabberwocky) Sourcebooks, Inc.

Funk, Tara. Newton & His Laws. 2005. (J). pap. (978-1-4108-4622-8(9)) Benchmark Education Co.

Gianopoulos, Andrea & Barnett, Charles, III. Isaac Newton & the Laws of Motion, 1 vol. Miller, Phil, illus. 2007. (Inventions & Discovery Ser.). (ENG.). 32p. (gr. 3-4). pap. 8.10 (978-0-7368-7899-9(8), 1264949, Graphic Library) Capstone Press of Coughlan Cos.

Gianopoulos, Andrea & Barnett III, Charles. Isaac Newton & the Laws of Motion [Scholastic]. Miller, Phil, illus. 2010. (Inventions & Discovery Ser.). 32p. pap. 0.45 (978-1-4296-5969-7(6), Capstone Interactive Library) Capstone Digital.

Gordon, Fernando. Sir Isaac Newton, 1 vol. 2016. (ENG., Illus.). 24p. (J). (978-1-68078-158-8(8)) ABDO Publishing Co.

Graham, Ian. You Wouldn't Want to Be Sir Isaac Newton! A Lonely Life You'd Rather Not Lead. Antram, David, illus. 2013. (You Wouldn't Want to... Ser.). (ENG.). 32p. (J). 29.00 (978-0-531-25943-6(9)); pap. 9.95 (978-0-531-23040-4(6)) Scholastic Library Publishing. (Watts, Franklin).

—You Wouldn't Want to Be Sir Isaac Newton! A Lonely Life You'd Rather Not Lead. 2013. (You Wouldn't Want To... Ser.). lib. bdg. 20.80 (978-0-606-31632-3(9), Turtleback) Turtleback Bks.

Hollihan, Kerrie Logan. Isaac Newton & Physics for Kids: His Life & Ideas with 21 Activities. 2009. (For Kids Ser.). (ENG., Illus.). 144p. (J). (gr. 4-7). pap. 16.95 (978-1-55652-778-4(0)) Chicago Review Pr., Inc.

Hunter, Nick. Gravity. 2017. (Great Scientific Theories Ser.). (ENG.). 32p. (gr. 4-6). lib. bdg. 30.65 **(978-1-4109-8729-7(9)**, Raintree Perspectives) Heinemann-Raintree.

Isaac Newton: Organizing the Universe. 2004. (Great Scientists Ser.). (Illus.). 144p. (YA). (gr. 6-12). 26.95 (978-1-931798-01-3(X)) Reynolds, Morgan Inc.

Kramer, Alan & Kramer, Candice. Isaac Newton: The World in Motion. 2005. (J). pap. (978-1-4108-4222-0(3)) Benchmark Education Co.

Krull, Kathleen. Isaac Newton. Kulikov, Boris, illus. 2008. (Giants of Science Ser.). (ENG.). 128p. (J). (gr. 3-7). 7.99 (978-0-14-240820-9(4), Puffin Books) Penguin Young Readers Group.

Lasky, Kathryn. Newton's Rainbow: The Miraculous Discoveries of a Young Scientist. Hawkes, Kevin, illus. 2017. (ENG.). 48p. (J). 17.99 (978-0-374-35513-5(4), 9780374355135, Farrar, Straus & Giroux (BYR)) Farrar, Straus & Giroux.

Lin, Yoming S. Isaac Newton & Gravity. 2012. (Eureka! Ser.). (Illus.). 24p. (YA). (gr. 3-6). lib. bdg. 22.60 (978-1-4488-5032-7(0)) Rosen Publishing Group, Inc., The.

Losure, Mary. Isaac the Alchemist: Secrets of Isaac Newton, Reveal'd. 2017. (ENG.). 176p. (J). (gr. 5). 19.99 (978-0-7636-7063-4(4)) Candlewick Pr.

McNeil, Niki, et al. HOCPP 1059 Isaac Newton. 2006. spiral bd. 18.50 (978-1-60308-059-0(7)) In the Hands of a Child.

Meyer, Susan. Isaac Newton. 2017. (Leaders of the Scientific Revolution Ser.). 112p. (J). (gr. 12-13). 37.10 **(978-1-5081-7470-7(9)**, Rosen Young Adult) Rosen Publishing Group, Inc., The.

Mooney, Carla. Isaac Newton: Genius Mathematician & Physicist, 1 vol. 2014. (Great Minds of Science Ser.). (ENG.). 48p. (gr. 8-12). lib. bdg. 32.79 (978-1-62403-382-7(2)) ABDO Publishing Co.

Novelli, Luca. Newton & the Antigravity Formula. 2017. (Flashes of Genius Ser.). (ENG., Illus.). 112p. (J). (gr. 2). pap. 9.99 **(978-1-61373-861-0(7))** Chicago Review Pr., Inc.

O'Donnell, Kerri. Sir Isaac Newton: Using the Laws of Motion to Solve Problems. (Math for the Real World Ser.). 32p. 2009. (ENG., Illus.). (gr. 6-7). pap. 10.00 (978-1-4042-6079-5(X)) 2009. (gr. 5-5). 47.90 (978-1-60851-366-6(1), PowerKids Pr.) 2006. (Illus.). (YA). (gr. 5-9). lib. bdg. 25.25 (978-1-4042-3363-8(6)) Rosen Publishing Group, Inc., The.

O'Leary, Denyse. What Are Newton's Laws of Motion? 2010. (Shaping Modern Science Ser.). (ENG.). 64p. (J). (gr. 5-8). pap. (978-0-7787-7207-1(1)) Crabtree Publishing Co.

Pascal, Janet. Who Was Isaac Newton? Foley, Tim & Harrison, Nancy, illus. 2014. (Who Was? Ser.). (ENG.). 112p. (J). (gr. 3-7). pap. 5.99 (978-0-448-47913-2(3), Grosset & Dunlap) Penguin Young Readers Group.

—Who Was Isaac Newton? 2014. (Who Was... ? Ser.). lib. bdg. 16.00 (978-0-606-36174-3(X)) Turtleback Bks.

Petersen, Kristen. Understanding the Laws of Motion. 2015. (J). lib. bdg. (978-1-62713-427-9(1)) Cavendish Square Publishing.

Phelan, Glen. Newton's Laws. 2007. (Reading Expeditions Ser.). (ENG., Illus.). 32p. (J). pap. 17.95 (978-0-7922-4584-1(9)) CENGAGE Learning.

Royston, Angela. Sir Isaac Newton: Overlord of Gravity. 2015. (Superheroes of Science Ser.). (ENG., Illus.). 48p. (J). (gr. 6-6). pap. 14.05 (978-1-4824-3153-7(X)) Stevens, Gareth Publishing LLLP.

Salas, Laura Purdie. Discovering Nature's Laws: A Story about Isaac Newton. Reynolds, Emily C. S., tr. Reynolds, Emily C. S., illus. 2003. (Creative Minds Biographies Ser.). (ENG.). 64p. (gr. 4-8). pap. 8.95 (978-1-57505-606-7(2)); lib. bdg. 22.60 (978-1-57505-183-3(4)) Lerner Publishing Group.

Steele, Philip. Isaac Newton: Mi Mejor Amigo Es la Verdad. 2007. (SPA., Illus.). 416p. (J). (gr. 4-8). pap. 14.99 (978-970-58-0222-5(X)) Altea, Ediciones, S.A. - Grupo Santillana ESP. Dist: Two Rivers Distribution.

Sullivan, Anne Marie. Sir Isaac Newton: Famous English Scientist. (Illus.). 32p. (J). 2013. (People of Importance Ser.: 21). (gr. 4-18). 19.95 (978-1-4222-2856-2(8)) 2004. (Great Names Ser.). (gr. 3-18). lib. bdg. 19.95 (978-1-59084-139-6(5)) Mason Crest.

Weir, Jane. Isaac Newton & the Laws of the Universe, 1 vol. 2007. (Science Readers Ser.). (ENG.). 32p. (J). (gr. 3-3). pap. 8.99 (978-0-7439-0574-9(1)) Shell Educational Publishing.

NEWTS

Goldish, Meish. Little Newts. 2010. (Amphibiana Ser.). (Illus.). 24p. (YA). (gr. k-3). lib. bdg. 22.61 (978-1-936087-38-9(3)) Bearport Publishing Co., Inc.

Kolpin, Molly. Newts. 2010. (Amphibians Ser.). (ENG.). 24p. (gr. k-1). pap. 41.70 (978-1-4296-5090-8(7), Pebble Plus) Capstone Press of Coughlan Cos.

NIAGARA FALLS (N.Y. AND ONT.)

Bauer, Marion Dane. Niagara Falls. Wallace, John, illus. 2006. (Wonders of America Ser.). (ENG.). 32p. (J). (gr. -1-1). pap. 3.99 (978-0-689-86944-0(4), Simon Spotlight) Simon Spotlight.

Butcher, Timothy. ABACA Flows over Niagara Falls: An Illustrated History. 2006. (Illus.). 48p. (J). lib. bdg. 16.95 (978-0-9786473-0-8(0)) Amoeba Bks.

Leigh, Autumn. Niagara Falls. 2008. (Real Readers - Upper Emergent Ser.). (ENG., Illus.). 12p. (gr. 1-2). pap. 5.90 (978-0-8239-8195-3(9)) Rosen Publishing Group, Inc., The.

Marsh, Carole. The Wild Water Mystery of Niagra Falls. 2009. (Real Kids, Real Places Ser.). (J). (gr. 2-9). lib. bdg. 18.99 (978-0-635-06831-6(1)) Gallopade International.

Sisk, Siobhan. Would You Dare Walk Across Niagara Falls? 2016. (Would You Dare? Ser.). 00032p. (J). pap. 10.50 **(978-1-4824-5830-5(6))**; lib. bdg. 26.60 **(978-1-4824-5832-9(2))** Stevens, Gareth Publishing LLLP.

Stine, Megan. Where Is Niagara Falls? 2015. (Where Is... ? Ser.). lib. bdg. 16.00 (978-0-606-37548-1(1)) Turtleback Bks.

Stine, Megan & dePaola, Tomie. Where Is Niagara Falls? 2015. (Where Is? Ser.). (ENG., Illus.). 112p. (J). (gr. 3-7). 5.99 (978-0-448-48425-9(0), Grosset & Dunlap) Penguin Young Readers Group.

Tieck, Sarah. Niagara Falls, 1 vol. 2008. (All Aboard America Ser.). (ENG.). 24p. (J). (gr. 1-4). 25.65 (978-1-59928-938-0(5)) ABDO Publishing Co.

Tokunaga, Wendy. Niagara Falls. 2003. (Illus.). 48p. (J). 26.20 (978-0-7377-2056-3(5), Greenhaven Pr., Inc.) Cengage Gale.

Van Allsburg, Chris. Queen of the Falls. 2011. (ENG., Illus.). 40p. (J). (gr. 1-4). 18.99 (978-0-547-31581-2(3)) Houghton Mifflin Harcourt Publishing Co.

NICARAGUA

Brimson, Samuel. Korea, North-Nicaragua, 8 vols., Vol. 5. 2003. (Nations of the World Ser.: Vol. 5). (Illus.). 64p. (gr. 5-12). lib. bdg. 31.00 (978-0-8368-5489-3(6), Gareth Stevens Secondary Library) Stevens, Gareth Publishing LLLP.

Kallen, Stuart A. The Aftermath of the Sandinista Revolution. 2009. (Aftermath of History Ser.). 160p. (YA). (gr. 7-12). 38.60 (978-0-8225-9091-0(3)) Twenty First Century Bks.

Kott, Jennifer & Streiffert, Kristi. Nicaragua. 2nd rev. ed. 2005. (Cultures of the World Ser.). (Illus.). 144p. (gr. 6-10). lib. bdg. 42.79 (978-0-7614-1969-3(1), Benchmark Bks.) Marshall Cavendish Corp.

Mara, Wil. Nicaragua. 2017. (Enchantment of the World(tm) Ser.). (ENG., Illus.). 144p. (J). lib. bdg. 40.00 (978-0-531-22090-0(7), Children's Pr.) Scholastic Library Publishing.

Mundera, Kristina. A Day in Pueblo Nuevo. 2012. 40p. pap. 9.75 (978-1-937314-36-1(7)) ABREN (A Bk. to Read Empowers Nicaraguans).

Owings, Lisa. Nicaragua. 2014. (Exploring Countries Ser.). (ENG., Illus.). 32p. (J). (gr. 3-7). lib. bdg. 26.95 (978-1-60014-985-6(5), Blastoff! Readers) Bellwether Media.

Shields, Charles J. Nicaragua. 2010. (Central America Today Ser.). 63p. (YA). (gr. 7-18). pap. 9.95 (978-1-4222-0717-8(X)); (Illus.). (gr. 9-12). 21.95 (978-1-4222-0650-8(5)) Mason Crest.

—Nicaragua, Vol. 8. Henderson, James D., ed. 2015. (Discovering Central America: History, Politics, & Culture Ser.). (Illus.). 64p. (J). (gr. 7). lib. bdg. 22.95 (978-1-4222-3291-0(3)) Mason Crest.

Torres, John Albert. Meet Our New Student from Nicaragua. 2009. (Meet Our New Student Ser.). 48p. (J). (gr. 2-5). 29.95 (978-1-58415-834-9(4)) Mitchell Lane Pubs., Inc.

NICHOLAS, SAINT, BISHOP OF MYRA

Collins, Janet Ann. Secret Service Saint. Ruble, Eugene, illus. 2009. 16p. pap. 9.95 (978-1-935137-98-6(0)) Guardian Angel Publishing, Inc.

Demi. The Legend of Saint Nicholas. Demi, illus. 2003. (ENG., Illus.). 40p. (J). (gr. k-5). 21.99 (978-0-689-84681-6(9), McElderry, Margaret K. Bks.) McElderry, Margaret K. Bks.

Forest, Jim. Saint Nicholas & the Nine Gold Coins. Andrejev, Vladislav, illus. 2015. (J). (978-0-88141-511-7(1)) St. Vladimir's Seminary Pr.

Grün, Anselm, et al. The Legend of Saint Nicholas. Ferri, Giuliano, illus. 2014. (ENG.). 26p. (J). 16.00 (978-0-8028-5434-6(6), Eerdmans Bks For Young Readers) Eerdmans, William B. Publishing Co.

Stiegemeyer, Julie. Saint Nicholas: The Real Story of the Christmas Legend. Ellison, Chris, illus. (J). 2005. 16p. (gr. -1-17). bds. 7.49 (978-0-7586-0688-4(5)) 2003. 32p. 13.49 (978-0-7586-0376-0(2)) Concordia Publishing Hse.

Tompert, Ann. Saint Nicholas. Garland, Michael, illus. 2005. (ENG.). 32p. (J). (gr. 1-7). pap. 8.95 (978-1-59078-336-8(0)) Boyds Mills Pr.

NICHOLAS, SAINT, BISHOP OF MYRA—FICTION

Mackall, Dandi Daley. The Legend of St. Nicholas: A Story of Christmas Giving, 1 vol. Cowdrey, Richard, illus. 2014. (ENG.). 32p. (J). 16.99 (978-0-310-73115-3(1)) Zonderkidz.

Stiegemeyer, Julie. Saint Nicholas: The Real Story of the Christmas Legend. Ellison, Chris, illus. 2007. 32p. (J). (gr. -1). per. 7.49 (978-0-7586-1341-7(5)) Concordia Publishing Hse.

NICHOLAS II, EMPEROR OF RUSSIA, 1868-1918

Fleming, Candace. The Family Romanov: Murder, Rebellion, & the Fall of Imperial Russia. 2014. (ENG., Illus.). 304p. (YA). (gr. 7). 19.99 (978-0-375-86782-8(1)); lib. bdg. 21.99 (978-0-375-96782-5(6)) Random Hse. Children's Bks. (Schwartz & Wade Bks.).

NIGER RIVER

Behnke, Alison. Niger in Pictures. 2008. (Visual Geography (Lerner) Ser.). (Illus.). 80p. (YA). (gr. 7-12). lib. bdg. 31.93 (978-0-8225-7147-6(1)) Twenty First Century Bks.

Seffal, Rabah & Spilling, Jo-Ann. Niger. 2nd rev. ed. 2010. (Cultures of the World 20 Ser.). 144p. (gr. 6). 42.79 (978-1-60870-026-4(7)) Marshall Cavendish GBR. Dist: Marshall Cavendish Corp.

NIGERIA

Brownlie Bojang, Ali. Discover Nigeria. 2012. (Discover Countries Ser.). (Illus.). 32p. (YA). (gr. 4-7). lib. bdg. 26.50 (978-1-4488-5270-3(6)) Rosen Publishing Group, Inc., The.

Brownlie Bojang, Ali & Bowden, Rob. Focus on Nigeria. 2006. (World in Focus Ser.). (Illus.). 64p. (gr. 5-12). pap. 14.05 (978-0-8368-6239-3(2)); lib. bdg. 34.00 (978-0-8368-6220-1(1)) Stevens, Gareth Publishing LLLP. (Gareth Stevens Secondary Library).

Gibson, Karen. We Visit Nigeria. 2012. (J). lib. bdg. 33.95 (978-1-61228-309-8(8)) Mitchell Lane Pubs., Inc.

Graham, Ian. Nigeria. 2004. (Country File Ser.). (J). lib. bdg. 27.10 (978-1-58340-498-0(8)) Black Rabbit Bks.

Hamilton, Janice. Nigeria in Pictures. 2nd ed. 2003. (Visual Geography Series, Second Ser.). (ENG., Illus.). 80p. (gr. 5-12). 31.93 (978-0-8225-0373-6(5)) Lerner Publishing Group.

Heinrichs, Ann. Nigeria. 2009. (Enchantment of the World Ser.). (ENG.). 144p. (J). (gr. 5-9). 40.00 (978-0-531-20653-9(X)) Scholastic Library Publishing.

Jay, Ruth Johnson. Mary Slessor: Missionary to Calabar. 2006. (Illus.). 143p. (J). (978-1-56265-077-3(7)) Accelarated Christian Education, Inc.

Lynch, Annabelle. Nigeria. 2017. (Living In Ser.). (ENG., Illus.). 24p. (J). (gr. k-2). 16.99 (978-1-4451-4865-6(X), Franklin Watts) Hachette Children's Group GBR. Dist: Hachette Bk. Group.

Ogunnaike, Anna M. Meet Our New Student from Nigeria. 2008. (Meet Our New Student Ser.). (Illus.). 47p. (YA). (gr. 2-5). lib. bdg. 29.95 (978-1-58415-655-0(4)) Mitchell Lane Pubs., Inc.

Oluonye, Mary. Nigeria. 2008. pap. 40.95 (978-0-8225-9306-5(8)) Lerner Publishing Group.

Oluonye, Mary N. Nigeria. 2007. (Country Explorers Ser.). (Illus.). 48p. (J). (gr. 4-8). lib. bdg. 27.93 (978-0-8225-7131-5(5), Lerner Pubns.) Lerner Publishing Group.

Orr, Tamra. Nigeria. 2006. (A to Z Ser.). (ENG., Illus.). 40p. (J). (gr. 2-4). pap. 6.95 (978-0-516-24954-4(1), Children's Pr.) Scholastic Library Publishing.

Phillips, Douglas A. Nigeria. 2003. (Modern World Nations Ser.). (Illus.). 150p. (gr. 6-12). 35.00 (978-0-7910-7475-6(7), Chelsea Hse.) Facts On File, Inc.

Powell, Jillian. Looking at Nigeria. 2007. (Looking at Countries Ser.). (Illus.). 32p. (gr. 1-5). pap. 10.50 (978-0-8368-7678-9(4)); lib. bdg. 26.00 (978-0-8368-7671-0(7)) Stevens, Gareth Publishing LLLP. (Gareth Stevens Learning Library).

Rau, Dana Meachen. Nigeria. 2010. (Explorer Library: Social Studies Explorer Ser.). (ENG.). 48p. (gr. 4-8). lib. bdg. 31.36 (978-1-60279-830-4(3), 200526) Cherry Lake Publishing.

Walker, Ida. Nigeria. Rotberg, Robert I., ed. 2012. (Evolution of Africa's Major Nations Ser.). (Illus.). 80p. (J). (gr. 7). 22.95 (978-1-4222-2200-3(4)) Mason Crest.

—Nigeria. 2011. (J). pap. (978-1-4222-2228-7(4)) Mason Crest.

Zocchi, Judy. In Nigeria. Brodie, Neale, illus. 2005. (Global Adventures II Ser.). 32p. (J). per. 10.95 (978-1-59646-144-4(6)) Dingles & Co.

—In Nigeria/en Nigeria. Brodie, Neale, illus. 2005. (Global Adventures II Ser.).Tr. of En Nigeria. (ENG & SPA.). 32p. (J). per. 10.95 (978-1-59646-146-8(2)) Dingles & Co.

NIGERIA—FICTION

Achebe, Chinua. Chike & the River. Rodriguez, Edel, illus. 2011. (ENG.). 96p. (YA). pap. 12.00 (978-0-307-47386-8(4), Penguin Books) Penguin Publishing Group.

Alakija, Polly. Catch That Goat! A Market Day in Nigeria. Alakija, Polly, illus. 2007. (ENG., Illus.). 40p. (J). (gr. -1-3). 8.99 (978-1-84686-057-7(1)) Barefoot Bks., Inc.

Bodden, Michelle, adapted by. Obara the Gatekeeper. 2007. (J). 14.95 (978-0-9753089-1-2(2)) Water Daughter Publishing.

Holman, Nedra. Beautiful Queen. Velitchenko, Olga, illus. 2008. 40p. (J). (978-1-4363-5461-5(7)) Xlibris Corp.

Okorafor, Nnedi. Akata Witch. (ENG.). (YA). (gr. 7). 2017. 384p. pap. 10.99 **(978-0-14-242091-1(3)**, Speak) 2011. 368p. 17.99 (978-0-670-01196-4(7), Viking Books for Young Readers) Penguin Young Readers Group.

Onyefulu, Ifeoma & Quarto Generic Staff. The Girl Who Married a Ghost: And Other Tales from Nigeria. 2010. (ENG., Illus.). 112p. (J). (gr. 3-6). 15.95 (978-1-84780-176-0(5), Frances Lincoln Children's Bks.) Quarto Publishing Group UK GBR. Dist: Hachette Bk. Group.

Saint-Lot, Katia Novet & Tokunbo, Dimitrea. Amadi's Snowman. 2008. (ENG., Illus.). 32p. (gr. 1-6). 16.95 *(978-0-88448-298-7(7),* 884298) Tilbury Hse. Pubs.

Unobagha, Uzo. Grandma, How Do You Say I Love You? Krassa, Victoria, illus. 2007. 28p. (J). 16.95 *(978-0-9773180-0-1(1))* Adonoke Inc.

NIGERIA—HISTORY

Giles, Bridget. Nigeria. 2007. (Countries of the World Ser.). (ENG., Illus.). 64p. (J). (gr. 5-9). lib. bdg. 27.90 *(978-1-4263-0124-7(3),* National Geographic Children's Bks.) National Geographic Society.

Kelly, Terri B. Mary Slessor: Missionary Mother. 2014. (Illus.). 164p. (J). *(978-1-60682-630-0(1))* BJU Pr.

Leavitt, Amie Jane. Discovering the Kingdom of Benin. 2013. (Exploring African Civilizations Ser.). 64p. (J). (gr. 5-8). 31.95 *(978-1-4777-1884-1(2),* Rosen Reference) Rosen Publishing Group, Inc., The.

Owings, Lisa. Nigeria. 2011. (Exploring Countries Ser.). (ENG., Illus.). 32p. (YA). (gr. 3-7). lib. bdg. 26.95 *(978-1-60014-619-0(8),* Blastoff! Readers) Bellwether Media.

Rogers Seavey, Lura. Nigeria. 2016. (Enchantment of the World(tm) Ser.). (ENG., Illus.). 144p. (J). lib. bdg. 40.00 *(978-0-531-21886-0(4),* Children's Pr.) Scholastic Library Publishing.

UNESCO. Funmilayo Ransome-Kuti. 2016. (ENG., Illus.). 112p. (J). (gr. 3-7). 13.95 *(978-0-00-815006-8(0))* HarperCollins Pubs. Ltd. GBR. Dist: Independent Pubs. Group.

Wiseman, Blaine. Nigeria. 2014. (J). *(978-1-4896-3058-2(9))* Weigl Pubs., Inc.

Zocchi, Judy. In Nigeria. Brodie, Neale, illus. 2005. (Global Adventures I Ser.). 32p. (J). pap. 10.95 *(978-1-59646-143-7(8));* lib. bdg. 21.65 *(978-1-59646-010-2(5))* Dingles & Co.

—In Nigeria/en Nigeria. Brodie, Neale, illus. 2005. (Global Adventures I Ser.).Tr. of En Nigeria. (ENG & SPA.). 32p. (J). pap. 10.95 *(978-1-59646-145-1(4));* lib. bdg. 21.65 *(978-1-59646-011-9(3))* Dingles & Co.

NIGHT

Branley, Franklyn M. What Makes Day & Night? 2015. (Let's Read & Find Out Science Stage 2 Ser.). (J). lib. bdg. 17.20 *(978-0-606-37738-6(7))* Turtleback Bks.

Clark, Claire. How Long Is a Day?, 1 vol. 2012. (Calendar Ser.). (ENG.). 24p. (J). (gr. k-1). lib. bdg. 26.65 *(978-1-4296-7591-8(8),* Pebble Plus) Capstone Press of Coughlan Cos.

Evans, Shira. Day & Night. 2016. (Readers Ser.). (ENG., Illus.). 48p. (J). (-k). pap. 4.99 *(978-1-4263-2470-3(7),* National Geographic Children's Bks.) National Geographic Society.

Green, Jen. Day & Night. 2008. (Our Earth Ser.). (Illus.). 24p. (J). (gr. 1-4). lib. bdg. 22.60 *(978-1-4042-4275-3(9))* Rosen Publishing Group, Inc., The.

Havener, Katherine. Nursies When the Sun Shines: A Little Book on Night Weaning. Burrier, Sara, illus. 2nd ed. 2013. 20p. (J). pap. 9.99 *(978-0-615-75642-4(5))* Elea Pr.

Hughes, Tom. Day & Night. 2016. (All about Opposites Ser.). (Illus.). 24p. (J). pap. 9.35 *(978-0-7660-8082-9(X))* Enslow Pubs., Inc.

Katirgis, Jane. Day & Night. 2011. (All about Opposites Ser.). (Illus.). 24p. (J). (gr. -1-18). pap. 7.95 *(978-1-59845-262-4(2),* Enslow Elementary); (gr. k-3). lib. bdg. 22.60 *(978-0-7660-3915-5(3))* Enslow Pubs., Inc.

Kochanoff, Peggy. Be a Night Detective: Solving the Mysteries of Twilight, Dusk, & Nightfall, 1 vol. 2017. (ENG., Illus.). 56p. (J). (gr. -1-3). pap. 14.95 ***(978-1-77108-464-2(2))*** Nimbus Publishing, Ltd. CAN. Dist: Orca Bk. Pubs. USA.

Llewellyn, Claire. Day & Night. 2006. (I Know That, Cycles of Nature Set Ser.). (Illus.). 24p. (J). (gr. -1-3). lib. bdg. 22.80 *(978-1-59771-018-3(0))* Sea-To-Sea Pubns.

Low, William & Cobalt Illustrations Studio Staff. Daytime Nighttime. Low, William & Cobalt Illustrations Studio Staff, illus. (ENG., Illus.). (J). (gr. -1-3). 2015. 28p. bds. 7.99 *(978-1-62779-172-4(8),* 9781627791724) 2014. 40p. 16.99 *(978-0-8050-9751-1(1),* 9780805097511) Holt, Henry & Co. (Holt, Henry & Co. Bks. For Young Readers).

Marsico, Katie. The Darkest & the Brightest. 2015. (True Book(tm), a — Extreme Places Ser.). (ENG., Illus.). 48p. (J). lib. bdg. 31.00 *(978-0-531-21848-8(1),* Children's Pr.) Scholastic Library Publishing.

Meithrin, Mudiad Ysgolion. Llyfr Lliwio Dydd a Nos. 2005. (WEL & ENG., Illus.). 26p. pap. *(978-1-870222-48-8(2))* Mudiad Ysgolion Meithrin.

Murphy, Stuart J. It's about Time! Speirs, John, illus. 2005. (MathStart Ser.). 40p. (J). 16.99 *(978-0-06-055768-3(0));* (ENG.). (gr. -1). pap. 5.99 *(978-0-06-055769-0(9))* HarperCollins Pubs.

—It's about Time! Speirs, John, illus. 2005. (Mathstart Ser.). 33p. (gr. -1-3). 16.00 *(978-0-7569-5224-2(7))* Perfection Learning Corp.

Neumeyer, Peter F. & Gorey, Edward. Why We Have Day & Night. 2011. (Illus.). 36p. (J). (gr. -1-1). 12.95 *(978-0-7649-5886-1(0))* Pomegranate Communications, Inc.

O'DellKathryn. THE SCIENCE OF DARKNESS LOW INTERMEDIATE BOOK WITH ONLINE ACCESS. 2014. (ENG., Illus.). 28p. (J). pap. 9.50 *(978-1-107-65493-8(9))* Cambridge Univ. Pr.

¿Por Que Es Oscura la Noche? (Coleccion Primeros Pasos en la Ciencia). (SPA., Illus.). (J). (gr. 1-3). pap. *(978-950-724-112-3(4),* LMA8218) Lumen ARG. Dist: Lectorum Pubns., Inc.

Sasso, Sandy Eisenberg. Adam & Eve's New Day. Rothenberg, Joani Keller, illus. 2006. (ENG.). 24p. (gr. -1). bds. 7.99 *(978-1-59473-205-8(1),* 9781594732058, Skylight Paths Publishing) LongHill Partners, Inc.

Smith, Alastair. Nighttime. 2004. (Lift-the-Flap Learners Ser.). (Illus.). 16p. (J). (gr. 1-18). pap. 8.95 *(978-0-7945-0366-6(7),* Usborne) EDC Publishing.

Smith, Sian. Night & Day, 1 vol. 2014. (Opposites Ser.). (ENG.). 24p. (gr. -1-1). pap. 5.99 *(978-1-4846-0336-9(2),* Acorn) Heinemann-Raintree.

Tagholm, Sally. The Complete Book of the Night. 2006. (Illus.). 96p. (J). (gr. 4-8). reprint ed. 19.00 *(978-1-4223-5329-5(X))* DIANE Publishing Co.

NIGHT—FICTION

Abrahams, Peter, et al. Up All Night: A Short Story Collection. 2008. (Illus.). 240p. (J). (gr. 7). lib. bdg. 17.89 *(978-0-06-137077-9(0));* 16.99 *(978-0-06-137076-2(2))* HarperCollins Pubs. (Geringer, Laura Book).

Allgood, Jean. Come Follow Me Bk. 1: Understanding One's Worth: Color Orange. Smith, Sandra, illus. l.t. ed. 2004. 23p. (J). 14.95 *(978-0-9741627-3-7(6))* PricePoint+Publications.

Anderson, Sara. Noisy City Night (2015 Board Book) Anderson, Sara, illus. 2015. (ENG., Illus.). 12p. (J). (gr. -1-1). bds. 10.95 *(978-1-943459-01-8(0))* Sara Anderson Children's Bks.

Ashman, Linda. How to Make a Night. Tusa, Tricia, illus. Date not set. 32p. (J). (gr. -1-3). pap. 5.99 *(978-0-06-443699-1(3))* HarperCollins Pubs.

Awdry, Wilbert V. Blue Train, Green Train. Stubbs, Tommy, illus. 2006. (Bright & Early Books(R) Ser.). (ENG.). 36p. (J). (gr. k-k). 8.99 *(978-0-375-83463-9(X),* Random Hse. Bks. for Young Readers) Random Hse. Children's Bks.

Awdry, Wilbert V. & Awdry, W. Blue Train, Green Train. Stubbs, Tommy, illus. 2007. (Bright & Early Board Books(TM) Ser.). (ENG.). 24p. (J). (— 1). bds. 4.99 *(978-0-375-83984-9(4),* Random Hse. Bks. for Young Readers) Random Hse. Children's Bks.

Babbitt, Natalie. The Something. 40p. (J). (gr. k-2). pap. 2.95 *(978-0-8072-1333-9(0),* Listening Library) Random Hse. Audio Publishing Group.

Baldwin, Christy. Nine Things Nathan Noticed at Night. Barnes, Sarah, illus. 2005. 24p. (J). per. 13.00 *(978-0-9765072-1-5(8))* Tribute Bks.

Ban Breathnach, Sarah. The Best Part of the Day. Edelson, Wendy, illus. 2014. (ENG.). 40p. (J). (-k). 16.99 *(978-1-62157-252-7(8),* Regnery Kids) Regnery Publishing, Inc., An Eagle Publishing Co.

Banks, Kate. The Night Worker. Hallensleben, Georg, illus. 2007. (ENG.). 40p. (J). (gr. -1-1). 8.99 *(978-0-374-40000-2(8),* 9780374400002) Square Fish.

—Night Worker. 2014. 19.00 *(978-1-63419-674-1(0))* Perfection Learning Corp.

Barlics, Brian. Brady Needs a Nightlight. Jones, Gregory Burgess, illus. 2013. (ENG.). 32p. (J). pap. 18.95 *(978-1-61296-195-8(9))* Black Rose Writing.

Barnett, Mac. Noisy Night. Biggs, Brian, illus. 2017. (ENG.). 32p. (J). 16.99 *(978-1-59643-967-2(X),* 9781596439672) Roaring Brook Pr.

Bartoletti, Susan Campbell. Naamah & the Ark at Night. Meade, Holly, illus. 2011. (ENG.). 32p. (J). (gr. -1-3). 16.99 *(978-0-7636-4242-6(8))* Candlewick Pr.

Bauer, Marion Dane. The Longest Night. Lewin, Ted, illus. 2009. (ENG.). 40p. (J). (gr. -1-3). 17.95 *(978-0-8234-2054-4(X))* Holiday Hse., Inc.

Bayless, Julie. Roar! 2015. (ENG., Illus.). 32p. (J). (gr. -1-17). 16.95 *(978-0-7624-5750-2(3),* Running Pr. Kids) Running Pr. Bk. Pubs.

Bean, Jonathan. At Night. Bean, Jonathan, illus. 2007. (ENG., Illus.). 32p. (J). (gr. -1-3). 17.99 *(978-0-374-30446-1(7),* 9780374304461, Farrar, Straus & Giroux (BYR)) Farrar, Straus & Giroux.

Bell, Taj. The Little Night Fairy: Written & illustrated by Taj Bell graphic design & co-illustration by Lisa. 2008. 40p. pap. 20.99 *(978-1-4389-2602-5(2))* AuthorHouse.

Bentley, Dawn. Goodnight Bear: A Book & Night Light. Couri, Kathryn A., illus. 2005. (Stories to Share Ser.). 12p. (J). 12.95 *(978-1-58117-034-4(3),* Intervisual/Piggy Toes) Bendon, Inc.

Berenstain, Jan & Berenstain, Mike. The Berenstain Bears Go Out to Eat. Berenstain, Jan & Berenstain, Mike, illus. 2009. (Berenstain Bears Ser.). (ENG., Illus.). 32p. (J). (gr. -1-2). pap. 3.99 *(978-0-06-057393-5(7),* HarperFestival) HarperCollins Pubs.

Blackall, Sophie. Are You Awake? Blackall, Sophie, illus. 2011. (ENG., Illus.). 40p. (J). (gr. -1-k). 12.99 *(978-0-8050-7858-9(4),* 9780805078589, Holt, Henry & Co. Bks. For Young Readers) Holt, Henry & Co.

Bond, Felicia. Poinsettia & the Firefighters. Bond, Felicia, illus. 2003. (Illus.). (J). *(978-0-06-056871-9(2))* HarperCollins Pubs.

Boyd, Lizi. Flashlight. 2014. (ENG., Illus.). 40p. (J). (gr. -1-1). 16.99 *(978-1-4521-1894-9(9))* Chronicle Bks. LLC.

Boynton, Sandra. The Going to Bed Book. Boynton, Sandra, illus. (ENG., Illus.). (J). 2006. 14p. bds. 12.95 *(978-1-4169-2794-5(8))* 30th anniv. ed. 2012. 18p. (gr. -1-3). bds. 7.99 *(978-1-4424-5409-5(1))* Little Simon. (Little Simon).

Bradbury, Ray. Switch on the Night. Dillon, Leo & Dillon, Diane, illus. 2004. (ENG.). 40p. (J). (gr. -1-2). reprint ed. pap. 7.99 *(978-0-553-11244-3(9),* Dragonfly Bks.) Random Hse. Children's Bks.

Bradford, William. Jeremy Mcbright Was Afraid of the Night. 2006. (Illus.). 36p. (J). lib. bdg. 13.95 *(978-0-9672585-2-2(9))* CyPress Pubns.

Brand, Brandon. Lily Is... Wide Awake. 2008. 32p. (J). 16.00 *(978-0-9802329-0-5(2))* Upside Down Tree Publishing.

Brown, Marc. Good Night, D. W. Brown, Marc, illus. 2004. (ENG., Illus.). 24p. (J). (gr. -1-1). pap. 3.99 *(978-0-316-73385-4(7))* Little, Brown Bks. for Young Readers.

Brown, Margaret Wise. Buenas Noches, Luna, 1 vol. Mlawer, Teresa, tr. from ENG. Hurd, Clement, illus. 2006.Tr. of Goodnight Moon. (SPA.). 32p. (J). (gr. -1-3). 17.99 *(978-0-06-026214-3(1),* HC0528, Rayo) HarperCollins Pubs.

—Goodnight Moon 1 2 3: A Counting Book. Hurd, Clement, illus. 2008. (ENG.). 30p. (J). (gr. -1-k). bds. 8.99 *(978-0-06-112597-3(0),* HarperFestival) HarperCollins Pubs.

Buchanan, Nelda. The Hall Closet Light. 2009. 36p. (J). pap. 13.95 *(978-1-4327-4584-4(0))* Outskirts Pr., Inc.

Burleigh, Robert. Night Train, Night Train. Minor, Wendell, illus. 2017. (J). lib. bdg. ***(978-1-58089-717-4(7))*** Charlesbridge Publishing, Inc.

Butterworth, Nick. One Snowy Night. Butterworth, Nick, illus. 2008. (Tales from Percy's Park Ser.). (ENG., Illus.). 32p. (J). (gr. k-2). pap. 12.95 incl. audio compact disk *(978-0-00-726024-9(5))* HarperCollins Pubs.

—One Snowy Night. Butterworth, Nick, illus. 2007. (ENG., Illus.). 32p. (J). 24.00 *(978-0-00-725942-7(5))* HarperCollins Pubs. Ltd. GBR. Dist: Independent Pubs. Group.

Carroll, James Christopher. The Boy & the Moon. Carroll, James Christopher, illus. 2010. (ENG., Illus.). 32p. (J). (gr. 1-4). 19.99 *(978-1-58536-521-0(1),* 202209) Sleeping Bear Pr.

Carter, Anne Laurel. Night Boy, 1 vol. Pelletier, Ninon, illus. 2012. (ENG.). 32p. (J). (gr. -1-3). 19.95 *(978-1-55469-402-0(7))* Orca Bk. Pubs. USA.

Castro, Edmund Lee. Crystal & the Not-So-Scary Night. 2008. 36p. pap. 24.95 *(978-1-60672-236-7(0))* America Star Bks.

Catran, Ken. Tomorrow the Dark. 2005. 208p. pap. *(978-0-7344-0417-6(4),* Lothian Children's Bks.) Hachette Australia.

Charest, Emily MacLachlan & MacLachlan, Patricia. Before You Came. Diaz, David, illus. 2011. 32p. (J). (gr. -1-3). (ENG.). 16.99 *(978-0-06-051234-7(2));* lib. bdg. 17.89 *(978-0-06-051235-4(0))* HarperCollins Pubs. (Tegen, Katherine Bks).

Chouette Publishing Staff. Baby Caillou: Good Night! Brignaud, Pierre, illus. 2013. (Baby Caillou Ser.). (ENG.). 10p. (J). (gr. -1 — 1). 7.99 *(978-2-89718-099-7(4))* Filmer Ltd.

Cinderfella's Big Night: Individual Title Six-Packs. (Action Packs Ser.). 104p. (gr. 3-5). 44.00 *(978-0-7635-2984-0(2))* Rigby Education.

Condon, Tom. The Sandman: Stories to Read to Children. 2003. 136p. (J). pap. 11.95 *(978-0-595-27291-4(6))* iUniverse, Inc.

Costales, Amy. Hello Night/Hola Noche. McDonald, Mercedes, illus. 2007. (ENG, SPA & MUL.). 24p. (J). (gr. -1 — 1). 14.95 *(978-0-87358-927-7(0))* Cooper Square Publishing Llc.

Crawford, Deborah. Tyler the Turtle Is Afraid of the Dark. Balzer, Jeremy, illus. 2006. 32p. (J). 14.95 *(978-0-9770516-1-8(7))* Laffin Minor Pr.

Crimi, Carolyn. Where's My Mummy? Manders, John, illus. 2009. (ENG.). 32p. (J). (gr. -1-3). 7.99 *(978-0-7636-4337-9(8))* Candlewick Pr.

Crowther, Kitty, creator. Scritch Scratch Scraww Plop. 2015. (ENG., Illus.). 40p. (J). (gr. -1-3). 16.95 *(978-1-59270-179-7(5))* Enchanted Lion Bks., LLC.

Crummel, Susan Stevens. All in One Hour, 0 vols. Donohue, Dorothy, illus. 2009. (ENG.). 40p. (J). (gr. k-3). pap. 9.99 *(978-0-7614-5537-0(X),* 9780761455370, Amazon Children's Publishing) Amazon Publishing.

Delacroix, Sibylle. Blanche Hates the Night. Morelli, Christelle, tr. from FRE. 2016. (ENG., Illus.). 32p. (J). (gr. -1-2). 16.95 *(978-1-77147-158-9(1),* Owlkids) Owlkids Bks. Inc. CAN. Dist: Publishers Group West (PGW).

Disney Publishing Staff. Piglet's Night Lights, 15 vols. 2003. (It's Fun to Learn Ser.). (Illus.). 32p. (J). (gr. -1-3). 3.99 *(978-1-57973-127-4(9))* Advance Pubs. LLC.

Feiffer, Kate. No Go Sleep! Feiffer, Jules, illus. 2012. (ENG.). 32p. (J). (gr. -1-2). 16.99 *(978-1-4424-1683-3(1),* Simon & Schuster/Paula Wiseman Bks.) Simon & Schuster/Paula Wiseman Bks.

Ford, Bernette G. & Ford, Bernette. First Snow. Braun, Sebastien, illus. 2005. (ENG.). 32p. (J). (gr. -1-3). 16.95 *(978-0-8234-1937-1(1))* Holiday Hse., Inc.

Fox, Sabrina. Who Can Help Me Sleep? Rothan, Ann, illus. 2004. 32p. (gr. -1-3). 16.95 *(978-1-885394-36-1(5))* Amber Lotus Publishing.

Fraley, Patty. Fear at Night: To Matthew. 2011. 24p. (gr. -1). pap. 12.79 *(978-1-4567-5555-3(2))* AuthorHouse.

Gayatri Stein, Mari. Puddle Moon. 2010. (ENG., Illus.). 32p. 17.95 *(978-0-9793840-0-4(1),* Riverwood Bks.) White Cloud Pr.

Gerstein, Mordicai. The Night World. 2015. (ENG., Illus.). 40p. (J). (gr. -1-3). 18.00 *(978-0-316-18822-7(0))* Little Brown & Co.

Gomez, Lorena. Nightlights. Alvarez, Lorena, illus. 2017. (ENG.). 56p. (gr. 3). 18.95 *(978-1-910620-13-7(0))* Nobrow Ltd. GBR. Dist: Consortium Bk. Sales & Distribution.

Grey, Mini. Toys in Space. 2013. (ENG.). 32p. (J). (gr. k-3). 16.99 *(978-0-307-97812-7(5),* Knopf Bks. for Young Readers) Random Hse. Children's Bks.

Grover, Neha Lamba. Shaurya's Adventures. 2010. 43p. pap. 17.40 *(978-0-557-12636-1(3))* Lulu Pr., Inc.

Guilloppé, Antoine. One Scary Night. 2007. (ENG., Illus.). 32p. (J). (gr. 4-7). 15.95 *(978-1-59687-185-4(7))* IBks., Inc.

Gutierrez, Lorna. Hello, Mr. Moon. Watkins, Laura, illus. 2016. (J). ***(978-1-4351-6412-3(1))*** Barnes & Noble, Inc.

Gwanas, Bethan. Ramboy. 2009. (ENG.). 112p. (J). pap. 7.95 *(978-0-86243-993-4(0))* Y Lolfa GBR. Dist: Dufour Editions, Inc.

Hadland, W. Into the Night. 2010. 312p. (gr. 4-6). pap. 19.13 *(978-1-4251-4187-5(0))* Trafford Publishing.

Harris, Sally M. Rainbow Nights. Grady, Kit, illus. 2009. 20p. pap. 9.95 *(978-1-61633-002-6(3))* Guardian Angel Publishing, Inc.

Harshman, Marc. All the Way to Morning. Dávalos, Felipe, illus. 2006. (J). per. 7.95 *(978-1-891852-49-7(3))* Quarrier Pr.

Harwood, Beth. One Snowy Night. Ronchi, Susanna, illus. 2005. 12p. (J). *(978-1-84011-627-4(7))* Templar Publishing.

Hawkins, Colin & Hawkins, Jacqui. Snap! Snap! 2005. (ENG., Illus.). 32p. (J). pap. 7.99 *(978-1-4052-1099-7(0))* Egmont Bks., Ltd. GBR. Dist: Trafalgar Square Publishing.

Hegarty, Patricia. Who's There? Beware! 2015. (Amazing Changing Pictures! Ser.). (ENG.). 14p. (J). (gr. -1-3). 12.99 *(978-1-68010-000-6(9))* Tiger Tales.

Heine, Helme. El Maravilloso Viaje a Traves de la Noche. 3rd ed. 2003. (SPA., Illus.). 250p. *(978-84-85334-62-9(0))* Lóguez Ediciones ESP. Dist: Lectorum Pubns., Inc.

—Wunderbare Reise Durch Die Na. 12.95 *(978-3-7876-9528-7(1))* Middelhauve Verlags GmbH DEU. Dist: Distribooks, Inc.

Heo, Yumi, illus. Sun & Moon Have a Tea Party. 2016. (J). *(978-0-385-39033-0(5),* Schwartz & Wade Bks.) Random Hse. Children's Bks.

Hodge, Rosamund. Crimson Bound. 2016. 464p. (YA). (gr. 8). pap. 9.99 *(978-0-06-222477-4(8))* HarperCollins Pubs.

Hood, Karen Jean Matsko. Goodnight, I Wish You Goodnight, Bilingual English & Icelandic, Vol. 1. Whispering Pine Press International, ed. Hatakeyama, Hiroshi, illus. 2015. (Hood Picture Book Ser.). (ENG & ICE.). 60p. (J). 34.95 *(978-1-59649-920-1(6));* pap. 29.95 *(978-1-59649-919-5(2))* Whispering Pine Pr. International, Inc.

Hopgood, Tim. Wow! Said the Owl. Hopgood, Tim, illus. 2009. (ENG., Illus.). 32p. (J). (gr. -1-k). 16.99 *(978-0-374-38518-7(1),* 9780374385187, Farrar, Straus & Giroux (BYR)) Farrar, Straus & Giroux.

Hornsby, Ashley. Pretty Little Lilly & the Magical Light. Couch, Greg, illus. 2007. 32p. (J). 15.95 *(978-0-9777241-0-9(7))* Cepia LLC.

Hornsby, Ashley Brooke. Pretty Little Lilly & the Magical Night (paperback) 2006. (Illus.). (J). *(978-0-9777241-1-6(5))* Cepia LLC.

Horwitz, Elinor Lander. When the Sky Is Like Lace, 1 vol. Cooney, Barbara, illus. 2015. (ENG.). 32p. 17.95 *(978-1-939017-47-5(5),* 3ee48b7a-7a20-4033-ab13-196c42256117) Islandport Pr., Inc.

Hosta, Dar. I Love the Night. Hosta, Dar, illus. l.t. ed. 2003. (Illus.). 32p. (J). (gr. k-3). 16.95 *(978-0-9721967-0-3(6))* Brown Dog Bks.

Ibarrola, Begonia. Crisol & His Star. Herranz, Yésica, ed. Pita, Lorena, illus. 2013. (ENG.). 40p. (J). (gr. k-2). 13.95 *(978-84-95923-50-9(5))* Primera Persona ESP. Dist: Independent Pubs. Group.

Iriyama, Satoshi. Good Night, Chirp. 2015. (Chirp the Chick Ser.). (ENG., Illus.). 36p. (J). (— 1). 8.99 *(978-0-544-35994-9(1),* HMH Books For Young Readers) Houghton Mifflin Harcourt Publishing Co.

Jeffers, Dawn. Beautiful Moon. Leick, Bonnie, illus. 2009. (ENG.). 32p. (J). (gr. -1-3). 16.95 *(978-1-934960-05-9(5),* Raven Tree Pr.,Csi) Continental Sales, Inc.

Juan, Ana. The Night Eater. 2004. (Illus.). (J). *(978-0-439-48892-1(3),* Levine, Arthur A. Bks.) Scholastic, Inc.

Kemble, Mai S. The Moon & the Night Sweeper. Kemble, Mai S., illus. 2008. (Illus.). (J). pap. 6.95 *(978-1-60108-023-3(9))* Red Cygnet Pr.

Kemble, Mai S., illus. The Moon & the Night Sweeper. 2007. 30p. (J). (gr. -1-2). 15.95 *(978-1-60108-013-4(1))* Red Cygnet Pr.

Kessler, Ethel & Kessler, Leonard. Night Story. 2008. (ENG.). 52p. (J). (gr. -1-3). 10.99 *(978-1-4169-9030-7(5),* Simon & Schuster Bks. For Young Readers) Simon & Schuster Bks. For Young Readers.

Krensky, Stephen. Fraidy Cats. Lewin, Betsy, illus. 2015. (Scholastic Reader, Level 2 Ser.). (ENG.). 32p. (J). (gr. -1-3). pap. 3.99 *(978-0-545-79966-9(X),* Cartwheel Bks.) Scholastic, Inc.

La Coccinella. At Night. 2015. (Peekaboo! Ser.). (ENG., Illus.). 26p. (J). (gr. -1-k). bds. 6.95 *(978-1-4549-1583-6(8))* Sterling Publishing Co., Inc.

Lacoursiere, Patrick. Dream Songs Night Songs: From China to Senegal. Bourbonnière, Sylvie, illus. 2006. (ENG.). 36p. (J). (gr. -1-2). 16.95 *(978-2-923163-24-6(9))* La Montagne Secrete CAN. Dist: Independent Pubs. Group.

Laplante, Carole. Night Noises. Byrne-Walker, Mary Ann, illus. 2012. 40p. pap. 9.95 *(978-1-62006-046-9(9))* Sunbury Press, Inc.

Lewis, Rose A. Sweet Dreams. Corace, Jen, illus. 2012. (ENG.). 32p. (J). (gr. -1-k). 16.95 *(978-1-4197-0189-4(4),* Abrams Bks. for Young Readers) Abrams, Inc.

Listening with Zachary. (J). pap. 13.75 *(978-0-8136-4655-8(3))* Modern Curriculum Pr.

Loewer, Peter. The Moonflower, 1 vol. Loewer, Jean, illus. 2004. (ENG.). 32p. (J). (gr. 1-5). pap. 7.95 *(978-1-56145-314-6(5))* Peachtree Pubs.

Low, J. H. Night in the Gardens. 2017. (ENG.). 40p. 10.00 *(978-981-4751-42-1(1))* Marshall Cavendish International (Asia) Private Ltd. SGP. Dist: National Bk. Network.

Marlar, Debra L. Morgan's Sleepover at Grandma's. 2010. 36p. 16.99 *(978-1-4520-6496-3(2))* AuthorHouse.

Matheson, Christie. Touch the Brightest Star. Matheson, Christie, illus. (Illus.). (J). (gr. -1-3). 2017. 42p. bds. 7.99 *(978-0-06-227448-9(1))* 2015. (ENG., 40p. 15.99 *(978-0-06-227447-2(3))* HarperCollins Pubs. (Greenwillow Bks.).

McKay, Amanda S. The New Night Sky. 2012. 28p. pap. 19.99 *(978-1-4685-2517-5(4))* AuthorHouse.

McMillan, Dawn. Awake in the Dark! Fino, Roberto, illus. 2009. (Rigby PM Stars Bridge Bks.). (ENG.). 24p. (gr. 2-3). pap. 8.70 *(978-1-4190-5527-0(5))* Rigby Education.

Mellgren, Jöns. Elsa & the Night. 2014. (ENG., Illus.). 32p. (J). (gr. -1-3). 19.95 *(978-3-89955-716-9(6))* Die Gestalten Verlag DEU. Dist: Penguin Random Hse. LLC.

Miller, Jules, illus. When Night Became Day. 2015. (ENG.). 32p. (J). (gr. -1-k). 16.95 *(978-1-62914-632-4(3),* Sky Pony Pr.) Skyhorse Publishing Co., Inc.

Montardre, Hélène. Night & Day. 2003. (Illus.). 8p. (J). bds. 7.95 *(978-1-58728-481-6(2),* Two-Can Publishing) T&N Children's Publishing.

Morales, Yuyi. Little Night / Nochecita. 2016. (ENG & SPA.). (J). lib. bdg. 18.40 *(978-0-606-38443-8(X))* Turtleback Bks.

Moulton, Mark Kimball. The Visit. Winget, Susan, tr. Winget, Susan, illus. 2003. (ENG.). 56p. (J). 14.95 *(978-0-8249-5859-6(4),* Ideal Pubns.) Worthy Publishing.

Padur, Simone. Things That Go Bump in the Night. 2012. 20p. pap. 19.99 *(978-0-9847831-7-5(2))* Big Country Publishing, LLC.

Paraskevas, Michael. Mr. Moon. 2016. (ENG., Illus.). 40p. (J). (gr. -1-2). 17.99 *(978-0-399-54992-2(7),* Crown Books For Young Readers) Random Hse. Children's Bks.

Parker, Amy. Night Night, Train, 1 vol. Allyn, Virginia, illus. 2017. (Night Night Ser.). (ENG.). 20p. (J). bds. 9.99 ***(978-0-7180-8932-0(4))*** Nelson, Thomas Inc.

Pearson, Anthony. Baby Bear Eats the Night, 0 vols. Leick, Bonnie, illus. 2012. (ENG.). 32p. (J). (gr. -1-k). 16.99 *(978-0-7614-6103-6(5),* 9780761461036, Amazon Children's Publishing) Amazon Publishing.

Peters, Lisa Westberg. Frankie Works the Night Shift. Taylor, Jennifer, illus. 2010. (ENG.). 32p. (J). (gr. -1-k). 16.99 *(978-0-06-009095-1(2),* Greenwillow Bks.) HarperCollins Pubs.

Pilkey, Dav. The Paperboy. 2015. 32p. pap. 7.00 *(978-1-61003-556-9(9))* Center for the Collaborative Classroom.

Poppele, Jonathan. Sophie's Night Sky Adventure. 2015. (ENG.). 32p. (J). 12.95 *(978-1-59193-419-6(2))* Adventure Pubns.

Priddy, Roger. Night Night Farm. 2017. (ENG., Illus.). 20p. (J). bds. 9.99 *(978-0-312-52163-9(4),* 9780312521639, Priddy Bks.) St. Martin's Pr.

Reilly, Carmel & Ashforth, Kate. A Night Out. 2008. (Rigby Focus Forward: Level E Ser.). (Illus.). 24p. (J). (gr. 4-7). pap. *(978-1-4190-3678-1(5),* Rigby) Pearson Education Australia.

Rey, H. A. A Winter's Nap. 2010. (Curious George Ser.). (ENG., Illus.). 24p. (J). (gr. -1-3). pap. 3.99

MNO

(978-0-547-23590-5(9)) Houghton Mifflin Harcourt Publishing Co.

Ricci, Christine. Buenas Noches, Dora! Cuento Para Levantar la Tapita. Hall, Susan, illus. 2004. (Dora the Explorer Ser.).Tr. of Good Night, Dora! (SPA.). 16p. (J). pap. 5.99 *(978-0-689-86648-7(8),* Libros Para Ninos) Libros Para Ninos.

Rimland, Mark, illus. The Secret Night World of Cats. 2008. 32p. (YA). 15.00 *(978-0-9740360-6-9(4))* Autism Research Institute.

Rodgers, Frank. Ruidos en la Noche. (SPA.). 64p. (J). (gr. 3). 7.95 *(978-84-88061-85-0(4))* Serres, Ediciones, S. L. ESP. Dist: Lectorum Pubns., Inc.

Roscoe, Lily. The Night Parade. Walker, David, illus. 2014. (ENG.). 32p. (J). (— 1). 16.99 *(978-0-545-39623-3(9),* Orchard Bks.) Scholastic, Inc.

Rosenthal, Amy Krouse. Little Hoot. Corace, Jen, illus. 2016. (ENG.). 28p. (J). (gr. -1-k). bds. 7.99 *(978-1-4521-5207-3(1))* Chronicle Bks. LLC.

Ross, Melanie H. & Willis, Jeanne. Mayfly Day. Ross, Tony, illus. 2012. (ENG.). 32p. (J). (gr. -1-k). pap. 10.99 *(978-1-84270-606-0(3))* Andersen Pr. GBR. Dist: Independent Pubs. Group.

Runton, Andy. Owly & Wormy, Bright Lights & Starry Nights. Runton, Andy, illus. 2012. (ENG., Illus.). 40p. (J). (gr. -1-3). 17.99 *(978-1-4169-5775-1(8),* Atheneum Bks. for Young Readers) Simon & Schuster Children's Publishing.

Ryder, Joanne. The Night Flight. Schwartz, Amy, illus. 2014. (ENG.). 32p. (J). (gr. k-2). 16.99 *(978-1-4814-2521-6(8),* Simon & Schuster Bks. For Young Readers) Simon & Schuster Bks. For Young Readers.

Rylant, Cynthia. Mr. Putter & Tabby See the Stars. Howard, Arthur, illus. 2008. (Mr. Putter & Tabby Ser.). (ENG.). 44p. (J). (gr. 1-4). pap. 5.99 *(978-0-15-206366-5(8))* Houghton Mifflin Harcourt Publishing Co.

—Night in the Country. Szilagyi, Mary, illus. 2014. 32p. pap. 7.00 *(978-1-61003-359-6(0))* Center for the Collaborative Classroom.

Sakai, Komako. Hannah's Night. 2014.Tr. of Hanna-chan ga Me wo Samashitara. (ENG., Illus.). 32p. (J). (gr. -1-2). 17.95 *(978-1-877579-54-7(8))* Gecko Pr. NZL. Dist: Lerner Publishing Group.

Sanroman, Susana. Senora Reganona: A Mexican Bedtime Story. Domi, illus. 2006. 20p. (J). (gr. k-4). reprint ed. 15.00 *(978-1-4223-5466-7(0))* DIANE Publishing Co.

Scillian, Devin. Cosmo's Moon. Braught, Mark, illus. 2003. (ENG.). 40p. (J). (gr. 1-4). 15.95 *(978-1-58536-123-6(2),* 201966) Sleeping Bear Pr.

Sendak, Maurice. La Cocina de Noche. Sendak, Maurice, illus. 2003. (Picture Books Collection). (SPA., Illus.). 40p. (J). (gr. k-3). 10.95 *(978-84-204-4570-0(3))* Ediciones Alfaguara ESP. Dist: Santillana USA Publishing Co., Inc.

Sergeant, Kate. It's a Very Good Night. 2005. (J). *(978-0-9770158-5-6(8))* BeachWalk Bks. Inc.

Shulevitz, Uri. Dusk. Shulevitz, Uri, illus. 2013. (ENG., Illus.). 32p. (J). (gr. -1-3). 17.99 *(978-0-374-31903-6(0),* 9780374319038, Farrar, Straus & Giroux (BYR)) Farrar, Straus & Giroux.

Simon, Mary Manz. God Made the Moon. Walkley, Lizzie, illus. 2016. (J). *(978-0-8249-1981-8(5),* Ideal Pubns.) Worthy Publishing.

Sparks, Fredda. One October Night. 2012. 20p. pap. 17.99 *(978-1-4772-5656-5(3))* AuthorHouse.

Spider Night! (Early Intervention Levels Ser.). 28.38 *(978-0-7362-0411-8(3))* CENGAGE Learning.

Srinivasan, Divya. Little Owl's 1-2-3. Srinivasan, Divya, illus. 2015. (ENG., Illus.). 18p. (J). (— 1). 5.99 *(978-0-451-47454-4(6),* Viking Books for Young Readers) Penguin Young Readers Group.

—Little Owl's Night. (ENG., 32p. (J). 2013. Illus.). (— 1). bds. 6.99 *(978-0-670-01579-5(2))* 2011. (gr. -1-k). 16.99 *(978-0-670-01295-4(5))* Penguin Young Readers Group. (Viking Books for Young Readers).

Swanson, Susan Marie. The House in the Night. Krommes, Beth, illus. (ENG.). (J). 2011. 36p. (gr. k — 1). bds. 7.99 *(978-0-547-57769-2(9))* 2008. 40p. (gr. -1-3). 17.99 *(978-0-618-86244-3(7))* Houghton Mifflin Harcourt Publishing Co.

Thompson, Lauren. Little Quack's Bedtime. Anderson, Derek, illus. 2005. (ENG.). 32p. (J). (gr. -1-3). 17.99 *(978-0-689-86894-8(4),* Simon & Schuster Bks. For Young Readers) Simon & Schuster Bks. For Young Readers.

—Polar Bear Night. Savage, Stephen, illus. (ENG.). 32p. (J). (gr. -1 — 1). 2013. bds. 8.99 *(978-0-545-48558-6(4),* Cartwheel Bks.) 2004. 17.99 *(978-0-439-49524-0(5),* Scholastic Pr.) Scholastic, Inc.

Thomson, Sarah L. Imagine a Night. Gonsalves, Rob, illus. 2003. (Imagine A... Ser.). (ENG.). 40p. (J). (gr. -1-3). 19.99 *(978-0-689-85218-3(5),* Atheneum Bks. for Young Readers) Simon & Schuster Children's Publishing.

Tibo, Gilles. Le Voyage du Funambule. 2004. (Mon Roman Ser.). (FRE., Illus.). 64p. (J). (gr. 2). pap. *(978-2-89021-701-0(9))* Diffusion du livre Mirabel (DLM).

Tremblay, Carole. Floop in the Dark. Beshwaty, Steve, illus. 2009. (Floop Ser.). 24p. (J). (gr. -1-k). 22.60 *(978-1-60754-341-1(9));* pap. 8.15 *(978-1-60754-342-8(7))* Windmill Bks.

Wargin, Kathy-jo. Frank & Beans. 1 vol. Lewis, Anthony, illus. 2010. (I Can Read! / Frank & Beans Ser.). (ENG.). 32p. (J). pap. 3.99 *(978-0-310-71847-5(3))* Zondervan.

Waring, Geoff. Oscar & the Moth: A Book about Light & Dark. Waring, Geoff, illus. 2008. (Start with Science Ser.). (ENG., Illus.). 32p. (J). (gr. -1-3). pap. 6.99 *(978-0-7636-4031-6(X))* Candlewick Pr.

Warner, Gertrude Chandler, creator. The Midnight Mystery. 2003. (Boxcar Children Mysteries Ser.: 95). (ENG., Illus.). 128p. (J). (gr. 1-5). pap. 5.99 *(978-0-8075-5538-5(X))* Whitman, Albert & Co.

Watson, Clyde. Midnight Moon. Natti, Susanna, illus. 2006. (ENG.). 24p. (J). (gr. -1-k). *(978-1-59692-162-7(5))* MacAdam/Cage Publishing, Inc.

Weston, Carrie. If a Chicken Stayed for Supper. Fatus, Sophie, illus. 2007. (ENG.). 32p. (J). (gr. -1-3). 16.95 *(978-0-8234-2067-4(1))* Holiday Hse., Inc.

Wilson, Sarah & Thompson Bros. Estrellita. Thompson Brothers Studio Staff, illus. 2003. (Dora la Exploradora Ser.).Tr. of Little Star. (SPA.). 24p. (J). pap. 3.99 *(978-0-689-86307-3(1),* Libros Para Ninos) Libros Para Ninos.

Wilson, Karma. Mama, Why? Mendez, Simon, illus. 2011. (ENG.). 40p. (J). (gr. -1-2). 16.99 *(978-1-4169-4205-4(X),* McElderry, Margaret K. Bks.) McElderry, Margaret K. Bks.

Wormell, Chris. Molly & the Night Monster. Wormell, Chris, illus. 2011. (ENG., Illus.). 32p. (J). (gr. -1-k). pap. 9.99 *(978-1-86230-185-6(9),* Red Fox) Random House Children's Books GBR. Dist: Independent Pubs. Group.

Yee, Wong Herbert. Summer Days & Nights. Yee, Wong Herbert, illus. 2012. (ENG., Illus.). 32p. (J). (gr. -1-1). 16.99 *(978-0-8050-9078-9(9),* 9780805090789, Holt, Henry & Co. Bks. For Young Readers) Holt, Henry & Co.

Zschock, Heather. Whoo's There? A Bedtime Shadow Book. Zschock, Martha Day, illus. 2005. (Activity Book Ser.). 16p. (J). (gr. -1-4). 12.99 *(978-1-59359-904-1(8))* Peter Pauper Pr. Inc.

NIGHT—POETRY

Andrew, Moira, et al, selected by. Night Poems & Ghost Poems. 2008. (Illus.). 32p. (J). pap. 10.95 *(978-1-59646-623-4(5))* Dingles & Co.

Andrew, Moira, et al. Night Poems & Ghost Poems. 2008. (Illus.). 32p. (J). lib. bdg. 23.65 *(978-1-59646-622-7(7))* Dingles & Co.

Dromgoole, Glenn. Good Night Cowboy. Clack, Barbra, illus. 2006. (ENG.). 24p. (J). (gr. -1-k). 15.95 *(978-1-931721-51-6(3),* 1a919f96-6211-41bc-a0b4-ea4ca94e5e4d) Bright Sky Pr.

Karas, G. Brian, illus. Switching on the Moon: A Very First Book of Bedtime Poems. 2010. (ENG.). 96p. (J). (gr. k-12). 21.99 *(978-0-7636-4249-5(5))* Candlewick Pr.

Sidman, Joyce. Dark Emperor & Other Poems of the Night. Allen, Rick, illus. 2010. (ENG.). 32p. (J). (gr. 1-4). 16.99 *(978-0-547-15228-8(0))* Houghton Mifflin Harcourt Publishing Co.

NIGHTINGALE, FLORENCE, 1820-1910

Alexander, Carol. Florence Nightingale. (Rookie Biographies(tm) Ser.). (ENG., Illus.). 32p. (J). 2015. lib. bdg. 25.00 *(978-0-531-21412-1(5))* 2005. (gr. 1-2). pap. 4.95 *(978-0-516-25828-7(1))* Scholastic Library Publishing. (Children's Pr.).

Alexander, Carol & Vargus, Nanci Reginelli. Florence Nightingale. 2004. (Rookie Biography Ser.). (J). 20.50 *(978-0-516-24406-8(X))* Scholastic Library Publishing.

Aller, Susan Bivin. Florence Nightingale. 2008. pap. 52.95 *(978-0-8225-9389-8(0))* Lerner Publishing Group.

—Florence Nightingale. Butler, Tad, illus. 2007. (History Maker Biographies Ser.). (ENG.). 48p. (gr. 3-6). lib. bdg. 27.93 *(978-0-8225-7609-9(0),* Lerner Pubns.) Lerner Publishing Group.

Connors, Kathleen. The Life of Florence Nightingale, Vol. 1. 2014. (Famous Lives Ser.). (ENG.). 24p. (J). (gr. 1-2). 22.60 *(978-1-4824-0405-0(2))* Stevens, Gareth Publishing LLLP.

Cooke, Tim. Florence Nightingale. 2016. (Meet the Greats Ser.). 00048p. (J). pap. 14.05 ***(978-1-4824-5948-7(5))*** Stevens, Gareth Publishing LLLP.

Davis, Marc. Florence Nightingale: Founder of the Nightingale School of Nursing. 2003. (Our People Ser.). (ENG., Illus.). 32p. (J). (gr. 3-6). 29.93 *(978-1-59296-003-3(0),* 200636) Child's World, Inc., The.

Demi. Florence Nightingale. Demi, illus. 2014. (ENG., Illus.). 40p. (J). (gr. -1-3). 17.99 *(978-0-8050-9729-0(5),* 9780805097290, Holt, Henry & Co. Bks. For Young Readers) Holt, Henry & Co.

Edison, Erin. Florence Nightingale, 1 vol. 2014. (Great Women in History Ser.). (ENG.). 24p. (gr. k-1). lib. bdg. 21.99 *(978-1-4765-4214-0(7),* Pebble Bks.) Capstone Press of Coughlan Cos.

Garnett, Emmeline. Florence Nightingale's Nuns. 2009. (Saints for Youth: Ser.). 150p. pap. 9.95 *(978-1-58617-297-8(2))* Ignatius Pr.

Gorrell, Gena K. Heart & Soul: The Story of Florence Nightingale. 2005. (ENG., Illus.). 152p. (J). (gr. 5). pap. 11.95 *(978-0-88776-703-6(6),* Tundra Bks.) Tundra Bks. CAN. Dist: Penguin Random Hse. LLC.

Hinman, Bonnie. Florence Nightingale & the Advancement of Nursing. 2004. (Uncharted, Unexplored, & Unexplained Ser.). (Illus.). 48p. (J). (gr. 4-8). lib. bdg. 29.95 *(978-1-58415-257-6(5))* Mitchell Lane Pubs., Inc.

Howell, Izzi & Wayland Publishers Staff. Florence Nightingale. 2016. (Fact Cat: History Ser.). (ENG., Illus.). 24p. (J). (gr. k-2). 14.99 *(978-1-5263-0168-0(7),* Wayland) Hachette Children's Group GBR. Dist: Hachette Bk. Group.

Reef, Catherine. Florence Nightingale: The Courageous Life of the Legendary Nurse. 2016. (ENG., Illus.). 192p. (YA). (gr. 7). 18.99 *(978-0-544-53580-0(4))* Houghton Mifflin Harcourt Publishing Co.

Richter, Sandy. The Life of Florence Nightingale. 2009. (Real Life Readers Ser.). 16p. (gr. 2-3). pap. 7.05 *(978-1-4358-0225-4(X),* Rosen Classroom) Rosen Publishing Group, Inc., The.

Robbins, Trina. Florence Nightingale: Lady with the Lamp, 1 vol. Timmons, Anne, illus. 2007. (Graphic Biographies Ser.). (ENG.). 32p. (gr. 3-4). per. 8.10 *(978-0-7368-7902-6(1),* 1264942, Graphic Library) Capstone Press of Coughlan Cos.

Robbins, Trina & Capstone Press Staff. Florence Nightingale: Lady with the Lamp, 1 vol. Timmons, Anne, illus. 2007. (Graphic Biographies Ser.). (ENG.). 32p. (gr. 3-4). 30.65 *(978-0-7368-6850-1(X),* Graphic Library) Capstone Press of Coughlan Cos.

Ross, Stewart. Don't Say No to Flo: The Story of Florence Nightingale. Shields, Susan, illus. 32p. (J). pap. *(978-0-7502-3273-9(0),* Wayland) Hachette Children's Group.

Tieck, Sarah. Florence Nightingale, 1 vol. 2006. (First Biographies Ser.). (ENG., Illus.). 32p. (gr. -1-3). 27.07 *(978-1-59679-786-4(X),* Buddy Bks.) ABDO Publishing Co.

Webb, Robert N. The How & Why Wonder Book of Florence Nightingale. Vosburgh, Leonard, illus. 2011. 50p. 35.95 *(978-1-258-09107-1(0))* Literary Licensing, LLC.

Wood, Jill G. Florence Nightingale: Called to Serve with Buffalo Biff & Farley's Raiders. Cox, Brian T., illus. 2006. (Time Traveler's Adventure Ser.). 56p. (J). 13.50 incl. audio compact disk *(978-1-932332-29-2(4))* Toy Box Productions.

Zemlicka, Shannon. Florence Nightingale. Debon, Nicolas, illus. (On My Own Biographies Ser.). 48p. (gr. 2-5). 2005. 23.93 *(978-0-87614-917-1(4))* 2003. (ENG.). pap. 6.95 *(978-0-87614-102-1(5),* Carolrhoda Bks.) Lerner Publishing Group.

NIGHTINGALE, FLORENCE, 1820-1910—FICTION

Dunlap, Susanne. In the Shadow of the Lamp. 2012. (ENG., Illus.). 320p. (YA). (gr. 7). pap. 9.99 *(978-1-59990-753-6(4),* 9781599907536, Bloomsbury USA Childrens) Bloomsbury Publishing USA.

Osborne, Mary Pope. High Time for Heroes. Murdocca, Sal, illus. (ENG.). (J). (gr. 2-5). 2016. (Magic Tree House Merlin Mission Ser.: 23). 144p. 5.99 *(978-0-307-98052-6(9))* 2014. (Magic Tree House Merlin Missions Ser.: No. 23). 128p. 12.99 *(978-0-307-98049-6(9))* 2014. (Magic Tree House Merlin Mission Ser.: No. 23). 128p. lib. bdg. 15.99 *(978-0-307-98050-2(2))* Random Hse. Children's Bks. (Random Hse. Bks. for Young Readers).

—High Time for Heroes. 2016. (Magic Tree House Merlin Missions Ser.: 23). lib. bdg. 16.00 *(978-0-606-38464-3(2))* Turtleback Bks.

Springer, Nancy. The Case of the Cryptic Crinoline. 2011. (Enola Holmes Mystery Ser.: 5). (ENG.). 176p. (J). (gr. 5-7). 6.99 *(978-0-14-241690-7(8),* Puffin Books) Penguin Young Readers Group.

NIGHTMARES

Apel, Melanie Ann. Let's Talk about Nightmares. 2009. (Let's Talk Library). 24p. (gr. 2-3). 42.50 *(978-1-60853-446-3(4),* PowerKids Pr.) Rosen Publishing Group, Inc., The.

NIGHTMARES—FICTION

Adams, Mark Wayne. Good NightMare. 2007. (ENG.). 32p. (J). (gr. -1-1). lib. bdg. 12.99 *(978-1-59616-001-9(2),* SYP Kids) Southern Yellow Pine (SYP) Publishing LLC.

Alloway, Kit. Dreamfever: A Novel. 2016. (Dream Walker Trilogy Ser.: 2). (ENG.). 320p. (J). 19.99 *(978-1-250-07811-7(3),* 9781250078117, St. Martin's Griffin) St. Martin's Pr.

—Dreamfire. 2015. (Dream Walker Trilogy Ser.: 1). (ENG.). 368p. (YA). (gr. 8-12). 18.99 *(978-1-250-06366-3(3),* 9781250063663, St. Martin's Griffin) St. Martin's Pr.

Andersen, Hans Christian. The Emperor & the Nightingale, 1 vol. Van Nutt, Robert, illus. 2007. (Rabbit Ears: A Classic Tale Ser.).Tr. of Nattergalen. (ENG.). 40p. (gr. -1-3). 25.65 *(978-1-59961-307-9(7))* Spotlight.

Arnold, Tedd. Fly Guy & the Frankenfly. 2013. (Fly Guy Ser.: 13). (ENG., Illus.). 32p. (J). (gr. -1-3). 6.99 *(978-0-545-49328-4(5),* Cartwheel Bks.) Scholastic, Inc.

—Fly Guy & the Frankenfly. 2013. (Fly Guy Ser.: 13). lib. bdg. 17.20 *(978-0-606-32440-3(2),* Turtleback) Turtleback Bks.

Baker, Monica S. Freestyle, 1 vol. 2010. (ENG., Illus.). 160p. (J). 14.99 *(978-0-7643-3538-9(3),* 9780764335389) Schiffer Publishing, Ltd.

Balzola, Asun. Munia y el Cocolilo Naranja. (SPA.). 32p. (J). *(978-84-233-1335-8(2))* Ediciones Destino ESP. Dist: Lectorum Pubns., Inc.

Barker, Kathryn. In the Skin of a Monster. 2016. (ENG.). 304p. (YA). (gr. 10). pap. 12.99 *(978-1-76011-171-7(6))* Allen & Unwin AUS. Dist: Independent Pubs. Group.

Begler, Peter. The Fearless Travelers' Guide to Wicked Places. 2017. (ENG., Illus.). 384p. (gr. 4-8). 14.95 *(978-1-62370-799-6(4))* Capstone Young Readers of Coughlan Cos.

Berenstain, Stan & Berenstain, Jan. The Berenstain Bears & the Bad Dream. 2004. (Berenstain Bears First Time Bks.). (J). (gr. -1-2). spiral bd. *(978-0-616-01555-1(0));* spiral bd. *(978-0-616-01556-8(9))* Canadian National Institute for the Blind/Institut National Canadien pour les Aveugles.

Bour, Daniele. Petit ours brun fait un Cauche. pap. 12.95 *(978-2-227-70921-8(9))* Bayard Editions FRA. Dist: Distribooks, Inc.

Busby, Cylin. Blink Once. 2012. (ENG.). 304p. (YA). (gr. 7-12). 17.99 *(978-1-59990-818-2(2),* 9781599908182, Bloomsbury USA Childrens) Bloomsbury Publishing USA.

Butler, Darren J. The Secret of Crybaby Hollow. 2004. (YA). mass mkt. 6.99 *(978-0-9753367-5-5(4))* Onstage Publishing, LLC.

Cach, Lisa. Wake unto Me. 2011. (ENG.). 320p. (YA). (gr. 7-18). 8.99 *(978-0-14-241436-1(0),* Speak) Penguin Young Readers Group.

Carnevale, Michael. The Hotel Coolidge. 2007. 91p. pap. 10.95 *(978-0-7414-3752-5(X))* Infinity Publishing.

Carter, Rebecca. Moonlit Daydreams. 2010. 71p. pap. 11.99 *(978-0-557-35588-4(5))* Lulu Pr., Inc.

Chalmers, Jason. Fall Nightmares 101: A Parody. 2011. 72p. pap. 19.95 *(978-1-4626-2883-4(4))* America Star Bks.

Christenson, Debra. Hairy Harry, 1 vol. 2010. 38p. pap. 24.95 *(978-1-4489-2549-0(5))* PublishAmerica, Inc.

Cordero, Silvia Jaeger & Cordero, Silvia Jaegar. El Huevo Azul. Sunset Producciones & Producciones, Sunset, illus. rev. ed. 2005. (Castillo de la Lectura Verde Ser.). (SPA & ENG.). 136p. (J). (gr. -1-7). pap. 7.95 *(978-970-20-0127-0(7))* Castillo, Ediciones, S. A. de C. V. MEX. Dist: Macmillan.

Corentin, Philippe. Papa! (SPA.). 32p. *(978-84-95150-38-7(7))* Corimbo, Editorial S.L.

—Papa. 2003. (SPA.). (J). (gr. -1-k). 19.99 *(978-84-8470-094-4(1))* Corimbo, Editorial S.L. ESP. Dist: Lectorum Pubns., Inc.

Darke, J. A. The Grin in the Dark. Evergreen, Nelson, illus. 2015. (Spine Shivers Ser.). (ENG.). 128p. (gr. 3-4). lib. bdg. 26.65 *(978-1-4965-0217-9(5))* Stone Arch Bks.

Drouin, Véronique. L'Île D'Aurélie. 2004. (Mon Roman Ser.). (FRE.). 304p. (J). (gr. 2). pap. *(978-2-89021-690-7(X))* Diffusion du livre Mirabel (DLM).

Grunberg, Greg. Nightmare Escape. Tumbloom, Lucas, illus. 2016. (Dream Jumper Ser.: 1). (ENG.). 208p. (J). (gr. 3-7). 24.99 *(978-0-545-82603-7(9),* Graphix) Scholastic, Inc.

Gutierrez, Debbi Miller. Cactus Factory. 2007. (J). pap. 5.99 *(978-0-9740173-4-1(5))* Prints By Mail.

Hill, Andrew G. The Song of the Seraphim. 2009. 196p. pap. 13.95 *(978-1-60860-194-3(3),* Strategic Bk. Publishing) Strategic Book Publishing & Rights Agency (SBPRA).

Hinchcliffe, L. T. For the Love of Prudence Possum. 2008. 76p. pap. 15.50 *(978-1-60693-136-3(9),* Eloquent Bks.) Strategic Book Publishing & Rights Agency (SBPRA).

The Iris House. 2006. (YA). per. 12.95 *(978-0-9677047-7-7(4))* Marble Hse. Editions.

Johnson, Linda & Hodges, Quae. 21st Century Parables: A Child's Book. 2006. 48p. pap. 14.95 *(978-1-60145-071-5(0))* Booklocker.com, Inc.

Joseph, Curtis. Fairy Tales of the Forbidden & Untold. 2011. 24p. pap. 24.95 *(978-1-4626-3485-9(0))* America Star Bks.

Joy, Judith Bourassa. A Doorway Through Space: Winner of Mayhaven Award for Children's Fiction. 2008. (ENG.). 224p. (YA). 14.95 *(978-1-932278-17-0(6))* Mayhaven Publishing, Inc.

Joyce, William. E. Aster Bunnymund & the Warrior Eggs at the Earth's Core!, Bk. 2. Joyce, William, illus. 2012. (Guardians Ser.: 2). (ENG., Illus.). 272p. (J). (gr. 2-6). 15.99 *(978-1-4424-3050-1(8),* Atheneum Bks. for Young Readers) Simon & Schuster Children's Publishing.

Kitami, Yoko. Cactus. 2005. (Los Especiales de A la Orilla del Viento Ser.).Tr. of Cactus. (SPA., Illus.). 36p. (J). (gr. 2-4). *(978-968-16-7386-4(7),* FC15223) Fondo de Cultura Economica.

Klavan, Andrew. Nightmare City, 1 vol. 2013. (ENG.). 320p. (YA). 14.99 *(978-1-59554-797-2(5))* Nelson, Thomas Inc.

Lawrence, Dionne L. The Story of Her?! 2012. 28p. (-18). pap. 16.95 *(978-1-62709-253-1(6))* America Star Bks.

Lois, Lowry. Gossamer. 2006. (ENG.). 144p. (J). (gr. 5-7). 17.99 *(978-0-618-68550-9(2))* Houghton Mifflin Harcourt Publishing Co.

—Gossamer. 2008. (ENG.). 176p. (J). (gr. 3-7). 6.99 *(978-0-385-73416-5(6),* Yearling) Random Hse. Children's Bks.

MacKenzie, Ross. Zac & the Dream Stealers. (J). 2013. 297p. *(978-0-545-40107-4(0))* 2012. (ENG.). 304p. (gr. 3-7). 16.99 *(978-0-545-40106-7(2))* Scholastic, Inc. (Chicken Hse., The).

Mayer, Jeffrey J. Il y a Cauchemar dans Mon Placard.Tr. of There's a Nightmare in My Cupboard. (FRE.). (J). pap. 10.95 *(978-2-07-050611-8(8))* Gallimard, Editions FRA. Dist: Distribooks, Inc.

McMann, Lisa. Don't Close Your Eyes: Wake; Fade; Gone. 2013. (ENG., Illus.). 720p. (YA). (gr. 9). pap. 12.99 *(978-1-4424-9913-3(3),* Simon Pulse) Simon Pulse.

Moffett, Rodney. The Eighth Crest. 2006. (ENG.). 228p. per. 24.95 *(978-1-4241-3907-1(4))* PublishAmerica, Inc.

Nero, Molly. Smarty Pig & the Test Taking Terror. Turchan, Monique, illus. 2012. 28p. pap. 12.95 *(978-1-61244-055-2(X))* Halo Publishing International.

Night, P. J. Together Forever. 2012. (Creepover Ser.: 8). lib. bdg. 16.00 *(978-0-606-26339-9(X),* Turtleback) Turtleback Bks.

—Your Worst Nightmare. 2013. (You're Invited to a Creepover Ser.: 17). (ENG., Illus.). 160p. (J). (gr. 3-7). pap. 6.99 *(978-1-4424-8235-7(4),* Simon Spotlight) Simon Spotlight.

Nixon, Joan Lowery. Nightmare. 2005. 166p. (gr. 5-7). 17.00 *(978-0-7569-5239-6(5))* Perfection Learning Corp.

Perez, Marlene. Dead Is Just a Dream. (Dead Is Ser.: 8). (ENG.). 176p. (YA). (gr. 7). 2014. pap. 7.99 *(978-0-544-33634-6(8),* HMH Books For Young Readers) 2013. 16.99 *(978-0-544-10262-0(2))* Houghton Mifflin Harcourt Publishing Co.

—Dead Is Just a Dream. 2014. (Dead Is Ser.: 8). lib. bdg. 18.40 *(978-0-606-35990-0(7))* Turtleback Bks.

Peters, Robert. Da Goodie Monsta: Chase Dem Nightmares Away. Peters, Robert, illus. 2009. (Illus.). 28p. (YA). lib. bdg. *(978-0-9823906-7-2(X))* Wiggles Pr.

Piggy Toes Press Staff. All the Way's I Love You Mini. Downing, Julie, illus. 2005. (ENG.). 10p. (J). 4.95 *(978-1-58117-437-3(3),* Intervisual/Piggy Toes) Bendon, Inc.

Plum, Amy. Dreamfall. 2017. (Dreamfall Ser.: 1). 288p. (YA). (gr. 9). 17.99 *(978-0-06-242987-2(6),* HarperTeen) HarperCollins Pubs.

Randall, Thomas. The Waking: Dreams of the Dead. 2nd ed. 2010. (ENG., Illus.). 304p. (YA). (gr. 7-18). pap. 8.99 *(978-1-59990-585-3(X),* 9781599905853, Bloomsbury USA Childrens) Bloomsbury Publishing USA.

Rey, H. A. Sweet Dreams, Curious George. 2013. (Curious George Ser.). (ENG., Illus.). 24p. (J). (gr. -1-3). 9.99 *(978-0-544-03880-6(0))* Houghton Mifflin Harcourt Publishing Co.

Richardson, Tracy. The Field. unabr. ed. 2013. (ENG.). 200p. (YA). (gr. 7-12). pap. 11.95 *(978-1-935462-82-8(2))* Luminis Bks., Inc.

Rippin, Sally. The Night Fright. Fukuoka, Aki, illus. 2015. 43p. (J). *(978-1-61067-451-5(0))* Kane Miller.

—The Night Fright: Billie B Brown. Fukuoka, Aki, illus. 2016. (ENG.). 48p. (J). pap. 4.99 *(978-1-61067-391-4(3))* Kane Miller.

Roe, D. J. The Impossible Dream. 2008. 59p. pap. 16.95 *(978-1-60610-173-5(0))* America Star Bks.

Roman, Stacey. Some of Us Want Wrinkles. Wurster, Laurie, illus. 2005. (J). per. 16.95 *(978-1-59858-033-4(7))* Dog Ear Publishing, LLC.

Schraff, Anne. The Very Bad Dream, 1 vol. unabr. ed. 2010. (Q Reads Ser.). (ENG.). 32p. (YA). (gr. 9-12). pap. 6.95 *(978-1-61651-187-6(7))* Saddleback Educational Publishing, Inc.

Schroeder, Lisa. Chasing Brooklyn. (ENG.). 432p. (YA). (gr. 9). 2011. pap. 11.99 *(978-1-4169-9174-8(3))* 2010. 15.99 *(978-1-4169-9168-7(9))* Simon Pulse. (Simon Pulse).

Schwartz, Alvin. Scary Stories 3: More Tales to Chill Your Bones. Helquist, Brett, illus. 2011. (Scary Stories Ser.). (ENG.). 128p. (J). (gr. 4-18). 16.99 *(978-0-06-083523-1(0));* pap. 5.99 *(978-0-06-083524-8(9))* HarperCollins Pubs.

Segel, Jason & Miller, Kirsten. The Lost Lullaby. Kwasny, Karl, illus. 2016. (Nightmares! Ser.: 3). (ENG.). 336p. (J). (gr. 3-7). lib. bdg. 19.99 *(978-0-375-99159-2(X),* Delacorte Bks. for Young Readers) Random Hse. Children's Bks.

—Nightmares! Kwasny, Karl, illus. (Nightmares! Ser.). (ENG.). (J). (gr. 3-7). 2015. 400p. 7.99 *(978-0-385-74426-3(9),* Yearling) 2014. 368p. 16.99 *(978-0-385-74425-6(0),* Delacorte Bks. for Young Readers) 2014. 368p. lib. bdg. 19.99 *(978-0-375-99157-8(3),* Delacorte Bks. for Young Readers) Random Hse. Children's Bks.

—The Sleepwalker Tonic. Kwasny, Karl, illus. 2016. (Nightmares! Ser.: 2). (ENG.). 384p. (J). (gr. 3-7). 18.40 *(978-0-606-39350-8(1))* Turtleback Bks.

Sewell, Byron W. Alix's Adventures in Wonderland: Lewis Carroll's Nightmare. 2011. (Illus.). 130p. pap. *(978-1-904808-72-5(7))* Evertype.

Spring, Manda. Emerald & the Withered Willow. 2007. 148p. pap. 18.00 *(978-1-4303-1353-3(6))* Lulu Pr., Inc.

Stine, R. L. Don't Stay up Late: A Fear Street Novel. 2015. (Fear Street Ser.). (ENG.). 304p. (YA). (gr. 7-12). 17.99 *(978-1-250-05162-2(2)*, 9781250051622, St. Martin's Griffin) St. Martin's Pr.

—Fear Street Super Thriller: Party Games & Don't Stay up Late. 2015. (Fear Street Ser.). (ENG.). 592p. (YA). (gr. 7-12). pap. 11.99 *(978-1-250-07693-9(5)*, 9781250076939, St. Martin's Griffin) St. Martin's Pr.

—Welcome to Camp Nightmare. 2010. (Classic Goosebumps Ser.: 14). (ENG.). 160p. (J). (gr. 3-7). 6.99 *(978-0-545-15889-3(3)*, Scholastic Paperbacks) Scholastic, Inc.

Stolarz, Laurie Faria. Red Is for Remembrance. l.t. ed. 2008. (Blue Is for Nightmares Ser.: Bk. 4). 385p. (YA). (gr. 7). 22.95 *(978-1-4104-0339-1(4))* Thorndike Pr.

Taft, Christopher C. The Witch of Green Spring. 2013. 120p. pap. 11.00 *(978-1-61204-198-8(1)*, Strategic Bk. Publishing) Strategic Book Publishing & Rights Agency (SBPRA).

Teare, Nellie. Celia & the Witches. Senkel, Nicholas, illus. 2008. 24p. (J). 13.95 *(978-0-9820852-0-2(6))* Harmon Creek Pr.

Tibo, Gilles. Le Gardien du Sommeil. Jorisch, Stéphane, illus. 2004. (Mon Roman Ser.). (FRE.). 64p. (J). (gr. 2). pap. *(978-2-89021-691-4(8))* Diffusion du livre Mirabel (DLM).

Timroth, Stephen. Dreamhawk. 2009. 24p. pap. 12.00 *(978-1-60860-501-9(9)*, Strategic Bk. Publishing) Strategic Book Publishing & Rights Agency (SBPRA).

Van Zant, Dawn. No More Night Mares: A Dream of Freedom. McElroy, Kim, illus. 2005. (J). pap. 9.99 *(978-0-9761768-1-7(5))* Wild Heart Ranch, Inc.

Vernon, Ursula. Nightmare of the Iguana. 2013. (Dragonbreath Ser.: 8). (ENG., Illus.). 208p. (J). (gr. 3-7). 12.99 *(978-0-8037-3846-1(3)*, Dial Bks) Penguin Publishing Group.

Villoro, Carmen & Perez, Federico. Amarina y el Viejo Pesadilla y Otros Cuentos. (Torre de Papel Ser.). (SPA.). (J). (gr. 2). 7.95 *(978-958-04-3650-8(9))* Norma S.A. COL. Dist: Distribuidora Norma, Inc.

Walsh, Ann. The Doctor's Apprentice. 2005. 160p. (YA). (gr. 3-8). pap., tchr. ed. 8.95 *(978-0-88878-389-9(2))* Beach Holme Pubs., Ltd. CAN. Dist: Literary Pr. Group of Canada.

—The Doctor's Apprentice: A Barkerville Mystery. 2007. (Barkerville Mystery Ser.: 2). (ENG.). 160p. (J). pap. 9.99 *(978-1-55002-633-7(X)*, Sandcastle Bks.) Dundurn CAN. Dist: Ingram Publisher Services.

Weston, Paula. Shadows. 2013. (Rephaim Ser.). (ENG.). 400p. (YA). (gr. 9). 17.99 *(978-1-77049-547-0(9)*, Tundra Bks.) Tundra Bks. CAN. Dist: Penguin Random Hse. LLC.

Williams, Harland, illus. The Kid with Too Many Nightmares. 2004. (J). *(978-0-8431-1582-6(3)*, Price Stern Sloan) Penguin Publishing Group.

Wynne-Jones, Tim. Stephen Fair. (J). pap. 6.95 *(978-0-88899-360-1(9))* Groundwood Bks. CAN. Dist: Publishers Group West (PGW).

NIKOLAEVA, VALENTINA VLADIMIROVNA TERESHKOVA, 1937-

Feldman, Heather. Valentina Tereshkova: The First Woman in Space. 2009. (Space Firsts Ser.). 24p. (gr. 3-4). 42.50 *(978-1-60853-114-1(7)*, PowerKids Pr.) Rosen Publishing Group, Inc., The.

NILE RIVER AND VALLEY

Aloian, Molly. The Nile: River in the Sand. 2010. (Rivers Around the World Ser.). (ENG., Illus.). 32p. (J). (gr. 5-8). pap. *(978-0-7787-7468-6(6))*; lib. bdg. *(978-0-7787-7445-7(7))* Crabtree Publishing Co.

Banting, Erinn. The Nile River. (Natural Wonders Ser.). (Illus.). 32p. (J). 2007. per. 8.95 *(978-1-59036-275-4(6))* 2005. (gr. 4-6). lib. bdg. 26.00 *(978-1-59036-269-3(1))* Weigl Pubs., Inc.

Gagne, Tammy. The Nile River. 2012. (Illus.). 47p. (J). lib. bdg. 29.95 *(978-1-61228-294-7(6))* Mitchell Lane Pubs., Inc.

Gregory, Stefan. Life along the Nile. 2009. (Real Life Readers Ser.). 16p. (gr. 2-4). pap. 7.05 *(978-1-4358-0226-1(8)*, Rosen Classroom) Rosen Publishing Group, Inc., The.

Heinrichs, Ann. The Nile River. 2008. (Nature's Wonders Ser.). 96p. (gr. 6-18). lib. bdg. 35.64 *(978-0-7614-2854-1(2)*, Benchmark Bks.) Marshall Cavendish Corp.

Lonely Planet Publications Staff. Secrets of the Nile, 1 vol. 2017. (Lonely Planet Kids Ser.). (ENG., Illus.). 16p. (J). pap. 17.99 ***(978-1-78657-538-8(8)***, 5376) Lonely Planet Pubns.

Manning, Paul. Nile River. 2014. (River Adventures Ser.). (J). lib. bdg. 31.35 *(978-1-59920-917-3(9))* Black Rabbit Bks.

The Nile. 2011. (River Journey Ser.). (ENG.). 48p. (YA). (gr. 5-8). 27.95 *(978-1-4488-6012-8(1)*, Rosen Reference) Rosen Publishing Group, Inc., The.

Parks, Peggy J. Aswan High Dam. (Building World Landmarks Ser.). (J). 2004. 26.19 *(978-1-4103-0204-5(0))* 2003. (Illus.). 48p. 24.95 *(978-1-56711-329-7(X))* Cengage Gale. (Blackbirch Pr., Inc.).

Publishers, Wayland & Newland, Sonya. Journey along the Nile. 2016. (Travelling Wild Ser.). (ENG., Illus.). 32p. (J). (gr. 4-6). 17.99 *(978-0-7502-9861-2(8)*, Wayland) Hachette Children's Group GBR. Dist: Hachette Bk. Group.

Simon, Charnan. The Secrets of the Nile. 2004. (Geography of the World Ser.). (ENG., Illus.). 32p. (J). (gr. 3-6). 28.50 *(978-1-59296-340-9(4)*, 200274) Child's World, Inc., The.

Throp, Claire. The Nile River, 1 vol. 2012. (Explorer Tales Ser.). (ENG.). 32p. (gr. 1-3). 29.99 *(978-1-4109-4784-0(X)*, Read Me!) Heinemann-Raintree.

Weintraub, Aileen. The Nile: The Longest River. 2009. (Great Record Breakers in Nature Ser.). 24p. (gr. 3-4). 42.50 *(978-1-61513-184-6(1)*, PowerKids Pr.) Rosen Publishing Group, Inc., The.

NINO CURRENT

see El Nino Current

NIXON, RICHARD M. (RICHARD MILHOUS), 1913-1994

Archer, Jules. Watergate: A Story of Richard Nixon & the Shocking 1972 Scandal. rev. ed. 2015. (Jules Archer History for Young Readers Ser.). (ENG., Illus.). 344p. (J). (gr. 6). 16.99 *(978-1-63220-606-0(4)*, Sky Pony Pr.) Skyhorse Publishing Co., Inc.

Aronson, Billy. Richard M. Nixon. 2007. (Presidents & Their Times Ser.). (Illus.). 96p. (J). (gr. 4-7). lib. bdg. 34.21 *(978-0-7614-2428-4(8)*, Benchmark Bks.) Marshall Cavendish Corp.

Barron, Rachel Stiffler. Richard Nixon: American Politician. rev. exp. ed. 2003. (Notable Americans Ser.). (Illus.). 128p. (J). (gr. 6-12). 23.95 *(978-1-931798-30-3(3))* Reynolds, Morgan Inc.

Britton, Tamara L. Richard Nixon, 1 vol. 2009. (United States Presidents Ser.). (ENG., Illus.). 40p. (YA). (gr. 3-6). 27.07 *(978-1-60453-468-9(0))* ABDO Publishing Co.

Donaldson, Madeline. Richard Nixon. 2009. pap. 52.95 *(978-0-7613-4956-3(1))* 2008. (ENG.). 48p. (gr. 3-6). 27.93 *(978-0-8225-8896-2(X)*, Lerner Pubns.) Lerner Publishing Group.

Dunn, Joeming & Dunn, Ben. Richard Nixon: 37th U. S. President, 1 vol. 2011. (Presidents of the United States Bio-Graphics Ser.). (ENG., Illus.). 32p. (YA). (gr. 3-6). 28.50 *(978-1-61641-647-8(5))* Magic Wagon.

Elish, Dan. The Watergate Scandal. 2004. (Cornerstones of Freedom Ser.). (ENG., Illus.). 48p. (J). 26.00 *(978-0-516-24239-2(3)*, Children's Pr.) Scholastic Library Publishing.

Fremon, David K. The Watergate Scandal in United States History. 2014. (In United States History Ser.). (Illus.). 96p. (J). (gr. 5-12). 27.94 *(978-0-7660-6107-1(8))*; pap. 10.95 *(978-0-7660-6108-8(6))* Enslow Pubs., Inc.

Gaines, Ann Graham. Richard M. Nixon. 2008. (Presidents of the U. S. A. Ser.). (ENG., Illus.). 48p. (J). (gr. 3-6). 32.79 *(978-1-60253-065-2(3)*, 200704) Child's World, Inc., The.

Hasselius, Michelle M. Richard M. Nixon, 1 vol. 2014. (Presidential Biographies Ser.). (ENG.). 24p. (gr. k-1). lib. bdg. 26.65 *(978-1-4765-9612-9(3)*, Pebble Plus) Capstone Press of Coughlan Cos.

Lewis K., Parker. How to Draw the Life & Times of Richard M. Nixon. 2007. (Kid's Guide to Drawing the Presidents of the United States of America Ser.). (Illus.). 32p. (YA). (gr. 2-5). 26.50 *(978-1-4042-3013-2(0))* Rosen Publishing Group, Inc., The.

Marquez, Heron. Richard M. Nixon. 2003. (Presidential Leaders Ser.). (Illus.). 112p. (J). 29.27 *(978-0-8225-0098-8(1)*, Lerner Pubns.) Lerner Publishing Group.

Parker, Lewis. How to Draw the Life & Times of Richard M. Nixon. 2009. (Kid's Guide to Drawing the Presidents of the United States of America Ser.). 32p. (gr. 4-4). 50.50 *(978-1-61511-157-2(3)*, PowerKids Pr.) Rosen Publishing Group, Inc., The.

Schultz, Randy. Richard M. Nixon: A MyReportLinks. Com Book. 2003. (Presidents Ser.). (Illus.). 48p. (J). (gr. 4-10). lib. bdg. 25.26 *(978-0-7660-5104-1(8)*, MyReportLinks.com Bks.) Enslow Pubs., Inc.

Schuman, Michael A. Richard M. Nixon. rev. ed. 2003. (United States Presidents Ser.). (Illus.). 128p. (J). (gr. 5-12). lib. bdg. 27.94 *(978-0-7660-2031-3(2))* Enslow Pubs., Inc.

Smith, Don. Political Power: Richard Nixon. 2012. (ENG.). 32p. pap. 3.99 *(978-0-9855911-3-7(7))* Bluewater Productions, Inc.

Tracy, Kathleen. The Watergate Scandal. 2006. (Monumental Milestones Ser.). (Illus.). 48p. (YA). (gr. 4-7). lib. bdg. 29.95 *(978-1-58415-470-9(5))* Mitchell Lane Pubs., Inc.

Uschan, Michael V. Watergate. 2009. (American History Ser.). (ENG., Illus.). 104p. 39.40 *(978-1-4205-0135-3(6)*, Lucent Bks.) Cengage Gale.

Van Meter, Larry A. United States V. Nixon: The Question of Executive Privilege. 2007. (Great Supreme Court Decisions Ser.). (Illus.). 112p. (YA). (gr. 5-9). lib. bdg. 32.95 *(978-0-7910-9381-8(6))* Facts On File, Inc.

Venezia, Mike. Richard M. Nixon: Thirty-Seventh President, 1969-1974. Venezia, Mike, illus. 2007. (Getting to Know the U. S. Presidents Ser.). (Illus.). 32p. (J). (gr. 3-4). (ENG.). pap. 7.95 *(978-0-531-17949-9(4))*; 28.00 *(978-0-516-22641-5(X))* Scholastic Library Publishing. (Children's Pr.).

Wheeler, Jill C. Patricia Nixon, 1 vol. 2010. (First Ladies Set 2 Ser.). (ENG., Illus.). 32p. (YA). (gr. 1-4). 27.07 *(978-1-60453-632-4(2))* ABDO Publishing Co.

Wittekind, Erika & Gerhardt, Michael J. The United States v. Nixon: The Watergate Scandal & Limits to Us Presidential Power, 1 vol. 2012. (Landmark Supreme Court Cases Ser.). (ENG., Illus.). 160p. (J). (gr. 6-12). 37.07 *(978-1-61783-478-3(5))* ABDO Publishing Co.

NOAH'S ARK

Adams, Michelle Medlock. The Story of Noah Activity Book. Reed, Lisa, illus. 2014. 18p. (J). 4.99 *(978-0-8249-5660-8(5)*, Ideal Pubns.) Worthy Publishing.

Amery, H. Noah's Ark. rev. ed. 2004. (Bible Tales Readers Ser.). (Illus.). 16p. (J). pap. 4.95 *(978-0-7945-0416-8(7))*; lib. bdg. 12.95 *(978-1-58086-542-5(9))* EDC Publishing.

The Answer Book for Kids: 25 Questions on Dinosaurs & the Flood of Noah. 2008. 60p. (J). pap. 7.99 *(978-0-89051-527-3(1))* Master Bks.

The Ark. (J). bds. 9.95 *(978-0-87162-415-4(X))* Warner Pr., Inc.

Barker, Stephen, illus. Noah's Ark. 2016. (ENG.). 12p. (J). (-k). bds. 9.99 *(978-1-62686-814-4(X)*, Silver Dolphin Bks.) Readerlink Distribution Services, LLC.

Barry, Bruce. The Roach Approach, Noah's Journey of Faith. 2003. (Illus.). (J). per. 16.99 *(978-0-9742997-0-9(7))* Wacky World Studios LLC.

Beaton, Clare. Make Your Own Noah's Ark. Beaton, Clare, illus. 2007. (Illus.). (J). (gr. k-3). 9.95 *(978-0-8198-4862-8(X))* Pauline Bks. & Media.

—Noah's Ark. 2014. (Make Your Own Ser.). (ENG.). 20p. (J). (gr. k-2). pap. 7.99 *(978-1-905710-25-6(9))* B Small Publishing GBR. Dist: Independent Pubs. Group.

Blyton, Enid. Noah & the Ark: See the Picture & Say the Word. 2012. (ENG.). 24p. (J). pap. 9.95 *(978-1-84135-746-1(4))* Award Pubns. Ltd. GBR. Dist: Parkwest Pubns., Inc.

Bower, Gary. A Patch on the Peak of Ararat. Chotiner, Barbara, illus. 2017. (Faith That God Built Book Ser.). (ENG.). 32p. (J). 14.99 *(978-1-4964-1744-2(5)*, Tyndale Kids) Tyndale Hse. Pubs.

Box, Su. The First Rainbow. Poole, Susie, illus. 2009. (ENG.). 24p. (J). (gr. -1-k). bds. 6.95 *(978-0-7459-6904-6(6)*, Lion Children's) Lion Hudson PLC GBR. Dist: Independent Pubs. Group.

—Noah's Ark. East, Jacqueline, illus. 2014. (Bible Dial-A-Picture Bks.). (ENG.). 8p. (J). (gr. -1-k). bds. 6.99 *(978-0-7641-6695-2(6))* Barron's Educational Series, Inc.

Brayley, Genevieve. Noah Saves the Tigers. 2010. 28p. pap. 28.03 *(978-1-4500-3077-9(7))* Xlibris Corp.

Carlson, Melody. Noah & the Incredible Flood, 5 vols. Francisco, Wendy, illus. 2003. (Bible Adventure Club Ser.). 36p. wbk. ed. 19.99 incl. audio, cd-rom *(978-1-58134-336-6(1))* Crossway.

Coburn, Claudia. Did the Aardvarks Say "No Ark"? Hoard, Angela, illus. 2004. 32p. (J). *(978-0-9759343-1-9(7))* Purfect Promises.

Copenhagen Publishing Company, prod. Noah's Big Boat. 2015. (ENG.). 10p. (J). 4.99 *(978-1-4964-0463-3(7)*, Tyndale Kids) Tyndale Hse. Pubs.

Cousins, Lucy. Noah's Ark. Cousins, Lucy, illus. 2004. (ENG., Illus.). 22p. (J). (gr. k-k). bds. 6.99 *(978-0-7636-2446-0(2))* Candlewick Pr.

Dalmatian Press Staff. Noah's Ark. 2004. (ENG., Illus.). 24p. (J). 2.99 *(978-1-4037-0968-4(8)*, Spirit Pr.) Bendon, Inc.

David, Juliet. All Aboard with Noah: Pop-Up, 1 vol. Canuso, Julie & Canuso, Jackie, illus. 2016. (ENG.). 12p. (J). 14.99 *(978-1-78128-249-6(8)*, Candle Bks.) Lion Hudson PLC GBR. Dist: Kregel Pubns.

—The Great Flood, 1 vol. Parry, Jo, illus. 2014. (ENG.). 12p. (J). bds. 3.99 *(978-1-85985-991-9(7)*, Candle Bks.) Lion Hudson PLC GBR. Dist: Kregel Pubns.

David, Juliet & Embleton-Hall, Chris. Noah's Amazing Ark: A Lift-The-Flap Adventure, 1 vol. 2017. (ENG., Illus.). 14p. (J). 9.99 ***(978-1-78128-317-2(6)***, Candle Bks.) Lion Hudson PLC GBR. Dist: Kregel Pubns.

David, R. Noahs Ark. 2010. 12p. *(978-965-91286-1-7(4))* Sifrei Bet Shearim Ltd.

De Graaf, A. M. Noe y el Arca. (Divertidas Historias Biblicas para Ninos Ser.). (SPA.). (J). 3.49 *(978-0-7899-0524-6(8)*, 496641) Editorial Unilit.

DeVries, Catherine & Zondervan Staff. All Aboard with Noah!, 1 vol. Pulley, Kelly, illus. 2009. (Beginner's Bible Ser.). (ENG.). 12p. (J). bds. 7.99 *(978-0-310-71726-3(4))* Zonderkidz.

Dowley, Tim. Noah & His Big Boat. 2005. (Magnetic Adventures Ser.). (Illus.). 10p. (J). (gr. -1-3). 15.99 *(978-0-8254-7294-7(6)*, Candle Bks.) Lion Hudson PLC GBR. Dist: Kregel Pubns.

—Noah's Ark Pop-Up. Martin, Stuart, illus. 2007. 6p. (J). bds. 14.99 *(978-0-8254-7330-2(6)*, Candle Bks.) Lion Hudson PLC GBR. Dist: Kregel Pubns.

Dudley, Becki. Remarkable Rescue: Saved on Noah's Ark. 2016. (ENG.). 12p. (J). bds. 7.99 *(978-0-89051-976-9(5))* Master Bks.

Falken, Linda & The Metropolitan Museum of Art, The Metropolitan. Noah's Ark. 2015. (ENG., Illus.). 32p. (J). (gr. -1-3). 17.95 *(978-1-4197-1361-3(2)*, Abrams Bks. for Young Readers) Abrams, Inc.

Froeb, Lori C. Noah's Ark, 1 vol. Rinaldo, Luana, illus. 2008. 12p. (J). bds. 7.99 *(978-0-8254-5546-9(4))* Kregel Pubns.

Golden, William Lee. Noah, Didn't It Rain. Looney, Bill, illus. 2008. 29p. (J). (gr. -1-3). 13.99 incl. audio compact disk *(978-0-89221-683-3(2))* New Leaf Pub. Group.

Goldsack, Gaby & Dawson, Peter. Noah's Ark: My Little Bible Book. Lawson, Peter, illus. 2003. 12p. (J). bds. 10.99 *(978-0-8254-7266-4(0)*, Candle Bks.) Lion Hudson PLC GBR. Dist: Kregel Pubns.

Goodings, Christina. Guess Who? Noah's Ark: A Flip-The-Flap Book. Muss, Angela, illus. 2014. (ENG.). 6p. (J). (— 1). bds. 9.99 *(978-0-7459-6496-6(6))* Lion Hudson PLC GBR. Dist: Independent Pubs. Group.

—My Noah's Ark Jigsaw Book. Elliott, Rebecca, illus. 2009. (ENG.). 12p. (J). (gr. -1-k). bds. 9.99 *(978-0-7459-6096-8(0)*, Lion Children's) Lion Hudson PLC GBR. Dist: Independent Pubs. Group.

—Noah's Ark. Carletti, Emanuela, illus. 2015. (ENG.). 16p. (J). (gr. -1-k). pap. 6.99 *(978-0-7459-6569-7(5))* Lion Hudson PLC GBR. Dist: Independent Pubs. Group.

Ham, Ken. A Special Door. Looney, Bill, illus. 2016. (ENG.). 24p. (J). 14.99 *(978-0-89051-977-6(3))* Master Bks.

Hartman, Bob. Noah's Big Boat. Samuel, Janet, illus. 2007. (ENG.). 32p. (J). (gr. -1-k). pap. 9.95 *(978-0-7459-4995-6(9))* Lion Hudson PLC GBR. Dist: Independent Pubs. Group.

Hawksley, Gerald. Amazing Journey of Noah & His Incredible Ark. 2004. 20p. pap. 11.99 *(978-0-8254-7275-6(X))* Kregel Pubns.

Hazen, Barbara Shook. Noah's Ark. Catusanu, Mircea, illus. 2003. (Little Golden Book Ser.). (ENG.). 24p. (J). (gr. -1-2). 4.99 *(978-0-307-10440-3(0)*, Golden Bks.) Random Hse. Children's Bks.

James, Annabelle. Noah's Ark: Story in a Box. 2003. (J). bds. 8.99 *(978-1-883043-51-3(4))* Straight Edge Pr., The.

Josephs, Mary. All Aboard Noah's Ark! Bratun, Katy, illus. 2007. (Chunky Book Ser.). (ENG.). 22p. (J). (— 1). bds. 3.99 *(978-0-679-86054-9(1)*, Golden Inspirational) Random Hse. Children's Bks.

Karr, Lily. Noah's Ark. Berg, Michelle, illus. 2007. (ENG.). 6p. (J). (gr. -1). bds. 12.99 *(978-0-439-86396-4(1))* Scholastic, Inc.

Kneen, Maggie. Two by Two: The Story of Noah & the Ark. 2008. (ENG., Illus.). 12p. (J). *(978-1-55168-324-9(5))* Fenn, H. B. & Co., Ltd.

Knudsen, Michelle. Noah's Ark. Santoro, Christopher, illus. 2016. (Lift-The-Flap Ser.). (ENG.). 14p. (J). (gr. -1 — 1). bds. 6.99 *(978-0-553-53537-2(4)*, Random Hse. Bks. for Young Readers) Random Hse. Children's Bks.

Ladybird Books Staff. Noah's Ark. (Bible Stories Ser.: No. S846-2). (Illus.). (J). (gr. -1-2). pap. 3.95 *(978-0-7214-5065-0(2)*, Dutton Juvenile) Penguin Publishing Group.

Larcombe, Jennifer Rees. The Best Boat Ever Built. Björkman, Steve, illus. 2004. (Best Bible Stories Ser.). 24p. (gr. -1-3). pap. 2.99 *(978-1-58134-148-5(2))* Crossway.

MacDonald, Mindy. Noah's Crew Came 2 By 2. 2004. (GodCounts Ser.). (ENG.). 24p. bds. 12.99 *(978-1-59052-409-1(8)*, Multnomah Bks.) Crown Publishing Group.

MacKenzie, Carine. Bible Heroes - Noah. 2013. (Bible Art Ser.). (ENG.). 16p. (J). pap., act. bk. ed. 1.99 *(978-1-85792-823-5(7)*, 68bc0ad9-0c11-4662-b243-81a7a41e4b52) Christian Focus Pubns. GBR. Dist: Bookmasters Distribution.

Make Believe Ideas. Noah. 2006. (Illus.). 32p. (J). (gr. -1-3). 8.97 *(978-1-59145-526-4(X))* Nelson, Thomas Inc.

Martin, Jr., Bill & Sampson, Michael. Noah, Noah, What Do You See?, 1 vol. 2017. (ENG., Illus.). 30p. (J). bds. 7.99 *(978-0-7180-8949-8(9))* Nelson, Thomas Inc.

Martin, Oscar, Jr., creator. Noah l.t. ed. 2003. (Illus.). 25p. (J). E-Book 19.95 incl. cd-rom *(978-0-9748416-1-8(7))* Build Your Story.

McCombs, Margi. Noah's Ark. Fox, Lisa, illus. 2014. (ENG.). 10p. (J). (gr. -1-k). bds. 7.99 *(978-0-545-60557-1(1)*, Little Shepherd) Scholastic, Inc.

Mitter, Matt. Guess Who Noah's Boat, 1 vol. Jarzabek, Ela, illus. 2014. 10p. (J). 11.99 *(978-0-8254-4205-6(2))* Kregel Pubns.

Mitzo Thompson, Kim, et al. Rise & Shine: Sing-A-Story Book with CD. 2017. (Let's Share a Story Ser.). (ENG.). 16p. (J). (-5). bds. 9.99 ***(978-1-68322-199-9(0))*** Barbour Publishing, Inc.

Nilsen, Lenie. The Elephant & the Dove. 2013. (Illus.). 42p. (J). 18.99 *(978-1-940473-04-8(7))* Stonebridge Pubns.

Noah & the Ark. 2004. 5.95 *(978-1-57264-240-9(8))* Parsons Technology.

Noah & the Ark. Date not set. (J). 8.95 *(978-0-88271-533-9(X)*, 10521) Regina Pr., Malhame & Co.

Noah's Ark. Date not set. (Illus.). (J). bds. 9.98 *(978-1-4054-2048-8(0))* Parragon, Inc.

Noah's Ark: A Bible Story to Color. (Illus.). 16p. (J). pap. 1.50 *(978-0-87162-823-7(6)*, E6017) Warner Pr., Inc.

Noah's Ark Bible Sticker Book. 2003. (Illus.). 16p. (J). 2.98 *(978-1-4054-1558-3(4))* Parragon, Inc.

Noah's Ark Fun Book. (Illus.). 16p. (J). pap. 1.50 *(978-0-87162-977-7(1)*, E4982) Warner Pr., Inc.

Noble, Marty. Fun with Noah's Ark Stencils. 2006. (Dover Stencils Ser.). (ENG., Illus.). 6p. (J). (gr. -1-5). pap. 1.50 *(978-0-486-44881-7(9))* Dover Pubns., Inc.

Page, Nick & Claire. Noah & the Ark. 2006. (Read with Me (Make Believe Ideas) Ser.). (Illus.). 32p. (J). (gr. k-2). *(978-1-84610-168-7(9))* Make Believe Ideas.

Pingry, Patricia A. Bible Story Cards: The Story of Noah. 2006. (ENG., Illus.). 10p. 7.95 *(978-0-8249-1703-6(0)*, Ideal Pubns.) Worthy Publishing.

—The Story of Noah. Venturi-Pickett, Stacy, illus. 2007. (ENG.). 32p. (J). (gr. -1-3). per. 3.99 *(978-0-8249-5569-4(2)*, Ideal Pubns.) Worthy Publishing.

Pinkney, Jerry. Noah's Ark. 2004. (J). (gr. k-3). 29.95 *(978-1-55592-533-8(2))* Weston Woods Studios, Inc.

Prestofillipo, Mary Nazarene, tr. The Story of Noah's Ark. Flamini, Lorella, illus. 2003. 38p. (J). 9.95 *(978-0-8198-7084-1(6)*, 332-380) Pauline Bks. & Media.

Priddy, Roger & Priddy Books Staff. Noah's Ark. 2012. (ENG., Illus.). 10p. (J). (gr. -1 — 1). bds. 4.95 *(978-0-312-51456-3(5)*, 9780312514563, Priddy Bks.) St. Martin's Pr.

Publications International Ltd. Staff, ed. Look & Find - Noah's Arc & Other Bible Stories. 2011. 24p. (J). 3.75 net. *(978-1-4508-1554-3(5))* Phoenix International Publications, Inc.

Pulley, Kelly & Zondervan Staff. Noah & the Ark, 1 vol. Pulley, Kelly, illus. 2009. (I Can Read! / the Beginner's Bible / ¡Yo Sé Leer! Ser.). (SPA & ENG., Illus.). 32p. (J). pap. 3.99 *(978-0-310-71886-4(4))* Zonderkidz.

Reed, Avery & Bader, Bonnie. Noah's Ark. Costa, Marta, illus. 2016. (Penguin Young Readers, Level 2 Ser.). (ENG.). 32p. (J). (gr. 1-2). 3.99 *(978-0-448-48967-4(8)*, Penguin Young Readers) Penguin Young Readers Group.

Reinhart, Matthew. The Ark: A Pop-up Book. Reinhart, Matthew, illus. 2006. (Illus.). 12p. (J). (gr. k-4). reprint ed. 17.00 *(978-1-4223-5673-9(6))* DIANE Publishing Co.

Rivadeneira, Caryn Dahlstrand. The Story of Noah's Ark: A Spark Bible Story. Grosshauser, Peter, illus. 2016. (Spark Story Bibles Ser.). (ENG.). 32p. (J). (gr. -1-3). 12.99 *(978-1-5064-1767-7(1))* Augsburg Fortress, Pubs.

Rock, Lois. The First Rainbow. Allsopp, Sophie, illus. 2010. (ENG.). 28p. (J). (gr. k-2). 12.99 *(978-0-7459-6055-5(3))* Lion Hudson PLC GBR. Dist: Independent Pubs. Group.

—Noah's Ark. Allsopp, Sophie, illus. 2014. (ENG.). 32p. (J). (gr. k-2). 6.99 *(978-0-7459-6321-1(8))* Lion Hudson PLC GBR. Dist: Independent Pubs. Group.

—Noah's Ark: A Spot-the-Difference Jigsaw Book. Bolam, Emily, illus. 2014. (Bible Stories for Little Hands Ser.). (ENG.). 8p. (J). (gr. -1 — 1). bds. 8.99 *(978-0-7459-6442-3(7))* Lion Hudson PLC GBR. Dist: Independent Pubs. Group.

Rowlands, Avril. All the Tales from the Ark. 2003. (Illus.). 446p. pap. 13.99 *(978-0-7459-4835-5(9)*, Lion Books) Lion Hudson PLC GBR. Dist: Trafalgar Square Publishing.

Rutherford, Peter, illus. Noah's Ark. 2015. (ENG.). 24p. bds. 6.99 *(978-1-86147-644-9(2)*, Armadillo) Anness Publishing GBR. Dist: National Bk. Network.

Simon, Mary Manz. Noah's Ark: Read & Learn the Bible. 2005. (ENG., Illus.). 24p. (J). pap. 2.99 *(978-1-4037-1157-1(7)*, Spirit Pr.) Bendon, Inc.

Smart Kids Publishing Staff. Noah's Ark Story of Being Thankful. 2007. (ENG.). 16p. (J). 19.99 *(978-0-8249-6703-1(8)*, Ideal Pubns.) Worthy Publishing.

Smart Kids Publishing Staff, creator. Noah & the Ark: A Story about Being Thankful. 2005. (I Can Read the Bible Ser.). (Illus.). 12p. (J). (gr. -1-3). 19.95 *(978-0-8249-6658-4(9)*, Ideal Pubns.) Worthy Publishing.

Smith, Brendan Powell. Noah's Ark: The Brick Bible for Kids. (Brick Bible for Kids Ser.). (ENG., Illus.). 32p. (J). (gr. -1-k). 2015. 3.99 *(978-1-63450-054-8(7))* 2012. 12.95 *(978-1-61608-737-1(4)*, 608737, Skyhorse Publishing Co., Inc. (Sky Pony Pr.).

Smith, Dororthy. Noah's Ark Coloring Book. 2007. (Illus.). 16p. (J). pap. 1.89 *(978-1-59317-188-9(9))* Warner Pr., Inc.

Snellenberger, Earl & Snellenberger, Bonita. Noah's Ark Pre-School Activity Book. Snellenberger, Earl & Snellenberger, Bonita, illus. 2014. (ENG., Illus.). 98p. (J). (gr. -1-3). pap. 8.99 *(978-0-89051-832-8(7))* Master Bks.

Stewig, John Warren. The Animals Watched: An Alphabet Book. Litzinger, Rosanne, illus. 2007. (ENG.). 32p. (J). (gr. -1-3). 16.95 *(978-0-8234-1906-7(1))* Holiday Hse., Inc.

Strauss, Ed. Know Your Bible for Kids: Noah's Ark: My First Bible Reference for 5-8 Year Olds. 2015. (ENG., Illus.). 128p. (J). pap. 4.99 *(978-1-63058-913-4(6)*, Barbour Bks.) Barbour Publishing, Inc.

Suter, Janine. Noah's Floating Animal Park. Gunther, Richard, illus. 2009. 32p. (J). 10.99 *(978-0-89051-576-1(X))* Master Bks.

The Book Company, prod. Noah's Ark 3-D Pop-ups. 2016. (ENG.). 10p. (J). bds. 19.99 (978-1-4964-0454-1(8)) Tyndale Hse. Pubs.

Thomas Nelson. Noah's Noisy Friends, 1 vol. 2016. (God's Little Ones Ser.). (ENG., Illus.). 12p. (J). (gr. -1). bds. 5.99 (978-0-7180-8533-9(7)) Nelson, Thomas Inc.

Turgeon, Stephane, illus. Noah's Ark. 2007. 16p. (J). (gr. -1-3). (978-2-7641-0340-1(9)) Tormont Pubns.

Twin Sisters(r) Staff, et al. Noah & the Ark Padded Board Book & CD, 1 vol. 2014. (Let's Share a Story Ser.). 16p. (J). (-5). bds. 9.99 incl. audio compact disk (978-1-63058-847-2(4)) Barbour Publishing, Inc.

—Play & Learn Bible Stories: Noah's Ark: Wipe-Clean Storybook. 2015. (I'm Learning the Bible Activity Book Ser.). (ENG.). 16p. (J). (gr. -1-k). pap. 6.99 (978-1-63058-894-6(6)) Barbour Publishing, Inc.

Umansky, Kaye. Noah's Ark, Vol. 7. 2nd ed. 2003. (Curtain Up Ser.: Vol. 7). (ENG., Illus.). 48p. (J). (gr. 1-4). pap. (978-0-7136-4340-4(4), A&C Black) Bloomsbury Publishing Plc.

Wedeven, Carol. El arca de Noé (Noah's 2-by-2 Adventure) - Bilingual. 2011. 16p. pap. 2.99 (978-0-7586-3072-8(7)) Concordia Publishing Hse.

Williamson, Karen. Play-Time Noah, 1 vol. Anglicas, Louise, illus. 2014. (ENG.). 8p. (J). bds. 9.99 (978-1-78128-111-6(4), Candle Bks.) Lion Hudson PLC GBR. Dist: Kregel Pubns.

Winch, John. Two by Two. 2004. (ENG., Illus.). 32p. (J). (gr. k-3). tchr. ed. 16.95 (978-0-8234-1840-4(5)) Holiday Hse., Inc.

Winkler, Jude. Noah & the Flood. 2004. (Illus.). (J). (978-0-89942-718-8(9)) Catholic Bk. Publishing Corp.

Wolf, Gita, adapted by. The Enduring Ark. 2013. (ENG., Illus.). 34p. (J). (gr. k). 21.95 (978-93-80340-18-0(4)) Tara Books Agency IND. Dist: Publishers Group West (PGW).

Zondervan. The Beginner's Bible Noah & the Noisy Ark, 1 vol. 2017. (Beginner's Bible Ser.). (ENG., Illus.). 18p. (J). bds. 8.99 (978-0-310-75957-7(9)) Zonderkidz.

Zondervan Bibles Staff. Noah's Voyage, 1 vol. Miles, David, illus. 2015. (I Can Read! / Adventure Bible Ser.). (ENG.). 32p. (J). pap. 3.99 (978-0-310-74683-6(3)) Zonderkidz.

Zondervan Staff. All Aboard the Ark, 1 vol. 2016. (ENG., Illus.). 24p. (J). bds. 6.99 (978-0-310-75377-3(5)) Zonderkidz.

NOAH'S ARK—FICTION

Adams, Georgie. Noah's Ark. Leplar, Anna C., illus. 2013. (ENG.). 64p. (J). (gr. -1-k). pap. 7.99 (978-1-4440-0789-3(0), Orion Children's Bks.) Hachette Children's Group GBR. Dist: Hachette Bk. Group.

Amoss, Berthe. Draw Yourself into the Ark with Noah & His Family. 2003. 32p. (J). spiral bd. 12.95 (978-1-59325-003-4(7)) Word Among Us Pr.

Auerbach, Annie. Traveling in Two's: The Journey to Noah's Ark. Dillard, Sarah, illus. 2005. 8p. (J). 10.95 (978-1-58117-236-2(2), Intervisual/Piggy Toes) Bendon, Inc.

Award, Anna. Noah & the Ark. 2012. (ENG., Illus.). 24p. (J). pap. 6.50 (978-1-84135-603-7(4)) Award Pubns. Ltd. GBR. Dist: Parkwest Pubns., Inc.

B&H Kids Editorial Staff. Noah's Ark. Conger, Holli, illus. 2015. (Little Words Matter(tm) Ser.). (ENG.). 24p. (J). (— 1). bds. 8.99 (978-1-4336-8649-8(X), B&H Kids) B&H Publishing Group.

Bartoletti, Susan Campbell. Naamah & the Ark at Night. Meade, Holly, illus. 2011. (ENG.). 32p. (J). (gr. -1-3). 16.99 (978-0-7636-4242-6(8)) Candlewick Pr.

Bell, Bill. Noah: The Incredible Voyager. Bell, Bill, illus. 2004. (Illus.). 48p. (J). (gr. -1-3). per. 14.99 (978-0-88092-801-4(8)) Royal Fireworks Publishing Co.

Bently, Peter. A Lark in the Ark. Chapman, Lynne, illus. 2015. (ENG.). 24p. (J). (gr. -1-k). pap. 12.99 (978-1-4052-7508-8(1)) Egmont Bks., Ltd. GBR. Dist: Independent Pubs. Group.

Booth, Bradley. Noah: The End of the World. 2010. (J). pap. 19.99 (978-0-8163-2407-1(7)) Pacific Pr. Publishing Assn.

Brett, Jan. On Noah's Ark. Brett, Jan, illus. (ENG., Illus.). (J). (gr. -1 — 1). 2009. 34p. bds. 7.99 (978-0-399-25220-4(7)) 2003. 32p. 17.99 (978-0-399-24028-7(4)) Penguin Young Readers Group. (G.P. Putnam's Sons Books for Young Readers).

Brooks, Felicity. Noisy Noah's Ark. 2013. (Noisy Bks). 10p. (J). ring bd. 19.99 (978-0-7945-3347-2(7), Usborne) EDC Publishing.

Coplestone, Lis & Coplestone, Jim. Noah's Bed. 2005. (ENG., Illus.). 32p. (J). (gr. -1-1). pap. 7.95 (978-1-84507-107-3(7), Frances Lincoln) Quarto Publishing Group UK GBR. Dist: Hachette Bk. Group.

Corman, Dick. Noah Knows. 2006. 183p. (YA). pap. 12.95 (978-0-9655749-3-8(8)) Corman Productions.

Cote, Jenny. The Ark, the Reed & the Fire Cloud: The Amazing Tales of Max & Liz Book One, 2 bks, Bk 1. 2008. (Amazing Tales of Max & Liz Ser.: 1). (ENG., Illus.). 432p. (J). (gr. 5-11). pap. 16.99 (978-0-89957-198-0(0), Living Ink Bks.) AMG Pubs.

Cullen, Lynn. Little Scraggly Hair: A Dog on Noah's Ark. Rogers, Jacqueline, illus. 2003. (ENG.). 32p. (J). (gr. k-3). tchr. ed. 16.95 (978-0-8234-1772-8(7)) Holiday Hse., Inc.

Curry, Kenneth. Mandu & Minka. 2007. (Illus.). 22p. (J). 10.95 (978-0-9798364-7-3(6)) Curry Brothers Publishing Group.

Dardik, Helen. The Story of Noah's Ark. 2017. (ENG., Illus.). 24p. (J). (gr. -1-1). bds. 9.95 **(978-0-7624-6184-4(5),** Running Pr.) Running Pr. Bk. Pubs.

David, Juliet. Noah & His Boat, 1 vol. Denham, Gemma, illus. 2008. (Candle Playbook Ser.). 18p. (J). bds. 7.99 (978-0-8254-7378-4(0), Candle Bks.) Lion Hudson PLC GBR. Dist: Kregel Pubns.

Emberley, Barbara. One Wide River to Cross. Emberley, Barbara, ed. 2015. (ENG., Illus.). 32p. 17.95 (978-1-62326-059-0(0)) AMMO Bks., LLC.

Falewee, Samantha. The Stowaway aboard Noah's Ark. 2004. (YA). per. 8.95 (978-1-59712-001-2(4)) Catawba Publishing Co.

Farrer, Vashti & Curtis, Neil. Mr. Noah & the Cats. 2005. (Illus.). 62p. (J). (gr. -1 — 1). pap. (978-0-7344-0630-9(4), Lothian Children's Bks.) Hachette Australia.

Froeb, Lori C. The Boat Noah Built. Sakamoto, Miki, illus. 2014. (Pop & Play Ser.: 3). (ENG.). 10p. (J). (gr. -1-1). 12.99 (978-0-7944-3156-3(9), Reader's Digest Children's Bks.) Studio Fun International.

—Fisher-Price Little People Noah & the Animals. 2016. (Lift-The-Flap Ser.: 18). (ENG.). 10p. (J). (gr. -1-k). bds. 9.99 (978-0-7944-3667-4(6)) Studio Fun International.

Goodwin, John. An Arkful of Animal Stories. Macnaughton, Tina, illus. 2008. 32p. (J). (gr. k-3). 13.95 (978-0-8198-0782-3(6)) Pauline Bks. & Media.

Ham, Ken & Ham, Mally. N Is for Noah Coloring Book. 2016. (Illus.). 32p. (J). pap. 4.99 **(978-1-68344-016-1(1))** Master Bks.

Harrah, Judith. Come Inside the Ark. Foster, Jack, illus. 2012. (J). pap. 17.99 (978-1-937331-12-2(1)) ShadeTree Publishing, LLC.

Hub, Ulrich. Be at the Ark by Eight. Mühle, Jörg, illus. 2012. (ENG.). 68p. (J). 12.00 (978-0-8028-5410-0(9), Eerdmans Bks For Young Readers) Eerdmans, William B. Publishing Co.

Jennings, Arleen Naish. God Is in the Rain. 2012. 64p. (gr. 1-2). pap. 8.95 (978-1-4759-3292-8(8)) iUniverse, Inc.

Jones, Liz. Noah's Bed. Copplestone, Jim, illus. 2004. 32p. (J). (978-1-84507-002-1(X)) ReiseArt Buchhandlung GmbH.

Krensky, Stephen. Noah's Bark. Girard, Roger, illus. 2010. (ENG.). 32p. (J). (gr. -1-2). lib. bdg. 16.95 (978-0-8225-7645-7(7)) Lerner Publishing Group.

Lane, W. Seth. Riley Rabbit's Quest to the Ark. 2011. 32p. (gr. -1 — 1). pap. 17.25 (978-1-4269-6178-6(2)) Trafford Publishing.

L'Engle, Madeleine. Many Waters. 2007. (Wrinkle in Time Quintet Ser.: 3). (ENG.). 368p. (J). (gr. 5-9). per. 6.99 (978-0-312-36857-9(7), 9780312368579) Square Fish.

Lodge, Yvette. Noah's Ark: Baby's First Pop-up! Lodge, Ali, illus. gif. ed. 2006. 8p. (J). 19.95 (978-1-57791-217-0(9)) Brighter Minds Children's Publishing.

Marks, Allison & Marks, Wayne. Og's Ark. Peluso, Martina, illus. 2016. (ENG.). 32p. (J). (gr. -1-3). 17.99 (978-1-4677-6149-9(4), Kar-Ben Publishing) Lerner Publishing Group.

McCardell, Ken. BibleRhymes' Noah & the Ark, bk. 2. Chirco, Antonella, illus. 2007. (BibleRhymes Ser.: 2). 28p. (J). 17.95 (978-0-9790605-1-9(6), BibleRhymes) BibleRhymes Publishing, L.L.C.

McCaughrean, Geraldine. Not the End of the World. 2005. 256p. (YA). (gr. 5-8). (ENG.). 16.99 (978-0-06-076030-4(3)); lib. bdg. 17.89 (978-0-06-076031-1(1)) HarperCollins Pubs. (HarperTeen).

Mitton, Tony. All Afloat on Noah's Boat. Parker-Rees, Guy, illus. 2017. (ENG.). 32p. (J). (gr. -1-k). pap. 7.99 (978-1-84616-242-8(4), Orchard Bks.) Hachette Children's Group GBR. Dist: Hachette Bk. Group.

Molchadsky, Yael. The Chameleon That Saved Noah's Ark. Bergman, Orit, illus. 2016. (ENG.). 32p. (J). (gr. k-3). 16.99 (978-1-101-99676-8(5), Nancy Paulsen Books) Penguin Young Readers Group.

Monroe, Colleen. A Is for Ark: Noah's Journey. Monroe, Michael Glenn, illus. 2004. 38p. (gr. -1-1). pap. 17.95 (978-0-9754942-0-2(1)) Storytime Pr., Inc.

Munter, June. Noah's Ark: The Animals Story. 2011. 20p. pap. 10.03 (978-1-4634-4992-6(5)) AuthorHouse.

Myers, Bill. Choices: A Truth Seekers Novel. 2014. (Truth Seekers Ser.). (ENG.). 224p. (J). (gr. 4-8). 10.99 (978-1-4336-9081-5(0), B&H Kids) B&H Publishing Group.

Napoli, Donna Jo. Storm. 2014. (ENG., Illus.). 368p. (YA). (gr. 9). 17.99 (978-1-4814-0302-3(8), Simon & Schuster/Paula Wiseman Bks.) Simon & Schuster/Paula Wiseman Bks.

Nolan, Allia Zobel. God's Rainbow. Chung, Chi, illus. 2007. 16p. (J). 12.99 (978-0-8254-5537-7(5)) Kregel Pubns.

Okrant, Mark. Judson's Island. 2006. per. 10.95 (978-0-9791757-2-5(0)) Oak Manor Publishing, Inc.

Parry, Jo. Under the Rainbow. 2009. (Wow! Bks.). (Illus.). (J). bds. 12.99 (978-1-934650-04-2(8)) Just For Kids Pr., LLC.

Peters, E. G. The Voyage of Noah's Ark. 2011. 166p. 29.99 (978-1-4653-4080-1(7)); pap. 19.99 (978-1-4653-4079-5(3)) Xlibris Corp.

Price, Olivia. All Aboard Noah's Ark: A Touch & Feel Book. Mitchell, Melanie, illus. 2008. (ENG.). 12p. (J). (gr. -1). 12.95 (978-1-58117-778-7(X), Intervisual/Piggy Toes) Bendon, Inc.

Racklin-Siegel, Carol, illus. Noah's Ark. 2003. 32p. (J). per. 10.95 (978-0-939144-42-6(5)) EKS Publishing Co.

Rangel, Graciela. Anthony's Journey to God's Ark. 2007. 84p. pap. 8.95 (978-1-59526-907-2(X), Llumina Christian Bks.) Aeon Publishing Inc.

Ranson, Erin. The Story of Noah's Ark. Petrlik, Andrea, illus. 2007. (Interactive Magnetic Book Ser.). 10p. (J). (gr. -1). (978-1-84666-359-8(8), Tide Mill Pr.) Top That! Publishing PLC.

Reynolds, Loralyn & Caldwell, Christiana Marie Melvin. Animals of the Ark: (for a boy named Clay) Foster, Trista, photos by. 2011. (Illus.). 36p. pap. 15.14 (978-1-4634-3328-4(X)) AuthorHouse.

Richardson, Robert. Twin Hicks Noah's Ark. Hicks, Alan and Aaron, illus. 2008. 36p. pap. 16.95 (978-1-4389-1809-9(7)) AuthorHouse.

Rouss, Sylvia A. The Littlest Pair. Hannon, Holly, illus. 2005. 32p. (J). (gr. -1-1). 14.95 (978-1-930143-17-3(6), Devora Publishing) Simcha Media Group.

Rouss, Sylviaa01. The Littlest Pair. Hannon, Holly, illus. 2015. (ENG.). 32p. (J). pap. 9.99 (978-1-68115-505-0(2), Apples & Honey Pr.) Behrman Hse., Inc.

Rowlands, Avril. All the Tales from the Ark. 2nd ed. 2017. (ENG.). 416p. (J). (gr. 2-4). pap. 9.99 **(978-0-7459-7682-2(4))** Lion Hudson PLC GBR. Dist: Independent Pubs. Group.

Santore, Charles. A Stowaway on Noah's Ark. 2015. (ENG., Illus.). 56p. (J). (gr. -1). 17.95 (978-1-60433-543-9(2), Applesauce Pr.) Cider Mill Pr. Bk. Pubs., LLC.

Sassi, Laura. Goodnight, Ark, 1 vol. Chapman, Jane, illus. (ENG.). (J). 2015. 24p. bds. 8.99 (978-0-310-74938-7(7)) 2014. 32p. 16.99 (978-0-310-73784-1(2)) Zonderkidz.

Saxon, Terrill. Baby's Noah's Ark. 2006. (Baby Blessings Ser.). (Illus.). 6p. 15.99 (978-0-7847-1430-0(4), 04013) Standard Publishing.

Schultz, Doreen. The Days of Noah. 2013. 26p. pap. 9.99 (978-1-62697-228-5(1)) Salem Author Services.

Singer, Isaac Bashevis. Why Noah Chose the Dove. 2013. (J). lib. bdg. 18.40 (978-0-606-28425-7(7), Turtleback) Turtleback Bks.

Smith, E. Boyd. Noah's Ark: The Story of the Flood & After. 2011. (Dover Children's Classics Ser.). (ENG., Illus.). 112p. (gr. -1-5). pap. 15.00 (978-0-486-47745-9(2)) Dover Pubns., Inc.

Swinson, Joyce Ann. Noah's Boat. Clark, Casey, illus. 2007. 32p. per. 24.95 (978-1-4241-9012-6(6)) America Star Bks.

Tebbs, Victoria. See & Say! Noah's Ark Story. Mitchell, Melanie, illus. 2009. (See & Say! Ser.). (ENG.). 20p. (J). (gr. k — 1). 6.95 (978-0-7459-4901-7(0)) Lion Hudson PLC GBR. Dist: Independent Pubs. Group.

Titan Books Staff & Korman, Susan. Noah - Ila's Story. 2014. (ENG., Illus.). 128p. (J). (gr. 7). 6.99 (978-1-78329-258-5(X), Titan Bks.) Titan Bks. Ltd. GBR. Dist: Penguin Random Hse. LLC.

Torseter, Øyvind & Steven, Kenneth. Why Dogs Have Wet Noses. 2015. (ENG., Illus.). 40p. (J). (gr. -1-3). 17.95 (978-1-59270-173-5(6)) Enchanted Lion Bks., LLC.

Townsend, Stephanie Z. Not Too Small at All: A Mouse Tale. Looney, Bill, illus. 2008. 30p. (J). (gr. -1). 13.99 (978-0-89051-524-2(7)) Master Bks.

Travis, Lucille. Timna. 2009. (ENG.). 168p. (J). (gr. 3-9). pap. 9.99 (978-0-8361-9484-5(5)) Herald Pr.

Veggietales. Noah's Ark: A Lesson in Trusting God. 2015. (ENG.). 32p. (J). pap. 6.99 (978-1-61795-550-1(7)) Worthy Publishing.

Wells, Janet F. For Petey's Sake! 2013. 24p. pap. 10.99 (978-1-4525-8297-9(1), Balboa Pr.) Author Solutions, Inc.

Whyte, Hugh, illus. Rock Steady: A Story of Noah's Ark. 2006. 28p. (J). (gr. k-4). reprint ed. 17.00 (978-1-4223-5556-5(X)) DIANE Publishing Co.

Widner, Jan. Then Came the Rains. 2013. 28p. pap. 16.95 (978-1-4497-9456-9(4), WestBow Pr.) Author Solutions, Inc.

Wildsmith, Brian. Professor Noah's Spaceship, 1 vol. Wildsmith, Brian, illus. 2008. (ENG., Illus.). 32p. (J). 16.95 (978-1-59572-124-2(X)) Star Bright Bks., Inc.

Wilkie, E. m. The Noah's Ark Adventure. 2013. 38p. pap. 9.99 (978-0-9887048-3-1(8)) IndieGo Publishing LLC.

Wilkinson, Simon. Noah's Ark Black & White Visual Development Book for Babies. 2008. 34p. pap. 17.95 (978-1-4092-4702-9(3)) Lulu Pr., Inc.

Zondervan Staff. Noah & God's Great Promise, 1 vol. Jones, Dennis, illus. 2010. (I Can Read! / Dennis Jones Ser.). (ENG.). 32p. (J). (gr. -1-2). pap. 3.99 (978-0-310-71884-0(8)) Zonderkidz.

NOBEL, ALFRED BERNHARD, 1833-1896

Wargin, Kathy-jo. Alfred Nobel: The Man Behind the Peace Prize. Pullen, Zachary, illus. 2009. (ENG.). 32p. (J). (gr. k-6). 17.95 (978-1-58536-281-3(6)) Sleeping Bear Pr.

NOBEL PRIZES

Anderson, Dale. Al Gore: A Wake-Up Call to Global Warming. 2009. (Voices for Green Choices Ser.). (ENG., Illus.). 48p. (J). (gr. 5-9). pap. (978-0-7787-4679-9(8)) Crabtree Publishing Co.

Benjamin, Michelle & Mooney, Maggie. Nobel's Women of Peace, 1 vol. 2008. (Women's Hall of Fame Ser.). (ENG., Illus.). 120p. (J). (gr. 4-8). pap. 10.95 (978-1-897187-38-8(6)) Second Story Pr. CAN. Dist: Orca Bk. Pubs. USA.

Brexel, Bernadette. Yasser Arafat. 2009. (Middle East Leaders Ser.). 112p. (gr. 5-8). 66.50 (978-1-61514-649-9(0), Rosen Reference) Rosen Publishing Group, Inc., The.

Cefery, Holly. Yasser Arafat. 2004. (Middle East Leaders Ser.). (Illus.). 112p. (J). (gr. 5-8). lib. bdg. 34.60 (978-0-8239-4469-9(7), Rosen Reference) Rosen Publishing Group, Inc., The.

Cullen, J. Heather. Barbara McClintock. 2003. (Women in Science Ser.). (Illus.). 112p. (gr. 6-12). 30.00 (978-0-7910-7248-6(7), Chelsea Hse.) Facts On File, Inc.

Darraj, Susan Muaddi. Mairead Corrigan & Betty Williams: Partners in Peace in Northern Ireland. 2006. (Modern Peacemakers Ser.). (Illus.). 106p. (J). (gr. 9-12). lib. bdg. 30.00 (978-0-7910-9001-5(9)) Facts On File, Inc.

Frisch, Aaron. Albert Einstein. 2005. (Genius Ser.). (Illus.). 48p. (J). (gr. 5-9). lib. bdg. 21.95 (978-1-58341-328-9(6), Creative Education) Creative Co., The.

Hasday, Judy L. Albert Einstein: The Giant of 20th Century Science. 2004. (Nobel Prize-Winning Scientists Ser.). (Illus.). 128p. (J). lib. bdg. 26.60 (978-0-7660-2185-3(8)) Enslow Pubs., Inc.

Houghton, Sarah. Elie Wiesel: A Holocaust Survivor Cries Out for Peace. 2003. (High Five Reading - Green Ser.). (ENG., Illus.). 48p. (J). (gr. 3-4). per. 9.00 (978-0-7368-2833-8(8), High Five Reading (RBL)) Capstone Press of Coughlan Cos.

—Elie Wiesel Set: A Holocaust Survivor Cries Out for Peace, 6. 2003. (High Five Reading - Green Ser.). (ENG.). 48p. (gr. 3-4). pap. 54.00 (978-0-7368-2843-7(5), High Five Reading (RBL)) Capstone Press of Coughlan Cos.

Jane Addams, 34 bks., Set. Incl. Air Pollution. Lopez, Gary. 32p. (gr. 2-12). 1992. lib. bdg. (978-0-88682-427-3(3)); Cells. George, Michael. 40p. (gr. 2-7). 1992. lib. bdg. 23.95 (978-0-88682-437-2(0)); Clouds. Markert, Jenny. 40p. (gr. 2-12). 1997. lib. bdg. 23.95 (978-0-88682-435-8(4)); Coral Reef. George, Michael. 32p. (gr. 2-12). 1992. lib. bdg. (978-0-88682-430-3(3)); Deserts. George, Michael. 40p. (gr. 2-12). 1992. lib. bdg. 23.95 (978-0-88682-434-1(6)); Earthquakes. George, Michael. 30p. (gr. 2-12). 1997. lib. bdg. 23.95 (978-0-88682-709-0(4)); Fungi. Rotter, Charles M. 40p. (gr. 2-12). 1993. lib. bdg. 23.95 (978-0-88682-593-5(8)); Galaxies. George, Michael. 40p. (gr. 2-12). 1993. lib. bdg. 23.95 (978-0-88682-433-4(8)); Glaciers. George, Michael. 32p. (gr. 2-12). 1992. lib. bdg. (978-0-88682-401-3(X)); Life. George, Michael. 32p. (gr. 2-12). 1994. lib. bdg. (978-0-88682-602-4(0)); Mars. George, Michael. 32p. (gr. 3-7). 1992. lib. bdg. (978-0-88682-432-7(X)); Moon. George, Michael. 40p. (gr. 2-12). 1993. lib. bdg. 23.95 (978-0-88682-436-5(2)); Mountains. Rotter, Charles M. 40p. (gr. 2-12). 1994. lib. bdg. 23.95 (978-0-88682-596-6(2)); Ocean Resources. Markert, Jenny. 40p. (gr. 2-12). 1994. lib. bdg. 23.95 (978-0-88682-599-7(7)); Prairie. Rotter, Charles M. 40p. (gr. 2-12). 1994. lib. bdg. 17.95 (978-0-88682-598-0(9)); Rain Forest. George, Michael. 40p. (gr. 2-12). 1992. lib. bdg. 23.95 (978-0-88682-483-9(4)); Sequoias. George, Michael. 32p. (gr. 2-12). 1992. lib. bdg. (978-0-88682-482-2(6)); Space Exploration. George, Michael. 32p. (gr. 2-12). 1993. lib. bdg. (978-0-88682-481-5(8)); Stars. George, Michael. 40p. (gr. 2-12). 1992. lib. bdg. 17.95 (978-0-88682-400-6(1)); Sun. George, Michael. 40p. (gr. 2-12). 1992. lib. bdg. 23.95 (978-0-88682-402-0(8)); Volcanoes. George, Michael. 32p. (gr. 3-12). 1992. lib. bdg. (978-0-88682-403-7(6)); Water. Markert, Jenny. 32p. (gr. 2-12). 1992. lib. bdg. (978-0-88682-431-0(1)); (Illus.). (J). (Women of America Ser.). 32p. Set lib. bdg. 576.30 o.p. (978-0-88682-165-4(7), Creative Education) Creative Co., The.

Johnson, Jen Cullerton. Seeds of Change. Sadler, Sonia Lynn, illus. 2013. (ENG.). 40p. (J). (gr. 1-6). 18.95 (978-1-60060-367-9(X)) Lee & Low Bks., Inc.

Kent, Deborah. Mario Molina: Chemist & Nobel Prize Winner. 2004. (Proud Heritage: the Hispanic Library). (ENG., Illus.). 40p. (J). (gr. 3-6). 29.93 (978-1-59296-170-2(3), 200011) Child's World, Inc., The.

Kepnes, Caroline. Stephen Crane. 2004. (Classic Storytellers Ser.). (Illus.). 48p. (J). (gr. 4-8). lib. bdg. 29.95 (978-1-58415-272-9(9)) Mitchell Lane Pubs., Inc.

Labrecque, Ellen. Gertrude B. Elion & Pharmacology. 2017. (21st Century Junior Library: Women Innovators Ser.). (ENG., Illus.). 24p. (J). (gr. 2-5). pap. 12.79 (978-1-63472-314-5(7), 209301) Cherry Lake Publishing.

MacBain, Jennifer. Gertrude Elion: Nobel Prize Winner in Physiology & Medicine. 2009. (Women Hall of Famers in Mathematics & Science Ser.). 112p. (gr. 5-8). 63.90 (978-1-60854-811-8(2), Rosen Reference) Rosen Publishing Group, Inc., The.

Pasachoff, Naomi E. Linus Pauling: Advancing Science, Advocating Peace. 2004. (Nobel Prize-Winning Scientists Ser.). (Illus.). 128p. (J). lib. bdg. 26.60 (978-0-7660-2130-3(0)) Enslow Pubs., Inc.

—Niels Bohr: Physicist & Humanitarian. 2003. (Great Minds of Science Ser.). (Illus.). 128p. (J). (gr. 4-10). lib. bdg. 27.94 (978-0-7660-1997-3(7)) Enslow Pubs., Inc.

Publishers, Chelsea House, creator. Modern Peacemakers Set, 12-Volumes. 2007. (Modern Peacemakers Ser.). (C). (gr. 9). 360.00 (978-0-7910-9701-4(3), Chelsea Hse.) Facts On File, Inc.

Stiekel, Bettina, ed. The Nobel Book of Answers: A the Dalai Lama, Mikhail Gorbachev, Shimon Peres. 2010. (ENG.). 272p. (J). (gr. 5-9). pap. 12.99 (978-1-4424-2193-6(2), Atheneum Bks. for Young Readers) Simon & Schuster Children's Publishing.

Stiekel, Bettina, et al. The Nobel Book of Answers: The Dalai Lama, Mikhail Gorbachev, Shimon Peres, & Other Nobel Prize Winners Answer Some of Life's Most Intriguing Questions for Young People. Stiekel, Bettina, ed. 2003. (ENG., Illus.). 255p. 16.00 (978-0-689-86310-3(1)) Chemical Heritage Foundation.

Stux, Erica. Enrico Fermi: Trailblazer in Nuclear Physics. 2004. (Nobel Prize-Winning Scientists Ser.). (Illus.). 128p. (J). lib. bdg. 27.94 (978-0-7660-2177-8(7)) Enslow Pubs., Inc.

Tracy, Kathleen. John Steinbeck. 2004. (Classic Storytellers Ser.). (Illus.). 48p. (J). (gr. 4-8). lib. bdg. 29.95 (978-1-58415-271-2(0)) Mitchell Lane Pubs., Inc.

—Robert Koch & the Study of Anthrax. 2004. (Uncharted, Unexplored, & Unexplained Ser.). (Illus.). 48p. (J). (gr. 4-8). lib. bdg. 29.95 (978-1-58415-261-3(3)) Mitchell Lane Pubs., Inc.

Wargin, Kathy-jo. Alfred Nobel: The Man Behind the Peace Prize. Pullen, Zachary, illus. 2009. (ENG.). 32p. (J). (gr. k-6). 17.95 (978-1-58536-281-3(6)) Sleeping Bear Pr.

Whiting, Jim. Otto Hahn & the Story of Nuclear Fission. 2003. (Unlocking the Secrets of Science Ser.). (Illus.). 56p. (gr. 4-10). lib. bdg. 25.70 (978-1-58415-204-0(4)) Mitchell Lane Pubs., Inc.

NOCTURNAL ANIMALS

Animals of the Night. 2015. (Animals of the Night Ser.). (ENG.). 32p. (J). (gr. 3-4). pap., pap., pap. 63.12 (978-0-7660-7053-0(0)) Enslow Pubs., Inc.

Bedoyere, Camilla. Creatures of the Night. 2014. (ENG., Illus.). 80p. (J). (gr. 3-6). pap. 9.95 (978-1-77085-459-8(2), 9781770854598) Firefly Bks., Ltd.

Clarke, Ginjer L. Black Out! Animals That Live in the Dark. Mueller, Pete, illus. 2008. (Penguin Young Readers, Level 3 Ser.). (ENG.). 48p. (J). (gr. 1-3). mass mkt. 3.99 (978-0-448-44824-4(6), Penguin Young Readers) Penguin Young Readers Group.

De la Bédoyère, Camilla. Nocturnal Animals. 2010. (100 Things You Should Know About Ser.). 48p. (YA). (gr. 4-6). lib. bdg. 19.95 (978-1-4222-1523-4(7)) Mason Crest.

de Lambilly-Bresson, Elisabeth. Animales de la Noche. 2007. (Los animales nos cuentan su vida (Animal Show & Tell) Ser.). (SPA., Illus.). 16p. (gr. -1-3). lib. bdg. 19.00 (978-0-8368-8105-9(2), Gareth Stevens Learning Library) Stevens, Gareth Publishing LLLP.

—Animals of the Night. 2007. (Animal Show & Tell Ser.). (Illus.). 16p. (gr. -1-3). lib. bdg. 19.00 (978-0-8368-7833-2(7), Gareth Stevens Learning Library) Stevens, Gareth Publishing LLLP.

Dorling Kindersley Publishing Staff. DK Readers L0: Nighttime Animals: Nighttime Animals. 2015. (DK Readers Ser.). (ENG., Illus.). 32p. (J). (gr. -1-1). 14.99 (978-1-4654-2853-0(4), DK Children) Dorling Kindersley Publishing, Inc.

—Nighttime Animals. 2015. (DK Readers Ser.). (ENG., Illus.). 32p. (J). (gr. -1-1). pap. 3.99 (978-1-4654-2852-3(6), DK Children) Dorling Kindersley Publishing, Inc.

Dunn, Mary R. Hedgehogs, 1 vol. 2011. (Nocturnal Animals Ser.). (ENG., Illus.). 24p. (gr. k-1). pap. 7.29 (978-1-4296-6191-1(7), Pebble Plus) Capstone Press of Coughlan Cos.

—Opossums, 1 vol. 2011. (Nocturnal Animals Ser.). (ENG., Illus.). 24p. (gr. k-1). pap. 7.29 (978-1-4296-6192-8(5), Pebble Plus) Capstone Press of Coughlan Cos.

—Porcupines, 1 vol. 2011. (Nocturnal Animals Ser.). (ENG., Illus.). 24p. (gr. k-1). pap. 7.29 (978-1-4296-6193-5(3), Pebble Plus) Capstone Press of Coughlan Cos.

Dunne, Abbie. Nocturnal Animals. 2016. (Life Science Ser.). (ENG., Illus.). 24p. (gr. k-1). lib. bdg. 26.65 (978-1-5157-0946-6(9), Pebble Plus) Capstone Press of Coughlan Cos.

Eck, Thomas Van. Tarsiers in the Dark. 2012. (Creatures of the Night Ser.). (Illus.). 24p. (J). (gr. 1-3). pap. 8.15 (978-1-4339-6382-7(5)); lib. bdg. 22.60 (978-1-4339-6380-3(9)) Stevens, Gareth Publishing LLLP.

Esbaum, Jill. Explore My World Nighttime. 2015. (Explore My World Ser.). (ENG.). 32p. (J). (gr. -1-2). pap. 4.99 (978-1-4263-2048-4(5), National Geographic Children's Bks.) National Geographic Society.

Golding, Elizabeth. Moonlight Ocean. Lodge, Ali, illus. 2012. (ENG.). 12p. (J). (gr. -1-3). 12.95 *(978-0-7624-4486-1(X))* Running Pr. Bk. Pubs.

Gonzales, Doreen. Raccoons in the Dark. 2009. 24p. (YA). pap. 8.25 *(978-1-4358-3259-6(0))*; (Illus.). (J). (gr. 1-3). 22.60 *(978-1-4042-8101-1(0))* Rosen Publishing Group, Inc., The.

—Scorpions in the Dark. 2009. 24p. (YA). pap. 8.25 *(978-1-4358-3257-2(4))*; (Illus.). (J). (gr. 1-3). 22.60 *(978-1-4042-8100-4(2))* Rosen Publishing Group, Inc., The.

Harasymiw, Therese. Hedgehogs in the Dark. 2012. (Creatures of the Night Ser.). (Illus.). 24p. (J). (gr. 1-3). pap. 8.15 *(978-1-4339-6374-2(4))* Stevens, Gareth Publishing LLLP.

Heliadore. Animals at Night. Heliadore, illus. 2013. (ENG., Illus.). 36p. (J). (gr. -1-k). 12.99 *(978-1-85103-413-0(7))* Moonlight Publishing, Ltd. GBR. Dist: Independent Pubs. Group.

Hicks, Kelli L. Nocturnal Animals, 1 vol. 2012. (Learn about Animal Behavior Ser.). (ENG.). 24p. (gr. 1-2). pap. 7.29 *(978-1-4296-9312-7(6))*; pap. 41.70 *(978-1-4296-9313-4(4)*, First Facts); lib. bdg. 25.32 *(978-1-4296-8268-8(X))* Capstone Press of Coughlan Cos.

Hirschmann, Kris. Owls, Bats, Wolves & Other Nocturnal Animals. 2003. (World Discovery Science Readers Ser.). (Illus.). 32p. (J). *(978-0-439-56628-5(2))* Scholastic, Inc.

Hoff, Mary. Life at Night. 2003. (Illus.). 32p. (J). lib. bdg. *(978-1-58341-267-1(0)*, Creative Education) Creative Co., The.

Honders, Christine. How Cats & Other Animals See at Night. 2015. (Superior Animal Senses Ser.). (ENG., Illus.). 24p. (J). (gr. 3-4). pap. 8.25 *(978-1-4994-0989-5(3)*, PowerKids Pr.) Rosen Publishing Group, Inc., The.

Johnson, J. Angelique. Raccoons, 1 vol. 2011. (Nocturnal Animals Ser.). (ENG., Illus.). 24p. (gr. k-1). pap. 7.29 *(978-1-4296-6194-2(1)*, Pebble Plus) Capstone Press of Coughlan Cos.

—Red Foxes, 1 vol. 2011. (Nocturnal Animals Ser.). (ENG., Illus.). 24p. (gr. k-1). pap. 7.29 *(978-1-4296-6195-9(X)*, Pebble Plus) Capstone Press of Coughlan Cos.

Johnson, J. Angelique & Dunn, Mary R. Nocturnal Animals. 2011. (Nocturnal Animals Ser.). (ENG.). 24p. (gr. k-1). pap. 51.03 *(978-1-4296-7123-1(8))*; pap. 333.60 *(978-1-4296-7124-8(6))*; lib. bdg. 53.30 *(978-1-4296-6650-3(1))* Capstone Press of Coughlan Cos. (Pebble Plus).

Kalman, Bobbie. Night Animals. 2011. (ENG.). 16p. (J). lib. bdg. *(978-0-7787-9558-2(6))*; pap. *(978-0-7787-9583-4(7))* Crabtree Publishing Co.

Klepeis, Alicia. Nocturnal & Diurnal Animals Explained. 2016. (Distinctions in Nature Ser.). 32p. (J). pap. 10.58 *(978-1-5026-2173-3(8))* Cavendish Square Publishing.

Kochanoff, Peggy. Be a Night Detective: Solving the Mysteries of Twilight, Dusk, & Nightfall, 1 vol. 2017. (ENG., Illus.). 56p. (J). (gr. -1-3). pap. 14.95 ***(978-1-77108-464-2(2))*** Nimbus Publishing, Ltd. CAN. Dist: Orca Bk. Pubs. USA.

Kudlinski, Kathleen V. The Sunset Switch. Burnett, Lindy, illus. 2005. (Picture Book Ser.). (ENG.). 32p. (J). (gr. k-3). 15.95 *(978-1-55971-916-2(8))* Cooper Square Publishing Llc.

Landau, Elaine. Hunters of the Night. 2012. (Illus.). 96p. (J). (gr. 3-4). pap. 10.99 *(978-1-4644-0033-9(4))* Enslow Pubs., Inc.

Lang, Diane. Daytime Nighttime, All Through the Year, 1 vol. Gabriel, Andrea, illus. 2017. (ENG.). 32p. (J). (gr. -1-3). 16.95 ***(978-1-58469-606-3(0))***; pap. 8.95 ***(978-1-58469-607-0(9))*** Dawn Pubns.

Lewis, Kelly. Animals by Day, Animals by Night. 2016. (Spring Forward Ser.). (J). (gr. 1). *(978-1-4900-3727-1(6))* Benchmark Education Co.

Lockerd, Jodi. Nocturnal Animals: Represent & Solve Problems Involving Multiplication. 2014. (Rosen Common Core Math Readers Ser.). 24p. (J). (gr. 3-4). (ENG.). pap. 49.50 *(978-1-4777-4969-2(1)*, Rosen Classroom); (ENG., Illus.). pap. 8.25 *(978-1-4777-4968-5(3)*, PowerKids Pr.); (Illus.). lib. bdg. 23.60 *(978-1-4777-6447-3(X)*, PowerKids Pr.) Rosen Publishing Group, Inc., The.

Maximus, Sofia. Badgers in the Dark. 2012. (Creatures of the Night Ser.). (Illus.). 24p. (J). (gr. 1-3). pap. 8.15 *(978-1-4339-6362-9(0))*; lib. bdg. 22.60 *(978-1-4339-6480-0(5))* Stevens, Gareth Publishing LLLP.

Meredith, S. Night Animals. 2004. (Beginners Ser.). (ENG.). 32p. (J). (gr. 1-18). pap. 4.95 *(978-0-7945-0383-3(7))* EDC Publishing.

Meredith, Sue. Night Animals: Level 1. Donaera, Patrizia & Larkum, Adam, illus. 2007. (Beginners Ser.). 32p. (J). 4.99 *(978-0-7945-1656-7(4)*, Usborne) EDC Publishing.

Minor, Wendell & Airgood, Ellen. Daylight Starlight Wildlife. Minor, Wendell, illus. 2015. (ENG., Illus.). 32p. (J). (gr. -1-k). 17.99 *(978-0-399-24662-3(2)*, Nancy Paulsen Books) Penguin Young Readers Group.

Niver, Heather Moore. Bull Sharks after Dark. 2016. (Animals of the Night Ser.). (Illus.). 32p. (J). (gr. 3-3). 25.27 *(978-0-7660-7712-6(8))* Enslow Pubs., Inc.

Nocturnal Animals. (Nocturnal Animals Ser.). (ENG.). 24p. (gr. k-1). 2011. pap. 250.20 *(978-1-4296-6365-6(0))* 2010. pap. 36.45 *(978-1-4296-6196-6(8))* Capstone Press of Coughlan Cos. (Pebble Plus).

Nocturnal Animals, 8 vols., Set. Incl. Fireflies. Dunn, Mary R. 2011. lib. bdg. 26.65 *(978-1-4296-6649-7(8))*; Hedgehogs. Dunn, Mary R. 2010. lib. bdg. 26.65 *(978-1-4296-5284-1(5))*; Owls. Dunn, Mary R. 2011. lib. bdg. 26.65 *(978-1-4296-5997-0(1))*; Raccoons. Johnson, J. Angelique. 2010. lib. bdg. 26.65 *(978-1-4296-5288-9(8))*; Red Foxes. Johnson, J. Angelique. 2010. lib. bdg. 26.65 *(978-1-4296-5285-8(3))*; (gr. k-1). (Nocturnal Animals Ser.). (ENG.). 24p. 2011. Set lib. bdg. 133.25 *(978-1-4296-6651-0(X)*, Pebble Plus) Capstone Press of Coughlan Cos.

O'Mara, Jean Claude. Raccoons in the Dark. 2012. (Creatures of the Night Ser.). (Illus.). 24p. (J). (gr. 1-3). pap. 8.15 *(978-1-4339-6378-0(7))*; lib. bdg. 22.60 *(978-1-4339-6376-6(0))* Stevens, Gareth Publishing LLLP.

O'Shaughnessy, Ruth. Bats after Dark. 2015. (Animals of the Night Ser.). (ENG., Illus.). 32p. (J). (gr. 3-4). 25.27 *(978-0-7660-6752-3(1))* Enslow Pubs., Inc.

—Big Cats after Dark. 2015. (Animals of the Night Ser.). (ENG.). 32p. (J). (gr. 3-4). pap. 10.52 *(978-0-7660-7044-8(1))*; (Illus.). 25.27 *(978-0-7660-7046-2(8))* Enslow Pubs., Inc.

—Crocodiles & Alligators after Dark. 2015. (Animals of the Night Ser.). (ENG.). 32p. (J). (gr. 3-4). pap. 10.52 *(978-0-7660-6754-7(8))*; (Illus.). 25.27 *(978-0-7660-6756-1(4))* Enslow Pubs., Inc.

—Raccoons after Dark. 2015. (Animals of the Night Ser.). (ENG.). 32p. (J). (gr. 3-4). pap. 10.52 *(978-0-7660-6762-2(9))*; (Illus.). 25.27 *(978-0-7660-6764-6(5))* Enslow Pubs., Inc.

—Snakes after Dark. 2015. (Animals of the Night Ser.). (ENG.). 32p. (J). (gr. 3-4). pap. 10.52 *(978-0-7660-6766-0(1))*; (Illus.). 25.27 *(978-0-7660-6768-4(8))* Enslow Pubs., Inc.

Pearson, Jane & Bryan, Philip. Creatures of the Dark. 2007. (Literacy 2000 Satellites: Stage 6 Ser.). (Illus.). 24p. (J). (gr. -1-3). pap. *(978-0-7327-1731-5(0)*, Rigby) Pearson Education Australia.

Petrie, Kristin. Aye-Ayes, 1 vol. 2010. (Nocturnal Animals Ser.). (ENG.). 24p. (J). (gr. 3-6). 25.65 *(978-1-60453-735-2(3))* ABDO Publishing Co.

Rissman, Rebecca. Hedgehogs: Nocturnal Foragers, 1 vol. 2014. (Night Safari Ser.). (ENG., Illus.). 24p. (gr. k-2). 23.32 *(978-1-4846-0313-0(3)*, Heinemann Read & Learn) Heinemann-Raintree.

—Mice: Nocturnal Explorers, 1 vol. 2014. (Night Safari Ser.). (ENG., Illus.). 24p. (gr. k-2). 23.32 *(978-1-4846-0311-6(7)*, Heinemann Read & Learn) Heinemann-Raintree.

—Red Foxes: Nocturnal Predators, 1 vol. 2014. (Night Safari Ser.). (ENG., Illus.). 24p. (gr. k-2). 23.32 *(978-1-4846-0312-3(5)*, Heinemann Read & Learn) Heinemann-Raintree.

Robinson, Martyn & Thomson, Bruce. Australian Wildlife after Dark. 2016. (ENG., Illus.). 156p. pap. 24.95 *(978-1-4863-0072-3(3))* CSIRO Publishing AUS. Dist: Stylus Publishing, LLC.

Shea, Therese. Bobcats in the Dark. 2012. (Creatures of the Night Ser.). (Illus.). 24p. (J). (gr. 1-3). pap. 8.15 *(978-1-4339-6366-7(3))*; lib. bdg. 22.60 *(978-1-4339-6364-3(7))* Stevens, Gareth Publishing LLLP.

Ward, Jennifer. Forest Bright, Forest Night. Henterly, Jamichael, illus. (Simply Nature Book Ser.). (J). 2007. 26p. (gr. -1 — 1). bds. 7.95 *(978-1-58469-089-4(5))* 2005. 32p. (gr. k-3). 16.95 *(978-1-58469-066-5(6))* 2005. (ENG.). 32p. (gr. k-3). pap. 8.95 *(978-1-58469-067-2(4))* Dawn Pubns.

Wood, Alix. Amazing Animals at Night. 2012. (Wow! Wildlife Ser.). (ENG., Illus.). 24p. (J). (gr. k-5). 22.60 *(978-1-4488-8102-4(1))*; pap. 8.25 *(978-1-4488-8165-9(X))* Windmill Bks.

Wren, Jenny, illus. Night Animals. 2017. (First Explorers Ser.). (ENG.). 10p. (J). (— 1). bds. 8.95 ***(978-1-4549-2657-3(0))*** Sterling Publishing Co., Inc.

NOISE

Brasch, Nicolas. Why Does Sound Travel? All about Sound. 2010. (Illus.). 24p. (J). 49.50 *(978-1-61531-909-1(3)*, 1307169, PowerKids Pr.) Rosen Publishing Group, Inc., The.

—Why Is It So Loud? 2010. (Solving Science Mysteries Ser.). (Illus.). 24p. (J). pap. 8.25 *(978-1-61531-908-4(5)*, PowerKids Pr.); (YA). (gr. 3-6). lib. bdg. 22.60 *(978-1-61531-888-9(7))* Rosen Publishing Group, Inc., The.

Johnson, Marion. Caillou, What's That Noise. CINAR Corporation Staff, illus. 2004. (Clubhouse Usa Ser.). (ENG.). 24p. (J). pap. 3.95 *(978-2-89450-489-5(6))* Ellipsis Pr.

Jordan, Appie. Noisy Quiet. 2nd rev. ed. 2011. (Bookworms 2nd Edition: Opposites Ser.). 16p. (gr. k-1). 21.36 *(978-1-60870-421-7(1))* Marshall Cavendish Corp.

Lonely Planet Publications Staff. Adventures in Noisy Places: Packed Full of Activities & over 250 Stickers, 1 vol. 2015. (Lonely Planet Kids Ser.). (ENG., Illus.). 48p. (J). pap. 9.99 *(978-1-74360-780-0(6)*, 4982) Lonely Planet Pubns.

The something Noise: Individual Title Six-Packs. (gr. 1-2). 25.00 *(978-0-7635-9130-4(0))* Rigby Education.

Thomson, Ruth. Ruidos. (Coleccion Mi Primer Libro). (SPA.). 32p. (J). 13.95 *(978-84-207-3779-9(8)*, ANY872) Grupo Anaya, S.A. ESP. Dist: Continental Bk. Co., Inc.

NOISE—FICTION

Alizadeh, Kate. Quiet! Alizadeh, Kate, illus. 2017. (Child's Play Library). (ENG., Illus.). 32p. (J). pap. *(978-1-84643-888-2(8))* Child's Play International Ltd.

Anderson, Sara. Noisy City Night (2015 Board Book) Anderson, Sara, illus. 2015. (ENG., Illus.). 12p. (J). (gr. -1-1). bds. 10.95 *(978-1-943459-01-8(0))* Sara Anderson Children's Bks.

Banks, Steven. The Song That Never Ends. DePorter, Vince, illus. 2004. (Spongebob Squarepants Ser.). 32p. (J). (gr. k-2). 11.65 *(978-0-7569-5374-4(X))* Perfection Learning Corp.

Beckstrand, Karl. Sounds in the House! A Mystery. Jones, Channing, illus. 2004.Tr. of Sonidos en la Casa. (ENG.). 24p. (J). per. 4.00 *(978-0-9672012-5-2(X))* Premio Publishing & Gozo Bks., LLC.

Burleigh, Robert. Clang! Clang! Beep! Beep! Listen to the City. Giacobbe, Beppe, illus. 2009. (ENG.). 32p. (J). (gr. -1-2). 17.99 *(978-1-4169-4052-4(9)*, Simon & Schuster/Paula Wiseman Bks.) Simon & Schuster/Paula Wiseman Bks.

—Zoom! Zoom! Sounds of Things That Go in the City. Carpenter, Tad, illus. 2014. (ENG.). 32p. (J). (gr. -1-3). 17.99 *(978-1-4424-8315-6(6)*, Simon & Schuster Bks. For Young Readers) Simon & Schuster Bks. For Young Readers.

Cameron, Kristy. Behind the Door of Timothy Moore. Schickle, Ian, illus. 2013. 28p. pap. *(978-0-9859790-1-0(1))* LP Publishing.

Crimi, Carolyn. The Louds Move In!, 1 vol. Dunnick, Regan, illus. 2006. (ENG.). 32p. (J). (gr. -1-3). 14.95 *(978-0-7614-5221-8(4))* Marshall Cavendish Corp.

Desautels, Jodi. There Were Always Noises. 2012. 20p. pap. 24.95 *(978-1-4626-8628-5(1))* PublishAmerica, Inc.

Donegan, Noel & Donegan, Luz. The Noisy Blue Drum. 2013. (Magical Mozart & His Musical Ser.). (ENG.). 32p. (J). pap. 8.95 *(978-1-84730-391-2(9))* Veritas Pubns. IRL. Dist: Dufour Editions, Inc.

DOYLE, Malachy. Too Noisy! Vere, Ed, illus. 2012. (ENG.). 32p. (J). (gr. -1-2). 15.99 *(978-0-7636-6226-4(7))* Candlewick Pr.

Ebbeler, Jeffrey. Click! 2015. (ENG., Illus.). 32p. (J). (gr. -1-1). 16.95 *(978-0-8234-3295-0(5))* Holiday Hse., Inc.

Eves, Sue. The Quiet Woman & the Noisy Dog. Busby, Allie, illus. 2010. (ENG.). 32p. (J). (gr. k-k). pap. 10.99 *(978-1-84270-939-9(9))* Andersen Pr. GBR. Dist: Independent Pubs. Group.

Franco, Betsy. Summer Beat. Middleton, Charlotte, illus. 2011. (ENG.). 36p. (J). (gr. -1-1). 14.99 *(978-1-4424-4339-6(1)*, McElderry, Margaret K. Bks.) McElderry, Margaret K. Bks.

Garcia, Emma. Toot Toot Beep Beep. 2013. (ENG., Illus.). 26p. (J). (— 1). bds. 6.95 *(978-1-906250-84-3(7))* Boxer Bks., Ltd. GBR. Dist: Sterling Publishing Co., Inc.

Gibson, Ginger Foglesong. Tiptoe Joe. Rankin, Laura, illus. 2013. (ENG.). 32p. (J). (gr. -1-k). 17.99 *(978-0-06-177203-0(8)*, Greenwillow Bks.) HarperCollins Pubs.

Goss, Leon. By the Light of the Moon. Luo, Shiyin Sean, illus. 2005. (J). pap. *(978-1-933156-12-5(0))*; per. 16.99 *(978-1-933156-05-7(8))* GSVQ Publishing. (VisionQuest Kids).

Harris, Robie H. When Lions Roar. Raschka, Chris, illus. 2013. (ENG.). 32p. (J). (gr. -1-k). 16.99 *(978-0-545-11283-3(4)*, Orchard Bks.) Scholastic, Inc.

Herbauts, Anne. Prince Silencio. Bedrick, Claudia Z., tr. from FRE. 2006. (ENG., Illus.). 32p. (J). (gr. -1-3). 14.95 *(978-1-59270-055-4(1))* Enchanted Lion Bks., LLC.

Higgins, Ryan T. Be Quiet! Higgins, Ryan T., illus. 2017. (ENG., Illus.). 40p. (J). (gr. -1-k). 17.99 *(978-1-4847-3162-8(X))* Hyperion Bks. for Children.

Holden, Pam. The Long, Long Ride, 6 pack. Storey, Jim, illus. 2009. (Red Rocket Readers Ser.). (ENG.). 16p. (gr. 2-2). pap. *(978-1-877363-76-4(6))* Flying Start Bks.

Hopgood, Tim. Here Comes Frankie! 2008. (ENG., Illus.). 32p. (J). (gr. 2-6). 23.95 *(978-1-4050-9271-5(8)*, Macmillan) Pan Macmillan GBR. Dist: Trans-Atlantic Pubns., Inc.

Inkpen, Mick. Lullabyhullaballoo! Inkpen, Mick, illus. 2007. (ENG., Illus.). 32p. (gr. 13-17). pap. 10.99 *(978-0-340-93108-0(6))* Hodder & Stoughton GBR. Dist: Hachette Bk. Group.

Keep, Richard. A Thump from Upstairs: Starring Mr. Boo & Max, 1 vol. Keep, Richard, illus. 2005. (ENG., Illus.). 36p. (J). (gr. -1-3). 15.95 *(978-1-56145-348-1(X))* Peachtree Pubs.

Kohuth, Jane. Ducks Go Vroom. Garofoli, Viviana, illus. 2011. (Step into Reading Ser.). (ENG.). 32p. (J). (gr. -1-1). pap. 3.99 *(978-0-375-86560-2(8)*, Random Hse. Bks. for Young Readers) Random Hse. Children's Bks.

Kramer, Alan & Kramer, Candice. Brer Rabbit Hears a Big Noise in the Woods: An African /American Folktale. 2006. (J). pap. *(978-1-4108-7163-3(0))* Benchmark Education Co.

Landry, Leo. Space Boy. Landry, Leo, illus. 2007. (ENG., Illus.). 32p. (J). (gr. -1-3). 16.99 *(978-0-618-60568-2(1))* Houghton Mifflin Harcourt Publishing Co.

Lemniscates. Silence. 2012. (Illus.). (J). 28p. 14.95 *(978-1-4338-1137-1(5))*; 29p. pap. 9.95 *(978-1-4338-1136-4(7))* American Psychological Assn. (Magination Pr.).

Light, Steve. Diggers Go. 2013. (ENG., Illus.). 16p. (J). (gr. -1 — 1). bds. 9.99 *(978-1-4521-1864-2(7))* Chronicle Bks. LLC.

Long, Ethan. One Drowsy Dragon. 2010. (Illus.). (J). *(978-0-545-23412-2(3)*, Orchard Bks.) Scholastic, Inc.

—Pig Has a Plan. Long, Ethan, illus. 2012. (I Like to Read(r) Ser.). (ENG., Illus.). 24p. (J). (gr. -1-3). 14.95 *(978-0-8234-2428-3(6))* Holiday Hse., Inc.

Maier, Inger M. When Fuzzy Was Afraid of Big & Loud Things. Candon, Jennifer, illus. 2005. (Fuzzy the Little Sheep Ser.). (J). (gr. -1-3). 32p. 14.95 *(978-1-59147-322-0(5))*; 30p. per. 9.95 *(978-1-59147-323-7(3))* American Psychological Assn. (Magination Pr.).

Mandy and Ness Staff, et al. Hattie's House: A First Book about Sound. 2005. (Senses Ser.). (URD, ENG, VIE, CHI & BEN., Illus.). 16p. (J). pap. 9.95 *(978-1-84059-156-9(0))* Milet Publishing.

Mayo, Margaret. Choo Choo Clickety-Clack! Ayliffe, Alex, illus. 2005. (ENG.). 32p. (J). (gr. k-3). 16.95 *(978-1-57505-819-1(7))* Lerner Publishing Group.

McGovern, Ann. Too Much Noise. 2014. 16.95 *(978-1-63419-746-5(1))* Perfection Learning Corp.

Medearis, Angela Shelf. Lucy's Quiet Book. Ernst, Lisa Campbell, illus. 2004. (Green Light Readers Level 2 Ser.). (ENG.). 24p. (J). (gr. -1-3). pap. 3.95 *(978-0-15-205143-3(0))* Houghton Mifflin Harcourt Publishing Co.

—Lucy's Quiet Book. Ernst, Lisa Campbell, illus. 2004. (Green Light Readers Level 2 Ser.). (gr. k-2). 13.95 *(978-0-7569-4310-3(8))* Perfection Learning Corp.

Molitoris, Cathy. I've Got Music! McConnell, Sarah, illus. 2006. (J). *(978-0-439-88620-8(1))* Scholastic, Inc.

Moore, Nicholas & Murton, Gareth. Princess Lydia & the wailing Monster. 2008. 32p. pap. 18.95 *(978-1-4092-4993-1(X))* Lulu Pr., Inc.

Morris, Eileen. The Original "Shnoozles" Starring in "and Next Came a Roar" 2005. (ENG.). 16p. pap. *(978-0-9768852-0-7(4))* Sirene Enterprises.

Mortimer, Rachael. The Three Billy Goats Fluff. Pichon, Liz, illus. 2013. (ENG.). 32p. (J). (gr. -1-2). pap. 7.95 *(978-1-58925-439-8(2))* Tiger Tales.

Morton, Christine. No Te Preocupes, Guille. McMullen, Nigel, illus. (Buenas Noches Ser.). (SPA.). 26p. (J). (gr. k-3). 8.95 *(978-958-04-5088-7(9))* Norma S.A. COL. Dist: Distribuidora Norma, Inc.

Newton, Jill. Don't Wake Mr Bear! Newton, Jill, illus. 2011. (ENG., Illus.). 32p. (J). (gr. -1). 17.99 *(978-1-4052-4965-2(X))*; pap. 9.99 *(978-1-4052-4966-9(8))* Egmont Bks., Ltd. GBR. Dist: Independent Pubs. Group.

Newton, Jill, illus. Crash Bang Donkey! 2015. 32p. (J). *(978-1-4896-3858-8(X))* Weigl Pubs., Inc.

Patricelli, Leslie. Be Quiet, Mike! 2011. (ENG., Illus.). 40p. (J). (gr. -1-2). 14.99 *(978-0-7636-4477-2(3))* Candlewick Pr.

Pearson, Debora. Big City Song. Reed, Lynn Rowe, illus. 2006. (ENG.). 32p. (J). (gr. -1-3). 16.95 *(978-0-8234-1988-3(6))* Holiday Hse., Inc.

Pennypacker, Sara. Sparrow Girl. Tanaka, Yoko, illus. 2009. (ENG.). 40p. (J). (gr. k-4). 16.99 *(978-1-4231-1187-0(7))* Hyperion Pr.

Pizzoli, Greg. Good Night Owl. Pizzoli, Greg, illus. 2016. (ENG., Illus.). 48p. (J). (gr. -1-k). 16.99 *(978-1-4847-1275-7(7))* Disney Pr.

Rauss, Ron. Can I Just Take a Nap? Shepperson, Rob, illus. 2012. (ENG.). 32p. (J). (gr. -1-1). 15.99 *(978-1-4424-3497-4(X)*, Simon & Schuster/Paula Wiseman Bks.) Simon & Schuster/Paula Wiseman Bks.

Roques, Dominique. Sleep Tight, Anna Banana! Dormal, Alexis, illus. 2014. (Anna Banana Ser.). (ENG.). 28p. (J). (gr. -1-2). 15.99 *(978-1-62672-019-0(3)*, 9781626720190, First Second Bks.) Roaring Brook Pr.

Rosen, Michael. Bear's Day Out. Reynolds, Adrian, illus. 2007. (ENG.). 32p. (J). (gr. k-3). 16.95 *(978-1-59990-007-0(6)*, 9781599900070, Bloomsbury USA Childrens) Bloomsbury Publishing USA.

Scharer, Niko. Emily's House, 1 vol. Fitzgerald, Joanne, illus. 2010. (ENG.). 22p. (J). (gr. k — 1). bds. 7.95 *(978-0-88899-831-6(7))* Groundwood Bks. CAN. Dist: Publishers Group West (PGW).

Schotter, Roni. When the Wizzy Foot Goes Walking. Wohnoutka, Mike, illus. 2007. (J). *(978-5-525-47791-9(2)*, Dutton Juvenile) Penguin Publishing Group.

Singer, Marilyn. City Lullaby. Cneut, Carll, illus. 2007. (ENG.). 32p. (J). (gr. -1-3). 16.99 *(978-0-618-60703-7(X))* Houghton Mifflin Harcourt Publishing Co.

Sosin, Deborah. Charlotte & the Quiet Place. Woolley, Sara, illus. 2015. (ENG.). 40p. (J). (gr. -1-2). 16.95 *(978-1-941529-02-7(X)*, Plum Blossom Bks.) Parallax Pr.

Sullivan-Ringe, Laurie. Noise in the Night. Matiuzzo, Nick, illus. 2008. 37p. pap. 24.95 *(978-1-60672-476-7(2))* America Star Bks.

Teal, Val. The Little Woman Wanted Noise. Lawson, Robert, illus. 2013. (ENG.). 48p. (J). (gr. -1-2). 14.95 *(978-1-59017-711-2(8)*, NYR Children's Collection) New York Review of Bks., Inc., The.

Tyler, Jenny & Hawthorn, Phillip. Who's Making That Noise? 2008. (Luxury Flap Bks). 16p. (J). 9.99 *(978-0-7945-1695-6(5)*, Usborne) EDC Publishing.

Underwood, Deborah. The Loud Book! Liwska, Renata, illus. 2011. (ENG.). 32p. (J). (gr. -1-3). 12.99 *(978-0-547-39008-6(4))* Houghton Mifflin Harcourt Publishing Co.

Urey, Gary. Super Schnoz Boxed Set #1-3. Long, Ethan & Frawley, Keith, illus. 2017. (Super Schnoz Ser.). (ENG.). 480p. (J). (gr. 3-7). pap., pap., pap. 19.99 *(978-0-8075-9989-1(1))* Whitman, Albert & Co.

Van Biesen, Koen & Watkinson, Laura. Roger Is Reading a Book. 2015. (ENG., Illus.). 42p. (J). 16.00 *(978-0-8028-5442-1(7)*, Eerdmans Bks For Young Readers) Eerdmans, William B. Publishing Co.

Willis, Jeanne. The Really Rude Rhino. Ross, Tony, illus. 2007. (ENG.). 32p. (J). (gr. -1-k). per. 12.99 *(978-1-84270-571-1(7))* Andersen Pr. GBR. Dist: Independent Pubs. Group.

Willson, Sarah. Do Not Wake Jake. Johnson, Meredith, illus. 2006. (Step-By-Step Readers Ser.). (J). *(978-1-59939-059-8(0)*, Reader's Digest Young Families, Inc.) Studio Fun International.

Wilson, Karma. Who Goes There? Currey, Anna, illus. 2013. (ENG.). 40p. (J). (gr. -1-3). 16.99 *(978-1-4169-8002-5(4)*, McElderry, Margaret K. Bks.) McElderry, Margaret K. Bks.

NOMADS

Eggleton, Jill. Nomads. 2007. (Connectors Ser.). (gr. 2-5). pap. *(978-1-877453-12-0(9))* Global Education Systems Ltd.

Hinds, Kathryn. Huns. 2009. (Barbarians! Ser.). 80p. (gr. 6). 35.64 *(978-0-7614-4066-6(6))* Marshall Cavendish GBR. Dist: Marshall Cavendish Corp.

—Scythians & Sarmatians. 2009. (Barbarians! Ser.). 80p. (gr. 6). 35.64 *(978-0-7614-4072-7(0))* Marshall Cavendish GBR. Dist: Marshall Cavendish Corp.

Kocienda, Genevieve. On the Move: The Lives of Nomads. 2014. (ENG., Illus.). 28p. pap. 9.50 *(978-1-107-63293-6(5))* Cambridge Univ. Pr.

Rice, Earle. The Life & Times of Attila the Hun. 2009. (Biography from Ancient Civilizations Ser.). 48p. (J). (gr. 4-8). 29.95 *(978-1-58415-741-0(0))* Mitchell Lane Pubs., Inc.

Sepahban, Lois. Mongol Warriors. 2015. (Ancient Warriors Ser.). (ENG.). 32p. (J). (gr. 2-5). 28.50 *(978-1-63143-756-4(9)*, 208588) Child's World, Inc., The.

NONOBJECTIVE ART

see Art, Abstract

NONSENSE VERSES

see also Limericks

Adams, Pam, illus. There Was an Old Lady Who Swallowed a Fly. 2003. (Classic Books with Holes 8x8 Ser.). (ENG.). 16p. (J). pap. *(978-0-85953-134-4(1))* Child's Play International Ltd.

Barrett, Judi. I Knew Two Who Said Moo: A Counting & Rhyming Book. Moreton, Daniel, illus. 2003. (ENG.). 32p. (J). (gr. -1-3). 7.99 *(978-0-689-85935-9(X)*, Atheneum Bks. for Young Readers) Simon & Schuster Children's Publishing.

Baxter, Nicola & Shuttleworth, Cathie. Silly Rhymes & Limericks. 2013. (ENG., Illus.). 64p. (J). (gr. -1-12). pap. 8.99 *(978-1-84322-866-0(1)*, Armadillo) Anness Publishing GBR. Dist: National Bk. Network.

Belloc, Hilaire. A Moral Alphabet: In Words of from One T. 2006. (Illus.). pap. 16.95 *(978-1-4286-1934-0(8))* Kessinger Publishing, LLC.

—More Beasts for Worse Children. B. T. B., illus. 2008. 48p. pap. *(978-1-4099-1329-0(5))* Dodo Pr.

Canetti, Yanitzia. Trabalenguas Científicos. 2010. 32p. (J). pap. 6.99 *(978-1-59835-264-1(4)*, BrickHouse Education) Cambridge BrickHouse, Inc.

Carroll, Lewis, pseud. The Hunting of the Snark. Peake, Mervyn, illus. 2004. 64p. *(978-0-413-74380-0(2))* Methuen Publishing Ltd.

—The Hunting of the Snark: An Agony in Eight Fits. Lipchenko, Oleg, illus. 2012. (ENG.). 48p. (J). (gr. k-12). 17.95 *(978-1-77049-407-7(3)*, Tundra Bks.) Tundra Bks. CAN. Dist: Penguin Random Hse. LLC.

—Jabberwocky. Jorisch, Stéphane, illus. 2004. (Visions in Poetry Ser.). (ENG.). 40p. (J). (gr. 2-9). 16.95 *(978-1-55337-079-6(1))* Kids Can Pr., Ltd. CAN. Dist: Hachette Bk. Group.

Chaudet, Annette. The Nose Book. 2007. (Illus.). 56p. (J). pap. 16.95 *(978-1-932636-36-9(6))* Pronghorn Pr.

Chwast, Seymour. She Sells Sea Shells: World Class Tongue Twisters. 2008. (ENG., Illus.). 64p. (J). (gr. 1). 19.95 *(978-1-60433-009-0(0)*, Applesauce Pr.) Cider Mill Pr. Bk. Pubs., LLC.

Colandro, Lucille. There Was an Old Lady Who Swallowed a Clover. Lee, Jared, illus. 2012. (There Was an Old Lady Ser.). (ENG.). 32p. (J). (gr. -1-k). pap. 6.99 *(978-0-545-35222-2(3),* Cartwheel Bks.) Scholastic, Inc.
—There Was an Old Lady Who Swallowed a Rose! Lee, Jared, illus. 2012. (There Was an Old Lad Ser.). (ENG.). 32p. (J). (gr. -1-k). pap. 6.99 *(978-0-545-35223-9(1))* Scholastic, Inc.
—There Was an Old Lady Who Swallowed Some Books! Lee, Jared, illus. 2012. (ENG.). 32p. (J). (gr. -1-k). 6.99 *(978-0-545-40287-3(5),* Cartwheel Bks.) Scholastic, Inc.
Dalmatian Press Staff. I Know an Old Lady Who Swallow. 2008. (ENG.). 12p. (J). bds. 4.95 *(978-1-58117-710-7(0),* Intervisual/Piggy Toes) Bendon, Inc.
Densmore, Don. The Tongue Twister Experiments Student Workbook. Evans, Andrew, illus. 2007. 60p. per. 20.00 *(978-0-9787113-5-1(1),* Ithaca Pr.) Authors & Artists Publishers of New York, Inc.
Dowell, Ruth I. Move over, Mother Goose! Finger Plays, Action Verses & Funny Rhymes. Charner, Kathleen, ed. Scott, Concetta C., illus. 2004. 126p. (Orig.). (gr. -1-1). pap. 12.95 *(978-0-87659-113-0(6),* 10006) Gryphon Hse., Inc.
Downing, Johnette, illus. & adapted by. There Was an Old Lady Who Swallowed Some Bugs, 1 vol. Downing, Johnette, adapted by. 2010. (ENG.). 32p. (J). (gr. k-3). 16.99 *(978-1-58980-858-4(4))* Pelican Publishing Co., Inc.
Foster, John, ed. Seriously Scary Poems. 2011. (ENG., Illus.). 96p. (J). (gr. k-4). pap. 5.99 *(978-0-00-714801-1(1))* HarperCollins Pubs. Ltd. GBR. Dist: HarperCollins Pubs.
Foster, John, ed. & compiled by. Completely Crazy Poems. Foster, John, compiled by. 2011. (ENG., Illus.). 96p. (J). (gr. k-4). pap. 5.99 *(978-0-00-714802-8(X))* HarperCollins Pubs. Ltd. GBR. Dist: HarperCollins Pubs.
Gorey, Edward & Lear, Edward, illus. The Dong with the Luminous Nose. 2010. 48p. 14.95 *(978-0-7649-5427-6(X))* Pomegranate Communications, Inc.
—Jumblies. 2010. 48p. 14.95 *(978-0-7649-5426-9(1))* Pomegranate Communications, Inc.
Guarino, Deborah & Kellogg, Steven. Ta Maman Est-Elle un Lama? (FRE., Illus.). (J). pap. 7.99 *(978-0-590-74555-0(7))* Scholastic, Inc.
Guinness, Louise, ed. & intro. The Everyman Book of Nonsense Verse. Guinness, Louise, intro. 2005. (Everyman's Library Children's Classics Ser.). (ENG., Illus.). 256p. (gr. -1-17). 16.95 *(978-1-4000-4425-2(1),* Everyman's Library) Knopf Doubleday Publishing Group.
Hample, Stuart E. & Hample, Stoo. The Silly Book. Hample, Stoo, illus. 2004. (ENG., Illus.). 32p. (J). (gr. k-12). 15.99 *(978-0-7636-2256-5(7))* Candlewick Pr.
Harris, Tony. There's a Wombat in My Bed. 2nd rev. ed. 2012. (Illus.). 32p. (J). *(978-1-875763-00-9(7))* ThinkSoft.
Ingersoll, Donna. Ten Tempting Tongue Twisters. 2012. 28p. 24.95 *(978-1-4626-8217-1(0))* America Star Bks.
Kralovansky, Susan Holt. There Was a Tall Texan Who Swallowed a Flea, 1 vol. Kadair, Deborah Ousley, illus. 2013. (ENG.). 32p. (J). (gr. -1-k). 16.99 *(978-1-4556-1717-3(2))* Pelican Publishing Co., Inc.
Lear, Edward. Nonsense Poems. 2011. (Dover Children's Thrift Classics Ser.). (ENG., Illus.). 96p. (Orig.). (J). (gr. 3-8). reprint ed. pap. 4.00 *(978-0-486-28031-8(4))* Dover Pubns., Inc.
—Nonsense Song. l.t. ed. 2006. 108p. pap. *(978-1-84637-276-6(3))* Echo Library.
Lee, Dennis. Garbage Delight. 2014. (Illus.). 64p. (J). 17.99 *(978-0-06-231350-8(9))* HarperCollins Pubs.
Miller, Connie Colwell, et al. Tickles, Pickles, & Floofing Persnickles: Reading & Writing Nonsense Poems, 1 vol. Smith, Simon et al, illus. 2014. (Poet in You Ser.). (ENG.). 32p. (gr. 2-4). pap. 9.95 *(978-1-4795-2949-0(4));* lib. bdg. 27.32 *(978-1-4795-2198-2(1))* Picture Window Bks.
Rosen, Michael. Nonsense. Mackie, Clare, illus. 2003. 48p. pap. *(978-0-7500-2671-0(5),* Wayland) Hachette Children's Group.
Seuss, Dr. Fox in Socks, Bricks & Blocks. Gerardi, Jan, illus. 2011. (Dr. Seuss Nursery Collection). (ENG.). 14p. (J). (gr. -1 — 1). 7.99 *(978-0-375-87209-9(4),* Random Hse. Bks. for Young Readers) Random Hse. Children's Bks.
Twin Sisters(r) Staff. Down by the Bay. 2010. (J). (gr. k-2). pap. 4.99 *(978-1-59922-505-0(0))* Twin Sisters IP, LLC.
Walrus Books. Children's Treasure Chest: Fairy Tales, Nursery Rhymes, & Nonsense Verse. 2004. (ENG., Illus.). 386p. (J). (gr. k-12). 29.95 *(978-1-55285-579-9(1))* Whitecap Bks., Ltd. CAN. Dist: Graphic Arts Ctr. Publishing Co.
Ward, Jennifer. There Was an Odd Princess Who Swallowed a Pea, 0 vols. Calderon, Lee, illus. 2011. (ENG.). 32p. (J). (gr. -1-3). 16.99 *(978-0-7614-5822-7(0),* 9780761458227, Amazon Children's Publishing) Amazon Publishing.
—There Was an Old Monkey Who Swallowed a Frog, 0 vols. Gray, Steve, illus. 2010. (ENG.). 40p. (J). (gr. k-3). 16.99 *(978-0-7614-5580-6(9),* 9780761455806, Amazon Children's Publishing) Amazon Publishing.
Westcott, Nadine Bernard. I Know an Old Lady Who Swallowed a Fly, 3 vols. 2003. (ENG., Illus.). 11p. (J). (gr. -1 — 1). bds. 6.99 *(978-0-316-93084-0(9),* Tingley, Megan Bks.) Little, Brown Bks. for Young Readers.

NONVIOLENCE

Gandhi, Mahatma. My Experiments with Truth. Chougule, Shailja Jain, illus. 2016. (ENG.). 64p. pap. 6.95 *(978-1-906230-88-3(9))* Real Reads Ltd. GBR. Dist: Casemate Pubs. & Bk. Distributors, LLC.
Haldy, Emma E. Martin Luther King, Jr. Bane, Jeff, illus. 2016. (My Early Library: My Itty-Bitty Bio Ser.). (ENG.). 24p. (J). (gr. k-1). 28.50 *(978-1-63470-477-9(0),* 207639) Cherry Lake Publishing.
Kuhn, Betsy. The Force Born of Truth: Mohandas Gandhi & the Salt March, India, 1930. 2010. (Civil Rights Struggles around the World Ser.). (ENG., Illus.). 160p. (gr. 9-12). lib. bdg. 38.60 *(978-0-8225-8968-6(0))* Lerner Publishing Group.
Meltzer, Brad. I Am Martin Luther King, Jr. Eliopoulos, Christopher, illus. 2016. (Ordinary People Change the World Ser.). (ENG.). 40p. (J). (gr. k-3). 14.99 *(978-0-525-42852-7(6),* Dial Bks) Penguin Young Readers Group.
Vander Hook, Sue. Mahatma Gandhi: Proponent of Peace, 1 vol. 2010. (Essential Lives Set 5 Ser.). (ENG.). 112p. (J). (gr. 6-12). lib. bdg. 35.64 *(978-1-61613-515-7(8))* ABDO Publishing Co.

NONVIOLENT NONCOOPERATION

see Passive Resistance

NORMANDY (FRANCE)—FICTION

Myers, Walter Dean. Invasion. 2015. (ENG.). 224p. (J). (gr. 6). pap. 8.99 *(978-0-545-38429-2(X))* 2013. (YA). *(978-0-545-57659-8(8))* 2013. (ENG.). 224p. (J). (gr. 7). 17.99 *(978-0-545-38428-5(1))* Scholastic, Inc. (Scholastic Pr.).
Osborne, Mary Pope. Danger in the Darkest Hour. Murdocca, Sal, illus. 2015. (Stepping Stone Book Ser.: No. 1). (ENG.). 192p. (J). (gr. 2-5). 14.99 *(978-0-553-49772-4(3),* Random Hse. Bks. for Young Readers) Random Hse. Children's Bks.
Stein, Evaleen. Our Little Norman Cousin of Long Ago. Goss, John, illus. 2007. 112p. per. 8.95 *(978-1-59915-245-5(2))* Yesterday's Classics.
Yonge, Charlotte M. The Little Duke. 2005. 26.95 *(978-1-4218-0318-0(6));* 164p. pap. 11.95 *(978-1-4218-0418-7(2))* 1st World Publishing, Inc. (1st World Library - Literary Society).
—The Little Duke. 2004. reprint ed. pap. 1.99 *(978-1-4179-9908-8(X));* pap. 15.95 *(978-1-4179-9958-3(6))* Kessinger Publishing, LLC.
—The Little Duke. 2008. 112p. pap. 9.05 *(978-1-60459-557-4(4))* Wilder Pubns., Corp.
Zafón, Carlos Ruiz. The Watcher in the Shadows. (ENG.). (YA). (gr. 7-17). 2014. 288p. pap. 10.99 *(978-0-316-04475-2(X))* 2013. 272p. 18.00 *(978-0-316-04476-9(8))* Little, Brown Bks. for Young Readers.

NORMANS

see also Northmen

Abbott, Jacob. History of William the Conqueror. 2003. 291p. 89.00 *(978-0-7950-4508-0(5))* New Library Press LLC.
Hamilton, Janice. The Norman Conquest of England. 2007. (Pivotal Moments in History Ser.). (ENG., Illus.). 160p. (J). (gr. 9-12). lib. bdg. 38.60 *(978-0-8225-5902-3(1))* Lerner Publishing Group.
Harkins, Susan Sales & Harkins, William H. The Life & Times of William the Conqueror. 2008. (Biography from Ancient Civilizations Ser.). (Illus.). 48p. (J). (gr. 4-8). lib. bdg. 29.95 *(978-1-58415-700-7(3))* Mitchell Lane Pubs., Inc.
Hilliam, Paul. William the Conqueror: First Norman King of England. 2009. (Leaders of the Middle Ages Ser.). 112p. (gr. 5-8). 66.50 *(978-1-61513-903-3(6),* Rosen Reference) Rosen Publishing Group, Inc., The.
HOCPP 1101 the Norman Conquest. 2006. spiral bd. 23.50 *(978-1-60308-101-6(1))* In the Hands of a Child.

NORMANS—FICTION

Henty, George Alfred. Wulf the Saxon: A Story of the Norman Conquest. Peacock, Ralph, illus. 2010. (Dover Children's Classics Ser.). (ENG.). 352p. (YA). (gr. 3-8). pap. 8.95 *(978-0-486-47595-0(6))* Dover Pubns., Inc.
Leighton-Porter, Wendy. The Shadow of the Norman Arrow. 2013. 270p. pap. *(978-1-909411-07-4(8))* Mauve Square Publishing.

NORSEMEN

see Northmen

NORTH AFRICA

see Africa, North

NORTH AMERICA

Adasiewicz, Sue. Your Papers, Please: Crossing Borders. 2007. (Shockwave: People & Communities Ser.). (ENG., Illus.). 36p. (J). (gr. 3-5). 25.00 *(978-0-531-17572-9(3),* Children's Pr.) Scholastic Library Publishing.
Allgor, Marie. Endangered Animals of North America. 2011. (Save Earth's Animals! Ser.). (Illus.). 24p. (J). pap. 8.25 *(978-1-4488-2648-3(9));* (gr. 3-4). 22.60 *(978-1-4488-2532-5(6))* Rosen Publishing Group, Inc., The. (PowerKids Pr.).
Aloian, Molly & Kalman, Bobbie. Explore North America. 2007. (Explore the Continents Ser.). (ENG., Illus.). 32p. (J). (gr. 4-7). lib. bdg. *(978-0-7787-3075-0(1));* (gr. 1-5). pap. *(978-0-7787-3089-7(1))* Crabtree Publishing Co.
Alter, Judy. Discovering North America's Land, People, & Wildlife: A MyReportLinks. com Book. 2004. (Continents of the World Ser.). (Illus.). 48p. (J). lib. bdg. 25.26 *(978-0-7660-5206-2(0),* MyReportLinks.com Bks.) Enslow Pubs., Inc.
Banting, Erinn. North America. (J). 2016. ***(978-1-4896-5725-1(8))*** 2005. (Illus.). 32p. (gr. -1-7). pap. 9.95 *(978-1-59036-328-7(0))* 2005. (Illus.). 32p. (gr. 4-6). lib. bdg. 26.00 *(978-1-59036-321-8(3))* Weigl Pubs., Inc.
Benchmark Education Co., LLC. Ancient Cultures of North America. 2014. (PRIME Ser.). (J). (gr. 6-8). pap. *(978-1-4509-9483-5(0))* Benchmark Education Co.
—The Geography of North & South America. 2014. (PRIME Ser.). (J). (gr. 6-8). pap. *(978-1-4509-9505-4(5))* Benchmark Education Co.
Catt, Thessaly. Migrating with the Caribou. 2011. (Animal Journeys Ser.). (Illus.). 24p. (YA). (gr. 1-4). 22.60 *(978-1-4488-2541-7(5))* Rosen Publishing Group, Inc., The.
Dahl, Michael. Wolves, 1 vol. 2012. (North American Animals Ser.). (ENG.). 24p. (gr. k-1). lib. bdg. 26.65 *(978-1-4296-7701-1(5),* Pebble Plus) Capstone Press of Coughlan Cos.
Donaldson, Madeline. North America. 2005. (Pull Ahead Bks.). (Illus.). 32p. (J). (gr. k-3). lib. bdg. 22.60 *(978-0-8225-4722-8(8))* Lerner Publishing Group.
Donaldson, Madeline & National Geographic Learning Staff. North America. 2012. (ENG., Illus.). 32p. (C). (gr. k-3). pap. 12.95 *(978-0-8225-2494-6(5))* National Geographic School Publishing, Inc.
Dutcher, Jim & Dutcher, Jamie. Living with Wolves! True Stories of Adventures with Animals. 2016. (NGK Chapters Ser.). (ENG., Illus.). 112p. (J). (gr. 2-5). pap. 5.99 *(978-1-4263-2563-2(0),* National Geographic Children's Bks.) National Geographic Society.
Encyclopaedia Britannica, Inc. Staff, compiled by. My First Britannica: The Americas. 2008. (gr. 7-12). *(978-1-59339-409-7(8))* Encyclopaedia Britannica, Inc.
Encyclopaedia Britannica Publishers, Inc. Staff. Views of the Americas. 2003. (Britannica Learning Library). (Illus.). 14.95 *(978-1-59339-012-9(2))* Encyclopaedia Britannica, Inc.
Esbensen, Barbara Juster. Playful Slider: The North American River Otter. Brown, Mary Barrett, illus. 2011. (Fesler-Lampert Minnesota Heritage Ser.). (ENG.). 32p. pap. 11.95 *(978-0-8166-7765-8(4))* Univ. of Minnesota Pr.
Gamble, Adam. Good Night Lake. Kelly, Cooper, illus. 2008. (Good Night Our World Ser.). (ENG.). 28p. (J). (gr. k — 1). bds. 9.95 *(978-1-60219-028-3(3))* Good Night Bks.
Gardner, Jane P. Timber & Forest Products, Vol. 12. 2015. (North American Natural Resources Ser.). (Illus.). 64p. (J). (gr. 7). 23.95 *(978-1-4222-3389-4(8))* Mason Crest.
Hansen, Grace. Animals of North America. 2016. (Animals of North America Ser.: 6). (ENG.). 24p. (J). (gr. k-2). lib. bdg. 171.00 *(978-1-68080-106-4(6))* ABDO Publishing Co.
Hovanec, Erin M. An Online Visit to North America. 2009. (Internet Field Trips Ser.). 24p. (gr. 3-3). 45.00 *(978-1-61513-606-3(1),* PowerKids Pr.) Rosen Publishing Group, Inc., The.
Johnson, Jinny. Brown Bear. 2014. (North American Mammals Ser.). 24p. (gr. 2-5). 28.50 *(978-1-62588-032-1(4))* Black Rabbit Bks.
King, Colin, illus. Jigsaw Atlas of North America. 2006. (Usborne Jigsaw Bks.). 14p. (J). (gr. k-3). bds. 14.99 *(978-0-7945-1242-2(9),* Usborne) EDC Publishing.
Koponen, Libby. North America. 2009. (True Bks.). (ENG., Illus.). 48p. (J). pap. 6.95 *(978-0-531-21830-3(9),* Children's Pr.) Scholastic Library Publishing.
Kuskowski, Alex. Super Simple Native American Art: Fun & Easy Art from Around the World, 1 vol. 2012. (ENG.). 32p. 27.07 *(978-1-61783-214-7(6),* Super SandCastle) ABDO Publishing Co.
Lindeen, Mary. Welcome to North America, 1 vol. 2011. (Wonder Readers Fluent Level Ser.). (ENG.). 32p. (gr. -1-2). pap. 5.99 *(978-1-4296-7974-9(3),* Wonder Readers) Capstone Press of Coughlan Cos.
Mattern, Joanne, et al. North American Animals. 2012. (North American Animals Ser.). (ENG.). 24p. (gr. k-1). pap. 250.20 *(978-1-4296-8363-0(5),* Pebble Plus) Capstone Press of Coughlan Cos.
Max And Steven Oscherwitz. Gilbert's Adventure. 2008. 56p. pap. 27.99 *(978-1-4257-4577-6(6))* Xlibris Corp.
McAneney, Caitlin. North American Birds: Represent & Solve Problems Involving Multiplication. 2014. (Rosen Common Core Math Readers Ser.). (Illus.). 24p. (J). (gr. 3-4). (ENG.). pap. 8.25 *(978-1-4777-4971-5(3));* lib. bdg. 23.60 *(978-1-4777-6445-9(3))* Rosen Publishing Group, Inc., The. (PowerKids Pr.).
McNeil, Niki, et al. North America. 2007. (In the Hands of a Child: Project Pack Continent Study Ser.). (Illus.). 104p. spiral bd. 24.00 *(978-1-60308-076-7(7))* In the Hands of a Child.
Migrating with the Caribou. 2011. (Animal Journeys Ser.). (Illus.). 24p. (J). pap. 8.25 *(978-1-4488-2666-7(7),* PowerKids Pr.) Rosen Publishing Group, Inc., The.
Minnesota Historical Society & Mille Lacs Indian Museum. Ojibwe Shoulder Bag Kit. 2013. (ENG., Illus.). 24p. (J). (gr. 1-6). 18.95 *(978-0-87351-825-3(X))* Minnesota Historical Society Pr.
Nagle, Garrett. North America. 2005. (Continents of the World Ser.). 64p. (gr. 5-12). pap. 14.05 *(978-0-8368-5921-8(9));* (Illus.). lib. bdg. 34.00 *(978-0-8368-5914-0(6))* Stevens, Gareth Publishing LLLP. (Gareth Stevens Secondary Library).
Nelson, Maria. The Pan-American Highway. 2016. (Road Trip Ser.). (Illus.). 24p. (J). (gr. 3-2). 22.60 *(978-1-4824-4669-2(3))* Stevens, Gareth Publishing LLLP.
North American Historical Atlases - Group 2, 5 bks., Set. 135.36 *(978-0-7614-1344-8(8),* Benchmark Bks.) Marshall Cavendish Corp.
Parker, Steve. Coal, Vol. 12. 2015. (North American Natural Resources Ser.). 64p. (J). (gr. 7). 23.95 *(978-1-4222-3379-5(0))* Mason Crest.
Pero, Denis & Auzou Publishing Staff. My Book of Animals: A Walk Through the National Parks. 2013. (ENG., Illus.). 96p. (J). (gr. 2). 16.95 *(978-2-7338-2315-6(9))* Auzou, Philippe Editions FRA. Dist: Consortium Bk. Sales & Distribution.
Potts, Steve, et al. North American Animals. 2012. (North American Animals Ser.). (ENG.). 24p. (gr. k-1). pap. 41.70 *(978-1-4296-8362-3(7));* lib. bdg. 159.90 *(978-1-4296-8142-1(X))* Capstone Press of Coughlan Cos. (Pebble Plus).
Ring, Susan. We Live in North America. 2005. (Yellow Umbrella Fluent Level Ser.). (ENG.). 16p. (gr. k-1). pap. 35.70 *(978-0-7368-5311-8(1),* Yellow Umbrella Bks.) Capstone Press of Coughlan Cos.
Sayre, April Pulley. Welcome to North America! 2003. 32p. (J). (gr. 2-5). pap. 7.95 *(978-0-7613-1988-7(3));* (Illus.). lib. bdg. 21.90 *(978-0-7613-2150-7(0))* Lerner Publishing Group. (Millbrook Pr.).
Strauss, Bob. A Field Guide to Dinosaurs of North America: And Prehistoric Megafauna. 2015. (ENG., Illus.). 224p. (YA). (gr. 8-17). pap. 22.95 *(978-1-4930-0925-1(7))* Globe Pequot Pr., The.
Tarbox, A. D. A Prairie Food Chain: Nature's Bounty. 2015. (Illus.). 80p. (J). *(978-1-60818-542-9(7),* Creative Education) Creative Co., The.
Vierow, Wendy. North America. (Atlas of the Seven Continents Ser.). 24p. 2009. (gr. 3-3). 42.50 *(978-1-61511-481-8(5))* 2004. (Illus.). (J). lib. bdg. 22.60 *(978-0-8239-6692-9(5))* Rosen Publishing Group, Inc., The. (PowerKids Pr.).
Wallace, Marianne D. America's Forests: Guide to Plants & Animals. 2009. (America's Ecosystems Ser.). (ENG.). 48p. (J). (gr. 1-5). pap. 11.95 *(978-1-55591-595-7(7))* Fulcrum Publishing.
Wojahn, Rebecca Hogue & Wojahn, Donald. A Desert Food Chain: A Who-Eats-What Adventure in North America. 2009. (Follow That Food Chain Ser.). (ENG.). 64p. (gr. 3-5). 30.60 *(978-0-8225-7501-6(9))* Lerner Publishing Group.
—A Temperate Forest Food Chain: A Who-Eats-What Adventure in North America. 2009. (Follow That Food Chain Ser.). (ENG., Illus.). 64p. (J). (gr. 3-5). 30.60 *(978-0-8225-7496-5(9))* Lerner Publishing Group.
Wolny, Philip. Muslims Around the World Today. 2009. (Understanding Islam Ser.). 64p. (gr. 6-6). 58.50 *(978-1-60854-626-8(8))* Rosen Publishing Group, Inc., The.
Woods, Michael & Woods, Mary B. Seven Natural Wonders of North America. 2009. (Seven Wonders Ser.). (ENG., Illus.). 80p. (gr. 5-8). lib. bdg. 33.26 *(978-0-8225-9069-9(7))* Lerner Publishing Group.

NORTH AMERICA—ANTIQUITIES

Harrison, David L. Mammoth Bones & Broken Stones: The Mystery of North America's First People. Hilliard, Richard, illus. 2010. (ENG.). 48p. (J). (gr. 4-6). 18.95 *(978-1-59078-561-4(4))* Boyds Mills Pr.
Woods, Mary B. & Woods, Michael. Seven Wonders of Ancient North America. 2008. (Seven Wonders Ser.). (ENG., Illus.). 80p. (gr. 5-8). lib. bdg. 33.26 *(978-0-8225-7572-6(8))* Lerner Publishing Group.

NORTH AMERICA—DISCOVERY AND EXPLORATION

see America—Discovery and Exploration

NORTH AMERICA—HISTORY

Aloian, Molly & Kalman, Bobbie. Explora America del Norte. 2007. (Explora Los Continentes Ser.). (SPA & ENG., Illus.). 32p. (J). (gr. 4-7). pap. *(978-0-7787-8300-8(6))* Crabtree Publishing Co.
Banting, Erinn. North America. 2012. (J). pap. 13.95 *(978-1-61913-452-2(7));* 28.55 *(978-1-61913-451-5(9))* Weigl Pubs., Inc.
Benchmark Education Company, LLC Staff, compiled by. Historical Communities: Theme Set. 2006. (J). 121.00 *(978-1-4108-7097-1(9))* Benchmark Education Co.
Boyd, Judy. North America, Vol. 10. 2016. (Social Progress & Sustainability Ser.). (Illus.). 80p. (J). (gr. 7). 24.95 *(978-1-4222-3498-3(3))* Mason Crest.
Coletti, Sharon. Everything You Need to Teach North America. 2005. (YA). ring bd. 149.95 *(978-1-933558-05-9(9))* InspirEd Educators.
Daly, Ruth. North America. 2014. (J). *(978-1-4896-0954-0(7))* Weigl Pubs., Inc.
Desaulniers, Kristi. Northern America. Gritzner, Charles F., ed. 2006. (Modern World Cultures Ser.). (Illus.). 128p. (gr. 6-12). lib. bdg. 30.00 *(978-0-7910-8141-9(9),* Chelsea Hse.) Facts On File, Inc.
Exploring North America, 1800-1900, Revised Edition. 2nd rev. ed. 2009. (Discovery & Exploration Ser.). (Illus.). 152p. (YA). (gr. 7-12). 35.00 *(978-1-60413-194-9(2))* Facts On File, Inc.
Fox, Mary Virginia. North America. 2016. (Continents Ser.). (ENG.). 32p. pap. 8.29 *(978-1-4846-3821-7(2),* Heinemann First Library) Heinemann-Raintree.
Guiberson, Brenda Z. Mummy Mysteries: Tales from North America. Guiberson, Brenda Z., illus. 2013. (My Readers Ser.). (ENG., Illus.). 48p. (J). (gr. 1-3). pap. 3.99 *(978-1-250-01047-6(0),* 9781250010476) Square Fish.
Hall, Derek. North America. 2009. (FAYFT: Countries Ser.). (Illus.). 64p. (gr. 4-10). lib. bdg. 39.95 *(978-1-933834-07-8(2))* Brown Bear Bks.
Hirsch, Rebecca E. North America. 2012. (Rookie Read-About(tm) Geography — Continents Ser.). (ENG.). 32p. (J). lib. bdg. 25.00 *(978-0-531-28980-8(X));* (Illus.). pap. 5.95 *(978-0-531-29280-8(0))* Scholastic Library Publishing.
In North & South America. (J). (gr. 5). 3.80 *(978-0-8374-1454-6(7),* 405) Weekly Reader Corp.
Jankowski, Emily. Mapping North America. 2013. 24p. (J). (gr. 2-5). 22.60 *(978-1-4339-9114-1(4));* pap. 48.90 *(978-1-4339-9116-5(0));* (ENG., Illus.). pap. 8.15 *(978-1-4339-9115-8(2))* Stevens, Gareth Publishing LLLP.
Johnston, Lissa. A Brief Political & Geographic History of North America: Where Are... New France, New Netherland, & New Sweden. 2007. (Places in Time Ser.). (Illus.). 112p. (YA). (gr. 5-9). lib. bdg. 37.10 *(978-1-58415-627-7(9))* Mitchell Lane Pubs., Inc.
Kalman, Bobbie. L'Amérique du Nord. 2012. (FRE.). 32p. (J). pap. 9.95 *(978-2-89579-460-8(X))* Bayard Canada CAN. Dist: Crabtree Publishing Co.
Kjelle, Marylou Morano. Pre-Columbian America. 2009. (How'd They Do That? Ser.). (Illus.). 64p. (J). (gr. 4-8). lib. bdg. 33.95 *(978-1-58415-826-4(3))* Mitchell Lane Pubs., Inc.
Koenig, Emily C. North America, 1 vol. 2013. (Continents Ser.). (ENG.). 48p. (J). (gr. 3-6). lib. bdg. 32.79 *(978-1-61783-933-7(7))* ABDO Publishing Co.
Koponen, Libby. North America. 2008. (True Book(tm), A — Continents Ser.). (ENG., Illus.). 48p. (J). (gr. 2-5). 31.00 *(978-0-531-16868-4(9))* Scholastic Library Publishing.
Lindeen, Mary. Welcome to North America, 1 vol. (Wonder Readers: Social Studies). (ENG.). (gr. -1-2). 2012. 20p. lib. bdg. 22.65 *(978-1-4296-9617-3(6))* 2011. 16p. pap. 35.94 *(978-1-4296-8204-6(3))* Capstone Press of Coughlan Cos. (Wonder Readers).
Looye, Juliette, text. I Live on the Earth. 2004. (Illus.). 16p. (J). pap. *(978-0-7367-1931-5(8))* Zaner-Bloser, Inc.
Lucas, Bruce. North America on the Map. 2013. (InfoMax Readers Ser.). (ENG.). 24p. (J). (gr. 2-3). pap. 49.50 *(978-1-4777-2432-3(X));* (Illus.). pap. 8.25 *(978-1-4777-2431-6(1))* Rosen Publishing Group, Inc., The. (Rosen Classroom).
MacLeod, Elizabeth. Secrets Underground: North America's Buried Past. 2014. (ENG., Illus.). 96p. (YA). (gr. 5-12). 24.95 *(978-1-55451-631-5(5),* 9781554516315); pap. 14.95 *(978-1-55451-630-8(7),* 9781554516308) Annick Pr., Ltd. CAN. Dist: Publishers Group West (PGW).
McClish, Bruce. New World Continents & Land Bridges: North & South America. 2016. (Continents Ser.). (ENG.). 32p. (gr. 4-6). pap. 8.99 *(978-1-4846-3639-8(2),* NA-h) Heinemann-Raintree.
North America: Regions of the World. 2003. spiral bd. 16.95 *(978-1-56004-160-3(9))* Social Studies Schl. Service.
North American Historical Atlases - Group 2, 5 bks., Set. 135.36 *(978-0-7614-1344-8(8),* Benchmark Bks.) Marshall Cavendish Corp.
Oachs, Emily Rose. North America. (North America Ser.). 24p. (J). (gr. k-3). 2017. pap. 6.99 ***(978-1-61891-259-6(3))*** 2016. (ENG., Illus.). lib. bdg. 25.95 *(978-1-62617-328-6(1))* Bellwether Media. (Blastoff! Readers).
O'Brien, Cynthia. Explore with Sieur de la Salle. 2014. (ENG., Illus.). 32p. (J). *(978-0-7787-1430-9(6))* Crabtree Publishing Co.
Oxlade, Chris. Introducing North America, 1 vol. 2013. (Introducing Continents Ser.). (ENG.). 32p. (gr. 1-3). 27.32 *(978-1-4329-8043-6(2));* pap. 8.95 *(978-1-4329-8051-1(3))* Heinemann-Raintree. (Heinemann First Library).
Petersen, Christine. Learning about North America. 2015. (ENG., Illus.). 40p. (J). (gr. 3-5). 29.32 *(978-1-4677-8020-9(0),* Lerner Pubns.) Lerner Publishing Group.

Peterson, Cris. Birchbark Brigade: A Fur Trade History. 2009. (ENG.). 136p. (J). (gr. 4-18). 18.95 *(978-1-59078-426-6(X),* Calkins Creek) Boyds Mills Pr.

Phelps, Bonnie. Map Facts: North America. 2013. (Rosen Readers Ser.). (ENG.). 24p. (J). (gr. 2-3). pap. 49.50 *(978-1-4777-2282-4(3))*; pap. 8.25 *(978-1-4777-2281-7(5))* Rosen Publishing Group, Inc., The. (Rosen Classroom).

Rockett, Paul. Mapping North America. 2016. (Illus.). 32p. (J). *(978-0-7787-2616-6(9))* Crabtree Publishing Co.

Roumanis, Alexis. North America. 2014. (Illus.). 24p. (J). *(978-1-4896-3042-1(2))* Weigl Pubs., Inc.

Stanley, George Edward. The European Settlement of North America (1492-1754) 2005. (Primary Source History of the United States Ser.). (Illus.). 48p. (gr. 5-12). pap. 14.05 *(978-0-8368-5833-4(6))*; lib. bdg. 31.00 *(978-0-8368-5824-2(7))* Stevens, Gareth Publishing LLLP. (Gareth Stevens Secondary Library).

Steffof, Rebecca. Cities & Towns. 2007. (ENG., Illus.). 96p. (C). (gr. 6-18). lib. bdg. 140.00 *(978-0-7656-8109-6(9),* Y181735) Routledge.

Weird America: Set 2. 2016. (Weird America Ser.). 00032p. (J). pap. 63.00 ***(978-1-4824-5835-0(7))*** Stevens, Gareth Publishing LLLP.

Wingate, Philippa & Reid, Struan. Who Were the First North Americans? 2004. (Starting Point History Ser.). (Illus.). 32p. (J). pap. 4.99 *(978-0-7945-0397-0(7),* Usborne); lib. bdg. 12.95 *(978-1-58086-512-8(7))* EDC Publishing.

NORTH AMERICAN INDIANS

see Indians of North America

NORTH ATLANTIC TREATY ORGANIZATION

Richardson, Erik. NATO, the Warsaw Pact, & the Iron Curtain. 2017. (J). ***(978-1-5026-2727-8(2))*** Cavendish Square Publishing.

NORTH CAROLINA

Alex, Nan. North Carolina. 2008. (From Sea to Shining Sea, Second Ser.). (ENG., Illus.). 80p. (J). (gr. 3-5). pap. 7.95 *(978-0-531-18808-8(6),* Children's Pr.) Scholastic Library Publishing.

Alter, Judy. North Carolina: A MyReportLinks. Com Book. 2003. (States Ser.). (Illus.). 48p. (J). (gr. 4-10). lib. bdg. 25.26 *(978-0-7660-5135-5(8),* MyReportLinks.com Bks.) Enslow Pubs., Inc.

Bird, Janice W. Freddy in the City: Center City Sites. Bird, Richard E., photos by. Date not set. (Illus.). 32p. (J). (gr. 2-5). pap. 5.95 *(978-0-9710071-1-6(X))* JFW, Ltd.

Browning, Wilt, ed. Nothing Finer: North Carolina's Sports History & the People Who Made It. 2014. 416p. pap. 35.00 *(978-1-61163-608-6(6))* Carolina Academic Pr.

Crane, Carol. T Is for Tar Heel: A North Carolina Alphabet. Palmer, Gary, illus. 2003. (Discover America State by State Ser.). (ENG.). 40p. (J). 17.95 *(978-1-58536-082-6(1))* Sleeping Bear Pr.

—Wright Numbers: A North Carolina Number Book. Palmer, Gary, illus. 2005. (Count Your Way Across the USA Ser.). (ENG.). 40p. (J). (gr. k-5). 16.95 *(978-1-58536-196-0(8))* Sleeping Bear Pr.

Galiano, Dean. North Carolina. 2009. (Bilingual Library of the United States of America Ser.). (ENG & SPA.). 32p. (gr. 2-2). 47.90 *(978-1-60853-377-0(8),* Editorial Buenas Letras) Rosen Publishing Group, Inc., The.

—North Carolina/Carolina del Norte. Brusca, Maria Cristina, tr. from ENG. 2006. (Bilingual Library of the United States of America Ser.: Set 2). (ENG & SPA., Illus.). 32p. (J). (gr. 3-6). lib. bdg. 25.25 *(978-1-4042-3098-9(X))* Rosen Publishing Group, Inc., The.

George, Pamela & Brown, Walter M. The North Carolina Alphabet. 2005. 60p. (J). *(978-0-932112-50-7(1))* Carolina Wren Pr.

Greene, Melanie W., et al. Goodnight, Boone. Marlowe, Susan B., illus. 2012. (J). *(978-1-933251-80-6(8))* Parkway Pubs., Inc.

Heinrichs, Ann. North Carolina. 144p. (J). 2014. (America the Beautiful Ser.: 3). (ENG.). lib. bdg. 40.00 *(978-0-531-24896-6(8))* 2011. (America the Beautiful, Third Ser.). pap. 12.95 *(978-0-531-22917-0(3),* Children's Pr.) Scholastic Library Publishing.

Hyman, Teresa L. North Carolina. 2003. (Seeds of a Nation Ser.). (Illus.). 48p. (J). 23.70 *(978-0-7377-1420-3(4))* Cengage Gale.

Jerome, Kate Boehm. North Carolina: What's So Great about This State? 2011. (Arcadia Kids Ser.). (ENG.). 48p. (J). pap. 7.99 *(978-1-58973-017-5(8))* Arcadia Publishing.

Maine, Tyler. North Carolina. 2016. (States Ser.). (ENG., Illus.). 32p. (gr. 3-4). lib. bdg. 27.32 *(978-1-5157-0420-1(3))* Next Page Pr., The.

Marsh, Carole. My First Book about North Carolina. 2004. (North Carolina Experience! Ser.). 32p. (J). (gr. k-4). pap. 7.95 *(978-0-7933-9518-7(6))* Gallopade International.

—The Nifty North Carolina Coloring Book. 2004. (North Carolina Experience! Ser.). (Illus.). 32p. (J). (gr. k-2). pap. 3.95 *(978-0-7933-9472-2(4))* Gallopade International.

—North Carolina Current Events Projects: 30 Cool, Activities, Crafts, Experiments & More for Kids to Do to Learn about Your State! 2003. (North Carolina Experience Ser.). 32p. (gr. k-8). pap. 5.95 *(978-0-635-02052-9(1),* Marsh, Carole Bks.) Gallopade International.

—The North Carolina Experience Pocket Guide. 2004. (North Carolina Experience! Ser.). (Illus.). 96p. (J). (gr. 3-8). pap. 6.95 *(978-0-7933-9452-4(X))* Gallopade International.

—North Carolina Geography Projects: 30 Cool, Activities, Crafts, Experiments & More for Kids to Do to Learn about Your State! 2003. (North Carolina Experience Ser.). 32p. (gr. k-5). pap. 5.95 *(978-0-635-01852-6(7),* Marsh, Carole Bks.) Gallopade International.

—North Carolina Government Projects: 30 Cool, Activities, Crafts, Experiments & More for Kids to Do to Learn about Your State! 2003. (North Carolina Experience Ser.). 32p. (gr. k-5). pap. 5.95 *(978-0-635-01952-3(3),* Marsh, Carole Bks.) Gallopade International.

—North Carolina Jeopardy! Answers & Questions about Our State! 2004. (North Carolina Experience! Ser.). (Illus.). 32p. (J). (gr. 3-8). pap. 7.95 *(978-0-7933-9519-4(4))* Gallopade International.

—North Carolina "Jography" A Fun Run Through the Tarheel State! 2004. (North Carolina Experience! Ser.). (Illus.). 32p. (J). (gr. 3-8). pap. 7.95 *(978-0-7933-9520-0(8))* Gallopade International.

—North Carolina People Projects: 30 Cool, Activities, Crafts, Experiments & More for Kids to Do to Learn about Your State! 2003. (North Carolina Experience Ser.). 32p. (gr. k-5). pap. 5.95 *(978-0-635-02002-4(5),* Marsh, Carole Bks.) Gallopade International.

—North Carolina Symbols & Facts Projects: 30 Cool, Activities, Crafts, Experiments & More for Kids to Do to Learn about Your State! 2003. (North Carolina Experience Ser.). 32p. (gr. k-8). pap. 5.95 *(978-0-635-01902-8(7),* Marsh, Carole Bks.) Gallopade International.

—North Carolina's Big Activity Book. 2004. (North Carolina Experience! Ser.). (Illus.). 96p. (J). (gr. 2-6). pap. 9.95 *(978-0-7933-9462-3(7))* Gallopade International.

McNeil, Niki, et al. HOCPP 1080 North Carolina. 2006. spiral bd. 24.00 *(978-1-60308-080-4(5))* In the Hands of a Child.

Meyer, John H. Wilmington Today: A Guide to Cape Fear Leisure. 2003. Orig. Title: A Guide to Cape Fear Leisure. (Illus.). 60p. 13.95 *(978-0-9729573-0-4(8))* Wilmington Today LLC.

Murray, Julie. North Carolina. 1 vol. 2006. (Buddy Book Ser.). (ENG., Illus.). 32p. (gr. 2-4). 27.07 *(978-1-59197-692-9(8),* Buddy Bks.) ABDO Publishing Co.

Peters, S. True. How to Draw North Carolina's Sights & Symbols. 2009. (Kid's Guide to Drawing America Ser.). 32p. (gr. k-k). 50.50 *(978-1-61511-084-1(4),* PowerKids Pr.) Rosen Publishing Group, Inc., The.

Schulz, Andrea. North Carolina. (J). 2012. lib. bdg. 25.26 *(978-0-7613-4549-7(3),* Lerner Pubns.) 2nd exp. rev. ed. 2003. (Illus.). 84p. (gr. 3-6). pap. 6.95 *(978-0-8225-4137-0(8))* Lerner Publishing Group.

Sermons, Faye. My Granma Lives at the Airport. 2012. 20p. pap. 12.00 *(978-1-4490-1893-1(9))* AuthorHouse.

Shirley, David & Hart, Joyce. North Carolina. 2nd rev. ed. 2009. (Celebrate the States 10 Ser.). 144p. (gr. 6). 42.79 *(978-0-7614-4729-0(6))* Marshall Cavendish Corp.

Sullivan, E. J. N Is for North Carolina. Eldredge, Ernie, illus. 2007. (State Alphabet Bks.). 20p. *(978-1-58173-625-0(8))* Sweetwater Pr.

NORTH CAROLINA—FICTION

Anybody Shining. 2014. (ENG., Illus.). 240p. (J). (gr. 5-7). 16.99 *(978-1-4424-3292-5(6),* Atheneum Bks. for Young Readers) Simon & Schuster Children's Publishing.

Asim, Jabari. The Road to Freedom: A Story of the Reconstruction. 2004. 131p. (J). lib. bdg. 16.92 *(978-1-4242-0765-7(7))* Fitzgerald Bks.

Averette, Sonya M. Aunt Ruby's Kisses. 1 vol. Proulx, Denis, illus. 2009. 35p. pap. 24.95 *(978-1-60749-045-6(5))* America Star Bks.

Baker, Mary. Amy's Apple Butter Granny. 2009. 48p. pap. 16.95 *(978-1-61582-032-0(9))* America Star Bks.

Bare, Bart. Girl. 2010. 188p. (YA). pap. 11.95 *(978-0-9825396-4-4(9))* Canterbury Hse. Publishing, Ltd.

Beatty, Robert. Serafina & the Black Cloak. (Serafina Ser.). (ENG.). (J). (gr. 3-7). 2016. 320p. pap. 7.99 *(978-1-4847-1187-3(4))* 2015. 304p. 16.99 *(978-1-4847-0901-6(2))* Hyperion Bks. for Children.

—Serafina & the Black Cloak. 2016. (J). lib. bdg. 18.40 *(978-0-606-38336-3(0))* Turtleback Bks.

—Serafina & the Splintered Heart. 2017. (Serafina Ser.: bk.3). (ENG.). 368p. (J). (gr. 3-7). 16.99 ***(978-1-4847-7504-2(X))*** Hyperion Bks. for Children.

Beatty, Robert. Serafina & the Twisted Staff. (Serafina Ser.). (ENG.). (J). (gr. 3-7). 2017. 400p. pap. 7.99 ***(978-1-4847-7806-7(5))*** 2016. 384p. 16.99 *(978-1-4847-7503-5(1))* Hyperion Bks. for Children.

—Serafina & the Twisted Staff. 2017. (J). lib. bdg. 18.40 ***(978-0-606-39977-7(1))*** Turtleback Bks.

Bennett, Amy Culbertson. The Little Donkey & the Shadow of the Cross. 2008. 15p. pap. 24.95 *(978-1-60563-545-3(6))* America Star Bks.

Bird, Janie. Freddy in the City: Memorable Monday. Treffeisen, Brian, photos by. 2nd rev. ed. 2005.Tr. of Freddy en la Ciudad un Lunes Memorble. (SPA., Illus.). 32p. (J). 10.95 *(978-1-59494-005-7(3))* CPCC Pr.

Bond, Gwenda. Strange Alchemy. 2017. (ENG.). 336p. (gr. 9-12). 17.95 ***(978-1-63079-076-9(1))*** Switch Pr.

Bradfield, Carl. The Sullivans of Little Horsepen Creek: A Tale of Colonial North Carolina's Regulator Era, Circa: 1760s. (Illus.). 350p. (YA). (gr. 8-12). *(978-0-9632319-2-5(8))* ASDA Publishing, Inc.

Burnell, Pamela H. The Light Keeper: An Epps Kids Mystery. 2008. 76p. pap. 19.95 *(978-1-60474-847-5(8))* America Star Bks.

Calonita, Jen. Belles. 2012. (Belles Ser.: 1). (ENG.). 384p. (YA). (gr. 7-17). pap. 8.99 *(978-0-316-09112-1(X),* Poppy) Little, Brown Bks. for Young Readers.

—The Grass Is Always Greener. 2014. (Belles Ser.: 3). (ENG.). 320p. (YA). (gr. 7-17). pap. 10.00 *(978-0-316-09109-1(X),* Poppy) Little, Brown Bks. for Young Readers.

Carmichael, Clay. Brother, Brother. 2013. (ENG.). 320p. (YA). (gr. 7). 17.99 *(978-1-59643-743-2(X))* Roaring Brook Pr.

Carris, Joan D. A Ghost of a Chance. 2003. (Legends of the Carolinas Ser.). 155p. (J). 8.95 *(978-1-928556-40-4(X))* Coastal Carolina Pr.

Church, Bryan. The Dreamcatcher Bowl. 2009. 54p. pap. 9.99 *(978-0-557-07517-1(3))* Lulu Pr., Inc.

Collins, Yozette Yogi & Jennings, Marlis. Goodnight, Boone. Ziolkowski, Ania, illus. 2012. 24p. pap. 11.95 *(978-1-937376-18-5(4))* All Star Pr.

Doherty, Patrick. Waves of Grace. Ordaz, Frank, illus. 2007. 160p. (J). (gr. 9-12). pap. 11.95 *(978-0-9744446-6-6(9))* All About Kids Publishing.

Dowell, Frances O'Roark. Anybody Shining. Wachter, Jill, photos by. 2015. (ENG., Illus.). 256p. (J). (gr. 5-7). pap. 7.99 *(978-1-4424-3293-2(4),* Atheneum Bks. for Young Readers) Simon & Schuster Children's Publishing.

—Anybody Shining. 2015. lib. bdg. 18.40 *(978-0-606-37849-9(9))* Turtleback Bks.

—Ten Miles Past Normal. (ENG., 224p. (YA). (gr. 7). 2012. Illus.). pap. 9.99 *(978-1-4169-9586-9(2))* 2011. 16.99 *(978-1-4169-9585-2(4))* Simon & Schuster Children's Publishing. (Atheneum Bks. for Young Readers).

Draper, Sharon M. Stella by Starlight. (ENG., Illus.). (J). (gr. 4-8). 2016. 352p. pap. 8.99 *(978-1-4424-9498-5(0))* 2015. 336p. 17.99 *(978-1-4424-9497-8(2),* Atheneum Bks. for Young Readers) Simon & Schuster Children's Publishing.

—Stella by Starlight. 2016. lib. bdg. 18.40 *(978-0-606-38255-7(0))* Turtleback Bks.

Edgerton, Martha. Civility Matters: Anna Moves to the Big City. 2011. 38p. pap. 16.95 *(978-1-4626-4211-3(X))* America Star Bks.

Edward, J. P. Truckin with Rocky. 1 vol. 2010. 22p. 24.95 *(978-1-4512-9082-0(9))* PublishAmerica, Inc.

Ernst, Kathleen. Highland Fling. 2006. (ENG.). 192p. (J). (gr. 3-8). 15.95 *(978-0-8126-2742-8(3))* Cricket Bks.

Flowers, Fran. Rosita: The Journey Home. 2012. 108p. (gr. 4-6). 28.95 *(978-1-4497-3505-0(3))*; pap. 11.95 *(978-1-4497-3503-6(7))* Author Solutions, Inc. (WestBow Pr.).

Furman, Ben. Sam's Quest. 2008. 240p. pap. 8.95 *(978-0-9778731-4-2(5))* Black Hawk Pr., Inc., The.

—Sam's Quest for the Crimson Crystal. 2007. 189p. (J). per. 8.95 *(978-0-9778731-8-0(8))* Black Hawk Pr., Inc., The.

Gamble, Adam. Good Night North Carolina. Rosen, Anne, illus. 2009. (Good Night Our World Ser.). (ENG.). 20p. (J). (gr. k — 1). bds. 9.95 *(978-1-60219-033-7(X))* Good Night Bks.

Garza, Amy Ammons. Sterlen: And a Mosaic of Mountain Women. Ammons, David F. & Ammons, Sherilyn, eds. Cain, Doreyl Ammons, illus. 2005. 308p. (YA). per. 16.00 *(978-0-9753023-2-3(9),* Catch the Spirit of Appalachia) Ammons Communications, Ltd.

Griffin, Kitty. The Ride: The Legend of Betsy Dowdy. Priceman, Marjorie, illus. 2010. (ENG.). 40p. (J). (gr. -1-3). 16.99 *(978-1-4169-2816-4(2),* Atheneum Bks. for Young Readers) Simon & Schuster Children's Publishing.

Griffith, Gretchen. When Christmas Feels Like Home. Farias, Carolina, illus. 2013. (ENG.). 32p. (J). (gr. -1-3). 16.99 *(978-0-8075-8872-7(5))* Whitman, Albert & Co.

Guo, Amy. Vhonk. 2012. 588p. pap. 34.95 *(978-1-4626-9981-0(2))* America Star Bks.

Gutenberg, S. R. Abby Longbotham & the Quilt. 2008. 28p. pap. 24.95 *(978-1-4241-9428-5(8))* America Star Bks.

Gutman, Dan. Race for the Sky: The Kitty Hawk Diaries of Johnny Moore. 2003. (ENG., Illus.). 192p. (J). (gr. 5-9). 19.99 *(978-0-689-84554-3(5),* Simon & Schuster Bks. For Young Readers) Simon & Schuster Bks. For Young Readers.

Haddix, Margaret Peterson. Sabotaged. (Missing Ser.: 3). (ENG.). (J). (gr. 3-7). 2011. 400p. pap. 8.99 *(978-1-4169-5425-5(2))* 2010. 384p. 17.99 *(978-1-4169-5424-8(4))* Simon & Schuster Bks. For Young Readers. (Simon & Schuster Bks. For Young Readers).

Hall, Terri L. Denny & Denise: A Story of Two Ducks: Introducing Pretty Boy & Fella. 1 vol. Hall, Terri L. & Babeaux, Dennis, photos by. 2009. (Illus.). 42p. pap. 24.95 *(978-1-60749-609-0(7))* America Star Bks.

Hall, Tessa Emily. Purple Moon. 2013. 328p. pap. 13.95 *(978-1-938499-87-6(5))* Lighthouse Publishing of the Carolinas.

Harvell, Richard Brian. Adventures of the Book Battling Kids: The Carson Corners Chronicles. 2006. (J). per. 5.99 *(978-0-9769044-7-2(0))* Waterwood Publishing Group.

Harvey, Jeanne Walker. My Hands Sing the Blues: Romare Bearden's Childhood Journey. 0 vols. Zunon, Elizabeth, illus. 2011. (ENG.). 40p. (J). (gr. k-3). 17.99 *(978-0-7614-5810-4(7),* 9780761458104, Amazon Children's Publishing) Amazon Publishing.

Hemingway, Edith M. Road to Tater Hill. 2011. (ENG.). 224p. (J). (gr. 3-7). 7.99 *(978-0-375-84544-4(5),* Yearling) Random Hse. Children's Bks.

Hostetter, Joyce Moyer. Aim. 2016. (Bakers Mountain Stories Ser.). (ENG.). 288p. (J). (gr. 3-7). 17.99 *(978-1-62979-673-4(5),* Calkins Creek) Boyds Mills Pr.

—Blue. 2006. (ENG.). 200p. (J). (gr. 5). 16.95 *(978-1-59078-389-4(1),* Calkins Creek) Boyds Mills Pr.

—Comfort. 2011. (ENG.). 312p. (J). (gr. 5-12). pap. 7.95 *(978-1-59078-895-0(8),* Calkins Creek) Boyds Mills Pr.

Hutton, John. Flowers for Mr. President. 2012. (Illus.). (J). *(978-0-9789608-3-4(1))* Salem Academy & College.

Jacobs, Lily. The Littlest Bunny in North Carolina: An Easter Adventure. Dunn, Robert, illus. 2015. (ENG.). 32p. (J). (-3). 9.99 *(978-1-4926-1156-1(5),* Sourcebooks Jabberwocky) Sourcebooks, Inc.

James, Eric. A Halloween Scare in North Carolina. Le Ray, Marina, illus. 2015. (ENG.). 32p. (J). (-5). 9.99 *(978-1-4926-2855-2(7),* 9781492628552, Sourcebooks Jabberwocky) Sourcebooks, Inc.

—A Halloween Scare in the Carolinas. Le Ray, Marina, illus. 2014. (ENG.). 32p. (J). (-5). 9.99 *(978-1-4926-0576-8(X),* 9781492605768, Sourcebooks Jabberwocky) Sourcebooks, Inc.

—Santa's Sleigh Is on Its Way to North Carolina. Dunn, Robert, illus. 2015. (ENG.). 32p. (J). (-2). 12.99 *(978-1-4926-2750-0(X),* Sourcebooks Jabberwocky) Sourcebooks, Inc.

Johnson, Denise Donna. The Veridical Circle. 2011. 78p. pap. 19.95 *(978-1-4626-0472-2(2))* America Star Bks.

Johnson, Harriet McBryde. Accidents of Nature. rev. ed. 2006. (ENG.). 240p. (YA). (gr. 7-12). 19.99 *(978-0-8050-7634-9(4),* Holt, Henry & Co. Bks. For Young Readers) Holt, Henry & Co.

—Accidents of Nature. rev. l.t. ed. 2007. (Thorndike Literacy Bridge Ser.). 273p. (YA). (gr. 7-12). 22.95 *(978-0-7862-9182-3(6))* Thorndike Pr.

Johnson, T. The Beach Club: Magic Beach, Vol. 1. 2012. (ENG.). 131p. pap. 11.95 *(978-1-4327-9316-6(0))* Outskirts Pr., Inc.

Jolley, Dan. Wrapped up in You. Nourigat, Natalie, illus. 2012. (My Boyfriend Is a Monster Ser.: 6). (ENG.). 128p. (YA). (gr. 7-12). pap. 9.95 *(978-0-8225-9425-3(0))*; lib. bdg. 29.27 *(978-0-7613-6856-4(6))* Lerner Publishing Group. (Graphic Universe™).

Klein, Lisa. Cate of the Lost Colony. 2012. (ENG.). 336p. (YA). (gr. 9-12). pap. 9.99 *(978-1-59990-739-0(9),* 9781599907390, Bloomsbury USA Childrens) Bloomsbury Publishing USA.

Krisher, Trudy. Fallout. 2006. (ENG.). 272p. (J). (gr. 3-7). 17.95 *(978-0-8234-2035-3(3))* Holiday Hse., Inc.

Lau, Barbara & Nesbitt, Kris. Sokita Celebrates the New Year: A Cambodian American Holiday. Chatterley, Cedric N., photos by. 2004. (Illus.). 32p. (J). per. 9.95 *(978-0-9747456-0-2(X))* Greensboro Historical Museum, Inc.

Lawrence, Donna. Susie's Tale Hand with Paw We Changed the Law. Coble, Lynn Berner, ed. Cappoen, Jennifer Tipton, illus. 2012. 64p. 24.95 *(978-0-9846724-1-7(9))* Paws and Claws Publishing, LLC.

Lawrenson, Judith. Petunia the Pirate of Port Royal Sound. 2007. (Illus.). (J). 14.95 *(978-0-9767278-0-4(3))* Mrs. L's Reading Room.

LeBrun, Barbie. Porter Horse Finds Blackbeard's Treasure. 2013. (ENG.). 24p. (J). pap. 21.95 *(978-1-4787-1604-4(5))* Outskirts Pr., Inc.

Leppard, Lois Gladys. The Mandie Collection. (ENG.). (J). (gr. 3-8). 2011. 368p. pap. 12.99 *(978-0-7642-0932-1(9))* 2011. 384p. pap. 13.00 *(978-0-7642-0878-2(0))* 2011. 368p. pap. 10.99 *(978-0-7642-0689-4(3))* 2011. 368p. pap. 12.99 *(978-0-7642-0877-5(2))* Vol. 1. 2007. 544p. pap. 15.99 *(978-0-7642-0446-3(7))* Vol. 2. 2008. (Illus.). 576p. pap. 15.99 *(978-0-7642-0538-5(2))* Bethany Hse. Pubs.

—Mandie Collection, Vol. 3. 2008. (ENG.). 608p. (J). pap. 15.99 *(978-0-7642-0593-4(5))* Bethany Hse. Pubs.

Lipsyte, Robert. Yellow Flag. 2009. (ENG.). 256p. (YA). (gr. 8). pap. 9.99 *(978-0-06-055709-6(5),* Tegen, Katherine Bks) HarperCollins Pubs.

Looper, Grace W. Molasses Making Time. l.t. ed. 2004. 152p. (YA). pap. 8.95 *(978-0-9747685-5-7(3))* Bella Rosa Bks.

Madden, Kerry. Gentle's Holler. 2007. (Maggie Valley Ser.). 237p. (gr. 4-7). 17.00 *(978-0-7569-8090-0(9))* Perfection Learning Corp.

Marsh, Carole. The Mystery at Kill Devil Hills. 2009. (Real Kids, Real Places Ser.). (Illus.). 145p. (J). lib. bdg. 18.99 *(978-0-635-06999-3(7),* Marsh, Carole Mysteries) Gallopade International.

—The Mystery of Blackbeard the Pirate. Marsh, Carole, photos by. 2009. (Real Kids, Real Places Ser.). (Illus.). 150p. (J). 18.99 *(978-0-635-06992-4(X),* Marsh, Carole Mysteries) Gallopade International.

—The Mystery of the Biltmore House. 25th ed. 2009. (Real Kids, Real Places Ser.). 148p. (J). 18.99 *(978-0-635-06989-4(X),* Marsh, Carole Mysteries) Gallopade International.

—The Mystery of the Lost Colony. 2010. (Real Kids, Real Places Ser.). (Illus.). 158p. (J). 24.99 *(978-0-635-07607-6(1))*; pap. 18.99 *(978-0-635-07595-6(4))* Gallopade International. (Marsh, Carole Mysteries).

The Marsh Runners. 2004. (J). per. 14.95 *(978-0-9761178-0-3(0))* Maritime Kids Quest Pr.

Martin, Amy. As You Wake. 2013. 294p. pap. 10.93 *(978-0-9882051-2-3(2))* Martin, Amy.

Martone, Ginny. Trapped in Dead Man's Cave. 2007. 61p. pap. 19.95 *(978-1-60474-227-5(5))* America Star Bks.

McDavid-Jones, Elizabeth. The Night Flyers. 2009. (Mysteries Through Time Ser.). 144 - 176p. (YA). (gr. 4-8). 31.95 *(978-1-60754-197-4(1))*; pap. 15.25 *(978-1-60754-198-1(X))* Windmill Bks.

McDonald, Megan. Judy Moody & Stink: La Loca, Loca Busqueda del Tesoro. Reynolds, Peter, illus. 2011. (SPA.). 256p. (J). (gr. 2-5). pap. 14.95 *(978-1-61605-137-2(X))* Ediciones Alfaguara ESP. Dist: Two Rivers Distribution.

—Judy Moody & Stink: The Mad, Mad, Mad, Mad Treasure Hunt. Reynolds, Peter H., illus. 2009. (Judy Moody Ser.: No. 2). (ENG.). 128p. (J). (gr. 1-4). 14.99 *(978-0-7636-3962-4(1))* Candlewick Pr.

—The Mad, Mad, Mad, Mad Treasure Hunt. Reynolds, Peter H., illus. 2010. (Judy Moody Ser.: Bk. 2). (ENG.). 128p. (J). (gr. 1-4). pap. 7.99 *(978-0-7636-4351-5(3))* Candlewick Pr.

—The Mad, Mad, Mad, Mad Treasure Hunt. 2010. (Judy Moody & Stink Ser.: 2). lib. bdg. 18.40 *(978-0-606-01311-6(3),* Turtleback) Turtleback Bks.

McGougan, Kathy. Fixin' Buddy's Little Red Wagon. Hale, Sally, illus. 2009. 16p. pap. 9.95 *(978-1-4251-8975-4(X))* Trafford Publishing.

McKay, Laurie. Quest Maker. 2016. (Last Dragon Charmer Ser.: 2). (Illus.). 352p. (J). (gr. 3-7). 16.99 *(978-0-06-230846-7(7))* HarperCollins Pubs.

—The Villain Keeper. (Last Dragon Charmer Ser.: 1). (J). (gr. 3-7). 2016. 368p. pap. 6.99 *(978-0-06-230844-3(0))* 2015. (ENG.). 352p. 16.99 *(978-0-06-230843-6(2))* HarperCollins Pubs.

Michaels, Craig. Blackbeard's Treasure. 2008. (J). *(978-0-936389-99-8(0))* Tudor Pubs., Inc.

Milburn, Trish. White Witch. 2012. 188p. pap. 12.95 *(978-1-61194-083-1(4),* Bell Bridge Bks.) BelleBks., Inc.

Moses, Shelia P. The Baptism. (ENG., 144p. 2008. Illus.). (J). (gr. 5-9). pap. 5.99 *(978-1-4169-5833-8(9))* 2007. (YA). (gr. 7-12). 15.99 *(978-1-4169-0671-1(1))* McElderry, Margaret K. Bks. (McElderry, Margaret K. Bks.).

—The Legend of Buddy Bush. 2004. (ENG., Illus.). 224p. (YA). (gr. 7). 19.99 *(978-0-689-85839-0(6),* McElderry, Margaret K. Bks.) McElderry, Margaret K. Bks.

—The Legend of Buddy Bush. 2005. (Illus.). 211p. (gr. 7-12). 17.00 *(978-0-7569-5459-8(2))* Perfection Learning Corp.

—The Legend of Buddy Bush, 3 vols. unabr. ed. 2005. (YA). (gr. 3-7). 54.75 *(978-1-4193-3575-4(8),* 42043) Recorded Bks., Inc.

Mr. Bud's Country Store: A Story of Family & Community. 2003. (J). per. 18.95 *(978-0-9711534-1-7(8))* Hidden Path Pubn., Inc.

No Place to Fall. 2014. (ENG.). 368p. (YA). (gr. 9). 17.99 *(978-0-06-227099-3(0))* HarperCollins Pubs.

O'Connor, Barbara. Greetings from Nowhere. 2008. (ENG.). 208p. (J). (gr. 5-8). 17.99 *(978-0-374-39937-5(9),* 9780374399375, Farrar, Straus & Giroux (BYR)) Farrar, Straus & Giroux.

—How to Steal a Dog. 2009. (ENG.). 192p. (J). (gr. 3-7). pap. 6.99 *(978-0-312-56112-3(1),* 9780312561123) Square Fish.

Patterson, Nancy Ruth. A Simple Gift. 2009. 128p. (gr. 3-7). pap. 10.95 *(978-1-4401-1206-5(1))* iUniverse, Inc.

Pearson, Joanna. The Rites & Wrongs of Janice Wills. 2011. (YA). pap. *(978-0-545-19774-8(0))*; (ENG.). 224p. (J). (gr. 9-7). 16.99 *(978-0-545-19773-1(2))* Scholastic, Inc. (Levine, Arthur A. Bks.).

Penn, Audrey. The Whistling Tree. Gibson, Barbara, illus. 2003. 32p. 16.95 *(978-0-87868-852-4(8),* 8528, Child & Family Pr.) Child Welfare League of America, Inc.

—The Whistling Tree. Gibson, Barbara Leonard, illus. 2006. (ENG.). 32p. (J). (gr. -1-3). 16.95 (978-0-9749303-9-8(3)) Tanglewood Pr.
Penn, Audrey & Miller, Joshua. Blackbeard & the Gift of Silence. 2009. (ENG.). 350p. (J). (gr. 2-7). pap. 8.95 (978-1-933718-32-3(3)) Tanglewood Pr.
—Blackbeard & the Sandstone Pillar: When Lightning Strikes. 2009. (ENG.). 350p. (J). (gr. 2-7). pap. 8.95 (978-1-933718-31-6(5)) Tanglewood Pr.
Pfaff, Eugene E. Guns at Guilford Court House. 2008. 132p. (YA). (gr. 6-9). pap. 14.95 (978-0-936389-97-4(4)) Tudor Pubs., Inc.
Pickett, Anola. Whisper Island. 2013. (ENG.). 235p. (J). (gr. 3-7). pap. 14.99 (978-1-4621-1167-1(X), Sweetwater Bks.) Cedar Fort, Inc./CFI Distribution.
Poehler, S. Applecheeks & the Pop E. Tree. 2012. 12p. pap. 15.99 (978-1-4772-8180-2(0)) AuthorHouse.
Posey, S. A. M. The Last Station Master: A Boy, a Terroist, a Secret, & Trouble. 2013. (ENG.). 200p. (-12). pap. 19.99 (978-1-926780-22-1(1)) Key Publishing Hse., Inc., The CAN. Dist: Bookmasters Distribution.
Propst, Milam McGraw. The Further Adventures of Ociee Nash. 2009. 146p. pap. 14.95 (978-0-9841258-0-7(9), Bell Bridge Bks.) BelleBks., Inc.
Pyron, Bobbie. A Dog's Way Home. 2012. (ENG.). 336p. (J). (gr. 3-7). pap. 6.99 (978-0-06-198672-7(0), Tegen, Katherine Bks) HarperCollins Pubs.
—A Dog's Way Home. Jessell, Tim, illus. 2011. (ENG.). 336p. (J). (gr. 3-7). 16.99 (978-0-06-198674-1(7), Tegen, Katherine Bks) HarperCollins Pubs.
Ransom, Candice. The Life-Saving Adventure of Sam Deal, Shipwreck Rescuer. 2010. pap. 51.02 (978-0-7613-6918-9(X)) Lerner Publishing Group.
—The Life-Saving Adventure of Sam Deal, Shipwreck Rescuer. Trover, Zachary, illus. 2010. (History's Kid Heroes Ser.). (ENG.). 32p. (gr. 3-5). pap. 8.95 (978-0-7613-6196-1(0), Graphic Universe™); lib. bdg. 26.60 (978-0-7613-6177-0(4)) Lerner Publishing Group.
Ridley, R. W. Banshee Worm King. 2012. 242p. pap. 9.99 (978-0-9792067-5-7(8)) Middleburry Hse. Publishing.
Ritch, Catherine. Zipper Finds a Job. Trexler, Jennifer Suther, illus. 2014. (White Squirrel Parables Ser.: Vol. 2). (ENG.). 32p. (J). (gr. -1-3). 13.95 (978-1-933341-40-8(8)) CRM.
Rose, Caroline Starr & McPike, Elizabeth. Blue Birds. 2015. (ENG., Illus.). 400p. (J). (gr. 5). bds. 16.99 (978-0-399-16810-9(9), G.P. Putnam's Sons Books for Young Readers) Penguin Young Readers Group.
Salter, Kay. Fifteenth Summer: The Sarah Bowers Series. 2011. 188p. (gr. -1). 24.99 (978-1-4567-6380-0(6)); pap. 15.99 (978-1-4567-6381-7(4)) AuthorHouse.
—Fourteenth Summer: So begins the search for a suitable Bride. Noe, Amy, ed. 2009. 287p. pap. 14.95 (978-0-9842517-2-8(3)) Bartlett Park.
—Thirteenth Summer: More fun & adventure on the Carolina Coast. Noe, Amy, ed. 2009. 293p. pap. 14.95 (978-0-9842517-1-1(5)) Bartlett Park.
—Twelfth Summer: Coming of age in a time of War. Noe, Amy, ed. 2009. 297p. pap. 14.95 (978-0-9842517-0-4(7)) Bartlett Park.
Scott, Lisa Ann. School of Charm. 2014. (ENG.). 304p. (J). (gr. 3-7). 16.99 (978-0-06-220758-6(X), Tegen, Katherine Bks) HarperCollins Pubs.
Silvano, Wendi. Love Is All Around North Carolina. Czemichowska, Joanna, illus. 2016. (ENG.). 32p. (J). (-6). 12.99 (978-1-4926-2947-4(2), Sourcebooks Jabberwocky) Sourcebooks, Inc.
Simpson, N. J. Not So Random. 2011. 200p. pap. 13.67 (978-0-557-83059-6(1)) Lulu Pr., Inc.
Smallman, Steve. Santa Is Coming to Asheville. Dunn, Robert, illus. 2013. (ENG.). 32p. (J). (-3). 9.99 (978-1-4022-9030-5(6), Sourcebooks Jabberwocky) Sourcebooks, Inc.
—Santa Is Coming to Charlotte. Dunn, Robert, illus. 2014. (ENG.). 32p. (J). (-3). 9.99 (978-1-4926-0697-0(9), Sourcebooks Jabberwocky) Sourcebooks, Inc.
—Santa Is Coming to North Carolina. Dunn, Robert, illus. 2014. (ENG.). 32p. (J). (-3). 9.99 (978-1-4926-0682-6(0), Sourcebooks Jabberwocky) Sourcebooks, Inc.
—Santa Is Coming to Raleigh-Durham. Dunn, Robert, illus. 2015. (ENG.). 32p. (J). (-3). 9.99 (978-1-4926-2642-8(2), Sourcebooks Jabberwocky) Sourcebooks, Inc.
—Santa Is Coming to the Carolinas. Dunn, Robert, illus. 2012. (ENG.). 32p. (J). (-3). 9.99 (978-1-4022-7586-9(2), Sourcebooks Jabberwocky) Sourcebooks, Inc.
Smith, Donna Campbell. An Independent Spirit: The Tale of Betsy Dowdy & Black Bess. 2006. (Illus.). 182p. (J). per. 11.95 (978-0-9779889-0-7(2)) Faithful Publishing.
Smith, Roland. Kitty Hawk. 2012. (I, Q Ser.: Bk. 3). (ENG., Illus.). 240p. (J). (gr. 5). pap. 8.95 (978-1-58536-604-0(8)); lib. bdg. 15.95 (978-1-58536-605-7(6)) Sleeping Bear Pr.
Solomon, Jef. Right in My Own Neighborhood. 2009. 53p. pap. 15.50 (978-0-557-05790-0(6)) Lulu Pr., Inc.
Stead, Judy. The Twelve Days of Christmas in North Carolina. Stead, Judy, illus. 2009. (Twelve Days of Christmas in America Ser.). (ENG., Illus.). 40p. (J). (gr. k). 12.95 (978-1-4027-4467-9(6)) Sterling Publishing Co., Inc.
Stead, Judy, illus. The Twelve Days of Christmas in North Carolina. 2017. (Twelve Days of Christmas in America Ser.). (ENG.). 22p. (J). (— 1). bds. 7.95 **(978-1-4549-2285-8(0))** Sterling Publishing Co., Inc.
Surviving the Applewhites. (J). tchr. ed. (978-0-06-058369-9(X)) HarperCollins Pubs.
Taylor, Theodore. The Odyssey of Ben O'Neal. 2004. (ENG., Illus.). 264p. (J). (gr. 2-5). pap. 15.95 (978-0-15-205295-9(X)) Houghton Mifflin Harcourt Publishing Co.
—Teetoncey. 2004. (ENG., Illus.). 228p. (J). (gr. 2-5). pap. 13.95 (978-0-15-205294-2(1)) Houghton Mifflin Harcourt Publishing Co.
—Teetoncey & Ben O'Neal. 2004. (ENG., Illus.). 240p. (J). (gr. 2-5). pap. 15.95 (978-0-15-205297-3(6)) Houghton Mifflin Harcourt Publishing Co.
—The Weirdo. 2006. (Illus.). 292p. (gr. 7-12). 18.00 (978-0-7569-6752-9(X)) Perfection Learning Corp.
Taylor, Theodore & Taylor, Theodore. The Weirdo. 2006. (ENG., Illus.). 304p. (YA). (gr. 7-12). pap. 8.99 (978-0-15-205666-7(1)) Houghton Mifflin Harcourt Publishing Co.
Thomas, Blair L. The Sabatini Prophecy. 2008. (ENG.). 496p. (YA). 8.99 (978-0-9760237-4-6(1)) Axiom Hse.
Tolan, Stephanie S. Applewhites at Wit's End. (Applewhites Ser.: 2). (J). (gr. 5). 2013. (ENG.). 288p. pap. 6.99 (978-0-06-057940-1(4)) 2012. (ENG.). 272p. 16.99 (978-0-06-057938-8(2)) 2012. 272p. lib. bdg. 17.89 (978-0-06-057939-5(0)) HarperCollins Pubs.
Tuck, Pamela M. As Fast As Words Could Fly, 1 vol. Velasquez, Eric, illus. 2013. (ENG.). 40p. (J). 18.95 (978-1-60060-348-8(3)) Lee & Low Bks., Inc.
Tucker, Valerie Neil. The Hermit's Box. 2009. 36p. pap. 15.49 (978-1-4490-2285-3(5)) AuthorHouse.
Turnage, Sheila. The Ghosts of Tupelo Landing. (ENG.). 368p. (J). (gr. 5). 2015. 7.99 (978-0-14-242571-8(0), Puffin Books) 2014. 16.99 (978-0-8037-3671-9(1), Kathy Dawson Books) Penguin Young Readers Group.
—The Ghosts of Tupelo Landing. 2015. lib. bdg. 18.40 (978-0-606-36773-8(X)) Turtleback Bks.
—The Odds of Getting Even. 2015. (ENG., Illus.). 352p. (J). (gr. 5). 16.99 (978-0-8037-3961-1(3), Kathy Dawson Books) Penguin Young Readers Group.
—Three Times Lucky. (ENG.). (J). (gr. 5). 2013. 336p. pap. 7.99 (978-0-14-242605-0(9), Puffin Books) 2012. 314p. 16.99 (978-0-8037-3670-2(3), Dial Bks) Penguin Young Readers Group.
—Three Times Lucky. 2013. lib. bdg. 18.40 (978-0-606-34168-4(4), Turtleback) Turtleback Bks.
Waddell, Barbara. If I Could Catch a Train. 2009. 20p. pap. 9.15 (978-1-4251-8667-8(X)) Trafford Publishing.
Walker, Melissa. Let's Pretend We Never Met. 2017. 240p. (J). (gr. 3-7). 16.99 (978-0-06-256716-1(0)) HarperCollins Pubs.
Weatherford, Carole Boston. Freedom on the Menu: The Greensboro Sit-Ins. Lagarrigue, Jerome Lagarrigue, illus. 2007. (ENG.). 32p. (J). (gr. -1-3). pap. 5.99 (978-0-14-240894-0(8), Puffin Books) Penguin Young Readers Group.
—Freedom on the Menu: The Greensboro Sit-Ins. Lagarrigue, Jerome, illus. 2007. (gr. 4-7). 16.00 (978-0-7569-8160-0(3)) Perfection Learning Corp.
Wright, Barbara. Crow. 2013. (ENG.). 320p. (J). (gr. 5-7). pap. 7.99 (978-0-375-87367-6(8), Yearling) Random Hse. Children's Bks.

NORTH CAROLINA—HISTORY

Bartram, Pat. Guide to New Bern NC History. 2009. (ENG., Illus.). 56p. (J). pap. 7.50 (978-0-615-31220-0(9)) Bartram Team, The.
Bauer, Marion Dane. Celebrating North Carolina: 50 States to Celebrate. Canga, C. B., illus. 2014. (Green Light Readers Level 3 Ser.). (ENG.). 40p. (J). (gr. 1-4). 12.99 (978-0-544-28875-1(0), HMH Books For Young Readers) Houghton Mifflin Harcourt Publishing Co.
—Celebrating North Carolina: 50 States to Celebrate. C.B. Canga, C. B., illus. 2014. (Green Light Readers Level 3 Ser.). (ENG.). 40p. (J). (gr. 1-4). pap. 3.99 (978-0-544-28827-0(0), HMH Books For Young Readers) Houghton Mifflin Harcourt Publishing Co.
Boehm Jerome, Kate. Charlotte & the State of North Carolina: Cool Stuff Every Kid Should Know. 2011. (Arcadia Kids Ser.). (ENG., Illus.). 48p. (J). (gr. 3-6). pap. 9.99 (978-1-4396-0097-9(X)) Arcadia Publishing.
—Raleigh & the State of North Carolina: Cool Stuff Every Kid Should Know. 2011. (Arcadia Kids Ser.). (ENG., Illus.). 48p. (J). (gr. 3-6). pap. 9.99 (978-1-4396-0096-2(1)) Arcadia Publishing.
Brickey, Peter, creator. Coastal Impressions... A photographic journey along the North Carolina Coast. 2004. (Illus.). 186p. cd-rom (978-0-9758964-1-9(5)) Brickey E-Publishing.
—From Currituck to Oak Island... A Photo Tour of North Carolina's Lighthouses. 2004. (Illus.). 88p. cd-rom 10.00 net. (978-0-9758964-0-2(7)) Brickey E-Publishing.
Cannavale, Matthew C. North Carolina, 1524-1776. 2007. (National Geographic Voices from ColonialAmerica Ser.). (ENG., Illus.). 112p. (J). (gr. 5-9). 21.95 (978-1-4263-0032-5(8)); lib. bdg. 32.90 (978-1-4263-0033-2(6)) National Geographic Society. (National Geographic Children's Bks.).
Crane, Carol. Little North Carolina. Brett, Jeannie, illus. 2011. (My Little State Ser.). (ENG.). 20p. 9.95 (978-1-58536-545-6(9)) Sleeping Bear Pr.
Cunningham, Kevin. The North Carolina Colony. 2011. (True Bk Ser.). (ENG., Illus.). 48p. (J). pap. 6.95 (978-0-531-26608-3(7)); lib. bdg. 29.00 (978-0-531-25395-3(3)) Scholastic Library Publishing. (Children's Pr.).
Daly, Ruth. Biltmore Estate. 2015. (Illus.). 24p. (J). (978-1-4896-3388-0(X)) Weigl Pubs., Inc.
Davidson, Tish. Atlantic: North Carolina, Virginia, West Virginia, Vol. 19. 2015. (Let's Explore the States Ser.). (Illus.). 64p. (J). (gr. 5). 23.95 (978-1-4222-3320-7(0)) Mason Crest.
Englar, Xavier & Niz, Xavier W. The Mystery of the Roanoke Colony, 1 vol. Denton, Shannon E., illus. 2006. (Graphic History Ser.). (ENG.). 32p. (gr. 3-4). per. 8.10 (978-0-7368-9657-3(0), Graphic Library) Capstone Press of Coughlan Cos.
Ervin, C. H. Hummingbird,Hummingbird. 2012. 20p. pap. 13.77 (978-1-4669-5912-5(6)) Trafford Publishing.
Foran, Jill. North Carolina. 2011. (Guide to American States Ser.). (Illus.). 48p. (YA). (gr. 3-6). 29.99 (978-1-61690-805-8(X)); (J). 29.99 (978-1-61690-481-4(X)) Weigl Pubs., Inc.
—North Carolina: The Tar Heel State. 2016. (J). (978-1-4896-4914-0(X)) Weigl Pubs., Inc.
Gaines, Ann & Steinitz, Andy. North Carolina. 2014. (It's My State! (r) Ser.). 80p. (J). (gr. 4-8). lib. bdg. 34.21 (978-1-62712-754-7(2)) Cavendish Square Publishing.
—North Carolina. 2nd rev. ed. 2010. (It's My State! Ser.). 80p. (gr. 3-18). lib. bdg. 31.36 (978-1-60870-057-8(7)) Marshall Cavendish Corp.
Gunderson, Jessica. Exploring the North Carolina Colony. 2016. (Exploring the 13 Colonies Ser.). (ENG., Illus.). 48p. (gr. 3-4). lib. bdg. 31.99 (978-1-5157-2233-5(3)) Capstone Press of Coughlan Cos.
Harcourt School Publishers Staff. Horizons: North Carolina Edition. 3rd ed. 2003. (Illus.). (gr. 4). 73.50 (978-0-15-321347-2(7)) Harcourt Schl. Pubs.
Harkins, Susan. The Carolinas: Sir George Carteret & Sir Anthony Ashley Cooper. 2006. (J). lib. bdg. (978-1-58415-464-8(0)) Mitchell Lane Pubs., Inc.
Jerome, Kate B. Lucky to Live in North Carolina. 2017. (Arcadia Kids Ser.). (ENG., Illus.). 32p. (J). 16.99 **(978-0-7385-2783-3(1))** Arcadia Publishing.
—The Wise Animal Handbook North Carolina. 2017. (Arcadia Kids Ser.). (ENG., Illus.). 32p. (J). 16.99 **(978-0-7385-2835-9(8))** Arcadia Publishing.
Knoke, Paul. The Storm on Godfather Mountain: A True Story. 2010. 24p. pap. 14.99 (978-1-4490-5773-2(X)) AuthorHouse.
Lew, Kristi. North Carolina: Past & Present. 2010. (United States: Past & Present Ser.). (ENG.). 48p. (YA). pap. 11.75 (978-1-4358-9518-8(5)); lib. bdg. 29.25 (978-1-4358-9491-4(X)) Rosen Publishing Group, Inc., The. (Rosen Reference).
Living in Our World, Grade 5: Its Land & People, 2 vols. 2nd ed. 2003. 586p. (J). tchr. ed., spiral bd. (978-1-885647-42-9(5)) North Carolina State Univ. Humanities Extension Pubns./Program.
Margulies, Philip. The Colony of North Carolina. 2006. (Primary Sources of the Thirteen Colonies & the Lost Colony Ser.). (ENG., Illus.). 64p. (gr. 4-8). per. 12.95 (978-1-4042-0666-3(3)) Rosen Publishing Group, Inc., The.
—A Primary Source History of the Colony of North Carolina. 2006. (Primary Sources of the Thirteen Colonies & the Lost Colony Ser.). (Illus.). 64p. (YA). (gr. 4-7). lib. bdg. 31.95 (978-1-4042-0432-4(6)) Rosen Publishing Group, Inc., The.
Margulies, Phillip. A Primary Source History of the Colony of North Carolina. 2009. (Primary Sources of the Thirteen Colonies & the Lost Colony Ser.). 64p. (gr. 5-8). 58.50 (978-1-60851-886-9(8)) Rosen Publishing Group, Inc., The.
Marsh, Carole. Exploring North Carolina Through Project-Based Learning: Geography, History, Government, Economics & More. 2016. (North Carolina Experience Ser.). (ENG.). (J). pap. 9.99 (978-0-635-12357-2(6)) Gallopade International.
—North Carolina History Projects: 30 Cool, Activities, Crafts, Experiments & More for Kids to Do to Learn about Your State! 2003. (North Carolina Experience Ser.). 32p. (gr. k-5). pap. 5.95 (978-0-635-01802-1(0), Marsh, Carole Bks.) Gallopade International.
Mayr, Diane. North Carolina. 2005. (Portraits of the States Ser.). (Illus.). 32p. (gr. 2-6). pap. 10.50 (978-0-8368-4650-8(8)); lib. bdg. 26.00 (978-0-8368-4631-7(1)) Stevens, Gareth Publishing LLLP. (Gareth Stevens Learning Library).
Miller, Jake. The Lost Colony of Roanoke: A Primary Source History. 2006. (Primary Source Library of the Thirteen Colonies & the Lost Colony Ser.). (Illus.). 24p. (J). (gr. 3-7). lib. bdg. 22.60 (978-1-4042-3027-9(0), PowerKids Pr.) Rosen Publishing Group, Inc., The.
Mis, Melody S. The Colony of North Carolina: A Primary Source History. (Primary Source Library of the Thirteen Colonies & the Lost Colony Ser.). 24p. (gr. 3-4). 2009. 42.50 (978-1-60854-150-8(9)) 2006. (Illus.). (J). lib. bdg. 22.60 (978-1-4042-3436-9(5)) Rosen Publishing Group, Inc., The. (PowerKids Pr.).
Murray, Julie. North Carolina, 1 vol. 2012. (Explore the United States Ser.). (ENG., Illus.). 32p. (J). (gr. 2-5). lib. bdg. 28.50 (978-1-61783-371-7(1), Big Buddy Bks.) ABDO Publishing Co.
Phipps, Shane. The Carter Journals: Time Travels in Early U.S. History. 2015. (Illus.). xii, 189p. (J). pap. (978-0-87195-364-3(1)) Indiana Historical Society.
Reed, Jennifer. Cape Hatteras National Seashore: Adventure, Explore, Discover. 2008. (America's National Parks Ser.). (Illus.). 128p. (J). (gr. 5-9). lib. bdg. 34.60 (978-1-59845-086-6(7)) Enslow Pubs., Inc.
Rodriguez, Cindy. North Carolina: The Tar Heel State. 2012. (J). (978-1-61913-385-3(7)); pap. (978-1-61913-386-0(5)) Weigl Pubs., Inc.
Silcox, Diane. A Light to Keep. Moates, Carol Meetze, illus. 2013. 30p. pap. 14.95 (978-1-938101-36-6(7)) Indigo Sea Pr., LLC.
Smith, Rich. North Carolina, 1 vol. 2009. (United States Ser.). (ENG., Illus.). 48p. (YA). (gr. 2-5). 27.07 (978-1-60453-668-3(3)) ABDO Publishing Co.
Taylor, Michaelle. Singing Across the Old North State: Story-Songs of North Carolina. 2004. 44p. (J). pap. (978-1-880970-89-8(9)) Aerial Photography Services, Inc.
Traylor, Waverley. Indian Legends of the Great Dismal Swamp. Traylor, Margaret, ed. Hancock, Stefanie, illus. 2004. 72p. (gr. 8-18). pap. 9.95 (978-0-9715068-3-1(3)) Traylor, Waverley Publishing.
Truette, Charlotte. Adam's Adventure: Walking in the Footsteps of History in His Hometown. 2012. 224p. pap. 24.95 (978-1-4626-7630-9(8)) America Star Bks.
Walser, Richard & Street, Julia Montgomery. North Carolina Parade: Stories of History & People. Browning, Dixie Burrus, illus. 2012. (ENG.). 216p. pap. 47.50 (978-0-8078-3708-5(3)) Univ. of North Carolina Pr.
What's Great about North Carolina? 2014. (Our Great States Ser.). (ENG.). 32p. (gr. 2-5). lib. bdg. 26.60 (978-1-4677-3339-7(3)) Lerner Publishing Group.
Wimmer, Teresa. North Carolina. 2009. (This Land Called America Ser.). (Illus.). 32p. (YA). (gr. 3-6). 19.95 (978-1-58341-786-7(9)) Creative Co., The.
Yasuda, Anita. What's Great about North Carolina? 2014. (Our Great States Ser.). (ENG., Illus.). 32p. (gr. 2-5). pap. 7.95 (978-1-4677-4529-1(4)) Lerner Publishing Group.
Zepke, Terrance. Pirates of the Carolinas for Kids. 2009. (Carolinas for Kids Ser.). (ENG.). 71p. (J). (gr. 4-18). pap. 9.95 (978-1-56164-459-9(5)) Pineapple Pr., Inc.

NORTH CENTRAL STATES

see Middle West

NORTH DAKOTA

Bailer, Darice. What's Great about North Dakota? 2014. (Our Great States Ser.). (ENG.). 32p. (gr. 2-5). lib. bdg. 26.60 (978-1-4677-3389-2(X), Lerner Pubns.) Lerner Publishing Group.
Brown, Vanessa. North Dakota. 2009. (Bilingual Library of the United States of America Ser.). (ENG & SPA.). 32p. (gr. 2-2). 47.90 (978-1-60853-378-7(6), Editorial Buenas Letras) Rosen Publishing Group, Inc., The.
—North Dakota/Dakota del Norte. Brusca, Maria Cristina, tr. from ENG. 2006. (Bilingual Library of the United States of America Ser.: Set 2). (ENG & SPA., Illus.). 32p. (J). (gr. 3-6). lib. bdg. 25.25 (978-1-4042-3099-6(8)) Rosen Publishing Group, Inc., The.
Hoena, Blake. North Dakota. 2013. (Exploring the States Ser.). (ENG., Illus.). 32p. (J). (gr. 3-7). lib. bdg. 26.95 (978-1-62617-033-9(9), Blastoff! Readers) Bellwether Media.
Knapp, Ron. North Dakota: A MyReportLinks. Com Book. 2003. (States Ser.). (Illus.). 48p. (J). (gr. 4-10). lib. bdg. 25.26 (978-0-7660-5119-5(6), MyReportLinks.com Bks.) Enslow Pubs., Inc.
Maine, Tyler. North Dakota. 2016. (States Ser.). (ENG., Illus.). 32p. (gr. 3-4). lib. bdg. 27.32 (978-1-5157-0421-8(1)) Next Page Pr., The.
Marsh, Carole. North Dakota Current Events Projects: 30 Cool, Activities, Crafts, Experiments & More for Kids to Do to Learn about Your State! 2003. (North Dakota Experience Ser.). 32p. (gr. k-8). pap. 5.95 (978-0-635-02053-6(X), Marsh, Carole Bks.) Gallopade International.
—North Dakota Geography Projects: 30 Cool, Activities, Crafts, Experiments & More for Kids to Do to Learn about Your State! 2003. (North Dakota Experience Ser.). 32p. (gr. k-5). pap. 5.95 (978-0-635-01853-3(5), Marsh, Carole Bks.) Gallopade International.
—North Dakota Government Projects: 30 Cool, Activities, Crafts, Experiments & More for Kids to Do to Learn about Your State! 2003. (North Dakota Experience Ser.). 32p. (gr. k-5). pap. 5.95 (978-0-635-01953-0(1), Marsh, Carole Bks.) Gallopade International.
—North Dakota People Projects: 30 Cool, Activities, Crafts, Experiments & More for Kids to Do to Learn about Your State! 2003. (North Dakota Experience Ser.). 32p. (gr. k-5). pap. 5.95 (978-0-635-02003-1(3), Marsh, Carole Bks.) Gallopade International.
McDaniel, Melissa & Kras, Sara Louise. North Dakota. 2nd rev. ed. 2009. (Celebrate the States 11 Ser.). 144p. (gr. 6). 42.79 (978-0-7614-4733-7(4)) Marshall Cavendish GBR. Dist: Marshall Cavendish Corp.
Mis, M. S. How to Draw North Dakota's Sights & Symbols. 2009. (Kid's Guide to Drawing America Ser.). 32p. (gr. k-k). 50.50 (978-1-61511-087-2(9), PowerKids Pr.) Rosen Publishing Group, Inc., The.
Murray, Julie. North Dakota, 1 vol. 2006. (Buddy Book Ser.). (ENG., Illus.). 32p. (gr. 2-4). 27.07 (978-1-59197-693-6(6), Buddy Bks.) ABDO Publishing Co.
Salonen, Roxane B. P Is for Peace Garden: A North Dakota Alphabet. Yardley, Joanna, illus. 2005. (Discover America State by State Ser.). (ENG.). 40p. (J). (gr. -1-7). 17.95 (978-1-58536-142-7(9)) Sleeping Bear Pr.
Severin, E. Hoover. North Dakota. 2006. (Portraits of the States Ser.). 32p. (gr. 2-6). pap. 10.50 (978-0-8368-4723-9(7)); (Illus.). lib. bdg. 26.00 (978-0-8368-4706-2(7)) Stevens, Gareth Publishing LLLP. (Gareth Stevens Learning Library).
Silverman, Robin Landew. North Dakota. 2003. (From Sea to Shining Sea Ser.: 2). (ENG., Illus.). 80p. (J). 30.50 (978-0-516-22365-8(2), Children's Pr.) Scholastic Library Publishing.
Verba, Joan Marie. North Dakota. 2012. (J). lib. bdg. 25.26 (978-0-7613-4189-5(7), Lerner Pubns.) Lerner Publishing Group.
Zollman, Pam. North Dakota. 2005. (Rookie Read-About Geography Ser.). (ENG., Illus.). 32p. (J). (gr. 1-2). lib. bdg. 20.50 (978-0-516-25259-9(3), Children's Pr.) Scholastic Library Publishing.

NORTH DAKOTA—FICTION

Baum, L. Frank & Bancroft, Laura. Twinkle & Chubbins. 2011. 106p. 22.95 (978-1-4638-9604-1(2)) Rodgers, Alan Bks.
Bergstrom, Candace. People of the Prairie. 2008. 12.95 (978-0-9787648-1-4(1)) Bergstrom Bks.
DeFelice, Cynthia. Wild Life. 2011. (ENG.). 192p. (J). (gr. 3-7). 17.99 (978-0-374-38001-4(5), 9780374380014, Farrar, Straus & Giroux (BYR)) Farrar, Straus & Giroux.
—Wild Life. 2013. (ENG.). 208p. (J). (gr. 3-7). pap. 7.99 (978-1-250-03407-6(8), 9781250034076) Square Fish.
Fournier, Kevin Mark. Sandbag Shuffle. 2007. (ENG.). 240p. (gr. 8-13). per. 12.95 (978-1-897235-22-5(4)) Thistledown Pr., Ltd. CAN. Dist: Univ. of Toronto Pr.
Gunderson, Jessica. Emma's New Beginning. Foti, Anthony J., illus. 2015. (U. S. Immigration in The 1900s Ser.). (ENG.). 96p. (gr. 3-4). pap. 7.95 (978-1-4965-0501-9(8)) Stone Arch Bks.
Jacobs, Lily. The Littlest Bunny in North Dakota: An Easter Adventure. Dunn, Robert, illus. 2015. (ENG.). 32p. (J). (-3). 9.99 (978-1-4926-1159-2(X), Sourcebooks Jabberwocky) Sourcebooks, Inc.
James, Eric. A Halloween Scare in North Dakota. Le Ray, Marina, illus. 2015. (ENG.). 32p. (J). (-5). 9.99 (978-1-4926-2390-8(3), 9781492623908, Sourcebooks Jabberwocky) Sourcebooks, Inc.
—Santa's Sleigh Is on Its Way to North Dakota: A Christmas Adventure. Dunn, Robert, illus. 2016. (ENG.). 32p. (J). (-2). 12.99 (978-1-4926-4345-6(9), 9781492643456, Sourcebooks Jabberwocky) Sourcebooks, Inc.
Kurtz, Jane. River Friendly, River Wild. Brennan, Neil, illus. 2007. (ENG.). 40p. (J). (gr. -1-3). 7.99 (978-1-4169-3487-5(1), Simon & Schuster/Paula Wiseman Bks.) Simon & Schuster/Paula Wiseman Bks.
Martin, Rebecca. Blossoms on the Roof. 2015. (Amish Frontier Ser.). (ENG.). 160p. (J). (gr. 2-7). pap. 8.99 (978-0-7369-6367-1(7)) Harvest Hse. Pubs.
Peterson, Esther Allen. Will Spring Come? 2009. (Illus.). 157p. (J). (978-0-88092-768-0(2)) Royal Fireworks Publishing Co.
Pyke, Helen Godfrey. Julia. 2012. (J). pap. (978-0-8163-3400-1(5)) Pacific Pr. Publishing Assn.
Rylander, Chris. Codename Zero. 2015. (Codename Conspiracy Ser.: 1). (ENG.). 384p. (J). (gr. 3-7). pap. 6.99 (978-0-06-212009-0(3), Walden Pond Pr.) HarperCollins Pubs.
Schuman, Burt E. Chanukah on the Prairie. Kaye, Rosalind Charney, illus. 2004. (gr. k-3). 13.95 (978-0-8074-0814-8(X), 381780) URJ Pr.
Silvano, Wendi. Love Is All Around North Dakota. Czemichowska, Joanna, illus. 2016. (ENG.). 32p. (J). (-6). 12.99 (978-1-4926-2948-1(0), Sourcebooks Jabberwocky) Sourcebooks, Inc.

Smallman, Steve. Santa Is Coming to North Dakota. Dunn, Robert, illus. 2013. (ENG.). 32p. (J). (-3). 9.99 *(978-1-4022-9514-0(6)*, Sourcebooks Jabberwocky) Sourcebooks, Inc.

Tooke, Wes. King of the Mound: My Summer with Satchel Paige. (ENG.). 160p. (J). (gr. 3-7). 2013. pap. 7.99 *(978-1-4424-3347-2(7))* 2012. (Illus.). 17.99 *(978-1-4424-3346-5(9))* Simon & Schuster Bks. For Young Readers. (Simon & Schuster Bks. For Young Readers).

Wilder, Laura Ingalls. By the Shores of Silver Lake. (Little House Ser.). (J). (gr. 3-6). lib. bdg. 23.95 *(978-0-8488-2117-3(3))* Amereon Ltd.

—By the Shores of Silver Lake. Williams, Garth, illus. 2004. (Little House Ser.: 5). (ENG.). 304p. (J). (gr. 3-7). pap. 8.99 *(978-0-06-058184-8(0))* HarperCollins Pubs.

NORTH DAKOTA—HISTORY

Bailer, Darice. What's Great about North Dakota? 2014. (Our Great States Ser.). (ENG., Illus.). 32p. (gr. 2-5). pap. 7.95 *(978-1-4677-4539-0(1))* Lerner Publishing Group.

Blauvelt, Marie. Sacajawea. 2011. (Early Connections Ser.). (J). *(978-1-61672-616-4(4))* Benchmark Education Co.

Draper, Penny. Red River Raging, 1 vol. 2014. (Disaster Strikes! Ser.: 8). (ENG.). 168p. (J). (gr. 5-8). pap. 8.95 *(978-1-55050-584-9(X))* Coteau Bks. CAN. Dist: Orca Bk. Pubs. USA.

Hamilton, John. Theodore Roosevelt National Park. 2008. (National Parks Set II Ser.). 32p. (gr. 4-9). 27.07 *(978-1-60453-095-7(2)*, Abdo & Daughters) ABDO Publishing Co.

Lewis, Mark J. North Dakota: Past & Present. 2010. (United States: Past & Present Ser.). (ENG.). 48p. (YA). pap. 11.75 *(978-1-4358-9519-5(3))*; lib. bdg. 29.25 *(978-1-4358-9492-1(8))* Rosen Publishing Group, Inc., The. (Rosen Reference).

Lusted, Marcia Amidon. North Dakota: The Peace Garden State. 2010. (Our Amazing States Ser.). (ENG.). 24p. (J). pap. 8.25 *(978-1-4488-0764-2(6))*; lib. bdg. 22.60 *(978-1-4488-0664-5(X))* Rosen Publishing Group, Inc., The. (PowerKids Pr.).

Marsh, Carole. Exploring North Dakota Through Project-Based Learning: Geography, History, Government, Economics & More. 2016. (North Dakota Experience Ser.). (ENG.). (J). pap. 9.99 *(978-0-635-12358-9(4))* Gallopade International.

—I'm Reading about North Dakota. 2014. (North Dakota Experience Ser.). (ENG., Illus.). (J). pap., pap. 8.99 *(978-0-635-11309-2(0))* Gallopade International.

—North Dakota History Projects: 30 Cool, Activities, Crafts, Experiments & More for Kids to Do to Learn about Your State! 2003. (North Dakota Experience Ser.). 32p. (gr. k-5). pap. 5.95 *(978-0-635-01803-8(9)*, Marsh, Carole Bks.) Gallopade International.

Murray, Julie. North Dakota, 1 vol. 2012. (Explore the United States Ser.). (ENG., Illus.). 32p. (J). (gr. 2-5). lib. bdg. 28.50 *(978-1-61783-372-4(X)*, Big Buddy Bks.) ABDO Publishing Co.

Ollhoff, Jim. North Dakota, 1 vol. 2009. (United States Ser.). (ENG., Illus.). 48p. (YA). (gr. 2-5). 27.07 *(978-1-60453-669-0(1))* ABDO Publishing Co.

Peterson, Sheryl. North Dakota. 2009. (This Land Called America Ser.). (Illus.). 32p. (YA). (gr. 3-6). 19.95 *(978-1-58341-787-4(7))* Creative Co., The.

Rodriguez, Cindy. North Dakota: The Peach Garden State. 2012. (J). *(978-1-61913-387-7(3))*; pap. *(978-1-61913-388-4(1))* Weigl Pubs., Inc.

Sanders, Doug. North Dakota. 2014. (J). pap. *(978-1-62712-483-6(7))*; (Illus.). 80p. *(978-1-62712-223-8(0))* Cavendish Square Publishing.

Sanders, Doug & Bjorklund, Ruth. North Dakota. 2016. (It's My State! (r) Ser.). 80p. (J). (gr. 4-4). 34.21 *(978-1-62713-250-3(3))* Cavendish Square Publishing.

Silverman, Robin Landew. North Dakota. 2009. (From Sea to Shining Sea, Second Ser.). (ENG.). 80p. (J). pap. 7.95 *(978-0-531-21140-3(1)*, Children's Pr.) Scholastic Library Publishing.

Stille, Darlene R. North Dakota (Revised Edition) 2014. (America the Beautiful, Third Ser. (Revised Edition) Ser.). (ENG.). 144p. (J). lib. bdg. 40.00 *(978-0-531-28286-1(4))* Scholastic Library Publishing.

Watson, Galadriel Findlay. North Dakota. 2011. (Guide to American States Ser.). (Illus.). 48p. (YA). (gr. 3-6). 29.99 *(978-1-61690-806-5(8))* Weigl Pubs., Inc.

—North Dakota: The Peace Garden State. 2016. (J). *(978-1-4896-4917-1(4))* Weigl Pubs., Inc.

Westcott, Jim. Upper Plains: Montana, North Dakota, South Dakota, Vol. 19. 2015. (Let's Explore the States Ser.). (Illus.). 64p. (J). (gr. 5). 23.95 *(978-1-4222-3336-8(7))* Mason Crest.

NORTH POLE

see also Arctic Regions

Aboff, Marcie. Do You Really Want to Meet a Polar Bear? Fabbri, Daniele, illus. 2015. (Do You Really Want to Meet... ? Ser.). 24p. (J). 27.10 *(978-1-60753-455-6(X))* Amicus Publishing.

Bedesky, Baron. Peary & Henson: The Race to the North Pole. 2006. (In the Footsteps of Explorers Ser.). (ENG., Illus.). 32p. (J). (gr. 4-7). pap. *(978-0-7787-2462-9(X))*; lib. bdg. *(978-0-7787-2426-1(3))* Crabtree Publishing Co.

Blaisdell, Molly. If You Were a Comma, 1 vol. Gray, Sara, illus. 2009. (Word Fun Ser.). (ENG.). 24p. (gr. 2-4). pap. 7.95 *(978-1-4048-5321-8(9))* Picture Window Bks.

—If You Were a Comma [LTD Commodities]. Gray, Sara, illus. 2010. (Word Fun Ser.). 24p. pap. 3.50 *(978-1-4048-6251-7(X)*, Nonfiction Picture Bks.) Picture Window Bks.

Bluthenthal, Todd. The North Pole. 2017. (Where on Earth? Mapping Parts of the World Ser.). 24p. (gr. 1-2). pap. 8.15 ***(978-1-4824-6429-0(2))*** Stevens, Gareth Publishing LLLP.

Chapman, Simon. At the North Pole. 2005. (Illus.). 115p. (J). lib. bdg. 20.00 *(978-1-4242-0629-2(4))* Fitzgerald Bks.

Cooke, Tim. The Exploration of the North & South Poles. 2013. (Explorers Discovering the World Ser.). (Illus.). 48p. (J). (gr. 4-6). 31.95 *(978-1-4339-8631-4(0))*; pap. 14.05 *(978-1-4339-8632-1(9))* Stevens, Gareth Publishing LLLP. (Gareth Stevens Learning Library).

DuBose, Judy. Santa's Count down 'Til Christmas. 2011. 36p. (gr. -1). pap. 16.00 *(978-1-4269-6545-6(1))* Trafford Publishing.

Dunn, Joeming W. Reaching the North Pole, 1 vol. Espinosa, Rod, illus. 2008. (Graphic History Ser.). (ENG.). 32p. 28.50 *(978-1-60270-185-4(7)*, Graphic Planet- Nonfiction) ABDO Publishing Co.

Hopkinson, Deborah. Keep On! The Story of Matthew Henson, Co-Discoverer of the North Pole, 1 vol. Alcorn, Stephen, illus. (ENG.). 36p. (J). (gr. 1-5). 2015. pap. 7.95 *(978-1-56145-886-8(4))* 2009. 17.95 *(978-1-56145-473-0(7))* Peachtree Pubs.

Hyde, Natalie. Expedition to the Arctic. 2013. (ENG., Illus.). 48p. (J). *(978-0-7787-1169-8(2))*; pap. *(978-0-7787-1177-3(3))* Crabtree Publishing Co.

Isaacs, Sally. Helen Thayer's Arctic Adventure: A Woman & a Dog Walk to the North Pole. Sasheva, Iva, illus. 2016. (Encounter: Narrative Nonfiction Picture Bks.). (ENG.). 32p. (gr. 4-5). lib. bdg. 28.65 *(978-1-4914-8044-1(0))* Encounter Bks.

Isaacs, Sally Senzell. Helen Thayer's Arctic Adventure: A Woman & a Dog Walk to the North Pole. Sasheva, Iva, illus. 2017. (Encounter: Narrative Nonfiction Picture Bks.). (ENG.). 32p. (gr. 4-5). pap. 7.95 *(978-1-4914-8045-8(9))* Capstone Press of Coughlan Cos.

Johnson, Dolores. Onward: A Photobiography of African-American Polar Explorer Matthew Henson. 2005. (Photobiographies Ser.). (ENG., Illus.). 64p. (gr. k-3). 27.90 *(978-0-7922-7915-0(8))*; 17.95 *(978-0-7922-7914-3(X))* National Geographic Society. (National Geographic Children's Bks.).

Mattern, Joanne. Will Steger, 1 vol. 2014. (Conservationists Ser.). (ENG., Illus.). 32p. (gr. 3-6). lib. bdg. 27.07 *(978-1-62403-096-3(3)*, Checkerboard Library) ABDO Publishing Co.

Petrie, Kristin. Robert Peary, 1 vol. 2007. (Explorers Set 2 Ser.). (ENG., Illus.). 32p. (gr. 4-5). 27.07 *(978-1-59679-746-8(0)*, Checkerboard Library) ABDO Publishing Co.

Roxburgh, Ellis. Robert Peary vs. Frederick Cook: Race to the North Pole. 2016. (History's Greatest Rivals Ser.). (ENG., Illus.). 48p. (J). (gr. 6-8). pap. 14.05 *(978-1-4824-4231-1(0))* Stevens, Gareth Publishing LLLP.

Scraper, Katherine. Matthew Henson. 2011. (Early Connections Ser.). (J). *(978-1-61672-563-1(X))* Benchmark Education Co.

Stamper, Judith Bauer, et al. Polar Bear Patrol. Haefele, Steve, illus. 2003. (Magic School Bus Ser.: No. 13). (ENG.). 96p. (J). (gr. -1-3). pap. 4.99 *(978-0-439-31433-6(X)*, Scholastic Paperbacks) Scholastic, Inc.

Wade, Mary Dodson. Amazing Arctic Explorer Matthew Henson. (Amazing Americans Ser.). (Illus.). 24p. (J). 2013. (gr. k-3). pap. 7.95 *(978-0-7660-5974-0(X)*, Enslow Elementary) 2009. (gr. 1-3). lib. bdg. 22.60 *(978-0-7660-3286-6(8))* Enslow Pubs., Inc.

Weidt, Maryann N. Matthew Henson. 2003. (History Maker Bios Ser.). (Illus.). 48p. (J). (gr. 2-4). 26.60 *(978-0-8225-0397-2(2)*, Lerner Pubns.) Lerner Publishing Group.

Worth, Bonnie. Ice Is Nice! All about the North & South Poles. Ruiz, Aristides & Mathieu, Joe, illus. 2010. (Cat in the Hat's Learning Library). (ENG.). 48p. (J). (gr. -1-3). 9.99 *(978-0-375-82885-0(0)*, Random Hse. Bks. for Young Readers) Random Hse. Children's Bks.

NORTH POLE—FICTION

Adair, Dick. The Story of Aloha Bear. Britt, Stephanie, illus. 2008. 24p. (J). 12.95 *(978-1-59700-492-3(8))* Island Heritage Publishing.

Ashman, Linda. Sailing off to Sleep. Winter, Susan, illus. 2010. (ENG.). 32p. (J). (gr. -1-1). pap. 9.99 *(978-1-4424-1435-8(9)*, Simon & Schuster Bks. For Young Readers) Simon & Schuster Bks. For Young Readers.

Bamford, Desmond Nicholas. Beekemose. 2012. (Illus.). 54p. (gr. 2-4). pap. 13.66 *(978-1-4685-7773-0(5))* AuthorHouse.

Bigalow, Stephen W. Who Is Santa? And How Did He Get to the North Pole? Megenhardt, Bill, illus. 2013. (ENG.). 144p. (J). (gr. 4-7). 19.95 *(978-0-9773757-3-8(0))* Profit Publishing.

Briggs, Raymond. The Snowman & the Snowdog. 2015. (Step into Reading Ser.). (ENG., Illus.). 32p. (J). (gr. -1-1). 12.99 *(978-0-385-38735-4(0)*, Random Hse. Bks. for Young Readers) Random Hse. Children's Bks.

Brinkley, Lonnie. I Believe: Lost at the North Pole. 2008. (Illus.). 450p. (J). 29.95 *(978-0-9801215-3-7(1))* Big Bear Publishing U.S.

Brooks, Walter R. Freddy & the North Pole. Wiese, Kurt, illus. 2013. (ENG.). 322p. (gr. 4-13). pap. 10.99 *(978-1-4683-0320-9(1)*, 460320) Overlook Pr., The.

Depken, Kristen L. Rudolph the Red-Nosed Reindeer. Karl, Linda, illus. 2014. (My Readers Ser.). (ENG.). 32p. (J). (gr. k-2). 15.99 *(978-1-250-05044-1(8)*, 9781250050441) Square Fish.

Dineen, Kaite. What Santa Wants You to Know: A Story of Santa's Love for Jesus, 1 vol. 2010. 34p. pap. 24.95 *(978-1-4489-7071-1(7))* PublishAmerica, Inc.

Eaton, Kay A. Gleason, the Christmas Giraffe. 2009. 28p. pap. 12.50 *(978-1-4389-3010-7(0))* AuthorHouse.

Fearne, Peter. My Week with Father Christmas. 2006. 176p. per. *(978-1-84667-021-3(7))* Derwent Pr., The.

Feldman, Thea. Rudolph the Red-Nosed Reindeer - The Classic Story. Madrid, Erwin, illus. 50th ed. 2014. (Rudolph the Red-Nosed Reindeer Ser.). (ENG.). 40p. (J). (gr. -1-3). 12.99 *(978-1-250-04760-1(9)*, 9781250047601) Square Fish.

Green, Rod. Santa Claus: The Magical World of Father Christmas. 2014. (ENG., Illus.). 32p. (J). (gr. 1). 12.95 *(978-1-78312-076-5(2))* Carlton Bks., Ltd. GBR. Dist: Sterling Publishing Co., Inc.

Hansen, Eric. Ian, Ceo, North Pole. 2008. 108p. pap. 9.95 *(978-1-60693-554-5(2)*, Eloquent Bks.) Strategic Book Publishing & Rights Agency (SBPRA).

Hatfield, Kara. The Real Story of Sant. 2011. 30p. pap. 16.95 *(978-1-4626-1022-8(6))* America Star Bks.

Head, Jean. Andrew's Christmas Dream. 2012. 28p. pap. 5.00 *(978-1-937260-19-4(4))* Sleepytown Pr.

Higginson, Sheila Sweeny. A Very McStuffins Christmas. 2014. (Doc Mcstuffins 8X8 Ser.). (J). lib. bdg. 16.00 *(978-0-606-35908-5(7))* Turtleback Bks.

Horse, Harry. The Last Polar Bears. Horse, Harry, illus. 2007. (ENG., Illus.). 128p. (J). (gr. 1-5). 12.95 *(978-1-56145-379-5(X)*, Peachtree Junior) Peachtree Pubs.

Hurst, Joshua. One Day at the North Pole. Johnson, Jared, illus. 2008. 44p. pap. 24.95 *(978-1-60703-327-1(5))* America Star Bks.

Ianieri, Tom. Polar Pals. 2011. 28p. pap. 15.99 *(978-1-4628-5403-5(6))* Xlibris Corp.

James, Brian. Yo-Ho-Ho! Zivoin, Jennifer, illus. 2008. (Pirate School Ser.: 7). (ENG.). 64p. (J). (gr. 1-3). pap. 3.99 *(978-0-448-44887-9(4)*, Grosset & Dunlap) Penguin Young Readers Group.

Jones, Carl. Rudy the Rangifer & Why Her Nose Turned Orange. 2007. 64p. pap. 14.99 *(978-0-9748266-3-9(4))* Grampa Jones's Publishing Co.

Judge, Chris. The Great Explorer. 2012. (ENG., Illus.). 32p. (J). (gr. -1-2). pap. 13.99 *(978-1-84939-401-7(6))* Andersen Pr. GBR. Dist: Independent Pubs. Group.

King, Lisa. The Gingerbread Baby in Search of a Family. 2013. 28p. pap. 24.95 *(978-1-63004-147-2(5))* America Star Bks.

Kramer, Candice. Matthew Henson en el Polo Norte & Matthew Henson at the North Pole. 2005. spiral bd. 76.00 *(978-1-4108-5790-3(5))* Benchmark Education Co.

Kurtz, John. Claus Kids Christmas Coloring Book. 2011. (Dover Holiday Coloring Book Ser.). (ENG.). 32p. (J). (gr. k-5). pap. 3.99 *(978-0-486-48292-7(8))* Dover Pubns., Inc.

La Porte, Mary Ellen. The Almost Christmas Story. 2011. 44p. pap. 18.99 *(978-1-4520-9946-0(4))* AuthorHouse.

LePage, Michaele L. & Lovass-Nagy, Nicole. A Year at the North Pole. 2009. 31p. 16.95 *(978-0-557-06430-4(9))* Lulu Pr., Inc.

Mitcham Davis, Zipporah. The Fox & Emily's Long Migration. 2008. 28p. pap. 13.99 *(978-1-4389-0326-2(X))* AuthorHouse.

Patterson, James. SantaKid. Garland, Michael, illus. 2004. (ENG.). 48p. (J). (gr. -1-1). 17.99 *(978-0-316-00061-1(2)*, Jimmy Patterson) Little Brown & Co.

Primavera, Elise. Auntie Claus & the Key to Christmas. 2011. (ENG., Illus.). 40p. (J). (gr. -1-3). pap. 7.99 *(978-0-547-57679-4(X))* Houghton Mifflin Harcourt Publishing Co.

—Auntie Claus Gift Edition. Primavera, Elise, illus. 2015. (ENG., Illus.). 40p. (J). (gr. -1-3). 17.99 *(978-0-544-53872-6(2)*, HMH Books For Young Readers) Houghton Mifflin Harcourt Publishing Co.

Schomer-Wendel, Gretchen & Schomer, Adam Anthony. Becka Goes to the North Pole. 2009. (Becka & the Big Bubble Ser.). (Illus.). 32p. (J). (gr. -1-3). pap. 10.55 *(978-1-60754-117-2(3))* Windmill Bks.

Shepherd, Anita. The Santa Genie. 2012. 50p. pap. 7.95 *(978-0-9882368-0-6(X))* New Eden Publishing.

Smallman, Steve. Santa Is Coming to My House. Dunn, Robert, illus. 2012. (ENG.). 32p. (J). (-3). 9.99 *(978-1-4022-7775-7(X)*, Sourcebooks Jabberwocky) Sourcebooks, Inc.

Snedeker, Erin. The Littlest Elf: Marvin Mcgee & the Candle of Fate. Drotleff, David J., illus. 2010. 44p. pap. 15.50 *(978-1-60911-194-6(X)*, Eloquent Bks.) Strategic Book Publishing & Rights Agency (SBPRA).

Sonnebom, Scott. The Computer Meltdown. Lozano, Omar, illus. 2015. (North Police Ser.). (ENG.). 32p. (gr. k-2). lib. bdg. 21.32 *(978-1-4795-6485-9(0))* Picture Window Bks.

—Meet the South Police. Lozano, Omar, illus. 2015. (North Police Ser.). (ENG.). 32p. (gr. k-2). lib. bdg. 21.32 *(978-1-4795-6486-6(9))* Picture Window Bks.

—The Mystery of Santa's Sleigh. Lozano, Omar, illus. 2015. (North Police Ser.). (ENG.). 32p. (gr. k-2). lib. bdg. 21.32 *(978-1-4795-6484-2(2))* Picture Window Bks.

—The North Police. Lozano, Omar, illus. 2015. (North Police Ser.). (ENG.). 32p. (gr. k-2). 85.28 *(978-1-4795-7929-7(7))* Picture Window Bks.

—The Reindeer Games. Lozano, Omar, illus. 2015. (North Police Ser.). (ENG.). 32p. (gr. k-2). lib. bdg. 21.32 *(978-1-4795-6487-3(7))* Picture Window Bks.

Sullivan, E. J. Bubba the Redneck Reindeer. Eldredge, Ernie, illus. 2007. 32p. (J). (gr. 4-7). 12.95 *(978-1-60261-008-8(8))* Cliff Road Bks.

Van Allsburg, Chris. The Polar Express. 30th anniv. ed. 2015. (ENG., Illus.). 32p. (J). (gr. -1-3). 19.99 *(978-0-544-58014-5(1)*, HMH Books For Young Readers) Houghton Mifflin Harcourt Publishing Co.

—The Polar Express: Sam's Edition. annot. ed. 2006. (J). (gr. k-3). 35.00 *(978-0-618-83659-8(4))* Houghton Mifflin Harcourt Trade & Reference Pubs.

—The Polar Express Big Book. 2014. (ENG., Illus.). 32p. (J). (gr. -1-3). 29.99 *(978-0-544-45798-0(6)*, HMH Books For Young Readers) Houghton Mifflin Harcourt Publishing Co.

Verne, Jules. The English at the North Pole. 2009. 160p. 24.95 *(978-1-60664-684-7(2))*; pap. 13.95 *(978-1-60664-313-6(4))* Rodgers, Alan Bks.

Wendel, Gretchen Schomel, et al. Becka Goes to the North Pole. Renthrope, Damon, illus. 2007. (ENG.). 28p. (J). 11.99 *(978-1-933754-11-6(7))* Waterside Publishing.

Wendel, Gretchen Schomer & Schomer, Adam Anthony. Becka Goes to the North Pole. Renthrope, Damon, illus. 2009. (Becka & the Big Bubble Ser.). 32p. (J). (gr. -1-2). lib. bdg. 22.60 *(978-1-60754-116-5(5))* Windmill Bks.

Wrecks, Billy. The Super Friends Save Christmas/Race to the North Pole! Random House Staff, illus. 2012. (Pictureback(R) Ser.). (ENG.). 32p. (J). (gr. -1-2). pap. 4.99 *(978-0-307-97946-9(6)*, Random Hse. Bks. for Young Readers) Random Hse. Children's Bks.

Wynne-Jones, Tim. Zoom, 1 vol. Beddows, Eric, illus. 2009. (ENG.). 96p. (J). (gr. -1-2). 25.00 *(978-0-88899-936-8(4))* Groundwood Bks. CAN. Dist: Publishers Group West (PGW).

Yoon, Salina. Penguin's Big Adventure. 2015. (Penguin Ser.). (ENG., Illus.). 40p. (J). (gr. -1-1). 14.99 *(978-0-8027-3828-8(1)*, 9780802738288, Bloomsbury USA Childrens) Bloomsbury Publishing USA.

Zurcher, Corina. Growing up Claus. 2007. 188p. 21.99 *(978-1-60477-046-9(5))*; per. 13.99 *(978-1-60266-917-8(1))* Salem Author Services.

NORTHMEN

Here are entered works on the inhabitants of Scandinavia prior to the 10th century. Works on the Scandinavian sea-warriors who plundered the northern and western coasts of Europe from the 8th to the 10th centuries are entered under Vikings. Works on the inhabitants of Scandinavia since the 10th century are entered under Scandinavians.

see also Normans; Vikings

Dowling, Lucy. Why Why Why... Were Vikings So Fierce? 2010. (Why Why Why Ser.). 32p. (YA). (gr. 1-3). lib. bdg. 18.95 *(978-1-4222-1591-3(1))* Mason Crest.

Hindley, Judy, et al. Time Traveler: Visit Medieval Times, the Viking Age, the Roman World & Ancient Egypt. rev. ed. 2004. (Time Travelers Bks.). (Illus.). 130p. (J). (gr. 3-6). 22.95 *(978-0-7460-3365-4(6))* EDC Publishing.

Hinds, Kathryn. Vikings: Masters of the Sea. 2009. (Barbarians! Ser.). 80p. (gr. 6-8). 35.64 *(978-0-7614-4074-1(7))* Marshall Cavendish Corp.

Hopkins, Andrea. Viking Families & Farms. 2009. (Viking Library). 24p. (gr. 3-3). 42.50 *(978-1-60854-257-4(2)*, PowerKids Pr.) Rosen Publishing Group, Inc., The.

—Viking Raiders & Traders. 2009. (Viking Library). 24p. (gr. 3-3). 42.50 *(978-1-60854-260-4(2)*, PowerKids Pr.) Rosen Publishing Group, Inc., The.

Macdonald, Fiona. The Medieval Chronicles: Vikings, Knights, & Castles. Antram, David, illus. 2013. 92p. (J). *(978-1-4351-5067-6(8))* Barnes & Noble, Inc.

—Vikings. 2010. (Remarkable Man & Beast Ser.). (Illus.). 48p. (J). (gr. 3-18). lib. bdg. 19.95 *(978-1-4222-1977-5(1))* Mason Crest.

MacDonald, Fiona. Vikings: Dress, Eat, Write & Play Just Like the Vikings. 2008. (Hands-on History Ser.). (ENG., Illus.). 32p. (J). (gr. 3-7). pap. *(978-0-7787-4072-8(2))* Crabtree Publishing Co.

McLeese, Don. Vikings. 2009. 32p. pap. 7.99 *(978-0-8249-1445-5(7)*, Ideal Pubns.) Worthy Publishing.

Nardo, Don. The Vikings. 2010. (World History Ser.). (ENG.). 96-128p. 34.95 *(978-1-4205-0316-6(2)*, Lucent Bks.) Cengage Gale.

Toth, Henrietta. Viking Explorers. 2016. (Spotlight on Explorers & Colonization Ser.). 48p. (J). (gr. 6-6). pap. 11.75 *(978-1-4777-8832-5(8))* Rosen Publishing Group, Inc., The.

Trueit, Trudi Strain. The Vikings. 2011. (Technology of the Ancients Ser.). 64p. (gr. 5). 32.79 *(978-1-60870-769-0(5))* Marshall Cavendish Corp.

NORTHMEN—FICTION

Brown, Abbie Farwell. In the Days of Giants. Smith, E. Boyd, illus. 2008. 204p. per. 9.95 *(978-1-59915-044-4(1))* Yesterday's Classics.

NORTHWEST, OLD

see also Middle West

O'Maley, Elizabeth. Bones on the Ground. 2014. (J). *(978-0-87195-362-9(5))* Indiana Historical Society.

NORTHWEST, PACIFIC

Benchmark Education Company. The Pacific Northwest Region (Teacher Guide) 2005. *(978-1-4108-4646-4(6))* Benchmark Education Co.

Blomgren, Jennifer. Why Do I Sing? Animal Songs of the Pacific Northwest. Gabriel, Andrea, illus. 2013. (ENG.). 32p. (J). (gr. -1-2). 16.99 *(978-1-57061-845-1(3)*, Little Bigfoot) Sasquatch Bks.

Brannon, Barbara. Discover the Pacific Northwest Region. 2005. (J). pap. *(978-1-4108-5150-5(8))* Benchmark Education Co.

Connery-Boyd, Peg. Totally Pacific Northwest! 2016. (Hawk's Nest Activity Bks.: 0). (ENG.). 64p. (J). (-3). pap. 8.99 *(978-1-4926-3969-5(9)*, 9781492639695, Sourcebooks Jabberwocky) Sourcebooks, Inc.

Goddu, Krystyna Poray. Native Peoples of the Northwest. 2016. (North American Indian Nations Ser.). (ENG., Illus.). 48p. (J). (gr. 3-5). 33.32 *(978-1-4677-7939-5(3))* Lerner Publishing Group.

Johnson, Michael & Clarke, Duncan. Native Tribes of the Great Basin & Plateau. 2004. (Native Tribes of North America Ser.). (Illus.). 64p. (gr. 5-12). lib. bdg. 34.00 *(978-0-8368-5610-1(4)*, Gareth Stevens Secondary Library) Stevens, Gareth Publishing LLLP.

Leonardo, Victoria. The Pacific Northwest Region. 2005. (J). pap. *(978-1-4108-4598-6(2))* Benchmark Education Co.

Mullen, Amy. Colors of the Pacific Northwest. 2017. (Naturally Local Ser.). (ENG., Illus.). 20p. (J). (gr. -1 — 1). bds. 8.95 ***(978-1-938093-80-7(1)**, Duo Pr. Llc (US)) Duo Pr. LLC.*

O'Dell, Kathryn L., et al. My Coast Is Better Than Yours! 2017. (Text Connections Guided Close Reading Ser.). (J). (gr. 2). *(978-1-4900-1852-2(2))* Benchmark Education Co.

Shallop, Laura. The Pacific Northwest: Set Of 6. 2011. (Navigators Ser.). (J). pap. 48.00 net. *(978-1-4108-6255-6(0))* Benchmark Education Co.

—The Pacific Northwest: Text Pairs. 2008. (Bridges/Navigators Ser.). (J). (gr. 4). 89.00 *(978-1-4108-8395-7(7))* Benchmark Education Co.

NORTHWEST, PACIFIC—FICTION

Allen, Quinc. The Outdoor Chums after Big Game (Illust. 2006. pap. *(978-1-4065-0780-5(6))* Dodo Pr.

Anderson, Margaret J. Olla-Piska: Tales of David Douglas. 2006. (ENG., Illus.). 144p. 19.95 *(978-0-87595-297-0(6))* Univ. of Washington Pr.

Banerjee, Anjali. Looking for Bapu. 2008. (ENG.). 176p. (J). (gr. 3-7). 6.50 *(978-0-553-49425-9(2)*, Yearling) Random Hse. Children's Bks.

Blomgren, Jennifer. The Tale of Alice's Quilt. 2008. (That Patchwork Place Ser.). (ENG., Illus.). 95p. (YA). (gr. 8-12). per. 14.95 *(978-1-56477-833-8(9)*, That Patchwork Place) Martingale & Co.

Capeci, Anne. Daredevils, 1 vol. Casale, Paul, illus. 2004. (Cascade Mountain Railroad Mysteries Ser.). (ENG.). 144p. (J). (gr. 2-5). 12.95 *(978-1-56145-307-8(2))* Peachtree Pubs.

—Ghost Train, 1 vol., Vol. 3. Casale, Paul, illus. 2004. (Cascade Moutain Railroad Mystery Ser.: 3). (ENG.). 144p. (J). (gr. 2-5). 12.95 *(978-1-56145-324-5(2))* Peachtree Pubs.

—Missing!, 1 vol. Casale, Paul, illus. 2005. (Cascade Mountain Railroad Mysteries Ser.). (ENG.). 144p. (J). (gr. 2-5). 12.95 *(978-1-56145-334-4(X))* Peachtree Pubs.

Challenger, Robert James. Eagle's Reflection: And Other Northwest Coast Stories, 1 vol. Challenger, Robert James,

M
N
O

illus. 2009. (ENG., Illus.). 48p. (J). (gr. k-3). pap. 9.95 *(978-1-895811-07-0(4))* Heritage Hse. CAN. Dist: Orca Bk. Pubs. USA.

Ellis, Sarah & Suzuki, David. Salmon Forest. Lott, Sheena, illus. 2006. (ENG.). 32p. (J). (gr. k-3). pap. 9.95 *(978-1-55365-163-5(4))* Greystone Books Ltd. CAN. Dist: Publishers Group West (PGW).

Fernandez, Joy C. Rockman. 2010. 36p. pap. 16.45 *(978-1-4520-6751-3(1))* AuthorHouse.

Hanson, Thor. Bartholomew Quill: A Crow Learns to Tell Who's Who in the Animal World. Amim, Dana, illus. 2016. (ENG.). 32p. (J). (gr. -1-3). 17.99 *(978-1-63217-046-0(9)*, Little Bigfoot) Sasquatch Bks.

Harper, Charise Mericle. Alien Encounter. Harper, Charise Mericle, illus. 2014. (Sasquatch & Aliens Ser.: 1). (ENG., Illus.). 208p. (J). (gr. 2-5). 12.99 *(978-0-8050-9621-7(3)*, 9780805096217, Holt, Henry & Co. Bks. For Young Readers) Holt, Henry & Co.

—Super Sasquatch Showdown. Harper, Charise Mericle, illus. 2015. (Sasquatch & Aliens Ser.: 2). (ENG., Illus.). 176p. (J). (gr. 2-5). 13.99 *(978-0-8050-9622-4(1)*, 9780805096224, Holt, Henry & Co. Bks. For Young Readers) Holt, Henry & Co.

Jolby, illus. Monsters under Bridges. 2013. (ENG.). 32p. (J). (gr. -1-3). 16.99 *(978-1-57061-856-7(9)*, Little Bigfoot) Sasquatch Bks.

LaCour, Nina. The Disenchantments. (ENG.). (YA). (gr. 9). 2013. 336p. pap. 10.99 *(978-0-14-242391-2(2)*, Speak) 2012. 320p. 16.99 *(978-0-525-42219-8(6)*, Dutton Books for Young Readers) Penguin Young Readers Group.

London, Jonathan. Bella, Bella. London, Sean, illus. 2016. (Aaron's Wilderness Ser.: 2). (ENG.). 180p. (J). pap. 12.99 *(978-0-88240-923-8(9)*, West Winds Pr.) Graphic Arts Ctr. Publishing Co.

—Bella Bella. London, Sean, illus. 2016. (Aaron's Wilderness Ser.: 2). (ENG.). 180p. (YA). 23.99 *(978-1-943328-33-8(1)*, West Winds Pr.) Graphic Arts Ctr. Publishing Co.

Mackey, Heather. Dreamwood. 2014. (ENG.). 352p. (J). (gr. 5). 16.99 *(978-0-399-25067-5(0)*, G.P. Putnam's Sons Books for Young Readers) Penguin Young Readers Group.

Meyers, Haily & Meyers, Kevin. All Aboard! Pacific Northwest, 1 vol. 2017. (ENG., Illus.). 22p. (J). bds. 9.99 *(978-1-4236-4601-3(0))* Gibbs Smith, Publisher.

Nickerson, Sara. How to Disappear Completely & Never Be Found. Comport, Sally Wern, illus. 2003. (ENG.). 288p. (J). (gr. 5-18). pap. 5.99 *(978-0-06-441027-4(7))* HarperCollins Pubs.

Norris, David A. The CBARCs of Cannon Bay: Storm Clouds over Cannon Bay, 5 bks, Bk.3. Norris, Judy-Jo Harris, illus. 2012. 128p. (YA). pap. 16.95 *(978-1-937493-30-1(X))* Dancing Moon Pr.

Parry, Rosanne. Written in Stone. 2014. (ENG., Illus.). 208p. (J). (gr. 4-7). pap. 6.99 *(978-0-375-87135-1(7)*, Yearling) Random Hse. Children's Bks.

Sanderson, Whitney. Golden Sun. Sanderson, Ruth, illus. 2010. (Horse Diaries). (ENG.). 160p. (J). (gr. 3-7). pap. 7.99 *(978-0-375-86194-9(7)*, Random Hse. Bks. for Young Readers) Random Hse. Children's Bks.

Spalding, Andrea & Scow, Alfred. Secret of the Dance, 1 vol. Gait, Darlene, illus. 2009. (ENG.). 32p. (J). (gr. -1-3). 9.95 *(978-1-55469-129-6(X))* Orca Bk. Pubs. USA.

Vanasse, Patricia. Resilient. Shalaby, Asharaf, illus. 2013. (ENG.). 328p. (YA). pap. 13.99 *(978-0-9860373-2-0(X))* Pants On Fire Pr.

Vaughan, Richard Lee. Eagle Boy: A Pacific Northwest Native Tale. Christiansen, Lee, illus. 2008. (ENG.). 32p. (J). (gr. -1-3). pap. 10.99 *(978-1-57061-592-4(6)*, Little Bigfoot) Sasquatch Bks.

NORTHWEST PASSAGE

Cooke, Tim. Explore with Henry Hudson. 2014. (ENG., Illus.). 32p. (J). *(978-0-7787-1246-6(X))*; pap. *(978-0-7787-1258-9(3))* Crabtree Publishing Co.

Donohue, Moira Rose. Jacques Cartier. 2013. (Illus.). 24p. (J). *(978-1-938813-03-0(0))* State Standards Publishing, LLC.

Foran, Jill. Search for the Northwest Passage. 2004. (Great Journeys Ser.). (Illus.). 32p. (J). lib. bdg. 26.00 *(978-1-59036-205-1(5))* Weigl Pubs., Inc.

—The Search for the Northwest Passage. 2005. (Great Journeys Ser.). (Illus.). 32p. (J). (gr. -1-3). per. 9.95 *(978-1-59036-259-4(4))* Weigl Pubs., Inc.

Gleason, Carrie. Henry Hudson: Seeking the Northwest Passage. 2005. (In the Footsteps of Explorers Ser.). (ENG., Illus.). 32p. (J). (gr. -1-9). pap. *(978-0-7787-2444-5(1))* Crabtree Publishing Co.

Hyde, Natalie. Expedition to the Arctic. 2013. (ENG., Illus.). 48p. (J). *(978-0-7787-1169-8(2))*; pap. *(978-0-7787-1177-3(3))* Crabtree Publishing Co.

Keranen, Rachel. The Northwest Passage. 2017. (J). ***(978-1-5026-2695-0(0))*** Cavendish Square Publishing.

Knudsen, Anders. Sir John Franklin: The Search for the Northwest Passage. 2007. (In the Footsteps of Explorers Ser.). (ENG., Illus.). 32p. (J). (gr. 4-7). lib. bdg. *(978-0-7787-2420-9(4))*; pap. *(978-0-7787-2456-8(5))* Crabtree Publishing Co.

O'Brien, Cynthia. Explore with John Franklin. 2015. (Travel with the Great Explorers Ser.). (ENG., Illus.). 32p. (J). (gr. 3-6). *(978-0-7787-1703-4(8))* Crabtree Publishing Co.

Rogers, Stan. Northwest Passage, 1 vol. James, Matt, illus. 2013. (ENG.). 56p. (J). (gr. k). 24.95 *(978-1-55498-153-3(0))* Groundwood Bks. CAN. Dist: Publishers Group West (PGW).

Sherman, Josepha. Henry Hudson: English Explorer of the Northwest Passage. (Library of Explorers & Exploration Ser.). 112p. (gr. 5-8). 2009. 66.50 *(978-1-60853-605-4(X))* 2003. (Illus.). (J). lib. bdg. 34.60 *(978-0-8239-3620-5(1))* Rosen Publishing Group, Inc., The. (Rosen Reference).

—Henry Hudson: Exploring the Northwest Passage. 2015. *(Incredible Explorers Ser.). (ENG., Illus.). 64p. (J). (gr. 7-7).* 34.21 *(978-1-5026-0127-8(3))* Cavendish Square Publishing.

Warrick, Karen Clemens. The Perilous Search for the Fabled Northwest Passage in American History. 2004. (In American History Ser.). (Illus.). 128p. (J). lib. bdg. 26.60 *(978-0-7660-2148-8(3))* Enslow Pubs., Inc.

NORTHWEST TERRITORIES

Laws, Gordon D. & Laws, Lauren M. The Northwest Territories. 2003. (Exploring Canada Ser.). (ENG., Illus.). 112p. (J). 30.85 *(978-1-59018-049-5(6)*, Lucent Bks.) Cengage Gale.

NORTHWEST TERRITORIES—FICTION

Fletcher, Archibald Lee. Boy Scouts in Northern Wilds. 2006. (ENG.). 124p. pap. 18.99 *(978-1-4264-6161-3(5))*; 134p. pap. 19.99 *(978-1-4264-6216-0(6))* Creative Media Partners, LLC.

Football, Virginia. How the Fox Saved the People. Wedzin, James, illus. 2009. (Fox Ser.). (ENG & DGR.). 56p. (gr. k-6). 26.95 *(978-1-894778-75-6(8))* Theytus Bks., Ltd. CAN. Dist: Univ. of Toronto Pr.

Football, Virginia & Mantla, Rosa. How the Fox Got His Crossed Legs. Siemens, Mary, tr. Wedzin, James, illus. 2009. (Fox Ser.). (ENG & DGR.). 32p. (gr. 2-3). 20.95 *(978-1-894778-74-9(X))* Theytus Bks., Ltd. CAN. Dist: Univ. of Toronto Pr.

Wilson, John. Across Frozen Seas. 2006. (ENG.). 128p. (J). (gr. 6-8). pap., tchr. ed. 12.99 *(978-0-88878-381-3(7))* Dundurn CAN. Dist: Ingram Publisher Services.

—The Alchemist's Dream. 2009. (ENG.). 248p. (YA). (gr. 7-18). pap. *(978-1-55470-101-8(5))* Me to We.

NORTHWESTERN STATES

Here are entered works on the northern part of the United States between the Great Lakes or Mississippi River and the Pacific Ocean.

Holmes, Parker. Amazing Snakes of the Northwest. 2014. (Amazing Snakes Ser.). (Illus.). 24p. (J). (gr. 3-6). 23.60 *(978-1-4777-6507-4(7)*, PowerKids Pr.) Rosen Publishing Group, Inc., The.

NORWAY

Bodden, Valerie. To the South Pole. 2012. (Great Expeditions Ser.). (ENG.). 48p. (J). (gr. 4-7). pap. 12.00 *(978-0-89812-667-9(3)*, Creative Paperbacks) Creative Co., The.

Discover Norway. 2012. (Discover Countries Ser.). (ENG., Illus.). 32p. (J). (gr. 3-5). 25.25 *(978-1-4488-6623-6(5)*, PowerKids Pr.) Rosen Publishing Group, Inc., The.

Fouberg, Erin Hogan & Hogan, Edward Patrick, trs. Norway. 2003. (Modern World Nations Ser.). (Illus.). 150p. (gr. 6-12). 35.00 *(978-0-7910-7479-4(X)*, Chelsea Hse.) Facts On File, Inc.

Ganeri, Anita. How to Live Like a Viking Warrior. Epelbaum, Mariano, illus. 2015. (How to Live Like... Ser.). (ENG.). 32p. (J). (gr. 3-6). lib. bdg. 26.65 *(978-1-4677-6354-7(3))* Lerner Publishing Group.

Hand, Carol. Norway, 1 vol. 2013. (Countries of the World Set 2 Ser.). (ENG.). 144p. (J). (gr. 6-12). lib. bdg. 37.07 *(978-1-61783-633-6(8)*, Essential Library) ABDO Publishing Co.

Kagda, Sakina & Cooke, Barbara. Norway. 2nd rev. ed. 2006. (Cultures of the World Ser.). (Illus.). 144p. (gr. 6-7). lib. bdg. 42.79 *(978-0-7614-2067-5(3)*, Benchmark Bks.) Marshall Cavendish Corp.

Kagda, Sakina, et al. Norway. 2016. (Cultures of the World (r) Ser.). (ENG.). 144p. (J). (gr. 5-5). lib. bdg. 47.07 *(978-1-5026-1848-1(6))* Cavendish Square Publishing.

Lunge-Larsen, Lise. The Race of the Birkebeiners. Azarian, Mary, illus. 2007. (ENG.). 32p. (J). (gr. k — 1). 7.99 *(978-0-618-91599-6(0))* Houghton Mifflin Harcourt Publishing Co.

Manning, Jack. Christmas in Norway, 1 vol. 2013. (Christmas Around the World Ser.). (ENG.). 24p. (gr. 1-2). 25.32 *(978-1-4765-3101-4(3)*, First Facts) Capstone Press of Coughlan Cos.

Mara, Wil. Norway. 2017. (Enchantment of the World(tm) Ser.). (ENG., Illus.). 144p. (J). lib. bdg. 40.00 *(978-0-531-22091-7(5)*, Children's Pr.) Scholastic Library Publishing.

Mis, Melody S. How to Draw Norway's Sights & Symbols. 2009. (Kid's Guide to Drawing the Countries of the World Ser.). 48p. (gr. 4-4). 53.00 *(978-1-61511-119-0(0)*, PowerKids Pr.) Rosen Publishing Group, Inc., The.

Murray, Julie. Norway, 1 vol. 2014. (Explore the Countries Set 2 Ser.). (ENG.). 40p. (gr. 7-11). lib. bdg. 29.93 *(978-1-62403-345-2(8)*, Big Buddy Bks.) ABDO Publishing Co.

Rose, Elizabeth. A Primary Source Guide to Norway. (Countries of the World). 24p. 2009. (gr. 2-3). 42.50 *(978-1-61512-041-3(6))* 2004. (Illus.). (J). lib. bdg. 22.60 *(978-0-8239-6732-2(8))* Rosen Publishing Group, Inc., The. (PowerKids Pr.).

Undset, Sigrid, ed. True & Untrue & Other Norse Tales. Chapman, Frederick T., illus. 2013. (ENG.). 264p. pap. 16.95 *(978-0-8166-7828-0(6))* Univ. of Minnesota Pr.

Yomtov, Nel. Roald Amundsen Explores the South Pole. 2015. (Extraordinary Explorers Ser.). (ENG., Illus.). 24p. (J). (gr. 3-7). lib. bdg. 29.95 *(978-1-62617-295-1(1)*, Black Sheep) Bellwether Media.

Zobel, Derek. Norway. 2011. (Exploring Countries Ser.). (ENG., Illus.). 32p. (YA). (gr. 3-7). lib. bdg. 26.95 *(978-1-60014-620-6(1)*, Blastoff! Readers) Bellwether Media.

NORWAY—FICTION

Asbjørnsen, Peter Christen. The Three Billy Goats Gruff. Vohra, Sibi, illus. 2010. (J). *(978-1-60617-149-3(6))* Teaching Strategies, LLC.

Bentley, Sue. Snowy Wishes. 2013. (Magic Puppy Ser.). lib. bdg. 16.00 *(978-0-606-32124-2(1)*, Turtleback) Turtleback Bks.

D'Aulaire, Edgar Parin & D'Aulaire, Ingri. Ola. 2013. (ENG., Illus.). 56p. 16.95 *(978-0-8166-9017-6(0))* Univ. of Minnesota Pr.

D'Aulaire, Ingri, et al. The Terrible Troll-Bird. 2007. (ENG., Illus.). 52p. (J). (gr. k-4). 15.95 *(978-1-59017-252-0(3)*, NYR Children's Collection) New York Review of Bks., Inc., The.

Endicott, Megan. In the Hall of the Mountain King. 2013. 48p. pap. 20.95 *(978-1-4582-0789-0(7)*, Abbott Pr.) Author Solutions, Inc.

A Foal Is Born. 2007. (J). *(978-1-933343-46-4(X)*, PONY) Stabenfeldt Inc.

Golding, Julia. The Silver Sea, 0 vols. 2013. (ENG.). 352p. (YA). (gr. 7-11). pap. 9.99 *(978-1-4778-1598-4(8)*, 9781477815984, Amazon Children's Publishing) Amazon Publishing.

Gulliksen, Anne. A Boy from Nøtterøy. 2009. 108p. pap. 13.00 *(978-1-59858-939-9(3))* Dog Ear Publishing, LLC.

Haig, Matt. Samuel Blink & the Forbidden Forest. 2008. (ENG.). 352p. (J). (gr. 3-7). 7.99 *(978-0-14-241191-9(4)*, Puffin Books) Penguin Young Readers Group.

—Shadow Forest. 2009. pap. 1.00 *(978-1-4074-4391-1(7))* Recorded Bks., Inc.

Halse, Leif. The Boys from Vangen: Vangsgutane. Huntrods, Alexander Knud, tr. Nilssen, Jens R., illus. 2009. (ENG & NNO.). 176p. (J). 19.95 *(978-0-9760541-5-3(9))* Astri My Astri Publishing.

Haugaard, Erik Christian. Hakon of Rogen's Saga. Dillon, Leo & Dillon, Diane, illus. 2013. (ENG.). 144p. pap. 11.95 *(978-0-8166-8127-3(9))* Univ. of Minnesota Pr.

Hayes, Tracey J. Bartina in Trouble Again. 2009. 64p. pap. 15.99 *(978-1-4415-2050-0(3))* Xlibris Corp.

Hole, Stian. Garmann's Secret. Hole, Stian, illus. 2011. (ENG., Illus.). 56p. (J). 17.00 *(978-0-8028-5400-1(1)*, Eerdmans Bks For Young Readers) Eerdmans, William B. Publishing Co.

Inger's Promise: Evaluation Guide. 2006. (J). *(978-1-55942-409-7(5))* Witcher Productions.

Jacobsen, Annie. The Terrible Troll Cat. Hanson, Susan Jo, illus. 2012. 32p. (J). 9.98 *(978-0-9778276-4-0(X))* Pickled Herring Pr.

Jennewein, James & Parker, Tom S. RuneWarriors. 2008. (RuneWarriors Ser.). 320p. (J). (gr. 3-7). lib. bdg. 17.89 *(978-0-06-144937-6(7)*, Geringer, Laura Book) HarperCollins Pubs.

Johnson, Lois Walfrid. The Raider's Promise. 2006. (Viking Quest Ser.: 5). (ENG., Illus.). 304p. (J). (gr. 3-7). per. 8.99 *(978-0-8024-3116-5(X))* Moody Pubs.

Louise, Märtha. Why Kings & Queens Don't Wear Crowns. Sevig-Fajardo, Mari Elise, tr. from NOR. Nyhus, Svein, illus. 2005. Orig. Title: Hvorfor de kongelige ikke har krone på Hodet. 32p. (J). 17.95 *(978-1-57534-037-1(2)*, CSC 100) Skandisk, Inc.

Lund, Celia. Square Sails & Dragons. 2006. 284p. pre. 19.95 *(978-1-4120-5758-5(2))* Trafford Publishing.

MacHale, D. J. East of the Sun, West of the Moon, 1 vol. Flesher, Vivienne, illus. 2007. (Rabbit Ears: A Classic Tale Ser.). (ENG.). 36p. (gr. -1-3). 25.65 *(978-1-59961-306-2(9))* Spotlight.

Nesbø, Jo. Doctor Proctor's Fart Powder. Chace, Tara F., tr. Lowery, Mike, illus. 2010. (Doctor Proctor's Fart Powder Ser.). (ENG.). 288p. (J). (gr. 3-7). pap. 7.99 *(978-1-4169-7973-9(5)*, Aladdin) Simon & Schuster Children's Publishing.

—Doctor Proctor's Fart Powder. Chace, Tara, tr. from GER. Lowery, Mike, illus. 2009. (Doctor Proctor's Fart Powder Ser.). (ENG.). 272p. (J). (gr. 3-7). 17.99 *(978-1-4169-7972-2(7)*, Aladdin) Simon & Schuster Children's Publishing.

—Doctor Proctor's Fart Powder. 2010. (Dr. Proctor's Fart Powder Ser.: 1). lib. bdg. 18.40 *(978-0-606-15419-2(1)*, Turtleback) Turtleback Bks.

—Silent (but Deadly) Night. Lowery, Mike, illus. 2017. (J). pap. ***(978-1-5344-1000-8(7)***, Simon & Schuster/Paula Wiseman Bks.) Simon & Schuster/Paula Wiseman Bks.

Nesbø, Jo. Who Cut the Cheese? Chace, Tara F., tr. Lowery, Mike, illus. 2012. (Doctor Proctor's Fart Powder Ser.). (ENG.). 464p. (J). (gr. 3-7). pap. 7.99 *(978-1-4424-3308-3(6)*, Aladdin) Simon & Schuster Children's Publishing.

—Who Cut the Cheese? Chace, Tara, tr. from NOR. Lowery, Mike, illus. 2012. (Doctor Proctor's Fart Powder Ser.). (ENG.). 464p. (J). (gr. 3-7). 17.99 *(978-1-4424-3307-6(8)*, Aladdin) Simon & Schuster Children's Publishing.

Paulson, Ingrid. Valkyrie Rising. 2012. (Valkyrie Rising Ser.). (ENG.). 352p. (YA). (gr. 8). 17.99 *(978-0-06-202572-2(4)*, HarperTeen) HarperCollins Pubs.

Peers, Bobbie. William Wenton & the Impossible Puzzle. 2017. (William Wenton Ser.: 1). (ENG., Illus.). 272p. (J). (gr. 3-7). 16.99 ***(978-1-4814-7825-0(7)***, Aladdin) Simon & Schuster Children's Publishing.

Preus, Margi. Shadow on the Mountain. 2012. (ENG., Illus.). 304p. (YA). (gr. 3-7). 17.95 *(978-1-4197-0424-6(9)*, Amulet Bks.) Abrams, Inc.

—West of the Moon. 2014. (ENG., Illus.). 224p. (J). (gr. 3-7). 16.95 *(978-1-4197-0896-1(1)*, Amulet Bks.) Abrams, Inc.

Rossing, Nina. Fjord Blue. 2016. (ENG., Illus.). (YA). 27.99 ***(978-1-63533-016-8(5))***; 256p. (J). pap. 16.99 *(978-1-63476-385-1(8))* Dreamspinner Pr. (Harmony Ink Pr.).

Røssland, Ingelin. Minus Me. Dawkin, Deborah, tr. from NOR. 2015. (ENG.). 288p. (J). (gr. 4-9). pap. 10.99 *(978-1-78074-694-4(6))* Oneworld Pubns. GBR. Dist: Publishers Group West (PGW).

Sharp, Margery. The Rescuers. Williams, Garth, illus. 2016. (ENG.). 160p. (J). (gr. 4-7). pap. 9.99 *(978-1-68137-007-1(7)*, NYRB Kids) New York Review of Bks., Inc., The.

Thorne-Thomsen, Gudrun. East O' the Sun & West O' the Moon. Richardson, Frederick, illus. 2009. 148p. pap. 8.95 *(978-1-59915-337-7(8))* Yesterday's Classics.

—East O' the Sun & West O' the Moon: With Other Norwegian Folk Tales. 2007. (ENG.). 104p. pap. 18.99 *(978-1-4346-0058-5(0))*; 114p. pap. 19.99 *(978-1-4346-0062-2(9))* Creative Media Partners, LLC.

Undset, Sigrid. Sigurd & His Brave Companions: A Tale of Medieval Norway. Bull Teilman, Gunvor, illus. 2013. (ENG.). 152p. pap. 16.95 *(978-0-8166-7826-6(X))* Univ. of Minnesota Pr.

NORWAY—HISTORY—FICTION

Casanova, Mary. The Klipfish Code. 2012. (ENG.). 240p. (J). (gr. 5-7). pap. 6.99 *(978-0-547-74447-6(1))* Houghton Mifflin Harcourt Publishing Co.

Kaurin, Marianne. Almost Autumn. Hedger, Rosie, tr. from NOR. 2017. (ENG.). 288p. (J). (gr. 7). 17.99 *(978-0-545-88965-0(0)*, Levine, Arthur A. Bks.) Scholastic, Inc.

McSwigan, Marie. Snow Treasure. Reardon, Mary, illus. 2006. (ENG.). 208p. (J). (gr. 3-7). 6.99 *(978-0-14-240224-5(9)*, Puffin Books) Penguin Young Readers Group.

Preus, Margi. Shadow on the Mountain. 2014. (ENG., Illus.). 320p. (YA). (gr. 3-7). pap. 8.95 *(978-1-4197-1159-6(8)*, Amulet Bks.) Abrams, Inc.

Simpson, Craig. Resistance. 2007. (ENG., Illus.). 368p. (YA). (gr. 7). pap. 15.99 *(978-0-552-55571-5(1))* Transworld Publishers Ltd. GBR. Dist: Independent Pubs. Group.

NORWEGIAN LANGUAGE

Hippocrene Books Staff, ed. Norwegian Children's Picture Dictionary: English-Norwegian/Norwegian-English. 2006. (ENG., Illus.). 114p. pap. 14.95 *(978-0-7818-1164-4(3))* Hippocrene Bks., Inc.

Modéré, Armelle. My First English/Norwegian Dictionary of Sentences. 2008. (NOR & ENG., Illus.). 128p. (J). *(978-1-57534-048-7(8))* Skandisk, Inc.

NORWEGIANS—UNITED STATES—FICTION

Peterson, Esther Allen. Coming of Age. 2010. (J). pap. *(978-0-88092-485-6(3))* Royal Fireworks Publishing Co.

—The House That Cared. 2010. (J). pap. *(978-0-88092-505-1(1))* Royal Fireworks Publishing Co.

—A Long Journey to a New Home. 2006. (J). pap. *(978-0-88092-470-2(5))*; lib. bdg. *(978-0-88092-469-6(1))* Royal Fireworks Publishing Co.

—Will Spring Come? 2009. (Illus.). 157p. (J). *(978-0-88092-768-0(2))* Royal Fireworks Publishing Co.

Push to the West (Norwegians) 76p. (YA). (gr. 6-12). pap. 9.95 *(978-0-8224-3678-2(7))* Globe Fearon Educational Publishing.

NOTATION, MUSICAL

see Musical Notation

NOVA SCOTIA

Beckett, Harry. Nova Scotia. 2003. (Eye on Canada Ser.). (Illus.). 32p. (J). pap. 9.95 *(978-1-894705-05-9(X))* Weigl Pubs., Inc.

Boudreau, Hélène. Life in a Fishing Community. 2009. (Learn about Rural Life Ser.). (ENG., Illus.). 32p. (J). (gr. 3-6). pap. *(978-0-7787-5085-7(X))* Crabtree Publishing Co.

Grant, Vicki. The Halifax Citadel. Pilsworth, Graham, illus. 2003. (Dreadful Truth Ser.). (ENG.). 80p. (J). (gr. 3-8). *(978-0-88780-599-8(X))* Formac Publishing Co., Ltd.

Hammer, Maxwell. Sidney Crosby: NHL MVP & Champion. 2015. (Today's MVPs & Champions Ser.). (ENG.). 24p. (J). (gr. 2-5). 27.07 *(978-1-63143-740-3(2)*, 208575) Child's World, Inc., The.

Joyce, Jaime. A Fatal Fall: Was It an Accident or Murder? 2011. (J). pap. *(978-0-545-32809-8(8))* Scholastic, Inc.

Kyi, Tanya Lloyd. Nova Scotia, 1 vol. 2003. (Canada Ser.). (ENG., Illus.). 96p. *(978-1-55285-418-1(3))* Whitecap Bks., Ltd.

Lamb, Lee. Oak Island Family: The Restall Hunt for Buried Treasure. 2012. (ENG., Illus.). 136p. (YA). pap. 19.99 *(978-1-4597-0342-1(1))* Dundurn CAN. Dist: Ingram Publisher Services.

—Oak Island Family: The Restall Hunt for Buried Treasure (Large Print 16pt) 2013. 204p. pap. *(978-1-4596-6324-4(1))* ReadHowYouWant.com, Ltd.

Redmond, Shirley Raye. The Oak Island Treasure Pit. 2011. (Mysterious Encounters Ser.). 48p. lib. bdg. 29.00 *(978-0-7377-5140-6(1)*, Kidhaven) Cengage Gale.

Stanbridge, Joanne. Maurice Ruddick: Un Survivant. 2004. (FRE., Illus.). (J). *(978-2-7650-0744-9(6))* Les Editions de la Cheneliere, Inc.

Tooke, Susan. B Is for Bluenose: A Nova Scotia Alphabet. Tooke, Susan, illus. 2008. (Discover Canada Province by Province Ser.). (ENG., Illus.). 40p. (J). 17.95 *(978-1-58536-362-9(6))* Sleeping Bear Pr.

Walker, Sally M. Blizzard of Glass: The Halifax Explosion Of 1917. 2011. (ENG., Illus.). 160p. (YA). (gr. 5-9). 18.99 *(978-0-8050-8945-5(4)*, 9780805089455, Holt, Henry & Co. Bks. For Young Readers) Holt, Henry & Co.

—Blizzard of Glass: The Halifax Explosion Of 1917. 2014. (ENG., Illus.). 160p. (YA). (gr. 5-9). pap. 14.99 *(978-1-250-04008-4(6)*, 9781250040084) Square Fish.

NOVA SCOTIA—FICTION

Aker, Don. The Fifth Rule. 2014. 256p. (YA). (gr. 8). pap. 8.99 *(978-0-06-231348-5(7))* HarperCollins Pubs.

—The First Stone. 2004. (ENG.). 304p. (J). mass mkt. 6.99 *(978-0-00-639286-6(5)*, Harper Trophy) HarperCollins Pubs.

Amoss, Berthe. The Loup Garou, 1 vol. Amoss, Berthe, illus. 2011. (ENG., Illus.). 48p. (J). (gr. 1-3). pap. 11.99 *(978-1-58980-893-5(2))* Pelican Publishing Co., Inc.

Ashby, Freya Katrina. Summer at the Dunes: A Deirdre Carlisle Mystery. 2007. 108p. per. 9.95 *(978-0-595-43663-7(3))* iUniverse, Inc.

Barkhouse, Joyce. Pit Pony, 1 vol. 2nd ed. 2010. (ENG., Illus.). 136p. (J). (gr. 3-5). 12.95 *(978-0-88780-924-8(3)*, 9780887809248) Formac Publishing Co., Ltd. CAN. Dist: Casemate Pubs. & Bk. Distributors, LLC.

Barkhouse, Joyce & Barkhouse, Janet. Pit Pony: The Picture Book. Smith, Sydney, illus. 2012. (ENG.). 32p. (J). (gr. -1-2). 14.95 *(978-1-4595-0143-0(8)*, 9781459501430) Formac Publishing Co., Ltd. CAN. Dist: Casemate Pubs. & Bk. Distributors, LLC.

Bass, Karen. Two Times a Traitor. 2017. (ENG.). 288p. (J). (gr. 4-8). 15.95 ***(978-1-77278-031-4(6))***; pap. 10.95 ***(978-1-77278-024-6(3))*** Pajama Pr. CAN. Dist: Ingram Publisher Services.

Bawtree, Michael. Joe Howe to the Rescue, 1 vol. Smith, David Preston, illus. 2004. (ENG.). 152p. (J). (gr. 4-7). pap. 12.95 *(978-1-55109-495-3(9))* Nimbus Publishing, Ltd. CAN. Dist: Orca Bk. Pubs. USA.

Choyce, Lesley. Hell's Hotel, 1 vol. rev. ed. 2008. (Lorimer SideStreets Ser.). (ENG.). 224p. (YA). (gr. 9-12). 9.95 *(978-1-55277-022-1(2)*, 9781552770221) Lorimer, James & Co., Ltd., Pubs. CAN. Dist: Casemate Pubs. & Bk. Distributors, LLC.

Coates, Jan. King of Keji, 1 vol. MacKinnon, Patsy, illus. 2015. (ENG.). 32p. (J). (gr. k-3). pap. 12.95 *(978-1-77108-281-5(X))* Nimbus Publishing, Ltd. CAN. Dist: Orca Bk. Pubs. USA.

Dale, Mitzi. The Great & Awful Summer, 1 vol. 2007. (ENG.). 192p. (YA). (gr. 8-12). pap. 9.95 *(978-1-55109-614-8(5))* Nimbus Publishing, Ltd. CAN. Dist: Orca Bk. Pubs. USA.

Dinsdale, Christopher. Betrayed: The Legend of Oak Island. 2009. (Stories of Canada Ser.). (ENG., Illus.). 304p. (J). (gr. 6-8). pap. 10.95 *(978-1-894917-91-9(X)*, Napoleon & Co.) Dundurn CAN. Dist: Ingram Publisher Services.

Gunnery, Sylvia. Personal Best, 1 vol. 2005. (Lorimer Sports Stories Ser.). (ENG.). 112p. (J). (gr. 4-8). 16.95 *(978-1-55028-897-1(0)*, 9781550288971) Lorimer, James &

Co., Ltd., Pubs. CAN. Dist: Casemate Pubs. & Bk. Distributors, LLC.
Halsey, Jacqueline. Explosion News. Migani, Loretta, illus. 2015. (ENG.). 32p. (J). (gr. -1-4). 16.95 *(978-1-4595-0401-1(1),* 9781459504011) Formac Publishing Co., Ltd. CAN. Dist: Casemate Pubs. & Bk. Distributors, LLC.
Hull, Maureen. The View from a Kite, 1 vol. 2007. (ENG., Illus.). 320p. (YA). (gr. 8-12). pap. 15.95 *(978-1-55109-591-2(2),* Vagrant Pr.) Nimbus Publishing, Ltd. CAN. Dist: Orca Bk. Pubs. USA.
Larson, Hope. Mercury. Larson, Hope, illus. 2010. (ENG., Illus.). 240p. (YA). (gr. 7-18). 19.99 *(978-1-4169-3585-8(1));* pap. 15.99 *(978-1-4169-3588-9(6))* Simon & Schuster Children's Publishing. (Atheneum Bks. for Young Readers).
Lightburn, Sandra. Pumpkin People, 1 vol. Lightburn, Ron, illus. 2009. (ENG.). 32p. (J). (gr. -1-5). 17.95 *(978-1-55109-681-0(1))* Nimbus Publishing, Ltd. CAN. Dist: Orca Bk. Pubs. USA.
May, Maggie. Pilot, Swaydy & Friends. Larade, April, illus. 2011. 30p. pap. 24.95 *(978-1-4560-8499-8(2))* America Star Bks.
Montgomery, L. M. Anne of the Island. 2006. (ENG.). pap. *(978-1-4068-2171-0(3));* pap. *(978-1-4068-3175-7(1))* Echo Library.
—Anne of the Island. 2004. reprint ed. pap. 1.99 *(978-1-4192-0718-1(0));* pap. 30.95 *(978-1-4179-0885-1(8))* Kessinger Publishing, LLC.
—Anne of the Island. l.t. ed. 2004. 396p. 26.00 *(978-1-58287-640-5(1))* North Bks.
—Anne of the Island. 2010. (Puffin Classics Ser.). (ENG.). 368p. (J). (gr. 5-7). pap. 5.99 *(978-0-14-132736-5(7),* Puffin Books) Penguin Young Readers Group.
Nervelle, Rosemarie. The Witch of Beaver Creek Mine. 2007. (ENG.). 160p. (J). (gr. 3-7). 14.95 *(978-0-89272-741-4(1));* 2nd ed. pap. 9.95 *(978-0-89272-763-6(2))* Down East Bks.
Payzant, Joan M. Who's a Scaredy Cat! A Story of the Halifax Explosion, 1 vol. Simons, Marijke, tr. Simons, Marijke, illus. 2005. (ENG.). 85p. (J). (gr. 4-7). pap. 11.95 *(978-1-55109-456-4(8))* Nimbus Publishing, Ltd. CAN. Dist: Orca Bk. Pubs. USA.
Perkyns, Dorothy. Last Days in Africville. 2005. (Illus.). 144p. (YA). pap., tchr. ed. *(978-0-88878-446-9(5),* Sandcastle Bks.) Dundurn.
—Last Days in Africville. 2006. (ENG.). 120p. (J). (gr. 4-7). pap. 10.99 *(978-1-55002-630-6(5),* Dundurn Pr.) Dundurn CAN. Dist: Ingram Publisher Services.
Poplawska, Yolanda, illus. Halifax Harbour 123 (BB) A Counting Book about Halifax Harbour, 1 vol. 2014. (ENG.). 12p. (J). (gr. -1-k). bds. 9.95 *(978-1-77108-002-6(7))* Nimbus Publishing, Ltd. CAN. Dist: Orca Bk. Pubs. USA.
Ryan, Tom. Way to Go, 1 vol. 2012. (ENG.). 224p. (YA). (gr. 8-12). pap. 12.95 *(978-1-4598-0077-9(X))* Orca Bk. Pubs. USA.
Schwarzkopf, Tom. Danger at Mason's Island, 1 vol. 2007. (ENG.). 128p. (J). (gr. 4-7). pap. 10.95 *(978-1-55109-562-2(9))* Nimbus Publishing, Ltd. CAN. Dist: Orca Bk. Pubs. USA.
Shaw, Tucker. Anxious Hearts. (ENG.). 272p. (YA). (gr. 7-17). 2011. pap. 6.95 *(978-0-8109-9711-0(8))* 2010. 16.95 *(978-0-8109-8718-0(X))* Abrams, Inc. (Amulet Bks.).
Smallman, Steve. Santa Is Coming to Nova Scotia. 2014. (ENG.). 32p. (J). (-3). 11.99 *(978-1-4926-0709-0(6),* Sourcebooks Jabberwocky) Sourcebooks, Inc.
Thompson, Lisa. Digging for Buried Treasure. Cantell, Brenda, illus. 2006. (Treasure Trackers Ser.). 80p. (J). (gr. 3-4). lib. bdg. 19.00 *(978-0-7910-8872-2(3),* Chelsea Hse.) Facts On File, Inc.
—Search for the Lost Cavern. 2007. (Illus.). 56p. (J). pap. *(978-1-4207-0718-2(3))* Sundance/Newbridge Educational Publishing.
Trenowden, Mark. The Miracle of Bean's Bullion. 2012. 192p. pap. *(978-1-84667-041-1(1))* Derwent Pr., The.
Vaughan, Garth. Tommy's New Block Skates, 1 vol. Smith, David Preston, illus. 2007. (ENG.). 32p. (J). (gr. -1-3). pap. 12.95 *(978-1-55109-620-9(X))* Nimbus Publishing, Ltd. CAN. Dist: Orca Bk. Pubs. USA.
Viva, Frank. Sea Change. Viva, Frank, illus. 2016. (ENG., Illus.). 120p. (J). (gr. 2-7). 18.95 *(978-1-935179-92-4(6))* TOON Books / RAW Junior, LLC.
Wilson, Budge. A Fiddle for Angus. Tooke, Susan, illus. 2006. (ENG.). 32p. (J). (gr. 1-4). pap. 13.95 *(978-0-88776-785-2(0),* Tundra Bks.) Tundra Bks. CAN. Dist: Penguin Random Hse. LLC.
—The Leaving, 1 vol. (ENG.). 176p. (J). mass mkt. 6.95 *(978-0-7736-7363-2(6))* Stoddart Kids CAN. Dist: Fitzhenry & Whiteside, Ltd.
Wishinsky, Frieda. Halifax Explodes! Lewis-MacDougall, Patricia Ann & Owlkids Books Inc. Staff, illus. 2011. (Canadian Flyer Adventures Ser.: 17). (ENG.). 96p. (J). (gr. 1-4). pap. 7.95 *(978-1-926818-98-6(9),* Maple Tree Pr.) Owlkids Bks. Inc. CAN. Dist: Publishers Group West (PGW).

NOVELISTS

see Authors

NUCLEAR ENERGY

Bailey, Diane. Harnessing Energy: Nuclear Power. 2015. (Harnessing Energy Ser.). (ENG.). 48p. (J). (gr. 5-8). pap. 12.00 *(978-0-89812-997-7(4),* Creative Paperbacks) Creative Co., The.
Benduhn, Tea. Energía Nuclear. 2008. (Energía para el presente (Energy for Today) Ser.). (SPA.). 24p. (gr. 2-6). (J). lib. bdg. 22.00 *(978-0-8368-9268-0(2));* pap. 8.15 *(978-0-8368-9367-0(0))* Stevens, Gareth Publishing LLLP. (Weekly Reader Leveled Readers).
—Nuclear Power. 2008. (Energy for Today Ser.). 24p. (gr. 2-6). (J). lib. bdg. 22.00 *(978-0-8368-9262-8(3));* pap. 8.15 *(978-0-8368-9361-8(1))* Stevens, Gareth Publishing LLLP. (Weekly Reader Leveled Readers).
Benoit, Peter. The Nuclear Age. 2012. (Cornerstones of Freedom, Third Ser.). (ENG., Illus.). 64p. (J). pap. 8.95 *(978-0-531-28162-8(0));* (gr. 4-6). lib. bdg. 30.00 *(978-0-531-23062-6(7))* Scholastic Library Publishing. (Children's Pr.).
—Nuclear Meltdowns. 2011. (True Book(tm), A — Disasters Ser.). (Illus.). 48p. (J). lib. bdg. 31.00 *(978-0-531-25422-6(4));* (ENG., pap. 6.95 *(978-0-531-26627-4(3))* Scholastic Library Publishing. (Children's Pr.).
Carson, Jill. Nuclear Power. 2010. (Compact Research Ser.). (YA). (gr. 7-12). 26.95 *(978-1-60152-123-1(5))* ReferencePoint Pr., Inc.
Derkins, Susie. The Meltdown at Three Mile Island. 2009. (When Disaster Strikes! Ser.). 48p. (gr. 5-8). 53.00 *(978-1-60854-781-4(7),* Rosen Reference) Rosen Publishing Group, Inc., The.
Dickmann, Nancy. Energy from Nuclear Fission: Splitting the Atom. 2015. (Next Generation Energy Ser.). (ENG., Illus.). 32p. (J). *(978-0-7787-1981-6(2))* Crabtree Publishing Co.
Doeden, Matt. Finding Out about Nuclear Energy. 2014. (Searchlight Books — What Are Energy Sources? Ser.). (Illus.). 40p. (gr. 3-4). pap. 8.95 *(978-1-4677-4556-7(1));* (ENG., lib. bdg. 27.93 *(978-1-4677-3655-8(4),* Lerner Pubns.) Lerner Publishing Group.
Duke, Shirley Smith. Nuclear Power. 2013. (J). *(978-1-61080-971-9(8));* (ENG.). 32p. (gr. 4-8). 28.50 *(978-1-61080-896-5(7),* 202563); (ENG.). 32p. (gr. 4-8). pap. 14.21 *(978-1-61080-921-4(1),* 202565) Cherry Lake Publishing.
Follett, Katherine. Energy Sources for the 21st Century. 2011. (Readers' & Writers' Genre Workshop Ser.). (J). pap. *(978-1-4509-3029-1(8))* Benchmark Education Co.
Friedman, Lauri S. Nuclear Power. 2009. (Introducing Issues with Opposing Viewpoints Ser.). (ENG., Illus.). 144p. (gr. 10-12). 42.00 *(978-0-7377-4482-8(0))* Cengage Gale.
Grady, Colin. Nuclear Energy. 2016. (Saving the Planet Through Green Energy Ser.). 24p. (J). pap. 9.35 *(978-0-7660-8288-5(1))* Enslow Pubs., Inc.
Greeley, August. Fallout: Nuclear Disasters in Our World. 2003. (Man-Made Disasters Ser.). (Illus.). 24p. (J). lib. bdg. 22.60 *(978-0-8239-6484-0(1),* PowerKids Pr.) Rosen Publishing Group, Inc., The.
Greenhaven Press Staff, ed. Nuclear Power. 2012. (Opposing Viewpoints Ser.). (ENG., Illus.). 240p. (gr. 10-12). pap. 29.45 *(978-0-7377-6063-7(X));* lib. bdg. 42.95 *(978-0-7377-6062-0(1))* Cengage Gale. (Greenhaven Pr., Inc.).
Haney, Johannah. Nuclear Energy. 2011. (Debating the Issues Ser.). 64p. (gr. 6). 32.79 *(978-0-7614-4976-8(0))* Marshall Cavendish Corp.
Hansen, Amy. Nuclear Energy: Amazing Atoms. 2010. (Powering Our World Ser.). (ENG.). 24p. (J). pap. 8.25 *(978-1-4358-9744-1(7),* PowerKids Pr.) Rosen Publishing Group, Inc., The.
Hansen, Amy S. Nuclear Energy: Amazing Atoms. 2010. (Powering Our World Ser.). 24p. (J). (gr. 2-5). E-Book 42.50 *(978-1-4488-0201-2(6));* (Illus.). lib. bdg. 22.60 *(978-1-4358-9328-3(X),* PowerKids Pr.) Rosen Publishing Group, Inc., The.
Hantula, Richard, et al. Nuclear Power. 2010. (Energy Today Ser.). 48p. (J). (gr. 3-6). 30.00 *(978-1-60413-784-2(3))* Facts On File, Inc.
Harrison Adams, Troon & Adams, Troon Harrison. Nuclear Energy: Power from the Atom. 2010. (ENG., Illus.). 32p. (J). pap. *(978-0-7787-2935-8(4));* lib. bdg. *(978-0-7787-2921-1(4))* Crabtree Publishing Co.
Hillstrom, Kevin. Nuclear Energy. Greenhaven Press Editors, ed. 2013. (Hot Topics Ser.). (ENG., Illus.). 128p. (gr. 7-10). lib. bdg. 39.40 *(978-1-4205-0874-1(1),* Lucent Bks.) Cengage Gale.
Holt, Rinehart and Winston Staff. Holt Science & Technology Chapter 16: Physical Science: Atomic Energy. 5th ed. 2004. (Illus.). pap. 12.86 *(978-0-03-030413-2(X))* Holt McDougal.
Hulick, Kathryn. Real-World STEM: Develop Fusion Energy. 2017. (ENG.). 80p. (YA). (gr. 5-12). ***(978-1-68282-245-6(1))*** ReferencePoint Pr., Inc.
Lusted, Marcia Amidon. Nuclear Energy, 1 vol. 2013. (Innovative Technologies Ser.). (ENG.). 112p. (J). (gr. 6-12). 35.64 *(978-1-61783-466-0(1))* ABDO Publishing Co.
—The Three Mile Island Nuclear Disaster, 1 vol. 2012. (Essential Events Set 8 Ser.). (ENG.). 112p. (J). (gr. 6-12). lib. bdg. 35.64 *(978-1-61783-311-3(8))* ABDO Publishing Co.
Manatt, Kathleen. Nuclear Energy. 2007. (21st Century Skills Library: Power Up! Ser.). (ENG.). 32p. (gr. 4-8). pap. 14.21 *(978-1-60279-099-5(X),* 200660) Cherry Lake Publishing.
Mara, Wil. The Chernobyl Disaster: Legacy & Impact on the Future of Nuclear Energy. 2010. (Perspectives on 2 Ser.). 112p. (gr. 7). 39.93 *(978-0-7614-4984-3(1))* Marshall Cavendish Corp.
McLean, Adam. What Is Atomic Theory? 2010. (Shaping Modern Science Ser.). (ENG.). 64p. (J). (gr. 5-8). lib. bdg. *(978-0-7787-7197-5(0))* Crabtree Publishing Co.
McLeish, Ewan. The Pros & Cons of Nuclear Power. 2007. (Energy Debate Ser.). (Illus.). 48p. (YA). (gr. 5-9). lib. bdg. 29.25 *(978-1-4042-3740-7(2))* Rosen Publishing Group, Inc., The.
Miller, Debra A. Nuclear Energy. Gale Editors, ed. 2010. (Current Controversies Ser.). (ENG.). 224p. (gr. 10-12). 46.40 *(978-0-7377-4917-5(2));* pap. 32.00 *(978-0-7377-4918-2(0))* Cengage Gale. (Greenhaven Pr., Inc.).
Morris, Neil. Nuclear Power. 2010. (J). 34.25 *(978-1-59920-341-6(3))* 2007. (Illus.). 32p. (YA). (gr. 4-7). lib. bdg. 28.50 *(978-1-58340-907-7(6))* Black Rabbit Bks.
Olhoff, Jim. Nuclear Energy, 1 vol. 2010. (Future Energy Ser.). (ENG.). 32p. (YA). (gr. 4-7). 27.07 *(978-1-60453-936-3(4))* ABDO Publishing Co.
Owen, Ruth. Energy from Atoms: Nuclear Power. 2013. (Power: Yesterday, Today, Tomorrow Ser.). (ENG., Illus.). 32p. (J). (gr. 3-6). 25.25 *(978-1-4777-0272-7(5));* pap. 11.75 *(978-1-4777-0283-3(0))* Rosen Publishing Group, Inc., The. (PowerKids Pr.).
Oxlade, Chris. Nuclear Energy, 1 vol. 2011. (Tales of Invention Ser.). (ENG.). 32p. (gr. 3-5). pap. 8.95 *(978-1-4329-4888-7(1),* NA-h) Heinemann-Raintree.
—Nuclear Power. 2010. (J). 34.25 *(978-1-59920-320-1(0))* Black Rabbit Bks.
Paley, Caitlyn. The Pros & Cons of Nuclear Power. 2016. (Economics of Energy Ser.). (ENG., Illus.). 80p. (J). (gr. 7-7). 35.64 *(978-1-5026-0950-2(9))* Cavendish Square Publishing.
Parker, Steve. Nuclear Energy. 2004. (Science Files Ser.). (Illus.). 32p. (gr. 2-6). lib. bdg. 26.00 *(978-0-8368-4030-8(5),* Gareth Stevens Learning Library) Stevens, Gareth Publishing LLLP.
Pipe, Jim. Nuclear Power. 2010. (J). 28.50 *(978-1-59604-210-0(9))* Black Rabbit Bks.
Reynoldson, Fiona. Understanding Nuclear Power. 2010. (World of Energy Ser.). (ENG.). 48p. (J). (gr. 6-8). lib. bdg. 31.95 *(978-1-4339-4124-5(4),* Gareth Stevens Learning Library) Stevens, Gareth Publishing LLLP.
Richards, Julie. Nuclear Energy. 2009. (J). 19.95 *(978-0-7614-4433-6(5))* Marshall Cavendish GBR. Dist: Marshall Cavendish Corp.
Rosinsky, Natalie M. The Story of the Atomic Bomb: How It Changed the World, 1 vol. 2010. (World Transformed Ser.). (ENG.). 64p. (gr. 6-7). lib. bdg. 33.99 *(978-0-7565-4316-7(9),* CPB Grades 4-8) Compass Point Bks.
Spilsbury, Richard & Spilsbury, Louise. Nuclear Power. 2012. (Let's Discuss Energy Resources Ser.). (Illus.). 32p. (YA). (gr. 4-7). lib. bdg. 26.50 *(978-1-4488-5291-8(9))* Rosen Publishing Group, Inc., The.
Tiner, John Hudson. Uranium & Plutonium Make Nuclear Power. 2003. (From Resource to Energy Source Ser.). (J). *(978-1-58417-288-8(6));* pap. *(978-1-58417-289-5(4))* Lake Street Pubs.
Venezia, Mike. Lise Meitner: Had the Right Vision about Nuclear Fission. Venezia, Mike, illus. 2010. (Getting to Know the World's Greatest Inventors & Scientists Ser.). (ENG., Illus.). 32p. (J). (gr. 3-4). pap. 6.95 *(978-0-531-20776-5(5),* Children's Pr.) Scholastic Library Publishing.
Wheeler, Jill C. Nuclear Power, 1 vol. 2008. (Eye on Energy Ser.). (ENG., Illus.). 32p. (gr. k-6). 27.07 *(978-1-59928-807-9(9),* Checkerboard Library) ABDO Publishing Co.
Young-Brown, Fiona. Nuclear Fusion & Fission. 2016. (Great Discoveries in Science Ser.). (Illus.). 128p. (J). (gr. 9-9). 45.64 *(978-1-5026-1949-5(0))* Cavendish Square Publishing.

NUCLEAR ENGINEERING

see also Nuclear Reactors

Bailey, Diane. Harnessing Energy: Nuclear Power. 2015. (Harnessing Energy Ser.). (ENG.). 48p. (J). (gr. 5-8). pap. 12.00 *(978-0-89812-997-7(4),* Creative Paperbacks) Creative Co., The.
Friedman, Lauri S. Nuclear Power. 2009. (Introducing Issues with Opposing Viewpoints Ser.). (ENG., Illus.). 144p. (gr. 10-12). 42.00 *(978-0-7377-4482-8(0))* Cengage Gale.
Jakubiak, David J. What Can We Do about Nuclear Waste? 2012. (Illus.). 24p. (J). 49.50 *(978-1-4488-5115-7(7),* PowerKids Pr.); (J). pap. 8.25 *(978-1-4488-5114-0(9),* PowerKids Pr.); (YA). (gr. 2-5). lib. bdg. 22.60 *(978-1-4488-4983-3(7))* Rosen Publishing Group, Inc., The.
Morris, Neil. Nuclear Power. 2007. (Energy Sources Ser.). (Illus.). 32p. (YA). (gr. 4-7). lib. bdg. 28.50 *(978-1-58340-907-7(6))* Black Rabbit Bks.
Olhoff, Jim. Nuclear Energy, 1 vol. 2010. (Future Energy Ser.). (ENG.). 32p. (YA). (gr. 4-7). 27.07 *(978-1-60453-936-3(4))* ABDO Publishing Co.
Oxlade, Chris. Nuclear Power. 2010. (J). 34.25 *(978-1-59920-320-1(0))* Black Rabbit Bks.
Paley, Caitlyn. The Pros & Cons of Nuclear Power. 2016. (Economics of Energy Ser.). (ENG., Illus.). 80p. (J). (gr. 7-7). 35.64 *(978-1-5026-0950-2(9))* Cavendish Square Publishing.
Richards, Julie. Nuclear Energy. 2009. (J). 19.95 *(978-0-7614-4433-6(5))* Marshall Cavendish GBR. Dist: Marshall Cavendish Corp.

NUCLEAR PHYSICS

see also Chemistry, Physical and Theoretical; Electrons; Nuclear Engineering; Nuclear Reactors; Radioactivity

Barron, Rachel Stiffler. Lise Meitner: Discoverer of Nuclear Fission. 2004. (Profiles in Science Ser.). (Illus.). 112p. (YA). (gr. 6-12). lib. bdg. 23.95 *(978-1-883846-52-7(8),* First Biographies) Reynolds, Morgan Inc.
Bortz, Fred. Understanding the Large Hadron Collider. 2015. (Exploring the Subatomic World Ser.). (ENG., Illus.). 64p. (J). (gr. 8-8). lib. bdg. 34.21 *(978-1-5026-0552-8(X))* Cavendish Square Publishing.
Cooper, Christopher. The Basics of Nuclear Physics. 2014. (Core Concepts Ser.). 96p. (YA). (gr. 7-12). 35.60 *(978-1-4777-7770-1(9))* Rosen Publishing Group, Inc., The.
Jackson, Tom. The Basics of Atoms & Molecules. 2013. (Core Concepts Ser.). 96p. (YA). (gr. 7-12). 34.60 *(978-1-4777-2715-7(9))* Rosen Publishing Group, Inc., The.
Morris, Neil. Nuclear Power. 2010. (J). 34.25 *(978-1-59920-341-6(3))* Black Rabbit Bks.
Oxlade, Chris. Nuclear Power. 2010. (J). 34.25 *(978-1-59920-320-1(0))* Black Rabbit Bks.
Parker, Katie. Splitting the Atom. 2009. (Big Ideas in Science Ser.). (Illus.). 48p. (gr. 5-8). 31.36 *(978-0-7614-4399-5(1))* Marshall Cavendish Corp.
Rock, Meghan. String Theory. 2016. (Great Discoveries in Science Ser.). 128p. (J). (gr. 9-9). 45.64 *(978-1-5026-1961-7(X))* Cavendish Square Publishing.
Singer, Neal. Wonders of Nuclear Fusion: Creating an Ultimate Energy Source. 2011. (World's of Wonder Ser.). (ENG., Illus.). 130p. (J). (gr. 4-18). 34.95 *(978-0-8263-4778-7(9))* Univ. of New Mexico Pr.
Slade, Suzanne. The Structure of Atoms. (Library of Physical Science Ser.). 24p. (gr. 4-4). 2009. 42.50 *(978-1-60853-795-2(1))* 2007. (ENG., Illus.). pap. 7.05 *(978-1-4042-2161-1(1))* Rosen Publishing Group, Inc., The. (PowerKids Pr.).
Spiro, Ruth & Chan, Irene. Baby Loves Quarks! 2016. (Baby Loves Science Ser.). (ENG., Illus.). 20p. (J). (— 1). bds. 8.95 *(978-1-58089-540-8(9))* Charlesbridge Publishing, Inc.
Venezia, Mike. Lise Meitner: Had the Right Vision about Nuclear Fission. Venezia, Mike, illus. 2009. (Getting to Know the World's Greatest Inventors & Scientists Ser.). (ENG., Illus.). 32p. (J). (gr. 2-5). 28.00 *(978-0-531-23702-1(8))* Scholastic Library Publishing.
Walliman, Dominic. Professor Astro Cat's Atomic Adventure. Newman, Ben, illus. 2016. (ENG.). 56p. (J). (gr. 1-6). 24.00 *(978-1-909263-60-4(5))* Flying Eye Bks. GBR. Dist: Consortium Bk. Sales & Distribution.
Whiting, Jim. Mysteries of the Universe: Mass & Matter. 2013. (Mysteries of the Universe Ser.). (ENG., Illus.). 48p. (J). (gr. 4-7). pap. 12.00 *(978-0-89812-916-8(8),* Creative Paperbacks) Creative Co., The.
Young-Brown, Fiona. Nuclear Fusion & Fission. 2016. (Great Discoveries in Science Ser.). (Illus.). 128p. (J). (gr. 9-9). 45.64 *(978-1-5026-1949-5(0))* Cavendish Square Publishing.

NUCLEAR PHYSICS—HISTORY

Pasachoff, Naomi E. Ernest Rutherford: Father of Nuclear Science. 2005. (Great Minds of Science Ser.). (Illus.). 128p. (J). lib. bdg. 26.60 *(978-0-7660-2441-0(5))* Enslow Pubs., Inc.

NUCLEAR POWER

see also Atomic Bomb; Nuclear Engineering; Nuclear Reactors

Bailey, Diane. Nuclear Power. 2014. (Harnessing Energy Ser.). 35.65 *(978-1-60818-411-8(0))* Creative Co., The.
Gillard, Arthur, ed. Nuclear Power. 2011. (Issues That Concern You Ser.). (Illus.). 144p. (YA). (gr. 9-12). 36.95 *(978-0-7377-5696-8(9))* Cengage Gale.
Kidd, Renee A. Nuclear Power: The Study of Quarks & Sparks. 2nd rev. ed. 2006. (Science & Society Ser.). (Illus.). 176p. (gr. 6-12). 35.00 *(978-0-8160-5606-4(4))* Facts On File, Inc.
Lopatka, Michael. Nuclear Power Facility Virtual Field Trip. 2003. (YA). cd-rom 15.95 *(978-0-9723218-8-4(8))* Awesome Guides, Inc.
Metcalf, Tom & Metcalf, Gena, eds. Nuclear Power. 2006. (Fueling the Future Ser.). (ENG., Illus.). 244p. (J). (gr. 9-18). lib. bdg. 39.35 *(978-0-7377-3587-1(2),* 1256645, Greenhaven Pr., Inc.) Cengage Gale.
Parker, Steve. Nuclear Energy. 2004. (Science Files Ser.). (Illus.). 32p. (gr. 2-6). lib. bdg. 26.00 *(978-0-8368-4030-8(5),* Gareth Stevens Learning Library) Stevens, Gareth Publishing LLLP.

NUCLEAR POWER—FICTION

Beard, Linda P. Remember ... Remember Your Name. 2011. 24p. (gr. 4-6). pap. 14.99 *(978-1-4269-6859-4(0))* Trafford Publishing.
Hesse, Karen. Phoenix Rising. 2009. (ENG.). 208p. (J). (gr. 6-11). pap. 9.99 *(978-0-312-53562-9(7),* 9780312535629) Square Fish.

NUCLEAR POWER PLANTS

Arato, Rona. Fukushima Nuclear Disaster. 2013. (ENG., Illus.). 32p. (J). *(978-0-7787-1192-6(7));* pap. *(978-0-7787-1194-0(3))* Crabtree Publishing Co.
Benoit, Peter. Nuclear Meltdowns. 2011. (True Book(tm), A — Disasters Ser.). (Illus.). 48p. (J). lib. bdg. 31.00 *(978-0-531-25422-6(4));* (ENG., pap. 6.95 *(978-0-531-26627-4(3))* Scholastic Library Publishing. (Children's Pr.).
Derkins, Susie. The Meltdown at Three Mile Island. (When Disaster Strikes! Ser.). 48p. (gr. 5-8). 2009. 53.00 *(978-1-60854-781-4(7),* Rosen Reference) 2005. (Illus.). (YA). lib. bdg. 29.25 *(978-0-8239-3678-6(3))* Rosen Publishing Group, Inc., The.
Feigenbaum, Aaron. Emergency at Three Mile Island. 2007. (Code Red Ser.). (Illus.). 32p. (YA). (gr. 2-5). lib. bdg. 25.27 *(978-1-59716-364-4(3))* Bearport Publishing Co., Inc.
Greeley, August. Fallout: Nuclear Disasters in Our World. 2009. (Man-Made Disasters Ser.). 24p. (gr. 3-3). 42.50 *(978-1-61514-348-1(3),* PowerKids Pr.) Rosen Publishing Group, Inc., The.
Haney, Johannah. Nuclear Energy. 2011. (Debating the Issues Ser.). 64p. (gr. 6). 32.79 *(978-0-7614-4976-8(0))* Marshall Cavendish Corp.
Hulick, Kathryn. Real-World STEM: Develop Fusion Energy. 2017. (ENG.). 80p. (YA). (gr. 5-12). ***(978-1-68282-245-6(1))*** ReferencePoint Pr., Inc.
Ingram, Scott. The Chernobyl Nuclear Disaster. 2005. (Environmental Disasters Ser.). (Illus.). 112p. (J). (gr. 6-12). 35.00 *(978-0-8160-5755-9(9))* Facts On File, Inc.
Larson, Kirsten. Nuclear Meltdowns. 2015. (ENG.). 48p. (gr. 3-6). 35.64 *(978-1-63430-428-3(4))* Rourke Educational Media.
Lusted, Greg & Lusted, Marcia Amidon. A Nuclear Power Plant. 2005. (Building History Ser.). (ENG., Illus.). 112p. (YA). (gr. 7-12). lib. bdg. 32.45 *(978-1-59018-392-2(4))* Cengage Gale.
Lusted, Marcia Amidon. The Chernobyl Disaster, 1 vol. 2011. (Essential Events Set 6 Ser.). (ENG., Illus.). 112p. (J). (gr. 6-12). lib. bdg. 35.64 *(978-1-61714-763-0(X))* ABDO Publishing Co.
—The Three Mile Island Nuclear Disaster, 1 vol. 2012. (Essential Events Set 8 Ser.). (ENG.). 112p. (J). (gr. 6-12). lib. bdg. 35.64 *(978-1-61783-311-3(8))* ABDO Publishing Co.
Marquardt, Meg. The Science of a Nuclear Plant Explosion. 2015. (21st Century Skills Library: Disaster Science Ser.). (ENG., Illus.). 32p. (J). (gr. 4-8). 29.93 *(978-1-63362-480-1(3),* 206828) Cherry Lake Publishing.
Olhoff, Jim. Nuclear Energy, 1 vol. 2010. (Future Energy Ser.). (ENG.). 32p. (YA). (gr. 4-7). 27.07 *(978-1-60453-936-3(4))* ABDO Publishing Co.
Rissman, Rebecca. Chernobyl Disaster, 1 vol. 2013. (History's Greatest Disasters Ser.). (ENG.). 48p. (J). (gr. 3-6). lib. bdg. 32.79 *(978-1-61783-955-9(8))* ABDO Publishing Co.
—Chernobyl Disaster Paperback. 2013. (J). pap. 15.64 *(978-1-62403-020-8(3),* Core Library) ABDO Publishing Co.
Smith, Jim & Beresford, Nicholas A. Chernobyl: Catastrophe & Consequences, 1 vol. 2005. (Springer Praxis Bks.). (ENG., Illus.). xxvi, 310p. 249.99 *(978-3-540-23866-9(2),* 9783540238669) Springer.
Woods, Michael & Woods, Mary B. Environmental Disasters. 2008. (Disasters up Close Ser.). (ENG., Illus.). 64p. (gr. 4-8). lib. bdg. 27.93 *(978-0-8225-6774-5(1),* Lerner Pubns.) Lerner Publishing Group.

NUCLEAR REACTORS

Cruise, Robin. The Nuclear Disaster at Chernobyl. Taylor, Marjorie, illus. rev. ed. 2003. (Take Ten Ser.). 46p. (J). (gr. 4-18). pap. 4.95 *(978-1-58659-022-2(7))* Artesian Pr.
Mahaffey, James A. Nuclear Fission Reactors. 2011. (Nuclear Power Ser.). (Illus.). 160p. (C). (gr. 9). 45.00 *(978-0-8160-7651-2(0))* Facts On File, Inc.

NUCLEAR SUBMARINES

Amato, William. Nuclear Submarines. 2009. (High-Tech Vehicles Ser.). 24p. (gr. 2-3). 42.50 *(978-1-61513-306-2(2),* PowerKids Pr.) Rosen Publishing Group, Inc., The.
—Submarinos Nucleares. 2004. (Vehículos de Alta Tecnología (High-Tech Vehicles) Ser.). (SPA & ENG., Illus.). 24p. (J). (gr. 3-6). lib. bdg. 22.60 *(978-0-8239-6882-4(0),* Editorial Buenas Letras) Rosen Publishing Group, Inc., The.

M N O

—Submarinos nucleares (Nuclear Submarines) 2009. (Vehículos de alta tecnología (High-Tech Vehicles) Ser.). (SPA.). 24p. (gr. 2-3). 42.50 *(978-1-60854-720-3(5),* Editorial Buenas Letras) Rosen Publishing Group, Inc., The.

Loveless, Antony. Nuclear Submariners. 2009. (World's Most Dangerous Jobs Ser.). (ENG., Illus.). 32p. (J). (gr. 3-6). pap. *(978-0-7787-5111-3(2));* lib. bdg. *(978-0-7787-5097-0(3))* Crabtree Publishing Co.

NUCLEAR SUBMARINES—FICTION

Riley, Clifford. Spymasters. 2013. (39 Clues: the Cahill Files Ser.). (ENG., Illus.). 256p. (J). (gr. 3-7). 12.99 *(978-0-545-56468-7(9))* Scholastic, Inc.

NUCLEAR TEST BAN

see Disarmament

NUCLEAR WARFARE

Beyer, Mark. Nuclear Weapons & the Cold War. (Library of Weapons of Mass Destruction Ser.). 64p. 2009. (gr. 5-5). 58.50 *(978-1-60853-953-6(9))* 2005. (Illus.). (J). lib. bdg. 31.95 *(978-1-4042-0290-0(0))* Rosen Publishing Group, Inc., The.

Bougie, Matt. Strategic Inventions of the Cold War. 2016. (Tech in the Trenches Ser.). (ENG., Illus.). 112p. (J). (gr. 9-9). 42.79 *(978-1-5026-1022-5(1))* Cavendish Square Publishing.

Freese, Susan M. Nuclear Weapons, 1 vol. 2011. (Essential Issues Set 3 Ser.). (ENG., Illus.). 112p. (J). (gr. 6-12). lib. bdg. 35.64 *(978-1-61783-137-9(9))* ABDO Publishing Co.

Gerdes, Louise, ed. Nuclear Weapons. 2009. (At Issue Ser.). (ENG.). 128p. (gr. 10-12). 39.40 *(978-0-7377-4308-1(5));* pap. 27.80 *(978-0-7377-4307-4(7))* Cengage Gale. (Greenhaven Pr., Inc.).

Maus, Derek C., ed. Living under the Threat of Nuclear War. 2005. (Living Through the Cold War Ser.). (ENG., Illus.). 143p. (YA). (gr. 10-12). lib. bdg. 37.90 *(978-0-7377-2130-0(8),* Greenhaven Pr., Inc.) Cengage Gale.

Minneus, Steve. Nukes: The Spread of Nuclear Weapons. 2007. (In the News Ser.). (Illus.). 64p. (YA). (gr. 7-12). lib. bdg. 31.95 *(978-1-4042-1916-8(1))* Rosen Publishing Group, Inc., The.

Orr, Tamra. The Hydrogen Bomb: Unleashing the Nuclear Age & Arms Race. 2009. (Library of Weapons of Mass Destruction Ser.). 64p. (gr. 5-5). 58.50 *(978-1-60853-956-7(3))* Rosen Publishing Group, Inc., The.

—The Hydrogen Bomb: Unleashing the Nuclear & Arms Race. 2004. (Library of Weapons of Mass Destruction Ser.). (Illus.). 64p. (J). lib. bdg. 31.95 *(978-1-4042-0293-1(5))* Rosen Publishing Group, Inc., The.

Spalding, Frank. Nuclear Annihilation. 2010. (Doomsday Scenarios: Separating Fact from Fiction Ser.). 64p. (YA). (ENG.). pap. 12.95 *(978-1-4358-8522-6(8),* Rosen Reference); (gr. 5-8). E-Book 58.50 *(978-1-4488-1208-0(9));* (Illus.). (gr. 5-8). lib. bdg. 31.95 *(978-1-4358-3560-3(3),* Rosen Reference) Rosen Publishing Group, Inc., The.

NUCLEAR WARFARE—FICTION

Bodeen, S. A. The Fallout. 2013. (Compound Ser.: 2). (ENG.). 336p. (YA). (gr. 7). 18.99 *(978-0-312-65011-7(6),* 9780312650117) Feiwel & Friends.

Higgins, Jack & Richards, Justin. First Strike. 2011. (Rich & Jade Ser.: Bk. 4). (ENG.). 240p. (YA). (gr. 7-18). 8.99 *(978-0-14-241909-0(5),* Speak) Penguin Young Readers Group.

O'Brien, Robert C. Z for Zachariah. 2007. (ENG.). 240p. (YA). (gr. 7-12). pap. 10.99 *(978-1-4169-3921-4(0),* Simon Pulse) Simon Pulse.

Reedy, Trent. The Last Full Measure. 2016. (Divided We Fall Ser.: 3). (ENG.). 464p. (YA). (gr. 9). 17.99 *(978-0-545-54877-9(2),* Levine, Arthur A. Bks.) Scholastic, Inc.

Strasser, Todd. Fallout. 2013. (ENG.). 272p. (J). (gr. 5). 16.99 *(978-0-7636-5534-1(1))* Candlewick Pr.

Zorn, Claire. The Sky So Heavy. 2014. (ENG.). 302p. (gr. 7). 16.00 *(978-0-7022-4976-1(9))* Univ. of Queensland Pr. AUS. Dist: Independent Pubs. Group.

NUCLEAR WEAPONS AND DISARMAMENT

see Disarmament

NUMBER CONCEPT

ABDO Publishing Company Staff. Numbers 1-20. 2014. (Numbers 1-20 Ser.: 6). (ENG.). 24p. (J). (gr. k-3). lib. bdg. 145.26 *(978-1-62403-263-9(X),* SandCastle) ABDO Publishing Co.

Aboff, Marcie. If You Were an Even Number, 1 vol. Dillard, Sarah, illus. 2008. (Math Fun Ser.). (ENG.). 24p. (gr. 2-4). 27.99 *(978-1-4048-4796-5(0));* pap. 7.95 *(978-1-4048-4797-2(9))* Picture Window Bks.

Accord Publishing Staff. Numbers: A Caterpillar-Shaped Book. 2012. (ENG.). 24p. (J). 11.99 *(978-1-4494-1736-9(1))* Andrews McMeel Publishing.

Ackland, Nick. Numbers. Bradley, Jennie, illus. 2016. (Baby Sparkler Ser.). (ENG.). 10p. (J). (gr. -1 — 1). bds. 5.99 *(978-0-7641-6857-4(6))* Barron's Educational Series, Inc.

—Numbers. 2015. (Bright Beginnings Ser.). (ENG., Illus.). 20p. (J). (gr. -1 — 1). bds. 5.99 *(978-0-7641-6744-7(8))* Barron's Educational Series, Inc.

Adamson, Thomas K. and Heather. Fun with Numbers. 2012. (Fun with Numbers Ser.). (ENG.). 32p. (gr. 1-2). pap. 16.20 *(978-1-4296-8453-8(4));* pap. 190.80 *(978-1-4296-8454-5(2));* lib. bdg. 81.96 *(978-1-4296-8105-6(5))* Capstone Press of Coughlan Cos. (Aplus Bks.).

Adler, David A. Millions, Billions, & Trillions: Understanding Big Numbers. Miller, Edward, illus. (ENG.). 32p. (J). (gr. -1-3). 2014. 7.99 *(978-0-8234-3049-9(9))* 2013. 17.95 *(978-0-8234-2403-0(0))* Holiday Hse., Inc.

Allen, Susan & Lindaman, Jane. Used Any Numbers Lately? Enright, Vicky, illus. 2008. 32p. (J). (gr. k-4). 16.95 *(978-0-8225-8658-6(4),* Millbrook Pr.) Lerner Publishing Group.

Alvarez, Lourdes M. Mi Primer Libro Numeros. Brooks, David, illus. 2005. (Mi primer libro Ser.). (SPA.). 9p. (J). (gr. -1 — 1). bds. 3.95 *(978-1-933050-00-3(4))* Sweetwater Pr.

—My First Book Numbers. Brooks, David, illus. 2005. (My First Book Ser.). 9p. (J). (gr. -1-1). bds. 3.95 *(978-1-933050-06-5(3))* Sweetwater Pr.

Anastasio, Dina. Number Games: Set Of 6. 2011. (Early Connections Ser.). (J). pap. 37.00 net. *(978-1-4108-1082-3(8))* Benchmark Education Co.

Anderson, Joanna. Cooking with My Dad: Number Names & Count Sequence. 2013. (InfoMax Math Readers Ser.). (ENG.). 16p. (J). (gr. k-1). pap. 42.00 *(978-1-4777-1998-5(9));* (Illus.). pap. 7.00 *(978-1-4777-1997-8(0))* Rosen Publishing Group, Inc., The. (Rosen Classroom).

Anthony, Susan C. Casting Nines Quick Check For. 2004. pap. 8.00 *(978-1-879478-09-1(9))* Instructional Resources Co.

Aryai, Sia, photos by. 1 2 3s. (Baby Bright Board Bks.). (Illus.). 10p. (J). (gr. -1). 5.95 *(978-1-56565-824-0(8),* 08248W, Roxbury Park Juvenile) Lowell Hse. Juvenile.

Atwood, Megan. Balancing Bears: Comparing Numbers, 1 vol. Holm, Sharon, illus. 2012. (Count the Critters Ser.). (ENG.). 24p. (J). (gr. k-3). 27.07 *(978-1-61641-851-9(6))* Magic Wagon.

Aufbau des Zahlensystems, Vollstaendige Induktion. (Duden-Schuelerhilfen Ser.). (GER.). 80p. (YA). (gr. 7-10). *(978-3-411-02625-8(1))* Bibliographisches Institut & F. A. Brockhaus AG DEU. Dist: International Bk. Import Service, Inc.

Austen, Amy. Endangered Animals: Develop Understanding of Fractions & Numbers. 2014. (Rosen Common Core Math Readers Ser.). (ENG.). 24p. (J). (gr. 3-4). pap. 8.25 *(978-1-4777-4921-0(7),* PowerKids Pr.) Rosen Publishing Group, Inc., The.

AWARD & Award, Anna. Bumper Dot to Dot. 2015. (ENG.). 64p. (J). pap. 7.99 *(978-1-78270-158-3(3))* Award Pubns. Ltd. GBR. Dist: Parkwest Pubns., Inc.

Bambi727 & Bambi727. Having Fun with Colors' & Numbers' I wrote this book in hopes our younger children would enjoy & have fun learning their colors' & Numbers' 2009. 32p. pap. 14.49 *(978-1-4389-6226-9(6))* AuthorHouse.

Berenstain, Jan, et al. The Berenstain Bears' Count on Numbers Coloring Book. 2014. (ENG.). 48p. (J). (gr. -1). pap. 4.99 *(978-0-486-49469-2(1))* Dover Pubns., Inc.

Beveridge, Dorothy. Counting Belize Frogs & Toads. Beveridge, Jim, photos by. 2012. (Illus.). 26p. pap. *(978-976-8142-47-4(2))* Producciones de la Hamaca.

Blechmann, R. O. The One & Only 1, 2, 3 Book. Blechmann, R. O., illus. 2013. (ENG., Illus.). 24p. (J). (gr. -1-k). 15.99 *(978-1-56846-245-5(X),* Creative Editions) Creative Co., The.

Boye, B. D. Easy As 1, 2, 3. Boye, B. D., illus. l.t. ed. 2005. (Illus.). 22p. (J). per. 4.99 *(978-0-9768078-0-3(7))* Innerchild Publishing, Inc.

Brainy Baby Quad Book. 2005. (Brainy Baby Ser.). 40p. (J). bds. 10.39 *(978-1-59394-240-3(0))* Bendon, Inc.

Brallier, Max. The Numbers Field Guide. 2012. (ENG.). (J). pap. *(978-0-8118-7771-8(X))* Chronicle Bks. LLC.

Brinker, Spencer. Odd or Even in a Monstrous Season. 2015. (Illus.). 32p. (J). lib. bdg. *(978-1-62724-331-5(3))* Bearport Publishing Co., Inc.

Brocket, Jane. 1 Cookie, 2 Chairs, 3 Pears: Numbers Everywhere. 2013. 32p. 26.60 *(978-1-4677-1702-1(9))* Lerner Publishing Group.

—1 Cookie, 2 Chairs, 3 Pears: Numbers Everywhere. Brocket, Jane, photos by. 2013. (Jane Brocket's Clever Concepts Ser.). (ENG., Illus.). 32p. (gr. -1-2). lib. bdg. 26.60 *(978-1-4677-0232-4(3),* Millbrook Pr.) Lerner Publishing Group.

Brooks, F. & Litchfield, J. Primeros Numeros. 2004.Tr. of First Numbers. (SPA., Illus.). 48p. (J). (gr. -1-18). lib. bdg. 20.95 *(978-1-58086-352-0(3))* EDC Publishing.

Burnett, James & Irons, Calvin. The Flower Pot Hen: A Book about Representing Data. 2012. (J). *(978-1-921358-60-9(2))* Origo Education.

—Scaredy Cats: A Book about Combinations of Ten. 2012. (J). *(978-1-921358-98-2(X))* Origo Education.

—Stella's Store: Book about Skip Counting by Five. 2012. (J). *(978-1-921358-61-6(0))* Origo Education.

—Sweet Dreams: A Book about Counting Quantities to Ten. 2012. (J). *(978-1-921358-96-8(3))* Origo Education.

Burton, Margie, et al. We Use Numbers. 2011. (Early Connections Ser.). (J). *(978-1-61672-511-2(7))* Benchmark Education Co.

Bussiere, Desireé. Tennis by the Numbers, 1 vol. 2013. (Sports by the Numbers Ser.). (ENG.). 24p. (J). (gr. k-3). lib. bdg. 24.21 *(978-1-61783-847-7(0),* SandCastle) ABDO Publishing Co.

Butler, Nathalie. Numbers Parade. 2017. (Learning with Stories Ser.). 24p. (gr. 4-6). pap. 8.25 ***(978-1-5081-6233-9(6),*** PowerKids Pr.) Rosen Publishing Group, Inc., The.

Cameron, Antonia & Fosnot, Catherine Twomey. Games for Early Number Sense. 2008. (ENG.). 96p. (gr. k-1). pap. 31.25 *(978-0-325-01009-0(9),* E01009, Firsthand) Heinemann.

Capote, Lori. Monster Knows More Than, Less Than, 1 vol. Wass, Chip, illus. 2013. (Monster Knows Math Ser.). (ENG.). (gr. 3-4). 20p. bds. 7.95 *(978-1-4048-8039-9(9));* 24p. lib. bdg. 24.65 *(978-1-4048-7947-8(1))* Picture Window Bks.

—Monster Knows Numbers, 1 vol. Wass, Chip, illus. 2013. (Monster Knows Math Ser.). (ENG.). 24p. (gr. 3-4). lib. bdg. 24.65 *(978-1-4048-7946-1(3))* Picture Window Bks.

Carroll, Danielle. Place Value. 2005. (Yellow Umbrella Fluent Level Ser.). (ENG., Illus.). 16p. (gr. k-1). pap. 35.70 *(978-0-7368-5324-8(3),* Yellow Umbrella Bks.) Capstone Press of Coughlan Cos.

Carson-Dellosa Publishing Staff. Numbers 1 to 100 (Numeros del 1 al 100) 2006. (ENG & SPA., Illus.). 54p. (gr. k-3). 2.99 *(978-0-7696-4799-9(5),* Brighter Child) Carson-Dellosa Publishing, LLC.

Carter, David A. The Glittery Crittery Pop-up Counting Book. 2007. (ENG., Illus.). 10p. (gr. -1). bds. 16.95 *(978-1-58117-651-3(1),* Intervisual/Piggy Toes) Bendon, Inc.

Cernek, Kim & Williams, Rozanne Lanczak. Build-a-Skill Instant Books Color, Shape & Number Words. Shiotsu, Vicky & Faulkner, Stacey, eds. Campbell, Jenny & Tom, Darcy, illus. 2007. (J). 4.99 *(978-1-59198-411-5(4))* Creative Teaching Pr., Inc.

Chapman, Joan. Count the Ways to Get Around: Learning to Count To 5. 2009. (Math for the Real World Ser.). (ENG., Illus.). 8p. (gr. k-1). pap. 5.15 *(978-0-8239-8841-9(4))* Rosen Publishing Group, Inc., The.

Child's Play, ed. 5 Little Men in a Flying Saucer. 2006. (Classic Books with Holes Big Book Ser.). (ENG., Illus.). 16p. (J). *(978-1-84643-007-7(0))* Child's Play International Ltd.

Coe, Layla. At the Art Store: Compare Numbers. 2013. (Rosen Math Readers Ser.). (ENG.). 16p. (J). (gr. k-1). pap. 42.00 *(978-1-4777-1663-2(7));* (Illus.). pap. 7.00 *(978-1-4777-1662-5(9))* Rosen Publishing Group, Inc., The. (Rosen Classroom).

Corcorane, Ann. Numbers Are Everywhere, 1 vol. 2011. (Wonder Readers Emergent Level Ser.). (ENG.). (gr. -1-1). 32p. pap. 5.99 *(978-1-4296-7846-9(1));* 8p. pap. 35.94 *(978-1-4296-8233-6(7))* Capstone Press of Coughlan Cos. (Wonder Readers).

Craig, Diane & Doudna, Kelly. No One Slumbers When We Use Numbers!, 1 vol. 2007. (Science Made Simple Ser.). (ENG., Illus.). 24p. (J). (gr. k-3). lib. bdg. 24.21 *(978-1-59928-612-9(2),* SandCastle) ABDO Publishing Co.

Crane, Carol. Net Numbers: A South Carolina Numbers Book. Palmer, Gary, illus. 2006. (Count Your Way Across the U. S. A. Ser.). (ENG.). 40p. (J). (gr. -1-3). 17.95 *(978-1-58536-202-8(6))* Sleeping Bear Pr.

Crews, G. Ellen G Goes Fishing. marion, designs & proctor, brian, illus. 2007. 28p. pap. 4.99 *(978-0-9795236-0-1(5))* Crews Pubns., LLC.

Dahl, Michael. From the Garden: A Counting Book about Growing Food, 1 vol. Ouren, Todd, illus. 2004. (Know Your Numbers Ser.). (ENG.). 24p. (gr. -1-2). per. 8.95 *(978-1-4048-1116-4(8))* Picture Window Bks.

Daybell, Chad. Book of Mormon Numbers. Bonham, Bob, illus. 2004. (J). bds. 8.95 *(978-1-55517-755-3(7),* 77557) Cedar Fort, Inc./CFI Distribution.

Deen, Marilyn. Odd & Even. 2011. (Wonder Readers Fluent Level Ser.). (ENG.). 16p. (gr. -1-2). pap. 35.94 *(978-1-4296-8133-9(0),* Wonder Readers) Capstone Press of Coughlan Cos.

Dennison, Matt. Building with Blocks: Work with 11-19 to Gain Foundations for Place Value. 2013. (InfoMax Math Readers Ser.). (ENG.). 16p. (J). (gr. k-1). pap. 42.00 *(978-1-4777-1962-6(8));* (Illus.). pap. 7.00 *(978-1-4777-1961-9(X))* Rosen Publishing Group, Inc., The. (Rosen Classroom).

Diaz, James & Gerth, Melanie, illus. Numbers: Learning Fun for Little Ones! 2007. 10p. (J). reprint ed. *(978-1-4223-6683-7(9))* DIANE Publishing Co.

Dingles, Molly. Number 1 What Grows in the Sun?/Número 1 Qué crece en el Sol? Wallis, Rebecca, illus. 2005. (Community of Counting Ser.).Tr. of Número 1 Qué crece en el Sol?. (ENG & SPA.). 32p. (J). per. 10.95 *(978-1-59646-275-5(2))* Dingles & Co.

—Number 10 Where Is the Hen? Wallis, Rebecca, illus. 2005. (Community of Counting Ser.). 32p. (J). per. 10.95 *(978-1-59646-309-7(0))* Dingles & Co.

—Number 10 Where Is the Hen?/Número 10 en dónde está la Gallina? Wallis, Rebecca, illus. 2005. (Community of Counting Ser.). (ENG & SPA.). 32p. (J). per. 10.95 *(978-1-59646-311-0(2))* Dingles & Co.

—Number 2 Let's Go to the Zoo! Wallis, Rebecca, illus. 2005. (Community of Counting Ser.). 32p. (J). 10.95 *(978-1-59646-277-9(9))* Dingles & Co.

—Number 2 Let's Go to the Zoo!/Número 2 Vamos al Zoologico! Wallis, Rebecca, illus. 2005. (Community of Counting Ser.).Tr. of Número 2 Vamos al Zoologico! (ENG & SPA.). 32p. (J). per. 10.95 *(978-1-59646-279-3(5))* Dingles & Co.

—Number 3 What's in the Sea? Wallis, Rebecca, illus. 2005. (Community of Counting Ser.). 32p. (J). per. 10.95 *(978-1-59646-281-6(7))* Dingles & Co.

—Number 3 What's in the Sea?/Número 3 Qué hay en el Mar? Wallis, Rebecca, illus. 2005. (Community of Counting Ser.).Tr. of Número 3 Qué hay en el Mar? (ENG & SPA.). 32p. (J). pap. 10.95 *(978-1-59646-282-3(5));* per. 10.95 *(978-1-59646-283-0(3))* Dingles & Co.

—Number 4 Shop at the Store! Wallis, Rebecca, illus. 2005. (Community of Counting Ser.). 32p. (J). per. 10.95 *(978-1-59646-285-4(X))* Dingles & Co.

—Number 4 Shop at the Store!/Número 4 Vamos de compras a la Tienda! Wallis, Rebecca, illus. 2005. (Community of Counting Ser.).Tr. of Número 4 Vamos de compras a la Tienda! (ENG & SPA.). 32p. (J). per. 10.95 *(978-1-59646-287-8(6))* Dingles & Co.

—Number 5 Let's Go for a Drive! Wallis, Rebecca, illus. 2005. (Community of Counting Ser.). 32p. (J). per. 10.95 *(978-1-59646-289-2(2))* Dingles & Co.

—Number 5 Let's Go for a Drive!/Número 5 Vamos a viajar en Coche! Wallis, Rebecca, illus. 2005. (Community of Counting Ser.).Tr. of Número 5 Vamos a viajar en Coche! (ENG & SPA.). 32p. (J). per. 10.95 *(978-1-59646-291-5(4))* Dingles & Co.

—Number 6 What Can We Mix? Wallis, Rebecca, illus. 2005. (Community of Counting Ser.). 32p. (J). per. 10.95 *(978-1-59646-293-9(0))* Dingles & Co.

—Number 6 What Can We Mix?/Número 6 Qué podemos Mezclar? Wallis, Rebecca, illus. 2005. (Community of Counting Ser.).Tr. of Número 6 Qué podemos Mezclar? (ENG & SPA.). 32p. (J). per. 10.95 *(978-1-59646-295-3(7))* Dingles & Co.

—Number 7 Stars in the Heaven. Wallis, Rebecca, illus. 2005. (Community of Counting Ser.). 32p. (J). per. 10.95 *(978-1-59646-297-7(3))* Dingles & Co.

—Number 7 Stars in the Heaven/Número 7 Estrellas en el Cielo. Wallis, Rebecca, illus. (Community of Counting Ser.).Tr. of Número 7 Estrellas en el Cielo. (ENG & SPA.). 32p. (J). 2005. per. 10.95 *(978-1-59646-299-1(X))* 2004. lib. bdg. 21.65 *(978-1-891997-83-9(1))* Dingles & Co.

—Number 8 Let's Stay up Late! Wallis, Rebecca, illus. 2005. (Community of Counting Ser.). 32p. (J). per. 10.95 *(978-1-59646-301-1(5))* Dingles & Co.

—Number 8 Let's Stay up Late!/Número 8 Vamos a quedarnos en vela hasta muy Noche! Wallis, Rebecca, illus. (Community of Counting Ser.).Tr. of Número 8 Vamos a quedarnos en vela hasta muy Noche! (ENG & SPA.). 32p. (J). 2005. per. 10.95 *(978-1-59646-303-5(1))* 2004. lib. bdg. 21.65 *(978-1-891997-82-2(3))* Dingles & Co.

—Number 9 Dress up to Dine! Wallis, Rebecca, illus. 2005. (Community of Counting Ser.). 32p. (J). per. 10.95 *(978-1-59646-305-9(8))* Dingles & Co.

—Number 9 Dress up to Dine!/Número 9 Vestirse con elegancia para Cenar! Wallis, Rebecca, illus. 2005. (Community of Counting Ser.).Tr. of Número 9 Vestirse con elegancia para Cenar! (ENG & SPA.). 32p. (J). per. 10.95 *(978-1-59646-307-3(4))* Dingles & Co.

Donahue, Peter. Build a Poster Coloring Book — ABC & 123. 2010. (Dover Build a Poster Coloring Book Ser.). (ENG., Illus.). 48p. (J). (gr. 3-5). pap. 4.99 *(978-0-486-47946-0(3))* Dover Pubns., Inc.

Dorling Kindersley Publishing Staff. My First Number Board Book. Ward, Kristin, ed. 2004. (My First Bks.). (ENG., Illus.). 36p. (J). (gr. -1 — 1). bds. 5.99 *(978-0-7894-9903-5(7),* DK Children) Dorling Kindersley Publishing, Inc.

—My First Numbers: Let's Get Counting! 2008. (Tab Board Bks.). (ENG.). 28p. (J). (gr. -1-k). bds. 9.99 *(978-0-7566-3604-3(3),* DK Children) Dorling Kindersley Publishing, Inc.

—Numbers. 2013. (Baby Touch & Feel Ser.). (ENG.). 14p. (J). (gr. -1 — 1). bds. 5.99 *(978-1-4654-1432-8(0),* DK Children) Dorling Kindersley Publishing, Inc.

Dot-to-Dot Numbers 1-100 (Gr. 1-2) 2003. (J). *(978-1-58232-069-4(1))* ECS Learning Systems, Inc.

Dot-to-Dot Numbers 1-25 (Gr. K-1) 2003. (J). *(978-1-58232-068-7(3))* ECS Learning Systems, Inc.

Dowdy, Penny. Money. 2008. (My Path to Math Ser.). (ENG., Illus.). 24p. (J). (gr. k-3). pap. *(978-0-7787-4360-6(8));* lib. bdg. *(978-0-7787-4342-2(X))* Crabtree Publishing Co.

—Place Value. 2008. (My Path to Math Ser.). (ENG., Illus.). 24p. (J). (gr. k-3). pap. *(978-0-7787-4361-3(6))* Crabtree Publishing Co.

Ekeland, Ivar. The Cat in Numberland. O'brien, John, illus. 2006. (ENG.). 56p. (J). (gr. 3-9). 19.95 *(978-0-8126-2744-2(X))* Cricket Bks.

Encycbrita. Revisiting Numbers Mic 2006 G. 6th ed. 2005. pap. 10.60 *(978-0-03-038568-1(7))* Harcourt Schl. Pubs.

Encyclopaedia Britannica Publishers, Inc. Staff. Math in Context: Picturing Numbers. 6th ed. 2005. (Math in Context Ser.). (gr. 6). pap. 10.60 *(978-0-03-042402-1(X))* Harcourt Schl. Pubs.

Etringer, Kathy. Mrs. E's Extraordinary Number Activities. Mitchell, Judy & Sussman, Ellen, eds. Rojas, Mary Galan, illus. 2006. 128p. (J). pap. 13.95 *(978-1-57310-506-4(6))* Teaching & Learning Co.

Feldman, Jean. Highway Letters, Numbers & Shapes: PreK-1. 2010. 80p. pap. 22.99 *(978-1-61601-036-2(3))* Creative Teaching Pr., Inc.

First Number Skills (Gr. K-1) 2003. (J). *(978-1-58232-081-6(0))* ECS Learning Systems, Inc.

Fisher, Valorie. Everything I Need to Know Before I'm Five. Fisher, Valorie, illus. 2011. (ENG., Illus.). 40p. (J). (gr. k-k). 17.99 *(978-0-375-86865-8(8),* Schwartz & Wade Bks.) Random Hse. Children's Bks.

Flash Kids Editors, ed. Place Value: Grade 1 (Flash Skills) 2010. (Flash Skills Ser.). (ENG.). 64p. (J). pap. 3.95 *(978-1-4114-3455-4(2),* Spark Publishing Group) Sterling Publishing Co., Inc.

—Place Value: Grade 2 (Flash Skills) 2010. (Flash Skills Ser.). (ENG.). 64p. (J). pap. 3.95 *(978-1-4114-3459-2(5),* Spark Publishing Group) Sterling Publishing Co., Inc.

Freeman, Marcia S. My Sister Is in Third Grade: Putting Numbers in Order. 2007. (Math Focal Points (Discovery Library) Ser.). (Illus.). 24p. (J). (gr. 3-7). lib. bdg. 22.79 *(978-1-60044-638-2(8))* Rourke Educational Media.

Gagliano, Eugene M. Four Wheels West: A Wyoming Number Book. Guy, Sue, illus. 2006. (Count Your Way Across the U. S. A. Ser.). (ENG.). 40p. (J). (gr. -1-3). 17.95 *(978-1-58536-210-3(7))* Sleeping Bear Pr.

Galvin, Laura Gates. Tracing 123s. rev. ed. 2005. (Trace & Learn Ser.). (ENG., Illus.). 28p. (J). (gr. -1-3). 16.49 *(978-1-59069-446-6(5),* 1A601) Studio Mouse LLC.

Goldstone, Bruce. 100 Ways to Celebrate 100 Days. Goldstone, Bruce, illus. 2010. (ENG., Illus.). 48p. (J). (gr. -1-3). 16.99 *(978-0-8050-8997-4(7),* 9780805089974, Holt, Henry & Co. Bks. For Young Readers) Holt, Henry & Co.

—100 Ways to Celebrate 100 Days. Goldstone, Bruce, illus. 2013. (ENG., Illus.). 48p. (J). (gr. -1-3). 7.99 *(978-1-250-03369-7(1),* 9781250033697) Square Fish.

Granger, Ronald. A Day at the Zoo: Compare Numbers. 2013. (InfoMax Math Readers Ser.). (ENG.). 16p. (J). (gr. k-1). pap. 42.00 *(978-1-4777-1986-2(5));* (Illus.). pap. 7.00 *(978-1-4777-1985-5(7))* Rosen Publishing Group, Inc., The. (Rosen Classroom).

Hammelef, Danielle S. Numbers Big & Small. 2006. (Early Explorers Ser.). (J). pap. *(978-1-4108-6130-6(9))* Benchmark Education Co.

Harcourt, creator. I Know Numbers: Math Concept Reader. 2007. (Illus.). (J). pap. 31.53 *(978-0-15-379893-1(9))* Houghton Mifflin Harcourt School Pubs.

Harcourt School Publishers Staff. Math Program Development, Grades K-2: Number Sense Binder Package. 3rd ed. 2003. ring bd. 355.40 *(978-0-15-340574-7(0))* Harcourt Schl. Pubs.

Harris, Nancy. Sticky Fingers: Exploring the Number 5. 2007. (Math Focal Points (Discovery Library) Ser.). (Illus.). 24p. (J). (gr. 3-7). lib. bdg. 22.79 *(978-1-60044-639-9(6))* Rourke Educational Media.

Harris, Trudy. Splitting the Herd: A Corral of Odds & Evens. Julian, Russell, illus. 2008. (Math Is Fun! Ser.). (ENG.). 32p. (gr. k-2). 16.95 *(978-0-8225-7466-8(7),* Millbrook Pr.) Lerner Publishing Group.

Hawley, Ella. The Number 1. 2010. (Numbers in My World Ser.). (ENG.). 16p. (J). bds. 11.95 *(978-1-4358-9319-1(0),* PowerKids Pr.) Rosen Publishing Group, Inc., The.

—The Number 2. 2010. (Numbers in My World Ser.). (ENG.). 16p. (J). bds. 11.95 *(978-1-4358-9320-7(4),* PowerKids Pr.) Rosen Publishing Group, Inc., The.

—The Number 3. 2010. (Numbers in My World Ser.). (ENG.). 16p. (J). bds. 11.95 *(978-1-4358-9321-4(2),* PowerKids Pr.) Rosen Publishing Group, Inc., The.

—The Number 4. 2010. (Numbers in My World Ser.). (ENG.). 16p. (J). bds. 11.95 *(978-1-4358-9322-1(0),* PowerKids Pr.) Rosen Publishing Group, Inc., The.

—The Number 5. 2010. (Numbers in My World Ser.). (ENG.). 16p. (J). bds. 11.95 *(978-1-4358-9323-8(9),* PowerKids Pr.) Rosen Publishing Group, Inc., The.

—Numbers 1, 2, 3, 4, 5. 2010. (Numbers in My World Ser.). (ENG.). (J). bds. 11.95 *(978-1-4358-9324-5(7),* PowerKids Pr.) Rosen Publishing Group, Inc., The.

Head, Debby & Pollett, Libby. Bby Practice Pages: 02-Modeling Numbers 0-100. 2004. (ENG., Illus.). spiral bd.

37.00 *(978-1-885775-19-1(9))* bby Publications at The University of West Alabama.
—Bby Practice Pages: 06-Numbers & Words 0-10. 2004. (ENG., Illus.). spiral bd. 37.00 *(978-1-885775-22-1(9))* bby Publications at The University of West Alabama.
—Bby Practice Pages: 07-Making Ten. 2004. (ENG., Illus.). spiral bd. 37.00 *(978-1-885775-23-8(7))* bby Publications at The University of West Alabama.
—Bby Practice Pages: 09-Numbers & Words 11-20. 2004. (ENG., Illus.). spiral bd. 37.00 *(978-1-885775-25-2(3))* bby Publications at The University of West Alabama.
Heinst, Marie. My First Number Book. (Illus.). (J). pap. 16.95 *(978-0-590-74282-5(5))* Scholastic, Inc.
—My First Number Book. Scholastic, Inc. Staff, ed. (FRE., Illus.). 48p. (J). 19.99 *(978-0-590-74416-4(X))* Scholastic, Inc.
Hickman, Debbie. The Exasperated Clock. Taylor, Adam, illus. 2013. 40p. pap. *(978-1-4602-1811-2(6))* FriesenPress.
Highlights for Children Editorial Staff, creator. My First 123. 2016. (Highlights(tm) My First Write-On Wipe-off Board Bks.). (ENG.). 28p. (J). (gr. -1-k). bds. 9.99 *(978-1-62979-707-6(3),* Highlights) Boyds Mills Pr.
Hill, Eric. S. S. Happiness Crew: Book of Numbers. (Illus.). 11p. (J). (gr. -1). *(978-0-915696-65-9(7))* Determined Productions, Inc.
Hinkler Books Staff. 1 2 3. rev. ed. 2006. (ENG., Illus.). 12p. (J). (gr. -1-1). bds. 7.95 *(978-1-74157-603-0(2))* Hinkler Bks. Pty, Ltd. AUS. Dist: Penton Overseas, Inc.
Hoffman, Joan. Nursery Rhymes. 2008. (ENG.). 32p. (J). pap. 3.99 *(978-1-60159-115-9(2))* School Zone Publishing Co.
Holden, Pam. Name the Numbers. 2015. (ENG., Illus.). 16p. (-1). pap. *(978-1-77654-117-1(0),* Red Rocket Readers) Flying Start Bks.
HOP, LLC. Hooked on Numbers. 2006. 24.99 *(978-1-60143-034-2(5))* HOP, LLC.
In Step with the Standards - Number Sense. 2005. (J). spiral bd. 15.95 *(978-1-58123-375-9(2))* Larson Learning, Inc.
It's Counting Time. 2004. (J). per. 15.99 *(978-0-9744205-2-3(2))* Golden Eagle Publishing Hse., Inc.
Jerome, Kate Boehm. Number Know-How. 2007. (Reading Expeditions Ser.). (ENG., Illus.). 24p. (J). pap. 14.95 *(978-0-7922-4591-9(1))* CENGAGE Learning.
Kelly, Jodi. At the Race: Count to Tell the Number of Objects. 2013. (InfoMax Math Readers Ser.). (ENG.). 16p. (J). (gr. k-1). pap. 42.00 *(978-1-4777-1971-8(7));* (Illus.). pap. 7.00 *(978-1-4777-1970-1(9))* Rosen Publishing Group, Inc., The. (Rosen Classroom).
Kenyon, Dolores. The History of Complex Numbers - A Genealogy. 2007. spiral bd. 8.95 net. *(978-1-60402-110-3(1))* Independent Pub.
Kernan, Elizabeth. Counting at the Store: Learning to Count from 6 To 10. 2009. (Math for the Real World: Early Emergent Ser.). (ENG., Illus.). 8p. (gr. k-1). pap. 5.15 *(978-0-8239-8842-6(2))* Rosen Publishing Group, Inc., The.
King, Zelda. The Story of Our Numbers: The History of Arabic Numerals. 2009. (PowerMath Ser.). (ENG., Illus.). 24p. (gr. 3-4). pap. 8.25 *(978-0-8239-8870-9(8),* PowerKids Pr.) Rosen Publishing Group, Inc., The.
Kleinberg, Naomi. 1, 2, 3 Count with Me. Moroney, Christopher, illus. 2005. (ENG.). 20p. (J). (gr. k — 1). bds. 7.99 *(978-0-375-83227-7(0),* Random Hse. Bks. for Young Readers) Random Hse. Children's Bks.
La Jars, David. One, Two, Red & Blue. rev. ed. 2004. (Talk Together Ser.). (Illus.). 24p. (J). (gr. -1-k). pap. 5.95 *(978-1-58728-019-1(1),* Two-Can Publishing) T&N Children's Publishing.
Lamb, Stacey, illus. Wipe Clean 123 Book. 2011. (Wipe-Clean Bks). 20p. (J). pap. 7.99 *(978-0-7945-3075-4(3),* Usborne) EDC Publishing.
Larousse Color ABC y 123 (Amarillo), Vol. 1. 2003. (SPA., Illus.). 6p. (J). 2.98 *(978-970-22-0163-2(2))* Larousse, Ediciones, S. A. de C. V. MEX. Dist: Giron Bks.
Learn Your Numbers. 2003. (Illus.). 10p. (J). bds. *(978-1-74047-003-2(6))* Book Co. Publishing Pty, Ltd., The.
Let's Say Our Numbers. 2007. (Simple First Words Ser.). (Illus.). 14p. (J). *(978-1-84332-520-8(9))* Priddy Bks.
Levine, Julia Pimsleur. Little Pim: Numbers. 2012. (ENG.). 10p. (J). (gr. -1-k). bds. 8.95 *(978-1-4197-0175-7(4))* Abrams, Inc.
El Libro de Contar de los Chocolates M & M's Brand. 2004. 32p. (J). pap. 6.95 *(978-1-57091-370-9(6))* Charlesbridge Publishing, Inc.
Linda, Winder. Glitter: My First Book of Shapes Numbers Colors & the Alphabet Gods Way. 2003. *(978-1-892354-85-3(3))* Educational Publishing Concepts, Inc.
Litchfield, Felicity. Primeros Numeros. 2004.Tr. of First Numbers. (SPA., Illus.). 48p. (J). (gr. -1-18). 12.95 *(978-0-7460-4508-4(5))* EDC Publishing.
Litchfield, Jo, illus. First Picture 123. 2005. (First Picture Board Books Ser.). 16p. (J). 11.95 *(978-0-7945-0939-2(8),* Usborne) EDC Publishing.
Litton, Jonathan. Touch & Feel Numbers. Galloway, Fhiona, illus. 2017. (My Little World Ser.). (ENG.). 10p. (J). (gr. -1-k). bds. 8.99 ***(978-1-68010-511-7(6))*** Tiger Tales.
Lluch, Alex A. I Like to Learn Numbers: Hungry Chameleon. 2011. (ENG.). 32p. (J). (gr. -1-k). bds. 4.95 *(978-1-934386-01-9(4))* WS Publishing.
—Let's Leap Ahead Numbers. 2012. (ENG.). 80p. (J). (gr. -1). spiral bd. 9.95 *(978-1-936061-60-0(0))* WS Publishing.
—Trace & Learn The 123s. 2014. (ENG., Illus.). 28p. (J). (-k). bds. 8.95 *(978-1-61351-088-9(8))* WS Publishing.
LoPresti, Angeline Sparagna. A Place for Zero. Hornung, Phyllis, illus. alt. ed. 2003. (Math Adventures Ser.). (ENG.). 32p. (J). (gr. 1-4). pap. 7.95 *(978-1-57091-196-5(7))* Charlesbridge Publishing, Inc.
Lucy Ladybug Learns Numbers. (Board Bks.). (Illus.). 6p. (J). (gr. -1-k). 4.99 *(978-0-7847-1119-4(4),* 03529, Bean Sprouts) Standard Publishing.
Madden, Jean Griffing. Digger Digs Digits. 2011. 36p. pap. *(978-1-4269-9587-3(3))* Trafford Publishing (UK) Ltd.
Make Believe Ideas. Bubble Buddies 123. 2014. (ENG.). 12p. (J). bds. 9.99 *(978-1-78235-972-2(9))* Make Believe Ideas GBR. Dist: Nelson, Thomas Inc.
Make Believe Ideas, creator. Busy Baby 123: First Concepts. 2007. (Busy Baby Ser.). (Illus.). 12p. (gr. -1-k). per., bds. *(978-1-84610-468-8(8))* Make Believe Ideas.
Makeeff, Cyndi Sue. Inky Winky Spider 1,2,3,4. Riley, Kevin, illus. 2006. 32p. (J). pap. 7.99 *(978-0-9778310-1-2(9))* New Vision Entertainment, LLC.
Mattern, Joanne. At the Football Game: Learning the Symbols , And = 2009. (Math for the REAL World Ser.). 16p. (gr. 2-3). pap. 7.05 *(978-0-8239-8875-4(9),* Rosen Classroom) Rosen Publishing Group, Inc., The.
—Sequence It! 2011. (ENG., Illus.). 24p. (gr. -1-1). pap. 8.95 *(978-1-61741-966-9(4))* Rourke Educational Media.
Meachen Rau, Dana. Cinco. 2008. (¡Cuenta con Ello! Ser.). (SPA.). 24p. (gr. k-1). lib. bdg. 15.95 *(978-0-7614-3449-8(6),* Benchmark Bks.) Marshall Cavendish Corp.
—Cuatro. 2008. (¡Cuenta con Ello! Ser.). (SPA.). 24p. (gr. k-1). lib. bdg. 15.95 *(978-0-7614-3448-1(8),* Benchmark Bks.) Marshall Cavendish Corp.
—Diez. 2008. (¡Cuenta con Ello! Ser.). (SPA.). 24p. (gr. k-1). lib. bdg. 15.95 *(978-0-7614-3452-8(6),* Benchmark Bks.) Marshall Cavendish Corp.
—Dos. 2008. (¡Cuenta con Ello! Ser.). (SPA.). 24p. (gr. k-1). lib. bdg. 15.95 *(978-0-7614-3445-0(3),* Benchmark Bks.) Marshall Cavendish Corp.
—Five. 2004. (Count on It! Ser.). 24p. (gr. k-1). lib. bdg. 15.95 *(978-0-7614-2970-8(0),* Benchmark Bks.) Marshall Cavendish Corp.
—Five/Cinco. 2008. (Count on It!/¡Cuenta con Ello! Ser.). (SPA & ENG.). 24p. (gr. k-1). lib. bdg. 15.95 *(978-0-7614-3477-1(1),* Benchmark Bks.) Marshall Cavendish Corp.
—Four. 2004. (Count on It! Ser.). 24p. (gr. k-1). lib. bdg. 15.95 *(978-0-7614-2969-2(7),* Benchmark Bks.) Marshall Cavendish Corp.
—Four/Cuatro. 2008. (Count on It!/¡Cuenta con Ello! Ser.). (SPA & ENG.). 24p. (gr. k-1). lib. bdg. 15.95 *(978-0-7614-3476-4(3),* Benchmark Bks.) Marshall Cavendish Corp.
—One. 2004. (Count on It! Ser.). 24p. (gr. k-1). lib. bdg. 15.95 *(978-0-7614-2966-1(2),* Benchmark Bks.) Marshall Cavendish Corp.
—One/Uno. 2008. (Count on It!/¡Cuenta con Ello! Ser.). (SPA & ENG.). 24p. (gr. k-1). lib. bdg. 15.95 *(978-0-7614-3472-6(0),* Benchmark Bks.) Marshall Cavendish Corp.
—Ten. 2004. (Count on It! Ser.). 24p. (gr. k-1). lib. bdg. 15.95 *(978-0-7614-2971-5(9),* Benchmark Bks.) Marshall Cavendish Corp.
—Ten/Diez. 2008. (Count on It!/¡Cuenta con Ello! Ser.). (SPA & ENG.). 24p. (gr. k-1). lib. bdg. 15.95 *(978-0-7614-3478-8(X),* Benchmark Bks.) Marshall Cavendish Corp.
—Three. 2004. (Count on It! Ser.). 24p. (gr. k-1). lib. bdg. 15.95 *(978-0-7614-2968-5(9),* Benchmark Bks.) Marshall Cavendish Corp.
—Three/Tres. 2008. (Count on It!/¡Cuenta con Ello! Ser.). (SPA & ENG.). 24p. (gr. k-1). lib. bdg. 15.95 *(978-0-7614-3475-7(5),* Benchmark Bks.) Marshall Cavendish Corp.
—Tres. 2008. (¡Cuenta con Ello! Ser.). (SPA.). 24p. (gr. k-1). lib. bdg. 15.95 *(978-0-7614-3446-7(1),* Benchmark Bks.) Marshall Cavendish Corp.
—Two. 2004. (Count on It! Ser.). 24p. (gr. k-1). lib. bdg. 15.95 *(978-0-7614-2967-8(0),* Benchmark Bks.) Marshall Cavendish Corp.
—Two/Dos. 2008. (Count on It!/¡Cuenta con Ello! Ser.). (SPA & ENG.). 24p. (gr. k-1). lib. bdg. 15.95 *(978-0-7614-3474-0(7),* Benchmark Bks.) Marshall Cavendish Corp.
—Uno. 2008. (¡Cuenta con Ello! Ser.). (SPA.). 24p. (gr. k-1). lib. bdg. 15.95 *(978-0-7614-3444-3(5),* Benchmark Bks.) Marshall Cavendish Corp.
Medcalf, Carol, et al. Numbers, Age 3-5. 2014. (Letts Monster Practice Ser.). (ENG.). 32p. (J). (gr. -1-k). pap. 6.99 *(978-1-84419-770-5(0))* HarperCollins Pubs. Ltd. GBR. Dist: Independent Pubs. Group.
Mega Jumbo ABC And 123. 2006. (J). per. 9.95 *(978-1-885920-13-3(X))* Pyramid Publishing, Inc.
Meredith, Susan. Half or Whole? 2010. (ENG., Illus.). 24p. (gr. k-2). pap. 8.95 *(978-1-61590-532-4(4))* Rourke Educational Media.
Meyers, Nancy. Doodles 123. Meyers, Nancy, illus. 2012. (Doodles Ser.). (ENG., Illus.). 64p. (J). (gr. k-5). pap. 7.95 *(978-1-61608-664-0(5),* 608664, Sky Pony Pr.) Skyhorse Publishing Co., Inc.
Miles Kelly Staff & Nilsen, Anna. Numbers: Let's Learn. 2003. (Let's Learn Ser.). (Illus.). 20p. (J). 7.95 *(978-1-84236-018-7(3))* Miles Kelly Publishing, Ltd. GBR. Dist: Independent Pubs. Group.
Moon, Jo, illus. Making Numbers. 2006. (Making... Ser.). 14p. (J). (gr. -1-3). bds. 7.95 *(978-1-57791-249-1(7))* Brighter Minds Children's Publishing.
Morris, Charlie. Avery's Art Supplies: Compare Numbers. 2013. (InfoMax Math Readers Ser.). (ENG.). 16p. (J). (gr. k-1). pap. 42.00 *(978-1-4777-1953-4(9));* (Illus.). pap. 7.00 *(978-1-4777-1952-7(0))* Rosen Publishing Group, Inc., The. (Rosen Classroom).
Napier, Matt. Hat Tricks Count: A Hockey Number Book. Rose, Melanie, illus. rev. ed. 2005. (Sports Ser.). (ENG.). 40p. (J). (gr. k-5). 16.95 *(978-1-58536-163-2(1))* Sleeping Bear Pr.
—Hockey Numbers. Rose, Melanie, illus. (Numbers & Counting Ser.). (ENG.). 2009. 14p. 11.75 *(978-1-58536-495-4(9))* 2007. 22p. (J). (gr. -1-1). 7.99 *(978-1-58536-346-9(4))* Sleeping Bear Pr.
Nickelodeon Staff, ed. 1-2-3 - Go Diego Go! 2010. (Write, Slide & Learn Ser.). 14p. (J). (gr. -1-1). 9.99 *(978-1-74184-521-1(1))* Hinkler Bks. Pty, Ltd. AUS. Dist: Ideals Pubns.
Nimble with Numbers: Student Practice Book. 2003. (Nimble with Numbers Ser.). 11.95 *(978-0-7690-2824-8(1));* 11.95 *(978-0-7690-2823-1(3));* (J). (gr. 4). 11.95 *(978-0-7690-2821-7(7));* (J). (gr. 5). 11.95 *(978-0-7690-2820-0(9));* (J). (gr. 6). 11.95 *(978-0-7690-2819-4(5))* Seymour, Dale Pubns.
Norton, Grace R. Count Us in Too. 2005. (Illus.). 32p. (J). (gr. -1-4). 14.95 *(978-1-889506-03-6(6))* Kendar Publishing, Inc.
Nouvian, Judith. Numbers. 2016. (Picture This Ser.). (ENG., Illus.). 24p. (J). (gr. -1-3). bds. 7.99 *(978-0-544-51265-8(0),* HMH Books For Young Readers) Houghton Mifflin Harcourt Publishing Co.
Novick, Mary & Hale, Jenny. Numbers. Harlin, Sybel, illus. 2010. (Double Delight Ser.). (ENG.). 24p. (J). (gr. -1 — 1). pap. 8.99 *(978-1-877003-57-8(3))* Little Hare Bks. AUS. Dist: Independent Pubs. Group.
Novick, Mary & Peterson, Jenna. Numbers. Miesen, Christina, illus. 2008. (Mini Marvels Ser.). (ENG.). 12p. (J). (gr. k — 1). 6.95 *(978-1-921049-61-3(8))* Little Hare Bks. AUS. Dist: Independent Pubs. Group.
Number Facts To 10 (Gr. 1-2) 2003. (J). *(978-1-58232-083-0(7))* ECS Learning Systems, Inc.
Number Facts to 10 Spanish Version. 2007. (J). per. *(978-1-58232-152-3(3))* ECS Learning Systems, Inc.
Number Fun. 2005. (Little Celebrations Thematic Packages Ser.). (J). (gr. k-3). 133.50 *(978-0-673-75381-6(6))* Celebration Pr.
Numbers. 2003. (J). per. *(978-1-884907-43-2(1));* per. *(978-1-884907-47-0(4))* Paradise Pr., Inc.
Numbers. 2004. (Early Days Ser.). (Illus.). 18p. (J). bds. *(978-1-84229-973-9(5))* Top That! Publishing PLC.
Numbers - Book 2. 2005. (J). per. 8.95 *(978-1-59566-158-6(1))* QEB Publishing Inc.
Numbers: English & Spanish Book 3. 2006. (SPA.). (J). bds. *(978-0-9785744-3-7(5))* LTL Media LLC.
Numbers & More. 2005. (J). bds. *(978-1-4194-0051-3(7))* Paradise Pr., Inc.
Numbers Book 1. 2005. (J). per. 8.95 *(978-1-59566-154-8(9))* QEB Publishing Inc.
Numbers Count. 2003. (J). per. *(978-1-57657-951-0(4))* Paradise Pr., Inc.
Numeracy Through Spreadsheets. (Illus.). 48p. (J). (gr. 4-6). pap. *(978-1-876367-63-3(6))* Wizard Bks.
Oquendo, Lisa, illus. Números - Numbers. 2006. (ENG & SPA.). (J). bds. 5.99 *(978-1-934113-01-1(8))* Little Cubans, LLC.
Penn, M. W. Comparing Numbers!, 1 vol. 2012. (Pebble Math Ser.). (ENG.). 24p. (gr. k-1). pap. 6.29 *(978-1-4296-7874-2(7));* pap. 35.70 *(978-1-4296-8307-4(4));* lib. bdg. 21.99 *(978-1-4296-7561-1(6))* Capstone Press of Coughlan Cos. (Pebble Bks.).
Phillips, Dee. Colors. 2009. (Christmas Lift the Flap Ser.). (ENG.). 10p. (J). (gr. -1-k). bds. 5.95 *(978-1-84696-966-9(2),* TickTock Books) Octopus Publishing Group GBR. Dist: Independent Pubs. Group.
—First Addition. 2009. (Christmas Lift the Flap Ser.). (ENG.). 10p. (J). (gr. -1-k). bds. 5.95 *(978-1-84696-967-6(0),* TickTock Books) Octopus Publishing Group GBR. Dist: Independent Pubs. Group.
—Numbers. 2009. (Christmas Lift the Flap Ser.). (ENG.). 10p. (J). (gr. -1-k). bds. 5.95 *(978-1-84696-969-0(7),* TickTock Books) Octopus Publishing Group GBR. Dist: Independent Pubs. Group.
Phillips, Sarah & Tattam, Mark. Numbers. 2005. (Baby See a Shape Ser.). (Illus.). 12p. (gr. -1-k). per., bds. *(978-1-905051-91-5(3))* Make Believe Ideas.
Poitier, Anton, illus. Numbers. 2015. (Twisters Ser.). (ENG.). 10p. (J). (gr. -1 — 1). bds. 7.99 *(978-0-7641-6809-3(6))* Barron's Educational Series, Inc.
Priddy Books Staff. First Concepts: Numbers. 2003. (Illus.). (J). bds. *(978-0-312-49232-8(4),* Priddy Bks.) St. Martin's Pr.
Priddy, Roger. First 100 Board Books First 100 Numbers. 2012. (First 100 Ser.). (ENG., Illus.). 14p. (J). (gr. -1 — 1). bds. 8.95 *(978-0-312-51376-4(3),* 9780312513764, Priddy Bks.) St. Martin's Pr.
—Numbers. 2016. (Little Friends Ser.). (ENG., Illus.). 12p. (J). bds. 14.99 *(978-0-312-52006-9(9),* 9780312520069, Priddy Bks.) St. Martin's Pr.
—Sticker Early Learning: Numbers. 2016. (ENG., Illus.). 24p. (J). pap. 4.99 *(978-0-312-52017-5(4),* 9780312520175, Priddy Bks.) St. Martin's Pr.
Professor Q's Chinese-English Language Books: Shu' Zi' - Numbers. 2006. (J). *(978-0-9743359-6-4(7))* Murdock Publishing Co.
Publications International Ltd. Staff, ed. Eric Carle Counting Write & Erase Sound. 2011. 16p. (J). bds. 16.98 *(978-1-4508-1373-0(9),* 89ea66b2-f0ff-4240-b53e-290c676c9925) Phoenix International Publications, Inc.
—My Numbers Book. 2011. 32p. (J). bds. *(978-1-4508-1021-0(7))* Publications International, Ltd.
—Numbers Learning Board. 2011. 1p. (J). bds. *(978-1-4508-1431-7(X))* Publications International, Ltd.
—Numbers (Listen & Learn Sound Book) 2011. 19p. (J). bds. 11.98 *(978-1-4508-1705-9(X))* Phoenix International Publications, Inc.
QEB Maths Club National Book Stores Edition: Using Numbers Book 1. 2006. (J). per. *(978-1-59566-286-6(3))* QEB Publishing Inc.
QEB Maths Club National Book Stores Edition: Using Numbers Book 2. 2006. (J). per. *(978-1-59566-290-3(1))* QEB Publishing Inc.
QEB Start Math Book National Book Stores Edition: Numbers - Book 1. 2006. (J). per. *(978-1-59566-272-9(3))* QEB Publishing Inc.
QEB Start Math Book Stores Edition: Numbers - Book 2. 2006. (J). per. *(978-1-59566-276-7(6))* QEB Publishing Inc.
Really Big Numbers. 2014. (Illus.). 192p. (J). pap. 25.00 *(978-1-4704-1425-2(2))* American Mathematical Society.
Rebman, Nick. What Comes First? A Book about Sequences. 2016. (Concept Fun Ser.). (ENG.). 16p. (J). (gr. -1-2). 25.64 *(978-1-5038-0763-1(0),* 210611) Child's World, Inc., The.
—Which One Is Not Like the Others? A Book about Differences. 2016. (Concept Fun Ser.). (ENG.). 16p. (J). (gr. -1-2). 25.64 *(978-1-5038-0768-6(1),* 210616) Child's World, Inc., The.
Reynolds, Cynthia Furlong. Fishing for Numbers: A Maine Number Book. Brett, Jeannie, illus. 2005. (Count Your Way Across the USA Ser.). (ENG.). 40p. (J). (gr. k-5). 16.95 *(978-1-58536-035-2(X))* Sleeping Bear Pr.
Rigol, Francesc, illus. Dan & Din Learn Numbers. 2009. (Learning with Dan & Din Ser.). 12p. (J). (gr. -1-k). bds. 11.40 *(978-1-60754-402-9(4))* Windmill Bks.
Ripley's Believe It Or Not! Staff, compiled by. Wacky 1, 2, 3: Ripley's Believe It or Not! 2017. (Little Bks.: 1). (ENG.). 26p. (J). bds. 6.99 *(978-1-60991-181-2(4))* Ripley Entertainment, Inc.
Robinson, C. L. MATH1on1 Numbers & Operations. 2006. (YA). per. 9.99 *(978-0-9786767-0-4(X))* Robinson, Consuelo.
Robleda, Margarita. Los Numeros Tragaldabas. Gurovich, Natalia, illus. 2004. (SPA.). 24p. (J). 12.95 *(978-970-690-807-0(2))* Planeta Mexicana Editorial S. A. de C. V. MEX. Dist: Lectorum Pubns., Inc.
Rosa-Mendoza, Gladys. Numbers. Cifuentes, Carolina, ed. Noiset, Michele, illus. 2004. (English-Spanish Foundations Ser.).Tr. of Los Numeros. (ENG & SPA.). 20p. (J). bds. 6.95 *(978-0-9679748-2-8(8))* Me+Mi Publishing.
Rosario, Sherwin, illus. Meet the Numbers Lift the Flap Book. 2005. 12p. (J). bds. 9.99 *(978-0-9767008-1-4(6))* Preschool Prep Co.
—Meet the Numbers One to Ten. 2005. 10p. (J). bds. 7.99 *(978-0-9767008-3-8(2))* Preschool Prep Co.
Rosen, Michael J. Mind-Boggling Numbers. Patton, Julia, illus. 2016. (ENG.). 32p. (gr. 2-5). 38.65 *(978-1-5124-1108-9(6),* Millbrook Pr.) Lerner Publishing Group.
—Mind-Boggling Numbers: Math for the Curious. Patton, Julia, illus. 2016. (ENG.). 32p. (J). (gr. 2-5). 19.99 *(978-1-4677-3489-9(6),* Millbrook Pr.) Lerner Publishing Group.
Rosenberg, Pam. Is It Still a Number? 2006. (Rookie Read-About Math Ser.). (ENG., Illus.). 32p. (J). (gr. 1-2). lib. bdg. 20.50 *(978-0-516-25443-2(X))* Scholastic Library Publishing.
Roy, Jennifer Rozines & Roy, Gregory. Numbers on the Street. 2005. (Math All Around Ser.). (Illus.). 32p. (gr. 2-7). lib. bdg. 29.93 *(978-0-7614-2002-6(9),* Benchmark Bks.) Marshall Cavendish Corp.
Roza, Greg. The Hubble Space Telescope: Understanding & Representing Numbers in the Billions. 2005. (PowerMath: Proficiency Plus Ser.). (Illus.). 32p. (J). (gr. 3-6). lib. bdg. 25.25 *(978-1-4042-2931-0(0),* PowerKids Pr.) Rosen Publishing Group, Inc., The.
—The Hubble Space Telescope: Understanding & Representing Numbers up to 1 Billion. 2009. (Math for the REAL World Ser.). (ENG., Illus.). 32p. (gr. 5-6). pap. 10.00 *(978-1-4042-5129-8(4))* Rosen Publishing Group, Inc., The.
Santillana & Dorling Kindersley Publishing Staff. Numeros. (Show Me Ser.). (SPA., Illus.). 16p. (J). (gr. -1-k). bds. 6.95 *(978-1-58986-326-2(7))* Santillana USA Publishing Co., Inc.
Sargent, Daina. Colors & the Number 1, 11 vols. Lenoir, Jane, illus. 2005. (Learn to Read Ser.: 11). 24p. (J). pap. 10.95 *(978-1-59381-031-3(8))* Ozark Publishing.
—Colors & the Number 10/Los Colores y el Número 10, 11 vols. Lenoir, Jane, illus. 2005. (Learn to Read Ser.: 11). (ENG & SPA.). 24p. (J). pap. 10.95 *(978-1-59381-147-1(0));* lib. bdg. 20.95 *(978-1-59381-146-4(2))* Ozark Publishing.
—Colors & the Number 2, 11 vols. Lenoir, Jane, illus. l.t. ed. 2004. (Learn to Read Ser.). 24p. (J). lib. bdg. 20.95 *(978-1-59381-032-0(6))* Ozark Publishing.
—Colors & the Number 4, 11 vols. Lenoir, Jane, illus. 2005. (Learn to Read Ser.). 24p. (J). pap. 10.95 *(978-1-59381-037-5(7))* Ozark Publishing.
—Colors & the Number 6, 11 vols. Lenoir, Jane, illus. l.t. ed. 2004. (Learn to Read Ser.). 24p. (J). lib. bdg. 20.95 *(978-1-59381-040-5(7))* Ozark Publishing.
—Colors & the Number 6/Los Colores y el Número 6, 11 vols. Lenoir, Jane, illus. 2005. (Learn to Read Ser.: 11). (ENG & SPA.). 24p. (J). pap. 10.95 *(978-1-59381-139-6(X))* Ozark Publishing.
—Colors & the Number 7, 11 vols. Lenoir, Jane, illus. l.t. ed. 2004. (Learn to Read Ser.). 24p. (J). lib. bdg. 20.95 *(978-1-59381-042-9(3))* Ozark Publishing.
—Colors & the Number 8, 11 vols. Lenoir, Jane, illus. l.t. ed. 2004. (Learn to Read Ser.). 24p. (J). lib. bdg. 20.95 *(978-1-59381-044-3(X))* Ozark Publishing.
—Colors & the Number 9, 11 vols. Lenoir, Jane, illus. l.t. ed. 2004. (Learn to Read Ser.). 24p. (J). lib. bdg. 20.95 *(978-1-59381-046-7(6))* Ozark Publishing.
—Introduction to Colors & Numbers, 11 vols. Lenoir, Jane, illus. l.t. ed. 2004. (Learn to Read Ser.: 11). 24p. (J). lib. bdg. 20.95 *(978-1-59381-050-4(4))* Ozark Publishing.
—Introduction to Colors & Numbers/Introduccion a los Colores Numeros, 11 vols. Lenoir, Jane, illus. l.t. ed. 2005. (Learn to Read Ser.: 11). (SPA & ENG.). 24p. (J). pap. 10.95 *(978-1-59381-149-5(7))* Ozark Publishing.
Sargent, Daina & Lenoir, Jane. Colors & the Number 6/Los colores y el Número 6, 11 vols. 2005. (Learn to Read Ser.).Tr. of Los colores y el Número 6. (ENG & SPA., Illus.). 24p. (J). lib. bdg. 20.95 *(978-1-59381-138-9(1))* Ozark Publishing.
Scholastic Teaching Resources Staff. Kindergarten Basic Skills: Alphabet & Fine-Motor Skills. 2012. (Kindergarten Basic Skills Ser.). (ENG.). 48p. pap. 6.99 *(978-0-545-42964-1(1))* Teacher's Friend Pubns., Inc.
—Kindergarten Basic Skills: Numbers & Counting. 2012. (Kindergarten Basic Skills Ser.). (ENG.). 48p. pap. 6.99 *(978-0-545-42965-8(X))* Teacher's Friend Pubns., Inc.
School Zone Publishing Company Staff. Bilingual 1-25 Dot to Dots. rev. ed. 2007. (ENG.). 64p. (J). (gr. k). pap. 3.99 *(978-1-58947-971-5(8))* School Zone Publishing Co.
—Numbers & Shapes. 2008. (ENG.). (J). 5.99 *(978-1-60159-102-9(0))* School Zone Publishing Co.
School Zone Staff. Bilingual Numbers 1-100. 2004. (ENG.). (J). 2.99 *(978-1-58947-983-8(1))* School Zone Publishing Co.
—Numbers 0-25. rev. ed. 2005. (ENG.). (J). 2.99 *(978-1-58947-478-9(3))* School Zone Publishing Co.
Schrier, Allyson Valentine. First in Line. 2008. (Discovering & Exploring Science Ser.). (Illus.). 16p. (J). (gr. -1-3). lib. bdg. 12.95 *(978-0-7569-8437-3(8))* Perfection Learning Corp.
Schwartz, David M. How Much Is a Million? Kellogg, Steven, illus. 20th anniv. ed. 2004. (Reading Rainbow Bks.). (ENG.). 40p. (J). (gr. -1-3). pap. 7.99 *(978-0-688-09933-6(5))* HarperCollins Pubs.
—How Much Is a Million? 2004. (J). (gr. k-3). 18.40 *(978-0-8085-7914-4(2),* Turtleback) Turtleback Bks.
Schwartz, Richard Evan. The Gallery of the Infinite. 2016. (Illus.). 187p. (J). pap. 29.00 *(978-1-4704-2557-9(2))* American Mathematical Society.
—You Can Count on Monsters: The First 100 Numbers & Their Characters. 2015. (Illus.). 242p. (J). pap. 25.00 *(978-1-4704-2209-7(3))* American Mathematical Society.
Sevaly, Karen, ed. Match, Trace, & Write Numbers Mats: 30 Activities. 2006. (Scholastic Hands-on Learning Ser.). (ENG., Illus.). 14.99 *(978-0-439-82384-5(6),* Teaching Resources) Scholastic, Inc.
Shea. Working with Numbers. 2004. (Steck-Vaughn Working with Numbers Ser.). (ENG., Illus.). 160p. (gr. 5-5). pap. 18.85 *(978-0-7398-9160-5(X));*Level D. (gr. 4-4). pap. 18.85

M
N
O

(978-0-7398-9159-6(6));Level F. (gr. 6-6). pap. 18.85 (978-0-7398-9161-2(8)) Houghton Mifflin Harcourt Publishing Co.

Silver Dolphin en Español Editors. Disney Tesoro de libros de Calcomanias: Disney Sticker Book Treasury, Spanish-Language Edition. 2007. (Illus.). 48p. (J). (978-970-718-447-3(7), Silver Dolphin en Español) Advanced Marketing, S. de R. L. de C. V.

Slaughter, Tom. 1 2 3. 2005. (SPA.). (J). (gr. k-18). pap. 7.95 (978-968-7381-54-1(X)) Tecolote, Ediciones, S.A. de C.V. MEX. Dist: Iaconi, Mariuccia Bk. Imports.

Steck-Vaughn Staff. At-Home Workbooks: Numbers. 2004. (Illus.). pap., wbk. ed. (978-0-7398-8529-1(4)) Steck-Vaughn.

—Early Math: Number Sense, 10 Pack. 2005. pap. 29.95 (978-1-4190-0343-1(7)); pap. 2.99 (978-1-4190-0319-6(4)); pap. 29.95 (978-1-4190-0343-1(7)) Steck-Vaughn.

—How Much Is 100? 2003. pap. 4.10 (978-0-7398-7661-9(9)) Steck-Vaughn.

—Math Remediation: Number Concepts. 2005. pap. 5.49 (978-1-4190-0366-0(6)) Harcourt Schl. Pubs.

Sterling Publishing Co., Inc. Numbers. 2012. (Say & Play Ser.). (ENG., Illus.). 28p. (J). (gr. k — 1). bds. 4.95 (978-1-4027-9891-7(1)) Sterling Publishing Co., Inc.

Studio Mouse Staff, creator. Write-with-Me Numbers. rev. ed. 2008. (Illus.). 28p. (J). 14.99 (978-1-59069-617-0(4)) Studio Mouse LLC.

Tabletop Pocket Chart Counting & Numbers Card Set. 2004. (J). pap. 8.95 (978-1-56911-169-7(3)) Learning Resources, Inc.

Teach-Me-Bears Learn Numbers. 2003. (J). per. (978-1-884907-62-3(8)) Paradise Pr., Inc.

Teaching Resources Corporation Staff, creator. Number Puzzles. 2006. (Scholastic Hands-on Learning Ser.). (ENG.). 12.99 (978-0-439-82391-3(9), Teaching Resources) Scholastic, Inc.

TestSMART Plus Whole Numbers, Level B-1. 2004. (J). (978-1-57022-489-8(7)) ECS Learning Systems, Inc.

TestSMART Plus Whole Numbers, Level B-2. 2004. (J). (978-1-57022-490-4(0)) ECS Learning Systems, Inc.

TestSMART Plus Whole Numbers, Level C-1. 2004. (J). (978-1-57022-491-1(9)) ECS Learning Systems, Inc.

TestSMART Plus Whole Numbers, Level C-2. 2004. (J). (978-1-57022-492-8(7)) ECS Learning Systems, Inc.

TestSMART Plus Whole Numbers, Level D-1. 2004. (J). (978-1-57022-493-5(5)) ECS Learning Systems, Inc.

TestSMART Plus Whole Numbers, Level D-2. 2004. (J). (978-1-57022-494-2(3)) ECS Learning Systems, Inc.

TestSMART Plus Whole Numbers, Level E. 2004. (J). (978-1-57022-495-9(1)) ECS Learning Systems, Inc.

TestSMART Plus Whole Numbers, Level F. 2004. (J). (978-1-57022-496-6(X)) ECS Learning Systems, Inc.

TestSMART Plus Whole Numbers, Level G. 2004. (J). (978-1-57022-497-3(8)) ECS Learning Systems, Inc.

TestSMART Plus Whole Numbers, Level H. 2004. (J). (978-1-57022-498-0(6)) ECS Learning Systems, Inc.

TestSMART Plus Whole Numbers, Level I. 2004. (YA). (978-1-57022-499-7(4)) ECS Learning Systems, Inc.

Thomas, Sheeba P. Fun with Numbers. 2011. 28p. pap. 24.95 (978-1-4560-7923-9(9)) America Star Bks.

Thomson, Ruth. 1, 2, 3. (Coleccion Mi Primer Libro). (SPA., Illus.). 32p. (J). 13.95 (978-84-207-3777-5(1), ANY876) Grupo Anaya, S.A. ESP. Dist: Continental Bk. Co., Inc.

The TI Math Mate Calculator. 2004. suppl. ed. 265.50 (978-0-201-25341-2(0)); suppl. ed. 91.50 (978-0-201-25340-5(2)) Addison-Wesley Educational Pubs., Inc. (Scott Foresman).

Tipton, Stacey. The Complete Musical Spanish: With New Bonus Verbs Learning CD, 1. 2nd ed. 2005. (SPA., Illus.). 112p. 49.99 (978-0-9706829-7-0(2)) Musical Linguist, The.

Tourville, Amanda Doering. Buzzing Bees: Discovering Odd Numbers, 1 vol. Holm, Sharon Lane, illus. 2008. (Count the Critters Ser.). (ENG.). 24p. (J). (gr. k-3). 27.07 (978-1-60270-262-2(4)) Magic Wagon.

—Sunning Sea Lions: Discovering Even Numbers, 1 vol. Holm, Sharon Lane, illus. 2008. (Count the Critters Ser.). (ENG.). 24p. (J). (gr. k-3). 27.07 (978-1-60270-267-7(5)) Magic Wagon.

Twine, Alice. My Favorite Book of Numbers. 2008. (Board Bks.). (Illus.). 14p. (J). (gr. -1-k). bds. 11.95 (978-1-4042-4256-2(2)) Rosen Publishing Group, Inc., The.

Watson, Craig. Maddie Counts Marbles: Number Names & Count Sequence. 2013. (InfoMax Math Readers Ser.). (ENG.). 16p. (J). (gr. k-1). pap. 42.00 (978-1-4777-1950-3(4)); (Illus.). pap. 7.00 (978-1-4777-1949-7(0)) Rosen Publishing Group, Inc., The. (Rosen Classroom).

Watt, Fiona & Wells, Rachel. Adding II. 2004. (Usborne Sticker Math Ser.). (ENG., Illus.). 1p. (J). (gr. 1-2). pap., act. bk. ed. 6.95 (978-0-7460-4080-5(6)) EDC Publishing.

Weakland, Mark. Scooby-Doo! a Number Comparisons Mystery: The Case of the Lunchroom Gobbler, 1 vol. Gross, Scott, illus. 2014. (Solve It with Scooby-Doo!: Math Ser.). (ENG.). 24p. (gr. k-2). lib. bdg. 27.99 (978-1-4914-1542-9(8)) Capstone Press of Coughlan Cos.

—Scooby-Doo! an Even or Odd Mystery: The Case of the Oddzilla, 1 vol. Gross, Scott, illus. 2014. (Solve It with Scooby-Doo!: Math Ser.). (ENG.). 24p. (gr. k-2). lib. bdg. 27.99 (978-1-4914-1541-2(X)) Capstone Press of Coughlan Cos.

Weatherly. Working with Numbers. 2004. (Steck-Vaughn Working with Numbers Ser.). (ENG., Illus.). Level D. 160p. (gr. 3-3). pap. 18.85 (978-0-7398-9158-2(8));Level A. 144p. (gr. 1-1). pap., stu. ed. 18.85 (978-0-7398-9156-8(1));Level B. 144p. (gr. 2-2). pap. 18.85 (978-0-7398-9157-5(X)) Houghton Mifflin Harcourt Publishing Co.

Weekly Reader Early Learning Library Staff, contrib. by. I Know Numbers/Los Números. 2006. (I'm Ready for Math/ Ya puedo aprender matemáticas Ser.). (ENG & SPA., Illus.). 16p. (gr. -1-2). pap. 5.30 (978-0-8368-6490-8(5), Weekly Reader Leveled Readers) Stevens, Gareth Publishing LLLP.

Weekly Reader Editorial Staff. I Know Numbers. 2006. (I'm Ready for Math Ser.). (Illus.). 16p. (gr. -1-2). lib. bdg. 19.00 (978-0-8368-6475-5(1), Weekly Reader Leveled Readers) Stevens, Gareth Publishing LLLP.

—Los Numeros. 2006. (I'm Ready for Math/YA Puedo Aprender Matematicas Ser.). (ENG & SPA., Illus.). 16p. (gr. -1-2). lib. bdg. 19.00 (978-0-8368-6485-4(9), Weekly Reader Leveled Readers) Stevens, Gareth Publishing LLLP.

Weekly Reader Editorial Staff, contrib. by. I Know Numbers. 2006. (I'm Ready for Math Ser.). (Illus.). 16p. (gr. -1-2). pap. 5.30 (978-0-8368-6480-9(8), Weekly Reader Leveled Readers) Stevens, Gareth Publishing LLLP.

Weston Woods Staff, creator. How Much Is a Million? 2011. 38.75 (978-0-439-84576-2(9)) 2004. 18.95 (978-1-55592-106-4(X)) 2004. 29.95 (978-1-55592-124-8(8)) Weston Woods Studios, Inc.

White, Ella. I Can Write Numbers! Number Names & Count Sequence. 2013. (Rosen Math Readers Ser.). (ENG., Illus.). 16p. (J). (gr. k-1). pap. 7.00 (978-1-4777-1590-1(8), Rosen Classroom) Rosen Publishing Group, Inc., The.

White, Ella & White, Emma. I Can Write Numbers! Number Names & Count Sequence. 2013. (Rosen Math Readers Ser.). (ENG.). 16p. (J). (gr. k-1). pap. 42.00 (978-1-4777-1591-8(6), Rosen Classroom) Rosen Publishing Group, Inc., The.

World Book, Inc Staff, contrib. by. Numbers. 2012. (J). (978-0-7166-1436-4(7)); pap. (978-0-7166-1477-7(4)) World Bk., Inc.

The World of Eric Carle My Numbers Activity Kit. 2007. (J). 16.99 (978-0-9794445-1-7(9)) Loew-Cornell, Inc.

Yates, Gene. The Giraffe Numbers Book. 2003. (Illus.). 18p. (J). (978-1-58865-107-5(X)) Kidsbooks, LLC.

Yegoryan, Kristina & Yegoryan, Rubik. I Know Digits & Shapes. 2009. 108p. pap. 33.49 (978-1-4389-5444-8(1)) AuthorHouse.

Yoyo Books Staff. Numbers: Mini Baby's First Library. 2005. 42p. bds. (978-90-5843-804-1(X)) YoYo Bks.

Zakiyyah & Zakiyyah. Chatterworld My Numbers in Spanish/My Numbers in French: MIS Numeros en Espanol/Mes Mombres en Francais. 2006. (Illus.). 40p. (J). (gr. -1-3). 14.99 (978-0-9777085-0-5(0)) Little Linguists Press.

Zinsmeister, Elke, illus. Ten Fat Sausages. 2006. (Classic Books with Holes Big Book Ser.). (ENG.). 16p. (J). (gr. -1-3). (978-1-84643-008-4(9)) Child's Play International Ltd.

1, 2, 3. (Coleccion Picaros Peluchines). (SPA.). (J). 5.50 (978-950-11-0399-1(4), SGM399); (Illus.). 10p. pap. 5.50 (978-950-11-0791-3(4), SGM914) Sigmar ARG. Dist: Continental Bk. Co., Inc.

NUMBER THEORY

Adams, Colleen. Magic Squares: Learning the Inverse Relationships Between Addition & Subtraction. 2009. (Math for the REAL World Ser.). 16p. (gr. 2-3). pap. 7.05 (978-0-8239-8907-2(0), Rosen Classroom); 37.50 (978-1-60851-374-1(2), PowerKids Pr.) Rosen Publishing Group, Inc., The.

Allen, Susan & Lindaman, Jane. Used Any Numbers Lately? Enright, Vicky, illus. 2013. (ENG.). 32p. (J). (gr. k-3). pap. 6.95 (978-1-4677-0864-7(X), Millbrook Pr.) Lerner Publishing Group.

Arias, Lisa. Magical Mathematical Properties: Commutative, Associative, & Distributive. 2014. (ENG.). 32p. (gr. 3-6). 32.79 (978-1-62717-705-4(1)) Rourke Educational Media.

Burns, Kylie. Roman Numerals & Ordinals. 2010. (ENG., Illus.). 24p. (J). (978-0-7787-5250-9(X)); pap. (978-0-7787-5297-4(6)) Crabtree Publishing Co.

Carlton Publishing Group, illus. Magical Designs & Color-By-Numbers. 2016. (Cool & Calm Coloring for Kids Ser.). (ENG.). 48p. (J). (gr. 2-6). pap. 6.99 (978-1-4380-0927-8(5)) Barron's Educational Series, Inc.

Carson-Dellosa Publishing Staff. Number Play, Grade K. 2010. (Home Workbooks Ser.). (ENG.). 64p. (gr. k-k). pap. 4.49 (978-1-60418-777-9(8)) Carson-Dellosa Publishing, LLC.

—Numbers 0-20, Grades PK - K. 2010. (Home Workbooks Ser.). (ENG.). 64p. (gr. -1-k). pap. 4.49 (978-1-60418-762-5(X)) Carson-Dellosa Publishing, LLC.

—Numbers 0-30, Grades K - 1. 2010. (Home Workbooks Ser.). (ENG.). 64p. (gr. k-1). pap. 4.49 (978-1-60418-783-0(2)) Carson-Dellosa Publishing, LLC.

—Numbers 0-30, Grades Pk - K: Dot-to-Dot. 2010. (Home Workbooks Ser.). (ENG.). 64p. (gr. -1-k). pap. 4.49 (978-1-60418-763-2(8)) Carson-Dellosa Publishing, LLC.

Carson-Dellosa Publishing Staff, compiled by. Numbers 0-10, Grades PK - K. 2010. (Home Workbooks Ser.). (ENG.). 64p. (gr. -1-k). pap. 4.49 (978-1-60418-761-8(1)) Carson-Dellosa Publishing, LLC.

Downey, Tika. The History of Zero: Exploring Our Place-Value Number System. 2009. (PowerMath Ser.). (ENG., Illus.). 32p. (gr. 4-5). pap. 10.00 (978-0-8239-8869-3(4), PowerKids Pr.) Rosen Publishing Group, Inc., The.

Emerson-Stonnell, Sharon. Number Systems. 2006. 372p. pap. 35.95 (978-1-59800-658-2(4)) Outskirts Pr., Inc.

Faulkner, Nicholas & Hosch, William L. Numbers & Measurements. 2017. (J). lib. bdg. **(978-1-68048-778-7(7)**, Britannica Educational Publishing) Rosen Publishing Group, Inc., The.

Lundy, Miranda & Mcnaughton, Phoebe. Sacred Number: The Secret Quality of Quantities. Lundy, Miranda et al, illus. 2005. (Wooden Bks.). (ENG.). 64p. 14.00 (978-0-8027-1456-5(0), 9780802714565) Bloomsbury Publishing USA.

Marzollo, Jean. Help Me Learn Numbers 0-20. Phillips, Chad, illus. Phillips, Chad, photos by. 2011. (ENG.). 32p. (J). (gr. -1-k). 15.95 (978-0-8234-2334-7(4)) Holiday Hse., Inc.

Numbers. 2004. (J). 12p. bds. 3.99 (978-1-85997-813-9(4)); 24p. 4.99 (978-1-85997-979-2(3)) Byeway Bks.

Numbers. (People's Bible Commentary Ser.). 264p. 14.99 (978-0-7586-0418-7(1)) Concordia Publishing Hse.

Numbers. 2003. (J). per. (978-1-57657-918-3(2)) Paradise Pr., Inc.

Numbers. (Rainbow Ryhmes Ser.). (J). 12p. bds. (978-2-7643-0175-3(8)); 8p. bds. (978-2-7643-0184-5(7)) Phidal Publishing, Inc./Editions Phidal, Inc.

Phidal Publishing Staff, ed. Numbers. (Turn & Learn Ser.). 12p. (J). (978-2-7643-0139-5(1)) Phidal Publishing, Inc./Editions Phidal, Inc.

Scholastic, Inc. Staff. Write-and-Learn Number Practice Pages: Help Kids Recognize, Write, & Really Learn the Numbers 1-30. 2003. (ENG.). 72p. (gr. -1-1). pap., tchr. ed. 12.99 (978-0-439-45865-8(X), Teaching Resources) Scholastic, Inc.

School Zone Publishing Co. Numbers Bingo Game. 2006. (ENG.). (J). (gr. -1-k). 5.99 (978-1-58947-495-6(3)) School Zone Publishing Co.

Sterling, Kristin. Ordinal Numbers. 2008. pap. 22.95 (978-0-8225-9362-1(9)); (ENG.). 8p. (gr. -1-1). pap. 4.95 (978-0-8225-8846-7(3)) Lerner Publishing Group.

TestSMART Plus Number Theory, Level A/B. 2004. (J). (978-1-57022-482-9(X)) ECS Learning Systems, Inc.

TestSMART Plus Number Theory, Level C/D. 2004. (J). (978-1-57022-483-6(8)) ECS Learning Systems, Inc.

TestSMART Plus Number Theory, Level E/F. 2004. (J). (978-1-57022-484-3(6)) ECS Learning Systems, Inc.

TestSMART Plus Number Theory, Level G. 2004. (J). (978-1-57022-485-0(4)) ECS Learning Systems, Inc.

TestSMART Plus Number Theory, Level H. 2004. (J). (978-1-57022-486-7(2)) ECS Learning Systems, Inc.

TestSMART Plus Number Theory, Level I. 2004. (YA). (978-1-57022-487-4(0)) ECS Learning Systems, Inc.

Wipe-Clean Writing Numbers. 2017. (Wipe-Clean Bks.). (ENG.). (J). pap. 7.99 **(978-0-7945-3697-8(2)**, Usborne) EDC Publishing.

NUMISMATICS

see also Coins

Bekkering, Annalise. Seals. 2008. (U. S. Sites & Symbols Ser.). (Illus.). 48p. (J). (gr. 3-5). pap. 10.95 (978-1-59036-893-0(2)); lib. bdg. 29.05 (978-1-59036-892-3(4)) Weigl Pubs., Inc.

Whitman Publishing, ed. Adventure Across the States: Collecting State Quarters & Other Coins. 2006. (Official Whitman Guidebook Ser.). (Illus.). 92p. per. 4.99 (978-0-7948-2050-3(6)) Whitman Publishing LLC.

Yeoman, R. S. The Official Blue Book(r) Handbook of United States CoinsTM: With Premium List. Bressett, Ken, ed. 62nd ed. 2004. (Illus.). 224p. pap. 9.95 (978-0-7948-1787-9(4)) Whitman Publishing LLC.

NUNEZ CABEZA DE VACA, ALVAR, ACTIVE 16TH CENTURY

Marsh, Carole. Alvar Nunez Cabeza de Vaca:Explorer & Survivor: Explorer & Survivor. 2003. 12p. (gr. k-4). 2.95 (978-0-635-02135-9(8)) Gallopade International.

Peppas, Lynn. Why Cabeza de Vaca Matters to Texas. 2014. (Illus.). 32p. (J). lib. bdg. 26.25 (978-1-4777-0913-9(4)) Rosen Publishing Group, Inc., The.

Waldman, Stuart. We Asked for Nothing. McNally, Tom, illus. 2014. (ENG.). 208p. (J). (gr. 5-7). pap. 8.95 (978-1-931414-50-0(5), 9781931414500) Mikaya Pr.

NUNS

Fitzpatrick, Anne. Mother Teresa. 2005. (Genius Ser.). (Illus.). 48p. (J). (gr. 5-9). lib. bdg. 21.95 (978-1-58341-330-2(8), Creative Education) Creative Co., The.

Ganeri, Anita. Mother Teresa's Alms Bowl. Radford, Karen & Noyes, Leighton, illus. 2008. (Stories of Great People Ser.). (ENG.). 40p. (J). (gr. 3-8). pap. (978-0-7787-3712-4(8)) Crabtree Publishing Co.

Ganeri, Anita & Bailey, Gerry. Mother Teresa's Alms Bowl. 2008. (Stories of Great People Ser.). (ENG., Illus.). 40p. (J). (gr. 3-8). lib. bdg. (978-0-7787-3690-5(3)) Crabtree Publishing Co.

Gigliotti, Jim & dePaola, Tomie. Who Was Mother Teresa? Harrison, Nancy, illus. 2015. (Who Was? Ser.). (ENG.). 112p. (J). (gr. 3-7). 5.99 (978-0-448-48299-6(1), Grosset & Dunlap) Penguin Young Readers Group.

Glavich, Mary Kathleen. Blessed Teresa of Calcutta: Missionary of Charity. Kiwak, Barbara, tr. Kiwak, Barbara, illus. 2003. (Encounter the Saints Ser.: Vol. 17). 136p. (J). pap. 7.95 (978-0-8198-1160-8(2), 332-024) Pauline Bks. & Media.

Harrison, Paul. Mother Teresa. 2017. (ENG., Illus.). 32p. (J). (gr. 4-6). pap. 6.99 (978-0-7502-9877-3(4), Wayland) Hachette Children's Group GBR. Dist: Hachette Bk. Group.

Helfand, Lewis. Mother Teresa: Saint of the Slums. Banerjee, Sankha & Nagar, Sachin, illus. 2013. (Campfire Graphic Novels Ser.). (ENG.). 88p. (YA). (gr. 5). pap. 11.99 (978-93-80028-70-5(9), Campfire) Steerforth Pr.

Jones, Brenn. Learning about Love from the Life of Mother Teresa. 2009. (Character Building Book Ser.). 24p. (gr. 2-3). 42.50 (978-1-61511-001-8(1), PowerKids Pr.) Rosen Publishing Group, Inc., The.

Lazaro, Georgina. Juana Ines. Preza, Bruno Gonzalez, illus. 2007. (SPA.). 32p. (J). (gr. 3-5). 14.99 (978-1-930332-57-7(2)) Lectorum Pubns., Inc.

Martinez, Elsie & Stelly, Colette. Henriette Delille: Rebellious Saint, 1 vol. Reppel, Phyllis, illus. 2010. (ENG.). 200p. (J). (gr. 3-7). 19.95 (978-1-58980-839-3(8)) Pelican Publishing Co., Inc.

Murphy, Sally. Meet Mary MacKillop. Martinez, Sonia, illus. 2013. (Meet... Ser.). (ENG.). 32p. (J). (gr. -1). 18.99 (978-1-74275-721-6(9)) Random Hse. Australia AUS. Dist: Independent Pubs. Group.

Nelson, Robin. Mother Teresa: A Life of Caring. (Pull Ahead Books-Biographies Ser.). (Illus.). 32p. 2007. (ENG.). (gr. k-3). pap. 7.95 (978-0-8225-6433-1(5)) 2006. (J). (gr. 3-7). lib. bdg. 22.60 (978-0-8225-6384-6(3), Lerner Pubns.) Lerner Publishing Group.

Price, Sean Stewart & Price, Sean. Attila the Hun: Leader of the Barbarian Hordes. 2009. (Wicked History Ser.). (ENG., Illus.). 128p. (J). (gr. 6-12). 31.00 (978-0-531-21801-3(5), Watts, Franklin) Scholastic Library Publishing.

Slavicek, Louise Chipley. Mother Teresa: Caring for the World's Poor. 2007. (Modern Peacemakers Ser.). (Illus.). 113p. (YA). (gr. 9-12). lib. bdg. 30.00 (978-0-7910-9433-4(2)) Facts On File, Inc.

Sullivan, Anne Marie. Mother Theresa: Religious Humanitarian. 2004. (Great Names Ser.). (Illus.). 32p. (J). (gr. 3-18). lib. bdg. 19.95 (978-1-59084-142-6(5)) Mason Crest.

Trussell-Cullen, Alan. Mother Teresa. 2009. pap. 13.25 (978-1-60559-066-0(5)) Hameray Publishing Group, Inc.

Valentine, Emily. Mother Teresa: With a Discussion of Compassion. 2004. (Values in Action Ser.). (J). (978-1-59203-070-5(X)) Learning Challenge, Inc.

NUNS—FICTION

Ahern, Dianne. Curse of the Coins: Adventures with Sister Philomena, Special Agent to the Pope. 2007. (J). pap. 11.95 (978-0-9679437-7-0(9)) Aunt Dee's Attic, Inc.

Blagden, Scott. Dear Life, You Suck: A Novel. 2015. (ENG.). 320p. (YA). (gr. 9). pap. 9.99 (978-0-544-33621-6(6), HMH Books For Young Readers) Houghton Mifflin Harcourt Publishing Co.

Carville, Declan. The Incredible Sister Brigid. Black, Kieron, illus. 29p. pap. 7.95 (978-0-9538222-5-2(2)) Discovery Pubns. GBR. Dist: Irish Bks. & Media, Inc.

Clark, Kathy. Guardian Angel House, 1 vol. 2009. (Holocaust Remembrance Ser.). (ENG., Illus.). 180p. (J). (gr. 4-8). pap. 14.95 (978-1-897187-58-6(0)) Second Story Pr. CAN. Dist: Orca Bk. Pubs. USA.

Hooper, Mary. Round the Rainbow. Harker, Lesley, illus. 2008. (Two Naughty Angels Ser.). (ENG.). 96p. (J). (gr. 2-4). pap. 11.95 (978-0-7475-9062-0(1)) Bloomsbury Publishing Plc GBR. Dist: Independent Pubs. Group.

Jarzab, Anna. The Opposite of Hallelujah. 2013. (ENG.). 464p. (YA). (gr. 7). pap. 10.99 (978-0-375-85529-0(7), Ember) Random Hse. Children's Bks.

Keffer, Ann. The Seventh Chair. 2007. 76p. (J). per. 8.95 (978-0-595-45917-9(X)) iUniverse, Inc.

Marie, Cynthia. Sister Aggie Goes Surfing. 2012. 50p. pap. 20.95 (978-1-4497-5404-4(X), WestBow Pr.) Author Solutions, Inc.

Murphy, Jim. Revenge of the Green Banana. 2017. (ENG.). 224p. (J). (gr. 5-7). 16.99 (978-0-544-78677-6(7), Clarion Bks.) Houghton Mifflin Harcourt Trade & Reference Pubs.

Nogar, Anna M. & Lamadrid, Enrique R. Sisters in Blue: Sor María de Ágreda Comes to New Mexico = Hermanas de Azul: Sor María de Ágreda Viene a Nuevo México. Córdova, Amy, illus. 2017. (SPA & ENG.). 88p. (J). **(978-0-8263-5821-9(7))** Univ. of New Mexico Pr.

Shofner, Corabel. Almost Paradise. 2017. (ENG.). 304p. (J). 16.99 (978-0-374-30378-5(9), 9780374303785, Farrar, Straus & Giroux (BYR)) Farrar, Straus & Giroux.

The Year We Sailed the Sun. 2015. (ENG., Illus.). 432p. (J). (gr. 3-7). 17.99 (978-0-689-85827-7(2), Atheneum/Richard Jackson Bks.) Simon & Schuster Children's Publishing.

NUREMBERG TRIAL OF MAJOR GERMAN WAR CRIMINALS, NUREMBERG, GERMANY, 1945-1946

DiPalma, Emilio & Chetkowski, Emily DiPalma. Just a Kid: A Guard at the Nuremberg Trials. 2004. (Illus.). 69p. per. 9.95 (978-0-9744803-3-6(9)) PublishingWorks.

NUREYEV, RUDOLF, 1939-1993

Fandel, Jennifer. Rudolf Nureyev. 2005. (Extraordinary Artists Ser.). (Illus.). 48p. (J). (gr. 5-9). lib. bdg. 21.95 (978-1-58341-380-7(4), Creative Education) Creative Co., The.

NURSERY RHYMES

A&C Black, A&C. The Wheels on the Bus: And Other Illustrated Songs & Nursery Rhymes to Sing Together. 2017. (ENG.). 32p. (J). pap. 10.99 **(978-1-4729-3439-0(3))** HarperCollins Pubs. Ltd. GBR. Dist: Independent Pubs. Group.

—The Wheels on the Bus (Big Book) And Other Illustrated Songs & Nursery Rhymes to Sing Together. 2017. (ENG.). 32p. (J). pap. 29.95 **(978-1-4729-3438-3(5))** HarperCollins Pubs. Ltd. GBR. Dist: Independent Pubs. Group.

Abel, Simone, illus. Cuddly Critters: Animal Nursery Rhymes, 1 vol. 2007. (Mother Goose Rhymes Ser.). (ENG.). 32p. (gr. -1-2). lib. bdg. 25.99 (978-1-4048-2344-0(1), 1265749, Nonfiction Picture Bks.) Picture Window Bks.

—Mother Goose Rhymes, 6 bks., Set. Incl. Cuddly Critters: Animal Nursery Rhymes. (ENG., Illus.). 32p. (gr. -1-2). 2007. lib. bdg. 25.99 (978-1-4048-2344-0(1), 1265749, Nonfiction Picture Bks.); (Mother Goose Rhymes Ser.). (ENG.). 32p. 2007. Set lib. bdg. 51.98 (978-1-4048-3512-2(1)) Picture Window Bks.

Adams, Pam, illus. Old Macdonald. 2004. (Classic Books with Holes Board Book Ser.). (ENG.). 16p. (J). bds. (978-0-85953-317-1(4)) Child's Play International Ltd.

—This Is the House That Jack Built. 2007. (Classic Books with Holes 8x8 with CD Ser.). (ENG.). 16p. (J). (gr. -1-1). pap. incl. audio compact disk (978-1-904550-65-5(7)) Child's Play International Ltd.

Ahlberg, Allan. Everybody Was a Baby Once: And Other Poems. Ingman, Bruce, illus. 2010. (ENG.). 64p. (J). (gr. -1-k). 15.99 (978-0-7636-4682-0(2)) Candlewick Pr.

Aizen, Marina, illus. Mary Had a Little Lamb. 2015. (Classic Books with Holes Ser.). (ENG.). 16p. (J). pap. incl. audio compact disk (978-1-84643-679-6(6)) Child's Play International Ltd.

Alvarez, Mrinali, illus. Pon, Pon: ¡A Jugar con el Bebé! 2005. (SPA.). 28p. (J). 8.95 (978-0-8477-1550-3(7)) Univ. of Puerto Rico Pr.

Anderson, Airlie, illus. Cows in the Kitchen. (Classic Books with Holes 8x8 with CD Ser.). (ENG.). (J). 2013. 16p. (gr. -1). pap. incl. audio compact disk (978-1-84643-625-3(7)) 2007. 14p. (gr. -1-1). bds. (978-1-84643-110-4(7)) 2007. 16p. (gr. 1-1). pap. (978-1-84643-106-7(9)) Child's Play International Ltd.

—Ten Little Ducks. 2008. (Activity Bks.). (ENG.). 24p. (J). (gr. -1-1). (978-1-84643-182-1(4)) Child's Play International Ltd.

Andrews, Jackie. Old Macdonald His Farm. Bennett, John, illus. 2012. (ENG.). 32p. pap. 6.50 (978-1-84135-195-7(4)) Award Pubns. Ltd. GBR. Dist: Parkwest Pubns., Inc.

Anness Publishing Staff. Nursery Rhymes for Little Ones: Mother Goose Collection, 3 vols. 2013. (ENG., Illus.). 72p. (J). (gr. -1-1). bds. 9.99 (978-1-86147-318-9(4), Armadillo) Anness Publishing GBR. Dist: National Bk. Network.

Applesauce Press Staff. Twinkle Twinkle Little Star: A Spinning Star Pop-up Book. 2015. (ENG., Illus.). 8p. (J). 12.95 (978-1-60433-597-2(1), Applesauce Pr.) Cider Mill Pr. Bk. Pubs., LLC.

Archer, Dosh. Urgency Emergency!, 4, Set. Archer, Dosh, illus. 2016. (Urgency Emergency! Ser.). (ENG., Illus.). 192p. (J). (gr. -1-3). pap. 19.99 (978-0-8075-9991-4(3)) Whitman, Albert & Co.

Arenson, Roberta. One, Two, Skip a Few! First Number Rhymes. Arenson, Roberta, illus. 2005. (Illus.). 32p. (J). pap. 6.99 (978-1-84148-130-2(0)) Barefoot Bks., Inc.

Armadillo Publishing Staff. This Little Pig. Lewis, Jan, illus. 2015. (ENG.). 24p. bds. 6.99 (978-1-86147-486-5(5), Armadillo) Anness Publishing GBR. Dist: National Bk. Network.

Atkins, Alison, illus. Humpty Dumpty & Friends. 2005. 10p. bds. (978-1-84510-767-3(5)) Top That! Publishing PLC.

—Incy Wincy Spider & Friends. 2005. 10p. bds. (978-1-84510-768-0(3)) Top That! Publishing PLC.

Atkinson, Ruth & Atkinson, Brett. Rhyme Templates. Atkinson, Ruth & Atkinson, Brett, illus. (Illus.). (J). (gr. k-2). pap. (978-1-875739-74-5(2)) Wizard Bks.

—Traditional Rhyme Templates. Atkinson, Ruth & Atkinson, Brett, illus. (Illus.). (J). (gr. k-2). pap. *(978-1-875739-94-3(7))* Wizard Bks.

Avril, Lynne, illus. Five Little Monkeys. 2010. (Favorite Children's Songs Ser.). (ENG.). 16p. (J). (gr. -1-2). 25.64 *(978-1-60253-530-5(2),* 200112) Child's World, Inc., The.

Award, Anna. My First Nursery Rhymes. 2012. (ENG., Illus.). 10p. (J). pap. 9.95 *(978-1-84135-570-2(4));* bds. 6.50 *(978-1-84135-569-6(0))* Award Pubns. Ltd. GBR. Dist: Parkwest Pubns., Inc.

Baby Jamz Color & Fun Book: Posters of Solange & Beyonce' Inside. 2008. (J). per. 2.57 *(978-0-9796536-2-9(2),* EPI Kid Bks.) EPI Bks.

Baby's Book of Rhymes. 2008. (Nursery Rhyme Boards with CD Sliding Tray Ser.). 48p. *(978-1-4075-3199-1(9))* Parragon, Inc.

Baggott, Stella. Baby's Very First Noisy Nursery Rhymes. 2013. (Baby's Very First Noisy Book Ser.). 10p. (J). ring bd. 14.99 *(978-0-7945-3317-5(5),* Usborne) EDC Publishing.

Baker, Keith. La Gallina Grande/Big Fat Hen. Campoy, F. Isabel, tr. 2014. (SPA & ENG., Illus.). 30p. (J). (— 1). bds. 4.99 *(978-0-544-17398-9(8),* HMH Books For Young Readers) Houghton Mifflin Harcourt Publishing Co.

Balmer, Paul. Big Nursery Rhyme Songbook. 2009. pap. 12.95 *(978-1-84772-579-0(1),* AM993828) Wise Pubns. GBR. Dist: Music Sales Corp.

Barefoot Books Staff. Clare Beaton's Animal Rhymes. Beaton, Clare, illus. 2014. 14p. (J). (gr. -1-k). bds. 6.99 *(978-1-78285-080-9(5))* Barefoot Bks., Inc.

—Clare Beaton's Garden Rhymes. Beaton, Clare, illus. 2014. 14p. (J). (gr. -1-k). bds. 6.99 *(978-1-78285-081-6(3))* Barefoot Bks., Inc.

Baring-Gould, Sabine. A Book of Nursery Songs & Rhymes. 2009. 216p. pap. *(978-1-4099-5663-1(6))* Dodo Pr.

Barnum-Newman, Winifred. Old King Cole. 2009. (Favorite Mother Goose Rhymes Ser.). (ENG., Illus.). 16p. (J). (gr. -1-2). 25.64 *(978-1-60253-301-1(6),* 200249) Child's World, Inc., The.

—To Market, to Market. Newman, Winifred Barnum & Barnum-Newman, Winifred, illus. 2010. (Favorite Children's Songs Ser.). (ENG.). 16p. (J). (gr. -1-2). 25.64 *(978-1-60253-532-9(9),* 200114) Child's World, Inc., The.

Barritt, Margaret. Hickory Dickory Dock. East, Jacqueline, illus. 2006. (ENG.). 7p. (J). (gr. -1-7). bds. 7.95 *(978-1-59354-153-8(8),* Handprint Bks.) Chronicle Bks. LLC.

Baxter, Nicola. Classic Nursery Rhymes. Shuttleworth, Cathie, illus. 2012. (ENG.). 80p. (J). (gr. -1-k). 9.99 *(978-1-84322-837-0(8))* Anness Publishing GBR. Dist: National Bk. Network.

—Head, Shoulders, Knees & Toes & Other Action Rhymes. Buckingham, Gabriella, illus. 2013. (ENG.). 16p. (J). (gr. -1-6). bds. 7.99 *(978-1-84322-829-5(7),* Armadillo) Anness Publishing GBR. Dist: National Bk. Network.

—Rhymes for Playtime Fun. Shuttleworth, Cathie, illus. 2013. (ENG.). 80p. (J). (gr. -1-k). pap. 9.99 *(978-1-84322-921-6(8))* Anness Publishing GBR. Dist: National Bk. Network.

Beacon, Dawn. Peter Piper. Beacon, Dawn, illus. 2011. (Favorite Mother Goose Rhymes Ser.). (ENG., Illus.). 16p. (J). (gr. -1-2). lib. bdg. 25.64 *(978-1-60954-282-5(7),* 200234) Child's World, Inc., The.

Beall, Mary Kay. Sleep Tight with Angels Tonight. 2008. (ENG.). 84p. pap. 17.95 incl. audio compact disk *(978-1-59235-230-2(8),* 1592352308) Shawnee Pr., Inc.

Beall, Pamela Conn & Nipp, Susan Hagen. Wee Sing Nursery Rhymes & Lullabies, 1 vol. 2005. (Wee Sing Ser.). (ENG.). 64p. (J). (gr. -1-2). 10.99 *(978-0-8431-1360-0(X),* Price Stern Sloan) Penguin Young Readers Group.

Beaton, Clare. Baby's First Book. 2008. (ENG., Illus.). 64p. (J). (gr. -1-k). 19.99 *(978-1-84686-143-7(8))* Barefoot Bks., Inc.

—Clare Beaton's Bedtime Rhymes. Beaton, Clare, illus. 2012. (ENG., Illus.). 14p. (J). (gr. -1-k). 6.99 *(978-1-84686-737-8(1))* Barefoot Bks., Inc.

—Clare Beaton's Farmyard Rhymes. Beaton, Clare, illus. 2012. (ENG., Illus.). 14p. (J). (gr. -1-k). 6.99 *(978-1-84686-736-1(3))* Barefoot Bks., Inc.

—Playtime Rhymes for Little People. 2008. (ENG., Illus.). 64p. (J). (gr. -1-k). 19.99 *(978-1-84686-156-7(X))* Barefoot Bks., Inc.

Beaton, Clare, illus. Clare Beaton's Action Rhymes. 2010. (ENG.). 14p. (J). (gr. -1-k). 6.99 *(978-1-84686-473-5(9))* Barefoot Bks., Inc.

—Clare Beaton's Nursery Rhymes. 2010. (ENG.). 14p. (J). (gr. -1-k). 6.99 *(978-1-84686-472-8(0))* Barefoot Bks., Inc.

Benchmark Education Company, LLC Staff, compiled by. Reader's Theater Nursery Rhymes & Songs Big Books. 2009. (Reader's Theater Nursery Rhymes & Songs Ser.). (J). (gr. k-1). 665.00 *(978-1-4108-8454-1(6))* Benchmark Education Co.

Bentley, Dawn, et al. Rhyme Time: Rhyme-and-Learn. Schwaeber, Barbie H. & Williams, Tracee, eds. 2008. (ENG., Illus.). 24p. (J). (gr. -1). 4.99 *(978-1-59069-653-8(0))* Studio Mouse LLC.

Billin-Frye, Paige. Pease Porridge Hot. Billin-Frye, Paige & Frye, Paige, illus. 2011. (Favorite Children's Songs Ser.). (ENG.). 16p. (J). (gr. -1-2). lib. bdg. 25.64 *(978-1-60954-293-1(2),* 200097) Child's World, Inc., The.

Bixley, Donovan, illus. Pussycat, Pussycat: Purrfect Nursery Rhymes. 2016. (ENG.). 24p. (J). (— 1). pap. 9.99 *(978-1-927262-28-3(3))* Upstart Pr. NZL. Dist: Independent Pubs. Group.

Blake, Quentin. Quentin Blake's Nursery Rhyme Book. 2013. (ENG., Illus.). 32p. (J). (gr. k-2). pap. 12.99 *(978-1-84941-690-0(7),* Red Fox) Random House Children's Books GBR. Dist: Independent Pubs. Group.

—Quentin Blake's Nursery Rhyme Book. 2013. (Illus.). 32p. lib. bdg. 24.50 *(978-0-606-31771-9(6),* Turtleback) Turtleback Bks.

Bleck, Linda, illus. A Children's Treasury of Mother Goose. 2015. (ENG.). 32p. (J). (-k). pap. 6.95 *(978-1-4549-1473-0(4))* Sterling Publishing Co., Inc.

Blyton, Enid. Mother Goose: Treasury of Favourite Rhymes. Barnes-Murphy, Rowan, illus. 2012. (ENG.). 160p. 24.95 *(978-1-84135-591-7(7))* Award Pubns. Ltd. GBR. Dist: Parkwest Pubns., Inc.

Blyton, Enid, et al. Magical Creatures. 2013. (ENG.). 10p. (J). bds. 9.95 *(978-1-84135-725-6(1))* Award Pubns. Ltd. GBR. Dist: Parkwest Pubns., Inc.

Bodden, Valerie. Nursery Rhymes. 2011. (Poetry Basics Ser.). (ENG.). 32p. (J). (gr. 4-7). pap. 9.99 *(978-1-926722-46-7(9),* Creative Paperbacks) Creative Co., The.

—Poetry Basics - Nursery Rhymes. 2009. (Poetry Basics Ser.). 32p. 19.95 *(978-1-58341-778-2(8),* Creative Education) Creative Co., The.

Bonnet, Rosaline. Very First Nursery Rhymes. Bonnet, Rosaline, illus. 2010. (Very First Words Board Bks). (Illus.). 12p. (J). bds. 6.99 *(978-0-7945-2723-5(X),* Usborne) EDC Publishing.

Borreguita Negra: Poems, Rhymes, & Songs Listening Packs. 2003. 34.50 *(978-0-673-58629-2(4))* Celebration Pr.

Bourdeau, Marje. Baby's 1st Times, Baby's 1st Rhymes. 2011. 56p. pap. 15.99 *(978-1-4628-4641-2(6))* Xlibris Corp.

Bousquet, Anthea. Lucy's St. Lucian Alphabet: The ABCs of Caribbean Culture in Upbeat Rhyming Verse. Sandiford, Ted, illus. 2012. 20p. (J). pap. *(978-976-8238-02-3(X))* Maryli Pubs.

Boynton, Sandra. Belly Button Book! 2005. (ENG., Illus.). 24p. (J). (gr. k — 1). bds. 6.95 *(978-0-7611-3799-3(8),* 13799) Workman Publishing Co., Inc.

Brilla, Brilla Estrellita: Poems, Rhymes & Songs Listening Packs. 2003. 34.50 *(978-0-673-58608-7(1))* Celebration Pr.

Britton, April Spring. Alphabet Rhymes. 2011. 24p. pap. 15.99 *(978-1-4653-4897-5(2))* Xlibris Corp.

Brooke, L. Leslie. Ring o' Roses, a Nursery Rhyme Picture Book. Brooke, L. Leslie, illus. 2012. (Illus.). 102p. pap. 9.99 *(978-1-61720-438-8(2))* Wilder Pubns., Corp.

—The Ring o' Roses Treasury: Nursery Rhymes & Stories. 2015. (Calla Editions Ser.). (ENG., Illus.). 232p. (J). (gr. -1-6). 30.00 *(978-1-60660-074-0(5))* Dover Pubns., Inc.

Brooks, Felicity. Animal Rhymes. 2010. (Look & Say Board Bks). (Illus.). 12p. (J). bds. 8.99 *(978-0-7945-2817-1(1),* Usborne) EDC Publishing.

—Counting Rhymes. Gregorio, Giuliana, illus. 2010. (Look & Say Board Bks). 12p. (J). bds. 8.99 *(978-0-7945-2779-2(5),* Usborne) EDC Publishing.

—Finger Rhymes. Gregorio, Giuliana, illus. 2010. (Rhyming Look & Say Ser.). 12p. (J). bds. 8.99 *(978-0-7945-2780-8(9),* Usborne) EDC Publishing.

Brown, Jean. My Treasure Book of Nursery Rhymes & Hymns. 2007. (Illus.). 56p. per. *(978-1-84748-087-3(X))* Athena Pr.

Brown, Marc. Marc Brown's Playtime Rhymes: A Treasury for Families to Learn & Play Together. 2013. (ENG.). 48p. (J). (gr. -1-3). 18.00 *(978-0-316-20735-5(7))* Little, Brown Bks. for Young Readers.

Brown, Marc, illus. Read-Aloud Rhymes for the Very Young. 2016. (ENG.). 112p. (J). (gr. -1-2). 15.99 *(978-0-399-55357-8(6),* Dragonfly Bks.) Random Hse. Children's Bks.

Brown, Michelle Haney. My First Book of Japanese Words: An ABC Rhyming Book. Padron, Aya, illus. 2013. (ENG & JPN.). 32p. (J). (gr. -1-3). 12.95 *(978-4-8053-1201-8(7))* Tuttle Publishing.

Bruriah, D. Around the Yamim Tovim. 14p. 13.99 *(978-1-58330-620-8(X))* Feldheim Pubs.

—Let's Welcome Shabbos. 24p. 12.99 *(978-1-58330-591-1(2))* Feldheim Pubs.

Bunton, M. Catherine. The Fairy Tale Keeper. 2012. 134p. pap. 8.95 *(978-1-60594-783-9(0))* Aeon Publishing Inc.

Bush, Timothy, illus. Teddy Bear, Teddy Bear: A Traditional Rhyme. 2005. 32p. (J). 14.99 *(978-0-06-057835-0(1));* (gr. -1 — 1). lib. bdg. 15.89 *(978-0-06-057836-7(X))* HarperCollins Pubs.

Butler, John. Ten in the Den, 1 vol. Butler, John, illus. 2016. (ENG., Illus.). 32p. (J). (gr. -1-1). pap. 7.95 *(978-1-56145-965-0(8))* Peachtree Pubs.

Byeway Books, creator. Rhymes. 2011. (My First Picture Fun Bks.). (ENG., Illus.). 24p. (J). (gr. -1). bds. 5.99 *(978-1-60176-022-7(1))* Byeway Bks.

Byrne, Mike, illus. Twinkle, Twinkle, Little Star; and, Spaceship, Spaceship, Zooming. 2013. (ENG.). 24p. (J). pap. *(978-0-7787-1150-6(1))* Crabtree Publishing Co.

—Twinkle, Twinkle, Little Star; and, Spaceship, Spaceship, Zooming High. 2013. (ENG.). 24p. (J). *(978-0-7787-1132-2(3))* Crabtree Publishing Co.

Cabrera, Jane. Old Mother Hubbard. 2008. (Jane Cabrera Board Bks.). (ENG., Illus.). 24p. (J). (gr. -1-k). bds. 6.95 *(978-0-8234-2132-9(5))* Holiday Hse., Inc.

Caldecott, Randolph. Come Lasses & Lads. 2006. pap. *(978-1-4065-1220-5(6))* Dodo Pr.

—The Farmer's Boy. 2006. (Illus.). pap. *(978-1-4065-1223-6(0))* Dodo Pr.

—Hey Diddle Diddle & Baby Bunting. 2006. pap. *(978-1-4065-1226-7(5))* Dodo Pr.

—The House That Jack Built. 2006. pap. *(978-1-4065-1227-4(3))* Dodo Pr.

—The Queen of Hearts, & Sing a Song for Sixpence. 2006. pap. *(978-1-4065-1228-1(1))* Dodo Pr.

—Ride a Cock-Horse to Banbury Cross, & a Farmer Went Trotting upon His Grey Mare. 2006. pap. *(978-1-4065-1229-8(X))* Dodo Pr.

—The Three Jovial Huntsmen. 2007. pap. *(978-1-4065-1230-4(3))* Dodo Pr.

Carleton, Will. Rhymes of Our Planet, by Will Carleton. 2006. 216p. per. 20.99 *(978-1-4255-1746-5(3))* Michigan Publishing.

Carpenter, Stephen, illus. Mary Had a Little Jam, & Other Silly Rhymes. 2004. 32p. (J). *(978-0-88166-470-6(7))* Meadowbrook Pr.

Carpenter, Stephen, illus. Mary Had a Little Jam & Other Silly Rhymes: Expanded with Twice As Many Rhymes. 2016. 80p. (J). ***(978-0-88166-597-0(5))*** Meadowbrook Pr.

Caswell, Kelly, illus. Hickory Dickory Dock. 2012. (Classic Books with Holes Board Book Ser.). (ENG.). (J). 14p. bds. *(978-1-84643-510-2(2));* 16p. pap. *(978-1-84643-499-0(8))* Child's Play International Ltd.

Chambers, Mark, illus. Five Little Monkeys; and, Five Little Penguins. 2013. (ENG.). 24p. (J). *(978-0-7787-1133-9(1))* Crabtree Publishing Co.

—Five Little Monkeys; Five Little Penguins. 2013. (ENG.). 24p. (J). pap. *(978-0-7787-1151-3(X))* Crabtree Publishing Co.

Chiesa, Lynn. Guess What? 2011. 20p. pap. 10.03 *(978-1-4634-8754-6(1))* AuthorHouse.

Chorao, Kay. Baby's Lap Book. Chorao, Kay, illus. 2004. (ENG., Illus.). 64p. (J). (gr. -1 — 1). 18.99 *(978-0-525-47330-5(0),* Dutton Books for Young Readers) Penguin Young Readers Group.

Christelow, Eileen. Five Little Monkeys Jumping on the Bed. Ortiz, Victoria, tr. 2014. (Five Little Monkeys Story Ser.). (ENG & SPA., Illus.). 30p. (J). (— 1). bds. 7.99 *(978-0-544-08900-6(6),* HMH Books For Young Readers) Houghton Mifflin Harcourt Publishing Co.

—Five Little Monkeys Jumping on the Bed. 25th ed. 2014. (Five Little Monkeys Story Ser.). (ENG., Illus.). 40p. (J). (gr. -1-3). 16.99 *(978-0-544-28329-9(5))* Houghton Mifflin Harcourt Publishing Co.

Chronicle Books Staff. Nick Jr. Nursery Rhyme Time: A Touch-and-See Activity Book. (J). 15.95 *(978-0-8118-4726-1(8))* Chronicle Bks. LLC.

Church, Caroline Jayne. Twinkle, Twinkle, Little Star. Church, Caroline Jayne, illus. 2014. (ENG., Illus.). 12p. (J). (— 1). bds. 6.99 *(978-0-545-51806-2(7),* Cartwheel Bks.) Scholastic, Inc.

Cleary, Brian P. Pre- & Re-, Mis- & Dis- What Is a Prefix? Goneau, Martin, illus. 2015. (ENG.). 32p. (gr. 2-5). pap. 6.95 *(978-1-4677-9383-4(3),* Millbrook Pr.) Lerner Publishing Group.

Cloke, Rene, illus. My First Picture Book of Nursery Rhymes. 2012. (ENG.). 24p. 9.95 *(978-1-84135-581-8(X))* Award Pubns. Ltd. GBR. Dist: Parkwest Pubns., Inc.

Close, Laura Ferraro. Grey Squirrel. 2009. (Favorite Children's Songs Ser.). (ENG., Illus.). 16p. (J). (gr. -1-2). 25.64 *(978-1-60253-189-5(7),* 200102) Child's World, Inc., The.

Codell, Esmé Raji. Maybe Mother Goose. Chavarri, Elisa, illus. 2016. (ENG.). 32p. (J). (gr. -1-3). 17.99 *(978-1-4814-4036-3(5),* Aladdin) Simon & Schuster Children's Publishing.

Cole, Joanna & Calmenson, Stephanie, eds. Tons of Fun: Over 300 Action Rhymes, Old & New Riddles, Tongue Twisters, & Play Rhymes. Tiegren, Alan, illus. 2004. 229p. (J). (gr. k-4). reprint ed. pap. 15.00 *(978-0-7567-8222-1(8))* DIANE Publishing Co.

Collier-Morales, Roberta. Where Is Thumbkin? 2009. (Favorite Children's Songs Ser.). (ENG., Illus.). 16p. (J). (gr. -1-2). 25.64 *(978-1-60253-196-3(X),* 200109) Child's World, Inc., The.

Collins, Heather, illus. Hey Diddle Diddle. 2003. (Traditional Nursery Rhymes Ser.). (ENG.). 12p. (J). (gr. -1 — 1). bds. 3.95 *(978-1-55337-078-9(3))* Kids Can Pr., Ltd. CAN. Dist: Hachette Bk. Group.

—Jack & Jill. 2003. (Traditional Nursery Rhymes Ser.). (ENG.). 12p. (J). (gr. -1 — 1). bds. 3.95 *(978-1-55337-075-8(9))* Kids Can Pr., Ltd. CAN. Dist: Hachette Bk. Group.

—Little Miss Muffet. 2003. (Traditional Nursery Rhymes Ser.). (ENG.). 12p. (J). (gr. -1 — 1). bds. 3.95 *(978-1-55337-076-5(7))* Kids Can Pr., Ltd. CAN. Dist: Hachette Bk. Group.

—Pat-a-Cake. 2003. (Traditional Nursery Rhymes Ser.). (ENG.). 12p. (J). (gr. -1 — 1). bds. 3.95 *(978-1-55337-077-2(5))* Kids Can Pr., Ltd. CAN. Dist: Hachette Bk. Group.

Collins, Mark, et al. Mother Goose's Bedtime Rhymes, 2 vols. Scheffler, Axel, illus. 2008. (ENG.). 32p. (J). (gr. 2-6). 19.95 *(978-0-230-70842-6(0,* Macmillan) Pan Macmillan GBR. Dist: Trans-Atlantic Pubns., Inc.

Conway, David. The Great Nursery Rhyme Disaster. Williamson, Melanie, illus. 2009. 32p. (J). (gr. -1-2). 15.95 *(978-1-58925-080-2(X))* Tiger Tales.

Corvaisier, Laurent, illus. Songs in the Shade of the Flamboyant Tree: French Creole Lullabies & Nursery Rhymes, 1 vol. 2012. (ENG.). 52p. (J). (gr. -1-k). 16.95 *(978-2-923163-82-6(6))* La Montagne Secrete CAN. Dist: Independent Pubs. Group.

Cousins, Lucy. Treasury of Nursery Rhymes. 2015. (ENG., Illus.). 22p. (J). (-k). 15.99 *(978-1-4472-7724-8(4))* Pan Macmillan GBR. Dist: Independent Pubs. Group.

Cousins, Lucy, illus. Bedtime Rhymes. 2015. (First Nursery Rhymes Ser.). (ENG.). 16p. (J). (-k). bds. 9.99 *(978-1-4472-6106-3(2))* Pan Macmillan GBR. Dist: Independent Pubs. Group.

—Nursery Rhymes. 2015. (First Nursery Rhymes Ser.). (ENG.). 16p. (J). (-k). bds. 9.99 *(978-1-4472-6105-6(4))* Pan Macmillan GBR. Dist: Independent Pubs. Group.

Cowle, Ken. Harold Can't Stand to Be Alone. Dorland, Andrew, illus. 2006. 24p. per. *(978-0-9781338-3-2(8))* Soul Asylum Poetry.

Crane, Walter, et al, illus. Mother Goose's Nursery Rhymes: A Collection of Alphabets, Rhymes, Tales, & Jingles. 2010. (ENG.). 324p. (gr. -1-k). pap. 19.95 *(978-1-4290-9005-6(7))* Applewood Bks.

Crews, Nina. Neighborhood Mother Goose. Crews, Nina, illus. 2003. (ENG., Illus.). 64p. (J). (gr. -1-3). 17.99 *(978-0-06-051573-7(2),* Greenwillow Bks.) HarperCollins Pubs.

Cricket Books Staff. Favorite Mother Goose Rhymes. Wenzel, David, illus. 2007. (ENG.). 20p. (J). (gr. k-k). bds. 7.95 *(978-0-8126-7935-9(0))* Cricket Bks.

Crisp, Dan. The Ants Go Marching. 2013. (Classic Books with Holes 8x8 Ser.). (ENG., Illus.). 16p. (J). (gr. -1). pap. *(978-1-84643-618-5(4))* Child's Play International Ltd.

Crisp, Dan, illus. The Ants Go Marching. 2007. (Classic Books with Holes Board Book Ser.). (ENG.). (J). 14p. bds. *(978-1-84643-109-8(3));* 16p. (gr. 1-2). pap. *(978-1-84643-105-0(0))* Child's Play International Ltd.

Currey, Anna, illus. Hush-a-Bye, Baby: And Other Nursery Rhymes. 2003. (ENG.). 14p. (J). bds. 8.99 *(978-0-333-78086-2(8))* Macmillan Pubs., Ltd. GBR. Dist: Trafalgar Square Publishing.

—Pat-a-Cake: And Other Nursery Rhymes. 2003. (ENG.). 14p. (J). bds. 6.95 *(978-0-333-78083-1(3))* Macmillan Pubs., Ltd. GBR. Dist: Trafalgar Square Publishing.

—Ring-a-Ring O' Roses: And Other Nursery Rhymes. 2003. (ENG.). 14p. (J). bds. 6.95 *(978-0-333-78084-8(1))* Macmillan Pubs., Ltd. GBR. Dist: Trafalgar Square Publishing.

Dalmatian Press Staff. My First Nursery Rhymes. 2008. (ENG.). 5p. bds. 4.95 *(978-1-58117-716-9(X),* Intervisual/Piggy Toes) Bendon, Inc.

David C. Cook Publishing Company Staff. Nursery Rhymes. 2003. (My Jesus Pocket Bks.). (Illus.). 32p. (J). pap., pap. 8.90 *(978-1-55513-102-9(6),* 1555131026) Cook, David C.

Davidson, Susanna. Baby & Toddler Treasury. Furukawa, Masumi et al, illus. 2007. (Baby & Toddler Treasury Ser.). 95p. (J). (gr. -1-k). 19.99 *(978-0-7945-1150-0(3),* Usborne) EDC Publishing.

—Nursery Rhyme Treasury. Kolanovic, Dubravka, illus. 2006. 96p. (J). 19.99 *(978-0-7945-1281-1(X),* Usborne) EDC Publishing.

Davies, Caroline, tr. & illus. Hey, Diddle Diddle. Davies, Caroline, illus. 2004. (Baby's First Nursery Rhymes Ser.). 12p. (J). bds. 3.99 *(978-1-85854-622-3(2))* Brimax Books Ltd. GBR. Dist: Byeway Bks.

—Humpty Dumpty. Davies, Caroline, illus. 2004. (Baby's First Nursery Rhymes Ser.). 12p. (J). bds. 3.99 *(978-1-85854-610-0(9))* Brimax Books Ltd. GBR. Dist: Byeway Bks.

—Little Miss Muffet. Davies, Caroline, illus. 2004. (Baby's First Nursery Rhymes Ser.). 12p. (J). bds. 3.99 *(978-1-85854-623-0(0))* Brimax Books Ltd. GBR. Dist: Byeway Bks.

—Pat-A-Cake. Davies, Caroline, illus. 2004. (Baby's First Nursery Rhymes Ser.). 12p. (J). bds. 3.99 *(978-1-85854-611-7(7))* Brimax Books Ltd. GBR. Dist: Byeway Bks.

Davies, Gill. My Nursery Rhyme Pop-up Book. Guile, Gill, illus. 2005. 20p. (J). (gr. k-4). reprint ed. 20.00 *(978-0-7567-8704-2(1))* DIANE Publishing Co.

Davis, David. Southern Mother Goose, 1 vol. Leonhard, Herb, illus. 2013. (ENG.). 40p. (J). (gr. k-4). 17.99 *(978-1-4556-1760-9(1))* Pelican Publishing Co., Inc.

—Texas Mother Goose, 1 vol. Ward, Sue Marshall, illus. 2006. (ENG.). 40p. (J). (gr. k-3). 17.99 *(978-1-58980-369-5(8))* Pelican Publishing Co., Inc.

Davis, Jimmie. We Love to Sing Along! Church, Caroline Jayne, illus. 2016. (ENG.). 18p. (J). (gr. -1 — 1). bds. 8.99 *(978-0-545-90137-6(5),* Cartwheel Bks.) Scholastic, Inc.

—You Are My Sunshine. Church, Caroline Jayne, illus. 2011. (ENG.). 12p. (J). (gr. k — 1). bds. 6.99 *(978-0-545-07552-7(1),* Cartwheel Bks.) Scholastic, Inc.

de La Cour, Gary, et al, illus. Twinkle Twinkle: And Other Sleepy-Time Rhymes. 2005. (Mother Goose Ser.). (ENG.). 36p. (J). (gr. -1-k). 12.95 *(978-1-59249-464-4(1),* 10016) Soundprints.

Deacon, Melissa. I Have a Monkey in My Tub! 2011. 32p. pap. 24.95 *(978-1-4626-2001-2(9))* America Star Bks.

Dean, James. Twinkle, Twinkle, Little Star. 2014. (Pete the Cat Ser.). (ENG.). 32p. (J). *(978-0-06-235967-4(3))* Harper & Row Ltd.

Delacre, Lulu, illus. & compiled by. Arrorro Mi Nino: Latino Lullabies & Gentle Games, 1 vol. Delacre, Lulu, compiled by. 2004. (ENG & SPA.). 32p. (J). 16.95 *(978-1-58430-159-2(7))* Lee & Low Bks., Inc.

Dellas, Melanie & Woodworth, John. Pat-A-Cake, Pat-a-Cake... We Made a Mistake! Sun, Antuanette, illus. 2012. 24p. pap. 9.95 *(978-0-9830163-2-8(1))* Dellas, Melanie.

Denslow, W. W. Denslow's Mother Goose. 2011. (Dover Children's Classics Ser.). (ENG., Illus.). 96p. (J). (gr. k-3). 20.00 *(978-0-486-48466-2(1))* Dover Pubns., Inc.

Denton, Kady MacDonald. A Child's Treasury of Nursery Rhymes. 2004. (J). (gr. -1-2). spiral bd. *(978-0-616-01640-4(9))* Canadian National Institute for the Blind/Institut National Canadien pour les Aveugles.

—A Child's Treasury of Nursery Rhymes. 2004. (ENG., Illus.). 90p. (J). (gr. -1-k). pap. 12.99 *(978-0-7534-5710-8(5),* 9780753457108, Kingfisher) Roaring Brook Pr.

Denton, Kady MacDonald, illus. A Child's Treasury of Nursery Rhymes. 2004. (J). (gr. k). audio compact disk 12.95 *(978-0-618-49306-7(9))* Houghton Mifflin Harcourt Trade & Reference Pubs.

dePaola, Tomie. Baa, Baa, Black Sheep & Other Rhymes. dePaola, Tomie, illus. 2004. (ENG., Illus.). 32p. (J). (gr. -1 — 1). bds. 7.99 *(978-0-399-24326-4(7),* G.P. Putnam's Sons Books for Young Readers) Penguin Young Readers Group.

—More Mother Goose Favorites. dePaola, Tomie, illus. 2007. (Illus.). (gr. -1-3). 14.00 *(978-0-7569-8138-9(7))* Perfection Learning Corp.

Disney Book Group Staff. Nursery Rhymes. 2011. (Read-Along Storybook & CD Ser.). (ENG.). 32p. (J). (gr. -1-k). bds. 10.99 *(978-1-4231-3743-6(4))* Disney Pr.

Dodge, Mary Mapes. Rhymes & Jingles. 2006. 288p. per. 23.99 *(978-1-4255-2592-7(X))* Michigan Publishing.

Dolby, Karen. Oranges & Lemons: Rhymes from Past Times. (ENG., Illus.). 192p. 2016. pap. 13.95 *(978-1-78243-485-6(2))* 2013. 15.95 *(978-1-84317-959-7(8))* O'Mara, Michael Bks., Ltd. GBR. Dist: Independent Pubs. Group.

Domain Public Staff. The Tall Book of Mother Goose. Ivanov, Aleksey & Ivanov, Olga, illus. 2006. (Harper Tall Book Ser.). (ENG.). 80p. (J). (gr. -1-2). 6.99 *(978-0-06-054373-0(6))* HarperCollins Pubs.

Donaldson, Julia. Goat Goes to Playgroup. Sharratt, Nick, illus. 2012. (ENG.). 32p. (J). (gr. -1). 16.99 *(978-0-330-51228-2(5))* Pan Macmillan GBR. Dist: Independent Pubs. Group.

Dorling Kindersley Publishing Staff. Things That Go. 2007. (My 1st T&F Picture Cards Ser.). (ENG.). 16p. (J). (gr. -1 — 1). 9.99 *(978-0-7566-1970-1(X),* DK Children) Dorling Kindersley Publishing, Inc.

Dovidija-Budney, Elizabeth. My Little Red Mittens. 2011. 32p. pap. 16.39 *(978-1-4634-3735-0(8))* AuthorHouse.

Dowell, Ruth I. Move over, Mother Goose! Finger Plays, Action Verses & Funny Rhymes. Charner, Kathleen, ed. Scott, Concetta C., illus. 2004. 126p. (Orig.). (gr. -1-1). pap. 12.95 *(978-0-87659-113-0(6),* 10006) Gryphon Hse., Inc.

Downes, Belinda. Baby Days: A Quilt of Rhymes & Pictures. Downes, Belinda, illus. 2006. (ENG., Illus.). 32p. (J). (— 1). 14.99 *(978-0-7636-2786-7(0))* Candlewick Pr.

Doyle, Mick & Doyle, Laura. My Rhyming Abc. 2011. (Illus.). 32p. pap. *(978-0-7552-0656-8(8))* Authors OnLine, Ltd.

Dunn, Opal. Un Deux Trois: First French Rhymes. Aggs, Patrice, illus. 2006. (FRE & ENG.). 24p. (J). (gr. k-3). pap. 9.99 *(978-1-84507-623-8(0),* Frances Lincoln Children's Bks.) Quarto Publishing Group UK GBR. Dist: Hachette Bk. Group.

Dwyer, Anne, tr. from RUS. The Silly Parade & Other Topsy-Turvy Poems: Russian Folk Nursery Rhymes, Tongue Twisters, & Lullabies. Popov, Nikolai, illus. 2017. (ENG.).

M
N
O

48p. (J). (gr. -1-12). 19.95 ***(978-0-9845867-6-9(8))*** Rovakada, LLC.

Eagle, Kin. Humpty Dumpty. 2004. (Illus.). (J). (gr. 1-18). spiral bd., bds. *(978-0-616-14612-5(4))* Canadian National Institute for the Blind/Institut National Canadien pour les Aveugles.

Early Macken, JoAnn. Read, Recite, & Write Nursery Rhymes. 2014. (ENG., Illus.). 32p. (J). *(978-0-7787-0411-9(4))* Crabtree Publishing Co.

East, Jacqueline, et al, illus. Hickory Dickory Dock: And Other Silly-Time Rhymes. 2005. (Mother Goose Rhymes Ser.). (ENG.). 36p. (J). (gr. -1-k). 12.95 *(978-1-59249-463-7(3),* 1D019) Soundprints.

Education.com. Nursery Rhymes & More: A Workbook of Letter Tracing, Letter Recognition, & Rhymes. 2015. (ENG.). 128p. (J). (gr. -1-k). pap. 7.99 *(978-0-486-80255-8(8))* Dover Pubns., Inc.

Ellwand, David, photos by. Row, Row, Row Your Boat. 2016. (Teddy Bear Sing-Along Ser.). (ENG., Illus.). 14p. (J). bds. 14.99 *(978-1-62686-654-6(6),* Silver Dolphin Bks.) Readerlink Distribution Services, LLC.

Elya, Susan Middleton. La Madre Goose: Nursery Rhymes for Niños. Martinez-Neal, Juana, illus. 2016. (ENG.). 32p. (J). (gr. k-3). 16.99 *(978-0-399-25157-3(X),* G.P. Putnam's Sons Books for Young Readers) Penguin Young Readers Group.

Engel, Christiane. Knick Knack Paddy Whack. 2009. (ENG., Illus.). (J). pap. 9.99 *(978-1-84686-304-2(X))* Barefoot Bks., Inc.

—Knick Knack Paddy Whack. Songs, Steve, illus. 2009. (ENG.). 24p. (J). pap. 6.99 *(978-1-84686-305-9(8))* Barefoot Bks., Inc.

Engelbreit, Mary. Mary Engelbreit's Mother Goose. Engelbreit, Mary, illus. 2008. (ENG., Illus.). 128p. (J). (gr. -1-3). 26.99 *(978-0-06-143153-1(2))* HarperCollins Pubs.

Esparz, Esther LaMadrid. Rocking Horse Rhymes. 3rd ed. 2003.Tr. of Rimas Del Caballo Mecedor, Edicion 3. (SPA & ENG.). (J). lib. bdg. 24.95 *(978-1-879817-32-6(2))* Star Light Pr.

Esparza, Thomas, Jr., prod. Esther's Playhouse, Disk G. 2004. (Illus.). (J). cd-rom *(978-1-879817-48-7(9),* Children) Star Light Pr.

Evans, Michael, illus. Over in the Meadow. 2004. (Classic Books with Holes 8x8 Ser.). (ENG.). 16p. (J). pap. *(978-0-85953-692-9(0))* Child's Play International Ltd.

Evans, Michael, Jr., illus. Over in the Meadow. 2007. (Classic Books with Holes 8x8 Ser.). (ENG.). 16p. (J). (gr. -1-1). pap. *(978-1-84643-136-4(0))* Child's Play International Ltd.

Everett, Melissa. Baa, Baa, Black Sheep. Imodraj, illus. 2013. (ENG.). 20p. (J). (gr. -1-3). bds. 8.99 *(978-1-77093-537-2(1))* Flowerpot Children's Pr. Inc. CAN. Dist: Cardinal Pubs. Group.

—Diddle Diddle Dumpling. Imodraj, illus. 2013. (ENG.). 20p. (J). (gr. -1-1). bds. 8.99 *(978-1-77093-522-8(3))* Flowerpot Children's Pr. Inc. CAN. Dist: Cardinal Pubs. Group.

—Hey Diddle Diddle. Manning, Mary, illus. 2013. (ENG.). 20p. (J). (gr. -1-3). 8.99 *(978-1-77093-536-5(3))* Flowerpot Children's Pr. Inc. CAN. Dist: Cardinal Pubs. Group.

—I Wish I Was a Little. Paiva, Johannah Gilman, ed. Manning, Mary, illus. 2014. (ENG.). 20p. (J). 8.99 *(978-1-77093-844-1(3))* Flowerpot Children's Pr. Inc. CAN. Dist: Cardinal Pubs. Group.

—Jack & Jill. Paiva, Johannah Gilman, ed. Imodraj, illus. 2014. (ENG.). 20p. (J). (gr. -1-1). 8.99 *(978-1-77093-843-4(5))* Flowerpot Children's Pr. Inc. CAN. Dist: Cardinal Pubs. Group.

—One, Two, Buckle My Shoe. Morgan, Christopher, illus. 2013. (ENG.). 20p. (J). 8.99 *(978-1-77093-523-5(1))* Flowerpot Children's Pr. Inc. CAN. Dist: Cardinal Pubs. Group.

—Pat-A-Cake. Kummer, Mark, illus. 2013. (ENG.). 20p. (J). (gr. -1-1). 8.99 *(978-1-77093-521-1(5))* Flowerpot Children's Pr. Inc. CAN. Dist: Cardinal Pubs. Group.

—Rain, Rain, Go Away. Wendel, Carrie, illus. 2013. (ENG.). 20p. (J). (gr. -1-1). 8.99 *(978-1-77093-524-2(X))* Flowerpot Children's Pr. Inc. CAN. Dist: Cardinal Pubs. Group.

—Rock-A-Bye Baby. Wendel, Carrie, illus. 2013. (Record-A-Story Ser.). (ENG.). 18p. (J). (gr. -1). bds. *(978-1-77093-464-1(2))* Flowerpot Children's Pr. Inc.

—Rock-A-Bye Baby. Wendel, Carie, illus. 2013. (ENG.). 20p. (J). (gr. -1-3). bds. 8.99 *(978-1-77093-668-3(8))* Flowerpot Children's Pr. Inc. CAN. Dist: Cardinal Pubs. Group.

—Twinkle, Twinkle, Little Star. Pasishnychenko, Oksana, illus. 2013. (ENG.). 20p. (J). (gr. -1-3). bds. 8.99 *(978-1-77093-534-1(7))* Flowerpot Children's Pr. Inc. CAN. Dist: Cardinal Pubs. Group.

Everitt, Anne. Hush Little Baby. Flowerpot Press, ed. 2012. (Illus.). 18p. (J). *(978-1-77093-463-4(4))* Flowerpot Children's Pr. Inc.

Ezozo, Wanda. According to the Book of Genesis Nursery Rhyme. 2005. (Illus.). 24p. (J). 13.50 *(978-1-4120-4425-7(1))* Trafford Publishing.

Farias, Carolina & Lewis, Anthony, illus. Sing-Along Nursery Rhymes. 2017. (Rookie Nursery Rhymes(tm) Ser.). (ENG.). 32p. (J). pap. 12.00 *(978-0-531-23048-0(1),* Children's Pr.) Scholastic Library Publishing.

Farmer in Dell. 2005. (Mother Goose Ser.). (ENG., Illus.). 32p. (J). 15.95 *(978-1-59249-387-6(4),* 1D006) Soundprints.

Faundez, Anne. One, Two, Buckle My Shoe. 2004. (QEB Start Talking Ser.). (Illus.). 24p. (J). lib. bdg. 15.95 *(978-1-59566-007-7(0))* QEB Publishing Inc.

Faurot, Kimberly. Mother Goose Rhyme Time Animals. Cox, Steve, illus. 2006. 68p. (gr. -1-1). pap. 16.95 *(978-1-932146-66-0(0),* Upstart Bks.) Highsmith Inc.

—Mother Goose Rhyme Time Night. Cox, Steve, illus. 2006. 72p. (gr. -1-1). pap. 16.95 *(978-1-932146-65-3(2),* Upstart Bks.) Highsmith Inc.

—Mother Goose Rhyme Time People. Cox, Steve, illus. 2006. 66p. (gr. -1-1). pap. 16.95 *(978-1-932146-67-7(9),* Upstart Bks.) Highsmith Inc.

Favret, Hafida & Lerasle, Magdeleine. Songs In the Shade of the Olive Tree. Novi, Nathalie, illus. 2012. (ENG.). 52p. (J). (gr. -1-k). 16.95 *(978-2-923163-84-0(2))* La Montagne Secrete CAN. Dist: Independent Pubs. Group.

Ferraro Close, Laura. Little Boy Blue. 2010. (Favorite Mother Goose Rhymes Ser.). (ENG., Illus.). 16p. (J). (gr. -1-2). 25.64 *(978-1-60253-537-4(X),* 200241) Child's World, Inc., The.

Figuerola & Alonso. Sal, Caracol. 2005. (SPA.). 8p. 5.99 *(978-84-263-4739-8(8))* Juventud, Editorial ESP. Dist: Lectorum Pubns., Inc.

—Tengo Tres Ovejas. 2005. (SPA.). 8p. 5.99 *(978-84-263-4735-0(5))* Vives, Luis Editorial (Edelvives) ESP. Dist: Lectorum Pubns., Inc.

First Nursery Rhymes. 2004. (Baby's First Nursery Rhymes Gift Set Ser.). 12p. (J). bds. 12.99 *(978-1-85854-693-3(1))* Brimax Books Ltd. GBR. Dist: Byeway Bks.

Fisher Wright, Blanche. The Real Mother Goose. 2007.Tr. of 160. 160p. per. 11.45 *(978-1-59462-888-7(2),* Book Jungle) Standard Pubns., Inc.

Flor Ada, Alma & Campoy, F. Isabel. ¡Muu, Moo! Rimas de Animales. Escrivá, Viví, illus. 2010. (SPA & ENG.). 48p. (J). (gr. -1-2). 16.99 *(978-0-06-134613-2(6),* Rayo) HarperCollins Pubs.

—Muu, Moo! Rimas de Animales - Animal Nursery Rhymes. Escrivá, Viví, illus. 2010. (SPA & ENG.). 48p. (J). (gr. -1-2). lib. bdg. 17.89 *(978-0-06-134614-9(4),* Rayo) HarperCollins Pubs.

—Ten Little Puppies/Diez Perritos. Wensell, Ulises, illus. 2011. (SPA & ENG.). 32p. (J). (gr. -1-3). 16.99 *(978-0-06-147043-1(0),* Rayo) HarperCollins Pubs.

Flor Ada, Alma, et al. Pio Peep! Traditional Spanish Nursery Rhymes. Escrivá, Viví, illus. 2003. (ENG & SPA.). 64p. (J). (gr. -1-1). 15.99 *(978-0-688-16019-7(0),* Rayo) HarperCollins Pubs.

Flying Frog Pub, creator. Hey Diddle Diddle. 2011. (Read along with Elmo Bks.). (ENG., Illus.). 14p. (gr. -1-k). bds. 3.99 *(978-1-60745-083-2(6))* Flying Frog Publishing.

—Mary Had a Little Lamb. 2011. (Read along with Elmo Bks.). (ENG., Illus.). 14p. (J). (gr. -1-3). bds. 3.99 *(978-1-60745-080-1(1))* Flying Frog Publishing.

—Rock-A-Bye, Baby. 2011. (Read along with Elmo Bks.). (ENG., Illus.). 14p. (gr. -1-k). bds. 3.99 *(978-1-60745-081-8(X))* Flying Frog Publishing.

—This Little Piggy. 2011. (Read along with Elmo Bks.). (ENG., Illus.). 14p. (gr. -1-k). bds. 3.99 *(978-1-60745-082-5(8))* Flying Frog Publishing.

—Twinkle, Twinkle, Little Star. 2011. (Read along with Elmo Bks.). (ENG., Illus.). 14p. (J). (gr. -1-3). bds. 3.99 *(978-1-60745-079-5(8))* Flying Frog Publishing.

Fontanez, Edwin. Hadas, Sirenas y Sapos: Un ramito de poemas Encantados. Fontanez, Edwin, illus. 2008. (SPA., Illus.). 32p. (J). lib. bdg. 19.99 *(978-0-9640868-8-3(3))* Exit Studio.

Foote, Samuel. Great Panjandrum Himself. 2006. (Illus.). pap. *(978-1-4065-1225-0(7))* Dodo Pr.

Foster, John. See You Later, Escalator: Rhymes for the Very Young. 2011. (ENG., Illus.). 96p. (YA). pap. 10.95 *(978-0-19-273183-8(1))* Oxford Univ. Pr., Inc.

Fox, Mem. Good Night, Sleep Tight. Horacek, Judy, illus. 2013. (ENG.). 32p. (J). (gr. -1-k). 16.99 *(978-0-545-53370-6(8),* Orchard Bks.) Scholastic, Inc.

—Ten Little Fingers & Ten Little Toes. Oxenbury, Helen, illus. (ENG.). (J). 2010. 38p. (gr. k — 1). bds. 8.99 *(978-0-547-36620-3(5))* 2008. 40p. (gr. -1 — 1). 17.99 *(978-0-15-206057-2(X))* Houghton Mifflin Harcourt Publishing Co.

Franck, Charlotte. Little Rhymes for Quiet Times. Garvin, Sheri, illus. 2006. 29p. per. 15.95 *(978-1-60002-116-9(6),* 4029) Mountain Valley Publishing, LLC.

Free Spirit Publishing Staff & Stein, Deborah Jiang. Fingerplays & Rhymes. 2009. (In a Jar(r) Ser.). (ENG.). (J). 9.99 *(978-1-57542-954-0(3))* Free Spirit Publishing, Inc.

Freed, Herb. Sing & Learn Spanish. 2004. 271p. (J). pap. 14.95 *(978-0-9760472-0-9(9))* Global Village Kids, LLC.

Freeman, Tina, tr. & illus. Ten Little Monkeys Jumping on the Bed. Freeman, Tina, illus. 2003. (Classic Books with Holes 8x8 Ser.). (ENG.). 16p. (J). pap. *(978-0-85953-137-5(6))* Child's Play International Ltd.

Fuentes, José. Paisaje del eco/EchoLandscape. 2008. 16p. pap. *(978-84-934160-0-3(2))* Atalante.

—Paisaje infantil/Children Landscape. 2008. 16p. pap. *(978-84-934160-1-0(0))* Atalante.

Fujikawa, Gyo, illus. Mother Goose. 2007. (ENG.). 130p. (J). (gr. -1-2). 9.95 *(978-1-4027-5064-9(1))* Sterling Publishing Co., Inc.

Gache, Stephen Vance. The Real Mother Goose Coloring Book. Wright, Blanche Fisher, illus. 2009. (Dover Classic Stories Coloring Book Ser.). (ENG.). 32p. (J). (gr. k-5). pap. 3.99 *(978-0-486-46991-1(3))* Dover Pubns., Inc.

Galdone, Paul. Three Little Kittens. (Paul Galdone Classics Ser.). (ENG., Illus.). (J). (gr. -1-3). 2013. 32p. 26.99 *(978-0-547-99480-2(X))* 2011. 40p. 8.99 *(978-0-547-57575-9(0))* Houghton Mifflin Harcourt Publishing Co.

—Three Little Kittens, 1 vol. Galdone, Paul, illus. 2007. (Paul Galdone Classics Ser.). (ENG., Illus.). 32p. (J). (gr. -1-3). audio compact disk 10.99 *(978-0-618-85285-7(9))* Houghton Mifflin Harcourt Publishing Co.

Gallagher, Belinda & Maccuish, Isla, eds. 100 Best-Loved Nursery Rhymes. 2007. (Illus.). 128p. (J). (gr. -1-3). *(978-1-84236-123-8(6))* Miles Kelly Publishing, Ltd.

Gentry, J. Richard & Craddock, Richard S. Nursery Rhyme Time. 2005. (ENG.). 6.95 *(978-1-931181-98-3(5))* Universal Publishing.

Gerlings, Rebecca, ed. Hey, Diddle, Diddle & Other Best-Loved Rhymes. Ulkutay Design Group Staff, illus. 2009. (Nursery Rhymes Ser.). 32p. (J). (gr. -1-2). lib. bdg. 22.60 *(978-1-60754-125-7(4))* Windmill Bks.

—Hey, Diddle, Diddle & Other Best-loved Rhymes. Ulkutay & Co Ltd, illus. 2009. (Nursery Rhymes Ser.). 32p. (J). (gr. -1-2). pap. 10.55 *(978-1-60754-126-4(2))* Windmill Bks.

—Itsy Bitsy Spider & Other Best-Loved Rhymes. Ulkutay Design Group Staff, illus. 2009. (Nursery Rhymes Ser.). 32p. (J). (gr. -1-2). lib. bdg. 22.60 *(978-1-60754-128-8(9))* Windmill Bks.

—Itsy Bitsy Spider & Other Best-loved Rhymes. Ulkutay & Co Ltd, illus. 2009. (Nursery Rhymes Ser.). 32p. (J). (gr. -1-2). pap. 10.55 *(978-1-60754-129-5(7))* Windmill Bks.

—Little Miss Muffet & Other Best-Loved Rhymes. Ulkutay Design Group Staff, illus. 2009. (Nursery Rhymes Ser.). 32p. (J). (gr. -1-2). lib. bdg. 22.60 *(978-1-60754-131-8(9))* Windmill Bks.

—Little Miss Muffet & Other Best-loved Rhymes. Ulkutay & Co Ltd, illus. 2009. (Nursery Rhymes Ser.). 32p. (J). (gr. -1-2). pap. 10.55 *(978-1-60754-132-5(7))* Windmill Bks.

—Mary Had a Little Lamb & Other Best-Loved Rhymes. Ulkutay Design Group Staff, illus. 2009. (Nursery Rhymes Ser.). 32p. (J). (gr. -1-2). lib. bdg. 22.60 *(978-1-60754-134-9(3))* Windmill Bks.

—Mary Had a Little Lamb & Other Best-loved Rhymes. Ulkutay & Co Ltd, illus. 2009. (Nursery Rhymes Ser.). 32p. (J). (gr. -1-2). pap. 10.55 *(978-1-60754-135-6(1))* Windmill Bks.

—Wee Willie Winkie & Other Best-Loved Rhymes. Ulkutay Design Group Staff, illus. 2009. (Nursery Rhymes Ser.). 32p. (J). (gr. -1-2). lib. bdg. 22.60 *(978-1-60754-137-0(8))* Windmill Bks.

—Wee Willie Winkie & Other Best-loved Rhymes. Ulkutay & Co Ltd & Ulkutay & Co Ltd, illus. 2009. (Nursery Rhymes Ser.). 32p. (J). (gr. -1-2). pap. 10.55 *(978-1-60754-138-7(6))* Windmill Bks.

—Yankee Doodle & Other Best-Loved Rhymes. Ulkutay Design Group Staff, illus. 2009. (Nursery Rhymes Ser.). 32p. (J). (gr. -1-2). lib. bdg. 22.60 *(978-1-60754-122-6(X))* Windmill Bks.

—Yankee Doodle & Other Best-loved Rhymes. Ulkutay & Co Ltd, illus. 2009. (Nursery Rhymes Ser.). 32p. (J). (gr. -1-2). pap. 10.55 *(978-1-60754-123-3(8))* Windmill Bks.

Giuffre, Mary & Clark, Paul L. Scribble & Grin: 53 Rhymes for Inspiring Times. Sullivan, Troy, illus. 2013. 142p. *(978-0-9919101-0-6(9))* inspirtainment ink.

Goembel, Ponder. Animal Fair, 0 vols. Goembel, Ponder, illus. 2012. (ENG., Illus.). 24p. (J). (gr. -1 — 1). bds. 7.99 *(978-0-7614-6205-7(8),* 9780761462057, Amazon Children's Publishing) Amazon Publishing.

Goldsmith, Oliver. Elegy on the Death of A Mad Dog. 2006. (Illus.). pap. *(978-1-4065-1221-2(4))* Dodo Pr.

—Elegy on the Glory of Her Sex Mrs Mary B. 2006. (Illus.). pap. *(978-1-4065-1222-9(2))* Dodo Pr.

Goodnight, Rosemary. Dear Old Granny's Nursery Rymes for the 21st Century. Turner, Michael W., illus. 2009. 64p. (J). 14.99 *(978-0-9816282-7-1(3))* Recipe Pubs.

—Dear Old Granny's Nursery Rymes for the 21st Century. 2010. (ENG.). (J). 9.95 *(978-0-9826424-3-6(1))* Recipe Pubs.

Gowar, Mick. Baa Baa, Black Sheep & Baa Baa, Pink Sheep. 2012. (ENG., Illus.). 24p. (J). pap. *(978-0-7787-7895-0(9))* Crabtree Publishing Co.

Gray, E. Travis. Ridalin Phymes: Poetry for the ADHD Generation. 2012. (ENG.). pap. 10.95 *(978-1-4675-1962-5(6))* Independent Pub.

Grimly, Gris. Gris Grimly's Wicked Nursery Rhymes III. 2017. (ENG., Illus.). 32p. 16.95 *(978-1-61404-014-9(1))* Baby Tattoo Bks.

Grimly, Gris & Last, First. Gris Grimly's Wicked Nursery Rhymes. Grimly, Gris, illus. 2003. (ENG., Illus.). 32p. 16.95 *(978-0-9729388-7-7(7))* Baby Tattoo Bks.

Grudzina, Rebecca. Mary, Mary, Quite Contrary. Harrington, David, illus. 2010. (Rising Readers Ser.). (J). 3.49 *(978-1-60719-704-1(9))* Newmark Learning LLC.

Guile, Gill, illus. In My Garden. 20p. (J). *(978-1-932209-38-9(7))* Bendon, Inc.

—My Nursery Rhyme Pop-up Book. 20p. (J). *(978-1-59394-119-2(6))* Bendon, Inc.

Gustafson, Scott. Classic Bedtime Stories. 2016. (ENG., Illus.). 84p. (J). (gr. k-3). 19.95 *(978-1-57965-760-4(5))* Artisan.

—Favorite Nursery Rhymes from Mother Goose. 2016. (ENG., Illus.). 100p. (J). 19.95 *(978-1-57965-698-0(6))* Artisan.

Hal Leonard Corp. Staff, creator. First Nursery Rhymes: Fun Repertoire for Beginner Pianists Complementing Any Piano Course. 2005. (ENG.). 32p. pap. 5.99 *(978-0-87718-022-7(9),* 0877180229) Willis Music Co.

—211. the Big Book of Nursery Rhymes & Children's Songs. 2012. (ENG.). 240p. pap. 12.99 *(978-1-4584-4071-6(0),* 1458440710) Music Sales Corp.

Hall, Dee. Can You Imagine? Hall, Dee & Hesselbein, Kent, illus. 2013. 64p. pap. 8.95 *(978-1-935786-59-7(8))* St. Clair Pubns.

Hall, Pamela. Rena & Rio Build a Rhyme. Pilo, Cary, illus. 2011. (Poetry Builders Ser.). 32p. (J). (gr. 2-4). lib. bdg. 25.27 *(978-1-59953-439-8(8))* Norwood Hse. Pr.

Halverson, Lydia, illus. Nursery Rhymes. 2004. (Elements of Reading: Phonics Ser.). 24p. pap. 40.00 *(978-0-7398-9014-1(X))* Houghton Mifflin Harcourt Supplemental Pubs.

Hammill, Elizabeth, ed. Over the Hills & Far Away: A Treasury of Nursery Rhymes. 2015. (ENG., Illus.). 160p. (J). (gr. -1-2). 21.99 *(978-0-7636-7729-9(9))* Candlewick Pr.

Harbo, Christopher. Flip-Side Nursery Rhymes. Jack, Colin & Chatzikonstantinou, Danny, illus. 2015. (Flip-Side Nursery Rhymes Ser.). (ENG.). 24p. (gr. -1-2). lib. bdg. 109.28 *(978-1-4795-6022-6(7))* Picture Window Bks.

Harbo, Christopher L. Humpty Dumpty Flip-Side Rhymes. Chatzikonstantinou, Danny, illus. 2015. (Flip-Side Nursery Rhymes Ser.). (ENG.). 24p. (gr. -1-2). lib. bdg. 27.32 *(978-1-4795-5986-2(5))* Picture Window Bks.

—Jack & Jill Flip-Side Rhymes. Jack, Colin, illus. 2015. (Flip-Side Nursery Rhymes Ser.). (ENG.). 24p. (gr. -1-2). lib. bdg. 27.32 *(978-1-4795-5988-6(1))* Picture Window Bks.

—Little Bo Peep Flip-Side Rhymes. Chatzikonstantinou, Danny, illus. 2015. (Flip-Side Nursery Rhymes Ser.). (ENG.). 24p. (gr. -1-2). lib. bdg. 27.32 *(978-1-4795-5989-3(X))* Picture Window Bks.

—Little Miss Muffet Flip-Side Rhymes. Jack, Colin, illus. 2015. (Flip-Side Nursery Rhymes Ser.). (ENG.). 24p. (gr. -1-2). lib. bdg. 27.32 *(978-1-4795-5987-9(3))* Picture Window Bks.

Harcourt School Publishers Staff. Big Book of Rhymes. 3rd ed. 2003. (Trophies Reading Program Ser.). (gr. -1). pap. 70.10 *(978-0-15-340344-6(6))* Harcourt Schl. Pubs.

—Trophies Reading Program: Nursery Rhymes Anthology. 3rd ed. 2003. (Illus.). (gr. k). pap. 47.70 *(978-0-15-340345-3(4))* Harcourt Schl. Pubs.

Harker, Lesley. Baby's Book of Rhymes. (Book of Rhymes & CD Ser.). 10p. *(978-1-4054-9663-6(0))* Parragon, Inc.

Harris, Brooke. Twinkle, Twinkle, Little Star. Harrington, David, illus. 2010. (Rising Readers Ser.). (J). 3.49 *(978-1-60719-697-6(2))* Newmark Learning LLC.

Harvey, Barbara. Inner City Nursery Rhymes. 2004. 48p. (J). per. 11.95 *(978-1-56167-863-1(5))* American Literary Pr.

Havener, Katherine. Nursies When the Sun Shines: A Little Book on Night Weaning. Burrier, Sara, illus. 2nd ed. 2013. 20p. (J). pap. 9.99 *(978-0-615-75642-4(5))* Elea Pr.

Head Shoulders Knees & Toes. 2005. (Mother Goose Ser.). (ENG., Illus.). 36p. (J). 12.95 *(978-1-59249-381-4(5),* 1D007) Soundprints.

Hefferan, Rob, illus. My Pop-up Nursery Rhymes. 2006. (ENG.). 10p. (J). (gr. -1-3). 4.95 *(978-1-58117-439-7(X),* Intervisual/Piggy Toes) Bendon, Inc.

—My Sparkling Nursery Rhymes. 2005. (ENG.). 10p. (J). 8.95 *(978-1-58117-295-9(8),* Intervisual/Piggy Toes) Bendon, Inc.

Henley, Ralph. Action Rhymes & Active Games: Over 200 Bible Story Activities for Ages 2 To 5. 2004. (J). tchr. ed., per. 19.99 *(978-1-933803-02-9(9))* Child Sensitive Communication, LLC.

Hentley, Sheila Rose. Nursery Rhymes & Nursery Riddles for All Ages. 2007. 28p. per. 21.99 *(978-1-4257-9011-0(9))* Xlibris Corp.

Heras, Theo. What Will We Do with the Baby-O? Herbert, Jennifer, illus. 2004. (ENG.). 32p. (J). (gr. k-k). 12.95 *(978-0-88776-689-3(7),* Tundra Bks.) Tundra Bks. CAN. Dist: Penguin Random Hse. LLC.

Herz, Henry, et al. Monster Goose Nursery Rhymes, 1 vol. Larson, Abigail, illus. 2015. (ENG.). 32p. (J). (gr. k-3). 16.99 *(978-1-4556-2032-6(7))* Pelican Publishing Co., Inc.

Hey Diddle Diddle. 2004. (J). per. *(978-1-57657-428-7(8))* Paradise Pr., Inc.

Highlights for Children Editorial Staff, creator. Favorite Nursery Rhymes. 2016. (Story Puzzle Fun Ser.). (ENG.). 24p. (J). (gr. -1-k). pap. 4.99 *(978-1-62979-547-8(X),* Highlights) Boyds Mills Pr.

—Nursery Rhymes. 2015. (Highlights(tm) Write-On Wipe-off Hidden Pictures(r) Ser.). (ENG.). 28p. (J). (gr. -1). pap. 8.99 *(978-1-62979-418-1(X),* Highlights) Boyds Mills Pr.

Hillenbrand, Will. Mother Goose Picture Puzzles, 0 vols. Hillenbrand, Will, illus. 2011. (ENG., Illus.). 40p. (J). (gr. k-3). 17.99 *(978-0-7614-5808-1(5),* 9780761458081, Amazon Children's Publishing) Amazon Publishing.

Hillenbrand, Will & Cabrera, Jane. Baa, Baa, Black Sheep. 2016. (ENG.). 32p. (J). (gr. -1-k). 6.99 *(978-0-8234-3683-5(7))* Holiday Hse., Inc.

Hoberman, Mary Ann. Miss Mary Mack. Bernard Westcott, Nadine & Westcott, Nadine Bernard, illus. 2003. (ENG.). 32p. (J). (gr. -1-1). pap. 7.99 *(978-0-316-07614-2(7),* Tingley, Megan Bks.) Little, Brown Bks. for Young Readers.

—You Read to Me, I'll Read to You: Very Short Mother Goose Tales to Read Together. Emberley, Michael, illus. 3rd rev. ed. 2005. (ENG.). 32p. (J). (gr. -1-3). 16.99 *(978-0-316-14431-5(2))* Little, Brown Bks. for Young Readers.

—You Read to Me, I'll Read to You: Very Short Mother Goose Tales to Read Together. 2012. (J). lib. bdg. 18.40 *(978-0-606-26684-0(4),* Turtleback) Turtleback Bks.

—You Read to Me, I'll Read to You - Very Short Mother Goose Tales to Read Together. Emberley, Michael, illus. 3rd ed. 2012. (You Read to Me, I'll Read to You Ser.). (ENG.). 32p. (J). (gr. -1-3). pap. 7.99 *(978-0-316-20715-7(2))* Little, Brown Bks. for Young Readers.

Hone, Brettell. My African Bedtime Rhymes. 2009. (ENG., Illus.). 32p. *(978-0-620-40992-6(4))* Shamwari Publishing.

Hooper, Caroline & Danes, Emma. Little Book of Nursery Rhymes. 2005. 64p. (J). 6.99 *(978-0-7945-0954-5(1),* Usborne) EDC Publishing.

Hopkins, Lee Bennett. The Lee Bennett Hopkins Mother Goose. 2005. (Poetry Ser.). (gr. -1-2). 270.00 *(978-0-8215-0459-8(2))* Sadlier, William H. Inc.

—Mother Goose Through the Seasons. Fehlau, Dagmar et al, illus. 2005. (Lee Bennett Hopkins Mother Goose Ser.). (YA). (gr. -1-1). 76.50 *(978-0-8215-0480-2(0))* Sadlier, William H. Inc.

Howard, Jennie & Howard, Akime. Creepy Colored Creatures. 2007. 28p. per. 15.95 *(978-1-4327-0723-1(X))* Outskirts Pr., Inc.

Huliska-Beith, Laura, et al, illus. Dream-Along Nursery Rhymes. (Rookie Nursery Rhymes(tm) Ser.). (ENG.). 32p. (J). 2016. pap. 25.00 *(978-0-531-22877-7(0))* 2017. pap. 12.00 *(978-0-531-23045-9(7))* Scholastic Library Publishing. (Children's Pr.).

—Move-Along Nursery Rhymes. (Rookie Nursery Rhymes(tm) Ser.). (ENG.). 32p. (J). 2016. pap. 25.00 *(978-0-531-22878-4(9))* 2017. pap. 12.00 *(978-0-531-23047-3(3))* Scholastic Library Publishing. (Children's Pr.).

Humpty Dumpty: 6 Small Books. (gr. k-2). 23.00 *(978-0-7635-8498-6(3))* Rigby Education.

Humpty Dumpty at Sea. 2003. (J). per. *(978-1-57657-800-1(3))* Paradise Pr., Inc.

Hunter, Emily. The Bible-Time Nursery Rhyme Book. 2013. (ENG.). 98p. pap. 30.95 *(978-1-4787-1182-7(5))* Outskirts Pr., Inc.

Iglesias González, Natalia. Nursery rhymes for the English Classroom. 2009. 51p. pap. 28.50 *(978-1-4092-6513-9(7))* Lulu Pr., Inc.

Itchyka-Dana. Asian Nursery Rhymes. 2004. (J). *(978-1-85269-701-3(6))* Mantra Lingua.

Ives, Penny. 5 Little Ducks W. 2007. (Classic Books with Holes 8x8 with CD Ser.). (ENG., Illus.). 16p. (J). audio compact disk *(978-1-84643-137-1(9))* Child's Play International Ltd.

Ives, Penny, illus. Five Little Ducks. 2005. (Classic Books with Holes 8x8 Ser.). (ENG.). 16p. (J). pap. *(978-0-85953-447-5(2))* Child's Play International Ltd.

Ives, Penny & Hilb, Nora, illus. Itsy Bitsy Spider. 2017. (Classic Books with Holes 8x8 Ser.). (ENG.). 16p. (J). pap. ***(978-1-84643-974-2(4))*** Child's Play International Ltd.

Izuora, Ikechukwu. Dazzle-Kids Book of Nursery Rhymes & Poems: Book of Nursery Rhymes & Poems. 2012. (Illus.). 40p. pap. 21.99 *(978-1-4653-0366-0(9))* Xlibris Corp.

Jack & Jill. 2003. (J). per. *(978-1-57657-801-8(1))* Paradise Pr., Inc.

Jack & Jill: 6 Small Books. (gr. k-2). 23.00 *(978-0-7635-8492-4(4))* Rigby Education.

Jackson, Marilyn Malloy, ed. Mother Goose on the Loose in Guam A Chamorro Adaptation of Traditional Nursery Rhymes. Tayama, Thomas, illus. 2006. (J). 6.50 net. *(978-0-9790111-5-3(9))* M-m-mauleg Publishing.

James, Diane. Baa, Baa, Black Sheep. 2004. (Jigsaw Nursery Rhymes Ser.). (Illus.). 12p. (J). (gr. -1-k). 9.95

(978-1-58728-625-4(4), Two-Can Publishing) T&N Children's Publishing.
—Pat-a-Cake. 2004. (Jigsaw Nursery Rhymes Ser.). (Illus.). 12p. (J). (gr. -1-k). 9.95 (978-1-58728-623-0(8), Two-Can Publishing) T&N Children's Publishing.
—Three Blind Mice. 2004. (Jigsaw Nursery Rhymes Ser.). (Illus.). 12p. (J). (gr. -1-k). 9.95 (978-1-58728-626-1(2), Two-Can Publishing) T&N Children's Publishing.
Jerrold, Walter, ed. The Big Book of Nursery Rhymes. Robinson, Charles, illus. 2012. (Calla Editions Ser.). (ENG.). 352p. (gr. -1). 40.00 (978-1-60660-030-6(3)) Dover Pubns., Inc.
Jigsaw Nursery Rhymes. Blow, Wind, Blow. 2003. (Jigsaw Nursery Rhymes Ser.). 12p. (J). (gr. -1). bds. 9.95 (978-1-58728-640-7(8), Two-Can Publishing) T&N Children's Publishing.
—Jack & Jill. 2003. (Jigsaw Nursery Rhymes Ser.). 12p. (J). (gr. -1). bds. 9.95 (978-1-58728-641-4(6), Two-Can Publishing) T&N Children's Publishing.
—Old King Cole. 2003. (Jigsaw Nursery Rhymes Ser.). 12p. (J). (gr. -1). bds. 9.95 (978-1-58728-642-1(4), Two-Can Publishing) T&N Children's Publishing.
—Rub-a-Dub-Dub. 2003. (Jigsaw Nursery Rhymes Ser.). 12p. (J). bds. 9.95 (978-1-58728-643-8(2), Two-Can Publishing) T&N Children's Publishing.
John Knapp, Ii. A Pillar of Pepper & Other Bible Rhymes. Turner-Deckert, Dianne, illus. 2012. 130p. 29.99 (978-0-912290-34-8(X)) Ephemeron Pr.
Jones, Latoya. My Learning Rhythms: Book 1. 2012. 20p. pap. 13.77 (978-1-4669-3267-8(8)) Trafford Publishing.
—My Learning Rhythms: Book 3. 2012. 20p. pap. 13.77 (978-1-4669-3599-0(5)) Trafford Publishing.
—My Learning Rhythms: Book 4. 2012. 20p. pap. 13.77 (978-1-4669-3602-7(9)) Trafford Publishing.
Kays, Judy. ABC Rhymes by Grammy. 2010. 36p. pap. 19.95 (978-1-4520-5154-3(2)) AuthorHouse.
Keith, Barbara Benson, illus. & compiled by. The Girls & Boys of Mother Goose. Keith, Barbara Benson, compiled by. 2006. 32p. (J). per. 7.99 (978-0-9789688-0-9(8)) Brownian Bee Pr.
Kemp, Moira. Hey Diddle Diddle. Kemp, Moira, illus. 2009. (Favorite Mother Goose Rhymes Ser.). (ENG., Illus.). 16p. (J). (gr. -1-2). 25.64 (978-1-60253-289-2(3), 200245) Child's World, Inc., The.
—Pat-a-Cake, Pat-a-Cake. Kemp, Moira, illus. 2009. (Favorite Children's Songs Ser.). (ENG., Illus.). 16p. (J). (gr. -1-2). 25.64 (978-1-60253-194-9(3), 200105) Child's World, Inc., The.
—Round & Round the Garden. Kemp, Moira, illus. 2009. (Favorite Children's Songs Ser.). (ENG., Illus.). 16p. (J). (gr. -1-2). 25.64 (978-1-60253-195-6(1), 200106) Child's World, Inc., The.
Kessey, K.O. Rhythms of African Drums: Rhymes & Lyrics for School Children & Youngsters. 2011. 232p. (gr. -1). pap. 22.87 (978-1-4567-8610-6(5)) AuthorHouse.
Kole, Ted & Genet, John, eds. Katoufs in Nursery Rhymes Chapbook: Mother Goose. (Illus.). 48p. (Orig.). (J). (gr. 1-4). pap. 3.95 (978-0-9641381-0-0(7)) Kreative Character Kreations, Inc.
Krumwiede, Lana. Just Itzy. Pizzoli, Greg, illus. 2015. (ENG.). 40p. (J). (-k). 15.99 (978-0-7636-5811-3(1)) Candlewick Pr.
Kubler, Annie. Baa Baa, Black Sheep! 2005. (Sign & Signalong Ser.). (ENG., Illus.). 12p. (J). (gr. -1-k). bds. (978-1-904550-41-9(X)) Child's Play International Ltd.
—Head, Shoulders, Knees & Toes. (Illus.). 10p. (J). 2004. (ENG & TUR.). bds. (978-1-84444-156-3(3)) 2004. (ENG & TAM., bds. (978-1-84444-155-6(5)) 2004. (ENG & SPA., bds. (978-1-84444-154-9(7)) 2004. (ENG & SOM., bds. (978-1-84444-153-2(9)) 2004. (ENG & POR., bds. (978-1-84444-152-5(0)) 2004. (ENG & PAN., bds. (978-1-84444-151-8(2)) 2004. (ENG & GUJ., bds. (978-1-84444-150-1(4)) 2004. (ENG & PER., bds. (978-1-84444-148-8(2)) 2004. (FRE & ENG., bds. (978-1-84444-149-5(0)) 2004. (ENG & CHI., bds. (978-1-84444-147-1(4)) 2004. (ENG & ARA., bds. (978-1-84444-145-7(8)) 2004. (ENG & ALB., bds. (978-1-84444-144-0(X)) 2003. (BEN & ENG., bds. (978-1-84444-146-4(6)) Mantra Lingua.
—Hey Diddle Diddle. 2007. (Baby Board Bks.). (ENG., Illus.). 12p. (J). (gr. 1-1). bds. (978-1-84643-121-0(2)) Child's Play International Ltd.
—Itsy, Bitsy Spider. 2005. (Sign & Singalong Ser.). (ENG., Illus.). 12p. (J). (gr. k-k). bds. (978-1-904550-43-3(6)) Child's Play International Ltd.
—Ring Around a Rosie. 2003. (Baby Board Bks.). (ENG., Illus.). 12p. (J). bds. (978-0-85953-578-6(9)) Child's Play International Ltd.
—Row, Row, Row Your Boat. 2003. (Baby Board Bks.). (ENG., Illus.). 12p. (J). bds. (978-0-85953-658-5(0)) Child's Play International Ltd.
—Ten Little Fingers. 2003. (Baby Board Bks.). (ENG., Illus.). 12p. (J). (gr. k-1). bds. (978-0-85953-610-3(6)) Child's Play International Ltd.
—This Little Piggy. 2007. (Baby Board Bks.). (ENG., Illus.). 12p. (J). (gr. k-1). bds. (978-1-84643-120-3(4)) Child's Play International Ltd.
—Wee Willie Winkie. 2007. (Baby Board Bks.). (ENG., Illus.). 12p. (J). (gr. 1-1). bds. (978-1-84643-119-7(0)) Child's Play International Ltd.
Kubler, Annie, illus. Baa, Baa, Black Sheep! 2005. (ENG.). 12p. (J). bds. (978-1-904550-01-3(0)) Child's Play International Ltd.
—Head, Shoulders, Knees & Toes../Cabeza, Hombros, Piernas, Pies... 2009. (Baby Board Bks.). (SPA & ENG.). 12p. (J). bds. (978-1-84643-311-5(8)) Child's Play International Ltd.
—Hickory Dickory Dock. 2014. (Classic Books with Holes Big Book Ser.). (ENG.). 16p. (J). (978-1-84643-667-3(2)) Child's Play International Ltd.
—Humpty Dumpty. 2010. (Baby Board Bks.). (ENG.). 12p. (J). bds. (978-1-84643-339-9(8)) Child's Play International Ltd.
—I'm a Little Teapot. 2007. (Baby Board Bks.). (ENG.). 12p. (J). (gr. k-1). bds. (978-1-84643-122-7(0)) Child's Play International Ltd.
—Itsy Bitsy Spider. 2014. (Classic Books with Holes Big Book Ser.). (ENG.). 16p. (J). (978-1-84643-666-6(4)) Child's Play International Ltd.
—Mary Had a Little Lamb. 2014. (Classic Books with Holes Big Book Ser.). (ENG.). 16p. (J). (978-1-84643-669-7(9)) Child's Play International Ltd.
—Pat-A-Cake! 2010. (Baby Board Bks.). (ENG.). 12p. (J). bds. (978-1-84643-338-2(X)) Child's Play International Ltd.
—Pussy Cat, Pussy Cat. 2010. (Baby Board Bks.). (ENG.). 12p. (J). bds. (978-1-84643-340-5(1)) Child's Play International Ltd.
—Teddy Bear, Teddy Bear. 2005. (Sign & Singalong Ser.). (ENG.). 12p. (J). (gr. k-1). bds. (978-1-904550-40-2(1)) Child's Play International Ltd.
—This Little Piggy / Este Cochinito. 2009. (Baby Board Bks.). (SPA & ENG.). 12p. (J). bds. (978-1-84643-313-9(4)) Child's Play International Ltd.
—Twinkle, Twinkle, Little Star. 2005. (Sign & Singalong Ser.). (ENG.). 12p. (J). (gr. k-k). bds. (978-1-904550-42-6(8)); bds. (978-1-904550-02-0(9)) Child's Play International Ltd.
—The Wheels on the Bus. 2007. (Classic Books with Holes 8x8 with CD Ser.). (ENG.). 16p. (J). (gr. -1-1). pap. incl. audio compact disk (978-1-904550-66-2(5)) Child's Play International Ltd.
—The Wheels on the Bus Go Round & Round. 2003. (Classic Books with Holes 8x8 Ser.). (ENG.). 16p. (J). (978-0-85953-136-8(8)) Child's Play International Ltd.
Kubler, Annie & Nascimbeni, Barbara, illus. Little Miss Muffet. 2014. (Classic Books with Holes Big Book Ser.). (ENG.). 16p. (J). (978-1-84643-668-0(0)) Child's Play International Ltd.
Kumon Publishing, ed. My Book of Rhyming Words. 2004. (Illus.). 80p. (J). per. 7.95 (978-4-7743-0761-9(0)) Kumon Publishing North America, Inc.
—My Book of Rhyming Words & Phrases. 2004. (ENG., Illus.). 82p. (J). per. 7.95 (978-4-7743-0762-6(9)) Kumon Publishing North America, Inc.
Lacome, Julie. Walking Through the Jungle Big Book. Lacome, Julie, illus. 2004. (Big Books! Ser.). (ENG., Illus.). 32p. (J). (gr. k-k). pap. 24.99 (978-0-7636-2471-2(3)) Candlewick Pr.
Ladybird Books Staff. Nursery Rhymes. (First Bks.: No. S808-5). (Illus.). (J). (gr. -1). pap. 3.95 (978-0-7214-5056-8(3), Dutton Juvenile) Penguin Publishing Group.
Landon, Angela. What Is Freedom? How Does It Ring? 2011. 40p. (gr. 1-2). 16.59 (978-1-4567-4538-7(7)) AuthorHouse.
Language Works Rhyme Time. 8p. (J). (978-0-8136-3519-4(5)) Modern Curriculum Pr.
Lansky, Bruce. Mary Had a Little Jam: And Other Silly Rhymes. Expanded Edition with Twice As Many Rhymes. Carpenter, Stephen, illus. 2016. (Giggle Poetry Ser.). (ENG.). 80p. (J). (gr. -1-1). pap. 8.95 (978-1-4814-9278-2(0)) Meadowbrook Pr.
Le Ray, Marina, illus. Row, Row, Row Your Boat; and, Ride, Ride, Ride Your Bike. 2013. (ENG.). 24p. (J). (978-0-7787-1149-0(8)) Crabtree Publishing Co.
Lenton, Steven, illus. Teddy Bear, Teddy Bear: And Other Favorite Nursery Rhymes. 2013. (ENG.). 22p. (gr. -1). bds. 8.95 (978-1-58925-601-9(8)) Tiger Tales.
Leonard, Barry, ed. Humpty Dumpty & Other Rhymes. 2003. (Illus.). 12p. (J). (gr. k-5). reprint ed. 17.00 (978-0-7567-6855-3(1)) DIANE Publishing Co.
—Mary Had a Little Lamb & Other Rhymes. 2003. (Illus.). 12p. (J). (gr. k-4). reprint ed. 17.00 (978-0-7567-6861-4(6)) DIANE Publishing Co.
—Mary, Mary, Quite Contrary & Other Rhymes. 2003. (Illus.). 12p. (J). (gr. k-5). reprint ed. 17.00 (978-0-7567-6857-7(8)) DIANE Publishing Co.
—Rock-a-Bye, Baby & Other Rhymes. 2003. (Illus.). 12p. (J). (gr. k-4). reprint ed. 17.00 (978-0-7567-6863-8(2)) DIANE Publishing Co.
—See-Saw Margery Daw & Other Rhymes. 2003. (Illus.). 12p. (J). (gr. k-5). reprint ed. 17.00 (978-0-7567-6866-9(7)) DIANE Publishing Co.
—Wee Willie Winkie & Other Rhymes. 2003. (Illus.). 12p. (J). (gr. k-4). reprint ed. 17.00 (978-0-7567-6859-1(4)) DIANE Publishing Co.
Lewis, Anthony. Sing-Along Nursery Rhymes. Farias, Carolina, illus. 2016. (Rookie Nursery Rhymes(tm) Ser.). (ENG.). 32p. (J). pap. 25.00 (978-0-531-22876-0(2), Children's Pr.) Scholastic Library Publishing.
Lewis, Anthony, illus. Five Little Ducks. 2013. (Hands-On Songs Ser.). (ENG.). 12p. (J). (gr. -1). bds. (978-1-84643-630-7(3)) Child's Play International Ltd.
—Jack & Jill. 2013. (Hands-On Songs Ser.). (ENG.). 12p. (J). (gr. -1). bds. (978-1-84643-629-1(X)) Child's Play International Ltd.
—Old MacDonald. 2013. (Hands-On Songs Ser.). (ENG.). 12p. (J). (gr. -1). bds. (978-1-84643-628-4(1)) Child's Play International Ltd.
—The Wheels on the Bus: Asl. 2013. (Hands-On Songs Ser.). (ENG.). 12p. (J). bds. (978-1-84643-626-0(5)) Child's Play International Ltd.
Lewis, Jan. Best-Ever Rhymes. 2015. (ENG., Illus.). 24p. bds. 6.99 (978-1-86147-499-5(7), Armadillo) Anness Publishing GBR. Dist: National Bk. Network.
—Mother Goose Nursery Rhymes. 2015. (ENG., Illus.). 48p. bds. 9.99 (978-1-86147-649-4(3), Armadillo) Anness Publishing GBR. Dist: National Bk. Network.
Lewis, Jan, illus. Mother Goose Action Rhymes: Old MacDonald Had a Farm; One, Two, Buckle My Shoe; Round & Round the Garden; This Little Pig. 2004. 90p. (J). vinyl bd. (978-1-902272-32-0(3)) Tucker Slingsby, Ltd.
—Mother Goose Rhymes: One, Two, Buckle My Shoe. 2015. (ENG.). 24p. bds. 6.99 (978-1-86147-637-1(X), Armadillo) Anness Publishing GBR. Dist: National Bk. Network.
—My Favourite Nursery Rhyme Collection, Set. 2017. (ENG.). 1p. bds. 14.99 (978-1-86147-740-8(6), Armadillo) Anness Publishing GBR. Dist: National Bk. Network.
—My Little Nursery Rhymes. 2015. (ENG.). 24p. bds. 6.99 (978-1-86147-469-8(5), Armadillo) Anness Publishing GBR. Dist: National Bk. Network.
—Old Macdonald Had a Farm. 2015. (ENG.). 24p. bds. 6.99 (978-1-86147-468-1(7), Armadillo) Anness Publishing GBR. Dist: National Bk. Network.
—Round & Round the Garden. 2015. (ENG.). 24p. bds. 6.99 (978-1-86147-636-4(1), Armadillo) Anness Publishing GBR. Dist: National Bk. Network.
Linder, Dorothy Perillo. A Vegetable Collection: Recipes & Rhymes to Conquer Kids of All Ages. 2008. (Illus.). (J). 35.00 (978-0-9753334-2-6(9)) Sanctuary Bks.
Lipchenko, Oleg, selected by. Humpty Dumpty & Friends: Nursery Rhymes for the Young at Heart. 2010. (ENG.). 24p. (J). (gr. -1-2). 17.95 (978-1-77049-205-9(4), Tundra Bks.) Tundra Bks. CAN. Dist: Penguin Random Hse. LLC.
Listen! Listen! Letter Sounds in Rhyme: Blends & Digraphs Set. (gr. k-1). 89.95 (978-0-322-02639-1(3)) Wright Group/McGraw-Hill.
Listen! Listen! Letter Sounds in Rhyme: Consonants Set. (gr. k-1). 84.95 (978-0-322-02637-7(7)) Wright Group/McGraw-Hill.
Listen! Listen! Letter Sounds in Rhyme: Vowels Set. (gr. k-1). 52.95 (978-0-322-02638-4(5)) Wright Group/McGraw-Hill.
Litchfield, Jo, illus. First Picture Nursery Rhymes. 2005. (Usborne First Book Ser.). 16p. (J). (gr. -1-k). per. 11.99 (978-0-7945-1014-5(0), Usborne) EDC Publishing.
Litchfield, Jo & Allen, Francesca, illus. First Picture Nursery Rhymes With. 2006. 18p. (J). bds. 18.99 (978-0-7945-1489-1(8), Usborne) EDC Publishing.
Little Bee Books Staff. Humpty Dumpty. 2016. (ENG., Illus.). 12p. (J). (gr. -1 — 1). 8.99 (978-1-4998-0213-9(7)) Little Bee Books Inc.
Little Jack Horner: 6 Small Books. (gr. k-2). 23.00 (978-0-7635-8500-6(9)) Rigby Education.
Locatelli, Ellen, illus. Filastrocche Italiane- Italian Nursery Rhymes. 2013. 54p. (978-1-938712-08-1(0)) Roxby Media Ltd.
Long, Sylvia. Twinkle, Twinkle, Little Star: A Traditional Lullaby. Long, Sylvia, illus. 2006. (ENG., Illus.). 26p. (J). (gr. -1-7). bds. 6.99 (978-0-8118-5230-2(X)) Chronicle Bks. LLC.
Loper, Kathleen. Angelina Katrina: Builds Troy Snowman. Waltz, Dan, illus. l.t. ed. 2004. 36p. (J). 17.95 (978-0-9741774-5-8(6)) D. W. Publishing.
Low, Elizabeth Cothen. Big Book of Seasons, Holidays, & Weather: Rhymes, Fingerplays, & Songs for Children. 2011. (ENG., Illus.). 156p. E-Book (978-1-59884-624-9(8), Libraries Unlimited) ABC-CLIO, LLC.
Mabie, Hamilton Wright, et al, eds. Childhood's Favorites & Fairy Stories. 2007. (Illus.). 660p. per. (978-1-4065-2960-9(5)) Dodo Pr.
Magee, Wes. Itsy Bitsy Spider & Itsy Bitsy Beetle. 2012. (ENG., Illus.). 24p. (J). (978-0-7787-7886-8(X)); pap. (978-0-7787-7898-1(3)) Crabtree Publishing Co.
Make Believe Ideas. Hey Diddle Diddle & Other Nursery Rhymes. 2015. (ENG.). 24p. (J). bds. 7.99 (978-1-78393-436-2(0)) Make Believe Ideas GBR. Dist: Nelson, Thomas Inc.
—Treasures Five-Minute Bedtime Stories. 2014. (ENG.). 192p. (J). 19.99 (978-1-78235-872-5(2)) Make Believe Ideas GBR. Dist: Nelson, Thomas Inc.
—Twinkle Twinkle Little Star. 2015. (ENG.). 12p. (J). bds. 8.99 (978-1-78393-532-1(4)) Make Believe Ideas GBR. Dist: Nelson, Thomas Inc.
Malley, Barbara. Read Me A Rhyme Please. 2006. (Illus.). 236p. per. 19.95 (978-0-89334-414-6(1), Humanics Learning) Green Dragon Bks.
Manousos, Dave. Life Is Good & Other Reasons for Rhyme. Manousos, Dave, illus. 2008. (Illus.). 36p. pap. 16.95 (978-1-59858-590-2(8)) Dog Ear Publishing, LLC.
MansBach, Sara. Round & Round the Garden, Finger Games in English & Spanish. Arroyave, Heidy, tr. Landau, Donna, illus. 2007. 42p. spiral bd. (978-0-9785477-2-1(1)) BladeRunner Publishing.
Marinaro, Stacy. Nap Time. 2009. 34p. pap. 16.50 (978-0-557-06881-4(9)) Lulu Pr., Inc.
Marks, Alan. The People of the Town: Nursery-Rhyme Friends for You & Me. 2016. (ENG., Illus.). 40p. (J). (-k). lib. bdg. 16.95 (978-1-58089-726-6(6)) Charlesbridge Publishing, Inc.
Marshall, Natalie. Five Little Monkeys: A Fingers & Toes Nursery Rhyme Book. 2015. (ENG.). 12p. (J). (— 1). bds. 6.99 (978-0-545-76762-0(8), Cartwheel Bks.) Scholastic, Inc.
—This Little Piggy: A Fingers & Toes Nursery Rhyme Book. Marshall, Natalie, illus. 2015. (ENG., Illus.). 12p. (J). (— 1). bds. 6.99 (978-0-545-76761-3(X), Cartwheel Bks.) Scholastic, Inc.
Marten, Luanne. There Was an Old Woman Who Lived in a Shoe. Marten, Luanne, illus. 2011. (Favorite Mother Goose Rhymes Ser.). (ENG., Illus.). 16p. (J). (gr. -1-2). lib. bdg. 25.64 (978-1-60954-284-9(3), 200236) Child's World, Inc., The.
Mathers, Petra, illus. & compiled by. The McElderry Book of Mother Goose: Revered & Rare Rhymes. Mathers, Petra, compiled by. 2012. (ENG.). 96p. (J). (gr. k-5). 21.99 (978-0-689-85605-1(9), McElderry, Margaret K. Bks.) McElderry, Margaret K. Bks.
Mavor, Salley. Pocketful of Posies: A Treasury of Nursery Rhymes. 2010. (ENG., Illus.). 72p. (J). (gr. k — 1). 21.99 (978-0-618-73740-6(5)) Houghton Mifflin Harcourt Publishing Co.
Mayo, Diana. House That Jack Built. 2007. (ENG., Illus.). 24p. (J). pap. 9.99 (978-1-84686-076-8(8)) Barefoot Bks., Inc.
McDermott, Mustafa Yusuf. Muslim Nursery Rhymes. rev. ed. 2015. (ENG., Illus.). 30p. (J). 14.95 (978-0-86037-563-0(3)) Kube Publishing Ltd. GBR. Dist: Consortium Bk. Sales & Distribution.
McDonald, Jill. Over in the Meadow. (J). 2012. (ENG., Illus.). 24p. (gr. -1-2). 9.99 (978-1-84686-747-7(9)) 2011. (978-1-84686-542-8(5)) Barefoot Bks., Inc.
McKay-Lawton, Toni. In Bloom. Manning, Eddie, illus. 2007. (Just in Rhyme Ser.). (ENG.). 12p. (J). (gr. -1-3). pap. (978-1-84167-030-0(8)) Ransom Publishing Ltd.
McPhail, David. My Mother Goose: A Collection of Favorite Rhymes, Songs, & Concepts. McPhail, David, illus. 2013. (ENG., Illus.). 96p. (J). (gr. -1-k). 19.99 (978-1-59643-526-1(7), 9781596435261) Roaring Brook Pr.
Mendonca, Angela. Nursery Rhymes Island Style. Mendonca, Angela, illus. 2013. (Illus.). 24p. pap. 9.99 (978-0-9843125-6-6(0)) Wealth of Wisdom LLC, A.
Monreal, Violeta & Violeta, Monreal. Mio, Mio! el Huevo Es Mio. 2003. (Coleccion Pictogramas Pictogramns Ser.). (SPA.). 36p. (J). (gr. k-3). pap. 8.50 (978-84-241-8102-4(6)) Everest Editora ESP. Dist: Lectorum Pubns., Inc.
Moore, Colin. Modern Nursery Rhymes: For Grown-Ups. 2012. (Illus.). 100p. pap. 13.95 (978-1-4678-9029-8(4)) AuthorHouse.
Moran, Erin. Colorful Spring. Pickett, Danny, illus. 2005. 32p. (J). mass mkt. 15.95 (978-0-9763778-0-1(2)) Seal Rock Publishing, LLC.
Moreillon, Judi. Vamos a Leer. Mercado, Mary M., tr. from ENG. Teis, Kyra, illus.Tr. of Read to Me. (SPA.). 12p. (J). 2005. bds. 6.95 (978-1-59572-015-3(4)) 2004. 6.95 (978-1-932065-50-3(4)) Star Bright Bks., Inc.
Morgan, Richard, illus. The Wheels on the Bus - The Boat on the Waves. 2013. (ENG.). 24p. (J). (978-0-7787-1148-3(X)) Crabtree Publishing Co.
—The Wheels on the Bus; The Boat on the Waves. 2013. (ENG.). 24p. (J). pap. (978-0-7787-1152-0(8)) Crabtree Publishing Co.
Moroney, Trace, creator. Baa, Baa, Black Sheep. 2008. (Illus.). 10p. (gr. -1-1). bds. 4.99 (978-1-74178-526-5(X)) Gardner Pubns.
Morris, Jackie. The Cat & the Fiddle: A Treasury of Nursery Rhymes. Morris, Jackie, illus. 2011. (ENG., Illus.). 64p. (J). (gr. -1-1). 19.95 (978-1-84507-987-1(6), Frances Lincoln) Quarto Publishing Group UK GBR. Dist: Hachette Bk. Group.
Moses, Brian. Hey Diddle Diddle & Hey Diddle Doodle. 2012. (ENG., Illus.). 24p. (J). pap. (978-0-7787-7896-7(7)) Crabtree Publishing Co.
—Humpty Dumpty & Humpty Dumpty at Sea. 2012. (ENG., Illus.). 24p. (J). (978-0-7787-7885-1(1)); pap. (978-0-7787-7897-4(5)) Crabtree Publishing Co.
Mother Goose, ed. Nursery Rhyme Classics. 2006. (ENG., Illus.). 12p. (J). 17.95 (978-1-59069-472-5(4)) Soundprints.
—Nursery Rhyme Songs. 2006. (ENG., Illus.). 12p. 17.95 (978-1-59069-473-2(2)) Soundprints.
La Muneca Azul: Poems, Rhymes, & Songs Listening Packs. 2003. 34.50 (978-0-673-58631-5(6)) Celebration Pr.
Music Sales. The Nursery Rhyme Songbook. 2009. (ENG.). 104p. (J). 9.95 (978-1-84772-580-6(5), AM993839) Wise Pubns. GBR. Dist: Music Sales Corp.
Nascimbeni, Barbara, illus. Little Miss Muffet. (Classic Books with Holes Ser.). (ENG.). (J). 2015. 16p. pap. incl. audio compact disk (978-1-84643-678-9(8)) 2012. 14p. bds. (978-1-84643-511-9(0)) 2012. 16p. pap. (978-1-84643-500-3(5)) Child's Play International Ltd.
Nippert, Brenda & Nippert, George. An Alphabet of Catholic Saints, bks. 13000. Nippert, Brenda & Nippert, George, illus. 3rd ed. 2006. (ENG., Illus.). 64p. (J). pap. 11.95 (978-0-9787035-1-6(0)) Joseph's Heartprint.
—An Alphabet of Mary, bks. 3000. Nippert, Brenda & Nippert, George, illus. 2012. (ENG., Illus.). 64p. (J). pap. 12.95 (978-0-9787035-0-9(2)) Joseph's Heartprint.
NO AUTHORSHIP. Hey Diddle Diddle. 2013. (ENG.). 12p. (gr. -1-1). pap. 5.95 (978-1-62169-094-8(6)) Rourke Educational Media.
—Hickory Dickory Dock. 2013. (ENG.). 12p. (gr. -1-1). pap. 5.95 (978-1-62169-091-7(1)) Rourke Educational Media.
—Humpty Dumpty. 2013. (ENG.). 12p. (gr. -1-1). pap. 5.95 (978-1-62169-088-7(1)) Rourke Educational Media.
—I'm a Little Tea Pot. 2013. (ENG.). 12p. (gr. -1-1). pap. 5.95 (978-1-62169-093-1(8)) Rourke Educational Media.
—Itsy Bitsy Spider. 2013. (ENG.). 12p. (gr. -1-1). pap. 5.95 (978-1-62169-092-4(X)) Rourke Educational Media.
—Jack & Jill. 2013. (ENG.). 12p. (gr. -1-1). pap. 5.95 (978-1-62169-090-0(3)) Rourke Educational Media.
—This Old Man. 2013. (ENG.). 12p. (gr. -1-1). pap. 5.95 (978-1-62169-089-4(X)) Rourke Educational Media.
—Twinkle Twinkle. 2013. (ENG.). 12p. (gr. -1-1). pap. 5.95 (978-1-62169-087-0(3)) Rourke Educational Media.
Noe, David C. Tres Mures Caeci. Thoburn, Michelle, illus. 2005. (LAT.). 48p. (J). (gr. k-12). 11.99 (978-0-9714458-1-9(8)) Patrick Henry College Pr.
Nosy Crow Staff. Happy Birthday. Huang, Yu-Hsuan, illus. 2017. (Sing along with Me! Ser.). (ENG.). 10p. (J). (-k). bds. 8.99 (978-0-7636-9505-7(X), Nosy Crow) Candlewick Pr.
—Hey Diddle Diddle: Sing along with Me! Huang, Yu-Hsuan, illus. 2017. (Sing along with Me! Ser.). (ENG.). 10p. (J). (-k). bds. 8.99 (978-0-7636-9320-6(0), Nosy Crow) Candlewick Pr.
—Row, Row, Row Your Boat: Sing along with Me! Huang, Yu-Hsuan, illus. 2017. (Sing along with Me! Ser.). (ENG.). 10p. (J). (-k). bds. 8.99 (978-0-7636-9240-7(9), Nosy Crow) Candlewick Pr.
Novick, Mary. Double Delight - Nursery Rhymes. Hale, Jenny, illus. 2011. (Double Delight Ser.). (ENG.). 16p. (J). (gr. -1 — 1). pap. 8.99 (978-1-877003-06-6(9)) Little Hare Bks. AUS. Dist: Independent Pubs. Group.
—Nursery Songs. Hale, Jenny, illus. 2003. 16p. (Orig.). pap. (978-1-877003-33-2(6)) Little Hare Bks. AUS. Dist: HarperCollins Pubs. Australia.
Nursery Rhyme Treasury. 2008. (Treasuries Ser.). 192p. (978-1-4075-2857-1(2)) Parragon, Inc.
Nursery Rhymes. (My First Sing-Alongs Ser.). (J). 7.99 incl. audio (978-1-55723-603-6(8)) Walt Disney Records.
Nursery Rhymes - Jack & Jill. 2005. (J). bds. (978-1-4194-0077-3(0)) Paradise Pr., Inc.
Nursery Rhymes - Old Mcdonald. 2005. (J). bds. (978-1-4194-0076-6(2)) Paradise Pr., Inc.
Nursery Rhymes - One, Two, Buckle my Shoe. 2005. (J). bds. (978-1-4194-0078-0(9)) Paradise Pr., Inc.
NUrsery rhymes- Bah,Bah black Sheep. 2005. (J). bds. (978-1-4194-0079-7(7)) Paradise Pr., Inc.
Nursery Rhymes Set 800783, 5. 2005. (J). bds. (978-1-59794-018-4(6)) Environments, Inc.
Nursery Rhymes Book. 2005. (J). bds. (978-1-4194-0070-4(3)) Paradise Pr., Inc.
Nursery Songs & Rhyms Gift Book. 2006. (J). 9.99 (978-1-934004-03-6(0)) Byeway Bks.
O'Brien, Eileen. This Little Piggy. Tyler, Jenny, ed. Edward, Linda, illus. 2004. (Carry-Me Bks.). 16p. (J). 5.95 (978-0-7945-0125-9(7), Usborne) EDC Publishing.
Oelschlager, Vanita. Ivy in Bloom: The Poetry of Spring from Great Poets & Writers from the Past. Blackwood, Kristin, illus. 2009. (ENG.). 40p. (J). (gr. -1-3). 17.95 (978-0-9800162-7-7(4)) VanitaBooks.
—Mother Goose/Other Goose. Hegan, Robin, illus. 2008. (ENG.). 32p. (J). (gr. -1-3). 17.95 (978-0-9800162-6-0(6)) VanitaBooks.
Olowoyeye, Ola. Rhythm & Motion: Volume 2. 2011. 28p. pap. 12.03 (978-1-4634-3256-0(9)) AuthorHouse.

M
N
O

Opie, Ian, ed. My Very First Mother Goose. Wells, Rosemary, illus. 2004. 107p. (J). reprint ed. 17.00 (978-0-7567-8384-6(4)) DIANE Publishing Co.

Opie, Iona. Mother Goose's Little Treasures. Wells, Rosemary, illus. 2007. (My Very First Mother Goose Ser.). (ENG.). 56p. (J). (gr. -1-2). 17.99 (978-0-7636-3655-5(X)) Candlewick Pr.

—My Very First Mother Goose. Wells, Rosemary, illus. 2016. (My Very First Mother Goose Ser.). (ENG.). 108p. (J). (gr. k-12). 24.99 (978-0-7636-8891-2(6)) Candlewick Pr.

—One, Two, Three, Mother Goose. Wells, Rosemary, illus. 2016. (ENG.). (J). (— 1). bds. 8.99 (978-0-7636-8766-3(9)) Candlewick Pr.

Opie, Iona, ed. Snuggle up with Mother Goose. Wells, Rosemary, illus. 2015. (My Very First Mother Goose Ser.). (ENG.). 26p. (J). (— 1). bds. 8.99 (978-0-7636-7867-8(8)) Candlewick Pr.

Osborne, Nancy. Rhyming Words: Cut & Paste. l.t. ed. 2007. (Illus.). 52p. ring bd. 9.95 (978-1-928856-07-8(1)) Osborne Pr.

Oscar: Poems, Rhymes, & Songs Listening Packs. 2003. 34.50 (978-0-673-58622-3(7)) Celebration Pr.

Pagnoni, Roberta, illus. Humpty Dumpty's Nursery Rhymes. 2010. (ENG.). 10p. (J). (gr. -1-k). bds. 7.99 (978-0-7641-6278-7(0)) Barron's Educational Series, Inc.

Paraclete Press, Paraclete. Praying with My Fingers: An Easy Way to Talk with God. 2014. (ENG., Illus.). 18p. (J). bds. 7.99 (978-1-61261-525-7(2)) Paraclete Pr., Inc.

Parekh, R. Nursery Rhymes. 2004. (Flashcards Ser.). (ENG., Illus.). 48p. (J). pap. 8.95 (978-0-7945-0530-1(9)) EDC Publishing.

Pat-a-Cake. 2003. (J). per. (978-1-57657-802-5(X)) Paradise Pr., Inc.

Pedro, Pedrito: Poems, Rhymes, & Songs Listening Packs. 2003. 34.50 (978-0-673-58632-2(4)) Celebration Pr.

Penner, Fred. Here We Go Round the Mulberry Bush. Fatus, Sophie, illus. 2008. (ENG.). 24p. (J). 6.99 (978-1-84686-189-5(6)) Barefoot Bks., Inc.

Pernice, Clare. The Real Mother Goose. 2017. (ENG., Illus.). 40p. (gr. -1-3). 14.95 (978-1-927018-83-5(8)) Simply Read Bks. CAN. Dist: Ingram Publisher Services.

Petelinsek, Kathleen. Little Jack Horner. Petelinsek, Kathleen, illus. 2011. (Favorite Mother Goose Rhymes Ser.). (ENG., Illus.). 16p. (J). (gr. -1-2). lib. bdg. 25.64 (978-1-60954-280-1(0), 200232) Child's World, Inc., The.

Phonics Songs & Rhymes Flip Chart. 2004. (gr. k-18). suppl. ed. 109.15 (978-0-328-02213-7(6)); (gr. 1-18). suppl. ed. 109.15 (978-0-673-59716-8(4)); (gr. 3-18). suppl. ed. 109.50 (978-0-673-59718-2(0)) Addison-Wesley Educational Pubs., Inc.

Pi Kids, creator. Mother Goose. 2007. (My First Treasury Ser.). (Illus.). 38p. (J). bds. 7.98 (978-1-4127-8713-0(0), PIL Kids) Publications International, Ltd.

Pinkney, Jerry. Three Little Kittens. Pinkney, Jerry, illus. 2010. (ENG., Illus.). 40p. (J). (gr. -1-k). 16.99 (978-0-8037-3533-0(2), Dial Bks) Penguin Young Readers Group.

—Twinkle, Twinkle, Little Star. 2011. (ENG., Illus.). 40p. (gr. -1 — 1). 16.99 (978-0-316-05696-0(0)) Little, Brown Bks. for Young Readers.

Poplin, Isaac E. A-Z's of Ancient Rome: A Rhyming Introduction to Roman History. 2011. 60p. (gr. 1-2). pap. 9.99 (978-1-4567-6931-4(6)) AuthorHouse.

Potter, Beatrix. Beatrix Potter's Nursery Rhyme Book. 2007. (Peter Rabbit Ser.). (ENG., Illus.). 80p. (J). (gr. -1-2). 12.99 (978-0-7232-5771-4(X), Warne) Penguin Young Readers Group.

Potter, Debra, illus. I am the Music Man. 2005. (Classic Books with Holes Board Book Ser.). (ENG.). 14p. (J). bds. (978-1-904550-60-0(6)) Child's Play International Ltd.

—I Am the Music Man. 2005. (Classic Books with Holes Soft Cover Ser.). (ENG.). 16p. (J). pap. (978-1-904550-34-1(7)) Child's Play International Ltd.

Power, Eloise. The Apple Tree Inside of Me. 2012. 36p. pap. 16.95 (978-1-4525-5522-5(2)) Balboa Pr.

Priddy Books Staff. My Bedtime Book of Favorite Nursery Rhymes: Including Ladybug, Baa Baa Black Sheep, I Had a Nut Tree, Plus Many More... 2003. (Illus.). (J). bds. (978-0-312-49174-1(3), Priddy Bks.) St. Martin's Pr.

Priddy, Roger. Nursery Rhymes. (Baby Boxsets Ser.). (ENG.). (J). (gr. -1-1). 2013. 32p. 14.99 (978-0-312-51563-8(4), 9780312515638) 2006. (Illus.). 28p. 12.95 (978-0-312-49808-5(X), 9780312498085) St. Martin's Pr. (Priddy Bks.).

La Primavera: Poems, Rhymes, & Songs Listening Packs. 2003. 34.50 (978-0-673-58633-9(2)) Celebration Pr.

Profiri, Charline. Rain, Rain, Stay Today: Southwestern Nursery Rhymes. Watson, Laura, illus. 2014. (J). (978-1-933855-85-1(1)) Rio Nuevo Pubs.

Publications International Ltd. Staff. Mother Goose. 2009. 320p. (J). lib. bdg. 19.98 (978-1-4127-4528-4(4)) Phoenix International Publications, Inc.

Publications International Ltd. Staff, creator. Mother Goose. 2006. (Keepsake Collection). (Illus.). 96p. (J). (gr. -1-3). 12.98 (978-1-4127-6061-4(5), PIL Kids) Publications International, Ltd.

Publications International Ltd. Staff, ed. BABY EINSTEIN(tm) under the Sea with Me! 2014. 12p. (J). bds. 7.98 (978-1-4508-6813-6(4), 1450868134) Phoenix International Publications, Inc.

—Happy Baby. 2011. 8p. (J). bds. 7.98 (978-1-4508-1243-6(0)) Publications International, Ltd.

The Puffin Book of Nursery Rhymes. 2016. (ENG., Illus.). 160p. (J). (gr. -1-k). 24.99 **(978-0-14-137016-3(5))** Penguin Bks., Ltd. GBR. Dist: Independent Pubs. Group.

Quattlebaum, Mary. Jo MacDonald Hiked in the Woods. Bryant, Laura J., illus. 2013. (ENG.). 32p. (J). (gr. -1-3). 16.95 (978-1-58469-334-5(7)); pap. 8.95 (978-1-58469-335-2(5)) Dawn Pubns.

Ralles, H. J. Looking Out My Window. 2013. (Illus.). 38p. (J). lib. bdg. 16.00 (978-1-935722-80-9(8), TOP) Top Pubns., Ltd.

Random House. My First Songs (Sesame Street) Brannon, Tom, illus. 2017. (ENG.). 26p. (J). (-k). bds. 8.99 **(978-1-5247-1770-4(3)**, Random Hse. Bks. for Young Readers) Random Hse. Children's Bks.

Read along Nursery Rhymes - Student Books. 2005. (J). pap. 19.95 (978-1-58970-701-6(X)) Lakeshore Learning Materials.

Read along Nursery Rhymes Big Book. 2005. (J). pap. 16.95 (978-1-58970-700-9(1)) Lakeshore Learning Materials.

Reading 2000 Phonics Songs & Rhymes Flip Chart. 2004. (gr. 2-18). suppl. ed. 109.15 (978-0-673-59717-5(2)) Addison-Wesley Educational Pubs., Inc.

Reasoner, Charles. Hey, Diddle, Diddle, 1 vol. Le Ray, Marina, illus. 2014. (Charles Reasoner Nursery Rhymes Ser.). (ENG.). 10p. (gr. -1 — 1). bds. 4.99 (978-1-4795-3807-2(8)) Picture Window Bks.

—Hickory, Dickory, Dock. Le Ray, Marina, illus. 2014. (Charles Reasoner Nursery Rhymes Ser.). (ENG.). 10p. (gr. -1 — 1). bds. 4.99 (978-1-4795-3805-8(1)) Picture Window Bks.

—Itsy Bitsy Spider, 1 vol. Le Ray, Marina, illus. 2013. (Charles Reasoner Nursery Rhymes Ser.). (ENG.). 10p. (gr. -1 — 1). bds. 4.99 (978-1-4795-1691-9(0)) Picture Window Bks.

—Jack & Jill, 1 vol. Le Ray, Marina, illus. 2014. (Charles Reasoner Nursery Rhymes Ser.). (ENG.). 10p. (gr. -1 — 1). bds. 4.99 (978-1-4795-3806-5(X)) Picture Window Bks.

—Little Bo Peep, 1 vol. Le Ray, Marina, illus. 2014. (Charles Reasoner Nursery Rhymes Ser.). (ENG.). 10p. (gr. -1 — 1). bds. 4.99 (978-1-4795-3804-1(3)) Picture Window Bks.

—Twinkle, Twinkle, Little Star, 1 vol. Le Ray, Marina, illus. 2013. (Charles Reasoner Nursery Rhymes Ser.). (ENG.). 10p. (gr. -1 — 1). bds. 4.99 (978-1-4795-1693-3(7)) Picture Window Bks.

Reid, Michael, et al, illus. Laugh-Along Nursery Rhymes. (Rookie Nursery Rhymes(tm) Ser.). (ENG.). 32p. (J). 2016. pap. 25.00 (978-0-531-22879-1(7)) 2017. pap. 12.00 (978-0-531-23046-6(5)) Scholastic Library Publishing. (Children's Pr.).

Reinhart, Matthew. A Pop-Up Book of Nursery Rhymes. Reinhart, Matthew, illus. 2009. (ENG., Illus.). 12p. (J). (gr. -1-3). 29.99 (978-1-4169-1825-7(6), Little Simon) Little Simon.

Rešcek, Sanja, illus. One Elephant Went Out to Play. 2007. (Classic Books with Holes Board Book Ser.). (ENG.). 14p. (J). (gr. -1-1). bds. (978-1-84643-111-1(5)) Child's Play International Ltd.

Rhatigan, Joe. The Itsy Bitsy Spider. Farias, Carolina, illus. 2017. (Classic Nursery Rhymes Retold Ser.). (ENG.). 32p. (J). (gr. -1-k). 12.95 (978-1-63322-160-4(1), Moondance) Quarto Publishing Group USA.

Rhyme Time. 2006. (J). bds. (978-1-4194-0144-2(0)) Paradise Pr., Inc.

Richardson, Frederick, illus. Mother Goose: A Classic Collection of Children's Nursery Rhymes. 2008. (ENG.). 24p. (J). 19.95 (978-1-58117-687-2(2), Intervisual/Piggy Toes) Bendon, Inc.

Rigby Education Staff. Humpty Dumpty Bigbook: Rhyme 2. (gr. k-2). 21.00 (978-0-7635-2410-4(7)) Rigby Education.

—Jack & Jill Big Book: Rhyme 1. (gr. k-2). 21.00 (978-0-7635-2404-3(2)) Rigby Education.

—Little Jack. (gr. k-2). 21.00 (978-0-7635-2412-8(3)) Rigby Education.

—Mary Big Book: Rhyme 2. (gr. k-2). 21.00 (978-0-7635-2411-1(5)) Rigby Education.

—Old King: Rhyme 1. (gr. k-2). 21.00 (978-0-7635-2405-0(0)) Rigby Education.

Riley, James Whitcomb. Riley Child-Rhymes. 2007. 64p. per. (978-1-4068-3909-8(4)) Echo Library.

—Riley Child-Rhymes with Hoosier Pictures. Vawter, Will, illus. 4th ed. 2010. (Library of Indiana Classics Ser.). (ENG.). 192p. 17.95 (978-0-253-35569-0(9), 9780253355690) Indiana Univ. Pr.

—Riley Farm-Rhymes. 2007. 60p. per. (978-1-4068-3912-8(4)) Echo Library.

Ritter-Henley, Sharlene. 123 Count Drive Nursery Rhyme, 1 vol. 2010. 20p. pap. 24.95 (978-1-4489-8141-0(7)) PublishAmerica, Inc.

Robleda, Margarita. Rebeca. Suarez, Maribel, illus. (Rana, Rema, Rimas Ser.).Tr. of Rebecca. (SPA.). 16p. (J). (gr. k-3). 7.95 (978-1-59437-819-5(3)) Santillana USA Publishing Co., Inc.

—Suenos. Suarez, Maribel, illus. (Rana, Rema, Rimas Ser.). (SPA.). 16p. (J). (gr. k-3). 7.95 (978-1-59437-821-8(5)) Santillana USA Publishing Co., Inc.

Roetzheim, William, ed. Modern Nursery Rhymes. 2009. (ENG., Illus.). 76p. pap. 7.95 (978-1-933769-43-1(2)) Level 4 Press, Inc.

Roger, Priddy. Nursery Rhymes. 2016. (ENG., Illus.). 18p. (J). bds. 12.99 (978-0-312-51963-6(X), 9780312519636, Priddy Bks.) St. Martin's Pr.

Rooney, Ronnie. There Was a Crooked Man. Rooney, Ronnie, illus. 2011. (Favorite Mother Goose Rhymes Ser.). (ENG., Illus.). 16p. (J). (gr. -1-2). lib. bdg. 25.64 (978-1-60954-283-2(5), 200235) Child's World, Inc., The.

Rossetti, Christina Georgina. Speaking Likenesses / by Christina Rossetti; with Pictures Thereof by Arthur Hughes. 2006. 112p. per. 16.99 (978-1-4255-0744-2(1)) Michigan Publishing.

Rossitter, Derek. The Greedy Pigeon & the Hungry Porcupine & Friends. 2008. (Illus.). 60p. (J). (gr. 4-7). pap. (978-0-7552-0406-9(9)) Authors OnLine, Ltd.

—Greedy Pigeon the Hungry Porcupine & Friends. Home, Grace, illus. 2004. 60p. pap. (978-0-7552-0142-6(6)) Authors OnLine, Ltd.

Rudisill, J. J. Hickory Dickory Dock, 1 vol. 2012. (Early Childhood Themes Ser.). (ENG.). 16p. (J). (gr. -1-2). pap. 6.99 (978-1-4333-3493-1(3)); pap. 19.99 (978-1-4333-3494-8(1)) Teacher Created Materials, Inc.

Sacred Friends. I Found the Answer. 2013. 16p. pap. 7.95 (978-1-4525-8515-4(6), Balboa Pr.) Author Solutions, Inc.

Salgado, Tono. Versos y Rimas para Ninos.Tr. of Verses & Ryhmes for Children. (SPA.). (J). 7.98 (978-968-403-880-6(1)) Selector, S.A. de C.V. MEX. Dist: AIMS International Bks., Inc.

Salzmann, Ann. Rainbow Rhymes. 2012. (ENG.). pap. (978-1-4675-1531-3(0)) Independent Pub.

Sanders, Nancy I. A Pirate's Mother Goose. Jack, Colin, illus. 2015. (ENG.). 32p. (J). (gr. -1-3). 16.99 (978-0-8075-6559-9(8)) Whitman, Albert & Co.

Schecter, Deborah. Nursery Rhymes: Adorable Art Projects with Easy Directions & Rebus Support That Build Beginning Reading Skills. 2009. (Follow-the-Directions Ser.). (ENG.). 80p. (gr. -1-1). pap. 12.99 (978-0-545-10219-3(7), Teaching Resources) Scholastic, Inc.

Scheffler, Axel. Mother Goose's Action Rhymes, 1 vol. 2017. (ENG., Illus.). 26p. (J). (-k). 9.99 **(978-1-5098-2064-1(7))** Pan Macmillan GBR. Dist: Independent Pubs. Group.

—Mother Goose's Bedtime Rhymes, 2 vols. 2017. (ENG., Illus.). 26p. (J). (-k). 9.99 **(978-1-5098-2062-7(0))** Pan Macmillan GBR. Dist: Independent Pubs. Group.

Scheffler, Axel & Green, Alison. Mother Goose's Nursery Rhymes: And How She Came to Tell Them. Scheffler, Axel, illus. 2006. (ENG., Illus.). 128p. (978-0-333-96136-0(6), Macmillan Children's Bks.) Pan Macmillan.

—Mother Goose's Storytime Nursery Rhymes. 2007. (J). (978-0-439-90307-3(6), Levine, Arthur A. Bks.) Scholastic, Inc.

Scholastic, Inc. Staff. The Real Mother Goose. Maccarone, Grace, ed. Wright, Blanche Fisher, illus. anniv. ed. 2006. (ENG.). 144p. (J). (gr. 3-7). 10.99 (978-0-439-85875-5(5), Cartwheel Bks.) Scholastic, Inc.

Scholastic, Inc. Staff, contrib. by. What Rhymes? 2013. (ENG.). 12p. (J). bds. 6.95 (978-0-531-27257-2(5)) Scholastic Library Publishing.

Schwartz, Carol. Old Mother Hubbard. Schwartz, Carol, illus. 2010. (Favorite Mother Goose Rhymes Ser.). (ENG., Illus.). 16p. (J). (gr. -1-2). 25.64 (978-1-60253-538-1(8), 200242) Child's World, Inc., The.

Scieszka, Jon. Truckery Rhymes. 2009. (Jon Scieszka's Trucktown Ser.). (ENG., Illus.). 24p. (J). (gr. k). pap. 6.25 (978-0-328-50050-5(X), Scott Foresman) Addison Wesley Schl.

—Truckery Rhymes. Gordon, David et al, illus. 2009. (Jon Scieszka's Trucktown Ser.). (ENG.). 64p. (J). (gr. -1-3). 17.99 (978-1-4169-4135-4(5), Simon & Schuster Bks. For Young Readers) Simon & Schuster Bks. For Young Readers.

Seibold, J. Otto. Other Goose: Re-Nurseried!! & Re-Rhymed!! Childrens Classics. 2010. (ENG., Illus.). 80p. (J). (gr. -1-17). 19.99 (978-0-8118-6882-2(6)) Chronicle Bks. LLC.

Sellers, Amy. Miss Amy's: Hurray for Rhyme It's Story Time: Contemporary Rhyming Stories for Children of All Ages. 2007. 32p. (J). pap. 19.95 (978-0-9787632-0-6(3)) Sellers, Amy.

Senor Cascaron: Poems, Rhymes, & Songs Listening Packs. 2003. (SPA.). 34.50 (978-0-673-58623-0(5)) Celebration Pr.

Settel, Jim. The Things I See & the Things I Do. Han, Mylene, illus. 2013. 52p. pap. 19.95 (978-1-4787-0879-7(4)) Outskirts Pr., Inc.

Shearer, Susan. Wacky Rhymes: Three-Letter A, E, I, O & U Words. 2007. 141p. pap. 24.95 (978-1-60441-498-1(7)) America Star Bks.

Sickler, Jonas & Pixton, Kaaren, illus. Hickory Dickory Dock: Hey Baby! Look at the Mouse that Went up the Clock — Big Ben in London! 2011. (Indestructibles Ser.). (ENG.). 12p. (J). (gr. k — 1). pap. 5.95 (978-0-7611-5921-6(5), 15921) Workman Publishing Co., Inc.

Silver Dolphin Staff, ed. My Wonderful Nursery Rhyme Collection. 2016. (ENG., Illus.). 192p. (J). (-k). 14.99 (978-1-62686-683-6(X), Silver Dolphin Bks.) Readerlink Distribution Services, LLC.

Slegers, Liesbet. Hooray, I Am a Boy! 2013. (My Baby Bks.). (ENG.). 56p. (— 1). 19.95 (978-1-60537-146-7(7)) Cobblestone Publishing Co.

—Hooray, I Am a Girl! 2013. (My Baby Bks.). (ENG.). 56p. (— 1). 19.95 (978-1-60537-145-0(9)) Cobblestone Publishing Co.

Smart Kidz, creator. I'm a Little Teapot. 2013. (Sing N Play Songs Ser.). (ENG., Illus.). 12p. (J). bds. 12.99 (978-1-891100-07-9(6), Smart Kids) Penton Overseas, Inc.

Smee, Nicola. Sleepyhead. Smee, Nicola, illus. 2004. (ENG & URD., Illus.). 10p. (J). bds. (978-1-85269-097-7(6)); bds. (978-1-85269-095-3(X)) Mantra Lingua.

—Sleepyhead. 2004. (ENG & PAN., Illus.). 10p. (J). bds. (978-1-85269-096-0(8)) Mantra Lingua.

Smith, Eric, et al, illus. This Little Piggy: And Other Favorite Rhymes. 2005. (Mother Goose Rhymes Ser.). (ENG.). 36p. (J). (gr. -1-k). 12.95 (978-1-59249-466-8(8), 1D013) Soundprints.

Smith, L. & Mcgee, B. Clappity clap all through the Town. 2009. (J). pap. 9.95 (978-1-61584-680-1(8)) Independent Pub.

Smith, Lesley, illus. My Big Book of Rhymes. 2012. (ENG.). 96p. (J). 13.50 (978-1-84135-134-6(2)) Award Pubns. Ltd. GBR. Dist: Parkwest Pubns., Inc.

Smith, Marie & Smith, Roland. T Is for a Time. Graef, Renee, illus. 2015. (ENG.). 40p. (J). (gr. 2-5). 16.99 (978-1-58536-512-8(2), 203809) Sleeping Bear Pr.

Snyder, Susan E. Grandma's Crazy Chickens. Richardson, Mike, illus. 2012. 34p. (J). 14.95 (978-0-9846428-8-5(9)) FireFly Publishings & Entertainment LLC.

Sommers, Faith & Burkholder, Diane. Helping Mama. 2003. (Illus.). 24p. (J). (978-0-87813-608-7(8)) Christian Light Pubns., Inc.

Soundprints Staff. Farmer in Dell. 2005. (Mother Goose Ser.). (ENG., Illus.). 32p. (J). 12.95 (978-1-59249-380-7(7), 1D005) Soundprints.

—Hey Diddle Diddle & Other Favorites. (Mother Goose Nursery Rhymes Ser.). (ENG., Illus.). 36p. (J). 14.95 (978-1-59069-221-9(7), MPD1110) Studio Mouse LLC.

—Hey Diddle Diddle & Other Favorites. (Mother Goose Nursery Rhymes Ser.). (Illus.). 36p. (J). 10.95 (978-1-59069-219-6(5), MD1110); 2003. bds. 8.95 (978-1-59069-218-9(7)) Studio Mouse LLC.

—I'm a Little Teapot & Other Favorites. 2003. (Nursery Sing-a-Longs Ser.). (Illus.). 36p. (J). 8.95 (978-1-59069-202-8(0)) Studio Mouse LLC.

—I've Been Workin on Railroad. 2005. (Mother Goose Ser.). (ENG., Illus.). 36p. (J). 12.95 (978-1-59249-379-1(3), 1D003) Soundprints.

—Mother Goose Bitsy Board Book Travel Pack, Vol. 2. 2005. (Studio Mouse Ser.). (ENG., Illus.). 10p. (J). 9.95 (978-1-59069-360-5(4)) Studio Mouse LLC.

—Mother Goose's Hide n' Seek Book. 2005. (Studio Mouse Ser.). (ENG., Illus.). 24p. (J). 12.95 (978-1-59069-376-6(0)) Studio Mouse LLC.

—Nursery Rhymes: Story Time Treasury. 2005. (Studio Mouse Ser.). (Illus.). 256p. (J). (gr. -1-2). 14.95 (978-1-59069-228-8(4), MT1001) Studio Mouse LLC.

Soundprints Staff, creator. Head, Shoulders, Knees & Toes: And Other Move-along Rhymes. 2004. (Mother Goose Ser.). (ENG., Illus.). 34p. (J). 15.95 (978-1-59249-386-9(6), 1D008) Soundprints.

Sourcebooks, Inc Staff. Star Light, Star Bright: A Mother Goose Bedtime Collection. 2013. (ENG., Illus.). 16p. (J). bds. 8.99 (978-1-4022-9291-0(0), Sourcebooks Jabberwocky) Sourcebooks, Inc.

Soy La Cafetera: Poems, Rhymes, & Songs Listening Packs. 2003. 34.50 (978-0-673-58634-6(0)) Celebration Pr.

Spenceley, Annabel. Faber Book of Nursery Rhymes. 2003. (Faber Edition Ser.). (ENG., Illus.). 1p. pap. 12.25 (978-0-571-10099-6(6)) Faber & Faber, Ltd. GBR. Dist: Alfred Publishing Co., Inc.

Spengler, Margaret, illus. One, Two, Buckle My Shoe. 2004. (J). bds. 6.99 (978-1-890647-12-4(8)) TOMY International, Inc.

Spradlin, Michael P. Jack & Jill Went up to Kill: A Book of Zombie Nursery Rhymes. Weigel, Jeff, illus. 2011. (ENG.). 96p. pap. 9.99 (978-0-06-208359-3(7), William Morrow Paperbacks) HarperCollins Pubs.

Squillace, Elisa, illus. Down in the Jungle. (Classic Books with Holes 8x8 with CD Ser.). (ENG.). 16p. (J). 2013. (gr. -1). pap. incl. audio compact disk (978-1-84643-623-9(0)) 2005. pap. (978-1-904550-32-7(0)) Child's Play International Ltd.

Stanley, Mandy. This Little Piggy & Other Action Rhymes. 2010. (Time for a Rhyme Ser.). (ENG., Illus.). 24p. (J). (gr. k — 1). pap. 5.99 (978-0-00-731565-9(1)) HarperCollins Pubs. Ltd. GBR. Dist: Independent Pubs. Group.

—Three Little Kittens & Other Number Rhymes. 2010. (Time for a Rhyme Ser.). (ENG., Illus.). 24p. (J). (gr. k — 1). pap. 5.99 (978-0-00-731566-6(X)) HarperCollins Pubs. Ltd. GBR. Dist: Independent Pubs. Group.

Stanley, Mandy, illus. Jack & Jill & Other Nursery Favourites. 2010. (Time for a Rhyme Ser.). (ENG.). 24p. (J). (gr. k — 1). 6.99 (978-0-00-731564-2(3)) HarperCollins Pubs. Ltd. GBR. Dist: Independent Pubs. Group.

Stone, Julia. The Lion Book of Nursery Rhymes. 2014. (ENG., Illus.). 96p. (J). (gr. -1 — 1). 17.99 (978-0-7459-6467-6(2)) Lion Hudson PLC GBR. Dist: Independent Pubs. Group.

Stoop, Naoko. Sing with Me! Stoop, Naoko, illus. 2016. (ENG., Illus.). 32p. (J). 16.99 (978-0-8050-9904-1(2), 9780805099041, Holt, Henry & Co. Bks. For Young Readers) Holt, Henry & Co.

Strevens-Marzo, Bridget. Bridget's Book of Nursery Rhymes. 2008. (ENG., Illus.). 24p. (J). (gr. -1-k). pap. 7.95 (978-1-921272-12-7(0)) Little Hare Bks. AUS. Dist: Independent Pubs. Group.

Studio Mouse. Nursery Rhymes. 2003. (ENG., Illus.). 22p. (J). 16.95 (978-1-59069-392-6(2)) Studio Mouse LLC.

—Sesame Street Abby Cadabby's Nursery Rhymes. 2008. (ENG.). 20p. (J). 9.99 (978-1-59069-658-3(1)) Studio Mouse LLC.

Studio Mouse, creator. Let's Listen: Nursery Rhymes for Listening & Learning. 2005. (Mother Goose Ser.). (ENG., Illus.). 36p. (J). (gr. -1-k). 7.95 (978-1-59249-533-7(8), 1D203) Soundprints.

Studio Mouse Staff. Five Little Monkeys: And Other Counting Rhymes. Elliott, Rebecca et al, illus. rev. ed. 2007. (ENG.). 24p. (J). (gr. -1-k). 4.99 (978-1-59069-608-8(5)) Studio Mouse LLC.

—Let's Listen: Nursery Rhymes for Listening & Learning. 2008. (Mother Goose Ser.). (ENG., Illus.). 36p. (gr. -1-k). 7.99 (978-1-59249-795-9(0)) Studio Mouse LLC.

—Let's Move: Nursery Rhymes for Moving & Learning. 2008. (ENG., Illus.). 36p. (gr. -1-k). 7.99 (978-1-59249-796-6(9)) Studio Mouse LLC.

—Let's Play: Nursery Rhymes for Playing & Learning. 2008. (Mother Goose Ser.). (ENG.). 36p. (gr. -1-k). 7.99 (978-1-59249-797-3(7)) Studio Mouse LLC.

—Princess Rhyme Time. 2006. (Learn-Aloud Bks.). (ENG., Illus.). 36p. (gr. -1). 12.99 (978-1-59069-495-4(3), 1A802) Studio Mouse LLC.

Sullivan, Cheryl. The New Nursery Rhymes. 2011. 24p. pap. (978-1-4269-7332-1(2)) Trafford Publishing (UK) Ltd.

Sullivan, Kevin. The Best Hawaiian Style Mother Goose Ever! Aoki, Deb, illus. 2006. 40p. 16.95 incl. cd-rom (978-0-9644149-6-9(1)) Hawaya, Inc.

Taback, Simms. This Is the House That Jack Built. Taback, Simms, illus. 2004. (ENG., Illus.). 32p. (J). (gr. k-3). reprint ed. 6.99 (978-0-14-240200-9(1), Puffin Books) Penguin Young Readers Group.

Taggart, Katy, et al, illus. Workin' on the Railroad: And Other Favorite Rhymes. 2004. (Mother Goose Ser.). (ENG.). 32p. (J). 15.95 (978-1-59249-385-2(8), 1D004) Soundprints.

Tanner, Suzy-Jane, illus. Nursery Rhymes. 2012. (ENG.). 24p. (J). pap. 9.95 (978-1-84135-743-0(X)) Award Pubns. Ltd. GBR. Dist: Parkwest Pubns., Inc.

Taplin, Sam. The Usborne Book of Bedtime Rhymes. Luraschi, Anna, illus. 2008. (Usborne Book Of... Ser.). 12p. (J). (gr. -1-3). bds. 12.99 (978-0-7945-1898-1(2), Usborne) EDC Publishing.

Taylor, Jane. Twinkle, Twinkle, Little Star. Holm, Sharon Lane, illus. 2010. (Favorite Children's Songs Ser.). (ENG.). 16p. (J). (gr. -1-2). 25.64 (978-1-60253-533-6(7), 200115) Child's World, Inc., The.

Teel, Karen. Robot Rhymes. Teets, Ashley, illus. 2013. (ENG.). 31p. (J). (gr. -1-3). 16.95 (978-0-938467-79-3(4)) Headline Bks., Inc.

Thaler, Mike. Seven Little Hippos. Smath, Jerry, illus. 2014. (ENG.). 36p. (J). (gr. -1-1). 16.99 (978-1-4814-2541-4(2), Simon & Schuster Bks. For Young Readers) Simon & Schuster Bks. For Young Readers.

Thienes-Schunemann, Mary. Lavender's Blue Dilly Dilly, 1 bk, 1 CD. 2004. (J). spiral bd. 21.95 incl. audio compact disk (978-0-9708397-7-0(4)) Naturally You Can Sing.

Thom, Marie & Walton, Elizabeth. Make Nursery Rhymes: Ten Very Easy Crafts for Toddlers. 2005. (Little Fingers Ser.). (ENG., Illus.). 32p. (J). (gr. -1-k). pap. 8.99 **(978-1-85714-332-4(9))** Ragged Bears USA.

Thompson, Carol. Mockingbird Song. 2011. (ENG., Illus.). 24p. (J). (978-1-84643-446-4(7)) Child's Play International Ltd.

Thompson, Carol & Newman, Lesléa. Daddy, Papa, & Me. Thompson, Carol, illus. 2009. (ENG., Illus.). 20p. (J). (gr. -1 — 1). bds. 7.99 (978-1-58246-262-2(3), Tricycle Pr.) Random Hse. Children's Bks.

—Mommy, Mama, & Me. Thompson, Carol, illus. 2009. (ENG., Illus.). 20p. (J). (gr. -1-2). bds. 7.99 (978-1-58246-263-9(1), Tricycle Pr.) Random Hse. Children's Bks.

Thomson, Sarah L. Around the Neighborhood: A Counting Lullaby, 0 vols. Christy, Jana, illus. 2012. (ENG.). 32p. (J). (gr. -1-3). 16.99 (978-0-7614-6164-7(7), 9780761461647, Amazon Children's Publishing) Amazon Publishing.

Thornhill, Jan. Over in the Meadow. Thornhill, Jan, illus. rev. ed. 2012. (ENG., Illus.). 32p. (J). (gr. -1-1). pap. 7.95 (978-1-926973-06-7(2), Owlkids) Owlkids Bks. Inc. CAN. Dist: Publishers Group West (PGW).

Tian, Elli. Silly nursery Rhymes. Tian, Elli, illus. 2007. (Illus.). 12p. (J). 9.49 (978-0-9798611-5-4(2)) Byte Me! Inc.

Tiger Tales, ed. Nursery Rhymes Sticker Book. Galloway, Fhiona, illus. 2015. (My Little World Ser.). (ENG.). 14p. (J). (gr. -1-3). 3.99 (978-1-58925-452-7(X)) Tiger Tales.

Tiger, Tales, ed. Twinkle, Twinkle Little Star 10th Anniversary. Rescek, Sanja, illus. 2016. (ENG.). 10p. (J). (gr. -1-k). 14.99 (978-1-58925-230-1(6)) Tiger Tales.

Tiger Tales Staff. 5 Minute Nursery Rhymes. 2013. (ENG.). 292p. (J). 14.95 (978-1-58925-506-7(2)) Tiger Tales Pubns.

Tiger Tales Staff, ed. Hickory, Dickory, Dock: And Other Favorite Nursury Rhymes. Rescek, Sanja, illus. 2006. (ENG.). 22p. (J). bds. 7.95 (978-1-58925-786-3(3)) Tiger Tales.

—This Little Piggy. Hannah, Wood, illus. 2010. (ENG.). 24p. (J). (gr. -1-k). bds. 8.95 (978-1-58925-849-5(5)) Tiger Tales.

—Twinkle, Twinkle Little Star: And Other Favorite Bedtime Rhymes. Rescek, Sanja, illus. 2006. (ENG.). 22p. (J). bds. 7.95 (978-1-58925-787-0(1)) Tiger Tales.

Tildes, Phyllis Limbacher. Will You Be Mine? A Nursery Rhyme Romance. Tildes, Phyllis Limbacher, illus. 2011. (ENG., Illus.). 32p. (J). (gr. -1-2). pap. 7.95 (978-1-58089-245-2(0)) Charlesbridge Publishing, Inc.

Traditional & Cloke, Rene. My Book of Favourite Tales & Rhymes. 2013. (ENG., Illus.). 93p. (J). 16.50 (978-1-84135-812-3(6)) Award Pubns. Ltd. GBR. Dist: Parkwest Pubns., Inc.

Trapani, Iza. Jingle Bells. Trapani, Iza, illus. 2007. (ENG., Illus.). 32p. (J). (gr. -1-k). 7.95 (978-1-58089-096-0(2)) Charlesbridge Publishing, Inc.

—Little Miss Muffet. Trapani, Iza, illus. (ENG., Illus.). 32p. (J). (gr. -1-k). 2015. 6.95 (978-1-62914-616-4(1)) 2013. 16.95 (978-1-62087-986-3(7), 620986) Skyhorse Publishing Co., Inc. (Sky Pony Pr.).

—Old King Cole. Trapani, Iza, illus. 2015. (ENG., Illus.). 32p. (J). (-k). lib. bdg. 15.95 (978-1-58089-632-0(4)) Charlesbridge Publishing, Inc.

—Rufus & Friends: Rhyme Time. Trapani, Iza, illus. 2008. (ENG., Illus.). 40p. (J). (gr. -1-3). pap. 7.95 (978-1-58089-207-0(8)) Charlesbridge Publishing, Inc.

—Rufus & Friends: School Days. Trapani, Iza, illus. 2010. (ENG., Illus.). 36p. (J). (gr. -1-3). 16.95 (978-1-58089-248-3(5)); pap. 7.95 (978-1-58089-249-0(3)) Charlesbridge Publishing, Inc.

Tugeau, Jeremy, illus. Making Friends with Mother Goose, 1 vol. 2011. (Mother Goose Nursery Rhymes Ser.). (ENG.). 32p. (gr. -1-2). 28.50 (978-1-61641-145-9(7), Looking Glass Library) ABDO Publishing Co.

—Mother Goose Nursery Rhymes, 6 vols., Set. Incl. Animal Tales from Mother Goose. Hedlund, Stephanie, adapted by. (gr. -1-2). 28.50 (978-1-61641-142-8(2)); Bedtime with Mother Goose. Hedlund, Stephanie. (gr. k-2). 28.50 (978-1-61641-143-5(0)); Count along with Mother Goose. Hedlund, Stephanie, adapted by. (gr. -1-2). 28.50 (978-1-61641-144-2(9)); Making Friends with Mother Goose. Hedlund, Stephanie F., compiled by. (gr. -1-2). 28.50 (978-1-61641-145-9(7)); Seeing Colors with Mother Goose. Hedlund, Stephanie, adapted by. (gr. -1-2). 28.50 (978-1-61641-146-6(5)); Weather Fun with Mother Goose. Hedlund, Stephanie, adapted by. (gr. -1-2). 28.50 (978-1-61641-147-3(3)); (Mother Goose Nursery Rhymes Ser.). (Illus.). 32p. 2011. 171.00 (978-1-61641-141-1(4), Looking Glass Library) ABDO Publishing Co.

—Weather Fun with Mother Goose, 1 vol. 2011. (Mother Goose Nursery Rhymes Ser.). (ENG.). 32p. (gr. -1-2). 28.50 (978-1-61641-147-3(3), Looking Glass Library) ABDO Publishing Co.

Twin Sister Produtions & Galvin, Laura Gates. Sesame Street Abby Cadabby's Nursery Rhymes. 2010. (J). (gr. k-2). 14.99 (978-1-59922-636-1(7)) Twin Sisters IP, LLC.

Twin Sisters(r) Staff. Abc Nursery Rhymes. 2010. (J). (gr. k-2). pap. 4.99 (978-1-59922-507-4(7)) Twin Sisters IP, LLC.

—Humpty Dumpty & More. 2010. (J). (gr. k-2). pap. 4.99 (978-1-59922-506-7(9)) Twin Sisters IP, LLC.

—30 Nursery Rhymes Songs CD. 2008. 6.99 (978-1-59922-156-4(X)) Twin Sisters IP, LLC.

Twin Sisters(r) Staff, et al. Five Little Bunnies. 2010. (J). (gr. k-1). 14.99 (978-1-59922-421-3(6)); 14.99 (978-1-59922-629-3(4)) Twin Sisters IP, LLC.

Twinkle Twinkle Little Star. 2012. (Nursery Rhymes (Little Birdie) Ser.). 10p. (J). (gr. -1-k). bds. 6.99 (978-1-61236-979-2(0)) Rourke Educational Media.

Various Authors Staff. Nursery Rhyme Comics: 50 Timeless Rhymes from 50 Celebrated Cartoonists. Duffy, Chris, ed. Chast, Roz & Feiffer, Jules, illus. 2011. (ENG.). 128p. (J). (gr. -1-3). 19.99 (978-1-59643-600-8(X), 9781596436008, First Second Bks.) Roaring Brook Pr.

Verrett, Michael. The Rhymes of the Gray Beard Tree. 2010. 185p. pap. 15.95 (978-0-557-57957-0(0)) Lulu Pr., Inc.

Wadsworth, Olive A. Over in the Meadow: A Counting Rhyme. Vojtech, Anna, illus. 2003. (Cheshire Studio Book Ser.). (ENG.). 32p. (J). pap. 7.95 (978-0-7358-1871-2(1)) North-South Bks., Inc.

Walrus Books. Children's Treasure Chest: Fairy Tales, Nursery Rhymes, & Nonsense Verse. 2004. (ENG., Illus.). 386p. (J). (gr. k-12). 29.95 (978-1-55285-579-9(1)) Whitecap Bks., Ltd. CAN. Dist: Graphic Arts Ctr. Publishing Co.

Walter Foster Jr. Creative Team. Nursery Rhyme Clues & Crimes: Complete the Puzzle to Solve the Nursery Rhyme Mystery. 2016. (ENG.). 16p. (J). (gr. -1-1). bds. 14.95 (978-1-63322-068-3(0)) Quarto Publishing Group USA.

Watt, Fiona. Nursery Rhymes Touchy-Feely Board Book. Meyer, Kerry, illus. 2010. (Luxury Touchy-Feely Board Bks). 10p. (J). bds. 15.99 (978-0-7945-2662-7(4), Usborne) EDC Publishing.

—Sing-along Nursery Rhymes. Bordoni, Chiara, illus. 2009. (Baby Board Books w/CD Ser.). 12p. (J). (gr. -1). bds. 15.99 (978-0-7945-2351-0(X), Usborne) EDC Publishing.

Weaver, Joyce Mckissick. Little Rhymes for Little Minds, 1 vol. 2010. 38p. 24.95 (978-1-4489-9622-3(8)) PublishAmerica, Inc.

Webb, Sarah & Ranson, Claire. Sally Go Round the Stars: Favourite Rhymes for an Irish Childhood. McCarthy, Steven, illus. 2012. (ENG.). 64p. (J). 26.00 (978-1-84717-211-2(3)) O'Brien Pr., Ltd., The IRL. Dist: Dufour Editions, Inc.

—Sally Go Round the Stars: Favourite Rhymes from an Irish Childhood. McCarthy, Steve, illus. 2015. (ENG.). 64p. (J). pap. 17.00 (978-1-84717-675-2(5)) O'Brien Pr., Ltd., The IRL. Dist: Dufour Editions, Inc.

Weidner, Teri. Three Little Kittens. Weidner, Teri, illus. 2011. (Favorite Mother Goose Rhymes Ser.). (ENG., Illus.). 16p. (J). (gr. -1-2). lib. bdg. 25.64 (978-1-60954-285-6(1), 200237) Child's World, Inc., The.

Weidner, Teri, illus. Five Little Ducks. 2010. (Favorite Children's Songs Ser.). (ENG.). 16p. (J). (gr. -1-2). 25.64 (978-1-60253-528-2(0), 200111) Child's World, Inc., The.

White, Jill & White, Robbin. Can Starfish Make A Wish. 2nd ed. 2008. (Illus.). 26p. (J). 4.95 (978-0-9746613-1-5(7)) Starfish Aquatics Institute.

White, Larisa. Teacup Rhymes for Teacup Humans. 2012. 24p. pap. 17.99 (978-1-4685-5784-8(X)) AuthorHouse.

Williams, Brenda & Mayo, Diana. The House That Jack Built. 2006. (Barefoot Paperback Ser.). (ENG., Illus.). 24p. (J). (gr. -1-1). pap. 6.99 (978-1-84686-051-5(2)) Barefoot Bks., Inc.

Williams, Shannon. Songs of Science: Physics in the Bathtub. 2012. 20p. pap. 13.77 (978-1-4669-3021-6(7)) Trafford Publishing.

—Songs of Science: Physics in the Car. 2012. 20p. pap. 13.77 (978-1-4669-4967-6(8)) Trafford Publishing.

Winburn, William B., illus. Knees & Toes. 2009. (Rookie Toddler: Sing along Toddler Ser.). (ENG.). 12p. (J). (gr. -1). bds. 6.95 (978-0-531-24546-0(2)) Scholastic Library Publishing.

Wohnoutka, Mike, illus. This Little Piggy. 2005. (J). (978-1-58987-106-9(5)) Kindermusik International.

Wong, JoyLynn Charity. Carried Away: A Collection of Wrapscapes & Nursery Rhymes. 2014. (Illus.). 40p. pap. (978-1-4600-0406-7(X)) Essence Publishing.

Wood, Hannah, illus. Hey, Diddle, Diddle & More Favorite Nursery Rhymes. 2012. (ENG.). 20p. (J). bds. (978-1-58925-870-9(3)) Tiger Tales.

Woodruff, Liza. Mary Had a Little Lamb. Woodruff, Liza, illus. 2011. (Favorite Mother Goose Rhymes Ser.). (ENG., Illus.). 16p. (J). (gr. -1-2). lib. bdg. 25.64 (978-1-60954-281-8(9), 200233) Child's World, Inc., The.

Wright, Blanche Fisher. Mother Goose Nursery Rhymes. 2013. (ENG., Illus.). 128p. (J). (gr. -1-2). 16.95 (978-1-4549-0980-4(3), Fall River) Sterling Publishing Co., Inc.

Wright, Blanche Fisher, illus. The Real Mother Goose. 2017. (J). pap. (978-1-5124-2602-1(4)) Lerner Publishing Group.

—Real Mother Goose Clock Book. 22p. (J). (gr. -1-2). 6.95 (978-1-56288-095-8(0)) Checkerboard Pr., Inc.

Wright, Danielle. Korean Nursery Rhymes: Wild Geese, Land of Goblins & Other Favorite Songs & Rhymes. Acraman, Helen, illus. 2013. (ENG & KOR.). 32p. (J). (gr. -1-3). 16.95 (978-0-8048-4227-3(2)) Tuttle Publishing.

Wu, Faye-Lynn. Chinese & English Nursery Rhymes: Share & Sing in Two Languages. Dutcher, Kieren, illus. 2010. (ENG & CHI.). 32p. (J). (gr. -1-3). 16.95 (978-0-8048-4094-1(6)) Tuttle Publishing.

Yaccarino, Dan. Dan Yaccarino's Mother Goose. Yaccarino, Dan, illus. 2003. (Little Golden Book Ser.). (ENG., Illus.). 24p. (J). (gr. -1-2). 4.99 (978-0-375-82571-2(1), Golden Bks.) Random Hse. Children's Bks.

Yolen, Jane. Wee Rhymes: Baby's First Poetry Book. Dyer, Jane, illus. 2013. (ENG.). 112p. (J). (gr. -1-3). 19.99 (978-1-4169-4898-8(8), Simon & Schuster/Paula Wiseman Bks.) Simon & Schuster/Paula Wiseman Bks.

Zinsmeister, Elke, illus. Ten Fat Sausages. 2005. (Classic Books with Holes Soft Cover Ser.). (ENG.). 16p. (J). pap. (978-1-904550-31-0(2)) Child's Play International Ltd.

NURSERY SCHOOLS

see also Kindergarten

Anderson, Pamela. My New School: Blonde Girl. Lee, Han & Wu, Stacie, illus. 2004. (J). 12.95 (978-1-932555-04-2(8)) Watch Me Grow Kids.

Beylon, Cathy. Fun at Nursery School. 2006. (Dover Coloring Bks.). (ENG., Illus.). 30p. (J). (gr. -1-1). pap. 4.99 (978-0-486-44536-6(4)) Dover Pubns., Inc.

Bridges, Doreen. Music, Young Children & You: A Parent-Teacher Guide to Music for 0 -5 Year Olds. (Illus.). 160p. (J). (gr. -1-k). pap. (978-0-86806-530-4(7), Hale & Iremonger) GHR Pr., The.

Bunnett, Rochelle. Amigos en la Escuela, 1 vol. Muñoz, Yenny, tr. from ENG. Brown, Matt, photos by. 2007.Tr. of Friends at School. (SPA., Illus.). 32p. (J). (gr. -1). pap. 5.95 (978-1-59572-041-2(3)) Star Bright Bks., Inc.

Burton, Marilee R. Kindergarten Scholar. Boyer, Robin, illus. 2004. (ENG.). 32p. (J). pap. 2.99 (978-1-58947-455-0(4)) School Zone Publishing Co.

Campos, Maria de Fatima. Victoria's Day. 2015. (ENG., Illus.). 32p. (J). (gr. -1-1). pap. 10.99 (978-1-84780-424-2(1), Frances Lincoln) Quarto Publishing Group UK GBR. Dist: Hachette Bk. Group.

Cleveland, Alexandra, et al. Camino al Primer Grado. Franco, Sharon, tr. from ENG. Koeller, Carol, illus. 2004. (SPA.). 128p. (Orig.). (J). pap. 14.95 (978-0-943452-35-7(X)) Building Blocks, LLC.

Codell, Esmé Raji. It's Time for Preschool! Ramá, Sue, illus. 2012. 40p. (J). (gr. -1-k). (ENG.). 15.99 (978-0-06-145518-6(0)); lib. bdg. 16.89 (978-0-06-145519-3(9)) HarperCollins Pubs. (Greenwillow Bks.).

Contando. 2005. (SPA.). (J). (gr. -1-18). pap. 6.95 (978-950-11-0903-0(8)) Sigmar ARG. Dist: Iaconi, Mariuccia Bk. Imports, Lectorum Pubns., Inc.

Douglas, Vincent. Everything for Early Learning, Grade Preschool Vol. 1. 2004. (Everything for Early Learning Ser.: Vol. 1). (ENG., Illus.). 320p. (gr. -1 — 1). pap. 7.95 (978-0-7696-3347-3(1)) Carson-Dellosa Publishing, LLC.

Equipo Staff. La Escuela Infantil. (Coleccion Mundo Maravilloso). (SPA., Illus.). 36p. (J). (gr. 2-4). (978-84-348-7228-8(5), SM31363) SM Ediciones ESP. Dist: Lectorum Pubns., Inc.

Haley, Amanda. 3-2-1 School Is Fun! 2009. (Rookie Preschool Ser.). (ENG.). 24p. (J). (gr. -1). 23.00 (978-0-531-24405-0(9)) Scholastic Library Publishing.

Heinemann Educational Ltd. Publishing Staff. Minbeasts Up Close Package. 2004. pap. 243.00 (978-1-4109-1386-9(4)) Harcourt Schl. Pubs.

Hoffman, Joan. Kindergarten Basics. Boyer, Robin, illus. 2004. (ENG.). 32p. (J). pap. 2.99 (978-1-58947-436-9(8)) School Zone Publishing Co.

—Nursery Rhymes. 2008. (ENG.). 32p. (J). pap. 3.99 (978-1-60159-115-9(2)) School Zone Publishing Co.

—Preschool Practice. 2007. (ENG.). 32p. (J). pap. 3.99 (978-1-60159-116-6(0)) School Zone Publishing Co.

—Preschool Scholar: Scholar Series Workbooks. 2008. (ENG.). 32p. (J). pap. 2.99 (978-1-58947-454-3(6)) School Zone Publishing Co.

Kannenberg, Stacey. Let's Get Ready for Kindergarten! rev. ed. 2006. (Let's Get Ready Ser.). (Illus.). 30p. (J). (gr. -1-1). per. 19.00 (978-1-933476-00-1(1)) Cedar Valley Publishing.

Key Porter Books, creator. Face Painting: Enchanting Designs for Faces & Bodies. rev. ed. 2007. (Gymboree Play & Music Ser.). (ENG., Illus.). 36p. (J). (gr. -1-2). bds. (978-1-55263-962-7(2)) Magma.

—Music Play: Inspired Ways to Explore Music. rev. ed. 2007. (Gymboree Play & Music Ser.). (ENG., Illus.). 36p. (J). (gr. -1-2). bds. (978-1-55263-964-1(9)) Magma.

Key Porter Books Staff. Gymboree in a Princess Castle. rev. ed. 2007. (ENG., Illus.). 1p. (J). (978-1-55263-923-8(1)) Magma.

—Gymboree on a Pirate Ship. rev. ed. 2007. (ENG., Illus.). 1p. (J). (978-1-55263-921-4(5)) Magma.

Kilodavis, Cheryl. My Princess Boy. DeSimone, Suzanne, illus. 2010. (ENG.). 36p. (J). (gr. -1-3). 17.99 (978-1-4424-2988-8(7), Aladdin) Simon & Schuster Children's Publishing.

Légaré, Gisèle & L'Heureux, Christine. Day Care. Brignaud, Pierre & Depratto, Marcel, illus. 2008. (Big Dipper Ser.). (ENG.). 24p. (J). (gr. -1-k). pap. 3.95 (978-2-89450-657-8(0)) Caillouet, Gerry.

Mason, Jane B. & Stephens, Sarah Hines. Gymboree Dance Play. rev. ed. 2007. (ENG., Illus.). 36p. (J). (gr. -1-2). bds. (978-1-55263-960-3(6)) Magma.

Scholastic, Inc. Staff. Preschool Basic Skills: Visual Perception & Drawing Activities. 2003. (Preschool Basic Skills Ser.). (ENG.). 48p. 6.99 (978-0-439-50026-5(5), Teaching Resources) Scholastic, Inc.

School Zone Interactive Staff. Kindergarten. 2006. (ENG.). (J). cd-rom 24.99 (978-1-58947-682-0(4)) School Zone Publishing Co.

The Mailbox Books Staff. Totally for Twos: Art Age 2. 2010. (Illus.). 128p. (J). 18.95 (978-1-56234-934-9(1), Mailbox Bks., The) Education Ctr., Inc.

NURSERY SCHOOLS—FICTION

Ashdown, Rebecca. Bob & Flo. 2015. (ENG., Illus.). 32p. (J). (gr. -1-3). 16.99 (978-0-544-44430-0(2), HMH Books For Young Readers) Houghton Mifflin Harcourt Publishing Co.

Cousins, Lucy. Maisy Goes to Preschool: A Maisy First Experiences Book. Cousins, Lucy, illus. 2010. (Maisy Ser.). (ENG., Illus.). 32p. (J). (gr. k-k). pap. 6.99 (978-0-7636-5086-5(2)) Candlewick Pr.

Dewdney, Anna. Llama Llama Misses Mama. 2009. (Llama Llama Ser.). (ENG., Illus.). 40p. (J). (gr. -1-k). 17.99 (978-0-670-06198-3(0), Viking Books for Young Readers) Penguin Young Readers Group.

Dorsey, Maggie. My Hero, My Dad, the Nurse. 2008. (ENG.). 36p. pap. 16.99 (978-1-4196-9476-9(6)) CreateSpace Independent Publishing Platform.

Edwards, Becky. My First Day at Nursery School. Flintoft, Anthony, illus. 2004. (ENG.). 32p. (J). (gr. -1-1). pap. 7.99 (978-1-58234-909-1(6), 9781582349091, Bloomsbury USA Childrens) Bloomsbury Publishing USA.

Henkes, Kevin. Prudencia Se Preocupa. 2017.Tr. of Wemberly Worried. (SPA.). (J). pap. **(978-1-63245-666-3(4))** Lectorum Pubns., Inc.

Henkes, Kevin. Wemberly Worried. Henkes, Kevin, illus. 2010. (ENG., Illus.). 32p. (J). (gr. -1-4). pap. 6.99 (978-0-06-185776-8(9), Greenwillow Bks.) HarperCollins Pubs.

—Wemberly Worried. Henkes, Kevin, illus. (Illus.). pap. 18.95 incl. audio compact disk (978-1-59112-359-0(3)); pap. 39.95 incl. audio compact disk (978-1-59112-561-7(8)); pap. 16.95 incl. audio (978-0-87499-806-1(9)); pap. incl. audio (978-0-87499-808-5(5)) Live Oak Media.

Huber, Mike. All in One Day. Cowman, Joseph, illus. 2014. (ENG.). 32p. (gr. -1-k). 15.95 (978-1-60554-207-2(5)) Redleaf Pr.

Hudson, Wade. Puddin', Jeffrey & Leah. 2008. (Illus.). 16p. (gr. -1). 6.95 (978-1-60349-006-1(X), Marimba Bks.) Hudson Publishing Group, The.

Kehret, Peg. Race to Disaster. 2008. (ENG.). 128p. (J). (gr. 3-7). pap. 7.99 (978-1-4169-9108-3(5), Simon & Schuster/Paula Wiseman Bks.) Simon & Schuster/Paula Wiseman Bks.

Kelly, Mij. Preschool Time. McQuillan, Mary, illus. 2014. (ENG.). 32p. (J). (gr. -1 — 1). 14.99 (978-0-7641-6655-6(7)) Barron's Educational Series, Inc.

Korngold, Jamie. Sadie & the Big Mountain. Fortenberry, Julie, illus. 2012. (Lag B'Omer & Shavuot Ser.). (ENG.). 32p. (J). (gr. -1-1). pap. 7.95 (978-0-7613-6494-8(3), Kar-Ben Publishing) Lerner Publishing Group.

Onyefulu, Ifeoma. Deron Goes to Nursery School. Onyefulu, Ifeoma, photos by. 2010. (First Experiences Ser.). (ENG., Illus.). 32p. (J). (gr. -1-2). 17.95 (978-1-84507-864-5(0), Frances Lincoln) Quarto Publishing Group UK GBR. Dist: Hachette Bk. Group.

Publications International Ltd. Staff, ed. Sesame St Let's Go to School First Look & Find. 2013. 18p. (J). bds. 7.98 (978-1-4508-2933-5(3), 1450829333) Phoenix International Publications, Inc.

Radlauer. Molly. 2007. (ENG.). 32p. (J). (gr. -1-2). 11.99 (978-1-4169-6836-8(9), Simon & Schuster/Paula Wiseman Bks.) Simon & Schuster/Paula Wiseman Bks.

Rankin, Joan E. First Day. Rankin, Joan E., illus. 2007. (ENG., Illus.). 32p. (J). (gr. -1-2). 10.99 (978-1-4169-6848-1(2), Simon & Schuster/Paula Wiseman Bks.) Simon & Schuster/Paula Wiseman Bks.

Rockwell, Anne F. My Preschool. Rockwell, Anne F., illus. 2008. (ENG., Illus.). 32p. (J). (gr. -1-k). 17.99 (978-0-8050-7955-5(6), 9780805079555, Holt, Henry & Co. Bks. For Young Readers) Holt, Henry & Co.

Schwartz, Amy. The Boys Team. Schwartz, Amy, illus. 2014. (ENG., Illus.). 40p. (J). (gr. -1-1). 19.99 (978-1-4814-2534-6(X), Atheneum Bks. for Young Readers) Simon & Schuster Children's Publishing.

Shea, Bob. Dinosaur vs. School. Shea, Bob, illus. 2014. (Dinosaur vs. Book Ser.). (ENG., Illus.). 40p. (J). (gr. -1-k). 16.99 (978-1-4231-6087-8(8)) Hyperion Bks. for Children.

Wing, Natasha. The Night Before Preschool. Wummer, Amy, illus. (Night Before Ser.). (ENG.). 32p. (J). (gr. -1-k). 2014. 12.99 (978-0-448-48254-5(1)) 2011. pap. 4.99 (978-0-448-45451-1(3)) Penguin Young Readers Group. (Grosset & Dunlap).

NURSES

see also Children—Health and Hygiene; First Aid; Hospitals; School Nursing

Alexander, Carol. Florence Nightingale. (Rookie Biographies(tm) Ser.). (ENG., Illus.). 32p. (J). 2015. lib. bdg. 25.00 (978-0-531-21412-1(5)) 2005. (gr. 1-2). pap. 4.95 (978-0-516-25828-7(1)) Scholastic Library Publishing. (Children's Pr.).

Alexander, Carol & Vargus, Nanci Reginelli. Florence Nightingale. 2004. (Rookie Biography Ser.). (J). 20.50 (978-0-516-24406-8(X)) Scholastic Library Publishing.

Aller, Susan Bivin. Florence Nightingale. 2008. pap. 52.95 (978-0-8225-9389-8(0)) Lerner Publishing Group.

—Florence Nightingale. Butler, Tad, illus. 2007. (History Maker Biographies Ser.). (ENG.). 48p. (gr. 3-6). lib. bdg. 27.93 (978-0-8225-7609-9(0), Lerner Pubns.) Lerner Publishing Group.

Arnold, Quinn M. Nurses. 2017. (J). **(978-1-60818-874-1(4)**, Creative Education) Creative Co., The.

Batten, Jack. Silent in an Evil Time: The Brave War of Edith Cavell. 2007. (ENG., Illus.). 144p. (J). (gr. 5-18). pap. 16.95 (978-0-88776-737-1(0), Tundra Bks.) Tundra Bks. CAN. Dist: Penguin Random Hse. LLC.

Bickerstaff, Linda. What Degree Do I Need to Pursue a Career in Nursing?, 1 vol. 2015. (ENG., Illus.). 80p. (J). 34.60 (978-1-4777-7857-9(8), Rosen Young Adult) Rosen Publishing Group, Inc., The.

Blount, Rachel. Nurse. 2017. (Here to Help Ser.). (ENG., Illus.). 24p. (J). (gr. k-2). 16.99 (978-1-4451-4011-7(X), Franklin Watts) Hachette Children's Group GBR. Dist: Hachette Bk. Group.

Braun, Eric. Trapped Behind Enemy Lines: The Story of the U. S. Army Air Force 807th Medical Evacuation Squadron. 2016. (Encounter: Narrative Nonfiction Stories Ser.). (ENG.). 224p. (gr. 4-6). 14.95 (978-1-62370-605-0(X)); (Illus.). lib. bdg. 32.65 (978-1-4914-8042-7(4), 1400082) Encounter Bks.

Brill, Marlene Targ. Nurses. 2005. (Pull Ahead Bks.). 32p. (Illus.). (J). (gr. 3-7). lib. bdg. 22.60 (978-0-8225-1692-7(6)); (ENG.). (gr. k-3). pap. 7.95 (978-0-8225-5476-9(3)) Lerner Publishing Group.

Campbell, Candy. My Mom Is A Nurse, 1 vol. 2010. (ENG.). 208p. pap., pap. 27.95 (978-0-578-02360-1(1)) New Year Publishing.

Caviezel, Giovanni. Nurse. Mesturini, C., illus. 2011. (Mini People Shape Bks.). (ENG.). 10p. (J). bds. 5.99 (978-0-7641-6440-8(6)) Barron's Educational Series, Inc.

Clark, Sarah Kartchner. Nurses Then & Now, 1 vol. 2006. (Primary Source Readers Ser.). (ENG.). 32p. (J). (gr. 1-1). pap. 8.99 (978-0-7439-9374-6(8)) Shell Educational Publishing.

Connors, Kathleen. The Life of Clara Barton, Vol. 1. 2014. (Famous Lives Ser.). (ENG.). 24p. (J). (gr. 1-2). 22.60 (978-1-4824-0375-6(7)) Stevens, Gareth Publishing LLLP.

—The Life of Florence Nightingale, Vol. 1. 2014. (Famous Lives Ser.). (ENG.). 24p. (J). (gr. 1-2). 22.60 (978-1-4824-0405-0(2)) Stevens, Gareth Publishing LLLP.

Crompton, Samuel Williard. Clara Barton. 2009. (Women of Achievement Ser.). (Illus.). 144p. (J). (gr. 6-12). 35.00 (978-1-60413-492-6(5), Chelsea Hse.) Facts On File, Inc.

Cunningham, Kevin. Nurse. (21st Century Skills Library: Cool STEAM Careers Ser.). (ENG., Illus.). 32p. (gr. 4-7). 2015. (J). 29.93 (978-1-63362-561-7(3), 206428) 2008. lib. bdg. 28.50 (978-1-60279-299-9(2), 200138) Cherry Lake Publishing.

Davis, Marc. Florence Nightingale: Founder of the Nightingale School of Nursing. 2003. (Our People Ser.). (ENG., Illus.). 32p. (J). (gr. 3-6). 29.93 (978-1-59296-003-3(0), 200636) Child's World, Inc., The.

Dell, Pamela. Memoir of Susie King Taylor: A Civil War Nurse. 2017. (First-Person Histories Ser.). (ENG.). 32p. (gr. 3-4). pap. 8.95 (978-1-5157-3356-0(4)); (Illus.). lib. bdg. 27.32 (978-1-5157-3354-6(8)) Capstone Press of Coughlan Cos. (Fact Finders).

Demi. Florence Nightingale. Demi, illus. 2014. (ENG., Illus.). 40p. (J). (gr. -1-3). 17.99 (978-0-8050-9729-0(5), 9780805097290, Holt, Henry & Co. Bks. For Young Readers) Holt, Henry & Co.

Devillier, Christy. Clara Barton, 1 vol. 2004. (First Biographies Set Iv Ser.). (ENG., Illus.). 32p. (gr. k-4). 27.07 (978-1-59197-511-3(5), Buddy Bks.) ABDO Publishing Co.

Ditchfield, Christin. Clara Barton: Founder of the American Red Cross. 2004. (Great Life Stories Ser.). (ENG., Illus.). 111p. (J). 30.50 (978-0-531-12276-1(X), Watts, Franklin) Scholastic Library Publishing.

Dunn, Joeming W. Clara Barton, 1 vol. Espinosa, Rod, illus. 2008. (Bio-Graphics Ser.). (ENG.). 32p. (gr. 3-5). 28.50 (978-1-60270-170-0(9), Graphic Planet- Nonfiction) ABDO Publishing Co.

Edison, Erin. Clara Barton, 1 vol. 2013. (Great Women in History Ser.). (ENG.). 24p. (gr. k-1). pap. 6.29 (978-1-62065-857-4(7)); pap. 35.70 (978-1-62065-858-1(5)); (Illus.). lib. bdg. 21.99 (978-1-62065-076-9(2)) Capstone Press of Coughlan Cos. (Pebble Bks.).

—Florence Nightingale, 1 vol. 2014. (Great Women in History Ser.). (ENG.). 24p. (gr. k-1). lib. bdg. 21.99 (978-1-4765-4214-0(7), Pebble Bks.) Capstone Press of Coughlan Cos.

Farrell, Mary Cronk. Pure Grit: How American World War II Nurses Survived Battle & Prison Camp in the Pacific. 2014. (ENG., Illus.). 160p. (J). (gr. 3-7). 24.95 (978-1-4197-1028-5(1), Abrams Bks. for Young Readers) Abrams, Inc.

Favor, Lesli J. Women Doctors & Nurses of the Civil War. 2009. (American Women at War Ser.). 112p. (gr. 8-8). 63.90 (978-1-61511-404-7(1)) Rosen Publishing Group, Inc., The.

Favor, Leslie. Women Doctors & Nurses of the Civil War. 2009. 112p. (YA). (gr. 7-12). pap. 12.95 (978-1-4358-3273-2(6)) Rosen Publishing Group, Inc., The.

Ferguson, Amanda. American Women of the Vietnam War. 2004. (American Women at War Ser.). (Illus.). 112p. (YA). (gr. 7-12). lib. bdg. 34.60 (978-0-8239-4448-4(4)) Rosen Publishing Group, Inc., The.

Fields, J. Choosing a Career as a Nurse-Midwife. 2009. (World of Work Ser.). 64p. (gr. 5-5). 58.50 (978-1-60854-323-6(4)) Rosen Publishing Group, Inc., The.

Garnett, Emmeline. Florence Nightingale's Nuns. 2009. (Saints for Youth: Ser.). 150p. pap. 9.95 (978-1-58617-297-8(2)) Ignatius Pr.

Garrett, Winston. What Does the School Nurse Do? (¿Qué Hace la Enfermera de la Escuela?) de la Vega, Eida, ed. 2014. (Oficios en Mi Escuela / Jobs in My School Ser.). (SPA & ENG.). 24p. (J). (gr. k-2). lib. bdg. 23.60 (978-1-4777-6801-3(7), PowerKids Pr.) Rosen Publishing Group, Inc., The.

Glasscock, Sarah, et al. How Nurses Use Math. 2009. (Math in the Real World Ser.). 32p. (gr. 4-6). 28.00 (978-1-60413-607-4(3), Chelsea Clubhouse) Facts On File, Inc.

Gogerly, Liz. Doctors & Nurses. 2016. (Play the Part Ser.). (ENG., Illus.). 24p. (J). (gr. k-2). pap. 10.99 (978-0-7502-9705-9(0), Wayland) Hachette Children's Group GBR. Dist: Hachette Bk. Group.

Guillain, Charlotte. Brave Nurses. 2015. (Collins Big Cat Ser.). (ENG.). 32p. (J). (gr. 2-2). pap. 7.95 (978-0-00-759124-4(1)) HarperCollins Pubs. Ltd. GBR. Dist: Independent Pubs. Group.

Hamen, Susan E. Clara Barton: Civil War Hero & American Red Cross Founder, 1 vol. 2010. (Military Heroes Ser.). (ENG.). 112p. (J). (gr. 6-12). lib. bdg. 35.64 (978-1-60453-960-8(7)) ABDO Publishing Co.

Harkins, Susan Sales & Harkins, William H. The Life & Times of Clara Barton. 2008. (Profiles in American History Ser.). (Illus.). 48p. (J). (gr. 4-8). lib. bdg. 29.95 (978-1-58415-667-3(8)) Mitchell Lane Pubs., Inc.

Hinman, Bonnie. Florence Nightingale & the Advancement of Nursing. 2004. (Uncharted, Unexplored, & Unexplained Ser.). (Illus.). 48p. (J). (gr. 4-8). lib. bdg. 29.95 (978-1-58415-257-6(5)) Mitchell Lane Pubs., Inc.

Howell, Izzi. Edith Cavell. 2016. (Fact Cat: History Ser.). (ENG., Illus.). 24p. (J). (gr. k-2). 14.99 (978-0-7502-9772-1(7), Wayland) Hachette Children's Group GBR. Dist: Hachette Bk. Group.

—Mary Seacole. 2016. (Fact Cat: History Ser.). (ENG., Illus.). 24p. (J). (gr. k-2). 14.99 (978-0-7502-9854-4(5), Wayland) Hachette Children's Group GBR. Dist: Hachette Bk. Group.

Howell, Izzi & Wayland Publishers Staff. Florence Nightingale. 2016. (Fact Cat: History Ser.). (ENG., Illus.). 24p. (J). (gr. k-2). 14.99 (978-1-5263-0168-0(7), Wayland) Hachette Children's Group GBR. Dist: Hachette Bk. Group.

Jeffries, Joyce. Meet the Nurse. 2012. (People Around Town Ser.). (Illus.). 24p. (gr. k-2). 69.20 (978-1-4339-8061-9(4)); (J). 22.60 (978-1-4339-7332-1(4)); (J). pap. 8.15 (978-1-4339-7333-8(2)) Stevens, Gareth Publishing LLLP.

—Meet the Nurse / Te Presento A Los Enfermeros. 2012. (People Around Town / Gente de mi ciudad Ser.). (SPA & ENG., Illus.). 24p. (J). (gr. k-2). 22.60 (978-1-4339-7388-8(X)) Stevens, Gareth Publishing LLLP.

Jones, Carrie. Sarah Emma Edmonds Was a Great Pretender: The True Story of a Civil War Spy. Oldroyd, Mark, illus. 2011. (Carolrhoda Picture Bks.). (ENG.). 32p. (J). (gr. 2-5). 17.95 (978-0-7613-5399-7(2)) Lerner Publishing Group.

Kenney, Karen L. Nurses at Work, 1 vol. Dumm, Brian Caleb, illus. 2009. (Meet Your Community Workers Ser.). (ENG.). 32p. (J). (gr. -1-2). 28.50 (978-1-60270-651-4(4)) Magic Wagon.

Kishel, Ann-Marie & Rivera, Sheila. Nurse. 2007. (First Step Nonfiction - Work People Do Ser.). (ENG.). 8p. (gr. -1-1). pap. 4.95 (978-0-8225-6846-9(2)) Lerner Publishing Group.

Lakin, Patricia. Clara Barton: Spirit of the American Red Cross. Sullivan, Simon, illus. 2004. (Ready-To-read SOFA Ser.). (ENG.). 48p. (J). (gr. 1-3). pap. 3.99 (978-0-689-86513-8(9), Simon Spotlight) Simon Spotlight.

Liebman, Dan. Infirmiere. Lior, Tsipora, tr. from ENG. 2006. (Je Veux Etre Ser.). (FRE., Illus.). 24p. (J). (gr. -1-2). pap. 5.95 (978-1-55407-107-4(0), 9781554071074) Firefly Bks., Ltd.

Macken, JoAnn Early. Nurses. 2010. (People in My Community Ser.). (ENG.). 24p. (J). (gr. k-3). pap. 8.15 (978-1-4339-3807-8(3)); lib. bdg. 22.60 (978-1-4339-3806-1(5)) Stevens, Gareth Publishing LLLP.

Mara, Wil. Clara Barton. 2003. (Rookie Biographies Ser.). (ENG., Illus.). 32p. (J). (gr. 1-2). pap. 4.95 (978-0-516-27339-6(6), Children's Pr.) Scholastic Library Publishing.

Marko, Eve. Clara Barton & the American Red Cross. Marcos, Pablo, illus. 2005. (Heroes of America Ser.). 237p. (gr. 3-8). 27.07 (978-1-59679-255-5(8), Abdo & Daughters) ABDO Publishing Co.

Marsh, Carole. Clara Barton. 2003. 12p. (gr. k-4). 2.95 (978-0-635-02353-7(9)) Gallopade International.

McDoniel, Estelle. Registered Nurse to Rear Admiral: A First for Navy Women. 2003. (Illus.). viii, 81p. (J). 16.95 (978-1-57168-766-1(1), Eakin Pr.) Eakin Pr.

Mills, Nathan & Machajewski, Sarah. Nurses Are There to Help. 2012. (Rosen Readers Ser.). (ENG., Illus.). 24p. (J). (gr. 1-2). pap. 8.25 (978-1-4488-8782-8(8), Rosen Classroom) Rosen Publishing Group, Inc., The.

Minden, Cecilia & Armantrout, Linda M. Nurses. 2014. (People in Our Community Ser.). (ENG.). 24p. (J). (gr. k-3). 27.07 (978-1-62687-015-4(2), 206805) Child's World, Inc., The.

Morris, Ann. That's Our Nurse! Linenthal, Peter, illus. Linenthal, Peter, photos by. 2003. (That's Our School Ser.). (ENG.). 32p. (gr. k-3). lib. bdg. 22.60 (978-0-7613-2402-7(X), Millbrook Pr.) Lerner Publishing Group.

Moss, Marissa. Nurse, Soldier, Spy: The Story of Sarah Edmonds, a Civil War Hero. Hendrix, John, illus. 2011. (ENG.). 48p. (J). (gr. 3-7). 19.95 (978-0-8109-9735-6(5), Abrams Bks. for Young Readers) Abrams, Inc.

Murray, Aaron R. Nurses Help Us. 2012. (All about Community Helpers Ser.). (Illus.). 24p. (J). (gr. -1-1). 22.60 (978-0-7660-4044-1(5), Enslow Elementary) Enslow Pubs., Inc.

Murray, Julie. Nurses, 1 vol. 2010. (Buddy Bks.). (ENG.). 32p. (J). (gr. 2-5). 27.07 (978-1-61613-507-2(7)) ABDO Publishing Co.

Nardo, Don. Clara Barton: Face Danger, but Never Fear It. 2008. (Americans—the Spirit of a Nation Ser.). (Illus.). 128p. (J). (gr. 3-7). lib. bdg. 33.27 (978-0-7660-3024-4(5)) Enslow Pubs., Inc.

Parkes, Elle. Hooray for Nurses! 2016. (Bumba Books (tm) — Hooray for Community Helpers! Ser.). (ENG., Illus.). 24p. (J). (gr. -1-1). lib. bdg. 25.32 (978-1-5124-1444-8(1)) Lerner Publishing Group.

Parkes, Elle. Que Vivan Las Enfermeras! 2017. (Bumba Books (tm) en Español — ¡Que Vivan Los Ayudantes Comunitarios! (Hooray for Community Helpers!) Ser.). (SPA.). 24p. (J). (gr. -1-1). 25.32 **(978-1-5124-4139-0(2))** Lerner Publishing Group.

Polacco, Patricia. Clara & Davie. 2014. (ENG.). 40p. (J). (gr. -1-k). 18.99 (978-0-545-35477-6(3), Scholastic Pr.) Scholastic, Inc.

Ransom, Candice. Clara Barton. 2003. (History Maker Bios Ser.). (Illus.). 48p. (J). (gr. 3-5). lib. bdg. 26.60 (978-0-8225-4677-1(9)) Lerner Publishing Group.

Ready, Dee. Nurses Help, 1 vol. 2013. (Our Community Helpers Ser.). (ENG.). 24p. (gr. k-1). pap. 6.29 (978-1-62065-849-9(6)); pap. 35.70 (978-1-62065-850-5(X)); lib. bdg. 21.99 (978-1-62065-080-6(0)) Capstone Press of Coughlan Cos. (Pebble Bks.).

Reef, Catherine. Florence Nightingale: The Courageous Life of the Legendary Nurse. 2016. (ENG., Illus.). 192p. (YA). (gr. 7). 18.99 (978-0-544-53580-0(4)) Houghton Mifflin Harcourt Publishing Co.

Richter, Sandy. The Life of Florence Nightingale. 2009. (Real Life Readers Ser.). 16p. (gr. 2-3). pap. 7.05 (978-1-4358-0225-4(X), Rosen Classroom) Rosen Publishing Group, Inc., The.

Riggs, Kate. Seedlings: Nurses. 2017. (Seedlings Ser.). (ENG.). 24p. (J). (gr. -1-1). pap. 7.99 **(978-1-62832-489-1(9)**, Creative Paperbacks) Creative Co., The.

Robbins, Trina. Florence Nightingale: Lady with the Lamp, 1 vol. Timmons, Anne, illus. 2007. (Graphic Biographies Ser.). (ENG.). 32p. (gr. 3-4). per. 8.10 (978-0-7368-7902-6(1), 1264942, Graphic Library) Capstone Press of Coughlan Cos.

Robbins, Trina & Capstone Press Staff. Florence Nightingale: Lady with the Lamp, 1 vol. Timmons, Anne, illus. 2007. (Graphic Biographies Ser.). (ENG.). 32p. (gr. 3-4). 30.65 (978-0-7368-6850-1(X), Graphic Library) Capstone Press of Coughlan Cos.

Rose, Mary Catherine. Clara Barton: Soldier of Mercy. Johnson, E. Harper, illus. 2011. 80p. 37.95 (978-1-258-07364-0(1)) Literary Licensing, LLC.

Ross, Stewart. Don't Say No to Flo: The Story of Florence Nightingale. Shields, Susan, illus. 32p. (J). pap. (978-0-7502-3273-9(0), Wayland) Hachette Children's Group.

Simon, Samantha. Nurses. 2017. (Careers in Healthcare Ser.: Vol. 13). (ENG.). (YA). (gr. 7-12). 23.95 **(978-1-4222-3800-4(8))** Mason Crest.

Simons, Rae & Gommer, Viola Ruelke. Nurse. Riggs, Ernestine G. & Gholar, Cheryl, eds. 2013. (Careers with Character Ser.: 18). 96p. (J). (gr. 7-18). 22.95 (978-1-4222-2761-9(8)) Mason Crest.

Spinner, Stephanie. Who Was Clara Barton? Groff, David, illus. 2014. 103p. (J). lib. bdg. (978-1-4844-3355-3(6), Grosset & Dunlap) Penguin Publishing Group.

—Who Was Clara Barton? Harrison, Nancy & Groff, David, illus. 2014. (Who Was? Ser.). (ENG.). 112p. (J). (gr. 3-7). 5.99 (978-0-448-47953-8(2), Grosset & Dunlap) Penguin Young Readers Group.

Strange, Cordelia. Physicians Assistants & Nurses: New Opportunities in the 21st-Century Health System. 2010. (New Careers for the 21st Century Ser.). 64p. (YA). (gr. 7-18). pap. 9.95 (978-1-4222-2041-2(9)); lib. bdg. 22.95 (978-1-4222-1820-4(1)) Mason Crest.

Tieck, Sarah. Florence Nightingale, 1 vol. 2006. (First Biographies Ser.). (ENG., Illus.). 32p. (gr. -1-3). 27.07 (978-1-59679-786-4(X), Buddy Bks.) ABDO Publishing Co.

Time for Kids Editors. Clara Barton: Angel of the Battlefield. 2008. (Time for Kids Ser.). (ENG., Illus.). 48p. (J). (gr. 2-4). pap. 3.99 (978-0-06-057622-6(7), Collins) HarperCollins Pubs.

Trumbauer, Lisa. What Does a Nurse Do? 2006. (What Does a Community Helper Do? Ser.). (Illus.). 24p. (J). (gr. 1-3). lib. bdg. 22.60 (978-0-7660-2325-3(7), Enslow Elementary) Enslow Pubs., Inc.

Vogel, Elizabeth. Meet the School Nurse. 2009. (My School Ser.). 24p. (gr. 1-2). 37.50 (978-1-61514-708-3(X), PowerKids Pr.) Rosen Publishing Group, Inc., The.

Wade, Mary Dodson. Amazing Civil War Nurse Clara Barton. (Amazing Americans Ser.). (Illus.). 24p. (J). 2013. (gr. k-3). pap. 7.95 (978-0-7660-5977-1(4), Enslow Elementary) 2009. (gr. 1-3). lib. bdg. 22.60 (978-0-7660-3281-1(7)) Enslow Pubs., Inc.

Wohlrabe, Sarah C. Helping You Heal: A Book about Nurses, 1 vol. Thomas, Eric, illus. 2003. (Community Workers Ser.). (ENG.). 24p. (gr. -1-3). per. 8.95 (978-1-4048-0480-7(3)) Picture Window Bks.

Zeiger, Jennifer. What Do They Do? Nurses. 2010. (Community Connections: What Do They Do? Ser.). (ENG.). 24p. (gr. 2-5). lib. bdg. 25.64 (978-1-60279-808-3(7), 200506) Cherry Lake Publishing.

Zemlicka, Shannon. Florence Nightingale. Debon, Nicolas, illus. 2003. (On My Own Biography Ser.). (ENG.). 48p. (gr. 2-4). pap. 6.95 (978-0-87614-102-1(5), Carolrhoda Bks.) Lerner Publishing Group.

NURSES—FICTION

Binger, Christine. Show Me Some Urgency, I'm an Emergency: A trip to the ER. 2010. 16p. 8.49 (978-1-4490-9318-1(3)) AuthorHouse.

Bloch, Robert. The Crowded Earth. 2009. 112p. 22.95 (978-1-60664-648-9(6)); pap. 9.95 (978-1-60664-273-3(1)) Rodgers, Alan Bks.

Brand, Christianna. Nurse Matilda Goes to Hospital. Ardizzone, Edward, illus. (ENG.). 128p. (978-0-7475-7678-5(5)) Bloomsbury Publishing Plc GBR. Dist: Macmillan.

Daley, Robert. What Color Are You? 2007. (Illus.). 34p. (J). pap. 8.75 (978-0-9800839-1-0(5)) Daley, Robert.

Davidson, Michele R. Stowaways to Smith Island: Hayden & Chloe's Enchanted Journey with the Nurses to Maryland's Mysterious Smith Island. Watjen, Laureen, illus. 2004. 128p. (J). pap. 8.95 (978-0-9754170-1-0(0)) Smith Island Foundation.

Dunlap, Susanne. In the Shadow of the Lamp. 2012. (ENG., Illus.). 320p. (YA). (gr. 7). pap. 9.99 (978-1-59990-753-6(4), 9781599907536, Bloomsbury USA Childrens) Bloomsbury Publishing USA.

Eleanor Hallowell Abbott. The White Linen Nurse. l.t. ed. 2007. (ENG.). 156p. pap. 21.99 (978-1-4264-8087-4(3)) Creative Media Partners, LLC.

Farenhorst, Christine. A Cup of Cold Water: The Compassion of Nurse Edith Cavell. 2007. 222p. (J). (gr. 3-7). per. 11.99 (978-1-59638-026-4(8)) P & R Publishing.

Gutman, Dan. Mrs. Cooney Is Loony! Paillot, Jim, illus. 2005. (My Weird School Ser.: 7). (ENG.). 112p. (J). (gr. 1-5). pap. 4.99 (978-0-06-074522-6(3)) HarperCollins Pubs.

Hammock, Mary B. Msn Cpnp. Princess Reagan & the Paci Fairy. 2012. 24p. pap. 15.99 (978-1-4797-1074-4(1)) Xlibris Corp.

Hendry, Frances. Quest for a Queen: The Falcon. 2006. pap. (978-1-905665-06-8(7)) Pollinger In Print.

Hill, Maree. Nurse Nerid. 2011. 28p. pap. 28.03 (978-1-4568-5419-5(4)) Xlibris Corp.

Hooper, Mary. Poppy. 2016. (ENG.). 288p. (YA). 17.99 (978-1-61963-496-1(1), 9781619634961, Bloomsbury USA Childrens) Bloomsbury Publishing USA.

Howat, Irene. On His Majesty's Service. 2008. (Trailblazers Ser.). (ENG.). 176p. (J). (gr. 4-9). per. 8.99 (978-1-84550-259-1(0), bea45fc4-969e-4e89-84fe-2abf3d4baa6d) Christian Focus Pubns. GBR. Dist: Bookmasters Distribution.

Jackson, Kathryn. Nurse Nancy. Malvern, Corinne, illus. 2005. (Little Golden Book Ser.). (ENG.). 24p. (J). (gr. -1-2). 4.99 (978-0-375-83262-8(9), Golden Bks.) Random Hse. Children's Bks.

Jacobs, Evan. FatherSonFather, 1 vol. 2015. (Gravel Road Ser.). (ENG.). (YA). (gr. 9-12). pap. 9.95 (978-1-68021-038-5(6)) Saddleback Educational Publishing, Inc.

—Fathersonfather. 2015. (Gravel Road Ser.). (YA). lib. bdg. 20.80 (978-0-606-37959-5(2)) Turtleback Bks.

James, Simon. Nurse Clementine. 2013. (ENG.). 40p. (J). (gr. -1-2). 15.99 (978-0-7636-6382-7(4)) Candlewick Pr.

Juslin, Lee. Nurse Frosty & the Four Paws Retirement Home. 2009. 36p. pap. 20.00 (978-1-4357-5568-0(5)) Lulu Pr., Inc.

Kemnitz, Dianna. Mia, Jack & Nurse Olivi. 2012. 40p. pap. 24.95 (978-1-4626-8795-4(4)) America Star Bks.

Ladd, Debbie. Nurse Robin's Hats. Nakasone, Shaun, illus. 2006. 52p. (J). 16.95 (978-0-9727615-3-6(5)) Deb on Air Bks.

LeSourd, Nancy. Secrets of Civil War Spies, 1 vol. 2008. (Liberty Letters Ser.). (ENG.). 224p. (J). pap. 7.99 (978-0-310-71390-6(0)) Zonderkidz.

Machajewski, Sarah. My Dad Is a Nurse. 2012. (InfoMax Readers Ser.). (ENG., Illus.). 24p. (J). (gr. 1-2). pap. 8.25 (978-1-4488-9001-9(2), Rosen Classroom) Rosen Publishing Group, Inc., The.

McDaniel, Lurlene. Losing Gabriel: a Love Story. 2017. (ENG.). 336p. (YA). (gr. 7). pap. 9.99 **(978-0-385-74422-5(6)**, Ember) Random Hse. Children's Bks.

Nancy St. Paul-Martin. Go to the Nurse: Peanut Puffs & Snicker-Doodles. 2009. 28p. pap. 15.49 (978-1-4389-7653-2(4)) AuthorHouse.

Norman, Thelma G. A Wife Called Tommie. 2005. 226p. per. 14.95 (978-1-57258-295-8(2)) TEACH Services, Inc.

Nurse, B. A. Outrageously Cool Nurses. 2007. 84p. per. 8.95 (978-0-595-43530-2(0)) iUniverse, Inc.

Osborne, Mary Pope. High Time for Heroes. Murdocca, Sal, illus. 2016. (Magic Tree House Merlin Mission Ser.: 23). (ENG.). 144p. (J). (gr. 2-5). 5.99 (978-0-307-98052-6(9), Random Hse. Bks. for Young Readers) Random Hse. Children's Bks.

Paul, Bette. Nurses: Claire's Conquests & Jan's Journey. 2007. 312p. per. (978-1-905665-43-3(1)) Pollinger In Print.

—Nurses: Katie Goes to College (Large Pri. 2006. pap. (978-1-905665-09-9(1)) Pollinger In Print.

—Nurses: Nikki, Barbara & Nick. 2007. 488p. per. (978-1-905665-44-0(X)) Pollinger In Print.

Rothstein, Evelyn. My Great Grandpa Dave. 2007. (J). per. 12.95 (978-0-9786745-1-9(0)) Marble Hse. Editions.

Sawyer, Ruth. The Primrose Ring. 2007. 104p. per. (978-1-4065-3881-6(7)) Dodo Pr.

Siebold, Jan. Doing Time Online. 2004. 88p. (gr. 4-7). 17.50 (978-0-7569-3612-9(8)) Perfection Learning Corp.

Spanyol, Jessica. Clive Is a Nurse. Spanyol, Jessica, illus. 2017. (Clive's Jobs Ser.: 4). (ENG., Illus.). 14p. (J). bds. **(978-1-84643-991-9(4))** Child's Play International Ltd.

Stevens, Serita. The Adventure Begins. 2004. (Illus.). 182p. (978-0-9753548-1-0(7)) Palm Publishing LLC.

Thaler, Mike. The School Nurse from the Black Lagoon, 1 vol. Lee, Jared, illus. 2011. (Black Lagoon Set 1 Ser.: No. 1). (ENG.). 32p. (gr. -1-2). lib. bdg. 24.21 (978-1-59961-798-5(6)) Spotlight.

Van Dyne, Edith. Aunt Jane's Nieces in the Red Cross. rev. ed. 2006. 180p. 26.95 (978-1-4218-1724-8(1)); pap. 11.95 (978-1-4218-1824-5(8)) 1st World Publishing, Inc. (1st World Library - Literary Society).

Wells, Helen. Cherry Ames, Army Nurse. 2005. (Cherry Ames Nurse Stories Ser.: Bk. 3). 224p. (J). (gr. 4-7). 14.95 (978-0-9771597-2-7(8)) Springer Publishing Co., Inc.

—Cherry Ames at Hilton Hospital: Book 13. 2007. (Cherry Ames Nurse Stories Ser.). 224p. (J). (gr. 3-7). 14.95 (978-0-8261-0421-2(5)) Springer Publishing Co., Inc.

—Cherry Ames, Boarding School Nurse. 10th ed. 2007. (Cherry Ames Nurse Stories Ser.). 224p. (YA). (gr. 7-12). 14.95 (978-0-8261-0413-7(4)) Springer Publishing Co., Inc.

—Cherry Ames Boxed Set: Volumes 17-20. 2007. 896p. (J). 39.95 (978-0-8261-0439-7(8)) Springer Publishing Co., Inc.

—Cherry Ames, Camp Nurse. 2007. (Cherry Ames Nurse Stories Ser.). 224p. (YA). (gr. 7-12). 14.95 (978-0-8261-0417-5(7)) Springer Publishing Co., Inc.

—Cherry Ames, Chief Nurse. 2005. (Cherry Ames Nurse Stories Ser.: Bk. 4). 224p. (YA). (gr. 8-12). 14.95 (978-0-9771597-3-4(6)) Springer Publishing Co., Inc.

—Cherry Ames, Companion Nurse. 2007. (Cherry Ames Nurse Stories Ser.). 224p. (J). (gr. 3-7). 14.95 (978-0-8261-0431-1(2)) Springer Publishing Co., Inc.

—Cherry Ames, Cruise Nurse. 2007. (Cherry Ames Nurse Stories Ser.). 232p. (YA). (gr. 7-12). 14.95 (978-0-8261-0411-3(8)) Springer Publishing Co., Inc.

—Cherry Ames, Department Store Nurse. 2007. (Cherry Ames Nurse Stories Ser.). 224p. (YA). (gr. 8-12). 14.95 (978-0-8261-0415-1(0)) Springer Publishing Co., Inc.

—Cherry Ames, Flight Nurse. 2006. (Cherry Ames Nurse Stories Ser.). 224p. (J). (gr. 3-7). 14.95 (978-0-8261-0397-0(9)) Springer Publishing Co., Inc.

—Cherry Ames, Island Nurse. 2007. (Cherry Ames Nurse Stories Ser.). 224p. (J). (gr. 3-7). 14.95 (978-0-8261-0423-6(1)) Springer Publishing Co., Inc.

—Cherry Ames Jungle Nurse. 2007. (Cherry Ames Nurse Stories Ser.). 224p. (J). (gr. 3-7). 14.95 (978-0-8261-0433-5(9)) Springer Publishing Co., Inc.

—Cherry Ames, Private Duty Nurse. 2006. (Cherry Ames Nurse Stories Ser.). 224p. (J). (gr. 3-7). 14.95 (978-0-8261-0398-7(7)) Springer Publishing Co., Inc.

—Cherry Ames, Rural Nurse. 2007. (Cherry Ames Nurse Stories Ser.). 224p. (J). (gr. 3-7). 14.95 (978-0-8261-0425-0(8)) Springer Publishing Co., Inc.

—Cherry Ames, Senior Nurse. 2005. (Cherry Ames Nurse Stories Ser.: Bk. 2). 224p. (J). (gr. 4-7). 14.95 (978-0-9771597-1-0(X)) Springer Publishing Co., Inc.

—Cherry Ames, Ski Nurse Mystery. 2007. (Cherry Ames Nurse Stories Ser.). 224p. (J). (gr. 3-7). 14.95 (978-0-8261-0437-3(1)) Springer Publishing Co., Inc.

—Cherry Ames, Staff Nurse. 2007. (Cherry Ames Nurse Stories Ser.). 176p. (J). (gr. 3-7). 14.95 (978-0-8261-0427-4(4)) Springer Publishing Co., Inc.

—Cherry Ames, Student Nurse. 2005. (Cherry Ames Nurse Stories Ser.: Bk. 1). 224p. (J). (gr. 4-7). 14.95 (978-0-9771597-0-3(1)) Springer Publishing Co., Inc.

—Cherry Ames, the Mystery in the Doctor's Office. 2007. (Cherry Ames Nurse Stories Ser.). 224p. (J). (gr. 3-7). 14.95 (978-0-8261-0435-9(5)) Springer Publishing Co., Inc.

—Cherry Ames Veteran's Nurse. 2006. (Cherry Ames Nurse Stories Ser.). 224p. (J). (gr. 3-7). 14.95 (978-0-8261-0400-7(2)) Springer Publishing Co., Inc.

—Cherry Ames, Visiting Nurse. 2006. (Cherry Ames Nurse Stories Ser.). 224p. (J). (gr. 3-7). 14.95 (978-0-8261-0399-4(5)) Springer Publishing Co., Inc.

Wick, Elaine. It's MY Future: Should I Be a Nurse Practitioner? Tremaine, Michele, illus. 2004. 64p. (J). lib. bdg. 12.95 (978-0-9749769-0-7(3)) NAPNAP.

Yonge, Charlotte M. Little Lucy's Wonderful Globe. 2007. 52p. per. (978-1-4065-5529-5(0)) Dodo Pr.

—Little Lucy's Wonderful Globe. 2007. 156p. per. 21.95 (978-0-548-67542-7(2)) 2004. reprint ed. pap. 15.95 (978-1-4191-3079-3(X)) Kessinger Publishing, LLC.

NURSES AND NURSING

see Nurses; Nursing

NURSING

Arnold, Quinn M. Nurses. 2017. (J). **(978-1-60818-874-1(4)**, Creative Education) Creative Co., The.

Bickerstaff, Linda. What Degree Do I Need to Pursue a Career in Nursing?, 1 vol. 2015. (ENG., Illus.). 80p. (J). 34.60 (978-1-4777-7857-9(8), Rosen Young Adult) Rosen Publishing Group, Inc., The.

Blount, Rachel. Nurse. 2017. (Here to Help Ser.). (ENG., Illus.). 24p. (J). (gr. k-2). 16.99 (978-1-4451-4011-7(X), Franklin Watts) Hachette Children's Group GBR. Dist: Hachette Bk. Group.

Careers in Focus - Nursing. 4th rev. ed. 2011. (Careers in Focus Ser.). (Illus.). 224p. (gr. 6-12). 32.95 (978-0-8160-8034-2(8), Ferguson Publishing Co.) Facts On File, Inc.

Caviezel, Giovanni. Nurse. Mesturini, C., illus. 2011. (Mini People Shape Bks.). (ENG.). 10p. (J). bds. 5.99 (978-0-7641-6440-8(6)) Barron's Educational Series, Inc.

Cunningham, Kevin. Nurse. 2015. (21st Century Skills Library: Cool STEAM Careers Ser.). (ENG., Illus.). 32p. (J). (gr. 4-7). 29.93 (978-1-63362-561-7(3), 206428) Cherry Lake Publishing.

Greenhaven Press Editors & Craig, Lizabeth. The History of Nursing. Hardman, Lizabeth, ed. 2013. (World History Ser.). (ENG., Illus.). 128p. (gr. 7-10). lib. bdg. 39.90 (978-1-4205-0823-9(7), Lucent Bks.) Cengage Gale.

Jeffries, Joyce. Meet the Nurse. 2012. (People Around Town Ser.). (Illus.). 24p. (gr. k-2). 69.20 (978-1-4339-8061-9(4)); (J). 22.60 (978-1-4339-7332-1(4)); (J). pap. 8.15 (978-1-4339-7333-8(2)) Stevens, Gareth Publishing LLLP.

—Meet the Nurse / Te Presento A Los Enfermeros. 2012. (People Around Town / Gente de mi ciudad Ser.). (SPA & ENG., Illus.). 24p. (J). (gr. k-2). 22.60 (978-1-4339-7388-8(X)) Stevens, Gareth Publishing LLLP.

Minden, Cecilia & Armantrout, Linda M. Nurses. 2014. (People in Our Community Ser.). (ENG.). 24p. (J). (gr. k-3). 27.07 (978-1-62687-015-4(2), 206805) Child's World, Inc., The.

Murray, Aaron R. Nurses Help Us. 2012. (All about Community Helpers Ser.). (Illus.). 24p. (J). (gr. -1-1). 22.60 (978-0-7660-4044-1(5), Enslow Elementary) Enslow Pubs., Inc.

Nursing. 2nd rev. ed. 2007. (What Can I Do Now? Ser.). 208p. (YA). (gr. 7-12). 29.95 (978-0-8160-6028-3(2)) Facts On File, Inc.

Parkes, Elle. Hooray for Nurses! 2016. (Bumba Books (tm) — Hooray for Community Helpers! Ser.). (ENG., Illus.). 24p. (J). (gr. -1-1). lib. bdg. 25.32 (978-1-5124-1444-8(1)) Lerner Publishing Group.

Riggs, Kate. Seedlings: Nurses. 2017. (Seedlings Ser.). (ENG.). 24p. (J). (gr. -1-1). pap. 7.99 **(978-1-62832-489-1(9)**, Creative Paperbacks) Creative Co., The.

Simons, Rae & Gommer, Viola Ruelke. Nurse. Riggs, Ernestine G. & Gholar, Cheryl, eds. 2013. (Careers with

Character Ser.: 18). 96p. (J). (gr. 7-18). 22.95 *(978-1-4222-2761-9(8))* Mason Crest.
Wasson, E. & Strausser, A. Mommies & Daddies Are Nurses. Ebert, Roey, illus. 2011. 32p. pap. 15.99 *(978-1-4634-3451-9(0))* AuthorHouse.

NURSING—FICTION

James, Simon. Nurse Clementine. 2013. (ENG.). 40p. (J). (gr. -1-2). 15.99 *(978-0-7636-6382-7(4))* Candlewick Pr.
Repkin, Mark. Mommy Breastfeeds My Baby Brother/ Mama Amamanta A Mi Hermanito. Moneysmith, David, illus. 2011.Tr. of Mama Amamanta A Mi Hermanito. 24p. (J). pap. 9.99 *(978-0-9816538-1-5(2))* Istoria Hse.
Stier, Catherine. What's Bugging Nurse Penny? A Story about Lice. Beaky, Suzanne, illus. 2013. (ENG.). 32p. (J). (gr. -1-3). 16.99 *(978-0-8075-8803-1(2))* Whitman, Albert & Co.
Wakem, Samantha. Milly's Magic Play House: The Hospital, 1 vol. Herridge, Debbie, illus. 2010. 20p. 24.95 *(978-1-4489-5114-7(3))* PublishAmerica, Inc.

NUTRITION

see also Diet; Digestion; Food; Metabolism; Vitamins

ABDO Publishing Company Staff. Mission: Nutrition, 1 vol. 2012. (Mission: Nutrition Ser.: 6). (ENG., Illus.). 32p. 162.42 *(978-1-61783-079-2(8),* Checkerboard Library) ABDO Publishing Co.
ABDO Publishing Company Staff & Rondeau, Amanda. What Should I Eat?, 1 vol. 2003. (What Should I Eat? Ser.: 6). (ENG., Illus.). 24p. (J). (gr. k-3). lib. bdg. 145.26 *(978-1-57765-831-3(0),* SandCastle) ABDO Publishing Co.
Adams, Julia. Proteins. 2011. (Good Food Ser.). (ENG.). 24p. (J). lib. bdg. 22.60 *(978-1-4488-3272-9(1),* PowerKids Pr.) Rosen Publishing Group, Inc., The.
Alexander's Enrichment Activties. 2006. (J). pap. 5.95 *(978-0-9742806-6-0(6))* Heart to Heart Publishing, Inc.
Allsop, Marcus. We Like to Help Cook: Nos Gusta Ayudar a Cocinar. Iverson, Diane, illus. 2015. (ENG.). 32p. (J). (gr. -1-1). pap. 9.95 *(978-1-890772-70-3(4))* Hohm Pr.
—We Like to Help Cook: Nos Gusta Ayudar a Cocinar. Iverson, Diane, illus. (We Like To Ser.). 32p. 2011. (SPA & ENG.). pap. 10.95 *(978-1-935826-00-2(X))* 2011th alt. ed. 2012. (ENG.). pap. 9.95 *(978-1-935826-05-7(0))* Kalindi Pr.
Allsop, Marcus & Iverson, Diane. Nos Gusta Ayudar a Cocinar: We Like to Help Cook. Iverson, Diane, illus. 2009. (SPA & ENG., Illus.). (J). pap. *(978-1-890772-97-0(6))* Hohm Pr.
Aloian, Molly. Why We Need Carbohydrates. 2011. (Science of Nutrition Ser.). (ENG.). 48p. (J). (gr. 5-9). lib. bdg. *(978-0-7787-1686-0(4))*; pap. *(978-0-7787-1693-8(7))* Crabtree Publishing Co.
—Why We Need Fats. 2011. (Science of Nutrition Ser.). (ENG.). 48p. (J). (gr. 5-9). *(978-0-7787-1687-7(2))*; pap. *(978-0-7787-1694-5(5))* Crabtree Publishing Co.
Anthony, Mark, et al. Gut Instinct: Diet's Missing Link. 2003. (Illus.). 216p. per. 19.95 *(978-0-9743664-0-1(4))* Leap Forward Pubns.
Antill, Sara. 10 Ways I Can Live A Healthy Life. 2012. (I Can Make a Difference Ser.). (ENG., Illus.). 24p. (J). (gr. 2-5). 22.60 *(978-1-4488-6207-8(8))*; pap. 8.25 *(978-1-4488-6373-0(2))* Rosen Publishing Group, Inc., The. (PowerKids Pr.).
April, Elyse. We Like to Eat Well. Agrell, Lewis, illus. 2010th rev. ed. 2013. (We Like To Ser.). (ENG.). 32p. pap. 9.95 *(978-1-935826-04-0(2))* Kalindi Pr.
—We Like to Eat Well/Nos Gusta Comer Bien. Agrell, Lewis, illus. 2011th alt. ed. 2011. (We Like To Ser.). (ENG.). 32p. pap. 10.95 *(978-1-935826-01-9(8))* Kalindi Pr.
Ayer, Paula & Banyard, Antonia. Eat Up! An Infographic Exploration of Food. Wuthrich, Belle, illus. 2017. (Visual Exploration Ser.). (ENG.). 72p. (gr. 3-7). 22.95 *(978-1-55451-884-5(9))* Annick Pr., Ltd. CAN. Dist: Publishers Group West (PGW).
—Eat Up! An Infographic Exploration of Food. Wuthrich, Belle, illus. 2017. (Visual Exploration Ser.). (ENG.). 72p. (gr. 3-7). pap. 12.95 *(978-1-55451-883-8(0))* Annick Pr., Ltd. CAN. Dist: Publishers Group West (PGW).
Barraclough, Sue & Lanz, Helen. Eat & Drink. 2012. (Healthy Habits Ser.). 24p. (gr. 1-3). lib. bdg. 24.25 *(978-1-59771-307-8(4))* Sea-To-Sea Pubns.
Beck, Leslie. Healthy Eating for Preteens & Teens: The Ultimate Guide to Diet Nutrition & Food. 2005. (ENG.). 304p. (J). (gr. 7-18). 25.50 *(978-0-14-301720-2(9),* Penguin Canada) Penguin Canada CAN. Dist: Penguin Random Hse. LLC.
Bellisario, Gina. Choose Good Food! My Eating Tips. Conger, Holli, illus. 2014. (Cloverleaf Books — My Healthy Habits Ser.). (ENG.). 24p. (gr. k-2). lib. bdg. 23.93 *(978-1-4677-1350-4(3),* Millbrook Pr.) Lerner Publishing Group.
Benchmark Education Company, LLC Staff, compiled by. Nutrition & Exercise. 2006. (J). 91.00 *(978-1-4108-7036-0(7))* Benchmark Education Co.
Benduhn, Tea. Fruit: Fruta. 2007. (Find Out about Food/ Conoce la comida Ser.). (SPA & ENG.). 24p. (gr. k-3). pap. 8.15 *(978-0-8368-8462-3(0),* Weekly Reader Leveled Readers) Stevens, Gareth Publishing LLLP.
—Fruit/Fruta. 2007. (Find Out about Food/Conoce la Comida Ser.). (SPA & ENG., Illus.). 24p. (gr. k-3). lib. bdg. 22.00 *(978-0-8368-8455-5(8),* Weekly Reader Leveled Readers) Stevens, Gareth Publishing LLLP.
Berger, Melvin & Berger, Gilda. Healthy Eating. 2007. (Now I Know Ser.). (Illus.). 32p. (J). *(978-0-439-02446-4(3))* Scholastic, Inc.
Bickerstaff, Linda. Careers in Nutrition. 2009. (Careers in the New Economy Ser.). 144p. (gr. 7-7). 63.90 *(978-1-61511-818-2(7))* Rosen Publishing Group, Inc., The.
Bodden, Valerie. Eating Healthy. 2015. (J). *(978-1-60818-507-8(9),* Creative Education) Creative Co., The.
—Grains. 2015. (J). *(978-1-60818-510-8(9),* Creative Education) Creative Co., The.
—Healthy Plates: Eating Healthy. 2015. (Healthy Plates Ser.). (ENG.). 24p. (J). (gr. 1-3). pap. 9.99 *(978-1-62832-107-4(5),* Creative Paperbacks) Creative Co., The.
—Healthy Plates: Fruits. 2015. (Healthy Plates Ser.). (ENG.). 24p. (J). (gr. 1-3). pap. 9.99 *(978-1-62832-109-8(1),* Creative Paperbacks) Creative Co., The.
—Healthy Plates: Grains. 2015. (Healthy Plates Ser.). (ENG.). 24p. (J). (gr. 1-3). pap. 9.99 *(978-1-62832-110-4(5),* Creative Paperbacks) Creative Co., The.
—Healthy Plates: Proteins. 2015. (Healthy Plates Ser.). (ENG.). 24p. (J). (gr. 1-3). pap. 9.99 *(978-1-62832-111-1(3),* Creative Paperbacks) Creative Co., The.
—Healthy Plates: Vegetables. 2015. (Healthy Plates Ser.). (ENG.). 24p. (J). (gr. 1-3). pap. 9.99 *(978-1-62832-112-8(1),* Creative Paperbacks) Creative Co., The.
Boothroyd, Jennifer. Taste Something New! Giving Different Foods a Try. 2016. (Lightning Bolt Books — Healthy Eating Ser.). (ENG., Illus.). 32p. (J). (gr. 1-3). 26.65 *(978-1-4677-9472-5(4),* Lerner Pubns.) Lerner Publishing Group.
—What's on My Plate? 2016. (Lightning Bolt Books — Healthy Eating Ser.). (ENG., Illus.). 32p. (J). (gr. 1-3). 26.65 *(978-1-4677-9470-1(8),* Lerner Pubns.) Lerner Publishing Group.
—What's on My Plate? Choosing from the Five Food Groups. 2016. (Lightning Bolt Books — Healthy Eating Ser.). (ENG., Illus.). 32p. (gr. 1-3). 39.99 *(978-1-5124-1669-5(X),* Lerner Digital); (J). (gr. 2-3). E-Book 39.99 *(978-1-4677-9672-9(7),* 9781467796729, Lerner Pubns.) Lerner Publishing Group.
Borgert-Spaniol, Megan. Dairy Group. 2012. (Eating Right with Myplate Ser.). (ENG., Illus.). 24p. (J). (gr. k-3). lib. bdg. 25.95 *(978-1-60014-754-8(2),* Blastoff! Readers) Bellwether Media.
—Fruit Group. 2012. (Eating Right with Myplate Ser.). (ENG., Illus.). 24p. (J). (gr. k-3). lib. bdg. 25.95 *(978-1-60014-755-5(0),* Blastoff! Readers) Bellwether Media.
—Healthy Eating. 2012. (Eating Right with Myplate Ser.). (ENG., Illus.). 24p. (J). (gr. k-3). lib. bdg. 25.95 *(978-1-60014-757-9(7),* Blastoff! Readers) Bellwether Media.
—Protein Foods Group. 2012. (Eating Right with Myplate Ser.). (ENG., Illus.). 24p. (J). (gr. k-3). lib. bdg. 25.95 *(978-1-60014-759-3(3),* Blastoff! Readers) Bellwether Media.
—Vegetable Group. 2012. (Eating Right with Myplate Ser.). (ENG., Illus.). 24p. (J). (gr. k-3). lib. bdg. 25.95 *(978-1-60014-760-9(7),* Blastoff! Readers) Bellwether Media.
Bow, James. Why We Need Minerals. 2011. (Science of Nutrition Ser.). (ENG.). 48p. (J). (gr. 5-9). lib. bdg. *(978-0-7787-1688-4(0))*; pap. *(978-0-7787-1695-2(3))* Crabtree Publishing Co.
Brancato, Robin F. Food Choices: The Ultimate Teen Guide. 2010. (It Happened to Me Ser.: 28). (ENG.). 240p. (gr. 7-10). 50.00 *(978-0-8108-6109-1(7))* Scarecrow Pr., Inc.
Brew Ed.D., Ranelle L. Healthy Days. 2013. 24p. pap. 10.96 *(978-1-4669-6005-3(1))* Trafford Publishing.
Burstein, John. Delicious Dairy. 2009. (Slim Goodbody's Nutrition Edition Ser.). (ENG., Illus.). 24p. (J). (gr. k-3). pap. *(978-0-7787-5056-7(6))*; lib. bdg. *(978-0-7787-5041-3(8))* Crabtree Publishing Co.
—Fabulous Fruits. 2009. (Slim Goodbody's Nutrition Edition Ser.). (ENG., Illus.). 24p. (J). (gr. k-3). pap. *(978-0-7787-5057-4(4))*; lib. bdg. *(978-0-7787-5042-0(6))* Crabtree Publishing Co.
—Glorious Grains. 2009. (Slim Goodbody's Nutrition Edition Ser.). (ENG., Illus.). 24p. (J). (gr. k-3). pap. *(978-0-7787-5058-1(2))*; lib. bdg. *(978-0-7787-5043-7(4))* Crabtree Publishing Co.
—Marvelous Meats & More. 2009. (Slim Goodbody's Nutrition Edition Ser.). (ENG., Illus.). 24p. (J). (gr. k-3). pap. *(978-0-7787-5059-8(0))*; lib. bdg. *(978-0-7787-5044-4(2))* Crabtree Publishing Co.
—Outstanding Oils & Wonderful Water. 2009. (Slim Goodbody's Nutrition Edition Ser.). (ENG., Illus.). 24p. (J). (gr. k-3). pap. *(978-0-7787-5061-1(2))*; lib. bdg. *(978-0-7787-5046-8(9))* Crabtree Publishing Co.
—Vital Vegetables. 2009. (Slim Goodbody's Nutrition Edition Ser.). (ENG., Illus.). 24p. (J). (gr. k-3). pap. *(978-0-7787-5060-4(4))*; lib. bdg. *(978-0-7787-5045-1(0))* Crabtree Publishing Co.
Burton, Margie, et al. Your Body. 2011. (Early Connections Ser.). (J). *(978-1-61672-549-5(4))* Benchmark Education Co.
Butterworth, Christine. How Did That Get in My Lunchbox? The Story of Food. Gaggiotti, Lucia, illus. 2011. (ENG.). 32p. (J). (gr. k-3). 12.99 *(978-0-7636-5005-6(6))* Candlewick Pr.
Byrd, Tracy. Fruits & Vegetables & How They Grow: A to Z. 2012. 60p. pap. 24.99 *(978-1-4772-4897-3(8))* AuthorHouse.
Canavan, Thomas. Fueling the Body: Digestion & Nutrition. 2015. (How Your Body Works). (ENG.). 32p. (J). (gr. 4-4). pap. 10.00 *(978-1-4994-1227-7(4),* PowerKids Pr.) Rosen Publishing Group, Inc., The.
Candlewick Press Staff. Fizzy's Lunch Lab: Super Supper Throwdown. Lunch Lab Staff, illus. 2014. (Fizzy's Lunch Lab Ser.). (ENG.). 64p. (J). (gr. 1-4). pap. 5.99 *(978-0-7636-6883-9(4),* Candlewick Entertainment) Candlewick Pr.
CATTCH Kids Club Nutrition. 2005. per. *(978-1-932032-19-2(3))* Flaghouse, Inc.
Centore, Michael. Fiber. 2017. (J). ***(978-1-4222-3735-9(4))*** Mason Crest.
—Salt. 2017. (J). ***(978-1-4222-3742-7(7))*** Mason Crest.
Chancellor, Deborah. Healthy Eating. 2009. (Now We Know About... Ser.). (ENG., Illus.). 24p. (J). (gr. k-3). pap. *(978-0-7787-4737-6(9))*; lib. bdg. *(978-0-7787-4720-8(4))* Crabtree Publishing Co.
Chilson, Martin. Carmen Cooks Healthy! Represent & Solve Problems Involving Division. 2014. (Math Masters: Operations & Algebraic Thinking Ser.). 24p. (J). (gr. 3-4). 23.60 *(978-1-4777-6410-7(0))*; (ENG.). pap. 8.25 *(978-1-4777-4965-4(9))* Rosen Publishing Group, Inc., The. (Rosen Classroom).
Clark, Katie. Balanced Meals. 2013. (Healthy Eating with Myplate Ser.). (ENG.). 24p. (J). (gr. 1-4). 28.50 *(978-1-62323-599-4(5),* 206401) Child's World, Inc., The.
—The Dairy Group. 2013. (Healthy Eating with Myplate Ser.). (ENG.). 24p. (J). (gr. 1-4). 28.50 *(978-1-62323-602-1(9),* 206404) Child's World, Inc., The.
Cleary, Brian P. Macaroni & Rice & Bread by the Slice: What Is in the Grains Group? Goneau, Martin, illus. 2011. (Food Is CATegorical Ser.). (ENG.). 32p. (gr. k-3). pap. 7.95 *(978-0-7613-6386-6(6))* Lerner Publishing Group.
Cleary, Brian P. & Goneau, Martin. Macaroni & Rice & Bread by the Slice: What Is in the Grains Group? 2011. (Food Is CATegorical Ser.). pap. 45.32 *(978-0-7613-8351-2(4),* Millbrook Pr.) Lerner Publishing Group.
Cleary, Brian P. & Nelson, Jennifer K. Apples, Cherries, Red Raspberries: What Is in the Fruits Group? Goneau, Martin, illus. 2010. (Food Is CATegorical Ser.). (ENG.). 32p. (gr. k-3). lib. bdg. 25.26 *(978-1-58013-589-4(7))* Lerner Publishing Group.
—Green Beans, Potatoes, & Even Tomatoes: What Is in the Vegetables Group? Goneau, Martin, illus. 2010. (Food Is CATegorical Ser.). (ENG.). 32p. (gr. k-3). 25.26 *(978-1-58013-588-7(9))* Lerner Publishing Group.
—Macaroni & Rice & Bread by the Slice: What Is in the Grains Group? Goneau, Martin, illus. 2010. (Food Is CATegorical Ser.). (ENG.). 32p. (gr. k-3). lib. bdg. 25.26 *(978-1-58013-587-0(0))* Lerner Publishing Group.
—Yogurt & Cheeses & Ice Cream That Pleases: What Is the Milk Group? Goneau, Martin, illus. 2010. (Food Is CATegorical Ser.). (ENG.). 32p. (gr. k-3). lib. bdg. 25.26 *(978-1-58013-590-0(0))* Lerner Publishing Group.
Coan, Sharon. Bueno para Mí - Comida Saludable (Good for Me - Healthy Food) 2016. (TIME for KIDS(r) Nonfiction Readers Ser.). (SPA.). 12p. (J). (gr. k-k). 4.99 *(978-1-4938-3032-9(5))* Teacher Created Materials, Inc.
—Good for Me: Healthy Food. 2015. (TIME for KIDS(r) Nonfiction Readers Ser.). (ENG., Illus.). 12p. (gr. k-k). 4.99 *(978-1-4938-2151-8(2))* Teacher Created Materials, Inc.
Cohen, Marina. Why We Need Vitamins. 2011. (Science of Nutrition Ser.). (ENG.). 48p. (J). (gr. 5-9). lib. bdg. *(978-0-7787-1690-7(2))*; pap. *(978-0-7787-1697-6(X))* Crabtree Publishing Co.
Colored Nuts about Nutrition: Ages 7-11, 12 activity books. 2005. (J). 9.95 *(978-1-57175-176-8(9),* 6508-C) Learning ZoneXpress.
Colored Nuts about Nutrition Activity Books: Ages 2-6, 12 activity books. 2005. (J). 9.95 *(978-1-57175-174-4(2),* 6507-C) Learning ZoneXpress.
Colored Snack Attack Activity Books: Ages 2-6, 12 activity books. 2005. (J). 9.95 *(978-1-57175-169-0(6),* 6503-C) Learning ZoneXpress.
Colored Snack Attack Activity Books: Ages 7-11, 12 activity books. 2005. (J). 9.95 *(978-1-57175-171-3(8),* 6504-C) Learning ZoneXpress.
Conklin, Wendy. Safe & Sound: Our Health. 2017. (J). pap. 9.99 ***(978-1-4938-3629-1(3))*** Teacher Created Materials, Inc.
Crabtree Publishing, creator. Slim Goodbody's Lighten Up. 2008. (ENG.). 32p. (J). pap. *(978-0-7787-3929-6(5))* Crabtree Publishing Co.
Crawford, Greg. Super Hero Foods & the Abc's of Nutrition. 2013. 108p. pap. 21.95 *(978-0-9890227-0-5(6))* It's a Lifestyle Fitness.
Creighton, Judith Matlock, et al. Health Education Primer. 2nd ed. 2006. (Illus.). 76p. (J). spiral bd. 29.95 *(978-0-9773228-0-0(7))* WHA Publishing.
—Nutrition Lessons for Kids: (and Their Parents) 2006. (J). spiral bd. 19.95 *(978-0-9773228-3-1(1))* WHA Publishing.
Crockett, Kyle A. Managing Your Weight with Nutrition. Borus, Joshua, ed. 2013. (Understanding Nutrition: a Gateway to Physical & Mental Health Ser.: 11). (Illus.). 48p. (J). (gr. 5-18). 19.95 *(978-1-4222-2881-4(9))* Mason Crest.
—Navigating Your School Cafeteria & Convenience Store. Borus, Joshua, ed. 2013. (Understanding Nutrition: a Gateway to Physical & Mental Health Ser.: 11). (Illus.). 48p. (J). (gr. 5-18). 19.95 *(978-1-4222-2882-1(7))* Mason Crest.
—Nutrition & Your Future. Borus, Joshua, ed. 2013. (Understanding Nutrition: a Gateway to Physical & Mental Health Ser.: 11). (Illus.). 48p. (J). (gr. 5-18). 19.95 *(978-1-4222-2885-2(1))* Mason Crest.
—Nutrition for Achievement in Sports & Academics. Borus, Joshua, ed. 2013. (Understanding Nutrition: a Gateway to Physical & Mental Health Ser.). (Illus.). 48p. (J). (gr. 5-18). pap. 9.95 *(978-1-4222-2990-3(4))*; 19.95 *(978-1-4222-2884-5(3))* Mason Crest.
Danger Zone: Dieting & Eating Disorders, 6 bks., Set. Incl. Anorexia. Watson, Stephanie. 2006. lib. bdg. 31.95 *(978-1-4042-1996-0(X))*; Binge Eating. Watson, Stephanie. 2006. lib. bdg. 31.95 *(978-1-4042-1998-4(6))*; Bulimia. Watson, Stephanie. 2007. lib. bdg. 31.95 *(978-1-4042-1997-7(8))*; Diet Drugs. Williams, Kara. 2006. lib. bdg. 31.95 *(978-1-4042-1994-6(3))*; Diet Fads. Zahensky, Barbara A. 2007. lib. bdg. 31.95 *(978-1-4042-1999-1(4))*; Negative Body Image. Willett, Edward. 2006. lib. bdg. 31.95 *(978-1-4042-1995-3(1))*; (Illus.). 64p. (YA). (gr. 7-12). 2007. Set lib. bdg. 167.70 *(978-1-4042-1061-5(X))* Rosen Publishing Group, Inc., The.
Davis, Sheila & Williams, Nadia. Claudia & Grammy Lose Weight: A Mississippi Grammy & California Granddaughter Lose Weight. 2012. 48p. (-18). pap. 31.99 *(978-1-4771-3594-5(4))* Xlibris Corp.
Deal, Darlene. Play with Your Food & Learn How to Eat Right: Nutritional Book about Fruits & Vegetables. 2004. (ENG & SPA., Illus.). 22p. (J). (gr. 1-4). pap. 9.95 *(978-0-9747299-0-9(6))* Deal, Darlene.
Dell, Helen Sue. The Thinker's Pizza Cookbook. 2003. (Illus.). 64p. (J). pap. 5.99 *(978-0-9747247-0-6(X))* Food Enhancement Enterprises.
Dickmann, Nancy. Protein. 2012. (Healthy Eating with Myplate Ser.). (ENG.). 24p. (gr. -1-1). pap. 6.29 *(978-1-4329-6983-7(8))*; lib. bdg. 22.65 *(978-1-4329-6976-9(5))* Heinemann-Raintree. (Acorn).
—Vegetables. 2012. (Healthy Eating with Myplate Ser.). (ENG.). 24p. (gr. -1-1). pap. 6.29 *(978-1-4329-6981-3(1),* Acorn) Heinemann-Raintree.
Doeden, Matt. Eat Right! How You Can Make Good Food Choices. 2009. pap. 52.95 *(978-0-7613-4684-5(8))* Lerner Publishing Group.
—Eat Right! How You Can Make Good Food Choices. Desrocher, Jack, illus. 2008. (Health Zone Ser.). (ENG.). 64p. (gr. 4-7). lib. bdg. 30.60 *(978-0-8225-7552-8(3))* Lerner Publishing Group.
Dole Nutrition Institute Staff. The Dole Counting Book. 2011. (ENG., Illus.). 10p. (J). (gr. -1-k). bds. 5.99 *(978-1-60961-044-9(X),* 9781609610449) Rodale Pr., Inc.
Dorling Kindersley Publishing Staff. Are You What You Eat? 2015. (ENG.). 96p. (J). (gr. 3-7). 16.99 *(978-1-4654-2944-5(1),* DK Children) Dorling Kindersley Publishing, Inc.
Dru Tecco, Betsy. Food for Fuel: The Connection Between Food & Physical Activity. 2008. (Library of Nutrition Ser.). (Illus.). 48p. (YA). (gr. 8-12). lib. bdg. 29.25 *(978-1-4042-1871-0(8),* Rosen Reference) Rosen Publishing Group, Inc., The.
Durrie, Karen. Health. 2011. (J). 27.13 *(978-1-61690-950-5(1))* Weigl Pubs., Inc.
—Health: Arabic-English Bilingual Edition. 2016. (Community Helpers Ser.). (ENG.). (J). (gr. -1-3). 29.99 ***(978-1-61913-903-9(0))*** Weigl Pubs., Inc.
Durrie, Karen. Salud. 2012. (SPA.). (J). *(978-1-61913-210-8(9))* Weigl Pubs., Inc.
Dyer, Janice. Get into Smart Snacks. 2017. (Illus.). 32p. (J). ***(978-0-7787-3642-4(3))*** Crabtree Publishing Co.
Eating Your Colors. 2010. (Eat Your Colors Ser.). 32p. lib. bdg. 155.94 *(978-1-4296-5196-7(2),* Aplus Bks.) Capstone Press of Coughlan Cos.
Edwards, Hazel & Alexander, Goldie. Talking about What You Eat. 2010. (Healthy Living Ser.). (Illus.). 32p. (YA). (gr. 3-6). lib. bdg. 26.00 *(978-1-4339-3656-2(9))* Stevens, Gareth Publishing LLLP.
Esbaum, Jill. Apples for Everyone. 2009. (Picture the Seasons Ser.). (ENG., Illus.). 16p. (J). (gr. -1-3). pap. 5.95 *(978-1-4263-0523-8(0),* National Geographic Children's Bks.) National Geographic Society.
Etingoff, Kim. Diet Myths: Sorting Through the Hype. Borus, Joshua, ed. 2013. (Understanding Nutrition: a Gateway to Physical & Mental Health Ser.: 11). (Illus.). 48p. (J). (gr. 5-18). 19.95 *(978-1-4222-2876-0(2))* Mason Crest.
—Eating Out: How to Order in Restaurants. Borus, Joshua, ed. 2013. (Understanding Nutrition: a Gateway to Physical & Mental Health Ser.: 11). (Illus.). 48p. (J). (gr. 5-18). 19.95 *(978-1-4222-2877-7(0))* Mason Crest.
—Healthy Alternatives to Sweets & Snacks. Borus, Joshua, ed. 2013. (Understanding Nutrition: a Gateway to Physical & Mental Health Ser.). (Illus.). 48p. (J). (gr. 5-18). pap. 9.95 *(978-1-4222-2992-7(0))*; 19.95 *(978-1-4222-2878-4(9))* Mason Crest.
—Healthy Fast Foods. Borus, Joshua, ed. 2013. (Understanding Nutrition: a Gateway to Physical & Mental Health Ser.). (Illus.). 48p. (J). (gr. 5-18). pap. 9.95 *(978-1-4222-2988-0(2))*; 19.95 *(978-1-4222-2879-1(7))* Mason Crest.
—How to Read Food Product Labels. Borus, Joshua, ed. 2013. (Illus.). 48p. (J). (gr. 5-18). pap. 9.95 *(978-1-4222-2993-4(9))*; (Understanding Nutrition: a Gateway to Physical & Mental Health Ser.: 11). 19.95 *(978-1-4222-2880-7(0))* Mason Crest.
—Understanding Nutrition: A Gateway to Physical & Mental Health, 11 vols. 2014. (Illus.). 11p. (J). *(978-1-4222-2874-6(6))* Mason Crest.
Favor, Lesli J. & Freed, Kira. Food As Foe: Nutrition & Eating Disorders. 2009. (Benchmark Rockets Ser.). 32p. (gr. 5-18). 28.50 *(978-0-7614-4364-3(9))* Marshall Cavendish Corp.
Favor, Lesli J. & Massie, Elizabeth. Weighing In: Nutrition & Weight Management. 2009. (Benchmark Rockets Ser.). 32p. (gr. 5-18). 28.50 *(978-0-7614-4367-4(3))* Marshall Cavendish Corp.
Feeding the Baby: Individual Title Six-Packs. (gr. -1-2). 23.00 *(978-0-7635-8790-1(7))* Rigby Education.
Feldman, Julie, creator. The No Diet Diet: Healthy Meals in 5 Minutes. 2003. (YA). spiral bd. 19.95 *(978-0-615-12437-7(2))* Creative Nutrition & Wellness.
Figtree, Dale. Eat Smarter: The Smarter Choice for Healthier Kids. 2006. (Illus.). 120p. (YA). (gr. 7-12). 19.95 *(978-0-8329-7001-6(8),* Z Health Bks.) New Win Publishing.
Fisher, Beverly. Mental Toughness for Weight Management: Workbook for Life. 2004. (Illus.). 60p. pap. 10.99 *(978-0-9745066-1-6(3))* Sports In Mind.
Food Friends: How to Make Friends Out of Food. 2016. (J). *(978-0-87659-713-2(4))* Gryphon Hse., Inc.
Fordham, Henrietta. Healthy Food for Young Children Inernet-Referenced. 2010. (Parent's Guides). 128p. (J). pap. 12.99 *(978-0-7945-1925-4(3),* Usborne) EDC Publishing.
Friddle-Ponder, Alma. Chile Pepper Unit Study Comprehensive Edition. 2007. (Illus.). 93p. spiral bd. 19.95 *(978-1-934627-00-6(3))* Fish Head Pubns., LLC.
—Chile Pepper Unit Study Graphic Edition. 2007. (Illus.). 63p. spiral bd. 14.95 *(978-1-934627-01-3(1))* Fish Head Pubns., LLC.
—Chile Pepper Unit Study Reading Enhanced Edition. 2007. (Illus.). 68p. spiral bd. 14.95 *(978-1-934627-02-0(X))* Fish Head Pubns., LLC.
Furgang, Kathy. Having Healthful Habits & Tener hábitos Sanos: 6 English, 6 Spanish Adaptations. 2011. (ENG & SPA.). (J). 97.00 net. *(978-1-4108-5710-1(7))* Benchmark Education Co.
Gardner, Robert, et al. Ace Your Exercise & Nutrition Science Project: Great Science Fair Ideas. 2009. (Ace Your Biology Science Project Ser.). (Illus.). 128p. (J). (gr. 5-9). lib. bdg. 33.27 *(978-0-7660-3218-7(3))* Enslow Pubs., Inc.
Gay, Kathlyn. Do You Know What to Eat? 2015. (Got Issues? Ser.). (ENG., Illus.). 128p. (J). (gr. 7-7). 37.27 *(978-0-7660-6987-9(7))* Enslow Pubs., Inc.
—The Scoop on What to Eat: What You Should Know about Diet & Nutrition. 2009. (Issues in Focus Today Ser.). (Illus.). 112p. (J). (gr. 6-12). lib. bdg. 33.27 *(978-0-7660-3066-4(0))* Enslow Pubs., Inc.
Giddens, Sandra. Making Smart Choices about Food, Nutrition, & Lifestyle. 2009. (Making Smart Choices Ser.). 48p. (gr. 5-5). 53.00 *(978-1-61514-339-9(4),* Rosen Reference) Rosen Publishing Group, Inc., The.
Giddens, Sandra & Giddens, Owen. Making Smart Choices about Food, Nutrition, & Lifestyle. 2008. (Making Smart Choices Ser.). (Illus.). 48p. (YA). (gr. 5-9). lib. bdg. 29.25 *(978-1-4042-1389-0(9))* Rosen Publishing Group, Inc., The.
Gilpin, Rebecca. 30 Healthy Things to Cook & Eat. 2010. (Children's Cooking Ser.). (ENG., Illus.). 30p. (J). (gr. 1). 9.99 *(978-0-7945-2396-1(X),* Usborne) EDC Publishing.
Gleisner, Jenna Lee. My Body Needs Food. 2015. (Healthy Me Ser.). (Illus.). 24p. (J). 27.10 *(978-1-60753-587-4(4))* Amicus Publishing.
Gogerly, Liz. Eating Well. Gordon, Mike, illus. 2008. (Looking after Me Ser.). (ENG.). 32p. (J). (gr. -1-3). pap. *(978-0-7787-4117-6(6))* Crabtree Publishing Co.
Goldsmith, Connie. Dietary Supplements. 2015. (ENG., Illus.). 96p. (J). (gr. 7-12). lib. bdg. 34.65 *(978-1-4677-3848-4(4),* Twenty-First Century Bks.) Lerner Publishing Group.
Good Times with Good Foods Activity Books: Ages 2-6, 12 vols. 2005. (J). 9.95 *(978-1-57175-172-0(6),* 6505-C) Learning ZoneXpress.

M N O

Good Times with Good Foods Activity Books: Ages 7-11, 12 vols. 2005. (J). 9.95 (978-1-57175-173-7(4), 6506-C) Learning ZoneXpress.

Goodacre, Sonia, et al. Cambridge VCE Health & Human Development Units 3 & 4 Bundle. 2nd ed. 2013. (ENG.). pap. (978-1-107-68809-4(4)) Cambridge Univ. Pr.

Goodbody, Slim. Eating Right. McGinnis, Ben, illus. Pinchbeck, Chris, photos by. 2007. (Slim Goodbody's Good Health Guides Ser.). 32p. (J). (gr. 2-6). lib. bdg. 26.00 (978-0-8368-7740-3(3), Gareth Stevens Learning Library) Stevens, Gareth Publishing LLLP.

Goodbody, Slim & Burstein, John. Energy In, Energy Out: Food As Fuel. 2008. (Slim Goodbody's Lighten Up! Ser.). (ENG., Illus.). 32p. (J). (gr. 3-7). lib. bdg. (978-0-7787-3914-2(7)) Crabtree Publishing Co.

—Fast Food: Slowing Us All Down. 2008. (Slim Goodbody's Lighten Up! Ser.). (ENG., Illus.). 32p. (J). (gr. 3-7). pap. (978-0-7787-3933-3(3)); lib. bdg. (978-0-7787-3915-9(5)) Crabtree Publishing Co.

—Grocery Shopping: It's in the Bag. 2008. (Slim Goodbody's Lighten Up! Ser.). (ENG., Illus.). 32p. (J). (gr. 3-7). pap. (978-0-7787-3934-0(1)); lib. bdg. (978-0-7787-3916-6(3)) Crabtree Publishing Co.

—Looking at Labels: The Inside Story. 2008. (Slim Goodbody's Lighten Up! Ser.). (ENG., Illus.). 32p. (J). (gr. 3-7). pap. (978-0-7787-3935-7(X)); lib. bdg. (978-0-7787-3917-3(1)) Crabtree Publishing Co.

—The Shape of Good Nutrition: The Food Pyramid. 2008. (Slim Goodbody's Lighten Up! Ser.). (ENG., Illus.). 32p. (J). (gr. 3-7). pap. (978-0-7787-3937-1(6)); lib. bdg. (978-0-7787-3919-7(8)) Crabtree Publishing Co.

—Snack Attack: Unhealthy Treats. 2008. (Slim Goodbody's Lighten Up! Ser.). (ENG., Illus.). 32p. (J). (gr. 3-7). pap. (978-0-7787-3936-4(8)); lib. bdg. (978-0-7787-3918-0(X)) Crabtree Publishing Co.

Gordon, Sharon. You Are What You Eat. 2003. (Rookie Read-About Health Ser.). (ENG., Illus.). 32p. (J). (gr. k-2). pap. 5.95 (978-0-516-26952-8(6), Children's Pr.) Scholastic Library Publishing.

Graham, Gillian. The Rainbow Cookbook for Kids. 2011. 64p. pap. 26.49 (978-1-4567-5209-5(X)) AuthorHouse.

Graimes, Nicola. Kids' Fun & Healthy Cookbook. Shooter, Howard, photos by. 2007. (ENG., Illus.). 128p. (J). (gr. 2-5). 17.99 (978-0-7566-2916-8(0), DK Children) Dorling Kindersley Publishing, Inc.

Greathouse, Lisa. Eat Healthy, 1 vol. 2011. (Science Readers: a Closer Look Ser.). (ENG., Illus.). 32p. (J). (gr. 3-3). pap. 8.99 (978-1-4333-3087-2(3)) Teacher Created Materials, Inc.

—Make It Healthy, 1 vol. 2011. (Science Readers: a Closer Look Ser.). (ENG.). 32p. (J). (gr. 2-2). pap. 8.99 (978-1-4333-3088-9(1)) Teacher Created Materials, Inc.

Green, Emily K. Fruits. 2006. (Blastoff! Readers Ser.). (ENG., Illus.). 24p. (J). (gr. k-3). lib. bdg. 24.95 (978-1-60014-005-1(X), Blastoff! Readers) Bellwether Media.

—Fruits. 2011. (Blastoff! Readers: New Food Guide Pyramid Ser.). (Illus.). 24p. (J). pap. 5.95 (978-0-531-25850-7(5), Children's Pr.) Scholastic Library Publishing.

—Grains. 2006. (Blastoff! Readers Ser.). (ENG., Illus.). 24p. (J). (gr. k-3). lib. bdg. 24.95 (978-1-60014-003-7(3), Blastoff! Readers) Bellwether Media.

—Grains. 2011. (Blastoff! Readers Ser.). (Illus.). 24p. (J). pap. 5.95 (978-0-531-25851-4(3), Children's Pr.) Scholastic Library Publishing.

—Healthy Eating. 2006. (Blastoff! Readers Ser.). (ENG., Illus.). 24p. (J). (gr. k-3). lib. bdg. 24.95 (978-1-60014-007-5(6)) Bellwether Media.

—Meat & Beans. 2006. (Blastoff! Readers Ser.). (ENG., Illus.). 24p. (J). (gr. k-3). lib. bdg. 24.95 (978-1-60014-004-4(1), Blastoff! Readers) Bellwether Media.

—Meat & Beans. 2011. (Blastoff! Readers: New Food Guide Pyramid Ser.). (Illus.). 24p. (J). pap. 5.95 (978-0-531-25854-5(8), Children's Pr.) Scholastic Library Publishing.

—Milk, Yogurt, & Cheese. 2006. (Blastoff! Readers Ser.). (ENG., Illus.). 24p. (J). (gr. k-3). lib. bdg. 24.95 (978-1-60014-000-6(9), Blastoff! Readers) Bellwether Media.

—Milk, Yogurt, & Cheese. 2011. (Blastoff! Readers Ser.). (Illus.). 24p. (J). pap. 5.95 (978-0-531-25855-2(6), Children's Pr.) Scholastic Library Publishing.

—Oils. 2006. (Blastoff! Readers Ser.). (ENG., Illus.). 24p. (J). (gr. k-3). lib. bdg. 24.95 (978-1-60014-001-3(7), Blastoff! Readers) Bellwether Media.

—Oils. 2011. (Blastoff! Readers: New Food Guide Pyramid Ser.). (Illus.). 24p. (J). pap. 5.95 (978-0-531-25856-9(4), Children's Pr.) Scholastic Library Publishing.

—Vegetables. 2006. (Blastoff! Readers Ser.). (ENG., Illus.). 24p. (J). (gr. k-3). lib. bdg. 24.95 (978-1-60014-002-0(5), Blastoff! Readers) Bellwether Media.

—Vegetables. 2011. (Blastoff! Readers Ser.). (Illus.). 24p. (J). pap. 5.95 (978-0-531-25857-6(2), Children's Pr.) Scholastic Library Publishing.

Greenhaven Press Staff. What Should We Eat? Greenhaven Press, ed. 2016. (At Issue Ser.). (ENG.). 128p. (gr. 10-12). 39.40 (978-0-7377-7390-3(1), Greenhaven Pr., Inc.) Cengage Gale.

Gregory, Helen. Healthy Eating, 1 vol. (Wonder Readers Next Steps: Science Ser.). (ENG.). (gr. -1-1). 2013. 20p. lib. bdg. 22.65 (978-1-4765-0036-2(3)) 2011. 32p. pap. 5.99 (978-1-4296-7828-5(3)) 2011. 16p. pap. 35.94 (978-1-4296-8094-3(6)) Capstone Press of Coughlan Cos. (Wonder Readers).

Grossman, Rena. Eating the Rainbow, 1 vol. 2009. (ENG.). 32p. (J). (gr. -1). bds. 6.95 (978-1-59572-174-7(6)) Star Bright Bks., Inc.

Hamilton, Bethany. Body & Soul: A Girl's Guide to a Fit, Fun & Fabulous Life, 1 vol. 2014. (ENG.). 160p. (J). pap. 19.99 (978-0-310-73105-4(4)) Zondervan.

Hardyman, Robyn. Eating Well. 2012. (Healthy & Happy Ser.). (Illus.). 32p. (J). (gr. 1-4). lib. bdg. 26.50 (978-1-4488-5273-4(0)) Rosen Publishing Group, Inc., The.

Harris, Pj. Fat, Fat, What's Wrong with That? The Importance of Diet & Exercise. 2009. 36p. pap. 15.49 (978-1-4490-2345-4(2)) AuthorHouse.

Hartman, Eve & Meshbesher, Wendy. Digestion & Nutrition: What Happens to the Food We Eat?, 1 vol. 2014. (Show Me Science Ser.). (ENG., Illus.). 32p. (gr. 3-5). lib. bdg. 30.65 (978-1-4329-8748-0(8), Raintree Perspectives) Heinemann-Raintree.

Hasler, Doris, et al. Nutrition & Wellness, 2 vols. 7th l.t. ed. 2003. (NUTRITION & WELLNESS Ser.). (ENG., Illus.). 576p. (gr. 5-8). stu. ed. 79.44 (978-0-07-846332-7(7), 0078463327) McGraw-Hill Education.

Hassan, Masood. Madeline & Friends: Fruits & Veggies vs Candy. Lady Josephine, illus. 2010. (978-0-9812600-6-8(3)) Sapphira Pubns.

Hau, Stephanie. I Can Live To 100! Secrets Just for Kids. Hau, Joseph, illus. 2005. 60p. (J). per. 9.95 (978-0-9767324-0-2(8), Kids Can) Proactive Publishing.

Haugen, David M. Nutrition. 2011. (Opposing Viewpoints Ser.). (ENG., Illus.). 224p. (gr. 10-12). 48.80 (978-0-7377-5751-4(5)); pap. 33.80 (978-0-7377-5752-1(3), Greenhaven Pr., Inc.) Cengage Gale.

Having a Healthy Baby - Diet & Nutrition. 2004. (YA). pap. 4.00 net. (978-1-930996-57-1(8)) Planned Parenthood Federation of America, Inc.

Hawley, Ella. Exploring Food & Nutrition. 2012. (Let's Explore Life Science Ser.). (ENG., Illus.). 24p. (J). (gr. 3-6). pap. 8.25 (978-1-4488-6310-5(4)); lib. bdg. 22.60 (978-1-4488-6176-7(4)) Rosen Publishing Group, Inc., The. (PowerKids Pr.).

Head, Honor. Healthy Eating. 2013. (Let's Read & Talk about Ser.). (Illus.). 32p. (gr. 2-5). 28.50 (978-1-59771-394-8(5)) Sea-To-Sea Pubns.

Health & Your Body. 2010. (Health & Your Body Ser.). (ENG.). 24p. (gr. k-1). lib. bdg. 106.60 (978-1-4296-5926-0(2), Pebble Plus) Capstone Press of Coughlan Cos.

Healthy Eating with Mypyramid [US Toy]. 2010. (Healthy Eating with Mypyramid Ser.). pap. 34.75 (978-1-4296-5566-8(6), Pebble Plus) Capstone Press of Coughlan Cos.

Hewitt, Sally. Keeping Healthy. 2015. (ENG.). 24p. (gr. -1-2). 23.99 (978-1-939581-82-2(6)) QEB Publishing Inc.

Hidalgo-Robert, Alberto. Fat No More: A Teenager's Victory over Obesity. 2012. (J). pap. 16.95 (978-1-55885-745-2(1), Piñata Books) Arte Publico Pr.

Hovius, Christopher. Fitness & Nutrition. McDonnell, Mary Ann & Forman, Sara, eds. 2013. (Young Adult's Guide to the Science of Health Ser.: 15). 128p. (J). (gr. 7-18). 24.95 (978-1-4222-2809-8(6)) Mason Crest.

Hulme, Janet A. Bladder & Bowel Issues for Kids: A Handy Guide for Kids Ages 4-12. 2003. (Illus.). 92p. pap. 14.95 (978-1-928812-05-0(8), 4000-07) Phoenix Publishing.

Incredibly Disgusting Food, 4 vols., Set. Incl. Carbonated Beverages: The Incredibly Disgusting Story. Furgang, Adam. (YA). lib. bdg. 29.25 (978-1-4488-1266-0(6)); Fake Foods: Fried, Fast, & Processed: The Incredibly Disgusting Story. Johanson, Paula. (YA). lib. bdg. 29.25 (978-1-4488-1269-1(0)); Mystery Meat: Hot Dogs, Sausages, & Lunch Meats. Watson, Stephanie. (J). lib. bdg. 29.25 (978-1-4488-1268-4(2), 1323609); Salty & Sugary Snacks: The Incredibly Disgusting Story. Furgang, Adam. (YA). lib. bdg. 29.25 (978-1-4488-1267-7(4)); (gr. 5-9). 2011. (Incredibly Disgusting Food Ser.). (Illus.). 48p. 2011. Set lib. bdg. 106.00 (978-1-4488-1390-2(5), Rosen Reference) Rosen Publishing Group, Inc., The.

Ingredients for a Healthy Life. 2014. (Ingredients for a Healthy Life Ser.). 24p. (J). (gr. 2-5). pap. 48.90 (978-1-4824-1543-8(7)) Stevens, Gareth Publishing LLLP.

Innovative Kids Staff. In the Garden. Phillips, Jillian, illus. 2009. (ENG.). 20p. (J). (gr. -1-1). 8.99 (978-1-58476-810-4(X)) Innovative Kids.

Johnson, Katherine. Nutrition Education for Kids: Health Science Series. 2013. 62p. pap. 24.99 (978-1-4817-0099-3(5)) AuthorHouse.

Jones, Susan Smith & Warren, Dianne. Vegetable Soup - The Fruit Bowl. Lindman, Amy Sorvaag, illus. rev. ed. 2006. 64p. (J). (gr. -1-3). per. 14.95 (978-0-9652736-0-2(1)) Oasis Pubns.

Jones, Tammy. I Am Active. 2009. (Sight Word Readers Set A Ser.). (J). (978-1-60719-139-1(3)) Newmark Learning LLC.

Jukes, Mavis, et al. Be Healthy! It's a Girl Thing: Food, Fitness, & Feeling Great! Ziss, Debra, illus. 2003. (It's a Girl Thing Ser.). (ENG.). 128p. (J). (gr. 3-7). pap. 12.99 (978-0-679-89029-4(7), Knopf Bks. for Young Readers) Random Hse. Children's Bks.

Kalman, Bobbie. I Eat a Rainbow. 2010. (ENG., Illus.). 16p. (J). (gr. k-2). (978-0-7787-9412-7(1)); pap. (978-0-7787-9456-1(3)) Crabtree Publishing Co.

—I Eat a Rainbow: Me Como un Arco Iris. 2010. (SPA, ENG & MUL.). 16p. (J). pap. (978-0-7787-8263-6(8)); lib. bdg. (978-0-7787-8270-4(0)) Crabtree Publishing Co.

—Me Como un Arco Iris. 2010. (SPA.). 16p. (J). pap. (978-0-7787-8578-1(5)); lib. bdg. (978-0-7787-8552-1(1)) Crabtree Publishing Co.

Kalz, Jill. Fruits. 2003. 24p. (J). lib. bdg. 21.35 (978-1-58340-299-3(3)) Black Rabbit Bks.

—Grains. 2003. 24p. (J). lib. bdg. 21.35 (978-1-58340-301-3(9)) Black Rabbit Bks.

—Meats & Protein. 2003. 24p. (J). lib. bdg. 21.35 (978-1-58340-298-6(5)) Black Rabbit Bks.

—Vegetables. 2003. 24p. (J). lib. bdg. 21.35 (978-1-58340-300-6(0)) Black Rabbit Bks.

Katirgis, Jane. STEM Jobs in Food & Nutrition. 2014. (ENG., Illus.). 48p. (gr. 4-8). 35.64 (978-1-62717-703-0(5)) Rourke Educational Media.

Keepin, William, et al. Divine Duality: The Power of Reconciliation Between Women & Men. 2015. (SPA & ENG.). 300p. per. 19.95 (978-1-890772-74-1(7)) Hohm Pr.

Kerr, J. B. Food - Ethical Debates in What We Eat. 2008. (Dilemmas in Modern Science Ser.). (ENG., Illus.). 48p. (J). 23.99 (978-0-237-53367-0(7)) Evans Brothers, Ltd. GBR. Dist: Independent Pubs. Group.

Kesselman, Robin & Kesselman, Marc. Nerdel's ABC Book. Martinez, Natali, illus. 2009. 38p. (J). 16.99 (978-0-9823357-2-7(5)) Nerdel Co., The.

Kesselring, Susan. Eat a Rainbow: Healthy Foods, 1 vol. Avakyan, Tatevik, illus. 2012. (Move & Get Healthy Ser.). (ENG.). 32p. (J). (gr. k-3). 28.50 (978-1-61641-858-8(3)) Magic Wagon.

—Make a Meal Plan: Smart Food Shopping, 1 vol. 2012. (Move & Get Healthy Ser.). (ENG.). 32p. (J). (gr. k-3). 28.50 (978-1-61641-863-2(X)) Magic Wagon.

Kids Mypyramid Tablet. 2005. (J). pap. 9.95 (978-1-57175-091-4(6), 4275-T) Learning ZoneXpress.

Knighton, Kate. Why Shouldn't I Eat Junk Food? Larkum, Adam, illus. 2008. (Usborne Ser.). 48p. (J). (gr. 4-7). pap. 6.99 (978-0-7945-1953-7(9), Usborne) EDC Publishing.

Koellhoffer, Tara, ed. Food & Nutrition. 2006. (Science News for Kids Ser.). (Illus.). 128p. (gr. 4-6). lib. bdg. 30.00 (978-0-7910-9121-0(X), Chelsea Clubhouse) Facts On File, Inc.

Kreisman, Rachelle. You Want Me to Eat That? A Kids' Guide to Eating Right. Haggerty, Tim, illus. 2014. (Start Smart: Health Ser.). 32p. (J). (gr. 1-3). pap. 7.95 (978-1-937529-70-3(3)) Red Chair Pr.

Kuskowski, Alex. Cool Eating: Healthy & Fun Ways to Eat Right, 1 vol. 2012. (Cool Health & Fitness Ser.). (ENG.). 32p. (J). (gr. 3-6). lib. bdg. 27.07 (978-1-61783-426-4(2), Checkerboard Library) ABDO Publishing Co.

Landau, Elaine. A Healthy Diet. 2003. (Watts Library). (ENG., Illus.). 64p. (J). 25.50 (978-0-531-12027-9(9), Watts, Franklin) Scholastic Library Publishing.

Lanser, Amanda. Food Science: You Are What You Eat, 1 vol. 2014. (History of Science Ser.). (ENG.). 112p. (J). (gr. 6-12). lib. bdg. 35.64 (978-1-62403-560-9(4), Essential Library) ABDO Publishing Co.

Lee, Sally. Healthy Snacks, Healthy You!, 1 vol. Swift, Gary, illus. 2011. (First Graphics: Myplate & Healthy Eating Ser.). (ENG.). 24p. (gr. 1-2). pap. 6.29 (978-1-4296-7162-0(9)); pap. 35.70 (978-1-4296-7168-2(8)) Capstone Press of Coughlan Cos.

—Healthy Snacks, Healthy You! [Scholastic]. Swift, Gary, illus. 2013. (First Graphics: Myplate & Healthy Eating Ser.). (ENG.). (gr. 1-2). pap. 0.50 (978-1-4765-3129-8(3)) Capstone Press of Coughlan Cos.

Leedy, Loreen. The Edible Pyramid: Good Eating Every Day. Leedy, Loreen, illus. rev. ed. 2007. (Reading Rainbow Bks.). (ENG., Illus.). 32p. (J). (gr. -1-3). 6.95 (978-0-8234-2075-9(2)) Holiday Hse., Inc.

Lin, Grace & McKneally, Ranida T. Our Food. Zong, Grace, illus. 2016. (ENG.). 40p. (J). (gr. k-3). lib. bdg. 16.95 (978-1-58089-590-3(5)) Charlesbridge Publishing, Inc.

Llewellyn, Claire. Your Food. 2008. (Look after Yourself Ser.). (Illus.). 30p. (J). (gr. 1-4). lib. bdg. 28.50 (978-1-59771-098-5(9)) Sea-To-Sea Pubns.

Lori A. Smolin, ed. Eating Right: An Introduction to Human Nutrition. 2005. (Eating Right: an Introduction to Human Nutrition Ser.). (Illus.). 160p. (C). (gr. 9-13). 105.00 (978-0-7910-7849-5(3), Chelsea Hse.) Facts On File, Inc.

Love. Why Do I Take Vitamins? a Book for Children with Autism. 2010. 20p. pap. 9.99 (978-1-60911-169-4(9), Eloquent Bks.) Strategic Book Publishing & Rights Agency (SBPRA).

Madison, Lynda. Food & You: Eat Right, Being Strong & Feeling Great. 2008. (ENG.). 64p. (YA). (gr. 3-18). spiral bd. 8.95 (978-1-59369-415-9(6)) American Girl Publishing, Inc.

Maile, Ruby. Why Should I Eat Fruit? 2014. (Little Books of Answers: Level a Ser.). (Illus.). 16p. (gr. k-2). pap. 7.95 (978-1-927136-03-4(2)) Three Crows Media NZL. Dist: RiverStream Publishing.

Manolis, Kay. Blastoff! Readers - Body Systems, 6 vols., Set. Incl. Circulatory System. 20.00 (978-0-531-21701-6(9)); Digestive System. 20.00 (978-0-531-21702-3(7)); Muscular System. 20.00 (978-0-531-21703-0(5)); Nervous System. 20.00 (978-0-531-21704-7(3)); Respiratory System. 20.00 (978-0-531-21705-4(1)); Skeletal System. 20.00 (978-0-531-21706-1(X)); (Illus.). 24p. (J). (gr. k-3). 2009. 2009. Set lib. bdg. 120.00 (978-0-531-27900-7(6), Children's Pr.) Scholastic Library Publishing.

Mansbach, Adam. Seriously, You Have to Eat. Brozman, Owen, illus. 2015. (ENG.). 32p. (J). 15.95 (978-1-61775-408-1(0)) Akashic Bks.

Marsico, Katie. Eat a Balanced Diet! 2015. (21st Century Junior Library: Your Healthy Body Ser.). (ENG., Illus.). 24p. (J). (gr. 2-5). 27.07 (978-1-63188-983-7(4), 205844) Cherry Lake Publishing.

—Your Healthy Plate - Dairy. 2012. (21st Century Basic Skills Library: Your Healthy Plate Ser.). (ENG., Illus.). 24p. (J). (gr. k-3). lib. bdg. 22.79 (978-1-61080-350-2(7), 201288) Cherry Lake Publishing.

—Your Healthy Plate - Grains. 2012. (21st Century Basic Skills Library: Your Healthy Plate Ser.). (ENG.). 24p. (J). (gr. k-3). lib. bdg. 22.79 (978-1-61080-348-9(5), 201294) Cherry Lake Publishing.

—Your Healthy Plate - Oils & Fats. 2012. (21st Century Basic Skills Library: Your Healthy Plate Ser.). (ENG., Illus.). 24p. (J). (gr. k-3). lib. bdg. 22.79 (978-1-61080-351-9(5), 201296) Cherry Lake Publishing.

—Your Healthy Plate - Protein. 2012. (21st Century Basic Skills Library: Your Healthy Plate Ser.). (ENG., Illus.). 24p. (J). (gr. k-3). lib. bdg. 22.79 (978-1-61080-349-6(3), 201298) Cherry Lake Publishing.

—Your Healthy Plate - Vegetables. 2012. (21st Century Basic Skills Library: Your Healthy Plate Ser.). (ENG.). 24p. (gr. k-3). lib. bdg. 22.79 (978-1-61080-347-2(7), 201290) Cherry Lake Publishing.

—Your Healthy Plate: Dairy. 2012. (21st Century Basic Skills Library: Your Healthy Plate Ser.). (ENG.). 24p. (gr. k-3). pap. 12.79 (978-1-61080-398-4(1), 201333) Cherry Lake Publishing.

—Your Healthy Plate: Fruits. 2012. (21st Century Basic Skills Library: Your Healthy Plate Ser.). (ENG., Illus.). 24p. (J). (gr. k-3). pap. 12.79 (978-1-61080-400-4(7), 201335) Cherry Lake Publishing.

—Your Healthy Plate: Grains. 2012. (21st Century Basic Skills Library: Your Healthy Plate Ser.). (ENG.). 24p. (J). (gr. k-3). pap. 12.79 (978-1-61080-401-1(5), 201336) Cherry Lake Publishing.

—Your Healthy Plate: Oils & Fats. 2012. (21st Century Basic Skills Library: Your Healthy Plate Ser.). (ENG., Illus.). 24p. (J). (gr. k-3). pap. 12.79 (978-1-61080-402-8(3), 201337) Cherry Lake Publishing.

—Your Healthy Plate: Protein. 2012. (21st Century Basic Skills Library: Your Healthy Plate Ser.). (ENG., Illus.). 24p. (J). (gr. k-3). pap. 12.79 (978-1-61080-403-5(1), 201338) Cherry Lake Publishing.

—Your Healthy Plate: Vegetables. 2012. (21st Century Basic Skills Library: Your Healthy Plate Ser.). (ENG.). 24p. (gr. k-3). pap. 12.79 (978-1-61080-399-1(X), 201334) Cherry Lake Publishing.

Mayo Clinic Center for Social Media Staff. Mayo Clinic Kids' 50 Favorite Recipes for Fun & Healthy Eating. 2012. (ENG., Illus.). 128p. (gr. -1-7). 19.95 (978-1-56148-751-6(1), Da Capo Lifelong) Da Capo Pr., Inc.

Mayo Clinic Staff, contrib. by. Eating Out: Your Pocket Guide to Healthy Dining. 2004. (Mayo Clinic on Health Ser.). (Illus.). 36,52p. (YA). (gr. 8-18). lib. bdg. 15.95 (978-1-59084-249-2(9)) Mason Crest.

—Healthy Meals for Hurried Lives. 2004. (Mayo Clinic on Health Ser.). (Illus.). 36,52p. (YA). (gr. 8-18). lib. bdg. 15.95 (978-1-59084-252-2(9)) Mason Crest.

McCarthy, Rose. Food Labels: Using Nutrition Information to Create a Healthy Diet. 2008. (Library of Nutrition Ser.). (ENG., Illus.). 48p. (gr. 5-8). per. 11.75 (978-1-4042-1633-4(2)) Rosen Publishing Group, Inc., The.

—Food Labels: Using Nutritional Information to Create a Healthy Diet. 2004. (Library of Nutrition). (Illus.). 48p. (J). lib. bdg. 26.50 (978-1-4042-0300-6(1)) Rosen Publishing Group, Inc., The.

McCurry, Chris & Waddington, Emma. Why Do I Have to Eat My Greens? Big Issues for Little People Around Health & Well-Being. Thomas, Louis, illus. 2016. (Life & Soul Library). (ENG.). 32p. (J). (gr. -1-3). 12.99 (978-1-84780-865-3(4), Frances Lincoln Children's Bks.) Quarto Publishing Group UK GBR. Dist: Hachette Bk. Group.

Meiners, Cheri J. & Allen, Elizabeth. Grow Strong! A Book about Healthy Habits. 2016. (Being the Best Me Ser.). (ENG., Illus.). 40p. (J). (gr. -1-2). pap. 9.99 (978-1-63198-085-5(8)) Free Spirit Publishing, Inc.

Miller, Edward. The Monster Health Book: A Guide to Eating Healthy, Being Active & Feeling Great for Monsters & Kids! (ENG., Illus.). 40p. (J). (gr. 2-5). 2008. 7.99 (978-0-8234-2139-8(2)) 2006. 17.95 (978-0-8234-1956-2(8)) Holiday Hse., Inc.

Minden, Cecilia. Cooking by the Numbers. 2007. (21st Century Skills Library: Real World Math Ser.). (ENG., Illus.). 32p. (gr. 4-8). lib. bdg. 28.50 (978-1-60279-007-0(8), 200061) Cherry Lake Publishing.

Mooney, Carla. Healthy Weight Loss for Teens. 2013. (Nutrition & Health Ser.). (ENG., Illus.). 128p. (gr. 7-10). lib. bdg. 35.70 (978-1-4205-1021-8(5), Lucent Bks.) Cengage Gale.

MyPyramid for Kids Tablet. 2005. (J). pap. 9.95 (978-1-57175-179-9(3), 4281-T) Learning ZoneXpress.

Nardo, Don. Vegan Diets. Greenhaven Press Editors, ed. 2014. (Nutrition & Health Ser.). (ENG., Illus.). 128p. (gr. 7-10). lib. bdg. 35.70 (978-1-4205-1151-2(3), Lucent Bks.) Cengage Gale.

Needham, Kate. Why Do People Eat? Spenceley, Annabel & Chen, Kuo Kang, illus. rev. ed. 2007. (Starting Point Science Ser.). 24p. (J). (gr. 1-4). pap. 4.99 (978-0-7945-1623-9(8), Usborne) EDC Publishing.

Nelson, Robin. Dairy. 2003. (First Step Nonfiction - Food Groups Ser.). (ENG., Illus.). 24p. (gr. k-2). lib. bdg. 23.93 (978-0-8225-4632-0(9)) Lerner Publishing Group.

—Fats, Oils, & Sweets. 2003. (First Step Nonfiction - Food Groups Ser.). (ENG., Illus.). 24p. (gr. k-2). lib. bdg. 23.93 (978-0-8225-4634-4(5)) Lerner Publishing Group.

—Fruits. 2003. (First Step Nonfiction Ser.). (Illus.). 24p. (J). (gr. k-2). lib. bdg. 18.60 (978-0-8225-4624-5(8)) Lerner Publishing Group.

—Grains. 2003. (First Step Nonfiction - Food Groups Ser.). (ENG., Illus.). 24p. (gr. k-2). lib. bdg. 23.93 (978-0-8225-4628-3(0)) Lerner Publishing Group.

—Vegetables. 2003. (First Step Nonfiction - Food Groups Ser.). (ENG., Illus.). 24p. (gr. k-2). lib. bdg. 23.93 (978-0-8225-4626-9(4)) Lerner Publishing Group.

The Nutraceutical Reference Guide. 2005. (YA). per. 14.95 (978-1-59872-184-3(4)) Instant Pub.

O'Donnell, Sallie. Animals, Vegetables & Minerals from A to Z. Plumley, Alea, illus. l.t. ed. 2005. 60p. pap. 9.95 (978-0-9764982-5-4(1)) Legacy Publishing Services, Inc.

Olmstead, Lucinda. But Not on My Ice Cream, Please. 2008. (Illus.). 20p. pap. 13.99 (978-1-4389-0917-2(9)) AuthorHouse.

Olson, Gillia M. MyPlate & You, 1 vol. 2011. (Health & Your Body Ser.). (ENG.). 24p. (gr. k-1). pap. 7.29 (978-1-4296-7129-3(7)); lib. bdg. 26.65 (978-1-4296-6809-5(1)); pap. 41.70 (978-1-4296-7135-4(1)) Capstone Press of Coughlan Cos. (Pebble Plus).

Oramasionwu, Angela. Sammy the Cell & the Healthy 1s: Let's Learn about Nutrition. 2004. 33p. pap. 24.95 (978-1-4137-3449-2(9)) PublishAmerica, Inc.

Orme, Helen. Healthy Eating. 2010. (Science Everywhere! Ser.). 24p. 24.25 (978-1-84898-289-5(5)) Black Rabbit Bks.

Orr, Tamra. Playing Safe, Eating Right: Making Healthy Choices, 1 vol. 2008. (Essential Health: Strong Beautiful Girls Set 1 Ser.). (ENG.). 112p. (J). (gr. 6-12). lib. bdg. 35.64 (978-1-60453-103-9(7)) ABDO Publishing Co.

Orr, Tamra B. Growing Nutritious Food. 2015. (Explorer Library: Science Explorer Ser.). (ENG., Illus.). 32p. (J). (gr. 4-8). 29.93 (978-1-63362-392-7(0), 206988) Cherry Lake Publishing.

Pappas, Diane H. & Covey, Richard D. I'm a Healthy Eater. Estrada, Ric, illus. 2007. (J). (978-0-545-01424-3(7)) Scholastic, Inc.

—My Healthy Food Pyramid. Estrada, Ric, illus. 2007. (J). pap. (978-0-545-01429-8(8)) Scholastic, Inc.

Paris, Stephanie. Straight Talk: The Truth about Food, 1 vol. 2nd rev. ed. 2013. (Nonfiction Readers Ser.). (ENG., Illus.). 48p. (J). (gr. 4-4). pap. 29.96 (978-1-4807-1109-9(8)) Shell Educational Publishing.

—Straight Talk - The Truth about Food , 1 vol. 2nd rev. ed. 2012. (Nonfiction Readers Ser.). (ENG.). 48p. (J). (gr. 4-4). pap. 9.99 (978-1-4333-4857-0(8)) Teacher Created Materials, Inc.

Parker, Chance. Nutrition & Science. 2014. (ENG., Illus.). 112p. 42.79 (978-1-62524-072-9(4), Village Earth Pr.) Harding Hse. Publishing Sebice Inc.

Parker, Vic. Breakfast: Healthy Food Choices, 1 vol. 2014. (Healthy Food Choices Ser.). (ENG.). 32p. (gr. 1-3). lib. bdg. 27.32 (978-1-4329-9116-6(7), Heinemann First Library) Heinemann-Raintree.

—Dinner: Healthy Food Choices, 1 vol. 2014. (Healthy Food Choices Ser.). (ENG.). 32p. (gr. 1-3). lib. bdg. 27.32

(978-1-4329-9118-0(3), Heinemann First Library) Heinemann-Raintree.

—Healthy Food Choices, 1 vol. 2014. (Healthy Food Choices Ser.). (ENG.). 32p. (gr. 1-3). lib. bdg. 109.28 (978-1-4329-9120-3(5), Heinemann First Library) Heinemann-Raintree.

—Lunch: Healthy Food Choices, 1 vol. 2014. (Healthy Food Choices Ser.). (ENG.). 32p. (gr. 1-3). lib. bdg. 27.32 (978-1-4329-9117-3(5), Heinemann First Library) Heinemann-Raintree.

—Snacks: Healthy Food Choices, 1 vol. 2014. (Healthy Food Choices Ser.). (ENG.). 32p. (gr. 1-3). lib. bdg. 27.32 (978-1-4329-9119-7(1), Heinemann First Library) Heinemann-Raintree.

Parsons, William B., Jr. Tough Talk about Fat! How to Reach & Maintain Your Ideal Weight. 2003. 134p. per. 12.95 (978-0-9662568-9-5(1)) Lilac Pr.

Perritano, John. Fats & Cholesterol. 2017. (J). **(978-1-4222-3734-2(6))** Mason Crest.

—Sugar & Sweeteners. 2017. (J). **(978-1-4222-3744-1(3))** Mason Crest.

Peters, Celeste A. Food. 2009. (Science Q & A Ser.). (Illus.). 48p. (YA). (gr. 5-8). pap. 10.95 (978-1-60596-075-3(6)); lib. bdg. 29.05 (978-1-60596-074-6(8)) Weigl Pubs., Inc.

—Food Q & A. 2014. (Science Discovery Ser.). (ENG., Illus.). 48p. (J). (gr. 5-8). pap. 13.95 (978-1-4896-0689-1(0), AV2 by Weigl) Weigl Pubs., Inc.

Petrie, Kristin. Food & Energy: Striking a Healthy Balance, 1 vol. 2012. (Mission: Nutrition Ser.). (ENG., Illus.). 32p. (YA). (gr. 3-6). 27.07 (978-1-61783-080-8(1)) ABDO Publishing Co.

—Food Buzz: Nutrition in the News, 1 vol. 2012. (Mission: Nutrition Ser.). (ENG., Illus.). 32p. (YA). (gr. 3-6). 27.07 (978-1-61783-082-2(8)) ABDO Publishing Co.

—Food Culture: Celebrating Diverse Traditions, 1 vol. 2012. (Mission: Nutrition Ser.). (ENG., Illus.). 32p. (YA). (gr. 3-6). 27.07 (978-1-61783-083-9(6)) ABDO Publishing Co.

—Food Options: Following Special Diets, 1 vol. 2012. (Mission: Nutrition Ser.). (ENG., Illus.). 32p. (YA). (gr. 3-6). 27.07 (978-1-61783-084-6(4)) ABDO Publishing Co.

—The Food Pyramid. 2004. (Nutrition Ser.). (Illus.). 32p. (J). (gr. k-6). lib. bdg. 22.78 (978-1-59197-403-1(8)) ABDO Publishing Co.

Priest, Bonnie. Nancy & the Nutrition Tree. 2008. 28p. pap. 12.95 (978-1-934925-86-7(1), Strategic Bk. Publishing) Strategic Book Publishing & Rights Agency (SBPRA).

Que Debo Comer Hoy? 2005. (SPA.). (J). 10.99 (978-0-9770756-1-4(3)) Family Nutrition Ctr. P.C.

Quinlan, Julia J. & Furgang, Adam. The Truth Behind Soft Drinks. 2017. (J). **(978-1-4777-8992-6(8))** Rosen Publishing Group, Inc., The.

Rau, Dana Meachen. Going Organic: A Healthy Guide to Making the Switch, 1 vol. 2012. (Food Revolution Ser.). (ENG.). 64p. (gr. 6-7). 34.65 (978-0-7565-4523-9(4)); pap. 9.10 (978-0-7565-4528-4(5)) Compass Point Bks. (CPB Grades 4-8).

—Going Vegetarian: A Healthy Guide to Making the Switch, 1 vol. 2012. (Food Revolution Ser.). (ENG., Illus.). 64p. (gr. 6-7). 34.65 (978-0-7565-4522-2(6)); pap. 9.10 (978-0-7565-4530-7(7)) Compass Point Bks. (CPB Grades 4-8).

—Sports Nutrition for Teen Athletes: Eat Right to Take Your Game to the Next Level. 2012. (Sports Training Zone Ser.). (ENG.). 48p. (gr. 4-5). pap. 47.70 (978-1-4296-8488-0(7)) Capstone Press of Coughlan Cos.

Rau, Dana Meachen, et al. Sports Training Zone. 2012. (Sports Training Zone Ser.). (ENG.). 48p. (gr. 4-5). pap. 190.80 (978-1-4296-8492-7(5)); pap. 24.57 (978-1-4296-8491-0(7)); lib. bdg. 127.96 (978-1-4296-8182-7(9)) Capstone Press of Coughlan Cos.

Reese, Brandon. Draw Me Healthy! Reese, Brandon, illus. 2012. (Illus.). 32p. (J). 7.99 (978-0-8280-2680-2(7)) Review & Herald Publishing Assn.

Reinke, Beth Bence. Healthy Snacks. 2013. (Healthy Eating with Myplate Ser.). (ENG.). 24p. (J). (gr. 1-4). 28.50 (978-1-62323-600-7(2), 206402) Child's World, Inc., The.

Rice, Dona Herweck. Comer Bien, 1 vol. 2nd rev. ed. 2012. (Nonfiction Readers Ser.). (SPA.). 20p. (J). (gr. 1-1). pap. 4.99 (978-1-4333-4430-5(0)) Teacher Created Materials, Inc.

—Delicious & Nutritious, 1 vol. 2011. (Early Childhood Themes Ser.). (ENG.). 16p. (J). (gr. -1-2). pap. 19.99 (978-1-4333-2370-6(2)); pap. 6.99 (978-1-4333-2369-0(9)) Teacher Created Materials, Inc.

—Eating Right, 1 vol. 2nd rev. ed. 2014. (TIME for KIDS(r) Nonfiction Readers Ser.). (ENG., Illus.). 20p. (J). (gr. 1-1). pap. 19.96 (978-1-4807-1030-6(X)) Shell Educational Publishing.

Rice, Dona Herwick. Eating Right, 1 vol. 2nd rev. ed. 2011. (Nonfiction Readers Ser.). (ENG.). 20p. (J). (gr. 1-1). pap. 4.99 (978-1-4333-3597-6(2)) Teacher Created Materials, Inc.

Rissman, Rebecca. Using Myplate. 2012. (Healthy Eating with Myplate Ser.). (ENG.). 24p. (gr. -1-1). pap. 6.29 (978-1-4329-6985-1(4), Acorn) Heinemann-Raintree.

Rissman, Rebecca & Smith, Sian. Eating Well, 1 vol. 2012. (Take Care of Yourself! Ser.). (ENG.). 24p. (gr. -1-1). pap. 6.29 (978-1-4329-6718-5(5), Acorn) Heinemann-Raintree.

Ritchie, Scot. See What We Eat! A First Book of Healthy Eating. Ritchie, Scot, illus. 2017. (ENG., Illus.). 32p. (J). (gr. -1-2). 16.99 **(978-1-77138-618-0(5))** Kids Can Pr., Ltd. CAN. Dist: Hachette Bk. Group.

Rizzo, Nicholas. Championship Nutrition & Performance: The Wrestler's Guide to Lifestyle, Diet & Healthy Weight Control. rev. ed. 2004. (Illus.). 114p. 15.95 (978-0-9748220-1-3(9), Executive Performances Publishing) Executive Performances, Inc.

Rondeau, Amanda. Food Pyramid, 1 vol. 2003. (What Should I Eat? Ser.). (ENG., Illus.). 24p. (J). (gr. k-3). lib. bdg. 24.21 (978-1-57765-832-0(9), SandCastle) ABDO Publishing Co.

—Grains Are Good, 1 vol. 2003. (What Should I Eat? Ser.). (ENG., Illus.). 24p. (J). (gr. k-3). lib. bdg. 24.21 (978-1-57765-833-7(7), SandCastle) ABDO Publishing Co.

—Milk Is Magnificent, 1 vol. 2003. (What Should I Eat? Ser.). (ENG., Illus.). 24p. (J). (gr. k-3). lib. bdg. 24.21 (978-1-57765-837-5(X), SandCastle) ABDO Publishing Co.

—Proteins Are Powerful, 1 vol. 2003. (What Should I Eat? Ser.). (ENG., Illus.). 24p. (J). (gr. k-3). lib. bdg. 24.21 (978-1-57765-836-8(1), SandCastle) ABDO Publishing Co.

—Vegetables Are Vital, 1 vol. 2003. (What Should I Eat? Ser.). (ENG., Illus.). 24p. (J). (gr. k-3). lib. bdg. 24.21 (978-1-57765-835-1(3), SandCastle) ABDO Publishing Co.

Rose, Elizabeth. Food & Nutrition. 24p. 2009. (Illus.). (J). (gr. 3-6). pap. 8.25 (978-1-4358-3264-0(7)) 2009. (gr. 3-4). 42.50 (978-1-60854-001-3(4)) 2006. (Illus.). (J). (gr. -1-3). lib. bdg. 21.25 (978-1-4042-2821-4(7)) Rosen Publishing Group, Inc., The. (PowerKids Pr.).

Rosen, Michael J. & Kassoy, Ben. Strange Foods. Jones, Doug, illus. 2013. (No Way! Ser.). (ENG.). 32p. (J). (gr. 3-5). lib. bdg. 26.60 (978-0-7613-8984-2(9), Millbrook Pr.) Lerner Publishing Group.

Rothenberg, Annye. I Like to Eat Treats. Wenzel, David T., illus. 2010. 48p. (J). pap. 9.95 (978-0-9790420-2-7(X)) Perfecting Parenting Pr.

Rotner, Shelley & Kelly, Sheila M. Yummy! Rotner, Shelley, photos by. 2013. (ENG., Illus.). 32p. (J). (gr. -1-1). 16.95 (978-0-8234-2426-9(X)) Holiday Hse., Inc.

Royston, Angela. Diet. 2010. (Being Healthy, Feeling Great Ser.). (ENG.). 32p. (J). pap. 10.60 (978-1-61532-372-2(4), PowerKids Pr.); (YA). (gr. 3-6). lib. bdg. 26.50 (978-1-61532-367-8(8)) Rosen Publishing Group, Inc., The.

—Why We Need Proteins. 2011. (Science of Nutrition Ser.: No. 4). (ENG., Illus.). 48p. (J). (gr. 5-8). pap. (978-0-7787-1696-9(1)) Crabtree Publishing Co.

—Why We Need Water & Fiber. 2011. (Science of Nutrition Ser.: No. 6). (ENG., Illus.). 48p. (J). (gr. 5-8). pap. (978-0-7787-1698-3(8)) Crabtree Publishing Co.

Rustad, Martha E. H. I Eat Well. 2017. (Healthy Me Ser.). (ENG., Illus.). 24p. (gr. k-1). lib. bdg. 21.99 (978-1-5157-3983-8(X)) Capstone Press of Coughlan Cos.

Salzmann, Mary Elizabeth. Eat Your Vegetables! Healthy Eating Habits, 1 vol. 2014. (Healthy Habits Ser.). (ENG.). 24p. (J). (gr. -1-3). 24.21 (978-1-62403-529-6(9)) ABDO Publishing Co.

—Healthy Habits, 1 vol. 2014. (Healthy Habits Ser.: 6). (ENG.). 24p. (J). (gr. -1-3). lib. bdg. 145.26 (978-1-62403-527-2(2), SandCastle) ABDO Publishing Co.

Samson, Tess. Snack Time. 2010. (Sight Word Readers Ser.). (J). 3.49 (978-1-60719-618-1(2)) Newmark Learning LLC.

Sayer, Melissa & Naik, Anita. Too Fat? Too Thin? The Healthy Eating Handbook. 2009. (Really Useful Handbooks Ser.). (ENG., Illus.). 48p. (J). (gr. 5-11). pap. (978-0-7787-4405-4(1)); lib. bdg. (978-0-7787-4392-7(6)) Crabtree Publishing Co.

Schaefer, Adam. Alimentos Saludables, 1 vol. 2010. (Salud y el Estado Fisico Ser.).Tr. of Healthy Food. (SPA.). 32p. (gr. 1-3). 27.32 (978-1-4329-4444-5(4)); pap. 8.29 (978-1-4329-4449-0(5)) Heinemann-Raintree.

Scherer, Lauri S. Artificial Ingredients. Friedman, Lauri S., ed. 2012. (Issues That Concern You Ser.). (ENG., Illus.). 144p. (gr. 7-10). lib. bdg. 42.00 (978-0-7377-6284-6(5)) Cengage Gale.

Schrier, Allyson Valentine. Eat Right: Your Guide to Maintaining a Healthy Diet. 2011. (Healthy Me Ser.). (ENG.). 32p. (gr. 3-4). pap. 47.70 (978-1-4296-7292-4(7)); lib. bdg. 27.99 (978-1-4296-6544-5(0)) Capstone Press of Coughlan Cos. (Snap Bks.).

Schuh, Mari. Dairy on Myplate, 1 vol. 2012. (What's on Myplate? Ser.). (ENG., Illus.). 24p. (gr. k-1). pap. 7.29 (978-1-4296-9410-0(6), Pebble Plus) Capstone Press of Coughlan Cos.

—Healthy Snacks on Myplate, 1 vol. 2012. (What's on Myplate? Ser.). (ENG., 24p. (gr. k-1). Illus.). pap. 7.29 (978-1-4296-9418-6(1)); pap. 41.70 (978-1-4296-9419-3(X)) Capstone Press of Coughlan Cos. (Pebble Plus).

—Protein on Myplate, 1 vol. 2012. (What's on Myplate? Ser.). (ENG., 24p. (gr. k-1). Illus.). pap. 7.29 (978-1-4296-9420-9(3)); pap. 41.70 (978-1-4296-9421-6(1)) Capstone Press of Coughlan Cos. (Pebble Plus).

—Sugars & Fats, 1 vol. 2012. (What's on Myplate? Ser.). (ENG., 24p. (gr. k-1). Illus.). pap. 7.29 (978-1-4296-9422-3(X)); pap. 41.70 (978-1-4296-9423-0(8)) Capstone Press of Coughlan Cos. (Pebble Plus).

—Vegetables on Myplate, 1 vol. 2012. (What's on Myplate? Ser.). (ENG., 24p. (gr. k-1). Illus.). pap. 7.29 (978-1-4296-9424-7(6)); pap. 41.70 (978-1-4296-9425-4(4)) Capstone Press of Coughlan Cos. (Pebble Plus).

—What's on Myplate? 2012. (What's on Myplate? Ser.). (ENG.). 24p. (gr. k-1). pap. 333.60 (978-1-4296-9427-8(0)); pap. 55.60 (978-1-4296-9426-1(2)); lib. bdg. 213.20 (978-1-4296-9168-0(9)) Capstone Press of Coughlan Cos. (Pebble Plus).

Schuh, Mari C. Antojitos para Dientes Sanos. 2010. (Dientes Sanos/Healthy Teeth Ser.).Tr. of Snacks for Healthy Teeth. (MUL, ENG & SPA.). 24p. (gr. k-1). lib. bdg. 26.65 (978-1-4296-4599-7(7)) Capstone Press of Coughlan Cos.

—Dairy on Myplate, 1 vol. 2012. (What's on Myplate? Ser.). (ENG., Illus.). 24p. (gr. k-1). lib. bdg. 26.65 (978-1-4296-8744-7(4), Pebble Plus) Capstone Press of Coughlan Cos.

—Healthy Snacks on Myplate, 1 vol. 2012. (What's on Myplate? Ser.). (ENG., Illus.). 24p. (gr. k-1). lib. bdg. 26.65 (978-1-4296-8748-5(7), Pebble Plus) Capstone Press of Coughlan Cos.

—Protein on Myplate, 1 vol. 2012. (What's on Myplate? Ser.). (ENG., Illus.). 24p. (gr. k-1). lib. bdg. 26.65 (978-1-4296-8745-4(2), Pebble Plus) Capstone Press of Coughlan Cos.

—Proteínas en MiPlato. Strictly Spanish LLC. Staff, tr. 2013. (¿Qué Hay en Miplato?/What's on My Plate? Ser.).Tr. of Protein on MyPlate. (SPA, ENG & MUL.). 24p. (gr. k-1). lib. bdg. 26.65 (978-1-62065-945-8(X)) Capstone Press of Coughlan Cos.

—Snacks for Healthy Teeth, 1 vol. Saunders-Smith, Gail, ed. 2008. (Healthy Teeth Ser.). (ENG., Illus.). 24p. (gr. k-1). pap. 7.29 (978-1-4296-1785-7(3), Pebble Plus) Capstone Press of Coughlan Cos.

—Sugars & Fats, 1 vol. 2012. (What's on Myplate? Ser.). (ENG., Illus.). 24p. (gr. k-1). lib. bdg. 26.65 (978-1-4296-8746-1(0), Pebble Plus) Capstone Press of Coughlan Cos.

—Vegetables on Myplate, 1 vol. 2012. (What's on Myplate? Ser.). (ENG., Illus.). 24p. (gr. k-1). lib. bdg. 26.65 (978-1-4296-8743-0(6), Pebble Plus) Capstone Press of Coughlan Cos.

Science stories foss spanish food & nutrition ea Cr05. 2005. (J). (978-1-59242-596-9(8)) Delta Education, LLC.

Scott, Celicia. My Daily Diet: Proteins. Prock, Lisa Albers, ed. 2014. (On My Plate Ser.: 6). 48p. (J). (gr. 5-18). 20.95 (978-1-4222-3099-2(6)) Mason Crest.

—My Daily Diet: Vegetables. Prock, Lisa Albers, ed. 2014. (On My Plate Ser.: 6). 48p. (J). (gr. 5-18). 20.95 (978-1-4222-3100-5(3)) Mason Crest.

Seaborn, Ron. The Children's Health Food Book. rev. ed. 2006. 40p. 16.95 (978-0-9647089-2-1(2)) Life Line, Inc.

Senker, Cath. Healthy Eating. 2008. (Healthy Choices Ser.). (Illus.). 24p. (J). (gr. 3-7). lib. bdg. 22.60 (978-1-4042-4303-3(8), PowerKids Pr.) Rosen Publishing Group, Inc., The.

Sertori, Trisha. Dairy Foods. 2008. (Body Fuel for Healthy Bodies Ser.). 32p. (gr. 4-18). lib. bdg. 18.56 (978-0-7614-3797-0(5), Benchmark Bks.) Marshall Cavendish Corp.

—Fats & Oils. 2008. (Body Fuel for Healthy Bodies Ser.). 32p. (gr. 4-18). lib. bdg. 18.56 (978-0-7614-3798-7(3), Benchmark Bks.) Marshall Cavendish Corp.

—Fruits, Vegetables, & Legumes. 2008. (Body Fuel for Healthy Bodies Ser.). 32p. (gr. 4-18). lib. bdg. 18.56 (978-0-7614-3799-4(1), Benchmark Bks.) Marshall Cavendish Corp.

—Grains, Bread, Cereal & Pasta. 2008. (Body Fuel for Healthy Bodies Ser.). 32p. (gr. 4-18). lib. bdg. 18.56 (978-0-7614-3800-7(9), Benchmark Bks.) Marshall Cavendish Corp.

—Meats, Fish, Eggs, Nuts, & Beans. 2008. (Body Fuel for Healthy Bodies Ser.). 32p. (gr. 4-18). lib. bdg. 18.56 (978-0-7614-3801-4(7), Benchmark Bks.) Marshall Cavendish Corp.

—Vitamins & Minerals. 2008. (Body Fuel for Healthy Bodies Ser.). 32p. (gr. 4-18). lib. bdg. 18.56 (978-0-7614-3802-1(5), Benchmark Bks.) Marshall Cavendish Corp.

Sesame's: A Giant Coloring Book that teaches Healthy Eating Habits. 2006. (J). 6.99 (978-1-59949-499-9(X)) Food Marketing Consultants, Inc.

Shryer, Donna. Body Fuel: A Guide to Good Nutrition. 2007. (Food & Fitness Ser.). (Illus.). 128p. (YA). (gr. 7-12). lib. bdg. 38.50 (978-0-7614-2552-6(7)) Marshall Cavendish Corp.

Shryer, Donna & Dawson, Stephen. Body Fuel: A Guide to Good Nutrition. 2009. (Benchmark Rockets Ser.). 32p. (gr. 5-18). 28.50 (978-0-7614-4362-9(2)) Marshall Cavendish Corp.

Shryer, Donna & Forschmiedt, Jodi. Peak Performance: Sports Nutrition. 2009. (Benchmark Rockets Ser.). 32p. (gr. 5-18). 28.50 (978-0-7614-4366-7(5)) Marshall Cavendish Corp.

Sieving Pelkki, Jane. Healthy Eating. 2016. (True Book(tm), A — Health Ser.). (ENG., Illus.). 48p. (J). lib. bdg. 31.00 (978-0-531-22848-7(7), Children's Pr.) Scholastic Library Publishing.

Silate, Jennifer. Planning & Preparing Healthy Meals & Snacks: A Day-to-Day Guide to a Healthier Diet. (Library of Nutrition Ser.). 48p. 2009. (gr. 5-8). 53.00 (978-1-60853-776-1(5), Rosen Reference) 2008. (ENG., Illus.). (gr. 5-8). per. 11.75 (978-1-4042-1634-1(0)) 2004. (Illus.). (J). lib. bdg. 26.50 (978-1-4042-0302-0(8)) Rosen Publishing Group, Inc., The.

Sjonger, Rebecca. How to Choose Foods Your Body Will Use. 2016. (ENG.). 24p. (J). (978-0-7787-2350-9(X)) Crabtree Publishing Co.

—On a Mission for Good Nutrition! 2015. (ENG., Illus.). 24p. (J). (978-0-7787-1880-2(8)) Crabtree Publishing Co.

Slim Goodbody Corp. What's on Myplate? A Guide to Good Nutrition. 2011. (Illus.). 40p. (J). 14.95 (978-1-887028-63-9(3)) Slim Goodbody Corp.

Slim Goodbody Corp., creator. What's on Myplate? A Guide to Good Nutrition. 2011. (Illus.). 40p. (J). pap. 9.95 (978-1-887028-62-2(5)) Slim Goodbody Corp.

Sly, Stacey. What Should I Eat? Gentry, Susana, photos by. 2010. (Illus.). 26p. pap. 12.95 (978-1-60911-432-9(9), Eloquent Bks.) Strategic Book Publishing & Rights Agency (SBPRA).

Smalley, Carol Parenzan. Fats, Oils, & Sweets. (Rookie Read-About Health Ser.). (ENG., Illus.). 32p. (J). (gr. k-2). 2006. pap. 5.95 (978-0-516-24759-5(X)) 2005. lib. bdg. 20.50 (978-0-516-25289-6(5)) Scholastic Library Publishing. (Children's Pr.).

Smallwood, Sally. We Are What We Eat! 2008. (Things I Eat Ser.). (ENG., Illus.). 24p. (J). (gr. -1-k). (978-1-84089-523-0(3)) Zero to Ten, Ltd.

Smith, Alastair. What Happens to Your Food. Wheatley, Maria, illus. 2003. 16p. (J). (gr. 2-18). pap. 7.95 (978-0-7945-0643-8(7), Usborne) EDC Publishing.

Smolin, Lori A. & Grosvenor, Mary B. Nutrition & Eating Disorders. 2nd rev. ed. 2010. (Healthy Eating: A Guide to Nutrition Ser.). 136p. (C). (gr. 9). 35.00 (978-1-60413-802-3(5), Chelsea Hse.) Facts On File, Inc.

Snow, Todd. You Are Healthy (PB) Strong, Melodee, illus. 2008. (ENG.). 24p. (J). pap. 8.99 (978-1-934277-22-5(3)) Marn Green Publishing, Inc.

Sohn, Emily & Bair, Diane. Food & Nutrition: Eating to Win. 2011. (IScience Readers Ser.). 48p. (J). (gr. 5-6). lib. bdg. 23.94 (978-1-59953-424-4(X)) Norwood Hse. Pr.

Solway, Andrew. Food & Digestion. 2011. (Your Body Inside & Out Ser.). (Illus.). 32p. (J). (gr. 3-6). lib. bdg. 28.50 (978-1-59771-264-4(7)) Sea-To-Sea Pubns.

Spilsbury, Richard, et al. Your Body for Life. 2013. (Your Body for Life Ser.). (ENG.). 64p. (gr. 7-8). pap. 59.94 (978-1-4329-7095-6(X)) Heinemann-Raintree.

Staniford, Linda. Food & Drink. 2015. (Wants vs Needs Ser.). (ENG., Illus.). 24p. (gr. k-2). 23.32 (978-1-4846-0943-9(3), Heinemann Read & Learn) Heinemann-Raintree.

Stille, Darlene R. Lunch Lady Science: Understanding the Food That Goes in Your Body, 1 vol. 2011. (Everyday Science Ser.). (ENG.). 64p. (gr. 5-7). pap. 9.10 (978-0-7565-4502-4(1), CPB Grades 4-8) Compass Point Bks.

Storper, Barbara. Janey Junkfood's Fresh Adventure! Making Good Eating Great Fun! Schneid, Frances E., illus. 2008. 32p. (J). (gr. 3-7). 15.95 (978-0-9642858-5-9(1)) FoodPlay Productions.

Sullivan, Jaclyn. What's in Your Soda? 2012. (What's in Your Fast Food Ser.). (ENG., Illus.). 24p. (J). (gr. 2-5). pap. 8.25 (978-1-4488-6379-2(1), PowerKids Pr.); lib. bdg. 22.60 (978-1-4488-6210-8(8)) Rosen Publishing Group, Inc., The.

Sundance/Newbridge LLC Staff. You Are What You Eat. 2007. (Early Science Ser.). (gr. k-3). 18.95 (978-1-4007-6432-7(7)); pap. 6.10 (978-1-4007-6428-0(9)) Sundance/Newbridge Educational Publishing.

Tabletop Pocket Chart Nutrition Card Set. 2004. (J). 8.95 (978-1-56911-171-0(5)) Learning Resources, Inc.

Tecco, Betsy Dru. Food for Fuel: The Connection Between Food & Physical Activity. (Library of Nutrition Ser.). 48p. 2009. (gr. 5-8). 53.00 (978-1-60853-766-2(8), Rosen Reference) 2008. (ENG., Illus.). (gr. 5-8). per. 11.75 (978-1-4042-1635-8(9)) 2004. (Illus.). (J). lib. bdg. 26.50 (978-1-4042-0303-7(6)) Rosen Publishing Group, Inc., The.

Thomas, Patsy E. A Camp Carrot Cheer for Good Nutrition. 2011. 16p. (gr. 2-4). pap. 10.67 (978-1-4269-6200-4(2)) Trafford Publishing.

Thompson, Helen. Cookies or Carrots? You Are What You Eat. 2010. (Kids & Obesity Ser.). (Illus.). 48p. (YA). lib. bdg. 19.95 (978-1-4222-1707-8(8)) Mason Crest.

Thomson, Sarah L. What's for Lunch? Aye, Nila, illus. 2016. (Let's-Read-And-Find-Out Science 1 Ser.). 40p. (J). (gr. -1-3). pap. 6.99 (978-0-06-233137-3(X)) HarperCollins Pubs.

Tieck, Sarah. Eat Well, 1 vol. 2012. (ENG.). 32p. 27.07 (978-1-61783-232-1(4), Buddy Bks.) ABDO Publishing Co.

Tomczyk, Tara & Smith, Terry L. Nutrition & Food Safety. 2010. (Healthy Eating: A Guide to Nutrition Ser.). 184p. (C). (gr. 9). 35.00 (978-1-60413-776-7(2), Chelsea Hse.) Facts On File, Inc.

Tourville, Amanda Doering. Alimenta Tu Cuerpo. Rooney, Ronnie, illus. 2011. (Cómo Mantenernos Saludables/How to Be Healthy Ser.).Tr. of Fuel the Body. (SPA, MUL & ENG.). 24p. (gr. k-2). 26.65 (978-1-4048-6890-8(9)) Picture Window Bks.

—Fuel the Body: Eating Well, 1 vol. Rooney, Ronnie, illus. 2008. (How to Be Healthy! Ser.). (ENG.). 24p. (gr. k-2). 26.65 (978-1-4048-4814-6(2)) Picture Window Bks.

Troupe, Thomas Kingsley. Kitanai & Hungry Hare Eat Healthfully. Christoph, Jamey, illus. 2015. (Kitanai's Healthy Habits Ser.). (ENG.). 24p. (gr. k-2). pap. 8.95 (978-1-4795-6114-8(2)) Picture Window Bks.

Turnbull, Stephanie. Why Do We Eat? Haggerty, Tim, illus. 2006. (Usborne Beginners Ser.). 32p. (J). (gr. 4-7). lib. bdg. 12.99 (978-1-58086-933-1(5), Usborne) EDC Publishing.

Ureel, Jessica Mary. Allergy Express: Food Allergy Coloring & Activity Book. 2007. (J). per. 6.95 (978-0-9745033-1-8(2)) Main Street Pubns.

Ventura, Marne. Nutrition Myths, Busted! 2017. (Science Myths, Busted! Ser.). (ENG., Illus.). 32p. (J). (gr. 3-6). 21.95 (978-1-63235-304-7(0)) Pr. Room Editions LLC.

—12 Tips for a Healthy Diet. 2017. (J). (978-1-62143-507-5(5)) Pr. Room Editions LLC.

Ventura, Marne & Ringstad, Arnold. 12 Tips for a Healthy Diet. 2016. (Healthy Living Ser.). (ENG., Illus.). 32p. (J). pap. 9.95 (978-1-63235-383-2(0)) Pr. Room Editions LLC.

Vogel, Elizabeth. ¡A comer sanamente! (Eating Right) 2009. (Limpieza y salud todo el día (Clean & Healthy All Day Long) Ser.). (SPA.). 24p. (gr. 1-1). 37.50 (978-1-61514-290-3(8), Editorial Buenas Letras) Rosen Publishing Group, Inc., The.

—A Comer Sanamente! 2004. (Limpieza y Salud Todo el Dia Ser.). (SPA & ENG., Illus.). 24p. (J). (gr. -1-2). lib. bdg. 18.75 (978-0-8239-6612-7(7)) Rosen Publishing Group, Inc., The.

—Eating Right. 2009. (Clean & Healthy All Day Long Ser.). 24p. (gr. 1-1). 37.50 (978-1-61511-865-6(9), PowerKids Pr.) Rosen Publishing Group, Inc., The.

Wallach, Joel Dennis & Ma, Ian. Hell's Kitchen. 2005. 386p. (YA). pap. 19.95 (978-0-9748581-1-1(0)) Wellness Pubn.

Waters, Rosa. My Daily Diet: Fruits. Prock, Lisa Albers, ed. 2014. (On My Plate Ser.: 6). 48p. (J). (gr. 5-18). 20.95 (978-1-4222-3097-8(X)) Mason Crest.

—My Daily Diet: Grains. Prock, Lisa Albers, ed. 2014. (On My Plate Ser.: 6). 48p. (J). (gr. 5-18). 20.95 (978-1-4222-3098-5(8)) Mason Crest.

Weintraub, Aileen. Everything You Need to Know about Eating Smart. 2005. (Need to Know Library). (Illus.). 64p. (YA). (gr. 7-12). lib. bdg. 31.95 (978-0-8239-3082-1(3), NTEASM) Rosen Publishing Group, Inc., The.

West, Dorothy F. Nutrition, Food, & Fitness. 3rd ed. 2006. (ENG., Illus.). 510p. (gr. 9-12). 62.64 (978-1-59070-527-8(0)) Goodheart-Willcox Pub.

Where Does My Food Go. 2005. (J). 6.95 (978-0-9776850-0-4(4)) Sundback, Ruth.

Williams, Kara. Frequently Asked Questions about My Pyramid: Eating Right. 2009. (FAQ: Teen Life Ser.). 64p. (gr. 5-6). 58.50 (978-1-61512-583-8(3)) Rosen Publishing Group, Inc., The.

—Mypyramid: Eating Right. 2007. (FAQ: Teen Life Ser.). (Illus.). 64p. (YA). (gr. 7-12). lib. bdg. 31.95 (978-1-4042-1974-8(9)) Rosen Publishing Group, Inc., The.

Wilson, Scott & Wilkinson, Jody. Eating Healthy, Eating Right. 2004. 200p. 18.99 (978-0-8307-3022-3(2), Gospel Light) Gospel Light Pubns.

World Book, Inc Staff, contrib. by. Good Food for You. 2010. (J). (978-0-7166-7739-0(3)) World Bk., Inc.

NUTS

Benduhn, Tea. Meat & Beans (Carne y Frijoles) 2007. (Find Out about Food/ Conoce la comida Ser.). (SPA & ENG.). 24p. (gr. k-3). pap. 8.15 (978-0-8368-8463-0(9), Weekly Reader Leveled Readers) Stevens, Gareth Publishing LLLP.

—Meat & Beans/Carne y Legumbres. 2007. (Find Out about Food/Conoce la Comida Ser.). (SPA & ENG., Illus.). 24p. (gr. k-3). lib. bdg. 22.00 (978-0-8368-8456-2(6), Weekly Reader Leveled Readers) Stevens, Gareth Publishing LLLP.

Dilkes, D. H. Beans, Nuts, & Oils. 2011. (All about Good Foods We Eat Ser.). (Illus.). 24p. (J). (gr. -1-18). pap. 7.95 (978-1-59845-256-3(8), Enslow Elementary); (gr. k-3). lib. bdg. 22.60 (978-0-7660-3928-5(5)) Enslow Pubs., Inc.

Head, Honor. Beans & Nuts: On Your Plate. 2010. (J). 24.25 (978-1-59920-336-2(7)) Black Rabbit Bks.

Hughes, Meredith Sayles. Hard to Crack: Nut Trees. 2005. (Plants We Eat Ser.). (Illus.). 104p. (gr. 6-9). 26.60 (978-0-8225-2838-8(X)) Lerner Publishing Group.

Sayre, April Pulley. Let's Go Nuts! Seeds We Eat. Sayre, April Pulley, illus. 2013. (ENG., Illus.). 32p. (J). (gr. -1-3). 16.99 (978-1-4424-6728-6(2), Beach Lane Bks.) Beach Lane Bks.

Sertori, Trisha. Meats, Fish, Eggs, Nuts, & Beans. 2008. (Body Fuel for Healthy Bodies Ser.). 32p. (gr. 4-18). lib. bdg. 18.56

(978-0-7614-3601-4(7), Benchmark Bks.) Marshall Cavendish Corp.

NUVOLARI, TAZIO, 1892-1953

Briggs, Raymond. Nuvolari & the Alfa Romeo. 2006. (Illus.). (J). *(978-0-9766683-1-2(9))* Racemaker Pr.

NYERERE, JULIUS K. (JULIUS KAMBARAGE), 1922-1999

Maillu, David G. Julius Nyerere: Father of Ujamaa. 2005. (Lion Book Ser.). (Illus.). ix, 81p. (J). *(978-9966-951-32-8(6))* Sasa Sema Publications Ltd.

O

OAK

Berne, Emma. From Acorn to Oak Tree. 2017. (Start to Finish, Second Ser.). (ENG.). (J). (gr. k-3). pap. 6.99 ***(978-1-5124-5621-9(7))*** Lerner Publishing Group.

Berne, Emma Carlson. From Acorn to Oak Tree. 2017. (Start to Finish, Second Ser.). (ENG.). 24p. (J). (gr. k-3). 23.99 ***(978-1-5124-3440-8(X))*** Lerner Publishing Group.

Cain, Marie Mowery. Tiny Acorns, Majestic Oaks. 2013. (Big Books, Red Ser.). (ENG & SPA., Illus.). 16p. pap. 33.00 *(978-1-59246-218-6(9))* Big Books, by George!

De la Bédoyère, Camilla. Acorn to Oak Tree. 2013. (Illus.). 24p. (J). *(978-1-4351-4711-9(1))* Barnes & Noble, Inc.

Dickmann, Nancy. An Oak Tree's Life, 1 vol. 2010. (Watch It Grow Ser.). (ENG., Illus.). 24p. (gr. -1-1). pap. 6.29 *(978-1-4329-4152-9(6)*, Acorn) Heinemann-Raintree.

—La Vida del Roble. 2011. (¡Mira Cómo Crece! Ser.). (ENG & SPA.). 24p. (gr. -1-1). pap. 6.29 *(978-1-4329-5288-4(9)*, Bellota) Heinemann-Raintree.

Glaser, Rebecca. Oak Trees. 2012. (ENG., Illus.). 24p. (J). lib. bdg. 25.65 *(978-1-62031-027-4(9))* Jump! Inc.

Héliadore, et al. Let's Look at the Oak Close Up. Héliadore, illus. 2013. (ENG., Illus.). 36p. (J). (gr. 1-4). pap. 11.99 *(978-1-85103-352-2(1))* Moonlight Publishing, Ltd. GBR. Dist: Independent Pubs. Group.

Herrington, Lisa M. Acorn to Oak Tree. 2014. (Rookie Read-About(r) Science - Life Cycles Ser.). (ENG.). 32p. (J). lib. bdg. 23.00 *(978-0-531-21054-3(5))* Scholastic Library Publishing.

Hipp, Andrew. Oak. 2004. (Getting into Nature Ser.). (Illus.). 32p. (J). lib. bdg. 25.25 *(978-0-8239-4206-0(6))* Rosen Publishing Group, Inc., The.

—Oak Trees: Inside & Out. 2009. (Getting into Nature Ser.). 32p. (gr. 3-4). 47.90 *(978-1-61512-722-1(4)*, PowerKids Pr.) Rosen Publishing Group, Inc., The.

—El Roble: Por dentro y por fuera (Oak Tree: Inside & Out) 2009. (Explora la Naturaleza (Getting into Nature) Ser.). (SPA.). 32p. (gr. 3-4). 47.90 *(978-1-61512-338-4(5)*, Editorial Buenas Letras) Rosen Publishing Group, Inc., The.

Huseby, Victoria. Oak Tree. 2008. (J). 25.65 *(978-1-59920-178-8(X))* Black Rabbit Bks.

Johnson, Jinny. Oak Tree. Rosewarne, Graham, illus. 2010. (J). 28.50 *(978-1-59920-356-0(1))* Black Rabbit Bks.

Lowery, Lawrence F. Our Very Own Tree. 2015. (I Wonder Why Ser.). (ENG., Illus.). 36p. (J). (gr. k-3). pap. 11.95 *(978-1-941316-24-5(7))* National Science Teachers Assn.

Markovics, Joyce L. Oak Tree. 2015. (See It Grow Ser.). (ENG.). 24p. (J). (gr. -1-3). lib. bdg. 23.93 *(978-1-62724-844-0(7))* Bearport Publishing Co., Inc.

Mitchell, Melanie S. Oak Trees. (First Step Nonfiction Ser.). (Illus.). (gr. k-2). 2005. 24p. lib. bdg. 17.27 *(978-0-8225-4610-8(8))* 2003. 23p. (J). pap. 5.95 *(978-0-8225-4611-5(6)*, Lerner Pubns.) Lerner Publishing Group.

Pfeffer, Wendy. A Log's Life. Brickman, Robin, illus. 2007. (ENG.). 32p. (J). (gr. -1-3). 6.99 *(978-1-4169-3483-7(9)*, Aladdin) Simon & Schuster Children's Publishing.

Pugliano-Martin, Carol. Discover the Life Cycle of Oak Trees. 2006. (English Explorers Ser.). (J). pap. *(978-1-4108-6472-7(3))* Benchmark Education Co.

—The Life Cycle of Oak Trees. 2006. (English Explorers Ser.). (J). pap. *(978-1-4108-6469-7(3))* Benchmark Education Co.

Reid, Barbara. Acorn to Oak Tree. braille ed. 2004. (J). (gr. 1). spiral bd., bds. *(978-0-616-03085-1(1))* Canadian National Institute for the Blind/Institut National Canadien pour les Aveugles.

Schaefer, Lola M. & Schaefer, Adam. Acorn. Preston-Gannon, Frann, illus. 2016. (ENG.). 36p. (J). (gr. -1-k). 16.99 *(978-1-4521-1242-8(8))* Chronicle Bks. LLC.

Stockland, Patricia M. Look at an Oak Tree. 2012. (First Step Nonfiction - Look at Trees Ser.). (ENG., Illus.). 8p. (gr. -1-1). pap. 4.95 *(978-1-4677-0521-9(7)*, Lerner Pubns.) Lerner Publishing Group.

Thomson, Ruth. The Life Cycle of an Oak Tree. 2009. (Learning about Life Cycles Ser.). 24p. (J). (ENG.). (gr. k-5). pap. 8.25 *(978-1-4358-2888-9(7)*, PowerKids Pr.); (gr. 2-5). lib. bdg. 22.60 *(978-1-4358-2838-4(0))* Rosen Publishing Group, Inc., The.

OAK—FICTION

Albam, Jessica. The Boy in the Oak. 2010. (ENG., Illus.). 40p. (J). (gr. k-4). 17.95 *(978-1-897476-52-9(3))* Simply Read Bks. CAN. Dist: Ingram Publisher Services.

Barry, Debra R. The Loneliest Leaf. Baker, David, illus. 2011. 28p. pap. 24.95 *(978-1-4560-1002-7(6))* America Star Bks.

Beausoleil, Dana. The Elf in the Oak Tree. 2010. 32p. pap. 17.99 *(978-1-4251-1572-2(1))* Trafford Publishing.

Clauson, Marilyn & Drake, Lana. Woody Acorn. Drake, Lana, illus. 2012. (Illus.). 48p. pap. 24.95 *(978-1-4626-7946-1(3))* America Star Bks.

De Fombelle, Timothée. Toby & the Secrets of the Tree. Ardizzone, Sarah, tr. from FRE. Place, Francois, illus. 2010. (ENG.). 432p. (J). (gr. 4-7). 16.99 *(978-0-7636-4655-4(5))* Candlewick Pr.

Emerson, Carl. The Cold Winter Day, 1 vol. Doerrfeld, Cori, illus. 2008. (Read-It! Readers: Science Ser.). (ENG.). 32p. (gr. k-2). lib. bdg. 21.32 *(978-1-4048-2627-4(0)*, Easy Readers) Picture Window Bks.

George, Lindsay Barrett. That Pup! George, Lindsay Barrett, illus. 2011. (ENG., Illus.). 32p. (J). (gr. -1-k). 16.99 *(978-0-06-200413-0(1)*, Greenwillow Bks.) HarperCollins Pubs.

Hansen, Jeff. Albriana Visits the Branch Office. 2009. 36p. pap. 16.99 *(978-1-4389-4534-7(5))* AuthorHouse.

Hellier, Lorraine. The Wayward Wagon. 2010. 114p. pap. 10.99 *(978-1-4520-3232-0(7))* AuthorHouse.

Hilgendorf, L. B. Orville Oak & Friends. Dow, S. B., illus. 2005. 26p. (gr. -1-1). bds. 11.95 *(978-1-58275-149-8(8))* Black Forest Pr.

Karas, G. Brian. As an Oak Tree Grows. Karas, G. Brian, illus. 2014. (ENG., Illus.). 32p. (J). (gr. k-3). 17.99 *(978-0-399-25233-4(9)*, Nancy Paulsen Books) Penguin Young Readers Group.

Kimball, Lucy. Big Oak, Little Oak. 2016. (Spring Forward Ser.). (J). (gr. k). *(978-1-4900-6019-4(7))* Benchmark Education Co.

La Flamme Beighey, Carole. The Waddodles of Hollow Lake: The Mighty Oak. 2009. 344p. 28.49 *(978-1-4389-4037-3(8))* 2008. 340p. pap. 17.99 *(978-1-4343-8201-6(X))* AuthorHouse.

Lough, Erin & Duke, Mave Lough. The Spirit Tree at Toomer's Corner. 2012. (J). 19.95 *(978-1-62086-122-6(4))* Mascot Bks., Inc.

Lucado, Max. The Oak Inside the Acorn, 1 vol. Angelini, George, illus. 2006. (ENG.). 48p. 16.99 *(978-1-4003-0601-5(9))* Nelson, Thomas Inc.

Mitchell, Laurence. The Mean Root of Crowteal Pond: Inside a Hollow Oak Tree, Book #4. 2009. 28p. pap. 12.49 *(978-1-4389-5406-6(9))* AuthorHouse.

Mollis Lindquist, Melody Rose. Oak Tree. 2009. 16p. pap. 10.99 *(978-1-4490-0859-8(3))* AuthorHouse.

Parker, Lucy. Acorn Meadow has a Secret. 2010. (ENG., Illus.). 80p. pap. *(978-1-84748-600-4(2))* Athena Pr.

Penson, Mary. Billy Bardin & the Witness Tree. 2004. (Chaparral Bks.). (ENG.). 146p. (J). pap. 11.95 *(978-0-87565-283-2(2))* Texas Christian Univ. Pr.

Pride, Wallace. The Mighty Christmas Oak. 2008. 19p. pap. 24.95 *(978-1-60672-752-2(4))* PublishAmerica, Inc.

Taylor, Alice. Secrets of the Oak. Barnett, Russell, illus. 32p. 4.99 *(978-0-86322-138-5(6))* Penguin Publishing Group.

Violet Mackerel's Pocket Protest. 2014. (Violet Mackerel Ser.). (ENG., Illus.). 128p. (J). (gr. 1-5). 17.99 *(978-1-4424-9458-9(1)*, Atheneum Bks. for Young Readers) Simon & Schuster Children's Publishing.

Walsh, Ellen Stoll. Dot & Jabber & the Great Acorn Mystery. 2016. (Green Light Readers Level 2 Ser.). (ENG., Illus.). 32p. (J). (gr. -1-3). 12.99 *(978-0-544-79164-0(9)*, HMH Books For Young Readers) Houghton Mifflin Harcourt Publishing Co.

OAKLAND ATHLETICS (BASEBALL TEAM)

Gilbert, Sara. The Story of the Oakland Athletics. 2011. (Baseball: the Great American Game Ser.). (Illus.). 48p. (J). (gr. 5-8). lib. bdg. 34.25 *(978-1-60818-050-9(6)*, Creative Education) Creative Co., The.

Howell, Brian. Oakland Athletics, 1 vol. (Inside MLB Ser.). (ENG., 48p. (gr. 3-6). 2011. Illus.). (YA). lib. bdg. 32.79 *(978-1-61714-053-2(8))* 2014. lib. bdg. 32.79 *(978-1-62403-479-4(9)*, SportsZone) ABDO Publishing Co.

Pueschner, Gordon. The Story of the Oakland Athletics. 2007. (Baseball, the Great American Game Ser.). (Illus.). 48p. (YA). (gr. 4-7). lib. bdg. 32.80 *(978-1-58341-496-5(7))* Creative Co., The.

Stewart, Mark. The Oakland Athletics. 2012. (Team Spirit Ser.). 48p. (J). (gr. 3-6). lib. bdg. 29.27 *(978-1-59953-491-6(6))* Norwood Hse. Pr.

OAKLAND RAIDERS (FOOTBALL TEAM)

Burgess, Zack. Meet the Oakland Raiders. 2016. (Big Picture Sports Ser.). (ENG., Illus.). 24p. (J). (gr. k-3). lib. bdg. 22.60 *(978-1-59953-743-6(5))* Norwood Hse. Pr.

Caffrey, Scott. The Story of the Oakland Raiders. 2009. (NFL Today Ser.). (Illus.). 48p. (YA). (gr. 5-9). 22.95 *(978-1-58341-765-2(6))* Creative Co., The.

Frisch, Aaron. The History of the Oakland Raiders. 2003. (NFL Today Ser.). (Illus.). 32p. (YA). (gr. 5-9). 18.95 *(978-1-58341-308-1(1))* Creative Co., The.

—Oakland Raiders. (Super Bowl Champions Ser.). (J). (gr. 1-3). 2011. 24.25 *(978-1-60818-025-7(5))* 2005. (Illus.). 24p. lib. bdg. 16.95 *(978-1-58341-388-3(X)*, Creative Education) Creative Co., The.

—Oakland Raiders. 2014. (Illus.). 24p. (J). *(978-1-60818-384-5(X)*, Creative Education) Creative Co., The.

Frisch, Nate. NFL Today: Oakland Raiders. 2013. (NFL Today Ser.). (ENG.). 48p. (J). (gr. 4-7). pap. 12.00 *(978-0-89812-867-3(6)*, Creative Paperbacks) Creative Co., The.

—The Story of the Oakland Raiders. 2013. (J). 35.65 *(978-1-60818-314-2(9)*, Creative Education) Creative Co., The.

Howell, Brian. Oakland Raiders. 2015. (Insider's Guide to Pro Football Ser.). (ENG.). 32p. (J). (gr. k-3). 28.50 *(978-1-63407-001-0(1)*, 208836) Child's World, Inc., The.

Morey, Allan. The Oakland Raiders Story. 2016. (NFL Teams Ser.). (ENG., Illus.). 24p. (J). (gr. 3-7). lib. bdg. 26.95 *(978-1-62617-377-4(X)*, Torque Bks.) Bellwether Media.

Wyner, Zach. Oakland Raiders. (Illus.). 32p. (J). 2015. pap. *(978-1-4896-0871-0(0))* 2014. (ENG., (gr. 4-7). lib. bdg. 28.55 *(978-1-4896-0870-3(2)*, AV2 by Weigl) Weigl Pubs., Inc.

Zappa, Marcia. Oakland Raiders, 1 vol. 2014. (NFL's Greatest Teams Set 2 Ser.). (ENG.). 32p. (gr. 2-5). 28.50 *(978-1-62403-590-6(6))* ABDO Publishing Co.

OAKLEY, ANNIE, 1860-1926

Annie Oakley. 2010. (Legends of the Wild West Ser.). (Illus.). 104p. (gr. 6-12). 35.00 *(978-1-60413-594-7(8)*, Chelsea Hse.) Facts On File, Inc.

Annie Oakley. 2009. 48p. pap. 8.95 *(978-0-8225-5788-3(6))* Lerner Publishing Group.

Blair, Eric. Annie Oakley, 1 vol. Silverman, Dianne, illus. 2011. (My First Classic Story Ser.). (ENG.). 32p. (gr. k-3). lib. bdg. 22.65 *(978-1-4048-6577-8(2)*, My First Classic Story) Picture Window Bks.

DiVito, Anna. Annie Oakley Saves the Day. DiVito, Anna, illus. 2004. (Ready-To-read COFA Ser.). (ENG., Illus.). 32p. (J). (gr. k-2). pap. 3.99 *(978-0-689-86520-6(1)*, Simon Spotlight) Simon Spotlight.

Feinstein, Stephen. Read about Annie Oakley. 2006. (I Like Biographies! Ser.). (Illus.). 24p. (J). (gr. 1-3). lib. bdg. 22.60 *(978-0-7660-2583-7(7)*, Enslow Elementary) Enslow Pubs., Inc.

Flynn, Jean. Annie Oakley: Sharpshooter & Entertainer. 2015. (J). pap. *(978-0-7660-6441-6(7))* Enslow Pubs., Inc.

Gilbert, Sara. Annie Oakley. 2005. (Legends of the West (Creative Education) Ser.). (Illus.). 48p. (J). (gr. 5-9). lib. bdg. 21.95 *(978-1-58341-334-0(0)*, Creative Education) Creative Co., The.

Graves, Charles P. Annie Oakley: The Shooting Star. Cary, illus. 2011. 80p. (gr. 4-7). 37.95 *(978-1-258-01390-5(8))* Literary Licensing, LLC.

Herwick Rice, Dona & Greathouse, Lisa. Annie Oakley, 1 vol. 2009. (Building Fluency Through Reader's Theater Ser.). (ENG.). 24p. (J). (gr. 2-4). pap. 6.99 *(978-1-4333-0997-7(1))* Teacher Created Materials, Inc.

Kunstler, James Howard. Annie Oakley, 1 vol. Warter, Fred, illus. 2004. (Rabbit Ears-A Classic Tale Ser.). (ENG.). 36p. (gr. k-5). 25.65 *(978-1-59197-759-9(2))* Spotlight.

Landau, Elaine. Annie Oakley: Wild West Sharpshooter. 2004. (Best of the West Biographies Ser.). (Illus.). 48p. (J). lib. bdg. 23.93 *(978-0-7660-2205-8(6))* Enslow Pubs., Inc.

Link, Theodore. Annie Oakley: Wild West Sharpshooter. 2004. (Primary Sources of Famous People in American History Ser.). (ENG., Illus.). 32p. (gr. 4-8). pap. 10.00 *(978-0-8239-4174-2(4))* Rosen Publishing Group, Inc., The.

Macy, Sue. Bull's Eye: A Photobiography of Annie Oakley. 2015. (Photobiographies Ser.). (ENG.). 64p. (J). (gr. 5). pap. 7.99 *(978-1-4263-2218-1(6)*, National Geographic Children's Bks.) National Geographic Society.

Miller, Dean & Talbot, Jeffrey. Annie Oakley. 2014. (Illus.). 32p. (J). 28.50 *(978-1-62712-286-3(9))* Cavendish Square Publishing.

Porterfield, Jason. Annie Oakley: Tiradora del Lejano Oeste (Annie Oakley: Wild West Sharpshooter) 2009. (Grandes personajes en la historia de los Estados Unidos (Famous People in American History) Ser.). 32p. (gr. 2-3). 47.90 *(978-1-61512-789-4(5)*, Editorial Buenas Letras) Rosen Publishing Group, Inc., The.

—Annie Oakley: Wild West Sharpshooter. 2009. (Primary Sources of Famous People in American History Ser.). 32p. (gr. 2-3). 47.90 *(978-1-60851-651-3(2))* Rosen Publishing Group, Inc., The.

—Annie Oakley: Wild West Sharpshooter / Tiradora del Lejano Oeste. 2009. (Famous People in American History/Grandes personajes en la historia de los Estados Unidos Ser.). 32p. (gr. 2-3). 47.90 *(978-1-61512-537-1(X)*, Editorial Buenas Letras) Rosen Publishing Group, Inc., The.

Rose, Katherine. Annie Oakley. 2014. (Illus.). 32p. (J). pap. *(978-1-62712-287-0(7))* Cavendish Square Publishing.

Silate, Jennifer. Little Sure Shot: Annie Oakley & Buffalo Bill's Wild West Show. 2009. (Great Moments in American History Ser.). 32p. (gr. 3-3). 47.90 *(978-1-61513-147-1(7))* Rosen Publishing Group, Inc., The.

Spinner, Stephanie. Who Was Annie Oakley? Day, Larry, illus. 2003. (Who Was... ? Ser.). 109p. (gr. 4-7). 15.00 *(978-0-7569-1588-9(0))* Perfection Learning Corp.

Wadsworth, Ginger. Annie Oakley. 2005. (History Maker Bios Ser.). (Illus.). 48p. (J). (gr. 3-7). lib. bdg. 26.60 *(978-0-8225-2940-8(8)*, Lerner Pubns.) Lerner Publishing Group.

Whiting, Jim. Annie Oakley. 2006. (What's So Great About... ? Ser.). (Illus.). 32p. (J). (gr. 2-4). lib. bdg. 25.70 *(978-1-58415-477-8(2))* Mitchell Lane Pubs., Inc.

Wills, Chuck. Annie Oakley. 2007. (DK Biography Ser.). (ENG., Illus.). 128p. (J). (gr. 5-12). per. 6.99 *(978-0-7566-2997-7(7)*, DK Children) Dorling Kindersley Publishing, Inc.

OAKLEY, ANNIE, 1860-1926—FICTION

Dell, Pamela. Tag-along Tay: A Story about Annie Oakley & Buffalo Bill's Wild West Show. 2003. (Scrapbooks of America Ser.). (ENG., Illus.). 48p. (J). (gr. 3-6). 32.79 *(978-1-59187-039-5(9)*, 200812) Child's World, Inc., The.

Verral, Charles Spain. Annie Oakley, Sharpshooter. Dreany, E. Joseph, illus. 2011. 28p. pap. 35.95 *(978-1-258-06762-5(5))* Literary Licensing, LLC.

OBAMA, BARACK, 1961-

ABDO Publishing Company Staff & Wheeler, Jill C. Barack Obama, 1 vol. 2009. (United States Presidents Ser.). (ENG., Illus.). 40p. (YA). (gr. 3-6). 27.07 *(978-1-60453-481-8(8))* ABDO Publishing Co.

Amédékanya, Ben-Kofi. Pillars of Pride. 2011. 32p. pap. 15.99 *(978-1-4567-3458-9(X))* AuthorHouse.

B. Yes I Can for Kids. 2009. 36p. pap. 17.95 *(978-1-4490-1585-5(9))* AuthorHouse.

Bahadur, Gaiutra. Family Ties. 2011. (J). pap. *(978-0-531-22554-7(2))* Scholastic, Inc.

Barack Obama. 2007. (Political Profiles Ser.). (Illus.). 128p. (YA). (gr. 5-9). lib. bdg. 27.95 *(978-1-59935-045-5(9))* Reynolds, Morgan Inc.

Bartlett, Mel. Meet President Obama. 2012. (InfoMax Readers Ser.). (ENG., Illus.). 24p. (J). (gr. 1-2). pap. 8.25 *(978-1-4488-9058-3(6)*, Rosen Classroom) Rosen Publishing Group, Inc., The.

Besel, Jennifer M. Malia & Sasha Obama. 2012. (Star Biographies Ser.). (ENG.). 32p. (gr. 3-4). pap. 47.70 *(978-1-4296-9463-6(7)*, Snap Bks.) Capstone Press of Coughlan Cos.

Biskup, Agnieszka. Obama: The Historic Election of America's 44th President, 1 vol. Hayden, Seitu, illus. 2011. (American Graphic Ser.). (ENG.). 32p. (gr. 3-4). pap. 8.10 *(978-1-4296-7339-6(7))*; pap. 47.70 *(978-1-4296-7340-2(0))*; lib. bdg. 30.65 *(978-1-4296-6016-7(3))* Capstone Press of Coughlan Cos. (Graphic Library).

Bourcier, Cammy S. Barack Obama. 2009. (Sharing the American Dream Ser.). (Illus.). 64p. (YA). (gr. 7-12). 22.95 *(978-1-4222-0574-7(6))* Mason Crest.

Brill, Marlene Targ. Barack Obama: Working to Make a Difference. 2006. (J). pap. 6.95 *(978-0-8225-6056-2(9)*, First Avenue Editions); (Illus.). 48p. 23.93 *(978-0-8225-3417-4(7))* Lerner Publishing Group.

—Barack Obama (Revised Edition) 2009. pap. 52.95 *(978-0-7613-5031-6(4))* Lerner Publishing Group.

Britton, Tamara L. Barack Obama, 1 vol. 2013. (United States Presidents Ser.). (ENG.). 40p. (gr. 3-6). lib. bdg. 27.07 *(978-1-61783-492-9(0)*, Checkerboard Library) ABDO Publishing Co.

Brophy, David B. Michelle Obama: Meet the First Lady. 2008. 128p. (J). pap. 6.99 *(978-0-06-177990-9(3))* HarperCollins Pubs.

Brophy, David Bergen. Michelle Obama: Meet the First Lady. 2009. (ENG.). 128p. (J). (gr. 3-7). 16.99 *(978-0-06-177991-6(1)*, Collins) HarperCollins Pubs.

Burgan, Michael. Barack Obama. 2016. (Front-Page Lives Ser.). (ENG.). 112p. (gr. 6-9). pap. 11.99 *(978-1-4846-3813-2(1)*, NA-h) Heinemann-Raintree.

Carney-Nunes, Charisse & Williams, Ann Marie. I Am Barack Obama. 2009. (ENG., Illus.). 36p. (J). (gr. k-2). 16.95 *(978-0-9748142-4-7(5)*, Brand Nu Words) Nunes Productions, LLC.

Carolan, Joanna & Carolan, Terry. A President from Hawaii. Zunon, Elizabeth, illus. 2012. (ENG.). 24p. (J). (gr. 2-5). 15.99 *(978-0-7636-5230-2(X))*; pap. 7.99 *(978-0-7636-6282-0(8))* Candlewick Pr.

Conklin, Blane. Barack Obama: President of the United States. 2011. (Primary Source Readers Focus On Ser.). (ENG.). 32p. (J). (gr. 4-4). pap. 8.99 *(978-1-4333-1522-0(X))* Teacher Created Materials, Inc.

Corey, Shana. Barack Obama: Out of Many, One. Bernardin, James, illus. 2009. (Step into Reading Ser.). (ENG.). 48p. (J). (gr. k-3). pap. 3.99 *(978-0-375-86339-4(7)*, Random Hse. Bks. for Young Readers) Random Hse. Children's Bks.

—Barack Obama: Out of Many, One. 2014. (Step into Reading Ser.). (ENG., Illus.). 48p. (J). (gr. k-3). lib. bdg. 12.99 *(978-0-375-97371-0(0)*, Random Hse. Bks. for Young Readers) Random Hse. Children's Bks.

Davis, William Michael. Barack Obama: The Politics of Hope. 2007. (Illus.). 168p. (J). (gr. 10-18). lib. bdg. 25.95 *(978-1-59556-024-7(6))*; (YA). (gr. 8-18). pap. 16.99 *(978-1-59556-032-2(7))* OTTN Publishing.

De Medeiros, Michael. Barack Obama. (J). 2013. *(978-1-62127-388-2(1))* 2008. (Illus.). 24p. (gr. 4-6). pap. 8.95 *(978-1-59036-989-0(0))* 2008. (Illus.). 24p. (gr. 4-6). lib. bdg. 24.45 *(978-1-59036-988-3(2))* Weigl Pubs., Inc.

Devaney, Sherri, et al. Barack Obama. 2009. (People in the News Ser.). (ENG.). 104p. (YA). (gr. 7-12). lib. bdg. 33.45 *(978-1-4205-0206-0(9)*, LML02109-248525) Cengage Gale.

Doak, Robin S. Barack Obama. 2013. (True Book(tm), A — Biographies Ser.). (ENG., Illus.). 48p. (J). lib. bdg. 31.00 *(978-0-531-21904-1(6))*; pap. 6.95 *(978-0-531-23875-2(X))* Scholastic Library Publishing.

Dunn, Joeming. Barack Obama: 44th U. S. President, 1 vol. Espinosa, Rod, illus. 2011. (Presidents of the United States Bio-Graphics Ser.). (ENG.). 32p. (YA). (gr. 3-6). 28.50 *(978-1-61641-648-5(3))* Magic Wagon.

Edwards, Roberta. Barack Obama: Presidente de Estados Unidos. Call, Ken, illus. 2009.Tr. of Barack Obama: United States President. (SPA.). 64p. (J). (gr. 2-5). pap. 9.99 ***(978-1-63113-956-7(8)***, Loqueleo) Santillana USA Publishing Co., Inc.

—Barack Obama: United States President. Call, Ken, illus. rev. exp. ed. 2009. (ENG.). 64p. (J). (gr. 1-3). mass mkt. 5.99 *(978-0-448-45234-0(0)*, Grosset & Dunlap) Penguin Young Readers Group.

—Hail to the Chiefs, 5 vols. 2013. (Who Was? Ser.). (ENG.). 560p. (J). (gr. 3-7). pap. 24.95 *(978-0-448-48122-7(7)*, Grosset & Dunlap) Penguin Young Readers Group.

—Michelle Obama: Primera Dama y Primera Mama. Call, Ken, illus. 2010. (SPA.). 48p. (gr. 3-5). pap. 9.99 *(978-1-60396-946-8(2))* Santillana USA Publishing Co., Inc.

—Who Is Barack Obama? Harrison, Nancy & O'brien, John, illus. 2009. (Who Was? Ser.). (ENG.). 112p. (J). (gr. 3-7). pap. 5.99 *(978-0-448-45330-9(4)*, Grosset & Dunlap) Penguin Young Readers Group.

Epstein, Brad M. Barack Obama 101. l.t. ed. 2009. (My First Presidential Board Book Ser.). (Illus.). 28p. (J). (gr. -1-1). bds. *(978-1-60730-044-1(3)*, 101 Bk.) Michaelson Entertainment.

Falk, Laine. Meet President Barack Obama. Childrens Press Staff, ed. 2009. (Scholastic News Nonfiction Readers Ser.). (ENG., Illus.). 24p. (J). (gr. 1-2). pap. 6.95 *(978-0-531-23524-9(6)*, Children's Pr.) Scholastic Library Publishing.

—Meet President Barack Obama. 2009. (Scholastic News Nonfiction Readers Ser.). (ENG.). 24p. (J). (gr. 1-2). 20.00 *(978-0-531-23403-7(7)*, Children's Pr.) Scholastic Library Publishing.

Feinstein, Stephen. Barack Obama. 2008. (African-American Heroes Ser.). (Illus.). 24p. (J). (gr. 1-3). lib. bdg. 22.60 *(978-0-7660-2893-7(3)*, Enslow Elementary) Enslow Pubs., Inc.

Garner, Lama. A Children's Book of Barack Obama Our 44th President. Garner, Essex, illus. 2009.Tr. of Children's Book of Barack Obama Our 44th President. 24p. pap. 7.95 *(978-0-615-31464-8(3))* Art Of Essex Fine Art, The.

Gibson, Karen Bush. The Historic Fight for the 2008 Democratic Presidential Nomination: The Obama View. 2009. (Monumental Milestones Ser.). (Illus.). 48p. (YA). (gr. 4-7). lib. bdg. 29.95 *(978-1-58415-732-8(1))* Mitchell Lane Pubs., Inc.

Gormley, Beatrice. Barack Obama: Our 44th President. 2015. (Real-Life Story Ser.). (ENG., Illus.). 272p. (J). (gr. 3-7). 17.99 *(978-1-4814-4648-8(7)*, Aladdin) Simon & Schuster Children's Publishing.

Grimes, Nikki. Barack Obama: Son of Promise, Child of Hope. Collier, Bryan, illus. 2012. (ENG.). 48p. (J). (gr. k-3). pap. 9.99 *(978-1-4424-5077-6(0)*, Little Simon) Little Simon.

—Barack Obama: Son of Promise, Child of Hope. Collier, Bryan, illus. (ENG.). 48p. (J). (gr. k-3). 2012. 9.99 *(978-1-4424-4092-0(9))* 2008. 16.99 *(978-1-4169-7144-3(0))* Simon & Schuster Bks. For Young Readers. (Simon & Schuster Bks. For Young Readers).

Hansen, Grace. Barack Obama, 1 vol. 2014. (United States President Biographies Ser.). (ENG.). 24p. (J). (gr. 4-8). lib. bdg. 28.50 *(978-1-62970-086-1(X))* ABDO Publishing Co.

—Barack Obama. 2015. (Biografías de Los Presidentes de Los Estados Unidos Ser.). (SPA., Illus.). 24p. (gr. k-1). pap. 7.95 *(978-1-4966-0403-3(2))* Capstone Classroom.

Harkness, Karen. Obama, Our Hero. 2008. (Illus.). 32p. (J). lib. bdg. 12.99 *(978-0-9800934-1-4(4))* H&W Publishing Inc.

Hoe, Susan. Rosa Parks. 2007. (Sharing the American Dream Ser.). 64p. (YA). (gr. 7-18). pap. 9.95 *(978-1-4222-0760-4(9))* Mason Crest.

Hollar, Sherman, contrib. by. Barack Obama. 2012. (Pivotal Presidents: Profiles in Leadership Ser.). (ENG.). 80p. (gr. 7-12). (J). lib. bdg. 32.90 *(978-1-61530-945-0(4))*; (Illus.). (YA). 65.80 *(978-1-61530-955-9(1))* Rosen Publishing Group, Inc., The.

Hopkinson, Deborah. First Family. Ford, A. G., illus. 2009. (ENG.). 32p. (J). (gr. -1-2). 17.99 *(978-0-06-189680-4(2)*, Tegen, Katherine Bks) HarperCollins Pubs.

Hoppe, Ludwig Augustin. Die Epiklesis Der Griechischen Und Orientalischen Liturgieen Und Der Römische Consekrationskanon (German Edition) 2010. 350p. pap. 32.75 *(978-1-142-96440-5(X))* Creative Media Partners, LLC.

Horn, Geoffrey M. Barack Obama. 2009. (People We Should Know Ser.). 32p. (gr. 3-5). (J). lib. bdg. 31.00 *(978-1-4339-0017-4(3))*; pap. 10.50 *(978-1-4339-0157-7(9))* Stevens, Gareth Publishing LLLP. (Gareth Stevens Learning Library).

Katirgis, Jane. Celebrating President Barack Obama in Pictures. 2009. (Obama Family Photo Album Ser.). (Illus.). 32p. (J). (gr. 2-5). lib. bdg. 23.94 *(978-0-7660-3651-2(0))* Enslow Pubs., Inc.

—Celebrating the Inauguration of Barack Obama in Pictures. 2009. (Obama Family Photo Album Ser.). (Illus.). 32p. (J). (gr. 2-5). lib. bdg. 23.94 *(978-0-7660-3650-5(2))* Enslow Pubs., Inc.

—Celebrating the Obama Family in Pictures. 2009. (Obama Family Photo Album Ser.). (Illus.). 32p. (J). (gr. 2-5). lib. bdg. 23.94 *(978-0-7660-3653-6(7))* Enslow Pubs., Inc.

Kawa, Katie. Barack Obama: First African American President. 2012. (Beginning Biographies Ser.). (ENG., Illus.). 24p. (J). (gr. 1-3). 22.60 *(978-1-4488-8595-4(7)*, PowerKids Pr.) Rosen Publishing Group, Inc., The.

Klein, Adria F. Barack Obama. 2009. pap. 13.25 *(978-1-60559-055-4(X))* Hameray Publishing Group, Inc.

Krensky, Stephen & Dorling Kindersley Publishing Staff. Biography Barack Obama: A Photographic Story of Life. 2009. (DK Biography Ser.). (ENG.). 128p. (J). (gr. 5-12). 6.99 *(978-0-7566-5805-2(5)*, DK Children) Dorling Kindersley Publishing, Inc.

Lee, T. S. The Obama Story: The Boy with the Biggest Dream! Shin, Janet Jaywan, tr. from KOR. 2009. 207p. (J). (gr. 6-18). pap. 14.95 *(978-0-9819542-0-2(0))* DASANBOOKS.

Lowery, Zoe, ed. Barack Obama & the Idea of a Postracial Society. 2015. (African American Experience: from Slavery to the Presidency Ser.). (ENG.). 80p. (YA). (gr. 7-8). 65.80 *(978-1-68048-052-8(9)*, Britannica Educational Publishing) Rosen Publishing Group, Inc., The.

Mansfield, Cheryl. Barack Obama. 2016. (Premier Presidents Ser.). (ENG.). 24p. (J). (gr. 1-4). 27.07 *(978-1-5038-0846-1(7)*, 210696) Child's World, Inc., The.

Marcovitz, Hal. Barack. 2007. (Obamas Ser.). (Illus.). 64p. (YA). (gr. 3-6). pap. 9.95 *(978-1-4222-1484-8(2))*; (gr. 4-7). lib. bdg. 19.95 *(978-1-4222-1477-0(X))* Mason Crest.

—The Obama Family Tree. 2007. (Obamas Ser.). (Illus.). 64p. (YA). (gr. 3-6). pap. 9.95 *(978-1-4222-1488-6(5))*; (gr. 4-7). lib. bdg. 19.95 *(978-1-4222-1481-7(8))* Mason Crest.

—Obama Mania. 2007. (Obamas Ser.). (Illus.). 64p. (YA). (gr. 3-6). pap. 9.95 *(978-1-4222-1489-3(3))*; (gr. 4-7). lib. bdg. 19.95 *(978-1-4222-1482-4(6))* Mason Crest.

Marsh, Carole. Barack Obama: Biography FunBook. 2009. (J). (gr. 2-9). pap. 3.99 *(978-0-635-07053-1(7))* Gallopade International.

—Barack Obama - America's 44th President. 2009. (Here & Now Ser.). 40p. (J). (gr. 2-9). 29.99 *(978-0-635-06983-2(0))* Gallopade International.

—Barack Obama Presidential Coloring Book! 2008. (Here & Now Ser.). (J). 5.99 *(978-0-635-07050-0(2))* Gallopade International.

—Michelle Obama: Biography FunBook. 2009. (J). (gr. 2-9). pap. 3.99 *(978-0-635-07054-8(5))* Gallopade International.

—The Obama Family - Life in the White House: President Barack Obama, First Lady Michelle Obama, First Children Malia & Sasha. 2008. (Here & Now Ser.). 32p. (J). (gr. 2-9). pap. 8.99 *(978-0-635-07051-7(0))* Gallopade International.

Mattern, Joanne. Barack Obama. 2013. (Rookie Biographies(r) Ser.). (ENG.). 32p. (J). pap. 5.95 *(978-0-531-24701-3(5))*; lib. bdg. 23.00 *(978-0-531-24735-8(X))* Scholastic Library Publishing.

McCaffrey, Paul. Michelle Obama. 2010. (Women of Achievement Ser.). 144p. (gr. 6-12). 35.00 *(978-1-60413-911-2(0)*, Chelsea Hse.) Facts On File, Inc.

Mendell, David & Thomson, Sarah L. Obama: A Promise of Change. 2008. (ENG., Illus.). 192p. (J). (gr. 3-7). pap. 6.99 *(978-0-06-169700-5(1)*, Amistad) HarperCollins Pubs.

Michelle Obama. 2009. (Political Profiles Ser.). 112p. (YA). (gr. 5-9). lib. bdg. 28.95 *(978-1-59935-090-5(4))* Reynolds, Morgan Inc.

Miller, Moses. The Barack in Me: An Inspirational Novel for Young African American Males. 2009. 116p. pap. 10.99 *(978-0-9786929-2-6(6))* Mind Candy, LLC.

Mills, Nathan & Kawa, Katie. Barack Obama: First African American President. 2012. (Rosen Readers Ser.). (ENG., Illus.). 24p. (J). (gr. 1-2). pap. 8.25 *(978-1-4488-8845-0(X)*, Rosen Classroom) Rosen Publishing Group, Inc., The.

"Miss Nancy" Sorensen. President Barack Obam. 2009. 16p. pap. 8.50 *(978-1-4389-4604-7(X))* AuthorHouse.

National Geographic Kids Staff & Gilpin, Caroline Crosson. National Geographic Readers: Barack Obama. 2014. (Readers Bios Ser.). (ENG.). 32p. (J). (gr. k-3). pap. 3.99 *(978-1-4263-1759-0(X)*, National Geographic Children's Bks.) National Geographic Society.

Obama, Barack. Our Enduring Spirit: President Barack Obama's First Words to America. Ruth, Greg, illus. 2009. 48p. lib. bdg. 18.89 *(978-0-06-183456-1(4))* HarperCollins Pubs.

Obama, Barack & Nelson, Kadir. Change Has Come: An Artist Celebrates Our American Spirit. Nelson, Kadir, illus. 2009. (ENG., Illus.). 64p. (J). (gr. 1). 12.99 *(978-1-4169-8955-4(2)*, Simon & Schuster Bks. For Young Readers) Simon & Schuster Bks. For Young Readers.

O'Neal, Claire. What's So Great about Barack Obama. 2009. (What's So Great About... ? Ser.). 32p. (J). (gr. 2-4). lib. bdg. 25.70 *(978-1-58415-830-1(1))* Mitchell Lane Pubs., Inc.

Phillips, Alonzo. Follow the Course! an Action Book. 2010. 50p. pap. 15.99 *(978-1-4535-3702-2(3))* Xlibris Corp.

Robinson, Tom. Barack Obama: 44th U. S. President. 2009. (J). lib. bdg. 32.79 *(978-1-60453-528-0(8)*, Essential Library) ABDO Publishing Co.

Schuetz, Rachael Law. The Long Road to Change: An American Story of Civil Rights & Barack Obama's Journey to the White House. 2009. 36p. (J). 16.00 *(978-0-615-27983-1(X))* NRS Enterprises.

Schuman, Michael A. Barack Obama: We Are One People. 2008. (African-American Biography Library). (Illus.). 128p. (J). (gr. 3-7). lib. bdg. 33.27 *(978-0-7660-2891-3(7))* Enslow Pubs., Inc.

—Barack Obama: We Are One People, Revised & Expanded. rev. ed. 2009. (African-American Biography Library). (Illus.). 160p. (J). (gr. 6). lib. bdg. 33.27 *(978-0-7660-3649-9(9))* Enslow Pubs., Inc.

Shepherd, Jodie. Barack Obama: Groundbreaking President. 2016. (Rookie Biographies(tm) Ser.). (ENG., Illus.). 32p. (J). lib. bdg. 25.00 *(978-0-531-21681-1(0)*, Children's Pr.) Scholastic Library Publishing.

Sherman, Patrice. What It's Like to Be President Barack Obama? Vega, Eida de la, tr. 2009. (What It's Like to Be/Que se Siente al Ser Ser.). (SPA & ENG., Illus.). 32p. (J). (gr. -1-2). 25.70 *(978-1-58415-843-1(3))* Mitchell Lane Pubs., Inc.

Sirvaitis, Karen. Barack Obama: A Leader in a Time of Change. 2009. (USA TODAY Lifeline Biographies Ser.). (ENG.). 112p. (gr. 6-12). lib. bdg. 34.60 *(978-0-7613-4235-9(4))* Lerner Publishing Group.

Snyder, Gail. Malia. 2007. (Obamas Ser.). 64p. (YA). (gr. 3-6). pap. 9.95 *(978-1-4222-1486-2(9))*; (gr. 4-7). lib. bdg. 19.95 *(978-1-4222-1479-4(6))* Mason Crest.

—Sasha. 2007. (Obamas Ser.). (Illus.). 64p. (YA). (gr. 3-6). pap. 9.95 *(978-1-4222-1487-9(7))*; (gr. 4-7). lib. bdg. 19.95 *(978-1-4222-1480-0(X))* Mason Crest.

Stille, Darlene R. Barack Obama: 44th U.S. President, 1 vol. Stergulz, Richard, illus. 2013. (Beginner Biographies Set 2 Ser.). (ENG.). 32p. (J). (gr. -1-4). 28.50 *(978-1-61641-939-4(3))* Magic Wagon.

Sutcliffe, Jane. Barack Obama. 2010. (History Maker Biographies Ser.). (ENG.). 48p. (gr. 3-6). lib. bdg. 27.93 *(978-0-7613-5205-1(8)*, Lerner Pubns.) Lerner Publishing Group.

Taylor, Charlotte & Feinstein, Stephen. Barack Obama: First African-American President. 2015. (Exceptional African Americans Ser.). (ENG.). 24p. (J). (gr. 3-4). pap. 9.35 *(978-0-7660-7122-3(7))*; (Illus.). 22.60 *(978-0-7660-7124-7(3))* Enslow Pubs., Inc.

Thomas, Garen. Yes We Can: A Biography of President Barack Obama. 2nd rev. ed. 2008. (ENG., Illus.). 256p. (J). (gr. 3-7). pap. 12.99 *(978-0-312-58639-3(6)*, 9780312586393) Feiwel & Friends.

Tieck, Sarah. Barack Obama, 1 vol. 2010. (First Biographies Set 6 Ser.). (ENG.). 32p. (J). (gr. 1-4). 27.07 *(978-1-60453-985-1(2))* ABDO Publishing Co.

—Sasha & Malia Obama: Historic First Kids, 1 vol. 2009. (Big Buddy Biographies Set 3 Ser.). (ENG., Illus.). 32p. (J). (gr. 2-5). 28.50 *(978-1-60453-710-9(8))* ABDO Publishing Co.

—Sasha & Malia Obama: Historic First Kids CD & Book. 2010. (Big Buddy Biographies CD+Book Ser.). 32p. (gr. 2-5). audio compact disk 57.00 *(978-1-61613-310-8(4)*, Big Buddy Bks.) ABDO Publishing Co.

—Sasha & Malia Obama: Historic First Kids Site CD & Book. 2010. (Big Buddy Biographies Site CD+Book Ser.). 32p. (gr. 2-5). cd-rom 85.57 *(978-1-61613-282-8(5)*, Big Buddy Bks.) ABDO Publishing Co.

Tolliver, Julia. The Distinguishable Gentleman & the Presidential Race Of '08. 2011. 202p. (gr. 1-1). 29.99 *(978-1-4535-8791-1(8))*; pap. 19.99 *(978-1-4535-8790-4(X))* Xlibris Corp.

Torres, John. How Barack Obama Fought the War on Terrorism. 2017. (Presidents at War Ser.). 128p. (J). (gr. 8-8). lib. bdg. 37.27 ***(978-0-7660-8535-0(X))*** Enslow Pubs., Inc.

Wagner, Heather Lehr. Barack Obama. 2008. (Black Americans of Achievement: Legacy Edition Ser.). 104p. (gr. 6-12). pap. 11.95 *(978-1-60413-324-0(4)*, Checkmark Bks.) Facts On File, Inc.

—Barack Obama: Politician. 2008. (Black Americans of Achievement Ser.). (Illus.). 104p. (YA). (gr. 7-12). lib. bdg. 35.00 *(978-0-7910-9716-8(1))* Facts On File, Inc.

Winter, Jonah. Barack. Ford, A. G., illus. 32p. (J). (gr. -1-2). 2010. (ENG.). pap. 7.99 *(978-0-06-170396-6(6)*, Tegen, Katherine Bks) 2008. lib. bdg. 18.89 *(978-0-06-170393-5(1))* 2008. (ENG.). 17.99 *(978-0-06-170392-8(3)*, Tegen, Katherine Bks) HarperCollins Pubs.

—Barack, 2 vols. 2009. (J). 38.75 *(978-1-4407-3624-7(3))*; 40.75 *(978-1-4407-3622-3(7))*; 40.75 *(978-1-4407-3618-6(9))*; 38.75 *(978-1-4407-3620-9(0))*; 222.75 *(978-1-4407-3619-3(7))*; 1.25 *(978-1-4407-3625-4(1))* Recorded Bks., Inc.

Wong, Angi Ma. Barack Obama: Historymaker. 2009. (Illus.). 104p. (J). *(978-1-928753-86-5(8))* Pacific Heritage Bks.

Wong, Angi Ma, illus. Meet President Obama: America's 44th President. 2009. 32p. (J). *(978-1-928753-28-5(0))* Pacific Heritage Bks.

Zaboly, Gary. Barack Obama Coloring Book. 2009. (Dover History Coloring Book Ser.). (ENG., Illus.). 32p. (J). (gr. 3-6). pap. 3.99 *(978-0-486-47320-8(1))* Dover Pubns., Inc.

Zeiger, Jennifer. Barack Obama. 2012. (Cornerstones of Freedom, Third Ser.). (ENG.). 64p. (J). (gr. 4-6). pap. 8.95 *(978-0-531-28150-5(7))*; lib. bdg. 30.00 *(978-0-531-23050-3(3))* Scholastic Library Publishing. (Children's Pr.).

Zumbusch, Amelie von. Barack Obama: Man of Destiny. 2010. (Making History: the Obamas Ser.). (Illus.). 24p. (J). pap. 8.25 *(978-1-4358-9866-0(4))*; (gr. 2-3). lib. bdg. 22.60 *(978-1-4358-9387-0(5))* Rosen Publishing Group, Inc., The. (PowerKids Pr.).

—Barack Obama's Family Tree: Roots of Achievement. 2010. (Making History: the Obamas Ser.). (Illus.). 24p. (J). pap. 8.25 *(978-1-4358-9872-1(9))*; (gr. 2-3). lib. bdg. 22.60 *(978-1-4358-9390-0(5))* Rosen Publishing Group, Inc., The. (PowerKids Pr.).

—First Family: The Obamas in the White House. 2010. (Making History: the Obamas Ser.). (Illus.). 24p. (J). pap. 8.25 *(978-1-4358-9870-7(2))*; (gr. 2-3). lib. bdg. 22.60 *(978-1-4358-9389-4(1))* Rosen Publishing Group, Inc., The. (PowerKids Pr.).

—Making History: The Obamas, 4 vols., Set. Incl. Barack Obama: Man of Destiny. lib. bdg. 22.60 *(978-1-4358-9387-0(5))*; Barack Obama's Family Tree: Roots of Achievement. lib. bdg. 22.60 *(978-1-4358-9390-0(5))*; First Family: The Obamas in the White House. lib. bdg. 22.60 *(978-1-4358-9389-4(1))*; Michelle Obama: Our First Lady. lib. bdg. 22.60 *(978-1-4358-9388-7(3))*; (J). (gr. 2-3). (Illus.). 24p. 2010. 85.00 *(978-1-4358-9407-5(3)*, PowerKids Pr.) Rosen Publishing Group, Inc., The.

OBAMA, MICHELLE, 1964-

Bodden, Valerie. Michelle Obama: First Lady & Role Model, 1 vol. 2009. (Essential Lives Set 4 Ser.). (ENG., Illus.). 112p. (J). (gr. 6-12). lib. bdg. 35.64 *(978-1-60453-703-1(5))* ABDO Publishing Co.

Brill, Marlene Targ. Michelle Obama. 2009. (Illus.). 48p. (J). pap. 8.95 *(978-0-7613-5053-8(5))* Lerner Publishing Group.

—Michelle Obama: From Chicago's South Side to the White House. 2009. (Gateway Biographies Ser.). (ENG., Illus.). 48p. (gr. 4-8). 26.60 *(978-0-7613-5033-0(0))* Lerner Publishing Group.

Brophy, David B. Michelle Obama: Meet the First Lady. 2008. 128p. (J). pap. 6.99 *(978-0-06-177990-9(3))* HarperCollins Pubs.

Brophy, David Bergen. Michelle Obama: Meet the First Lady. 2009. (ENG.). 128p. (J). (gr. 3-7). 16.99 *(978-0-06-177991-6(1)*, Collins) HarperCollins Pubs.

Colbert, David. Michelle Obama: An American Story. 2008. (ENG., Illus.). 160p. (J). (gr. 2-5). pap. 6.99 *(978-0-547-24770-0(2))* Houghton Mifflin Harcourt Publishing Co.

Doak, Robin S. Michelle Obama, 1 vol. 2014. (Extraordinary Women Ser.). (ENG., Illus.). 48p. (gr. 6-6). lib. bdg. 32.65 *(978-1-4109-5940-9(6))* Heinemann-Raintree.

Edwards, Roberta. Michelle Obama: Primera Dama y Primera Mama. Call, Ken, illus. 2010. (SPA.). 48p. (gr. 3-5). pap. 9.99 *(978-1-60396-946-8(2))* Santillana USA Publishing Co., Inc.

Endsley, Kezia. Michelle Obama: 44th First Lady & Health & Education Advocate. 2014. (Leading Women Ser.). 112p. (YA). (gr. 7-11). lib. bdg. 39.93 *(978-1-62712-975-6(8))* Cavendish Square Publishing.

Gourley, Robbin. First Garden: The White House Garden & How It Grew. 2011. (ENG., Illus.). 48p. (J). (gr. 1-4). 16.99 *(978-0-547-48224-8(8))* Houghton Mifflin Harcourt Publishing Co.

Hopkinson, Deborah. Michelle. Ford, A. G., illus. 2009. 32p. (J). (gr. -1-2). 17.99 *(978-0-06-182739-6(8))* HarperCollins Pubs.

Hudson, Amanda. Michelle Obama. 2009. (People We Should Know Ser.). (ENG.). 48p. (J). (gr. 3-5). pap. 10.50 *(978-1-4339-2192-6(8))*; lib. bdg. 31.00 *(978-1-4339-2187-2(1))* Stevens, Gareth Publishing LLLP. (Gareth Stevens Learning Library).

Katirgis, Jane. Celebrating First Lady Michelle Obama in Pictures. 2009. (Obama Family Photo Album Ser.). (Illus.). 32p. (J). (gr. 2-5). lib. bdg. 23.94 *(978-0-7660-3652-9(9))* Enslow Pubs., Inc.

Machajewski, Sarah. Michelle Obama. 2016. (Superwomen Role Models Ser.). (Illus.). 32p. (J). (gr. 4-3). 26.25 *(978-1-5081-4812-8(0)*, PowerKids Pr.) Rosen Publishing Group, Inc., The.

Marcovitz, Hal. Michelle. 2007. (Obamas Ser.). 64p. (YA). (gr. 3-6). pap. 9.95 *(978-1-4222-1485-5(0))*; (gr. 4-7). lib. bdg. 19.95 *(978-1-4222-1478-7(8))* Mason Crest.

Marsh, Carole. Michelle Obama: Biography FunBook. 2009. (J). (gr. 2-9). pap. 3.99 *(978-0-635-07054-8(5))* Gallopade International.

—The Obama Family - Life in the White House: President Barack Obama, First Lady Michelle Obama, First Children Malia & Sasha. 2008. (Here & Now Ser.). 32p. (J). (gr. 2-9). pap. 8.99 *(978-0-635-07051-7(0))* Gallopade International.

Mattern, Joanne. What's So Great about Michelle Obama. 2009. (What's So Great About... ? Ser.). 32p. (J). (gr. 2-4). lib. bdg. 25.70 *(978-1-58415-833-2(6))* Mitchell Lane Pubs., Inc.

McCaffrey, Paul. Michelle Obama. 2010. (Women of Achievement Ser.). 144p. (gr. 6-12). 35.00 *(978-1-60413-911-2(0)*, Chelsea Hse.) Facts On File, Inc.

Michelle Obama. 2009. (Political Profiles Ser.). 112p. (YA). (gr. 5-9). lib. bdg. 28.95 *(978-1-59935-090-5(4))* Reynolds, Morgan Inc.

Nault, Jennifer. Michelle Obama. 2009. (Remarkable People Ser.). (Illus.). 24p. (J). (gr. 4-6). pap. 8.95 *(978-1-60596-666-3(5))*; lib. bdg. 24.45 *(978-1-60596-665-6(7))* Weigl Pubs., Inc.

Raatma, Lucia. Michelle Obama, 1 vol. 2010. (First Ladies Ser.). (ENG.). 24p. (gr. k-1). lib. bdg. 26.65 *(978-1-4296-5008-3(7)*, Pebble Plus) Capstone Press of Coughlan Cos.

Stine, Megan. Who Is Michelle Obama? O'brien, John & Harrison, Nancy, illus. 2013. (Who Was? Ser.). (ENG.). 112p. (J). (gr. 3-7). 5.99 *(978-0-448-47863-0(3)*, Grosset & Dunlap) Penguin Young Readers Group.

—Who Is Michelle Obama? 2013. (Who Is... ? Ser.). lib. bdg. 14.75 *(978-0-606-32131-0(4)*, Turtleback) Turtleback Bks.

Taylor-Butler, Christine. Michelle Obama. 2015. (ENG.). 48p. (J). pap. 6.95 *(978-0-531-21206-6(8)*, Orchard Bks.) Scholastic Library Publishing.

Uschan, Michael V. Michelle Obama. 2010. (People in the News Ser.). (Illus.). 128p. (YA). (gr. 8-10). 33.95 *(978-1-4205-0209-1(3)*, Lucent Bks.) Cengage Gale.

Zumbusch, Amelie von. First Family: The Obamas in the White House. 2010. (Making History: the Obamas Ser.). (Illus.). 24p. (J). pap. 8.25 *(978-1-4358-9870-7(2))*; (gr. 2-3). lib. bdg. 22.60 *(978-1-4358-9389-4(1))* Rosen Publishing Group, Inc., The. (PowerKids Pr.).

—Making History: The Obamas, 4 vols., Set. Incl. Barack Obama: Man of Destiny. lib. bdg. 22.60 *(978-1-4358-9387-0(5))*; Barack Obama's Family Tree: Roots of Achievement. lib. bdg. 22.60 *(978-1-4358-9390-0(5))*; First Family: The Obamas in the White House. lib. bdg. 22.60 *(978-1-4358-9389-4(1))*; Michelle Obama: Our First Lady. lib. bdg. 22.60 *(978-1-4358-9388-7(3))*; (J). (gr. 2-3). (Illus.). 24p. 2010. 85.00 *(978-1-4358-9407-5(3)*, PowerKids Pr.) Rosen Publishing Group, Inc., The.

—Michelle Obama: Our First Lady. 2010. (Making History: the Obamas Ser.). (Illus.). 24p. (J). pap. 8.25 *(978-1-4358-9868-4(0))*; (gr. 2-3). lib. bdg. 22.60 *(978-1-4358-9388-7(3))* Rosen Publishing Group, Inc., The. (PowerKids Pr.).

OBEDIENCE

Berry, Joy. Help Me Be Good Disobeying. Bartholomew, illus. 2010. (Help Me Be Good Ser.). (ENG.). 32p. (J). (gr. -1-2). pap. 4.99 *(978-1-60577-137-3(6))* Berry, Joy Enterprises.

Berry, Joy Wilt. A Children's Book about Disobeying. 2005. (Illus.). (J). *(978-0-7172-8593-8(6))* Scholastic, Inc.

Bloom, Paul. Rules in the Classroom. 2015. (School Rules Ser.). (ENG., Illus.). 24p. (J). (gr. k-k). pap. 8.15 *(978-1-4824-2641-0(2))* Stevens, Gareth Publishing LLLP.

—Rules in the Gym. 2015. (School Rules Ser.). (ENG., Illus.). 24p. (J). (gr. k-k). pap. 8.15 *(978-1-4824-2645-8(5))* Stevens, Gareth Publishing LLLP.

Gordon, Sharon. Respetamos las Reglas. 2006. (Bookworms Ser.). (SPA & ENG., Illus.). 24p. (gr. k-1). lib. bdg. 15.95 *(978-0-7614-2358-4(3)*, Benchmark Bks.) Marshall Cavendish Corp.

—We Follow the Rules. (Bookworms: Ready for School Ser.). (Illus.). (J). (gr. 3-7). 2007. 23p. pap. 6.99 *(978-0-7614-3273-9(6))* 2005. (ENG & SPA., 24p. lib. bdg. *(978-0-7614-1995-2(0))* Marshall Cavendish Corp. (Benchmark Bks.).

—We Follow the Rules/Respetamos Las Reglas. 2006. (Bookworms Ser.). (ENG & SPA., Illus.). 24p. (gr. k-1). lib. bdg. 15.95 *(978-0-7614-2438-3(5))* Marshall Cavendish Corp.

Leventhal-Belfer, Laurie. Why Do I Have To? A Book for Children Who Find Themselves Frustrated by Everyday Rules. Montaini-Klovdahl, Luisa, illus. 2008. (ENG.). 80p. pap. 10.95 *(978-1-84310-891-7(7)*, 5918) Kingsley, Jessica Pubs. GBR. Dist: Macmillan Distribution Ltd.

MacKenzie, Carine. Glorifying God: Obedient Lives from the Bible. 2013. (ENG., Illus.). 96p. (J). pap. 7.99 *(978-1-78191-124-2(X)*, 404a70e4-6acf-4784-85be-df8caceea0fa) Christian Focus Pubns. GBR. Dist: Bookmasters Distribution.

Mayer, Cassie. Following Rules, 1 vol. Beech, Mark, illus. 2007. (Citizenship Ser.). (ENG.). 24p. (gr. -1-3). pap. 6.29 *(978-1-4034-9495-5(9)*, Acorn) Heinemann-Raintree.

—Seguir las Reglas. 2007. (Civismo Ser.). (SPA., Illus.). 24p. (gr. -1-1). pap. 6.29 *(978-1-4329-0410-4(8)*, Bellota) Heinemann-Raintree.

Meiners, Cheri J. Know & Follow Rules. Johnson, Meredith, illus. (Learning to Get Along(r) Ser.). (ENG, SPA & MUL.). (J). (gr. -1-3). 2015. 48p. pap. 12.45 *(978-1-57542-498-9(3))* 2005. 40p. pap. 10.95 *(978-1-57542-130-8(5))* Free Spirit Publishing, Inc.

Nelson, Robin. Following Rules. 2003. (First Step Nonfiction - Citizenship Ser.). (ENG., Illus.). 24p. (gr. k-2). pap. 6.95 *(978-0-8225-1321-6(8))*; lib. bdg. 23.93 *(978-0-8225-1284-4(X))* Lerner Publishing Group.

Robak, Raelinda. Herbie the Hippo. 2007. (J). *(978-0-8127-0465-5(7))* Autumn Hse. Publishing Co.

OBEDIENCE—FICTION

A. L. O. E. The Triumph over Midian. 2006. 344p. per. 23.99 *(978-1-4255-3466-0(X))* Michigan Publishing.

Bauer, Marion Dane. On My Honor. 2012. lib. bdg. 18.40 *(978-0-606-24717-7(3)*, Turtleback) Turtleback Bks.

Bolton, Robin. Sunny Goes Out to Play. 2011. 28p. pap. 12.03 *(978-1-4634-2530-2(9))* AuthorHouse.

Clara Mulholland. Naughty Miss Bunny. 2007. 128p. per. 10.95 *(978-1-4218-3938-7(5)*, 1st World Library - Literary Society) 1st World Publishing, Inc.

Cook, Julia. I Just Don't Like the Sound of No! My Story about Accepting No for an Answer & Disagreeing the Right Way. De Weerd, Kelsey, illus. 2011. (ENG.). 32p. (J). *(978-1-934490-26-6(1))* Boys Town Pr.

—I Just Don't Like the Sound of No! My Story about Accepting 'No' for an Answer & Disagreeing the Right Way!: My Story about Accepting 'No' for an Answer & Disagreeing... the Right Way! De Weerd, Kelsey, illus. 2011. (ENG.). 32p. (J). 10.95 *(978-1-934490-25-9(3))* Boys Town Pr.

Crouch, Cheryl. Troo's Big Climb, 1 vol. Zimmer, Kevin, illus. 2011. (I Can Read! / Rainforest Friends Ser.). (ENG.). 32p. (J). (gr. -1-2). pap. 3.99 *(978-0-310-71808-6(2))* Zonderkidz.

Dean, Walter. How Leo the Lion Learned to Roar. 2013. 44p. pap. 12.95 *(978-0-9844342-6-8(7))* C&K Publishing Co.

Feiffer, Jules. I'm Not Bobby! Feiffer, Jules, illus. 2006. (Illus.). 28p. (J). (gr. k-4). reprint ed. 16.00 *(978-0-7567-9853-6(1))* DIANE Publishing Co.

Ferrier, Charlotte. Goldilocks & the Three Bears. 2016. (Fairytale Cottages Ser.). (ENG., Illus.). 12p. (J). (gr. -1-k). bds. 8.99 *(978-0-7641-6817-8(7))* Barron's Educational Series, Inc.

Frye, Timea Csonka. Wishing Star: Lost in the Woods. 2013. 32p. pap. 24.95 *(978-1-63000-931-1(8))* America Star Bks.

Gaichies, Sarah. Mirabelle the Lost Kitten. 2010. (Illus.). 76p. pap. 24.99 *(978-1-4490-5593-6(1))* AuthorHouse.

Gallegos, Eligio Stephen. Nothing Is Nothing. 2013. 144p. pap. 6.99 *(978-0-944164-24-2(2))* Moon Bear Pr.

Hamilton, Elizabeth L. Little Zoh's Submissive Trunk. 2003. (Character Critters Ser.: No. 3). (Illus.). 32p. (J). (gr. -1-3). per. 5.95 *(978-0-9713749-9-7(6)*, Character-in-Action) Quiet Impact, Inc.

Holub, Joan. Be Patient, Pandora! Patricelli, Leslie, illus. 2014. (Mini Myths Ser.). (ENG.). 24p. (J). (gr. -1 — 1). bds. 6.95 *(978-1-4197-0951-7(8)*, Abrams Appleseed) Abrams, Inc.

Jacqueline, Thomas. Birthday Picnic. 2010. 24p. pap. 9.99 *(978-0-88144-493-3(6))* Yorkshire Publishing Group.

Knudsen, Michelle. Library Lion. Hawkes, Kevin, illus. 2006. (ENG.). 48p. (J). (gr. -1-3). 16.99 *(978-0-7636-2262-6(1))* Candlewick Pr.

—Library Lion. Hawkes, Kevin, illus. 2009. (ENG.). 48p. (J). (gr. -1-3). pap. 6.99 *(978-0-7636-3784-2(X))* Candlewick Pr.

—Library Lion. 2009. lib. bdg. 17.20 *(978-0-606-06666-2(7)*, Turtleback) Turtleback Bks.

Laboy, Gloria J. Freddie Learns Obedience. 2008. 24p. pap. 13.95 *(978-1-4327-1906-7(8))* Outskirts Pr., Inc.

Larosa, Marjanita. Mosquit: The Very Disobedient Mosquito. 2012. 36p. pap. 16.95 *(978-1-4497-3283-7(6)*, WestBow Pr.) Author Solutions, Inc.

MNO

Mulholland, Clara. Naughty Miss Bunny. 2007. 128p. 25.95 (978-1-4218-3838-0(9), 1st World Library - Literary Society) 1st World Publishing, Inc.

Richards, Christine. Bobby the Busy Body Boy. 2011. 24p. pap. 14.93 (978-1-4269-5913-4(3)) Trafford Publishing.

Ries, Lori. Good Dog, Aggie. Dormer, Frank W., illus. 2009. (ENG.). 48p. (J). (gr. -1-3). 12.95 (978-1-57091-645-8(4)) Charlesbridge Publishing, Inc.

Rutland, J. I Love You No Matter What: A Prince Chirpio Story, 1 vol. 2013. (ENG.). 32p. (J). 9.99 (978-1-4003-2195-7(6)) Nelson, Thomas Inc.

Snowballs & Coconuts. 2006. 56p. pap. 7.75 (978-0-8341-2295-6(2), 083-412-2952) Beacon Hill Pr. of Kansas City.

Sonberg, Caryn. Six Dogs & a Police Officer. Dorenkamp, Michelle, illus. 2006. 31p. pap. 8.40 (978-1-55501-776-7(2)) Ballard & Tighe Pubs.

Sorenson, Toni. I Will Go, I Will Do: A Book of Mormon Story. 2008. (Illus.). (J). (978-1-59811-627-4(4)) Covenant Communications.

Tamburri, Pasqualino. Alex & the Trampoline. 2008. 32p. (J). (gr. -1-2). 14.95 (978-1-60227-473-0(8)) Above the Clouds Publishing.

Twin Sisters(r) Staff, et al. Jonah & the Whale Padded Board Book & CD, 1 vol. 2014. (Let's Share a Story Ser.). 16p. (J). (-5). bds. 9.99 incl. audio compact disk (978-1-63058-783-3(4)) Barbour Publishing, Inc.

Werntz, Terry. Grace the Church Mouse. 2010. (ENG.). 28p. pap. 9.95 (978-1-4564-4191-3(4)) CreateSpace Independent Publishing Platform.

Weston Woods Staff, creator. Goldilocks & the Three Bears. 2011. 18.95 (978-0-439-72679-5(4)); 29.95 (978-0-439-73471-4(1)); 38.75 (978-0-439-72682-5(4)) Weston Woods Studios, Inc.

OBESITY

see Weight Control

OBI-WAN KENOBI (FICTITIOUS CHARACTER)—FICTION

see Kenobi, Obi-Wan (Fictitious Character)—Fiction

OBSCENITY (LAW)

Axelrod-Contrada, Joan. Reno V. ACLU Internet Censorship. 2006. (Supreme Court Milestones Ser.). (Illus.). 128p. (gr. 7-7). lib. bdg. 42.79 (978-0-7614-2144-3(0), Benchmark Bks.) Marshall Cavendish Corp.

OBSERVATORIES, ASTRONOMICAL

see Astronomical Observatories

OBSTETRICS

see Childbirth

OCCULT SCIENCES

see Occultism

OCCULTISM

see also Alchemy; Astrology; Clairvoyance; Divination; Fortune-Telling; Magic; Superstition; Witchcraft

Acer, David. Gotcha! 18 Amazing Ways to Freak Out Your Friends. MacEachern, Stephen, illus. 2008. (ENG.). 48p. (J). (gr. 3-7). 16.95 (978-1-55453-194-3(2)); pap. 8.95 (978-1-55453-195-0(0)) Kids Can Pr., Ltd. CAN. Dist: Hachette Bk. Group.

Belanger, Jeff. Real-Life Ghost Encounters. 2013. 208p. (YA). (gr. 7-12). 37.25 (978-1-4777-0678-7(X)) Rosen Publishing Group, Inc., The.

Blohm, Craig E. The Possessed. 2007. (Mysterious Encounters Ser.). (ENG., Illus.). 48p. (gr. 4-8). lib. bdg. 33.60 (978-0-7377-3781-3(6), LML02109-234481, Kidhaven) Cengage Gale.

Chandler, Matt. The World's Most Haunted Places, 1 vol. 2011. (Ghost Files Ser.). (ENG.). 32p. (gr. 3-4). lib. bdg. 27.99 (978-1-4296-6518-6(1), Edge Bks.) Capstone Press of Coughlan Cos.

Coronet Instructional Media (Firm) Staff, contrib. by. Counterpoint Reader: Myth, Magic & Mystery. (Illus.). (J). (978-0-388-30353-5(0)) Steck-Vaughn.

Cox, Barbara & Forbes, Scott. Haunted Homes, Vol. 1. 2014. (Creepy Chronicles Ser.). (ENG.). 32p. (J). (gr. 5-6). 26.60 (978-1-4824-0230-8(0)) Stevens, Gareth Publishing LLLP.

Ellis, Carol. New Orleans Voodoo. 2015. (J). (978-1-61900-068-1(7)) Eldorado Ink.

Everett, J. H. & Scott-Waters, Marilyn. Haunted Histories: Creepy Castles, Dark Dungeons, & Powerful Palaces. 2012. (ENG., Illus.). 160p. (J). (gr. 4-7). 14.99 (978-0-8050-8971-4(3), 9780805089714, Holt, Henry & Co. Bks. For Young Readers) Holt, Henry & Co.

Guiley, Rosemary Ellen. Ghosts & Haunted Places. 2008. (Mysteries, Legends, & Unexplained Phenomena Ser.). (Illus.). 144p. (YA). (gr. 7-12). 29.95 (978-0-7910-9392-4(1)) Facts On File, Inc.

—Spirit Communications. 2009. (Mysteries, Legends, & Unexplained Phenomena Ser.). (Illus.). 128p. (YA). (gr. 7-12). 29.95 (978-0-7910-9391-7(3)) Facts On File, Inc.

Hart, Chris. Manga Mania Romance: Drawing Shojo Girls & Bishie Boys. 2008. (Manga Mania(tm) Ser.). (ENG., Illus.). 144p. (gr. 5-18). pap. 19.95 (978-1-933027-43-2(6), Hart, Chris Bks.) Sixth&Spring Bks.

Haunted: Ghosts & the Paranormal: Set 3. 2013. (Haunted: Ghosts & the Paranormal Ser.). 208p. (YA). (gr. 7-12). 149.00 (978-1-4777-0686-2(0)) Rosen Publishing Group, Inc., The.

Haunted: Ghosts & the Paranormal: Sets 1 - 3. 2013. (Haunted: Ghosts & the Paranormal Ser.). 208p. (YA). (gr. 7-12). 414.65 (978-1-4777-0734-0(4)) Rosen Publishing Group, Inc., The.

Herbst, Judith. Hoaxes. 2004. (Unexplained Ser.). (Illus.). 48p. (J). pap. 7.95 (978-0-8225-2406-9(6), Lerner Pubns.); (ENG., (gr. 5-12). lib. bdg. 26.60 (978-0-8225-1629-3(2)) Lerner Publishing Group.

Kolpin, Molly. Eerie Haunted Places, 1 vol. 2013. (Scared! Ser.). (ENG.). 32p. (gr. 3-4). 27.99 (978-1-4296-9980-8(9), Snap Bks.) Capstone Press of Coughlan Cos.

Krull, Kathleen. They Saw the Future: Oracles, Psychics, Scientists, Great Thinkers, & Pretty Good Guessers. Brooker, Kyrsten, illus. 2014. (ENG.). 112p. (J). (gr. -1-3). pap. 45.99 (978-1-4814-3623-6(6), Atheneum Bks. for Young Readers) Simon & Schuster Children's Publishing.

Lassiter, Rhiannon. The Supernatural. 2006. (Unexplained Ser.). (Illus.). 36p. (gr. 3-6). lib. bdg. 26.00 (978-0-8368-6267-6(8), Gareth Stevens Learning Library) Stevens, Gareth Publishing LLLP.

Mattern, Joanne. Mystics & Psychics. 2011. (World Religions & Beliefs Ser.). 128p. (gr. 7-12). 28.95 (978-1-59935-148-3(X)) Reynolds, Morgan Inc.

McIntosh, Kenneth. Prophecies & End-Time Speculations: The Shape of Things to Come. 2007. (Religion & Modern Culture Ser.). (Illus.). 112p. (YA). (gr. 3-7). lib. bdg. 22.95 (978-1-59084-979-8(5), 1248068) Mason Crest.

Miles, Liz. Terrifying Tales: Ghosts, Ghouls, & Other Things That Go Bump in the Night. 2010. (Culture in Action Ser.). (ENG., Illus.). 32p. (gr. 3-6). 30.65 (978-1-4109-3926-5(X), NA-r) Heinemann-Raintree.

Peterson, Megan Cooley. Super Scary Stories. 2016. (Super Scary Stuff Ser.). (ENG., Illus.). 24p. (gr. 1-2). lib. bdg. 25.32 (978-1-5157-0279-5(0), First Facts) Capstone Press of Coughlan Cos.

Place, Robert M. Astrology & Divination. 2008. (Mysteries, Legends, & Unexplained Phenomena Ser.). (Illus.). 136p. (YA). (gr. 7-12). lib. bdg. 29.95 (978-0-7910-9385-6(9)) Facts On File, Inc.

Rosen Publishing Staff. Understanding the Paranormal, 1 vol. 2015. (Understanding the Paranormal Ser.). (ENG.). 48p. (YA). 155.10 (978-1-62275-813-5(7), Britannica Educational Publishing) Rosen Publishing Group, Inc., The.

Shecter, Vicky Alvear. Anubis Speaks! A Guide to the Afterlife by the Egyptian God of the Dead. Revoy, Antoine, illus. 2013. (Secrets of the Ancient Gods Ser.). (ENG.). 128p. (J). (gr. 4-6). 16.95 (978-1-59078-995-7(4)) Boyds Mills Pr.

Stern, Steven L. Cursed Grounds. 2011. (Scary Places Ser.). 32p. (YA). (gr. 4-7). lib. bdg. 25.27 (978-1-61772-147-2(6)) Bearport Publishing Co., Inc.

Understanding the Paranormal: Set 2. 2016. (Understanding the Paranormal Ser.). 48p. (gr. 5-5). 161.10 (978-1-5081-0219-9(8)); pap. 84.30 (978-1-68048-602-5(0)) Rosen Publishing Group, Inc., The. (Britannica Educational Publishing).

Walker, Kathryn. Mysterious Predictions. 2009. (Unsolved! Ser.). (ENG., Illus.). 32p. (J). (gr. 3-5). pap. (978-0-7787-4164-0(8)); (gr. 4-6). (978-0-7787-4151-0(6)) Crabtree Publishing Co.

Williams, Dinah. Monstrous Morgues of the Past. 2011. (Scary Places Ser.). 32p. (YA). (gr. 4-7). lib. bdg. 25.27 (978-1-61772-149-6(2)) Bearport Publishing Co., Inc.

OCCULTISM—FICTION

Aguirre, Ann. Public Enemies. 2015. (ENG.). 384p. (YA). (978-1-250-07420-1(7)) St. Martin's Pr.

Arnowitz, Lisa. Until Beth. 2015. (ENG.). 260p. (YA). (gr. 10-12). pap. 9.95 (978-1-63392-033-0(X)) Spencer Hill Pr.

Anonymous. Jay's Journal. Sparks, Beatrice, ed. (ENG.). 240p. (YA). 2012. (gr. 9). 17.99 (978-1-4424-8094-0(7)) 2010. (gr. 7). pap. 10.99 (978-1-4424-1993-3(8)) Simon Pulse. (Simon Pulse).

Argyle, Amber. Winter Queen. 2013. 256p. 21.99 (978-0-9857394-4-7(4)) Starling Publishing.

Bitterman, Albert. Fortune Cookies. Raschka, Chris, illus. 2011. (ENG.). 28p. (J). (gr. -1-k). 14.99 (978-1-4169-6814-6(8), Beach Lane Bks.) Beach Lane Bks.

Black, Yelena. Dance of Shadows. (Dance of Shadows Ser.). (ENG., Illus.). 384p. (YA). (gr. 7). 2014. pap. 9.99 (978-1-61963-185-4(7), 9781619631854) 2013. 17.99 (978-1-59990-940-0(5), 9781599909400) Bloomsbury Publishing USA. (Bloomsbury USA Childrens).

Buckingham, Royce. Demonkeeper. 2007. 216p. (J). (978-1-4287-4608-4(0)) Penguin Publishing Group.

Byars, Betsy. Tarot Says Beware. (Herculeah Jones Mystery Ser.). 160p. (J). (gr. 4-6). pap. 3.99 (978-0-8072-1498-5(1), Listening Library) Random Hse. Audio Publishing Group.

Cast, P. C. & Cast, Kristin. Awakened. (House of Night Novels Ser.: 8). (ENG.). 304p. (YA). (gr. 7-12). 2012. pap. 10.99 (978-0-312-38797-6(0), 9780312387976) 2011. 17.99 (978-0-312-65024-7(8), 9780312650247) St. Martin's Pr. (St. Martin's Griffin).

—Awakened. l.t. ed. 2011. (House of Night Ser.). (ENG.). 436p. 23.99 (978-1-4104-3776-1(0)) Thorndike Pr.

—Betrayed. 2009. (House of Night Novels Ser.: 2). (ENG.). 320p. (YA). (gr. 7-12). 19.99 (978-0-312-59629-3(4), 9780312596293) St. Martin's Pr.

—Burned. l.t. ed. 2011. (House of Night Ser.). (ENG.). 552p. 23.99 (978-1-4104-3440-1(0)) Thorndike Pr.

—Chosen. 2010. (House of Night Novels (Quality) Ser.). (CHI.). 367p. pap. (978-957-0316-42-1(X)) Locus Publishing Co.

—Chosen. 2008. (House of Night Novels Ser.: 3). (ENG.). 320p. (YA). (gr. 8-12). pap. 10.99 (978-0-312-36030-6(4), 9780312360306, St. Martin's Griffin) St. Martin's Pr.

—Chosen. l.t. ed. 2009. (House of Night Ser.: Bk. 3). (ENG.). 406p. (YA). 23.95 (978-1-4104-1608-7(9)) Thorndike Pr.

—Destined. 2013. (House of Night Novels Ser.: 9). (ENG.). 336p. (YA). (gr. 7-12). pap. 10.99 (978-0-312-38798-3(9), 9780312387983, St. Martin's Griffin) St. Martin's Pr.

—House of Night: the Beginning: Marked & Betrayed. 2013. (House of Night Novels Ser.). (ENG.). 640p. (YA). (gr. 7-12). pap. 11.99 (978-1-250-03723-7(9), 9781250037237, St. Martin's Griffin) St. Martin's Pr.

—Hunted. (House of Night Novels Ser.: 5). (ENG.). 336p. (YA). (gr. 7-12). 2013. mass mkt. 9.99 (978-1-250-04696-3(3), 9781250046963, St. Martin's Paperbacks) 2010. pap. 10.99 (978-0-312-57799-5(0), 9780312577995, St. Martin's Griffin) St. Martin's Pr.

—Hunted. l.t. ed. 2010. (House of Night Ser.: Bk. 5). (ENG.). 548p. 23.95 (978-1-4104-1951-4(7)) Thorndike Pr.

—Marked. (House of Night Novels Ser.: 1). (ENG.). 320p. (YA). (gr. 8-12). 2009. 19.99 (978-0-312-36025-2(8), 9780312360252) 2007. pap. 10.99 (978-0-312-36026-9(6), 9780312360269, St. Martin's Griffin) St. Martin's Pr.

—Marked. l.t. ed. 2008. (House of Night Ser.: No. 1). (ENG.). 442p. (YA). 23.95 (978-1-4104-1021-4(8)) Thorndike Pr.

—Marked. 2007. (House of Night Ser.: 1). 306p. (YA). lib. bdg. 22.10 (978-1-4178-0853-3(5), Turtleback) Turtleback Bks.

—Tempted. (House of Night Novels Ser.: 6). (ENG.). 336p. (YA). (gr. 7-12). 2011. pap. 10.99 (978-0-312-60938-2(8), 9780312609382) 2009. 17.99 (978-0-312-56748-4(0), 9780312567484) St. Martin's Pr. (St. Martin's Griffin).

—Tempted. l.t. ed. 2010. (House of Night Novel Ser.). (ENG.). 552p. 23.99 (978-1-4104-3141-7(X)) Thorndike Pr.

Curley, Marianne. Fearless. 2015. (Avena Ser.). (ENG.). 384p. (YA). (gr. 7). pap. 13.99 (978-1-4088-2264-7(4), 9781408822647, Bloomsbury USA Childrens) Bloomsbury Publishing USA.

DeSpain, Pleasant. Tales of Enchantment. 2016. (ENG., Illus.). 80p. (J). (gr. 3-4). pap. 9.95 (978-1-941460-37-5(2)) August Hse. Pubs., Inc.

Donnelly, Jennifer. Waterfire Saga, Book Three Dark Tide. 2016. (Waterfire Saga Ser.). (ENG.). 416p. (YA). (gr. 7-12). pap. 9.99 (978-1-4847-1302-0(8)) Hyperion Bks. for Children.

Dunning, John Harris & Singh, Nikhil. Salem Brownstone: All along the Watchtowers. Singh, Nikhil, illus. 2010. (ENG., Illus.). 96p. (YA). (gr. 7-18). 18.99 (978-0-7636-4735-3(7)) Candlewick Pr.

Elfgren, Sara B. & Strandberg, Mats. The Circle: The Engelsfors Trilogy — Book 1. 2013. (Engelsfors Trilogy Ser.: 1). (ENG.). 608p. (gr. 9-13). 18.99 (978-1-4683-0658-3(8), 460658) Overlook Pr., The.

Feasey, Steve. Dark Moon. 2011. (Wereling Ser.: 2). (ENG.). 336p. (YA). (gr. 7-18). pap. 18.99 (978-0-312-64643-1(7), 9780312646431) Feiwel & Friends.

Fleischman, Paul. Graven Images. Ibatoulline, Bagram, illus. (ENG.). 128p. (YA). 2005. (gr. 5-9). per. 6.99 (978-0-7636-2984-7(7)) 2006. (gr. 7-9). reprint ed. 16.99 (978-0-7636-2775-1(5)) Candlewick Pr.

Galante, Cecilia. Be Not Afraid. 2015. (ENG.). 352p. (YA). (gr. 7). 17.99 (978-0-385-37274-9(4), Random Hse. Bks. for Young Readers) Random Hse. Children's Bks.

Gayle, Emi. Night & Day. 2014. 132p. (YA). (978-1-937744-55-7(8)) J. Taylor Publishing.

Ghent, Natale. Book of Living & Dying. 2006. (ENG.). 288p. (J). mass mkt. 6.99 (978-0-00-639350-4(0), Harper Trophy) HarperCollins Pubs.

Glanville, K. L. The Realm: The Awakening Begins, bk. 1. 2008. (ENG.). 314p. (YA). pap. 12.99 (978-0-9821199-1-4(7)) Luminations Media Group, Inc.

Green, Sally. Half Lost. 2016. (Half Bad Trilogy: Bk. 3). (ENG.). 352p. (YA). (gr. 9). 18.99 (978-0-670-01714-0(0), Viking Books for Young Readers) Penguin Young Readers Group.

Hamel-Mcevoy, Kristen & Chin, Jonathan L. My Little Leo. 2011. 28p. pap. 12.50 (978-1-61204-104-9(3), Strategic Bk. Publishing) Strategic Book Publishing & Rights Agency (SBPRA).

Hansen, Tevin. C. K. & the Worm of Wisdom. 2016. (ENG.). 128p. (YA). pap. 6.99 (978-1-941429-35-8(1)) Handersen Publishing.

—The Complete Saga One: Evil Mouse Chronicles. 2016. (ENG.). 346p. (YA). pap. 12.99 (978-1-941429-39-6(4)) Handersen Publishing.

—An Evening of Temptation & the Ultimate Sacrifice. 2017. 231p. (YA). 19.99 **(978-1-941429-68-6(8))** Handersen Publishing.

—Mr. B Presents: An Evening of Temptation & the Ultimate Sacrifice. 2014. (ENG.). 231p. (YA). pap. 8.95 (978-1-941429-01-3(7)) Handersen Publishing.

—Mummy Mouse: A Tail of Evil. 2015. (ENG.). 78p. pap. 8.95 (978-1-941429-19-8(X)) Handersen Publishing.

—Psycho Kim. 2016. (ENG.). 70p. pap. 5.99 (978-1-941429-30-3(0)) Handersen Publishing.

—Rhomby the Skater Zombie. Hansen, Tevin, illus. 2016. (ENG., Illus.). 134p. (J). pap. 7.99 (978-1-941429-32-7(7)) Handersen Publishing.

—Snickers. 2015. (ENG.). 76p. pap. 7.95 (978-1-941429-20-4(3)) Handersen Publishing.

—A Sunday Demon Drive & a Gathering of Friends. 2014. (ENG.). 210p. (YA). pap. 8.95 (978-1-941429-08-2(4)) Handersen Publishing.

Hatton, L. J. Sing down the Stars, 0 vols. 2015. (Sing down the Stars Ser.: 1). (ENG.). 380p. (YA). (gr. 8-13). pap. 9.99 (978-1-5039-4656-9(8), 9781503946569, Skyscape) Amazon Publishing.

Havard, Amanda. The Survivors. 2011. (ENG.). (YA). 294p. 21.99 (978-0-9833190-0-9(6)); 300p. pap. 11.99 (978-0-9833190-2-3(2)) Chafie Pr., LLC.

Horowitz, Anthony. Evil Star. 2006. (ENG.). 320p. (YA). (gr. 4-7). 26.87 (978-1-4156-7833-6(2), Follettbound) Follett School Solutions.

—Evil Star. 2007. (Gatekeepers Ser.: 2). (ENG.). 320p. (J). (gr. 3-7). 8.99 (978-0-439-68008-0(5)) Scholastic, Inc.

—Necropolis, 9 vols. 2009. (Gatekeepers Ser.: 4). (J). 92.75 (978-1-4407-0430-7(9)); 122.75 (978-1-4407-0434-5(1)); 120.75 (978-1-4407-0436-9(8)); 90.75 (978-1-4407-0432-1(5)); 1.25 (978-1-4407-0439-0(2)); 254.75 (978-1-4407-0431-4(7)) Recorded Bks., Inc.

—Necropolis. (Gatekeepers Ser.: 4). (ENG.). 400p. (J). (gr. 3-7). 2011. pap. 8.99 (978-0-439-68006-6(9), Scholastic Paperbacks) 2009. 17.99 (978-0-439-68003-5(4), Scholastic Pr.) Scholastic, Inc.

—Necropolis. 2009. 400p. pap. (978-1-4063-2108-1(7)) Walker Bks., Ltd.

—Oblivion. 2014. (Gatekeepers Ser.: 5). lib. bdg. 20.85 (978-0-606-36035-7(2)) Turtleback Bks.

Hunter, C. C. Unspoken: Shadow Falls: after Dark. 2015. (Shadow Falls: after Dark Ser.: 3). (ENG.). 416p. (YA). (gr. 7-12). pap. 9.99 (978-1-250-06709-8(X), 9781250067098, St. Martin's Griffin) St. Martin's Pr.

—Whispers at Moonrise. 2013. (Shadow Falls Novel Ser.: 4). (ENG.). 400p. (YA). (gr. 7-12). mass mkt. 9.99 (978-1-250-04682-6(3), 9781250046826, St. Martin's Paperbacks) St. Martin's Pr.

Hunter, Erin. The Last Hope. Richardson, Owen & Douglas, Allen, illus. 2012. (Warriors: Omen of the Stars Ser.: 6). (ENG.). 384p. (J). (gr. 3-7). 16.99 (978-0-06-155527-5(4)) HarperCollins Pubs.

Kahler, A. R. Echoes of Memory. 2017. (Ravenborn Ser.: 2). (ENG., Illus.). 336p. (YA). (gr. 9). 17.99 (978-1-4814-3260-3(5), Simon Pulse) Simon Pulse.

—Shades of Darkness. 2016. (Ravenborn Ser.: 1). (ENG., Illus.). 304p. (YA). (gr. 9). 17.99 (978-1-4814-3257-3(5), Simon Pulse) Simon Pulse.

Keay, Ben. Perfect Solution. Hsu, Florence, illus. 2009. (YA). (978-1-933791-09-8(8)) Finial Publishing.

Kress, Adrienne. Outcast. 2013. (ENG.). 326p. pap. 18.99 (978-1-62681-092-1(3)) Diversion Publishing Corp.

LaFevers, R. L. Theodosia & the Serpents of Chaos. Tanaka, Yoko, illus. 2008. (ENG.). 352p. (J). (gr. 2-5). pap. 7.99 (978-0-618-99976-7(0)) Houghton Mifflin Harcourt Publishing Co.

Lancaster, Susan. The Diamond Talisman. 2004. 168p. pap. (978-0-9730350-0-1(5)) Snosrap Publishing.

Larcombe, Jennifer Rees. Stone of Evil. 173p. pap. (978-0-340-58754-6(7)) Hodder & Stoughton.

Laurie, Victoria. Oracles of Delphi Keep. 2010. (Oracles of Delphi Keep Ser.). (ENG.). 576p. (J). (gr. 3-7). 7.99 (978-0-440-42258-7(2), Yearling) Random Hse. Children's Bks.

Lilleland, Ingrid. A Demon's Touch. 2017. (ENG.). 124p. pap. 11.95 **(978-1-78554-775-1(5)**, 9e376bfe-ad89-4807-a9c2-0b5372f8b144) Austin, Stan AUS. Dist: Bookmasters Distribution.

Loewer, Peter. The Moonflower, 1 vol. Loewer, Jean, illus. 2004. (ENG.). 32p. (J). (gr. 1-5). pap. 7.95 (978-1-56145-314-6(5)) Peachtree Pubs.

Maguire, Eden. Arizona. 2010. (Beautiful Dead Ser.: 2). (ENG.). 288p. (YA). (gr. 8-12). pap. 11.99 (978-1-4022-3945-8(9)) Sourcebooks, Inc.

Mak, Olha. Stones under the Scythe. Kaczmarskyj, Vera, tr. from UKR. 2011. 184p. 23.95 (978-1-4620-1038-7(5)); pap. 13.95 (978-1-4620-1037-0(7)) iUniverse, Inc.

McDonald, Megan. Judy Moody Predicts the Future. Reynolds, Peter H., illus. 2010. (Judy Moody Ser.: 4). (ENG.). 160p. (J). (gr. 1-4). 15.99 (978-0-7636-4858-9(2)); pap. 5.99 (978-0-7636-4857-2(4)) Candlewick Pr.

McKenzie, Paige. Sacrifice of Sunshine Girl. 2017. (Haunting of Sunshine Girl Ser.: 3). (ENG.). 336p. (gr. 7-17). 17.99 **(978-1-60286-298-2(2)**, Weinstein Bks.) Perseus Bks. Group.

Mlynowski, Sarah. If the Shoe Fits. 2013. (Whatever After Ser.: 2). (ENG.). 176p. (J). (gr. 3-7). 14.99 (978-0-545-41567-5(5), Scholastic Pr.) Scholastic, Inc.

Murphy, Shirley Rousseau & Murphy, Pat J. J. The Cat, the Devil, the Last Escape: A Novel. 2015. (ENG., Illus.). 320p. 24.99 (978-0-06-226910-2(0), Morrow, William & Co.) HarperCollins Pubs.

Myers, Bill. Invisible Terror Collection, 1 vol., Vol. 2. 2011. (Forbidden Doors Ser.). (ENG.). 368p. (YA). pap. 12.99 (978-0-310-72904-4(1)) Zondervan.

—My Life as a Haunted Hamburger, Hold the Pickles, 1 vol. 2006. (Incredible Worlds of Wally Mcdoogle Ser.: 27). (ENG., Illus.). 128p. (gr. 3-7). per. 6.99 (978-1-4003-0636-7(1)) Nelson, Thomas Inc.

Myracle, Lauren. Bliss. 2008. (ENG.). 464p. (YA). (gr. 9-17). 16.95 (978-0-8109-7071-7(6), Amulet Bks.) Abrams, Inc.

Noël, Alyson. Fated. 2012. (Soul Seekers Ser.: 1). (ENG.). 368p. (YA). (gr. 7). pap. 10.99 (978-0-312-57565-6(3), 9780312575656, St. Martin's Griffin) St. Martin's Pr.

O'Connor, Jane. Sees the Future. Glasser, Robin Preiss, illus. 2014. (Nancy Clancy Ser.: 3). (ENG.). 144p. (J). (gr. 1-5). pap. 5.99 (978-0-06-208421-7(6)) HarperCollins Pubs.

Odentz, Howard. Dead. 2013. 272p. pap. 14.95 (978-1-61194-299-6(3), Bell Bridge Bks.) BelleBks., Inc.

Oh, Ellen. Warrior. 2015. (Prophecy Ser.: 2). (ENG.). 352p. (YA). (gr. 8). pap. 9.99 (978-0-06-209113-0(1), HarperTeen) HarperCollins Pubs.

Older, Daniel José. Shadowhouse Fall. 2017. (Shadowshaper Cypher Ser.). (ENG.). 368p. (J). (gr. 7-7). 18.99 **(978-0-545-95282-8(4)**, Levine, Arthur A. Bks.) Scholastic, Inc.

Ormand, Kate. The Wanderers. 2015. (ENG.). 320p. (J). (gr. 6). 16.99 (978-1-63450-201-6(9), Sky Pony Pr.) Skyhorse Publishing Co., Inc.

Osborne, Mary Pope. Haunted Castle on Hallows Eve. 2010. (Magic Tree House Merlin Missions Ser.: 2). lib. bdg. 16.00 (978-0-606-13992-2(3), Turtleback) Turtleback Bks.

Parker, Daniel. December. 2014. (Countdown Ser.: 12). (ENG.). 144p. (YA). (gr. 7). pap. 13.99 (978-1-4814-2597-1(8), Simon Pulse) Simon Pulse.

Payne, Mary Jennifer. Finding Jade. 2017. (Daughters of Light Ser.: 1). (ENG.). 216p. (YA). pap. 12.99 (978-1-4597-3500-2(5)) Dundurn CAN. Dist: Ingram Publisher Services.

Phillips, Ruby Ann. Krystal Ball. 2015. (Krystal Ball Ser.). (ENG.). 112p. (gr. 2-3). 101.28 (978-1-4795-6274-9(2)) Picture Window Bks.

Pillsworth, Anne M. Summoned. 2014. (Redemption's Heir Ser.: 1). (ENG.). 320p. (YA). (gr. 8-7). 17.99 (978-0-7653-3589-0(1), 9780765335890, Tor Teen) Doherty, Tom Assocs., LLC.

Plante, Raymond. Marilou Forecasts the Future, 1 vol. Cummins, Sarah, tr. from FRE. Favreau, Marie-Claude, illus. 2003. (Formac First Novels Ser.: 49). (ENG.). 64p. (J). (gr. 1-5). 4.95 (978-0-88780-614-8(7), 9780887806148); (gr. 2-5). 14.95 (978-0-88780-615-5(5), 9780887806155) Formac Publishing Co., Ltd. CAN. Dist: Casemate Pubs. & Bk. Distributors, LLC.

Poole, Gabriella. Blood Ties. 2010. (ENG.). 304p. (YA). (gr. 7-17). pap. 9.99 (978-0-340-98925-8(4)) Hodder & Stoughton GBR. Dist: Hachette Bk. Group.

Portman, Frank. Andromeda Klein. 2010. (ENG.). 432p. (YA). (gr. 9). pap. 9.99 (978-0-385-73526-1(X), Delacorte Bks. for Young Readers) Random Hse. Children's Bks.

Powers, J. L. & Powers, M. A. Broken Circle. 2017. (ENG.). 320p. (J). (gr. 6). pap. 14.95 **(978-1-61775-580-4(X)**, Black Sheep) Akashic Bks.

Preussler, Otfried. Krabat & the Sorcerer's Mill. Bell, Anthea, tr. from GER. 2014. (ENG.). 264p. (J). (gr. 3-7). 17.95 (978-1-59017-778-5(9), NYR Children's Collection) New York Review of Bks., Inc., The.

Richardson, Sharde. Watched. 2011. (ENG.). 290p. (YA). pap. 12.99 (978-0-9831498-0-4(1)) Jolt.

Rinehart, J. D. Crown of Three. 2016. (Crown of Three Ser.: 1). (ENG., Illus.). 432p. (J). (gr. 4-8). pap. 7.99 (978-1-4814-2444-8(0), Aladdin) Simon & Schuster Children's Publishing.

Roberts, Rachel. Circles in the Stream. 2007. (Avalon Ser.: Bk. 1). 175p. (J). 9.99 (978-1-933164-64-9(6)) Seven Seas Entertainment, LLC.

Scott, Michael. The Alchemyst. 2009. (ENG., Illus.). 375p. (gr. 6-10). 19.00 (978-1-60686-514-9(5)) Perfection Learning Corp.

—The Alchemyst. (Secrets of the Immortal Nicholas Flamel Ser.: Bk. 1). (ENG.). 400p. (YA). (gr. 7). 2008. pap. 10.99 (978-0-385-73600-8(2), Ember) 2007. (Illus.). 16.99

(978-0-385-73357-1(7), Delacorte Bks. for Young Readers) Random Hse. Children's Bks.

Shouoto, Aya. He's My Only Vampire, Vol. 10. 2017. (He's My Only Vampire Ser.: 10). (ENG., Illus.). 176p. (gr. 11-17). pap. 13.00 *(978-0-316-39912-8(4)*, Yen Pr.) Orbit.

Showalter, Gena. Red Handed. 2007. (ENG.). 288p. (gr. 7-12). pap. 11.99 *(978-1-4165-3224-8(2)*, MTV Bks.) MTV Books.

Smith, L. J. The Initiation & the Captive. movie tie-in ed. 2011. (Secret Circle Ser.). (ENG.). 416p. (YA). (gr. 8). pap. 9.99 *(978-0-06-211900-1(1)*, HarperTeen) HarperCollins Pubs.

Smith, L. J. & Williamson, Kevin. The Compelled. 2012. (Vampire Diaries: Stefan's Diaries: 6). (ENG.). 256p. (YA). (gr. 9). pap. 10.99 *(978-0-06-211398-6(4)*, HarperTeen) HarperCollins Pubs.

Smith, Ronald L. The Mesmerist. 2017. (ENG.). 272p. (J). (gr. 5-7). 16.99 *(978-0-544-44528-4(7)*, Clarion Bks.) Houghton Mifflin Harcourt Trade & Reference Pubs.

Stiefvater, Maggie. Blue Lily, Lily Blue. (Raven Cycle Ser.: 3). (ENG.). 400p. (J). (gr. 9). 2015. pap. 9.99 *(978-0-545-42497-4(6))* 2014. 18.99 *(978-0-545-42496-7(8))* Scholastic, Inc. (Scholastic Pr.).

—Blue Lily, Lily Blue. 2015. (Raven Cycle Ser.: 3). lib. bdg. 20.85 *(978-0-606-38004-1(3))* Turtleback Bks.

—The Dream Thieves. (Raven Cycle Ser.: 2). (ENG.). 448p. (J). (gr. 9). 2014. pap. 9.99 *(978-0-545-42495-0(X)*, Scholastic Paperbacks) 2013. 18.99 *(978-0-545-42494-3(1)*, Scholastic Pr.) Scholastic, Inc.

—The Dream Thieves. 2014. (Raven Cycle Ser.: 2). lib. bdg. 20.85 *(978-0-606-36029-6(8))* Turtleback Bks.

—The Raven Boys. 2015. 50.87 *(978-1-320-56337-6(6))* Blurb, Inc.

—The Raven Boys. 2013. (Raven Cycle Ser.: 1). 20.00 *(978-1-62765-119-6(5))* Perfection Learning Corp.

—The Raven Boys. (Raven Cycle Ser.: 1). (ENG.). 416p. (J). (gr. 9). 2013. pap. 10.99 *(978-0-545-42493-6(3)*, Scholastic Paperbacks) 2012. 18.99 *(978-0-545-42492-9(5)*, Scholastic Pr.) 2012. E-Book *(978-0-545-46979-1(1))* Scholastic, Inc.

—The Raven Boys. 2016. (CHI.). 448p. (YA). (gr. 7). pap. *(978-986-361-180-6(8))* Sitak Group Holding, Ltd.

—The Raven Boys. 2013. (Raven Cycle Ser.: 1). lib. bdg. 20.85 *(978-0-606-32028-3(8)*, Turtleback) Turtleback Bks.

Stine, R. L. Nightmare Hour. movie tie-in ed. 2011. (ENG.). 160p. (J). (gr. 3). pap. 5.99 *(978-0-06-210692-6(9))* HarperCollins Pubs.

Tanabe, Yellow. Kekkaishi, Vol. 22. Tanabe, Yellow, illus. 2010. (ENG., Illus.). 192p. pap. 9.99 *(978-1-4215-3069-7(4))* Viz Media.

—Kekkaishi, Vol. 23. Tanabe, Yellow, illus. 2010. (ENG., Illus.). 192p. pap. 9.99 *(978-1-4215-3200-4(X))* Viz Media.

Templeman, McCormick. The Glass Casket. 2015. (ENG.). 352p. (YA). (gr. 9). pap. 9.99 *(978-0-385-74343-3(2)*, Ember) Random Hse. Children's Bks.

Tiernan, Cate. A Chalice of Wind - A Circle of Ashes - A Feather of Stone - A Necklace of Water. 2011. (Balefire Ser.). (ENG.). 976p. (YA). (gr. 7-18). 9.99 *(978-1-59514-411-9(0)*, Razorbill) Penguin Young Readers Group.

—Awakening. 2007. (Sweep Ser.: 5). (ENG.). 192p. (YA). (gr. 7-18). pap. 7.99 *(978-0-14-241020-2(9)*, Speak) Penguin Young Readers Group.

—Book of Shadows, Bk. 1. 2007. (Sweep Ser.: 1). (ENG.). 192p. (YA). (gr. 7-18). pap. 7.99 *(978-0-14-240986-2(3)*, Speak) Penguin Young Readers Group.

—Book of Shadows - The Coven - Blood Witch. 2010. (Sweep Ser.: 1). (ENG.). 592p. (YA). (gr. 7-18). 8.99 *(978-0-14-241717-1(3)*, Speak) Penguin Young Readers Group.

—The Calling, Bk. 7. 2008. (Sweep Ser.: 7). (ENG.). 192p. (YA). (gr. 7-18). 7.99 *(978-0-14-241022-6(5)*, Speak) Penguin Young Readers Group.

—Dark Magick, Bk. 4. 2007. (Sweep Ser.: 4). (ENG.). 192p. (YA). (gr. 7-18). 7.99 *(978-0-14-240989-3(8)*, Speak) Penguin Young Readers Group.

—Dark Magick - Awakening - Spellbound, 2 vols., Vol. 2. 2010. (Sweep Ser.: 2). (ENG.). 576p. (YA). (gr. 7-18). pap. 9.99 *(978-0-14-241897-0(8)*, Speak) Penguin Young Readers Group.

—Immortal Beloved. (Immortal Beloved Ser.: 1). (ENG.). (YA). (gr. 7-17). 2012. 432p. pap. 9.99 *(978-0-316-03591-0(2))* 2010. 416p. 16.99 *(978-0-316-03592-7(0))* Little, Brown Bks. for Young Readers.

—Sweep Vol. 3: The Calling - Changeling - Strife, 3 vols. 2011. (Sweep Ser.: 3). (ENG.). 576p. (YA). (gr. 7-18). 9.99 *(978-0-14-241955-7(9)*, Speak) Penguin Young Readers Group.

Troupe, Thomas Kingsley. Wandering Wagon. Faber, Rudy, illus. 2016. (Hauntiques Ser.). (ENG.). 128p. (gr. 4-6). lib. bdg. 25.32 *(978-1-4965-3547-4(2))* Stone Arch Bks.

Vajda, Tibor Timothy. The End of the World. 2008. 96p. pap. 9.95 *(978-0-595-52914-8(3))* iUniverse, Inc.

Voelkel, J. P. The Lost City. 2015. (Jaguar Stones Ser.: 4). (ENG., Illus.). 368p. (J). (gr. 5-12). 16.99 *(978-1-5124-0184-4(6)*, Darby Creek) Lerner Publishing Group.

Ward, John. Le Secret de l'Alchimiste. Guitard, Agnes & Pineau, Severine, trs. from ENG. 2004. (FRE., Illus.). 336p. (J). pap. *(978-2-89021-672-3(1))* Diffusion du livre Mirabel (DLM).

Whyman, Matt. Street Runners. 2008. (ENG.). 272p. (J). (gr. 4-7). pap. 11.95 *(978-1-84738-282-5(7))* Simon & Schuster, Ltd. GBR. Dist: Simon & Schuster, Inc.

Wilson, Diane Lee. Raven Speak. 2010. (ENG.). 256p. (YA). (gr. 7-9). 16.99 *(978-1-4169-8653-9(7)*, McElderry, Margaret K. Bks.) McElderry, Margaret K. Bks.

OCCUPATION, CHOICE OF

see Vocational Guidance

OCCUPATIONAL THERAPY—VOCATIONAL GUIDANCE

Amidon Lusted, Marcia. Jump-Starting a Career in Physical Therapy & Rehabilitation. 2013. (Health Care Careers in 2 Years Ser.). 80p. (YA). (gr. 7-12). 33.25 *(978-1-4777-1695-3(5))* Rosen Publishing Group, Inc., The.

Flath, Camden. Therapy Jobs in Educational Settings: Speech, Physical, Occupational & Audiology. 2010. (New Careers for the 21st Century Ser.). (Illus.). 64p. (YA). (gr. 7-18). pap. 9.95 *(978-1-4222-2047-4(8))*; lib. bdg. 22.95 *(978-1-4222-1826-6(0))* Mason Crest.

Hunsaker, Jennifer. Occupational Therapists. 2017. (Careers in Healthcare Ser.: Vol. 13). (ENG.). (YA). (gr. 7-12). 23.95 ***(978-1-4222-3801-1(6))*** Mason Crest.

OCCUPATIONS

see also Professions; Vocational Guidance

also names of countries, cities, etc. with the subdivision Occupations (e.g. U. S.—Occupations); also such headings as Law—Vocational Guidance

ABDO Publishing Company Staff. Extreme Jobs, 1 vol. 2011. (Extreme Jobs Ser.). (ENG., Illus.). 32p. 171.00 *(978-1-61783-023-5(2)*, Big Buddy Bks.) ABDO Publishing Co.

Adamson, Heather. A Day in the Life of a Construction Worker, 1 vol. 2004. (Community Helpers at Work Ser.). (ENG., Illus.). 24p. (gr. 1-2). 25.32 *(978-0-7368-2505-4(3)*, First Facts) Capstone Press of Coughlan Cos.

—A Day in the Life of a Police Officer, 1 vol. 2003. (Community Helpers at Work Ser.). (ENG., Illus.). 24p. (gr. 1-2). 25.32 *(978-0-7368-2285-5(2)*, First Facts) Capstone Press of Coughlan Cos.

Aksomitis, Linda. Choosing a Career. 2008. (Issues That Concern You Ser.). (ENG., Illus.). 144p. (gr. 10-12). lib. bdg. 42.00 *(978-0-7377-4184-1(8)*, LML02109-243088, Greenhaven Pr., Inc.) Cengage Gale.

Alexander, Richard. Zoo Workers, 01 vols., 1. 2016. (Hands-On Jobs Ser.). (ENG., Illus.). 24p. (J). pap. 8.25 *(978-1-5081-4375-8(7)*, PowerKids Pr.) Rosen Publishing Group, Inc., The.

Antill, Sara. 10 Ways I Can Help My Community. 2012. (I Can Make a Difference Ser.). (ENG., Illus.). 24p. (J). (gr. 2-5). pap. 8.25 *(978-1-4488-6363-1(5))*; lib. bdg. 22.60 *(978-1-4488-6202-3(7))* Rosen Publishing Group, Inc., The. (PowerKids Pr.).

Antram, David, illus. You Wouldn't Want To..., 4 vols., Set. Incl. Be in the Forbidden City! A Sheltered Life You'd Rather Avoid. Morley, Jacqueline. (gr. 4-7). 29.00 *(978-0-531-18749-4(7)*, Children's Pr.); Live in Pompeii! A Volcanic Eruption You'd Rather Avoid. Malam, John. (gr. 2-5). 29.00 *(978-0-531-18748-7(9))*; Sail on an Irish Famine Ship! A Trip Across Teh Atlantic You'd Rather Not Make. Pipe, Jim. (gr. 4-7). 29.00 *(978-0-531-13913-4(1))*; You Wouldn't Want to Be Mary Queen of Scots: A Ruler Who Really Lost Her Head. MacDonald, Fiona. (gr. 4-7). 29.00 *(978-0-531-13912-7(3))*; (Illus.). 32p. (J). 2008. Set lib. bdg. 116.00 o.p. *(978-0-531-24349-7(4)*, Watts, Franklin) Scholastic Library Publishing.

Appleby, Alex. I Can Be a Ballerina. 2014. (When I Grow Up Ser.). (Illus.). 24p. (J). (gr. k-2). 22.60 *(978-1-4824-0745-7(0))* Stevens, Gareth Publishing LLLP.

—Puedo Ser Presidente / I Can Be the President. 2014. (Cuando Sea Grande / When I Grow Up Ser.). (SPA.). 24p. (J). (gr. k-2). 22.60 *(978-1-4824-0867-6(8))* Stevens, Gareth Publishing LLLP.

—Puedo Ser un Artista / I Can Be an Artist. 2014. (Cuando Sea Grande / When I Grow Up Ser.). (SPA.). 24p. (J). (gr. k-2). 22.60 *(978-1-4824-0861-4(9))* Stevens, Gareth Publishing LLLP.

—Puedo Ser una Cantante / I Can Be a Singer. 2014. (Cuando Sea Grande / When I Grow Up Ser.). (SPA.). 24p. (J). (gr. k-2). 22.60 *(978-1-4824-0865-2(1))* Stevens, Gareth Publishing LLLP.

Barber, Nicola. Ancient Roman Jobs. 2010. (Ancient Communities: Roman Life Ser.). (Illus.). 32p. (J). pap. 10.60 *(978-1-61532-317-3(1))*; (gr. 3-6). lib. bdg. 26.50 *(978-1-61532-307-4(4))* Rosen Publishing Group, Inc., The. (PowerKids Pr.).

Baxter, Roberta. Bomb Squad Technicians in Action. 2017. (Dangerous Jobs in Action Ser.). (ENG.). 32p. (J). (gr. 3-6). lib. bdg. 27.07 *(978-1-5038-1627-5(3)*, 211143) Child's World, Inc., The.

Beaver, Simon. Dangerous & Dirty Jobs Low Intermediate Book with Online Access. 2014. (ENG., Illus.). 28p. pap. 9.50 *(978-1-107-64567-7(0))* Cambridge Univ. Pr.

Benchmark Education Company, LLC Staff, compiled by. Jobs. 2006. (J). 118.00 *(978-1-4108-7041-4(3))* Benchmark Education Co.

Berendes, Mary. Careers/Las Carreras. Petelinsek, Kathleen, illus. 2008. (WordBooks/Libros de Palabras Ser.). (SPA & ENG.). 24p. (J). (gr. k-3). 25.64 *(978-1-59296-988-3(7)*, 201088) Child's World, Inc., The.

Berlatsky, Noah. Manufacturing Jobs in the U. S. Greenhaven Press Staff, ed. 2015. (At Issue Ser.). (ENG.). 128p. (gr. 10-12). lib. bdg. 39.40 *(978-0-7377-7173-2(9)*, Greenhaven Pr., Inc.) Cengage Gale.

Boothroyd, Jennifer. From Assembly Lines to Home Offices: How Work Has Changed. 2011. (Comparing Past & Present Ser.). pap. 7.95 *(978-0-7613-7842-6(1))*; pap. 45.32 *(978-0-7613-8389-5(1))*; (ENG., Illus.). 32p. lib. bdg. 26.60 *(978-0-7613-6748-2(9))* Lerner Publishing Group.

Bowman-Kruhm, Mary. A Day in the Life of a Firefighter. 2009. (Kids' Career Library). 24p. (gr. 3-3). 42.50 *(978-1-60853-437-1(5)*, PowerKids Pr.) Rosen Publishing Group, Inc., The.

Boyd, Nicole. A Doctor's Busy Day. 2009. (Reading Room Collection 2 Ser.). 24p. (gr. 3-4). 42.50 *(978-1-60851-952-1(X)*, PowerKids Pr.) Rosen Publishing Group, Inc., The.

Bozak, Kristin & Cohen, Judith Love. You Can Be a Woman Botanist. Katz, David Arthur, illus. Date not set. 40p. (J). (gr. 3-6). 13.95 *(978-1-880599-41-9(4))* Cascade Pass, Inc.

Brezina, Corona. Getting a Job in Health Care. 2013. 80p. (YA). (gr. 9-12). 33.25 *(978-1-4488-9610-3(X))* Rosen Publishing Group, Inc., The.

Brill, Marlene Targ. Doctors. (Pull Ahead Bks.). (Illus.). 32p. (J). 2005. lib. bdg. 22.60 *(978-0-8225-1689-7(6))* 2004. pap. 5.95 *(978-0-8225-2531-8(3)*, Lerner Pubns.) Lerner Publishing Group.

Brooks, Felicity. Daisy Doctor. Litchfield, Jo, illus. 2005. 24p. (J). pap. 6.95 *(978-0-7945-0724-4(7)*, Usborne) EDC Publishing.

—Frank the Farmer. Litchfield, Jo, illus. 2005. (Jobs People Do Ser.). 23p. (J). (gr. -1-7). pap. 6.95 *(978-0-7945-0723-7(9)*, Usborne) EDC Publishing.

—Vicky the Vet. Litchfield, Jo, illus. 2004. (Jobs People Do Ser.). 24p. (J). pap. 6.95 *(978-0-7945-0726-8(3)*, Usborne) EDC Publishing.

Brooks, Shunda K. What Should I Be? It's All up to Me! The Opportunities Are Endless! 2013. 48p. 28.99 *(978-1-4582-0906-1(7))*; pap. 20.99 *(978-1-4582-0907-8(5))* Author Solutions, Inc. (Abbott Pr.).

Brown, Janet Allison. My First Book of Jobs. 2004. (Early Learning Ser.). (Illus.). 18p. (J). bds. 5.99 *(978-1-85854-429-8(7))* Brimax Books Ltd. GBR. Dist: Byeway Bks.

Bryan, Nichol. The National Guard, 1 vol. 2003. (Everyday Heroes Ser.). (ENG., Illus.). 32p. (gr. k-6). 27.07 *(978-1-57765-858-0(2)*, Checkerboard Library) ABDO Publishing Co.

—Paramedics, 1 vol. 2003. (Everyday Heroes Ser.). (ENG., Illus.). 32p. (gr. k-6). 27.07 *(978-1-57765-856-6(6)*, Checkerboard Library) ABDO Publishing Co.

—Police Officers, 1 vol. 2003. (Everyday Heroes Ser.). (ENG., Illus.). 32p. (gr. k-6). 27.07 *(978-1-57765-860-3(4)*, Checkerboard Library) ABDO Publishing Co.

Burchett. When I Grow Up: Level A. 2004. (Illus.). (J). pap. 6.00 *(978-0-7398-8154-5(X))* Steck-Vaughn.

Burton, Margie, et al. Doing My Job. 2011. (Early Connections Ser.). (J). *(978-1-61672-521-1(4))* Benchmark Education Co.

—What Will I Be? 2011. (Early Connections Ser.). (J). *(978-1-61672-315-6(7))* Benchmark Education Co.

Butz, Christopher. I Go to Work as a Letter Carrier. 2003. (I Go to Work As Ser.). (Illus.). (J). pap. *(978-1-58417-104-1(9))*; lib. bdg. *(978-1-58417-041-9(7))* Lake Street Pubs.

Byrd-Hill, Ida. Me & My Big Career, Hill, Karen, ed. Hill, Kevin, illus. 2010. (ENG.). 24p. (J). 14.95 *(978-0-9829610-0-1(6))* Upheaval Media, Inc.

Calling All Innovators: A Career for You (Fall 2014 Set Of 4) 2014. (Calling All Innovators: a Career for You Ser.). (J). lib. bdg. 120.00 *(978-0-531-24352-7(4))* Scholastic Library Publishing.

Calling All Innovators: A Career for You (Fall 2016 Set Of 4) 2016. (Calling All Innovators: a Career for You Ser.). (J). lib. bdg. 120.00 *(978-0-531-22057-3(5)*, Children's Pr.) Scholastic Library Publishing.

Cannon, Shannon. The Letter Uu Set: Jobs, 6. 2004. (Letter Bks.). (ENG.). 8p. (gr. k-1). pap. 29.70 *(978-0-7368-4120-7(2)*, Letter Bks.) Capstone Press of Coughlan Cos.

Careers in Focus - Politics. 2nd rev. ed. 2011. (Careers in Focus Ser.). (Illus.). 194p. (gr. 6-12). 32.95 *(978-0-8160-8035-9(6)*, Ferguson Publishing Co.) Facts On File, Inc.

Carson, J. You Can Do It! Learning the Y Sound. 2009. (PowerPhonics Ser.). 24p. (gr. 1-1). 39.90 *(978-1-60851-481-6(1)*, PowerKids Pr.) Rosen Publishing Group, Inc., The.

Chambers, Catherine, et al. The Coolest Jobs on the Planet, 1 vol. 2014. (Coolest Jobs on the Planet Ser.). (ENG.). 48p. (gr. 6-6). 97.95 *(978-1-4109-6644-5(5))* Heinemann-Raintree.

Christopher, Nick. Que Hacen Los Carteros? / What Do Mail Carriers Do? 2015. (Ayudantes de la Comunidad / Helping the Community Ser.). (ENG & SPA.). 24p. (J). (gr. 1-1). 23.60 *(978-1-4994-0633-7(9)*, PowerKids Pr.) Rosen Publishing Group, Inc., The.

Christy, Lee Louis. I Go to Work as a Firefighter. 2003. (I Go to Work As Ser.). (Illus.). (J). *(978-1-58417-039-6(5))* Lake Street Pubs.

—I Go to Work as a Police Officer. 2003. (I Go to Work As Ser.). (Illus.). (J). *(978-1-58417-040-2(9))*; pap. *(978-1-58417-103-4(0))* Lake Street Pubs.

Clerks & Administrative Workers. 2nd rev. ed. 2010. (Careers in Focus Ser.). (Illus.). 176p. (gr. 6-12). 32.95 *(978-0-8160-8017-5(8)*, Ferguson Publishing Co.) Facts On File, Inc.

Coan, Sharon. Trabajadores de Mi Ciudad (Workers in My City) 2016. (TIME for KIDS(r) Nonfiction Readers Ser.). (SPA.). 12p. (J). (gr. k-k). 4.99 *(978-1-4938-3027-5(9))* Teacher Created Materials, Inc.

—Workers at My School (Foundations Plus) 2015. (TIME for KIDS(r) Nonfiction Readers Ser.). (ENG., Illus.). 12p. (gr. k-k). 4.99 *(978-1-4938-2145-7(8))* Teacher Created Materials, Inc.

—Workers in My City (Foundations Plus) 2015. (TIME for KIDS(r) Nonfiction Readers Ser.). (ENG., Illus.). 12p. (gr. k-k). 4.99 *(978-1-4938-2146-4(6))* Teacher Created Materials, Inc.

—Workers Who Take Care of Me (Foundations Plus) 2015. (TIME for KIDS(r) Nonfiction Readers Ser.). (ENG., Illus.). 12p. (gr. k-k). 4.99 *(978-1-4938-2147-1(4))* Teacher Created Materials, Inc.

Coffey, Michele. A Park Ranger's Day. 2008. (Rosen Real Readers: Upper Emergent Ser.). (ENG., Illus.). 12p. (gr. 1-2). pap. 5.90 *(978-0-8239-8200-4(9))* Rosen Publishing Group, Inc., The.

Cohn, Jessica. Pest Control Worker. 2010. (Benchmark Rockets: Dirty & Dangerous Jobs Ser.). 32p. (J). (gr. 3-6). 28.50 *(978-1-60870-176-6(X))* Marshall Cavendish GBR. Dist: Marshall Cavendish Corp.

Coldfeather, Suzanne D. Places to Work, 1 vol. 2011. (Wonder Readers Early Level Ser.). (ENG.). (gr. -1-1). 32p. pap. 5.99 *(978-1-4296-7806-3(2))*; 16p. pap. 35.94 *(978-1-4296-8198-8(5))* Capstone Press of Coughlan Cos. (Wonder Readers).

Community Helpers & Their Tools. 2015. (Community Helpers & Their Tools Ser.). (ENG.). 24p. (J). (gr. 2-3). pap., pap., pap. 297.00 *(978-1-4994-1278-9(9)*, PowerKids Pr.) Rosen Publishing Group, Inc., The.

Community Helpers at Work. 2016. (Community Helpers at Work Ser.). (ENG.). 24p. (gr. 1-2). lib. bdg. 101.28 *(978-1-5157-4026-1(9)*, First Facts) Capstone Press of Coughlan Cos.

Cool Arts Careers, 8 vols., Set. Incl. Actor. Somervill, Barbara. lib. bdg. 28.50 *(978-1-61080-129-4(6)*, 201136); Choreographer. Marsico, Katie. lib. bdg. 28.50 *(978-1-61080-136-2(9)*, 201150); Dancer. Marsico, Katie. lib. bdg. 28.50 *(978-1-61080-130-0(X)*, 201138); Fashion Designer. Wooster, Patricia. lib. bdg. 28.50 *(978-1-61080-131-7(8)*, 201140); Music Producer. Wooster, Patricia. lib. bdg. 28.50 *(978-1-61080-133-1(4)*, 201144); Musician. Somervill, Barbara. lib. bdg. 28.50 *(978-1-61080-132-4(6)*, 201142); Scriptwriter. Mullins, Matt. lib. bdg. 28.50 *(978-1-61080-135-5(0)*, 201148); Special Effects Technician. Mullins, Matt. lib. bdg. 28.50 *(978-1-61080-134-8(2)*, 201146); 32p. (gr. 4-8). 2011. Set lib. bdg. 228.00 *(978-1-61080-150-8(4))* Cherry Lake Publishing.

Cool Careers. 2011. 32p. lib. bdg. 478.80 *(978-1-60279-998-1(9)*, 200936) Cherry Lake Publishing.

Coulter, Laurie. Ballplayers & Bonesetters: One Hundred Ancient Aztec & Maya Jobs You Might Have Adored or Abhorred. Newbigging, Martha, illus. 2008. (Jobs in History Ser.). (ENG.). 96p. (J). (gr. 4-7). 25.95 *(978-1-55451-141-9(0)*, 9781554511419); pap. 16.95 *(978-1-55451-140-2(2)*, 9781554511402) Annick Pr., Ltd. CAN. Dist: Publishers Group West (PGW).

—Kings & Carpenters: One Hundred Bible Land Jobs You Might Have Praised or Panned. Newbigging, Martha, illus. 2010. (Jobs in History Ser.). (ENG.). 96p. (J). (gr. 3-6). 25.95 *(978-1-55451-227-0(1)*, 9781554512270); pap. 16.95 *(978-1-55451-226-3(3)*, 9781554512263) Annick Pr., Ltd. CAN. Dist: Publishers Group West (PGW).

Craats, Rennay. The Blacksmith: Pioneers of Canada. 2011. 24p. (YA). (gr. 2-4). *(978-1-77071-681-0(5))*; pap. *(978-1-77071-685-8(8))* Weigl Educational Pubs. Ltd.

—Le Forgeron: Le Début de la Colonie. Karvonen, Tanjah, tr. from ENG. 2011. (FRE., Illus.). 24p. (gr. 3-6). *(978-1-77071-418-2(9))* Weigl Educational Pubs. Ltd.

Crane, Natalie. I Go to Work as a Teacher. 2003. (I Go to Work As Ser.). (Illus.). (J). pap. *(978-1-58417-106-5(5))*; lib. bdg. *(978-1-58417-044-0(1))*; lib. bdg. *(978-1-58417-043-3(3))* Lake Street Pubs.

Crowson, Andrew. Flip Flap People. 2003. (Illus.). 12p. bds. *(978-1-85602-443-3(1)*, Pavilion Children's Books) Pavilion Bks.

Currie, Stephen. Teen Guide to Jobs & Taxes. 2016. (ENG.). 64p. (J). (gr. 5-12). lib. bdg. *(978-1-68282-082-7(3))* ReferencePoint Pr., Inc.

Cutcher, Jenai. Gotta Dance! The Rhythms of Jazz & Tap. (Curtain Call Library of Dance Ser.). 48p. (gr. 5-8). 2009. 53.00 *(978-1-60853-421-0(9))* 2004. (Illus.). (J). lib. bdg. 29.25 *(978-0-8239-4554-2(5))* Rosen Publishing Group, Inc., The. (Rosen Reference).

Dahlman, Tricia, ed. MnCareers 2005. 2004. (Illus.). 112p. (YA). per. 12.95 *(978-0-9670505-7-7(X)*, ES-90508-09) Minnesota Dept. Employment & Economic Development.

Dalton, Sarah, et al, eds. Encyclopedia of Careers & Vocational Guidance, 5 vols., Set. 15th rev. ed. 2010. 4128p. (C). (gr. 9). 249.95 *(978-0-8160-8313-8(4)*, Ferguson Publishing Co.) Facts On File, Inc.

Deedrick, Tami & Ready, Dee. Our Community Helpers, 1 vol. 2014. (Our Community Helpers Ser.). (ENG.). 24p. (gr. k-1). lib. bdg. 87.96 *(978-1-4765-7069-3(8)*, Pebble Bks.) Capstone Press of Coughlan Cos.

Dorling Kindersley Publishing Staff. Careers. 2015. (ENG.). 320p. (J). (gr. 8-12). pap. 19.99 *(978-1-4654-2973-5(5)*, DK Children) Dorling Kindersley Publishing, Inc.

Dunn, Mary R. Dream Jobs, 6 vols., Set 2. Incl. I Want to Be a Ballet Dancer. lib. bdg. 22.60 *(978-1-4042-4469-6(7))*; I Want to Be a Chef. lib. bdg. 22.60 *(978-1-4042-4471-9(9))*; I Want to Be a Fashion Designer. lib. bdg. 22.60 *(978-1-4042-4472-6(7))*; I Want to Be in Musicals. lib. bdg. 22.60 *(978-1-4042-4470-2(0))*; I Want to Make Movies. lib. bdg. 22.60 *(978-1-4042-4473-3(5))*; I Want to Write Books. lib. bdg. 22.60 *(978-1-4042-4474-0(3))*; (Illus.). 24p. (YA). (gr. 2-5). 2009. 2008. Set lib. bdg. 127.50 *(978-1-4358-2551-2(9)*, PowerKids Pr.) Rosen Publishing Group, Inc., The.

—I Want to Be a Chef. 2009. (Dream Jobs Ser.). 24p. (gr. 2-3). 42.50 *(978-1-61512-205-9(2)*, PowerKids Pr.) Rosen Publishing Group, Inc., The.

—Quiero Ser Chef. 2009.Tr. of I Want to Be a Chef. (SPA., Illus.). 24p. pap. 8.25 *(978-1-4358-3427-9(5)*, Editorial Buenas Letras) Rosen Publishing Group, Inc., The.

—Quiero Ser Diseñador de Modas. 2009.Tr. of I Want to Be a Fashion Designer. (SPA., Illus.). 24p. pap. 8.25 *(978-1-4358-3433-0(X))*; (J). (gr. 2-4). lib. bdg. 22.60 *(978-1-4042-8154-7(1))* Rosen Publishing Group, Inc., The. (Editorial Buenas Letras).

Early Macken, JoAnn. Mail Carriers. Andersen, Gregg, photos by. 2010. (People in My Community Ser.). (Illus.). 24p. (gr. k-3). pap. 8.15 *(978-1-4339-3345-5(4))* Stevens, Gareth Publishing LLLP.

—Mail Carriers / Carteros. Andersen, Gregg, photos by. 2010. (People in My Community / Mi comunidad Ser.). (SPA., Illus.). 24p. (gr. k-3). pap. 8.15 *(978-1-4339-3763-7(8))* Stevens, Gareth Publishing LLLP.

—Teachers. Andersen, Gregg, photos by. 2010. (People in My Community Ser.). (Illus.). 24p. (gr. k-3). pap. 8.15 *(978-1-4339-3348-6(9))* Stevens, Gareth Publishing LLLP.

—Teachers / Maestros. Andersen, Gregg, photos by. 2010. (People in My Community / Mi comunidad Ser.). (SPA., Illus.). 24p. (gr. k-3). pap. 8.15 *(978-1-4339-3766-8(2))* Stevens, Gareth Publishing LLLP.

English, Melissa. Caution: Why You Need to Think about Careers NOW! 2004. (YA). per. 12.95 *(978-0-9754148-0-4(1))* Caution Bks.

Essential Careers: Set 3. 2013. (Essential Careers Ser.). 80p. (YA). (gr. 7-12). 199.50 *(978-1-4488-9485-7(9))* Rosen Publishing Group, Inc., The.

Essential Careers: Set 4. 2013. (Essential Careers Ser.). 80p. (YA). (gr. 7-12). 166.25 *(978-1-4777-1800-1(1))* Rosen Publishing Group, Inc., The.

Essential Careers: Sets 1 - 3. 2013. (Essential Careers Ser.). 80p. (YA). (gr. 7-12). 731.50 *(978-1-4777-0615-2(1))* Rosen Publishing Group, Inc., The.

Extreme Careers, 8 bks. Incl. Demolition Experts: Life Blowing Things Up. Beyer, Mark. 31.95 *(978-0-8239-3365-5(2))*; Race Car Drivers: Life on the Fast Track. Cefrey, Holly. 31.95 *(978-0-8239-3367-9(9))*; Smokejumpers: Life Fighting Fires. Beyer, Mark. 31.95 *(978-0-8239-3370-9(9))*; Stunt Performers: Life Before the Camera. Turner, Cherie. 26.50 *(978-0-8239-3371-6(7))*; 64p. (YA). (gr. 5-8). (Illus.). 2005. 212.00 *(978-0-8239-9422-9(8))* Rosen Publishing Group, Inc., The.

Extreme Careers, 8 bks., Set 5. Incl. Disaster Relief Workers. Roza, Greg. (J). (gr. 3-7). 2007. lib. bdg. 31.95 *(978-1-4042-0943-5(3))*; First Responders. Cobb, Allan B. (J). (gr. 3-7). 2007. lib. bdg. 26.50 *(978-1-4042-0944-2(1))*; Homeland Security Officers. Meyer, Jared. (J). (gr. 3-7).

2007. lib. bdg. 31.95 *(978-1-4042-0945-9(X))*; Hostage Rescuers. Poolos, Jamie. (gr. 5-8). 2007. lib. bdg. 31.95 *(978-1-4042-0941-1(7))*; Refugee Workers. Levy, Janey. (J). (gr. 5-8). 2006. lib. bdg. 31.95 *(978-1-4042-0960-2(3))*; U. S. Air Marshals. Broyles, Matthew. (J). (gr. 3-7). 2007. lib. bdg. 31.95 *(978-1-4042-0942-8(5))*; Working in a War Zone: Military Contractors. Meyer, Jared. (J). (gr. 5-8). 2006. lib. bdg. 31.95 *(978-1-4042-0959-6(X))*; (Illus.). 64p. 2007. Set lib. bdg. 212.00 *(978-1-4042-1042-4(3))* Rosen Publishing Group, Inc., The.

Extreme Careers, 5 vols., Set 6. Incl. Brain Surgeons. Bailey, Diane. 62p. lib. bdg. 31.95 *(978-1-4042-1787-4(8))*; High Risk Construction Work: Life Building Skyscrapers, Bridges, & Tunnels. Wolny, Philip. 64p. lib. bdg. 31.95 *(978-1-4042-1789-8(4))*; Manga Artists. Orr, Tamra. 64p. lib. bdg. 31.95 *(978-1-4042-1854-3(8))*; Search & Rescue Swimmers. La Bella, Laura. 64p. lib. bdg. 31.95 *(978-1-4042-1786-7(X))*; Treasure Hunters. Brezina, Corona. 64p. lib. bdg. 31.95 *(978-1-4042-1788-1(6))*; (Illus.). (YA). (gr. 5-9). 2008. 2008. Set lib. bdg. 146.25 *(978-1-4042-1875-8(0)*, Rosen Reference) Rosen Publishing Group, Inc., The.

Facts on File, Inc. Staff. Food. 2012. (Discovering Careers Ser.). (Illus.). 122p. (gr. 4-9). 24.95 *(978-0-8160-8057-1(7)*, Ferguson Publishing Co.) Facts On File, Inc.

Farrell, Courtney. Green Jobs, 1 vol. 2011. (Inside the Industry Ser.). (ENG., Illus.). 112p. (J). (gr. 6-12). lib. bdg. 35.64 *(978-1-61714-801-9(6)*, Essential Library) ABDO Publishing Co.

Ferguson Publishing. Encyclopedia of Careers & Vocational Guidance, 16th Edition, 5-Volume Set, 5 vols. 16th ed. 2014. (ENG., Illus.). 4128p. (J). lib. bdg. 249.95 *(978-0-8160-8503-3(X))* Facts On File, Inc.

Ferguson Publishing Staff, contrib. by. Encyclopedia of Careers & Vocational Guidance. 2017. (J). ***(978-0-8160-8514-9(5)***, Ferguson Publishing Co.) Facts On File, Inc.

Ferry, Francis. Job-O E: Elementary. Ellis, Amy, illus. 3rd ed. 2003. (Job-O Ser.). (J). *(978-1-887481-43-4(5))* CFKR Career Materials, Inc.

Fields, J. Choosing a Career as a Nurse-Midwife. 2009. (World of Work Ser.). 64p. (gr. 5-5). 58.50 *(978-1-60854-323-6(4))* Rosen Publishing Group, Inc., The.

Flath, Camden. 21st-Century Counselors: New Approaches to Mental Health & Substance Abuse. 2010. (New Careers for the 21st Century Ser.). 64p. (YA). (gr. 7-18). pap. 9.95 *(978-1-4222-2046-7(X))*; (Illus.). lib. bdg. 22.95 *(978-1-4222-1825-9(2))* Mason Crest.

Franks, Katie. Dream Jobs, 6 bks., Set. Incl. I Want to Be a Baseball Player. (J). lib. bdg. 22.60 *(978-1-4042-3622-6(8))*; I Want to Be a Basketball Player. (J). lib. bdg. 22.60 *(978-1-4042-3621-9(X))*; I Want to Be a Movie Star. (YA). lib. bdg. 22.60 *(978-1-4042-3619-6(8))*; I Want to Be a Race Car Driver. (J). lib. bdg. 22.60 *(978-1-4042-3623-3(6))*; (Illus.). 24p. (gr. 2-5). 2007. Set lib. bdg. 127.50 *(978-1-4042-3598-4(1))* Rosen Publishing Group, Inc., The.

Freed, Kira. Making Things, Doing Things. 2017. (Text Connections Guided Close Reading Ser.). (J). (gr. k). *(978-1-4900-1779-2(8))* Benchmark Education Co.

French, Cathy. Jobs up High. 2011. (Early Connections Ser.). (J). *(978-1-61672-231-9(2))* Benchmark Education Co.

—Using Numbers at Work. 2011. (Early Connections Ser.). (J). *(978-1-61672-242-5(8))* Benchmark Education Co.

Fronczak, Emerson. Who Works at My School? 2012. (InfoMax Readers Ser.). (ENG., Illus.). 16 pp.p. (J). (gr. k-1). pap. 7.00 *(978-1-4488-8938-9(3)*, Rosen Classroom) Rosen Publishing Group, Inc., The.

Galloway, Priscilla. Archers, Alchemists, & 98 Other Medieval Jobs You Might Have Loved or Loathed. Newbigging, Martha, illus. 5th ed. 2003. (Jobs in History Ser.). (ENG.). 96p. (J). (gr. 4-7). pap. 16.95 *(978-1-55037-810-8(4)*, 9781550378108) Annick Pr., Ltd. CAN. Dist: Publishers Group West (PGW).

Garbe, Suzanne. Killer Jobs: History's Most Dangerous Jobs. 2013. (Dangerous History Ser.). (ENG.). 32p. (gr. 3-4). 27.99 *(978-1-4765-0127-7(0)*, Edge Bks.) Capstone Press of Coughlan Cos.

Gardiner, Lisa. Big Dreams. Flowerpot Press, ed. 2012. (Illus.). 20p. (J). *(978-1-926988-04-7(3))* Flowerpot Children's Pr. Inc.

—People. Flowerpot Press, ed. 2012. (Illus.). 20p. (J). *(978-1-926988-06-1(X))* Flowerpot Children's Pr. Inc.

Gerry, Lisa M. 100 Things to Be When You Grow Up. 2017. (ENG., Illus.). 256p. (J). (gr. 3-7). pap. 9.99 *(978-1-4263-2711-7(0)*, National Geographic Children's Bks.) National Geographic Society.

Giacobello, John. Bodyguards: Life Protecting Others. 2009. (Extreme Careers Ser.). 64p. (gr. 5-5). 58.50 *(978-1-61512-385-8(7)*, Rosen Reference) Rosen Publishing Group, Inc., The.

Gifford, Clive. Ancient Rome. 2017. (Best & Worst Jobs Ser.). (ENG., Illus.). 32p. (J). (gr. 4-6). 17.99 *(978-0-7502-8738-8(1)*, Wayland) Hachette Children's Group GBR. Dist: Hachette Bk. Group.

Gillis, Jennifer B. Jobs on Wheels. 2006. (My Neighborhood Ser.). (Illus.). 24p. (J). (gr. -1-3). 16.15 *(978-0-7569-6928-8(X))* Perfection Learning Corp.

Gonzalez, Lissette. Bomb Squads in Action. 2009. (Dangerous Jobs Ser.). 24p. (gr. 2-3). 42.50 *(978-1-61512-133-5(1)*, PowerKids Pr.) Rosen Publishing Group, Inc., The.

Gorman, Jacqueline Laks. Bus Drivers. Andersen, Gregg, photos by. 2010. (People in My Community Ser.). (Illus.). 24p. (gr. k-3). pap. 8.15 *(978-1-4339-3336-3(5))* Stevens, Gareth Publishing LLLP.

—Police Officers. Andersen, Gregg, photos by. 2010. (People in My Community Ser.). (Illus.). 24p. (gr. k-3). pap. 8.15 *(978-1-4339-3351-6(9))* Stevens, Gareth Publishing LLLP.

Gorman, Jacqueline Laks & Laks Gorman, Jacqueline. Firefighters. Andersen, Gregg, photos by. 2010. (People in My Community Ser.). (Illus.). 24p. (gr. k-3). 22.60 *(978-1-4339-3338-7(1))* Stevens, Gareth Publishing LLLP.

—Police Officers. Andersen, Gregg, photos by. 2010. (People in My Community Ser.). (Illus.). 24p. (gr. k-3). 22.60 *(978-1-4339-3350-9(0))* Stevens, Gareth Publishing LLLP.

Gray, Leon. Horrible Jobs of the Industrial Revolution, Vol. 1. 2014. (History's Most Horrible Jobs Ser.). (ENG.). 48p. (J). (gr. 5-6). 31.95 *(978-1-4824-0343-5(9))* Stevens, Gareth Publishing LLLP.

Green Careers, 6 vols., Set. 2010. (Green Careers Ser.). (C). (gr. 9). 197.70 *(978-0-8160-8291-9(X)*, Ferguson Publishing Co.) Facts On File, Inc.

Gregory, Helen. Places to Work, 1 vol. 2013. (Wonder Readers Next Steps: Social Studies). (ENG.). 20p. (gr. -1-1). lib. bdg. 22.65 *(978-1-4765-0043-0(6)*, Wonder Readers) Capstone Press of Coughlan Cos.

Guerrero, Pablo. Mi Laberinto. Urberuaga, Emilio, illus. 2004.Tr. of My Labyrinth. (SPA.). (J). 21.99 *(978-84-88342-42-3(X))* S.A. Kokinos ESP. Dist: Lectorum Pubns., Inc.

Guillain, Charlotte. History, 1 vol. 2012. (Jobs If You Like... Ser.). (ENG.). 32p. (gr. 1-3). pap. 8.29 *(978-1-4329-6818-2(1))*; lib. bdg. 27.32 *(978-1-4329-6807-6(6))* Heinemann-Raintree. (Heinemann First Library).

Hammelef, Danielle S. Behind the Glamour. 2017. (Behind the Glamour Ser.). (ENG.). 64p. (gr. 4-5). 125.28 *(978-1-5157-4900-4(2))* Capstone Press of Coughlan Cos.

Harcourt School Publishers Staff. Jobs People Do, No. 6. 2nd ed. 2003. (Illus.). pap. 139.70 *(978-0-15-337561-3(2))* Harcourt Schl. Pubs.

Harea, Maria. Who Does That? Jobs in Your Community. 2009. (Real Life Readers Ser.). 16p. (gr. 2-3). pap. 7.05 *(978-1-4358-0115-8(6)*, Rosen Classroom) Rosen Publishing Group, Inc., The.

Harms, Julia. Recipe & Craft Guide to Italy. 2011. (World Crafts & Recipes Ser.). (ENG., Illus.). 64p. (J). (gr. 4-7). lib. bdg. 33.95 *(978-1-61228-083-7(8))* Mitchell Lane Pubs., Inc.

Hatanaka, Kellen. Work: An Occupational ABC, 1 vol. 2014. (ENG., Illus.). 40p. (J). (gr. -1-2). 16.95 *(978-1-55498-409-1(2))* Groundwood Bks. CAN. Dist: Publishers Group West (PGW).

Health Care Careers in 2 Years. 2013. (Health Care Careers in 2 Years Ser.). 80p. (YA). (gr. 7-12). 232.75 *(978-1-4777-1705-9(6))* Rosen Publishing Group, Inc., The.

Heiman, Diane & Suneby, Liz. See What You Can Be: Explore Careers That Could Be for You! Wood, Tracey, illus. 2009. (ENG.). 108p. (gr. 4-7). spiral bd. 9.95 *(978-1-59369-277-3(3))* American Girl Publishing, Inc.

Heling, Kathryn. Clothesline Clues to Jobs People Do. 2014. 17.95 *(978-1-63419-654-3(6))* Perfection Learning Corp.

Heling, Kathryn & Hembrook, Deborah. Clothesline Clues to Jobs People Do. Davies, Andy Robert, illus. (ENG.). 40p. (J). (gr. -1-2). 2014. pap. 7.95 *(978-1-58089-252-0(3))* 2012. 14.95 *(978-1-58089-251-3(5))* Charlesbridge Publishing, Inc.

Henry, Claire. The World's Deadliest Jobs, 1 vol., 1. 2014. (World's Deadliest Ser.). (ENG.). 32p. (J). (gr. 3-6). 26.25 *(978-1-4777-6161-8(6)*, PowerKids Pr.) Rosen Publishing Group, Inc., The.

Heos, Bridget. Getting a Job in Hair Care & Makeup. 2013. 80p. (YA). (gr. 9-12). 33.25 *(978-1-4488-9611-0(8))* Rosen Publishing Group, Inc., The.

Hibbert, Clare. Seaside Jobs. 2016. (Beside the Seaside Ser.). (ENG., Illus.). 24p. (J). (gr. k-2). 16.99 *(978-1-4451-3763-6(1)*, Franklin Watts) Hachette Children's Group GBR. Dist: Hachette Bk. Group.

High-Tech Jobs. 2015. (High-Tech Jobs Ser.). (ENG.). 96p. (J). (gr. 7-7). 256.74 *(978-1-5026-0295-4(4))* Cavendish Square Publishing.

Hill, Christina. Community Leaders Then & Now, 1 vol. 2006. (Primary Source Readers Ser.). (ENG., Illus.). 32p. (J). (gr. 1-1). pap. 8.99 *(978-0-7439-9385-2(3))* Shell Educational Publishing.

Holden, Pam. Jobs People Do Big Book Edition. 2014. (ENG.). 16p. (gr. 1-1). Beta *(978-1-77654-046-4(8)*, Red Rocket Readers) Flying Start Bks.

—When I Grow Up. East, Jacqueline, illus. 2009. (Red Rocket Readers Ser.). (ENG.). 16p. (gr. -1-1). pap. *(978-1-877363-06-1(5)*, Red Rocket Readers) Flying Start Bks.

I Can Be Anything! 2017. (I Can Be Anything! Ser.). 24p. (gr. k-k). pap. 48.90 ***(978-1-5382-0241-8(7))***; lib. bdg. 135.60 ***(978-1-5382-0240-1(9))*** Stevens, Gareth Publishing LLLP.

I Want to Be a Construction Worker. 2008. (Magnetic Board Books Ser.). 7p. bds. *(978-1-4075-1415-4(6))* Parragon, Inc.

Ingalls, Ann. Isabella & Ivan Build an Interview. Siegel, Melanie, illus. 2012. (Writing Builders Ser.). 32p. (J). (gr. 2-4). pap. 11.94 *(978-1-60357-389-4(5))*; lib. bdg. 25.27 *(978-1-59953-509-8(2))* Norwood Hse. Pr.

Iosa, Ann, illus. Jobs in My Neighborhood. 2010. (My World Ser.). (ENG.). 24p. (J). (gr. -1-1). pap. 8.15 *(978-1-61533-037-9(2))*; lib. bdg. 22.60 *(978-1-60754-952-9(2))* Windmill Bks.

Ivy, Darlene Sigda. Working in Sports. 2018. (ENG.). 32p. (gr. 3-6). ***(978-1-63235-449-5(7)***, 12-Story Library) Pr. Room Editions LLC.

Jango-Cohen, Judith. Librarians. 2005. (Pull Ahead Books: Community Helpers Ser.). 32p. (gr. k-3). (ENG.). pap. 7.95 *(978-0-8225-2533-2(X))*; (Illus.). (J). lib. bdg. 22.60 *(978-0-8225-1691-0(8))* Lerner Publishing Group.

Jarrell, Jane & Saathoff, Deborah. Off to Work We Go. 2004. 50p. (gr. -1-18). pap., act. bk. ed. 6.99 *(978-0-8054-0823-2(1))* B&H Publishing Group.

Jeffries, Joyce. Meet the Construction Worker. 2013. 24p. (J). (gr. k-2). 22.60 *(978-1-4339-9364-0(3))*; pap. 48.90 *(978-1-4339-9363-3(5))*; pap. 8.15 *(978-1-4339-9362-6(7))* Stevens, Gareth Publishing LLLP.

—Meet the Construction Worker / Conoce a Los Trabajadores de la Construccin. 2013. (People Around Town / Gente de Mi Ciudad Ser.). (SPA & ENG., Illus.). 24p. (J). (gr. k-2). 22.60 *(978-1-4339-9464-7(X))* Stevens, Gareth Publishing LLLP.

—Meet the Farmer. 2013. (People Around Town Ser.). (Illus.). 24p. (J). (gr. k-2). pap. 48.90 *(978-1-4339-9369-5(4))*; pap. 8.15 *(978-1-4339-9368-8(6))*; (ENG., lib. bdg. 22.60 *(978-1-4339-9367-1(8))* Stevens, Gareth Publishing LLLP.

—Meet the Farmer / Conoce a Los Granjeros. 2013. (People Around Town / Gente de Mi Ciudad Ser.). (SPA & ENG., Illus.). 24p. (J). (gr. k-2). 22.60 *(978-1-4339-9466-1(6))* Stevens, Gareth Publishing LLLP.

—Meet the Mayor. 2013. (People Around Town Ser.). 24p. (J). (gr. k-2). pap. 48.90 *(978-1-4339-9379-4(1))*; pap. 8.15 *(978-1-4339-9378-7(3))*; (ENG., Illus.). lib. bdg. 22.60 *(978-1-4339-9377-0(5))* Stevens, Gareth Publishing LLLP.

—Meet the Mayor / Conoce a Los Alcaldes. 2013. (People Around Town / Gente de Mi Ciudad Ser.). (SPA & ENG., Illus.). 24p. (J). (gr. k-2). 22.60 *(978-1-4339-9470-8(4))* Stevens, Gareth Publishing LLLP.

JIST Publishing Editors. Young Person's Occupational Outlook Handbook. 7th ed. 2010. (ENG.). 336p. (J). pap. 19.95 *(978-1-59357-743-8(5)*, JIST Works) JIST Publishing.

JIST Publishing Staff, creator. Young Person's Career Skills Handbook. 2006. (JIST's Young Person's Handbook Ser.). (Illus.). 250p. per. 19.95 *(978-1-59357-243-3(3)*, J2433, JIST Works) JIST Publishing.

JIST Works. People at Work! Second Edition: A Student's A-Z Guide to 350 Jobs. 2nd ed. 2005. (Early Start Career Ser.). (Illus.). 432p. (J). 27.95 *(978-1-59357-078-1(3)*, 1237657, JIST Works) JIST Publishing.

—Young Person's Occupational Outlook Handbook, Fifth Edition. 5th ed. 2004. (Illus.). 336p. pap. 19.95 *(978-1-59357-125-2(9)*, J1259, JIST Works) JIST Publishing.

Job Basics: Getting the Job You Need. 2013. (Job Basics: Getting the Job You Need Ser.). 80p. (YA). (gr. 9-12). 266.00 *(978-1-4488-9621-9(5))* Rosen Publishing Group, Inc., The.

Job Basics: Getting the Job You Need: Set 2. 2016. (Job Basics: Getting the Job You Need Ser.). 80p. (gr. 8-8). 250.25 *(978-1-4777-8550-8(7)*, Rosen Young Adult) Rosen Publishing Group, Inc., The.

Jobs in My School. 2014. (Jobs in My School Ser.). 24p. (J). (gr. k-2). pap. 49.50 *(978-1-4777-7226-3(X)*, PowerKids Pr.) Rosen Publishing Group, Inc., The.

Johnson, Jeremy. Unusual & Awesome Jobs in Sports: Pro Team Mascot, Pit Crew Member, & More. 2015. (You Get Paid for THAT? Ser.). (ENG.). 32p. (gr. 3-4). lib. bdg. 27.99 *(978-1-4914-2032-4(4)*, Edge Bks.) Capstone Press of Coughlan Cos.

Jones, Molly. Top 10 Tips for Planning for a Career. 2012. (Tips for Success Ser.). (ENG., Illus.). 64p. (J). (gr. 7-12). 31.95 *(978-1-4488-6863-6(7))* Rosen Publishing Group, Inc., The.

Jones, Tammy. Jobs Around Town. 2009. (Sight Word Readers Set A Ser.). (J). 3.49 net. *(978-1-60719-158-2(X))* Newmark Learning LLC.

Jordan, Anna Louise. Lo Que Hacen Los EMT/What EMTs Do. 2007. (What Does a Community Helper Do? Bilingual Ser.). (ENG & SPA., Illus.). 24p. (J). (gr. 1-3). lib. bdg. 22.60 *(978-0-7660-2825-8(9)*, Enslow Elementary) Enslow Pubs., Inc.

Kalman, Bobbie. Community Helpers Then & Now. 2013. (ENG., Illus.). 24p. (J). *(978-0-7787-0115-6(8))*; pap. *(978-0-7787-0143-9(3))* Crabtree Publishing Co.

Kamberg, Mary-Lane. Getting a Job in Law Enforcement, Security, & Corrections. 2013. 80p. (YA). (gr. 9-12). 33.25 *(978-1-4488-9605-9(3))* Rosen Publishing Group, Inc., The.

Kidde, Rita. What Does a Janitor Do? 2014. (Jobs in My School Ser.). (Illus.). 24p. (J). (gr. k-2). pap. 8.25 *(978-1-4777-6544-9(1)*, PowerKids Pr.) Rosen Publishing Group, Inc., The.

Kimbrell, Grady, et al. Entering the World of Work. 4th ed. 2006. (Exploring the World of Work Ser.). (ENG., Illus.). 464p. (gr. 9-12). stu. ed. 88.24 *(978-0-07-861458-3(9)*, 0078614589) McGraw-Hill Education.

Koh, Frederick. Danger at Work. 2007. (Steck-Vaughn BOLDPRINT Anthologies Ser.). (ENG., Illus.). 48p. (gr. 6-9). pap. 16.90 *(978-1-4190-4027-6(8))* Houghton Mifflin Harcourt Publishing Co.

Koosmann, Melissa. Recipe & Craft Guide to South Africa. 2011. (World Crafts & Recipes Ser.). (ENG., Illus.). 64p. (J). (gr. 4-7). lib. bdg. 33.95 *(978-1-61228-080-6(3))* Mitchell Lane Pubs., Inc.

Krasinski, Jay. Who Works at the Store? 2012. (InfoMax Readers Ser.). (ENG., Illus.). 16 pp.p. (J). (gr. k-1). pap. 7.00 *(978-1-4488-8956-3(1)*, Rosen Classroom) Rosen Publishing Group, Inc., The.

Krebs, Laurie. A Day in the Life of a Colonial Miller. 2004. (Library of Living & Working in Colonial Times). (Illus.). 24p. (J). lib. bdg. 19.95 *(978-0-8239-6230-3(X)*, PowerKids Pr.) Rosen Publishing Group, Inc., The.

Laks Gorman, Jacqueline. Bus Drivers / Conductores de Autobuses. Andersen, Gregg, photos by. 2010. (People in My Community / Mi comunidad Ser.). (SPA., Illus.). 24p. (gr. k-3). pap. 8.15 *(978-1-4339-3754-5(9))* Stevens, Gareth Publishing LLLP.

—Firefighters / Bomberos. Andersen, Gregg, photos by. 2010. (People in My Community / Mi comunidad Ser.). (SPA., Illus.). 24p. (gr. k-3). pap. 8.15 *(978-1-4339-3757-6(3))* Stevens, Gareth Publishing LLLP.

—Librarians. Andersen, Gregg, photos by. 2010. (People in My Community Ser.). (Illus.). 24p. (gr. k-3). pap. 8.15 *(978-1-4339-3342-4(X))* Stevens, Gareth Publishing LLLP.

—Librarians / Bibliotecarios. Andersen, Gregg, photos by. 2010. (People in My Community / Mi comunidad Ser.). (SPA., Illus.). 24p. (gr. k-3). pap. 8.15 *(978-1-4339-3760-6(3))* Stevens, Gareth Publishing LLLP.

—Police Officers / Policías. Andersen, Gregg, photos by. 2010. (People in My Community / Mi comunidad Ser.). (SPA., Illus.). 24p. (gr. k-3). pap. 8.15 *(978-1-4339-3769-9(7))* Stevens, Gareth Publishing LLLP.

Landau, Elaine. Deadly High-Risk Jobs. 2013. (ShockZone — Deadly & Dangerous Ser.). (ENG., Illus.). 32p. (gr. 5-8). pap. 8.95 *(978-1-4677-0891-3(7))*; lib. bdg. 26.60 *(978-1-4677-0603-2(5)*, Lerner Pubns.) Lerner Publishing Group.

Latou, Pierre. Who Works Here? 2014. (Little Books of Answers: Level C Ser.). (Illus.). 16p. (gr. k-2). pap. 7.95 *(978-1-927136-22-5(9))* Three Crows Media NZL. Dist: RiverStream Publishing.

Leake, Diyan. People in the Community, 6 bks., Set. Incl. Teachers. (ENG., Illus.). 24p. (gr. -1-1). 2008. 21.99 *(978-1-4329-1191-1(0)*, Acorn); (People in the Community Ser.). (ENG.). 24p. 2008. Set lib. bdg. 21.99 o.p. *(978-1-4329-1193-5(7)*, Acorn) Heinemann-Raintree.

LeBoutillier, Linda. Unusual & Awesome Jobs Using Technology: Roller Coaster Designer, Space Robotics Engineer, & More. 2015. (You Get Paid for THAT? Ser.). (ENG.). 32p. (gr. 3-4). 27.99 *(978-1-4914-2029-4(4))* Capstone Press of Coughlan Cos.

Lerner Publishing Group Staff. Work People Do: Classroom Set. 2005. (Illus.). (J). (gr. -1-1). 24.95 *(978-0-8225-5356-4(2))* Lerner Publishing Group.

LernerClassroom Editors. First Step Nonfiction-Work People Do Set I Teaching Guide. 2009. pap. 7.95 *(978-0-8225-5398-4(8))* Lerner Publishing Group.

—First Step Nonfiction-Work People Do Set Ii Teaching Guide. 2009. pap. 7.95 *(978-0-8225-3858-5(X))* Lerner Publishing Group.

Litchfield, Jo. Jobs. Litchfield, Jo & Allen, Francesca, illus. 2006. (Usborne Look & Say Ser.). 10p. (J). (gr. -1-k). bds. 7.99 *(978-0-7945-1353-5(0)*, Usborne) EDC Publishing.

Lonely Planet Publications Staff. World Search - Amazing Jobs, 1 vol. 2014. (Lonely Planet Kids Ser.). (ENG., Illus.). 16p. (J). 14.99 *(978-1-74321-920-1(2)*, 4640) Lonely Planet Pubns.

Lopez, Eduardo. 20 Great Career-Building Activities Using Instagram & Snapchat. 2016. (Social Media Career Building Ser.). 00064p. (J). (gr. 7-7). 34.45 *(978-1-5081-7272-7(2))* Rosen Publishing Group, Inc., The.

Lost Jobs: Individual Title Six-Packs. (Bookweb Ser.). 32p. (gr. 6-18). 34.00 *(978-0-7578-0909-5(X))* Rigby Education.

Luebke, Gayle M. When I Grow Up. 2005. 19p. 9.88 *(978-1-4116-2790-1(3))* Lulu Pr., Inc.

Lüsted, Marcia Amidon. What Are Jobs & Earnings? 2016. (Let's Find Out! Ser.). 32p. (J). (gr. 3-2). lib. bdg. 24.45 *(978-1-68048-401-4(X))* Rosen Publishing Group, Inc., The.

MacDonald, Margaret. Working as a Team. 2011. (Learn-Abouts Ser.). (Illus.). 16p. (J). pap. 7.95 *(978-1-59920-648-6(X))* Black Rabbit Bks.

Macken, JoAnn Early. Teachers. 2010. (People in My Community Ser.). (Illus.). 24p. (J). (gr. k-3). 22.60 *(978-1-4339-3347-9(0))* Stevens, Gareth Publishing LLLP.

Mahaney, Ian F. The Best Job Ever, 1 vol. 2015. (Best Job Ever Ser.). (ENG.). 24p. (J). 49.50 *(978-1-4994-0302-2(X)*, PowerKids Pr.) Rosen Publishing Group, Inc., The.

Maile, Ruby. Why Do You Live Here? 2014. (Little Books of Answers: Level C Ser.). (Illus.). 16p. (gr. k-2). pap. 7.95 *(978-1-927136-25-6(3))* Three Crows Media NZL. Dist: RiverStream Publishing.

Mangrum, Allison. Jobs from A to Z. Capaldi, Gina, illus. 2006. 28p. pap. 9.50 *(978-1-55501-675-3(8))* Ballard & Tighe Pubs.

Marsh, Carole. Job Tracks: 60 Great Careers & How to Get from Where You Are... to Where You Want to Go! 2012. (Carole Marsh's Careers Curriculum Ser.). (ENG., Illus.). 130p. (J). pap. 19.99 *(978-0-635-10552-3(7))* Gallopade International.

—Work Words: Job/Business/Career Words & Terms You Need to Know! 2012. (Carole Marsh's Careers Curriculum Ser.). (ENG., Illus.). 58p. (J). pap. 19.99 *(978-0-635-10556-1(X))* Gallopade International.

—Would You Hire This Person? A Look at Getting Hired (or Not!)... from the Point of View of Your (Possible!) Future Employer. 2012. (Carole Marsh's Careers Curriculum Ser.). (ENG., Illus.). 82p. (J). pap. 19.99 *(978-0-635-10553-0(5))* Gallopade International.

Martin, Bobi. Working As an Electrician in Your Community. 2015. (Careers in Your Community Ser.). (ENG., Illus.). 80p. (YA). (gr. 7-8). 34.25 *(978-1-4994-6111-4(9)*, Rosen Young Adult) Rosen Publishing Group, Inc., The.

Mattern, Joanne. Astronauts. 2009. (Working Together Ser.). 24p. (gr. 1-2). 42.50 *(978-1-60854-828-6(7)*, PowerKids Pr.) Rosen Publishing Group, Inc., The.

—Chefs. 2009. (Working Together Ser.). 24p. (gr. 1-2). 42.50 *(978-1-60854-829-3(5)*, PowerKids Pr.) Rosen Publishing Group, Inc., The.

—Cocineros (Chefs) 2009. (Trabajo en grupo (Working Together) Ser.). (SPA.). 24p. (gr. 1-2). 42.50 *(978-1-60854-576-6(8)*, Editorial Buenas Letras) Rosen Publishing Group, Inc., The.

—Emt. 2009. (Working Together Ser.). 24p. (gr. 1-2). 42.50 *(978-1-60854-830-9(9)*, PowerKids Pr.) Rosen Publishing Group, Inc., The.

—Pilotos (Pilots) 2009. (Trabajo en grupo (Working Together) Ser.). (SPA.). 24p. (gr. 1-2). 42.50 *(978-1-60854-577-3(6)*, Editorial Buenas Letras) Rosen Publishing Group, Inc., The.

—Pilots. 2009. (Working Together Ser.). 24p. (gr. 1-2). 42.50 *(978-1-60854-832-3(5)*, PowerKids Pr.) Rosen Publishing Group, Inc., The.

—Técnicos en emergencias Médicas (EMT) 2009. (Trabajo en grupo (Working Together) Ser.). (SPA.). 24p. (gr. 1-2). 42.50 *(978-1-60854-579-7(2)*, Editorial Buenas Letras) Rosen Publishing Group, Inc., The.

Matthews, Sheelagh. Canadian Shield. 2010. (Illus.). 32p. *(978-1-55388-628-0(3))*; pap. *(978-1-55388-629-7(1))* Weigl Educational Pubs. Ltd.

Maxwell, Scott, et al. The Coolest Jobs on the Planet. 2013. (Coolest Jobs on the Planet Ser.). (ENG.). 48p. (gr. 5-8). pap. 35.96 *(978-1-4109-5492-3(7))*; lib. bdg. 130.60 *(978-1-4109-5487-9(0))* Heinemann-Raintree.

Meister, Cari. Chefs. 2014. (Illus.). 24p. (J). lib. bdg. 25.65 *(978-1-62031-089-2(9)*, Bullfrog Bks.) Jump! Inc.

—Construction Workers. 2014. (Illus.). 24p. (J). lib. bdg. 25.65 *(978-1-62031-090-8(2)*, Bullfrog Bks.) Jump! Inc.

—Farmers. 2014, (Illus.). 24p. (J). lib. bdg. 25.65 *(978-1-62031-092-2(9)*, Bullfrog Bks.) Jump! Inc.

—Mechanics. 2014. (Illus.). 24p. (J). lib. bdg. 25.65 *(978-1-62031-093-9(7)*, Bullfrog Bks.) Jump! Inc.

—Nurses. 2014. (Illus.). 24p. (J). lib. bdg. 25.65 *(978-1-62031-094-6(5)*, Bullfrog Bks.) Jump! Inc.

—Veterinarians. 2014. (Illus.). 24p. (J). lib. bdg. 25.65 *(978-1-62031-096-0(1)*, Bullfrog Bks.) Jump! Inc.

Metz, L. On the Job: Learning the O Sound. 2009. (PowerPhonics Ser.). 24p. (gr. 1-1). 39.90 *(978-1-60851-466-3(8)*, PowerKids Pr.) Rosen Publishing Group, Inc., The.

Meyer, Susan. Getting a Job in Sanitation. 2013. 80p. (YA). (gr. 9-12). 33.25 *(978-1-4488-9607-3(X))* Rosen Publishing Group, Inc., The.

Milet Publishing Staff. Jobs. 2012. (My First Bilingual Book Ser.). (Illus.). 24p. (J). (gr. k — 1). (ENG & ITA.). bds. 7.99 *(978-1-84059-706-6(2))*; (ENG & SOM., bds. 7.99 *(978-1-84059-711-0(9))*; (FRE & ENG., bds. 7.99 *(978-1-84059-704-2(6))* Milet Publishing.

—Jobs - Berufe. 2012. (My First Bilingual Book Ser.). (ENG & GER., Illus.). 24p. (J). (gr. k — 1). bds. 7.99 *(978-1-84059-705-9(4))* Milet Publishing.

—Jobs - My First Bilingual Book. 2012. (My First Bilingual Book Ser.). (ENG & BEN., Illus.). 24p. (J). (gr. k — 1). bds. 7.99 (978-1-84059-701-1(1)) Milet Publishing.

—Jobs Empregos. 2012. (My First Bilingual Book Ser.). (ENG & POR., Illus.). 24p. (J). (gr. k — 1). bds. 7.99 (978-1-84059-709-7(7)) Milet Publishing.

—Jobs Profesiones. 2012. (My First Bilingual Book Ser.). (SPA & ENG., Illus.). 24p. (J). (gr. k — 1). bds. 7.99 (978-1-84059-712-7(7)) Milet Publishing.

—My First Bilingual Book - Jobs. 2012. (My First Bilingual Book Ser.). (ENG, POL & POR., Illus.). 24p. (J). (gr. k — 1). bds. 7.99 (978-1-84059-708-0(9)) Milet Publishing.

—My First Bilingual Book-Jobs. 2012. (My First Bilingual Book Ser.). (ENG & PER., Illus.). 24p. (J). (gr. k — 1). bds. 7.99 (978-1-84059-703-5(8)); bds. 7.99 (978-1-84059-700-4(3)) Milet Publishing.

—My First Bilingual Book-Jobs (English-Korean) 2012. (My First Bilingual Book Ser.). (ENG & KOR., Illus.). 24p. (J). (gr. k — 1). bds. 7.99 (978-1-84059-707-3(0)) Milet Publishing.

—My First Bilingual Book-Jobs (English-Russian) 2012. (My First Bilingual Book Ser.). (ENG & RUS., Illus.). 24p. (J). (gr. k — 1). bds. 7.99 (978-1-84059-710-3(0)) Milet Publishing.

—My First Bilingual Book-Jobs (English-Turkish) 2012. (My First Bilingual Book Ser.). (ENG & TUR., Illus.). 24p. (J). (gr. k — 1). bds. 7.99 (978-1-84059-713-4(5)) Milet Publishing.

—My First Bilingual Book-Jobs (English-Urdu) 2012. (My First Bilingual Book Ser.). (ENG & URD., Illus.). 24p. (J). (gr. k — 1). bds. 7.99 (978-1-84059-714-1(3)) Milet Publishing.

—My First Bilingual Book-Jobs (English-Vietnamese) 2012. (My First Bilingual Book Ser.). (ENG & VIE., Illus.). 24p. (J). (gr. k — 1). bds. 7.99 (978-1-84059-715-8(1)) Milet Publishing.

Miller, Connie Colwell. The Deadliest Jobs on Earth. 2010. (World's Deadliest Ser.). (ENG.). 32p. (gr. 1-2). lib. bdg. 26.65 (978-1-4296-3931-6(8), Blazers) Capstone Press of Coughlan Cos.

—Disgusting Jobs. 2016. (That's Disgusting! Ser.). (ENG.). 32p. pap. 7.95 (978-1-5157-6268-3(8), Blazers) Capstone Press of Coughlan Cos.

Miller, Mirella S. Oil Worker. 2015. (Gross Jobs Ser.). (ENG.). 24p. (J). (gr. 2-5). 27.07 (978-1-63143-690-1(2), 208523) Child's World, Inc., The.

Mitchell, Melanie. Principals. (Pull Ahead Bks.). (J). 2005. (Illus.). 32p. lib. bdg. 22.60 (978-0-8225-1694-1(2)) 2004. pap. 6.95 (978-0-8225-2535-6(6), Lerner Pubns.) Lerner Publishing Group.

—Teachers. 2005. (Pull Ahead Bks.). (Illus.). 32p. (J). lib. bdg. 22.60 (978-0-8225-1696-5(9)); (ENG., pap. 7.95 (978-0-8225-2536-3(4)) Lerner Publishing Group.

Mitchell, Missy. Ballet: Pointe by Pointe. (Curtain Call Library of Dance Ser.). 48p. (gr. 5-8). 2009. 53.00 (978-1-60853-418-0(9), Rosen Reference) 2004. (Illus.). (YA). lib. bdg. 29.25 (978-0-8239-4555-9(3)) Rosen Publishing Group, Inc., The.

Moncure, Jane Belk. What Can We Play Today? A Book about Community Helpers. Gallagher-Cole, Mernie, illus. 2013. (Magic Castle Readers Ser.). (ENG.). 32p. (J). (gr. -1-2). 25.64 (978-1-62323-587-1(1), 206322) Child's World, Inc., The.

Monroe, Judy. A Day in the Life of a Librarian, 1 vol. 2004. (Community Helpers at Work Ser.). (ENG., Illus.). 24p. (gr. 1-2). 25.32 (978-0-7368-2630-3(0), First Facts) Capstone Press of Coughlan Cos.

Moore, Elizabeth. Keeping Us Safe, 1 vol. 2011. (Wonder Readers Emergent Level Ser.). (ENG.). (gr. -1-1). 32p. pap. 5.99 (978-1-4296-7845-2(3)); 8p. pap. 35.94 (978-1-4296-8232-9(9)) Capstone Press of Coughlan Cos. (Wonder Readers).

Moore, Elizabeth & Gregory, Helen. Where Do People Work?, 1 vol. 2011. (Wonder Readers Emergent Level Ser.). (ENG.). 32p. (gr. -1-1). pap. 5.99 (978-1-4296-7879-7(8), Wonder Readers) Capstone Press of Coughlan Cos.

Moore, Philip. How Can You Use A Computer? 2014. (Little Books of Answers: Level d Ser.). (Illus.). 16p. (gr. k-2). pap. 7.95 (978-1-927136-32-4(6)) Three Crows Media NZL. Dist: RiverStream Publishing.

Morgand, Virginie. What Do Grown-Ups Do All Day? Morgand, Virginie, illus. 2016. (ENG., Illus.). 64p. (J). 22.99 (978-1-84780-809-7(3), Wide Eyed Editions) Quarto Publishing Group UK GBR. Dist: Littlehampton Bk Services, Ltd.

Morris, Ann. That's Our Custodian! Linenthal, Peter, illus. Linenthal, Peter, photos by. 2003. (That's Our School Ser.). (ENG.). 32p. (gr. k-3). lib. bdg. 22.60 (978-0-7613-2401-0(1), Millbrook Pr.) Lerner Publishing Group.

—That's Our Gym Teacher! Linenthal, Peter, illus. Linenthal, Peter, photos by. 2003. (That's Our School Ser.). (ENG.). 32p. (gr. k-3). lib. bdg. 22.60 (978-0-7613-2403-4(8), Millbrook Pr.) Lerner Publishing Group.

—That's Our Nurse! Linenthal, Peter, illus. Linenthal, Peter, photos by. 2003. (That's Our School Ser.). (ENG.). 32p. (gr. k-3). lib. bdg. 22.60 (978-0-7613-2402-7(X), Millbrook Pr.) Lerner Publishing Group.

Mullins, Matt. Surgical Technologist. 2010. (21st Century Skills Library: Cool Careers Ser.). (ENG.). 32p. (gr. 4-8). lib. bdg. 28.50 (978-1-60279-939-4(3), 200623) Cherry Lake Publishing.

Murdico, Suzanne J. Bomb Squad Experts: Life Defusing Explosive Devices. 2009. (Extreme Careers Ser.). 64p. (gr. 5-5). 58.50 (978-1-61512-386-5(5), Rosen Reference) Rosen Publishing Group, Inc., The.

Murphy, Patricia J. Investigating Insects with a Scientist. 2004. (I Like Science! Ser.). (Illus.). 24p. (J). (gr. 1-3). lib. bdg. 22.60 (978-0-7660-2270-6(6)) Enslow Pubs., Inc.

Murray, Amy. The Character & Career Connection. 2005. (Illus.). 76p. (J). per. 19.95 (978-1-931636-45-2(1)) National Ctr. For Youth Issues.

Nelson, Robin. Coaches. 2005. (Pull Ahead Bks.). (Illus.). 32p. (J). (gr. 3-7). lib. bdg. 22.60 (978-0-8225-1686-6(1)) Lerner Publishing Group.

—Custodians. 2005. (Pull Ahead Bks.). (Illus.). 32p. (J). 22.60 (978-0-8225-1687-3(X)) Lerner Publishing Group.

—Jobs. 2004. (First Step Nonfiction - Basic Human Needs Ser.). (ENG., Illus.). 8p. (gr. -1-1). pap. 4.95 (978-0-8225-3929-2(2), Lerner Pubns.) Lerner Publishing Group.

—Working Then & Now. 2008. pap. 34.95 (978-0-8225-9486-4(2)); (ENG., Illus.). 24p. lib. bdg. 23.93 (978-0-8225-8604-3(5)) Lerner Publishing Group.

Ollhoff, Jim. Hazmat. 2012. (Emergency Workers Ser.). 32p. (J). (gr. 5-9). lib. bdg. 27.07 (978-1-61783-514-8(5), Abdo & Daughters) ABDO Publishing Co.

—Swat. 2012. (Emergency Workers Ser.). 32p. (J). (gr. 5-9). lib. bdg. 27.07 (978-1-61783-517-9(X), Abdo & Daughters) ABDO Publishing Co.

On the Edge: Individual Title Six-Packs. (Action Packs Ser.). 104p. (gr. 3-5). 44.00 (978-0-7635-2995-6(8)) Rigby Education.

Owaki, Takashi. Dreams Around the World. 2012. (ENG., Illus.). 32p. 16.95 (978-1-935548-11-9(5)) One Peace Bks., Inc.

Owen, Ann & National Geographic Learning Staff. Delivering Your Mail: A Book about Mail Carriers. Thomas, Eric, illus. 2003. (Community Workers Ser.). (ENG.). 24p. (gr. -1-3). per. 8.95 (978-1-4048-0485-2(4)) Picture Window Bks.

Paige, Joy. Cool Careers Without College for People Who Love to Build Things. 2009. (Cool Careers Without College Ser.). 144p. (gr. 6-6). 66.50 (978-1-61511-970-7(1)) Rosen Publishing Group, Inc., The.

Parks, Peggy J. Doctor. 2003. (Exploring Careers Ser.). (ENG., Illus.). 48p. (J). (gr. 3-5). 27.50 (978-0-7377-1484-5(0), Kidhaven) Cengage Gale.

—Firefighter. 2004. (EXPLORING CAREERS Ser.). (ENG., Illus.). 48p. (J). 27.50 (978-0-7377-2066-2(2), Greenhaven Pr., Inc.) Cengage Gale.

Paul, Miranda. Whose Hands Are These? A Community Helper Guessing Book. 2016. (ENG., Illus.). 32p. (J). (gr. -1-3). 19.99 (978-1-4677-5214-5(2)); 38.65 (978-1-4677-9726-9(X)) Lerner Publishing Group. (Millbrook Pr.).

—Whose Hands Are These? A Community Helper Guessing Book. Powell, Luciana Navarro, illus. 2016. (Millbrook Picture Bks). (ENG.). 32p. (gr. -1-3). 38.65 (978-1-5124-0738-9(0)) Lerner Publishing Group.

Pavolino, Amy. When I Grow Up. 2010. (ENG., Illus.). 30p. (J). pap. 16.00 (978-1-4349-9917-7(3), RoseDog Bks.) Dorrance Publishing Co., Inc.

Pelos, Rebecca & Greenberger, Robert. Cool Careers Without College for People Who Love Planning & Organizing. 2017. (Cool Careers Without College Ser.). 112p. (gr. 12-12). 38.45 **(978-1-5081-7540-7(3)**, Rosen Young Adult) Rosen Publishing Group, Inc., The.

Perish, Patrick. Disgusting Jobs. 2014. (Totally Disgusting Ser.). (ENG., Illus.). 24p. (J). (gr. 3-7). 25.95 (978-1-62617-131-2(9), Epic Bks.) Bellwether Media.

Perritano, John. The Most Disgusting Jobs on the Planet, 1 vol. 2012. (Disgusting Stuff Ser.). (ENG., Illus.). 48p. (gr. 3-4). lib. bdg. 31.99 (978-1-4296-7532-1(2)) Capstone Press of Coughlan Cos.

Pratt, Laura. Plains. 2010. (Illus.). 32p. (978-1-55388-625-9(9)); pap. (978-1-55388-626-6(7)) Weigl Educational Pubs. Ltd.

Price-Wright, Heather. Life in Numbers: Choose Your Career (Level 5) 2017. (Exploring Reading Ser.). (Illus.). 48p. (J). (gr. 5-5). pap. 10.99 **(978-1-4258-4985-6(7))** Teacher Created Materials, Inc.

Priddy Books Staff. I Want to Be a Builder & Firefighter, 2 bks. (Illus.). (J). bds. (978-0-312-49163-5(8), Priddy Bks.) St. Martin's Pr.

Raum, Elizabeth. Work: From Plows to Robots. 2010. (Timeline History Ser.). (ENG., Illus.). 32p. (gr. 3-5). 29.99 (978-1-4329-3806-2(1), NA-h) Heinemann-Raintree.

Ready, Dee. Nurses Help. 2013. (Our Community Helpers Ser.). (ENG.). 24p. (gr. k-1). pap. 35.70 (978-1-62065-850-5(X)); pap. 6.29 (978-1-62065-849-9(6)); lib. bdg. 21.99 (978-1-62065-080-6(0)) Capstone Press of Coughlan Cos. (Pebble Bks.).

Reeves, Diane Lindsey. Career Ideas for Kids Who Like Art. Bond, Nancy, illus. 2nd rev. ed. 2007. (Career Ideas for Kids Ser.). 208p. (gr. 4-9). 32.95 (978-0-8160-6541-7(1), Ferguson Publishing Co.) Facts On File, Inc.

—Career Ideas for Kids Who Like Talking. Bond, Nancy, illus. 2nd rev. ed. 2007. (Career Ideas for Kids Ser.). 208p. (gr. 4-9). 32.95 (978-0-8160-6553-0(5), Checkmark Bks.) Facts On File, Inc.

—Career Ideas for Teens Set. 2005. (Career Ideas for Teens Ser.). 192p. (gr. 6-12). 120.00 (978-0-8160-5287-5(5), Ferguson Publishing Co.) Facts On File, Inc.

—Glamorous Jobs. 2009. (Way Out Work Ser.). (Illus.). 48p. (gr. 3-5). 29.95 (978-1-60413-129-1(2), Ferguson Publishing Co.) Facts On File, Inc.

—Goofy Jobs. 2009. (Way Out Work Ser.). (Illus.). 48p. (gr. 3-5). 29.95 (978-1-60413-130-7(6), Ferguson Publishing Co.) Facts On File, Inc.

—Gross Jobs. 2009. (Way Out Work Ser.). (Illus.). 48p. (gr. 3-5). 29.95 (978-1-60413-131-4(4), Ferguson Publishing Co.) Facts On File, Inc.

—Gutsy Jobs. 2009. (Way Out Work Ser.). (Illus.). 48p. (gr. 3-5). 29.95 (978-1-60413-133-8(0), Ferguson Publishing Co.) Facts On File, Inc.

—Manufacturing. 2017. (Bright Futures Press: World of Work Ser.). (ENG., Illus.). 32p. (J). (gr. 4-7). lib. bdg. 29.93 (978-1-63472-627-6(8), 209542) Cherry Lake Publishing.

—Way Out Work Set, 6-Volumes. 2009. (Way Out Work Ser.). (gr. 3-5). 179.70 (978-1-60413-831-3(9), Ferguson Publishing Co.) Facts On File, Inc.

Reina, Mary. Earn Money. 2015. (Money & You Ser.). (ENG.). 24p. (gr. k-1). pap. 5.95 (978-1-4914-2299-1(8), Pebble Bks.) Capstone Press of Coughlan Cos.

Rice, Dona Herweck. Trabajadores, 1 vol. 2nd rev. ed. 2011. (Nonfiction Readers Ser.). (SPA.). 12p. (J). (gr. 1-1). pap. 4.99 (978-1-4333-4411-4(4)) Teacher Created Materials, Inc.

—Workers, 1 vol. 2nd rev. ed. 2013. (Nonfiction Readers Ser.). (ENG., Illus.). 12p. (J). (gr. 1-1). pap. 15.96 (978-1-4807-1011-5(3)) Shell Educational Publishing.

—Workers, 1 vol. 2nd rev. ed. 2011. (TIME for KIDS(r) Nonfiction Readers Ser.). (ENG.). 12p. (gr. 1-1). 4.99 (978-1-4333-3572-3(7)) Teacher Created Materials, Inc.

Rosa-Mendoza, Gladys. Jobs Around My Neighborhood/Oficios en Mi Vecindario. Iosa, Ann, illus. 2007. (English Spanish Foundations Ser.). 20p. (gr. -1-k). pap. 19.95 (978-1-931398-81-7(X)) Me+Mi Publishing.

Rosa-Mendoza, Gladys, creator. Jobs Around My Neighborhood. 2004. (English-Spanish Foundations Ser.: Vol. 9).Tr. of Officios en Mi Vecindario. (SPA & ENG., Illus.). 20p. (J). bds. 6.95 (978-1-931398-09-1(7)) Me+Mi Publishing.

Rosen, Michael J. & Kassoy, Ben. Weird Jobs. Sandy, Pat, illus. 2013. (No Way! Ser.). (ENG.). 32p. (gr. 3-5). lib. bdg. 26.60 (978-0-7613-8983-5(0), Millbrook Pr.) Lerner Publishing Group.

Rosen Publishing Staff. The Best Job Ever, 1 vol. 2015. (Best Job Ever Ser.). (ENG.). 24p. (J). 141.60 (978-1-4777-5737-6(6), PowerKids Pr.) Rosen Publishing Group, Inc., The.

Rosenberg, Aaron. Cryptologists: Life Making & Breaking Codes. 2009. (Extreme Careers Ser.). 64p. (gr. 5-5). 58.50 (978-1-61512-388-9(1), Rosen Reference) Rosen Publishing Group, Inc., The.

Ross, Kathy. Community Workers. Barger, Jan, illus. 2005. (Crafts for Kids Who Are Learning about Ser.). (ENG.). 48p. (gr. k-3). lib. bdg., tchr. ed. 26.60 (978-0-7613-2743-1(6)) Lerner Publishing Group.

Royston, Angela. Diary of A... 2013. (Diary of A... Ser.). (ENG.). 32p. (gr. 1-3). pap. 44.75 (978-1-4329-7592-0(7)); lib. bdg. 136.60 (978-1-4329-7585-2(4)) Heinemann-Raintree. (Heinemann First Library).

Sanders, Michael J. Preteen Challenges: Hurdling to Your Success. 2010. 64p. pap. 12.50 (978-1-60911-113-7(3), Eloquent Bks.) Strategic Book Publishing & Rights Agency (SBPRA).

Saul, Laya. Recipe & Craft Guide to Israel. 2011. (World Crafts & Recipes Ser.). (ENG., Illus.). 64p. (J). (gr. 4-7). lib. bdg. 33.95 (978-1-61228-081-3(1)) Mitchell Lane Pubs., Inc.

Scarry, Richard. Richard Scarry's What Do People Do All Day? 2015. (ENG., Illus.). 96p. (J). (gr. -1-2). 15.99 (978-0-553-52059-0(8), Golden Bks.) Random Hse. Children's Bks.

Schuh, Mari. Community Helpers at a Fire. 2016. (Community Helpers on the Scene Ser.). (ENG., Illus.). 24p. (gr. k-1). lib. bdg. 21.99 (978-1-5157-2399-8(2), Pebble Bks.) Capstone Press of Coughlan Cos.

—Community Helpers on the Scene. 2016. (Community Helpers on the Scene Ser.). (ENG.). 24p. (gr. k-1). 87.96 (978-1-5157-2433-9(6), Pebble Bks.) Capstone Press of Coughlan Cos.

Scraper, Katherine. Kids Can Have Jobs. 2006. (Early Explorers Ser.). (J). pap. (978-1-4108-6034-7(5)) Benchmark Education Co.

Selwyn, Josephine. Who Uses This Machine? 2014. (Little Books of Answers: Level C Ser.). (Illus.). 16p. (gr. k-2). pap. 7.95 (978-1-927136-29-4(6)) Three Crows Media NZL. Dist: RiverStream Publishing.

Shone, Rob. Crime Scene Investigators. 2009. (Graphic Forensic Science Ser.). (ENG.). 48p. (YA). (gr. 5-5). 58.50 (978-1-61512-947-8(2), Rosen Reference) Rosen Publishing Group, Inc., The.

Siemens, Jared. Construction Worker. 2015. (J). (978-1-4896-4217-2(X)) Weigl Pubs., Inc.

—Police Officers. 2015. (Illus.). 24p. (J). (978-1-4896-3653-9(6)) Weigl Pubs., Inc.

Silate, Jennifer. Your Mayor: Local Government in Action. 2009. (Primary Source Library of American Citizenship Ser.). 32p. (gr. 5-5). 47.90 (978-1-61511-237-1(5), Rosen Reference) Rosen Publishing Group, Inc., The.

Simons, Lisa M. Bolt. Unusual & Awesome Jobs Using Math: Stunt Coordinator, Cryptologist, & More. 2015. (You Get Paid for THAT? Ser.). (ENG., Illus.). 32p. (gr. 3-4). 27.99 (978-1-4914-2030-0(8)) Capstone Press of Coughlan Cos.

Skills for Success. 2017. (Skills for Success Ser.). 64p. (gr. 12-12). 172.25 **(978-1-4994-6636-2(6)**, Rosen Young Adult) Rosen Publishing Group, Inc., The.

Small, Cathleen. 20 Great Career-Building Activities Using Facebook. 2016. (Social Media Career Building Ser.). 00064p. (J). (gr. 7-7). 34.45 (978-1-5081-7262-8(5)) Rosen Publishing Group, Inc., The.

Smith, Ben. Who Listens to the Weather Forecast? 2014. (Little Books of Answers: Level d Ser.). (Illus.). 16p. (gr. k-2). pap. 7.95 (978-1-927136-36-2(9)) Three Crows Media NZL. Dist: RiverStream Publishing.

Smith, Carrie. Jobs at School. 2006. (Early Explorers Ser.). (J). pap. (978-1-4108-6032-3(9)) Benchmark Education Co.

Souter, Gerry. Secret Service Agent: And Careers in Federal Protection. 2006. (Homeland Security & Counterterrorism Careers Ser.). (Illus.). 128p. (J). (gr. 5-9). lib. bdg. 33.27 (978-0-7660-2651-3(5)) Enslow Pubs., Inc.

St. Clair, Noel. The Unofficial Divergent Aptitude Test: Discover Your True Faction! 2015. (ENG.). 208p. pap. 14.99 (978-1-4405-8514-2(8)) Adams Media Corp.

Suen, Anastasia. Getting a Job in Child Care. 2013. (Job Basics: Getting the Job You Need Ser.). 80p. (YA). (gr. 9-12). 33.25 (978-1-4488-9612-7(6)) Rosen Publishing Group, Inc., The.

Sundance/Newbridge LLC Staff. World of Work. 2004. (Reading PowerWorks Ser.). (gr. 1-3). 37.50 (978-0-7608-9269-5(5)); pap. 6.10 (978-0-7608-9270-1(9)) Sundance/Newbridge Educational Publishing.

Swinburne, Stephen R. Whose Shoes? A Shoe for Every Job. 2010. (ENG., Illus.). 32p. (J). (gr. k-2). 16.95 (978-1-59078-569-0(X)) Boyds Mills Pr.

Tech Track: Building Your Career in IT. 2017. (Tech Track: Building Your Career in IT Ser.). 80p. (gr. 12-12). 286.00 **(978-1-4994-6637-9(4)**, Rosen Young Adult) Rosen Publishing Group, Inc., The.

Thomas, William David. Mountain Rescuer. 2008. (Cool Careers Ser.). 32p. (gr. 5-8). pap. 10.50 (978-0-8368-9328-1(X)); lib. bdg. 26.00 (978-0-8368-9195-9(3)) Stevens, Gareth Publishing LLLP.

Trumbauer, Lisa. Lo Que Hacen los Carteros. 2007. (What Does a Community Helper Do? Bilingual Ser.).Tr. of What Mail Carriers Do. (ENG & SPA., Illus.). 24p. (J). (gr. 1-3). lib. bdg. 22.60 (978-0-7660-2827-2(5), Enslow Elementary) Enslow Pubs., Inc.

Vastola, P. What I Think: Learning the TH Sound. 2009. (PowerPhonics Ser.). 24p. (gr. 1-1). 39.90 (978-1-60851-479-3(X), PowerKids Pr.) Rosen Publishing Group, Inc., The.

Verderosa, Laura. When I Grow Up. 2010. (Sight Word Readers Ser.). (J). 3.49 (978-1-60719-608-2(5)) Newmark Learning LLC.

Vogel, Elizabeth. Meet My Teacher. 2009. (My School Ser.). 24p. (gr. 1-2). 37.50 (978-1-61514-704-5(7), PowerKids Pr.) Rosen Publishing Group, Inc., The.

—Meet the Cafeteria Workers. 2009. (My School Ser.). 24p. (gr. 1-2). 37.50 (978-1-61514-705-2(5), PowerKids Pr.) Rosen Publishing Group, Inc., The.

—Meet the Librarian. 2009. (My School Ser.). 24p. (gr. 1-2). 37.50 (978-1-61514-706-9(3), PowerKids Pr.) Rosen Publishing Group, Inc., The.

—Meet the Principal. 2009. (My School Ser.). 24p. (gr. 1-2). 37.50 (978-1-61514-707-6(1), PowerKids Pr.) Rosen Publishing Group, Inc., The.

Weiss, Ellen & Fremont, Elenor. Odd Jobs: The Wackiest Jobs You've Never Heard Of. Ross, Damon, photos by. 2012. (ENG., Illus.). 80p. (J). (gr. 4-6). pap. 33.99 (978-0-689-82934-5(5), Simon & Schuster/Paula Wiseman Bks.) Simon & Schuster/Paula Wiseman Bks.

Wendinger, Jennifer. Unusual & Awesome Jobs Using Science: Hollywood Animal Trainer, Cave Diver, & More. 2015. (You Get Paid for THAT? Ser.). (ENG.). 32p. (gr. 3-4). 27.99 (978-1-4914-2031-7(6)) Capstone Press of Coughlan Cos.

Wheeler, Jill C. Firefighters, 1 vol. 2003. (Everyday Heroes Ser.). (ENG., Illus.). 32p. (gr. k-6). 27.07 (978-1-57765-855-9(8), Checkerboard Library) ABDO Publishing Co.

When I Grow Up. 2003. (J). per. (978-1-884907-56-2(3)); per. (978-1-884907-75-3(X)) Paradise Pr., Inc.

When I Grow Up. 2014. (When I Grow Up Ser.). 24p. (J). (gr. k-2). 135.00 (978-1-4824-1035-8(4)) Stevens, Gareth Publishing LLLP.

White, Nancy. Paramedics to the Rescue. 2011. (Work of Heroes: First Responders in Action Ser.). (Illus.). 32p. (J). (gr. 1-4). lib. bdg. 25.27 (978-1-61772-282-0(0)) Bearport Publishing Co., Inc.

Wigu Publishing. When I Grow up I Want to Be... a Teacher! Carlee Learns a Surprising Lesson! 2013. (When I Grow Up I Want To Be....Ser.). (Illus.). 62p. pap. 12.95 (978-1-939973-08-5(2), Wigu Publishing) Wigu Publishing.

Willett, Edward. Careers in Outer Space: New Business Opportunities. (Career Resource Library). 192p. (gr. 7-12). 2009. 63.90 (978-1-60853-401-2(4)) 2005. (Illus.). (YA). lib. bdg. 34.60 (978-0-8239-3358-7(X)) Rosen Publishing Group, Inc., The.

Williams, Jack S. Sailors, Merchants, & Muleteers of the California Mission Frontier. 2009. (People of the California Missions Ser.). 64p. (gr. 4-4). 58.50 (978-1-60851-159-4(6), PowerKids Pr.) Rosen Publishing Group, Inc., The.

Williams, Jack S. & Davis, Thomas L. Sailors, Merchants, & Muleteers. 2004. (People of the California Missions Ser.). (Illus.). 64p. (J). lib. bdg. 26.50 (978-0-8239-6282-2(2)) Rosen Publishing Group, Inc., The.

Williams, Judith. Exploring the Rain Forest Treetops with a Scientist. 2004. (I Like Science! Ser.). (Illus.). 24p. (J). lib. bdg. 22.60 (978-0-7660-2294-2(3)) Enslow Pubs., Inc.

—Saving Endangered Animals with a Scientist. 2004. (I Like Science! Ser.). (Illus.). 24p. (J). (gr. 2-4). lib. bdg. 21.26 (978-0-7660-2276-8(5)) Enslow Pubs., Inc.

Winning at Work Readiness. 2014. (Winning at Work Readiness Ser.). 64p. (YA). (gr. 9-12). pap. 64.75 (978-1-4777-8116-6(1)) Rosen Publishing Group, Inc., The.

Wood, Alexander. Our Jobs. 2009. (Real Life Readers Ser.). 8p. (gr. k-1). pap. 5.15 (978-1-4042-8011-3(1), Rosen Classroom) Rosen Publishing Group, Inc., The.

Wood, Alix. Test Pilot, 1 vol., 1. 2014. (World's Coolest Jobs Ser.). (ENG.). 32p. (J). (gr. 3-6). 26.25 (978-1-4777-6019-2(9), PowerKids Pr.) Rosen Publishing Group, Inc., The.

Wunderlich, Richard. Math on the Job. 2016. (ENG., Illus.). 32p. (J). lib. bdg. (978-0-7787-2360-8(7)) Crabtree Publishing Co.

Yanuchi, Lori & Yanuchi, Jeff. Ranger Trails: Jobs of Adventure in America's Parks. Morris, James R., illus. 2005. 64p. (J). per. 12.95 (978-0-9670177-2-3(6)) Ridge Rock Pr.

You Wouldn't Want To..., 4 vols., Set. Incl. Be a Salem Witch! Bizarre Accusations You'd Rather Not Face. Pipe, Jim. 29.00 (978-0-531-20821-2(4)); Be a Skyscraper Builder! A Hazardous Job You'd Rather Not Take. Malam, John. 29.00 (978-0-531-20824-3(9)); Be on the Hindenburg! A Transatlantic Trip You'd Rather Skip. Graham, Ian. 29.00 (978-0-531-20823-6(0)); Meet a Body Snatcher! Criminals & Murderers You'D Rather Avoid. MacDonald, Fiona. 29.00 (978-0-531-20822-9(2)); (Illus.). 32p. (J). (gr. 3-18). 2009. 2009. Set lib. bdg. 116.00 (978-0-531-26141-5(7), Watts, Franklin) Scholastic Library Publishing.

8-deck Careers for Kids Box Set. (Careers for Kids Ser.). 7.00 (978-1-57281-409-7(8), CFKS8) U.S. Games Systems, Inc.

21st Century Junior Library: Careers. 2011. 24p. lib. bdg. 287.20 (978-1-61080-000-6(1), 200934) Cherry Lake Publishing.

OCCUPATIONS—FICTION

Aiken, Zora & Aiken, David. A to Z: Pick What You'll Be. Aiken, David, illus. 2011. (ENG., Illus.). 32p. (J). 14.99 (978-0-7643-3701-7(7), 9780764337017, Schiffer Publishing Ltd) Schiffer Publishing, Ltd.

Aunt Judy. Chickens in the Know! Chickens of Different Occupations. Aunt Judy, illus. 2007. (Illus.). 40p. (J). pap. 7.00 (978-0-9780693-1-5(5)) McEwen, Judith A.

Baker, Keith. LMNO Pea-Quel. Baker, Keith, illus. 2017. (Peas Ser.). (ENG., Illus.). 40p. (J). (gr. -1-3). 17.99 **(978-1-4814-5856-6(6)**, Beach Lane Bks.) Beach Lane Bks.

Baker, Keith. LMNO Peas. Baker, Keith, illus. 2010. (Peas Ser.). (ENG., Illus.). 40p. (J). (gr. -1-3). 17.99 (978-1-4169-9141-0(7), Beach Lane Bks.) Beach Lane Bks.

—LMNO Peas. Baker, Keith, illus. 2014. (Peas Ser.). (ENG., Illus.). 36p. (J). (gr. -1-k). bds. 7.99 (978-1-4424-8978-3(2), Little Simon) Little Simon.

Bedrick, Claudia Z. People. 2011. (ENG., Illus.). 208p. (J). (gr. -1). 22.95 (978-1-59270-110-0(8)) Enchanted Lion Bks., LLC.

Berenstain, Mike. The Berenstain Bears: When I Grow Up. Berenstain, Mike, illus. 2015. (Berenstain Bears Ser.). (ENG., Illus.). 24p. (J). (gr. -1-3). pap. 3.99 (978-0-06-235005-3(6), HarperFestival) HarperCollins Pubs.

—When I Grow Up. 2015. (Berenstain Bears Ser.). (J). lib. bdg. 13.55 *(978-0-606-37606-8(2))* Turtleback Bks.
Berenstain, Stan, et al. Jobs Around Town, 1 vol. 2011. (Berenstain Bears/Living Lights Ser.). (ENG.). 32p. (J). (gr. -1-2). pap. 3.99 *(978-0-310-72286-1(1))* Zonderkidz.
Birney, Betty G. Humphrey's Mixed-Up Magic Trick. Burris, Priscilla, illus. 2016. (Humphrey's Tiny Tales Ser.: 5). (ENG.). 96p. (J). (gr. k-3). 4.99 *(978-0-14-751461-5(4)*, Puffin Books) Penguin Young Readers Group.
Blackstone, Stella. Bear at Work. Harter, Debbie, illus. 2011. (ENG & SPA.). 24p. (J). (gr. -1-k). pap. 6.99 *(978-1-84686-554-1(9))* Barefoot Bks., Inc.
—Bear at Work (Oso en el Trabajo) 2012. (ENG & SPA., Illus.). (J). 6.99 *(978-1-84686-769-9(X))* Barefoot Bks., Inc.
—L'Ours au Travail. 2012.Tr. of Bear at Work. (FRE & ENG.). (J). 6.99 *(978-1-84686-770-5(3))* Barefoot Bks., Inc.
Blackstone, Stella & Harter, Debbie. Bear at Work. Harter, Debbie, illus. 2008. (Bear Ser.). (ENG., Illus.). 24p. (J). (gr. -1-1). pap. 6.99 *(978-1-84686-110-9(1))* Barefoot Bks., Inc.
Blance, Ellen & Cook, Tony. Monster Gets a Job. Date not set. (Illus.). 40p. pap. 129.15 *(978-0-582-19307-9(9))* Addison-Wesley Longman, Ltd. GBR. Dist: Trans-Atlantic Pubns., Inc.
Blyton, Enid, et al. The Fairies' Shoemaker & Other Stories. 2013. (ENG., Illus.). 192p. (J). 9.99 *(978-1-84135-458-3(9))* Award Pubns. Ltd. GBR. Dist: Parkwest Pubns., Inc.
Bradman, Tony. Mr. Wolf Bounces Back, 1 vol. Warburton, Sarah, illus. 2009. (After Happily Ever After Ser.). (ENG.). 56p. (gr. 2-3). 25.32 *(978-1-4342-1306-8(4)*, After Happily Ever After) Stone Arch Bks.
Brooks, Felicity. Jobs People Do. Litchfield, Jo, illus. 2008. (Jobs People Do Ser.). 143p. (J). (gr. -1-3). 22.99 *(978-0-7945-1998-8(9)*, Usborne) EDC Publishing.
Brown, Ruby. I Want to Be ... an Astronaut. Coburn, Alisa, illus. 2016. (ENG.). 22p. (J). bds. 8.99 *(978-1-61067-406-5(5))* Kane Miller.
Bunting, Eve. Girls A to Z. Bloom, Suzanne, illus. 2013. (ENG.). 32p. (J). (gr. k-2). pap. 6.95 *(978-1-62091-028-3(4))* Boyds Mills Pr.
Caletti, Deb. The Fortunes of Indigo Skye. 2009. (ENG.). 320p. (YA). (gr. 7). pap. 9.99 *(978-1-4169-1008-4(5)*, Simon Pulse) Simon Pulse.
Canetti, Yanitzia. Abecedario de Profesiones y Oficios. 2009. (SPA.). 40p. (J). pap. 8.99 *(978-1-59835-122-4(2)*, BrickHouse Education) Cambridge BrickHouse, Inc.
Carpenter, Tad. When I Grow Up. 2015. (Who's That? Ser.). (ENG., Illus.). 16p. (J). (— 1). bds. 7.95 *(978-1-4549-1228-6(6))* Sterling Publishing Co., Inc.
Catalanotto, Peter. Kitten Red, Yellow, Blue. Catalanotto, Peter, illus. 2005. (ENG., Illus.). 32p. (J). (gr. -1-k). 18.99 *(978-0-689-86562-6(7)*, Atheneum/Richard Jackson Bks.) Simon & Schuster Children's Publishing.
Clark, Carol. Eternity Express. 2009. 32p. pap. 10.95 *(978-0-9818488-6-0(9))* Ajoyin Publishing, Inc.
Cohn, Diana. iSi, Se Puede! Delgado, Francisco, illus. 2009.Tr. of Yes, We Can! (SPA & ENG.). 32p. (J). (gr. k-2). pap. 7.95 *(978-0-938317-89-0(X))* Cinco Puntos Pr.
Cooley, Judy. I Want to Be a Mommy. 2012. (Illus.). (J). 17.99 *(978-1-60908-910-8(3))* Deseret Bk. Co.
Crow, Sara. Even Superheroes Have to Sleep. Record, Adam, illus. 2017. (ENG.). 32p. (J). (-k). 16.99 *(978-0-399-55806-1(3)*, Doubleday Bks. for Young Readers) Random Hse. Children's Bks.
Cunliffe, John. Postman Pat & the Beast of Greendale, Bk. 12. (Illus.). 32p. (J). *(978-0-340-67816-9(X))* Hodder & Stoughton.
—Postman Pat Has Too Many Parcels, Pt. 8. (Illus.). 32p. (J). *(978-0-340-67812-1(7))* Hodder & Stoughton.
DeLand, M. Maitland. Busy Bees at Work & Play. 2010. (Illus.). 32p. (J). 14.95 *(978-1-60832-028-8(6)*, Greenleaf Book Group Pr.) Greenleaf Book Group.
Derrick, David G., Jr. Sid the Squid: And the Search for the Perfect Job. 2010. (ENG., Illus.). 36p. (J). (gr. -1-3). 15.95 *(978-1-59702-021-3(4))* Immedium.
Dipucchio, Kelly. Dress-Up Mess-Up. Ross, Heather, illus. 2013. (Crafty Chloe Ser.). (ENG.). 40p. (J). (gr. -1-3). 16.99 *(978-1-4424-2124-0(X))* Simon & Schuster Children's Publishing.
Dorsey, Maggie. My Hero, My Dad, the Nurse. 2008. (ENG.). 36p. pap. 16.99 *(978-1-4196-9476-9(6))* CreateSpace Independent Publishing Platform.
Edwards, Michelle. Chicken Man. 2008. (J). *(978-1-58838-237-5(0))*; 3rd ed. (Illus.). 32p. 16.95 *(978-1-58838-223-8(0))* NewSouth, Inc. (Junebug Bks.).
Ferguson, Sally. What Will I Be When I Grow Up? 2005. (J). pap. 1.69 *(978-1-59317-118-6(8))* Warner Pr., Inc.
Friedman, Laurie. Honestly, Mallory! 2009. pap. 34.95 *(978-0-7613-4788-0(7))* Lerner Publishing Group.
—Honestly, Mallory! Pollak, Barbara, illus. (Mallory Ser.: 8). (ENG.). 160p. (J). (gr. 2-5). 2008. pap. 5.95 *(978-1-58013-840-6(3)*, First Avenue Editions) 2007. 15.95 *(978-0-8225-6193-4(X)*, Carolrhoda Bks.) Lerner Publishing Group.
Garton, Sam. Otter: the Best Job Ever! Garton, Sam, illus. 2016. (My First I Can Read Ser.). (Illus.). 32p. (J). (gr. -1-3). pap. 3.99 *(978-0-06-236654-2(8))* HarperCollins Pubs.
Gregorowski, Christopher. Fly, Eagle, Fly: An African Tale. Daly, Niki, illus. 2008. (ENG.). 36p. (J). (gr. -1-3). 12.99 *(978-1-4169-7599-1(3)*, Aladdin) Simon & Schuster Children's Publishing.
Guggenheim, Jaenet. Next Week When I'm Big. Verelst, Suana, illus. I.t. ed. 2005. 32p. (J). (gr. -1-2). 19.95i *(978-1-929115-13-6(X))* Azro Pr., Inc.
Hallinan, P. K. When I Grow Up. (J). 24p. 7.95 *(978-0-8249-5392-8(4))*; 2008. (ENG., Illus.). 26p. (gr. -1-k). bds. 7.95 *(978-0-8249-6677-5(5))* Worthy Publishing. (Ideal Pubns.).
Handy, Libby & Newnham, Jack. Boss for a Week.Tr. of C'Est Moi Qui Mene. (FRE., Illus.). (J). 13.99 incl. audio *(978-0-590-73908-5(5))* Scholastic, Inc.
Harley, Bill. Charlie Bumpers vs. His Big Blabby Mouth, 1 vol. Gustavson, Adam, illus. 2017. (Charlie Bumpers Ser.). (ENG.). 186p. (J). (gr. 2-4). 14.95 ***(978-1-56145-940-7(2))*** Peachtree Pubs.
Horn, Peter. When I Grow Up... Kadmon, Cristina, illus. 2014. 32p. pap. 8.00 *(978-1-61003-370-1(1))* Center for the Collaborative Classroom.
K. Maurice Strickland. I Want to Be a Bucket. 2009. 32p. pap. 15.99 *(978-1-4389-7015-8(3))* AuthorHouse.
Kirkova, Milena & Hannigan, Paula. When I'm Big. 2010. (ENG.). 12p. (J). (gr. -1-1). bds. 14.99 *(978-0-7407-9727-9(1))* Andrews McMeel Publishing.
Kittinger, Jo S. Cuando Sea Grande. Lucas, Margeaux, illus. 2005. (Rookie Reader Español Ser.). (SPA & ESP.). 23p. (J). (gr. k-2). per. 4.95 *(978-0-516-24692-5(5)*, Children's Pr.) Scholastic Library Publishing.
Kleinhenz, Sydnie Meltzer. Trabajar y Jugar. Reasor, Mick, illus. 2006. (Rookie Reader Español Ser.). (SPA.). 23p. (J). (gr. k-2). lib. bdg. 19.50 *(978-0-516-25306-0(9))* Scholastic Library Publishing.
Krulik, Nancy. Lice Check, No. 12. Blecha, Aaron, illus. 2014. (George Brown, Class Clown Ser.: 12). (ENG.). 128p. (J). (gr. 2-4). 4.99 *(978-0-448-46112-0(9)*, Grosset & Dunlap) Penguin Young Readers Group.
—Lice Check. 2014. (George Brown, Class Clown Ser.: 12). lib. bdg. 14.75 *(978-0-606-34144-8(7)*, Turtleback) Turtleback Bks.
Kupchella, Rick. Girls Can! Make it Happen. Brown, Marilyn, illus. 2004. (ENG.). 40p. (J). 16.95 *(978-0-9726504-3-4(1))* TRISTAN Publishing, Inc.
Kusmierski, Janet & Colin, Paul. Snowman's Big Job. 2004. (Illus.). (J). *(978-0-439-58392-3(6))* Scholastic, Inc.
LaFleur, John & Dubin, Shawn. Dreary & Naughty: The ABCs of Being Dead, 1 vol. 2013. (ENG., Illus.). 72p. (J). 14.99 *(978-0-7643-4496-1(X)*, 9780764344961) Schiffer Publishing, Ltd.
Lang, Sheri. My Mom Can Code: Careers in Computers. 2017. (Computer Science for the Real World Ser.). 16p. (gr. 7-8). pap. 7.95 ***(978-1-5383-5226-7(5)***, Rosen Classroom) Rosen Publishing Group, Inc., The.
Liberto, Lorenzo. Matt the Rat & His Sister Maggie (Raton Mateo y Su Hermana Maggie) When I Grow Up (Cuando Yo Crezca) Gomez, Rocio, ed. Torres, Irving, illus. 2003. (Matt the Rat Ser. / La Serie de Ratón Mateo). (SPA & ENG.). 40p. (J). lib. bdg. 20.00 *(978-0-9743668-1-4(1))* Harvest Sun Pr., LLC.
Manushkin, Fran. Katie Finds a Job, 1 vol. Lyon, Tammie, illus. 2011. (Katie Woo Ser.). (ENG.). 32p. (gr. k-2). pap. 5.95 *(978-1-4048-6614-0(0))*; lib. bdg. 21.32 *(978-1-4048-6513-6(6))* Picture Window Bks.
Marsh, Carole. The Adventure Diaries of Felipe, the Fearless Firefighter!, 12 vols. 2003. 48p. (J). (gr. 1-4). pap. 5.95 *(978-0-635-01096-4(8))* Gallopade International.
—The Adventure Diaries of Hannah, the Humanitarian Aid Worker!, 6 vols. 2003. 48p. (J). (gr. 1-4). pap. 5.95 *(978-0-635-01153-4(0))* Gallopade International.
—The Adventure Diaries of Haz Matt, the Hazardous Materials Worker!, 11 vols. 2003. 48p. (J). (gr. 1-4). pap. 5.95 *(978-0-635-01152-7(2))* Gallopade International.
—The Adventure Diaries of Li, the Excellent EMT!, 7 vols. 2004. 48p. (J). (gr. 1-4). pap. 5.95 *(978-0-635-01145-9(X))* Gallopade International.
—The Adventure Diaries of P. J., the Photo-Journalist!, 10 vols. 2003. 48p. (J). (gr. 1-4). pap. 5.95 *(978-0-635-01154-1(9))* Gallopade International.
—The Adventure Diaries of Vicki, the Volunteer!, 12 vols. 2003. 48p. (J). (gr. 1-4). pap. 5.95 *(978-0-635-01158-9(1))* Gallopade International.
Mayer, Mercer. Going to the Firehouse. Mayer, Mercer, illus. 2008. (My First I Can Read Ser.). (ENG., Illus.). 32p. (J). (gr. -1-3). 16.99 *(978-0-06-083546-0(X))*; pap. 3.99 *(978-0-06-083545-3(1))* HarperCollins Pubs.
—When I Grow Up. 2003. (Look-Look Ser.). (ENG., Illus.). 24p. (J). (gr. -1-k). pap. 3.99 *(978-0-375-82632-0(7)*, Random Hse. Bks. for Young Readers) Random Hse. Children's Bks.
—When I Grow Up. 2003. (Little Critter Ser.). (gr. -1-2). lib. bdg. 13.55 *(978-0-613-82737-9(6)*, Turtleback) Turtleback Bks.
McGill, Erin. I Do Not Like Al's Hat. McGill, Erin, illus. 2017. (Illus.). 32p. (J). (gr. -1-3). 17.99 *(978-0-06-245576-5(1)*, Greenwillow Bks.) HarperCollins Pubs.
McMullan, Kate. Bulldog's Big Day. Lemaître, Pascal, illus. 2011. (J). *(978-0-545-17156-4(3)*, Orchard Bks.) Scholastic, Inc.
—I'm Dirty! McMullan, Jim, illus. 2006. (ENG.). 40p. (J). (gr. -1-3). 16.99 *(978-0-06-009293-1(9))* HarperCollins Pubs.
McNamara, Margaret. Dad Goes to School. Gordon, Mike, illus. 2007. (Robin Hill School Ser.). (ENG.). 32p. (J). (gr. -1-1). pap. 3.99 *(978-1-4169-1541-6(9)*, Simon Spotlight) Simon Spotlight.
Meltzer Kleinhenz, Sydnie. Work & Play. Reasor, Mick, illus. 2011. (Rookie Ready to Learn — Out & about: in My Community Ser.). 32p. (J). (gr. -1-k). lib. bdg. 25.00 *(978-0-531-27179-7(X))*; (ENG.). pap. 5.95 *(978-0-531-26829-2(2))* Scholastic Library Publishing. (Children's Pr.).
Miller, Sibley. A Horse, of Course! Chang, Tara Larsen & Gershman, Jo, illus. 2009. (Wind Dancers Ser.: 7). (ENG.). 80p. (J). (gr. 1-4). pap. 16.99 *(978-0-312-56402-5(3)*, 9780312564025) Feiwel & Friends.
Miller, Suzanne. You Can Be... 2010. 24p. pap. 12.99 *(978-1-4520-4697-6(2))* AuthorHouse.
Morris, Bridgette. I Wish I Was All Grown-up. 2004. 20p. pap. 8.99 *(978-1-4116-1719-3(3))* Lulu Pr., Inc.
Nikola-Lisa, W. My Teacher Can Teach... Anyone! Galindo, Felipe, illus. 2004. (ENG.). 32p. (J). (gr. -1-2). 16.95 *(978-1-58430-163-9(5))* Lee & Low Bks., Inc.
O'Donnell, Kerri. Whose Hat Is That? 2006. (Neighborhood Readers Ser.). (ENG.). 8p. (gr. -1-3). pap. 5.15 *(978-1-4042-5647-7(4)*, Rosen Classroom) Rosen Publishing Group, Inc., The.
Olsen, Jan Z. Mat Man Hats. Delaney, Molly, illus. 2008. (ENG.). 36p. stu. ed. 13.75 *(978-1-891627-93-4(7))* Handwriting Without Tears.
Parish, Herman. Amelia Bedelia Chapter Book #9: Amelia Bedelia on the Job. Avril, Lynne, illus. 2016. (Amelia Bedelia Ser.). 160p. (J). (gr. 1-5). pap. 4.99 *(978-0-06-233412-1(3)*, Greenwillow Bks.) HarperCollins Pubs.
Park, Barbara. Junie B. Jones y Su Gran Bocota. Brunkus, Denise, illus. 2005. (Junie B. Jones Ser.).Tr. of Junie B. Jones & Her Big Fat Mouth. (SPA.). 80p. (J). (gr. 2-5). pap. 4.99 *(978-0-439-42516-2(6)*, Scholastic en Espanol) Scholastic, Inc.
Patrick, Wendy. When Passion Wins. 2012. 186p. (gr. 4-6). pap. 14.50 *(978-1-4669-7131-8(2))* Trafford Publishing.
Phillips, Dee. What Can I Be? 2010. (Look at Me! Ser.). (ENG.). 5p. (J). (gr. -1-k). bds. 6.95 *(978-1-84696-199-1(8)*, TickTock Books) Octopus Publishing Group GBR. Dist: Independent Pubs. Group.
—Who Can I Be? 2010. (Look at Me! Ser.). (ENG.). 5p. (J). (gr. -1-k). bds. 6.95 *(978-1-84696-200-4(5)*, TickTock Books) Octopus Publishing Group GBR. Dist: Independent Pubs. Group.
Pierce, Heather Vowell. What Does Your Daddy Do? Price, Dana, illus. 2010. 32p. pap. 16.49 *(978-1-4520-1723-5(9))* AuthorHouse.
Publications International Ltd. Staff, ed. A Days Work. 2005. (J). 6.50 *(978-1-4127-3708-1(7))* Phoenix International Publications, Inc.
Rey, H. A. Curious George Neighborhood Friends. 2010. (Curious George Ser.). (ENG., Illus.). 12p. (J). (gr. -1 — 1). bds. 6.99 *(978-0-547-23875-3(4))* Houghton Mifflin Harcourt Publishing Co.
Rey, H. A. & Rey, Margret. Curious George Takes a Job. 2007. (Curious George Ser.). (ENG., Illus.). 48p. (J). (gr. -1-3). audio compact disk 10.99 *(978-0-618-72406-2(0))* Houghton Mifflin Harcourt Publishing Co.
Roach, Sandra & Torowski, Dave. Alina's Options: Careers from A to Z. 2008. (ENG., Illus.). 52p. pap. 12.99 *(978-0-9801426-0-0(1))* Options Galore.
Rosenstiehl, Agnes. Silly Lilly in What Will I Be Today?, 1 vol. 2013. (Toon Bks). (ENG.). 36p. (J). (gr. k-1). lib. bdg. 27.07 *(978-1-61479-156-0(2))* Spotlight.
—Silly Lilly in What Will I Be Today? Mouly, Francoise, ed. 2011. (ENG., Illus.). 32p. (J). (gr. -1-3). 12.95 *(978-1-935179-08-5(X))* TOON Books / RAW Junior, LLC.
Scarry, Patsy. The Bunny Book. Scarry, Richard, illus. 2016. (Little Golden Board Book Ser.). (ENG.). 26p. (J). (— 1). bds. 7.99 *(978-0-553-53587-7(0)*, Random Hse. Bks. for Young Readers) Random Hse. Children's Bks.
—Richard Scarry's the Bunny Book. Scarry, Richard, illus. 2015. (Big Golden Book Ser.). (ENG.). 32p. (J). (-k). 9.99 *(978-0-385-39090-3(4)*, Golden Bks.) Random Hse. Children's Bks.
Scarry, Richard. Richard Scarry's Busiest People Ever. 2017. (ENG., Illus.). 48p. (J). (gr. -1-2). 15.99 *(978-0-394-83293-7(0)*, Golden Bks.) Random Hse. Children's Bks.
—Richard Scarry's Postman Pig & His Busy Neighbors. Scarry, Richard, illus. 2015. (Pictureback(R) Ser.). (ENG., Illus.). 32p. (J). (gr. -1-2). pap. 4.99 *(978-0-385-38419-3(X)*, Random Hse. Bks. for Young Readers) Random Hse. Children's Bks.
Schulz, Charles. You Can Be Anything! 2009. (ENG.). 48p. (J). (gr. -1-3). 12.95 *(978-0-7624-3583-8(6)*, Running Pr. Kids) Running Pr. Bk. Pubs.
Shaw, Natalie. I Can Do Anything! 2016. (Illus.). (J). *(978-1-5182-0411-1(2))* Simon & Schuster Children's Publishing.
Shea, Therese. The Summer Job. 2006. (Neighborhood Readers Ser.). (ENG., Illus.). 12p. (gr. 1-3). pap. 5.90 *(978-1-4042-6855-5(3)*, Rosen Classroom) Rosen Publishing Group, Inc., The.
Sommer, Carl. Your Job Is Easy. James, Kennon, illus. 2003. (Another Sommer-Time Story Ser.). (ENG.). 48p. (J). (gr. -1-4). 9.95 *(978-1-57537-018-7(2))*; (gr. 1-4). 16.95 incl. audio compact disk *(978-1-57537-517-5(6))*; (gr. 2-4). lib. bdg. 16.95 *(978-1-57537-067-5(0))* Advance Publishing, Inc.
—Your Job Is Easy. 2003. (Another Sommer-Time Story Ser.). (Illus.). 48p. (J). (gr. 1-4). 16.95 incl. audio *(978-1-57537-566-3(4))* Advance Publishing, Inc.
Spinelli, Eileen. Boy, Can He Dance! Yalowitz, Paul, illus. 2012. (ENG.). 32p. (J). (gr. -1-3). 16.99 *(978-1-4424-7441-3(6)*, Simon & Schuster Bks. For Young Readers) Simon & Schuster Bks. For Young Readers.
Standish, Burt L. Frank Merriwell's First Job. Rudman, Jack, ed. 2003. (Frank Merriwell Ser.). 29.95 *(978-0-8373-9330-8(2))*; (YA). (gr. 9-18). pap. 9.95 *(978-0-8373-9030-7(3))* Merriwell, Frank Inc.
Tong, Kevin. The Earth Machine. Tong, Kevin, illus. 2007. (Illus.). 32p. (J). (gr. -1-3). 15.95 *(978-1-60108-001-1(8))* Red Cygnet Pr.
Traylor, Marci. What Will I Be? 2008. 40p. pap. 19.50 *(978-1-4389-0247-0(6))* AuthorHouse.
Wang, Margaret C. When I Grow Up: A Touch & Feel Book. Gévry, Claudine, illus. 2005. (ENG.). 12p. (J). bds. 10.95 *(978-1-58117-423-6(3)*, Intervisual/Piggy Toes) Bendon, Inc.
Wess, Robert, illus. & photos by. Friends at Work & Play. Wess, Robert, photos by. Bunnett, Rochelle, photos by. 2003. 32p. (J). 14.95 *(978-0-9660884-2-7(5))*; pap. *(978-0-9660884-1-0(7))* Our Kids Pr.
Yankovic, Al, pseud. When I Grow Up. Hargis, Wes, illus. 2011. (ENG.). 32p. (J). (gr. -1-3). 17.99 *(978-0-06-192691-4(4))* HarperCollins Pubs.
Zoboli, Giovanna. Professional Crocodile. Di Giorgio, Mariachiara, illus. 2017. (ENG.). 32p. (J). (gr. k-3). 17.99 ***(978-1-4521-6506-6(8))*** Chronicle Bks. LLC.

OCEAN

see also Icebergs; Oceanography; Seashore; Storms; Tides

Acampora, Courtney & DiPerna, Kaitlyn. Read with Me! Pre, Level 1. 2016. (Smithsonian Readers Ser.). (ENG., Illus.). 200p. (J). (gr. -1). 14.95 *(978-1-62686-571-6(X)*, Silver Dolphin Bks.) Readerlink Distribution Services, LLC.
Aitken, Stephen. Fever in the Oceans, 1 vol. 2011. (Climate Change Ser.). (ENG., Illus.). 32p. (J). (gr. k-3). 28.50 *(978-1-61641-672-0(6))* Magic Wagon.
—Ocean Life. 2013. (Climate Crisis Ser.). (Illus.). 64p. (J). (gr. 5-8). 31.36 *(978-1-60870-460-6(2))*; pap. 15.28 *(978-1-62712-040-1(8))* Cavendish Square Publishing.
Allaby, Michael. Oceans: A Scientific History of Oceans & Marine Life. Garratt, Richard, illus. 2009. (Discovering the Earth Ser.). 208p. (J). (gr. 9-18). 39.95 *(978-0-8160-6099-3(1))* Facts On File, Inc.
American Girl Editors & Magruder, Trula, eds. Oodles of Ocean Fun: A Collection of Posters, Puzzles, Doodles, Cards, Crafts, Stickers, Frames. 2011. (ENG.). 80p. (YA). (gr. 3-18). spiral bd. 12.95 *(978-1-59369-771-6(6))* American Girl Publishing, Inc.
Arlon, Penelope. Really? Ocean. 2015. (ENG.). 64p. (J). (gr. 2-5). pap. 8.99 *(978-0-545-80650-3(X)*, Scholastic Nonfiction) Scholastic, Inc.
Arnold, Quinn M. & Riggs, Kate. Oceans. 2017. (Seedlings Ser.). (ENG., Illus.). 24p. (J). (gr. k-2). pap. 7.99 *(978-1-62832-339-9(6)*, Creative Paperbacks) Creative Co., The.
Arnov Jr., Boris. Oceans of the World. 2011. 190p. 42.95 *(978-1-258-08168-3(7))* Literary Licensing, LLC.
Austen, Amy. Earth's Oceans. 2016. (Spotlight on Earth Science Ser.). 00024p. (J). (gr. 4-6). pap. 10.00 *(978-1-4994-2501-7(5)*, PowerKids Pr.) Rosen Publishing Group, Inc., The.
AZ Books Staff. Exploring the Ocean. Vasilkova, Elena, ed. 2012. (Wild Theater Ser.). (ENG.). 8p. (J). (gr. -1-3). bds. 17.95 *(978-1-61889-020-7(4))* AZ Bks. LLC.
—Living Book of the Ocean. Aksinovich, Natalia, ed. 2012. (Our Amazing World Ser.). (ENG.). 12p. (J). (gr. 1-3). bds. 19.95 *(978-1-61889-021-4(2))* AZ Bks. LLC.
—Visiting the Ocean. Lukjanenko, Anna, ed. 2012. (Lively Pictures Ser.). (ENG.). 10p. (J). (gr. -1-1). bds. 9.95 *(978-1-61889-180-8(4))* AZ Bks. LLC.
Banks, Christopher. Oceans of the World. 2009. (Real Life Readers Ser.). 16p. (gr. 2-3). pap. 7.05 *(978-1-4358-0061-8(3)*, Rosen Classroom) Rosen Publishing Group, Inc., The.
Barnes, Julia. 101 Facts about Oceans. 2003. (One Hundred One Facts about Our World Ser.). (Illus.). 32p. (gr. 1-4). lib. bdg. 26.00 *(978-0-8368-3709-4(6)*, Gareth Stevens Learning Library) Stevens, Gareth Publishing LLLP.
Bayrock, Fiona. The Ocean Explorer's Handbook. 2005. (Undersea University Ser.). (Illus.). 48p. (J). pap. *(978-0-439-71184-5(3))* Scholastic, Inc.
Becker, Helaine. The Big Green Book of the Big Blue Sea. Dawson, Willow, illus. 2012. (ENG.). 80p. (J). (gr. 3-7). 15.95 *(978-1-55453-746-4(0))*; pap. 9.95 *(978-1-55453-747-1(9))* Kids Can Pr., Ltd. CAN. Dist: Hachette Bk. Group.
Benchmark Education Company. Ocean Pollution (Teacher Guide) 2005. *(978-1-4108-4678-5(4))* Benchmark Education Co.
Bennett, Paul. Ocean Habitats. 2006. (Exploring Habitats Ser.). (Illus.). 36p. (gr. 3-7). lib. bdg. 26.00 *(978-0-8368-7255-2(X)*, Gareth Stevens Learning Library) Stevens, Gareth Publishing LLLP.
Benoit, Peter. Oceans. 2011. (True Bk Ser.). 48p. (J). (ENG.). pap. 6.95 *(978-0-531-28105-5(1))*; (gr. 3-5). 29.00 *(978-0-531-20556-3(8))* Scholastic Library Publishing. (Children's Pr.).
—The Titanic Disaster. 2011. (J). pap. *(978-0-531-29026-2(3))* Children's Pr., Ltd.
—The Titanic Disaster. 2011. (True Bks.). 48p. (J). (gr. 3-5). 29.00 *(978-0-531-20627-0(0)*, Children's Pr.) Scholastic Library Publishing.
Bessesen, Brooke. Look Who Lives in the Ocean: Splashing & Dashing, Nibbling & Quibbling, Blending & Fending. 2009. (Illus.). 48p. (J). (gr. k-4). 19.95 *(978-1-932082-82-1(4))* Arizona Highways.
Boatner, Kay. Funny Fill-In - My Ocean Adventure. 2013. (ENG., Illus.). 48p. (J). (gr. 3-7). pap. 4.99 *(978-1-4263-1643-2(7)*, National Geographic Children's Bks.) National Geographic Society.
Bodden, Valerie. Oceans. 2006. (Our World Ser.). (Illus.). 24p. (J). (gr. -1-3). 16.95 *(978-1-58341-464-4(9)*, Creative Education) Creative Co., The.
Bonder, Dianna. A, B, Sea: A Deep Sea Symphony, 1 vol. 2013. (ENG.). 32p. (J). *(978-1-77050-043-3(X))* Whitecap Bks., Ltd.
Boothroyd, Jennifer. Let's Visit the Ocean. 2016. (Lightning Bolt Books (tm) — Biome Explorers Ser.). (ENG., Illus.). 32p. (J). (gr. 1-3). 26.65 *(978-1-5124-1194-2(9))* Lerner Publishing Group.
Boughton, Samantha. Under the Sea Adventure Coloring Book. 2013. (ENG., Illus.). 48p. (J). (gr. k-5). pap. 4.99 *(978-0-486-49166-0(8))* Dover Pubns., Inc.
Bowsher, Alice, illus. Lift-The-Flap & Color Ocean. 2017. (Lift-The-flap & Color Ser.). (ENG.). 10p. (J). (gr. -1-k). pap. 8.99 ***(978-1-84780-932-2(4)***, Frances Lincoln Children's Bks.) Quarto Publishing Group UK GBR. Dist: Hachette Bk. Group.
Brannon, Barbara. Discover Ocean Pollution. 2005. (J). pap. *(978-1-4108-5140-6(0))* Benchmark Education Co.
Buchanan, Shelly. The Powerful Ocean. 2015. (Science Readers: Content & Literacy Ser.). (Illus.). 32p. (J). (gr. 5-5). pap. 8.99 *(978-1-4807-4726-5(2))* Teacher Created Materials, Inc.
Bulletpoints Oceans & Rivers. 2005. (Illus.). (J). per. 4.99 *(978-1-933581-01-9(8))* Byeway Bks.
Burlingame, Jeff. The Titanic Tragedy. 2011. (Perspectives on 3 Ser.). 112p. (gr. 7). 39.93 *(978-1-60870-450-7(5))* Marshall Cavendish Corp.
Casado, Dami. El Mar. 2005. (Yo Te Hablare De... Ser.). (SPA., Illus.). 14p. (J). per., bds. 8.99 *(978-84-272-7298-9(7))* Molino, Editorial ESP. Dist: Santillana USA Publishing Co., Inc.
Cecchini, Marie E. Under the Sea: A Cross-Curricular Unit for Grades 1-3. Mitchell, Judy & Lindeen, Mary, eds. Armbrust, Janet & Skiles, Janet, illus. 2007. 32p. (J). pap. 6.95 *(978-1-57310-529-3(5))* Teaching & Learning Co.
Cefrey, Holly. Oceans. (Biomes Ser.). 24p. 2009. (gr. 2-3). 42.50 *(978-1-61511-592-1(7))* 2003. (Illus.). (J). lib. bdg. 22.60 *(978-0-8239-6453-6(1))* Rosen Publishing Group, Inc., The. (PowerKids Pr.).
Chambers, Catherine. Stickmen's Guide to Oceans in Layers. Dean, Venitia & De Quay, John Paul, illus. 2016. (Stickmen's Guides to This Incredible Earth Ser.). (ENG.). 32p. (J). (gr. 3-6). 26.65 *(978-1-5124-0619-1(8))* Lerner Publishing Group.
Channing, Margot. Seas & Oceans. 2014. (Closer Look At... Ser.). (Illus.). 32p. (gr. 3-6). 31.35 *(978-1-905087-07-5(1))* Book Hse. GBR. Dist: Black Rabbit Bks.
Clarke, Phillip. Seas & Oceans Sticker Atlas. Le Rolland, Leonard, illus. 2006. 24p. (J). pap. 8.95 *(978-0-7945-1218-7(6)*, Usborne) EDC Publishing.
Cobb, Allan B. Super Science Projects about Oceans. 2005. (Psyched for Science Ser.). (Illus.). 48p. (YA). (gr. 5-8). lib. bdg. 29.25 *(978-0-8239-3174-3(9)*, SCOCEA) Rosen Publishing Group, Inc., The.

Cole, Joanna & Carson, Mary Kay. Ocean Adventure. 2014. (Magic School Bus Scholastic Readers Ser.). lib. bdg. 13.55 *(978-0-606-36040-1(9))* Turtleback Bks.
Collins. Collins Fascinating Facts - Oceans. 2016. (Collins Fascinating Facts Ser.). (ENG.). 72p. (J). (gr. 1-3). pap. 10.99 *(978-0-00-816924-4(1))* HarperCollins Pubs. Ltd. GBR. Dist: Independent Pubs. Group.
Dale, Jay. Taking Care of the Ocean, 1 vol. 2012. (Engage Literacy Blue Ser.). (ENG.). 32p. (gr. k-2). pap. 5.99 *(978-1-4296-8837-6(8),* Engage Literacy) Capstone Press of Coughlan Cos.
Davies, Nicola. Discover Science: Oceans & Seas. 2013. (Discover Science Ser.). (ENG., Illus.). 56p. (J). (gr. k-3). 7.99 *(978-0-7534-6776-3(3),* 9780753467763, Kingfisher) Roaring Brook Pr.
—Oceans & Seas. 2014. 48p. pap. 7.00 *(978-1-61003-360-2(4))* Center for the Collaborative Classroom.
De la Bédoyère, Camilla. Deep Ocean. 2010. (Unpredictable Nature Ser.). (Illus.). 48p. (J). (gr. 3-18). lib. bdg. 19.95 *(978-1-4222-1997-3(6))* Mason Crest.
—Oceans. 2010. (Ripley Twists Ser.). (Illus.). 48p. (J). (gr. 3-18). lib. bdg. 19.95 *(978-1-4222-1632-7(5))* Mason Crest.
Denne, B. First Encyclopedia of Seas & Oceans. 2004. (First Encyclopedias Ser.). (Illus.). 64p. (J). (gr. 3-18). lib. bdg. 17.95 *(978-1-58086-380-3(9))* EDC Publishing.
—First Encyclopedia of Seas & Oceans II. rev. ed. 2011. (First Encyclopedias Ser.). 64p. (J). pap. 9.99 *(978-0-7945-3048-8(6),* Usborne) EDC Publishing.
Denne, Ben. First Encyclopedia of Seas & Oceans. 2004. (First Encyclopedias Ser.). (ENG., Illus.). 1p. (J). (gr. 3-18). pap. 9.99 *(978-0-7945-0111-2(7),* Usborne) EDC Publishing.
Desonie, Dana. Oceans: How We Use the Seas. 2007. (Our Fragile Planet Ser.). (Illus.). 215p. (YA). (gr. 7-12). lib. bdg. 35.00 *(978-0-8160-6216-4(1))* Facts On File, Inc.
Dipper, F. D. & Dipper, Frances. Misterios de los Oceanos. (Coleccion Misterios De). (SPA., Illus.). 48p. (YA). (gr. 5-8). 19.95 *(978-84-348-5691-2(3),* SM6117) SM Ediciones ESP. Dist: AIMS International Bks., Inc., Lectorum Pubns., Inc.
Dorling Kindersley Publishing Staff. Ocean. 2010. (ENG.). 96p. (J). (gr. k-4). pap. 12.99 *(978-0-7566-6304-9(0),* DK Children) Dorling Kindersley Publishing, Inc.
—Ocean: a Visual Encyclopedia: A Visual Encyclopedia. 2015. (Visual Encyclopedia Ser.). (ENG.). 256p. (J). (gr. 3-7). pap. 19.99 *(978-1-4654-3594-1(8),* DK Children) Dorling Kindersley Publishing, Inc.
—Oceans. 2015. (Eye Wonder Ser.). (ENG., Illus.). 56p. (J). (gr. k-4). 10.99 *(978-1-4654-1852-4(0),* DK Children) Dorling Kindersley Publishing, Inc.
—Squeaky Baby Bath: at the Beach. 2017. (ENG.). 8p. (J). (— 1). 5.99 *(978-1-4654-5600-7(7),* DK Children) Dorling Kindersley Publishing, Inc.
—Ultimate Sticker Book: Ocean. 2016. (Ultimate Sticker Bks.). (ENG.). 32p. (J). (gr. k-3). pap. 6.99 *(978-1-4654-4882-8(9),* DK Children) Dorling Kindersley Publishing, Inc.
Editors of Kingfisher. Ocean Wonders: Come Face to Face with Life in the Ocean Deep. 2016. (Fast Facts Ser.). (ENG., Illus.). 32p. (J). pap. 6.99 *(978-0-7534-7299-6(6),* 9780753472996, Kingfisher) Roaring Brook Pr.
Endres, Hollie J. The Letter Ww Set: The Ocean, 6 vols. 2004. (Letter Bks.). (ENG.). 8p. (gr. k-1). pap. 29.70 *(978-0-7368-4122-1(9),* Letter Bks.) Capstone Press of Coughlan Cos.
Foxxe, Ellen. The Rising Seas: Shorelines under Threat. 2006. (Extreme Environmental Threats Ser.). (Illus.). 64p. (YA). (gr. 5-9). lib. bdg. 31.95 *(978-1-4042-0742-4(2))* Rosen Publishing Group, Inc., The.
Franklin, Yvonne. Los Océanos, 1 vol. rev. ed. 2010. (Science Readers: a Closer Look Ser.). (SPA., Illus.). 32p. (J). (gr. 2-3). pap. 8.99 *(978-1-4333-2142-9(4))* Shell Educational Publishing.
Friedman, Lauri S. Oceans. 2011. (Introducing Issues with Opposing Viewpoints Ser.). (ENG.). 144p. (gr. 10-10). lib. bdg. 42.00 *(978-0-7377-5200-7(9),* Greenhaven Pr., Inc.) Cengage Gale.
Friesen, Helen Lepp. Indian Ocean. 2016. (J). *(978-1-4896-4737-5(6))* Weigl Pubs., Inc.
Gabbi & Somaschini. Los Oceanos. (SPA.). 242p. (YA). (gr. 5-8). *(978-84-7131-935-7(7))* Editex, Editorial S.A. ESP. Dist: Lectorum Pubns., Inc.
Gallagher, Belinda. Why Why Why... Are There Schools in the Sea? 2010. (Why Why Why Ser.). (Illus.). 32p. (J). (gr. 1-3). lib. bdg. 18.95 *(978-1-4222-1572-2(5))* Mason Crest.
Galloway, Fhiona, illus. Look Through: Sea. 2016. (ENG.). 10p. (J). bds. 8.99 *(978-1-62686-658-4(9),* Silver Dolphin Bks.) Readerlink Distribution Services, LLC.
Ganeri, Anita. Esos Inmensos Oceanos. (Coleccion Esa Horrible Geografia).Tr. of Odious Oceans. (SPA., Illus.). 160p. (YA). (gr. 5-8). *(978-84-272-2152-9(5),* ML3927) Molino, Editorial ESP. Dist: Lectorum Pubns., Inc.
—I Wonder Why the Sea Is Salty. 2014. 32p. pap. 7.00 *(978-1-61003-352-7(3))* Center for the Collaborative Classroom.
—I Wonder Why the Sea Is Salty: And Other Questions about the Oceans. 2011. (I Wonder Why Ser.). (ENG., Illus.). 32p. (J). (gr. k-3). pap. 6.99 *(978-0-7534-6521-9(3),* 9780753465219, Kingfisher) Roaring Brook Pr.
—Protecting Ocean Habitats. 2005. (Protecting Habitats Ser.). (Illus.). 32p. (gr. 4-7). lib. bdg. 26.00 *(978-0-8368-4992-9(2),* Gareth Stevens Learning Library) Stevens, Gareth Publishing LLLP.
Gardeski, Christina Mia. All about Oceans. 2017. (Habitats Ser.). (ENG.). 24p. (gr. k-1). lib. bdg. 21.99 ***(978-1-5157-7644-4(1),*** Pebble Bks.) Capstone Press of Coughlan Cos.
Gareth Stevens Editorial Staff. Oceans. 2004. (Discovery Channel School Science Ser.). (Illus.). 32p. (gr. 4-8). lib. bdg. 26.00 *(978-0-8368-3383-6(X),* Gareth Stevens Learning Library) Stevens, Gareth Publishing LLLP.
Goldsack, Gaby. Ocean Animals. Bampton, Bob, illus. (J). *(978-1-57755-508-7(2))* Flying Frog Publishing, Inc.
Goldstein, Natalie. How Do We Know the Nature of the Ocean? 2005. (Great Scientific Questions & the Scientists Who Answered Them Ser.). (Illus.). 112p. (J). (gr. 7-12). lib. bdg. 34.60 *(978-1-4042-0079-1(7))* Rosen Publishing Group, Inc., The.
—How Do We Know the Nature of the Ocean. 2009. (Great Scientific Questions & the Scientists Who Answered Them Ser.). 112p. (gr. 7-12). 63.90 *(978-1-61513-204-1(X))* Rosen Publishing Group, Inc., The.
Gonzales, Doreen. The Mighty Atlantic Ocean. 2013. (Our Earth's Oceans Ser.). 48p. (J). (gr. 3-4). pap. 8.95 *(978-1-4644-0152-7(7),* Enslow Elementary) Enslow Pubs., Inc.
—The Southern Ocean: A MyReportLinks. com Book. 2004. (Oceans of the World Ser.). (Illus.). 48p. (J). lib. bdg. 25.26 *(978-0-7660-5196-6(X),* MyReportLinks.com Bks.) Enslow Pubs., Inc.
—The Tropical Indian Ocean. 2013. (Our Earth's Oceans Ser.). 48p. (J). (gr. 3-4). pap. 8.95 *(978-1-4644-0150-3(0),* Enslow Elementary); 25.27 *(978-0-7660-4089-2(5))* Enslow Pubs., Inc.
Gordon, Sharon. At Home by the Ocean. 2005. (Bookworms Ser.). (Illus.). 32p. (J). (gr. 3-7). lib. bdg. *(978-0-7614-1959-4(4),* Benchmark Bks.) Marshall Cavendish Corp.
Gosman, Gillian. What Do You Know about Earth's Oceans? 2013. (20 Questions: Earth Science Ser.). 24p. (J). (gr. 3-6). pap. 49.50 *(978-1-4488-9859-6(5));* lib. bdg. 22.60 *(978-1-4488-9700-1(9));* (ENG., Illus.). pap. 8.25 *(978-1-4488-9858-9(7))* Rosen Publishing Group, Inc., The. (PowerKids Pr.).
Gould, Jane H. The Flying Dutchman. 2014. (Jr. Graphic Ghost Stories Ser.). 24p. (J). (gr. 3-6). lib. bdg. 26.25 *(978-1-4777-7088-7(7),* PowerKids Pr.) Rosen Publishing Group, Inc., The.
Gray, Leon. Oceans. 2015. (Amazing Biomes Ser.). (Illus.). 32p. (gr. 3-6). 31.35 *(978-1-78121-243-1(0),* 1389630) Brown Bear Bks.
Green, Emily K. Oceans. 2006. (Learning about the Earth Ser.). (ENG., Illus.). 24p. (J). (gr. k-3). lib. bdg. 25.95 *(978-1-60014-039-6(4))* Bellwether Media.
Green, Jen. Arctic Ocean. 2006. (Oceans & Seas Ser.). (Illus.). 48p. (gr. 5-12). pap. 14.05 *(978-0-8368-6278-2(3));* lib. bdg. 31.00 *(978-0-8368-6270-6(8))* Stevens, Gareth Publishing LLLP. (Gareth Stevens Secondary Library).
—Atlantic Ocean. 2006. (Oceans & Seas Ser.). (Illus.). 48p. (gr. 5-12). pap. 14.05 *(978-0-8368-6279-9(1));* lib. bdg. 31.00 *(978-0-8368-6271-3(6))* Stevens, Gareth Publishing LLLP. (Gareth Stevens Secondary Library).
—Indian Ocean. 2006. (Oceans & Seas Ser.). (Illus.). 48p. (gr. 5-12). pap. 14.05 *(978-0-8368-6281-2(3));* lib. bdg. 31.00 *(978-0-8368-6273-7(2))* Stevens, Gareth Publishing LLLP. (Gareth Stevens Secondary Library).
—Mediterranean Sea. 2006. (Oceans & Seas Ser.). (Illus.). 48p. (gr. 5-12). pap. 14.05 *(978-0-8368-6282-9(1));* lib. bdg. 31.00 *(978-0-8368-6274-4(0))* Stevens, Gareth Publishing LLLP. (Gareth Stevens Secondary Library).
—The World's Oceans. 2009. (Amazing Planet Earth Ser.). 32p. (gr. 4-7). 31.35 *(978-1-59920-373-7(1))* Black Rabbit Bks.
Gregory, Joy. Atlantic Ocean. 2016. (J). *(978-1-4896-4735-1(X))* Weigl Pubs., Inc.
Group/McGraw-Hill, Wright. Our World's Oceans, 6 vols. (Book2WebTM Ser.). (gr. 4-8). 36.50 *(978-0-322-04447-0(2))* Wright Group/McGraw-Hill.
Hall, Stephen. Exploring the Oceans. 2012. (ENG., Illus.). 48p. (J). 15.00 *(978-1-899762-79-8(5))* Award Pubns. Ltd. GBR. Dist: Parkwest Pubns., Inc.
Hansen, Grace. Ocean Life, 1 vol. 2014. (Ocean Life Ser.: 6). (ENG.). 24p. (J). (gr. -1-2). lib. bdg. 171.00 *(978-1-62970-707-5(4))* ABDO Publishing Co.
Harris, Nicholas, text. Panoramas: Ocean Life. 2006. (Illus.). 23p. (J). *(978-0-7607-8156-2(7))* backpackbooks.
Harrison, David L. Oceans: The Vast, Mysterious Deep. Nathan, Cheryl, illus. 2003. (Earth Works). (ENG.). 32p. (J). (gr. k-2). 15.95 *(978-1-59078-018-3(3))* Boyds Mills Pr.
Hasselfeldt, Lori. The under the Ocean Alphabet Book. Hasselfeldt, Lori, illus. 2013. (Illus.). 32p. 24.95 *(978-1-61493-155-3(0));* pap. 14.95 *(978-1-61493-154-6(2))* Peppertree Pr., The.
Heinrichs, Ann. Oceans. 2009. (21st Century Skills Library: Real World Math Ser.). (ENG.). 32p. (gr. 4-8). lib. bdg. 28.50 *(978-1-60279-496-2(0),* 200317) Cherry Lake Publishing.
Holland, Gini. I Live near the Ocean. 2004. (Weekly Reader Early Learning Library). (Illus.). 24p. (gr. k-3). pap. 8.15 *(978-0-8368-4089-6(5),* Weekly Reader Leveled Readers) Stevens, Gareth Publishing LLLP.
—I Live near the Ocean/Vivo cerca del Mar. Coffey, Colleen & Carrillo, Consuelo, trs. 2004. (Weekly Reader Early Learning Library). (SPA & ENG., Illus.). 24p. (gr. k-3). pap. 8.15 *(978-0-8368-4137-4(9));* lib. bdg. 22.00 *(978-0-8368-4130-5(1))* Stevens, Gareth Publishing LLLP. (Weekly Reader Leveled Readers).
Holland, Simon. Oceans: Can You Tell the Facts from the Fibs? Cosgrove, Lee, illus. 2015. (Lie Detector Ser.). (ENG.). 32p. (gr. k-3). lib. bdg. 27.32 *(978-1-4795-8512-0(2))* Picture Window Bks.
Horn, Susan & Richardson, Phillip. Message in a Bottle. Björkman, Steve, illus. 2009. (ENG.). 72p. (J). pap. 19.95 *(978-1-60433-001-4(5),* Applesauce Pr.) Cider Mill Pr. Bk. Pubs., LLC.
Hudak, Heather C. Oceans. (Illus.). 32p. (J). 2017. ***(978-1-5105-0878-1(3))*** 2016. *(978-1-5105-0876-7(7))* SmartBook Media, Inc.
—Oceans. 2013. (Illus.). 32p. (J). 13.95 *(978-1-61913-237-5(0));* 28.55 *(978-1-61913-074-6(2))* Weigl Pubs., Inc.
Hughes, Catherine D. First Big Book of the Ocean. 2013. (National Geographic Little Kids First Big Bks.). (ENG., Illus.). 128p. (J). (gr. -1-3). 14.95 *(978-1-4263-1368-4(3));* lib. bdg. 23.90 *(978-1-4263-1369-1(1))* National Geographic Society. (National Geographic Children's Bks.).
Hunter, Nick. Seas. 2013. (Explorer Travel Guides). (ENG., Illus.). 48p. (gr. 3-6). 29.99 *(978-1-4109-5433-6(1));* pap. 8.95 *(978-1-4109-5440-4(4))* Heinemann-Raintree. (NA-r).
James, Ian, ed. Oceans. (Illus.). 32p. *(978-0-7540-9031-1(0))* Cherrytree Bks.
Jedicke, Peter. Exploring the Ocean Depths. 2003. (Hot Science Ser.). (J). lib. bdg. 28.50 *(978-1-58340-367-9(1))* Black Rabbit Bks.
Jewitt, Kathryn. 3D Theater: Oceans. Dogi, Fiametta, illus. 2011. (3D Theater Ser.). (ENG.). 20p. (J). (gr. -1-3). 19.99 *(978-0-7534-6466-3(7),* 9780753464663, Kingfisher) Roaring Brook Pr.
Johnson, Rebecca L. A Journey into the Ocean. Saroff, Phyllis V., illus. 2004. (Biomes of North America Ser.). (ENG.). 48p. (gr. 3-6). pap. 8.95 *(978-0-8225-2046-7(X),* l); lib. bdg. 23.93 *(978-1-57505-591-6(0))* Lerner Publishing Group.
Johnson, Rebecca L., et al. Ocean Exploration. 2007. (Avenues Ser.). (ENG., Illus.). 36p. (J). pap. 18.95 *(978-0-7922-5430-0(9))* CENGAGE Learning.
Johnson, Robin. Oceans Inside Out. 2014. (ENG.). 32p. (J). *(978-0-7787-0635-9(4))* Crabtree Publishing Co.
Jordano, Kimberly & Corcoran, Tebra. Oceans of Fun. Fisch, Teri L., ed. Campbell, Jenny, illus. 2003. (Stepping into Standards Theme Ser.). 64p. (J). (gr. k-2). pap. 10.99 *(978-1-57471-946-8(7),* 2474) Creative Teaching Pr., Inc.
K/H (Pathways). Pathways: Grade 4 Where the Waves Break: Life at the Edge of the Sea Trade Book. rev. ed. 2011. (ENG.). 48p. pap. 10.50 *(978-0-7575-4072-1(4))* Kendall Hunt Publishing Co.
Kalman, Bobbie. The ABCs of Oceans. 2007. (ABCs of the Natural World Ser.). (ENG., Illus.). 32p. (J). (gr. 1-4). lib. bdg. *(978-0-7787-3412-3(9));* pap. *(978-0-7787-3432-1(3))* Crabtree Publishing Co.
—Explore Earth's Five Oceans. 2010. (Explore the Continents Ser.). (ENG., Illus.). 32p. (J). (gr. 1-5). lib. bdg. *(978-0-7787-3077-4(8))* Crabtree Publishing Co.
—Los Océanos de la Tierra. 2009. (SPA.). 32p. (J). *(978-0-7787-8243-8(3));* pap. *(978-0-7787-8260-5(3))* Crabtree Publishing Co.
—What Is an Ocean? 2010. (My World Ser.). (ENG.). 24p. (J). (gr. k-3). *(978-0-7787-9515-5(2));* pap. *(978-0-7787-9540-7(3))* Crabtree Publishing Co.
Kalman, Bobbie & MacAulay, Kelley. Earth's Oceans. 2008. (Looking at Earth Ser.). (ENG., Illus.). 32p. (J). (gr. 3-7). pap. *(978-0-7787-3214-3(2));* lib. bdg. *(978-0-7787-3204-4(5))* Crabtree Publishing Co.
Kalman, Bobbie & Macaulay, Kelly. Les Mers Tropicales. Briere, Marie-Josee, tr. from ENG. 2008. (Petit Monde Vivant Ser.). (FRE., Illus.). 32p. (J). (gr. 3-7). pap. 9.95 *(978-2-89579-182-9(1))* Bayard Canada Livres CAN. Dist: Crabtree Publishing Co.
Karas, G. Brian. Atlantic. Karas, G. Brian, illus. 2004. (Rise & Shine Ser.). (ENG., Illus.). 32p. (J). (gr. -1-3). reprint ed. pap. 6.99 *(978-0-14-240027-2(0),* Puffin Books) Penguin Young Readers Group.
Kerrod, Robin. Find Out about the Sea: With 20 Projects & More Than 260 Pictures. 2013. (ENG., Illus.). 64p. (J). (gr. 3-7). 9.99 *(978-1-84322-896-7(3))* Anness Publishing GBR. Dist: National Bk. Network.
Kids: Explore Oceans & Activity Booklet. 2003. (J). 1.00 *(978-1-888631-26-5(0))* Project WET Foundation.
Kingfisher Editors & Murrell, Deborah. Lift & Explore: Oceans. Bull, Peter, illus. 2013. (Lift & Explore Ser.). (ENG.). 16p. (J). (gr. -1-1). bds. 12.99 *(978-0-7534-7081-7(0),* 9780753470817, Kingfisher) Roaring Brook Pr.
Koll, Hilary & Mills, Steve. A Math Journey under the Ocean. 2016. (ENG., Illus.). 32p. (J). *(978-0-7787-2315-8(1))* Crabtree Publishing Co.
Kortemeier, Todd. Exploring the Depths of the Ocean. 2017. (Science Frontiers Ser.). (ENG., Illus.). 32p. (J). (gr. 3-6). 21.95 *(978-1-63235-377-1(6))* Pr. Room Editions LLC.
Labrecque, Ellen. Deep Oceans, 1 vol. 2014. (Earth's Last Frontiers Ser.). (ENG., Illus.). 32p. (gr. 1-3). lib. bdg. 29.99 *(978-1-4109-6178-5(8),* Read Me!) Heinemann-Raintree.
—Earth's Last Frontiers, 1 vol. 2014. (Earth's Last Frontiers Ser.). (ENG.). 32p. (gr. 1-3). lib. bdg. 119.96 *(978-1-4109-6181-5(8),* Read Me!) Heinemann-Raintree.
—Living Beside the Ocean. 2015. (Places We Live Ser.). (ENG., Illus.). 32p. (gr. 1-3). 27.32 *(978-1-4846-0803-6(8),* Heinemann First Library) Heinemann-Raintree.
Laval, Thierry, et al. Look & Find - Oceans. 2016. (Look & Find Ser.). (ENG., Illus.). 14p. (J). 18.99 *(978-0-531-22236-2(5),* Children's Pr.) Scholastic Library Publishing.
Leake, Diyan. Oceans & Seas, 1 vol. 2014. (Water, Water Everywhere! Ser.). (ENG., Illus.). 24p. (gr. -1-1). 22.65 *(978-1-4846-0449-6(0),* Acorn) Heinemann-Raintree.
Leardi, Jeanette. Protecting Our Oceans: Set Of 6. 2011. (Navigators Ser.). (J). pap. 50.00 net. *(978-1-4108-5092-8(7))* Benchmark Education Co.
—Protecting Our Oceans: Text Pairs. 2008. (Bridges/Navigators Ser.). (J). (gr. 6). 89.00 *(978-1-4108-8447-3(3))* Benchmark Education Co.
Leonhardt, Alice. Why the Ocean Is Salty. 2009. (Steck-Vaughn Pair-It Books Proficiency Stage 5 Ser.). (ENG.). 40p. (gr. 4-4). pap. 9.10 *(978-0-7398-0868-9(0))* Steck-Vaughn.
Levete, Sarah. Save the Oceans. 2011. (ENG.). 24p. (J). pap. *(978-0-7787-7879-0(7));* (gr. 3-6). *(978-0-7787-7857-8(6))* Crabtree Publishing Co.
Lindeen, Carol K. Life in an Ocean. 2016. (Living in a Biome Ser.). (ENG.). 24p. (gr. k-1). pap. 7.29 *(978-1-5157-3693-6(8),* Pebble Plus) Capstone Press of Coughlan Cos.
Llewellyn, Claire. Oceans, 1 vol. 2012. (Habitat Survival Ser.). (ENG.). 32p. (gr. 2-4). pap. 8.29 *(978-1-4109-4607-2(X));* lib. bdg. 30.65 *(978-1-4109-4598-3(7))* Heinemann-Raintree. (Raintree Perspectives).
—The Sea. 2003. (Starters Ser.). 24p. (J). lib. bdg. 21.35 *(978-1-58340-262-7(4))* Black Rabbit Bks.
Lonely Planet Publications Staff, et al. Let's Explore... Ocean, 1 vol. 2016. (Lonely Planet Kids Ser.). (ENG.). 48p. (J). pap. 9.99 *(978-1-76034-040-7(5),* 5146) Lonely Planet Pubns.
Look Who's Popping Up: Under the Sea. 2003. (J). (gr. -1-k). 4.98 *(978-0-7525-8904-6(0))* Parragon, Inc.
Lynch, Seth. There's an Ocean in My Backyard! 2016. (Backyard Biomes Ser.). 00024p. (J). pap. 8.15 ***(978-1-4824-5567-0(6))*** Stevens, Gareth Publishing LLLP.
MacAulay, Kelley & Kalman, Bobbie. Tropical Oceans. 2005. (Living Ocean Ser.). (ENG., Illus.). 32p. (J). (gr. 3-4). lib. bdg. *(978-0-7787-1300-5(8))* Crabtree Publishing Co.
Macken, JoAnn Early. Seas. 2006. (Where on Earth? World Geography Ser.). (Illus.). 24p. (gr. 1-4). lib. bdg. 22.00 *(978-0-8368-6398-7(4),* Weekly Reader Leveled Readers) Stevens, Gareth Publishing LLLP.
MacQuitty, Miranda. DK Eyewitness Books: Ocean: Ocean. 2014. (DK Eyewitness Bks.). (ENG., Illus.). 72p. (J). (gr. 3-7). pap. 9.99 *(978-1-4654-2054-1(1),* DK Children) Dorling Kindersley Publishing, Inc.
Make It Work Geography, 4 vol. set. 2003. (gr. 4-8). 59.00 *(978-0-7166-5124-6(6))* World Bk., Inc.
Mara, Wil. Deep-Sea Exploration: Science, Technology, & Engineering. 2015. (ENG., Illus.). 64p. (J). pap. 8.95 *(978-0-531-21173-1(8),* Orchard Bks.) Scholastic Library Publishing.
Marshall, Natalie, illus. Colors in the Ocean. 2017. (Touch & Learn Bks.). (ENG.). 12p. (J). (gr. -1 — 1). bds. 5.99 ***(978-1-4380-5001-0(1))*** Barron's Educational Series, Inc.
Martin, Claudia. Complete Guides Ocean Life. 2012. (ENG.). 144p. (J). *(978-1-4351-4408-8(2))* Barnes & Noble, Inc.
Marx, Christy. Life in the Ocean Depths. 2009. 64p. (gr. 5-8). (YA). pap. 12.95 *(978-1-4358-3265-7(5));* 53.00 *(978-1-61514-272-9(X))* Rosen Publishing Group, Inc., The. (Rosen Reference).
Mason, Paul. Oceans under Threat. 2016. (World in Peril Ser.). (ENG.). 32p. (gr. 3-5). pap. 7.99 *(978-1-4846-4023-4(3),* NA-h) Heinemann-Raintree.
McCune, Jamie. First Look at Ocean Animals. 2010. (First Look At Ser.). (ENG.). 16p. (J). (gr. -1). 6.95 *(978-1-60727-138-3(9))* Soundprints.
McFadzean, Lesley. Ocean Habitats. 2013. (Discovery Education: Habitats Ser.). 32p. (J). (gr. 3-6). 25.25 *(978-1-4777-1322-8(0));* pap. 10.00 *(978-1-4777-1479-9(0));* pap. 60.00 *(978-1-4777-1480-5(4))* Rosen Publishing Group, Inc., The. (PowerKids Pr.).
McKissack, Fredrick L. & McKissack, Lisa Beringer. Counting in the Oceans. 2009. (Counting in the Biomes Ser.). (Illus.). 32p. (J). (gr. 1-3). lib. bdg. 23.94 *(978-0-7660-2994-1(8),* Enslow Elementary) Enslow Pubs., Inc.
McMillan, Beverly & Musick, John A. Oceans. 2007. (Insiders Ser.). (ENG., Illus.). 64p. (J). (gr. 3-7). 17.99 *(978-1-4169-3859-0(1),* Simon & Schuster Bks. For Young Readers) Simon & Schuster Bks. For Young Readers.
Meachen Rau, Dana. Los Océanos. 2008. (Planeta Es Importante Ser.). (SPA.). 32p. (gr. 1-2). lib. bdg. 15.95 *(978-0-7614-3469-6(0),* Benchmark Bks.) Marshall Cavendish Corp.
—Oceans. 2008. (Earth Matters Ser.). 32p. (gr. 1-2). lib. bdg. 15.95 *(978-0-7614-3048-3(2),* Benchmark Bks.) Marshall Cavendish Corp.
—Oceans/Los Oceanos. 2008. (Earth Matters/El Planeta Es Importante Ser.). (SPA & ENG.). 32p. (gr. k-1). lib. bdg. 15.95 *(978-0-7614-3494-8(1),* Benchmark Bks.) Marshall Cavendish Corp.
Moore, Elizabeth. Oceans, 1 vol. (Wonder Readers Next Steps: Science Ser.). (ENG.). (gr. -1-1). 2013. 20p. lib. bdg. 22.65 *(978-1-4765-0038-6(X))* 2011. 16p. pap. 35.94 *(978-1-4296-8132-2(2))* 2011. 32p. pap. 5.99 *(978-1-4296-7829-2(1))* Capstone Press of Coughlan Cos. (Wonder Readers).
Morey, Allan. Ocean Food Chains. 2003. (What Eats What? Ser.). (J). pap. *(978-1-58417-219-2(3));* lib. bdg. *(978-1-58417-218-5(5))* Lake Street Pubs.
Morgan, Sally. Encyclopedia of Ocean Life. 2012. (Illus.). 224p. (J). *(978-1-4351-4351-7(5))* Barnes & Noble, Inc.
Nadeau, Isaac. Water in Oceans. (Water Cycle Ser.). 24p. 2009. (gr. 4-4). 42.50 *(978-1-60854-269-7(6))* 2003. (Illus.). (J). lib. bdg. 22.60 *(978-0-8239-6267-9(9))* Rosen Publishing Group, Inc., The. (PowerKids Pr.).
National Geographic Editors & Rizzo, Johnna. Oceans: Dolphins, Sharks, Penguins, & More! 2010. (ENG., Illus.). 64p. (J). (gr. 3-7). 24.90 *(978-1-4263-0724-9(1),* National Geographic Children's Bks.) National Geographic Society.
National Geographic Kids Staff & Rizzo, Johnna. Oceans: Dolphins, Sharks, Penguins, & More! 2010. (ENG., Illus.). 64p. (J). (gr. 3-7). 14.95 *(978-1-4263-0686-0(5),* National Geographic Children's Bks.) National Geographic Society.
Natural History Museum. Ocean Sticker Book. 2013. (ENG.). 14p. (J). (gr. -1-1). pap. 6.99 *(978-0-565-09257-3(X))* Natural History Museum Pubns. GBR. Dist: Independent Pubs. Group.
Nelson, Robin. From Sea to Salt. 2003. (Start to Finish Ser.). (ENG., Illus.). 24p. (J). (gr. k-3). 19.93 *(978-0-8225-0946-2(6),* Lerner Pubns.) Lerner Publishing Group.
Nemeth, Jason D. Rivers, Lakes, & Oceans. 2012. (Our Changing Earth Ser.). (ENG.). 24p. (J). (gr. 3-6). pap. 8.25 *(978-1-4488-6300-6(7),* PowerKids Pr.); lib. bdg. 22.60 *(978-1-4488-6171-2(3))* Rosen Publishing Group, Inc., The.
Nugent, Samantha. Arctic Ocean. 2016. (J). *(978-1-4896-4733-7(3))* Weigl Pubs., Inc.
Oachs, Emily Rose. Arctic Ocean. 2017. (Arctic Ocean Ser.). 24p. (J). (gr. k-3). pap. 6.99 ***(978-1-61891-261-9(5),*** Blastoff! Readers) Bellwether Media.
—Atlantic Ocean. 2017. (Atlantic Ocean Ser.). 24p. (J). (gr. k-3). pap. 6.99 ***(978-1-61891-262-6(3),*** Blastoff! Readers) Bellwether Media.
—Indian Ocean. (Indian Ocean Ser.). 24p. (J). (gr. k-3). 2017. pap. 6.99 ***(978-1-61891-263-3(1))*** 2016. (ENG., Illus.). lib. bdg. 25.95 ***(978-1-62617-332-3(X))*** Bellwether Media. (Blastoff! Readers).
—Southern Ocean. 2017. (Southern Ocean Ser.). 24p. (J). (gr. k-3). pap. 6.99 ***(978-1-61891-279-4(8),*** Blastoff! Readers) Bellwether Media.
Ocean. 2003. (J). per. *(978-1-57657-886-5(0))* Paradise Pr., Inc.
The Ocean. 2004. (Illus.). lib. bdg. 7.95 *(978-0-8225-4535-4(7))* Lerner Publishing Group.
Ocean Facts, 4 vols., Set. 2005. (Ocean Facts Ser.). (Illus.). 24p. (gr. 2-4). 92.00 *(978-0-7910-7284-4(3),* Chelsea Hse.) Facts On File, Inc.
Ocean (Gr. PreK-5) 2003. (J). *(978-1-58232-024-3(1))* ECS Learning Systems, Inc.
Oceans Instructional Guide. 2009. (Grade 8: Science Exit Project Kits Ser.). spiral bd. *(978-1-4042-4025-4(X),* Rosen Classroom) Rosen Publishing Group, Inc., The.
O'Neill, Michael Patrick, photos by. Ocean Magic. O'Neill, Michael Patrick, . 2008. (Illus.). 48p. (J). (gr. 1-4). 19.95 *(978-0-9728653-5-7(7))* Batfish Bks.
Orme, David. Sea Killers. 2009. (Fact to Fiction Ser.). (Illus.). 36p. (J). pap. 6.95 *(978-0-7891-7905-0(9))* Perfection Learning Corp.
Orr, Tamra B. The Undersea World. 2016. (True Book(tm), a — Greatest Discoveries & Discoverers Ser.). (ENG., Illus.).

48p. (J). lib. bdg. 31.00 *(978-0-531-21859-4(7),* Children's Pr.) Scholastic Library Publishing.

Ostopowich, Melanie. Oceans, Lakes, & Rivers. 2015. (Illus.). 24p. (J). *(978-1-5105-0052-5(9))* SmartBook Media, Inc.

—Oceans, Lakes, & Rivers. 2010. (Water Science Ser.). (Illus.). 24p. (gr. 3-5). (J). pap. 11.95 *(978-1-61690-007-6(5));* (YA). lib. bdg. 25.70 *(978-1-61690-001-4(6))* Weigl Pubs., Inc.

—Oceans, Rivers, & Lakes. 2005. (Science Matters Ser.). (Illus.). 24p. (J). (gr. 3-7). lib. bdg. 24.45 *(978-1-59036-304-1(3))* Weigl Pubs., Inc.

Parker, Steve. Ocean & Sea. 2012. (J). lib. bdg. *(978-0-531-22959-0(9))* Scholastic, Inc.

Parker, Steven. In Focus: Oceans & Seas. 2017. (In Focus Ser.). (ENG.). 64p. (J). 17.99 *(978-0-7534-7347-4(X),* 9780753473474, Kingfisher) Roaring Brook Pr.

Parsons, Michelle Hyde. Ocean Pollution. 2005. (J). pap. *(978-1-4108-4630-3(X))* Benchmark Education Co.

Patchett, Fiona. Under the Sea. Kushii, Tetsuo & Wray, Zoe, illus. 2006. (Beginners Nature: Level 1 Ser.). 32p. (J). (gr. k-2). 4.99 *(978-0-7945-1336-8(0),* Usborne) EDC Publishing.

—Under the Sea. Kushii, Tetsuo, illus. 2006. (Usborne Beginners Ser.). 32p. (J). (gr. 1). lib. bdg. 12.99 *(978-1-58086-931-7(9),* Usborne) EDC Publishing.

Penguin Books Staff, ed. The Sea. (Information Activity Ser.). 24p. (J). 3.50 *(978-0-7214-3442-1(8),* Dutton Juvenile) Penguin Publishing Group.

Plisson, Phillip. Mar Explicado a los ninos. 2005. 80p. *(978-970-651-911-5(4))* Editorial Oceano De Mexico, S.A. DE C.V.

¿Que Hay Debajo del Mar? (Coleccion Primeros Pasos en la Ciencia). (SPA., Illus.). (J). (gr. 1-3). pap. *(978-950-724-419-3(0),* LMA8226) Lumen ARG. Dist: Lectorum Pubns., Inc.

Rabe, Tish. Clam-I-Am! All about the Beach. Ruiz, Aristides & Mathieu, Joe, illus. 2005. (Cat in the Hat's Learning Library). (ENG.). 48p. (J). (gr. -1-3). 9.99 *(978-0-375-82280-3(1),* Random Hse. Bks. for Young Readers) Random Hse. Children's Bks.

Rake, Jody Sullivan. Endangered Oceans: Investigating Oceans in Crisis. 2015. (Endangered Earth Ser.). (ENG.). 32p. (gr. 3-4). lib. bdg. 27.32 *(978-1-4914-2038-6(3),* Fact Finders) Capstone Press of Coughlan Cos.

Rau, Dana Meachen. By the Ocean. 2007. (J). pap. 6.99 *(978-0-7614-3312-5(0))* Marshall Cavendish Corp.

Rettore. Sea: A Soft Book & Mirror for Baby! 2017. (Baby Sees Cloth Bks.). (ENG., Illus.). 6p. (J). (gr. -1 — 1). 10.99 *(978-1-4380-7761-1(0))* Barron's Educational Series, Inc.

Rice, Bill. Survival! Ocean. 1 vol. 2nd rev. ed. 2013. (Nonfiction Readers Ser.). (ENG., Illus.). 48p. (J). (gr. 4-4). pap. 29.96 *(978-1-4807-1095-5(4))* Shell Educational Publishing.

Rice, Dona Herweck. La Vida Marina. 1 vol. 2nd rev. ed. 2012. (Nonfiction Readers Ser.). (SPA.). 20p. (J). (gr. 1-1). pap. 4.99 *(978-1-4333-4423-7(8))* Teacher Created Materials, Inc.

Rice, William. ¡Supervivencia! Océano. 2017. (TIME for Kids en Español - Level 4 Ser.). (SPA., Illus.). 48p. (gr. 4-4). lib. bdg. 31.99 *(978-1-5157-5124-3(4))* Time for Kids Inc AUS. Dist: Capstone Pub.

Rice, William & Franklin, Yvonne. Oceans. 1 vol. 2009. (Science Readers: a Closer Look Ser.). (ENG.). 32p. (J). (gr. 2-2). pap. 8.99 *(978-1-4333-0320-3(5))* Teacher Created Materials, Inc.

Rice, William B. Survival! Ocean. 1 vol. 2nd rev. ed. 2012. (Nonfiction Readers Ser.). (ENG., Illus.). 48p. (J). (gr. 4-4). pap. 9.99 *(978-1-4333-4819-8(5))* Teacher Created Materials, Inc.

Richmond, Benjamin. Why Is the Sea Salty? And Other Questions about the Ocean. Azhderian, Cecelia, illus. 2014. (Good Question! Ser.). (ENG.). 32p. (J). (gr. 1). pap. 5.95 *(978-1-4549-0677-3(4))* Sterling Publishing Co., Inc.

—Why Is the Sea Salty? And Other Questions about the Oceans. Azhderian, Cecelia, illus. 2014. (Good Question! Ser.). (ENG.). 40p. (J). (gr. 1). 12.95 *(978-1-4549-0676-6(6))* Sterling Publishing Co., Inc.

Richter, A. By the Ocean: Learning the Long O Sound. 2009. (PowerPhonics Ser.). 24p. (gr. 1-1). 39.90 *(978-1-60851-436-6(6),* PowerKids Pr.) Rosen Publishing Group, Inc., The.

Riggs, Kate. Oceans. 2016. (Illus.). 24p. *(978-1-60818-743-0(8),* Creative Education) Creative Co., The.

Ring, Susan. The Ocean, 6 vols., Set. 2003. (Yellow Umbrella Early Level Ser.). (ENG.). 16p. (gr. k-1). pap. 35.70 *(978-0-7368-2997-7(0),* Yellow Umbrella Bks.) Capstone Press of Coughlan Cos.

Ripley's Believe It Or Not! Staff, et al. Oceans: Believe It or Not!, 4 vols. 2010. (Twist Ser.: 6). (ENG., Illus.). 48p. (J). 12.95 *(978-1-893951-81-5(2))* Ripley Entertainment, Inc.

Rivera, Sheila. Ocean. 2005. (First Step Nonfiction - Habitats Ser.). (ENG., Illus.). 24p. (gr. k-2). lib. bdg. 23.93 *(978-0-8225-2795-4(2),* Lerner Pubns.) Lerner Publishing Group.

Rivers, Lakes, & Oceans. 2008. (Restless Earth Ser.). 112p. (YA). (gr. 5-9). 35.00 *(978-0-7910-9797-7(8))* Facts On File, Inc.

RodríGuez, Ana María. Leatherback Turtles, Giant Squids, & Other Mysterious Animals of the Deepest Seas. 2012. (Extreme Animals in Extreme Environments Ser.). (Illus.). 48p. (J). (gr. 5-18). pap. 8.95 *(978-1-4644-0019-3(9))* Enslow Pubs., Inc.

Rodriguez, Ana Maria. Leatherback Turtles, Giant Squids, & Other Mysterious Animals of the Deepest Seas. 2012. (Extreme Animals in Extreme Environments Ser.). (Illus.). 48p. (J). (gr. 5-18). 25.27 *(978-0-7660-3696-3(0))* Enslow Pubs., Inc.

Rosa-Mendoza, Gladys. Who Lives in the Sea?/Quí'n Vive en el Mar? O'Neil, Sharron, illus. 2007. (English Spanish Foundations Ser.). (ENG & SPA.). 20p. (J). (gr. -1-k). bds. 6.95 *(978-1-931398-24-4(0))* Me+Mi Publishing.

Roumanis, Alexis. Oceans. 2014. (Illus.). 24p. (J). *(978-1-4896-3014-8(7))* Weigl Pubs., Inc.

Roydhouse, Sandy. Oceans of the World. 2009. (Our Planet Ser.). (YA). (gr. 3-6). lib. bdg. 25.25 *(978-1-4358-2814-8(3))* Rosen Publishing Group, Inc., The.

Royston, Angela. Ocean - It's My Home! 2011. (ENG., Illus.). 24p. (J). pap. *(978-0-7787-7873-8(8))* Crabtree Publishing Co.

—Ocean Explorer! 2011. (ENG., Illus.). 24p. (J). pap. *(978-0-7787-7864-6(9));* (gr. 3-6). *(978-0-7787-7842-4(8))* Crabtree Publishing Co.

—Ocean It's My Home! 2011. (Crabtree Connections Ser.). (ENG., Illus.). 24p. (J). (gr. 3-6). *(978-0-7787-7851-6(7))* Crabtree Publishing Co.

—Oceans. 2015. (Research on the Edge Ser.). (ENG., Illus.). 32p. (J). (gr. 3-8). 31.35 *(978-1-62588-157-1(6))* Black Rabbit Bks.

Running Press Staff. Posters to Color: Oceans. 2016. (ENG., Illus.). 24p. (J). (gr. -1-17). pap. 9.95 *(978-0-7624-5998-8(0),* Running Pr. Kids) Running Pr. Bk. Pubs.

Salas, Laura Purdie. Colors of the Ocean. (Colors All Around Ser.). (ENG.). 32p. (gr. 1-2). 2011. pap. 47.70 *(978-1-4296-6156-0(9))* 2010. lib. bdg. 27.32 *(978-1-4296-5257-5(8))* Capstone Press of Coughlan Cos. (Aplus Bks.).

—Océanos: Mundos Submarinos. Abello, Patricia, tr. from ENG. Yesh, Jeff, illus. 2008. (Ciencia Asombrosa: Ecosistemas Ser.). (SPA.). 24p. (gr. k-4). lib. bdg. 26.65 *(978-1-4048-3864-2(3))* Picture Window Bks.

Schier, Helga. Endangered Oceans. Gale, G., ed. 2014. (Opposing Viewpoints Ser.). (ENG., Illus.). 224p. (gr. 7-12). lib. bdg. 48.80 *(978-0-7377-6052-1(4),* Greenhaven Pr., Inc.) Cengage Gale.

The Sea. (Eyes on Adventure Ser.). 32p. (J). (gr. 1). pap. *(978-1-882210-81-7(6))* Action Publishing, Inc.

The Sea & its Marvels. (Action Bks.). 64p. (J). (gr. 3-7). pap. *(978-1-882210-66-4(2))* Action Publishing, Inc.

Sea into the Sea: Tidal Zone. 2007. (Illus.). 16p. (J). 3.99 *(978-0-9792820-1-0(2))* Toe The Line.

Shackleton, Caroline. Deep Blue: Discovering the Sea Intermediate Book with Online Access. 2014. (ENG., Illus.). 28p. (J). pap. 9.50 *(978-1-107-69705-8(0))* Cambridge Univ. Pr.

Shea, Therese. The Dead Sea. 2014. (Scariest Places on Earth Ser.). 24p. (J). (gr. 2-5). 22.60 *(978-1-4824-1166-9(0))* Stevens, Gareth Publishing LLLP.

Sill, Cathryn. About Habitats-Oceans, 1 vol. Sill, John, illus. 2012. (ENG.). 48p. (J). 16.95 *(978-1-56145-618-5(7))* Peachtree Pubs.

—Oceans, 1 vol. Sill, John, illus. 2016. (About Habitats Ser.). (ENG.). 48p. (J). (gr. -1-2). pap. 7.95 *(978-1-56145-960-5(7))* Peachtree Pubs.

Simon, Seymour. Oceans. 2006. (ENG., Illus.). 40p. (J). (gr. k-4). 6.99 *(978-0-06-088999-9(3),* Collins) HarperCollins Pubs.

—Oceans. 2006. (Illus.). 31p. (gr. k-4). 17.00 *(978-0-7569-6749-9(X))* Perfection Learning Corp.

—Seymour Simon's Extreme Oceans. 2013. (ENG., Illus.). 60p. (J). (gr. 4-7). 17.99 *(978-1-4521-0833-9(1))* Chronicle Bks. LLC.

Sloan, Andy & Benchmark Education Co., LLC. Opinions about Ocean Health. 2014. (Text Connections Ser.). (J). (gr. 3). *(978-1-4509-9653-2(1))* Benchmark Education Co.

Smith, Ben. How Are Oceans & Lakes Alike? 2014. (Little Books of Answers: Level F Ser.). (Illus.). 16p. (gr. k-2). pap. 7.95 *(978-1-927136-55-3(5))* Three Crows Media NZL. Dist: RiverStream Publishing.

Smith, Marie & Smith, Roland. W Is for Waves: An Ocean Alphabet. Megahan, John & Rose, Melanie, illus. 2008. (ENG.). 32p. (J). (gr. k-6). 17.95 *(978-1-58536-254-7(9))* Sleeping Bear Pr.

Smithyman, Kathryn & Kalman, Bobbie. El Bioma Marino. 2006. (Libro de Bobbie Kalman Ser.). (SPA., Illus.). 32p. (J). (gr. 3-7). pap. *(978-0-7787-8414-2(2));* lib. bdg. *(978-0-7787-8400-5(2))* Crabtree Publishing Co.

Spilsbury, Louise. Surviving the Sea. 2016. (Sole Survivor Ser.). 48p. (gr. 5-4). pap. 14.05 *(978-1-4824-5071-2(2))* Stevens, Gareth Publishing LLLP.

Spilsbury, Louise & Spilsbury, Richard. Oceans of the World. 2015. (Oceans of the World Ser.). (ENG.). 32p. (gr. 1-3). lib. bdg. 136.60 *(978-1-4846-0775-6(9),* Heinemann First Library) Heinemann-Raintree.

Stewart, Melissa. Is the Bermuda Triangle Really a Dangerous Place? And Other Questions about the Ocean. 2011. (Is That a Fact? Ser.). (ENG.). 40p. (gr. 4-6). 26.60 *(978-0-7613-6097-1(2))* Lerner Publishing Group.

Stone, Lynn M. Oceans. 2003. (Illus.). 24p. (J). 20.64 *(978-1-58952-686-0(4))* Rourke Educational Media.

Sullivan, Laura L. 24 Hours in the Ocean. 2017. (J). ***(978-1-5026-2478-9(8))*** Cavendish Square Publishing.

Tahta, Sophie. What's under the Sea? Trotter, Stuart, illus. rev. ed. 2006. (Starting Point Science Ser.). 24p. (J). (gr. 4-7). pap. 4.99 *(978-0-7945-1409-9(X),* Usborne) EDC Publishing.

Tallarico, Tony. Under the Sea. 2003. (Ultimate Hidden Pictures Ser.). (ENG., Illus.). 48p. (J). (gr. -1-3). mass mkt. 5.99 *(978-0-8431-0266-6(7),* Price Stern Sloan) Penguin Young Readers Group.

Taylor, Barbara. Oceans. 2004. (Make It Work! Geography Ser.). (Illus.). 48p. (J). (gr. 3-6). 12.95 *(978-1-58728-255-3(0),* Two-Can Publishing) T&N Children's Publishing.

Taylor, Trace & Zorzi, Gina. This Is an Ocean. 2011. (Power 100 - Ecosystems Ser.). 28p. pap. 45.32 *(978-1-61541-241-9(7))* American Reading Co.

Taylor, Trace, et al. In the Ocean. Reese, Jonathan, illus. 2006. (1-3Y Ecosystems Ser.). (ENG.). 16p. (J). (gr. k-1). pap. 5.99 *(978-1-59301-438-4(4))* American Reading Co.

Tocci, Salvatore. Marine Habitats: Life in Saltwater. 2004. (Watts Library). (ENG.). (J). 25.50 *(978-0-531-12306-5(5),* Watts, Franklin) Scholastic Library Publishing.

Troupe, Thomas Kingsley. The Pilgrims' Voyage to America: a Fly on the Wall History. Tejido, Jomike, illus. 2017. (Fly on the Wall History Ser.). (ENG.). 32p. (gr. 1-3). lib. bdg. 27.32 *(978-1-4795-9786-4(4))* Picture Window Bks.

Twist, Clint. 1000 Things You Should Know about Oceans. 2008. (1000 Things You Should Know about (Miles Kelley) Ser.). (Illus.). 61p. (J). pap. *(978-1-84236-852-7(4))* Miles Kelly Publishing, Ltd.

Ventura, Marne. Exploring the Depths of the Ocean. 2016. (Science Frontiers Ser.). (ENG., Illus.). 32p. (J). pap. 9.95 *(978-1-63235-394-8(6),* 12-Story Library) Pr. Room Editions LLC.

Wade, Laura. Sea & Sealife. 2003. (Knowledge Masters Ser.). (Illus.). 32p. (YA). pap. incl. cd-rom *(978-1-903954-10-2(X),* Pavilion Children's Books) Pavilion Bks.

Waldendorf, Kurt. How Deep Is the Ocean? 2017. (Comparison Fun Ser.). (ENG.). 24p. (J). (gr. -1-2). lib. bdg. 27.07 *(978-1-5038-1676-3(1),* 211511) Child's World, Inc., The.

Walker, Rachel. Help Our Oceans. 2015. (ENG., Illus.). 16p. (-2). pap. *(978-1-77654-138-6(3),* Red Rocket Readers) Flying Start Bks.

West, Krista, ed. Critical Perspectives on the Oceans. (Scientific American Critical Anthologies on Environment & Climate Ser.). 2009. 208p. (gr. 9-9). 63.90 *(978-1-60853-070-0(1))* 2006. (Illus.). 200p. (J). (gr. 3-7). 37.95 *(978-1-4042-0692-2(2))* Rosen Publishing Group, Inc., The.

Wilsdon, Christina. Ultimate Oceanpedia. 2016. (ENG., Illus.). 272p. (J). (gr. 2-5). 24.99 *(978-1-4263-2550-2(9),* National Geographic Children's Bks.) National Geographic Society.

Wood, A. J. Lift & Learn: in the Ocean. Pledger, Maurice, illus. 2017. (ENG.). 18p. (J). bds. 14.99 ***(978-1-62686-943-1(X),*** Silver Dolphin Bks.) Readerlink Distribution Services, LLC.

Woods, Michael & Woods, Mary B. Seven Natural Wonders of the Arctic, Antarctica, & the Oceans. 2009. (Seven Wonders Ser.). (ENG., Illus.). 80p. (gr. 5-8). 33.26 *(978-0-8225-9075-0(1))* Lerner Publishing Group.

Woodward, John. Oceans. 2004. (Geography Fact Files Ser.). (J). lib. bdg. 28.50 *(978-1-58340-427-0(9))* Black Rabbit Bks.

—Oceans. (Illus.). 64p. (YA). (gr. 4-18). lib. bdg. 29.95 *(978-1-59389-125-1(3))* Chrysalis Education.

World Book, Inc. Staff, contrib. by. Oceans & Climate Change. 2015. (Illus.). 44p. (J). *(978-0-7166-2710-4(8))* World Bk., Inc.

World Book, Inc Staff, contrib. by. Treasures of the Ocean. 2017. (J). ***(978-0-7166-3370-9(1))*** World Bk., Inc.

Young, Karen Romano. No Bones! 2016. (Smithsonian Ser.). (ENG., Illus.). 48p. (J). (gr. 1-3). pap. 3.99 *(978-0-399-54131-5(4),* Penguin Young Readers) Penguin Young Readers Group.

Zoehfeld, Kathleen Weidner. How Deep Is the Ocean? Puybaret, Eric, illus. 2016. (Let's-Read-And-Find-Out Science 2 Ser.). 40p. (J). (gr. -1-3). pap. 6.99 *(978-0-06-232819-9(0))* HarperCollins Pubs.

Zondervan Staff & Schriemer, Peter. Ocean Adventures, Volume 1: Whales, Waves, & Ocean Wonders, 1 vol. 2013. (Nature of God Ser.). (ENG.). (J). 7.99 *(978-0-310-88832-1(8))* Zonderkidz.

—Ocean Adventures, Volume 2: Fins, Foliage, & Shoreline Fun, 1 vol. 2013. (Nature of God Ser.). (ENG.). (J). 7.99 *(978-0-310-88838-3(7))* Zonderkidz.

Zorzi, Gina & Sanchez, Lucia M. OcéAnos: This Is an Ocean. 2011. (poder de 100 - Ecosistemas (Power 100 - Ecosystems) Ser.). (SPA.). 28p. (J). pap. 7.95 *(978-1-61541-428-4(2))* American Reading Co.

OCEAN—ECONOMIC ASPECTS

see Marine Resources

OCEAN—FICTION

Altbacker, E. J. Enemy of Oceans. 2013. (Shark Wars Ser.: 5). (ENG., Illus.). 256p. (J). (gr. 3-7). 12.99 *(978-1-59514-476-8(5),* Razorbill) Penguin Young Readers Group.

Anderson, Carolyn. Water Queen & the Sea of Kings. 2013. 28p. pap. 24.95 *(978-1-63000-446-0(4))* America Star Bks.

Appelt, Kathi. Keeper. Hall, August, illus. (ENG.). (J). (gr. 3-7). 2012. 432p. pap. 8.99 *(978-1-4169-5061-5(3))* 2010. 416p. 17.99 *(978-1-4169-5060-8(5))* Simon & Schuster Children's Publishing. (Atheneum Bks. for Young Readers).

Aureliani, Franco. Dino-Mike & the Underwater Dinosaurs. Aureliani, Franco, illus. 2015. (Dino-Mike! Ser.). (ENG., Illus.). 128p. (gr. 1-3). lib. bdg. 25.32 *(978-1-4342-9629-0(6))* Stone Arch Bks.

Averill, Esther. Jenny Goes to Sea. Averill, Esther, illus. 2005. (New York Review Children's Collection). (ENG., Illus.). 140p. (J). (gr. k-4). reprint ed. 17.95 *(978-1-59017-155-4(1),* NYR Children's Collection) New York Review of Bks., Inc., The.

Berkes, Marianne. Over in the Ocean: In a Coral Reef. Canyon, Jeanette, illus. 2006. (Simply Nature Bks.). (ENG.). 26p. (J). (gr. -1). bds. 7.95 *(978-1-58469-082-5(8))* Dawn Pubns.

Bozanich, Tony L. & Wight, Joe. Nazi Zombies. Isaksen, Patricia, ed. Isaksen, Lisa A., illus. 2013. (ENG.). 112p. (gr. -1-4). pap. 14.95 *(978-0-930655-00-6(1),* 9780930655006) Antarctic Pr., Inc.

Brezenoff, Steve. Overboard, 1 vol. Murphy, Scott, illus. 2012. (Return to Titanic Ser.). (ENG.). 112p. (gr. 2-3). pap. 6.95 *(978-1-4342-3912-9(8));* lib. bdg. 25.32 *(978-1-4342-3302-8(2))* Stone Arch Bks. (Return to Titanic).

—Stowaways, 1 vol. Murphy, Scott, illus. 2012. (Return to Titanic Ser.). (ENG.). 112p. (gr. 2-3). pap. 6.95 *(978-1-4342-3910-5(1));* lib. bdg. 25.32 *(978-1-4342-3300-4(6))* Stone Arch Bks. (Return to Titanic).

—Time Voyage, 1 vol. Murphy, Scott, illus. 2012. (Return to Titanic Ser.). (ENG.). 112p. (gr. 2-3). pap. 6.95 *(978-1-4342-3909-9(8));* lib. bdg. 25.32 *(978-1-4342-3299-1(9))* Stone Arch Bks. (Return to Titanic).

—An Unsinkable Ship, 1 vol. Murphy, Scott, illus. 2012. (Return to Titanic Ser.). (ENG.). 112p. (gr. 2-3). lib. bdg. 25.32 *(978-1-4342-3301-1(4),* Return to Titanic) Stone Arch Bks.

Brouillette, Kathy. What Makes me Smile. 2010. 16p. 8.99 *(978-1-4520-1112-7(5))* AuthorHouse.

Buckingham, Matt. Bright Stanley. 2006. (Illus.). 32p. (J). (gr. -1-3). 15.95 *(978-1-58925-059-8(1))* Tiger Tales.

Case, Julie. Emma & the Whale. White, Lee, illus. 2017. (ENG.). 40p. (J). (gr. -1-3). 17.99 *(978-0-553-53847-2(0),* Schwartz & Wade Bks.) Random Hse. Children's Bks.

Cassano, Carol E. A Journey to the Bottom of the Ocean: Heavenly Adventures Volume 2. 2011. 20p. pap. *(978-1-4269-7335-2(7))* Trafford Publishing (UK) Ltd.

Corwin, Katherine A. R. Greg the Bearded Dragon & Thomas the Sea Turtle: A Tale of Adventure, Discovery, & Friendship. 2012. 28p. pap. 19.99 *(978-1-4685-7958-1(4))* AuthorHouse.

Cowan, Catherine. My Life with the Wave. 2004. (Illus.). (J). (gr. k-3). spiral bd. *(978-0-616-01621-3(2))* Canadian National Institute for the Blind/Institut National Canadien pour les Aveugles.

—My Life with the Wave. Buehner, Mark, illus. 2004. (ENG.). 32p. (J). (gr. -1-3). reprint ed. pap. 7.99 *(978-0-06-056200-7(5))* HarperCollins Pubs.

Croteau, Marie-Danielle & St. Aubin, Bruno. Des Fantomes Sous la Mer. 2003. (Roman Jeunesse Ser.). (FRE., Illus.). 96p. (J). (gr. 4-7). pap. *(978-2-89021-610-5(1))* Diffusion du livre Mirabel (DLM).

Davis, Caroline. Sparkly Ocean. Davis, Caroline, illus. 2008. (Tiger Tales Ser.). (Illus.). 8p. (J). (gr. -1). bds. 6.95 *(978-1-58925-832-7(0))* Tiger Tales.

Disney. Disney Moana: Call of the Ocean. 2016. (ENG.). 12p. (J). (gr. -1-1). 8.99 *(978-0-7944-3797-8(4),* Reader's Digest Children's Bks.) Studio Fun International.

Disney Editors. Ocean of Color. 2016. (Step into Reading Level 1 Ser.). lib. bdg. 14.75 *(978-0-606-38890-0(7))* Turtleback Bks.

Duey, Kathleen & Bale, Karen A. Titanic: April 1912. 2014. (Survivors Ser.). (ENG., Illus.). 192p. (J). (gr. 3-7). pap. 7.99 *(978-1-4424-9051-2(9),* Aladdin) Simon & Schuster Children's Publishing.

Engler, Zoe. The Lonely Starfish, 1 vol. 2010. 26p. 24.95 *(978-1-4489-2929-0(6))* PublishAmerica, Inc.

Floerchinger, Lori Liddic. Ocean of Dreams. Floerchinger, Jeremy, illus. 2008. 36p. pap. 24.95 *(978-1-60703-003-4(9))* America Star Bks.

Flynn, Pat. To the Light. Stewart, Chantal, illus. 2005. 120p. (Orig.). (YA). pap. *(978-0-7022-3492-7(3))* Univ. of Queensland Pr.

Fontes, Justine & Fontes, Ron. Casebook: The Bermuda Triangle. 2009. (Top Secret Graphica Mysteries Ser.). (Illus.). 48p. (YA). (gr. 2-6). 29.25 *(978-1-60754-591-0(8));* pap. 11.75 *(978-1-60754-592-7(6))* Windmill Bks.

Fuson, Robin Densmore. Rosita Valdez: And the Giant Sea Turtle. 2012. 108p. 28.99 *(978-1-4497-6487-6(8));* pap. 11.99 *(978-1-4497-6486-9(X))* Author Solutions, Inc. (WestBow Pr.).

Gillingham, Sara. In My Ocean. Siminovich, Lorena, illus. 2011. (ENG.). 12p. (J). (gr. -1 — 1). bds. 8.99 *(978-0-8118-7717-6(5))* Chronicle Bks. LLC.

Glennon, Michelle. My Big Green Teacher: Don't Rock the Boat: Saving Our Oceans. Glennon, Michelle, illus. 2008. (Illus.). 32p. (J). 19.95 *(978-0-9796625-2-2(4))* GDG Publishing.

Groves. Bee & the Sea, Bk. 9. Date not set. (Illus.). 32p. (J). pap. 129.15 *(978-0-582-18770-2(2))* Addison-Wesley Longman, Ltd. GBR. Dist: Trans-Atlantic Pubns., Inc.

Hanton, Sophie. Colors by the Sea. 2009. (Mag-NUT-Tics! Ser.). (Illus.). (J). bds. 9.99 *(978-1-934650-73-8(0))* Just For Kids Pr., LLC.

Haydon, Elizabeth. The Tree of Water. Dorman, Brandon, illus. 2014. (Lost Journals of Ven Polypheme Ser.: 4). (ENG.). 400p. (J). (gr. 5-9). 17.99 *(978-0-7653-2059-9(2),* 9780765320599, Starscape) Doherty, Tom Assocs., LLC.

Hayes, Karel. The Amazing Journey of Lucky the Lobster Buoy. 2009. (ENG.). 32p. (J). (gr. -1-3). 16.95 *(978-0-89272-791-9(8))* Down East Bks.

Hogan, Barbara. How Ryan & Aiden Saved the Ocean. 2013. 36p. pap. 16.99 *(978-1-4525-7776-0(5),* Balboa Pr.) Author Solutions, Inc.

Holloway, Christina. Irish Selkie. 2008. 12p. pap. 24.95 *(978-1-60610-693-8(7))* America Star Bks.

Holub, Joan & Williams, Suzanne. Poseidon & the Sea of Fury. 2012. (Heroes in Training Ser.: 2). lib. bdg. 16.00 *(978-0-606-26904-9(5),* Turtleback) Turtleback Bks.

Holyoke, Polly. The Neptune Challenge. 2015. (ENG.). 352p. (J). (gr. 3-7). 16.99 *(978-1-4847-1345-7(1))* Hyperion Bks. for Children.

Homberg, Ruth. Across the Sea. 2016. (Disney Princess Step into Reading Ser.). lib. bdg. 14.75 *(978-0-606-38472-8(3))* Turtleback Bks.

Howells, Amanda. The Summer of Skinny Dipping. 2010. (ENG.). 304p. (YA). (gr. 7-12). pap. 9.99 *(978-1-4022-3862-8(2),* Sourcebooks Jabberwocky) Sourcebooks, Inc.

Inches, Alison. I Can Save the Ocean! The Little Green Monster Cleans up the Beach. Garofoli, Viviana, illus. 2010. (Little Green Bks.). (ENG.). 24p. (J). (gr. -1-1). 7.99 *(978-1-4169-9514-2(5),* Little Simon) Little Simon.

Isabel, Michelle. Murtle the Sea Turtle. Isabel, Michelle & Thomas, Franselica, illus. 2011. 24p. pap. 24.95 *(978-1-4626-0114-1(6))* America Star Bks.

Jasper, Mark & Kelly, Cooper. Good Night Ocean. Veno, Joe & Kelly, Cooper, illus. 2009. (Good Night Our World Ser.). (ENG.). 20p. (J). (gr. k — 1). bds. 9.95 *(978-1-60219-036-8(4))* Good Night Bks.

Joy, Linda. Little Wave & the Mission of Laura Hawksbill. 2012. 24p. pap. 15.99 *(978-1-4691-9178-2(4))* Xlibris Corp.

Jupin, David Perez, illus. Love. 2013. 20p. pap. 11.95 *(978-1-937504-67-0(0))* Worthy Shorts.

Karas, G. Brian. Atlantic. 2014. 32p. pap. 7.00 *(978-1-61003-315-2(9))* Center for the Collaborative Classroom.

Kerr, Gordon. Story of Robinson Crusoe. 2006. 100p. per. *(978-1-4067-2131-7(X),* Hesperides Pr.) Read Bks.

Kruse, Robyn A. Sammy the Sea Turtle, 1 vol. Litteral, Christopher, illus. 2010. 18p. 24.95 *(978-1-4489-4020-2(6))* PublishAmerica, Inc.

Lewis, Anthony, illus. Little Ocean Explorers. 2007. (Little Explorers Ser.). (ENG.). 14p. (J). (gr. 1-1). bds. *(978-1-84643-039-8(9))* Child's Play International Ltd.

Maclear, Kyo. The Specific Ocean. Maurey, Katty, illus. 2015. (ENG.). 32p. (J). (gr. -1-3). 17.95 *(978-1-894786-35-5(1))* Kids Can Pr., Ltd. CAN. Dist: Hachette Bk. Group.

Mae, Darcie. Sammy & Robert. 2008. 24p. pap. 24.95 *(978-1-60474-811-6(7))* America Star Bks.

—Sammy & Robert Discover the Ocean, 1 vol. 2009. 39p. pap. 24.95 *(978-1-61546-827-0(7))* America Star Bks.

Maine, Margarita. Un Mar Muy Mojado. (SPA.). pap. 8.95 *(978-950-07-1985-8(1))* Editorial Sudamericana S.A. ARG. Dist: Distribooks, Inc.

Marsh, Carole. The Mystery of the Graveyard of the Atlantic. 2009. (Real Kids, Real Places Ser.). (Illus.). 144p. (J). lib. bdg. 18.99 *(978-0-635-07046-3(4),* Marsh, Carole Mysteries) Gallopade International.

Marshall, Edward & Marshall, James. Three by the Sea. 48p. (J). (gr. k-3). pap. 3.99 *(978-0-8072-1342-1(X),* Listening Library) Random Hse. Audio Publishing Group.

Mayer, Mercer. Little Critter: 5-Minute Little Critter Stories. Mayer, Mercer, illus. 2017. (Little Critter Ser.). (Illus.). 192p. (J). (gr. -1-3). 12.99 ***(978-0-06-265525-7(6)***, HarperFestival) HarperCollins Pubs.

Mayer, Mercer. Little Critter: Just an Adventure at Sea. Mayer, Mercer, illus. 2017. (My First I Can Read Ser.). (Illus.). 32p. (J). (gr. -1-3). pap. 3.99 *(978-0-06-243140-0(4))* HarperCollins Pubs.

McCarthy, Jenna & Evans, Carolyn. Maggie Malone Makes a Splash. 2015. (Maggie Malone Ser.: 3). (ENG.). 192p. (J). (gr. 4-7). pap. 8.99 *(978-1-4022-9312-2(7)*, Sourcebooks Jabberwocky) Sourcebooks, Inc.

McGinnis, Mindy. Given to the Sea. 2017. (Given Duet Ser.). (ENG.). 352p. (YA). (gr. 9). 17.99 *(978-0-399-54461-3(5)*, G.P. Putnam's Sons Books for Young Readers) Penguin Young Readers Group.

Meadows, Daisy. Courtney the Clownfish Fairy. 2011. (Illus.). 62p. (J). *(978-0-545-28877-4(0))* Scholastic, Inc.

Meister, Cari. Ocean Tales. Harpster, Steve, illus. 2013. (Ocean Tales Ser.). (ENG.). 32p. (gr. -1-3). 158.55 *(978-1-4342-8844-8(7))* Stone Arch Bks.

Meyer, L. A. Rapture of the Deep: Being an Account of the Further Adventures of Jacky Faber, Soldier, Sailor, Mermaid, Spy. 2009. (Bloody Jack Adventures Ser.: 7). (ENG., Illus.). 464p. (YA). (gr. 9-18). 17.00 *(978-0-15-206501-0(6))* Houghton Mifflin Harcourt Publishing Co.

Milbourne, Anna. How Deep Is the Sea? Riglietti, Serena, illus. 2010. (Picture Bks). 24p. (J). 10.99 *(978-0-7945-2311-4(0))* EDC Publishing.

Miller, Jay. Sal & Sally. 2008. 52p. pap. 20.49 *(978-1-935028-13-0(8))* AuthorHouse.

Morgan, G. A. Chantarelle, 1 vol. 2015. (Five Stones Trilogy Ser.: 2). (ENG.). 316p. (J). pap. 18.95 *(978-1-939017-63-5(7)*, a178678b-3da7-4c5c-96c5-09386c28787e) Islandport Pr., Inc.

O'Neill, Michael Patrick. Fishy Friends: A Journey Through the Coral Kingdom. O'Neill, Michael Patrick, photos by. 2003. (Illus.). 64p. (J). 19.95 *(978-0-9728653-0-2(6))* Batfish Bks.

Pallotta, Jerry. Dory Story. Biedrzycki, David, illus. 2006. (ENG.). 32p. (J). (gr. -1-3). pap. 7.95 *(978-0-88106-076-8(3))* Charlesbridge Publishing, Inc.

Pallotta, Jerry, et al. Dory Story. Biedrzycki, David, illus. 2003. (Avenues Ser.). (ENG.). 32p. (C). (gr. -1-3). pap. 27.95 *(978-0-88106-075-1(5))* National Geographic School Publishing, Inc.

PAN Macmillan, P. A. N. Pirates. Van De Leijgraaf, Deborah, illus. 2015. (First Sticker Story Fun Ser.). (ENG.). 30p. (J). (gr. -1-k). pap. 9.99 ***(978-1-4472-8674-5(X))*** Pan Macmillan GBR. Dist: Independent Pubs. Group.

Pearce, Jackson. Fathomless. 2013. (Fairy Tale Retelling Ser.). (ENG.). 320p. (YA). (gr. 10-17). pap. 8.99 *(978-0-316-20777-5(2))* Little, Brown Bks. for Young Readers.

Peck, Jan. Way down Deep in the Deep Blue Sea. Petrone, Valeria, illus. 2004. (ENG.). 32p. (J). (gr. -1-3). 17.99 *(978-0-689-85110-0(3)*, Simon & Schuster Bks. For Young Readers) Simon & Schuster Bks. For Young Readers.

Pelosi, Vincent L. The Magical Underwater Kingdom of Balenarium. 2012. 200p. 46.72 *(978-1-4797-1951-8(X))*; pap. 28.03 *(978-1-4797-1950-1(1))* Xlibris Corp.

Piano, Maureen. When Flamingos Fly: Discovering the Wonders of the World. 2006. (Illus.). 44p. (J). (gr. -1-3). pap. 12.99 incl. audio compact disk *(978-1-59092-362-7(6))* Blue Forge Pr.

Picard, Matthias. Jim Curious: A Voyage to the Heart of the Sea in 3-D Vision. 2014. (ENG., Illus.). 52p. (J). (gr. 1-4). 19.95 *(978-1-4197-1043-8(5)*, Abrams Bks. for Young Readers) Abrams, Inc.

Pitt, Sarah. Peek a Boo! Ocean. 2009. (Little Peek a Boo Bks.). (Illus.). (J). bds. 9.99 *(978-1-934650-58-5(7))* Just For Kids Pr., LLC.

Plourde, Lynn. The First Feud: Between the Mountain & the Sea. Sollers, Jim, illus. 2003. (ENG.). 30p. (J). (gr. k-17). 15.95 *(978-0-89272-611-0(3))* Down East Bks.

Porta, Bill K. Adventures of Henry the Little Boat. 2011. 24p. (gr. -1). pap. 11.32 *(978-1-4520-4448-4(1))* AuthorHouse.

The Quest for Courage. 2006. (Amazing Travels of Wannabeb Ser.). (Illus.). 32p. (J). (gr. -1-3). 8.99 *(978-0-7847-1801-8(6)*, 04127) Standard Publishing.

Rash, Ron. The Shark's Tooth. Martin, Cecile L. K., illus. 2015. (Young Palmetto Bks.). (ENG.). 40p. (J). pap. 12.95 *(978-1-61117-527-1(5))* Univ. of South Carolina Pr.

Reasoner, Charles. Numbers under the Sea. Pitt, Sarah, illus. 2009. (3D Board Bks.). 12p. (J). (gr. -1-k). bds. 9.99 *(978-1-934650-37-0(4))* Just For Kids Pr., LLC.

Rey, H. A. Curious George Discovers the Ocean (Science Storybook) 2015. (Curious George Ser.). (ENG., Illus.). 32p. (J). (gr. -1-3). 6.99 *(978-0-544-43065-5(4)*, HMH Books For Young Readers) Houghton Mifflin Harcourt Publishing Co.

RH Disney. Moana: the Deluxe Junior Novelization (Disney Moana) RH Disney, illus. 2016. (Deluxe Junior Novel Ser.). (ENG., Illus.). 144p. (J). (gr. 2-5). 9.99 *(978-0-7364-3574-1(3)*, RH/Disney) Random Hse. Children's Bks.

—An Ocean Adventure. RH Disney, illus. 2016. (Magnetic Play Book Ser.). (ENG., Illus.). 8p. (J). (-k). bds. 9.99 *(978-0-7364-3626-7(X)*, Random Hse. Bks. for Young Readers) Random Hse. Children's Bks.

Roth, Megan. Bright Books: Bubble's Ocean Friends. Hayashi, Emiri, illus. 2016. (Bright Bks.). (ENG.). 12p. (J). bds. 14.99 *(978-1-62686-716-1(X)*, Silver Dolphin Bks.) Readerlink Distribution Services, LLC.

Ryan, Pam Muñoz. Hello Ocean. Astrella, Mark, illus. 2014. 32p. pap. 8.00 *(978-1-61003-319-0(1))* Center for the Collaborative Classroom.

—Hello, Ocean / Hola Mar. Canetti, Yanitzia, tr. from ENG. Astrella, Mark, illus. 2003. (ENG & SPA.). 32p. (J). (gr. -1-2). pap. 7.95 *(978-1-57091-372-3(2))* Charlesbridge Publishing, Inc.

Santillo, LuAnn. Flap. Santillo, LuAnn, ed. 2003. (Half-Pint Kids Readers Ser.). (Illus.). 7p. (J). (gr. -1-1). pap. 1.00 *(978-1-59256-096-7(2))* Half-Pint Kids, Inc.

Santoro, Lucio & Santoro, Meera. Wild Oceans: A Pop-Up Book with Revolutionary Technology. 2010. (ENG.). 12p. (J). (gr. 1-5). 29.99 *(978-1-4169-8467-2(4)*, Little Simon) Little Simon.

Sconyers, Jennifer. John Bunny Goes on Vacation. 2010. 20p. pap. 12.99 *(978-1-4490-7774-7(9))* AuthorHouse.

Scott, Jeff. The Discovery of Monkey Island. 2008. 64p. pap. 19.95 *(978-1-60610-921-2(9))* America Star Bks.

Seven, John. The Ocean Story, 1 vol. Christy, Jana, illus. 2011. (Fiction Picture Bks.). (ENG.). 32p. (gr. k-2). lib. bdg. 23.99 *(978-1-4048-6785-7(6)*, Fiction Picture Bks.) Picture Window Bks.

Shasha, Mark. Night of the Moonjellies: 15th Anniversary Edition. 2007. (Illus.). 32p. (J). (gr. -1-2). 12.95 *(978-1-930900-34-9(1))* Purple Hse. Pr.

Simmons, Derek. Flash of Life. 2006. 85p. pap. 16.95 *(978-1-4241-3890-6(6))* PublishAmerica, Inc.

Simpson, Dorothy. Visitors from the Sea. Date not set. 188p. (J). 20.95 *(978-0-8488-2632-1(9))* Amereon Ltd.

small world creations ltd. Blubb, Blubb! 2017. (Magic Bath Bks.). (ENG.). 8p. (J). (gr. -1 — 1). 5.99 ***(978-1-4380-7843-4(9))*** Barron's Educational Series, Inc.

Smith, Sindy. Dadu the Dolphin. Smith, Sindy, illus. 2012. (Illus.). 24p. 29.95 *(978-1-4626-9862-2(X))* America Star Bks.

Sollinger, Emily. Diego's Ocean Adventure: A Book of Facts about Ocean Animals. Mawhinney, Art, illus. 2008. (Go, Diego, Go! Ser.). (ENG.). 16p. (J). (gr. -1-2). pap. 6.99 *(978-1-4169-4781-3(7)*, Simon Spotlight/Nickelodeon) Simon Spotlight/Nickelodeon.

Spradlin, Michael P. Into the Killing Seas. 2015. (ENG.). 224p. (J). (gr. 3-7). 16.99 *(978-0-545-72602-3(6)*, Scholastic Pr.) Scholastic, Inc.

St. Pierre, Stephanie. What the Sea Saw, 1 vol. Doyle, Beverly, illus. 2006. (ENG.). 48p. (J). (gr. k-3). 16.95 *(978-1-56145-359-7(5))* Peachtree Pubs.

Stevenson, William. Ricky's Dream Trip under the Sea. 2013. 38p. pap. 13.50 *(978-1-936517-85-5(X))* Micro Publishing Media, Inc.

Stilton, Thea. The Treasure of the Sea. 5th ed. 2016. (Thea Stilton Special Edition Ser.: 5). (ENG.). 320p. (J). (gr. 2-5). 14.99 *(978-1-338-03290-1(9)*, Scholastic Paperbacks) Scholastic, Inc.

Stratemeyer, Edward. The Rover Boys on the Ocean: Or, a Chase for a Fortune. 2007. (ENG.). 158p. pap. 19.99 *(978-1-4264-2766-4(2))*; 170p. pap. 21.99 *(978-1-4264-2804-3(9))* Creative Media Partners, LLC.

ToyBox Innovations, creator. Disney's the Little Mermaid. abr. ed. 2006. (Disney's Read along Collection). (ENG.). (J). (gr. -1-3). pap. *(978-0-7634-2184-7(7))* Walt Disney Records.

Twins, Pope, illus. Poke-A-Dot!: Who's in the Ocean? (30 Poke-able Poppin' Dots) 2012. (ENG.). 1p. (J). (gr. -1-1). 14.99 *(978-1-60169-270-2(2))* Innovative Kids.

Under the Sea Magic Painting Book. 2017. (Magic Painting Bks.). (ENG.). (J). pap. 9.99 ***(978-0-7945-3958-0(0)***, Usborne) EDC Publishing.

Van Tassel, Mary. Beach Ball's Journey, 1 vol. 2010. 18p. pap. 24.95 *(978-1-4489-9618-6(X))* America Star Bks.

Villoldo, Alberto. Skeleton Woman. 2008. (ENG.). 36p. (J). (gr. -1-3). 12.99 *(978-1-4169-8962-2(5)*, Simon & Schuster Bks. For Young Readers) Simon & Schuster Bks. For Young Readers.

Viva, Frank. A Long Way Away. 2013. (ENG., Illus.). 40p. (J). (gr. -1-3). 16.99 *(978-0-316-22196-2(1))* Little, Brown Bks. for Young Readers.

What's under the Sea? 2003. (J). per. *(978-1-57657-934-3(4))* Paradise Pr., Inc.

Williams, Greg. Salty the Sea Gull. 2011. 38p. pap. 19.00 *(978-1-60746-205-7(2))* FastPrncil, Inc.

Worthington, Michelle. Start of the Ocean. Finn, Ann-Marie, illus. 2013. 32p. pap. *(978-0-9874160-1-8(4))* Wybble Publishing.

Wright, Mary. Co-Man & Poppa Meet Kanka. Dewitt, Levi, illus. 2013. 24p. pap. 24.95 *(978-1-62709-328-6(1))* America Star Bks.

Yee, Paul. The Jade Necklace. Lin, Grace, illus. 2006. 29p. (J). (gr. 4-8). reprint ed. 16.00 *(978-1-4223-5135-2(1))* DIANE Publishing Co.

OCEAN BOTTOM

Aleshire & Peter. Ocean Ridges & Trenches. 2007. (Extreme Earth Ser.). (Illus.). 176p. (J). (gr. 7-12). 35.00 *(978-0-8160-5919-5(5))* Facts On File, Inc.

Cerullo, Mary M. Sharks of the Deep: A Shark Photographer's Search for Sharks at the Bottom of the Sea, 1 vol. Rotman, Jeffrey L., illus. Rotman, Jeffrey L., photos by. 2014. (Shark Expedition Ser.). (ENG.). 40p. (gr. 5-7). lib. bdg. 31.99 *(978-0-7565-4886-5(1))* Compass Point Bks.

Cole, Joanna. On the Ocean Floor. Degen, Bruce, illus. 2010. (Magic School Bus Ser.). (ENG.). (J). (gr. 2-5). 9.99 *(978-0-545-22751-3(8))* Scholastic, Inc.

Macken, JoAnn Early. Ocean Floors. 2005. (Water Habitats Ser.). (Illus.). 24p. (gr. k-3). lib. bdg. 22.00 *(978-0-8368-4885-4(3)*, Weekly Reader Leveled Readers) Stevens, Gareth Publishing LLLP.

—Ocean Floors (Fondos Oceánicos) 2005. (Water Habitats/ Habitats acuaticos Ser.). (SPA., Illus.). 24p. (gr. k-3). pap. 8.15 *(978-0-8368-6037-5(3)*, Weekly Reader Leveled Readers) Stevens, Gareth Publishing LLLP.

Macken, JoAnn Early & Early Macken, JoAnn. Ocean Floors/Fondos Oceánicos. 2005. (Water Habitats/ Habitats acuaticos Ser.). (SPA., Illus.). 24p. (gr. k-3). lib. bdg. 22.00 *(978-0-8368-6030-6(6)*, Weekly Reader Leveled Readers) Stevens, Gareth Publishing LLLP.

Woodward, John. On the Seabed. 2010. (Oceans Alive! Ser.). 32p. lib. bdg. 28.50 *(978-1-933834-64-1(1))* Brown Bear Bks.

OCEAN LIFE

see Marine Biology

OCEAN ROUTES

see Trade Routes

OCEAN TRAVEL

Amato, William. Cruceros. 2004. (Vehículos de Alta Tecnología (High-Tech Vehicles) Ser.). (SPA & ENG., Illus.). 24p. (J). (gr. 2-4). lib. bdg. 22.60 *(978-0-8239-6884-8(7))* Rosen Publishing Group, Inc., The.

Bailey, Gerry. Sea Transportation. 2008. (Simply Science Ser.). (Illus.). 32p. (YA). (gr. 3-6). lib. bdg. 26.00 *(978-0-8368-9230-7(5))* Stevens, Gareth Publishing LLLP.

Brook, Henry. True Sea Stories. 2005. (True Adventure Stories Ser.). (Illus.). 154p. (J). (gr. 5). lib. bdg. 12.95 *(978-1-58086-693-4(X))* EDC Publishing.

Disney Editions, creator. Birnbaum's Disney Cruise Line. 2006. (Birnbaum's Disney Cruise Line Ser.). (ENG., Illus.). 224p. (gr. -1-17). per. 13.95 *(978-1-4231-0052-2(2)*, Disney Editions) Disney Pr.

Gregory, Josh. If You Were a Kid Aboard the Titanic. 2017. (If You Were a Kid Ser.). (ENG., Illus.). 32p. (J). lib. bdg. 26.00 *(978-0-531-22382-6(5)*, Children's Pr.) Scholastic Library Publishing.

Macdonald, Fiona. You Wouldn't Want to Sail with Christopher Columbus! (Revised Edition) 2014. (You Wouldn't Want to... Ser.). (ENG.). 32p. (J). lib. bdg. 29.00 *(978-0-531-21177-9(0)*, Watts, Franklin) Scholastic Library Publishing.

Parker, Steven. On Water. 2011. (Future Transport Ser.). (Illus.). 32p. (J). (gr. 4). 28.50 *(978-1-60870-780-5(6))* Marshall Cavendish Corp.

Paulsen, Gary. Caught by the Sea: My Life on Boats. 2003. (Illus.). 103p. (gr. 7). 16.00 *(978-0-7569-1635-0(6))* Perfection Learning Corp.

—Caught by the Sea: My Life on Boats. 2003. (ENG., Illus.). 112p. (YA). (gr. 7). mass mkt. 5.99 *(978-0-440-40716-4(8)*, Laurel Leaf) Random Hse. Children's Bks.

West, David. Ten of the Best Adventures on the Seas. 2015. (Ten of the Best: Stories of Exploration & Adventure Ser.). (ENG., Illus.). 24p. (J). (gr. 3-6). *(978-0-7787-1839-0(5))* Crabtree Publishing Co.

Zimmermann, Karl. Ocean Liners: Crossing & Cruising the Seven Seas. 2008. (ENG., Illus.). 48p. (J). (gr. 4-7). 17.95 *(978-1-59078-552-2(5))* Boyds Mills Pr.

OCEAN TRAVEL—FICTION

Abbott, Jacob. Rollo on the Atlantic. 2008. 116p. 23.95 *(978-1-60664-822-3(5))*; pap. 9.95 *(978-1-60664-067-8(4))* Aegypan.

Alger, Horatio. Brave & Bold. 2005. 28.95 *(978-1-4218-1452-0(8))*; 280p. pap. 13.95 *(978-1-4218-1552-7(4))* 1st World Publishing, Inc. (1st World Library - Literary Society).

—Brave & Bold. 2006. 152p. per. 12.95 *(978-1-59818-652-9(3))*; 24.95 *(978-1-59818-570-6(5))* Aegypan.

—Brave & Bold: The Fortunes of Robert Rushton. 2007. (ENG.). 188p. per. 19.99 *(978-1-4346-4411-4(1))*; 208p. per. 22.99 *(978-1-4346-4412-1(X))* Creative Media Partners, LLC.

Boisrobert, Anouck & Rigaud, Louis. Under the Ocean. 2014. (ENG., Illus.). 10p. (gr. -1-17). 19.95 *(978-1-84976-159-8(0))* Tate Publishing, Ltd. GBR. Dist: Abrams, Inc.

Buckey, Sarah Masters. The Stolen Sapphire. 2007. (American Girl Mysteries Ser.). (Illus.). 181p. (gr. 4-7). 17.45 *(978-0-7569-8278-2(2))* Perfection Learning Corp.

Bunting, Eve. S. O. S. Titanic. 2012. (ENG.). 256p. (YA). (gr. 7-12). pap. 7.99 *(978-0-15-201305-9(9))* Houghton Mifflin Harcourt Publishing Co.

Coatsworth, Elizabeth Jane. The Fair American. Sewell, Helen, illus. 2005. (Sally (Bethlehem Books) Ser.). 137p. (J). pap. 11.95 *(978-1-883937-85-0(X))* Bethlehem Bks.

Deutsch, Neil. Rose & the Pelican. 2013. 32p. pap. 19.99 *(978-1-4817-0947-7(X))* AuthorHouse.

Else, Barbara. The Traveling Restaurant: Jasper's Voyage in Three Parts. 2012. (Gecko Press Titles Ser.). (ENG.). 304p. (J). (gr. 5-8). 17.95 *(978-1-877579-03-5(3))* Gecko Pr. NZL. Dist: Lerner Publishing Group.

George, Jessica Day. Saturdays at Sea. 2017. (Tuesdays at the Castle Ser.). (ENG.). 272p. (J). 16.99 *(978-1-61963-957-7(2)*, 9781619639577, Bloomsbury USA Childrens) Bloomsbury Publishing USA.

Jorgensen, Norman. Smuggler's Curse The. 2017. (ENG.). 356p. (J). (gr. 4-7). 8.95 ***(978-1-925164-19-0(5))*** Fremantle Pr. AUS. Dist: Independent Pubs. Group.

Keene, Carolyn. Curse of the Arctic Star. 2013. (Nancy Drew Diaries: 1). (ENG.). 208p. (J). (gr. 3-7). 15.99 *(978-1-4424-6610-4(3)*, Aladdin) Simon & Schuster Children's Publishing.

—Nancy Drew Diaries: Curse of the Arctic Star; Strangers on a Train; Mystery of the Midnight Rider; Once upon a Thriller. 2013. (Nancy Drew Diaries). (ENG., Illus.). 768p. (J). (gr. 3-7). pap. 27.99 *(978-1-4424-8896-0(4)*, Aladdin) Simon & Schuster Children's Publishing.

—Once upon a Thriller. 2013. (Nancy Drew Diaries: 4). (ENG., Illus.). 144p. (J). (gr. 3-7). 15.99 *(978-1-4424-6612-8(X))*; pap. 6.99 *(978-1-4169-9074-1(7))* Simon & Schuster Children's Publishing. (Aladdin).

Kehret, Peg. Secret Journey. 2008. (ENG.). 144p. (J). (gr. 3-7). pap. 8.99 *(978-1-4169-9112-0(3)*, Simon & Schuster/Paula Wiseman Bks.) Simon & Schuster/Paula Wiseman Bks.

Kisko, Stephen. Sailing the Puddles. 2013. 36p. pap. 12.95 *(978-1-62838-002-6(0))* Page Publishing Inc.

Klise, Kate. The Circus Goes to Sea. Klise, M. Sarah, illus. 2014. (Three-Ring Rascals Ser.: Book 3). (ENG.). 160p. (J). 15.95 *(978-1-61620-365-8(X)*, 73365) Algonquin Bks. of Chapel Hill.

Lalicki, Tom. Shots at Sea: A Houdini & Nate Mystery. 2011. (Houdini & Nate Mysteries Ser.). 224p. (J). pap. 6.99 *(978-0-312-65920-2(2))* Square Fish.

Lawrence, Iain. The Convicts. 2006. 15.10 *(978-0-7569-6901-1(8))* Random House Children's Books GBR. Dist: Perfection Learning Corp.

Manus, Willard. A Dog Called Leka. 2007. (ENG.). 122p. pap. 7.99 *(978-0-9740551-3-8(1))* Smith, Viveca Publishing.

Mumford, Carole. Caribbean Cruise Summer Vacation: A Magnificent Six Adventure, 1 vol. 2009. 96p. pap. 16.95 *(978-1-61546-760-0(2))* PublishAmerica, Inc.

Neale, Cynthia G. The Irish Dresser: A Story of Hope During the Great Hunger (an Gorta Mor, 1845-1850) 2003. 148p. (J). pap. 7.95 *(978-1-57249-344-5(5)*, White Mane Kids) White Mane Publishing Co., Inc.

Parker, Danny. Lola's Toybox: on the Story Sea. 2017. (Lola's Toy Box Ser.: 2). (ENG.). 96p. (J). (gr. k-2). pap. 6.99 *(978-1-76012-437-3(0))* Hardie Grant Egmont Pty, Ltd. AUS. Dist: Independent Pubs. Group.

Peck, Richard. Secrets at Sea. 2012. (ENG.). 272p. (J). (gr. 3-7). pap. 7.99 *(978-0-14-242183-3(9)*, Puffin Books) Penguin Young Readers Group.

—Secrets at Sea. Murphy, Kelly, illus. 2011. (ENG.). 256p. (J). (gr. 3-7). 16.99 *(978-0-8037-3455-5(7)*, Dial Bks) Penguin Young Readers Group.

Penn, Audrey & Miller, Joshua. Blackbeard & the Gift of Silence. 2009. (ENG.). 350p. (J). (gr. 2-7). pap. 8.95 *(978-1-933718-32-3(3))* Tanglewood Pr.

Redbank, Tennant. Treasure: Ariel's Curious Kitten. 2015. (Disney Princess Palace Pets Ser.). lib. bdg. 16.00 *(978-0-606-36392-1(0))* Turtleback Bks.

—Treasure: Ariel's Curious Kitten (Disney Princess: Palace Pets) RH Disney Staff et al, illus. 2015. (Stepping Stone Book(TM) Ser.). (ENG.). 64p. (J). (gr. 1-4). 5.99 *(978-0-7364-3346-4(5)*, RH/Disney) Random Hse. Children's Bks.

Roy, Lillian Elizabeth. Polly's Southern Cruise: The Polly Brewster Series. Barbour, H. S., illus. 2011. 294p. 48.95 *(978-1-258-10514-3(4))* Literary Licensing, LLC.

Schliewen, Richard. Paulina's Teddy Bear Journey. Visaya, Artemio, illus. 2012. 104p. 24.95 *(978-1-62709-055-1(X))* America Star Bks.

Shusterman, Neal. Challenger Deep. 2016. (YA). lib. bdg. 20.85 *(978-0-606-38734-7(X))* Turtleback Bks.

Smithwick, John W. Drift. 2012. 36p. pap. 13.95 *(978-1-61897-972-8(8)*, Strategic Bk. Publishing) Strategic Book Publishing & Rights Agency (SBPRA).

Snider, Jesse Blaze. Toy Story: Toy Overboard. Watson, Nathan, illus. 2011. 128p. (J). pap. 9.99 *(978-1-60886-605-2(X))* Boom! Studios.

Snow, Alan. Worse Things Happen at Sea! A Tale of Pirates, Poison, & Monsters. Snow, Alan, illus. 2013. (Ratbridge Chronicles Ser.: 2). (ENG., Illus.). 352p. (J). (gr. 3-9). 17.99 *(978-0-689-87049-1(3)*, Atheneum Bks. for Young Readers) Simon & Schuster Children's Publishing.

Staniszewski, Anna. Once upon a Cruise: a Wish Novel. 2016. (ENG.). 256p. (J). (gr. 3-7). pap. 6.99 *(978-0-545-87986-6(8)*, Scholastic Paperbacks) Scholastic, Inc.

Stewart, Paul & Riddell, Chris. Far-Flung Adventures: Corby Flood. 2012. (Far-Flung Adventures Ser.). (ENG.). 256p. (J). (gr. 3-7). 7.99 *(978-0-385-75097-4(8)*, Yearling) Random Hse. Children's Bks.

Stier, Catherine. Welcome to America, Champ. Ettinger, Doris, illus. 2013. (Tales of the World Ser.). (ENG.). 32p. (J). (gr. 1-4). 17.95 *(978-1-58536-606-4(4)*, 202360) Sleeping Bear Pr.

Tanner, Lian. Icebreaker. 2015. (Hidden Ser.: Bk. 1). (ENG.). 304p. (J). (gr. 4-7). 16.99 *(978-1-250-05216-2(5)*, 9781250052162) Feiwel & Friends.

—Sunker's Deep. 2016. (Icebreaker Trilogy Ser.: 2). (ENG.). 304p. (J). 16.99 *(978-1-250-05217-9(3)*, 9781250052179) Feiwel & Friends.

Tarshis, Lauren. I Survived the Sinking of the Titanic 1912. 2010. (I Survived Ser.: 1). (ENG., Illus.). 112p. (J). (gr. 2-5). 4.99 *(978-0-545-20694-5(4)*, Scholastic Paperbacks) Scholastic, Inc.

—I Survived the Sinking of the Titanic 1912. 2010. (I Survived Ser.: No. 1). lib. bdg. 14.75 *(978-0-606-23741-3(0)*, Turtleback) Turtleback Bks.

Wilson, John. Lost, 1 vol. 2016. (Orca Currents Ser.). (ENG.). 144p. (J). (gr. 5-9). pap. 9.95 *(978-1-4598-1195-9(X))* Orca Bk. Pubs. USA.

Winfield, Arthur M. The Rover Boys on Land & Sea or the Crusoes of Seven Islands. 2006. (ENG.). 284p. per. 28.95 *(978-1-4286-4097-9(5))* Kessinger Publishing, LLC.

Yin. Coolies. Soentpiet, Chris K., illus. 2003. (ENG.). 40p. (J). (gr. 2-5). 7.99 *(978-0-14-250055-2(0)*, Puffin Books) Penguin Young Readers Group.

Zaugg, Sandra L. Hidden Notes & High Seas. 2005. (Illus.). 95p. (J). *(978-0-8163-2052-3(7))* Pacific Pr. Pubns.

OCEAN WAVES

Dougherty, Terri. The Worst Tsunamis of All Time, 1 vol. 2012. (Epic Disasters Ser.). (ENG.). 32p. (gr. 3-4). lib. bdg. 27.99 *(978-1-4296-8416-3(X))* Capstone Press of Coughlan Cos.

Hawkins, John. Tsunami Disasters. 2011. (Catastrophe! Ser.). (ENG., Illus.). 48p. (J). (gr. 5-9). lib. bdg. 29.25 *(978-1-4488-6005-0(9))* Rosen Publishing Group, Inc., The.

Ingram, Scott. Tsunami! The 1946 Hilo Wave of Terror. 2005. (X-Treme Disasters That Changed America Ser.). (Illus.). 32p. (J). lib. bdg. 25.27 *(978-1-59716-010-0(5))* Bearport Publishing Co., Inc.

Mason, Janeen. Ocean Commotion: Caught in the Currents, 1 vol. Mason, Janeen, illus. 2012. (ENG., Illus.). 32p. (J). (gr. k-3). 16.99 *(978-1-58980-862-1(2))* Pelican Publishing Co., Inc.

Peppas, Lynn. Ocean, Tidal & Wave Energy: Power from the Sea. 2008. (Energy Revolution Ser.). (ENG., Illus.). 32p. (J). (gr. 3-8). pap. *(978-0-7787-2933-4(8))*; lib. bdg. *(978-0-7787-2919-8(2))* Crabtree Publishing Co.

Prokos, Anna & Keedle, Jayne. Tsunamis & Floods. 2008. (Ultimate 10 Ser.). (Illus.). 48p. (J). (gr. 5-9). lib. bdg. 31.00 *(978-0-8368-9154-6(6))* Stevens, Gareth Publishing LLLP.

Vogel, Carole G. Shifting Shores. 2003. (Restless Sea Ser.). (ENG., Illus.). 80p. (J). (gr. 5-8). 30.50 *(978-0-531-12322-5(7)*, Watts, Franklin) Scholastic Library Publishing.

Wendorff, Anne. Tsunamis. 2008. (Extreme Weather Ser.). (ENG., Illus.). 24p. (J). (gr. 2-5). lib. bdg. 25.95 *(978-1-60014-188-1(9))* Bellwether Media.

OCEANIA

see Islands of the Pacific

OCEANOGRAPHIC RESEARCH

see Oceanography—Research

OCEANOGRAPHY

see also Marine Biology; Marine Resources; Navigation; Ocean Waves; Submarine Geology

Anderson, Michael. Investigating Earth's Oceans. 2011. (Illus.). 88p. (J). lib. bdg. 31.70 *(978-1-61530-497-4(5))* Rosen Publishing Group, Inc., The.

Arlon, Penelope. Really? Ocean. 2015. (ENG.). 64p. (J). (gr. 2-5). pap. 8.99 *(978-0-545-80650-3(X)*, Scholastic Nonfiction) Scholastic, Inc.

Aronnax, Pierre. The Oceanology Handbook: A Course for Underwater Explorers. Hawkins, Emily & Twist, Clint, eds. 2010. (Ologies Ser.). (ENG., Illus.). 80p. (J). (gr. 4-7). 14.99 *(978-0-7636-4874-9(4))* Candlewick Pr.

M N O

Austen, Amy. Earth's Oceans. 2016. (Spotlight on Earth Science Ser.). 00024p. (J). (gr. 4-6). pap. 10.00 (978-1-4994-2501-7(5), PowerKids Pr.) Rosen Publishing Group, Inc., The.

Bailey, Gerry. Swept Away by the Storm. 2014. (ENG., Illus.). 32p. (J). (978-0-7787-0431-7(9)) Crabtree Publishing Co.

Barnes, Julia. 101 Facts about Oceans. 2003. (One Hundred One Facts about Our World Ser.). (Illus.). 32p. (gr. 1-4). lib. bdg. 26.00 (978-0-8368-3709-4(6), Gareth Stevens Learning Library) Stevens, Gareth Publishing LLLP.

Basher, Simon & Green, Dan. Oceans: Making Waves! Basher, Simon, illus. 2012. (Basher Science Ser.). (ENG., Illus.). 128p. (J). (gr. 5-9). pap. 8.99 (978-0-7534-6822-7(0), 9780753468227, Kingfisher) Roaring Brook Pr.

Bayrock, Fiona. The Ocean Explorer's Handbook. 2005. (Undersea University Ser.). (Illus.). 48p. (J). pap. (978-0-439-71184-5(3)) Scholastic, Inc.

Becker, Helaine. The Big Green Book of the Big Blue Sea. Dawson, Willow, illus. 2012. (ENG.). 80p. (J). (gr. 3-7). 15.95 (978-1-55453-746-4(0)); pap. 9.95 (978-1-55453-747-1(9)) Kids Can Pr., Ltd. CAN. Dist: Hachette Bk. Group.

Belcher, Angie & Belcher, Andy. Oceans Alive: Band 14. Belcher, Angie, illus. 2007. (Collins Big Cat Ser.). (ENG., Illus.). 48p. (J). (gr. 3-4). pap. 8.99 (978-0-00-723092-1(3)) HarperCollins Pubs. Ltd. GBR. Dist: Independent Pubs. Group.

Benoit, Peter. Oceans. 2011. (True Bk Ser.). 48p. (J). (ENG.). pap. 6.95 (978-0-531-28105-5(1)); (gr. 3-5). 29.00 (978-0-531-20556-3(8)) Scholastic Library Publishing. (Children's Pr.).

Buchanan, Shelly. The Powerful Ocean. 2015. (Science Readers: Content & Literacy Ser.). (Illus.). 32p. (J). (gr. 5-5). pap. 8.99 (978-1-4807-4726-5(2)) Teacher Created Materials, Inc.

Burns, Loree Griffin. Tracking Trash: Flotsam, Jetsam, & the Science of Ocean Motion. 2010. (Scientists in the Field Ser.). (ENG., Illus.). 64p. (J). (gr. 5-7). pap. 9.99 (978-0-547-32860-7(5)) Houghton Mifflin Harcourt Publishing Co.

Cardenas, Ernesto A. Oceans. 2009. pap. 4.95 (978-1-60698-086-6(6)) Milo Educational Bks. & Resources.

Chambers, Catherine. Stickmen's Guide to Oceans in Layers. Dean, Venitia & De Quay, John Paul, illus. 2016. (Stickmen's Guides to This Incredible Earth Ser.). (ENG.). 32p. (J). (gr. 3-6). 26.65 (978-1-5124-0619-1(8)) Lerner Publishing Group.

Collard, Sneed B., III. The Deep-Sea Floor. Wenzel, Gregory, illus. 2003. (ENG.). 32p. (J). (gr. 1-4). pap. 7.95 (978-1-57091-403-4(6)) Charlesbridge Publishing, Inc.

La Conservacion del Mar. (Colección Biblioteca Juvenil de Ecología). (SPA., Illus.). (YA). (gr. 5-8). pap. (978-958-04-2405-5(5), 80424055) Norma S.A. COL. Dist: Lectorum Pubns., Inc.

Croce, Nicholas, ed. Oceanography & Hydrology. 2016. (Study of Science Ser.). 96p. (gr. 8-8). 72.50 (978-1-68048-234-8(3));1. (ENG.). (J). 36.25 (978-1-68048-235-5(1)) Rosen Publishing Group, Inc., The. (Britannica Educational Publishing).

Desonie, Dana. Oceans: How We Use the Seas. 2007. (Our Fragile Planet Ser.). (Illus.). 215p. (YA). (gr. 7-12). lib. bdg. 35.00 (978-0-8160-6216-4(1)) Facts On File, Inc.

Diamond, Claudia. What's under the Sea? 2009. (Reading Room Collection 2 Ser.). 24p. (gr. 3-4). 42.50 (978-1-60852-002-2(1), PowerKids Pr.) Rosen Publishing Group, Inc., The.

Douglas. Reading Explorer. 4th ed. 2010. (ENG., Illus.). 224p. (J). pap., stu. ed. incl. cd-rom (978-1-4240-2939-6(2)) Cengage Heinle.

Franks, Sharon E. & Cohen, Judith Love. You Can Be A Woman Oceanographer. Katz, David Arthur, illus. 2004. (J). 40p. 19.95 incl. DVD (978-1-880599-67-9(8)); pap. 13.95 incl. DVD (978-1-880599-66-2(X)) Cascade Pass, Inc.

Gallagher, Belinda. Why Why Why... Are There Schools in the Sea? 2010. (Why Why Why Ser.). (Illus.). 32p. (J). (gr. 1-3). lib. bdg. 18.95 (978-1-4222-1572-2(5)) Mason Crest.

Garbe, Suzanne. The Science Behind Wonders of the Water: Exploding Lakes, Ice Circles, & Brinicles. 2016. (Science Behind Natural Phenomena Ser.). (ENG., Illus.). 32p. (gr. 3-4). lib. bdg. 27.99 (978-1-5157-0776-9(8), Edge Bks.) Capstone Press of Coughlan Cos.

Gareth Stevens Editorial Staff. Oceans. 2004. (Discovery Channel School Science Ser.). (Illus.). 32p. (gr. 4-8). lib. bdg. 26.00 (978-0-8368-3383-6(X), Gareth Stevens Learning Library) Stevens, Gareth Publishing LLLP.

Goldstein, Natalie. How Do We Know the Nature of the Ocean? 2005. (Great Scientific Questions & the Scientists Who Answered Them Ser.). (Illus.). 112p. (J). (gr. 7-12). lib. bdg. 34.60 (978-1-4042-0079-1(7)) Rosen Publishing Group, Inc., The.

—How Do We Know the Nature of the Ocean. 2009. (Great Scientific Questions & the Scientists Who Answered Them Ser.). 112p. (gr. 7-12). 63.90 (978-1-61513-204-1(X)) Rosen Publishing Group, Inc., The.

Gonzales, Doreen. The Arctic Ocean: A MyReportLinks. com Book. 2004. (Oceans of the World Ser.). (Illus.). 48p. (J). lib. bdg. 26.60 (978-0-7660-5193-5(5), MyReportLinks.com Bks.) Enslow Pubs., Inc.

—The Atlantic Ocean: A MyReportLinks. com Book. 2004. (Oceans of the World Ser.). (Illus.). 48p. (J). lib. bdg. 26.60 (978-0-7660-5194-2(3), MyReportLinks.com Bks.) Enslow Pubs., Inc.

—The Indian Ocean: A MyReportLinks. com Book. 2004. (Oceans of the World Ser.). (Illus.). 48p. (J). lib. bdg. 26.60 (978-0-7660-5195-9(1), MyReportLinks.com Bks.) Enslow Pubs., Inc.

—The Pacific Ocean: A MyReportLinks. com Book. 2004. (Oceans of the World Ser.). (Illus.). 48p. (J). lib. bdg. 26.60 (978-0-7660-5192-8(7), MyReportLinks.com Bks.) Enslow Pubs., Inc.

Gordon, Sharon. At Home by the Ocean. 2005. (Bookworms Ser.). (Illus.). 32p. (J). (gr. 3-7). lib. bdg. (978-0-7614-1959-4(4), Benchmark Bks.) Marshall Cavendish Corp.

—At Home by the Ocean/Mi Casa Junto Al Mar. 2006. (Bookworms Ser.). (ENG & SPA., Illus.). 32p. (gr. k-2). lib. bdg. 15.95 (978-0-7614-2456-7(3)) Marshall Cavendish Corp.

—Mi Casa Junto al Mar. 2006. (Bookworms Ser.). (SPA & ENG., Illus.). 32p. (gr. k-2). lib. bdg. 15.95 (978-0-7614-2377-5(X)) Marshall Cavendish Corp.

Gray, Susan Heinrichs. Oceanography: The Study of Oceans. 2012. (True Book Ser.). (ENG., Illus.). 48p. (J). pap. 6.95 (978-0-531-28273-1(2)); lib. bdg. 29.00 (978-0-531-24679-5(5)) Scholastic Library Publishing. (Children's Pr.).

Hall, Stephen. Exploring the Oceans. 2012. (ENG., Illus.). 48p. (J). 15.00 (978-1-899762-79-8(5)) Award Pubns. Ltd. GBR. Dist: Parkwest Pubns., Inc.

Heinrichs, Ann. Oceans. 2009. (21st Century Skills Library: Real World Math Ser.). (ENG.). 32p. (gr. 4-8). lib. bdg. 28.50 (978-1-60279-496-2(0), 200317) Cherry Lake Publishing.

Holmes, Parker. Oceanographers, 01 vols., 1. 2016. (Out of the Lab: Extreme Jobs in Science Ser.). (ENG., Illus.). 32p. (J). pap. 10.00 (978-1-5081-4517-2(2), PowerKids Pr.) Rosen Publishing Group, Inc., The.

Holt, Rinehart and Winston Staff. Holt Science & Technology Chapter 13: Earth Science: Exploring the Oceans. 5th ed. 2004. (Illus.). pap. 12.86 (978-0-03-030319-7(2)) Holt McDougal.

—Holt Science & Technology Chapter 14: Earth Science: Movement of the Ocean. 5th ed. 2004. (Illus.). pap. 12.86 (978-0-03-030321-0(4)) Holt McDougal.

Hudak, Heather C. Oceans. (Illus.). 32p. (J). 2017. **(978-1-5105-0878-1(3))** 2016. (978-1-5105-0876-7(7)) SmartBook Media, Inc.

Jakubiak, David J. Protecting Our Planet: What Can We Do about Oil Spills & Ocean Pollution? 2012. (Protecting Our Planet Ser.). (Illus.). 24p. (J). (gr. 2-5). lib. bdg. 22.60 (978-1-4488-4982-6(9)) Rosen Publishing Group, Inc., The.

Jedicke, Peter. Exploring the Ocean Depths. 2003. (Hot Science Ser.). (J). lib. bdg. 28.50 (978-1-58340-367-9(1)) Black Rabbit Bks.

Johnson, Rebecca L., et al. Ocean Exploration. 2007. (Avenues Ser.). (ENG., Illus.). 36p. (J). pap. 18.95 (978-0-7922-5430-0(9)) CENGAGE Learning.

Johnson, Robin. Oceans Inside Out. 2014. (ENG.). 32p. (J). (978-0-7787-0635-9(4)) Crabtree Publishing Co.

Kalman, Bobbie. Explore Earth's Five Oceans. 2010. (Explore the Continents Ser.). (ENG., Illus.). 32p. (J). (gr. 1-5). pap. (978-0-7787-3091-0(3)); lib. bdg. (978-0-7787-3077-4(8)) Crabtree Publishing Co.

—What Is an Ocean? 2010. (My World Ser.). (ENG.). 24p. (J). (gr. k-3). (978-0-7787-9515-5(2)); pap. (978-0-7787-9540-7(3)) Crabtree Publishing Co.

Kerrod, Robin. Find Out about the Sea: With 20 Projects & More Than 260 Pictures. 2013. (ENG., Illus.). 64p. (J). (gr. 3-7). 9.99 (978-1-84322-896-7(3)) Anness Publishing GBR. Dist: National Bk. Network.

Koll, Hilary & Mills, Steve. A Math Journey under the Ocean. 2016. (ENG., Illus.). 32p. (J). (978-0-7787-2315-8(1)) Crabtree Publishing Co.

Kranking, Kathy & Carrano, Matthew T. Swimming with Saurs. 2006. 32p. (J). (978-0-439-83875-7(4)) Scholastic, Inc.

Labrecque, Ellen. Deep Oceans, 1 vol. 2014. (Earth's Last Frontiers Ser.). (ENG., Illus.). 32p. (gr. 1-3). lib. bdg. 29.99 (978-1-4109-6178-5(8), Read Me!) Heinemann-Raintree.

—Earth's Last Frontiers, 1 vol. 2014. (Earth's Last Frontiers Ser.). (ENG.). 32p. (gr. 1-3). lib. bdg. 119.96 (978-1-4109-6181-5(8), Read Me!) Heinemann-Raintree.

Levete, Sarah. Save the Oceans. 2011. (ENG.). 24p. (J). pap. (978-0-7787-7879-0(7)); (gr. 3-6). (978-0-7787-7857-8(6)) Crabtree Publishing Co.

Life on an Ocean Planet Laboratory & Activity Manual. 2005. (YA). spiral bd. (978-1-878663-35-1(6)) Current Publishing Corp.

Littlefield, Cindy A. Awesome Ocean Science. 2006. (Williamson Kids Can! Ser.). (ENG., Illus.). 120p. (J). (gr. 4-7). 16.95 (978-0-8249-6797-0(6), Ideal Pubns.) Worthy Publishing.

Llewellyn, Claire. The Sea. 2003. (Starters Ser.). 24p. (J). lib. bdg. 21.35 (978-1-58340-262-7(4)) Black Rabbit Bks.

Louisy, Patrick. My Encyclopedia of the Sea. 2016. (My Encyclopedia Ser.). (ENG., Illus.). 128p. (J). lib. bdg. 34.00 (978-0-531-22473-1(2), Children's Pr.) Scholastic Library Publishing.

Make It Work Geography, 4 vol. set. 2003. (gr. 4-8). 59.00 (978-0-7166-5124-6(6)) World Bk., Inc.

Mallory, Kenneth. Adventure Beneath the Sea: Living in an Underwater Science Station. Skerry, Brian, photos by. 2010. (ENG., Illus.). 48p. (J). (gr. 4-6). 18.95 (978-1-59078-607-9(6)) Boyds Mills Pr.

Mara, Wil. The Four Oceans. 2005. (Rookie Read-About Geography Ser.). (ENG., Illus.). 32p. (J). (gr. 1-2). per. 5.95 (978-0-516-25817-1(6), Children's Pr.) Scholastic Library Publishing.

McAneney, Caitie. Freaky Stories from Beneath the Sea. 2015. (Freaky True Science Ser.). (ENG.). 32p. (J). (gr. 4-5). pap. 10.50 (978-1-4824-2964-0(0)); lib. bdg. 26.60 (978-1-4824-2966-4(7)) Stevens, Gareth Publishing LLLP.

Montgomery, Sy. The Octopus Scientists. Ellenbogen, Keith, illus. 2015. (Scientists in the Field Ser.). (ENG.). 80p. (J). (gr. 5-7). 18.99 (978-0-544-23270-9(4), HMH Books For Young Readers) Houghton Mifflin Harcourt Publishing Co.

Myers, Janet Nuzum. Water Wonders of the World: From Killer Waves to Monsters of the Deep. 2006. (Illus.). 96p. (J). pap. (978-1-59336-729-9(5)) Mondo Publishing.

Nelson, John. Polar Ice Caps in Danger: Expedition to Antarctica. 2008. (Jr. Graphic Environmental Dangers Ser.). (ENG.). 24p. (J). 47.90 (978-1-61532-097-4(0)); (Illus.). (gr. 3-6). lib. bdg. 25.25 (978-1-4042-4227-2(9)) Rosen Publishing Group, Inc., The. (PowerKids Pr.).

Nelson, John & Obregón, José María. Casquetes Polares en Riesgo: Expedición a la Antártida. 2009. (Historietas Juveniles: Peligros Del Medioambiente (Jr. Graphic Environmental Dangers) Ser.). (SPA., Illus.). 24p. (gr. 3-6). (YA). lib. bdg. 25.25 (978-1-4358-8474-8(4)); pap. 10.60 (978-1-4358-8475-5(2)) Rosen Publishing Group, Inc., The.

Nivola, Claire A. Life in the Ocean: The Story of Oceanographer Sylvia Earle, 1 vol. Nivola, Claire A., illus. 2012. (ENG., Illus.). 32p. (J). (gr. -1-3). 18.99 (978-0-374-38068-7(6), 9780374380687, Farrar, Straus & Giroux (BYR)) Farrar, Straus & Giroux.

Ostopowich, Melanie. Oceans, Lakes, & Rivers. 2016. **(978-1-4896-5794-7(0))** Weigl Pubs., Inc.

Padilla-Gamino, Jacqueline L. Kupe & the Corals. Leggitt, Marjorie, illus. 2014. (Long Term Ecological Research Ser.). (ENG.). 32p. (J). (gr. 3-7). 15.95 (978-1-58979-753-6(1)) Taylor Trade Publishing.

Rauf, Don & Vescia, Monique. Virtual Apprentice: Oceanographer. 2009. (Virtual Apprentice Ser.). 64p. (gr. 4-9). pap. 9.95 (978-0-8160-7895-0(5), Checkmark Bks.) Facts On File, Inc.

Richmond, Benjamin. Why Is the Sea Salty? And Other Questions about the Ocean. Azhderian, Cecelia, illus. 2014. (Good Question! Ser.). (ENG.). 32p. (J). (gr. 1). pap. 5.95 (978-1-4549-0677-3(4)) Sterling Publishing Co., Inc.

—Why Is the Sea Salty? And Other Questions about the Oceans. Azhderian, Cecelia, illus. 2014. (Good Question! Ser.). (ENG.). 40p. (J). (gr. 1). 12.95 (978-1-4549-0676-6(6)) Sterling Publishing Co., Inc.

Riggs, Kate. Oceans. 2016. (Illus.). 24p. (978-1-60818-743-0(8), Creative Education) Creative Co., The.

Royston, Angela. Ocean Explorer! 2011. (ENG., Illus.). 24p. (J). pap. (978-0-7787-7864-6(9)); (gr. 3-6). (978-0-7787-7842-4(8)) Crabtree Publishing Co.

Sheehan, Robert. The Undersea Lab: Exploring the Oceans, 1 vol., 1. 2014. (Discovery Education: Earth & Space Science Ser.). (ENG.). 32p. (gr. 3-6). 26.25 (978-1-4777-6166-3(7), PowerKids Pr.) Rosen Publishing Group, Inc., The.

Sherwin, Frank. The Ocean Book. 2006. (Wonders of Creation Ser.). 72p. pap. 3.99 (978-1-893345-62-1(9)) Answers in Genesis Ministries.

—The Ocean Book. 2004. (Wonders of Creation Ser.). (Illus.). 80p. (J). 15.99 (978-0-89051-401-6(1)) Master Bks.

Sjonger, Rebecca. Ocean Engineering & Designing for the Deep Sea. 2016. (Engineering in Action Ser.). (ENG., Illus.). 32p. (J). (gr. 5-8). (978-0-7787-7536-2(4)) Crabtree Publishing Co.

Spilsbury, Louise. What Are Rivers, Lakes, & Oceans?, 1 vol., 1. 2014. (Let's Find Out! Ser.). (ENG.). 32p. (gr. 3-6). 23.45 (978-1-62275-281-2(3)) Rosen Publishing Group, Inc., The.

Spilsbury, Louise & Spilsbury, Richard. Arctic Ocean. 2015. (Oceans of the World Ser.). (ENG., Illus.). 32p. (gr. 1-3). 27.32 (978-1-4846-0774-9(0), Heinemann First Library) Heinemann-Raintree.

—Atlantic Ocean. 2015. (Oceans of the World Ser.). (ENG., Illus.). 32p. (gr. 1-3). 27.32 (978-1-4846-0770-1(8), Heinemann First Library) Heinemann-Raintree.

—Indian Ocean. 2015. (Oceans of the World Ser.). (ENG., Illus.). 32p. (gr. 1-3). 27.32 (978-1-4846-0772-5(4), Heinemann First Library) Heinemann-Raintree.

—Pacific Ocean. 2015. (Oceans of the World Ser.). (ENG., Illus.). 32p. (gr. 1-3). 27.32 (978-1-4846-0771-8(6), Heinemann First Library) Heinemann-Raintree.

—Southern Ocean. 2015. (Oceans of the World Ser.). (ENG., Illus.). 32p. (gr. 1-3). 27.32 (978-1-4846-0773-2(2), Heinemann First Library) Heinemann-Raintree.

Sundance/Newbridge LLC Staff. Exploring Our Oceans. 2004. (Reading PowerWorks Ser.). (gr. 1-3). 37.50 (978-0-7608-9759-1(X)); pap. 6.10 (978-0-7608-9760-7(3)) Sundance/Newbridge Educational Publishing.

Thompson, Lisa. Wild Waves. 2003. (Real Deal Ser.). (Illus.). 32p. (J). pap. (978-0-7608-6690-0(2)) Sundance/Newbridge Educational Publishing.

Vogel, Carole G. Savage Waters. 2003. (Restless Sea Ser.). (ENG., Illus.). 80p. (J). 30.50 (978-0-531-12321-8(9), Watts, Franklin) Scholastic Library Publishing.

Walker, Pam & Wood, Elaine. The Open Ocean. 2005. (Life in the Sea Ser.). (Illus.). 144p. (YA). (gr. 7-12). 35.00 (978-0-8160-5705-4(2)) Facts On File, Inc.

—People & the Sea. 2005. (Life in the Sea Ser.). (Illus.). 144p. (YA). (gr. 7-12). 35.00 (978-0-8160-5706-1(0)) Facts On File, Inc.

West, Krista. Hands-on Projects about Oceans. 2009. (Great Earth Science Projects Ser.). 24p. (gr. 3-3). 42.50 (978-1-61513-112-9(4), PowerKids Pr.) Rosen Publishing Group, Inc., The.

Wilsdon, Christina. Ultimate Oceanpedia. 2016. (ENG., Illus.). 272p. (J). (gr. 2-5). lib. bdg. 34.90 (978-1-4263-2551-9(7), National Geographic Children's Bks.) National Geographic Society.

Wohlers, Bob. Life on an Ocean Planet Student Text Book. 2005. (Illus.). lib. bdg. (978-1-878663-34-4(8)) Current Publishing Corp.

Wood, Lisa. Marine Science, Vol. 3. 2005. 80p. 12.95 (978-1-59363-098-0(0)) Prufrock Pr.

Woodward, John. The Deep, Deep Ocean. 2010. (Oceans Alive! Ser.). 32p. lib. bdg. 28.50 (978-1-933834-63-4(3)) Brown Bear Bks.

—Oceans. 2004. (Geography Fact Files Ser.). (J). lib. bdg. 28.50 (978-1-58340-427-0(9)) Black Rabbit Bks.

—Oceans. (Illus.). 64p. (YA). (gr. 4-18). lib. bdg. 29.95 (978-1-59389-125-1(3)) Chrysalis Education.

—Under the Waves. 2010. (Oceans Alive! Ser.). lib. bdg. 28.50 (978-1-933834-62-7(5)) Brown Bear Bks.

World Book, Inc Staff, contrib. by. The Sea & Its Marvels. 2011. (J). (978-0-7166-1791-4(9)) World Bk., Inc.

Yomtov, Nelson. Polar Ice Caps in Danger: Expedition to Antarctica. 2009. (Jr. Graphic Environmental Dangers Ser.). (ENG., Illus.). 24p. (gr. 3-8). pap. 10.60 (978-1-4042-4594-5(4), PowerKids Pr.) Rosen Publishing Group, Inc., The.

Zoehfeld, Kathleen Weidner. How Deep Is the Ocean? Puybaret, Eric, illus. 2016. (Let's-Read-And-Find-Out Science 2 Ser.). 40p. (J). (gr. -1-3). pap. 6.99 (978-0-06-232819-9(0)) HarperCollins Pubs.

OCEANOGRAPHY—BIOGRAPHY

Hodgkins, Fran. Champions of the Ocean, 1 vol. Arbo, Cris, illus. 2009. (Earth Heroes Ser.). (ENG.). 144p. (J). (gr. 5-9). pap. 11.95 (978-1-58469-119-8(0)) Dawn Pubns.

Zronik, John Paul & Zronik, John. Jacques Cousteau: Conserving Underwater Worlds. 2007. (In the Footsteps of Explorers Ser.). (ENG., Illus.). 32p. (J). (gr. 3-7). lib. bdg. (978-0-7787-2419-3(0)); pap. (978-0-7787-2455-1(7)) Crabtree Publishing Co.

OCEANOGRAPHY—FICTION

Hatton, Libby. Pete Puffin's Wild Ride Cruising Alaska's Currents. Hatton, Libby, illus. 2008. (Illus.). (J). pap. 16.95 (978-0-930931-92-6(0)) Alaska Geographic Assn.

Osborne, Mary Pope. Dark Day in the Deep Sea. 2009. (Magic Tree House Merlin Missions Ser.: 11). lib. bdg. 16.00 (978-0-606-01778-7(X), Turtleback) Turtleback Bks.

Osborne, Mary Pope & Osborne, Magic Tree. Dark Day in the Deep Sea. Murdocca, Sal, illus. 2009. (Magic Tree House Merlin Mission Ser.: 11). (ENG.). 144p. (J). (gr. 2-5). 5.99 (978-0-375-83732-6(9), Random Hse. Bks. for Young Readers) Random Hse. Children's Bks.

Ricci, Christine. Dora in the Deep Sea. Roper, Robert, illus. 2003. (Dora the Explorer Ser.: Vol. 3). (ENG.). 24p. (J). pap. 3.99 (978-0-689-85845-1(0), Simon Spotlight/Nickelodeon) Simon Spotlight/Nickelodeon.

OCEANOGRAPHY—RESEARCH

see also Bathyscaphe; Skin Diving; Underwater Exploration

Diagram Group Staff. Marine Science: An Illustrated Guide to Science. 2006. (Science Visual Resources Ser.). (Illus.). 208p. (gr. 6-12). 49.50 (978-0-8160-6166-2(1)) Facts On File, Inc.

Yount, Lisa. Modern Marine Science: Exploring the Deep. 2006. (Milestones in Discovery & Invention Ser.). (Illus.). 224p. (J). (gr. 6-12). 35.00 (978-0-8160-5747-4(8)) Facts On File, Inc.

OCEANOGRAPHY—VOCATIONAL GUIDANCE

Ferguson Publishing. Careers in Focus: Oceanography. 2010. (Careers in Focus Ser.). (Illus.). 202p. (gr. 6-12). 32.95 (978-0-8160-8026-7(7), Ferguson Publishing Co.) Facts On File, Inc.

Mara, Wil. Deep-Sea Exploration: Science, Technology, & Engineering. 2015. (ENG., Illus.). 64p. (J). pap. 8.95 (978-0-531-21173-1(8), Orchard Bks.) Scholastic Library Publishing.

Oceanographer. 2008. (Virtual Apprentice Ser.). 64p. (gr. 4-9). 29.95 (978-0-8160-6762-6(7), Ferguson Publishing Co.) Facts On File, Inc.

OCEANOLOGY

see Oceanography

OCELOT

Randall, Henry. Ocelots. 2011. (Cats of the Wild Ser.). (ENG.). 24p. (J). pap. 8.25 (978-1-4488-2623-0(3)); lib. bdg. 22.60 (978-1-4488-2519-6(9)) Rosen Publishing Group, Inc., The. (PowerKids Pr.).

—Ocelots: Ocelotes. 2011. (Cats of the Wild / Felinos Salvajes Ser.). (SPA & ENG., Illus.). 24p. lib. bdg. 22.60 (978-1-4488-3131-9(8), PowerKids Pr.) Rosen Publishing Group, Inc., The.

OCTOPUSES

Allyn, Daisy. Deadly Blue-Ringed Octopuses. 2011. (Small but Deadly Ser.). (Illus.). 24p. (J). (gr. 2-5). pap. 8.15 (978-1-4339-5736-9(1)); lib. bdg. 22.60 (978-1-4339-5734-5(5)) Stevens, Gareth Publishing LLLP. (Gareth Stevens Learning Library).

Andover, Max. Octopuses & Squid. 2011. (Illus.). 16p. (J). pap. (978-0-545-24792-4(6)) Scholastic, Inc.

Berger, Melvin & Berger, Gilda. Octopus. 2003. (Scholastic Reader Ser.). (Illus.). (J). pap. (978-0-439-47391-0(8)) Scholastic, Inc.

Blaine, John. The Wailing Octopus: A Rick Brant Science Adventure Story. 2011. 218p. 44.95 (978-1-258-10006-3(1)) Literary Licensing, LLC.

Claybourne, Anna. Octopuses, 1 vol. 2013. (Animal Abilities Ser.). (ENG.). 32p. (gr. 2-4). 29.99 (978-1-4109-5240-0(1)); pap. 8.95 (978-1-4109-5247-9(9)) Heinemann-Raintree. (Raintree Perspectives).

Coldiron, Deborah. Octopuses, 1 vol. 2007. (Underwater World Ser.). (ENG.). 32p. (gr. 3-7). 27.07 (978-1-59928-815-4(X), Buddy Bks.) ABDO Publishing Co.

Gish, Melissa. Living Wild: Octopuses. 2014. (Living Wild Ser.). (ENG., Illus.). 48p. (J). (gr. 4-7). pap. 12.00 (978-0-89812-842-0(0), Creative Paperbacks) Creative Co., The.

—Octopuses. 2013. (Illus.). 46p. (J). 35.65 (978-1-60818-289-3(4), Creative Education) Creative Co., The.

Gordon, Sharon. Adivina Quien Atrapa. 2006. (Bookworms Ser.). (SPA & ENG., Illus.). 32p. (gr. k-2). lib. bdg. 15.95 (978-0-7614-2383-6(4)) Marshall Cavendish Corp.

—Guess Who Grabs. 2007. (Bookworms: Guess Who Ser.). (Illus.). 31p. (J). (gr. -1-3). pap. 6.99 (978-0-7614-3320-0(1), Benchmark Bks.) Marshall Cavendish Corp.

—Guess Who Grabs/Adivina Quien Atrapa. 2006. (Bookworms Ser.). (ENG & SPA., Illus.). 32p. (gr. k-2). lib. bdg. 15.95 (978-0-7614-2464-2(4)) Marshall Cavendish Corp.

Gray, Leon. Giant Pacific Octopus: The World's Largest Octopus. 2013. (Even More SuperSized! Ser.). 24p. (J). (gr. k-3). lib. bdg. 23.93 (978-1-61772-730-6(X)) Bearport Publishing Co., Inc.

The Greedy Gray Octopus: 6 Small Books. (gr. k-3). 24.00 (978-0-7635-6235-9(1)) Rigby Education.

Gross, Miriam J. The Octopus. (Weird Sea Creatures Ser.). 2009. 24p. (gr. 3-3). 42.50 (978-1-60854-755-5(8)) 2006. (Illus.). 23p. (J). lib. bdg. 22.60 (978-1-4042-3188-7(9)) Rosen Publishing Group, Inc., The. (PowerKids Pr.).

Hansen, Grace. Octopuses, 1 vol. 2014. (Ocean Life Ser.). (ENG.). 24p. (J). (gr. 2-4). lib. bdg. 28.50 (978-1-62970-710-5(4)) ABDO Publishing Co.

Herriges, Ann. Octopuses. 2006. (Oceans Alive Ser.). (ENG., Illus.). 24p. (J). (gr. k-3). lib. bdg. 25.95 (978-1-60014-019-8(X)) Bellwether Media.

Jackson, Ellen. Octopuses One to Ten. Page, Robin, illus. 2016. (ENG.). 32p. (J). (gr. -1-3). 17.99 (978-1-4814-3182-8(X), Beach Lane Bks.) Beach Lane Bks.

James, Helen Foster. Discover Octopuses. 2015. (21st Century Basic Skills Library: Splash! Ser.). (ENG., Illus.). 24p. (J). (gr. 2-4). pap. 12.79 (978-1-63362-692-8(X), 206593) Cherry Lake Publishing.

Jango-Cohen, Judith. Octopuses. 2003. (Animals Animals Ser.). (Illus.). 48p. (gr. 3-18). lib. bdg. 29.93 (978-0-7614-1614-2(5)) Marshall Cavendish Corp.

John, Gee. The Octopus. 2011. (Power 100 - Marine Life Ser.). 20p. pap. 39.62 (978-1-61541-238-9(7)) American Reading Co.

Johnson, Elizabeth R. Octopus. 2016. (Sea Life Ser.). (ENG.). 24p. (gr. k-1). lib. bdg. 26.65 (978-1-5157-2080-5(2)) Capstone Press of Coughlan Cos.

Johnson, Gee. The Octopus. Johnson, Gee, illus. 2010. (2G Marine Life Ser.). (ENG., Illus.). 20p. (J). (gr. k-2). pap. 5.99 (978-1-61541-221-1(2)) American Reading Co.
Johnson, Gee & Sánchez, Lucía M. El Pulpo. 2011. (2G Vida Marina Ser.). (SPA., Illus.). 20p. (J). (gr. k-2). pap. 6.99 (978-1-61541-452-9(5)) American Reading Co.
Kalman, Bobbie & Sjonger, Rebecca. The Amazing Octopus. 2003. (Living Ocean Ser.). (ENG., Illus.). 32p. (J). (gr. 2-9). pap. (978-0-7787-1321-0(0)) Crabtree Publishing Co.
Kalman, Bobbie, et al. Les Pieuvres. 2009. (FRE., Illus.). 32p. (J). pap. 9.95 (978-2-89579-247-5(X)) Bayard Canada Livres CAN. Dist: Crabtree Publishing Co.
Laughlin, Kara L. Octopuses. 2017. (In the Deep Blue Sea Ser.). (ENG.). 24p. (J). (gr. k-3). lib. bdg. 27.07 (978-1-5038-1687-9(7), 211521) Child's World, Inc., The.
Leaf, Christina. Octopuses. 2016. (Ocean Life up Close Ser.). (ENG., Illus.). 24p. (J). (gr. k-3). 25.95 (978-1-62617-419-1(9), Blastoff! Readers) Bellwether Media.
Lunis, Natalie. Blue-Ringed Octopus: Small but Deadly. (Afraid of the Water Ser.). 24p. 2016. (ENG.). (J). (gr. 1-6). pap. 7.95 **(978-1-944998-61-5(6))** 2009. (Illus.). (YA). (gr. 2-5). lib. bdg. 22.61 (978-1-59716-944-8(7)) Bearport Publishing Co., Inc.
Macheske, Felicia. Awesome Arms. 2016. (Guess What Ser.). (ENG., Illus.). 24p. (J). (gr. k-2). 28.50 (978-1-63470-718-3(4), 207583) Cherry Lake Publishing.
Markle, Sandra. Los Pulpos. Translations.com Staff, tr. from ENG. 2008. (Animales Presa (Animal Prey) Ser.). (SPA.). 40p. (gr. 3-6). 25.26 (978-0-7613-3898-7(5)) Lerner Publishing Group.
—Los Pulpos (Octopuses) 2009. (SPA.). pap. 46.95 (978-0-7613-4721-7(6)) Lerner Publishing Group.
—Octopuses. 2008. pap. 46.95 (978-0-8225-9321-8(1)) 2008. (ENG., Illus.). 40p. (gr. 3-6). per. 7.95 (978-0-8225-6066-1(6), First Avenue Editions) 2007. (Illus.). 40p. (J). (gr. 4-7). lib. bdg. 25.26 (978-0-8225-6063-0(1)) Lerner Publishing Group.
—Los Pulpos (Octopuses) Translations.com Staff, tr. 2008. (Animales Presa (Animal Prey) Ser.). (SPA.). 40p. (gr. 3-6). pap. 7.95 (978-0-7613-3902-1(7), Ediciones Lerner) Lerner Publishing Group.
Meister, Cari. Octopuses. 2012. (Illus.). 24p. (J). lib. bdg. 25.65 (978-1-62031-010-6(4)) Jump! Inc.
Miller, Tori. Octopuses & Squid. 2009. (Freaky Fish Ser.). 24p. (ENG., Illus.). (J). (gr. 2-5). pap. 8.25 (978-1-4358-3174-2(8), PowerKids Pr.); (gr. 2-3). 42.50 (978-1-61512-640-8(6), PowerKids Pr.); (J). (gr. 1-4). lib. bdg. 22.60 (978-1-4358-2757-8(0)) Rosen Publishing Group, Inc., The.
Mitchell, Susan K. Biggest vs. Smallest Sea Creatures. 2010. (Biggest vs. Smallest Animals Ser.). (Illus.). 24p. (J). 22.60 (978-0-7660-3580-5(8), Enslow Elementary) Enslow Pubs., Inc.
Montgomery, Sy. The Octopus Scientists. Ellenbogen, Keith, illus. 2015. (Scientists in the Field Ser.). (ENG.). 80p. (J). (gr. 5-7). 18.99 (978-0-544-23270-9(4), HMH Books For Young Readers) Houghton Mifflin Harcourt Publishing Co.
Octopus. 2004. (J). 5.99 (978-0-7566-0251-2(3)) Dorling Kindersley Publishing, Inc.
Olsen, Alana. Look Out for the Blue-Ringed Octopus! 2015. (Surprisingly Scary! Ser.). (ENG., Illus.). 24p. (J). (gr. 2-3). pap. 8.25 (978-1-4994-0877-5(3), PowerKids Pr.) Rosen Publishing Group, Inc., The.
Owen, Ruth. Giant Squid & Octopuses, 1 vol., 1. 2014. (Real Life Sea Monsters Ser.). (ENG.). 32p. (J). (gr. k-5). 26.25 (978-1-4777-6261-5(2), PowerKids Pr.) Rosen Publishing Group, Inc., The.
—Octopuses. 2011. (World's Smartest Animals Ser.). (ENG., Illus.). 32p. (J). (gr. k-5). pap. 11.75 (978-1-61533-412-4(2)); lib. bdg. 26.50 (978-1-61533-374-5(6)) Windmill Bks.
Pearce, Kevin. Being an Octopus. 2013. (Can You Imagine Ser.). (Illus.). 32p. (J). (gr. 2-3). pap. 10.50 (978-1-4824-3281-7(1)) Rosen Publishing Group, Inc., The.
—Being an Octopus, Vol. 1. 2014. (Can You Imagine? Ser.). (ENG., Illus.). 32p. (J). (gr. 2-3). 25.25 (978-1-4824-0136-3(3)) Stevens, Gareth Publishing LLLP.
Phillips, Jillian. What to Doodle? At the Aquarium. 2011. (Dover Doodle Bks.). (ENG., Illus.). 64p. (J). (gr. k-3). pap. 1.99 (978-0-486-47819-7(X)) Dover Pubns., Inc.
Plattner, Josh. Octopus: Master of Disguise, 1 vol. 2016. (ENG., Illus.). 24p. (J). (978-1-62403-737-5(2)) ABDO Publishing Co.
Pringle, Laurence. Octopuses! Strange & Wonderful. Henderson, Meryl, illus. 2015. (ENG.). 32p. (J). (gr. 1-4). 16.95 (978-1-59078-928-5(8)) Boyds Mills Pr.
Raum, Elizabeth. Blue-Ringed Octopuses. 2015. (Poisonous Animals Ser.). (ENG., Illus.). 32p. (J). (gr. 2-4). 19.95 (978-1-60753-785-4(0)) Amicus Publishing.
Rhodes, Mary Jo & Hall, David. Octopuses & Squids. Hall, David, photos by. 2006. (Undersea Encounters Ser.). (ENG., Illus.). 48p. (J). (gr. 3-7). per. 6.95 (978-0-516-25350-3(6), Children's Pr.) Scholastic Library Publishing.
Riggs, Kate. Octopuses. 2016. (Amazing Animals Ser.). (Illus.). 24p. (J). (ENG.). (gr. 1-3). pap. 8.99 (978-1-62832-219-4(5), Creative Paperbacks); 28.95 (978-1-60818-613-6(X), Creative Education) Creative Co., The.
Riggs, Kate. Seedlings: Octopuses. 2017. (Seedlings Ser.). (ENG., Illus.). 24p. (J). (gr. -1-1). pap. 7.99 **(978-1-62832-399-3(X)**, Creative Paperbacks) Creative Co., The.
Roumanis, Alexis. Giant Octopus. 2014. (J). (978-1-4896-1070-6(7)) Weigl Pubs., Inc.
Shaskan, Trisha Speed. I Am an Octopus: The Life of a Common Octopus, 1 vol. Ouren, Todd, illus. 2008. (I Live in the Ocean Ser.). (ENG.). 24p. (gr. -1-2). lib. bdg. 26.65 (978-1-4048-4729-3(4)) Picture Window Bks.
Shea, Therese. The Bizarre Life Cycle of an Octopus. 2012. (Strange Life Cycles Ser.). (Illus.). 24p. (J). (gr. 2-5). 22.60 (978-1-4339-7055-9(4)); pap. 8.15 (978-1-4339-7056-6(2)) Stevens, Gareth Publishing LLLP. (Gareth Stevens Learning Library).
Shoemaker, Kate. Octopus Ink. 2015. (Nature's Grossest Ser.). (ENG.). 24p. (J). (gr. 1-2). pap. 8.15 (978-1-4824-1846-0(0)); (Illus.). 22.60 (978-1-4824-1845-3(2)) Stevens, Gareth Publishing LLLP.
Spilsbury, Louise. Octopus, 1 vol. 2010. (Day in the Life: Sea Animals Ser.). (ENG.). 24p. (gr. k-2). pap. 6.79 (978-1-4329-4011-9(2), Heinemann Read & Learn) Heinemann-Raintree.
Spirn, Michele. Octopuses. 2006. (Smart Animals! Ser.). (Illus.). 32p. (YA). (gr. 2-5). lib. bdg. 25.27 (978-1-59716-250-0(7)) Bearport Publishing Co., Inc.
Stone, Tanya Lee. Octopuses. 2003. (Wild Wild World Ser.). 24p. (YA). 24.94 (978-1-56711-817-9(8), Blackbirch Pr., Inc.) Cengage Gale.
Sullivan, Laura L. Blue-Ringed Octopus. 2017. (J). **(978-1-5026-2580-9(6))** Cavendish Square Publishing.
Thomas, Elizabeth. Octopuses. 2014. (21st Century Skills Library: Exploring Our Oceans Ser.). (ENG., Illus.). 32p. (J). (gr. 3-6). 28.50 (978-1-62431-601-2(8), 203188) Cherry Lake Publishing.
Trueit, Trudi Strain. Octopuses. 2010. (Benchmark Rebus: Ocean Life Ser.). 24p. (gr. k-1). 15.95 (978-0-7614-4892-1(6)) Marshall Cavendish GBR. Dist: Marshall Cavendish Corp.
Wearing, Judy. Octopuses. 2011. (J). (gr. 2-4). pap. 12.95 (978-1-61690-693-1(6), AV2 by Weigl); (Illus.). 24p. (gr. 3-6). 27.13 (978-1-61690-689-4(8)) Weigl Pubs., Inc.
Weber, Valerie J. Octopuses & Squids. 2008. (Animals That Live in the Ocean Ser.). (Illus.). 24p. (J). (gr. -1-3). lib. bdg. 22.60 (978-0-8368-9242-0(9), Weekly Reader Leveled Readers) Stevens, Gareth Publishing LLLP.
—Octopuses & Squids/Pulpos y Calamares. 2008. (Animals That Live in the Ocean/Animales Que Viven en el Oceano Ser.). (SPA & ENG.). 24p. (gr. -1-3). (J). lib. bdg. 22.60 (978-0-8368-9248-2(8)); pap. 8.15 (978-0-8368-9347-2(6)) Stevens, Gareth Publishing LLLP. (Weekly Reader Leveled Readers).

OCTOPUSES—FICTION

Aldrich, Sandra D. Trouble in the Park. 2012. 28p. 19.95 (978-1-4626-8818-0(7)) America Star Bks.
—Willie's Lesson. 2012. 28p. 19.95 (978-1-4626-9663-5(5)) America Star Bks.
Allen, Elanna. Poor Little Guy. 2016. (ENG., Illus.). 40p. (J). (-k). 16.99 (978-0-525-42825-1(9), Dial Bks) Penguin Young Readers Group.
Angus, Laurie Ellen. Octopus Escapes Again!, 1 vol. Angus, Laurie Ellen, illus. 2016. (ENG., Illus.). 32p. (J). (gr. k-4). 16.95 (978-1-58469-577-6(3)) Dawn Pubns.
Anton, Amy Way. Ina the Octopus & Her Shipwreck Adventure. Way, MaryFaye, illus. 2008. 28p. pap. 13.99 (978-1-4389-2177-8(2)) AuthorHouse.
Arroyo, Yvonne. How the Octopus Got Eight Arms: Two Arms Are Never Enough. 2013. (ENG., Illus.). 45p. (J). pap. 31.95 (978-1-4327-9644-0(5)); pap. 23.95 (978-1-4327-9369-2(1)) Outskirts Pr., Inc.
Baker, Keith. My Octopus Arms. Baker, Keith, illus. 2013. (ENG., Illus.). 40p. (J). (gr. -1-3). 16.99 (978-1-4424-5843-7(7), Beach Lane Bks.) Beach Lane Bks.
Baron, Andrew, illus. The Adventures of Octopus Rex. 2003. (J). per. 17.95 (978-0-9760348-0-3(8)) BaHart Pubns. / Eight Legs Publishing.
Brett, Jan. The Mermaid. Brett, Jan, illus. 2017. (ENG., Illus.). 32p. (J). (gr. -1-3). 18.99 **(978-0-399-17072-0(3)**, G.P. Putnam's Sons Books for Young Readers) Penguin Young Readers Group.
Calfee, Pat. Issy Books Set 2, 5 bks. Gee, Isybilla, illus. 2013. 60p. (J). pap. 24.95 (978-1-938406-14-0(1), Compass) Raphel Marketing, Inc.
Cazet, Denys. Grandpa Spanielson's Chicken Pox Stories No. 1: The Octopus. Cazet, Denys, illus. 2005. (I Can Read Bks.). (Illus.). 48p. (J). (gr. -1-3). lib. bdg. 16.89 (978-0-06-051089-3(7)) HarperCollins Pubs.
—The Octopus. Cazet, Denys, illus. 2008. (Grandpa Spanielson's Chicken Pox Stories Ser.). (Illus.). (J). (gr. -1-3). pap. 16.95 incl. audio (978-1-4301-0455-1(4));Set. pap. 29.95 incl. audio (978-1-4301-0457-5(0));Set. pap. 31.95 incl. audio compact disk (978-1-4301-0460-5(0)) Live Oak Media.
Clough, Julie, illus. The Octopus. 2008. (Seaside Bath Bks.). (ENG.). 6p. (J). (gr. -1-k). 6.99 (978-0-7641-9530-3(1)) Barron's Educational Series, Inc.
Cox, Amy. Odetta the Octopus Teacher. 2013. 28p. pap. 24.95 (978-1-63000-491-0(X)) America Star Bks.
Dahl, Michael. The Night Octopus: And Other Scary Tales. Bonet, Xavier, illus. 2017. (Michael Dahl's Really Scary Stories Ser.). (ENG.). 72p. (gr. 2-3). lib. bdg. 25.32 **(978-1-4965-4899-3(X))** Stone Arch Bks.
Daniels, Lucy. Oscar's Best Friends. 2005. 57p. (978-0-439-68199-5(5)) Scholastic, Inc.
DeLorge, Jaqueline. Giffinton under the Sea. 2005. (Illus.). 28p. (J). per. 7.99 (978-1-932338-97-3(7)) Lifevest Publishing, Inc.
Diller, Kevin & Lowe, Justin. Hello, My Name Is Octicorn. Talib, Binny, illus. 2016. 48p. (J). (gr. -1-3). 17.99 (978-0-06-238793-6(6)) HarperCollins Pubs.
Douglas, Babette. Oscarpus. Rockwell, Barry, illus. 2006. (Kiss a Me Teacher Creature Stories Ser.). (J). (gr. -1-3). 9.99 (978-1-890343-30-9(7)) Kiss A Me Productions, Inc.
Estes, Allison & Stark, Dan. Izzy & Oscar. Dockray, Tracy, illus. 2015. (ENG.). 40p. (J). (-2). 16.99 (978-1-4926-0150-0(0), 9781492601500, Sourcebooks Jabberwocky) Sourcebooks, Inc.
Farrell, Darren. Thank You, Octopus. 2014. (ENG.). 40p. (J). (gr. -1-k). 16.99 (978-0-8037-3438-8(7), Dial Bks) Penguin Young Readers Group.
Flaherty, Kathleen Marion. An Octopus Named Mom. Donehey, Jennifer Caulfield, illus. 2012. (ENG.). 32p. (J). 16.95 (978-0-9767276-8-2(4)) Three Bean Pr.
Fraioli, James O. Polar Ice Expedition: With Jean-Michel Cousteau. 2009. (J). (gr. 4-7). (978-1-4236-0550-8(0)) Gibbs Smith, Publisher.
Friendly Octopus. 2004. (J). per. (978-1-57657-373-0(7)) Paradise Pr., Inc.
Gaffney, K. Ollie the Octopus. 2012. 12p. pap. 12.68 (978-1-4669-7023-6(5)) Trafford Publishing.
Gaines, Pat. O. O. Octopus: Sheriff of Blue Ribbon Sound. 2008. (Illus.). 24p. (J). lib. bdg. (978-0-9801376-4-4(0)); per. (978-0-9801376-5-1(9)) Dragonfly Publishing, Inc.
Galloway, Ruth. Clumsy Crab. Galloway, Ruth, illus. 2005. (Illus.). 32p. (J). (gr. -1-2). 15.95 (978-1-58925-050-5(8)) Tiger Tales.
—Tickly Octopus. Galloway, Ruth, illus. 2007. (Illus.). 15.95 (978-1-58925-064-2(8)) Tiger Tales.
Green, Judy. The Little Blue Octopus. 2009. 28p. pap. 21.99 (978-1-4415-3393-7(1)) Xlibris Corp.
Hart, J. Tristan. The Adventures of Friendly & Barnackel: Book 3 Ollie the Octopus. 2011. 32p. 12.77 (978-1-4567-2602-7(1)) AuthorHouse.
Holmes, Steve, illus. Animales Marinos: Mezcla y Diviertete. 2005. (Mezcla y Diviertete Ser.). (SPA.). 5p. (J). (gr. -1-7). (978-970-718-291-2(1), Silver Dolphin en Español) Advanced Marketing, S. de R. L. de C. V.
Kesinger, Brian. Coloring with Your Octopus: A Coloring Book for Domesticated Cephalopods. 2014. (ENG., Illus.). 48p. pap. 12.00 (978-1-61404-010-1(9)) Baby Tattoo Bks.
Knox, Dahk. Zander, Friend of the Se. 2008. 32p. pap. 7.95 (978-1-58275-229-7(X)) Black Forest Pr.
Kompelien, Tracy. Octopus's Garden, 1 vol. 2007. (Critter Chronicles Ser.). (ENG., Illus.). 24p. (J). (gr. k-3). lib. bdg. 24.21 (978-1-59928-456-9(1), SandCastle) ABDO Publishing Co.
Lee, Shari. Mandie's & Mindie's Adventure under the Sea, 1 vol. 2009. 63p. pap. 19.95 (978-1-4489-9977-4(4)) America Star Bks.
Making Waves. 2004. (J). per. (978-1-57657-460-7(1)) Paradise Pr., Inc.
Mayer, Mercer. Octopus Soup, 0 vols. Mayer, Mercer, illus. 2011. (ENG., Illus.). 24p. (J). (gr. k-3). 16.99 (978-0-7614-5812-8(3), 9780761458128, Amazon Children's Publishing) Amazon Publishing.
Mcintyre Brister, Mary. Ollie the Orange Octopus. 2009. 24p. pap. 12.99 (978-1-4389-8372-1(7)) AuthorHouse.
McKenna, Martin. The Octopuppy. 2015. (ENG., Illus.). 32p. (J). (gr. -1-k). 16.99 (978-0-545-75140-7(3), Scholastic Pr.) Scholastic, Inc.
Meister, Cari. The Fancy Octopus, 1 vol. Harpster, Steve, illus. 2011. (Ocean Tales Ser.). (ENG.). 32p. (gr. 2-3). pap. 6.25 (978-1-4342-3392-9(8)); lib. bdg. 22.65 (978-1-4342-3201-4(8)) Stone Arch Bks.
Menard, Lucille. The Top of the Bottom: Inky to the Rescue, Volume 1. 2013. 38p. pap. 12.50 (978-0-9887969-6-6(1)) Four Menards, The.
Michie, Brandon J. Ollie the Octopus: Animal Lessons. 2011. 20p. 13.49 (978-1-4567-4782-4(7)) AuthorHouse.
Morano, John. Makoona. 2nd rev. ed. 2005. (Morano Eco-Adventure Ser.: 2). 236p. (YA). (gr. 8-12). per. 14.99 (978-1-59092-111-1(9)) Blue Forge Pr.
Nyeu, Tao. Squid & Octopus: Friends for Always. 2012. (ENG., Illus.). 40p. (J). (gr. -1-k). 16.99 (978-0-8037-3565-1(0), Dial Bks) Penguin Young Readers Group.
October the Octopus: A Huggable Concept Book about the Months of the Year. 2014. (ENG., Illus.). 28p. (J). (gr. -1-k). 24.99 (978-1-4814-2047-1(X), Simon & Schuster/Paula Wiseman Bks.) Simon & Schuster/Paula Wiseman Bks.
Pendergrass, Daphne. Meet the Penguins! Style Guide, Style, illus. 2014. (Penguins of Madagascar Ser.). (ENG.). 24p. (J). (gr. -1-3). pap. 3.99 (978-1-4814-3734-9(8), Simon Spotlight) Simon Spotlight.
Pichard, Alexandra. Pen Pals. Pichard, Alexandra, illus. 2017. (ENG., Illus.). 48p. (J). (gr. -1-2). 17.99 (978-1-4814-7247-0(X), Simon & Schuster/Paula Wiseman Bks.) Simon & Schuster/Paula Wiseman Bks.
Pitcher, Caroline. Nico's Octopus. Mistry, Nilesh, illus. 2003. (ENG.). 32p. (J). (gr. k-3). 15.95 (978-1-56656-483-0(2), Crocodile Bks.) Interlink Publishing Group, Inc.
Pollard, Mary Jean. Octrina the Octopus. 2011. 28p. pap. 15.99 (978-1-4568-4778-4(3)) Xlibris Corp.
Puckett, A. J., creator. If I Had a Pet Octopus. 2005. (Illus.). 24p. (J). (978-0-9764938-0-8(2)) Puckett Publishing, Inc.
Ramos, Angelica. If My Mommy Was an Octopus. 2008. 12p. pap. 24.95 (978-1-60563-821-8(8)) PublishAmerica, Inc.
Rathmell, Donna & Rathmell, Doreen. Octavia & Her Purple Ink Cloud, 1 vol. McLennan, Connie, illus. 2006. (ENG.). 32p. (J). (gr. -1-2). 15.95 (978-0-9764943-5-5(3)); pap. 9.95 (978-1-60718-586-4(5)) Arbordale Publishing.
Reed, Lynn Rowe. Shark Kiss, Octopus Hug. Cornell, Kevin, illus. 2014. (ENG.). 32p. (J). (gr. -1-3). 14.99 (978-0-06-220320-5(7)) HarperCollins Pubs.
Roby, Ian. Surface Diver Tommy & the Sea Critters, 1 vol. 2010. 40p. 24.95 (978-1-4489-6161-0(0)) PublishAmerica, Inc.
Rouss, Sylvia & Avalone, C. The Littlest Fish. 2008. 32p. 12.95 (978-1-934440-53-7(1), Pitspopany Pr.) Simcha Media Group.
Rylant, Cynthia. The Octopus. McDaniels, Preston, illus. 2005. (Lighthouse Family Ser.: 5). (ENG.). 64p. (J). (gr. 1-5). 15.99 (978-0-689-86246-5(6), Simon & Schuster Bks. For Young Readers) Simon & Schuster Bks. For Young Readers.
Shernock, Judith. Sammi the Seahorse. 2012. 28p. pap. 15.99 (978-1-4691-3293-8(1)) Xlibris Corp.
Srinivasan, Divya. Octopus Alone. 2013. (ENG., Illus.). 40p. (J). (gr. -1-k). 16.99 (978-0-670-78515-5(6), Viking Books for Young Readers) Penguin Young Readers Group.
Starr, Ringo, pseud. Octopus's Garden. Cort, Ben, illus. 2014. (ENG.). 32p. (J). (gr. -1-3). 17.99 (978-1-4814-0362-7(1), Aladdin) Simon & Schuster Children's Publishing.
Strub, Scott Richard. Otto the Outerspace Octopus. 2007. (J). per. 10.00 (978-1-59872-782-1(6)) Instant Pub.
Tauililli, Pemerika L. The Rat & the Bat: And Other Short Stories. 2009. 88p. pap. 16.99 (978-1-4490-4389-6(5)); pap. 32.49 (978-1-4389-2700-8(2)) AuthorHouse.
Tokuda-Hall, Maggie. Also an Octopus. Davies, Benji, illus. 2016. (ENG.). 32p. (J). (gr. -1-2). 16.99 (978-0-7636-7084-9(7)) Candlewick Pr.
Trimble, Marcia. The Adventure of Pushy Octopus & His Friends. Sprague, Dean, illus. 2005. 18p. (J). (gr. k-2). 4.95 (978-1-891577-61-1(1), SAN2994844) Images Pr.
Ullrich, Nai D. Octo-Annie: Home-Help Super Star. 2012. 24p. pap. 15.99 (978-1-4797-0928-1(X)) Xlibris Corp.
Ungerer, Tomi. Emile. 2009. 32p. 16.95 (978-0-7148-4973-7(1)) Phaidon Pr., Inc.
Voake, Charlotte. Melissa's Octopus & Other Unsuitable Pets. Voake, Charlotte, illus. 2015. (ENG., Illus.). 32p. (J). (gr. -1-2). 16.99 (978-0-7636-7481-6(8)) Candlewick Pr.
Vosailagi, Jo, illus. Pentapus. 2006. 120p. per. 12.56 (978-1-4120-9272-2(8)) Trafford Publishing.
Wrecks, Billy. Crime Wave! 2012. (Step into Reading Level 2 Ser.). lib. bdg. 13.55 (978-0-606-23739-0(9), Turtleback) Turtleback Bks.
—Crime Wave! (DC Super Friends) Schoening, Dan, illus. 2012. (Step into Reading Ser.). (ENG.). 32p. (J). (gr. -1-1). pap. 3.99 (978-0-375-86898-6(4), Random Hse. Bks. for Young Readers) Random Hse. Children's Bks.

ODYSSEUS (GREEK MYTHOLOGY)

Capaldi, Mario, illus. Odysseus & the Wooden Horse: A Greek Legend. 2003. (Dominie Collection of Myths & Legends). (SPA.). 20p. (J). lib. bdg. (978-0-7685-2425-3(3)) Dominie Pr., Inc.
—Odysseus & the Wooden Horse: A Greek Legend. 2004. (SPA & ENG.). 20p. (J). (gr. 3-3). pap. 6.47 net. (978-0-7685-2128-3(9), Dominie Elementary) Pearson Schl.
Church, Alfred J. The Story of the Odyssey. 2007. 128p. per. (978-1-4065-1370-7(9)) Dodo Pr.
Church, Alfred John. The Story of the Odyssey. 2004. reprint ed. pap. 19.95 (978-1-4191-8412-3(1)); pap. 1.99 (978-1-4192-8412-0(6)) Kessinger Publishing, LLC.
Clayboume, A. & Khanduri, K. Greek Myths: Ulysses & the Trojan War: Mini-Edition. 2004. (Spotter's Guides). 160p. (J). 8.95 (978-0-7945-0535-6(X)) EDC Publishing.
Colum, Padraic. The Adventures of Odysseus & the Tale of Troy. Pogány, Willy, illus. 2004. (Dover Children's Classics Ser.). (ENG.). 176p. (J). (gr. 3-8). pap. 6.95 (978-0-486-43455-1(9)) Dover Pubns., Inc.
—The Adventures of Odysseus & the Tale of Troy. Pogány, Willy, illus. 2008. 164p. pap. (978-1-4068-2730-9(4)) Echo Library.
—The Adventures of Odysseus & the Tales of Troy. 2007. (ENG.). 200p. pap. 19.99 (978-1-4346-0573-3(6)); 220p. pap. 22.99 (978-1-4346-0648-8(1)) Creative Media Partners, LLC.
—The Children's Homer: The Adventures of Odysseus & the Tale of Troy. 2011. 144p. pap. 7.95 (978-1-61382-004-9(6)) Simon & Brown.
Freeberg, Eric, illus. Greek Myths. 2011. (Classic Starts(tm) Ser.). (ENG.). 160p. (J). (gr. 2-4). 6.95 (978-1-4027-7312-9(9)) Sterling Publishing Co., Inc.
Hoena, Blake. The Epic Adventures of Odysseus: An Interactive Mythological Adventure. Azzalin, Stefano, illus. 2016. (You Choose: Ancient Greek Myths Ser.). (ENG.). 112p. (gr. 3-4). lib. bdg. 31.99 (978-1-4914-8114-1(5), You Choose Bks.) Capstone Press of Coughlan Cos.
Hoena, Blake, retold by. The Voyages of Odysseus: A Graphic Retelling. 2015. (Ancient Myths Ser.). (ENG., Illus.). 32p. (gr. 3-4). lib. bdg. 30.65 (978-1-4914-2076-8(6), Graphic Library) Capstone Press of Coughlan Cos.
Homer. The Odyssey. Freeberg, Eric, illus. 2011. (Classic Starts(tm) Ser.). (ENG.). 160p. (J). (gr. 2-4). 6.95 (978-1-4027-7334-1(X)) Sterling Publishing Co., Inc.
—The Odyssey. Tsilis, Thanos, illus. 2013. (Greek Classics Ser.). (ENG.). 64p. pap. 6.95 (978-1-906230-54-8(4)) Real Reads Ltd. GBR. Dist: Casemate Pubs. & Bk. Distributors, LLC.
Homer. The Odyssey. Gelev, Penko & Sidong, Li, illus. 2009. (Barron's Graphic Classics Ser.). (ENG.). (J). (gr. 5-11). lib. bdg. 21.10 **(978-1-62765-645-0(6))** Perfection Learning Corp.
Jeffrey, Gary. Odysseus & the Odyssey. 2012. (Graphic Mythical Heroes Ser.). (Illus.). 24p. (J). (gr. 3-5). pap. 8.15 (978-1-4339-7520-2(3)); lib. bdg. 23.95 (978-1-4339-7519-6(X)) Stevens, Gareth Publishing LLLP.
Jolley, Dan. Odysseus: Escaping Poseidon's Curse. 2009. pap. 52.95 (978-0-7613-4759-0(3)) Lerner Publishing Group.
—Odysseus: Escaping Poseidon's Curse. Yeates, Thomas, illus. (Graphic Myths & Legends Ser.). (ENG.). 48p. (gr. 4-8). 2008. pap. 8.95 (978-0-8225-8515-2(4)) 2007. (J). lib. bdg. 27.93 (978-0-8225-6208-5(1), Graphic Universe™) Lerner Publishing Group.
—Odysseus: Escaping Poseidon's Curse [a Greek Legend]. Yeates, Thomas, illus. 2015. (Graphic Myths & Legends Ser.). (ENG.). 48p. (gr. 4-8). 21.32 (978-1-4677-5983-0(X), Lerner Digital) Lerner Publishing Group.
Jonas, Anne. Ulises y Casimiro. (SPA.). 32p. (J). (gr. 2-4). (978-84-8418-043-2(3)) Zendrera Zariquiey, Editorial ESP. Dist: Lectorum Pubns., Inc.
LaFontaine, Bruce. The Adventures of Ulysses. 2014. (Dover Classic Stories Coloring Book Ser.). (ENG., Illus.). 32p. (J). (gr. 4-6). pap. 3.99 (978-0-486-43328-8(5)) Dover Pubns., Inc.
Lamb, Charles. Adventures of Ulysses. 2006. pap. (978-1-4068-1416-3(4)) Echo Library.
Lupton, Hugh & Morden, Daniel. The Adventures of Odysseus. Balit, Christina, illus. 2012. (ENG.). 96p. (J). 23.99 (978-1-84686-703-3(7)) Barefoot Bks., Inc.
Lupton, Hugh, et al. The Adventures of Odysseus. 2006. (ENG., Illus.). 96p. (J). (gr. 3-7). 19.99 (978-1-84148-800-4(3)) Barefoot Bks., Inc.
Osborne, Mary Pope. Tales from the Odyssey, 3 vols. 2010. (Tales from the Odyssey Ser.). (ENG., Illus.). (J). (gr. 3-7). Pt. 1. 288p. pap. 5.99 (978-1-4231-2864-9(8))Pt. 2. 304p. pap. 5.99 (978-1-4231-2610-2(6)) Disney Pr.
Spies, Karen Bornemann. Mythology of the Iliad & the Odyssey. 2014. (Mythology, Myths, & Legends Ser.). 96p. (J). (gr. 6-12). 27.94 (978-0-7660-6172-9(8)) Enslow Pubs., Inc.
Sutcliff, Rosemary. The Wanderings of Odysseus: The Story of the Odyssey. 2005. (ENG.). 160p. (YA). (gr. 7). mass mkt. 7.99 (978-0-553-49482-2(1), Laurel Leaf) Random Hse. Children's Bks.
Takvorian, Nadine, illus. Odysseus & the Cyclops, 1 vol. 2011. (Greek Myths Ser.). (ENG.). 32p. (gr. 4-5). lib. bdg. 28.65 (978-1-4048-6666-9(3), 1329959) Picture Window Bks.
Tracy, Kathleen. Odysseus. 2008. (Profiles in Greek & Roman Mythology Ser.). (Illus.). 48p. (J). (gr. 4-7). lib. bdg. 29.95 (978-1-58415-705-2(4)) Mitchell Lane Pubs., Inc.
Weiss, Lynne. The Voyage of Odysseus, 1 vol., 1. 2014. (Jr. Graphic Myths: Greek Heroes Ser.). (ENG., Illus.). 24p. (J). (gr. 3-6). 26.25 (978-1-4777-6244-8(2), PowerKids Pr.) Rosen Publishing Group, Inc., The.

OFFICE WORK—TRAINING

see Business Education

OFFICIALS

see Civil Service
see names of countries, cities, etc. and organizations with subdivision Officials and Employees, e.g. United States—Officials and Employees

OGLETHORPE, JAMES EDWARD, 1696-1785

Bennett, Doraine. Tomochichi. 2008. (J). *(978-1-935077-06-0(6))*; pap. *(978-1-935077-13-8(9))* State Standards Publishing, LLC.

Blackburn, Joyce. James Edward Oglethorpe. 2004. (ENG., Illus.). 192p. (J). per. 15.95 *(978-1-57736-332-3(9))* Turner Publishing Co.

Schwartz, Heather E. Tomochichi: A Chief & a Friend. 2016. (Primary Source Readers Ser.). (Illus.). 32p. (gr. 2-2). 8.99 *(978-1-4938-2556-1(9))* Teacher Created Materials, Inc.

OHIO

Barker, Charles Ferguson. Under Ohio: The Story of Ohio's Rocks & Fossils. Barker, Charles Ferguson, illus. 2007. (Illus.). 56p. (J). (gr. 3-7). 26.95 *(978-0-8214-1755-3(X))* Ohio Univ. Pr.

Birle, Pete. Cleveland Cavaliers. 2014. (On the Hardwood Ser.). (gr. 3-8). pap. 8.95 *(978-1-61570-901-4(0))* Scobre Pr. Corp.

Birle, Peter. Cleveland Cavaliers. 2014. (On the Hardwood Ser.). 48p. (gr. 3-8). 27.93 *(978-1-61570-902-1(9))* Scobre Pr. Corp.

Brown, Dottie. Ohio. (J). 2012. lib. bdg. 25.26 *(978-0-7613-4550-3(7)*, Lerner Pubns.) 2nd exp. rev. ed. 2003. (Illus.). 84p. (gr. 3-6). pap. 6.95 *(978-0-8225-4134-9(3))* Lerner Publishing Group.

Gibbs Smith & Padavick, Nate. Know Your State Ohio, 1 vol. 2016. (ENG., Illus.). 272p. (J). pap. 14.99 *(978-1-4236-4225-1(2))* Gibbs Smith, Publisher.

Hart, Joyce. Ohio. 2006. (It's My State! Ser.). (Illus.). 80p. (J). (gr. 4-7). lib. bdg. *(978-0-7614-1907-5(1)*, Benchmark Bks.) Marshall Cavendish Corp.

Houghton, Gillian. Mildred Taylor. 2005. (Library of Author Biographies Ser.). (Illus.). 112p. (YA). 34.60 *(978-1-4042-0330-3(3))* Rosen Publishing Group, Inc., The.

Kurtz, Jane. Celebrating Ohio. Canga, C. B., illus. 2015. (Green Light Readers Level 3 Ser.). (ENG.). 40p. (J). (gr. 1-4). pap. 3.99 *(978-0-544-41979-7(0)*, HMH Books For Young Readers) Houghton Mifflin Harcourt Publishing Co.

Lew, Kristi. Ohio: Past & Present. 2009. (J). 70.50 *(978-1-4358-5571-7(X))*; (J). pap. 11.75 *(978-1-4358-5570-0(1))*; (ENG., Illus.). 48p. (YA). lib. bdg. 29.25 *(978-1-4358-5286-0(9))* Rosen Publishing Group, Inc., The. (Rosen Reference).

Lusted, Marcia Amidon. Ohio: The Buckeye State. (Illus.). 24p. (J). 2010. pap. 8.25 *(978-1-4358-3370-8(8))* 2009. lib. bdg. 22.60 *(978-1-4042-8122-6(3))* Rosen Publishing Group, Inc., The. (PowerKids Pr.).

Maine, Tyler. Ohio. 2016. (States Ser.). (ENG., Illus.). 32p. (gr. 3-4). lib. bdg. 27.32 *(978-1-5157-0422-5(X))* Next Page Pr., The.

Marsh, Carole. Ohio Current Events Projects: 30 Cool, Activities, Crafts, Experiments & More for Kids to Do to Learn about Your State! 2003. (Ohio Experience Ser.). 32p. (gr. k-5). pap. 5.95 *(978-0-635-02054-3(8)*, Marsh, Carole Bks.) Gallopade International.

—Ohio Experience Book (HC) 2004. 64p. 29.95 *(978-0-635-02505-0(1))* Gallopade International.

—Ohio Experience Book (PB) 2004. 64p. pap. 14.95 *(978-0-635-02504-3(3))* Gallopade International.

—Ohio Geography Projects: 30 Cool, Activities, Crafts, Experiments & More for Kids to Do to Learn about Your State! 2003. (Ohio Experience Ser.). 32p. (gr. k-5). pap. 5.95 *(978-0-635-01854-0(3)*, Marsh, Carole Bks.) Gallopade International.

—Ohio Government Projects: 30 Cool, Activities, Crafts, Experiments & More for Kids to Do to Learn about Your State! 2003. (Ohio Experience Ser.). 32p. (gr. k-5). pap. 5.95 *(978-0-635-01954-7(X)*, Marsh, Carole Bks.) Gallopade International.

—Ohio History Projects: 30 Cool, Activities, Crafts, Experiments & More for Kids to Do to Learn about Your State! 2003. (Ohio Experience Ser.). 32p. (gr. k-5). pap. 5.95 *(978-0-635-01804-5(7)*, Marsh, Carole Bks.) Gallopade International.

—Ohio People Projects: 30 Cool, Activities, Crafts, Experiments & More for Kids to Do to Learn about Your State! 2003. (Ohio Experience Ser.). 32p. (gr. k-5). pap. 5.95 *(978-0-635-02004-8(1)*, Marsh, Carole Bks.) Gallopade International.

—Ohio Symbols & Facts Projects: 30 Cool, Activities, Crafts, Experiments & More for Kids to Do to Learn about Your State! 2003. (Ohio Experience Ser.). 32p. (gr. k-5). pap. 5.95 *(978-0-635-01904-2(3)*, Marsh, Carole Bks.) Gallopade International.

—Ohio's Big Activity Book. 2004. (Ohio Experience! Ser.). (Illus.). 96p. (J). (gr. 2-6). pap. 9.95 *(978-0-7933-9464-7(3))* Gallopade International.

McHugh, Erin. Ohio. Schrier, Alfred, illus. 2007. (ENG.). 48p. (J). (gr. -1-17). 9.95 *(978-1-57912-702-2(9)*, 81702, Black Dog & Leventhal Pubs. Inc.) Hachette Bks.

Murray, Julie. Ohio, 1 vol. 2006. (Buddy Book Ser.). (ENG., Illus.). 32p. (gr. 2-4). 27.07 *(978-1-59197-694-3(4)*, Buddy Bks.) ABDO Publishing Co.

Oehler, David A. The Cincinnati Zoo & Botanical Garden. 2003. (Great Zoos of the United States Ser.). (Illus.). 24p. (J). lib. bdg. 22.60 *(978-0-8239-6320-1(9)*, PowerKids Pr.) Rosen Publishing Group, Inc., The.

Rexroth, Sharon. Ohio from the Sky. 2006. (ENG., Illus.). (J). 9.95 *(978-1-57166-420-4(3))* Quixote Pr.

Roe-Pimm, Nancy. Colo's Story. 2011. (ENG.). 80p. (gr. 4-8). 18.95 *(978-0-9841554-4-6(9))*; pap. 8.95 *(978-0-9841554-5-3(7))* Columbus Zoo & Aquarium, The.

Schonberg, Marcia. The Ohio Reader. Darnell, K. L., illus. rev. ed. 2007. (State Readers Ser.). (ENG.). 96p. (J). (gr. 1-5). 12.95 *(978-1-58536-321-6(9))* Sleeping Bear Pr.

Sherrow, Victoria. Ohio. 2nd ed. 2007. (Celebrate the States Ser.). (J). lib. bdg. 42.79 *(978-0-7614-2558-8(6)*, Benchmark Bks.) Marshall Cavendish Corp.

Swainston, Jeani. Grandma Stuff: ... it's what love Is made Of. 2006. (J). *(978-0-9791384-0-9(X))* Rock Cliff Media.

Taylor-Butler, Christine. Ohio. 2007. (Rookie Read-About Geography Ser.). (Illus.). 31p. (J). (gr. 1-2). 20.50 *(978-0-531-12573-1(4)*, Children's Pr.) Scholastic Library Publishing.

Way, Jennifer. Ohio. 2009. (Bilingual Library of the United States of America Ser.). (ENG & SPA.). 32p. (gr. 2-2). 47.90 *(978-1-60853-379-4(4)*, Editorial Buenas Letras) Rosen Publishing Group, Inc., The.

—Ohio. Brusca, Maria Cristina, tr. from ENG. 2006. (Bilingual Library of the United States of America Ser.: Set 2). (ENG & SPA., Illus.). 32p. (J). (gr. 3-6). lib. bdg. 25.25 *(978-1-4042-3100-9(5))* Rosen Publishing Group, Inc., The.

Weintraub, A. How to Draw Ohio's Sights & Symbols. 2009. (Kid's Guide to Drawing America Ser.). 32p. (gr. k-k). 50.50 *(978-1-61511-088-9(7)*, PowerKids Pr.) Rosen Publishing Group, Inc., The.

Woodyard, Chris. Haunted Ohio V: 200 Years of Ghosts. 2003. (Illus.). 240p. pap. *(978-0-9628472-8-8(3))* Kestrel Pubns.

OHIO—BIOGRAPHY

Andreasen, Dan. The Giant of Seville: A Tall Tale Based on a True Story. 2007. (ENG., Illus.). 32p. (J). (gr. -1-3). 16.95 *(978-0-8109-0988-5(X)*, Abrams Bks. for Young Readers) Abrams, Inc.

Georgiady, Nicholas P., et al. Ohio Men, Vol. 2. Collins, Julia B., illus. 2nd rev. ed. Date not set. 44p. (J). (gr. 4-8). pap. 4.50 *(978-0-917961-04-5(8))* Argee Pubs.

Huey, Lois Miner. Floodwaters & Flames: The 1913 Disaster in Dayton, Ohio. 2016. (ENG., Illus.). 56p. (gr. 4-8). 50.65 *(978-1-4677-9728-3(6)*, Millbrook Pr.) Lerner Publishing Group.

Mangal, Melina. Mildred Taylor. 2004. (Classic Storytellers Ser.). (Illus.). 48p. (J). (gr. 4-8). lib. bdg. 29.95 *(978-1-58415-311-5(3))* Mitchell Lane Pubs., Inc.

Sims, Rudine. Bishop Daniel A. Payne: Great Black Leader. 2009. (Illus.). 70p. (J). (gr. 3-7). pap. 12.95 *(978-1-933491-15-8(9))* Just Us Bks., Inc.

Sowash, Rick. Heroes of Ohio: 23 True Tales of Courage & Character. 2003. (J). 19.95 *(978-0-9762412-5-6(0))*; pap. 11.95 *(978-0-9762412-4-9(2))* Sowash, Rick Publishing Co.

—Heroes of Ohio Coloring Book. 2003. (J). 5.95 *(978-0-9762412-6-3(9))* Sowash, Rick Publishing Co.

Tait, Leia. Emi the Sumatran Rhino. 2008. (Inspiring Animals Ser.). (Illus.). 24p. (J). (gr. 2-4). pap. 8.95 *(978-1-59036-857-2(6))*; lib. bdg. 24.45 *(978-1-59036-856-5(8))* Weigl Pubs., Inc.

Williams, Dave. Windgalore Farm. 2005. (Illus.). 182p. pap. 21.95 *(978-0-937921-56-2(4))* Acorn Publishing.

OHIO—FICTION

Adams, James D. Creepy Campfire Tales: Halloween Campout, Vol. 1. 2008. 132p. (J). per. 12.95 *(978-1-60404-103-3(X))* Owl Creek Media Ltd.

—Creepy Campfire Tales Vol. 1: Halloween Campout. 2008. 132p. (YA). 26.95 *(978-1-60404-104-0(8))* Owl Creek Media Ltd.

Alpine, Rachele. A Void the Size of the World. 2017. (ENG., Illus.). 368p. (YA). (gr. 9). 17.99 ***(978-1-4814-8571-5(7)**, Simon Pulse)* Simon Pulse.

Altsheler, Joseph A. The Border Watch: A Story of the Great Chief's Last Stand. 2008. 320p. pap. *(978-1-4099-0579-0(9))* Dodo Pr.

—The Border Watch: A Story of the Great Chief's Last Stand. 2008. 232p. pap. *(978-1-84830-132-0(4))* Echo Library.

—The Border Watch: A Story of the Great Chief's Last Stand. 2010. (Young Trailers Ser.: Vol. 8). (Illus.). 206p. (J). (gr. 4-7). reprint ed. pap. 20.31 *(978-1-153-78841-0(1))* General Bks. LLC.

—The Border Watch: A Story of the Great Chief's Last Stand. 2012. (Young Trailers Ser.: Vol. 8). 340p. (J). (gr. 4-7). reprint ed. pap. *(978-3-8472-2486-0(7))* Tredition GmbH.

Anderson, Jennifer. Honey Creek Royalty. 2013. 246p. pap. 12.99 *(978-1-62237-148-8(8))* Turquoise Morning Pr.

Anderson, Laurie Halse. Twisted. 2014. (ENG.). 288p. (YA). (gr. 7-12). 14.24 *(978-1-63245-343-3(6))* Lectorum Pubns., Inc.

—Twisted. 2011. 11.04 *(978-0-7848-3388-9(5)*, Everbind) Marco Bk. Co.

—Twisted. 2008. (ENG.). 288p. (YA). (gr. 7-18). 9.99 *(978-0-14-241184-1(1)*, Speak) Penguin Young Readers Group.

—Twisted. l.t. ed. 2007. (Literacy Bridge Young Adult Ser.). 299p. (YA). (gr. 7-12). 23.95 *(978-0-7862-9885-3(5))* Thorndike Pr.

Aryal, Aimee. Hello, Brutus! De Angel, Miguel & Moore, D., illus. 2006. 24p. (J). lib. bdg. 14.95 *(978-1-932888-51-5(9))* Mascot Bks., Inc.

Barker, Charles Ferguson. Under Ohio: The Story of Ohio's Rocks & Fossils. 2016. (ENG.). 56p. pap. 17.95 *(978-0-8214-2195-6(6))* Ohio Univ. Pr.

Barnes, John. Tales of the Madman Underground. 2011. (ENG.). 544p. (YA). (gr. 9-18). 9.99 *(978-0-14-241702-7(5)*, Speak) Penguin Young Readers Group.

Basham, Tom. Accidental Evie. Calvert, Lissa, illus. 2012. 120p. *(978-1-77097-373-2(7))*; pap. *(978-1-77097-374-9(5))* FriesenPress.

Beil, Michael D. Summer at Forsaken Lake. Kneen, Maggie, illus. 2013. (ENG.). 336p. (J). (gr. 5). pap. 8.99 *(978-0-375-86496-4(2)*, Yearling) Random Hse. Children's Bks.

Berten, Jinny Powers & Holt, Norah. Littsie of Cincinnati. 2003. (Illus.). 125p. (J). per. 9.95 *(978-0-9724421-0-7(3))* Fountain Square Publishing.

Bogel, Rachel Anne. A Ride on the Monster's Back. Greenfelder, Jill, illus. 2008. 28p. pap. 15.99 *(978-1-59858-752-4(8))* Dog Ear Publishing, LLC.

Borntrager, Mary Christner. Andy. 2015. (Ellie's People Ser.: Vol. 6). (ENG.). 200p. (YA). (gr. 7-18). pap. 9.99 *(978-0-8361-3633-3(0))* Herald Pr.

—Ellie. 2014. (Ellie's People, Book One Ser.: Vol. 1). (ENG.). 193p. (J). (gr. 3-7). pap. 9.99 *(978-0-8361-3468-1(0))* Herald Pr.

—Rebecca. 2014. (Ellie's People, Book Two Ser.: Vol. 2). (ENG.). 234p. (J). (gr. 4-7). pap. 9.99 *(978-0-8361-3500-8(8))* Herald Pr.

Bowditch, Eden Unger. The Atomic Weight of Secrets or the Arrival of the Mysterious Men in Black. 2011. (Young Inventors Guild Ser.: 1). (ENG.). 320p. (YA). 19.95 *(978-1-61088-002-2(1)*, 33471904-45bf-4a52-9f65-44ef10fff3b6) Bancroft Pr.

Brenner, Vida. The Magic Music Shop. Sharp, Mary, ed. Sharpnack, Joe, illus. 2013. 102p. pap. 12.95 *(978-1-57216-094-1(2))* Penfield Bks.

Brunstetter, Wanda E. Humble Pie. Madden, Colleen M., illus. 2014. 158p. (J). *(978-1-63058-967-7(5))* Barbour Publishing, Inc.

Charlton-Trujillo, E. E. Fat Angie. 2013. (ENG.). 272p. (YA). (gr. 9). 16.99 *(978-0-7636-6119-9(8))* Candlewick Pr.

Clements, Andrew. Lost & Found. Elliott, Mark, illus. 2010. (ENG.). 192p. (J). (gr. 3-7). pap. 7.99 *(978-1-4169-0986-6(9)*, Atheneum Bks. for Young Readers) Simon & Schuster Children's Publishing.

Cohen-Spence, Susan. An Amazing Adventure Back in Time. Scott, Susan, illus. 2013. 32p. pap. 14.99 *(978-0-9886360-4-0(2))* Kids At Heart Publishing, LLC.

Coolidge, Susan. What Katy Did. 2012. 246p. pap. *(978-1-78139-262-1(5))* Benediction Classics.

—What Katy Did. 2012. 302p. pap. 29.75 *(978-1-286-07372-8(3))* 2012. 300p. pap. 29.75 *(978-1-286-00091-5(2))* 2011. 290p. (gr. 3-7). pap. 28.75 *(978-1-179-65265-8(7))* 2010. (ENG.). 300p. pap. 29.75 *(978-1-178-00783-1(9))* 2010. (ENG.). 282p. (gr. 3-7). pap. 28.75 *(978-1-177-27477-7(9))* 2010. 302p. pap. 29.75 *(978-1-145-74830-9(9))* 2008. 164p. (gr. 4-7). 22.99 *(978-0-554-37937-1(6))* 2008. 164p. (gr. 4-7). 25.99 *(978-0-554-28634-1(3))* 2007. (ENG.). 144p. pap. 18.99 *(978-1-4346-5943-9(7))* 2007. (ENG.). 160p. pap. 21.99 *(978-1-4346-5944-6(5))* Creative Media Partners, LLC.

—What Katy Did. 2007. (ENG.). 148p. per. *(978-1-4065-1527-5(2))* Dodo Pr.

—What Katy Did. 2006. (Dover Children's Classics Ser.). (ENG., Illus.). 160p. (J). (gr. 3-8). per. 6.95 *(978-0-486-44760-5(X))* Dover Pubns., Inc.

—What Katy Did. 2007. (ENG.). 104p. per. *(978-1-4068-4855-7(7))* Echo Library.

—What Katy Did. 2010. (Illus.). 92p. (gr. 3-7). pap. 19.99 *(978-1-153-74507-9(0))* 2009. 104p. pap. 6.40 *(978-0-217-53637-0(9))* General Bks. LLC.

—What Katy Did. 2010. 132p. pap. *(978-1-4076-5115-6(3))* HardPr.

—What Katy Did. Ledyard, Addie, illus. 284p. 2010. 35.16 *(978-1-163-85079-4(9))* 2010. pap. 23.16 *(978-1-163-77965-1(2))* 2007. 43.95 *(978-0-548-53870-8(0))* 2007. per. 28.95 *(978-0-548-48700-6(6))* Kessinger Publishing, LLC.

—What Katy Did. 2010. (Puffin Classics Ser.). (ENG., Illus.). 240p. (J). (gr. 5-7). pap. 5.99 *(978-0-14-132671-9(9)*, Puffin Books) Penguin Young Readers Group.

—What Katy Did. 2013. (ENG., Illus.). 256p. (J). (gr. 4-7). pap. 12.99 *(978-0-09-957312-8(1))* Random Hse. GBR. Dist: Independent Pubs. Group.

—What Katy Did. 2007. (ENG.). 192p. pap. 12.45 *(978-1-60424-403-8(8)*, Book Jungle) Standard Pubns., Inc.

—What Katy Did. 2011. 162p. (gr. 3-7). pap. *(978-3-8424-6664-7(1))* Tredition GmbH.

—What Katy Did. 2010. 144p. pap. 4.99 *(978-1-61720-100-4(6))* Wilder Pubns., Corp.

Coolidge, Susan & Ledyard, Addie. What Katy Did. 2010. (ENG.). 292p. pap. 28.75 *(978-1-172-34659-2(3))* Creative Media Partners, LLC.

Cooper, Jennifer. Guardian Angel. 2009. 155p. pap. 12.87 *(978-0-557-09330-4(9))* Lulu Pr., Inc.

Cvetkovic, Judith. Mandy & Star's Sheep Ranch Getaway, 1 vol. 2010. 108p. pap. 19.95 *(978-1-4489-5673-9(0))* America Star Bks.

DeSio, Delores. Annie's Journey Through the Golden Door, 1 vol. 2009. 114p. pap. 19.95 *(978-1-4489-8470-1(X))* America Star Bks.

Draper, Sharon M. Double Dutch. 2004. 183p. (gr. 6-9). 17.00 *(978-0-7569-2934-3(2))* Perfection Learning Corp.

—Double Dutch. 2004. (ENG.). 192p. (J). (gr. 5-9). pap. 7.99 *(978-0-689-84231-3(7)*, Atheneum Bks. for Young Readers) Simon & Schuster Children's Publishing.

Evatt, Harriet. The Secret of the Old Coach Inn. Stone, David, illus. 2011. 190p. 42.95 *(978-1-258-08239-0(X))* Literary Licensing, LLC.

FitzGerald, Dawn. Getting in the Game. 2007. (ENG.). 144p. (J). (gr. 4-8). pap. 16.99 *(978-0-312-37753-3(3)*, 9780312377533) Square Fish.

—Soccer Chick Rules. 2007. (ENG.). 160p. (J). (gr. 5-9). per. 9.99 *(978-0-312-37662-8(6)*, 9780312376628) Square Fish.

Gabel, Stacey. The New Blue Tractor. Neuman, Richard, illus. 2007. 24p. per. 13.95 *(978-1-59858-424-0(3))* Dog Ear Publishing, LLC.

Garrott, Dawn E. How Riley Tamed the Invisible Monster. 2008. (J). pap. *(978-0-87743-709-3(2))* Baha'i Publishing Trust, U.S.

Garsee, Jeannine. The Unquiet. 2012. (ENG.). 400p. (YA). (gr. 9). 16.99 *(978-1-59990-723-9(2)*, 9781599907239, Bloomsbury USA Childrens) Bloomsbury Publishing USA.

Gerber, Carole. The Twelve Days of Christmas in Ohio. Ebbeler, Jeffrey, illus. 2014. (Twelve Days of Christmas in America Ser.). (ENG.). 40p. (J). (gr. k). 12.95 *(978-1-4549-0890-6(4))* Sterling Publishing Co., Inc.

Goon, Geraldine. Grandma Tells Dozens of Stories. 2008. 64p. pap. *(978-1-84748-515-1(4))* Athena Pr.

Greenburg, Dan. Secrets of Dripping Fang: Attack of the Giant Octopus. Fischer, Scott M., illus. 2009. (Secrets of Dripping Fang Ser.). (ENG.). 160p. 25.65 *(978-1-59961-537-0(1))* Spotlight.

—Secrets of Dripping Fang: Fall of the House of Mandible. Fischer, Scott M., illus. 2009. (Secrets of Dripping Fang Ser.). (ENG.). 160p. 25.65 *(978-1-59961-535-6(5))* Spotlight.

—Secrets of Dripping Fang: Please Don't Eat the Children: Book 7: Book 7. Fischer, Scott M., illus. 2009. (Secrets of Dripping Fang Ser.). (ENG.). 160p. 25.65 *(978-1-59961-538-7(X))* Spotlight.

—Secrets of Dripping Fang: The Onts. Fischer, Scott M., illus. 2009. (Secrets of Dripping Fang Ser.). (ENG.). 144p. 25.65 *(978-1-59961-532-5(0))* Spotlight.

—Secrets of Dripping Fang: The Shluffmuffin Boy Is History. Fischer, Scott M., illus. 2009. (Secrets of Dripping Fang Ser.). (ENG.). 176p. 25.65 *(978-1-59961-536-3(3))* Spotlight.

—Secrets of Dripping Fang: The Vampire's Curse: Book 3: Book 3. Fischer, Scott M., illus. 2009. (Secrets of Dripping Fang Ser.). (ENG.). 144p. 25.65 *(978-1-59961-534-9(7))* Spotlight.

—Secrets of Dripping Fang: Treachery & Betrayal at Jolly Days. Fischer, Scott M., illus. 2009. (Secrets of Dripping Fang Ser.). (ENG.). 144p. 25.65 *(978-1-59961-533-2(9))* Spotlight.

—Secrets of Dripping Fang: When Bad Snakes Attack Good Children. Fischer, Scott M., illus. 2009. (Secrets of Dripping Fang Ser.). (ENG.). 144p. 25.65 *(978-1-59961-539-4(8))* Spotlight.

—Secrets of Dripping Fang, Book Seven: Please Don't Eat the Children. Fischer, Scott M., illus. 2007. (Secrets of Dripping Fang Ser.: Bk. 7). (ENG.). 160p. (J). (gr. 2-5). 11.95 *(978-0-15-206047-3(2))* Houghton Mifflin Harcourt Publishing Co.

Greene, Stephanie. Queen Sophie Hartley. 2011. (ENG.). 144p. (J). (gr. 2-5). pap. 5.99 *(978-0-547-55021-3(9))* Houghton Mifflin Harcourt Publishing Co.

Haddix, Margaret Peterson. Full Ride. (ENG.). (YA). (gr. 7). 2014. 368p. pap. 12.99 *(978-1-4424-4279-5(4))* 2013. 352p. 16.99 *(978-1-4424-4278-8(6))* Simon & Schuster Bks. For Young Readers. (Simon & Schuster Bks. For Young Readers).

—Takeoffs & Landings. 2004. 201p. (gr. 5-9). 17.00 *(978-0-7569-4255-7(1))* Perfection Learning Corp.

Hamilton, Virginia. The House of Dies Drear. 8.97 *(978-0-13-437491-8(6))* Prentice Hall PTR.

—M. C. Higgins, the Great. 2006. 271p. (gr. 8-12). 18.00 *(978-0-7569-6809-0(7))* Perfection Learning Corp.

—M. C. Higgins, the Great, 6 vols. 3rd ed. (J). pap. 23.70 *(978-0-13-620220-2(9))*; pap. 3.95 *(978-0-13-800137-7(5))* Prentice Hall (Schl. Div.).

—M. C. Higgins, the Great. 2006. (ENG., Illus.). 288p. (J). (gr. 3-7). pap. 7.99 *(978-1-4169-1407-5(2)*, Aladdin) Simon & Schuster Children's Publishing.

Harwood, Kelsey. Still Alive. 2012. 144p. pap. 9.99 *(978-1-60820-746-6(3))* MLR Pr., LLC.

Hayes, Christine. The Mothman's Curse. Hindle, James K., illus. 2015. (ENG.). 320p. (J). (gr. 3-7). 15.99 *(978-1-62672-027-5(4)*, 9781626720275) Roaring Brook Pr.

—Mothman's Curse. 2016. (J). lib. bdg. 18.40 *(978-0-606-39560-1(1))* Turtleback Bks.

Holm, M. S. How Mohammed Saved Miss Liberty: The Story of a Good Muslim Boy. 2008. (ENG., Illus.). 270p. (YA). (gr. 7-12). pap. 12.00 *(978-0-9796199-0-8(4)*, Sentry Bks.) Great West Publishing.

Jacobs, Lily. The Littlest Bunny in Cincinnati: An Easter Adventure. Dunn, Robert, illus. 2015. (ENG.). 32p. (J). (-3). 9.99 *(978-1-4926-1054-0(2)*, Sourcebooks Jabberwocky) Sourcebooks, Inc.

—The Littlest Bunny in Ohio: An Easter Adventure. Dunn, Robert, illus. 2015. (ENG.). 32p. (J). (-3). 9.99 *(978-1-4926-1162-2(X)*, Sourcebooks Jabberwocky) Sourcebooks, Inc.

James, Eric. A Halloween Scare in Cincinnati. Le Ray, Marina, illus. 2015. (ENG.). 32p. (J). (-5). 9.99 *(978-1-4926-2369-4(5)*, 9781492623694, Sourcebooks Jabberwocky) Sourcebooks, Inc.

—A Halloween Scare in Ohio. Le Ray, Marina, illus. 2014. (ENG.). 32p. (J). (-5). 9.99 *(978-1-4926-0624-6(3)*, 9781492606246, Sourcebooks Jabberwocky) Sourcebooks, Inc.

—Santa's Sleigh Is on Its Way to Ohio. Dunn, Robert, illus. 2015. (ENG.). 32p. (J). (-2). 12.99 *(978-1-4926-2742-5(9)*, Sourcebooks Jabberwocky) Sourcebooks, Inc.

—Santa's Sleigh Is on Its Way to Cincinnati: A Christmas Adventure. Dunn, Robert, illus. 2016. (ENG.). 32p. (J). (-2). 12.99 *(978-1-4926-4324-1(6)*, 9781492643241, Sourcebooks Jabberwocky) Sourcebooks, Inc.

Jones, Patrick. Out of the Tunnel. 2014. (Red Zone Ser.: 1). (ENG.). 104p. (YA). (gr. 6-12). pap. 7.95 *(978-1-4677-4471-3(9)*, Darby Creek); lib. bdg. 27.93 *(978-1-4677-2126-4(3))* Lerner Publishing Group.

Keenan-Bolger, Andrew, et al. Jack & Louisa - Act 1. Webster, Kyle T., illus. 2015. (Jack & Louisa Ser.: 1). (ENG.). 240p. (J). (gr. 3-7). bds. 16.99 *(978-0-448-47839-5(0)*, Grosset & Dunlap) Penguin Young Readers Group.

Kennedy, Marlane. Me & the Pumpkin Queen. 2009. (ENG.). 192p. (J). (gr. 3-7). pap. 5.99 *(978-0-06-114024-2(4)*, Greenwillow Bks.) HarperCollins Pubs.

Kuhlman, Evan. The Last Invisible Boy. Coovert, J. P., illus. (ENG.). 240p. (J). (gr. 5-9). 2010. pap. 6.99 *(978-1-4169-6089-8(9))* 2008. 16.99 *(978-1-4169-5797-3(9))* Simon & Schuster Children's Publishing. (Atheneum Bks. for Young Readers).

Levine, Phyllis. At the Skylight with Matilda. 2007. (ENG.). 160p. per. 12.95 *(978-1-60047-089-9(0))* Wasteland Pr.

Levine, Susan Sachs. Harriett's Homecoming: A High-Flying Tour of Cincinnati. Burchwell, Erin, illus. 2012. (ENG.). 32p. (J). (gr. -1-3). 19.95 *(978-1-933197-97-5(8))* Orange Frazer Pr.

Lore, Pittacus. I Am Number Four. (YA). (gr. 9). 2016. (Lorien Legacies: the Lost Files Ser.). 416p. pap. 9.99 *(978-0-06-238771-4(5))* 2011. (Lorien Legacies Ser.: 1). (ENG.). 496p. pap. 9.99 *(978-0-06-196957-7(5))* 2010. (Lorien Legacies Ser.: 1). (ENG.). 448p. 17.99 *(978-0-06-196955-3(9))* 2011. (Lorien Legacies Ser.: 1). (ENG.). 496p. pap. 9.99 *(978-0-06-211655-0(X))* 2011. (Lorien Legacies Ser.: 1). (ENG.). 480p. 17.99 *(978-0-06-202624-8(0))* HarperCollins Pubs.

—I Am Number Four. 2009. (Lorien Legacies Ser.: Bk. 1). 11.04 *(978-0-7848-3715-3(5)*, Everbind) Marco Bk. Co.

—I Am Number Four. 2011. (I Am Number Four Ser.: Vol. 1). (ENG.). 440p. (gr. 9-12). 20.00 *(978-1-61383-207-3(9))* Perfection Learning Corp.

—I Am Number Four. 2011. (Lorien Legacies Ser.: 1). (YA). lib. bdg. 20.85 *(978-0-606-23545-7(0)*, Turtleback) Turtleback Bks.

—I Am Number Four: The Lost Files: Rebel Allies. 2015. (Lorien Legacies: the Lost Files Ser.). (ENG.). 416p. (YA). (gr. 9). pap. 9.99 *(978-0-06-236404-3(9))* HarperCollins Pubs.

—I Am Number Four: The Lost Files: Secret Histories. 2013. (Lorien Legacies: the Lost Files Ser.). (ENG.). 416p. (YA). (gr. 9). pap. 9.99 *(978-0-06-222367-8(4))* HarperCollins Pubs.

—Secret Histories. 2013. (Lorien Legacies: the Lost Files Ser.). (YA). lib. bdg. 20.85 *(978-0-606-31823-5(2)*, Turtleback) Turtleback Bks.

Magsamen, Sandra. I Love Ohio (an ABC Adventure) 2015. (ENG.). 40p. (J). (-5). 12.99 *(978-1-4926-2836-1(0),* Sourcebooks Jabberwocky) Sourcebooks, Inc.
Marie, Leann. The Ghost of Oberlin. 2008. pap. 16.95 *(978-1-4241-9597-8(7))* America Star Bks.
Marquez, Sofia. Pepe Perez Mexican Mouse: Pepe Perez Comes to the United States: Book 1, 1 vol. Marquez, Sofia, illus. 2009. (Illus.). 20p. pap. 24.95 *(978-1-61546-496-8(4))* America Star Bks.
—Pepe Perez Mexican Mouse: Pepe Perez Comes to the United States: Book 1, 1 vol. 2010. 20p. 24.95 *(978-1-4489-6600-4(0))* PublishAmerica, Inc.
Martin, Maggie Ann. The Big F. 2017. (ENG.). 304p. (YA). pap. 10.99 *(978-1-250-12321-3(6),* 9781250123213) Feiwel & Friends.
Martin, Rebecca. Joanna's Journey. Yoder, Laura & Weaver, Lisa, illus. 2006. 168p. (YA). pap. 9.99 *(978-1-933753-01-0(3))* Carlisle Pr.- Walnut Creek.
McBride, Kristina. One Moment. 2017. (ENG.). 272p. (YA). (gr. 8). pap. 9.99 *(978-1-5107-1455-7(3),* Sky Pony Pr.) Skyhorse Publishing Co., Inc.
Mullen, Paul Michael. The Day I Hit a Home Run at Great American Ball Park. 2007. 146p. (J). *(978-1-933197-30-2(7))* Orange Frazer Pr.
Murphy, Buelina. Boke. 2003. 32p. pap. 8.00 *(978-0-8059-5524-8(0))* Dorrance Publishing Co., Inc.
Oneill, Elizabeth. Alfred Visits Ohio. 2006. 24p. pap. 12.00 *(978-0-9771836-4-7(5))* Global Business Information Strategies, Inc.
Osorio, Rick. The Great Adventure of Sally Rock & the Cretaceous Chicken. 2006. 65p. pap. 16.95 *(978-1-4241-0971-5(X))* PublishAmerica, Inc.
Ottman, Frank. Not Wanted: The Memories of Cain Mann. 2005. 194p. pap. 24.95 *(978-1-4241-0163-4(8))* PublishAmerica, Inc.
Pearsall, Shelley. Crooked River. 2007. (ENG.). 272p. (J). (gr. 3-7). 7.99 *(978-0-440-42101-6(2),* Yearling) Random Hse. Children's Bks.
Phillips, Raelene. Towpath to Truth: Finding Family on the Miami & Erie Canal. 2009. (Illus.). 112p. (J). pap. *(978-0-7880-2229-6(6),* Fairway Pr.) CSS Publishing Co.
Pilkey, Dav. Captain Underpants & the Preposterous Plight of the Purple Potty People. Pilkey, Dav, illus. 2006. (Captain Underpants Ser.: 8). (ENG., Illus.). 176p. (J). (gr. 2-5). 18.99 *(978-0-439-37613-6(0))* Scholastic, Inc.
Price, Roxanne M. Buckeyes Bow Ties & Sweater Vests. 2010. (Illus.). 20p. pap. *(978-1-4251-8537-4(1))* Trafford Publishing (UK) Ltd.
Revenge of the Bully. 2014. (How to Beat the Bully Ser.). (ENG., Illus.). 288p. (J). (gr. 3-7). 17.99 *(978-1-4424-5677-8(9),* Simon & Schuster/Paula Wiseman Bks.) Simon & Schuster/Paula Wiseman Bks.
Rexroth, Sharon. Ohio. 2006. (ENG., Illus.). (J). per. 19.95 *(978-1-57166-421-1(1))* Quixote Pr.
Rininger, Alyce. Ka-Boom. Lucas, Diane, illus. 2012. 46p. pap. 13.95 *(978-1-61244-069-9(X))* Halo Publishing International.
Roos, Stephen. Recycling George. 2010. (ENG.). 144p. (J). (gr. 3-7). pap. 8.99 *(978-1-4424-2941-3(0),* Simon & Schuster Bks. For Young Readers) Simon & Schuster Bks. For Young Readers.
Rosen, Michael J. Don't Shoot! Chase R.'S Top Ten Reasons Not to Move to the Country. 2007. (ENG., Illus.). 160p. (YA). (gr. 7). per. 6.99 *(978-0-7636-2088-2(2))* Candlewick Pr.
Sanders, Scott Russell. Warm as Wool. Cogancherry, Helen, illus. 2007. (J). lib. bdg. 18.00 *(978-1-59098-421-5(8))* Wooster Bk. Co., The.
Saturen, Myra. Journey to a New World: Mystic River of the West. 2006. (J). pap. *(978-0-88092-495-5(0))* Royal Fireworks Publishing Co.
Shoup, Andrew J. Andy & Elmer's Apple Dumpling Adventure. 2nd ed. 2007. (J). 16.95 *(978-0-9720436-3-2(2))* TokoBooks, LLC.
—Andy & Elmer's Apple Dumpling Adventure Coloring & Activity Book. Shoup, Andrew J., illus. 2007. (Illus.). 36p. (J). 3.95 *(978-0-9720436-2-5(4))* TokoBooks, LLC.
Silvano, Wendi. Love Is All Around Cincinnati. Czernichowska, Joanna, illus. 2016. (ENG.). 32p. (J). (-6). 12.99 *(978-1-4926-2913-9(8),* Sourcebooks Jabberwocky) Sourcebooks, Inc.
—Love Is All Around Ohio. Czernichowska, Joanna, illus. 2016. (ENG.). 32p. (J). (-6). 12.99 *(978-1-4926-2949-8(9),* Sourcebooks Jabberwocky) Sourcebooks, Inc.
Skovron, Jon. Struts & Frets. (ENG.). 304p. (YA). 2011. (gr. 9-17). pap. 7.95 *(978-1-4197-0028-6(6))* 2009. (gr. 7-11). 16.95 *(978-0-8109-4174-8(0))* Abrams, Inc. (Amulet Bks.).
Smallman, Steve. Santa Is Coming to Cincinnati. Dunn, Robert, illus. 2013. (ENG.). 32p. (J). (-3). 9.99 *(978-1-4022-8997-2(9),* Sourcebooks Jabberwocky) Sourcebooks, Inc.
—Santa Is Coming to Columbus. Dunn, Robert, illus. 2013. (ENG.). 32p. (J). (-3). 9.99 *(978-1-4022-9036-7(5),* Sourcebooks Jabberwocky) Sourcebooks, Inc.
—Santa Is Coming to Madison. Dunn, Robert, illus. 2014. (ENG.). 32p. (J). (-3). 9.99 *(978-1-4926-0706-9(1),* Sourcebooks Jabberwocky) Sourcebooks, Inc.
—Santa Is Coming to Ohio. Dunn, Robert, illus. 2012. (ENG.). 32p. (J). (-3). 9.99 *(978-1-4022-7554-8(4),* Sourcebooks Jabberwocky) Sourcebooks, Inc.
—Santa Is Coming to Toledo. Dunn, Robert, illus. 2015. (ENG.). 32p. (J). (-3). 9.99 *(978-1-4926-2654-1(6),* Sourcebooks Jabberwocky) Sourcebooks, Inc.
Smallman, Steve, et al. My First Santa's Coming to Ohio. Dunn, Robert, illus. 2015. (ENG.). 18p. (J). bds. 9.99 *(978-1-4926-2876-7(X),* Sourcebooks Jabberwocky) Sourcebooks, Inc.
Sowach, Rick. Critters, Flitters & Spitters: 24 Amazing Ohio Animal Tales. 2003. (J). 19.95 *(978-0-9762412-3-2(4))* Sowash, Rick Publishing Co.
Sowash, Rick. Critters, Flitters & Spitters: 24 Amazing Ohio Animal Tales. 2003. (J). pap. 11.95 *(978-0-9762412-2-5(6))* Sowash, Rick Publishing Co.
—Ripsnorting Whoppers! A Book of Ohio Tall Tales. 2003. (J). 19.95 *(978-0-9762412-1-8(8))*; pap. 11.95 *(978-0-9762412-0-1(X))* Sowash, Rick Publishing Co.
Springstubb, Tricia. What Happened on Fox Street. Ross, Heather, illus. 2011. (Fox Street Ser.: 1). (ENG.). 240p. (J). (gr. 3-7). pap. 6.99 *(978-0-06-198636-9(4))* HarperCollins Pubs.
Starkey, Scott. How to Beat the Bully Without Really Trying. (How to Beat the Bully Ser.). (ENG.). 272p. (J). (gr. 3-7). 2013. pap. 7.99 *(978-1-4424-8473-3(X))* 2012. 15.99 *(978-1-4424-1685-7(8))* Simon & Schuster/Paula Wiseman Bks. (Simon & Schuster/Paula Wiseman Bks.).
Stilton, Geronimo & Stilton, Thea. Thea Stilton & the Dragon's Code. 2009. (Thea Stilton Ser.: 1). (ENG.). 176p. (J). (gr. 2-5). pap. 8.99 *(978-0-545-10367-1(3),* Scholastic Paperbacks) Scholastic, Inc.
Sully, Katherine. Night-Night Ohio. Kolanovic, Dubravka & Poole, Helen, illus. 2016. (ENG.). 20p. (J). (-1). bds. 9.99 *(978-1-4926-4220-6(7),* 9781492642206, Sourcebooks Jabberwocky) Sourcebooks, Inc.
Tama. Black Cow. 2012. 116p. pap. 14.95 *(978-1-4685-6680-2(6))* AuthorHouse.
Wilsdon, Christina. An Amusement Park Mystery in Ohio. Ebert, Len, illus. 2006. 26p. (J). 7.99 *(978-1-59939-013-0(2))* Cornerstone Pr.
Wolf, Sara. Forget Me Always. 2016. (Lovely Vicious Ser.: 2). (ENG.). 250p. (YA). pap. 9.99 *(978-1-63375-317-4(4),* 9781633753174) Entangled Publishing, LLC.
Wood, David. A Year in the Life of the Kingwood Bunnies. Floeter, Nell, illus. 2010. 54p. pap. 15.95 *(978-1-936343-07-2(X))* Peppertree Pr., The.

OHIO—HISTORY

Bailer, Darice. What's Great about Ohio? 2015. (ENG., Illus.). 32p. (J). (gr. 2-5). 26.65 *(978-1-4677-3885-9(9))* Lerner Publishing Group.
Boehm Jerome, Kate. Columbus & the State of Ohio: Cool Stuff Every Kid Should Know. 2011. (Arcadia Kids Ser.). (ENG., Illus.). 48p. (J). (gr. 3-6). pap. 9.99 *(978-1-4396-0087-0(2))* Arcadia Publishing.
Cafmeyer, Judy. Ready, Set, Show What You Know(r) on the Ohio Acheivement Test for Gr. 3: Student Edition. 2004. (J). per. 10.95 *(978-1-59230-062-4(6))* Englefield & Assocs., Inc.
Dalton, Curt. Dayton Inventions: Fact & Fiction. 2003. (Illus.). 74p. per. 12.95 *(978-0-9720965-1-5(5))* Montgomery County Historical Society.
Deady, Kathleen W. Ohio. 2005. (Portraits of the States Ser.). (Illus.). 32p. (gr. 2-6). pap. 10.50 *(978-0-8368-4651-5(6))*; lib. bdg. 26.00 *(978-0-8368-4632-4(X))* Stevens, Gareth Publishing LLLP. (Gareth Stevens Learning Library).
Gamble, Adam. Good Night Ohio. Jasper, Mark, illus. 2013. (Good Night Our World Ser.). (ENG.). 20p. (J). (— 1). bds. 9.95 *(978-1-60219-076-4(3))* Good Night Bks.
Gray, Susan. All Across Ohio: A Bird's Eye View with Worthington Cardinal, 7 bks. Messer, Celia, illus. 2003. 24p. (J). 7.95 *(978-0-9742862-0-4(6))* Two's Company.
—Colorful Ohio! A Bird's Eye View with Worthington Cardinal, 7 bks. Gray, Susan & Messer, Celia, illus. 2003. 28p. (J). 4.95 *(978-0-9742862-5-9(7))* Two's Company.
—Plain & Simple: A Bird's Eye View with Worthington Cardinal, 7 bks. Messer, Celia, illus. 2003. 24p. (J). 7.95 *(978-0-9742862-4-2(9))* Two's Company.
—A River Ride: A Bird's Eye View with Worthington Cardinal, 7 bks. Messer, Celia, illus. 2003. 24p. (J). 7.95 *(978-0-9742862-3-5(0))* Two's Company.
—Wagon-O! A Bird's Eye View with Worthington Cardinal, 7 bks. Messer, Celia, illus. 2003. 24p. (J). 7.95 *(978-0-9742862-2-8(2))* Two's Company.
—We Can Fly! A Bird's Eye View with Worthington Cardinal, 7 bks. Messer, Celia, illus. 2003. 24p. (J). 7.95 *(978-0-9742862-1-1(4))* Two's Company.
Gunderson, Jessica. Ohio. 2009. (This Land Called America Ser.). 32p. (YA). (gr. 3-6). 19.95 *(978-1-58341-788-1(5))* Creative Co., The.
Hart, Joyce & Herrington, Lisa M. Ohio. 2nd rev. ed. 2011. (It's My State! 2 Ser.). 80p. (gr. 3). 31.36 *(978-1-60870-524-5(2))* Marshall Cavendish GBR. Dist: Marshall Cavendish Corp.
Hart, Joyce, et al. Ohio. 2016. (It's My State! (r) Ser.). (Illus.). 80p. (J). (gr. 4-4). 34.21 *(978-1-62713-169-8(8))* Cavendish Square Publishing.
Helweg, Laura. Eastern Great Lakes: Indiana, Michigan, Ohio, Vol. 19. 2015. (Let's Explore the States Ser.). 64p. (J). (gr. 5). 23.95 *(978-1-4222-3323-8(5))* Mason Crest.
Huey, Lois Miner. Floodwaters & Flames: The 1913 Disaster in Dayton, Ohio. 2016. (ENG., Illus.). 56p. (J). (gr. 4-8). lib. bdg. 33.32 *(978-1-4677-9432-9(5),* Millbrook Pr.) Lerner Publishing Group.
Jensen, Niels R. Ohio, 1 vol. 2009. (United States Ser.). (ENG., Illus.). 48p. (YA). (gr. 2-5). 27.07 *(978-1-60453-670-6(5))* ABDO Publishing Co.
Jerome, Kate B. Lucky to Live in Ohio. 2017. (Arcadia Kids Ser.). (ENG., Illus.). 32p. (J). 16.99 ***(978-0-7385-2773-4(4))*** Arcadia Publishing.
—The Wise Animal Handbook Ohio. 2017. (Arcadia Kids Ser.). (ENG., Illus.). 32p. (J). 16.99 ***(978-0-7385-2837-3(4))*** Arcadia Publishing.
Jerome, Kate Boehm. Cincinnati, Oh: Cool Stuff Every Kid Should Know. 2010. (Arcadia Kids Ser.). (ENG., Illus.). 48p. (J). (gr. 3-6). pap. 9.99 *(978-1-4396-0068-9(6))* Arcadia Publishing.
Kandel, Megan. Let's Celebrate Ohio. 2003. pap. 10.95 *(978-1-931334-20-4(X),* CLC0287) Pieces of Learning.
Kline, Nancy. Ohio. 2009. (From Sea to Shining Sea, Second Ser.). (ENG.). 80p. (J). pap. 7.95 *(978-0-531-21141-0(X),* Children's Pr.) Scholastic Library Publishing.
Lawton, Val. Ohio. 2011. (Guide to American States Ser.). (Illus.). 48p. (YA). (gr. 3-6). 29.99 *(978-1-61690-807-2(6))* Weigl Pubs., Inc.
Lawton, Val. Ohio: The Buckeye State. 2016. (J). ***(978-1-5105-2091-2(0))*** SmartBook Media, Inc.
—Ohio: The Buckeye State. 2016. (J). *(978-1-4896-4920-1(4))* Weigl Pubs., Inc.
Leebrick, Kristal. The Lucky Buckeye: A Story about Ohio, 1 vol. 2008. (Fact & Fable: State Stories Ser.). (ENG., Illus.). 24p. (J). (gr. -1-2). 25.65 *(978-1-60453-185-5(1))* ABDO Publishing Co.
Levine, Susan Sachs. Packard Takes Flight: A Bird's-Eye View of Columbus, Ohio. Burchwell, Erin McCauley, illus. 2010. (ENG.). 32p. 17.99 *(978-1-60949-051-5(7),* History Pr., The) Arcadia Publishing.
Lucht, Susan & Wilson, Mollie. Olden Days of Medina: A Children's Guide to Medina History. Allman, Cynthia, illus. 2013. iii, 30p. (J). pap. *(978-0-578-10958-9(1))* U. S. ISBN Agency.
Marsh, Carole. Exploring Ohio Through Project-Based Learning: Geography, History, Government, Economics & More. 2016. (Ohio Experience Ser.). (ENG.). (J). pap. 9.99 *(978-0-635-12359-6(2))* Gallopade International.
McNeese, Tim. Ohio River. 2004. (Rivers in American Life & Times Ser.). (Illus.). 120p. (C). (gr. 9-13). 32.50 *(978-0-7910-7725-2(X),* Chelsea Hse.) Facts On File, Inc.
Moore, Cyd. Diary of a Ohio Kid. 2010. (State Journal Ser.). (ENG.). 128p. (J). (gr. 4-8). pap. 9.95 *(978-1-58536-540-1(8),* 202218) Sleeping Bear Pr.
Murray, Julie. Ohio, 1 vol. 2012. (Explore the United States Ser.). (ENG.). 32p. (J). (gr. 2-5). lib. bdg. 28.50 *(978-1-61783-373-1(8),* Big Buddy Bks.) ABDO Publishing Co.
Ohio Historical Society Staff. Ohio, A Sentimental Journey Study Guide, 1 CD. 2004. (Illus.). 102p. (YA). cd-rom *(978-0-9747666-1-4(5))* American Retrospects, LLC.
Raizk, Mary Ann. Happy Birthday, Ohio: Celebrating Ohio's Bicentennial 1803-2003, 1. Raizk, Leyla Marie, illus. 2003. 32p. (J). pap. 14.95 *(978-1-882203-97-0(6))* Orange Frazer Pr.
Rodriguez, Cindy. Ohio: The Buckeye State. 2012. (J). *(978-1-61913-389-1(X))*; pap. *(978-1-61913-390-7(3))* Weigl Pubs., Inc.
Schonberg, Marcia. Little Ohio. Monroe, Michael Glenn, illus. 2011. (My Little State Ser.). (ENG.). 20p. (J). 9.95 *(978-1-58536-527-2(0))* Sleeping Bear Pr.
Sipp, Leora Janson. Nathan & Tori Visit Ohio: And Learn about Wild Animals. 2012. 40p. pap. 14.50 *(978-1-4669-3822-9(6))* Trafford Publishing.
Snyder, Sally. Hold the Fort. Snyder, Sally, illus. 2003. (Illus.). 45p. (J). 20.00 *(978-1-882203-99-4(2))* Orange Frazer Pr.
Stille, Darlene R. Ohio (Revised Edition) 2014. (America the Beautiful, Third Ser. (Revised Edition) Ser.). (ENG.). 144p. (J). lib. bdg. 40.00 *(978-0-531-28287-8(2))* Scholastic Library Publishing.
Weymouth Seguin, Marilyn. The Freedom Stairs: The Story of Adam Lowry Rankin, Underground Railroad Conductor. 2004. (Illus.). 93p. (J). (gr. 3-7). per. 12.95 net. *(978-0-8283-2084-9(5))* Branden Bks.

OHIO—HISTORY—FICTION

Clark, Henry. The Book That Proves Time Travel Happens. 2015. (ENG., Illus.). 416p. (J). (gr. 3-7). 17.00 *(978-0-316-40617-8(1))* Little Brown & Co.
Hulme, Lucy V. Passages, 1 bk. Redpath, Dale, illus. 2005. 40p. (J). 7.95 *(978-0-9769804-0-2(3),* 001) Combs-Hulme Publishing.
Long, Loren & Bildner, Phil. Magic in the Outfield. Long, Loren, illus. 2009. (Sluggers Ser.: 1). (ENG., Illus.). 160p. (J). (gr. 3-7). pap. 8.99 *(978-1-4169-1884-4(1),* Simon & Schuster Bks. For Young Readers) Simon & Schuster Bks. For Young Readers.
McGinnis, Mindy. A Madness So Discreet. 2015. (ENG.). 384p. (YA). (gr. 9). 17.99 *(978-0-06-232086-5(6))* HarperCollins Pubs.
Pearsall, Shelley. Crooked River. 2007. 249p. (gr. 5-9). 17.00 *(978-0-7569-7771-9(1))* Perfection Learning Corp.
Raven, Margot Theis. Night Boat to Freedom. Lewis, E. B., illus. 2008. (ENG.). 40p. (J). (gr. 1-4). pap. 8.99 *(978-0-312-55018-9(9),* 9780312550189) Square Fish.
Reed, Stephanie. The Light Across the River, 1 vol. 2008. (Illus.). 216p. (J). (gr. 4-7). pap. 10.99 *(978-0-8254-3574-4(9))* Kregel Pubns.
Saturen, Myra. Journey to a New World: Mystic River of the West. 2006. (J). pap. *(978-0-88092-495-5(0))* Royal Fireworks Publishing Co.
Van Leeuwen, Jean. Cabin on Trouble Creek. 2008. (ENG.). 224p. (J). (gr. 3-7). 7.99 *(978-0-14-241164-3(7),* Puffin Books) Penguin Young Readers Group.

OHIO RIVER AND VALLEY—FICTION

Hemphill, Kris. Ambush in the Wilderness. 2003. (Adventures in America Ser.). (Illus.). 90p. (gr. 4). 14.95 *(978-1-893110-34-2(6))* Silver Moon Pr.
Rush, Barbara & Stratton, Jane. The Boat in the Attic. 2012. (ENG.). 30p. pap. 15.00 *(978-1-938002-02-1(4),* Hummingbird World Media) Double Edge Pr.
Shoemaker, E. W. Mother Nature & the Tales of North Fork. 2009. 220p. pap. 18.75 *(978-1-4389-8604-3(1))* AuthorHouse.
Winfield, Arthur M. The Rover Boys on the River or the Search for the Missing. 2006. (ENG.). 272p. per. 27.95 *(978-1-4286-4115-0(7))* Kessinger Publishing, LLC.

OIL

see Petroleum

OIL ENGINES

see Internal Combustion Engines

OIL FUEL

see Petroleum As Fuel

OIL SPILLS

Beech, Linda Ward. The Exxon Valdez's Deadly Oil Spill. 2007. (Code Red Ser.). (Illus.). 32p. (YA). (gr. 2-5). lib. bdg. 25.27 *(978-1-59716-366-8(X))* Bearport Publishing Co., Inc.
Benchmark Education Company. Oil Spills (Teacher Guide) 2005. *(978-1-4108-4671-6(7))* Benchmark Education Co.
Benoit, Peter. The BP Oil Spill. 2011. (J). pap. *(978-0-531-29029-3(8))* Children's Pr., Ltd.
—The BP Oil Spill. 2011. (True Bks.). 48p. (J). (gr. 3-5). lib. bdg. 29.00 *(978-0-531-20630-0(0))*; (ENG., Illus.). pap. 6.95 *(978-0-531-28999-0(0))* Scholastic Library Publishing. (Children's Pr.).
—The Exxon Valdez Oil Spill. 2011. (J). pap. *(978-0-531-29028-6(X))* Children's Pr., Ltd.
—The Exxon Valdez Oil Spill. 2011. (True Bks.). 48p. (J). (gr. 3-5). 29.00 *(978-0-531-20629-4(7),* Children's Pr.) Scholastic Library Publishing.
—The EXXON Valdez Oil Spill. 2011. (True Bk Ser.). (ENG., Illus.). 48p. (J). pap. 6.95 *(978-0-531-28998-3(2),* Children's Pr.) Scholastic Library Publishing.
Bogart, Jon. Animals & Oil Spills. 2013. (Animal 911: Environmental Threats Ser.). 48p. (J). (gr. 3-5). pap. 84.30 *(978-1-4339-9712-9(6))*; pap. 14.05 *(978-1-4339-9711-2(8))*; (ENG., Illus.). lib. bdg. 31.95 *(978-1-4339-9710-5(X))* Stevens, Gareth Publishing LLLP.
Brannon, Barbara. Discover Oil Spills. 2005. (J). pap. *(978-1-4108-5139-0(7))* Benchmark Education Co.
Brennan, Linda Crotta. Gulf Oil Spill, 1 vol. 2013. (History's Greatest Disasters Ser.). (ENG.). 48p. (J). (gr. 3-6). lib. bdg. 32.79 *(978-1-61783-957-3(4))* ABDO Publishing Co.
—Gulf Oil Spill Paperback. 2013. (J). 15.65 *(978-1-62403-022-2(X),* Core Library) ABDO Publishing Co.
Chiang, Mona. Oil Spill: Disaster in the Gulf. 2010. (Illus.). 32p. (J). pap. *(978-0-545-31128-1(4))* Scholastic, Inc.
Dalton, Anna. Examining Oil Spills. 2015. (ENG., Illus.). 48p. (J). lib. bdg. 24.95 net. *(978-1-934545-65-2(1))* Oliver Pr., Inc.
Farrell, Courtney. The Gulf of Mexico Oil Spill, 1 vol. 2011. (Essential Events Set 6 Ser.). (ENG., Illus.). 112p. (J). (gr. 6-12). lib. bdg. 35.64 *(978-1-61714-765-4(6))* ABDO Publishing Co.
Faust, Daniel R. Desastres Ecológicos: Los Derrames de Petróleo y el Medio Ambiente = Sinister Sludge: Oil Spills & the Environment. 2009. (Historietas Juveniles: Peligros Del Medioambiente (Jr. Graphic Environmental Dangers) Ser.). (Illus.). 24p. (gr. 3-6). (SPA.). (YA). lib. bdg. 25.25 *(978-1-4358-8468-7(X))*; (ENG & SPA., pap. 10.60 *(978-1-4358-8469-4(8),* PowerKids Pr.) Rosen Publishing Group, Inc., The.
—Sinister Sludge: Oil Spills & the Environment. (Jr. Graphic Environmental Dangers Ser.). (ENG., 24p. 2009. Illus.). (gr. 3-8). pap. 10.60 *(978-1-4042-4597-6(9))* 2008. (J). 47.90 *(978-1-61532-100-1(4))* 2008. (Illus.). (J). (gr. 3-6). lib. bdg. 25.25 *(978-1-4042-4230-2(9))* Rosen Publishing Group, Inc., The. (PowerKids Pr.).
Goldish, Meish. Oil Spill: Deepwater Horizon. 2017. (Eco-Disasters Ser.). (ENG.). 32p. (J). (gr. 2-7). 19.95 ***(978-1-68402-226-7(6))*** Bearport Publishing Co., Inc.
Greeley, August. Sludge & Slime: Oil Spills in Our World. (Man-Made Disasters Ser.). 24p. 2009. (gr. 3-3). 42.50 *(978-1-61514-352-8(1))* 2003. (Illus.). (J). lib. bdg. 22.60 *(978-0-8239-6485-7(X))* Rosen Publishing Group, Inc., The. (PowerKids Pr.).
Haugen, David M. The BP Oil Spill. 2011. (At Issue Ser.). (ENG.). 128p. (gr. 10-12). pap. 27.80 *(978-0-7377-5569-5(5),* Greenhaven Pr., Inc.) Cengage Gale.
—Drilling in the Gulf of Mexico. 2011. (At Issue Ser.). (ENG.). 128p. (gr. 10-12). 39.40 *(978-0-7377-5568-8(7))* Cengage Gale.
Hunter, Nick. Offshore Oil Drilling, 1 vol. 2011. (Hot Topics Ser.). (ENG., Illus.). 56p. (gr. 7-8). 34.65 *(978-1-4329-5176-4(9),* NA-h) Heinemann-Raintree.
Jakubiak, David J. Protecting Our Planet: What Can We Do about Oil Spills & Ocean Pollution? 2012. (Illus.). 24p. (J). 49.50 *(978-1-4488-5113-3(0),* PowerKids Pr.); pap. 8.25 *(978-1-4488-5112-6(2),* PowerKids Pr.); (gr. 2-5). lib. bdg. 22.60 *(978-1-4488-4982-6(9))* Rosen Publishing Group, Inc., The.
Landau, Elaine. Oil Spill! Disaster in the Gulf of Mexico. 2011. (Exceptional Science Titles for Intermediate Grades Ser.). (ENG.). 32p. (gr. 3-5). 25.26 *(978-0-7613-7485-5(X),* Millbrook Pr.) Lerner Publishing Group.
Leacock, Elspeth. Exxon Valdez Oil Spill. 2005. (Environmental Disasters Ser.). (Illus.). 112p. (J). (gr. 6-12). 35.00 *(978-0-8160-5754-2(0))* Facts On File, Inc.
Margulies, Philip. The Exxon Valdez Oil Spill: When Disaster Strikes! 2005. (When Disaster Strikes! Ser.). (Illus.). 48p. (YA). (gr. 5-8). lib. bdg. 29.25 *(978-0-8239-3675-5(9))* Rosen Publishing Group, Inc., The.
Margulies, Phillip. The Exxon Valdez Oil Spill. 2009. (When Disaster Strikes! Ser.). 48p. (gr. 5-8). 53.00 *(978-1-60854-780-7(9),* Rosen Reference) Rosen Publishing Group, Inc., The.
Markle, Sandra. The Great Penguin Rescue: Saving the African Penguins. 2017. (ENG.). 48p. (J). (gr. 4-6). 30.65 ***(978-1-5124-1315-1(1),*** Millbrook Pr.) Lerner Publishing Group.
Nardo, Don. Oil Spills. 2011. (Hot Topics Ser.). (ENG., Illus.). 128p. (gr. 7-10). lib. bdg. 39.40 *(978-1-4205-0624-2(2))* Cengage Gale.
Parsons, Michelle Hyde. Oil Spills. 2005. (J). pap. *(978-1-4108-4623-5(7))* Benchmark Education Co.
Peppas, Lynn. Gulf Oil Spill. 2011. (ENG., Illus.). 32p. (J). *(978-0-7787-1592-4(2))*; (Disaster Alert! Ser.: No. 20). (gr. 3-6). pap. *(978-0-7787-1625-9(2))* Crabtree Publishing Co.
Person, Stephen. Saving Animals from Oil Spills. 2011. (Rescuing Animals from Disasters Ser.). 32p. (YA). (gr. 2-5). lib. bdg. 25.27 *(978-1-61772-288-2(X))* Bearport Publishing Co., Inc.
The Science of an Oil Spill. 2014. (21st Century Skills Library: Disaster Science Ser.). (ENG.). 32p. (J). (gr. 4-8). 28.50 *(978-1-63137-630-6(6),* 205303) Cherry Lake Publishing.
Smith, Steven Michael. New Carissa: The Ship That Refused to Die. 2010. 52p. pap. 22.99 *(978-1-4520-6612-7(4))* AuthorHouse.
Stone, Adam. The Deepwater Horizon Oil Spill. 2014. (Disaster Stories Ser.). (ENG., Illus.). 24p. (J). (gr. 3-8). 29.95 *(978-1-62617-152-7(1),* Black Sheep) Bellwether Media.
Thompson, Tamara. Oil Spills. Greenhaven Press Editors & Gale, A. G., eds. 2014. (Current Controversies Ser.). (ENG., Illus.). 224p. (gr. 7-12). pap. 32.00 *(978-0-7377-6881-7(9),* Greenhaven Pr., Inc.) Cengage Gale.
—Oil Spills. Greenhaven Press Editors & Gale Editors, eds. 2014. (Current Controversies Ser.). (ENG., Illus.). 224p. (gr. 7-12). lib. bdg. 46.40 *(978-0-7377-6880-0(0),* Greenhaven Pr., Inc.) Cengage Gale.

OIL WELLS

see Petroleum

OKEFENOKEE SWAMP (GA. AND FLA.)

Bateman, Donna M. Deep in the Swamp. Lies, Brian, illus. 2007. (ENG.). 32p. (J). (gr. -1-3). pap. 7.95 *(978-1-57091-597-0(0))* Charlesbridge Publishing, Inc.

OKEFENOKEE SWAMP (GA. AND FLA.)—FICTION

Jackson's Plan: Evaluation Guide. 2006. (J). *(978-1-55942-410-3(9))* Witcher Productions.
Lettrick, Robert. The Murk. Disney Storybook Art Team, illus. 2015. (ENG.). 320p. (J). (gr. 5-9). 16.99 *(978-1-4231-8695-3(8))* Hyperion Bks. for Children.
Marsh, Carole. The Secret of Skullcracker Swamp. 2009. (Pretty Darn Scary Mysteries Ser.). (Illus.). 113p. (YA). lib.

MNO

bdg. 18.99 (978-0-635-07020-3(0), Marsh, Carole Mysteries) Gallopade International.

OKINAWA ISLAND (JAPAN)—FICTION

Mazer, Harry. Heroes Don't Run. 2007. (Aladdin Historical Fiction Ser.). 113p. (gr. 3-7). 16.00 (978-0-7569-8111-2(5)) Perfection Learning Corp.

OKLAHOMA

Baldwin, Guy & Hart, Joyce. Oklahoma. 2nd rev. ed. 2009. (Celebrate the States 9 Ser.). 144p. (gr. 6). 42.79 (978-0-7614-4032-1(1)) Marshall Cavendish Corp.

Boys and Girls Club of Oklahoma County. O Is for Oklahoma: Written by Kids for Kids. McCann, Michelle, ed. 2013. (See My State Ser.). (ENG., Illus.). 32p. (J). (gr. -1-3). 14.99 (978-0-88240-911-5(5), West Winds Pr.) Graphic Arts Ctr. Publishing Co.

Brown, Jonatha A. Oklahoma. 2006. (Portraits of the States Ser.). (Illus.). 32p. (gr. 2-6). pap. 10.50 (978-0-8368-4691-1(5)); lib. bdg. 26.00 (978-0-8368-4672-0(9)) Stevens, Gareth Publishing LLLP. (Gareth Stevens Learning Library).

Brown, Vanessa. Oklahoma. 2009. (Bilingual Library of the United States of America Ser.). (ENG & SPA.). 32p. (gr. 2-2). 47.90 (978-1-60853-380-0(8), Editorial Buenas Letras) Rosen Publishing Group, Inc., The.

—Oklahoma. Brusca, Maria Cristina, tr. from ENG. 2006. (Bilingual Library of the United States of America Ser.: Set 2). (ENG & SPA., Illus.). 32p. (J). (gr. 3-6). lib. bdg. 25.25 (978-1-4042-3101-6(3)) Rosen Publishing Group, Inc., The.

Brownell, Richard. The Oklahoma City Bombing. 2007. (Crime Scene Investigations Ser.). (ENG., Illus.). 104p. (YA). (gr. 7-12). lib. bdg. 35.45 (978-1-59018-843-9(8)) Cengage Gale.

Fein, E. How to Draw Oklahoma's Sights & Symbols. 2009. (Kid's Guide to Drawing America Ser.). 32p. (gr. k-k). 50.50 (978-1-61511-089-6(5), PowerKids Pr.) Rosen Publishing Group, Inc., The.

Giordano, Geraldine. The Oklahoma City Bombing. 2009. (Terrorist Attacks Ser.). 64p. (gr. 5-5). 58.50 (978-1-60853-318-3(2)) Rosen Publishing Group, Inc., The.

Hinkle, Donald Henry. Oklahoma: A MyReportLinks. Com Book. 2003. (States Ser.). (Illus.). 48p. (J). lib. bdg. 25.26 (978-0-7660-5138-6(2), MyReportLinks.com Bks.) Enslow Pubs., Inc.

Hoena, Blake. Oklahoma. 2013. (Exploring the States Ser.). (ENG., Illus.). 32p. (J). (gr. 3-7). lib. bdg. 26.95 (978-1-62617-035-3(5), Blastoff! Readers) Bellwether Media.

Labella, Susan. Oklahoma. 2007. (Rookie Read-About Geography Ser.). (Illus.). 31p. (J). (gr. 1-2). 20.50 (978-0-516-25468-5(5), Children's Pr.) Scholastic Library Publishing.

LaDoux, Rita. Oklahoma. 2012. (J). lib. bdg. 25.26 (978-0-7613-4551-0(5), Lerner Pubns.) Lerner Publishing Group.

Maine, Tyler. Oklahoma. 2016. (States Ser.). (ENG., Illus.). 32p. (gr. 3-4). lib. bdg. 27.32 (978-1-5157-0423-2(8)) Next Page Pr., The.

Marsh, Carole. My First Book about Oklahoma. 2004. (Oklahoma Experience! Ser.). (Illus.). 32p. (J). (gr. k-4). pap. 7.95 (978-0-7933-9595-8(X)) Gallopade International.

—My First Pocket Guide: Oklahoma. 2004. (Oklahoma Experience! Ser.). (Illus.). 96p. (J). (gr. 3-8). per. 6.95 (978-0-7933-9594-1(1)) Gallopade International.

—Oklahoma Current Events Projects: 30 Cool, Activities, Crafts, Experiments & More for Kids to Do to Learn about Your State! 2003. (Oklahoma Experience Ser.). 32p. (gr. k-8). pap. 5.95 (978-0-635-02055-0(6), Marsh, Carole Bks.) Gallopade International.

—Oklahoma Geography Projects: 30 Cool, Activities, Crafts, Experiments & More for Kids to Do to Learn about Your State! 2003. (Oklahoma Experience Ser.). 32p. (gr. k-5). pap. 5.95 (978-0-635-01855-7(1), Marsh, Carole Bks.) Gallopade International.

—Oklahoma Government Projects: 30 Cool, Activities, Crafts, Experiments & More for Kids to Do to Learn about Your State! 2003. (Oklahoma Experience Ser.). 32p. (gr. k-5). pap. 5.95 (978-0-635-01955-4(8), Marsh, Carole Bks.) Gallopade International.

—Oklahoma History Projects: 30 Cool, Activities, Crafts, Experiments & More for Kids to Do to Learn about Your State! 2003. (Oklahoma Experience Ser.). 32p. (gr. k-5). pap. 5.95 (978-0-635-01805-2(5), Marsh, Carole Bks.) Gallopade International.

—Oklahoma Jeopardy! Answers & Questions about Our State. 2004. (Oklahoma Experience! Ser.). (Illus.). 32p. (J). (gr. 3-12). pap. 7.95 (978-0-7933-9596-5(8)) Gallopade International.

—Oklahoma Jography! A Fun Run Thru Our State. 2004. (Oklahoma Experience! Ser.). (Illus.). 32p. (J). (gr. 3-8). pap. 7.95 (978-0-7933-9597-2(6)) Gallopade International.

—Oklahoma People Projects: 30 Cool, Activities, Crafts, Experiments & More for Kids to Do to Learn about Your State! 2003. (Oklahoma Experience Ser.). 32p. (gr. k-5). pap. 5.95 (978-0-635-02005-5(X), Marsh, Carole Bks.) Gallopade International.

—Oklahoma Symbols Projects: 30 Cool Activities, Crafts, Experiments & More for Kids to Do! 2003. (Oklahoma Experience Ser.). (Illus.). 32p. (J). (gr. k-5). pap. 5.95 (978-0-635-01905-9(1), Marsh, Carole Bks.) Gallopade International.

—The Out-of-This-World Oklahoma Coloring Book! 2004. (Oklahoma Experience! Ser.). (Illus.). 32p. (J). (gr. k-2). 3.95 (978-0-7933-9599-6(2)) Gallopade International.

Murray, Julie. Oklahoma, 1 vol. 2006. (Buddy Book Ser.). (ENG., Illus.). 32p. (gr. 2-4). 27.07 (978-1-59197-695-0(2), Buddy Bks.) ABDO Publishing Co.

Orr, Tamra B. Oklahoma. 2014. (America the Beautiful Ser.: 3). (ENG.). 144p. (J). lib. bdg. 40.00 (978-0-531-24897-3(6)) Scholastic Library Publishing.

Sanders, Doug. Oklahoma. 2013. (It's My State 2nd Ed 5 Ser.). 80p. (J). (gr. 4-8). pap. 17.64 (978-1-62712-102-6(1)) Cavendish Square Publishing.

—Oklahoma. 2006. (It's My State! Ser.). (Illus.). 80p. (J). (gr. 4-7). lib. bdg. 19.95 (978-0-7614-1906-8(3), Benchmark Bks.) Marshall Cavendish Corp.

Savage, Jeff. Kevin Durant. 2011. (Amazing Athletes Set VIII Ser.). pap. 45.32 (978-0-7613-8602-5(5)); (ENG.). 32p. (gr. 2-5). pap. 7.95 (978-0-7613-7819-8(7)) Lerner Publishing Group.

Saylor-Marchant, Linda. From Sea to Shining Sea: Oklahoma. 2008. (ENG.). 80p. (J). pap. 7.95 (978-0-531-20810-6(9), Children's Pr.) Scholastic Library Publishing.

—Oklahoma. 2003. (From Sea to Shining Sea Ser.: 2). (ENG., Illus.). 80p. (J). 30.50 (978-0-516-22393-3(3), Children's Pr.) Scholastic Library Publishing.

Scillian, Devin. S Is for Sooner: An Oklahoma Alphabet. Doner, Kim & Radzinski, Kandy, illus. 2003. (Discover America State by State Ser.). (ENG.). 40p. (J). 17.95 (978-1-58536-062-8(7)) Sleeping Bear Pr.

Wheeler, Jill C. Pioneer Practices with Ree Drummond, 1 vol. 2016. (ENG., Illus.). 32p. (J). (978-1-62403-819-8(0)) ABDO Publishing Co.

OKLAHOMA—FICTION

Angelique, A. J. Rose Petals & Ash: Curse of the Red Rose Killer, 1 vol. 2010. 94p. pap. 19.95 (978-1-4489-5316-5(2)) America Star Bks.

Beard, Darleen Bailey. The Flimflam Man. Christelow, Eileen, illus. 2003. (ENG.). 96p. (J). (gr. 2-5). per. 10.99 (978-0-374-42345-2(8), 9780374423452, Farrar, Straus & Giroux (BYR)) Farrar, Straus & Giroux.

Blom, Jen K. Possum Summer. Rayyan, Omar, illus. 2011. (ENG.). 256p. (J). (gr. 3-7). 17.95 (978-0-8234-2331-6(X)) Holiday Hse., Inc.

Bonner, Gayle. Life on Peavine Creek: Sam's Story. Johnson, Brandon, illus. 2008. 33p. pap. 24.95 (978-1-60610-624-2(4)) America Star Bks.

Daly, Jerald James. An Early Snow (the Visions Come) 2008. 180p. pap. 24.95 (978-1-60703-610-4(X)) America Star Bks.

Fazenbaker, Jo Ann. Daisy & Duke, 1 vol. 2010. 18p. 24.95 (978-1-4512-1483-3(9)) PublishAmerica, Inc.

Gensler, Sonia. The Revenant. 2013. (ENG.). 354p. (YA). (gr. 7). pap. 9.99 (978-0-375-86139-0(4), Ember) Random Hse. Children's Bks.

Griffis, Molly Levite. The Rachel Resistance. 224p. 8.95 (978-1-57168-553-7(7)) Eakin Pr.

Hartgraves, Richard. Little Cedar. 2006. 130p. pap. 24.95 (978-1-4241-4603-1(8)) PublishAmerica, Inc.

Hay, Barbara. Lesson of the White Eagle. Hay, Peter, illus. 2012. (ENG.). 144p. (YA). pap. 11.99 (978-1-937054-01-4(2)) RoadRunner Pr.

Hesse, Karen. Out of the Dust. 240p. (YA). (gr. 5-18). pap. 4.99 (978-0-8072-1526-5(0), Listening Library) Random Hse. Audio Publishing Group.

—Out of the Dust. 2009. (gr. 5-8). 18.40 (978-0-613-11953-5(3), Turtleback) Turtleback Bks.

Honderich, Lou. Ricki. 2013. 170p. pap. 10.99 (978-0-9856906-6-3(6)) Mockingbird Lane Pr.

Hudson, Marilyn A. Annie Oklahoma: Tales of the Plains. 2007. (YA). per. (978-0-9778850-3-9(8)) Whorl Bks.

—Elephant Hips Are Expensive! A Tale of the Sooner State. Fulco, Haley, illus. 2007. 50p. (J). per. (978-0-9778850-2-2(X), WhorlBooks Thumbprints) Whorl Bks.

Hudson, Tara. Arise. (Hereafter Trilogy Ser.: 2). (ENG.). (YA). (gr. 8). 2013. 432p. pap. 9.99 (978-0-06-202680-4(1)) 2012. 416p. 17.99 (978-0-06-202679-8(8)) HarperCollins Pubs. (HarperTeen).

—Elegy. 2013. (Hereafter Trilogy Ser.: 3). (ENG.). 400p. (YA). (gr. 8). 17.99 (978-0-06-202681-1(X), HarperTeen) HarperCollins Pubs.

—Hereafter. 2012. (Hereafter Trilogy Ser.: 1). (ENG.). 432p. (YA). (gr. 8). pap. 8.99 (978-0-06-202678-1(X), HarperTeen) HarperCollins Pubs.

I'm Not Afraid of Needles. 2004. (J). 4.99 (978-0-9776144-0-0(9)) Kidstalk, LLC.

Jacobs, Lily. The Littlest Bunny in Oklahoma: An Easter Adventure. Dunn, Robert, illus. 2015. (ENG.). 32p. (J). (-3). 9.99 (978-1-4926-1165-3(4), Sourcebooks Jabberwocky) Sourcebooks, Inc.

—The Littlest Bunny in Tulsa: An Easter Adventure. Dunn, Robert, illus. 2015. (ENG.). 32p. (J). (-3). 9.99 (978-1-4926-1216-2(2), Sourcebooks Jabberwocky) Sourcebooks, Inc.

James, Eric. A Halloween Scare in Oklahoma. Le Ray, Marina, illus. 2015. (ENG.). 32p. (J). (-5). 9.99 (978-1-4926-2391-5(1), 9781492623915, Sourcebooks Jabberwocky) Sourcebooks, Inc.

—A Halloween Scare in Tulsa. Le Ray, Marina, illus. 2015. (ENG.). 32p. (J). (-5). 9.99 (978-1-4926-2404-2(7), 9781492624042, Sourcebooks Jabberwocky) Sourcebooks, Inc.

—Santa's Sleigh Is on Its Way to Oklahoma: A Christmas Adventure. Dunn, Robert, illus. 2016. (ENG.). 32p. (J). (-2). 12.99 (978-1-4926-4346-3(7), 9781492643463, Sourcebooks Jabberwocky) Sourcebooks, Inc.

—Santa's Sleigh Is on Its Way to Tulsa: A Christmas Adventure. Dunn, Robert, illus. 2016. (ENG.). 32p. (J). (-2). 12.99 (978-1-4926-4359-3(9), 9781492643593, Sourcebooks Jabberwocky) Sourcebooks, Inc.

Jones, Jenny B. So Not Happening, 1 vol. 2009. (Charmed Life Ser.: 1). (ENG.). 336p. (YA). (gr. 7-18). pap. 12.99 (978-1-59554-541-1(7)) Nelson, Thomas Inc.

Kennedy, Marlane. Tornado Alley. 2014. (Disaster Strikes Ser.: 2). lib. bdg. 14.75 (978-0-606-35828-6(5)) Turtleback Bks.

Krueger, Kathryn L. Road to Grandma's House. 2005. 128p. pap. 13.95 (978-1-59800-366-6(6)) Outskirts Pr., Inc.

Lansdale, Joe R. All the Earth, Thrown to the Sky. 2012. (ENG.). 252p. (YA). (gr. 7). pap. 8.99 (978-0-385-73932-0(X), Ember) Random Hse. Children's Bks.

Latham, Jennifer. Dreamland Burning. 2017.Tr. of s. (ENG.). 384p. (YA). (gr. 9-17). 18.99 (978-0-316-38493-3(3)) Little, Brown Bks. for Young Readers.

Leech, Richard W. Adventures of Button Broken Tail, Bk. II. 2011. 249p. (J). 29.99 (978-1-4535-5219-3(7)); pap. 19.99 (978-1-4535-5218-6(9)) Xlibris Corp.

Mary, Agnes. The Story of Sammie. 2011. 28p. pap. 15.99 (978-1-4568-7771-2(2)) Xlibris Corp.

Mills, Timothy. The Mystery Kids: the Phantom Camper. 2010. 88p. pap. 14.95 (978-0-557-55089-0(0)) Lulu Pr., Inc.

Morrow, John. Ostrich Egg Omelets. 2017. (ENG., Illus.). (J). 19.99 (978-0-9790832-1-1(4)) 405 Pubns.

Oklahoma Energy Resoures Board, creator. The Road to Petroville: Petro Pete's Adventure. 2008. 15.00 (978-0-615-19844-6(9)) Oklahoma Energy Resources Board.

Onley, Sandra. Halley the Sheepdog. 2011. (Illus.). 28p. pap. 12.50 (978-1-61204-237-4(6), Strategic Bk. Publishing) Strategic Book Publishing & Rights Agency (SBPRA).

Paulsen, Gary. The Legend of Bass Reeves: Being the True & Fictional Account of the Most Valiant Marshal in the West. 2008. (ENG., Illus.). 160p. (YA). (gr. 7-9). mass mkt. 6.99 (978-0-553-49429-7(5), Laurel Leaf) Random Hse. Children's Bks.

Penn, Linda M. Is Kentucky in the Sky? 2012. 36p. pap. 9.95 (978-0-9852488-0-2(7)) Racing to Joy Pr. LLC.

Rand, Johnathan. American Chillers #26 Oklahoma Outbreak. 2009. 208p. (J). pap. 5.99 (978-1-893699-99-1(4)) AudioCraft Publishing, Inc.

Robinson, Gary. Paranormal: A Billy Buckhorn Supernatural Adventure. 2014. (PathFinders Ser.). (ENG.). 147p. (J). pap. (978-1-939053-08-4(0)) Book Publishing Co.

—Supranormal. 2015. (ENG.). 128p. (J). pap. (978-1-939053-12-1(9)) Book Publishing Co.

Sala, Sharon. Lunatic Detective. 2011. 164p. (YA). pap. 11.95 (978-1-61194-043-5(5)) BelleBks., Inc.

Sauer, Tammi. The Twelve Days of Christmas in Oklahoma. Hutto, Victoria, illus. 2012. (Twelve Days of Christmas in America Ser.). (ENG.). 40p. (J). (gr. k-3). 12.95 (978-1-4027-9224-3(7)) Sterling Publishing Co., Inc.

Schabram, Dennis W. Sugar & Me, 1 vol. 2010. 92p. pap. 19.95 (978-1-4489-2761-6(7)) America Star Bks.

Schuck, Philip. A Ricochet from Circumstance. 2005. (YA). 19.95 (978-0-9764670-0-7(3)) Smithfield Capital Corp.

Silvano, Wendi. Love Is All Around Oklahoma. Czernichowska, Joanna, illus. 2016. (ENG.). 32p. (J). (-6). 12.99 (978-1-4926-2950-4(2), Sourcebooks Jabberwocky) Sourcebooks, Inc.

—Love Is All Around Tulsa. Czernichowska, Joanna, illus. 2016. (ENG.). 32p. (J). (-6). 12.99 (978-1-4926-2967-2(7), Sourcebooks Jabberwocky) Sourcebooks, Inc.

Singh, Navneet. The Key to Light & Darkness: Everything Can Feel Like a Dream... 2013. 344p. pap. 19.92 (978-1-4907-0948-2(7)) Trafford Publishing.

Sisco, Joann Ellen. Midnight at Faraway Farm. 2008. 79p. pap. 19.95 (978-1-60474-777-5(3)) America Star Bks.

Skye, obert. The Eyes of the Want. Sowards, Ben, illus. 2008. (Leven Thumps Ser.: 3). (ENG.). 464p. (J). (gr. 3-7). pap. 9.99 (978-1-4169-4719-6(1), Aladdin) Simon & Schuster Children's Publishing.

Smallman, Steve. Santa Is Coming to Oklahoma. Dunn, Robert, illus. 2013. (ENG.). 32p. (J). (-3). 9.99 (978-1-4022-9012-1(8), Sourcebooks Jabberwocky) Sourcebooks, Inc.

—Santa Is Coming to Oklahoma City. Dunn, Robert, illus. 2015. (ENG.). 32p. (J). (-3). 9.99 (978-1-4926-2637-4(6), Sourcebooks Jabberwocky) Sourcebooks, Inc.

—Santa Is Coming to Tulsa. Dunn, Robert, illus. 2013. (ENG.). 32p. (J). (-3). 9.99 (978-1-4022-9039-8(X), Sourcebooks Jabberwocky) Sourcebooks, Inc.

Smith, Darshiel & Haddi, Javon. Introducing the Rollies. 2013. 28p. pap. 24.95 (978-1-63000-582-5(7)) America Star Bks.

Tharp, Tim. Knights of the Hill Country. 2008. 233p. 17.00 (978-1-60686-365-7(7)) Perfection Learning Corp.

—Knights of the Hill Country. 2013. (ENG.). 240p. (YA). (gr. 7). pap. 8.99 (978-0-449-81287-7(1), Ember) Random Hse. Children's Bks.

—The Spectacular Now. (ENG.). 304p. (YA). (gr. 9). 2010. pap. 8.99 (978-0-375-86502-2(0), Knopf Bks. for Young Readers) 2013. pap. 9.99 (978-0-385-75430-9(2), Ember) Random Hse. Children's Bks.

Tingle, Tim. How I Became a Ghost: A Choctaw Trail of Tears Story, 1 vol. l.t. ed. 2013. (ENG., Illus.). 160p. (J). 18.95 (978-1-937054-53-3(5)) RoadRunner Pr.

Townsend, Una Belle. Grady's in the Silo, 1 vol. Artley, Bob, illus. 2003. (ENG.). 32p. (J). (gr. k-3). 16.99 (978-1-58980-098-4(2)) Pelican Publishing Co., Inc.

—The Great Elephant Escape, 1 vol. Hechter, Janice, illus. 2012. (ENG.). 32p. (J). (gr. k-3). 16.99 (978-1-4556-1582-7(X)) Pelican Publishing Co., Inc.

Wallace, Bill. The Dog Who Thought He Was Santa. 2007. (ENG., Illus.). 224p. (J). (gr. 4-7). 17.95 (978-0-8234-2114-5(7)) Holiday Hse., Inc.

Wallace, Sharolyn. The Adventures of Bruce, Ben & Gerry: Bruce's Dream. 2012. 28p. pap. 17.99 (978-1-4772-0249-4(8)) AuthorHouse.

Worley, Carla. Freedom Choice: A Book that Allows You to Consider Your Options. 2010. 76p. pap. 23.50 (978-1-60860-624-5(4), Strategic Bk. Publishing) Strategic Book Publishing & Rights Agency (SBPRA).

OKLAHOMA—HISTORY

Boehme, Gerry, et al. Oklahoma. 2015. (It's My State! (r) Ser.). (ENG., Illus.). 80p. (J). (gr. 4-4). 34.21 (978-1-62713-213-8(9)) Cavendish Square Publishing.

Bolden, Tonya. Searching for Sarah Rector: The Richest Black Girl in America. 2014. (ENG., Illus.). 80p. (J). (gr. 3-7). 21.95 (978-1-4197-0846-6(5), Abrams Bks. for Young Readers) Abrams, Inc.

Brean, Alta. Dear Grandchildren: Growing up on the Frontier. 2003. (Illus.). 144p. 18.95 (978-0-9726360-0-1(5), (408) 718-5654) Alta Omnimedia.

Calhoun, Sharon Cooper & English, Billie Joan. Oklahoma Adventure. 2007. (Illus.). 444p. (J). (978-1-934397-00-8(8)) Apple Corps Pubs.

Coleman, Miriam. Oklahoma: The Sooner State. 2010. (Our Amazing States Ser.). (ENG.). 24p. (J). pap. 8.25 (978-1-4488-0746-8(8)); lib. bdg. 22.60 (978-1-4488-0657-7(7)) Rosen Publishing Group, Inc., The. (PowerKids Pr.).

Dillard, Sheri. What's Great about Oklahoma? 2015. (Our Great States Ser.). (ENG.). 32p. (J). (gr. 2-5). pap. 7.95 (978-1-4677-6087-4(0)); (Illus.). 26.60 (978-1-4677-3863-7(8)) Lerner Publishing Group. (Lerner Pubns.).

Dorman, Robert L. Oklahoma: Past & Present. 2010. (United States: Past & Present Ser.). (ENG.). 48p. (YA). pap. 11.75 (978-1-4358-9520-1(7)); lib. bdg. 29.25 (978-1-4358-9493-8(6)) Rosen Publishing Group, Inc., The. (Rosen Reference).

Douglas, Bettye. Portrait of a People: The Bettye Douglas Forum, Inc. Multicultural Resource Book. Douglas, Bettye, ed. Douglas, Ana & Douglas, Garbrielle, illus. 222p. (YA). (gr. 5-13). 100.00 (978-0-9703183-1-2(6)) Douglas, Bettye Forum, Inc., The.

—Safari Oklahoma Presents: God Bless America Historical. Douglas, Garbrielle, illus. 2003. 22p. (J). (gr. 2-7). wbk. ed. 19.95 (978-0-9703183-6-7(7)) Douglas, Bettye Forum, Inc., The.

Durrett, Deanne. Oklahoma. 2003. (Seeds of a Nation Ser.). (Illus.). 48p. (J). (gr. 3-5). 23.70 (978-0-7377-1479-1(4), Kidhaven) Cengage Gale.

Friesen, Helen Lepp. Oklahoma: The Sooner State. 2012. (J). (978-1-61913-391-4(1)); pap. (978-1-61913-392-1(X)) Weigl Pubs., Inc.

Gish, Melissa. Oklahoma. 2009. (This Land Called America Ser.). 32p. (YA). (gr. 3-6). 19.95 (978-1-58341-789-8(3)) Creative Co., The.

Jerome, Kate B. Lucky to Live in Oklahoma. 2017. (Arcadia Kids Ser.). (ENG., Illus.). 32p. (J). 16.99 **(978-0-7385-2799-4(8))** Arcadia Publishing.

—The Wise Animal Handbook Oklahoma. 2017. (Arcadia Kids Ser.). (ENG., Illus.). 32p. (J). 16.99 **(978-0-7385-2838-0(2))** Arcadia Publishing.

Laird, Johnna M. Southwest: New Mexico, Oklahoma, Texas, Vol. 19. 2015. (Let's Explore the States Ser.). (Illus.). 64p. (J). (gr. 5). 23.95 (978-1-4222-3334-4(0)) Mason Crest.

LeBoutillier, Nate. The Story of the Oklahoma City Thunder. 2010. (NBA — A History of Hoops Ser.). 48p. (YA). (gr. 5-18). 23.95 (978-1-58341-962-5(4), Creative Education) Creative Co., The.

Marsh, Carole. Exploring Oklahoma Through Project-Based Learning: Geography, History, Government, Economics & More. 2016. (Oklahoma Experience Ser.). (ENG.). (J). pap. 9.99 (978-0-635-12360-2(6)) Gallopade International.

Murray, Julie. Oklahoma, 1 vol. 2012. (Explore the United States Ser.). (ENG., Illus.). 32p. (J). (gr. 2-5). lib. bdg. 28.50 (978-1-61783-374-8(6), Big Buddy Bks.) ABDO Publishing Co.

Nelson, Vaunda Micheaux. Bad News for Outlaws: The Remarkable Life of Bass Reeves, Deputy U. S. Marshall. Christie, R. Gregory, illus. 2009. (Exceptional Social Studies Titles for Intermediate Grades). (ENG.). 40p. (J). (gr. 3-6). lib. bdg. 17.95 (978-0-8225-6764-6(4)) Lerner Publishing Group.

Paul, Michael. Oklahoma City & Anti-Government Terrorism. 2006. (Terrorism in Today's World Ser.). (Illus.). 48p. (gr. 5-12). pap. 14.05 (978-0-8368-6565-3(0)); lib. bdg. 31.00 (978-0-8368-6558-5(8)) Stevens, Gareth Publishing LLLP. (Gareth Stevens Secondary Library).

Rigby. When Day Turned to Night. 2014. (Rigby LIteracy Ser.). (ENG.). 32p. (gr. 4-4). pap. 11.10 (978-0-7578-2002-1(6)) Rigby Education.

Sanders, Doug & Horn, Geoffrey M. Oklahoma. 2nd ed. 2013. 80p. (J). (gr. 4-8). 31.36 (978-0-7614-8001-3(3)) Cavendish Square Publishing.

Smith, Rich. Oklahoma, 1 vol. 2009. (United States Ser.). (ENG., Illus.). 48p. (YA). (gr. 2-5). 27.07 (978-1-60453-671-3(3)) ABDO Publishing Co.

Strudwick, Leslie. Oklahoma. 2011. (Guide to American States Ser.). (Illus.). 48p. (YA). (gr. 3-6). 29.99 (978-1-61690-808-9(4)); (J). 29.99 (978-1-61690-484-5(4)) Weigl Pubs., Inc.

—Oklahoma: The Sooner State. 2016. (J). (978-1-4896-4923-2(9)) Weigl Pubs., Inc.

Zuchora-Walske, Christine. The Dust Bowl: A History Perspectives Book. 2013. (Perspectives Library). (ENG., Illus.). 32p. (J). (gr. 4-8). 28.50 (978-1-62431-417-9(1), 202788); pap. 14.21 (978-1-62431-493-3(7), 202790) Cherry Lake Publishing.

OKLAHOMA—HISTORY—FICTION

Davis, Russell G. & Ashabranner, Brent. The Choctaw Code. 2006. 121p. (J). (gr. 3-7). per. 8.99 (978-1-59166-621-9(X)) BJU Pr.

Griffis, Molly Levite. Simon Says. 2004. vi, 263p. (J). 22.95 (978-1-57168-836-1(6)); pap. (978-1-57168-847-7(1)) Eakin Pr. (Eakin Pr.).

Kirby, Susan E. A No-Fuss Christmas. 2010. (J). (978-1-60682-059-9(1)) BJU Pr.

Love, D. Anne. Semiprecious. (ENG.). 304p. (J). (gr. 5-9). 2009. pap. 6.99 (978-0-689-87389-8(1)) 2006. (Illus.). 17.99 (978-0-689-85638-9(5)) McElderry, Margaret K. Bks. (McElderry, Margaret K. Bks.).

McCaughrean, Geraldine. Stop the Train! 2003. (ENG.). 304p. (J). (gr. 5-18). 16.99 (978-0-06-050749-7(7)) HarperCollins Pubs.

Mitchell, Saundra. The Springsweet. 2013. (ENG.). 304p. (YA). (gr. 7). pap. 8.99 (978-0-544-00327-9(6)) Houghton Mifflin Harcourt Publishing Co.

Myers, Anna. Tulsa Burning. 2004. (Illus.). 184p. (J). (gr. 3-7). 16.95 (978-0-8027-8829-0(7)) Walker & Co.

Scillian, Devin. Pappy's Handkerchief. Ellison, Chris, illus. rev. ed. 2007. (Tales of Young Americans Ser.). (ENG.). 32p. (J). (gr. 3-7). 17.95 (978-1-58536-316-2(2)) Sleeping Bear Pr.

Scillian, Devin & Young, Judy. Westward Journeys. Ellison, Chris et al, illus. 2013. (American Adventures Ser.). (ENG.). 96p. (J). (gr. 3-6). pap. 6.99 (978-1-58536-860-0(1), 202367) Sleeping Bear Pr.

Sowards, Ben. Asleep on the Hay: A Dust Bowl Christmas. Sowards, Ben, illus. 2015. (Illus.). (J). 17.99 (978-1-62972-067-8(4), Ensign Peak) Deseret Bk. Co.

Stanley, George E. Night Fires. 2009. (ENG.). 192p. (J). (gr. 3-7). 15.99 (978-1-4169-7559-5(4), Simon & Schuster/Paula Wiseman Bks.) Simon & Schuster/Paula Wiseman Bks.

Stanley, George Edward. Night Fires. 2011. (ENG.). 192p. (J). (gr. 3-7). pap. 6.99 (978-1-4169-1250-7(9), Simon & Schuster/Paula Wiseman Bks.) Simon & Schuster/Paula Wiseman Bks.

Townsend, Una Belle. The Oklahoma Land Run, 1 vol. Henriquez, Emile, illus. 2008. (ENG.). 32p. (J). (gr. k-3). 16.99 (978-1-58980-566-8(6)) Pelican Publishing Co., Inc.

Wallace, Bill. The Dog Who Thought He Was Santa. 2008. (ENG.). 192p. (J). (gr. 3-7). pap. 5.99 (978-1-4169-4816-2(3), Aladdin) Simon & Schuster Children's Publishing.

OLD AGE

see also Older People

Birmingham, Maria. A Beginner's Guide to Immortality: from Alchemy to Avatars. Holinaty, Josh, illus. 2015. (ENG.). 48p. (J). (gr. 3-7). 16.95 (978-1-77147-045-2(3), Owlkids) Owlkids Bks. Inc. CAN. Dist: Publishers Group West (PGW).

Bregoli, Jane. The Goat Lady. Bregoli, Jane, illus. 2008. (ENG., Illus.). 32p. (gr. 2-6). pap. 8.95 *(978-0-88448-309-0(6),* 884309) Tilbury Hse. Pubs.

McCurry, Chris & Waddington, Emma. Why Are People Different Colors? Big Issues for Little People Around Identity & Diversity. Thomas, Louis, illus. 2016. (Life & Soul Library). (ENG.). 32p. (J). (gr. -1-3). 12.99 *(978-1-84780-864-6(6),* Frances Lincoln Children's Bks.) Quarto Publishing Group UK GBR. Dist: Hachette Bk. Group.

Naughton, Diane. Secrets to a Long Life Intermediate Book with Online Access. 2014. (ENG., Illus.). 28p. (J). pap. 9.50 *(978-1-107-68378-5(5))* Cambridge Univ. Pr.

Panno, Joseph. Aging. 2nd rev. ed. 2010. (New Biology Ser.). 264p. (gr. 6-12). 40.00 *(978-0-8160-6846-3(1))* Facts On File, Inc.

—The Science of Aging: Theories & Potential Therapies. 2006. (New Biology Ser.). (Illus.). 157p. (gr. 6-12). per. 18.95 *(978-0-8160-6930-9(1),* Checkmark Bks.) Facts On File, Inc.

Thompson, Tamara. Expanding the Human Lifespan. Greenhaven Press Editors, ed. 2013. (At Issue Ser.). (ENG.). 128p. (gr. 10-12). 39.40 *(978-0-7377-6836-7(3),* Greenhaven Pr., Inc.) Cengage Gale.

OLD AGE—FICTION

Almond, David. Kit's Wilderness. unabr. ed. 2004. 240p. (J). (gr. 7-18). pap. 36.00 incl. audio *(978-0-8072-8216-8(2),* Listening Library) Random Hse. Audio Publishing Group.

Altés, Marta. My Grandpa. 2013. (ENG., Illus.). 32p. (J). (gr. k-2). 16.95 *(978-1-4197-0588-5(1),* Abrams Bks. for Young Readers) Abrams, Inc.

Auch, M. J. Wing Nut. 2008. (ENG.). 256p. (J). (gr. 5-9). pap. 14.99 *(978-0-312-38420-3(3),* 9780312384203) Square Fish.

Baker, Matthew. If You Find This. 2015. (ENG.). 368p. (J). (gr. 3-7). 17.00 *(978-0-316-24008-6(7))* Little, Brown Bks. for Young Readers.

Bauer, Joan. Best Foot Forward. 2006. (ENG.). 192p. (YA). (gr. 7-18). reprint ed. 7.99 *(978-0-14-240690-8(2),* Speak) Penguin Young Readers Group.

—Best Foot Forward. 2006. 183p. (gr. 7-12). 18.00 *(978-0-7569-6767-3(8))* Perfection Learning Corp.

—Rules of the Road. 2005. (ENG.). 208p. (YA). (gr. 7-7). pap. 8.99 *(978-0-14-240425-6(X),* Speak) Penguin Young Readers Group.

Blythe, Carolita. Revenge of a Not-So-Pretty Girl. 2013. (ENG.). 336p. (YA). (gr. 7). 19.99 *(978-0-375-99081-6(X),* Delacorte Bks. for Young Readers) Random Hse. Children's Bks.

Boné, Thomas H., illus. The Teacher Who Would Not Retire Retires. 2017. (J). ***(978-0-9885295-7-1(2))*** Blue Marlin Pubns.

Bosak, Susan V. Something to Remember Me By. 2015. 32p. pap. 8.00 *(978-1-61003-553-8(4))* Center for the Collaborative Classroom.

Brooks, Mel & Reiner, Carl. The 2000 Year Old Man Goes to School. Bennett, James, illus. 2006. 32p. (J). (gr. 4-8). reprint ed. 18.00 *(978-1-4223-5622-7(1))* DIANE Publishing Co.

—The 2000 Year Old Man Goes to School. Bennett, James, illus. 2005. (ENG.). 40p. (J). (gr. -1-3). 17.99 *(978-0-06-076676-4(X))* HarperCollins Pubs.

Buckley-Archer, Linda. The Many Lives of John Stone. 2015. (ENG., Illus.). 544p. (YA). (gr. 7). 17.99 *(978-1-4814-2637-4(0))* Simon & Schuster Children's Publishing.

Bundy, Tamara. Walking with Miss Millie. 2017. (ENG.). 240p. (J). (gr. 5). 16.99 ***(978-0-399-54456-9(9),*** Nancy Paulsen Books) Penguin Young Readers Group.

Burns, Catherine Lloyd. The Half-True Lies of Cricket Cohen. 2017. (ENG.). 256p. (J). 16.99 *(978-0-374-30041-8(0),* 9780374300418, Farrar, Straus & Giroux (BYR)) Farrar, Straus & Giroux.

Caletti, Deb. Honey, Baby, Sweetheart. 2008. (ENG.). 336p. (YA). (gr. 7-12). pap. 9.99 *(978-1-4169-5783-6(9),* Simon Pulse) Simon Pulse.

Cannon, Janell. Verdi. pap. 24.95 *(978-85-325-1343-4(3))* Rocco, Editora, Ltda BRA. Dist: Distribooks, Inc.

Cannon, Janell & Cannon. Verdi. 2003. (SPA., Illus.). 48p. (J). (gr. 1-3). *(978-84-261-3042-6(9),* JV7591) Juventud, Editorial ESP. Dist: Lectorum Pubns., Inc.

Cascone, Annette & Cascone, Gina. Grave Secrets. 2014. (Deadtime Stories Ser.). (ENG.). 192p. (J). (gr. 3-7). pap. 6.99 *(978-0-7653-3071-0(7),* 9780765330710, Starscape) Doherty, Tom Assocs., LLC.

Cherry, Alison. The Classy Crooks Club. 2016. (ENG., Illus.). 336p. (J). (gr. 3-7). 16.99 *(978-1-4814-4637-2(1),* Aladdin) Simon & Schuster Children's Publishing.

Christiansen, Candace. The Mitten Tree. Greenstein, Elaine, illus. 2009. (ENG.). 32p. (J). (gr. -1-1). pap. 10.95 *(978-1-55591-733-3(X))* Fulcrum Publishing.

Condon, Bill. Riley & the Fantastic Plan. Hopgood, Andrew, illus. 2015. (Legends in Their Own Lunchbox Ser.). (ENG.). 56p. (gr. 2-3). pap. 7.99 *(978-1-4966-0252-7(8),* Legends in Their Own Lunchbox) Capstone Classroom.

Cooney, Caroline B. Hit the Road. rev. l.t. ed. 2007. (Thorndike Literacy Bridge Ser.). 259p. (YA). (gr. 7-12). 23.95 *(978-0-7862-9429-9(9))* Thorndike Pr.

Corriell, Shelley. Welcome, Caller, This Is Chloe. 2013. (ENG.). 320p. (YA). (gr. 7-17). pap. 7.95 *(978-1-4197-0545-8(8),* Amulet Bks.) Abrams, Inc.

Currim, Nazli. Grandma Lives with Us. Tung, Kadhima Ren, illus. 2010. 46p. (J). 16.95 *(978-0-9814629-5-0(2))* Acacia Publishing, Inc.

De Baun, Hillary Hall. The Last Stop Before Heaven. Cooper, Floyd, illus. 2012. (ENG.). 236p. (J). pap. 9.00 *(978-0-8028-5398-1(6),* Eerdmans Bks For Young Readers) Eerdmans, William B. Publishing Co.

dePaola, Tomie. Nana Upstairs & Nana Downstairs. unabr. ed. 2006. (J). (gr. k-3). pap. 17.95 incl. audio *(978-0-8045-6943-9(6));* pap. 19.95 incl. audio compact disk *(978-0-8045-4157-2(4))* Spoken Arts, Inc.

Dion. Fishing with Balloons. 2004. (Illus.). 57p. (J). pap. 4.95 *(978-1-881929-34-5(5))* Oxton Hse., Pubs.

Dyan, Penelope. Great Grandma Is Getting Old. Dyan, Penelope, illus. 2010. (Illus.). 42p. pap. 11.95 *(978-1-935118-97-8(8))* Bellissima Publishing, LLC.

Edwards, Michelle. A Hat for Mrs. Goldman: A Story about Knitting & Love. Karas, G. Brian, illus. 2016. (ENG.). 40p. (J). (gr. -1-3). 17.99 *(978-0-553-49710-6(3),* Schwartz & Wade Bks.) Random Hse. Children's Bks.

Fitzpatrick, Huntley. What I Thought Was True. 2014. (ENG.). 416p. (YA). (gr. 9). 17.99 *(978-0-8037-3909-3(5),* Dial Bks) Penguin Young Readers Group.

Flood, Pansie Hart. Sometimey Friend. Marshall, Felicia, illus. 2005. 124p. (J). (gr. 3-7). 15.95 *(978-1-57505-866-5(9))* Lerner Publishing Group.

—Sylvia & Miz Lula Maye. Marshall, Felicia, illus. 2003. (Middle Grade Fiction Ser.). 120p. (J). (gr. 3-6). 15.95 *(978-0-87614-204-2(8),* Carolrhoda Bks.) Lerner Publishing Group.

Gantos, Jack. Dead End in Norvelt. 2011. (Norvelt Ser.: 1). (ENG., Illus.). 352p. (J). (gr. 5-9). 15.99 *(978-0-374-37993-3(9),* 9780374379933, Farrar, Straus & Giroux (BYR)) Farrar, Straus & Giroux.

—Dead End in Norvelt. 2013. (Norvelt Ser.: 1). (ENG., Illus.). 384p. (J). (gr. 5-9). pap. 8.99 *(978-1-250-01023-0(3),* 9781250010230) Square Fish.

—Dead End in Norvelt. 2013. (J). lib. bdg. 18.40 *(978-0-606-31901-0(8),* Turtleback) Turtleback Bks.

—From Norvelt to Nowhere. 2015. (J). lib. bdg. 18.40 *(978-0-606-37280-0(6))* Turtleback Bks.

Gardiner, John Reynolds. General Butterfingers. Smith, Cat Bowman & Smith, Catharine Bowman, illus. 2007. (ENG.). 96p. (J). (gr. 5-7). 7.95 *(978-0-618-75922-4(0))* Houghton Mifflin Harcourt Publishing Co.

Giff, Patricia Reilly. Pictures of Hollis Woods. 2014. (ENG.). 176p. (J). (gr. 3-7). 11.24 *(978-1-63245-318-1(5))* Lectorum Pubns., Inc.

—Pictures of Hollis Woods. 2004. (ENG.). 176p. (J). (gr. 3-7). 7.99 *(978-0-440-41578-7(0),* Yearling) Random Hse. Children's Bks.

Greene, Stephanie. Queen Sophie Hartley. 2011. (ENG.). 144p. (J). (gr. 2-5). pap. 5.99 *(978-0-547-55021-3(9))* Houghton Mifflin Harcourt Publishing Co.

Henson, Heather. Grumpy Grandpa. MacDonald, Ross, illus. 2009. (ENG.). 40p. (J). (gr. -1-3). 16.99 *(978-1-4169-0811-1(0),* Atheneum Bks. for Young Readers) Simon & Schuster Children's Publishing.

Hest, Amy. Mr. George Baker. Muth, Jon J., illus. 2007. (Reading Rainbow Bks.). (ENG.). 32p. (J). (gr. k-3). 6.99 *(978-0-7636-3308-0(9))* Candlewick Pr.

—Mr. George Baker. 2007. lib. bdg. 17.20 *(978-1-4177-9067-8(9),* Turtleback) Turtleback Bks.

Holt, Kimberly Willis. Dancing in Cadillac Light. 2003. (ENG.). 176p. (J). (gr. 5-9). 5.99 *(978-0-698-11970-3(3),* Puffin Books) Penguin Young Readers Group.

—Dancing in Cadillac Light. 2004. 176p. (J). (gr. 4-7). pap. 36.00 incl. audio *(978-0-8072-2095-5(7),* Listening Library) Random Hse. Audio Publishing Group.

Howland, Naomi. The Better-Than-Best Purim. 0 vols. 2012. (ENG.). 32p. (J). (gr. -1-2). 16.99 *(978-0-7614-6203-3(1),* 9780761462033, Amazon Children's Publishing) Amazon Publishing.

Jeffers, Dawn. Vegetable Dreams/Huerto Sonado. de La Vega, Eida, tr. Schneider, Claude, illus. 2006. (SPA & ENG.). 32p. (J). (gr. -1-3). 16.95 *(978-0-9741992-9-0(X),* 626999, Raven Tree Pr.,Csi) Continental Sales, Inc.

Joyce, William. The Leaf Men: And the Brave Good Bugs. Joyce, William, illus. 2017. (World of William Joyce Ser.). (ENG., Illus.). 40p. (J). (gr. -1-3). 17.99 ***(978-1-4814-8955-3(0),*** Atheneum/Caitlyn Dlouhy Books) Simon & Schuster Children's Publishing.

Kennedy, Marlane. The Dog Days of Charlotte Hayes. 2009. (ENG., Illus.). 240p. (J). (gr. 3-7). 15.99 *(978-0-06-145241-3(6),* Greenwillow Bks.) HarperCollins Pubs.

Kimmel, Eric A. Hanukkah Bear. Wohnoutka, Mike, illus. (ENG.). 32p. (J). (gr. -1-3). 2014. 6.99 *(978-0-8234-3169-4(X))* 2013. 17.95 *(978-0-8234-2855-7(9))* Holiday Hse., Inc.

Klise, Kate. Stay: A Girl, a Dog, a Bucket List. Klise, M. Sarah, illus. 2017. (ENG.). 32p. (J). 17.99 *(978-1-250-10714-5(8),* 9781250107145) Feiwel & Friends.

Korngold, Jamie. Sadie & Ori & the Blue Blanket. Fortenberry, Julie, illus. 2015. (ENG.). 32p. (J). (gr. -1-2). 17.99 *(978-1-4677-1191-3(8),* Kar-Ben Publishing) Lerner Publishing Group.

Lakritz, Deborah. Say Hello, Lily. Avilés, Martha, illus. 2010. (Jewish Identity Ser.). 32p. (J). (gr. -1-3). lib. bdg. 17.95 *(978-0-7613-4511-4(6));* (ENG.). pap. 7.95 *(978-0-7613-4512-1(4))* Lerner Publishing Group. (Kar-Ben Publishing).

Levin, Betty. The Unmaking of Duncan Veerick. 2007. (ENG.). 212p. (J). (gr. 9-12). 16.95 *(978-1-932425-96-3(9),* Front Street) Boyds Mills Pr.

Levine, Arthur A. & Kath, Katie. What a Beautiful Morning. 2016. (ENG., Illus.). 40p. (J). (gr. -1-17). 16.95 *(978-0-7624-5906-3(9),* Running Pr. Kids) Running Pr. Bk. Pubs.

Lindbergh, Reeve. My Little Grandmother Often Forgets. Brown, Kathryn, illus. 2007. (ENG.). 32p. (J). (gr. -1-1). 16.99 *(978-0-7636-1989-3(2))* Candlewick Pr.

Lynch, Chris. Kill Switch. (ENG., (YA). (gr. 7). 2013. Illus.). 192p. pap. 9.99 *(978-1-4424-5442-2(3))* 2012. 176p. 16.99 *(978-1-4169-2702-0(6))* Simon & Schuster Bks. For Young Readers. (Simon & Schuster Bks. For Young Readers).

Lyons, Kelly Starling. Tea Cakes for Tosh. Lewis, E. B., illus. 2012. (ENG.). 32p. (J). (gr. k-3). 16.99 *(978-0-399-25213-6(4),* G.P. Putnam's Sons Books for Young Readers) Penguin Young Readers Group.

MacLachlan, Patricia. Kindred Souls. (J). (gr. 1-5). 2013. (ENG.). 144p. pap. 5.99 *(978-0-06-052299-5(2))* 2012. (ENG.). 128p. 16.99 *(978-0-06-052297-1(6))* 2012. 128p. lib. bdg. 17.89 *(978-0-06-052298-8(4))* HarperCollins Pubs. (Tegen, Katherine Bks).

Maddox, Jake. Hoop Hustle. Aburto, Jesus, illus. 2015. (Jake Maddox Sports Stories Ser.). (ENG.). 72p. (gr. 2-3). lib. bdg. 25.32 *(978-1-4965-0494-4(1))* Stone Arch Bks.

Mazer, Norma Fox. Ten Ways to Make My Sister Disappear. 2007. (ENG.). 128p. (J). (gr. 4-7). 16.99 *(978-0-439-83983-9(1),* Levine, Arthur A. Bks.) Scholastic, Inc.

McCahan, Erin. The Lake Effect. 2017. (ENG.). 400p. (YA). (gr. 7). 17.99 ***(978-0-8037-4052-5(2),*** Dial Bks) Penguin Young Readers Group.

McCusker, Paul. Memory's Gate, 1 vol. 2009. (Time Thriller Trilogy Ser.: Bk. 3). (ENG.). 208p. (YA). (gr. 8-11). pap. 9.99 *(978-0-310-71438-5(9))* Zondervan.

Messner, Kate. The Brilliant Fall of Gianna Z. (ENG.). 224p. 2017. (J). pap. 8.99 ***(978-1-68119-547-6(X),*** 9781681195476) 2010. (YA). (gr. 3-6). pap. 8.99 *(978-0-8027-2173-0(7),* 9780802721730) Bloomsbury Publishing USA. (Bloomsbury USA Childrens).

—The Brilliant Fall of Gianna Z. 2017. (J). lib. bdg. 19.65 ***(978-0-606-40595-9(X))*** Turtleback Bks.

Mikaelsen, Ben. Petey. 2010. (ENG.). 256p. (J). (gr. 3-7). pap. 6.99 *(978-1-4231-3174-8(6))* Hyperion Pr.

—Petey. 2011. 8.32 *(978-0-7848-3604-0(3),* Everbind) Marco Bk. Co.

Murphy, Barbara Beasley & Wolkoff, Judie. Ace Hits Rock Bottom. 2003. (Can't Stop Ace Ser.: No. 2). 204p. (J). pap. 16.95 *(978-0-86534-408-2(6))* Sunstone Pr.

Myers, Walter Dean. Lockdown. (YA). (gr. 8). 2011. (ENG.). 272p. pap. 9.99 *(978-0-06-121482-0(5))* 2010. 256p. lib. bdg. 17.89 *(978-0-06-121481-3(7))* 2010. (ENG.). 256p. 16.99 *(978-0-06-121480-6(9))* HarperCollins Pubs. (Amistad).

Nelson, Vaunda Micheaux. Don't Call Me Grandma. Zunon, Elizabeth, illus. 2016. (ENG.). 32p. (gr. k-3). (J). 30.65 *(978-1-4677-9559-3(3));* 35.99 *(978-1-5124-0661-0(9))* Lerner Publishing Group. (Carolrhoda Bks.).

Newman, Jeff. The Boys. Newman, Jeff, illus. 2010. (ENG., Illus.). 40p. (J). (gr. -1-2). 17.99 *(978-1-4169-5012-7(5),* Simon & Schuster Bks. For Young Readers) Simon & Schuster Bks. For Young Readers.

Oboh, Rolic. Treasure Hunt. 2006. 108p. pap. 7.99 *(978-1-84426-318-9(5))* Upfront Publishing Ltd. GBR. Dist: Printondemand-worldwide.com.

Ørbeck-Nilssen, Constance. I'm Right Here. Düzakin, Akin, illus. 2015. (ENG.). 28p. (J). 16.00 *(978-0-8028-5455-1(9),* Eerdmans Bks For Young Readers) Eerdmans, William B. Publishing Co.

Paulsen, Gary. Fishbone's Song. 2016. (ENG., Illus.). 160p. (J). (gr. 5). 16.99 *(978-1-4814-5226-7(6),* Simon & Schuster Bks. For Young Readers) Simon & Schuster Bks. For Young Readers.

Pearsall, Shelley. Trouble Don't Last. 2003. (ENG.). 256p. (J). (gr. 3-7). reprint ed. 6.99 *(978-0-440-41811-5(9),* Yearling) Random Hse. Children's Bks.

Reynolds, Cynthia Furlong. Across the Reach. 2007. 269p. (J). (gr. 3-7). 16.95 *(978-1-58726-518-1(4),* Mitten Pr.) Ann Arbor Editions LLC.

Rubin, Adam. Those Darn Squirrels! Salmieri, Daniel, illus. 2008. (ENG.). 32p. (J). (gr. -1-3). 17.99 *(978-0-547-00703-8(5))* Houghton Mifflin Harcourt Publishing Co.

—Those Darn Squirrels Fly South. Salmieri, Daniel, illus. 2012. (ENG.). 32p. (J). (gr. -1-3). 17.99 *(978-0-547-67823-8(1))* Houghton Mifflin Harcourt Publishing Co.

Rylant, Cynthia. Henry & Mudge & the Great Grandpas. Stevenson, Suçie, illus. 2006. (Henry & Mudge Ser.). 40p. (gr. k-2). 14.00 *(978-0-7569-6793-2(7))* Perfection Learning Corp.

—Henry & Mudge & the Great Grandpas. Stevenson, Suçie, illus. 2006. (Henry & Mudge Ser.: 26). (ENG.). 40p. (J). (gr. k-2). pap. 3.99 *(978-0-689-83447-9(0),* Simon Spotlight) Simon Spotlight.

—Henry & Mudge & the Great Grandpas. Stevenson, Suçie & Stevenson, Suçie, illus. 2005. (Henry & Mudge Ser.: 26). (ENG.). 40p. (J). (gr. k-2). 15.99 *(978-0-689-81170-8(5),* Simon Spotlight) Simon Spotlight.

—Mr. Putter & Tabby Clear the Decks. Howard, Arthur, illus. alt. ed. 2011. (Mr. Putter & Tabby Ser.). (ENG.). 44p. (J). (gr. 1-4). pap. 5.99 *(978-0-547-57695-4(1))* Houghton Mifflin Harcourt Publishing Co.

—Mr. Putter & Tabby Dance the Dance. Howard, Arthur, illus. 2012. (Mr. Putter & Tabby Ser.: 21). (ENG.). 40p. (J). (gr. 1-4). 14.99 *(978-0-15-206415-0(X))* Houghton Mifflin Harcourt Publishing Co.

—Mr. Putter & Tabby Dance the Dance. 2013. (Mr. Putter & Tabby Ser.). lib. bdg. 16.00 *(978-0-606-32338-3(4),* Turtleback) Turtleback Bks.

—Mr. Putter & Tabby Drop the Ball. Howard, Arthur, illus. (Mr. Putter & Tabby Ser.). (ENG.). 44p. (J). (gr. 1-4). 2014. pap. 5.99 *(978-0-544-34115-9(5),* HMH Books For Young Readers) 2013. 14.99 *(978-0-15-205072-6(8))* Houghton Mifflin Harcourt Publishing Co.

—Mr. Putter & Tabby Drop the Ball. 2014. (Mr. Putter & Tabby Ser.). lib. bdg. 16.00 *(978-0-606-35985-6(0))* Turtleback Bks.

—Mr. Putter & Tabby Hit the Slope. Howard, Arthur, illus. 2016. (Mr. Putter & Tabby Ser.). (ENG.). 40p. (J). (gr. 1-4). 14.99 *(978-0-15-206427-3(3),* HMH Books For Young Readers) Houghton Mifflin Harcourt Publishing Co.

—Mr. Putter & Tabby Make a Wish. Howard, Arthur, illus. 2006. (Mr. Putter & Tabby Ser.). (ENG.). 44p. (J). (gr. -1-3). pap. 5.99 *(978-0-15-205443-4(X))* Houghton Mifflin Harcourt Publishing Co.

—Mr. Putter & Tabby Make a Wish. Howard, Arthur, illus. 2006. (Mr. Putter & Tabby Ser.). (gr. 1-4). 16.00 *(978-0-7569-6892-2(5))* Perfection Learning Corp.

—Mr. Putter & Tabby Ring the Bell. Howard, Arthur, illus. 2012. (Mr. Putter & Tabby Ser.). (ENG.). 44p. (J). (gr. 1-4). pap. 5.99 *(978-0-547-85075-7(1))* Houghton Mifflin Harcourt Publishing Co.

—Mr. Putter & Tabby Ring the Bell. Howard, Arthur, illus. 2012. (Mr. Putter & Tabby Ser.). lib. bdg. 16.00 *(978-0-606-26614-7(3),* Turtleback) Turtleback Bks.

—Mr. Putter & Tabby Spill the Beans. Howard, Arthur, illus. 2010. (Mr. Putter & Tabby Ser.). (ENG.). 44p. (J). (gr. 1-4). pap. 5.99 *(978-0-547-41433-1(1))* Houghton Mifflin Harcourt Publishing Co.

—Mr. Putter & Tabby Walk the Dog. Howard, Arthur, illus. 2007. (Mr. Putter & Tabby Ser.). pap. 7.93 *(978-1-4189-5209-9(5))* Houghton Mifflin Harcourt Trade & Reference Pubs.

—The Old Woman Who Named Things. Brown, Kathryn, illus. 2015. 32p. pap. 7.00 *(978-1-61003-498-2(8))* Center for the Collaborative Classroom.

—The Old Woman Who Named Things. Brown, Kathryn, illus. 2004. (gr. -1-3). 17.00 *(978-0-7569-4204-5(7))* Perfection Learning Corp.

Rylant, Cynthia & Howard, Arthur. Mr. Putter & Tabby Dance the Dance. Howard, Arthur, illus. 2013. (Mr. Putter & Tabby Ser.). (ENG., Illus.). 40p. (J). (gr. 1-4). pap. 5.99 *(978-0-544-10496-9(X))* Houghton Mifflin Harcourt Publishing Co.

Shanker, Myrna Gelman. Lazar, the Good Deed Dog. Robinson, Linda, illus. 2010. (J). *(978-0-9829273-0-4(4))* IGI Pr.

Siebold, Jan. Doing Time Online. 2004. 88p. (gr. 4-7). 17.50 *(978-0-7569-3612-9(8))* Perfection Learning Corp.

Smelcer, John. The Trap. 2007. (ENG.). 176p. (YA). (gr. 7-9). per. 9.99 *(978-0-312-37755-7(X),* 9780312377557) Square Fish.

Smith, Brian, Brian. Memory. 2014. (ENG.). 216p. (C). pap. 49.95 *(978-1-138-87117-5(6),* Y178984) Routledge.

Steinkellner, Elisabeth. My New Granny. Roher, Michael, illus. 2012. (ENG.). 32p. (J). (gr. -1-3). 16.95 *(978-1-62087-223-9(4),* 620223, Sky Pony Pr.) Skyhorse Publishing Co., Inc.

Stevens, Carla & Stevens, Chapman. Who's Knocking at the Door?, 1 vol. Chapman, Lee, illus. 2004. (ENG.). 32p. (J). 16.95 *(978-0-7614-5168-6(4))* Marshall Cavendish Corp.

Van Laan, Nancy. Forget Me Not. Graegin, Stephanie, illus. 2014. (ENG.). 40p. (J). (gr. -1-3). 16.99 *(978-0-449-81543-4(9),* Schwartz & Wade Bks.) Random Hse. Children's Bks.

Velásquez, Gloria. Rudy's Memory Walk. 2009. (Roosevelt High School Ser.). 140p. (YA). (gr. 6-18). pap. 9.95 *(978-1-55885-593-9(9))* Arte Publico Pr.

Walker, Sally M. Druscilla's Halloween. White, Lee, illus. 2009. (Carolrhoda Picture Bks.). (ENG.). 32p. (J). (gr. k-3). 16.95 *(978-0-8225-8941-9(9))* Lerner Publishing Group.

Weston Woods Staff, creator. Wilfrid Gordon Mcdonald Partridge. 2011. 38.75 *(978-0-439-72917-8(3));* 18.95 *(978-0-439-72916-1(5));* 29.95 *(978-0-439-73530-8(0))* Weston Woods Studios, Inc.

Wojciechowska, Maia & Manna, Sal. A Kingdom in a Horse. 2012. (ENG.). 160p. (J). (gr. 2-7). pap. 9.95 *(978-1-61608-481-3(2),* 608481, Sky Pony Pr.) Skyhorse Publishing Co., Inc.

Woods, Brenda. Saint Louis Armstrong Beach. 2012. lib. bdg. 16.00 *(978-0-606-26661-1(5),* Turtleback) Turtleback Bks.

Yep, Laurence. The Magic Paintbrush. Wang, Suling, illus. 2003. (ENG.). 96p. (J). (gr. 3-7). pap. 6.99 *(978-0-06-440852-3(3))* HarperCollins Pubs.

—The Magic Paintbrush. Wang, Suling, illus. 2003. 89p. (J). (gr. 3-7). 12.65 *(978-0-7569-1444-8(2))* Perfection Learning Corp.

OLD FORT NIAGARA (N.Y.)—FICTION

Smallman, Steve. Santa Is Coming to Niagara Falls. Dunn, Robert, illus. 2015. (ENG.). 32p. (J). (-3). 9.99 *(978-1-4926-2655-8(4),* Sourcebooks Jabberwocky) Sourcebooks, Inc.

OLD STURBRIDGE VILLAGE

Kauffman, Dorothy. Two Villages: Two Hundred Years Apart. 2005. (Oxford Picture Dictionary for the Content Areas Ser.). (ENG., Illus.). 22p. pap. 7.56 *(978-0-19-430952-3(5))* Oxford Univ. Pr., Inc.

OLD TESTAMENT

see Bible—*Old Testament*

OLDER PEOPLE

Engdahl, Sylvia. The Elderly. Gale Editors, ed. 2011. (Current Controversies Ser.). 240p. (J). pap. 28.45 *(978-0-7377-5180-2(0));* (ENG.). 224p. (gr. 12-12). lib. bdg. 46.40 *(978-0-7377-5179-6(7))* Cengage Gale. (Greenhaven Pr., Inc.).

Haerens, Margaret. The Aging Population. Greenhaven Press Editors & Gale Research Staff, eds. 2014. (Opposing Viewpoints Ser.). (ENG., Illus.). 224p. (gr. 7-12). pap. 33.80 *(978-0-7377-6944-9(0),* Greenhaven Pr., Inc.) Cengage Gale.

—The Aging Population. Greenhaven Press Editors & Gale Editors, eds. 2014. (Opposing Viewpoints Ser.). (ENG., Illus.). 224p. (gr. 7-12). lib. bdg. 48.80 *(978-0-7377-6943-2(2),* Greenhaven Pr., Inc.) Cengage Gale.

Holko, Suzanne L. Grampy & Me. 2012. 34p. pap. 13.95 *(978-1-4624-0080-5(9),* Inspiring Voices) Author Solutions, Inc.

Lüsted, Marcia Amidon. Supporting the Elderly Through Service Learning, 1 vol. 2015. (ENG.). 80p. (YA). 34.60 *(978-1-4777-7957-6(4),* Rosen Young Adult) Rosen Publishing Group, Inc., The.

Martz, Sandra, ed. When I Am an Old Woman I Shall Wear Purple: Petite Version. 2nd gif. rev. ed. 2006. (Illus.). 64p. (C). pap. 47.70 *(978-1-57601-093-8(7))* Nodin Pr.

Orr, Tamra. Ways to Help the Elderly: A Guide to Giving Back. 2010. (How to Help Ser.). (Illus.). 48p. (J). (gr. 4-8). lib. bdg. 29.95 *(978-1-58415-915-5(4))* Mitchell Lane Pubs., Inc.

Stranaghan, Crystal J. & Bzymek, Izabela. Safety Superheroes: Preventing Grandparents from Falling. 2010. *(978-0-9867103-0-8(X))* Feldman, Fabio.

OLDER PEOPLE—FICTION

Adams, Pam, illus. There Was an Old Lady Who Swallowed a Fly. 2005. (Classic Books with Holes Ser.). (ENG.). 20p. (J). (gr. -1-1). bds. *(978-0-85953-314-0(X))* Child's Play International Ltd.

—There Was an Old Lady Who Swallowed the Sea. 2007. (Classic Books with Holes Board Book Ser.). (ENG.). 14p. (J). (gr. -1-k). bds. *(978-1-84643-073-2(9))* Child's Play International Ltd.

Adderson, Caroline. Middle of Nowhere. 2013. 212p. pap. *(978-1-4596-6452-4(3))* ReadHowYouWant.com, Ltd.

Amon, Ras Ran. Gerald Fish of the Spirit! Activity Book. 2006. (J). act. bk. ed. 3.99 *(978-0-9776603-2-2(X))* One Love Assn. Bks.

Atkinson, Ruth & Atkinson, Brett. Story Templates. Atkinson, Ruth & Atkinson, Brett, illus. (Illus.). (J). (gr. k-2). pap. *(978-1-875739-73-8(4))* Wizard Bks.

Babbitt, Natalie. Tuck Everlasting. 2007. (ENG.). 160p. (J). (gr. 5-7). per. 7.99 *(978-0-312-36981-1(6),* 9780312369811) Square Fish.

Byars, Betsy. The Black Tower. 2007. (Herculeah Jones Mystery Ser.). (ENG.). 144p. (J). (gr. 3-7). 6.99 *(978-0-14-240937-4(5),* Puffin Books) Penguin Young Readers Group.

M N O

Colandro, Lucille. There Was an Old Lady Who Swallowed a Bell! Lee, Jared, illus. 2008. (ENG.). 32p. (J). (gr. -1-3). pap. 6.99 *(978-0-545-04361-8(1)*, Cartwheel Bks.) Scholastic, Inc.

—There Was an Old Lady Who Swallowed a Chick! Lee, Jared, illus. 2010. (ENG.). 32p. (J). (gr. -1-k). pap. 6.99 *(978-0-545-16181-7(9)*, Cartwheel Bks.) Scholastic, Inc.

—There Was an Old Lady Who Swallowed a Chick! 2009. (Illus.). (J). *(978-0-545-06059-2(1))* Scholastic, Inc.

—There Was an Old Lady Who Swallowed a Chick! Lee, Jared, illus. 2010. (There Was an Old Lady... Ser.). lib. bdg. 17.20 *(978-0-606-06821-5(X)*, Turtleback) Turtleback Bks.

—There Was an Old Lady Who Swallowed a Clover! 2012. (There Was an Old Lady Ser.). lib. bdg. 17.20 *(978-0-606-23937-0(5)*, Turtleback) Turtleback Bks.

—There Was an Old Lady Who Swallowed Some Books! Lee, Jared, illus. 2012. (There Was an Old Lady Ser.). lib. bdg. 17.20 *(978-0-606-26208-8(3)*, Turtleback) Turtleback Bks.

—There Was an Old Lady Who Swallowed Some Leaves! 2010. (There Was an Old Lady Ser.). lib. bdg. 17.20 *(978-0-606-15050-7(1)*, Turtleback) Turtleback Bks.

Diane Lair, Lair & Lair, Diane. Miss Muggles: The Comical Dog. 2010. 28p. pap. 16.09 *(978-1-4269-2844-4(0))* Trafford Publishing.

Elkeles, Simone. Leaving Paradise. 2007. 20.80 *(978-1-4177-8393-9(1)*, Turtleback) Turtleback Bks.

Fuerst, Jeffrey B. The Old Woman Who Lived in a Shoe. Greenhead, Bill, illus. 2010. (Rising Readers Ser.). (J). 3.49 *(978-1-60719-703-4(0))* Newmark Learning LLC.

Gaylord, Laurel Porter. Quiero a Mi Mama Porque. Wolff, Ashley, illus. 2004.Tr. of I Love My Mommy Because. (SPA & ENG.). 22p. (J). (gr. -1 — 1). bds. 6.99 *(978-0-525-47248-3(7)*, Dutton Books for Young Readers) Penguin Young Readers Group.

Haddix, Margaret Peterson. Turnabout. 2007. (ENG.). 240p. (YA). (gr. 7-12). mass mkt. 7.99 *(978-1-4169-3653-4(X)*, Simon Pulse) Simon Pulse.

Hawkins, June Morris. When Tony Caught a Fish. 2011. 28p. (gr. 1-2). 12.03 *(978-1-4567-5249-1(9))* AuthorHouse.

Howell, Ches Lee. The Old Lady's Story. 2010. 24p. pap. 12.99 *(978-1-4490-0715-7(5))* AuthorHouse.

Huser, Glen. Skinnybones & the Wrinkle Queen. 2013. 232p. pap. *(978-1-4596-6507-1(4))* ReadHowYouWant.com, Ltd.

Jeffs, Dixie. The Old Man. 2013. 20p. pap. 24.95 *(978-1-62709-344-6(3))* America Star Bks.

Johnston, Tony. A Small Thing ... but Big. Hooper, Hadley, illus. 2016. (ENG.). 40p. (J). 17.99 *(978-1-62672-256-9(0)*, 9781626722569) Roaring Brook Pr.

Kheiriyeh, Rashin, illus. There Was an Old Lady Who Swallowed a Fly. 2014. (ENG.). 32p. (J). 17.95 *(978-0-7358-4183-3(7))* North-South Bks., Inc.

Kiernan, Tim. Liams Luck & Finnegans Fortune. 2009. (ENG.). 144p. pap. 10.95 *(978-1-933916-48-4(6)*, Ferne Pr.) Nelson Publishing & Marketing.

Lancett, Peter. The Dark Dreams, 1 vol. unabr. ed. 2010. (Dark Man Ser.). (ENG.). 34p. (YA). (gr. 9-12). pap. 7.95 *(978-1-61651-017-6(X))* Saddleback Educational Publishing, Inc.

—The Dark Side of Magic, 1 vol. unabr. ed. 2010. (Dark Man Ser.). (ENG.). 34p. (YA). (gr. 9-12). pap. 7.95 *(978-1-61651-019-0(6))* Saddleback Educational Publishing, Inc.

Lane, Bruce Courand. The Friendly Little Martian. 2011. 28p. pap. 15.99 *(978-1-4568-6638-9(9))* Xlibris Corp.

Lloyd, Patricia. I Love Me 2! 2012. 20p. pap. 9.95 *(978-0-9771160-5-8(0)*, Vaughanworks) Vaughanworks Publishing.

Lovato, David C. The Little Old Man. 2013. 16p. pap. 12.68 *(978-1-4669-8292-5(6))* Trafford Publishing.

Malley, Gemma. The Declaration. 2008. (Declaration Ser.). (ENG., Illus.). 320p. (YA). (gr. 7). 10.99 *(978-1-59990-295-1(8)*, 9781599902951, Bloomsbury USA Childrens) Bloomsbury Publishing USA.

—The Declaration, 7 vols. (YA). 2008. 119.75 *(978-1-4281-7284-5(X))* 2007. 121.75 *(978-1-4281-7282-1(3))* 2007. 89.75 *(978-1-4281-7280-7(7))* 2007. 91.75 *(978-1-4281-7278-4(5))* 2007. 245.75 *(978-1-4281-7279-1(3))* 2007. 1.25 *(978-1-4281-7275-3(0))* Recorded Bks., Inc.

McCumbers, Jaime. Don't Step on the Flowers! 2008. 12p. per. 24.95 *(978-1-4241-9092-8(4))* America Star Bks.

Mejuto, Eva. Run Pumpkin, Run. 2007. (ENG., Illus.). 36p. (J). 17.95 *(978-84-96788-88-6(1))* OQO, Editora ESP. Dist: Baker & Taylor Bks.

The Old Woman in a Shoe: 6 Small Books. (gr. k-2). 23.00 *(978-0-7635-8501-3(7))* Rigby Education.

Patacrœa. BABY WHISKERS. 2007. (ENG., Illus.). 36p. (J). 17.95 *(978-84-96788-90-9(3))* OQO, Editora ESP. Dist: Baker & Taylor Bks.

Peyo. Benny Breakiron #2: Madame Adolphine. 2013. (Benny Breakiron Ser.). (ENG., Illus.). 64p. (J). (gr. 2-12). 11.99 *(978-1-59707-436-0(5)*, 9781597074360) Papercutz.

Pitcher, Caroline. Mariana & the Merchild: A Folk Tale from Chile. Morris, Jackie, illus. 2006. 24p. (J). (gr. k-4). reprint ed. 17.00 *(978-1-4223-5136-9(X))* DIANE Publishing Co.

Porter, Rhonda. Brody Learns about Strangers, 1 vol. 2009. 29p. pap. 19.95 *(978-1-61546-699-3(1))* PublishAmerica, Inc.

Rigby Education Staff. Jumble Tumble Old Woman. (gr. k-2). 21.00 *(978-0-7635-2413-5(1))* Rigby Education.

Rylant, Cynthia. Mr. Putter & Tabby Ring the Bell. Howard, Arthur, illus. 2011. (Mr. Putter & Tabby Ser.: 20). (ENG.). 44p. (J). (gr. 1-4). 14.99 *(978-0-15-205071-9(X))* Houghton Mifflin Harcourt Publishing Co.

Shawver, Margaret. What's Wrong with Grandma? A Family's Experience with Alzheimer's. Bagby, Jeffrey K., illus. 2003. (ENG.). 62p. (J). (gr. -1-3). pap. 16.99 *(978-1-59102-174-2(X))* Prometheus Bks., Pubs.

Stark, Ulf. Can You Whistle, Johanna? A Boy's Search for a Grandfather. Segerberg, Ebba, tr. from SWE. Hoglund, Anna, illus. 2004. 48p. (gr. 2-5). 16.95 *(978-1-57143-057-1(1))* RDR Bks.

Sullivan, Michael. Escapade Johnson & the Witches of Belknap County. Kolitsky, Joy, illus. 2008. (Escapade Johnson Ser.). (ENG.). 99p. (J). (gr. 2-4). pap. 3.95 *(978-1-929945-90-0(6))* Big Guy Bks., Inc.

Thompson, Kim. Eldritch Manor. 2013. 212p. pap. *(978-1-4596-6312-1(8))* ReadHowYouWant.com, Ltd.

Vanoosting, James. Walking Mary. 2005. 144p. (J). (gr. 7-18). lib. bdg. 16.89 *(978-0-06-028472-5(2))* HarperCollins Pubs.

Walters, Celeste. The Glass Mountain. 2003. 280p. (YA). pap. *(978-0-7022-3297-8(1))* Univ. of Queensland Pr.

Ward, Helen. Moon Dog. 2005. (Illus.). 40p. (J). *(978-1-84011-864-3(4))* Templar Publishing.

Watson, Anne-Marie. The Old Lady in the Woods. 2010. 24p. pap. 14.49 *(978-1-4520-5971-6(3))* AuthorHouse.

Weston Woods Staff, creator. The Little Old Lady Who Was Not Afraid of Anything. 2011. 18.95 *(978-0-545-37419-4(7))*; 38.75 *(978-0-545-37497-2(9))* Weston Woods Studios, Inc.

Wilson, Mark A. The Old Man's Secret Friend, 1 vol. 2009. 19p. pap. 19.95 *(978-1-61582-315-4(8))* PublishAmerica, Inc.

OLIVIA (FICTITIOUS CHARACTER: FALCONER)—FICTION

Barton, Elizabeth & Shaw, Natalie. Olivia Leaps! Osterhold, Jared, illus. 2009. (Olivia TV Tie-In Ser.). (ENG.). 12p. (J). (gr. -1-1). bds. 6.99 *(978-1-4169-8572-3(7)*, Simon Spotlight) Simon Spotlight.

Bryant, Megan E. Olivia Meets Olivia. Mawhinney, Art & Johnson, Shane L., illus. 2010. (Olivia TV Tie-In Ser.). (ENG.). 24p. (J). (gr. -1-2). 6.99 *(978-1-4169-9542-5(0)*, Simon Spotlight) Simon Spotlight.

Einhorn, Kama. Olivia Imagines: A Carryalong Treasury. 2011. (Olivia TV Tie-In Ser.). (ENG.). 22p. (J). (gr. -1-1). 14.99 *(978-1-4424-2048-9(0)*, Simon Spotlight) Simon Spotlight.

Evans, Cordelia. Olivia & Grandma's Visit. Johnson, Shane L., illus. 2013. (Olivia TV Tie-In Ser.). (ENG.). 24p. (J). (gr. -1-2). pap. 3.99 *(978-1-4424-4586-4(6)*, Simon Spotlight) Simon Spotlight.

—Olivia & the Easter Egg Hunt. 2013. (Olivia 8x8 Ser.). lib. bdg. 14.75 *(978-0-606-27062-5(0)*, Turtleback) Turtleback Bks.

—OLIVIA & the Fancy Party. Johnson, Shane L., illus. 2014. (Olivia TV Tie-In Ser.). (ENG.). 24p. (J). (gr. -1-2). pap. 3.99 *(978-1-4814-0364-1(8)*, Simon Spotlight) Simon Spotlight.

—Olivia & the Fancy Party. 2014. (Olivia 8x8 Ser.). lib. bdg. 13.55 *(978-0-606-35762-3(9))* Turtleback Bks.

—Olivia Takes Ballet: From the Fancy Keepsake Collection. Spaziante, Patrick, illus. 2013. (Olivia TV Tie-In Ser.). (ENG.). 28p. (J). (gr. -1-2). 6.99 *(978-1-4424-7394-2(0)*, Simon Spotlight) Simon Spotlight.

Falconer, Ian. Olivia. 2004. (Olivia Ser.). (J). (gr. k-3). (FRE., Illus.). spiral bd. *(978-0-616-14599-9(3))*; spiral bd. *(978-0-616-07233-2(3))*; spiral bd. *(978-0-616-07232-5(5))* Canadian National Institute for the Blind/Institut National Canadien pour les Aveugles.

—Olivia. (Olivia Ser.). (FRE.). pap. 29.95 *(978-2-02-041087-8(7))* Editions du Seuil FRA. Dist: Distribooks, Inc.

—Olivia. 2009. (Los Especiales de A la Orilla del Viento Ser.). (SPA.). 32p. (J). 13.99 *(978-968-16-6346-9(2))* Fondo de Cultura Económcia.

—Olivia. (Olivia Ser.). pap. 27.95 *(978-85-250-3380-2(4))* Globo, Editora SA BRA. Dist: Distribooks, Inc.

—Olivia. Mlawer, Teresa, tr. 2004. (Olivia Ser.). (SPA., Illus.). (J). (gr. k-2). 16.00 *(978-1-930332-20-1(3)*, LC5675) Lectorum Pubns., Inc.

—Olivia. (Olivia Ser.). *(978-3-7891-6504-7(2))* Oetinger, Friedrich GmbH Verlag.

—Olivia. Falconer, Ian, illus. 2009. (ENG., Illus.). 40p. (J). (gr. -1-3). 12.99 *(978-1-4169-8034-6(2)*, Atheneum Bks. for Young Readers) Simon & Schuster Children's Publishing.

—Olivia. High, Amy, tr. from ENG. Falconer, Ian, illus. 2007. (LAT., Illus.). 40p. (J). (gr. 3-7). 17.99 *(978-1-4169-4218-4(1)*, Atheneum Bks. for Young Readers) Simon & Schuster Children's Publishing.

—Olivia & the Fairy Princesses. Falconer, Ian, illus. 2012. (ENG., Illus.). 40p. (J). (gr. -1-3). 18.99 *(978-1-4424-5027-1(4)*, Atheneum Bks. for Young Readers) Simon & Schuster Children's Publishing.

—Olivia... & the Missing Toy. Falconer, Ian, illus. 2003. (ENG., Illus.). 42p. (J). (gr. -1-3). 18.99 *(978-0-689-85291-6(6)*, Atheneum Bks. for Young Readers) Simon & Schuster Children's Publishing.

—Olivia Forms a Band. Falconer, Ian, illus. 2009. (ENG., Illus.). 50p. (J). (gr. -1-3). 12.99 *(978-1-4169-8037-7(7)*, Atheneum Bks. for Young Readers) Simon & Schuster Children's Publishing.

—Olivia Helps with Christmas. Falconer, Ian, illus. 2007. (ENG., Illus.). 58p. (J). (gr. -1-3). 19.99 *(978-1-4169-0786-2(6)*, Atheneum Bks. for Young Readers) Simon & Schuster Children's Publishing.

—Olivia Saves the Circus. 2004. (Olivia Ser.). (J). (gr. k-2). spiral bd. *(978-0-616-11110-9(X))*; spiral bd. *(978-0-616-11111-6(8))* Canadian National Institute for the Blind/Institut National Canadien pour les Aveugles.

—Olivia Saves the Circus. Falconer, Ian, illus. 2010. (Classic Board Bks.). (ENG., Illus.). 36p. (J). (gr. -1-2). bds. 7.99 *(978-1-4424-1287-3(9)*, Atheneum Bks. for Young Readers) Simon & Schuster Children's Publishing.

—Olivia y Las Princesas. 2012. (SPA., Illus.). 32p. (J). (gr. -1-1). 17.99 *(978-1-933032-82-5(0))* Lectorum Pubns., Inc.

Falconer, Ian, et al. Olivia & Her Great Adventures. Osterhold, Jared & Johnson, Shane L., illus. 2012. (J). *(978-1-4351-4316-6(7)*, Simon Spotlight) Simon Spotlight.

Forte, Lauren. Olivia Goes to the Library. 2013. (Olivia Ready-To-Read Level 1 Ser.). lib. bdg. 13.55 *(978-0-606-35186-7(8))* Turtleback Bks.

Gallo, Tina. OLIVIA & the Christmas Party. Rose, Drew, illus. 2011. (Olivia TV Tie-In Ser.). (ENG.). 32p. (J). (gr. -1-1). 4.99 *(978-1-4424-3070-9(2)*, Simon Scribbles) Simon Scribbles.

—OLIVIA & the Puppy Wedding. Spaziante, Patrick, illus. 2012. (Olivia TV Tie-In Ser.). (ENG.). 24p. (J). (gr. -1-2). pap. 3.99 *(978-1-4424-5315-9(X)*, Simon Spotlight) Simon Spotlight.

—OLIVIA Plays Soccer. Osterhold, Jared, illus. 2013. (Olivia TV Tie-In Ser.). (ENG.). 24p. (J). (gr. -1-1). pap. 3.99 *(978-1-4424-7248-8(0)*, Simon Spotlight) Simon Spotlight.

—Olivia Plays Soccer. 2013. (Olivia Ready-To-Read Level 1 Ser.). lib. bdg. 13.55 *(978-0-606-32060-3(1)*, Turtleback) Turtleback Bks.

—Olivia Wishes on a Star. 2014. (Olivia 8x8 Ser.). lib. bdg. 13.55 *(978-0-606-36118-7(9))* Turtleback Bks.

Harvey, Alex. Olivia & the Kite Party. Spaziante, Patrick, illus. 2012. (Olivia Ready-To-Read Level 1 Ser.). lib. bdg. 13.55 *(978-0-606-26360-3(8)*, Turtleback) Turtleback Bks.

Johnson, Shane, illus. OLIVIA Paints a Mural. 2011. (Olivia TV Tie-In Ser.). (ENG.). 12p. (J). (gr. -1-1). bds. 5.99 *(978-1-4424-1674-1(2)*, Simon Spotlight) Simon Spotlight.

Johnson, Shane L., illus. Olivia & Her Ducklings. 2010. (Olivia TV Tie-In Ser.). (ENG.). 24p. (J). (gr. -1-1). 16.99 *(978-1-4424-1382-5(4)*, Simon Spotlight) Simon Spotlight.

—OLIVIA & the Christmas Present. 2011. (Olivia TV Tie-In Ser.). (ENG.). 24p. (J). (gr. -1-2). 9.99 *(978-1-4424-3624-4(7)*, Simon Spotlight) Simon Spotlight.

—OLIVIA & the Dog Wash. 2012. (Olivia TV Tie-In Ser.). (ENG.). 16p. (J). (gr. -1-1). pap. 5.99 *(978-1-4424-4638-0(2)*, Simon Spotlight) Simon Spotlight.

—OLIVIA & the Easter Egg Hunt. 2013. (Olivia TV Tie-In Ser.). (ENG.). 24p. (J). (gr. -1-2). pap. 4.99 *(978-1-4424-6022-5(9)*, Simon Spotlight) Simon Spotlight.

—Olivia & the Ice Show: A Lift-The-Flap Story. 2013. (Olivia TV Tie-In Ser.). (ENG.). 16p. (J). (gr. -1-2). pap. 6.99 *(978-1-4424-2083-0(9)*, Simon Spotlight) Simon Spotlight.

—OLIVIA & the Snow Day. 2010. (Olivia TV Tie-In Ser.). (ENG.). 24p. (J). (gr. -1-1). 15.99 *(978-1-4423-3638-4(2)*, Simon Spotlight) Simon Spotlight.

—OLIVIA Builds a House. 2012. (Olivia TV Tie-In Ser.). (ENG.). 24p. (J). (gr. -1-1). 15.99 *(978-1-4424-5323-4(0))*; pap. 3.99 *(978-1-4424-5322-7(2))* Simon Spotlight. (Simon Spotlight).

—Olivia Leads a Parade. 2011. (Olivia TV Tie-In Ser.). (ENG.). 24p. (J). (gr. -1-2). pap. 3.99 *(978-1-4424-2137-0(1)*, Simon Spotlight) Simon Spotlight.

—Olivia the Princess. 2011. (Olivia TV Tie-In Ser.). (ENG.). 24p. (J). (gr. -1-2). pap. 3.99 *(978-1-4424-3033-4(8)*, Simon Spotlight) Simon Spotlight.

—OLIVIA Trains Her Cat. 2009. (Olivia TV Tie-In Ser.). (ENG.). 24p. (J). (gr. -1-1). pap. 3.99 *(978-1-4169-8296-8(5)*, Simon Spotlight) Simon Spotlight.

—Star of the Show. 2014. (Olivia TV Tie-In Ser.). (ENG.). 24p. (J). (gr. -1-2). 7.99 *(978-1-4424-9860-0(9)*, Simon Spotlight) Simon Spotlight.

Mawhinney, Art, illus. Olivia the Magnificent: A Lift-the-Flap Story. 2009. (Olivia TV Tie-In Ser.). (ENG.). 16p. (J). (gr. -1-2). pap. 6.99 *(978-1-4169-8297-5(3)*, Simon Spotlight) Simon Spotlight.

McDoogle, Farrah. OLIVIA & the Sea Lions. Spaziante, Patrick, illus. 2013. (Olivia TV Tie-In Ser.). (ENG.). 16p. (J). (gr. -1-1). pap. 5.99 *(978-1-4424-7364-5(9)*, Simon Spotlight) Simon Spotlight.

—OLIVIA Makes a Charm Bracelet. Osterhold, Jared, illus. 2012. (Olivia TV Tie-In Ser.). (ENG.). 16p. (J). (gr. -1-2). pap. 6.99 *(978-1-4424-4163-7(1)*, Simon Spotlight) Simon Spotlight.

Mcdoogle, Farrah. Olivia Says Good Night. 2016. (Olivia 8x8 Ser.). lib. bdg. 13.55 *(978-0-606-39244-0(0))* Turtleback Bks.

McDoogle, Farrah. OLIVIA Talks Turkey. Osterhold, Jared, illus. 2011. (Olivia TV Tie-In Ser.). (ENG.). 16p. (J). (gr. -1-1). pap. 5.99 *(978-1-4424-3061-7(3)*, Simon Spotlight) Simon Spotlight.

—Olivia the Ballerina. Spaziante, Patrick, illus. 2013. (Olivia TV Tie-In Ser.). (ENG.). 24p. (J). (gr. -1-1). 16.99 *(978-1-4424-8515-0(9)*, Simon Spotlight) Simon Spotlight.

McDoogle, Farrah & Pulliam, Gabe. OLIVIA Says Good Night. Spaziante, Patrick, illus. 2011. (Olivia TV Tie-In Ser.). (ENG.). 24p. (J). (gr. -1-1). 16.99 *(978-1-4424-2947-5(X)*, Simon Spotlight) Simon Spotlight.

Mercer, Sienna. Date with Destiny. 2014. (My Sister the Vampire Ser.: 10). (ENG.). 224p. (J). (gr. 4-6). 6.99 *(978-1-4052-5985-9(X))* Egmont Bks., Ltd. GBR. Dist: Independent Pubs. Group.

—Flipping Out ! 2014. (My Sister the Vampire Ser.: 14). (ENG.). 256p. (J). (gr. 4-6). pap. 6.99 *(978-1-4052-6571-3(X))* Egmont Bks., Ltd. GBR. Dist: Independent Pubs. Group.

—Love Bites. 2014. (My Sister the Vampire Ser.: 6). (ENG.). 256p. (J). (gr. 4-6). pap. 6.99 *(978-1-4052-5698-8(2))* Egmont Bks., Ltd. GBR. Dist: Independent Pubs. Group.

—Lucky Break. 2014. (My Sister the Vampire Ser.: 7). (ENG.). 256p. (J). (gr. 4-6). 6.99 *(978-1-4052-5699-5(0))* Egmont Bks., Ltd. GBR. Dist: Independent Pubs. Group.

—My Sister the Vampire - Twin Spins! 2014. (My Sister the Vampire Ser.: 9). (ENG.). 224p. (J). (gr. 4-6). pap. 6.99 *(978-1-4052-5984-2(1))* Egmont Bks., Ltd. GBR. Dist: Independent Pubs. Group.

—Star Style. 2014. (My Sister the Vampire Ser.: 8). (ENG.). 256p. (J). (gr. 4-6). pap. 6.99 *(978-1-4052-5700-8(8))* Egmont Bks., Ltd. GBR. Dist: Independent Pubs. Group.

Mercer, Sienna & Miller, Sienna. Double Disaster! 2014. (My Sister the Vampire Ser.: 13). (ENG.). 256p. (J). (gr. 4-6). pap. 6.99 *(978-1-4052-6570-6(1))* Egmont Bks., Ltd. GBR. Dist: Independent Pubs. Group.

—Flying Solo. 2014. (My Sister the Vampire Ser.: 11). (ENG.). 224p. (J). (gr. 4-6). pap. 6.99 *(978-1-4052-5987-3(6))* Egmont Bks., Ltd. GBR. Dist: Independent Pubs. Group.

Oliver, Ilanit. OLIVIA & the Best Teacher Ever. Johnson, Shane L., illus. 2012. (Olivia TV Tie-In Ser.). (ENG.). 24p. (J). (gr. -1-2). pap. 3.99 *(978-1-4424-3599-5(2)*, Simon Spotlight) Simon Spotlight.

—Olivia & the Best Teacher Ever. 2012. (Olivia 8x8 Ser.). lib. bdg. 13.55 *(978-0-606-26367-2(5)*, Turtleback) Turtleback Bks.

Olivia's Sensational Stories: Olivia Helps Mother Nature; Olivia Goes to the Library; Olivia Plays Soccer; Olivia Measures Up; Olivia Builds a House; Olivia Becomes a Vet. 2014. (Olivia TV Tie-In Ser.). (ENG., Illus.). 144p. (J). (gr. -1-1). pap. 15.99 *(978-1-4814-2148-5(4)*, Simon Spotlight) Simon Spotlight.

Osterhold, Jared, illus. Olivia & the Babies. 2010. (Olivia TV Tie-In Ser.). (ENG.). 24p. (J). (gr. -1-2). pap. 3.99 *(978-1-4169-9529-6(3)*, Simon Spotlight) Simon Spotlight.

—OLIVIA Becomes a Vet. 2011. (Olivia TV Tie-In Ser.). (ENG.). 24p. (J). (gr. -1-1). 16.99 *(978-1-4424-2860-7(0))*; pap. 3.99 *(978-1-4424-2859-1(7))* Simon Spotlight. (Simon Spotlight).

—Olivia Claus. 2010. (Olivia TV Tie-In Ser.). (ENG.). 24p. (J). (gr. -1-1). 16.99 *(978-1-4424-0662-9(3)*, Simon Spotlight) Simon Spotlight.

—OLIVIA Goes Camping. 2011. (Olivia TV Tie-In Ser.). (ENG.). 24p. (J). (gr. -1-1). 15.99 *(978-1-4424-2253-7(X))*; pap. 3.99 *(978-1-4424-2135-6(5))* Simon Spotlight. (Simon Spotlight).

—OLIVIA Goes to the Library. 2013. (Olivia TV Tie-In Ser.). (ENG.). 24p. (J). (gr. -1-1). 16.99 *(978-1-4424-8479-5(9))*; pap. 3.99 *(978-1-4424-8478-8(0))* Simon Spotlight. (Simon Spotlight).

—OLIVIA Measures Up. 2013. (Olivia TV Tie-In Ser.). (ENG.). 24p. (J). (gr. -1-1). 15.99 *(978-1-4424-5974-8(3))*; pap. 3.99 *(978-1-4424-5973-1(5))* Simon Spotlight. (Simon Spotlight).

—Olivia Opens a Lemonade Stand. 2010. (Olivia TV Tie-In Ser.). (ENG.). 24p. (J). (gr. -1-2). pap. 3.99 *(978-1-4169-9932-4(9)*, Simon Spotlight) Simon Spotlight.

—OLIVIA Plants a Garden. 2011. (Olivia TV Tie-In Ser.). (ENG.). 24p. (J). (gr. -1-1). pap. 3.99 *(978-1-4424-1675-8(0)*, Simon Spotlight) Simon Spotlight.

—OLIVIA Plays Soccer. 2013. (Olivia TV Tie-In Ser.). (ENG.). 24p. (J). (gr. -1-1). 16.99 *(978-1-4424-7249-5(9)*, Simon Spotlight) Simon Spotlight.

—OLIVIA Takes a Trip. 2010. (Olivia TV Tie-In Ser.). (ENG.). 24p. (J). (gr. -1-1). 16.99 *(978-1-4424-1381-8(6)*, Simon Spotlight) Simon Spotlight.

—OLIVIA Wishes on a Star. 2014. (Olivia TV Tie-In Ser.). (ENG.). 24p. (J). (gr. -1-2). pap. 3.99 *(978-1-4814-1769-3(X)*, Simon Spotlight) Simon Spotlight.

Romay, Alexis, tr. OLIVIA Vende Galletas (OLIVIA Sells Cookies) Spaziante, Patrick, illus. 2013. (Olivia TV Tie-In Ser.). (SPA.). 24p. (J). (gr. -1-2). pap. 3.99 *(978-1-4424-5967-0(0)*, Libros Para Ninos) Libros Para Ninos.

Shaw, Natalie. A Guide to Being a Big Sister. 2014. (Olivia 8x8 Ser.). lib. bdg. 16.00 *(978-0-606-35761-6(0))* Turtleback Bks.

—A Guide to Being a Friend. 2014. (Olivia 8x8 Ser.). lib. bdg. 16.00 *(978-0-606-36117-0(0))* Turtleback Bks.

—A Guide to Life. Spaziante, Patrick, illus. 2015. (Olivia TV Tie-In Ser.). (ENG.). 16p. (J). (gr. -1-2). 5.99 *(978-1-4814-2788-3(1)*, Simon Spotlight) Simon Spotlight.

—OLIVIA & the Butterfly Adventure. Spaziante, Patrick, illus. 2012. (Olivia TV Tie-In Ser.). (ENG.). 36p. (J). (gr. -1-2). bds. 10.99 *(978-1-4424-3601-5(8)*, Simon Spotlight) Simon Spotlight.

—OLIVIA & the Perfect Valentine. Johnson, Shane L., illus. 2013. (Olivia TV Tie-In Ser.). (ENG.). 24p. (J). (gr. -1-2). pap. 4.99 *(978-1-4424-8484-9(5)*, Simon Spotlight) Simon Spotlight.

—Olivia & the Perfect Valentine. 2013. (Olivia 8x8 Ser.). lib. bdg. 14.75 *(978-0-606-35200-0(7))* Turtleback Bks.

—OLIVIA Dances for Joy. Spaziante, Patrick, illus. 2012. (Olivia TV Tie-In Ser.). (ENG.). 24p. (J). (gr. -1-1). 16.99 *(978-1-4424-5257-2(9)*, Simon Spotlight) Simon Spotlight.

—Olivia Leaps! Osterhold, Jared, illus. 2010. (Olivia TV Ser.). (ENG.). 12p. (J). bds. 8.99 *(978-1-84738-612-0(1))* Simon & Schuster Children's Publishing.

—A Special Day with Dad. Johnson, Shane L., illus. 2014. (Olivia TV Tie-In Ser.). (ENG.). 24p. (J). (gr. -1-2). pap. 4.99 *(978-1-4424-9751-1(3)*, Simon Spotlight) Simon Spotlight.

Shepherd, Jodie. Olivia & the Haunted Hotel. Spaziante, Patrick, illus. 2010. (Olivia TV Tie-In Ser.). (ENG.). 24p. (J). (gr. -1-2). pap. 4.99 *(978-1-4424-0182-2(6)*, Simon Spotlight) Simon Spotlight.

—Olivia & the Haunted Hotel. 2010. (Olivia 8x8 Ser.). lib. bdg. 14.75 *(978-0-606-26573-7(2)*, Turtleback) Turtleback Bks.

Silverhardt, Lauryn. OLIVIA Blasts Off! Wolek, Guy, illus. 2010. (Olivia TV Tie-In Ser.). (ENG.). 12p. (J). (gr. -1-1). 6.99 *(978-1-4169-9538-8(2)*, Simon Spotlight) Simon Spotlight.

Sollinger, Emily. OLIVIA Plants a Garden. Osterhold, Jared, illus. 2011. (Olivia TV Tie-In Ser.). (ENG.). 24p. (J). (gr. -1-1). 16.99 *(978-1-4424-2011-3(1)*, Simon Spotlight) Simon Spotlight.

Spaziante, Patrick, illus. Olivia Acts Out. 2009. (Olivia TV Tie-In Ser.). (ENG.). 24p. (J). (gr. -1-1). 16.99 *(978-1-4169-8571-6(9)*, Simon Spotlight) Simon Spotlight.

—OLIVIA & the Fashion Show. 2011. (Olivia TV Tie-In Ser.). (ENG.). 16p. (J). (gr. -1-1). pap. 5.99 *(978-1-4424-2028-1(6)*, Simon Spotlight) Simon Spotlight.

—OLIVIA & the Kite Party. 2012. (Olivia TV Tie-In Ser.). (ENG.). 24p. (J). (gr. -1-1). 16.99 *(978-1-4424-4650-2(1))*; pap. 3.99 *(978-1-4424-4649-6(8))* Simon Spotlight. (Simon Spotlight).

—OLIVIA Learns to Surf. 2010. (Olivia TV Tie-In Ser.). (ENG.). 12p. (J). (gr. -1-1). bds. 6.99 *(978-1-4424-0330-7(6)*, Simon Spotlight) Simon Spotlight.

—Olivia Plans a Tea Party: From the Fancy Keepsake Collection. 2011. (Olivia TV Tie-In Ser.). (ENG.). 28p. (J). (gr. -1-2). 6.99 *(978-1-4423-3962-0(4)*, Simon Spotlight) Simon Spotlight.

—OLIVIA Sells Cookies. 2013. (Olivia TV Tie-In Ser.). (ENG.). 24p. (J). (gr. -1-2). pap. 3.99 *(978-1-4424-5965-6(4)*, Simon Spotlight) Simon Spotlight.

—OLIVIA the Superhero. 2016. (Olivia TV Tie-In Ser.). (ENG.). 24p. (J). (gr. -1-2). pap. 3.99 *(978-1-4814-6055-2(2)*, Simon Spotlight) Simon Spotlight.

Testa, Maggie. OLIVIA & Her Favorite Things. Spaziante, Patrick, illus. 2013. (Olivia TV Tie-In Ser.). (ENG.). 12p. (J). (gr. -1-1). bds. 5.99 *(978-1-4424-6587-9(5)*, Simon Spotlight) Simon Spotlight.

—Olivia & the Rain Dance. 2012. (Olivia Ready-To-Read Level 1 Ser.). lib. bdg. 13.55 *(978-0-606-23688-1(0)*, Turtleback) Turtleback Bks.

—OLIVIA Counts down to Christmas. Johnson, Shane L., illus. 2012. (Olivia TV Tie-In Ser.). (ENG.). 16p. (J). (gr. -1-1). pap. 6.99 *(978-1-4424-5747-8(3)*, Simon Spotlight) Simon Spotlight.

—OLIVIA Loves Halloween. Osterhold, Jared, illus. 2014. (Olivia TV Tie-In Ser.). (ENG.). 24p. (J). (gr. -1-1). pap. 3.99 *(978-1-4814-0462-4(8)*, Simon Spotlight) Simon Spotlight.

Various, illus. OLIVIA Loves to Read: Olivia Trains Her Cat; Olivia & Her Ducklings; Olivia Takes a Trip; Olivia & the Snow Day; Olivia Plants a Garden; Olivia Goes Camping. 2012. (Olivia TV Tie-In Ser.). (ENG.). 144p. (J). (gr. -1-1). pap. 15.99 *(978-1-4424-5879-6(8)*, Simon Spotlight) Simon Spotlight.

—Olivia Ready-To-Read Value Pack #2: Olivia & the Kite Party; Olivia & the Rain Dance; Olivia Becomes a Vet; Olivia Builds a House; Olivia Measures up; Olivia Trains Her Cat. 2013. (Olivia TV Tie-In Ser.). (ENG.). 144p. (J). (gr. -1-k).

pap. 15.96 (978-1-4424-9438-1(7), Simon Spotlight) Simon Spotlight.
—Story Time with Princess OLIVIA: Olivia the Princess; Olivia & the Puppy Wedding; Olivia Sells Cookies; Olivia & the Best Teacher Ever; Olivia Meets Olivia; Olivia & Grandma's Visit. 2013. (Olivia TV Tie-In Ser.). (ENG.). 144p. (J). (gr. -1-2). pap. 15.99 (978-1-4424-9370-4(4), Simon Spotlight) Simon Spotlight.
Various Authors. OLIVIA on the Go: Dinner with OLIVIA; OLIVIA & the Babies; OLIVIA & the School Carnival; OLIVIA Opens a Lemonade Stand; OLIVIA Cooks up a Surprise; OLIVIA Leads a Parade. 2012. (Olivia TV Tie-In Ser.). (ENG.). 144p. (J). (gr. -1-2). pap. 15.99 (978-1-4424-4358-7(8), Simon Spotlight) Simon Spotlight.
The Very Best of OLIVIA: A Storybook Treasury. 2013. (Olivia TV Tie-In Ser.). (ENG., Illus.). 248p. (J). (gr. -1-1). 15.99 (978-1-4424-8597-6(3), Simon Spotlight) Simon Spotlight.
Wolek, Guy, illus. OLIVIA & the Rain Dance. 2012. (Olivia TV Tie-In Ser.). (ENG.). 24p. (J). (gr. -1-1). 15.99 (978-1-4424-3543-8(7)); pap. 3.99 (978-1-4424-3542-1(9)) Simon Spotlight. (Simon Spotlight).
—OLIVIA & the School Carnival. 2010. (Olivia TV Tie-In Ser.). (ENG.). 24p. (J). (gr. -1-2). pap. 3.99 (978-1-4424-0870-8(7), Simon Spotlight) Simon Spotlight.
—OLIVIA Builds a Snowlady. 2011. (Olivia TV Tie-In Ser.). (ENG.). 24p. (J). (gr. -1-2). pap. 4.99 (978-1-4424-3286-4(1), Simon Spotlight) Simon Spotlight.

OLMSTED, FREDERICK LAW, 1822-1903

Dunlap, Julie & Olmsted, Frederick Law. Parks for the People: The Life of Frederick Law Olmsted. 2011. (ENG., Illus.). 112p. (J). (gr. 4-7). pap. 12.95 (978-1-55591-470-7(5)) Fulcrum Publishing.
Wishinsky, Frieda. The Man Who Made Parks: The Story of Parkbuilder Frederick Law Olmsted. Zhang, Song Nan, illus. 2009. (ENG.). 32p. (J). (gr. k-12). pap. 10.95 (978-0-88776-902-3(0), Tundra Bks.) Tundra Bks. CAN. Dist: Penguin Random Hse. LLC.

OLSEN TWINS (FICTITIOUS CHARACTERS)—FICTION

Butcher, Nancy, et al. It's Snow Problem, 3 vols. 2003. (ENG., Illus.). 112p. (978-0-00-714466-2(0), HarperCollins Children's Bks.) HarperCollins Pubs. Ltd.
—Two for the Road. 2003. (ENG., Illus.). 112p. (978-0-00-714463-1(6), HarperCollins Children's Bks.) HarperCollins Pubs. Ltd.
Katschke, Judy, et al. Shore Thing. 2003. (ENG., Illus.). 112p. (978-0-00-714464-8(4), HarperCollins Children's Bks.) HarperCollins Pubs. Ltd.
Olsen, Mary-Kate & Olsen, Ashley. Calling All Boys. 2003. (ENG., Illus.). 112p. (978-0-00-714472-3(5), HarperCollins Children's Bks.) HarperCollins Pubs. Ltd.
—The Cool Club. 2003. (ENG., Illus.). 112p. (978-0-00-714469-3(5), HarperCollins Children's Bks.) HarperCollins Pubs. Ltd.
—Dare to Scare. 2005. (ENG., Illus.). 112p. (978-0-00-715887-4(4)) HarperCollins Pubs. Australia.
—Dating Game, 2 vols. 2003. (ENG., Illus.). 128p. (978-0-00-714447-1(4), HarperCollins Children's Bks.) HarperCollins Pubs. Ltd.
—A Girl's Guide to Guys. 2003. (ENG., Illus.). 128p. (978-0-00-714455-6(5), HarperCollins Children's Bks.) HarperCollins Pubs. Ltd.
—Let's Party, 3 vols. 2003. (ENG., Illus.). 112p. (978-0-00-714473-0(3)) HarperCollins Pubs. Australia.
—Love, Set, Match. 2005. (ENG., Illus.). 112p. (978-0-00-715885-0(8)) HarperCollins Pubs. Australia.
—P. S Wish You Were Here. 2003. (ENG., Illus.). 112p. (978-0-00-714470-9(9), HarperCollins Children's Bks.) HarperCollins Pubs. Ltd.
—Santa Girls, 3 vols. 2005. (ENG., Illus.). 112p. (978-0-00-715888-1(2)) HarperCollins Pubs. Australia.
—Two of a Kind Diaries: Winner Take All. 2003. (ENG., Illus.). 112p. (978-0-00-714471-6(7), HarperCollins Children's Bks.) HarperCollins Pubs. Ltd.
Stine, Megan, et al. Girl Talk. 2003. (ENG., Illus.). 128p. (978-0-00-714453-2(9), HarperCollins Children's Bks.) HarperCollins Pubs. Ltd.
—Likes Me, Likes Me Not. 2003. (ENG., Illus.). 112p. (978-0-00-714465-5(2), HarperCollins Children's Bks.) HarperCollins Pubs. Ltd.
—War of the Wardrobes. 2003. (ENG., Illus.). 112p. (978-0-00-714468-6(7), HarperCollins Children's Bks.) HarperCollins Pubs. Ltd.

OLYMPICS

ABDO Publishing Company Staff. Great Moments in Olympic Sports. 2014. (Great Moments in Olympic Sports Ser.: 8). (ENG.). 64p. (gr. 10-14). lib. bdg. 262.32 (978-1-62403-392-6(X), SportsZone) ABDO Publishing Co.
Amstutz, Lisa J. The Science Behind Track & Field. 2016. (Science of the Summer Olympics Ser.). (ENG., Illus.). 32p. (gr. 3-4). lib. bdg. 27.99 (978-1-4914-8158-5(7), Edge Bks.) Capstone Press of Coughlan Cos.
Bailey, Tom. Jennifer Chandler: Olympic Champion Diver. 2005. (Alabama Roots Biography Ser.). (Illus.). 112p. (J). pap. (978-1-59421-014-3(4)) Seacoast Publishing, Inc.
Barnas, Jo-Ann. Great Moments in Olympic Skating, 1 vol. 2014. (Great Moments in Olympic Sports Ser.). (ENG.). 64p. (gr. 10-14). lib. bdg. 32.79 (978-1-62403-396-4(2), SportsZone) ABDO Publishing Co.
Barnas, Jo-Ann. Olympics Record Breakers, 1 vol. 2016. (ENG., Illus.). 48p. (J). **(978-1-62403-849-5(2)**, 1391441, SportsZone) ABDO Publishing Co.
Belval, Brian. Olympic Track & Field. (Great Moments in Olympic History Ser.). 2009. 48p. (gr. 5-6). 53.00 (978-1-61513-163-1(9), Rosen Reference) 2007. (Illus.). 52p. (gr. 3-7). pap. 26.50 (978-1-4358-3779-9(7)) 2007. (Illus.). 48p. (YA). (gr. 5-9). lib. bdg. 29.25 (978-1-4042-0971-8(9)) Rosen Publishing Group, Inc., The.
Bobrick, Benson. A Passion for Victory: The Story of the Olympics in Ancient & Early Modern Times. (ENG.). 160p. (J). (gr. 5). 2014. pap. 14.99 (978-0-375-87252-5(3)) 2012. (Illus.). 19.99 (978-0-375-86869-6(0)) Random Hse. Children's Bks. (Knopf Bks. for Young Readers).
Brassey, Richard. The Story of the Olympics. 2017. (ENG., Illus.). 32p. (J). (gr. 1-3). pap. 10.99 (978-1-5101-0138-8(1), Orion Children's Bks.) Hachette Children's Group GBR. Dist: Hachette Bk. Group.
Brown, Daniel James. The Boys in the Boat (Young Readers Adaptation) The True Story of an American Team's Epic Journey to Win Gold at the 1936 Olympics. (ENG., Illus.). (J). (gr. 5). 2016. 256p. 10.99 (978-0-14-751685-5(4), Puffin Books) 2015. 240p. 17.99 (978-0-451-47592-3(5), Viking Books for Young Readers) Penguin Young Readers Group.
—The Boys in the Boat (Young Readers Adaptation) The True Story of an American Team's Epic Journey to Win Gold at the 1936 Olympics. 2016. lib. bdg. 22.10 (978-0-606-39312-6(9)) Turtleback Bks.
Burgan, Michael. Miracle on Ice: How a Stunning Upset United a Country. 2016. (Captured History Sports Ser.). (ENG.). 64p. (gr. 5-7). pap. 8.95 (978-0-7565-5294-7(X), CPB Grades 4-8) Compass Point Bks.
Butterfield, Moira. The Olympics - History. 2011. (Olympics Ser.). 32p. (YA). (gr. 4-7). lib. bdg. 28.50 (978-1-59771-319-1(8)) Sea-To-Sea Pubns.
Butterfield, Moira & Hachette Children's Group. The Olympics Events. 2011. (Olympics Ser.). 32p. (YA). (gr. 4-7). 28.50 (978-1-59771-321-4(X)) Sea-To-Sea Pubns.
—The Olympics Scandals. 2011. (Olympics Ser.). 32p. (YA). (gr. 4-7). 28.50 (978-1-59771-320-7(1)) Sea-To-Sea Pubns.
Butterfield, Moira, et al. The Olympics Records. 2011. (Olympics Ser.). 32p. (YA). (gr. 4-7). 28.50 (978-1-59771-322-1(8)) Sea-To-Sea Pubns.
Carmichael, L. E. The Science Behind Gymnastics. 2016. (Illus.). 32p. (J). (978-1-4747-1142-5(1)) Capstone Press of Coughlan Cos.
Christopher, Matt. Great Moments in the Summer Olympics. 2012. (ENG., Illus.). 128p. (J). (gr. 3-7). pap. 9.99 (978-0-316-19579-9(0)) Little Brown & Co.
—The Olympics: Unforgettable Moments of the Games. 2008. (ENG., Illus.). 112p. (J). (gr. 3-7). pap. 15.99 (978-0-316-01118-1(5)) Little, Brown Bks. for Young Readers.
Christopher, Matt & Peters, Stephanie. Great Moments in the Summer Olympics. 2012. (J). lib. bdg. 16.00 (978-0-606-26159-3(1), Turtleback) Turtleback Bks.
Clarkson, Stephanie. Let's Get Moving with Wenlock & Mandeville! 2012. (London 2012 Ser.). (ENG., Illus.). 32p. (J). (gr. -1-k). pap. 10.99 (978-1-84732-645-4(5)) Carlton Bks., Ltd. GBR. Dist: Independent Pubs. Group.
Conway, Hollis. Grasshopper: The Hollis Conway Story. 2004. 30p. (J). per. (978-1-59196-584-8(5)) Instant Pub.
Crabtree Publishing, compiled by. The Olympic Sports. 2008. (ENG.). 32p. (J). (gr. -1-3). (978-0-7787-4011-7(0)) Crabtree Publishing Co.
Doeden, Matt. Combat Sports. 2015. (Summer Olympic Sports Ser.). (ENG., Illus.). 32p. (J). (gr. 2-4). 19.95 (978-1-60753-807-3(5)) Amicus Publishing.
—Track & Field. 2015. (Summer Olympic Sports Ser.). (ENG., Illus.). 32p. (J). (gr. 2-4). 19.95 (978-1-60753-810-3(5)) Amicus Publishing.
—Volleyball. 2015. (Summer Olympic Sports Ser.). (ENG., Illus.). 32p. (J). (gr. 2-4). 19.95 (978-1-60753-811-0(3)) Amicus Publishing.
Dublin, Anne. Bobbie Rosenfeld: The Olympian Who Could Do Everything, 1 vol. 2004. (ENG., Illus.). 148p. (J). (gr. 4-8). pap. 14.95 (978-1-896764-82-5(7)) Second Story Pr. CAN. Dist: Orca Bk. Pubs. USA.
Dunn, Joe. Miracle on Ice, 1 vol. Dunn, Ben, illus. 2007. (Graphic History Ser.). (ENG.). 32p. (gr. 3-6). 28.50 (978-1-60270-077-2(X), Graphic Planet- Nonfiction) ABDO Publishing Co.
Dyan, Penelope. The Rain in Spain — -A Kid's Guide to Barcelona, Spain. Weigand, John D., photos by. 2011. (Illus.). 38p. pap. 12.95 (978-1-935630-56-2(3)) Bellissima Publishing, LLC.
—The Squeaky Wheel Gets to Greece — -A Kid's Guide to Athens, Greece. Weigand, John D., photos by. 2011. (Illus.). 36p. pap. 11.95 (978-1-935630-58-6(X)) Bellissima Publishing, LLC.
Dzidrums, Christine. Yuna Kim: Ice Queen. Rendon, Leah, ed. Dzidrums, Joseph et al, photos by. 2011. (Skate Stars Ser.: Vol. 2). (Illus.). 72p. (YA). pap. 10.99 (978-0-9826435-9-4(4)) Creative Media Publishing.
Dzidrums, Christine & Rendon, Leah. Joannie Rochette: Canadian Ice Princess. Allison, Elizabeth, ed. Adeff, Jay & Mittan, J. Barry, photos by. 2nd exp. rev. ed. 2010. (Skate Stars Ser.: Vol. 1). (Illus.). 100p. (YA). pap. 12.99 (978-0-9826435-0-1(0)) Creative Media Publishing.
Farbs, C. Olympic Ice Skating. 2009. (Great Moments in Olympic History Ser.). 48p. (gr. 5-6). 53.00 (978-1-61513-161-7(2), Rosen Reference) Rosen Publishing Group, Inc., The.
Farrell, Courtney. Terror at the Munich Olympics, 1 vol. 2010. (Essential Events Set 4 Ser.). (ENG.). 112p. (J). (gr. 6-12). lib. bdg. 35.64 (978-1-60453-945-5(3)) ABDO Publishing Co.
Faster, Higher, Stronger: The Olympics, 6 vols. (Book2WebTM Ser.). (gr. 4-8). 36.50 (978-0-322-02984-2(8)) Wright Group/McGraw-Hill.
Fishman, Jon M. Michael Phelps. 2017. (Sports All-Stars Ser.). (ENG.). 32p. (J). (gr. 2-5). 12.99 **(978-1-5124-5400-0(1)**, Lerner Pubns.); 39.99 **(978-1-5124-5398-0(6)**, Lerner Pubns.); 39.99 **(978-1-5124-5397-3(8)**, Lerner Pubns.); (Illus.). pap. 8.99 **(978-1-5124-5401-7(X))**; (Illus.). lib. bdg. 26.65 **(978-1-5124-5396-6(X))** Lerner Publishing Group.
Fishman, Jon M. Mikaela Shiffrin. 2014. (Amazing Athletes Ser.). (ENG., Illus.). 32p. (gr. 2-5). lib. bdg. 25.26 (978-1-4677-5780-5(2), Lerner Pubns.) Lerner Publishing Group.
Ford, Jeanne Marie. The 12 Most Influential Athletes of All Time. 2018. (ENG.). 32p. (gr. 3-6). 31.35 **(978-1-63235-407-5(1)**, 12-Story Library) Pr. Room Editions LLC.
Ford, Michael. You Wouldn't Want to Be a Greek Athlete! (Revised Edition) 2014. (You Wouldn't Want to... Ser.). (ENG.). 32p. (J). lib. bdg. 29.00 (978-0-531-21175-5(4), Watts, Franklin) Scholastic Library Publishing.
Ford, Michael & Salariya, David. You Wouldn't Want to Be a Greek Athlete! Races You'd Rather Not Run. Antram, David, illus. 2004. (You Wouldn't Want to Ser.). (ENG.). 32p. (J). 29.00 (978-0-531-12352-2(9)) Scholastic Library Publishing.
Frederick, Shane. Boxing. 2012. (Illus.). 48p. (J). 35.65 (978-1-60818-209-1(6), Creative Education) Creative Co., The.
—Track & Field. 2012. (Illus.). 48p. (J). 35.65 (978-1-60818-212-1(6), Creative Education) Creative Co., The.
Fullman, Joe. Ancient & Modern. 2017. (Olympics Ser.). (ENG., Illus.). 32p. (J). (gr. 4-6). pap. 12.99 (978-0-7502-9779-0(4), Wayland) Hachette Children's Group GBR. Dist: Hachette Bk. Group.
Gifford, Clive. Ball Sports. 2011. (Olympic Sports Ser.). 32p. (YA). (gr. 4-7). 19.95 (978-1-60753-188-3(7)) Amicus Publishing.
—Basketball & Other Ball Sports. 2011. (ENG., Illus.). 32p. (J). pap. 10.95 (978-1-77092-035-4(8)) Saunders Bk. Co. CAN. Dist: RiverStream Publishing.
—Combat Sports. 2011. (ENG., Illus.). 32p. (J). pap. 10.95 (978-1-77092-036-1(6)) Saunders Bk. Co. CAN. Dist: RiverStream Publishing.
—Cycling. 2011. (ENG., Illus.). 32p. (J). pap. 10.95 (978-1-77092-037-8(4)) Saunders Bk. Co. CAN. Dist: RiverStream Publishing.
—Gymnastics. 2011. (ENG., Illus.). 32p. (J). pap. 10.95 (978-1-77092-038-5(2)) Saunders Bk. Co. CAN. Dist: RiverStream Publishing.
—So You Think You Know the Olympics. 2012. (ENG., Illus.). 176p. (YA). (gr. 7-17). pap. 8.99 (978-1-4449-0685-1(2)) Hodder & Stoughton GBR. Dist: Hachette Bk. Group.
—Swimming & Diving. 2011. (Olympic Sports Ser.). 32p. (YA). (gr. 4-7). 19.95 (978-1-60753-192-0(5)) Amicus Publishing.
—Swimming & Diving. 2011. (ENG., Illus.). 32p. (J). pap. 10.95 (978-1-77092-039-2(0)) Saunders Bk. Co. CAN. Dist: RiverStream Publishing.
—Track & Field. 2011. (ENG., Illus.). 32p. (J). pap. 10.95 (978-1-77092-040-8(4)) Saunders Bk. Co. CAN. Dist: RiverStream Publishing.
Girginov, Vassill, et al. The Olympic Games Explained: A Student Guide to the Evolution of the Modern Olympic Games. 2005. (Student Sport Studies). (ENG., Illus.). 288p. (C). 55.95 (978-0-415-34604-7(5)); 185.00 (978-0-415-34603-0(7), RU27967) Routledge.
Gitlin, Martin. The 1980 U. S. Olympic Boycott: A History Perspectives Book. 2014. (Perspectives Library). (ENG., Illus.). 32p. (J). (gr. 4-8). 28.50 (978-1-62431-663-0(8), 203216) Cherry Lake Publishing.
Goldish, Meish. Michael Phelps: Anything Is Possible! 2009. (Defining Moments Ser.). (Illus.). 32p. (YA). (gr. 2-5). lib. bdg. 25.27 (978-1-59716-855-7(6)) Bearport Publishing Co., Inc.
Great Moments in Olympic History, 6 bks., Set. Incl. Olympic Basketball. Hofstetter, Adam B. (YA). (gr. 5-9). lib. bdg. 29.25 (978-1-4042-0967-1(0)); Olympic Gymnastics. Hofstetter, Adam B. (J). (gr. 3-7). lib. bdg. 29.25 (978-1-4042-0968-8(9), Rosen Reference); Olympic Ice Skating. Farbs, C. (J). (gr. 3-7). lib. bdg. 26.50 (978-1-4042-0969-5(7)); Olympic Swimming & Diving. Kehm, Greg. (YA). (gr. 5-9). lib. bdg. 29.25 (978-1-4042-0970-1(0)); Olympic Track & Field. Belval, Brian. (YA). (gr. 5-9). lib. bdg. 29.25 (978-1-4042-0971-8(9)); Olympic Wrestling. Linde, Barbara M. (YA). (gr. 5-9). lib. bdg. 29.25 (978-1-4042-0972-5(7)); (Illus.). 48p. 2007. 2007. Set lib. bdg. 159.00 (978-1-4042-0933-6(6)) Rosen Publishing Group, Inc., The.
Gustaitis, Joseph. Snowboard. 2009. (Winter Olympic Sports Ser.). (ENG., Illus.). 32p. (J). (gr. 3-6). lib. bdg. (978-0-7787-4026-1(9)) Crabtree Publishing Co.
—Speed Skating. 2009. (Winter Olympic Sports Ser.). (ENG., Illus.). 32p. (J). (gr. 3-6). lib. bdg. (978-0-7787-4027-8(7)) Crabtree Publishing Co.
Hatton, Caroline. The Night Olympic Team: Fighting to Keep Drugs Out of the Games. 2008. (ENG., Illus.). 56p. (YA). (gr. 9-12). 17.95 (978-1-59078-566-9(5)) Boyds Mills Pr.
Herman, Gail. What Are the Summer Olympics? Marchesi, Stephen & McVeigh, Kevin, illus. 2016. (What Was? Ser.). (ENG.). 112p. (J). (gr. 3-7). 5.99 (978-0-448-48834-9(5), Grosset & Dunlap) Penguin Young Readers Group.
—What Are the Summer Olympics? 2016. (What Is... . ? Ser.). lib. bdg. 16.00 (978-0-606-38413-1(8)) Turtleback Bks.
Hernandez, Laurie. I Got This: To Gold & Beyond. 240p. (J). (gr. 3-7). 2018. (ENG.). pap. 8.99 **(978-0-06-267732-7(2))** 2017. 17.99 **(978-0-06-267731-0(4))** HarperCollins Pubs.
Herzog, Brad. G Is for Gold Medal: An Olympics Alphabet. Bowles, Doug, illus. 2015. (Av2 Fiction Readalong 2016 Ser.). (ENG.). (J). (gr. 1-4). lib. bdg. 34.28 (978-1-4896-3738-3(9), AV2 by Weigl) Weigl Pubs., Inc.
Herzog, Brad & Bowles, Doug. G Is for Gold Medal: An Olympics Alphabet. Bowles, Doug, illus. 2011. (ENG., Illus.). 32p. (gr. k-5). 15.95 (978-1-58536-462-6(2)) Sleeping Bear Pr.
Hess, Debra & Olson, Tod. The Modern Olympics: Battling for Peace. 2006. (Lynx2 Social Studies). (ENG., Illus.). 32p. (J). (gr. 6-8). pap. 13.60 (978-1-4190-2308-8(X)) Heinemann-Raintree.
Hofstetter, Adam. Olympic Basketball. 2007. 52p. pap. 26.50 (978-1-4358-3778-2(9)) Rosen Publishing Group, Inc., The.
Hofstetter, Adam B. Olympic Basketball. 2009. (Great Moments in Olympic History Ser.). 48p. (gr. 5-6). 53.00 (978-1-61513-157-0(4), Rosen Reference) Rosen Publishing Group, Inc., The.
—Olympic Gymnastics. (Great Moments in Olympic History Ser.). 48p. 2009. (gr. 5-6). 53.00 (978-1-61513-160-0(4)) 2007. (Illus.). (J). (gr. 3-7). lib. bdg. 29.25 (978-1-4042-0968-8(9)) Rosen Publishing Group, Inc., The. (Rosen Reference).
Hotchkiss, Ron. The Matchless Six: The Story of Canada's First Women's Olympic Team. 2006. (ENG., Illus.). 200p. (J). (gr. 5). pap. 16.95 (978-0-88776-738-8(9), Tundra Bks.) Tundra Bks. CAN. Dist: Penguin Random Hse. LLC.
Howell, Brian. Great Moments in Olympic Snowboarding, 1 vol. 2014. (Great Moments in Olympic Sports Ser.). (ENG.). 64p. (gr. 10-14). lib. bdg. 32.79 (978-1-62403-398-8(9), SportsZone) ABDO Publishing Co.
Hunter, Nick. Winter Olympics. 2013. (ENG.). 32p. (gr. 3-5). pap. 5.95 (978-1-4329-7700-9(8)); 30.65 (978-1-4329-7699-6(0)) Heinemann-Raintree. (NA-h).
—The World of Olympics, 1 vol. 2011. (Olympics Ser.). (ENG.). 32p. (gr. 3-5). 30.65 (978-1-4109-4120-6(5), NA-h) Heinemann-Raintree.
—The 2012 London Olympics. 2011. (Olympics Ser.). (ENG.). 32p. (gr. 3-5). pap. 7.99 (978-1-4109-4125-1(6)); 30.65 (978-1-4109-4119-0(1)) Heinemann-Raintree. (NA-h).
Johnson, Robin. Bobsleigh, Luge, & Skeleton. 2009. (Winter Olympic Sports Ser.). (ENG., Illus.). 32p. (J). (gr. 3-6). lib. bdg. (978-0-7787-4024-7(2)) Crabtree Publishing Co.
—Olympic Heroes & Zeroes. 2012. (ENG.). 48p. (J). (978-0-7787-7930-8(0)); pap. (978-0-7787-7939-1(4)) Crabtree Publishing Co.
Keen, Marian. Lexi & Hippocrates: Find Trouble at the Olympics. Jodie, Dias & Wendy, Watson, illus. 2014. (ENG.). 92p. pap. (978-1-77141-026-7(4), Influence Publishing) Lean Marketing Pr.
Kehm, Greg. Olympic Swimming & Diving. (Great Moments in Olympic History Ser.). 48p. (gr. 5-6). 2009. 53.00 (978-1-61513-162-4(0), Rosen Reference) 2007. (Illus.). (YA). lib. bdg. 29.25 (978-1-4042-0970-1(0)) Rosen Publishing Group, Inc., The.
Kennedy, Mike. Michael Phelps. 2009. (People We Should Know Ser.). (ENG.). 48p. (J). (gr. 3-5). pap. 10.50 (978-1-4339-2151-3(0)); lib. bdg. 31.00 (978-1-4339-1950-3(8)) Stevens, Gareth Publishing LLLP. (Gareth Stevens Learning Library).
Lacey, Minna. Story of the Olympics. 2008. (Young Reading Series 2 Gift Bks). 64p. (J). 8.99 (978-0-7945-1934-6(2), Usborne) EDC Publishing.
Lanser, Amanda. The Science Behind Swimming, Diving, & Other Water Sports. 2016. (Illus.). 32p. (J). (978-1-4914-8169-1(2)) Capstone Press of Coughlan Cos.
Lawrence, Blythe. Great Moments in Olympic Gymnastics, 1 vol. 2014. (Great Moments in Olympic Sports Ser.). (ENG.). 64p. (gr. 10-14). lib. bdg. 32.79 (978-1-62403-394-0(6), SportsZone) ABDO Publishing Co.
LeBoutillier, Nate. Basketball. 2012. (J). 35.65 (978-1-60818-208-4(8), Creative Education) Creative Co., The.
—Gymnastics. 2012. (J). 35.65 (978-1-60818-210-7(X), Creative Education) Creative Co., The.
—Swimming. 2012. (J). 35.65 (978-1-60818-211-4(8), Creative Education) Creative Co., The.
—Volleyball. 2012. (Illus.). 48p. (J). 35.65 (978-1-60818-213-8(4), Creative Education) Creative Co., The.
Levin, Ina. Journey to Athens: Grades 4-6. 2004. (U. S. Olympic Committee's Activity Book Ser.). 64p. (J). pap. 9.99 (978-1-58000-121-2(1)) Griffin Publishing Group.
Levin, Ina & Siskind, Ellyn. Journey to Athens: Grades 1-3. 2004. (U. S. Olympic Committee's Activity Book Ser.). (Illus.). 32p. (J). pap. 7.99 (978-1-58000-120-5(3)) Griffin Publishing Group.
Linde, Barbara. Olympic Wrestling. 2009. (Great Moments in Olympic History Ser.). 48p. (gr. 5-6). 53.00 (978-1-61513-166-2(3), Rosen Reference) Rosen Publishing Group, Inc., The.
Linde, Barbara M. Olympic Wrestling. 2007. (Great Moments in Olympic History Ser.). (Illus.). 48p. (YA). (gr. 5-9). lib. bdg. 29.25 (978-1-4042-0972-5(7)) Rosen Publishing Group, Inc., The.
Macy, Sue. Freeze Frame: A Photographic History of the Winter Olympics. 2006. (ENG., Illus.). 96p. (gr. 5-18). 28.90 (978-0-7922-7888-7(7), National Geographic Children's Bks.) National Geographic Society.
—Swifter, Higher, Stronger: A Photographic History of the Summer Olympics. 2008. (ENG., Illus.). 96p. (J). (gr. 5-9). 18.95 (978-1-4263-0290-9(8)); lib. bdg. 27.90 (978-1-4263-0302-9(5)) National Geographic Society. (National Geographic Children's Bks.).
Marsh, Carole. Greece: A Volcanic Land of Ancient Olympic Origins! 2009. (It's Your World Ser.). 48p. (J). (gr. 2-9). pap. 7.99 (978-0-635-06818-7(4)) Gallopade International.
Mason, Tyler. Incredible Olympic Records. 2016. (Incredible Sports Records Ser.). (ENG.). 24p. (J). (gr. 2-5). 28.50 (978-1-5038-0890-4(4), 210679) Child's World, Inc., The.
McCarthy, Meghan. The Wildest Race Ever: The Story of the 1904 Olympic Marathon. McCarthy, Meghan, illus. 2016. (ENG., Illus.). 48p. (J). (gr. -1-3). 17.99 (978-1-4814-0639-0(6), Simon & Schuster/Paula Wiseman Bks.) Simon & Schuster/Paula Wiseman Bks.
Michael Phelps. rev. ed. 2009. (Amazing Athletes Ser.). (gr. 2-5). pap. 6.95 (978-0-7613-4138-3(2), First Avenue Editions) Lerner Publishing Group.
Moore, Kaitlin. Kerri Strug & & the Magnificent Seven. 2016. (Totally True Adventures Ser.). (ENG., Illus.). 112p. (J). (gr. 1-4). pap. 4.99 (978-0-553-52174-0(8), Random Hse. Bks. for Young Readers) Random Hse. Children's Bks.
Morey, Allan. Basketball. 2016. (Summer Olympic Sports Ser.). (ENG., Illus.). 32p. (J). (gr. 2-4). pap. 9.99 (978-1-68152-047-6(8)) Amicus.
—Basketball. 2015. (Summer Olympic Sports Ser.). (ENG., Illus.). 32p. (J). (gr. 2-4). 19.95 (978-1-60753-806-6(7)) Amicus Publishing.
—Gymnastics. 2015. (Summer Olympic Sports Ser.). (ENG., Illus.). 32p. (J). (gr. 2-4). 19.95 (978-1-60753-808-0(3)) Amicus Publishing.
—Swimming & Diving. 2015. (Summer Olympic Sports Ser.). (ENG., Illus.). 32p. (J). (gr. 2-4). 19.95 (978-1-60753-809-7(1)) Amicus Publishing.
Nardo, Don. Massacre in Munich: How Terrorists Changed the Oylmpics & the World. 2016. (Captured History Sports Ser.). (ENG., Illus.). 64p. (gr. 5-7). lib. bdg. 34.65 (978-0-7565-5292-3(3), CPB Grades 4-8) Compass Point Bks.
Newsham, Gavin. The London 2012 Games Fact File. 2012. (London 2012 Ser.). (ENG., Illus.). 64p. (J). (gr. k-3). 13.99 (978-1-84732-929-5(2)) Carlton Bks., Ltd. GBR. Dist: Independent Pubs. Group.
Osborne, Mary Pope & Boyce, Natalie Pope. Ancient Greece & the Olympics: A Nonfiction Companion to Hour of the Olympics. Murdocca, Sal, tr. Murdocca, Sal, illus. 2004. (Magic Tree House - Fact Tracker Ser.: 10). (ENG.). 128p. (J). (gr. 2-5). pap. 6.99 (978-0-375-82378-7(6), Random Hse. Bks. for Young Readers) Random Hse. Children's Bks.
Page, Jason. Basketball, Soccer, & Other Ball Games. 2008. (Olympic Sports Ser.). (ENG., Illus.). 32p. (J). (gr. 4-7). pap. (978-0-7787-4029-2(3)); lib. bdg. (978-0-7787-4012-4(9)) Crabtree Publishing Co.
—Cycling, Shooting, & Show Jumping: Archery, Weightlifting, & a Whole Lot More. 2008. (Olympic Sports Ser.). (ENG., Illus.). 32p. (J). (gr. 3-7). pap. (978-0-7787-4030-8(7)); (gr.

4-7). lib. bdg. *(978-0-7787-4013-1(7))* Crabtree Publishing Co.
—Decathlon, High Jump, & Other Field Events. 2008. (Olympic Sports Ser.). (ENG., Illus.). 32p. (J). (gr. 3-7). pap. *(978-0-7787-4031-5(5))*; lib. bdg. *(978-0-7787-4014-8(5))* Crabtree Publishing Co.
—Gymnastics Events. 2008. (Olympic Sports Ser.). (ENG., Illus.). 32p. (J). (gr. 3-7). pap. *(978-0-7787-4032-2(3))*; lib. bdg. *(978-0-7787-4015-5(3))* Crabtree Publishing Co.
—Martial Arts, Boxing, & Other Combat Sports: Fencing, Judo, Wrestling, Taekwondo, & a Whole Lot More. 2008. (Olympic Sports Ser.). (ENG., Illus.). 32p. (J). (gr. 3-7). pap. *(978-0-7787-4033-9(1))*; lib. bdg. *(978-0-7787-4016-2(1))* Crabtree Publishing Co.
—Rowing, Sailing, & Other Sports on the Water. 2008. (Olympic Sports Ser.). (ENG., Illus.). 32p. (J). (gr. 3-7). pap. *(978-0-7787-4034-6(X))*; lib. bdg. *(978-0-7787-4017-9(X))* Crabtree Publishing Co.
—Sprints, Hurdles, & Other Track Events. 2008. (Olympic Sports Ser.). (ENG., Illus.). 32p. (J). (gr. 3-7). pap. *(978-0-7787-4035-3(8))*; lib. bdg. *(978-0-7787-4018-6(8))* Crabtree Publishing Co.
—Swimming, Diving, & Other Water Sports. 2008. (Olympic Sports Ser.). (ENG., Illus.). 32p. (J). (gr. 3-7). pap. *(978-0-7787-4036-0(6))*; lib. bdg. *(978-0-7787-4019-3(6))* Crabtree Publishing Co.
Patrick, Jean L. S. & Gustavson, Adam. Long-Armed Ludy & the First Women's Olympics: Based on the True Story of Lucile Ellerbe Godbold. 2017. (ENG., Illus.). 32p. (J). (gr. 1-4). lib. bdg. 16.99 *(978-1-58089-546-0(8))* Charlesbridge Publishing, Inc.
Pemu, Dennis. The Complete Guide to Sports. 2015. (Illus.). 144p. (J). *(978-1-4351-6166-5(1))* Barnes & Noble, Inc.
Peters, Andrew, et al. Winter Olympics. 2014. (Collins Big Cat Progress Ser.). (ENG., Illus.). 32p. (YA). (gr. 7). pap. 7.99 *(978-0-00-751924-8(9))* HarperCollins Pubs. Ltd. GBR. Dist: Independent Pubs. Group.
Peters, Chris. Great Moments in Olympic Ice Hockey, 1 vol. 2014. (Great Moments in Olympic Sports Ser.). (ENG.). 64p. (gr. 10-14). lib. bdg. 32.79 *(978-1-62403-395-7(4),* SportsZone) ABDO Publishing Co.
Peterson, Christine. The Science Behind Swimming, Diving, & Other Water Sports. 2016. (Science of the Summer Olympics Ser.). (ENG., Illus.). 32p. (gr. 3-4). lib. bdg. 27.99 *(978-1-4914-8157-8(9),* Edge Bks.) Capstone Press of Coughlan Cos.
Peterson, Christine, et al. Science of the Summer Olympics. 2016. (Science of the Summer Olympics Ser.). (ENG.). 32p. (gr. 3-4). 111.96 *(978-1-4914-8173-8(0),* Edge Bks.) Capstone Press of Coughlan Cos.
Phelps, Michael & Abrahamson, Alan. How to Train with a T. Rex & Win 8 Gold Medals. Jenkins, Ward, illus. 2009. (ENG.). 32p. (J). (gr. -1-3). 17.99 *(978-1-4169-8669-0(3),* Simon & Schuster Bks. For Young Readers) Simon & Schuster Bks. For Young Readers.
Powell, Jillian. Olympic Heroes. 2012. (Collins Big Cat Ser.). (ENG., Illus.). 24p. (J). (gr. k-1). pap. 6.99 *(978-0-00-746190-5(9))* HarperCollins Pubs. Ltd. GBR. Dist: Independent Pubs. Group.
Reeves, Diane Lindsey & Kelley, K. C. Choose Your Own Career Adventure at the Olympics. 2016. (Bright Futures Press: Choose Your Own Career Adventure Ser.). (ENG., Illus.). 32p. (J). (gr. 4-6). 29.93 *(978-1-63471-914-8(X),* 208977) Cherry Lake Publishing.
Rose, Simon. Canada's Olympic Torch. 2010. (Illus.). 24p. *(978-1-77071-580-6(0))*; pap. *(978-1-77071-587-5(8))* Weigl Educational Pubs. Ltd.
—Le Flambeau Olympique: Les Emblèmes Canadiens. McMann, Julie, tr. from ENG. 2011. (FRE.). 24p. (YA). (gr. 2-4). *(978-1-77071-411-3(1))* Weigl Educational Pubs. Ltd.
Rosen, Karen. Great Moments in Olympic Swimming & Diving, 1 vol. 2014. (Great Moments in Olympic Sports Ser.). (ENG.). 64p. (gr. 10-14). lib. bdg. 32.79 *(978-1-62403-399-5(7),* SportsZone) ABDO Publishing Co.
—Great Moments in Olympic Track & Field, 1 vol. 2014. (Great Moments in Olympic Sports Ser.). (ENG.). 64p. (gr. 10-14). lib. bdg. 32.79 *(978-1-62403-400-8(4),* SportsZone) ABDO Publishing Co.
Roza, Greg. Olympic Math: Working with Percentages & Decimals. 2009. (PowerMath: Advanced Proficiency Plus Ser.). 32p. (gr. 5-5). 47.90 *(978-1-60851-363-5(7),* PowerKids Pr.) Rosen Publishing Group, Inc., The.
—Olympic Math: Working with Percents & Decimals. (Math for the Real World Ser.). (Illus.). 32p. 2009. (ENG.). (gr. 6-7). pap. 10.00 *(978-1-4042-6057-3(9))* 2006. (J). lib. bdg. 23.95 *(978-1-4042-3352-2(0))* Rosen Publishing Group, Inc., The.
Sévigny, Eric, illus. Caillou - Backyard Olympics. 2016. (Clubhouse Ser.). (ENG.). 24p. (J). (gr. -1-k). pap. 3.99 *(978-2-89718-311-0(X))* Caillouet, Gerry.
Sherrow, Victoria. Wilma Rudolph. Johnson, Larry, illus. 2006. (Yo Solo Biografías Ser.). (ENG & SPA.). 48p. (J). (gr. 2-3). lib. bdg. 23.93 *(978-0-8225-6260-3(X),* Ediciones Lerner) Lerner Publishing Group.
Simon, Francesca. Gold Medal Games. Ross, Tony, illus. 2017. (Horrid Henry Ser.). (ENG.). 24p. (J). (gr. 1-3). pap. 8.99 ***(978-1-5101-0127-2(6),*** Orion Children's Bks.) Hachette Children's Group GBR. Dist: Hachette Bk. Group.
Simonds, Lucy. The Olympics. 2007. (Trackers-Math Ser.). (gr. 2-5). pap. 5.00 *(978-1-59055-911-6(8))* Pacific Learning, Inc.
Simons, Lisa M. Bolt. The First Olympics of Ancient Greece, 1 vol. 2014. (Ancient Greece Ser.). (ENG., Illus.). 24p. (gr. 1-2). 25.32 *(978-1-4914-0273-3(3))* Capstone Press of Coughlan Cos.
Smith-Llera, Danielle. Black Power Salute: How a Photograph Captured a Political Protest. 2017. (Captured History Sports Ser.). (ENG.). 64p. (gr. 5-7). lib. bdg. 34.65 *(978-0-7565-5526-9(4),* CPB Grades 4-8) Compass Point Bks.
Smith, Nikkolas, illus. The Golden Girls of Rio. 2016. (ENG.). 32p. (J). (gr. -1-3). 16.99 *(978-1-5107-2247-7(5),* Sky Pony Pr.) Skyhorse Publishing Co., Inc.
Sonneborn, Liz. Murder at the 1972 Olympics in Munich. 2009. (Terrorist Attacks Ser.). 64p. (gr. 5-5). 58.50 *(978-1-60853-308-4(5))* Rosen Publishing Group, Inc., The.
Stewart, Mark. The Olympics. 2009. (Ultimate 10: Sports Ser.). 48p. (ENG.). (J). (gr. 4-8). pap. 10.50 *(978-1-4339-2208-4(8))*; (YA). (gr. 5-9). lib. bdg. 31.00 *(978-0-8368-9160-7(0))* Stevens, Gareth Publishing LLLP.
Sullivan, Erin Ash. Math at the Olympics & Matemáticas en las Olimpiadas: 6 English, 6 Spanish Adaptations. 2011. (ENG & SPA.). (J). 97.00 net. *(978-1-4108-5707-1(7))* Benchmark Education Co.
Sylvester, Kevin. Gold Medal for Weird. Sylvester, Kevin, illus. 2007. (ENG., Illus.). 112p. (J). (gr. 2-6). 7.95 *(978-1-55453-021-2(0))* Kids Can Pr., Ltd. CAN. Dist: Hachette Bk. Group.
Tieck, Sarah. Michael Phelps: Olympic Champion, 1 vol. 2009. (Big Buddy Biographies Set 2 Ser.). (ENG., Illus.). 32p. (J). (gr. 2-5). 28.50 *(978-1-60453-550-1(4))* ABDO Publishing Co.
—Michael Phelps: The Greatest Olympian, 1 vol. 2013. (Big Buddy Biographies Set 9 Ser.). (ENG.). 32p. (J). (gr. 2-5). lib. bdg. 28.50 *(978-1-61783-753-1(9),* Big Buddy Bks.) ABDO Publishing Co.
Torsiello, David P. Michael Phelps: Swimming for Olympic Gold. 2009. (Hot Celebrity Biographies Ser.). (Illus.). 48p. (J). (gr. 5-9). pap. 8.95 *(978-0-7660-3630-7(8))* Enslow Pubs., Inc.
Trusdell, Brian. Great Moments in Olympic Skiing, 1 vol. 2014. (Great Moments in Olympic Sports Ser.). (ENG.). 64p. (gr. 10-14). lib. bdg. 32.79 *(978-1-62403-397-1(0),* SportsZone) ABDO Publishing Co.
Watson, Stephanie. The Science Behind Soccer, Volleyball, Cycling, & Other Popular Sports. 2016. (Science of the Summer Olympics Ser.). (ENG., Illus.). 32p. (gr. 3-4). lib. bdg. 27.99 *(978-1-4914-8160-8(9),* Edge Bks.) Capstone Press of Coughlan Cos.
Waxman, Laura Hamilton. Bobsled & Luge. 2017. (Winter Olympic Sports Ser.). (ENG.). 32p. (J). (gr. 2-5). pap. 9.99 *(978-1-68152-181-7(4))* Amicus.
—Bobsled & Luge. 2017. (Winter Olympic Sports Ser.). (ENG.). 32p. (gr. 1-4). 20.95 *(978-1-68151-150-4(9))* Amicus Publishing.
—Figure Skating. 2017. (Winter Olympic Sports Ser.). (ENG.). 32p. (J). (gr. 2-5). pap. 9.99 *(978-1-68152-179-4(2))* Amicus.
—Figure Skating. 2017. (Winter Olympic Sports Ser.). (ENG.). 32p. (gr. 1-4). 20.95 *(978-1-68151-148-1(7))* Amicus Publishing.
—Ice Hockey & Curling. 2017. (Winter Olympic Sports Ser.). (ENG.). 32p. (J). (gr. 2-5). pap. 9.99 *(978-1-68152-180-0(6))* Amicus.
—Skiing. 2017. (Winter Olympic Sports Ser.). (ENG.). 32p. (J). (gr. 1-4). 20.95 ***(978-1-68151-151-1(7),*** Amicus High Interest) Amicus Publishing.
—Speed Skating: By Laura Hamilton Waxman. 2017. (Winter Olympic Sports Ser.). (ENG.). 32p. (J). (gr. 2-5). pap. 9.99 ***(978-1-68152-184-8(9))*** Amicus.
—Speed Skating: By Laura Hamilton Waxman. 2017. (Winter Olympic Sports Ser.). (ENG.). 32p. (gr. 1-4). 20.95 ***(978-1-68151-153-5(3))*** Amicus Publishing.
—Winter Olympic Sports: Skiing. 2017. (Winter Olympic Sports Ser.). (ENG.). 32p. (J). (gr. 2-5). pap. 9.99 ***(978-1-68152-182-4(2))*** Amicus.
Whitfield, Simon & Dheensaw, Cleve. Simon Says Gold: Simon Whitfield's Pursuit of Athletic Excellence, 1 vol. 2009. (ENG., Illus.). 128p. (J). (gr. 5-12). pap. 14.00 *(978-1-55469-141-8(9))* Orca Bk. Pubs. USA.
Williams, Doug. Great Moments in Olympic Basketball, 1 vol. 2014. (Great Moments in Olympic Sports Ser.). (ENG.). 64p. (gr. 10-14). lib. bdg. 32.79 *(978-1-62403-393-3(8),* SportsZone) ABDO Publishing Co.
Zuehlke, Jeffrey. Michael Phelps. (First Step Nonfiction Ser.). 32p. 2005. (Illus.). (J). (gr. 2-5). per. 5.95 *(978-0-8225-2631-5(X))* 2005. (Illus.). (J). (gr. 3-7). lib. bdg. 23.93 *(978-0-8225-2431-1(7))* 2009. (ENG.). (gr. 2-5). 25.26 *(978-0-7613-4055-3(6))* Lerner Publishing Group.

OLYMPICS—FICTION

Ahearn, Dan & Ahearn, Janet. Olympic Dreams. 2011. (Navigators Ser.). (J). pap. *(978-1-61672-964-6(3))* Benchmark Education Co.
Arena, Felice & Kettle, Phil. Olympics. Cox, David, illus. 2004. (J). pap. *(978-1-59336-374-1(5))* Mondo Publishing.
Boiger, Alexandra. Max & Marla. Boiger, Alexandra, illus. 2015. (ENG., Illus.). 32p. (J). (-k). 17.99 *(978-0-399-17504-6(0),* G.P. Putnam's Sons Books for Young Readers) Penguin Young Readers Group.
Carter, Caela. Tumbling. 2016. (ENG.). 432p. (YA). (gr. 7). 17.99 *(978-0-451-47300-4(0),* Viking Books for Young Readers) Penguin Young Readers Group.
Charles, Norma. Chasing a Star. 2009. (ENG., Illus.). 182p. (YA). (gr. 5-8). pap. *(978-1-55380-077-4(X))* Ronsdale Pr.
Debnam, Mio. Animalympics, 5 BK Set. 2010. (ENG.). 140p. (J). (gr. -1-3). pap. 23.00 *(978-988-98819-0-0(X))* Haven Bks.
Farmer, Tom. Once upon a Daydream: The Story of Patrick & the Clumsy Camel. 2013. 44p. pap. 17.44 *(978-1-4669-6912-4(1))* Trafford Publishing.
Feinstein, John. Rush for the Gold: Mystery at the Olympics. 2013. (Sports Beat Ser.). (ENG.). 336p. (J). (gr. 5). pap. 7.99 *(978-0-375-87168-9(3),* Yearling) Random Hse. Children's Bks.
Freitas, Donna. Gold Medal Winter. 2014. (ENG.). 320p. (J). (gr. 4-7). 16.99 *(978-0-545-64377-1(5))* Scholastic, Inc.
Golub, Osu. Penguins Go for the Gold. 2009. 16p. pap. 10.00 *(978-1-4490-3907-3(3))* AuthorHouse.
Goscinny, René. Asterix aux jeux Olympiques. 21.95 *(978-2-01-210012-1(0))* Hachette Groupe Livre FRA. Dist: Distribooks, Inc.
Holub, Joan & Williams, Suzanne. Artemis the Loyal. 2013. (Goddess Girls Ser.: 7). (ENG., Illus.). 288p. (J). (gr. 3-7). 16.99 *(978-1-4424-8594-5(9),* Aladdin) Simon & Schuster Children's Publishing.
—The Girl Games. 2014. (Goddess Girls Ser.). (ENG., Illus.). 320p. (J). (gr. 3-7). 17.99 *(978-1-4424-9575-3(8),* Aladdin) Simon & Schuster Children's Publishing.
—The Girl Games: Super Special. 2012. (Goddess Girls Ser.). (ENG.). 320p. (J). (gr. 3-7). pap. 7.99 *(978-1-4424-4933-6(0),* Aladdin) Simon & Schuster Children's Publishing.
—The Girls' Games. 2012. (Goddess Girls Ser.). lib. bdg. 18.40 *(978-0-606-26349-8(7),* Turtleback) Turtleback Bks.
Jamieson, Victoria. Olympig! 2016. lib. bdg. 19.65 *(978-0-606-38844-3(3))* Turtleback Bks.
Keene, Carolyn. Gold Medal Murder. 2010. (Nancy Drew/Hardy Boys Ser.: 4). (ENG.). 176p. (J). (gr. 3-7). pap. 6.99 *(978-1-4424-0326-0(8),* Aladdin) Simon & Schuster Children's Publishing.
Kelly, David A. The Gold Medal Mess. Brundage, Scott, illus. 2016. (Most Valuable Players Ser.: 1). (ENG.). 128p. (J). (gr. 1-4). 4.99 *(978-0-553-51319-6(2),* Random Hse. Bks. for Young Readers) Random Hse. Children's Bks.
Khalili, Davood. Developing Olympian Character, 1 vol. 2010. 32p. pap. 24.95 *(978-1-4489-5281-6(6))* PublishAmerica, Inc.
Lewis, Beverly. Girls Only! 2008. (Girls Only (Go!) Ser.: Vols. 5-8). (ENG.). (J). (gr. 4-7). 510p. pap. 20.00 *(978-0-7642-0462-3(9))*;Vols. 1-4. 512p. pap. 16.00 *(978-0-7642-0461-6(0))* Bethany Hse. Pubs.
MacGregor, Roy. Murder at the Winter Games, No. 18. 2004. (Screech Owls Ser.: No. 18). (ENG., Illus.). 128p. (YA). mass mkt. 4.95 *(978-0-7710-5647-5(8),* Screech Owls) McClelland & Stewart CAN. Dist: Penguin Random Hse. LLC.
Malaspina, Ann. Touch the Sky: Alice Coachman, Olympic High Jumper. Velasquez, Eric, illus. 2012. (ENG.). 32p. (J). (gr. 1-3). 16.99 *(978-0-8075-8035-6(X))* Whitman, Albert & Co.
Meadows, Daisy. Alice the Tennis Fairy. 2010. (Sports Fairies Ser.: 6). (ENG.). 80p. (J). (gr. 2-5). 4.99 *(978-0-545-20257-2(4),* Scholastic Paperbacks) Scholastic, Inc.
—Brittany the Basketball Fairy. 2010. (Sports Fairies Ser.: 4). (ENG.). 80p. (J). (gr. 2-5). 4.99 *(978-0-545-20255-8(8),* Scholastic Paperbacks) Scholastic, Inc.
—Gemma the Gymnastics Fairy. 2010. (Sports Fairies Ser.: 7). (ENG.). 80p. (J). (gr. 2-5). 4.99 *(978-0-545-20258-9(2),* Scholastic Paperbacks) Scholastic, Inc.
—Helena the Horse-Riding Fairy. 2010. (Sports Fairies Ser.: 1). (ENG.). 80p. (J). (gr. 2-5). 4.99 *(978-0-545-20252-7(3),* Scholastic Paperbacks) Scholastic, Inc.
—Samantha the Swimming Fairy. 2010. (Sports Fairies Ser.: 5). (ENG.). 80p. (J). (gr. 2-5). 4.99 *(978-0-545-20256-5(6),* Scholastic Paperbacks) Scholastic, Inc.
—Stacey the Soccer Fairy. 2010. (Sports Fairies Ser.: 2). (ENG.). 80p. (J). (gr. 2-5). 4.99 *(978-0-545-20253-4(1),* Scholastic Paperbacks) Scholastic, Inc.
—Zoe the Skating Fairy. 2010. (Sports Fairies Ser.: 3). (ENG.). 80p. (J). (gr. 2-5). 4.99 *(978-0-545-20254-1(X),* Scholastic Paperbacks) Scholastic, Inc.
Morgan, Winter. Attack on Minecrafters Academy. 2017. (Unofficial Minecrafters Academy Ser.: 4). lib. bdg. 18.40 ***(978-0-606-40309-2(4))*** Turtleback Bks.
Nicholson, Lorna Schultz. Puckster Goes to the Olympics. Findley, Kelly, illus. 2013. (ENG.). 24p. (J). (gr. -1-3). pap. 6.99 *(978-1-77049-594-4(0),* Fenn-Tundra) Tundra Bks. CAN. Dist: Penguin Random Hse. LLC.
Osborne, Mary Pope. La Hora de Los Juegos Olímpicos. Brovelli, Marcela, tr. Murdocca, Sal, illus. 2007. (Casa del Arbol Ser.: 16).Tr. of Hour of the Olympics Games. (ENG & SPA.). 68p. (J). per. 5.99 *(978-1-933032-22-1(7))* Lectorum Pubns., Inc.
—Hour of the Olympics. unabr. ed. 2004. (Magic Tree House Ser.: No. 16). 70p. (J). (gr. k-3). pap. 17.00 incl. audio *(978-0-8072-0785-7(3),* LFTR 244 SP, Listening Library) Random Hse. Audio Publishing Group.
Panayotis. Junior & Bo's Trip to the Olympics. Theophilopoulos, Andrew, illus. 2007. 104p. per. 10.95 *(978-1-934246-26-9(3))* Peppertree Pr., The.
Peyo. The Smurf Championship Games. 2012. (Simon & Schuster Ready-To-Read Level 2 Ser.). lib. bdg. 13.55 *(978-0-606-26363-4(2),* Turtleback) Turtleback Bks.
—The Smurfs Graphic Novels Boxed Set: Vol. #10-12. 2013. (Smurfs Graphic Novels Ser.). (ENG., Illus.). 168p. (J). (gr. 2-5). 17.99 *(978-1-59707-386-8(5),* 9781597073868) Papercutz.
Peyo & Delporte, Yvan. The Smurf Olympics. 2012. (Smurfs Graphic Novels Ser.). (ENG., Illus.). 56p. (J). (gr. 2-5). 10.99 *(978-1-59707-302-8(4),* 9781597073028); pap. 7.99 *(978-1-59707-301-1(6),* 9781597073011) Papercutz.
Richards, Jean. The First Olympic Games: A Gruesome Greek Myth with a Happy Ending. Thacker, Kat, illus. 2004. 32p. pap. 10.95 *(978-0-7613-2443-0(7),* Millbrook Pr.) Lerner Publishing Group.
Riley, Lehman & Austin, Megan. The Life of Babe Didrikson: "Greatness Is Never Forgotten" Wallace, Joshua, illus. 2005. 47p. (J). pap. *(978-0-9760523-2-6(6))* Matter of Africa America Time.
Stilton, Geronimo. Geronimo & the Gold Medal Mystery. 2008. (Geronimo Stilton Ser.). (Illus.). 87p. (J). (gr. 2-5). lib. bdg. 14.65 *(978-0-7569-8803-6(9))* Perfection Learning Corp.
—Geronimo & the Gold Medal Mystery. 2008. (Geronimo Stilton Ser.: 33). (ENG., Illus.). 128p. (J). (gr. 2-5). pap. 7.99 *(978-0-545-02133-3(2),* Scholastic Paperbacks) Scholastic, Inc.
Terrell, Brandon. Grit & Gold. Max, Iman & Garcia, Eduardo, illus. 2016. (Time Machine Magazine Ser.). (ENG.). 128p. (gr. 3-4). lib. bdg. 22.65 *(978-1-4965-2597-0(3))* Capstone Press of Coughlan Cos.
—Harmony & Hoops. Max, Iman & Garcia, Eduardo, illus. 2016. (Time Machine Magazine Ser.). (ENG.). 128p. (gr. 3-4). lib. bdg. 22.65 *(978-1-4965-2596-3(5))* Capstone Press of Coughlan Cos.
—Pluck & Perfection. Max, Iman, illus. 2016. (Time Machine Magazine Ser.). (ENG.). 128p. (gr. 3-4). lib. bdg. 22.65 *(978-1-4965-2595-6(7))* Capstone Press of Coughlan Cos.
—Valor & Victory. Max, Iman, illus. 2016. (Time Machine Magazine Ser.). (ENG.). 128p. (gr. 3-4). lib. bdg. 22.65 *(978-1-4965-2594-9(9))* Capstone Press of Coughlan Cos.
Tobey, Carole A. The Frog Olympics. 2005. (Illus.). 70p. (J). per. 12.00 *(978-0-9773648-3-1(6))* Legend eXpress Publishing.
Uderzo, Albert & Goscinny, René. Asterix at the Olympic Games. Uderzo, Albert, illus. 2004. (ENG., Illus.). 48p. pap. 12.99 *(978-0-7528-6627-7(3),* Orion) Orion Publishing Group, Ltd. GBR. Dist: Hachette Bk. Group.
Yardley Hastings Primary School. Tim & Holly's Olympic Adventure. 2012. 74p. pap. *(978-1-909039-52-0(7))* Legend Pr.

OMAN

Barnett, Tracy. Oman. 2003. (Modern Middle East Nations & Their Strategic Place in the World Ser.). (Illus.). 112,128p. (YA). (gr. 7-18). lib. bdg. *(978-1-59084-517-2(X))* Mason Crest.
Ejaz, Khadija. We Visit Oman. 2011. (Your Land & My Land Ser.). (Illus.). 64p. (J). (gr. 4-7). lib. bdg. 33.95 *(978-1-58415-962-9(6))* Mitchell Lane Pubs., Inc.
Issac, Michael. A Historical Atlas of Oman. (Historical Atlases of South Asia, Central Asia, & the Middle East Ser.). 64p. 2009. (gr. 6-6). 61.20 *(978-1-61513-326-0(7))* 2004. (Illus.). (gr. 7-12). lib. bdg. 31.95 *(978-0-8239-4500-9(6))* Rosen Publishing Group, Inc., The.
King, David C. Oman. 2008. (Cultures of the World Ser.). (Illus.). 144p. (gr. 6-18). lib. bdg. 42.79 *(978-0-7614-3120-6(9),* Benchmark Bks.) Marshall Cavendish Corp.
Rinaldo, Denise. Lost City Spotted from Space! Is There a Hidden Land under the Sand? 2011. (J). pap. *(978-0-545-32929-3(9))* Scholastic, Inc.

ONASSIS, JACQUELINE KENNEDY, 1929-1994

Agins, Donna Brown. Jacqueline Kennedy Onassis: Legendary First Lady. 2004. (People to Know Ser.). (Illus.). 128p. (J). lib. bdg. 26.60 *(978-0-7660-2186-0(6))* Enslow Pubs., Inc.
Bader, Bonnie. Who Was Jackie Kennedy? Qiu, Joseph J. M., illus. 2016. (Who Was? Ser.). (ENG.). 112p. (J). (gr. 3-7). lib. bdg. 15.99 *(978-0-399-54242-8(6),* Grosset & Dunlap) Penguin Young Readers Group.
Mattern, Joanne. Jacqueline Kennedy, 1 vol. 2008. (First Ladies Set 1 Ser.). (ENG., Illus.). 32p. (YA). (gr. 1-4). 27.07 *(978-1-59928-796-6(X))* ABDO Publishing Co.
Raatma, Lucia. Jacqueline Kennedy, 1 vol. 2010. (First Ladies Ser.). (ENG.). 24p. (gr. k-1). pap. 7.29 *(978-1-4296-5601-6(8))*; pap. 41.70 *(978-1-4296-5602-3(6))*; lib. bdg. 26.65 *(978-1-4296-5009-0(5))* Capstone Press of Coughlan Cos. (Pebble Plus).

ONE-ACT PLAYS

Sacco, Christopher & Haehnel, Alan. The Education of Janet O'Malley: One-Act Comedy Play. 2003. (YA). pap. 4.25 *(978-1-932404-10-4(4),* 728) Brooklyn Pubs.

O'NEILL, EUGENE, 1888-1953

Bloom, Harold, ed. Long Day's Journey into Night - Eugene O'Neill, New Edition. 2nd rev. ed. 2009. (Bloom's Modern Critical Interpretations Ser.). 248p. (C). (gr. 9-18). 45.00 *(978-1-60413-390-5(2),* Chelsea Hse.) Facts On File, Inc.
Hermann, Spring. Reading & Interpreting the Works of Eugene O'Neill. 2016. (Lit Crit Guides). 176p. (J). (gr. 6-6). 39.93 *(978-0-7660-7913-7(9))* Enslow Pubs., Inc.
—A Student's Guide to Eugene O'Neill. 2009. (Understanding Literature Ser.). (Illus.). 176p. (YA). (gr. 9-12). lib. bdg. 29.27 *(978-0-7660-2886-9(0))* Enslow Pubs., Inc.

ONTARIO

Adams, Carly. Queens of the Ice: They Were Fast, They Were Fierce, They Were Teenage Girls, 1 vol. 2011. (Lorimer Recordbooks Ser.). (ENG., Illus.). 136p. (YA). (gr. 7-12). 9.95 *(978-1-55277-720-6(0),* 9781552777206) Lorimer, James & Co., Ltd., Pubs. CAN. Dist: Casemate Pubs. & Bk. Distributors, LLC.
Brignall, Richard. Big Train: The Legendary Ironman of Sport, Lionel Conacher, 1 vol. 2009. (Lorimer Recordbooks Ser.). (ENG., Illus.). 168p. (YA). (gr. 6-12). 16.95 *(978-1-55277-451-9(1),* 9781552774519); 9.95 *(978-1-55277-450-2(3),* 9781552774502) Lorimer, James & Co., Ltd., Pubs. CAN. Dist: Casemate Pubs. & Bk. Distributors, LLC.
Cooper, John, Jr. Season of Rage: Hugh Burnett & the Struggle for Civil Rights. 2005. (ENG., Illus.). 80p. (J). (gr. 5-12). pap. 9.95 *(978-0-88776-700-5(1),* Tundra Bks.) Tundra Bks. CAN. Dist: Penguin Random Hse. LLC.
Gorman, Lovenia. A Is for Algonquin: An Ontario Alphabet. Rose, Melanie, illus. rev. ed. 2005. (Discover Canada Province by Province Ser.). (ENG.). 40p. (J). (gr. k-5). 17.95 *(978-1-58536-263-9(8))* Sleeping Bear Pr.

ONTARIO—FICTION

Autio, Karen. Saara's Passage, 1 vol. 2009. (ENG.). 256p. (J). (gr. 4-12). pap. 10.95 *(978-1-55039-168-8(2))* Sono Nis Pr. CAN. Dist: Orca Bk. Pubs. USA.
—Sabotage, 1 vol. 2014. (ENG.). 293p. (J). (gr. 4-8). pap. 10.95 *(978-1-55039-208-1(5))* Sono Nis Pr. CAN. Dist: Orca Bk. Pubs. USA.
Awad, Shelley. The Greenhouse Kids: Dan Delion's Secret. Zonta, Rose, illus. 2009. 127p. (J). pap. *(978-0-88887-379-8(4))* Borealis Pr.
Batchelor, Rhonda. She Loves You. 2008. (ENG.). 136p. (YA). (gr. 7-8). pap. 11.99 *(978-1-55002-789-1(1),* Sandcastle Bks.) Dundurn CAN. Dist: Ingram Publisher Services.
Bell, Aaron. Jak's Story. 2010. (ENG., Illus.). 96p. (YA). (gr. 4). pap. 10.99 *(978-1-55488-710-1(0))* Dundurn CAN. Dist: Ingram Publisher Services.
Bow, James. The Young City: The Unwritten Books. 2008. (Unwritten Bks.: 3). (ENG.). 264p. (YA). (gr. 7). pap. 12.99 *(978-1-55002-846-1(4))* Dundurn CAN. Dist: Ingram Publisher Services.
Bow, Patricia. The Prism Blade. 2008. (Passage to Mythrin Ser.: 2). (ENG.). 272p. (YA). (gr. 7-12). pap. 12.99 *(978-1-55002-809-6(X),* Boardwalk Bks.) Dundurn CAN. Dist: Ingram Publisher Services.
—The Ruby Kingdom. 2007. (Passage to Mythrin Ser.: 1). (ENG.). 256p. (YA). (gr. 7). pap. 12.99 *(978-1-55002-667-2(4),* Boardwalk Bks.) Dundurn CAN. Dist: Ingram Publisher Services.
Brouwer, Sigmund. Timberwolf Chase, 1 vol. Griffiths, Dean, illus. 2006. (Orca Echoes Ser.). (ENG.). 64p. (J). (gr. 2-3). per. 6.95 *(978-1-55143-548-0(9))* Orca Bk. Pubs. USA.
Charles, Rie. No More Dragons. 2010. (ENG., Illus.). 112p. (J). (gr. 5-7). pap. 9.95 *(978-1-926607-12-2(0),* Napoleon & Co.) Dundurn CAN. Dist: Ingram Publisher Services.
Clavette, Taylor. Shapeshifter's Mark. 2012. 168p. (gr. 10-12). 22.95 *(978-1-4697-9266-8(4))*; pap. 12.95 *(978-1-4697-9264-4(8))* iUniverse, Inc.
Cliffe, Susan. Thread of Deceit, 1 vol. 2005. (ENG., Illus.). 200p. (YA). (gr. 7-12). pap. *(978-1-894549-38-7(4),* Sumach Pr.) Canadian Scholars.
Crawley, Oksanna. So, You Be Keon & I'll Be Mahovlich. 2009. 28p. pap. 13.99 *(978-1-4490-0243-5(9))* AuthorHouse.
Croza, Laurel. From There to Here, 1 vol. James, Matt, illus. 2014. (ENG.). 36p. (J). (gr. -1-2). 18.95

(978-1-55498-365-0(7)) Groundwood Bks. CAN. Dist: Publishers Group West (PGW).
Curtis, Christopher Paul. Elijah of Buxton. (ENG.). (J). (gr. 3-7). 2009. 368p. 7.99 *(978-0-439-02345-0(9)*, Scholastic Paperbacks) 2007. 352p. 16.99 *(978-0-439-02344-3(0)*, Scholastic Pr.) Scholastic, Inc.
Desclouds, Rick. My Year with the ESL Boys. 2009. 280p. pap. 22.92 *(978-1-4269-0621-3(8))* Trafford Publishing.
Donoghue, Emma. The Lotterys Plus One. Hadiiaksono, Caroline, illus. 2017. (ENG.). 320p. (J). (gr. 3-7). 17.99 *(978-0-545-92581-5(9))* Scholastic, Inc.
Doyle, Brian. Pure Spring, 1 vol. 2008. (ENG.). 160p. (J). (gr. 5-9). pap. 8.95 *(978-0-88899-775-3(2))* Groundwood Bks. CAN. Dist: Publishers Group West (PGW).
Draper, Penny. Peril at Pier Nine, 1 vol. 2007. (Disaster Strikes! Ser.: 3). (ENG.). 208p. (J). (gr. 4-7). pap. 7.95 *(978-1-55050-376-0(6))* Coteau Bks. CAN. Dist: Orca Bk. Pubs. USA.
Dublin, Anne. 44 Hours or Strike!, 1 vol. 2015. (ENG., Illus.). 112p. (J). (gr. 6-8). pap. 11.95 *(978-1-927583-76-0(4))* Second Story Pr. CAN. Dist: Orca Bk. Pubs. USA.
Etienne, Doris. Jewels of Sofia Tate. 2009. (ENG.). 272p. (J). (gr. 6). pap. 12.99 *(978-1-55488-230-4(3)*, Dundurn Pr.) Dundurn CAN. Dist: Ingram Publisher Services.
Freedman, Zelda. Rosie's Dream Cape. Bevilacqua, Silvana, illus. 2005. (ENG.). 116p. (J). pap. 6.95 *(978-1-55380-025-5(7))* Ronsdale Pr. CAN. Dist: Literary Pr. Group of Canada.
Gamble, Adam & Jasper, Mark. Good Night Toronto. Veno, Joe & Kelly, Cooper, illus. 2011. (Good Night Our World Ser.). (ENG.). 20p. (J). (gr. k — 1). bds. 9.95 *(978-1-60219-048-1(8))* Good Night Bks.
Girard, M-E. Girl Mans Up. 2016. 384p. (YA). (gr. 9). 17.99 *(978-0-06-240417-6(2)*, HarperTeen) HarperCollins Pubs.
Gromosiak, Paul. Owahonton: Maid of the Mist. 2012. (ENG.). (J). pap. 12.95 *(978-1-4675-4107-7(9))* Independent Pub.
Guest, Jacqueline & Leavey, Peggy Dymond. Growing up Ivy. 2010. (ENG.). 256p. (YA). (gr. 4-8). pap. 10.99 *(978-1-55488-723-1(2))* Dundurn CAN. Dist: Ingram Publisher Services.
Henighan, Tom. Doom Lake Holiday. 2009. (ENG.). 240p. (YA). (gr. 6). pap. 12.99 *(978-1-55002-847-8(2))* Dundurn CAN. Dist: Ingram Publisher Services.
Hill, James. Larry the Lunker. 2004. 35p. pap. 24.95 *(978-1-4137-2972-6(X))* PublishAmerica, Inc.
Hopkinson, Nalo. The Chaos. 2013. (ENG., Illus.). 256p. (YA). (gr. 9). pap. 9.99 *(978-1-4424-5926-7(3)*, McElderry, Margaret K. Bks.) McElderry, Margaret K. Bks.
Ibbitson, John. The Landing. 2008. (ENG.). 160p. (J). (gr. 7-9). 17.95 *(978-1-55453-234-6(5))*; pap. 7.95 *(978-1-55453-238-4(8))* Kids Can Pr., Ltd. CAN. Dist: Hachette Bk. Group.
Jacobs, Lily. The Littlest Bunny in Ottawa: An Easter Adventure. Dunn, Robert, illus. 2015. (ENG.). 32p. (J). (-3). 11.99 *(978-1-4926-1174-5(3)*, Sourcebooks Jabberwocky) Sourcebooks, Inc.
—The Littlest Bunny in Toronto: An Easter Adventure. Dunn, Robert, illus. 2015. (ENG.). 32p. (J). (-3). 11.99 *(978-1-4926-1213-1(8)*, Sourcebooks Jabberwocky) Sourcebooks, Inc.
James, Eric. A Halloween Scare in Ottawa. Le Ray, Marina, illus. 2015. (ENG.). 32p. (J). (-5). 11.99 *(978-1-4926-2394-6(6)*, 9781492623946, Sourcebooks Jabberwocky) Sourcebooks, Inc.
—A Halloween Scare in Toronto. Le Ray, Marina, illus. 2015. (ENG.). 32p. (J). (-5). 11.99 *(978-1-4926-2403-5(9)*, 9781492624035, Sourcebooks Jabberwocky) Sourcebooks, Inc.
Jocelyn, Marthe. Mable Riley: A Reliable Record of Humdrum, Peril, & Romance. 2007. 279p. (gr. 4-7). 17.00 *(978-0-7569-8183-9(2))* Perfection Learning Corp.
Johnston, E. K. Exit, Pursued by a Bear. 2016. (ENG.). 256p. (YA). (gr. 9). 17.99 *(978-1-101-99458-0(4)*, Dutton Books for Young Readers) Penguin Young Readers Group.
Johnston, Julie. A Very Fine Line. (ENG.). 208p. (gr. 5). 2008. (YA). pap. 10.95 *(978-0-88776-829-3(6))* 2006. (J). 18.95 *(978-0-88776-746-3(X))* Tundra Bks. CAN. (Tundra Bks.). Dist: Penguin Random Hse. LLC.
Kerbel, Deborah. Lure. 2010. (ENG.). 200p. (YA). (gr. 9). pap. 12.99 *(978-1-55488-754-5(2))* Dundurn CAN. Dist: Ingram Publisher Services.
Koehler, Hanne Lore & Laraya-Coutts, Corie. A Tale of a Malipayon Warrior. 2010. 128p. 21.95 *(978-1-4502-1344-8(8))*; pap. 11.95 *(978-1-4502-1346-2(4))* iUniverse, Inc.
Leznoff, Glenda. Heartache & Other Natural Shocks. 2015. (ENG., Illus.). 382p. (YA). (gr. 9). 19.99 *(978-1-77049-836-5(2)*, Tundra Bks.) Tundra Bks. CAN. Dist: Penguin Random Hse. LLC.
Lo, Catherine. How It Ends. 2016. (ENG.). 304p. (YA). (gr. 9). 17.99 *(978-0-544-54006-4(9)*, HMH Books For Young Readers) Houghton Mifflin Harcourt Publishing Co.
MacDonald, Frances. The Screaming Tunnel. 2012. (ENG.). 140p. (YA). pap. 15.99 *(978-1-926780-23-8(X))* Key Publishing Hse., Inc., The CAN. Dist: Bookmasters Distribution.
MacGregor, Roy. The Ghost of the Stanley Cup. 2013. (Screech Owls Ser.). (ENG.). 176p. (J). (gr. 4-7). pap. 8.99 *(978-1-77049-416-9(2)*, Tundra Bks.) Tundra Bks. CAN. Dist: Penguin Random Hse. LLC.
—Peril at the World's Biggest Hockey Tournament. 2008. (ENG.). 160p. (YA). (gr. 3-7). mass mkt. 6.99 *(978-0-7710-5607-9(9)*, Screech Owls) McClelland & Stewart CAN. Dist: Penguin Random Hse. LLC.
Malik, Katherine. Giselle's Magical World, 1 vol. 2009. 150p. pap. 24.95 *(978-1-4489-1902-4(9))* America Star Bks.
Martin, Mary. Grandma's Goose. Hoover, Charity, illus. 2012. 188p. *(978-0-7399-2452-5(4))* Rod & Staff Pubs., Inc.
Maruno, Jennifer. Cherry Blossom Winter. 2012. (Cherry Blossom Book Ser.: 2). (ENG.). 176p. (J). pap. 9.99 *(978-1-4597-0211-0(5))* Dundurn CAN. Dist: Ingram Publisher Services.
—Cherry Blossom Winter. 2013. 208p. pap. *(978-1-4596-6307-7(1))* ReadHowYouWant.com, Ltd.
—When the Cherry Blossoms Fell. 2009. (Cherry Blossom Book Ser.: 1). (ENG.). 144p. (J). (gr. 4-7). pap. 9.95 *(978-1-894917-83-4(9)*, Napoleon & Co.) Dundurn CAN. Dist: Ingram Publisher Services.
Matthews, Curtis. Boots Meets the Grizzly Bears. 2007. 164p. per. 13.95 *(978-1-4343-3372-8(8))* AuthorHouse.
McClintock, Norah. From the Dead, 1 vol. 2014. (Seven Sequels Ser.). (ENG., Illus.). 288p. (J). (gr. 5-10). pap. 10.95 *(978-1-4598-0537-8(2))* Orca Bk. Pubs. USA.
McFarlane, Leslie. McGonigle Scores! 2006. (ENG.). 256p. (J). pap. 9.95 *(978-1-55263-834-7(0))* Leaf Storm Pr.
McNamee, Graham. Bonechiller. 2012. (ENG.). 304p. (YA). (gr. 7). pap. 9.99 *(978-0-307-97593-5(2)*, Ember) Random Hse. Children's Bks.
McNaughton, Janet. To Dance at the Palais Royale. 2006. (ENG.). 252p. (J). mass mkt. 6.99 *(978-0-00-639541-6(4)*, Harper Trophy) HarperCollins Pubs.
Milord, Susan. The Ghost on the Hearth. Dabcovich, Lydia, illus. 2003. (Vermont Folklife Center Children's Book Ser.). (ENG.). 32p. (J). (gr. -1-3). 15.95 *(978-0-916718-18-3(2))* Vermont Folklife Ctr.
Montague, Gay & Wise, Erin. Peace Is a Bright Delight. 2008. 28p. pap. 13.99 *(978-1-4389-2153-2(5))* AuthorHouse.
Montgomery, L. M. Jane of Lantern Hill. 2014. (ENG.). 272p. (YA). (gr. 5-12). pap. 11.99 *(978-1-4022-8930-9(8))* Sourcebooks, Inc.
Norman, C. S. The Lockview Logans: Fire One. 2012. 316p. (gr. 4-6). pap. 18.95 *(978-1-4697-9840-0(9))* iUniverse, Inc.
Peacock, Shane. Double You, 1 vol. 2014. (Seven Sequels Ser.). (ENG., Illus.). 272p. (J). (gr. 5-10). pap. 10.95 *(978-1-4598-0534-7(8))* Orca Bk. Pubs. USA.
Pearce, Jacqueline. Siege, 1 vol. 2014. (Orca Currents Ser.). (ENG.). 136p. (J). (gr. 5-9). pap. 9.95 *(978-1-4598-0751-8(0))* Orca Bk. Pubs. USA.
Pearl, Beverly. Poison Ivy. 2008. 98p. pap. 9.99 *(978-1-4357-1386-4(9))* Lulu Pr., Inc.
—Poison Ivy, the Pocket Book. 2008. 105p. pap. 14.95 *(978-1-4357-2328-3(7))* Lulu Pr., Inc.
Pollock, Beth. Harley's Gift, 1 vol. 2007. (Lorimer Streetlights Ser.). (ENG.). 128p. (J). (gr. 2-5). 7.95 *(978-1-55028-992-3(6)*, 9781550289923) Lorimer, James & Co., Ltd., Pubs. CAN. Dist: Casemate Pubs. & Bk. Distributors, LLC.
Posesorski, Sherie. Escape Plans. Pearcey, Dawn, illus. 2005. 272p. (J). (gr. 5). 8.95 *(978-1-55050-177-3(1))* Coteau Bks. CAN. Dist: Fitzhenry & Whiteside, Ltd.
Radford, Heather. The Asquinn Twins: Frontier Life. Oakley, Darlene, ed. 2012. 104p. *(978-1-77097-693-1(0))*; pap. *(978-1-77097-694-8(9))* FriesenPress.
Ridge, Yolanda. Road Block, 1 vol. 2012. (Orca Young Readers Ser.). (ENG.). 168p. (J). (gr. 3-6). pap. 7.95 *(978-1-4598-0045-8(1))* Orca Bk. Pubs. USA.
Scrimger, Richard. The Wolf & Me, 1 vol. 2014. (Seven Sequels Ser.). (ENG., Illus.). 256p. (J). (gr. 5-10). pap. 10.95 *(978-1-4598-0531-6(3))* Orca Bk. Pubs. USA.
Shawyer, Jo. Legend of the Paymaster's Gold. 2012. (ENG., Illus.). 136p. (YA). (gr. 6). pap. 12.99 *(978-1-55488-990-7(1)*, 9781554889907) Dundurn CAN. Dist: Ingram Publisher Services.
Sherrard, Valerie. Watcher. 2009. (ENG.). 224p. (YA). (gr. 6-18). pap. 10.99 *(978-1-55488-431-5(4)*, Dundurn Pr.) Dundurn CAN. Dist: Ingram Publisher Services.
Silvano, Wendi. Love Is All Around Ottawa. Czernichowska, Joanna, illus. 2016. (ENG.). 32p. (J). (-6). 12.99 *(978-1-4926-2953-5(7)*, Sourcebooks Jabberwocky) Sourcebooks, Inc.
—Love Is All Around Toronto. Czernichowska, Joanna, illus. 2016. (ENG.). 32p. (J). (-6). 12.99 *(978-1-4926-2966-5(9)*, Sourcebooks Jabberwocky) Sourcebooks, Inc.
Smallman, Steve. Santa Is Coming to Toronto. Dunn, Robert, illus. 2012. (ENG.). 32p. (J). (-3). 9.99 *(978-1-4022-7521-0(8)*, Sourcebooks Jabberwocky) Sourcebooks, Inc.
Staunton, Ted. Coda, 1 vol. 2014. (Seven Sequels Ser.). (ENG., Illus.). 224p. (J). (gr. 5-10). pap. 10.95 *(978-1-4598-0549-1(6))* Orca Bk. Pubs. USA.
—Jump Cut, 1 vol. 2012. (Seven (the Series) Ser.). (ENG., Illus.). 232p. (J). (gr. 5-10). pap. 9.95 *(978-1-55469-947-6(9))* Orca Bk. Pubs. USA.
Stevenson, Steve. The Heist at Niagara Falls. Turconi, Stefano, illus. 2013. (Agatha: Girl of Mystery Ser.: 4). (ENG.). 144p. (J). (gr. 2-5). 6.99 *(978-0-448-46221-9(4)*, Grosset & Dunlap) Penguin Young Readers Group.
—The Heist at Niagara Falls. 2013. (Agatha Girl of Mystery Ser.: 4). lib. bdg. 16.00 *(978-0-606-32128-0(4)*, Turtleback) Turtleback Bks.
Stinson, Kathy. One Year Commencing. 2006. (ENG.). 152p. pap. 11.95 *(978-1-895449-65-5(0))* Thistledown Pr., Ltd. CAN. Dist: Univ. of Toronto Pr.
Sutherland, Suzanne. When We Were Good, 1 vol. 2013. (ENG.). 240p. (YA). (gr. 9-12). pap. *(978-1-927513-11-8(1)*, Sumach Pr.) Canadian Scholars.
Taylor, Drew Hayden. The Night Wanderer: A Native Gothic Novel. Wyatt, Michael, illus. 2007. (ENG.). 228p. (YA). (gr. 7-12). 21.95 *(978-1-55451-100-6(3)*, 9781554511006); 5th ed. pap. 12.95 *(978-1-55451-099-3(6)*, 9781554510993) Annick Pr., Ltd. CAN. Dist: Publishers Group West (PGW).
Towell, Ann. Grease Town. 2010. (ENG.). 240p. (YA). (gr. 5-9). 17.95 *(978-0-88776-983-2(7)*, Tundra Bks.) Tundra Bks. CAN. Dist: Penguin Random Hse. LLC.
Vandervelde, Beatrice. Home Ice, 1 vol. 2004. (Lorimer Sports Stories Ser.: 76). (ENG.). 104p. (J). (gr. 4-8). 16.95 *(978-1-55028-863-6(6)*, 9781550288636) Lorimer, James & Co., Ltd., Pubs. CAN. Dist: Casemate Pubs. & Bk. Distributors, LLC.
Walmsley, Tom. Kid Stuff: A Novel. 2004. (ENG.). 288p. 17.95 *(978-1-55152-153-4(9)*, 187) Arsenal Pulp Pr. CAN. Dist: Consortium Bk. Sales & Distribution.
Westley, William. Charlie & Crow. 2011. 66p. 24.99 *(978-1-4628-6802-5(9))*; pap. 15.99 *(978-1-4628-6801-8(0))* Xlibris Corp.
Wilson, David. The Adventures of Jack Bennett Winter Rescue. 2013. 116p. pap. *(978-0-9919509-0-4(9))* Wilson, David.
Wilson, John. Broken Arrow, 1 vol. 2014. (Seven Sequels Ser.). (ENG., Illus.). 240p. (J). (gr. 5-10). pap. 10.95 *(978-1-4598-0540-8(2))* Orca Bk. Pubs. USA.
—Ghosts of James Bay. 2nd ed. 2009. (ENG.). 128p. (J). (gr. 6). pap. 11.99 *(978-1-55002-827-0(8)*, Sandcastle Bks.) Dundurn CAN. Dist: Ingram Publisher Services.
Wishinsky, Frieda. Stop That Stagecoach! Eid, Jean-Paul & Owlkids Books Inc. Staff, illus. 2009. (Canadian Flyer Adventures Ser.: 13). (ENG.). 96p. (J). (gr. 1-4). pap. 7.95 *(978-1-897349-63-2(7)*, Maple Tree Pr.) Owlkids Bks. Inc. CAN. Dist: Publishers Group West (PGW).
Young, Jennifer Hayman. Aliens, Eh!. 2011. 248p. (gr. 4-6). pap. 16.95 *(978-1-4620-0588-8(8))* iUniverse, Inc.

OPERA

see also Ballet

Battaglia, Stephen. Mr. Mcsymphony's It's All about Opera. 2008. (ENG.). 30p. pap. 9.99 *(978-1-4196-8091-5(9))* CreateSpace Independent Publishing Platform.
Cohan, George M. & Schwaeber, Barbie. Give My Regards to Broadway. Newsom, Carol, illus. 2008. (American Favorites Ser.). (ENG.). 32p. (J). (gr. -1-3). 8.95 *(978-1-59249-727-0(6))*; 14.95 *(978-1-59249-726-3(8))* Soundprints.
Dunn, Mary R. I Want to Be in Musicals. 2009. (Dream Jobs Ser.). 24p. (gr. 2-3). 42.50 *(978-1-61512-215-8(X)*, PowerKids Pr.); (Illus.). (YA). lib. bdg. 22.60 *(978-1-4042-4470-2(0))* Rosen Publishing Group, Inc., The.
Dunn, Mary R. & Alamán, Eduardo. Quiero Trabajar en Los Musicales. 2009. (Trabajos de ensueño (Dream Jobs) Ser.). (SPA.). 24p. pap. 8.25 *(978-1-4358-3435-4(6))*; (Illus.). (J). (gr. 2-4). lib. bdg. 22.60 *(978-1-4042-8153-0(3))* Rosen Publishing Group, Inc., The. (PowerKids Pr.).
Kushner, Tony. Brundibar. Sendak, Maurice, illus. 2003. (ENG.). 56p. (J). (gr. -1-17). 24.99 *(978-0-7868-0904-2(3)*, di Capua, Michael Bks.) Hyperion Bks. for Children.
Lindsay, Liddy. Opera a to Z: A Beginner's Guide to Opera. 2013. (ENG., Illus.). 60p. (J). pap. 24.95 *(978-0-9854248-3-1(4))* Pinwheel Bks.
Raum, Elizabeth. Song & Dance: A Journey Through Musical Theater. 2010. (Culture in Action Ser.). (ENG.). 32p. (gr. 3-6). 30.65 *(978-1-4109-3921-0(9)*, NA-r) Heinemann-Raintree.
Riggs, Kate. Opera Music. 2008. (World of Music Ser.). (Illus.). 24p. (J). (gr. -1). lib. bdg. 24.25 *(978-1-58341-568-9(8)*, Creative Education) Creative Co., The.
Walker, Geof. William Shakespeare's 'the Tempest' - a playscript for younger Students. 2006. 40p. pap. 19.46 *(978-1-4116-7138-6(4))* Lulu Pr., Inc.
—William Shakespeare's 'Twelfth Night' - a playscript for younger Students. 2006. 52p. pap. 19.51 *(978-1-4116-7137-9(6))* Lulu Pr., Inc.

OPERA—FICTION

Amaury. The Phantom of the Opera: Based on the Novel by Gaston Leroux. Rosner, Gillian, tr. Druvert, Hélène, illus. 2016. (ENG.). 40p. (J). (gr. 2). 19.95 *(978-1-4197-2086-4(4)*, Abrams Bks. for Young Readers) Abrams, Inc.
Brian, Janeen. Cat-Astrophe at the Opera, 1 vol. rev. ed. 2013. (Fiction Readers Ser.). (ENG., Illus.). 28p. (J). (gr. 3-3). pap. 8.99 *(978-1-4333-5597-4(3))* Shell Educational Publishing.
—Cat-Astrpohe at the Opera. rev. ed. 2013. (Fiction Readers Ser.). (ENG., Illus.). 28p. (gr. 3-3). pap. 19.96 *(978-1-4807-1719-0(3))* Teacher Created Materials, Inc.
Clement, Gary. The Great Poochini. 2004. (J). (gr. 1-4). spiral bd. *(978-0-616-03027-1(4))* Canadian National Institute for the Blind/Institut National Canadien pour les Aveugles.
Fleming, Candace. Westward Ho, Carlotta! Catrow, David, illus. 2009. (ENG.). 36p. (J). (gr. -1-2). 10.99 *(978-1-4424-0218-8(0)*, Atheneum Bks. for Young Readers) Simon & Schuster Children's Publishing.
Francis, Pauline, retold by. The Phantom of the Opera. 2010. (Essential Classics - Horror Ser.). (Illus.). 56p. pap. *(978-0-237-54095-1(9))* Evans Brothers, Ltd.
Howard, A. G. RoseBlood. 2017. (ENG.). (gr. 8-17). 400p. (J). pap. 8.95 ***(978-1-4197-2342-1(1))***; 432p. (YA). 18.95 *(978-1-4197-1909-7(2)*, Amulet Bks.) Abrams, Inc.
—RoseBlood. 2018. lib. bdg. 20.85 ***(978-0-606-40729-8(4))*** Turtleback Bks.
Husain, Shahrukh & Barefoot Books. Barefoot Books Stories from the Opera. Mayhew, James, illus. 2015. 96p. (J). (gr. 2-6). 16.99 *(978-1-78285-253-7(0))* Barefoot Bks., Inc.
Huser, Glen. The Golden Touch, 1 vol. Béha, Philippe, illus. 2015. (ENG.). 64p. (J). (gr. 1-6). 18.00 *(978-1-896580-73-9(4))* Tradewind Bks. CAN. Dist: Orca Bk. Pubs. USA.
Knighton, Kate, retold by. Phantom of the Opera. 2008. (Young Reading Series 2 Gift Bks). 64p. (J). 8.99 *(978-0-7945-2082-3(0)*, Usborne) EDC Publishing.
Rigby Education Staff. The Night Out. (Sails Literacy Ser.). (Illus.). 16p. (gr. 2-3). 27.00 *(978-0-7635-9952-2(2)*, 699522C99) Rigby Education.
Thomas, Novene. The Enchanted Opera: Supernaturally Enchanting & Spiritually Enlightening. 2013. 192p. pap. 13.95 *(978-1-62212-986-7(5)*, Strategic Bk. Publishing) Strategic Book Publishing & Rights Agency (SBPRA).
Turnbull, Ann. Mary Ann & Miss Mozart. 2009. (Historical House Ser.). 166p. (YA). (gr. 5-18). pap. 5.99 *(978-0-7945-2332-9(3)*, Usborne) EDC Publishing.

OPERA HOUSES

see Theaters

OPERAS—STORIES, PLOTS, ETC.

Balfe, Roberta Rymer, et al. A Young Person's Introduction to the Arts Featuring the Opera La Cenerentola (Cinderella) by Gioachino [sic] Rossini: Music, Drama, Language, Costumes, Games, Puzzles. 2008. (Illus.). 24p. (J). *(978-0-9785364-0-4(1))* Young Patronesses of the Opera, The.
Bredin, Henrietta & McEwen, Priscilla. The Prince & the Goosegirl: A Story with Activities Based on the Opera by Humperdinck. 2006. (Illus.). 30p. (J). (gr. k-4). reprint ed. pap. 17.00 *(978-1-4223-5538-1(1))* DIANE Publishing Co.
Husain, Shahrukh & Mayhew, James. The Barefoot Book of Stories from the Opera. 2007. (ENG., Illus.). 80p. (J). pap. 16.99 *(978-1-84686-098-0(9))* Barefoot Bks., Inc.
Teis, Kyra, adapted by. The Magic Flute: An Opera by Mozart, 1 vol. 2008. (ENG., Illus.). 32p. (J). (gr. k-9). 17.95 *(978-1-59572-058-0(8))* Star Bright Bks., Inc.

OPIATES

see Narcotics

OPINION, PUBLIC

see Public Opinion

OPOSSUMS

Berne, Emma Carlson. Opossums. 2014. (Scavengers: Eating Nature's Trash Ser.). (Illus.). 24p. (J). (gr. k-5). lib. bdg. 23.60 *(978-1-4777-6602-6(2)*, PowerKids Pr.) Rosen Publishing Group, Inc., The.
Doudna, Kelly. It's a Baby Opossum!, 1 vol. 2008. (Baby Mammals Ser.). (ENG., Illus.). 24p. (J). (gr. k-3). lib. bdg. 24.21 *(978-1-60453-028-5(6))* ABDO Publishing Co.
Dunn, Mary R. Opossums, 1 vol. 2011. (Nocturnal Animals Ser.). (ENG., 24p. (gr. k-1). Illus.). pap. 7.29 *(978-1-4296-6192-8(5))*; pap. 41.70 *(978-1-4296-6361-8(8))* Capstone Press of Coughlan Cos. (Pebble Plus).
Green, Emily. Opossums. 2011. (Backyard Wildlife Ser.). (ENG., Illus.). 24p. (J). (gr. k-3). lib. bdg. 25.95 *(978-1-60014-561-2(2)*, Blastoff! Readers) Bellwether Media.
—Opossums. 2011. (Backyard Wildlife Ser.). 24p. (J). (gr. k-1). lib. bdg. 22.00 *(978-0-531-20137-4(6)*, Children's Pr.) Scholastic Library Publishing.
Kenney, Karen. Sugar Glider. 2015. (ENG.). 32p. (gr. 3-6). 32.79 *(978-1-63430-436-8(5))* Rourke Educational Media.
Kissock, Heather. Opossums. 2016. (J). ***(978-1-4896-5396-3(1))*** Weigl Pubs., Inc.
Linde, Barbara M. The Life Cycle of an Opossum. 2011. (Nature's Life Cycles Ser.). (Illus.). 24p. (J). (gr. 2-5). pap. 8.15 *(978-1-4339-4680-6(7))*; lib. bdg. 22.60 *(978-1-4339-4679-0(3))* Stevens, Gareth Publishing LLLP. (Gareth Stevens Learning Library).
Macken, JoAnn Early. Opossums. 2nd rev. ed. 2009. (Animals That Live in the Forest Ser.). (ENG.). 24p. (J). (gr. -1-3). pap. 8.15 *(978-1-4339-2481-1(1))*; lib. bdg. 22.60 *(978-1-4339-2405-7(6))* Stevens, Gareth Publishing LLLP.
—Opossums/Zarigüeyas. 2nd rev. ed. 2009. (Animals That Live in the Forest/Animales del bosque Ser.). 24p. (J). (gr. -1-3). (SPA & ENG.). pap. 8.15 *(978-1-4339-2488-0(9))*; (ENG & SPA.). lib. bdg. 22.60 *(978-1-4339-2437-8(4))* Stevens, Gareth Publishing LLLP. (Weekly Reader Leveled Readers).
McGill, Jordan. Opossums. 2011. (J). *(978-1-61690-579-8(4))*; 27.13 *(978-1-61690-933-8(1))* Weigl Pubs., Inc.
Moore Niver, Heather. Opossums after Dark. 2016. (Animals of the Night Ser.). (ENG.). 32p. (J). (gr. 3-3). pap. 10.52 *(978-0-7660-7302-9(5))*; (Illus.). lib. bdg. 25.27 *(978-0-7660-7304-3(1))* Enslow Pubs., Inc.
Nichols, Catherine. Tricky Opossums. 2008. (Gross-Out Defenses Ser.). (Illus.). 24p. (J). (gr. k-3). lib. bdg. 21.28 *(978-1-59716-718-5(5))* Bearport Publishing Co., Inc.
Petrie, Kristin. Sugar Gliders, 1 vol. 2012. (Unique Pets Ser.). (ENG.). 24p. (J). (gr. 3-6). lib. bdg. 25.65 *(978-1-61783-443-1(2)*, Checkerboard Library) ABDO Publishing Co.
Quinlivan, Ada. Opossums. 2016. (Creatures of the Forest Habitat Ser.). 00024p. (J). (gr. 3-3). 23.60 *(978-1-4994-2928-2(2)*, PowerKids Pr.) Rosen Publishing Group, Inc., The.
Schuh, Mari. Opossums. 2016. (My First Animal Library). 24p. (J). (gr. k-2). lib. bdg. 25.65 *(978-1-62031-289-6(1)*, Bullfrog Bks.) Jump! Inc.
Tatlock, Ann. Backyard Jungle Safari Opossums: Opossums. 2015. (ENG., Illus.). 32p. (J). 26.50 *(978-1-62469-100-3(5))* Purple Toad Publishing, Inc.
Terhune, Charlotte. There's a Possum in the Pillows. 2005. (Illus.). 14p. (J). 12.00 *(978-0-9764893-1-3(7))* Where-I-Live / Foster Pr.
Walker, Sally M. Opossums. 2008. (Early Bird Nature Bks.). (ENG., Illus.). 48p. (J). (gr. 2-5). lib. bdg. 26.60 *(978-0-8225-3055-8(4))* Lerner Publishing Group.
Webster, Christine. Opossums. (J). 2012. *(978-1-61913-264-1(8))* 2012. *(978-1-61913-067-8(X))* 2007. (Illus.). 24p. (gr. -1-3). lib. bdg. 24.45 *(978-1-59036-677-6(8))* Weigl Pubs., Inc.
—Opossums. Hudak, Heather C., ed. 2007. (Backyard Animals Ser.). (Illus.). 24p. (J). (gr. -1-3). pap. 8.95 *(978-1-59036-678-3(6))* Weigl Pubs., Inc.
Whitehouse, Patricia. La Zarigüeya, 1 vol. 2010. (¿Qué Está Despierto? Ser.). (SPA.). 24p. (gr. k-2). 23.32 *(978-1-4329-4207-6(7))*; pap. 6.79 *(978-1-4329-4216-8(6))* Heinemann-Raintree.

OPOSSUMS—FICTION

Ballard, John E. & Shiply, Lyn. What Is That Sound! 2011. 40p. pap. 24.95 *(978-1-4560-0988-5(5))* America Star Bks.
Bannister, Barbara. Possum's Three Fine Friends. Baron, Kathy, illus. 2006. (ENG.). 32p. (J). pap. 9.95 *(978-1-57874-096-3(7)*, Kaeden Bks.) Kaeden Corp.
Berkes, Marianne. Anybody Home?, 1 vol. Dickinson, Rebecca, illus. 2013. (ENG.). 32p. (J). (gr. -1-3). 17.95 *(978-1-60718-618-2(7)*, 9781607186182); pap. 9.95 *(978-1-60718-630-4(6))* Arbordale Publishing.
—Hay Alguien en Casa?, 1 vol. Dickinson, Rebecca, illus. 2013. (SPA.). 32p. (J). (gr. -1-3). 17.95 *(978-1-60718-714-1(0))* Arbordale Publishing.
Blom, Jen K. Possum Summer. Rayyan, Omar, illus. 2011. (ENG.). 256p. (J). (gr. 3-7). 17.95 *(978-0-8234-2331-6(X))* Holiday Hse., Inc.
Bogue, Gary. There's an Opossum in My Backyard. Todd, Chuck, illus. 2007. 40p. (J). (gr. -1-3). 15.95 *(978-1-59714-059-1(7))* Heyday.
Burgess, Thornton W. The Adventures of Unc' Billy Possum. 2007. 140p. (gr. 4-7). per. 13.95 *(978-1-60312-337-2(7))*; 24.95 *(978-1-60312-675-5(9))* Aegypan.
—The Adventures of Unc' Billy Possum. (J). 18.95 *(978-0-8488-0382-7(5))* Amereon Ltd.
—The Adventures of Unc' Billy Possum. Cady, Harrison & Stewart, Pat Ronson, trs. Cady, Harrison & Stewart, Pat Ronson, illus. 2003. (Dover Children's Thrift Classics Ser.). (ENG.). 96p. (J). (gr. 3-8). pap. 3.00 *(978-0-486-43031-7(6))* Dover Pubns., Inc.
—The Adventures of Unc' Billy Possum. 2011. 140p. 24.95 *(978-1-4638-9563-1(1))* Rodgers, Alan Bks.
Chaconas, Dori. The Babysitters. McCue, Lisa, illus. 2014. (Cork & Fuzz Ser.: 6). (ENG.). 32p. (J). (gr. 1-3). pap. 3.99 *(978-0-448-48050-3(6)*, Penguin Young Readers) Penguin Young Readers Group.
—The Collectors, 4 vols. McCue, Lisa, illus. 2010. (Cork & Fuzz Ser.: 4). (ENG.). 32p. (J). (gr. 1-3). mass mkt. 3.99

M
N
O

(978-0-14-241714-0(9), Penguin Young Readers) Penguin Young Readers Group.

—Cork & Fuzz. McCue, Lisa, illus. 2005. (Cork & Fuzz Ser.: 1). (ENG.). 32p. (J). (gr. 1-3). 13.99 *(978-0-670-03602-8(1)*, Viking Books for Young Readers) Penguin Young Readers Group.

—Finders Keepers, 5 vols. McCue, Lisa, illus. 2011. (Cork & Fuzz Ser.: 5). (ENG.). 32p. (J). (gr. 1-3). mass mkt. 3.99 *(978-0-14-241869-7(2)*, Penguin Young Readers) Penguin Young Readers Group.

—Good Sports. McCue, Lisa, illus. 2010. (Cork & Fuzz Ser.: 3). (ENG.). 32p. (J). (gr. 1-3). mass mkt. 3.99 *(978-0-14-241713-3(0)*, Penguin Young Readers) Penguin Young Readers Group.

—Merry Merry Holly Holly. McCue, Lisa, illus. 2015. (Cork & Fuzz Ser.: 11). (ENG.). 32p. (J). (gr. -1-k). 16.99 *(978-0-451-47501-5(1)*, Viking Books for Young Readers) Penguin Young Readers Group.

—Short & Tall No. 2, 2 vols. McCue, Lisa, illus. 2010. (Cork & Fuzz Ser.: 2). (ENG.). 32p. (J). (gr. 1-3). mass mkt. 3.99 *(978-0-14-241594-8(4)*, Penguin Young Readers) Penguin Young Readers Group.

—Swimming Lesson, 7 vols. McCue, Lisa, illus. 2011. (Cork & Fuzz Ser.: 7). (ENG.). 32p. (J). (gr. 1-3). 13.99 *(978-0-670-01281-7(5)*, Viking Books for Young Readers) Penguin Young Readers Group.

—The Swimming Lesson. McCue, Lisa, illus. 2014. (Cork & Fuzz Ser.: 7). (ENG.). 32p. (J). (gr. 1-3). pap. 3.99 *(978-0-448-48051-0(4)*, Penguin Young Readers) Penguin Young Readers Group.

Chaconas, Dori & Bader, Bonnie. Spring Cleaning. McCue, Lisa, illus. 2015. (Cork & Fuzz Ser.: 10). (ENG.). 32p. (J). (gr. 1-3). 14.99 *(978-0-670-01686-0(1)*, Penguin Young Readers) Penguin Young Readers Group.

—Wait a Minute. McCue, Lisa, illus. 2015. (Cork & Fuzz Ser.: 9). (ENG.). 32p. (J). (gr. 1-3). 3.99 *(978-0-14-750856-0(8)*, Penguin Young Readers) Penguin Young Readers Group.

Collins, Nafessa. Mrs. Precious & the Possum. 2012. 56p. (gr. -1). pap. 8.95 *(978-1-4759-1273-9(0))* iUniverse, Inc.

deGroat, Diane. Ants in Your Pants, Worms in Your Plants! Gilbert Goes Green. deGroat, Diane, illus. 2011. (Gilbert Ser.). (ENG., Illus.). 32p. (J). (gr. -1-3). 16.99 *(978-0-06-176511-7(2))* HarperCollins Pubs.

—Gilbert & the Lost Tooth. deGroat, Diane, illus. 2012. (I Can Read Level 2 Ser.). (ENG., Illus.). 32p. (J). (gr. k-3). 16.99 *(978-0-06-125214-3(X))*; pap. 3.99 *(978-0-06-125216-7(6))* HarperCollins Pubs.

—Gilbert, the Surfer Dude. deGroat, Diane, illus. 2010. (I Can Read Level 2 Ser.). (ENG., Illus.). 32p. (J). (gr. k-3). pap. 3.99 *(978-0-06-125213-6(1))* HarperCollins Pubs.

—Gilbert, the Surfer Dude. 2009. (Illus.). 31p. (J). lib. bdg. 18.89 *(978-0-06-125212-9(3))* HarperCollins Pubs.

—Last One in Is a Rotten Egg! deGroat, Diane, illus. 2011. (Gilbert Ser.). (ENG., Illus.). 32p. (J). (gr. -1-3). pap. 6.99 *(978-0-06-089296-8(X))* HarperCollins Pubs.

Desmet, Sara. Scared Silly. Desmet, Sara, illus. 2006. (Illus.). 32p. (J). (gr. -1-3). 15.95 *(978-1-60108-009-7(3))* Red Cygnet Pr.

Emerson, Carl. Opie the Opossum Wakes Up, 1 vol. Trover, Zachary, illus. 2007. (Animal Underdogs Ser.). (ENG.). 32p. (gr. -1-4). 28.50 *(978-1-60270-017-8(6)*, Looking Glass Library) ABDO Publishing Co.

Hinchcliffe, L. T. For the Love of Prudence Possum. 2008. 76p. pap. 15.50 *(978-1-60693-136-3(9)*, Eloquent Bks.) Strategic Book Publishing & Rights Agency (SBPRA).

Holtam, Elizabeth T. A Possum in My Pocket. 2013. 28p. pap. 21.99 *(978-1-4797-7889-8(3))* Xlibris Corp.

Jones, Birdy. Blossom Plays Possum: (Because She's Shy) McDonnell, Janet, illus. 2017. 32p. (J). 15.95 ***(978-1-4338-2735-8(2)***, Magination Pr.) American Psychological Assn.

Kasza, Keiko. No Te Rias, Pepe. (Buenas Noches Ser.). (SPA.). (J). (gr. k-3). *(978-958-04-3623-2(1))* Norma S.A.

Landry, Leo. What's up, Chuck? 2016. (ENG., Illus.). 48p. (J). (gr. k-3). lib. bdg. 12.95 *(978-1-58089-698-6(7))* Charlesbridge Publishing, Inc.

Lang, Valerie E. Jet's Day: A Whisker Team Story. 2011. 32p. pap. 13.00 *(978-1-61204-178-0(7)*, Strategic Bk. Publishing) Strategic Book Publishing & Rights Agency (SBPRA).

Martin, Anne E. Midnight Kitties. 2007. (Illus.). 35p. (J). per. 13.99 *(978-1-59879-245-4(8))* Lifevest Publishing, Inc.

Osmond, Jimmy. The Awesome Possum Family Band. 2014. (ENG., Illus.). 40p. (J). (gr. -1-3). 16.99 *(978-1-62157-211-4(0)*, Regnery Kids) Regnery Publishing, Inc., An Eagle Publishing Co.

Salley, Coleen. Epossumondas Plays Possum. Stevens, Janet, illus. 2009. (ENG.). 40p. (J). (gr. -1-3). 17.99 *(978-0-15-206420-4(6))* Houghton Mifflin Harcourt Publishing Co.

Sanders, Cecilia. Wanted Dead or Alive. 2010. 36p. pap. 16.99 *(978-1-4520-7023-0(7))* AuthorHouse.

Sargent, Dave & Sargent, Pat. Pokey Opossum: I'm Kinda Slow, 15 vols., Vol. 18. Huff, Jeane, illus. 2nd rev. ed. 2003. (Animal Pride Ser.: 18). 42p. (J). pap. 10.95 *(978-1-56763-794-6(9))*; lib. bdg. 20.95 *(978-1-56763-793-9(0))* Ozark Publishing.

Sloan, Holly Goldberg. Appleblossom the Possum. Rosen, Gary, illus. 2015. (ENG.). 288p. (J). (gr. 3-7). 16.99 *(978-0-8037-4133-1(2)*, Dial Bks) Penguin Young Readers Group.

Tashlin, Frank. The Possum That Didn't. 2016. (ENG., Illus.). 64p. (gr. 5-5). pap. 3.99 *(978-0-486-80080-6(6))* Dover Pubns., Inc.

Tingwald, July Ann. Orrie's Christmas. Powell, James, illus. 2007. 42p. 9.00 *(978-0-9706728-5-8(3))* New Millenium Pr., The.

Walker, Sally M. Opossum at Sycamore Road. Snyder, Joel, illus. 2011. (Smithsonian's Backyard Ser.). (ENG.). 32p. (J). (gr. -1-3). 8.95 *(978-1-60727-640-1(2))* Soundprints.

Weston Woods Staff, *creator*. Possum Magic. 2011. 18.95 *(978-0-545-08634-9(5))*; 38.75 *(978-0-545-14784-2(0))* Weston Woods Studios, Inc.

OPPENHEIMER, J. ROBERT, 1904-1967

Allman, Toney. J. Robert Oppenheimer: Theoretical Physicist, Atomic Pioneer. 2005. (Giants of Science Ser.). (ENG., Illus.). 64p. (J). (gr. 3-7). lib. bdg. 28.35 *(978-1-56711-889-6(5)*, Blackbirch Pr., Inc.) Cengage Gale.

Scherer, Glenn & Fletcher, Marty. J. Robert Oppenheimer: The Brain Behind the Bomb. 2007. (Inventors Who Changed the World Ser.). (Illus.). 128p. (J). (gr. 5-9). lib. bdg. 34.60 *(978-1-59845-050-7(6)*, MyReportLinks.com Bks.) Enslow Pubs., Inc.

OPPOSITES

see Polarity

OPTICAL ILLUSIONS

Cobb, Vicki. On Stage. 2008. pap. 52.95 *(978-0-8225-9450-5(1))* Lerner Publishing Group.

—On Stage. Gold, Michael, photos by. 2005. (Where's the Science Here? Ser.). (ENG., Illus.). 48p. (gr. 3-5). lib. bdg. 23.93 *(978-0-7613-2774-5(6)*, Millbrook Pr.) Lerner Publishing Group.

Dorling Kindersley Publishing Staff. Optical Illusions. 2012. (ENG., Illus.). 32p. (J). (gr. 2-5). 19.99 *(978-0-7566-9789-1(1)*, DK Children) Dorling Kindersley Publishing, Inc.

Einhorn, Nicholas. Stand-up Magic & Optical Illusions. 2010. (Inside Magic Ser.). (Illus.). 64p. (YA). 31.95 *(978-1-4358-9452-5(9)*, Rosen Reference) Rosen Publishing Group, Inc., The.

Gifford, Clive. Eye Benders: The Science of Seeing & Believing. 2014. (ENG.). 64p. (J). (gr. 5-9). pap. 9.99 *(978-1-4380-0366-5(8))* Barron's Educational Series, Inc.

Hanson, Anders & Mann, Elissa. Cool Optical Illusions: Creative Activities That Make Math & Science Fun for Kids!, 1 vol. 2013. (Cool Art with Math & Science Ser.). (ENG.). 32p. (J). (gr. 3-6). lib. bdg. 28.50 *(978-1-61783-822-4(5)*, Checkerboard Library) ABDO Publishing Co.

Honeycutt, Brad. Exceptional Eye Tricks. 2013. (ENG., Illus.). 128p. pap. 9.95 *(978-1-936140-73-2(X)*, Imagine Publishing) Charlesbridge Publishing, Inc.

IllusionWorks Staff. Amazing Optical Illusions. 2004. (ENG., Illus.). 32p. (J). (gr. 1-3). 16.95 *(978-1-55297-961-7(X)*, 9781552979617); pap. 6.95 *(978-1-55297-962-4(8)*, 9781552979624) Firefly Bks., Ltd.

Kay, Keith. Optical Illusions. 2007. (ENG., Illus.). 352p. (J). (gr. 3-7). pap. 6.95 *(978-1-4027-4971-1(6))* Sterling Publishing Co., Inc.

Kuskowski, Alex. Science Experiments with Sight & Sound, 1 vol. 2013. (More Super Simple Science Ser.). (ENG.). 32p. (gr. k-4). lib. bdg. 27.07 *(978-1-61783-854-5(3)*, Super SandCastle) ABDO Publishing Co.

Magic Eye, Inc. Staff. Harry Potter Magic Eye Book: 3D Magical Moments. 2011. (ENG.). 32p. 16.99 *(978-1-4494-0141-2(4))* Andrews McMeel Publishing.

Moore, Gareth. Seeing Is Believing. 2015. (Brain Benders Ser.). (ENG., Illus.). 32p. (J). (gr. 3-6). pap. 7.99 *(978-1-4677-7201-3(1)*, Lerner Pubns.) Lerner Publishing Group.

Muir, Duncan. Optical Illusions. 2003. (Knowledge Masters Ser.). (Illus.). 32p. (YA). pap. incl. cd-rom *(978-1-903954-61-4(4)*, Pavilion Children's Books) Pavilion Bks.

National Geographic Kids Staff. Look Again: Fun-Tastic Photo Puzzles for Curious Minds. 2015. (ENG., Illus.). 48p. (J). (gr. 3-7). 16.99 *(978-1-4263-2080-4(9)*, National Geographic Children's Bks.) National Geographic Society.

—What in the World? 2014. (ENG., Illus.). 48p. (J). (gr. 3-7). 16.99 *(978-1-4263-1517-6(1)*, National Geographic Children's Bks.) National Geographic Society.

—Xtreme Illusions 2. 2015. (ENG.). 48p. (J). (gr. 3-7). 16.99 *(978-1-4263-1974-7(6)*, National Geographic Children's Bks.) National Geographic Society.

Sacks, Janet. The Optical Illusion Pack. 2013. (ENG.). 36p. (J). 12.99 *(978-0-7641-6617-4(4))* Barron's Educational Series, Inc.

Taplin, Sam. Optical Illusions Tin. 2013. (Activity Tins Ser.). 80p. (J). 14.99 *(978-0-7945-3338-0(8)*, Usborne) EDC Publishing.

—50 Optical Illusions. Seckel, Al, illus. 2010. (Activity Cards Ser.). 50p. (J). 9.99 *(978-0-7945-2664-1(0)*, Usborne) EDC Publishing.

Vry, Silke. Trick of the Eye: Art & Illusion. 2010. (ENG., Illus.). 96p. (J). (gr. 1-4). 14.95 *(978-3-7913-7026-2(X))* Prestel Verlag GmbH & Co KG. DEU. Dist: Penguin Random Hse. LLC.

Wick, Walter. Optical Tricks. Wick, Walter, illus. 10th anniv. ed. 2008. (ENG., Illus.). 48p. (J). (gr. -1-3). 14.99 *(978-0-439-85520-4(9)*, Cartwheel Bks.) Scholastic, Inc.

OPTICAL MASERS

see Lasers

OPTICS

see also Color; Light; Perspective; Radiation; Vision

Bodach, Vijaya Khisty. Reflection. 2008. (Discovering & Exploring Science Ser.). (Illus.). 16p. (J). (gr. -1-3). lib. bdg. 12.95 *(978-0-7569-8428-1(9))* Perfection Learning Corp.

Boothroyd, Jennifer. Sensing Light & Sound. 2014. (First Step Nonfiction - Light & Sound Ser.). (ENG., Illus.). 24p. (gr. k-2). lib. bdg. 23.93 *(978-1-4677-3915-3(4)*, Lerner Pubns.) Lerner Publishing Group.

Brasch, Nicolas. Why Do Shadows Lengthen? 2010. (Solving Science Mysteries Ser.). (Illus.). 24p. (J). pap. 8.25 *(978-1-61531-913-8(1)*, PowerKids Pr.); (YA). (gr. 3-6). lib. bdg. 22.60 *(978-1-61531-891-9(7))* Rosen Publishing Group, Inc., The.

—Why Do Shadows Lengthen? All about Light. 2010. (Illus.). 24p. (J). 49.50 *(978-1-61531-914-5(X)*, PowerKids Pr.) Rosen Publishing Group, Inc., The.

Cobb, Allan B. Super Science Projects about Light & Optics. 2005. (Psyched for Science Ser.). (Illus.). 48p. (YA). (gr. 5-8). lib. bdg. 29.25 *(978-0-8239-3177-4(3)*, SCLIOP) Rosen Publishing Group, Inc., The.

Ferrie, Chris. Optical Physics for Babies. 2017. (J). ***(978-1-4926-5606-7(2))***; (Baby University Ser.: 0). (ENG., Illus.). 24p. bds. 9.99 ***(978-1-4926-5621-0(6)***, Sourcebooks Jabberwocky) Sourcebooks, Inc.

Fink, Charles. Light Show: Reflection & Absorption. 2009. (Amazing Science Ser.). 24p. (gr. 3-3). 42.50 *(978-1-61511-329-3(0)*, PowerKids Pr.) Rosen Publishing Group, Inc., The.

Hamilton, Gina L. Light. 2016. (J). ***(978-1-5105-2239-8(5))*** SmartBook Media, Inc.

—Light. 2008. (Science Q & A Ser.). (Illus.). 48p. (YA). (gr. 5-8). pap. 10.95 *(978-1-59036-947-0(5))*; lib. bdg. 29.05 *(978-1-59036-946-3(7))* Weigl Pubs., Inc.

—Light Q & A. 2013. (J). *(978-1-62127-415-5(2))*; pap. *(978-1-62127-421-6(7))* Weigl Pubs., Inc.

Hawkins, Jay. Bright Ideas: The Science of Light. 2013. (Big Bang Science Experiments Ser.). (ENG., Illus.). 32p. (gr. 3-6). 26.50 *(978-1-4777-0320-5(9))*; pap. 11.75 *(978-1-4777-0362-5(4))* Windmill Bks.

Hewitt, Sally. Amazing Light. 2007. (Amazing Science Ser.). (ENG.). 32p. (J). pap. *(978-0-7787-3626-4(1))* Crabtree Publishing Co.

Hughes, Susan. Is It Transparent or Opaque? 2012. (ENG., Illus.). 24p. (J). *(978-0-7787-2052-2(7))*; pap. *(978-0-7787-2059-1(4))* Crabtree Publishing Co.

Jennings, Terry. Light & Dark. 2009. (Science Alive Ser.). (Illus.). 32p. (J). (gr. 4-7). pap. *(978-1-897563-56-4(6))* Saunders Bk. Co.

Jennings, Terry J. Light & Dark. 2009. (J). 28.50 *(978-1-59920-270-9(0))* Black Rabbit Bks.

Jensen Shaffer, Jody. Vampires & Light, 6 vols. Gervasio, illus. 2013. (Monster Science Ser.). (ENG.). 32p. (gr. 3-4). 47.70 *(978-1-62065-821-5(6)*, Graphic Library) Capstone Press of Coughlan Cos.

Kenney, Karen Latchana. The Science of Color: Investigating Light, 1 vol. 2016. (Science in Action Ser.). (ENG., Illus.). 32p. (J). (gr. 3-6). 27.07 *(978-1-62403-960-7(X))* ABDO Publishing Co.

Levy, Janey. Renaissance Paintings: Using Perspective to Represent Three-Dimensional Objects. 2005. (Math for the REAL World Ser.). 32p. 47.50 *(978-1-4042-5220-2(7)*, Rosen Classroom) Rosen Publishing Group, Inc., The.

Nunn, Daniel. Shadows & Reflections, 1 vol. 2012. (Light All Around Us Ser.). (ENG.). 24p. (gr. -1-1). pap. 6.29 *(978-1-4329-6629-4(4))*; lib. bdg. 22.65 *(978-1-4329-6624-9(3))* Heinemann-Raintree. (Acorn).

O'Dea, Lori. Tools for Seeing. 2017. (Text Connections Guided Close Reading Ser.). (J). (gr. k). *(978-1-4900-1767-9(4))* Benchmark Education Co.

Richards, Roy. En Optica. (Coleccion 101 Trucos Cientificos). (SPA., Illus.). (J). (gr. 3-5). pap. *(978-950-724-175-8(2)*, LMA8751) Lumen ARG. Dist: Lectorum Pubns., Inc.

Romero, Libby. Ibn Al-Haytham. 2016. (Illus.). 48p. (J). *(978-1-4263-2616-5(5))* National Geographic Society.

—Ibn Al-Haytham: The Man Who Discovered How We See. 2016. (Readers Bios Ser.). (ENG., Illus.). 48p. (J). (gr. 1-4). pap. 3.99 *(978-1-4263-2500-7(2)*, National Geographic Children's Bks.) National Geographic Society.

Rooney, Anne. Optical Engineering & the Science of Light. 2013. (ENG.). 32p. (J). *(978-0-7787-1228-2(1))*; (Illus.). pap. *(978-0-7787-1232-9(X))* Crabtree Publishing Co.

Shaffer, Jody Jensen. Vampires & Light, 1 vol. Gervasio, illus. 2013. (Monster Science Ser.). (ENG.). 32p. (gr. 3-4). lib. bdg. 30.65 *(978-1-4296-9928-0(0)*, Graphic Library) Capstone Press of Coughlan Cos.

Spilsbury, Louise & Spilsbury, Richard. Light & Sound, 1 vol. 2013. (Essential Physical Science Ser.). (ENG.). 48p. (gr. 4-6). 33.32 *(978-1-4329-8146-4(3)*, Heinemann InfoSearch) Heinemann-Raintree.

—Reflecting Light. 2015. (Exploring Light Ser.). (ENG., Illus.). 32p. (gr. 2-4). 30.65 *(978-1-4109-7943-8(1))* Heinemann-Raintree.

Spilsbury, Richard & Spilsbury, Louise. What Is Light? Exploring Science with Hands-on Activities. 2008. (In Touch with Basic Science Ser.). (Illus.). 32p. (J). (gr. 3-4). lib. bdg. 23.94 *(978-0-7660-3097-8(0)*, Enslow Elementary) Enslow Pubs., Inc.

Strom, Laura Layton. Mirror Power. 2007. (Shockwave: Technology & Manufacturing Ser.). (ENG., Illus.). 36p. (J). (gr. 3-5). 25.00 *(978-0-531-17588-0(X)*, Children's Pr.) Scholastic Library Publishing.

Torrence, Jack. Light Show: Reflection & Absorption. 2009. (Real Life Readers Ser.). 24p. (gr. 3-4). pap. 8.25 *(978-1-4358-0096-0(6)*, Rosen Classroom) Rosen Publishing Group, Inc., The.

Tullet, Hervé. The Game of Mirrors. 2014. (ENG., Illus.). 14p. (gr. -1-17). 12.95 *(978-0-7148-6687-1(3))* Phaidon Pr., Inc.

Turner, Matt. Genius Optical Inventions: From the X-Ray to the Telescope. Conner, Sarah, illus. 2017. (Incredible Inventions Ser.). (ENG.). 32p. (J). (gr. 3-6). 26.65 ***(978-1-5124-3208-4(3))*** Lerner Publishing Group.

Walker, Sally M. Light. 2006. (Illus.). 48p. (J). pap. 8.95 *(978-0-8225-2842-5(8))* Lerner Publishing Group.

—Light. King, Andy, photos by. 2005. (Early Bird Energy Ser.). (ENG., Illus.). 48p. (gr. 2-5). lib. bdg. 26.60 *(978-0-8225-2925-5(4)*, Lerner Pubns.) Lerner Publishing Group.

Whitfield, David. Rainbows. (Sky Science (Library) Ser.). (J). 2012. (ENG., Illus.). 24p. (gr. 3-5). pap. 12.95 *(978-1-61913-546-8(9)*, 1346030, AV2 by Weigl) 2006. (Illus.). 24p. (gr. 3-7). pap. 24.45 *(978-1-59036-414-7(7))* 2006. pap. 8.95 *(978-1-59036-420-8(1))* Weigl Pubs., Inc.

Williams, Brian. The Science of a Pair of Glasses: The Science of Light. 2009. (Science of... Ser.). (Illus.). 32p. (YA). (gr. 3-6). lib. bdg. 26.00 *(978-1-4339-0044-0(0))* Stevens, Gareth Publishing LLLP.

Yasuda, Anita. Explore Light & Optics! With 25 Great Projects. Stone, Bryan, illus. 2016. (Explore Your World Ser.). (ENG.). 96p. (gr. 1-5). 19.95 *(978-1-61930-376-8(0))*; pap. 14.95 *(978-1-61930-380-5(9))* Open City Bks.

OPTICS—EXPERIMENTS

Cobb, Allan B. Super Science Projects about Light & Optics. 2005. (Psyched for Science Ser.). (Illus.). 48p. (YA). (gr. 5-8). lib. bdg. 29.25 *(978-0-8239-3177-4(3)*, SCLIOP) Rosen Publishing Group, Inc., The.

Jackson, Tom. Experiments with Light & Color. 2010. (Cool Science Ser.). (Illus.). 32p. (J). (gr. 5-6). pap. 10.50 *(978-1-4339-3454-4(X))*; lib. bdg. 28.00 *(978-1-4339-3453-7(1)*, 1309304) Stevens, Gareth Publishing LLLP. (Gareth Stevens Learning Library).

Kessler, Colleen. A Project Guide to Light & Optics. 2011. (Physical Science Projects for Kids Ser.). (Illus.). 48p. (J). (gr. 3-6). lib. bdg. 29.95 *(978-1-58415-969-8(3)*, 1327831) Mitchell Lane Pubs., Inc.

Kuskowski, Alex. Science Experiments with Sight & Sound, 1 vol. 2013. (More Super Simple Science Ser.). (ENG.). 32p. (gr. k-4). lib. bdg. 27.07 *(978-1-61783-854-5(3)*, Super SandCastle) ABDO Publishing Co.

Rau, Dana Meachen. Super Cool Science Experiments: Light. 2009. (Explorer Library: Science Explorer Ser.). (ENG., Illus.). 32p. (gr. 4-8). lib. bdg. 28.50 *(978-1-60279-531-0(2)*, 200285) Cherry Lake Publishing.

OPTIONS (FINANCE)

see Stock Exchanges

OPTOMETRY

see also Eye

Nixon, James. Optician. 2016. (ENG., Illus.). 24p. (J). (gr. k-2). 16.99 *(978-1-4451-4020-9(9)*, Franklin Watts) Hachette Children's Group GBR. Dist: Hachette Bk. Group.

ORANGES

Brannon, Cecelia H. Oranges. 2017. (All about Food Crops Ser.). 24p. (gr. k-1). lib. bdg. 22.60 ***(978-0-7660-8581-7(3))*** Enslow Pubs., Inc.

deMarin, Layne. Oranges: from Fruit to Juice. 2011. (Wonder Readers Fluent Level Ser.). (ENG.). (gr. -1-2). 16p. pap. 35.94 *(978-1-4296-8135-3(7))*; 32p. pap. 5.99 *(978-1-4296-7926-8(3))* Capstone Press of Coughlan Cos. (Wonder Readers).

Hill, Christina. Lue Gim Gong: The Citrus Wizard (Florida) 2016. (Primary Source Readers Ser.). (Illus.). 32p. (J). (gr. 4-4). pap. 8.99 *(978-1-4938-3549-2(1))* Teacher Created Materials, Inc.

Jacobson, Ryan. Orange Juice. 2016. (J). *(978-1-4896-4535-7(7))* Weigl Pubs., Inc.

—Orange Juice Before the Store. McGeehan, Dan, illus. 2012. (Before the Store Ser.). (ENG.). 32p. (J). (gr. 2-5). lib. bdg. 29.93 *(978-1-60973-678-1(8)*, 201253) Child's World, Inc., The.

Snyder, Inez. Oranges to Orange Juice: How Things Are Made. 2003. (Welcome Bks.). (ENG., Illus.). 24p. (J). (gr. -1-2). pap. 4.95 *(978-0-516-24357-3(8)*, Watts, Franklin) Scholastic Library Publishing.

Staniford, Linda. Where Does Fruit Come From? 2016. (From Farm to Fork: Where Does My Food Come From? Ser.). (ENG.). 24p. (gr. k-2). lib. bdg. 23.99 *(978-1-4846-3352-6(0))* Heinemann-Raintree.

Stockland, Patricia M. Orange, 1 vol. Woolf, Julia, illus. 2011. (Colors Set 2 Ser.). (ENG.). 24p. (gr. -1-2). 27.07 *(978-1-61641-137-4(6)*, Looking Glass Library- Nonfiction) Magic Wagon.

Turning Oranges into Juice. 2014. (Step-By-Step Transformations Ser.). 24p. (J). (gr. k-2). lib. bdg. 24.21 *(978-1-62713-016-5(0))* Cavendish Square Publishing.

ORANGUTANS

Borgert-Spaniol, Megan. Orangutans. 2013. (Animal Safari Ser.). (ENG., Illus.). 24p. (J). (gr. k-3). lib. bdg. 25.95 *(978-1-60014-913-9(8)*, Blastoff! Readers) Bellwether Media.

Bredeson, Carmen. Orangutans up Close. (Zoom in on Animals! Ser.). (Illus.). 24p. (J). 2012. (gr. k-18). pap. 7.95 *(978-1-59845-419-2(6))* 2008. (gr. 1-3). lib. bdg. 22.60 *(978-0-7660-3078-7(4))* Enslow Pubs., Inc. (Enslow Elementary).

Davis, Jill. Orangutans Are Ticklish: Fun Facts from an Animal Photographer. Grubman, Steve, photos by. 2016. (ENG., Illus.). 40p. (J). (gr. -1-2). 7.99 *(978-0-553-53393-4(2)*, Dragonfly Bks.) Random Hse. Children's Bks.

Davis, Patricia. Orangutans. 2009. (Illus.). 52p. (J). *(978-0-7172-8030-8(6))* Grolier, Ltd.

De la Bédoyère, Camilla. Why Why Why Are Orang-Utans So Hairy? 2008. (Why Why Why Ser.). (Illus.). 32p. (J). (gr. 4-7). pap. *(978-1-84810-003-9(5))* Miles Kelly Publishing, Ltd.

De Medeiros, Michael. Orangutans. 2008. (Amazing Animals Ser.). (Illus.). 24p. (J). (gr. 2-4). pap. 8.95 *(978-1-59036-967-8(X))*; lib. bdg. 24.45 *(978-1-59036-966-1(1))* Weigl Pubs., Inc.

Dennard, Deborah. Apes & Monkeys. McGee, John F., illus. 2003. (Our Wild World Ser.). (ENG.). 192p. (J). (gr. 2-5). 16.95 *(978-1-55971-863-9(3))* Cooper Square Publishing Llc.

Eason, Sarah. Save the Orangutan. Geeson, Andrew & Veldhoven, Marijke, illus. 2009. (Save the... Ser.). 32p. (J). (gr. 2-5). lib. bdg. 25.25 *(978-1-4358-2811-7(9))* Rosen Publishing Group, Inc., The.

Eszterhas, Suzi. Orangutan Orphanage. 2016. (Wildlife Rescue Ser.: 2). (ENG., Illus.). 44p. (J). (gr. 2-5). 17.95 *(978-1-77147-141-1(7)*, Owlkids) Owlkids Bks. Inc. CAN. Dist: Publishers Group West (PGW).

Ganeri, Anita. Orangutan, 1 vol. 2010. (Day in the Life: Rain Forest Animals Ser.). (ENG.). 24p. (gr. k-2). pap. 6.79 *(978-1-4329-4118-5(6)*, Heinemann Read & Learn) Heinemann-Raintree.

—Survival in the Jungle. 2011. (ENG.). 24p. (J). pap. *(978-0-7787-7880-6(0))*; (gr. 3-6). *(978-0-7787-7858-5(4))* Crabtree Publishing Co.

Goldish, Meish. Orangutans. 2008. (Smart Animals! Ser.). (Illus.). 32p. (J). (gr. 2-5). lib. bdg. 25.27 *(978-1-59716-578-5(6))* Bearport Publishing Co., Inc.

Harkrader, Lisa. The Orangutan: A Myreportlinks. com Book. 2005. (Endangered & Threatened Animals Ser.). (Illus.). 48p. (J). (gr. 4-10). lib. bdg. 26.60 *(978-0-7660-5068-6(8)*, MyReportLinks.com Bks.) Enslow Pubs., Inc.

Katirgis, Jane & Harkrader, Lisa. Endangered Orangutans. 2015. (Wildlife at Risk Ser.). (ENG.). 48p. (J). (gr. 6-6). pap. 11.70 *(978-0-7660-6884-1(6))*; (Illus.). 27.93 *(978-0-7660-6886-5(2))* Enslow Pubs., Inc.

Knudsen, Shannon. Climbing Orangutans. 2007. (Pull Ahead Books-Animals Ser.). (ENG., Illus.). 32p. (gr. k-3). (J). lib. bdg. 22.60 *(978-0-8225-6704-2(0)*, Lerner Pubns.); per. 7.95 *(978-0-8225-6708-0(3)*, First Avenue Editions) Lerner Publishing Group.

Knudson, Shannon. Climbing Orangutans. 2009. pap. 40.95 *(978-0-8225-9317-1(3))* Lerner Publishing Group.

Kueffner, Sue. Orangutans. 2006. (Illus.). 45p. (J). *(978-1-59939-113-7(9)*, Reader's Digest Young Families, Inc.) Studio Fun International.

Kueffner, Sue & Kueffner, Susan. Orangutans. 2008. (Amazing Animals Ser.). 48p. (YA). (gr. 3-6). lib. bdg. 28.00 *(978-0-8368-9099-0(X))* Stevens, Gareth Publishing LLLP.

Kueffner, Susan. Orangutans. 2009. (Amazing Animals Ser.). 48p. (gr. 2-6). pap. 10.50 *(978-1-4339-2016-5(6)*, Gareth Stevens Learning Library) Stevens, Gareth Publishing LLLP.

Laman, Tim & Knott, Cheryl. Face to Face with Orangutans. 2009. (Face to Face with Animals Ser.). (ENG., Illus.). 32p. (J). (gr. 2-5). lib. bdg. 25.90 *(978-1-4263-0465-1(X)*, National Geographic Children's Bks.) National Geographic Society.

Lawrence, Ellen. Tiny Fingers & Fuzzy Orange Hair (Orangutan) 2015. (Whose Little Baby Are You? Ser.). (ENG.). 24p. (J). (gr. -1-3). lib. bdg. 23.93 *(978-1-910549-26-1(6))* Bearport Publishing Co., Inc.

Leaf, Christina. Baby Orangutans. 2015. (Super Cute! Ser.). (ENG., Illus.). 24p. (J). (gr. k-3). lib. bdg. 25.95 *(978-1-62617-171-8(8)*, Blastoff! Readers) Bellwether Media.

Morey, Allan. Orangutans Are Awesome! 2015. (Awesome Asian Animals Ser.). (ENG., Illus.). 32p. (gr. 1-2). lib. bdg. 27.32 *(978-1-4914-3907-4(6))* Capstone Press of Coughlan Cos.

Morgan, Sally. Orangutans. 2006. (QEB Animal Lives Ser.). (Illus.). 32p. (J). (gr. 4-7). lib. bdg. 19.95 *(978-1-59566-204-0(9))* QEB Publishing Inc.

Murray, Julie. Orangutans, 1 vol. (Asian Animals Ser.). (ENG.). 2013. 32p. (J). (gr. 2-5). 28.50 *(978-1-61783-556-8(0))* 2005. (Illus.). 24p. (gr. k-4). 25.65 *(978-1-59197-327-0(9)*, Buddy Bks.) ABDO Publishing Co.

Orme, Helen. Orangutans in Danger. 2006. (Wildlife Survival Ser.). (Illus.). 32p. (J). (gr. 2-5). lib. bdg. 25.27 *(978-1-59716-263-0(9))* Bearport Publishing Co., Inc.

Owen, Ruth. Orangutans. 2011. (World's Smartest Animals Ser.). (ENG., Illus.). 32p. (J). (gr. k-5). pap. 11.75 *(978-1-61533-419-3(X))*; lib. bdg. 26.50 *(978-1-61533-381-3(9))* Windmill Bks.

Raum, Elizabeth. Los Osos y Sus Guaridas (Bears Make Dens) Romina Martí, illus. 2017. (Animal Builders Ser.). (ENG & SPA.). 24p. (J). (gr. 1-4). 20.95 ***(978-1-68151-282-2(3)***, Amicus Illustrated) Amicus Publishing.

—Orangutans Build Tree Nests. Romina Martí, illus. 2017. (Animal Builders Ser.). (ENG.). 24p. (J). (gr. 1-4). 20.95 ***(978-1-68151-172-6(X)***, Amicus Illustrated) Amicus Publishing.

Riehecky, Janet. Orangutans, 1 vol. 2012. (Endangered & Threatened Animals Ser.). (ENG., Illus.). 32p. (gr. 3-4). lib. bdg. 27.99 *(978-1-4296-8587-0(5)*, Snap Bks.) Capstone Press of Coughlan Cos.

Ring, Susan. Elok. 2009. (J). *(978-1-60596-660-1(6))*; *(978-1-60596-659-5(2))* Weigl Pubs., Inc.

—Project Orangutan. Marshall, Diana & Nault, Jennifer, eds. 2003. (Zoo Life Ser.). (Illus.). 24p. (J). pap. 8.95 *(978-1-59036-058-3(3))* Weigl Pubs., Inc.

Sabatino, Michael. Being an Orangutan. 2013. (Can You Imagine Ser.). (Illus.). 32p. (J). (gr. 2-3). pap. 10.50 *(978-1-4824-3283-1(8))* Rosen Publishing Group, Inc., The.

—Being an Orangutan. 2014. (Illus.). 32p. (J). lib. bdg. ***(978-1-4824-0137-0(1))*** Stevens, Gareth Publishing LLLP.

Shively, Julie. Baby Orangutan. Johnson, Meredith, illus. 2005. (San Diego Zoo Animal Library: Vol. 9). (ENG.). 24p. (J). bds. 6.95 *(978-0-8249-6578-5(7)*, Ideal Pubns.) Worthy Publishing.

Silverman, Buffy. Orangutans, 1 vol. 2012. (Living in the Wild: Primates Ser.). (ENG.). 48p. (gr. 3-6). lib. bdg. 33.32 *(978-1-4329-5866-4(6)*, Heinemann InfoSearch) Heinemann-Raintree.

Soundprints, creator. Orang Utan's Playtime. 2011. (Let's Go to the Zoo! Ser.). (ENG., Illus.). 16p. (gr. -1). 5.95 *(978-1-60727-456-8(6))* Soundprints.

Taylor, Trace. Orangutan. 2008. (1-3Y Animals Ser.). (ENG.). 20p. (J). (gr. k-2). pap. 5.99 *(978-1-59301-442-1(2))* American Reading Co.

ORANGUTANS—FICTION

Antle, Bhagavan. Suryia & Roscoe: The True Story of an Unlikely Friendship. Antle, Bhagavan & Bland, Barry, illus. 2011. (ENG.). 32p. (J). (gr. -1-3). 18.99 *(978-0-8050-9316-2(8)*, 9780805093162, Holt, Henry & Co. Bks. For Young Readers) Holt, Henry & Co.

Burchett, Jan & Vogler, Sara. Rainforest Rescue, 1 vol. Le Feyer, Diane, illus. 2012. (Wild Rescue Ser.). (ENG.). 152p. (gr. 3-6). 9.95 *(978-1-4342-4595-3(0))*; lib. bdg. 25.32 *(978-1-4342-3768-2(0))* Stone Arch Bks.

Daddo, Andrew. Goodnight, Me. Quay, Emma, illus. 2007. (ENG.). 32p. (J). (gr. -1-k). 14.99 *(978-1-59990-153-4(6)*, 9781599901534, Bloomsbury USA Childrens) Bloomsbury Publishing USA.

Komalasan, Arie. Kiki the Orangutan: The Big Banana Festival. 2017. (ENG., Illus.). 32p. (J). (gr. -1-3). 8.95 *(978-0-8048-4811-4(4))* Tuttle Publishing.

Law, Felicia. Olivia the Orangutan: A Tale of Helpfulness. Spoor, Mike, illus. 2010. (Animal Fair Values Ser.). (ENG.). 32p. (J). (gr. -1-3). pap. 10.55 *(978-1-60754-917-8(4))*; lib. bdg. 22.60 *(978-1-60754-906-2(9))* Windmill Bks.

Lumry, Amanda & Hurwitz, Laura. Operation Orangutan. 2007. (Adventures of Riley (Unnumbered) Ser.). (Illus.). 36p. (J). (gr. -1-3). 15.95 *(978-0-9748411-4-4(5))* Eaglemont Pr.

McNaney, Jeanne. Miracle in Sumatra: The Story of Gutsy Gus. Cochard, David, illus. 2009. (ENG.). 32p. (J). (gr. -1-3). 16.95 *(978-0-9814534-6-0(5))* Ovation Bks.

Romanelli, Serena. El Pequeno Coco. Lamas, Blanca Rosa, tr. from GER. de Beer, Hans, illus. 2004.Tr. of Kleiner Dodo was Spielst du? (SPA.). 24p. (J). (gr. k-4). reprint ed. 16.00 *(978-0-7567-7707-4(0))* DIANE Publishing Co.

Schrefer, Eliot. Rescued. 2016. (ENG.). 272p. (J). (gr. 7). 18.99 *(978-0-545-65503-3(X)*, Scholastic Pr.) Scholastic, Inc.

Wurge, B. B. The Last Notebook of Leonardo. 2010. (LeapKids Ser.). (ENG., Illus.). 154p. (J). (gr. 1-7). pap. 9.95 *(978-1-935248-14-9(6))* Leapfrog Pr.

ORATORY

see Public Speaking

ORBITING VEHICLES

see Artificial Satellites

ORCHARDS

see Fruit Culture

ORCHESTRA

see also Bands (Music); Orchestral Music

Almeida, Artie. The Ultimate Game & Activity Pack for Orchestra: Grades 3-6. 2004. act. bk. ed. 39.95 *(978-0-89328-006-2(2)*, 30/1966H) Heritage Music Pr.

Claudio, Abbado. Yo Sere Director de Orquesta. 2007. (SPA.). 48p. (J). (gr. 4-5). 23.99 *(978-84-8470-052-4(6))* Corimbo, Editorial S.L. ESP. Dist: Lectorum Pubns., Inc.

Fullman, Joe. The Ultimate Guide to Music. 2016. (ENG., Illus.). 96p. (J). (gr. 3). 19.95 *(978-1-78312-091-8(6))* Carlton Kids GBR. Dist: Sterling Publishing Co., Inc.

Hood, Susan. Ada's Violin: The Story of the Recycled Orchestra of Paraguay. Comport, Sally Wern, illus. 2016. (ENG.). 40p. (J). (gr. -1-3). 17.99 *(978-1-4814-3095-1(5)*, Simon & Schuster Bks. For Young Readers) Simon & Schuster Bks. For Young Readers.

—El Violín de Ada (Ada's Violin) La Historia de la Orquesta de Reciclados Del Paraguay. McConnell, Shelley, tr. from ENG. Comport, Sally Wern, illus. 2016. (SPA.). 40p. (J). (gr. -1-3). 17.99 *(978-1-4814-6657-8(7)*, Simon & Schuster Bks. For Young Readers) Simon & Schuster Bks. For Young Readers.

Rubin, Daniel. Orchestra. (ENG.). 48p. (J). pap. 9.95 *(978-0-88899-051-8(0))* Groundwood Bks. CAN. Dist: Publishers Group West (PGW).

Swalin, Benjamin. Hard Circus Road: The Odyssey of the North Carolina Symphony. McVaugh, Julia A., ed. (Illus.). 158p. (YA). 24.95 *(978-0-9618952-0-4(9))* North Carolina Symphony Society, Inc., The.

Ustinov, Peter. The Orchestra. (J). (gr. -1-18). 19.98 incl. audio Music for Little People, Inc.

ORCHESTRA—FICTION

Barnes, Peter W. Maestro Mouse: And the Mystery of the Missing Baton. Barnes, Cheryl Shaw, illus. 2005. 32p. (J). 16.95 *(978-1-893622-17-3(7)*, VSP Bks.) Vacation Spot Publishing.

Barnes, Peter W. & Barnes, Cheryl S., illus. Maestro Mouse: And the Mystery of the Missing Baton. 2013. (ENG.). 40p. (J). (gr. k-5). 16.95 *(978-1-62157-036-3(3)*, Little Patriot Pr.) Regnery Publishing, Inc., An Eagle Publishing Co.

Brezenoff, Steve. The Symphony That Was Silent, 1 vol. Calo, Marcos, illus. 2011. (Field Trip Mysteries Ser.). (ENG.). 88p. (gr. 2-3). pap. 6.10 *(978-1-4342-3429-2(0))*; lib. bdg. 25.32 *(978-1-4342-3226-7(3))* Stone Arch Bks.

Chinese, the Singapore. Musical Adventures with Quek Quek: Discover the Sounds of the Chinese Orchestra. Fong, Lee Kow, illus. 2016. (ENG.). 96p. pap. 25.00 incl. cd-rom *(978-981-4677-23-3(X))* Marshall Cavendish International (Asia) Private Ltd. SGP. Dist: National Bk. Network.

Gantry, Chris. The Underwater Orchestra. Burns, Theresa, illus. 2013. 38p. 16.98 *(978-1-940224-19-0(5))* Taylor and Seale Publishing, LLC.

Huthmaker, Dixie. Trapped in Half Position. 2005. pap. 10.95 *(978-1-59330-317-4(3))* Aventine Pr.

King, Dedie. I See the Sun in Russia. Ossipova, Irina, tr. Inglese, Judith, illus. 2012. (I See the Sun Ser.: 0). (RUS & ENG.). 40p. (J). (gr. 1-2). 12.95 *(978-1-935874-08-9(X))* Satya Hse. Pubns.

Legrand, Claire. The Year of Shadows. Kwasny, Karl, illus. 2013. (ENG.). 416p. (J). (gr. 3-7). 16.99 *(978-1-4424-4294-8(8)*, Simon & Schuster Bks. For Young Readers) Simon & Schuster Bks. For Young Readers.

Scollon, William, et al. Easter Bonnet Parade. Disney Storybook Artists Staff, illus. 2013. (ENG.). 24p. (J). (gr. -1-k). pap. 5.99 *(978-1-4231-6416-6(4))* Disney Pr.

Snicket, Lemony, pseud & Stookey, Nathaniel. The Composer Is Dead. Ellis, Carson, illus. 2009. (ENG.). 40p. (J). (gr. k-5). 17.99 *(978-0-06-123627-3(6))* HarperCollins Pubs.

Taplin, Sam. Noisy Orchestra. 2013. (Noisy Bks). 10p. (J). ring bd. 19.99 *(978-0-7945-3334-2(5)*, Usborne) EDC Publishing.

Tripp, Paul. Tubby the Tuba. Cole, Henry, illus. 2006. (ENG.). 32p. (J). (gr. -1-3). 16.99 *(978-0-525-47717-4(9)*, Dutton Books for Young Readers) Penguin Young Readers Group.

Wilson, Budge. A Fiddle for Angus. 2004. (Illus.). (J). (gr. k-3). spiral bd. *(978-0-616-11140-6(1))* Canadian National Institute for the Blind/Institut National Canadien pour les Aveugles.

Wright, Johanna. The Orchestra Pit. Wright, Johanna, illus. 2014. (ENG., Illus.). 32p. (J). (gr. -1-1). 16.99 *(978-1-59643-769-2(3)*, 9781596437692) Roaring Brook Pr.

Wu, Mike. Ellie in Concert. Wu, Mike, illus. 2017. (ENG., Illus.). 40p. (J). (gr. -1-k). 16.99 *(978-1-4847-1238-2(2))* Hyperion Bks. for Children.

ORCHESTRAL MUSIC

Heyens, Gudrun, et al. Fun & Games with the Alto Recorder Bk. 1: Tune. 2004. (ENG.). 46p. pap. 9.95 *(978-1-902455-14-3(2)*, 1902455142) Schott Music Corp.

—Fun & Games with the Alto Recorder Bk. 1: Tuto. 2004. (ENG.). 80p. pap. 14.95 *(978-1-902455-13-6(4)*, 1902455134) Schott Music Corp.

—Fun & Games with the Alto Recorder Bk. 2: Tune. 2005. (ENG.). 92p. pap. 10.95 *(978-1-902455-16-7(9)*, 1902455169) Schott Music Corp.

Levin, Herbert & Levin, Gail. Symphonics R Us. 2006. spiral bd. 16.00 *(978-1-891278-41-9(X))* Barcelona Pubs.

Masters of Music, 12 bks., Set. 2004. (Masters of Music Ser.). (Illus.). 7p. (gr. 4-8). lib. bdg. 239.40 *(978-1-58415-253-8(2))* Mitchell Lane Pubs., Inc.

ORCHIDS

Wallace, Ian. The Slippers' Keeper, 1 vol. 2015. (ENG., Illus.). 36p. (J). (gr. k-3). 18.95 *(978-1-55498-414-5(9))* Groundwood Bks. CAN. Dist: Publishers Group West (PGW).

ORDNANCE

see also names of general and specific military ordnance, e.g. Atomic Weapons; also names of armies with the subdivision Ordnance and Ordnance Stores, e.g. U. S. Army—Ordnance and Ordnance Stores

Adams, Simon. Artillery. 2009. (War Machines Ser.). (YA). (gr. 5-9). 28.50 *(978-1-59920-226-6(3))* Black Rabbit Bks.

Finn, Denny Von. M109A6 Paladins. 2012. (Military Vehicles Ser.). (ENG., Illus.). 24p. (J). (gr. 3-7). lib. bdg. 25.95 *(978-1-60014-820-0(4)*, Epic Bks.) Bellwether Media.

Gilpin, Daniel & Pang, Alex. Military Fighting Machines. 2010. (Machines Close-Up Ser.). 32p. (J). (gr. 4-7). 28.50 *(978-1-60870-109-4(3))* Marshall Cavendish Corp.

Peak, Doris-Jean. Wernher Von Braun: Alabama's Rocket Scientist. 2009. (Alabama Roots Biography Ser.). (Illus.). 112p. (J). *(978-1-59421-044-0(6))* Seacoast Publishing, Inc.

OREGON

Aronin, Miriam. How Many People Traveled the Oregon Trail? And Other Questions about the Trail West. 2012. (Six Questions of American History Ser.). (ENG.). 48p. (gr. 4-6). pap. 56.72 *(978-0-7613-9237-8(8))*; pap. 9.95 *(978-0-7613-8566-0(5))* Lerner Publishing Group.

Bjorklund, Ruth, et al. Oregon. 2015. (Illus.). 80p. (J). *(978-1-62713-172-8(8))* Hudson Hills Pr. LLC.

Bratvold, Gretchen. Oregon. 2012. (J). lib. bdg. 25.26 *(978-0-7613-4552-7(3)*, Lerner Pubns.) Lerner Publishing Group.

Hart, Joyce. Oregon. 2006. (It's My State! Ser.). (Illus.). 80p. (J). (gr. 4-7). lib. bdg. 21.95 *(978-0-7614-1908-2(X)*, Benchmark Bks.) Marshall Cavendish Corp.

Labella, Susan. Oregon. 2006. (Rookie Read-About Geography Ser.). (ENG., Illus.). 32p. (J). (gr. 1-2). lib. bdg. 20.50 *(978-0-516-25386-2(7))* Scholastic Library Publishing.

Lusted, Marcia Amidon. Oregon: The Beaver State. 2010. (Our Amazing States Ser.). (ENG.). 24p. (J). pap. 8.25 *(978-1-4358-9786-1(2))*; lib. bdg. 22.60 *(978-1-4358-9346-7(8))* Rosen Publishing Group, Inc., The. (PowerKids Pr.).

Maine, Tyler. Oregon. 2016. (States Ser.). (ENG., Illus.). 32p. (gr. 3-4). lib. bdg. 27.32 *(978-1-5157-0424-9(6))* Next Page Pr., The.

Marsh, Carole. Oregon Current Events Projects: 30 Cool, Activities, Crafts, Experiments & More for Kids to Do to Learn about Your State! 2003. (Oregon Experience Ser.). 32p. (gr. k-5). pap. 5.95 *(978-0-635-02056-7(4)*, Marsh, Carole Bks.) Gallopade International.

—Oregon Geography Projects: 30 Cool, Activities, Crafts, Experiments & More for Kids to Do to Learn about Your State! 2003. (Oregon Experience Ser.). 32p. (gr. k-5). pap. 5.95 *(978-0-635-01856-4(X)*, Marsh, Carole Bks.) Gallopade International.

—Oregon Government Projects: 30 Cool, Activities, Crafts, Experiments & More for Kids to Do to Learn about Your State! 2003. (Oregon Experience Ser.). 32p. (gr. k-5). pap. 5.95 *(978-0-635-01956-1(6)*, Marsh, Carole Bks.) Gallopade International.

—Oregon People Projects: 30 Cool, Activities, Crafts, Experiments & More for Kids to Do to Learn about Your State! 2003. (Oregon Experience Ser.). 32p. (gr. k-5). pap. 5.95 *(978-0-635-02006-2(8)*, Marsh, Carole Bks.) Gallopade International.

—Oregon Symbols & Facts Projects: 30 Cool, Activities, Crafts, Experiments & More for Kids to Do to Learn about Your State! 2003. (Oregon Experience Ser.). 32p. (gr. k-5). pap. 5.95 *(978-0-635-01906-6(X)*, Marsh, Carole Bks.) Gallopade International.

Murray, Julie. Oregon, 1 vol. 2006. (United States Ser.). (ENG., Illus.). 32p. (gr. 2-4). 27.07 *(978-1-59197-696-7(0)*, Buddy Bks.) ABDO Publishing Co.

Peters, S. True. How to Draw Oregon's Sights & Symbols. 2009. (Kid's Guide to Drawing America Ser.). 32p. (gr. k-k). 50.50 *(978-1-61511-090-2(9)*, PowerKids Pr.) Rosen Publishing Group, Inc., The.

Peterson del Mar, David & Del Mar, David Peterson. Oregon's Promise: An Interpretive History. 2003. (ENG., Illus.). 320p. pap. 19.95 *(978-0-87071-558-7(5))* Oregon State Univ. Pr.

Smith, Marie & Smith, Roland. B Is for Beaver: An Oregon Alphabet. Roydon, Michael, illus. 2003. (Discover America State by State Ser.). (ENG.). 40p. (J). 17.95 *(978-1-58536-071-0(6))* Sleeping Bear Pr.

Sonneborn, Liz. Oregon. 2006. (Portraits of the States Ser.). (Illus.). 32p. (gr. 2-6). pap. 10.50 *(978-0-8368-4692-8(3))*; lib. bdg. 26.00 *(978-0-8368-4673-7(7))* Stevens, Gareth Publishing LLLP. (Gareth Stevens Learning Library).

Stefoff, Rebecca. Oregon. 2nd rev. ed. 2005. (Celebrate the States Ser.). (Illus.). 144p. (gr. 6-7). lib. bdg. 42.79 *(978-0-7614-2022-4(3)*, Benchmark Bks.) Marshall Cavendish Corp.

Way, Jennifer. Oregon. Brusca, Maria Cristina, tr. from ENG. 2006. (Bilingual Library of the United States of America Ser.: Set 2). (ENG & SPA., Illus.). 32p. (J). (gr. 3-6). lib. bdg. 25.25 *(978-1-4042-3102-3(1))* Rosen Publishing Group, Inc., The.

Winterhaven Elementary Staff. O Is for Oregon. 2008. (See My State Ser.). (ENG., Illus.). 32p. (J). (gr. -1-3). 13.95 *(978-0-88240-747-0(3)*, West Winds Pr.) Graphic Arts Ctr. Publishing Co.

OREGON—FICTION

Adrian, Emily. Like It Never Happened. 2015. (ENG.). 368p. (J). (gr. 9). 17.99 *(978-0-525-42823-7(2)*, Dial Bks) Penguin Young Readers Group.

Angstrom, Gwen R. Silent, Snowy Night in Sunriver, Book 2: The Eemlets & Grandma Eema Stories. 2007. 76p. per. 19.95 *(978-1-4241-9000-3(2))* America Star Bks.

Archer, Nick & McDonald, Megan. Rule of Three. 2010. (Sisters Club Ser.: 2). (ENG., Illus.). 240p. (J). (gr. 3-7). pap. 5.99 *(978-0-7636-4830-5(2))* Candlewick Pr.

—Rule of Three. Consolazio, Pamela A., illus. 2009. (Sisters Club Ser.: 2). (ENG.). 240p. (J). (gr. 3-7). 15.99 *(978-0-7636-4153-5(7))* Candlewick Pr.

Arnold, Elana K. The Question of Miracles. 2016. (ENG.). 256p. (J). (gr. 5-7). pap. 6.99 *(978-0-544-66852-2(9)*, HMH Books For Young Readers) Houghton Mifflin Harcourt Publishing Co.

Asher, Jay. What Light. 2016. (ENG.). 272p. (YA). (gr. 7). 18.99 *(978-1-59514-551-2(6)*, Razorbill) Penguin Young Readers Group.

—What Light. 2017. lib. bdg. 22.10 ***(978-0-606-40488-4(0))*** Turtleback Bks.

Beatty, Cherie B. Meet Lewis the Duck. 2009. 24p. pap. 12.99 *(978-1-4389-5116-4(7))* AuthorHouse.

Bernal, Estela. Can You See Me Now? 2014. (ENG.). (YA). pap. 10.95 *(978-1-55885-783-4(4)*, Piñata Books) Arte Publico Pr.

Blackaby, Susan. The Twelve Days of Christmas in Oregon. Conahan, Carolyn Digby, illus. 2014. (Twelve Days of Christmas in America Ser.). (ENG.). 40p. (J). (gr. k). 12.95 *(978-1-4549-0891-3(2))* Sterling Publishing Co., Inc.

Boat, Patty. A Disappointing Homecoming: (A Soldier's Story), 1 vol. 2009. 158p. pap. 24.95 *(978-1-61546-997-0(4))* PublishAmerica, Inc.

Bowen, Carl. Fire Front. Lee, Marc, illus. 2016. (Firestormers Ser.). (ENG.). 112p. (gr. 4-8). lib. bdg. 26.65 *(978-1-4965-3308-1(9))* Stone Arch Bks.

Buyer, Robert L. & Coute, Ursula T. Following the North Star. 2013. 52p. pap. 23.95 *(978-1-4624-0611-1(4)*, Inspiring Voices) Author Solutions, Inc.

Caletti, Deb. The Six Rules of Maybe. (ENG.). (YA). (gr. 7). 2011. 352p. pap. 9.99 *(978-1-4169-7971-5(9))* 2010. 336p. 16.99 *(978-1-4169-7969-2(7))* Simon Pulse. (Simon Pulse).

Carlson, Melody. Girl Power, 1 vol. 2016. (Faithgirlz / Girls of Harbor View Ser.). (ENG.). 272p. (J). pap. 9.99 *(978-0-310-75361-2(9))* Zonderkidz.

Castro, Shirley. The Pelican Family Series — Stelly & the Sticky, Gooey Taffy. Castro, Christopher, illus. 2011. 36p. (J). 15.00 *(978-0-9790307-3-4(0))* Castro, Shirley.

Cereghino, Sandy. Oscar: The Short Legged Reindeer. 2006. (ENG., Illus.). 48p. (J). 24.95 *(978-1-59299-248-5(X))* Inkwater Pr.

Christie, Ed. The Sweet Smell of Rotten Eggs: Volume Two, the Dude Ranch Rangers. 2009. 108p. pap. 10.95 *(978-1-4401-3764-8(1))* iUniverse, Inc.

Cleary, Beverly. Emily's Runaway Imagination. Krush, Beth et al, illus. 2008. (Cleary Reissue Ser.). (ENG.). 288p. (J). (gr. 3-7). pap. 6.99 *(978-0-380-70923-6(6))* HarperCollins Pubs.

—Emily's Runaway Imagination. 221p. (J). (gr. 2-4). pap. 4.95 *(978-0-8072-1416-9(7)*, Listening Library) Random Hse. Audio Publishing Group.

Daneshvari, Gitty. The Ghouls Rule Boxed Set, Set. 2013. (ENG., Illus.). 816p. (J). (gr. 3-7). 39.00 *(978-0-316-32361-1(6))* Little, Brown Bks. for Young Readers.

Davis, Susan Page. Sarah's Long Ride. 2007. (Piper Ranch Ser.). 173p. (J). (gr. 3-7). per. 8.99 *(978-1-59166-737-7(2))* BJU Pr.

Dickson, Darnell G. Small Town, Big Dreams: A Dane Jordan Sports Novel. 2008. pap. 14.99 *(978-1-59955-229-3(9))* Cedar Fort, Inc./CFI Distribution.

Elliott, Jenny. Save Me. 2015. (ENG.). 336p. (YA). (gr. 7-12). pap. 9.99 *(978-1-250-06147-8(4)*, 9781250061478) Feiwel & Friends.

Forman, Gayle. If I Stay. 2011. (If I Stay Ser.: BK.1). (YA). 10.36 *(978-0-7848-3573-9(X)*, Everbind) Marco Bk. Co.

—If I Stay. movie tie-in ed. 2014. (If I Stay Ser.: BK.1). (ENG.). 304p. (YA). (gr. 9). pap. 10.99 *(978-0-14-751453-0(3))* Penguin Publishing Group.

—If I Stay. (If I Stay Ser.: BK.1). (ENG.). (YA). (gr. 9-18). 2010. 320p. 10.99 *(978-0-14-241543-6(X)*, Speak) 2009. 208p. 17.99 *(978-0-525-42103-0(3)*, Dutton Books for Young Readers) 2014. 304p. 17.99 *(978-0-451-47464-3(3)*, Viking Books for Young Readers) Penguin Young Readers Group.

—If I Stay. 2010. (If I Stay Ser.: BK.1). (ENG.). 262p. (YA). (gr. 9-12). 18.45 *(978-1-60686-742-6(3))* Perfection Learning Corp.

—If I Stay. l.t. ed. 2014. (If I Stay Ser.: BK.1). (ENG.). (YA). 482p. 23.99 *(978-1-4104-7543-5(3))*; 480p. pap. 12.99 *(978-1-59413-814-0(1)*, Large Print Pr.) Thorndike Pr.

—If I Stay. 2010. (If I Stay Ser.: BK.1). (YA). lib. bdg. 22.10 *(978-0-606-14395-0(5)*, Turtleback) Turtleback Bks.

Grandpa & Little Guy. 2004. (J). 15.95 *(978-0-9764012-0-9(7))* Rockmill Publishing Co.

Hancock, Dennis & Uyen. The Tree House on the Bluff. Hancock, Uyen, illus. 2012. 36p. pap. 24.95 *(978-1-4626-7318-6(X))* America Star Bks.

Harrison, Lisi. Back & Deader Than Ever. 2013. (Monster High Ser.: 4). (ENG.). 256p. (YA). (gr. 7-17). pap. 9.99 *(978-0-316-18667-4(8)*, Poppy) Little, Brown Bks. for Young Readers.

—The Ghoul Next Door. (Monster High Ser.: 2). (ENG.). 256p. (YA). (gr. 7-17). 2012. pap. 8.99 *(978-0-316-18666-7(X))* 2011. 16.99 *(978-0-316-09911-0(2))* Little, Brown Bks. for Young Readers. (Poppy).

—Monster High. 2010. (SPA.). 448p. (YA). (gr. 8-12). mass mkt. 19.99 *(978-607-11-0641-4(9))* Aguilar, Altea, Taurus, Alfaguara, S.A. de C.V MEX. Dist: Two Rivers Distribution.

—Monster High. (Monster High Ser.: 1). (ENG.). 272p. (YA). (gr. 7-17). 2011. pap. 8.99 *(978-0-316-17621-7(4))* 2010. 16.99 *(978-0-316-09918-9(X))* Little, Brown Bks. for Young Readers. (Poppy).

—Monster High. 2011. (Monster High Ser.: 1). (YA). lib. bdg. 19.65 *(978-0-606-23459-7(4)*, Turtleback) Turtleback Bks.

—Monster High: Where There's a Wolf, There's a Way. 2011. (Monster High Ser.: 3). (ENG., Illus.). 256p. (YA). (gr. 7-17). 17.99 *(978-0-316-09919-6(8)*, Poppy) Little, Brown Bks. for Young Readers.

—Where There's a Wolf, There's a Way. 2012. (Monster High Ser.: 3). (ENG., Illus.). 272p. (YA). (gr. 7-17). pap. 9.99 *(978-0-316-18668-1(6)*, Poppy) Little, Brown Bks. for Young Readers.

Henry, April. The Night She Disappeared. 2013. (ENG.). 256p. (YA). (gr. 7-12). pap. 10.99 *(978-1-250-01674-4(6)*, 9781250016744) Square Fish.

Hensley, Nathaniel. The Strange Tale of Hector & Hannah Crowe. 2015. (ENG.). 222p. (J). (gr. 8-18). 13.95 *(978-1-937240-49-3(5))* Casa de Snapdragon LLC.

Hermes, Patricia. The Wild Year Bk. 3: Joshua's Oregon Trail Diary. 2003. (My America Ser.). (ENG., Illus.). 112p. (J). 12.95 *(978-0-439-37055-4(8))* Scholastic, Inc.

Herrick, Ann. Walk Softly & Watch Out for Bigfoot. 2006. (YA). pap. 9.95 *(978-0-7599-4489-3(X))* Hard Shell Word Factory.

Houck, Colleen. Tiger's Quest. (Tiger's Curse Ser.: Bk. 2). (ENG.). (J). (gr. 7). 2013. 512p. pap. 9.95 *(978-1-4549-0358-1(9))* 2011. 496p. 17.95 *(978-1-4027-8404-0(X))* Sterling Publishing Co., Inc.

Humphrey, Matthew J. Coastal Magic. 2007. lib. bdg. 21.95 *(978-1-59872-997-9(7))* Instant Pub.

Hutchens, Calvin. The Adventures of Otis Possum. 2007. 52p. per. 16.95 *(978-1-4241-7065-4(6))* America Star Bks.

Jacobs, Lily. The Littlest Bunny in Oregon: An Easter Adventure. Dunn, Robert, illus. 2015. (ENG.). 32p. (J). (-3). 9.99 *(978-1-4926-1171-4(9)*, Sourcebooks Jabberwocky) Sourcebooks, Inc.

James, Eric. A Halloween Scare in Oregon. Le Ray, Marina, illus. 2015. (ENG.). 32p. (J). (-5). 9.99 *(978-1-4926-2393-9(8)*, 9781492623939, Sourcebooks Jabberwocky) Sourcebooks, Inc.

—Santa's Sleigh Is on Its Way to Oregon: A Christmas Adventure. Dunn, Robert, illus. 2016. (ENG.). 32p. (J). (-2). 12.99 *(978-1-4926-4348-7(3)*, 9781492643487, Sourcebooks Jabberwocky) Sourcebooks, Inc.

—Santa's Sleigh Is on Its Way to Portland: A Christmas Adventure. Dunn, Robert, illus. 2016. (ENG.). 32p. (J). (-2). 12.99 *(978-1-4926-4352-4(1)*, 9781492643524, Sourcebooks Jabberwocky) Sourcebooks, Inc.

Jessell, Tim, illus. Mystery of the Fallen Treasure. 2013. (Boxcar Children Mysteries Ser.: 132). (ENG.). 128p. (J). (gr.

M N O

1-5). 5.99 *(978-0-8075-5506-4(1))*; 15.99 *(978-0-8075-5508-8(8))* Whitman, Albert & Co.
Kehret, Peg. Escaping the Giant Wave. 2004. (ENG., Illus.). 160p. (J). (gr. 3-7). pap. 7.99 *(978-0-689-85273-2(8)*, Aladdin) Simon & Schuster Children's Publishing.
Kelly, Tara. The Foxglove Killings. 2015. (ENG.). 320p. (J). 16.99 *(978-1-63375-165-1(1)*, 9781633751651) Entangled Publishing, LLC.
Kelso, Mary Jean. One Family's Christmas. Snider, K. C., illus. 2008. 24p. pap. 10.95 *(978-1-935137-05-4(0))* Guardian Angel Publishing, Inc.
Kerley, Barbara. Portland Baby. Cleland, Josh, illus. 2017. (Local Baby Ser.). (ENG.). 22p. (J). (gr. -1-k). bds. 8.95 ***(978-1-946064-05-9(X))*** Duo Pr. LLC.
Kopp, J. J. Aurora, Daughter of the Dawn: A Story of New Beginnings. Will, Clark Moor, illus. 2012. (ENG.). 72p. (gr. 6-12). pap. 12.95 *(978-0-87071-671-3(9))* Oregon State Univ. Pr.
Lazebnik, Claire. The Trouble with Flirting. 2013. (ENG.). 336p. (YA). (gr. 8). pap. 9.99 *(978-0-06-192127-8(0)*, HarperTeen) HarperCollins Pubs.
Lucier, Makiia. A Death-Struck Year. 2014. (ENG.). 288p. (J). (gr. 7-12). 17.99 *(978-0-544-16450-5(4)*, HMH Books For Young Readers) Houghton Mifflin Harcourt Publishing Co.
Manning, Lisa C. Falcons in the City. Manning, Lisa C., illus. 2013. (ENG., Illus.). 40p. (J). pap. 14.95 *(978-1-59299-886-9(0))* Inkwater Pr.
Margolin, Phillip & Rome, Ami Margolin. Vanishing Acts. 2012. (ENG.). 176p. (J). (gr. 3-7). pap. 8.99 *(978-0-06-188558-7(4))* HarperCollins Pubs.
Martha, Morales. Ariana Leaves San Francisco. Chiu, Bessie, illus. 2011. 28p. pap. 8.50 *(978-1-61170-017-6(5))* Robertson Publishing.
McCarthy, Dan & Rosen, Anne. Good Night Oregon. Veno, Joe, illus. 2010. (Good Night Our World Ser.). (ENG.). 20p. (J). (gr. k — 1). bds. 9.95 *(978-1-60219-041-2(0))* Good Night Bks.
McCollum, Lynn Tragesser. The Green School Caper: The Adventures of the Five Amigos. 2008. 164p. pap. 9.95 *(978-1-4327-2564-8(5))* Outskirts Pr., Inc.
McDonald, Megan. Cloudy with a Chance of Boys. (Sisters Club Ser.: 3). (ENG., Illus.). 272p. (J). (gr. 3-7). 2012. pap. 5.99 *(978-0-7636-5577-8(5))* 2011. 15.99 *(978-0-7636-4615-8(6))* Candlewick Pr.
—The Sisters Club. 2008. (Sisters Club Ser.: 1). (ENG., Illus.). 208p. (J). (gr. 3-7). pap. 5.99 *(978-0-7636-3251-9(1))* Candlewick Pr.
—The Sisters Club. 2008. (Sisters Club Ser.: 1). lib. bdg. 16.00 *(978-1-4178-1785-6(2)*, Turtleback) Turtleback Bks.
Meloy, Colin. Under Wildwood. Ellis, Carson, illus. (Wildwood Chronicles Ser.: 2). (ENG.). (J). (gr. 3). 2013. 592p. pap. 9.99 *(978-0-06-202473-2(6))* 2012. 576p. 17.99 *(978-0-06-202471-8(X))* HarperCollins Pubs.
—Wildwood. Ellis, Carson, illus. (Wildwood Chronicles Ser.: 1). (ENG.). (J). (gr. 3). 2012. 576p. pap. 9.99 *(978-0-06-202470-1(1))* 2011. 560p. 17.99 *(978-0-06-202468-8(X))* HarperCollins Pubs.
—Wildwood. Ellis, Carson, illus. 2012. (Wildwood Chronicles Ser.: 1). (J). lib. bdg. 20.85 *(978-0-606-26864-6(2)*, Turtleback) Turtleback Bks.
—Wildwood Imperium: The Wildwood Chronicles, Book III. Ellis, Carson, illus. 2015. (Wildwood Chronicles Ser.: 3). (ENG.). 592p. (J). (gr. 3). pap. 9.99 *(978-0-06-202476-3(0))* HarperCollins Pubs.
Morrow, Dj. Charlie & Joe. 2013. 28p. pap. 24.95 *(978-1-62709-833-5(X))* America Star Bks.
Nelson, Blake. The New Rules of High School. 2004. (ENG.). 240p. (YA). (gr. 7-18). reprint ed. 7.99 *(978-0-14-240242-9(7)*, Speak) Penguin Young Readers Group.
—Paranoid Park. 2008. (ENG.). 192p. (YA). (gr. 7-18). 6.99 *(978-0-14-241156-8(6)*, Puffin Books) Penguin Young Readers Group.
Noe, Katherine Schlick. Something to Hold. 2011. (ENG., Illus.). 256p. (J). (gr. 5-7). 17.99 *(978-0-547-55813-4(9))* Houghton Mifflin Harcourt Publishing Co.
Ockler, Sarah. The Summer of Chasing Mermaids. 2015. (ENG., Illus.). 416p. (YA). (gr. 9). 17.99 *(978-1-4814-0127-2(0)*, Simon Pulse) Simon Pulse.
O'Dell, Kathryn L. From Wagon to Train. Chalik, Chris, illus. 2017. (Text Connections Guided Close Reading Ser.). (J). (gr. 2). *(978-1-4900-1854-6(9))* Benchmark Education Co.
Oneill, Elizabeth. Alfred Visits Oregon. 2008. 24p. pap. 12.00 *(978-0-9799121-8-4(0))* Global Business Information Strategies, Inc.
Palmer, Connie. I Will Run Free No More, 1 vol. 2009. 49p. pap. 16.95 *(978-1-4489-7122-0(5))* America Star Bks.
Parenteau, Shirley. Ship of Dolls. 2014. (ENG.). 272p. (J). (gr. 3-7). 16.99 *(978-0-7636-7003-0(0))* Candlewick Pr.
Parnell, Robyn. The Mighty Quinn. DeYoe, Katie & DeYoe, Aaron, illus. 2013. (ENG.). 272p. (gr. 2-7). pap. 10.95 *(978-1-938063-10-7(4)*, Mighty Media Junior Readers) Mighty Media Pr.
Parry, Rosanne. The Turn of the Tide. 2016. (ENG., Illus.). 304p. (J). (gr. 3-7). 16.99 *(978-0-375-86972-3(7)*, Random Hse. Bks. for Young Readers) Random Hse. Children's Bks.
Platt, Randall. Incommunicado. 2014. (ENG.). 336p. (J). (gr. 4-7). 14.95 *(978-1-62914-646-1(3)*, Sky Pony Pr.) Skyhorse Publishing Co., Inc.
Rand, Johnathan. American Chillers #29 Oregon Oceanauts. 2010. 208p. (J). pap. 5.99 *(978-1-893699-24-3(2))* AudioCraft Publishing, Inc.
Reece, Colleen L. Wilderness Warriors. 2012. 114p. 18.95 *(978-1-61633-309-6(X))*; pap. 8.95 *(978-1-61633-310-2(3))* Guardian Angel Publishing, Inc.
Reed, Amy Lynn. The Nowhere Girls. 2017. (YA). pap. ***(978-1-4814-8174-8(6)***, Simon Pulse) Simon Pulse.
Rescue Flight! 2003. 150p. (J). (gr. 4-6). per. 12.95 *(978-0-9740202-0-4(6))* Skyword Pr.
Rice, Dona Herwick & Shannon, Catherine. Narcissa Whitman & the Westward Movement, 1 vol. 2009. (Building Fluency Through Reader's Theater Ser.). (ENG., Illus.). 32p. (J). (gr. 3-5). pap. 7.99 *(978-1-4333-0542-9(9))* Teacher Created Materials, Inc.
Ryan, Sara. Bad Houses. Hahn, Sierra, ed. 2013. (ENG., Illus.). 152p. pap. 19.99 *(978-1-59582-993-1(8))* Dark Horse Comics.
Schroeder, Lisa. All We Have Is Now. 2015. (ENG.). 272p. (J). (gr. 7). 17.99 *(978-0-545-80253-6(9))* Scholastic, Inc.
—The Day Before. (ENG.). (YA). (gr. 9). 2012. 336p. pap. 9.99 *(978-1-4424-1744-1(7))* 2011. 320p. 16.99 *(978-1-4424-1743-4(9))* Simon Pulse. (Simon Pulse).
—It's Raining Cupcakes. (ENG., Illus.). 208p. (J). (gr. 3-7). 2011. pap. 6.99 *(978-1-4169-9085-7(2))* 2010. 17.99 *(978-1-4169-9084-0(4))* Simon & Schuster Children's Publishing. (Aladdin).
Scofield, Chris. The Shark Curtain. 2015. (ENG., Illus.). 320p. (J). (gr. 6). pap. 13.95 *(978-1-61775-313-8(0)*, Black Sheep) Akashic Bks.
Sheley, Kristen. Partners in Time #5: A Change of Course. 2010. 236p. 25.95 *(978-1-4502-6658-1(4))*; pap. 15.95 *(978-1-4502-6657-4(6))* iUniverse, Inc.
Silvano, Wendi. Love Is All Around Oregon. Czernichowska, Joanna, illus. 2016. (ENG.). 32p. (J). (-6). 12.99 *(978-1-4926-2952-8(9)*, Sourcebooks Jabberwocky) Sourcebooks, Inc.
—Love Is All Around Portland. Czernichowska, Joanna, illus. 2016. (ENG.). 32p. (J). (-6). 12.99 *(978-1-4926-2957-3(X)*, Sourcebooks Jabberwocky) Sourcebooks, Inc.
Smallman, Steve. Santa Is Coming to Oregon. Dunn, Robert, illus. 2013. (ENG.). 32p. (J). (-3). 9.99 *(978-1-4022-9075-6(6)*, Sourcebooks Jabberwocky) Sourcebooks, Inc.
—Santa Is Coming to Portland. Dunn, Robert, illus. 2012. (ENG.). 32p. (J). (-3). 9.99 *(978-1-4022-7772-6(5)*, Sourcebooks Jabberwocky) Sourcebooks, Inc.
Stelljes, Susan. Wonder Dog: The Story of Silverton Bobbie. 2005. (Illus.). 167p. (YA). pap. 14.95 *(978-0-9761124-7-1(7))* For The Love of Dog Bks.
Walton, Rick. 10 Little Monsters Visit Oregon. Smiley, Jess Smart, illus. 2014. (ENG.). 32p. (J). 16.95 *(978-1-939629-29-6(2)*, 9781939629296) Familius LLC.
Watson, Renée. This Side of Home. (ENG.). (YA). 2017. 352p. pap. 9.99 *(978-1-61963-930-0(0)*, 9781619639300) 2015. 336p. (gr. 7). 17.99 *(978-1-59990-668-3(6)*, 9781599906683) Bloomsbury Publishing USA. (Bloomsbury USA Childrens).
Waugh, Peter. Cannon Beach Mouse Caper. 2007. 128p. per. 13.95 *(978-0-944638-68-2(6))* Educare Pr.
Westover, Steve. Crater Lake: Battle for Wizard Island. 2012. pap. 14.99 *(978-1-59955-960-5(9))* Cedar Fort, Inc./CFI Distribution.
—Return of the Mystic Gray. 2013. 15.99 *(978-1-4621-1187-9(4))* Cedar Fort, Inc./CFI Distribution.
Whitney, Barbara I. Barbara's Quest to Find a Messenger: Journeys I & II. 2009. 40p. pap. 19.49 *(978-1-4415-0159-2(2))* Xlibris Corp.
Winters, Cat. The Cure for Dreaming. (ENG., Illus.). (YA). 2016. 384p. (gr. 8-17). pap. 9.95 *(978-1-4197-1941-7(6))* 2014. 368p. (gr. 7-17). 17.95 *(978-1-4197-1216-6(0))* Abrams, Inc. (Amulet Bks.).
—The Steep & Thorny Way. (ENG.). (YA). (gr. 8-17). 2017. 368p. pap. 9.99 ***(978-1-4197-2350-6(2))*** 2016. (Illus.). 352p. 17.95 *(978-1-4197-1915-8(7))* Abrams, Inc. (Amulet Bks.).
Wolff, Virginia Euwer. Bat 6. 256p. (J). (gr. 4-6). pap. 4.99 *(978-0-8072-8223-6(5))*; 2004. (gr. 5-9). pap. 36.00 incl. audio *(978-0-8072-8222-9(7)*, YYA144SP) Random Hse. Audio Publishing Group. (Listening Library).
Young, Judy. A Book for Black-Eyed Susan. Ettinger, Doris, illus. 2011. (Tales of Young Americans Ser.). (ENG.). 32p. (J). (gr. k-6). lib. bdg. 16.95 *(978-1-58536-463-3(0))* Sleeping Bear Pr.

OREGON—HISTORY

Aronin, Miriam. How Many People Traveled the Oregon Trail? And Other Questions about the Trail West. 2012. (Six Questions of American History Ser.). (ENG.). 48p. (gr. 4-6). lib. bdg. 30.60 *(978-0-7613-5332-4(1))* Lerner Publishing Group.
Bodden, Valerie. Oregon. 2009. (This Land Called America Ser.). 32p. (YA). (gr. 3-6). 19.95 *(978-1-58341-790-4(7))* Creative Co., The.
Boekhoff, P. M. & Kallen, Stuart A. Oregon. 2003. (Seeds of a Nation Ser.). (Illus.). 48p. (J). (gr. 3-5). 23.70 *(978-0-7377-1482-1(4)*, Kidhaven) Cengage Gale.
Crewe, Sabrina & Uschan, Michael V. The Oregon Trail. 2004. (Events That Shaped America Ser.). (Illus.). 32p. (gr. 3-6). lib. bdg. 26.00 *(978-0-8368-3405-5(4)*, Gareth Stevens Learning Library) Stevens, Gareth Publishing LLLP.
The Famous Oregon Events Guide ~ 2006. 2005. (YA). per. 15.95 *(978-1-881005-50-6(X))* Gail's Guides.
Felix, Rebecca. What's Great about Oregon? 2015. (Our Great States Ser.). (ENG., Illus.). 32p. (J). (gr. 2-5). pap. 7.95 *(978-1-4677-6090-4(0))*; lib. bdg. 26.60 *(978-1-4677-3866-8(2))* Lerner Publishing Group. (Lerner Pubns.).
Friesen, Helen Lepp. Oregon: The Beaver State. 2012. (J). *(978-1-61913-393-8(8))*; pap. *(978-1-61913-394-5(6))* Weigl Pubs., Inc.
Harness, Cheryl. The Tragic Tale of Narcissa Whitman & a Faithful History of the Oregon Trail. Harness, Cheryl, illus. 2006. (Cheryl Harness Histories Ser.). (ENG., Illus.). 144p. (J). (gr. 5-9). 16.95 *(978-0-7922-5920-6(3))*; lib. bdg. 25.90 *(978-0-7922-5921-3(1))* National Geographic Society. (National Geographic Children's Bks.).
Hart, Joyce & Gorman, Jacqueline Laks. Oregon. 2nd rev. ed. 2011. (It's My State! 2 Ser.). 80p. (gr. 3). 31.36 *(978-1-60870-525-2(0))* Marshall Cavendish Corp.
Jerome, Kate B. Lucky to Live in Oregon. 2017. (Arcadia Kids Ser.). (ENG., Illus.). 32p. (J). 16.99 ***(978-0-7385-2791-8(2))*** Arcadia Publishing.
—The Wise Animal Handbook Oregon. 2017. (Arcadia Kids Ser.). (ENG., Illus.). 32p. (J). 16.99 ***(978-0-7385-2839-7(0))*** Arcadia Publishing.
Kent, Deborah. Oregon (Revised Edition) 2014. (America the Beautiful, Third Ser. (Revised Edition) Ser.). (ENG., Illus.). 144p. (J). lib. bdg. 40.00 *(978-0-531-28288-5(0))* Scholastic Library Publishing.
Leedom, Karen L. A Is for Astoria. Bailey, Sally, illus. 2010. 32p. 15.00 *(978-0-9826252-0-0(0))* Riverride Publishing.
Ludwig, Trudy. Gifts from the Enemy. Orback, Craig, illus. 2014. (HumanKIND Project Ser.). (ENG.). 32p. (gr. 2-7). 16.95 *(978-1-935952-97-8(8))* White Cloud Pr.
Marsh, Carole. Exploring Oregon Through Project-Based Learning: Geography, History, Government, Economics & More. 2016. (Oregon Experience Ser.). (ENG.). (J). pap. 9.99 *(978-0-635-12361-9(4))* Gallopade International.
—I'm Reading about Oregon. 2014. (Oregon Experience Ser.). (ENG., Illus.). (J). pap., pap. 8.99 *(978-0-635-11312-2(0))* Gallopade International.
—Oregon History Projects: 30 Cool, Activities, Crafts, Experiments & More for Kids to Do to Learn about Your State! 2003. (Oregon Experience Ser.). 32p. (gr. k-5). pap. 5.95 *(978-0-635-01806-9(3)*, Marsh, Carole Bks.) Gallopade International.
Matchette, Katharine E. Discovering Oregon. Comfort, Mike & Baisley, Stephen, illus. Matchette, Dennis, photos by. (YA). (gr. 5-9). spiral bd. 13.00 *(978-0-9645045-4-7(5))* Deka Pr.
Maynard, Charles W. Fort Clatsop. 2009. (Famous Forts Throughout American History Ser.). 24p. (gr. 3-4). 42.50 *(978-1-61512-515-9(9)*, PowerKids Pr.) Rosen Publishing Group, Inc., The.
Olson, Steven P. The Oregon Trail. 2004. (Primary Sources in American History Ser.). (Illus.). 64p. (gr. 5-8). lib. bdg. 31.95 *(978-0-8239-4512-2(X)*, Rosen Reference) Rosen Publishing Group, Inc., The.
Publications International Ltd. Staff. Yesterday & Today Portland. 2009. 192p. 24.95 *(978-1-4127-7793-3(3))* Publications International, Ltd.
Roza, Greg. Oregon: Past & Present. 2010. (United States: Past & Present Ser.). (ENG., Illus.). 48p. (J). pap. 11.75 *(978-1-4358-8480-9(9))*; lib. bdg. 29.25 *(978-1-4358-3515-3(8))* Rosen Publishing Group, Inc., The. (Rosen Reference).
Shannon, Terry Miller. Oregon. 2009. (From Sea to Shining Sea, Second Ser.). (ENG.). 80p. (J). pap. 7.95 *(978-0-531-21142-7(8)*, Children's Pr.) Scholastic Library Publishing.
Skewes, John. Larry Loves Portland! Skewes, John, illus. 2014. (Larry Gets Lost Ser.). (ENG., Illus.). 20p. (J). (— 1). bds. 9.99 *(978-1-57061-935-9(2)*, Little Bigfoot) Sasquatch Bks.
Skewes, John, illus. Portland ABC. 2014. (Larry Gets Lost Ser.). (ENG.). 32p. (J). (gr. -1-k). 14.99 *(978-1-57061-920-5(4)*, Little Bigfoot) Sasquatch Bks.
Skewes, John & Mullin, Michael. Larry Gets Lost in Portland. Skewes, John, illus. 2012. (Larry Gets Lost Ser.). (ENG., Illus.). 32p. (J). (gr. -1-2). 17.99 *(978-1-57061-679-2(5)*, Little Bigfoot) Sasquatch Bks.
Skogen, J. M. Portland Trail Blazers. 2013. (On the Hardwood Ser.). (ENG., Illus.). 47p. (gr. 3-8). pap. 8.95 *(978-1-61570-838-3(3))* Scobre Pr. Corp.
Smith, Rich. Oregon, 1 vol. 2009. (United States Ser.). (ENG., Illus.). 48p. (YA). (gr. 2-5). 27.07 *(978-1-60453-672-0(1))* ABDO Publishing Co.
Smith, Steven Michael. New Carissa: The Ship That Refused to Die. 2010. 52p. pap. 22.99 *(978-1-4520-6612-7(4))* AuthorHouse.
Spenser & Mom. Spenser Goes to Portland. Jacobsen, Amie, illus. 2008. 32p. 14.95 *(978-0-9817598-0-7(7))* Simple Fish Bk. Co., LLC.
Tieck, Sarah. Oregon, 1 vol. 2012. (Explore the United States Ser.). (ENG.). 32p. (J). (gr. 2-5). lib. bdg. 28.50 *(978-1-61783-375-5(4)*, Big Buddy Bks.) ABDO Publishing Co.
Way, Jennnifer. Oregon. 2009. (Bilingual Library of the United States of America Ser.). (ENG & SPA.). 32p. (gr. 2-2). 47.90 *(978-1-60853-381-7(6)*, Editorial Buenas Letras) Rosen Publishing Group, Inc., The.
Williams, Jack. The Modoc of California. 2009. (Library of Native Americans Ser.). 64p. (gr. 4-4). 58.50 *(978-1-60853-754-9(4)*, PowerKids Pr.) Rosen Publishing Group, Inc., The.
—The Mojave of California. 2009. (Library of Native Americans Ser.). 64p. (gr. 4-4). 58.50 *(978-1-60853-755-6(2)*, PowerKids Pr.) Rosen Publishing Group, Inc., The.
Winans, Jay D. Oregon. 2011. (Guide to American States Ser.). (Illus.). 48p. (YA). (gr. 3-6). 29.99 *(978-1-61690-809-6(2))*; (J). *(978-1-61690-485-2(2))* Weigl Pubs., Inc.
—Oregon: The Beaver State. 2016. (J). *(978-1-4896-4926-3(3))* Weigl Pubs., Inc.
Ziff, John. Northwest: Idaho, Oregon, Washington, Vol. 19. 2015. (Let's Explore the States Ser.). (Illus.). 64p. (J). (gr. 5). 23.95 *(978-1-4222-3331-3(6))* Mason Crest.

OREGON NATIONAL HISTORIC TRAIL

Aronin, Miriam. How Many People Traveled the Oregon Trail? And Other Questions about the Trail West. 2012. (Six Questions of American History Ser.). (ENG.). 48p. (gr. 4-6). pap. 56.72 *(978-0-7613-9237-8(8))*; pap. 9.95 *(978-0-7613-8566-0(5))*; lib. bdg. 30.60 *(978-0-7613-5332-4(1))* Lerner Publishing Group.
Crewe, Sabrina & Uschan, Michael V. The Oregon Trail. 2004. (Events That Shaped America Ser.). (Illus.). 32p. (gr. 3-6). lib. bdg. 26.00 *(978-0-8368-3405-5(4)*, Gareth Stevens Learning Library) Stevens, Gareth Publishing LLLP.
Dean, Arlan. The Oregon Trail: From Independence, Missouri to Oregon City, Oregon. (Famous American Trails Ser.). 24p. 2009. (gr. 3-3). 42.50 *(978-1-61512-490-9(X))* 2003. (Illus.). (J). lib. bdg. 22.60 *(978-0-8239-6478-9(7))* Rosen Publishing Group, Inc., The. (PowerKids Pr.).
Doeden, Matt. Oregon Trail: An Interactive History Adventure. 2013. (You Choose: History Ser.). (ENG.). 112p. (gr. 3-4). pap. 6.95 *(978-1-4765-3607-1(4))*; 31.99 *(978-1-4765-0254-0(4))* Capstone Press of Coughlan Cos. (You Choose Bks.).
Dunn, Joeming W. The Oregon Trail, 1 vol. Smith, Tim, illus. 2008. (Graphic History Ser.). (ENG.). 32p. 28.50 *(978-1-60270-183-0(0)*, Graphic Planet- Nonfiction) ABDO Publishing Co.
Figley, Marthy Rhodes. Clara Morgan & the Oregon Trail Journey. Orback, Craig, illus. 2011. (History Speaks: Picture Books Plus Reader's Theater Ser.). 48p. pap. 56.72 *(978-0-7613-7631-6(3))* Lerner Publishing Group.
Figley, Marthy Rhodes & Figley, Marty Rhodes. Clara Morgan & the Oregon Trail Journey. Orback, Craig, illus. 2011. (History Speaks: Picture Books Plus Reader's Theater Ser.). (ENG.). 48p. (gr. 2-4). pap. 9.95 *(978-0-7613-7115-1(X))* Lerner Publishing Group.
Freedman, Jeri. Life As a Pioneer on the Oregon Trail. 2016. (Life As... Ser.). (ENG., Illus.). 32p. (J). (gr. 3-3). pap. 10.58 *(978-1-5026-1075-1(2))* Cavendish Square Publishing.
Friedman, Mel. The Oregon Trail. (Cornerstones of Freedom, Third Ser.). (ENG.). (J). 2012. Illus.). 64p. pap. 8.95 *(978-0-531-28163-5(9))* 2012. (Illus.). 64p. lib. bdg. 30.00 *(978-0-531-23063-3(5))* 2010. 48p. pap. 6.95 *(978-0-531-21247-9(5)*, Children's Pr.) Scholastic Library Publishing.
Graham, Amy. The Oregon Trail & the Daring Journey West by Wagon. 2006. (Wild History of the American West Ser.). (Illus.). 128p. (J). (gr. 5-9). lib. bdg. 34.60 *(978-1-59845-021-7(2)*, MyReportLinks.com Bks.) Enslow Pubs., Inc.
Group/McGraw-Hill, Wright. History: The Oregon Trail, 6 vols. (Book2WebTM Ser.). (gr. 4-8). 36.50 *(978-0-322-04452-4(9))* Wright Group/McGraw-Hill.
Gunderson, Jessica. Your Life As a Pioneer on the Oregon Trail. Dougherty, Rachel, illus. 2012. (Way It Was Ser.). (ENG.). 32p. (gr. 2-3). pap. 8.95 *(978-1-4048-7250-9(7))*; lib. bdg. 26.65 *(978-1-4048-7157-1(8))* Picture Window Bks.
Harness, Cheryl. The Tragic Tale of Narcissa Whitman & a Faithful History of the Oregon Trail. Harness, Cheryl, illus. 2006. (Cheryl Harness Histories Ser.). (ENG., Illus.). 144p. (J). (gr. 5-9). 16.95 *(978-0-7922-5920-6(3))*; lib. bdg. 25.90 *(978-0-7922-5921-3(1))* National Geographic Society. (National Geographic Children's Bks.).
Jeffrey, Gary. The Oregon Trail. Poluzzi, Allesandro, illus. 2012. (Graphic History of the American West Ser.). (ENG.). 24p. (J). (gr. 3-8). pap. 8.15 *(978-1-4339-6745-0(6)*, Gareth Stevens Learning Library); (gr. 4-7). lib. bdg. 23.95 *(978-1-4339-6743-6(X))* Stevens, Gareth Publishing LLLP.
Kravitz, Danny. Surviving the Journey: The Story of the Oregon Trail, 1 vol. 2014. (Adventures on the American Frontier Ser.). (ENG.). 32p. (gr. 3-4). 27.32 *(978-1-4914-0187-3(7)*, Fact Finders) Capstone Press of Coughlan Cos.
Landau, Elaine. The Oregon Trail. 2006. (True Bks.). (ENG., Illus.). 48p. (J). (gr. 3-7). pap. 6.95 *(978-0-516-27903-9(3)*, Children's Pr.) Scholastic Library Publishing.
Lusted, Marcia Amidon. The Oregon Trail, 1 vol. 2011. (Essential Events Set 7 Ser.). (ENG., Illus.). 112p. (J). (gr. 6-12). lib. bdg. 35.64 *(978-1-61783-102-7(6))* ABDO Publishing Co.
Lynette, Rachel. The Oregon Trail. 2013. (Pioneer Spirit: the Westward Expansion Ser.). 24p. (J). (gr. 3-6). 22.60 *(978-1-4777-0786-9(7))*; (ENG., Illus.). pap. 8.25 *(978-1-4777-0905-4(3))* Rosen Publishing Group, Inc., The. (PowerKids Pr.).
Marciniak, Kristin. The Oregon Trail & Westward Expansion: A History Perspectives Book. 2013. (Perspectives Library). (ENG., Illus.). 32p. (J). (gr. 4-8). 28.50 *(978-1-62431-419-3(8)*, 202796); pap. 14.21 *(978-1-62431-495-7(3)*, 202798) Cherry Lake Publishing.
Nash, Nancy. Mama's Books: An Oregon Trail Story. Burke, Ruth Anne, illus. 2013. (J). pap. 9.95 *(978-0-9838653-6-0(1))* Doorlight Pubns.
Olson, Steven. The Oregon Trail: A Primary Source History of the Route to the American West. 2009. (Primary Sources in American History Ser.). 64p. (gr. 5-8). 58.50 *(978-1-60851-501-1(X))* Rosen Publishing Group, Inc., The.
Olson, Steven P. The Oregon Trail. 2004. (Primary Sources in American History Ser.). (Illus.). 64p. (gr. 5-8). lib. bdg. 31.95 *(978-0-8239-4512-2(X)*, Rosen Reference) Rosen Publishing Group, Inc., The.
The Oregon Trail. 2013. (Pioneer Spirit: the Westward Expansion Ser.). 24p. (J). (gr. 3-6). pap. 49.50 *(978-1-4777-0906-1(1)*, PowerKids Pr.) Rosen Publishing Group, Inc., The.
Proudfit, Benjamin. The Oregon Trail. 2016. (Road Trip Ser.). (Illus.). 24p. (J). (gr. 3-2). pap. 8.15 *(978-1-4824-4675-3(8))* Stevens, Gareth Publishing LLLP.
Stefoff, Rebecca. Surviving the Oregon Trail. 2012. (Stories in American History Ser.). (Illus.). 128p. (J). (gr. 5-18). 33.27 *(978-0-7660-3955-1(2))* Enslow Pubs., Inc.
—Surviving the Oregon Trail: Stories in American History. 2012. (Stories in American History Ser.). (Illus.). 128p. (J). (gr. 5-18). pap. 10.95 *(978-1-4644-0025-4(3))* Enslow Pubs., Inc.
Tieck, Sarah. Oregon Trail, 1 vol. 2008. (All Aboard America Ser.). (ENG.). 24p. (J). (gr. 1-4). 25.65 *(978-1-59928-939-7(3))* ABDO Publishing Co.
Uschan, Michael V. The Oregon Trail. 2004. (Great Cities of the World Ser.). (Illus.). 48p. (gr. 5-12). pap. 14.05 *(978-0-8368-5414-5(4)*, Gareth Stevens Secondary Library) Stevens, Gareth Publishing LLLP.

OREGON NATIONAL HISTORIC TRAIL—FICTION

Bly, Stephen A. The Lost Wagon Train. 2005. (Retta Barre's Oregon Trail Ser.: Vol. 1). 110p. pap. 5.99 *(978-1-58134-391-5(4)*, Crossway Bibles) Crossway.
Carr, Mary Jane. Children of the Covered Wagon. 2007. (Illus.). 266p. per. 9.95 *(978-1-932971-50-7(5))* Christian Liberty Pr.
Kelso, Mary Jean. The Christmas Angel. Snider, K. C., illus. 2007. 32p. (J). 11.95 *(978-1-933090-58-0(8))* Guardian Angel Publishing, Inc.
Lee, Stacey. Under a Painted Sky. 2015. (ENG.). 384p. (YA). (gr. 7). 16.99 *(978-0-399-16803-1(6)*, G.P. Putnam's Sons Books for Young Readers) Penguin Young Readers Group.
—Under a Painted Sky. 2016. lib. bdg. 22.10 *(978-0-606-38391-2(3))* Turtleback Bks.
Marsh, Carole. The Mystery on the Oregon Trail. 2010. (Real Kids, Real Places Ser.). (Illus.). 158p. (J). 18.99 *(978-0-635-07440-9(0)*, Marsh, Carole Mysteries) Gallopade International.
—The Mystery on the Oregon Trail. Friedlander, Randolyn, illus. 2010. (Real Kids, Real Places Ser.). 32p. pap. 7.99 *(978-0-635-07441-6(9)*, Marsh, Carole Mysteries) Gallopade International.
Messner, Kate. Rescue on the Oregon Trail. McMorris, Kelley, illus. 2015. (Ranger in Time Ser.: 1). (ENG.). 144p. (J). (gr. 2-5). pap. 5.99 *(978-0-545-63914-9(X)*, Scholastic Pr.) Scholastic, Inc.
Olson, Tod. How to Get Rich on the Oregon Trail. Allred, Scott & Proch, Gregory, illus. 2009. (How to Get Rich Ser.). (ENG.). 48p. (J). (gr. 5-9). 18.95 *(978-1-4263-0412-5(9)*, National Geographic Children's Bks.) National Geographic Society.
—How to Get Rich on the Oregon Trail. Proch, Gregory & Allred, Scott, illus. 2009. (How to Get Rich Ser.). (ENG.). 48p. (J). (gr. 5-9). lib. bdg. 27.90 *(978-1-4263-0413-2(7)*,

National Geographic Children's Bks.) National Geographic Society.
Pierpoint, Eric. The Last Ride of Caleb O'Toole. 2013. (ENG.). 304p. (J). (gr. 4-7). pap. 7.99 *(978-1-4022-8171-6(4),* 9781402281716, Sourcebooks Jabberwocky) Sourcebooks, Inc.
Scillian, Devin & Young, Judy. Westward Journeys. Ellison, Chris et al, illus. 2013. (American Adventures Ser.). (ENG.). 96p. (J). (gr. 3-6). pap. 6.99 *(978-1-58536-860-0(1),* 202367) Sleeping Bear Pr.
Wilson, Laura. How I Survived the Oregon Trail: The Journal of Jesse Adams. 2006. (Illus.). 37p. (J). (gr. 4-8). reprint ed. pap. 10.00 *(978-0-7567-9925-0(2))* DIANE Publishing Co.
Winters, Kay. Voices from the Oregon Trail. Day, Larry, illus. 2014. (ENG.). 48p. (J). (gr. 2-4). 17.99 *(978-0-8037-3775-4(0),* Dial Bks) Penguin Young Readers Group.

OREGON TRAIL
see Oregon National Historic Trail

ORGANIC CHEMISTRY
see Chemistry, Organic

ORGANIC FARMING
Barker, David M. Organic Foods. 2016. (Growing Green Ser.). (ENG., Illus.). 64p. (J). (gr. 6-8). lib. bdg. 34.65 *(978-1-4677-9391-9(4));* 51.99 *(978-1-4677-9712-2(X),* Lerner Pubns.) Lerner Publishing Group.
Centore, Michael. Organic Foods. 2017. (J). ***(978-1-4222-3740-3(0))*** Mason Crest.
Flounders, Anne. Growing Good Food. 2014. (Our Green Earth Ser.). (Illus.). 32p. (gr. 2-4). pap. 8.95 *(978-1-939656-31-5(1))* Red Chair Pr.
Francis, Amy. The Local Food Movement. 2010. (At Issue Ser.). (ENG.). 128p. (gr. 10-12). 39.40 *(978-0-7377-4888-8(5));* pap. 27.80 *(978-0-7377-4889-5(3),* Greenhaven Pr., Inc.) Cengage Gale.
Hodge, Deborah. Up We Grow! A Year in the Life of a Small, Local Farm. Harris, Brian, illus. 2010. (ENG.). 32p. (J). (gr. -1-2). 16.95 *(978-1-55453-561-3(1))* Kids Can Pr., Ltd. CAN. Dist: Hachette Bk. Group.
Hurt, Avery Elizabeth. Corporate Farming. 2017. (J). pap. ***(978-1-5345-0049-5(9))*** Greenhaven Publishing LLC.
Mickelson, Trina. Free-Range Farming. 2016. (Growing Green Ser.). (ENG., Illus.). 64p. (J). (gr. 6-8). lib. bdg. 34.65 *(978-1-4677-9389-6(2));* 51.99 *(978-1-4677-9710-8(3),* Lerner Pubns.) Lerner Publishing Group.
Orr, Tamra. Organic Farmer. 2009. (21st Century Skills Library: Cool Careers Ser.). (ENG.). 32p. (gr. 4-8). lib. bdg. 28.50 *(978-1-60279-500-6(2),* 200312) Cherry Lake Publishing.
Reilly, Kathleen M. Food - 25 Amazing Projects: Investigate the History & Science of What We Eat. Carbaugh, Samuel, illus. 2010. (Build It Yourself Ser.). (ENG.). 128p. (J). (gr. 3-7). 21.95 *(978-1-934670-60-6(X))* Octavio Publishing.
—Food - 25 Amazing Projects: Investigate the History & Science of What We Eat. Carbaugh, Samuel & Rizvi, Farah, illus. 2010. (Build It Yourself Ser.). (ENG.). 128p. (J). (gr. 3-7). pap. 15.95 *(978-1-934670-59-0(6))* Octavio Publishing.
ShackletonCaroline. MONEY TREE: THE BUSINESS OF ORGANICS HIGH INTERMEDIATE BOOK WITH ONLINE ACCESS, 1 vol. 2014. (ENG., Illus.). 28p. (J). pap. 9.50 *(978-1-107-63678-1(7))* Cambridge Univ. Pr.
Squire, Ann O. Organic Food. 2017. (True Book(tm), a — Farm to Table Ser.). (ENG., Illus.). 48p. (J). lib. bdg. 31.00 *(978-0-531-22934-7(3),* Children's Pr.) Scholastic Library Publishing.

ORGANIC GARDENING
Aloian, Molly. Green Gardening & Composting. 2013. (ENG.). 24p. (J). *(978-0-7787-0262-7(6));* pap. *(978-0-7787-0276-4(6))* Crabtree Publishing Co.
Dunn-Georgiou, Elisha. Everything You Need to Know about Organic Foods. (Need to Know Library). 64p. 2009. (gr. 5-5). 58.50 *(978-1-60854-079-2(0))* 2005. (Illus.). (YA). (gr. 4-6). lib. bdg. 31.95 *(978-0-8239-3551-2(5))* Rosen Publishing Group, Inc., The.
Korrow, Chris. The Organic Bug Book. Korrow, Chris, illus. 2013. (ENG., Illus.). 44p. (J). pap. 11.95 *(978-1-58420-145-8(2),* Lindisfarne Bks.) SteinerBooks, Inc.
Loh-Hagan, Virginia. Organic Garden. 2016. (D. I. Y. Make It Happen Ser.). (ENG.). 32p. (J). (gr. 4-8). 29.93 *(978-1-63471-102-9(5),* 208519, 45th Parallel Press) Cherry Lake Publishing.
McKenzie, Precious. Our Organic Garden. 2011. (ENG., Illus.). 24p. (gr. k-2). pap. 8.95 *(978-1-61741-969-0(9))* Rourke Educational Media.
Scholl, Elizabeth. Organic Gardening for Kids. 2009. (Gardening for Kids Ser.). (Illus.). 48p. (YA). (gr. 1-4). lib. bdg. 29.95 *(978-1-58415-815-8(8))* Mitchell Lane Pubs., Inc.
Siddals, Mary McKenna. Compost Stew: An a to Z Recipe for the Earth. Wolff, Ashley, illus. 2014. (ENG.). 40p. (J). (gr. -1-2). 7.99 *(978-0-385-75538-2(4),* Dragonfly Bks.) Random Hse. Children's Bks.
Spilsbury, Louise. How Community Gardens Work. 2013. (EcoWorks Ser.). 32p. (J). (gr. 3-5). pap. 10.50 *(978-1-4339-9557-6(3));* pap. 63.00 *(978-1-4339-9558-3(1));* (ENG., Illus.). lib. bdg. 26.60 *(978-1-4339-9556-9(5))* Stevens, Gareth Publishing LLLP.
Squire, Ann O. Organic Food. 2017. (True Book(tm), a — Farm to Table Ser.). (ENG., Illus.). 48p. (J). lib. bdg. 31.00 *(978-0-531-22934-7(3),* Children's Pr.) Scholastic Library Publishing.
Winckler, Suzanne. Planting the Seed: A Guide to Gardening. 2005. (Illus.). 64p. (gr. 5-12). 25.76 *(978-0-8225-0081-0(7))* Lerner Publishing Group.

ORGANICULTURE
see Organic Farming; Organic Gardening

ORGANIZATION, INTERNATIONAL
see International Organization

ORGANIZATION AND MANAGEMENT
see Management

ORGANIZATION OF AFRICAN UNITY
Badejo, Diedre L. The African Union. 2008. (Global Organizations Ser.). (Illus.). 128p. (YA). (gr. 7-12). 35.00 *(978-0-7910-9543-0(6))* Facts On File, Inc.

ORGANIZED CRIME
see Racketeering

ORGANIZED LABOR
see Labor Unions

ORIENTATION
Champion, Neil. Finding Your Way. 2010. (Survive Alive Ser.). 32p. (J). (gr. 3-6). 28.50 *(978-1-60753-038-1(4))* Amicus Publishing.
Champion, Neil & Ganeri, Anita. Finding Food & Water. 2011. (How the World Makes Music Ser.). 32p. (gr. 4-7). lib. bdg. 31.35 *(978-1-59920-478-9(9))* Black Rabbit Bks.
De Capua, Sarah. Como Nos Orientamos? 2005. (Rookie Reader Español Ser.). (SPA., Illus.). 32p. (J). (gr. k-2). lib. bdg. 19.50 *(978-0-516-24442-6(6),* Children's Pr.) Scholastic Library Publishing.
Katirgis, Jane. Up & Down. 2011. (All about Opposites Ser.). (Illus.). 24p. (J). (gr. -1-18). pap. 7.95 *(978-1-59845-258-7(4),* Enslow Elementary); (gr. k-3). lib. bdg. 22.60 *(978-0-7660-3913-1(7))* Enslow Pubs., Inc.
Nelson, Robin. Staying Clean. 2005. (Pull Ahead Books: Health Ser.). (ENG., Illus.). 32p. (gr. k-3). lib. bdg. 22.60 *(978-0-8225-2638-4(7))* Lerner Publishing Group.
Oxlade, Chris. Be an Explorer. Sassin, Eva, illus. 2015. (Go Wild Ser.). (ENG.). 32p. (J). (gr. 3-6). lib. bdg. 26.65 *(978-1-4677-6358-5(6))* Lerner Publishing Group.
Rivera, Sheila. Above & Below. 2005. (First Step Nonfiction - Location Ser.). (ENG.). 8p. (gr. -1-1). pap. 4.95 *(978-0-8225-5355-7(4),* Lerner Pubns.) Lerner Publishing Group.
—Behind & in Front. 2005. (First Step Nonfiction - Location Ser.). (ENG.). 8p. (gr. -1-1). pap. 4.95 *(978-0-8225-5352-6(X),* Lerner Pubns.) Lerner Publishing Group.
—Left & Right. 2004. (First Step Nonfiction Ser.). (J). pap. 3.95 *(978-0-8225-5351-9(1),* Lerner Pubns.) Lerner Publishing Group.
Savage, Jeff. Carly Patterson. 2005. (Amazing Athletes Ser.). (Illus.). 32p. (J). 23.93 *(978-0-8225-2639-1(5),* Lerner Pubns.) Lerner Publishing Group.
Woods, Michael & Woods, Mary B. The History of Medicine. 2005. (Major Inventions Through History Ser.). (ENG., Illus.). 56p. (gr. 5-8). lib. bdg. 26.60 *(978-0-8225-2636-0(0),* Twenty-First Century Bks.) Lerner Publishing Group.

ORIGAMI
see also Paper Work
Akass, Susan. My First Origami Book. 2011. (ENG., Illus.). 128p. (J). (gr. 7-11). pap. 14.95 *(978-1-907563-70-6(9),* 1907563709, CICO Books) Ryland Peters & Small GBR. Dist: WIPRO.
Amazing Geogami. 2007. *(978-1-884270-11-6(5));* *(978-1-884270-10-9(7))* Hall, Nancy Inc.
Amazing Origami. 2013. (Amazing Origami Ser.). 32p. (J). (gr. 2-5). pap. 378.00 *(978-1-4339-9814-0(9));* pap. 63.00 *(978-1-4339-9813-3(0))* Stevens, Gareth Publishing LLLP.
Amazing Origami: Set 2. 2015. (Amazing Origami Ser.). (ENG.). 32p. (J). (gr. 2-3). 159.60 *(978-1-4824-2198-9(4))* Stevens, Gareth Publishing LLLP.
Amazing Origami: Set 4. 2016. (Amazing Origami Ser.). 00032p. (J). lib. bdg. 159.60 ***(978-1-4824-5848-0(9))*** Stevens, Gareth Publishing LLLP.
Angleberger, Tom. Art2-D2's Guide to Folding & Doodling. (Origami Yoda Ser.). (ENG., Illus.). (J). (gr. 3-7). 2016. 192p. pap. 7.95 *(978-1-4197-2028-4(7))* 2013. 176p. 12.95 *(978-1-4197-0534-2(2))* Abrams, Inc. (Amulet Bks.).
—Darth Paper Strikes Back. 2015. (Origami Yoda Ser.). (ENG., Illus.). 176p. (J). (gr. 3-7). pap. 7.95 *(978-1-4197-1640-9(9),* Amulet Bks.) Abrams, Inc.
Animal Kingdom Origami. 2017. (Animal Kingdom Origami Ser.). 32p. (gr. 8-8). 165.00 ***(978-1-4994-3398-2(0));*** pap. 70.50 ***(978-1-5081-5370-2(1))*** Rosen Publishing Group, Inc., The. (PowerKids Pr.).
Ard, Catherine. Origami Bugs. 2015. (Amazing Origami Ser.). (ENG.). 32p. (J). (gr. 2-3). 26.60 *(978-1-4824-2199-6(2))* Stevens, Gareth Publishing LLLP.
—Origami Holidays. 2015. (Amazing Origami Ser.). (ENG.). 32p. (J). (gr. 2-3). 26.60 *(978-1-4824-2200-9(X))* Stevens, Gareth Publishing LLLP.
—Origami Monsters. 2015. (Amazing Origami Ser.). (ENG.). 32p. (J). (gr. 2-3). 26.60 *(978-1-4824-2201-6(8))* Stevens, Gareth Publishing LLLP.
—Origami on the Move. 2015. (Amazing Origami Ser.). (ENG.). 32p. (J). (gr. 2-3). 26.60 *(978-1-4824-2202-3(6))* Stevens, Gareth Publishing LLLP.
—Origami Planes. 2015. (Amazing Origami Ser.). (ENG.). 32p. (J). (gr. 2-3). 26.60 *(978-1-4824-2203-0(4))* Stevens, Gareth Publishing LLLP.
—Origami Space. 2015. (Amazing Origami Ser.). (ENG.). 32p. (J). (gr. 2-3). 26.60 *(978-1-4824-2204-7(2))* Stevens, Gareth Publishing LLLP.
Amstein, Bennett Roy. The Saturday Afternoon Public Library Origami Club Manual: Not Just Another Origami Book. 2004. (Illus.). 69p. 11.95 *(978-0-9620058-2-4(7))* Amstein, Bennett.
Azzità, Emanuele. Origami Arts & Crafts. 2017. (Exciting Origami Ser.). 48p. (J). (gr. 3-3). pap. 11.70 ***(978-0-7660-8761-3(1));*** lib. bdg. 27.93 ***(978-0-7660-8646-3(1))*** Enslow Pubs., Inc.
—Origami Birds. 2017. (Exciting Origami Ser.). 48p. (J). (gr. 3-3). pap. 11.70 ***(978-0-7660-8759-0(X));*** lib. bdg. 27.93 ***(978-0-7660-8648-7(8))*** Enslow Pubs., Inc.
—Origami Land & Sea Animals. 2017. (Exciting Origami Ser.). 48p. (J). (gr. 3-3). lib. bdg. 27.93 ***(978-0-7660-8718-7(2))*** Enslow Pubs., Inc.
Behar, Susan & Robinson, Nick. Origami XOXO, 1 vol. 2012. (Secret Origami Ser.). (ENG.). 48p. (gr. 4-5). pap. 12.95 *(978-1-4296-9852-8(7))* Capstone Press of Coughlan Cos.
Biddle, Steve & Biddle, Megumi. Paper Capers — a First Book of Paper-Folding Fun: Includes 24 Sheets of Origami Paper. 2014. (ENG.). 64p. (J). (gr. 4-4). pap. 9.99 *(978-0-486-49164-6(1))* Dover Pubns., Inc.
Bolitho, Mark. Fold Your Own Origami Air Force. 2013. 32p. (J). (gr. 3-6). 26.50 *(978-1-4777-1319-8(0));* pap. 11.75 *(978-1-4777-1469-0(3))* Rosen Publishing Group, Inc., The. (PowerKids Pr.).
—Fold Your Own Origami Army. 2013. 32p. (J). (gr. 3-6). 26.50 *(978-1-4777-1317-4(4));* pap. 11.75 *(978-1-4777-1465-2(0))* Rosen Publishing Group, Inc., The. (PowerKids Pr.).
—Fold Your Own Origami Navy. 2013. 32p. (J). (gr. 3-6). 26.50 *(978-1-4777-1318-1(2));* pap. 11.75 *(978-1-4777-1467-6(7))* Rosen Publishing Group, Inc., The. (PowerKids Pr.).
—Fold Your Own Origami Weapons. 2013. 32p. (J). (gr. 3-6). 26.50 *(978-1-4777-1320-4(4));* pap. 11.75 *(978-1-4777-1471-3(5))* Rosen Publishing Group, Inc., The. (PowerKids Pr.).
Boursin, Didier. Easy Origami. 2005. (ENG., Illus.). 64p. (J). (gr. 2-8). pap. 9.95 *(978-1-55297-939-6(3),* 9781552979396) Firefly Bks., Ltd.
Braun, Eric. Let's Rock! Science Adventures with Rudie the Origami Dinosaur, 1 vol. Christoph, Jamey, illus. 2013. (Origami Science Adventures Ser.). (ENG.). 24p. (gr. 3-4). pap. 6.95 *(978-1-4048-8068-9(2));* lib. bdg. 27.32 *(978-1-4048-7971-3(4))* Picture Window Bks.
—Lookin' for Light: Science Adventures with Manny the Origami Moth, 1 vol. Christoph, Jamey, illus. 2014. (Origami Science Adventures Ser.). (ENG.). 24p. (gr. 3-4). lib. bdg. 27.32 *(978-1-4795-2186-9(8))* Picture Window Bks.
—Simply Sound: Science Adventures with Jasper the Origami Bat, 1 vol. Christoph, Jamey, illus. 2014. (Origami Science Adventures Ser.). (ENG.). 24p. (gr. 3-4). lib. bdg. 27.32 *(978-1-4795-2187-6(6))* Picture Window Bks.
Braun, Eric & Troupe, Thomas Kingsley. Origami Science Adventures, 1 vol. Christoph, Jamey, illus. 2014. (Origami Science Adventures Ser.). (ENG.). 24p. (gr. 3-4). lib. bdg. 109.28 *(978-1-4795-3365-7(3))* Picture Window Bks.
Butler, Tom. Origami Animals. 2016. (Mastering Origami Ser.). 48p. (gr. 6-5). pap. 11.70 *(978-0-7660-7944-1(9))* Enslow Pubs., Inc.
—Origami Toys & Games. 2016. (Mastering Origami Ser.). 48p. (gr. 6-5). pap. 11.70 *(978-0-7660-7948-9(1))* Enslow Pubs., Inc.
—Origami Vehicles. 2016. (Mastering Origami Ser.). 48p. (gr. 6-5). pap. 11.70 *(978-0-7660-7952-6(X))* Enslow Pubs., Inc.
—Practical Origami. 2016. (Mastering Origami Ser.). 48p. (gr. 6-5). pap. 11.70 *(978-0-7660-7955-7(4))* Enslow Pubs., Inc.
Cook, Trevor & Henry, Sally. Origami: A Step-By-Step Introduction to the Art of Paper Folding. 2012. (ENG., Illus.). 96p. (J). pap. 12.95 *(978-1-84858-650-5(7),* 9781848586505) Arcturus Publishing GBR. Dist: Bookmasters Distribution.
Dare, Sterling. Money Menagerie: A Collection of Wild or Strange Animals. 2004. 15.00 *(978-0-9727938-3-4(6))* H & R Magic Bks.
Diaz, James. Popigami: When Everyday Paper Pops! Diaz, Francesca, illus. 2007. (ENG.). 8p. (J). (gr. -1). 19.95 *(978-1-58117-641-4(4),* Intervisual/Piggy Toes) Bendon, Inc.
Easy Origami. 2010. (Easy Origami Ser.). (ENG.). 24p. (gr. 1-2). lib. bdg. 101.28 *(978-1-4296-5388-6(4),* First Facts) Capstone Press of Coughlan Cos.
Everything Origami. 2015. (Everything Origami Ser.). (ENG.). 32p. (J). (gr. 3-4). pap., pap., pap. 423.00 *(978-1-4777-5677-5(9),* Windmill Bks.) Rosen Publishing Group, Inc., The.
Exciting Origami. 2017. (Exciting Origami Ser.). 48p. (gr. 3-3). pap. 46.80 ***(978-0-7660-8807-8(3));*** lib. bdg. 111.72 ***(978-0-7660-8592-3(9))*** Enslow Pubs., Inc.
Fold Your Own Origami Air Force. 2013. (Origami Army Ser.). 32p. (J). (gr. 3-6). pap. 70.50 *(978-1-4777-1470-6(7),* PowerKids Pr.) Rosen Publishing Group, Inc., The.
Fold Your Own Origami Army. 2013. (Origami Army Ser.). 32p. (J). (gr. 3-6). pap. 70.50 *(978-1-4777-1466-9(9),* PowerKids Pr.) Rosen Publishing Group, Inc., The.
Fold Your Own Origami Navy. 2013. (Origami Army Ser.). 32p. (J). (gr. 3-6). pap. 70.50 *(978-1-4777-1468-3(5),* PowerKids Pr.) Rosen Publishing Group, Inc., The.
Fold Your Own Origami Weapons. 2013. (Origami Army Ser.). 32p. (J). (gr. 3-6). pap. 70.50 *(978-1-4777-1472-0(3),* PowerKids Pr.) Rosen Publishing Group, Inc., The.
Fullman, Joe. Arctic Origami. 2016. (Amazing Origami Ser.). 00032p. (J). pap. 10.50 ***(978-1-4824-5920-3(5))*** Stevens, Gareth Publishing LLLP.
—Desert Origami. 2016. (Amazing Origami Ser.). 00032p. (J). pap. 10.50 ***(978-1-4824-5924-1(8))*** Stevens, Gareth Publishing LLLP.
—Floating Origami. 2016. (Amazing Origami Ser.). (ENG.). 32p. (J). (gr. 2-3). lib. bdg. 26.60 *(978-1-4824-4167-3(5))* Stevens, Gareth Publishing LLLP.
—Flying Origami. 2016. (Amazing Origami Ser.). (ENG.). 32p. (J). (gr. 2-3). pap. 10.50 *(978-1-4824-4155-0(1))* Stevens, Gareth Publishing LLLP.
—Jungle Origami. 2016. (Amazing Origami Ser.). 00032p. (J). pap. 10.50 ***(978-1-4824-5928-9(0))*** Stevens, Gareth Publishing LLLP.
—Ocean Origami. 2016. (Amazing Origami Ser.). 00032p. (J). pap. 10.50 ***(978-1-4824-5932-6(9))*** Stevens, Gareth Publishing LLLP.
—Origami Games. 2016. (Amazing Origami Ser.). (ENG.). 32p. (J). (gr. 2-3). pap. 10.50 *(978-1-4824-4159-8(4))* Stevens, Gareth Publishing LLLP.
—Origami Magic. 2016. (Amazing Origami Ser.). (ENG.). 32p. (J). (gr. 2-3). pap. 10.50 *(978-1-4824-4163-5(2))* Stevens, Gareth Publishing LLLP.
—Safari Origami. 2016. (Amazing Origami Ser.). 00032p. (J). pap. 10.50 ***(978-1-4824-5936-4(1))*** Stevens, Gareth Publishing LLLP.
—Snapping & Speaking Origami. 2016. (Amazing Origami Ser.). (ENG.). 32p. (J). (gr. 2-3). pap. 10.50 *(978-1-4824-4175-8(6))* Stevens, Gareth Publishing LLLP.
Fullman, Joe. Woodland Origami. 2016. (Amazing Origami Ser.). 00032p. (J). pap. 10.50 ***(978-1-4824-5940-1(X))*** Stevens, Gareth Publishing LLLP.
Gardiner, Matthew. Everything Origami Set. 2015. (Everything Origami Ser.). (ENG., Illus.). 32p. (J). pap., pap., pap. 70.50 *(978-1-4777-5678-2(7),* Windmill Bks.) Rosen Publishing Group, Inc., The.
Hanson, Anders & Mann, Elissa. Cool Paper Folding: Creative Activities That Make Math & Science Fun for Kids!, 1 vol. 2013. (Cool Art with Math & Science Ser.). (ENG.). 32p. (J). (gr. 3-6). lib. bdg. 28.50 *(978-1-61783-823-1(3),* Checkerboard Library) ABDO Publishing Co.
Harbo, Christopher. Easy Origami Decorations: An Augmented Reality Crafting Experience. 2017. (Origami Crafting 4D Ser.). (ENG., Illus.). 24p. (gr. 1-2). lib. bdg. 26.65 *(978-1-5157-3585-4(0),* First Facts) Capstone Press of Coughlan Cos.
—Easy Origami Greeting Cards: An Augmented Reality Crafting Experience. 2017. (Origami Crafting 4D Ser.). (ENG., Illus.). 24p. (gr. 1-2). lib. bdg. 26.65 *(978-1-5157-3587-8(7),* First Facts) Capstone Press of Coughlan Cos.
—Easy Origami Ornaments: An Augmented Reality Crafting Experience. 2017. (Origami Crafting 4D Ser.). (ENG., Illus.). 24p. (gr. 1-2). lib. bdg. 26.65 *(978-1-5157-3586-1(9),* First Facts) Capstone Press of Coughlan Cos.
—Easy Origami Scrapbooking: An Augmented Reality Crafting Experience. 2017. (Origami Crafting 4D Ser.). (ENG., Illus.). 24p. (gr. 1-2). lib. bdg. 26.65 *(978-1-5157-3584-7(2),* First Facts) Capstone Press of Coughlan Cos.
—Origami Crafting 4D. 2017. (Origami Crafting 4D Ser.). (ENG.). 24p. (gr. 1-2). 106.60 *(978-1-5157-3588-5(5),* First Facts) Capstone Press of Coughlan Cos.
—Origami Paperpalooza. 2015. (Origami Paperpalooza Ser.). (ENG.). 32p. (gr. 3-4). lib. bdg. 111.96 *(978-1-4914-2548-0(2),* Edge Bks.) Capstone Press of Coughlan Cos.
Harbo, Christopher L. Easy Animal Origami, 1 vol. 2010. (Easy Origami Ser.). (ENG.). 24p. (gr. 1-2). lib. bdg. 25.32 *(978-1-4296-5384-8(1),* First Facts) Capstone Press of Coughlan Cos.
—Easy Holiday Origami, 1 vol. 2010. (Easy Origami Ser.). (ENG.). 24p. (gr. 1-2). lib. bdg. 25.32 *(978-1-4296-5387-9(6),* First Facts) Capstone Press of Coughlan Cos.
—Easy Magician Origami, 1 vol. 2011. (Easy Origami Ser.). (ENG.). 24p. (gr. 1-2). lib. bdg. 25.32 *(978-1-4296-6000-6(7),* First Facts) Capstone Press of Coughlan Cos.
—Easy Ocean Origami, 1 vol. 2010. (Easy Origami Ser.). (ENG.). 24p. (gr. 1-2). lib. bdg. 25.32 *(978-1-4296-5385-5(X),* First Facts) Capstone Press of Coughlan Cos.
—Easy Origami. 2011. (Easy Origami Ser.). (ENG.). 24p. (gr. 1-2). lib. bdg. 50.64 *(978-1-4296-6136-2(4),* First Facts) Capstone Press of Coughlan Cos.
—Easy Origami, 6 vols., Set. Incl. Easy Animal Origami. 2010. lib. bdg. 25.32 *(978-1-4296-5384-8(1));* Easy Holiday Origami. 2010. lib. bdg. 25.32 *(978-1-4296-5387-9(6));* Easy Magician Origami. 2011. lib. bdg. 25.32 *(978-1-4296-6000-6(7));* Easy Ocean Origami. 2010. lib. bdg. 25.32 *(978-1-4296-5385-5(X));* Easy Origami Toys. 2010. lib. bdg. 25.32 *(978-1-4296-5386-2(8));* Easy Space Origami. 2011. lib. bdg. 25.32 *(978-1-4296-6001-3(5));* (gr. 1-2). (Easy Origami Ser.). (ENG.). 24p. 2011. Set lib. bdg. 151.92 *(978-1-4296-6137-9(2),* First Facts) Capstone Press of Coughlan Cos.
—Easy Origami Toys, 1 vol. 2010. (Easy Origami Ser.). (ENG.). 24p. (gr. 1-2). lib. bdg. 25.32 *(978-1-4296-5386-2(8),* First Facts) Capstone Press of Coughlan Cos.
—Easy Space Origami, 1 vol. 2011. (Easy Origami Ser.). (ENG.). 24p. (gr. 1-2). lib. bdg. 25.32 *(978-1-4296-6001-3(5),* First Facts) Capstone Press of Coughlan Cos.
—Origami Explosion: Scorpions, Whales, Boxes, & More! 2015. (Origami Paperpalooza Ser.). (ENG.). 32p. (gr. 3-4). lib. bdg. 27.99 *(978-1-4914-2023-2(5))* Capstone Press of Coughlan Cos.
—Origami Folding Frenzy: Boats, Fish, Cranes, & More! 2015. (Origami Paperpalooza Ser.). (ENG.). 32p. (gr. 3-4). lib. bdg. 27.99 *(978-1-4914-2021-8(9))* Capstone Press of Coughlan Cos.
—Origami Palooza: Dragons, Turtles, Birds, & More! 2015. (Origami Paperpalooza Ser.). (ENG.). 32p. (gr. 3-4). lib. bdg. 27.99 *(978-1-4914-2024-9(3))* Capstone Press of Coughlan Cos.
—Origami Paperpalooza! 2015. (ENG., Illus.). 144p. (gr. 3-4). pap. 14.95 *(978-1-62370-227-4(5))* Capstone Press of Coughlan Cos.
—Origami Papertainment: Samurai, Owls, Ninja Stars, & More! 2015. (Origami Paperpalooza Ser.). (ENG.). 32p. (gr. 3-4). lib. bdg. 27.99 *(978-1-4914-2022-5(7))* Capstone Press of Coughlan Cos.
Hardyman, Roby. Origami Fun: Pets. 2017. (Origami Fun Ser.). (ENG., Illus.). 24p. (YA). (gr. 3-7). lib. bdg. 25.95 ***(978-1-62617-714-7(7),*** Express Bks.) Bellwether Media.
Hardyman, Robyn. Origami Fun: Aircraft. 2017. (Origami Fun Ser.). (ENG., Illus.). 24p. (YA). (gr. 3-7). lib. bdg. 25.95 ***(978-1-62617-707-9(4))*** Bellwether Media.
—Origami Fun: Birds. 2017. (Origami Fun Ser.). (ENG., Illus.). 24p. (YA). (gr. 3-7). lib. bdg. 25.95 ***(978-1-62617-708-6(2),*** Express Bks.) Bellwether Media.
—Origami Fun: Dinosaurs. 2017. (Origami Fun Ser.). (ENG., Illus.). 24p. (YA). (gr. 3-7). lib. bdg. 25.95 ***(978-1-62617-709-3(0),*** Express Bks.) Bellwether Media.
—Origami Fun: Farm Animals. 2017. (Origami Fun Ser.). (ENG., Illus.). 24p. (YA). (gr. 3-7). lib. bdg. 25.95 ***(978-1-62617-710-9(4),*** Express Bks.) Bellwether Media.
—Origami Fun: Holidays. 2017. (Origami Fun Ser.). (ENG., Illus.). 24p. (YA). (gr. 3-7). lib. bdg. 25.95 ***(978-1-62617-711-6(2))*** Bellwether Media.
—Origami Fun: Jungle Animals. 2017. (Origami Fun Ser.). (ENG., Illus.). 24p. (YA). (gr. 3-7). lib. bdg. 25.95 ***(978-1-62617-712-3(0),*** Express Bks.) Bellwether Media.
—Origami Fun: Ocean Animals. 2017. (Origami Fun Ser.). (ENG., Illus.). 24p. (YA). (gr. 3-7). 25.95 ***(978-1-62617-713-0(9),*** Express Bks.) Bellwether Media.
Henry, Sally & Cook, Trevor. Origami. 2010. (Make Your Own Art Ser.). 32p. (J). (ENG.). pap. 11.75 *(978-1-4488-1619-4(X));* (Illus.). (gr. 3-6). lib. bdg. 26.50 *(978-1-4488-1586-9(X))* Rosen Publishing Group, Inc., The.
Hinkler Books. Day of the Dead Origami. 2017. (ENG.). 240p. pap. 12.99 ***(978-1-4380-1100-4(8))*** Barron's Educational Series, Inc.
Idea Network LA Inc. Origami: 15 Easy & Fun Origami Designs. 2006. (CHI & SPA.). (J). DVD 24.95 *(978-0-9773301-0-2(9))* Idea Network LA Inc.
Imamori, Mitsuhiko. Everybody Kirigami! 2014. (ENG., Illus.). 88p. pap. 18.95 *(978-1-939130-17-4(4),* Vertical) Kodansha America, Inc.
Johnson, Anne Akers. Origami. 88p. (J). 2005. (SPA., Illus.). spiral bd. 19.95 *(978-987-1078-26-4(9))* 2004. (ENG.). spiral bd. 19.95 *(978-987-1078-15-8(3))* Klutz Latino MEX. Dist: Independent Pubs. Group.
Kallevig, Christine P. Nature Fold-along Stories: Quick & Easy Origami Tales about Plants & Animals. 2009. (ENG., Illus.). 80p. (Orig.). (J). (gr. k-8). pap. 11.95 *(978-0-9628769-2-9(5))* Storytime Ink International.
LaFosse, Michael. Making Origami Cards Step by Step. 2004. (Kid's Guide to Origami Ser.). (Illus.). 24p. (J). lib. bdg. 25.25

M
N
O

(978-0-8239-6701-8(8), PowerKids Pr.) Rosen Publishing Group, Inc., The.

—Making Origami Science Experiments Step by Step. 2004. (Kid's Guide to Origami Ser.). (Illus.). 24p. (J). lib. bdg. 25.25 (978-0-8239-6705-6(0), PowerKids Pr.) Rosen Publishing Group, Inc., The.

LaFosse, Michael G. Making Origami Cards Step by Step. 2009. (Kid's Guide to Origami Ser.). 24p. (gr. 3-4). 47.90 (978-1-61511-183-1(2), PowerKids Pr.) Rosen Publishing Group, Inc., The.

—Making Origami Masks Step by Step. 2009. (Kid's Guide to Origami Ser.). 24p. (gr. 3-4). 47.90 (978-1-61511-188-6(3), PowerKids Pr.) Rosen Publishing Group, Inc., The.

—Making Origami Puzzles Step by Step. 2009. (Kid's Guide to Origami Ser.). 24p. (gr. 3-4). 47.90 (978-1-61511-194-7(8), PowerKids Pr.) Rosen Publishing Group, Inc., The.

—Making Origami Science Experiments Step by Step. 2009. (Kid's Guide to Origami Ser.). 24p. (gr. 3-4). 47.90 (978-1-61511-195-4(6), PowerKids Pr.) Rosen Publishing Group, Inc., The.

—Origami Activities: Create Secret Boxes, Good-Luck Animals, & Paper Charms with the Japanese Art of Origami. 2003. (Asian Arts & Crafts for Creative Kids Ser.). (ENG., Illus.). 64p. (gr. 2-6). 15.95 (978-0-8048-3497-1(0)) Tuttle Publishing.

LaFosse, Michael G. & Alexander, Richard L. Story-Gami Kit: Creating Origami Using Folding Stories. 2010. (ENG., Illus.). 1p. (gr. 1-4). 16.95 (978-0-8048-4134-4(9)) Tuttle Publishing.

Lim, Annalees. Origami Crafts, 01 vols., 1. 2016. (10-Minute Crafts Ser.). (ENG., Illus.). 24p. (J). pap. 10.60 (978-1-5081-9097-4(6), 1397688, Windmill Bks.) Rosen Publishing Group, Inc., The.

Linde, Barbara M. Origami: Identifying Right Angles in Geometric Figures. (PowerMath Ser.). 24p. 2009. (ENG., Illus.). (gr. 3-4). pap. 8.25 (978-0-8239-8882-2(1)) 2009. (gr. 3-4). 45.00 (978-1-60851-382-6(3)) 2004. (Illus.). (J). lib. bdg. 22.50 (978-0-8239-8968-3(2)) Rosen Publishing Group, Inc., The. (PowerKids Pr.).

Maekawa, Jun & Origami. Genuine Japanese Origami: 33 Mathematical Models Based upon √2. Hatori, Koshiro, tr. from JPN. 2012. (Dover Origami Papercraft Ser.). (ENG.). 160p. (gr. 7). pap. 19.95 (978-0-486-48331-3(2)) Dover Pubns., Inc.

Mastering Origami. 2016. (Mastering Origami Ser.). 48p. (gr. 6-5). pap. 46.80 (978-0-7660-7985-4(6)); lib. bdg. 111.72 (978-0-7660-7943-4(0)) Enslow Pubs., Inc.

Meinking, Mary. Easy Origami, 1 vol. 2008. (Origami Ser.). (ENG.). 32p. (gr. 3-4). 27.99 (978-1-4296-2020-8(X), Snap Bks.) Capstone Press of Coughlan Cos.

—Not-Quite-So-Easy Origami, 1 vol. 2008. (Origami Ser.). (ENG.). 32p. (gr. 3-4). 27.99 (978-1-4296-2021-5(8), Snap Bks.) Capstone Press of Coughlan Cos.

Meinking, Mary & Alexander, Chris. Easy Origami: A Step-by-Step Guide for Kids. 2010. (Origami Ser.). (ENG.). 112p. (gr. 3-4). pap. 12.95 (978-1-4296-5034-2(6), Snap Bks.) Capstone Press of Coughlan Cos.

Miles, Lisa. Origami Birds & Butterflies. 2013. (Amazing Origami Ser.). 32p. (J). (gr. 2-5). pap. 63.00 (978-1-4339-9646-7(4)); pap. 10.50 (978-1-4339-9645-0(6)); (ENG., Illus.). lib. bdg. 26.60 (978-1-4339-9644-3(8)) Stevens, Gareth Publishing LLLP.

—Origami Dinosaurs. 2013. (Amazing Origami Ser.). 32p. (J). (gr. 2-5). pap. 10.50 (978-1-4339-9649-8(9)); pap. 63.00 (978-1-4339-9650-4(2)); (ENG., Illus.). lib. bdg. 26.60 (978-1-4339-9648-1(0)) Stevens, Gareth Publishing LLLP.

—Origami Farm Animals. 2013. (Amazing Origami Ser.). 32p. (J). (gr. 2-5). pap. 63.00 (978-1-4339-9654-2(5)); pap. 10.50 (978-1-4339-9653-5(7)); (ENG., Illus.). lib. bdg. 26.60 (978-1-4339-9652-8(9)) Stevens, Gareth Publishing LLLP.

—Origami Pets. 2013. (Amazing Origami Ser.). 32p. (J). (gr. 2-5). pap. 10.50 (978-1-4339-9657-3(X)); pap. 63.00 (978-1-4339-9658-0(8)); (ENG., Illus.). lib. bdg. 26.60 (978-1-4339-9656-6(1)) Stevens, Gareth Publishing LLLP.

—Origami Sea Creatures. 2013. (Amazing Origami Ser.). 32p. (J). (gr. 2-5). pap. 63.00 (978-1-4339-9662-7(6)); pap. 10.50 (978-1-4339-9661-0(8)); (ENG., Illus.). lib. bdg. 26.60 (978-1-4339-9660-3(X)) Stevens, Gareth Publishing LLLP.

—Origami Wild Animals. 2013. (Amazing Origami Ser.). 32p. (J). (gr. 2-5). pap. 10.50 (978-1-4339-9665-8(0)); pap. 63.00 (978-1-4339-9666-5(9)); (ENG., Illus.). lib. bdg. 26.60 (978-1-4339-9664-1(2)) Stevens, Gareth Publishing LLLP.

Montroll, John. Batman Origami: Amazing Folding Projects for the Dark Knight. Ku, Min Sung, illus. 2015. (DC Origami Ser.). (ENG.). 48p. (gr. 4-5). lib. bdg. 27.99 (978-1-4914-1786-7(2)) Capstone Press of Coughlan Cos.

—DC Origami. Ku, Min Sung, illus. 2015. (DC Origami Ser.). (ENG.). 48p. (gr. 4-5). 111.96 (978-1-4914-1790-4(0), DC Super Heroes) Stone Arch Bks.

—DC Super Heroes Origami: 21 Folding Projects for Batman, Superman, & More! 2017. (J). lib. bdg. **(978-1-5157-5930-0(X))** Capstone Young Readers of Coughlan Cos.

—DC Super Heroes Origami: 46 Folding Projects for Batman, Superman, Wonder Woman, & More! Ku, Min Sung, illus. 2015. (DC Super Heroes Ser.). (ENG.). 448p. (gr. 4-5). pap. 14.95 (978-1-62370-217-5(8)) Capstone Young Readers of Coughlan Cos.

—Dollar Bill Origami. 2003. (Illus.). 120p. (YA). per. 14.94 net. (978-1-877656-17-0(8)) Antroll Publishing Co.

—Justice League Origami: Amazing Folding Projects for the JLA. Ku, Min Sung, illus. 2015. (DC Origami Ser.). (ENG.). 48p. (gr. 4-5). lib. bdg. 27.99 (978-1-4914-1789-8(7)) Capstone Press of Coughlan Cos.

—Superman Origami: Amazing Folding Projects for the Man of Steel. Ku, Min Sung, illus. 2015. (DC Origami Ser.). (ENG.). 48p. (gr. 4-5). lib. bdg. 27.99 (978-1-4914-1787-4(0)) Capstone Press of Coughlan Cos.

—*Wonder Woman Origami: Amazing Folding Projects for the* Warrior Princess. Ku, Min Sung, illus. 2015. (DC Origami Ser.). (ENG.). 48p. (gr. 4-5). lib. bdg. 27.99 (978-1-4914-1788-1(9)) Capstone Press of Coughlan Cos.

Ng, Cindy. Girligami: Fun & Fashionable Origami! 2012. (ENG., Illus.). 72p. (J). (gr. 2). spiral bd. 14.95 (978-1-60710-327-1(3), Silver Dolphin Bks.) Readerlink Distribution Services, LLC.

O'Brien, Eileen & Needham, Kate. Origami Pack. 2004. (Activity Kits Ser.). 24p. (J). act. bk. ed. 14.95 (978-0-7945-0460-1(4)) EDC Publishing.

Ono, Mari & Ono, Roshin. Origami for Children, Pack. 2009. (ENG., Illus.). 128p. (J). (gr. 3-11). pap. 19.95 (978-1-906525-80-4(3), CICO Books) Ryland Peters & Small GBR. Dist: WIPRO.

—Origami for Children: 35 Easy-to-Follow Step-by-Step Projects. 2008. (ENG., Illus.). 128p. (978-1-906094-38-6(1), CICO Books) Ryland Peters & Small.

Ono, Mari & Shingu, Fumiaki. Fun Origami for Kids - Wild! 12 Amazing Animals to Fold! 2017. (ENG., Illus.). 32p. (J). (gr. 5-7). pap. 12.95 **(978-1-78249-467-6(7)**, 1782494677, Cico Kidz) Ryland Peters & Small GBR. Dist: WIPRO.

Ono, Mari & Takai, Hiroaki. Easy Origami for Kids - Dino! 12 Daring Dinosaurs to Fold! 2017. (ENG., Illus.). 32p. (J). (gr. 5-7). pap. 12.95 **(978-1-78249-466-9(9)**, 1782494669, Cico Kidz) Ryland Peters & Small GBR. Dist: WIPRO.

Origami Army. 2013. (Origami Army Ser.). 32p. (J). (gr. 3-6). 106.00 (978-1-4777-1548-2(7)); pap. 47.00 (978-1-4777-2732-4(9)); pap. 282.00 (978-1-4777-2733-1(7)) Rosen Publishing Group, Inc., The. (PowerKids Pr.).

Origami Holidays. 2016. (Origami Holidays Ser.). 32p. (gr. 3-3). 165.00 (978-1-4994-2252-8(0)); pap. 70.50 (978-1-4994-2452-2(3)) Rosen Publishing Group, Inc., The. (PowerKids Pr.).

Origami Safari. 2014. (Origami Safari Ser.). 32p. (J). (gr. 3-6). 165.00 (978-1-4777-9113-4(2)) Windmill Bks.

Owen, Ruth. Christmas & Hanukkah Origami. 2012. (Holiday Origami Ser.). (ENG., Illus.). 32p. (J). (gr. 3-6). 26.50 (978-1-4488-7860-4(8)); pap. 11.75 (978-1-4488-7919-9(1)) Rosen Publishing Group, Inc., The. (PowerKids Pr.).

—Desert Animals. 2014. (Origami Safari Ser.). (Illus.). 32p. (J). (gr. 3-6). pap. 11.75 (978-1-4777-9242-1(2)) Windmill Bks.

—Easter Origami. 2012. (Holiday Origami Ser.). (ENG., Illus.). 32p. (J). (gr. 3-6). 26.50 (978-1-4488-7861-1(6)); pap. 11.75 (978-1-4488-7920-5(5)) Rosen Publishing Group, Inc., The. (PowerKids Pr.).

—Grassland Animals. 2014. (Origami Safari Ser.). (Illus.). 32p. (J). (gr. 3-6). lib. bdg. 27.50 (978-1-4777-9253-7(8)) Windmill Bks.

—Halloween Origami. 2012. (Holiday Origami Ser.). (ENG., Illus.). 32p. (J). (gr. 3-6). 26.50 (978-1-4488-7862-8(4)); pap. 11.75 (978-1-4488-7921-2(3)) Rosen Publishing Group, Inc., The. (PowerKids Pr.).

—Independence Day Origami. 2012. (Holiday Origami Ser.). (ENG., Illus.). 32p. (J). (gr. 3-6). 26.50 (978-1-4488-7863-5(2)); pap. 11.75 (978-1-4488-7922-9(1)) Rosen Publishing Group, Inc., The. (PowerKids Pr.).

—Jungle Animals. 2014. (Origami Safari Ser.). (Illus.). 32p. (J). (gr. 3-6). lib. bdg. 27.50 (978-1-4777-9238-4(4)) Windmill Bks.

—More Christmas Origami, 1 vol. 2015. (Holiday Origami Ser.). (ENG., Illus.). 32p. (J). 27.50 (978-1-4777-5706-2(6), 1384074, PowerKids Pr.) Rosen Publishing Group, Inc., The.

—More Halloween Origami, 1 vol. 2015. (Holiday Origami Ser.). (ENG.). 32p. (J). 27.50 (978-1-4777-5702-4(3), PowerKids Pr.) Rosen Publishing Group, Inc., The.

—More Hanukkah Origami, 1 vol. 2015. (Holiday Origami Ser.). (ENG., Illus.). 32p. (J). 27.50 (978-1-4777-5714-7(7), 1384076, PowerKids Pr.) Rosen Publishing Group, Inc., The.

—More Thanksgiving Origami, 1 vol. 2015. (Holiday Origami Ser.). (ENG.). 32p. (J). 27.50 (978-1-4777-5710-9(4), PowerKids Pr.) Rosen Publishing Group, Inc., The.

—More Valentine's Day Origami, 1 vol. 2015. (Holiday Origami Ser.). (ENG.). 32p. (J). 27.50 (978-1-4777-5698-0(1), PowerKids Pr.) Rosen Publishing Group, Inc., The.

—Mountain Animals. 2014. (Origami Safari Ser.). (Illus.). 32p. (J). (gr. 3-6). lib. bdg. 27.50 (978-1-4777-9257-5(0)) Windmill Bks.

—Ocean Animals. 2014. (Origami Safari Ser.). (Illus.). 32p. (J). (gr. 3-6). lib. bdg. 27.50 (978-1-4777-9249-0(X)) Windmill Bks.

—Polar Animals. 2014. (Origami Safari Ser.). (Illus.). 32p. (J). (gr. 3-6). lib. bdg. 27.50 (978-1-4777-9245-2(7)) Windmill Bks.

—St. Patrick's Day Origami, 1 vol. 2015. (Holiday Origami Ser.). (ENG.). 32p. (J). 27.50 (978-1-4777-5718-5(X), PowerKids Pr.) Rosen Publishing Group, Inc., The.

—Thanksgiving Origami. 2012. (Holiday Origami Ser.). (ENG., Illus.). 32p. (J). (gr. 3-6). 26.50 (978-1-4488-7864-2(0)); pap. 11.75 (978-1-4488-7923-6(X)) Rosen Publishing Group, Inc., The. (PowerKids Pr.).

—Valentine's Day Origami. 2012. (Holiday Origami Ser.). (ENG., Illus.). 32p. (J). (gr. 3-6). 26.50 (978-1-4488-7865-9(9)); pap. 11.75 (978-1-4488-7924-3(8)) Rosen Publishing Group, Inc., The. (PowerKids Pr.).

Palacios, Vicente. Origami Animals. 2012. (Dover Origami Papercraft Ser.). (ENG., Illus.). 64p. (gr. 7). pap. 9.95 (978-0-486-47874-6(2)) Dover Pubns., Inc.

Play Pen Books Staff. Animals: Easy Instructions Make Bringing Your Origami to Life Fun from Start to Finish! 2010. (ENG.). 24p. (J). pap. 12.95 (978-1-60433-153-0(4), Applesauce Pr.) Cider Mill Pr. Bk. Pubs., LLC.

Rau, Dana Meachen. Folding Origami. Petelinsek, Kathleen, illus. 2013. (How-To Library). (ENG.). 32p. (J). (gr. 3-6). 28.50 (978-1-62431-145-1(8), 202900); pap. 14.21 (978-1-62431-277-9(2), 202902) Cherry Lake Publishing.

Robinson, Nick. The Awesome Origami Pack: With Waterproof & Foil Papers, Plus 50 Sheets of Origami Papers. 2014. (ENG., Illus.). 48p. (J). (gr. 4-8). 14.99 (978-0-7641-6726-3(X)) Barron's Educational Series, Inc.

—My First Origami Book — Christmas: With 24 Sheets of Origami Paper! 2013. (Dover Origami Papercraft Ser.). (ENG.). 96p. (J). (gr. 2). pap. 12.99 (978-0-486-49182-0(X)) Dover Pubns., Inc.

—*Origami Adventures:* Animals. Quigley, Sebastian, illus. 2014. (Origami Adventures Ser.). (ENG.). 76p. (J). (gr. 1). spiral bd. 15.95 (978-1-60710-763-7(5), Silver Dolphin Bks.) Readerlink Distribution Services, LLC.

Rosen Publishing Staff. Holiday Origami: Set 2, 1 vol. 2015. (Holiday Origami Ser.). (ENG.). 32p. (J). 165.00 (978-1-4777-5722-2(8), PowerKids Pr.) Rosen Publishing Group, Inc., The.

Schultz, Walter-Alexandre. Origami Dinosaurs. 2017. (Exciting Origami Ser.). 48p. (J). (gr. 3-3). lib. bdg. 27.93 **(978-0-7660-8650-0(X))** Enslow Pubs., Inc.

Shingu, Fumiaki. Easy Origami. 2007. (Illus.). 64p. (J). (978-1-60311-000-6(3)) Mud Puddle, Inc.

Smith, Soonboke. Origami. 2004. (For the First Time(r) Ser.). (ENG., Illus.). 112p. pap. 9.95 (978-1-4027-1767-3(9), Chapelle) Sterling Publishing Co., Inc.

Song, Sok. Everyday Origami: A Foldable Fashion Guide. Song, Sok, illus. 2016. (Fashion Origami Ser.). (ENG., Illus.). 48p. (gr. 4-5). lib. bdg. 31.99 (978-1-5157-1630-3(9)) Capstone Press of Coughlan Cos.

—Fashion Origami. Song, Sok, illus. 2016. (Fashion Origami Ser.). (ENG., Illus.). 48p. (gr. 4-5). 95.97 (978-1-5157-1653-2(8)) Capstone Press of Coughlan Cos.

—Origami Accessories: A Foldable Fashion Guide. Song, Sok, illus. 2016. (Fashion Origami Ser.). (ENG., Illus.). 48p. (gr. 4-5). lib. bdg. 31.99 (978-1-5157-1623-5(6)) Capstone Press of Coughlan Cos.

—Origami Chic: A Guide to Foldable Fashion. Song, Sok, illus. 2016. (ENG., Illus.). 240p. (gr. 3-3). pap. 14.95 (978-1-62370-771-2(4)) Capstone Young Readers of Coughlan Cos.

—Origami Outfits: A Foldable Fashion Guide. Song, Sok, illus. 2016. (Fashion Origami Ser.). (ENG., Illus.). 48p. (gr. 4-5). lib. bdg. 31.99 (978-1-5157-1631-0(7)) Capstone Press of Coughlan Cos.

Stadler, Charlotte. Origami. 2011. (Early Connections Ser.). (J). (978-1-61672-614-0(8)) Benchmark Education Co.

Sterling Children's, Sterling & Woodroffe, David. I Heart Origami. 2016. (ENG., Illus.). 240p. (J). (gr. 3). pap. 12.95 (978-1-4549-2289-6(3)) Sterling Publishing Co., Inc.

Terry, Nicolas. Origami Adventures: Oceans. Quigley, Sebastian, illus. 2015. (Origami Adventures Ser.). (ENG.). 76p. (J). (gr. 1). spiral bd. 15.95 (978-1-62686-251-7(6), Silver Dolphin Bks.) Readerlink Distribution Services, LLC.

Troupe, Thomas Kingsley. Diggin' Dirt: Science Adventures with Kitanai the Origami Dog, 1 vol. Christoph, Jamey, illus. 2013. (Origami Science Adventures Ser.). (ENG.). 24p. (gr. 3-4). pap. 6.95 (978-1-4048-8066-5(6)); lib. bdg. 27.32 (978-1-4048-7969-0(2)) Picture Window Bks.

—Glowing with Electricity: Science Adventures with Glenda the Origami Firefly, 1 vol. Christoph, Jamey, illus. 2014. (Origami Science Adventures Ser.). (ENG.). 24p. (gr. 3-4). lib. bdg. 27.32 (978-1-4795-2189-0(2)) Picture Window Bks.

—Magnet Power! Science Adventures with MAG-3000 the Origami Robot, 1 vol. Christoph, Jamey, illus. 2013. (Origami Science Adventures Ser.). (ENG.). 24p. (gr. 3-4). pap. 6.95 (978-1-4048-8070-2(4)); lib. bdg. 27.32 (978-1-4048-7972-0(2)) Picture Window Bks.

—Wild Weather: Science Adventures with Sonny the Origami Bird, 1 vol. Christoph, Jamey, illus. 2014. (Origami Science Adventures Ser.). (ENG.). 24p. (gr. 3-4). lib. bdg. 27.32 (978-1-4795-2188-3(4)) Picture Window Bks.

Troupe, Thomas Kingsley & Braun, Eric. Origami Science Adventures. Christoph, Jamey, illus. 2013. (Origami Science Adventures Ser.). (ENG.). 24p. (gr. 3-4). pap. 23.80 (978-1-4048-8074-0(7)); lib. bdg. 109.28 (978-1-4048-7973-7(0)) Picture Window Bks.

Tsin, Justin. What Would You Imagine? 2008. (Illus.). 32p. (gr. k-3). per. 19.95 (978-1-60396-039-7(2)) Santillana USA Publishing Co., Inc.

Yates, Jane. Dollar Bill Origami. 2016. (Cool Crafts for Kids Ser.). 00032p. (J). (gr. 3-3). pap. 11.75 (978-1-4994-8226-3(4), Windmill Bks.) Rosen Publishing Group, Inc., The.

Yee, Tammy. Easy Butterfly Origami. 2015. (Dover Origami Papercraft Ser.). (ENG.). 64p. (gr. 3). pap. 9.99 (978-0-486-78457-1(6)) Dover Pubns., Inc.

ORIGIN OF HUMAN BEINGS

see Human Beings—Origin

ORIGIN OF SPECIES

see Evolution

ORNAMENT

see Decoration and Ornament

ORNAMENTAL ALPHABETS

see Lettering

ORNAMENTAL DESIGN

see Design, Decorative

ORNITHOLOGY

see Birds

ORPHANAGES

Benge, Janet & Benge, Geoff. Christian Heroes - Then & Now - Lillian Trasher: The Greatest Wonder in Egypt. 2003. (Christian Heroes Ser.). (ENG.). 190p. (YA). pap. 9.99 (978-1-57658-305-0(8)) YWAM Publishing.

Jocelyn, Marthe. A Home for Foundlings. 2005. (Lord Museum Book Ser.). (ENG., Illus.). 120p. (J). (gr. k-12). pap. 16.95 (978-0-88776-709-8(5), Tundra Bks.) Tundra Bks. CAN. Dist: Penguin Random Hse. LLC.

Richards, Laurae. Coming Home. 2013. 28p. pap. 16.95 (978-1-4624-0769-9(2), Inspiring Voices) Author Solutions, Inc.

Skrypuch, Marsha Forchuk. Last Airlift: A Vietnamese Orphan's Rescue from War. 2013. (ENG., Illus.). 120p. (J). (gr. 3-7). pap. 9.95 (978-0-9869495-1-7(5)) Pajama Pr. CAN. Dist: Ingram Publisher Services.

ORPHANAGES—FICTION

Alders, Willa. Leafy Finds a Home. Burns, Sandra, illus. 2013. 24p. pap. 8.99 (978-1-938768-13-2(2)) Gypsy Pubns.

Authords, D. K. Being Alone. 2013. 120p. pap. 19.95 (978-1-63000-114-8(7)) America Star Bks.

Barnaby, Hannah. Wonder Show. (ENG., 288p. (YA). (gr. 7). 2013. Illus.). pap. 8.99 (978-0-544-10483-9(8)) 2012. 16.99 (978-0-547-59980-9(3)) Houghton Mifflin Harcourt Publishing Co.

Bass, Guy. The Spider's Lair. Williamson, Pete, illus. 2015. (Stitch Head Ser.). (ENG.). 208p. (gr. 3-4). 10.95 (978-1-62370-192-5(9)) Capstone Young Readers of Coughlan Cos.

Bastian, Kimberlee Ann. The Orphan, the Soulcatcher, & the Black Blizzard. 2012. 258p. pap. 22.50 (978-1-105-06633-7(9)) Lulu.com GBR. Dist: Lulu Pr., Inc.

Bragg, Jane. Teddy Bears Christmas Miracle. 2009. 49p. pap. 18.70 (978-0-557-22087-8(4)) Lulu Pr., Inc.

Brezenoff, Steve. The Sleeper, 1 vol. Percival, Tom, illus. 2012. (Ravens Pass Ser.). (ENG.). 96p. (gr. 2-3). pap. 6.15 (978-1-4342-4211-2(0)); lib. bdg. 25.32 (978-1-4342-3792-7(3)) Stone Arch Bks.

Burch, Genny. My Name Is Bobby Claus: A fictional Christmas story for Children. 2009. 36p. pap. 15.99 (978-1-4490-4233-2(3)) AuthorHouse.

Chapmon, Rachelle. Mari. 2009. 148p. pap. 11.99 (978-1-4389-6310-5(6)) AuthorHouse.

Conlon-McKenna, Marita. A Girl Called Blue. 2nd rev. ed. 2004. (ENG.). 224p. (J). pap. 12.95 (978-0-86278-887-2(0)) O'Brien Pr., Ltd., The IRL. Dist: Dufour Editions, Inc.

Darke, J. A. The Screaming Bridge. Evergreen, Nelson, illus. 2015. (Spine Shivers Ser.). (ENG.). 128p. (gr. 3-4). lib. bdg. 26.65 (978-1-4965-0219-3(1)) Stone Arch Bks.

Doty, Kathryn Adams. Wild Orphan. 2006. (ENG.). 144p. (gr. 3-7). per. 14.95 (978-1-889020-20-4(6)) Edinborough Pr.

Flores-Galbis, Enrique. 90 Miles to Havana. 2010. (ENG.). 304p. (J). (gr. 4-7). 18.99 (978-1-59643-168-3(7), 9781596431683) Roaring Brook Pr.

—90 Miles to Havana. 2012. (ENG.). 304p. (J). (gr. 4-7). pap. 7.99 (978-1-250-00559-5(0), 9781250005595) Square Fish.

Freeman, Martha. The Orphan & the Mouse. McPhail, David, illus. 2014. (ENG.). 176p. (J). (gr. 3-7). 16.95 (978-0-8234-3167-0(3)) Holiday Hse., Inc.

Gazdag, Adam. The Non Born Heir. 2010. 313p. pap. 19.27 (978-0-557-17709-7(X)) Lulu Pr., Inc.

Griser, Carol. Breona's New Life. 2009. 24p. pap. 14.00 (978-1-4389-4975-8(8)) AuthorHouse.

Grizzard, Sue H. Princess Caylee: An Incredible Birthday Wish Come True. 2009. 44p. pap. 19.95 (978-1-4490-4001-7(2)) AuthorHouse.

Harvey, Pam & Panckridge, Michael. Ghost of a Chance. 2007. 208p. (978-0-207-20063-2(7)) HarperCollins Pubs. Australia.

Hueller, Andy. Skipping Stones at the Center of the Earth: A Middle Grade Novel. 2011. (J). pap. 8.99 (978-1-59955-488-4(7), Bonneville Bks.) Cedar Fort, Inc./CFI Distribution.

Johnson, D. C. & Rowan, Ron. The Secret of MeadowBrook Orphanage. 2012. 528p. (gr. -1). pap. 18.30 (978-1-4669-1866-5(7)) Trafford Publishing.

Khan, Rukhsana. Wanting Mor, 1 vol. 2010. (ENG.). 192p. (J). (gr. 4-9). pap. 9.95 (978-0-88899-862-0(7)) Groundwood Bks. CAN. Dist: Publishers Group West (PGW).

Laurie, Victoria. Oracles of Delphi Keep. 2010. (Oracles of Delphi Keep Ser.). (ENG.). 576p. (J). (gr. 3-7). 7.99 (978-0-440-42258-7(2), Yearling) Random Hse. Children's Bks.

Legrand, Claire. The Cavendish Home for Boys & Girls. Watts, Sarah, illus. (ENG.). (J). (gr. 5). 2013. 368p. pap. 7.99 (978-1-4424-4292-4(1)) 2012. 352p. 16.99 (978-1-4424-4291-7(3)) Simon & Schuster Bks. For Young Readers. (Simon & Schuster Bks. For Young Readers).

Mandeville, Terry M. Just Waiting for My Family. l.t. ed. 2005. (Illus.). 52p. (J). 14.95 (978-0-9762475-0-0(X)) Mandeville, Terry M.

Montgomery, L. PENGUIN ACTIVE READING 2: ANNE OF GREEN GABLES BOOK AND CD-ROM PACK. 2007. (ENG.). 64p. pap. 17.32 (978-1-4058-5205-0(4)) Pearson Education.

Patterson, Valerie O. Operation Oleander. (ENG.). 192p. (J). (gr. 5-7). 2015. pap. 7.99 (978-0-544-43935-1(X), HMH Books For Young Readers) 2013. 16.99 (978-0-547-24437-2(1)) Houghton Mifflin Harcourt Publishing Co.

Peacock, Carol Antoinette. Red Thread Sisters. 2012. (ENG.). 240p. (J). (gr. 3-7). 15.99 (978-0-670-01386-9(2), Viking Books for Young Readers) Penguin Young Readers Group.

Pinkney, Andrea Davis. Bird in a Box. Qualls, Sean, illus. 2012. (ENG.). 288p. (J). (gr. 3-7). pap. 8.99 (978-0-316-07402-5(0)) Little, Brown Bks. for Young Readers.

—Bird in a Box. Qualls, Sean, illus. 2012. (J). lib. bdg. 18.45 (978-0-606-26157-9(5), Turtleback) Turtleback Bks.

Riggs, Ransom. Hollow City. 2015. (Miss Peregrine's Peculiar Children Ser.: Bk. 2). (ENG., Illus.). 416p. (YA). pap. 10.99 (978-1-59474-735-9(0)) Quirk Bks.

—Hollow City. Riggs, Ransom, illus. 2014. (ENG., Illus.). 352p. (YA). (gr. 9). 18.99 (978-1-59474-612-3(5)) Quirk Bks.

—Hollow City. Riggs, Ransom, illus. 2015. (Miss Peregrine's Peculiar Children Ser.: 2). (Illus.). lib. bdg. 22.10 (978-0-606-36394-5(7)) Turtleback Bks.

—Miss Peregrine's Home for Peculiar Children. (ENG., Illus.). (YA). (gr. 9). 2013. 368p. pap. 10.99 (978-1-59474-603-1(6)) 2011. (Miss Peregrine's Peculiar Children Ser.: 1). 352p. 18.99 (978-1-59474-476-1(9)) 2016. (Miss Peregrine's Peculiar Children Ser.: 1). 392p. pap. 11.99 (978-1-59474-902-5(7)) Quirk Bks.

—Miss Peregrine's Home for Peculiar Children. l.t. ed. 2012. (ENG.). 484p. (J). (gr. 8-12). 23.99 (978-1-4104-5023-4(6)) Thorndike Pr.

—Miss Peregrine's Home for Peculiar Children. 2013. (Miss Peregrine's Peculiar Children Ser.: 1). lib. bdg. 22.10 (978-0-606-32081-8(4), Turtleback) Turtleback Bks.

Riggs, Ransom & Jean, Cassandra. Hollow City: the Graphic Novel. 2016. (Miss Peregrine's Peculiar Children: the Graphic Novel Ser.: 2). (ENG., Illus.). 272p. (J). (gr. 8-17). 20.00 (978-0-316-30679-9(7), Yen Pr.) Orbit.

Riggs, Ransom, et al. Miss Peregrine's Home for Peculiar Children. 2011. pap. (978-1-59474-574-4(9)) Quirk Bks.

Roesti, Delores. Mareena Maree Mulligan & the Flying Wheel Chair: Book 1: School Days. 2007. 81p. pap. 9.95 (978-0-7414-4048-8(2)) Infinity Publishing.

Roesti, Delores Anne. Mareena Maree Mulligan & the Flying Wheelchair Book #3: Temptation's Talking, 1 vol. 2010. 93p. pap. 16.95 (978-1-4489-6692-9(2)) PublishAmerica, Inc.

Stewart, Trenton Lee. The Extraordinary Education of Nicholas Benedict. Sudyka, Diana, illus. (Mysterious Benedict Society Ser.). (ENG.). (J). (gr. 3-7). 2013. 496p. pap. 9.99 (978-0-316-17620-0(6)) 2012. 480p. 18.99 (978-0-316-17619-4(2)) Little, Brown Bks. for Young Readers.

—The Extraordinary Education of Nicholas Benedict. 2013. (Mysterious Benedict Society Ser.: 0). (J). lib. bdg. 19.65 (978-0-606-31743-6(0), Turtleback) Turtleback Bks.

Thompson-Swift, Joseph. The Adventures of Primrose Perfect. 2011. 248p. pap. *(978-1-907652-88-2(4))* Grosvenor Hse. Publishing Ltd.

Tripp, Valerie. Nellie's Promise. England, Tamara, ed. Andreasen, Dan, illus. 2004. (ENG.). 96p. (gr. 2-18). pap. 6.95 *(978-1-58485-890-4(7))* American Girl Publishing, Inc.

Williams, Karen Lynn. Lubuto Means Light. Grifalconi, Ann, illus. 2010. (ENG.). 32p. 16.95 *(978-1-59078-716-8(1))* Boyds Mills Pr.

Woodell, Rejoice. Kohara, the White Veiled City. 2011. 138p. pap. 19.99 *(978-1-4568-7969-3(3))* Xlibris Corp.

The Year We Sailed the Sun. 2015. (ENG., Illus.). 432p. (J). (gr. 3-7). 17.99 *(978-0-689-85827-7(2),* Atheneum/Richard Jackson Bks.) Simon & Schuster Children's Publishing.

ORPHANS

Amis, Nancy. The Orphans of Normandy: A True Story of World War II Told Through Drawings by Children. 2016. (ENG., Illus.). 48p. (J). (gr. 3-7). pap. 13.99 *(978-1-4814-9470-0(8),* Atheneum Bks. for Young Readers) Simon & Schuster Children's Publishing.

Deprince, Michaela & DePrince, Elaine. Ballerina Dreams: From Orphan to Dancer. Morrison, Frank, illus. 2014. (Step into Reading Ser.). (ENG.). 48p. (J). (gr. 2-4). 3.99 *(978-0-385-75515-3(5),* Random Hse. Bks. for Young Readers) Random Hse. Children's Bks.

Gutwein, Austin & Hillard, Todd. Take Your Best Shot: Do Something Bigger Than Yourself, 1 vol. 2009. (ENG.). 240p. (gr. 7-12). pap. 14.99 *(978-1-4003-1515-4(8))* Nelson, Thomas Inc.

Johnson, Kristin F. The Orphan Trains, 1 vol. 2012. (Essential Events Set 8 Ser.). (ENG., Illus.). 112p. (J). (gr. 6-12). lib. bdg. 35.64 *(978-1-61783-103-4(4))* ABDO Publishing Co.

Langston-George, Rebecca. Orphan Trains: Taking the Rails to a New Life. 2016. (Encounter: Narrative Nonfiction Stories Ser.). (ENG., Illus.). 128p. (gr. 3-4). lib. bdg. 30.65 *(978-1-4914-8551-4(5))* Capstone Press of Coughlan Cos.

—Orphan Trains: Taking the Rails to a New Life. 2016. (Encounter: Narrative Nonfiction Stories Ser.). (ENG., Illus.). 128p. (gr. 3-4). pap. 6.95 *(978-1-62370-630-2(0))* Encounter Bks.

Littlefield, Holly. Children of the Orphan Trains. 2005. (Picture the American Past Ser.). (Illus.). 48p. (gr. 2-5). lib. bdg. 22.60 *(978-1-57505-466-7(3))* Lerner Publishing Group.

Lynette, Rachel. Ana Dodson: Advocate for Peruvian Orphans. 2007. (Young Heroes Ser.). (ENG., Illus.). 48p. (J). (gr. 3-7). lib. bdg. 30.50 *(978-0-7377-3865-0(0),* Kidhaven) Cengage Gale.

MacKenzie, Catherine. Helen Roseveare: What's in the Parcel? 2012. (Little Lights Ser.). (ENG.). 24p. (J). 7.99 *(978-1-84550-383-3(X),* 30e4822e-2a72-488e-8b19-1af61b42efe4) Christian Focus Pubns. GBR. Dist: Bookmasters Distribution.

Naidoo, Beverley, intro. Making It Home: Real-Life Stories from Children Forced to Flee. 2005. (ENG., Illus.). 128p. (J). (gr. 3-7). 6.99 *(978-0-14-240455-3(1),* Puffin Books) Penguin Young Readers Group.

Raum, Elizabeth. Orphan Trains: An Interactive History Adventure, 1 vol. (You Choose: History Ser.). (ENG.). 112p. (gr. 3-4). 2011. pap. 6.95 *(978-1-4296-6273-4(5))* 2011. pap. 41.70 *(978-1-4296-6441-7(X))* 2010. 31.99 *(978-1-4296-5479-1(1))* Capstone Press of Coughlan Cos. (You Choose Bks.).

Richards, Laurae. Coming Home. 2013. 28p. pap. 16.95 *(978-1-4624-0769-9(2),* Inspiring Voices) Author Solutions, Inc.

Robertson, David Alexander. Scars. Henderson, Scott B., illus. 2010. (7 Generations Ser.: 2). (ENG.). 32p. (YA). pap. *(978-1-55379-228-4(9),* 4ae83eb9-baca-4c13-a381-ea5771ba95b7, HighWater Pr.) Portage & Main Pr.

Ruckel, Izidor. Abandoned for Life: The Incredible Story of One Romanian Orphan, Hidden from the World. His Life. His Words. Bramsch, Joan, ed. 2003. (YA). mass mkt. 19.97 *(978-0-934334-13-6(7))* JB Information Station.

Shames, Stephen. Transforming Lives: Turning Uganda's Forgotten Children into Leaders. Shames, Stephen, photos by. 2009. (Illus.). 40p. (YA). pap. 12.95 *(978-1-59572-213-3(0))* Star Bright Bks., Inc.

Skrypuch, Marsha Forchuk. Last Airlift: A Vietnamese Orphan's Rescue from War. 2013. (ENG., Illus.). 120p. (J). (gr. 3-7). pap. 9.95 *(978-0-9869495-1-7(5))* Pajama Pr. CAN. Dist: Ingram Publisher Services.

—One Step at a Time: A Vietnamese Child Finds Her Way. (ENG., Illus.). 128p. (J). (gr. 3-7). 2014. pap. 12.95 *(978-1-927485-02-6(9))* 2013. 13.95 *(978-1-927485-01-9(0))* Pajama Pr. CAN. Dist: Ingram Publisher Services.

Stevens, Dylan. Wooded Sanctuary. 2004. 136p. (YA). pap. 13.95 *(978-0-595-31093-7(1))* iUniverse, Inc.

Uschan, Michael V. Matt Dalio: China Care Founder. 2007. (Young Heroes Ser.). (ENG., Illus.). 64p. (gr. 4-8). lib. bdg. 35.70 *(978-0-7377-3670-0(4),* Kidhaven) Cengage Gale.

Warren, Andrea. We Rode the Orphan Trains. 2004. (ENG., Illus.). 144p. (J). (gr. 5-7). reprint ed. pap. 9.95 *(978-0-618-43235-6(3))* Houghton Mifflin Harcourt Publishing Co.

Warren, Andrea & National Geographic Learning Staff. Escape from Saigon: How a Vietnam War Orphan Became an American Boy. 2008. (ENG., Illus.). 128p. (J). (gr. 5-9). pap. 12.99 *(978-0-374-40023-1(7),* 9780374400231) Square Fish.

ORPHANS—FICTION

Abbott, E. F. Nettie & Nellie Crook: Orphan Train Sisters. 2016. (Based on a True Story Ser.). (ENG., Illus.). 176p. (J). 15.99 *(978-1-250-06835-4(5),* 9781250068354) Feiwel & Friends.

Acosta, Marta. Dark Companion. 2013. (ENG.). 368p. (YA). (gr. 8-12). pap. 10.99 *(978-0-7653-2965-3(4),* 9780765329653, Tor Teen) Doherty, Tom Assocs., LLC.

Adams, W. Royce. Jay. 2005. viii, 115p. (YA). pap. *(978-1-58832-120-6(7))* Unlimited Publishing LLC.

Aguila, Priscilla. As Different As Can Be. 2006. 48p. pap. 17.96 *(978-1-4116-5609-3(1))* Lulu Pr., Inc.

Akita, Yoshinobu. Orphen, Vol. 4. 2006. (Orphen Ser.). (Illus.). 168p. (YA). pap. 9.99 *(978-1-4139-0269-3(3))* ADV Manga.

Alcott, Louisa May. Eight Cousins. 2005. 29.95 *(978-1-4218-0976-2(1),* 1st World Library - Literary Society) 1st World Publishing, Inc.

—Eight Cousins. 2013. (Works of Louisa May Alcott). 291p. reprint ed. lthr. 79.00 *(978-0-7812-1633-3(8))* Reprint Services Corp.

—Eight Cousins, or, the Aunt-Hill. 2010. 250p. pap. 16.95 *(978-1-60444-100-0(3))* IndoEuropeanPublishing.com.

—Little Men: Life at Plumfield with Jo's Boys. 2013. (Works of Louisa May Alcott). 292p. reprint ed. lthr. 79.00 *(978-0-7812-1629-6(X))* Reprint Services Corp.

Alexander, Lloyd. The Book of Three. Wyatt, David, illus. 2006. (Chronicles of Prydain Ser.: 1). (ENG.). 224p. (J). (gr. 3-7). pap. 7.99 *(978-0-8050-8048-3(1),* 9780805080483) Square Fish.

Alger, Horatio. Facing the World. 2006. pap. *(978-1-4065-0704-1(0))* Dodo Pr.

—Fame & Fortune: Or: the Progress of Richard Hunter. 2007. (ENG.). 160p. per. 19.99 *(978-1-4346-5061-0(8));* 176p. per. 21.99 *(978-1-4346-5062-7(6))* Creative Media Partners, LLC.

—Frank & Fearless or the Fortunes of Jasper Kent. 2007. 228p. 20.99 *(978-1-4280-7465-1(1));* per. 14.99 *(978-1-4280-7470-5(8))* IndyPublish.com.

—Frank Fowler, the Cash Boy. reprint ed. pap. 79.00 *(978-1-4047-3558-3(5))* Classic Textbooks.

—Frank Fowler, the Cash Boy. 2013. (Works of Horatio Alger Jr.). 254p. reprint ed. lthr. 79.00 *(978-0-7812-3558-7(8))* Reprint Services Corp.

—Joe's Luck. 2005. 28.95 *(978-1-4218-1455-1(2));* 264p. pap. 13.95 *(978-1-4218-1555-8(9))* 1st World Publishing, Inc. (1st World Library - Literary Society).

—Joe's Luck: Or, Always Wide Awake. 2006. (ENG.). 176p. pap. 19.99 *(978-1-4264-0883-0(8))* 2006. (ENG.). 172p. pap. 19.99 *(978-1-4264-6426-3(6))* 2007. 186p. pap. 21.99 *(978-1-4264-6500-0(9))* 2006. (ENG.). 170p. pap. 21.99 *(978-1-4264-0864-9(1))* Creative Media Partners, LLC.

—Joe's Luck: Or, Always Wide Awake. 2006. pap. *(978-1-4065-0713-3(X))* Dodo Pr.

—The Young Outlaw: Or, Adrift in the Streets. 2004. (Illus.). 15.90 *(978-1-4145-0294-6(X))* Pavilion Pr., Inc.

Alice B. Emerson. Ruth Fielding of the Red Mill: Or Jasper Parloe's Secret. 2007. (ENG.). 134p. per. 18.99 *(978-1-4346-3930-1(4));* 146p. per. 19.99 *(978-1-4346-3931-8(2))* Creative Media Partners, LLC.

Anderson, Natalie C. City of Saints & Thieves. 2017. (ENG.). 432p. (YA). (gr. 7). 18.99 *(978-0-399-54758-4(4),* G.P. Putnam's Sons Books for Young Readers) Penguin Young Readers Group.

Anne of Green Gables. 2008. (Charm Boook Classics Ser.). 32p. *(978-1-4075-1583-0(7))* Parragon, Inc.

Annie S. Swan. Thankful Rest. 2007. 98p. pap. 16.99 *(978-1-4346-1978-5(8));* (ENG.). 102p. pap. 19.99 *(978-1-4346-1888-7(9))* Creative Media Partners, LLC.

Aronson, Sarah. Believe. 2013. (ENG.). 296p. (YA). (gr. 7-12). 17.95 *(978-1-4677-0697-1(3),* Carolrhoda Lab™) Lerner Publishing Group.

Atwood, Megan. Beat the Odds. 2016. (Contest Ser.: 2). (ENG.). 104p. (YA). (gr. 6-12). lib. bdg. 27.99 *(978-1-4677-7507-6(X),* Darby Creek) Lerner Publishing Group.

—Break the Code. 2016. (Contest Ser.: 4). (ENG.). 104p. (YA). (gr. 6-12). lib. bdg. 27.99 *(978-1-4677-7509-0(6),* Darby Creek) Lerner Publishing Group.

—Stay in the Game. 2016. (Contest Ser.: 1). (ENG.). 104p. (YA). (gr. 6-12). pap. 7.99 *(978-1-4677-8101-5(0))* Lerner Publishing Group.

—Turn the Tables. 2016. (Contest Ser.: 5). (ENG.). 112p. (J). (gr. 4-4). E-Book 20.99 *(978-1-4677-8835-9(X),* 9781467788359, Darby Creek) Lerner Publishing Group.

Auerbach, Annie, adapted by. Despicable Me 2: The Junior Novel. movie tie-in ed. 2013. (ENG.). 144p. (J). (gr. 3-7). pap. 6.99 *(978-0-316-23432-0(X))* Little, Brown Bks. for Young Readers.

Auxier, Jonathan. The Night Gardener. (ENG.). (YA). (gr. 3-7). 2015. 384p. pap. 8.95 *(978-1-4197-1531-0(3))* 2014. 368p. 16.95 *(978-1-4197-1144-2(X))* Abrams, Inc. (Amulet Bks.).

—The Night Gardener. 2015. (J). lib. bdg. 19.60 *(978-0-606-36891-9(4))* Turtleback Bks.

—Peter Nimble & His Fantastic Eyes. (ENG.). 400p. (J). (gr. 3-7). 2012. pap. 9.95 *(978-1-4197-0421-5(4))* 2011. 19.95 *(978-1-4197-0025-5(1))* Abrams, Inc. (Amulet Bks.).

Avi. Crispin: La Cruz de Plomo. 2004.Tr. of Crispin: The Cross of Lead. (SPA., Illus.). (YA). pap. 7.99 *(978-84-348-9601-7(X))* SM Ediciones ESP. Dist: Lectorum Pubns., Inc.

—Crispin: The Cross of Lead. 2004. (Crispin Ser.). (ENG.). 320p. (J). (gr. 3-7). reprint ed. pap. 7.99 *(978-0-7868-1658-3(9))* Hyperion Pr.

—The End of Time. 2011. (ENG.). 240p. (J). (gr. 5). pap. 6.99 *(978-0-06-174083-1(7))* HarperCollins Pubs.

—Murder at Midnight. (ENG.). (J). (gr. 3-7). 2011. 256p. pap. 6.99 *(978-0-545-08091-0(6),* Scholastic Paperbacks) 2009. 272p. 17.99 *(978-0-545-08090-3(8),* Scholastic Pr.) Scholastic, Inc.

Aviation Book Company Staff. Crispin: The Cross of Lead. 2004. (J). (gr. 3-6). 18.40 *(978-0-613-74965-7(0),* Turtleback) Turtleback Bks.

Aviles, Donna Nordmark. Fly Little Bird, Fly! 2004. 80p. per. 10.00 *(978-1-932852-07-3(7))* Wasteland Pr.

Axelrod, Amy & Axelrod, David. The Bullet Catch. 2015. (ENG.). 320p. (J). (gr. 5-9). 17.95 *(978-0-8234-2858-8(3))* Holiday Hse., Inc.

Ayres, Katherine. Under Copp's Hill. 2009. (Mysteries Through Time Ser.). 176p. (YA). (gr. 4-8). 31.95 *(978-1-60754-185-1(8));* pap. 15.25 *(978-1-60754-186-8(6))* Windmill Bks.

Babbitt, Natalie. The Moon over High Street. 2012. (J). (ENG.). 160p. (gr. 5-9). 15.95 *(978-0-545-37636-5(X),* Di Capua, Michael); 148p. pap. *(978-0-545-46740-7(3))* Scholastic, Inc.

Bacigalupi, Paolo. The Drowned Cities. 2013. (ENG.). 464p. (J). (gr. 10-17). pap. 10.99 *(978-0-316-05622-9(7))* 2012. 448p. (YA). 17.99 *(978-0-316-20037-0(9))* Little, Brown Bks. for Young Readers.

—The Drowned Cities. 2012. 352p. *(978-1-59606-506-2(0))* Subterranean Pr.

—The Drowned Cities. 2013. (J). lib. bdg. 22.10 *(978-0-606-31749-8(X),* Turtleback) Turtleback Bks.

Baggott, Julianna. The Prince of Fenway Park. 2011. (ENG.). 352p. (J). (gr. 3-7). pap. 6.99 *(978-0-06-087244-1(6))* HarperCollins Pubs.

Bailey, Em. Shift. 2016. (ENG.). 288p. (YA). (gr. 9). pap. 17.99 ***(978-1-76012-698-8(5))*** Hardie Grant Egmont Pty, Ltd. AUS. Dist: Independent Pubs. Group.

Bailey, Kristin. Legacy of the Clockwork Key. (Secret Order Ser.: 1). (ENG., (YA). (gr. 9). 2014. Illus.). 432p. pap. 9.99 *(978-1-4424-4027-2(9))* 2013. 416p. 17.99 *(978-1-4424-4026-5(0))* Simon Pulse. (Simon Pulse).

—Shadow of the War Machine. 2015. (Secret Order Ser.: 3). (ENG., Illus.). 448p. (YA). (gr. 9). 17.99 *(978-1-4424-6805-4(X),* Simon Pulse) Simon Pulse.

Banks, Kimberly E. Mask Man. Wroe, Dameon K., ed. 2003. 57p. (YA). pap. 9.99 *(978-0-9740685-0-3(0))* Another Ep Publishing.

Baratz-Logsted, Lauren. The Education of Bet. 2011. (ENG.). 192p. (YA). (gr. 7). pap. 11.99 *(978-0-547-55024-4(3))* Houghton Mifflin Harcourt Publishing Co.

Bardugo, Leigh. Ruin & Rising. 2014. (Grisha Trilogy: Vol. 3). (ENG., Illus.). 432p. (YA). (gr. 7-12). 19.99 *(978-0-8050-9461-9(X),* 9780805094619, Holt, Henry & Co. Bks. For Young Readers) Holt, Henry & Co.

—Shadow & Bone. 2012. (Shadow & Bone Trilogy Ser.: 1). (ENG.). 368p. (YA). (gr. 7-12). 19.99 *(978-0-8050-9459-6(8),* 9780805094596, Holt, Henry & Co. Bks. For Young Readers) Holt, Henry & Co.

—Shadow & Bone. 2013. (Shadow & Bone Trilogy Ser.: 1). (ENG.). 416p. (YA). (gr. 7-12). pap. 10.99 *(978-1-250-02743-6(8),* 9781250027436) Square Fish.

—Shadow & Bone. 2013. (Grisha Trilogy Ser.: 1). (YA). lib. bdg. 22.10 *(978-0-606-31903-4(4),* Turtleback) Turtleback Bks.

—Siege & Storm. 2013. (Shadow & Bone Trilogy Ser.: 2). (ENG., Illus.). 448p. (YA). (gr. 7). 19.99 *(978-0-8050-9460-2(1),* 9780805094602, Holt, Henry & Co. Bks. For Young Readers) Holt, Henry & Co.

—Siege & Storm. 2014. (Shadow & Bone Trilogy Ser.: 2). (ENG.). 496p. (YA). (gr. 7). pap. 10.99 *(978-1-250-04443-3(X),* 9781250044433) Square Fish.

Barker, M. P. Mending Horses. 2014. (ENG.). 320p. (J). (gr. 5). 17.95 *(978-0-8234-2948-6(2))* Holiday Hse., Inc.

Barrie, J. M. Peter Pan & Wendy: Centenary Edition. Ingpen, Robert R., illus. 2010. (Sterling Illustrated Classics Ser.). (ENG.). 216p. (J). (gr. 5-18). 19.95 *(978-1-4027-2868-6(9))* Sterling Publishing Co., Inc.

Barry, Dave & Pearson, Ridley. Peter & the Starcatchers. Call, Greg, illus. rev. ed. 2006. (Peter & the Starcatchers Ser.). (ENG.). 480p. (J). (gr. 5-9). reprint ed. pap. 9.99 *(978-0-7868-4907-9(X),* Disney Editions) Disney Pr.

Barwin, Steven. Hurricane Heat, 1 vol. 2013. (Orca Sports Ser.). (ENG.). 176p. (YA). (gr. 6-10). pap. 9.95 *(978-1-4598-0213-1(6))* Orca Bk. Pubs. USA.

Bass, Guy. The Spider's Lair. Williamson, Pete, illus. 2015. (Stitch Head Ser.). (ENG.). 208p. (gr. 3-4). 10.95 *(978-1-62370-192-5(9))* Capstone Young Readers of Coughlan Cos.

Bath, K. P. The Secret of Castle Cant. 2005. 1.00 *(978-1-4237-3189-4(1))* Recorded Bks., Inc.

Bayard, Louis. Lucky Strikes. 2016. (ENG., Illus.). 320p. (YA). 16.99 *(978-1-62779-390-2(9),* 9781627793902, Holt, Henry & Co. Bks. For Young Readers) Holt, Henry & Co.

—Lucky Strikes. 2017. (YA). lib. bdg. 20.85 ***(978-0-606-39951-7(8))*** Turtleback Bks.

Beake, Lesley. Home Now. Littlewood, Karin, illus. 2007. 32p. (J). (ENG.). (gr. -1-3). pap. 6.95 *(978-1-58089-163-9(2));* (gr. k-3). 16.95 *(978-1-58089-162-2(4))* Charlesbridge Publishing, Inc.

Beard, Robert W. A Boy Named Shawn. 2009. (A Shawn Barton Adventure Ser.). 116p. (J). pap. 12.95 *(978-1-935083-07-8(4))* CyPress Pubns.

—Halcyon. 2009. (J). pap. *(978-1-935083-08-5(2))* CyPress Pubns.

Beasley, Cassie. Circus Mirandus. 2016. (SPA.). 25.99 *(978-84-246-5686-7(5))* La Galera, S.A. Editorial ESP. Dist: Lectorum Pubns., Inc.

—Circus Mirandus. (ENG., Illus.). 304p. (J). (gr. 4-7). 2016. pap. 8.99 *(978-0-14-751554-4(8),* Puffin Books) 2015. 17.99 *(978-0-525-42843-5(7),* Dial Bks) Penguin Young Readers Group.

—Circus Mirandus. 2016. (ENG.). 304p. (J). (gr. 3-7). 19.65 *(978-0-606-39311-9(0))* Turtleback Bks.

Bemelmans, Ludwig. Madeline, 1 vol. 2007. (Madeline Ser.). (ENG., Illus.). 48p. (J). (gr. -1-2). 9.99 *(978-0-14-240871-1(9),* Puffin Books) Penguin Young Readers Group.

Bemis, John Claude. The Nine Pound Hammer. 2010. (Clockwork Dark Ser.: Bk. 1). (ENG.). 384p. (J). (gr. 3-7). pap. 7.99 *(978-0-375-85565-8(3),* Yearling) Random Hse. Children's Bks.

Bennion, Jay B. From Here to There. 2013. 136p. pap. 9.99 *(978-0-9826175-0-2(X))* Pearl Publishing, LLC.

Bergstrom, Sarah. Desert Dwellers Born by Fire: The First Book in the Paintbrush Saga. 2015. (ENG.). 312p. (YA). (gr. 8-17). pap. 12.95 *(978-1-78279-587-2(1),* Lodestone Bks.) Hunt, John Publishing Ltd. GBR. Dist: National Bk. Network.

Berkeley, Jon. Between the Light. Dorman, Brandon, illus. 2008. (Julie Andrews Collection). (J). lib. bdg. 17.89 *(978-0-06-075514-0(8))* HarperCollins Pubs.

—The Palace of Laughter. Dorman, Brandon, illus. (Wednesday Tales Ser.: No. 1). (J). (gr. 3-7). 2007. (ENG.). 464p. pap. 8.99 *(978-0-06-075509-6(1))* 2006. 427p. 16.99 *(978-0-06-075507-2(5),* Julie Andrews Collection) HarperCollins Pubs.

—The Tiger's Egg. Dorman, Brandon, illus. (Wednesday Tales Ser.: No. 2). (J). 2009. (ENG.). 432p. pap. 7.99 *(978-0-06-075512-6(1),* Harper Trophy) 2007. 416p. (gr. 3-7). 16.99 *(978-0-06-075510-2(5),* Julie Andrews Collection) HarperCollins Pubs.

Berry, Julie. The Amaranth Enchantment. (ENG.). (YA). (gr. 5-8). 2010. 336p. pap. 7.99 *(978-1-59990-449-8(7),* 9781599904498) 2009. 320p. 16.99 *(978-1-59990-334-7(2),* 9781599903347) Bloomsbury Publishing USA. (Bloomsbury USA Childrens).

—Secondhand Charm. 2010. (ENG.). 352p. (YA). (gr. 5-8). 16.99 *(978-1-59990-511-2(6),* 9781599905112, Bloomsbury USA Childrens) Bloomsbury Publishing USA.

Berryman, Chelsea. Missing Pages. 2007. 77p. pap. 19.95 *(978-1-60441-747-0(1))* America Star Bks.

Besser, Kenneth/R. Amie Carver & the Plague of Demeverde. 2007. (Illus.). x, 338p. (J). *(978-1-934316-02-3(4))* RTMC Organization, LLC.

Bethers, Linda, retold by. Christmas Oranges. 2004. 13p. pap. 3.95 *(978-1-57734-546-6(0),* 01114387) Covenant Communications, Inc.

Biedrzycki, David. Ace Lacewing, Bug Detective: The Big Swat. Biedrzycki, David, illus. 2010. (ENG., Illus.). 44p. (J). (gr. k-4). 16.95 *(978-1-57091-747-9(7))* Charlesbridge Publishing, Inc.

Biggs, Suzanne K. Charlie Christmas. 2012. 124p. (gr. 4-6). 20.95 *(978-1-4759-4157-9(9));* pap. 10.95 *(978-1-4759-4155-5(2))* iUniverse, Inc.

Billingsley, Franny. The Folk Keeper. unabr. ed. 2004. 176p. (J). (gr. 5-9). pap. 36.00 incl. audio *(978-0-8072-0662-1(8),* Listening Library) Random Hse. Audio Publishing Group.

Binns, B. A. Pull. 2010. 310p. (YA). (gr. 9-18). 16.95 *(978-1-934813-43-0(5))* Westside Bks.

Black, Peter Jay. Blackout. 2015. (Urban Outlaws Ser.: 2). (ENG.). 304p. (YA). (gr. 5-8). 16.99 *(978-1-61963-592-0(5),* 9781619635920, Bloomsbury USA Childrens) Bloomsbury Publishing USA.

—Lockdown. 2016. (Urban Outlaws Ser.: 3). (ENG.). 272p. (J). 16.99 *(978-1-61963-834-1(7),* 9781619638341, Bloomsbury USA Childrens) Bloomsbury Publishing USA.

—Urban Outlaws. (Urban Outlaws Ser.: 1). (ENG.). (gr. 5-8). 2015. 304p. (YA). pap. 7.99 *(978-1-61963-572-2(0),* 9781619635722) 2014. (Illus.). 288p. (J). 16.99 *(978-1-61963-400-8(7),* 9781619634008) Bloomsbury Publishing USA. (Bloomsbury USA Childrens).

Blackwood, Sage. Jinx. (Jinx Ser.: 3). 400p. (J). (gr. 3-7). 2016. pap. 7.99 *(978-0-06-212997-0(X))* 2015. (ENG.). 16.99 *(978-0-06-212996-3(1))* 2014. (ENG.). 16.99 *(978-0-06-212993-2(7))* HarperCollins Pubs. (Tegen, Katherine Bks).

Blagden, Scott. Dear Life, You Suck: A Novel. 2015. (ENG.). 320p. (YA). (gr. 9). pap. 9.99 *(978-0-544-33621-6(6),* HMH Books For Young Readers) Houghton Mifflin Harcourt Publishing Co.

Bloodworth, Mark, illus. The Castle Mystery. 2010. (Boxcar Children Graphic Novels Ser.: 12). (ENG.). 32p. (J). (gr. 1-5). pap. 6.99 *(978-0-8075-1080-3(7))* Whitman, Albert & Co.

Booher, Brock. The Charity Chip. 2015. pap. 16.99 *(978-1-4621-1669-0(8))* Cedar Fort, Inc./CFI Distribution.

Boone, Martina. Illusion. 2016. (Heirs of Watson Island Ser.). (ENG., Illus.). 480p. (YA). (gr. 9). 17.99 *(978-1-4814-1128-8(4),* Simon Pulse) Simon Pulse.

Bouani, Jennifer. Tyler & His Solve-A-Matic Machine: (1st Edition) 2006. (Future Business Leaders' Ser.). (Illus.). 118p. (J). (gr. 4-7). per. 6.99 *(978-0-9779265-0-3(8))* Bouje Publishing, LLC.

Bow, Erin. Plain Kate. (ENG.). 320p. (J). (gr. 7-7). 2012. pap. 9.99 *(978-0-545-16665-2(9))* 2010. 17.99 *(978-0-545-16664-5(0))* Scholastic, Inc. (Levine, Arthur A. Bks.).

Boyne, John. The Boy at the Top of the Mountain. 2017. (J). lib. bdg. 18.40 ***(978-0-606-39937-1(2))*** Turtleback Bks.

Bradbury, Jennifer. Outside In. 2017. (ENG., Illus.). 288p. (J). (gr. 3-7). 16.99 ***(978-1-4424-6827-6(0),*** Atheneum/Caitlyn Dlouhy Books) Simon & Schuster Children's Publishing.

Braden, Stephanie. The Wishing Well. 2012. 48p. pap. 16.95 *(978-1-62709-450-4(4))* America Star Bks.

Bradford, Chris. The Way of the Warrior, Bk. 1. 2008. (Young Samurai Ser.: 1). (ENG., Illus.). 352p. (J). (gr. 6-10). pap. 12.99 ***(978-0-14-132430-2(9))*** Penguin Bks., Ltd. GBR. Dist: Independent Pubs. Group.

—Young Samurai: the Way of the Sword. 2011. 448p. pap. 7.99 *(978-1-4231-2937-0(7))* Hyperion Pr.

—Young Samurai the Way of the Sword. l.t. ed. 2012. (Young Samurai Ser.). (ENG.). 547p. (J). (gr. 6-9). 23.99 *(978-1-4104-4404-2(X))* Thorndike Pr.

Bredsdorff, Bodil. The Crow-Girl: The Children of Crow Cove. Ingwersen, Faith, tr. from DAN. 2007. (Illus.). 155p. (gr. 3-7). 18.00 *(978-0-7569-8186-0(7))* Perfection Learning Corp.

—The Crow-Girl: The Children of Crow Cove. Ingwersen, Faith, tr. 2006. (Children of Crow Cove Ser.: 1). (ENG., Illus.). 160p. (J). (gr. 3-7). reprint ed. pap. 8.99 *(978-0-374-40003-3(2),* 9780374400033, Farrar, Straus & Giroux (BYR)) Farrar, Straus & Giroux.

Brewer, Heather. Chronicles of Vladimir Tod, 2 vols. 2009. (Chronicles of Vladimir Tod Ser.: 2). (ENG.). 288p. (YA). (gr. 7-18). 8.99 *(978-0-14-241342-5(9),* Speak) Penguin Young Readers Group.

—Eighth Grade Bites. Laud, Julia, illus. 2013. (Chronicles of Vladimir Tod Ser.: 1). (ENG.). 144p. (YA). (gr. 7). pap. 12.99 *(978-0-8037-3811-9(0),* Dial Bks) Penguin Young Readers Group.

—Eighth Grade Bites. 2008. (Chronicles of Vladimir Tod Ser.: 1). (ENG.). 192p. (YA). (gr. 7). 8.99 *(978-0-14-241187-2(6),* Speak) Penguin Young Readers Group.

—Eleventh Grade Burns, 4 vols. 2010. (Chronicles of Vladimir Tod Ser.: 4). (ENG.). 320p. (YA). (gr. 7-18). 8.99 *(978-0-14-241647-1(9),* Speak); 4th ed. 16.99 *(978-0-525-42243-3(9),* Dutton Books for Young Readers) Penguin Young Readers Group.

—Tenth Grade Bleeds. Preseault, N., ed. 2010. (Chronicles of Vladimir Tod Ser.: 3). (ENG.). 304p. (YA). (gr. 7-18). pap. 8.99 *(978-0-14-241560-3(X),* Speak) Penguin Young Readers Group.

—Tenth Grade Bleeds. 2009. (Chronicles of Vladimir Tod Ser.: 3). (ENG., Illus.). 304p. (YA). (gr. 7-18). 16.99 *(978-0-525-42135-1(1),* Dutton Books for Young Readers) Penguin Young Readers Group.

—Tenth Grade Bleeds. 2010. (Chronicles of Vladimir Tod Ser.: 03). lib. bdg. 19.65 *(978-0-606-10594-1(8),* Turtleback) Turtleback Bks.

Brockway, Stephanie. Mystic Phyles: Beasts. Masiello, Ralph, illus. 2011. (ENG.). 144p. (J). (gr. 4-7). 15.95 *(978-1-57091-718-9(3))* Charlesbridge Publishing, Inc.

Brontë, Charlotte. Jane Eyre. 2006. (Reader's Workshop Ser.). (ENG.). 120p. (C). pap. 19.95 *(978-0-7362-3137-4(4))* CENGAGE Learning.

Brooks, Walter R. The Clockwork Twin: A Freddy the Pig Book on Everything. Wiese, Kurt, illus. 2013. (ENG.). 256p. (gr.

M
N
O

4-13). pap. 10.99 (978-1-4683-0349-0(X), 460349) Overlook Pr., The.

Bross, Lee. Tangled Webs. 2016. (Tangled Webs Ser.). (ENG., Illus.). 400p. (YA). (gr. 9-17). pap. 9.99 (978-1-4231-9467-5(5)) Hyperion Bks. for Children.

Brouwer, Sigmund. Cobra Strike, 1 vol. 2007. (Orca Sports Ser.). (ENG.). 176p. (YA). (gr. 6-10). per. 9.95 (978-1-55143-725-5(2)) Orca Bk. Pubs. USA.

Brown, Jeff. The True Joy of Christmas. 2012. 28p. pap. 16.99 (978-1-4624-0365-3(4), Inspiring Voices) Author Solutions, Inc.

Bruchac, Joseph. Whisper in the Dark. Comport, Sally Wern, illus. 2009. (ENG.). 192p. (J). (gr. 5). pap. 6.99 (978-0-06-058089-6(5)) HarperCollins Pubs.

Buck, Alicia. Out of the Ashes. 2015. 281p. (YA). pap. 17.99 (978-1-4621-1727-7(9)) Cedar Fort, Inc./CFI Distribution.

Buckey, Sarah Masters. Clue in the Castle Tower: A Samantha Mystery. Ross, Peg, ed. Giovine, Sergio, illus. 2011. (ENG.). 184p. (YA). (gr. 4-18). pap. 6.95 (978-1-59369-752-5(X)) American Girl Publishing, Inc.

—The Stolen Sapphire. 2007. (American Girl Mysteries Ser.). (Illus.). 181p. (gr. 4-7). 17.45 (978-0-7569-8278-2(2)) Perfection Learning Corp.

Buckley, Michael. The Fairy-Tale Detectives. Ferguson, Peter, illus. 2005. (ENG.). 288p. (J). (gr. 3-7). 16.95 (978-0-8109-5925-5(9), Abrams Bks. for Young Readers) Abrams, Inc.

—The Fairy-Tale Detectives. (Sisters Grimm Ser.: 1). (J). 2008. 81.45 (978-1-4361-0398-5(3)) 2007. 214.75 (978-1-4193-6197-5(X)) 2007. 1.25 (978-1-4193-6193-7(7)) 2006. 71.75 (978-1-4193-6198-2(8)) 2006. 86.75 (978-1-4193-8749-4(9)) 2006. 74.75 (978-1-4193-6196-8(1)) 2006. 89.75 (978-1-4193-8747-0(2)) Recorded Bks., Inc.

—The Fairy-Tale Detectives: And the Unusual Suspects. Ferguson, Peter, illus. 2012. 580p. (J). (978-1-4351-4487-3(2), Amulet Bks.) Abrams, Inc.

—The Problem Child. Ferguson, Peter, illus. 2006. (Sisters Grimm Ser.). (ENG.). 320p. (J). (gr. 3-7). 16.95 (978-0-8109-4914-0(8), Amulet Bks.) Abrams, Inc.

—The Sisters Grimm: The Fairy-Tale Detectives. Ferguson, Peter, illus. 10th anniv. ed. 2017. (Sisters Grimm Ser.). (ENG.). 288p. (J). (gr. 3-7). pap. 8.95 (978-1-4197-2005-5(8), Amulet Bks.) Abrams, Inc.

—A Very Grimm Guide. Ferguson, Peter, illus. 2012. (Sisters Grimm Ser.). (ENG.). 128p. (J). (gr. 3-7). 16.95 (978-1-4197-0201-3(7), Amulet Bks.) Abrams, Inc.

Bunce, Elizabeth C. A Curse Dark as Gold. (ENG.). 400p. (J). (gr. 7). 2010. 9.99 (978-0-439-89577-4(4), Scholastic Paperbacks) 2008. 17.99 (978-0-439-89576-7(6), Levine, Arthur A. Bks.) Scholastic, Inc.

Bunney, Ron. No One Owns Me. 2004. (Illus.). 256p. (YA). pap. 13.50 (978-1-920731-86-1(5)) Fremantle Pr. AUS. Dist: Independent Pubs. Group.

Bunting, Eve. Forbidden. 2015. (ENG.). 224p. (YA). (gr. 7). 17.99 (978-0-544-39092-8(X)) Houghton Mifflin Harcourt Publishing Co.

—Train to Somewhere. Himler, Ronald, illus. 2004. 32p. (gr. -1-3). 18.00 (978-0-7569-4260-1(8)) Perfection Learning Corp.

Burgess, Melvin. Nicholas Dane. 2013. (ENG.). 432p. (YA). (gr. 9-13). pap. 9.99 (978-0-312-55146-9(0), 9780312551469) Square Fish.

Burnett, Frances Hodgson. A Little Princess. 2008. 156p. 25.95 (978-1-60664-768-4(7)); pap. 13.95 (978-1-60664-141-5(7)) Aegypan.

—A Little Princess. 2008. 212p. (gr. 2-4). 27.99 (978-0-554-29155-0(X)); 24.99 (978-0-554-38458-0(2)) Creative Media Partners, LLC.

—A Little Princess. Aldous, Kate, illus. 2005. 62p. (J). (gr. 4-7). 8.95 (978-0-7945-1123-4(6), Usborne) EDC Publishing.

—A Little Princess. 2012. 212p. pap. 8.99 (978-1-60796-454-4(6)) Meirovich, Igal.

—A Little Princess. 2012. (ENG., Illus.). 280p. (978-1-905716-04-3(4), Collector's Library, The) Pan Macmillan.

—A Little Princess. 2012. (Puffin Classics Ser.). (ENG., Illus.). 320p. (J). (gr. 5-7). 16.99 (978-0-14-134171-2(8), Puffin Books) Penguin Young Readers Group.

—A Little Princess. Gill, Margery, illus. 2008. (Puffin Classics Ser.). (ENG.). 320p. (J). (gr. 5-7). 5.99 (978-0-14-132112-7(1), Puffin Books) Penguin Young Readers Group.

—A Little Princess. 188p. 2009. pap. 13.95 (978-1-4385-0876-4(X)) 2008. pap. 13.45 (978-1-4385-0194-9(3)) Standard Pubns., Inc. (Book Jungle).

—A Little Princess. McKowen, Scott, illus. 2004. (Sterling Unabridged Classics Ser.). (ENG.). 208p. (J). (gr. 5). 9.95 (978-1-4027-1454-2(8)) Sterling Publishing Co., Inc.

—A Little Princess. Engelbreit, Mary, illus. 2007. (Mary Engelbreit's Classic Library). (ENG.). 304p. (J). (gr. 3-7). 9.99 (978-0-06-008137-9(6), HarperFestival) HarperCollins Pubs.

—A Little Princess. 2012. (Children's Classics Ser.). (ENG.). 186p. pap. 19.99 (978-1-909438-52-1(9), Sovereign) Bollinger, Max GBR. Dist: Lightning Source UK, Ltd.

—A Little Princess. Kliros, Thea, illus. abr. ed. 2012. (Dover Children's Thrift Classics Ser.). (ENG.). 96p. (J). (gr. 3-8). pap. 3.00 (978-0-486-29171-0(5)) Dover Pubns., Inc.

—A Little Princess: Being the whole story of Sara Crewe now told for T. 2007. 196p. per. 19.99 (978-1-4346-7028-1(7)); (ENG.). 210p. per. 22.99 (978-1-4346-7029-8(5)) Creative Media Partners, LLC.

—A Little Princess: The Story of Sara Crewe. (J). 16.95 (978-0-8488-1253-9(0)) Amereon Ltd.

—A Little Princess: The Story of Sara Crewe. Warren, Eliza, ed. Marcos, Pablo, illus. 2006. 239p. (YA). reprint ed. 10.00 (978-0-7567-9835-2(3)) DIANE Publishing Co.

—A Little Princess: The Story of Sara Crewe. 2005. 112p. per. 4.95 (978-1-4209-2529-6(6)) Digireads.com Publishing.

—A Little Princess: The Story of Sara Crewe. 2006. pap. (978-1-4065-0559-7(5)) Dodo Pr.

—A Little Princess: The Story of Sara Crewe. l.t. ed. 2005. 376p. pap. (978-1-84637-117-2(1)) Echo Library.

—A Little Princess: The Story of Sara Crewe. 2004. reprint ed. pap. 1.99 (978-1-4192-0213-1(8)); pap. 22.95 (978-1-4191-0213-4(3)) Kessinger Publishing, LLC.

—A Little Princess: The Story of Sara Crewe. 2006. 204p. (YA). 19.95 (978-1-934169-20-9(X)); pap. 7.95 (978-1-934169-21-6(8)) Norilana Bks.

—A Little Princess: The Story of Sara Crewe. 2005. (Twelve-Point Ser.). lib. bdg. 25.00 (978-1-58287-320-6(8)); lib. bdg. 26.00 (978-1-58287-814-0(5)) North Bks.

—A Little Princess: The Story of Sara Crewe. Rust, Graham, illus. (J). pap. 22.95 (978-0-590-24079-6(X)) Scholastic, Inc.

—A Little Princess: The Story of Sara Crewe. l.t. ed. 2003. 342p. pap. 10.95 (978-0-7862-6247-2(8)) Thorndike Pr.

—A Little Princess: With a Discussion of Generosity. Gribbon, Sean & Jael, trs. Gribbon, Sean & Jael, illus. 2003. (Values in Action Illustrated Classics Ser.). (J). (978-1-59203-050-7(5)) Learning Challenge, Inc.

—Petite Princess. pap. 19.95 (978-2-07-051994-1(5)) Gallimard, Editions FRA. Dist: Distribooks, Inc.

—Sara Crewe. l.t. ed. 2006. 92p. pap. (978-1-84637-263-6(1)) Echo Library.

—Sara Crewe. 2009. 68p. pap. 7.95 (978-1-60664-388-4(6)) Rodgers, Alan Bks.

—Sara Crewe or What Happened at Miss Minc. 2005. pap. 20.95 (978-0-7661-9708-4(5)) Kessinger Publishing, LLC.

—Sara Crewe or What Happened at Miss Minchin's. 2006. (ENG.). 88p. per. 8.95 (978-1-59462-359-2(7), 395, Book Jungle) Standard Pubns., Inc.

—Sara Crewe, or What Happened at Miss Minchin's. 2007. 48p. per. (978-1-4068-4489-4(6)) Echo Library.

—The Secret Garden. 2012. (Illus.). 304p. (978-1-4351-4212-1(8)) Barnes & Noble, Inc.

—The Secret Garden. Robinson, Charles, illus. 2011. 304p. (J). (978-1-4351-3344-0(7)) Barnes & Noble, Inc.

—The Secret Garden. Moore, Inga, illus. 2008. (ENG.). 272p. (J). (gr. 1-4). 22.99 (978-0-7636-3161-1(2)) Candlewick Pr.

—The Secret Garden. 2003. (ENG., Illus.). 288p. (gr. 12-18). mass mkt. 5.95 (978-0-451-52883-4(2), Signet) Penguin Publishing Group.

—The Secret Garden. Lawrie, Robin, illus. 2008. (Puffin Classics Ser.). (ENG.). 368p. (J). (gr. 3-7). 5.99 (978-0-14-132106-6(7), Puffin Books) Penguin Young Readers Group.

—The Secret Garden. 2003. (Modern Library Classics Ser.). (ENG.). 288p. (J). (gr. 3-7). pap. 7.95 (978-0-8129-6998-6(7), Modern Library) Random House Publishing Group.

—The Secret Garden. 2013. (ENG.). 384p. (J). (gr. 4-7). pap. 11.99 (978-0-09-957295-4(8)) Random Hse. GBR. Dist: Independent Pubs. Group.

—The Secret Garden. Ingpen, Robert R., illus. 2011. (Sterling Illustrated Classics Ser.). (ENG.). 240p. (J). (gr. 5-18). 19.95 (978-1-4027-7872-8(4)) Sterling Publishing Co., Inc.

—The Secret Garden. Moore, Inga, illus. 2010. (ENG.). 272p. (J). (gr. 1-4). pap. 16.99 (978-0-7636-4732-2(2)) Candlewick Pr.

—The Secret Garden, 1 vol. Simon, Ute, illus. 2011. (Calico Illustrated Classics Ser.: No. 3). (ENG.). 112p. (J). (gr. 3-6). 27.07 (978-1-61641-108-4(2)) Magic Wagon.

—The Secret Garden. Corvino, Lucy, illus. 2005. (Classic Starts(tm) Ser.). (ENG.). 160p. (J). (gr. 2-4). 6.95 (978-1-4027-1319-4(3)) Sterling Publishing Co., Inc.

—The Secret Garden. Tudor, Tasha, illus. 100th anniv. ed. 2010. (Trophy Bk.). (ENG.). 384p. (J). (gr. 4-18). reprint ed. pap. 6.99 (978-0-06-440188-3(X)) HarperCollins Pubs.

—The Secret Garden. Hunt, Peter, ed. 2011. (Oxford World's Classics Ser.). (ENG.). 304p. (gr. 7-18). pap. 8.95 (978-0-19-958822-0(8)) Oxford Univ. Pr., Inc.

—The Secret Garden: A Young Reader's Edition of the Classic Story. (J). 22.95 (978-0-8488-0692-7(1)) Amereon Ltd.

—The Secret Garden: A Young Reader's Edition of the Classic Story. 2004. (Illus.). (J). (gr. 1-4). spiral bd. (978-0-616-14565-4(9)); spiral bd. (978-0-616-14566-1(7)) Canadian National Institute for the Blind/Institut National Canadien pour les Aveugles.

—The Secret Garden: A Young Reader's Edition of the Classic Story. (English As a Second Language Bk.). (Illus.). 92p. pap. 4.46 net. (978-0-582-53417-9(8)) Longman Publishing Group.

—The Secret Garden: With a Discussion of Compassion. Lauter, Richard, illus. 2003. (Values in Action Illustrated Classics Ser.). 191p. (J). (978-1-59203-037-8(8)) Learning Challenge, Inc.

—The Secret Garden Book & Charm. Tudor, Tasha, illus. deluxe ed. 2005. (Charming Classics). 368p. (J). 9.99 (978-0-06-075771-7(X), HarperFestival) HarperCollins Pubs.

Burnett, Frances Hodgson & Naxos of America Staff. The Secret Garden. 3rd ed. 2008. (Hear It Read It Classics Ser.: 0). (ENG., Illus.). 144p. (J). (gr. 2-4). 9.95 (978-1-4022-1244-4(5), Sourcebooks Jabberwocky) Sourcebooks, Inc.

Bush, Suzanne & Takes, Deb. Time Will Tell. 2004. 279p. (YA). lib. bdg. 15.95 (978-0-9747426-0-1(0)) Imagining Possibilities.

Byng, Georgia. Molly Moon & the Morphing Mystery. 2011. (Molly Moon Ser.: 5). (ENG.). 416p. (J). (gr. 3-7). pap. 7.99 (978-0-06-166162-4(7)) HarperCollins Pubs.

—Molly Moon Detiene el Mundo. 2004. (SPA.). 358p. (gr. 5-8). 18.99 (978-84-348-9610-9(9)) SM Ediciones ESP. Dist: Lectorum Pubns., Inc.

—Molly Moon Stops the World. (J). 2004. (Illus.). 384p. 16.99 (978-0-06-051410-5(8)) 2005. (Molly Moon Ser.: 2). (ENG.). 416p. (gr. 3-7). reprint ed. pap. 7.99 (978-0-06-051415-0(9)) HarperCollins Pubs.

—Molly Moon y el Increible Libro. 2003. (SPA.). 349p. (J). 18.99 (978-84-348-9076-3(3)) SM Ediciones ESP. Dist: Lectorum Pubns., Inc.

—Molly Moon's Incredible Book of Hypnotism. 2003. 135.92 (978-0-06-057217-4(5)) 2003. (Molly Moon Ser.: 1). (Illus.). 384p. (J). (gr. 3-7). 17.99 (978-0-06-051406-8(X)) 2004. (Molly Moon Ser.: 1). (ENG., Illus.). 384p. (J). (gr. 3-7). reprint ed. pap. 7.99 (978-0-06-051409-9(4)) HarperCollins Pubs.

—Molly Moon's Incredible Book of Hypnotism. 2004. (Molly Moon Ser.). 371p. (gr. 3-7). 18.00 (978-0-7569-3484-2(2)) Perfection Learning Corp.

Byrne, Michael. Lottery Boy. 2016. (ENG.). 304p. (YA). (gr. 7). 16.99 (978-0-7636-7996-5(8)) Candlewick Pr.

Calhoun, Dia. After the River the Sun. Slater, Kate, illus. 2013. (ENG.). 368p. (J). (gr. 4-7). 16.99 (978-1-4424-3985-6(8)) Simon & Schuster Children's Publishing.

Campbell, H. David. Merribell: A Comforting Story. 2011. 218p. (gr. 2-2). 23.95 (978-1-4620-4477-1(8)); pap. 13.95 (978-1-4620-4476-4(X)) iUniverse, Inc.

Cardarelli, Mario. Bunny, an Orphan's Story. 2008. 44p. pap. 18.99 (978-1-4389-1597-5(7)) AuthorHouse.

Carey, Anna. Eve. (Eve Ser.: 1). (ENG.). (YA). (gr. 8). 2012. 352p. pap. 9.99 (978-0-06-204851-6(1)) 2011. 336p. 17.99 (978-0-06-204850-9(3)) HarperCollins Pubs.

—Eve. 2012. (SPA.). 224p. (YA). pap. 20.95 (978-84-9918-434-0(0)) Roca Editorial ESP. Dist: Spanish Pubs., LLC.

Carey, Edward. Heap House. 2014. (Iremonger Trilogy Ser.: 1). (ENG.). 416p. (gr. 4-13). 16.99 (978-1-4683-0953-9(6), 460953) Overlook Pr., The.

—Lungdon: The Iremonger Trilogy: Book Three. 2015. (Iremonger Trilogy Ser.: 0). (ENG., Illus.). 512p. (gr. 5-12). 17.99 (978-1-4683-0955-3(2), 460955) Overlook Pr., The.

Carlon, Mick. Riding on Duke's Train. 2011. (LeapKids Ser.). (ENG.). 160p. (J). (gr. k-7). pap. 9.95 (978-1-935248-06-4(5)) Leapfrog Pr.

Carlson-Voiles, Polly. Summer of the Wolves. 2013. (ENG.). 352p. (J). (gr. 5-7). pap. 7.99 (978-0-544-02276-8(9)) Houghton Mifflin Harcourt Publishing Co.

Carman, Patrick. The House of Power. 2008. (Atherton Ser.: 1). (ENG., Illus.). 384p. (J). (gr. 3-7). pap. 9.99 (978-0-316-16671-3(5)) Little, Brown Bks. for Young Readers.

—Rivers of Fire. 2009. (Atherton Ser.: 2). (ENG., Illus.). 336p. (J). (gr. 3-7). pap. 9.99 (978-0-316-16673-7(1)) Little Brown & Co.

Carmichael, Clay. Wild Things. (ENG.). (J). 2012. 184p. (gr. 5-8). pap. 9.95 (978-1-59078-914-8(8)) 2009. 248p. (gr. 4-6). 18.95 (978-1-59078-627-7(0), Front Street) Boyds Mills Pr.

—Wild Things, 6 vols. 2010. (J). 77.75 (978-1-4498-0632-3(5)) Recorded Bks., Inc.

Carolyn, Reeder. Shades of Gray. 2014. (ENG.). 160p. (J). (gr. 5-12). 11.24 (978-1-63245-242-9(1)) Lectorum Pubns., Inc.

Carr, Pat. Border Ransom. 2006. (Chaparral Bks.). (ENG., Illus.). 178p. (J). (gr. 3-7). per. 11.95 (978-0-87565-332-7(4)) Texas Christian Univ. Pr.

Casey, Barbara. The Cadence of Gypsies. 2011. (ENG.). 272p. (J). (gr. 7-12). 16.95 (978-0-9820812-8-0(6), Hungry Goat Pr.) Gauthier Pubns. Inc.

Cashore, Kristin. Jane, Unlimited. 2017. (ENG.). 464p. (YA). (gr. 9). 18.99 **(978-0-8037-4149-2(9)**, Kathy Dawson Books) Penguin Young Readers Group.

Cavanagh, Peter J. Fungie: The Dingle Dolphin. 2008. 48p. per. 24.95 (978-1-4241-8356-2(1)) America Star Bks.

Chee, Traci. The Reader. (Sea of Ink & Gold Ser.: 1). (ENG.). 464p. (YA). (gr. 7). 2017. pap. 10.99 **(978-0-14-751805-7(9)**, Speak)Bk. 1. 2016. 19.99 (978-0-399-17677-7(2), G.P. Putnam's Sons Books for Young Readers) Penguin Young Readers Group.

—The Reader. 2017. (Sea of Ink & Gold Ser.: 1). lib. bdg. 22.10 **(978-0-606-40001-5(X))** Turtleback Bks.

Chima, Cinda Williams. The Wizard Heir. 2008. (Heir Chronicles Ser.). (ENG.). 480p. (J). (gr. 5-9). pap. 9.99 (978-1-4231-0488-9(9)) Hyperion Pr.

Chimombo, S. The Bird Boy's Song. 2004. 96p. pap. (978-99908-48-07-6(6)) Wasi Pubns. ZWE. Dist: Michigan State Univ. Pr.

Ching, Lorilei. He Ping: An Orphan's Destiny. 2013. 32p. pap. 13.95 (978-1-4624-0807-8(9), Inspiring Voices) Author Solutions, Inc.

Chriss, Granddad. The Adventures of Barazaburg. 2011. 54p. 24.99 (978-1-4568-7988-4(X)); pap. 15.99 (978-1-4568-7987-7(1)) Xlibris Corp.

Christopher, Matt. Dirt Bike Runaway. 2008. (New Matt Christopher Sports Library). 176p. (J). (gr. 4-6). lib. bdg. 26.60 (978-1-59953-215-8(8)) Norwood Hse. Pr.

Chronicles of Avonlea. 2004. 142p. (YA). pap. 7.95 (978-1-57646-893-7(3)) Quiet Vision Publishing.

City of a Thousand Dolls. 2014. (ENG.). 384p. (YA). (gr. 8). pap. 9.99 (978-0-06-212132-5(4)) HarperCollins Pubs.

Clare, Cassandra. Clockwork Angel. (Infernal Devices Ser.: Bk. 1). (ENG., Illus.). (YA). (gr. 9). 2015. 544p. pap. 13.99 (978-1-4814-5602-9(4)) 2010. 496p. 24.99 (978-1-4169-7586-1(1)) McElderry, Margaret K. Bks. (McElderry, Margaret K. Bks.).

—Clockwork Angel. 2012. (Infernal Devices Ser.: 1). (ENG.). 240p. (gr. 8-17). pap. 13.00 (978-0-316-20098-1(0), Yen Pr.) Orbit.

—Clockwork Angel. 2015. (Infernal Devices Ser.: Bk. 1). 544p. (YA). lib. bdg. 25.75 (978-0-606-37737-9(9)) 2012. (Infernal Devices Graphic Novel Ser.: 1). lib. bdg. 24.55 (978-0-606-32257-7(4), Turtleback) Turtleback Bks.

—Clockwork Prince. (Infernal Devices Ser.: Bk. 2). (YA). 2015. (ENG., Illus.). 560p. (gr. 9). pap. 13.99 (978-1-4814-5601-2(6)) 2011. (ENG., Illus.). 528p. (gr. 9-18). 24.99 (978-1-4169-7588-5(8)) 2011. 502p. (978-1-4424-5174-2(2)) McElderry, Margaret K. Bks. (McElderry, Margaret K. Bks.).

—Clockwork Prince. 2013. (Infernal Devices Ser.: 2). (ENG., Illus.). 256p. (gr. 8-17). pap. 13.00 (978-0-316-20096-7(4), Yen Pr.) Orbit.

—Clockwork Prince. 2015. (Infernal Devices Ser.: Bk. 2). 560p. (YA). lib. bdg. 25.75 (978-0-606-37895-6(2)) 2013. (Infernal Devices Graphic Novel Ser.: 2). lib. bdg. 24.55 (978-0-606-32258-4(2), Turtleback) Turtleback Bks.

—Clockwork Princess. 2013. (YA). (Infernal Devices Ser.: 3). (ENG., Illus.). 592p. (gr. 9). 24.99 (978-1-4169-7590-8(X)); 570p. (978-1-4424-8541-9(8)) McElderry, Margaret K. Bks. (McElderry, Margaret K. Bks.).

—The Infernal Devices: Clockwork Angel; Clockwork Prince; Clockwork Princess. 2013. (Infernal Devices Ser.: Bks. 1-3). (ENG.). 1520p. (YA). (gr. 9). 74.99 (978-1-4424-8372-9(5), McElderry, Margaret K. Bks.) McElderry, Margaret K. Bks.

Clark, Brenda. Spiro & Zinger Rescue the Orphans: Spiro the Shooting Star - Book Three, 1 vol. 2010. 70p. pap. 19.95 (978-1-4489-3992-3(5)) America Star Bks.

Coats, J. Anderson. The Many Reflections of Miss Jane Deming. 2017. (ENG., Illus.). 288p. (J). (gr. 5-7). 16.99 (978-1-4814-6496-3(5), Atheneum Bks. for Young Readers) Simon & Schuster Children's Publishing.

Coatsworth, Elizabeth Jane. The Fair American. Sewell, Helen, illus. 2005. (Sally (Bethlehem Books) Ser.). 137p. (J). pap. 11.95 (978-1-883937-85-0(X)) Bethlehem Bks.

Colfer, Eoin. The Forever Man. (Warp Ser.). (ENG.). (YA). (gr. 7-12). 2016. 368p. pap. 9.99 (978-1-4847-2616-7(2)) 2015. 352p. 17.99 (978-1-4847-2603-7(0)) Hyperion Bks. for Children.

—The Supernaturalist. 2012. (Supernaturalist Ser.). (ENG.). 272p. (J). (gr. 5-9). pap. 7.99 (978-1-4231-4679-7(4)) Hyperion Pr.

Collier, James Lincoln. Me & Billy, 0 vols. unabr. ed. 2013. (ENG.). 194p. (J). (gr. 5-7). pap. 9.99 (978-1-4778-1706-3(9), 9781477817063, Amazon Children's Publishing) Amazon Publishing.

Collingwood, Harry. The Log of a Privateersman. 2008. 216p. 26.95 (978-1-60664-899-5(3)); pap. 15.95 (978-1-60664-018-0(6)) Aegypan.

Collins, Pat Lowery. Hidden Voices: The Orphan Musicians of Venice. 2009. (ENG., Illus.). 352p. (YA). (gr. 7). 17.99 (978-0-7636-3917-4(6)) Candlewick Pr.

Collins, Sonny. Mouse Tails. 2006. (ENG.). 52p. per. 16.95 (978-1-4241-4589-8(9)) PublishAmerica, Inc.

Conlon-McKenna, Marita. A Girl Called Blue. 2nd rev. ed. 2004. (ENG.). 224p. (J). pap. 12.95 (978-0-86278-887-2(0)) O'Brien Pr., Ltd., The IRL. Dist: Dufour Editions, Inc.

Constable, Cathryn. The Wolf Princess. (ENG.). 320p. (J). (gr. 5-9). 2014. pap. 6.99 (978-0-545-52841-2(0)) 2013. 16.99 (978-0-545-52839-9(9)) Scholastic, Inc. (Chicken Hse., The).

Cook, Kristi. Eternal. (ENG., Illus.). (YA). (gr. 9). 2014. 432p. pap. 9.99 (978-1-4424-8531-0(0)) 2013. 416p. 16.99 (978-1-4424-8532-7(9)) Simon Pulse. (Simon Pulse).

—Haven. (ENG.). (YA). (gr. 9). 2012. 448p. pap. 9.99 (978-1-4424-0761-9(1)) 2011. 416p. 16.99 (978-1-4424-0760-2(3)) Simon Pulse. (Simon Pulse).

—Mirage. (ENG., (YA). (gr. 9). 2013. Illus.). 416p. pap. 9.99 (978-1-4424-4300-6(6)) 2012. 384p. 16.99 (978-1-4424-4299-3(9)) Simon Pulse. (Simon Pulse).

Cooney, Caroline B. If the Witness Lied. 2010. (ENG.). 224p. (YA). (gr. 7). pap. 8.99 (978-0-385-73449-3(2), Ember) Random Hse. Children's Bks.

Cooper, Paul Fenimore. Tal, His Marvelous Adventures with Noom-Zor-Noom. Reeves, Ruth, illus. 80th ed. 2009. 305p. (J). pap. 12.95 (978-1-930900-41-7(4)) Purple Hse. Pr.

Cormier, Robert. Heroes. 2006. (York Notes Ser.). (ENG., Illus.). 112p. pap. (978-1-4058-3559-6(1)) Pearson Education, Ltd.

Couloumbis, Audrey. Maude March on the Run! Or Trouble Is Her Middle Name. 2008. (Maude March Ser.). (ENG., Illus.). 320p. (J). (gr. 3-7). pap. 7.99 (978-0-375-83248-2(3), Yearling) Random Hse. Children's Bks.

—The Misadventures of Maude March: Or Trouble Rides a Fast Horse. 2007. (Illus.). 295p. (gr. 3-7). 18.00 (978-0-7569-7770-2(3)) Perfection Learning Corp.

—The Misadventures of Maude March: Or Trouble Rides a Fast Horse. 2007. (Maude March Ser.). (ENG., Illus.). 320p. (J). (gr. 3-7). 7.99 (978-0-375-83247-5(5), Yearling) Random Hse. Children's Bks.

Coville, Katherine. Ivy. 2017. (ENG.). 144p. (J). (gr. 2-5). lib. bdg. 19.99 (978-0-553-53976-9(0), Knopf Bks. for Young Readers) Random Hse. Children's Bks.

Cowling, Douglas. Vivaldi's Ring of Mystery. Fernandez, Laura & Jacobson, Rick, illus. 2004. (ENG.). 44p. (J). (978-0-439-96904-8(2), North Winds Pr) Scholastic Canada, Ltd.

Crawford, Clint. The Rag Tag Gang, 1 vol. 2009. 83p. pap. 19.95 (978-1-4489-9697-1(X)) America Star Bks.

Creech, Sharon. The Castle Corona. Diaz, David, illus. (J). 2013. (ENG.). 352p. (gr. 3-7). pap. 7.99 (978-0-06-206395-3(2)) 2007. 336p. (gr. 4-7). lib. bdg. 19.89 (978-0-06-084622-0(4), Cotler, Joanna Books) HarperCollins Pubs.

—The Great Unexpected. (J). (gr. 3-7). 2013. (ENG.). 256p. pap. 6.99 (978-0-06-189234-9(3)) 2012. (ENG., Illus.). 240p. 16.99 (978-0-06-189232-5(7)) 2012. (Illus.). 240p. lib. bdg. 17.89 (978-0-06-189233-2(5)) HarperCollins Pubs.

—Ruby Holler. 2012. (ENG.). 288p. (J). (gr. 3-7). pap. 6.99 (978-0-06-056015-7(0)) HarperCollins Pubs.

—Ruby Holler. 2004. (Joanna Cotler Bks.). 310p. (gr. 3-7). 17.00 (978-0-7569-1940-5(1)) Perfection Learning Corp.

—Ruby Holler. 2012. (J). (gr. 3-6). 17.20 (978-0-613-86272-1(4), Turtleback) Turtleback Bks.

—The Unfinished Angel. 2013. (ENG.). 160p. (J). (gr. 3-7). pap. 6.99 (978-0-06-143097-8(8)) HarperCollins Pubs.

Crocker, Carter & Swift, Jonathan. The Last of the Gullivers. 2012. (ENG.). 224p. (J). (gr. 4-7). 16.99 (978-0-399-24231-1(7), Philomel Bks.) Penguin Young Readers Group.

Croggon, Alison. The Singing: Book Four of Pellinor. 2017. (Pellinor Ser.). (ENG.). 496p. (J). (gr. 7). pap. 9.99 (978-0-7636-9446-3(0)) Candlewick Pr.

Cuevas, Michelle. Beyond the Laughing Sky. Morstad, Julie, illus. 2014. (ENG.). 160p. (J). (gr. 3-7). 16.99 (978-0-8037-3867-6(6), Dial Bks) Penguin Young Readers Group.

Cullen, Seán. Hamish X & the Hollow Mountain. 2008. (ENG.). 288p. (J). (gr. 7-18). 9.99 (978-0-14-305312-5(4), Puffin Canada) Penguin Random House Canada Young Readers CAN. Dist: Penguin Random Hse. LLC.

Cummins, Maria S. The Lamplighter. 2011. 308p. pap. 16.99 (978-1-61203-228-3(1)) Bottom of the Hill Publishing.

Cushman, Karen. Rodzina. 2016.Tr. of Rodzina. (ENG.). 224p. (J). (gr. 5-7). pap. 6.99 (978-0-544-54029-3(8), HMH Books For Young Readers) Houghton Mifflin Harcourt Publishing Co.

Cusick, Richie Tankersley. The Unseen 1 It Begins. 2005. (Unseen Ser.: 1). (ENG.). 304p. (YA). (gr. 7-7). 8.99 (978-0-14-240463-8(2), Speak) Penguin Young Readers Group.

Dahl, Roald. The BFG. 2016. (CHI.). 112p. (J). (gr. 3-6). pap. **(978-986-479-012-8(9))** Commonwealth Publishing Co., Ltd.

—The BFG. 30th rev. ed. 2014. (ENG.). 208p. (J). (gr. 2-12). 11.24 (978-1-63245-341-9(X)) Lectorum Pubns., Inc.

—The BFG. 2009. 9.00 (978-0-7848-2054-4(6), Everbind) Marco Bk. Co.

—The BFG. Dahl, Roald & Blake, Quentin, illus. 2007. 17.00 (978-0-7569-8233-1(2)) Penguin Publishing Group.

—The BFG. movie tie-in ed. 2016. (ENG., Illus.). 224p. (J). (gr. 3-7). 7.99 (978-1-101-99769-7(9), Puffin Books) Penguin Young Readers Group.

—The BFG. Blake, Quentin, illus. 30th anniv. ed. 2007. (ENG.). 224p. (J). (gr. 3-7). 7.99 (978-0-14-241038-7(1), Puffin Books) Penguin Young Readers Group.
—The BFG. 2005. (J). 1.25 (978-1-4193-5995-8(9)) Recorded Bks., Inc.
—The BFG. 2007. 18.40 (978-1-4177-8612-1(4), Turtleback) Turtleback Bks.
Dalmatian Press Staff, adapted by. Heidi. (SPA., Illus.). (YA). 11.95 (978-84-7281-082-2(8), AF1082) Auriga, Ediciones S.A. ESP. Dist: Continental Bk. Co., Inc.
—Heidi. (Young Collector's Illustrated Classics Ser.). (Illus.). 192p. (J). (gr. 3-7). 9.95 (978-1-56156-455-2(9)) Kidsbooks, LLC.
—Oliver Twist. Date not set. (C). pap. (978-0-7593-9612-8(4), Cengage Learning) CENGAGE Learning.
La Dama de Cobre (the Copper Lady) 2006. (J). pap. 6.95 (978-0-8225-6616-8(8), Ediciones Lerner) Lerner Publishing Group.
Danforth, Emily M. The Miseducation of Cameron Post. 2012. (ENG.). 480p. (YA). (gr. 9). 17.99 (978-0-06-202056-7(0)) HarperCollins Pubs.
D'Arcy, Megan. Be Happy. Gawthrop, Shaughn, illus. 2011. 32p. (J). 14.95 (978-1-879094-95-6(9)) Momentum Bks., LLC.
Daunis, Marcia Prosco. Miller's Ben. 2008. 159p. pap. 24.95 (978-1-60672-759-1(1)) America Star Bks.
Davidson, Jenny. The Explosionist. 2008. 464p. (YA). (gr. 7-18). lib. bdg. 18.89 (978-0-06-123976-2(3), HarperTeen) HarperCollins Pubs.
Davies, Anna. Wrecked. (ENG., Illus.). 336p. (YA). (gr. 9). 2013. pap. 9.99 (978-1-4424-3279-6(9)) 2012. 16.99 (978-1-4424-3278-9(0)) Simon & Schuster Bks. For Young Readers. (Simon & Schuster Bks. For Young Readers).
Davis, Susan Page. Sarah's Long Ride. 2007. (Piper Ranch Ser.). 173p. (J). (gr. 3-7). per. 8.99 (978-1-59166-737-7(2)) BJU Pr.
De Haven, Tom. The Orphan's Tent. 2005. (Illus.). 192p. mass mkt. 5.99 (978-0-7434-9772-5(4)) ibooks, Inc.
De Leeuw, Cateau. Fear in the Forest. Vosburgh, Leonard, illus. 2014. (ENG.). 123p. (J). pap. 14.95 (978-1-932350-43-2(8)) Bethlehem Bks.
de Lint, Charles. The Cats of Tanglewood Forest. 2014. (J). lib. bdg. 22.10 (978-0-606-36532-1(X)) Turtleback Bks.
De Stefano, Lauren. A Curious Tale of the In-Between. 2016. (J). lib. bdg. 18.40 (978-0-606-39553-3(9)) Turtleback Bks.
DeFelice, Cynthia C. The Apprenticeship of Lucas Whitaker. 2007. (ENG.). 160p. (J). (gr. 5-9). per. 9.99 (978-0-374-40014-9(8), 9780374400149) Square Fish.
del Rio, Tania. Warren the 13th & the All-Seeing Eye. Staehle, Will, illus. 2015. (Warren The 13th Ser.: 1). (ENG.). 224p. (J). (gr. 5). 16.95 (978-1-59474-803-5(9)) Quirk Bks.
Delaney, Joseph. Ghost Prison. (ENG.). 112p. (YA). (gr. 6-12). 2014. pap. 5.99 (978-1-4926-0174-6(8)) 2013. 12.99 (978-1-4022-9318-4(6), 9781402293184) Sourcebooks, Inc.
D'Elia, Amy & Clerman, Lisa. Dreams Come True: A story about the blessing of Adoption. 2007. (978-0-9777744-1-8(4)) Finneran, Lisa.
Denenberg, Barry. A True Patriot: The Journal of William Thomas Emerson, a Revolutionary War Patriot. 2012. lib. bdg. 17.20 (978-0-606-26736-6(0), Turtleback) Turtleback Bks.
Denton, Shannon Eric & Warner, Gertrude Chandler. The Boxcar Children, 1 vol. Dubisch, Michael, illus. 2009. (Boxcar Children Graphic Novels Ser.). (ENG.). 32p. (J). (gr. 2-5). lib. bdg. 28.50 (978-1-60270-586-9(0)) ABDO Publishing Co.
Desio, Delores. The Legend of Ruby O'Grady: Grandma Was A Hippie. 2011. 122p. pap. 19.95 (978-1-4560-7039-7(8)) America Star Bks.
DeStefano, Lauren. A Curious Tale of the In-Between. 2015. (ENG.). 240p. (YA). (gr. 3-6). 16.99 (978-1-61963-600-2(X), 9781619636002, Bloomsbury USA Childrens) Bloomsbury Publishing USA.
—Fever, 7 vols. 2012. (Chemical Garden Trilogy: Bk. 2). (YA). 102.75 (978-1-4640-1914-2(2)) Recorded Bks., Inc.
—Fever. (Chemical Garden Trilogy Ser.: 2). (ENG., (YA). (gr. 9). 2013. Illus.). 368p. pap. 9.99 (978-1-4424-0908-8(8)) 2012. 352p. 17.99 (978-1-4424-0907-1(X)) Simon & Schuster Bks. For Young Readers. (Simon & Schuster Bks. For Young Readers).
—Fiebre. (Chemical Garden Trilogy: Bk. 2).Tr. of Fever. (SPA.). 352p. pap. (978-84-96886-28-5(X)) Ediciones Urano S. A.
—The Peculiar Night of the Blue Heart. 2016. (ENG.). 208p. (J). 16.99 (978-1-61963-643-9(3), 9781619636439, Bloomsbury USA Childrens) Bloomsbury Publishing USA.
—Sever. 2013. (Chemical Garden Trilogy Ser.: 3). (ENG.). 400p. (YA). (gr. 9). pap. 9.99 (978-1-4424-0910-1(X)) Simon & Schuster.
—Sever. 2013. (Chemical Garden Trilogy Ser.: 3). (ENG.). 384p. (YA). (gr. 9). 17.99 (978-1-4424-0909-5(6), Simon & Schuster Bks. For Young Readers) Simon & Schuster Bks. For Young Readers.
—Wither, 9 vols. (Chemical Garden Ser.: 1). (YA). 256.75 (978-1-4561-2059-7(X)); 1.25 (978-1-4561-2064-1(6)); 90.75 (978-1-4561-2060-3(3)); 2011. 122.75 (978-1-4561-2061-0(1)); 2011. 120.75 (978-1-4561-2063-4(8)) Recorded Bks., Inc.
—Wither. 2011. (Chemical Garden Trilogy Ser.: 1). (ENG.). (YA). (gr. 9). 384p. pap. 10.99 (978-1-4424-0906-4(1)); 368p. 19.99 (978-1-4424-0905-7(3)) Simon & Schuster Bks. For Young Readers. (Simon & Schuster Bks. For Young Readers).
DiCamillo, Kate. The Magician's Elephant. Tanaka, Yoko, illus. (ENG.). (J). (gr. 3-7). 2015. 224p. pap. 7.99 (978-0-7636-8088-6(5)) 2009. 208p. 16.99 (978-0-7636-4410-9(2)) Candlewick Pr.
—The Magician's Elephant. l.t. ed. 2010. (ENG.). 242p. 23.95 (978-1-4104-2493-8(6)) Thorndike Pr.
—The Magician's Elephant. 2015. lib. bdg. 17.20 (978-0-606-37891-8(X)) 2011. lib. bdg. 17.20 (978-0-606-15375-1(6), Turtleback) Turtleback Bks.
Dickens, Charles. David Copperfield. 2006. (ENG.). 130p. per. 18.95 (978-1-84002-570-5(0)) Consortium Bk. Sales & Distribution.
—David Copperfield. 2008. (Bring the Classics to Life Ser.). (Illus.). 72p. (gr. 4-12). pap., act. bk. ed. 10.95 (978-1-55576-322-0(7), EDCTR-408B) EDCON Publishing Group.
—David Copperfield. 2009. 186p. pap. 19.99 (978-1-4590-4328-2(6)) General Bks. LLC.
—David Copperfield, 1 vol. McWilliam, Howard, illus. 2011. (Calico Illustrated Classics Ser.). (ENG.). 112p. (YA). (gr. 3-6). 27.07 (978-1-60270-745-0(6)) Magic Wagon.
—David Copperfield. 2009. (Foundation Classics Ser.). 56p. (J). (gr. 5-9). lib. bdg. 27.95 (978-1-60754-852-2(6)) Windmill Bks.
—David Copperfield. 2006. (Oxford Progressive English Readers Ser.). (ENG., Illus.). 103p. (J). (gr. 4-7). per. (978-0-19-597140-8(X)) Oxford Univ. Pr.
—Great Expectations. Freeberg, Eric, illus. 2010. (Classic Starts(tm) Ser.). (ENG.). 160p. (J). (gr. 2-4). 6.95 (978-1-4027-6645-9(9)) Sterling Publishing Co., Inc.
—Great Expectations. Donnelly, Karen, illus. 2013. (Charles Dickens Ser.). (ENG.). 64p. pap. 6.95 (978-1-906230-01-2(3)) Real Reads Ltd. GBR. Dist: Casemate Pubs. & Bk. Distributors, LLC.
—Great Expectations. 2011. (Puffin Classics Ser.). (ENG.). 432p. (J). (gr. 5-7). pap. 4.99 (978-0-14-133013-6(9), Puffin Books) Penguin Young Readers Group.
—Great Expectations. 2014. (Differentiated Timeless Classics Ser.). (ENG.). 80p. (YA). (gr. 9-12). 12.95 (978-1-62250-718-4(5)) Saddleback Educational Publishing, Inc.
—Great Expectations: The Graphic Novel. 2010. (Classic Graphic Novel Collection). (ENG.). 160p. (YA). (gr. 7-12). 34.80 (978-1-4205-0372-2(3)) Cengage Gale.
—Oliver Twist. 2009. (Foundation Classics Ser.). (Illus.). 56p. (J). (gr. 5-9). lib. bdg. 27.95 (978-1-60754-542-2(X)) Windmill Bks.
—Oliver Twist. Andreasen, Dan, illus. 2006. (Classic Starts(tm) Ser.). (ENG.). 160p. (J). (gr. 2-4). 6.95 (978-1-4027-2665-1(1)) Sterling Publishing Co., Inc.
—Oliver Twist. Donnelly, Karen, illus. 2013. (Charles Dickens Ser.). (ENG.). 64p. pap. 6.95 (978-1-906230-00-5(5)) Real Reads Ltd. GBR. Dist: Casemate Pubs. & Bk. Distributors, LLC.
—Oliver Twist, 1 vol. McWilliam, Howard, illus. 2011. (Calico Illustrated Classics Ser.: No. 3). (ENG.). 112p. (J). (gr. 3-6). 27.07 (978-1-61641-106-0(6)) Magic Wagon.
—Oliver Twist. abr. ed. Date not set. (Nelson Readers Ser.). (J). pap. (978-0-17-557020-1(5)) Addison-Wesley Longman, Inc.
—Oliver Twist. Volpari, Daniela, illus. 2014. (Big Picture Book Ser.). (ENG.). 48p. (J). (gr. 1). 16.95 (978-2-7338-2529-7(1)) Auzou, Philippe Editions FRA. Dist: Consortium Bk. Sales & Distribution.
—Oliver Twist. 2014. (Graphic Classics Ser.). 48p. (gr. 2-7). pap. 8.95 (978-1-905087-97-6(7)) Book Hse. GBR. Dist: Black Rabbit Bks.
—Oliver Twist. 2013. 274p. pap. 14.99 (978-1-4837-0319-0(3)) Bottom of the Hill Publishing.
—Oliver Twist. Belli, Alfredo, illus. 2008. (Green Apple Step Two Ser.). (ENG.). 96p. (J). (gr. 5). pap. incl. audio compact disk (978-88-530-0580-9(7)) Cideb.
—Oliver Twist. 2008. (Bring the Classics to Life Ser.). (ENG., Illus.). 72p. (gr. 3-12). pap., act. bk. ed. 10.95 (978-1-55576-325-1(1), EDCTR-308B) EDCON Publishing Group.
—Oliver Twist. abr. ed. (J). 9.95 (978-1-56156-372-2(2)) Kidsbooks, LLC.
—Oliver Twist. 2013. (ENG., Illus.). 722p. (J). (gr. 4-7). pap. 12.99 (978-0-09-958263-2(5)) Random Hse. GBR. Dist: Independent Pubs. Group.
—Oliver Twist. Morgan, Richard & Fennell, Tracy, illus. 2008. 48p. (J). (gr. 4-7). pap. 10.00 (978-1-4190-5075-6(3)) Steck-Vaughn.
—Oliver Twist. 2009. (Real Reads Ser.). (Illus.). 64p. (YA). (gr. 4-8). pap. 13.55 (978-1-60754-153-0(X)) Windmill Bks.
—Oliver Twist: With a Discussion of Honesty. 2003. (Values in Action Illustrated Classics Ser.). (J). (978-1-59203-051-4(3)) Learning Challenge, Inc.
Dickens, Charles & Dauvillier, Loïc. Oliver Twist. 70th anniv. ed. 2012. (Classics Illustrated Deluxe Graphic Nove Ser.). (ENG., Illus.). 240p. (J). (gr. 3-9). pap. 19.99 (978-1-59707-307-3(5), 9781597073073) Papercutz.
Dimpel, Matt. The War of the Serpent Swords. 2011. 230p. pap. 24.95 (978-1-4626-3169-8(X)) PublishAmerica, Inc.
Dinerstein, Eric. What Elephants Know. 2016. (ENG.). 288p. (J). (gr. 3-7). 16.99 (978-1-4847-2854-3(8)) Disney Publishing Worldwide.
Dixon, John. Phoenix Island. 2014. (ENG.). 320p. pap. 11.99 (978-1-4767-3865-9(3), Gallery Bks.) Gallery Bks.
Doder, Joshua. Grk Smells a Rat. 2009. (J). (978-0-385-90654-8(4), Delacorte Pr) Random House Publishing Group.
Domínguez, José A. Mamerto: A Children's Story. 2006. (J). mass mkt. 12.50 (978-1-59835-022-7(6)) Cambridge BrickHouse, Inc.
dos Santos, Steven. The Culling. 2013. (Torch Keeper Ser.: 1). (ENG.). 432p. (YA). pap. 9.99 (978-0-7387-3537-5(X), Flux) North Star Editions.
Dowell, Frances O'Roark. Where I'd Like to Be. 2004. (Aladdin Fiction Ser.). 232p. (gr. 5-9). 17.00 (978-0-7569-4357-8(4)) Perfection Learning Corp.
—Where I'd Like to Be. (ENG., (J). (gr. 5-9). 2003. Illus.). 240p. 17.99 (978-0-689-84420-1(4)) 2004. 256p. reprint ed. pap. 7.99 (978-0-689-87067-5(1)) Simon & Schuster Children's Publishing. (Atheneum Bks. for Young Readers).
—Where I'd Like to Be. l.t. ed. 2003. 162p. (J). 22.95 (978-0-7862-5741-6(5)) Thorndike Pr.
Dower, Laura. Maggie's Magic Chocolate Moon. Lazuli, Lilly, illus. 2016. (Dessert Diaries). (ENG.). 160p. (gr. 4-5). pap. 5.95 (978-1-4965-4141-3(3)); lib. bdg. 26.65 (978-1-4965-3121-6(3)) Stone Arch Bks.
Dowswell, Paul. The Auslander. 2011. (ENG.). 304p. (YA). 17.99 (978-1-59990-633-1(3), 9781599906331, Bloomsbury USA Childrens) Bloomsbury Publishing USA.
Doyle, Brian. Easy Avenue, 1 vol. 2nd ed. 2004. (ENG.). 122p. (YA). pap. 6.95 (978-0-88899-605-3(5)) Groundwood Bks. CAN. Dist: Publishers Group West (PGW).
Doyle, Sheldon. Purple Mountain's Majesty. 2008. 224p. pap. 21.95 (978-1-4357-2017-6(2)) Lulu Pr., Inc.
Du Jardin, Rosamond. Young & Fair. 2003. (YA). pap. 12.95 (978-1-930009-79-0(8), 800-691-7779) Image Cascade Publishing.
Dubisch, Mike, illus. The Haunted Cabin Mystery. 2009. (Boxcar Children Graphic Novels Ser.: 9). (ENG.). 32p. (J). (gr. 1-5). pap. 6.99 (978-0-8075-3180-8(4)) Whitman, Albert & Co.
—The Pizza Mystery. 2010. (Boxcar Children Graphic Novels Ser.: 11). (ENG.). 32p. (J). (gr. 1-5). pap. 6.99 (978-0-8075-6537-7(7)) Whitman, Albert & Co.
—Tree House Mystery. 2009. (Boxcar Children Graphic Novels Ser.: 8). (ENG.). 32p. (J). (gr. 1-5). pap. 6.99 (978-0-8075-8088-2(0)) Whitman, Albert & Co.
Dubisch, Mike & Bloodworth, Mark, illus. The Amusement Park Mystery. 2010. (Boxcar Children Graphic Novels Ser.: 10). (ENG.). 32p. (J). (gr. 1-5). pap. 6.99 (978-0-8075-0321-8(5)) Whitman, Albert & Co.
Duble, Kathleen Benner. Madame Tussaud's Apprentice: An Untold Story of Love in the French Revolution. 2014. (ENG.). 224p. (YA). 17.99 (978-1-4405-8116-8(9), Simon Pulse) Simon Pulse.
—Phantoms in the Snow. 2011. (ENG.). 240p. (J). (gr. 7-7). 17.99 (978-0-545-19770-0(8), Scholastic Pr.) Scholastic, Inc.
Dublin, Anne. The Baby Experiment: A Novel (Large Print 16pt) 2013. 172p. pap. (978-1-4596-6337-4(3)) ReadHowYouWant.com, Ltd.
Dunkle, Clare B. The Hollow Kingdom. 2006. (Hollow Kingdom Trilogy Ser.: 1). (ENG.). 240p. (J). (gr. 6-9). reprint ed. pap. 10.99 (978-0-8050-8108-4(9), 9780805081084, Holt, Henry & Co. Bks. For Young Readers) Holt, Henry & Co.
—The House of Dead Maids. Arrasmith, Patrick, illus. 2011. (ENG.). 176p. (YA). (gr. 7-12). pap. 16.99 (978-0-312-55155-1(X), 9780312551551) Square Fish.
Dunn, Joeming & Dunn, Ben, illus. Houseboat Mystery. 2011. (Boxcar Children Graphic Novels Ser.: 16). (ENG.). 32p. (J). (gr. 1-5). pap. 6.99 (978-0-8075-3395-6(5)) Whitman, Albert & Co.
Dunn, Joeming & Warner, Gertrude Chandler. The Lighthouse Mystery, 1 vol., Bk. 14. Dunn, Ben, illus. 2011. (Boxcar Children Graphic Novels Ser.). (ENG.). 32p. (J). (gr. 2-5). 28.50 (978-1-61641-122-0(8)) ABDO Publishing Co.
—The Woodshed Mystery, 1 vol., Bk. 13. Dunn, Ben, illus. 2011. (Boxcar Children Graphic Novels Ser.). (ENG.). 32p. (J). (gr. 2-5). 28.50 (978-1-61641-121-3(X)) ABDO Publishing Co.
Edge, Christopher. The Black Crow Conspiracy. 2015. (Penelope Tredwell Mysteries Ser.: 3). (ENG.). 272p. (J). (gr. 3-7). 16.99 (978-0-8075-0780-3(6)) Whitman, Albert & Co.
—Shadows of the Silver Screen. 2014. (Penelope Tredwell Mysteries Ser.: 2). (ENG.). 256p. (J). (gr. 3-7). 16.99 (978-0-8075-7319-8(1)) Whitman, Albert & Co.
—Twelve Minutes to Midnight. 2014. (Penelope Tredwell Mysteries Ser.: Book 1). (ENG.). 256p. (J). (gr. 3-7). 16.99 (978-0-8075-8133-9(X)) Whitman, Albert & Co.
Edwards, Garth. Escape from Mercy Hall. 2012. (Thorn Gate Trilogy Ser.). (Illus.). 192p. (J). (gr. 4-6). pap. 7.99 (978-0-9567122-4-0(X)) Lerner Publishing Group.
Edwards, Judith. Invasion on the Mountain: The Adventures of Will Ryan & the Civilian Conservation Corps 1933. 2011. (ENG., Illus.). 90p. (J). (gr. 3-7). pap. 12.50 (978-1-884592-55-3(4)) Images from the Past, Inc.
—Trouble on the Mountain: The Adventures of Will Ryan & the Civilian Conservation Corps, 1934-35. 2012. (ENG., Illus.). 118p. (J). (gr. 3-7). pap. 12.50 (978-1-884592-60-7(0)) Images from the Past, Inc.
Edwards, Julie Andrews. Mandy. Westerman, Johanna, illus. 2nd ed. 2006. (Julie Andrews Collection). (ENG.). 320p. (J). (gr. 3-7). 17.99 (978-0-06-113162-2(8)); pap. 6.99 (978-0-06-120707-5(1)) HarperCollins Pubs.
Edwards, S. Neil. My Dog, Digger. 2006. 122p. pap. 19.95 (978-1-4241-0514-4(5)) America Star Bks.
Eliot, Ethel. The Little House in the Fairy Wood. 2006. 108p. per. 9.95 (978-1-59818-097-8(5)); 22.95 (978-1-59818-343-6(5)) Aegypan.
Elliott, Rebecca. Zoo Girl. Elliott, Rebecca, illus. 2013. (ENG., Illus.). 32p. (J). (gr. k-2). pap. 8.99 (978-0-7459-6270-2(X)) Lion Hudson PLC GBR. Dist: Independent Pubs. Group.
Ellis, Deborah. No Ordinary Day, 1 vol. (ENG.). (J). (gr. 3-7). 2014. 160p. pap. 9.95 (978-1-55498-108-3(5)) 2011. 144p. 16.95 (978-1-55498-134-2(4)) Groundwood Bks. CAN. Dist: Publishers Group West (PGW).
—No Ordinary Day. 2013. 164p. pap. (978-1-4596-6451-7(5)) ReadHowYouWant.com, Ltd.
Ellis, Mary. Elephant Child. Denton, Kady MacDonald, illus. 2010. (ENG.). 128p. (J). (gr. 2-4). pap. 7.99 (978-0-00-712820-4(7), HarperCollins Children's Bks.) HarperCollins Pubs. Ltd. GBR. Dist: HarperCollins Pubs.
Ellis, Sarah. The Several Lives of Orphan Jack, 1 vol. St-Aubin, Bruno, illus. 2005. (ENG.). 88p. (J). pap. 8.95 (978-0-88899-618-3(7)) Groundwood Bks. CAN. Dist: Publishers Group West (PGW).
Emerson, Alice B. Ruth Fielding at Snow Camp or Lost in the Backwoods. 2005. reprint ed. pap. 24.95 (978-1-4179-3132-3(9)) Kessinger Publishing, LLC.
—Ruth Fielding in the Red Cross or Doing. 2005. pap. 24.95 (978-1-4179-1799-0(7)) Kessinger Publishing, LLC.
—Ruth Fielding on Cliff Island: Or the Old Hunter's Treasure Box. 2007. (ENG.). 136p. pap. 18.99 (978-1-4346-2493-2(5)) Creative Media Partners, LLC.
—Ruth Fielding on the St. Lawrence or the. 2005. pap. 24.95 (978-0-7661-9911-8(8)) Kessinger Publishing, LLC.
Emery, Joanna. Brothers of the Falls. Erickson, David, illus. 2004. (Adventures in America Ser.). (gr. 4). 14.95 (978-1-893110-37-3(0)) Silver Moon Pr.
Everest, D. D. Archie Greene & the Magician's Secret. 2015. (Archie Greene Ser.: 1). (ENG.). 320p. (J). (gr. 3-7). 16.99 (978-0-06-231211-2(1)) HarperCollins Pubs.
Falkner, John Meade. Moonfleet: A Classic Tale of Smuggling. Marks, Alan, illus. 2007. (Young Reading Series 3 Gift Bks). 63p. (J). (gr. 4-7). 8.99 (978-0-7945-1906-3(7), Usborne) EDC Publishing.
Fenn, G. Manville. Brownsmith's Boy. 2008. 260p. 29.95 (978-1-60664-780-6(6)) Aegypan.
Ferguson, M. J. The Mirror in the Box: A Children's Story & a Parable. 2013. 66p. (gr. 4-6). pap. 9.99 (978-1-4497-7804-0(6), WestBow Pr.) Author Solutions, Inc.
Ficklin, Jonene H. The Garden Gate. 2005. (YA). 14.95 (978-0-9761188-2-4(3)) Victor's Crown Publishing.
Fiona Fox Staff, ed. The Secret Garden. 2012. (ENG., Illus.). 64p. 15.00 (978-1-84135-837-6(1)) Award Pubns. Ltd. GBR. Dist: Parkwest Pubns., Inc.
Fisher, Dorothy Canfield. Understood Betsy. 2004. reprint ed. pap. 1.99 (978-1-4192-9201-9(3)); pap. 24.95 (978-1-4179-0955-1(2)) Kessinger Publishing, LLC.
Ford, Martyn. The Imagination Box. 2016. (ENG.). 240p. (J). (gr. 4-7). 16.99 (978-1-101-93627-6(4), Delacorte Pr.) Random Hse. Children's Bks.
Forman, M. L. Adventurers Wanted, Book 1: Slathbog's Gold. 2011. 400p. mass mkt. 7.99 (978-1-60641-681-5(2)) Deseret Bk. Co.
—Adventurers Wanted, Book 2: The Horn of Moran. 2012. (J). pap. 7.99 (978-1-60908-911-5(1)) 2011. 400p. 39.99 (978-1-60641-255-8(8)) Deseret Bk. Co.
—Adventurers Wanted, Book 3: Albrek's Tomb. 2013. (Adventurers Wanted Ser.: 3). (ENG.). 504p. (J). (gr. 5). pap. 9.99 (978-1-60907-339-8(8), Shadow Mountain) Shadow Mountain Publishing.
—Adventurers Wanted, Book 4: Sands of Nezza. 2013. (Adventurers Wanted Ser.: 4). (ENG.). 400p. (J). (gr. 5). 19.99 (978-1-60907-329-9(0), Shadow Mountain) Shadow Mountain Publishing.
—Adventures Wanted, Book 3: Albrek's Tomb. 2012. (YA). 19.99 (978-1-60908-892-7(1)) Deseret Bk. Co.
Forman, Mark. The Horn of Moran. 2011. 400p. (YA). (gr. 3-18). 18.99 (978-1-60641-226-8(4), Shadow Mountain) Shadow Mountain Publishing.
—Slathbog's Gold. 2009. (Adventurers Wanted Ser.: Bk. 1). 432p. (J). 17.95 (978-1-60641-029-5(6), Shadow Mountain) Shadow Mountain Publishing.
Forster, Miriam. City of a Thousand Dolls. 2013. (ENG.). 368p. (YA). (gr. 8). 17.99 (978-0-06-212130-1(8), HarperTeen) HarperCollins Pubs.
Forte, Joseph. At the Window. 2013. 32p. pap. (978-1-4602-2190-7(7)) FriesenPress.
Foster, Stewart. Bubble. 2017. (ENG., Illus.). 352p. (J). (gr. 3-5). 16.99 (978-1-4814-8742-9(6), Simon & Schuster Bks. For Young Readers) Simon & Schuster Bks. For Young Readers.
Fox, Jennifer. Meet the Boxtrolls. 2014. (Passport to Reading Level 2 Ser.). (J). lib. bdg. 13.55 (978-0-606-36529-1(X)) Turtleback Bks.
Francis, Pauline, retold by. The Turn of the Screw. 2010. (Essential Classics - Horror Ser.). (Illus.). 48p. pap. (978-0-237-54110-1(6)) Evans Brothers, Ltd.
Frazier, Neta. The Stout-Hearted Seven: Orphaned on the Oregon Trail. 2017. (Great Leaders & Events Ser.). (ENG.). (J). (gr. 4-8). lib. bdg. 35.99 (978-1-942875-43-7(6)) Quarto Publishing Group USA.
Frazier, Neta Lohnes. The Stout-Hearted Seven: Orphaned on the Oregon Trail. 2016. (Young Voyageur Ser.). (ENG., Illus.). 224p. (J). (gr. 4-9). pap. 12.99 (978-0-7603-5224-3(0), Voyageur Pr.) Quarto Publishing Group USA.
—The Stout-Hearted Seven: Orphaned on the Oregon Trail. 2006. (Sterling Point Books(r) Ser.). (ENG., Illus.). 208p. (J). (gr. 4-7). pap. 6.95 (978-1-4027-3617-9(7)) Sterling Publishing Co., Inc.
Frederick Marryat. The Children of the New Forest. 2007. 412p. per. 17.95 (978-1-4218-4823-5(6)); 33.95 (978-1-4218-4726-9(4)) 1st World Publishing, Inc. (1st World Library - Literary Society).
Freeman, Martha. The Orphan & the Mouse. McPhail, David, illus. 2014. (ENG.). 176p. (J). (gr. 3-7). 16.95 (978-0-8234-3167-0(3)) Holiday Hse., Inc.
French, Vivian. The Bag of Bones: The Second Tale from the Five Kingdoms. Collins, Ross, illus. 2009. (Tales from the Five Kingdoms Ser.: 2). (ENG.). 256p. (J). (gr. 3-7). 14.99 (978-0-7636-4255-6(X)) Candlewick Pr.
Frost, C. Amethyst. Mourning under the Bridge. 2012. 280p. pap. 9.99 (978-0-9847236-2-1(5)) Frost, C. A.
Funaro, Gregory. Alistair Grim's Odd Aquaticum. 2016. (Alistair Grim Ser.). (ENG.). 448p. (J). (gr. 3-7). pap. 7.99 (978-1-4847-0900-9(4)) Hyperion Bks. for Children.
—Alistair Grim's Odd Aquaticum. 2016. (Alistair Grim Ser.). (ENG., Illus.). 448p. (J). (gr. 3-7). 16.99 (978-1-4847-0007-5(4)) Hyperion Pr.
—Alistair Grim's Odditorium. 2015. (Alistair Grim Ser.). (ENG.). (J). (gr. 3-7). 448p. pap. 7.99 (978-1-4847-0899-6(7)); (Illus.). 432p. 16.99 (978-1-4847-0006-8(6)) Hyperion Bks. for Children.
—Alistair Grim's Odditorium. 2015. (J). lib. bdg. 18.40 (978-0-606-37399-9(3)) Turtleback Bks.
Funke, Cornelia. Thief Lord. Birmingham, Christian, illus. 2010. (ENG.). 376p. (J). (gr. 3-7). 7.99 (978-0-545-22770-4(4), Chicken Hse., The) Scholastic, Inc.
Fusco, Kimberly Newton. Beholding Bee. 2015. (ENG.). 336p. (J). (gr. 3-7). 7.99 (978-0-375-86808-5(9), Yearling) Random Hse. Children's Bks.
Gaiman, NEil. The Graveyard Book. McKean, Dave, illus. (J). 2014. (ENG.). 352p. (gr. 5-7). pap. 9.99 (978-0-06-234918-7(X)) 2010. (ENG.). 352p. (gr. 5). pap. 8.99 (978-0-06-053094-5(4)) 2008. 552p. pap. 17.99 (978-0-06-170912-8(3)) 2008. (ENG.). 320p. (gr. 5-7). 17.99 (978-0-06-053092-1(8)) 2008. 320p. (gr. 5-7). lib. bdg. 18.89 (978-0-06-053093-8(6)) HarperCollins Pubs.
—The Graveyard Book. 2009. 19.00 (978-1-60686-823-2(3)) Perfection Learning Corp.
—The Graveyard Book. 2011. (Literature Kit Ser.). (ENG., Illus.). 55p. pap. 12.95 (978-1-55319-559-7(0), Classroom Complete Pr.) Rainbow Horizons Publishing, Inc.
—The Graveyard Book, 7 vols. 2008. (J). 256.75 (978-1-4361-5882-4(6)); 100.75 (978-1-4361-5887-9(7)) Recorded Bks., Inc.
—The Graveyard Book. l.t. ed. 2009. (ENG.). 373p. (YA). 23.95 (978-1-4104-1441-0(8)) Thorndike Pr.
—The Graveyard Book. 2010. (J). lib. bdg. 19.65 (978-0-606-14883-2(3), Turtleback) Turtleback Bks.
—EL LIBRO DEL CEMENTERIO. (SPA.). 2010. 256p. pap. 20.95 (978-84-9918-146-2(5)) 2009. 306p. (YA). 20.95 (978-84-9918-030-4(2)) Roca Editorial ESP. Dist: Spanish Pubs., LLC.
Gaiman, NEil & Russell, P. Craig. The Graveyard Book Graphic Novel. Russell, P. Craig, illus. 2014. (ENG., Illus.). (J). (gr. 3-7). Vol. 1. 192p. 19.99 (978-0-06-219481-7(X)) Vol. 2. 176p. 19.99 (978-0-06-219483-1(6)) HarperCollins Pubs.

MNO

Galdós, Benito Pérez. Tristana. Jull Costa, Margaret, tr. from FRE. 2014. (NYRB Classics Ser.). (ENG.). 192p. pap. 14.95 (978-1-59017-765-5(7), NYRB Classics) New York Review of Bks., Inc., The.
Gardner, Sally. The Red Necklace. 2009. (ENG.). 400p. (YA). (gr. 7-18). 8.99 (978-0-14-241488-0(3), Speak) Penguin Young Readers Group.
—The Red Necklace: A Story of the French Revolution. l.t. ed. 2008. 583p. 23.95 (978-1-4104-1016-0(1)) Thorndike Pr.
Garinger, Alan K. Alone: The Journey of the Boy Sims. 2008. (J). 15.95 (978-0-87195-266-0(1)); pap. 7.95 (978-0-87195-267-7(X)) Indiana Historical Society.
Garlick, Nicholas. Storm Horse. 2017. (J). pap. (978-0-545-90415-5(3)) Scholastic, Inc.
Gemeinhart, Dan. Some Kind of Courage. 2016. (ENG.). 240p. (J). (gr. 3-7). 16.99 (978-0-545-66577-3(9), Scholastic Pr.) Scholastic, Inc.
George, Jessica Day. Dragon Slippers. (Dragon Slippers Ser.). (ENG., (YA). 2008. Illus.). 352p. (gr. 5). pap. 8.99 (978-1-59990-275-3(3), 9781599902753) 2007. 336p. (gr. 4-7). 16.95 (978-1-59990-057-5(2), 9781599900575) Bloomsbury Publishing USA. (Bloomsbury USA Childrens).
—Dragon Slippers. l.t. ed. 2008. (Thorndike Literacy Bridge Middle Reader Ser.). 391p. (J). (gr. 4-7). 22.95 (978-1-4104-0337-7(8)) Thorndike Pr.
Giff, Patricia Reilly. Eleven. 2009. (ENG.). 176p. (J). (gr. 3-7). 7.99 (978-0-440-23802-7(1), Yearling) Random Hse. Children's Bks.
—Gingersnap. 2014. (ENG.). 160p. (J). (gr. 3-7). 6.99 (978-0-440-42178-8(0), Yearling) Random Hse. Children's Bks.
—Pictures of Hollis Woods. 2014. (ENG.). 176p. (J). (gr. 3-7). 11.24 (978-1-63245-318-1(5)) Lectorum Pubns., Inc.
—Pictures of Hollis Woods. 2004. (ENG.). 176p. (J). (gr. 3-7). 7.99 (978-0-440-41578-7(0), Yearling) Random Hse. Children's Bks.
Gildea, Kathy. The Adventures of Baylee Beagle — Annabelle Beagle. Larson, Amanda, illus. 2005. 28p. (J). 7.95 (978-0-9767096-1-9(9)) Maxim Pr.
—The Adventures of Baylee Beagle — Greenville. 2005. (Illus.). 20p. (J). 7.95 (978-0-9767096-0-2(0)) Maxim Pr.
—The Adventures of Baylee Beagle — Hurricane Hound. Larson, Amanda, illus. 2005. 28p. (J). 7.95 (978-0-9767096-2-6(7)) Maxim Pr.
Gleitzman, Morris. Then. 2013. (Once Ser.: 2). (ENG.). 224p. (YA). (gr. 7). pap. 9.99 (978-1-250-00341-6(5), 9781250003416) Square Fish.
—Then. 2013. (YA). lib. bdg. 20.85 (978-0-606-31904-1(2), Turtleback) Turtleback Bks.
Godden, Rumer. The Story of Holly & Ivy. Birmingham, Christian, illus. 2017. (ENG.). 80p. (J). (gr. 2-4). pap. 8.99 (978-1-5098-0505-1(2)) Pan Macmillan GBR. Dist: Independent Pubs. Group.
—The Story of Holly & Ivy. Cooney, Barbara, illus. 2006. (ENG.). 32p. (J). (gr. k-3). 17.99 (978-0-670-06219-5(7), Viking Books for Young Readers) Penguin Young Readers Group.
Golding, Julia. Cat among the Pigeons. 2010. (Cat Royal Adventure Ser.: 2). (ENG.). 400p. (J). (gr. 5-9). pap. 22.99 (978-0-312-60215-4(4), 9780312602154) Square Fish.
—The Diamond of Drury Lane. 2009. (Cat Royal Adventure Ser.: 1). (ENG., Illus.). 448p. (J). (gr. 5-9). pap. 11.99 (978-0-312-56123-9(7), 9780312561239) Square Fish.
Gonick, Larry. Kokopelli & Company in Attack of the Smart Pies. 2005. (ENG., Illus.). 192p. (J). 15.95 (978-0-8126-2740-4(7)) Cricket Bks.
Goudge, Elizabeth. The Little White Horse. movie tie-in ed. 2008. (ENG., Illus.). 248p. (J). (gr. 4-7). pap. (978-0-7459-6118-7(5)) Lion Hudson PLC GBR. Dist: Independent Pubs. Group.
Graff, Lisa. A Tangle of Knots. 2013. (ENG.). 240p. (J). (gr. 3-7). 16.99 (978-0-399-25517-5(6), Philomel Bks.) Penguin Young Readers Group.
Grant, Holly. The Dastardly Deed. Portillo, Josie, illus. 2016. (League of Beastly Dreadfuls Ser.: Bk. 2). (ENG.). 368p. (J). (gr. 3-7). 16.99 (978-0-385-37025-7(3), Random Hse. Bks. for Young Readers) Random Hse. Children's Bks.
—The League of Beastly Dreadfuls. (League of Beastly Dreadfuls Ser.: Bk. 1). (ENG., Illus.). (J). (gr. 3-7). 2016. 336p. 7.99 (978-0-385-37010-3(5), Yearling) 2015. 320p. 16.99 (978-0-385-37007-3(5), Random Hse. Bks. for Young Readers) Random Hse. Children's Bks.
Gratton, Tessa. Blood Magic. 2011. (YA). pap. (978-0-375-86486-5(5)) Random Hse. Children's Bks.
Gray, Claudia. Defy the Stars. 2017. (Defy the Stars Ser.: 1). (ENG.). 512p. (YA). (gr. 10-17). 17.99 (978-0-316-39403-1(3)) Little, Brown Bks. for Young Readers.
Great, Alex. Balkan Tales. 2009. 134p. pap. 18.36 (978-1-4452-4363-4(6)) Lulu Pr., Inc.
Greenburg, Dan. Secrets of Dripping Fang: Attack of the Giant Octopus. Fischer, Scott M., illus. 2009. (Secrets of Dripping Fang Ser.). (ENG.). 160p. 25.65 (978-1-59961-537-0(1)) Spotlight.
—Secrets of Dripping Fang: Fall of the House of Mandible. Fischer, Scott M., illus. 2009. (Secrets of Dripping Fang Ser.). (ENG.). 160p. 25.65 (978-1-59961-535-6(5)) Spotlight.
—Secrets of Dripping Fang: Please Don't Eat the Children: Book 7: Book 7. Fischer, Scott M., illus. 2009. (Secrets of Dripping Fang Ser.). (ENG.). 160p. 25.65 (978-1-59961-538-7(X)) Spotlight.
—Secrets of Dripping Fang: The Onts. Fischer, Scott M., illus. 2009. (Secrets of Dripping Fang Ser.). (ENG.). 144p. 25.65 (978-1-59961-532-5(0)) Spotlight.
—Secrets of Dripping Fang: The Shluffmuffin Boy Is History. Fischer, Scott M., illus. 2009. (Secrets of Dripping Fang Ser.). (ENG.). 176p. 25.65 (978-1-59961-536-3(3)) Spotlight.
—Secrets of Dripping Fang: The Vampire's Curse: Book 3: Book 3. Fischer, Scott M., illus. 2009. (Secrets of Dripping Fang Ser.). (ENG.). 144p. 25.65 (978-1-59961-534-9(7)) Spotlight.
—Secrets of Dripping Fang: Treachery & Betrayal at Jolly Days. Fischer, Scott M., illus. 2009. (Secrets of Dripping Fang Ser.). (ENG.). 144p. 25.65 (978-1-59961-533-2(9)) Spotlight.
—Secrets of Dripping Fang: When Bad Snakes Attack Good Children. Fischer, Scott M., illus. 2009. (Secrets of Dripping Fang Ser.). (ENG.). 144p. 25.65 (978-1-59961-539-4(8)) Spotlight.
—Secrets of Dripping Fang, Book One: The Onts. Fischer, Scott M., illus. 2005. (Secrets of Dripping Fang Ser.: Bk. 1). (ENG.). 144p. (J). (gr. 2-5). 12.99 (978-0-15-205457-1(X)) Houghton Mifflin Harcourt Publishing Co.
Greenland, Shannon. Down to the Wire. 2007. (Specialists Ser.: Vol. 2). (ENG.). 224p. (YA). (gr. 7-18). pap. 7.99 (978-0-14-240917-6(0), Speak) Penguin Young Readers Group.
—The Winning Element, Vol. 3. 2008. (Specialists Ser.). (ENG.). 224p. (YA). (gr. 7-18). 6.99 (978-0-14-241052-3(7), Speak) Penguin Young Readers Group.
Grew, David. The Wild Dog of Edmonton. Segner, Ellen, illus. 2011. 208p. 44.95 (978-1-258-09902-2(0)) Literary Licensing, LLC.
Grey, Jacob. Ferals #2: the Swarm Descends. 2016. (Ferals Ser.: 2). 288p. (J). (gr. 3-7). 16.99 (978-0-06-232106-0(4)) HarperCollins Pubs.
Griffin, A. C. America's Child. 2008. (J). pap. 9.99 (978-0-88092-492-4(6)) Royal Fireworks Publishing Co.
Griffith, A. J. America's Child. 2008. (J). pap. 9.99 (978-0-88092-493-1(4)) Royal Fireworks Publishing Co.
Grogan, Joy. Into the Fold. 2003. 156p. per. 15.00 (978-0-9740321-6-0(6)) Open Bk. Publishing.
The Guardians. 2014. (ENG., Illus.). 288p. (J). (gr. 4-8). pap. 7.99 (978-1-4814-1834-8(3), Aladdin) Simon & Schuster Children's Publishing.
Gustafson, Scott. Eddie: The Lost Youth of Edgar Allan Poe. Gustafson, Scott, illus. (ENG., Illus.). 208p. (J). (gr. 3-7). 2012. pap. 6.99 (978-1-4169-9765-8(2)) 2011. 15.99 (978-1-4169-9764-1(4)) Simon & Schuster Bks. For Young Readers. (Simon & Schuster Bks. For Young Readers).
Guzman, Lila & Guzman, Rick. Lorenzo's Revolutionary Quest. 2003. 176p. (J). pap. 9.95 (978-1-55885-392-8(8), Piñata Books) Arte Publico Pr.
—Lorenzo's Secret Mission. 2005. 153p. (gr. 4-7). 19.95 (978-0-7569-5599-1(8)) Perfection Learning Corp.
Haas, Jessie & Wedekind, Annie. Mercury's Flight: The Story of a Lipizzaner Stallion. 2011. (Breyer Horse Collection: 4). (ENG.). 128p. (J). (gr. 4-7). pap. 9.99 (978-0-312-64451-2(5), 9780312644512) Feiwel & Friends.
Habel, Lia. Dearly, Departed. 2012. (ENG.). 496p. (YA). (gr. 8-12). pap. 10.99 (978-0-345-52332-7(6), Del Rey) Random House Publishing Group.
Haberdasher, Violet. Knightley Academy. 2011. (ENG.). 512p. (J). (gr. 3-7). pap. 5.99 (978-1-4169-9144-1(1), Aladdin) Simon & Schuster Children's Publishing.
—Knightley Academy. 2010. (ENG.). 480p. (J). (gr. 3-7). 16.99 (978-1-4169-9143-4(3), Simon & Schuster/Paula Wiseman Bks.) Simon & Schuster/Paula Wiseman Bks.
—The Secret Prince. 2011. (ENG.). 512p. (J). (gr. 3-7). 16.99 (978-1-4169-9145-8(X), Simon & Schuster/Paula Wiseman Bks.) Simon & Schuster/Paula Wiseman Bks.
—The Secret Prince: A Knightley Academy Book. 2012. (ENG.). 512p. (J). (gr. 3-7). pap. 7.99 (978-1-4169-9146-5(8), Simon & Schuster/Paula Wiseman Bks.) Simon & Schuster/Paula Wiseman Bks.
Haddix, Margaret Peterson. Palace of Mirrors. 2010. (Palace Chronicles Ser.: 2). (ENG.). 320p. (J). (gr. 5-9). pap. 7.99 (978-1-4424-0667-4(4), Simon & Schuster Bks. For Young Readers) Simon & Schuster Bks. For Young Readers.
Hagman, Harvey Dixon. Majesty from Assateague, 1 vol. Aiken, David, illus. 2009. (ENG.). 80p. (J). pap. 8.95 (978-0-87033-552-5(9), 9780870335525, Cornell Maritime Pr./Tidewater Pubs.) Schiffer Publishing, Ltd.
Hahn, Mary Downing. The Ghost of Crutchfield Hall. (ENG.). 160p. (J). (gr. 5-7). 2011. pap. 6.99 (978-0-547-57715-9(X)) 2010. 17.00 (978-0-547-38560-0(9)) Houghton Mifflin Harcourt Publishing Co.
—Promises to the Dead. 2009. (ENG.). 208p. (J). (gr. 5-7). pap. 7.99 (978-0-547-25838-6(0)) Houghton Mifflin Harcourt Publishing Co.
Hale, Bruce. Ends of the Earth. Dorman, Brandon, illus. 2015. (School for Spies Novel Ser.). (ENG.). 304p. (J). (gr. 3-7). 16.99 (978-1-4231-6852-2(6)) Disney Pr.
—School for SPIES Book 2 Thicker Than Water. Dorman, Brandon, illus. 2014. (School for Spies Novel Ser.). (ENG.). 352p. (J). (gr. 3-7). 16.99 (978-1-4231-6851-5(8)) Hyperion Bks. for Children.
—School for SPIES Book One Playing with Fire. Dorman, Brandon, illus. 2014. (School for Spies Novel Ser.). (ENG.). 336p. (J). (gr. 3-7). pap. 6.99 (978-1-4231-7105-8(5)) Hyperion Bks. for Children.
—School for SPIES Thicker Than Water. Dorman, Brandon, illus. 2015. (ENG.). 368p. (J). (gr. 3-7). pap. 6.99 (978-1-4231-7106-5(3)) Hyperion Bks. for Children.
Hall, C. Aubrey. The Call of Eirian, 0 vols. 2012. (Faelin Chronicles Ser.: 2). (ENG.). 352p. (YA). (gr. 7-11). 17.99 (978-0-7614-6262-0(7), 9780761462620, Amazon Children's Publishing) Amazon Publishing.
Halpern, Jake & Kujawinski, Peter. Edgeland. 2017. (ENG., Illus.). 272p. (J). (gr. 5). 17.99 (978-0-399-17581-7(4), G.P. Putnam's Sons Books for Young Readers) Penguin Young Readers Group.
Hannigan, Kate. The Detective's Assistant. 2015. (ENG.). 368p. (J). (gr. 3-7). 17.00 (978-0-316-40351-1(2)) Little Brown & Co.
Hansen, Joyce. One True Friend. Giblin, James Cross, ed. 2005. (ENG.). 160p. (J). (gr. 5-7). pap. 11.95 (978-0-618-60991-8(1)) Houghton Mifflin Harcourt Publishing Co.
Hardinge, Frances. Fly Trap. 2012. 592p. (J). (gr. 5). pap. 7.99 (978-0-06-088046-0(5)) HarperCollins Pubs.
Hardy, Janice. A Blue Fire, Bk. 2. 2010. (Healing Wars Ser.: II). (ENG.). 384p. (J). (gr. 5-18). 16.99 (978-0-06-174741-0(6)) HarperCollins Pubs.
—The Healing Wars: Book II: Blue Fire. 2011. (Healing Wars Ser.: II). (ENG.). 400p. (J). (gr. 5). pap. 7.99 (978-0-06-174744-1(0)) HarperCollins Pubs.
—The Shifter. (J). (gr. 5). 2010. (Healing Wars Ser.: I). (ENG.). 400p. pap. 7.99 (978-0-06-174708-3(4)) 2009. (Healing Wars Ser.). 384p. lib. bdg. 17.89 (978-0-06-176177-5(X)) HarperCollins Pubs.
Harley, Bill. The Amazing Flight of Darius Frobisher, 1 vol. 2006. (ENG., Illus.). 160p. (J). (gr. 3-7). 14.95 (978-1-56145-381-8(1)) Peachtree Pubs.
Harlow, Joan Hiatt. Midnight Rider. 2006. (ENG.). 384p. (J). (gr. 4-9). pap. 8.99 (978-0-689-87010-1(8), McElderry, Margaret K. Bks.) McElderry, Margaret K. Bks.
—Thunder from the Sea. 2004. (ENG., Illus.). 208p. (J). (gr. 3-7). 17.99 (978-0-689-86403-2(5), McElderry, Margaret K. Bks.) McElderry, Margaret K. Bks.
Harris, Christine. Undercover Girl #5: Twisted. 2007. (ENG.). 136p. (J). per. 10.95 (978-1-59594-151-0(7), Wingspan Pr.) WingSpan Publishing.
Harrison, Michelle. 13 Curses. 2011. (13 Treasures Trilogy Ser.: 2). (ENG.). 496p. (J). (gr. 5-9). 15.99 (978-0-316-04150-8(5)) Little Brown & Co.
—13 Curses. 2012. (13 Treasures Trilogy Ser.: 2). (ENG.). 512p. (J). (gr. 5-9). pap. 8.99 (978-0-316-04149-2(1)) Little, Brown Bks. for Young Readers.
—13 Curses. 2012. (13 Treasures Ser.: 2). (J). lib. bdg. 19.65 (978-0-606-26160-9(5), Turtleback) Turtleback Bks.
Harvey, Gill. Orphan of the Sun. 2006. (ENG., Illus.). 320p. (YA). (gr. 3-7). 16.95 (978-1-58234-685-4(2), 9781582346854, Bloomsbury USA Childrens) Bloomsbury Publishing USA.
Hawes, Charles Boardman. The Dark Frigate. 2005. pap. 27.95 (978-1-4179-3209-2(0)) Kessinger Publishing, LLC.
Hawthorne, Rachel. Shadow of the Moon. 2010. (Dark Guardian Ser.: 4). (ENG.). 256p. (YA). (gr. 9-18). pap. 8.99 (978-0-06-196290-5(2), HarperTeen) HarperCollins Pubs.
Heimerdinger, Chris. Escape from Zarahemla. 2011. 263p. (YA). pap. (978-1-60861-539-1(1)) Covenant Communications.
Helldorfer, M. C. Anne of Green Gables. Beier, Ellen, illus. 2003. (ENG.). 40p. (J). (gr. -1-2). pap. 7.99 (978-0-440-41614-2(0), Dragonfly Bks.) Random Hse. Children's Bks.
Helvig, Kristi. Burn Out. 2015. (ENG., Illus.). 272p. (gr. 9). pap. 9.99 (978-1-60684-569-1(1), Carolrhoda Lab™) Lerner Publishing Group.
—Strange Skies, Bk. 2. 2015. (ENG.). 272p. (gr. 9). 17.99 (978-1-60684-481-6(4), Carolrhoda Lab™) Lerner Publishing Group.
Hembree, G. Wil. The Willisby Orphans: In the Keys to the Bottomless Pit. 2011. 552p. (gr. -1 — 1). 44.95 (978-1-4497-2366-8(7)); pap. 34.95 (978-1-4497-2365-1(9)) Author Solutions, Inc. (WestBow Pr.).
Hemphill, Kris. Ambush in the Wilderness. 2003. (Adventures in America Ser.). (Illus.). 90p. (gr. 4). 14.95 (978-1-893110-34-2(6)) Silver Moon Pr.
Hendershot, Eric. At Season's End. 2012. pap. 13.99 (978-1-59955-995-7(1)) Cedar Fort, Inc./CFI Distribution.
Henderson, Lauren. Kiss Me Kill Me. 2009. (ENG.). 272p. (YA). (gr. 9). pap. 8.99 (978-0-385-73488-2(3), Delacorte Pr.) Random Hse. Children's Bks.
—Kiss of Death. 2012. (ENG.). 318p. (YA). (gr. 9). pap. 9.99 (978-0-385-73780-7(7), Ember) Random Hse. Children's Bks.
Henderson, Leah. One Shadow on the Wall. 2017. (ENG., Illus.). 448p. (J). (gr. 3-7). 16.99 (978-1-4814-6295-2(4), Atheneum Bks. for Young Readers) Simon & Schuster Children's Publishing.
Heneghan, Judith. The Magician's Apprentice. 2008. (Illus.). 168p. (J). (gr. 3-7). 16.95 (978-0-8234-2150-3(3)) Holiday Hse., Inc.
Henry, April. The Girl I Used to Be. 2016. (ENG., Illus.). 240p. (YA). 17.99 (978-1-62779-332-2(1), 9781627793322, Holt, Henry & Co. Bks. For Young Readers) Holt, Henry & Co.
Herbert, Bethany Zohner. The Perfect Fool. 2015. 279p. (YA). pap. 17.99 (978-1-4621-1620-1(5)) Cedar Fort, Inc./CFI Distribution.
Hering, Marianne. Trouble on the Orphan Train. 2016. (AIO Imagination Station Bks.: 18). (ENG.). 144p. (J). pap. 4.99 (978-1-58997-805-8(6)) Focus on the Family Publishing.
Hershenhorn, Esther. Fancy That. Lloyd, Megan, illus. 2003. (ENG.). 32p. (J). (gr. k-3). tchr. ed. 16.95 (978-0-8234-1605-9(4)) Holiday Hse., Inc.
Hest, Amy. When Jessie Came Across the Sea. 2003. 17.20 (978-0-613-69484-1(8), Turtleback) Turtleback Bks.
Hicks, Jamara. Calvin Gets a Family. 2009. 24p. pap. 12.00 (978-1-4490-4754-2(8)) AuthorHouse.
Higgins, Simon. Moonshadow #2: the Nightmare Ninja. 2012. (Moonshadow Ser.: 2). (ENG.). 384p. (J). (gr. 3-7). pap. 6.99 (978-0-316-05534-5(4)) Little, Brown Bks. for Young Readers.
Hill, Kirkpatrick. Bo at Ballard Creek. Pham, LeUyen, illus. 2014. (ENG.). 304p. (J). (gr. 3-7). pap. 7.99 (978-1-250-04425-9(1), 9781250044259) Square Fish.
Hoban, Julia. Willow. 2010. (ENG.). 336p. (YA). (gr. 9-18). 8.99 (978-0-14-241666-2(5), Speak) Penguin Young Readers Group.
Hobbs, Valerie. Maggie & Oliver or a Bone of One's Own. Thermes, Jennifer, illus. 2013. (ENG.). 208p. (J). (gr. 3-7). pap. 6.99 (978-1-250-01672-0(X), 9781250016720) Square Fish.
Hobbs, William. Jason's Gold. unabr. ed. 2004. 240p. (J). (gr. 5-9). pap. 38.00 incl. audio (978-0-8072-8229-8(4), Listening Library) Random Hse. Audio Publishing Group.
Holm, Jennifer L. The Claim. 2010. (Boston Jane Ser.: No. 2). (ENG.). 224p. (J). (gr. 3-7). pap. 7.99 (978-0-375-86206-9(4), Yearling) Random Hse. Children's Bks.
—Wilderness Days. 2004. (Boston Jane Ser.: No. 2). 256p. (J). (gr. 5-18). pap. 5.99 (978-0-06-440881-3(7), Harper Trophy) HarperCollins Pubs.
—Wilderness Days. 2010. (Boston Jane Ser.: No. 2). (ENG.). 256p. (J). (gr. 3-7). pap. 7.99 (978-0-375-86205-2(6), Yearling) Random Hse. Children's Bks.
Hooper, Mary. Velvet. 2012. (ENG.). 336p. (YA). (gr. 7-12). 16.99 (978-1-59990-912-7(X), 9781599909127, Bloomsbury USA Childrens) Bloomsbury Publishing USA.
Hooper, R. M. J. The Secret of Crescent Grey. 2009. 340p. pap. 19.99 (978-1-4363-3206-4(0)) Xlibris Corp.
Hopkinson, Deborah. The Great Trouble: A Mystery of London, the Blue Death, & a Boy Called Eel. 2013. (ENG.). 256p. (J). (gr. 5). 16.99 (978-0-375-84818-6(5), Knopf Bks. for Young Readers) Random Hse. Children's Bks.
—Into the Firestorm: A Novel of San Francisco 1906. 2008. (Yearling Bks.). (ENG.). 208p. (J). (gr. 3-7). per. 6.99 (978-0-440-42129-0(2), Yearling) Random Hse. Children's Bks.
Hoppenstedt, Elbert M. President Harrison's Horse Race. 2006. (ENG.). 48p. per. 16.95 (978-1-4241-5017-5(5)) PublishAmerica, Inc.
Horatio Alger Jr. Cast upon the Breakers. l.t. ed. 2007. 226p. pap. 22.99 (978-1-4264-8224-3(8)) Creative Media Partners, LLC.
Horowitz, Anthony. Ark Angel. (Alex Rider Ser.: Bk. 6). (ENG.). (J). (gr. 5-18). 2007. 352p. 8.99 (978-0-14-240738-7(0), Puffin Books) 2006. 336p. 17.99 (978-0-399-24152-9(3), Philomel Bks.) Penguin Young Readers Group.
—Ark Angel. 2007. (Alex Rider Ser.: Bk. 6). 326p. (gr. 5-9). 19.00 (978-0-7569-8134-1(4)) Perfection Learning Corp.
—Ark Angel. 2007. (Alex Rider Ser.: 6). 326p. lib. bdg. 19.65 (978-1-4177-7664-1(1), Turtleback) Turtleback Bks.
—Eagle Strike. (Alex Rider Ser.). (ENG.). (J). (gr. 5-18). 2006. 368p. 8.99 (978-0-14-240613-7(9), Puffin Books) 2004. (Illus.). 272p. 17.99 (978-0-399-23979-3(0), Philomel Bks.) Penguin Young Readers Group.
—The Falcon's Malteser. 2004. (Diamond Brothers Ser.: No. 1). (ENG.). 208p. (J). (gr. 3-7). 6.99 (978-0-14-240219-1(2), Puffin Books) Penguin Young Readers Group.
—Point Blanc. 2004. (Alex Rider Ser.: Bk. 2). (SPA.). 264p. pap. 7.95 (978-84-414-1410-5(6)) Editorial Edaf, S.L. ESP. Dist: Spanish Pubs., LLC.
—Point Blank. 2006. (Alex Rider Ser.). (ENG.). 320p. (J). (gr. 5-18). 8.99 (978-0-14-240612-0(0), Puffin Books) Penguin Young Readers Group.
—Russian Roulette. 2014. (Alex Rider Ser.: 10). lib. bdg. 19.65 (978-0-606-36189-7(8)) Turtleback Bks.
—Russian Roulette: The Story of an Assassin. 2014. (Alex Rider Ser.). (ENG.). 432p. (J). (gr. 5). pap. 8.99 (978-0-14-751231-4(X), Puffin Books) Penguin Young Readers Group.
—Scorpia. (Alex Rider Ser.). (ENG.). (J). (gr. 5-18). 2006. 416p. pap. 8.99 (978-0-14-240578-9(7), Puffin Books) 2005. 336p. 17.99 (978-0-399-24151-2(5), Philomel Bks.) Penguin Young Readers Group.
—Scorpia Rising. (Alex Rider Ser.). (ENG.). (J). (gr. 5-18). 2012. 432p. 8.99 (978-0-14-241985-4(0), Puffin Books) 2011. 416p. 17.99 (978-0-399-25057-6(3), Philomel Bks.) Penguin Young Readers Group.
—Scorpia Rising. (J). 2012. 1.25 (978-1-4640-0577-0(X)) 2012. 256.75 (978-1-4561-3362-7(4)) 2012. 90.75 (978-1-4561-3363-4(2)) 2011. 122.75 (978-1-4561-3365-8(9)) 2011. 120.75 (978-1-4561-3367-2(5)) Recorded Bks., Inc.
—Scorpia Rising. 2012. (Alex Rider Ser.: 9). lib. bdg. 19.65 (978-0-606-23638-6(4), Turtleback) Turtleback Bks.
—Skeleton Key. Kanako & Yuzuru, illus. 2009. (Alex Rider Ser.: Bk. 3). (ENG.). 176p. (J). (gr. 5-18). pap. 14.99 (978-0-399-25418-5(8), Philomel Bks.) Penguin Young Readers Group.
—Skeleton Key. (Alex Rider Ser.: Bk. 3). (ENG.). (J). (gr. 5-18). 2006. 368p. 8.99 (978-0-14-240614-4(7), Puffin Books) 2003. 240p. 17.99 (978-0-399-23777-5(1), Philomel Bks.) Penguin Young Readers Group.
—Snakehead. (Alex Rider Ser.: Bk. 7). (ENG.). (gr. 5-18). 2008. 432p. (J). pap. 8.99 (978-0-14-241212-1(0), Puffin Books) 2007. 400p. (YA). 17.99 (978-0-399-24161-1(2), Philomel Bks.) Penguin Young Readers Group.
—Stormbreaker. Damerum, Kanako et al, illus. 2006. (Alex Rider Ser.). (ENG.). 144p. (J). (gr. 5-18). pap. 14.99 (978-0-399-24633-3(9), Philomel Bks.) Penguin Young Readers Group.
—Stormbreaker. 2006. (Alex Rider Ser.: Bk. 1). (ENG.). 304p. (J). (gr. 5-18). 8.99 (978-0-14-240611-3(2), Puffin Books) Penguin Young Readers Group.
—Stormbreaker. 2004. (Alex Rider Ser.: Bk. 1). 208p. (J). (gr. 4-7). pap. 38.00 incl. audio (978-0-8072-2277-5(1), Listening Library) Random Hse. Audio Publishing Group.
Houck, Colleen. Tiger's Curse, Bk. 1. 2012. (Tiger's Curse Ser.: Bk. 1). (ENG.). 456p. (J). (gr. 7). pap. 9.95 (978-1-4549-0249-2(3)) Sterling Publishing Co., Inc.
—Tiger's Curse. 2012. (Tiger's Curse Ser.: Bk. 1). lib. bdg. 20.80 (978-0-606-23822-9(0), Turtleback) Turtleback Bks.
—Tiger's Destiny. 2015. (Tiger's Curse Ser.: Bk. 4). (ENG.). 464p. (J). (gr. 7). pap. 9.95 (978-1-4549-0356-7(2)) Sterling Publishing Co., Inc.
—Tiger's Quest. (Tiger's Curse Ser.: Bk. 2). (ENG.). (J). (gr. 7). 2013. 512p. pap. 9.95 (978-1-4549-0358-1(9)) 2011. 496p. 17.95 (978-1-4027-8404-0(X)) Sterling Publishing Co., Inc.
—Tiger's Voyage. (Tiger's Curse Ser.: Bk. 3). (ENG.). (J). (gr. 7). 2014. 568p. pap. 9.95 (978-1-4549-0357-4(0))Bk. 3. 2011. 560p. 17.95 (978-1-4027-8405-7(8)) Sterling Publishing Co., Inc.
Howard, Ellen. Edith Herself. 2007. (ENG.). 144p. (J). (gr. 3-7). pap. 10.95 (978-1-4169-6454-4(1), Simon & Schuster/Paula Wiseman Bks.) Simon & Schuster/Paula Wiseman Bks.
—The Gate in the Wall. 2007. (ENG.). 160p. (J). (gr. 3-7). pap. 9.95 (978-1-4169-6796-5(6), Simon & Schuster/Paula Wiseman Bks.) Simon & Schuster/Paula Wiseman Bks.
Howell, Robert. Third Times the Charm. 2007. (ENG.). 224p. (gr. 4-7). per. 12.95 (978-1-897235-20-1(8)) Thistledown Pr., Ltd. CAN. Dist: Univ. of Toronto Pr.
Huber, Morgan. Nanite. 2013. 140p. pap. 19.95 (978-1-63004-633-0(7)) America Star Bks.
Hue, Wendy. Tópé Arrives. 2011. (Illus.). 100p. pap. 12.10 (978-1-4567-7640-4(1)) AuthorHouse.
Hull, Norman. Robin's Big Brother. 2011. 56p. (gr. 4-6). pap. 9.99 (978-1-4634-3691-9(2)) AuthorHouse.
Hussey, Charmian. The Valley of Secrets. Crump, Christopher, illus. 2006. (ENG.). 400p. (J). (gr. 7-12). per. 17.99 (978-1-4169-0015-3(2), Simon Pulse) Simon Pulse.
Hutchinson, Shaun David. The Five Stages of Andrew Brawley. Larsen, Christine, illus. 2015. (ENG.). 304p. (YA). (gr. 7). 17.99 (978-1-4814-0310-8(9), Simon Pulse) Simon Pulse.
Ibbotson, Eva. Dial-a-Ghost. Hawkes, Kevin, illus. 2003. (ENG.). 224p. (J). (gr. 3-7). pap. 6.99 (978-0-14-250018-7(6), Puffin Books) Penguin Young Readers Group.
—Journey to the River Sea. Hawkes, Kevin, illus. 2003. 298p. (gr. 3-7). 18.00 (978-0-7569-1552-0(X)) Perfection Learning Corp.
—Journey to the River Sea. Hawkes, Kevin, illus. 2003. (ENG.). 304p. (J). (gr. 3-7). pap. 8.99

(978-0-14-250184-9(0), Puffin Books) Penguin Young Readers Group.
—Journey to the River Sea. 5th unabr. ed. 2008. (ENG.). 304p. (J). (gr. 10-14). 14.95 (978-0-330-39715-5(X), Macmillan) Pan Macmillan GBR. Dist: Trans-Atlantic Pubns., Inc.
—The Ogre of Oglefort. 2012. (ENG.). 272p. (J). (gr. 3-7). pap. 6.99 (978-0-14-242135-2(9), Puffin Books) Penguin Young Readers Group.
Iinuma, Yuuki. Itsuwaribito , Vol. 14. 2015. (ENG.). 192p. pap. 9.99 (978-1-4215-6525-5(0)) Viz Media.
Imbemón, Maite & Dickens, Charles. Oliver Twist. 2003. (Timeless Classics Ser.). (SPA., Illus.). 92p. (J). pap. 10.95 (978-84-204-5750-5(7)) Santillana USA Publishing Co., Inc.
In a World Just Right. 2015. (ENG., Illus.). 432p. (YA). (gr. 7). 18.99 (978-1-4814-1660-3(X)) Simon & Schuster Children's Publishing.
Inman, Robert. The Christmas Bus. Baskin, Lyle, illus. 2006. 77p. 19.95 (978-0-9760963-6-8(6)) Novello Festival Pr.
Ireland, Justina. Vengeance Bound. 2013. (ENG.). 320p. (YA). (gr. 9). 17.99 (978-1-4424-4462-1(2), Simon & Schuster Bks. For Young Readers) Simon & Schuster Bks. For Young Readers.
Isbell, Tom. The Capture. 2016. (Prey Trilogy Ser.: 2). 448p. (YA). (gr. 8). 17.99 (978-0-06-221605-2(8), HarperTeen) HarperCollins Pubs.
—The Prey. 2015. (Prey Trilogy Ser.: 1). (ENG.). 416p. (YA). (gr. 8). 17.99 (978-0-06-221601-4(5), HarperTeen) HarperCollins Pubs.
Jacobson, Jennifer Richard. Paper Things. 2015. (ENG.). 384p. (J). (gr. 5). 16.99 (978-0-7636-6323-0(9)) Candlewick Pr.
—Paper Things. 2017. (ENG.). (J). (gr. 5). lib. bdg. 19.65 **(978-0-606-39841-1(4))** Turtleback Bks.
Jacques, Brian. Voyage of Slaves: A Tale from the Castaways of the Flying Dutchman. 2007. (ENG.). 320p. (gr. 12-18). 7.99 (978-0-441-01528-3(X), Ace Bks.) Penguin Publishing Group.
James-Carde, Genice. A Father for Me. Thomas, Michael Lee, illus. 2011. 20p. pap. 24.95 (978-1-4560-3951-6(2)) America Star Bks.
James, Helen Foster & Loh, Virginia Shin-Mui. Paper Son: Lee's Journey to America. Ong, Wilson, illus. 2013. (Tales of Young Americans Ser.). (ENG.). 32p. (J). (gr. 1-4). 16.99 (978-1-58536-833-4(4), 202366) Sleeping Bear Pr.
James, Will. Cowboy in the Making. rev. ed. (Illus.). 104p. (J). (gr. 4-6). pap. 15.00 (978-0-87842-439-9(3), 811) Mountain Pr. Publishing Co., Inc.
Jarvis, Robin. The Whitby Witches. 2017. (Modern Classics Ser.). (ENG., Illus.). 336p. (YA). (gr. 6). pap. 9.99 **(978-1-4052-8540-7(0))** Egmont Bks., Ltd. GBR. Dist: Independent Pubs. Group.
Jennings, Patrick. Wish Riders. 2008. (ENG.). 288p. pap. 6.99 (978-1-4231-0015-7(8)) Hyperion Pr.
Jennings, Sharon. Home Free, 1 vol. 2009. (Gutsy Girl Ser.). (ENG., Illus.). 160p. (J). (gr. 4-7). pap. 8.95 (978-1-897187-55-5(6)) Second Story Pr. CAN. Dist: Orca Bk. Pubs. USA.
Jessell, Tim. The Boardwalk Mystery. Dunn, Robert, illus. 2013. (Boxcar Children Mysteries Ser.: 131). (ENG.). 144p. (J). (gr. 1-5). 15.99 (978-0-8075-0802-2(0)); pap. 5.99 (978-0-8075-0803-9(9)) Whitman, Albert & Co.
—The Mystery of the Stolen Snowboard. 2014. (Boxcar Children Mysteries Ser.: 134). (ENG.). 128p. (J). (gr. 1-5). 15.99 (978-0-8075-8728-7(1)) Whitman, Albert & Co.
—The Mystery of the Wild West Bandit. 2014. (Boxcar Children Mysteries Ser.: 135). (ENG.). 128p. (J). (gr. 1-5). 15.99 (978-0-8075-8725-6(7)) Whitman, Albert & Co.
Jessell, Tim, illus. The Boxcar Children, Set. 2013. (Boxcar Children Mysteries Ser.). (ENG.). 538p. (J). (gr. 1-5). 45.00 (978-0-8075-0864-0(0)) Whitman, Albert & Co.
—Mystery of the Fallen Treasure. 2013. (Boxcar Children Mysteries Ser.: 132). (ENG.). 128p. (J). (gr. 1-5). 5.99 (978-0-8075-5506-4(1)); 15.99 (978-0-8075-5508-8(8)) Whitman, Albert & Co.
—The Return of the Graveyard Ghost. 2013. (Boxcar Children Mysteries Ser.: 133). (ENG.). 128p. (J). (gr. 1-5). 5.99 (978-0-8075-6936-8(4)); 15.99 (978-0-8075-6935-1(6)) Whitman, Albert & Co.
Jinks, Catherine. Babylonne. 2008. (ENG., Illus.). 400p. (YA). (gr. 7). 18.99 (978-0-7636-3650-0(9)) Candlewick Pr.
—The Last Bogler. (How to Catch a Bogle Ser.: 3). (ENG.). 336p. (J). (gr. 5-7). 2017. pap. 7.99 (978-0-544-81309-0(X)) 2016. (Illus.). 16.99 (978-0-544-08696-8(1)) Houghton Mifflin Harcourt Publishing Co. (HMH Books For Young Readers).
—A Plague of Bogles. 2015. (How to Catch a Bogle Ser.: 2). (ENG.). 336p. (J). (gr. 5-7). pap. 6.99 (978-0-544-54067-5(0)); (Illus.). 16.99 (978-0-544-08747-7(X)) Houghton Mifflin Harcourt Publishing Co. (HMH Books For Young Readers).
Johnson, Gerald J. J. Misty's Christmas Present, 1 vol. Miltenberger, Jeri & Miltenberger, Dave, illus. 2010. 32p. 24.95 (978-1-4512-1330-0(1)) PublishAmerica, Inc.
Johnson, Mary L. Flinthills Frannie, 1 vol. 2009. 43p. pap. 24.95 (978-1-61546-886-7(2)) America Star Bks.
Johnson, Nancy. A Sweet-Sounding Place: A Civil War Story. 2008. (ENG.). 128p. (J). (gr. 3-7). pap. 10.95 (978-0-89272-770-4(5)) Down East Bks.
Johnson, Sarah Blake. Crossings. 2017. (YA). pap. 17.99 **(978-1-4621-1957-8(3))** Cedar Fort, Inc./CFI Distribution.
Jonell, Lynne. The Secret of Zoom. 2009. (ENG.). 304p. (J). (gr. 4-7). 16.99 (978-0-8050-8856-4(3), 9780805088564, Holt, Henry & Co. Bks. For Young Readers) Holt, Henry & Co.
—The Secret of Zoom. 2011. (ENG.). 320p. (J). (gr. 4-7). pap. 7.99 (978-0-312-65933-2(4), 9780312659332) Square Fish.
Jones, Chris. Cameron Jack & the Ghosts of World War 2. 2010. 120p. pap. 12.49 (978-1-4520-2839-2(7)) AuthorHouse.
Jones, Diana Wynne. Earwig & the Witch. Zelinsky, Paul O., illus. 2012. 128p. (J). (gr. 3-7). 15.99 (978-0-06-207511-6(X), Greenwillow Bks.) HarperCollins Pubs.
—Enchanted Glass. 304p. (J). (gr. 3-7). 2011. pap. 6.99 (978-0-06-186685-2(7)) 2010. 16.99 (978-0-06-186684-5(9)) HarperCollins Pubs. (Greenwillow Bks.).
Jones, Patrick. The Gamble. 2014. (Bareknuckle Ser.). 104p. (YA). (gr. 6-12). lib. bdg. 27.93 (978-1-4677-1462-4(3), Darby Creek) Lerner Publishing Group.
Jones, Sandra. Sasha's Little Red Box: An Adoption Story. 2008. 27p. pap. 24.95 (978-1-60703-187-1(6)) America Star Bks.
Jones, Sandy. Anya's Gift: A Tale of Two Christmases, 1 vol. Yourell, Pam, illus. 2009. 48p. pap. 24.95 (978-1-61546-129-5(9)) America Star Bks.
Joyce, Kelley A. Amos the Elf & His Magical Pajamas. Beckman, Jeff & Aguirre, Diego, illus. 2012. 38p. pap. 9.95 (978-0-9881822-0-2(3)) Elf Garb.
Kacer, Kathy. Stones on a Grave, 1 vol. 2015. (Secrets Ser.). (ENG.). 240p. (YA). (gr. 8-12). pap. 14.95 (978-1-4598-0659-7(X)) Orca Bk. Pubs. USA.
Kares, P. S. Hole-in-the-Wall with the Prairie Orphans. 2009. 32p. pap. 24.95 (978-1-60813-521-9(7)) America Star Bks.
Kehoe, Tim. Furious Jones & the Assassin's Secret. 2014. (ENG., Illus.). 336p. (J). (gr. 3-7). 16.99 (978-1-4424-7337-9(1), Simon & Schuster Bks. For Young Readers) Simon & Schuster Bks. For Young Readers.
Kellogg, Elijah. Charlie Bell, the Waif of Elm Island by Rev Elijah Kellogg. 2006. 352p. per. 23.99 (978-1-4255-3559-9(3)) Michigan Publishing.
Kennedy, Emma. The Case of the Fatal Phantom, 3 vols. Marc, Sylvain, illus. 2012. (Wilma Tenderfoot Ser.: 3). (ENG.). 368p. (J). (gr. 3-7). 16.99 (978-0-8037-3542-2(1), Dial Bks) Penguin Young Readers Group.
—The Case of the Frozen Hearts. 2012. (Wilma Tenderfoot Ser.: 1). (ENG.). 368p. (J). (gr. 3-7). 7.99 (978-0-14-242140-6(5), Puffin Books) Penguin Young Readers Group.
—The Case of the Putrid Poison, 2 vols. Marc, Sylvain & Dorman, Brandon, illus. 2011. (Wilma Tenderfoot Ser.: 2). (ENG.). 336p. (J). (gr. 3-7). 16.99 (978-0-8037-3541-5(3), Dial Bks) Penguin Young Readers Group.
—Wilma Tenderfoot - The Case of the Frozen Hearts. Marc, Sylvain et al, illus. 2011. (Wilma Tenderfoot Ser.: 1). (ENG.). 352p. (J). (gr. 3-7). 16.99 (978-0-8037-3540-8(5), Dial Bks) Penguin Young Readers Group.
—Wilma Tenderfoot: the Case of the Fatal Phantom. Marc, Sylvain, illus. 2013. (Wilma Tenderfoot Ser.: 3). (ENG.). 384p. (J). (gr. 3-7). pap. 7.99 (978-0-14-242609-8(1), Puffin Books) Penguin Young Readers Group.
Kerr, Esme. Mischief at Midnight. 2016. (ENG.). 272p. (J). (gr. 3-7). 16.99 (978-0-545-90403-2(X), Chicken Hse., The) Scholastic, Inc.
Kessler, Deirdre & Montgomery, L. M. Anne of Green Gables, 1 vol. Smith, David Preston, illus. 2008. (ENG.). 46p. (J). (gr. k-5). pap. 10.95 (978-1-55109-662-9(5)) Nimbus Publishing, Ltd. CAN. Dist: Orca Bk. Pubs. USA.
Key, Watt. Alabama Moon. (Alabama Moon Ser.: 1). (ENG.). (J). (gr. 5-9). 2008. 304p. pap. 8.99 (978-0-312-38428-9(9), 9780312384289) 2010. 320p. pap. 8.99 (978-0-312-64480-2(9), 9780312644802) Square Fish.
Kieffer, Jean-Francois. The Adventures of Loupio, Volume 3: The Tournament. Chevrier, Janet, tr. 2013. (ENG., Illus.). 40p. (J). (gr. 4-7). pap. 6.99 (978-1-58617-853-6(9)) Ignatius Pr.
Kimmel, Elizabeth Cody. The Boxtrolls: A Novel. 2014. (Illus.). 246p. (J). (978-0-316-33263-7(1)) Little Brown & Co.
Kindl, Patrice. Goose Chase. 2010. (ENG.). 240p. (J). (gr. 5-7). pap. 6.99 (978-0-547-33164-5(9)) Houghton Mifflin Harcourt Publishing Co.
King, Emily R. The Hundredth Queen. 2017. (Hundredth Queen Ser.: 1). (YA). (ENG.). 300p. pap. 9.99 **(978-1-5039-4365-0(8)**, 9781503943650, Amazon Children's Publishing); **(978-1-5039-9865-0(7))** Amazon Publishing.
King, Wesley. The Incredible Space Raiders from Space! 2015. (ENG., Illus.). 304p. (J). (gr. 3-7). 16.99 (978-1-4814-2319-9(3), Simon & Schuster Bks. For Young Readers) Simon & Schuster Bks. For Young Readers.
Kinra, Richa, illus. The Princess Panda Tea Party: A Cerebral Palsy Fairy Tale. 2014. 45p. (J). pap. 14.95 (978-1-61599-219-5(7)) Loving Healing Pr., Inc.
Kipling, Rudyard. Kim. 2008. (Bring the Classics to Life Ser.). (ENG., Illus.). 72p. (gr. 5-12). pap., act. bk. ed. 10.95 (978-0-931334-69-6(1), EDCTR-503B) EDCON Publishing Group.
Kirby, Jessi. In Honor. (ENG., (YA). (gr. 9). 2013. Illus.). 256p. pap. 9.99 (978-1-4424-1698-7(X)) 2012. 240p. 16.99 (978-1-4424-1697-0(1)) Simon & Schuster Bks. For Young Readers. (Simon & Schuster Bks. For Young Readers).
Kirby, Susan E. A No-Fuss Christmas. 2010. (J). (978-1-60682-059-9(1)) BJU Pr.
Klein, Lisa. Cate of the Lost Colony. 2012. (ENG.). 336p. (YA). (gr. 9-12). pap. 9.99 (978-1-59990-739-0(9), 9781599907390, Bloomsbury USA Childrens) Bloomsbury Publishing USA.
Kline, Christina Baker. Orphan Train Girl. 2017. 240p. (J). (gr. 3-7). 17.99 (978-0-06-244594-0(4)) HarperCollins Pubs.
Koertge, Ronald. Strays. (ENG., 176p. (YA). (gr. 9). 2010. Illus.). pap. 7.99 (978-0-7636-4377-5(7)) 2007. 16.99 (978-0-7636-2705-8(4)) Candlewick Pr.
Koja, Kathe. Buddha Boy. 2004. (ENG.). 128p. (YA). (gr. 7-11). reprint ed. 6.99 (978-0-14-240209-2(5), Speak) Penguin Young Readers Group.
—Buddha Boy. 2004. 117p. (gr. 3-7). 16.00 (978-0-7569-3117-9(7)) Perfection Learning Corp.
Konigbagbe, Olutobi. Joy in the Morning. 2012. (Illus.). 100p. pap. (978-1-908064-14-1(5)) Grace Publishing Group.
Korman, Gordon. The Medusa Plot. 2011. (39 Clues: Cahills vs. Vespers Ser.: 1). (ENG., Illus.). 224p. (J). (gr. 3-7). 12.99 (978-0-545-32409-0(2), Scholastic Pr.); 12.99 (978-0-545-29839-1(3)) Scholastic, Inc.
Kovalkova-McKenna, Svetlana & McKenna, Konstantin. Oberon. 2009. 44p. pap. 7.26 (978-0-557-06114-3(8)) Lulu Pr., Inc.
Kraegel, Kenneth. The Song of Delphine. Kraegel, Kenneth, illus. 2015. (ENG., Illus.). 40p. (J). (gr. k-3). 15.99 (978-0-7636-7001-6(4)) Candlewick Pr.
Krisp, Caleb. Anyone but Ivy Pocket. Cantini, Barbara, illus. 2015. (Ivy Pocket Ser.: 1). 400p. (J). (gr. 3-7). 17.99 (978-0-06-236434-0(0), Greenwillow Bks.) HarperCollins Pubs.
Kuehn, Stephanie. Complicit. (ENG.). 256p. (YA). 2016. pap. 10.99 (978-1-250-04460-0(X), 9781250044600) 2014. (gr. 8-12). 19.99 (978-1-250-04459-4(6), 9781250044594) St. Martin's Pr. (St. Martin's Griffin).
Kurtagich, Dawn. The Dead House. 2015. (ENG., Illus.). 432p. (J). (gr. 10-17). 18.00 (978-0-316-29868-1(9)) Little, Brown Bks. for Young Readers.
Laar-Yond C.T. Six Fingers & the Blue Warrior. Playcrib, illus. 2013. 36p. pap. 14.00 (978-1-62212-177-9(5), Strategic Bk. Publishing) Strategic Book Publishing & Rights Agency (SBPRA).
Lackey, Mercedes & Edghill, Rosemary. Conspiracies. 2011. (Shadow Grail Ser.: 2). (ENG.). 352p. (YA). (gr. 8-12). pap. 19.99 (978-0-7653-1762-9(1), 9780765317629, Tor Teen) Doherty, Tom Assocs., LLC.
—Legacies, No. 1. 2010. (Shadow Grail Ser.: 1). (ENG.). 320p. (YA). (gr. 8-12). pap. 11.99 (978-0-7653-1761-2(3), Tor Teen) Doherty, Tom Assocs., LLC.
—Shadow Grail #3: Sacrifices. 2013. (Shadow Grail Ser.: 3). (ENG.). 304p. (YA). (gr. 8-12). pap. 14.99 (978-0-7653-1763-6(X), 9780765317636, Tor Teen) Doherty, Tom Assocs., LLC.
LaFaye, A. Stella Stands Alone. 2010. (ENG.). 256p. (YA). (gr. 7). pap. 7.99 (978-1-4169-8647-8(2), Simon & Schuster Bks. For Young Readers) Simon & Schuster Bks. For Young Readers.
—Water Steps. 2009. (ENG., Illus.). 208p. (J). (gr. 2-7). 16.95 (978-1-57131-687-5(6)); pap. 6.95 (978-1-57131-686-8(8)) Milkweed Editions.
—Worth. unabr. ed. 2006. (Live Oak Histories Ser.). (J). (gr. 3-6). pap. 28.95 incl. audio compact disk (978-1-59519-767-2(2)) Live Oak Media.
—Worth. 2006. 144p. (J). (gr. 4-7). 13.65 (978-0-7569-6614-0(0)) Perfection Learning Corp.
—Worth. 2004. (ENG., Illus.). 160p. (J). (gr. 3-7). 17.99 (978-0-689-85730-0(6), Simon & Schuster Bks. For Young Readers) Simon & Schuster Bks. For Young Readers.
LaFevers, R. L. The Basilisk's Lair. Murphy, Kelly, illus. 2011. (Nathaniel Fludd, Beastologist Ser.: 2). (ENG.). 160p. (J). (gr. 1-4). pap. 6.99 (978-0-547-54957-6(1)) Houghton Mifflin Harcourt Publishing Co.
—Flight of the Phoenix Bk. 1. Murphy, Kelly, illus. 2010. (Nathaniel Fludd, Beastologist Ser.: 1). (ENG.). 144p. (J). (gr. 1-4). pap. 5.99 (978-0-547-40845-3(5)) Houghton Mifflin Harcourt Publishing Co.
—The Wyverns' Treasure. 2012. (Nathaniel Fludd, Beastologist Ser.: 3). lib. bdg. 16.00 (978-0-606-24516-6(2), Turtleback) Turtleback Bks.
LaFleur, Suzanne. Eight Keys. 2012. (ENG.). 224p. (J). (gr. 4-7). 6.99 (978-0-375-87213-6(2), Yearling) Random Hse. Children's Bks.
Landers, Ace. Darth Maul's Mission. White, David A., illus. 2011. (Lego Star Wars Ser.). (ENG.). 24p. (J). (gr. -1-3). pap. 3.99 (978-0-545-30441-2(5)) Scholastic, Inc.
Landman, Tanya. I Am Apache. 2008. (ENG., Illus.). 320p. (YA). (gr. 7-18). 17.99 (978-0-7636-3664-7(9)) Candlewick Pr.
Landowne, Youme. Selavi, That Is Life: A Haitian Story of Hope. Landowne, Youme, illus. 2005. (ENG., Illus.). 40p. (J). (gr. k-2). pap. 8.95 (978-0-938317-95-1(4)) Cinco Puntos Pr.
Langrish, Katherine. Troll Fell. 2004. (Illus.). 272p. (J). (gr. 5-18). (ENG.). 16.99 (978-0-06-058304-0(5)); lib. bdg. 16.89 (978-0-06-058305-7(3)) HarperCollins Pubs.
—Troll Mill. 2008. (ENG., Illus.). 336p. (YA). (gr. 7). pap. 7.99 (978-0-06-058309-5(6), Eos) HarperCollins Pubs.
Lansdale, Joe R. All the Earth, Thrown to the Sky. 2012. (ENG.). 252p. (YA). (gr. 7). pap. 8.99 (978-0-385-73932-0(X), Ember) Random Hse. Children's Bks.
Larson, Kirby. Audacity Jones Steals the Show (Audacity Jones #2) 2017. (Audacity Jones Ser.: 2). (ENG.). 192p. (J). (gr. 3-7). 16.99 (978-0-545-84065-1(1), Scholastic Pr.) Scholastic, Inc.
—Audacity Jones to the Rescue. 2016. (Audacity Jones Ser.: 1). (ENG.). 224p. (J). (gr. 3-7). pap. 6.99 (978-0-545-84060-6(0)); 16.99 (978-0-545-84056-9(2)) Scholastic, Inc. (Scholastic Pr.).
—Audacity Jones to the Rescue. 2016. (Audacity Jones Ser.: 1). lib. bdg. 17.20 **(978-0-606-39708-7(6))** Turtleback Bks.
—Hattie Big Sky. (ENG.). (YA). (gr. 7-7). 2008. 304p. 7.99 (978-0-385-73595-7(2), Yearling) 2007. 320p. pap. 8.99 (978-0-440-23941-3(9), Ember) Random Hse. Children's Bks.
—Hattie Big Sky. l.t. ed. 2007. (Literacy Bridge Young Adult Ser.). 381p. (YA). (gr. 7-12). 23.95 (978-0-7862-9697-2(6)) Thorndike Pr.
—Hattie Ever After. 2014. (ENG.). 256p. (YA). (gr. 7). pap. 8.99 (978-0-375-85090-5(2), Ember) Random Hse. Children's Bks.
Lasky, Kathryn. Christmas after All. 2012. (Dear America Ser.). (ENG.). 192p. (J). (gr. 3-7). 12.99 (978-0-545-38177-2(0)) Scholastic, Inc.
—Hannah. 2011. (Daughters of the Sea Ser.: 1). (ENG.). 320p. (J). (gr. 7-7). pap. 9.99 (978-0-545-23803-8(X)) Scholastic, Inc.
Laurie, Victoria. The Curse of Deadman's Forest. 2011. (ENG.). 432p. (J). (gr. 3-7). 8.99 (978-0-440-42259-4(0), Yearling) Random Hse. Children's Bks.
—Oracles of Delphi Keep. 2010. (Oracles of Delphi Keep Ser.). (ENG.). 576p. (J). (gr. 3-7). 7.99 (978-0-440-42258-7(2), Yearling) Random Hse. Children's Bks.
Lavender, William. Just Jane: A Daughter of England Caught in the Struggle of the American Revolution. 2005. (Great Episodes Ser.). (ENG.). 336p. (YA). (gr. 7-12). pap. 15.95 (978-0-15-205472-4(3)) Houghton Mifflin Harcourt Publishing Co.
Lawrence, Caroline. P. K. Pinkerton & the Deadly Desperados. 2013. (P. K. Pinkerton Ser.: 1). (ENG.). 304p. (J). (gr. 3-7). pap. 7.99 (978-0-14-242381-3(5), Puffin Books) Penguin Young Readers Group.
—P. K. Pinkerton & the Pistol-Packing Widows. 2015. (P. K. Pinkerton Ser.: 3). (ENG.). 320p. (J). (gr. 3-7). 7.99 (978-0-14-751130-0(5), Puffin Books) Penguin Young Readers Group.
Le Feuvre, Amy. Harebell's Friend. 2004. (Golden Inheritance Ser.: Vol. 8). (Illus.). 140p. (J). pap. (978-0-921100-84-3(1)) Inheritance Pubns.
Lee, Y. S. The Agency: A Spy in the House. 2016. (Agency Ser.). (ENG.). 352p. (YA). (gr. 7). pap. 7.99 (978-0-7636-8748-9(0)) Candlewick Pr.
—The Body at the Tower. 2010. (Agency Ser.: 2). (ENG., Illus.). 352p. (YA). (gr. 7-18). 16.99 (978-0-7636-4968-5(6)) Candlewick Pr.
—Rivals in the City. 2015. (Agency Ser.). (ENG.). 304p. (YA). (gr. 7). 16.99 (978-0-7636-5914-1(2)) Candlewick Pr.
—The Traitor in the Tunnel. 2012. (Agency Ser.: 3). (ENG., Illus.). 384p. (YA). (gr. 7). 16.99 (978-0-7636-5316-3(0)) Candlewick Pr.
L'Engle, Madeleine. Meet the Austins. 2008. (Austin Family Ser.: 1). (ENG., Illus.). 240p. (J). (gr. 6-12). pap. 8.99 (978-0-312-37931-5(5), 9780312379315) Square Fish.
—The Moon by Night, Bk. 2. 2008. (Austin Family Ser.: 2). (ENG.). 288p. (J). (gr. 6-12). pap. 9.99 (978-0-312-37932-2(3), 9780312379322) Square Fish.
Leppard, Lois Gladys. The Mandie Collection. (ENG.). (J). (gr. 3-8). 2011. 368p. pap. 12.99 (978-0-7642-0932-1(9)) 2011. 384p. pap. 13.00 (978-0-7642-0878-2(0)) 2011. 368p. pap. 12.99 (978-0-7642-0877-5(2)) 2011. 368p. pap. 10.99 (978-0-7642-0689-4(3)) Vol. 1. 2007. 544p. pap. 15.99 (978-0-7642-0446-3(7)) Vol. 2. 2008. (Illus.). 576p. pap. 15.99 (978-0-7642-0538-5(2)) Bethany Hse. Pubs.
—Mandie Collection, Vol. 3. 2008. (ENG.). 608p. (J). pap. 15.99 (978-0-7642-0593-4(5)) Bethany Hse. Pubs.
Lethcoe, Jason, illus. You Wish. 2007. 215p. (J). (978-1-4287-1806-7(0), Grosset & Dunlap) Penguin Publishing Group.
Levine, Gail Carson. Dave at Night. 2006. (ENG.). 304p. (J). (gr. 3-7). reprint ed. pap. 7.99 (978-0-06-440747-2(0)) HarperCollins Pubs.
—Dave at Night. 2004. 281p. (gr. 3-7). 17.00 (978-0-7569-4101-7(6)) Perfection Learning Corp.
—Dave at Night. unabr. ed. 2004. 278p. (J). (gr. 4-7). pap. 38.00 incl. audio (978-0-8072-8379-0(7), YA174SP, Listening Library) Random Hse. Audio Publishing Group.
Lincoln Collier, James. The Corn Raid. 2004. 142p. (J). lib. bdg. 16.92 (978-1-4242-0768-8(1)) Fitzgerald Bks.
Lindgren, Astrid & Crampton, Patricia. The Red Bird. Tornqvist, Marit, illus. 2005. (J). 5.99 (978-0-439-62797-9(4), Levine, Arthur A. Bks.) Scholastic, Inc.
Lindner, April. Jane. 2011. (ENG.). 400p. (YA). (gr. 10-17). pap. 8.99 (978-0-316-08419-2(0), Poppy) Little, Brown Bks. for Young Readers.
Lindren, Astrid. Rasmus & the Vagabond. Bothmer, Gerry, tr. from SWE. Palmquist, Eric, illus. 2014. (ENG.). 180p. pap. 9.95 (978-0-87486-597-4(2)) Plough Publishing Hse.
Lindstrom, Eric. Not If I See You First. 2015. (ENG.). 320p. (YA). (gr. 10-17). 18.00 (978-0-316-25985-9(3)) Little Brown & Co.
Lisle, Janet Taylor. The Crying Rocks. 2005. 281p. (YA). (gr. 7-12). 14.65 (978-0-7569-5507-6(6)) Perfection Learning Corp.
Literature Connections English: Jane Eyre. 2004. (gr. 6-12). (978-0-395-77557-8(4), 2-80126) Holt McDougal.
Llorente, Pilar Molina. Aura Gris. (SPA.). 192p. (YA). (gr. 5-8). (978-84-216-0993-4(9), BU3870) Bruño, Editorial ESP. Dist: Lectorum Pubns., Inc.
Lloyd, Natalie. The Key to Extraordinary. (ENG.). 240p. (J). (gr. 3-7). 2017. pap. 6.99 **(978-0-545-55276-9(1))** 2016. 16.99 (978-0-545-55274-5(5)) Scholastic, Inc. (Scholastic Pr.).
Lo, Malinda. Ash. 2010. (ENG.). 272p. (gr. 10-17). pap. 10.99 (978-0-316-04010-5(X)) Little, Brown Bks. for Young Readers.
Lockhart, E. Genuine Fraud. 2017. (YA). **(978-1-5247-7067-9(1)**, Delacorte Pr) Random House Publishing Group.
—Genuine Fraud, 9 vols. 2017. (ENG.). (YA). 170.91 **(978-0-525-50205-0(X))**; 75.96 **(978-0-525-50207-4(6))**; 170.91 **(978-0-525-50206-7(8))**; 288p. (gr. 7). 18.99 **(978-0-385-74477-5(3))**; 288p. (gr. 7). lib. bdg. 21.99 **(978-0-375-99184-4(0))** Random Hse. Children's Bks. (Delacorte Pr.).
Lois, Lowry. Gathering Blue. (Giver Quartet Ser.: 2). (ENG.). 256p. (YA). (gr. 7). 2013. pap. 9.99 (978-0-547-90414-6(2)) 2012. 17.99 (978-0-547-99568-7(7)) Houghton Mifflin Harcourt Publishing Co.
—Gathering Blue. unabr. ed. 2004. (Middle Grade Cassette Librariestm Ser.). 224p. (J). (gr. 5-9). pap. 38.00 incl. audio (978-0-8072-0989-9(9), S YA 250 SP, Listening Library) Random Hse. Audio Publishing Group.
—Gathering Blue. 2013. (Giver Quartet Ser.: 2). lib. bdg. 20.85 (978-0-606-31673-6(6), Turtleback) Turtleback Bks.
—The Willoughbys. Lois, Lowry, illus. 2008. (ENG., Illus.). 176p. (J). (gr. 1-4). 17.99 (978-0-618-97974-5(3)) Houghton Mifflin Harcourt Publishing Co.
—The Willoughbys. 2010. (ENG.). 176p. (J). (gr. 3-7). 6.99 (978-0-385-73776-0(9), Yearling) Random Hse. Children's Bks.
London, J. A. After Daybreak. 2013. (Darkness Before Dawn Ser.: 3). (ENG., Illus.). 336p. (YA). (gr. 9). pap. 9.99 (978-0-06-202067-3(6), HarperTeen) HarperCollins Pubs.
—Darkness Before Dawn. 2012. (Darkness Before Dawn Ser.: 1). (ENG., Illus.). 368p. (YA). (gr. 9). pap. 9.99 (978-0-06-202065-9(X), HarperTeen) HarperCollins Pubs.
London, Victoria. Emily Cobbs & the Naked School Bk. 1: A Gifted Girls Series. 2005. (Gifted Girls Ser.). (J). per. 7.99 (978-1-59748-857-0(7)) Sparklesoup LLC.
—Emily Cobbs Collection, Bks. 1 & 2. 2nd ed. 2005. (Gifted Girls Ser.). 164p. (J). pap. 10.95 (978-1-59748-358-2(3)) Sparklesoup LLC.
—Emily Cobbs Collection Bk. 1 & Bk. 2: A Gifted Girls Series. 2005. (Gifted Girls Ser.). (J). per. 12.95 (978-1-59748-859-4(3)) Sparklesoup LLC.
Long, Christopher E. & Warner, Gertrude Chandler. Tree House Mystery, 1 vol. Bloodworth, Mark, illus. 2010. (Boxcar Children Graphic Novels Ser.). (ENG.). 32p. (J). (gr. 2-5). 28.50 (978-1-60270-716-0(2)) ABDO Publishing Co.
Love, D. Anne. The Puppeteer's Apprentice. 2004. (ENG., Illus.). 192p. (J). (gr. 3-7). reprint ed. pap. 9.99 (978-0-689-84425-6(5), McElderry, Margaret K. Bks.) McElderry, Margaret K. Bks.

—The Puppeteer's Apprentice. 2004. (Aladdin Historical Fiction Ser.). 185p. (gr. 3-7). 17.00 *(978-0-7569-4323-3(X))* Perfection Learning Corp.

Lovric, Michelle. The Undrowned Child. 2012. (ENG.). 464p. (J). (gr. 5). 7.99 *(978-0-375-86597-8(7)*, Yearling) Random Hse. Children's Bks.

Lunievicz, Joe. Open Wounds. 2011. 352p. (YA). (gr. 9-18). 16.95 *(978-1-934813-51-5(6))* Westside Bks.

Lupica, Mike. Fast Break. 2015. (ENG.). 272p. (J). (gr. 5-8). 17.99 *(978-0-399-25606-6(7)*, Philomel Bks.) Penguin Publishing Group.

—Fast Break. 2016. (ENG.). 288p. (J). (gr. 5). pap. 8.99 *(978-1-101-99783-3(4)*, Puffin Books) Penguin Young Readers Group.

—Fast Break. 2016. (ENG.). 288p. (J). (gr. 5). 19.65 *(978-0-606-39313-3(7))* Turtleback Bks.

—Heat. 2007. (ENG.). 256p. (J). (gr. 5-18). 7.99 *(978-0-14-240757-8(7)*, Puffin Books) Penguin Young Readers Group.

—Heat. 2007. 220p. (gr. 5-9). 18.00 *(978-0-7569-8131-0(X))* Perfection Learning Corp.

—Heat. 2007. 18.40 *(978-1-4177-7264-3(6)*, Turtleback) Turtleback Bks.

—Safe at Home. 1 vol. 2012. (Comeback Kids Ser.). (ENG.). 192p. (J). (gr. 4-8). lib. bdg. 27.07 *(978-1-59961-177-8(5))* Spotlight.

Luxa, Sue. Denver Days. 2004. (Illus.). 82p. (J). pap. 8.95 *(978-1-890437-98-5(0)*, 1234247) Western Reflections Publishing Co.

Lyle, Cindy. The Creation Chronicles - the Dragon Within. 2013. 320p. *(978-1-4602-2618-6(6))* FriesenPress.

MacColl, Michaela & Chronicle Books Staff. A Novel of Intrigue & Romance. 2010. (ENG., Illus.). 368p. (YA). (gr. 7-17). 16.99 *(978-0-8118-7300-0(5))* Chronicle Bks. LLC.

MacColl, Michaela & Nichols, Rosemary. Rory's Promise. 2014. (Hidden Histories Ser.). (ENG.). 288p. (J). (gr. 4-7). 16.95 *(978-1-62091-623-0(1)*, Calkins Creek) Boyds Mills Pr.

MacDonald, Bailey. Wicked Will: A Mystery of Young William Shakespeare. 2009. (ENG.). 208p. (J). (gr. 4-7). 16.99 *(978-1-4169-8660-7(X)*, Simon & Schuster/Paula Wiseman Bks.) Simon & Schuster/Paula Wiseman Bks.

MacDonald, Betty Bard. Nancy & Plum. GrandPré, Mary, illus. 2011. (ENG.). 240p. (J). (gr. 3-7). 7.99 *(978-0-375-85986-1(1)*, Yearling) Random Hse. Children's Bks.

MacLean, Betty. Jiali's Traveling Heart. Kinra, Richa, illus. 2013. 34p. (J). 17.95 *(978-1-60131-157-3(5)*, Castlebridge Bks.) Big Tent Bks.

Maguire, Gregory. Missing Sisters. 2009. 192p. (J). 16.99 *(978-0-06-123204-6(1))*; (ENG.). (gr. 3-7). pap. 6.99 *(978-0-06-123203-9(3))* HarperCollins Pubs.

—What-the-Dickens: The Story of a Rogue Tooth Fairy. 2008. (ENG., Illus.). 304p. (gr. 4-7). pap. 8.99 *(978-0-7636-4147-4(2))* Candlewick Pr.

—What-the-Dickens: The Story of a Rogue Tooth Fairy. 2007. (ENG.). 304p. (J). (gr. 4-8). 24.80 *(978-1-4287-6555-9(7)*, Follettbound) Follett School Solutions.

Mahoney, Karen. The Iron Witch. 2011. (Iron Witch Ser.: 1). (ENG.). 312p. (YA). (gr. 7-18). pap. 9.95 *(978-0-7387-2582-6(X)*, Flux) North Star Editions.

Malam, John, retold by. Oliver Twist. 2014. (Graphic Classics Ser.). 48p. (gr. 3-6). 37.10 *(978-1-908973-89-4(7))* Book Hse. GBR. Dist: Black Rabbit Bks.

Mallory, Alex. Wild. 2014. (ENG.). 448p. (YA). (gr. 8). 17.99 *(978-0-06-221874-2(3)*, HarperTeen) HarperCollins Pubs.

Malot, Hector & Crewe-Jones, Florence. Nobody's Boy: Companion Story to Nobody's Girl. Gooch, Thelma & Gruelle, Johnny, illus. 2006. 237p. (J). pap. *(978-1-894666-75-6(5))* Inheritance Pubns.

—Nobody's Girl: Companion Story to Nobody's Boy. Gooch, Thelma, illus. 2006. 220p. (J). pap. *(978-1-894666-76-3(3))* Inheritance Pubns.

Mama Jamie. I Will Call Myself Future. 2012. 34p. pap. 15.95 *(978-1-4497-5500-3(3)*, WestBow Pr.) Author Solutions, Inc.

Manale, Shizumi Shigeto & Marshall, Richard. Running with Cosmos Flowers: The Children of Hiroshima. 1 vol. 2014. (ENG., Illus.). 152p. (YA). (gr. 8-8). 16.99 *(978-1-4556-1966-5(3))* Pelican Publishing Co., Inc.

Mantchev, Lisa. Eyes Like Stars. 2010. (Theatre Illuminata Ser.: 1). (ENG.). 384p. (YA). (gr. 7-12). pap. 11.99 *(978-0-312-60866-8(7)*, 9780312608668) Square Fish.

—Perchance to Dream. 2011. (Theatre Illuminata Ser.: 2). (ENG.). 368p. (YA). (gr. 7-12). pap. 9.99 *(978-0-312-67510-3(0)*, 9780312675103) Square Fish.

Marciano, John Bemelmans. Madeline & Her Dog. 2011. (Madeline Ser.). (ENG.). 32p. (J). (gr. 1-2). pap. 3.99 *(978-0-448-45438-2(6)*, Penguin Young Readers) Penguin Young Readers Group.

—Madeline & the Old House in Paris. 2013. (Madeline Ser.). (ENG.). 48p. (J). (gr. -1-2). 17.99 *(978-0-670-78485-1(0)*, Viking Books for Young Readers) Penguin Young Readers Group.

—Madeline at the White House. (Madeline Ser.). (ENG., (J). (gr. -1-2). 2016. Illus.). 48p. 8.99 *(978-1-101-99780-2(X)*, Puffin Books) 2011. 45p. 17.99 *(978-0-670-01228-2(9)*, Viking Books for Young Readers) Penguin Young Readers Group.

—Madeline at the White House. 2016. (Madeline Ser.). lib. bdg. 19.65 *(978-0-606-38845-0(1))* Turtleback Bks.

—Madeline's Tea Party. 2012. (Madeline Ser.). (ENG.). 32p. (J). (gr. 1-2). pap. 3.99 *(978-0-448-45439-9(4)*, Penguin Young Readers) Penguin Young Readers Group.

—The Nine Lives of Alexander Baddenfield. Blackall, Sophie, illus. 2013. (ENG.). 144p. (J). (gr. 5). 16.99 *(978-0-670-01406-4(0)*, Viking Books for Young Readers) Penguin Young Readers Group.

Mariconda, Barbara. Lucy at Sea. 2013. (Voyage of Lucy P. Simmons Ser.: 2). (ENG.). 320p. (J). (gr. 3-7). 16.99 *(978-0-06-211993-3(1)*, Tegen, Katherine Bks) HarperCollins Pubs.

—The Voyage of Lucy P. Simmons. 2074. (ENG.). 256p. (J). (gr. 3-7). 6.99 *(978-0-06-211980-3(X)*, Tegen, Katherine Bks) HarperCollins Pubs.

Marillier, Juliet. Raven Flight. (ENG.). 416p. (YA). (gr. 7). 2014. pap. 9.99 *(978-0-375-87197-9(7)*, Ember) 2013. 16.99 *(978-0-375-86955-6(7)*, Knopf Bks. for Young Readers) Random Hse. Children's Bks.

—Shadowfell. 2013. (ENG.). 416p. (YA). (gr. 7). pap. 10.99 *(978-0-375-87196-2(9)*, Ember) Random Hse. Children's Bks.

Marks, Alan, illus. The Story of Heidi. 2007. (Picture Book Classics Ser.). 24p. (J). (gr. -1-3). 9.99 *(978-0-7945-1716-8(1)*, Usborne) EDC Publishing.

Marmell, Ari. Covenant's End: A Widdershins Adventure. 2015. (ENG.). 271p. (YA). (gr. 7). 17.99 *(978-1-61614-986-4(8)*, Pyr Bks.) Prometheus Bks., Pubs.

Marryat. The Children of the New Forest, Level 2. Bassett, Jennifer, ed. 3rd ed. 2008. (ENG., Illus.). 64p. pap. 10.00 *(978-0-19-479054-3(1))* Oxford Univ. Pr., Inc.

Marryat, Captian. The Children of the New Forest. 2008. 332p. (gr. 8-12). 28.99 *(978-0-554-38541-9(4))*; 29.99 *(978-0-554-29238-0(6))* Creative Media Partners, LLC.

—The Children of the New Forest. 2007. 312p. per. *(978-1-4065-5647-6(5))* Dodo Pr.

—The Children of the New Forest. 2006. 216p. pap. *(978-1-84637-527-9(4))*; pap. *(978-1-84702-355-1(X))* Echo Library.

—The Children of the New Forest. 2004. reprint ed. pap. 28.95 *(978-1-4191-5655-7(1))*; pap. 1.99 *(978-1-4192-5655-4(6))* Kessinger Publishing, LLC.

—The Children of the New Forest. 2008. 292p. pap. 16.95 *(978-1-60597-491-0(9)*, Book Jungle) Standard Pubns., Inc.

Marryat, Frederick. Children of the New Forest (Yesterday's Classics) 2007. (J). pap. 12.95 *(978-1-59915-050-5(6))* Yesterday's Classics.

Marsden, Carolyn. Take Me with You. 2010. (ENG., Illus.). 176p. (J). (gr. 5-18). 14.99 *(978-0-7636-3739-2(4))* Candlewick Pr.

Marsh, Katherine. The Door by the Staircase. 2016. (ENG., Illus.). 284p. (J). (gr. 3-7). 16.99 *(978-1-4231-3499-2(0))* Disney Pr.

—The Door by the Staircase. Murphy, Kelly, illus. 2017. (ENG.). 288p. (J). (gr. 5-9). pap. 7.99 *(978-1-4231-3785-6(X))* Hyperion Bks. for Children.

Marshall, G. Skies of Dawn. 2007. 160p. per. 12.95 *(978-0-595-42946-2(7))* iUniverse, Inc.

Martin, Ann M. Best Friends. 2008. (Illus.). 195p. (J). pap. *(978-0-545-05062-3(6))* Scholastic, Inc.

—Needle & Thread. Andreasen, Dan, illus. 2007. 205p. (J). pap. *(978-0-545-03660-3(7))* Scholastic, Inc.

Martin, Jenny. Marked. 2016. (ENG.). 368p. (YA). (gr. 7). 17.99 *(978-0-525-42871-8(2)*, Dial Bks) Penguin Young Readers Group.

—Tracked. 2015. (ENG.). 400p. (YA). (gr. 7). 17.99 *(978-0-8037-4012-9(3)*, Dial Bks) Penguin Young Readers Group.

Maruno, Jennifer. Totem. 0 vols. 2014. (ENG.). 168p. (YA). pap. 10.99 *(978-1-4597-1934-7(4)*, 9781459719347) Dundurn CAN. Dist: Ingram Publisher Services.

—Warbird. 2010. (ENG., Illus.). 120p. (J). (gr. 4-7). pap. 9.95 *(978-1-926607-11-5(2)*, Napoleon & Co.) Dundurn CAN. Dist: Ingram Publisher Services.

Mason, Conrad. The Watchmen of Port Fayt. 2015. (ENG.). 400p. (J). (gr. 3-7). 17.99 *(978-0-545-83308-0(6))* Scholastic, Inc.

Mason, Mike. The Blue Umbrella. 2009. (ENG.). 448p. (YA). pap. 10.99 *(978-1-4347-6526-0(1))* Cook, David C.

Matthews, L. S. Lexi. 2008. 200p. (J). pap. *(978-0-385-73575-9(8)*, Delacorte Pr) Random House Publishing Group.

Matute, Ana María. El Polizón del Ulises. (SPA.). 96p. (J). *(978-84-264-3401-2(0)*, LM4015) Editorial Lumen ESP. Dist: Lectorum Pubns., Inc.

McCaughrean, Geraldine. Monacello: The Little Monk. Diemberger, Jana, illus. 2013. (Monacello Trilogy Ser.: 1). (ENG.). 64p. (J). (gr. 4-7). pap. 12.99 *(978-1-907912-03-0(7))* Phoenix Yard Bks. GBR. Dist: Independent Pubs. Group.

McClure, Wendy. Wanderville. 2014. (Wanderville Ser.: 1). (ENG.). (J). (gr. 3-7). 240p. pap. 7.99 *(978-1-59514-701-1(2))*; 224p. 16.99 *(978-1-59514-700-4(4))* Penguin Young Readers Group. (Razorbill).

McDougal-Littell Publishing Staff. Literature Connections Spanish. 2004. (McDougal Littell Literature Connections Ser.). (SPA.). 576p. (gr. 12-12). stu. ed. 16.90 *(978-0-395-81741-4(2)*, 2-70491) Great Source Education Group, Inc.

McEnroe, Jim. The Rabbit King: Kingdom Leporidae. 2011. 32p. pap. 15.95 *(978-1-4520-9199-0(4))* AuthorHouse.

McGowan, Jennifer. Maid of Secrets. (Maids of Honor Ser.). (ENG.). (YA). (gr. 7). 2014. 432p. pap. 9.99 *(978-1-4424-4139-2(9))* 2013. 416p. 17.99 *(978-1-4424-4138-5(0))* Simon & Schuster Bks. For Young Readers. (Simon & Schuster Bks. For Young Readers).

McGowan, Maureen. Deviants. 0 vols. 2014. (Dust Chronicles Ser.: 1). (ENG.). 322p. (YA). (gr. 9-12). pap. 9.99 *(978-1-4778-1032-3(3)*, 9781477810323, Skyscape) Amazon Publishing.

McKenzie, Sophie. Every Second Counts. 2016. 405p. (YA). pap. *(978-1-4814-3927-5(8))* Simon & Schuster Children's Publishing.

—In a Split Second. 2015. (ENG., Illus.). 368p. (YA). (gr. 7). 17.99 *(978-1-4814-1394-7(5))* Simon & Schuster Children's Publishing.

McKernan, Victoria. The Devil's Paintbox. (ENG.). (YA). (gr. 9). 2013. 384p. pap. 9.99 *(978-0-449-81655-4(9)*, Ember) 2010. 368p. mass mkt. 8.99 *(978-0-440-23962-8(1)*, Laurel Leaf) Random Hse. Children's Bks.

McNichol, John. The Tripods Attack! 2008. (Young Chesterton Chronicles Ser.). 367p. (YA). (gr. 8-12). pap. 17.95 *(978-1-933184-26-5(4))* Sophia Institute Pr.

McQuestion, Karen. Life on Hold. 0 vols. unabr. ed. 2011. (ENG.). 196p. (gr. 4-6). pap. 9.95 *(978-1-935597-27-8(2)*, 9781935597278, Skyscape) Amazon Publishing.

Meade, L. T. The Children's Pilgrimage. 2007. (ENG.). 254p. pap. 21.99 *(978-1-4346-4863-1(X))*; 280p. pap. 23.99 *(978-1-4346-4864-8(8))* Creative Media Partners, LLC.

Meehan, Thomas. Annie. 2013. (Annie Book Ser.). (ENG.). 272p. (J). (gr. 5). pap. 7.99 *(978-0-14-751114-0(3)*, Puffin Books) Penguin Young Readers Group.

Meigs, Elizabeth Bleecker. The White Winter: A Story of Scarlet Hill. Chapman, Frederick T., illus. 2011. 208p. 44.95 *(978-1-258-08230-7(6))* Literary Licensing, LLC.

Meloy, Colin. Wildwood Imperium: The Wildwood Chronicles, Book III. Ellis, Carson, illus. 2015. (Wildwood Chronicles Ser.: 3). (ENG.). 592p. (J). (gr. 3). pap. 9.99 *(978-0-06-202476-3(0))* HarperCollins Pubs.

Messenger, Shannon. Let the Sky Fall. 2013. (Sky Fall Ser.: 1). (ENG., (YA). (gr. 7). Illus.). 432p. pap. 10.99 *(978-1-4424-5042-4(8))*; 416p. 17.99 *(978-1-4424-5041-7(X))* Simon Pulse. (Simon Pulse).

—Let the Storm Break. 2014. (Sky Fall Ser.: 2). (ENG., Illus.). 400p. (YA). (gr. 7). 17.99 *(978-1-4424-5044-8(4)*, Simon Pulse) Simon Pulse.

Messner, Kate. Spitfire. 2007. (J). *(978-1-59531-018-7(5))* North Country Bks., Inc.

Meyer, Carolyn. Duchessina: A Novel of Catherine de' Medici. 2009. (Young Royals Ser.). (ENG., Illus.). 272p. (J). (gr. 9). pap. 8.99 *(978-0-15-206620-8(9))* Houghton Mifflin Harcourt Publishing Co.

Meyer, Kai. Dark Reflections: The Water Mirror - The Stone Light; the Glass Word. Crawford, Elizabeth D., tr. from GER. 2010. (Dark Reflections Trilogy Ser.). (ENG.). 896p. (YA). (gr. 7). pap. 9.99 *(978-1-4424-0938-5(X)*, McElderry, Margaret K. Bks.) McElderry, Margaret K. Bks.

—The Glass Word. Crawford, Elizabeth D., tr. from GER. 2008. (ENG.). 288p. (YA). (gr. 7). (Dark Reflections Trilogy Ser.: 3). pap. 9.99 *(978-0-689-87792-6(7))*; (Dark Reflections Trilogy: Bk. 3). 16.99 *(978-0-689-87791-9(9))* McElderry, Margaret K. Bks. (McElderry, Margaret K. Bks.).

—The Stone Light. Crawford, Elizabeth D., tr. 2007. (Dark Reflections Trilogy Ser.: 2). (ENG.). 384p. (YA). (gr. 7-12). pap. 8.99 *(978-0-689-87790-2(0)*, McElderry, Margaret K. Bks.) McElderry, Margaret K. Bks.

Meyer, L. A. In the Belly of the Bloodhound: Being an Account of a Particularly Peculiar Adventure in the Life of Jacky Faber. 2008. (Bloody Jack Adventures Ser.: 4). (ENG., Illus.). 528p. (YA). (gr. 7-12). pap. 7.95 *(978-0-15-206166-1(5))* Houghton Mifflin Harcourt Publishing Co.

—Mississippi Jack: Being an Account of the Further Waterborne Adventures of Jacky Faber, Midshipman, Fine Lady, & the Lily of the West. 2nd ed. 2010. (Bloody Jack Adventures Ser.: 5). (ENG., Illus.). 624p. (J). (gr. 7). pap. 8.99 *(978-0-15-206632-1(2))* Houghton Mifflin Harcourt Publishing Co.

—My Bonny Light Horseman: Being an Account of the Further Adventures of Jacky Faber, in Love & War. (Bloody Jack Adventures Ser.: 6). (ENG., Illus.). 448p. (YA). (gr. 7). 2010. pap. 9.99 *(978-0-547-32794-5(3))* 2008. 17.00 *(978-0-15-206187-6(8))* Houghton Mifflin Harcourt Publishing Co.

—Rapture of the Deep: Being an Account of the Further Adventures of Jacky Faber, Soldier, Sailor, Mermaid, Spy. 2011. (Bloody Jack Adventures Ser.: 7). (ENG.). 464p. (YA). (gr. 9). pap. 9.99 *(978-0-547-55120-3(7))* Houghton Mifflin Harcourt Publishing Co.

—Under the Jolly Roger: Being an Account of the Further Nautical Adventures of Jacky Faber. 2010. (Bloody Jack Adventures Ser.: 3). (ENG., Illus.). 528p. (YA). (gr. 7). pap. 9.99 *(978-0-15-205873-9(7))* Houghton Mifflin Harcourt Publishing Co.

—The Wake of the Lorelei Lee: Being an Account of the Further Adventures of Jacky Faber, on Her Way to Botany Bay. (Bloody Jack Adventures Ser.: 8). (ENG.). (YA). (gr. 9). 2012. 576p. pap. 9.99 *(978-0-547-72194-1(3))* 2010. 560p. 17.00 *(978-0-547-32768-6(4))* Houghton Mifflin Harcourt Publishing Co.

—The Wake of the Lorelei Lee: Being an Account of the Further Adventures of Jacky Faber, on Her Way to Botany Bay. 2010. (Bloody Jack Adventures Ser.: Bk. 8). audio compact disk 29.95 *(978-1-59316-484-3(X))* Listen & Live Audio, Inc.

Michaelis, Antonia. The Secret of the Twelfth Continent. Hosmer-Dillard, Mollie, tr. from GER. Nievelstein, Ralf, illus. 2013. (ENG.). 288p. (J). (gr. 2-7). 14.95 *(978-1-62087-539-1(X)*, 620539, Sky Pony Pr.) Skyhorse Publishing Co., Inc.

—The Secret Room. 2012. (ENG., Illus.). 208p. (J). (gr. 2-7). 14.95 *(978-1-61608-960-3(1)*, 608960, Sky Pony Pr.) Skyhorse Publishing Co., Inc.

Michaels, Rune. Fix Me. 2011. (ENG., Illus.). 160p. (YA). (gr. 9). 16.99 *(978-1-4169-5772-0(3)*, Atheneum Bks. for Young Readers) Simon & Schuster Children's Publishing.

Miklowitz, Gloria D. Secrets in the House of Delgado. 2004. 192p. (J). (gr. 4-18). pap. 8.00 *(978-0-8028-5210-6(6))* Eerdmans, William B. Publishing Co.

Milford, Kate. The Broken Lands. Offermann, Andrea, illus. 2012. (ENG.). 464p. (YA). (gr. 7). 16.99 *(978-0-547-73966-3(4))* Houghton Mifflin Harcourt Publishing Co.

Molesworth, Mary Louisa. The Cuckoo Clock. 2004. reprint ed. pap. 1.99 *(978-1-4192-5839-8(7))*; pap. 19.95 *(978-1-4191-5839-1(2))* Kessinger Publishing, LLC.

Montgomery, L. M. Akin to Anne: Tales of Other Orphans. (YA). 22.95 *(978-0-8488-2656-7(6))* Amereon Ltd.

—Ana la de Avonlea. García Díaz, José, tr. 5th ed. (Ana la de Tejas Verdes Ser.: 2).Tr. of Anne of Avonlea. (SPA., Illus.). 254p. (J). (gr. 5-8). *(978-84-7888-632-6(X)*, SAL3943) Emece Editores ESP. Dist: Lectorum Pubns., Inc.

—Ana la de Ingleside. 2nd ed. (Ana la de Tejas Verdes Ser.: 6).Tr. of Anne of Ingleside. (SPA., Illus.). 288p. (J). (gr. 5-8). *(978-84-7888-634-0(6)*, SAL3088) Emece Editores ESP. Dist: Lectorum Pubns., Inc.

—Ana la de Isla. 4th ed. (Ana la de Tejas Verdes Ser.: 3).Tr. of Anne of the Island. (SPA., Illus.). 240p. (YA). (gr. 5-8). *(978-84-7888-635-7(4)*, SAL5036) Emece Editores ESP. Dist: Lectorum Pubns., Inc.

—Ana la de Tejas Verdes. García Díaz, José, tr. 7th ed. (Ana la de Tejas Verdes Ser.: 1).Tr. of Anne of Green Gables. (SPA., Illus.). 288p. (J). (gr. 5-8). *(978-84-7888-633-3(8))* Emece Editores ESP. Dist: Lectorum Pubns., Inc.

—Anne of Avonlea. 2004. 352p. per. 15.95 *(978-1-59540-109-0(1))* 1st World Publishing, Inc.

—Anne of Avonlea. 2005. pap. *(978-1-905432-15-8(1))* Dodo Pr.

—Anne of Avonlea. 2011. (Oxford Children's Classics Ser.). (ENG.). 336p. (YA). (gr. 3-18). 9.95 *(978-0-19-276359-4(8))* Oxford Univ. Pr., Inc.

—Anne of Avonlea. 2005. (Aladdin Classics Ser.). (ENG., Illus.). 416p. (J). (gr. 4-7). pap. 5.99 *(978-1-4169-0328-4(3)*, Aladdin) Simon & Schuster Children's Publishing.

—Anne of Avonlea. Andreasen, Dan, illus. 2009. (Classic Starts(tm) Ser.). (ENG.). 160p. (J). (gr. 2-4). 6.95 *(978-1-4027-5424-1(8))* Sterling Publishing Co., Inc.

—Anne of Avonlea. McKowen, Scott, illus. 2008. (Sterling Unabridged Classics Ser.). (ENG.). 256p. (J). 9.95 *(978-1-4027-5428-9(0))* Sterling Publishing Co., Inc.

—Anne of Avonlea. 2012. (World Classics Ser.). (ENG.). 228p. pap. 19.99 *(978-1-909438-94-1(4)*, Sovereign) Bollinger, Max GBR. Dist: Lightning Source UK, Ltd., Gardners Bks. Ltd.

—Anne of Avonlea. l.t. ed. 2006. (ENG.). pap. *(978-1-4068-3173-3(5))* Echo Library.

—Anne of Green Gables. 400p. 2005. 33.95 *(978-1-4218-0660-0(6)*, 1st World Library - Literary Society) 2004. per. 16.95 *(978-1-59540-110-6(5))* 1st World Publishing, Inc.

—Anne of Green Gables. 2009. 292p. 27.99 *(978-1-60512-375-2(7))*; pap. 14.99 *(978-1-60512-475-9(3))* Akasha Publishing, LLC. (Akasha Classics).

—Anne of Green Gables. 2008. 316p. 28.99 *(978-0-554-32848-5(8))* 2008. 316p. 29.99 *(978-0-554-23545-5(5))* 2007. (ENG.). 312p. pap. 24.99 *(978-1-4264-4662-7(4))* Creative Media Partners, LLC.

—Anne of Green Gables. 2008. (Anne of Green Gables Ser.). (ENG.). 366p. (J). (gr. 4-7). pap. 9.95 *(978-0-9782552-6-8(7))* Davenport Pr. CAN. Dist: Independent Pubs. Group.

—Anne of Green Gables. 2007. per. 6.99 *(978-1-4209-2922-5(4))* Digireads.com Publishing.

—Anne of Green Gables. 2007. 284p. per. *(978-1-4065-6399-3(4))* Dodo Pr.

—Anne of Green Gables. 2007. 572p. *(978-1-84702-773-3(3))* 2006. pap. *(978-1-4068-2170-3(5))* Echo Library.

—Anne of Green Gables. 2008. 316p. pap. 16.95 *(978-1-60096-101-4(0))*; pap. 16.95 *(978-1-60096-565-4(2))* Editorium, The.

—Anne of Green Gables. 2009. 242p. pap. 8.58 *(978-0-217-43952-7(7))* General Bks. LLC.

—Anne of Green Gables. 2005. (My First Classics Ser.). 112p. (J). (gr. k-3). pap., pap. 4.99 *(978-0-06-079147-6(0)*, HarperFestival) HarperCollins Pubs.

—Anne of Green Gables. 2005. 21.99 *(978-1-4142-5125-7(4))* IndyPublish.com.

—Anne of Green Gables. 2008. (ENG.). 376p. (gr. k-12). pap. 14.95 *(978-0-7710-9368-5(3)*, New Can Library) McClelland & Stewart CAN. Dist: Penguin Random Hse. LLC.

—Anne of Green Gables. 1 vol. 2016. (ENG.). 352p. (J). (gr. 2-5). pap. 10.95 *(978-1-55109-249-2(2))* Nimbus Publishing, Ltd. CAN. Dist: National Bk. Network.

—Anne of Green Gables. Rubio, Mary Henley & Waterston, Elizabeth, eds. 2007. (Norton Critical Editions Ser.: 0). (ENG., Illus.). 464p. (C). (gr. 9-12). per. 15.02 *(978-0-393-92695-8(8)*, 92695) Norton, W. W. & Co., Inc.

—Anne of Green Gables. 2003. (ENG.). 320p. (gr. 5-7). 5.95 *(978-0-451-52882-7(4)*, Signet) Penguin Publishing Group.

—Anne of Green Gables. 2008. (Puffin Classics Ser.). (ENG., Illus.). 464p. (J). (gr. 3-7). 5.99 *(978-0-14-132159-2(8)*, Puffin Books) Penguin Young Readers Group.

—Anne of Green Gables. 2003. 320p. (J). (gr. 4-7). 12.60 *(978-0-7569-1848-4(0))* Perfection Learning Corp.

—Anne of Green Gables. 2013. (Word Cloud Classics Ser.). (ENG.). 264p. pap. 14.99 *(978-1-60710-728-6(7)*, Thunder Bay Pr.) Readerlink Distribution Services, LLC.

—Anne of Green Gables. 2009. 224p. pap. 15.45 *(978-1-4385-1847-3(1)*, Book Jungle) Standard Pubns., Inc.

—Anne of Green Gables. McKowen, Scott, illus. 2004. (Sterling Unabridged Classics Ser.). (ENG.). 312p. (J). (gr. 5). 9.95 *(978-1-4027-1451-1(3))* Sterling Publishing Co., Inc.

—Anne of Green Gables. Corvino, Lucy, illus. 2005. (Classic Starts(tm) Ser.). (ENG.). 160p. (J). (gr. 2-4). 6.95 *(978-1-4027-1130-5(1))* Sterling Publishing Co., Inc.

—Anne of Green Gables. 2008. (Modern Library Classics Ser.). (ENG.). 320p. pap. 9.00 *(978-0-8129-7903-9(6)*, Modern Library) Random House Publishing Group.

—Anne of Green Gables. 2012. (World Classics Ser.). (ENG.). 260p. pap. 19.99 *(978-1-909438-96-5(0)*, Sovereign) Bollinger, Max GBR. Dist: Lightning Source UK, Ltd.

—Anne of Green Gables. rev. ed. 2007. 280p. pap. 21.99 *(978-1-4264-4611-5(X))* Creative Media Partners, LLC.

—Anne of Green Gables. l.t. ed. 2006. pap. *(978-1-4068-3174-0(3))* Echo Library.

—Anne of Green Gables. 2004. reprint ed. pap. 27.95 *(978-1-4191-0717-7(8))*; pap. 1.99 *(978-1-4192-0717-4(2))* Kessinger Publishing, LLC.

—Anne of Green Gables. l.t. ed. 2009. (World Classics Ser.). 288p. pap. 21.95 *(978-1-59688-123-5(2))* Large Print Bk. Co., The.

—The Anne of Green Gables Collection: Six Complete & Unabridged Novels in One Volume. 2013. 1140p. *(978-1-78139-344-4(3))* Benediction Classics.

—Anne of the Green Gables. 2014. (Anne of Green Gables Ser.: 1). (ENG.). 352p. (YA). (gr. 5-12). pap. 9.99 *(978-1-4022-8894-4(8))* Sourcebooks, Inc.

—Anne of the Island. 2012. (World Classics Ser.). (ENG.). 212p. pap. 19.99 *(978-1-909438-92-7(8)*, Sovereign) Bollinger, Max GBR. Dist: Lightning Source UK, Ltd.

—Anne of the Island. 2008. (Anne of Green Gables Ser.). (ENG.). 272p. (J). (gr. 4-7). pap. 9.95 *(978-0-9782552-8-2(3))* Davenport Pr. CAN. Dist: Independent Pubs. Group.

—Anne of the Island. 2006. (ENG.). pap. *(978-1-4068-2171-0(3))*; pap. *(978-1-4068-3175-7(1))* Echo Library.

—Anne of the Island. 2004. reprint ed. pap. 1.99 *(978-1-4192-0718-1(0))*; pap. 30.95 *(978-1-4179-0885-1(8))* Kessinger Publishing, LLC.

—Anne of the Island. l.t. ed. 2004. 396p. 26.00 *(978-1-58287-640-5(1))* North Bks.

—Anne of the Island. 2010. (Puffin Classics Ser.). (ENG.). 368p. (J). (gr. 5-7). pap. 5.99 *(978-0-14-132736-5(7)*, Puffin Books) Penguin Young Readers Group.

—Emily Climbs. 2009. (ENG.). 376p. pap. 16.95 *(978-0-7710-9382-1(9)*, New Can Library) McClelland & Stewart CAN. Dist: Random Hse., Inc.

—Emily Climbs: Emily of New Moon Series. 2014. (Emily Ser.: 2). (ENG.). 368p. (YA). (gr. 5-12). pap. 8.99 (978-1-4022-8915-6(4)) Sourcebooks, Inc.

—Emily's Quest. 2009. (ENG.). 272p. pap. 19.95 (978-0-7710-9383-8(7), New Can Library) McClelland & Stewart CAN. Dist: Random Hse., Inc.

—Emily's Quest. 2014. (Emily Ser.: 3). (ENG.). 256p. (YA). (gr. 5-12). pap. 8.99 (978-1-4022-8918-7(9)) Sourcebooks, Inc.

Montgomery, L. M & Castelao, Patricia. Anne of Green Gables, 1 vol. 2012. (Calico Illustrated Classics Ser.: No. 4). (ENG., Illus.). 112p. (J). (gr. 3-6). 27.07 (978-1-61641-612-6(2)) Magic Wagon.

Montgomery, R. A. Chinese Dragons. Semionov, Vladimir, illus. 2009. (Choose Your Own Adventure Ser.: No. 30). 144p. (J). (gr. 2-7). pap. 6.99 (978-1-933390-30-7(1)) Chooseco LLC.

Moore, Stephanie. Better Than Picture Perfect. 2014. (Sharp Sisters Ser.: 2). (ENG.). 160p. (YA). (gr. 6-12). pap. 7.95 (978-1-4677-4486-7(7), Darby Creek) Lerner Publishing Group.

Moore, Stephanie Perry. Better Than Picture Perfect. 2014. (Sharp Sisters Ser.: 2). (ENG.). 160p. (YA). (gr. 6-12). lib. bdg. 27.93 (978-1-4677-3725-8(9)) Lerner Publishing Group.

Moreton, Clara. Frank & Fanny: A Rural Story. 2007. (ENG.). 66p. per. 16.99 (978-1-4346-2717-9(9)); per. 18.99 (978-1-4346-2723-0(3)) Creative Media Partners, LLC.

Morgan, Clay. The Boy Who Returned from the Sea. 2009. (ENG.). 256p. (J). (gr. 3-7). pap. 7.99 (978-0-14-241395-1(X), Puffin Books) Penguin Young Readers Group.

—The Boy Who Spoke Dog. 2005. (ENG.). 176p. (J). (gr. 3-7). 5.99 (978-0-14-240343-3(1), Puffin Books) Penguin Young Readers Group.

Morpurgo, Michael. Kaspar the Titanic Cat. Foreman, Michael, illus. 2012. 208p. (J). (gr. 3-7). 16.99 (978-0-06-200618-9(5)) HarperCollins Pubs.

Mosher, Richard. Zazoo. 2004. (ENG.). 272p. (YA). (gr. 7-18). reprint ed. pap. 15.95 (978-0-618-43904-1(8)) Houghton Mifflin Harcourt Publishing Co.

Motomi, Kyousuke. Dengeki Daisy , Vol. 16. 2015. (ENG.). 192p. pap. 9.99 (978-1-4215-7771-5(2)) Viz Media.

Moulton, Mark Kimball. A Cricket's Carol. Blowers, Lisa, illus. 2004. 32p. (J). 14.95 (978-0-8249-5488-8(2), Ideal Pubns.) Worthy Publishing.

Mourlevat, Jean-Claude. Winter's End. Bell, Anthea, tr. from FRE. 2009. (ENG., Illus.). 432p. (YA). (gr. 9-18). 17.99 (978-0-7636-4450-5(1)) Candlewick Pr.

Muchamore, Robert. The Dealer. (Cherub Ser.: 2). (ENG.). (YA). (gr. 7). 2011. 336p. pap. 11.99 (978-1-4424-1361-0(1)) 2010. 320p. 18.99 (978-1-4169-9941-6(8)) Simon Pulse. (Simon Pulse).

—Maximum Security. 2012. (Cherub Ser.: 3). (ENG.). 320p. (YA). (gr. 7). pap. 9.99 (978-1-4424-1362-7(X), Simon Pulse) Simon Pulse.

Murdock, Catherine Gilbert. Wisdom's Kiss. 2013. (ENG.). 320p. (YA). (gr. 7). pap. 8.99 (978-0-547-85540-0(0)) Houghton Mifflin Harcourt Publishing Co.

—Wisdom's Kiss: A Thrilling & Romantic Adventure, Incorporating Magic, Villany, & a Cat. 2011. (ENG.). 304p. (YA). (gr. 7). 16.99 (978-0-547-56687-0(5)) Houghton Mifflin Harcourt Publishing Co.

Murphy, Jim. On Enemy Soil: The Journal of James Edmond Pease, a Civil War Union Soldier. 2012. (ENG.). 176p. (J). (gr. 3-7). pap. 6.99 (978-0-545-39887-9(8)) Scholastic, Inc.

Murray, Kirsty. Vulture's Wake. 2010. (ENG.). 256p. (YA). (gr. 7-18). pap. 17.95 (978-0-8234-2282-1(8)) Holiday Hse., Inc.

Muschla, Gary Robert. Crusader. 2006. (YA). pap. (978-0-88092-491-7(8)) Royal Fireworks Publishing Co.

Myhre, Jennifer. A Chameleon, a Boy, & a Quest. 2015. (ENG., Illus.). 160p. (J). pap. 15.99 (978-1-942572-08-4(5)) New Growth Pr.

Myklusch, Matt. The Accidental Hero. 2011. (Jack Blank Adventure Ser.: 1). (ENG., Illus.). 496p. (J). (gr. 3-7). pap. 7.99 (978-1-4169-9562-3(5), Aladdin) Simon & Schuster Children's Publishing.

—Jack Blank & the Imagine Nation. 2010. (Jack Blank Adventure Ser.: Bk. 1). (ENG., Illus.). 480p. (J). (gr. 3-7). 16.99 (978-1-4169-9561-6(7), Aladdin) Simon & Schuster Children's Publishing.

—The Secret War. 2012. (Jack Blank Adventure Ser.: 2). (ENG., Illus.). 560p. (J). (gr. 3-7). pap. 7.99 (978-1-4169-9565-4(X), Aladdin) Simon & Schuster Children's Publishing.

—The Secret War. 2011. (Jack Blank Adventure Ser.: 2). (ENG., Illus.). 544p. (J). (gr. 3-7). lib. bdg. 16.99 (978-1-4169-9564-7(1), Simon & Schuster/Paula Wiseman Bks.) Simon & Schuster/Paula Wiseman Bks.

Nadol, Jen. The Mark. (ENG.). (YA). (gr. 9-12). 2011. 256p. pap. 8.99 (978-1-59990-660-7(0), 9781599906607) 2010. 240p. 16.99 (978-1-59990-431-3(4), 9781599904313) Bloomsbury Publishing USA. (Bloomsbury USA Childrens).

Nannestad, Katrina. When Mischief Came to Town. 2016. (ENG.). 192p. (J). (gr. 5-7). 16.99 (978-0-544-53432-2(8), HMH Books For Young Readers) Houghton Mifflin Harcourt Publishing Co.

Napoli, Donna Jo. Dark Shimmer. 2015. (ENG., Illus.). 368p. (YA). (gr. 9). 16.99 (978-0-385-74655-7(5), Lamb, Wendy Bks.) Random Hse. Children's Bks.

Naylor, Phyllis Reynolds. Emily & Jackson Hiding Out. (ENG.). 176p. (J). (gr. 2-5). 2013. 6.99 (978-0-375-87185-6(3), Yearling) 2012. (Illus.). 14.99 (978-0-385-74097-5(2), Delacorte Bks. for Young Readers) Random Hse. Children's Bks.

—Emily's Fortune. 2011. (ENG.). 160p. (J). (gr. 3-7). 6.99 (978-0-375-84492-8(9), Yearling) Random Hse. Children's Bks.

—Sang Spell. 224p. (YA). (gr. 5-18). pap. 4.99 (978-0-8072-8294-6(4), Listening Library) Random Hse. Audio Publishing Group.

—Sang Spell. 2013. (ENG., Illus.). 224p. (YA). (gr. 7). pap. 13.99 (978-1-4814-1589-7(1), Atheneum Bks. for Young Readers) Simon & Schuster Children's Publishing.

Nelson, Suzanne. Serendipity's Footsteps. 2015. (ENG.). 368p. (YA). (gr. 7). 17.99 (978-0-385-39212-9(5), Knopf Bks. for Young Readers) Random Hse. Children's Bks.

Nibali, Ellen Cook. Secret of St. Nicholas. 2010. 32p. 16.95 (978-0-9818154-1-1(3)) Fairland Bks.

Nielsen, Jennifer A. The False Prince. 2012. (Ascendance Trilogy: Bk. 1). (ENG.). (J). (gr. 5-8). 64.99 (978-1-61707-596-4(5)) Findaway World, LLC.

—The False Prince. 2013. (False Prince Ser.: Bk. 1). (ENG.). 352p. (J). (gr. 5-9). pap. 7.99 (978-0-545-28414-1(7), Scholastic Paperbacks) 2012. (Ascendance Trilogy Ser.: 1). (ENG., Illus.). 352p. (J). (gr. 4-7). 17.99 (978-0-545-28413-4(9), Scholastic Pr.) 2012. (Ascendance Trilogy: Bk. 1). 352p. pap. 17.99 (978-0-545-39249-5(7)) 2012. (Ascendance Trilogy: Bk. 1). (Illus.). 342p. (J). pap. (978-0-545-43347-1(9), Scholastic Pr.) Scholastic, Inc.

—The False Prince. 2013. (Ascendance Trilogy Ser.: 1). lib. bdg. 18.40 (978-0-606-31491-6(1), Turtleback) Turtleback Bks.

Novak, Ali. My Life with the Walter Boys. 2014. (ENG.). 368p. (YA). (gr. 7-12). pap. 10.99 (978-1-4022-9786-1(6), 9781402297861) Sourcebooks, Inc.

Nye, Bill & Mone, Gregory. Jack & the Geniuses: At the Bottom of the World. Iluzada, Nicholas, illus. 2017. (ENG.). 256p. (J). (gr. 3-7). 13.95 (978-1-4197-2303-2(0), Amulet Bks.) Abrams, Inc.

Ogilvy, Ian. Measle & the Wrathmonk. 2004. 224p. (J). (gr. 4-6). 15.99 (978-0-06-058685-0(0)) HarperCollins Pubs.

Oladokun, Alexander. Acrux Manor: The Prodigal's Curse (Hardcover) 2013. 206p. 28.50 (978-1-300-68651-4(0)) Lulu Pr., Inc.

Olds, Barbara Anne. Haven House. Amatrula, Michele, illus. 2007. (ENG.). 141p. (J). pap. 8.95 (978-0-9744446-0-4(X)) All About Kids Publishing.

Oliveira, Luis. The DogMan 2. 2009. 60p. pap. 15.50 (978-0-578-02385-4(7)) Desktop Prepress Services.

Oliver, Jana. The Demon Trapper's Daughter. 2011. (Demon Trappers Ser.: 1). (ENG.). 368p. (YA). (gr. 7-18). pap. 9.99 (978-0-312-61478-2(0), 9780312614782, St. Martin's Griffin) St. Martin's Pr.

Oliver, Lauren. Delirium. (Delirium Trilogy Ser.: 1). (ENG.). 480p. (YA). (gr. 9-18). 2016. pap. 9.99 (978-0-06-172683-5(4)) 2011. 17.99 (978-0-06-211243-9(0)) HarperCollins Pubs.

—Delirium. 2016. (Delirium Ser.: 1). (YA). lib. bdg. 20.85 (978-0-606-23575-4(2), Turtleback) Turtleback Bks.

—Delirium Stories: Hana, Annabel, Raven & Alex. (Delirium Story Ser.). 224p. (YA). (gr. 9). 2016. pap. 9.99 (978-0-06-248432-1(X)) 2013. (ENG.). pap. 9.99 (978-0-06-226778-8(7)) HarperCollins Pubs.

—Delirium Stories: Hana, Annabel, Raven & Alex. (Delirium Ser.). (YA). 2016. lib. bdg. 20.85 (978-0-606-38920-4(2)) 2013. lib. bdg. 20.85 (978-0-606-31834-1(8), Turtleback) Turtleback Bks.

—Liesl & Po. Acedera, Kei, illus. (ENG.). (J). (gr. 3-7). 2012. 336p. pap. 6.99 (978-0-06-201452-8(8)) 2011. 320p. 16.99 (978-0-06-201451-1(X)) HarperCollins Pubs.

—Liesl & Po. 2012. (J). lib. bdg. 17.20 (978-0-606-26853-0(7), Turtleback) Turtleback Bks.

Oliver, Lauren & Chester, H. C. The Screaming Statue. 2017. (Curiosity House Ser.: 2). 384p. (J). (gr. 3-7). pap. 6.99 (978-0-06-227085-6(0)) HarperCollins Pubs.

—The Shrunken Head. Lacombe, Benjamin, illus. 2015. (Curiosity House Ser.: 1). (ENG.). 368p. (J). (gr. 3-7). 16.99 (978-0-06-227081-8(8)) HarperCollins Pubs.

Oliver, Lin & Baker, Theo. The Shadow Mask, No. 2. 2013. (Sound Bender Ser.: 2). (ENG.). 368p. (J). (gr. 5-9). 16.99 (978-0-545-19694-9(9), Scholastic Pr.) Scholastic, Inc.

—Sound Bender. 2011. (ENG.). 272p. (J). (gr. 5-9). 16.99 (978-0-545-19692-5(2), Scholastic Pr.) Scholastic, Inc.

Olmstead, Kathleen & Porter, Eleanor H. Pollyanna. Akib, Jamel, illus. 2007. (Classic Starts Ser.). 154p. (J). (978-1-4287-4209-3(3)) Sterling Publishing Co., Inc.

Olswanger, Anna. Greenhorn. Nerlove, Miriam, illus. 2012. (ENG.). (J). E-Book 9.99 (978-1-60306-159-9(2)); 48p. 17.95 (978-1-58838-235-1(4)) NewSouth, Inc. (NewSouth Bks.).

Orenstein, Denise Gosliner. Unseen Companion. 2003. 368p. (J). 15.99 (978-0-06-052056-4(6)); lib. bdg. 16.89 (978-0-06-052057-1(4)) HarperCollins Pubs.

Orenstein, Denise Gosliner & Orenstein, Denise G. Unseen Companion. 2005. (ENG.). 368p. (YA). (gr. 8). reprint ed. pap. 7.99 (978-0-06-052058-8(2), Tegen, Katherine Bks) HarperCollins Pubs.

Orlean, Susan & Bradford, Chris. Young Samurai the Way of the Warrior. l.t. ed. 2011. (Young Samurai Ser.). (ENG.). 628p. (J). 23.99 (978-1-4104-4329-8(9)) Thorndike Pr.

Ormsbee, K. E. The Doorway & the Deep. 2016. (ENG., Illus.). 480p. (J). (gr. 3-7). 16.99 (978-1-4521-3636-3(X)) Chronicle Bks. LLC.

—The Water & the Wild. Mora, Elsa, illus. 2015. (ENG.). 448p. (J). (gr. 3-7). 16.99 (978-1-4521-1386-9(6)) Chronicle Bks. LLC.

Osborne, Jill. Riley Mae & the Sole Fire Safari, 1 vol. 2014. (Faithgirlz / the Good News Shoes Ser.). (ENG.). 256p. (J). pap. 7.99 (978-0-310-74283-8(8)) Zonderkidz.

Otis, James. Peter of New Amsterdam: A story of Old New York. 2007. 136p. per. 9.95 (978-0-9790876-2-2(7)) Living Bks. Pr.

Ott, Alexandra. Rules for Thieves. 2017. (Rules for Thieves Ser.: 1). (ENG., Illus.). 320p. (J). (gr. 3-7). 17.99 **(978-1-4814-7274-6(7)**, Aladdin) Simon & Schuster Children's Publishing.

—Rules for Thieves. 2017. (J). pap. **(978-1-4814-7275-3(5)**, Simon & Schuster/Paula Wiseman Bks.) Simon & Schuster/Paula Wiseman Bks.

Otten, Charlotte F. Home in a Wilderness Fort: Copper Harbor 1844. 2006. (Illus.). 232p. (J). (gr. 2-7). per. 14.95 (978-0-9766104-5-8(0)) Arbutus Pr.

Palmer, Pamela. Horse of the Dawn. 2005. 89p. pap. 16.95 (978-1-4137-9545-5(5)) PublishAmerica, Inc.

Papemy, Myra. The Greenies. 2007. (ENG.). 304p. (J). mass mkt. 6.99 (978-0-00-639356-6(X), Harper Trophy) HarperCollins Pubs.

Papp, Robert, illus. The Amazing Mystery Show. 2010. (Boxcar Children Mysteries Ser.: 123). (ENG.). 128p. (J). (gr. 1-5). pap. 6.99 (978-0-8075-0315-7(0));No. 123. 14.99 (978-0-8075-0314-0(2)) Whitman, Albert & Co.

—The Clue in the Recycling Bin. 2011. (Boxcar Children Mysteries Ser.: 126). (ENG.). 128p. (J). (gr. 1-5). pap. 6.99 (978-0-8075-1209-8(5)) Whitman, Albert & Co.

—The Clue in the Recycling Bin. 2011. (Boxcar Children Mysteries Ser.: 126). (ENG.). 128p. (J). (gr. 1-5). lib. bdg. 14.99 (978-0-8075-1208-1(7)) Whitman, Albert & Co.

—The Creature in Ogopogo Lake. 2006. (Boxcar Children Mysteries Ser.: 108). (ENG.). 128p. (J). (gr. 1-5). per. 6.99 (978-0-8075-1337-8(7)) Whitman, Albert & Co.

—The Ghost of the Chattering Bones. 2007. (Boxcar Children Ser.). 120p. 15.00 (978-0-7569-7611-8(1)) Perfection Learning Corp.

—The Ghost of the Chattering Bones. 2005. (Boxcar Children Mysteries Ser.: 102). (ENG.). 128p. (J). (gr. 1-5). pap. 5.99 (978-0-8075-0874-9(8)) Whitman, Albert & Co.

—The Giant Yo-Yo Mystery. 2006. (Boxcar Children Mysteries Ser.: 107). (ENG.). 128p. (J). (gr. 1-5). per. 5.99 (978-0-8075-0879-4(9)) Whitman, Albert & Co.

—The Great Detective Race. 2008. (Boxcar Children Mysteries Ser.: 115). (ENG.). 128p. (J). (gr. 1-5). 14.99 (978-0-8075-5573-6(8)) Whitman, Albert & Co.

—The Great Detective Race. 2008. (Boxcar Children Mysteries Ser.: 115). (ENG.). 128p. (J). (gr. 1-5). pap. 5.99 (978-0-8075-5574-3(6)) Whitman, Albert & Co.

—The Great Turkey Heist. 2011. (Boxcar Children Mysteries Ser.: 129). (ENG.). (J). (gr. 1-5). 144p. 6.99 (978-0-8075-3051-1(4)); 128p. lib. bdg. 14.99 (978-0-8075-3050-4(6)) Whitman, Albert & Co.

—Monkey Trouble. 2011. (Boxcar Children Mysteries Ser.: 127). (ENG.). 128p. (J). (gr. 1-5). pap. 5.99 (978-0-8075-5240-7(2)) Whitman, Albert & Co.

—Monkey Trouble. 2011. (Boxcar Children Mysteries Ser.: 127). (ENG.). 128p. (J). (gr. 1-5). lib. bdg. 14.99 (978-0-8075-5239-1(9)) Whitman, Albert & Co.

—The Rock 'n' Roll Mystery. 2006. (Boxcar Children Mysteries Ser.: 109). (ENG.). 128p. (J). (gr. 1-5). lib. bdg. 14.99 (978-0-8075-7089-0(3)); per. 5.99 (978-0-8075-7090-6(7)) Whitman, Albert & Co.

—The Seattle Puzzle. 2007. (Boxcar Children Mysteries Ser.: 111). (ENG.). 128p. (J). (gr. 1-5). lib. bdg. 14.99 (978-0-8075-5560-6(6)); per. 5.99 (978-0-8075-5561-3(4)) Whitman, Albert & Co.

—Spooktacular Special. 2013. (Boxcar Children Mysteries Ser.). (ENG.). 400p. (J). (gr. 1-5). 9.99 (978-0-8075-7605-2(0)) Whitman, Albert & Co.

—The Spy in the Bleachers. 2010. (Boxcar Children Mysteries Ser.: 122). (ENG.). 128p. (J). (gr. 1-5). 14.99 (978-0-8075-7606-9(9));No. 122. pap. 6.99 (978-0-8075-7607-6(7)) Whitman, Albert & Co.

—The Sword of the Silver Knight. 2005. (Boxcar Children Mysteries Ser.: 103). (ENG.). 128p. (J). (gr. 1-5). per. 6.99 (978-0-8075-0876-3(4)) Whitman, Albert & Co.

—The Vanishing Passenger. 2006. (Boxcar Children Mysteries Ser.: 106). (ENG.). 128p. (J). (gr. 1-5). 14.99 (978-0-8075-1066-7(1)) Whitman, Albert & Co.

—The Zombie Project. 2011. (Boxcar Children Mysteries Ser.: 128). (ENG.). 128p. (J). (gr. 1-5). 6.99 (978-0-8075-9493-3(8)); lib. bdg. 14.99 (978-0-8075-9492-6(X)) Whitman, Albert & Co.

Papp, Robert L., illus. The Dog-Gone Mystery. 2009. (Boxcar Children Mysteries Ser.: 119). (ENG.). 128p. (J). (gr. 1-5). lib. bdg. 14.99 (978-0-8075-1658-4(9)) Whitman, Albert & Co.

—The Spy Game. 2009. (Boxcar Children Mysteries Ser.: 118). (ENG.). 128p. (J). (gr. 1-5). 14.99 (978-0-8075-7603-8(4)) Whitman, Albert & Co.

Parker, Richard. Voyage to Tasmani. Seward, Prudence, illus. 2011. 128p. 40.95 (978-1-258-08572-8(0)) Literary Licensing, LLC.

Parry, Rosanne. Written in Stone. 2014. (ENG., Illus.). 208p. (J). (gr. 4-7). pap. 6.99 (978-0-375-87135-1(7), Yearling) Random Hse. Children's Bks.

Patterson, James. Armageddon. 2012. (Daniel X Ser.: 5). (ENG.). 304p. (J). (gr. 3-7). 16.99 (978-0-316-10179-0(6), Jimmy Patterson) Little Brown & Co.

—The Dangerous Days of Daniel X. 2014. lthr. 79.00 (978-1-62715-506-9(6)) Leatherbound Bestsellers.

—The Dangerous Days of Daniel X. (Daniel X Ser.: 1). (ENG.). 2010. 272p. (J). (gr. 3-7). pap. 8.00 (978-0-316-11970-2(9), Jimmy Patterson) 2008. 304p. pap. 20.99 (978-0-316-03025-0(2)) Little Brown & Co.

—The Dangerous Days of Daniel X. 2010. (Daniel X Ser.: 1). (J). lib. bdg. 18.45 (978-0-606-14720-0(9), Turtleback) Turtleback Bks.

—Demons & Druids. 2011. (Daniel X Ser.: 3). (ENG.). 304p. (J). (gr. 3-7). pap., pap. 8.00 (978-0-316-03830-0(X), Jimmy Patterson) Little Brown & Co.

—Watch the Skies. 2014. lthr. 79.00 (978-1-62715-571-7(6)) Leatherbound Bestsellers.

—Watch the Skies. l.t. ed. 2009. (Daniel X Ser.: 2). (ENG.). 352p. pap. 21.99 (978-0-316-04363-2(X)) Little Brown & Co.

—Watch the Skies. 2010. (Daniel X Ser.: 2). (J). lib. bdg. 18.45 (978-0-606-10550-7(6), Turtleback) Turtleback Bks.

Patterson, James & Grabenstein, Chris. Armageddon. 2013. (Daniel X Ser.: 5). (ENG.). 320p. (J). (gr. 3-7). pap. 8.00 (978-0-316-10177-6(X), Jimmy Patterson) Little Brown & Co.

—Armageddon. 2013. (Daniel X Ser.: 5). (J). lib. bdg. 18.45 (978-0-606-31747-4(3), Turtleback) Turtleback Bks.

—Daniel X: Lights Out. 2015. (Daniel X Ser.: 6). (ENG.). 272p. (J). (gr. 3-7). 17.00 (978-0-316-20745-4(4), Jimmy Patterson) Little Brown & Co.

Patterson, James & Ledwidge, Michael. The Dangerous Days of Daniel X. 2009. (Daniel X Ser.: 1). (ENG.). 288p. mass mkt. 7.99 (978-0-446-50913-8(2), Jimmy Patterson) Little Brown & Co.

Patterson, James & Rust, Ned. Game Over. 2012. (Daniel X Ser.: 4). (J). lib. bdg. 18.45 (978-0-606-26165-4(6), Turtleback) Turtleback Bks.

—Watch the Skies. 2010. (Daniel X Ser.: 2). (ENG.). 288p. (J). (gr. 3-7). pap. 8.00 (978-0-316-11969-6(5), Jimmy Patterson) Little Brown & Co.

Patterson, James & Sadler, Adam. Demons & Druids. l.t. ed. 2010. (Daniel X Ser.: 3). (ENG.). 320p. 29.99 (978-0-316-08731-5(9), Jimmy Patterson) Little Brown & Co.

Peart, Hendry. Red Falcons of Tremoine. Brevannes, Maurice, illus. 2007. (Living History Library (Bethlehem Books) Ser.). 239p. (YA). (gr. 8-12). pap. 12.95 (978-1-932350-15-9(2)) Bethlehem Bks.

Peart, Jane. Orphan Train West Trilogy. 2004. (Orphan Train West Ser.). pap. 11.98 (978-0-8007-5843-1(9)) Baker Publishing Group.

Peck, Robert Newton. Horse Thief. 2003. 277p. (YA). (gr. 7). 13.65 (978-0-7569-1461-5(2)) Perfection Learning Corp.

Peters, Julie Anne. Rage: A Love Story. 2010. (ENG.). 306p. (YA). (gr. 9). pap. 9.99 (978-0-375-84411-9(2), Knopf Bks. for Young Readers) Random Hse. Children's Bks.

Petersen, Alicia. A Sparrow Alone. 2004. 154p. (YA). 8.99 (978-1-59166-204-4(4)) BJU Pr.

Peterson Haddix, Margaret. EL DESAFÍO FINAL: THE 39 CLUES 10. 2013. (SPA.). 304p. (J). pap. 14.99 (978-84-08-10876-4(X)) Noguer y Caralt Editores, S. A. ESP. Dist: Lectorum Pubns., Inc.

Petrucha, Stefan. Ripper. 2013. (ENG.). 432p. (YA). (gr. 7). pap. 9.99 (978-0-14-242418-6(8), Speak) Penguin Young Readers Group.

Pfeffer, Susan Beth. Revenge of the Aztecs. 2004. 118p. (J). lib. bdg. 16.92 (978-1-4242-0763-3(0)) Fitzgerald Bks.

Philbrick, Rodman. The Mostly True Adventures of Homer P. Figg. (ENG.). (J). (gr. 3-7). 2011. 240p. pap. 7.99 (978-0-439-66821-7(2), Scholastic Paperbacks) 2009. 224p. 16.99 (978-0-439-66818-7(2), Blue Sky Pr., The) Scholastic, Inc.

Phillips, Dixie. One Noble Journey. Sponaugle, Kim, illus. 2009. 16p. pap. 9.95 (978-1-935137-86-3(7)) Guardian Angel Publishing, Inc.

Pickett, Lanaya A. Walking with Angels. 2011. 192p. 23.95 (978-1-4620-2306-6(1)); pap. 13.95 (978-1-4620-2307-3(X)) iUniverse, Inc.

Pierpoint, Eric. The Last Ride of Caleb O'Toole. 2013. (ENG.). 304p. (J). (gr. 4-7). pap. 7.99 (978-1-4022-8171-6(4), 9781402281716, Sourcebooks Jabberwocky) Sourcebooks, Inc.

Pinkney, Andrea Davis. Bird in a Box. Qualls, Sean, illus. 2012. (J). lib. bdg. 18.45 (978-0-606-26157-9(5), Turtleback) Turtleback Bks.

Poblocki, Dan. No Way Out. 2017. (Shadow House Ser.: 3). (ENG.). 224p. (J). (gr. 3-7). lib. bdg. 16.99 **(978-1-338-14859-6(1))**; (Illus.). 12.99 **(978-0-545-92552-5(5))** Scholastic, Inc.

Polonsky, Ami. Gracefully Grayson. 2016. (ENG., Illus.). 250p. (J). (gr. 5-9). pap. 8.99 (978-1-4847-2365-4(1)) Hyperion Bks. for Children.

—Gracefully Grayson. 2014. (ENG.). 256p. (J). (gr. 5-9). 16.99 (978-1-4231-8527-7(7)) Hyperion Pr.

Porter, Eleanor H. Pollyanna. (J). 21.95 (978-0-8488-1445-8(2)) Amereon Ltd.

—Pollyanna. 2007. (ENG.). 184p. pap. 19.99 (978-1-4346-0972-4(3)) Creative Media Partners, LLC.

—Pollyanna. 2005. 104p. per. 4.95 (978-1-4209-2555-5(5)) Digireads.com Publishing.

—Pollyanna. Date not set. (J). 14.99 (978-0-06-028226-4(6)); 32p. pap. 4.99 (978-0-06-443536-9(9)) HarperCollins Pubs.

—Pollyanna. 2016. (J). pap. (978-1-5124-2614-4(8)) Lerner Publishing Group.

—Pollyanna. McKowen, Scott, illus. 2013. (Sterling Unabridged Classics Ser.). (ENG.). 208p. (J). (gr. 5). 9.95 (978-1-4027-9718-7(4)) Sterling Publishing Co., Inc.

—Pollyanna. Akib, Jamel, illus. 2007. (Classic Starts(tm) Ser.). (ENG.). 160p. (J). (gr. 2-4). 6.95 (978-1-4027-3692-6(4)) Sterling Publishing Co., Inc.

—Pollyanna. abr. ed. 2006. 210p. (J). (gr. 3-7). per. 8.99 (978-1-59166-669-1(4)) BJU Pr.

—Pollyanna. l.t. ed. 2007. (ENG.). 206p. pap. 22.99 (978-1-4346-1071-3(3)) Creative Media Partners, LLC.

—Pollyanna. 2011. (Dover Children's Evergreen Classics Ser.). (ENG.). 208p. (J). (gr. 3-8). pap. 4.99 (978-0-486-43206-9(8)) Dover Pubns., Inc.

—Pollyanna & Pollyanna Grows Up. 2004. pap. 11.95 (978-1-4145-0603-6(1)) Pavilion Pr., Inc.

Porter, Pamela. I'll Be Watching. 2013. 336p. pap. (978-1-4596-6449-4(3)) ReadHowYouWant.com, Ltd.

Potter, Ellen. The Humming Room. 2012. (ENG.). 192p. (J). (gr. 4-7). 16.99 (978-0-312-64438-3(8), 9780312644383) Feiwel & Friends.

—The Humming Room. 2013. (ENG.). 208p. (J). (gr. 4-7). pap. 6.99 (978-1-250-01666-9(5), 9781250016669) Square Fish.

—Slob. 2009. (ENG.). 208p. (J). (gr. 3-7). 16.99 (978-0-399-24705-7(X), Philomel Bks.) Penguin Young Readers Group.

Price, Lissa. Starters. (ENG.). (YA). (gr. 7). 2013. 384p. pap. 9.99 (978-0-385-74248-1(7), Ember) 2012. 352p. 17.99 (978-0-385-74237-5(1), Delacorte Pr.) Random Hse. Children's Bks.

Price, Roy. The Gnome Guardian: Polly's Adventure. 2012. 64p. pap. 13.66 (978-1-4678-9701-3(9)) AuthorHouse.

Priestley, Chris. The Dead of Winter. 2012. (ENG., Illus.). 224p. (YA). (gr. 7-12). 16.99 (978-1-59990-745-1(3), 9781599907451, Bloomsbury USA Childrens) Bloomsbury Publishing USA.

Prineas, Sarah. Found. Caparo, Antonio Javier, illus. 2011. (Magic Thief Ser.: 3). (ENG.). 384p. (J). (gr. 5). pap. 7.99 (978-0-06-137595-8(0)) HarperCollins Pubs.

Puckett, Kelley. Batman's Dark Secret. Muth, Jon J., illus. 2015. (ENG.). 32p. (J). (gr. k-2). 17.99 (978-0-545-86755-9(X), Scholastic Pr.) Scholastic, Inc.

Pullman, Philip. The Ruby in the Smoke. 2009. 9.84 (978-0-7848-2919-6(5), Everbind) Marco Bk. Co.

—The Ruby in the Smoke. (Sally Lockhart Ser.: Bk. 1). (YA). 2008. (ENG.). 256p. (gr. 7). pap. 9.99 (978-0-375-84516-1(X), Ember) 2003. (Illus.). pap. 9.95 (978-0-375-82545-3(2), Knopf Bks. for Young Readers) Random Hse. Children's Bks.

Qualey, Marsha. Thin Ice. 2007. (YA). (978-0-9793444-0-4(9)) Quercus Pr.

Raasch, Sara. Frost Like Night. (Snow Like Ashes Ser.: 3). (YA). (gr. 9). 2017. 512p. pap. 9.99 **(978-0-06-228699-4(4))** 2016. (Illus.). 496p. 17.99 (978-0-06-228698-7(6)) HarperCollins Pubs.

—Ice Like Fire. (YA). 2016. (Snow Like Ashes Ser.: 2). 512p. (gr. 9). pap. 9.99 (978-0-06-228696-3(X)) 2015. (Snow Like Ashes Ser.: Bk. 2). (ENG., Illus.). 496p. (gr. 9-12). 17.99 (978-0-06-228695-6(1)) 2015. (Illus.). 496p. pap. **(978-0-06-242793-9(8))** HarperCollins Pubs.

—Snow Like Ashes. (Snow Like Ashes Ser.: 1). (ENG., Illus.). (YA). (gr. 9). 2015. 448p. pap. 9.99 (978-0-06-228693-2(5)) 2014. 432p. 17.99 (978-0-06-228692-5(7)) HarperCollins Pubs.

Rand, Edward A. The Knights of the White Shield: Up-the-Ladder Club Series Round One Play. 2007. 166p. pap. 19.99 *(978-1-4264-8273-1(6))*; (ENG.). 184p. pap. 21.99 *(978-1-4264-8310-3(4))* Creative Media Partners, LLC.

—The Knights of the White Shield; or, up-the-Ladder Club Series, Round One Play. 2007. 120p. per. *(978-1-4068-3739-1(3))* Echo Library.

Randall, Alice. The Diary of B. B. Bright, Possible Princess. 2012. (J). *(978-1-61858-016-0(7))* Turner Publishing Co.

Randall, Alice & Williams, Caroline Randall. The Diary of B. B. Bright, Possible Princess. Strickland, Shadra, illus. 2012. (ENG.). 192p. (J). (gr. 2-6). 19.95 *(978-1-61858-015-3(9))* Turner Publishing Co.

Redding, LaTisha. Calling the Water Drum, 1 vol. Boyd, Aaron, illus. 2016. (ENG.). 32p. (J). (gr. 1-4). 17.95 *(978-1-62014-194-6(9))* Lee & Low Bks., Inc.

Reh, Rusalka. Pizzicato: The Abduction of the Magic Violin, 0 vols. Wilson, David Henry, tr. from GER. 2011. (ENG.). 132p. (J). (gr. 4-6). pap. 9.95 *(978-1-61109-004-8(0)*, 9781611090048) Amazon Publishing.

Resau, Laura. Red Glass. 2009. (ENG.). 304p. (YA). (gr. 7). pap. 8.99 *(978-0-440-24025-9(5)*, Delacorte Bks. for Young Readers) Random Hse. Children's Bks.

Rewa. Molly May on the High Seas. (Illus.). 9.95 *(978-0-9726375-1-0(6))* Little Red Cat Publishing.

Richards, Laura E. Captain January. 2004. reprint ed. pap. 1.99 *(978-1-4192-1199-7(4))*; pap. 15.95 *(978-1-4191-1199-0(X))* Kessinger Publishing, LLC.

Richardson, Arleta. Across the Border. 2016. (Beyond the Orphan Train Ser.: 4). (ENG.). 192p. (J). (gr. 3-6). pap. 7.99 *(978-0-7814-1358-9(3))* Cook, David C.

—Prairie Homestead. 2016. (Beyond the Orphan Train Ser.: 3). (ENG.). 192p. (J). pap. 7.99 *(978-0-7814-1357-2(5))* Cook, David C.

—Whistle Stop West. 2003. (Orphans' Journey Ser.: Vol. 2). 144p. (J). (gr. 3-7). pap., pap. 5.99 *(978-0-7814-3537-6(4)*, 0781435374) Cook, David C.

Riggs, Ransom. Library of Souls. 2015. (Miss Peregrine's Peculiar Children Ser.: Bk. 3). (ENG., Illus.). 464p. (YA). (gr. 9). 18.99 *(978-1-59474-758-8(X))* Quirk Bks.

—Library of Souls. 2017. (Miss Peregrine's Peculiar Children Ser.: 3). (ENG.). (YA). (gr. 9). lib. bdg. 23.30 ***(978-0-606-39808-4(2))*** Turtleback Bks.

Rigsby, Annelle & Raffa, Edwina. Race to Kitty Hawk. 2003. (Adventures in America Ser.). (Illus.). 84p. (gr. 4). 14.95 *(978-1-893110-33-5(8))* Silver Moon Pr.

Riley, Clifford. Operation Trinity. 2012. (39 Clues: the Cahill Files Ser.). (ENG.). 144p. (J). (gr. 3-7). 9.99 *(978-0-545-43143-9(3))* Scholastic, Inc.

Rinaldi, Ann. Juliet's Moon. 2010. (ENG., Illus.). 256p. (YA). (gr. 7). pap. 14.99 *(978-0-547-25874-4(7))* Houghton Mifflin Harcourt Publishing Co.

Rioux, Jo. The Golden Twine. Rioux, Jo, illus. 2012. (Cat's Cradle Ser.: 1). (ENG., Illus.). 112p. (J). (gr. 4-7). 9.95 *(978-1-55453-637-5(5))* Kids Can Pr., Ltd. CAN. Dist: Hachette Bk. Group.

Ritter, John H. Desperado Who Stole Baseball. 2010. (ENG.). 288p. (J). (gr. 5-18). 7.99 *(978-0-14-241507-8(3)*, Puffin Books) Penguin Young Readers Group.

Roberts, Kelly Hughes. The Road to Chianti. 2012. 214p. (gr. 4-6). 33.99 *(978-1-4525-5963-6(5))*; pap. 15.99 *(978-1-4525-5961-2(9))* Balboa Pr.

Robins, Eleanor. The Secret Message, 1 vol. unabr. ed. 2011. (Carter High Mysteries Ser.). (ENG.). 48p. (YA). (gr. 9-12). 7.95 *(978-1-61651-568-3(6))* Saddleback Educational Publishing, Inc.

Roesti, Delores. Mareena Maree Mulligan & the Flying Wheel Chair: Book 1: School Days. 2007. 81p. pap. 9.95 *(978-0-7414-4048-8(2))* Infinity Publishing.

Roman, Annette. 1 World Manga, Vol. 5. Ng, Leandro, illus. 2007. (1 World Manga Ser.). (ENG.). 240p. pap. 3.99 *(978-1-4215-1169-6(X))* Viz Media.

Rosen, Lev Ac & Rosen, Ellis J. Woundabout. Rosen, Lev Ac & Rosen, Ellis J., illus. 2015. (ENG., Illus.). 288p. (J). (gr. 3-7). 17.00 *(978-0-316-37078-3(9))* Little Brown & Co.

Ross, Alice & Ross, Kent. La Dama de Cobre. Bowman, Leslie, illus. 2006. (Yo Solo - Historia (on My Own - History) Ser.). (SPA.). 48p. (gr. 2-4). lib. bdg. 25.26 *(978-0-8225-6262-7(6))* Lerner Publishing Group.

Ross, Joel. The Fog Diver. 2015. (Fog Diver Ser.: 1). (ENG.). 336p. (J). (gr. 3-7). 16.99 *(978-0-06-235293-4(8))* HarperCollins Pubs.

—The Fog Diver. 2016. (J). lib. bdg. 17.20 *(978-0-606-38745-3(5))* Turtleback Bks.

—The Lost Compass. 2016. (Fog Diver Ser.: 2). 352p. (J). (gr. 3-7). 16.99 *(978-0-06-235297-2(0))* HarperCollins Pubs.

Rossell, Judith. Withering-By-Sea. Rossell, Judith, illus. 2017. (ENG., Illus.). 288p. (J). (gr. 3-7). pap. 7.99 *(978-1-4814-4368-5(2))* Simon & Schuster Children's Publishing.

Rossell, Judith. Wormwood Mire. Rossell, Judith, illus. 2017. (ENG., Illus.). 288p. (J). (gr. 3-7). 16.99 ***(978-1-4814-4370-8(4)***, Atheneum Bks. for Young Readers) Simon & Schuster Children's Publishing.

Rubright, Lynn. Mama's Window. Smith, Duane, illus. 2005. 89p. (J). 16.95 *(978-1-57480-160-6(0))* Lee & Low Bks., Inc.

Rudden, Dave. Knights of the Borrowed Dark. (Knights of the Borrowed Dark Ser.: 1). (ENG.). (J). (gr. 5). 2017. 400p. 7.99 ***(978-0-553-52300-3(7)***, Yearling) 2016. 384p. 16.99 *(978-0-553-52297-6(3)*, Random Hse. Bks. for Young Readers) Random Hse. Children's Bks.

Rue, Nancy N. Sophie Steps Up, 1 vol. 2009. (Faithgirlz! Ser.: No. 4). (ENG.). 128p. (J). pap. 6.99 *(978-0-310-71841-3(4))* Zonderkidz.

Rundell, Katherine. Cartwheeling in Thunderstorms. Castrillón, Melissa, illus. 2014. (ENG.). 256p. (J). (gr. 3-7). 17.99 *(978-1-4424-9061-1(6)*, Simon & Schuster Bks. For Young Readers) Simon & Schuster Bks. For Young Readers.

—Cartwheeling in Thunderstorms. 2016. lib. bdg. 18.40 *(978-0-606-38273-1(9))* Turtleback Bks.

Russell, Christopher. Dogboy. 2006. 272p. (J). (gr. 5). 15.99 *(978-0-06-084116-4(8)*, Greenwillow Bks.) HarperCollins Pubs.

Ryan, Carrie. Daughter of Deep Silence. 2015. (ENG.). 384p. (YA). (gr. 9). 17.99 *(978-0-525-42650-9(7)*, Dutton Books for Young Readers) Penguin Young Readers Group.

Ryan, Frank P. The Snowmelt River. 2013. (Three Powers Ser.: 1). (ENG.). 720p. (J). (gr. 7-17). 15.95 *(978-1-62365-048-3(8)*, Jo Fletcher Books) Quercus NA.

Ryan, Margaret. Magic Mistakes! Murfin, Teresa, illus. 2010. (Airy Fairy Ser.). (ENG.). 80p. (gr. 2-4). lib. bdg. 24.21 *(978-1-59961-499-1(5))* Spotlight.

Salerni, Dianne K. The Eighth Day. McClellan, David, illus. (Eighth Day Ser.: 1). (ENG.). (J). (gr. 3-7). 2015. 336p. pap. 6.99 *(978-0-06-227216-4(0))* 2014. 320p. 16.99 *(978-0-06-227215-7(2))* HarperCollins Pubs.

—The Inquisitor's Mark. 2015. (Eighth Day Ser.: 2). (ENG.). 352p. (J). (gr. 3-7). 16.99 *(978-0-06-227218-8(7))* HarperCollins Pubs.

—The Morrigan's Curse. 2016. (Eighth Day Ser.: 3). 400p. (J). (gr. 3-7). 16.99 *(978-0-06-227221-8(7))* HarperCollins Pubs.

Sanchez, Jenny Torres. Because of the Sun. 2017. (ENG.). 272p. (YA). (gr. 7). 17.99 *(978-0-399-55145-1(X)*, Delacorte Pr.) Random Hse. Children's Bks.

Sandwall-Bergstrom, Martha. Goldie at the Farm. Stalsjo, Eva, illus. 24p. 17.95 *(978-0-86315-485-0(9))* Floris Bks. GBR. Dist: SteinerBooks, Inc.

Sandwall-Bergström, Martha. Goldie at the Orphanage, 1 vol. Stålsjö, Eva, illus. 2004. (ENG.). 24p. (J). 16.95 *(978-0-86315-443-0(3))* Floris Bks. GBR. Dist: SteinerBooks, Inc.

Saunders, Margaret Marshall. Tilda Jane: A Rambunctious Orphan's Misadventures Finding a Home in the Early 1900s. 2008. (Fiction Treasures Ser.). (ENG.). 318p. pap. 16.95 *(978-0-88780-780-0(1)*, 9780887807800) Formac Publishing Co., Ltd. CAN. Dist: Casemate Pubs. & Bk. Distributors, LLC.

Savage, Melissa. Lemons. 2017. (ENG.). 320p. (J). (gr. 3-7). 16.99 ***(978-1-5247-0012-6(6))***; lib. bdg. 19.99 ***(978-1-5247-0013-3(4))*** Random Hse. Children's Bks. (Crown Books For Young Readers).

Scarrow, Kristine. Throwaway Girl. 2014. (ENG.). 176p. (YA). pap. 12.99 *(978-1-4597-1407-6(5))* Dundurn CAN. Dist: Ingram Publisher Services.

Scattergood, Augusta. The Way to Stay in Destiny. 2015. (ENG.). 192p. (J). (gr. 3-7). 16.99 *(978-0-545-53824-4(6)*, Scholastic Pr.) Scholastic, Inc.

Scheier, Leah. Secret Letters. 2013. (ENG., Illus.). 320p. (J). (gr. 5-17). pap. 8.99 *(978-1-4231-2758-1(7))* Hyperion Pr.

Schlitz, Laura Amy. Splendors & Glooms. (ENG.). 400p. (J). 2014. (gr. 5-9). pap. 8.99 *(978-0-7636-6926-3(1))* 2012. (Illus.). (gr. 4-7). 17.99 *(978-0-7636-5380-4(2))* Candlewick Pr.

—Splendors & Glooms. 2014. (ENG.). (J). (gr. 4-7). lib. bdg. 18.60 ***(978-1-62765-443-2(7))*** Perfection Learning Corp.

—Splendors & Glooms. 2014. lib. bdg. 18.40 *(978-0-606-35170-6(1))* Turtleback Bks.

Schmid, Susan Maupin. Ghost of a Chance. Marlin, Lissy, illus. 2017. (100 Dresses Ser.: 2). (ENG.). 320p. (J). (gr. 3-7). 16.99 *(978-0-553-53373-6(8)*, Random Hse. Bks. for Young Readers) Random Hse. Children's Bks.

Schmid, Susan Maupin. If the Magic Fits. (100 Dresses Ser.: 1). (ENG.). (J). (gr. 3-7). 2017. 320p. 7.99 ***(978-0-553-53369-9(X)***, Yearling) 2016. (Illus.). 304p. 16.99 *(978-0-553-53366-8(5)*, Random Hse. Bks. for Young Readers) Random Hse. Children's Bks.

Scholastic, Inc. Staff & Glass, Calliope. Annie - A True Family. 2014. (ENG., Illus.). 32p. (J). (gr. 1-3). pap. 3.99 *(978-0-545-79752-8(7))* Scholastic, Inc.

Scholastic, Inc. Staff & Ryals, Lexi. Annie. movie tie-in ed. 2014. (ENG., Illus.). 144p. (J). (gr. 2-5). pap. 5.99 *(978-0-545-79751-1(9))* Scholastic, Inc.

Schrefer, Eliot. Threatened. 2014. (ENG., Illus.). 288p. (J). (gr. 7). 17.99 *(978-0-545-55143-4(9)*, Scholastic Pr.) Scholastic, Inc.

Scott, Elaine. Secrets of the Cirque Medrano. 2008. (ENG., Illus.). 216p. (J). (gr. 5-9). 15.95 *(978-1-57091-712-7(4))* Charlesbridge Publishing, Inc.

—The Spanish Web: An Encounter with Picasso. 2004. (Art Encounters Ser.). (J). 15.95 *(978-0-8230-0410-2(4))*; pap. 6.99 *(978-0-8230-0413-3(9))* Watson-Guptill Pubns., Inc.

Seabag-Montefiore, Mary, retold by. David Copperfield. 2008. (Young Reading Series 3 Gift Books - Famous Lives Ser.). 64p. (J). 8.99 *(978-0-7945-2097-7(9)*, Usborne) EDC Publishing.

Seabrooke, Brenda. Stonewolf. 2004. (ENG.). 240p. (J). (gr. 7-18). tchr. ed. 16.95 *(978-0-8234-1848-0(0))* Holiday Hse., Inc.

Sedgwick, Julian. The Black Dragon. Moffett, Patricia, illus. 2016. (Mysterium Ser.: 1). (ENG.). 352p. (gr. 4-8). 18.99 *(978-1-4677-7567-0(3))*; 38.65 *(978-1-4677-9555-5(0))* Lerner Publishing Group. (Carolrhoda Bks.).

Sedgwick, Marcus. The Book of Dead Days. 2006. (ENG.). 288p. (YA). (gr. 5-12). reprint ed. per. 7.99 *(978-0-385-74704-2(7)*, Lamb, Wendy Bks.) Random Hse. Children's Bks.

Seidler, Tor. The Dulcimer Boy. Selznick, Brian, illus. 2003. 160p. (J). (gr. 3-7). lib. bdg. 16.89 *(978-0-06-623610-0(X))* HarperCollins Pubs.

—The Dulcimer Boy. Selznick, Brian, illus. 2004. 153p. (gr. 5-7). 17.00 *(978-0-7569-3520-7(2))* Perfection Learning Corp.

Seki, Sunny. Yuko-Chan & the Daruma Doll: The Adventures of a Blind Japanese Girl Who Saves Her Village. 2012. (ENG., Illus.). 32p. (J). (gr. -1-3). 15.95 *(978-4-8053-1187-5(8))* Tuttle Publishing.

Selznick, Brian. The Invention of Hugo Cabret. 2007. (CHI., Illus.). 534p. (J). *(978-957-570-894-8(6))* Eastern Publishing Co., Ltd., The.

—The Invention of Hugo Cabret. 2008. (CHI., Illus.). 465p. (J). pap. *(978-7-5448-0279-6(5))* Jieli Publishing Hse.

—The Invention of Hugo Cabret. Selznick, Brian, illus. 2007. (Illus.). (ENG.). 544p. (J). (gr. 4-7). 24.99 *(978-0-439-81378-5(6)*, Scholastic Pr.); 534p. *(978-1-4071-0348-8(2))* Scholastic, Inc.

Seredy, Kate. Philomena. Seredy, Kate, illus. 2008. (Illus.). 93p. (J). pap. 11.95 *(978-1-932350-19-7(5))* Bethlehem Bks.

Seydou, Garba B. The One Man Army. 2012. 58p. pap. 16.95 *(978-1-4626-8958-3(2))* America Star Bks.

Shapiro, David L. Sara's Journey. 2005. (ENG.). 224p. (gr. 7-12). per. 16.95 *(978-0-8276-0776-7(8))* Jewish Pubn. Society.

Sharenow, Robert. The Girl in the Torch. 2015. (ENG.). 304p. (J). (gr. 3-7). 16.99 *(978-0-06-222795-9(5))* HarperCollins Pubs.

Sharplin, Emory. Scrap. 2013. 352p. (J). pap. 10.95 *(978-1-938416-35-4(X))* River Grove Bks.

Shearer, Alex. Sky Run. 2014. (Cloud Hunters Ser.). (ENG.). 288p. (J). (gr. 2-7). 14.95 *(978-1-62873-593-2(7)*, Sky Pony Pr.) Skyhorse Publishing Co., Inc.

Shefelman, Janice Jordan. Anna Maria's Gift. Papp, Robert, illus. 2011. (Stepping Stone Book Ser.). (ENG.). 112p. (J). (gr. 2-5). pap. 4.99 *(978-0-375-85882-6(2)*, Random Hse. Bks. for Young Readers) Random Hse. Children's Bks.

Showalter, Gena. Alice in Zombieland. 2013. lib. bdg. 20.85 *(978-0-606-31712-2(0)*, Turtleback) Turtleback Bks.

Silver, Shana & Shane, Rachel. Alice in Wonderland High. 2015. (ENG.). 300p. (YA). 17.99 *(978-1-4405-8466-4(4)*, Simon Pulse) Simon Pulse.

Simmons, Andrew & Averdonz, N. R. I Was an Eighth-Grade Ninja, 1 vol. Padilla, Ariel, illus. 2007. (Z Graphic Novels / Tomo Ser.). (ENG.). 160p. (J). (gr. 3-7). pap. 6.99 *(978-0-310-71300-5(5))* Zondervan.

Simon, Nadine. Flickers of True Destiny. 2010. 58p. pap. 11.95 *(978-1-60860-948-2(0)*, Eloquent Bks.) Strategic Book Publishing & Rights Agency (SBPRA).

Skot, Joelle. The Legend of the Blue Squid. 2008. (Illus.). (J). per. 16.99 *(978-1-933156-16-3(3)*, Visikid Bks.) GSVQ Publishing.

Skrypuch, Marsha Forchuk. Nobody's Child. 2003. (ENG.). 200p. (YA). (gr. 7). pap. 8.99 *(978-1-55002-442-5(6))* Dundurn CAN. Dist: Ingram Publisher Services.

Sleiman, Dina L. Dauntless. 2015. (Valiant Hearts Ser.: 1). (ENG.). 368p. (YA). pap. 13.99 *(978-0-7642-1312-0(1))* Bethany Hse. Pubs.

Sloan, Holly Goldberg. Counting by 7s. 2015. (CHI.). 392p. (J). pap. *(978-986-6104-68-8(0))* DaskoviK, Izdatel'sko-torgovaja korporacija.

—Counting by 7s. 2013. (ENG.). 384p. (YA). (gr. 5). 17.99 *(978-0-8037-3855-3(2)*, Dial Bks) Penguin Publishing Group.

—Counting by 7s. 2014. (ENG.). 400p. (J). (gr. 5). 8.99 *(978-0-14-242286-1(X)*, Puffin Books) Penguin Young Readers Group.

—Counting by 7s. 2014. (ENG.). (J). (gr. 5). lib. bdg. 19.60 ***(978-1-62765-616-0(2))*** Perfection Learning Corp.

—Counting by 7s. 2014. (gr. 5-8). lib. bdg. 19.65 *(978-0-606-36583-3(4))* Turtleback Bks.

Smelcer, John. The Great Death. 2009. (ENG.). 176p. (YA). (gr. 5-9). 17.99 *(978-0-8050-8100-8(3)*, 9780805081008, Holt, Henry & Co. Bks. For Young Readers) Holt, Henry & Co.

Smith, Cynthia Leitich. Blessed. (Tantalize Ser.). (ENG., Illus.). (YA). (gr. 9). 2012. 464p. pap. 8.99 *(978-0-7636-5479-5(5))* 2011. 480p. 17.99 *(978-0-7636-4326-3(2))* Candlewick Pr.

—Tantalize. 2007. (Tantalize Ser.). (ENG., Illus.). 336p. (YA). (gr. 9-12). 16.99 *(978-0-7636-2791-1(7))* Candlewick Pr.

Smith, Sarah. The Other Side of Dark. (ENG., 320p. (YA). (gr. 7). 2011. Illus.). pap. 11.99 *(978-1-4424-0281-2(4))* 2010. 16.99 *(978-1-4424-0280-5(6))* Simon & Schuster Children's Publishing. (Atheneum Bks. for Young Readers).

Smithem, Beth. Cocoa Bean & Squirt. 2010. 68p. pap. 10.49 *(978-1-4520-1929-1(0))* AuthorHouse.

Snedeker, Caroline. Downright Dencey. Barney, Maginel Wright, illus. 2003. (Young Adult Library). 268p. (YA). pap. 12.95 *(978-1-883937-79-9(5))* Bethlehem Bks.

Snicket, Lemony, pseud. El Ascensor Artificioso. 2004. (Coleccion Una Serie de Catastroficas Desdichas A Series of Unfortunate Events Ser.). (SPA., Illus.). 232p. (YA). 12.95 *(978-84-8441-215-1(6))* Grijalbo Mondadori, S.A.-Montena ESP. Dist: Lectorum Pubns., Inc.

—The Austere Academy. Helquist, Brett, illus. 2008. (Series of Unfortunate Events Ser.: Bk. 5). (ENG.). 240p. (J). (gr. 5-18). pap. 6.99 *(978-0-06-114634-3(X)*, Harper Trophy) HarperCollins Pubs.

—The Bad Beginning. 2007. (Ser. of Unfortunate Events Ser.: 1). (J). lib. bdg. 17.20 *(978-1-4177-8840-8(2)*, Turtleback) Turtleback Bks.

—The Bad Beginning No. 1: Or, Orphans! Helquist, Brett & Kupperman, Michael, illus. 2007. (Series of Unfortunate Events Ser.: 1). (ENG.). 176p. (J). (gr. 5-9). pap. 7.99 *(978-0-06-114630-5(7))* HarperCollins Pubs.

—Una Funesta Finestra. pap. 21.95 *(978-88-7782-953-5(2))* Salani ITA. Dist: Distribooks, Inc.

—The Gloom Looms, Bks. 10-12. Helquist, Brett, illus. 2005. (Series of Unfortunate Events Ser.: Bks. 10-12). (J). (gr. 5). 41.99 *(978-0-06-083909-3(0))* HarperCollins Pubs.

—The Grim Grotto. Helquist, Brett & Kupperman, Michael, illus. 2004. (Series of Unfortunate Events Ser.: 11). (ENG.). 352p. (J). (gr. 5-6). 13.99 *(978-0-06-441014-4(5))* HarperCollins Pubs.

—Un Infausto Inizio. pap. 23.95 *(978-88-7782-951-1(6))* Salani ITA. Dist: Distribooks, Inc.

—The Loathsome Library, Bks. 1-6. Helquist, Brett, illus. 2005. (Series of Unfortunate Events Ser.: Bks. 1-6). (J). (gr. 5). 65.00 *(978-0-06-083353-4(X))* HarperCollins Pubs.

—The Miserable Mill, 13 vols. Helquist, Brett, illus. 2008. (Series of Unfortunate Events Ser.: Bk. 4). (ENG.). 208p. (J). (gr. 5-18). pap. 6.99 *(978-0-06-114632-9(3)*, Harper Trophy) HarperCollins Pubs.

—Piege au College. pap. 24.95 *(978-2-09-282599-0(2))* Nathan, Fernand FRA. Dist: Distribooks, Inc.

—The Reptile Room: Or, Murder! Helquist, Brett & Kupperman, Michael, illus. 2007. (Series of Unfortunate Events Ser.: 2). (ENG.). 192p. (J). (gr. 5-9). pap. 6.99 *(978-0-06-114631-2(5))* HarperCollins Pubs.

—The Slippery Slope. Helquist, Brett, illus. 2003. (Series of Unfortunate Events Ser.: Bk. 10). (YA). (gr. 5-18). 197.82 *(978-0-06-057743-8(6))*; 352p. (J). (gr. 3-6). lib. bdg. 15.89 *(978-0-06-029641-4(0))* HarperCollins Pubs.

—The Slippery Slope. Helquist, Brett & Kupperman, Michael, illus. 2003. (Series of Unfortunate Events Ser.: 10). (ENG.). 352p. (J). (gr. 5-6). 13.99 *(978-0-06-441013-7(7))* HarperCollins Pubs.

—The Trouble Begins. Helquist, Brett, illus. movie tie-in ed. 2004. (Series of Unfortunate Events Ser.: Bks. 1-3). (J). 35.99 *(978-0-06-075773-1(6))* HarperCollins Pubs.

—The Wide Window - Or, Disappearance! Helquist, Brett & Kupperman, Michael, illus. 2007. (Series of Unfortunate Events Ser.: 3). (ENG.). 208p. (J). (gr. 5). pap. 6.99 *(978-0-06-114633-6(1))* HarperCollins Pubs.

Sniegoski, Thomas E. Aerie & Reckoning. 2010. (Fallen Ser.: 2). (ENG.). 576p. (YA). (gr. 11-18). pap. 9.99 *(978-1-4424-0863-0(4)*, Simon Pulse) Simon Pulse.

—End of Days Vol. 3. 2011. (Fallen Ser.: 3). (ENG.). 384p. (YA). (gr. 9). pap. 9.99 *(978-1-4424-2349-7(8)*, Simon Pulse) Simon Pulse.

—The Fallen & Leviathan. 2010. (Fallen Ser.: 1). (ENG.). 544p. (YA). (gr. 11). pap. 11.99 *(978-1-4424-0862-3(6)*, Simon Pulse) Simon Pulse.

Snowe, Olivia. Hansen & Gracie, 1 vol. Lamoreaux, Michelle, illus. 2014. (Twicetold Tales Ser.). (ENG.). 128p. (gr. 3-4). pap. 5.95 *(978-1-4342-9150-9(2))* Stone Arch Bks.

Snyder, Laurel. Orphan Island. 2017. 288p. (J). (gr. 3-7). 16.99 *(978-0-06-244341-0(0)*, Waldon Pond Pr.) HarperCollins Pubs.

Soileau, Hodges, illus. The Black Widow Spider Mystery. 2004. (Boxcar Children Special Ser.). 130p. (gr. 2-7). 15.50 *(978-0-7569-3266-4(1))* Perfection Learning Corp.

—The Comic Book Mystery. 2003. (Boxcar Children Ser.). 106p. (gr. 4-7). 15.00 *(978-0-7569-1611-4(9))* Perfection Learning Corp.

—The Great Shark Mystery. 2003. (Boxcar Children Special Ser.). 130p. (gr. 4-7). 15.50 *(978-0-7569-1616-9(X))* Perfection Learning Corp.

—The Mystery at Skeleton Point. 2003. (Boxcar Children Ser.). 120p. (gr. 4-7). 15.00 *(978-0-7569-1609-1(7))* Perfection Learning Corp.

Sonneborn, Scott. Feet First. Banks, Timothy, illus. 2014. (Frankenstein Journals). (ENG.). 80p. (gr. 2-3). 22.65 *(978-1-4342-8999-5(0))* Stone Arch Bks.

—The Frankenstein Journals, 1 vol. Banks, Timothy, illus. 2014. (Frankenstein Journals). (ENG.). 160p. (gr. 2-3). 9.95 *(978-1-4342-9130-1(8))* Stone Arch Bks.

—I for an Eye. Banks, Timothy, illus. 2014. (Frankenstein Journals). (ENG.). 80p. (gr. 2-3). 22.65 *(978-1-4342-9000-7(X))* Stone Arch Bks.

—No Guts, No Gloria. Banks, Timothy, illus. 2015. (Frankenstein Journals). (ENG.). 80p. (gr. 2-3). 22.65 *(978-1-4965-0221-6(3))* Stone Arch Bks.

—A Pain in the Butt. Banks, Timothy, illus. 2015. (Frankenstein Journals). (ENG.). 80p. (gr. 2-3). 22.65 *(978-1-4965-0222-3(1))* Stone Arch Bks.

Sowards, Ben, illus. Christmas Oranges. 2004. 32p. 17.95 *(978-1-59156-098-2(5))* Covenant Communications, Inc.

Spence, Eleanor. Jamberoo Road. 2007. (Living History Library). 183p. (YA). (gr. 8-12). pap. 12.95 *(978-1-932350-17-3(9))* Bethlehem Bks.

—The Switherby Pilgrims: A Tale of the Australian Bush. 2005. (Living History Library). 195p. (YA). (gr. 8-12). pap. 12.95 *(978-1-883937-99-7(X))* Bethlehem Bks.

Spies, Ben. Weirdo. Spies, Robert, illus. 2015. (ENG.). 54p. (J). pap. *(978-0-473-33563-2(8))* Spies Publishing.

Spinale, Wendy. Everland. (ENG.). (J). (gr. 7). 2017. (Everland Ser.: 1). 336p. pap. 9.99 *(978-1-338-09553-1(6)*, Scholastic Paperbacks) 2016. 320p. 17.99 *(978-0-545-83694-4(8)*, Scholastic Pr.) Scholastic, Inc.

Springer, Audrey. Rusty's Gift. Richards, Kris, illus. 2012. 28p. 24.95 *(978-1-4626-6589-1(6))* America Star Bks.

Spyri, Johanna. Heidi. 2014. (ENG.). 345p. 17.50 *(978-1-78270-044-9(7))* Award Pubns. Ltd. GBR. Dist: Parkwest Pubns., Inc.

—Heidi. 2008. (Bring the Classics to Life Ser.). (Illus.). 72p. (gr. 1-12). pap., act. bk. ed. 10.95 *(978-1-55576-178-3(X)*, EDCTR-107B) EDCON Publishing Group.

—Heidi. 2003. pap. *(978-1-84637-585-9(1))* Echo Library.

—Heidi. 2013. (ENG., Illus.). 336p. (J). (gr. 2-7). 14.95 *(978-1-62087-686-2(8)*, 620686, Sky Pony Pr.) Skyhorse Publishing Co., Inc.

—Heidi. Akib, Jamel, illus. 2007. (Classic Starts(tm) Ser.). (ENG.). 160p. (J). (gr. 2-4). 6.95 *(978-1-4027-3691-9(6))* Sterling Publishing Co., Inc.

—Heidi: With a Discussion of Optimism. Clift, Eva, illus. 2003. (Values in Action Illustrated Classics Ser.). 190p. (J). *(978-1-59203-030-9(0))* Learning Challenge, Inc.

Spyri, Johanna & Blaisdell, Robert. Heidi: Adapted for Young Readers. Kliros, Thea, illus. 2011. (Dover Children's Thrift Classics Ser.). (ENG.). 80p. (J). (gr. 3-8). pap. 3.00 *(978-0-486-40166-9(9))* Dover Pubns., Inc.

Spyri, Johanna & Lacey, Mike. Heidi, 1 vol. 2012. (Calico Illustrated Classics Ser.: No. 4). (ENG., Illus.). 112p. (J). (gr. 3-6). 27.07 *(978-1-61641-613-3(0))* Magic Wagon.

Spyri, Johanna & Stork, Elisabeth P. Heidi. Kirk, Maria L., illus. 2014. (J). 13.32 *(978-1-4677-5846-8(9)*, First Avenue Editions) Lerner Publishing Group.

St. Crow, Lili. Betrayals. 2009. (Strange Angels Ser.: 2). (ENG., Illus.). 304p. (YA). (gr. 7-18). 9.99 *(978-1-59514-252-8(5)*, Razorbill) Penguin Young Readers Group.

—Betrayals, 10 vols. 2010. (Strange Angels Ser.: 2). (YA). 95.75 *(978-1-4407-7156-9(1))* Recorded Bks., Inc.

—Betrayals. 2009. (Strange Angels Ser.: 2). lib. bdg. 20.85 *(978-0-606-09020-9(7)*, Turtleback) Turtleback Bks.

—Jealousy. 2010. (Strange Angels Ser.: 3). (ENG.). 320p. (YA). (gr. 7-18). 9.99 *(978-1-59514-290-0(8)*, Razorbill) Penguin Young Readers Group.

—Jealousy, 10 vols. 2010. (Strange Angels Ser.: 3). (J). 86.75 *(978-1-4498-2776-8(8))*; 83.75 *(978-1-4498-2776-2(4))*; 68.75 *(978-1-4498-2773-1(X))*; 1.25 *(978-1-4498-2777-9(2))*; 209.75 *(978-1-4498-2772-4(1))* Recorded Bks., Inc.

—Jealousy. 2010. (Strange Angels Ser.: 3). lib. bdg. 20.85 *(978-0-606-14566-4(4)*, Turtleback) Turtleback Bks.

—Strange Angels. 2009. (Strange Angels Ser.: 1). (ENG., Illus.). 304p. (YA). (gr. 7-18). pap. 9.99 *(978-1-59514-251-1(7)*, Razorbill) Penguin Young Readers Group.

—Strange Angels, 9 vols. 2009. (Strange Angels Ser.: 1). (J). 84.75 *(978-1-4407-6195-9(7))*; 114.75 *(978-1-4407-6199-7(X))*; 117.75 *(978-1-4407-6197-3(3))*; 87.75 *(978-1-4407-6193-5(0))*; 181.75 *(978-1-4407-6194-2(9))* Recorded Bks., Inc.

—Strange Angels. 2009. (Strange Angels Ser.: 1). lib. bdg. 20.85 *(978-0-606-08957-9(8)*, Turtleback) Turtleback Bks.

St. Jean, Alan. Aidan of Oren: The Journey Begins. Friedman, Judith, illus. 2004. (ENG.). 208p. (J). (gr. 4-7). 19.95 *(978-0-9724853-5-7(X))* Keene Publishing.

St. John, Lauren. Dolphin Song. 2009. (ENG.). 272p. (J). (gr. 3-7). 7.99 (978-0-14-241375-3(5), Puffin Books) Penguin Young Readers Group.

—The Elephant's Tale. 2011. (ENG.). 240p. (J). (gr. 3-7). 6.99 (978-0-14-241879-6(X), Puffin Books) Penguin Young Readers Group.

—The White Giraffe. 2008. (ENG., Illus.). 208p. (J). (gr. 2-5). 7.99 (978-0-14-241152-0(3), Puffin Books) Penguin Young Readers Group.

Stanley, Diane. Raising Sweetness, 4 bks. Karas, G. Brian, illus. 2004. (J). pap. 39.95 incl. audio compact disk (978-1-59112-524-2(3)) Live Oak Media.

—Raising Sweetness. 2003. (Illus.). (J). 28.95 incl. audio compact disk (978-1-59112-516-7(2)); 25.95 incl. audio (978-1-59112-266-1(X)) Live Oak Media.

—Raising Sweetness, 4 bks. Stanley, Diane, illus. 2003. (Illus.). (J). pap. 37.95 incl. audio (978-1-59112-267-8(8)) Live Oak Media.

—Sweetness Series. Karas, G. Brian, illus. 2003. pap. 30.95 incl. audio (978-1-59112-847-2(1)); pap. 34.95 incl. audio compact disk (978-1-59112-860-1(9)) Live Oak Media.

Stentiford, Tyler Michael. A Darker Secret. 2009. (ENG.). 128p. (YA). pap. 9.99 (978-1-60138-315-0(0)) Atlantic Publishing Group, Inc.

Stevenson, Chris. The Drum of Destiny. 2016. (Middle-Grade Novels Ser.). (ENG., Illus.). 224p. (gr. 4-7). lib. bdg. 26.65 (978-1-4965-2673-1(2)) Stone Arch Bks.

Stevenson, James. Runaway Horse! Date not set. (J). 15.99 (978-0-06-051978-0(9)); 16.89 (978-0-06-051979-7(7)) HarperCollins Pubs.

Stevermer, Caroline. Magic below Stairs. 2011. (ENG.). 208p. (J). (gr. 3-7). 6.99 (978-0-14-241871-0(4), Puffin Books) Penguin Young Readers Group.

Stewart, Paul. Far-Flung Adventures: Hugo Pepper. 2012. (Far-Flung Adventures Ser.). (ENG.). 272p. (J). (gr. 3-7). 7.99 (978-0-385-75223-7(7), Yearling) Random Hse. Children's Bks.

Stewart, Paul & Riddell, Chris. Last of the Sky Pirates. 2009. (Edge Chronicles Ser.). (ENG.). 384p. (J). (gr. 3-7). 8.99 (978-0-440-42100-9(4), Yearling) Random Hse. Children's Bks.

Stewart, Trenton Lee. The Extraordinary Education of Nicholas Benedict. Sudyka, Diana, illus. 2013. (Mysterious Benedict Society Ser.). (ENG.). 496p. (J). (gr. 3-7). pap. 9.99 (978-0-316-17620-0(6)) Little, Brown Bks. for Young Readers.

—The Extraordinary Education of Nicholas Benedict. 2013. (Mysterious Benedict Society Ser.: 0). (J). lib. bdg. 19.65 (978-0-606-31743-6(0), Turtleback) Turtleback Bks.

—The Mysterious Benedict Society. Tingley, Megan, ed. Sudyka, Diana, illus. 2010. (Mysterious Benedict Society Ser.: 3). (ENG.). 400p. (J). (gr. 3-7). pap. 8.99 (978-0-316-04550-6(0)) Little, Brown Bks. for Young Readers.

—The Mysterious Benedict Society. Ellis, Carson, illus. (Mysterious Benedict Society Ser.: 1). (ENG.). (J). (gr. 3-7). 2008. 512p. pap. 9.99 (978-0-316-00395-7(6)) 2007. 496p. 19.00 (978-0-316-05777-6(0), Tingley, Megan Bks.) 2015. 512p. 12.99 (978-0-316-26501-0(2)) Little, Brown Bks. for Young Readers.

—The Mysterious Benedict Society. unabr. ed. 2007. (Mysterious Benedict Society Ser.: Bk. 1). (ENG.). (J). (gr. 3-7). 25.50 (978-0-307-28440-2(9), Listening Library (Audio)) Penguin Random House Audio Publishing Group.

—The Mysterious Benedict Society. 2009. 17.45 (978-1-60686-527-9(7)) Perfection Learning Corp.

—The Mysterious Benedict Society. 2010. (Mysterious Benedict Society Ser.: 3). (J). lib. bdg. 19.65 (978-0-606-15117-7(6), Turtleback) Turtleback Bks.

—The Mysterious Benedict Society. Ellis, Carson, illus. 2008. (Mysterious Benedict Society Ser.: 1). 485p. (J). (gr. 3-7). lib. bdg. 19.65 (978-1-4178-1817-4(4), Turtleback) Turtleback Bks.

—The Mysterious Benedict Society & the Prisoner's Dilemma. Sudyka, Diana, illus. 2009. (Mysterious Benedict Society Ser.: 3). (ENG.). 400p. (J). (gr. 3-7). 18.99 (978-0-316-04552-0(7)) Little, Brown Bks. for Young Readers.

Stiefvater, Maggie. The Scorpio Races. (ENG.). (J). (gr. 9). 2013. 448p. pap. 10.99 (978-0-545-22491-8(8), Scholastic Paperbacks) 2011. 416p. 17.99 (978-0-545-22490-1(X), Scholastic Pr.) Scholastic, Inc.

—The Scorpio Races. 2013. lib. bdg. 22.10 (978-0-606-31501-2(2), Turtleback) Turtleback Bks.

Stokes, Paula. Vicarious. 2016. (Vicarious Ser.). (ENG.). 336p. (YA). 17.99 (978-0-7653-8094-4(3), 9780765380944, Tor Teen) Doherty, Tom Assocs., LLC.

Stone, Jeff. Five Ancestors Out of the Ashes: Phoenix. 2013. (Five Ancestors Out of the Ashes Ser.: 1). (ENG.). 304p. (J). (gr. 4-7). 6.99 (978-0-375-87097-2(0), Yearling) Random Hse. Children's Bks.

—Five Ancestors Out of the Ashes #1: Phoenix. 2012. (Five Ancestors Out of the Ashes Ser.). (ENG.). 288p. (J). (gr. 4-7). 16.99 (978-0-375-87018-7(0), Random Hse. Bks. for Young Readers) Random Hse. Children's Bks.

Stone, Marie. On Their Own: A Journey to Jamestown. 2006. (Illus.). 166p. (J). (gr. 3-7). per. 8.95 (978-1-57249-385-8(2), White Mane Kids) White Mane Publishing Co., Inc.

Stork, Francisco X. The Last Summer of the Death Warriors. 2010. (ENG.). 352p. (J). (gr. 9-7). 18.99 (978-0-545-15133-7(3), Levine, Arthur A. Bks.) Scholastic, Inc.

Stratton, Allan. Chanda's Wars. 2009. (ENG.). 416p. (YA). (gr. 8). pap. 8.99 (978-0-06-087265-6(9), HarperTeen) HarperCollins Pubs.

—Chanda's Wars. 2011. 10.36 (978-0-7848-3486-2(5), Everbind) Marco Bk. Co.

Stratton-Porter, Gene. Freckles. (J). reprint ed. lib. bdg. 24.95 (978-0-89190-949-1(4), Rivercity Pr.) Amereon Ltd.

—Freckles. (ENG., 2015. Illus.). (J). 27.95 **(978-1-297-91217-7(9))** 2015. (Illus.). (J). 27.95 **(978-1-297-66159-4(1))** 2007. 248p. pap. 22.99 (978-1-4264-5654-1(9)) Creative Media Partners, LLC.

—Freckles. 2006. 236p. (YA). 19.95 (978-1-934169-32-2(3)); pap. 8.95 (978-1-934169-33-9(1)) Norilana Bks.

Sumerak, Marc. Ororo: Before the Storm. Barberi, Carlo, illus. 2012. (Ororo: Before the Storm Ser.). 24p. (J). (gr. 2-6). lib. bdg. 24.21 (978-1-61479-025-9(6)); lib. bdg. 24.21 (978-1-61479-024-2(8)); lib. bdg. 24.21 (978-1-61479-026-6(4)); lib. bdg. 24.21 (978-1-61479-027-3(2)) Spotlight.

Surget, Alain. The Ghost Ship. 2015. (Jolly Roger Ser.). (Illus.). 96p. (gr. 3-6). 28.50 (978-1-909645-41-7(9)) Book Hse. GBR. Dist: Black Rabbit Bks.

Sutton, Kelsey. Where Silence Gathers. 2014. (ENG.). 360p. (YA). pap. 9.99 (978-0-7387-3947-2(2), Flux) North Star Editions.

Swan, Bill. Corner Kick, 1 vol. 2004. (Lorimer Sports Stories Ser.: 66). (ENG.). 144p. (J). (gr. 4-8). 16.95 (978-1-55028-817-9(2), 9781550288179) Lorimer, James & Co., Ltd., Pubs. CAN. Dist: Casemate Pubs. & Bk. Distributors, LLC.

Tavner, Gill & Dickens, Charles. David Copperfield. Donnelly, Karen, illus. 2009. (Real Reads Ser.). 64p. (J). (gr. 4-8). pap. 13.55 (978-1-60754-383-1(4)) Windmill Bks.

Taylor, G. P. The First Escape. 2008. (Dopple Ganger Chronicles Ser.: 1). (ENG., Illus.). 288p. (J). (gr. 3-7). 19.99 (978-1-4143-1947-6(9), SaltRiver) Tyndale Hse. Pubs.

—The Great Mogul Diamond. 2011. (Dopple Ganger Chronicles Ser.: 3). (ENG.). 304p. (J). (gr. 3-7). 19.99 (978-1-4143-1949-0(5), SaltRiver) Tyndale Hse. Pubs.

—The Secret of Indigo Moon. 2009. (Dopple Ganger Chronicles Ser.: 2). (ENG., Illus.). 304p. (J). (gr. 3-7). 19.99 (978-1-4143-1948-3(7), SaltRiver) Tyndale Hse. Pubs.

Taylor, Laini. Strange the Dreamer. 2017. 536p. (YA). **(978-0-316-43120-0(6))** Little Brown & Co.

—Strange the Dreamer. 2017. (ENG.). (J). 544p. (gr. 10-17). 18.99 (978-0-316-34168-4(1)); 704p. (gr. 9-17). 20.99 (978-0-316-46427-7(9)) Little, Brown Bks. for Young Readers.

Taylor, Richard A. Ships of Children. 2nd rev. ed. 2006. (Illus.). 191p. (YA). lib. bdg. 37.95 (978-0-9764403-7-6(7)) Klare Taylor Pubs.

Taylor, S. S. The Expeditioners & the Treasure of Drowned Man's Canyon. Roy, Katherine, illus. 2013. (ENG.). 384p. pap. 12.95 (978-1-938073-71-7(1)) McSweeney's Publishing.

Taylor, Shirley A. The Stable Boy. Hall, Wendell E., illus. 2012. (ENG.). 40p. (J). (gr. 2-17). 17.95 (978-1-935166-79-5(4)) Parkhurst Brothers, Inc., Pubs.

Teele, Elinor. The Mechanical Mind of John Coggin. 2016. (Illus.). 352p. (J). (gr. 3-7). 16.99 (978-0-06-234510-3(9), Waldon Pond Pr.) HarperCollins Pubs.

Tewee, Laqaixit. Winterbloom & the Magical Swan: Book 1 Discovery of the Moon Treasure. 2012. 68p. pap. 31.99 (978-1-4653-9933-5(X)) Xlibris Corp.

Thompson, Michelle. Taming the Wind. 2010. 176p. pap. 12.99 (978-1-59955-379-5(1)) Cedar Fort, Inc./CFI Distribution.

Thoms, Gigi. Noble Pocket. 2016. (YA). pap. 18.99 (978-1-4621-1773-4(2), Horizon Pubs.) Cedar Fort, Inc./CFI Distribution.

Tiernan, Cate. Darkest Fear. 2014. (Birthright Ser.: 1). (ENG., Illus.). 368p. (YA). (gr. 9). pap. 9.99 (978-1-4424-8245-6(1), Simon Pulse) Simon Pulse.

Tollefson, Carol. McTavich That Rascal Squirrel. 2015. (ENG., Illus.). 20p. pap. 12.00 (978-1-62288-101-7(X)) Austin, Stephen F. State Univ. Pr.

Townsend, Daniel. Trumpet. 2008. 24p. pap. 24.95 (978-1-4241-9387-5(7)) America Star Bks.

Tucker, David J. The Fourth Gift. 2010. 96p. 12.99 (978-1-59955-438-9(0)) Cedar Fort, Inc./CFI Distribution.

Ungerer, Tomi. The Three Robbers. 2009. (ENG., Illus.). 40p. (gr. -1-3). 16.95 (978-0-7148-4877-8(8)) Phaidon Pr., Inc.

Unsworth, Tania. The One Safe Place. 2014. (ENG.). 304p. (J). (gr. 5-8). 15.95 (978-1-61620-329-0(3), 73329) Algonquin Bks. of Chapel Hill.

Ure, Jean. Daisy May. Donnelly, Karen, illus. 2011. (ENG.). 96p. (J). pap. 5.99 (978-0-00-713369-7(3), HarperCollins Children's Bks.) HarperCollins Pubs. Ltd. GBR. Dist: HarperCollins Pubs.

—Ice Lolly. 2010. (ENG., Illus.). 208p. (J). (gr. 4-7). 9.99 (978-0-00-728173-2(0), HarperCollins Children's Bks.) HarperCollins Pubs. Ltd. GBR. Dist: HarperCollins Pubs.

van Arsdale, Peternelle. The Beast Is an Animal. 2017. (ENG., Illus.). 352p. (YA). (gr. 9). 17.99 (978-1-4814-8841-9(4), McElderry, Margaret K. Bks.) McElderry, Margaret K. Bks.

Van Draanen, Wendelin. Runaway. 2012. (ENG.). 272p. (YA). (gr. 5). pap. 9.99 (978-0-307-97597-3(5), Ember) Random Hse. Children's Bks.

Van Hamme, Jean. The Heir. Francq, Philippe, illus. 2008. (Largo Winch Ser.: 1). (ENG.). 96p. pap. 19.95 (978-1-905460-48-9(1)) CineBook GBR. Dist: National Bk. Network.

VanArsdale, Anthony, illus. The Sleepy Hollow Mystery. 2015. 111p. (J). **(978-1-4806-9407-1(X))** Whitman, Albert & Co.

Vander Zee, Ruth. Always with You. Himler, Ronald, illus. 2008. (ENG.). 32p. (J). (gr. -1-3). 17.00 (978-0-8028-5295-3(5), Eerdmans Bks For Young Readers) Eerdmans, William B. Publishing Co.

Verrico, Susan. The Privateer's Apprentice, 1 vol. 2012. (ENG.). 224p. (J). 15.95 (978-1-56145-633-8(0)) Peachtree Pubs.

Verrone, Patric C. W. Sharktooth. 2009. 229p. pap. 14.76 (978-0-557-09535-3(2)) Lulu Pr., Inc.

Viguie, Debbie & Holder, Nancy. Unleashed. 2012. (Wolf Spring Chronicles Ser.). (ENG.). 400p. (YA). (gr. 7). pap. 9.99 (978-0-385-74099-9(9), Ember) Random Hse. Children's Bks.

Vincent, Victoria. The City of Kind Words: A Story by Tory. l.t. ed. 2006. (Illus.). 56p. (J). per. 19.95 (978-0-9788950-0-6(2)) All Over Creation.

Voisin, Mandy Madson. Star of Deliverance. 2014. pap. 17.99 (978-1-4621-1454-2(7)) Cedar Fort, Inc./CFI Distribution.

Wait, Lea. Stopping to Home. 2003. (ENG.). 160p. (J). (gr. 3-7). pap. 8.99 (978-0-689-83849-1(2), Simon & Schuster/Paula Wiseman Bks.) Simon & Schuster/Paula Wiseman Bks.

Walker, Keegan Holmes. Sebastianus: The War Begins. 2010. 304p. pap. 18.95 (978-1-4502-5580-6(9)) iUniverse, Inc.

Wallace, Barbara Brooks. The Perils of Peppermints. 2005. (ENG., Illus.). 272p. (J). (gr. 3-7). pap. 12.99 (978-0-689-85045-5(X), Simon & Schuster/Paula Wiseman Bks.) Simon & Schuster/Paula Wiseman Bks.

Walsh, Pat. The Crowfield Curse. (ENG.). (J). (gr. 3-7). 2012. 352p. pap. 7.99 (978-0-545-23103-9(5)) 2010. 336p. 16.99 (978-0-545-22922-7(7)) Scholastic, Inc. (Chicken Hse., The).

—The Crowfield Demon. (J). 2013. 360p. (978-0-545-37350-0(6)) 2012. (ENG.). 368p. (gr. 3-7). 16.99 (978-0-545-31769-6(X), Chicken Hse., The) Scholastic, Inc.

Walter, Jon. Close to the Wind. 2015. (ENG.). 304p. (J). (gr. 5-9). 17.99 (978-0-545-81662-5(9)) Scholastic, Inc.

—My Name Is Not Friday. 2017. (ENG.). 400p. (J). (gr. 7). pap. 9.99 **(978-1-338-16064-2(8))** Scholastic, Inc.

Walter, Jon. My Name's Not Friday. 2016. (ENG.). 384p. (YA). (gr. 7). 18.99 (978-0-545-85522-8(5)) Scholastic, Inc.

Wang, Holman & Wang, Jack. Charles Dickens's Great Expectations. 2016. (ENG., Illus.). 24p. (J). (gr. -1 — 1). bds. 9.95 (978-1-4521-5243-1(8)) Chronicle Bks. LLC.

Wang, Jack, et al. Victor Hugo's les Misérables. 2016. (ENG., Illus.). 24p. (J). (gr. -1 — 1). bds. 9.95 (978-1-4521-5251-6(9)) Chronicle Bks. LLC.

Ward, Rachel. The Chaos. 2011. (Numbers Ser.: 2). (ENG.). 352p. (J). (gr. 9-9). 17.99 (978-0-545-24269-1(X), Chicken Hse., The) Scholastic, Inc.

—Numbers. 2010. (Numbers Ser.: 1). (ENG.). 336p. (J). (gr. 7-12). 17.99 (978-0-545-14299-1(7), Chicken Hse., The) Scholastic, Inc.

Warner, Gertrude Chandler. Blue Bay Mystery, 1 vol. Dubisch, Michael, illus. 2009. (Boxcar Children Graphic Novels Ser.). (ENG.). 32p. (J). (gr. 2-5). 28.50 (978-1-60270-591-3(7)) ABDO Publishing Co.

—The Boxcar Children. Date not set. (Boxcar Children Ser.: No. 1). (J). (gr. 2-5). lib. bdg. 18.95 (978-0-8488-1712-1(5)) Amereon Ltd.

—The Boxcar Children. (Boxcar Children Ser.: No. 1). 154p. (J). (gr. 2-5). pap. 3.95 (978-0-8072-1447-3(7), Listening Library) Random Hse. Audio Publishing Group.

—The Boxcar Children Guide to Adventure: A How-To for Mystery Solving, Make-It-Yourself Projects, & More. 2014. (Boxcar Children Mysteries Ser.). (ENG.). 144p. (J). (gr. 1-5). 12.99 (978-0-8075-0905-0(1)) Whitman, Albert & Co.

—The Haunted Cabin Mystery, 1 vol. Bloodworth, Mark, illus. 2010. (Boxcar Children Graphic Novels Ser.). (ENG.). 32p. (J). (gr. 2-5). 28.50 (978-1-60270-717-7(0)) ABDO Publishing Co.

—The Lighthouse Mystery. (Boxcar Children Ser.: No. 8). 147p. (J). (gr. 2-5). pap. 3.95 (978-0-8072-1474-9(4), Listening Library) Random Hse. Audio Publishing Group.

—Mike's Mystery. (Boxcar Children Ser.: No. 5). 128p. (J). (gr. 2-5). pap. 3.95 (978-0-8072-1462-6(0), Listening Library) Random Hse. Audio Publishing Group.

—Mike's Mystery, 1 vol. Dubisch, Michael, illus. 2009. (Boxcar Children Graphic Novels Ser.). (ENG.). 32p. (J). (gr. 2-5). 28.50 (978-1-60270-590-6(9)) ABDO Publishing Co.

—The Mystery of the Grinning Gargoyle. VanArsdale, Anthony, illus. 2014. (Boxcar Children Mysteries Ser.: 137). (ENG.). 128p. (J). (gr. 1-5). pap. 5.99 (978-0-8075-0893-0(4)) Whitman, Albert & Co.

—The Mystery of the Runaway Ghost. Soileau, Hodges, illus. 2004. (Boxcar Children Ser.). 135p. (J). 12.65 (978-0-7569-3264-0(5)) Perfection Learning Corp.

—The Mystery of the Soccer Snitch. VanArsdale, Anthony, illus. 2014. (Boxcar Children Mysteries Ser.: 136). (ENG.). 128p. (J). (gr. 1-5). pap. 5.99 (978-0-8075-0896-1(9)) Whitman, Albert & Co.

—Mystery Ranch. (Boxcar Children Ser.: No. 4). 128p. (J). (gr. 2-5). pap. 3.95 (978-0-8072-1450-3(7), Listening Library) Random Hse. Audio Publishing Group.

—Mystery Ranch, 1 vol. Dubisch, Michael, illus. 2009. (Boxcar Children Graphic Novels Ser.). (ENG.). 32p. (J). (gr. 2-5). 28.50 (978-1-60270-589-0(5)) ABDO Publishing Co.

—Snowbound Mystery. Dubisch, Mike, illus. 2009. (Boxcar Children Graphic Novels Ser.: 7). (ENG.). 32p. (J). (gr. 1-5). pap. 6.99 (978-0-8075-7515-4(1)) Whitman, Albert & Co.

—Snowbound Mystery, 1 vol. Dubisch, Mike, illus. 2010. (Boxcar Children Graphic Novels Ser.). (ENG.). 32p. (J). (gr. 2-5). 28.50 (978-1-60270-715-3(4)) ABDO Publishing Co.

—The Yellow House Mystery. (Boxcar Children Ser.: No. 3). 191p. (J). (gr. 2-5). pap. 3.95 (978-0-8072-1449-7(3), Listening Library) Random Hse. Audio Publishing Group.

—The Yellow House Mystery, 1 vol. Dubisch, Michael, illus. 2009. (Boxcar Children Graphic Novels Ser.). (ENG.). 32p. (J). (gr. 2-5). 28.50 (978-1-60270-588-3(7)) ABDO Publishing Co.

—The Yellow House Mystery, No. 3. Dubisch, Mike, illus. 2009. (Boxcar Children Graphic Novels Ser.). (ENG.). 32p. (J). (gr. 2-5). 6.99 (978-0-8075-2869-3(2)) Whitman, Albert & Co.

Warner, Gertrude Chandler, creator. The Creature in Ogopogo Lake. 2006. (Boxcar Children Mysteries Ser.: 108). (ENG., Illus.). 128p. (J). (gr. 1-5). lib. bdg. 14.99 (978-0-8075-1336-1(9)) Whitman, Albert & Co.

—The Garden Thief. 2012. (Boxcar Children Mysteries Ser.: 130). (ENG., Illus.). 128p. (J). (gr. 1-5). 5.99 (978-0-8075-2752-8(1)) Whitman, Albert & Co.

—The Garden Thief 2012. (Boxcar Children Mysteries Ser.: 130). (ENG., Illus.). 128p. (J). (gr. 1-5). 15.99 (978-0-8075-2751-1(3)) Whitman, Albert & Co.

—The Ghost at the Drive-In Movie. 2008. (Boxcar Children Mysteries Ser.: 116). (ENG.). 128p. (J). (gr. 1-5). 14.99 (978-0-8075-5577-4(0)) Whitman, Albert & Co.

—The Ghost-Hunting Special. 2015. (Boxcar Children Mysteries Ser.). (ENG.). 352p. (J). (gr. 1-5). 9.99 (978-0-8075-2846-4(3)) Whitman, Albert & Co.

—The Haunted Legends Special. 2016. (Boxcar Children Mysteries Ser.). (ENG.). 368p. (J). (gr. 1-5). 9.99 (978-0-8075-0724-7(5)) Whitman, Albert & Co.

—The Legend of the Irish Castle. 2016. (Boxcar Children Mysteries Ser.: 142). (ENG., Illus.). 128p. (J). (gr. 1-5). 15.99 (978-0-8075-0705-6(9)) Whitman, Albert & Co.

—The Mystery at the Calgary Stampede. 2015. (Boxcar Children Mysteries Ser.: 140). (ENG.). 128p. (J). (gr. 1-5). 15.99 (978-0-8075-2840-2(4)) Whitman, Albert & Co.

—The Mystery of the Missing Pop Idol. 2015. (Boxcar Children Mysteries Ser.: 138). (ENG., Illus.). 128p. (J). (gr. 1-5). 15.99 (978-0-8075-5605-4(X)) Whitman, Albert & Co.

—The Mystery of the Stolen Dinosaur Bones. 2015. (Boxcar Children Mysteries Ser.: 139). (ENG., Illus.). 128p. (J). (gr. 1-5). 15.99 (978-0-8075-5608-5(4)) Whitman, Albert & Co.

—The Sleepy Hollow Mystery. 2015. (Boxcar Children Mysteries Ser.: 141). (ENG., Illus.). 128p. (J). (gr. 1-5). 15.99 (978-0-8075-2843-3(9)) Whitman, Albert & Co.

—The Vanishing Passenger. 2006. (Boxcar Children Mysteries Ser.: 106). (ENG., Illus.). 112p. (J). (gr. 1-5). per. 6.99 (978-0-8075-1067-4(X)) Whitman, Albert & Co.

Waters, Zack C. Blood Moon Rider. 2006. (Florida Historical Fiction for Youth Ser.). (ENG.). 126p. (J). (gr. 4-9). 13.95 (978-1-56164-350-9(5)) Pineapple Pr., Inc.

Watson, Jude. Loot. (ENG.). 272p. (J). (gr. 3-7). 2015. pap. 6.99 (978-0-545-46803-9(5), Scholastic Paperbacks) 2014. 17.99 (978-0-545-46802-2(7), Scholastic Pr.) Scholastic, Inc.

Watson, Renée. What Momma Left Me. (ENG.). 240p. (YA). 2012. pap. 7.99 (978-1-59990-704-8(6), 9781599907048) 2010. (gr. 5-8). 16.99 (978-1-59990-446-7(2), 9781599904467) Bloomsbury Publishing USA. (Bloomsbury USA Childrens).

Watts, Irene N. When the Bough Breaks. 2007. (ENG.). 152p. (YA). (gr. 4-7). pap. 9.95 (978-0-88776-821-7(0), Tundra Bks.) Tundra Bks. CAN. Dist: Penguin Random Hse. LLC.

Webb, Holly. Return to the Secret Garden. 2016. (ENG.). 224p. (J). (gr. 3-7). 16.99 (978-1-4926-3909-1(5), 9781492639091) Sourcebooks, Inc.

—Rose. 2013. (Rose Ser.: 1). (ENG.). 240p. (J). (gr. 3-6). pap. 6.99 (978-1-4022-8581-3(7), 9781402285813, Sourcebooks Jabberwocky) Sourcebooks, Inc.

—Rose & the Lost Princess. 2011. (ENG.). 272p. (J). (gr. 4-6). pap. 8.99 (978-1-4083-0448-8(1)) Hodder & Stoughton GBR. Dist: Hachette Bk. Group.

—Rose & the Lost Princess. 2014. (Rose Ser.: 2). (ENG.). 256p. (J). (gr. 3-6). pap. 6.99 (978-1-4022-8584-4(1), Sourcebooks Jabberwocky) Sourcebooks, Inc.

—Rose & the Magician's Mask. 2014. (Rose Ser.: 3). (ENG.). 224p. (J). (gr. 3-6). pap. 6.99 (978-1-4926-0430-3(5), 9781492604303, Sourcebooks Jabberwocky) Sourcebooks, Inc.

Weber, John. Orphan. 2010. 266p. (YA). (gr. 7-18). 16.95 (978-1-934813-38-6(9)) Westside Bks.

Webster, Jean. Daddy-Long-Legs. (J). 19.95 (978-0-8488-0323-0(X)) Amereon Ltd.

—Daddy-Long-Legs. 2004. reprint ed. pap. 1.99 (978-1-4192-1490-5(X)); pap. 19.95 (978-1-4191-1490-8(5)) Kessinger Publishing, LLC.

—Daddy-Long-Legs. 2011. (Puffin Classics Ser.). (ENG., Illus.). 192p. (J). (gr. 5-7). pap. 5.99 (978-0-14-133111-9(9), Puffin Books) Penguin Young Readers Group.

—Dear Enemy. (J). 21.95 (978-0-8488-0324-7(8)) Amereon Ltd.

—Dear Enemy. 2013. (Best Sellers of 1916 Ser.). 425p. reprint ed. lthr. 69.00 (978-0-7426-1275-4(9)) Classic Bks.

—Dear Enemy. 2004. reprint ed. pap. 31.95 (978-1-4179-1744-0(X)) Kessinger Publishing, LLC.

Welsh, Charles. Goody Two Shoes. 2005. reprint ed. pap. 22.95 (978-1-4179-6775-9(7)) Kessinger Publishing, LLC.

West, Temple. Velvet. 2015. (ENG.). 416p. (YA). (gr. 8). pap. 9.99 (978-1-250-05708-2(6), 9781250057082) Feiwel & Friends.

Westley, William. Charlie & Crow. 2011. 66p. 24.99 (978-1-4628-6802-5(9)); pap. 15.99 (978-1-4628-6801-8(0)) Xlibris Corp.

Wexler, Django. The Forbidden Library. 2015. (ENG., Illus.). 400p. (J). (gr. 5). 8.99 (978-0-14-242681-4(4), Puffin Books) Penguin Young Readers Group.

—The Mad Apprentice. Jansson, Alexander, illus. 2015. (Forbidden Library). (ENG.). 352p. (J). (gr. 5). 16.99 (978-0-8037-3976-5(1), Kathy Dawson Books) Penguin Young Readers Group.

Wheeler, Kim. The Adventures of Jonny Plumb. 2013. 174p. pap. (978-0-7552-1568-3(0), Bright Pen) Authors OnLine, Ltd.

Whelan, Gloria. Listening for Lions. 2006. (ENG.). 208p. (J). (gr. 5-9). pap. 6.99 (978-0-06-058176-3(X)) HarperCollins Pubs.

—Listening for Lions. 2007. 194p. (gr. 5-9). 16.00 (978-0-7569-7800-6(9)) Perfection Learning Corp.

White, Andrea. Windows on the World. 2011. 238p. (J). 18.95 (978-1-60898-105-2(3)); pap. 9.95 (978-1-60898-106-9(1)) namelos llc.

White, Ellen Emerson. Voyage on the Great Titanic. 2010. (Dear America Ser.). (ENG., Illus.). 208p. (J). (gr. 3-7). 12.99 (978-0-545-23834-2(X), Scholastic Pr.) Scholastic, Inc.

White, Ruth. The Treasure of Way down Deep. 2013. (ENG.). 176p. (J). (gr. 5-9). 16.99 (978-0-374-38067-0(8), 9780374380670, Farrar, Straus & Giroux (BYR)) Farrar, Straus & Giroux.

—Way down Deep. 2011. (ENG.). 224p. (J). (gr. 5-8). pap. 7.99 (978-0-312-66096-3(0), 9780312660963) Square Fish.

Wicke, Ed. The Muselings. Douglas, Janine, illus. 2012. 212p. pap. 9.99 (978-0-9840718-8-3(1)) Blacknblue Pr.

Williams, Mary. Brothers in Hope: The Story of the Lost Boys of Sudan, 1 vol. Christie, R. Gregory, illus. 2013. (ENG.). 32p. (J). 18.95 (978-1-58430-232-2(1)) Lee & Low Bks., Inc.

Wilson, Laurie Harman. The Treasures of Destiny. 2012. 72p. pap. 7.95 (978-0-9848050-3-7(6), Little Creek Bks.) Jan-Carol Publishing, INC.

Winter, Barbara. Trapped in Gallipoli. 2007. (Illus.). 48p. (YA). lib. bdg. 15.00 (978-1-4242-1643-7(5)) Dingles & Co.

Wolk, Lauren. Beyond the Bright Sea. 2017. (ENG.). 304p. (J). (gr. 5). 16.99 **(978-1-101-99485-6(1)**, Dutton Books for Young Readers) Penguin Young Readers Group.

Wood, Francis Eusene. The Christmas Letter. Wood, Christine & Marken, Jon, eds. McDermott, Robert, illus. Wood, Christine, photos by. 2007. pap. 9.95 (978-0-9746372-6-6(2)) Tip-Of-The-Moon Publishing Co.

Wood, Maryrose. The Hidden Gallery. Klassen, Jon, illus. (J). (gr. 3-7). 2015. (Incorrigible Children of Ashton Place Ser.: 2). (ENG.). 336p. pap. 6.99 (978-0-06-236694-8(7)) 2011. (Incorrigible Children of Ashton Place Ser.: 2). (ENG.). 320p. 16.99 (978-0-06-179112-3(1)) 2011. (Incorrigible Children of Ashton Place Ser.: Bk. 2). 16.89 (978-0-06-179114-7(8)) HarperCollins Pubs.

—The Incorrigible Children of Ashton Place Bk. 4: The Interrupted Tale. Wheeler, Eliza, illus. 2015. (Incorrigible Children of Ashton Place Ser.: 4). (ENG.). 400p. (J). (gr. 3-7). pap. 6.99 (978-0-06-179123-9(7)) HarperCollins Pubs.

—The Incorrigible Children of Ashton Place: Book V: The Unmapped Sea. Wheeler, Eliza, illus. 2016. (Incorrigible

M
N
O

Children of Ashton Place Ser.: 5). 416p. (J). (gr. 3-7). pap. 7.99 (978-0-06-211042-8(X)) HarperCollins Pubs.

—The Mysterious Howling. Klassen, Jon, illus. (Incorrigible Children of Ashton Place Ser.: 1). (ENG.). (J). (gr. 3-7). 2015. 288p. pap. 6.99 (978-0-06-236693-1(9))Bk. I. 2010. 272p. 16.99 (978-0-06-179105-5(9)) HarperCollins Pubs.

—The Unseen Guest. Klassen, Jon, illus. 2015. (Incorrigible Children of Ashton Place Ser.: 3). (ENG.). 352p. (J). (gr. 3-7). pap. 6.99 (978-0-06-236695-5(5)) HarperCollins Pubs.

Woodruff, Elvira. Fearless. 2011. (ENG.). 240p. (J). (gr. 3-7). pap. 6.99 (978-0-439-67704-2(1), Scholastic Pr.) Scholastic, Inc.

Woodson, Jacqueline. Miracle's Boys. 2010. (ENG.). 176p. (YA). (gr. 7-18). 8.99 (978-0-14-241553-5(7), Speak) Penguin Young Readers Group.

—Peace, Locomotion. (ENG.). (J). 2010. 176p. (gr. 5-18). 8.99 (978-0-14-241512-2(X), Puffin Books) 2009. 144p. (gr. 4-7). 15.99 (978-0-399-24655-5(X), G.P. Putnam's Sons Books for Young Readers) Penguin Young Readers Group.

Woolston, Blythe. MARTians. 2015. (ENG.). 224p. (YA). (gr. 7). 16.99 (978-0-7636-7756-5(6)) Candlewick Pr.

Worley, Rob M. & Warner, Gertrude Chandler. Surprise Island, 1 vol. Dubisch, Michael, illus. 2009. (Boxcar Children Graphic Novels Ser.). (ENG.). 32p. (J). (gr. 2-5). 28.50 (978-1-60270-587-6(9)) ABDO Publishing Co.

Wright, Betty Ren. Crandalls' Castle. 2005. (ENG.). 184p. (YA). (gr. 4-6). tchr. ed. 17.95 (978-0-8234-1726-1(3)) Holiday Hse., Inc.

Wulf, Linda Press. The Night of the Burning. 2007. (ENG.). 224p. pap. (978-0-7475-9051-4(6)) Bloomsbury Publishing Plc.

Yancey, Rick. Alfred Kropp: the Seal of Solomon. 2015. (Alfred Kropp Ser.). (ENG.). 352p. (YA). (gr. 7). pap. 9.99 (978-1-61963-917-1(3), 9781619639171, Bloomsbury USA Childrens) Bloomsbury Publishing USA.

—Alfred Kropp: the Thirteenth Skull. 2015. (Alfred Kropp Ser.). (ENG.). 304p. (YA). (gr. 7). pap. 9.99 (978-1-61963-918-8(1), 9781619639188, Bloomsbury USA Childrens) Bloomsbury Publishing USA.

—The Curse of the Wendigo. 2011. (Monstrumologist Ser.: 2). (ENG.). 464p. (YA). (gr. 9). pap. 12.99 (978-1-4169-8451-1(8), Simon & Schuster Bks. For Young Readers) Simon & Schuster Bks. For Young Readers.

—The Final Descent. 2013. (Monstrumologist Ser.: 4). (ENG., Illus.). 320p. (YA). (gr. 9). 18.99 (978-1-4424-5153-7(X), Simon & Schuster Bks. For Young Readers) Simon & Schuster Bks. For Young Readers.

—The Isle of Blood. (Monstrumologist Ser.: 3). (ENG.). 560p. (YA). (gr. 9). 2012. pap. 12.99 (978-1-4169-8453-5(4)) 2011. (Illus.). 18.99 (978-1-4169-8452-8(6)) Simon & Schuster Bks. For Young Readers. (Simon & Schuster Bks. For Young Readers).

—The Monstrumologist. (Monstrumologist Ser.: 1). (ENG.). (YA). (gr. 9). 2010. 464p. pap. 11.99 (978-1-4169-8449-8(6)) 2009. 448p. 21.99 (978-1-4169-8448-1(8)) Simon & Schuster Bks. For Young Readers. (Simon & Schuster Bks. For Young Readers).

—The Thirteenth Skull. (Alfred Kropp Ser.). (ENG.). 304p. (YA). (gr. 7). 2009. mass mkt. 6.99 (978-1-59990-363-7(6), 9781599903637) 2008. 16.99 (978-1-59990-114-5(5), 9781599901145) Bloomsbury Publishing USA. (Bloomsbury USA Childrens).

Yates, Alexander. The Winter Place. 2015. (ENG., Illus.). 448p. (YA). (gr. 9). 17.99 (978-1-4814-1981-9(1)) Simon & Schuster Children's Publishing.

The Year We Sailed the Sun. 2015. (ENG., Illus.). 432p. (J). (gr. 3-7). 17.99 (978-0-689-85827-7(2), Atheneum/Richard Jackson Bks.) Simon & Schuster Children's Publishing.

Yep, Laurence. The Magic Paintbrush. Wang, Suling, illus. 2003. (ENG.). 96p. (J). (gr. 3-7). pap. 6.99 (978-0-06-440852-3(3)) HarperCollins Pubs.

—The Magic Paintbrush. Wang, Suling, illus. 2003. 89p. (J). (gr. 3-7). 12.65 (978-0-7569-1444-8(2)) Perfection Learning Corp.

—The Tiger's Apprentice. 2005. (Tiger's Apprentice Ser.: Bk. 1). 184p. (J). lib. bdg. 24.62 (978-1-4242-0449-6(6)) Fitzgerald Bks.

—The Tiger's Apprentice. 2005. (Tiger's Apprentice (Tandem Library) Ser.). 184p. (gr. 5-9). 17.00 (978-0-7569-5074-3(0)) Perfection Learning Corp.

Young, Moira. Blood Red Road. (Dust Lands Ser.: 1). (ENG.). (YA). (gr. 9). 2012. 480p. pap. 10.99 (978-1-4424-2999-4(2)) 2011. (Illus.). 464p. 17.99 (978-1-4424-2998-7(4)) McElderry, Margaret K. Bks. (McElderry, Margaret K. Bks.).

—Blood Red Road, 9 vols. 2011. (YA). 122.75 (978-1-4618-0629-5(1)); 286.75 (978-1-4618-0634-9(8)); 120.75 (978-1-4618-0630-1(5)); 120.75 (978-1-4618-0633-2(X)); 1.25 (978-1-4640-2632-4(7)) Recorded Bks., Inc.

—Raging Star. (Dust Lands Ser.: 3). (ENG., Illus.). 448p. (YA). (gr. 9). 2015. pap. 10.99 (978-1-4424-3003-7(6)) 2014. 17.99 (978-1-4424-3002-0(8)) McElderry, Margaret K. Bks. (McElderry, Margaret K. Bks.).

—Rebel Heart. 2013. (Dust Lands Ser.: 2). (ENG., Illus.). 448p. (YA). (gr. 9). pap. 11.99 (978-1-4424-3001-3(X), McElderry, Margaret K. Bks.) McElderry, Margaret K. Bks.

Zafón, Carlos Ruiz. The Midnight Palace. 2012. (ENG.). 320p. (YA). (gr. 7-17). pap. 10.00 (978-0-316-04474-5(1)) Little, Brown Bks. for Young Readers.

Zahler, Diane. Baker's Magic. Price, Mina, illus. 2016. (Middle-Grade Novels Ser.). (ENG.). 336p. (gr. 4-7). lib. bdg. 26.65 (978-1-4965-2724-0(0)) Stone Arch Bks.

Zamorsky, Tania & Burnett, Frances Hodgson. A Little Princess. Corvino, Lucy, illus. 2005. (Classic Starts(tm) Ser.). (ENG.). 160p. (J). (gr. 2-4). 6.95 (978-1-4027-1275-3(8)) Sterling Publishing Co., Inc.

Zdunich, Terrance. The Molting: Issue #1 Guilty Susie. 2009. pap. 7.99 (978-1-61623-120-0(3)) Independent Pub.

Zettel, Sarah. Palace of Spies. 2013. (Palace of Spies Ser.: 1). (ENG.). 368p. (YA). (gr. 7). 16.99 (978-0-544-07411-8(4)) Houghton Mifflin Harcourt Publishing Co.

Zink, Michelle. A Temptation of Angels. 2013. (ENG.). 448p. (YA). (gr. 7). pap. 9.99 (978-0-14-242423-0(4), Speak) Penguin Young Readers Group.

Zweig, Eric. Fever Season. 2009. (ENG.). 256p. (YA). (gr. 4-18). pap. 10.99 (978-1-55488-432-2(2), Dundurn Pr.) Dundurn CAN. Dist: Ingram Publisher Services.

ORWELL, GEORGE, 1903-1950

Boerst, William J. Generous Anger: The Story of George Orwell. 2004. (World Writers Ser.). (Illus.). 112p. (YA). (gr. 6-12). 23.95 (978-1-883846-74-9(9), First Biographies) Reynolds, Morgan Inc.

Borus, Audrey. Reading & Interpreting the Works of George Orwell. 2016. (Lit Crit Guides). (Illus.). 176p. (J). 39.93 (978-0-7660-8354-7(3)) Enslow Pubs., Inc.

George Orwell 1984: The Political Pen. 2014. (ENG.). 180p. (J). (gr. 3-7). pap. 13.95 (978-1-59077-354-3(3)) Evans, M. & Co., Inc.

Orwell, George. 1984. Orwell, George & Bloom, Harold, eds. 2nd rev. ed. 2006. (Bloom's Modern Critical Interpretations Ser.). 216p. (C). (gr. 9-18). lib. bdg. 45.00 (978-0-7910-9300-9(X), Chelsea Hse.) Facts On File, Inc.

OSCEOLA, SEMINOLE CHIEF, 1804-1838

Hunt, Santana. Osceola. 2015. (Native American Heroes Ser.). (ENG., Illus.). 24p. (J). (gr. 1-2). pap. 8.15 (978-1-4824-2689-2(7)) Stevens, Gareth Publishing LLLP.

Sanford, William R. Seminole Chief Osceola. 2013. (Native American Chiefs & Warriors Ser.). 48p. (J). (gr. 5-18). lib. bdg. 22.60 (978-0-7660-4117-2(4)); pap. 8.95 (978-1-4644-0263-0(9)) Enslow Pubs., Inc.

OSTEOLOGY

see Bones

OSTRICHES

Awesome Ostriches. 2013. (Great Big Animals Ser.). 24p. (J). (gr. k-2). pap. 48.90 (978-1-4339-9418-0(6)) Stevens, Gareth Publishing LLLP.

Calhoun, Kelly. Fast & Flightless: Ostrich. 2015. (Guess What Ser.). (ENG., Illus.). 24p. (J). (gr. k-2). 28.50 (978-1-63362-627-0(X), 206664) Cherry Lake Publishing.

—Velocidad Sin Vuelo (Fast & Flightless) Avestruz (Ostrich) 2016. (Adivina (Guess What) Ser.). (SPA.). 24p. (J). (gr. k-2). 28.50 (978-1-63471-446-4(6), 208847) Cherry Lake Publishing.

Cunningham, Kevin. Zebras & Ostriches. 2016. (21st Century Junior Library: Better Together Ser.). (ENG.). 24p. (J). (gr. 2-5). 27.07 (978-1-63471-082-4(7), 208407) Cherry Lake Publishing.

Davin, Rose. Ostriches. 2017. (Meet Desert Animals Ser.). (ENG., Illus.). 24p. (gr. k-1). lib. bdg. 26.65 (978-1-5157-4603-4(8), Pebble Plus) Capstone Press of Coughlan Cos.

Gibbs, Maddie. Ostriches. 2011. (Safari Animals Ser.). (ENG.). 24p. (J). pap. 8.25 (978-1-4488-2600-1(4)); lib. bdg. 22.60 (978-1-4488-2509-7(1)) Rosen Publishing Group, Inc., The. (PowerKids Pr.).

—Ostriches: Avestruces. 2011. (Safari Animals / Animales de Safari Ser.). (SPA & ENG.). 24p. (J). (gr. -1-2). lib. bdg. 22.60 (978-1-4488-3121-0(0)) Rosen Publishing Group, Inc., The.

Gish, Melissa. Ostriches. (Living Wild Ser.). (Illus.). (J). 2017. (ENG.). 48p. (gr. 4-7). pap. 12.00 (978-1-62832-302-3(7), Creative Paperbacks) 2016. 46p. (978-1-60818-706-5(3), Creative Education) Creative Co., The.

Harasymiw, Therese. Ostriches. 2010. (Animals That Live in the Grasslands Ser.). (ENG.). 24p. (J). (gr. -1-3). pap. 8.15 (978-1-4339-3879-5(0)); lib. bdg. 22.60 (978-1-4339-3878-8(2)) Stevens, Gareth Publishing LLLP.

Herriott, Charlotte. Cheetah vs. Ostrich. 2015. (Bizarre Beast Battles Ser.). (ENG., Illus.). 24p. (J). (gr. 2-3). pap. 8.15 (978-1-4824-2784-4(2)) Stevens, Gareth Publishing LLLP.

Jacobs, Liza. Ostriches. 2003. (Wild Wild World Ser.). (Illus.). 24p. (J). 21.20 (978-1-4103-0040-9(4), Blackbirch Pr., Inc.) Cengage Gale.

Lawrence, Ellen. A Giant Egg & Fluffy Feathers (Ostrich) 2015. (Whose Little Baby Are You? Ser.). (ENG.). 24p. (J). (gr. -1-3). lib. bdg. 23.93 (978-1-910549-20-9(7)) Bearport Publishing Co., Inc.

Lunis, Natalie. Ostrich: The World's Biggest Bird. 2007. (SuperSized! Ser.). (Illus.). 24p. (J). (gr. k-3). lib. bdg. 21.28 (978-1-59716-394-1(5), 1265939) Bearport Publishing Co., Inc.

Markovics, Joyce. My Legs Are Long & Strong (Ostrich) 2014. (Zoo Clues Ser.). 24p. (J). (gr. -1-3). lib. bdg. 23.93 (978-1-62724-108-3(6)) Bearport Publishing Co., Inc.

Markovics, Joyce L. MIS Patas Son Largas y Fuertes. 2015. (Pistas de Animales Ser.). (SPA.). 24p. (J). (gr. -1-3). lib. bdg. 23.93 (978-1-62724-582-1(0)) Bearport Publishing Co., Inc.

Nagelhout, Ryan. Awesome Ostriches. 2013. (Great Big Animals Ser.). (ENG., Illus.). 24p. (J). (gr. k-2). lib. bdg. 22.60 (978-1-4339-9416-6(X)) Stevens, Gareth Publishing LLLP.

—Awesome Ostriches / Avestruces Increbles. 2013. (Great Big Animals / Superanimales Ser.). (SPA.). 24p. (J). (gr. k-2). 22.60 (978-1-4339-9450-0(X)) Stevens, Gareth Publishing LLLP.

Nagelhout, Ryan, ed. Awesome Ostriches. 2013. (Great Big Animals Ser.). 24p. (J). (gr. k-2). pap. 8.15 (978-1-4339-9417-3(8)) Stevens, Gareth Publishing LLLP.

Niver, Heather Moore. Ostriches Are Not Pets! 2013. (When Pets Attack! Ser.). 32p. (J). (gr. 3-6). pap. 10.50 (978-1-4339-9284-1(1)) Stevens, Gareth Publishing LLLP.

Niver, Heather Moore & Moore Niver, Heather. Ostriches Are Not Pets! 2013. 32p. (J). (gr. 3-6). 26.60 (978-1-4339-9283-4(3)) Stevens, Gareth Publishing LLLP.

Ostriches Are Not Pets! 2013. (When Pets Attack! Ser.). 32p. (J). (gr. 3-6). pap. 63.00 (978-1-4339-9285-8(X)) Stevens, Gareth Publishing LLLP.

Powell, Marie. Meet a Baby Ostrich. 2015. (ENG., Illus.). 32p. (J). (gr. k-2). 26.65 (978-1-4677-7971-5(7), Lerner Pubns.) Lerner Publishing Group.

Schuetz, Kari. Ostriches. 2013. (Animal Safari Ser.). (ENG., Illus.). 24p. (J). (gr. k-3). lib. bdg. 25.95 (978-1-60014-866-8(2), Blastoff! Readers) Bellwether Media.

Silverman, Buffy. Can You Tell an Ostrich from an Emu. 2012. (Animal Look-Alikes Ser.). (Illus.). 32p. (J). (gr. k-2). lib. bdg. 25.26 (978-0-7613-6741-3(1), Lerner Pubns.) Lerner Publishing Group.

—Can You Tell an Ostrich from an Emu? 2012. (Lightning Bolt Books (tm) — Animal Look-Alikes Ser.). 32p. (gr. k-2). (ENG.). pap. 7.95 (978-0-7613-8555-4(X)); pap. 45.32 (978-0-7613-9258-3(0)) Lerner Publishing Group.

Spilsbury, Louise. Ostrich, 1 vol. 2011. (Day in the Life: Grassland Animals Ser.). (ENG., Illus.). 24p. (gr. k-2). 23.32 (978-1-4329-4730-9(3)); pap. 6.79 (978-1-4329-4740-8(0)) Heinemann-Raintree. (Heinemann Read & Learn).

Stout, Frankie. Ostriches: Nature's Biggest Birds. 2009. (Things with Wings Ser.). 24p. (gr. 2-3). 42.50 (978-1-60854-353-3(6)); (Illus.). (J). lib. bdg. 22.60 (978-1-4042-4498-6(0)) Rosen Publishing Group, Inc., The. (PowerKids Pr.).

Ward, Finn. Avestruces / Ostriches at the Zoo. 2015. (Animales Del Zoológico / Zoo Animals Ser.). (ENG & SPA.). 24p. (J). (gr. k-k). lib. bdg. 22.60 (978-1-4824-3233-6(1)) Stevens, Gareth Publishing LLLP.

—Ostriches at the Zoo. 2015. (Zoo Animals Ser.). (ENG., Illus.). 24p. (J). (gr. k-k). pap. 8.15 (978-1-4824-2601-4(3)) Stevens, Gareth Publishing LLLP.

Waxman, Laura Hamilton. Ostriches: Fast Flightless Birds. 2016. (Comparing Animal Traits Ser.). (ENG., Illus.). 32p. (J). (gr. 2-4). 26.65 (978-1-4677-9509-8(7), Lerner Pubns.) Lerner Publishing Group.

Yasuda, Anita. Avestruces. 2013. (Animales en la Granja Ser.). (SPA., Illus.). 24p. (J). (gr. -1-3). lib. bdg. 27.13 (978-1-62127-589-3(2), AV2 by Weigl) Weigl Pubs., Inc.

—Ostriches. 2012. (J). 27.13 (978-1-61913-277-1(X)); (ENG., Illus.). 24p. pap. 12.95 (978-1-61913-281-8(8), AV2 by Weigl) Weigl Pubs., Inc.

OSTRICHES—FICTION

Belonie, Shannon. Teaching an Ostrich to Fly. 2008. 16p. pap. 8.74 (978-1-4343-5519-5(5)) AuthorHouse.

Brown, Ken. Why Can't I Fly? (Illus.). 32p. (J). pap. 9.99 (978-1-84270-017-4(0)) Andersen Pr. GBR. Dist: Trafalgar Square Publishing.

Del Riego, Erica. The Heart of Life. 2010. 36p. pap. 17.75 (978-1-4389-7572-6(4)) AuthorHouse.

Harrison, Casey. I'm an Ostrich. 2012. 24p. pap. 9.99 (978-0-9853650-4-2(8)) Mindstir Media.

Henderson, Susan Sinclair. Penelope's Journey Home. 2013. 48p. pap. 9.99 (978-1-4908-0420-0(X), WestBow Pr.) Author Solutions, Inc.

Idle, Molly. Flora & the Ostrich: An Opposites Book. 2017. (ENG., Illus.). 20p. (J). (gr. -1 — 1). bds. 9.99 (978-1-4521-4658-4(6)) Chronicle Bks. LLC.

Kok, Gemma. Scribble. 2008. 42p. pap. 17.94 (978-1-4092-2060-2(5)) Lulu Pr., Inc.

—Scribble (Printed in black & White) 2008. 42p. pap. 7.96 (978-1-4092-2531-7(3)) Lulu Pr., Inc.

Moncure, Jane Belk. Little Too-Tall: A Book about Friendship. DeSantis, Susan, illus. 2013. (Magic Castle Readers Ser.). (ENG.). 32p. (J). (gr. -1-2). 25.64 (978-1-62323-568-0(5), 206303) Child's World, Inc., The.

Morrow, John. Ostrich Egg Omelets. 2017. (ENG., Illus.). (J). 19.99 (978-0-9790832-1-1(4)) 405 Pubns.

Nelson, Marilyn. Ostrich & Lark. Artists of the Kuru Art Project in Botswana, San, illus. 2012. (ENG.). 32p. (J). (gr. k-4). 16.95 (978-1-59078-702-1(1)) Boyds Mills Pr.

Rea, Monique. Toulouse the Moose & the Mystery Guests. 2012. 34p. pap. 13.99 (978-0-9788926-4-7(X)) Trails of Discovery.

Stockton, Lucille. Hallo, Mallo & Pallo: The Ostracized Ostrich Family. Sampson, April, illus. 2005. 31p. (J). 19.95 (978-1-59408-511-6(0)) Cork Hill Pr.

Wallace, Karen. Flash Harriet & the Outrageous Ostrich Egg Mystery. (Illus.). 64p. (J). pap. (978-0-340-61961-2(9)) Hodder & Stoughton.

Wilson, D. Arthur. Little Red Rhupert. 2006. 15.95 (978-0-9785144-0-2(8)) Ostrageous Publishing.

OTTERS

Costain, Meredith. Otter. Hanna, Gary, illus. 2016. (Wild World Ser.). 00032p. (J). (gr. 1-2). pap. 10.00 (978-1-4994-8218-8(3), Windmill Bks.) Rosen Publishing Group, Inc., The.

Drumlin, Sam. Sea Otters. 2013. (PowerKids Readers: Sea Friends Ser.). (ENG., Illus.). 24p. (J). (gr. k-2). pap. 8.25 (978-1-4488-9744-5(0)); lib. bdg. 22.60 (978-1-4488-9643-1(6)) Rosen Publishing Group, Inc., The. (PowerKids Pr.).

—Sea Otters: Las Nutrias Marinas. Alamán, Eduardo, tr. from ENG. 2013. (PowerKids Readers: Sea Friends / Los Amigos Del Mar Ser.). (SPA & ENG., Illus.). 24p. (J). (gr. k-2). lib. bdg. 22.60 (978-1-4488-9976-0(1), PowerKids Pr.) Rosen Publishing Group, Inc., The.

Esbaum, Jill. Explore My World Sea Otters. 2017. (Explore My World Ser.). (ENG.). 32p. (J). (gr. -1-2). lib. bdg. 14.90 **(978-1-4263-2826-8(5))**; (Illus.). pap. 4.99 **(978-1-4263-2825-1(7))** National Geographic Society. (National Geographic Children's Bks.).

Esbensen, Barbara Juster. Playful Slider: The North American River Otter. Brown, Mary Barrett, illus. 2011. (Fesler-Lampert Minnesota Heritage Ser.). (ENG.). 32p. pap. 11.95 (978-0-8166-7765-8(4)) Univ. of Minnesota Pr.

Eszterhas, Suzi, photos by. Sea Otter Rescue. 2016. (Wildlife Rescue Ser.: 3). (ENG., Illus.). 44p. (J). (gr. k-5). 17.95 (978-1-77147-175-6(1), Owlkids) Owlkids Bks. Inc. CAN. Dist: Publishers Group West (PGW).

Gates, Margo. Sea Otters. 2013. (Animal Safari Ser.). (ENG., Illus.). 24p. (J). (gr. k-3). lib. bdg. 25.95 (978-1-60014-915-3(4), Blastoff! Readers) Bellwether Media.

Goldsworthy, Kaite. Otters. 2011. (J). (gr. 2-4). pap. 12.95 (978-1-61690-627-6(8), AV2 by Weigl); (Illus.). 24p. 27.13 (978-1-61690-621-4(9)) Weigl Pubs., Inc.

Green, Jen. River Otters. 2008. (Illus.). 52p. (J). (978-0-7172-6283-0(9)) Grolier, Ltd.

—Sea Otter. 2013. (Science Slam: the Deep End-Animal Life Underwater Ser.). 24p. (J). (gr. -1-3). lib. bdg. 23.93 (978-1-61772-922-5(1)) Bearport Publishing Co., Inc.

Hutchison, Patricia. Sea Otters. 2015. (Endangered Animals Ser.). (ENG.). 24p. (J). (gr. 1-4). 27.07 (978-1-63143-972-8(3), 208807) Child's World, Inc., The.

Johnson, Jinny. Sea Otter. 2014. (North American Mammals Ser.). (Illus.). 24p. (gr. 2-5). 28.50 (978-1-62588-037-6(5)) Black Rabbit Bks.

King, Zelda. Sea Otters. 2012. (Illus.). 24p. (J). 49.50 (978-1-4488-5140-9(8), PowerKids Pr.); pap. 8.25 (978-1-4488-5139-3(4), PowerKids Pr.); lib. bdg. 22.60 (978-1-4488-5004-4(5)) Rosen Publishing Group, Inc., The.

Laughlin, Kara L. Sea Otters. 2017. (In the Deep Blue Sea Ser.). (ENG.). 24p. (J). (gr. k-3). lib. bdg. 27.07 (978-1-5038-1689-3(3), 211522) Child's World, Inc., The.

Lawrence, Ellen. Giant Otter. 2017. (Apex Predators of the Amazon Rain Forest Ser.). (ENG., Illus.). 24p. (J). (gr. -1-3). 17.95 **(978-1-68402-034-8(4))** Bearport Publishing Co., Inc.

Lawrence, Ellen. River Otter. 2016. (Swamp Things: Animal Life in a Wetland Ser.). (ENG.). 24p. (J). (gr. -1-3). 17.95 (978-1-944102-54-8(X)) Bearport Publishing Co., Inc.

Leach, Michael. Otter. (Animal Neighbors Ser.). (gr. k-5). 2009. 32p. pap. 10.60 (978-1-4042-4570-9(7), Rosen Classroom) 2008. (J). 25.25 (978-1-4358-4993-8(0)) Rosen Publishing Group, Inc., The.

Leaf, Christina. Baby Sea Otters. 2014. (Super Cute! Ser.). (ENG., Illus.). 24p. (J). (gr. k-3). lib. bdg. 25.95 (978-1-60014-976-4(6), Blastoff! Readers) Bellwether Media.

Levine, Michelle. Let's Look at Sea Otters. 2010. pap. 45.32 (978-0-7613-6978-3(3)) Lerner Publishing Group.

Levine, Michelle & Waxman, Laura. Let's Look at Sea Otters. 2010. (Lightning Bolt Books — Animal Close-Ups Ser.). (ENG., Illus.). 32p. (gr. k-2). lib. bdg. 26.60 (978-0-8225-7896-3(4), Lerner Pubns.) Lerner Publishing Group.

Litwin, Stephanie K. Raising Otter. 2011. 32p. pap. 14.99 (978-1-4634-2595-1(3)) AuthorHouse.

London, Jonathan. Otters Love to Play. So, Meilo, illus. 2016. (ENG.). 32p. (J). (gr. k-3). 16.99 (978-0-7636-6913-3(X)) Candlewick Pr.

Lynette, Rachel. Giant River Otters. 2013. (Jungle Babies of the Amazon Rain Forest Ser.). 24p. (J). (gr. -1-3). lib. bdg. 21.32 (978-1-61772-754-2(7)) Bearport Publishing Co., Inc.

Mara, Wil. Otters. 2007. (Animals Animals Ser.). 48p. (gr. 3-7). lib. bdg. 29.93 (978-0-7614-2527-4(6), Benchmark Bks.) Marshall Cavendish Corp.

Marsh, Laura. Sea Otters. 2014. (Readers Ser.). (ENG., Illus.). 32p. (J). (gr. -1-1). pap. 3.99 (978-1-4263-1751-4(4), National Geographic Children's Bks.) National Geographic Society.

Marsico, Katie. Otters. 2015. (ENG.). 48p. (J). pap. 6.95 (978-0-531-21190-8(8), Orchard Bks.) Scholastic Library Publishing.

Mason, Adrienne. Otters. Ogle, Nancy Gray & Ogle, Nancy, illus. 2003. (Kids Can Press Wildlife Ser.). (ENG.). 32p. (J). (gr. k-5). 5.95 (978-1-55337-407-7(X)) Kids Can Pr., Ltd. CAN. Dist: Hachette Bk. Group.

Miles, Victoria. Sea Otter Pup, 1 vol. Gatt, Elizabeth, illus. (ENG.). (J). (gr. -1-k). 2017. 28p. 6.95 (978-1-4598-1506-3(8)) 2013. 26p. bds. 9.95 (978-1-4598-0467-8(8)) Orca Bk. Pubs. USA.

Miller, Sara Swan. Otters. (Paws & Claws Ser.). 24p. 2009. (gr. 2-3). 42.50 (978-1-60851-151-8(0)) 2008. (Illus.). (J). (gr. 3-7). lib. bdg. 22.60 (978-1-4042-4162-6(0)) Rosen Publishing Group, Inc., The. (PowerKids Pr.).

National Geographic Kids. National Geographic Readers: Peek, Otter. 2016. (Readers Ser.). (ENG.). 24p. (J). (-k). pap. 3.99 (978-1-4263-2436-9(7), National Geographic Children's Bks.) National Geographic Society.

National Geographic Kids Staff. Peek, Otter. 2016. (Readers Ser.). (ENG.). 24p. (J). (-k). lib. bdg. 13.90 (978-1-4263-2437-6(5), National Geographic Children's Bks.) National Geographic Society.

Newman, Patricia. Sea Otter Heroes: The Predators That Saved an Ecosystem. 2017. (Nonfiction — Grades 4-8 Ser.). (ENG.). 56p. (J). (gr. 4-8). 16.99 **(978-1-5124-3884-0(7))**; 47.99 **(978-1-5124-2844-5(2))**; 47.99 **(978-1-5124-3885-7(5))**; (Illus.). 31.99 (978-1-5124-2631-1(8)) Lerner Publishing Group. (Millbrook Pr.).

Pingry, Patricia A. Baby Sea Otter. Rose, Drew, illus. Seaworld, photos by. 2006. (SeaWorld Library: Vol. 7). 26p. (J). (gr. -1-k). bds. 6.95 (978-0-8249-6646-1(5), Ideal Pubns.) Worthy Publishing.

Ring, Susan. Project Otter. Kissock, Heather & Marshall, Diana, eds. 2003. (Zoo Life Ser.). (Illus.). 24p. (J). pap. 8.95 (978-1-59036-059-0(1)) Weigl Pubs., Inc.

Rustad, Martha E. H. A Baby Sea Otter Story. 2011. (Baby Animals Ser.). (ENG.). 24p. (gr. k-1). pap. 41.70 (978-1-4296-7101-9(7), Pebble Plus) Capstone Press of Coughlan Cos.

Schuh, Mari. Sea Otters. 2015. (Illus.). 24p. (J). lib. bdg. (978-1-62031-191-2(7), Bullfrog Bks.) Jump! Inc.

Slade, Suzanne. What If There Were No Sea Otters? A Book about the Ocean Ecosystem, 1 vol. Schwartz, Carol, illus. 2010. (Food Chain Reactions Ser.). (ENG.). 24p. (gr. 2-4). pap. 9.95 (978-1-4048-6397-2(4)) Picture Window Bks.

Wendorff, Anne. Sea Otters. 2008. (Oceans Alive Ser.). (ENG., Illus.). 24p. (J). (gr. k-3). lib. bdg. 25.95 (978-1-60014-207-9(9)) Bellwether Media.

Wilsdon, Christina. Otters. 2007. (J). (978-1-59939-138-0(4), Reader's Digest Young Families, Inc.) Studio Fun International.

OTTERS—FICTION

Anderson, Dee, retold by. Otter Gets Tricked! A Cherokee Trickster Story. l.t. ed. 2004. (Illus.). 32p. (J). pap. 6.00 (978-0-9755934-1-7(2)) Colonel Davenport Historical Foundation.

Autio, Karen. Kah-Lan the Adventurous Sea Otter, 1 vol. Lott, Sheena, illus. 2016. (ENG.). 64p. (J). (gr. 2-5). 9.95 (978-1-55039-244-9(1)) Sono Nis Pr. CAN. Dist: Orca Bk. Pubs. USA.

Bleu, Kennedy. Cotter Otter in Treasure Water. Goembel, Ponder, illus. 2014. (ENG.). 24p. (J). pap. 24.95 (978-1-63004-814-3(3)) America Star Bks.

Burgess, Thornton W. Little Joe Otter. (J). 18.95 (978-0-8488-0398-8(1)) Amereon Ltd.

Casanova, Mary. Utterly Otterly Day. Hoyt, Ard, illus. 2008. (ENG.). 40p. (J). (gr. -1-3). 17.99 (978-1-4169-0868-5(4), Simon & Schuster Bks. For Young Readers) Simon & Schuster Bks. For Young Readers.

—Utterly Otterly Night. Hoyt, Ard, illus. 2011. (ENG.). 40p. (J). (gr. -1-1). 16.99 (978-1-4169-7562-5(4), Simon & Schuster Bks. For Young Readers) Simon & Schuster Bks. For Young Readers.

Collins, Yvonne & Rideout, Sandy. The Black Sheep. 2007. 348p. (J). (978-1-4287-4665-7(X)) Hyperion Pr.

Cosgrove, Stephen. Gnome from Nome. James, Robin, illus. 2012. (Paws IV Ser.). (ENG.). 32p. (J). (gr. -1-2). pap. 10.99 (978-1-57061-777-5(5), Little Bigfoot) Sasquatch Bks.

Curtis, Jennifer Keats. Saving Squeak: The Otter Tale, 1 vol. Ramsey, Marcy Dunn, illus. 2010. (ENG.). 31p. (J). 14.99 (978-0-7643-3588-4(X), 9780764335884) Schiffer Publishing, Ltd.

Dana, Katherine. Never Invite an Otter to Stay the Night. 2011. 60p. 29.95 *(978-1-60844-956-9(4))*; pap. 19.95 *(978-1-4575-0158-6(9))* Dog Ear Publishing, LLC.

deRubertis, Barbara. Oliver Otter's Own Office. Alley, R. W., illus. 2011. (Animal Antics A to Z Ser.). 32p. (J). pap. 45.32 *(978-0-7613-7661-3(5))*; lib. bdg. 22.60 *(978-1-57565-336-5(2))*; (gr. -1-3). pap. 7.95 *(978-1-57565-327-3(3))* Kane Press, Inc.

deRubertis, Barbara & DeRubertis, Barbara. Oliver Otter's Own Office. Alley, R. W., illus. 2012. (Animal Antics A to Z Ser.). 32p. (J). (gr. 2 — 1). cd-rom 7.95 *(978-1-57565-408-9(3))* Kane Press, Inc.

Dodd, Emma. Together. Dodd, Emma, illus. 2016. (Emma Dodd's Love You Bks.). (ENG., Illus.). 24p. (J). (-k). 12.99 *(978-0-7636-8940-7(8))*, Nosy Crow) Candlewick Pr.

Dohlke, Nora. The Wonderful Adventures of Ozzie Sea Otter (Spanish) Stearns, Forest, illus. 2009. (ENG.). 98p. 19.95 *(978-0-9822046-2-7(0))* Bay Publishing.

—The Wonderful Adventures of Ozzie the Sea Otter. Stearns, Forest, illus. 2009. 98p. (J). 19.95 *(978-0-9822046-0-3(4))* Bay Publishing.

—The Wonderful Adventures of Ozzie the Sea Otter (Book & CD) Stearns, Forest, illus. 2009. (ENG.). 98p. 26.95 *(978-0-9822046-1-0(2))* Bay Publishing.

Eagle, Golden. You Can Play All Day If You Know the Way: Otter Medicine. 2005. (Illus.). 18p. (J). per. 12.99 *(978-1-932338-64-5(0))* Lifevest Publishing, Inc.

Ealy, Gerald & Ealy, Gerald. I Made a Wish to Be a Fish. 2012. 32p. pap. 9.95 *(978-0-9843837-5-7(1))* G340 Publishing.

Galvin, Laura. River Otter at Autumn Lane. Leeper, Christopher, illus. 2003. (ENG.). 32p. (J). (gr. -1-3). 9.95 *(978-1-931465-66-3(5)*, PB5073) Soundprints.

Galvin, Laura Gates. River Otter at Autumn Lane. Leeper, Christopher J., illus. 2011. (Smithsonian's Backyard Ser.). (ENG.). 32p. (J). (gr. -1-3). 8.95 *(978-1-60727-642-5(9))*; 19.95 *(978-1-60727-641-8(0))* Soundprints.

—River Otter at Autumn Lane. Leeper, Christopher, illus. 2005. (Smithsonian's Backyard Ser.). (ENG.). 32p. (J). (gr. -1-2). 19.95 *(978-1-931465-63-2(0)*, BC5023); 15.95 *(978-1-931465-61-8(4)*, B5023) Soundprints.

Garton, Sam. I Am Otter. Garton, Sam, illus. (Illus.). (J). (gr. -1 — 1). 2016. 34p. bds. 7.99 *(978-0-06-240908-9(5))* 2014. (ENG., 32p. 16.99 *(978-0-06-224775-9(1))* HarperCollins Pubs.

—Otter Goes to School. Garton, Sam, illus. 2016. (Illus.). 32p. (J). (gr. -1-3). 17.99 *(978-0-06-235225-5(3))* HarperCollins Pubs.

—Otter: Hello, Sea Friends! Garton, Sam, illus. 2016. (My First I Can Read Ser.). (Illus.). 32p. (J). (gr. -1-3). pap. 3.99 *(978-0-06-236660-3(2))* HarperCollins Pubs.

—Otter: Let's Go Swimming! Garton, Sam, illus. 2017. (My First I Can Read Ser.). (Illus.). 32p. (J). (gr. -1-3). pap. 3.99 *(978-0-06-236663-4(7))* HarperCollins Pubs.

—Otter Loves Easter! Garton, Sam, illus. 2017. (Illus.). 32p. (J). (gr. -1-3). 9.99 *(978-0-06-236667-2(X))* HarperCollins Pubs.

—Otter Loves Halloween! Garton, Sam, illus. 2015. (ENG., Illus.). 32p. (J). (gr. -1-3). 9.99 *(978-0-06-236666-5(1)*, Balzer & Bray) HarperCollins Pubs.

—Otter: Oh No, Bath Time! Garton, Sam, illus. 2016. (My First I Can Read Ser.). (Illus.). 32p. (J). (gr. -1-3). pap. 3.99 *(978-0-06-236657-3(2))* HarperCollins Pubs.

—Otter: the Best Job Ever! Garton, Sam, illus. 2016. (My First I Can Read Ser.). (Illus.). 32p. (J). (gr. -1-3). pap. 3.99 *(978-0-06-236654-2(8))* HarperCollins Pubs.

Grandpa & Little Guy. 2004. (J). 15.95 *(978-0-9764012-0-9(7))* Rockmill Publishing Co.

Halfmann, Janet. Good Night, Little Sea Otter, 1 vol. Williams, Wish, illus. (ENG.). (J). 2012. 24p. 15.95 *(978-1-59572-277-5(7))* 2010. 32p. (gr. -1-3). pap. 5.95 *(978-1-59572-254-6(8))* Star Bright Bks., Inc.

—Good Night, Little Sea Otter (Burmese Karen/English), 1 vol. Williams, Wish, illus. 2012. (KAR & ENG.). 24p. (J). 5.95 *(978-1-59572-371-0(4))* Star Bright Bks., Inc.

—Good Night, Little Sea Otter (Burmese/English), 1 vol. Williams, Wish, illus. 2012. (ENG.). 24p. (J). pap. 5.95 *(978-1-59572-370-3(6))* Star Bright Bks., Inc.

—Good Night, Little Sea Otter (Hmong/English), 1 vol. Williams, Wish, illus. 2012. (ENG.). 24p. (J). pap. 5.95 *(978-1-59572-365-9(X))* Star Bright Bks., Inc.

—Good Night, Little Sea Otter (Portuguese/English), 1 vol. Williams, Wish, illus. 2012. (ENG.). 24p. (J). pap. 5.95 *(978-1-59572-359-8(5))* Star Bright Bks., Inc.

—Good Night, Little Sea Otter (Spanish/English), 1 vol. Williams, Wish, illus. 2012. (ENG.). 24p. (J). pap. 5.95 *(978-1-59572-347-5(1))* Star Bright Bks., Inc.

Hedderwick, Mairi. The Utterly Otterleys. 2006. (ENG., Illus.). 32p. (J). (gr. -1-k). pap. 9.99 *(978-0-340-87369-4(8)*, Hodder Children's Books) Hachette Children's Group GBR. Dist: Hachette Bk. Group.

Hicks, Aniya & Hicks, Michelle. Fun Back in Ruskin Town. 2012. 24p. pap. 24.95 *(978-1-4626-8245-4(6))* America Star Bks.

Howe, James. Otter & Odder: A Love Story. Raschka, Chris, illus. 2012. (ENG.). 40p. (J). (gr. 1-4). 14.00 *(978-0-7636-4174-0(X))* Candlewick Pr.

Jacques, Brian. Taggerung. Standley, Peter & Chalk, Gary, illus. 2003. (Redwall Ser.). (ENG.). 448p. (J). (gr. 5-18). pap. 8.99 *(978-0-14-250154-2(9)*, Firebird) Penguin Young Readers Group.

—*Taggerung. 2003. (Redwall Ser.). 1.00 (978-1-4175-5326-6(X))* Recorded Bks., Inc.

Jones, Kari. Out of Season, 1 vol. 2012. (Orca Currents Ser.). (ENG.). 128p. (J). (gr. 5-9). 16.95 *(978-1-4598-0097-7(4))*; pap. 9.95 *(978-1-4598-0096-0(6))* Orca Bk. Pubs. USA.

Keiser, Frances R. Annie the River Otter: The Adventures of Pelican Pete. Keiser, Hugh M., illus. l.t. ed. 2006. (ENG.). 34p. (J). 19.99 *(978-0-9668845-4-8(X))* Sagaponack Bks.

Keller, Laurie. Do unto Otters: A Book about Manners. Keller, Laurie, illus. 2007. (ENG., Illus.). 40p. (J). (gr. k-3). 18.99 *(978-0-8050-7996-8(3)*, 9780805079968, Holt, Henry & Co. Bks. For Young Readers) Holt, Henry & Co.

—Do unto Otters: A Book about Manners. Keller, Laurie, illus. 2009. (ENG., Illus.). 40p. (J). (gr. k-3). pap. 7.99 *(978-0-312-58140-4(8)*, 9780312581404) Square Fish.

LeapFrog Staff. Ozzie & Mack. 2008. (J). pap. 39.99 *(978-1-59319-976-0(7))*; pap. 49.99 *(978-1-59319-924-1(4))* LeapFrog Enterprises, Inc.

Leavy, Diana C. Backstroke the Sea Otter & the Perfect Day. 2003. 32p. (J). per. *(978-1-59196-258-8(7))* Instant Pub.

London, Jonathan. Ollie's First Year. Van Zyle, Jon, illus. 2014. (ENG.). 32p. (J). 15.95 *(978-1-60223-228-0(8))* Univ. of Alaska Pr.

—Pup the Sea Otter. London, Sean, illus. 2017. (ENG.). 32p. (J). (gr. -1-3). 16.99 *(978-1-943328-87-1(0)*, West Winds Pr.) Graphic Arts Ctr. Publishing Co.

McSorley, Paul J. & Bearss, Patricia. The Adventures of Forealdo: Finding Millie. 2012. 34p. 24.95 *(978-1-4626-6721-5(X))* America Star Bks.

Meadows, Daisy. Chloe Slipperside's Secret. 2016. (Magic Animal Friends Ser.: 11). (ENG., Illus.). 112p. (J). (gr. 2-5). pap. 4.99 *(978-0-545-94078-8(8)*, Scholastic Paperbacks) Scholastic, Inc.

—Chloe Slipperslide's Secret. 2016. (Magic Animal Friends Ser.: 11). lib. bdg. 14.75 *(978-0-606-38801-6(X))* Turtleback Bks.

Morrow, Dj. Charlie & Joe. 2013. 28p. pap. 24.95 *(978-1-62709-833-5(X))* America Star Bks.

OHora, Zachariah. Stop Snoring, Bernard! OHora, Zachariah, illus. 2012. (ENG., Illus.). 32p. (J). (gr. -1-2). pap. 7.99 *(978-1-250-00717-9(8)*, 9781250007179) Square Fish.

Otter, Otter. (J). 26.20 *(978-0-8136-8416-1(1))*; (gr. -1-3). 59.50 *(978-0-8136-7954-9(0))* Modern Curriculum Pr.

Paul J McSorley; Illustrated By Patricia. The Adventures of Forealdo. Bearss, Patricia, illus. 2011. 36p. pap. 24.95 *(978-1-4560-8429-5(1))* America Star Bks.

Reminick, Gerald. Ollie Otter's Special Gift: A Story from Quiet Pond. Quintero, michelle, illus. 2013. 32p. (J). 10.00 *(978-1-889901-60-2(1)*, Palo Alto Bks.) Glencannon Pr.

RH Disney Staff & Posner-Sanchez, Andrea. Treasure's Day at Sea (Disney Princess: Palace Pets) RH Disney Staff & DiCicco, Sue, illus. 2015. (Little Golden Book Ser.). (ENG.). 24p. (J). (-k). 4.99 *(978-0-7364-3335-8(X)*, Golden/Disney) Random Hse. Children's Bks.

Rylant, Cynthia. The Otter. McDaniels, Preston, illus. 2016. (Lighthouse Family Ser.: 6). (ENG.). 48p. (J). (gr. 1-5). 15.99 *(978-1-4814-6045-3(5)*, Beach Lane Bks.) Beach Lane Bks.

Skewes, John & Ode, Eric. Elliott the Otter: The Totally Untrue Story of Elliott Bay. Skewes, John, illus. 2015. (ENG., Illus.). 32p. (J). (gr. -1-2). 16.99 *(978-1-57061-952-6(2)*, Little Bigfoot) Sasquatch Bks.

Soundprints Staff. Smithsonian Oceanic Collection Micro 4 Book Set. 2007. (ENG.). 32p. 14.95 *(978-1-59249-748-5(9))*; 14.95 *(978-1-59249-749-2(7))* Soundprints.

Springer, Susan Woodward. Seldovia Sam & the Sea Otter Rescue. Meissner, Amy, illus. 2003. (Misadventures of Seldovia Sam Ser.: Vol. 2). (ENG.). 64p. (J). (gr. -1-4). pap. 6.95 *(978-0-88240-571-1(3))* Graphic Arts Ctr. Publishing Co.

Steven, Kenneth. Fergus Finds a Friend, 1 vol. Crowe, Louise, illus. 2010. (ENG.). 32p. (J). (gr. -1-1). 11.95 *(978-0-86315-778-3(5))* Floris Bks. GBR. Dist: SteinerBooks, Inc.

Swenson, Lynn. Rollie & Mollie: Disappearing Act. Baker, David, illus. 2012. 26p. 24.95 *(978-1-4626-5277-8(8))* America Star Bks.

Tomlinson, Jill. The Otter Who Wanted to Know. Howard, Paul, illus. 2014. (ENG.). 96p. (J). (gr. -1-2). pap. 8.99 *(978-1-4052-7194-3(9))* Egmont Bks., Ltd. GBR. Dist: Independent Pubs. Group.

Voake, Steve. Daisy Dawson & the Secret Pond. Meserve, Jessica, illus. 2010. (Daisy Dawson Ser.: 2). (ENG.). 96p. (J). (gr. 1-4). pap. 5.99 *(978-0-7636-4730-8(6))* Candlewick Pr.

Webster, Christine. Otter Everywhere: Brand New Readers. Nihoff, Tim, illus. 2007. (Brand New Readers Ser.). (ENG.). 48p. (J). (gr. -1-3). pap. 5.99 *(978-0-7636-2922-9(7))* Candlewick Pr.

OUTBOARD MOTORS

see Motorboats

OUTDOOR COOKERY

see Outdoor Cooking

OUTDOOR COOKING

Conners, Christine & Conners, Tim. Scout's Deck of Outdoor Recipe Cards. 2015. (ENG., Illus.). 64p. 14.95 *(978-1-4930-0811-7(0)*, Falcon Guides) Globe Pequot Pr., The.

Jorgensen, Katrina. Food, Football, & Fun! Sports Illustrated Kids' Football Recipes. 2015. (Sports Illustrated Kids Ser.). (ENG., Illus.). 144p. (gr. 3-6). pap. 15.95 *(978-1-62370-230-4(5))* Capstone Press of Coughlan Cos.

—Football Tailgating Recipes: Tasty Treats for the Stadium Crowd. 2015. (Football Cookbooks Ser.). (ENG.). 48p. (gr. 3-6). lib. bdg. 31.32 *(978-1-4914-2137-6(1))* Capstone Press of Coughlan Cos.

Labat, Yancey C., illus. Let's Have a Cookout! 2007. 56p. (J). *(978-0-439-83228-1(4))* Scholastic, Inc.

Ornoth, Tyler. Grill Master: Finger-Licking Grilled Recipes. 2017. (Kids Can Cook! Ser.). (ENG., Illus.). 32p. (gr. 3-4). lib. bdg. 27.99 *(978-1-5157-3815-2(9))* Capstone Press of Coughlan Cos.

White, Kate. Cooking in a Can: More Campfire Recipes for Kids, 1 vol. Dixon, Debra, illus. 2006. (ENG.). 64p. (J). (gr. 4-7). pap. 9.99 *(978-1-58685-814-8(9)*, 1255566) Gibbs Smith, Publisher.

OUTDOOR LIFE

see also Camping; Country Life; Hiking; Mountaineering; Nature Study; Sports; Wilderness Survival

Aloian, Molly. The Yangtze: China's Majestic River. 2010. (Rivers Around the World Ser.). (ENG., Illus.). 32p. (J). (gr. 5-8). pap. *(978-0-7787-7472-3(4))*; lib. bdg. *(978-0-7787-7449-5(X))* Crabtree Publishing Co.

Barclay, Adrian. Outdoor Adventure Doodles: Amazing Scenes to Complete & Create. Running Press Staff, ed. 2014. (ENG., Illus.). 160p. (J). (gr. -1-17). pap. 12.95 *(978-0-7624-5218-7(8)*, Running Pr. Kids) Running Pr. Bk. Pubs.

Brennan, Finn. The Adventurous Boy's Handbook: For Ages 9 to 99. Brennan, Stephen & Brennan, Finn, eds. 2nd ed. 2011. (ENG., Illus.). 224p. (J). (gr. 2-5). pap. 12.95 *(978-1-61608-163-8(5)*, 608163) Skyhorse Publishing Co., Inc.

Brennan, Stephen & Brennan, Finn. The Adventurous Boy's Handbook. Brennan, Stephen & Brennan, Finn, eds. 2014. (ENG., Illus.). 320p. 17.95 *(978-1-62873-707-3(7))* Skyhorse Publishing Co., Inc.

Brennan, Stephen & Brennan, Lara. The Adventurous Girl's Handbook. Brennan, Stephen & Brennan, Lara, eds. 2014. (ENG., Illus.). 320p. 17.95 *(978-1-62873-708-0(5))* Skyhorse Publishing Co., Inc.

Butterfield, Moira. Survive & Thrive: A Pocket Guide to Wilderness Safety Skills. 2016. (ENG.). 112p. (J). (gr. 3-7). pap. 11.99 *(978-1-4380-0842-4(2))* Barron's Educational Series, Inc.

Cain, Marie Mowery. Beyond the Backyard. 2013. (Big Books, Blue Ser.). (ENG & SPA., Illus.). 16p. pap. 33.00 *(978-1-59246-022-9(4))* Big Books, by George!

—Let's Move. 2013. (Big Books, Blue Ser.). (ENG & SPA., Illus.). 16p. pap. 33.00 *(978-1-59246-012-0(7))* Big Books, by George!

Chandler, Matt, et al. Into the Great Outdoors. 2013. (Into the Great Outdoors Ser.). (ENG.). 32p. (gr. 3-4). pap. 31.80 *(978-1-62065-697-6(3))*; pap. 71.55 *(978-1-62065-698-3(1))* Capstone Press of Coughlan Cos. (Edge Bks.).

Dalton, Kippy. Outdoor Fun. 2016. (Spring Forward Ser.). (J). (gr. 1). *(978-1-4900-3712-7(8))* Benchmark Education Co.

Dybvik, Tina & Meister, Cari. Take It Outside. Record, Adam, illus. 2013. (Take It Outside Ser.). (ENG.). 24p. (gr. k-2). pap. 31.80 *(978-1-4795-1998-9(7))*; lib. bdg. 109.28 *(978-1-4048-8142-6(5))* Picture Window Bks.

Dymock, Melissa. Sliding in the Snow: Winter Activities for Kids, 1 vol. Lee, Frances Cook, illus. 2015. (ENG.). 64p. (J). pap. 9.99 *(978-1-4236-3893-3(X))* Gibbs Smith, Publisher.

Eggerling, Kristin J. Breath of Wilderness: The Life of Sigurd Olson. 2014. (ENG., Illus.). 112p. (J). (gr. 4-7). pap. 12.95 *(978-1-938486-10-4(2))* Fulcrum Publishing.

Encyclopaedia Britannica, Inc. Staff, compiled by. Discover English with Ben & Bella: Series 1: Outdoors. 2010. 180.00 *(978-1-61535-348-4(8))* Encyclopaedia Britannica, Inc.

Field & Stream's Guide to the Outdoors. 2015. (Field & Stream's Guide to the Outdoors Ser.). (ENG.). 96p. (J). (gr. 6-8). 143.80 *(978-1-4824-2306-8(5))* Stevens, Gareth Publishing LLLP.

Field & Stream's Guide to the Outdoors: Set 2. 2015. (Field & Stream's Guide to the Outdoors Ser.). (ENG.). 96p. (J). (gr. 6-8). 107.85 *(978-1-4824-2563-5(7))* Stevens, Gareth Publishing LLLP.

Free Spirit Publishing. Kids & Nature: Easy Ways to Love & Learn about the Outdoors. 2014. (In a Jar(r) Ser.). (ENG.). (J). 9.99 *(978-1-57542-462-0(2))* Free Spirit Publishing, Inc.

Gamble, Adam, et al. Good Night Mountains. 2013. (Good Night Our World Ser.). (ENG., Illus.). 26p. (J). (— 1). bds. 9.95 *(978-1-60219-090-0(9))* Good Night Bks.

Get Outdoors, 4 vols., Set 1. Incl. Canoeing & Kayaking. Rock, Lois. (J). lib. bdg. 25.25 *(978-1-4358-3041-7(5)*, PowerKids Pr.); Fishing. Ross, Nick. (YA). lib. bdg. 25.25 *(978-1-4358-3042-4(3))*; Orienteering. Champion, Neil. (YA). lib. bdg. 25.25 *(978-1-4358-3044-8(X))*; Rock Climbing. Champion, Neil. (YA). lib. bdg. 25.25 *(978-1-4358-3043-1(1))*; (gr. 4-7). 2009. (Illus.). 32p. 2009. Set lib. bdg. 95.80 *(978-1-4358-3231-2(0)*, PowerKids Pr.) Rosen Publishing Group, Inc., The.

Heidtke, John. Family Outdoor Journal. 2008. (YA). pap. *(978-0-9792739-4-0(3))* Ajoyin Publishing, Inc.

Hoenecke, Karen. At the Park. Biddle, Bruce, illus. 2003. (Bridging School to Home Series B). (ENG.). 8p. (gr. k-1). pap. 7.95 *(978-1-879835-37-5(1)*, Kaeden Bks.) Kaeden Corp.

Honovich, Nancy & Beer, Julie. National Geographic Kids Get Outside Guide: All Things Adventure, Exploration, & Fun! 2014. (ENG., Illus.). 160p. (J). (gr. 4-7). pap. 14.99 *(978-1-4263-1502-2(3)*, National Geographic Children's Bks.) National Geographic Society.

Jenson-Elliott, Cindy & Mebane, Jeanie. Wild Outdoors. 2011. (Wild Outdoors Ser.). (ENG.). 32p. (gr. 1-2). lib. bdg. 79.95 *(978-1-4296-6513-1(0)*, Blazers) Capstone Press of Coughlan Cos.

Johnson, Rich & James, Robert F. Outdoor Life's Disaster Survival Guide. 2015. (Field & Stream's Guide to the Outdoors Ser.). (ENG.). 96p. (J). (gr. 6-8). lib. bdg. 35.95 *(978-1-4824-3189-6(0))* Stevens, Gareth Publishing LLLP.

Kallen, Stuart A. Careers If You Like the Outdoors. 2017. (ENG.). 80p. (YA). (gr. 5-12). 39.93 ***(978-1-68282-140-4(4))*** ReferencePoint Pr., Inc.

Let's Go Outdoors! 2015. (Let's Go Outdoors! Ser.). (ENG.). 24p. (J). (gr. k-k). 135.60 *(978-1-4824-2540-6(8))*; pap., pap., pap. 293.40 *(978-1-4824-3483-5(0))*; pap., pap., pap. 48.90 *(978-1-4824-3484-2(9))* Stevens, Gareth Publishing LLLP.

Lowrie, Paul. Hooray for Minnesota Lakes. 2008. 19.95 *(978-0-9755801-8-9(3))* Questmarc Publishing.

—Hooray for Minnesota Winters. 2008. 19.95 *(978-0-9755801-9-6(1))* Questmarc Publishing.

Manning, Mick & Granström, Brita. Wild Adventures. 2015. (ENG., Illus.). 48p. (J). (gr. 1-5). 19.99 *(978-1-84780-436-5(5)*, Frances Lincoln) Quarto Publishing Group UK GBR. Dist: Hachette Bk. Group.

National Trust Staff. 50 Things to Do Before You're 11 3/4: Night-Time Adventure Notebook. 2016. (ENG., Illus.). 96p. (J). (gr. 1-5). 14.99 *(978-1-909881-48-8(1))* National Trust, Aylesbury GBR. Dist: Independent Pubs. Group.

Navarre, Gabrielle. Cool Careers Without College for People Who Love Nature. 2013. (New Cool Careers Without College Ser.). (Illus.). 144p. (J). (gr. 7-12). 35.95 *(978-1-4777-1821-6(4))* Rosen Publishing Group, Inc., The.

Nickens, T. Eward. Field & Stream's Guide to Outdoor Survival. 2015. (Field & Stream's Guide to the Outdoors Ser.). (ENG.). 96p. (J). (gr. 6-8). 35.95 *(978-1-4824-2304-4(9))* Stevens, Gareth Publishing LLLP.

Outdoor Adventure. 2014. (Outdoor Adventure Ser.). 32p. (J). (gr. 3-6). 151.50 *(978-1-4824-1175-1(X))* Stevens, Gareth Publishing LLLP.

Outdoor Book IR. 2017. (Outdoor Book Ser.). (ENG.). (J). 9.99 ***(978-0-7945-3968-9(8)**,* Usborne) EDC Publishing.

Paulsen, Gary. Puppies, Dogs, & Blue Northers: Reflections on Being Raised by a Pack of Sled Dogs. 2007. (ENG., Illus.). 80p. (J). (gr. 5-7). pap. 5.95 *(978-0-15-206103-6(7))* Houghton Mifflin Harcourt Publishing Co.

—Woodsong. 2007. (ENG., Illus.). 144p. (J). (gr. 5-9). pap. 7.99 *(978-1-4169-3939-9(3)*, Simon & Schuster Bks. For Young Readers) Simon & Schuster Bks. For Young Readers.

Pipe, Jim. How to Survive on a Desert Island. 2012. (Tough Guides). (ENG., Illus.). 32p. (J). (gr. 4-6). pap. 10.00 *(978-1-4488-7935-9(3))*; lib. bdg. 25.25 *(978-1-4488-7870-3(5))* Rosen Publishing Group, Inc., The. (PowerKids Pr.).

Reeves, Diane Lindsey. Career Ideas for Kids Who Like Animals & Nature. Bond, Nancy, illus. 2nd rev. ed. 2007. (Career Ideas for Kids Ser.). 208p. (gr. 4-9). 32.95 *(978-0-8160-6539-4(X)*, Ferguson Publishing Co.) Facts On File, Inc.

Rice, William B. Survival! Desert, 1 vol. 2nd rev. ed. 2012. (Nonfiction Readers Ser.). (ENG., Illus.). 48p. (J). (gr. 4-4). pap. 9.99 *(978-1-4333-4818-1(7))* Teacher Created Materials, Inc.

—Survival! Jungle, 1 vol. 2nd rev. ed. 2012. (Nonfiction Readers Ser.). (ENG., Illus.). 48p. (J). (gr. 4-4). pap. 9.99 *(978-1-4333-4820-4(9))* Teacher Created Materials, Inc.

Royston, Angela. How to Survive in the Desert. 2012. (Tough Guides). (ENG., Illus.). 32p. (J). (gr. 4-6). pap. 10.00 *(978-1-4488-7932-8(9))*; lib. bdg. 25.25 *(978-1-4488-7867-3(5))* Rosen Publishing Group, Inc., The. (PowerKids Pr.).

—How to Survive in the Rain Forest. 2012. (Tough Guides). (ENG., Illus.). 32p. (J). (gr. 4-6). pap. 10.00 *(978-1-4488-7934-2(5))*; lib. bdg. 25.25 *(978-1-4488-7869-7(1))* Rosen Publishing Group, Inc., The. (PowerKids Pr.).

Slade, Suzanne. Adventures Outdoors, 6 bks., Set. Incl. Let's Go Camping. lib. bdg. 25.25 *(978-1-4042-3650-9(3))*; Let's Go Canoeing & Kayaking. lib. bdg. 25.25 *(978-1-4042-3649-3(X))*; Let's Go Fishing. lib. bdg. 25.25 *(978-1-4042-3647-9(3))*; Let's Go Hiking. lib. bdg. 25.25 *(978-1-4042-3651-6(1))*; Let's Go Snowboarding. lib. bdg. 25.25 *(978-1-4042-3648-6(1))*; (Illus.). 32p. (J). (gr. 3-7). 2007. 2007. Set lib. bdg. 143.70 *(978-1-4042-3603-5(1)*, PowerKids Pr.) Rosen Publishing Group, Inc., The.

Sole Survivor. 2016. (Sole Survivor Ser.). 48p. (gr. 5-4). pap. 84.30 *(978-1-4824-5302-7(9))*; lib. bdg. 191.70 *(978-1-4824-4974-7(9))* Stevens, Gareth Publishing LLLP.

Spilsbury, Louise. Surviving the Ice. 2016. (Sole Survivor Ser.). 48p. (gr. 5-4). pap. 14.05 *(978-1-4824-5087-3(9))* Stevens, Gareth Publishing LLLP.

—Surviving the Mountain. 2016. (Sole Survivor Ser.). 48p. (gr. 5-4). pap. 14.05 *(978-1-4824-5083-5(6))* Stevens, Gareth Publishing LLLP.

Ward, Jennifer. Let's Go Outside! Outdoor Activities & Projects to Get You & Your Kids Closer to Nature. 2009. (ENG., Illus.). 144p. (gr. 3-7). pap. 14.00 *(978-1-59030-698-7(8)*, Roost Books) Shambhala Pubns., Inc.

Weakland, Mark. Yogi Bear's Guide to the Great Outdoors. Beach, Bryan & Cornia, Christian, illus. 2015. (Yogi Bear's Guide to the Great Outdoors Ser.). (ENG.). 32p. (gr. 1-2). 111.96 *(978-1-4914-6967-5(6))* Capstone Press of Coughlan Cos.

Wild Outdoors. 2011. (Wild Outdoors Ser.). (ENG.). 32p. (gr. 1-2). lib. bdg. 133.25 *(978-1-4296-6514-8(9)*, Blazers) Capstone Press of Coughlan Cos.

Young, Jeff C., et al. Into the Great Outdoors. 2013. (Into the Great Outdoors Ser.). (ENG.). 32p. (gr. 3-4). lib. bdg. 279.90 *(978-1-4296-9905-1(1))*; lib. bdg. 111.96 *(978-1-4296-9904-4(3))* Capstone Press of Coughlan Cos. (Edge Bks.).

OUTDOOR LIFE—FICTION

Aimard, Gustave. The Indian Scout: a Story of the Aster City. 2006. (ENG.). 464p. per. 37.95 *(978-1-4286-1776-6(0))* Kessinger Publishing, LLC.

Allen, Quinc. The Outdoor Chums. 2006. pap. *(978-1-4065-0782-9(2))* Dodo Pr.

—The Outdoor Chums after Big Game (Illust. 2006. pap. *(978-1-4065-0780-5(6))* Dodo Pr.

—The Outdoor Chums on the Gulf. 2006. pap. *(978-1-4065-0781-2(4))* Dodo Pr.

Ballantyne, R. M. Red Rooney: Or, the Last of the Crew. 2007. (R. M. Ballantyne Collection). (Illus.). 408p. 22.00 *(978-1-934554-08-1(1))* Vision Forum, Inc., The.

Ballantyne, Robert Michael. Red Rooney: The Last of the Crew. 2007. (ENG.). 270p. pap. 21.99 *(978-1-4346-3693-5(3))*; 302p. pap. 24.99 *(978-1-4346-3741-3(7))* Creative Media Partners, LLC.

Bentley, Sue. Moonlight Mischief. 2009. (Magic Kitten Ser.: 5). lib. bdg. 14.75 *(978-0-606-06016-5(2)*, Turtleback) Turtleback Bks.

Byrne, Marlene. Kick the Can. Graber, Jesse, illus. 2009. 61p. pap. 9.99 *(978-0-9777135-3-0(9))* Celtic Marketing Inc.

Clark, Henry Scott. The Legionaires: A Story of the Great Raid. 2005. reprint ed. pap. 34.95 *(978-1-4191-3923-9(1))* Kessinger Publishing, LLC.

Cole, Henry. On the Way to the Beach. Cole, Henry, illus. 2003. (ENG., Illus.). 32p. (J). (gr. -1-3). 16.99 *(978-0-688-17515-3(5)*, Greenwillow Bks.) HarperCollins Pubs.

Dilz, Ric. My Grandma Could Do Anything in the Great Outdoors! 2008. (Illus.). 32p. (J). 14.95 *(978-0-9758704-6-4(7))* Ric Design LLC.

Grant, Robert. Jack in the Bush or A Summer on a Salmon River. 2005. pap. 33.95 *(978-1-4179-5573-2(2))* Kessinger Publishing, LLC.

Keough, Rob. Wolf Summer. 2009. (Gem Lakes Ser.: 2). (ENG.). 192p. pap. 14.95 *(978-1-894283-87-8(2)*, Great Plains Teen Fiction) Great Plains Pubns. CAN. Dist: Publishers Group Canada.

London, Jonathan. Grizzly Peak. London, Sean, illus. 2017. (Aaron's Wilderness Ser.). (ENG.). 174p. (YA). pap. 12.99 *(978-1-943328-77-2(3)*, West Winds Pr.) Graphic Arts Ctr. Publishing Co.

Longstreth, Galen Goodwin. Yes, Let's. Wicks, Maris, illus. 2013. (ENG.). 32p. (J). (gr. -1-3). 15.95 *(978-1-933718-87-3(0))* Tanglewood Pr.

Mullendore, Bryan L. Scott's Many Adventures. 2010. 54p. pap. 22.95 *(978-0-557-63648-8(5))* Lulu Pr., Inc.

Peep for Keeps. 2005. 43p. (J). 3.99 *(978-0-9763213-4-7(3))* OHC Group LLC.

Pringle, Cindy & Pringle, Kirby. Happy Tails: The Call of Nature. 2008. (ENG., Illus.). 32p. (J). (gr. 2-7). *(978-0-9777126-1-8(3))* Dogtown Artworks.

M
N
O

Santillo, LuAnn. Mike. Santillo, LuAnn, ed. 2003. (Half-Pint Kids Readers Ser.). (Illus.). 7p. (J). (gr. -1-1). pap. 1.00 (978-1-59256-100-1(4)) Half-Pint Kids, Inc.
Schimler, Amy. Splish Splash! A Touch & Hear Book. Schimler, Amy, illus. 2011. (ENG., Illus.). 14p. (J). (gr. -1 — 1). bds. 6.99 (978-1-4424-1354-2(9), Little Simon) Little Simon.
Sedita, Francesco. Miss Popularity Goes Camping. 2009. (ENG.). 142p. (J). lib. bdg. 15.38 (978-1-4242-4383-9(1)) Fitzgerald Bks.
Seton, Ernest Thompson. Two Little Savages. 2011. (Dover Children's Classics Ser.). (ENG., Illus.). 320p. (J). (gr. 3-8). pap. 14.95 (978-0-486-20985-2(7)) Dover Pubns., Inc.
—Two Little Savages: The Adventures of Two Boys Who Lived As American Indians. Seton, Ernest Thompson, illus. 2010. (ENG., Illus.). 313p. (J). (gr. 4-7). pap. 18.00 (978-1-60419-033-5(7)) Axios Pr.
Thornes, William Henry. The Bushrangers a Yankee's Adventures During His Second Visit to Australia by William H Thornes. 2006. 420p. per. 26.99 (978-1-4255-4567-3(X)) Michigan Publishing.
Walker, Lane. The Boss on Redemption Road. 2014. 176p. pap. 9.99 (978-1-58169-563-2(2), Evergreen Pr.) Genesis Communications, Inc.
Wang, Adria. My World: My Outdoors. Nicholls, Paul, illus. 2005. (My World Bks.). 10p. (J). 4.95 (978-1-58117-249-2(4), Intervisual/Piggy Toes) Bendon, Inc.
Wright, Caleb E. Marcus Blair A Story of Provincial Times. 2006. pap. 22.95 (978-1-4286-6303-9(7)) Kessinger Publishing, LLC.

OUTDOOR SURVIVAL

see Wilderness Survival

OUTER SPACE

Aguilar, David A. Planets, Stars, & Galaxies: A Visual Encyclopedia of Our Universe. Aguilar, David A., illus. 2007. (ENG., Illus.). 192p. (J). (gr. 5-18). lib. bdg. 38.90 (978-1-4263-0171-1(5)); 24.95 (978-1-4263-0170-4(7)) National Geographic Society. (National Geographic Children's Bks.).
Aldrin, Buzz. Look to the Stars. Minor, Wendell, illus. 2009. (ENG.). 40p. (J). (gr. 1-3). 17.99 (978-0-399-24721-7(1), G.P. Putnam's Sons Books for Young Readers) Penguin Young Readers Group.
Arlon, Penelope & Gordon-Harris, Tory. Planets. 2012. (J). lib. bdg. (978-0-531-22957-6(2)) Scholastic, Inc.
Asimov, Isaac & Hantula, Richard. Asteroides. Porras, Carlos & D'Andrea, Patricia, trs. from ENG. 2003. (Isaac Asimov's Biblioteca del Universo del Siglo XXI).Tr. of Asteroids. (SPA., Illus.). 32p. (gr. 2-6). lib. bdg. 26.00 (978-0-8368-3853-4(X), Gareth Stevens Learning Library) Stevens, Gareth Publishing LLLP.
AZ Books Staff. Amazing Space. Ivinskaya, Snezhana, ed. 2012. (Encyclopedia with Flaps Ser.). (ENG.). 22p. (J). (gr. 1-3). bds. 13.95 (978-1-61889-150-1(2)) AZ Bks. LLC.
Becker, Helaine. Space: Blast off for a Universe of Photos, Facts, & Fun! 2015. (National Geographic Kids Everything Ser.). (ENG., Illus.). 64p. (J). (gr. 3-7). pap. 12.99 (978-1-4263-2074-3(4), National Geographic Children's Bks.) National Geographic Society.
Berkowitz, Jacob. Out of This World: The Amazing Search for an Alien Earth. 2009. (ENG., Illus.). 40p. (J). (gr. 3-7). 8.95 (978-1-55453-198-1(5)); 16.95 (978-1-55453-197-4(7)) Kids Can Pr., Ltd. CAN. Dist: Hachette Bk. Group.
Bow, James. Deep Space Extremes. 2008. (Extreme Nature Ser.). (ENG., Illus.). 32p. (J). (gr. 2-3). pap. (978-0-7787-4522-8(8)) Crabtree Publishing Co.
Bowman, Donna H. What Is the Moon Made Of? And Other Questions Kids Have about Space, 1 vol. Lubach, Peter, illus. (Kids' Questions Ser.). (ENG.). 24p. (gr. 1-2). 2011. pap. 7.49 (978-1-4048-6726-0(0)) 2009. lib. bdg. 26.65 (978-1-4048-5529-8(7)) Picture Window Bks.
Britannica, Learning Library. Exploring Space. 2003. (Illus.). 64p. 14.95 (978-1-59339-031-0(9)) Encyclopaedia Britannica, Inc.
Cain, Marie Mowery. Wide Open Space. 2013. (Big Books, Blue Ser.). (ENG & SPA., Illus.). 16p. pap. 33.00 (978-1-59246-002-1(X)) Big Books, by George!
Canavan, Thomas. Why Are Black Holes Black? Questions & Answers about Space. 2013. (Science F. A. Q. Ser.). 32p. (gr. 3-6). 31.35 (978-1-78212-395-8(4)) Arcturus Publishing GBR. Dist: Black Rabbit Bks.
Carson, Mary Kay. Exploring the Solar System: A History with 22 Activities. rev. ed. 2008. (For Kids Ser.). (ENG., Illus.). 176p. (J). (gr. 4-7). pap. 19.99 (978-1-55652-715-9(2)) Chicago Review Pr., Inc.
Conrad, David. Exploring Space. 2011. (Earth & Space Science Ser.). (ENG.). 24p. (gr. k-1). pap. 41.70 (978-1-4296-7143-9(2), Pebble Plus) Capstone Press of Coughlan Cos.
Coupper, Heather. Atlas Visual del Espacio. (Colección Atlas Visual). (SPA., Illus.). 64p. (YA). (gr. 5-8). (978-84-216-1816-5(4), BU5067) Bruño, Editorial ESP. Dist: Lectorum Pubns., Inc.
Creese, Sarah. Mad about Rockets Stars & Outer Space. 2009. (Mad About Ser.). (ENG., Illus.). 24p. (J). (gr. -1-3). pap. 3.99 (978-1-84879-007-0(4)) Make Believe Ideas GBR. Dist: Nelson, Thomas Inc.
Dakota, Heather. Space. Myers, Lawrence E., illus. 2008. 64p. (J). pap. (978-0-545-08503-8(9)) Scholastic, Inc.
Daynes, Katie. Living in Space. Fox, Christyan & Pang, Alex, illus. 2003. (Usborne Beginners Ser.). 32p. (J). (gr. 1). lib. bdg. 12.99 (978-1-58086-930-0(0), Usborne) EDC Publishing.
—See Inside Space. Allen, Peter, illus. 2009. (See Inside Board Bks). 16p. (J). (gr. 2). bds. 12.99 (978-0-7945-2088-5(X), Usborne) EDC Publishing.
Daynes, Katie & Wray, Zoe. Life in Space. Fox, Christyan & Pang, Alex, illus. 2008. (Usborne Beginners Ser.). 32p. (J). (978-0-545-06963-2(7)) Scholastic, Inc.
DiSiena, Laura Lyn & Eliot, Hannah. Saturn Could Sail: And Other Fun Facts. Oswald, Pete & Spurgeon, Aaron, illus. 2014. (Did You Know? Ser.). (ENG.). 32p. (J). (gr. -1-3). 17.99 (978-1-4814-1429-6(1)); pap. 6.99 (978-1-4814-1428-9(3)) Little Simon. (Little Simon).
Dorling Kindersley Publishing Staff. Sticker Encyclopedia Space. 2009. (ENG.). 96p. (J). (gr. k-2). pap. 12.99 (978-0-7566-5839-7(X), DK Children) Dorling Kindersley Publishing, Inc.
—Ultimate Factivity Collection: Space. 2016. (ENG., Illus.). 96p. (J). (gr. 1-4). pap. 12.99 (978-1-4654-4430-1(0), DK Children) Dorling Kindersley Publishing, Inc.
—Ultimate Sticker Book: Space. 2016. (Ultimate Sticker Bks.). (ENG.). 32p. (J). (gr. k-3). pap. 6.99 (978-1-4654-4881-1(0), DK Children) Dorling Kindersley Publishing, Inc.
Dowswell, Paul. Mi Primera Enciclopedia del Espacio. 2004. (Titles in Spanish Ser.).Tr. of First Encyclopedia of Space. (SPA.). (J). pap. 9.95 (978-0-7460-5075-0(5)) EDC Publishing.
—The Usborne Little Encyclopedia of Space. Bines, Gary & Hancock, David, illus. 2005. 64p. (J). (gr. -1-3). 6.95 (978-0-7945-1091-6(4), Usborne) EDC Publishing.
Doyle, Bill. The Space Explorer's Guide to the Universe. Labat, Yancey C., illus. 2003. (Space University Ser.). 48p. (J). (978-0-439-55739-9(9)) Scholastic, Inc.
Duhamel, Megan. Space. 2010. (Illus.). 16p. (J). (978-0-545-13723-2(3)) Scholastic, Inc.
Dyer, Alan. Space. 2007. (Insiders Ser.). (ENG., Illus.). 64p. (J). (gr. 3-7). 17.99 (978-1-4169-3860-6(5), Simon & Schuster Bks. For Young Readers) Simon & Schuster Bks. For Young Readers.
Earth & Space. (Illus.). (J). Date not set. 48p. 5.98 (978-1-4054-0206-4(7)) 2003. 256p. 12.98 (978-1-4054-1543-9(6)) Parragon, Inc.
Editors of TIME For Kids Magazine. Space. 2014. (TIME for Kids X-WHY-Z Ser.). (ENG., Illus.). 96p. (J). (gr. -1-1). 14.95 (978-1-61893-126-9(1)) Time Inc. Bks.
—Stellar Space. 2014. (TIME for Kids Big Books of WHY Ser.). (ENG., Illus.). 48p. (J). (gr. 3-17). pap. 4.99 (978-1-60320-985-4(9)) Time Inc. Bks.
Explore Outer Space: Set 2. 2013. (Explore Outer Space Ser.). 32p. (J). (gr. 3-6). 277.75 (978-1-4777-1541-3(X)) Windmill Bks.
First Discovery Staff & Grant, Donald. Atlas of Space. Grant, Donald, illus. 2006. (ENG., Illus.). 36p. (J). (gr. k-3). pap. 11.99 (978-1-85103-245-7(2)) Moonlight Publishing, Ltd. GBR. Dist: Independent Pubs. Group.
Flynn, Mike. Outer Space Explained, 1 vol. 2015. (ENG.). 136p. (J). 38.25 (978-1-4777-8128-9(5), Rosen Young Adult) Rosen Publishing Group, Inc., The.
Ford, Harry & Barnham, Kay. Outer Space. 2003. (Knowledge Masters Ser.). (Illus.). 32p. (YA). pap. incl. cd-rom (978-1-903954-09-6(6), Pavilion Children's Books) Pavilion Bks.
Fun Fact File: Space! 2014. (Fun Fact File: Space! Ser.). 32p. (J). (gr. 2-5). 151.50 (978-1-4824-0995-6(X)) Stevens, Gareth Publishing LLLP.
The Geek's Guide to Space. 2017. (Geek's Guide to Space Ser.). 192p. (gr. 12-14). 223.00 **(978-1-4994-6664-5(1)**, Rosen Young Adult) Rosen Publishing Group, Inc., The.
Goldsmith, Mike & Taylor, Barbara. Earth & Space: A Thrilling Adventure from Planet Earth into the Universe. 2016. (ENG., Illus.). 80p. 15.99 (978-0-7534-7279-8(1), 9780753472798, Kingfisher) Roaring Brook Pr.
Goldstein, Margaret J. Garbage in Space. 2017. (Space Discovery Guides). (ENG., Illus.). 48p. (J). (gr. 4-6). 31.99 (978-1-5124-2590-1(7)) Lerner Publishing Group.
Grego, Peter. My Little Book of Space. 2014. (Illus.). 64p. (J). (978-1-4351-5530-5(0)) Barnes & Noble, Inc.
Gregoire, Maryellen. Things in Space. 2011. (Wonder Readers Emergent Level Ser.). (ENG.). 8p. (gr. -1-1). pap. 35.94 (978-1-4296-8235-0(3), Wonder Readers) Capstone Press of Coughlan Cos.
Harrison, Paul. Space. (Up Close Ser.). 24p. (gr. 3-3). 2009. 47.90 (978-1-60854-704-3(3), PowerKids Pr.) 2008. (Illus.). (J). lib. bdg. 25.25 (978-1-4042-4221-0(X)) Rosen Publishing Group, Inc., The.
Hartson, Tamara & Super Explorers. Space, 1 vol. 2017. (Super Explorers Ser.). (ENG., Illus.). 64p. (J). pap. 6.99 **(978-1-926700-72-4(4)**, 9781926700724) Blue Bike Bks. CAN. Dist: Lone Pine Publishing USA.
Haslam, Andrew, et al. Space. (Make It Work! Ser.). (Illus.). 48p. (J). pap. 7.99 (978-0-590-24690-3(9)) Scholastic, Inc.
Hirschmann, Kris. Space & the Planets. Bollinger, Peter, illus. 2003. (Magic School Bus Fact Finder Ser.). (ENG.). 96p. (J). pap. 4.99 (978-0-439-38175-8(4)) Scholastic, Inc.
Hofer, Charles. Spacecraft. 2008. (World's Fastest Machines Ser.). (Illus.). 24p. lib. bdg. 22.60 (978-1-4042-4178-7(7), PowerKids Pr.) Rosen Publishing Group, Inc., The.
Howell, Laura & Rogers, Kirsteen. Earth & Space. 2004. (Library of Science Ser.). 64p. (J). lib. bdg. 17.95 (978-1-58086-373-5(6)) EDC Publishing.
Hubbard, Ben & Langley, Andrew. Adventures in Space. 2015. (Adventures in Space Ser.). (ENG.). 48p. (gr. 4-6). lib. bdg. 133.28 (978-1-4846-2518-7(8), Heinemann InfoSearch) Heinemann-Raintree.
Jefferis, David. Star Spotters: Telescopes & Observatories. 2008. (Exploring Our Solar System Ser.). (ENG., Illus.). 32p. (J). (gr. 4-9). pap. (978-0-7787-3742-1(X)) Crabtree Publishing Co.
Jerome, Kate Boehm & National Geographic Learning Staff. Exploring Space. 2006. (Nonfiction Reading & Writing Workshops Ser.). (ENG., Illus.). 32p. (J). pap. 17.95 (978-0-7922-8870-1(X)) CENGAGE Learning.
Jones, Rob Lloyd. Look Inside Space. 2012. (Look Inside Board Bks). 14p. (J). bds. 14.99 (978-0-7945-3282-6(9), Usborne) EDC Publishing.
Knapman, Timothy. Space. Canby, Kelly, illus. 2016. (Early Reader Non Fiction Ser.). (ENG.). 64p. (J). (gr. k-2). 6.99 (978-1-4440-1575-1(3), Orion Children's Bks.) Hachette Children's Group GBR. Dist: Hachette Bk. Group.
Kortenkamp, Steve. Show Me Space: My First Picture Encyclopedia, 1 vol. 2013. (My First Picture Encyclopedias Ser.). (ENG., Illus.). 32p. (gr. 1-2). 7.95 (978-1-62065-922-9(0), Aplus Bks.) Capstone Press of Coughlan Cos.
Kuligowski, Stephanie. 22nd Century: Future of Space, 1 vol. 2nd rev. ed. 2013. (Nonfiction Readers Ser.). (ENG., Illus.). 64p. (J). (gr. 5-5). pap. 31.96 (978-1-4333-7424-1(2)) Teacher Created Materials, Inc.
LaBaff, Stephanie. Draw Aliens & Space Objects in 4 Easy Steps: Then Write a Story. LaBaff, Tom, illus. 2012. (Drawing in 4 Easy Steps Ser.). 48p. (J). (gr. 3-18). lib. bdg. 25.27 (978-0-7660-3841-7(6)) Enslow Pubs., Inc.
Launch into Space! 2015. (Launch into Space! Ser.). (ENG.). 32p. (J). (gr. 3-4). 151.62 (978-0-7660-6682-3(7)) Enslow Pubs., Inc.
Let's Find Out! Space. 2014. (Let's Find Out! Ser.). 32p. (J). (gr. 3-6). 281.40 (978-1-62275-757-2(2)) Rosen Publishing Group, Inc., The.
Little & Large Sticker Activity - Space. 2006. (J). 3.99 (978-1-933581-36-1(0)) Byeway Bks.
Looking at Space. (Jump Ser.). 36p. (J). (gr. 2-7). pap. (978-1-882210-20-6(4)) Action Publishing, Inc.
Martin, Ruth. Little Explorers: Outer Space. Sanders, Allan, illus. 2016. (Little Explorers Ser.). (ENG.). 18p. (J). (gr. -1-3). 9.99 (978-1-4998-0250-4(1)) Little Bee Books Inc.
McGill, Jordan, ed. Space. 2011. (gr. 3-5). (J). pap. 13.95 (978-1-61690-865-2(3), AV2 by Weigl); (Illus.). 32p. (YA). 28.55 (978-1-61690-859-1(9)) Weigl Pubs., Inc.
Media, Cont. Sun Moon Stars. 2008. (ENG., Illus.). 48p. (YA). 12.99 (978-1-931703-09-3(4)) Creative Publishing Consultants.
Miles, Lisa. Astronomy & Space. 2010. (Complete Bks). 96p. (J). pap. 14.99 (978-0-7945-2626-9(8), Usborne) EDC Publishing.
Miller, Ron. Space Exploration. 2007. (Space Innovations Ser.). (ENG., Illus.). 112p. (gr. 6-8). lib. bdg. 31.93 (978-0-8225-7155-1(2)) Lerner Publishing Group.
Morris, Neil. What Does Space Exploration Do for Us?, 1 vol. 2011. (Earth, Space, & Beyond Ser.). (ENG.). 48p. (gr. 6-6). 34.65 (978-1-4109-4159-6(0), Raintree Freestyle) Heinemann-Raintree.
Morris, Ting & Morris, Neil. Space. Turvey, Raymond, illus. 2006. (Sticky Fingers Ser.). 32p. (J). lib. bdg. 27.10 (978-1-59771-032-9(6)) Sea-To-Sea Pubns.
Nardo, Don. Destined for Space: Our Story of Exploration, 1 vol. 2012. (Smithsonian Ser.). (ENG.). 64p. (gr. 4-5). pap. 8.95 (978-1-4296-8024-0(5)) Capstone Press of Coughlan Cos.
Nicolson, Cynthia Pratt & Bourgeois, Paulette. The Jumbo Book of Space. Nicolson, Cynthia Pratt & Slavin, Bill, illus. 2007. (Jumbo Bks.). (ENG.). 208p. (J). 17.95 (978-1-55453-020-5(2)) Kids Can Pr., Ltd. CAN. Dist: Hachette Bk. Group.
O'Brien, Eileen. Space. 2008. (Discovery Nature Ser.). 48p. (YA). (gr. 3-18). 8.99 (978-0-7945-2242-1(4), Usborne) EDC Publishing.
O'Hearn, Michael. Awesome Space Robots. 2013. (Robots Ser.). (ENG.). 32p. (gr. 3-4). pap. 47.70 (978-1-62065-779-9(1), Edge Bks.) Capstone Press of Coughlan Cos.
Ortler, Brett. Outer Space Activity Book. Juliano, Phil, illus. 2017. (Color & Learn Ser.). (ENG.). 64p. (J). (gr. k-5). pap. 6.95 (978-1-59193-708-1(6)) Adventure Pubns.
Outer Space. Date not set. (Illus.). 12p. (J). 3.98 (978-1-4054-0498-3(1)) Parragon, Inc.
Outer Space. 2014. (Ken Jennings' Junior Genius Guides). (ENG., Illus.). 160p. (J). (gr. 3-5). pap. 7.99 (978-1-4814-0170-8(X), Little Simon) Little Simon.
Oxlade, Chris. Why Why Why... Do Astronauts Float in Space? 2010. (Why Why Why Ser.). 32p. (J). (gr. 1-3). lib. bdg. 18.95 (978-1-4222-1578-4(4)) Mason Crest.
Parisi, Anthony. First Look at Space. Pindroh, Paula, illus. 2011. (ENG.). 16p. (J). (978-1-60727-225-0(3), Blackbirch Pr., Inc.) Soundprints.
Parker. Space Mysteries - Space Busters. 2004. (YA). pap. 48.30 (978-1-4109-0293-1(5)) Harcourt Schl. Pubs.
Parker, Steve & Oxlade, Chris. Earth & Space. 2007. (J). 159.00 (978-1-4042-1103-2(9), Rosen Reference) Rosen Publishing Group, Inc., The.
Penguin Books Staff, ed. Space. (Learners Ser.). (Illus.). 48p. (J). 3.50 (978-0-7214-1702-8(7), Dutton Juvenile) Penguin Publishing Group.
Pulliam, Christine & Daniels, Patricia. Space Encyclopedia: A Tour of Our Solar System & Beyond. Aguilar, David A., illus. 2013. 191p. (J). (978-1-4263-1629-6(1)) National Geographic Society.
¿Que Hay en el Espacio? (Coleccion Primeros Pasos en la Ciencia). (SPA., Illus.). (J). (gr. 1-3). pap. (978-950-724-099-7(3), LMA8217) Lumen ARG. Dist: Lectorum Pubns., Inc.
Rabe, Tish. Super Rover's Space Adventure (Dr. Seuss/Cat in the Hat) Brannon, Tom, illus. 2016. (Pictureback(R) Ser.). (ENG.). 24p. (J). (gr. -1-2). 4.99 (978-0-399-55204-5(9), Random Hse. Bks. for Young Readers) Random Hse. Children's Bks.
Red Bird Press Staff. Space. 2004. (Mission Xtreme 3D Ser.). 18p. (J). pap. 5.95 (978-1-902626-62-8(1)) Red Bird Publishing GBR. Dist: Weatherhill, Inc.
Redfern, Nick. True Stories of Space Exploration Conspiracies. 2014. (Off the Record! Ser.). 248p. (YA). (gr. 7-12). 38.25 (978-1-4777-7833-3(0)) Rosen Publishing Group, Inc., The.
Ripley's Believe It Or Not! Staff. Ripley Twists: Space PORTRAIT EDN. 2014. (Twist Ser.). (ENG.). 48p. (J). 12.95 (978-1-893951-87-7(1)) Ripley Entertainment, Inc.
Ripley's Inc. Staff. Zoom! Graziano, John, illus. 2012. (Ripley's Shout Outs Ser.: 2). (ENG.). 96p. (J). (gr. 2-5). pap. 4.99 (978-0-545-38076-8(6)) Scholastic, Inc.
Robertson, Ann E. The Militarization of Space. 2011. (Global Issues Ser.). 408p. (C). (gr. 9). 45.00 (978-0-8160-7873-8(4)) Facts On File, Inc.
Rockett, Paul. 70 Thousand Million, Million, Million Stars in Space. Ruffle, Mark, illus. 2015. (Big Countdown Ser.). (ENG.). 32p. (gr. 3-5). 29.99 (978-1-4109-6875-3(8), Raintree Perspectives) Heinemann-Raintree.
Rooney, Anne. A Math Journey Through Space. 2014. (ENG.). 32p. (J). (978-0-7787-0730-1(X)) Crabtree Publishing Co.
Royston, Angela. Space. 2015. (Research on the Edge Ser.). (ENG., Illus.). 32p. (gr. 3-8). 31.35 (978-1-62588-158-8(4)) Black Rabbit Bks.
Roytman, Arkady & Coloring Books Staff. Outer Space. 2011. (Build Window Stained Glass Coloring Book Ser.). (ENG., Illus.). 32p. (J). (gr. 3-5). pap. 6.99 (978-0-486-48392-4(4)) Dover Pubns., Inc.
Roza, Greg. Space Math. (Reading Room Collection 2 Ser.). 24p. 2009. (gr. 3-4). 42.50 (978-1-60851-989-7(9), PowerKids Pr.) 2003. (Illus.). (J). lib. bdg. 22.60 (978-0-8239-3705-9(4)) Rosen Publishing Group, Inc., The.
Russell, Harriet. Drawing in Space. 2017. (ENG.). 64p. (J). (gr. 1-3). pap. 18.95 (978-1-61689-497-9(0)) Princeton Architectural Pr.
Rustad, Martha E. H. Exploring Space. 2012. (Exploring Space Ser.). (ENG.). 24p. (gr. k-1). pap. 250.20 (978-1-4296-8333-3(3)); pap. 21.87 (978-1-4296-8332-6(5)); lib. bdg. 159.90 (978-1-4296-8113-1(6)) Capstone Press of Coughlan Cos. (Pebble Plus).
Samuel, Nigel. The 10 Coolest Wonders of the Universe. 2008. (Illus.). (J). 14.99 (978-1-55448-490-4(1)) Scholastic Library Publishing.
Science, Punk & Punk Science Staff. Punk Science - Intergalactic, Supermassive Space Book, Vol. 1. unabr. ed. 2015. (ENG., Illus.). 96p. (J). (gr. 2). pap. 7.99 (978-1-4472-5384-6(1)) Pan Macmillan GBR. Dist: Independent Pubs. Group.
Science Readers Staff & Jankowski, Connie. From Hubble to Hubble: Astromers & Outer Space, 1 vol. 2007. (Science Readers Ser.). (ENG., Illus.). 32p. (J). (gr. 3-3). pap. 8.99 (978-0-7439-0564-0(4)) Shell Educational Publishing.
—The Wonder of Outer Space, 1 vol. 2007. (Science Readers Ser.). (SPA & ENG., Illus.). 32p. (J). (gr. 4-4). pap. 8.99 (978-0-7439-0563-3(6)) Shell Educational Publishing.
Secrets of Space, 3 vols. lib. bdg. 50.94 (978-0-8050-5022-6(1), Twenty-First Century Bks.) Lerner Publishing Group.
Smith, A. Book of Astronomy & Space. 2004. (Complete Bks.). (SPA., Illus.). 96p. (J). lib. bdg. 22.95 (978-1-58086-385-8(X)) EDC Publishing.
Smithsonian Institution Staff, contrib. by. Destined for Space: Our Story of Exploration, 1 vol. 2012. (Smithsonian Ser.). (ENG.). 64p. (gr. 4-5). lib. bdg. 34.65 (978-1-4296-7540-6(3)) Capstone Press of Coughlan Cos.
Spilsbury, Louise. Projects with Space. 2014. (Make & Learn Ser.). (Illus.). 32p. (J). (gr. 3-6). lib. bdg. 27.50 (978-1-4777-7177-8(8), PowerKids Pr.) Rosen Publishing Group, Inc., The.
Spilsbury, Louise & Spilsbury, Richard. In Space. 2016. (Science on Patrol Ser.). 00048p. (J). pap. 14.05 **(978-1-4824-5972-2(8))** Stevens, Gareth Publishing LLLP.
Stone, Lynn. Space (Skywatch) 2008. (ENG.). 24p. (gr. k-3). pap. 8.95 (978-1-60472-957-3(0)) Rourke Educational Media.
Stott, Carole. Eye Wonder: Space. 2016. (Eye Wonder Ser.). (ENG., Illus.). 56p. (J). (gr. k-4). 10.99 (978-1-4654-1856-2(3), DK Children) Dorling Kindersley Publishing, Inc.
—Mission: Space: Explore the Galaxy. 2016. (Illus.). 128p. (J). (978-1-4654-5376-1(8)) Dorling Kindersley Publishing, Inc.
Stuart, Colin. Why Space Matters to Me. 2015. (ENG., Illus.). 48p. (J). (gr. 2-4). 12.99 (978-1-60684-589-9(6), Millbrook Pr.) Lerner Publishing Group.
The Sun. (Eyes on Adventure Ser.). (J). 32p. (gr. 1). pap. (978-1-882210-62-6(X)); 42p. (gr. 4-8). pap. (978-1-882210-49-7(2)) Action Publishing, Inc.
The Sun. 2009. (FACT ATLAS Ser.). 72p. (J). (gr. 3-7). pap. 13.99 (978-0-8437-1896-6(X)) Hammond World Atlas Corp.
Turner, Tracey & Kindberg, Sally. The Comic Strip Big Fat Book of Knowledge. 2012. (ENG., Illus.). 288p. (J). (gr. 6-9). pap. 18.99 (978-1-4088-0824-5(2), 9781408808245, Bloomsbury USA Childrens) Bloomsbury Publishing USA.
Wadsworth, Pamela. Amser a Gofod. 2005. (WEL., Illus.). 24p. pap. (978-1-85596-241-5(1)) Dref Wen.
—Rhagor Am Amser a Gofod. 2005. (WEL., Illus.). 24p. pap. (978-1-85596-242-2(X)) Dref Wen.
Walsh, Kenneth. Outer Space, 1 vol. 2nd rev. ed. 2013. (Nonfiction Readers Ser.). (ENG., Illus.). 28p. (J). (gr. 2-2). pap. 23.96 (978-1-4807-1053-5(9)) Shell Educational Publishing.
—Outer Space, 1 vol. 2nd rev. ed. 2011. (Nonfiction Readers Ser.). (ENG.). 28p. (J). (gr. 2-2). pap. 6.99 (978-1-4333-3632-4(4)) Teacher Created Materials, Inc.
Walsh, Kieran. Space Math. 2005. (Math & My World Ser.). (Illus.). 48p. (J). (gr. 4-6). lib. bdg. 20.95 (978-1-59515-494-1(9)) Rourke Educational Media.
Willett, Edward. Space Q&a. 2014. (Science Discovery Ser.). (ENG., Illus.). 48p. (J). (gr. 4-7). lib. bdg. 28.55 (978-1-4896-0692-1(0), AV2 by Weigl) Weigl Pubs., Inc.
Wolny, Philip. Weapons Satellites. 2009. (Library of Satellites Ser.). 64p. (gr. 5-8). 58.50 (978-1-60853-834-8(6), Rosen Reference) Rosen Publishing Group, Inc., The.
Wooster, Patricia. An Illustrated Timeline of Space Exploration, 1 vol. Doty, Eldon, illus. 2011. (Visual Timelines in History Ser.). (ENG.). 32p. (gr. 3-4). lib. bdg. 28.65 (978-1-4048-6660-7(4)) Picture Window Bks.
World Book, Inc Staff, contrib. by. Human Space Exploration. 2010. (J). (978-0-7166-9543-1(X)) World Bk., Inc.
Wynne, Patricia J. & Silver, Donald M. My First Book about Outer Space. 2015. (ENG.). 48p. (J). (gr. 3-8). pap. 4.99 (978-0-486-78329-1(4)) Dover Pubns., Inc.

OUTER SPACE—COMMUNICATION

see Interstellar Communication

OUTER SPACE—EXPLORATION

Adamson, Thomas K. & Kortenkamp, Steve. You Choose: Space. 2016. (You Choose: Space Ser.). (ENG.). 112p. (gr. 3-4). 127.96 (978-1-4914-8365-7(2), You Choose Bks.) Capstone Press of Coughlan Cos.
Alexander, Florence & Alexander, Stanley. Space Exploration. l.t. ed. 2003. (Come with Me & See Ser.). (ENG & SPA., Illus.). 32p. (J). 7.99 (978-0-915960-75-0(3)) Ebon Research Systems Publishing, LLC.
Anderson, Amy & Anderson, Brian. Space Dictionary for Kids: The Everything Guide for Kids Who Love Space. 2016. (ENG., Illus.). 200p. (J). (gr. 4-7). 13.95 (978-1-61821-515-4(9), 9781618215154) Prufrock Pr.
Angelo, Joseph A., Jr. Human Spaceflight. 2007. (Frontiers in Space Ser.). (Illus.). 272p. (C). (gr. 9-10). 45.00 (978-0-8160-5775-7(3)) Facts On File, Inc.
Arnold, Tedd. Space. 2013. (Fly Guy Presents Ser.). lib. bdg. 13.55 (978-0-606-32353-6(8), Turtleback) Turtleback Bks.
Asimov, Isaac & Hantula, Richard. Global Space Programs: Past & Present. 2005. (Isaac Asimov's 21st Century Library of the Universe). (Illus.). 32p. (gr. 2-6). lib. bdg. 26.00 (978-0-8368-3982-1(X), Gareth Stevens Learning Library) Stevens, Gareth Publishing LLLP.
Bailey, Diane. The Future of Space Exploration. 2012. (What's Next? Ser.). (Illus.). 48p. (J). (gr. 5-12). 23.95

(978-1-60818-223-7(1), Creative Education) Creative Co., The.

Bailey, Gerry. Space Challenge. 2011. (Planet SOS Ser.). (Illus.). 48p. (J). (gr. 3-6). pap. 14.05 *(978-1-4339-4983-8(0)*, Gareth Stevens Learning Library) Stevens, Gareth Publishing LLLP.

Baker, David. Satellites. 2008. (Exploring Space Ser.). (Illus.). 32p. (J). (gr. 4-6). lib. bdg. 26.00 *(978-1-59036-777-3(4))* Weigl Pubs., Inc.

—The Shuttle. 2008. (Exploring Space Ser.). (Illus.). 32p. (J). (gr. 4-6). lib. bdg. 26.00 *(978-1-59036-767-4(7))* Weigl Pubs., Inc.

Baker, David & Kissock, Heather. The International Space Station. 2016. (J). ***(978-1-4896-5824-1(6)***, AV2 by Weigl) Weigl Pubs., Inc.

—Rockets. 2016. (J). ***(978-1-4896-5821-0(1)***, AV2 by Weigl) Weigl Pubs., Inc.

—Satellites. 2008. (Exploring Space Ser.). (Illus.). 32p. (J). (gr. 4-6). pap. 9.95 *(978-1-59036-778-0(2))* Weigl Pubs., Inc.

—The Shuttle. 2008. (Exploring Space Ser.). (Illus.). 32p. (J). (gr. 4-6). pap. 9.95 *(978-1-59036-768-1(5))* Weigl Pubs., Inc.

Banquieri, Eduardo. Space. 2005. (Our Planet Ser.). (Illus.). 32p. (gr. 4-6). lib. bdg. 28.00 *(978-0-7910-9009-1(4)*, Chelsea Clubhouse) Facts On File, Inc.

Barchers, Suzanne I. Revolution in Space. 2009. (It Works! Ser.). 32p. (gr. 3). 28.50 *(978-0-7614-4377-3(0))* Marshall Cavendish Corp.

Basher, Simon. Basher Basics: Space Exploration. Basher, Simon, illus. 2013. (Basher Basics Ser.). (ENG., Illus.). 64p. (J). (gr. 3-7). pap. 7.99 *(978-0-7534-7165-4(5)*, 9780753471654, Kingfisher) Roaring Brook Pr.

Bellisario, Gina. To the Stars! Moran, Mike, illus. 2017. (Cloverleaf Books (tm) — Space Adventures Ser.). (ENG.). 24p. (J). (gr. k-2). 25.32 *(978-1-5124-2537-6(0))*; 6.99 ***(978-1-5124-3897-0(9))***; 38.65 ***(978-1-5124-2834-6(5))***; 38.65 ***(978-1-5124-3896-3(0))*** Lerner Publishing Group. (Millbrook Pr.).

Berne, Emma Carlson. Totally Wacky Facts about Exploring Space. 2015. (Mind Benders Ser.). (ENG., Illus.). 112p. (gr. 1-3). lib. bdg. 23.32 *(978-1-4914-6524-0(7))* Capstone Press of Coughlan Cos.

—Totally Wacky Facts about Space. 2015. (Mind Benders Ser.). (ENG., Illus.). 240p. (gr. 1-3). pap. 7.95 *(978-1-4914-6526-4(3))* Capstone Press of Coughlan Cos.

Block, Dakota. Exploring the Solar System. 2012. (Exploring Earth & Space Ser.). (ENG., Illus.). 24p. (J). (gr. 1-3). 22.60 *(978-1-4488-8572-5(8)*, PowerKids Pr.) Rosen Publishing Group, Inc., The.

Bortz, Fred. Envisioning Outer Space: Where Science & Fiction Meet. 2015. (J). *(978-1-4677-6305-9(5))*; lib. bdg. *(978-1-4677-3740-1(2))* Twenty First Century Bks.

—Seven Wonders of Space Technology. 2011. (Seven Wonders Ser.). (ENG., Illus.). 80p. (gr. 5-8). 33.26 *(978-0-7613-5453-6(0))* Lerner Publishing Group.

Bow, James. Deep Space Extremes. 2008. (Extreme Nature Ser.). (ENG., Illus.). 32p. (J). (gr. 2-4). lib. bdg. *(978-0-7787-4505-1(8))* Crabtree Publishing Co.

Bredeson, Carmen & Dyson, Marianne. Astronauts Explore the Galaxy. 2015. (Launch into Space! Ser.). (ENG.). 32p. (J). (gr. 3-4). pap. 10.52 *(978-0-7660-6813-1(7))* Enslow Pubs., Inc.

—Exploring the Solar System. 2015. (Launch into Space! Ser.). (ENG.). 32p. (J). (gr. 3-4). pap. 10.52 *(978-0-7660-6825-4(0))* Enslow Pubs., Inc.

Bredeson, Carmen, et al. Astronauts Explore the Galaxy. 2015. (Launch into Space! Ser.). (ENG., Illus.). 32p. (J). (gr. 3-4). 25.27 *(978-0-7660-6815-5(3))* Enslow Pubs., Inc.

—Exploring the Solar System. 2015. (Launch into Space! Ser.). (ENG., Illus.). 32p. (J). (gr. 3-4). 25.27 *(978-0-7660-6827-8(7))* Enslow Pubs., Inc.

Bright, Michael. Journey into Space. 2017. (Planet Earth Ser.). 32p. (gr. 9-10). 26.25 ***(978-1-5081-5393-1(0)***, PowerKids Pr.) Rosen Publishing Group, Inc., The.

Brownell, Richard, ed. Space Exploration. 2012. (World History Ser.). (ENG., Illus.). 128p. (gr. 7-10). lib. bdg. 34.95 *(978-1-4205-0875-8(X)*, Lucent Bks.) Cengage Gale.

Bryant, Ray, illus. The Book of Space. 2013. (Questions Ser.). (ENG.). 64p. (J). (gr. k-3). 7.99 *(978-0-7534-7099-2(3)*, 9780753470992, Kingfisher) Roaring Brook Pr.

Buckley, James, Jr. Space Exploration, Vol. 7. 2016. (Solar System Ser.: Vol. 7). (ENG., Illus.). 48p. (J). (gr. 5-8). 20.95 *(978-1-4222-3644-4(7))* Mason Crest.

Carroll, Jillian. Hot Spot. 2003. (J). pap. *(978-1-58417-235-2(5))*; lib. bdg. *(978-1-58417-234-5(7))* Lake Street Pubs.

—Zoom Around a Moon. 2003. (J). pap. *(978-1-58417-241-3(X))*; lib. bdg. *(978-1-58417-240-6(1))* Lake Street Pubs.

Carson, Mary Kay. The Mission to Pluto: The First Visit to an Ice Dwarf & the Kuiper Belt. Uhlman, Tom, photos by. 2017. (Scientists in the Field Ser.). (ENG., Illus.). 80p. (J). (gr. 5-7). 18.99 *(978-0-544-41671-0(6)*, HMH Books For Young Readers) Houghton Mifflin Harcourt Publishing Co.

Castaldo, Nancy F. Leap into Space: Exploring the Universe & Your Place in It. McRae, Patrick, illus. 2008. (ENG.). 128p. (J). (gr. 3-7). 16.99 *(978-0-8249-6815-1(8))*; pap. 12.99 *(978-0-8249-6816-8(6))* Worthy Publishing. (Ideal Pubns.).

Cerullo, Mary M. & Nardo, Don. Smithsonian. 2012. (Smithsonian Ser.). (ENG.). (gr. 2-6). 63.97 *(978-1-4296-8100-1(4))*; pap. 107.40 *(978-1-4296-8526-9(3))*; pap. 17.90 *(978-1-4296-8525-2(5))* Capstone Press of Coughlan Cos.

Clarke, Penny. The Story of the Exploration of Space. Antram, David et al, illus. 2013. 64p. (J). *(978-1-4351-5030-0(9))* Barnes & Noble, Inc.

Clay, Kathryn. Astronaut in Training. 2017. (Little Astronauts Ser.). (ENG., Illus.). 32p. (gr. 1-2). lib. bdg. 27.99 *(978-1-5157-3660-8(1))* Capstone Press of Coughlan Cos.

—Living in Space. 2017. (Little Astronauts Ser.). (ENG., Illus.). 32p. (gr. 1-2). lib. bdg. 27.99 *(978-1-5157-3657-8(1))* Capstone Press of Coughlan Cos.

—Space Flights. 2017. (Little Astronauts Ser.). (ENG., Illus.). 32p. (gr. 1-2). lib. bdg. 27.99 *(978-1-5157-3659-2(8))* Capstone Press of Coughlan Cos.

—Spacewalks. 2017. (Little Astronauts Ser.). (ENG., Illus.). 32p. (gr. 1-2). lib. bdg. 27.99 *(978-1-5157-3658-5(X))* Capstone Press of Coughlan Cos.

Cole, Joanna. Lost in the Solar System. Degen, Bruce, illus. 2010. (Magic School Bus Ser.). (ENG.). (J). (gr. -1-3). 18.95 *(978-0-545-22337-9(7))* Scholastic, Inc.

Conrad, David. Exploring Space, 1 vol. 2011. (Earth & Space Science Ser.). (ENG.). 24p. (gr. k-1). pap. 7.29 *(978-1-4296-7139-2(4))*; lib. bdg. 26.65 *(978-1-4296-6810-1(5))* Capstone Press of Coughlan Cos. (Pebble Plus).

Countdown to Space, 40 bks. , Set. (Illus.). (YA). (gr. 4-10). lib. bdg. 758.00 *(978-0-89490-562-9(7))* Enslow Pubs., Inc.

Currie, Stephen & National Geographic Learning Staff. Missions in Space. 2007. (Reading Expeditions Ser.). (ENG., Illus.). 32p. (J). pap. 17.95 *(978-0-7922-4546-9(6))* CENGAGE Learning.

(Del) Space Mysteries: Set 2. 2013. (Space Mysteries Ser.). 32p. (J). (gr. 2-5). 279.80 *(978-1-4824-0003-8(0))* Stevens, Gareth Publishing LLLP.

Dickmann, Nancy. Exploring Beyond the Solar System. 2015. (Spectacular Space Science Ser.). (ENG., Illus.). 48p. (J). (gr. 5-6). 30.25 *(978-1-4994-3641-9(6)*, Rosen Central) Rosen Publishing Group, Inc., The.

—Exploring Comets, Asteroids, & Other Objects in Space. 2015. (Spectacular Space Science Ser.). (ENG., Illus.). 48p. (J). (gr. 5-6). 30.25 *(978-1-4994-3637-2(8)*, Rosen Central) Rosen Publishing Group, Inc., The.

—Exploring the Inner Planets. 2015. (Spectacular Space Science Ser.). (ENG., Illus.). 48p. (J). (gr. 5-6). 30.25 *(978-1-4994-3629-7(7)*, Rosen Central) Rosen Publishing Group, Inc., The.

—Exploring the Outer Planets. 2015. (Spectacular Space Science Ser.). (ENG., Illus.). 48p. (J). (gr. 5-6). 30.25 *(978-1-4994-3633-4(5)*, Rosen Central) Rosen Publishing Group, Inc., The.

Doeden, Matt. Human Travel to the Moon & Mars: Waste of Money or Next Frontier? 2011. (USA TODAY's Debate: Voices & Perspectives Ser.). (ENG., Illus.). 112p. (gr. 9-12). lib. bdg. 35.93 *(978-0-7613-6436-8(6)*, Twenty-First Century Bks.) Lerner Publishing Group.

Dorling Kindersley Publishing Staff. DK Eyewitness Books: Universe: Universe. 2015. (DK Eyewitness Bks.). (ENG., Illus.). 72p. (J). (gr. 3-7). 19.99 *(978-1-4654-3362-6(7)*, DK Children) Dorling Kindersley Publishing, Inc.

—Eyewitness - Universe. 2015. (DK Eyewitness Bks.). (ENG.). 72p. (J). (gr. 3-7). pap. 9.99 *(978-1-4654-3187-5(X)*, DK Children) Dorling Kindersley Publishing, Inc.

Dugan, Christine. La Exploración Del Espacio. 2017. (TIME for Kids en Español - Level 3 Ser.). (SPA.). 32p. (gr. 3-3). lib. bdg. 31.99 ***(978-1-5157-5181-6(3))*** Time for Kids Inc AUS. Dist: Capstone Pub.

—Space Exploration, 1 vol. 2nd rev. ed. 2014. (TIME for KIDS(r) Nonfiction Readers Ser.). (ENG., Illus.). 32p. (J). (gr. 3-3). pap. 25.96 *(978-1-4807-1083-2(0))* Shell Educational Publishing.

—Space Exploration, 1 vol. 2nd rev. ed. 2012. (Nonfiction Readers Ser.). (ENG.). 32p. (J). (gr. 3-3). pap. 8.99 *(978-1-4333-3674-4(X))* Teacher Created Materials, Inc.

Dugan, Christine. La Vida en el Espacio. 2017. (TIME for Kids en Español - Level 3 Ser.). (SPA.). 32p. (gr. 3-3). lib. bdg. 31.99 ***(978-1-5157-5182-3(1))*** Time for Kids Inc AUS. Dist: Capstone Pub.

Einspruch, Andrew. Mysteries of the Universe: How Astronomers Explore Space. 2006. (Science Chapters Ser.). (ENG., Illus.). 48p. (J). (gr. 1-4). lib. bdg. 17.90 *(978-0-7922-5956-5(4)*, National Geographic Children's Bks.) National Geographic Society.

Elish, Dan. NASA. 2006. (Kaleidoscope Space Ser.). (Illus.). 48p. (gr. 3-7). lib. bdg. 20.95 *(978-0-7614-2046-0(0)*, Benchmark Bks.) Marshall Cavendish Corp.

Encyclopaedia Britannica, Inc. Staff, compiled by. Britannica Illustrated Science Library: Space Exploration, 16 vols. 2008. (Illus.). (J). 29.95 *(978-1-59339-397-7(0))* Encyclopaedia Britannica, Inc.

—Exploring Space. 2003. (Britannica Learning Library). (gr. 2-5). 14.95 *(978-1-59339-000-6(9)*, 049901-EN-REF) Encyclopaedia Britannica, Inc.

—Space Exploration. 2008. 49.95 *(978-1-59339-689-3(9))* Encyclopaedia Britannica, Inc.

Explore Outer Space: Sets 1 - 2. 2013. (Explore Outer Space Ser.). 32p. (J). (gr. 3-6). 429.25 *(978-1-61533-869-6(1))*; pap. 1020.00 *(978-1-61533-883-2(7))*; pap. 170.00 *(978-1-61533-882-5(9))* Windmill Bks.

Explore Space. (Color & Learn Ser.). 36p. (J). (gr. 1-5). pap. *(978-1-882210-13-8(1))* Action Publishing, Inc.

Exploring Space. 2004. (J). cd-rom *(978-0-9764218-3-2(6))* Dawasoft.

Exploring Space. (Eyes on Adventure Ser.). (Illus.). 32p. (J). (gr. 1-18). 7.95 *(978-1-56156-488-0(5))* Kidsbooks, LLC.

Exploring Space, 6 vols. (Sunshinetm Science Ser.). 24p. (gr. 1-2). 31.50 *(978-0-7802-0294-8(5))* Wright Group/McGraw-Hill.

Exploring Space, Revised Edition. 2nd rev. ed. 2009. (Discovery & Exploration Ser.). (Illus.). 120p. (gr. 5-8). 35.00 *(978-1-60413-188-8(8)*, Chelsea Hse.) Facts On File, Inc.

Eyewitness - Space Exploration. 2014. (DK Eyewitness Bks.). (ENG., Illus.). 72p. (J). (gr. 3-7). lib. bdg. 19.99 *(978-1-4654-2621-5(3)*, DK Children) Dorling Kindersley Publishing, Inc.

Faust, Daniel R. After Earth: Living on a Different Planet. 2008. (Jr. Graphic Environmental Dangers Ser.). (ENG.). 24p. (J). 47.90 *(978-1-61532-099-8(7)*, PowerKids Pr.) Rosen Publishing Group, Inc., The.

—Más Allá de la Tierra: Vivir en Otro Planeta. 2009. (Historietas Juveniles: Peligros Del Medioambiente (Jr. Graphic Environmental Dangers) Ser.). (SPA., Illus.). 24p. (gr. 3-6). (YA). lib. bdg. 25.25 *(978-1-4358-8471-7(X))*; pap. 10.60 *(978-1-4358-8472-4(8))* Rosen Publishing Group, Inc., The.

Felix, Rebecca. 12 Things to Know about Space Exploration. 2015. (ENG., Illus.). 32p. (J). *(978-1-63235-032-9(7))* Pr. Room Editions LLC.

From Earth to the Stars. 2017. (From Earth to the Stars Ser.). 48p. (gr. 10-12). 107.40 ***(978-1-5081-0527-5(8))***; pap. 56.20 ***(978-1-5081-0529-9(4))*** Rosen Publishing Group, Inc., The. (Britannica Educational Publishing).

Furgang, Adam. Human Spaceflight. 2017. (From Earth to the Stars Ser.). 48p. (gr. 10-12). pap. 14.05 ***(978-1-68048-669-8(1)***, Britannica Educational Publishing) Rosen Publishing Group, Inc., The.

Furgang, Kathy. Rocket Science & Spacecraft Fundamentals. 2017. (From Earth to the Stars Ser.). 48p. (gr. 10-12). pap. 14.05 ***(978-1-68048-673-5(X)***, Britannica Educational Publishing) Rosen Publishing Group, Inc., The.

Furstinger, Nancy. Robots in Space. 2014. (Lightning Bolt Books Robots Everywhere! Ser.). (Illus.). 32p. (gr. k-2). (J). lib. bdg. 26.60 *(978-1-4677-4055-5(1)*, Lerner Pubns.); pap. 7.95 *(978-1-4677-4510-9(3))* Lerner Publishing Group.

Gareth Stevens Publishing Staff, contrib. by. Space Exploration. 2003. (Discovery Channel School Science Ser.). (Illus.). 32p. (gr. 4-8). lib. bdg. 26.00 *(978-0-8368-3373-7(2)*, Gareth Stevens Learning Library) Stevens, Gareth Publishing LLLP.

Gifford, Clive. Astronomy, Astronauts, & Space Exploration. 2015. (Watch This Space! Ser.). (ENG., Illus.). 32p. (J). (gr. 3-7). lib. bdg. *(978-0-7787-2021-8(7))* Crabtree Publishing Co.

Goldsworthy, Steve. Famous Explorers. 2011. (J). (gr. 4-6). pap. 13.95 *(978-1-61690-636-8(7)*, AV2 by Weigl); (Illus.). 32p. (YA). (gr. 2-5). 28.55 *(978-1-61690-632-0(4))* Weigl Pubs., Inc.

Goldsworthy, Steve. Space Explorers. 2017. (J). ***(978-1-4896-5815-9(7)***, AV2 by Weigl) Weigl Pubs., Inc.

Green, Jen. The Story of the Race to the Moon. Mark Bergin, illus. 2017. (Explorers Ser.). 32p. (gr. 3-6). 31.35 ***(978-1-910706-92-3(2))*** Book Hse. GBR. Dist: Black Rabbit Bks.

Gregory, Josh. If You Were a Kid Docking at the International Space Station. 2017. (If You Were a Kid Ser.). (ENG.). 32p. (J). lib. bdg. 26.00 ***(978-0-531-23746-5(X)***, Children's Pr.) Scholastic Library Publishing.

—If You Were a Kid Docking at the International Space Station. Raish, Jason, illus. 2017. (If You Were a Kid Ser.). (ENG.). 32p. (J). pap. 7.95 ***(978-0-531-23947-6(0)***, Children's Pr.) Scholastic Library Publishing.

Greve, Tom. Thanks, Nasa! 2012. (ENG.). 48p. (gr. 4-6). pap. 10.95 *(978-1-61810-253-9(2))* Rourke Educational Media.

Gross, Miriam. All about Space Missions. 2009. (Blast Off! Ser.). 24p. (gr. 2-3). 42.50 *(978-1-61511-623-2(0)*, PowerKids Pr.) Rosen Publishing Group, Inc., The.

Gross, Miriam J. All about Space Missions. 2009. (Blast Off! Ser.). 24p. (J). (gr. 2-5). (ENG.). pap. 8.25 *(978-1-4358-3138-4(1))*; lib. bdg. 22.60 *(978-1-4358-2740-0(6))* Rosen Publishing Group, Inc., The. (PowerKids Pr.).

Group/McGraw-Hill, Wright. History: Space Exploration, 6 vols. (Book2WebTM Ser.). (gr. 4-8). 36.50 *(978-0-322-04456-2(1))* Wright Group/McGraw-Hill.

Hamilton, S. L. Astronaut Firsts. 2011. (Xtreme Space Ser.). (Illus.). 32p. (gr. 3-9). 27.07 *(978-1-61714-736-4(2)*, A&D Xtreme) ABDO Publishing Co.

—Exploration. 2011. (Xtreme Space Ser.). (Illus.). 32p. (gr. 3-9). 27.07 *(978-1-61714-737-1(0)*, A&D Xtreme) ABDO Publishing Co.

Hamilton, Tracy Brown. All about Spacecraft. 2016. (Let's Find Out! Ser.). 32p. (J). (gr. 3-2). lib. bdg. 24.45 *(978-1-68048-445-8(1))* Rosen Publishing Group, Inc., The.

Harmon, Daniel E. The Early Days of Space Exploration. 2017. (From Earth to the Stars Ser.). 48p. (gr. 10-12). pap. 14.05 ***(978-1-68048-665-0(9)***, Britannica Educational Publishing) Rosen Publishing Group, Inc., The.

Harris, Joseph. Space Exploration: The Impact of Science & Technology. 2009. (Pros & Cons Ser.). (ENG.). 64p. (YA). (gr. 5-9). lib. bdg. 35.00 *(978-1-4339-1989-3(3))* Stevens, Gareth Publishing LLLP.

Hartson, Tamara & Super Explorers. Space, 1 vol. 2017. (Super Explorers Ser.). (ENG., Illus.). 64p. (J). pap. 6.99 ***(978-1-926700-72-4(4)***, 9781926700724) Blue Bike Bks. CAN. Dist: Lone Pine Publishing USA.

Haugen, David M., ed. Space Exploration. 2011. (At Issue Ser.). 128p. pap. 24.45 *(978-0-7377-5597-8(0)*, Greenhaven Pr., Inc.); (YA). (gr. 9-12). 34.45 *(978-0-7377-5596-1(2))* Cengage Gale.

Hermsen, Sarah. Space Exploration Library Cumulative Index. 2004. (Space Exploration Reference Library). (ENG.). 42p. (J). lib. bdg. 5.00 *(978-0-7876-9214-8(X)*, UXL) Cengage Gale.

Hofer, Charles. Spacecraft. 2009. (World's Fastest Machines Ser.). 24p. (gr. 2-3). 42.50 *(978-1-60854-855-2(4)*, PowerKids Pr.) Rosen Publishing Group, Inc., The.

Holcroft, John & Candlewick Press Staff. Space Exploration: Panorama Pops. Holcroft, John, illus. 2015. (ENG., Illus.). 30p. (J). (gr. k-4). 8.99 *(978-0-7636-7699-5(3))* Candlewick Pr.

Hopping, Lorraine Jean. Space Rocks: The Story of Planetary Geologist Adriana Ocampo. 2006. (ENG., Illus.). 128p. (gr. 7-9). per. 19.95 *(978-0-309-09555-6(7)*, Joseph Henry Pr.) National Academies Pr.

Hunter, Nick. Space, 1 vol. 2012. (Explorer Tales Ser.). (ENG.). 32p. (gr. 1-3). 29.99 *(978-1-4109-4782-6(3)*, Read Me!) Heinemann-Raintree.

Hwang, William Liang & Mian, Matthew K., eds. InnoWorks: Explorations, Student Edition. 2006. (YA). spiral bd. *(978-0-9771380-4-3(6))* United InnoWorks Academy.

Ingebretsen, Karen, et al. Human Space Exploration. 2006. (World Book's Solar System & Space Exploration Library). (Illus.). 63p. (J). *(978-0-7166-9509-7(X))* World Bk., Inc.

Jackson, Tom. The Universe: An Illustrated History of Astronomy. 2012. (Illus.). 144p. (J). *(978-0-9853230-2-8(7))* Shelter Harbor Pr.

Jedicke, Peter. Great Moments in Space Exploration. 2007. (Scientific American Ser.). (Illus.). 72p. (YA). (gr. 5-9). lib. bdg. 30.00 *(978-0-7910-9046-6(9))* Facts On File, Inc.

Jemison, Mae & Rau, Dana Meachen. Journey Through Our Solar System. 2013. (True Book™—Dr. Mae Jemison & 100 Year Starship™ Ser.). (ENG., Illus.). 48p. (J). pap. 6.95 *(978-0-531-24061-8(4))*; lib. bdg. 29.00 *(978-0-531-25501-8(8))* Scholastic Library Publishing.

Jenkins, Martin. Exploring Space: from Galileo to the Mars Rover & Beyond. Biesty, Stephen, illus. 2017. (ENG.). 64p. (J). (gr. 3-7). 17.99 *(978-0-7636-8931-5(9))* Candlewick Pr.

Jones, Tom. Ask the Astronaut: A Galaxy of Astonishing Answers to Your Questions on Spaceflight. 2016. (ENG., Illus.). 224p. (YA). (gr. 5-12). pap. 12.95 *(978-1-58834-537-0(8)*, Smithsonian Bks.) Smithsonian Institution Scholarly Pr.

Keiser, Cody. Exploring Uranus. 2017. (J). ***(978-1-5345-2253-4(0)***, KidHaven Publishing) Greenhaven Publishing LLC.

Kelley, K. C. Astronauts!, Vol. 10. 2015. (Scientists in Action Ser.). (Illus.). 48p. (J). (gr. 5). 20.95 *(978-1-4222-3418-1(5))* Mason Crest.

Kerrod, Robin. Space. 2003. 48p. (J). lib. bdg. 27.10 *(978-1-58340-351-8(5))* Black Rabbit Bks.

Khan, Hena. The Space Explorer's Guide to Earth's Neighborhood. 2003. (Space University Ser.). (Illus.). 48p. (J). *(978-0-439-55741-2(0))* Scholastic, Inc.

Khan, Hena & Dyson, Marianne J. The Space Explorer's Guide to Out-Of-This-World Science. 2004. (Space University Ser.). (Illus.). 48p. (J). *(978-0-439-55747-4(X))* Scholastic, Inc.

Koontz, Robin. Our Place in Space. 2016. (Let's Explore Science Ser.). (ENG., Illus.). 48p. (gr. 5-8). 35.64 *(978-1-68191-390-2(9))* Rourke Educational Media.

Kortemeier, Todd. Searching for Alien Life. 2017. (Science Frontiers Ser.). (ENG., Illus.). 32p. (J). (gr. 3-6). 21.95 *(978-1-63235-380-1(6))* Pr. Room Editions LLC.

Kortenkamp, Steve. Future Explorers: Robots in Space. 2015. (Exploring Space & Beyond Ser.). (ENG., Illus.). 48p. (gr. 3-4). lib. bdg. 29.32 *(978-1-4914-4163-3(1))* Capstone Press of Coughlan Cos.

—Show Me Space: My First Picture Encyclopedia, 1 vol. 2013. (My First Picture Encyclopedias Ser.). (ENG.). 32p. (gr. 1-2). pap. 8.10 *(978-1-4765-3790-0(9)*, Aplus Bks.); lib. bdg. 27.32 *(978-1-62065-058-5(4))* Capstone Press of Coughlan Cos.

Kranz, Rachel. La exploración del Espacio. 2011. (SPA.). 32p. (J). pap. 49.00 net. *(978-1-4108-2344-1(X)*, A2344X) Benchmark Education Co.

Krieger, Emily. Funny Fill-In - My Space Adventure. Sipple, Dan, illus. 2013. (ENG.). 48p. (J). (gr. 3-7). pap. 4.99 *(978-1-4263-1354-7(3)*, National Geographic Children's Bks.) National Geographic Society.

Kruesi, Liz. Discover Space Exploration. 2016. (Searchlight Books (tm) — What's Cool about Science? Ser.). (ENG., Illus.). 40p. (J). (gr. 3-5). 30.65 *(978-1-5124-0811-9(5))* Lerner Publishing Group.

Krumm, Brian. Shuttle in the Sky: The Story of the Space Shuttle Columbia. 2015. (Exploring Space & Beyond Ser.). (ENG., Illus.). 48p. (gr. 3-4). lib. bdg. 29.32 *(978-1-4914-4161-9(5))* Capstone Press of Coughlan Cos.

Labrecque, Ellen. Yvonne Brill & Satellite Propulsion. 2017. (21st Century Junior Library: Women Innovators Ser.). (ENG., Illus.). 24p. (J). (gr. 2-5). lib. bdg. 27.07 *(978-1-63472-184-4(5)*, 209308) Cherry Lake Publishing.

Lakin, Patricia. The Stellar Story of Space Travel. Burroughs, Scott, illus. 2016. (History of Fun Stuff Ser.). (ENG.). 48p. (J). (gr. 1-3). pap. 3.99 *(978-1-4814-5623-4(7)*, Simon Spotlight) Simon Spotlight.

Langley, Andrew. Chris Hadfield & Living on the International Space Station. 2015. (Adventures in Space Ser.). (ENG., Illus.). 48p. (gr. 4-6). 33.32 *(978-1-4846-2517-0(X))* Heinemann-Raintree.

—Sally Ride & the Shuttle Missions. 2015. (Adventures in Space Ser.). (ENG., Illus.). 48p. (gr. 4-6). 33.32 *(978-1-4846-2516-3(1))* Heinemann-Raintree.

Larson, Kirsten W. Space Robots. 2017. (Robotics in Our World Ser.). (ENG.). 32p. (gr. 1-4). 20.95 ***(978-1-68151-147-4(9))*** Amicus Publishing.

Lassieur, Allison. International Space Station: An Interactive Space Exploration Adventure. 2016. (You Choose: Space Ser.). (ENG., Illus.). 112p. (gr. 3-4). lib. bdg. 31.99 *(978-1-4914-8104-2(8)*, You Choose Bks.) Capstone Press of Coughlan Cos.

Launch into Space! 2015. (Launch into Space! Ser.). (ENG.). 32p. (J). (gr. 3-4). pap., pap., pap. 378.72 *(978-0-7660-6683-0(5))* Enslow Pubs., Inc.

Law, Felicia. Trouble in Space. 2015. (Science to the Rescue Ser.). (ENG., Illus.). 32p. (J). (gr. 3-6). *(978-0-7787-1676-1(7))* Crabtree Publishing Co.

little bee books, little bee. Listopia: Space. 2016. (ENG., Illus.). 208p. (J). (gr. 2-4). pap. 9.99 *(978-1-4998-0280-1(3))* Little Bee Books Inc.

The Magic School Bus: Lost in the Solar System. 2011. (J). audio compact disk 9.99 *(978-0-545-22880-0(8))* Scholastic, Inc.

Mallick, Nita. Space Exploration. 2016. (Study of Science Ser.). 00104p. (J). (gr. 8-8). lib. bdg. 36.25 *(978-1-5081-0427-8(1))* Rosen Publishing Group, Inc., The.

McMahon, Michael. Why Do Stars Twinkle? 2010. (Solving Science Mysteries Ser.). (Illus.). 24p. (J). pap. 8.25 *(978-1-61531-921-3(2)*, PowerKids Pr.); (YA). (gr. 3-6). lib. bdg. 22.60 *(978-1-61531-895-7(X))* Rosen Publishing Group, Inc., The.

Meet NASA Inventor Robert Hoyt & His Team's Web-Spinning Space Spiders. 2017. (J). ***(978-0-7166-6157-3(8))*** World Bk., Inc.

Miller, Gary. The Outer Limits: The Future of Space Exploration. 2009. (Current Science Ser.). (ENG.). 48p. (gr. 4-7). (YA). lib. bdg. 31.00 *(978-1-4339-2242-8(8))*; (J). pap. 8.95 *(978-1-4339-2246-6(0)*, Gareth Stevens Learning Library) Stevens, Gareth Publishing LLLP.

Mills, Nathan & Block, Dakota. Exploring the Solar System. 2012. (Rosen Readers Ser.). (ENG., Illus.). 24p. (J). (gr. 1-2). pap. 8.25 *(978-1-4488-8857-3(3)*, Rosen Classroom) Rosen Publishing Group, Inc., The.

Mills, Nathan & Stiegler, Lorraine. Space Probes. 2012. (Rosen Readers Ser.). (ENG., Illus.). 24p. (J). (gr. 1-2). pap. 8.25 *(978-1-4488-8869-6(7)*, Rosen Classroom) Rosen Publishing Group, Inc., The.

Moore, Philip. When Did American Astronauts Explore Space? 2014. (Little Books of Answers: Level C Ser.). (Illus.). 16p. (gr. k-2). pap. 7.95 *(978-1-927136-26-3(1))* Three Crows Media NZL. Dist: RiverStream Publishing.

Morey, Allan. The Hubble Space Telescope. 2017. (Space Tech Ser.). (ENG., Illus.). 24p. (J). (gr. 3-7). lib. bdg. 25.95 ***(978-1-62617-700-0(7)***, Epic Bks.) Bellwether Media.

—Mars Rovers. 2017. (Space Tech Ser.). (ENG., Illus.). 24p. (J). (gr. 3-7). lib. bdg. 25.95 ***(978-1-62617-703-1(1)***, Epic Bks.) Bellwether Media.

—Robonauts. 2017. (Space Tech Ser.). (ENG., Illus.). 24p. (J). (gr. 3-7). lib. bdg. 25.95 **(978-1-62617-704-8(X)**, Epic Bks.) Bellwether Media.

—Rockets. 2017. (Space Tech Ser.). (ENG., Illus.). 24p. (J). (gr. 3-7). lib. bdg. 25.95 **(978-1-62617-705-5(8)**, Epic Bks.) Bellwether Media.

Morris, Neil. What Does Space Exploration Do for Us?, 1 vol. 2011. (Earth, Space, & Beyond Ser.). (ENG.). 48p. (gr. 3-3). pap. 9.49 (978-1-4109-4183-1(3), Raintree Freestyle Express); (gr. 6-6). pap. 9.49 (978-1-4109-4165-7(5), Raintree Freestyle); (gr. 3-3). 34.65 (978-1-4109-4177-0(9), Raintree Freestyle Express) Heinemann-Raintree.

Moskal, Greg. The History of Space Exploration: Sequencing Events Chronologically on a Timeline. 2009. (PowerMath Ser.). (ENG., Illus.). 24p. (gr. 3-4). pap. 8.25 (978-0-8239-8850-1(3), PowerKids Pr.) Rosen Publishing Group, Inc., The.

Murphy, Patricia J. Explorando el Espacio con una Astronauta/Exploring Space with an Astronaut. 2008. (I Like Science! Bilingual Ser.). (ENG & SPA., Illus.). 24p. (J). (gr. 1-3). lib. bdg. 22.60 (978-0-7660-2977-4(8), Enslow Elementary) Enslow Pubs., Inc.

—Exploring Space with an Astronaut. 2004. (I Like Science! Ser.). (Illus.). 24p. (J). lib. bdg. 22.60 (978-0-7660-2268-3(4)) Enslow Pubs., Inc.

Nagel, Rob. Space Exploration - Almanac, 2 vols. 2004. (Space Exploration Reference Library). (ENG., Illus.). 400p. lib. bdg. 191.00 (978-0-7876-9209-4(3), UXL) Cengage Gale.

Nagelhout, Ryan. Astronauts, 01 vols., 1. 2016. (Out of the Lab: Extreme Jobs in Science Ser.). (ENG., Illus.). 32p. (J). pap. 10.00 (978-1-5081-4509-7(1), PowerKids Pr.) Rosen Publishing Group, Inc., The.

—Space Robots. 2016. (Robots & Robotics Ser.). 32p. (J). (gr. 5-5). 26.25 (978-1-4994-2183-5(4), PowerKids Pr.) Rosen Publishing Group, Inc., The.

Nardo, Don. Destined for Space: Our Story of Exploration. 2012. (Smithsonian Ser.). (ENG.). 64p. (gr. 4-5). pap. 53.70 (978-1-4296-8524-5(7)) Capstone Press of Coughlan Cos.

Nardo, Don. Hubble Deep Field: How a Photo Revolutionized Our Understanding of the Universe. 2017. (Captured Science History Ser.). (ENG.). 64p. (gr. 5-7). lib. bdg. 34.65 **(978-0-7565-5643-3(0)**, CPB Grades 4-8) Compass Point Bks.

Newland, Sonya. Space Exploration: Triumphs & Tragedies. 2016. (ENG., Illus.). 48p. (J). pap. (978-0-7787-2231-1(7)) Crabtree Publishing Co.

Nicolson, Cynthia. Discover Space. Slavin, Bill, illus. 2005. 32p. (J). lib. bdg. 15.38 (978-1-4242-1193-7(X)) Fitzgerald Bks.

Nicolson, Cynthia Pratt. Discover Space. Slavin, Bill, illus. 2005. (Kids Can Read! Ser.). (ENG.). 32p. (J). (gr. 1-3). 3.95 (978-1-55337-824-2(5)) Kids Can Pr., Ltd. CAN. Dist: Hachette Bk. Group.

O'Brien, Eileen & Denne, Ben. Space. 2004. (Discovery Program Ser.). (SPA., Illus.). 48p. (J). pap. 8.95 (978-0-7945-0126-6(5), Usborne); lib. bdg. 16.95 (978-1-58086-388-9(4)) EDC Publishing.

O'Hearn, Michael. Awesome Space Robots, 1 vol. 2013. (Robots Ser.). (ENG.). 32p. (gr. 3-4). lib. bdg. 27.99 (978-1-4296-9918-1(3)); (Illus.). pap. 8.29 (978-1-62065-778-2(3)) Capstone Press of Coughlan Cos.

Owen, David. Final Frontier: Voyages into Outer Space. 2004. (ENG., Illus.). 128p. (J). (gr. 6-9). pap. 9.95 (978-1-55297-775-0(7), 9781552977750) Firefly Bks., Ltd.

Paris, Stephanie. Siglo Xxi: Misterios Del Espacio Sideral. 2016. (TIME for Kids en Español - Level 5 Ser.). (SPA.). 64p. (gr. 5-5). lib. bdg. 31.99 (978-1-5157-2937-2(0)) Time for Kids Inc AUS. Dist: Capstone Pub.

—Siglo Xxii: El Futuro Del Espacio. 2016. (TIME for Kids en Español - Level 5 Ser.). (SPA.). 64p. (gr. 5-5). lib. bdg. 31.99 (978-1-5157-2936-5(2)) Time for Kids Inc AUS. Dist: Capstone Pub.

—20th Century: Race to the Moon, 1 vol. 2nd rev. ed. 2013. (Nonfiction Readers Ser.). (ENG.). 64p. (J). (gr. 5-5). pap. 10.99 (978-1-4333-4899-0(3)) Teacher Created Materials, Inc.

—21st Century: Mysteries of Deep Space, 1 vol. 2nd rev. ed. 2013. (TIME for KIDS(r) Nonfiction Readers Ser.). (ENG.). 64p. (J). (gr. 5-5). pap. 10.99 (978-1-4333-4900-3(0)); (Illus.). pap. 31.96 (978-1-4333-7423-4(4)) Teacher Created Materials, Inc.

Paris, Stephanie & Kuligowski, Stephanie. 22nd Century - Future of Space, 1 vol. 2nd rev. ed. 2013. (Nonfiction Readers Ser.). (ENG.). 64p. (J). (gr. 5-5). pap. 10.99 (978-1-4333-4901-0(9)) Teacher Created Materials, Inc.

Parker, Steve. In Space. 2010. (J). 28.50 (978-1-59920-285-3(9)) Black Rabbit Bks.

—In Space. 2011. (Future Transport Ser.). (Illus.). 32p. (J). (gr. 4). 28.50 (978-1-60870-778-2(4)) Marshall Cavendish GBR. Dist: Marshall Cavendish Corp.

—Looking Beyond. West, David, illus. 2015. (Story of Space Ser.). (ENG.). 32p. (J). (gr. 3-6). 31.35 (978-1-62588-076-5(6), 1389436) Black Rabbit Bks.

—Space Exploration. 2010. (How It Works Ser.). 40p. (J). (gr. 3-18). lib. bdg. 19.95 (978-1-4222-1799-3(X)) Mason Crest.

—Space Stations. West, David, illus. 2015. (Story of Space Ser.). (ENG.). 32p. (gr. 3-6). 31.35 (978-1-62588-081-9(2)) Black Rabbit Bks.

Parker, Steve & Snedding, Robert. A Brief Illustrated History of Space Exploration. 2017. (Brief Illustrated History Ser.). (ENG.). 32p. (gr. 3-5). lib. bdg. 27.32 (978-1-5157-2519-0(7), Fact Finders) Capstone Press of Coughlan Cos.

Parker, Steve & Twist, Clint. Exploring Space. 2013. (Illus.). 48p. (J). (978-1-4351-5088-1(0)) Barnes & Noble, Inc.

Parks, Peggy J. Space Research. 2010. (Inside Science Ser.). (Illus.). 96p. (J). (gr. 7-12). 26.95 (978-1-60152-111-8(1), 1316146) ReferencePoint Pr., Inc.

Patenaude, Jeremy & Lock, Peter. Space Quest: Mission to Mars. 2014. (DK Readers Ser.). (ENG.). 32p. (J). (gr. 1-3). 14.99 (978-1-4654-2002-2(9), DK Children) Dorling Kindersley Publishing, Inc.

Peters, Elisa. Outer Space. 2012. (PowerKids Readers: the Universe Ser.). (ENG., Illus.). 24p. (J). (gr. k-2). 22.60 (978-1-4488-7390-6(8)); pap. 8.25 (978-1-4488-7469-9(6)) Rosen Publishing Group, Inc., The. (PowerKids Pr.).

—Outer Space: El Espacio Exterior. 2012. (PowerKids Readers: the Universe / el universo Ser.). (SPA & ENG., Illus.). 24p. (J). (gr. k-2). lib. bdg. 22.60 (978-1-4488-7826-0(8), PowerKids Pr.) Rosen Publishing Group, Inc., The.

Peterson, Judy Monroe. Exploring Space: Astronauts & Astronomers. 2009. (Extreme Scientists Ser.). 24p. (gr. 2-3). 42.50 (978-1-61512-451-0(9), PowerKids Pr.); (Illus.). (YA). lib. bdg. 22.60 (978-1-4042-4528-0(6)) Rosen Publishing Group, Inc., The.

Peterson, Megan Cooley & Rustad, Martha E. H. The First Space Missions, 1 vol. 2014. (Famous Firsts Ser.). (ENG., Illus.). 24p. (gr. k-1). 26.65 (978-1-4914-0576-5(7)); pap. 6.95 (978-1-4914-0644-1(5)) Capstone Press of Coughlan Cos. (Pebble Plus).

Petrikowski, Nicki Peter. Critical Perspectives on the Viability of Human Life on Other Planets. 2016. (Analyzing the Issues Ser.). 208p. (J). (gr. 8-8). 47.93 (978-0-7660-7674-7(1)) Enslow Pubs., Inc.

Phelan, Glen & National Geographic Learning Staff. Stars. 2007. (Language, Literacy, & Vocabulary - Reading Expeditions Ser.). (ENG., Illus.). 36p. (J). pap. 18.95 (978-0-7922-5433-1(3)) CENGAGE Learning.

Porterfield, Jason. The Benefits of Spaceflight & Space Exploration. 2017. (From Earth to the Stars Ser.). 48p. (gr. 10-12). pap. 14.05 **(978-1-68048-661-2(6)**, Britannica Educational Publishing) Rosen Publishing Group, Inc., The.

Rauf, Don & Vescia, Monique. Choose Your Own Career Adventure at NASA. 2016. (Bright Futures Press: Choose Your Own Career Adventure Ser.). (ENG., Illus.). 32p. (J). (gr. 4-6). 29.93 (978-1-63471-913-1(1), 208973) Cherry Lake Publishing.

Reynolds, Toby & Calver, Paul. Space. 2016. (Visual Explorers Ser.). (ENG., Illus.). 32p. (J). (gr. 3-7). pap. 6.99 (978-1-4380-0829-5(5)) Barron's Educational Series, Inc.

Rich, Mari. Space, Vol. 10. Gilmore, Malinda & Pouson, Mel, eds. 2016. (Black Achievement in Science Ser.). (Illus.). 64p. (J). (gr. 7). 23.95 (978-1-4222-3563-8(7)) Mason Crest.

Riley, Peter & Lorimer, Lawrence. The Solar System. 2013. (Jigsaw Journey Ser.). (ENG., Illus.). 48p. (J). (gr. k). 15.95 (978-1-60710-949-5(2), Silver Dolphin Bks.) Readerlink Distribution Services, LLC.

Robots Exploring Space. 2016. (Robots Exploring Space Ser.). 32p. (gr. 5-5). 157.50 (978-1-4994-2253-5(9)); pap. 60.00 (978-1-5081-5254-5(3)) Rosen Publishing Group, Inc., The. (PowerKids Pr.).

Ross, Jerry L. & Gunderson, Susan G. Becoming a Spacewalker: My Journey to the Stars. 2014. (ENG., Illus.). 40p. (J). 16.95 (978-1-55753-693-8(7), e5b8fc3c-8198-4711-bb0a-bd7f87ffa1b0) Purdue Univ. Pr.

Royston, Angela. Space Blog. 2010. (ENG., Illus.). 32p. (J). (978-0-7787-9910-8(7)); pap. (978-0-7787-9931-3(X)) Crabtree Publishing Co.

Roza, Greg. The Hubble Space Telescope: Understanding & Representing Numbers in the Billions. (PowerMath: Proficiency Plus Ser.). 32p. 2009. (gr. 4-5). 47.90 (978-1-60851-422-9(6)) 2005. (Illus.). (J). (gr. 3-6). lib. bdg. 25.25 (978-1-4042-2931-0(0)) Rosen Publishing Group, Inc., The. (PowerKids Pr.).

—The Hubble Space Telescope: Understanding & Representing Numbers up to 1 Billion. 2009. (Math for the REAL World Ser.). (ENG., Illus.). 32p. (gr. 5-6). pap. 10.00 (978-1-4042-5129-8(4)) Rosen Publishing Group, Inc., The.

Rustad, Martha E. H. NASA, 1 vol. 2012. (Exploring Space Ser.). (ENG.). 24p. (gr. k-1). pap. 7.29 (978-1-4296-7894-0(1)); pap. 41.70 (978-1-4296-8329-6(5)); lib. bdg. 26.65 (978-1-4296-7581-9(0)) Capstone Press of Coughlan Cos. (Pebble Plus).

Salzano, Tammi J. Destination, Space. 2006. (Illus.). 30p. (J). (978-0-439-88736-6(4)) Scholastic, Inc.

Salzmann, Mary Elizabeth. Astronauts, 1 vol. 2015. (ENG., Illus.). 24p. (J). 17.95 (978-1-62403-742-9(9)) ABDO Publishing Co.

Saunders-Smith, Gail. Robots in Space, 1 vol. 2014. (Cool Robots Ser.). (ENG., Illus.). 24p. (gr. k-1). 26.65 (978-1-4914-0585-7(6), Pebble Plus) Capstone Press of Coughlan Cos.

Schmermund, Elizabeth. Telescopes, Probes, Spacecraft, & the Future of Space Exploration. 2016. (Space Systems Ser.). 112p. (J). lib. bdg. 42.79 (978-1-5026-2293-8(9)) Cavendish Square Publishing.

The Science of Space. 2016. (Illus.). 48p. (J). (978-1-4222-3515-7(7)) Mason Crest.

Science Readers Staff & Jankowski, Connie. From Hubble to Hubble: Astromers & Outer Space, 1 vol. 2007. (Science Readers Ser.). (ENG., Illus.). 32p. (J). (gr. 3-3). pap. 8.99 (978-0-7439-0564-0(4)) Shell Educational Publishing.

ShackletonCaroline. LIFT OFF: EXPLORING THE UNIVERSE HIGH INTERMEDIATE BOOK WITH ONLINE ACCESS. 2014. (ENG., Illus.). 28p. (J). pap. 9.50 (978-1-107-69249-7(0)) Cambridge Univ. Pr.

Smibert, Angie. Space Myths, Busted! 2017. (Science Myths, Busted! Ser.). (ENG., Illus.). 32p. (J). (gr. 3-6). 21.95 (978-1-63235-305-4(9)) Pr. Room Editions LLC.

Snedden, Robert. Exploring Space. 2016. (Sci-Hi: Earth & Space Science Ser.). (ENG.). 48p. (gr. 4-4). pap. 8.99 (978-1-4109-8522-4(9), Sci-Hi) Heinemann-Raintree.

—How Do Scientists Explore Space?, 1 vol. 2011. (Earth, Space, & Beyond Ser.). (ENG.). 48p. (gr. 6-6). pap. 9.49 (978-1-4109-4164-0(7), Raintree Freestyle); (gr. 3-3). 34.65 (978-1-4109-4176-3(0), Raintree Freestyle Express); (gr. 6-6). 34.65 (978-1-4109-4158-9(2), Raintree Freestyle) Heinemann-Raintree.

Space Exploration. 2011. (New Discovering Careers for Your Future Ser.). (Illus.). 128p. (gr. 4-9). 24.95 (978-0-8160-8054-0(2), Ferguson Publishing Co.) Facts On File, Inc.

Space Exploration. 2014. (DK Eyewitness Bks.). (ENG., Illus.). 72p. (J). (gr. 3-7). pap. 9.99 (978-1-4654-2616-1(7), DK Children) Dorling Kindersley Publishing, Inc.

Space Exploration: Science Technology Engineering. 2014. (Calling All Innovators: a Career for You Ser.). (ENG.). 64p. (J). lib. bdg. 32.00 (978-0-531-20615-7(7)) Scholastic Library Publishing.

Sparrow, Giles. Exploring the Universe. 2006. (Secrets of the Universe Ser.). (Illus.). 48p. (gr. 6-12). lib. bdg. 31.00 (978-0-8368-7276-7(2), Gareth Stevens Secondary Library) Stevens, Gareth Publishing LLLP.

—Probing Deep Space. 2006. (Secrets of the Universe Ser.). (Illus.). 48p. (gr. 6-12). lib. bdg. 31.00 (978-0-8368-7279-8(7), Gareth Stevens Secondary Library) Stevens, Gareth Publishing LLLP.

—Space Exploration. 2011. (Exploring Space: Space Travel Guides). 32p. (gr. 3-6). lib. bdg. 31.35 (978-1-59920-665-3(X)) Black Rabbit Bks.

Sparrow, Giles & John, Judith. Exploring Space. 2016. (Discoveries in Space Science Ser.). (ENG., Illus.). 80p. (YA). (gr. 9-9). lib. bdg. 35.64 (978-1-5026-1012-6(4), 1398704) Cavendish Square Publishing.

—Shuttles & Space Missions. 2016. (Discoveries in Space Science Ser.). (ENG., Illus.). 80p. (YA). (gr. 9-9). lib. bdg. 35.64 (978-1-5026-1016-4(7), 1398739) Cavendish Square Publishing.

Spilsbury, Louise & Spilsbury, Richard. Fly to Mars! Forces in Space. 2015. (Feel the Force Ser.). (ENG., Illus.). 48p. (gr. 3-6). 33.32 (978-1-4846-2600-9(1)) Heinemann-Raintree.

Squishy, Fishy Robot Explorers: Meet NASA Inventor Mason Peck & His Team's. 2017. (J). **(978-0-7166-6156-6(X))** World Bk., Inc.

Stefoff, Rebecca. Space Race: An Interactive Space Exploration Adventure. 2016. (You Choose: Space Ser.). (ENG.). 112p. (gr. 3-4). lib. bdg. 31.99 (978-1-4914-8101-1(3), You Choose Bks.) Capstone Press of Coughlan Cos.

Stiegler, Lorraine. Space Probes. 2012. (Exploring Earth & Space Ser.). (ENG., Illus.). 24p. (J). (gr. 1-3). 22.60 (978-1-4488-8580-0(9), PowerKids Pr.) Rosen Publishing Group, Inc., The.

Teitelbaum, Michael. Mars & Venus Space Exploration: Set Of 6. 2011. (Navigators Ser.). (J). pap. 50.00 net. (978-1-4108-6243-3(7)) Benchmark Education Co.

—Mars & Venus: Space Exploration: Text Pairs. 2008. (Bridges/Navigators Ser.). (J). (gr. 6). 94.00 (978-1-4108-8445-9(7)) Benchmark Education Co.

Telescopes & Space Probes. 2006. (World Book's Solar System & Space Exploration Library). (Illus.). 63p. (J). (978-0-7166-9510-3(3)) World Bk., Inc.

Trotman, Felicity. Exploration of Space. 2010. (History of Exploration Ser.). 48p. 32.80 (978-1-84898-302-1(6)) Black Rabbit Bks.

Walliman, Dominic. Professor Astro Cat's Frontiers of Space. Newman, Ben, illus. 2013. (ENG.). 64p. (J). (gr. 2-6). 24.00 (978-1-909263-07-9(9)) Flying Eye Bks. GBR. Dist: Consortium Bk. Sales & Distribution.

Waxman, Laura Hamilton. Exploring Black Holes. 2011. (Searchlight Books Whats Amazing about Space Ser.). (ENG., Illus.). 40p. (gr. 3-5). pap. 8.95 (978-0-7613-7877-8(4)) Lerner Publishing Group.

Way, Steve & Bailey, Gerry. Space. 2008. (Simply Science Ser.). (Illus.). 32p. (YA). (gr. 3-6). lib. bdg. 26.00 (978-0-8368-9232-1(1)) Stevens, Gareth Publishing LLLP.

Wilson, Hannah. Kingfisher Readers L2: Sun, Moon, & Stars. Feldman, Thea, ed. 2014. (Kingfisher Readers Ser.). (ENG., Illus.). 32p. (J). (gr. k-3). 12.99 (978-0-7534-7146-3(9), 9780753471463, Kingfisher) Roaring Brook Pr.

Wimmer, Teresa. National Aeronautics & Space Administration. (Agents of Government Ser.). 48p. 2016. (ENG.). (J). (gr. 5-9). pap. 12.00 (978-1-62832-148-7(2), Creative Paperbacks) 2015. (Illus.). (YA). (978-1-60818-547-4(8), Creative Education) Creative Co., The.

Windham, Ryder. Journey Through Space. 2015. (DK Readers Ser.). (ENG.). 48p. (J). (gr. 1-3). 14.99 (978-1-4654-3389-3(9), DK Children) Dorling Kindersley Publishing, Inc.

World Book, contrib. by. Human Space Exploration. 2nd ed. 2006. (World Book's Solar System & Space Exploration Library). (Illus.). 64p. (J). (978-0-7166-9514-1(6)) World Bk., Inc.

World Book, Inc Staff, contrib. by. Encyclopedia of Space. 2013. (J). (978-0-7166-7523-5(4)) World Bk., Inc.

—Space Exploration. 2011. (J). (978-0-7166-1792-1(7)) World Bk., Inc.

World Book, Inc. Staff, contrib. by. Stargazing to Space Travel: A Timeline of Space Exploration. 2016. (J). (978-0-7166-3545-1(3)) World Bk.-Childcraft International.

World Book, Inc Staff, contrib. by. Telescopes & Space Probes. 2nd ed. 2006. (Illus.). 64p. (J). (978-0-7166-9520-2(0)) World Bk., Inc.

Zappa, Marcia. Space Exploration, 1 vol. 2011. (Universe Set 2 Ser.). (ENG., Illus.). 32p. (gr. 3-5). 27.07 (978-1-61714-692-3(7), Buddy Bks.) ABDO Publishing Co.

Zobel, Derek. NASA. 2010. (Exploring Space Ser.). (ENG., Illus.). 24p. (J). (gr. k-3). lib. bdg. 25.95 (978-1-60014-293-2(1), Blastoff! Readers) Bellwether Media.

OUTER SPACE—FICTION

Act-Two Staff. Space Mission. 2004. (Illus.). (J). pap. 8.99 incl. cd-rom (978-0-7868-3418-1(8)) Hyperion Bks. for Children.

Adventures Beyond the Solar System: Planetron & Me. 2005. (J). audio, cd-rom 24.95 (978-0-9771381-5-9(1)) Williams, Geoffrey T.

Adventures in the Solar System: Planetron & Me. 2005. (J). audio, cd-rom 24.95 (978-0-9771381-4-2(3)) Williams, Geoffrey T.

Anholt, Laurence. Hansel & Gretel & the Space Witch. 2016. (Seriously Silly: Scary Fairy Tales Ser.). (ENG., Illus.). 48p. (J). (gr. k-17). pap. 6.99 (978-1-4083-2960-3(3), Orchard Bks.) Hachette Children's Group GBR. Dist: Hachette Bk. Group.

The Annoying Crush. 2014. (Galaxy Zack Ser.: 9). (ENG., Illus.). 128p. (J). (gr. k-4). 16.99 (978-1-4424-9364-3(X)); pap. 5.99 (978-1-4424-9363-6(1)) Little Simon. (Little Simon).

Auerbach, Annie. My Race into Space! A Water Wonder Book. Garofoli, Viviana, illus. 2005. 18p. (J). 9.95 (978-1-58117-351-2(2), Intervisual/Piggy Toes) Bendon, Inc.

Bean, Raymond. First Family in Space. 2016. (Out of This World Ser.). (ENG., Illus.). 112p. (gr. 2-5). lib. bdg. 32.65 (978-1-4965-3617-4(7)) Out of this World GBR. Dist: Capstone Pub.

—Journey to the Moon. 2016. (Out of This World Ser.). (ENG., Illus.). 112p. (gr. 2-5). lib. bdg. 32.65 (978-1-4965-3616-7(9)) Out of this World GBR. Dist: Capstone Pub.

—Trouble on Venus. 2016. (Out of This World Ser.). (ENG., Illus.). 112p. (gr. 2-5). lib. bdg. 32.65 (978-1-4965-3614-3(2)) Out of this World GBR. Dist: Capstone Pub.

Beecroft, Simon. Stand Aside-Bounty Hunters! 2009. (Star Wars: the Clone Wars DK Readers Ser.). lib. bdg. 13.55 (978-0-606-07065-2(6), Turtleback) Turtleback Bks.

Bloomsbury USA. Lift & Look: in Space. 2016. (ENG., Illus.). 12p. (J). (— 1). bds. 8.99 (978-1-61963-826-6(6), 9781619638266, Bloomsbury Activity Bks.) Bloomsbury Publishing USA.

Boyce, Frank Cottrell. Cosmic. 2011. 336p. (J). (gr. 3-7). pap. 6.99 (978-0-06-183688-6(5), Waldon Pond Pr.) HarperCollins Pubs.

—Cosmic. Lenton, Steven, illus. unabr. ed. 2008. (ENG.). 320p. (J). (gr. 10-13). 23.95 (978-1-4050-5464-5(6), Macmillan) Pan Macmillan GBR. Dist: Trans-Atlantic Pubns., Inc.

Brophy, Ann. Novus 3 & Me: Six Short Stories about Friendship. 2010. 44p. pap. 18.49 (978-1-4490-7132-5(5)) AuthorHouse.

Camper, Cathy. Low Riders in Space. Raúl, III, illus. 2014. (ENG & SPA.). 112p. (J). (gr. 3-7). pap. 9.99 (978-1-4521-2869-6(3));Bk. 1. 22.99 (978-1-4521-2155-0(9)) Chronicle Bks. LLC.

Carson, Penny & Hess, Amy. Simon Goes Camping. 2008. 19p. 10.95 (978-1-4357-1560-8(8)) Lulu Pr., Inc.

Castellan, Andrea. Mickey Mouse & the Orbiting Nightmare. 2011. (ENG., Illus.). 128p. (J). pap. (978-1-60886-630-4(0)) Boom! Studios.

Chang, Ifay, as told by. Outopians. 2007. (Illus.). 27p. (YA). pap. (978-0-9771594-1-3(8)) TLC Information Services.

Chiaramonti, Gregory. Probie: the Space Probe, Mission One: the Ocean of Europa. 2007. 32p. (J). 16.72 (978-0-615-13848-0(9)) Chiaramonti, Gregory.

Connely, Chris L. & Vaughan, Mark. An Alien from Earth. 2003. 175p. per. 9.95 (978-0-9745544-0-2(5)) Lewis Lynn Bks.

Cook, Julia. Personal Space Camp. Hartman, Carrie, illus. 2008. 32p. (J). (gr. -1-3). pap. 9.95 (978-1-931636-87-2(7)) National Ctr. For Youth Issues.

Courtenay, L. A. Space Penguins Cosmic Crash! Davies, James, illus. 2015. (Space Penguins Ser.). (ENG.). 112p. (gr. 2-3). lib. bdg. 22.65 (978-1-4342-9785-3(3)) Stone Arch Bks.

—Space Penguins Galaxy Race! Davies, James, illus. 2015. (Space Penguins Ser.). (ENG.). 112p. (gr. 2-3). lib. bdg. 22.65 (978-1-4342-9783-9(7)) Stone Arch Bks.

—Space Penguins Meteor Madness! Davies, James, illus. 2015. (Space Penguins Ser.). (ENG.). 112p. (gr. 2-3). lib. bdg. 22.65 (978-1-4342-9782-2(9)) Stone Arch Bks.

—Space Penguins Star Attack! Davies, James, illus. 2015. (Space Penguins Ser.). (ENG.). 112p. (gr. 2-3). lib. bdg. 22.65 (978-1-4342-9784-6(5)) Stone Arch Bks.

Dahl, Roald. Charlie & the Great Glass Elevator. Blake, Quentin, illus. 2007. (ENG.). 192p. (J). (gr. 3-7). 7.99 (978-0-14-241032-5(2), Puffin Books) Penguin Young Readers Group.

—Charlie & the Great Glass Elevator. Blake, Quentin, illus. 2005. (Puffin Modern Classics Ser.). (ENG.). 176p. (J). (gr. 3-7). pap. 7.99 (978-0-14-240412-6(8), Puffin Books) Penguin Young Readers Group.

—Charlie & the Great Glass Elevator. 2007. 18.40 (978-1-4177-8610-7(8), Turtleback) Turtleback Bks.

Dale, Penny. Dinosaur Rocket! Dale, Penny, illus. 2015. (ENG., Illus.). 32p. (J). (-k). 15.99 (978-0-7636-7999-6(2), Nosy Crow) Candlewick Pr.

Disney Book Group. Miles from Tomorrowland: Who Stole the Stellosphere? Disney Storybook Art Team, illus. 2015. (World of Reading Ser.). (ENG.). 32p. (J). (gr. -1-k). pap. 3.99 (978-1-4847-1610-6(8)) Disney Pr.

—Miles from Tomorrowland the Haunted Ship. Disney Storybook Art Team, illus. 2016. (ENG.). 24p. (J). (gr. -1-k). pap. 5.99 (978-1-4847-2953-3(6)) Disney Pr.

Disney Press Editors. Ewoks Join the Fight. 2015. (Star Wars: World of Reading Ser.). (J). lib. bdg. 13.55 (978-0-606-36912-1(0)) Turtleback Bks.

Dolan, Elys. Nuts in Space. Dolan, Elys, illus. 2015. (ENG., Illus.). 32p. (J). (gr. k-3). 17.99 (978-0-7636-7609-4(8), Nosy Crow) Candlewick Pr.

Edick, Grant. Space Station. 2004. (Two Boys Adventure Story Ser.). 98p. (J). (gr. 3-6). 15.95 (978-0-9677839-9-4(2)) Wysteria Publishing.

Evans, D. L. & Sinclair, Valerie. How Rolly Robot Saved the Starbabies, 1 vol. 2012. (ENG., Illus.). 32p. (J). (978-1-55455-201-6(X)) Fitzhenry & Whiteside, Ltd.

Finn, Caitlin. Harold the Misfit. 2012. 24p. pap. 14.93 (978-1-4669-5131-0(1)) Trafford Publishing.

Freestone, Annie. The Little Mars Rovers. 2008. 36p. pap. 13.95 (978-1-59858-459-2(6)) Dog Ear Publishing, LLC.

George, Joshua. Space. Crisp, Dan, illus. 2017. (Search & Find Ser.). (ENG.). 48p. (J). (gr. k-2). pap. 6.99 **(978-1-78700-032-2(X))** Top That! Publishing PLC GBR. Dist: Independent Pubs. Group.

Gioseffi, Anthony P. Mainframe. 2007. 144p. per. 11.95 (978-0-595-44953-8(0)) iUniverse, Inc.

Girard, Philippe. Gustave et le Capitaine Planète. Girard, Philippe, illus. 2004. (Mon Roman Ser.). (FRE., Illus.). 96p. (J). (gr. 2). pap. (978-2-89021-649-5(7)) Diffusion du livre Mirabel (DLM).

Goguen, Martha M. Andromed: Dream Believe Achieve Series. Walker, Patricia M., illus. 2011. 36p. pap. (978-1-897435-35-9(5)) Agio Publishing Hse.

Golden Books Staff. Sponge in Space! (SpongeBob SquarePants) Martinez, Heather, illus. 2012. (Little Golden Book Ser.). (ENG.). 24p. (J). (gr. k-k). 4.99 (978-0-307-92990-7(6), Golden Bks.) Random Hse. Children's Bks.

Gonnard, Christel, et al. The Planet of Okidians. 2015. (Little Prince Ser.: 21). (ENG., Illus.). 48p. (J). (gr. 4-8). pap. 7.95 (978-1-4677-6024-9(2), Graphic Universe™) Lerner Publishing Group.

Granny J. Pinky Visits Outer Space: Pinky Frink's Adventures. 2012. 38p. pap. 17.99 (978-1-300-06064-2(6)) Lulu Pr., Inc.

Guibert, Emmanuel & Sfar, Joann. Sardine in Outer Space. Watson, Sasha, tr. from FRE. Sfar, Joann & Pezzali, Walter, illus. deluxe ed. 2006. (Sardine in Outer Space Ser.: 1). (ENG.). 128p. (J). (gr. 1-5). pap. 16.99 (978-1-59643-126-3(1), 9781596431263, First Second Bks.) Roaring Brook Pr.

—Sardine in Outer Space, Vol. 3. Brizzi, Elisabeth & Siegel, Alexis, trs. from FRE. Sfar, Joann & Pezzali, Walter, illus. 3rd rev. ed. 2007. (Sardine in Outer Space Ser.: 3). (ENG.). 112p. (J). (gr. 1-5). pap. 17.99 (978-1-59643-128-7(8), 9781596431287, First Second Bks.) Roaring Brook Pr.

Harber, Chris. Simon the Policeman on the Number Planet. Harber, Hulya, illus. 2013. 28p. pap. (978-0-7552-1560-7(5), Bright Pen) Authors OnLine, Ltd.

Harper, Benjamin. Star Wars: the Power of the Dark Side. 2015. (ENG.). 32p. (J). (gr. 1-4). 17.99 (978-0-7944-3532-5(7)) Reader's Digest Assn., Inc., The.

Harrison, Zac. Robot Warriors, 1 vol. 2013. (Hyperspace High Ser.). (ENG.). 288p. (gr. 4-8). pap. 8.95 (978-1-4342-6312-4(6)); 27.32 (978-1-4342-6308-7(8)) Stone Arch Bks.

Hawking, Lucy & Hawking, Stephen W. George's Cosmic Treasure Hunt. Parsons, Garry, illus. 2011. (George's Secret Key Ser.). (ENG.). 352p. (J). (gr. 3-7). pap. 11.99 (978-1-4424-2175-2(4), Simon & Schuster Bks. For Young Readers) Simon & Schuster Bks. For Young Readers.

Hawking, Stephen W. & Hawking, Lucy. George's Cosmic Treasure Hunt. Parsons, Garry, illus. 2009. (George's Secret Key Ser.). (ENG.). 320p. (J). (gr. 3-7). 19.99 (978-1-4169-8671-3(5), Simon & Schuster Bks. For Young Readers) Simon & Schuster Bks. For Young Readers.

—George's Secret Key to the Universe. Parsons, Garry, illus. l.t. ed. 2008. (Literacy Bridge Middle Reader Ser.). 359p. (J). (gr. 3-7). 24.95 (978-1-4104-0638-5(5)) Thorndike Pr.

Hoena, Blake A. Ooze Slingers from Outer Space. Harpster, Steve, illus. 2007. (Graphic Sparks Ser.). (ENG.). 40p. (gr. 1-3). per. 5.95 (978-1-59889-410-3(2), Graphic Sparks) Stone Arch Bks.

Hole, Stian. Garmann's Secret. Hole, Stian, illus. 2011. (ENG., Illus.). 56p. (J). 17.00 (978-0-8028-5400-1(1), Eerdmans Bks For Young Readers) Eerdmans, William B. Publishing Co.

Hunt, Meg, illus. Interstellar Cinderella. 2015. (ENG.). 40p. (J). (gr. -1-k). 16.99 (978-1-4521-2532-9(5)) Chronicle Bks. LLC.

Klein, Joel & Klein, Abby. The Night I Saved the Universe: From the Files of the Galactic Police Department. 2009. 126p. (J). (978-0-545-12933-6(8)) Scholastic, Inc.

Knife & Packer. Spash Mash. Knife & Packer, illus. 2016. (Illus.). 93p. (J). pap. 6.99 (978-1-61067-397-6(2)) Kane Miller.

Lehman, Seth. The Color Pets. 2006. (Illus.). 52p. (J). 7.00 net. (978-0-9787986-0-4(0)) 4All Ages LLC.

Long, Ethan. Clara & Clem in Outer Space. 2013. (Penguin Young Readers, Level 1 Ser.). (ENG.). 32p. (J). (gr. k-1). 14.99 (978-0-448-46722-1(4)); pap. 3.99 (978-0-448-46721-4(6)) Penguin Young Readers Group. (Penguin Young Readers).

Maihack, Mike. Target Practice. 2014. (Cleopatra in Space Ser.: 1). (ENG.). 176p. (J). (gr. 3-7). 22.99 (978-0-545-52842-9(9), Graphix) Scholastic, Inc.

McBride, Earvin, Jr. Space - M. D. 3001. McBride, Earvin, Jr., illus. 2nd unabr. ed. 2003. (Earvin MacBride's Amazing Sci-Fi & Adventure Heroes Ser.). (Illus.). 329p. (J). (gr. 7-12). pap. 4.95 (978-1-892511-09-6(6)) MacBride, E. J. Pubn., Inc.

McNamara, Margaret. The Three Little Aliens & the Big Bad Robot. Fearing, Mark, illus. 2011. (ENG.). 40p. (J). (gr. -1-3). 16.99 (978-0-375-86689-0(2), Schwartz & Wade Bks.) Random Hse. Children's Bks.

McNamee, Kevin. Just for Today. Movshina, Marina, illus. 2012. 16p. pap. 9.95 (978-1-61633-314-0(6)) Guardian Angel Publishing, Inc.

Meister, Cari. Buzz Beaker & the Outer Space Trip. McGuire, Bill, illus. 2010. (Buzz Beaker Bks.). (ENG.). 32p. (gr. 2-3). pap. 6.25 (978-1-4342-2800-0(2)) Stone Arch Bks.

Metz, Melinda. The Mars Mission Mayhem. McKenzie, Heath, illus. 2016. (S. M. A. R. T. S. Ser.). (ENG.). 128p. (gr. 3-6). pap. 9.95 (978-1-4965-3018-9(7)) Stone Arch Bks.

Miller, Bryan Q. Space Mountain: A Graphic Novel. 2014. (J). lib. bdg. 24.50 (978-0-606-35260-4(0)) Turtleback Bks.

Miller, Jeff. Close Encounters of the Nerd Kind. 2015. (Nerdy Dozen Ser.: 2). (ENG.). 272p. (J). (gr. 3-7). 16.99 (978-0-06-227265-2(9)) HarperCollins Pubs.

Molloy, Tom. Everything but the Beach: A Slice of Manchester Life. 2012. (Illus.). 192p. (J). pap. 9.60 (978-1-291-15817-5(0)) Lulu Pr., Inc.

Montgomery, R. A. Trouble on Planet Earth. 2007. 144p. (J). pap. (978-1-86504-933-5(6)) Chooseco LLC.

—Trouble on Planet Earth. Trod, Mariano et al, illus. 2006. (Choose Your Own Adventure Ser.: No. 11). 144p. (J). (gr. 4-8). per. 6.99 (978-1-933390-11-6(5), CHCL11) Chooseco LLC.

—Trouble on Planet Earth. 2005. (Illus.). 113p. (J). pap. (978-0-7608-9699-0(2)) Sundance/Newbridge Educational Publishing.

Moodey, Mary. Christopher Counts the Constellation, bks. 500, bk. 500. Shingle, Jude, illus. 500th l.t. ed. 2012. (ENG.). 37p. 16.99 (978-0-9853579-0-0(8)) MarMooWorks,LLC.

Moore, Brenna L. Out of Place in Outer Space. 2013. 28p. pap. 11.95 (978-1-4787-0706-6(2)) Outskirts Pr., Inc.

Oppel, Kenneth. Starclimber. 400p. (YA). (gr. 8). 2010. pap. 9.99 (978-0-06-085059-3(0)) 2009. (Illus.). 17.99 (978-0-06-085057-9(4)) HarperCollins Pubs.

O'Ryan, Ray. The Annoying Crush. 2014. (Galaxy Zack Ser.: 9). lib. bdg. 16.00 (978-0-606-36093-7(X)) Turtleback Bks.

—Drake Makes a Splash! Jack, Colin, illus. 2014. (Galaxy Zack Ser.: 8). (ENG.). 128p. (J). (gr. k-2). pap. 5.99 (978-1-4424-9360-5(7), Little Simon) Little Simon.

—A Galactic Easter! Jack, Colin, illus. 2014. (Galaxy Zack Ser.: 7). (ENG.). 128p. (J). (gr. k-4). pap. 5.99 (978-1-4424-9357-5(7), Little Simon) Little Simon.

—A Galactic Easter! 2014. (Galaxy Zack Ser.: 7). lib. bdg. 16.00 (978-0-606-35428-8(X)) Turtleback Bks.

—A Green Christmas! Jack, Colin, illus. 2013. (Galaxy Zack Ser.: 6). (ENG.). 128p. (J). (gr. k-2). 16.99 (978-1-4424-8225-8(7)); pap. 4.99 (978-1-4424-8224-1(9)) Little Simon. (Little Simon).

—A Green Christmas! 2013. (Galaxy Zack Ser.: 6). lib. bdg. 14.75 (978-0-606-35185-0(X)) Turtleback Bks.

Packer. Space Mash. Knife, illus. 2016. 93p. (J). (978-1-61067-477-5(4)) Kane Miller.

Park, Louise. Star Girl. May, Kyla & Matthews, Melanie, illus. 2015. (Star Girl Ser.). (ENG.). 80p. (gr. 1-4). 90.60 (978-1-4795-8292-1(1)) Picture Window Bks.

Parker, Danny. Crusts. 2016. (ENG., Illus.). 32p. (J). (gr. -1-k). 20.99 **(978-1-74297-983-0(1))** Little Hare Bks. AUS. Dist: Independent Pubs. Group.

Pilkey, Dav. Mighty Robot vs. the Naughty Nightcrawlers from Neptune. Santat, Dan, illus. 2016. (Ricky Ricotta Ser.: 8). (ENG.). 128p. (J). (gr. -1-3). 15.99 (978-0-439-37708-9(0)) Scholastic, Inc.

—Ricky Ricotta's Mighty Robot vs. the Naughty Nightcrawlers from Neptune. Santat, Dan, illus. 2016. (Ricky Ricotta Ser.: 8). (ENG.). 128p. (J). (gr. -1-3). pap. 5.99 (978-0-439-37709-6(9)) Scholastic, Inc.

Rand, Johnathan. Freddie Fernortner #9: Attack of the Dust Bunnies from Outer Space. 2008. 96p. (J). pap. 4.99 (978-1-893699-95-3(1)) AudioCraft Publishing, Inc.

Reeve, Philip. Starcross: A Stirring Adventure of Spies, Time Travel & Curious Hats. Wyatt, David, illus. 2007. (ENG.). 384p. (YA). (gr. 5-18). 16.95 (978-1-59990-121-3(8), 9781599901213, Bloomsbury USA Childrens) Bloomsbury Publishing USA.

Regan, Dian. Space Boy & His Dog. Neubecker, Robert, illus. 2015. (Space Boy Ser.). (ENG.). 32p. (J). (gr. k-5). 16.95 (978-1-59078-955-1(5)) Boyds Mills Pr.

—Space Boy & the Space Pirate. Neubecker, Robert, illus. 2016. (Space Boy Ser.). (ENG.). 40p. (J). (gr. k-5). 16.95 (978-1-59078-956-8(3)) Boyds Mills Pr.

Rockwell, Carey. The Revolt on Venus. 2007. 120p. per. (978-1-4068-3961-6(2)) Echo Library.

—The Space Pioneers. 2007. 120p. per. (978-1-4068-3962-3(0)) Echo Library.

Rosenthal, Adam. Adventures of Snizznsnozz. 2011. 24p. pap. 11.32 (978-1-4634-0736-0(X)) AuthorHouse.

Rouss, Sylvia A. Reach for the Stars. 2005. (Illus.). 40p. (J). (gr. 3-7). 16.95 (978-1-930143-82-1(6)); pap. 9.95 (978-1-930143-83-8(4)) Simcha Media Group. (Devora Publishing).

Santillo, LuAnn. The Big Job. Santillo, LuAnn, ed. 2003. (Half-Pint Kids Readers Ser.). (Illus.). 7p. (J). (gr. -1-1). pap. (978-1-59256-044-8(X)) Half-Pint Kids, Inc.

—Outerspace, 6 vols. Santillo, LuAnn, ed. 2003. (Half-Pint Kids Readers Ser.). (Illus.). 42p. (J). (gr. -1-1). pap. 6.95 (978-1-59256-042-4(3)) Half-Pint Kids, Inc.

Schooley, Bob & McCorkle, Mark. Liar of Kudzu. 2008. (ENG.). 192p. (J). (gr. 5-9). pap. 9.99 (978-1-4169-1489-1(7), Simon & Schuster Bks. For Young Readers) Simon & Schuster Bks. For Young Readers.

Scott, Janine. Café Cosmos. Wood, Hannah, illus. 2009. (Treasure Chest Readers Ser.). 24p. (J). (gr. -1-2). pap. 8.15 (978-1-60754-674-0(4)); lib. bdg. 22.60 (978-1-60754-673-3(6)) Windmill Bks.

—Mars Mouse. Wood, Hannah, illus. 2009. (Treasure Chest Readers Ser.). 24p. (J). (gr. -1-2). pap. 8.15 (978-1-60754-677-1(9)); lib. bdg. 22.60 (978-1-60754-676-4(0)) Windmill Bks.

Scribens, Sunny, et al. Space Song Rocket Ride. Sim, David, illus. 2014. 32p. (J). (gr. -1-2). 9.99 (978-1-78285-098-4(8)) Barefoot Bks., Inc.

Shannon, Ronnie Jay. Samurai Force: the Final Hope: The Junior Novel. 2007. (ENG.). 76p. per. 19.95 (978-1-4241-6528-5(8)) America Star Bks.

Silverhardt, Lauryn. OLIVIA Blasts Off! Wolek, Guy, illus. 2010. (Olivia TV Tie-In Ser.). (ENG.). 12p. (J). (gr. -1-1). 6.99 (978-1-4169-9538-8(2), Simon Spotlight) Simon Spotlight.

Smiley, Mark. A Journey Far Away. 2006. 164p. pap. 13.95 (978-1-59526-494-7(9)) Aeon Publishing Inc.

Spoonmore, Scott. Seymour the Semi- Space Truckin' Sponaugle, Kim, illus. 2012. 24p. 19.95 (978-1-61633-282-2(4)); pap. 11.95 (978-1-61633-283-9(2)) Guardian Angel Publishing, Inc.

Stilton, Geronimo. Beware! Space Junk! 2016. (Geronimo Stilton Spacemice Ser.: 7). (ENG.). 128p. (J). (gr. 2-5). pap. 7.99 (978-0-545-87245-4(6), Scholastic Paperbacks) Scholastic, Inc.

—Ice Planet Adventure. 2015. (Geronimo Stilton Spacemice Ser.: 3). (ENG., Illus.). 128p. (J). (gr. 2-5). pap. 7.99 (978-0-545-74619-9(1), Scholastic Paperbacks) Scholastic, Inc.

—Rescue Rebellion. 2015. (Geronimo Stilton Spacemice Ser.: 5). lib. bdg. 17.20 (978-0-606-37775-1(1)) Turtleback Bks.

—The Underwater Planet. 2016. (Geronimo Stilton Spacemice Ser.: 6). (ENG., Illus.). 128p. (J). (gr. 2-5). pap. 7.99 (978-0-545-87243-0(X), Scholastic Paperbacks) Scholastic, Inc.

—You're Mine, Captain! 2014. (Geronimo Stilton Spacemice Ser.: 2). (ENG., Illus.). 128p. (J). (gr. 2-5). pap. 7.99 (978-0-545-64652-9(9), Scholastic Paperbacks) Scholastic, Inc.

Strub, Scott Richard. Otto the Outerspace Octopus. 2007. (J). per. 10.00 (978-1-59872-782-1(6)) Instant Pub.

Sutton, Laurie S. The Dark Side of the Apokolips. Vecchio, Luciano, illus. 2015. (Superman: Comic Chapter Bks.). (ENG.). 88p. (gr. 3-7). lib. bdg. 21.32 (978-1-4965-0509-5(3)) Stone Arch Bks.

Thompson, Craig. Space Dumplins. 2015. (ENG.). 320p. (J). (gr. 3-7). 24.99 (978-0-545-56541-7(3)); pap. 14.99 (978-0-545-56543-1(X)) Scholastic, Inc. (Graphix).

Trine, Greg. Willy Maykit in Space. Burks, James, illus. (ENG.). 208p. (J). (gr. 2-5). 2016. pap. 7.99 (978-0-544-66848-5(0)) 2015. 13.99 (978-0-544-31351-4(8)) Houghton Mifflin Harcourt Publishing Co. (HMH Books For Young Readers).

Tucker, Susan K. Ridiculously Ridiculous. Foster, Jack, illus. 2012. 16p. pap. 9.95 (978-1-61633-346-1(4)) Guardian Angel Publishing, Inc.

Viva, Frank. A Long Way Away. 2013. (ENG., Illus.). 40p. (J). (gr. -1-3). 16.99 (978-0-316-22196-2(1)) Little, Brown Bks. for Young Readers.

Winn, L. B. Butterpod Jerome & the Planet of Gabool. Winn, L. B., illus. 2007. (Illus.). (J). pap. 18.95 (978-0-9791884-0-4(7)) Winn, Lynnette.

Wyneken, Cherise. Spaceship Lands in Africa, 1 vol. 2010. 50p. pap. 16.95 (978-1-4489-5417-9(7)) America Star Bks.

Yaccarino, Dan. Zorgoochi Intergalactic Pizza: Delivery of Doom. Yaccarino, Dan, illus. 2014. (ENG., Illus.). 336p. (J). (gr. 3-7). 16.99 (978-1-250-00844-2(1), 9781250008442) Feiwel & Friends.

Young, Craig. Arrr Marks the Spot. 2011. 32p. pap. (978-1-926959-06-1(X)) 1889 Labs Ltd.

Zucker, Jonny. Mission 2: Supersonic. Woodman, Ned, illus. 2013. (Max Flash Ser.: 2). (ENG.). 144p. (gr. 2-5). pap. 7.95 (978-1-4677-1482-2(8)); lib. bdg. 27.93 (978-1-4677-1208-8(6)) Lerner Publishing Group. (Darby Creek).

OUTLAWS

see Robbers and Outlaws

OVERLAND JOURNEYS TO THE PACIFIC

Arnez, Lynda. My Wagon Train Adventure. 2016. (My Place in History Ser.). (ENG., Illus.). 24p. (J). (gr. 2-3). pap. 8.15 (978-1-4824-4002-7(4)) Stevens, Gareth Publishing LLLP.

Aronin, Miriam. How Many People Traveled the Oregon Trail? And Other Questions about the Trail West. 2012. (Six Questions of American History Ser.). (ENG.). 48p. (gr. 4-6). pap. 56.72 (978-0-7613-9237-8(8)); pap. 9.95 (978-0-7613-8566-0(5)); lib. bdg. 30.60 (978-0-7613-5332-4(1)) Lerner Publishing Group.

Braidich, Victoria. Making History: A Covered Wagon. 2006. (Tony Stead Nonfiction Independent Reading Collection). (ENG.). 24p. (gr. 3-6). pap. 8.85 (978-1-4042-5589-0(3)) Rosen Publishing Group, Inc., The.

Bryant, Jill. Wagon Train. 2003. (Real Life Stories Ser.). (Illus.). 24p. (J). lib. bdg. 24.45 (978-1-59036-082-8(6)) Weigl Pubs., Inc.

Crewe, Sabrina & Uschan, Michael V. The Oregon Trail. 2004. (Events That Shaped America Ser.). (Illus.). 32p. (gr. 3-6). lib. bdg. 26.00 (978-0-8368-3405-5(4), Gareth Stevens Learning Library) Stevens, Gareth Publishing LLLP.

Dean, Arlan. The Old Spanish Trail: From Santa Fe, New Mexico to Los Angeles, California. 2009. (Famous American Trails Ser.). 24p. (gr. 3-3). 42.50 (978-1-61512-489-3(6), PowerKids Pr.) Rosen Publishing Group, Inc., The.

—The Oregon Trail: From Independence, Missouri to Oregon City, Oregon. (Famous American Trails Ser.). 24p. 2009. (gr. 3-3). 42.50 (978-1-61512-490-9(X)) 2003. (Illus.). (J). lib. bdg. 22.60 (978-0-8239-6478-9(7)) Rosen Publishing Group, Inc., The. (PowerKids Pr.).

—The Overland Trail: From Atchison, Kansas, to Fort Bridger, Wyoming. 2003. (Famous American Trails Ser.). (Illus.). 24p. (J). lib. bdg. 22.60 (978-0-8239-6479-6(5), PowerKids Pr.) Rosen Publishing Group, Inc., The.

—The Overland Trail: From Atchison, Kansas to Ft. Bridger, Wyoming. 2009. (Famous American Trails Ser.). 24p. (gr. 3-3). 42.50 (978-1-61512-491-6(8), PowerKids Pr.) Rosen Publishing Group, Inc., The.

Doeden, Matt. Oregon Trail: An Interactive History Adventure. 2013. (You Choose: History Ser.). (ENG.). 112p. (gr. 3-4). pap. 6.95 (978-1-4765-3607-1(4)); 31.99 (978-1-4765-0254-0(4)) Capstone Press of Coughlan Cos. (You Choose Bks.).

Domnauer, Teresa. Westward Expansion. 2010. (True Book Ser.). (ENG., Illus.). 48p. (J). pap. 6.95 (978-0-531-21249-3(1)); (gr. 2-5). 29.00 (978-0-531-20586-0(X)) Scholastic Library Publishing.

Dunn, Joeming W. The Oregon Trail, 1 vol. Smith, Tim, illus. 2008. (Graphic History Ser.). (ENG.). 32p. 28.50 (978-1-60270-183-0(0), Graphic Planet- Nonfiction) ABDO Publishing Co.

Figley, Marthy Rhodes. Clara Morgan & the Oregon Trail Journey. Orback, Craig, illus. 2011. (History Speaks: Picture Books Plus Reader's Theater Ser.). 48p. pap. 56.72 (978-0-7613-7631-6(3)) Lerner Publishing Group.

Figley, Marthy Rhodes & Figley, Marty Rhodes. Clara Morgan & the Oregon Trail Journey. Orback, Craig, illus. 2011. (History Speaks: Picture Books Plus Reader's Theater Ser.). (ENG.). 48p. (gr. 2-4). pap. 9.95 (978-0-7613-7115-1(X)) Lerner Publishing Group.

Francis, Dorothy Brenner. Courage on the Oregon Trail. 2003. (Reading Essentials in Social Studies). (Illus.). 40p. pap. 8.00 (978-0-7891-5872-7(8)) Perfection Learning Corp.

Freedman, Jeri. Life As a Pioneer on the Oregon Trail. 2016. (Life As... Ser.). (ENG., Illus.). 32p. (J). (gr. 3-3). pap. 10.58 (978-1-5026-1075-1(2)) Cavendish Square Publishing.

Friedman, Mel. The Oregon Trail. (Cornerstones of Freedom, Third Ser.). (ENG., (J). 2012. Illus.). 64p. pap. 8.95 (978-0-531-28163-5(9)) 2012. (Illus.). 64p. lib. bdg. 30.00 (978-0-531-23063-3(5)) 2010. 48p. pap. 6.95 (978-0-531-21247-9(5), Children's Pr.) 2010. (Illus.). 48p. (gr. 2-5). 29.00 (978-0-531-20584-6(3)) Scholastic Library Publishing.

Gingrich, Callista. From Sea to Shining Sea. Arciero, Susan, illus. 2014. (Ellis the Elephant Ser.). (ENG.). 40p. (J). (gr. -1-3). 14.99 (978-1-62157-253-4(6), Regnery Kids) Regnery Publishing, Inc., An Eagle Publishing Co.

Graham, Amy. The Oregon Trail & the Daring Journey West by Wagon. 2006. (Wild History of the American West Ser.). (Illus.). 128p. (J). (gr. 5-9). lib. bdg. 34.60 (978-1-59845-021-7(2), MyReportLinks.com Bks.) Enslow Pubs., Inc.

Gregory, Josh. If You Were a Kid on the Oregon Trail. Farré, Lluís, illus. 2016. (If You Were a Kid Ser.). (ENG.). 32p. (J). lib. bdg. 26.00 (978-0-531-21970-6(4), Children's Pr.) Scholastic Library Publishing.

Gunderson, Jessica. Your Life As a Pioneer on the Oregon Trail. Dougherty, Rachel, illus. 2012. (Way It Was Ser.). (ENG.). 32p. (gr. 2-3). pap. 8.95 (978-1-4048-7250-9(7)); lib. bdg. 26.65 (978-1-4048-7157-1(8)) Picture Window Bks.

Hale, Nathan. Donner Dinner Party. 2013. (Nathan Hale's Hazardous Tales Ser.). (ENG., Illus.). 128p. (J). (gr. 3-7). 12.99 (978-1-4197-0856-5(2), Amulet Bks.) Abrams, Inc.

Harberts, Bernie. Woody & Maggie Walk Across America. 2006. (Illus.). 40p. (J). 16.96 (978-0-9787722-9-1(6)) RiverEarth.

Harkins, Susan Sales & Harkins, William H. The Donner Party. 2008. (What's So Great About... ? Ser.). (Illus.). 32p. (J). (gr. 2-4). lib. bdg. 25.70 (978-1-58415-669-7(4)) Mitchell Lane Pubs., Inc.

Harness, Cheryl. The Tragic Tale of Narcissa Whitman & a Faithful History of the Oregon Trail. Harness, Cheryl, illus. 2006. (Cheryl Harness Histories Ser.). (ENG., Illus.). 144p. (J). (gr. 5-9). 16.95 (978-0-7922-5920-6(3)); lib. bdg. 25.90 (978-0-7922-5921-3(1)) National Geographic Society. (National Geographic Children's Bks.).

Hill, William E. The California Trail: Yesterday & Today. 2017. **(978-0-87004-604-9(7))** Caxton Pr.

Jeffrey, Gary. The Gold Rush. Boccanfuso, Emanuele, illus. 2012. (Graphic History of the American West Ser.). (ENG.). 24p. (J). (gr. 3-8). pap. 8.15 (978-1-4339-6741-2(3), Gareth Stevens Learning Library) Stevens, Gareth Publishing LLLP.

—The Oregon Trail. Poluzzi, Allesandro, illus. 2012. (Graphic History of the American West Ser.). (ENG.). 24p. (J). (gr. 3-8). pap. 8.15 (978-1-4339-6745-0(6), Gareth Stevens Learning Library); (gr. 4-7). lib. bdg. 23.95 (978-1-4339-6743-6(X)) Stevens, Gareth Publishing LLLP.

Kravitz, Danny. Surviving the Journey: The Story of the Oregon Trail, 1 vol. 2014. (Adventures on the American Frontier Ser.). (ENG.). 32p. (gr. 3-4). 27.32 (978-1-4914-0187-3(7), Fact Finders) Capstone Press of Coughlan Cos.

LaClair, Teresa. Americans Move West (1846-1860) 2013. (Illus.). 48p. (J). pap. (978-1-4222-2417-5(1)) Mason Crest.

—Americans Move West (1846-1860) Rakove, Jack N., ed. 2012. (How America Became America Ser.). (Illus.). 48p. (J). (gr. 3-4). 19.95 (978-1-4222-2403-8(1)) Mason Crest.

Landau, Elaine. The Oregon Trail. 2006. (True Bks.). (ENG., Illus.). 48p. (J). (gr. 3-7). pap. 6.95 (978-0-516-27903-9(3), Children's Pr.) Scholastic Library Publishing.

Levy, Janey. Life on a Wagon Train. 2003. (Rosen Real Readers Big Bookstm Ser.). (ENG.). 16p. (gr. 2-3). 37.95 (978-1-4042-6224-9(5)) Rosen Publishing Group, Inc., The.

Lynette, Rachel. The Oregon Trail. 2013. (Pioneer Spirit: the Westward Expansion Ser.). 24p. (J). (gr. 3-6). 22.60 (978-1-4777-0786-9(7)); (ENG., Illus.). pap. 8.25 (978-1-4777-0905-4(3)) Rosen Publishing Group, Inc., The. (PowerKids Pr.).

Marciniak, Kristin. The Oregon Trail & Westward Expansion: A History Perspectives Book. 2013. (Perspectives Library). (ENG., Illus.). 32p. (J). (gr. 4-8). 28.50 (978-1-62431-419-3(8), 202796); pap. 14.21 (978-1-62431-495-7(3), 202798) Cherry Lake Publishing.

McNeese, Tim. The Oregon Trail. 2009. (Milestones in American History Ser.). (Illus.). 152p. (gr. 6-12). 35.00 (978-1-60413-027-0(X), Chelsea Hse.) Facts On File, Inc.

Morley, Jacqueline. You Wouldn't Want to... Be an American Pioneer! Antram, David, illus. rev. ed. 2012. (ENG.). (J). 40p. pap. 9.95 (978-0-531-28025-6(X)); 32p. lib. bdg. 29.00 (978-0-531-27500-9(0)) Scholastic Library Publishing.

Nolan, Frederick. Trailblazing the Way West. 2015. (Wild West Ser.). (Illus.). 64p. (J). (gr. 9-12). 39.95 (978-1-78404-081-9(9)) Arcturus Publishing GBR. Dist: Black Rabbit Bks.

Oachs, Emily Rose. Death in the Donner Party: A Cause-And-Effect Investigation. 2016. (Cause-And-Effect Disasters Ser.). (ENG., Illus.). 40p. (J). (gr. 4-6). 30.65 (978-1-5124-1115-7(9)) Lerner Publishing Group.

Olson, Steven. The Oregon Trail: A Primary Source History of the Route to the American West. 2009. (Primary Sources in American History Ser.). 64p. (gr. 5-8). 58.50 (978-1-60851-501-1(X)) Rosen Publishing Group, Inc., The.

Olson, Steven P. The Oregon Trail. 2004. (Primary Sources in American History Ser.). (Illus.). 64p. (gr. 5-8). lib. bdg. 31.95 (978-0-8239-4512-2(X), Rosen Reference) Rosen Publishing Group, Inc., The.

The Oregon Trail. 2013. (Pioneer Spirit: the Westward Expansion Ser.). 24p. (J). (gr. 3-6). pap. 49.50 (978-1-4777-0906-1(1), PowerKids Pr.) Rosen Publishing Group, Inc., The.

Quasha, Jennifer. Covered Wagons: Hands-on Projects about America's Westward Expansion. 2009. (Great Social Studies Projects Ser.). 24p. (gr. 3-3). 42.50 (978-1-61513-208-9(2), PowerKids Pr.) Rosen Publishing Group, Inc., The.

Rajczak, Kristen. The Donner Party. 2015. (Doomed! Ser.). (ENG., Illus.). 32p. (J). (gr. 4-5). pap. 10.50 (978-1-4824-2928-2(4)) Stevens, Gareth Publishing LLLP.

—Life on a Wagon Train. 2013. (What You Didn't Know about History Ser.). (Illus.). 24p. (J). (gr. 2-5). pap. 8.15 (978-1-4339-8445-7(8)); lib. bdg. 22.60 (978-1-4339-8444-0(X)) Stevens, Gareth Publishing LLLP.

Schwartz, Heather E. The Foul, Filthy American Frontier: The Disgusting Details about the Journey Out West. 2011. (Disgusting History Ser.). (ENG.). 32p. (gr. 3-4). pap. 47.70 (978-1-4296-6478-3(9), Fact Finders) Capstone Press of Coughlan Cos.

Sechrist, Darren. Westward, Ho! 2008. (ENG.). 32p. (J). pap. (978-0-7787-4217-3(2)) Crabtree Publishing Co.

Smith-Llera, Danielle. Stranded in the Sierra Nevada: The Story of the Donner Party. 2015. (Adventures on the American Frontier Ser.). (ENG., Illus.). 32p. (gr. 3-4). pap. 7.95 (978-1-4914-4912-7(8)) Capstone Press of Coughlan Cos.

Steele, Christy. Famous Wagon Trails. 2005. (America's Westward Expansion Ser.). (Illus.). 48p. (gr. 5-12). pap. 14.05 (978-0-8368-5795-5(X)); lib. bdg. 31.00 (978-0-8368-5788-7(7)) Stevens, Gareth Publishing LLLP. (Gareth Stevens Secondary Library).

Stefoff, Rebecca. Surviving the Oregon Trail. 2012. (Stories in American History Ser.). (Illus.). 128p. (J). (gr. 5-18). 33.27 (978-0-7660-3955-1(2)) Enslow Pubs., Inc.

—Surviving the Oregon Trail: Stories in American History. 2012. (Stories in American History Ser.). (Illus.). 128p. (J). (gr. 5-18). pap. 10.95 (978-1-4644-0025-4(3)) Enslow Pubs., Inc.

Stuckey, Rachel. Wagon Trains Heading West. 2015. (True History of the Wild West Ser.). (ENG., Illus.). 32p. (J). (gr. 5-5). pap. 10.00 (978-1-4994-1179-9(0), PowerKids Pr.) Rosen Publishing Group, Inc., The.

Tieck, Sarah. Oregon Trail, 1 vol. 2008. (All Aboard America Ser.). (ENG.). 24p. (J). (gr. 1-4). 25.65 (978-1-59928-939-7(3)) ABDO Publishing Co.

Wadsworth, Ginger. Survival in the Snow. Orback, Craig, illus. 48p. 2011. (J). pap. 6.95 (978-0-7613-3941-0(8), First Avenue Editions) 2009. (ENG.). (gr. 2-4). 25.26 (978-0-8225-7892-5(1)) Lerner Publishing Group.

Welveart, Scott R. & Welvaert, Scott R. The Donner Party, 1 vol. Frenz, Ron et al, illus. 2006. (Disasters in History Ser.). (ENG.). 32p. (gr. 3-4). 30.65 (978-0-7368-5479-5(7), Graphic Library) Capstone Press of Coughlan Cos.

OVERLAND JOURNEYS TO THE PACIFIC—FICTION

Applegate, Katherine. The Buffalo Storm. Ormerod, Jan, illus. 2014. (ENG.). 32p. (J). (gr. -1-3). pap. 7.99 (978-0-544-33921-7(5), HMH Books For Young Readers) Houghton Mifflin Harcourt Publishing Co.

Bly, Stephen A. The Lost Wagon Train. 2005. (Retta Barre's Oregon Trail Ser.: Vol. 1). 110p. pap. 5.99 (978-1-58134-391-5(4), Crossway Bibles) Crossway.

MNO

Carson, Rae. Walk on Earth a Stranger. 2015. (Gold Seer Trilogy Ser.: 1). (ENG.). 448p. (YA). (gr. 8). 17.99 (978-0-06-224291-4(1), Greenwillow Bks.) HarperCollins Pubs.
Coerr, Eleanor. The Josefina Story Quilt. Degen, Bruce, illus. 2003. (I Can Read! Level 3 Ser.). 64p. (J). (gr. 2-4). lib. bdg. 13.55 (978-0-8335-2723-3(1), Turtleback) Turtleback Bks.
Crawford, Neil. The Journeyers. 2006. (ENG.). 248p. (J). per. (978-0-9778205-4-2(8)) Helm Publishing.
Fitzgerald, John D. Brave Buffalo Fighter. 2003. (Young Adult Historical Library). 178p. (YA). pap. 11.95 (978-1-883937-59-1(0)) Bethlehem Bks.
Frazier, Neta. The Stout-Hearted Seven: Orphaned on the Oregon Trail. 2017. (Great Leaders & Events Ser.). (ENG.). (J). (gr. 4-8). lib. bdg. 35.99 (978-1-942875-43-7(6)) Quarto Publishing Group USA.
Frazier, Neta Lohnes. The Stout-Hearted Seven: Orphaned on the Oregon Trail. 2016. (Young Voyageur Ser.). (ENG., Illus.). 224p. (J). (gr. 4-9). pap. 12.99 (978-0-7603-5224-3(0), Voyageur Pr.) Quarto Publishing Group USA.
—The Stout-Hearted Seven: Orphaned on the Oregon Trail. 2006. (Sterling Point Books(r) Ser.). (ENG., Illus.). 208p. (J). (gr. 4-7). pap. 6.95 (978-1-4027-3617-9(7)) Sterling Publishing Co., Inc.
Hallowell, George & Holub, Joan. Wagons Ho! Avril, Lynne, illus. 2011. (ENG.). 32p. (J). (gr. 1-3). 16.99 (978-0-8075-8612-9(9)) Whitman, Albert & Co.
Hopkinson, Deborah. Apples to Oregon. 2014. 17.00 (978-1-63419-642-0(2)) Perfection Learning Corp.
—Apples to Oregon: Being the (Slightly) True Narrative of How a Brave Pioneer Father Brought Apples, Peaches, Pears, Plums, Grapes, & Cherries (and Children) Across the Plains. Carpenter, Nancy, illus. 2008. (ENG.). 40p. (J). (gr. -1-3). 7.99 (978-1-4169-6746-0(X), Aladdin) Simon & Schuster Children's Publishing.
Hopkinson, Deborah & Carpenter, Nancy. Apples to Oregon: Being the (Slightly) True Narrative of How a Brave Pioneer Father Brought Apples, Peaches, Pears, Plums, Grapes, & Cherries (and Children) Across the Plains. 2004. (ENG., Illus.). 40p. (J). (gr. -1-3). 17.99 (978-0-689-84769-1(6), Atheneum Bks. for Young Readers) Simon & Schuster Children's Publishing.
Kimmel, E. Cody. West on the Wagon Train. Snow, Scott, illus. 2003. (Adventures of Young Buffalo Bill Ser.). (ENG.). 160p. (J). 15.99 (978-0-06-029113-6(3)) HarperCollins Pubs.
Lawlor, Laurie. He Will Go Fearless. (ENG.). 224p. (J). (gr. 5-9). 2012. pap. 10.99 (978-0-689-86580-0(5)) 2006. 15.95 (978-0-689-86579-4(1)) Simon & Schuster Bks. For Young Readers. (Simon & Schuster Bks. For Young Readers).
McKernan, Victoria. The Devil's Paintbox. (ENG.). (YA). (gr. 9). 2013. 384p. pap. 9.99 (978-0-449-81655-4(9), Ember) 2010. 368p. mass mkt. 8.99 (978-0-440-23962-8(1), Laurel Leaf) Random Hse. Children's Bks.
Napoli, Donna Jo. The Crossing. Madsen, Jim, illus. 2011. (ENG.). 40p. (J). (gr. -1-3). 16.99 (978-1-4169-9474-9(2), Atheneum Bks. for Young Readers) Simon & Schuster Children's Publishing.
Thompson, Gare. Our Journey West: An Adventure on the Oregon Trail. 2003. 40p. (J). pap. 6.99 (978-0-7922-5199-6(7)) CENGAGE Learning.
Wilson, Laura. How I Survived the Oregon Trail: The Journal of Jesse Adams. 2006. (Illus.). 37p. (J). (gr. 4-8). reprint ed. pap. 10.00 (978-0-7567-9925-0(2)) DIANE Publishing Co.
Winters, Kay. Voices from the Oregon Trail. Day, Larry, illus. 2014. (ENG.). 48p. (J). (gr. 2-4). 17.99 (978-0-8037-3775-4(0), Dial Bks) Penguin Young Readers Group.
Wolf, Allan. New Found Land: Lewis & Clark's Voyage of Discovery. 2007. (ENG., Illus.). 512p. (YA). (gr. 7-9). per. 14.99 (978-0-7636-3288-5(0)) Candlewick Pr.

OVERWEIGHT

see Weight Control

OWENS, JESSE, 1913-1980

Buckley, James. Who Was Jesse Owens? 2015. (Who Was... ? Ser.). lib. bdg. 16.00 (978-0-606-36754-7(3)) Turtleback Bks.
Buckley, James, Jr. & dePaola, Tomie. Who Was Jesse Owens? Copeland, Gregory, illus. 2015. (Who Was? Ser.). (ENG.). 112p. (J). (gr. 3-7). 5.99 (978-0-448-48307-8(6), Grosset & Dunlap) Penguin Young Readers Group.
Burgan, Michael. Olympic Gold 1936: How the Image of Jesse Owens Crushed Hitler's Evil Myth. 2017. (Captured History Sports Ser.). (ENG., Illus.). 64p. (gr. 5-7). lib. bdg. 34.65 (978-0-7565-5528-3(0), CPB Grades 4-8) Compass Point Bks.
Burlingame, Jeff. Jesse Owens: I Always Loved Running. 2011. (African-American Biography Library). (Illus.). 128p. (J). (gr. 7-12). lib. bdg. 33.27 (978-0-7660-3497-6(6)) Enslow Pubs., Inc.
Eboch, M. M. Jesse Owens: Young Record Breaker. Henderson, Meryl, illus. 2008. (Childhood of Famous Americans Ser.). (ENG.). 208p. (J). (gr. 3-7). pap. 6.99 (978-1-4169-3922-1(9), Aladdin) Simon & Schuster Children's Publishing.
Gentry, Tony. Jesse Owens: Champion Athlete. 2005. (Black Americans of Achievement Ser.). (Illus.). 112p. (gr. 6-12). 35.00 (978-0-7910-8252-2(0), Chelsea Hse.) Facts On File, Inc.
Hind, Devon & Bergstresser, Kate, trs. Jesse Owens: World's Fastest Human. 2003. (Alabama Roots Biography Ser.). (Illus.). 120p. (J). (978-1-878561-38-1(3)) Seacoast Publishing, Inc.
Jesse Owens. 2004. (Illus.). 112p. pap. 9.95 (978-0-8225-5318-2(X)) Lerner Publishing Group.
McDougall, Chros. Jesse Owens: Trailblazing Sprinter, 1 vol. 2011. (Legendary Athletes Ser.). (ENG., Illus.). 112p. (YA). (gr. 7-12). 34.22 (978-1-61714-758-6(3)) ABDO Publishing Co.
McKissack, Patricia C. & McKissack, Fredrick L. Jesse Owens: Legendary Track Star. 2013. (Famous African Americans Ser.). 24p. (J). (gr. k-3). pap. 7.95 (978-1-4644-0199-2(3), Enslow Elementary); (Illus.). 22.60 (978-0-7660-4104-2(2)) Enslow Pubs., Inc.
Shafer, Susan. Jesse Owens: Fastest Human. 2005. (J). pap. (978-1-4108-4207-7(X)) Benchmark Education Co.
Stanmyer, Jackie F. Jesse Owens: Facing down Hitler. 2016. (Game-Changing Athletes Ser.). (ENG., Illus.). 112p. (J). (gr. 9-9). lib. bdg. 42.79 (978-1-5026-1049-2(3)) Cavendish Square Publishing.
Streissguth, Tom. Jesse Owens. (Sports Heroes & Legends Ser.). (ENG., Illus.). 112p. (gr. 5-12). 2005. lib. bdg. 30.60 (978-0-8225-3070-1(8)) 2004. lib. bdg. 27.93 (978-0-8225-2256-0(X)) Lerner Publishing Group.
Sutcliffe, Jane. Jesse Owens. Porter, Janice Lee, illus. 2006. (On My Own Biographies Ser.). 48p. 17.00 (978-0-7569-6702-4(3)) Perfection Learning Corp.
Time for Kids Editors. Jesse Owens: Running into History. 2007. (Time for Kids Ser.). (ENG., Illus.). 48p. (J). (gr. 2-4). pap. 3.99 (978-0-06-057620-2(0), Collins) HarperCollins Pubs.

OWLS

Alinsky, Shelby. Hoot, Owl! (1 Hardcover/1 CD) 2017. (National Geographic Kids Ser.). (ENG.). (J). 29.95 (978-1-4301-2653-9(1)) Live Oak Media.
—Hoot, Owl! (1 Paperback/1 CD) 2017. (National Geographic Kids Ser.). (ENG.). (J). pap. 19.95 (978-1-4301-2652-2(3)) Live Oak Media.
—Hoot, Owl! (4 Paperbacks/1 CD), 4 vols. 2017. (National Geographic Kids Ser.). (ENG.). (J). pap., pap. 31.95 (978-1-4301-2654-6(X)) Live Oak Media.
Alinsky, Shelby. National Geographic Readers: Hoot, Owl! 2015. (Readers Ser.). (ENG., Illus.). 24p. (J). (-k). pap. 3.99 (978-1-4263-2125-2(2), National Geographic Children's Bks.) National Geographic Society.
Arjas, Pirkko & Butcher, Sally K., illus. Friend Owl: A Children's Book. 1000th ed. 2005. 48p. (J). 18.00 (978-0-9762132-0-8(6)) Old Bess Publishing Co.
Bodden, Valerie. Amazing Animals: Owls. 2013. (Amazing Animals Ser.). (ENG.). 24p. (J). (gr. 1-3). pap. 8.99 (978-0-89812-790-4(4), Creative Paperbacks) Creative Co., The.
—Owls. 2013. (Illus.). 24p. (J). 25.65 (978-1-60818-088-2(3), Creative Education) Creative Co., The.
Bone, Emily. Owls. Cooper, Jenny & Watson, Richard, illus. 2013. (Usborne Beginners Ser.). (ENG.). 32p. (J). 9.99 (978-0-7945-3401-1(5), Usborne) EDC Publishing.
Boothroyd, Jennifer. From Egg to Owl. 2016. (Start to Finish, Second Ser.). (ENG., Illus.). 24p. (J). (gr. k-3). 23.99 (978-1-5124-1831-6(6)) Lerner Publishing Group.
Camisa, Kathryn. Barn Owl. 2016. (Weird but Cute Ser.). (ENG., Illus.). 24p. (J). (gr. -1-3). 17.95 (978-1-943553-27-3(0)) Bearport Publishing Co., Inc.
Carr, Aaron. Owls. 2014. (Illus.). 24p. (J). (978-1-62127-213-7(3)) Weigl Pubs., Inc.
Courtauld, Sarah. Owls: Internet-Referenced. Hussey, Lorna, illus. 2009. (First Reading Level 3 Ser.). 48p. (J). (gr. 2). 6.99 (978-0-7945-2502-6(4), Usborne) EDC Publishing.
Dahlen, Noelle. Spark - Owls Coloring Book. 2015. (Dover Coloring Bks.). (ENG., Illus.). 64p. (J). (gr. 1-4). pap. 5.99 (978-0-486-80211-4(6)) Dover Pubns., Inc.
Danielson, Ethan. Owls, 01 vols., 1. 2016. (Raptors! Ser.). (ENG., Illus.). 24p. (J). 23.60 (978-1-5081-4252-2(1), PowerKids Pr.) Rosen Publishing Group, Inc., The.
Dibble, Traci. Where Can Owls Nest? 2016. (1-3Y Birds Ser.). (ENG., Illus.). 28p. (J). pap. 5.99 (978-1-63437-668-6(4)) American Reading Co.
Dieker, Wendy Strobel. El Búho (Owls) 2017. (Spot Backyard Animals Ser.). (ENG & SPA.). 16p. (J). (gr. k-3). 17.95 (978-1-68151-274-7(2), Amicus Readers) Amicus Publishing.
Dunn, Mary R. Owls, 1 vol. 2011. (Nocturnal Animals Ser.). (ENG.). 24p. (gr. k-1). pap. 7.29 (978-1-4296-7119-4(X)); pap. 41.70 (978-1-4296-7122-4(X)); lib. bdg. 26.65 (978-1-4296-5997-0(1)) Capstone Press of Coughlan Cos. (Pebble Plus).
Dyan, Penelope. The Comeback Kids, Book 8, the Antioch Burrowing Owl. Weigand, John D., photos by. 2009. (Illus.). 60p. pap. 22.00 (978-1-935118-86-2(2)) Bellissima Publishing, LLC.
Ford, Ansley Watson & Holt, Denver W. Snowy Owls: Whoo Are They?, 1 vol. Bohman, Jennifer White, illus. 2008. (ENG.). 64p. (J). (gr. 3-7). pap. 12.00 (978-0-87842-543-3(8)) Mountain Pr. Publishing Co., Inc.
Franks, Katie. Owls up Close. (Nature up Close Ser.). 24p. 2009. (gr. k-1). 42.50 (978-1-61514-827-1(2)) 2008. (Illus.). (J). (gr. 3-7). lib. bdg. 22.60 (978-1-4042-4140-4(X)) Rosen Publishing Group, Inc., The. (PowerKids Pr.).
—Owls up Close / Los Buhos. 2009. (Nature up Close / la naturaleza de cerca Ser.). (ENG & SPA.). 24p. (gr. k-1). 42.50 (978-1-61514-833-2(7), Editorial Buenas Letras) Rosen Publishing Group, Inc., The.
—Owls up Close/Los Buhos. Sanz, Pilar, tr. from ENG. 2008. (Nature up Close / la Naturaleza de Cerca Ser.). (Illus.). 24p. (J). (gr. 3-7). lib. bdg. 22.60 (978-1-4042-7678-9(5), Editorial Buenas Letras) Rosen Publishing Group, Inc., The.
Frick, Ivi. Hunting with Great Horned Owls. 2012. (Animal Attack! Ser.). (Illus.). 24p. (J). (gr. 2-5). pap. 8.15 (978-1-4339-7072-6(4)); lib. bdg. 22.60 (978-1-4339-7071-9(6)) Stevens, Gareth Publishing LLLP.
Frost, Helen. Snowy Owls [Scholastic]. 2009. (Polar Animals Ser.). 24p. (gr. k-1). pap. 0.34 (978-1-4296-4228-6(9), Pebble Bks.) Capstone Press of Coughlan Cos.
George, Jean Craighead. Winter Moon. 2003. (J). (gr. 3-7). 20.75 (978-0-8446-7244-1(0)) Smith, Peter Pub., Inc.
Gibbons, Gail. Owls. Gibbons, Gail, illus. 2006. (ENG., Illus.). 32p. (J). (gr. -1-3). 7.99 (978-0-8234-2014-8(0)) Holiday Hse., Inc.
—Owls. 2005. (ENG., Illus.). 32p. (J). (gr. -1-3). 17.95 (978-0-8234-1880-0(4)) Holiday Hse., Inc.
Gilbert, Betty. Buffy the Burrowing Owl. 2008. (Illus.). 40p. (J). 13.95 (978-0-942407-88-4(1)) Father & Son Publishing.
Gilkerson, Patricia. My Adventure with Owls. 2009. (ENG.). 44p. (J). 8.99 (978-1-59092-460-0(6)) Blue Forge Pr.
Gish, Melissa. Owls. 2012. (Living Wild Ser.). (J). (ENG.). 48p. (gr. 4-7). pap. 12.00 (978-0-89812-673-0(8), Creative Paperbacks); (Illus.). 46p. 35.65 (978-1-60818-081-3(6), Creative Education) Creative Co., The.
Gonzales, Doreen. Owls in the Dark. 2009. (Creatures of the Night Ser.). (Illus.). 24p. (J). pap. 8.25 (978-1-4358-3251-0(5), PowerKids Pr.); (gr. 1-3). 22.60 (978-1-4042-8097-7(9)) Rosen Publishing Group, Inc., The.
Gordon, Sharon. Adivina Quien Baja en Picada. 2006. (Bookworms Ser.). (SPA & ENG., Illus.). 32p. (gr. k-2). lib. bdg. 15.95 (978-0-7614-2387-4(7)) Marshall Cavendish Corp.
—Guess Who Swoops. 2007. (Bookworms: Guess Who Ser.). (Illus.). 31p. (J). (gr. -1-3). pap. 6.99 (978-0-7614-3323-1(6), Benchmark Bks.) Marshall Cavendish Corp.
—Guess Who Swoops/Adivina Quien Baja en Picada. 2006. (Bookworms Ser.). (SPA & ENG., Illus.). 32p. (gr. k-2). lib. bdg. 15.95 (978-0-7614-2468-0(7)) Marshall Cavendish Corp.
Gregory, Josh. Owls. 2013. (Nature's Children Ser.). (ENG.). 48p. (J). 28.00 (978-0-531-20979-0(2)); pap. 6.95 (978-0-531-24305-3(2)) Scholastic Library Publishing. (Children's Pr.).
Heos, Bridget. Do You Really Want to Meet an Owl? Fabbri, Daniele, illus. 2017. (Do You Really Want to Meet... Wild Animals? Ser.). (ENG.). 24p. (J). (gr. 1-3). pap. 8.99 (978-1-68152-119-0(9)) Amicus.
—Do You Really Want to Meet an Owl? 2016. (Do You Really Want to Meet... Wild Animals? Ser.). (ENG., Illus.). 24p. (J). (gr. k-3). 20.95 (978-1-60753-948-3(9)) Amicus Publishing.
Hill, Melissa. Barn Owls. 2015. (Owls Ser.). (ENG., Illus.). 24p. (gr. k-1). pap. 6.95 (978-1-4914-6051-1(2)) Capstone Press of Coughlan Cos.
—Burrowing Owls. 2015. (Owls Ser.). (ENG., Illus.). 24p. (gr. k-1). pap. 6.95 (978-1-4914-6052-8(0)) Capstone Press of Coughlan Cos.
—Great Horned Owls. 2015. (Owls Ser.). (ENG., Illus.). 24p. (gr. k-1). pap. 6.95 (978-1-4914-6053-5(9)) Capstone Press of Coughlan Cos.
—Owls. 2015. (Owls Ser.). (ENG.). 24p. (gr. k-1). 106.60 (978-1-4914-6942-2(0), Pebble Plus) Capstone Press of Coughlan Cos.
—Snowy Owls. 2015. (Owls Ser.). (ENG., Illus.). 24p. (gr. k-1). pap. 6.95 (978-1-4914-6054-2(7)) Capstone Press of Coughlan Cos.
Hirsch, Rebecca E. Snowy Owls. 2016. (Comparing Animal Traits Ser.). (ENG., Illus.). 32p. (J). (gr. 2-4). 26.65 (978-1-4677-9506-7(2)) Lerner Publishing Group.
—Snowy Owls: Stealthy Hunting Birds. 2016. (Comparing Animal Traits Ser.). (ENG., Illus.). 32p. (J). (gr. 2-4). 39.99 (978-1-4677-9628-6(X), Lerner Pubns.) Lerner Publishing Group.
Hiscock, Bruce. Ookpik: The Travels of a Snowy Owl. 2008. (ENG., Illus.). 32p. (J). (gr. 2-4). 16.95 (978-1-59078-461-7(8)) Boyds Mills Pr.
Holland, Mary. Otis, el Búho. 2017. (SPA., Illus.). 32p. (J). (gr. k-3). pap. 9.95 (978-1-62855-941-5(1)) Arbordale Publishing.
—Otis the Owl. 2017. (ENG & SPA., Illus.). 32p. (J). (gr. k-3). 17.95 (978-1-62855-939-2(X)) Arbordale Publishing.
Houghton, Gillian. Buhos: Por Dentro y Por Fuera. Gonzalez, Tomas, tr. Studio Stalio, illus. 2004. (Explora la Naturaleza (Getting into Nature) Ser.). (SPA.). 27p. (YA). (gr. 3-6). lib. bdg. 25.25 (978-1-4042-2866-5(7)) Rosen Publishing Group, Inc., The.
—Buhos: Por dentro y por fuera (Owls: Inside & Out) 2009. (Explora la Naturaleza (Getting into Nature) Ser.). (SPA.). 32p. (gr. 3-4). 47.90 (978-1-61512-335-3(0), Editorial Buenas Letras) Rosen Publishing Group, Inc., The.
—Owl. 2004. (Getting into Nature Ser.). (Illus.). 32p. (J). lib. bdg. 25.25 (978-0-8239-4208-4(2)) Rosen Publishing Group, Inc., The.
—Owls: Inside & Out. 2009. (Getting into Nature Ser.). 32p. (gr. 3-4). 47.90 (978-1-61512-724-5(0), PowerKids Pr.) Rosen Publishing Group, Inc., The.
Jacobs, Liza. Owls. 2003. (Wild Wild World Ser.). (Illus.). 24p. (J). 23.70 (978-1-4103-0050-8(1), Blackbirch Pr., Inc.) Cengage Gale.
Landau, Elaine. Owls: Hunters of the Night. 2007. (Animals after Dark Ser.). (Illus.). 32p. (J). (gr. 2-4). lib. bdg. 23.94 (978-0-7660-2768-8(6), Enslow Elementary) Enslow Pubs., Inc.
—Snowy Owls: Hunters of the Snow & Ice. 2010. (Animals of the Snow & Ice Ser.). (Illus.). 32p. (J). (gr. 1-3). 23.94 (978-0-7660-3464-8(X)) Enslow Pubs., Inc.
Lawrence, Riley. Snowy Owls of the Tundra. 2017. (J). (978-1-5345-2216-9(6), KidHaven Publishing) Greenhaven Publishing LLC.
Leaf, Christina. Baby Owls. 2015. (Super Cute! Ser.). (ENG., Illus.). 24p. (J). (gr. k-3). lib. bdg. 25.95 (978-1-62617-172-5(6), Blastoff! Readers) Bellwether Media.
—Great-Horned Owls. 2015. (North American Animals Ser.). (ENG., Illus.). 24p. (J). (gr. k-3). lib. bdg. 25.95 (978-1-62617-189-3(0), Blastoff! Readers) Bellwether Media.
Lundgren, Julie. Owls. 2009. (Illus.). 24p. (J). pap. 7.95 (978-1-60694-773-9(7)) Rourke Educational Media.
Lundgren, Julie & Lundgren, Julie. Owls. 2009. (Illus.). 24p. (J). (gr. 2-5). lib. bdg. 22.79 (978-1-60694-395-3(2)) Rourke Educational Media.
Lynch, Annabelle. Owls & Owlets. 2017. (Animals & Their Babies Ser.). (Illus.). 24p. (gr. k-3). 28.50 (978-1-62588-418-3(4), Smart Apple Media) Black Rabbit Bks.
Macken, JoAnn Early. Owls. 2nd rev. ed. 2009. (Animals That Live in the Forest Ser.). (ENG.). 24p. (J). (gr. -1-3). pap. 8.15 (978-1-4339-2482-8(X)); lib. bdg. 22.60 (978-1-4339-2406-4(4)) Stevens, Gareth Publishing LLLP.
—Owls;Búhos y Lechuzas. 2nd rev. ed. 2009. (Animals That Live in the Forest/Animales del bosque Ser.). (SPA & ENG.). 24p. (J). (gr. -1-3). pap. 8.15 (978-1-4339-2489-7(7)); lib. bdg. 22.60 (978-1-4339-2438-5(2)) Stevens, Gareth Publishing LLLP. (Weekly Reader Leveled Readers).
Mara, Wil. Owls. 2014. 32p. 28.50 (978-1-62712-298-6(2)) Cavendish Square Publishing.
Markle, Sandra. Owls. (Animal Predators Ser.). (ENG.). 40p. (gr. 3-6). 2005. pap. 7.95 (978-1-57505-745-3(X)) 2004. (Illus.). lib. bdg. 26.60 (978-1-57505-729-3(8)) Lerner Publishing Group.
Marsh, Laura. Owls. 2014. (Readers Ser.). (ENG., Illus.). 32p. (J). (gr. -1-1). pap. 3.99 (978-1-4263-1743-9(3), National Geographic Children's Bks.) National Geographic Society.
Mason, Adrienne. Owls. Ogle, Nancy Gray & Ogle, Nancy, illus. 2004. (Kids Can Press Wildlife Ser.). (ENG.). 32p. (J). (gr. k-5). 7.95 (978-1-55337-624-8(2)) Kids Can Pr., Ltd. CAN. Dist: Hachette Bk. Group.
Mattern, Joanne. Los Búhos Son Animales Nocturnos. 2007. (Night Animals/ Animales Nocturnos Ser.). (SPA & ENG., Illus.). 24p. (gr. k-3). pap. 8.15 (978-0-8368-8052-6(8), Weekly Reader Leveled Readers) Stevens, Gareth Publishing LLLP.
—Owls Are Night Animals. 2007. (Night Animals Ser.). (Illus.). 24p. (gr. k-3). pap. 8.15 (978-0-8368-7855-4(8)); lib. bdg. 22.00 (978-0-8368-7848-6(5)) Stevens, Gareth Publishing LLLP. (Weekly Reader Leveled Readers).
—Owls Are Night Animals/Los Buhos Son Animales Nocturnos. 2007. (Night Animals/ Animales Nocturnos Ser.). (SPA & ENG., Illus.). 24p. (gr. k-3). lib. bdg. 22.00 (978-0-8368-8045-8(5), Weekly Reader Leveled Readers) Stevens, Gareth Publishing LLLP.
Meinking, Mary. Owl vs. Mouse, 1 vol. 2011. (Predator vs. Prey Ser.). (ENG., Illus.). 32p. (gr. 1-2). 29.99 (978-1-4109-3936-4(7)); pap. 8.29 (978-1-4109-3945-6(6)) Heinemann-Raintree. (Read Me!).
Miller, Sara Swan. Owls. (Paws & Claws Ser.). 24p. 2009. (gr. 2-3). 42.50 (978-1-60851-152-5(9)) 2008. (Illus.). (J). (gr. 4-6). lib. bdg. 22.60 (978-1-4042-4165-7(5)) Rosen Publishing Group, Inc., The. (PowerKids Pr.).
Mudd-Ruth, Maria. Owls. 2004. (Animals Animals Ser.). (Illus.). 48p. (J). (gr. 3). 29.93 (978-0-7614-1752-1(4)) Marshall Cavendish Corp.
Murray, Julie. Owls, 1 vol. 2005. (Animal Kingdom Set Ii Ser.). (ENG., Illus.). 24p. (gr. k-4). 25.65 (978-1-59197-328-7(7), Buddy Bks.) ABDO Publishing Co.
Oddey the Owl. 2005. (J). 9.95 (978-0-9765502-0-4(2)) ONTRAK.
O'Shaughnessy, Ruth. Owls after Dark. 2015. (Animals of the Night Ser.). (ENG.). 32p. (J). (gr. 3-4). pap. 10.52 (978-0-7660-6758-5(0)); (Illus.). 25.27 (978-0-7660-6760-8(2)) Enslow Pubs., Inc.
Owen, Ruth. Snowy Owls. 2013. (Polar Animals: Life in the Freezer Ser.). (ENG., Illus.). 32p. (gr. k-5). 25.25 (978-1-4777-0223-9(7)); pap. 10.00 (978-1-4777-0233-8(4)) Windmill Bks.
Owls, 6 bks. 2005. (Animal Predators Ser.). (Illus.). 40p. (J). (gr. 3-6). pap. 46.95 (978-0-8225-5490-5(9)) Lerner Publishing Group.
Owls: Individual Title Six-Packs. (Story Steps Ser.). (gr. k-2). 32.00 (978-0-7635-9800-6(3)) Rigby Education.
Parker, Steve. Owls. Morandi, Andrea, illus. 2010. (I Love Animals Ser.). (ENG.). 24p. (J). (gr. 1-5). lib. bdg. 22.60 (978-1-61533-229-8(4)) Windmill Bks.
Patrick, Roman. Snowy Owls. 2010. (Animals That Live in the Tundra Ser.). (ENG.). 24p. (J). (gr. -1-3). pap. 8.15 (978-1-4339-3909-9(6)); lib. bdg. 22.60 (978-1-4339-3908-2(8)) Stevens, Gareth Publishing LLLP.
Phillips, Dee. Burrowing Owl's Hideaway. 2015. (Illus.). 24p. (J). lib. bdg. (978-1-62724-307-0(0)) Bearport Publishing Co., Inc.
—Spotted Owl. 2013. (Science Slam: Treed-Animal Life in the Trees Ser.). 24p. (J). (gr. -1-3). lib. bdg. 23.93 (978-1-61772-910-2(8)) Bearport Publishing Co., Inc.
Pringle, Laurence. Owls! Strange & Wonderful. Henderson, Meryl, illus. 2016. (Strange & Wonderful Ser.). (ENG.). 32p. (J). (gr. 1-4). 16.95 (978-1-62091-651-3(7)) Boyds Mills Pr.
Quality Productions Staff. Lechuzas. Rountree, Monica, tr. 2003. (Zoobooks Ser.). Orig. Title: Owls. (SPA., Illus.). 24p. (J). (gr. 1-7). lib. bdg. 15.95 (978-1-888153-81-1(4)) Wildlife Education, Ltd.
—Owls. rev. ed. 2003. (Illus.). 24p. (J). (gr. 1-7). 10.95 (978-1-888153-93-4(8), Zoo Bks.) Wildlife Education, Ltd.
Read, Tracy C. Exploring the World of Owls. 2011. (Exploring the World Of Ser.). (ENG., Illus.). 24p. (J). (gr. 3-7). 16.95 (978-1-55407-883-7(0), 9781554078837); pap. 6.95 (978-1-55407-957-5(8), 9781554079575) Firefly Bks., Ltd.
Reher, Matt. Farmers Like Barn Owls. 2016. (1G Predator Animals Ser.). (ENG., Illus.). 28p. (J). pap. 5.99 (978-1-63437-675-4(7)) American Reading Co.
Richardson, Adele D. Owls, 1 vol. 2012. (Birds Ser.). (ENG., Illus.). 24p. (gr. 1-2). lib. bdg. 25.32 (978-1-4296-8684-6(7)) Capstone Press of Coughlan Cos.
Riley, Joelle. Quiet Owls. 2004. (Pull Ahead Bks.). (Illus.). 32p. (J). 22.60 (978-0-8225-3771-7(0), Carolrhoda Bks.); (ENG., pap. 7.95 (978-0-8225-9889-3(2)) Lerner Publishing Group.
Rissman, Rebecca. Barn Owls: Nocturnal Hunters, 1 vol. 2014. (Night Safari Ser.). (ENG., Illus.). 24p. (gr. k-2). 23.32 (978-1-4846-0310-9(9), Heinemann Read & Learn) Heinemann-Raintree.
Rustad, Martha E. H. Owls. 2013. (ENG., Illus.). 24p. (J). lib. bdg. 25.65 (978-1-62031-071-7(6)) Jump! Inc.
Sandoval, Gustavo. Owls & Owlets. 2017. (Animal Family Ser.). 24p. (gr. k-k). pap. 8.15 (978-1-4824-6385-9(7)) Stevens, Gareth Publishing LLLP.
Schuetz, Kari. Owls. 2011. (Backyard Wildlife Ser.). (ENG., Illus.). 24p. (J). (gr. k-3). lib. bdg. 25.95 (978-1-60014-598-8(1)) Bellwether Media.
Smalley, Carol Parenzan. Threat to the Spotted Owl. 2008. (On the Verge of Extinction Ser.). (Illus.). 32p. (YA). (gr. 2-5). lib. bdg. 25.70 (978-1-58415-687-1(2)) Mitchell Lane Pubs., Inc.
Sollinger, Emily. Owls: Birds of the Night. Rallis, Chris, illus. 2014. (Penguin Young Readers, Level 3 Ser.). (ENG.). 48p. (J). (gr. 1-3). pap. 3.99 (978-0-448-48135-7(9), Penguin Young Readers) Penguin Young Readers Group.
Taylor, Trace & Cline, Gina. Owls. Taylor, Trace, illus. 2011. (2G Predator Animals Ser.). (ENG., Illus.). 32p. (J). pap. 5.99 (978-1-61406-133-5(5)) American Reading Co.
Thomson, Ruth. The Life Cycle of an Owl. 2009. (Learning about Life Cycles Ser.). 24p. (J). (ENG., Illus.). (gr. k-5). pap. 8.25 (978-1-4358-2883-4(6), PowerKids Pr.); (gr. 2-5). lib. bdg. 22.60 (978-1-4358-2833-9(X)) Rosen Publishing Group, Inc., The.
Warhol, Tom. Owls. 2007. (Animalways Ser.). (Illus.). 104p. (gr. 6-3). lib. bdg. 24.95 (978-0-7614-2537-3(3), Benchmark Bks.) Marshall Cavendish Corp.
Wechsler, Doug. Great Horned Owls. 2009. (Really Wild Life of Animals Ser.). 24p. (gr. 3-4). 42.50 (978-1-60854-194-2(0), PowerKids Pr.) Rosen Publishing Group, Inc., The.
Winnick, Nick. Owls. 2010. (Backyard Animals Ser.). (Illus.). 24p. (J). (gr. 2-4). pap. 11.95 (978-1-60596-953-4(2)); lib. bdg. 25.70 (978-1-60596-952-7(4)) Weigl Pubs., Inc.
Wyatt, Laura. Those Outrageous Owls. Weaver, Steve, illus. Moore, H G, III, photos by. 2006. (Those Amazing Animals Ser.). (ENG.). 55p. (J). (gr. 3-7). 14.95 (978-1-56164-365-3(3)); per. 9.95 (978-1-56164-366-0(1)) Pineapple Pr., Inc.

Zeiger, Jennifer. Snowy Owls. 2014. (Nature's Children Ser.). (ENG.). 48p. (J). lib. bdg. 28.00 *(978-0-531-21228-8(9))* Scholastic Library Publishing.

OWLS—FICTION

Accord Publishing Staff & Stone, Kate. One Spooky Night: A Halloween Adventure. 2011. (ENG.). 36p. (J). pap. 11.99 *(978-1-4494-0330-0(1))* Andrews McMeel Publishing.

Alexander, Heather. Wallace & Grace & the Cupcake Caper. Zarrin, Laura, illus. 2017. (Wallace & Grace Ser.). (ENG.). 80p. (J). 9.99 *(978-1-68119-010-5(9)*, 9781681190105, Bloomsbury USA Childrens) Bloomsbury Publishing USA.

—Wallace & Grace & the Lost Puppy. Zarrin, Laura, illus. 2017. (Wallace & Grace Ser.). (ENG.). 80p. (J). 9.99 ***(978-1-68119-012-9(5)***, 9781681190129, Bloomsbury USA Childrens) Bloomsbury Publishing USA.

Alexander, Heather. Wallace & Grace Take the Case. Zarrin, Laura, illus. 2017. (Wallace & Grace Ser.). (ENG.). 80p. (J). 9.99 *(978-1-61963-988-1(2)*, 9781619639881, Bloomsbury USA Childrens) Bloomsbury Publishing USA.

Allen, Jonathan. I'm Not Reading! 2013. (Baby Owl Ser.). (ENG., Illus.). 32p. (J). (gr. -1-k). 16.95 *(978-1-907967-44-3(3))* Boxer Bks., Ltd. GBR. Dist: Sterling Publishing Co., Inc.

—I'm Not Ready! 2011. (Baby Owl Ser.). (ENG., Illus.). 32p. (J). (gr. -1-k). 16.95 *(978-1-907967-05-4(2))* Boxer Bks., Ltd. GBR. Dist: Sterling Publishing Co., Inc.

—I'm Not Sleepy! 2012. (Baby Owl Ser.). (ENG., Illus.). 26p. (J). (gr. k — 1). bds. 6.95 *(978-1-907967-37-5(0))* Boxer Bks., Ltd. GBR. Dist: Sterling Publishing Co., Inc.

Anastasio, Dina. How Raven Became Black & Owl Got Its Spots & Por qué el cuervo es negro y el búho tiene Manchitas: 6 English, 6 Spanish Adaptations. 2011. (ENG & SPA.). (J). 75.00 net. *(978-1-4108-5626-5(7))* Benchmark Education Co.

Anastasio, Dina, retold by. How Raven Became Black & Owl Got Its Spots: Set Of 6. 2010. (Early Connections Ser.). (J). pap. 37.00 net. *(978-1-4108-1093-9(3))* Benchmark Education Co.

Avi. Poppy. Floca, Brian, illus. 2006. (Poppy Stories Ser.). (ENG.). 192p. (J). (gr. 3-7). pap. 6.99 *(978-0-380-72769-8(2))* HarperCollins Pubs.

—Poppy. 2006. (Poppy Stories Ser.: 2). (J). (gr. 3-6). lib. bdg. 17.20 *(978-0-613-03338-1(8)*, Turtleback) Turtleback Bks.

Bailey, Arthur Scott. Tuck-Me-in Tales: The Tale of Solomon Ow. 2006. (Illus.). pap. *(978-1-4065-0452-1(1))* Dodo Pr.

Balboni, Mary. The Birds of Winslow. 2010. 20p. 10.49 *(978-1-4490-2712-4(1))* AuthorHouse.

Beatty, Connie. Why Owls Say Who. Beatty, Connie & Phillippi, Faith, illus. 2008. 20p. per. 24.95 *(978-1-4137-6715-5(X))* America Star Bks.

Bertagnolli, Daniel. Whooo Turned Out the Lights? Bertagnolli, Daniel, illus. 2009. (Illus.). 20p. pap. 9.14 *(978-1-4269-0590-2(4))* Trafford Publishing.

Billows, Denis. Down in Bluebell Wood. 2010. 164p. pap. 11.99 *(978-1-4490-8822-4(8))* AuthorHouse.

Bingamon-Haller, Mary. The Great Horned Owl. Burns, Sandra, illus. 2013. 28p. pap. 8.99 *(978-1-938768-12-5(4))* Gypsy Pubns.

Black, Cary & Schott, Gretchen Victoria. French Quarter Tori & the Red Owl. Travis, Caroline, illus. 2012. 38p. pap. 14.95 *(978-0-9754279-7-2(0))*; pap. 12.95 *(978-0-9754279-8-9(9))* Red Owl Pubns.

Bodoh, Tony. Hannah's Animal Farm. 2008. 28p. pap. 14.95 *(978-1-4327-2046-9(5))* Outskirts Pr., Inc.

Brodien-Jones, Christine. The Owl Keeper. Kneen, Maggie, illus. 2011. (ENG.). 320p. (J). (gr. 3-7). 8.99 *(978-0-385-73815-6(3)*, Yearling) Random Hse. Children's Bks.

Brown, Ruby. Cuddles for Mommy. Macnaughton, Tina, illus. 2016. (ENG.). 32p. (J). (gr. -1-3). 16.99 *(978-1-4998-0203-0(X))* Little Bee Books Inc.

Bruchac, Joseph. Wabi: A Hero's Tale. 2007. (ENG.). 208p. (YA). (gr. 7-18). pap. 7.99 *(978-0-14-240947-3(2)*, Speak) Penguin Young Readers Group.

Bunting, Sarah Clare. Why Are You So Lazy Owl? 2012. 16p. pap. 12.50 *(978-1-4709-4837-5(0))* Lulu Pr., Inc.

Burke, Maria. The Ark of Dun Ruah. 2013. (Ark of Dun Ruah Ser.: 01). (ENG., Illus.). 256p. (J). pap. 23.95 *(978-1-85607-794-1(2))* Currach Pr. IRL. Dist: Dufour Editions, Inc.

Callahan, Susan. A New Way. 2012. 20p. pap. 17.99 *(978-1-4772-4507-1(3))* AuthorHouse.

Carlson, Amie. The Owl That Was Afraid of the Dark. 2016. (Who's Afraid? Ser.). (ENG.). 18p. (J). 15.99 *(978-1-4964-1154-9(4))* Tyndale Hse. Pubs.

Cefalo, Maria Raffaella. If Dreams Could Talk. 2012. (ENG.). 25p. (J). pap. 17.95 *(978-1-4327-9623-5(2))*; pap. 27.95 *(978-1-4327-9708-9(5))* Outskirts Pr., Inc.

Chambers, Melinda. We Are Whoooo We Are. Spiker, Sue Ann, illus. 2006. 32p. (J). 16.95 *(978-0-929915-46-3(1))* Headline Bks., Inc.

Chandler, Tony. The Journey. 2013. 242p. pap. *(978-1-77115-091-0(2))* Double Dragon ebooks.

Chase, Kit. Oliver's Tree. Chase, Kit, illus. 2014. (ENG., Illus.). 32p. (J). (gr. -1-k). 16.99 *(978-0-399-25700-1(4)*, G.P. Putnam's Sons Books for Young Readers) Penguin Young Readers Group.

Clifton-Brown, Holly. Annie Hoot & the Knitting Extravaganza. Clifton-Brown, Holly, illus. 2010. (Andersen Press Picture Bks). (ENG., Illus.). 32p. (J). (gr. -1-3). 16.95 *(978-0-7613-6444-3(7))* Lerner Publishing Group.

Cochran, Randy. Critter Golf II: Chaos at Owl's Nest. 2013. 148p. pap. 10.95 *(978-1-4787-0302-0(4))* Outskirts Pr., Inc.

Councilman, Janet H. Rocky & His Responsible Band of Cowboys, 1 vol. 2009. pap. 24.95 *(978-1-60749-384-6(5))* America Star Bks.

Curtis, Jennifer Keats. Baby Owl's Rescue, 1 vol. Jacques, Laura, illus. 2009. (ENG.). 32p. (J). (gr. -1-3). 16.95 *(978-1-934359-95-2(5)*, 9781934359952) Arbordale Publishing.

Davies, Gill. Brave Little Owl. Twinney, Dick, illus. 2006. (ENG.). 24p. (J). *(978-1-55168-279-2(6))* Fenn, H. B. & Co., Ltd.

Davies, Nicola. White Owl, Barn Owl: Read & Wonder. Foreman, Michael, illus. 2009. (Read & Wonder Ser.). (ENG.). 32p. (J). (gr. -1-3). pap. 6.99 *(978-0-7636-4143-6(X))* Candlewick Pr.

—White Owl, Barn Owl with Audio, Peggable. Foreman, Michael, illus. 2009. (Read, Listen, & Wonder Ser.). (ENG.). 32p. (J). (gr. -1-3). pap. 9.99 *(978-0-7636-4194-8(4))* Candlewick Pr.

Debowski, Sharon. The Snowman, the Owl, & the Groundhog. 2007. (J). lib. bdg. 15.95 *(978-1-60227-468-6(1))*; (Illus.). 32p. (gr. -1-4). 14.95 *(978-1-60227-470-9(3))* Above the Clouds Publishing.

Del Riego, Erica. The Heart of Life. 2010. 36p. pap. 17.75 *(978-1-4389-7572-6(4))* AuthorHouse.

Dinardo, Jeff. The Sunrise Band: Cooperating. Palen, Debbie, illus. 2014. (Funny Bone Readers: Being a Friend Ser.). 24p. (gr. -1-1). pap. 4.99 *(978-1-939656-06-3(0))* Red Chair Pr.

Dodd, Emma. Happy. Dodd, Emma, illus. 2015. (Emma Dodd's Love You Bks.). (ENG., Illus.). 24p. (J). (-k). 12.99 *(978-0-7636-8008-4(7)*, Nosy Crow) Candlewick Pr.

Donald, George Mac. Cross Purposes. 2012. 104p. pap. 25.95 *(978-1-4474-5057-3(4))* Borah Pr.

Donaldson, Julia. The Further Adventures of the Owl & the Pussy-Cat. Voake, Charlotte, illus. 2017. (ENG.). 32p. (J). (gr. -1-2). 16.99 *(978-0-7636-9081-6(3))* Candlewick Pr.

Dyas, Amy. The Robins of St Lawrence Church. 2009. 128p. pap. 29.96 *(978-0-9786567-8-2(4))* Parson Place Pr., LLC.

Eagle, Golden. The Owl Who Lives in My House. l.t. ed. 2003. (Illus.). 24p. (J). per. 12.99 *(978-1-932338-34-8(9))* Lifevest Publishing, Inc.

Eisan, Daniel. The Lonely Peach. 2011. (Illus.). 48p. pap. 15.99 *(978-1-4628-5634-3(9))* Xlibris Corp.

Eisele, Barbara. Miss Thistle & Friends. 2009. 48p. pap. 12.99 *(978-1-4490-2007-1(0))* AuthorHouse.

Elliott, Rebecca. Baxter Is Missing - A Branches Book. Elliott, Rebecca, illus. 2017. (Owl Diaries: 6). (ENG., Illus.). 80p. (J). (gr. k-2). pap. 4.99 ***(978-1-338-04284-9(X))*** Scholastic, Inc.

—Eva & the New Owl. 2016. (Owl Diaries: 4). (ENG., Illus.). 80p. (J). (gr. k-2). pap. 4.99 *(978-0-545-82559-7(8))* Scholastic, Inc.

—Eva Sees a Ghost. 2015. (Owl Diaries: 2). (ENG., Illus.). 80p. (J). (gr. k-2). 15.99 *(978-0-545-78784-0(X))*; pap. 4.99 *(978-0-545-78783-3(1))* Scholastic, Inc.

—Eva's Treetop Festival. Bk. 1. Elliott, Rebecca, illus. 2015. (Owl Diaries: 1). (ENG., Illus.). 80p. (J). (gr. k-2). pap. 4.99 *(978-0-545-68362-3(9))* Scholastic, Inc.

—Warm Hearts Day: A Branches Book. Elliott, Rebecca, illus. 2016. (Owl Diaries: 5). (ENG., Illus.). 80p. (J). (gr. k-2). pap. 4.99 *(978-1-338-04280-1(7))* Scholastic, Inc.

—A Woodland Wedding. Elliott, Rebecca, illus. 2016. (Owl Diaries: 3). (ENG., Illus.). 80p. (J). (gr. k-2). 15.99 *(978-0-545-82558-0(X))* Scholastic, Inc.

Fabrizio, Anthony. The Last Forest, 1 vol. 2009. 64p. pap. 19.95 *(978-1-61546-861-4(7))* America Star Bks.

Feeney, Tatyana. Little Owl's Orange Scarf. 2013. (ENG.). 32p. (J). (— 1). 16.99 *(978-0-449-81411-6(4)*, Knopf Bks. for Young Readers) Random Hse. Children's Bks.

Fields, Jan. Meet the Mothman, 1 vol. Brundage, Scott, illus. 2016. (ENG.). 80p. (J). lib. bdg. *(978-1-62402-153-4(0))* Magic Wagon.

Filoche, Eric. Hey ! We're Talking about Ourselves ! 2013. 68p. pap. *(978-2-9538737-4-0(0))* Koshkindom.

Fitzpatrick, Marie-Louise. Owl Bat Bat Owl. Fitzpatrick, Marie-Louise, illus. 2017. (ENG., Illus.). 32p. (J). (gr. -1-2). 15.99 *(978-0-7636-9161-5(5))* Candlewick Pr.

Frank, Rochelle. So What, Saw-Whet? Gast, Linda, photos by. 2004. (Illus.). (J). per. 9.95 *(978-0-9746792-0-4(8))* Hummingbird Mountain Pr.

Freedman, Claire. The Monster of the Woods! Julian, Russell, illus. 2013. (ENG.). 32p. (J). pap. *(978-0-545-51571-9(8)*, Cartwheel Bks.) Scholastic, Inc.

French, Jennifer Pratt. Hoot Owl Shares the Dawn 2004. 128p. (YA). per. 9.95 *(978-0-9709104-4-8(4))* Hickory Tales Publishing.

Friester, Paul. Owl Howl. Goossens, Philippe, illus. 2014. (ENG.). 32p. (J). 15.95 *(978-0-7358-4188-8(8))* North-South Bks., Inc.

—Owl Howl & the BLU-BLU. Goossens, Philippe, illus. 2016. (ENG.). 32p. (J). 15.95 *(978-0-7358-4246-5(9))* North-South Bks., Inc.

—Owl Howl Board Book. Goossens, Philippe, illus. 2nd rev. ed. 2016. (ENG.). 26p. (J). bds. 8.95 *(978-0-7358-4234-2(5))* North-South Bks., Inc.

Friester, Paul & Goossens, Philippe. Owl Howls Again! 2015. (ENG., Illus.). 32p. (J). 15.95 *(978-0-7358-4129-1(2))* North-South Bks., Inc.

Furuya, Michael, illus. Keoni's Special Gift. 2009. (J). *(978-1-56647-915-8(0))* Mutual Publishing LLC.

Gadsby, Maggie. Owl Be Home for Christmas. 2012. (J). 14.95 *(978-1-62086-064-9(3))* Mascot Bks., Inc.

Galante, Cecilia. The One & Only Willa Bean. Valiant, Kristi, illus. 2012. (Little Wings Ser.: 4). (ENG.). 112p. (J). (gr. 1-4). pap. 4.99 *(978-0-375-86950-1(6)*, Random Hse. Bks. for Young Readers) Random Hse. Children's Bks.

Gillingham, Sara & Siminovich, Lorena. In My Tree. 2009. (ENG., Illus.). 12p. (J). (gr. -1 — 1). bds. 8.99 *(978-0-8118-7052-8(9))* Chronicle Bks. LLC.

Glass, Shelby. Something Is Everything. 2012. 36p. pap. 19.99 *(978-1-4772-6581-9(3))* AuthorHouse.

Godwin, Laura & Dunlavey, Rob. Owl Sees Owl. 2016. (ENG., Illus.). 40p. (J). (gr. -1-2). 17.99 *(978-0-553-49782-3(0)*, Schwartz & Wade Bks.) Random Hse. Children's Bks.

Gordon, Pauline C. Animals in My Backyard! Joey, the Flying Squirrel. 2012. 28p. pap. 15.99 *(978-1-4771-1961-7(2))* Xlibris Corp.

Gram, Golden. Gail the Snail: Night Owl. 2008. 20p. pap. 11.95 *(978-1-59858-859-0(1))* Dog Ear Publishing, LLC.

Grandpa Dennis, as told by. George Washington's Smallest Army: The Miracle Before Trenton. 2009. 216p. (J). pap. 17.49 *(978-1-4389-3147-0(6))* AuthorHouse.

Grant, V. F. Stories from Grimley Forest. 2011. 48p. (gr. 1-2). pap. 19.50 *(978-1-4567-4709-1(6))* AuthorHouse.

Green, Joanne. Hootah's Baby. 2012. 46p. pap. *(978-1-897512-53-1(8))* Saga Bks.

Groce, Michelle. Jasper. Duis, Laura, illus. 2003. 174p. (J). 17.95 *(978-0-9708972-6-8(X))* Novello Festival Pr.

Gwyer, Gillian K. Podnockery Forest - Owl & the Trickster. 2013. 40p. *(978-1-4602-3974-2(1))* FriesenPress.

Hanson, Anders. Night Owl, 1 vol. Haberstroh, Anne, illus. 2006. (Animal Tales Ser.). 24p. (J). (gr. k-3). (ENG.). lib. bdg. 24.21 *(978-1-59679-953-0(6)*, SandCastle); pap. 48.42 *(978-1-59679-954-7(4))* ABDO Publishing Co.

Harary, Keith. The Owls of the Enchanted Forest. Gonina, Luba, illus. 2008. 52p. (J). pap. 15.88 *(978-0-9799196-8-8(1))* Owl Pals.

—The Owls of the Enchanted Forest - 2007 Special Collector's Edition. Gonina, Luba, illus. 2007. 50p. (J). 50.00 incl. DVD *(978-0-9799196-3-3(0))* Owl Pals.

Haughton, Chris. Little Owl Lost. Haughton, Chris, illus. (ENG., Illus.). (J). 2013. 30p. (-k). bds. 7.99 *(978-0-7636-6750-4(1))* 2010. 32p. (gr. -1-k). 14.99 *(978-0-7636-5022-3(6))* Candlewick Pr.

Hawkins, Linda J. Who Gives a Hoot? Hunter Hoot,the Great Horned Owl. 2012. (ENG., Illus.). 40p. (J). pap. 9.99 *(978-1-937008-06-2(1))* Heart to Heart Publishing, Inc.

Hemmings, Lisa & O'Keefe, Allan. Imagine Me with the Three Owls: Feeling Great. 2012. 32p. pap. 13.95 *(978-1-4525-0551-0(9))* Balboa Pr.

Hiaasen, Carl. Hoot. 2004. (ENG.). 304p. (YA). (gr. 7). reprint ed. pap. 8.99 *(978-0-375-82916-1(4)*, Ember) Random Hse. Children's Bks.

Hiaasen, Carl. Hoot. 2014. 17.00 *(978-1-63419-707-6(0))* Perfection Learning Corp.

Hillenbrand, Will. Asleep in the Stable. 2004. (ENG., Illus.). 32p. (J). (gr. k-3). tchr. ed. 16.95 *(978-0-8234-1824-4(3))* Holiday Hse., Inc.

Hills, Tad. Rocket Writes a Story. Hills, Tad, illus. 2012. (ENG., Illus.). 40p. (J). (gr. -1-3). 17.99 *(978-0-375-87086-6(5)*, Schwartz & Wade Bks.) Random Hse. Children's Bks.

Hopgood, Tim. Wow! Said the Owl. Hopgood, Tim, illus. 2009. (ENG., Illus.). 32p. (J). (gr. -1-k). 16.99 *(978-0-374-38518-7(1)*, 9780374385187, Farrar, Straus & Giroux (BYR)) Farrar, Straus & Giroux.

Huggins, Peter. Trosclair & the Alligator, 1 vol. Gardiner, Lindsey, illus. 2005. (ENG.). 32p. (J). (gr. -1-3). 15.95 *(978-1-932065-98-5(9))* Star Bright Bks., Inc.

Huxley, Aldous. The Crows of Pearblossom. Blackall, Sophie, illus. 2011. (ENG.). 40p. (J). (gr. k-2). 17.95 *(978-0-8109-9730-1(4)*, Abrams Bks. for Young Readers) Abrams, Inc.

I Am A Dog. 2008. (Illus.). 26p. 24.95 *(978-0-9801054-0-7(4))* Teahouse of Danger.

ImageBooks Staff. Little Owl Finger Puppet Book. 2011. (Little Finger Puppet Board Bks.). (ENG.). 12p. (J). (gr. -1 — 1). bds. 6.99 *(978-1-4521-0221-4(X))* Chronicle Bks. LLC.

Irvin-Marston, Hope. My Little Book of Burrowing Owls. Magdalena-Brown, Maria, illus. 2nd ed. 2004. 32p. (J). pap. 7.95 *(978-0-89317-054-7(2)*, WW-0542, Windward Publishing) Finney Co., Inc.

Jacquemain, Patti. Journey of the Great Bear: Through California's Golden Past. Jacquemain, Patti, illus. 2006. (Illus.). (J). *(978-0-929702-10-0(7))* Mission Creek Studios.

Johansen, Hanna & Barrett, John S. The Duck & the Owl. Bhend, Käthi, illus. 2005. (ENG.). 72p. (J). 17.95 *(978-1-56792-285-1(6))* Godine, David R. Pub.

Johnson, Jaime Gardner. The Ghost of Donley Farm, 1 vol. Klein, Laurie Allen, illus. 2015. (ENG.). 32p. (J). (gr. k-3). 17.95 *(978-1-62855-451-9(7))*; pap. 9.95 *(978-1-62855-459-5(2))* Arbordale Publishing.

Johnson, Tera. Berkeley's Barn Owl Dance. Howells, Tania, illus. 2008. (ENG.). 32p. (J). (gr. -1-2). 16.95 *(978-1-55453-263-6(9))* Kids Can Pr., Ltd. CAN. Dist: Hachette Bk. Group.

Judge, Lita. Hoot & Peep. 2016. (Hoot & Peep Ser.). (ENG., Illus.). 40p. (J). (-k). 17.99 *(978-0-525-42837-4(2)*, Dial Bks) Penguin Young Readers Group.

Kail, Leanna. The Owl Who Couldn't Whoo. Rottinger, Amy, illus. 2013. 24p. pap. 11.95 *(978-1-61244-129-0(7))* Halo Publishing International.

Kelly, Jacqueline. Who Gives a Hoot?: Calpurnia Tate, Girl Vet. Meyer, Jennifer L., illus. 2017. (Calpurnia Tate, Girl Vet Ser.). (ENG.). 112p. (J). 15.99 ***(978-1-62779-873-0(0)***, 9781627798730, Holt, Henry & Co. Bks. For Young Readers) Holt, Henry & Co.

Kim, Melissa & Fitch, Jada. A Snowy Owl Story, 1 vol. 2015. (ENG.). 12p. bds. 10.95 *(978-1-939017-48-2(3)*, a5d1799a-fc62-4c32-a6ff-01df8b39c260) Islandport Pr., Inc.

Kindl, Patrice. Owl in Love. 2004. (ENG.). 224p. (YA). (gr. 7-18). pap. 14.95 *(978-0-618-43910-2(2))* Houghton Mifflin Harcourt Publishing Co.

Kousky, Vern. Otto the Owl Who Loved Poetry. Kousky, Vern, illus. 2015. (ENG., Illus.). 32p. (J). (gr. k-3). 16.99 *(978-0-399-16440-8(5)*, Nancy Paulsen Books) Penguin Young Readers Group.

Lambert, Jonny. The Great AAA-OOO! Lambert, Jonny, illus. 2016. (ENG., Illus.). 32p. (J). (gr. -1-2). 16.99 *(978-1-68010-032-7(7))* Tiger Tales.

Lamm, C. Drew. Screech Owl at Midnight Hollow. Snyder, Joel, illus. 2011. (Smithsonian's Backyard Ser.). (ENG.). 32p. (J). (gr. -1-3). 19.95 *(978-1-60727-643-2(7))* Soundprints.

Lansdowne, Marcella. The Adventures of Patty & Annabel: The Javelinas & Releasing the Cords. 2009. 28p. pap. 15.95 *(978-1-4389-1645-3(0))* AuthorHouse.

Lasky, Kathryn. The Capture. 2003. (Guardians of Ga'hoole Ser.: 1). (ENG.). 240p. (J). (gr. 3-7). mass mkt. 6.99 *(978-0-439-40557-7(2)*, Scholastic Paperbacks) Scholastic, Inc.

—The Capture. l.t. ed. 2007. (Guardians of Ga'Hoole Ser.: Bk. 1). 228p. (YA). 22.95 *(978-0-7862-9865-5(0))* Thorndike Pr.

—The Capture. 2003. (Guardians of Ga'Hoole Ser.: 1). (gr. 3-6). lib. bdg. 17.20 *(978-0-613-67484-3(7)*, Turtleback) Turtleback Bks.

—The Coming of Hoole. 2006. (Guardians of Ga'hoole Ser.: 10). (ENG., Illus.). 240p. (J). (gr. 3-7). 6.99 *(978-0-439-79569-2(9)*, Scholastic Paperbacks) Scholastic, Inc.

—Exile. 2008. (Guardians of Ga'hoole Ser.: 14). (ENG., Illus.). 224p. (J). (gr. 3-7). 6.99 *(978-0-439-88808-0(5)*, Scholastic Paperbacks) Scholastic, Inc.

—The Golden Tree. 2007. (Guardians of Ga'Hoole Ser.: 12). (Illus.). 192p. lib. bdg. 17.20 *(978-1-4177-8260-4(9)*, Turtleback) Turtleback Bks.

—The Journey. l.t. ed. 2007. (Guardians of Ga'Hoole Ser.: Bk. 2). (Illus.). 271p. (J). (gr. 3-7). 22.95 *(978-1-4104-0293-6(2))* Thorndike Pr.

—Lost Tales of Ga'Hoole. Huang, Kathryn, illus. 2010. (Guardians of Ga'hoole Ser.). (ENG.). 192p. (J). (gr. 3-7). 6.99 *(978-0-545-10244-5(8)*, Scholastic Paperbacks) Scholastic, Inc.

—The Rescue. 2004. (Guardians of Ga'hoole Ser.: 3). (ENG., Illus.). 208p. (J). (gr. 4-7). 6.99 *(978-0-439-40559-1(9)*, Scholastic Paperbacks) Scholastic, Inc.

—The Rise of a Legend. (Guardians of Ga'hoole Ser.). (ENG.). 304p. (J). (gr. 3-7). 2015. pap. 6.99 *(978-0-545-50979-4(3))* 2013. 16.99 *(978-0-545-50978-7(5)*, Scholastic Pr.) Scholastic, Inc.

—The River of Wind. 2007. (Guardians of Ga'hoole Ser.: 13). (ENG., Illus.). 224p. (J). (gr. 3-7). 6.99 *(978-0-439-88807-3(7))* Scholastic, Inc.

—The River of Wind. 2007. (Guardians of Ga'Hoole Ser.: 13). lib. bdg. 17.20 *(978-1-4177-8261-1(7)*, Turtleback) Turtleback Bks.

—Shadow Wolf. 2010. (Wolves of the Beyond Ser.: 2). (ENG.). 272p. (J). (gr. 3-7). 17.99 *(978-0-545-09312-5(0)*, Scholastic Pr.) Scholastic, Inc.

—The Siege. 2004. (Guardians of Ga'hoole Ser.: 4). (ENG., Illus.). 224p. (J). (gr. 3-7). mass mkt. 6.99 *(978-0-439-40560-7(2)*, Scholastic Paperbacks) Scholastic, Inc.

—The War of the Ember. 2008. (Guardians of Ga'hoole Ser.: 15). (ENG.). 256p. (J). (gr. 3-7). pap. 6.99 *(978-0-439-88809-7(3)*, Scholastic Paperbacks) Scholastic, Inc.

Laurie, Peter. Mauby & the Hurricane. 2007. (Illus.). 56p. pap. 16.00 *(978-1-4050-7718-7(2))* Macmillan Caribbean GBR. Dist: Interlink Publishing Group, Inc.

Leadbetter, Lesley. Harold the Owl Who Couldn't Sleep. Leszek, Cedryll, illus. 2012. 30p. (J). pap. *(978-1-921869-89-1(5)*, Digital Publishing Centre) Interactive Pubns. Pty, Ltd.

Lear, Edward. Buho y la Gatita.Tr. of Owl & the Cat. (SPA., Illus.). 32p. (J). 14.95 *(978-84-261-3023-5(2))* Juventud, Editorial ESP. Dist: AIMS International Bks., Inc.

—The Owl & the Pussy-Cat & Other Stories. 2012. (ENG., Illus.). 80p. (J). (gr. 2). 12.99 *(978-0-7123-5876-7(5))* British Library, The GBR. Dist: Independent Pubs. Group.

Leist, Christina, illus. Jack the Bear. 2009. (ENG.). 40p. (J). (gr. -1-3). 16.95 *(978-1-894965-97-2(3))* Simply Read Bks. CAN. Dist: Ingram Publisher Services.

Litton, Jonathan. Hoot: A Hide-And-Seek Book of Counting. Galloway, Fhiona, illus. 2014. (My Little World Ser.). (ENG.). 16p. (J). (gr. -1-k). bds. 7.99 *(978-1-58925-595-1(X))* Tiger Tales.

Lodge, Jo. Bump! Little Owl. 2014. (Push, Pull, POP! Bks.). (ENG., Illus.). 10p. (J). (gr. -1 — 1). 6.99 *(978-0-7641-6667-9(0))* Barron's Educational Series, Inc.

London, Lewis. Wesley Owl. 2010. (Illus.). 36p. (J). pap. 16.99 *(978-1-4490-6122-7(2))* AuthorHouse.

Loyie, Larry & Brissenden, Constance. As Long As the Rivers Flow, 1 vol. Holmlund, Heather D., illus. 2005. (ENG.). 40p. (J). (gr. 4-7). pap. 9.95 *(978-0-88899-696-1(9))* Groundwood Bks. CAN. Dist: Publishers Group West (PGW).

Lucas, Ronne Kay. How the Cactus Got Its Thorns. 2013. 20p. pap. 24.95 *(978-1-4626-8915-6(9))* America Star Bks.

MacGregor, Roy. The Complete Screech Owls, Volume 2, Vol. 2. 2006. (ENG.). 592p. (J). (gr. 3-7). per. 15.95 *(978-0-7710-5486-0(6)*, Screech Owls) McClelland & Stewart CAN. Dist: Penguin Random Hse. LLC.

—The Kindergarten Caper: The Screech Owls Prequel. 2008. (ENG.). 144p. (YA). (gr. 3-7). mass mkt. 6.99 *(978-0-7710-5608-6(7)*, Screech Owls) McClelland & Stewart CAN. Dist: Penguin Random Hse. LLC.

—Trouble at the Top of the World. 2009. (ENG.). 136p. (YA). (gr. 3-7). mass mkt. 5.95 *(978-0-7710-5609-3(5)*, Screech Owls) McClelland & Stewart CAN. Dist: Penguin Random Hse. LLC.

MacGregor, Roy & MacGregor, Roy. The Complete Screech Owls, Vol. 5. 2007. (Complete Screech Owls Ser.). (ENG.). 488p. (J). (gr. 3-7). per. 15.95 *(978-0-7710-5497-6(1)*, Screech Owls) McClelland & Stewart CAN. Dist: Penguin Random Hse. LLC.

Maresca, Beth Anne, illus. Megan Owlet. 2015. (ENG.). 32p. (J). (gr. -1-k). 16.99 *(978-1-63220-404-2(5)*, Sky Pony Pr.) Skyhorse Publishing Co., Inc.

Marino, Gianna. Too Tall Houses. 2012. (ENG.). 40p. (J). (gr. -1-k). 16.99 *(978-0-670-01314-2(5)*, Viking Books for Young Readers) Penguin Young Readers Group.

Markowitz, Susan Meredith. The Great Green Forest & el gran bosque Verde: 6 English, 6 Spanish Adaptations. 2011. (ENG & SPA.). (J). 75.00 net. *(978-1-4108-5653-1(4))* Benchmark Education Co.

Masterson, Hoss. Owl Ball. Alves, Josh, illus. 2017. (Animal All-Stars Ser.). (ENG.). 56p. (gr. 1-3). lib. bdg. 25.32 *(978-1-4965-4309-7(2))* Stone Arch Bks.

Mcallister, Herb West. Doo West to Toadstool. 2011. 44p. pap. 21.99 *(978-1-4628-5530-8(X))* Xlibris Corp.

McMilin, Jack. Dodger the Dragon, 1 vol. Nevarez, Lisa, illus. 2009. pap. 24.95 *(978-1-60703-930-3(3))* PublishAmerica, Inc.

Mercer, M. J. O'No It's Henry. 2010. 24p. 12.99 *(978-1-4520-2125-6(2))* AuthorHouse.

Milton, Giles. Good Luck Baby Owls. Milton, Alexandra, illus. 2012. (ENG.). 32p. (J). (gr. -1-k). 16.95 *(978-1-907967-28-3(1))* Boxer Bks., Ltd. GBR. Dist: Sterling Publishing Co., Inc.

Modarressi, Mitra. Owlet's First Flight. Modarressi, Mitra, illus. 2012. (ENG., Illus.). 32p. (J). (gr. -1-k). 16.99 *(978-0-399-25526-7(5)*, G.P. Putnam's Sons Books for Young Readers) Penguin Young Readers Group.

Montgomery, R. A. The Owl Tree. 2010. (Illus.). 64p. (Orig.). (J). pap. 7.99 *(978-1-933390-80-2(8))* Chooseco LLC.

Moroney, Trace, creator. The Owl & the Pussy Cat. 2008. (Illus.). 10p. (gr. -1-1). bds. 4.99 *(978-1-74178-515-9(4))* Gardner Pubns.

Na, Il Sung. A Book of Sleep. 2011. (ENG.). 24p. (J). (gr. k — 1). bds. 6.99 *(978-0-375-86618-0(3)*, Knopf Bks. for Young Readers) Random Hse. Children's Bks.

Naughton, Geraldine. Owl's Birthday. 2010. 20p. 12.68 *(978-1-4269-4481-9(0))* Trafford Publishing.

Niddrie, June. Great Scott & Otis. 2010. 56p. pap. 23.30 *(978-0-557-31863-6(7))* Lulu Pr., Inc.

Orobosa-Ogbeide, Kathryn. The Owl That Couldn't Fly. 2012. 12p. pap. 12.68 *(978-1-4669-1892-4(6))* Trafford Publishing.

Paquet, Claudine, et al. Antonio, Plumero y Manchitas. 2006. (SPA., Illus.). 110p. (J). pap. (978-958-30-2016-2(8)) Panamericana Editorial.

Parrish, Emma. Little Owl Says Goodnight. 2016. (Slide-And-Seek Ser.). (ENG., Illus.). 10p. (J). (gr. -1-k). bds. 8.99 (978-1-4998-0406-5(7)) Little Bee Books Inc.

Pauline Wall & Shelley Smith. What the Owl Saw: (a Christmas Story) 2012. 20p. pap. 15.19 (978-1-4669-2813-8(1)) Trafford Publishing.

Perales, Alonso M. Brujas, Lechuzas y Espantos/Witches, Owls & Spooks. Pluecker, John, tr. from SPA. 2008. (ENG & SPA., Illus.). 96p. (J). (gr. 3-7). pap. 9.95 (978-1-55885-512-0(2), Piñata Books) Arte Publico Pr.

Peters, Lou. The Owl & the Turtle. 2010. 32p. pap. 15.95 (978-0-557-51727-5(3)) Lulu Pr., Inc.

Pevear, Ted F. & Pevear, Linda W. The Date in the Junk Yard. 2012. 28p. 24.95 (978-1-62709-781-9(3)); pap. 24.95 (978-1-4626-8994-1(9)) America Star Bks.

—Finding Little Feathers a Hub-A-Son. 2012. 24p. 24.95 (978-1-4626-5874-9(1)) America Star Bks.

Pinter, Karin. Niki Owl: Leap of Faith. 2012. 172p. (gr. 4-6). 27.99 (978-1-4772-8023-2(5)); pap. 16.95 (978-1-4772-8024-9(3)) AuthorHouse.

Pizzoli, Greg. Good Night Owl. Pizzoli, Greg, illus. 2016. (ENG., Illus.). 48p. (J). (gr. -1-k). 16.99 (978-1-4847-1275-7(7)) Disney Pr.

Potter, Alan Mitchell & Williams, Virginia. Hoo-Hoo Hooty-Hoo-Who. 2005. 9.00 (978-0-8059-9807-8(1)) Dorrance Publishing Co., Inc.

Preston-Gannon, Frann. What a Hoot! 2015. (ENG., Illus.). 20p. (J). (-k). bds. 12.95 (978-1-57687-758-6(2), powerHouse Bks.) powerHouse Cultural Entertainment, Inc.

Priddy, Roger. Home Sweet Home. 2014. (Little Friends Ser.). (ENG.). 10p. (J). (gr. -1 — 1). bds. 6.99 (978-0-312-51679-6(7), 9780312516796, Priddy Bks.) St. Martin's Pr.

Quay, Emma. Good Night, Sleep Tight: A Book about Bedtime. Walker, Anna, illus. 2011. (ENG.). 24p. (J). (gr. -1 — 1). bds. 5.99 (978-0-8037-3581-1(2), Dial Bks) Penguin Young Readers Group.

Reasoner, Charles & Wood, Steven. Owl's Halloween. 2015. (Charles Reasoner Halloween Bks.). (ENG., Illus.). 12p. (gr. -1 — 1). bds. 5.99 (978-1-4795-8500-7(9)) Picture Window Bks.

Rigo, L. Little Owl. 2011. (Look at Me Bks.). (ENG., Illus.). 10p. (J). bds. 8.99 (978-0-7641-6447-7(3)) Barron's Educational Series, Inc.

Rivers-Moore, Debbie. Owl. Larranaga, Ana Martin, illus. 2012. (Come Out & Play Bks.). (ENG.). 10p. (J). bds. 2.99 (978-0-7641-6518-4(6)) Barron's Educational Series, Inc.

Rixon, Denise. The Owl That Barked: Tammy, 1 vol. 2009. 203p. pap. 24.95 (978-1-4489-8472-5(6)) America Star Bks.

Rose, A. First Flight. 2011. 24p. pap. 15.99 (978-1-4628-7747-8(8)) Xlibris Corp.

Rosenthal, Amy Krouse. Little Hoot. Corace, Jen, illus. (ENG.). (J). (gr. -1-k). 2016. 28p. bds. 7.99 (978-1-4521-5207-3(1)) 2007. 36p. 15.99 (978-0-8118-6023-9(X)) Chronicle Bks. LLC.

Rounceville, Bibi. Gimbels & Gooseberries. 2010. 52p. pap. 9.50 (978-0-557-21585-0(4)) Lulu Pr., Inc.

Runton, Andy. Owly & Wormy, Bright Lights & Starry Nights. Runton, Andy, illus. 2012. (ENG., Illus.). 40p. (J). (gr. -1-3). 17.99 (978-1-4169-5775-1(8), Atheneum Bks. for Young Readers) Simon & Schuster Children's Publishing.

—Owly & Wormy, Friends All Aflutter! Runton, Andy, illus. 2011. (ENG., Illus.). 40p. (J). (gr. -1-2). 16.99 (978-1-4169-5774-4(X), Atheneum Bks. for Young Readers) Simon & Schuster Children's Publishing.

Russell, D. Z. The Amazing Adventures of Andy Owl: A Children's Guide to Understanding Music. Stone, John, illus. 2003. 34p. (J). per. 7.95 (978-0-9725398-0-7(8)) World Famous Children's Bks.

Sargent, Dave & Sargent, David, Jr. Hoot Owl: Mind Your Mamma, 19 vols., Vol. 9. Lenoir, Jane, illus. 2003. (Feather Tales Ser.: 9). 42p. (J). pap. 10.95 (978-1-56763-736-6(1)) Ozark Publishing.

Sargent, Dave & Sargent, David M., Jr. Hoot Owl: Mind Your Mamma, 20 vols., Vol. 9. Lenoir, Jane, illus. 2nd ed. 2003. (Feather Tales Ser.: 9). 42p. (J). lib. bdg. (978-1-56763-735-9(3)) Ozark Publishing.

Schatell, Brian. Owl Boy. 2015. (ENG., Illus.). 32p. (J). (gr. -1-1). 16.95 (978-0-8234-3208-0(4)) Holiday Hse., Inc.

Schmidt-Kyanka, Anita. Sapsucker Blues: The Story of an Endearing Family of Great Blue Herons. 2013. 48p. pap. 20.99 (978-1-4808-0250-6(6)) Archway Publishing.

Scull, Paul E. Los Animales Cuentan Su Histori. 2011. 20p. pap. (978-1-4269-7319-2(5)) Trafford Publishing (UK) Ltd.

The Secret Song & Other Stories: Individual Title Six-Pack. (Story Steps Ser.). (gr. k-2). 48.00 (978-0-7635-9808-2(9)) Rigby Education.

Seymour, Mary Sue. Friends in a Storm. Flynn, Samantha, illus. 2013. 20p. pap. 9.95 (978-1-61633-376-8(6)) Guardian Angel Publishing, Inc.

Shannon, Star Erian. Erian's Friend Jeremiah the Owl. 2003. (J). pap. 9.00 (978-0-8059-6068-6(5)) Dorrance Publishing Co., Inc.

Sharmat, Marjorie Weinman. Nate the Great on the Owl Express. Sharmat, Mitchell & Weston, Martha, illus. 2004. (Nate the Great Ser.: No. 24). (ENG.). 80p. (J). (gr. 1-4). 5.99 (978-0-440-41927-3(1), Yearling) Random Hse. Children's Bks.

Shaw, Stephanie. Under the Sleepy Stars. Harry, Rebecca, illus. 2015. (ENG.). 22p. (J). (gr. -1-3). bds. 8.99 (978-1-58925-204-2(7)) Tiger Tales.

Shirley, Alice. The Gentle Lion & the Little Owlet. Shirley, Alice, illus. 2013. Orig. Title: Owlet & Pussycat. (ENG., Illus.). 32p. (J). (gr. -1-k). pap. 8.99 (978-1-84365-199-4(8), Pavilion) Pavilion Bks. GBR. Dist: Independent Pubs. Group.

Silvey, Diane. Time of the Thunderbird. Mantha, John, illus. 2008. (ENG.). 88p. (J). (gr. 6-5). pap. 11.99 (978-1-55002-792-1(1), Sandcastle Bks.) Dundurn CAN. Dist: Ingram Publisher Services.

Smith, Jeffrey B. Stubby. 2006. 15p. 8.28 (978-1-4116-8215-3(7)) Lulu Pr., Inc.

Squires, R. L. Peaches & Cream, 1 vol. Collier, Kevin Scott, illus. 2009. 31p. pap. 24.95 (978-1-60749-164-4(8)) America Star Bks.

Squires, Ricky. Lily & Ike, 1 vol. 2010. 32p. 24.95 (978-1-4512-9308-1(9)) PublishAmerica, Inc.

Srinivasan, Divya. Little Owl's 1-2-3. Srinivasan, Divya, illus. 2015. (ENG., Illus.). 18p. (J). (— 1). 5.99 (978-0-451-47454-4(6), Viking Books for Young Readers) Penguin Young Readers Group.

—Little Owl's Colors. Srinivasan, Divya, illus. 2015. (ENG., Illus.). 18p. (J). (— 1). 5.99 (978-0-451-47456-8(2), Viking Books for Young Readers) Penguin Young Readers Group.

—Little Owl's Day. Srinivasan, Divya, illus. 2014. (ENG., Illus.). 32p. (J). (gr. -1-k). 16.99 (978-0-670-01650-1(0), Viking Books for Young Readers) Penguin Young Readers Group.

—Little Owl's Night. (ENG., 32p. (J). 2013. Illus.). (— 1). bds. 6.99 (978-0-670-01579-5(2)) 2011. (gr. -1-k). 16.99 (978-0-670-01295-4(5)) Penguin Young Readers Group. (Viking Books for Young Readers).

Staheli, Bee, ed. The Owl Who Couldn't Say Whoo. Clish, Lori, illus. Lt. ed. (J). (gr. k-5). pap. 7.95 (978-1-928632-50-4(5)) Writers Marketplace:Consulting, Critiquing & Publishing.

Stein, Renea. The Wise Old Owl & Those Tricky Times Tables. 2008. 36p. pap. 24.95 (978-1-60474-228-2(3)) America Star Bks.

Stewart, Bob. Baily Bumble Bee. 2009. 32p. pap. 14.49 (978-1-4389-7254-1(7)) AuthorHouse.

StJohn, Amanda. How to Check Out a Book. Ostrom, Bob, illus. 2012. (Library Skills Ser.). (ENG.). 24p. (J). (gr. -1-2). 28.50 (978-1-61473-249-5(3), 204951) Child's World, Inc., The.

—How to Find a Book. Ostrom, Bob, illus. 2012. (Library Skills Ser.). (ENG.). 24p. (J). (gr. -1-2). 28.50 (978-1-61473-250-1(7), 204952) Child's World, Inc., The.

—How to Find Information Online. Ostrom, Bob, illus. 2012. (Library Skills Ser.). (ENG.). 24p. (J). (gr. -1-2). 28.50 (978-1-61473-251-8(5), 204953) Child's World, Inc., The.

—How to Treat a Book. Ostrom, Bob, illus. 2012. (Library Skills Ser.). (ENG.). 24p. (J). (gr. -1-2). 28.50 (978-1-61473-252-5(3), 204954) Child's World, Inc., The.

Taylor, Sean. Hoot Owl, Master of Disguise. Jullien, Jean, illus. 2015. (ENG.). 48p. (J). (gr. -1-2). 15.99 (978-0-7636-7578-3(4)) Candlewick Pr.

Thomas Nelson. Oola the Owl Who Lost Her Hoot! 2016. (ENG.). 32p. (gr. -1-2). (978-1-78598-763-2(1)) Make Believe Ideas.

Timms, E. H. Ring of Nine. 2010. 156p. pap. 16.95 (978-1-4452-4512-6(4)) Lulu Pr., Inc.

Tomlinson, Jill. The Owl Who Was Afraid of the Dark. Howard, Paul, illus. 2014. (ENG.). 112p. (J). (gr. -1-2). pap. 9.99 (978-1-4052-7197-4(3)) Egmont Bks., Ltd. GBR. Dist: Independent Pubs. Group.

—Owl Who Was Afraid of the Dark. (Illus.). 95p. (J). pap. 6.99 (978-0-7497-0795-8(X)) Egmont Bks., Ltd. GBR. Dist: Trafalgar Square Publishing.

—The Owl Who Was Afraid of the Dark, Pack, Set. Howard, Paul, illus. 2015. (ENG.). 32p. (J). (gr. -1-2). 22.99 (978-1-4052-7554-5(5)) Egmont Bks., Ltd. GBR. Dist: Independent Pubs. Group.

Treml, Renee. Ten Little Owls. 2017. (ENG.). 24p. (J). (-k). bds. 9.99 (**978-0-14-378056-4(5)**) Random Hse. Australia AUS. Dist: Independent Pubs. Group.

Turner, Mary. The Quiet & Still Owl. 2012. 40p. pap. 21.99 (978-1-4691-2795-8(4)) Xlibris Corp.

Uihlein, Mary. Hello Little Owl. Uihlein, Mary, illus. 2012. (Illus.). 24p. 22.95 (978-1-61493-140-9(2)); pap. 12.95 (978-1-61493-139-3(9)) Peppertree Pr., The.

—Hello Little Owl, I Am Hermit Crab! Uihlein, Mary, illus. 2013. (Illus.). 28p. 24.95 (978-1-61493-159-1(3)); pap. 12.95 (978-1-61493-158-4(5)) Peppertree Pr., The.

Ulbrich, Jasper. The Little Owl. 2009. (Illus.). 32p. pap. 16.50 (978-1-60860-047-2(5), Eloquent Bks.) Strategic Book Publishing & Rights Agency (SBPRA).

Waddell, Martin. Owl Babies. (Illus.). 25p. (J). (CHI, ENG, URD, TUR & VIE.). (978-1-85430-343-1(0), 93441); (ENG, VIE, URD, TUR & CHI., (978-1-85430-348-6(1), 93442) Little Tiger Pr. Group.

—Owl Babies. Benson, Patrick, illus. 2015. (ENG.). 22p. (J). (— 1). bds. 6.99 (978-0-7636-7961-3(5)) Candlewick Pr.

—Owl Babies. Benson, Patrick, illus. 2017. (ENG.). 32p. (J). (gr. -1-2). 16.99 (**978-0-7636-9519-4(X)**) Candlewick Pr.

—Owl Babies Book & Toy Gift Set. Benson, Patrick, illus. 2016. (ENG.). (J). (-k). bds. 15.99 (978-0-7636-8898-1(3)) Candlewick Pr.

—Owl Babies: Candlewick Storybook Animations. Benson, Patrick, illus. 2008. (Candlewick Storybook Animations Ser.). (ENG.). 32p. (J). (gr. k-k). 14.99 (978-0-7636-3538-1(3)) Candlewick Pr.

Walchle, Donna Douglas. There's an Owl in the Closet. Galeano, Jose Daniel Oviedo, illus. 2013. (ENG.). 32p. (J). pap. 9.99 (978-1-4908-0932-8(5), WestBow Pr.) Author Solutions, Inc.

Walden, Libby. Noisy Touch & Feel: Owl Says Hoot. Enright, Amanda, illus. 2016. (Noisy Touch & Feel Ser.). (ENG.). 12p. (J). bds. 14.99 (978-1-62686-576-1(0), Silver Dolphin Bks.) Readerlink Distribution Services, LLC.

Walker, Mary. The Flower Tree. 2010. (Illus.). 50p. pap. 12.95 (978-1-4327-3588-3(8)) Outskirts Pr., Inc.

Wan, Joyce. Owl & Friends. Wan, Joyce, illus. 2013. (ENG., Illus.). 14p. (J). (gr. -1-k). bds. 6.99 (978-0-8431-7275-1(4), Price Stern Sloan) Penguin Young Readers Group.

West, Judy & Westerink, Gerda. The Christmas Owls. 2004. (Illus.). 32p. (J). 16.95 (978-0-86315-421-8(2)) Floris Bks. GBR. Dist: SteinerBooks, Inc.

Westerman, Robert. Alohalani Kalikimaka Auntie: Sheet Music & Lyrics. Westerman, Robert, . 2006. (Illus.). 12p. (J). 6.95 (978-0-9761992-1-2(1)) Gold Boy Music & Pubn.

Wildsmith, Brian. The Owl & the Woodpecker, 1 vol. Wildsmith, Brian, illus. 2006. (ENG., Illus.). 32p. (J). (gr. -1-3). 16.95 (978-1-59572-043-6(X)); pap. 6.95 (978-1-59572-050-4(2)) Star Bright Bks., Inc.

Willard, Gerald. Amy Firefly. 2009. 40p. pap. 18.50 (978-1-60693-448-7(1), Eloquent Bks.) Strategic Book Publishing & Rights Agency (SBPRA).

Williams, Raymond. Tales from the Willow Tree. 2012. (Illus.). 28p. pap. 8.50 (978-1-78035-343-2(X), Fastprint Publishing) Upfront Publishing Ltd. GBR. Dist: Printondemand-worldwide.com.

Willis, Jeanne. Fly, Chick, Fly! Ross, Tony, illus. 2012. (Andersen Press Picture Bks). (ENG.). 32p. (J). (gr. -1-3). 16.95 (978-1-4677-0314-7(1)) Lerner Publishing Group.

Wilson, Karma. Bear's New Friend. Chapman, Jane, illus. 2009. (Bear Bks.). (ENG.). 34p. (J). (gr. -1-2). bds. 7.99 (978-1-4169-5438-5(4), Little Simon) Little Simon.

—Bear's New Friend. Chapman, Jane, illus. 2006. (Bear Bks.). (ENG.). 40p. (J). (gr. -1-3). 17.99 (978-0-689-85984-7(8), McElderry, Margaret K. Bks.) McElderry, Margaret K. Bks.

Wilson, Robert. Pippy: The Miracle of A Dream. 2011. 136p. 21.95 (978-1-4620-6634-6(8)); pap. 11.95 (978-1-4620-6633-9(X)) iUniverse, Inc.

Winbolt-Lewis, Martin. Owliviah. Cressey, Roger, illus. 2013. 56p. (J). pap. (978-1-78222-075-6(5)) Paragon Publishing, Rothersthorpe.

Wolff, Susan. Quackers Wants to Fly. Currie, Justin, illus. 2013. 32p. pap. 8.95 (978-1-60653-074-0(7)) High Hill Pr.

Wolverton, Barry. Neversink. Nielson, Sam, illus. (ENG.). (J). (gr. 3-7). 2013. 320p. pap. 6.99 (978-0-06-202793-1(X)) 2012. 304p. 16.99 (978-0-06-202791-7(3)) HarperCollins Pubs. (Waldon Pond Pr.).

—Neversink. Nielson, Sam, illus. 2012. xiii, 287p. (J). (978-0-06-202792-4(1)) Longman Publishing.

Woman, Magpie Sleeping. Big Eyes: The Keeper of the Night. 2013. 24p. pap. 24.95 (978-1-4626-9569-0(8)) America Star Bks.

Won, Brian. Hooray for Today! 2016. (ENG., Illus.). 40p. (J). (gr. -1-3). 16.99 (978-0-544-74803-3(4), HMH Books For Young Readers) Houghton Mifflin Harcourt Publishing Co.

Wood, A. J. The Christmas Hat. Kneen, Maggie, illus. 2004. (ENG.). 24p. (J). (978-1-55168-267-9(2)) Fenn, H. B. & Co., Ltd.

Yolen, Jane. Owl Moon. 2013. lib. bdg. 18.40 (978-0-606-36222-1(3)) Turtleback Bks.

Young, Lynn. Adventures with Looka, 1 vol. 2009. 48p. pap. 16.95 (978-1-60813-959-0(X)) America Star Bks.

Yuly, Toni. Night Owl. Yuly, Toni, illus. 2015. (ENG., Illus.). 40p. (J). (— 1). 15.99 (978-1-250-05457-9(5), 9781250054579) Feiwel & Friends.

Zagiada, Vladimir. Gymmy the Owl & His Friends. 2012. 52p. pap. 24.99 (978-1-4772-0226-5(9)) AuthorHouse.

—Gymmy the Owl & His Friends: Tales in Rhyme about the Animal Kingdom's Natural Gymnasts. 2012. 52p. pap. 24.99 (978-1-4685-6011-4(5)) AuthorHouse.

OZ (IMAGINARY PLACE)—FICTION

Anfuso, Dennis & Lindsay, Alan. Oz House. 2012. (ENG.). 321p. pap. 19.95 (978-1-57433-041-0(1)) Interset Pr.

Baum, Frank. The Wonderful Wizard of Oz. 2008. (Oxford World's Classics Ser.). (ENG., Illus.). 336p. pap. 13.95 (978-0-19-954064-8(0)) Oxford Univ. Pr., Inc.

Baum, L. Frank. Adventures in Oz: Dorothy & the Wizard in Oz, the Road to Oz, the Emerald City of Oz. 2007. 296p. 24.95 (978-1-60459-016-6(5)); per. 12.95 (978-1-60459-017-3(3)) Wilder Pubns., Corp.

—Adventures in Oz: The Patchwork Girl of Oz, Little Wizard Stories of Oz, Tik-Tok of Oz. 2007. 268p. 24.95 (978-1-60459-019-7(X)); per. 12.99 (978-1-60459-018-0(1)) Wilder Pubns., Corp.

—Adventures in Oz: The Tin Woodman of Oz, the Magic of Oz, Glinda of Oz. 2007. 284p. 24.95 (978-1-60459-023-4(8)); per. 12.99 (978-1-60459-022-7(X)) Wilder Pubns., Corp.

—Adventures in Oz: The Wonderful Wizard of Oz, the Marvelous Land of Oz, Ozma of Oz. 2007. 264p. per. 12.99 (978-1-60459-014-2(9)); per. 24.95 (978-1-60459-015-9(7)) Wilder Pubns., Corp.

—Collected Short Stories of L. Frank Baum. 2006. (J). 29.95 (978-1-930764-14-9(6)) International Wizard of Oz Club, The.

—Complete Book of Oz: The Wonderful Wizard of Oz, the Marvelous Land of Oz, & Ozma of Oz, Vol. 1. 2009. 268p. (J). 24.95 (978-1-60459-711-0(9)) Wilder Pubns., Corp.

—Dorothy & the Wizard in Oz. 2004. reprint ed. pap. 20.95 (978-1-4191-1655-1(X)); pap. 1.99 (978-1-4192-1655-8(4)) Kessinger Publishing, LLC.

—Dorothy & the Wizard in Oz; the Road to Oz; the Emerald City of Oz, Vol. 2. 2013. (Oz, the Complete Collection: 2). (ENG.). 656p. (J). (gr. 3-7). pap. 12.99 (978-1-4424-8548-8(5), Aladdin) Simon & Schuster Children's Publishing.

—Dorothy & the Wizard of Oz. 2005. pap. (978-1-4065-0075-2(5)) Dodo Pr.

—Dorothy & the Wizard of Oz. l.t. ed. 2004. (Large Print Ser.). lib. bdg. 25.00 (978-1-58287-769-3(6)) North Bks.

—The Emerald City of Oz. 2007. 144p. per. 11.95 (978-1-60312-256-6(7)) Aegypan.

—The Emerald City of Oz. (Oz Ser.). (YA). (gr. 5-8). 21.95 (978-0-8488-0733-7(2)) Amereon Ltd.

—The Emerald City of Oz. 2003. (Twelve-Point Ser.). lib. bdg. 24.00 (978-1-58287-254-4(6)) North Bks.

—Glinda of Oz. rev. ed. 2006. 184p. 26.95 (978-1-4218-1786-6(1)); pap. 11.95 (978-1-4218-1886-3(8)) 1st World Publishing, Inc. (1st World Library - Literary Society).

—Glinda of Oz. 2007. 108p. 22.95 (978-1-60312-591-8(4)) Aegypan.

—Glinda of Oz. (Oz Ser.). (YA). (gr. 5-8). 21.95 (978-0-8488-0784-9(7)) Amereon Ltd.

—Glinda of Oz. (Twelve-Point Ser.). 2003. lib. bdg. 24.00 (978-1-58287-256-8(2)) 2004. 210p. 25.00 (978-1-58287-740-2(8)) North Bks.

—Glinda of Oz. John R Neill, illus. 2010. 144p. pap. 5.88 (978-1-60386-310-0(9), Merchant Bks.) Rough Draft Printing.

—Large Hardback 1: L. Frank Baum's Original Oz Series. Wonderful Wizard of Oz, Marvelous Land of Oz, Ozma of Oz, Dorothy & the Wizard I. 2011. 1194p. (978-1-905921-22-5(5)) Shoes & Ships & Sealing Wax Ltd.

—Little Wizard Stories of Oz. Neill, John R., illus. 2011. (Dover Children's Classics Ser.). (ENG.). 160p. (J). (gr. 3-5). pap. 14.99 (978-0-486-47644-5(8)) Dover Pubns., Inc.

—The Lost Princess of Oz. (Oz Ser.). (YA). (gr. 5-8). 22.95 (978-0-8488-0786-3(3)) Amereon Ltd.

—The Lost Princess of Oz. (Twelve-Point Ser.). 2003. lib. bdg. 24.00 (978-1-58287-255-1(4)) 2004. 241p. 25.00 (978-1-58287-739-6(4)) North Bks.

—The Magic of Oz. 2007. 108p. (gr. 4-7). per. 9.95 (978-1-60312-334-1(2)); 22.95 (978-1-60312-671-7(6)) Aegypan.

—The Magic of Oz. 2004. (Twelve-Point Ser.). lib. bdg. 24.00 (978-1-58287-279-7(1)); lib. bdg. 25.00 (978-1-58287-775-4(0)) North Bks.

—El Maravilloso Mago de Oz. (Oz Ser.).Tr. of Wonderful Wizard of Oz. (SPA., Illus.). 160p. (YA). (gr. 5-8). 14.95 (978-84-7281-184-3(0), AF1184) Auriga, Ediciones S.A. ESP. Dist: Continental Bk. Co., Inc.

—The Marvelous Land of Oz. 2007. 120p. per. 10.95 (978-1-60312-149-1(8)) Aegypan.

—The Marvelous Land of Oz. 2004. (Twelve-Point Ser.). lib. bdg. 24.00 (978-1-58287-272-8(4)); lib. bdg. 25.00 (978-1-58287-768-6(8)) North Bks.

—Michael Foreman's the Wonderful Wizard of Oz. Foreman, Michael, illus. 2010. (ENG.). 160p. (J). (gr. 2-7). 19.99 (978-1-84365-157-4(2), Pavilion Children's Books) Pavilion Bks. GBR. Dist: Independent Pubs. Group.

—Oz, the Complete Collection, Volume 1: The Wonderful Wizard of Oz; the Marvelous Land of Oz; Ozma of Oz. 2013. (Oz, the Complete Collection: 1). (ENG., Illus.). 592p. (J). (gr. 3-7). 19.99 (978-1-4424-8889-2(1), Aladdin) Simon & Schuster Children's Publishing.

—Oz, the Complete Collection, Volume 2: Dorothy & the Wizard in Oz; the Road to Oz; the Emerald City of Oz. 2013. (Oz, the Complete Collection: 2). (ENG.). 656p. (J). (gr. 3-7). 19.99 (978-1-4424-8890-8(5), Simon & Schuster/Paula Wiseman Bks.) Simon & Schuster/Paula Wiseman Bks.

—Oz, the Complete Collection, Volume 3: The Patchwork Girl of Oz; Tik-Tok of Oz; the Scarecrow of Oz. 2013. (Oz, the Complete Collection: 3). (ENG.). 720p. (J). (gr. 3-7). 19.99 (978-1-4424-8892-2(1), Aladdin) Simon & Schuster Children's Publishing.

—Oz, the Complete Collection, Volume 4: Rinkitink in Oz; the Lost Princess of Oz; the Tin Woodman of Oz. 2013. (Oz, the Complete Collection: 4). (ENG.). 656p. (J). (gr. 3-7). 19.99 (978-1-4424-8893-9(X), Aladdin) Simon & Schuster Children's Publishing.

—Oz, the Complete Hardcover Collection. 2013. (Oz, the Complete Collection). (ENG.). 3200p. (J). (gr. 3-7). 99.99 (978-1-4424-8903-5(0), Aladdin) Simon & Schuster Children's Publishing.

—Ozma of Oz. 2007. 108p. (gr. 4-7). per. 9.95 (978-1-60312-150-7(1)) Aegypan.

—Ozma of Oz. (Twelve-Point Ser.). 2003. lib. bdg. 24.00 (978-1-58287-252-0(X)) 2004. 210p. 25.00 (978-1-58287-736-5(X)) North Bks.

—The Patchwork Girl of Oz. 2007. 152p. (gr. -1-7). 24.95 (978-1-60312-632-8(5)); per. 12.95 (978-1-60312-374-7(1)) Aegypan.

—The Patchwork Girl of Oz. (Oz Ser.). (YA). (gr. 5-8). 25.95 (978-0-8488-0705-4(7)) Amereon Ltd.

—The Patchwork Girl of OZ. l.t. ed. 2004. (Large Print Ser.). lib. bdg. 25.00 (978-1-58287-771-6(8)) North Bks.

—Rinkitink in Oz. rev. ed. 2006. 216p. 27.95 (978-1-4218-1791-0(8)); pap. 12.95 (978-1-4218-1891-7(4)) 1st World Publishing, Inc. (1st World Library - Literary Society).

—Rinkitink in Oz. (Oz Ser.). (YA). (gr. 5-8). 22.95 (978-0-8488-0735-1(9)) Amereon Ltd.

—Rinkitink in Oz. 2004. reprint ed. pap. 20.95 (978-1-4191-6718-8(9)); pap. 1.99 (978-1-4192-6718-5(3)) Kessinger Publishing, LLC.

—Rinkitink in Oz. 2004. (Twelve-Point Ser.). lib. bdg. 24.00 (978-1-58287-278-0(3)); lib. bdg. 25.00 (978-1-58287-774-7(2)) North Bks.

—Rinkitink in Oz; the Lost Princess of Oz; the Tin Woodman of Oz, Vol. 4. 2013. (Oz, the Complete Collection: 4). (ENG.). 656p. (J). (gr. 3-7). pap. 11.99 (978-1-4424-8550-1(7), Aladdin) Simon & Schuster Children's Publishing.

—The Road to Oz. (Oz Ser.). (YA). (gr. 5-8). 20.95 (978-0-8488-0788-7(X)) Amereon Ltd.

—The Road to Oz. 2004. (Twelve-Point Ser.). lib. bdg. 24.00 (978-1-58287-274-2(0)); lib. bdg. 25.00 (978-1-58287-770-9(X)) North Bks.

—The Scarecrow of Oz. (Oz Ser.). (YA). (gr. 5-8). 20.95 (978-0-8488-0707-8(3)) Amereon Ltd.

—The Scarecrow of Oz. 2004. (Twelve-Point Ser.). lib. bdg. 24.00 (978-1-58287-277-3(5)); lib. bdg. 25.00 (978-1-58287-773-0(4)) North Bks.

—The Patchwork Girl of Oz; Tik-Tok of Oz; the Scarecrow of Oz, Vol. 3. 2013. (Oz, the Complete Collection: 3). (ENG.). 720p. (J). (gr. 3-7). pap. 12.99 (978-1-4424-8549-5(3), Aladdin) Simon & Schuster Children's Publishing.

—The Wonderful Wizard of Oz; the Marvelous Land of Oz; Ozma of Oz. 2013. (Oz, the Complete Collection: 1). (ENG., Illus.). 592p. (J). (gr. 3-7). pap. 12.99 (978-1-4424-8547-1(7), Aladdin) Simon & Schuster Children's Publishing.

—Tik-Tok of Oz. 2007. 128p. (gr. -1-7). per. 10.95 (978-1-60312-333-4(4)); 23.95 (978-1-60312-670-0(8)) Aegypan.

—Tik-Tok of Oz. 2004. (Twelve-Point Ser.). lib. bdg. 24.00 (978-1-58287-276-6(7)); lib. bdg. 25.00 (978-1-58287-772-3(6)) North Bks.

—The Tin Woodman of Oz. rev. ed. 2006. 204p. 27.95 (978-1-4218-1789-7(6)); pap. 12.95 (978-1-4218-1889-4(2)) 1st World Publishing, Inc. (1st World Library - Literary Society).

—The Tin Woodman of Oz. 2008. 116p. (gr. 4-7). 22.95 (978-1-60664-947-3(7)); per. 9.95 (978-1-60312-497-3(7)) Aegypan.

—The Tin Woodman of Oz. 2009. 174p. (gr. 4-7). 25.99 (978-1-60512-317-2(X)); pap. 12.99 (978-1-60512-417-9(6)) Akasha Publishing, LLC. (Akasha Classics).

—The Tin Woodman of Oz. (J). 20.95 (978-0-8488-0709-2(X)) Amereon Ltd.

—The Tin Woodman of Oz. 2008. 160p. 22.99 (978-0-554-37655-4(5)) 2008. 160p. 25.99 (978-0-554-28352-4(2)) 2007. (ENG.). 142p. pap. 18.99 (978-1-4346-5199-0(1)) 2007. (ENG.). 156p. pap. 21.99 (978-1-4346-5200-3(9)) Creative Media Partners, LLC.

—The Tin Woodman of Oz. 2005. pap. (978-1-4065-0079-0(8)) Dodo Pr.

—The Tin Woodman of Oz. l.t. ed. 2005. 256p. pap. (978-1-84637-112-7(0)) Echo Library.

—The Tin Woodman of Oz. (Twelve-Point Ser.). 2003. lib. bdg. 24.00 *(978-1-58287-257-5(0))* 2004. 230p. 25.00 *(978-1-58287-741-9(6))* North Bks.
—The Tin Woodman of Oz. 2009. 136p. pap. 10.95 *(978-1-4385-2196-1(0)*, Book Jungle) Standard Pubns., Inc.
—The Tin Woodman of Oz. 2008. 308p. (gr. 4-7). 32.95 *(978-1-4344-7192-5(6))*; pap. 19.95 *(978-1-4344-7191-8(8))* Wildside Pr., LLC.
—The Treasury of Oz. 2007. 784p. 49.99 *(978-1-60459-028-9(9))* Wilder Pubns., Corp.
—The Tresury of Oz: The Wonderful Wizard of Oz, the Marvelous Land of Oz, Ozma of Oz, Dorothy & the Wizard in Oz, the Road to Oz, the Emerald City Of. 2007. 548p. per. 19.49 *(978-1-60459-029-6(7))* Wilder Pubns., Corp.
—The Wizard of Oz. Evangelista, Mauro, illus. 2007. (Usborne Young Reading: Series Two Ser.). 64p. (J). (gr. 3-7). 8.99 *(978-0-7945-1457-0(X)*, Usborne) EDC Publishing.
—The Wizard of Oz. 2013. (ENG., Illus.). 176p. *(978-1-907360-90-9(5)*, Collector's Library, The) Pan Macmillan.
—The Wizard of Oz. 2012. (Puffin Classics Ser.). (ENG., Illus.). 224p. (J). (gr. 5). 16.99 *(978-0-14-134173-6(4)*, Puffin Books) Penguin Young Readers Group.
—The Wizard of Oz. (SPA.). 256p. (J). 9.95 *(978-84-204-3509-1(0))* Santillana USA Publishing Co., Inc.
—The Wizard of Oz. 2009. (Foundation Classics Ser.). (Illus.). 56p. (J). (gr. 5-9). lib. bdg. 27.95 *(978-1-60754-544-6(6))* Windmill Bks.
—The Wizard of Oz. 2012. (ENG., Illus.). (J). (gr. 4-7). 14.99 ***(978-1-61382-935-6(3))*** Simon & Brown.
—The Wizard of Oz. Zwerger, Lisbeth, illus. 2004. 103p. (J). (gr. 4-8). reprint ed. 20.00 *(978-0-7567-7708-1(9))* DIANE Publishing Co.
—The Wizard of Oz. 2004. reprint ed. pap. 19.95 *(978-1-4191-8832-9(1))* Kessinger Publishing, LLC.
—The Wizard of Oz: And Other Wonderful Books of Oz - The Emerald City of Oz & Glinda of Oz. Sumpter, Rachell, illus. deluxe ed. 2012. (Penguin Classics Deluxe Edition Ser.). (ENG.). 432p. (gr. 5). pap. 17.00 *(978-0-14-310663-0(5)*, Penguin Classics) Penguin Publishing Group.
—The Wizard of Oz Book & Charm. deluxe ed. 2005. (Charming Classics). 208p. (J). 9.99 *(978-0-06-075772-4(8)*, HarperFestival) HarperCollins Pubs.
—A Wonderful Welcome to Oz: The Marvelous Land of Oz, Ozma of Oz, & the Emerald City of Oz. Maguire, Gregory, ed. Neill, John R., illus. 2006. (Modern Library Classics Ser.). (ENG.). 624p. per. 17.00 *(978-0-8129-7494-2(8)*, Modern Library) Random House Publishing Group.
—The Wonderful Wizard of Oz. 180p. 2005. 26.95 *(978-1-4218-0652-5(5))* 2004. pap. 11.95 *(978-1-59540-102-1(4))* 1st World Publishing, Inc. (1st World Library - Literary Society).
—The Wonderful Wizard of Oz. (Oz Ser.). (YA). (gr. 5-8). 20.95 *(978-0-88411-772-8(3))* Amereon Ltd.
—The Wonderful Wizard of Oz. 2014. (ENG., Illus.). 167p. 17.50 *(978-1-78270-042-5(0))* Award Pubns. Ltd. GBR. Dist: Parkwest Pubns., Inc.
—The Wonderful Wizard of Oz. 2007. (ENG.). 134p. pap. 19.99 *(978-1-4264-4884-3(8))*; 374p. pap. 18.99 *(978-1-4264-4841-6(4))* Creative Media Partners, LLC.
—The Wonderful Wizard of Oz. Denslow, W. W., illus. 2015. (Dover Children's Classics Ser.). (ENG.). 308p. (J). (gr. 3-6). reprint ed. pap. 14.99 *(978-0-486-20691-2(2))* Dover Pubns., Inc.
—The Wonderful Wizard of Oz. 2003. (Modern Library Classics Ser.). (ENG., Illus.). 224p. pap. 15.00 *(978-0-8129-7011-1(X)*, Modern Library) Random House Publishing Group.
—The Wonderful Wizard of Oz. (ENG., Illus.). (J). (gr. 1-7). 2012. 14.99 ***(978-1-61382-939-4(6))*** 2011. 14.99 ***(978-1-61382-942-4(6))*** Simon & Brown.
—The Wonderful Wizard of Oz. Baum, L. Frank & McKowen, Scott, illus. 2005. (Sterling Unabridged Classics Ser.). (ENG.). 176p. (J). (gr. 5). 9.95 *(978-1-4027-2504-3(3))* Sterling Publishing Co., Inc.
—The Wonderful Wizard of Oz: A Classic Story about Cooperation. 2003. (Illus.). 32p. per. 3.95 *(978-0-9747133-5-9(X)*, Values to Live By Classic Stories) Thomas, Frederic Inc.
—The Wonderful Wizard of Oz: The Marvelous Land of Oz - Ozma of Oz. 2013. (Oz, the Complete Collection). (ENG.). 3200p. (J). (gr. 3-7). pap. 54.99 *(978-1-4424-8902-8(2)*, Aladdin) Simon & Schuster Children's Publishing.
—7 Books In: L. Frank Baum's Original Oz Series, Volume 1 of 2. the Wonderful Wizard of Oz, the Marvelous Land of Oz, Ozma of Oz, Dorothy & the W. 2008. 820p. *(978-1-905921-02-7(0))* Shoes & Ships & Sealing Wax Ltd.
—7 Books In: L. Frank Baum's Oz Series, volume 1 of 2. the Wonderful Wizard of Oz, the Marvelous Land of Oz, Ozma of Oz, Dorothy & the Wizard In. 2008. 824p. pap. *(978-1-905921-01-0(2))* Shoes & Ships & Sealing Wax Ltd.
—8 Books In: L. Frank Baum's Original Oz Series, volume 2 of 2. Little Wizard Stories of Oz, Tik-Tok of Oz, the Scarecrow of Oz, Rinkitink in Oz, T. 2008. 764p. *(978-1-905921-03-4(9))* Shoes & Ships & Sealing Wax Ltd.
Baum, L. Frank, told to. The Emerald City of Oz. l.t. ed. 2004. (Large Print Ser.). 285p. 25.00 *(978-1-58287-738-9(6))* North Bks.
Baum, L. Frank & Denslow, W. W. The Wonderful Wizard of Oz. 2012. (Illus.). 232p. *(978-1-4351-3973-2(9))* Barnes & Noble, Inc.
Baum, L. Frank & Neill, John R., illus. The Emerald City of Oz: Novels 6 Through 10 of the Oz Series. 2014. viii, 791p. (J). ***(978-1-4351-5615-9(3))*** Barnes & Noble, Inc.
Baum, L. Frank & Thompson, Ruth Plumly. Oz - The Complete Collection Vol. 5: The Magic of Oz; Glinda of Oz; The Royal Book of Oz. 2013. (Oz, the Complete Collection: 5). (ENG.). 576p. (J). (gr. 3-7). 19.99 *(978-1-4424-8894-6(8)*, Aladdin) Simon & Schuster Children's Publishing.
—The Magic of Oz; Glinda of Oz; the Royal Book of Oz. 2013. (Oz, the Complete Collection: 5). (ENG.). 576p. (J). (gr. 3-7). pap. 12.99 *(978-1-4424-8551-8(5)*, Aladdin) Simon & Schuster Children's Publishing.
Baum, L. Frank & Zwerger, Lisbeth. The Wizard of Oz. 2011. (ENG., Illus.). 160p. (J). (gr. 4-3). 22.95 *(978-0-7358-4042-3(3))* North-South Bks., Inc.
Baum, Roger S. The Lion of Oz & the Badge of Courage. Coons, Dean, illus. 2nd ed. 2003. 247p. (J). 24.95 *(978-1-57072-255-4(2))* Overmountain Pr.
—The Oz Odyssey. Seitzinger, Victoria, illus. 2006. 176p. (J). 19.95 *(978-1-57072-299-8(4))* Overmountain Pr.
—Toto of Oz & the Surprise Party. Seitzinger, Victoria, illus. 2004. (ENG.). 32p. (J). 13.95 *(978-1-57072-284-4(6)*, 1233723) Overmountain Pr.
Blossom, Maggie. Wizard of Oz. Pearse, Asha, illus. 2014. (ENG.). 16p. (J). (gr. -1-4). 7.99 *(978-1-4867-0009-7(8))* Flowerpot Children's Pr. Inc. CAN. Dist: Cardinal Pubs. Group.
Bracken, Beth. The Wizard of Oz, 1 vol. 2013. (Wizard of Oz Ser.). (ENG., Illus.). 32p. (gr. k-3). 14.95 *(978-1-62370-026-3(4))* Capstone Young Readers of Coughlan Cos.
Burns, Laura J. Bewitched in Oz, 1 vol. Peters, Liam, illus. 2014. (Bewitched in Oz Ser.). (ENG.). 256p. (gr. 4-8). 12.95 *(978-1-62370-129-1(5))*; lib. bdg. 30.65 *(978-1-4342-9207-0(X))* Stone Arch Bks.
—Magic Below. 2016. (Bewitched in Oz Ser.). (ENG.). 240p. (gr. 4-8). lib. bdg. 30.65 *(978-1-4965-2603-8(1))* Stone Arch Bks.
Conlon, Mara, adapted by. Scratch & Sketch Wizard of Oz: An Art Activity Story Book for Artists on Both Sides of the Rainbow. 2005. (Activity Book Ser.). (Illus.). 64p. (J). 14.99 *(978-1-59359-906-5(4))* Peter Pauper Pr. Inc.
Einhorn, Edward. The Living House of Oz. Shanower, Eric, illus. 2005. 239p. (J). 27.95 *(978-1-929527-08-3(X))* Hungry Tiger Pr.
Evans, Robert J. Dorothy's Mystical Adventures in Oz. 2004. reprint ed. pap. 1.99 *(978-1-4192-1658-9(9))* Kessinger Publishing, LLC.
Gardner, Martin & Nye, Russel B. The Wizard of Oz & Who He Was. 2011. 220p. 44.95 *(978-1-258-00799-7(1))* Literary Licensing, LLC.
Kirshenblatt, Shane. Dorothy Gale - Journey to Oz. 2005. 64p. Vol. 2. 7.99 *(978-1-894998-89-5(8))* Vol. 3. 7.99 *(978-1-894998-90-1(1))* Lake, Jack Productions, Inc. CAN. Dist: Hushion Hse. Publishing, Ltd.
Landes, William-Alan & Standish, Marilyn. The Wizard of Oz. rev. ed. 2003. (Wondrawhopper Ser.). 40p. (J). (gr. 3-12). pap. 6.00 *(978-0-88734-105-2(5))* Players Pr., Inc.
Martin, Dick. The Ozmapolitan of Oz. 2006. (J). 24.95 *(978-1-930764-11-8(1))* International Wizard of Oz Club, The.
McGraw, Eloise Jarvis & McGraw, Lauren Lynn. The Forbidden Fountain of Oz. 2006. (J). 24.95 *(978-1-930764-12-5(X))* International Wizard of Oz Club, The.
Michiko Florence, Debbi. Dorothy & Toto. Roe, Monika, illus. 2016. (Dorothy & Toto Ser.). (ENG.). 40p. (gr. k-2). 85.28 *(978-1-4795-8714-8(1))* Capstone Press of Coughlan Cos.
Mula, Tom. The Hackers of Oz. 2012. 272p. (-18). 21.95 *(978-1-4575-1562-0(8))*; pap. 14.99 *(978-1-4575-1564-4(4))* Dog Ear Publishing, LLC.
Paige, Danielle. Dorothy Must Die. (Dorothy Must Die Ser.: 1). (ENG.). (gr. 9). 2015. 480p. (J). pap. 9.99 *(978-0-06-228068-8(6))* 2014. 464p. (YA). 17.99 *(978-0-06-228067-1(8)*, HarperTeen) HarperCollins Pubs.
—Dorothy Must Die. 2015. (Dorothy Must Die Ser.: 1). (YA). lib. bdg. 20.85 *(978-0-606-36510-9(9))* Turtleback Bks.
—Dorothy Must Die 2-Book Box Set: Dorothy Must Die, the Wicked Will Rise. 2016. (Dorothy Must Die Ser.). 800p. (YA). (gr. 9). pap. 19.98 *(978-0-06-256982-0(1))* HarperCollins Pubs.
—Dorothy Must Die Stories: No Place Like Oz - The Witch Must Burn; the Wizard Returns. 2015. (Dorothy Must Die Novella Ser.). (ENG., Illus.). 416p. (YA). (gr. 9). pap. 9.99 *(978-0-06-228079-4(1))* HarperCollins Pubs.
—Dorothy Must Die Stories: No Place Like Oz, the Witch Must Burn, the Wizard Returns. 2015. (Dorothy Must Die Ser.). (YA). lib. bdg. 20.85 *(978-0-606-37248-0(2))* Turtleback Bks.
—Dorothy Must Die Stories Volume 2. 2016. (Dorothy Must Die Novella Ser.). 336p. (YA). (gr. 9). pap. 9.99 *(978-0-06-240397-1(4))* HarperCollins Pubs.
—The End of Oz. 2017. (Dorothy Must Die Ser.: 4). 304p. (YA). (gr. 9). 18.99 *(978-0-06-242377-1(0))* HarperCollins Pubs.
—The Wicked Will Rise. (Dorothy Must Die Ser.: 2). (YA). (gr. 9). 2016. 320p. pap. 9.99 *(978-0-06-228071-8(6))* 2015. (ENG.). 304p. 17.99 *(978-0-06-228070-1(8))* HarperCollins Pubs.
—The Wicked Will Rise. 2016. (Dorothy Must Die Ser.: 2). (YA). lib. bdg. 20.85 *(978-0-606-38170-3(8))* Turtleback Bks.
—Yellow Brick War. 2016. *(978-0-06-245860-5(4))*; (Dorothy Must Die Ser.: 3). (ENG.). 288p. (YA). (gr. 9-12). 18.99 *(978-0-06-228073-2(2))* HarperCollins Pubs.
Price, Nick, illus. The Wonderful Wizard of Oz. 2009. (ENG.). 12p. (J). 8.95 *(978-1-58117-856-2(5)*, Intervisual/Piggy Toes) Bendon, Inc.
Rayburn, Tricia. Ruby's Slippers. 2010. (ENG.). 352p. (J). (gr. 4-8). pap. 7.99 *(978-1-4169-8701-7(0)*, Aladdin) Simon & Schuster Children's Publishing.
Ridley, R. W. Banshee Worm King. 2012. 242p. pap. 9.99 *(978-0-9792067-5-7(8))* Middlebury Hse. Publishing.
Robertson, Barny & Smith, Jeff. Pirates of the "I Don't Care" -Ibbean: A Kids' Musical about Storing up Treasures in Heaven. 2007. (ENG.). 104p. pap. 7.99 *(978-0-8341-7595-2(9)*, 0834175959) Lillenas Publishing Co.
Robinson, Robin, illus. L. Frank Baum's Wizard of Oz. 2013. (Penguin Young Readers, Level 4 Ser.). (ENG.). 48p. (J). (gr. 3-4). mass mkt. 3.99 *(978-0-448-45588-4(9)*, Penguin Young Readers) Penguin Young Readers Group.
Santore, Charles, illus. The Wizard of Oz Coloring Book. 2017. (ENG.). 96p. (J). pap. 10.99 ***(978-1-60433-706-8(0)***, Applesauce Pr.) Cider Mill Pr. Bk. Pubs., LLC.
Shanower, Eric. Adventures in Oz. Shanower, Eric, illus. 2007. (Illus.). 256p. (J). (gr. 5-7). 75.00 *(978-1-60010-071-0(6))* Idea & Design Works, LLC.
—Adventures in Oz Volume 1. 2014. (Adventures in Oz Ser.). (ENG., Illus.). 160p. (J). (gr. 2-5). 34.99 *(978-1-63140-150-3(5)*, 9781631401503) Idea & Design Works, LLC.
—Marvelous Land of Oz: Vol. 1, 1 vol. 2014. (ENG.). 24p. 24.21 *(978-1-61479-235-2(6))* ABDO Publishing Co.
—Marvelous Land of Oz: Vol. 2, 1 vol. 2014. (ENG.). 24p. 24.21 *(978-1-61479-236-9(4))* ABDO Publishing Co.
—Marvelous Land of Oz: Vol. 3, 1 vol. 2014. (ENG.). 24p. 24.21 *(978-1-61479-237-6(2))* ABDO Publishing Co.
—Oz: Dorothy & the Wizard in Oz. 2014. (ENG., Illus.). 184p. (J). (gr. -1-17). pap. 19.99 *(978-0-7851-9114-8(3))* Marvel Worldwide, Inc.
—Oz: The Emerald City of Oz. 2014. (ENG., Illus.). 120p. (J). (gr. -1-17). 24.99 *(978-0-7851-8388-4(4))* Marvel Worldwide, Inc.
—The Salt Sorcerer of Oz & Other Stories. Shanower, Eric, illus. 2003. (Oz Ser.). (Illus.). 288p. (J). 24.95 *(978-1-929527-06-9(3))* Hungry Tiger Pr.
Shanower, Eric & Baum, L. Frank. The Marvelous Land of Oz: Adapted from the Novel by L. Frank Baum, 1 vol. Young, Skottie, illus. 2014. (ENG.). 24p. (J). *(978-1-61479-238-3(0))* Spotlight.
—The Wonderful Wizard of Oz, 1 vol. Young, Skottie, illus. 2014. (ENG.). 24p. (J). *(978-1-61479-229-1(1))* Spotlight.
Smith, Sherwood. The Emerald Wand of Oz. Stout, William, illus. 2007. 262p. (J). 17.00 *(978-1-4223-6710-0(X))* DIANE Publishing Co.
—The Emerald Wand of Oz. Stout, William, illus. 2005. (ENG.). 272p. (J). (gr. -1-17). 16.99 *(978-0-06-029607-0(0))* HarperCollins Pubs.
Stine, R. L. Lizard of Oz. 2016. (Goosebumps: Most Wanted Ser.: 10). (ENG.). 160p. (J). (gr. 3-7). pap. 6.99 *(978-0-545-82549-8(0)*, Scholastic Paperbacks) Scholastic, Inc.
—Lizard of Oz. 2016. (Goosebumps Most Wanted Ser.: 10). (ENG.). 160p. (J). (gr. 3-7). 17.20 *(978-0-606-39142-9(8))* Turtleback Bks.
Sundstrom, Dainel H. The Return of Oz. 2007. pap. 10.00 *(978-0-8059-8944-1(7))* Dorrance Publishing Co., Inc.
Thompson, Ruth Plumly. The Enchanted Island of Oz. 2006. (J). 24.95 *(978-1-930764-10-1(3))* International Wizard of Oz Club, The.
—The Royal Book of Oz. 2004. reprint ed. pap. 1.99 *(978-1-4192-8123-5(2))*; pap. 20.95 *(978-1-4191-8123-8(8))* Kessinger Publishing, LLC.
—The Wonder Book. 2006. (J). 24.95 *(978-1-930764-15-6(4))* International Wizard of Oz Club, The.
—Yankee in Oz. 2006. (J). 24.95 *(978-1-930764-13-2(8))* International Wizard of Oz Club, The.
Thompson, Ruth Plumly & Baum, L. Frank. The Silver Princess in Oz. Neill, John R., illus. 2011. 248p. 46.95 *(978-1-258-01166-6(2))* Literary Licensing, LLC.
The Wizard of Oz. 2016. (First Favourite Tales Ser.). (ENG., Illus.). 32p. (J). (gr. -1-k). 7.99 *(978-0-7232-9219-7(1))* Penguin Bks., Ltd. GBR. Dist: Independent Pubs. Group.
The Wizard of OZ. 2008. (Charm Book Classics Ser.). 32p. *(978-1-4075-1582-3(9))* Parragon, Inc.
Young, Skottie, illus. Oz: The Marvelous Land of Oz. 2011. (ENG.). 200p. (J). (gr. -1-17). pap. 19.99 *(978-0-7851-4087-0(5))* Marvel Worldwide, Inc.

OZARK MOUNTAINS REGION

Arnold, Jude. The Lipizzan Reunion: A True Story. 2009. 48p. pap. 19.49 *(978-1-4389-7060-8(9))* AuthorHouse.

OZARK MOUNTAINS REGION—FICTION

Ellis, Edward Sylvester & Coghlan, John. The Camp in the Mountains. 2004. (Illus.). 200p. (J). pap. 19.95 *(978-0-9713470-8-3(5))* Phoenix International, Inc.
—The Hunters of the Ozark. 2004. (Illus.). 224p. (J). pap. 19.95 *(978-0-9713470-2-1(6))* Phoenix International, Inc.
Fields, Jan. Hunt the Ozark Howler, 1 vol. Brundage, Scott, illus. 2016. (ENG.). 80p. (J). lib. bdg. *(978-1-62402-152-7(2))* Magic Wagon.
Jones, Don. When the Firewood Comes. 2009. 86p. pap. 19.95 *(978-1-4489-9667-4(8))* America Star Bks.
McDougal-Littell Publishing Staff. Literature Connections English: Where the Red Fern Grows. 2004. (McDougal Littell Literature Connections Ser.). (ENG.). 328p. (gr. 7-7). 16.90 *(978-0-395-77528-8(0)*, 2-80097) Great Source Education Group, Inc.
Rawls, Wilson. Where the Red Fern Grows. 249p. (YA). (gr. 5-18). pap. 5.99 *(978-0-8072-1467-1(1))*; pap. 5.99 *(978-0-8072-1358-2(6))* Random Hse. Audio Publishing Group. (Listening Library).
—Where the Red Fern Grows. l.t. ed. 2005. 376p. pap. 10.95 *(978-0-7862-7312-6(7)*, Large Print Pr.) Thorndike Pr.

P

PACIFIC ISLANDS

see Islands of the Pacific

PACIFIC NORTHWEST

see Northwest, Pacific

PACIFIC OCEAN

Cerullo, Mary M. Journey to Shark Island: A Shark Photographer's Close Encounters, 1 vol. Rotman, Jeffrey L., illus. Rotman, Jeffrey L., photos by. 2014. (Shark Expedition Ser.). (ENG.). 40p. (gr. 5-7). lib. bdg. 31.99 *(978-0-7565-4887-2(X))* Compass Point Bks.
Cerullo, Mary M. & Simmons, Beth E. Sea Secrets. Carlson, Kirsten, illus. 2015. (Long Term Ecological Research Ser.). (ENG.). 32p. (J). (gr. 1-5). pap. 9.95 *(978-1-63076-075-5(7))* Taylor Trade Publishing.
Cooke, Tim. The Exploration of Australasia & the Pacific. 2013. (Explorers Discovering the World Ser.). (Illus.). 48p. (J). (gr. 4-6). 31.95 *(978-1-4339-8619-2(1))*; pap. 14.05 *(978-1-4339-8620-8(5))* Stevens, Gareth Publishing LLLP. (Gareth Stevens Learning Library).
Freed, Kira. The Terrific Pacific. 2017. (Text Connections Guided Close Reading Ser.). (J). (gr. 1). *(978-1-4900-1807-2(7))* Benchmark Education Co.
Gonzales, Doreen. The Huge Pacific Ocean. 2013. (Our Earth's Oceans Ser.). 48p. (J). (gr. 3-4). pap. 8.95 *(978-1-4644-0151-0(9)*, Enslow Elementary); 25.27 *(978-0-7660-4090-8(9))* Enslow Pubs., Inc.
—The Pacific Ocean: A MyReportLinks.com Book. 2004. (Oceans of the World Ser.). (Illus.). 48p. (J). lib. bdg. 26.60 *(978-0-7660-5192-8(7)*, MyReportLinks.com Bks.) Enslow Pubs., Inc.
Green, Jen. Pacific Ocean. 2006. (Oceans & Seas Ser.). (Illus.). 48p. (gr. 5-12). pap. 14.05 *(978-0-8368-6283-6(X))*; lib. bdg. 31.00 *(978-0-8368-6275-1(9))* Stevens, Gareth Publishing LLLP. (Gareth Stevens Secondary Library).
Jeffrey, Gary. War in the Pacific. 2012. (ENG., Illus.). 48p. (J). *(978-0-7787-4197-8(4))*; pap. *(978-0-7787-4204-3(0))* Crabtree Publishing Co.
Kopp, Megan. Pacific Ocean. 2016. (J). *(978-1-4896-4739-9(2))* Weigl Pubs., Inc.
Mara, Wil. The Four Oceans. 2005. (Rookie Read-About Geography Ser.). (ENG., Illus.). 32p. (J). (gr. 1-2). per. 5.95 *(978-0-516-25817-1(6)*, Children's Pr.) Scholastic Library Publishing.
Nagelhout, Ryan. Vasco Núñez de Balboa. 2016. (Spotlight on Explorers & Colonization Ser.). 48p. (J). (gr. 6-6). pap. 11.75 *(978-1-4777-8828-8(X))* Rosen Publishing Group, Inc., The.
Oachs, Emily Rose. Pacific Ocean. 2016. (Discover the Oceans Ser.). (ENG., Illus.). 24p. (J). (gr. k-3). lib. bdg. 25.95 *(978-1-62617-333-0(8)*, Blastoff! Readers) Bellwether Media.
Olson, Tod. Lost in the Pacific, 1942: Not a Drop to Drink. 2016. (Lost Ser.: 1). (ENG., Illus.). 176p. (J). (gr. 4-7). 12.99 *(978-0-545-92811-3(7)*, Scholastic Nonfiction) Scholastic, Inc.
Petrie, Kristin. Vasco Núñez de Balboa, 1 vol. 2007. (Explorers Set 2 Ser.). (ENG., Illus.). 32p. (gr. 4-7). 27.07 *(978-1-59679-740-6(1)*, Checkerboard Library) ABDO Publishing Co.
Ray, Deborah Kogan. The Impossible Voyage of Kon-Tiki. Ray, Deborah Kogan, illus. 2015. (ENG., Illus.). 40p. (J). (gr. 2-5). lib. bdg. 16.95 *(978-1-58089-620-7(0))* Charlesbridge Publishing, Inc.
Sandler, Michael. Oceans: Surviving in the Deep Sea. 2005. (X-treme Places Ser.). (Illus.). 32p. (J). (gr. 2-5). lib. bdg. 25.27 *(978-1-59716-087-2(3))* Bearport Publishing Co., Inc.
Spilsbury, Louise & Spilsbury, Richard. Pacific Ocean. 2015. (Oceans of the World Ser.). (ENG., Illus.). 32p. (gr. 1-3). 27.32 *(978-1-4846-0771-8(6)*, Heinemann First Library) Heinemann-Raintree.
Tarbox, A. D. An Ocean Food Chain: Nature's Bounty. 2015. (Illus.). 80p. (J). *(978-1-60818-541-2(9)*, Creative Education) Creative Co., The.
Webb, Sophie. Far from Shore: Chronicles of an Open Ocean Voyage. 2011. (ENG., Illus.). 80p. (J). (gr. 5-7). 17.99 *(978-0-618-59729-1(8))* Houghton Mifflin Harcourt Publishing Co.
Weintraub, Aileen. The Pacific Ocean: The Largest Ocean. 2009. (Great Record Breakers in Nature Ser.). 24p. (gr. 3-4). 42.50 *(978-1-61513-185-3(X)*, PowerKids Pr.) Rosen Publishing Group, Inc., The.

PACIFIC RAILROADS

Behnke, Alison. A Timeline History of the Transcontinental Railroad. 2015. (ENG., Illus.). 48p. (J). (gr. 5-8). 30.65 *(978-1-4677-8581-5(4))* Lerner Publishing Group.
Caswell, Max. My Life As a Chinese Immigrant. 2017. (My Place in History Ser.). 24p. (J). (gr. 2-3). pap. 8.15 ***(978-1-5382-0293-7(X))*** Stevens, Gareth Publishing LLLP.
Coleman, Wim & Perrin, Pat. The Transcontinental Railroad & the Great Race to Connect the Nation. 2006. (Wild History of the American West Ser.). (Illus.). 128p. (J). (gr. 4-10). lib. bdg. 34.60 *(978-1-59845-014-9(X)*, MyReportLinks.com Bks.) Enslow Pubs., Inc.
Fine, Jil. The Transcontinental Railroad: Tracks Across America. 2005. (High Interest Bks.). (ENG., Illus.). 48p. (J). (gr. 4-7). per. 6.95 *(978-0-516-25098-4(1)*, Children's Pr.) Scholastic Library Publishing.
Gimpel, Diane. The Transcontinental Railroad, 1 vol. 2011. (Essential Events Set 6 Ser.). (ENG., Illus.). 112p. (J). (gr. 6-12). lib. bdg. 35.64 *(978-1-61714-768-5(0))* ABDO Publishing Co.
Halpern, Monica. Building the Transcontinental Railroad. 2007. (Reading Expeditions Ser.). (ENG., Illus.). 40p. (J). pap. 19.95 *(978-0-7922-8690-5(1))* CENGAGE Learning.
—Railroad Fever: Building the Transcontinental Railroad 1830-1870. 2004. (Crossroads America Ser.). (ENG., Illus.). 40p. (J). (gr. 5-9). 12.95 *(978-0-7922-6767-6(2)*, National Geographic Children's Bks.) National Geographic Society.
—Railroad Fever: Building the Transcontinental Railroad, 1830-1870. 2004. (Crossroads America Ser.). (ENG., Illus.). 40p. (J). (gr. 5-9). 21.90 *(978-0-7922-6993-9(4)*, National Geographic Children's Bks.) National Geographic Society.
Kraft, Eric. The Transcontinental Railroad & el ferrocarril Transcontinental: 6 English, 6 Spanish Adaptations. 2011. (ENG & SPA.). (J). 97.00 net. *(978-1-4108-5709-5(3))* Benchmark Education Co.
Lynette, Rachel. The Transcontinental Railroad. 2013. (Pioneer Spirit: the Westward Expansion Ser.). 24p. (J). (gr. 3-6). 22.60 *(978-1-4777-0785-2(9))*; (ENG., Illus.). pap. 8.25 *(978-1-4777-0903-0(7))* Rosen Publishing Group, Inc., The. (PowerKids Pr.).
McNeese, Tim. The Transcontinental Railroad & Westward Expansion: Chasing the American Frontier. 2006. (American Saga Ser.). (Illus.). 128p. (J). (gr. 5-9). lib. bdg. 33.27 *(978-0-7660-2572-1(1))* Enslow Pubs., Inc.
Nardo, Don. The Golden Spike: How a Photograph Celebrated a Connected Continent. 2015. (Captured History Ser.). (ENG.). 64p. (gr. 5-7). lib. bdg. 34.65 *(978-0-7565-4991-6(4))* Compass Point Bks.
Olson, Nathan. The Building of the Transcontinental Railroad, 1 vol. Dominguez, Richard et al, illus. 2006. (Graphic History Ser.). (ENG.). 32p. (gr. 3-4). 30.65 *(978-0-7368-6490-9(3)*, Graphic Library) Capstone Press of Coughlan Cos.
Otfinoski, Steven. Building the Transcontinental Railroad: An Interactive Engineering Adventure, 1 vol. 2014. (You Choose: Engineering Marvels Ser.). (ENG.). 112p. (gr. 3-4). 31.99 *(978-1-4914-0401-0(9)*, You Choose Bks.) Capstone Press of Coughlan Cos.
Perritano, John. The Transcontinental Railroad. 2010. 48p. (J). pap. 6.95 *(978-0-531-21248-6(3)*, Children's Pr.); (ENG.). (gr. 2-5). 29.00 *(978-0-531-20585-3(1))* Scholastic Library Publishing.
Rajczak, Michael. The Transcontinental Railroad, Vol. 1. 2014. (What You Didn't Know about History Ser.). (ENG., Illus.).

PQR

24p. (J). (gr. 2-3). 22.60 *(978-1-4824-0600-9(4))* Stevens, Gareth Publishing LLLP.

Redmond, Shirley Raye. Blind Tom: The Horse Who Helped Build the Great Railroad. Bradley, Lois, illus. 2009. (J). pap. 10.00 *(978-0-87842-558-7(6))* Mountain Pr. Publishing Co., Inc.

Roberts, Russell. The Railroad Fuels Westward Expansion (1870s) 2012. (Illus.). 47p. (J). lib. bdg. 29.95 *(978-1-61228-290-9(3))* Mitchell Lane Pubs., Inc.

Shea, Therese. The Transcontinental Railroad: Using Algebra to Represent Situations & Solve Problems. 2006. (Math Big Bookstm Ser.). (ENG.). 32p. (gr. 6-7). 47.50 *(978-1-4042-6365-9(9))* Rosen Publishing Group, Inc., The.

Stein, R. Conrad. The Incredible Transcontinental Railroad: Stories in American History. 2012. (Stories in American History Ser.). (Illus.). 128p. (J). (gr. 5-18). lib. bdg. 33.27 *(978-0-7660-3956-8(0))* Enslow Pubs., Inc.

The Transcontinental Railroad. 2013. (Pioneer Spirit: the Westward Expansion Ser.). 24p. (J). (gr. 3-6). pap. 49.50 *(978-1-4777-0904-7(5)*, PowerKids Pr.) Rosen Publishing Group, Inc., The.

Uschan, Michael V. The Transcontinental Railroad. 2009. (American History Ser.). pap. 24.10 *(978-1-4205-0303-6(0))*; (ENG.). 128p. (J). (gr. 7-10). 34.80 *(978-1-4205-0105-6(4))* Cengage Gale. (Lucent Bks.).

—The Transcontinental Railroad. 2003. (Landmark Events in American History Ser.). (Illus.). 48p. (J). (gr. 5-12). pap. 14.05 *(978-0-8368-5410-7(1)*, Gareth Stevens Secondary Library) Stevens, Gareth Publishing LLLP.

PACIFIC STATES

Here are entered works discussing collectively the states of California, Oregon, and Washington.

Bartley, Niccole. The West Coast. 2014. (Land That I Love: Regions of the United States Ser.). (Illus.). 32p. (J). (gr. 3-6). pap. 60.00 *(978-1-4777-6633-0(2)*, PowerKids Pr.) Rosen Publishing Group, Inc., The.

Connors, Kathleen. Let's Explore the Pacific Northwest. 2013. (Road Trip: Exploring America's Regions Ser.). 24p. (J). (gr. 2-5). pap. 8.15 *(978-1-4339-9140-0(3))*; (ENG., Illus.). lib. bdg. 22.60 *(978-1-4339-9139-4(X))* Stevens, Gareth Publishing LLLP.

Let's Explore the Pacific Northwest. 2013. (Road Trip: Exploring America's Regions Ser.). 24p. (J). (gr. 2-5). pap. 48.90 *(978-1-4339-9141-7(1))* Stevens, Gareth Publishing LLLP.

PACKAGING

Blaxland, Wendy. Cans. 2009. (How Are They Made? 2 Ser.). 32p. (gr. 4). lib. bdg. 18.56 *(978-0-7614-4753-5(9))* Marshall Cavendish Corp.

Chapman, Gillian & Robson, Pam. Making Art with Packaging. 2007. (Everyday Art Ser.). (Illus.). 32p. (YA). (gr. 4-7). lib. bdg. 26.50 *(978-1-4042-3724-7(0))* Rosen Publishing Group, Inc., The.

Walker, Kate. Metal Cans. 2010. (Recycling Ser.). (Illus.). 32p. (J). (gr. 1). 28.50 *(978-1-60870-131-5(X))* Marshall Cavendish Corp.

PACKAGING—FICTION

Rice, Franny L. Zip-Lock Zack. 2011. 28p. (gr. 1-2). 12.03 *(978-1-4567-1607-3(7))* AuthorHouse.

Santillo, LuAnn. Packing. Santillo, LuAnn, ed. 2003. (Half-Pint Kids Readers Ser.). (Illus.). 7p. (J). (gr. -1-1). pap. 1.00 *(978-1-59256-072-1(5))* Half-Pint Kids, Inc.

PACKING INDUSTRY

see Meat Industry and Trade

PADDINGTON BEAR (FICTITIOUS CHARACTER)—FICTION

Bond, Michael. Love from Paddington. Fortnum, Peggy & Alley, R. W., illus. (Paddington Ser.). 144p. (J). (gr. 3-7). 2016. pap. 5.99 *(978-0-06-242526-3(9))* 2014. (ENG.). 9.99 *(978-0-06-236816-4(8))* HarperCollins Pubs.

—More about Paddington. Fortnum, Peggy, illus. 2015. (Paddington Ser.). 176p. (J). (gr. 3-7). 9.99 *(978-0-06-231220-4(0))* HarperCollins Pubs.

—Paddington. Alley, R. W., illus. 2007. (Paddington Ser.). (ENG.). 32p. (J). (gr. -1-3). 17.99 *(978-0-06-117074-4(7))* HarperCollins Pubs.

—Paddington & the Christmas Surprise. Alley, R. W., illus. (Paddington Ser.). (ENG.). 32p. (J). (gr. -1-3). 2015. 17.99 *(978-0-06-231842-8(X))* 2008. 16.99 *(978-0-06-168740-2(5))* HarperCollins Pubs.

—Paddington at Large. Fortnum, Peggy, illus. 2016. (Paddington Ser.). 176p. (J). (gr. 3-7). 9.99 *(978-0-06-231224-2(3))* HarperCollins Pubs.

—Paddington at the Circus. Alley, R. W., illus. 2016. (Paddington Ser.). 32p. (J). (gr. -1-3). 17.99 *(978-0-06-231843-5(8))* HarperCollins Pubs.

—Paddington at Work. Fortnum, Peggy, illus. 2017. (Paddington Ser.). 176p. (J). (gr. 3-7). 9.99 *(978-0-06-231226-6(X))* HarperCollins Pubs.

—Paddington Bear All Day. braille ed. 2004. (Illus.). (J). (gr. 1). spiral bd., bds. *(978-0-616-01860-6(6))* Canadian National Institute for the Blind/Institut National Canadien pour les Aveugles.

—Paddington Bear All Day. Alley, R. W., illus. 2004. 12p. (J). *(978-1-85269-456-2(4))*; *(978-1-85269-442-5(4))*; *(978-1-85269-443-2(2))*; *(978-1-85269-444-9(0))*; *(978-1-85269-445-6(9))* Mantra Lingua.

—Paddington Bear Goes to Market. Alley, R. W., illus. 2004. 12p. (J). *(978-1-85269-451-7(3))*; *(978-1-85269-455-5(6))* Mantra Lingua.

—Paddington Helps Out. Fortnum, Peggy, illus. 2015. (Paddington Ser.). 160p. (J). (gr. 3-7). 9.99 *(978-0-06-231230-3(8))* HarperCollins Pubs.

—Paddington Here & Now. Alley, R. W., illus. 176p. (J). 2009. pap. 5.99 *(978-0-06-147366-1(9))* 2008. (ENG.). (gr. 3-7). 15.99 *(978-0-06-147364-7(2))* HarperCollins Pubs.

—Paddington Marches On. Fortnum, Peggy, illus. 2016. (Paddington Ser.). 176p. (J). (gr. 3-7). 9.99 *(978-0-06-231232-7(4))* HarperCollins Pubs.

—Paddington Takes the Test. Fortnum, Peggy, illus. 2016. (Paddington Ser.). 176p. (J). (gr. 3-7). 9.99 *(978-0-06-231240-2(5))* HarperCollins Pubs.

—The Paddington Treasury. Alley, R. W., illus. 2014. (Paddington Ser.). (ENG.). 160p. (J). (gr. -1-3). 21.99 *(978-0-06-231242-6(1))* HarperCollins Pubs.

—Paddington's Day Off. Alley, R. W., illus. 2017. (I Can Read Level 1 Ser.). 32p. (J). (gr. -1-3). pap. 3.99 *(978-0-06-243073-1(4))* HarperCollins Pubs.

—Paddington's Finest Hour. Fortnum, Peggy & Alley, R. W., illus. 2017. (Paddington Ser.). 144p. (J). (gr. 3-7). 9.99 ***(978-0-06-266972-8(9))*** HarperCollins Pubs.

Bond, Michael. Paddington's Prize Picture. Alley, R. W., illus. 2017. (I Can Read Level 1 Ser.). 32p. (J). (gr. -1-3). pap. 3.99 *(978-0-06-243076-2(9))* HarperCollins Pubs.

Collins, Harper & Harper Collins / LeapFrog. Paddington Bear. 2008. (J). 11.99 *(978-1-59319-989-0(9))* LeapFrog Enterprises, Inc.

HarperCollins Publishers Ltd. Staff & Auerbach, Annie. Paddington: Paddington's Adventures. 2014. (I Can Read Level 1 Ser.). (ENG., Illus.). 32p. (J). (gr. -1-3). pap. 3.99 *(978-0-06-235001-5(3))* HarperCollins Pubs.

—Paddington - Meet Paddington. 2014. (I Can Read Level 1 Ser.). (ENG., Illus.). 32p. (J). (gr. -1-3). pap. 3.99 *(978-0-06-234999-6(6))* HarperCollins Pubs.

HarperCollins Publishers Ltd. Staff, et al. Paddington: Paddington's World. 2014. (Paddington Ser.). (ENG., Illus.). 24p. (J). (gr. -1-3). pap. 3.99 *(978-0-06-234997-2(X))* HarperCollins Pubs.

PADEREWSKI, IGNACE JAN, 1860-1941

Roberto, Brother. Music for Millions: A Story of Ignace Paderewski. Jagodits, Carolyn Lee, illus. 2011. 94p. 38.95 *(978-1-258-09336-5(7))* Literary Licensing, LLC.

PAGANINI, NICOLO, 1782-1840

Frisch, Aaron. Dark Fiddler: The Life & Legend of Nicolo Paganini. Kelley, Gary, illus. 2008. (ENG.). 32p. (J). (gr. 1-3). 17.95 *(978-1-56846-200-4(X)*, Creative Editions) Creative Co., The.

PAIGE, SATCHEL, 1906-1982

Cline-Ransome, Lesa. Satchel Paige. Ransome, James E., illus. 2004. 31p. (J). (gr. k-4). reprint ed. pap. 7.00 *(978-0-7567-7799-9(2))* DIANE Publishing Co.

—Satchel Paige. Ransome, James E., illus. 2003. (ENG.). 40p. (J). (gr. 1-5). 8.99 *(978-0-689-85681-5(4)*, Simon & Schuster/Paula Wiseman Bks.) Simon & Schuster/Paula Wiseman Bks.

Frystak, Timothy D. Jackie Robinson: With Profiles of Satchel Paige & & Branch Rickey. 2006. (Biographical Connections Ser.). (Illus.). 112p. (J). *(978-0-7166-1828-7(1))* World Bk., Inc.

Skead, Robert. Something to Prove: Rookie Joe Dimaggio vs. the Great Satchel Paige. Cooper, Floyd, illus. 2013. (ENG.). 32p. (J). (gr. 2-5). lib. bdg. 16.95 *(978-0-7613-6619-5(9)*, Carolrhoda Bks.) Lerner Publishing Group.

PAINE, THOMAS, 1737-1809

Aldritt, Jeremy. Thomas Paine & the Power of Common Sense. 2015. (Spotlight on American History Ser.). (ENG., Illus.). 24p. (J). (gr. 4-6). pap. 10.00 *(978-1-4994-1765-4(9)*, PowerKids Pr.) Rosen Publishing Group, Inc., The.

Crompton, Samuel Willard. Thomas Paine: Fighting for American Independence. 2017. (Rebels with a Cause Ser.). 128p. (gr. 8-8). lib. bdg. 37.27 ***(978-0-7660-8515-2(5))*** Enslow Pubs., Inc.

Crompton, Samuel Willard. Thomas Paine & the Fight for Liberty. 2005. (Leaders of the American Revolution Ser.). (Illus.). 100p. (J). (gr. 5-8). lib. bdg. 30.00 *(978-0-7910-8625-4(9))* Facts On File, Inc.

Jeffrey, Gary. Thomas Paine Writes Common Sense. 2011. (Graphic Heroes of the American Revolution Ser.). 24p. (gr. 3-6). (YA). lib. bdg. 23.95 *(978-1-4339-6028-4(1))*; (J). pap. 8.15 *(978-1-4339-6029-1(X)*, Gareth Stevens Learning Library) Stevens, Gareth Publishing LLLP.

Marrin, Albert. Thomas Paine: Crusader for Liberty: an Adventure in the History of Ideas. 2014. (ENG., Illus.). 176p. (YA). (gr. 7). lib. bdg. 20.99 *(978-0-375-96674-3(9)*, Knopf Bks. for Young Readers) Random Hse. Children's Bks.

—Thomas Paine: Crusader for Liberty: How One Man's Ideas Helped Form a New Nation. (ENG.). (YA). (gr. 7). 2016. 144p. pap. 15.99 *(978-0-375-85969-4(1)*, Ember) 2014. (Illus.). 176p. 17.99 *(978-0-375-86674-6(4)*, Knopf Bks. for Young Readers) Random Hse. Children's Bks.

Marsh, Carole. Thomas Paine. 2004. 12p. (gr. k-4). 2.95 *(978-0-635-02369-8(5))* Gallopade International.

McCartin, Brain. Thomas Paine: "Common Sense" & Revolutionary Pamphleteering. 2005. (Library of American Lives & Times). (Illus.). 112p. (J). (gr. 4-8). lib. bdg. 34.60 *(978-0-8239-5729-3(2))* Rosen Publishing Group, Inc., The.

McCartin, Brian. Thomas Paine: Common Sense, & Revolutionary Pamphleteering. 2009. (Library of American Lives & Times Ser.). 112p. (gr. 5-5). 69.20 *(978-1-60853-509-5(6))* Rosen Publishing Group, Inc., The.

Nagelhout, Ryan. Thomas Paine's Common Sense. 2013. 32p. (J). (gr. 4-6). 26.60 *(978-1-4339-9013-7(X))*; pap. 10.50 *(978-1-4339-9014-4(8))* Stevens, Gareth Publishing LLLP.

Rauf, Don. Thomas Paine: Author of Common Sense. 2017. (J). ***(978-1-5383-8100-7(1))***; pap. ***(978-1-5383-8097-0(8))*** Rosen Publishing Group, Inc., The.

Thomas Paine's Common Sense. 2013. (Documents That Shaped America Ser.). 32p. (J). (gr. 4-6). pap. 63.00 *(978-1-4339-9015-1(6))* Stevens, Gareth Publishing LLLP.

Waxman, Laura Hamilton. An Uncommon Revolutionary: A Story about Thomas Paine. Orback, Craig, illus. 2003. (Creative Minds Biography Ser.). (J). pap. 5.95 *(978-1-57505-608-1(9))*; (ENG.). 64p. (gr. 4-8). 22.60 *(978-1-57505-180-2(X))* Lerner Publishing Group. (Carolrhoda Bks.).

PAINTED GLASS

see Glass Painting and Staining

PAINTERS

see also Artists

also names of individual painters

Alvarez, Mateo. Diego Rivera: Famous Mexican Painter. 2015. (Exceptional Latinos Ser.). (ENG.). 24p. (J). (gr. 3-4). pap. 9.35 *(978-0-7660-6702-8(5))* Enslow Pubs., Inc.

Bacon, Dolores. Pictures Every Child Should Know (Illust. 2006. pap. *(978-1-4065-0424-8(6))* Dodo Pr.

Bankston, John. Diego Rivera. 2003. (Latinos in American History Ser.). (Illus.). 56p. (J). (gr. 4-8). lib. bdg. 29.95 *(978-1-58415-208-8(7))* Mitchell Lane Pubs., Inc.

Bassil, Andrea & van Gogh, Vincent. Vincent Van Gogh. 2004. (Lives of the Artists Ser.). (Illus.). 48p. (gr. 5-12). lib. bdg. 31.00 *(978-0-8368-5602-6(3)*, Gareth Stevens Secondary Library) Stevens, Gareth Publishing LLLP.

—Vincent van Gogh. 2004. (Lives of the Artists Ser.). (Illus.). 48p. (gr. 5-12). pap. 14.05 *(978-0-8368-5607-1(4)*, Gareth Stevens Secondary Library) Stevens, Gareth Publishing LLLP.

Bernier-Grand, Carmen. Diego: Bigger Than Life, 0 vols. Diaz, David, illus. 2009. (ENG.). 64p. (J). (gr. 8-13). 18.99 *(978-0-7614-5383-3(0))*, 9780761453833, Amazon Children's Publishing) Amazon Publishing.

Bodden, Valerie. Vincent Van Gogh. 2016. (Illus.). 80p. (J). *(978-1-60818-721-8(7)*, Creative Education) Creative Co., The.

Bogart, Jo Ellen. Capturing Joy: The Story of Maud Lewis. Lang, Mark, illus. 2011. (ENG.). 32p. (J). (gr. 3-7). pap. 8.95 *(978-1-77049-262-2(3)*, Tundra Bks.) Tundra Bks. CAN. Dist: Penguin Random Hse. LLC.

—Emily Carr: At the Edge of the World. Newhouse, Maxwell, illus. 2003. (ENG.). 40p. (J). (gr. 5-18). 22.95 *(978-0-88776-640-4(4)*, Tundra Bks.) Tundra Bks. CAN. Dist: Penguin Random Hse. LLC.

Bowen, Richard. Vincent Van Gogh: Modern Artist. 2013. (People of Importance Ser.: 21). (Illus.). 32p. (J). (gr. 4-18). 19.95 *(978-1-4222-2858-6(4))* Mason Crest.

Brown, Isobel. Klimt, Vol. 7. 2015. (Great Artists Collection). (Illus.). 64p. (J). (gr. 7). lib. bdg. 23.95 *(978-1-4222-3260-6(3))* Mason Crest.

Brown, Monica. Frida Kahlo & Her Animalitos. Parra, John, illus. 2017. (ENG.). 40p. (J). (gr. -1-3). 17.95 ***(978-0-7358-4269-4(8))*** North-South Bks., Inc.

Collard, Sneed B., III. Jacob Lawrence: A Painter's Story. 2009. (American Heroes Ser.). 48p. (gr. 3-18). 29.93 *(978-0-7614-4058-1(5))* Marshall Cavendish Corp.

Connolly, Sean. Botticelli. 2004. (Lives of the Artists Ser.). (Illus.). 48p. (gr. 5-12). lib. bdg. 31.00 *(978-0-8368-5648-4(1)*, Gareth Stevens Secondary Library) Stevens, Gareth Publishing LLLP.

Crabtree, Marc. Meet My Neighbor, the Artist. 2009. (Meet my Neighbor Ser.). (ENG., Illus.). 24p. (J). (gr. k-2). pap. *(978-0-7787-4579-2(1))*; lib. bdg. *(978-0-7787-4569-3(4))* Crabtree Publishing Co.

Crispino, Enrica. Van Gogh. 2008. (Art Masters Ser.). 64p. (YA). (gr. 6-18). lib. bdg. 24.95 net. *(978-1-934545-05-8(8))* Oliver Pr., Inc.

Debon, Nicolas. Four Pictures by Emily Carr, 1 vol. 2007. (ENG., Illus.). 40p. (J). (gr. 2-7). pap. 6.95 *(978-0-88899-814-9(7))* Groundwood Bks. CAN. Dist: Publishers Group West (PGW).

Devi, Dulari, illus. Following My Paint Brush. 2011. (ENG.). 32p. (J). (gr. 2-18). *(978-93-80340-11-1(7))* Tara Publishing.

Dickens, Rosie. Impressionists. Blackwood, Freyda, illus. 2009. (Young Reading Ser.). 64p. (J). 6.99 *(978-0-7945-2154-7(1)*, Usborne) EDC Publishing.

Fabiny, Sarah. Who Was Frida Kahlo? Hoare, Jerry, illus. 2013. (Who Was? Ser.). (ENG.). 112p. (J). (gr. 3-7). 5.99 *(978-0-448-47938-5(9)*, Grosset & Dunlap) Penguin Young Readers Group.

—Who Was Frida Kahlo? 2013. (Who Was... ? Ser.). lib. bdg. 16.00 *(978-0-606-34164-6(1)*, Turtleback) Turtleback Bks.

Flor Ada, Alma & Campoy, F. Isabel, contrib. by. Pasos. (Literature Collection of Puertas Al Sol Ser.).Tr. of Steps. (SPA.). 32p. (J). (gr. k-6). pap. 13.95 *(978-1-59437-704-4(9))* Santillana USA Publishing Co., Inc.

—Paths. (Literature Collection of Gateways to the Sun Ser.). 48p. (J). (gr. k-6). pap. 16.95 *(978-1-59437-722-8(7))* Santillana USA Publishing Co., Inc.

—Voces. (Literature Collection of Puertas Al Sol Ser.).Tr. of Voices. (SPA.). 32p. (J). (gr. k-6). pap. 13.95 *(978-1-59437-707-5(3))* Santillana USA Publishing Co., Inc.

Guzmán, Lila & Guzmán, Rick. Diego Rivera: Artist of Mexico. 2006. (Famous Latinos Ser.). (Illus.). 32p. (J). (gr. 3-4). lib. bdg. 23.94 *(978-0-7660-2641-4(8)*, Enslow Elementary) Enslow Pubs., Inc.

Guzman, Lila & Guzman, Rick. Frida Kahlo: Painting Her Life. 2006. (Famous Latinos Ser.). (Illus.). 32p. (J). (gr. 3-4). lib. bdg. 22.60 *(978-0-7660-2643-8(4)*, Enslow Elementary) Enslow Pubs., Inc.

Heine, Florian. 13 Painters Children Should Know. 2012. (ENG., Illus.). 48p. (J). (gr. 3-7). 14.95 *(978-3-7913-7086-6(3))* Prestel Verlag GmbH & Co KG. DEU. Dist: Penguin Random Hse. LLC.

Hersey, Bob, illus. Norman Rockwell: A Pop-Up Art Experience. 2004. 6p. (J). (gr. k-4). reprint ed. 19.00 *(978-0-7567-7642-8(2))* DIANE Publishing Co.

Hillstrom, Laurie. Frida Kahlo, Painter. 2008. (Twentieth Century Most Influential Hispanics Ser.). (ENG., Illus.). 96-128p. (YA). (gr. 7-12). 34.80 *(978-1-4205-0019-6(8))* Cengage Gale.

Holzhey, Magdalena. Frida Kahlo: The Artist in the Blue House. 2015. (ENG., Illus.). 32p. (J). (gr. 3-7). pap. 9.95 *(978-3-7913-7229-7(7))* Prestel Verlag GmbH & Co KG. DEU. Dist: Penguin Random Hse. LLC.

January, Brendan. Leonardo Da Vinci: Renaissance Painter. 2013. (People of Importance Ser.: 21). (Illus.). 32p. (J). (gr. 4-18). 19.95 *(978-1-4222-2848-7(7))* Mason Crest.

Kent, Deborah. Frida Kahlo: An Artist Celebrates Life. 2004. (Proud Heritage: the Hispanic Library). (ENG., Illus.). 40p. (J). (gr. 3-6). 29.93 *(978-1-59296-167-2(3)*, 200008) Child's World, Inc., The.

Klein, Adam G. Frida Kahlo, 1 vol. 2007. (Great Artists Set 2 Ser.). (ENG., Illus.). 32p. (gr. -1-3). 27.07 *(978-1-59679-731-4(2)*, Checkerboard Library) ABDO Publishing Co.

—Pieter Bruegel, 1 vol. 2007. (Great Artists Set 2 Ser.). (ENG., Illus.). 32p. (gr. -1-3). 27.07 *(978-1-59679-727-7(4)*, Checkerboard Library) ABDO Publishing Co.

—Raphael, 1 vol. 2007. (Great Artists Set 2 Ser.). (ENG., Illus.). 32p. (gr. -1-3). 27.07 *(978-1-59679-734-5(7)*, Checkerboard Library) ABDO Publishing Co.

Koja, Stephan. Gustav Klimt: A Painted Fairy Tale. 2007. (Adventures in Art Ser.). (Illus.). 28p. (J). (gr. 6-8). 14.95 *(978-3-7913-3704-3(1))* Prestel Publishing.

Kuiper, Kathleen, ed. The 100 Most Influential Painters & Sculptors of the Renaissance. 2009. (Britannica Guide to the World's Most Influential People Ser.). (Illus.). 376p. (YA). (gr. 9-12). lib. bdg. 53.00 *(978-1-61530-004-4(X))* Rosen Publishing Group, Inc., The.

Kuligowski, Stephanie. Leonardo Da Vinci: Renaissance Artist & Inventor, 1 vol. 2012. (Primary Source Readers Ser.). (ENG.). 32p. (J). (gr. 4-4). pap. 8.99 *(978-1-4333-5008-5(4))* Teacher Created Materials, Inc.

La Bella, Laura. Careers in Painting & Wall Covering, 01 vols., 1. 2016. (Essential Careers Ser.). (ENG.). 80p. (J). 34.25 *(978-1-4994-6219-7(0)*, Rosen Young Adult) Rosen Publishing Group, Inc., The.

Landau, Jennifer. Vincent Van Gogh: Master of Post-Impressionist Painting. 2015. (Britannica Beginner Bios Ser.). (ENG., Illus.). 32p. (J). 23.45 *(978-1-62275-946-0(X)*, Britannica Educational Publishing) Rosen Publishing Group, Inc., The.

Larsen, Wayne. A. Y. Jackson: A Love for the Land. 2003. (ENG., Illus.). 192p. pap. 15.95 *(978-1-894852-06-7(0))* Dundurn CAN. Dist: Ingram Publisher Services.

Larsson, Carl. A Family: Paintings from a Bygone Age. 2007. (Illus.). 30p. (J). (gr. 1). *(978-0-86315-583-3(9))* Floris Bks.

Litwin, Laura Baskes. Diego Rivera: Legendary Mexican Painter. 2005. (Latino Biography Library). (Illus.). 128p. (J). (gr. 6-13). lib. bdg. 33.27 *(978-0-7660-2486-1(5))* Enslow Pubs., Inc.

Lossani, Chiara & van Gogh, Vincent. Vincent Van Gogh & the Colors of the Wind. Monaco, Octavia, illus. 2011. (ENG.). 36p. (YA). (gr. 2). 19.00 *(978-0-8028-5390-5(0)*, Eerdmans Bks For Young Readers) Eerdmans, William B. Publishing Co.

Marín, Guadalupe Rivera. My Papá Diego & Me (Mi Papa Diego y Yo) Memories of My Father & His Art (Recuerdos de Mi Padre y Su Arte) Rivera, Diego, illus. 2013. (SPA & ENG.). 32p. (J). (gr. k-5). 18.95 *(978-0-89239-228-5(2))* Lee & Low Bks., Inc.

Marsh, Carole. Diego Rivera: Acclaimed Mural Painter: Acclaimed Mural Painter. 2003. 12p. (gr. k-4). 2.95 *(978-0-635-02137-3(4))* Gallopade International.

Mattern, Joanne. Diego Rivera, 1 vol. 2005. (Great Artists Set 1 Ser.). (ENG., Illus.). 32p. (gr. k-6). 27.07 *(978-1-59197-849-7(1)*, Checkerboard Library) ABDO Publishing Co.

—Jacob Lawrence, 1 vol. 2005. (Great Artists Set 1 Ser.). (ENG., Illus.). 32p. (gr. k-6). 27.07 *(978-1-59197-844-2(0)*, Checkerboard Library) ABDO Publishing Co.

—Sandro Botticelli, 1 vol. 2005. (Great Artists Set 1 Ser.). (ENG., Illus.). 32p. (gr. k-6). 27.07 *(978-1-59197-839-8(4)*, Checkerboard Library) ABDO Publishing Co.

Mecum, Shelly & Chun, Peggy. Watercolor Cat. 2007. 48p. 14.95 *(978-1-56647-838-0(3))* Mutual Publishing LLC.

Medina, Mariana & Wooten, Sara McIntosh. Frida Kahlo: Self-Portrait Artist. 2015. (Influential Latinos Ser.). (ENG., Illus.). 128p. (J). (gr. 7-7). 37.27 *(978-0-7660-6997-8(4))* Enslow Pubs., Inc.

Mes, Yvonne. Meet Sidney Nolan. Eterovic, Sandra, illus. 2016. (Meet... Ser.). (ENG.). 32p. (J). (gr. k-3). 22.99 *(978-0-85798-589-7(2))* Random Hse. Australia AUS. Dist: Independent Pubs. Group.

Mis, Melody S. Vermeer. 2009. (Meet the Artist Ser.). 24p. (gr. 2-3). 42.50 *(978-1-61514-633-8(4)*, PowerKids Pr.) Rosen Publishing Group, Inc., The.

Mofford, Juliet. Raphael. 2009. (Art Profiles for Kids Ser.). (Illus.). 48p. (YA). (gr. 4-7). lib. bdg. 29.95 *(978-1-58415-745-8(3))* Mitchell Lane Pubs., Inc.

Morales, Yuyi. Viva Frida. O'Meara, Tim, photos by. 2014. (ENG., Illus.). 40p. (J). (gr. -1-3). 17.99 *(978-1-59643-603-9(4)*, 9781596436039) Roaring Brook Pr.

Morrison, John. Frida Kahlo. 2nd rev. ed. 2010. (Great Hispanic Heritage Ser.). (Illus.). 128p. (J). (gr. 6-12). 35.00 *(978-1-60413-846-7(7)*, Chelsea Hse.) Facts On File, Inc.

Murray, Stuart A. P. John Trumbull: Painter of the Revolutionary War. 2008. (ENG., Illus.). 83p. (C). (gr. 6-18). lib. bdg. 158.00 *(978-0-7656-8150-8(1)*, Y182501) Routledge.

Nardo, Don, ed. Frida Kahlo. 2012. (Eye on Art Ser.). (ENG., Illus.). 128p. (J). (gr. 7-10). lib. bdg. 34.80 *(978-1-4205-0850-5(4)*, Lucent Bks.) Cengage Gale.

Nelson, Andy. The Renaissance Painters Coloring Book: Donatello, Raphael, Leonardo & Michelangelo. 2nd ed. 2004. (Illus.). 96p. (J). (gr. 1-6). pap. 8.95 *(978-0-929636-27-6(9))* Syren Bk. Co.

Nichols, Catherine. Vincent Van Gogh. 2006. (Primary Source Library of Famous Artists Ser.). (Illus.). 32p. (J). (gr. 3-7). lib. bdg. 23.95 *(978-1-4042-2766-8(0)*, PowerKids Pr.) Rosen Publishing Group, Inc., The.

—Vincent van Gogh. 2009. (Primary Source Library of Famous Artists Ser.). 32p. (gr. 3-4). 42.50 *(978-1-60854-105-8(3)*, PowerKids Pr.) Rosen Publishing Group, Inc., The.

Pezzi, Bryan. Emily Carr. 2010. (Illus.). 24p. *(978-1-77071-599-8(1))*; pap. *(978-1-77071-605-6(X))* Weigl Educational Pubs. Ltd.

Raczka, Bob & Vermeer, Johannes. The Vermeer Interviews: Conversations with Seven Works of Art. 2009. (Bob Raczka's Art Adventures Ser.). (ENG.). 32p. (gr. 3-12). 25.26 *(978-0-8225-9402-4(1)*, Millbrook Pr.) Lerner Publishing Group.

Raynham, Alex. Factfiles Leonardo da Vinci. 3rd ed. 2013. (ENG., Illus.). 64p. pap. 10.00 *(978-0-19-423670-6(6))* Oxford Univ. Pr., Inc.

Reef, Catherine. Frida & Diego: Art, Love, Life. 2014. (ENG., Illus.). 176p. (J). (gr. 7-12). 18.99 *(978-0-547-82184-9(0)*, Clarion Bks.) Houghton Mifflin Harcourt Publishing Co.

Restrepo, Felipe. Francis Bacon -Retrato de una Pesadilla. 2006. (SPA.). 136p. (YA). *(978-958-30-1693-6(4))* Panamericana Editorial.

Rockett, Paul. Pieter Bruegel, 01 vols., 1. 2016. (Inspiring Artists Ser.). (ENG.). 48p. (J). 30.25 *(978-1-5081-7060-0(6)*, Rosen Young Adult) Rosen Publishing Group, Inc., The.

Romeo, Francesca. Leonardo Da Vinci. 2008. (Art Masters Ser.). 64p. (YA). (gr. 6-18). lib. bdg. 24.95 net. *(978-1-934545-00-3(7))* Oliver Pr., Inc.

Rubin, Susan Goldman. Degas & the Dance: The Painter & the Petits Rats, Perfecting Their Art. 2005. (Illus.). 31p. (J). (gr. 4-8). reprint ed. 18.00 *(978-0-7567-9291-6(6))* DIANE Publishing Co.

—Diego Rivera: An Artist for the People. 2013. (ENG., Illus.). 56p. (J). (gr. 3-7). 22.95 *(978-0-8109-8411-0(3)*, Abrams Bks. for Young Readers) Abrams, Inc.

Salvi, Francesco. The Impressionists. 2008. (Art Masters Ser.). 64p. (YA). (gr. 6-18). lib. bdg. 24.95 net. *(978-1-934545-03-4(1))* Oliver Pr., Inc.

Sanchez Vegara, Isabel & Eng, Gee Fan. Frida Kahlo. 2016. (Little People, Big Dreams Ser.). (ENG.). 32p. (J). (gr. k-3). 14.99 *(978-1-84780-783-0(6),* Frances Lincoln Children's Bks.) Quarto Publishing Group UK GBR. Dist: Hachette Bk. Group.

Sanchez Vegara, Isabel & Fan, Eng Gee. Frida Kahlo. 2016. (Little People, Big Dreams Ser.). (ENG., Illus.). 32p. (J). 14.99 *(978-1-84780-770-0(4),* Frances Lincoln Children's Bks.) Quarto Publishing Group UK GBR. Dist: Littlehampton Bk Services, Ltd.

Sherman, Patrice & Wood, Elaine. John James Audubon. 2011. (Conservation Heroes Ser.). (Illus.). 152p. (YA). (gr. 6-12). 35.00 *(978-1-60413-953-2(6),* Chelsea Hse.) Facts On File, Inc.

Shull, Jodie A. Georgia O'Keeffe: Legendary American Painter. 2003. (People to Know Ser.). (Illus.). 112p. (J). lib. bdg. 27.94 *(978-0-7660-2104-4(1))* Enslow Pubs., Inc.

Soni, Jaymee & Schubert, Charles. A Kid at Art - Wassily Kandinsky. 2003. (J). pap. 14.99 *(978-0-9743760-2-8(7))* Little Noggin LLC.

Taylor, Charlotte. Get to Know Georgia O'Keeffe. 2016. (Famous Artists Ser.). (ENG.). 48p. (J). (gr. 3-4). pap. 11.70 *(978-0-7660-7224-4(X))* Enslow Pubs., Inc.

—Get to Know John Singer Sargent. 2016. (Famous Artists Ser.). (ENG., Illus.). 48p. (J). (gr. 3-4). 27.93 *(978-0-7660-7230-5(4))* Enslow Pubs., Inc.

—Get to Know Mary Cassatt. 2016. (Famous Artists Ser.). (ENG., Illus.). 48p. (J). (gr. 3-4). 27.93 *(978-0-7660-7234-3(7))* Enslow Pubs., Inc.

—Get to Know Norman Rockwell. 2016. (Famous Artists Ser.). (ENG., Illus.). 48p. (J). (gr. 3-4). 27.93 *(978-0-7660-7238-1(X))* Enslow Pubs., Inc.

Thomson, Ruth. Vincent Van Gogh, 01 vols., 1. 2016. (Inspiring Artists Ser.). (ENG.). 48p. (J). 30.25 *(978-1-5081-7056-3(8),* Rosen Young Adult) Rosen Publishing Group, Inc., The.

Tonatiuh, Duncan. Diego Rivera: His World & Ours. 2011. (ENG., Illus.). 40p. (J). (gr. 1-4). 17.95 *(978-0-8109-9731-8(2),* Abrams Bks. for Young Readers) Abrams, Inc.

van Gogh, Vincent. Make a Masterpiece — Van Gogh's Starry Night. 2014. (Dover Little Activity Bks.). (ENG.). 4p. (J). (gr. k-3). pap. 1.99 *(978-0-486-78950-7(0))* Dover Pubns., Inc.

—Vincent's Colors. 2005. (ENG., Illus.). 48p. (J). (gr. -1-17). 15.99 *(978-0-8118-5099-5(4))* Chronicle Bks. LLC.

van Gogh, Vincent & Lach, William. Vincent's Colors: Words & Pictures by Van Gogh. 2005. (Illus.). 48p. (J). 14.95 *(978-1-58839-155-1(8))* Metropolitan Museum of Art, The.

Venezia, Mike. Diego Velázquez. Venezia, Mike, illus. 2004. (Getting to Know the World's Greatest Artists Ser.). (ENG., Illus.). 32p. (J). (gr. 3-4). pap. 6.95 *(978-0-516-26980-1(1),* Children's Pr.) Scholastic Library Publishing.

—Frida Kahlo. Venezia, Mike, illus. 2015. (Getting to Know the World's Greatest Artists Ser.). (ENG., Illus.). 40p. (J). lib. bdg. 29.00 *(978-0-531-21259-2(9),* Children's Pr.) Scholastic Library Publishing.

—Georgia O'Keefe. Venezia, Mike, illus. 2015. (Getting to Know the World's Greatest Artists Ser.). (ENG., Illus.). 40p. (J). pap. 7.95 *(978-0-531-21291-2(2))* Scholastic Library Publishing.

—Horace Pippin. Venezia, Mike, illus. 2007. (Getting to Know the World's Greatest Artists Ser.). (ENG., Illus.). 32p. (J). (gr. 3-4). 28.00 *(978-0-531-18527-8(3),* Children's Pr.) Scholastic Library Publishing.

—Jackson Pollock. Venezia, Mike, illus. rev. ed. 2016. (Getting to Know the World's Greatest Artists Ser.). (ENG., Illus.). 40p. (J). pap. 7.95 *(978-0-531-22089-4(3),* Children's Pr.) Scholastic Library Publishing.

—Mary Cassatt. Venezia, Mike, illus. rev. ed. 2015. (Getting to Know the World's Greatest Artists Ser.). (ENG., Illus.). 40p. (J). pap. 7.95 *(978-0-531-21292-9(0))* Scholastic Library Publishing.

—Rembrandt. Venezia, Mike, illus. rev. ed. 2015. (Getting to Know the World's Greatest Artists Ser.). (ENG., Illus.). 40p. (J). pap. 7.95 *(978-0-531-21290-5(4))* Scholastic Library Publishing.

—Sandro Boticelli. Venezia, Mike, illus. rev. ed. 2016. (Getting to Know the World's Greatest Artists Ser.). (ENG., Illus.). 40p. (J). pap. 7.95 *(978-0-531-22086-3(9),* Children's Pr.) Scholastic Library Publishing.

Venezia, Mike & Magritte, Rene. René Magritte. Venezia, Mike, illus. 2003. (Getting to Know the World's Greatest Artists Ser.). (ENG., Illus.). 32p. (J). (gr. 3-4). pap. 6.95 *(978-0-516-27814-8(2),* Children's Pr.) Scholastic Library Publishing.

Wenzel, Angela. 13 Artists Children Should Know. 2009. (ENG., Illus.). 48p. (J). (gr. 3-7). 14.95 *(978-3-7913-4173-6(1))* Prestel Verlag GmbH & Co KG. DEU. Dist: Penguin Random Hse. LLC.

Whiting, Jim. Claude Monet. 2007. (Art Profiles for Kids Ser.). (Illus.). 48p. (YA). (gr. 4-7). lib. bdg. 29.95 *(978-1-58415-563-8(9))* Mitchell Lane Pubs., Inc.

—Vincent Van Gogh. 2007. (Art Profiles for Kids Ser.). (Illus.). 48p. (YA). (gr. 4-7). lib. bdg. 29.95 *(978-1-58415-564-5(7))* Mitchell Lane Pubs., Inc.

Wood, Alix. Johannes Vermeer. 2013. (Artists Through the Ages Ser.). (ENG., Illus.). 32p. (J). (gr. 3-6). pap. 10.00 *(978-1-61533-633-3(8));* lib. bdg. 25.25 *(978-1-61533-623-4(0))* Windmill Bks.

—Vincent Van Gogh. 2013. (Artists Through the Ages Ser.). (ENG., Illus.). 32p. (gr. 3-6). 25.25 *(978-1-61533-622-7(2));* pap. 10.00 *(978-1-61533-631-9(1))* Windmill Bks.

Wooten, Sara McIntosh. Frida Kahlo: Her Life in Paintings. 2005. (Latino Biography Library). (Illus.). 128p. (J). (gr. 6-13). lib. bdg. 31.93 *(978-0-7660-2487-8(3))* Enslow Pubs., Inc.

Zaczek, Iain. Edouard Manet. 2014. (Great Artists Ser.). 32p. (J). (gr. 3-6). pap. 10.50 *(978-1-4824-1217-8(9))* Stevens, Gareth Publishing LLLP.

—Vincent Van Gogh. 2014. (Great Artists Ser.). 32p. (J). (gr. 3-6). pap. 63.00 *(978-1-4824-1249-9(7))* Stevens, Gareth Publishing LLLP.

PAINTERS—FICTION

Bailie, James. The Steam Genie. 2005. 53p. (YA). 11.84 *(978-1-4116-3998-0(7))* Lulu Pr., Inc.

Blain, Christophe. Los Hielos, Vol. 2. 2005. (Isaac el Pirata Ser.). (SPA., Illus.). 48p. (YA). (gr. 8-17). 19.95 *(978-1-59497-114-3(5))* Public Square Bks.

Clancy, Kaycee. Sky Painters. 2007. 41p. per. 11.95 *(978-0-9776777-8-8(8))* Legacy Publishing Services, Inc.

Cullen, Lyn. I Am Rembrandt's Daughter. 2011. 8.88 *(978-0-7848-3491-6(1),* Everbind) Marco Bk. Co.

Greene, Sefton. Space Painters. 2003. 18p. bds. *(978-1-904502-30-2(X))* MediaWorld/BestBooks.

Hawes, Louise & Sharratt, Mary. The Vanishing Point. 2007. (ENG.). 240p. (J). (gr. 5-7). pap. 15.95 *(978-0-618-74788-7(5))* Houghton Mifflin Harcourt Publishing Co.

James, Wayan. My Friend the Painter. 2016. (Rosen REAL Readers: STEM & STEAM Collection). 12p. (gr. 1-k). pap. 6.33 *(978-1-5081-2661-4(5),* Rosen Classroom) Rosen Publishing Group, Inc., The.

Juliette, the Modern Art Monkey: Individual Title Six-Packs. (Bookweb Ser.). 32p. (gr. 5-18). 34.00 *(978-0-7635-3776-0(4))* Rigby Education.

Lamballe, Jérôme. The Curious Story of Pablo Picasslug. 2010. 28p. 16.95 *(978-1-4452-8949-6(0))* Lulu Pr., Inc.

The Magnificent Mural, 6 vols., Pack. (Bookweb Ser.). 32p. (gr. 6-18). 34.00 *(978-0-7578-0869-0(1))* Rigby Education.

McDougal-Littell Publishing Staff. Literature Connections Spanish: Yo, Juan de Pareja (I, Juan de Pareja) 2004. (McDougal Littell Literature Connections Ser.). (SPA.). 256p. (gr. 7-7). 16.90 *(978-0-395-84375-8(8),* 2-70788) Great Source Education Group, Inc.

Moss, Marissa. Caravaggio: Painter on the Run. Moss, Marissa, illus. 2016. (ENG., Illus.). 360p. (gr. 6). 16.95 *(978-1-939547-29-3(6))* Creston Bks.

Mullarkey, Lisa & Mullarkey, John. Monet Changes Mediums, 1 vol. Bernard, Courtney, illus. 2015. (ENG.). 128p. (J). *(978-1-62402-089-6(5))* Magic Wagon.

Osborne, Mary A. Nonna's Book of Mysteries. 2010. (ENG., Illus.). 352p. (gr. 8-17). pap. 16.95 *(978-1-936181-16-2(9))* Lake Street Pr.

Perkins, Mitali. Rickshaw Girl. Hogan, Jamie, illus. 2008. (ENG.). 96p. (J). (gr. 2-5). pap. 6.95 *(978-1-58089-309-1(0))* Charlesbridge Publishing, Inc.

Russo, Richard. Bridge of Sighs. 2007. *(978-0-7393-2751-7(8))* Random Hse. Large Print.

VAN HAERINGEN, Annemarie. Matisse. 2016. (ENG., Illus.). 32p. 16.95 *(978-0-7358-4263-2(9))* North-South Bks., Inc.

Verplancke, Klaas. Magritte's Apple. 2016. (ENG., Illus.). 40p. (J). (gr. -1-2). 19.95 *(978-1-63345-016-5(3))* Museum of Modern Art.

PAINTERS—FRANCE

Björk, Christina. Linnea in Monet's Garden. Sandin, Joan, tr. Anderson, Lena, illus. 2012. (ENG.). 48p. (J). (-3). 16.99 *(978-1-4022-7729-0(6),* Sourcebooks Jabberwocky) Sourcebooks, Inc.

Brooks, Susie. Claude Monet, 01 vols., 1. 2016. (Inspiring Artists Ser.). (ENG.). 48p. (J). 30.25 *(978-1-5081-7063-1(0),* Rosen Young Adult) Rosen Publishing Group, Inc., The.

Cernak, Linda. Vincent Van Gogh. Morrow, J. T., illus. 2014. (World's Greatest Artists Ser.). (ENG.). 24p. (J). (gr. 2-5). 28.50 *(978-1-62687-355-1(0),* 207195) Child's World, Inc., The.

Connolly, Sean & Monet, Claude. Claude Monet. 2004. (Lives of the Artists Ser.). (Illus.). 48p. (J). (gr. 5-12). pap. 14.05 *(978-0-8368-5655-2(4));* lib. bdg. 31.00 *(978-0-8368-5650-7(3))* Stevens, Gareth Publishing LLLP. (Gareth Stevens Secondary Library).

Dickins, Rosie & Ball, Karen. Leonardo Da Vinci. Unzner, Christa, illus. 2007. (Famous Lives Gift Bks). 63p. (J). (gr. 4-7). 8.99 *(978-0-7945-1594-2(0),* Usborne) EDC Publishing.

Harris, Nathaniel. Paul Cézanne. 2003. (Artists in Their Time Ser.). (ENG., Illus.). 48p. (J). 24.00 *(978-0-531-12242-6(5),* Watts, Franklin) Scholastic Library Publishing.

Kallen, Stuart A. Claude Monet. 2008. (Eye on Art Ser.). (ENG., Illus.). 112p. (YA). (gr. 7-10). lib. bdg. 34.80 *(978-1-4205-0074-5(0),* LML02109-242078, Lucent Bks.) Cengage Gale.

Kelley, True. Pierre-Auguste Renoir - Paintings That Smile. 2005. (Smart about Art Ser.). (ENG., Illus.). 32p. (J). (gr. k-4). mass mkt. 5.99 *(978-0-448-43371-4(0),* Grosset & Dunlap) Penguin Young Readers Group.

Klein, Adam G. Claude Monet, 1 vol. 2007. (Great Artists Set 2 Ser.). (ENG., Illus.). 32p. (gr. -1-3). 27.07 *(978-1-59679-732-1(0),* Checkerboard Library) ABDO Publishing Co.

—Paul Gauguin, 1 vol. 2007. (Great Artists Set 2 Ser.). (ENG., Illus.). 32p. (gr. -1-3). 27.07 *(978-1-59679-729-1(0),* Checkerboard Library) ABDO Publishing Co.

—Pierre-Auguste Renoir, 1 vol. 2007. (Great Artists Set 2 Ser.). (ENG., Illus.). 32p. (gr. -1-3). 27.07 *(978-1-59679-736-9(3),* Checkerboard Library) ABDO Publishing Co.

Lomberg, Michelle. Claude Monet. 2016. (Illus.). 32p. (J). *(978-1-4896-4619-4(1))* Weigl Pubs., Inc.

Markel, Michelle & Rousseau, Henri. The Fantastic Jungles of Henri Rousseau. Hall, Amanda, illus. 2012. (ENG.). 34p. (J). 17.00 *(978-0-8028-5364-6(1),* Eerdmans Bks For Young Readers) Eerdmans, William B. Publishing Co.

Mattern, Joanne. Edgar Degas, 1 vol. 2005. (Great Artists Set 1 Ser.). (ENG., Illus.). 32p. (gr. k-6). 27.07 *(978-1-59197-843-5(2),* Checkerboard Library) ABDO Publishing Co.

Merberg, Julie & Bober, Suzanne. A Picnic with Monet. 2003. (Mini Masters Ser.: MINI). (ENG., Illus.). 22p. (J). (gr. -1-7). bds. 6.99 *(978-0-8118-4046-0(8))* Chronicle Bks. LLC.

Mis, Melody S. Edgar Degas. (Meet the Artist Ser.). 24p. (gr. 2-3). 2009. 42.50 *(978-1-61514-628-4(8),* PowerKids Pr.) 2007. (Illus.). (YA). lib. bdg. 22.60 *(978-1-4042-3839-8(5))* Rosen Publishing Group, Inc., The.

—Edouard Manet. (Meet the Artist Ser.). 24p. (gr. 2-3). 2009. 42.50 *(978-1-61514-629-1(6),* PowerKids Pr.) 2007. (Illus.). (J). lib. bdg. 22.60 *(978-1-4042-3841-1(7))* Rosen Publishing Group, Inc., The.

—Paul Cezanne. (Meet the Artist Ser.). 24p. (gr. 2-3). 2009. 42.50 *(978-1-61514-631-4(8),* PowerKids Pr.) 2007. (Illus.). (YA). lib. bdg. 22.60 *(978-1-4042-3842-8(5))* Rosen Publishing Group, Inc., The.

Nichols, Catherine. Claude Monet. (Primary Source Library of Famous Artists Ser.). 32p. 2009. (gr. 3-4). 42.50 *(978-1-60854-100-3(2))* 2006. (Illus.). (J). (gr. -1-3). lib. bdg. 23.95 *(978-1-4042-2761-3(X))* Rosen Publishing Group, Inc., The. (PowerKids Pr.).

—Pierre-Auguste Renoir. (Primary Source Library of Famous Artists Ser.). 32p. 2009. (gr. 3-4). 42.50 *(978-1-60854-104-1(5))* 2006. (Illus.). (J). (gr. -1-3). lib. bdg. 23.95 *(978-1-4042-2765-1(2))* Rosen Publishing Group, Inc., The. (PowerKids Pr.).

Rubin, Susan Goldman. Matisse Dance for Joy. 2008. (ENG., Illus.). 26p. (J). (gr. -1 — 1). bds. 6.99 *(978-0-8118-6288-2(7))* Chronicle Bks. LLC.

Sánchez, Consuelo. Claudet Monet. 2005. (SPA.). 132p. (YA). *(978-958-30-1869-5(4))* Panamericana Editorial.

Somervill, Barbara A. Pierre-Auguste Renoir. 2007. (Art Profiles for Kids Ser.). (Illus.). 48p. (YA). (gr. 4-7). lib. bdg. 29.95 *(978-1-58415-566-9(3))* Mitchell Lane Pubs., Inc.

Spence, David. Gauguin. 2010. (Great Artists & Their World Ser.). (Illus.). 48p. (YA). 32.80 *(978-1-84898-316-8(6))* Black Rabbit Bks.

—Gauguin: Huida al Eden. (Coleccion Grandes Artistas).Tr. of Gauguin: Escape to Eden. (SPA.). 266p. (YA). (gr. 5-8). 12.76 *(978-84-8211-138-4(8))* Celeste Ediciones, S.A. ESP. Dist: Lectorum Pubns., Inc.

—Monet: Impresionismo. (Coleccion Grandes Artistas). (SPA.). 220p. (YA). (gr. 5-8). 12.76 *(978-84-8211-133-9(7))* Celeste Ediciones, S.A. ESP. Dist: Lectorum Pubns., Inc.

—Renoir. 2010. (Great Artists & Their World Ser.). 48p. 32.80 *(978-1-84898-317-5(4))* Black Rabbit Bks.

Stamford, Tasha. Monet, Vol. 7. 2015. (Great Artists Collection). (Illus.). 64p. (J). (gr. 7). lib. bdg. 23.95 *(978-1-4222-3261-3(1))* Mason Crest.

Swigelson, Kayce M. The Grand Adventures of Petit Louis. Swigelson, Kayce M., illus. 2013. (Illus.). 54p. 24.95 *(978-0-9889643-1-0(7))* MathisJones Communications, LLC.

Tracy, Kathleen. Edouard Manet. 2009. (Art Profiles for Kids Ser.). (Illus.). 48p. (YA). (gr. 4-7). lib. bdg. 29.95 *(978-1-58415-746-5(1))* Mitchell Lane Pubs., Inc.

—Paul Cezanne. 2007. (Art Profiles for Kids Ser.). (Illus.). 48p. (YA). (gr. 4-7). lib. bdg. 29.95 *(978-1-58415-565-2(5))* Mitchell Lane Pubs., Inc.

Venezia, Mike. Camille Pissarro. Venezia, Mike, illus. 2004. (Getting. . Know Artists Ser.). (ENG., Illus.). 32p. (J). (gr. 3-4). pap. 6.95 *(978-0-516-26977-1(1),* Children's Pr.) Scholastic Library Publishing.

—Camille Pissarro. 2003. (Getting to Know World Artists Ser.). (ENG., Illus.). 32p. (J). 28.00 *(978-0-516-22577-7(4),* Children's Pr.) Scholastic Library Publishing.

—Edgar Degas. Venezia, Mike, illus. rev. ed. 2016. (Getting to Know the World's Greatest Artists Ser.). (ENG., Illus.). 40p. (J). pap. 7.95 *(978-0-531-22087-0(7),* Children's Pr.) Scholastic Library Publishing.

—Eugene Delacroix. Venezia, Mike, illus. 2003. (Getting to Know World Artists Ser.). (ENG., Illus.). 32p. (J). 28.00 *(978-0-516-22576-0(6),* Children's Pr.) Scholastic Library Publishing.

—Paul Cezanne. 2016. (Getting to Know the World's Greatest Artists Ser.). (ENG.). 40p. (J). pap. 7.95 *(978-0-531-22108-2(3),* Children's Pr.) Scholastic Library Publishing.

—Paul Cezanne (Revised Edition) 2016. (Getting to Know the World's Greatest Artists Ser.). (ENG., Illus.). 40p. (J). lib. bdg. 29.00 *(978-0-531-21669-9(1),* Children's Pr.) Scholastic Library Publishing.

—Paul Gauguin. 2016. (Getting to Know the World's Greatest Artists Ser.). (ENG., Illus.). 40p. (J). pap. 7.95 *(978-0-531-22105-1(9),* Children's Pr.) Scholastic Library Publishing.

—Paul Gauguin (Revised Edition) 2016. (Getting to Know the World's Greatest Artists Ser.). (ENG., Illus.). 40p. (J). lib. bdg. 29.00 *(978-0-531-21666-8(7),* Children's Pr.) Scholastic Library Publishing.

—Pierre Auguste Renoir. 2016. (Getting to Know the World's Greatest Artists Ser.). (ENG.). 40p. (J). pap. 7.95 *(978-0-531-22107-5(5),* Children's Pr.) Scholastic Library Publishing.

—Pierre Auguste Renoir (Revised Edition) 2016. (Getting to Know the World's Greatest Artists Ser.). (ENG.). 40p. (J). lib. bdg. 29.00 *(978-0-531-21668-2(3),* Children's Pr.) Scholastic Library Publishing.

Waldron, Ann. Who Was Claude Monet? Harrison, Nancy & Marchesi, Stephen, illus. 2009. (Who Was? Ser.). (ENG.). 112p. (J). (gr. 3-7). pap. 5.99 *(978-0-448-44985-2(4),* Grosset & Dunlap) Penguin Young Readers Group.

—Who Was Claude Monet? 2009. (Who Was... ? Ser.). lib. bdg. 16.00 *(978-0-606-04028-0(5),* Turtleback) Turtleback Bks.

Winter, Jeanette. Henri's Scissors. Winter, Jeanette, illus. 2013. (ENG., Illus.). 40p. (J). (gr. k-3). 17.99 *(978-1-4424-6484-1(4),* Beach Lane Bks.) Beach Lane Bks.

Wood, Alix. Claude Monet. 2013. (Artists Through the Ages Ser.). (ENG., Illus.). 32p. (J). (gr. 3-6). pap. 10.00 *(978-1-61533-627-2(3));* lib. bdg. 25.25 *(978-1-61533-620-3(6))* Windmill Bks.

—Paul Cézanne. 2013. (Artists Through the Ages Ser.). (ENG., Illus.). 32p. (J). (gr. 3-6). pap. 10.00 *(978-1-61533-625-8(7));* lib. bdg. 25.25 *(978-1-61533-619-7(2))* Windmill Bks.

Zaczek, Iain. Georges Seurat. 2014. (Great Artists Ser.). 32p. (J). (gr. 3-6). pap. 63.00 *(978-1-4824-1248-2(9))* Stevens, Gareth Publishing LLLP.

—Paul Cézanne. 2014. (Great Artists Ser.). 32p. (J). (gr. 3-6). pap. 10.50 *(978-1-4824-1216-1(0))* Stevens, Gareth Publishing LLLP.

PAINTERS—SPAIN

Mis, Melody S. El Greco. (Meet the Artist Ser.). 24p. (gr. 2-3). 2009. 42.50 *(978-1-61514-630-7(X),* PowerKids Pr.) 2007. (Illus.). (YA). lib. bdg. 22.60 *(978-1-4042-3844-2(1))* Rosen Publishing Group, Inc., The.

Toyne, Jessica. Dali, Vol. 7. 2015. (Great Artists Collection). (Illus.). 64p. (J). (gr. 7). lib. bdg. 23.95 *(978-1-4222-3258-3(1))* Mason Crest.

Venezia, Mike. Francisco Goya. 2016. (Getting to Know the World's Greatest Artists Ser.). (ENG.). 40p. (J). pap. 7.95 *(978-0-531-22106-8(7),* Children's Pr.) Scholastic Library Publishing.

—Francisco Goya (Revised Edition) 2016. (Getting to Know the World's Greatest Artists Ser.). (ENG.). 40p. (J). lib. bdg. 29.00 *(978-0-531-21667-5(5),* Children's Pr.) Scholastic Library Publishing.

—El Greco. Venezia, Mike, illus. rev. ed. 2016. (Getting to Know the World's Greatest Artists Ser.). (ENG., Illus.). 40p. (J). pap. 7.95 *(978-0-531-22088-7(5),* Children's Pr.) Scholastic Library Publishing.

—Salvador Dali. Venezia, Mike, illus. 2015. (Getting to Know the World's Greatest Artists Ser.). (ENG., Illus.). 40p. (J). lib. bdg. 29.00 *(978-0-531-21262-2(9),* Children's Pr.) Scholastic Library Publishing.

PAINTERS—UNITED STATES

Abrams, Dennis. Georgia O'Keeffe. 2nd rev. ed. 2009. (Women of Achievement Ser.). (Illus.). 144p. (gr. 6-12). 35.00 *(978-1-60413-336-3(8),* Chelsea Hse.) Facts On File, Inc.

Berne, Emma Carlson. Frida Kahlo: Groundbreaking Artist, 1 vol. 2009. (Essential Lives Set 4 Ser.). (ENG., Illus.). 112p. (J). (gr. 6-12). lib. bdg. 35.64 *(978-1-60453-701-7(9))* ABDO Publishing Co.

Bryant, Jennifer. A Splash of Red: The Life & Art of Horace Pippin. Sweet, Melissa, illus. 2013. (ENG.). 40p. (J). (gr. k-3). 17.99 *(978-0-375-86712-5(0));* lib. bdg. 20.99 *(978-0-375-96712-2(5))* Random Hse. Children's Bks. (Knopf Bks. for Young Readers).

Burleigh, Robert. Edward Hopper Paints His World. Minor, Wendell, illus. 2014. (ENG.). 40p. (J). (gr. k-4). 17.99 *(978-0-8050-8752-9(4),* 9780805087529, Holt, Henry & Co. Bks. For Young Readers) Holt, Henry & Co.

Burleigh, Robert & Bellows, George. George Bellows: Painter with a Punch! 2012. (ENG., Illus.). 48p. (J). (gr. 3-7). 19.95 *(978-1-4197-0166-5(5),* Abrams Bks. for Young Readers) Abrams, Inc.

Christie, R. Gregory. It Jes' Happened: When Bill Traylor Started to Draw, 1 vol. Tate, Don, illus. 2012. (ENG.). 1p. (J). 17.95 *(978-1-60060-260-3(6))* Lee & Low Bks., Inc.

Davies, Jacqueline. The Boy Who Drew Birds: A Story of John James Audubon. Sweet, Melissa, illus. 2004. (ENG.). 32p. (J). (gr. -1-3). tchr. ed. 16.99 *(978-0-618-24343-3(7))* Houghton Mifflin Harcourt Publishing Co.

Dickinson, Stephanie. Jacob Lawrence. 2016. (Artists of the Harlem Renaissance Ser.). (ENG.). 128p. (YA). (gr. 9-9). 45.64 *(978-1-5026-1070-6(1))* Cavendish Square Publishing.

Greenberg, Jan & Jordan, Sandra. Action Jackson. Parker, Robert Andrew, illus. 2007. (ENG.). 32p. (J). (gr. 1-5). pap. 8.99 *(978-0-312-36751-0(1),* 9780312367510) Square Fish.

Harris, Lois V. Maxfield Parrish: Painter of Magical Make-Believe, 1 vol. 2011. (ENG., Illus.). 32p. (J). (gr. k-3). 16.99 *(978-1-4556-1472-1(6))* Pelican Publishing Co., Inc.

Igus, Toyomi. Going Back Home: An Artist Returns to the South. Wood, Michele, illus. 2013. (ENG.). 32p. (J). (gr. 1-18). pap. 9.95 *(978-0-89239-197-4(9),* Children's Book Press) Lee & Low Bks., Inc.

Jordan, Sandra & Greenberg, Jan. Action Jackson. Parker, Robert Andrew, illus. pap. incl. audio compact disk *(978-1-59112-965-3(6));* pap. incl. audio *(978-1-59112-961-5(3))* Live Oak Media.

Klein, Adam G. Grandma Moses, 1 vol. 2007. (Great Artists Set 2 Ser.). (ENG., Illus.). 32p. (J). (gr. -1-3). 27.07 *(978-1-59679-737-6(1),* Checkerboard Library) ABDO Publishing Co.

—Norman Rockwell, 1 vol. 2007. (Great Artists Set 2 Ser.). (ENG., Illus.). 32p. (gr. -1-3). 27.07 *(978-1-59679-738-3(X),* Checkerboard Library) ABDO Publishing Co.

Koerner, Henry. The Early Works of Henry Koerner 1945-1957. 2004. (Illus.). 96p. (YA). (gr. 13-18). pap. 35.00 *(978-0-9703425-5-3(1))* Frick Art & Historical Ctr.,The.

Kopp, Megan. Grandma Moses. 2016. (Illus.). 32p. (J). *(978-1-4896-4621-7(3))* Weigl Pubs., Inc.

Mattern, Joanne. Georgia O'Keeffe, 1 vol. 2005. (Great Artists Set 1 Ser.). (ENG., Illus.). 32p. (gr. k-6). 27.07 *(978-1-59197-846-6(7),* Checkerboard Library) ABDO Publishing Co.

—Jackson Pollock, 1 vol. 2005. (Great Artists Set 1 Ser.). (ENG.). 32p. (gr. k-6). 27.07 *(978-1-59197-847-3(5),* Checkerboard Library) ABDO Publishing Co.

McLellan, Richard A. The Land of Truth & Phantasy: Life & Painting at Ring Farm USA. Wyeth, Andrew N. & Kuerner, Karl J., illus. gif. ed. 2005. (ENG.). 187p. 24.00 *(978-0-9747536-0-7(2))* McLellan Bks.

O'Connor, Jane. Mary Cassatt: Family Pictures. Kalis, Jennifer, illus. 2003. (Smart about Art Ser.). (ENG.). 32p. (J). (gr. k-4). mass mkt. 5.99 *(978-0-448-43152-9(1),* Grosset & Dunlap) Penguin Young Readers Group.

Reich, Susanna. Painting the Wild Frontier: The Art & Adventures of George Catlin. 2008. (ENG., Illus.). 176p. (J). (gr. 5-7). 22.00 *(978-0-618-71470-4(7))* Houghton Mifflin Harcourt Publishing Co.

Rodriguez, Rachel Victoria. Through Georgia's Eyes. Paschkis, Julie, illus. rev. ed. 2006. (ENG.). 32p. (J). (gr. k-3). 18.99 *(978-0-8050-7740-7(5),* 9780805077407, Holt, Henry & Co. Bks. For Young Readers) Holt, Henry & Co.

Show Me America, 5 vols., Set. Incl. Dorothea Lange: Photographer of the People. King, David C. 88p. (C). 2009. lib. bdg. 158.00 *(978-0-7656-8154-6(4),* Y181941); George Catlin: Painter of Indian Life. Worth, Richard. 80p. (C). 2009. lib. bdg. 158.00 *(978-0-7656-8152-2(8),* Y182314); John Trumbull: Painter of the Revolutionary War. Murray, Stuart A. P. 83p. (C). 2008. lib. bdg. 158.00 *(978-0-7656-8150-8(1),* Y182501); Lewis Hine: Photographer of Americans at Work. Worth, Richard. 83p. (C). 2009. lib. bdg. 158.00 *(978-0-7656-8153-9(6),* Y182862); Mathew Brady: Photographer of Our Nation. Murray, Stuart A. P. 83p. 2009. lib. bdg. 158.00 *(978-0-7656-8151-5(X),* Y182957); (Illus.). (gr. 6-18). (ENG.). 2009. Set lib. bdg. 140.00 *(978-0-7656-8149-2(8),* Y183560) Routledge.

Stephens, Pamela Geiger. Dropping in on Romare Bearden. McNeill, Jim, illus. 2007. (ENG.). 32p. (J). 15.95 *(978-1-56290-539-2(2))* Crystal Productions.

Taylor, Charlotte. Get to Know Georgia O'Keeffe. 2016. (Famous Artists Ser.). (ENG., Illus.). 48p. (J). (gr. 3-4). 27.93 *(978-0-7660-7226-8(6))* Enslow Pubs., Inc.

Venezia, Mike. Horace Pippin. Venezia, Mike, illus. 2008. (Getting to Know the World's Greatest Artists Ser.). (ENG., Illus.). 32p. (J). (gr. 3-4). pap. 6.95 *(978-0-531-14758-0(4),* Children's Pr.) Scholastic Library Publishing.

—Winslow Homer. Venezia, Mike, illus. 2004. (Getting. . Know Artists Ser.). (ENG., Illus.). 32p. (J). (gr. 3-4). pap. 6.95

(978-0-516-26979-5(8), Children's Pr.) Scholastic Library Publishing.
Wallner, Alexandra, tr. & illus. Grandma Moses. Wallner, Alexandra, illus. 2004. (ENG.). 32p. (J). (gr. k-3). tchr. ed. 16.95 (978-0-8234-1538-0(4)) Holiday Hse., Inc.
Worth, Richard. George Catlin: Painter of Indian Life. 2009. (ENG., Illus.). 80p. (C). (gr. 6-18). lib. bdg. 158.00 (978-0-7656-8152-2(8), Y182314) Routledge.

PAINTING

see also Animal Painting and Illustration; Color; Composition (Art); Finger Painting; Flower Painting and Illustration; Impressionism (Art); Landscape Painting; Marine Painting; Perspective; Post-Impressionism (Art); Stencil Work; Textile Painting; Watercolor Painting

Aigner-Clark, Julie. Master Pieces. Zaidi, Nadeem, illus. 2004. (SPA.). 10p. (J). 9.95 (978-970-718-211-0(3), Silver Dolphin Bks.) Readerlink Distribution Services, LLC.
Alexander, Heather & Hamilton, Meredith. A Child's Introduction to Art: The World's Greatest Paintings & Sculptures. Hamilton, Meredith, illus. 2014. (ENG., Illus.). 96p. (J). (gr. -1-17). 19.99 (978-1-57912-956-9(0), 81956, Black Dog & Leventhal Pubs. Inc.) Hachette Bks.
Ancona, George. Murals: Walls That Sing, 1 vol. 2003. (ENG., Illus.). 32p. (YA). 17.95 (978-0-7614-5131-0(5)) Marshall Cavendish Corp.
Anderson, Robert. Paul Gauguin. 2003. (Artists in Their Time Ser.). (ENG., Illus.). 48p. (J). (gr. 5-7). pap. 6.95 (978-0-531-16647-5(3), Watts, Franklin) Scholastic Library Publishing.
Anholt, Laurence. Anholt's Artists Activity Book. 2012. (ENG.). 48p. (J). (gr. -1-3). pap. 11.99 (978-1-4380-0114-2(2)) Barron's Educational Series, Inc.
Armstrong, Carole. My Sticker Art Gallery: Monet. (Illus.). 12p. (J). (gr. 2-18). pap. (978-0-7112-0962-6(6)) ReiseArt Buchhandlung GmbH.
The Art of Glass Painting. 2004. (Classic Craft Cases Ser.). (Illus.). 64p. (978-1-84229-801-5(1)) Top That! Publishing PLC.
Ayres, Charlie. The Story of the World's Greatest Paintings. 2010. (ENG., Illus.). 96p. (J). (gr. 1-3). 19.95 (978-0-500-23880-6(4), 523880) Thames & Hudson.
Bacon, Dolores. Pictures Every Child Should Know (Illust. 2006. pap. (978-1-4065-0424-8(6)) Dodo Pr.
Barlowe, Dot. Flower Gardens to Paint or Color. 2007. (Dover Art Coloring Book Ser.). (ENG., Illus.). 48p. (gr. 3-5). 5.99 (978-0-486-46204-2(8)) Dover Pubns., Inc.
Barsony, Piotr. The Stories of the Mona Lisa: An Imaginary Museum Tale about the History of Modern Art. 2012. (ENG., Illus.). 56p. (J). (gr. 3-6). 19.95 (978-1-62087-228-4(5), 620228, Sky Pony Pr.) Skyhorse Publishing Co., Inc.
Binam, Sharyn. The Sidload: Garden. 2004. 64p. pap. 11.95 (978-1-57377-186-3(4), 0-1988-4-02500-9) Eas'l Pubns.
Bliss, John. Preening, Painting, & Piercing: Body Art. 2010. (Culture in Action Ser.). (ENG.). 32p. (gr. 3-6). 30.65 (978-1-4109-3924-1(3), NA-r) Heinemann-Raintree.
Bodden, Valerie. Brushes with Greatness: History Paintings. 2013. (Brushes with Greatness Ser.). (ENG.). 48p. (J). (gr. 4-7). pap. 12.00 (978-0-89812-763-8(7), Creative Paperbacks) Creative Co., The.
Booth, Elaine. This Painting Has Action! 2017. (Text Connections Guided Close Reading Ser.). (J). (gr. k). (978-1-4900-1764-8(X)) Benchmark Education Co.
Conway, Agnes Ethel & Conway, Martin. The Book of Art for Young People. 2007. (ENG., Illus.). 136p. per. (978-1-4065-1514-5(0)) Dodo Pr.
Conway, Agnes Ethel & Conway, William Martin. The Book of Art for Young People. 2007. (ENG.). 126p. pap. 18.99 (978-1-4346-4973-7(3)); 138p. pap. 19.99 (978-1-4346-4974-4(1)) Creative Media Partners, LLC.
Courtauld, Sarah. Story of Art Sticker Book. 2012. (Art Ser.). 42p. (J). pap. 9.99 (978-0-7945-3295-6(0), Usborne) EDC Publishing.
Crabtree, Marc. Meet My Neighbor, the Artist. 2009. (Meet my Neighbor Ser.). (ENG., Illus.). 24p. (J). (gr. k-2). pap. (978-0-7787-4579-2(1)); lib. bdg. (978-0-7787-4569-3(4)) Crabtree Publishing Co.
Crismon, Joy. Chinese Brush Painting. 84p. (J). (gr. 1-7). pap. (978-1-56861-049-8(1)) Swift Learning Resources.
Cuxart, Bernadette. Art Stamping Using Everyday Objects. 2015. (Art Painting Ser.). (ENG., Illus.). 36p. (J). (gr. k-3). pap. 6.99 (978-1-4380-0652-9(7)) Barron's Educational Series, Inc.
Davies, Carolyn. Josef Herman in Wales. 2004. (ENG., Illus.). 32p. pap. 15.95 (978-1-85902-999-2(X)) Beekman Bks., Inc.
D'Elia, Una. Painting in the Renaissance. 2009. (Renaissance World Ser.). (ENG., Illus.). 32p. (J). (gr. 5-8). pap. (978-0-7787-4612-6(7)); lib. bdg. (978-0-7787-4592-1(9)) Crabtree Publishing Co.
d'Harcourt, Claire. Masterpieces up Close: Western Painting from the 14th to 20th Centuries. 2016. (ENG., Illus.). 64p. (J). (gr. 1-3). 29.95 (978-1-61689-414-6(8)) Princeton Architectural Pr.
Dickens, Rosie. Famous Paintings: Internet-Linked. 2009. (Famous Paintings Ser.). 96p. (YA). (gr. 4-18). 16.99 (978-0-7945-2542-2(3), Usborne) EDC Publishing.
Disney Princess Paint n' Play with Sticker Rolls. 2005. (J). spiral bd. (978-1-59487-148-1(5)) Artist Studios, Ltd.
Dorling Kindersley Publishing Staff. My Art Book. 2011. (ENG., Illus.). 80p. (J). (gr. 2-5). 15.99 (978-0-7566-7582-0(0), DK Children) Dorling Kindersley Publishing, Inc.
Dubowski, Mark. Discovery in the Cave. Barnard, Bryn, illus. 2010. (Step into Reading Ser.). (ENG.). 48p. (J). (gr. 2-4). pap. 3.99 (978-0-375-85893-2(8), Random Hse. Bks. for Young Readers) Random Hse. Children's Bks.
Felix, Rebecca. Cool Crayons, Chalks, & Paints: Crafting Creative Toys & Amazing Games, 1 vol. 2016. (Cool Toys & Games Ser.). (ENG., Illus.). 32p. (J). (gr. 3-6). lib. bdg. 28.50 (978-1-68078-048-2(4), Checkerboard Library) ABDO Publishing Co.
Fisher, Diana. Rockin' Crafts: Everything You Need to Become a Rock-Painting Craft Star! 2012. (Craft Star Ser.). (Illus.). 64p. (J). (gr. 2-4). 32.80 (978-1-936309-40-5(8)) Quarto Publishing Group USA.
Fitzrandolph, Joyce. Learn to Paint with the Alexander Brush Club. (Illus.). 24p. (J). (gr. 4-6). pap. (978-1-883576-32-5(6), KT-220B) Alexander Art L.P.
Flor Ada, Alma & Campoy, F. Isabel, contrib. by. Blue & Green. (Literature Collection of Gateways to the Sun Ser.). 32p. (J). (gr. k-6). pap. 13.95 (978-1-59437-714-3(6)) Santillana USA Publishing Co., Inc.
Flower, Miri. Paint Book: Loads of Things You Can Make or Do with Paint. 2014. (ENG., Illus.). 128p. pap. 14.99 (978-0-7112-3583-0(X), Frances Lincoln) Quarto Publishing Group UK GBR. Dist: Hachette Bk. Group.
Foa, Emma. Edward Hopper. 2003. (Artists in Their Time Ser.). (ENG., Illus.). 48p. (J). 24.00 (978-0-531-12240-2(9)); (gr. 5-7). pap. 6.95 (978-0-531-16641-3(4)) Scholastic Library Publishing. (Watts, Franklin).
Foldvary-Anderson, Carol. 3-D Coloring Book — Hearts. 2012. (Dover 3-D Coloring Book Ser.). (ENG., Illus.). 32p. (J). (gr. 2-6). pap. 5.99 (978-0-486-49013-7(0)) Dover Pubns., Inc.
Fretland VanVoorst, Jenny. Painting. 2016. (Artist's Studio Ser.). 24p. (J). (gr. k-2). lib. bdg. 25.65 (978-1-62031-282-7(4), Bullfrog Bks.) Jump! Inc.
Frisch-Schmoll, Joy. Brushes with Greatness: Still Lifes. 2013. (Brushes with Greatness Ser.). (ENG.). 48p. (J). (gr. 4-7). pap. 12.00 (978-0-89812-766-9(1), Creative Paperbacks) Creative Co., The.
Gibson, Ray. What Shall I Paint? Everett, Felicity, ed. Kennard, Michaela, illus. 2006. (What Shall I Do Today? Ser.). 32p. (J). (gr. 2). lib. bdg. 15.95 (978-1-58086-549-4(6)) EDC Publishing.
Gluck, Larry. The Basic Painting Course. 2004. (YA). spiral bd. (978-1-929473-05-2(2)) Renaissance Pubns.
Golden Books. Bubble Bonanza! (Bubble Guppies) Golden Books, illus. 2013. (Color & Paint Plus Stickers Ser.). (ENG., Illus.). 128p. (J). (gr. -1-2). pap. 9.99 (978-0-449-81948-7(5), Golden Bks.) Random Hse. Children's Bks.
Gray, Savannah. We Can Feel Art! 2017. (Text Connections Guided Close Reading Ser.). (J). (gr. 1). (978-1-4900-1808-9(5)) Benchmark Education Co.
Guéry, Anne & Dussutour, Olivier. Alphab'art: Find the Letters Hidden in the Paintings. Parkin, Antonia, tr. from FRE. 2009. (ENG., Illus.). 64p. (J). (gr. -1-k). (978-1-84780-013-8(0)) Rough Guides, Ltd.
Handler, Daniel. Girls Standing on Lawns. Kalman, Maira, illus. 2014. (ENG.). 64p. (gr. 3-7). 14.95 (978-0-87070-908-1(9)) Museum of Modern Art.
Harron, Nancy. Harron's Nest Floor Decor & More. 2004. 68p. pap. 16.95 (978-1-57377-202-0(X), 0-1988-4-2524) Eas'l Pubns.
Henry, Sally. Make Your Own Art, 6 vols., Set 1. Incl. Card Making. lib. bdg. 26.50 (978-1-4358-2506-2(3)); Clay Modeling. lib. bdg. 26.50 (978-1-4358-2508-6(X)); Collage. lib. bdg. 26.50 (978-1-4358-2509-3(8)); Drawing. lib. bdg. 26.50 (978-1-4358-2510-9(1)); Painting. lib. bdg. 26.50 (978-1-4358-2511-6(X)); Paper Folding. lib. bdg. 26.50 (978-1-4358-2507-9(1)); (J). (gr. 3-6). 2009. (Make Your Own Art Ser.). (Illus.). 32p. 2008. Set lib. bdg. 151.50 (978-1-4358-2549-9(7), PowerKids Pr.) Rosen Publishing Group, Inc., The.
—Painting. 2009. (Make Your Own Art Ser.). (ENG., Illus.). 32p. (gr. 2-6). pap. 11.75 (978-1-4358-2644-1(2), PowerKids Pr.) Rosen Publishing Group, Inc., The.
Henry, Sally & Cook, Trevor. Make Your Own Art, 6 vols., Set 2. Incl. Eco Crafts. lib. bdg. 26.50 (978-1-4488-1582-1(7)); Making Masks. 26.50 (978-1-4488-1583-8(5)); Making Mosaics. 26.50 (978-1-4488-1585-2(1)); Making Puppets. 26.50 (978-1-4488-1584-5(3)); Papier-Mâché. 26.50 (978-1-4488-1587-6(8)); (J). (gr. 3-6). (Make Your Own Art Ser.). (Illus.). 32p. 2010. Set lib. bdg. 151.50 (978-1-4488-1625-5(4), PowerKids Pr.) Rosen Publishing Group, Inc., The.
Henry, Sandi. Using Color in Your Art! Choosing Colors for Impact & Pizzazz. Rakitin, Sarah, illus. 2005. (Kids Can Ser.). (ENG.). 128p. (J). (gr. 3-7). pap. 12.95 (978-0-8249-6754-3(2), Ideal Pubns.) Worthy Publishing.
Hill, Z. B. Painting. 2014. (Art Today! Ser.: 10). 64p. (J). (gr. 7-18). 23.95 (978-1-4222-3173-9(9)) Mason Crest.
Holden, Pam. I Like to Paint, 8, Set. 2009. (Red Rocket Readers Ser.). (ENG., Illus.). 16p. (gr. -1-1). pap. (978-1-877435-97-3(X)) Flying Start Bks.
Hyde, Margaret, ed. Van Gogh for Kids, 1 vol. 2nd ed. 2005. (Great Art for Kids Ser.). (ENG., Illus.). 12p. (J). (gr. -1 — 1). bds. 8.95 (978-1-58980-279-7(9)) Pelican Publishing Co., Inc.
Hyde, Margaret E., ed. Cassatt for Kids, 1 vol. 2003. (Great Art for Kids Ser.). (ENG., Illus.). 10p. (J). (gr. k-k). bds. 8.95 (978-1-58980-202-5(0)) Pelican Publishing Co., Inc.
—Matisse for Kids, 1 vol. 2003. (Great Art for Kids Ser.). (ENG., Illus.). 10p. (J). (gr. -1 — 1). bds. 8.95 (978-1-58980-204-9(7)) Pelican Publishing Co., Inc.
—Picasso for Kids, 1 vol. 2004. (Great Art for Kids Ser.). (ENG., Illus.). 12p. (J). 8.95 (978-1-58980-205-6(5)) Pelican Publishing Co., Inc.
—Renoir for Kids, 1 vol. 2003. (Great Art for Kids Ser.). (ENG., Illus.). 10p. (J). (gr. -1 — 1). bds. 8.95 (978-1-58980-206-3(3)) Pelican Publishing Co., Inc.
Jakopovich, Kathy. Paint on a Happy Face, Vol. 2. 2004. 68p. pap. 11.95 (978-1-57377-198-6(8), 0-1988-4-02516-0) Eas'l Pubns.
Jo Tuttle, Mary. Tuttles Touches. 2004. 60p. pap. 11.95 (978-1-57377-203-7(8), 0-1988-4-2526-9) Eas'l Pubns.
Klein, Carol Swartout. Painting for Peace in Ferguson. 2nd ed. 2015. (ENG.). 54p. (J). (gr. 2-3). 25.95 (978-0-9963901-0-1(3)); pap. 15.95 (978-0-9892079-9-7(4)) TreeHse. Publishing Group.
Kuiper, Kathleen, ed. The 100 Most Influential Painters & Sculptors of the Renaissance. 2009. (Britannica Guide to the World's Most Influential People Ser.). (Illus.). 376p. (YA). (gr. 9-12). lib. bdg. 53.00 (978-1-61530-004-4(X)) Rosen Publishing Group, Inc., The.
Kutschbach, Doris. The Art Treasure Hunt: I Spy with My Little Eye. 2012. (ENG., Illus.). 48p. (J). (gr. -1-3). 14.95 (978-3-7913-7097-2(9)) Prestel Verlag GmbH & Co KG. DEU. Dist: Penguin Random Hse. LLC.
—The Great Art Treasure Hunt: I Spy Red, Yellow, & Blue. 2013. (ENG., Illus.). 48p. (J). (gr. -1-3). 14.95 (978-3-7913-7106-1(1)) Prestel Verlag GmbH & Co KG. DEU. Dist: Penguin Random Hse. LLC.
la Valette, Desiree, et al. Keith Haring: I Wish I Didn't Have to Sleep! 2014. (ENG., Illus.). 32p. (J). (gr. 3-7). pap. 9.95 (978-3-7913-7219-8(X)) Prestel Verlag GmbH & Co KG. DEU. Dist: Penguin Random Hse. LLC.
Lang, Annie J. Who Let the Kids Out. 2003. 48p. pap. 10.95 (978-1-57377-168-9(6)) Eas'l Pubns.
Lappe, S. M. Street Painting: A Guide for Young Artists. 2011. 36p. pap. 13.95 (978-1-60976-963-5(5), Strategic Bk. Publishing) Strategic Book Publishing & Rights Agency (SBPRA).
Las pinturas de Pepe: Individual Title-Six Packs. (Chiquilibros Ser.). (SPA.). (gr. k-1). 23.00 (978-0-7635-8608-9(0)) Rigby Education.
Let's Paint! (Early Intervention Levels Ser.). 23.10 (978-0-7362-0012-7(6)) CENGAGE Learning.
Levy, Janey. Renaissance Paintings: Using Perspective to Represent Three-Dimensional Objects. (PowerMath Ser.). 32p. 2009. (ENG., Illus.). (gr. 5-6). pap. 10.00 (978-1-4042-5115-1(4)) 2009. (gr. 4-5). 47.90 (978-1-60851-416-8(1), PowerKids Pr.) 2005. (Illus.). (J). (gr. 3-6). lib. bdg. 25.25 (978-1-4042-2926-6(4), PowerKids Pr.) 2005. 47.50 (978-1-4042-5220-2(7), Rosen Classroom) Rosen Publishing Group, Inc., The.
Littlefield, Cindy A. Pop-Out & Paint Farm Animals. 2013. (ENG.). 48p. (J). (gr. 3-8). pap. 12.95 (978-1-61212-139-0(X)) Storey Publishing, LLC.
Make Your Own Art, 12 vols., Sets 1-2. Incl. Set 1. 2008. lib. bdg. 151.50 (978-1-4358-2549-9(7)); Set 2. 2010. lib. bdg. 151.50 (978-1-4488-1625-5(4)); (J). (gr. 3-6). (Make Your Own Art Ser.). 32p. 2010. Set lib. bdg. 303.00 (978-1-4488-1626-2(2), PowerKids Pr.) Rosen Publishing Group, Inc., The.
McCully, Emily Arnold. The Secret Cave: Discovering Lascaux. McCully, Emily Arnold, illus. 2010. (ENG., Illus.). 40p. (J). (gr. 1-4). 18.99 (978-0-374-36694-0(2), 9780374366940, Farrar, Straus & Giroux (BYR)) Farrar, Straus & Giroux.
McLean, Sandra. Monkey Business. 2004. (Illus.). 68p. pap. 10.95 (978-1-57377-187-0(2), 0-1988-4-02502-3) Eas'l Pubns.
McLewn, Sandra. Cuisine D'art. 2004. 60p. pap. 11.95 (978-1-57377-199-3(6), 0-1988-4-02518-4) Eas'l Pubns.
Medina, Sarah. Having Fun with Paint. 2007. (Fun Art Projects Ser.). (Illus.). 24p. (J). (gr. -1-3). lib. bdg. 25.25 (978-1-4042-3718-6(6), PowerKids Pr.) Rosen Publishing Group, Inc., The.
Meet the Artists, 6 vols., Pack. (Bookweb Ser.). 32p. (gr. 6-18). 34.00 (978-0-7578-0905-7(7)) Rigby Education.
Micklethwait, Lucy. I Spy Colors in Art. 2007. (ENG., Illus.). 40p. (J). (gr. -1-3). 19.99 (978-0-06-134837-2(6), Greenwillow Bks.) HarperCollins Pubs.
Munro, Roxie. Masterpiece Mix. 2017. (ENG., Illus.). 32p. (J). 16.95 (**978-0-8234-3699-6(3)**) Holiday Hse., Inc.
My Little Pony Paint n' Play. 2005. (J). spiral bd. (978-1-59487-072-9(1)) Artist Studios, Ltd.
My Little Pony Paint n' Play with Sticker Rolls. 2005. (J). spiral bd. (978-1-59487-143-6(4)) Artist Studios, Ltd.
Nardo, Don. Painting. Parks, Peggy, ed. 2012. (Eye on Art Ser.). (ENG., Illus.). 128p. (gr. 7-10). lib. bdg. 39.40 (978-1-4205-0549-8(1)) Cengage Gale.
Newlands, Anne & Thomson, Tom. The Group of Seven & Tom Thomson: An Introduction. 2008. (ENG., Illus.). 64p. (gr. 5-18). pap. 14.95 (978-1-895565-54-6(5), 9781895565546) Firefly Bks., Ltd.
Noble, Marty. Color Your Own Great Paintings by Women Artists. 2006. (Dover Art Coloring Book Ser.). (ENG., Illus.). 32p. (gr. 3-8). pap. 4.99 (978-0-486-45108-4(9)) Dover Pubns., Inc.
Nudelman, Edwar, ed. A Halloween Reader. 2004. (Illus.). 12p. 8.95 (978-1-58980-260-5(8)) Pelican Publishing Co., Inc.
O'Dea, Rory & Benchmark Education Co. Staff. Opinions about Art - a Study of Paintings from the Romantic Era. 2014. (Text Connections Ser.). (J). (gr. 5). (978-1-4900-1384-8(9)) Benchmark Education Co.
Paint. (Jump Ser.). (Illus.). 36p. (J). (gr. 2-6). pap. (978-1-882210-32-9(8)) Action Publishing, Inc.
Painting the Car: KinderConcepts Individual Title Six-Packs. (Kinderstarters Ser.). 8p. (gr. -1-1). 21.00 (978-0-7635-8732-1(X)) Rigby Education.
Palomaki, Kurt. Floating Men & Pale Faces: The Paintings of Kurt Palomaki. 2003. (Illus.). 48p. (YA). per. 19.99 (978-0-9645655-5-5(2)) BurnhillWolf.
Papel, Dibujos y Pinturas. (One Hundred One Things to Do Ser.).Tr. of Paper, Drawing & Painting. (SPA.). (J). (gr. 3-5). pap. 4.76 (978-950-724-204-5(X)) Lumen ARG. Dist: Lectorum Pubns., Inc.
Peel, Yana. Faces for Baby: An Art for Baby Book. 2013. (ENG., Illus.). 12p. (J). (gr. k — 1). bds. 21.99 (978-0-7636-6433-6(2), Templar) Candlewick Pr.
Pete Paints a Picture, 6 Packs. (Story Steps Ser.). (gr. k-2). 20.00 (978-0-7635-9602-6(7)) Rigby Education.
Peters, Scott. Painting Shapes. 2011. (Early Connections Ser.). (J). (978-1-61672-332-3(7)) Benchmark Education Co.
Powell, William F. Color Mixing Recipes for Portraits: More Than 500 Color Combinations for Skin, Eyes, Lips & Hair. 2006. (Color Mixing Recipes Ser.). (ENG., Illus.). 48p. 9.95 (978-1-56010-990-7(4), 1560109904) Quarto Publishing Group USA.
Price, Jamie Mills. Christmastime: Between the Vines, Vol. 3. 2004. 84p. pap. 12.95 (978-1-57377-195-5(3), 0-1988-4-02510-8) Eas'l Pubns.
QEB Learn Art National Book Stores Edition: Painting. 2006. (J). per. (978-1-59566-281-1(2)) QEB Publishing Inc.
QEB Let's Start! Art National Book Stores Edition: Painting. 2006. (J). per. (978-1-59566-303-0(7)) QEB Publishing Inc.
Raczka, Bob. Artful Reading. (Bob Raczka's Art Adventures Ser.). (ENG., Illus.). 32p. (gr. -1-3). 2009. pap. 9.95 (978-1-58013-880-2(2), First Avenue Editions) 2007. lib. bdg. 25.26 (978-0-8225-6754-7(7), Millbrook Pr.) Lerner Publishing Group.
—More Than Meets the Eye: Seeing Art with All Five Senses. 2003. (Bob Raczka's Art Adventures Ser.). (ENG., Illus.). 32p. (gr. k-12). pap. 9.95 (978-0-7613-1994-8(8), First Avenue Editions) Lerner Publishing Group.
Rau, Dana Meachen. Painting Rocks. 2012. (How-To Library). (ENG.). 32p. (gr. 3-6). 28.50 (978-1-61080-479-0(1), 202089); pap. 14.21 (978-1-61080-653-4(0), 202263) Cherry Lake Publishing.
Rendall, Richard & Abrams, Elise. Hand-Painted Porcelain Plates: Nineteenth Century to the Present, 1 vol. 2003. (ENG., Illus.). 240p. (gr. 10-13). 59.99 (978-0-7643-1692-0(3), 9780764316920) Schiffer Publishing, Ltd.
Riggs, Kate. What Is Realism? 2016. (Illus.). 24p. (J). (978-1-60818-628-0(8), Creative Education) Creative Co., The.
—What Is Romanticism? 2016. (Illus.). 24p. (J). (978-1-60818-629-7(6), Creative Education) Creative Co., The.
Rumsby, Anna, illus. The Painting-In Book. 2017. (ENG.). 64p. (J). (gr. -1-k). pap. 14.99 (978-1-78067-936-5(X)) King, Laurence Publishing GBR. Dist: Hachette Bk. Group.
Saxton, Jo. Snail Trail: In Search of a Modern Masterpiece. 2014. (ENG., Illus.). 32p. (J). (gr. -1-1). pap. 8.99 (978-1-84780-423-5(3), Frances Lincoln) Quarto Publishing Group UK GBR. Dist: Hachette Bk. Group.
Shirodkar, Suhag. Captured in Miniature. 2010. (ENG.). 56p. 16.95 (978-0-944142-61-5(3)) Mapin Publishing Pvt. Ltd IND. Dist: National Bk. Network.
Smith, Lucy. How to Draw Horses. Chapman, Chris et al, illus. rev. ed. 2006. (Kid Kits Ser.). 32p. (J). (gr. 4). pap. 13.99 (978-1-58086-969-0(6)) EDC Publishing.
Smith, Thomasina. Fantastic Faces to Paint Yourself! Become a Pirate, a Ghoul, a Spotty Dog & More. 2016. (ENG., Illus.). 64p. 9.99 (978-1-86147-470-4(9), Armadillo) Anness Publishing GBR. Dist: National Bk. Network.
Spence, David. The Impressionists: Monet, Cezanne, Renoir, Degas. 2010. (ENG.). 128p. (J). (gr. 4-7). pap. 12.95 (978-1-84696-217-2(X), TickTock Books) Octopus Publishing Group GBR. Dist: Independent Pubs. Group.
Spilsbury, Louise. Decorated Pottery. 2016. (Stories in Art Ser.). (ENG., Illus.). 32p. (J). (gr. 2-4). pap. 11.99 (978-0-7502-9445-4(0), Wayland) Hachette Children's Group GBR. Dist: Hachette Bk. Group.
Strawberry Shortcake Paint n' Play with Sticker Rolls. 2005. (J). spiral bd. (978-1-59487-146-7(9)) Artist Studios, Ltd.
Teenage Mutant Ninja Turtles Paint Master Activity Books. 2004. (J). act. bk. ed. 2.99 (978-0-7666-1301-0(1), 15330); act. bk. ed. 2.99 (978-0-7666-1302-7(X), 15330) Modern Publishing.
Thomas, Danita & Thomas, John E. The Ultimate Book of Holiday Kid Concoctions: More Than 50 Wacky, Wild, & Crazy Concoctions for All Occasions. 2006. (Ultimate Book of Kid Concoctions Ser.). (Illus.). 80p. (J). (gr. 4-7). per. 14.99 (978-0-8054-4445-2(9)) B&H Publishing Group.
—The Ultimate Book of Kid Concoctions. 2006. (Illus.). 80p. (J). (gr. 4-7). per. 14.99 (978-0-8054-4443-8(2)) B&H Publishing Group.
Thomas, John E. & Thomas, Danita. The Ultimate Book of Kid Concoctions 2. 2006. (Illus.). 80p. (J). (gr. 4-7). per. 14.99 (978-0-8054-4444-5(0)) B&H Publishing Group.
Thomson, Ruth. Portraits. 2003. (First Look at Art Ser.). (Illus.). 32p. (gr. 4-6). 23.00 (978-0-7910-7948-5(1), Chelsea Hse.) Facts On File, Inc.
Top That Publishing Staff, ed. Drawing with Pastels. 2006. 64p. (978-1-84510-615-7(6)) Top That! Publishing PLC.
—Glass Painting. 2004. (Creative Studios Ser.). (ENG., Illus.). 48p. (J). (978-1-84510-248-7(7)) Top That! Publishing PLC.
Torres, Laura. Rocas Pintadas. 2004. (SPA & ENG.). 64p. (J). spiral bd. 17.95 (978-968-5528-07-8(1)) Klutz Latino MEX. Dist: Independent Pubs. Group.
Toyne, Jessica. Dali, Vol. 7. 2015. (Great Artists Collection). (Illus.). 64p. (J). (gr. 7). lib. bdg. 23.95 (978-1-4222-3258-3(1)) Mason Crest.
VanVoorst, Jenny Fretland. La Pintura. 2016. (El Estudio del Artista (Artist's Studio)).Tr. of Painting. (SPA.). 24p. (J). (gr. k-2). lib. bdg. 25.65 (978-1-62031-325-1(1), Bullfrog Bks.) Jump! Inc.
Wagner, Lisa. Cool Painted Stuff, 1 vol. 2005. (Cool Crafts Ser.). (ENG., Illus.). 32p. (gr. k-6). 28.50 (978-1-59197-742-1(8), Checkerboard Library) ABDO Publishing Co.
Watt, Fiona. 50 Things to Draw & Paint. (50 Things to Make & Do Ser.). (J). 2009. 104p. spiral bd. 9.99 (978-0-7945-2463-0(X)) 2006. (Illus.). 50p. (gr. 1-4). 9.99 (978-0-7945-1215-6(1)) EDC Publishing. (Usborne).
Wenzel, Angela. 13 Art Mysteries Children Should Know. 2011. (ENG., Illus.). 48p. (J). (gr. 3-7). 14.95 (978-3-7913-7044-6(8)) Prestel Verlag GmbH & Co KG. DEU. Dist: Penguin Random Hse. LLC.
—13 Artists Children Should Know. 2009. (ENG., Illus.). 48p. (J). (gr. 3-7). 14.95 (978-3-7913-4173-6(1)) Prestel Verlag GmbH & Co KG. DEU. Dist: Penguin Random Hse. LLC.
—13 Paintings Children Should Know. 2009. (ENG., Illus.). 48p. (J). (gr. 3-7). 14.95 (978-3-7913-4323-5(8)) Prestel Verlag GmbH & Co KG. DEU. Dist: Penguin Random Hse. LLC.
Wilmes, Liz & Wilmes, Dick. Easel Art. Koeller, Carol, illus. 2004. 128p. (J). pap. 12.95 (978-0-943452-25-8(2)) Building Blocks, LLC.
Wisner, Karen. Country Seasons, Vol. 3. 2004. 60p. pap. 11.95 (978-1-57377-201-3(1), 0-1988-4-2522-1) Eas'l Pubns.
Wolfe, Gillian. Look! Zoom in on Art! 2007. (Look! Ser.). (ENG., Illus.). 40p. (J). (gr. 3-6). 16.95 (978-1-84507-796-9(2), Frances Lincoln) Quarto Publishing Group UK GBR. Dist: Hachette Bk. Group.
Zhang, Gui Jie. The Bamboo Forest: I Truly Love You, & God Loves You Too, 1 vol. 2009. 47p. pap. 24.95 (978-1-60836-292-9(2)) America Star Bks.

PAINTING, ABSTRACT

see Art, Abstract

PAINTING—COLOR REPRODUCTION

see Prints

PAINTING, DUTCH

Bassil, Andrea & van Gogh, Vincent. Vincent Van Gogh. 2004. (Lives of the Artists Ser.). (Illus.). 48p. (gr. 5-12). lib. bdg. 31.00 (978-0-8368-5602-6(3), Gareth Stevens Secondary Library) Stevens, Gareth Publishing LLLP.
—Vincent van Gogh. 2004. (Lives of the Artists Ser.). (Illus.). 48p. (gr. 5-12). pap. 14.05 (978-0-8368-5607-1(4), Gareth Stevens Secondary Library) Stevens, Gareth Publishing LLLP.
Geis, Patricia. Vincent Van Gogh. 2015. (ENG.). 16p. (J). (gr. 2-7). 24.95 (978-1-61689-456-6(3)) Princeton Architectural Pr.

Nichols, Catherine. Vincent Van Gogh. 2006. (Primary Source Library of Famous Artists Ser.). (Illus.). 32p. (J). (gr. 3-7). lib. bdg. 23.95 *(978-1-4042-2766-8(0),* PowerKids Pr.) Rosen Publishing Group, Inc., The.

—Vincent van Gogh. 2009. (Primary Source Library of Famous Artists Ser.). 32p. (gr. 3-4). 42.50 *(978-1-60854-105-8(3),* PowerKids Pr.) Rosen Publishing Group, Inc., The.

Raczka, Bob. The Vermeer Interviews: Conversations with Seven Works of Art. 2010. (Bob Raczka's Art Adventures Ser.). (ENG.). 32p. (gr. 3-12). pap. 9.95 *(978-1-58013-882-6(9),* First Avenue Editions) Lerner Publishing Group.

Wood, Alix. Vincent Van Gogh. 2013. (Artists Through the Ages Ser.). (ENG., Illus.). 32p. (gr. 3-6). 25.25 *(978-1-61533-622-7(2));* pap. 10.00 *(978-1-61533-631-9(1))* Windmill Bks.

PAINTING—FICTION

Aboff, Marcie. The Mystery of the Disappearing Painting. 2016. (Spring Forward Ser.). (J). (gr. 2). *(978-1-4900-9453-3(9))* Benchmark Education Co.

Adams, Adrienne. The Easter Egg Artists. 2017. (ENG.). 32p. (J). (gr. -1-3). 13.99 ***(978-1-5344-1245-3(X),*** Aladdin) Simon & Schuster Children's Publishing.

Adams, Jesse. Farmer Dillo Paints His Barn. Speer, Julie & Davis, Christopher Owen, illus. 2007. (J). (gr. -1-3). pap. 12.95 *(978-1-59166-808-4(5))* BJU Pr.

Agee, Jon. The Incredible Painting of Felix Clousseau. 2015. 32p. pap. 8.00 *(978-1-61003-620-7(4))* Center for the Collaborative Classroom.

Alphin, Elaine Marie. Simon Says. 2005. (ENG.). 264p. (YA). (gr. 9-12). pap. 14.95 *(978-0-15-204678-1(X))* Houghton Mifflin Harcourt Publishing Co.

Anholt, Laurence. Cezanne & the Apple Boy. 2009. (ENG., Illus.). 32p. (J). (gr. -1-2). 16.99 *(978-0-7641-6282-4(9))* Barron's Educational Series, Inc.

Ardwin, Juanita. Remember When, 1 vol. 2009. 40p. pap. 19.95 *(978-1-4489-2008-2(6))* PublishAmerica, Inc.

Arrigan, Mary. Mario's Angels: A Story about the Artist Giotto. McClure, Gillian, illus. 2006. (ENG.). 32p. (J). (gr. k-3). 15.95 *(978-1-84507-404-3(1),* Frances Lincoln) Quarto Publishing Group UK GBR. Dist: Hachette Bk. Group.

Asch, Frank. Bread & Honey. 2015. lib. bdg. 18.40 *(978-0-606-36290-0(8))* Turtleback Bks.

Austin, Rikey. Sandy Paints a Picture: Alice's Bear Shop. 2012. 28p. pap. *(978-1-78092-155-6(1))* MX Publishing, Ltd.

Baker, Keith. More Mr. & Mrs. Green, 1 vol. Baker, Keith, illus. 2007. (Mr. & Mrs. Green Ser.). (ENG., Illus.). 68p. (gr. 2-4). 27.07 *(978-1-59961-302-4(6))* Spotlight.

Bang, Molly. When Sophie's Feelings Are Really, Really Hurt. 2015. (ENG., Illus.). 40p. (J). (gr. -1-3). 17.99 *(978-0-545-78831-1(5),* Blue Sky Pr., The) Scholastic, Inc.

Barnett, Mac. Oh No! Not Again! Or How I Built a Time Machine to Save History - Or at Least My History Grade. Santat, Dan, illus. 2012. (Oh No! Picture Book Ser.). (ENG.). 40p. (J). (gr. -1-k). 17.99 *(978-1-4231-4912-5(2))* Hyperion Pr.

Barron, T. A. Ghost Hands. Low, William, illus. 2011. (ENG.). 40p. (J). (gr. k-3). 18.99 *(978-0-399-25083-5(2),* Philomel Bks.) Penguin Young Readers Group.

Beaumont, Karen. I Ain't Gonna Paint No More! Catrow, David, illus. (ENG.). (J). (gr. -1 — 1). 2012. 30p. bds. 11.99 *(978-0-547-87035-9(3))* 2005. 32p. 17.99 *(978-0-15-202488-8(3))* Houghton Mifflin Harcourt Publishing Co.

Benton, Jim. Piggy Paints. 2015. (ENG.). 16p. (J). (— 1). bds. 5.99 *(978-0-545-64785-4(1),* Cartwheel Bks.) Scholastic, Inc.

Blackaby, Susan & Jones, Christianne C. El Cuadro de Mary, 1 vol. Ruiz, Carlos, tr. Haugen, Ryan, illus. 2006. (Read-It! Readers en Español: Story Collection).Tr. of Mary's Art. (SPA.). 32p. (gr. -1-3). 21.32 *(978-1-4048-1649-7(6),* Easy Readers) Picture Window Bks.

Bledsoe, Michele & Bledsoe, Richard. The Secret Kingdom. 2013. 36p. 20.95 *(978-1-4787-0362-4(8))* Outskirts Pr., Inc.

Brennan-Nelson, Denise & Brennan, Rosemarie. Willow. Moore, Cyd, illus. 2008. (ENG.). 32p. (J). (gr. k-6). 16.95 *(978-1-58536-342-1(1))* Sleeping Bear Pr.

Bridges, Shirin Yim. The Umbrella Queen. Yoo, Taeeun, illus. 2008. (ENG.). 40p. (J). (gr. k-3). 16.99 *(978-0-06-075040-4(5),* Greenwillow Bks.) HarperCollins Pubs.

Buchholz, Quint. El Coleccionista de Momentos. 2nd ed. 2003. (Rosa y Manzana Ser.). (SPA., Illus.). 48p. (J). *(978-84-89804-16-6(8))* Lóguez Ediciones ESP. Dist: Lectorum Pubns., Inc.

Campoy, F. Isabel & Howell, Theresa. Maybe Something Beautiful: How Art Transformed a Neighborhood. López, Rafael, illus. 2016. (ENG.). 40p. (J). (gr. -1-3). 16.99 *(978-0-544-35769-3(8),* HMH Books For Young Readers) Houghton Mifflin Harcourt Publishing Co.

Capatti, Bérénice. Klimt & His Cat. Monaco, Octavia, illus. 2004. (ENG.). 40p. (J). 20.00 *(978-0-8028-5282-3(3))* Eerdmans, William B. Publishing Co.

Cardwell, Michelle. Seeing the World Through Different Eyes. 2009. 32p. pap. 12.99 *(978-1-4389-9776-6(0))* AuthorHouse.

Carle, Eric. The Artist Who Painted a Blue Horse. Carle, Eric, illus. (ENG., Illus.). (J). (gr. -1 — 1). 2013. 22p. bds. 7.99 *(978-0-399-16402-6(2))* 2011. 32p. 17.99 *(978-0-399-25713-1(6))* Penguin Young Readers Group. (Philomel Bks.).

Cohn, Diana. Mr Goethes Garden. Mirocha, Paul, illus. 2003. (ENG.). 32p. (J). 17.95 *(978-0-88010-521-7(6))* SteinerBooks, Inc.

Coulton, Mia. Danny Paints a Picture. Coulton, Mia, photos by. 2004. (ENG., Illus.). pap. 5.35 *(978-0-9746475-5-5(1))* Maryruth Bks., Inc.

Crain, Kira. SEK Statton. 2009. (GER.). 136p. 29.95 *(978-1-4092-6127-8(1))* Lulu Pr., Inc.

Crow, Melinda Melton. Let's Paint the Garage!, 1 vol. Thompson, Chad, illus. 2012. (Wonder Wheels Ser.). (ENG.). 32p. (gr. -1-1). pap. 6.25 *(978-1-4342-4238-9(2));* lib. bdg. 22.65 *(978-1-4342-4016-3(9))* Stone Arch Bks.

Davis, Chasta. The Easter Bunny & His Famous Painted Eggs. 2011. 28p. pap. 24.95 *(978-1-4512-1649-3(1))* America Star Bks.

Dean, James & Dean, Kimberly. A Pet for Pete. Dean, James, illus. 2014. (My First I Can Read Ser.). (ENG., Illus.). 32p. (J). (gr. -1-3). pap. 3.99 *(978-0-06-230379-0(1))* HarperCollins Pubs.

deRubertis, Barbara. Polly Porcupine's Painting Prize. Alley, R. W., illus. 2011. (Animal Antics A to Z Ser.). 32p. (J). pap. 45.32 *(978-0-7613-7662-0(3));* lib. bdg. 22.60 *(978-1-57565-337-2(0))* Kane Press, Inc.

—Polly Porcupine's Painting Prizes. Alley, R. W., illus. 2011. (Animal Antics A to Z Ser.). (ENG.). 32p. (J). (gr. -1-3). pap. 7.95 *(978-1-57565-328-0(1))* Kane Press, Inc.

deRubertis, Barbara & DeRubertis, Barbara. Polly Porcupine's Painting Prizes. Alley, R. W., illus. 2012. (Animal Antics A to Z Ser.). 32p. (J). (gr. 2 — 1). cd-rom 7.95 *(978-1-57565-409-6(1))* Kane Press, Inc.

Dolson, Carol Bland. Hattie & the Higgledy-Piggledy Hedge. Rabon, Elaine Hearn, illus. 2012. (ENG.). 32p. (J). 18.95 *(978-0-9827614-4-1(9),* 9780982761441) Moose Hill Bks., Inc.

Falwell, Cathryn. Butterflies for Kiri. Falwell, Cathryn, illus. 2003. (ENG., Illus.). 32p. (J). *(978-1-58430-100-4(7))* Lee & Low Bks., Inc.

Farish, Terry. Luis Paints the World. Dominguez, Oliver, illus. 2016. (ENG.). 32p. (J). (gr. k-4). 19.99 *(978-1-4677-5796-6(9),* Carolrhoda Bks.) Lerner Publishing Group.

Flavin, Teresa. The Blackhope Enigma. 2011. (ENG., Illus.). 304p. (J). (gr. 4-7). 15.99 *(978-0-7636-5694-2(1),* Templar) Candlewick Pr.

—The Crimson Shard. (ENG.). (J). (gr. 4-7). 2015. 288p. pap. 6.99 *(978-0-7636-7172-3(X))* 2012. (Illus.). 256p. 15.99 *(978-0-7636-6093-2(0))* Candlewick Pr. (Templar).

Fortune, Tracy. Kaila's Garden. 2009. 32p. pap. 14.98 *(978-0-557-02254-0(1))* Lulu Pr., Inc.

Froeb, Lori. I Am Picasso. Melman, Debra, illus. 2015. (Rescue Readers Ser.: 4). (ENG.). 32p. (J). (gr. 1-2). lib. bdg. 16.99 *(978-0-7944-3515-8(7))* Reader's Digest Assn., Inc., The.

Froeb, Lori C. ASPCA Rescue Readers - I Am Picasso! Melman, Debra, illus. 2015. (Rescue Readers Ser.). (ENG.). 32p. (J). (gr. k-2). pap. 3.99 *(978-0-7944-3514-1(9),* Reader's Digest Children's Bks.) Studio Fun International.

Frueh, Stacy. Jonah's Weird, but Totally Cool Field Tr. 2005. 50p. pap. 16.95 *(978-1-4137-9818-0(7))* PublishAmerica, Inc.

Fulton-Vengco, Aletha. Felicidad's Sidewalk Art. 2009. 36p. 14.80 *(978-0-578-00890-5(4))* Vengco, Aletha Fulton.

Gerstein, Mordicai. The First Drawing. 2013. (ENG., Illus.). 40p. (J). (gr. -1-3). 18.99 *(978-0-316-20478-1(1))* Little, Brown Bks. for Young Readers.

Gisbert, Montse & Gisbert, Montserrat. Salvador Dalí, Píntame un Sueño. 2004. (SPA., Illus.). (J). 19.99 *(978-84-8488-127-8(X))* Serres, Ediciones, S. L. ESP. Dist: Lectorum Pubns., Inc.

Golden Books. Snow Wonder! (Frosty the Snowman) Golden Books, illus. 2013. (Deluxe Paint Box Book Ser.). (ENG., Illus.). 128p. (J). (gr. -1-2). pap. 7.99 *(978-0-385-37179-7(9),* Golden Bks.) Random Hse. Children's Bks.

Graves, Sue. Oh, George! Collins, Ross, illus. 2005. (Reading Corner Ser.). 24p. (J). (gr. k-3). lib. bdg. 22.80 *(978-1-59771-000-8(8))* Sea-To-Sea Pubns.

Greve, Meg. Painting Party. Anglicas, Louise, illus. 2013. (ENG.). 24p. (gr. -1-1). pap. 8.95 *(978-1-62169-207-2(8))* Rourke Educational Media.

Gutierrez, Elisa. Picturescape. rev. ed. 2007. (ENG., Illus.). 40p. (J). (gr. -1-3). pap. 9.95 *(978-1-894965-65-1(5))* Simply Read Bks. CAN. Dist: Ingram Publisher Services.

Hahn, Blair. My Purple Toes. Nation, Tate, illus. 2010. 24p. (J). 10.99 *(978-0-9844556-4-5(7))* My Purple Toes, LLC.

Handford, Martin. Where's Waldo? the Great Picture Hunt. Handford, Martin, illus. 2010. (Where's Waldo? Ser.). (ENG., Illus.). 24p. (J). (gr. k-4). pap. 7.99 *(978-0-7636-4215-0(0))* Candlewick Pr.

Hardy, Sarah Frances. Paint Me! Hardy, Sarah Frances, illus. 2014. (ENG., Illus.). 32p. (J). (-k). 14.95 *(978-1-62873-813-1(8),* Sky Pony Pr.) Skyhorse Publishing Co., Inc.

Harris, Patricia. The Car of Many Colors. 2017. (Colorful Cars Ser.). 24p. (gr. 4-6). pap. 8.25 ***(978-1-5383-2087-7(8),*** PowerKids Pr.) Rosen Publishing Group, Inc., The.

Hewitt, Christine. A Mystical Journey. 2009. 80p. pap. 12.45 *(978-0-557-06314-7(0))* Lulu Pr., Inc.

Hicer, Nancy. Rosa's Painting. 2015. (Rosen REAL Readers: STEM & STEAM Collection). (ENG.). 8p. pap. 5.46 *(978-1-4994-9608-6(7),* Rosen Classroom) Rosen Publishing Group, Inc., The.

Hieber, Leanna Renee. Darker Still. 2011. (Magic Most Foul Ser.: 1). (ENG.). 336p. (YA). (gr. 7-12). pap. 8.99 *(978-1-4022-6052-0(0))* Sourcebooks, Inc.

Hoffman, Peter. A ferret in a Garret. Olson, Cindy, illus. 2008. 36p. (J). 24.99 *(978-0-9790247-6-4(5))* Artpacks.

Holden, Pam. Animal Art, 6 vols. Storey, Jim, illus. 2009. (Red Rocket Readers Ser.). (ENG.). 16p. (gr. 1-1). pap. *(978-1-877419-73-7(7),* Red Rocket Readers) Flying Start Bks.

I Love to Paint. 2003. (Illus.). (J). per. *(978-1-57657-961-9(1))* Paradise Pr., Inc.

Johnson, Angela. Daddy Calls Me Man. Mitchell, Rhonda, illus. 2014. 32p. pap. 7.00 *(978-1-61003-309-1(4))* Center for the Collaborative Classroom.

Johnson, D. B. Magritte's Marvelous Hat. Johnson, D. B., illus. 2012. (ENG., Illus.). 32p. (J). (gr. -1-3). 17.99 *(978-0-547-55864-6(3))* Houghton Mifflin Harcourt Publishing Co.

Johnson, Shane, illus. OLIVIA Paints a Mural. 2011. (Olivia TV Tie-In Ser.). (ENG.). 12p. (J). (gr. -1-1). bds. 5.99 *(978-1-4424-1674-1(2),* Simon Spotlight) Simon Spotlight.

Joseph, Danielle. Pure Red. 2011. (ENG.). 240p. (YA). pap. 9.95 *(978-0-7387-2743-1(1),* Flux) North Star Editions.

Kalar, Bonnie. Ann Paints & Plays. Spreen, Kathe, illus. Date not set. 12p. (J). (gr. -1-2). pap. *(978-1-891619-40-3(3))* Corona Pr.

King, Kirsty. My New Friends. 2005. 52p. pap. *(978-1-84401-576-4(9))* Athena Pr.

Kravetz, Nathan. A Horse of Another Color. 2011. 68p. (gr. 4-6). pap. 10.95 *(978-1-4620-0591-8(8))* iUniverse, Inc.

Larsen, Andrew. The Imaginary Garden. Luxbacher, Irene, illus. 2009. (ENG.). 32p. (J). (gr. -1-2). 16.95 *(978-1-55453-279-7(5))* Kids Can Pr., Ltd. CAN. Dist: Hachette Bk. Group.

Lodding, Linda Ravin. Painting Pepette. Fletcher, Claire, illus. 2016. (ENG.). 40p. (J). (gr. -1-3). 17.99 *(978-1-4998-0136-1(X))* Little Bee Books Inc.

Look, Lenore. Brush of the Gods. So, Meilo, illus. 2013. (ENG.). 40p. (J). (gr. -1-3). 17.99 *(978-0-375-87001-9(6),* Schwartz & Wade Bks.) Random Hse. Children's Bks.

Lukacs, Krisztian. Bud & Barnie: Let's Paint! 2011. 50p. pap. 19.99 *(978-1-4475-7901-4(1))* Lulu Pr., Inc.

MacLachlan, Patricia & MacLachlan, Emily. Painting the Wind. Schneider, Katy, illus. 2006. (Joanna Cotler Bks.). (ENG.). 40p. (J). (gr. -1-3). reprint ed. pap. 7.99 *(978-0-06-443825-4(2))* HarperCollins Pubs.

Markun, Patricia M. The Little Painter of Sabana Grande. Casilla, Robert, illus. 2014. (ENG.). 32p. (J). (gr. -1-3). 13.99 *(978-1-4814-4458-3(1),* Simon & Schuster Bks. For Young Readers) Simon & Schuster Bks. For Young Readers.

Mayhew, James. Katie & the Waterlily Pond. Mayhew, James, illus. 2015. (Katie Ser.). (ENG., Illus.). 32p. (J). (gr. -1-k). pap. 10.99 *(978-1-4083-3245-0(0))* Hodder & Stoughton GBR. Dist: Hachette Bk. Group.

Mayhew, James & McQuillan, Mary. Katie & the British Artists. Mayhew, James, illus. 2015. (Katie Ser.). (ENG., Illus.). 32p. (J). (gr. -1-k). 9.99 *(978-1-4083-3190-3(X))* Hodder & Stoughton GBR. Dist: Hachette Bk. Group.

McPhail, David. Big Brown Bear/El Gran Oso Pardo. Flor Ada, Alma & Campoy, F. Isabel, trs. 2007. (Green Light Readers Level 1 Ser.). (ENG & SPA., Illus.). 28p. (J). (gr. -1-3). pap. 3.95 *(978-0-15-205970-5(9))* Houghton Mifflin Harcourt Publishing Co.

Meadows, Daisy. Violet the Painting Fairy. 2015. (Illus.). (J). (Magical Crafts Fairies Ser.: 5). (ENG.). 80p. (gr. 2-5). pap. 4.99 *(978-0-545-70833-3(8),* Scholastic Paperbacks); 65p. *(978-0-545-72413-5(9))* Scholastic, Inc.

Meinderts, Koos. The Man in the Clouds. Fienieg, Annette, illus. 2012. (ENG.). 38p. (J). (gr. 1). 16.95 *(978-1-935954-13-2(X),* 9781935954132) Lemniscaat USA.

Merberg, Julie & Bober, Suzanne. Dreaming with Rousseau. 2007. (Mini Masters Ser.: MINI). (ENG., Illus.). 22p. (J). (gr. -1 — 1). bds. 6.99 *(978-0-8118-5712-3(3))* Chronicle Bks. LLC.

—Painting with Picasso. 2006. (Mini Masters Ser.: MINI). (ENG., Illus.). 22p. (J). (gr. -1 — 1). bds. 6.99 *(978-0-8118-5505-1(8))* Chronicle Bks. LLC.

Nez, John, illus. The Dragon Painter. 2006. (First Reading Level 4 Ser.). 48p. (J). (gr. 1-4). 8.99 *(978-0-7945-1275-0(5),* Usborne) EDC Publishing.

Numeroff, Laura Joffe & Evans, Nate. The Jellybeans & the Big Art Adventure. Munsinger, Lynn, illus. 2012. (ENG.). 32p. (J). (gr. -1-k). 17.95 *(978-1-4197-0171-9(1),* Abrams Bks. for Young Readers) Abrams, Inc.

Ortiz, Raquel M. & Ventura, Gabriela Baeza. Sofi & the Magic, Musical Mural. Dominguez, Maria, illus. 2015. (SPA & ENG.). (J). 17.95 *(978-1-55885-803-9(2),* Piñata Books) Arte Publico Pr.

Perdue, Gillian. Conor's Canvas. Connor, Michael, illus. 2007. (Pandas Ser.: 35). (ENG.). 64p. (J). pap. 9.95 *(978-1-84717-043-9(9))* O'Brien Pr., Ltd., The IRL. Dist: Dufour Editions, Inc.

Perkins, Mitali. Rickshaw Girl. Hogan, Jamie, illus. 2007. (ENG.). 96p. (J). (gr. 2-5). 14.95 *(978-1-58089-308-4(2))* Charlesbridge Publishing, Inc.

Plummer, David & Archambault, John. I Paint a Rainbow. Hollander, Sarah, illus. 2007. (J). *(978-1-58669-227-8(5));* *(978-1-58669-228-5(3))* Childcraft Education Corp.

Poulsen, David A. The Prisoners & the Paintings. 5th ed. 2008. (Salt & Pepper Chronicles: No. 5). (ENG.). 176p. (J). (gr. 2-7). *(978-1-55470-015-8(9))* Me to We.

Publications International Ltd. Staff. Play A Sound Video Fifi's Painting Party. 2008. 24p. 19.98 *(978-1-4127-9435-0(8),* PIL Kids) Publications International, Ltd.

Rabe, Tish. Chasing Rainbows. Ruiz, Aristides & Mathieu, Joe, illus. 2012. (Pictureback(R) Ser.). (ENG.). 16p. (J). (gr. -1-2). pap. 4.99 *(978-0-375-87124-5(1),* Random Hse. Bks. for Young Readers) Random Hse. Children's Bks.

Randolph, Joanne. A Rock for Mom. 2015. (Rosen REAL Readers: STEM & STEAM Collection). (ENG.). 8p. pap. 5.46 *(978-1-4994-9533-1(1),* Rosen Classroom) Rosen Publishing Group, Inc., The.

Rey, H. A. Time for School. 2011. (Curious George Ser.). (ENG., Illus.). 16p. (J). (gr. -1-3). 5.99 *(978-0-547-42230-5(X))* Houghton Mifflin Harcourt Publishing Co.

Reynolds, Peter H. Sky Color. Reynolds, Peter H., illus. 2012. (Creatrilogy Ser.). (ENG., Illus.). 32p. (J). (gr. k-12). 15.00 *(978-0-7636-2345-6(8))* Candlewick Pr.

Rigby Education Staff. Tom Sawyer: Jumbled Tumble. (gr. k-2). 26.00 *(978-0-7635-2424-1(7))* Rigby Education.

Robins, Eleanor. Art Show Mystery, 1 vol. unabr. ed. 2011. (Carter High Mysteries Ser.). (ENG.). 46p. (YA). (gr. 9-12). 7.95 *(978-1-61651-560-7(0))* Saddleback Educational Publishing, Inc.

Rogers, Gregory. The Hero of Little Street. Rogers, Gregory, illus. 2012. (ENG., Illus.). 32p. (J). (gr. k-3). 17.99 *(978-1-59643-729-6(4),* 9781596437296) Roaring Brook Pr.

Rorvik, Bjorn F. The Little Paintbrush. Hansen, Thore, illus. 2014. (ENG.). 32p. (J). (gr. -1-k). 12.95 *(978-1-62087-996-2(4),* 620996, Sky Pony Pr.) Skyhorse Publishing Co., Inc.

Ross, Donald. The Scribble Squad in the Weird Weird West. 2016. (ENG., Illus.). 256p. (J). 13.99 *(978-1-4494-6921-4(3))* Andrews McMeel Publishing.

Ross, Jill. What's the Matter, Mr. Ticklebritches? Pruitt, Gwendolyn, illus. 2010. (ENG.). 70p. (J). (gr. 3-7). pap. 9.95 *(978-1-59825-948-3(2))* Shenanigans Series.

Rouillard, Wendy W. Barnaby's Tree House. 2005. (Illus.). 30p. (J). *(978-0-9651070-4-4(3))* Barnaby & Co.

Rudolph, Tammy. Lucy's Mysterious Paint Brush. 2005. 17.00 *(978-0-8059-9765-1(2))* Dorrance Publishing Co., Inc.

Salter-Mathieson, Nigel C. S. Little Chief Mischief: From Tales of the Menehune. Gruen, Chuck, illus. 2011. 44p. pap. 35.95 *(978-1-258-10135-0(1))* Literary Licensing, LLC.

Schwartz, Amy. Begin at the Beginning: A Little Artist Learns about Life. Schwartz, Amy, illus. 2005. (Illus.). 40p. (J). (gr. -1-2). lib. bdg. 16.89 *(978-0-06-000112-4(7))* HarperCollins Pubs.

Seeger, Laura Vaccaro. One Boy. Seeger, Laura Vaccaro, illus. 2016. (ENG., Illus.). 48p. (J). 14.99 *(978-1-62672-252-1(8),* 9781626722521) Roaring Brook Pr.

Siminovich, Lorena. Alex & Lulu: Two of a Kind. Siminovich, Lorena, illus. 2009. (ENG., Illus.). 32p. (J). (gr. -1-3). 14.99 *(978-0-7636-4423-9(4),* Templar) Candlewick Pr.

Simko, Joe. The Sweet Rot, Book 2: Raiders of the Lost Art, 1 vol. 2011. (ENG., Illus.). 80p. (J). 19.99 *(978-0-7643-3828-1(5),* 9780764338281, Schiffer Publishing Ltd) Schiffer Publishing, Ltd.

Spencer, Hannah. With All Best Wishes, Mrs Butterbean. 2008. 28p. pap. 13.50 *(978-1-60693-138-7(5),* Eloquent Bks.) Strategic Book Publishing & Rights Agency (SBPRA).

St. Aubin, Anne. Drafus the Daring Dragon. 2008. 24p. pap. 16.49 *(978-1-4343-8875-9(1))* AuthorHouse.

Strauss, Victoria. Color Song, 0 vols. 2014. (Passion Blue Novel Ser.: 2). (ENG.). 344p. (J). (gr. 7-9). pap. 9.99 *(978-1-4778-2504-4(5),* 9781477825044, Skyscape) Amazon Publishing.

Tim's Paintings: Individual Title-Six Packs. (Chiquilibros Ser.). (gr. k-1). 23.00 *(978-0-7635-0430-4(0))* Rigby Education.

Tom Sawyer: 6 Small Books. (gr. k-2). 23.00 *(978-0-7635-8507-5(6))* Rigby Education.

Town, Vicky. Mayhem in the Museum. 2013. 74p. pap. 9.99 *(978-1-61720-974-1(0))* Wilder Pubns., Corp.

Twohy, Mike. Mouse & Hippo. Twohy, Mike, illus. 2017. (ENG., Illus.). 32p. (J). (gr. -1-3). 17.99 *(978-1-4814-5124-6(3),* Simon & Schuster/Paula Wiseman Bks.) Simon & Schuster/Paula Wiseman Bks.

Vance, Alexander. Behind the Canvas. 2016. (ENG.). 336p. (J). 16.99 *(978-1-250-02970-6(8),* 9781250029706) Feiwel & Friends.

Wells, Rosemary. Ruby's Rainbow. 2012. (Max Ruby Ser.). lib. bdg. 13.55 *(978-0-606-26091-6(9),* Turtleback) Turtleback Bks.

West, Jacqueline. The Shadows. 2011. (Books of Elsewhere Ser.: 1). (ENG.). 272p. (J). (gr. 5-7). 7.99 *(978-0-14-241872-7(2),* Puffin Books) Penguin Young Readers Group.

—The Shadows. Bernatene, Poly, illus. 2010. (Books of Elsewhere Ser.: 1). (ENG.). 256p. (J). (gr. 5-18). 16.99 *(978-0-8037-3440-1(9),* Dial Bks) Penguin Young Readers Group.

—The Shadows. l.t. ed. 2010. (Books of Elsewhere Ser.: Vol. 1). (ENG.). 268p. 23.99 *(978-1-4104-3139-4(8))* Thorndike Pr.

—The Shadows. 2011. (Books of Elsewhere Ser.: 1). lib. bdg. 17.20 *(978-0-606-23070-4(X),* Turtleback) Turtleback Bks.

Whipp, Jo. Otis & Baby Jean. Whipp, Katie, illus. 2012. 26p. 24.95 *(978-1-4626-5049-1(X))* America Star Bks.

Wiesner, David. Art & Max. 2012. (CHI.). 37p. (J). *(978-7-5434-9586-9(4))* Hebei Jiaoyu Chubanshe.

—Art & Max. 2010. (ENG., Illus.). 40p. (J). (gr. -1-3). 17.99 *(978-0-618-75663-6(9),* Clarion Bks.) Houghton Mifflin Harcourt Trade & Reference Pubs.

Wiggins, Thalia. Greg & the Mural, 1 vol. Tate, Don, illus. 2012. (Making Choices: the Mcnair Cousins Ser.). (ENG.). 64p. 27.07 *(978-1-61641-631-7(9),* Calico Chapter Bks) Magic Wagon.

Williams, John Joseph. The Frightened Garden. 2013. 98p. (J). pap. *(978-1-78299-167-0(0))* FeedARead.com.

Wilson, Martha. Latin Primer II - Student. 3rd ed. 2003. (ENG & LAT.). 138p. (gr. 3-6). spiral bd. 17.00 *(978-1-885767-52-3(8))* Canon Pr.

Zibart, Rosemary. I Have a Grandma Who ... Herzlich, Valori, illus. 2014. (J). *(978-1-929115-25-9(3))* Azro Pr., Inc.

Zuravicky, Orli. A Color for Sketch: A Book about Colors. Castellano, Giuseppe, illus. 2011. (Mister Doodle Ser.). (ENG.). 34p. (J). (gr. -1-k). bds. 7.99 *(978-1-4424-3154-6(7),* Little Simon) Little Simon.

PAINTING, FINGER

see Finger Painting

PAINTING—HISTORY

De Magalhaes, Roberto Carvalho. Claude Monet. 2003. (Great Artists Ser.). (Illus.). 40p. (J). 15.95 *(978-1-59270-009-7(8))* Enchanted Lion Bks., LLC.

Evans, Brooke DiGiovanni. Are You an Art Sleuth? Look, Discover, Learn! 2016. (ENG.). 104p. (J). (gr. -1-2). 17.99 *(978-1-63159-131-0(2),* Rockport Publishers) Quarto Publishing Group USA.

Fandel, Jennifer. Pablo Picasso. 2005. (Xtraordinary Artists Ser.). (Illus.). 48p. (J). (gr. 5-9). lib. bdg. 21.95 *(978-1-58341-331-9(6),* Creative Education) Creative Co., The.

Forte, Virginia. The History of Western Painting. 2015. (Britannica Guide to the Visual & Performing Arts Ser.). (ENG., Illus.). 128p. (J). (gr. 9-10). 45.00 *(978-1-68048-070-2(7),* Britannica Educational Publishing) Rosen Publishing Group, Inc., The.

Harris, Nathaniel. Paul Cézanne. 2003. (Artists in Their Time Ser.). (ENG., Illus.). 48p. (J). 24.00 *(978-0-531-12242-6(5),* Watts, Franklin) Scholastic Library Publishing.

Heine, Florian. 13 Painters Children Should Know. 2012. (ENG., Illus.). 48p. (J). (gr. 3-7). 14.95 *(978-3-7913-7086-6(3))* Prestel Verlag GmbH & Co KG. DEU. Dist: Penguin Random Hse. LLC.

Hodge, Susie & Picasso, P. Pablo Picasso. 2004. (Lives of the Artists Ser.). (Illus.). 48p. (gr. 5-12). pap. 14.05 *(978-0-8368-5606-4(6));* lib. bdg. 31.00 *(978-0-8368-5601-9(5))* Stevens, Gareth Publishing LLLP. (Gareth Stevens Secondary Library).

Lyons, Deborah. Edward Hopper: Summer at the Seaside. 2003. (Adventures in Art Ser.). (Illus.). 30p. (gr. 5-18). 14.95 *(978-3-7913-2737-2(2))* Prestel Publishing.

Manning, Mick. The Story of Paintings: A History of Art for Children. Granström, Brita, illus. 2017. (ENG.). 88p. (J). (gr. 3-9). 16.95 ***(978-1-4549-2702-0(X))*** Sterling Publishing Co., Inc.

Nichols, Catherine. Claude Monet. 2006. (Primary Source Library of Famous Artists Ser.). (Illus.). 32p. (J). (gr. -1-3). lib. bdg. 23.95 *(978-1-4042-2761-3(X),* PowerKids Pr.) Rosen Publishing Group, Inc., The.

—Pierre-Auguste Renoir. 2006. (Primary Source Library of Famous Artists Ser.). (Illus.). 32p. (J). (gr. -1-3). lib. bdg.

PQR

23.95 (978-1-4042-2765-1(2), PowerKids Pr.) Rosen Publishing Group, Inc., The.

Weller, Alan & Dover Publications Inc. Staff. Spot the Differences Bk. 2, Bk. 2. 2010. (Dover Children's Activity Bks.: Bk. 2). (ENG., Illus.). 64p. (J). (gr. 3-5). pap. 9.99 (978-0-486-47300-0(7)) Dover Pubns., Inc.

Wheatley, Abigail. The Story of Painting. Riley, Janis, ed. Mayer, Uwe & McNee, Ian, illus. 2007. (Story of Painting Ser.). 96p. (J). (gr. 4-7). pap. 10.99 (978-0-7945-1678-9(5), Usborne) EDC Publishing.

PAINTING, ITALIAN

Venezia, Mike. Getting to Know the World's Greatest Artists - Titian. Venezia, Mike, illus. 2003. (Getting to Know the World's Greatest Artists Ser.). (ENG., Illus.). 32p. (J). (gr. 3-4). pap. 6.95 (978-0-516-26975-7(5), Children's Pr.) Scholastic Library Publishing.

—Titian. Venezia, Mike, illus. 2003. (Getting to Know World Artists Ser.). (ENG., Illus.). 32p. (J). 28.00 (978-0-516-22575-3(8), Children's Pr.) Scholastic Library Publishing.

PAINTING—POETRY

Bernier-Grand, Carmen T. Frida: Viva la Vida! - Long Live Life!, 0 vols. Kahlo, Frida, illus. 2007. (ENG.). 64p. (YA). (gr. 7-11). lib. bdg. 18.99 (978-0-7614-5336-9(9), 9780761453369, Amazon Children's Publishing) Amazon Publishing.

PAINTING, RELIGIOUS

see Christian Art and Symbolism

PAINTING—TECHNIQUE

Boase, Petra. I Can Paint: Show Me How. 2016. (ENG., Illus.). 48p. 7.99 (978-1-86147-463-6(6), Armadillo) Anness Publishing GBR. Dist: National Bk. Network.

Bolte, Mari. Acrylics, 1 vol. Ice, D. C., illus. 2013. (Paint It Ser.). (ENG.). 32p. (gr. 3-4). 27.99 (978-1-4765-3109-0(9), Snap Bks.) Capstone Press of Coughlan Cos.

—Oil Paints, 1 vol. Becker, Pamela, illus. 2013. (Paint It Ser.). (ENG.). 32p. (gr. 3-4). 27.99 (978-1-4765-3110-6(2), Snap Bks.) Capstone Press of Coughlan Cos.

—Paint It. 2013. (Paint It Ser.). (ENG.). 32p. (gr. 3-4). lib. bdg. 111.96 (978-1-4765-3736-8(4), Snap Bks.) Capstone Press of Coughlan Cos.

—Paint It: The Art of Acrylics, Oils, Pastels, & Watercolors, 1 vol. Ice, D. C., illus. 2013. (Craft It Yourself Ser.). (ENG.). 144p. (gr. 3-4). pap. 14.95 (978-1-62370-009-6(4)) Capstone Young Readers of Coughlan Cos.

—Watercolors, 1 vol. Ice, D. C., illus. 2013. (Paint It Ser.). (ENG.). 32p. (gr. 3-4). 27.99 (978-1-4765-3108-3(0), Snap Bks.) Capstone Press of Coughlan Cos.

Brooks, Susie. Animals: Enjoy Great Art - Then Create Your Own! 2013. (Get into Art Ser.). (ENG., Illus.). 32p. (J). (gr. 2-9). 14.99 (978-0-7534-7058-9(6), 9780753470589, Kingfisher) Roaring Brook Pr.

—Get into Art Animals: Enjoy Great Art — Then Create Your Own! 2015. (Get into Art Ser.). (ENG., Illus.). 32p. (J). (gr. 2-9). 8.99 (978-0-7534-7217-0(1), 9780753472170, Kingfisher) Roaring Brook Pr.

Calver, Paul. Painting. 2014. (Mini Artist Ser.). (Illus.). 24p. (J). (gr. k-3). lib. bdg. 26.25 (978-1-4777-9119-6(1)) Windmill Bks.

Cuxart, Bernadette. Art Painting on Everyday Items. 2015. (Art Painting Ser.). (ENG., Illus.). 36p. (J). (gr. k-3). pap. 6.99 (978-1-4380-0651-2(9)) Barron's Educational Series, Inc.

—Art Painting with Different Tools. 2015. (Art Painting Ser.). (ENG.). 36p. (J). (gr. k-3). pap. 6.99 (978-1-4380-0653-6(5)) Barron's Educational Series, Inc.

—Art Painting with Everyday Materials. 2015. (Art Painting Ser.). (ENG., Illus.). 36p. (J). (gr. k-3). pap. 6.99 (978-1-4380-0654-3(3)) Barron's Educational Series, Inc.

Franco, Nick. Are You Ready to Paint? 2010. 17p. 19.25 (978-0-615-24474-7(2)) Franco, Nick Art.

Golden Books. Christmas Countdown (Team Umizoomi) Fruchter, Jason, illus. 2013. (Paint Box Book Ser.). (ENG.). 48p. (J). (gr. -1-2). pap. 3.99 (978-0-449-81853-4(5), Golden Bks.) Random Hse. Children's Bks.

Goldman, Ken. Beginner's Guide- Acrylic: Learn the Basics of Acrylic Painting, Bk. 1. 2003. (How to Draw & Paint Ser.). (ENG., Illus.). 32p. pap. 8.95 (978-1-56010-491-9(0), 1560104910) Quarto Publishing Group USA.

Hanson, Anders. Cool Painting: The Art of Creativity for Kids, 1 vol. 2009. (Cool Art Ser.). (ENG.). 32p. (gr. 3-6). 28.50 (978-1-60453-143-5(6), Checkerboard Library) ABDO Publishing Co.

Hendler, Muncie. Dover Masterworks: Color Your Own Modern Art Paintings. 2013. (Adult Coloring Ser.). (ENG.). 64p. (gr. 3). pap. 5.99 (978-0-486-78024-5(4)) Dover Pubns., Inc.

Henry, Sally. Painting. 2009. (Make Your Own Art Ser.). (Illus.). 32p. (J). (gr. 3-6). lib. bdg. 26.50 (978-1-4358-2511-6(X), PowerKids Pr.) Rosen Publishing Group, Inc., The.

Hewett, Angela, illus. Bumper Junior Art: Colour by Numbers. 2013. (ENG.). 64p. (J). (gr. -1-3). pap. 8.50 (978-1-84135-998-4(X)) Parkwest Pubns., Inc.

Hicks, Angie, illus. Alien. 2012. (ENG.). 24p. (J). 4.95 (978-1-84135-585-6(2)) Award Pubns. Ltd. GBR. Dist: Parkwest Pubns., Inc.

—Butterfly. 2012. (ENG.). 24p. (J). 4.95 (978-1-84135-582-5(8)) Award Pubns. Ltd. GBR. Dist: Parkwest Pubns., Inc.

—Colour by Numbers - Pirate. 2012. (ENG.). 16p. (J). 3.25 (978-1-84135-857-4(6)) Award Pubns. Ltd. GBR. Dist: Parkwest Pubns., Inc.

—Fish. 2012. (ENG.). 24p. (J). 4.95 (978-1-84135-584-9(4)) Award Pubns. Ltd. GBR. Dist: Parkwest Pubns., Inc.

—Pirate. 2012. (ENG.). 24p. (J). 4.95 (978-1-84135-583-2(6)) Award Pubns. Ltd. GBR. Dist: Parkwest Pubns., Inc.

Klutz Editors. Glitter Face Painting. 2016. (ENG.). 54p. (J). (gr. 3-7). 26.99 (978-1-338-03751-7(X)) Klutz.

Learn to Paint & Draw. 2009. (Reference Ser.). 128p. (978-1-4075-2106-0(3)) Parragon, Inc.

Long, Ethan, illus. Draw with Scribbles & Ink: Draw & Paint Your Own Masterpieces! 2014. (ENG.). 48p. (J). (gr. 1-3). 14.95 (978-1-60058-471-8(3)) Quarto Publishing Group USA.

Luxbacher, Irene. 123 I Can Paint! Luxbacher, Irene, illus. 2007. (Starting Art Ser.). (ENG., Illus.). 24p. (J). (gr. -1-2). 14.95 (978-1-55453-037-3(7)); pap. 5.95 (978-1-55453-150-9(0)) Kids Can Pr., Ltd. CAN. Dist: Hachette Bk. Group.

McGuinness, Denis E., ed. Painting: Materials, Technique, Styles, & Practice. 2016. (Britannica's Practical Guide to the Arts Ser.). 128p. (J). (gr. 10-10). lib. bdg. 36.25 (978-1-68048-373-4(0)) Rosen Publishing Group, Inc., The.

Mehtani, Henu. Handprint Animals. 2017. (Illus.). 32p. (J). **(978-0-7787-3108-5(1))** Crabtree Publishing Co.

—Handprint Garden. 2017. (Illus.). 32p. (J). **(978-0-7787-3110-8(3))** Crabtree Publishing Co.

—Handprint People. 2017. (Illus.). 32p. (J). **(978-0-7787-3111-5(1))** Crabtree Publishing Co.

—Handprint Transportation. 2017. (Illus.). 32p. (J). **(978-0-7787-3109-2(X))** Crabtree Publishing Co.

Nelson, Robin. De la cera a la crayon (from Wax to Crayon) 2006. (De Principio a Fin (Start to Finish) Ser.). (Illus.). 24p. (J). (gr. 4-7). per. 5.95 (978-0-8225-6635-9(4), Ediciones Lerner) Lerner Publishing Group.

—De la Cera Al Crayon. Translations.com Staff, tr. from ENG. 2006. (De Principio a Fin (Start to Finish) Ser.).Tr. of From Wax to Crayon. (SPA., Illus.). 24p. (gr. 3-5). lib. bdg. 19.93 (978-0-8225-6493-5(9), Ediciones Lerner) Lerner Publishing Group.

Noble, Marty. Dover Masterworks: Color Your Own Famous American Paintings. 2013. (Adult Coloring Ser.). (ENG.). 64p. (gr. 3). pap. 5.99 (978-0-486-77942-3(4)) Dover Pubns., Inc.

—Dover Masterworks: Color Your Own Impressionist Paintings. 2013. (Adult Coloring Ser.). (ENG.). 64p. (gr. 3). pap. 5.99 (978-0-486-78025-2(2)) Dover Pubns., Inc.

—Dover Masterworks: Color Your Own Monet Paintings. 2013. (Adult Coloring Ser.). (ENG.). 64p. (gr. 3). pap. 5.99 (978-0-486-77945-4(9)) Dover Pubns., Inc.

—Dover Masterworks: Color Your Own Renoir Paintings. 2013. (Adult Coloring Ser.). (ENG.). 64p. (gr. 3). pap. 5.99 (978-0-486-77946-1(7)) Dover Pubns., Inc.

—Dover Masterworks: Color Your Own Van Gogh Paintings. 2013. (Adult Coloring Ser.). (ENG.). 64p. (gr. 3). pap. 5.99 (978-0-486-77950-8(5)) Dover Pubns., Inc.

O'Brien, Gregory. Back & Beyond: New Zealand in Painting for the Young & Curious. 2008. (ENG., Illus.). 104p. 24.95 (978-1-86940-404-8(1)) Auckland Univ. Pr. NZL. Dist: Independent Pubs. Group.

Peot, Margaret. Inkblot: Drip, Splat, & Squish Your Way to Creativity. Peot, Margaret, illus. 2011. (ENG., Illus.). 56p. (J). (gr. 6-18). 19.95 (978-1-59078-720-5(X)) Boyds Mills Pr.

Robins, Deri. Painting: Amazing Ideas & Techniques to Help You Create Fabulous Art. 2006. (Art Smart Ser.). (ENG., Illus.). 32p. (J). (gr. -1-12). pap. 9.95 (978-1-58728-534-9(7), 1253682) Cooper Square Publishing Llc.

Sonneman, Alan. Clouds & Skyscapes: Explore Techniques for Painting Splendid Skies. 2011. (How to Draw & Paint Ser.). (ENG., Illus.). 32p. pap. 8.95 (978-1-60058-241-7(9), 1600582419) Quarto Publishing Group USA.

Thomas, Isabel. Painting, 1 vol. 2011. (Start with Art Ser.). (ENG.). 24p. (gr. k-2). 23.32 (978-1-4329-5018-7(5), Heinemann Read & Learn) Heinemann-Raintree.

Watt, Fiona. Complete Book of Art Ideas. rev. ed. 2011. (Art Ser.). 288p. (J). pap. 19.99 (978-0-7945-2642-9(X), Usborne) EDC Publishing.

—365 Things to Draw & Paint. 2011. (Activity Books Ser.). 128p. (J). pap. 24.99 (978-0-7945-2707-5(8), Usborne) EDC Publishing.

PAINTINGS

see Painting

PAIR SYSTEM

see Binary System (Mathematics)

PAKISTAN

Aykroyd, Clarissa. Pakistan. (Major Muslim Nations Ser.). (YA). 2010. 128p. (gr. 7-18). 25.95 (978-1-4222-1408-4(7)) 2008. pap. 14.95 (978-1-4222-1438-1(9)) Mason Crest.

Barker, Geoff. Discover Pakistan. 2012. (Discover Countries Ser.). 32p. (YA). (gr. 4-7). lib. bdg. 26.50 (978-1-4488-5271-0(4)) Rosen Publishing Group, Inc., The.

Brown, Dinah. Who Is Malala Yousafzai? Thomson, Andrew, illus. 2015. 105p. (J). (978-1-4844-6131-0(2), Grosset & Dunlap) Penguin Publishing Group.

—Who Is Malala Yousafzai? 2015. (Who Is... ? Ser.). lib. bdg. 16.00 (978-0-606-37551-1(1)) Turtleback Bks.

Donaldson, Madeline. Pakistan. 2009. pap. 52.95 (978-0-7613-4730-9(5)) Lerner Publishing Group.

Fazzi, Cindy. How to Draw Pakistan's Sights & Symbols. (Kid's Guide to Drawing the Countries of the World Ser.). 2009. 48p. (gr. 4-4). 53.00 (978-1-61511-120-6(4)) 2005. (J). 29.25 (978-1-4042-2739-2(3)) Rosen Publishing Group, Inc., The. (PowerKids Pr.).

Graham, Ian. Pakistan. 2003. (Country Files Ser.). 32p. (J). lib. bdg. 24.25 (978-1-58340-239-9(X)) Black Rabbit Bks.

Hansen, Grace. Malala Yousafzai: Education Activist, 1 vol. 2014. (History Maker Biographies Ser.). (ENG.). 24p. (J). (gr. 2-4). lib. bdg. 28.50 (978-1-62970-703-7(1)) ABDO Publishing Co.

Harmon, Daniel E. Pervez Musharraf: President of Pakistan. 2007. (Newsmakers Ser.). (Illus.). 112p. (YA). (gr. 7-12). lib. bdg. 34.60 (978-1-4042-1905-2(6)) Rosen Publishing Group, Inc., The.

Kiesbye, Stefan. How Should the U. S. Proceed in Afghanistan? 2009. (At Issue Ser.). (ENG., Illus.). 128p. (gr. 10-12). 24.45 (978-0-7377-4425-5(1)); 39.40 (978-0-7377-4424-8(3)) Cengage Gale. (Greenhaven Pr., Inc.).

Kumar, Monica & Kumar, Asha. The Great Desert Adventure. 2008. (HIN & ENG., Illus.). 32p. (J). (978-0-9797191-1-0(9)) MeeraMasi, Inc.

Labrecque, Ellen. Pakistan. 2010. (Explorer Library: Social Studies Explorer Ser.). (ENG.). 48p. (gr. 4-8). lib. bdg. 31.36 (978-1-60279-828-1(1), 200522) Cherry Lake Publishing.

Langston-George, Rebecca. For the Right to Learn: Malala Yousafzai's Story. Bock, Janna, illus. (Encounter: Narrative Nonfiction Picture Bks.). (ENG.). 40p. (gr. 3-4). 2016. pap. 7.95 (978-1-4914-6556-1(5)) 2015. lib. bdg. 28.65 (978-1-4914-6071-9(7)) Encounter Bks.

Martin, Claudia. Malala Yousafzai: Education Campaigner. 2017. (Inspirational Lives Ser.). (ENG., Illus.). 32p. (J). (gr. 4-6). pap. 12.99 **(978-0-7502-9314-3(4)**, Wayland) Hachette Children's Group GBR. Dist: Hachette Bk. Group.

Morgan, Sally. Focus on Pakistan. 2007. (World in Focus Ser.). 64p. (gr. 5-12). pap. 14.05 (978-0-8368-6759-6(9)); (Illus.). lib. bdg. 34.00 (978-0-8368-6752-7(1)) Stevens, Gareth Publishing LLLP. (Gareth Stevens Secondary Library).

Mortenson, Greg. Stones into Schools: Promoting Peace, One School at a Time. 2011. (ENG.). 240p. (J). (gr. 3-18). 16.99 (978-0-8037-3687-0(8), Dial) Penguin Publishing Group.

Mortenson, Greg & Relin, David Oliver. Three Cups of Tea: One Man's Journey to Change the World... One Child at a Time. 2009. (ENG.). 240p. (J). (gr. 3-7). 8.99 (978-0-14-241412-5(3), Puffin Books) Penguin Young Readers Group.

—Three Cups of Tea: One Man's Journey to Change the World... One Child at a Time. ed. 2009. lib. bdg. 19.65 (978-0-606-07164-2(4), Turtleback) Turtleback Bks.

Mortenson, Greg & Roth, Susan L. Listen to the Wind: The Story of Dr. Greg & Three Cups of Tea. Roth, Susan L., illus. 2009. (Rise & Shine Ser.). (ENG., Illus.). 32p. (J). (gr. 1-3). 16.99 (978-0-8037-3058-8(6), Dial Bks) Penguin Young Readers Group.

Mortenson, Greg, et al. Three Cups of Tea: One Man's Journey to Change the World... One Child at a Time. adapted ed. 2009. 10.36 (978-0-7848-3360-5(5), Everbind) Marco Bk. Co.

Murray, Julie. Pakistan, 1 vol. 2014. (Explore the Countries Set 2 Ser.). (ENG.). 40p. (gr. 7-11). 29.93 (978-1-62403-346-9(6)) ABDO Publishing Co.

O'Donnell, Kerri. A Primary Source Guide to Pakistan. (Countries of the World). 24p. 2009. (gr. 2-3). 42.50 (978-1-61512-042-0(4), PowerKids Pr.) 2003. (ENG., Illus.). (gr. 3-6). pap. 8.25 (978-0-8239-8079-6(0)) 2003. (Illus.). (J). lib. bdg. 22.60 (978-0-8239-6595-3(3)) Rosen Publishing Group, Inc., The.

Roraback, Amanda. Pakistan in a Nutshell. 2nd ed. 2004. (Nutshell Notes Ser.). (Illus.). 64p. pap. 7.95 (978-0-9702908-9-2(6)) Enisen Publishing.

Sheehan, Sean, et al. Pakistan. 2015. (Cultures of the World Ser.). (ENG., Illus.). 144p. (J). (gr. 6-6). 47.07 (978-1-5026-0082-0(X)) Cavendish Square Publishing.

Sheen, Barbara, ed. Foods of Pakistan. 2011. (Taste of Culture Ser.). (Illus.). 67p. (YA). (gr. 9-12). 30.45 (978-0-7377-5883-2(X)) Cengage Gale.

Simmons, Walter. Pakistan. 2011. (Illus.). 32p. (J). lib. bdg. (978-0-531-20958-5(X)); (ENG., (gr. 3-7). lib. bdg. 26.95 (978-1-60014-593-3(0), Blastoff! Readers) Bellwether Media.

Sonneborn, Liz. Pakistan. 2012. (Enchantment of the World, Second Ser.). (ENG., Illus.). 144p. (J). (gr. 5-8). lib. bdg. 40.00 (978-0-531-27544-3(2), Children's Pr.) Scholastic Library Publishing.

Taus-Bolstad, Stacy. Pakistan in Pictures. 2003. (Visual Geography Ser.). (Illus.). 80p. (J). (gr. 5-12). 27.93 (978-0-8225-4682-5(5)) Lerner Publishing Group.

Wang, Andrea. Malala Yousafzai: Nobel Peace Prize Winner & Education Activist, 1 vol. 2014. (Newsmakers Ser.). (ENG.). 48p. (gr. 3-6). lib. bdg. 32.79 (978-1-62403-646-0(5)) ABDO Publishing Co.

Worth, Richard. Pervez Musharraf. 2nd rev. ed. 2007. (Modern World Leaders Ser.). (Illus.). 104p. (YA). (gr. 7-12). lib. bdg. 30.00 (978-0-7910-9264-4(X)) Facts On File, Inc.

PAKISTAN—FICTION

Antieau, Kim. Broken Moon. 2007. (ENG.). 192p. (YA). (gr. 9-12). 16.99 (978-1-4169-1767-0(5), McElderry, Margaret K. Bks.) McElderry, Margaret K. Bks.

Ellis, Deborah. Mud City, 1 vol. 2015. (Breadwinner Ser.). (ENG., Illus.). 168p. (J). (gr. 4-9). pap. 9.95 (978-1-55498-773-3(3)) Groundwood Bks. CAN. Dist: Publishers Group West (PGW).

—Mud City. 2013. 156p. pap. (978-1-4596-6445-6(0)) ReadHowYouWant.com, Ltd.

Francesco, D'Adamo. Iqbal. 2014. (ENG.). 128p. (J). (gr. 3-7). 11.24 (978-1-63245-261-0(8)) Lectorum Pubns., Inc.

Hawke, Rosanne. Spirit of a Mountain Wolf. 2014. 216p. (Illus.). (YA). (gr. 9-12). pap. 10.95 (978-1-62324-034-9(4)); 18.95 (978-1-62324-033-2(6)) Enslow Pubs., Inc.

Hayes, Rosemary. Payback. 2009. (ENG.). 208p. (J). (gr. 7-10). pap. 8.95 (978-1-84507-935-2(3), Frances Lincoln) Quarto Publishing Group UK GBR. Dist: Hachette Bk. Group.

Khan, Rukhsana. King for a Day, 1 vol. Krömer, Christiane, illus. 2014. (ENG.). 32p. (J). 17.95 (978-1-60060-659-5(8)) Lee & Low Bks., Inc.

Laidlaw, S. J. An Infidel in Paradise. 2013. (ENG., Illus.). 314p. (YA). (gr. 7). 19.95 (978-1-77049-304-9(2), Tundra Bks.) Tundra Bks. CAN. Dist: Penguin Random Hse. LLC.

Mortenson, Greg & Husain, Farzana. Listen to the Children: The Story of Dr. Greg & Stones into Schools. Roth, Susan L., illus. 2011. (ENG.). 32p. (J). (gr. 1-3). 17.99 (978-0-8037-3593-4(6), Dial) Penguin Publishing Group.

Qamar, Amjed. Beneath My Mother's Feet. (ENG.). 208p. (YA). (gr. 7). 2011. pap. 10.99 (978-1-4424-1451-8(0)) 2008. 16.99 (978-1-4169-4728-8(0)) Simon & Schuster Children's Publishing. (Atheneum Bks. for Young Readers).

Saeed, Aisha & Airgood, Ellen. Written in the Stars. 2015. (ENG.). 304p. (YA). (gr. 9). 17.99 (978-0-399-17170-3(3), Nancy Paulsen Books) Penguin Young Readers Group.

Shea, Pegi Deitz & Deitz Shea, Pegi. The Carpet Boy's Gift, 1 vol. Morin, Leane, illus. 2005. (ENG.). 40p. (J). (gr. 3-6). 16.95 (978-0-88448-248-2(0)) Tilbury Hse. Pubs.

Smith, Roland. The Edge. 2015. (Peak Marcello Adventure Ser.). (ENG.). 240p. (YA). (gr. 7). 17.99 (978-0-544-34122-7(8), HMH Books For Young Readers) Houghton Mifflin Harcourt Publishing Co.

—The Edge. 2016. (Peak Marcello Adventure Ser.). (ENG.). 240p. (YA). (gr. 7). pap. 7.99 (978-0-544-81354-0(5), HMH Books For Young Readers) Houghton Mifflin Harcourt Publishing Co.

Staples, Suzanne Fisher. Haveli. 2012. (ENG.). 336p. (YA). (gr. 7). pap. 9.99 (978-0-307-97789-2(7), Ember) Random Hse. Children's Bks.

—Haveli. 2006. 21.50 (978-0-8446-7291-5(2)) Smith, Peter Pub., Inc.

—The House of Djinn. 2012. (ENG.). 222p. (YA). (gr. 7). pap. 8.99 (978-0-307-97642-0(4), Ember) Random Hse. Children's Bks.

—Shabanu: Daughter of the Wind. 3rd ed. (J). pap. 3.99 (978-0-13-800053-0(0)) Prentice Hall (Schl. Div.).

—Shabanu: Daughter of the Wind. 2012. (ENG.). 288p. (YA). (gr. 7). pap. 9.99 (978-0-307-97788-5(9), Ember) Random Hse. Children's Bks.

—Under the Persimmon Tree. 2008. (Illus.). 281p. (gr. 7-12). 20.00 (978-0-7569-9004-6(1)) Perfection Learning Corp.

—Under the Persimmon Tree. 2008. (ENG., Illus.). 304p. (YA). (gr. 7-12). pap. 9.99 (978-0-312-37776-2(2), 9780312377762) Square Fish.

PAKISTAN—HISTORY

Aretha, David. Malala Yousafzai & the Girls of Pakistan. 2014. (ENG.). (J). 27.45 (978-1-59935-454-5(3)) Reynolds, Morgan Inc.

Aykroyd, Clarissa. Pakistan, Vol. 13. 2015. (Major Nations of the Modern Middle East Ser.). (Illus.). 128p. (J). (gr. 7). lib. bdg. 25.95 (978-1-4222-3445-7(2)) Mason Crest.

Berlatsky, Noah, ed. East Pakistan. 2012. (Genocide & Persecution Ser.). (ENG.). 240p. (gr. 10-12). lib. bdg. 36.45 (978-0-7377-6256-3(X), Greenhaven Pr., Inc.) Cengage Gale.

Blashfield, Jean F. Pakistan, 1 vol. 2011. (Countries Around the World Ser.). (ENG.). 48p. (gr. 3-6). pap. 9.95 (978-1-4329-5239-6(0), NA-h) Heinemann-Raintree.

Cantor, Rachel Anne. Pakistan. 2017. (Countries We Come From Ser.). (ENG., Illus.). 32p. (J). (gr. -1-3). 19.95 **(978-1-68402-060-7(3))** Bearport Publishing Co., Inc.

Clements, Gillian. Indus Valley City. 2009. (Building History Ser.). (Illus.). 32p. (J). (gr. 3-5). lib. bdg. 27.10 (978-1-59771-144-9(6)) Sea-To-Sea Pubns.

Corey, Shana. Malala: A Hero for All. Sayles, Elizabeth, illus. 2016. (Step into Reading Ser.). (ENG.). 48p. (J). (gr. 2-4). pap. 3.99 (978-0-553-53761-1(X), Random Hse. Bks. for Young Readers) Random Hse. Children's Bks.

Donaldson, Madeline. Pakistan. 2009. (Country Explorers Ser.). (ENG., Illus.). 48p. (gr. 2-4). 29.27 (978-1-58013-599-3(4)) Lerner Publishing Group.

Greenberger, Robert. A Historical Atlas of Pakistan. 2009. (Historical Atlases of South Asia, Central Asia, & the Middle East Ser.). 64p. (gr. 6-6). 61.20 (978-1-61513-327-7(5)) Rosen Publishing Group, Inc., The.

HARMON, Daniel E. Pervez Musharraf: President of Pakistan. 2009. (Newsmakers Ser.). 112p. (gr. 9-10). 63.90 (978-1-60851-135-8(9)) Rosen Publishing Group, Inc., The.

Heiden, Pete. Pakistan, 1 vol. 2011. (Countries of the World Set 1 Ser.). (ENG., Illus.). 144p. (J). (gr. 6-12). lib. bdg. 37.07 (978-1-61783-117-1(4)) ABDO Publishing Co.

Hinman, Bonnie. We Visit Pakistan. 2011. (Your Land & My Land Ser.). (Illus.). 64p. (J). (gr. 4-7). lib. bdg. 33.95 (978-1-58415-960-5(X)) Mitchell Lane Pubs., Inc.

Kwek, Karen & Haque, Jameel. Pakistan. 2010. (Welcome to My Country Ser.). 48p. (gr. 3). 28.50 (978-1-60870-158-2(1)) Marshall Cavendish GBR. Dist: Marshall Cavendish Corp.

Langley, Andrew. Pakistan in Our World. 2011. (Countries in Our World Ser.). 32p. (YA). (gr. 4-7). lib. bdg. 28.50 (978-1-59920-392-8(8)) Black Rabbit Bks.

Malala, a Brave Girl from Pakistan/Iqbal, a Brave Boy from Pakistan. 2014. (ENG., Illus.). 40p. (J). (gr. 1-5). 17.99 (978-1-4814-2294-9(4), Beach Lane Bks.) Beach Lane Bks.

Mohiuddin, Yasmeen Niaz. Pakistan: A Global Studies Handbook, 1 vol. 2006. (Global Studies - Asia Ser.). (Illus.). 382p. (C). 61.00 (978-1-85109-801-9(1), PAKIGS1C) ABC-CLIO, LLC.

Naden, Corinne J. Benazir Bhutto. 2010. (Leading Women Ser.). 96p. (YA). (gr. 7-12). 39.93 (978-0-7614-4952-2(3)) Marshall Cavendish Corp.

Niver, Heather Moore. Malala Yousafzai, 01 vols., 1. 2016. (Britannica Beginner Bios Ser.). (ENG., Illus.). 32p. (J). lib. bdg. 23.45 (978-1-68048-253-9(X), Britannica Educational Publishing) Rosen Publishing Group, Inc., The.

Peters, Elisa. Malala Yousafzai: Pakistani Activist for Female Education. 2017. (J). **(978-1-5081-7749-4(X))** Rosen Publishing Group, Inc., The.

Rengel, Marian. Pakistan: A Primary Source Cultural Guide. 2009. (Primary Sources of World Cultures Ser.). 128p. (gr. 4-5). 79.90 (978-1-60851-928-6(7)) Rosen Publishing Group, Inc., The.

Simmons, Walter. Pakistan. 2011. (Illus.). 32p. (J). lib. bdg. (978-0-531-20958-5(X)) Bellwether Media.

Throp, Claire. Malala Yousafzai. 2015. (Against the Odds Biographies Ser.). (ENG., Illus.). 48p. (gr. 3-6). 33.32 (978-1-4846-2464-7(5)) Heinemann-Raintree.

World Book, Inc Staff, contrib. by. Independence of India & Pakistan. 2010. (J). (978-0-7166-1506-4(1)) World Bk., Inc.

Yousafzai, Malala. I Am Malala: The Girl Who Stood up for Education & Was Shot by the Taliban. (ENG.). (J). 2016. 256p. 98.91 (978-0-316-30398-9(4)) 2016. (Illus.). 256p. (gr. 5-17). pap. 10.99 (978-0-316-32791-6(3)) 2014. 256p. 153.00 (978-0-316-33917-9(2)) 2014. (Illus.). 240p. (gr. 5-17). 17.99 (978-0-316-32793-0(X)) 2015. 240p. (gr. 5-17). 17.00 (978-0-316-31119-9(7)) Little, Brown Bks. for Young Readers.

—I Am Malala: The Girl Who Stood up for Education & Was Shot by the Taliban. 2016. (J). lib. bdg. 22.10 (978-0-606-37164-3(8)) Turtleback Bks.

Yousafzai, Malala & McCormick, Patricia. I Am Malala: The Girl Who Stood up for Education & Was Shot by the Taliban. l.t. ed. 2017. (ENG., Illus.). 302p. 22.99 **(978-1-4104-9916-5(2))** Cengage Gale.

PALACES

Ball, Jacqueline A. Windsor Castle: England's Royal Fortress. 2005. (Castles, Palaces, & Tombs Ser.). (Illus.). 32p. (J). lib. bdg. 25.27 (978-1-59716-005-6(9)) Bearport Publishing Co., Inc.

Cullis, Megan. See Inside Famous Palaces. 2015. (See Inside Board Bks.). (ENG.). 16p. (J). (gr. k-5). 14.99 (978-0-7945-3477-6(5), Usborne) EDC Publishing.

Dyan, Penelope. A Royal Residence — A Kid's Guide to Windsor Castle. Weigand, John D., photos by. 2011. (Illus.). 40p. pap. 12.95 (978-1-935630-65-4(2)) Bellissima Publishing, LLC.

Hodge, Susie. The Forbidden City. 2005. (Places in History Ser.). (Illus.). 48p. (gr. 5-12). pap. 14.05 (978-0-8368-5817-4(4)); lib. bdg. 31.00 (978-0-8368-5810-5(7)) Stevens, Gareth Publishing LLLP. (World Almanac Library).

Lee, Sally. Castles & Palaces, 1 vol. 2013. (Royalty Ser.). (ENG.). 24p. (gr. k-1). lib. bdg. 26.65 (978-1-62065-121-6(1), Pebble Plus) Capstone Press of Coughlan Cos.

Mason, Anthony. Versailles. 2005. (Places in History Ser.). (Illus.). 48p. (gr. 5-12). lib. bdg. 31.00 (978-0-8368-5815-0(8), World Almanac Library) Stevens, Gareth Publishing LLLP.

Weil, Ann. The World's Most Amazing Palaces, 1 vol. 2011. (Landmark Top Tens Ser.). (ENG., Illus.). 32p. (gr. 3-5). pap. 8.29 (978-1-4109-4248-7(1)); 30.65 (978-1-4109-4237-1(6)) Heinemann-Raintree. (Raintree Perspectives).

PALACES—FICTION

Al-Zeheri, Ali. The Princess & the Gold. 2009. 32p. pap. 12.99 (978-1-4490-2091-0(7)) AuthorHouse.

Dadey, Debbie. The Crook & the Crown. Avakyan, Tatevik, illus. 2015. (Mermaid Tales Ser.: 13). (ENG.). 128p. (J). (gr. 1-4). pap. 5.99 (978-1-4814-4075-2(6), Aladdin) Simon & Schuster Children's Publishing.

Disney Book Group. Elena of Avalor a Palace Fit for a Princess. Disney Storybook Art Team, illus. 2016. (ENG.). 16p. (J). (gr. 1-3). 12.99 (978-1-4847-5872-4(2)) Disney Pr.

East, Jacqueline, illus. Princess Palace: A Three-Demensional Playset. 2006. 8p. (J). (gr. -1-3). 22.95 (978-1-58117-492-2(6), Intervisual/Piggy Toes) Bendon, Inc.

Fairy Palaces Magic Painting Book. 2017. (Magic Painting Bks.). (ENG.). (J). pap. 9.99 **(978-0-7945-3876-7(2)**, Usborne) EDC Publishing.

Feldman, Thea. Hooray for Palace Pets! Disney Storybook Artists Staff, illus. 2015. (ENG.). 12p. (J). (gr. -1-k). bds. 10.99 (978-0-7944-3389-5(8), Reader's Digest Children's Bks.) Studio Fun International.

Gil, Carmen. Que Fastidio Ser Princesa! 2012. (SPA & ENG., Illus.). 28p. (J). (gr. k-2). 14.95 (978-84-15241-14-0(3)) Eastern National.

Marsh, Carole. The Mystery at Mount Fuji: Tokyo, Japan. 2007. (Around the World in 80 Mysteries Ser.). (Illus.). 131p. (J). (gr. 3-5). per. 7.99 (978-0-635-06207-9(0)) Gallopade International.

—The Mystery at Mt. Fuji: Tokyo, Japan. 2007. (Around the World in 80 Mysteries Ser.). (Illus.). 131p. (J). (gr. 3-5). 14.95 (978-0-635-06211-6(9)) Gallopade International.

Muthu, Antony M. Athim. 2008. 48p. pap. 19.49 (978-1-4389-3074-9(7)) AuthorHouse.

Nicola Baxter Staff. Fairy Palace Pop up. 2009. (978-1-84322-574-4(3)) Bookmart Ltd.

Norman, Cook. Sam & the Glass Palace. 2005. (Illus.). 108p. pap. 8.00 (978-1-903087-42-8(2)) DayOne Pubns. GBR. Dist: Send The Light Distribution LLC.

Parker, Danny. Lola's Toybox: the Plastic Palace. Shield, Guy, illus. 2017. (Lola's Toy Box Ser.: 4). (ENG.). 96p. (J). (gr. k-2). pap. 6.99 **(978-1-76012-439-7(7))** Hardie Grant Egmont Pty, Ltd. AUS. Dist: Independent Pubs. Group.

Princess Protection Program Staff. The Palace of Mystery, No. 4. 2010. (Princess Protection Program Ser.). 144p. pap. 4.99 (978-1-4231-2727-7(7)) Disney Pr.

Wethington, Constance. The Butterfly's Ball. 2013. 20p. pap. 24.95 (978-1-4626-8640-7(0)) America Star Bks.

PALEOBOTANY

see Plants, Fossil

PALEOLITHIC PERIOD

see Stone Age

PALEONTOLOGISTS

Barnham, Kay. Mary Anning. 2017. (History VIPs Ser.). (ENG., Illus.). 32p. (J). (gr. 4-6). pap. 11.99 (978-0-7502-9914-5(2), Wayland) Hachette Children's Group GBR. Dist: Hachette Bk. Group.

Bennett, Leonie. Dinosaur Fossils. 2007. (I Love Reading Ser.). (Illus.). 24p. (J). (gr. -1-2). lib. bdg. 19.96 (978-1-59716-555-6(7)) Bearport Publishing Co., Inc.

—Dinosaur Hunting. 2007. (I Love Reading Ser.). (Illus.). 24p. (J). (gr. -1-2). lib. bdg. 19.96 (978-1-59716-554-9(9)) Bearport Publishing Co., Inc.

Butz, Steve. The Bone Race: A Quest for Dinosaur Fossils. 2007. (ENG.). 248p. (YA). (gr. 7). pap. (978-1-933255-30-9(7)) DNA Pr.

Capstone Press Staff, et al. Little Paleontologist, 1 vol. 2014. (Little Paleontologist Ser.). (ENG.). 32p. (gr. 1-3). 167.94 (978-1-4914-0838-4(3)) Capstone Press of Coughlan Cos.

Chrisp, Peter. Dinosaur Detectives, Level 4. 2009. (DK Readers Ser.). (ENG.). 48p. (J). (gr. 3-7). 3.99 (978-0-7566-5597-6(8), DK Children) Dorling Kindersley Publishing, Inc.

Close, Edward. Dinosaur Hunters. 2013. (Discovery Education: Discoveries & Inventions Ser.). 32p. (J). (gr. 3-6). pap. 60.00 (978-1-4777-1499-7(5), PowerKids Pr.) Rosen Publishing Group, Inc., The.

Collins Big Cat Staff. Fossil Hunter, Bd. 17. 2017. (ENG., Illus.). 56p. (J). pap. 8.95 **(978-0-00-820893-6(X))** HarperCollins Pubs. Ltd. GBR. Dist: Independent Pubs. Group.

Coupe, Robert. Dinosaur Hunters. 2013. (Discovery Education: Discoveries & Inventions Ser.). (ENG., Illus.). 32p. (J). (gr. 3-6). pap. 10.00 (978-1-4777-1498-0(7)); lib. bdg. 25.25 (978-1-4777-1328-0(X)) Rosen Publishing Group, Inc., The. (PowerKids Pr.).

Donald, Rhonda Lucas. Dino Treasures, 1 vol. Morrison, Cathy, illus. 2015. (ENG.). 32p. (J). (gr. 1-4). 17.95 (978-1-62855-450-2(9)) Arbordale Publishing.

Dowell, Lori. Be a Paleontologist. 2014. (Be a Scientist! Ser.). 32p. (J). (gr. 3-6). pap. 10.50 (978-1-4824-1209-3(8)); pap. 63.00 (978-1-4824-1200-0(4)) Stevens, Gareth Publishing LLLP.

Fern, Tracey E. Barnum's Bones: How Barnum Brown Discovered the Most Famous Dinosaur in the World, 1 vol. Kulikov, Boris, illus. 2012. (ENG.). 36p. (J). (gr. k-4). 17.99 (978-0-374-30516-1(1), 9780374305161, Farrar, Straus & Giroux (BYR)) Farrar, Straus & Giroux.

Goldish, Meish. The Fossil Feud: Marsh & Cope's Bone Wars. 2006. (Fossil Hunters Ser.). (Illus.). 32p. (YA). (gr. 2-5). lib. bdg. 25.27 (978-1-59716-256-2(6)) Bearport Publishing Co., Inc.

Greve, Tom. Paleontologists. 2015. (ENG.). 48p. (gr. 3-6). 35.64 (978-1-63430-411-5(X)) Rourke Educational Media.

Holmes, Thom. Dinosaur Scientist: Careers Digging up the Past. 2009. (Wild Science Careers Ser.). (Illus.). 128p. (J). (gr. 5-18). lib. bdg. 33.27 (978-0-7660-3053-4(9)) Enslow Pubs., Inc.

—Paleontologists: Searching for Dinosaur Bones. 2015. (Extreme Science Careers Ser.). (ENG., Illus.). 128p. (J). (gr. 7-7). 37.27 (978-0-7660-6964-0(8)) Enslow Pubs., Inc.

Holmes, Thom & Holmes, Laurie. Great Dinosaur Expeditions & Discoveries: Adventures with the Fossil Hunters. Skrepnick, Michael William, illus. 2003. (Dinosaur Library). 112p. (J). lib. bdg. 26.60 (978-0-7660-2078-8(9)) Enslow Pubs., Inc.

Kurtz, Jane. Mister Bones: Dinosaur Hunter. Haverfield, Mary, illus. 2004. (Ready-To-Reads Ser.). (ENG.). 32p. (J). (gr. -1-1). pap. 3.99 (978-0-689-85960-1(0), Simon Spotlight) Simon Spotlight.

Little Paleontologist, 1 vol. 2014. (Little Paleontologist Ser.). (ENG.). 32p. (gr. 1-3). 41.70 (978-1-4914-0841-4(3)); pap. 41.70 (978-1-4914-0839-1(1)) Capstone Press of Coughlan Cos.

Markarian, Margie. Who Cleans Dinosaur Bones? Working at a Museum. 2010. (Wild Work Ser.). (ENG.). 32p. (gr. 1-2). pap. 8.29 (978-1-4109-3857-2(3), Read Me!) Heinemann-Raintree.

McGowan, Chris. Dinosaur Discovery: Everything You Need to Be a Paleontologist. Schmidt, Erica Lyn, illus. 2011. (ENG.). 48p. (J). (gr. 2-6). 18.99 (978-1-4169-4764-6(7), Simon & Schuster Bks. For Young Readers) Simon & Schuster Bks. For Young Readers.

Miller, Connie Colwell. I'll Be a Paleontologist. Baroncelli, Silvia, illus. 2016. (When I Grow Up Ser.). (ENG.). 24p. (J). (gr. k-3). 20.95 (978-1-60753-763-2(X)) Amicus Publishing.

National Park Service Staff, ed. Junior Paleontologist Activity Book: Ages 5 to 12: Explore, Learn, Protect. Wood, Ethan, illus. rev. ed. 2012. (ENG.). 22p. (gr. k-6). 6.00 (978-0-16-090846-0(9)) National Park Service Div. of Pubns.

Owen, Ruth. Paleontologists & Archaeologists. 2013. (Out of the Lab: Extreme Jobs in Science Ser.). 32p. (J). (gr. 3-6). 25.25 (978-1-4777-1290-0(9)); pap. 60.00 (978-1-4777-1387-7(5)); pap. 10.00 (978-1-4777-1380-8(8)) Rosen Publishing Group, Inc., The. (PowerKids Pr.).

Peterson, Judy Monroe. Fossil Finders: Paleontologists. 2009. (Extreme Scientists Ser.). 24p. (gr. 2-3). 42.50 (978-1-61512-452-7(7), PowerKids Pr.) Rosen Publishing Group, Inc., The.

Walker, Sally M. Mary Anning: Fossil Hunter. Saroff, Phyllis V., illus. 2007. (On My Own Biographies Ser.). 48p. (J). (gr. 2-5). per. 6.95 (978-1-57505-457-5(4), First Avenue Editions) Lerner Publishing Group.

PALEONTOLOGY

see Fossils

PALESTINE

Carew-Miller, Anna. The Palestinians. 2010. (Major Muslim Nations Ser.). 135p. (YA). (gr. 5-18). lib. bdg. 25.95 (978-1-4222-1389-6(7)) Mason Crest.

Gonzales, Todd. Palestine in the News: Past, Present, & Future. 2006. (Middle East Nations in the News Ser.). (Illus.). 128p. (J). (gr. 5-9). lib. bdg. 34.60 (978-1-59845-029-3(8), MyReportLinks.com Bks.) Enslow Pubs., Inc.

Holy Land Caravan: The Holy Land in the Old Testament & the New Testament Funspirational Kit: Older Elementary. 2004. (BibleZone Ser.: No. 12). (gr. 4-6). 44.99 (978-0-687-08990-1(5)) Abingdon Pr.

Holy Land Caravan: The Holy Land in the Old Testament & the New Testament Funspirational Kit: Preschool. 2004. (BibleZone Ser.: No. 12). (gr. -1-k). 44.99 (978-0-687-08984-0(0)) Abingdon Pr.

Holy Land Caravan: The Holy Land in the Old Testament & the New Testament Funspirational Kit: Younger Elementary. 2004. (BibleZone Ser.: No. 12). (gr. 1-3). 44.99 (978-0-687-08987-1(5)) Abingdon Pr.

Katz, Samuel M. Jerusalem or Death: Palestinian Terrorism. 72p. (YA). (gr. 9-18). 19.95 (978-1-58013-208-4(1), Kar-Ben Publishing); 2003. (Illus.). (J). (gr. 6-12). 26.60 (978-0-8225-4033-5(9)) Lerner Publishing Group.

Lusted, Marcia. Understanding Palestine Today. 2014. (Illus.). 63p. (J). (gr. 3-6). 33.95 (978-1-61228-655-6(0)) Mitchell Lane Pubs., Inc.

PALESTINE—FICTION

Booth, Bradley. Escape from Egypt. 2009. (J). pap. 11.99 (978-0-8163-2305-0(4)) Pacific Pr. Publishing Assn.

Cohen, Deborah Bodin. Engineer Ari & the Hanukkah Mishap. Kober, Shahar, illus. 2011. (Hanukkah Ser.). (ENG.). 32p. (J). (gr. k-3). pap. 7.95 (978-0-7613-5146-7(9)); lib. bdg. 17.95 (978-0-7613-5145-0(0)) Lerner Publishing Group. (Kar-Ben Publishing).

Ellis, Deborah. The Cat at the Wall, 1 vol. (ENG., Illus.). (J). 2015. 152p. pap. 9.95 (978-1-55498-707-8(5)) 2014. 144p. (gr. 3-7). 16.95 (978-1-55498-491-6(2)) Groundwood Bks. CAN. Dist: Publishers Group West (PGW).

Evans, Loralee. The King's Heir. 2006. 287p. (YA). (gr. 8-12). per. 18.99 (978-1-55517-865-9(0), Bonneville Bks.) Cedar Fort, Inc./CFI Distribution.

Heimerdinger, Chris. Kingdoms & Conquerors: A Novel. 2005. 434p. (YA). (978-1-59156-740-0(8)) Covenant Communications.

Laurel Carter, Anne. The Shepherd's Granddaughter. 2013. 236p. pap. (978-1-4596-6490-6(6)) ReadHowYouWant.com, Ltd.

Martin, Gary & Zondervan Bibles Staff. The Sword of Revenge, 1 vol. Rogers, Bud, ed. Cariello, Sergio, illus. 2009. (Z Graphic Novels / Son of Samson Ser.). (ENG.). 160p. (J). pap. 6.99 (978-0-310-71285-5(8)) Zondervan.

Muñiz-Huberman, Angelina & Menton, Seymour. Dreaming of Safed. 2014. 126p. (YA). pap. (978-1-935604-61-7(9)) Gaon Bks.

Phillips, Dixie & Sharon, et al. Bethlehem's King Size Bed. 2013. 24p. pap. 7.95 (978-1-61633-423-9(1)) Guardian Angel Publishing, Inc.

Rucinski, Sandra. The Story of Jesus According to Tobin. 2009. 32p. pap. 14.50 (978-1-60860-372-5(5), Eloquent Bks.) Strategic Book Publishing & Rights Agency (SBPRA).

Silverberg, Selma Kritzer. Naomi's Song. 2009. (ENG.). 142p. (gr. 7-18). pap. 14.00 (978-0-8276-0886-3(1)) Jewish Pubn. Society.

Studer, Diana. The Tabby's Gift. 2009. 24p. pap. 12.55 (978-1-4389-5582-7(0)) AuthorHouse.

Travis, Lucille. Tirzah. Garber, S. David, ed. 2004. (ENG.). 160p. (YA). (gr. 4-7). pap. 9.99 (978-0-8361-3546-6(6)) Herald Pr.

Trodd, Mark. Hippo in the Stable. 2012. 36p. pap. 32.70 (978-1-4797-1561-9(1)) Xlibris Corp.

Zenatti, Valerie. A Bottle in the Gaza Sea. Hunter, Adriana, tr. from FRE. 2008. (ENG.). 160p. (YA). (gr. 7-13). 17.99 (978-1-59990-200-5(1), 9781599902005, Bloomsbury USA Childrens) Bloomsbury Publishing USA.

PALESTINE—HISTORY

Carew-Miller, Anna. The Palestinians, Vol. 13. 2015. (Major Nations of the Modern Middle East Ser.). (Illus.). 136p. (J). (gr. 7). lib. bdg. 25.95 (978-1-4222-3448-8(7)) Mason Crest.

Coulter, Laurie. Kings & Carpenters: One Hundred Bible Land Jobs You Might Have Praised or Panned. Newbigging, Martha, illus. 2010. (Jobs in History Ser.). (ENG.). 96p. (J). (gr. 3-6). 25.95 (978-1-55451-227-0(1), 9781554512270); pap. 16.95 (978-1-55451-226-3(3), 9781554512263) Annick Pr., Ltd. CAN. Dist: Publishers Group West (PGW).

Hayhurst, Chris. Israel's War of Independence. 2009. (War & Conflict in the Middle East Ser.). 64p. (gr. 5-5). 58.50 (978-1-60854-736-4(1)) Rosen Publishing Group, Inc., The.

—Israel's War of Independence: Al-Nakba. 2004. (War & Conflict in the Middle East Ser.). (Illus.). 64p. (gr. 7-12). lib. bdg. 31.95 (978-0-8239-4548-1(0)) Rosen Publishing Group, Inc., The.

Immell, Myra. The Creation of the State of Israel. 2009. (Perspectives on Modern World History Ser.). (Illus.). 224p. (YA). (gr. 10-18). 42.45 (978-0-7377-4556-6(8), Greenhaven Pr., Inc.) Cengage Gale.

Jones, Graham. How They Lived in Bible Times. Deverell, Richard, illus. 2003. 48p. 6.49 (978-1-85999-435-1(0)) Scripture Union GBR. Dist: Gabriel Resources.

Marabini, Sergio. Arafat. 2004. (Protagonistas Ser.). (SPA.). 96p. (YA). (978-987-1129-64-5(5)) Grupo Visor E.A.S.A.

Mason, Paul & Marshall Cavendish Staff. Israel & Palestine. 2008. (Global Hotspots Ser.). 32p. (gr. 5-18). lib. bdg. 18.56 (978-0-7614-3181-7(0), Benchmark Bks.) Marshall Cavendish Corp.

Olson, Marc. The World Jesus Knew: A Curious Kid's Guide to Life in First-Century Palestine. Maybank, Jem, illus. 2017. (ENG.). 64p. (J). (gr. 4-6). 19.99 **(978-1-5064-2500-9(3)**, Sparkhouse Family) Augsburg Fortress, Pubs.

Sanders, Nancy I. Mary, 1 vol. 2014. (Get to Know Ser.). (ENG.). 112p. (J). pap. 7.99 (978-0-310-74480-1(6)) Zonderkidz.

Wingate, Katherine. The Intifadas. (War & Conflict in the Middle East Ser.). 64p. 2009. (gr. 5-5). 58.50 (978-1-60854-738-8(8)) 2004. (Illus.). (gr. 7-12). lib. bdg. 31.95 (978-0-8239-4546-7(4)) Rosen Publishing Group, Inc., The.

PALMER, NATHANIEL BROWN, 1799-1877

Sanford, Candace. Captain Nathaniel Brown Palmer. Scala, Susan, illus. 2007. 96p. (YA). pap. 14.95 (978-0-9773725-9-1(6)) Flat Hammock Pr.

PALSY, CEREBRAL

see Cerebral Palsy

PANAMA

Adamson, Heather. Panama. 2016. (Exploring Countries Ser.). (ENG., Illus.). 32p. (J). (gr. 3-7). lib. bdg. 26.95 (978-1-62617-345-3(1), Blastoff! Readers) Bellwether Media.

Augustin, Byron. Panama. 2005. (Enchantment of the World Ser.). (ENG., Illus.). 144p. (YA). (gr. 5-9). 39.00 (978-0-516-23676-6(8)) Scholastic Library Publishing.

Blashfield, Jean F. Panama - Enchantment of the World. 2014. (ENG.). 144p. (J). lib. bdg. 40.00 (978-0-531-20789-5(7)) Scholastic Library Publishing.

Freire, Carolina. Panama. 2004. (Countries of the World Ser.). (Illus.). 96p. (gr. 5-12). lib. bdg. 31.00 (978-0-8368-3117-7(9)) Stevens, Gareth Publishing LLLP.

Gritzner, Charles F. & Swanson, Linnea C. Panama. 2008. (Modern World Nations Ser.). (Illus.). 114p. (gr. 6-12). lib. bdg. 35.00 (978-0-7910-9673-4(4), Chelsea Hse.) Facts On File, Inc.

Hassig, Susan M., et al. Panama. 3rd enl. ed. 2016. (Cultures of the World (Third Edition) (r) Ser.). 144p. (J). 47.07 (978-1-5026-2215-0(7)) Cavendish Square Publishing.

Hinman, Bonnie. We Visit Panama. 2010. (Your Land & My Land Ser.). (Illus.). 64p. (J). (gr. 3-6). lib. bdg. 33.95 (978-1-58415-893-6(X)) Mitchell Lane Pubs., Inc.

Matrishon, Maible. Island Experiences - Adventures in Bocas Del Toro, on the Caribbean Coast of Panama. 2013. 40p. pap. (978-0-9808653-9-4(5), Matrishon Media) Wider Vision Publishing.

Shields, Charles J. Panama. 2010. (Central America Today Ser.). 63p. (YA). (gr. 7-18). pap. 9.95 (978-1-4222-0718-5(8)); (Illus.). (gr. 9-12). 21.95 (978-1-4222-0651-5(3)) Mason Crest.

—Panama, Vol. 8. Henderson, James D., ed. 2015. (Discovering Central America: History, Politics, & Culture Ser.). (Illus.). 64p. (J). (gr. 7). lib. bdg. 22.95 (978-1-4222-3292-7(1)) Mason Crest.

Streissguth, Tom. Panama in Pictures. 2nd ed. 2005. (Visual Geography Series, Second Ser.). (ENG., Illus.). 80p. (gr. 5-12). 31.93 (978-0-8225-2395-6(7)) Lerner Publishing Group.

PANAMA—FICTION

Andrews, Carol. The Giggle Wind. 2003. (Illus.). 40p. 17.95 (978-0-9725609-2-4(0)) Diakonia Publishing.

Appleton, Victor. The Moving Picture Boys at Panama. 2005. 27.95 (978-1-4218-1499-5(4)); 208p. pap. 12.95 (978-1-4218-1599-2(0)) 1st World Publishing, Inc. (1st World Library - Literary Society).

—The Moving Picture Boys at Panama. 2004. reprint ed. pap. 1.99 (978-1-4192-7472-5(4)); pap. 20.95 (978-1-4191-7472-8(X)) Kessinger Publishing, LLC.

—The Moving Picture Boys at Panama: Stirring Adventures along the Great Canal. 2007. (ENG.). 140p. pap. 18.99 (978-1-4346-2170-2(7)); 152p. pap. 21.99 (978-1-4346-2230-3(4)) Creative Media Partners, LLC.

Engle, Margarita. Silver People: Voices from the Panama Canal. 2014. (ENG.). 272p. (J). (gr. 7-12). 17.99 (978-0-544-10941-4(4), HMH Books For Young Readers) Houghton Mifflin Harcourt Publishing Co.

Giménez Llort, Lydia. The man who wore a Panama Hat. 2009. 36p. pap. 20.50 (978-1-4092-7060-7(2)) Lulu Pr., Inc.

Markun, Patricia M. The Little Painter of Sabana Grande. Casilla, Robert, illus. 2014. (ENG.). 32p. (J). (gr. -1-3). 13.99 (978-1-4814-4458-3(1), Simon & Schuster Bks. For Young Readers) Simon & Schuster Bks. For Young Readers.

Payson, Howard. The Boy Scouts at the Panama Canal. 2007. 332p. per. 19.95 (978-1-60466-006-7(6)) Capricorn Hse. Publishing.

—The Boy Scouts at the Panama Canal. 2005. reprint ed. pap. 30.95 (978-1-4179-2457-8(8)) Kessinger Publishing, LLC.

—The Boy Scouts at the Panama Canal. 2005. pap. 30.95 (978-1-885529-44-2(9)) Stevens Publishing.

Popcorn, Socks, & Salvation. 2008. 32p. pap. 4.99 (978-0-8341-2350-2(9), 083-412-3509) Beacon Hill Pr. of Kansas City.

Ross, Jeff. Dawn Patrol, 1 vol. 2012. (Orca Sports Ser.). (ENG.). 160p. (YA). (gr. 6-10). pap. 9.95 (978-1-4598-0062-5(1)) Orca Bk. Pubs. USA.

Roy, Lillian Elizabeth. Polly's Southern Cruise: The Polly Brewster Series. Barbour, H. S., illus. 2011. 294p. 48.95 (978-1-258-10514-3(4)) Literary Licensing, LLC.

Wells, Helen. Cherry Ames, Army Nurse. 2005. (Cherry Ames Nurse Stories Ser.: Bk. 3). 224p. (J). (gr. 4-7). 14.95 (978-0-9771597-2-7(8)) Springer Publishing Co., Inc.

PANAMA CANAL (PANAMA)

Anderson, Dale. Building the Panama Canal. 2004. (Landmark Events in American History Ser.). (Illus.). 48p. (J). (gr. 5-12). pap. 14.05 (978-0-8368-5422-0(5), Gareth Stevens Secondary Library) Stevens, Gareth Publishing LLLP.

Benoit, Peter. The Panama Canal. 2013. (ENG.). 64p. (J). 30.00 (978-0-531-28205-2(8)); pap. 8.95 (978-0-531-27670-9(8)) Scholastic Library Publishing.

Crewe, Sabrina & Anderson, Dale. Building the Panama Canal. 2005. (Events That Shaped America Ser.). (Illus.). 32p. (gr. 3-6). lib. bdg. 26.00 (978-0-8368-3413-0(5), Gareth Stevens Learning Library) Stevens, Gareth Publishing LLLP.

Currie, Stephen. The Panama Canal. 2014. (History's Great Structures). (ENG., Illus.). 96p. (J). lib. bdg. (978-1-60152-710-3(1)) ReferencePoint Pr., Inc.

DuTemple, Lesley A. The Panama Canal: Great Building Feats Series. 2003. (Great Building Feats Ser.). (Illus.). 96p. (J). (gr. 5-9). 27.93 (978-0-8225-0079-7(5)) Lerner Publishing Group.

Hoffman, Mary Ann. The Panama Canal: Global Gateway. 2009. (Real Life Readers Ser.). 32p. (gr. 5-6). pap. 10.00 (978-1-4358-0207-0(1), Rosen Classroom) Rosen Publishing Group, Inc., The.

Mann, Elizabeth. The Panama Canal: The Story of How a Jungle Was Conquered & the World Made Smaller. Rangel, Fernando, illus. 2006. (Wonders of the World Book Ser.). (ENG.). 48p. (J). (gr. 4-8). pap. 12.95 (978-1-931414-14-2(9), 9781931414142) Mikaya Pr.

Miller, Heather. The Panama Canal. 2014. (Great Idea Ser.). (ENG., Illus.). 48p. (J). (gr. 4-6). lib. bdg. 26.60 (978-1-59953-594-4(7)) Norwood Hse. Pr.

Pascal, Janet. What Is the Panama Canal? 2014. (What Is... ? Ser.). lib. bdg. 16.00 (978-0-606-35688-6(6)) Turtleback Bks.

Pascal, Janet B. What Is the Panama Canal? Foley, Tim & Harper, Fred, illus. 2014. (What Was? Ser.). (ENG.). 112p. (J). (gr. 3-7). 5.99 (978-0-448-47899-9(4), Penguin Workshop) Penguin Young Readers Group.

Roberts, Russell. Building the Panama Canal. 2008. (Monumental Milestones Ser.). (Illus.). 48p. (YA). (gr. 4-7). lib. bdg. 29.95 (978-1-58415-692-5(9)) Mitchell Lane Pubs., Inc.

Ryckman, Tatiana. The Panama Canal. 2017. (J). **(978-1-5026-2692-9(6))** Cavendish Square Publishing.

Stefoff, Rebecca. Panama Canal. 2016. (Engineering Wonders Ser.). (ENG., Illus.). 32p. (gr. 3-4). lib. bdg. 27.32 (978-1-4914-8198-1(6), Fact Finders) Capstone Press of Coughlan Cos.

Vander Hook, Sue. Building the Panama Canal, 1 vol. 2010. (Essential Events Set 4 Ser.). (ENG.). 112p. (J). (gr. 6-12). lib. bdg. 35.64 (978-1-60453-942-4(9)) ABDO Publishing Co.

PANDAS

Allen, Kathy. Giant Pandas in a Shrinking Forest: A Cause & Effect Investigation, 1 vol. 2010. (Animals on the Edge Ser.). (ENG.). 32p. (gr. 3-4). lib. bdg. 27.32 (978-1-4296-5401-2(5), Fact Finders) Capstone Press of Coughlan Cos.

Anderson, AnnMarie. Giant Pandas. 2016. (Scholastic Reader, Level 2 Ser.). (ENG., Illus.). 32p. (J). (gr. 1-3). pap. 3.99 (978-0-545-93549-4(0), Scholastic Nonfiction) Scholastic, Inc.

Arnold, Caroline. A Panda's World. Arnold, Caroline, illus. 2015. (Caroline Arnold's Black & White Animals Ser.). (ENG., Illus.). 20p. (gr. -1-2). bds. 7.99 (978-1-4795-6354-8(4)) Picture Window Bks.

Austen, Mary. Panda Bears. 2016. (Bears of the World Ser.). 24p. (J). (gr. 3-3). 23.60 (978-1-4994-2040-1(4), PowerKids Pr.) Rosen Publishing Group, Inc., The.

Bell, Samantha. Giant Pandas Are Awesome. 2018. (ENG.). 32p. (gr. 3-6). 31.35 **(978-1-63235-435-8(7)**, 12-Story Library) Pr. Room Editions LLC.

Bodden, Valerie. Amazing Animals: Pandas. 2013. (Amazing Animals Ser.). (ENG.). 24p. (J). (gr. 1-3). pap. 8.99 (978-0-89812-791-1(2), Creative Paperbacks) Creative Co., The.

—Pandas. 2013. (Illus.). 24p. (J). 25.65 (978-1-60818-089-9(1), Creative Education) Creative Co., The.

Bodkin, Odds. Belly Button. 2003. (Illus.). 12p. (J). bds. (978-0-9657170-5-2(4)) Perkins Schl. for the Blind.

Boothroyd, Jennifer. From Cub to Panda. 2016. (Start to Finish, Second Ser.). (ENG., Illus.). 24p. (J). (gr. k-3). lib. bdg. 23.99 (978-1-5124-1828-6(5), Lerner Pubns.) Lerner Publishing Group.

Borgert-Spaniol, Megan. Red Pandas. 2015. (Animal Safari Ser.). (ENG., Illus.). 24p. (J). (gr. k-3). lib. bdg. 25.95 (978-1-62617-213-5(7), Blastoff! Readers) Bellwether Media.

Bortolotti, Dan. Panda Rescue: Changing the Future for Endangered Wildlife. 2003. (Firefly Animal Rescue Ser.). (ENG., Illus.). 64p. (J). (gr. 5-18). 19.95 (978-1-55297-598-5(3), 9781552975985); pap. 9.95 (978-1-55297-557-2(6), 9781552975572) Firefly Bks., Ltd.

Bredeson, Carmen. Giant Pandas up Close. 2006. (Zoom in on Animals! Ser.). (Illus.). 24p. (J). (gr. 1-3). lib. bdg. 22.60 (978-0-7660-2496-0(2), Enslow Elementary) Enslow Pubs., Inc.

Bright, Michael. Exploring Nature - Bears & Pandas: An Intriguing Insight into the Lives of Brown Bears, Polar Bears, Black Bears, Pandas & Others, with 190 Exciting Images: Bears & Pandas: Bears & Pandas. 2015. (ENG., Illus.). 64p. (J). (gr. -1-2). 12.99 (978-1-86147-389-9(3), Armadillo) Anness Publishing GBR. Dist: National Bk. Network.

PQR

Butterfield, Moira. Panda. (Who Am I? Ser.). (Illus.). 32p. lib. bdg. 24.25 (978-1-930643-91-8(8)) Chrysalis Education.

Cain, Marie Mowery. Look at That Face. 2013. (Big Books, Blue Ser.). (ENG & SPA., Illus.). 16p. pap. 33.00 (978-1-59246-004-5(6)) Big Books, by George!

Candy Cane Press, creator. Baby Panda Book & Toy Gift Set, Set. 2006. (Illus.). 26p. (J). bds. 16.95 (978-0-8249-6675-1(9), Ideal Pubns.) Worthy Publishing.

Caravan, Jill. Pandas: A Portrait of the Animal World. (Portrait of the Animal World Ser.). (Illus.). 72p. 2013. pap. 9.95 (978-1-59764-317-7(3)) 2nd rev. ed. 2012. 12.95 (978-1-59764-230-9(4)) New Line Bks.

Clark, Willow. Pandas. 2012. (Animals of Asia Ser.). (ENG., Illus.). 24p. (J). (gr. 1-5). pap. 8.25 (978-1-4488-7487-3(4)); lib. bdg. 22.60 (978-1-4488-7414-9(9)) Rosen Publishing Group, Inc., The. (PowerKids Pr.).

Costain, Meredith. Panda. Jackson-Carter, Stuart, illus. 2016. (Wild World Ser.). 00032p. (J). (gr. 1-2). 27.25 (978-1-4994-8221-8(3), Windmill Bks.) Rosen Publishing Group, Inc., The.

Craig, Diane. Panda, 1 vol. 2014. (Giant Animals Ser.). (ENG., Illus.). 24p. (J). (gr. -1-3). 24.21 (978-1-62403-060-4(2)) ABDO Publishing Co.

Crossingham, John & Kalman, Bobbie. Endangered Pandas. 2005. (Earth's Endangered Animals Ser.). (ENG., Illus.). 32p. (J). (gr. 3-5). pap. (978-0-7787-1904-5(9)) Crabtree Publishing Co.

Cruickshank, Don. Giant Pandas. 2006. (Amazing Animals Ser.). (Illus.). 24p. (J). (gr. 3-7). pap. 8.95 (978-1-59036-395-9(7)); lib. bdg. 24.45 (978-1-59036-389-8(2)) Weigl Pubs., Inc.

Dorling Kindersley Publishing Staff & Buller, Laura. The Great Panda Tale. 2014. (DK Readers Ser.). (ENG.). 32p. (J). (gr. 1-3). pap. 3.99 (978-1-4654-1718-3(4), DK Children) Dorling Kindersley Publishing, Inc.

Dudley, Karen. Giant Pandas with Code. 2012. (Animals on the Brink Ser.). (ENG., Illus.). 48p. (J). (gr. 4-7). pap. 14.95 (978-1-61913-434-8(9)); lib. bdg. 29.99 (978-1-61913-433-1(0)) Weigl Pubs., Inc. (AV2 by Weigl).

Eason, Sarah. Save the Panda. Geeson, Andrew & Veldhoven, Marijke, illus. 2009. (Save the... Ser.). 32p. (J). (gr. 2-5). lib. bdg. 25.25 (978-1-4358-2812-4(7)) Rosen Publishing Group, Inc., The.

Faundez, Anne. Animals in Danger. 2004. (QEB Start Reading Ser.). (Illus.). 24p. (J). lib. bdg. 15.95 (978-1-59566-009-1(7)) QEB Publishing Inc.

Firestone, Mary. Top 50 Reasons to Care about Giant Pandas: Animals in Peril. 2010. (Top 50 Reasons to Care about Endangered Animals Ser.). (Illus.). 104p. (J). (gr. 5-9). 33.27 (978-0-7660-3451-8(8)) Enslow Pubs., Inc.

Franks, Katie. Pandas. 2014. (Zoo's Who's Who Ser.). (Illus.). 24p. (J). (gr. k-2). pap. 49.50 (978-1-4777-6582-1(4), PowerKids Pr.) Rosen Publishing Group, Inc., The.

Furstinger, Nancy. Giant Pandas. 2015. (Endangered Animals Ser.). (ENG.). 24p. (J). (gr. 1-4). 27.07 (978-1-63143-969-8(3), 208804) Child's World, Inc., The.

Gallagher, Debbie. Pandas. 2009. (Zoo Animals 2 Ser.). 32p. (gr. 2). lib. bdg. 18.56 (978-0-7614-4745-0(8)) Marshall Cavendish Corp.

Gardner, Robert. How Heavy Is Heavy? Science Projects with Weight. 2015. (Hot Science Experiments Ser.). 48p. (J). (gr. 3-4). pap. 8.95 (978-0-7660-6601-4(0), Enslow Elementary) Enslow Pubs., Inc.

Gareth Stevens Editorial Staff. Pandas. 2004. (All about Wild Animals Ser.). (Illus.). 32p. (gr. k-4). lib. bdg. 26.00 (978-0-8368-4121-3(2), Gareth Stevens Learning Library) Stevens, Gareth Publishing LLLP.

Gervasio, Christine. Pandas Live to Eat. 2015. (1B Animal Behaviors Ser.). (ENG., Illus.). 32p. (J). pap. 5.99 (978-1-63437-015-8(5)) American Reading Co.

Gibbons, Gail. Giant Pandas. 2004. (ENG., Illus.). 32p. (J). (gr. k-3). pap. 7.99 (978-0-8234-1828-2(6)) Holiday Hse., Inc.

Gish, Melissa. Pandas. (Living Wild Ser.). 48p. (J). 2012. (ENG.). (gr. 4-7). pap. 12.00 (978-0-89812-674-7(6), Creative Paperbacks) 2011. (Illus.). 35.65 (978-1-60818-082-0(4), Creative Education) Creative Co., The.

Green, Carl R. The Giant Panda: A MyReportLinks. com Book. 2004. (Endangered & Threatened Animals Ser.). (Illus.). 48p. (J). lib. bdg. 26.60 (978-0-7660-5061-7(0), MyReportLinks.com Bks.) Enslow Pubs., Inc.

Gregory, Josh. Red Pandas. 2016. (Nature's Children Ser.). (ENG., Illus.). 48p. (J). pap. 6.95 (978-0-531-21936-2(4), Children's Pr.) Scholastic Library Publishing.

Greve, Tom. Giant Pandas. 2010. (ENG., Illus.). 24p. (gr. 3-6). pap. 8.95 (978-1-61590-512-6(X)) Rourke Educational Media.

Haugen, Brenda. Giant Pandas, 1 vol. 2012. (Endangered & Threatened Animals Ser.). (ENG., Illus.). 32p. (gr. 3-4). lib. bdg. 27.99 (978-1-4296-8663-1(4), Snap Bks.) Capstone Press of Coughlan Cos.

Imbriaco, Alison. The Giant Panda: Help Save This Endangered Species! 2006. (Saving Endangered Species Ser.). (Illus.). 128p. (J). (gr. 5-9). lib. bdg. 34.60 (978-1-59845-037-8(9), MyReportLinks.com Bks.) Enslow Pubs., Inc.

Jazynka, Kitson & National Geographic Kids Staff. Panda Rescue: All about Pandas & How to Save Them. 2016. (NG Kids Mission: Animal Rescue Ser.). (ENG., Illus.). 112p. (J). (gr. 5). pap. 12.99 (978-1-4263-2088-0(4), National Geographic Children's Bks.) National Geographic Society.

Katirgis, Jane & Green, Carl R. Endangered Giant Pandas. 2015. (Wildlife at Risk Ser.). (ENG.). 48p. (J). (gr. 6-6). pap. 11.70 (978-0-7660-6892-6(7)); (Illus.). 27.93 (978-0-7660-6894-0(3)) Enslow Pubs., Inc.

Keller, Susanna. Meet the Panda. 2010. (At the Zoo Ser.). 24p. (J). (ENG.). pap. 8.25 (978-1-4358-9726-7(9)); (Illus.). (gr. -1-1). lib. bdg. 22.60 (978-1-4358-9307-8(7)) Rosen Publishing Group, Inc., The. (PowerKids Pr.).

Kolpin, Molly. Giant Pandas, 1 vol. 2011. (Bears Ser.). (ENG.). 24p. (gr. 1-2). pap. 7.29 (978-1-4296-7185-9(8)); pap. 41.70 (978-1-4296-7186-6(6)); lib. bdg. 25.32 (978-1-4296-6132-4(1)) Capstone Press of Coughlan Cos. (First Facts).

Kueffner, Susan. Pandas. (Amazing Animals Ser.). 48p. 2009. (gr. 2-6). pap. 10.50 (978-1-4339-2017-2(4), Gareth Stevens Learning Library) 2008. (YA). (gr. 3-6). lib. bdg. 28.00 (978-0-8368-9100-3(7)) Stevens, Gareth Publishing LLLP.

—Pandas. 2007. (J). (978-1-59939-126-7(0), Reader's Digest Young Families, Inc.) Studio Fun International.

Lawrence, Ellen. Tiny Paws & Big Black Eyes (Giant Panda) 2015. (Whose Little Baby Are You? Ser.). (ENG.). 24p. (J). (gr. -1-3). lib. bdg. 23.93 (978-1-910549-28-5(2)) Bearport Publishing Co., Inc.

Levine, Michelle. Giant Pandas. 2006. (Pull Ahead Books-Animals Ser.). (ENG., Illus.). 32p. (gr. k-3). lib. bdg. 22.60 (978-0-8225-3482-2(7), Lerner Pubns.) Lerner Publishing Group.

Macheske, Felicia. Round & Rare: Giant Panda. 2017. (Guess What Ser.). (ENG., Illus.). 24p. (J). (gr. k-2). lib. bdg. 28.50 (978-1-63472-170-7(5), 209252) Cherry Lake Publishing.

Macleod, Steve. Panda Gigante. 2012. (SPA.). (J). 27.13 (978-1-61913-175-0(7)) Weigl Pubs., Inc.

Markle, Sandra. How Many Baby Pandas? / Scholastic Book Fair Edition. 2009. (Illus.). 32p. (J). pap. 4.99 (978-0-8027-2070-2(6)) Walker & Co.

Marsh, Laura & National Geographic Kids Staff. Red Pandas. 2015. (Readers Ser.). (ENG., Illus.). 32p. (J). (gr. -1-1). pap. 3.99 (978-1-4263-2121-4(X), National Geographic Children's Bks.) National Geographic Society.

Marsico, Katie. Bears. 2017. (True Book(tm) — The Most Endangered Ser.). (ENG., Illus.). 48p. (J). lib. bdg. 31.00 (978-0-531-22725-1(1), Children's Pr.) Scholastic Library Publishing.

Miller, Sara Swan. Red Pandas. (Paws & Claws Ser.). 24p. 2009. (gr. 2-3). 42.50 (978-1-60851-153-2(7)) 2008. (Illus.). (J). (gr. 3-7). lib. bdg. 22.60 (978-1-4042-4164-0(7)) Rosen Publishing Group, Inc., The. (PowerKids Pr.).

Min, Fang. The Giant Panda. Daggers, Ben, tr. 2011. (ENG., Illus.). 112p. (J). 16.95 (978-1-60220-130-9(7)) BetterLink Pr., Inc.

Moldovo, Eustacia. Baby Pandas at the Zoo. 2015. (All about Baby Zoo Animals Ser.). (ENG., Illus.). 24p. (J). (gr. -1-1). 22.60 (978-0-7660-7079-0(4)); pap. 9.35 (978-0-7660-7077-6(8)) Enslow Pubs., Inc.

Murray, Julie. Giant Pandas, 1 vol. 2013. (Asian Animals Ser.). (ENG.). 32p. (J). (gr. 2-5). 28.50 (978-1-61783-553-7(6)) ABDO Publishing Co.

—Pandas, 1 vol. 2005. (Animal Kingdom Set Ii Ser.). (ENG., Illus.). 24p. (gr. k-4). 25.65 (978-1-59197-329-4(5), Buddy Bks.) ABDO Publishing Co.

National Geographic Editors. Favorite Animals Collection. 2013. (Readers Ser.). (ENG., Illus.). 128p. (J). (gr. -1-1). pap. 7.99 (978-1-4263-1333-2(0), National Geographic Children's Bks.) National Geographic Society.

Olson, Bethany. Baby Pandas. 2013. (Super Cute! Ser.). (ENG., Illus.). 24p. (J). (gr. k-3). lib. bdg. 25.95 (978-1-60014-930-6(8), Blastoff! Readers) Bellwether Media.

Osborne, Mary Pope & Boyce, Natalie Pope. Pandas & Other Endangered Species: A Perfect Time for Pandas. Murdocca, Sal, illus. 2012. (Magic Tree House - Fact Tracker Ser.: 26). (ENG.). 128p. (J). (gr. 2-5). 6.99 (978-0-375-87025-5(3), Random Hse. Bks. for Young Readers) Random Hse. Children's Bks.

—Pandas & Other Endangered Species: A Perfect Time for Pandas. 2012. (Magic Tree House Fact Tracker Ser.: 26). lib. bdg. 16.00 (978-0-606-26400-6(0), Turtleback) Turtleback Bks.

Peterson, Megan Cooley & Rustad, Martha E. H. Giant Pandas Are Awesome! 2015. (Awesome Asian Animals Ser.). (ENG., Illus.). 32p. (gr. 1-2). lib. bdg. 27.32 (978-1-4914-3905-0(X)) Capstone Press of Coughlan Cos.

Pingry, Patricia A. Baby Panda. Sharp, Chris, illus. 2004. (San Diego Zoo Animal Library: Vol. 7). (ENG.). 26p. (J). bds. 6.95 (978-0-8249-6555-6(8), Ideal Pubns.) Worthy Publishing.

Pohl, Kathleen. Pandas. 2007. (Animals I See at the Zoo Ser.). 24p. (gr. k-3). pap. 8.15 (978-0-8368-8227-8(X)); (Illus.). lib. bdg. 22.00 (978-0-8368-8220-9(2)) Stevens, Gareth Publishing LLLP. (Weekly Reader Leveled Readers).

—Pandas/Pandas. 2007. (Animals I See at the Zoo/Animales que Veo en el Zoológico Ser.). (SPA & ENG., Illus.). 24p. (gr. k-3). lib. bdg. 22.00 (978-0-8368-8234-6(2), Weekly Reader Leveled Readers) Stevens, Gareth Publishing LLLP.

Portman, Michael. Pandas in Danger. 2011. (Animals at Risk Ser.). (Illus.). 24p. (J). (gr. 2-5). pap. 8.15 (978-1-4339-5800-7(7)); lib. bdg. 22.60 (978-1-4339-5798-7(1)) Stevens, Gareth Publishing LLLP. (Gareth Stevens Learning Library).

Potter, Alicia. Mrs. Harkness & the Panda. Sweet, Melissa, illus. 2012. (ENG.). 40p. (J). (gr. k-3). 16.99 (978-0-375-84448-5(1), Knopf Bks. for Young Readers) Random Hse. Children's Bks.

Quinton, Sasha. Root-A-Toot: A Phonics Reader. 2009. (Illus.). pap. (978-1-936199-01-3(7)) Book Shop, Ltd., The.

Riggs, Kate. Pandas. 2015. (J). (978-1-60818-514-6(1), Creative Education) Creative Co., The.

—Seedlings: Pandas. 2015. (Seedlings Ser.). (ENG.). 24p. (J). (gr. -1-1). pap. 7.99 (978-1-62832-114-2(8), Creative Paperbacks) Creative Co., The.

Royston, Angela. Save the Giant Panda, 1. 2014. (Animal SOS! Ser.). (ENG.). 32p. (J). (gr. k-5). pap. 10.00 (978-1-4777-6035-2(0), Windmill Bks.) Rosen Publishing Group, Inc., The.

Rudolph, Jessica. MIS Bigotes Son Largos y Blancos (Red Panda) 2016. (Pistas de Animales 2 Ser.). (SPA.). 24p. (J). (gr. -1-3). 17.95 (978-1-944102-79-1(5)) Bearport Publishing Co., Inc.

—My Whiskers Are Long & White (Red Panda) 2016. (Zoo Clues 2 Ser.). (ENG.). 24p. (J). (gr. -1-3). 17.95 (978-1-944102-61-6(2)) Bearport Publishing Co., Inc.

Ryder, Joanne. Little Panda: The World Welcomes Hua Mei at the San Diego Zoo. World-Famous San Diego Zoo Staff, photos by. 2004. (ENG., Illus.). 32p. (J). (gr. k-3). 7.99 (978-0-689-86616-6(X), Simon & Schuster Bks. For Young Readers) Simon & Schuster Bks. For Young Readers.

—Panda Kindergarten. Feng, Katherine, photos by. 2014. (Illus.). 32p. pap. 8.00 (978-1-61003-332-9(9)) Center for the Collaborative Classroom.

—Panda Kindergarten. Feng, Katherine, illus. (ENG.). 32p. (J). (gr. -1-3). 2015. pap. 6.99 (978-0-06-057852-7(1)) 2009. 17.99 (978-0-06-057850-3(5), Collins) HarperCollins Pubs.

Schreiber, Anne. Pandas. 2010. (Readers Ser.). (ENG., Illus.). 32p. (J). (gr. k-3). 13.90 (978-1-4263-0611-2(3)); pap. 3.99 (978-1-4263-0610-5(5)) National Geographic Society. (National Geographic Children's Bks.).

—Pandas (1 Hardcover/1 CD) 2017. (National Geographic Kids Ser.). (ENG.). (J). 29.95 **(978-1-4301-2661-4(2))** Live Oak Media.

—Pandas (1 Paperback/1 CD) 2017. (National Geographic Kids Ser.). (ENG.). (J). pap. 19.95 **(978-1-4301-2660-7(4))** Live Oak Media.

—Pandas (4 Paperbacks/1 CD), 4 vols. 2017. (National Geographic Kids Ser.). (ENG.). (J). pap., pap. 31.95 **(978-1-4301-2662-1(0))** Live Oak Media.

Schuetz, Kari. Giant Pandas. 2011. (Animal Safari Ser.). (ENG., Illus.). 24p. (J). (gr. k-3). lib. bdg. 25.95 (978-1-60014-603-9(1), Blastoff! Readers) Bellwether Media.

Schuh, Mari. Giant Pandas. 2017. (Black & White Animals Ser.). (ENG.). 24p. (gr. k-1). lib. bdg. 21.99 (978-1-5157-3372-0(6), Pebble Bks.) Capstone Press of Coughlan Cos.

Shaw, Gina & Bader, Bonnie. Welcome, Bao Bao. 2015. (Smithsonian Ser.). (ENG., Illus.). 48p. (J). (gr. 3-4). 3.99 (978-0-448-48225-5(8), Penguin Young Readers) Penguin Young Readers Group.

Shea, Bobby Kennedy. Patterns with Pandas. 2013. (Animal Math Ser.). 24p. (J). (gr. 1-3). pap. 48.90 (978-1-4339-9320-6(1)); (ENG., Illus.). lib. bdg. 22.60 (978-1-4339-9318-3(X)) Stevens, Gareth Publishing LLLP.

Shea, Bobby Kennedy & Kennedy Shea, Bobby. Patterns with Pandas. 2013. 24p. (J). (gr. 1-3). pap. 8.15 (978-1-4339-9319-0(8)) Stevens, Gareth Publishing LLLP.

Simon, Mary Manz. Panda Is Polite. 2006. (First Virtuestm for Toddlers Ser.). (Illus.). 20p. (J). 5.99 (978-0-7847-1577-2(7), 04071) Standard Publishing.

Sirota, Lyn A. Giant Pandas, 1 vol. 2010. (Asian Animals Ser.). (ENG.). 24p. (gr. k-1). pap. 7.29 (978-1-4296-4845-5(7)); 26.65 (978-1-4296-4028-2(6)); pap. 41.70 (978-1-4296-5095-3(8)) Capstone Press of Coughlan Cos. (Pebble Plus).

Soundprints, creator. Panda's Busy Day. 2011. (Let's Go to the Zoo! Ser.). (ENG., Illus.). 16p. (gr. -1). 5.95 (978-1-60727-455-1(8)) Soundprints.

Stone, Lynn M. Giant Pandas. Su, Keren, photos by. 2003. (Nature Watch Ser.). (ENG., Illus.). 48p. (gr. 4-8). 27.93 (978-1-57505-343-1(8), Carolrhoda Bks.) Lerner Publishing Group.

Torres, John. Threat to the Giant Panda. 2008. (On the Verge of Extinction Ser.). (Illus.). 32p. (YA). (gr. 2-5). lib. bdg. 25.70 (978-1-58415-689-5(9)) Mitchell Lane Pubs., Inc.

Trueit, Trudi Strain. Giant Pandas. 2015. (Wild Bears Ser.). (ENG., Illus.). 24p. (J). (gr. 1-4). 19.95 (978-1-60753-774-8(5)) Amicus Publishing.

Turnbull, Stephanie. Panda. 2015. (ENG., Illus.). 24p. (J). pap. 8.95 (978-1-77092-217-4(2)) RiverStream Publishing.

Volke, Gordon, et al, illus. Panda Patrol Sticker, Story & Activitity Book, Vol. 2. 2004. 16p. pap., act. bk. ed. 6.00 (978-1-84161-112-9(3)) Ravette Publishing, Ltd. GBR. Dist: Parkwest Pubns., Inc.

—Panda Patrol Sticker, Story & Activity Book. 2004. 16p. pap., act. bk. ed. 6.00 (978-1-84161-072-6(0)) Ravette Publishing, Ltd. GBR. Dist: Parkwest Pubns., Inc.

—Panda Patrol Travel Games with Stickers. 2004. 16p. pap., act. bk. ed. 6.00 (978-1-84161-110-5(7)) Ravette Publishing, Ltd. GBR. Dist: Parkwest Pubns., Inc.

Waring, Jamall & National Geographic Editors. Saving the Pandas. 2008. (Footprint Reading Library). (ENG., Illus.). 24p. cd-rom 16.95 **(978-1-4240-2348-6(3))** Cengage Heinle.

Zeiger, Jennifer. Pandas. 2012. (Nature's Children Ser.). (ENG.). 48p. (J). (gr. 3-5). lib. bdg. 28.00 (978-0-531-20905-9(9), Children's Pr.) Scholastic Library Publishing.

—Pandas - Nature's Children. 2012. (Nature's Children Ser.). (ENG.). 48p. (J). pap. 6.95 (978-0-531-21080-2(4), Children's Pr.) Scholastic Library Publishing.

PANDAS—FICTION

Ainsworth, Kimberly. Little Panda. Berg, Michelle, illus. 2008. (Little Green Bks.). (ENG.). 8p. (J). (gr. -1 — 1). 9.99 (978-1-4169-6173-4(9), Little Simon) Little Simon.

Alderfer, Lauren. Mindful Monkey, Happy Panda. MacLean, Kerry Lee, illus. 2011. (ENG.). 32p. (J). (gr. -1-3). 16.95 (978-0-86171-683-8(3)) Wisdom Pubns.

Alfred Sole. Pandi's Adventures in Afric. Patradol Kitcharoen, illus. 2012. 86p. pap. 23.97 (978-1-61897-493-8(9), Strategic Bk. Publishing) Strategic Book Publishing & Rights Agency (SBPRA).

Antony, Steve. I'll Wait, Mr. Panda. Antony, Steve, illus. 2016. (ENG., Illus.). 32p. (J). (gr. -1-k). 16.99 (978-1-338-02836-2(7), Scholastic Pr.) Scholastic, Inc.

—Please, Mr. Panda. 2014. (ENG.). 32p. (J). (gr. -1-k). 16.99 (978-0-545-78892-2(7), Scholastic Pr.) Scholastic, Inc.

Austin, Rikey. Ting Finds a Bell: Alice's Bear Shop. 2012. 28p. pap. (978-1-78092-158-7(6)) MX Publishing, Ltd.

Bamboo Zoo Set: Meet Lester Panda & his Friends. 2006. (J). 17.95 (978-0-9774493-1-6(9)) Bamboo Zoo, LLC.

Bell, Frank. Feng Suey's Special Garden. Seaman, Paul, illus. 2004. 24p. pap. 7.00 (978-1-84161-071-9(2)) Ravette Publishing, Ltd. GBR. Dist: Parkwest Pubns., Inc.

—How Slip Slap Slop Got His Name. Seaman, Paul, illus. 2004. 24p. pap. 7.00 (978-1-84161-069-6(0)) Ravette Publishing, Ltd. GBR. Dist: Parkwest Pubns., Inc.

—Ma Jong & the Magic Carpet. Seaman, Paul, illus. 2004. 24p. pap. 7.00 (978-1-84161-070-2(4)) Ravette Publishing, Ltd. GBR. Dist: Parkwest Pubns., Inc.

Bernal, Sandra Marie. I Want a Pand. 2011. 32p. pap. 24.95 (978-1-4626-2897-1(4)) America Star Bks.

Book Buddy: Panda with Story Book. Orig. Title: Child's Play. (Illus.). 10p. (J). (gr. -1-3). reprint ed. (978-1-881469-44-5(1)) Safari, Ltd.

Bowen, Sherry. Little Panda. Wallace, Chad, illus. 2003. (Books for Young Learners). (ENG.). 12p. (J). 5.75 net. (978-1-57274-673-2(4), 2459, Bks. for Young Learners) Owen, Richard C. Pubs., Inc.

Brennan, Sarah. The Tale of Pin Yin Panda. Harrison, Harry, illus. 2012. (ENG.). 32p. (J). 24.95 (978-1-937160-15-9(7)) Eliassen Creative.

Briant, Ed. A Day at the Beach, No. 1. Briant, Ed, illus. 2006. (Illus.). 32p. (J). (gr. -1). 17.89 (978-0-06-079982-3(X)) HarperCollins Pubs.

Brighter Minds, creator. Fact Book. 2008. (DreamWorks Kung Fu Panda Ser.). (Illus.). 10p. (J). (gr. -1-3). 9.95 (978-1-57791-420-4(1)) Brighter Minds Children's Publishing.

—Kung Fu Panda: Create-A-Story. 2008. (Illus.). 8p. (J). (gr. k-2). 9.95 (978-1-57791-419-8(8)) Brighter Minds Children's Publishing.

—Kung Fu Panda Magnetic Storybook. 2008. (DreamWorks Kung Fu Panda Ser.). (Illus.). 10p. (J). (gr. 1-3). bds. 12.95 (978-1-57791-421-1(X)) Brighter Minds Children's Publishing.

Buffomante, Maya. How Pandas Became Black & White. 2012. 24p. pap. (978-1-4602-0613-3(4)) FriesenPress.

Burchett, Jan & Vogler, Sara. Earthquake Escape, 1 vol. Le Feyer, Diane, illus. 2012. (Wild Rescue Ser.). (ENG.). 152p. (gr. 3-6). lib. bdg. 25.32 (978-1-4048-6891-5(7)) Picture Window Bks.

Capucilli, Alyssa Satin. Panda Kisses. Widdowson, Kay, illus. 2008. (Step into Reading Ser.). (ENG.). 32p. (J). (gr. -1-1). pap. 3.99 (978-0-375-84562-8(3), Random Hse. Bks. for Young Readers) Random Hse. Children's Bks.

Chihak, Sheena. Kung Fu Panda 3-D Puzzle Book. Salesse, Alain, illus. 2008. 10p. (J). 9.99 (978-0-696-23485-9(8)) Meredith Bks.

—Kung Fu Panda: Paws of Power Activity Kit. 2008. (Illus.). 32p. (J). 14.99 (978-0-696-23483-5(1)) Meredith Bks.

Chihak, Sheena & Loki. Kung Fu Panda. Mada Design Inc, illus. 2008. (I Can Find It Ser.). 22p. (J). 7.99 (978-0-696-23484-2(X)) Meredith Bks.

Child, Lauren. I Am Going to Save a Panda! 2010. (Charlie & Lola Ser.). lib. bdg. 13.55 (978-0-606-10628-3(6), Turtleback) Turtleback Bks.

Cook, Sherry & Johnson, Terri. Pressure Pete, 26 vols. Kuhn, Jesse, illus. l.t. ed. 2006. (Quirkles — Exploring Phonics through Science Ser.: 16). 32p. (J). 7.99 (978-1-933815-15-2(9), Quirkles, The) Creative 3, LLC.

Cornish, Linda Sowa Young. Pong's Birthday Journey. 2006. (J). pap. 15.00 (978-0-8059-6993-1(4)) Dorrance Publishing Co., Inc.

Crowley, Ashley. Officer Panda - Fingerprint Detective. Crowley, Ashley, illus. 2015. (Officer Panda Ser.: 1). (ENG., Illus.). 32p. (J). (gr. -1-3). 17.99 (978-0-06-236626-9(2)) HarperCollins Pubs.

—Officer Panda: Sky Detective. Crowley, Ashley, illus. 2016. (Officer Panda Ser.: 2). (Illus.). 32p. (J). (gr. -1-3). 17.99 (978-0-06-236627-6(0)) HarperCollins Pubs.

Dahl, Michael. Playdate for Panda. Vidal, Oriol, illus. 2016. (Hello Genius Ser.). (ENG.). 20p. (gr. 1-2). bds. 7.99 (978-1-4795-8741-4(9)) Picture Window Bks.

David, Erica. Po's Two Dads. 2015. (Kung Fu Panda Ready-To-Read Ser.). lib. bdg. 13.55 (978-0-606-38241-0(0)) Turtleback Bks.

Davies, Jacqueline. Panda Pants. Hanson, Sydney, illus. 2016. (ENG.). 32p. (J). (gr. -1-2). 17.99 (978-0-553-53576-1(5), Knopf Bks. for Young Readers) Random Hse. Children's Bks.

Dillard, Sarah. First Day at Zoo School. Dillard, Sarah, illus. 2014. (ENG., Illus.). 40p. (J). (gr. k-2). 14.99 (978-1-58536-890-7(3), 203670) Sleeping Bear Pr.

Disney Publishing Staff & Studiomouse Staff. Panda Cub Explores. 2011. (ENG.). 20p. (J). (978-1-59069-944-7(0)) Studio Mouse LLC.

Dowson, Nick. Tracks of a Panda. Rong, Yu, illus. 2007. (ENG.). 32p. (J). (gr. k-3). 16.99 (978-0-7636-3146-8(9)) Candlewick Pr.

—Tracks of a Panda: Read & Wonder. Rong, Yu, illus. 2010. (Read & Wonder Ser.). (ENG.). 32p. (J). (gr. -1-3). pap. 6.99 (978-0-7636-4737-7(3)) Candlewick Pr.

DreamWorks. Kung Fu Panda: Po's Tasty Training. 2008. (J). 13.99 (978-1-59319-981-4(3)) LeapFrog Enterprises, Inc.

DreamWorks & DreamWorks / LeapFrog. Kung Fu Panda: L'Entrainement Gourmand. 2008. (J). 20.79 (978-1-59319-946-3(5)) LeapFrog Enterprises, Inc.

Duncan, Randy. Miranda & Her Pand. 2009. 28p. pap. 12.49 (978-1-4389-6132-3(4)) AuthorHouse.

Evans, Ruth Todd. The Panda Who Would Not Eat. Evans, Ruth Todd, illus. 2007. (Illus.). 32p. (J). (gr. -1-3). per. 9.95 (978-0-932653-84-0(7)) Sunbelt Pubns., Inc.

Forsythe, Amanda J. The Contabulous Adventures of M E. 2012. 28p. 24.95 (978-1-4626-6531-0(4)) America Star Bks.

Franklin, Deborah. Annette's Christmas Gift. 2008. (Illus.). 24p. (YA). 7.00 (978-0-8059-7482-9(2)) Dorrance Publishing Co., Inc.

Gaiman, NEil. Chu's Day. Rex, Adam, illus. (ENG.). (J). (gr. -1-3). 2014. 40p. pap. 6.99 (978-0-06-201783-3(7)) 2013. 32p. 17.99 (978-0-06-201781-9(0)) HarperCollins Pubs.

—Chu's Day at the Beach. Rex, Adam, illus. 2015. (ENG.). 32p. (J). (gr. -1-3). 17.99 (978-0-06-222399-9(2)) HarperCollins Pubs.

—Chu's Day Board Book. Rex, Adam, illus. 2014. (ENG.). 36p. (J). (gr. -1 — 1). bds. 7.99 (978-0-06-234746-6(2), HarperFestival) HarperCollins Pubs.

—Chu's First Day of School. Rex, Adam, illus. 2014. (ENG.). 32p. (J). (gr. -1-3). 17.99 (978-0-06-222397-5(6)) HarperCollins Pubs.

—Chu's First Day of School Board Book. Rex, Adam, illus. 2015. (ENG.). 36p. (J). (gr. -1 — 1). bds. 7.99 (978-0-06-237149-2(5), HarperFestival) HarperCollins Pubs.

Gallo, Tina. Like Father, Like Po. 2015. (Kung Fu Panda 8x8 Ser.). lib. bdg. 13.55 (978-0-606-38257-1(7)) Turtleback Bks.

—Po's Awesomely Perfect Present. 2015. (Kung Fu Panda 8x8 Ser.). lib. bdg. 13.55 (978-0-606-37870-3(7)) Turtleback Bks.

Gallo, Tina, adapted by. Master of Manners. 2016. (Kung Fu Panda TV Ser.). (ENG., Illus.). 24p. (J). (gr. -1-2). pap. 3.99 (978-1-4814-6183-2(4), Simon Spotlight) Simon Spotlight.

—The Po Who Cried Ghost. 2014. (Kung Fu Panda TV Ser.). (ENG., Illus.). 24p. (J). (gr. -1-2). pap. 3.99 (978-1-4814-0491-4(1), Simon Spotlight) Simon Spotlight.

Gibbs, Lynne. Time to Share: A Story of Sharing. Mitchell, Melanie, illus. 2009. (Let's Grow Together Ser.). 32p. (J). (gr. -1-2). lib. bdg. 22.60 (978-1-60754-757-0(0)) Windmill Bks.

Gibbs, Stuart. Panda-Monium. 2017. (FunJungle Ser.). (ENG., Illus.). 352p. (J). (gr. 3-7). 16.99 (978-1-4814-4567-2(7), Simon & Schuster Bks. For Young Readers) Simon & Schuster Bks. For Young Readers.

Glass, Shelby. Something Is Everything. 2012. 36p. pap. 19.99 *(978-1-4772-6581-9(3))* AuthorHouse.
Green, John Patrick. Hippopotamister. 2016. (ENG., Illus.). 96p. (J). 17.99 *(978-1-62672-200-2(5),* 9781626722002, First Second Bks.) Roaring Brook Pr.
Hay DeSimone, Corkey. Panda Promise Activity & Coloring Book. Hay DeSimone, Corkey, illus. 2006. (Illus.). (J). 4.95 *(978-0-9747921-9-4(5))* Gentle Giraffe Pr.
Heston, L. L. The Story of Pan Doo: A Panda's Progress. 2012. 24p. pap. 15.99 *(978-1-4771-2392-8(X))* Xlibris Corp.
Hunt, Elizabeth Singer. The Puzzle of the Missing Panda, Bk. 7. Williamson, Brian, illus. 2008. (Secret Agent Jack Stalwart Ser.: 7). (ENG.). 128p. (J). (gr. 1-4). pap. 5.99 *(978-1-60286-020-9(3),* Weinstein Bks.) Perseus Bks. Group.
ImageBooks Staff & Mulligan, Lenz. Little Panda Finger Puppet Book. 2009. (Little Finger Puppet Board Bks.: FING). (ENG., Illus.). 12p. (J). (gr. -1 — 1). bds. 6.99 *(978-0-8118-6999-7(7))* Chronicle Bks. LLC.
Jarman, Julia. Two Shy Pandas. Varley, Susan, illus. 2013. (ENG.). 32p. (J). (gr. -1-3). 16.95 *(978-1-4677-1141-8(1))* Andersen Pr. GBR. Dist: Lerner Publishing Group.
Layman, Barbara. DreamWorks Kung Fu Panda 3: the Tao of Po. 2015. (ENG.). 56p. (J). (gr. -1-12). 10.99 *(978-0-7944-3521-9(1),* Reader's Digest Children's Bks.) Studio Fun International.
Lin, Chris. Mandy & Pandy Play Sports. Villalta, Ingrid, illus. 2008. 20p. (J). (gr. -1-3). bds. 9.99 *(978-0-9800156-7-6(7))* Mandy & Pandy Bks., LLC.
—Mandy & Pandy Visit China. Villalta, Ingrid, illus. 2008. 20p. (J). (gr. -1-3). bds. 9.99 *(978-0-9800156-6-9(9))* Mandy & Pandy Bks., LLC.
Lumry, Amanda & Hurwitz, Laura. Project Panda. 2008. (J). *(978-1-60040-008-7(6)); (978-1-60040-009-4(4))* Eaglemont Pr.
Lynn, Jeffrey. The Adventures of Pablo. . the Ecuadorian Panda. 2004. (YA). per. *(978-0-9763025-0-6(0))* Penner/Lynn Publishing.
Makura, Sho. Panda Man & the Treasure Hunt. Kato, Haruhi, illus. 2011. (ENG.). 96p. (J). (gr. 1-4). pap. 7.99 *(978-1-4215-3521-0(1))* Viz Media.
—Panda Man to the Rescue! Kato, Haruhi, illus. 2010. (ENG.). 96p. (J). pap. 7.99 *(978-1-4215-3520-3(3))* Viz Media.
—Panda Man vs. Chiwanda. Kato, Haruhi, illus. 2011. (ENG.). 96p. (J). (gr. 1-4). pap. 7.99 *(978-1-4215-3522-7(X))* Viz Media.
Martin, Bill, Jr. Panda Bear, Panda Bear, What Do You See? Carle, Eric, illus. rev. ed. 2003. (Brown Bear & Friends Ser.). (ENG.). 32p. (J). (gr. -1-k). 17.99 *(978-0-8050-1758-8(5),* 9780805017588, Holt, Henry & Co. Bks. For Young Readers) Holt, Henry & Co.
McDonald, Jill, illus. Ghoulish Gang. 2008. (ENG.). 12p. (J). 9.95 *(978-1-58117-782-4(8),* Intervisual/Piggy Toes) Bendon, Inc.
Meadows, Daisy. Mae the Panda Fairy. 2015. (Baby Animal Rescue Fairies Ser.: 1). (ENG.). 80p. (J). (gr. 2-5). pap. 4.99 *(978-0-545-70844-9(3),* Scholastic Paperbacks) Scholastic, Inc.
—Mae the Panda Fairy. 2015. (Rainbow Magic — Baby Animal Rescue Fairies Ser.: 1). lib. bdg. 14.75 *(978-0-606-37049-3(8))* Turtleback Bks.
Meldrum, Margaret. Peter Panda & His Friends. 2009. (Illus.). 24p. pap. 11.49 *(978-1-4343-7826-2(8))* AuthorHouse.
Meredith Books Staff, creator. Kung Fu Panda. 2008. (Illus.). 22p. (J). 15.95 *(978-0-696-23482-8(3))* Meredith Bks.
Milbourne, A. & Wells, R. Panda in the Park. 2004. (Look-Through Board Bks.). (Illus.). 10p. (J). (gr. -1-18). 4.95 *(978-0-7945-0158-7(3),* Usborne) EDC Publishing.
Moody-Luther, Jacqueline. Panda Bear Cub. Nelson, Will, illus. 2006. (ENG.). 32p. (J). pap. 3.95 *(978-1-59249-585-6(0))* Soundprints.
Mucklow, Hope. Rojo the Baby Red Panda at the Zoo: An Allegory about Self-Worth Through a Red Panda & Giant Panda Comparison. 2014. (ENG., Illus.). 32p. (J). (gr. -1-3). 14.95 *(978-1-62086-593-4(9))* Mascot Bks., Inc.
Murphy, Mary. Panda Foo & the New Friend. Murphy, Mary, illus. 2007. (ENG., Illus.). 32p. (J). (gr. k-k). 15.99 *(978-0-7636-3405-6(0))* Candlewick Pr.
Muth, Jon J. Zen Ghosts. 2010. (ENG.). 40p. (J). (gr. -1-3). 17.99 *(978-0-439-63430-4(X),* Scholastic Pr.) Scholastic, Inc.
—Zen Shorts. (ENG.). (J). (gr. -1-3). 2010. 18.99 *(978-0-545-22760-5(7))* 2008. (Illus.). 40p. 25.00 *(978-0-545-04087-7(6),* Scholastic) Scholastic, Inc.
—Zen Socks. 2015. (ENG., Illus.). 40p. (J). (gr. -1-3). 17.99 *(978-0-545-16669-0(1),* Scholastic Pr.) Scholastic, Inc.
—Zen Ties. Muth, Jon J., illus. 2008. (ENG., Illus.). 40p. (J). (gr. -1-3). 17.99 *(978-0-439-63425-0(3),* Scholastic Pr.) Scholastic, Inc.
Nagda, Ann Whitehead. A Home for Panda. Effler, Jim, illus. (Amazing Animal Adventures Ser.). (ENG.). 36p. (J). 2005. (gr. -1-2). 15.95 *(978-1-59249-045-5(X),* B7102) 2005. (gr. -1-2). pap. 6.95 *(978-1-59249-046-2(8),* S7102) 2005. (gr. 2-2). 8.95 *(978-1-59249-393-7(9),* SC7102) 2005. (gr. 2-2). 19.95 *(978-1-59249-392-0(0),* BC7102) 2003. (gr. -1-3). 2.95 *(978-1-59249-047-9(6),* S7152) Soundprints.
—A Home for Panda. Effler, Jim, illus. 2003. (ENG.). 36p. (J). (gr. -1-3). 9.95 *(978-1-59249-058-5(1),* PS7152) Soundprints.
—Time to Eat, Panda! 2005. (Soundprints' Read-and-Discover Ser.). (ENG., Illus.). 32p. (J). (gr. -1-1). 12.95 *(978-1-59249-148-3(0),* PS2011) Soundprints.
Nagda, Ann Whitehead, text. Time to Eat, Panda! 2005. (Soundprints' Read-and-Discover Ser.). (ENG., Illus.). 32p. (J). (gr. -1-1). pap. 3.95 *(978-1-59249-147-6(2),* S2011) Soundprints.
Nona Theresa Perez - Bayanin. The Birth of Nadia Mei. 2012. 24p. pap. 15.99 *(978-1-4771-0387-6(2))* Xlibris Corp.
O'Ryan, Ellie, adapted by. Panda School. 2015. (Kung Fu Panda TV Ser.). (ENG., Illus.). 32p. (J). (gr. k-2). pap. 3.99 *(978-1-4814-3707-3(0),* Simon Spotlight) Simon Spotlight.
Osborne, Mary Pope. A Perfect Time for Pandas. Murdocca, Sal, illus. (Magic Tree House Merlin Mission Ser.: No. 20). (ENG.). (J). (gr. 2-5). 2014. 144p. pap. 5.99 *(978-0-375-86798-9(8))* 2012. 128p. 12.99 *(978-0-375-86826-9(7))* 2012. 128p. lib. bdg. 15.99 *(978-0-375-96826-6(1))* Random Hse. Children's Bks. (Random Hse. Bks. for Young Readers).
—A Perfect Time for Pandas. 2014. (Magic Tree House Merlin Missions Ser.: 20). lib. bdg. 16.00 *(978-0-606-35564-3(2))* Turtleback Bks.
Panda, Jake G. The Case of the Cursed Dodo. 2014. (Illus.). 173p. (J). pap. 8.99 *(978-0-9909391-1-5(1))* Woolley Family Studios.
Pandas Are Coming! Fourth Grade Guided Comprehension Level O. (On Our Way to English Ser.). (gr. 4-18). 34.50 *(978-0-7578-7167-2(4))* Rigby Education.
Park, Linda Sue. Xander's Panda Party. Phelan, Matt, illus. 2013. (ENG.). 40p. (J). (gr. -1-3). 16.99 *(978-0-547-55865-3(1))* Houghton Mifflin Harcourt Publishing Co.
Paul, Ruth. Red Panda's Candy Apples. Paul, Ruth, illus. 2014. (ENG., Illus.). 32p. (J). (gr. -1-2). 14.99 *(978-0-7636-6758-0(7))* Candlewick Pr.
Pauley, Christa. Manda Panda & the Loons. 2013. 32p. pap. 19.99 *(978-1-62697-016-8(5))* Salem Author Services.
Pendergrass, Daphne. Secrets of the Secret Panda Village. 2015. (Kung Fu Panda 8x8 Ser.). lib. bdg. 16.00 *(978-0-606-38259-5(3))* Turtleback Bks.
Penelope Panda's Shooting Star. 2008. (Illus.). 32p. (J). (gr. k-3). pap. 14.99 *(978-0-9717290-3-2(4))* Adrema Pr.
Pett, Mark, illus. This Is My Book. 2016. (ENG.). 40p. (J). (gr. -1-2). 17.99 *(978-1-101-93790-7(4),* Knopf Bks. for Young Readers) Random Hse. Children's Bks.
Pickard, Chante. The Adventures of Louie the Panda. 2006. (ENG.). 32p. per. 19.99 *(978-1-4259-0490-6(4))* AuthorHouse.
Pignataro, Anna. Our Love Grows. 2016. (ENG.). 24p. (J). (-4). 16.99 *(978-1-4926-3418-8(2),* 9781492634188, Sourcebooks Jabberwocky) Sourcebooks, Inc.
Platt, Cynthia. Panda-Monium! Vasylenko, Veronica, illus. 2011. (ENG.). 32p. (J). (gr. -1-2). 15.95 *(978-1-58925-093-2(1));* pap. 7.95 *(978-1-58925-425-1(2))* Tiger Tales.
Pledger, Maurice, illus. Ping-Ping Panda's Bamboo Journey. 2015. (Friendship Tales Ser.). (ENG.). 16p. (J). (gr. -1). bds. 10.95 *(978-1-62686-345-3(8),* Silver Dolphin Bks.) Readerlink Distribution Services, LLC.
Powell, Richard. Peter Panda. Rhodes, Katie, illus. 2004. (Fuzzy Friends Ser.). 10p. (J). 7.95 *(978-1-58925-721-4(9))* Tiger Tales.
Quay, Emma. Good Night, Sleep Tight: A Book about Bedtime. Walker, Anna, illus. 2011. (ENG.). 24p. (J). (gr. -1 — 1). bds. 5.99 *(978-0-8037-3581-1(2),* Dial Bks) Penguin Young Readers Group.
Random House Staff. I Can Be... A Zoo Vet/I Can Be... A Cheerleader. Riley, Kellee, illus. 2011. (Pictureback(R) Ser.). (ENG.). 32p. (J). (gr. -1-2). pap. 4.99 *(978-0-375-87265-5(5),* Random Hse. Bks. for Young Readers) Random Hse. Children's Bks.
Ransom, Candice. Amanda Panda Quits Kindergarten. Grove, Christine, illus. 2017. (ENG.). 32p. (J). (gr. -1-2). 17.99 *(978-0-399-55455-1(6),* Doubleday Bks. for Young Readers) Random Hse. Children's Bks.
Rao, Lisa & Shea, Lisa. Littlest Pet Shop: the Perfect Pet Pageant: Starring Penny Ling. 2016. (ENG.). 160p. (J). (gr. 3-7). pap. 5.99 *(978-0-316-38985-3(4))* Little, Brown Bks. for Young Readers.
Rim, Sujean. Chee-Kee: A Panda in Bearland. 2017. (ENG., Illus.). 40p. (J). (gr. -1-3). 17.99 *(978-0-316-40744-1(5))* Little Brown & Co.
Rix, James. Panda Panic. 2013. (Awesome Animals Ser.). (ENG., Illus.). 192p. (J). (gr. 2-7). pap. 6.99 *(978-1-4380-0304-7(8))* Barron's Educational Series, Inc.
Rix, Jamie. Panda Panic: Running Wild. 2013. (Awesome Animals Ser.). (ENG., Illus.). 192p. (J). (gr. 2-6). pap. 6.99 *(978-1-4380-0308-5(0))* Barron's Educational Series, Inc.
Saltzberg, Barney. Chengdu Can Do. Saltzberg, Barney, illus. 2017. (Chengdu Ser.). (ENG., Illus.). 48p. (J). (gr. -1-k). 16.99 *(978-1-4847-5847-2(1))* Disney Pr.
Saltzberg, Barney. Chengdu Could Not, Would Not, Fall Asleep. Saltzberg, Barney, illus. (Chengdu Ser.). (ENG., Illus.). (J). (gr. -1-k). 2017. 32p. bds. 6.99 ***(978-1-4847-7565-3(1))*** 2014. 48p. 16.99 *(978-1-4231-6721-1(X))* Hyperion Bks. for Children.
Sang, Franchesca Ho, compiled by. Wisdom of Pandas. 2006. (Wisdom of Animals Ser.). (Illus.). 128p. (J). (gr. k). *(978-1-59258-253-2(2))* Hylas Publishing.
Schindel, John. Busy Pandas. Husar, Lisa & Husar, Mike, photos by. 2008. (Busy Book Ser.). (ENG., Illus.). 20p. (J). (gr. k — 1). bds. 6.99 *(978-1-58246-259-2(3),* Knopf Bks. for Young Readers) Random Hse. Children's Bks.
Scollon, Bill. Kung Fu Panda. Golden Books, illus. 2017. (Little Golden Book Ser.). (ENG.). 24p. (J). (-k). 4.99 ***(978-1-5247-6772-3(7),*** Golden Bks.) Random Hse. Children's Bks.
Sealed with a Kick. 2015. (Kung Fu Panda TV Ser.). (ENG., Illus.). 32p. (J). (gr. k-2). pap. 3.99 *(978-1-4814-1748-8(7),* Simon Spotlight) Simon Spotlight.
Shealeya, Mildred. Pookie Lookie: The Pink Spotted Panda Bear. Gang, Jobie, illus. 2007. 32p. (J). per. 12.95 *(978-0-9669595-7-4(4))* SMS Cos., Inc.
Sif, Birgitta. Where My Feet Go. 2016. (ENG., Illus.). 32p. (J). (-k). 16.99 *(978-0-553-51164-2(5),* Knopf Bks. for Young Readers) Random Hse. Children's Bks.
Sim, David. Panda's Pants. Sim, David, illus. 2006. (ENG., Illus.). 20p. (J). (gr. -1-k). 16.99 *(978-1-85707-663-9(X))* Tango Bks. GBR. Dist: Independent Pubs. Group.
Soundprints. Panda Cub in the Bamboo Forest: Wilderness Adventures. 2012. (ENG.). 32p. (J). pap. 3.95 *(978-1-60727-872-6(3))* Soundprints.
Style Guide Staff, illus. Good Po, Bad Po. 2014. (Kung Fu Panda TV Ser.). (ENG.). 24p. (J). (gr. -1-2). pap. 3.99 *(978-1-4814-0001-5(0),* Simon Spotlight) Simon Spotlight.
—Po's Secret Move. 2014. (Kung Fu Panda TV Ser.). (ENG.). 32p. (J). (gr. k-2). pap. 3.99 *(978-1-4424-9995-9(8),* Simon Spotlight) Simon Spotlight.
—Two to Kung Fu. 2014. (Kung Fu Panda TV Ser.). (ENG.). 96p. (J). (gr. 2-5). pap. 4.99 *(978-1-4424-9992-8(3),* Simon Spotlight) Simon Spotlight.
Testa, Maggie. Legendary Legends. Style Guide Staff, illus. 2014. (Kung Fu Panda TV Ser.). (ENG.). 16p. (J). (gr. -1-2). 5.99 *(978-1-4424-9998-0(2),* Simon Spotlight) Simon Spotlight.
—The Power of Po. 2015. (Kung Fu Panda 8x8 Ser.). lib. bdg. 13.55 *(978-0-606-38258-8(5))* Turtleback Bks.
Tipper, Sarah. Eviscerated Panda: Back in Bamboo. 2013. 346p. pap. 15.75 *(978-1-78035-624-2(2),* Fastprint Publishing) Upfront Publishing Ltd. GBR. Dist: Printondemand-worldwide.com.
Wacker, Eileen. Rainbow Panda & the Firecracker Fiasco. 2013. (Fujimini Adventure Ser.). (ENG.). 40p. (J). 10.99 *(978-1-4675-1749-2(6))* Oncekids.
Waldron, Kevin. Panda-Monium at Peek Zoo. Waldron, Kevin, illus. 2014. (ENG., Illus.). 40p. (J). (gr. -1-2). 16.99 *(978-0-7636-6658-3(0),* Templar) Candlewick Pr.
Wang, Kateri. Wang Ming: The Greatest of the Great Pandas. 2012. 32p. pap. 19.99 *(978-1-4772-9042-2(7))* AuthorHouse.
Watt, Fiona. That's Not My Panda. 2013. (Touchy-Feely Board Bks). 10p. (J). ring bd. 9.99 *(978-0-7945-3332-8(9),* Usborne) EDC Publishing.
Weatherstone, Hollie. When the Pandas Came to Scotland. 2012. (Illus.). 20p. pap. 19.82 *(978-1-4772-3528-7(0))* AuthorHouse.
Wehrmeijer, Annelien. Mimi & Ling. van de Leijgraaf, Deborah, illus. 2015. (My Best Friend & Me Ser.). (ENG.). 10p. (J). (gr. -1-k). bds. 6.99 *(978-0-7641-6765-2(0))* Barron's Educational Series, Inc.
West, Tracey. Kung Fu Panda 3 Movie Novelization. 2015. lib. bdg. 17.20 *(978-0-606-38260-1(7))* Turtleback Bks.
Yim, Natasha. Goldy Luck & the Three Pandas. Zong, Grace, illus. (ENG.). 32p. (J). (gr. -1-3). 2015. pap. 7.95 *(978-1-58089-653-5(7))* 2014. lib. bdg. 16.95 *(978-1-58089-652-8(9))* Charlesbridge Publishing, Inc.
Zhang, Crystal. Lil' P & His Big Problem, 1 vol. 2010. 32p. pap. 24.95 *(978-1-4489-8319-3(3))* PublishAmerica, Inc.

PANKHURST, EMMELINE, 1858-1928

Barnham, Kay. Emmeline Pankhurst. 2017. (History VIPs Ser.). (ENG., Illus.). 32p. (J). (gr. 4-6). 17.99 *(978-0-7502-8850-7(7),* Wayland) Hachette Children's Group GBR. Dist: Hachette Bk. Group.
—Emmeline Pankhurst - Votes for Women! Brilliant Biographies of the Dead Famous. 2017. (History VIPs Ser.). (ENG., Illus.). 32p. (J). (gr. 4-6). pap. 12.99 *(978-0-7502-9940-4(1),* Wayland) Hachette Children's Group GBR. Dist: Hachette Bk. Group.
Kaiser, Lisbeth. Emmeline Pankhurst. Sanfelippo, Ana, illus. 2017. (Little People, Big Dreams Ser.). (ENG.). 32p. (J). (gr. k-3). 14.99 ***(978-1-78603-020-7(9),*** Frances Lincoln Children's Bks.) Quarto Publishing Group UK GBR. Dist: Hachette Bk. Group.

PANTHERS

Cain, Marie Mowery. Big Bad Cats. 2013. (Big Books, Red Ser.). (ENG & SPA., Illus.). 16p. pap. 33.00 *(978-1-59246-209-4(X))* Big Books, by George!
Caper, William. Florida Panthers: Struggle for Survival. 2007. (America's Animal Comebacks Ser.). (Illus.). 32p. (YA). (gr. 2-5). lib. bdg. 25.27 *(978-1-59716-532-7(8))* Bearport Publishing Co., Inc.
Fletcher, Marty & Scherer, Glenn. The Florida Panther: Help Save This Endangered Species! 2006. (Saving Endangered Species Ser.). (Illus.). 128p. (J). (gr. 4-7). lib. bdg. 34.60 *(978-1-59845-034-7(4),* MyReportLinks.com Bks.) Enslow Pubs., Inc.
Group/McGraw-Hill, Wright. Panther Level: Adventure Journal Set. (Wildcats Ser.). (gr. 2-8). 31.95 *(978-0-322-05793-7(0))* Wright Group/McGraw-Hill.
—Panther Level: Wildcats Panther Complete Kit. (Wildcats Ser.). (gr. 2-8). 599.95 *(978-0-322-06490-4(2))* Wright Group/McGraw-Hill.
Somervill, Barbara. Florida Panther. 2009. (21st Century Skills Library: Road to Recovery Ser.). (ENG.). 32p. (gr. 4-8). lib. bdg. 28.50 *(978-1-60279-316-3(6),* 200212) Cherry Lake Publishing.
Wexo, John Bonnett. Panteras. Rountree, Monica, tr. 2003. (Zoobooks Ser.). Orig. Title: Bit Cats. (SPA., Illus.). 24p. (J). (gr. k-6). lib. bdg. 15.95 *(978-1-888153-80-4(6))* Wildlife Education, Ltd.

PANTHERS—FICTION

Aryal, Aimee. Let's Go Bengals! 2008. (J). 14.95 *(978-1-932888-23-2(3))* Mascot Bks., Inc.
Costello, Emily. Realm of the Panther: A Story of South Florida's Forest. 2005. (Soundprints' Wild Habitats Ser.). (ENG., Illus.). 32p. (J). (gr. 1-4). 8.95 *(978-1-59249-104-9(9))* Soundprints.
Graydon, William Murray. The Jungle Boy; or, Sexton Blake's Adventures in India. 2007. 120p. per. 14.99 *(978-1-4344-0189-2(8))* Wildside Pr., LLC.
Henderson, Milagros. Lulu the Bouncing Kangaroo. 2012. 36p. (-18). pap. 20.99 *(978-1-4772-8899-3(6))* AuthorHouse.
Johnson, Margaret. Running Wild Level 3 Lower-Intermediate. 2009. (ENG.). 80p. pap. 12.75 *(978-84-8323-501-0(3))* Cambridge Univ. Pr.
Orr, Wendy. The Princess & Her Panther. Stringer, Lauren, illus. 2010. (ENG.). 40p. (J). (gr. -1-3). 16.99 *(978-1-4169-9780-1(6),* Beach Lane Bks.) Beach Lane Bks.
Puerto, Carlos & Puerto, Carlos. Las Alas de la Pantera. (Barco de Vapor). (SPA.). 128p. (YA). (gr. 5-8). *(978-84-348-4667-8(5))* SM Ediciones.
Sargent, Pat. The Black Panther, 8 vols., Vol. 2. Lenoir, Jane, illus. 2003. (Barney the Bear Killer Ser.: Vol. 2). 137p. (J). lib. bdg. 26.25 *(978-1-56763-965-0(8))* Ozark Publishing.
Wallace, Bill. Danger on Panther Peak. 2008. (ENG., Illus.). 176p. (J). (gr. 3-7). pap. 6.99 *(978-1-4169-4110-1(X),* Simon & Schuster/Paula Wiseman Bks.) Simon & Schuster/Paula Wiseman Bks.

PAPACY—HISTORY

Caffery, Don R. Our Holy Father, the Pope: The Papacy from Saint Peter to the Present. Beaudesson, Emmanuel, illus. 2013. (ENG.). 44p. (J). (gr. -1-3). 14.95 *(978-1-58617-921-2(7))* Ignatius Pr.
Marchione, Margherita. Pope Pius XII: Bilingual Coloring Book. Elliott, John, illus. 2004. (SPA & ENG.). 32p. 1.00 *(978-0-8091-6721-0(2),* 6721-2) Paulist Pr.
Worth, Richard. Pope Francis: The People's Pope. 2016. (Influential Latinos Ser.). (ENG., Illus.). 128p. (J). (gr. 7-8). 37.27 *(978-0-7660-7328-9(9))* Enslow Pubs., Inc.

PAPER

Cardenas, Ernesto A. Wood or Paper? 2009. 23.95 *(978-1-60698-059-0(9));* pap. 4.95 *(978-1-60698-057-6(2))* Milo Educational Bks. & Resources.
Colich, Abby. Paper, 1 vol. 2013. (Exploring Materials Ser.). (ENG.). 24p. (gr. -1-1). 22.65 *(978-1-4329-8016-0(5));* pap. 6.95 *(978-1-4329-8024-5(6))* Heinemann-Raintree. (Acorn).
Costain, Meredith. The Life Cycle of Paper. 2012. (Discovery Education: the Environment Ser.). (ENG., Illus.). 32p. (J). (gr. 3-6). pap. 10.00 *(978-1-4488-7979-3(5));* lib. bdg. 25.25 *(978-1-4488-7891-8(8))* Rosen Publishing Group, Inc., The. (PowerKids Pr.).
De la Bédoyère, Camilla. The Science of a Piece of Paper: The Science of Materials. 2009. (Science of... Ser.). 32p. (YA). (gr. 3-6). lib. bdg. 26.00 *(978-1-4339-0045-7(9))* Stevens, Gareth Publishing LLLP.
Doney, Meryl. Paper Crafts. 2004. (Crafts from Many Cultures Ser.). (Illus.). 32p. (gr. 2-5). lib. bdg. 26.00 *(978-0-8368-4046-9(1),* Gareth Stevens Learning Library) Stevens, Gareth Publishing LLLP.
Grier, Paul. Recycling Paper. 2013. (InfoMax Readers Ser.). (ENG.). 24p. (J). (gr. 2-3). pap. 49.50 *(978-1-4777-2275-6(0));* (Illus.). pap. 8.25 *(978-1-4777-2274-9(2))* Rosen Publishing Group, Inc., The. (Rosen Classroom).
Herrington, Lisa M. Trees to Paper. 2013. (Rookie Read-About(r) Science Ser.). (ENG.). 32p. (J). pap. 5.95 *(978-0-531-24710-5(4));* lib. bdg. 23.00 *(978-0-531-24744-0(9))* Scholastic Library Publishing.
Hoffmann, Sara. Made of Paper. 2012. (First Step Nonfiction - Exploring Materials Ser.). (ENG., Illus.). 8p. (gr. -1-1). pap. 4.95 *(978-1-4677-0505-9(5),* Lerner Pubns.) Lerner Publishing Group.
Jackson, Demi. How Is Paper Made? 2016. (Everyday Mysteries Ser.). (ENG.). 24p. (J). (gr. 1-2). pap. 8.15 *(978-1-4824-3821-5(6))* Stevens, Gareth Publishing LLLP.
Langley, Andrew. Paper Products. 2008. (Everyday Materials Ser.). (ENG., Illus.). 24p. (J). (gr. k-3). pap. *(978-0-7787-4135-0(4))* Crabtree Publishing Co.
Laz, Ashley Ann. Totally Washi! More Than 45 Super Cute Washi Tape Crafts for Kids. 2014. (ENG., Illus.). 160p. pap. 15.99 *(978-1-4405-7941-7(5))* Adams Media Corp.
Levete, Sarah. Paper. 2006. (Material Matters Ser.). *(978-1-59389-271-5(3))* Chrysalis Education.
Lynette, Rachel. Toilet Paper. 2016. (J). *(978-1-4896-4545-6(4))* Weigl Pubs., Inc.
—Toilet Paper Before the Store. McGeehan, Dan, illus. 2012. (Before the Store Ser.). (ENG.). 32p. (gr. 2-5). lib. bdg. 29.93 *(978-1-60973-683-5(4),* 201258) Child's World, Inc., The.
Marshall, Pam. From Tree to Paper. 2013. (Start to Finish, Second Series: Everyday Products Ser.). (ENG., Illus.). 24p. (gr. k-3). pap. 6.95 *(978-1-4677-0797-8(X))* Lerner Publishing Group.
Moore, Phillip. Where Does Used Paper Go? 2014. (Little Books of Answers: Level F Ser.). (Illus.). 16p. (gr. k-2). pap. 7.95 *(978-1-927136-54-6(7))* Three Crows Media NZL. Dist: RiverStream Publishing.
Morris, Neil. Paper. 2010. (Materials That Matter Ser.). 32p. (YA). (gr. 4-7). 28.50 *(978-1-60753-067-1(8))* Amicus Publishing.
Paper. (Jump Ser.). (Illus.). 36p. (J). (gr. 2-6). pap. *(978-1-882210-33-6(6))* Action Publishing, Inc.
Petelinsek, Kathleen. Crafting with Tissue Paper. Petelinsek, Kathleen, illus. 2014. (How-To Library). (ENG., Illus.). 32p. (J). (gr. 3-6). 28.50 *(978-1-63137-779-2(5),* 205359) Cherry Lake Publishing.
Richards, Roy. En Papel. (Coleccion 101 Trucos Cientificos). (SPA., Illus.). (J). (gr. 3-5). pap. *(978-950-724-178-9(7),* LMA8752) Lumen ARG. Dist: Lectorum Pubns., Inc.
Smith, A. G. Cut & Assemble World War II Paper Soldiers. 2017. (ENG., Illus.). 32p. (J). pap. 12.95 *(978-0-486-40581-0(8))* Dover Pubns., Inc.
Smith, Terri Peterson. Paper. 2003. (Matter & Materials Ser.). (J). pap. *(978-1-58417-165-2(0));* lib. bdg. *(978-1-58417-159-1(6))* Lake Street Pubs.
Sohn, Emily & Wright, Pam. Paper from Wood: Dollhouse Decisions. 2011. (iScience Readers Ser.). 24p. (J). (gr. k-2). lib. bdg. 21.27 *(978-1-59953-412-1(6))* Norwood Hse. Pr.
Somervill, Barbara A. The Story Behind Paper, 1 vol. 2011. (True Stories Ser.). (ENG.). 32p. (gr. 3-3). 30.65 *(978-1-4329-5438-3(5),* NA-h) Heinemann-Raintree.
Turning Trees into Paper. 2014. (Step-By-Step Transformations Ser.). 24p. (J). (gr. k-2). lib. bdg. 24.21 *(978-1-62713-007-3(1))* Cavendish Square Publishing.

PAPER CRAFT

see Paper Work

PAPER FOLDING (HANDICRAFT)

see Paper Work

PAPER MAKING AND TRADE

see also Book Industries and Trade

Barraclough, Sue & Ridley, Sarah. A Paper Bag. 2006. (How It's Made Ser.). (Illus.). 32p. (gr. 1-4). lib. bdg. 26.00 *(978-0-8368-6703-9(3),* Gareth Stevens Learning Library) Stevens, Gareth Publishing LLLP.
Blaxland, Wendy. Paper. 2008. (How Are They Made? Ser.). 32p. (gr. 4-18). lib. bdg. 18.56 *(978-0-7614-3806-9(8),* Benchmark Bks.) Marshall Cavendish Corp.
Costain, Meredith. The Life Cycle of Paper. 2012. (Discovery Education: the Environment Ser.). (ENG., Illus.). 32p. (J). (gr. 3-6). pap. 10.00 *(978-1-4488-7979-3(5));* lib. bdg. 25.25 *(978-1-4488-7891-8(8))* Rosen Publishing Group, Inc., The. (PowerKids Pr.).
De la Bédoyère, Camilla. The Science of a Piece of Paper: The Science of Materials. 2009. (Science of... Ser.). 32p. (YA). (gr. 3-6). lib. bdg. 26.00 *(978-1-4339-0045-7(9))* Stevens, Gareth Publishing LLLP.
Draper, Allison Stark. Choosing a Career in the Pulp & Paper Industry. (World of Work Ser.). 64p. 2009. (gr. 5-5). 58.50 *(978-1-60854-340-3(4))* 2005. (Illus.). (YA). (gr. 7-12). lib. bdg. 31.95 *(978-0-8239-3333-4(4))* Rosen Publishing Group, Inc., The.
Hinkler Studios Staff., ed. The Big Bumper Book of Paper Models. 2011. 72p. pap. 9.99 *(978-1-74184-931-8(4))* Hinkler Bks. Pty, Ltd. AUS. Dist: Ideals Pubns.

PQR

Jackson, Demi. How Is Paper Made? 2016. (Everyday Mysteries Ser.). (ENG.). 24p. (J). (gr. 1-2). pap. 8.15 (978-1-4824-3821-5(6)) Stevens, Gareth Publishing LLLP.

Jackson, Steve. How Is Paper Recycled? 2013. (Rosen Readers Ser.). (ENG.). 24p. (J). (gr. 2-3). pap. 49.50 (978-1-4777-2255-8(6)); pap. 8.25 (978-1-4777-2254-1(8)) Rosen Publishing Group, Inc., The. (Rosen Classroom).

Langley, Andrew. Paper Products. 2008. (Everyday Materials Ser.). (ENG., Illus.). 24p. (J). (gr. k-3). pap. (978-0-7787-4135-0(4)) Crabtree Publishing Co.

Llewellyn, Claire. Paper. 2005. (I Know That! Ser.). (Illus.). 24p. (J). (gr. 1-3). lib. bdg. 22.80 (978-1-932889-54-3(X)) Sea-To-Sea Pubns.

Marshall, Pam. From Tree to Paper. 2013. (Start to Finish, Second Series: Everyday Products Ser.). (ENG., Illus.). 24p. (gr. k-3). pap. 6.95 (978-1-4677-0797-8(X)); lib. bdg. 23.93 (978-0-7613-9184-5(3), Lerner Pubns.) Lerner Publishing Group.

Radford, Tracey. Make Your Own Zoo: 35 Projects for Kids Using Everyday Cardboard Packaging. Turn Your Recycling into a Zoo! 2015. (ENG., Illus.). 128p. (J). (gr. 3-11). pap. 19.95 (978-1-78249-256-6(9), CICO Books) Ryland Peters & Small GBR. Dist: WIPRO.

Rau, Dana Meachen. Paper. 2011. (Bookworms Chapter Books: Use It! Reuse It! Ser.). 24p. (gr. 2-3). 22.79 (978-1-60870-517-7(X)) Marshall Cavendish Corp.

Snyder, Inez. Trees to Paper. 2003. (How Things Are Made Ser.). (ENG., Illus.). 24p. (J). 19.00 (978-0-516-24264-4(4), Children's Pr.) Scholastic Library Publishing.

Sohn, Emily & Wright, Pam. Paper from Wood: Dollhouse Decisions. 2011. (IScience Readers Ser.). 24p. (J). (gr. k-2). lib. bdg. 21.27 (978-1-59953-412-1(6)) Norwood Hse. Pr.

PAPER MONEY

Forest, Christopher. Dollar Bill in Translation: What It Really Means. 2016. (Kids' Translations Ser.). (ENG.). 32p. (gr. 3-4). pap. 8.10 (978-1-5157-6249-2(1), Fact Finders) Capstone Press of Coughlan Cos.

Hamilton, Robert M. Dolares - Dollar Bills. 2015. (Monedas y Billetes / Coins & Money Ser.). (ENG & SPA.). 24p. (J). (gr. 1-1). 23.60 (978-1-4994-0691-7(6), PowerKids Pr.) Rosen Publishing Group, Inc., The.

—Dollar Bills! 2015. (Coins & Money Ser.). (ENG., Illus.). 24p. (J). (gr. 1-1). 23.60 (978-1-4994-0499-9(9), PowerKids Pr.) Rosen Publishing Group, Inc., The.

Jozefowicz, Chris. 10 Fascinating Facts about Dollar Bills. 2016. (Rookie Star — Fact Finder Ser.). (ENG.). 32p. (J). lib. bdg. 25.00 (978-0-531-22815-9(0), Children's Pr.) Scholastic Library Publishing.

Kompelein, Tracy. We Have the Skills to Know U. S. Bills!, 1 vol. 2007. (Math Made Fun Ser.). (ENG., Illus.). 24p. (J). (gr. k-3). lib. bdg. 24.21 (978-1-59928-549-8(5), SandCastle) ABDO Publishing Co.

Meachen Rau, Dana. Los billetes (Paper Money) 2010. (Dinero y los Bancos (Money & Banks) Ser.). (SPA., Illus.). 24p. (gr. 2-5). pap. 8.15 (978-1-4339-3718-7(2)) Stevens, Gareth Publishing LLLP.

—Paper Money. 2010. (Money & Banks Ser.). (Illus.). 24p. (gr. 2-5). pap. 8.15 (978-1-4339-3384-4(5)) Stevens, Gareth Publishing LLLP.

Rau, Dana Meachen. Los Billetes. 2010. (Dinero y los Bancos Ser.). (SPA., Illus.). 24p. (J). (gr. 2-5). lib. bdg. 22.00 (978-1-4339-3717-0(4)) Stevens, Gareth Publishing LLLP.

—Paper Money. 2010. (Money & Banks Ser.). (Illus.). 24p. (J). (gr. 2-5). lib. bdg. 22.00 (978-1-4339-3383-7(7)) Stevens, Gareth Publishing LLLP.

Slade, Suzanne. A Dollar Bill's Journey, 1 vol. Swan, Susan, illus. 2010. (Follow It! Ser.). (ENG.). 24p. (gr. 1-3). lib. bdg. 26.65 (978-1-4048-6265-4(X)) Picture Window Bks.

Wingard-Nelson, Rebecca. I Can Name Bills & Coins. 2009. (I Like Money Math! Ser.). (Illus.). 24p. (J). pap. 7.95 (978-0-7660-3660-4(X), Enslow Elementary); (gr. 1-3). lib. bdg. 22.60 (978-0-7660-3140-1(3)) Enslow Pubs., Inc.

PAPER SCULPTURE

see Paper Work

PAPER WORK

see also names of paper crafts, e.g. Origami.

Accord Publishing Staff. Go Fun! Paper Airplanes. 2014. (ENG.). 108p. (J). pap. 10.99 (978-1-4494-3175-4(5)) Andrews McMeel Publishing.

Alexander, Chris. Sort-of-Difficult. 2008. (Origami Ser.). (ENG.). 32p. (gr. 3-4). 27.99 (978-1-4296-2023-9(4), Snap Bks.) Capstone Press of Coughlan Cos.

Baer, Sam. 100 Paper Dragons to Fold & Fly. 2015. (Tear-Off Papercraft Pads Ser.). (ENG.). 200p. (J). (gr. k-5). pap. 7.99 (978-0-7945-3593-3(3), Usborne) EDC Publishing.

Barker, Cicely Mary & Potter, Beatrix. Flower Fairies Paper Dolls. 2005. (Flower Fairies Ser.). (ENG.). 13p. (J). (gr. -1-2). 6.99 (978-0-7232-5432-4(X), Warne) Penguin Young Readers Group.

Bawden, Juliet & Moxley, Susan. Papier Mache. 2004. (Crafty Ideas Ser.). (SPA., Illus.). 32p. (J). (gr. 2-5). pap. 5.95 (978-1-58728-127-3(9), Two-Can Publishing) T&N Children's Publishing.

Beaton, Clare. Make & Colour Paper Planes. Beaton, Clare, illus. 2004. (ENG., Illus.). 24p. (J). (gr. 1-4). pap. 7.99 (978-1-874735-94-6(8)) B Small Publishing GBR. Dist: Independent Pubs. Group.

Bell-Myers, Darcy. Pretty Ponies Paper Dolls. 2015. (ENG.). 32p. (J). (gr. -1-2). pap. 7.99 (978-0-486-79100-5(9)) Dover Pubns., Inc.

Bergstrom, Matt. American Landmarks: Miniature Models to Cut & Assemble. 2012. (Dover Origami Papercraft Ser.). (ENG., Illus.). 32p. (gr. 5-8). pap. 12.95 (978-0-486-48281-1(2)) Dover Pubns., Inc.

Biddle, Steve & Biddle, Megumi. Make Your Own Greeting Cards. 2013. (ENG., Illus.). 48p. (J). (gr. 3-6). pap. 9.99 (978-0-486-49161-5(7)) Dover Pubns., Inc.

Blanchette, Peg & Thibault, Terri. Make Your Own Cool Cards: 40 Awesome Notes & Invitations! 2004. (ENG., Illus.). 64p. (J). 8.95 (978-1-885593-96-2(1), Ideal Pubns.) Worthy Publishing.

Bolte, Mari. Paper Presents You Can Make & Share. 2015. (Sleepover Girls Crafts Ser.). (ENG., Illus.). 32p. (gr. 3-4). lib. bdg. 27.99 (978-1-4765-7747-0(1), Snap Bks.) Capstone Press of Coughlan Cos.

Bounford, Trevor. Paper Gliders: To Cut Out, Make & Fly. 2004. (Illus.). 32p. 10.00 (978-1-899618-54-5(6)) Tarquin Pubns. GBR. Dist: Parkwest Pubns., Inc.

Boursin, Didier. Folding for Fun: Origami for Ages 4 & Up. 2007. (ENG., Illus.). 64p. (J). (gr. -1-12). pap. 9.95 (978-1-55407-252-1(2), 9781554072521) Firefly Bks., Ltd.

—Paper Folding Fun. 2005. (I Made It Myself! Ser.). (Illus.). 24p. (gr. k-3). lib. bdg. 23.00 (978-0-8368-5965-2(0), Gareth Stevens Learning Library) Stevens, Gareth Publishing LLLP.

Boyds Mills Press Staff & Highlights for Children Editorial Staff. Paper Planes That Soar. 2006. (ENG.). 256p. (J). (gr. 4-6). pap. 18.95 (978-1-59078-388-7(3)) Boyds Mills Pr.

Burke, Judy, ed. Look What You Can Make with Paper Bags: Creative Crafts from Everyday Objects. Schneider, Hank, photos by. 2013. (Look What You Can Make Ser.). (ENG., Illus.). 48p. (J). (gr. -1-7). pap. 6.95 (978-1-56397-717-6(6)) Boyds Mills Pr.

Cannon, Joanne Mary. Girlfriends Party Time Sticker Paper Dolls. 2006. (Dover Paper Dolls Ser.). (ENG., Illus.). 4p. (J). (gr. k-3). pap. 5.95 (978-0-486-44821-3(5)) Dover Pubns., Inc.

Carola, Leslie Conron & Grossman, Andrea. Mrs. Grossman's Sticker Magic. 2006. (Illus.). 132p. (978-0-88363-707-4(3)) Rizzoli International Pubns., Inc.

Carson-Dellosa Publishing Staff. I Can Trace. 2009. (Big Skills for Little Hands(r) Ser.). (ENG.). 80p. (gr. -1 — 1). pap. 6.95 (978-0-7696-6018-9(5)) Carson-Dellosa Publishing, LLC.

Castleforte, Brian. Papertoy Glowbots: 46 Glowing Robots You Can Make Yourself! 2016. (ENG., Illus.). 196p. (J). (gr. 5-12). pap. 18.95 (978-0-7611-7762-3(0)) Workman Publishing Co., Inc.

—Papertoy Monsters: 50 Cool Papertoys You Can Make Yourself! 2010. (ENG., Illus.). 124p. (J). pap. 18.95 (978-0-7611-5882-0(0), 15882) Workman Publishing Co., Inc.

Chapman, Gillian & Robson, Pam. Making Art with Packaging. 2007. (Everyday Art Ser.). (Illus.). 32p. (YA). (gr. 4-7). lib. bdg. 26.50 (978-1-4042-3724-7(0)) Rosen Publishing Group, Inc., The.

—Making Art with Paper. 2007. (Everyday Art Ser.). (Illus.). 32p. (YA). (gr. 4-7). lib. bdg. 26.50 (978-1-4042-3725-4(9)) Rosen Publishing Group, Inc., The.

Chorba, April. Dot Jewelry: Make Pretty Paper Bracelets & Necklaces. 2013. (ENG.). 56p. (J). (gr. 3). 19.99 (978-0-545-49278-2(5)) Klutz.

—Tissue Paper Crafts. 2014. (ENG.). 64p. (J). (gr. 3). 19.99 (978-0-545-64777-9(0)) Klutz.

Chronicle Books Staff. Port-A-Plant. 2013. (ENG.). 9p. 14.95 (978-1-4521-1078-3(6)) Chronicle Bks. LLC.

CICO Kidz Staff, compiled by. Let's Get Crafty with Paper & Glue: 25 Creative & Fun Projects for Kids Age 2 & Up. 2016. (ENG.). 80p. (J). (gr. 2-7). pap. 12.95 (978-1-78249-335-8(2), 1782493352, CICO Books) Ryland Peters & Small GBR. Dist: WIPRO.

COCHAE. Paper Sumo. 2015. (ENG., Illus.). 20p. (J). (gr. 1-17). 14.95 (978-1-4521-4485-6(0)) Chronicle Bks. LLC.

Collins, Francis. The Second Boys' Book of Model Aeroplanes. 2004. (Illus.). 262p. per. 16.95 (978-0-9758914-4-5(8)) Gustav's Library.

Collins, John M. The New World Champion Paper Airplane Book: Featuring the Guinness World Record-Breaking. 2013. (ENG., Illus.). 160p. pap. 16.99 (978-1-60774-388-0(4), Ten Speed Pr.) Potter/TenSpeed/Harmony.

Conigliaro, Phil. Colossal Paper Machines: Make 10 Giant Models That Move! 2015. (ENG., Illus.). 128p. (J). (gr. 4-12). pap. 24.95 (978-0-7611-7640-4(3)) Workman Publishing Co., Inc.

Cook, Lydia. Make a Mobile: 12 Cool Designs to Press Out & Hang. 2015. (ENG.). 76p. (J). (gr. 1-3). pap. 14.95 (978-1-63322-004-1(4)) Quarto Publishing Group USA.

Cool Things Press. 75 Cool Things to Cut Out. 2008. 152p. pap. 15.95 (978-0-615-20796-4(0)) Cool Things Pr.

Cryan, Mary Beth. Paper Shaper Forest Friends: 3-D Crafts to Make & Display. Anton, Carrie, ed. 2011. (ENG.). 64p. (J). spiral bd. 14.95 (978-1-59369-829-4(1)) American Girl Publishing, Inc.

—Paper Shapers Chic Boutique: 3-D Crafts to Make & Display. Anton, Carrie, ed. 2011. (ENG.). 64p. (J). spiral bd. 14.95 (978-1-59369-907-9(7)) American Girl Publishing, Inc.

Culley, Claire & Phipps, Amy. Paper Cutting: 20 Projects for Friends to Make. 2015. (ENG., Illus.). 144p. pap. 19.95 (978-1-86108-731-7(4), 9781861087317) GMC Distribution GBR. Dist: Ingram Publisher Services.

Curtis, Annabelle. Paper People: A Collection of Delightful Paper Characters to Make Yourself. 2004. (Illus.). 32p. (J). (gr. -1-3). 12.00 (978-0-906212-61-5(8)) Tarquin Pubns. GBR. Dist: Parkwest Pubns., Inc.

Dewar, Andrew. Ultimate Paper Airplanes for Kids: The Best Guide to Paper Airplanes - Complete Instructions + 48 Colorful Paper Planes! Vints, Kostya, illus. 2015. (ENG.). 160p. pap. 14.95 (978-4-8053-1363-3(3)) Tuttle Publishing.

Disney Frozen, Disney. Disney Frozen: Make It - Paper Dresses. 2015. (ENG.). 48p. (J). (gr. -1-2). 14.99 (978-0-7944-3356-7(1), Reader's Digest Children's Bks.) Studio Fun International.

Doney, Meryl. Paper Crafts. 2004. (Crafts from Many Cultures Ser.). (Illus.). 32p. (gr. 2-5). lib. bdg. 26.00 (978-0-8368-4046-9(1), Gareth Stevens Learning Library) Stevens, Gareth Publishing LLLP.

Dorling Kindersley Publishing Staff. Paper Craft. 2015. (ENG.). 224p. 20.00 (978-1-4654-3943-7(9), DK) Dorling Kindersley Publishing, Inc.

Eckel, Jessie. Doodle Dolls. 2013. (ENG., Illus.). 160p. (J). (gr. -1-17). pap. 12.95 (978-0-7624-5293-4(5), Running Pr. Kids) Running Pr. Bk. Pubs.

Elliot, Marion. Crafty Fun with Paper! 50 Fabulous Papercraft Projects to Make Yourself. 2014. (ENG., Illus.). 96p. (J). (gr. -1-7). 13.99 (978-1-86147-369-1(9), Armadillo) Anness Publishing GBR. Dist: National Bk. Network.

Falconer, Ian. Olivia Paper Doll Play Set. 2013. (ENG., Illus.). 5p. (J). (gr. -1-17). pap. 14.99 (978-1-4521-1171-1(5)) Chronicle Bks. LLC.

Fisher, Phyllis Mae Richardson, illus. Chrissy (#1 in the 1989 Family Friends Paper Doll Set) l.t. ed. 2004. 24p. (J). 10.00 (978-0-9745615-5-4(X)) PJs Corner.

—Janae, #3 in the 1989 Family Friends Paper Doll Set, Vol. 3. l.t. ed. 2003. 24p. (J). 10.00 (978-0-9745615-7-8(6)) PJs Corner.

—Melly, #2 in the 1989 Family Friends Paper Doll Set, Vols. 3, Vol. 2. l.t. ed. 2004. 24p. (J). 10.00 (978-0-9745615-6-1(8)) PJs Corner.

—Natasha, an International Friends Paper Doll from Russia. 2004. 15p. (J). 10.00 (978-0-9745615-8-5(4)) PJs Corner.

—Tess, an International Friends Paper Doll from Africa. 2004. (J). 10.00 (978-0-9745615-9-2(2)) PJs Corner.

Flying Frog Publishing, ed. Gigantic Paper Planes. 2012. 48p. (J). 14.99 (978-1-934967-81-2(5)) Flying Frog Publishing, Inc.

—Gigantic Sky Cruising Paper Planes. 2012. 48p. (J). 14.99 (978-1-60745-073-3(9)) Flying Frog Publishing, Inc.

Foley, Tim. Literary Greats Paper Dolls. 2011. (Dover Paper Dolls Ser.). (ENG.). 128p. (J). (gr. 6-8). pap. 12.99 (978-0-486-48117-3(4)) Dover Pubns., Inc.

Formaro, Amanda. Paper Fun Mania. 2015. (Mania Ser.: 4). (ENG., Illus.). 72p. (J). (gr. k-6). pap. 8.99 (978-0-7944-3338-3(3), Reader's Digest Children's Bks.) Studio Fun International.

Forte, Imogene. Holidays & Special Days. 2004. (Fun Things to Make & Do Ser.). (Illus.). 80p. (J). per. 9.95 (978-0-86530-616-5(8)) Incentive Pubns., Inc.

—Paper Capers. 2004. (Fun Things to Make & Do Ser.). (Illus.). 80p. (J). per. 9.95 (978-0-86530-615-8(X)) Incentive Pubns., Inc.

French, Cathy. Make a Paper Airplane & Haz un avión de Papel: 6 English, 6 Spanish Adaptations. 2011. (ENG & SPA.). (J). 75.00 net. (978-1-4108-5631-9(3)) Benchmark Education Co.

Garza, Carmen Lomas, illus. Making Magic Windows. 2014. (ENG & SPA.). 32p. (J). (gr. 4-7). pap. 11.95 (978-0-89239-159-2(6)) Lee & Low Bks., Inc.

Gaylord, Susan Kapuscinski & Jabbour, Joyce. Make, Draw, & Design Your Own Book. Labat, Yancey C., illus. 2006. 48p. (J). (978-0-439-81339-6(5)) Scholastic, Inc.

Gilpin, Rebecca. Fairy Things to Make & Do. 2004. (Usborne Activities Ser.). (Illus.). 31p. (J). (978-0-439-67250-4(3)) Scholastic, Inc.

Giulieri, Anne. Make Two Crocodiles, 1 vol. Kreinberg, Sylvia, photos by. 2012. (Engage Literacy Blue Ser.). (ENG., Illus.). 32p. (gr. k-2). pap. 5.99 (978-1-4296-8986-1(2), Engage Literacy) Capstone Press of Coughlan Cos.

Golden Books. Trolls Paper Doll Playset. Golden Books, illus. 2017. (Reusable Sticker & Paper Doll Ser.). (ENG., Illus.). 24p. (J). (gr. 1-4). pap. 9.99 **(978-1-5247-6396-1(9)**, Golden Bks.) Random Hse. Children's Bks.

Golding, Elizabeth. Make 24 Paper Planes: Includes Awesome Launcher Kit! Moerbeek, Kees, illus. 2015. (ENG.). 24p. (J). (gr. 2-6). pap. 10.99 (978-1-4380-0640-6(3)) Barron's Educational Series, Inc.

Green, Gail, et al. Paper Artist: Creations Kids Can Fold, Tear, Wear, or Share. 2013. (Craft It Yourself Ser.). (ENG., Illus.). 112p. (gr. 3-4). pap. 12.95 (978-1-62370-004-1(3)) Capstone Young Readers of Coughlan Cos.

Green, Gail D. Pretty Presents: Paper Creations to Share, 1 vol. 2013. (Paper Creations Ser.). (ENG.). 32p. (gr. 3-4). lib. bdg. 27.99 (978-1-62065-041-7(X), Snap Bks.) Capstone Press of Coughlan Cos.

Grimshaw, Melanie. The Toilet Roll Activity Book. Bigwood, John, illus. 2016. (ENG.). 96p. (J). (gr. 1). pap. 12.99 (978-1-78055-338-2(2)) O'Mara, Michael Bks., Ltd. GBR. Dist: Independent Pubs. Group.

Grumpy Cat, Grumpy. Grumpy Cat Paper Dolls. 2014. (ENG.). 32p. (J). (gr. 6-12). 9.99 (978-0-486-79162-3(9)) Dover Pubns., Inc.

—Grumpy Cat Sticker Paper Dolls. 2015. (ENG.). 4p. (J). (gr. 2-5). 1.99 (978-0-486-80320-3(1)) Dover Pubns., Inc.

Grumpy Cat, Grumpy & Bonogofsky-Gronseth, Jimi. Grumpy Cat's Miserable Papercraft Book. 2015. (ENG.). 64p. (J). (gr. 3-7). pap. 14.95 (978-0-486-80321-0(X)) Dover Pubns., Inc.

Gulliver, Amanda & Turnbull, Stephanie. Things to Make & Do with Paper. Sage, Molly, illus. 2004. (Activity Books). 32p. (J). pap. 6.95 (978-0-7945-0674-2(7), Usborne) EDC Publishing.

Hankin, Rosie. Cut & Paste Farm Animals. 2007. (Cut, Paste, & Create Ser.). (Illus.). 32p. (gr. k-3). lib. bdg. 26.00 (978-0-8368-7719-9(5), Gareth Stevens Learning Library) Stevens, Gareth Publishing LLLP.

—Cut & Paste Sea Creatures. 2007. (Cut, Paste, & Create Ser.). (Illus.). 32p. (gr. k-3). lib. bdg. 26.00 (978-0-8368-7720-5(9), Gareth Stevens Learning Library) Stevens, Gareth Publishing LLLP.

Hankinson, Kim, et al. Paper Pets: 10 Pets to Pop Out & Play With! 2015. (ENG.). 68p. (J). (gr. 3-7). pap. 9.95 (978-1-63322-007-2(9), Walter Foster Jr) Quarto Publishing Group USA.

Hanson, Anders & Mann, Elissa. Cool Flexagon Art: Creative Activities That Make Math & Science Fun for Kids!, 1 vol. 2013. (Cool Art with Math & Science Ser.). (ENG.). 32p. (J). (gr. 3-6). lib. bdg. 28.50 (978-1-61783-821-7(7), Checkerboard Library) ABDO Publishing Co.

—Cool Paper Folding: Creative Activities That Make Math & Science Fun for Kids!, 1 vol. 2013. (Cool Art with Math & Science Ser.). (ENG.). 32p. (J). (gr. 3-6). lib. bdg. 28.50 (978-1-61783-823-1(3), Checkerboard Library) ABDO Publishing Co.

Harbo, Christopher L. Co-Pilot, Level 2. 2010. (Paper Airplanes Ser.). (ENG.). 32p. (gr. 3-4). lib. bdg. 27.99 (978-1-4296-4742-7(6), Edge Bks.) Capstone Press of Coughlan Cos.

—Easy Origami Toys, 1 vol. 2010. (Easy Origami Ser.). (ENG.). 24p. (gr. 1-2). lib. bdg. 25.32 (978-1-4296-5386-2(8), First Facts) Capstone Press of Coughlan Cos.

—My First Guide to Paper Airplanes. 2015. (My First Guides). (ENG.). 24p. (gr. 1-2). lib. bdg. 25.32 (978-1-4914-2047-8(2)) Capstone Press of Coughlan Cos.

—Origami Paperpalooza! 2015. (ENG., Illus.). 144p. (gr. 3-4). pap. 14.95 (978-1-62370-227-4(5)) Capstone Press of Coughlan Cos.

—Paper Airplanes, Captain Level 4, 1 vol. 2010. (Paper Airplanes Ser.). (ENG.). 32p. (gr. 3-4). lib. bdg. 27.99 (978-1-4296-4744-1(2), Edge Bks.) Capstone Press of Coughlan Cos.

—Paper Airplanes, Flight School Level 1, 1 vol. 2010. (Paper Airplanes Ser.). (ENG.). 32p. (gr. 3-4). lib. bdg. 27.99 (978-1-4296-4741-0(8), Edge Bks.) Capstone Press of Coughlan Cos.

—Pilot, Level 3. 2010. (Paper Airplanes Ser.). (ENG.). 32p. (gr. 3-4). lib. bdg. 27.99 (978-1-4296-4743-4(4), Edge Bks.) Capstone Press of Coughlan Cos.

Hardyman, Robyn. Origami Fun: Aircraft. 2017. (Origami Fun Ser.). (ENG., Illus.). 24p. (YA). (gr. 3-7). lib. bdg. 25.95 **(978-1-62617-707-9(4))** Bellwether Media.

He, Xu. Happy Flight. 2007. 72p. per. 10.95 (978-1-4303-2326-6(4)) Lulu Pr., Inc.

Henry, Sally. Make Your Own Art, 6 vols., Set 1. Incl. Card Making. lib. bdg. 26.50 (978-1-4358-2506-2(3)); Clay Modeling. lib. bdg. 26.50 (978-1-4358-2508-6(X)); Collage. lib. bdg. 26.50 (978-1-4358-2509-3(8)); Drawing. lib. bdg. 26.50 (978-1-4358-2510-9(1)); Painting. lib. bdg. 26.50 (978-1-4358-2511-6(X)); Paper Folding. lib. bdg. 26.50 (978-1-4358-2507-9(1)); (J). (gr. 3-6). 2009. (Make Your Own Art Ser.). (Illus.). 32p. 2008. Set lib. bdg. 151.50 (978-1-4358-2549-9(7), PowerKids Pr.) Rosen Publishing Group, Inc., The.

—Paper Folding. 2009. (Make Your Own Art Ser.). 32p. (gr. 2-6). pap. 11.75 (978-1-4358-2640-3(X), Rosen Classroom); (Illus.). (J). (gr. 3-6). lib. bdg. 26.50 (978-1-4358-2507-9(1), PowerKids Pr.) Rosen Publishing Group, Inc., The.

Henry, Sally & Cook, Trevor. Make Your Own Art, 6 vols., Set 2. Incl. Eco Crafts. lib. bdg. 26.50 (978-1-4488-1582-1(7)); Making Masks. 26.50 (978-1-4488-1583-8(5)); Making Mosaics. 26.50 (978-1-4488-1585-2(1)); Making Puppets. 26.50 (978-1-4488-1584-5(3)); Papier-Mâché. 26.50 (978-1-4488-1587-6(8)); (J). (gr. 3-6). (Make Your Own Art Ser.). (Illus.). 32p. 2010. Set lib. bdg. 151.50 (978-1-4488-1625-5(4), PowerKids Pr.) Rosen Publishing Group, Inc., The.

—Making Mosaics. 2010. (Make Your Own Art Ser.). (Illus.). 32p. (J). pap. 11.75 (978-1-4488-1617-0(3)); (gr. 3-6). 26.50 (978-1-4488-1585-2(1)) Rosen Publishing Group, Inc., The. (PowerKids Pr.).

—Papier-Mâché. 2010. (Make Your Own Art Ser.). (Illus.). 32p. (J). pap. 11.75 (978-1-4488-1621-7(1)); (gr. 3-6). 26.50 (978-1-4488-1587-6(8)) Rosen Publishing Group, Inc., The. (PowerKids Pr.).

Higham, Cindy. Snowflakes for All Seasons: 72 Fold & Cut Paper Snowflakes, 1 vol. 2004. Orig. Title: Snowflakes Made Easy & Fun. (ENG., Illus.). 80p. pap. 9.99 (978-1-58685-528-4(X)) Gibbs Smith, Publisher.

Highlights for Children Editorial Staff & Boyds Mills Press Staff. Look What You Can Make with Paper Plates: Creative Crafts from Everyday Objects. Richmond, Margie Hayes, ed. Schneider, Hank, photos by. 2013. (Look What You Can Make Ser.). (ENG., Illus.). 48p. (J). (gr. k-7). pap., stu. ed. 6.95 (978-1-56397-643-8(9)) Boyds Mills Pr.

Hinkler Books, ed. Littlest Pet Shop Cat & Mouse. 2012. (Paper Models Ser.). 24p. (J). 3.99 (978-1-74185-743-6(0)) Hinkler Bks. Pty, Ltd. AUS. Dist: Ideals Pubns.

—Littlest Pet Shop Hamster & Dalmation. 2012. (Paper Models Ser.). 24p. (J). 3.99 (978-1-74185-744-3(9)) Hinkler Bks. Pty, Ltd. AUS. Dist: Ideals Pubns.

—Littlest Pet Shop Spaniel & Monkey. 2012. (Paper Models Ser.). 24p. (J). 3.99 (978-1-74185-745-0(7)) Hinkler Bks. Pty, Ltd. AUS. Dist: Ideals Pubns.

Hisao, Sato. Make & Move: Animals. 2016. (ENG., Illus.). 56p. (gr. 2-6). 14.95 (978-1-78067-741-5(3)) King, Laurence Publishing GBR. Dist: Hachette Bk. Group.

—Make & Move: Robots. 2016. (ENG., Illus.). 56p. (gr. 2-6). 14.95 (978-1-78067-739-2(1)) King, Laurence Publishing GBR. Dist: Hachette Bk. Group.

Hoffman, Joan. Preschool Practice. 2007. (ENG.). 32p. (J). pap. 3.99 (978-1-60159-116-6(0)) School Zone Publishing Co.

Holden, Pam. Paper Chains, 6 pack. 2009. (Red Rocket Readers Ser.). (ENG., Illus.). 16p. (gr. 2-2). pap. (978-1-877435-43-0(0)) Flying Start Bks.

Holland, Gini. Paper Crafts. 2013. (From Trash to Treasure Ser.). 32p. (J). (gr. 3-6). 26.50 (978-1-4777-1282-5(8)); pap. 11.75 (978-1-4777-1358-7(1)) Rosen Publishing Group, Inc., The. (PowerKids Pr.).

Humphrey, Paul. How to Make a Mask. Fairclough, Chris, photos by. 2007. (Crafty Kids Ser.). (Illus.). 24p. (J). (gr. -1-3). lib. bdg. 24.25 (978-1-59771-101-2(2)) Sea-To-Sea Pubns.

Indian Princess Paper Dolls. Date not set. (J). pap. 2.95 (978-1-57122-080-6(1)) Nickel Pr.

Irvine, Joan. How to Make Super Pop-Ups. Hendry, Linda, illus. 2008. (Dover Origami Papercraft Ser.). (ENG.). 96p. (gr. 3-7). per. 8.95 (978-0-486-46589-0(6)) Dover Pubns., Inc.

Issa, Joanna. I Can Make a Bunch of Flowers, 1 vol. 2014. (What Can I Make Today? Ser.). (ENG., Illus.). 24p. (gr. k-2). 22.65 (978-1-4846-0460-1(1), Heinemann Read & Learn) Heinemann-Raintree.

—I Can Make a Truck, 1 vol. 2014. (What Can I Make Today? Ser.). (ENG., Illus.). 24p. (gr. k-2). 22.65 (978-1-4846-0462-5(8), Heinemann Read & Learn) Heinemann-Raintree.

Jackson, Paul. Best Ever Paper Planes That Really Fly! (Illus.). 36p. pap. 8.95 (978-1-85479-334-8(9)) O'Mara, Michael Bks., Ltd. GBR. Dist: Independent Pubs. Group.

Johnson, Anne Akers. Twirly Q's: Make Irresistible Cardboard Creations. 2012. (ENG.). 60p. (J). (gr. 5-9). 19.99 (978-0-545-39624-0(7)) Klutz.

Johnson, Anne Akers & Murphy, Pat. Paper Flying Dragons: Design & Build Your Own Fantastic Flyers. Klutz Editors, ed. 2012. (ENG.). 48p. (J). (gr. 3). pap. 16.99 (978-0-545-44936-6(7)) Klutz.

Jones, Jen. Cool Crafts with Cardboard & Wrapping Paper: Green Projects for Resourceful Kids, 1 vol. 2010. (Green Crafts Ser.). (ENG.). 32p. (gr. 3-4). lib. bdg. 27.99 (978-1-4296-4765-6(5), Snap Bks.) Capstone Press of Coughlan Cos.

—Cool Crafts with Newspapers, Magazines, & Junk Mail: Green Projects for Resourceful Kids, 1 vol. 2010. (Green Crafts Ser.). (ENG.). 32p. (gr. 3-4). lib. bdg. 27.99 (978-1-4296-4764-9(7), Snap Bks.) Capstone Press of Coughlan Cos.

Kalama, Wayne & Fiedler, Heidi. Prehistoric Punch-Outs: Dinosaurs & Extinct Animals: Build Your Own 3-D Paper Models! 2015. (Paper Press Out Ser.). (ENG.). 80p. (J). (gr. 3-7). pap. 14.95 (978-1-63322-046-1(X)) Quarto Publishing Group USA.

Kelly, Emery J. Paper Airplanes: Models to Build & Fly. 2003. (Activities & Crafts Ser.). (Illus.). 64p. (J). (gr. 4-7). pap. 8.95 *(978-0-8225-9903-6(1))* Lerner Publishing Group.
Klutz Editors. Make Paper Lantern Animals. 2016. (ENG.). 48p. (J). (gr. 2-5). 19.99 *(978-1-338-03755-5(2))* Klutz.
—Paper Fashions. 2nd rev. ed. 2012. (ENG.). 60p. (J). (gr. 3-7). 21.99 *(978-0-545-44944-1(8))* Klutz.
—Smash Bot Battle. 2016. (ENG.). 40p. (J). (gr. 3-7). 19.99 *(978-0-545-90648-7(2))* Klutz.
Klutz Editors, contrib. by. The Cootie Catcher Book. 2009. (ENG.). 70p. (J). (gr. 1). 14.95 *(978-1-59174-680-5(9))* Klutz.
—Paper Fashions Fancy. 2008. (ENG., Illus.). 58p. (J). (gr. 3-18). 21.95 *(978-1-59174-519-8(5))* Klutz.
Klutz Editors, et al. Dress up Your Own Paper Pups. 2015. (ENG., Illus.). 48p. (J). (gr. 1). 16.99 *(978-0-545-79864-8(7))* Klutz.
Krcmár, Karol. Kirigami Greeting Cards: The Art of Paper Cutting & Folding. Simekova, Jela, ed. Chorvathova, Michaela, tr. Holoska, Jiri, photos by. 2005. (Kirigami Craft Books Ser.). (Illus.). 80p. (J). pap. 14.95 *(978-0-9715411-7-7(5))* Kotzig Publishing, Inc.
—Kirigami Paper Kingdom: The Art of Paper Cutting & Folding. Simekova, Jela, ed. Kovac, Stefan Patrik, tr. Holoska, Jiri, photos by. 2005. (Kirigami Craft Books Ser.). (Illus.). 112p. (J). pap. 14.95 *(978-0-9715411-6-0(7))* Kotzig Publishing, Inc.
Kumon Publishing, creator. Animals Lion & Mouse, 2 vols. 2005. (Kumon 3-D Paper Crafts Ser.). (Illus.). 16p. (J). (gr. 4-7). per. 5.95 *(978-1-933241-17-3(9))* Kumon Publishing North America, Inc.
—More Let's Cut Paper! 2006. (Kumon First Steps Workbooks Ser.). (Illus.). 40p. (gr. -1). per. 5.95 *(978-1-933241-33-3(0))* Kumon U.S.A., Inc.
—More Let's Fold! 2006. (Kumon First Steps Workbooks Ser.). (Illus.). 40p. (gr. -1). per. 5.95 *(978-1-933241-35-7(7))* Kumon U.S.A., Inc.
—My Book of Amazing Crafts: Ages 5-6-7. 2006. (Kumon Workbooks Ser.). (Illus.). 34p. (J). (gr. k-2). per. 7.95 *(978-1-933241-30-2(6))* Kumon Publishing North America, Inc.
Kumon Publishing, ed. Paper Playtime Vehicles. 2012. (Illus.). 64p. (J). pap. 7.95 *(978-4-7743-0006-1(3))* Kumon Publishing North America, Inc.
Kumon Staff. Let's Cut Paper!, 4 vols. 2005. (Kumon First Steps Workbooks Ser.). (Illus.). 40p. (J). (gr. -1). per. 5.95 *(978-1-933241-14-2(4))* Kumon Publishing North America, Inc.
Kurtz, John. Santa Claus Christmas Paper Dolls. 2013. (Dover Paper Dolls Ser.). (ENG.). 32p. (J). (gr. 1-5). pap. 9.99 *(978-0-486-49424-1(1))* Dover Pubns., Inc.
LaFosse, Michael. Making Origami Cards Step by Step. 2004. (Kid's Guide to Origami Ser.). (Illus.). 24p. (J). lib. bdg. 25.25 *(978-0-8239-6701-8(8),* PowerKids Pr.) Rosen Publishing Group, Inc., The.
—Making Origami Science Experiments Step by Step. 2004. (Kid's Guide to Origami Ser.). (Illus.). 24p. (J). lib. bdg. 25.25 *(978-0-8239-6705-6(0),* PowerKids Pr.) Rosen Publishing Group, Inc., The.
LaFosse, Michael G. Making Origami Cards Step by Step. 2009. (Kid's Guide to Origami Ser.). 24p. (gr. 3-4). 47.90 *(978-1-61511-183-1(2),* PowerKids Pr.) Rosen Publishing Group, Inc., The.
—Making Origami Masks Step by Step. 2009. (Kid's Guide to Origami Ser.). 24p. (gr. 3-4). 47.90 *(978-1-61511-188-6(3),* PowerKids Pr.) Rosen Publishing Group, Inc., The.
—Making Origami Puzzles Step by Step. 2009. (Kid's Guide to Origami Ser.). 24p. (gr. 3-4). 47.90 *(978-1-61511-194-7(8),* PowerKids Pr.) Rosen Publishing Group, Inc., The.
—Making Origami Science Experiments Step by Step. 2009. (Kid's Guide to Origami Ser.). 24p. (gr. 3-4). 47.90 *(978-1-61511-195-4(6),* PowerKids Pr.) Rosen Publishing Group, Inc., The.
Latno, Mark. The Paper Boomerang Book: Build Them, Throw Them, & Get Them to Return Every Time. 2010. (Science in Motion Ser.). (ENG., Illus.). 160p. (J). (gr. 4-18). pap. 12.95 *(978-1-56976-282-0(1))* Chicago Review Pr., Inc.
Laughlin, Kara L. Fun Things to Do with Paper Cups & Plates, 1 vol. 2014. (10 Things to Do Ser.). (ENG.). 32p. (gr. 1-2). 27.32 *(978-1-4765-9897-0(5))* Capstone Press of Coughlan Cos.
—Marvelous Memories: Paper Keepsake Creations, 1 vol. 2013. (Paper Creations Ser.). (ENG.). 32p. (gr. 3-4). lib. bdg. 27.99 *(978-1-62065-044-8(4),* Snap Bks.) Capstone Press of Coughlan Cos.
Laughlin, Kara L., et al. Paper Creations. 2013. (Paper Creations Ser.). (ENG.). 32p. (gr. 3-4). lib. bdg. 111.96 *(978-1-62065-045-5(2),* Snap Bks.) Capstone Press of Coughlan Cos.
Lee, Jacqueline. Twirled Paper. 2nd ed. 2012. (ENG.). 56p. (J). (gr. 3-7). 19.99 *(978-0-545-45991-4(5))* Klutz.
Lee, Kyong Hwa. Amazing Paper Airplanes: The Craft & Science of Flight. 2016. (ENG., Illus.). 184p. (J). pap. 19.95 *(978-0-8263-5664-2(8))* Univ. of New Mexico Pr.
Lim, Annalees. Fun with Paper. 2013. (Clever Crafts Ser.). (ENG., Illus.). 24p. (J). (gr. k-3). 25.25 *(978-1-4777-0183-6(4));* pap. 10.60 *(978-1-4777-0194-2(X))* Windmill Bks.
—Paper Crafts, Vol. 1. 2014. (Craft Attack! Ser.). 32p. (J). (gr. 3-3). (ENG.). 26.60 *(978-1-4824-0211-7(4));* pap. 10.50 *(978-1-4824-0213-1(0))* Stevens, Gareth Publishing LLLP.
Littlefield, Cindy A. Pop-Out & Paint Dogs & Cats. 2014. (ENG., Illus.). 48p. (J). (gr. 3-8). pap. 12.95 *(978-1-61212-140-6(3),* 622140) Storey Publishing, LLC.
—Pop-Out & Paint Horse Breeds: Create Paper Models of 10 Different Breeds. 2011. (ENG., Illus.). 48p. (J). (gr. 3-8). pap. 12.95 *(978-1-60342-963-4(8),* 62963) Storey Publishing, LLC.
Llimós, Anna. Easy Cardboard Crafts in 5 Steps. 2008. (Easy Crafts in 5 Steps Ser.). (Illus.). 32p. (J). (gr. 3-7). lib. bdg. 23.94 *(978-0-7660-3083-1(0),* Enslow Elementary) Enslow Pubs., Inc.
—Easy Paper Crafts in 5 Steps. 2008. (Easy Crafts in 5 Steps Ser.). (Illus.). 32p. (J). (gr. 3-7). lib. bdg. 23.94 *(978-0-7660-3087-9(3),* Enslow Elementary) Enslow Pubs., Inc.
—Easy Paper Crafts in 5 Steps. 2010. (Easy Crafts in 5 Steps Ser.). (Illus.). 32p. (J). pap. 7.95 *(978-0-7660-3762-5(2),* Enslow Elementary) Enslow Pubs., Inc.
Llimós Plomer, Anna. Earth-Friendly Papier-Mâché Crafts in 5 Easy Steps. 2013. (Earth-Friendly Crafts in 5 Easy Steps Ser.). (Illus.). 32p. (J). lib. bdg. 23.94 *(978-0-7660-4192-9(1))* Enslow Pubs., Inc.
Llimos Plomer, Anna. Paper. 2003. (Let's Create! Ser.). (Illus.). 32p. (gr. 1-4). lib. bdg. 26.00 *(978-0-8368-3747-6(9),* Gareth Stevens Learning Library) Stevens, Gareth Publishing LLLP.
Lo Monaco, Gérard. The Small World of Paper Toys. 2015. (ENG., Illus.). 24p. (J). (gr. -1-2). 24.95 *(978-3-89955-746-6(8))* Die Gestalten Verlag DEU. Dist: Penguin Random Hse. LLC.
Lonergan, Lei-Seu. The Great Paper Toy Book. 2004. (YA). spiral bd. *(978-0-9759014-0-3(0))* Stonechester, Inc.
Lum, Kwei-lin. Twisted Fairy Tales Paper Dolls. 2012. (Dover Paper Dolls Ser.). (ENG., Illus.). 32p. (gr. 6-8). pap. 9.99 *(978-0-486-48441-9(6))* Dover Pubns., Inc.
—Voodoo Paper Dolls. 2011. (Dover Paper Dolls Ser.). (ENG., Illus.). 32p. (J). (gr. 3-5). pap. 9.99 *(978-0-486-47785-5(1))* Dover Pubns., Inc.
Lum, Kwei-lin & Paper Dolls for Grownups Staff. Speakeasy Paper Dolls: Fabulous Flappers & More from the Roaring Twenties. 2012. (Dover Paper Dolls Ser.). (ENG., Illus.). 32p. (gr. 6-8). pap. 9.99 *(978-0-486-48639-0(7))* Dover Pubns., Inc.
Macdonald, Margaret. How Can You Re-Use an Egg Carton? 2014. (Little Books of Answers: Level d Ser.). (Illus.). 16p. (gr. k-2). pap. 7.95 *(978-1-927136-34-8(2))* Three Crows Media NZL. Dist: RiverStream Publishing.
Mackey, Dean. Paper Planes That Really Fly. 2012. 128p. (J). pap. 10.99 *(978-1-74308-787-9(X))* Hinkler Bks. Pty, Ltd. AUS. Dist: Ideals Pubns.
Make Your Own Art, 12 vols., Sets 1-2. Incl. Set 1. 2008. lib. bdg. 151.50 *(978-1-4358-2549-9(7));* Set 2. 2010. lib. bdg. 151.50 *(978-1-4488-1625-5(4));* (J). (gr. 3-6). (Make Your Own Art Ser.). (Illus.). 32p. 2010. Set lib. bdg. 303.00 *(978-1-4488-1626-2(2),* PowerKids Pr.) Rosen Publishing Group, Inc., The.
Mattox, Brenda Sneathen. Naughty Girls Paper Dolls. 2011. (Dover Celebrity Paper Dolls Ser.). (ENG.). 48p. (gr. 9). pap. 12.99 *(978-0-486-48397-9(5))* Dover Pubns., Inc.
Maurer, Tracy Nelson. Paper Crafts with Pizzazz. 2009. (Illus.). 32p. (J). pap. 8.95 *(978-1-60694-504-9(1))* Rourke Educational Media.
McGee, Randel. Celebrate Chinese New Year with Paper Crafts. 2015. (Celebrate Holidays with Paper Crafts Ser.). 48p. (J). (gr. 3-4). 25.27 *(978-0-7660-6350-1(X))* Enslow Pubs., Inc.
—Celebrate Christmas with Paper Crafts. 2015. (Celebrate Holidays with Paper Crafts Ser.). 48p. (J). (gr. 3-4). 25.27 *(978-0-7660-6355-6(0))* Enslow Pubs., Inc.
—Celebrate Day of the Dead with Paper Crafts. 2015. (Celebrate Holidays with Paper Crafts Ser.). 48p. (J). (gr. 3-4). 25.27 *(978-0-7660-6360-0(7))* Enslow Pubs., Inc.
—Celebrate Halloween with Paper Crafts. 2015. (Celebrate Holidays with Paper Crafts Ser.). 48p. (J). (gr. 3-4). 25.27 *(978-0-7660-6365-5(8))* Enslow Pubs., Inc.
—Celebrate Kwanzaa with Paper Crafts. 2015. (Celebrate Holidays with Paper Crafts Ser.). 48p. (J). (gr. 3-4). 25.27 *(978-0-7660-6370-9(4))* Enslow Pubs., Inc.
—Celebrate Valentine's Day with Paper Crafts. 2015. (Celebrate Holidays with Paper Crafts Ser.). 48p. (J). (gr. 3-4). 25.27 *(978-0-7660-6375-4(5))* Enslow Pubs., Inc.
—Paper Crafts for Chinese New Year. (Paper Craft Fun for Holidays Ser.). (Illus.). 48p. (J). (gr. 3-4). 2012. pap. 8.95 *(978-1-4644-0319-4(8))* 2008. lib. bdg. 25.27 *(978-0-7660-2950-7(6))* Enslow Pubs., Inc. (Enslow Elementary).
—Paper Crafts for Christmas. (Paper Craft Fun for Holidays Ser.). (Illus.). 48p. (J). (gr. 3-4). 2012. pap. 8.95 *(978-1-4644-0321-7(X))* 2009. lib. bdg. 25.27 *(978-0-7660-2952-1(2))* Enslow Pubs., Inc. (Enslow Elementary).
—Paper Crafts for Day of the Dead. (Paper Craft Fun for Holidays Ser.). (Illus.). 48p. (J). (gr. 3-4). 2012. pap. 8.95 *(978-1-4644-0323-1(6))* 2008. lib. bdg. 25.27 *(978-0-7660-2951-4(4))* Enslow Pubs., Inc. (Enslow Elementary).
—Paper Crafts for Easter. 2011. (Paper Craft Fun for Holidays Ser.). (Illus.). 48p. (J). (gr. 2-5). lib. bdg. 25.27 *(978-0-7660-3723-6(1));* (gr. 3-18). pap. 8.95 *(978-1-59845-335-5(1),* Enslow Elementary) Enslow Pubs., Inc.
—Paper Crafts for Halloween. (Paper Craft Fun for Holidays Ser.). (Illus.). 48p. (J). (gr. 3-4). 2012. pap. 8.95 *(978-1-4644-0325-5(2))* 2009. lib. bdg. 25.27 *(978-0-7660-2947-7(6))* Enslow Pubs., Inc. (Enslow Elementary).
—Paper Crafts for Kwanzaa. (Paper Craft Fun for Holidays Ser.). (Illus.). 48p. (J). (gr. 3-4). 2012. pap. 8.95 *(978-1-4644-0327-9(9))* 2008. lib. bdg. 25.27 *(978-0-7660-2949-1(2))* Enslow Pubs., Inc. (Enslow Elementary).
—Paper Crafts for Mardi Gras. 2011. (Paper Craft Fun for Holidays Ser.). (Illus.). 48p. (J). (gr. 2-5). lib. bdg. 25.27 *(978-0-7660-3724-3(X));* (gr. 3-18). pap. 8.95 *(978-1-59845-334-8(3),* Enslow Elementary) Enslow Pubs., Inc.
—Paper Crafts for Presidents' Day. 2011. (Paper Craft Fun for Holidays Ser.). (Illus.). 48p. (J). (gr. 2-5). lib. bdg. 25.27 *(978-0-7660-3726-7(6));* (gr. 3-18). pap. 8.95 *(978-1-59845-333-1(5),* Enslow Elementary) Enslow Pubs., Inc.
—Paper Crafts for St. Patrick's Day. 2011. (Paper Craft Fun for Holidays Ser.). (Illus.). 48p. (J). (gr. 2-5). lib. bdg. 25.27 *(978-0-7660-3725-0(8));* (gr. 3-18). pap. 8.95 *(978-1-59845-337-9(8),* Enslow Elementary) Enslow Pubs., Inc.
—Paper Crafts for Thanksgiving. 2011. (Paper Craft Fun for Holidays Ser.). (Illus.). 48p. (J). (gr. 2-5). lib. bdg. 25.27 *(978-0-7660-3722-9(3));* (gr. 3-18). pap. 8.95 *(978-1-59845-336-2(X),* Enslow Elementary) Enslow Pubs., Inc.
—Paper Crafts for the 4th of July. 2011. (Paper Craft Fun for Holidays Ser.). (Illus.). 48p. (J). (gr. 2-5). lib. bdg. 25.27 *(978-0-7660-3727-4(4));* (gr. 3-18). pap. 8.95 *(978-1-59845-332-4(7),* Enslow Elementary) Enslow Pubs., Inc.
—Paper Crafts for Valentine's Day. (Paper Craft Fun for Holidays Ser.). (Illus.). 48p. (J). (gr. 3-4). 2012. pap. 8.95 *(978-1-4644-0329-3(5))* 2008. lib. bdg. 25.27 *(978-0-7660-2948-4(4))* Enslow Pubs., Inc. (Enslow Elementary).
Medina, Conni. Make a Gingerbread Man, 1 vol. 2nd rev. ed. 2014. (TIME for KIDS(r) Nonfiction Readers Ser.). (ENG., Illus.). 20p. (J). (gr. 1-1). pap. 19.96 *(978-1-4807-1027-6(X))* Shell Educational Publishing.
—Make Papel Picado, 1 vol. 2nd rev. ed. 2014. (TIME for KIDS(r) Nonfiction Readers Ser.). (ENG., Illus.). 20p. (J). (gr. 1-1). pap. 19.96 *(978-1-4807-1025-2(3))* Shell Educational Publishing.
Medina, Sarah. Having Fun with Paper. 2007. (Fun Art Projects Ser.). (Illus.). 24p. (J). (gr. -1-3). lib. bdg. 25.25 *(978-1-4042-3716-2(X),* PowerKids Pr.) Rosen Publishing Group, Inc., The.
Menten, Ted. Evil Queens & Wicked Witches Paper Dolls. 2014. (ENG.). 32p. (J). (gr. 3-8). pap. 9.99 *(978-0-486-49497-5(7))* Dover Pubns., Inc.
—Little Goth Girl Sticker Paper Doll. 2011. (Dover Little Activity Books Paper Dolls Ser.). (ENG.). 4p. (J). (gr. 2-5). pap. 1.50 *(978-0-486-48172-2(7))* Dover Pubns., Inc.
—Victorian Vixens Paper Dolls. 2015. (ENG.). 32p. (gr. 6). pap. 11.99 *(978-0-486-79718-2(X))* Dover Pubns., Inc.
—Wizard of Oz Paper Dolls. 2008. (Dover Paper Dolls Ser.). (ENG., Illus.). 32p. (J). (gr. 1-5). pap. 6.99 *(978-0-486-46765-8(1))* Dover Pubns., Inc.
Mihaltchev, Atanas. Kid-Agami — Dinosaurs: Kiragami for Kids: Easy-To-Make Paper Toys. 2013. (Dover Children's Activity Bks.). (ENG.). 24p. (J). (gr. 1-5). pap. 9.99 *(978-0-486-49743-3(7))* Dover Pubns., Inc.
—Kid-Agami — Jungle Animals: Kirigami for Kids: Easy-To-Make Paper Toys. 2014. (ENG., Illus.). 24p. (J). (gr. 1-4). pap. 9.99 *(978-0-486-78938-5(1))* Dover Pubns., Inc.
—Kid-Agami — Sea Life: Kiragami for Kids: Easy-To-Make Paper Toys. 2013. (Dover Children's Activity Bks.). (ENG.). 24p. (J). (gr. 1-5). pap. 9.99 *(978-0-486-49744-0(5))* Dover Pubns., Inc.
Miller, Eileen Rudisill. Nutcracker Ballet Paper Dolls with Glitter! 2011. (Dover Paper Dolls Ser.). (ENG.). 32p. (J). (gr. 1-4). pap. 12.99 *(978-0-486-48390-0(8))* Dover Pubns., Inc.
Morris, Ting & Morris, Neil. Dinosaurs. Levy, Ruth & Cowne, Joanne, illus. 2006. (Sticky Fingers Ser.). 32p. (J). lib. bdg. 28.50 *(978-1-59771-029-9(6))* Sea-To-Sea Pubns.
Moslin, Helen. Fashion Studio. 2016. (ENG.). 32p. (J). (gr. 3-7). 19.99 *(978-0-7636-8222-4(5))* Candlewick Pr.
Naylor, Amy. Whoosh! Easy Paper Airplanes for Kids: Color, Fold & Fly! 2013. (ENG.). 48p. (J). (gr. -1-3). pap. 6.99 *(978-0-486-49231-5(1))* Dover Pubns., Inc.
Nemec, Nina. Play with Scissors & Little Miss Scribble. 2012. 20p. pap. 19.82 *(978-1-4772-4575-0(8))* AuthorHouse.
Newell, Keith. Models. 2005. (Art & Craft Skills (Sea-to-Sea) Ser.). (Illus.). 32p. (J). (gr. 3-6). lib. bdg. 27.10 *(978-1-932889-85-7(X),* 1247657) Sea-To-Sea Pubns.
Nguyen, Duy. Monstergami: Paper Folding for Your Inner Monster. 2015. (Sterling Children's Origami Ser.). (ENG., Illus.). 124p. (gr. 3-3). spiral bd. 12.95 *(978-1-4549-1439-6(4))* Sterling Publishing Co., Inc.
Nunn, Daniel. Cardboard, 1 vol. 2011. (From Trash to Treasures Ser.). (ENG.). 24p. (gr. k-2). 23.32 *(978-1-4329-5150-4(5),* Heinemann Read & Learn) Heinemann-Raintree.
—Paper, 1 vol. 2011. (From Trash to Treasures Ser.). (ENG.). 24p. (gr. k-2). 23.32 *(978-1-4329-5151-1(3),* Heinemann Read & Learn) Heinemann-Raintree.
Owen, Ruth. Paper Crafts. 2013. (From Trash to Treasure Ser.). 32p. (J). (gr. 3-6). pap. 70.50 *(978-1-4777-1359-4(X),* PowerKids Pr.) Rosen Publishing Group, Inc., The.
Paper Animals. 2004. (Art Rom Create Your Own... Ser.). (Illus.). 24p. (J). pap. incl. audio compact disk *(978-1-84229-771-1(6))* Top That! Publishing PLC.
Paper Dinosaurs. 2004. (Art Rom Create Your Own... Ser.). (Illus.). 24p. (J). pap. incl. audio compact disk *(978-1-84229-770-4(8))* Top That! Publishing PLC.
Paper Fliers. 2004. (Art Rom Create Your Own... Ser.). (Illus.). 24p. (J). pap. incl. audio compact disk *(978-1-84229-772-8(4))* Top That! Publishing PLC.
Paper Planes Boxed Kit. (J). 7.90 *(978-1-57755-401-1(9))* Flying Frog Publishing, Inc.
Papier Mache. (Jump Ser.). (Illus.). 36p. (J). (gr. 2-6). pap. *(978-1-882210-35-0(2))* Action Publishing, Inc.
Paprocki, Greg. Harajuku Paper Dolls: Japanese Street Fashions! 2015. (ENG.). 32p. (J). (gr. 3). pap. 7.99 *(978-0-486-79741-0(4))* Dover Pubns., Inc.
Parain, Nathalie. My Cut-Out Pictures. 2015. (ENG., Illus.). 24p. (gr. k-2). pap. 19.95 *(978-1-84976-258-8(9))* Tate Publishing, Ltd. GBR. Dist: Abrams, Inc.
Parramon's Editorial Team Staff. Papier-Mâché. Parramon's Editorial Team Staff, photos by. 2004. (Let's Create! Ser.). (Illus.). 32p. (gr. 1-4). lib. bdg. 26.00 *(978-0-8368-4017-9(8),* Gareth Stevens Learning Library) Stevens, Gareth Publishing LLLP.
Pasques, Patrick. Savanna Animals. 2013. (3D Paper Craft Ser.). (ENG & ITA., Illus.). 48p. (J). (gr. k). 14.95 *(978-84-92810-75-8(0))* Promotora de prensa internacional S.A ESP. Dist: Consortium Bk. Sales & Distribution.
Pereira, Diego Jourdan. Glow-In-the-Dark Fairy Princess Sticker Paper Doll. 2014. (ENG.). 4p. (J). (gr. 1-4). pap. 1.99 *(978-0-486-78123-5(2))* Dover Pubns., Inc.
—Glow-In-the-Dark Zombie Sticker Paper Doll. 2014. (ENG.). 4p. (J). (gr. 1-4). pap. 1.50 *(978-0-486-78122-8(4))* Dover Pubns., Inc.
Pérez-Reverte, Arturo. The Queen of the South. 2004. (Illus.). 384p. (J). (gr. 2-5). pap. *(978-0-9655018-2-8(5))* Knot Garden Pr.
Petelinsek, Kathleen. Crafting with Tissue Paper. Petelinsek, Kathleen, illus. 2014. (How-To Library). (ENG., Illus.). 32p. (J). (gr. 3-6). 28.50 *(978-1-63137-779-2(5),* 205359) Cherry Lake Publishing.
Phillips, Jennifer. Adorable Accessories: Paper Creations to Wear, 1 vol. 2013. (Paper Creations Ser.). (ENG.). 32p. (gr. 3-4). lib. bdg. 27.99 *(978-1-62065-043-1(6),* Snap Bks.) Capstone Press of Coughlan Cos.
—Snappy Style: Paper Decoration Creations, 1 vol. 2013. (Paper Creations Ser.). (ENG.). 32p. (gr. 3-4). lib. bdg. 27.99 *(978-1-62065-042-4(8),* Snap Bks.) Capstone Press of Coughlan Cos.
Phillips, Karen & Klutz Editors. Straw Shooter Jets: Make Your Own Mini Air Force. 2014. (ENG.). 60p. (J). (gr. 3). 16.99 *(978-0-545-64779-3(7))* Klutz.
Pixel, Marcel. Monsters: 11 Paper Finger Puppets to Punch Out, Cut, Fold, & Glue, with 10 Scenes to Color — Plus Stickers! 2017. (Make It Now! Ser.). (ENG., Illus.). 32p. (J). (gr. 1-4). pap. 8.99 *(978-0-544-91567-1(4),* HMH Books For Young Readers) Houghton Mifflin Harcourt Publishing Co.
Project Runway. Project Runway Fashion Paper Doll Kit - African American Girl. 2008. (J). mass mkt. *(978-0-9819053-2-7(3))* Westrim Crafts.
—Project Runway Fashion Paper Doll Kit - Asian Girl. 2008. (J). mass mkt. 12.99 *(978-0-9819053-3-4(1))* Westrim Crafts.
—Project Runway Fashion Paper Doll Kit - Blonde Girl. 2008. (J). mass mkt. 12.99 *(978-0-9819053-6-5(6))* Westrim Crafts.
—Project Runway Fashion Paper Doll Kit - Brunette Girl. 2008. (J). mass mkt. 12.99 *(978-0-9819053-4-1(X))* Westrim Crafts.
—Project Runway Fashion Paper Doll Kit - Caucasian Girl. 2008. (J). mass mkt. 12.99 *(978-0-9819053-0-3(7))* Westrim Crafts.
—Project Runway Fashion Paper Doll Kit - Latina Girl. 2008. (J). mass mkt. 12.99 *(978-0-9819053-1-0(5))* Westrim Crafts.
Quinn, Alice, et al, trs. My Town: A Little World for You to Build. 2013. (ENG., Illus.). 48p. (J). (gr. -1-3). pap. 15.95 *(978-1-926973-78-4(X))* Owlkids Bks. Inc. CAN. Dist: Publishers Group West (PGW).
Rau, Dana Meachen. Making a Paper Airplane & Other Paper Toys. 2012. (How-To Library). (ENG.). 32p. (gr. 3-6). 28.50 *(978-1-61080-473-8(2),* 202083); pap. 14.21 *(978-1-61080-647-3(6),* 202257) Cherry Lake Publishing.
Reynolds, Toby. Papercraft. 2014. (Mini Artist Ser.). 24p. (J). (gr. k-3). lib. bdg. 26.25 *(978-1-4777-9123-3(X))* Windmill Bks.
Robinson, Nick. My First Origami Book — Christmas: With 24 Sheets of Origami Paper! 2013. (Dover Origami Papercraft Ser.). (ENG.). 96p. (J). (gr. 2). pap. 12.99 *(978-0-486-49182-0(X))* Dover Pubns., Inc.
Robinson, Nick & Origami. My First Origami Book-Animals. 2012. (Dover Origami Papercraft Ser.). (ENG., Illus.). 96p. (J). (gr. 2). pap. 12.99 *(978-0-486-48706-9(7))* Dover Pubns., Inc.
—My First Origami Book-Things That Go. 2012. (Dover Origami Papercraft Ser.). (ENG., Illus.). 96p. (J). (gr. 2). pap. 12.99 *(978-0-486-48707-6(5))* Dover Pubns., Inc.
Rocky Mountain Snowflakes: New Edition. 2006. 8.95 *(978-0-9661572-3-9(0))* Dream Bee Pubns.
Ross, Kathy. Look What You Can Make with Recycled Paper. Schneider, Hank & Filipski, J. W., photos by. 2013. (Look What You Can Make Ser.). (ENG., Illus.). 48p. (J). (gr. k). pap. 6.95 *(978-1-62091-534-9(0))* Boyds Mills Pr.
—The Scrapbooker's Idea Book. Bosch, Nicole in den, illus. 2006. (Girl Crafts Ser.). 48p. (J). (gr. 3-7). per. 7.95 *(978-0-8225-6511-6(0),* First Avenue Editions) Lerner Publishing Group.
Rueben & Rachel's Paper Doll Book. 2003. (J). 10.00 *(978-0-9745615-3-0(3))* PJs Corner.
Ryall, Jeanette. Paper Art. 2012. (Awesome Art Ser.). (ENG., Illus.). 32p. (J). (gr. 3-6). 26.50 *(978-1-4488-8089-8(0));* pap. 11.75 *(978-1-4488-8142-0(0))* Windmill Bks.
Sabini, Oscar. Paper Zoo. 2015. (ENG., Illus.). 20p. (J). (gr. -1-3). 19.95 *(978-1-61689-439-9(3))* Princeton Architectural Pr.
Saltzberg, Barney. Andrew Drew & Drew. 2012. (ENG., Illus.). 40p. (J). (gr. -1-k). 16.95 *(978-1-4197-0377-5(3),* Abrams Appleseed) Abrams, Inc.
Sarris, Eno, ed. Animals: Dog & Cat, 4 vols. 2006. (Kumon 3-D Paper Crafts Ser.). (Illus.). 16p. (J). (gr. -1-3). per. 5.95 *(978-1-933241-18-0(7))* Kumon Publishing North America, Inc.
—Dinosaurs: Triceratops & Pteranodon, 4 vols. 2006. (Kumon 3-D Paper Crafts Ser.). (Illus.). 16p. (J). (gr. 4-7). per. 5.95 *(978-1-933241-19-7(5))* Kumon Publishing North America, Inc.
Scheunemann, Pam. Cool Paper Projects: Creative Ways to Upcycle Your Trash into Treasure, 1 vol. 2012. (Cool Trash to Treasure Ser.). (ENG.). 32p. (J). (gr. 3-6). 27.07 *(978-1-61783-436-3(X),* Checkerboard Library) ABDO Publishing Co.
Schmidt, Norman. Best Ever Paper Airplanes. 2007. (ENG., Illus.). 96p. (J). (gr. 5). pap. 7.95 *(978-1-895569-83-4(4))* Tamos Bks., Inc. CAN. Dist: Sterling Publishing Co., Inc.
Schwartz, Stephanie, ed. Disney Princess Make It - Paper Dresses. Froeb, photos by. 2016. (ENG., Illus.). 120p. (J). (gr. -1-2). 14.99 *(978-0-7944-3393-2(6),* Reader's Digest Children's Bks.) Studio Fun International.
Scraper, Katherine, et al. Boredom Busters! Try This! Free & Inexpensive Things to Make & Do. 2011. (J). pap. *(978-1-4509-5325-2(5))* Benchmark Education Co.
Seaman, Annalie. Build! - A Knight's Castle: Paper Toy Archaeology. 2015. (ENG., Illus.). 80p. (J). (gr. 3-8). pap. 12.95 *(978-1-61212-651-7(0))* Storey Publishing, LLC.
Shanahan, Sue. Cut & Color Paper Dolls: Maria & Megan. 2005. (Dover Paper Dolls Ser.). (ENG., Illus.). 32p. (J). (gr. -1-5). pap. 3.95 *(978-0-486-44122-1(9))* Dover Pubns., Inc.
Sjonger, Rebecca. Maker Projects for Kids Who Love Paper Engineering. 2016. (Be a Maker! Ser.). (ENG., Illus.). 32p. (J). (gr. 5-8). *(978-0-7787-2577-0(4))* Crabtree Publishing Co.
Smith, A. Papercraft. 2004. 96p. (J). pap. 14.95 *(978-0-7945-0140-2(0))* EDC Publishing.
Song, Sok. Everyday Origami: A Foldable Fashion Guide. Song, Sok, illus. 2016. (Fashion Origami Ser.). (ENG., Illus.). 48p. (gr. 4-5). lib. bdg. 31.99 *(978-1-5157-1630-3(9))* Capstone Press of Coughlan Cos.
—Origami Accessories: A Foldable Fashion Guide. Song, Sok, illus. 2016. (Fashion Origami Ser.). (ENG., Illus.). 48p. (gr. 4-5). lib. bdg. 31.99 *(978-1-5157-1623-5(6))* Capstone Press of Coughlan Cos.
—Origami Outfits: A Foldable Fashion Guide. Song, Sok, illus. 2016. (Fashion Origami Ser.). (ENG., Illus.). 48p. (gr. 4-5). lib. bdg. 31.99 *(978-1-5157-1631-0(7))* Capstone Press of Coughlan Cos.
Steadman, Barbara. Christmas Princess Sticker Paper Doll. 2005. (Dover Little Activity Books Paper Dolls Ser.). (ENG.,

P
Q
R

Illus.). 4p. (J). (gr. -1-5). pap. 1.50 *(978-0-486-44105-4(9))* Dover Pubns., Inc.

—Little Scandinavian Girls Sticker Paper Dolls. 2005. (Dover Little Activity Books Paper Dolls Ser.). (ENG., Illus.). 4p. (J). (gr. k-3). pap. 1.99 *(978-0-486-44450-5(3))* Dover Pubns., Inc.

—Storybook Princess. 2004. (Dover Little Activity Books Paper Dolls Ser.). (ENG., Illus.). 4p. (J). (gr. k-3). pap. 1.50 *(978-0-486-43726-2(4))* Dover Pubns., Inc.

—Sweet Valentine. 2004. (Dover Little Activity Books Paper Dolls Ser.). (ENG., Illus.). 4p. (J). (gr. -1-5). pap. 1.50 *(978-0-486-43751-4(5))* Dover Pubns., Inc.

Steadman, Barbara, creator. Glitter Ballerina Sticker Paper Doll. 2005. (Dover Little Activity Books Paper Dolls Ser.). (ENG., Illus.). 2p. (J). (gr. 1-4). pap. 1.99 *(978-0-486-44479-6(1))* Dover Pubns., Inc.

Stillerman, Robbie. Ballerina Friends Sticker Paper Dolls. 2008. (Dover Little Activity Books Paper Dolls Ser.). (ENG., Illus.). 4p. (J). (gr. k-3). pap. 1.99 *(978-0-486-46574-6(8))* Dover Pubns., Inc.

—Ghoulish Girls Paper Dolls. 2014. (ENG.). 32p. (J). (gr. 4-11). 7.99 *(978-0-486-49489-0(6))* Dover Pubns., Inc.

—Kati & Kayla. 2005. (Dover Paper Dolls Ser.). (ENG., Illus.). 32p. (J). (gr. -1-5). pap. 3.95 *(978-0-486-44146-7(6))* Dover Pubns., Inc.

—Kitty & Kid Sticker Paper Dolls. 2015. (ENG.). 4p. (J). (gr. k-3). pap. 1.50 *(978-0-486-78461-8(4))* Dover Pubns., Inc.

Stillerman, Robbie, creator. Glitter Pretty in Pink Sticker Paper Doll. 2005. (Dover Little Activity Books Paper Dolls Ser.). (ENG., Illus.). 2p. (J). (gr. 1-4). pap. 1.50 *(978-0-486-44475-8(9))* Dover Pubns., Inc.

Stillinger, Doug. The Klutz Book of Paper Airplanes. 2004. (ENG., Illus.). 56p. (J). (gr. 2-5). 16.95 *(978-1-57054-830-7(7))* Klutz.

Stohs, Anita Reith. Praise God with Paper Bags. 2004. (Illus.). 64p. (J). (gr. 2-5). 10.99 *(978-0-7586-0643-3(5))* Concordia Publishing Hse.

Storey, Rita. Make Your Own Creative Cards (Do It Yourself Projects!) 2010. 24p. pap. 9.40 *(978-1-61532-593-1(X))* Rosen Publishing Group, Inc., The.

—Make Your Own Toys (Do It Yourself Projects!) 2010. 24p. pap. 9.40 *(978-1-61532-594-8(8))* Rosen Publishing Group, Inc., The.

Stunt Planes. 2004. (Fantastic Fliers Ser.). (Illus.). 48p. (J). pap. *(978-1-84229-726-1(0))* Top That! Publishing PLC.

Sun, Ming-Ju. Godey's Fashions Paper Dolls 1860-1879. 2004. (Dover Victorian Paper Dolls Ser.). (ENG.). 32p. (J). (gr. 6-8). pap. 6.95 *(978-0-486-43424-7(9))* Dover Pubns., Inc.

Supercool Fliers. 2004. (Fantastic Fliers Ser.). (Illus.). 48p. (J). pap. *(978-1-84229-729-2(5))* Top That! Publishing PLC.

Tierney, Tom. Art Deco Fashions Paper Dolls. 2005. (Dover Paper Dolls Ser.). (ENG., Illus.). 32p. (J). (gr. 3-8). pap. 6.95 *(978-0-486-44158-0(X))* Dover Pubns., Inc.

—Brides from Around the World Paper Dolls. 2005. (Dover Paper Dolls Ser.). (ENG., Illus.). 32p. (gr. 3-5). pap. 6.95 *(978-0-486-44439-0(2))* Dover Pubns., Inc.

—The Dalai Lama Paper Doll. 2006. (Dover Paper Dolls Ser.). (ENG., Illus.). 32p. (gr. 7-8). pap. 6.95 *(978-0-486-45181-7(X))* Dover Pubns., Inc.

—Famous Torch Singers Paper Dolls. 2006. (Dover Celebrity Paper Dolls Ser.). (ENG., Illus.). 32p. (J). (gr. 6-8). pap. 6.95 *(978-0-486-44744-5(8))* Dover Pubns., Inc.

—Fashions of the First Ladies Paper Dolls. 2006. (Dover President Paper Dolls Ser.). (ENG., Illus.). 32p. (J). (gr. 3-8). pap. 8.95 *(978-0-486-44879-4(7))* Dover Pubns., Inc.

—French Film Stars Paper Dolls. 2005. (Dover Celebrity Paper Dolls Ser.). (FRE & ENG., Illus.). 32p. (J). (gr. 6-8). pap. 6.95 *(978-0-486-44132-0(6))* Dover Pubns., Inc.

—Glamorous Television Stars Paper Dolls. 2005. (Dover Celebrity Paper Dolls Ser.). (ENG., Illus.). 32p. (J). (gr. 7-5). pap. 6.95 *(978-0-486-44462-8(7))* Dover Pubns., Inc.

—Mae West Paper Doll. 2005. (Dover Celebrity Paper Dolls Ser.). (ENG., Illus.). 32p. (J). (gr. 7-8). pap. 5.95 *(978-0-486-44099-6(0))* Dover Pubns., Inc.

—Movie Mobsters Paper Dolls. 2011. (Dover Celebrity Paper Dolls Ser.). (ENG.). 32p. (J). (gr. 7-8). pap. 9.99 *(978-0-486-48049-7(6))* Dover Pubns., Inc.

—Newport Fashions of the Gilded Age Paper Dolls. 2005. (Dover Victorian Paper Dolls Ser.). (ENG., Illus.). 32p. (J). (gr. 6-5). pap. 6.95 *(978-0-486-44449-9(X))* Dover Pubns., Inc.

—Pin-Up Girls of World War II. 2009. (Dover Celebrity Paper Dolls Ser.). (ENG., Illus.). 32p. (gr. 6). pap. 9.99 *(978-0-486-47033-7(4))* Dover Pubns., Inc.

—Ziegfeld Girls Paper Dolls. 2004. (Dover Paper Dolls Ser.). (ENG., Illus.). 32p. (J). (gr. 6). pap. 5.95 *(978-0-486-43679-1(9))* Dover Pubns., Inc.

Top That! Team Staff, contrib. by. Design & Fly Paper Airplanes. 2003. (Illus.). 48p. (J). *(978-0-439-57192-0(8))* Scholastic, Inc.

Torres, Laura. Rock Your Party. 2012. (Illus.). 32p. (gr. 3-5). pap. 8.95 *(978-1-926853-86-4(5))* Saunders Bk. Co. CAN. Dist: RiverStream Publishing.

Tourenne, Virginie. Snow White & the Seven Dwarfs. 2013. (3D Paper Craft Ser.). (ENG & ITA., Illus.). 48p. (J). (gr. k). 14.95 *(978-84-92810-74-1(2)*, Promopress) Promotora de prensa internacional S.A ESP. Dist: Consortium Bk. Sales & Distribution.

Tremaine, Jon. Paper Tricks. 2012. (Illus.). 32p. (gr. 3-5). pap. 8.95 *(978-1-926853-84-0(9))* Saunders Bk. Co. CAN. Dist: RiverStream Publishing.

Tucker, Mary. Cut & Create! Ocean Life. Mitchell, Judy & Lindeen, Mary, eds. Rankin, Kim, illus. 2007. 80p. (J). pap. 9.95 *(978-1-57310-526-2(0))* Teaching & Learning Co.

—Cut & Create! Spring & Summer. Mitchell, Judy & Lindeen, Mary, eds. Rankin, Kim, illus. 2007. 80p. (J). pap. 9.95 *(978-1-57310-535-4(X))* Teaching & Learning Co.

Tudor, Andy, illus. 200 Paper Planes. 2013. (200 Paper Planes Ser.). 402p. (J). pap. 13.99 *(978-0-7945-3371-7(X)*, Usborne) EDC Publishing.

Turnbull, Stephanie. Cool Stuff to Make with Paper. 2015. (ENG., Illus.). 32p. (J). pap. 9.95 *(978-1-77092-223-5(7))* RiverStream Publishing.

—Papercraft. 2015. (Try This! Ser.). (ENG., Illus.). 24p. (J). (gr. 2-6). 27.10 *(978-1-62588-373-5(0)*, 1389462) Black Rabbit Bks.

Turnbull, Stephaniel & Turnbull, Stephanie. Cool Stuff to Make with Paper. 2014. (Cool Stuff Ser.). 32p. (gr. 2-5). 31.35 *(978-1-62588-189-2(4))* Black Rabbit Bks.

Ventura, Marne. Awesome Paper Projects You Can Create. 2015. (Imagine It, Build It Ser.). (ENG., Illus.). 32p. (gr. 3-4). lib. bdg. 27.99 *(978-1-4914-4293-7(X))* Capstone Press of Coughlan Cos.

—Cool Cardboard Projects You Can Create. 2015. (Imagine It, Build It Ser.). (ENG., Illus.). 32p. (gr. 3-4). lib. bdg. 27.99 *(978-1-4914-4291-3(3))* Capstone Press of Coughlan Cos.

Victorian Paper Dolls. Date not set. (J). pap. 2.95 *(978-1-57122-079-0(8))* Nickel Pr.

Vining, Diana. Flower Friends Paper Dolls. 2015. (Dover Paper Dolls Ser.). (ENG.). 32p. (J). (gr. -1-3). pap. 7.99 *(978-0-486-79758-8(9))* Dover Pubns., Inc.

Wallace, Holly. Paper. 2007. (How We Use Materials/Watts Ser.). (Illus.). 30p. (J). (gr. 4-7). lib. bdg. 28.50 *(978-1-59920-004-0(X))* Black Rabbit Bks.

Whatley, Charlotte. Peter Pan Paper Dolls. 2011. (Dover Paper Dolls Ser.). (ENG., Illus.). 32p. (J). (gr. 3-5). pap. 9.99 *(978-0-486-48231-6(6))* Dover Pubns., Inc.

Wilson, Tansy. Now I Can Paper Craft: 20 Hand-Crafted Projects to Make. 2017. (ENG., Illus.). 128p. pap. 17.95 *(978-1-78494-244-1(8)*, 9781784942441) GMC Distribution GBR. Dist: Ingram Publisher Services.

Woodroffe, David. Making Paper Airplanes: Make Your Own Aircraft & Watch Them Fly! 2012. (ENG., Illus.). 192p. (J). (gr. 4-7). pap. 12.95 *(978-1-62087-168-3(8)*, 620168, Sky Pony Pr.) Skyhorse Publishing Co., Inc.

Yates, Jane. Paper-Mache Masks. 2016. (Cool Crafts for Kids Ser.). 00032p. (J). (gr. 3-3). pap. 11.75 *(978-1-4994-8234-8(5)*, Windmill Bks.) Rosen Publishing Group, Inc., The.

—Tissue Paper Creations. 2016. (Cool Crafts for Kids Ser.). 00032p. (J). (gr. 3-3). pap. 11.75 *(978-1-4994-8240-9(X)*, Windmill Bks.) Rosen Publishing Group, Inc., The.

100 Birds to Fold & Fly. 2017. (Tear-Off Papercraft Pads Ser.). (ENG.). (J). pap. 7.99 ***(978-0-7945-3943-6(2)***, Usborne) EDC Publishing.

PAPERCRAFT

see Paper Work

PAPIER-MACHE

see Paper Work

PAPUA NEW GUINEA

Gascoigne, Ingrid. Papua New Guinea. 2nd rev. ed. 2008. (Cultures of the World Ser.). 144p. (gr. 6-18). lib. bdg. 42.79 *(978-0-7614-3416-0(X)*, Benchmark Bks.) Marshall Cavendish Corp.

PAPUA NEW GUINEA—FICTION

Carlson, Melody. Notes from a Spinning Planet: Papua New Guinea. 2007. (Notes from a Spinning Planet Ser.: 2). (ENG.). 240p. (YA). (gr. 7-12). per. 12.99 *(978-1-4000-7145-6(3)*, WaterBrook Pr.) Crown Publishing Group.

Jones, Lloyd. Mister Pip. 2010. 256p. 21.85 *(978-0-7569-9114-2(5))* Perfection Learning Corp.

Kuelinad, Marion. Little People's Little Happenings. 2013. 22p. pap. *(978-9980-87-916-5(5))* University of Papua New Guinea Press.

Mikaelsen, Ben. Jungle of Bones. 2014. (ENG.). 224p. (J). (gr. 3-7). 16.99 *(978-0-545-44287-9(7))* Scholastic, Inc.

Tago, Anita. Traditional Stories from Binandere in Oro Province, Papua New Guinea. 2012. 44p. pap. *(978-9980-945-71-6(0))* University of Papua New Guinea Press.

Trout, Richard. Devil's Breath Volcano, 1 vol. 2008. (MacGregor Family Adventure Ser.: 6). (ENG., Illus.). 208p. (YA). (gr. 6-10). 16.99 *(978-1-58980-558-3(5))* Pelican Publishing Co., Inc.

PARABLES

see also Allegories; Fables; Jesus Christ—Parables

Adeyemi, Sam. The Parable of Dollars: Proven Strategies for Your Financial Success. 2nd ed. 2004. Orig. Title: Parable of Dollars. 208p. per. 14.95 *(978-0-9746735-1-6(X))* Summit Hse. Pubs.

Ball, Liz, illus. Miracles & Parables of Jesus: Find-the-Picture Puzzles. 2004. (Find-the-Picture Puzzle Ser.: 2). 24p. (J). pap. 2.95 *(978-0-8198-4830-7(1)*, 332-221) Pauline Bks. & Media.

Berendes, Mary. The Lost Sheep. Squier, Robert, illus. 2011. (Parables Ser.). (ENG.). 24p. (J). (gr. k-3). lib. bdg. 28.50 *(978-1-60954-392-1(0)*, 201187) Child's World, Inc., The.

—The Prodigal Son. Squier, Robert, illus. 2011. (Parables Ser.). (ENG.). 24p. (J). (gr. k-3). lib. bdg. 28.50 *(978-1-60954-393-8(9)*, 201188) Child's World, Inc., The.

—The Sower & the Seeds. Squier, Robert, illus. 2011. (Parables Ser.). (ENG.). 24p. (J). (gr. k-3). lib. bdg. 28.50 *(978-1-60954-394-5(7)*, 201189) Child's World, Inc., The.

—The Ten Bridesmaids. Squier, Robert, illus. 2011. (Parables Ser.). (ENG.). 24p. (J). (gr. k-3). lib. bdg. 28.50 *(978-1-60954-395-2(5)*, 201190) Child's World, Inc., The.

—The Unmerciful Servant. Squier, Robert, illus. 2011. (Parables Ser.). (ENG.). 24p. (J). (gr. k-3). lib. bdg. 28.50 *(978-1-60954-396-9(3)*, 201191) Child's World, Inc., The.

Black, Peter A. Parables from the Pond. 2008. 232p. per. *(978-1-897373-21-7(X))* Word Alive Pr.

Bynum, Juanita, ed. A Parable about the King. 2004.Tr. of Una Parabola Sobre el Rey. (SPA.). 32p. 8.99 *(978-0-88419-998-4(3)*, Casa Creacion) Charisma Media.

Carlson, Melody. Farmer Brown's Field Trip. Björkman, Steve, illus. 2004. 40p. (gr. -1-3). 9.99 *(978-1-58134-142-3(3))* Crossway.

Clydesdale, David T., contrib. by. Acorns to Oaks: Planted, Rooted & Growing in Christ. 2007. (Illus.). 109p. pap. 6.95 *(978-5-557-71497-6(9)*, Word Music) Word Entertainment.

Eder, Enelle. Create & Take Bible Crafts: Parables & Miracles. 2004. (Create & Take Bible Crafts). (Illus.). 96p. (J). pap. 11.95 *(978-1-58411-007-1(4))* Rainbow Pubs. & Legacy Pr.

Ferguson, M. J. The Mirror in the Box: A Children's Story & a Parable. 2013. 66p. (gr. 4-6). pap. 9.99 *(978-1-4497-7804-0(6)*, WestBow Pr.) Author Solutions, Inc.

Gatty, Alfred. Parables from Nature (Yesterday's Classics) 2006. (Illus.). 456p. (J). per. 14.95 *(978-1-59915-005-5(0))* Yesterday's Classics.

Groenboom, Roger, et al. Sharable Parables. (Walk with Me Ser.). (gr. k-8). 24.95 *(978-1-59255-176-7(9)*, 017210) Faith Alive Christian Resources.

Higgs, Liz Curtis. The Pumpkin Patch Parable, 1 vol. 2006. (Parable Ser.). (ENG., Illus.). 36p. (gr. -1-2). 7.99 *(978-1-4003-0846-0(1))* Nelson, Thomas Inc.

Holmes, Wayne & Pelletier, Christine. Lost & Found Teaching Unit. Kalvoda, LeAnn, illus. rev. ed. 2003. 96p. (J). ring bd. 35.00 *(978-1-58302-232-0(5))* One Way St., Inc.

Koo, Rob, illus. More Great Buddhist Stories. 2012. (J). pap. *(978-1-935523-48-2(1))* World Tribune Pr.

Larcombe, Jennifer Rees. Danger on the Lonely Road. Björkman, Steve, illus. 2004. (Best Bible Stories Ser.). 24p. (gr. -1-3). pap. 2.99 *(978-1-58134-149-2(0))* Crossway.

Larsen, Sharon G. The Parable of the Chocolate Chips. 2008. (J). *(978-1-59038-912-6(3))* Deseret Bk. Co.

Littleton, Mark. Stories Jesus Told. Moroney, Trace, illus. 2004. 20p. (J). bds. 10.99 *(978-0-8254-5519-3(7))* Kregel Pubns.

Lucado, Max. You Are Special. Martinez, Sergio, illus. rev. ed. 2007. 32p. (J). (gr. -1-3). 19.99 *(978-1-58134-894-1(0))* Crossway.

Miller, Claire. The Parable of the Lost Sheep. van der Sterre, Johanna, illus. 2008. (Arch Bks.). 16p. (J). (gr. k-4). pap. 1.99 *(978-0-7586-1455-1(1))* Concordia Publishing Hse.

Phillips, Deborah. The Parable of the Princesses. 2008. 48p. (J). 19.99 *(978-1-59038-873-0(9))* Deseret Bk. Co.

Saunders, George. The Very Persistent Gappers of Frip. 2008. (ENG.). 88p. pap. 8.50 *(978-1-58342-557-2(8))* Dramatic Publishing Co.

—The Very Persistent Gappers of Frip. Smith, Lane, illus. 2015. (ENG.). 96p. 22.00 *(978-0-8129-8963-2(5)*, Random House) Random House Publishing Group.

Smith, Cyncie. The Joyful Shepherd. 2004. (Illus.). 32p. (J). 9.99 *(978-1-56309-484-2(3))* New Hope Pubs.

Sproul, R. C. The Priest with Dirty Clothes. Gerard, Justin, illus. 2nd ed. 2011. 45p. (J). *(978-1-56769-210-5(9))* Reformation Pubs.

—The Prince's Poison Cup. Gerard, Justin, illus. 2008. (J). *(978-1-56769-104-7(8))* Reformation Pubs.

Walker, John. Pioneer Parables. 2005. (Illus.). (YA). per. 11.99 *(978-0-9677379-1-1(5))* North Gap Publishing.

White, Anna. The Seed in My Pocket. 2009. 32p. pap. *(978-1-55452-391-7(5)*, Guardian Bks.) Essence Publishing.

Young, Jeanna Stolle & Johnson, Jacqueline. Princess Hope & the Hidden Treasure, 1 vol. Aranda, Omar, illus. 2012. (Princess Parables Ser.). (ENG.). 32p. (J). 14.99 *(978-0-310-72699-9(9))* Zonderkidz.

Zondervan Staff. The Good Samaritan, 1 vol. Miles, David, illus. 2015. (I Can Read! / Adventure Bible Ser.). (ENG.). 32p. (J). pap. 3.99 *(978-0-310-74662-1(0))* Zonderkidz.

PARACHUTE TROOPS

Harasymiw, M. Alexander. Pararescuemen. 2012. (US Special Forces Ser.). (ENG., Illus.). 32p. (J). (gr. 3-6). pap. 10.50 *(978-1-4339-6571-5(2))*; lib. bdg. 26.60 *(978-1-4339-6569-2(0))* Stevens, Gareth Publishing LLLP. (Gareth Stevens Learning Library).

Sandler, Michael. Pararescuemen in Action. 2008. (Special Ops Ser.). (Illus.). 32p. (J). (gr. 3-6). lib. bdg. 25.27 *(978-1-59716-633-1(2))* Bearport Publishing Co., Inc.

PARACHUTES

see also Parachute Troops

Boothroyd, Jennifer. How Do Parachutes Work? 2013. (Lightning Bolt Books (tm) — How Flight Works). (ENG., Illus.). 32p. (gr. k-2). pap. 7.95 *(978-1-4677-0787-9(2))*; lib. bdg. 26.60 *(978-0-7613-8968-2(7)*, Lerner Pubns.) Lerner Publishing Group.

Klutz Editors, contrib. by. SlingChute. (ENG.). (J). 14.95 *(978-1-57054-581-8(2))* Klutz.

PARACHUTING

see Skydiving

PARADES

Corcorane, Ann. Counting at the Parade, 1 vol. 2011. (Wonder Readers Emergent Level Ser.). (ENG.). (gr. -1-1). 32p. pap. 5.99 *(978-1-4296-7864-3(X))*; 16p. pap. 35.94 *(978-1-4296-8080-6(6))* Capstone Press of Coughlan Cos. (Wonder Readers).

Lyons, Shelly. If You Were an Exclamation Point, 1 vol. Gray, Sara, illus. 2009. (Word Fun Ser.). (ENG.). 24p. (gr. 2-4). lib. bdg. 27.99 *(978-1-4048-5326-3(X))* Picture Window Bks.

—If You Were an Exclamation Point [LTD Commodities]. Gray, Sara, illus. 2010. (Word Fun Ser.). 24p. pap. 3.50 *(978-1-4048-6254-8(4)*, Nonfiction Picture Bks.) Picture Window Bks.

—If You Were an Exclamation Point [Readers World]. Gray, Sara, illus. 2010. (Word Fun Ser.). 24p. pap. 2.72 *(978-1-4048-6707-9(4)*, Nonfiction Picture Bks.) Picture Window Bks.

McGahey, Suzanne. Winter Guard. 2006. (Team Spirit! Ser.). (Illus.). 64p. (J). (gr. 3-7). lib. bdg. 31.95 *(978-1-4042-0732-5(5))* Rosen Publishing Group, Inc., The.

Sweet, Melissa. Balloons over Broadway: The True Story of the Puppeteer of Macy's Parade. 2011. (ENG., Illus.). 40p. (J). (gr. -1-3). 17.99 *(978-0-547-19945-0(7))* Houghton Mifflin Harcourt Publishing Co.

Weill, Cynthia. Count Me In: A Parade of Mexican Folk Art Numbers in English & Spanish. Aguilar Sisters Staff, illus. 2012. (First Concepts in Mexican Folk Art Ser.). (ENG & SPA.). 32p. (J). (gr. k-k). 14.95 *(978-1-935955-39-9(X))* Cinco Puntos Pr.

PARADES—FICTION

Abramson, Jill & O'Connor, Jane. Puppy Parade. Melmon, Deborah, illus. 2013. (Penguin Young Readers, Level 2 Ser.). (ENG.). 32p. (J). (gr. 1-2). 14.99 *(978-0-448-46574-6(4))*; pap. 3.99 *(978-0-448-45676-8(1))* Penguin Young Readers Group. (Penguin Young Readers).

—Puppy Parade. 2013. (Penguin Young Readers Level 2 Ser.). lib. bdg. 13.55 *(978-0-606-31707-8(4)*, Turtleback) Turtleback Bks.

Anastos, Ernie. Ernie & the Big Newz. 2007. 32p. pap. 15.95 *(978-0-9705100-5-1(5))* NK Pubns.

Awdry, Wilbert V. & Random House Editors. Thomas & Percy & the Dragon. 2003. (Thomas & Friends Step into Reading Ser.). (gr. -1-2). lib. bdg. 13.55 *(978-0-613-89791-4(9)*, Turtleback) Turtleback Bks.

Balaban, Mariah. Scooby-Doo & the Thanksgiving Terror, 1 vol. Duendes Del Sur Staff, illus. 2012. (Scooby-Doo! Set 2 Ser.: No. 2). (ENG.). 24p. (J). (gr. k-3). lib. bdg. 24.21 *(978-1-59961-870-8(2))* Spotlight.

Barchers, Suzanne I. Main Street Parade, 1 vol. 2011. (Targeted Phonics Ser.). (ENG.). 16p. (J). (gr. k-2). pap. 5.99 *(978-1-4333-2921-0(2))* Teacher Created Materials, Inc.

Barner, Bob. Parade Day: Marching Through the Calendar Year. 2003. (ENG., Illus.). 32p. (J). (gr. k-3). tchr. ed. 16.95 *(978-0-8234-1690-5(9))* Holiday Hse., Inc.

Berenstain, Mike. The Berenstain Bears' Easter Parade. Berenstain, Mike, illus. 2014. (Berenstain Bears Ser.). (ENG., Illus.). 24p. (J). (gr. -1-3). pap. 3.99 *(978-0-06-207554-3(3)*, HarperFestival) HarperCollins Pubs.

Berenstain, Mike & Berenstain, Stan. The Berenstain Bears God Bless Our Country, 1 vol. 2015. (Berenstain Bears/Living Lights Ser.). (ENG.). 24p. (J). pap. 4.99 *(978-0-310-73485-7(1))* Zonderkidz.

Black, Michael Ian. A Pig Parade Is a Terrible Idea. Hawkes, Kevin, illus. 2010. (ENG.). 40p. (J). (gr. -1-3). 17.99 *(978-1-4169-7922-7(0)*, Simon & Schuster Bks. For Young Readers) Simon & Schuster Bks. For Young Readers.

Boswell, Addie & Addie, Boswell. The Rain Stomper, 0 vols. Velasquez, Eric, illus. 2008. (ENG.). 32p. (J). (gr. -1-3). 16.99 *(978-0-7614-5393-2(8)*, 9780761453932, Amazon Children's Publishing) Amazon Publishing.

Buzzeo, Toni. Fire up with Reading! Yoshikawa, Sachiko, illus. 2007. (Mrs. Skorupski Story Ser.). 32p. (J). (gr. -1-3). 17.95 *(978-1-932146-91-2(1)*, Upstart Bks.) Highsmith Inc.

Clark, Katie. Grandma Drove the Garbage Truck. Huntington, Amy, illus. 2006. (ENG.). 32p. (J). (gr. -1-17). 15.95 *(978-0-89272-698-1(9))* Down East Bks.

Corey, Shana. Milly & the Macy's Parade. Helquist, Brett, illus. 2006. 38p. (J). (gr. 4-8). reprint ed. 17.00 *(978-1-4223-5174-1(2))* DIANE Publishing Co.

—Milly & the Macy's Parade. Helquist, Brett, illus. 2006. (Scholastic Bookshelf Ser.). (ENG.). 40p. (J). (gr. -1-3). pap. 6.99 *(978-0-439-29755-4(9))* Scholastic, Inc.

Crimi, Carolyn. Pugs in a Bug. Buscema, Stephanie, illus. 2012. (ENG.). 32p. (J). (gr. -1-k). 16.99 *(978-0-8037-3320-6(8)*, Dial Bks) Penguin Young Readers Group.

Crow, Melinda Melton. Truck Parade, 1 vol. Thompson, Chad, illus. 2012. (Wonder Wheels Ser.). (ENG.). 32p. (gr. -1-1). pap. 6.25 *(978-1-4342-4240-2(4))*; lib. bdg. 22.65 *(978-1-4342-4017-0(7))* Stone Arch Bks.

De Laurentiis, Giada, et al. Rio de Janeiro! #5. Gambatesa, Francesca, illus. 2015. (Recipe for Adventure Ser.: 5). (ENG.). 160p. (J). (gr. 2-4). bds. 6.99 *(978-0-448-48204-0(5)*, Grosset & Dunlap) Penguin Young Readers Group.

Dipucchio, Kelly. Dress-Up Mess-Up. Ross, Heather, illus. 2013. (Crafty Chloe Ser.). (ENG.). 40p. (J). (gr. -1-3). 16.99 *(978-1-4424-2124-0(X))* Simon & Schuster Children's Publishing.

Dungy, Tony & Dungy, Lauren. Here Comes the Parade! Newton, Vanessa Brantley, illus. 2014. (Tony & Lauren Dungy Ready-To-Reads Ser.). (ENG.). 32p. (J). (gr. k-2). pap. 3.99 *(978-1-4424-5469-9(5)*, Simon Spotlight) Simon Spotlight.

Earhart, Kristin. Roscoe & the Pony Parade. Gurney, John Steven, illus. 2008. (Little Apple Ser.). 88p. (J). *(978-0-545-08094-1(0))* Scholastic, Inc.

Engelbreit, Mary. Queen of Easter. Engelbreit, Mary, illus. 2009. (Ann Estelle Stories Ser.). (ENG., Illus.). 32p. (J). (gr. -1-3). pap. 6.99 *(978-0-06-008186-7(4))* HarperCollins Pubs.

Estes, Don. Willy: The Little Jeep Who Wanted to Be a Fire Truck. Garrison, Sue, illus. 2003. 46p. (J). lib. bdg. 14.95 *(978-1-883551-47-6(1)*, ASP-471, Attic Studio Pr.) Attic Studio Publishing Hse.

—Willy & Friends traveling through the Seasons: The continuing story of Willy the little fire jeep. Glass, Eric, illus. 2006. (J). *(978-1-883551-75-9(7)*, Maple Corners Press) Attic Studio Publishing Hse.

Everett, Reese. Charlie's Big Break. 2015. (ENG.). 48p. (gr. k-3). 27.07 *(978-1-63430-376-7(8))* Rourke Educational Media.

Fisher-Price. Fisher-Price Little People: Halloween Is Here! 2016. (ENG.). 10p. (J). (gr. -1-k). bds. 9.99 *(978-0-7944-3756-5(7)*, Reader's Digest Children's Bks.) Studio Fun International.

French, Vivian. Princess Katie & the Silver Pony. Gibb, Sarah, illus. 2007. (Tiara Club Ser.: No.2). 80p. (J). (gr. 1-4). 15.99 *(978-0-06-112432-7(X)*, Tegen, Katherine Bks) HarperCollins Pubs.

Gerber, Carole. A Band of Babies. Dyer, Jane, illus. 2017. 32p. (J). (gr. -1-3). 17.99 *(978-0-06-168955-0(6))* HarperCollins Pubs.

Ginsberg, Mort. Ukey & His Magical Ukulele. 2008. 75p. pap. 19.95 *(978-1-60610-395-1(4))* America Star Bks.

Harimann, Sierra. Puppies on Parade. 2014. (Illus.). 30p. (J). pap. *(978-0-545-59211-6(9))* Scholastic, Inc.

Hoffman, Mary. Princess Grace. Van Wright, Cornelius & Hu, Ying-Hwa, illus. 2008. (ENG.). 32p. (J). (gr. -1-3). 18.99 *(978-0-8037-3260-5(0)*, Dial Bks) Penguin Young Readers Group.

Holub, Joan. Good Luck! A St. Patrick's Day Story. Terry, Will, illus. 2007. (Ant Hill Ser.). (ENG.). 24p. (J). (gr. -1-k). lib. bdg. 11.89 *(978-1-4169-2560-6(0)*, Aladdin Library) Simon & Schuster Children's Publishing.

—Good Luck! A St. Patrick's Day Story. Terry, Will, illus. 2007. (Ant Hill Ser.). (ENG.). 24p. (J). (gr. -1-k). pap. 3.99 *(978-1-4169-0955-2(9)*, Simon Spotlight) Simon Spotlight.

Jacobson, Jennifer Richard. Andy Shane, Hero at Last. Carter, Abby, illus. 2011. (Andy Shane Ser.: 6). (ENG.). 64p. (J). (gr. k-3). pap. 4.99 *(978-0-7636-5293-7(8))* Candlewick Pr.

—Hero at Last. Carter, Abby, illus. 2010. (Andy Shane Ser.: 6). (ENG.). 64p. (J). (gr. k-3). 14.99 *(978-0-7636-3600-5(2))* Candlewick Pr.

Janvier Gibeau, Claire. Here Comes Grandpa Now. 2009. 16p. pap. 8.49 *(978-1-4490-3829-8(8))* AuthorHouse.

Johnson, Angela. The Day Ray Got Away. LaMarca, Luke, illus. 2010. (ENG.). 40p. (J). (gr. k-3). 16.99 *(978-0-689-87375-1(1)*, Simon & Schuster Bks. For Young Readers) Simon & Schuster Bks. For Young Readers.

Johnson, Shane L., illus. Olivia Leads a Parade. 2011. (Olivia TV Tie-In Ser.). (ENG.). 24p. (J). (gr. -1-2). pap. 3.99 *(978-1-4424-2137-0(1)*, Simon Spotlight) Simon Spotlight.

Jonell, Lynne. Grasshopper Magic. Dorman, Brandon, illus. (Magical Mix-Ups Ser.: 3). (ENG.). 112p. (J). (gr. 1-4). 2014.

pap. 4.99 (978-0-307-93123-8(4)) 2013. 12.99 (978-0-375-87084-2(9)) Random Hse. Children's Bks. (Random Hse. Bks. for Young Readers).

Karr, Lily. Easter Parade! Richards, Kirsten, illus. 2013. (ENG.). 24p. (J). (gr. -1-k). pap. 4.99 (978-0-545-45824-5(2), Cartwheel Bks.) Scholastic, Inc.

—Easter Parade! 2013. lib. bdg. 14.75 (978-0-606-31494-7(6), Turtleback) Turtleback Bks.

Kerrin, Jessica Scott. Out of Orbit! Kelly, Joseph, illus. 2007. (Martin Bridge Ser.). (ENG.). 112p. (J). (gr. 2-5). 6.95 (978-1-55453-149-3(7)) Kids Can Pr., Ltd. CAN. Dist: Hachette Bk. Group.

Krulik, Nancy. Don't Be Such a Turkey! John and Wendy Staff, illus. 2010. (Katie Kazoo, Switcheroo Ser.). (ENG.). 160p. (J). (gr. 2-4). pap. 4.99 (978-0-448-45448-1(3), Grosset & Dunlap) Penguin Young Readers Group.

Kuphal, Shirley M. Flavor's Wild Wish. 2008. 36p. pap. 21.99 (978-1-4363-0656-0(6)) Xlibris Corp.

Leonard, Marcia. El Hombre de Hojalata. Handelman, Dorothy, photos by. 2005. (ENG & SPA., Illus.). 32p. (J). (gr. -1-1). pap. 4.99 (978-0-8225-3310-8(3)) Lerner Publishing Group.

London, Jonathan. Froggy Plays in the Band. Remkiewicz, Frank & Frank, Remkiewicz, illus. 2004. (Froggy Ser.). (ENG.). 32p. (J). (gr. -1-k). 6.99 (978-0-14-240051-7(3), Puffin Books) Penguin Young Readers Group.

—Froggy Plays in the Band. Remkiewicz, Frank, illus. 2004. (Froggy Ser.). (J). (gr. -1-3). 13.65 (978-0-7569-2955-8(5)) Perfection Learning Corp.

McCune, Susan. The Big Parade, 01 vols., 1. 2016. (Rosen REAL Readers: Social Studies Nonfiction / Fiction: Family, Community, & the World Ser.). (ENG.). 12p. (J). pap. 6.33 (978-1-5081-1967-8(8), Rosen Classroom) Rosen Publishing Group, Inc., The.

McGrath, Barbara Barbieri. The M & M's(r) Brand All-American Parade Book. Tagel, Peggy, illus. 2004. 12p. (J). (gr. -1-k). bds. 6.95 (978-1-57091-430-0(3)) Charlesbridge Publishing, Inc.

McGrath, Barbara Barbieri & Tagel, Peggy. Parade Colors. 2017. (First Celebrations Ser.). (ENG., Illus.). 12p. (J). (— 1). bds. 6.99 (978-1-58089-536-1(0)) Charlesbridge Publishing, Inc.

McKee, David. Elmer's Special Day. McKee, David, illus. 2009. (Andersen Press Picture Bks). (ENG., Illus.). 32p. (J). (gr. -1-3). 16.95 (978-0-7613-5154-2(X), Carolrhoda Bks.) Lerner Publishing Group.

Miller, Pat Zietlow. The Quickest Kid in Clarksville. Morrison, Frank, illus. 2016. (ENG.). 40p. (J). (gr. k-3). 16.99 (978-1-4521-2936-5(3)) Chronicle Bks. LLC.

Mishica, Clare. Here Comes the Parade. Richard, Ilene, illus. 2005. (Rookie Readers Ser.). (ENG.). 24p. (J). (gr. k-2). lib. bdg. 19.50 (978-0-516-24857-8(X), Children's Pr.) Scholastic Library Publishing.

—Vamos al Desfile. 2006. (Rookie Reader Español Ser.). (ENG & SPA., Illus.). 32p. (J). (gr. k-2). lib. bdg. 19.50 (978-0-516-25309-1(3)) Scholastic Library Publishing.

Nagaraj, Josephine. Giddy-Up, Guppies! (Bubble Guppies) Huxtable, John, illus. 2014. (Step into Reading Ser.). (ENG.). 32p. (J). (gr. -1-1). 3.99 (978-0-385-36974-9(3), Random Hse. Bks. for Young Readers) Random Hse. Children's Bks.

Nolan, Allia Zobel. Animal Parade. Maddocks, Maria, illus. 2011. (ENG.). 10p. (J). (gr. -1 — 1). 12.99 (978-0-547-55867-7(8)) Houghton Mifflin Harcourt Publishing Co.

Owen, Rob. Spy Boy, Cheyenne, & Ninety-Six Crayons: A "Mardi Gras" Indian's Story, 1 vol. Owen, Rob, illus. 2013. (ENG., Illus.). 32p. (J). (gr. k-3). 16.99 (978-1-4556-1799-9(7)) Pelican Publishing Co., Inc.

Pearson, Luke, illus. Hilda & the Bird Parade. 2013. (Hildafolk Ser.). (ENG.). 44p. (J). (gr. k). 24.00 (978-1-909263-06-2(0)) Flying Eye Bks. GBR. Dist: Consortium Bk. Sales & Distribution.

Pitman, Gayle E. This Day in June. Litten, Kristyna, illus. 2013. (J). (978-1-4338-1658-1(X)); pap. (978-1-4338-1659-8(8)) American Psychological Assn. (Magination Pr.).

Random House Staff. SpongeBob's Easter Parade (SpongeBob SquarePants) Random House Staff, illus. 2013. (Pictureback(R) Ser.). (ENG., Illus.). 24p. (J). (gr. -1-2). pap. 3.99 (978-0-449-81444-4(0), Random Hse. Bks. for Young Readers) Random Hse. Children's Bks.

Resnicoff, Stan. The BIG Parade: Los Angeles. 2012. (ENG.). (J). pap. (978-1-4675-1540-5(X)) Independent Pub.

—The BIG Parade: New York. 2012. (ENG.). (J). pap. (978-1-4675-1538-2(8)) Independent Pub.

—The BIG Parade: San Francisco. 2012. (ENG.). (J). pap. (978-1-4675-1539-9(6)) Independent Pub.

Rey, H. A. Curious George Parade Day. 2011. (Curious George Ser.). (ENG., Illus.). 14p. (J). (gr. -1 — 1). bds. 7.99 (978-0-547-47282-9(X)) Houghton Mifflin Harcourt Publishing Co.

Ricci, Christine. The Great Big Parade. Aikins, Dave, illus. 2007. (J). pap. (978-1-4127-8923-3(0)) Publications International, Ltd.

Roscoe, Lily. The Night Parade. Walker, David, illus. 2014. (ENG.). 32p. (J). (— 1). 16.99 (978-0-545-39623-3(9), Orchard Bks.) Scholastic, Inc.

Rowley, Julie P. The Little Purple Mardi Gras Bead, 1 vol. Paquette, John R., illus. 2016. (ENG.). 32p. (J). pap. 8.99 **(978-1-4556-2344-0(X))** Pelican Publishing Co., Inc.

Ryan, Pam Muñoz. Yo Ho Ho, Halloween! Fotheringham, Ed, illus. 2015. 39p. (J). pap. (978-0-545-91590-8(2)) Scholastic, Inc.

Schmauss, Judy Kentor. Parade Day. Chewning, Randy, illus. 2006. (Reader's Clubhouse Level 2 Reader Ser.). (ENG.). 24p. (J). (gr. 1-4). pap. 3.99 (978-0-7641-3293-3(8)) Barron's Educational Series, Inc.

Silverman, Erica. On the Morn of Mayfest. Frazee, Marla, illus. 2011. (ENG.). 32p. (J). (gr. -1-2). pap. 13.99 (978-1-4424-4341-9(3), Simon & Schuster Bks. For Young Readers) Simon & Schuster Bks. For Young Readers.

Steers, Billy. Tractor Mac Parade's Best. (Tractor Mac Ser.). (ENG.). (J). 2017. 24p. pap. 4.99 (978-0-374-30599-4(4), 9780374305994) 2015. (Illus.). 32p. (gr. -1-k). 8.99 (978-0-374-30106-4(9), 9780374301064) Farrar, Straus & Giroux. (Farrar, Straus & Giroux (BYR)).

Sulgit, Nicole. Caillou Leads the Parade. Poupart, Jean-Sébastien, illus. 2004. (J). (978-0-7853-9949-0(6)) Publications International, Ltd.

Thacker, Becky. The Chorus Kids' Memorial Day Parade. Thacker, Becky, illus. 2006. (Illus.). (J). 10.95 (978-0-9786276-1-4(X)) Mentzer Printing Ink.

Thaler, Mike. St. Patrick's Day from the Black Lagoon. Lee, Jared, illus. 2011. 61p. (J). (978-0-545-27328-2(5)) Scholastic, Inc.

—The Thanksgiving Day from the Black Lagoon. Lee, Jared, illus. 2009. 64p. (J). (978-0-545-16812-0(0)) Scholastic, Inc.

Wells, Rosemary. Max & the Fall Parade. 2014. (Max Ruby Ser.). lib. bdg. 13.55 (978-0-606-36192-7(8)) Turtleback Bks.

Zobel-Nolan, Allia. Animal Parade. Maddocks, Maria, illus. 2008. 10p. (J). (gr. -1). 12.95 (978-1-932915-63-1(X)) Sandvik Innovations, LLC.

PARAGUAY

Augustin, Byron. Paraguay. 2005. (Enchantment of the World Ser.). (ENG., Illus.). 144p. (YA). (gr. 5-9). 39.00 (978-0-516-23675-9(X)) Scholastic Library Publishing.

Behnke, Alison. Paraguay in Pictures. 2009. (Visual Geography Series, Second Ser.). (ENG.). 80p. (gr. 5-12). 31.93 (978-1-57505-962-4(2)) Lerner Publishing Group.

Hernández, Roger E. Paraguay. (South America Today Ser.). 64p. 2009. (J). (gr. 4-7). 21.95 (978-1-4222-0638-6(6)) 2007. (YA). (gr. 7-18). pap. 9.95 (978-1-4222-0705-5(6)) Mason Crest.

Hernandez, Roger E. Paraguay, Vol. 13. Henderson, James D., ed. 2015. (Discovering South America: History, Politics, & Culture Ser.). (Illus.). 64p. (J). (gr. 7). lib. bdg. 22.95 (978-1-4222-3301-6(4)) Mason Crest.

Jermyn, Leslie & Yong, Jui Lin. Paraguay. 2nd rev. ed. 2009. (Cultures of the World 19 Ser.). 144p. (gr. 6). 42.79 (978-0-7614-4858-7(6)) Marshall Cavendish Corp.

PARAPSYCHOLOGY

see also Apparitions; Clairvoyance; Extrasensory Perception; Ghosts; Hypnotism; Mind and Body; Thought Transference

Bodden, Valerie. Cemeteries. 2017. (J). (978-1-60818-806-2(X), Creative Education) Creative Co., The.

—Ghost Towns. 2017. (J). (978-1-60818-807-9(8), Creative Education) Creative Co., The.

—Old Jails. 2017. (J). (978-1-60818-809-3(4), Creative Education) Creative Co., The.

—Tombs. 2017. (J). (978-1-60818-810-9(8), Creative Education) Creative Co., The.

Breman, Billy & Watkins, Graham. Searching for Ghosts & Poltergeists. 2011. (J). 77.70 (978-1-4488-4778-5(8)); pap. 12.95 (978-1-4488-4770-9(2)); lib. bdg. 31.95 (978-1-4488-4762-4(1)) Rosen Publishing Group, Inc., The.

Centore, Michael. Psychic Abilities. 2017. (Freaky Phenomena Ser.: Vol. 8). (ENG., Illus.). (YA). (gr. 5-8). 20.95 **(978-1-4222-3779-3(6))** Mason Crest.

Coddington, Andrew. The Bermuda Triangle, Stonehenge, & Unexplained Places. 2017. (J). **(978-1-5026-2843-5(0))** Cavendish Square Publishing.

Cooley Peterson, Megan. Haunted Objects from Around the World. 2017. (It's Haunted! Ser.). (ENG., Illus.). 32p. (gr. 3-4). lib. bdg. 27.99 (978-1-5157-3859-6(0), Snap Bks.) Capstone Press of Coughlan Cos.

Dicker, Katie. Mysterious Messages. 2015. (Mystery! Ser.). 24p. (gr. 3-6). 28.50 (978-1-62588-203-5(3)) Black Rabbit Bks.

Diker, Katie. Missing! 2015. (ENG., Illus.). 24p. (J). pap. 8.95 (978-1-77092-232-7(6)) RiverStream Publishing.

—Mysterious Messages. 2015. (ENG., Illus.). 24p. (J). pap. 8.95 (978-1-77092-234-1(2)) RiverStream Publishing.

—Mysterious Places. 2015. (ENG., Illus.). 24p. (J). pap. 8.95 (978-1-77092-235-8(0)) RiverStream Publishing.

Ganeri, Anita & West, David. Lost in the Bermuda Triangle & Other Mysteries. 2011. (Incredible True Adventures Ser.). (ENG.). 48p. (YA). (gr. 5-8). pap. 11.75 (978-1-4488-6662-5(6)); lib. bdg. 29.25 (978-1-4488-6658-8(8)) Rosen Publishing Group, Inc., The. (Rosen Reference).

Green, Carl R. & Sanford, William R. Amazing Out-of-Body Experiences. Kelley, Gerald, illus. 2011. (Investigating the Unknown Ser.). 48p. (J). (gr. 5-18). pap. 8.95 (978-1-59845-307-2(6)); lib. bdg. 25.27 (978-0-7660-3822-6(X)) Enslow Pubs., Inc.

Gudgeon, Chris. Ghost Trackers: The Unreal World of Ghosts, Ghost-Hunting, & the Paranormal. 2010. (ENG.). 80p. (J). (gr. 4-7). pap. 14.95 (978-0-88776-950-4(0), Tundra Bks.) Tundra Bks. CAN. Dist: Penguin Random Hse. LLC.

Guiley, Rosemary Ellen. Spirit Communications. 2009. (Mysteries, Legends, & Unexplained Phenomena Ser.). (Illus.). 128p. (YA). (gr. 7-12). 29.95 (978-0-7910-9391-7(3)) Facts On File, Inc.

Harmon, Daniel E. Haunted Places & Ghostly Encounters. 2015. (J). (978-1-61900-066-7(0)) Eldorado Ink.

Henneberg, Susan. Investigating Ghosts & the Spirit World, 1 vol. 2015. (ENG.). 48p. (YA). 25.85 (978-1-62275-863-0(3), Britannica Educational Publishing) Rosen Publishing Group, Inc., The.

Herbst, Judith. Vanished. 2004. (Unexplained Ser.). (Illus.). 48p. (J). pap. 8.95 (978-0-8225-2404-5(X), Lerner Pubns.); (ENG., (gr. 5-12). lib. bdg. 26.60 (978-0-8225-1631-6(4)) Lerner Publishing Group.

Kallen, Stuart A. Time Travel. 2009. (Mysterious Encounters Ser.). 48p. (J). 29.00 (978-0-7377-4573-3(8), Kidhaven) Cengage Gale.

Kaplan, Debbie. When I Was Big. Osadchuk, Keit, illus. 2010. (J). pap. (978-1-57043-318-4(6)) Eckankar.

Lassiter, Rhiannon. The Supernatural. 2006. (Unexplained Ser.). (Illus.). 36p. (gr. 3-6). lib. bdg. 26.00 (978-0-8368-6267-6(8), Gareth Stevens Learning Library) Stevens, Gareth Publishing LLLP.

Marcovitz, Hal. Teens & the Supernatural & Paranormal. Developed in Association with the Gallup Organization Staff, ed. 2013. (Gallup Youth Survey: Major Issues & Trends Ser.: 14). (Illus.). 112p. (J). (gr. 7-18). 24.95 (978-1-4222-2959-0(9)) Mason Crest.

—Teens & the Supernatural & Paranormal. 2008. (Gallup Youth Survey, Major Issues & Trends Ser.). 112,128p. (J). (gr. 7-9). lib. bdg. 22.95 (978-1-59084-876-0(4)) Mason Crest.

Marvel, Robin. Awakening Consciousness: A Boy's Guide! 2009. (J). pap. 17.95 (978-1-932690-91-0(3)) Loving Healing Pr., Inc.

—Awakening Consciousness: A Girl's Guide. 2009. (J). pap. 16.95 (978-1-932690-80-4(8)) Loving Healing Pr., Inc.

Miles, Liz. Terrifying Tales: Ghosts, Ghouls, & Other Things That Go Bump in the Night. 2010. (Culture in Action Ser.). (ENG., Illus.). 32p. (gr. 3-6). 30.65 (978-1-4109-3926-5(X), NA-r) Heinemann-Raintree.

Mooney, Carla. Becoming Invisible: From Camouflage to Cloaks. 2010. (Great Idea Ser.). 48p. (J). (gr. 4-6). lib. bdg. 26.60 (978-1-59953-378-0(2)) Norwood Hse. Pr.

Olson, Elsie. Are You Psychic? Facts, Trivia, & Quizzes. 2017. (Mind Games Ser.). (ENG., Illus.). (J). (gr. 2-5). lib. bdg. 27.99 **(978-1-5124-3416-3(7))** Lerner Publishing Group.

Pearce, Q. L. Mysterious Disappearances. 2011. (Mysterious Encounters Ser.). (ENG., Illus.). 48p. (gr. 4-8). lib. bdg. 33.60 (978-0-7377-5840-5(6), Kidhaven) Cengage Gale.

Peterson, Megan Cooley. Super Scary Stories. 2016. (Super Scary Stuff Ser.). (ENG., Illus.). 24p. (gr. 1-2). lib. bdg. 25.32 (978-1-5157-0279-5(0), First Facts) Capstone Press of Coughlan Cos.

Place, Robert M. Astrology & Divination. 2008. (Mysteries, Legends, & Unexplained Phenomena Ser.). (Illus.). 136p. (YA). (gr. 7-12). lib. bdg. 29.95 (978-0-7910-9385-6(9)) Facts On File, Inc.

Rauf, Don. The Senses. 2017. (Freaky Phenomena Ser.: Vol. 8). (ENG., Illus.). (YA). (gr. 5-8). 20.95 **(978-1-4222-3780-9(X))** Mason Crest.

Rooney, Ann. Amazing Mysteries: Messages from Beyond. 2010. (Amazing Mysteries Ser.). (YA). (gr. 3-6). 28.50 (978-1-59920-363-8(4)) Black Rabbit Bks.

Schulte, Mary. Dover Demon. 2009. (Mysterious Encounters Ser.). (ENG., Illus.). 48p. (J). 29.00 (978-0-7377-4570-2(3), Greenhaven Pr., Inc.) Cengage Gale.

Seeley, M. H. Freaky Stories about the Paranormal. 2016. (Freaky True Science Ser.). (Illus.). 32p. (J). (gr. 5-4). pap. 10.50 (978-1-4824-4846-7(7)) Stevens, Gareth Publishing LLLP.

Terrell, Brandon. 12 Unsolved Mysteries. 2017. (Scary & Spooky Ser.). (ENG.). 32p. (J). (gr. 3-6). 21.95 (978-1-63235-298-9(2)) Pr. Room Editions LLC.

Townsend, John. Gone Missing. 2010. (Amazing Mysteries Ser.). (YA). (gr. 3-6). 28.50 (978-1-59920-364-5(2)) Black Rabbit Bks.

Walker, Kathryn. Mysterious Healing. 2009. (Unsolved! Ser.). (ENG., Illus.). 32p. (J). (gr. 3-5). pap. (978-0-7787-4163-3(X)); (gr. 4-6). lib. bdg. (978-0-7787-4150-3(8)) Crabtree Publishing Co.

PARAPSYCHOLOGY—FICTION

Alderson, Sarah. Losing Lila. 2013. (ENG.). 352p. (J). pap. 10.00 (978-0-85707-197-2(1), Simon & Schuster Children's) Simon & Schuster, Ltd. GBR. Dist: Simon & Schuster, Inc.

Allison, Jennifer. The Dead Drop. 2009. (Gilda Joyce Ser.). (ENG.). 320p. (J). (gr. 5-18). 16.99 (978-0-525-47980-2(5), Dutton Books for Young Readers) Penguin Young Readers Group.

Anastasiu, Heather. Override. 2013. (Glitch Novel Ser.: 2). (ENG.). 320p. (YA). (gr. 7-12). pap. 9.99 (978-1-250-00300-3(8), 9781250003003, St. Martin's Griffin) St. Martin's Pr.

Black, Michael Ian. The Purple Kangaroo. Brown, Peter, illus. 2009. (ENG.). 32p. (J). (gr. -1-3). 16.99 (978-1-4169-5771-3(5), Simon & Schuster Bks. For Young Readers) Simon & Schuster Bks. For Young Readers.

Blythe, Daniel. Shadow Breakers. 2013. (J). (978-0-545-47980-6(0)); (ENG.). 256p. (gr. 5-9). 16.99 (978-0-545-47979-0(7)) Scholastic, Inc. (Chicken Hse., The).

Bracken, Alexandra. The Darkest Minds. (Darkest Minds Novel Ser.). (ENG.). 2013. 528p. (YA). (gr. 9-17). pap. 9.99 (978-1-4231-5932-2(2)) 2012. 496p. (J). (gr. 5-9). 17.99 (978-1-4231-5737-3(0)) Hyperion Pr.

—The Darkest Minds. 2013. (Darkest Minds Ser.: 1). (YA). lib. bdg. 20.85 (978-0-606-36533-8(8)) Turtleback Bks.

—In the Afterlight. 2014. (Darkest Minds Novel Ser.). (ENG.). 544p. (YA). (gr. 7-12). 18.99 (978-1-4231-5752-6(4)) Hyperion Bks. for Children.

—Never Fade. 2014. (Darkest Minds Novel Ser.). (ENG.). 544p. (YA). (gr. 7-12). pap. 9.99 (978-1-4231-5933-9(0)) Hyperion Bks. for Children.

—Never Fade. 2013. (Darkest Minds Novel Ser.: Bk. 2). (ENG.). 512p. (J). (gr. 5-9). 17.99 (978-1-4231-5751-9(6)) Hyperion Pr.

—Never Fade. 2014. (Darkest Minds Ser.: 2). (YA). lib. bdg. 20.85 (978-0-606-36534-5(6)) Turtleback Bks.

Bradford, Rebecca. Delve. 2017. (ENG.). 192p. (YA). pap. 13.95 **(978-1-78710-008-4(1)**, 2d156507-81a8-4e51-bdee-e10b2ff8ef93) Austin, Stan AUS. Dist: Bookmasters Distribution.

Bray, Libba. The Diviners. 2012. 578p. (YA). 9.99 (978-0-316-23242-5(4)) Little Brown & Co.

—The Diviners. (Diviners Ser.: 1). (ENG.). (YA). (gr. 10-17). 2013. 496p. pap. 12.99 (978-0-316-12610-6(1)) 2012. 800p. 42.99 (978-0-316-22426-0(X)) Little, Brown Bks. for Young Readers.

—The Diviners. 2013. (Diviners Ser.: 1). (YA). lib. bdg. 24.50 (978-0-606-32284-3(1), Turtleback) Turtleback Bks.

Brignull, Irena. The Hawkweed Legacy. 2017. (Hawkweed Ser.: 2). (ENG.). 384p. (YA). 18.00 **(978-1-60286-314-9(8)**, Weinstein Bks.) Perseus Bks. Group.

Brockmann, Suzanne & Brockmann, Melanie. Night Sky. 2014. (Night Sky Ser.: 1). (ENG.). 496p. (YA). (gr. 8-12). 16.99 (978-1-4926-0144-9(6)) Sourcebooks, Inc.

Card, Orson Scott. Pathfinder. (ENG.). 672p. (YA). (gr. 7). 2011. pap. 12.99 (978-1-4169-9179-3(4)) 2010. 19.99 (978-1-4169-9176-2(X)) Simon Pulse. (Simon Pulse).

—Pathfinder. l.t. ed. 2011. (Pathfinder Ser.). (ENG.). 802p. 23.99 (978-1-4104-3681-8(0)) Thorndike Pr.

Carthage, Lynn. Avenged. 2017. (Arnaud Legacy Ser.: 3). (ENG.). 288p. (YA). (gr. 9). pap. 9.95 (978-1-61773-628-5(7)) Kensington Publishing Corp.

—Betrayed. 2016. (Arnaud Legacy Ser.: 2). (ENG.). 288p. (YA). (gr. 9). pap. 9.95 (978-1-61773-627-8(9)) Kensington Publishing Corp.

Chand, Emlyn. Farsighted. 2012. 260p. pap. 12.95 (978-0-9839308-3-9(X)) Blue Crown Pr.

Chen, Justina. Return to Me. 2013. (ENG.). 352p. (YA). (gr. 7-17). 17.99 (978-0-316-10255-1(5)) Little Brown & Co.

Epstein, Robin. Hear. 2016. (ENG., Illus.). 272p. (YA). (gr. 9). pap. 10.99 (978-1-61695-705-6(0), Soho Teen) Soho Pr., Inc.

Estep, Jennifer. Dark Heart of Magic. 2015. (Black Blade Ser.: 2). (ENG.). 368p. (J). (gr. 9). pap. 9.95 (978-1-61773-826-5(3)) Kensington Publishing Corp.

Everblaze. 2014. (Keeper of the Lost Cities Ser.: 3). (ENG., Illus.). 624p. (J). (gr. 3-7). 18.99 (978-1-4424-4599-4(8), Aladdin) Simon & Schuster Children's Publishing.

Flynn, Tatum. Hell's Belles. 2017. (d'Evil Diaries). (ENG., Illus.). 256p. (J). (gr. 4-6). pap. 7.99 (978-1-4083-3578-9(6), Orchard Bks.) Hachette Children's Group GBR. Dist: Hachette Bk. Group.

Garcia, Kami & Stohl, Margaret. Beautiful Darkness. 2010. (Beautiful Creatures Ser.: Bk. 2). (YA). 59.99 (978-1-60941-036-0(X)) Findaway World, LLC.

—Beautiful Darkness. (Beautiful Creatures Ser.: 2). 2011. (ENG.). 528p. (YA). (gr. 7-17). pap. 12.99 (978-0-316-07704-0(6)) 2010. (ENG.). 512p. (YA). (gr. 7-17). 17.99 (978-0-316-07705-7(4)) 2010. 512p. pap. 17.99 (978-0-316-09861-8(2)) Little, Brown Bks. for Young Readers.

—Beautiful Darkness. 2011. (Beautiful Creatures Ser.: 2). (YA). lib. bdg. 24.50 (978-0-606-26700-7(X), Turtleback) Turtleback Bks.

Garcia, Richard. Los Espiritus de Mi Tia Otilia. 2004. (ENG & SPA., Illus.). (J). (gr. k-3). spiral bd. (978-0-616-14606-4(X)) Canadian National Institute for the Blind/Institut National Canadien pour les Aveugles.

George, Elisabeth. The Edge of Nowhere. 2014. (Edge of Nowhere Ser.). (ENG.). 464p. (YA). (gr. 7). pap. 10.99 (978-0-14-242675-3(X), Speak) Penguin Young Readers Group.

—The Edge of the Water. 2014. (Edge of Nowhere Ser.). (ENG.). 448p. (YA). (gr. 7). 18.99 (978-0-670-01297-8(1), Viking Books for Young Readers) Penguin Young Readers Group.

Gibson, Marley. The Reason, Bk. 3. 2010. (ENG.). 240p. (YA). (gr. 7-18). pap. 8.99 (978-0-547-15095-6(4)) Houghton Mifflin Harcourt Publishing Co.

Harvey-Fitzhenry, Alyxandra. Broken, 1 vol. 2010. (ENG., Illus.). 176p. (YA). (gr. 7-12). pap. 12.95 (978-1-896580-41-8(6)) Tradewind Bks. CAN. Dist: Orca Bk. Pubs. USA.

Hendry, Frances. The Seer's Stone. l.t. ed. 2007. 160p. per. (978-1-905665-18-1(0)) Pollinger In Print.

The Iris House. 2006. (YA). per. 12.95 (978-0-9677047-7-7(4)) Marble Hse. Editions.

Kenny, Christopher D. Another World. 2017. (ENG.). 269p. pap. 13.95 **(978-1-78629-627-6(6)**, bf17030a-b424-442a-a077-3adb78cc431a) Austin, Stan AUS. Dist: Bookmasters Distribution.

Kenyon, Sherrilyn. Inferno. 2013. (Chronicles of Nick Ser.: 4). (ENG.). 464p. (YA). (gr. 7). 18.99 (978-1-250-00283-9(4), 9781250002839, St. Martin's Griffin) St. Martin's Pr.

Kessler, Liz. Haunt Me. 2017. (ENG.). (YA). (gr. 7). 17.99 **(978-0-7636-9162-2(3))** Candlewick Pr.

Mabry, Samantha. A Fierce & Subtle Poison. 2017. (ENG.). 288p. (YA). (gr. 8-12). pap. 9.95 (978-1-61620-698-7(5)) Algonquin Bks. of Chapel Hill.

Marr, Melissa & Pratt, Tim, eds. Rags & Bones: New Twists on Timeless Tales. 2015. (ENG.). 368p. (YA). (gr. 10-17). pap. 12.99 (978-0-316-21293-9(8)) Little, Brown Bks. for Young Readers.

McCune, D. J. Fault Lines. 2016. (Death & Co Ser.: 3). (ENG.). 352p. (YA). (gr. 8). pap. 11.99 (978-1-4714-0271-5(1)) Bonnier Publishing GBR. Dist: Independent Pubs. Group.

McDonald, Joyce. Shades of Simon Gray. 2003. (Readers Circle Ser.). 245p. (YA). 14.15 (978-0-7569-1880-4(4)) Perfection Learning Corp.

Mead, Richelle. Bloodlines: the Ruby Circle (book 6) 2015. (ENG.). 368p. (J). pap. (978-0-14-136131-4(X), Razorbill) Penguin Young Readers Group.

Messenger, Shannon. Exile. (Keeper of the Lost Cities Ser.: 2). (ENG., Illus.). (J). (gr. 3-7). 2014. 592p. pap. 9.99 (978-1-4424-4597-0(1)) 2013. 576p. 19.99 (978-1-4424-4596-3(3)) Simon & Schuster Children's Publishing. (Aladdin).

—Keeper of the Lost Cities. (Keeper of the Lost Cities Ser.: 1). (ENG., Illus.). (J). (gr. 3-7). 2013. 512p. pap. 8.99 (978-1-4424-4594-9(7)) 2012. 496p. 16.99 (978-1-4424-4593-2(9)) 2015. 1744p. pap. 26.99 (978-1-4814-5112-3(X)) Simon & Schuster Children's Publishing. (Aladdin).

—Lodestar. 2016. (Keeper of the Lost Cities Ser.: 5). (ENG., Illus.). 688p. (J). (gr. 3-7). 18.99 (978-1-4814-7495-5(2), Aladdin) Simon & Schuster Children's Publishing.

—Neverseen. (Keeper of the Lost Cities Ser.: 4). (ENG., Illus.). 688p. (J). (gr. 3-7). 2016. pap. 9.99 (978-1-4814-3230-6(3)) 2015. 19.99 (978-1-4814-3229-0(X)) Simon & Schuster Children's Publishing. (Aladdin).

Nelson, Marilyn. Pemba's Song. 2008. (ENG.). 112p. (J). (gr. 7-18). 16.99 (978-0-545-02076-3(X), Scholastic Pr.) Scholastic, Inc.

Noël, Alyson. Luna Azul. 2010. (Vintage Espanol Ser.).Tr. of Blue Moon. (SPA.). 368p. (YA). (gr. 7). pap. 13.95 (978-0-307-74116-5(8), Vintage Espanol) Knopf Doubleday Publishing Group.

Patten, E. J. The Legend Thief. Rocco, John, illus. 2014. (Hunter Chronicles Ser.: 2). (ENG.). 384p. (J). (gr. 3-7). pap. 7.99 (978-1-4424-2036-6(7), Simon & Schuster Bks. For Young Readers) Simon & Schuster Bks. For Young Readers.

Perez, Marlene. Dead Is Just a Rumor. 2010. (Dead Is Ser.: 4). (ENG., Illus.). 224p. (YA). (gr. 7-18). pap. 7.99 (978-0-547-34592-5(5)) Houghton Mifflin Harcourt Publishing Co.

Price, Charlie. Dead Investigation. 2015. (ENG.). 336p. (YA). (gr. 7). 18.99 (978-0-374-30227-6(8), 9780374302276, Farrar, Straus & Giroux (BYR)) Farrar, Straus & Giroux.

Rayne, C. M. Dark Oracle. Scythe, Adam, illus. 2016. (ENG.). (J). pap. **(978-615-80463-0-5(2))** GiziMap.

Rivers, Phoebe. Giving up the Ghost. 2013. (Saranormal Ser.: 6). (ENG.). 160p. (J). (gr. 3-7). 15.99 (978-1-4424-6616-6(2)); pap. 5.99 (978-1-4424-6617-3(0)) Simon Spotlight. (Simon Spotlight).

—Kindred Spirits. 2013. (Saranormal Ser.: 8). (ENG.). 160p. (J). (gr. 3-7). 15.99 (978-1-4424-6853-5(X)); (Illus.). pap. 5.99 (978-1-4424-6852-8(1)) Simon Spotlight. (Simon Spotlight).

Roderick, Timothy. Briar Blackwood's Grimmest of Fairytales. 2015. (ENG.). 279p. pap. 12.95 (978-1-78279-922-1(2), Lodestone Bks.) Hunt, John Publishing Ltd. GBR. Dist: National Bk. Network.

Rose, R. M. Guardians or Demons. 2017. (ENG.). 419p. (YA). pap. 15.95 **(978-1-78612-746-4(6)**, 9781786127464) Austin, Stan AUS. Dist: Bookmasters Distribution.

Smith, L. J. Dark Visions: The Strange Power - The Possessed - The Passion. 2009. (Dark Visions Ser.: Bks 1-3). (ENG.). 752p. (YA). (gr. 7). pap. 9.99 (978-1-4169-8956-1(0), Simon Pulse) Simon Pulse.

St. Crow, Lili. Betrayals. 2009. (Strange Angels Ser.: 2). (ENG., Illus.). 304p. (YA). (gr. 7-18). 9.99 (978-1-59514-252-8(5), Razorbill) Penguin Young Readers Group.

—Betrayals, 10 vols. 2010. (Strange Angels Ser.: 2). (YA). 95.75 (978-1-4407-7156-9(1)) Recorded Bks., Inc.

—Betrayals. 2009. (Strange Angels Ser.: 2). lib. bdg. 20.85 (978-0-606-09020-9(7), Turtleback) Turtleback Bks.

—Strange Angels. 2009. (Strange Angels Ser.: 1). (ENG., Illus.). 304p. (YA). (gr. 7-18). pap. 9.99 (978-1-59514-251-1(7), Razorbill) Penguin Young Readers Group.

—Strange Angels, 9 vols. 2009. (Strange Angels Ser.: 1). (J). 117.75 (978-1-4407-6197-3(3)); 84.75 (978-1-4407-6195-9(7)); 114.75 (978-1-4407-6199-7(X)); 87.75 (978-1-4407-6193-5(0)); 181.75 (978-1-4407-6194-2(9)) Recorded Bks., Inc.

—Strange Angels. 2009. (Strange Angels Ser.: 1). lib. bdg. 20.85 (978-0-606-08957-9(8), Turtleback) Turtleback Bks.

Stine, R. L. Help! We Have Strange Powers! 2009. (Goosebumps HorrorLand Ser.: 10). lib. bdg. 17.20 (978-0-606-05347-1(6), Turtleback) Turtleback Bks.

Vaughan, M. M. & Caletti, Deb. The Last Forever. Bruno, Iacapo, illus. 2016. (ENG.). 352p. (YA). (gr. 7-7). pap. 10.99 (978-1-4424-5002-8(9), Simon & Schuster Bks. For Young Readers) Simon & Schuster Bks. For Young Readers.

Weatherly, L. A. Angel Fever. 2014. (Angel Ser.). (ENG.). 496p. (YA). (gr. 9). pap. 8.99 (978-0-7636-7173-0(8)) Candlewick Pr.

White, Kiersten. Mind Games. 2013. (Mind Games Ser.: 1). (ENG.). (YA). (gr. 8). 304p. pap. 9.99 (978-0-06-213532-2(5)); 256p. 17.99 (978-0-06-213531-5(7)) HarperCollins Pubs. (HarperTeen).

—Paranormalcy. (Paranormalcy Ser.: 1). (ENG.). (YA). (gr. 8). 2011. 368p. pap. 9.99 (978-0-06-198585-0(6)) 2010. 352p. 16.99 (978-0-06-198584-3(8)) HarperCollins Pubs. (HarperTeen).

Winters, Cat. The Cure for Dreaming. 2016. (ENG., Illus.). 384p. (YA). (gr. 8-17). pap. 9.95 (978-1-4197-1941-7(6), Amulet Bks.) Abrams, Inc.

Young, Suzanne. Hotel for the Lost. 2016. (ENG., Illus.). 304p. (YA). (gr. 9). pap. 10.99 (978-1-4814-2301-4(0), Simon Pulse) Simon Pulse.

—A Need So Beautiful. 2012. (Need So Beautiful Ser.: No. 1). (ENG.). 288p. (YA). (gr. 9). pap. 8.99 (978-0-06-200825-1(0)) HarperCollins Pubs.

PARASITES

see also Bacteriology; Insect Pests

Alessi, Jolene. Zombie Grasshoppers. 2015. (Zombie Animals: Parasites Take Control! Ser.). (ENG.). 24p. (J). (gr. 2-3). 22.60 (978-1-4824-2846-9(6)) Stevens, Gareth Publishing LLLP.

—Zombie Snails. 2015. (Zombie Animals: Parasites Take Control! Ser.). (ENG., Illus.). 24p. (J). (gr. 2-3). pap. 8.15 (978-1-4824-2848-3(2)) Stevens, Gareth Publishing LLLP.

Artell, Mike. Backyard Bloodsuckers: Questions, Facts & Tongue Twisters about Creepy Crawlers. 2004. (Illus.). 80p. pap. 14.95 (978-0-673-59248-4(0)) Good Year Bks.

—Backyard Bloodsuckers: Questions, Facts & Tongue Twisters about Creepy, Crawly Creatures. 2008. (Illus.). 80p. (J). (gr. 4). pap. 14.95 (978-1-59647-271-6(5)) Good Year Bks.

Axelrod-Contrada, Joan. Body Snatchers: Flies, Wasps, & Other Creepy Crawly Zombie Makers. 2016. (Real-Life Zombies Ser.). (ENG., Illus.). 32p. (gr. 3-4). lib. bdg. 27.99 (978-1-5157-2480-3(8), Edge Bks.) Capstone Press of Coughlan Cos.

—Mini Mind Controllers: Fungi, Bacteria, & Other Tiny Zombie Makers. 2016. (Real-Life Zombies Ser.). (ENG.). 32p. (gr. 3-4). lib. bdg. 27.99 (978-1-5157-2478-0(6), Edge Bks.) Capstone Press of Coughlan Cos.

Bensinger, Lou. Tiny Invaders in Your Body. 2010. (Illus.). 24p. (J). 49.50 (978-1-4358-9851-6(6), 1307242); pap. 8.25 (978-1-4358-9850-9(8)); (gr. 1-5). lib. bdg. 22.60 (978-1-4358-9379-5(4)) Rosen Publishing Group, Inc., The. (PowerKids Pr.).

Christiansen, Per. Pests & Parasites. 2008. (Nature's Monsters Ser.). (Illus.). 32p. (YA). (gr. 3-6). lib. bdg. 26.00 (978-0-8368-9218-5(6)) Stevens, Gareth Publishing LLLP.

Ciletti, Barbara. Malaria Parasites. 2017. (Awful, Disgusting Parasites Ser.). (ENG.). 32p. (gr. 3-7). 31.35 **(978-1-68072-008-2(2))** Black Rabbit Bks.

—Tapeworms. 2017. (Awful, Disgusting Parasites Ser.). (ENG., Illus.). 32p. (J). (gr. 3-7). 31.35 **(978-1-68072-010-5(4))** Black Rabbit Bks.

Clark, Lisa. The 10 Most Revolting Parasites. 2008. (J). 14.99 (978-1-55448-521-5(5)) Scholastic Library Publishing.

Cohn, Jessica. Parasite Collector. 2010. (Benchmark Rockets: Dirty & Dangerous Jobs Ser.). 32p. (J). (gr. 3-6). 28.50 (978-1-60870-175-9(1)) Marshall Cavendish Corp.

Davies, Nicola. What's Eating You? Parasites — the Inside Story. Layton, Neal, illus. 2009. (Animal Science Ser.). (ENG.). 64p. (J). (gr. 3-7). pap. 7.99 (978-0-7636-4521-2(4)) Candlewick Pr.

Dlugos, Jenn & Hatton, Charlie. Odd Couples. 2016. (Things That Make You Go Yuck! Ser.: 0). (ENG., Illus.). 88p. (J). (gr. 4-7). pap. 7.95 (978-1-61821-566-6(3), 9781618215666) Prufrock Pr.

Fleisher, Paul. Parasites: Latching on to a Free Lunch. 2006. (Discovery! Ser.). (ENG., Illus.). 112p. (J). (gr. 6-12). lib. bdg. 31.93 (978-0-8225-3415-0(0)) Lerner Publishing Group.

Graham, Ian. Microscopic Scary Creatures. 2009. (Scary Creatures Ser.). (ENG.). 32p. (J). (gr. 3-5). pap. 8.95 (978-0-531-21044-4(8), Watts, Franklin); (Illus.). 27.00 (978-0-531-21673-6(X), Children's Pr.) Scholastic Library Publishing.

Harrison, Paul. Micro Bugs. (Up Close Ser.). 24p. (gr. 3-3). 2009. 47.90 (978-1-60854-696-1(9)) 2007. (Illus.). (J). lib. bdg. 25.25 (978-1-4042-3760-5(7)) Rosen Publishing Group, Inc., The. (PowerKids Pr.).

Jackson, Cari. Alien Invasion: Invasive Species Become Major Menaces. 2009. (Current Science Ser.). (ENG.). 48p. (J). (gr. 4-6). pap. 8.95 (978-1-4339-2128-5(6), Gareth Stevens Learning Library) Stevens, Gareth Publishing LLLP.

Johnson, Rebecca L. Zombie Makers: True Stories of Nature's Undead. (ENG., Illus.). 48p. (gr. 4-8). 2015. 34.65 (978-1-4677-5992-2(9), Lerner Digital) 2012. lib. bdg. 30.60 (978-0-7613-8633-9(5), Millbrook Pr.) Lerner Publishing Group.

Klepeis, Alicia Z. Brain Eaters: Creatures with Zombelike Diets. 2016. (Real-Life Zombies Ser.). (ENG., Illus.). 32p. (gr. 3-4). lib. bdg. 27.99 (978-1-5157-2479-7(4), Edge Bks.) Capstone Press of Coughlan Cos.

Kopp, Megan. Parasites. 2016. (J). **(978-1-4896-5782-4(7))** 2011. (J). (gr. 4-6). pap. 12.95 (978-1-61690-717-4(7), AV2 by Weigl) 2011. (Illus.). 24p. (YA). (gr. 2-5). 27.13 (978-1-61690-711-2(8)) Weigl Pubs., Inc.

Larson, Kirsten W. Zombies in Nature. 2015. (Freaky Nature Ser.). (ENG., Illus.). 32p. (J). (gr. 2-4). 19.95 (978-1-60753-783-0(4)) Amicus Publishing.

Marrin, Albert. Little Monsters: The Creatures That Live on Us & in Us. 2016. (ENG.). 208p. (J). (gr. 3-7). 8.99 (978-0-14-751913-9(6), Puffin Books) Penguin Young Readers Group.

Mincks, Margaret. Head Lice. 2017. (Awful, Disgusting Parasites Ser.). (ENG., Illus.). 32p. (J). (gr. 3-7). 31.35 **(978-1-68072-007-5(4))** Black Rabbit Bks.

—Ticks. 2017. (Awful, Disgusting Parasites Ser.). (ENG., Illus.). 32p. (J). (gr. 3-7). 31.35 **(978-1-68072-011-2(2))** Black Rabbit Bks.

Nagle, Frances. Zombie Ants. 2015. (Zombie Animals: Parasites Take Control! Ser.). (ENG.). 24p. (J). (gr. 2-3). pap. 8.15 (978-1-4824-2828-5(8)) Stevens, Gareth Publishing LLLP.

Newman, Mark. Sooper Yooper: Environmental Defender. Heckman, Mark, illus. 2010. 48p. (J). 17.95 (978-1-933272-26-9(0)) Thunder Bay Pr.

Owen, Ruth. Disgusting Food Invaders. (Up Close & Gross: Microscopic Creatures Ser.). 24p. 2016. (ENG.). (J). (gr. 1-6). pap. 7.95 **(978-1-944998-70-7(5))** 2011. (YA). (gr. 2-5). lib. bdg. 22.61 (978-1-61772-127-4(1)) Bearport Publishing Co., Inc.

Owen, Ruth. Gross Body Invaders. 2011. (Up Close & Gross Ser.). 24p. (YA). (gr. 2-5). lib. bdg. 22.61 (978-1-61772-126-7(3)) Bearport Publishing Co., Inc.

Parker, Barbara Keevil. Ticks. 2007. (Early Bird Nature Books). (Illus.). 48p. (J). (gr. 3-7). lib. bdg. 25.26 (978-0-8225-6464-5(5), Lerner Pubns.) Lerner Publishing Group.

Perritano, John. Bugs That Live on Us. 2008. (Bug Alert! Ser.). 32p. (gr. 3-2). lib. bdg. 28.50 (978-0-7614-3187-9(X), Benchmark Bks.) Marshall Cavendish Corp.

Rake, Matthew. Creepy, Crawly Creatures. Mendez, Simon, illus. 2015. (Real-Life Monsters Ser.). (ENG.). 32p. (J). (gr. 3-6). lib. bdg. 26.65 (978-1-4677-6362-2(4)) Lerner Publishing Group.

Rodger, Marguerite. Termites & Other Home Wreckers. 2010. (Creepy Crawlies Ser.). (ENG.). 32p. (J). (gr. 3-6). (978-0-7787-2503-9(0)); pap. (978-0-7787-2510-7(3)) Crabtree Publishing Co.

Spilsbury, Richard. Zoom in on Body Invaders. 2013. (Zoom in on... Ser.). 32p. (J). 23.94 (978-0-7660-4310-7(X)); (gr. 4-12). pap. 7.95 (978-1-4644-0565-5(4)) Enslow Pubs., Inc.

—Zoom in on House of Horrors. 2013. (Zoom in on... Ser.). 32p. (J). (gr. 4-12). pap. 7.95 (978-1-4644-0569-3(7)) Enslow Pubs., Inc.

Tilden, Thomasine E. Lewis. Worms! Parasites Plague a Village. 2011. (J). pap. (978-0-545-32804-3(7)) Scholastic, Inc.

Viegas, Jennifer. Parasites. (Germs: the Library of Disease-Causing Organisms Ser.). 48p. 2009. (gr. 5-5). 53.00 (978-1-61512-717-7(8)) 2004. (Illus.). (gr. 7-12). lib. bdg. 29.25 (978-0-8239-4494-1(8)) Rosen Publishing Group, Inc., The.

Viegas, Jennifer & Baum, Margaux. Parasites. 2016. (Germs: Disease Causing Organisms Ser.). 48p. (J). (gr. 5-5). pap. 11.75 (978-1-4777-8847-9(6), Rosen Reference) Rosen Publishing Group, Inc., The.

Weir, Kirsten. Bugs That Live on Animals. 2008. (Bug Alert! Ser.). 32p. (gr. 3-18). lib. bdg. 28.50 (978-0-7614-3189-3(6), Benchmark Bks.) Marshall Cavendish Corp.

Woodward, John. What Lives on Other Animals? 2007. (What Lives in... ? Ser.). (Illus.). 48p. (gr. 2-6). lib. bdg. 27.00 (978-0-8368-7860-8(4), Gareth Stevens Learning Library) Stevens, Gareth Publishing LLLP.

Zombie Animals: Parasites Take Control! 2015. (Zombie Animals: Parasites Take Control! Ser.). (ENG.). 24p. (J). (gr. 2-3). pap., pap., pap. 293.40 (978-1-4824-3500-9(4)) Stevens, Gareth Publishing LLLP.

PARATROOPS

see Parachute Troops

PARCEL POST

see Postal Service

PAREJA, JUAN DE, 1606-1670—FICTION

de Trevino, Elizabeth Borton. I, Juan de Pareja. 3rd ed. pap. 3.95 (978-0-13-800129-2(4)) Prentice Hall (Schl. Div.).

—I, Juan de Pareja. 2008. (ENG.). 192p. (YA). (gr. 7-12). pap. 7.99 (978-0-312-38005-2(4), 9780312380052) Square Fish.

—I, Juan de Pareja. l.t. ed. 2005. 244p. 20.95 (978-0-7862-7666-0(5)) Thorndike Pr.

I, Juan de Pareja. 3rd ed. (J). pap., stu. ed. (978-0-13-667452-8(6)) Prentice Hall (Schl. Div.).

PARENT AND CHILD

see also Child Rearing; Father and Child; Mother and Child

Arquette, Kerry. Daddy Promises. McCain, Kevin, illus. 2005. 32p. (J). pap. 7.49 (978-0-7586-0905-2(1)) Concordia Publishing Hse.

Astacio, Mrinali Alvarez, illus. Pon, Pon: A Jugar con el Bebé! 2007. (SPA.). 28p. 14.95 (978-0-8477-1575-6(2)) Univ. of Puerto Rico Pr.

Auld, Mary. My Mom. 2004. (Meet the Family Ser.). (Illus.). 24p. (gr. k-3). lib. bdg. 22.00 (978-0-8368-3927-2(7), Gareth Stevens Learning Library) Stevens, Gareth Publishing LLLP.

Beisswenger, Iffer & Eldred, Margaret. The Way We See Things: Middle Schoolers Look at Themselves & Issues They Face Everyday. Krusi, Carolynne, ed. 2004. 96p. pap. 14.95 (978-0-9759264-0-6(3)) Anemone Publishing.

Berry, Joy. I Love Mommies & Daddies. Regan, Dana, illus. 2010. (Teach Me About Ser.). (ENG.). 20p. (J). (gr. k — 1). pap. 5.99 (978-1-60577-001-7(9)) Berry, Joy Enterprises.

—Illness. 2009. (ENG.). 40p. (J). (gr. k — 1). bds. 7.95 (978-1-60577-012-3(4)) Berry, Joy Enterprises.

Bradley, Michael J. Yes, Your Parents Are Crazy! A Teen Survival Handbook. Glasbergen, Randy, illus. 2004. (ENG.). 432p. pap. 14.95 (978-0-936197-48-7(X)) Harbor Pr., Inc.

Brown, Tracy. Frequently Asked Questions about Same-Sex Marriage & When a Parent Is Gay. 2012. (FAQ: Teen Life Ser.). (ENG., Illus.). 64p. (J). (gr. 7-12). lib. bdg. 31.95 (978-1-4488-8330-1(X)) Rosen Publishing Group, Inc., The.

Burgen, Jim. What's the Big Deal about My Parents? Reeves, Dale, ed. 2006. (What's the Big Deal Ser.). 160p. (gr. 7-18). pap. 10.99 (978-0-7847-1252-8(2), 23335) Standard Publishing.

Carlton, Heather. Bobby's Lesson on Blessings. 2009. 36p. pap. 14.44 (978-0-557-12601-9(0)) Lulu Pr., Inc.

Cider Mill Press Staff & Copeland, Cynthia L. Secrets of Middle School: Everything You Need to Succeed. 2010. (ENG.). 144p. (J). pap. 12.95 (978-1-60433-195-0(X), Applesauce Pr.) Cider Mill Pr. Bk. Pubs., LLC.

Conversations with kids ages 7 To 10: A lovey bedtiem Book. 2007. (J). 9.95 (978-0-9747375-1-5(8)) Joanne Faye Pr.

Corey, Dorothy. You Go Away. Fox, Lisa, illus. 2010. (ENG.). 16p. (J). (gr. -1 — 1). bds. 7.99 (978-0-8075-9440-7(7)) Whitman, Albert & Co.

Dalton, Sommer. While You Sleep. Baker, David, illus. 2011. 28p. pap. 24.95 (978-1-4560-2360-7(8)) America Star Bks.

Donahue, Mary R. & Thornburgh, Gail. What's My Job? Helping Children Navigate the Rough Waters of Separation & Divorce. 2010. 32p. pap. 12.99 (978-1-4490-4669-9(X)) AuthorHouse.

Duffy, Betsy Smeltzer. I Am Beautiful Because... I Am Creative. 2013. 24p. pap. 17.99 (978-1-4817-0618-6(7)) AuthorHouse.

Ellis, Deborah. Our Stories, Our Songs: African Children Talk about AIDS, 1 vol. 2005. (ENG., Illus.). 104p. (J). (gr. 4-7). (978-1-55041-913-9(7)) Fitzhenry & Whiteside, Ltd.

Evans, Jane. Kit Kitten & the Topsy-Turvy Feelings: A Story about Parents Who Aren't Always Able to Care. Bean, Izzy, illus. 2015. (ENG.). 32p. (J). 16.95 (978-1-84905-602-1(1), 3206) Kingsley, Jessica Pubs. GBR. Dist: Macmillan Distribution Ltd.

Feldman, Rachel S. The Little Tree. 2010. 32p. pap. 14.99 (978-1-4520-0033-6(6)) AuthorHouse.

Fields, Julianna. Foster Families. 2010. (Changing Face of Modern Families Ser.). (Illus.). 64p. (YA). (gr. 5-18). lib. bdg. 22.95 (978-1-4222-1497-8(4)) Mason Crest.

Fink, Thad. I Want You to Know, Son. Robert, J. Martin, illus. 2007. 26p. (J). (gr. -1-3). per. 11.99 (978-1-59879-260-7(1)) Lifevest Publishing, Inc.

Flack, Judy. We're Having a Baby: A Story for Jack. 2010. 32p. pap. 12.99 (978-1-4490-6873-8(1)) AuthorHouse.

Flaherty, Patrick F. & Harper, Steven. Life's Lessons from Dad: Quotes for Life Book Series. McLaughlin, Patrick, ed. 2004. per. 12.95 (978-0-9724178-5-3(0)) Tecknì-Corp, Ltd.

Ford, Vikke. Angel Anya's Adventures: Anya's Magic Heart. 2009. 28p. pap. 15.95 (978-1-4490-0698-3(1)) AuthorHouse.

Fox-Lee, Kyme & Fox-Lee, Susan. What Are Parents? Jennings, Randy, illus. 2007. 32p. (J). 15.95 (978-0-9753699-1-3(1)) StoryTyme Publishing.

Garcia, Justine Marie. While You Were Gone Year Two. Robin, Gulack, illus. 2012. 26p. pap. 12.95 (978-0-9836913-5-8(5)) Rose Bud Publishing Co. LLC.

Ginsburg, Sara. Look What My Parents Give Me. David, Racheli, illus. 2014. 29p. (J). (978-1-4226-1489-1(1)) Mesorah Pubns., Ltd.

Gorbett, Danea. Adopted Teens Only: A Survival Guide to Adolescence. 2007. 120p. per. 9.95 (978-1-58348-481-4(7), iUniverse Star) iUniverse, Inc.

Grollman, Earl A. Talking about Divorce & Separation: A Dialogue Between Parent & Child. Pitzer, Suzanne, illus. 2005. (J). (978-1-56123-155-3(X)) Centering Corp.

Hahn, Donna M. Staying Safe When I Go Out. 2009. 24p. pap. 12.00 (978-1-4389-6498-0(6)) AuthorHouse.

Hallinan, P. K. How Do I Love You? Hallinan, P. K., illus. 2006. (ENG., Illus.). 26p. (J). (gr. -1-k). 12.95 (978-0-8249-6650-8(3), Ideal Pubns.) Worthy Publishing.

Hewitt, Sally. My Stepfamily. 2009. (J). 28.50 (978-1-59920-229-7(8)) Black Rabbit Bks.

—Our New Baby. 2009. (J). 28.50 (978-1-59920-232-7(8)) Black Rabbit Bks.

Hilton, Marilyn Copley. The Christian Girl's Guide to Your Mom. 2004. (Illus.). 176p. (J). pap. 9.99 (978-1-58411-045-3(7), Legacy Pr.) Rainbow Pubs. & Legacy Pr.

Hinds, Sandra A. I Love You Every. 2012. 32p. pap. 19.99 (978-1-4567-2418-4(5)) AuthorHouse.

Jareaux, Marlena. 26 Things to Teach Your Parents. 2007. (Illus.). 76p. (YA). per. 10.95 (978-0-9790415-1-8(1)) Inspired by the Beach Co.

Johnson, Alberta & Johnson, Errick C. Twelve Roses for Ann. 2008. 40p. pap. 16.99 (978-1-4389-2988-0(9)) AuthorHouse.

Jones, Marla F. Ponder Learns to Be Thankful. 2010. 28p. pap. 13.99 (978-1-4490-8570-4(9)) AuthorHouse.

Kerley, Barbara. You & Me Together: Moms, Dads, & Kids Around the World. 2010. (Barbara Kerley Photo Inspirations Ser.). (ENG., Illus.). 32p. (J). (gr. -1-3). pap. 7.95 (978-1-4263-0623-5(7), National Geographic Children's Bks.) National Geographic Society.

—You & Me Together: Moms, Dads, & Kids Arounds the World. 2005. (Barbara Kerley Photo Inspirations Ser.). (ENG., Illus.). 32p. (J). (gr. -1-3). 25.90 (978-0-7922-8298-3(1), National Geographic Children's Bks.) National Geographic Society.

Kiers, Erin L. I Have Chakras Just Like You. 2012. 24p. pap. (978-1-4602-0343-9(7)) FriesenPress.

Kiesbye, Stefan. Is Parenthood a Right or a Privilege? 2009. (At Issue Ser.). (ENG., Illus.). 128p. (J). (gr. 10-12). 34.45 (978-0-7377-4430-9(8), Greenhaven Pr., Inc.) Cengage Gale.

Krohn, Katherine E. Everything You Need to Know about Birth Order. 2005. (Need to Know Library). (Illus.). 64p. (YA). (gr. 7-12). 31.95 (978-0-8239-3228-3(1), NTBIOR) Rosen Publishing Group, Inc., The.

Lovegrove, Emily. Help! I'm Being Bullied. 2007. (Illus.). 167p. per. (978-1-905170-34-0(3)) Accent Pr. Ltd.

MacAdam, Lea. You & Rules in Your Family. 2009. (Family Matters Ser.). 48p. (gr. 5-8). 53.00 (978-1-61512-483-1(7), Rosen Reference) Rosen Publishing Group, Inc., The.

Marks, Jennifer L. Parents. rev. ed. 2009. (People Ser.). (ENG.). 24p. (gr. k-1). lib. bdg. 21.99 (978-1-4296-2240-0(7), Pebble Bks.) Capstone Press of Coughlan Cos.

—Parents, 1 vol. rev. ed. 2009. (People Ser.). (ENG.). 24p. (gr. k-1). pap. 6.29 (978-1-4296-3463-2(4), Pebble Bks.) Capstone Press of Coughlan Cos.

Martin-Finks, Nancy. Custody Battle: A Workbook for Children. Barber, David L., illus. 2005. 68p. per. 19.95 (978-1-931636-42-1(7)) National Ctr. For Youth Issues.

Martinez, Victor. Parrot in the Oven. Scott, Steve, illus. rev. ed. 2004. (ENG.). 240p. (YA). (gr. 8-18). pap. 8.99 (978-0-06-447186-2(1), Rayo) HarperCollins Pubs.

Maxwell, Shannon. Our Daddy Is Invincible! Biggers, Liza, illus. 40p. (J). 2011. 15.95 (978-1-61751-003-8(3)) 2010. pap. 9.95 (978-1-61751-002-1(5)) Kurdyla, E L Publishing LLC. (4th Division Pr.).

McCloud, Carol. Baby's Bucket Book. Zimmer, Glenn, illus. 2014. (ENG.). 16p. (J). (— 1). bds. 7.95 (978-0-9960999-2-9(1)) Bucket Fillers, Inc.

Okoronkwo, Stella. Communication with Children & Youth: A Guide for Parents, Social & Youth Workers. 2nd ed. 2012. (Illus.). 152p. (gr. 4-6). 23.99 (978-1-4678-8176-0(7)); pap. 14.95 (978-1-4678-8175-3(9)) AuthorHouse.

Peltier, Sylvia M. Nanny & I. Peltier, Sylvia M., illus. 2003. (Illus.). 32p. (YA). (gr. -1-18). 16.95 (978-0-9724394-0-4(4)) Sylables.

Phelan,, Thomas W. & Lee, Tracy M. 1-2-3 Magic for Kids: Helping Your Kids Understand the New Rules. 2nd ed. 2017. (ENG., Illus.). 128p. pap. 9.99 (978-1-4926-4786-7(1), 9781492647867) Sourcebooks, Inc.

Pinto, Marie Parks. Does It Still Hurt. Mazzei, Miriam, illus. 2012. 30p. pap. 16.95 (978-1-938812-02-6(6)) Full Court Pr.

—I Am Not Broken. Mazzei, Miriam, illus. 2012. (ENG.). 30p. pap. 16.95 (978-1-938812-00-2(X)) Full Court Pr.

—Where Is Daddy? Mazzei, Miriam, illus. 2012. 30p. pap. 16.95 (978-1-938812-06-4(9)) Full Court Pr.

Publishing, Sterling. Daddy & Me. 2008. (Illus.). 12p. (J). bds. (978-1-934618-44-8(6)) Begin Smart LLC.

Ramnath, Vianna. Daddy Loves You! 2006. 22p. 11.99 (978-1-4116-8867-4(8)) Lulu Pr., Inc.

Rešcek, Sanja, illus. Bounce & Jiggle. 2007. (Baby Gym Ser.). (ENG.). 12p. (J). (gr. -1). bds. (978-1-84643-131-9(X)) Child's Play International Ltd.

—Calm & Soothe. 2007. (Baby Gym Ser.). (ENG.). 12p. (J). (gr. -1). bds. (978-1-84643-133-3(6)) Child's Play International Ltd.

—Touch & Tickle. 2007. (Baby Gym Ser.). (ENG.). 12p. (J). (gr. -1). bds. (978-1-84643-130-2(1)) Child's Play International Ltd.

—Wiggle & Move. 2007. (Baby Gym Ser.). (ENG.). 12p. (J). (gr. -1). bds. (978-1-84643-132-6(8)) Child's Play International Ltd.

Ridley, Sarah. Family. 2017. (Tell Me What You Remember Ser.). (ENG., Illus.). 24p. (J). (gr. k-2). 17.99 (978-1-4451-3985-2(5), Franklin Watts) Hachette Children's Group GBR. Dist: Hachette Bk. Group.

Rigby Education Staff. Visiting My Mom's Office. (Illus.). 8p. (J). bds. 3.95 (978-0-7635-6452-0(4), 764524C99) Rigby Education.

Rissman, Rebecca. Foster Parents, 1 vol. 2011. (Families Ser.). (ENG., Illus.). 24p. (gr. -1-1). 22.65 (978-1-4329-4657-9(9)); pap. 6.29 (978-1-4329-4665-4(X)) Heinemann-Raintree. (Acorn).

Ritchie, Jon. Babies Are Boring. Ritchie, Alex, illus. 2008. 40p. (J). (978-0-9809970-0-2(3)) Purple Possum Publishing Inc.

Rosenfeld, Dina. It's Called Kibud Av Va'Eim: A Story about Honoring Parents. Ebert, Len, illus. 2014. 20p. (J). 10.95 (978-1-929628-78-0(1)) Hachai Publishing.

Ross, Allison J. Coping When a Parent Is Mentally Ill. (Coping Ser.). 192p. (gr. 7-12). 2009. 63.90 (978-1-61511-987-5(6)) 2005. (Illus.). (YA). lib. bdg. 34.60 (978-0-8239-3359-4(8)) Rosen Publishing Group, Inc., The.

Sanschagrin, Joceline. At Grandma & Grandpa's. Brignaud, Pierre & Depratto, Marcel, illus. 2008. (Big Dipper Ser.). (ENG.). 24p. (J). (gr. -1-k). pap. 3.99 (978-2-89450-656-1(2)) Caillouet, Gerry.

Searching for the Words. 2nd ed. 2003. (J). spiral bd. (978-0-9718626-2-3(1)) Holofcener, Mark.

Sermons, Faye. My Granma Lives at the Airport. 2012. 20p. pap. 12.00 (978-1-4490-1893-1(9)) AuthorHouse.

Sharp, Zoe. I Help My Dad. 2007. (Windows on Literacy Ser.). (ENG., Illus.). 12p. pap. 10.95 (978-0-7922-8464-2(X)) National Geographic School Publishing, Inc.

Sheldon, Annette. Big Brother Now: A Story about Me & Our New Baby. Maizel, Karen, illus. 2008. 32p. (J). (gr. -1-1). 14.95 (978-1-4338-0381-9(X)); pap. 9.95 (978-1-4338-0382-6(8)) American Psychological Assn. (Magination Pr.).

—Big Sister Now: A Story about Me & Our New Baby. Maizel, Karen, illus. 2005. 32p. (J). (gr. -1-1). per. 9.95 (978-1-59147-244-5(X)); 14.95 (978-1-59147-243-8(1)) American Psychological Assn. (Magination Pr.).

Sherman, Aliza. Everything You Need to Know about Placing Your Baby for Adoption. 2009. (Need to Know Library). 64p. (gr. 5-5). 58.50 (978-1-60854-082-2(0)) Rosen Publishing Group, Inc., The.

Sidman, Joyce & Swan, Susan. Just Us Two: Poems about Dads. 2003. (Single Titles Ser.: Vol. 3). 32p. pap. 7.95 (978-0-7613-1833-0(X), Millbrook Pr.) Lerner Publishing Group.

Smith, Andrea Joy. Gladys Blackmon-Morrow: Let the Words from My Mouth... Be Acceptable in Thy Sight, O Lord...

Psalms 19:14: the Woman, the Wife, the Mother. 2005. (YA). per. 14.95 *(978-0-9764396-1-5(1))* Smith, Andrea Joy.
Snow, Judith E. How It Feels to Have a Gay or Lesbian Parent: A Book by Kids for Kids of All Ages. 2004. (ENG., Illus.). (C). 136p. 140.00 *(978-1-56023-419-7(9)*, HW14434); 130p. pap. 35.95 *(978-1-56023-420-3(2)*, HW14375) Routledge.
Solomon, Andrew. Far from the Tree. 2017. (J). pap. *(978-1-4814-4091-2(8)*, Simon & Schuster Bks. For Young Readers) Simon & Schuster Bks. For Young Readers.
—Far from the Tree: Young Adult Edition. 2017. (ENG., Illus.). 464p. (YA). (gr. 9). 18.99 *(978-1-4814-4090-5(X)*, Simon & Schuster Bks. For Young Readers) Simon & Schuster Bks. For Young Readers.
Sportelli-Rehak, Angela. Uncle Sam's Kids: When Duty Calls. Hinlicky, Gregg, illus. 2004. (Uncle Sam's Kids Ser.: Bk. 1). 40p. (gr. k-6). 15.95 *(978-0-9714515-1-3(6))* Abidenme Bks.
Stanton, Brandon. Little Humans. Stanton, Brandon, photos by. 2014. (ENG., Illus.). 40p. (J). (gr. -1-1). 17.99 *(978-0-374-37456-3(2)*, 9780374374563, Farrar, Straus & Giroux (BYR)) Farrar, Straus & Giroux.
Steinkraus, Kyla. ¡Paren de Discutir! 2012.Tr. of Stop Arguing. (SPA & ENG.). 24p. (gr. 2-3). pap. 8.95 *(978-1-61810-542-4(6))* Rourke Educational Media.
Steverson, Sylvia. I LOVE YOU Means... 2010. 32p. pap. 16.99 *(978-0-557-36954-6(1))* Lulu Pr., Inc.
Stewart, Rachel M. The Angel Inside Me. 2012. 46p. pap. 17.45 *(978-1-4525-5047-3(6))* Balboa Pr.
Sullivan, James Kevin, illus. What Went Right Today? Journal: WWRT Journal. 2007. 72p. (J). spiral bd. 12.95 *(978-0-9766990-1-9(X))* Buz-Land Presentations, Inc.
Thomas, Natasha. Mommy & Daddy Is There Really Greatness in Me? 2013. (ENG.). 24p. (J). pap. 34.95 *(978-1-4327-8767-7(5))* Outskirts Pr., Inc.
Thumann, Robin K. Peaceful Thoughts: An Interactive Journey in Positive Thinking for Children & Their Parents. Thumann, Robin K., illus. 2003. (Illus.). 44p. (J). (gr. -1-4). 19.95 *(978-0-9725118-0-3(6))* Peaceful Thoughts Pr.
Tomories, K. G. Someone Special for You to Know. 2010. 28p. pap. 13.99 *(978-1-4389-9651-6(9))* AuthorHouse.
Towne, Isobel & MacAdam, Lea. Dealing with Family Rules, 01 vols., 1. 2016. (Family Issues & You Ser.). (ENG.). 48p. (J). pap. 11.75 *(978-1-4994-3697-6(1)*, Rosen Central) Rosen Publishing Group, Inc., The.
Tsioumanis, Marina. Mum & Dad Are Separating: A Practical Resource for Separating Families & Family Therapy Professionals, 2 vols. 2017. (ENG., Illus.). 176p. (C). pap. 51.95 ***(978-0-86388-669-0(8)***, Y329910) Routledge.
Verdick, Elizabeth. Sharing Time. Heinlen, Marieka, illus. 2009. (Toddler Tools Ser.). (ENG.). 24p. (J). (gr. -1). 7.95 *(978-1-57542-314-2(6))* Free Spirit Publishing, Inc.
—Sharing Time/Tiempo para Compartir. Heinlen, Marieka, illus. 2016. (Toddler Tools Ser.). (SPA, ENG & MUL.). 24p. (J). 7.95 *(978-1-63198-096-1(3))* Free Spirit Publishing, Inc.
Young, Diana S. Daddy Doesn't Live with Me Anymore. 2010. 20p. pap. 10.83 *(978-1-4490-7550-7(9))* AuthorHouse.

PARENT AND CHILD—FICTION

Abegg, Rainbow G. Peaches & Prayers. 2004. (Illus.). 17.95 *(978-1-59156-049-4(7))* Covenant Communications, Inc.
Adler, David A. It's Time to Sleep, It's Time to Dream. Chorao, Kay, illus. 2009. (ENG.). 32p. (J). (gr. -1-k). 16.95 *(978-0-8234-1924-1(X))* Holiday Hse., Inc.
Adler, Denise. Thank You for Looking for Me. 2010. 20p. 12.99 *(978-1-4520-2438-7(3))* AuthorHouse.
Adler, Victoria. All of Baby Nose to Toes. Nakata, Hiroe, illus. 2011. (ENG.). 30p. (J). (gr. k — 1). bds. 6.99 *(978-0-8037-3531-6(6)*, Dial Bks) Penguin Young Readers Group.
Ahlberg, Janet & Ahlberg, Allan. Adiós Pequeño! Ahlberg, Janet & Ahlberg, Allan, illus. (Historias Para Dormir Ser.).Tr. of Bye Bye Baby. (SPA., Illus.). 28p. (J). (gr. k-3). 9.95 *(978-968-19-1039-6(7))* Aguilar Editorial MEX. Dist: Santillana USA Publishing Co., Inc.
Akchurin, Sergo. Canadian Story. 2011. 16p. 12.99 *(978-1-4269-5215-9(5))* Trafford Publishing.
Al-Araimi, Saif & Al-Rawahi, Thuria. Smart Parents Meet Mr Motivation (V2) 2010. 85p. pap. 16.40 *(978-0-557-20544-8(1))* Lulu Pr., Inc.
Albert, Louise. Less Than Perfect. 2003. (ENG.). 224p. (J). (gr. 7-18). tchr. ed. 17.95 *(978-0-8234-1688-2(7))* Holiday Hse., Inc.
Alborough, Jez. Hug. Alborough, Jez, illus. (ENG., Illus.). 32p. (J). 2009. (gr. -1-k). pap. 3.99 *(978-0-7636-4510-6(9))* 2005. (— 1). bds. 11.99 *(978-0-7636-2893-2(X))* Candlewick Pr.
Aldis, Dorothy & Collins, Heather. Hiding. (FRE.). (J). pap. 7.99 *(978-0-590-24195-3(8))* Scholastic, Inc.
Ambrosio, Michael. It Takes a Lot of Love. Awes, Jennifer, illus. 2007. 32p. (J). 14.95 *(978-0-9716085-4-2(7))* LionX Publishing.
Amollo, Regina. When Mother Leaves Home. 2004. (Illus.). 35p. pap. *(978-9970-02-435-3(3))* Fountain Pubs. Ltd. UGA. Dist: Michigan State Univ. Pr.
Anastas, Margaret. A Hug for You. Winter, Susan, photos by. 2005. (ENG., Illus.). 32p. (J). (gr. -1-1). 15.99 *(978-0-06-623613-1(4))* HarperCollins Pubs.
—Mommy's Best Kisses. Winter, Susan, illus. 2003. (ENG.). 32p. (J). (gr. -1-1). 17.99 *(978-0-06-623601-8(0))* HarperCollins Pubs.
Anderson, Constance. Smelling Sunshine, 1 vol. Anderson, Constance, illus. 2013. (ENG., Illus.). 32p. (J). 16.99 *(978-1-59572-635-3(7))*; pap. 6.99 *(978-1-59572-636-0(5))* Star Bright Bks., Inc.
Anderson, Laurie Halse. Catalyst. 2003. (ENG.). 256p. (YA). (gr. 7-18). pap. 8.99 *(978-0-14-240001-2(7)*, Speak) Penguin Young Readers Group.
Anderson, Peggy Perry. I Can Help! 2015. (Green Light Readers Level 1 Ser.). (ENG., Illus.). 32p. (J). (gr. 1-4). pap. 3.99 *(978-0-544-52801-7(8)*, HMH Books For Young Readers) Houghton Mifflin Harcourt Publishing Co.
Andreae, Giles. Keep Love in Your Heart, Little One. Vulliamy, Clara, illus. 2007. 32p. (J). (gr. -1-3). 15.95 *(978-1-58925-066-6(4))* Tiger Tales.
Anholt, Laurence. Cezanne & the Apple Boy. 2009. (ENG., Illus.). 32p. (J). (gr. -1-2). 16.99 *(978-0-7641-6282-4(9))* Barron's Educational Series, Inc.
Ashman, Linda. All We Know. Dyer, Jane, illus. 2016. 40p. (J). (gr. -1-3). 17.99 *(978-0-06-168958-1(0))* HarperCollins Pubs.
Atteberry, Kevan. I Love You More Than the Smell of Swamp Gas. Atteberry, Kevan, illus. 2017. (Illus.). 40p. (J). (gr. -1-3). 17.99 ***(978-0-06-240871-6(2))*** HarperCollins Pubs.
Augustine, Kristen. Can I Tell You? 2005. 9.00 *(978-0-8059-8071-4(7))* Dorrance Publishing Co., Inc.
Ault, Kelly. Let's Sign, Baby! A Fun & Easy Way to Talk with Baby. Landry, Leo, illus. abr. ed. 2010. (ENG.). 40p. (J). (gr. k — 1). bds. 7.99 *(978-0-547-31596-6(1))* Houghton Mifflin Harcourt Publishing Co.
Babcock, Nabila. My Child, My Love. 2012. 24p. 24.95 *(978-1-4626-5214-3(X))* PublishAmerica, Inc.
Bacchus, Tamika D. Plain Jane Learns to Pray. 2011. 48p. pap. 19.99 *(978-1-61379-455-5(X))* Salem Author Services.
Baer, Julie. Love Me Later. 2005. (Illus.). 28p. (J). (gr. -1-3). 16.99 *(978-1-932188-03-5(7))* Bollix Bks.
Bailey, Tressie. The Little Box Kittens. 2009. 37p. pap. 20.50 *(978-0-557-02639-5(3))* Lulu Pr., Inc.
Baker, Liza, et al. I Love You: A Keepsake Storybook Collection. Bryan, Beth, ed. 2006. (ENG., Illus.). 144p. (J). (gr. -1-k). 10.99 *(978-0-439-84799-5(0)*, Cartwheel Bks.) Scholastic, Inc.
Balla, Trace. Shine: A Story about Saying Goodbye. Balla, Trace, illus. 2016. (ENG., Illus.). 24p. (J). (gr. -1-1). 15.99 *(978-1-74331-634-4(8))* Allen & Unwin AUS. Dist: Independent Pubs. Group.
Ballengee, Fran. Sara Elizabeth, an Adoption Story. 2008. 22p. pap. 24.95 *(978-1-60610-557-3(4))* PublishAmerica, Inc.
Balzac, Honoré De. Le Pere Goriot. (FRE.). (YA). (gr. 7-12). 9.95 *(978-0-88436-043-8(1)*, 40280) EMC/Paradigm Publishing.
Banting, Celia. I Only Said I Didn't Want You Because I Was Terrified. 2006. (I Only Said Ser.: 4). 240p. (YA). pap. 14.99 *(978-0-9786648-3-1(3))* Wighita Pr.
Barber, Barbara E. Saturday at the New You. Rich, Anna, illus. 2013. (ENG.). 32p. (J). (gr. -1-3). reprint ed. pap. 9.95 *(978-1-880000-43-4(1))* Lee & Low Bks., Inc.
Barkow, Henriette. That's My Mum. Brazell, Derek, illus. 2004. 28p. (J). (ENG & YOR.). pap. *(978-1-84444-381-9(7))*; (ALB & ENG.). pap. *(978-1-85269-595-8(1))* Mantra Lingua.
Bateman, Teresa. Hunting the Daddyosaurus. Huang, Benrei, illus. 2004. 29p. (J). (gr. k-4). reprint ed. 16.00 *(978-0-7567-7796-8(8))* DIANE Publishing Co.
Battle-Lavert, Gwendolyn. Papa's Mark. Bootman, Colin, illus. 2003. (ENG.). 32p. (J). (gr. k-3). tchr. ed. 17.95 *(978-0-8234-1650-9(X))* Holiday Hse., Inc.
Bauer, Joan. Tell Me. 2014. (ENG.). 272p. (J). (gr. 5). 16.99 *(978-0-451-47033-1(8)*, Viking Books for Young Readers) Penguin Young Readers Group.
Beaton, Kate. King Baby. 2016. (Dog Tags Ser.). (ENG., Illus.). 40p. (J). (gr. -1-3). 17.99 *(978-0-545-63754-1(6))* Scholastic, Inc.
Beaudette, Cathy. The Boss of Me. Beaudette, Michelle, illus. 2011. 32p. pap. *(978-1-77067-350-2(4))* FriesenPress.
Bechard, Margaret E. & Bechard, Margaret. Hanging on to Max. 2003. (ENG., Illus.). 176p. (YA). (gr. 7). pap. 9.99 *(978-0-689-86268-7(7)*, Simon Pulse) Simon Pulse.
Becker, Christie. You Will Be My Baby Even When. Brayton, Julie, illus. 2003. 32p. (J). (gr. -1-1). 14.95 *(978-0-9728116-0-6(5))* Becker, Christie.
Beckerman, Menucha. A Surprise for Mommy. 2003. (My Middos World Ser.: Vol. 4). (Illus.). 34p. (J). (gr. k-5). 5.95 *(978-1-931681-10-0(4))* Israel Bookshop Pubns.
Beckford, Avril. I Love You 65 Bulldozers. 2009. 36p. pap. 15.49 *(978-1-4389-4048-9(3))* AuthorHouse.
Bedford, David. Love Is a Magical Feeling. Butler, John, illus. 2016. (Snuggle Time Stories Ser.). (ENG.). 32p. (J). (gr. -1-k). 9.95 *(978-1-4549-1684-0(2))* Sterling Publishing Co., Inc.
Benson, Nicky. I Love You More & More. Lambert, Jonny, illus. 2016. (ENG.). 24p. (J). (gr. -1-k). bds. 9.99 *(978-1-58925-227-1(6))* Tiger Tales.
Bently, Peter. Meet the Parents. Ogilvie, Sara, illus. 2014. (ENG.). 32p. (J). (gr. -1-3). 17.99 *(978-1-4814-1483-8(6)*, Simon & Schuster/Paula Wiseman Bks.) Simon & Schuster/Paula Wiseman Bks.
Berenstain, Stan & Berenstain, Jan. The Berenstain Bears Meet Santa Bear (Deluxe Edition) 2016. (First Time Books(R) Ser.). (ENG., Illus.). 32p. (J). (gr. -1-2). pap. 6.99 *(978-0-399-55767-5(9)*, Random Hse. Bks. for Young Readers) Random Hse. Children's Bks.
Bess, Stacey. Planting More Than Pansies: A Fable about Love. Ricks, Melissa, illus. 2003. (J). 14.95 *(978-1-57008-893-3(4)*, Shadow Mountain) Shadow Mountain Publishing.
Beverly, Cleary. Dear Mr. Henshaw. 2014. (Cleary Reissue Ser.). (ENG.). 160p. (J). (gr. 7-12). 10.24 *(978-1-63245-195-8(6))* Lectorum Pubns., Inc.
Bigler, Ashley Hansen. Once upon a Time: An Adoption Story. Hintz, Amy, illus. 2010. (J). pap. 12.99 *(978-1-59955-310-8(4))* Cedar Fort, Inc./CFI Distribution.
Binch, Caroline. The Princess & the Castle. Binch, Caroline, illus. 2005. (ENG., Illus.). 32p. (J). (gr. k-2). 8.99 *(978-0-09-943236-4(6)*, Red Fox) Random House Children's Books GBR. Dist: Independent Pubs. Group.
Birkett, Georgie, illus. Fix It!/¡A Reparar! 2009. (Helping Hands English/Spanish Edition Ser.). (ENG & SPA.). 24p. (J). (gr. -1-k). pap. *(978-1-84643-571-3(4))* Child's Play International Ltd.
—Grow It!/¡A Sembrar! 2009. (Helping Hands English/Spanish Edition Ser.). (ENG & SPA.). 24p. (J). (gr. -1-k). pap. *(978-1-84643-570-6(6))* Child's Play International Ltd.
Blair, Candice. Rosie's Pink House, 1 vol. Cato, Andrea, illus. 2010. 18p. 24.95 *(978-1-4489-4619-8(0))* America Star Bks.
Blanks, Morgan Georgia. The Desert Island. 2008. 52p. pap. 20.49 *(978-1-4343-9006-6(3))* AuthorHouse.
Blocker, Adam P. Joshua & the Spider. Taylor, Josh, illus. 2013. (ENG.). 72p. 17.99 *(978-1-939418-08-1(9))* Writer of the Round Table Pr.
Bloom, Deb-b. The Bird Who Could Fly. 2008. 24p. pap. 24.95 *(978-1-60441-383-0(2))* America Star Bks.
Bonasia, Steve. Dominic & the Secret Ingredient. Van Norstrand, Kain, illus. 2012. (ENG.). 39p. (J). pap. 24.95 *(978-1-4327-9805-5(7))* Outskirts Pr., Inc.
Bondoux, Anne-Laure. The Princetta. Bell, Anthea, tr. 2008. (ENG.). 448p. (YA). (gr. 6-12). pap. 10.99 *(978-1-59990-098-8(X)*, 9781599900988, Bloomsbury USA Childrens) Bloomsbury Publishing USA.
Bonnell, Kris. A Walk with Dad. 2006. (J). pap. 5.95 *(978-1-933727-43-1(8))* Reading Reading Bks., LLC.
Borden, Louise. The Little Ships: The Heroic Rescue at Dunkirk in World War II. Foreman, Michael, illus. 2003. (ENG.). 32p. (J). (gr. 4-7). 7.99 *(978-0-689-85396-8(3)*, McElderry, Margaret K. Bks.) McElderry, Margaret K. Bks.
Borntrager, Mary Christner. Polly. 2015. (ENG.). 176p. (YA). (gr. 4-7). pap. 9.99 *(978-0-8361-3670-8(5))* Herald Pr.
Boyd, David. Closer to Hamlet. 2003. 120p. (YA). (gr. 6-9). pap. *(978-0-921156-93-2(6))* Rubicon Publishing, Inc.
Boynton, Sandra. Snuggle Puppy! 2003. (ENG., Illus.). 24p. (J). (gr. k — 1). bds. 6.95 *(978-0-7611-3067-3(5)*, 13067) Workman Publishing Co., Inc.
Bracken, Beth. Henry Helps Plant a Garden, 1 vol. Busby, Ailie, illus. 2012. (Henry Helps Ser.). (ENG.). 24p. (gr. -1 — 1). pap. 5.95 *(978-1-4048-7670-5(7))*; lib. bdg. 22.65 *(978-1-4048-7305-6(8))* Picture Window Bks. (Henry Helps).
Brandeis, Madeline. Mitz & Fritz of Germany. 2011. 164p. 41.95 *(978-1-258-10138-1(6))* Literary Licensing, LLC.
Braun, Sebastien. On Our Way Home. 2009. (ENG., Illus.). 32p. (J). (gr. -1-k). 14.95 *(978-1-906250-59-1(6))* Boxer Bks., Ltd. GBR. Dist: Sterling Publishing Co., Inc.
Brink Hull, Amanda. Maslyn: A Different Kind of Name for a Delightful Little Girl. 2009. (Illus.). 36p. pap. 16.99 *(978-1-4389-9338-6(2))* AuthorHouse.
Brooks, Bertha. The Big Fishing Trip. 2004. (Illus.). 32p. (J). 12.00 *(978-1-58374-086-6(4))* Chicago Spectrum Pr.
Brooks, Martha. Bone Dance, 1 vol. 2005. (ENG.). 184p. (J). (gr. 6-16). pap. 8.95 *(978-0-88899-336-6(6))* Groundwood Bks. CAN. Dist: Publishers Group West (PGW).
Brooks, Robert. Sonrieta. Urban, Helle, illus. 2008. 40p. (YA). 17.95 *(978-0-9792294-0-4(5))* Mystic Jaguar Publishing.
Brown, Jo. Where's My Mommy? 2004. (Illus.). 32p. (J). tchr. ed. 14.95 *(978-1-58925-019-2(2))* Tiger Tales.
Brown, Margaret Wise. The Runaway Bunny. Hurd, Clement, illus. 2017. (ENG.). (J). (gr. -1 — 1). 36p. bds. 12.99 *(978-0-694-01671-6(3))*; 34p. bds. 8.99 *(978-0-06-107429-5(2))* HarperCollins Pubs. (HarperFestival).
Brown, Petra. When the Wind Blew. Brown, Petra, illus. 2017. (ENG., Illus.). 32p. (J). (gr. k-3). 16.99 *(978-1-58536-969-0(1)*, 204234) Sleeping Bear Pr.
Brown, Susan Taylor. Oliver's Must-Do List. Sullivan, Mary, illus. 2005. (ENG.). 32p. (J). (gr. -1-1). 15.95 *(978-1-59078-198-2(8))* Boyds Mills Pr.
Brunell, Heather. Bedtime Monster. Adamson, Bonnie, illus. 2010. (ENG.). 32p. (J). (gr. -1-12). lib. bdg. 16.95 *(978-1-934960-03-5(9)*, Raven Tree Pr.,Csi) Continental Sales, Inc.
—Bedtime Monster/A Dormir, Monstruito! Del Risco, Eida & de la Vega, Eida, trs. 2010. (ENG & SPA., Illus.). 32p. (J). (gr. -1-3). pap. 7.95 *(978-1-932748-81-9(4)*, Raven Tree Pr.,Csi) Continental Sales, Inc.
—Bedtime Monster/A Dormir, Monstruito! de la Vega, Eida, tr. Adamson, Bonnie, illus. 2010. (ENG & SPA.). 32p. (J). (gr. -1-3). lib. bdg. 16.95 *(978-1-932748-80-2(6)*, Raven Tree Pr.,Csi) Continental Sales, Inc.
Bunting, Eve. Flower Garden. Hewitt, Kathryn, illus. 2004. 28p. (gr. -1-2). 17.00 *(978-0-7569-4113-0(X))* Perfection Learning Corp.
—My Mom's Wedding. Papp, Lisa, illus. 2006. (ENG.). 32p. (J). (gr. k-6). 16.95 *(978-1-58536-288-2(3))* Sleeping Bear Pr.
Burnett, Frances Hodgson. Editha's Burglar. Sandham, Henry, illus. 2005. reprint ed. pap. 15.95 *(978-1-4179-0135-7(7))* Kessinger Publishing, LLC.
Burns, Joanne. No Says the Baby When You Say Yes, a book about the terrible Twos. 2005. 1p. 5.68 *(978-1-4116-3386-5(5))* Lulu Pr., Inc.
Burton, Linda & Burton, Carl. Pay Attention, Emily Brown! Burton, Linda & Burton, Carl, illus. 2011. (Illus.). 32p. (J). *(978-1-60613-027-8(7))* Woodbine Hse.
Byrne, Barbara. Megan's Moon. 2004. 18p. 14.87 *(978-1-4116-1008-8(3))* Lulu Pr., Inc.
C., Brandi & Flanagan, Logan. City Mom Country Dad. 2009. pap. *(978-1-61584-398-5(1))* Independent Pub.
C. Larene Hall. Martha's Freedom Train. 2009. 100p. pap. 10.49 *(978-1-4389-7977-9(0))* AuthorHouse.
Cabrera, Jane. Mommy, Carry Me Please! Cabrera, Jane, illus. 2006. (ENG., Illus.). 32p. (J). (gr. 3-6). 16.95 *(978-0-8234-1935-7(5))* Holiday Hse., Inc.
A Cake for Mom: Individual Title Six-Packs. (gr. -1-2). 23.00 *(978-0-7635-8997-4(7))* Rigby Education.
Calabrese, Diane Marie. My Dad's off to War. Swope, Brenda, illus. 2011. 28p. pap. 24.95 *(978-1-4560-0942-7(7))* America Star Bks.
Calabrese, Dianne. The Inspirational Guide, 1 vol. 2010. 24p. 24.95 *(978-1-4489-4844-4(4))* PublishAmerica, Inc.
Calaf, Monica. How You Were Born. Fuentes, Mikel, illus. 2014. (ENG.). 48p. (J). (gr. -1-3). 9.99 *(978-1-78066-125-4(8))* Pinter & Martin Ltd. GBR. Dist: National Bk. Network.
Calvert, Patricia. Bigger. Minor, Wendell, illus. 2003. (ENG.). 144p. (J). (gr. 3-7). pap. 8.95 *(978-0-689-86003-4(X)*, Simon & Schuster/Paula Wiseman Bks.) Simon & Schuster/Paula Wiseman Bks.
Campbell, H. David. Merribell: A Comforting Story. 2011. 218p. (gr. 2-2). 23.95 *(978-1-4620-4477-1(8))*; pap. 13.95 *(978-1-4620-4476-4(X))* iUniverse, Inc.
Capucilli, Alyssa Satin. Panda Kisses. Widdowson, Kay, illus. 2008. (Step into Reading Ser.). (ENG.). 32p. (J). (gr. -1-1). pap. 3.99 *(978-0-375-84562-8(3)*, Random Hse. Bks. for Young Readers) Random Hse. Children's Bks.
Caraballo, Samuel. Mis Papitos: Heroes de la Cosecha. Gomez, Obed, illus. 2005. (ENG & SPA.). 32p. (J). (gr. -1-3). 16.95 *(978-1-55885-450-5(9)*, Piñata Books) Arte Publico Pr.
Carle, Eric. Mister Seahorse. Carle, Eric, illus. 2004. (ENG., Illus.). 32p. (J). (gr. -1-k). 18.99 *(978-0-399-24269-4(4)*, Philomel Bks.) Penguin Young Readers Group.
Carlson, Lavelle. Eek! I Hear a Squeak & the Scurrying of Little Feet. Loehr, Jenny, illus. 2006. (ENG.). 28p. (J). (gr. -1-3). 19.95 incl. audio compact disk *(978-0-9725803-8-0(7))* Children's Publishing.
Carlstrom, Nancy White & Saport, Linda. Before You Were Born. Saport, Linda, illus. 2004. (Illus.). 32p. (J). (gr. -1-k). 17.00 *(978-0-8028-5185-7(1))* Eerdmans, William B. Publishing Co.
Carolan, Jill. Sadie's Bargain. 2008. 148p. pap. 10.94 *(978-0-615-26231-4(7))* Never Quit Productions, Inc.
Carr, Dorothy. Snow Goes Home. 2011. 24p. pap. 15.99 *(978-1-4628-6701-1(4))* Xlibris Corp.
Carr, Karen. The Christmas Wishing Quilt. 2008. 24p. pap. 12.99 *(978-1-4389-1353-7(2))* AuthorHouse.
Casciano, Christie & Moziak, Rose Mary Casciano, illus. Haunted Hockey in Lake Placid. 2012. 72p. (J). pap. *(978-1-59531-040-8(1))* North Country Bks., Inc.
Cassidy, Colette. DIVCO, the Little Milk Truck. 2007. (Illus.). 28p. (J). pap. 7.99 *(978-0-615-17346-7(2))* Redcay Publishing.
Catalanotto, Peter. The Newbies. Catalanotto, Peter, illus. 2015. (ENG., Illus.). 40p. (J). (gr. -1-3). 17.99 *(978-1-4814-1892-8(0))* Simon & Schuster Children's Publishing.
Centeio, Tara Jaye. Mommy Loves Her Baby. Date not set. 32p. (J). (gr. -1-1). pap. 5.99 *(978-0-06-443715-8(9))* HarperCollins Pubs.
Cerrito, Dana. On the Day Love Was Born. Gallegos, Lauren, illus. 2011. 24p. (J). pap. 10.95 *(978-0-9835048-0-1(6))* Little Hill Pubs.
Chamberlain, Karen, et al. A Feather for the Queen. 2009. 28p. pap. 13.95 *(978-1-4490-3903-5(0))* AuthorHouse.
Charlip, Remy. A Perfect Day. 2007. (Illus.). 40p. (J). (gr. -1). lib. bdg. 17.89 *(978-0-06-051973-5(8))* HarperCollins Pubs.
Chayce, Jorden. How High Is Up? 2011. 36p. pap. 24.95 *(978-1-4560-6999-5(3))* America Star Bks.
Chronicle Books Staff. Thumbelina. Capdevila, Francesc, illus. 2004. (Bilingual Fairy Tales Ser.: BILI). (ENG & SPA.). 32p. (J). (gr. -1-7). pap. 6.99 *(978-0-8118-3928-0(1))* Chronicle Bks. LLC.
Church, Caroline Jayne. Giggle! Church, Caroline Jayne, illus. 2013. (ENG., Illus.). 10p. (J). (— 1). bds. 7.99 *(978-0-545-35082-2(4)*, Cartwheel Bks.) Scholastic, Inc.
—I Love You! Church, Caroline Jayne, illus. 2012. (ENG., Illus.). 6p. (J). (— 1). 12.99 *(978-0-545-46140-5(5)*, Cartwheel Bks.) Scholastic, Inc.
A City Garden, 6 Packs. (gr. -1-2). 27.00 *(978-0-7635-9441-1(5))* Rigby Education.
Clara Mulholland. Naughty Miss Bunny. 2007. 128p. per. 10.95 *(978-1-4218-3938-7(5)*, 1st World Library - Literary Society) 1st World Publishing, Inc.
Clarke, Judith. Al Capsella & Watchdogs. 164p. pap. *(978-0-7022-2294-8(1))* Univ. of Queensland Pr.
Cleary, Beverly. Ramona & Her Mother. Tiegreen, Alan et al, illus. 2013. (Ramona Ser.: 5). (ENG.). 224p. (J). (gr. 3-7). 16.99 *(978-0-688-22195-9(5))* HarperCollins Pubs.
—Ramona & Her Mother. Tiegreen, Alan & Rogers, Jacqueline, illus. 2013. (Ramona Ser.: 5). (ENG.). 224p. (J). (gr. 3-7). reprint ed. pap. 7.99 *(978-0-380-70952-6(X))* HarperCollins Pubs.
—Ramona & Her Mother. (Ramona Quimby Ser.). 208p. (J). (gr. 3-5). pap. 4.99 *(978-0-8072-1435-0(3)*, Listening Library) Random Hse. Audio Publishing Group.
Clements, Andrew. The Last Holiday Concert. Selznick, Brian, illus. 2004. (ENG.). 176p. (J). (gr. 3-7). 17.99 *(978-0-689-84516-1(2)*, Atheneum Bks. for Young Readers) Simon & Schuster Children's Publishing.
Cochran, Bill. My Parents Are Divorced My Elbows Have Nicknames & Other Fact. Björkman, Steve, illus. 2009. (ENG.). 32p. (J). (gr. -1-3). 17.99 *(978-0-06-053942-9(9))* HarperCollins Pubs.
Coffey, M. Carol. Zoe Lucky: And the Green Gables' Mystery. 2008. 156p. pap. 12.95 *(978-1-4327-3190-8(4))* Outskirts Pr., Inc.
Coleman, Evelyn. Mystery of the Dark Tower. 2009. (Mysteries Through Time Ser.). 160p. (YA). (gr. 4-8). 31.95 *(978-1-60754-188-2(2))*; pap. 15.25 *(978-1-60754-189-9(0))* Windmill Bks.
Collins, Yvonne & Rideout, Sandy. The Black Sheep. 2007. 348p. (J). *(978-1-4287-4665-7(X))* Hyperion Pr.
Conlon-McKenna, Marita. Under the Hawthorn Tree. Teskey, Donald, illus. 2003. 160p. pap. 5.95 *(978-0-86278-206-1(6))* O'Brien Pr., Ltd., The IRL. Dist: Independent Pubs. Group.
Cook, Julia. Scoop. Ventling, Elisabeth, illus. 2007. 32p. (J). 15.95 *(978-1-934073-07-0(5))* National Ctr. For Youth Issues.
Cooney, Caroline B. The Face on the Milk Carton. 2009. 9.14 *(978-0-7848-0397-4(8)*, Everbind) Marco Bk. Co.
—The Face on the Milk Carton. 2012. (ENG.). 208p. (YA). (gr. 7). pap. 9.99 *(978-0-385-74238-2(X)*, Ember) Random Hse. Children's Bks.
—The Face on the Milk Carton. 2012. (Janie Bks.: 1). lib. bdg. 20.85 *(978-0-606-26368-9(3)*, Turtleback) Turtleback Bks.
—The Voice on the Radio. 2012. (ENG.). 208p. (YA). (gr. 7). pap. 9.99 *(978-0-385-74240-5(1)*, Ember) Random Hse. Children's Bks.
—The Voice on the Radio. 2012. (Janie Bks.: 3). lib. bdg. 20.85 *(978-0-606-26369-6(1)*, Turtleback) Turtleback Bks.
—What Janie Found. 2012. (ENG.). 208p. (YA). (gr. 7). pap. 9.99 *(978-0-385-74241-2(X)*, Ember) Random Hse. Children's Bks.
—What Janie Found. 2012. (Janie Bks.: 4). lib. bdg. 20.85 *(978-0-606-26370-2(5)*, Turtleback) Turtleback Bks.
—Whatever Happened to Janie? 2012. (ENG.). 224p. (YA). (gr. 7). pap. 9.99 *(978-0-385-74239-9(8)*, Ember) Random Hse. Children's Bks.
Cooper, Judith. Many Moons. 2008. 28p. per. 24.95 *(978-1-4241-9284-7(6))* America Star Bks.
Corentin, Philippe. Papa! (SPA.). 32p. *(978-84-95150-38-7(7))* Corimbo, Editorial S.L.
—Papa. 2003. (SPA.). (J). (gr. -1-k). 19.99 *(978-84-8470-094-4(1))* Corimbo, Editorial S.L. ESP. Dist: Lectorum Pubns., Inc.
Cosmic Debris Etc., Inc. Staff & Chronicle Books Staff. Thumbelina. Max, illus. 2004. (Bilingual Fairy Tales Ser.: BILI). (ENG & SPA.). 32p. (J). (gr. -1-7). 14.99 *(978-0-8118-3927-3(3))* Chronicle Bks. LLC.
Cowell, Cressida & Mayhew, James. Emily Brown: Emily Brown & the Elephant Emergency. Layton, Neal, illus. 2015. (Emily Brown Ser.). (ENG.). 32p. (J). (gr. -1-k). pap. 10.99 *(978-1-4449-2343-8(9))* Hodder & Stoughton GBR. Dist: Hachette Bk. Group.
Coyle, Carmela Lavigna. Do Princesses Really Kiss Frogs? Gordon, Mike & Gordon, Carl, illus. 2005. (ENG.). 32p. (J).

(gr. -1-2). 15.95 *(978-0-87358-880-5(0))* Cooper Square Publishing Llc.

Creech, Sharon. Absolutely Normal Chaos. 2012. (Walk Two Moons Ser.: 2). (ENG.). 256p. (J). (gr. 4-18). pap. 7.99 *(978-0-06-440632-1(6))* HarperCollins Pubs.

—Fishing in the Air. Raschka, Chris, illus. 2003. (ENG.). 32p. (J). (gr. -1-3). pap. 6.99 *(978-0-06-051606-2(2))* HarperCollins Pubs.

—Fishing in the Air, 4 bks. Raschka, Chris, illus. 2003. (J). pap. 37.95 incl. audio *(978-1-59112-226-5(0))* Live Oak Media.

—Fishing in the Air. 2003. (J). (gr. k-3). 17.20 *(978-0-613-66967-2(3),* Turtleback) Turtleback Bks.

Crist-Evans, Craig. Moon over Tennessee: A Boy's Civil War Journal. Christensen, Bonnie, illus. 2003. (ENG.). 64p. (J). (gr. 5-7). pap. 8.95 *(978-0-618-31107-1(6))* Houghton Mifflin Harcourt Publishing Co.

Crosson, Denise D. Mommy's Gone to Treatment. Motz, Mike, illus. 2008. (ENG.). 44p. (J). (gr. k-3). pap. 14.95 *(978-0-9799869-1-8(5))* Central Recovery Pr.

Crowe, Chris. The Mississippi Trial 1955. 2003. (gr. 7-12). lib. bdg. 16.00 *(978-0-613-86522-7(7),* Turtleback) Turtleback Bks.

Cruise, Robin. Only You. Chodos-Irvine, Margaret, illus. 2016. (ENG.). 40p. (J). (— 1). 7.99 *(978-0-544-66832-4(4),* HMH Books For Young Readers) Houghton Mifflin Harcourt Publishing Co.

Crutcher, Chris. Ironman. 2004. (ENG.). 288p. (YA). (gr. 8). pap. 9.99 *(978-0-06-059840-2(9),* Greenwillow Bks.) HarperCollins Pubs.

Cummings, Suzy Lynch. Oh Goodness, Oh Gracious! What Have I Done to my Family? 2009. 28p. pap. 13.99 *(978-1-4490-2408-6(4))* AuthorHouse.

Currinder, Michael. Running Full Tilt. 2017. (ENG.). 336p. (YA). (gr. 7). lib. bdg. 17.99 ***(978-1-58089-802-7(5),*** Charlesbridge Teen) Charlesbridge Publishing, Inc.

Cushenberry, Lisa. No Tears for Teary. 2009. 84p. pap. 9.99 *(978-1-60860-556-9(6),* Strategic Bk. Publishing) Strategic Book Publishing & Rights Agency (SBPRA).

Cusimano Love, Maryann & Ichikawa, Satomi. You Are My Miracle (Tú Eres Mi Milagro) 2016. (SPA & ENG., Illus.). 28p. (J). (— 1). bds. 7.99 *(978-0-399-54734-8(7),* Philomel Bks.) Penguin Young Readers Group.

Daddy I Wanna Be A Lawyer: And Make Lots of Money. 2004. lib. bdg. 12.95 *(978-1-932762-08-2(6))* Elderberry Press, Inc.

Dannenbring, McKinsey. A Lemon Without the Sour. 2009. 32p. pap. 14.49 *(978-1-4389-2367-3(8))* AuthorHouse.

Danziger, Paula. Amber Brown Is Feeling Blue. 2010. (Amber Brown Ser.: 7). (ENG.). 160p. (J). (gr. 2-5). 5.99 *(978-0-14-241686-0(X),* Puffin Books) Penguin Young Readers Group.

—Amber Brown Is Feeling Blue. 2004. (Amber Brown Ser.: No. 7). 131p. (J). (gr. 2-4). pap. 17.00 incl. audio *(978-0-8072-2063-4(9),* Listening Library) Random Hse. Audio Publishing Group.

—Amber Brown Is Feeling Blue. 2010. (Amber Brown Ser.: 7). (gr. 3-6). lib. bdg. 16.00 *(978-0-613-20096-7(9),* Turtleback) Turtleback Bks.

—The Divorce Express. 2007. (ENG.). 208p. (J). (gr. 5-18). 8.99 *(978-0-14-240712-7(7),* Puffin Books) Penguin Young Readers Group.

—Es Dia de Feria, Ambar Dorado. Ross, Tony, illus. 2007. (de Ambar / a Is for Amber Easy-To-Read Ser.).Tr. of It's a Fair Day, Amber Brown. (SPA.). 48p. (gr. k-3). pap. 8.95 *(978-1-59820-596-1(X))* Santillana USA Publishing Co., Inc.

—I, Amber Brown. Ross, Tony, illus. 2011. (Amber Brown Ser.: 8). (ENG.). 160p. (J). (gr. 2-5). 5.99 *(978-0-14-241965-6(6),* Puffin Books) Penguin Young Readers Group.

—I, Amber Brown. 2004. (Amber Brown Ser.: No. 8). 144p. (J). (gr. 2-4). pap. 17.00 incl. audio *(978-0-8072-2064-1(7),* Listening Library) Random Hse. Audio Publishing Group.

—It's a Fair Day, Amber Brown. Ross, Tony, illus. 2003. pap. 31.95 incl. audio compact disk *(978-1-59112-564-8(2));* pap. 31.95 incl. audio compact disk *(978-1-59112-564-8(2));* (J). (gr. -1-2). audio compact disk 28.95 *(978-1-59112-565-5(0));* (J). (gr. -1-2). audio compact disk 28.95 *(978-1-59112-565-5(0))* Live Oak Media.

—It's a Fair Day, Amber Brown. Ross, Tony, illus. 2003. (Is for Amber Ser.). (ENG.). 48p. (J). (gr. 1-3). pap. 3.99 *(978-0-698-11982-6(7),* Penguin Young Readers) Penguin Young Readers Group.

—It's a Fair Day, Amber Brown. 2003. (Young Amber Brown Easy-To-Read Ser.: 4). (gr. k-3). lib. bdg. 13.55 *(978-0-613-61635-5(9),* Turtleback) Turtleback Bks.

Danziger, Paula & Mazer, Anne. Is Green with Envy. Ross, Tony, illus. 2004. (Amber Brown Ser.: 9). (ENG.). 160p. (J). (gr. 2-5). pap. 4.99 *(978-0-439-07171-0(2),* Scholastic Paperbacks) Scholastic, Inc.

David, Stuart. My Brilliant Idea (and How It Caused My Downfall) 2017. (ENG.). 240p. (YA). (gr. 7). pap. 9.99 *(978-0-544-93886-1(0),* HMH Books For Young Readers) Houghton Mifflin Harcourt Publishing Co.

Davidson, Barbara. Billys Most Difficult Choice. 2007. 49p. 16.95 *(978-1-4241-6153-9(3))* America Star Bks.

Davis, Helen J. Good Times with Gregory: Birds: Rescuing a Baby Bird. Davis, Robyn L., illus. 2008. (Good Times with Gregory Ser.). 54p. (J). (gr. -1-4). 12.95 *(978-1-935122-10-4(X))* K&B Products.

Davis, Melissa. Denny the Duck. 2008. 25p. pap. 24.95 *(978-1-60672-712-6(5))* America Star Bks.

Day, Kathleen. The Sweet Song of Rainbow Bird. 2012. 32p. pap. 14.75 *(978-1-4669-3555-6(3))* Trafford Publishing.

de Silva, Eugenie. The Adventures of Princess Eugenie. 2008. 35p. pap. 24.65 *(978-0-557-01213-8(9))* Lulu Pr., Inc.

De Smet, Marian. Anna's Tight Squeeze. Meijer, Marja, illus. 2003. Orig. Title: Op Slot. 32p. (J). pap. 5.95 *(978-1-58925-378-0(7))* Tiger Tales.

Deans, Sis Boulos. Racing the Past. 2005. (ENG.). 160p. (J). (gr. 3-7). reprint ed. 5.99 *(978-0-14-240308-2(3),* Puffin Books) Penguin Young Readers Group.

DeKeyser, Stacy. Jump the Cracks. 2008. (ENG.). 216p. (YA). (gr. 7-18). per. 9.95 *(978-0-7387-1274-1(4),* Flux) North Star Editions.

Delaney, Mark. Pepperland, 1 vol. 2004. (ENG.). 160p. (YA). (gr. 7-18). 14.95 *(978-1-56145-317-7(X))* Peachtree Pubs.

DeMeo, Kimberly F. One Little Egg. 2013. (ENG.). 25p. (J). pap. 20.95 *(978-1-4787-1084-4(5))* Outskirts Pr., Inc.

Dessen, Sarah. This Lullaby. 2004. (ENG.). 368p. (YA). (gr. 7-18). reprint ed. pap. 10.99 *(978-0-14-250155-9(7),* Speak) Penguin Young Readers Group.

Diggle, David Mark. Paco: The High-Performance Penguin. Preuss, Sarah Louise, illus. 2011. 24p. (J). pap. *(978-0-9871658-1-7(X))* Diggle de Doo Productions Pty, Ltd.

Dilz, Ric. My Grandma Could Do Anything! 2008. (J). 14.95 *(978-0-9758704-3-3(2))* Ric Design LLC.

—My Grandma Could Do Anything in the Great Outdoors! 2008. (Illus.). 32p. (J). 14.95 *(978-0-9758704-6-4(7))* Ric Design LLC.

Disney Book Group. Descendants: Mal's Diary. Disney Storybook Art Team, illus. 2015. (ENG.). 192p. (J). (gr. 3-7). 9.99 *(978-1-4847-2685-3(5))* Disney Pr.

—Descendants: Mal's Spell Book. Disney Storybook Art Team, illus. 2015. (ENG.). 192p. (J). (gr. 3-7). 11.99 *(978-1-4847-2638-9(3))* Disney Pr.

Disney Book Group Staff & Green, Rico. Descendants: Junior Novel. Disney Storybook Art Team, illus. 2015. (ENG.). 176p. (J). (gr. 5-9). 10.99 *(978-1-4847-2614-3(6))* Disney Pr.

DiTerlizzi, Angela. Baby Love. Hughes, Brooke Boynton, illus. 2015. (ENG.). 32p. (J). (gr. -1-3). 17.99 *(978-1-4424-3392-2(2),* Beach Lane Bks.) Beach Lane Bks.

—Say What? Chou, Joey, illus. 2011. (ENG.). 32p. (J). (gr. -1-k). 15.99 *(978-1-4169-8694-2(4),* Beach Lane Bks.) Beach Lane Bks.

Doan, Lisa. Jack & the Wild Life. Stevanovic, Ivica, illus. 2014. (Berenson Schemes Ser.: 2). (ENG.). 144p. (J). (gr. 4-6). 17.95 *(978-1-4677-1077-0(6))* Lerner Publishing Group.

—Jack the Castaway. Stevanovic, Ivica, illus. 2014. (Berenson Schemes Ser.: 1). (ENG.). 152p. (J). (gr. 4-6). 17.95 *(978-1-4677-1076-3(8),* Darby Creek) Lerner Publishing Group.

Doctor McGougain. Stevie's Dreams: Doctor Mcgougain. 2012. 16p. pap. 15.99 *(978-1-4685-5345-1(3))* AuthorHouse.

Dodd, Emma. Everything. Dodd, Emma, illus. 2015. (Emma Dodd's Love You Bks.). (ENG., Illus.). 24p. (J). (-k). 12.99 *(978-0-7636-7128-0(2),* Templar) Candlewick Pr.

—Forever. Dodd, Emma, illus. 2013. (Emma Dodd's Love You Bks.). (ENG., Illus.). 24p. (J). (-k). 12.99 *(978-0-7636-7132-7(0),* Templar) Candlewick Pr.

—More & More. Dodd, Emma, illus. 2014. (ENG., Illus.). 24p. (J). (-k). 12.99 *(978-0-7636-7543-1(1),* Templar) Candlewick Pr.

Doller, Trish. Where the Stars Still Shine. 2013. (ENG.). 352p. (YA). (gr. 9). 17.99 *(978-1-61963-144-1(X),* 9781619631441, Bloomsbury USA Childrens); 256p. 17.99 *(978-1-61963-145-8(8))* Bloomsbury Publishing USA.

Dorman, Brandon, illus. The Slippery Map. 2007. 288p. (J). (gr. 3-7). lib. bdg. 17.89 *(978-0-06-079109-4(8))* HarperCollins Pubs.

Dotlich, Rebecca Kai. Mama Loves. Brown, Kathryn, illus. 2004. 32p. (J). (gr. -1-2). lib. bdg. 15.89 *(978-0-06-029408-3(6))* HarperCollins Pubs.

Dower, Laura. For Emme, Baked with Love. Lazuli, Lilly, illus. 2016. (Dessert Diaries). (ENG.). 160p. (gr. 4-5). pap. 5.95 *(978-1-4965-4142-0(1));* lib. bdg. 26.65 *(978-1-4965-3122-3(1))* Stone Arch Bks.

Doyle, Patrick H. T. Edgar Font's Hunt for a House to Haunt: Adventure Three: the Flint Island Treehouse. 2008. (Illus.). 300p. (J). per. 7.99 *(978-0-9786132-2-8(8))* Armadillo Bks.

Doyle, Teresa J. The Dream Box: Big Dreams for Little Sleepers. 2008. 84p. pap. 26.95 *(978-1-4343-9086-8(1))* AuthorHouse.

Duble, Kathleen Benner. Pilot Mom. Marks, Alan, illus. 2004. 32p. (J). (gr. k-3). 15.95 *(978-1-57091-555-0(5))* Charlesbridge Publishing, Inc.

Duksta, Laura. I Love You More. Keesler, Karen, illus. 2007. (ENG.). 34p. (J). (gr. k-2). 16.99 *(978-1-4022-1126-3(0),* Sourcebooks Jabberwocky) Sourcebooks, Inc.

—I'll Hug You More. Iwai, Melissa, illus. 2017. (ENG.). (J). 22p. bds. 8.99 *(978-1-4926-4187-2(1),* 9781492641872); 32p. 16.99 *(978-1-4926-2618-3(X),* 9781492626183) Sourcebooks, Inc. (Sourcebooks Jabberwocky).

Dumble, Carol. R U My Friend? 2011. 20p. pap. 11.99 *(978-1-4567-1825-1(8))* AuthorHouse.

Dungy, Tony & Dungy, Lauren. A Team Stays Together! Newton, Vanessa Brantley, illus. 2011. (Tony & Lauren Dungy Ready-To-Reads Ser.). (ENG.). 32p. (J). (gr. k-2). pap. 3.99 *(978-1-4424-3539-1(9),* Simon Spotlight) Simon Spotlight.

Durrant, George D. Shakespeare's Best Work: A Novel of Unexpected Family Ties & Uncommon Faith. 2003. 130p. pap. 10.95 *(978-1-55517-709-6(3),* 77093) Cedar Fort, Inc./CFI Distribution.

Eareckson Tada, Joni. I'll Be with You Always. Nelson, Craig, illus. 2004. 32p. (gr. 8-12). 14.99 *(978-1-58134-000-6(1))* Crossway.

Eareckson Tada, Joni & Jensen, Steve. Tell Me the Promises. DiCianni, Ron, illus. 2004. 48p. (gr. 5-7). 17.99 *(978-0-89107-904-0(1))* Crossway.

Eaton, Kelly Toole. Kitten Trouble. 2011. 36p. pap. 21.99 *(978-1-4568-8937-1(0))* Xlibris Corp.

Edgeworth, Maria. The Parent's Assistant; or, Stories for Children. 2007. 468p. (gr. 4-7). per. *(978-1-4065-1649-4(X))* Dodo Pr.

Ehlert, Lois. Hands: Growing up to Be an Artist. 2004. (ENG., Illus.). 48p. (J). (gr. -1-3). 16.99 *(978-0-15-205107-5(4))* Houghton Mifflin Harcourt Publishing Co.

—Pie in the Sky. 2004. (ENG., Illus.). 40p. (J). (gr. -1-3). 17.99 *(978-0-15-216584-0(3))* Houghton Mifflin Harcourt Publishing Co.

Eldridge, Sherrie. Forever Fingerprints: An Amazing Discovery for Adopted Children. Williams, Rob, illus. 2014. (ENG.). 32p. 15.95 *(978-1-84905-778-3(8),* 3057) Kingsley, Jessica Pubs. GBR. Dist: Macmillan Distribution Ltd.

Elgert, C. J. The Elder Brothers & the Padstow Crystals. 2013. 208p. *(978-1-4602-1788-7(8));* pap. *(978-1-4602-1789-4(6))* FriesenPress.

Ellis, Ann Dee. You May Already Be a Winner. 2017. (ENG.). 352p. (J). (gr. 5-9). 16.99 ***(978-1-101-99385-9(5),*** Dial Bks) Penguin Young Readers Group.

Ennis, Nancy. When Mommy & Daddy Say No, They Still Love You. Meadows, Cynthia, illus. 2014. (ENG.). 24p. (J). 14.95 net. *(978-1-61254-198-3(4))* Brown Books Publishing Group.

Ethier, Vicki. Papa & the Hen. Ethier, Vicki, illus. 2004. (Illus.). 36p. (J). 7.00 *(978-1-928972-12-9(8))* Critter Pubns.

Eubank, Patti Reeder. Count Your Blessings! 2004. (ENG., Illus.). 14p. (J). bds. 9.95 *(978-0-8249-6544-0(2),* Ideal Pubns.) Worthy Publishing.

Falk, Jennifer & Morgan. A Heart Daddy for Chrissie. 2005. 43p. (J). pap. 16.00 *(978-1-4116-3585-2(X))* Lulu Pr., Inc.

Farrell, John. Dear Child. Manning, Maurie J., illus. 2008. (ENG.). 32p. (J). (gr. -1-k). 16.95 *(978-1-59078-495-2(2))* Boyds Mills Pr.

Fass, Tara. Turtlebird's Double Dip Shuffle. Conn, Alexandra, illus. 2013. 18p. pap. 10.00 *(978-0-9838120-4-3(7))* Huqua Pr.

Fehr, Signe. Mama Always Comes Back. 2008. 32p. pap. 14.99 *(978-1-4389-0036-0(8))* AuthorHouse.

Feldkamp, Jim And Cate. The Adventures of Tommy & Clara on Mount Catherine. 2008. 32p. pap. 14.49 *(978-1-4389-1366-7(4))* AuthorHouse.

Felker, Linda, et al. What If? 2013. 42p. pap. 13.95 *(978-1-938101-51-9(0))* Indigo Sea Pr., LLC.

Findlay, Chris. Ae Sma Voice. 2008. 152p. pap. *(978-1-84923-144-2(3))* YouWriteOn.

Fleischman, Paul. Seek. braille ed. 2003. (J). (gr. 2). spiral bd. *(978-0-616-15870-8(X))* Canadian National Institute for the Blind/Institut National Canadien pour les Aveugles.

—Seek. 2004. 176p. (J). (gr. 7-18). pap. 29.00 incl. audio *(978-0-8072-2285-0(2),* Listening Library) Random Hse. Audio Publishing Group.

—Seek. 2003. (ENG., Illus.). 176p. (YA). (gr. 7). pap. 9.99 *(978-0-689-85402-6(1),* Simon Pulse) Simon Pulse.

Fleming, Meg. I Heart You. Wright, Sarah Jane, illus. 2016. (ENG.). 40p. (J). (gr. -1-3). 17.99 *(978-1-4424-8895-3(6),* Beach Lane Bks.) Beach Lane Bks.

Flesher, Brandon. Shattered Dreams in Light. 2014. (J). *(978-1-938237-10-2(2))* Skywater Publishing Co.

Flinn, Alex. Breathing Underwater. unabr. ed. 2004. (Young Adult Cassette Librariestm Ser.). 272p. (J). (gr. 7-18). pap. 36.00 incl. audio *(978-0-8072-0992-9(9),* S YA 346 SP, Listening Library) Random Hse. Audio Publishing Group.

Ford, Jayme. The Adventures of Glop-A-Lopikins & the Pink Castle. 2013. 28p. pap. 24.95 *(978-1-62709-206-7(4))* America Star Bks.

Fox, Mem. Harriet, You'll Drive Me Wild! Frazee, Marla, illus. 2003. (ENG.). 32p. (J). (gr. -1-3). pap. 7.99 *(978-0-15-204598-2(8))* Houghton Mifflin Harcourt Publishing Co.

—Harriet, You'll Drive Me Wild! 2003. (gr. k-3). 17.20 *(978-0-613-59897-2(0),* Turtleback) Turtleback Bks.

Frederick, Heather Vogel. The Voyage of Patience Goodspeed. 2004. (ENG., Illus.). 224p. (J). (gr. 3-7). pap. 8.99 *(978-0-689-84869-8(2),* Simon & Schuster Bks. For Young Readers) Simon & Schuster Bks. For Young Readers.

Freedman, Claire. I Love You, Baby! Abbot, Judi, illus. 2017. (ENG.). 32p. (J). (gr. -1-3). 17.99 ***(978-1-4814-9904-0(1),*** Simon & Schuster/Paula Wiseman Bks.) Simon & Schuster/Paula Wiseman Bks.

Freeman, Marcia S. Catfish & Spaghetti. Stock, Rose, illus. 2013. (Maupin House Ser.). (ENG.). 48p. (gr. 3-5). pap. 4.50 *(978-0-929895-21-5(5))* Maupin Hse. Publishing.

Freeman, Suzanne. The Cuckoo's Child. 249p. (YA). (gr. 5-8). pap. 5.95 *(978-0-8072-1510-4(4),* Listening Library) Random Hse. Audio Publishing Group.

Friedman, Becky. Daniel Goes to School. 2014. (Daniel Tiger's Neighborhood 8X8 Ser.). lib. bdg. 13.55 *(978-0-606-35756-2(4))* Turtleback Bks.

—Daniel Tries a New Food. 2015. (Daniel Tiger's Neighborhood 8X8 Ser.). lib. bdg. 13.55 *(978-0-606-37874-1(X))* Turtleback Bks.

Friend, Natasha. Perfect. 2004. (ENG.). 232p. (J). pap. 7.95 *(978-1-57131-651-6(5))* Milkweed Editions.

Fruchter, Jason, illus. Daniel Feels Left Out. 2015. (Daniel Tiger's Neighborhood Ser.). (ENG.). 32p. (J). (gr. -1-k). 16.99 *(978-1-4814-3836-0(0),* Simon Spotlight) Simon Spotlight.

Frye, Timea Csonka. Wishing Star: Lost in the Woods. 2013. 32p. pap. 24.95 *(978-1-63000-931-1(8))* America Star Bks.

Gaffney, Linda. My Daddy Does GOOD Things, Too! Dabney, Undra & Goettling, Nickalas, illus. 2006. 55p. per. 10.99 *(978-0-9787501-0-7(1))* Gaffney, Linda.

Galassi, Isabel. I Want, 1 vol. 2009. 12p. pap. 24.95 *(978-1-61546-535-4(9))* America Star Bks.

Garisch, Dawn. Babyshoes. 2004. (ENG.). 288p. (J). pap. 9.99 *(978-0-689-83778-4(X))* Simon & Schuster, Ltd. GBR. Dist: Simon & Schuster, Inc.

Garner, Jazzy. The Cotton Tales of Pippa the Bunny. 2010. 20p. 12.49 *(978-1-4490-8699-2(3))* AuthorHouse.

Gasparro, Marie & Falletta, Bernadette. The Magnificent Hole. 2005. 13p. (J). 12.95 *(978-1-4116-5924-7(4))* Lulu Pr., Inc.

Gates, Josephine Scribner. The Story of Live Dolls: Being an Account of How, on a Certain June Morning. unabr. ed. 2012. (Illus.). 104p. 39.99 *(978-1-4622-8158-9(3))* Repressed Publishing LLC.

Gay, Michel. El Cochecito. 2003. (SPA.). 68p. *(978-84-8470-084-5(4))* Corimbo, Editorial S.L.

Geeslin, Campbell. Elena's Serenade. Juan, Ana, illus. 2004. (ENG.). 40p. (J). (gr. -1-2). 19.99 *(978-0-689-84908-4(7),* Atheneum Bks. for Young Readers) Simon & Schuster Children's Publishing.

Geise, Brenda & Merkle, Blair Geise. Love Spot. 2008. 28p. pap. 12.99 *(978-1-4389-1102-1(5))* AuthorHouse.

Gerber, Carole. Tuck-In Time. Pearson, Tracey Campbell, illus. 2014. (ENG.). 40p. (J). (gr. -1 — 1). 16.99 *(978-0-374-37860-8(6),* 9780374378608, Farrar, Straus & Giroux (BYR)) Farrar, Straus & Giroux.

Gershman, Jenifer. Where Did Mommy's Superpowers Go? Helping Kids Understand a Parent's Serious Illness. 2011. (ENG., Illus.). 36p. (J). pap. 16.95 *(978-0-9824461-9-5(5))* SDP Publishing.

Gerver, Jane E. I Love You. Brown, Jo, illus. 2015. (ENG.). 14p. (J). (— 1). bds. 4.99 *(978-1-62979-416-7(3),* Highlights) Boyds Mills Pr.

Gibbons, Alan. The Dying Photo. 2012. (Stoke Books Titles Ser.). 64p. (J). (gr. 5-8). pap. 45.32 *(978-0-7613-9217-0(3))* Stoke Bks.

Gibbs, Dreene. Am I Pretty, Momma? 2nd l.t. ed. 2004. (Illus.). 32p. (J). bds. 12.95 *(978-0-9741406-1-2(9),* 0138) Cranberry Quill Publishing Co.

Gibson, Donovan. The Ticker That Needed a Fixer. Rottinger, Amy, illus. 2011. 28p. pap. 12.95 *(978-1-935268-46-8(5))* Halo Publishing International.

Gilbert, George. George, Candy, & the Raccoon. Perez-Torres, Juliana, illus. 2008. 40p. pap. 16.99 *(978-1-4389-2848-7(3))* AuthorHouse.

Gilles, Almira Astudillo. Willie Wins, 1 vol. Angel, Carl, illus. 2013. (ENG.). 32p. (J). (gr. -1-3). 16.95 *(978-1-58430-023-6(X))* Lee & Low Bks., Inc.

Gillespie, Hollis. Unaccompanied Minor. 2014. (ENG.). 256p. (YA). 17.99 *(978-1-4405-6773-5(5))* Adams Media Corp.

Gliori, Debi. No Matter What. (ENG., Illus.). 24p. (J). (gr. -1 — 1). 2012. bds. 12.99 *(978-0-547-71905-4(1))* 2008. bds. 6.99 *(978-0-15-206343-6(9))* Houghton Mifflin Harcourt Publishing Co.

Goodman, Katie & Kisiel, Soren. The Night Our Parents Went Out. 2015. (ENG., Illus.). 32p. (J). (gr. -1-2). 16.95 *(978-1-57687-747-0(7),* powerHouse Bks.) powerHouse Cultural Entertainment, Inc.

Gormally, Eleanor. The Little One Asks. 2013. (ENG.). 32p. (J). pap. 12.95 *(978-1-84730-407-0(9))* Veritas Pubns. IRL. Dist: Dufour Editions, Inc.

Gove, Doris. My Mother Talks to Trees, 1 vol. Mallory, Marilynn H., illus. 2005. (ENG.). 32p. (J). (gr. k-3). pap. 7.95 *(978-1-56145-336-8(6),* Q31285) Peachtree Pubs.

Gownley, Jimmy. What Makes You Happy. Gownley, Jimmy, illus. 2009. (Amelia Rules! Ser.). (ENG., Illus.). 176p. (J). (gr. 2-7). pap. 12.99 *(978-1-4169-8605-8(7),* Atheneum Bks. for Young Readers) Simon & Schuster Children's Publishing.

Graff, Lisa. It Is Not Time for Sleeping. Castillo, Lauren, illus. 2016. (ENG.). 40p. (J). (gr. -1-3). 16.99 *(978-0-544-31930-1(3),* Clarion Bks.) Houghton Mifflin Harcourt Trade & Reference Pubs.

Graham, Bob. Home in the Rain. Graham, Bob, illus. 2017. (ENG., Illus.). 32p. (J). (gr. -1-2). 16.99 *(978-0-7636-9269-8(7))* Candlewick Pr.

Grandfeather Press. Roly Poly Napoleon Discovers Colors. 2011. (ENG., Illus.). 36p. (J). pap. 6.99 *(978-0-9832355-0-7(3))* Grandfeather Pr.

Graves, Jennifer. Ava's Awful Fright! 2009. 28p. pap. 15.99 *(978-1-4415-0482-1(6))* Xlibris Corp.

Greban, Quentin. Mommy, I Love You. Greban, Quentin, illus. 2005. (Illus.). 32p. *(978-0-689-03922-5(0),* Milk & Cookies) ibooks, Inc.

Greene, Marjorie. Cassie's Big Day. 2003. (Illus.). (J). 16.95 *(978-0-9741764-0-6(0))* Greene, Marjorie A.

Greenspan, Deborah. Kids' Day. 2004. (J). pap. 10.95 *(978-1-59526-197-7(4))* Aeon Publishing Inc.

Gregory, Dee. The Accidental Daughter: A Children's Story about Hope. 2008. 96p. pap. 10.49 *(978-1-4389-3338-2(X))* AuthorHouse.

Griffin, Donna. Dani & the Beans. 2008. 28p. pap. 13.50 *(978-1-4389-1175-5(0))* AuthorHouse.

Griffin, Michele. Picky, Picky Pete. 2010. (ENG.). 48p. (gr. -1). pap. 14.95 *(978-1-935567-21-9(7))* Sensory Resources.

Guest, Jacqueline & Leavey, Peggy Dymond. Growing up Ivy. 2010. (ENG.). 256p. (YA). (gr. 4-8). pap. 10.99 *(978-1-55488-723-1(2))* Dundurn CAN. Dist: Ingram Publisher Services.

Guion, Melissa. Baby Penguins Love Their Mama. Guion, Melissa, illus. 2014. (ENG., Illus.). 32p. (J). (gr. -1-k). 16.99 *(978-0-399-16365-4(4),* Philomel Bks.) Penguin Young Readers Group.

Gutman, Anne & Hallensleben, Georg. Daddy Cuddles. 2005. (ENG., Illus.). 14p. (J). (gr. -1 — 1). bds. 5.95 *(978-0-8118-4674-5(1))* Chronicle Bks. LLC.

Haddix, Margaret Peterson. Children of Exile. 2016. (Children of Exile Ser.: 1). (ENG., Illus.). 304p. (J). (gr. 5). 17.99 *(978-1-4424-5003-5(7),* Simon & Schuster Bks. For Young Readers) Simon & Schuster Bks. For Young Readers.

—Say What? Bernardin, James, illus. 2005. 91p. (J). 11.65 *(978-0-7569-5465-9(7))* Perfection Learning Corp.

Haislip, Phyllis Hall. Lottie's Courage: A Contraband Slave's Story. 2003. (Illus.). 120p. (J). pap. 7.95 *(978-1-57249-311-7(9),* White Mane Kids) White Mane Publishing Co., Inc.

Hall, John. What If I Pulled This Thread. Gilpin, Stephen, illus. 2006. 48p. 12.99 *(978-1-59379-067-7(8))* White Stone Bks.

Hall, Marjory. The Gold-Lined Box. 2003. 224p. 11.95 *(978-0-9714612-6-0(0))* Green Mansion Pr. LLC.

Hallensleben, Georg & Gutman, Anne. Mommy & Daddy Boxed Set, 4 vols. 2009. (ENG., Illus.). 56p. (J). (gr. -1 — 1). bds. 19.99 *(978-0-8118-7055-9(3))* Chronicle Bks. LLC.

Hallinan, P. K. ABC I Love You. 2003. (ENG., Illus.). 24p. (J). bds. 7.95 *(978-0-8249-5458-1(0),* Ideal Pubns.) Worthy Publishing.

—How Do I Love You? Hallinan, P. K., illus. 2014. (Illus.). 24p. (J). bds. 8.99 *(978-0-8249-1944-3(0),* Ideal Pubns.) Worthy Publishing.

—How Do I Love You? 2005. (ENG., Illus.). 32p. (J). (gr. -1-k). pap. 4.35 *(978-0-8249-5518-2(8),* Ideal Pubns.) Worthy Publishing.

—How Do I Love You/Como Te Amo. 2008. (SPA & ENG., Illus.). 30p. (J). pap. 4.35 *(978-0-8249-5471-0(8),* Ideal Pubns.) Worthy Publishing.

—We're Very Good Friends, My Mother & I. 24p. (J). 5.95 *(978-0-8249-5374-4(6));* 7.95 *(978-0-8249-5373-7(8))* Worthy Publishing. (Ideal Pubns.).

Halpern, Julie. Have a Nice Day. 2013. (ENG.). 352p. (YA). (gr. 7-12). pap. 10.99 *(978-1-250-03420-5(5),* 9781250034205) Square Fish.

Hanson, Anders. Iguana Mama, 1 vol. 2007. (Critter Chronicles Ser.). (ENG., Illus.). 24p. (J). (gr. k-3). lib. bdg. 24.21 *(978-1-59928-444-6(8),* SandCastle) ABDO Publishing Co.

Hao, K. T. Who Did This? Bernatene, Poly, illus. 2008. (ENG.). 32p. (J). (gr. -1). lib. bdg. 16.50 *(978-1-933327-33-4(2))* Purple Bear Bks., Inc.

—Who Did This? Bernatene, Poly, illus. 2008. (ENG.). 32p. (J). (gr. -1). 15.95 *(978-1-933327-32-7(4))* Purple Bear Bks., Inc.

Harber Freeman, Anna. Love You More Than Anything. Henry, Jed, illus. 2014. (Snuggle Time Stories Ser.). (ENG.). 24p. (J). (gr. -1-k). 9.95 *(978-1-4549-0021-4(0))* Sterling Publishing Co., Inc.

Harper, Jo. I Could Eat You Up! Chorao, Kay, illus. 2007. (ENG.). 32p. (J). (gr. -1-3). 16.95 *(978-0-8234-1733-9(6))* Holiday Hse., Inc.

Harrington, Claudia. My Military Mom, 1 vol. Persico, Zoe, illus. 2016. (ENG.). 32p. (J). *(978-1-62402-106-0(9))* Magic Wagon.
—My Two Homes, 1 vol. Persico, Zoe, illus. 2016. (ENG.). 32p. (J). *(978-1-62402-109-1(3))* Magic Wagon.
Harris, Teresa E. Summer Jackson: Grown Up. Ford, A. G., illus. 2011. (ENG.). 32p. (J). (gr. -1-2). 16.99 *(978-0-06-185757-7(2)*, Tegen, Katherine Bks) HarperCollins Pubs.
Hart, Melissa. Avenging the Owl. 2016. (ENG.). 224p. (J). (gr. 5-8). 15.99 *(978-1-63450-147-7(0)*, Sky Pony Pr.) Skyhorse Publishing Co., Inc.
Haughton, Emma. Rainy Day. Rinaldi, Angelo, illus. (Carolrhoda Picture Books Ser.). 32p. (J). 2004. pap. 6.95 *(978-1-57505-668-5(2))* 2003. (gr. -1-3). 6.95 *(978-1-57505-452-0(3)*, Carolrhoda Bks.) Lerner Publishing Group.
Haven, Gayle Jeanine. Love from Both Houses, My Parents Love. 2012. 28p. pap. 19.99 *(978-1-4685-9810-0(4))* AuthorHouse.
Haworth, Margaret. When Daddy Goes Away: Rusty Books. Edwards, Paul, illus. l.t. ed. 2003. (Books That Help Ser.: Vol. 2). 34p. (J). (gr. -1-5). pap. 9.95 *(978-0-9740313-1-6(3))* Haworth, Margaret.
Hayes, Geoffrey. A Night-Light for Bunny. Date not set. 32p. (J). (gr. -1-3). pap. 5.99 *(978-0-06-443728-8(0))* HarperCollins Pubs.
—A Night-Light for Bunny. Hayes, Geoffrey, illus. 2004. (Illus.). 32p. (J). (gr. -1-3). 14.99 *(978-0-06-029163-1(X))* HarperCollins Pubs.
Helakoski, Leslie. Woolbur. Harper, Lee, illus. 2008. (ENG.). 32p. (J). (gr. -1-3). 17.99 *(978-0-06-084726-5(3))* HarperCollins Pubs.
—Woolbur. 2008. (J). (gr. -1-2). 29.95 incl. audio *(978-0-8045-6971-2(1))* Spoken Arts, Inc.
Hemingway, Edith M. Road to Tater Hill. 2011. (ENG.). 224p. (J). (gr. 3-7). 7.99 *(978-0-375-84544-4(5)*, Yearling) Random Hse. Children's Bks.
Henkes, Kevin. Owen. 2017. (SPA.). (J). pap. ***(978-1-63245-665-6(6))*** Lectorum Pubns., Inc.
Henkes, Kevin & Kevin, Henkes. Owen. 2006. (Coleccion Rascacielos Ser.). (SPA., Illus.). 32p. (gr. k-1). pap. 9.99 *(978-84-241-1519-7(8))* Everest Editora ESP. Dist: Lectorum Pubns., Inc.
Henry, Nancy. Where's Papa? 2008. 24p. per. 24.95 *(978-1-60474-000-4(0))* America Star Bks.
Hest, Amy. Remembering Mrs. Rossi. Maione, Heather, illus. 2007. (ENG.). 192p. (J). (gr. 3-7). 14.99 *(978-0-7636-2163-6(3))* Candlewick Pr.
—Remembering Mrs. Rossi. Maione, Heather, illus. 2010. (ENG.). 192p. (J). (gr. 3-7). 6.99 *(978-0-7636-4089-7(1))* Candlewick Pr.
Hetzer, Michael. No More Handprints: Your Child's Handprint Completes the Story. Clayton, Kim, illus. 2nd ed. 2005. 32p. (J). 18.95 *(978-0-9728222-0-6(8))* Webster Henrietta Publishing.
Higgins, M. G. Family Fix-It Plan. Taylor, Jo, illus. 2016. (Sibling Split Ser.). (ENG.). 112p. (gr. 2-3). lib. bdg. 25.32 *(978-1-4965-2590-1(6))* Stone Arch Bks.
—The Impossible Wish. Taylor, Jo, illus. 2016. (Sibling Split Ser.). (ENG.). 112p. (gr. 2-3). lib. bdg. 25.32 *(978-1-4965-2593-2(0))* Stone Arch Bks.
—Party of Nine. Taylor, Jo, illus. 2016. (Sibling Split Ser.). (ENG.). 112p. (gr. 2-3). lib. bdg. 25.32 *(978-1-4965-2592-5(2))* Stone Arch Bks.
—Trouble in the City. Taylor, Jo, illus. 2016. (Sibling Split Ser.). (ENG.). 112p. (gr. 2-3). lib. bdg. 25.32 *(978-1-4965-2591-8(4))* Stone Arch Bks.
Hightman, Jason. The Saint of Dragons. 2004. (ENG.). 304p. (J). (gr. 7-18). 16.99 *(978-0-06-054011-1(7))* HarperCollins Pubs.
Hinbest, Wendy. Frizzy Tizzy Gets New Shoes. 2011. 24p. pap. 11.95 *(978-1-4583-5827-1(5))* Lulu Pr., Inc.
—Frizzy Tizzy Goes to the Park. 2011. 20p. pap. 11.95 *(978-1-4583-4346-8(4))* Lulu Pr., Inc.
Hines, Anna Grossnickle. Whistling. 2003. 40p. (J). 16.89 *(978-0-06-050236-2(3))* HarperCollins Pubs.
Hirsch, Jeff. Magisterium. 2012. (ENG.). 320p. (J). (gr. 7). 17.99 *(978-0-545-29018-0(X)*, Scholastic Pr.) Scholastic, Inc.
Hodges, Lynn & Buchanan, Sue. I Love You This Much, 1 vol. Bendall-Brunello, John, illus. 2010. (ENG.). 36p. (J). pap. 6.99 *(978-0-310-72265-6(9))* Zonderkidz.
Hodges, Lynn, et al. I Love You This Much, 1 vol. Bendall-Brunello, John, illus. 2005. (Songs of Gods Love Ser.). (ENG.). 16p. (J). (gr. -1). bds. 6.99 *(978-0-310-70961-9(X))* Zonderkidz.
Hodgkins, Fran. If You Were My Baby: A Wildlife Lullaby. Bryant, Laura J., illus. (Simply Nature Book Ser.). (J). (gr. -1 — 1). 2007. 26p. bds. 7.95 *(978-1-58469-090-0(9))* 2005. 32p. pap. 8.95 *(978-1-58469-075-7(5))* 2005. (ENG.). 32p. 16.95 *(978-1-58469-074-0(7))* Dawn Pubns.
Hofmeister, Nick. Adventures of Eli Deuce - SPECIAL EDITION - Fourth & Final Part Added. 2009. 360p. pap. 23.50 *(978-0-557-12192-2(2))* Lulu Pr., Inc.
Hofstad, Maryanne. Hi, Mommy & Daddy! I'm Here! 2009. 12p. pap. 9.99 *(978-1-4389-4887-4(5))* AuthorHouse.
Hogan, Janice M. As Big as the Sky. 2008. 32p. per. 24.95 *(978-1-4241-9181-9(5))* America Star Bks.
Holt, Kimberly Willis. My Louisiana Sky. 208p. (YA). (gr. 5-18). 4.99 *(978-0-8072-8291-5(X)*, Listening Library) Random Hse. Audio Publishing Group.
—My Louisiana Sky. 2011. (ENG.). 224p. (J). (gr. 4-7). pap. 7.99 *(978-0-312-66095-6(2)*, 9780312660956) Square Fish.
Hong, Denise & Hong, Andrew. Why I Love My Mom: The Ultimate Gift of the Heart. Lopez, Paul & Hong, Denise, illus. 2004. 32p. (J). lib. bdg. 17.95 *(978-0-9746503-4-0(X))* Platinum Bks.
Honowitz, Stacey & Brenner, Jordyn. My Privates Are Private. 2009. 24p. pap. 12.95 *(978-1-60844-281-2(0))* Dog Ear Publishing, LLC.
Hood, Tyline M. I Love You So Much, Goodnight. 2012. 26p. pap. 17.99 *(978-1-4685-6444-0(7))* AuthorHouse.
Hopkins, Ellen. The You I've Never Known. 2017. (ENG., Illus.). 608p. (YA). (gr. 9). 18.99 *(978-1-4814-4290-9(2)*, McElderry, Margaret K. Bks.) McElderry, Margaret K. Bks.
Horvath, Polly. Everything on a Waffle, 1 vol. (ENG., Illus.). 160p. (J). pap. 8.95 *(978-0-88899-442-4(7))* Groundwood Bks. CAN. Dist: Publishers Group West (PGW).
—Everything on a Waffle. 2008. (Illus.). 154p. (gr. 5-9). 18.00 *(978-0-7569-8776-3(8))* Perfection Learning Corp.
—Everything on a Waffle. 2008. (ENG., Illus.). 176p. (J). (gr. 5-9). pap. 7.99 *(978-0-312-38004-5(6)*, 9780312380045) Square Fish.
Hostetter, Joyce Moyer. Aim. 2016. (Bakers Mountain Stories Ser.). (ENG.). 288p. (J). (gr. 3-7). 17.99 *(978-1-62979-673-4(5)*, Calkins Creek) Boyds Mills Pr.
Houk, Amanda. Mommy's New Heart, 1 vol. 2010. 22p. 24.95 *(978-1-4512-9377-7(1))* PublishAmerica, Inc.
Hugger, M. A. Danny Malloy & His Mississippi River Samurai. 2008. 132p. 21.95 *(978-0-595-49382-1(3))*; pap. 11.95 *(978-0-595-48462-1(X))* iUniverse, Inc.
Hulslander, Dyan. God's Precious Gift. 2009. 24p. pap. 14.99 *(978-1-4389-6903-9(1))* AuthorHouse.
Humphrey, Lisa. A Mother's Promise. Danioth, David, illus. 2004. 32p. (J). per. 15.95 *(978-0-9701907-9-6(4))* Illumination Arts Publishing Co., Inc.
Ibeh, Chinwe. The Moment That Sandra Won. 2011. 28p. pap. 24.95 *(978-1-4626-2938-1(5))* PublishAmerica, Inc.
Inacio, Maria St. Katie's Big Move! 2013. 20p. pap. 17.99 *(978-1-4772-8703-3(5))* AuthorHouse.
Ingold, Jeanette. Mountain Solo. 2005. (ENG.). 320p. (YA). (gr. 7-12). pap. 15.95 *(978-0-15-205358-1(1))* Houghton Mifflin Harcourt Publishing Co.
Irvin, David. Rusty the Rainbow Trout: Moving Day. Irvin, Sioux, illus. 2007. 24p. per. 24.95 *(978-1-4241-8455-2(X))* America Star Bks.
Isol. The Menino: A Story Based on Real Events, 1 vol. Amado, Elisa, tr. from SPA. 2015. (ENG., Illus.). 60p. (J). (-k). 19.95 *(978-1-55498-778-8(4))* Groundwood Bks. CAN. Dist: Publishers Group West (PGW).
Jadoul, Émile. Good Night, Chickie. 2010. (ENG.). 26p. (J). (gr. -1-k). 14.00 *(978-0-8028-5378-3(1)*, Eerdmans Bks For Young Readers) Eerdmans, William B. Publishing Co.
Jameson, Catherine. Zoe & the Fawn. Flett, Julie, illus. 2006. (ENG.). 32p. pap. 11.95 *(978-1-894778-43-5(X))* Theytus Bks., Ltd. CAN. Dist: Univ. of Toronto Pr.
Jiries, Nariman. Grace-A-Lena Learns the Meaning of Self-Esteem. 2012. 36p. pap. 21.99 *(978-1-4771-0476-7(3))* Xlibris Corp.
Jobling, Curtis. My Daddy. Jobling, Curtis, illus. 2007. (ENG., Illus.). 32p. (J). (gr. -1-k). 9.99 *(978-0-00-722164-6(9)*, HarperCollins Children's Bks.) HarperCollins Pubs. Ltd. GBR. Dist: Independent Pubs. Group.
—My Daddy: Mini Edition. 2004. (Illus.). 32p. (J). 19.99 *(978-0-00-712254-7(3)*, HarperSport) HarperCollins Pubs. Ltd. GBR. Dist: Trafalgar Square Publishing.
—My Daddy: My Daddy Is the Best in the Universe! 2006. (ENG., Illus.). 32p. (J). (gr. -1-k). pap. 8.99 *(978-0-00-712255-4(1))* HarperCollins Pubs. Ltd. GBR. Dist: Independent Pubs. Group.
Jocham, Tammy. Smiley Meets Twinkle. 2008. 16p. pap. 8.49 *(978-1-4389-2615-5(4))* AuthorHouse.
Joel, Billy. Goodnight, My Angel: A Lullabye. Gilbert, Yvonne, illus. 2004. (J). pap. *(978-0-439-55378-0(4))* Scholastic, Inc.
Johnson, Angela. Heaven, 3 vols. 2006. (J). 44.75 *(978-1-4281-0237-8(X))* Recorded Bks., Inc.
—Heaven. 2010. (ENG.). 160p. (YA). (gr. 7). pap. 9.99 *(978-1-4424-0342-0(X)*, Simon & Schuster Bks. For Young Readers) Simon & Schuster Bks. For Young Readers.
Johnson, Antonia. Bianca's Light. 2009. 28p. pap. 14.99 *(978-1-4389-8951-8(2))* AuthorHouse.
Johnson, Pete. How to Train Your Parents. 2003. (ENG., Illus.). 208p. pap. *(978-0-440-86439-4(9)*, Yearling) Random Hse. Children's Bks.
Jones, Abigail. Still a Family. 2011. 24p. pap. 15.99 *(978-1-4568-7941-9(3))* Xlibris Corp.
Jones, Debbie Knatt. Maurice ... As Read to the Students in Room D183 & D184. 2013. 150p. pap. 13.95 *(978-1-62516-536-7(6)*, Strategic Bk. Publishing) Strategic Book Publishing & Rights Agency (SBPRA).
Jones, Jenny B. So Not Happening, 1 vol. 2009. (Charmed Life Ser.: 1). (ENG.). 336p. (YA). (gr. 7-18). pap. 12.99 *(978-1-59554-541-1(7))* Nelson, Thomas Inc.
Joosse, Barbara M. & Lavallee, Barbara. Papa, Do You Love Me? Lavallee, Barbara, illus. 2005. (Mama Ser.: MAMA). (ENG., Illus.). 36p. (J). (gr. -1-7). 15.99 *(978-0-8118-4265-5(7))* Chronicle Bks. LLC.
Kabat, Vicki Marsh. Will You Still Love Me? 2012. 28p. pap. 13.99 *(978-1-4624-0346-2(8)*, Inspiring Voices) Author Solutions, Inc.
Kalechofsky, Roberta. A Boy, a Chicken & the Lion of Judah: How Ari Became a Vegetarian. 2012. (ENG., Illus.). 50p. (J). pap. 12.00 *(978-0-916288-58-7(1))* Micah Pubns.
Kane, Sharon. Little Mommy. Kane, Sharon, illus. 2008. (Little Golden Book Ser.). (ENG., Illus.). 24p. (J). (gr. -1-2). 4.99 *(978-0-375-84820-9(7)*, Golden Bks.) Random Hse. Children's Bks.
Kathleen, Judith. Attila's Wobbly Birthday Box, 1 vol. 2010. 20p. pap. 24.95 *(978-1-4489-2451-6(0))* PublishAmerica, Inc.
Kavanagh, Peter. I Love My Mama. Chapman, Jane, tr. Chapman, Jane, illus. 2003. 32p. (J). 12.95 *(978-1-85430-806-1(8)*, Simon & Schuster Bks. For Young Readers) Simon & Schuster Bks. For Young Readers.
Keith, Donna. I Love You All the Same, 1 vol. Edgson, Allison, illus. 2014. (ENG.). 20p. (J). bds. 9.99 *(978-0-529-10204-1(8))* Nelson, Thomas Inc.
Kellerhals-Stewart, Heather. Brave Highland Heart. 2004. (Illus.). (J). (gr. k-3). spiral bd. *(978-0-616-01688-6(3))* Canadian National Institute for the Blind/Institut National Canadien pour les Aveugles.
Kelty, Colleen A. Spencer the Spectacular. 2011. 28p. pap. 24.95 *(978-1-4560-1033-1(6))* America Star Bks.
Kemp, Anna. Rhinos Don't Eat Pancakes. Ogilvie, Sara, illus. 2015. (ENG.). 32p. (J). (gr. -1-3). 17.99 *(978-1-4814-3845-2(X)*, Simon & Schuster/Paula Wiseman Bks.) Simon & Schuster/Paula Wiseman Bks.
Kerr, M. E., pseud. I'll Love You When You're More Like Me. 2014. (ENG.). 200p. (gr. 6). pap. 12.95 *(978-1-939601-06-3(1))* Ig Publishing, Inc.
Keun, Irmgard. Child of All Nations. Hofmann, Michael, tr. from GER. 2008. (ENG.). 208p. (gr. 4-13). 23.95 *(978-1-59020-099-5(3)*, 902099) Overlook Pr., The.
Key, Janet Rhyme. Rosa in Bloom. 2013. 86p. (J). pap. 13.95 *(978-1-4817-1956-8(4))* AuthorHouse.
Kim, Cecil. Mommy & Daddy Love You. Ladecka, Anna, illus. 2014. (MySELF Bookshelf Ser.). (ENG.). 32p. (J). (gr. k-2). pap. 11.94 *(978-1-60357-691-8(6))*; lib. bdg. 25.27 *(978-1-59953-656-9(0))* Norwood Hse. Pr.
Kimmel, Haven. Kaline Klattermaster's Tree House. Brown, Peter, illus. 2010. (ENG.). 160p. (J). (gr. 2-7). pap. 5.99 *(978-0-689-87403-1(0)*, Atheneum Bks. for Young Readers) Simon & Schuster Children's Publishing.
King-smith, Dick. Dinosaur Trouble. Bruel, Nick, illus. 2012. (ENG.). 128p. (J). (gr. 2-5). pap. 16.99 *(978-1-59643-935-1(1)*, 9781596439351) Roaring Brook Pr.
Kirkman, Rick & Scott, Jerry. Gross! A Baby Blues Collection. 2016. (Baby Blues Ser.: 40). (ENG., Illus.). 208p. pap. 18.99 *(978-1-4494-7781-3(X))* Andrews McMeel Publishing.
Kissell, Casey. Awaiting Your Arrival. 2013. 20p. pap. 24.95 *(978-1-62709-188-6(2))* America Star Bks.
Klingensmith, Ryan Lee & Klingensmith, Sherri Ann. Starlight Blue: A New Baby. Rollinger, Marsha, illus. 2012. 32p. pap. 24.95 *(978-1-4626-8219-5(7))* America Star Bks.
Knesek, Marian. Zane & the Armadillo. Leipsic, Regina, illus. 2012. 26p. 24.95 *(978-1-4626-6685-0(X))* America Star Bks.
Kormos, Lawrence A. There Is A Place I Go. 2007. (Illus.). (J). *(978-1-55452-245-3(5))* Essence Publishing.
—What Is Love Mama? 2007. (Illus.). (J). *(978-1-55452-190-6(4))* Essence Publishing.
Krossing, Karen. Pure, 1 vol. 2006. (ENG.). 245p. (YA). (gr. 7-9). per. 10.95 *(978-1-896764-96-2(7))* Second Story Pr. CAN. Dist: Orca Bk. Pubs. USA.
Krug, Ken. No, Silly! Krug, Ken, illus. 2015. (ENG., Illus.). 40p. (J). (gr. -1-3). 17.99 *(978-1-4814-0066-4(5)*, Beach Lane Bks.) Beach Lane Bks.
Kupchella, Rick. Tell Me What We Did Today. Hanson, Warren, illus. (ENG.). 32p. (J). 15.95 *(978-0-9726504-0-3(7))* TRISTAN Publishing, Inc.
Kurtz, Jane. Do Kangaroos Wear Seatbelts? Rossi, Ino, ed. Manning, Jane, illus. 2005. (ENG.). 32p. (J). (gr. -1-k). 16.99 *(978-0-525-47358-9(0)*, Dutton Books for Young Readers) Penguin Young Readers Group.
Kvasnosky, Laura McGee. Little Wolf's First Howling. Kvasnosky, Laura McGee & McGee, Kate Harvey, illus. 2017. (ENG.). 32p. (J). (gr. -1-2). 15.99 *(978-0-7636-8971-1(8))* Candlewick Pr.
Lambert, Teres. Mommy, Do You Love Me? 2008. 20p. pap. 24.95 *(978-1-60441-911-5(3))* America Star Bks.
Lane, Sandra & Miles, Brenda. The Moment You Were Born: A NICU Story for You & Your Preemie. Hehenberger, Shelly, illus. 2015. (J). *(978-1-4338-1964-3(3)*, Magination Pr.) American Psychological Assn.
Lapid, Koty. The Wild Virtual Enchanted Garden. 2005. 41p. (J). per. 16.18 *(978-1-4116-2068-1(2))* Lulu Pr., Inc.
LaRochelle, David. How Martha Saved Her Parents from Green Beans. Fearing, Mark, illus. 2013. (ENG.). 32p. (J). (gr. k-3). 16.99 *(978-0-8037-3766-2(1)*, Dial Bks) Penguin Young Readers Group.
—Monster & Son. Chou, Joey, illus. 2016. (ENG.). 32p. (J). (gr. -1 — 1). 16.99 *(978-1-4521-2937-2(1))* Chronicle Bks. LLC.
Larsen, Mylisa. How to Put Your Parents to Bed. Cole, Babette, illus. 2016. 32p. (J). (gr. -1-3). 17.99 *(978-0-06-232064-3(5))* HarperCollins Pubs.
Larson, Susan. Sam (a Pastoral) 2012. (ENG.). 220p. (YA). pap. 12.95 *(978-0-9826069-9-5(0))* Savvy Pr.
Lawler, Janet. If Kisses Were Colors. Jay, Alison, illus. (ENG.). (J). (gr. -1 — 1). 2010. 22p. bds. 6.99 *(978-0-8037-3530-9(8))* 2003. 32p. 16.99 *(978-0-8037-2617-8(1))* Penguin Young Readers Group. (Dial Bks).
Layne, Steven L. Over Land & Sea: The Story of International Adoption, 1 vol. Bower, Jan, illus. 2005. (ENG.). 32p. (J). (gr. k-3). 16.99 *(978-1-58980-182-0(2))* Pelican Publishing Co., Inc.
Leach, Sara. Count Me In, 1 vol. 2011. (ENG.). 176p. (J). (gr. 4-7). pap. 9.95 *(978-1-55469-404-4(3))* Orca Bk. Pubs. USA.
Ledwidge, Maria. My Salvation Birthday. 2011. 24p. (gr. 2-4). pap. 12.95 *(978-1-4497-1771-1(3)*, WestBow Pr.) Author Solutions, Inc.
Lee, Darrien. 16 Going on 21. 2008. (ENG., Illus.). 288p. (YA). (gr. 9). 9.95 *(978-1-933967-71-4(4)*, Urban Renaissance) Kensington Publishing Corp.
L'Engle, Madeleine. Camilla. 2009. (ENG.). 272p. (YA). (gr. 7-12). pap. 18.99 *(978-0-312-56132-1(6)*, 9780312561321) Square Fish.
Lester, Julius. Pharaoh's Daughter: A Novel of Ancient Egypt. 2009. (ENG., Illus.). 192p. (J). (gr. 7). pap. 6.99 *(978-0-15-206662-8(4))* Houghton Mifflin Harcourt Publishing Co.
—When Dad Killed Mom. 2003. (YA). (gr. 7-12). mass mkt. 6.95 *(978-0-15-524698-0(4)*, Silver Whistle) Harcourt Trade Pubs.
—When Dad Killed Mom. 2003. (ENG.). 216p. (YA). (gr. 7-12). pap. 13.95 *(978-0-15-204698-9(4))* Houghton Mifflin Harcourt Publishing Co.
Levine, Arthur A. Monday Is One Day. Hector, Julian, illus. 2015. (ENG.). 32p. (J). (gr. -1-k). 6.99 *(978-0-439-78925-7(7))* Scholastic, Inc.
Lewis, Anne Margaret. Sleeping Bear: Journey of the Cub Book 1. 2012. (ENG.). (J). pap. 8.00 *(978-1-4675-5260-8(7))* Independent Pub.
Lewis-Long, Carla. Why I'm So Special: A Book about Surrogacy. 2010. 44p. pap. 19.95 *(978-1-4389-9656-1(X))* AuthorHouse.
Lewis, Paeony. I'll Always Love You. Ives, Penny, illus. 2004. 32p. (J). pap. 5.95 *(978-1-58925-360-5(4))* Tiger Tales.
Lichtenheld, Tom. What Mess? 2012. (ENG., Illus.). 40p. (J). (gr. -1-3). pap. 7.00 *(978-0-316-20123-0(5))* Little, Brown Bks. for Young Readers.
—What Mess? 2012. (J). lib. bdg. 17.20 *(978-0-606-26686-4(0)*, Turtleback) Turtleback Bks.
Lilly, T. S. The Upgrade. 2008. 60p. pap. 16.95 *(978-1-60441-536-0(3))* America Star Bks.
Lindaman, Jane. Zip It! Carlson, Nancy, illus. 2012. (Carolrhoda Picture Bks.). (ENG.). 32p. (J). (gr. k-4). lib. bdg. 16.95 *(978-0-7613-5592-2(8))* Lerner Publishing Group.
Linden, Dianne. Peacekeepers. (J). 82p. stu. ed. 9.95 *(978-1-55050-297-8(2))*; 2003. (ENG., Illus.). 208p. (gr. 3-6). pap. 7.95 *(978-1-55050-271-8(9))* Coteau Bks. CAN. Dist: Fitzhenry & Whiteside, Ltd., Orca Bk. Pubs. USA.
Lindgren, Astrid. Mio, My Son. Wikland, Ilon, illus. 2003. Tr. of Mio, Min Mio. 179p. (J). 17.95 *(978-1-930900-23-3(6))* Purple Hse. Pr.
Line, Deirdre. All in the Dark. 2010. 24p. pap. 10.96 *(978-1-4251-4231-5(1))* Trafford Publishing.
Living the Life Prequel - Kurtis. 2003. (Living the Life Ser.: Vol. 2). 160p. (YA). pap. 14.00 *(978-0-9710398-3-4(6))* Michael-Christopher Bks.
Livingston, Juwuan. One Word for Good. 2011. 28p. pap. 15.99 *(978-1-4568-4341-0(9))* Xlibris Corp.
Livsey, John. '38: The Great Hurricane in Quonochontaug, Rhode Island. 2004. 288p. (YA). per. 15.49 *(978-0-9754979-2-0(8))* Big Wave Bks.
Lodding, Linda Ravin. The Busy Life of Ernestine Buckmeister. Beaky, Suzanne, illus. 2011. (ENG.). 32p. (J). (gr. -1-1). 16.95 *(978-0-9799746-9-4(0))* Flashlight Pr.
Lopez, Christopher P. The Absolute Truth about Lying. Racine, Victoria, illus. 2011. 36p. pap. 24.95 *(978-1-4626-3245-9(9))* America Star Bks.
Love, Maryann Cusimano. Sleep, Baby, Sleep. van Lieshout, Maria, illus. 2013. (ENG.). 30p. (J). (gr. -1-k). bds. 6.99 *(978-0-399-16144-5(9)*, Philomel Bks.) Penguin Young Readers Group.
—You Are My I Love You. Ichikawa, Satomi, illus. (Little Letters Ser.). (ENG.). (J). (gr. -1-k). 2012. 32p. 4.99 *(978-0-448-46307-0(5)*, Grosset & Dunlap) 2010. 30p. bds. 6.99 *(978-0-399-24395-0(X)*, Philomel Bks.) Penguin Young Readers Group.
—You Are My I Love You / Tú Eres Mi Te Quiero. Ichikawa, Satomi, illus. 2012. (SPA & ENG.). 28p. (J). (gr. -1 — 1). bds. 6.99 *(978-0-399-24396-7(8)*, Philomel Bks.) Penguin Young Readers Group.
—You Are My Miracle. Ichikawa, Satomi, illus. (ENG.). (J). (gr. -1 — 1). 2012. 28p. bds. 6.99 *(978-0-399-25791-9(8))* 2005. 32p. 16.99 *(978-0-399-24037-9(3))* Penguin Young Readers Group. (Philomel Bks.).
Lovins, Jennifer O. Opihi Baby. 2008. 32p. pap. 14.95 *(978-1-57306-285-5(5))* Bess Pr., Inc.
Lowe, Nakesha. Just Leave Me Alone. 2011. 16p. 10.70 *(978-1-4567-2641-6(2))* AuthorHouse.
Lowory, Brigid. Guitar Highway Rose. 2003. (ENG.). 208p. (YA). (gr. 7-12). tchr. ed. 16.95 *(978-0-8234-1790-2(5))* Holiday Hse., Inc.
Lowry, Brigid. Guitar Highway Rose. 2006. (ENG.). 208p. (YA). (gr. 8-12). reprint ed. pap. 18.99 *(978-0-312-34296-8(9)*, 9780312342968, St. Martin's Griffin) St. Martin's Pr.
Lubbe, Angela C. Don't Forget about Us. 2012. 16p. pap. 15.99 *(978-1-4685-9538-3(5))* AuthorHouse.
Lucado, Max. Just in Case You Ever Wonder, 1 vol. 32p. 2011. (ENG.). (J). 16.99 *(978-1-4003-1958-9(7))* 2009. (ENG.). (J). bds. 12.99 *(978-1-4003-8531-7(8))* 2005. 9.99 *(978-1-4003-0740-1(6))* Nelson, Thomas Inc.
Lupica, Mike. Safe at Home. 2009. (Comeback Kids Ser.). (ENG.). 192p. (J). (gr. 3-7). 6.99 *(978-0-14-241460-6(3)*, Puffin Books) Penguin Young Readers Group.
—Travel Team. 2004. (ENG.). 288p. (J). (gr. 3-7). 17.99 *(978-0-399-24150-5(7)*, Philomel Bks.) Penguin Young Readers Group.
Lynch, Chris. Iceman. 2013. (ENG.). (YA). (gr. 7). 160p. 16.99 *(978-1-4424-6002-7(4))*; 176p. pap. 9.99 *(978-1-4424-6001-0(6))* Simon & Schuster Bks. For Young Readers. (Simon & Schuster Bks. For Young Readers).
Macaulay, David. Black & White. 2005. (ENG., Illus.). 32p. (J). (gr. -1-3). 7.99 *(978-0-618-63687-7(0))* Houghton Mifflin Harcourt Publishing Co.
MacDonald, Annie. Bubbles for Poppo. 2011. 32p. pap. 19.95 *(978-1-4520-1720-4(4))* AuthorHouse.
MacDonald, Margaret Read. Tunjur! Tunjur! Tunjur! A Palestinian Folktale, 0 vols. Arzoumanian, Alik, illus. 2012. (ENG.). 32p. (J). (gr. -1-3). pap. 7.99 *(978-0-7614-6312-2(7)*, 9780761463122, Amazon Children's Publishing) Amazon Publishing.
Mace, Aubrey. My Fairy Grandmother. 2009. 270p. pap. 16.99 *(978-1-59955-217-0(5))* Cedar Fort, Inc./CFI Distribution.
Mack, Paulette. Cookout at Grandma's House: The Adventures of Mielle & Cheeky. 2006. (ENG., Illus.). 24p. per. 10.95 *(978-1-59800-998-9(2))* Outskirts Pr., Inc.
MacLachlan, Patricia. The Truth of Me. (J). (gr. 1-5). 2015. (ENG.). 144p. pap. 5.99 *(978-0-06-199861-4(3))* 2013. (ENG.). 128p. 16.99 *(978-0-06-199859-1(1))* 2013. 128p. lib. bdg. 17.89 *(978-0-06-199860-7(5))* HarperCollins Pubs. (Tegen, Katherine Bks).
MacLean, Christine. Even Firefighters Hug Their Moms. Reed, Mike, illus. 2004. (ENG.). 32p. (J). (gr. k-3). pap. 5.99 *(978-0-14-240191-0(9)*, Puffin Books) Penguin Young Readers Group.
MacPherson, Lorry. Lynne Woke Up! Alexander, Yvonne Rabdau, illus. 2007. 20p. per. 24.95 *(978-1-4137-2536-0(8))* America Star Bks.
Magnus, Kellie. Little Lion Goes to School. Robinson, Michael, illus. l.t. ed. 2003. 16p. (J). 9.99 *(978-0-9744211-0-0(3))* Media Magic New York.
Magsamen, Sandra. Good Night, My Love. 2013. (Padded Cloth Covers with Lift-The-Flaps Ser.). (ENG., Illus.). 10p. (J). (gr. -1-17). bds. 8.99 *(978-0-316-17691-0(5))* Little, Brown Bks. for Young Readers.
—I Love You, Honey Bunny. Magsamen, Sandra, illus. 2016. (ENG., Illus.). 12p. (J). (— 1). bds. 7.99 *(978-1-338-11084-5(5)*, Cartwheel Bks.) Scholastic, Inc.
—Welcome Little One. 2015. (ENG., Illus.). 32p. (J). (gr. 3-8). 16.99 *(978-1-4926-1930-7(2)*, Sourcebooks Jabberwocky) Sourcebooks, Inc.
Maier, Inger M. When Fuzzy Was Afraid: Of Losing His Mother. Candon, Jennifer, illus. 2004. 32p. (J). 14.95 *(978-1-59147-168-4(0))*; pap. 9.95 *(978-1-59147-169-1(9))* American Psychological Assn. (Magination Pr.).
Malone, Jen. Changes in Latitudes. 2017. 384p. (YA). (gr. 8). pap. 9.99 *(978-0-06-238017-3(6)*, HarperTeen) HarperCollins Pubs.
Mansfield, Creina. My Nutty Neighbours. 2006. (ENG., Illus.). 192p. (J). pap. 12.95 *(978-0-86278-788-2(2))* O'Brien Pr., Ltd., The IRL. Dist: Dufour Editions, Inc.

PQR

Martella, Liz. Izabella & her Wardrobe. 2007. 18p. 12.95 *(978-0-615-14941-7(3))* Martella, Liz.

Martin, Emily Winfield. The Wonderful Things You Will Be. Martin, Emily Winfield, illus. 2015. (ENG., Illus.). 36p. (J). (gr. -1-2). 17.99 *(978-0-385-37671-6(5),* Random Hse. Bks. for Young Readers) Random Hse. Children's Bks.

—The Wonderful Things You Will Be. 2015. (ENG., Illus.). 36p. (J). (gr. -1-2). lib. bdg. 20.99 *(978-0-375-97327-7(3),* Random Hse. Bks. for Young Readers) Random Hse. Children's Bks.

Martinez Jover, Carmen. The Twin Kangaroo Treasure Hunt, a Gay Parenting Story. Martinez, Rosemary, illus. 2013. 32p. pap. *(978-607-00-6545-3(X))* Martinez Jover, María del Carmen Dorotea.

Marzollo, Jean. Mama Mama - Papa Papa. Regan, Laura, illus. 2003. (Flip Boardbks.). (ENG.). 32p. (J). (gr. -1 — 1). bds. 7.99 *(978-0-06-051915-5(0),* HarperFestival) HarperCollins Pubs.

Massie, Elizabeth. Ameri-Scares: Virginia. 2013. 150p. pap. 12.99 *(978-1-937530-52-5(3))* Crossroad Pr.

Masurel, Claire. Two Homes. Denton, Kady MacDonald, illus. 2003. (ENG.). 40p. (J). (gr. -1-2). 6.99 *(978-0-7636-1984-8(1))* Candlewick Pr.

—Two Homes. 2003. 17.20 *(978-0-613-69470-4(8),* Turtleback) Turtleback Bks.

Mayes, Joanne. I'm Isaac: My Brain Is Green. 2008. 27p. pap. 24.95 *(978-1-60563-984-0(2))* America Star Bks.

Mazer, Norma Fox. What I Believe. 2007. (ENG., Illus.). 176p. (J). (gr. 5-9). pap. 12.95 *(978-0-15-206283-5(1))* Houghton Mifflin Harcourt Publishing Co.

—When We First Met. 2015. (ENG., Illus.). 208p. (YA). (gr. 7). pap. 14.99 *(978-1-4814-5103-1(0),* Atheneum Bks. for Young Readers) Simon & Schuster Children's Publishing.

McBratney, Sam. Guess How Much I Love You: Baby Book. Jeram, Anita, illus. 2014. (Guess How Much I Love You Ser.). (ENG.). 64p. (J). (gr. k-12). 14.99 *(978-0-7636-7023-8(5))* Candlewick Pr.

—Let's Play in the Snow. Jeram, Anita, illus. 2012. (Guess How Much I Love You Ser.). (ENG.). 24p. (J). (gr. k — 1). bds. 4.99 *(978-0-7636-6121-2(X))* Candlewick Pr.

—A Surprise for the Nutbrown Hares. Jeram, Anita, illus. 2009. (J). *(978-0-7636-4903-6(1))* Candlewick Pr.

—There, There. Bates, Ivan, illus. 2015. (ENG.). 32p. (J). (-k). bds. 7.99 *(978-0-7636-7565-3(2),* Templar) Candlewick Pr.

—You're All My Favorites. Jeram, Anita, illus. 2008. (ENG.). 32p. (J). (gr. k-k). bds. 7.99 *(978-0-7636-4297-6(5))* Candlewick Pr.

McCaughrean, Geraldine. Casting the Gods Adrift: A Tale of Ancient Egypt. Ludlow, Patricia D., illus. 2003. (ENG.). 112p. (J). (gr. 4-7). 15.95 *(978-0-8126-2684-1(2))* Cricket Bks.

Mccauley, Plum. It All Started with A Bicycle. 2011. (ENG.). 220p. pap. 11.95 *(978-1-4327-7412-7(3))* Outskirts Pr., Inc.

McCourt, Lisa. I Love You, Stinky Face. Moore, Cyd, illus. (ENG.). (J). 2004. 16p. (gr. 3-7). bds. 6.99 *(978-0-439-63572-1(1))* 2003. 32p. (gr. -1 — 1). pap. 6.99 *(978-0-439-63469-4(5))* Scholastic, Inc.

Mcghee, Alison. So Many Days. Yoo, Taeeun, illus. 2010. (ENG.). 40p. (J). (gr. k-2). 15.99 *(978-1-4169-5857-4(6),* Atheneum Bks. for Young Readers) Simon & Schuster Children's Publishing.

McGriff, Shawna A. Princess Pink: Princess Pink Helps Zion, Melinda, & Jasmine Learn to Communicate about Their Parents' Divorces. 2010. 56p. pap. 24.00 *(978-1-4520-3941-1(0))* AuthorHouse.

McKay, Lise Y. The Mysterious Well. 2012. 130p. pap. 14.95 *(978-1-59663-865-5(6),* Mount Helicon Pr.) Rock, James A. & Co. Pubs.

McKee, David. El Principe Pedro y el oso de Peluche. (SPA.). (J). 7.95 *(978-958-04-6258-3(5))* Norma S.A. COL. Dist: Distribuidora Norma, Inc.

McKellop, Holly R. To the Moon. 2012. 32p. pap. 24.95 *(978-1-4626-8034-4(8))* America Star Bks.

McLaughlin, Lauren. Wonderful You: An Adoption Story. So, Meilo, illus. 2017. (ENG.). 32p. (J). (gr. -1-2). 17.99 *(978-0-553-51001-0(0),* Random Hse. Bks. for Young Readers) Random Hse. Children's Bks.

McMahen, Chris. Box of Shocks. 1 vol. 2011. (ENG.). 168p. (J). (gr. 4-7). pap. 9.95 *(978-1-55469-917-9(7))* Orca Bk. Pubs. USA.

McNaney, Jeanne. Miracle in Sumatra: The Story of Gutsy Gus. Cochard, David, illus. 2009. (ENG.). 32p. (J). (gr. -1-3). 16.95 *(978-0-9814534-6-0(5))* Ovation Bks.

McNeal, Laura & McNeal, Tom. Crooked. 2007. (ENG.). 368p. (YA). (gr. 7-11). pap. 9.99 *(978-0-375-84191-0(1),* Ember) Random Hse. Children's Bks.

McOmber, Rachel B., ed. McOmber Phonics Storybooks: Mom & Dad Hop-Jig. rev. ed. (Illus.). (J). *(978-0-944991-16-9(5))* Swift Learning Resources.

McTrustry, Chris. Red Goes Green, 1 vol. rev. ed. 2013. (Fiction Readers Ser.). (ENG., Illus.). 32p. (J). (gr. 3-3). pap. 8.99 *(978-1-4333-5641-4(4))* Shell Educational Publishing.

McVicar, William E. Turtle Tries. 2008. 16p. pap. 24.95 *(978-1-60563-180-6(9))* America Star Bks.

Meagher, Ed. D. Zach & His Dog: A Story of Bonding, Love, & Loss for Children & Adults to Share Together. 2009. 56p. pap. 23.99 *(978-1-4389-4228-5(1))* AuthorHouse.

Mean Margaret. 2014. (ENG., Illus.). 176p. (J). (gr. 2-7). 16.99 *(978-1-4814-1014-4(8),* Atheneum Bks. for Young Readers) Simon & Schuster Children's Publishing.

Meron, Renato Mas. Why Corn Kernels Pop Up. 2012. 24p. pap. 24.95 *(978-1-62709-859-5(3))* America Star Bks.

Metzger, Steve. I Love You All Year Long. Keay, Claire, illus. 2009. 20p. (J). (gr. -1-k). 8.95 *(978-1-58925-847-1(9))* Tiger Tales.

Michaels, Kat. Gentle Is the Night. 2008. (J). 15.95 *(978-0-9745052-7-5(7))* Tree Of Life Publishing.

Middlestadt, Donna. Little Miss No Name. 2004. (ENG.). 218p. pap. 24.95 *(978-1-4137-0894-3(3))* America Star Bks.

Mike. New Pet. Mike, illus. l.t. ed. 2005. (ENG., Illus.). 32p. (J). lib. bdg. 14.95 *(978-0-9658365-8-6(4))* Beetle Bug Bks.

Millmann, Anita Sutherland. Zitta & Nelli. 2011. 24p. pap. 15.14 *(978-1-4634-0036-1(5))* AuthorHouse.

Mohler, Marie. Little Bird's Earth Nest. 2008. 32p. 18.95 *(978-1-4357-1711-4(2))* Lulu Pr., Inc.

Monte, Diane E. Coming Home: Welcome Home at Last. 2012. 24p. pap. 17.99 *(978-1-4772-5713-5(6))* AuthorHouse.

Montgomery, Arch. Hank. 2003. 171p. (YA). 19.95 *(978-1-890862-22-0(3))* Bancroft Pr.

Moore, Katherine Roberts. Is God Behind the Big Blue Sky? Moore, Kristen L., illus. 2010. 34p. pap. 13.95 *(978-1-60911-705-4(0),* Eloquent Bks.) Strategic Book Publishing & Rights Agency (SBPRA).

Moran, Alex & Sullivan, Paula. Todd's Box. Westcott, Nadine Bernard, illus. 2004. (Green Light Readers Level 1 Ser.). (ENG.). 24p. (J). (gr. -1-3). pap. 3.95 *(978-0-15-205094-8(9))* Houghton Mifflin Harcourt Publishing Co.

—Todd's Box. 2004. (Green Light Readers — Level 1 Ser.). (gr. -1-2). 13.50 *(978-0-613-81968-8(3),* Turtleback) Turtleback Bks.

Moreillon, Judi. Read to Me, 1 vol. Teis, Kyra, illus. (J). 2004. (ENG.). 32p. (gr. -1). bds. 6.95 *(978-1-59572-014-6(6))* 2003. 24p. 6.95 *(978-1-932065-49-7(0),* 1-718-784-9112) Star Bright Bks., Inc.

Moreira, Carol. Charged, 1 vol. 2008. (Lorimer SideStreets Ser.). (ENG.). 128p. (YA). (gr. 9-12). 9.95 *(978-1-55277-006-1(0),* 9781552770061); 16.95 *(978-1-55277-008-5(7),* 9781552770085) Lorimer, James & Co., Ltd., Pubs. CAN. Dist: Casemate Pubs. & Bk. Distributors, LLC.

Morgan, Melissa J. Alex's Challenge. 2005. (Camp Confidential Ser.: 4). (ENG.). 160p. (J). (gr. 3-7). mass mkt. 4.99 *(978-0-448-43876-4(3),* Grosset & Dunlap) Penguin Young Readers Group.

—Grace's Twist. 2005. (Camp Confidential Ser.: 3). (ENG.). 160p. (J). (gr. 3-7). mass mkt. 4.99 *(978-0-448-43875-7(5),* Grosset & Dunlap) Penguin Young Readers Group.

Morrow, Tara Jaye. Just Mommy & Me. Bratun, Katy, illus. 2004. 32p. (J). 13.89 *(978-0-06-000725-6(7))* HarperCollins Pubs.

Mossiano, Lilly. My New Mommy. Mossiano, Sage, illus. 2012. 28p. pap. 24.95 *(978-1-4626-8898-2(5))* PublishAmerica, Inc.

Mulholland, Clara. Naughty Miss Bunny. 2007. 128p. 25.95 *(978-1-4218-3838-0(9),* 1st World Library - Literary Society) 1st World Publishing, Inc.

Mulock, Dinah Maria. The Little Lame Prince & His Traveling Cloak. 2005. reprint ed. pap. 20.95 *(978-1-4179-1940-6(X))* Kessinger Publishing, LLC.

Munsch, Robert. Love You Forever. 2014. (ENG.). 32p. (J). (gr. 3-7). 10.20 *(978-1-63245-248-1(0))* Lectorum Pubns., Inc.

Murphy, Mary. I Like It When... Campoy, F. Isabel & Flor Ada, Alma, trs. from ENG. 2008. (ENG., Illus.). 22p. (J). (gr. k — 1). bds. 6.95 *(978-0-15-206045-9(6))* Houghton Mifflin Harcourt Publishing Co.

—I Like It When... 2005. (ENG., Illus.). 22p. (J). (gr. k — 1). bds. 6.95 *(978-0-15-205649-0(1))* Houghton Mifflin Harcourt Publishing Co.

—Utterly Lovely One. 2012. (ENG., Illus.). 32p. (J). (gr. -1-k). 16.99 *(978-0-7636-5267-8(9))* Candlewick Pr.

Murphy, Stuart J. Happy, Healthy Ajay! 2012. (I See I Learn Ser.). (ENG., Illus.). 32p. (J). (-k). 14.95 *(978-1-58089-470-8(4));* pap. 6.95 *(978-1-58089-471-5(2))* Charlesbridge Publishing, Inc.

My Dad Is Great. (My Great Relatives... Ser.). 32p. (J). *(978-1-84250-574-8(2),* Bright Sparks) Parragon, Inc.

My Father the Mad Professor: Individual Title Six-Packs. (Action Packs Ser.). 120p. (gr. 3-5). 44.00 *(978-0-7635-8424-5(X))* Rigby Education.

My Name Is Really Lucy! 2003. (J). pap. *(978-0-9745591-1-7(3))* Roehm, Nancy Jean.

Myers, Anna. Tulsa Burning. 2004. (Illus.). 184p. (J). (gr. 3-7). 16.95 *(978-0-8027-8829-0(7))* Walker & Co.

Myers, Walter Dean. The Dream Bearer. 2003. (ENG.). 192p. (J). (gr. 5-18). 15.99 *(978-0-06-029521-9(X),* Amistad) HarperCollins Pubs.

Nakawaki, Hatsue. Wait! Wait! Sakai, Komako, illus. 2013. (ENG.). 24p. (J). 14.95 *(978-1-59270-138-4(8))* Enchanted Lion Bks., LLC.

Nelson, Annabelle. Angelica's Hope: A Story for Young People & Their Parents about the Need to Talk about Things That No One Talks About. Palomares, Franz, illus. 2003. (SPA.). *(978-0-9656732-9-7(4))* WHEEL Council, Inc., The.

Nelson, Theresa. Ruby Electric. 2004. (ENG.). 272p. (J). (gr. 5-7). reprint ed. pap. 12.99 *(978-0-689-87146-7(5),* Atheneum Bks. for Young Readers) Simon & Schuster Children's Publishing.

Neufeld, John. Edgar Allan. 2007. 136p. (gr. 5-9). per. 11.95 *(978-0-595-45039-8(3),* Backinprint.com) iUniverse, Inc.

Nevin, Judy Carey. What Daddies Like. Six, Stephanie, illus. 2017. (ENG.). 32p. (J). (gr. -1-3). 16.99 *(978-1-4998-0197-2(1))* Little Bee Books Inc.

Newman, Lesléa. The Boy Who Cried Fabulous. Ferguson, Peter, illus. 2007. (ENG.). 32p. (J). (gr. -1-2). pap. 7.99 *(978-1-58246-224-0(0),* Tricycle Pr.) Random Hse. Children's Bks.

Newswanger, Rebecca. God Gave Us Fathers & Mothers. Steiner, Maria, illus. 2009. (Little Jewel Book Ser.). 24p. (J). (gr. 2). pap. 2.70 *(978-0-7399-2408-2(7))* Rod & Staff Pubs., Inc.

The Night Before Kindergarten. 2014. (Night Before Ser.). (ENG.). 32p. (J). (gr. 7-12). 8.24 *(978-1-63245-263-4(4))* Lectorum Pubns., Inc.

Nixon, Joan Lowery. John's Story, 1775. 2004. (J). *(978-0-87935-228-8(0))* Colonial Williamsburg Foundation.

—Will's Story, 1771. 2004. (J). *(978-0-87935-226-4(4))* Colonial Williamsburg Foundation.

Nkemayang, Chelsea. Split Ville. 2012. (Illus.). 36p. pap. 22.88 *(978-1-4772-4177-6(9))* AuthorHouse.

Nolan, Han. Born Blue. 2003. (ENG.). 308p. (YA). (gr. 9-12). pap. 7.99 *(978-0-15-204697-2(6))* Houghton Mifflin Harcourt Publishing Co.

Nolen, Jerdine. Hewitt Anderson's Great Big Life. Nelson, Kadir, illus. (ENG.). 40p. (J). (gr. k-3). 2013. 7.99 *(978-1-4424-6035-5(0))* 2005. 18.99 *(978-0-689-86866-5(9))* Simon & Schuster/Paula Wiseman Bks. (Simon & Schuster/Paula Wiseman Bks.).

North, Sherry. Because You Are My Baby. Hall, Marcellus, illus. 2008. (ENG.). 32p. (J). (gr. -1-1). 16.95 *(978-0-8109-9482-9(8),* Abrams Bks. for Young Readers) Abrams, Inc.

Numeroff, Laura Joffe. Would I Trade My Parents? Bernardin, James, illus. 2009. (ENG.). 32p. (J). (gr. k-2). 16.95 *(978-0-8109-0637-2(6),* Abrams Bks. for Young Readers) Abrams, Inc.

Oates, Joyce Carol. Freaky Green Eyes. 2003. 352p. (J). 16.99 *(978-0-06-623759-6(9))* 2005. (ENG.). 368p. (YA). (gr. 8). reprint ed. pap. 9.99 *(978-0-06-447348-4(1))* HarperCollins Pubs. (HarperTeen).

Ockun, Lisa C. Sammy the Tin Man. 2012. 32p. pap. 19.99 *(978-1-4685-4328-5(8))* AuthorHouse.

O'Connell, Rebecca. The Baby Goes Beep. Wilson-Max, Ken, illus. 2010. (ENG.). 16p. (J). (gr. -1 — 1). bds. 7.99 *(978-0-8075-0508-3(0))* Whitman, Albert & Co.

O'Connell, Rebecca. Baby Parade. Poole, Susie, illus. 2017. (ENG.). 24p. (J). (gr. -1 — 1). bds. 7.99 ***(978-0-8075-0515-1(3))*** Whitman, Albert & Co.

O'Dare, Helen. Love. O'Byrne, Nicola, illus. 2016. (ENG.). 26p. (J). bds. 6.99 *(978-1-62686-677-5(5),* Silver Dolphin Bks.) Readerlink Distribution Services, LLC.

Oelschlager, Vanita. Francesca. Blanc, Mike, illus. 2008. (ENG.). 32p. (J). (gr. -1-3). 17.95 *(978-0-9800162-4-6(X))* VanitaBooks.

On the Job: Individual Title Six-Packs. (gr. -1-2). 27.00 *(978-0-7635-9468-8(7))* Rigby Education.

Orgill, Rosanne Buhler. Mama Knows about Fences. 2008. 36p. 18.99 *(978-1-4343-2689-8(6))* AuthorHouse.

Orloff, Karen Kaufman. I Wanna Iguana. Catrow, David, illus. 2004. (ENG.). 32p. (J). (gr. -1-3). 16.99 *(978-0-399-23717-1(8),* G.P. Putnam's Sons Books for Young Readers) Penguin Young Readers Group.

Orr, Fran E. When Mommy Was a Soldier, 1 vol. 2008. (ENG.). 26p. 24.95 *(978-1-4241-9576-3(4))* America Star Bks.

Pallone, Robert. The Adventures of Main Man: A Child's View of the World. 2010. 28p. pap. 12.95 *(978-1-4490-5598-1(2))* AuthorHouse.

Palmer, Catherine. Fatal Harvest. l.t. ed. 2004. (Matthew 25 Ser.). 496p. (YA). 28.95 *(978-0-7862-6259-5(1))* Thorndike Pr.

Paratore, Coleen Murtagh. The Wedding Planner's Daughter. 2005. (Wedding Planner's Daughter Ser.). (ENG.). 208p. (J). (gr. 3-7). 15.95 *(978-0-689-87340-9(9),* Simon & Schuster Bks. For Young Readers) Simon & Schuster Bks. For Young Readers.

Parish, Herman. Amelia Bedelia Chapter Book #2: Amelia Bedelia Unleashed (Special Edition) 2013. (ENG., Illus.). 160p. (J). *(978-0-06-227056-6(7),* Collins Design) HarperCollins Pubs.

Parker, Marjorie Blain. I Love You near & Far. Henry, Jed, illus. 2015. (Snuggle Time Stories Ser.). (ENG.). 24p. (J). (gr. -1-1). 9.95 *(978-1-4549-0507-3(7))* Sterling Publishing Co., Inc.

Parker, Vicki Sue. The Get Well Soon... Balloon. Beebe, Susan, illus. 2005. 16p. (J). 15.00 *(978-1-931117-35-7(7),* BALL) Lash & Assocs. Publishing/Training, Inc.

Paterson, Katherine. El Signo del Crisantemo. 2003.Tr. of Sign of the Chrysanthemum. (SPA., Illus.). 142p. (YA). (gr. 5-8). *(978-84-348-6699-7(4),* SM30544) SM Ediciones ESP. Dist: Lectorum Pubns., Inc.

Patillo, D. L. Jessie's World: "the New Baby" 2012. 32p. pap. 21.99 *(978-1-4797-3142-8(0))* Xlibris Corp.

Pau Pau. Bird Bandit, 1 vol. 2010. 56p. pap. 16.95 *(978-1-4489-3991-6(7))* America Star Bks.

Paul, Ann Whitford. If Animals Kissed Good Night. Walker, David, illus. 2014. (ENG.). 34p. (J). (gr. -1-1). bds. 7.99 *(978-0-374-30021-0(6),* 9780374300210, Farrar, Straus & Giroux (BYR)) Farrar, Straus & Giroux.

Peck, J. L. Mr Crabby Pants & the Zoo. 2012. 24p. pap. 17.99 *(978-1-4685-7953-6(3))* AuthorHouse.

Pentz, Jane A. Horatio's Magical Journeys - Horatio's New Book. 2007. 108p. pap. 10.00 *(978-1-892426-10-9(2))* LMA Publishing.

Perryman, Kawanis. Gabrielle's Prayer: Gabrielle's Wish. 2011. 28p. pap. 13.59 *(978-1-4567-2731-4(1))* AuthorHouse.

Peters, Julie Anne. Define Normal. 2003. (ENG., Illus.). 196p. (J). (gr. 7-17). pap. 9.99 *(978-0-316-73489-9(6))* Little, Brown Bks. for Young Readers.

Pierre, Eileen. It's Not Easy Being Mean. 2010. 56p. pap. 10.00 *(978-1-60860-929-1(4),* Eloquent Bks.) Strategic Book Publishing & Rights Agency (SBPRA).

Pinkham, Mark Amaru. Love Me Later. 2005. 202p. 14.95 *(978-1-932188-02-8(9))* Adventures Unlimited Pr.

Pinkwater, Daniel M. Mrs. Noodlekugel. Stower, Adam, illus. 2013. (Mrs. Noodlekugel Ser.). (ENG.). 80p. (J). (gr. k-4). pap. 5.99 *(978-0-7636-6452-7(9))* Candlewick Pr.

Pinocchio: 6 Small Books. (gr. k-2). 23.00 *(978-0-7635-8513-6(0))* Rigby Education.

Piper, Sophie. From the Day You Were Born. Stephenson, Kristina, illus. 2014. (ENG.). 24p. (J). (— 1). bds. 6.99 *(978-0-7459-6237-5(8))* Lion Hudson PLC GBR. Dist: Independent Pubs. Group.

Pixton, Kaaren. Mama & Baby! 2010. (Indestructibles Ser.). (ENG., Illus.). 12p. (J). (gr. k — 1). pap. 5.95 *(978-0-7611-5859-2(6),* 15859) Workman Publishing Co., Inc.

Polacco, Patricia. Mommies Say Shhh! Polacco, Patricia, illus. 2005. (ENG., Illus.). 40p. (J). (gr. -1-1). 16.99 *(978-0-399-24341-7(0),* Philomel Bks.) Penguin Young Readers Group.

Porter-Gaylord, Laurel. I Love My Mommy Because... Wolff, Ashley, illus. 2004. (ENG.). 22p. (J). (gr. -1 — 1). bds. 6.99 *(978-0-525-47247-6(9),* Dutton Books for Young Readers) Penguin Young Readers Group.

Posner, Richard. Sweet Pain. 2014. (ENG.). 276p. (J). (gr. 5-12). pap. 16.95 *(978-1-59077-318-5(7))* Evans, M. & Co., Inc.

Powers, Elizabeth. Where Are You Taking Me? 2008. 28p. pap. 24.95 *(978-1-60563-033-5(0))* America Star Bks.

Powers, John. Seymour & the Big Red Rhino. Colavecchio, Alan, illus. 2005. 32p. (J). (gr. -1-3). 14.95 *(978-1-929039-21-0(2))* Ambassador Bks., Inc.

Preble, Joy. The Sweet Dead Life. 2014. (ENG., Illus.). 278p. (YA). (gr. 9). pap. 10.99 *(978-1-61695-368-3(3),* Soho Teen) Soho Pr., Inc.

Preiss, Thomas. The Boat under the Boat: A Story about the Golden Rule. 2nd rev. ed. 2004. (ENG., Illus.). 32p. (J). per. 14.95 *(978-0-9798620-1-4(9))* Peralta Publishing, LLC.

Prince, Mark E. I'm Happy When. 2009. 20p. pap. 12.99 *(978-1-4389-5523-0(5))* AuthorHouse.

Prins, Piet. Stefan Derksen's Polar Adventure. 2004. (Illus.). 237p. (J). pap. *(978-1-894666-67-1(4))* Inheritance Pubns.

Prochovnic, Dawn Babb. Hip Hip Hooray! It's Family Day! Sign Language for Family, 1 vol. Bauer, Stephanie, illus. 2012. (ENG.). 32p. 28.50 *(978-1-61641-837-3(0),* Looking Glass Library) Magic Wagon.

Propp, Vera W. When the Soldiers Were Gone: A Novel. 2006. 101p. (J). (gr. 4-8). reprint ed. 15.00 *(978-1-4223-5310-3(9))* DIANE Publishing Co.

Quillen, Donna Mc. I Can't Wait. 2011. 50p. 24.99 *(978-1-4628-8475-9(X));* pap. 15.99 *(978-1-4628-8474-2(1))* Xlibris Corp.

Quivers, Anthony S. Lil' Johnny's First Day of School. 2010. 24p. 13.99 *(978-1-4520-4149-0(0))* AuthorHouse.

Rabe, Tish. Love You, Hug You, Read to You! Endersby, Frank, illus. 2015. (ENG.). 32p. (J). (gr. -1 — 1). bds. 7.99 *(978-1-101-93655-9(X),* Random Hse. Bks. for Young Readers) Random Hse. Children's Bks.

—¡Te Amo, Te Abrazo, Leo Contigo!/Love You, Hug You, Read to You! Endersby, Frank, illus. 2015. (SPA & ENG.). 32p. (J). (gr. -1 — 1). bds. 7.99 *(978-1-101-93657-3(6),* Random Hse. Bks. for Young Readers) Random Hse. Children's Bks.

Rainwater, Crystal. Song the Slug: Book 1, 1 vol. 2010. 24p. pap. 24.95 *(978-1-4489-4215-2(2))* PublishAmerica, Inc.

Raisinghani, Jaya. Sweet Child of Mine. 2014. 16p. pap. 15.00 *(978-1-4828-9218-5(9))* Partridge Pub.

—Sweet Child of Mine. 2012. 16p. pap. 15.00 *(978-1-4669-3099-5(3))* Trafford Publishing.

Ramos, Jorge. I'm Just Like My Mom. Gutierrez, Akemi, illus. 2008.Tr. of Me Parezco Tanto a mi Papá. (ENG & SPA.). 40p. (J). (gr. -1-1). 16.99 *(978-0-06-123968-7(2),* Rayo) HarperCollins Pubs.

Rankin, Laura. Ruthie & the (Not So) Very Busy Day. Rankin, Laura, illus. 2014. (ENG., Illus.). 32p. (J). (gr. -1-1). 17.99 *(978-1-59990-052-0(1),* 9781599900520, Bloomsbury USA Childrens) Bloomsbury Publishing USA.

Rawlings, Marjorie Kinnan. The Yearling. Wyeth, N. C., illus. 2013. (Scribner Classics Ser.). (ENG.). 416p. (J). (gr. 5-9). 29.99 *(978-1-4424-8209-8(5),* Atheneum Bks. for Young Readers) Simon & Schuster Children's Publishing.

Reeve, Rosie. Lullaby Moon. Reeve, Rosie, illus. 2010. (ENG., Illus.). 20p. (J). (gr. k — 1). bds. 8.99 *(978-0-545-21146-8(8),* Cartwheel Bks.) Scholastic, Inc.

Reichert, Amy. While Mama Had a Quick Little Chat. Boiger, Alexandra, illus. 2005. (ENG.). 40p. (J). (gr. -1-2). 16.99 *(978-0-689-85170-4(7),* Atheneum/Richard Jackson Bks.) Simon & Schuster Children's Publishing.

Reiser, Lynn. You & Me, Baby. Gentieu, Penny, photos by. 2008. (ENG., Illus.). 32p. (J). (— 1). bds. 6.99 *(978-0-375-84420-1(1),* Knopf Bks. for Young Readers) Random Hse. Children's Bks.

Renninson, Lou. Frontalknutschen. pap. 17.95 *(978-3-570-30008-4(0))* Bertelsman, Verlagsgruppe C. GmbH DEU. Dist: Distribooks, Inc.

Restle, Hope Madeline. Brianna in Pink. 2007. 156p. per. 11.95 *(978-0-595-47401-1(2))* iUniverse, Inc.

RH Disney. Finding Dory. RH Disney, illus. 2016. (Junior Novel Ser.). (ENG., Illus.). 144p. (J). (gr. 2-5). 6.99 *(978-0-7364-3486-7(0),* RH/Disney) Random Hse. Children's Bks.

RH Disney Staff & Disney Enterprises Inc. Staff. Best Dad in the Sea. 2003. (Step into Reading Level 1 Ser.). (gr. k-3). lib. bdg. 13.55 *(978-0-613-73685-5(0),* Turtleback) Turtleback Bks.

Richmond, Marianne. I Love You So... (ENG.). 24p. (J). 2015. (Marianne Richmond Ser.: 0). bds. 8.99 *(978-1-4926-3381-5(X))* 2013. bds. 7.99 *(978-1-4022-7953-9(1))* Sourcebooks, Inc. (Sourcebooks Jabberwocky).

—If I Could Keep You Little. (ENG.). (J). 2012. 24p. bds. 8.99 *(978-1-4022-7237-0(5))* 2010. (Marianne Richmond Ser.: 0). 32p. 9.95 *(978-1-934082-92-8(9))* Sourcebooks, Inc. (Sourcebooks Jabberwocky).

—If I Could Keep You Little... 2010. (Marianne Richmond Ser.). (ENG.). 32p. (J). (gr. -1-2). 16.99 *(978-1-4022-5559-5(4),* Sourcebooks Jabberwocky) Sourcebooks, Inc.

—Si Pudiera Conservarte Pequeño... 2014. (SPA & ENG., Illus.). 24p. (J). bds. 6.99 *(978-1-4926-0369-6(4),* Sourcebooks Jabberwocky) Sourcebooks, Inc.

—You Are My Heart. 2015. (ENG., Illus.). 32p. (J). (-2). 16.99 *(978-1-4926-1542-2(0),* Sourcebooks Jabberwocky) Sourcebooks, Inc.

—You Are My Merry. 2015. (ENG.). 32p. (J). (-2). 16.99 *(978-1-4926-2894-1(8),* Sourcebooks Jabberwocky) Sourcebooks, Inc.

Rideau, Nicole. What Is a Pookalaka? 2009. 28p. pap. 13.99 *(978-1-4389-2275-1(2))* AuthorHouse.

Rigby Education Staff. Cinderella: Jumbled Tumble. (gr. k-2). 26.00 *(978-0-7635-2420-3(4))* Rigby Education.

—Pinocchio: Jumbled Tumble. (gr. k-2). 26.00 *(978-0-7635-2419-7(0))* Rigby Education.

—William Tell. (gr. k-2). 21.00 *(978-0-7635-2426-5(3))* Rigby Education.

Rigby, Jill. I Put It Right There! I Swear! The story of one boy's master plan to overcome executive functioning Difficulties! 2011. 28p. pap. 12.77 *(978-1-4634-3710-7(2))* AuthorHouse.

Riley-Collins, Jennifer. Daddy God. 2007. (J). pap. *(978-0-9791374-1-9(1))* Favored Publishing, Inc.

Rinaldi, Ann. The Secret of Sarah Revere. 2003. (Great Episodes Ser.). (ENG.). 336p. (J). (gr. 5-7). pap. 8.99 *(978-0-15-204684-2(4))* Houghton Mifflin Harcourt Publishing Co.

Roberts, Mary. Once upon A Monday. Lipe, Barbara, illus. 2004. 48p. (J). per. 19.95 *(978-0-9744412-0-7(1))* DinRo.

Roberts, Patricia Gaskins. My Friend Tommy Has a Daddy & a Mommy. 2012. 20p. pap. 17.99 *(978-1-4772-3273-6(7))* AuthorHouse.

Robinson, David. My Little Man. 2013. 20p. pap. 24.95 *(978-1-63004-427-5(X))* America Star Bks.

Rocha, K. E. Secrets of Bearhaven. 2016. (Bearhaven Ser.: 1). (ENG.). 256p. (J). (gr. 3-7). 14.99 *(978-0-545-81303-7(4),* Scholastic Pr.) Scholastic, Inc.

Rock, Brian. With All My Heart. Banta, Susan, illus. 2012. (ENG.). 24p. (J). *(978-1-58925-648-4(4))* Tiger Tales.

Rodgers, Mary. Freaky Friday. 2009. (Trophy Bk.). (ENG.). 192p. (J). (gr. 5-18). reprint ed. pap. 5.99 *(978-0-06-440046-6(8))* HarperCollins Pubs.

Rodriguez, Michelle. Never Far Away. 2013. 26p. pap. 9.99 *(978-0-9900061-0-7(7))* Rodriguez, Michelle.

Rokhsar, Lillian. Babytionary. Bell, Liesl, illus. 2012. (ENG.). 40p. 17.99 *(978-0-9884922-0-2(2))* Begoo Bks., LLC.

Rooney, Jodie C. Feather in Your Cap. vol 1. 2008. (ENG.). 19p. 24.95 *(978-1-60474-390-6(5))* America Star Bks.

Rosanbalm, Sunny, illus. A Gift for Baby. 2009. (SPA & ENG.). *(978-0-9685754-7-5(1))* Natural Child Project Society, The.

Rosen, Marvin. Becca in Cyberland, 1 vol. 2010. 48p. pap. 16.95 *(978-1-4489-9831-9(X))* America Star Bks.

Rossetti-Shustak, Bernadette. I Love You Through & Through. Church, Caroline Jayne, illus. 2005. (ENG.). 24p. (J). (gr. k — 1). bds. 8.95 *(978-0-439-67363-1(1),* Cartwheel Bks.) Scholastic, Inc.

—I Love You Through & Through: Board Book & Plush. Church, Caroline Jayne, illus. 2014. (ENG.). 24p. (J). (— 1). 14.99 *(978-0-545-64792-2(4),* Cartwheel Bks.) Scholastic, Inc.

—I Love You Through & Through (Te Quiero, Yo Te Quiero) Church, Caroline Jayne, illus. 2013. (Caroline Jayne Church Ser.). (ENG & SPA.). 24p. (J). (— 1). bds. 8.95 *(978-0-545-58416-6(7))* Scholastic, Inc.

Rovere, Amy. And Still They Bloom: A Family's Journey of Loss & Healing. Spector, Joel, illus. 2012. (ENG.). 48p. (J). (gr. 4-7). 14.95 *(978-1-60443-036-3(2))* American Cancer Society, Inc.

Rowland, Joanna & Weber, Penny. Always Mom, Forever Dad. 2014. (ENG., Illus.). 32p. (gr. -1-3). 16.95 *(978-0-88448-367-0(3),* 884367) Tilbury Hse. Pubs.

Rusackas, Francesca. I Love You All Day Long. Burris, Priscilla, illus. 2004. (ENG.). 32p. (J). (gr. -1-k). reprint ed. pap. 6.99 *(978-0-06-050278-2(9))* HarperCollins Pubs.

Salomon, Bob & Young, Rick. Beyond the Laces. 2015. (ENG., Illus.). (J). pap. 12.95 *(978-1-4951-5694-6(X))* Independent Pub.

Sammy's Sneeze: Individual Title Six-Packs. (gr. -1-2). 23.00 *(978-0-7635-9013-0(4))* Rigby Education.

Sanchez, Pete. A Friend for Petro. 2008. 73p. pap. 19.95 *(978-1-60474-902-1(4))* America Star Bks.

Santiago, Roberto. El Ultimo Sordo. 2003. (SPA., Illus.). 95p. *(978-84-236-3428-6(0),* ED7340) Edebé ESP. Dist: Lectorum Pubns., Inc.

Santucci, Barbara. Loon Summer. Shine, Andrea, illus. 2004. 32p. (J). (gr. k-3). 16.00 *(978-0-8028-5182-6(7))* Eerdmans, William B. Publishing Co.

Sam, Amélie & Trouillot, Virgile. A Day of Surprises. 2009. (Groove High Ser.). (Illus.). 112p. (YA). (gr. 5-8). 31.95 *(978-1-60754-209-4(9),* 1293912); pap. 15.25 *(978-1-60754-210-0(2),* 1293912) Windmill Bks.

Sawyer, Louise. Mother's Storybook Signs, Vol. 2. 2004. (YA). spiral bd. 19.95 *(978-0-9719842-8-8(X))* Martin & Brothers.

Schaumberg, Rose Mary & Schaumberg, Emily Rose. I'll Miss My Grandma, Wouldn't You? 2008. (Illus.). 40p. pap. 16.99 *(978-1-4389-1335-3(4))* AuthorHouse.

Schmid, Paul. A Pet for Petunia. 2011. (J). lib. bdg. 14.89 *(978-0-06-196332-2(1))* HarperCollins Pubs.

—A Pet for Petunia. Schmid, Paul, illus. 2011. (ENG., Illus.). 40p. (J). (gr. -1-2). 12.99 *(978-0-06-196331-5(3))* HarperCollins Pubs.

—Petunia Goes Wild. Schmid, Paul, illus. 2012. (ENG., Illus.). 40p. (J). (gr. -1-2). 12.99 *(978-0-06-196334-6(8))* HarperCollins Pubs.

Scholastic, Inc. Staff & Grimes, Nikki. A Day with Daddy. Tadgell, Nicole, illus. 2004. (Just for You Ser.). (ENG.). 32p. pap. 3.99 *(978-0-439-56850-0(1),* Teaching Resources) Scholastic, Inc.

Scholastic, Inc. Staff & Taylor-Butler, Christine. A Mom Like No Other. Devard, Nancy, illus. 2004. (Just for You Ser.). (ENG.). 32p. pap. 3.99 *(978-0-439-56853-1(6),* Teaching Resources) Scholastic, Inc.

Schwartz, Kristi. Divorced Together: For teh Sake of the Children. 2009. (ENG.). 32p. pap. 11.95 *(978-1-933916-47-7(8),* Ferne Pr.) Nelson Publishing & Marketing.

Scotton, Rob. The Perfect Present for Mom & Dad. Scotton, Rob, illus. 2012. (Splat the Cat Ser.). (ENG., Illus.). 24p. (J). (gr. k-3). pap. 4.99 *(978-0-06-210009-2(2),* HarperFestival) HarperCollins Pubs.

—The Perfect Present for Mom & Dad. 2012. (Splat the Cat 8X8 Ser.). (J). lib. bdg. 14.75 *(978-0-606-23579-2(5),* Turtleback) Turtleback Bks.

Sederman, Marty & Epstein, Seymour. The Magic Box: When Parents Can't Be There to Tuck You In. Brooks, Karen Stormer, illus. 2003. 32p. (J). (gr. -1-3). 14.95 *(978-1-55798-807-2(2),* Magination Pr.) American Psychological Assn.

Seevers, Tim. Love, Grandp. 2009. 28p. pap. 14.99 *(978-1-4389-3507-2(2))* AuthorHouse.

Segal, Howard. My Daddy the Lawyer: Mommy-Daddy Books. 2009. 16p. pap. 9.49 *(978-1-4343-0883-2(9))* AuthorHouse.

Shannon, David. Too Many Toys. Shannon, David, illus. 2008. (ENG., Illus.). 32p. (J). (gr. -1-3). 16.99 *(978-0-439-49029-0(4))* Scholastic, Inc.

Shaw, Mary. Brady Brady & the Singing Tree, 11 vols. Temple, Chuck, illus. l.t. ed. 2004. 32p. (J). per. *(978-0-9735557-3-8(4))* Brady Brady, Inc.

Sheets, Katherine. Captured by Henrey, 1 vol. 2010. 48p. pap. 16.95 *(978-1-4489-4538-2(0))* America Star Bks.

Sheinmel, Alyssa. Faceless. 2015. (ENG.). 352p. (J). (gr. 7). 18.99 *(978-0-545-67601-4(0),* Scholastic Pr.) Scholastic, Inc.

Shemtov, Yael. Sadie's Funny Feeling. 2009. 24p. pap. 16.99 *(978-1-4389-6023-4(9))* AuthorHouse.

Shields, Gillian. When the World Is Ready for Bed. Currey, Anna, illus. 2009. (ENG.). 32p. (J). (gr. -1-1). 14.99 *(978-1-59990-339-2(3),* 9781599903392, Bloomsbury USA Childrens) Bloomsbury Publishing USA.

Shollar, Leah Perl & Klineman, Harvey. The Key under the Pillow: A Story about Honoring Parents. 2004. (Illus.). 32p. (J). 10.95 *(978-1-929628-16-2(1))* Hachai Publishing.

Shoshan, Beth. That's When I'm Happy. East, Jacqueline, illus. 2011. *(978-1-4351-3618-2(7))* Barnes & Noble, Inc.

Shoup, Barbara. Wish You Were Here. 2008. (ENG.). 336p. (YA). (gr. 7). pap. 9.95 *(978-0-7387-1355-7(4),* Flux) North Star Editions.

Silves, Kate. Jamie the Giraffe Learns to Dance. 2013. 20p. pap. 13.77 *(978-1-4669-7305-3(6))* Trafford Publishing.

Siminovich, Lorena, illus. You Are My Baby: Meadow. 2015. (ENG.). 10p. (J). (gr. -1 — 1). bds. 8.99 *(978-1-4521-4011-7(1))* Chronicle Bks. LLC.

Simmons, Michael. Pool Boy. 2005. (ENG.). 192p. (YA). (gr. 7). reprint ed. pap. 7.99 *(978-0-385-73196-6(5),* Delacorte Bks. for Young Readers) Random Hse. Children's Bks.

Simon, Coco. Mia's Baker's Dozen. 2012. (Cupcake Diaries: 6). (ENG.). 160p. (J). (gr. 3-7). pap. 6.99 *(978-1-4424-4613-7(7),* Simon Spotlight) Simon Spotlight.

Simonds, William. Marcus; or, the Boy-Tamer by Walter Aimwell [Pseud.]. 2006. 336p. per. 23.99 *(978-1-4255-3348-9(5))* Michigan Publishing.

Simoneau, D. K. We're Having a Tuesday. Cornelius, Brad, illus. 2006. (ENG.). 32p. (J). 16.95 *(978-1-933302-13-3(5))* AC Pubns. Group LLC.

Skirvan, Pamela. The Bad Day. Skirvan, Ted, 3rd, illus. 2003. 12p. (J). (gr. k-6). pap. 4.95 *(978-0-9742943-0-8(6))* Skirvan, Pamela.

Slonim, David. I Loathe You. Slonim, David, illus. 2012. (ENG., Illus.). 24p. (J). (gr. -1-2). 15.99 *(978-1-4424-2244-5(0),* Aladdin) Simon & Schuster Children's Publishing.

Small, David. Eulalie & the Hopping Head. 2003. (Illus.). (J). 25.95 incl. audio *(978-1-59112-217-3(1))* Live Oak Media.

—Eulalie & the Hopping Head. Small, David, illus. 2003. (Illus.). (J). pap. 33.95 incl. audio *(978-1-59112-218-0(X))* Live Oak Media.

Smith, D. K. Sock 'n Boots - Share. 2010. 32p. pap. 13.60 *(978-0-557-52614-7(0))* Lulu Pr., Inc.

Smith, Jason. We Share When We Sleep. 2012. 28p. pap. 19.99 *(978-1-4772-5446-2(3))* AuthorHouse.

Smith, Rosie. My Dad's the Coolest. Whatley, Bruce, illus. 2017. (ENG.). 24p. (J). (gr. -1). bds. 6.95 ***(978-1-4549-2479-1(9))*** Sterling Publishing Co., Inc.

Smucker, Anna Egan. To Keep the South Manitou Light. 2004. (Great Lakes Books Ser.). (ENG., Illus.). 144p. (J). 23.95 *(978-0-8143-3235-1(8),* 1148, Painted Turtle) Wayne State Univ. Pr.

Snowe, Olivia. Beauty & the Basement, 1 vol. Lamoreaux, Michelle, illus. 2014. (Twicetold Tales Ser.). (ENG.). 128p. (gr. 3-4). 8.95 *(978-1-4342-9830-0(2))* Stone Arch Bks.

Sommer, Carl. The Donkey, Fox, & the Lion. Noé, Ignacio, illus. 2016. (ENG.). 32p. (J). (gr. k-4). lib. bdg. 16.95 *(978-1-57537-926-5(0),* Another Sommer-Time Story) Advance Publishing, Inc.

—I Am a Lion! Budwine, Greg, illus. 2014. (J). *(978-1-57537-403-1(X))* Advance Publishing, Inc.

—I Am a Lion!(Yo Soy un León!) Budwine, Greg, illus. 2009. (Another Sommer-Time Story Bilingual Ser.). (SPA & ENG.). 48p. (J). lib. bdg. 16.95 *(978-1-57537-153-5(7))* Advance Publishing, Inc.

Spellman, David & Lutz, Lisa. How to Negotiate Everything. Temairik, Jaime, illus. 2013. (ENG.). 32p. (J). (gr. -1-3). 16.99 *(978-1-4424-5119-3(X),* Simon & Schuster Bks. For Young Readers) Simon & Schuster Bks. For Young Readers.

Staehli, Melissa. I Love You to the Moon. 2013. 28p. 15.95 *(978-1-61244-205-1(6))* Halo Publishing International.

Stamps, Paula. Learning Makes Friends Fun, 1 vol. 2010. 22p. 24.95 *(978-1-4512-8765-3(8))* PublishAmerica, Inc.

Standish, Burt L. Frank Merriwell's Son. Rudman, Jack, ed. 2003. (Frank Merriwell Ser.). pap. 9.95 *(978-0-8373-9137-3(7))* Merriwell, Frank Inc.

Star, L. J. Lydia's First Christmas, 1 vol. 2010. 24p. 24.95 *(978-1-61546-593-4(6))* PublishAmerica, Inc.

Steig, William. Pedro Es una Pizza. (Buenas Noches Ser.). (SPA., Illus.). (J). (gr. -1-5). 7.95 *(978-958-04-6034-3(5))* Norma S.A. COL. Dist: Distribuidora Norma, Inc., Lectorum Pubns., Inc.

—Pete's a Pizza. 2004. (Illus.). 32p. (J). (gr. -1-2). 28.95 incl. audio compact disk *(978-1-59112-740-6(8))* Live Oak Media.

Stevens, Liza. Not Today, Celeste! A Dog's Tale about Her Human's Depression. 2016. (ENG., Illus.). 36p. (J). 17.95 *(978-1-78592-008-0(1),* 8254) Kingsley, Jessica Pubs. GBR. Dist: Macmillan Distribution Ltd.

Stever, Susan. When Fairies Die. 2010. 28p. pap. 13.99 *(978-1-4520-0912-4(0))* AuthorHouse.

Stewart, Kymberly M. Play It Again, Rachel. 2003. 74p. (J). pap. 10.95 *(978-0-9740653-0-4(7))* Neema's Children Literature Assn., Inc.

Stinson, June. Milton Hears a Train. 2012. 32p. pap. 24.95 *(978-1-4626-8192-1(1))* America Star Bks.

Stoehr, Shelley. Crosses. 2003. 161p. (YA). pap. 13.95 *(978-0-595-26952-5(4),* Writers Club Pr.) iUniverse, Inc.

Stratton, Allan. Leslie's Journal. rev. ed. 2008. (ENG.). 200p. (YA). (gr. 8-12). 21.95 *(978-1-55451-149-5(6),* 9781554511495) Annick Pr., Ltd. CAN. Dist: Publishers Group West (PGW).

Style Guide Staff & Fruchter, Jason, illus. Daniel Goes to School. 2014. (Daniel Tiger's Neighborhood Ser.). (ENG.). 24p. (J). (gr. -1-7). pap. 3.99 *(978-1-4814-0318-4(4),* Simon Spotlight) Simon Spotlight.

Sullivan, Therese M. & Bitner, Pamela. A Gift from Valentine. 2007. 24p. (J). per. 12.95 *(978-1-58939-981-5(1))* Virtualbookworm.com Publishing, Inc.

Sundberg, Angela M., et al. The Pottamus Family & the Unhappy Pottamus. Sundberg, Angela M. et al, illus. 2007. (J). pap. 16.00 *(978-0-8059-7478-2(4))* Dorrance Publishing Co., Inc.

Swanson, Julie A. Going for the Record. 2004. 223p. (YA). pap. 8.00 *(978-0-8028-5273-1(4))* Eerdmans, William B. Publishing Co.

Swayne Tidwell, Deborah. Magic Eraser & Camp Real. 2009. 16p. pap. 8.50 *(978-1-4343-8916-9(2))* AuthorHouse.

Tamburri, Pasqualino. Alex & the Trampoline. 2008. 32p. (J). (gr. -1-2). 14.95 *(978-1-60227-473-0(8))* Above the Clouds Publishing.

Tansil-Mitchell, Angela. Kimmie C Sunshine: When Mommy & Daddy Loses Their Jobs. 2011. 24p. pap. 13.79 *(978-1-4567-5666-6(4))* AuthorHouse.

Tashlikowich, Natasha. The Secret of the Seven Stones. 2009. 117p. pap. 18.97 *(978-0-557-03747-6(6))* Lulu Pr., Inc.

Thiel, Annie. Cosmos' Mom & Dad Are Moving Apart. Edwards, William M. & Marjoribanks, Karen, illus. 2006. (Playdate Kids Ser.). 32p. (J). (gr. -1-3). 14.95 *(978-1-933721-04-0(9))* Playdate Kids Publishing.

Thiel Annie. The Playdate Kids Cosmos' Mom & Dad are Moving Apart 2ED 2007. 2007. 32p. 12.95 *(978-1-933721-31-6(6));* pap. 6.95 *(978-1-933721-27-9(8))* Playdate Kids Publishing.

Thomas, Dalandra. Noonimals. 2006. (J). pap. 16.95 *(978-90-78473-02-2(9))* Nooni Publishing.

Thompson, Gwendolyn. Hayride to Heaven. 2009. 40p. pap. 16.99 *(978-1-4389-6741-7(1))* AuthorHouse.

Thompson, Lauren. A Christmas Gift for Mama. Burke, Jim, illus. 2003. (J). pap. 16.95 *(978-0-590-30726-0(6))* Scholastic, Inc.

Thompson, Vivian L. Neat! Said Jeremy. 2003. 33p. (J). pap. 8.95 *(978-0-7414-1579-0(8))* Infinity Publishing.

Tiller, Amy. My Sister Is Like a Baby Bird. Tiller, Amy, illus. 2009. (ENG., Illus.). 26p. (J). 12.95 *(978-1-935130-02-4(1))* Grateful Steps.

Tillman, Nancy. Wherever You Are: My Love Will Find You. Tillman, Nancy, illus. (ENG., Illus.). 32p. (J). (gr. -1-3). 2012. bds. 7.99 *(978-1-250-01797-0(1),* 9781250017970) 2010. 16.99 *(978-0-312-54966-4(0),* 9780312549664) Feiwel & Friends.

Time Slime. 2003. 156p. (YA). (gr. 5-12). pap. 7.95 *(978-0-9702176-3-9(3),* 0004) Night Howl Productions.

Toothman, Sherry. I'm Okay, Mommy. Toothman, Lindsey, illus. 2007. 20p. per. 24.95 *(978-1-4241-8733-1(8))* America Star Bks.

Townsend, Peter. Shelly & Muffin's Big Lesson Learned. 2008. 11p. pap. 24.95 *(978-1-60672-379-1(0))* America Star Bks.

Towson, Robert. The Wrong Bus, 1 vol. 2010. 34p. 24.95 *(978-1-4489-4345-6(0))* PublishAmerica, Inc.

Treiber, Jutta & Antoni, Birgit. Porque Siempre Va a Ser Asi. 2004. (SPA., Illus.). 28p. (J). 18.99 *(978-84-89804-54-8(0))* Lóguez Ediciones ESP. Dist: Lectorum Pubns., Inc.

Trent, Shanda. Farmers' Market Day. Dippold, Jane, illus. 2013. (ENG.). 32p. (J). (gr. -1-1). 12.95 *(978-1-58925-115-1(6))* Tiger Tales.

Trice, Linda. Kenya's Song. Johnson, Pamela, illus. 2013. (ENG.). 32p. (J). (gr. -1-3). pap. 7.95 *(978-1-57091-847-6(3));* lib. bdg. 17.95 *(978-1-57091-846-9(5))* Charlesbridge Publishing, Inc.

Tyle, Shirley. Where Is Time, 1 vol. 2010. 30p. 24.95 *(978-1-4489-5976-1(4))* PublishAmerica, Inc.

Ure, Daylene Mary. Today I'm Going to be a Hedgehog. 2008. 36p. 16.50 *(978-0-615-25326-8(1))* Ure, Daylene.

Valentino, Serena & Disney Book Group Staff. Fairest of All: A Tale of the Wicked Queen. Disney Storybook Artists Staff, illus. 2009. (Villains Ser.: 1). (ENG.). 256p. (J). (gr. 5-9). 15.99 *(978-1-4231-0629-6(6))* Disney Pr.

Van Buren, David. I Love You As Big As the World. Warnes, Tim, illus. 2013. (ENG.). 22p. (J). bds. *(978-1-58925-603-3(4))* Tiger Tales.

van Genechten, Guido. Because I Love You So Much. 2004. (Illus.). 32p. (J). tchr. ed. 15.95 *(978-1-58925-039-0(7))* Tiger Tales.

Van Steenwyk, Elizabeth. Prairie Christmas. Himler, Ronald, illus. 2006. 32p. (J). (gr. k). 17.00 *(978-0-8028-5280-9(7),* Eerdmans Bks For Young Readers) Eerdmans, William B. Publishing Co.

Van Wyk, Tasja. Twins: Meet the Doctor. 2011. (Illus.). 28p. pap. 13.78 *(978-1-4567-7813-2(7))* AuthorHouse.

Vandepeer, Helen. Gifts. 2008. 76p. pap. 35.80 *(978-0-557-03191-7(5))* Lulu Pr., Inc.

Vander Zee, Ruth. Erika's Story. Innocenti, Roberto, illus. 2013. (ENG.). 24p. (J). (gr. 1-3). pap. 10.99 *(978-0-89812-891-8(9),* Creative Paperbacks) Creative Co., The.

—Mississippi Morning. Cooper, Floyd, illus. 2004. 32p. (J). 16.00 *(978-0-8028-5211-3(4))* Eerdmans, William B. Publishing Co.

Vasquez, Paula. When I Grow Up, 1 vol. 2017. (ENG., Illus.). 40p. (J). 14.99 *(978-1-4236-4689-1(4))* Gibbs Smith, Publisher.

Vigna, Judith. When Eric's Mom Fought Cancer. 2004. (J). (gr. 1-5). spiral bd. *(978-0-616-03063-9(0))* Canadian National Institute for the Blind/Institut National Canadien pour les Aveugles.

Voyager, Beatrice Nambouy. Mama Minko: A Survival Quest. 2010. (Illus.). 28p. pap. 15.49 *(978-1-4490-5797-8(7))* AuthorHouse.

W. Parents Are Lucky: They Don't Have to Do Chores. 2010. 24p. pap. 12.49 *(978-1-4520-7671-3(5))* AuthorHouse.

Waber, Bernard. Ask Me. Lee, Suzy, illus. 2015. (ENG.). 40p. (J). (gr. -1-3). 16.99 *(978-0-547-73394-4(1),* HMH Books For Young Readers) Houghton Mifflin Harcourt Publishing Co.

Waddell, Martin. Owl Babies. (Illus.). 25p. (J). (ENG, VIE, URD, TUR & CHI.). *(978-1-85430-348-6(1),* 93442); (CHI, ENG, URD, TUR & VIE., *(978-1-85430-343-1(0),* 93441) Little Tiger Pr. Group.

Wadham, Tim. The Queen of France. Denton, Kady MacDonald, illus. 2011. (ENG.). 32p. (J). (gr. -1-3). 16.99 *(978-0-7636-4102-3(2))* Candlewick Pr.

Walker, G. L. Good Morning Baby. 2008. 24p. pap. 10.95 *(978-1-4327-0536-7(9))* Outskirts Pr., Inc.

Wallace, Bill. Skinny-Dipping at Monster Lake. 2004. (ENG., Illus.). 224p. (J). (gr. 3-7). pap. 6.99 *(978-0-689-85151-3(0),* Simon & Schuster/Paula Wiseman Bks.) Simon & Schuster/Paula Wiseman Bks.

Walsh, Melanie. Living with Mom & Living with Dad. Walsh, Melanie, illus. 2012. (ENG., Illus.). 40p. (J). (gr. -1-2). 15.99 *(978-0-7636-5869-4(3))* Candlewick Pr.

Walter, Lee. The Gifts That Are Forgotten. 2006. 60p. pap. 16.95 *(978-1-4137-9070-2(4))* PublishAmerica, Inc.

Walvoord, Linda. Razzamadaddy, 1 vol. Yoshikawa, Sachiko, tr. Yoshikawa, Sachiko, illus. 2004. (ENG.). 32p. (J). 14.95 *(978-0-7614-5158-7(7))* Marshall Cavendish Corp.

Wan, Joyce. We Belong Together. Wan, Joyce, illus. 2011. (ENG., Illus.). 14p. (J). (gr. k — 1). bds. 6.99 *(978-0-545-30740-6(6),* Cartwheel Bks.) Scholastic, Inc.

Ward, Jennifer. Because You Are My Baby. Long, Sylvia, illus. 2007. (ENG.). 32p. (J). (gr. -1-1). 15.95 *(978-0-87358-911-6(4))* Cooper Square Publishing Llc.

Ward, Ruth. The Adventures of Bloor Bone. 2005. (J). lib. bdg. 18.00 *(978-1-59094-105-8(5))* Jawbone Publishing Corp.

Wardlaw, Lee. 101 Ways to Bug Your Parents. 2005. (ENG.). 208p. (J). (gr. 5-3). pap. 6.99 *(978-0-14-240340-2(7),* Puffin Books) Penguin Young Readers Group.

Warwillow, Lucas D. Marick's Cross, 1 vol. 2010. 48p. pap. 16.95 *(978-1-61546-563-7(4))* America Star Bks.

Watt, Cliff. Jenny Brown & the Search for Eusebio's Star. 2008. 77p. pap. 19.95 *(978-1-60672-169-8(0))* America Star Bks.

Watts, Irene N. When the Bough Breaks. 2007. (ENG.). 152p. (YA). (gr. 4-7). pap. 9.95 *(978-0-88776-821-7(0),* Tundra Bks.) Tundra Bks. CAN. Dist: Penguin Random Hse. LLC.

Weeks, Sarah. Without You. Duranceau, Suzanne, illus. 40p. (J). (gr. -1-2). 2007. (ENG.). pap. 6.99 *(978-0-06-113998-7(X))* 2003. 16.99 *(978-0-06-027816-8(1),* Geringer, Laura Book) HarperCollins Pubs.

Weiss, Ellen. Whatever You Do, I Love You. Williams, Sam, illus. 2010. (ENG.). 16p. (J). (gr. -1 — 1). bds. 7.99 *(978-1-4424-0809-8(X),* Little Simon) Little Simon.

Wells, Charity. The Trouble with the Supernatural, 1 vol. 2010. 84p. pap. 19.95 *(978-1-4489-2117-1(1))* America Star Bks.

Wells, Rosemary. Hand in Hand. Wells, Rosemary, illus. 2016. (ENG., Illus.). 32p. (J). 17.99 *(978-1-62779-434-3(4),* 9781627794343, Holt, Henry & Co. Bks. For Young Readers) Holt, Henry & Co.

—Love Waves. Wells, Rosemary, illus. 2011. (ENG., Illus.). 32p. (J). (gr. -1-2). 15.99 *(978-0-7636-4989-0(9))* Candlewick Pr.

—Love Waves: Midi Edition. Wells, Rosemary, illus. 2012. (ENG., Illus.). 32p. (J). (gr. k — 1). 8.99 *(978-0-7636-6224-0(0))* Candlewick Pr.

Weston Woods Staff, creator. Owen. 2011. (SPA.). 18.95 *(978-0-439-02177-7(4));* 38.75 *(978-0-439-02178-4(2));* 29.95 *(978-0-439-02310-8(6))* Weston Woods Studios, Inc.

—Pete's a Pizza. 2011. 29.95 *(978-0-439-74519-2(5))* Weston Woods Studios, Inc.

—Too Many Toys! 2011. 29.95 *(978-0-545-37421-7(9))* Weston Woods Studios, Inc.

Whelan, Gloria. A Time to Keep Silent. 2004. 144p. (J). pap. 8.00 *(978-0-8028-5255-7(6))* Eerdmans, William B. Publishing Co.

Whelen-Banks, Jane. Liam Goes Poo in the Toilet: A Story about Trouble with Toilet Training. 2008. (ENG., Illus.). 32p. 12.95 *(978-1-84310-900-6(X),* 5371) Kingsley, Jessica Pubs. GBR. Dist: Macmillan Distribution Ltd.

White, James C. David Goes Fishing. Chapin, Patrick, illus. 2003. 32p. (J). 6.95 *(978-0-9747752-0-3(7))* White, James C.

Whybrow, Ian. Malicia para Principiantes: Una Aventura de Lobito y Apestosito. Quintana, Joela, tr. Ross, Tony, illus. 2005. (Libros Ilustrados (Picture Bks.)). (SPA.). 32p. (J). (gr. k-2). 16.95 *(978-0-8225-3211-8(5),* Ediciones Lerner) Lerner Publishing Group.

Whybrow, Ian & Ross, Tony. Badness for Beginners: A Little Wolf & Smellybreff Adventure. 2005. (Illus.). 32p. (J). (gr. -1-3). 16.95 *(978-1-57505-861-0(8),* Carolrhoda Bks.) Lerner Publishing Group.

Wicke, Ed. Nicklus. 2011. 184p. (J). per. 9.99 *(978-0-9677652-4-2(2),* BlacknBlue Pr. UK) Blacknblue Pr.

Wild, Margaret. Kiss Kiss! Strevens-Marzo, Bridget, illus. 2004. 26p. pap. *(978-1-877003-51-6(4))* Little Hare Bks. AUS. Dist: HarperCollins Pubs. Australia.

—Kiss Kiss! Strevens-Marzo, Bridget, illus. 2004. (ENG.). 24p. (J). (gr. -1-1). 14.99 *(978-0-689-86279-3(2),* Simon & Schuster Bks. For Young Readers) Simon & Schuster Bks. For Young Readers.

Wilkins, Rose. So Super-Starry. 2004. (ENG.). 256p. (J). pap. *(978-0-330-42086-0(0),* Macmillan Children's Bks.) Pan Macmillan.

Willems, Mo. Welcome: A Mo Willems Guide for New Arrivals. Willems, Mo, illus. 2017. (ENG., Illus.). 32p. (J). (gr. -1 — 1). 15.99 *(978-1-4847-6746-7(2))* Disney Pr.

William Tell: 6 Small Books. (gr. k-2). 23.00 *(978-0-7635-8506-8(8))* Rigby Education.

Williams-Garcia, Rita. P. S. Be Eleven. 2015. (ENG.). 304p. (J). (gr. 3-7). pap. 7.99 *(978-0-06-193864-1(5),* Amistad) HarperCollins Pubs.

Williams, Randy. A Hero Named Herman. 2007. 21p. pap. 24.95 *(978-1-4241-8648-8(X))* PublishAmerica, Inc.

Williams, T. H. Jo's Bright New Day. 2008. 20p. pap. 24.95 *(978-1-60474-949-6(0))* America Star Bks.

Wilson, Karma. Baby, I Love You. Williams, Sam, illus. 2009. (ENG.). 30p. (J). (gr. -1 — 1). bds., bds. 7.99 *(978-1-4169-1910-0(4),* Little Simon) Little Simon.

—Mama Always Comes Home. Dyer, Brooke, illus. 2005. 32p. (J). (gr. -1-1). 15.99 *(978-0-06-057505-2(0))* HarperCollins Pubs.

Wilson, Leonard W. Realms of Flimenia Jeremyæs Journey. 2008. 136p. pap. 11.95 *(978-0-595-51523-3(1))* iUniverse, Inc.

Winegar, Tracy. Keeping Keller. 2008. 207p. pap. 14.99 *(978-1-59955-115-9(2))* Cedar Fort, Inc./CFI Distribution.

Wojciechowski, Susan. The Best Halloween of All. Meddaugh, Susan, illus. 2012. (ENG.). 24p. (J). (gr. -1-3). pap. 3.99 *(978-0-7636-6008-6(6))* Candlewick Pr.

Wolfe, Myra & Monescillo, Maria. Charlotte Jane Battles Bedtime. Monescillo, Maria, illus. 2011. (ENG., Illus.). 32p. (J). (gr. -1-3). 16.99 *(978-0-15-206150-0(9))* Houghton Mifflin Harcourt Publishing Co.

Wolfe, Susan Markle. The Deer from Ponchatoula, 1 vol. Welch, Gracie, illus. 2009. 24p. pap. 24.95 *(978-1-60813-519-6(5))* America Star Bks.

Woodson, Jacqueline. Coming on Home Soon. Lewis, Earl & Lewis, E. B., illus. 2004. (ENG.). 32p. (J). (gr. k-3). 17.99 *(978-0-399-23748-5(8),* G.P. Putnam's Sons Books for Young Readers) Penguin Young Readers Group.

Wright, Gail R. The Adventures of Alfred in the Greatest Fruit of All: Conflicts & Resolutions. 2011. 112p. (gr. 1-2). 28.95 *(978-1-4497-1586-1(9));* pap. 11.95 *(978-1-4497-1585-4(0))* Author Solutions, Inc. (WestBow Pr.).

Yang, Gene Luen & Pham, Thien. Level Up. 2016. (YA). lib. bdg. 20.85 *(978-0-606-38563-3(0))* Turtleback Bks.

Yoo, Paula. Good Enough. 2012. (ENG.). 336p. (YA). (gr. 8). pap. 7.99 *(978-0-06-079090-5(3),* HarperTeen) HarperCollins Pubs.

Yvette, Sylvia. My Silly Imagination. 2012. 24p. (-18). pap. 15.99 *(978-1-4797-2966-1(3))* Xlibris Corp.

Zimmerman, Mary. The Secret in the Wings. 2014. (ENG., Illus.). 128p. pap. 16.00 *(978-0-8101-2987-0(6))* Northwestern Univ. Pr.

Zschock, Martha Day. Hello, Philadelphia! 2011. (Hello! Ser.). (ENG., Illus.). 16p. (J). (gr. -1-k). bds. 9.95 *(978-1-933212-64-7(0),* Commonwealth Editions) Applewood Bks.

—Hello, Rhode Island! 2011. (Hello! Ser.). (ENG., Illus.). 16p. (J). (gr. -1-k). bds. 9.95 (978-1-933212-62-3(4), Commonwealth Editions) Applewood Bks.

—Hello, San Francisco! 2012. (Hello! Ser.). (ENG., Illus.). 16p. (J). (gr. -1-k). bds. 9.95 (978-1-933212-65-4(9), Commonwealth Editions) Applewood Bks.

Zuckerman, Linda. I Will Hold You 'Til You Sleep. Muth, Jon J., illus. 2006. (J). (978-0-439-43421-8(1), Levine, Arthur A. Bks.) Scholastic, Inc.

PARENTS AND TEACHERS

see Home and School

PARIS (FRANCE)

Adams, Jennifer. My Little Cities: Paris. Pizzoli, Greg, illus. 2017. (ENG.). 22p. (J). (gr. -1 — 1). bds. 9.99 **(978-1-4521-5390-2(6))** Chronicle Bks. LLC.

Anastasio, Dina. Where Is the Eiffel Tower? 2017. (Where Is... ? Ser.). lib. bdg. 16.00 **(978-0-606-40102-9(4))** Turtleback Bks.

BeaverSimon. PARIS: CITY OF LIGHT BEGINNING BOOK WITH ONLINE ACCESS. 2014. (ENG.). 24p. (J). pap. 9.50 (978-1-107-64577-6(8)) Cambridge Univ. Pr.

Cooper, Sharon Katz. Gustave Eiffel's Spectacular Idea: The Eiffel Tower. Bock, Janna, illus. 2015. (Story Behind the Name Ser.). (ENG.). 32p. (gr. 2-3). lib. bdg. 28.65 (978-1-4795-7136-9(9)) Picture Window Bks.

Evans, June P. Michael in Paris. 2007. 10.00 (978-0-8059-8933-5(1)) Dorrance Publishing Co., Inc.

Evanson, Ashley. Paris: A Book of Shapes. Evanson, Ashley, illus. 2015. (Hello, World Ser.). (ENG., Illus.). 14p. (J). (— 1). bds. 6.99 (978-0-448-48915-5(5), Grosset & Dunlap) Penguin Young Readers Group.

Fowler, Gloria & Heo, Min. Come with Me to Paris. 2014. (ENG., Illus.). 56p. (J). 16.95 (978-1-62326-047-7(7)) AMMO Bks., LLC.

Friedman, Samantha & Pieropan, Cristina. What Degas Saw. 2016. (ENG., Illus.). 40p. (J). (gr. k-2). 19.95 (978-1-63345-004-2(X)) Museum of Modern Art.

Gardner, Alison. Passport to Paris. 2010. (Crabtree Connections Ser.). (ENG.). 24p. (J). (gr. 3-6). (978-0-7787-9955-9(7)); pap. (978-0-7787-9977-1(8)) Crabtree Publishing Co.

Herweck Rice, Dona. Engineering Marvels: The Eiffel Tower: Measurement (Grade 4) 2017. (Mathematics Readers Ser.). (Illus.). 32p. (J). (gr. 4-4). pap. 8.99 **(978-1-4258-5559-8(8))** Teacher Created Materials, Inc.

Howse, Jennifer. The Louvre. 2014. (J). (978-1-4896-1190-1(8)) Weigl Pubs., Inc.

Kissock, Heather, ed. Eiffel Tower. 2011. (J). (gr. 4-6). pap. 12.95 (978-1-61690-770-9(3), AV2 by Weigl); (Illus.). 24p. (gr. 2-5). 27.13 (978-1-61690-766-2(5)) Weigl Pubs., Inc.

Lamprell, Klay. Paris, 1 vol. 2012. (SPA & ENG.). 96p. (J). pap. 14.99 (978-84-08-10914-3(6), 103552) Lonely Planet Pubns.

Leboutillier, Nate. Eiffel Tower. 2006. (Modern Wonders of the World Ser.). (Illus.). 32p. (J). (gr. 4-7). 18.95 (978-1-58341-438-5(X), 1262895, Creative Education) Creative Co., The.

Lonely Planet & Mansfield, Andy. POP-UP PARIS, 1 vol. 2016. (Lonely Planet Kids Ser.). (ENG., Illus.). 16p. (J). 9.99 (978-1-76034-335-4(8), 5335) Lonely Planet Pubns.

Mason Crest. Paris, Vol. 8. 2016. (Major World Cities Ser.: Vol. 8). (ENG., Illus.). 48p. (J). (gr. 5-8). 20.95 (978-1-4222-3544-7(0)) Mason Crest.

Mattern, Joanne. Paris, 1 vol. 2007. (Cities Set 2 Ser.). (ENG., Illus.). 32p. (gr. -1-3). 27.07 (978-1-59679-720-8(7), Checkerboard Library) ABDO Publishing Co.

Meyers, Haily & Meyers, Kevin. All Aboard Paris, 1 vol. Meyers, Haily, illus. 2015. (ENG & FRE., Illus.). 22p. (J). bds. 9.99 (978-1-4236-4077-6(2), 1394332) Gibbs Smith, Publisher.

Nanji, Shenaaz. Notre Dame. 2014. (J). (978-1-4896-1146-8(0)) Weigl Pubs., Inc.

Pezzi, Bryan. Eiffel Tower. 2007. (Structural Wonders Ser.). (Illus.). 32p. (J). (gr. 4-7). lib. bdg. 26.00 (978-1-59036-719-3(7)); per. 9.95 (978-1-59036-720-9(0)) Weigl Pubs., Inc.

Prasadam-Halls, Smriti. Pairs! Underwater. Scobie, Lorna, illus. 2017. (Pairs Ser.). (ENG.). 12p. (J). (gr. -1-k). bds. 9.99 (978-1-84780-882-0(4), Frances Lincoln) Quarto Publishing Group UK GBR. Dist: Hachette Bk. Group.

Riggs, Kate. Eiffel Tower. 2009. (Now That's Big Ser.). 24p. (J). (gr. 1-5). lib. bdg. 24.25 (978-1-58341-702-7(8), Creative Education) Creative Co., The.

Rossi, Renzo. In the Sun King's Paris with Molière. Baldanzi, Alessandro, illus. 2008. (Come See My City Ser.). 48p. (gr. 4-8). lib. bdg. 28.50 (978-0-7614-4332-2(0), Benchmark Bks.) Marshall Cavendish Corp.

Rubbino, Salvatore. A Walk in Paris. Rubbino, Salvatore, illus. 2014. (ENG., Illus.). 40p. (J). (gr. -1-3). 17.99 (978-0-7636-6984-3(9)) Candlewick Pr.

Rudolph, Jessica. Paris. 2017. (Citified! Ser.). (ENG.). 24p. (J). (gr. k-3). 17.95 **(978-1-68402-233-5(9))** Bearport Publishing Co., Inc.

Sasek, Miroslav. This Is Paris. 2004. (This Is ... Ser.). (ENG., Illus.). 64p. (J). (gr. 2-12). 17.95 (978-0-7893-1063-7(5)) Universe Publishing.

Stacey, Gill. Paris. 2004. (Great Cities of the World Ser.). (Illus.). 48p. (gr. 5-12). lib. bdg. 31.00 (978-0-8368-5030-7(0), Gareth Stevens Secondary Library) Stevens, Gareth Publishing LLLP.

PARIS (FRANCE)—FICTION

Abbott, Jacob. Rollo in Paris. 2008. 116p. 22.95 (978-1-60664-943-5(4)); pap. 9.95 (978-1-60312-493-5(4)) Aegypan.

Abrahamson, Ruth Ann. Paris & the Purple Purse: Continuing Adventures of Magic Cookie Bean. 2011. 40p. (gr. 1-2). pap. 13.95 (978-1-4497-1665-3(2), WestBow Pr.) Author Solutions, Inc.

Adam D. Levine. Knights: Reign of Hellfire. 2010. (ENG.). 184p. 23.95 (978-1-4401-7614-2(0)); pap. 13.95 (978-1-4401-7618-0(3)) iUniverse, Inc.

Ahern, Carolyn L. Tino Turtle Travels to Paris, France. Burt Sullivan, Neallia, illus. 2007. 36p. (J). (gr. -1-4). 17.95 incl. audio compact disk (978-0-9793158-1-7(6)) Tino Turtle Travels, LLC.

Albon, Lucie, illus. Little Ballerina: A Children's Book Inspired by Edgar Degas. 2011. (ENG.). 32p. (J). (gr. -1-3). 14.95 (978-3-7913-7081-1(2)) Prestel Verlag GmbH & Co KG. DEU. Dist: Penguin Random Hse. LLC.

Alender, Katie. Marie Antoinette, Serial Killer. (ENG.). 304p. (J). (gr. 7). 2014. pap. 9.99 (978-0-545-46810-7(8), Scholastic Paperbacks) 2013. 18.99 (978-0-545-46809-1(4)) Scholastic, Inc.

Altsheler, Joseph A. The Forest of Swords: A Story of Paris & the Marne. 2006. (World War I Ser.: Vol. 3). 284p. (J). reprint ed. 28.95 (978-1-4218-1772-9(1)); pap. 13.95 (978-1-4218-1872-6(8)) 1st World Publishing, Inc. (1st World Library - Literary Society).

—The Forest of Swords: A Story of Paris & the Marne. l.t. ed. 2007. (World War I Ser.: Vol. 3). (ENG.). (J). 252p. pap. 23.99 (978-1-4264-8960-0(9)); 226p. reprint ed. pap. 20.99 (978-1-4264-8902-0(1)) Creative Media Partners, LLC.

—The Forest of Swords: A Story of Paris & the Marne. 2006. (World War I Ser.: Vol. 3). (J). reprint ed. pap. (978-1-4068-0742-4(7)) Echo Library.

—The Forest of Swords: A Story of Paris & the Marne. 2010. (World War I Ser.: Vol. 3). 216p. (J). reprint ed. pap. (978-1-4076-1521-9(1)) HardPr.

Amaury. The Phantom of the Opera: Based on the Novel by Gaston Leroux. Rosner, Gillian, tr. Druvert, Hélène, illus. 2016. (ENG.). 40p. (J). (gr. k-2). 19.95 (978-1-4197-2086-4(4), Abrams Bks. for Young Readers) Abrams, Inc.

Angel, Ido. Vipo in Paris: The Kings of Croissants & Baguettes. 2015. (AV2 Animated Storytime Ser.). (ENG.). (J). lib. bdg. 29.99 (978-1-4896-3902-8(0), AV2 by Weigl) Weigl Pubs., Inc.

Axelsson, Carina. Paris. 2014. (Model Undercover Ser.: 1). (ENG.). 368p. (J). (gr. 4-7). pap. 6.99 (978-1-4022-8587-5(6), Sourcebooks Jabberwocky) Sourcebooks, Inc.

Baccellia, Kim. Goddesses Can Wait. 2015. (YA). (978-1-61271-297-0(5)) Zumaya Pubns. LLC.

Barroux. Mr Leon's Paris. Ardizzone, Sarah, tr. from FRE. Barroux, illus. 2013. (ENG., Illus.). 32p. (J). (gr. k-2). pap. 9.99 (978-1-907912-08-5(8)) Phoenix Yard Bks. GBR. Dist: Independent Pubs. Group.

Barroux, Stephane-Yves. Mr Leon's Paris. 2013. (ENG., Illus.). 32p. (J). (gr. k-2). 17.99 (978-1-907912-07-8(X)) Phoenix Yard Bks. GBR. Dist: Independent Pubs. Group.

Beck, Andrea. Pierre in the Air!, 1 vol. Beck, Andrea, illus. 2011. (Pierre le Poof Ser.: 3). (ENG., Illus.). 32p. (J). (gr. -1-3). 19.95 (978-1-55469-032-9(3)) Orca Bk. Pubs. USA.

Bemelmans, Ludwig. Madeline. (Madeline Ser.). (ENG.). (J). (gr. -1-k). 2012. 36p. bds. 9.99 (978-0-670-01407-1(9), Viking Books for Young Readers) 2007. (Illus.). 48p. 9.99 (978-0-14-240871-1(9), Puffin Books) Penguin Young Readers Group.

—Madeline: Activity Book with Stickers. 2012. (Madeline Ser.). (ENG.). 32p. (J). (gr. k-3). act. bk. ed. 7.99 (978-0-448-45903-5(5), Grosset & Dunlap) Penguin Young Readers Group.

—Madeline's Christmas, 1 vol. Bemelmans, Ludwig, illus. 2007. (Madeline Ser.). (ENG., Illus.). 15p. (J). (gr. -1-2). 9.99 (978-0-14-240897-1(2), Puffin Books) Penguin Young Readers Group.

—Madeline's Rescue. 2004. (J). (gr. -1-2). spiral bd. (978-0-616-11864-1(3)) Canadian National Institute for the Blind/Institut National Canadien pour les Aveugles.

—Madeline's Rescue, 1 vol. 2009. (Madeline Ser.). (ENG.). 15p. (J). (gr. -1-2). 9.99 (978-0-14-241444-6(1), Puffin Books) Penguin Young Readers Group.

Blake, Robert J. Victor & Hugo. Blake, Robert J., illus. 2017. (ENG., Illus.). 40p. (J). (gr. -1-2). 16.99 (978-0-399-24324-0(0), Philomel Bks.) Penguin Young Readers Group.

Bowen, Carl & Poe, Edgar Allen. The Murders in the Rue Morgue, 1 vol. Dimaya, Emerson & Calero, Dennis, illus. 2013. (Edgar Allan Poe Graphic Novels Ser.). (ENG.). 72p. (gr. 2-3). 27.99 (978-1-4342-3033-1(3)); pap. 6.10 (978-1-4342-4259-4(5)) Stone Arch Bks.

Bradley, F. T. Double Vision. (Double Vision Ser.: 1). (ENG.). (J). (gr. 3-7). 2013. 272p. pap. 6.99 (978-0-06-210438-0(1)) 2012. (Illus.). 256p. 16.99 (978-0-06-210437-3(3)) HarperCollins Pubs.

—Double Vision - Code Name 711. 2013. (Double Vision Ser.: 2). (ENG.). 256p. (J). (gr. 3-7). 16.99 (978-0-06-210440-3(3)) HarperCollins Pubs.

Brannen, Sarah S. Madame Martine. Brannen, Sarah S., illus. 2014. (ENG., Illus.). 32p. (J). (gr. -1-3). 16.99 (978-0-8075-4905-6(3)) Whitman, Albert & Co.

—Madame Martine Breaks the Rules. Brannen, Sarah S., illus. 2015. (ENG., Illus.). 32p. (J). (gr. -1-3). 16.99 (978-0-8075-4907-0(X)) Whitman, Albert & Co.

Brannen, Sarah S., illus. Madame Martine. 2015. 32p. (J). (978-1-4896-3864-9(4)) Weigl Pubs., Inc.

Brian, Janeen. Cat-Astrophe at the Opera, 1 vol. rev. ed. 2013. (Fiction Readers Ser.). (ENG., Illus.). 28p. (J). (gr. 3-3). pap. 8.99 (978-1-4333-5597-4(3)) Shell Educational Publishing.

—Cat-Astrpohe at the Opera. rev. ed. 2013. (Fiction Readers Ser.). (ENG., Illus.). 28p. (gr. 3-3). pap. 19.96 (978-1-4807-1719-0(3)) Teacher Created Materials, Inc.

Brière-haquet, Alice & Csil. Mrs. Eiffel: The Love Story Behind the Eiffel Tower. 2015. (ENG., Illus.). 32p. (J). (gr. -1-3). 19.95 (978-3-89955-755-8(7)) Die Gestalten Verlag DEU. Dist: Penguin Random Hse. LLC.

Brown, Jeff. Framed in France. Pamintuan, Macky, illus. 2014. (Flat Stanley's Worldwide Adventures Ser.: 11). (ENG.). 128p. (J). (gr. 1-5). 15.99 (978-0-06-218985-1(9)); pap. 4.99 (978-0-06-218984-4(0)) HarperCollins Pubs.

—Framed in France. 2014. (Flat Stanley's Worldwide Adventures Ser.: 11). (J). lib. bdg. 14.75 (978-0-606-35480-6(8)) Turtleback Bks.

Bryant, Annie. Charlotte in Paris. 2008. (Beacon Street Girls Ser.: No. 1). (ENG.). 224p. (J). (gr. 5-8). pap. 8.99 (978-1-4169-6428-5(2), Aladdin) Simon & Schuster Children's Publishing.

Cameron, Sharon. Rook. (ENG.). 464p. (J). (gr. 7). 2016. pap. 9.99 (978-1-338-03246-8(1)) 2015. 17.99 (978-0-545-67599-4(5)) Scholastic, Inc. (Scholastic Pr.).

—A Spark Unseen. 2013. (ENG.). 352p. (J). (gr. 7). 17.99 (978-0-545-32813-5(6), Scholastic Pr.) Scholastic, Inc.

Cyr, Joe. Magical Trees & Crayons: Great Stories. 2006. (Illus.). pap. 9.95 (978-0-9778525-6-7(3)) Peppertree Pr., The.

de Brunhoff, Laurent. Babar's Guide to Paris. 2017. (ENG., Illus.). 48p. (J). (gr. k-2). 19.95 (978-1-4197-2289-9(1), Abrams Bks. for Young Readers) Abrams, Inc.

De La Barre De Nanteuil, Andrea. Mademoiselle Oiseau & the Letter from Her Past. 2015. (ENG., Illus.). 144p. (J). (gr. 3-7). 24.95 (978-3-89955-757-2(3)) Die Gestalten Verlag DEU. Dist: Penguin Random Hse. LLC.

De Laurentiis, Giada. Paris!, No. 2. Gambatesa, Francesca, illus. 2013. (Recipe for Adventure Ser.: 2). (ENG.). 144p. (J). (gr. 2-5). 6.99 (978-0-448-46257-8(5), Grosset & Dunlap) Penguin Young Readers Group.

—Paris! No. 2. Gambatesa, Francesca, illus. 2013. (Recipe for Adventure Ser.: 2). (ENG.). 144p. (J). (gr. 2-5). 16.99 (978-0-448-47854-8(4), Grosset & Dunlap) Penguin Young Readers Group.

de Vigan, Delphine. No & Me. Miller, George, tr. from FRE. 2010. (ENG.). 256p. (YA). (gr. 7-12). 16.99 (978-1-59990-479-5(9), 9781599904795, Bloomsbury USA Childrens) Bloomsbury Publishing USA.

Dennard, Susan. A Darkness Strange & Lovely. 2013. (Something Strange & Deadly Trilogy Ser.: 2). (ENG.). 416p. (YA). (gr. 9). 17.99 (978-0-06-208329-6(5), HarperTeen) HarperCollins Pubs.

Derrick, Patricia & O'Neil, Shirley. Rathbone the Rat. Martinez, J-P Loppo, illus. 2007. 32p. (J). (gr. -1-3). 18.95 incl. audio compact disk (978-1-933818-17-7(4)) Animalations.

Dixon, Franklin W. Passport to Danger. 2005. (Hardy Boys I Ser.: No. 179). 147p. (J). lib. bdg. 15.00 (978-1-59054-847-9(7)) Fitzgerald Bks.

Doder, Joshua. Grk Takes Revenge. 2010. (J). (978-0-385-90655-5(2)); (978-0-385-73723-4(8)) Random House Publishing Group. (Delacorte Pr).

Druvert, Hélène. Paris up, up & Away. 2016. (ENG., Illus.). 34p. (J). (gr. -1-1). 24.95 (978-0-500-65059-2(4), 565059) Thames & Hudson.

Eaton, Gordon J. Piebald & the Parade of Small Animals. 2009. 184p. pap. 14.99 (978-1-60791-991-9(5)) Salem Author Services.

Egan, Tim. Dodsworth in Paris. Egan, Tim, illus. 2010. (Dodsworth Book Ser.). (ENG., Illus.). 48p. (J). (gr. 1-4). pap. 3.99 (978-0-547-33192-8(4)) Houghton Mifflin Harcourt Publishing Co.

Eschberger, Beverly. The Elephants in the City of Light: An Elephant Family Adventure. Gower, Jim, illus. 2010. (J). per. 3.99 (978-1-932926-28-6(3), Kinkajou Pr.) Artemesia Publishing, LLC.

Francis, Pauline, retold by. The Phantom of the Opera. 2010. (Essential Classics - Horror Ser.). (Illus.). 56p. pap. (978-0-237-54095-1(9)) Evans Brothers, Ltd.

Frederick, Heather Vogel. Wish You Were Eyre. (Mother-Daughter Book Club Ser.). (ENG.). (J). (gr. 4-9). 2013. 480p. pap. 7.99 (978-1-4424-3065-5(6)) 2012. 464p. 16.99 (978-1-4424-3064-8(8)) Simon & Schuster Bks. For Young Readers. (Simon & Schuster Bks. For Young Readers).

Froman, Annabelle. Beezeur. 2013. 34p. pap. 9.95 (978-0-9842053-1-8(4)) Breathless Vintage Enterprises.

Fromental, Jean-Luc. Oops! Connors, Thomas, tr. from FRE. Jolivet, Joëlle, illus. 2010. (ENG.). 42p. (J). (gr. -1-k). 17.95 (978-0-8109-8749-4(X)) Abrams, Inc.

Ghislain, Gary. How I Stole Johnny Depp's Alien Girlfriend. 2011. (ENG., Illus.). 208p. (YA). (gr. 7-17). 16.99 (978-0-8118-7460-1(5)) Chronicle Bks. LLC.

Gibbs, Stuart. Traitor's Chase. 2012. (Last Musketeer Ser.: 2). (ENG.). 256p. (J). (gr. 3-7). 16.99 (978-0-06-204841-7(4)) HarperCollins Pubs.

Greene, Bette. Morning Is a Long Time Coming. l.t. ed. 2004. (Beeler Mystery Ser.). 35.95 (978-1-58118-122-7(1)) LRS.

Grimes, Nikki. On the Road to Paris. (Illus.). 224p. (J). 16.99 (978-0-8037-2817-2(4), Dial) Penguin Publishing Group.

Harris, L. Little Girl in Paris. 2004. (Madame Juliette & the Inchanded Crate Ser.: Vol. 1). (Illus.). 330p. (J). pap. 19.95 (978-0-9749950-2-1(9)) Granny's Pub Co.

Harvey, Jacqueline. Alice-Miranda in Paris. 2015. (Alice-Miranda Ser.: 7). (ENG.). 336p. (J). (gr. 3-7). 9.99 (978-1-74275-288-4(8)) Random Hse. Australia AUS. Dist: Independent Pubs. Group.

—Clementine Rose & the Paris Puzzle. 2016. (Clementine Rose Ser.: 12). (ENG.). 160p. (J). (gr. 1-3). pap. 8.99 (978-0-85798-788-4(7)) Random Hse. Australia AUS. Dist: Independent Pubs. Group.

Henty, George Alfred. At Agincourt: A Story of the White Hoods of Paris. 2007. (ENG.). 296p. pap. 21.99 (978-1-4264-2133-4(8)); 284p. pap. 23.99 (978-1-4264-2201-0(6)) Creative Media Partners, LLC.

Horowitz, Anthony. Three of Diamonds. 2005. (Diamond Brothers Ser.). (ENG.). 240p. (J). (gr. 3-7). 6.99 (978-0-14-240298-6(2), Puffin Books) Penguin Young Readers Group.

Howard, A. G. RoseBlood. 2017. (ENG.). (gr. 8-17). 400p. (J). pap. 8.95 **(978-1-4197-2342-1(1))**; 432p. (YA). 18.95 (978-1-4197-1909-7(2), Amulet Bks.) Abrams, Inc.

—RoseBlood. 2018. lib. bdg. 20.85 **(978-0-606-40729-8(4))** Turtleback Bks.

Hugo, Victor. The Hunchback of Notre Dame. 2008. (Bring the Classics to Life Ser.). (Illus.). 72p. (gr. 2-12). pap., act. bk. ed. 10.95 (978-1-55576-324-4(3), EDCTR-208B) EDCON Publishing Group.

—The Hunchback of Notre Dame: Illusrtrated Edition, 1 vol. 2012. (Calico Illustrated Classics Ser.: No. 4). (ENG., Illus.). 112p. (J). (gr. 3-6). 27.07 (978-1-61641-614-0(9)) Magic Wagon.

—The Hunchback of Notre Dame: With a Discussion of Compassion. Butterfield, Ned, tr. Butterfield, Ned, illus. 2003. (Values in Action Illustrated Classics Ser.). (J). (978-1-59203-049-1(1)) Learning Challenge, Inc.

The Hunchback of Notre Dame. (Read-Along Ser.). (J). 7.99 incl. audio (978-1-55723-992-1(4)) Walt Disney Records.

Hunt, Elizabeth Singer. The Mystery of the Mona Lisa, Bk. 3. Williamson, Brian, illus. 2007. (Secret Agent Jack Stalwart Ser.: 3). (ENG.). 128p. (J). (gr. 1-4). per. 5.99 (978-1-60286-001-8(7), Weinstein Bks.) Perseus Bks. Group.

Jacobus, Ann. Romancing the Dark in the City of Light: A Novel. 2015. (ENG.). 288p. (YA). (gr. 7-12). 18.99 (978-1-250-06443-1(0), 9781250064431) St. Martin's Pr.

Jeanne-Marie in Gay Paris. 2003. (Illus.). 32p. (J). mass mkt. 9.99 (978-0-9740599-1-4(9), 2) Omnibus Publishing.

Kaldor, Connie. A Poodle in Paris. Fil and Julie Staff, illus. 2006. (ENG.). 36p. (J). (gr. -1-2). 16.95 (978-2-923163-12-3(5)) La Montagne Secrete CAN. Dist: Independent Pubs. Group.

Kamata, Suzanne. Gadget Girl: The Art of Being Invisible. 2013. (ENG., Illus.). 256p. (YA). pap. 14.95 (978-1-936846-38-2(1)) GemmaMedia.

Kelly, Erin. The Mystery at the Eiffel Tower: Paris, France. 2005. (Carole Marsh Mysteries Ser.). (Illus.). 144p. (J). (gr. 3-5). pap. 7.99 (978-0-635-03468-7(9)) Gallopade International.

Kimmelman, Leslie. Everybody Bonjours! McMenemy, Sarah, illus. 2008. (ENG.). 40p. (J). (gr. -1-2). 16.99 (978-0-375-84443-0(0), Knopf Bks. for Young Readers) Random Hse. Children's Bks.

Kingfisher, Rupert. Madame Pamplemousse & Her Incredible Edibles. Hellard, Sue, illus. 2008. (ENG.). 144p. (YA). (gr. 3-6). 15.99 (978-1-59990-306-4(7), 9781599903064, Bloomsbury USA Childrens) Bloomsbury Publishing USA.

—Madame Pamplemousse & the Enchanted Sweet Shop. 2011. (ENG., Illus.). 176p. (YA). (gr. 3-6). 16.99 (978-1-4088-0505-3(7), 9781408805053, Bloomsbury USA Childrens) Bloomsbury Publishing USA.

Knighton, Kate, retold by. Phantom of the Opera. 2008. (Young Reading Series 2 Gift Bks). 64p. (J). 8.99 (978-0-7945-2082-3(0), Usborne) EDC Publishing.

Kraulis, Julie. An Armadillo in Paris. 2014. (ENG., Illus.). 32p. (J). (gr. k-4). 17.99 (978-1-77049-526-5(6), Tundra Bks.) Tundra Bks. CAN. Dist: Penguin Random Hse. LLC.

Kredensor, Diane. Ollie & Moon in Paris. Kress, Sandra, photos by. 2017. (Pictureback(R) Ser.). (ENG., Illus.). 32p. (J). (gr. -1-2). pap. 5.99 **(978-1-5247-1575-5(1)**, Random Hse. Bks. for Young Readers) Random Hse. Children's Bks.

Leroux, Gaston. The Phantom of the Opera. Howell, Troy, illus. 2008. (Classic Starts(tm) Ser.). (ENG.). 160p. (J). (gr. 2-4). 6.95 (978-1-4027-4580-5(X)) Sterling Publishing Co., Inc.

LeTourneau, Marie & Baty, Danielle Reed. The Mice of Bistrot des Sept Frères. LeTourneau, Marie, illus. 2006. (ENG., Illus.). 32p. (J). (gr. -1-3). 15.95 (978-0-9749303-6-7(9)) Tanglewood Pr.

Lodding, Linda Ravin. Painting Pepette. Fletcher, Claire, illus. 2016. (ENG.). 40p. (J). (gr. -1-3). 17.99 (978-1-4998-0136-1(X)) Little Bee Books Inc.

Mancuso, Jackie Clark. Paris-Chien: Adventures of an Ex-Pat Dog. 2013. (ENG., Illus.). 32p. (J). (gr. k-2). 17.95 (978-0-615-54542-4(4)) La Librairie Parisienne.

Marciano, John Bemelmans. Madeline & Her Dog. 2011. (Madeline Ser.). (ENG.). 32p. (J). (gr. 1-2). pap. 3.99 (978-0-448-45438-2(6), Penguin Young Readers) Penguin Young Readers Group.

—Madeline's Tea Party. 2012. (Madeline Ser.). (ENG.). 32p. (J). (gr. 1-2). pap. 3.99 (978-0-448-45439-9(4), Penguin Young Readers) Penguin Young Readers Group.

Marsh, Carole. The Mystery at the Eiffel Tower. 2009. (Around the World in 80 Mysteries Ser.). (Illus.). 132p. (J). 18.99 (978-0-635-07004-3(9), Marsh, Carole Mysteries) Gallopade International.

Mary John Lewis. Pookie in Paris. 2009. 24p. pap. 12.49 (978-1-4389-6514-7(1)) AuthorHouse.

Matuszak, Pat. Simone's Secret, 2, Bk 2. 2009. (Angel Light Ser.: 2). (ENG.). 192p. (gr. 11). pap. 12.99 (978-0-89957-876-7(4)) AMG Pubs.

McKnight, Gillian. To Catch a Prince: To Catch a Prince; the Frog Prince. 2011. (ENG., Illus.). 432p. (YA). (gr. 7). pap. 9.99 (978-1-4424-3139-3(3), Simon & Schuster Bks. For Young Readers) Simon & Schuster Bks. For Young Readers.

Meade, L. T. The Children's Pilgrimage. 2004. reprint ed. pap. 24.95 (978-1-4191-5659-5(4)); pap. 1.99 (978-1-4192-5659-2(9)) Kessinger Publishing, LLC.

—The Palace Beautiful: A Story for Girls. 2007. (ENG.). 288p. pap. 21.99 (978-1-4346-4867-9(2)); 310p. pap. 24.99 (978-1-4346-4868-6(0)) Creative Media Partners, LLC.

Miller, Kirsten. The Darkness Dwellers. 2013. (Kiki Strike Ser.). (ENG., Illus.). 416p. (YA). (gr. 7-12). 17.99 (978-1-59990-736-9(4), 9781599907369, Bloomsbury USA Childrens) Bloomsbury Publishing USA.

Minou: Evaluation Guide. 2006. (J). (978-1-55942-416-5(8)) Witcher Productions.

Modiano, Patrick. Catherine Certitude. (FRE.). pap. 17.95 (978-2-07-051608-7(3)) Gallimard, Editions FRA. Dist: Distribooks, Inc.

Mont, Eve Marie. A Phantom Enchantment. 2014. (Unbound Ser.). (ENG.). 288p. (YA). (gr. 13). pap. 9.95 (978-0-7582-6950-8(1), K-Teen) Kensington Publishing Corp.

Morgan, Page. The Beautiful & the Cursed. 2013. (Dispossessed Ser.). (ENG.). 352p. (YA). (gr. 7). 18.99 (978-0-385-74311-2(4), Delacorte Pr.) Random Hse. Children's Bks.

Nesbet, Anne. A Box of Gargoyles. 2013. (ENG.). 368p. (J). (gr. 3-7). 16.99 (978-0-06-210425-0(X)) HarperCollins Pubs.

—The Cabinet of Earths. 2013. (ENG.). 288p. (J). (gr. 3-7). pap. 6.99 (978-0-06-196319-3(4)) HarperCollins Pubs.

Nesbit, Sara E. Mary Wants to Be an Artist. 2009. 28p. pap. 12.49 (978-1-4490-2609-7(5)) AuthorHouse.

Nesbø, Jo. Bubble in the Bathtub. Chace, Tara F., tr. Lowery, Mike, illus. 2011. (Doctor Proctor's Fart Powder Ser.). (ENG.). 448p. (J). (gr. 3-7). pap. 7.99 (978-1-4169-7975-3(1), Aladdin) Simon & Schuster Children's Publishing.

—Bubble in the Bathtub. Chace, Tara, tr. from NOR. Lowery, Mike, illus. 2011. (Doctor Proctor's Fart Powder Ser.). (ENG.). 432p. (J). (gr. 3-7). 17.99 (978-1-4169-7974-6(3), Aladdin) Simon & Schuster Children's Publishing.

Neuschwander, Cindy. Pastry School in Paris: An Adventure in Capacity. Langdo, Bryan, illus. 2009. (ENG.). 32p. (J). (gr. 2-6). 18.99 (978-0-8050-8314-9(6), 9780805083149, Holt, Henry & Co. Bks. For Young Readers) Holt, Henry & Co.

Oliver, Lin. Splat! Another Messy Sunday 2. 2016. (Fantastic Frame Ser.: 2). (ENG., Illus.). 128p. (J). (gr. 2-4). 11.99

(978-0-448-48089-3(1), Grosset & Dunlap) Penguin Young Readers Group.

Orczy, Emmuska. Castles in the Air. 2008. 160p. 25.95 *(978-1-60664-927-5(2));* pap. 14.95 *(978-1-60664-047-0(X))* Aegypan.

Osborne, Mary Pope. Night of the New Magicians. Murdocca, Sal, illus. 2007. (Magic Tree House Merlin Mission Ser.: 7). (ENG.). 144p. (J). (gr. 2-5). 5.99 *(978-0-375-83036-5(7),* Random Hse. Bks. for Young Readers) Random Hse. Children's Bks.

Paris, Harper. The Mystery of the Stolen Painting. Calo, Marcos, illus. 2014. (Greetings from Somewhere Ser.: 3). (ENG.). 128p. (J). (gr. k-2). pap. 5.99 *(978-1-4814-0296-5(X),* Little Simon) Little Simon.

Parry, Rosanne. Second Fiddle. 2012. (ENG.). 240p. (J). (gr. 3-7). 6.99 *(978-0-375-86166-6(1),* Yearling) Random Hse. Children's Bks.

Patterson, James & Paetro, Maxine. Confessions: The Paris Mysteries. 2014. (Confessions Ser.). (ENG.). 320p. (YA). (gr. 7-17). 18.00 *(978-0-316-37084-4(3),* Jimmy Patterson) Little Brown & Co.

—The Paris Mysteries. l.t. ed. 2014. (Confessions Ser.: 3). (ENG.). 352p. (YA). (gr. 7-17). 30.99 *(978-0-316-40963-6(4),* Jimmy Patterson) Little Brown & Co.

—The Paris Mysteries. 2015. (Confessions Ser.: 3). (YA). lib. bdg. 20.85 *(978-0-606-37526-9(0))* Turtleback Bks.

Perkins, Stephanie. Anna & the French Kiss. 2010. (ENG.). 384p. (YA). (gr. 7-18). 16.99 *(978-0-525-42327-0(3),* Dutton Books for Young Readers) Penguin Young Readers Group.

—Isla & the Happily Ever After. 2015. (ENG.). 368p. (YA). (gr. 9-12). pap. 10.99 *(978-0-14-242627-2(X),* Speak) Penguin Publishing Group.

—Isla & the Happily Ever After. 2014. (ENG.). 352p. (YA). (gr. 9). 17.99 *(978-0-525-42563-2(2),* Dutton Books for Young Readers) Penguin Young Readers Group.

Plum, Amy. Die for Me. (Die for Me Ser.: 1). (ENG.). (YA). (gr. 9). 2012. 368p. pap. 8.99 *(978-0-06-200402-4(6))* 2011. 352p. 17.99 *(978-0-06-200401-7(8))* HarperCollins Pubs. (HarperTeen).

Ponnay, Brenda. Secret Agent Josephine in Paris. Ponnay, Brenda, illus. 2013. (Illus.). 32p. 19.99 *(978-1-62395-524-3(6))* Xist Publishing.

Ponnay, Brenda & Ponnay, Brenda. Secret Agent Josephine in Paris. 2013. 32p. pap. 9.99 *(978-1-62395-552-6(1))* Xist Publishing.

Reich, Susanna. Minette's Feast: The Delicious Story of Julia Child & Her Cat. Bates, Amy, illus. 2012. (ENG.). 40p. (J). (gr. -1-k). 17.95 *(978-1-4197-0177-1(0),* Abrams Bks. for Young Readers) Abrams, Inc.

Rohan, Margaret de. Celia & Granny Meg go to Paris: A survival Guide. 2011. (ENG., Illus.). 184p. pap. *(978-1-84876-650-1(5))* Troubador Publishing Ltd.

—Celia & Granny Meg Return to Paris: The man with no Face. 2012. (ENG., Illus.). 176p. pap. *(978-1-78088-243-7(2))* Troubador Publishing Ltd.

Rooftoppers. 2014. (ENG., Illus.). 304p. (J). (gr. 3-7). pap. 7.99 *(978-1-4424-9059-8(4),* Simon & Schuster Bks. For Young Readers) Simon & Schuster Bks. For Young Readers.

Rose, Phyllis & de Brunhoff, Laurent. Babar's Lost & Found. 2013. (ENG., Illus.). 22p. (J). (gr. -1 — 1). bds. 7.95 *(978-1-4197-0981-4(X),* Abrams Appleseed) Abrams, Inc.

Rue, Nancy N. Lily's Passport to Paris, 1 vol. 2003. (Lily Ser.). (ENG.). 160p. (J). pap. 6.99 *(978-0-310-70555-0(X))* Zonderkidz.

Rundell, Katherine. Rooftoppers. Fan, Terry, illus. 2013. (ENG.). 288p. (J). (gr. 3-7). 16.99 *(978-1-4424-9058-1(6),* Simon & Schuster Bks. For Young Readers) Simon & Schuster Bks. For Young Readers.

Ryan, Carrie. Divide & Conquer. 2015. (Infinity Ring Ser.: 2). (ENG.). 192p. (J). (gr. 3-7). pap. 6.99 *(978-0-545-90017-1(4))* Scholastic, Inc.

Schroeder, Lisa. My Secret Guide to Paris. (ENG.). 224p. (J). (gr. 3-7). 2016. pap. 6.99 *(978-0-545-70810-4(9))* 2015. 16.99 *(978-0-545-70808-1(7),* Scholastic Pr.) Scholastic, Inc.

Schwarz, Larry & Palmer, Iva-Marie. Romeo, Juliet & Jim, Bk. 1. 2017. (ENG., Illus.). 288p. (YA). 17.99 *(978-1-62779-250-9(3),* 9781627792509, Holt, Henry & Co. Bks. For Young Readers) Holt, Henry & Co.

Scott, Michael. The Magician. (Secrets of the Immortal Nicholas Flamel Ser.: Bk. 2). (ENG.). 496p. (YA). (gr. 7). 2009. pap. 10.99 *(978-0-385-73728-9(9),* Ember) 2008. 16.99 *(978-0-385-73358-8(5),* Delacorte Bks. for Young Readers) Random Hse. Children's Bks.

Seduction. 2014. (Legacy Ser.). (ENG., Illus.). 416p. (YA). (gr. 9). 17.99 *(978-1-4814-0023-7(1),* Simon & Schuster/Paula Wiseman Bks.) Simon & Schuster/Paula Wiseman Bks.

Smadja, Brigitte. Tarte aux Escargots. pap. 17.95 *(978-2-211-03633-7(3))* Archimede Editions FRA. Dist: Distribooks, Inc.

Smallman, Steve. Santa Is Coming to Notre Dame. Dunn, Robert, illus. 2013. (ENG.). 32p. (J). (-3). 9.99 *(978-1-4022-9024-4(1),* Sourcebooks Jabberwocky) Sourcebooks, Inc.

Snyder, Karen. Mona Lisa's Makeover. LaGrange, Tiffany, illus. 2010. 24p. pap. 12.95 *(978-1-936343-15-7(0))* Peppertree Pr., The.

Soriano, Osvaldo. El Negro de Paris. (Torre de Papel Ser.). (SPA.). (J). (gr. 4-18). 8.95 *(978-958-04-3450-4(6))* Norma S.A. COL. Dist: Distribuidora Norma, Inc.

Steel, Danielle. Pretty Minnie in Paris. Vaillant, Kristi, illus. 2014. (ENG.). 32p. (J). (gr. -1-2). 17.99 *(978-0-385-37000-4(8),* Doubleday Bks. for Young Readers) Random Hse. Children's Bks.

Stevenson, Steve. The Eiffel Tower Incident. 2014. (Agatha Girl of Mystery Ser.: 5). lib. bdg. 16.00 *(978-0-606-34153-0(6),* Turtleback) Turtleback Bks.

—The Eiffel Tower Incident #5. Turconi, Stefano, illus. 2014. (Agatha: Girl of Mystery Ser.: 5). (ENG.). 144p. (J). (gr. 2-5). 6.99 *(978-0-448-46223-3(0),* Grosset & Dunlap) Penguin Young Readers Group.

Stilton, Geronimo & Stilton, Thea. Thea Stilton & the Mystery in Paris. 2010. (Thea Stilton Ser.: 5). (ENG.). 176p. (J). (gr. 2-5). pap. 8.99 *(978-0-545-22773-5(9),* Scholastic Paperbacks) Scholastic, Inc.

—Thea Stilton & the Mystery on the Orient Express. 2012. (Thea Stilton Ser.: 13). (ENG.). 176p. (J). (gr. 2-5). pap. 8.99 *(978-0-545-34105-9(1),* Scholastic Paperbacks) Scholastic, Inc.

Stone, Phoebe. Paris for Two. 2016. (ENG.). 272p. (J). (gr. 3-7). 16.99 *(978-0-545-44362-3(8),* Levine, Arthur A. Bks.) Scholastic, Inc.

Strady, Sophie. The Memory of an Elephant: An Unforgettable Journey. Martin, Jean-Francois, illus. 2014. (ENG.). 38p. (J). (gr. k-3). 18.99 *(978-1-4521-2903-7(7))* Chronicle Bks. LLC.

Surget, Alain. The Ghost Ship. 2015. (Jolly Roger Ser.). (Illus.). 96p. (gr. 3-6). 28.50 *(978-1-909645-41-7(9))* Book Hse. GBR. Dist: Black Rabbit Bks.

Swank, Denise Grover. One Paris Summer, 1 vol. 2016. (ENG.). 352p. (YA). pap. 14.99 *(978-0-310-75516-6(6))* Blink.

A Tale of Two Cities. abr. ed. (ARA., Illus.). 48p. (J). 12.00 *(978-0-86685-627-0(7))* International Bk. Ctr., Inc.

Urbain, Christophe, photos by. Emma in Paris. 2013. (ENG., Illus.). 56p. (J). (gr. k). 17.95 *(978-1-59270-139-1(6))* Enchanted Lion Bks., LLC.

Ward, Christopher. Mac in the City of Light. 2013. 220p. pap. *(978-1-4596-6323-7(3))* ReadHowYouWant.com, Ltd.

Warner, Susan & Wetherell, Elizabeth. Queechy. 2008. 328p. per. 16.95 *(978-1-60312-446-1(2))* Aegypan.

Webb, Sarah. Bridesmaid Blitz. 2012. (Ask Amy Green Ser.: 3). (ENG., Illus.). 320p. (YA). (gr. 7). pap. 6.99 *(978-0-7636-5157-2(5))* Candlewick Pr.

Wells, Carolyn. Patty in Paris. 2004. reprint ed. pap. 21.95 *(978-1-4191-4034-1(5));* pap. 1.99 *(978-1-4192-4034-8(X))* Kessinger Publishing, LLC.

—Patty in Paris. 2011. 148p. 24.95 *(978-1-4638-9969-1(6));* pap. 12.95 *(978-1-4638-0166-3(1))* Rodgers, Alan Bks.

Weston Woods Staff, creator. Madeline's Rescue. 2011. 38.75 *(978-0-439-72772-3(3));* 29.95 *(978-0-439-73488-2(6));* 18.95 *(978-0-439-72770-9(7))* Weston Woods Studios, Inc.

Weyn, Suzanne. The Diamond Secret. 2009. (Once upon a Time Ser.). (ENG.). 240p. (YA). (gr. 7-18). mass mkt. 7.99 *(978-1-4169-7530-4(6),* Simon Pulse) Simon Pulse.

Whitby, Adele. Camille's Story 1910. 2015. (Secrets of the Manor Ser.: 7). (ENG., Illus.). 160p. (J). (gr. 3-7). pap. 6.99 *(978-1-4814-3988-6(X),* Simon Spotlight) Simon Spotlight.

Whitney, Daisy. Starry Nights. 2013. (ENG.). 288p. (YA). (gr. 7). 17.99 *(978-1-61963-133-5(4),* 9781619631335, Bloomsbury USA Childrens) Bloomsbury Publishing USA.

Willems, Mo. The Story of Diva & Flea. DiTerlizzi, Tony, illus. 2015. (ENG.). 80p. (J). (gr. 1-3). 14.99 *(978-1-4847-2284-8(1))* Disney Pr.

Wurge, B. B. Squiggle. 2009. (LeapKids Ser.). (ENG., Illus.). 152p. (J). (gr. 2-7). pap. 9.95 *(978-0-9815148-9-5(8))* Leapfrog Pr.

PARIS (FRANCE)—HISTORY—FICTION

Dennard, Susan. A Darkness Strange & Lovely. 2014. (Something Strange & Deadly Trilogy Ser.: 2). (ENG.). 432p. (YA). (gr. 9). pap. 9.99 *(978-0-06-208330-2(9),* HarperTeen) HarperCollins Pubs.

Dickens, Charles. A Tale of Two Cities: A Classic Retelling. 2006. (Classic Retelling Ser.). (Illus.). 240p. (YA). (gr. 8-12). *(978-0-618-03150-4(2),* 2-00144) Holt McDougal.

Dickens, Charles & Hawksley, L. Dickens. A Tale of Two Cities. 2004. (Paperback Classics Ser.). 144p. (J). pap. 4.95 *(978-0-7945-0390-1(X));* lib. bdg. 12.95 *(978-1-58086-515-9(1))* EDC Publishing.

Donnelly, Jennifer. Revolution. 2011. (ENG.). 512p. (YA). (gr. 9). pap. 9.99 *(978-0-385-73764-7(5),* Ember) Random Hse. Children's Bks.

Duble, Kathleen Benner. Madame Tussaud's Apprentice: An Untold Story of Love in the French Revolution. 2014. (ENG.). 224p. (YA). 17.99 *(978-1-4405-8116-8(9),* Simon Pulse) Simon Pulse.

Dunlap, Susanne. The Academie. 2012. (ENG.). 368p. (YA). 16.99 *(978-1-59990-586-0(8),* 9781599905860, Bloomsbury USA Childrens) Bloomsbury Publishing USA.

Fletcher, Susan E. A Little in Love. 2015. (ENG.). 288p. (J). (gr. 7). 17.99 *(978-0-545-82960-1(7),* Chicken Hse., The) Scholastic, Inc.

Fontes, Justine & Fontes, Ron. The Fifth Musketeer. Meconis, Dylan, illus. 2012. (Twisted Journeys Ser.: 19). (ENG.). 112p. (J). (gr. 4-7). pap. 45.32 *(978-0-7613-9289-7(0));* pap. 7.95 *(978-0-7613-8550-9(9));* lib. bdg. 27.93 *(978-0-7613-4594-7(9))* Lerner Publishing Group. (Graphic Universe™).

Gibbs, Stuart. Double Cross. 2013. (Last Musketeer Ser.: 3). (ENG.). 256p. (J). (gr. 3-7). 16.99 *(978-0-06-204844-8(9))* HarperCollins Pubs.

Henty, George Alfred. At Agincourt: A Tale of the White Hoods of Paris. 2011. 332p. pap. 19.95 *(978-1-61179-111-2(1))* Fireship Pr.

Hugo, Victor. The Hunchback of Notre-Dame. Corvino, Lucy, illus. 2008. (Classic Starts(tm) Ser.). (ENG.). 160p. (J). (gr. 2-4). 6.95 *(978-1-4027-4575-1(3))* Sterling Publishing Co., Inc.

The Hunchback of Notre Dame. (Read-Along Ser.). (J). 7.99 incl. audio *(978-1-55723-992-1(4))* Walt Disney Records.

Kesterson, Casie. The Goldfish in the Chandelier. Hovland, Gary, illus. 2012. (ENG.). 32p. 17.95 *(978-1-60606-094-0(5),* J. Paul Getty Museum) Getty Pubns.

McAlpine, Gordon. Mystery Box: A Novel about the Creators of Nancy Drew & the Hardy Boys. 2003. (ENG.). 190p. (YA). 16.95 *(978-0-8126-2680-3(X))* Cricket Bks.

Meyer, Carolyn. Marie, Dancing. 2007. (ENG., Illus.). 272p. (YA). (gr. 7-18). pap. 15.95 *(978-0-15-205879-1(6))* Houghton Mifflin Harcourt Publishing Co.

Montanari, Eva. Chasing Degas. 2009. (ENG., Illus.). 32p. (J). (gr. k-2). 18.95 *(978-0-8109-3878-6(2),* Abrams Bks. for Young Readers) Abrams, Inc.

Morgan, Page. The Beautiful & the Cursed. 2014. (Dispossessed Ser.). (ENG.). 352p. (YA). (gr. 7). pap. 9.99 *(978-0-385-74312-9(2),* Ember) Random Hse. Children's Bks.

Olshan, Matthew. The Mighty Lalouche. Blackall, Sophie, illus. 2013. (ENG.). 40p. (J). (gr. -1-3). 17.99 *(978-0-375-86225-0(0),* Schwartz & Wade Bks.) Random Hse. Children's Bks.

Osborne, Mary Pope. Night of the New Magicians. 2007. (Magic Tree House Merlin Missions Ser.: 7). lib. bdg. 16.00 *(978-1-4177-9108-8(X),* Turtleback) Turtleback Bks.

Ross, Elizabeth. Belle Epoque. 2014. (ENG.). 352p. (YA). (gr. 7). pap. 9.99 *(978-0-385-74147-7(2),* Ember) Random Hse. Children's Bks.

Ryan, Carrie. Divide & Conquer. 2012. (Infinity Ring Ser.: 2). (ENG.). 192p. (J). (gr. 3-7). 12.99 *(978-0-545-38697-5(7));* 16.99 *(978-0-545-48455-8(3))* Scholastic, Inc.

Scott, Elaine. Secrets of the Cirque Medrano. 2008. (ENG., Illus.). 216p. (J). (gr. 5-9). 15.95 *(978-1-57091-712-7(4))* Charlesbridge Publishing, Inc.

—The Spanish Web: An Encounter with Picasso. 2004. (Art Encounters Ser.). (J). 15.95 *(978-0-8230-0410-2(4));* pap. 6.99 *(978-0-8230-0413-3(9))* Watson-Guptill Pubns., Inc.

Selznick, Brian. The Invention of Hugo Cabret. 2007. (CHI., Illus.). 534p. (J). *(978-957-570-894-8(6))* Eastern Publishing Co., Ltd., The.

—The Invention of Hugo Cabret. 2008. (CHI., Illus.). 465p. (J). pap. *(978-7-5448-0279-6(5))* Jieli Publishing Hse.

—The Invention of Hugo Cabret. Selznick, Brian, illus. 2007. (Illus.). (ENG.). 544p. (J). (gr. 4-7). 24.99 *(978-0-439-81378-5(6),* Scholastic Pr.); 534p. *(978-1-4071-0348-8(2))* Scholastic, Inc.

Wang, Jack, et al. Victor Hugo's les Misérables. 2016. (ENG., Illus.). 24p. (J). (gr. -1 — 1). bds. 9.95 *(978-1-4521-5251-6(9))* Chronicle Bks. LLC.

Weyn, Suzanne. Faces of the Dead. 2014. (ENG.). 208p. (J). (gr. 7). 17.99 *(978-0-545-42531-5(X),* Scholastic Pr.) Scholastic, Inc.

PARKER, QUANAH, 1845?-1911

Sanford, William R. Comanche Chief Quanah Parker. 2013. (Native American Chiefs & Warriors Ser.). 48p. (J). (gr. 5-18). lib. bdg. 22.60 *(978-0-7660-4095-3(X));* pap. 8.95 *(978-1-4644-0255-5(8))* Enslow Pubs., Inc.

PARKS, GORDON, 1912-2006

Parr, Ann. Gordon Parks: No Excuses, 1 vol. Breidenthal, Kathryn, illus. Parks, Gordon, Jr., photos by. 2006. (ENG.). 32p. (J). (gr. k-3). 16.99 *(978-1-58980-411-1(2))* Pelican Publishing Co., Inc.

PARKS, ROSA, 1913-2005

Adler, David A. A Picture Book of Rosa Parks. Casilla, Robert, illus. 2015. 32p. pap. 8.00 *(978-1-61003-405-0(8))* Center for the Collaborative Classroom.

—A Picture Book of Rosa Parks. Casilla, Robert, illus. 2004. (J). (gr. -1-2). 28.95 incl. audio compact disk *(978-1-59112-762-8(9))* Live Oak Media.

Aretha, David. The Story of Rosa Parks & the Montgomery Bus Boycott in Photographs. 2014. (Story of the Civil Rights Movement in Photographs Ser.). 48p. (J). 25.27 *(978-0-7660-4234-6(0));* pap. 8.95 *(978-1-4644-0411-5(9))* Enslow Pubs., Inc.

Ashby, Ruth. Rosa Parks: Freedom Rider. 2008. (Sterling Biographies(r) Ser.). (ENG., Illus.). 128p. (J). (gr. 5). pap. 5.95 *(978-1-4027-4865-3(5))* Sterling Publishing Co., Inc.

Banting, Erinn. Rosa Parks. 2005. (Great African American Women for Kids Ser.). (Illus.). 24p. (J). (gr. 2-3). lib. bdg. 26.00 *(978-1-59036-336-2(1));* (gr. 3-7). per. 8.95 *(978-1-59036-342-3(6))* Weigl Pubs., Inc.

Bednar, Chuck. Rosa Parks. 2010. (Transcending Race in America Ser.). (Illus.). 64p. (YA). (gr. 5-18). lib. bdg. 22.95 *(978-1-4222-1615-6(2))* Mason Crest.

Bjornlund, Lydia. Rosa Parks & the Montgomery Bus Boycott. 2007. (Lucent Library of Black History Ser.). (ENG., Illus.). 128p. (gr. 8-12). lib. bdg. 39.40 *(978-1-4205-0010-3(4),* Lucent Bks.) Cengage Gale.

Brandt, Keith & Mattern, Joanne. Rosa Parks: Freedom Rider. Griffith, Gershom, illus. 2006. 54p. (J). pap. *(978-0-439-66045-7(9))* Scholastic, Inc.

Brown, Jonatha A. Rosa Parks. 2005. (Gente que hay que conocer (People We Should Know- Spanish edition) Ser.). (Illus.). 24p. (gr. 1-4). (ENG & SPA.). pap. 8.15 *(978-0-8368-4769-7(5));* pap. 8.15 *(978-0-8368-4755-0(5));* (ENG & SPA., lib. bdg. 22.00 *(978-0-8368-4762-8(8));* lib. bdg. 22.00 *(978-0-8368-4748-2(2))* Stevens, Gareth Publishing LLLP. (Weekly Reader Leveled Readers).

Collard, Sneed B., III. Rosa Parks: The Courage to Make a Difference. 2006. (American Heroes Ser.). (Illus.). 48p. (gr. 3-5). lib. bdg. 29.93 *(978-0-7614-2163-4(7),* Benchmark Bks.) Marshall Cavendish Corp.

Collins, James. Rosa Parks: Not Giving In with Buffalo Bill & Farley's Raiders. Cox, Brian T., illus. 2006. (Time Traveler's Adventure Ser.). 56p. (J). 13.50 incl. audio compact disk *(978-1-932332-17-9(0))* Toy Box Productions.

Connors, Kathleen. The Life of Rosa Parks, Vol. 1. 2014. (Famous Lives Ser.). (ENG.). 24p. (J). (gr. 1-2). 22.60 *(978-1-4824-0419-7(2))* Stevens, Gareth Publishing LLLP.

Daly, Ruth. Rosa Parks. 2014. (J). *(978-1-4896-2452-9(X))* Weigl Pubs., Inc.

Dubowski, Cathy East. Rosa Parks: Don't Give In! 2005. (Defining Moments Ser.). (Illus.). 32p. (J). (gr. 2-5). lib. bdg. 25.27 *(978-1-59716-078-0(4))* Bearport Publishing Co., Inc.

Edison, Erin. Rosa Parks. 2013. (Great Women in History Ser.). (ENG.). 24p. (gr. k-1). pap. 35.70 *(978-1-62065-864-2(X));* pap. 6.29 *(978-1-62065-863-5(1));* (Illus.). lib. bdg. 21.99 *(978-1-62065-071-4(1))* Capstone Press of Coughlan Cos. (Pebble Bks.).

Edwards, Pamela Duncan. The Bus Ride That Changed History: The Story of Rosa Parks. Shanahan, Danny, illus. 2009. (ENG.). 32p. (J). (gr. -1-3). pap. 6.99 *(978-0-547-07674-4(6))* Houghton Mifflin Harcourt Publishing Co.

Fine, Edith Hope. Rosa Parks: Meet a Civil Rights Hero. 2004. (Meeting Famous People Ser.). (Illus.). 32p. (J). lib. bdg. 23.94 *(978-0-7660-2099-3(1))* Enslow Pubs., Inc.

Giovanni, Nikki. Rosa. Collier, Bryan, illus. rev. ed. 2005. (ENG.). 40p. (J). (gr. -1-3). 17.99 *(978-0-8050-7106-1(7),* 9780805071061, Holt, Henry & Co. Bks. For Young Readers) Holt, Henry & Co.

—Rosa. Collier, Bryan, illus. 2007. (ENG.). 40p. (J). (gr. -1-3). per. 8.99 *(978-0-312-37602-4(2),* 9780312376024) Square Fish.

—Rosa. Collier, Bryan, illus. 2011. (J). (gr. 2-5). 29.95 *(978-0-545-04261-1(5))* Weston Woods Studios, Inc.

—Rosa Storytime Set, 1 vol. Collier, Bryan, illus. unabr. ed. 2014. (ENG.). 40p. (J). (gr. -1-3). 12.99 *(978-1-4272-4397-3(2),* 9781427243973) Macmillan Audio.

Haldy, Emma E. Rosa Parks. Bane, Jeff, illus. 2016. (My Early Library: My Itty-Bitty Bio Ser.). (ENG.). 24p. (J). (gr. k-1). 28.50 *(978-1-63470-481-6(9),* 207655) Cherry Lake Publishing.

Hoe, Susan C. Rosa Parks. 2009. (Sharing the American Dream Ser.). 64p. (YA). (gr. 7-12). 22.95 *(978-1-4222-0597-6(5))* Mason Crest.

Howell, Izzi. Rosa Parks. 2016. (Fact Cat: History Ser.). (ENG., Illus.). 24p. (J). (gr. k-2). 14.99 *(978-0-7502-9771-4(9),* Wayland) Hachette Children's Group GBR. Dist: Hachette Bk. Group.

Hull, Mary. Rosa Parks: Civil Rights Leader. 2nd rev. ed. 2006. (Black Americans of Achievement Ser.). (Illus.). 122p. (YA). (gr. 7-12). lib. bdg. 35.00 *(978-0-7910-9523-2(1))* Facts On File, Inc.

Hull, Mary & Gelfand, Dale Evva. Rosa Parks. 2nd rev. ed. 2008. (Black Americans of Achievement: Legacy Edition Ser.). 128p. (gr. 6-12). pap. 11.95 *(978-1-60413-325-7(2),* Checkmark Bks.) Facts On File, Inc.

Hurt, Avery Elizabeth. Rosa Parks: Civil Rights Activist. 2017. (J). ***(978-1-5383-8105-2(2));*** pap. ***(978-1-5383-8102-1(8))*** Rosen Publishing Group, Inc., The.

Jazynka, Kitson. National Geographic Readers: Rosa Parks. 2015. (Readers Bios Ser.). (ENG., Illus.). 32p. (J). (gr. k-3). pap. 3.99 *(978-1-4263-2141-2(4),* National Geographic Children's Bks.) National Geographic Society.

Jeffrey, Gary. Rosa Parks & the Montgomery Bus Boycott. 2012. (Graphic History of the Civil Rights Movement Ser.). (Illus.). 24p. (J). (gr. 3-8). pap. 8.15 *(978-1-4339-7500-4(9));* lib. bdg. 23.95 *(978-1-4339-7499-1(1))* Stevens, Gareth Publishing LLLP.

Kaiser, Lisbeth. Rosa Parks. Antelo, Marta, illus. 2017. (Little People, Big Dreams Ser.). (ENG.). 32p. (J). (gr. k-3). 14.99 ***(978-1-78603-018-4(7),*** Frances Lincoln Children's Bks.) Quarto Publishing Group UK GBR. Dist: Hachette Bk. Group.

Kemp, Kristin. Amazing Americans: Rosa Parks, 1 vol. rev. ed. 2014. (Primary Source Readers Content & Literacy Ser.). (ENG., Illus.). 32p. (gr. 3-3). pap. 8.99 *(978-1-4333-7375-6(0))* Teacher Created Materials, Inc.

Kishel, Ann-Marie. Rosa Parks: A Life of Courage. 2006. (Pull Ahead Books-Biographies Ser.). (ENG., Illus.). 32p. (gr. k-3). pap. 7.95 *(978-0-8225-5698-5(7));* lib. bdg. 22.60 *(978-0-8225-3478-5(9),* Lerner Pubns.) Lerner Publishing Group.

—Rosa Parks: Una Vida de Valentia. Translations.com Staff, tr. 2006. (Libros para Avanzar-Biografias (Pull Ahead Books-Biographies) Ser.). (ENG & SPA., Illus.). 32p. (gr. k-3). lib. bdg. 22.60 *(978-0-8225-6239-9(1))* Lerner Publishing Group.

—Rosa Parks: Una vida de valentia (A Life of Courage) 2006. (Libros para Avanzar-Biografias (Pull Ahead Books-Biographies Ser.). (Illus.). 32p. (gr. 3-7). per. 6.95 *(978-0-8225-6557-4(9),* Ediciones Lerner) Lerner Publishing Group.

Kittinger, Jo S. Rosa's Bus: The Ride to Civil Rights. Walker, Steven, illus. 2010. (ENG.). 40p. (J). (gr. 2-4). 17.95 *(978-1-59078-722-9(6))* Boyds Mills Pr.

Linde, Barbara M. Rosa Parks. 2011. (Civil Rights Crusaders Ser.). (Illus.). 24p. (gr. 2-5). (J). pap. 8.15 *(978-1-4339-5696-6(9),* Gareth Stevens Learning Library); (YA). lib. bdg. 22.60 *(978-1-4339-5694-2(2))* Stevens, Gareth Publishing LLLP.

Manolis, Kay & Leslie, Tonya. Rosa Parks: A Life of Courage. 2007. (People of Character Ser.). (ENG., Illus.). 24p. (J). (gr. 2-5). lib. bdg. 25.95 *(978-1-60014-088-4(2))* Bellwether Media.

Mara, Wil. Rosa Parks. (Rookie Biographies Ser.). (ENG., Illus.). 32p. (J). (gr. 1-2). 2004. pap. 4.95 *(978-0-516-27916-9(5))* 2007. pap. 4.95 *(978-0-531-12592-2(0))* Scholastic Library Publishing. (Children's Pr.).

—Rosa Parks: Mother of the Civil Rights Movement. 2014. (Rookie Biographies(tm) Ser.). (ENG.). 32p. (J). lib. bdg. 25.00 *(978-0-531-20561-7(4));* pap. 5.95 *(978-0-531-21204-2(1))* Scholastic Library Publishing.

McCormick, Anita Louise. Rosa Parks & the Montgomery Bus Boycott. 2017. (J). ***(978-1-5383-8061-1(7));*** pap. ***(978-1-5383-8062-8(5))*** Rosen Publishing Group, Inc., The.

McDonough, Yona Zeldis. Who Was Rosa Parks? Harrison, Nancy & Marchesi, Stephen, illus. 2010. (Who Was? Ser.). (ENG.). 112p. (J). (gr. 3-7). pap. 5.99 *(978-0-448-45442-9(4),* Grosset & Dunlap) Penguin Young Readers Group.

Meltzer, Brad. I Am Rosa Parks. Eliopoulos, Christopher, illus. 2014. (Ordinary People Change World Ser.). (ENG.). 40p. (J). (gr. -1-k). 14.99 *(978-0-8037-4085-3(9),* Dial Bks) Penguin Publishing Group.

Miller, Connie Colwell. Rosa Parks & the Montgomery Bus Boycott, 1 vol. Kalal, Dan, illus. 2006. (Graphic History Ser.). (ENG.). 32p. (gr. 3-4). 30.65 *(978-0-7368-6495-4(4),* Graphic Library) Capstone Press of Coughlan Cos.

—Rosa Parks & the Montgomery Bus Boycott, 1 vol. Kalal, Dan, illus. 2006. (Graphic History Ser.). (ENG.). 32p. (gr. 3-4). per. 8.10 *(978-0-7368-9658-0(9),* Graphic Library) Capstone Press of Coughlan Cos.

Mis, Melody S. Meet Rosa Parks. (Civil Rights Leaders Ser.). 24p. (gr. 2-3). 2009. 42.50 *(978-1-61511-855-7(1),* PowerKids Pr.) 2008. (Illus.). (YA). lib. bdg. 22.60 *(978-1-4042-4210-4(4))* Rosen Publishing Group, Inc., The.

Morretta, Alison. Rosa Parks & Civil Disobedience. 2016. (Primary Sources of the Civil Rights Movement Ser.). (Illus.). 64p. (J). (gr. 6-6). 34.21 *(978-1-5026-1870-2(2))* Cavendish Square Publishing.

Morris, Roz. Rosa Parks: Mother of the Civil Rights Movement. 2003. (Alabama Roots Biography Ser.). (Illus.). 109p. (J). *(978-1-878561-57-2(X))* Seacoast Publishing, Inc.

Pingry, Patricia A. Meet Rosa Parks. Walker, Steven, illus. 2008. (ENG.). 32p. (J). (gr. k-3). per. 7.99 *(978-0-8249-5578-6(1),* Ideal Pubns.) Worthy Publishing.

—The Story of Rosa Parks. Walker, Steven, illus. (J). 2016. *(978-0-8249-1987-0(4))* 2008. (ENG.). 24p. (gr. 3-7). bds. 7.69 *(978-0-8249-6687-4(2))* Worthy Publishing. (Ideal Pubns.).

Reed, Gregory J. Dear Mrs. Parks: A Dialogue with Today's Youth. 2013. (ENG., Illus.). 111p. (J). (gr. 3-7). reprint ed. per. 16.95 *(978-1-880000-61-8(X))* Lee & Low Bks., Inc.

Rinaldo, Denise. Rosa Parks: With a Discussion of Courage. 2003. (Values in Action Ser.). (J). *(978-1-59203-061-3(0))* Learning Challenge, Inc.

Ringgold, Faith. If a Bus Could Talk: The Story of Rosa Parks. Ringgold, Faith, illus. 2003. (ENG., Illus.). 32p. (J). (gr. k-4). pap. 7.99 (978-0-689-85676-1(8), Aladdin) Simon & Schuster Children's Publishing.

Roop, Peter. Take a Stand, Rosa Parks. 2005. (Illus.). 59p. (J). (978-0-439-67625-0(8)) Scholastic, Inc.

Ruiz, Rachel. When Rosa Parks Went Fishing. Fedele, Chiara, illus. 2017. (Leaders Doing Headstands Ser.). (ENG.). 32p. (gr. 2-3). lib. bdg. 27.99 **(978-1-5158-1574-7(9))** Picture Window Bks.

Schraff, Anne E. Rosa Parks: Tired of Giving In. 2005. (African-American Biography Library). (Illus.). 128p. (J). (gr. 6-12). lib. bdg. 33.27 (978-0-7660-2463-2(6)) Enslow Pubs., Inc.

Shea, Therese. Rosa Parks, 1 vol. 2015. (ENG., Illus.). 32p. (J). 23.45 (978-1-62275-697-1(5), Britannica Educational Publishing) Rosen Publishing Group, Inc., The.

Shone, Rob. Rosa Parks: The Life of a Civil Rights Heroine. 2009. (Graphic Nonfiction Biographies Ser.). (ENG.). 48p. (YA). (gr. 4-5). 58.50 (978-1-61513-026-9(8), Rosen Reference) Rosen Publishing Group, Inc., The.

—Rosa Parks: The Life of a Civil Rights Heroine. Spender, Nick, illus. 2007. (Graphic Nonfiction Biographies Ser.). (ENG.). 48p. (J). (gr. 4-7). lib. bdg. 31.95 (978-1-4042-0864-3(X)) Rosen Publishing Group, Inc., The.

—Rosa Parks: The Life of a Civil Rights Heroine. Spender, Nik, illus. 2007. (Graphic Biographies Ser.). (ENG.). 48p. (gr. 5-8). pap. 14.05 (978-1-4042-0927-5(1)) Rosen Publishing Group, Inc., The.

Summer, L. S. Rosa Parks. 2009. (Journey to Freedom Ser.). (ENG., Illus.). 32p. (J). (gr. 4-7). 29.93 (978-1-60253-133-8(1), 200399) Child's World, Inc., The.

Taylor-Butler, Christine. Rosa Parks. 2015. (ENG., Illus.). 48p. (J). pap. 6.95 (978-0-531-21209-7(2), Orchard Bks.) Scholastic Library Publishing.

Tieck, Sarah. Rosa Parks, 1 vol. 2006. (Buddy Book Ser.). (ENG., Illus.). 32p. (gr. -1-3). 27.07 (978-1-59679-788-8(6), Buddy Bks.) ABDO Publishing Co.

Time for Kids Editors. Rosa Parks: Civil Rights Pioneer. 2006. (Time for Kids Ser.). (ENG., Illus.). 48p. (J). (gr. 2-4). pap. 3.99 (978-0-06-057624-0(3), Collins) HarperCollins Pubs.

—Rosa Parks: Civil Rights Pioneer. 2007. (Time for Kids Biographies Ser.). (Illus.). 44p. (gr. 2-4). 14.00 (978-0-7569-8110-5(7)) Perfection Learning Corp.

Tracy, Kathleen. The Life & Times of Rosa Parks. 2008. (Illus.). 48p. (J). (gr. 4-8). lib. bdg. 29.95 (978-1-58415-666-6(X)) Mitchell Lane Pubs., Inc.

Turner-Barnes, Sandra. Beyond the Back of the Bus. Collins, Bernard, Jr., illus. 2011. (ENG.). 32p. (J). (gr. k-2). pap. 9.95 (978-0-88378-295-8(2)) Third World Press.

Weidt, Maryann N. Rosa Parks. (History Maker Bios Ser.). (Illus.). (J). 2004. 48p. pap. 8.95 (978-0-8225-4805-8(4)) 2003. 47p. 26.60 (978-0-8225-4673-3(6)) Lerner Publishing Group. (Lerner Pubns.).

Weston Woods Staff, creator. Rosa. 2011. 38.75 (978-0-545-14963-1(0)); 18.95 (978-0-545-14962-4(2)) Weston Woods Studios, Inc.

Wheeler, Jill C. Rosa Parks, Set II. 2003. (Breaking Barriers Ser.). 64p. (gr. 3-8). 27.07 (978-1-57765-640-1(7), Abdo & Daughters) ABDO Publishing Co.

Whiting, Jim. Rosa Parks. 2007. (What's So Great About...? Ser.). (Illus.). 32p. (YA). (gr. 2-4). lib. bdg. 25.70 (978-1-58415-573-7(6)) Mitchell Lane Pubs., Inc.

PARKS

Beck, Isabel L., et al. Trophies Kindergarten: The Park. 2003. (Trophies Ser.). (gr. k-6). 13.80 (978-0-15-329533-1(3)) Harcourt Schl. Pubs.

Beylon, Cathy. At the Amusement Park. 2004. (Dover Coloring Bks.). (ENG., Illus.). 32p. (J). (gr. -1-2). pap. 2.95 (978-0-486-43322-6(6)) Dover Pubns., Inc.

Cantor, Rachel Anne. Haunted Amusement Parks. 2017. (Tiptoe into Scary Places Ser.). (ENG., Illus.). 24p. (J). (gr. k-3). 18.95 **(978-1-68402-050-8(6))** Bearport Publishing Co., Inc.

Clark Sawyer, J. Patterns in the Park. 2015. (J). lib. bdg. (978-1-62724-339-1(9)) Bearport Publishing Co., Inc.

Dale, Jay. The Environment Park, 1 vol. Meldrum, Ned, photos by. 2012. (Engage Literacy Green Ser.). (ENG., Illus.). 32p. (gr. k-2). pap. 5.99 (978-1-4296-8997-7(8), Engage Literacy) Capstone Press of Coughlan Cos.

—I Am in the Park. Dybing, Michelle, illus. 2012. (Wonder Words Ser.). (ENG.). 32p. (gr. k-2). pap. 5.99 (978-1-4296-8890-1(4), Engage Literacy) Capstone Press of Coughlan Cos.

Disneyland Resort Then, Now & Forever: Remember the Moments - A Magical Souvenir. 2006. 192p. 24.95 (978-1-4231-0256-4(8), Disney Editions) Disney Pr.

Dorling Kindersley Publishing Staff. In the Park. 2004. (DK Readers Ser.). (ENG., Illus.). 32p. (J). (gr. -1-1). pap. 3.99 (978-0-7566-0537-7(7), DK Children) Dorling Kindersley Publishing, Inc.

—Park. 2010. (Baby Touch & Feel Ser.). (ENG.). 14p. (J). (gr. -1 — 1). bds. 5.99 (978-0-7566-7131-0(0), DK Children) Dorling Kindersley Publishing, Inc.

Dunlap, Julie & Olmsted, Frederick Law. Parks for the People: The Life of Frederick Law Olmsted. 2011. (ENG., Illus.). 112p. (J). (gr. 4-7). pap. 12.95 (978-1-55591-470-7(5)) Fulcrum Publishing.

Grandma Fudgie. A Walk to the Park. 2011. 24p. pap. 12.99 (978-1-4634-2695-8(X)) AuthorHouse.

Greathouse, Lisa. Cómo Funcionan los Parques de Diversiones, 1 vol. rev. ed. 2010. (Science Readers: a Closer Look Ser.). Orig. Title: How Amusement Parks Work. (SPA., Illus.). 32p. (J). (gr. 2-3). pap. 8.99 (978-1-4333-2149-8(1)) Shell Educational Publishing.

Gregory, Helen. The Park. 2011. (Wonder Readers Early Level Ser.). (ENG.). (gr. -1-1). 16p. pap. 35.94 (978-1-4296-8170-4(5)); 32p. pap. 5.99 (978-1-4296-7807-0(0)) Capstone Press of Coughlan Cos. (Wonder Readers).

Hamilton, Sue L. Water Parks. 2016. (Illus.). 32p. (J). **(978-1-62403-754-2(2)**, 1391385) ABDO Publishing Co.

Hengel, Katherine. Cool Parks & Trails: Great Things to Do in the Great Outdoors, 1 vol. 2016. (ENG., Illus.). 32p. (J). (978-1-62403-698-9(8)) ABDO Publishing Co.

Hill, Mary. Let's Go to a Park. 2004. (Welcome Bks.). 24p. (J). (gr. -1-2). pap. 4.95 (978-0-516-25918-5(0), Children's Pr.) Scholastic Library Publishing.

—Signs at the Park. 2003. (Welcome Bks.). (ENG., Illus.). 24p. (J). (gr. -1-2). pap. 4.95 (978-0-516-24365-8(9), Children's Pr.) Scholastic Library Publishing.

Hocking, Justin. Skate Parks. 2009. (Power Skateboarding Ser.). 24p. (gr. 3-4). 42.50 (978-1-60851-338-3(6), PowerKids Pr.) Rosen Publishing Group, Inc., The.

—Taking Action: How to Get Your City to Build a Public Skate Park. 2009. (Skateboarder's Guide to Skate Parks, Half-Pipes, Bowls, & Obstacles Ser.). 48p. (gr. 5-8). 53.00 (978-1-60854-234-5(3), Rosen Reference) Rosen Publishing Group, Inc., The.

—The World's Greatest Skate Parks. 2009. (Super Skateboarding Ser.). 48p. (Illus.). (J). (gr. 5-8). pap. 11.75 (978-1-4358-5390-4(3)); (YA). (gr. 4-7). lib. bdg. 29.25 (978-1-4358-5046-0(7)) Rosen Publishing Group, Inc., The.

—World's Greatest Skate Parks. 2009. (Super Skateboarding Ser.). 48p. (gr. 5-8). 53.00 (978-1-60853-222-3(4), Rosen Reference) Rosen Publishing Group, Inc., The.

Hutchings, Amy. What Happens at an Amusement Park?; ¿Qué pasa en un parque de Diversiones? 2009. (Where People Work/Dónde Trabaja la Gente? Ser.). (SPA & ENG.). 24p. (J). (gr. -1-3). pap. 8.15 (978-1-4339-0145-4(5), Weekly Reader Leveled Readers) Stevens, Gareth Publishing LLLP.

—What Happens at an Amusement Park?/¿Qué Pasa en un Parque de Diversiones? 2009. (Where People Work/Dónde Trabaja la Gente? Ser.). (SPA & ENG.). 24p. (J). (gr. -1-3). lib. bdg. 22.00 (978-1-4339-0081-5(5), Weekly Reader Leveled Readers) Stevens, Gareth Publishing LLLP.

Hutchings, Amy & Nations, Susan. What Happens at an Amusement Park? 2009. (Where People Work Ser.). 24p. (J). (gr. -1-3). lib. bdg. 22.00 (978-1-4339-0073-0(4), Weekly Reader Leveled Readers) Stevens, Gareth Publishing LLLP.

Leigh, Johanna. Spanish Words at the Park, Vol. 1. 2014. (Learn My Language! Spanish Ser.). 24p. (J). (gr. 1-2). (ENG.). pap. 8.15 (978-1-4824-0345-9(5)); 22.60 (978-1-4824-0346-6(3)) Stevens, Gareth Publishing LLLP.

Loh-Hagan, Virginia. Roller Coasters. 2017. (21st Century Junior Library: Extraordinary Engineering Ser.). (ENG., Illus.). 24p. (J). (gr. 2-5). lib. bdg. 27.07 (978-1-63472-164-6(0), 209228) Cherry Lake Publishing.

Lukeman, Noah. A Trip to the Amusement Park. 2015. (ENG., Illus.). 20p. (J). pap. 5.99 (978-1-63291-487-3(5)) Morgan Rice Bks.

Marsico, Katie. Working at a Park. 2008. (21st Century Junior Library: Careers Ser.). (ENG., Illus.). 24p. (gr. 2-5). lib. bdg. 25.64 (978-1-60279-267-8(4), 200172) Cherry Lake Publishing.

McCune, Susan. All about Our Park, 01 vols., 1. 2016. (Rosen REAL Readers: Social Studies Nonfiction / Fiction: Family, Community, & the World Ser.). (ENG.). 8p. (J). pap. 5.46 (978-1-5081-1722-3(5), Rosen Classroom) Rosen Publishing Group, Inc., The.

Nelson, Robin. How We Clean up a Park. 2014. (First Step Nonfiction - Responsibility in Action Ser.). (ENG., Illus.). 24p. (gr. k-2). pap. 6.95 (978-1-4677-3646-6(5)); lib. bdg. 23.93 (978-1-4677-3637-4(6), Lerner Pubns.) Lerner Publishing Group.

On a Roll: How Communities Build State Parks. 2005. (Book Treks Ser.). (J). 37.95 (978-0-7652-3254-0(5)) Celebration Pr.

A Park Ecosystem. 2012. (Nature Trail Ser.). (ENG., Illus.). 32p. (J). (gr. k-5). 23.95 (978-1-4488-6626-7(X), PowerKids Pr.) Rosen Publishing Group, Inc., The.

Parks Matter! 2004. (YA). (978-0-88441-673-9(9)) Girl Scouts of the USA.

Randall, Jory. My Day at the Park. 2009. (Kid's Life! Ser.). 24p. (J). (ENG.). pap. 8.25 (978-1-4358-2465-2(2)); (Illus.). lib. bdg. 22.60 (978-1-4042-8073-1(1)) Rosen Publishing Group, Inc., The. (PowerKids Pr.).

Reasoner, Charles. First Words at the Park. Pitt, Sarah, illus. 2009. (3D Board Bks.). 12p. (J). (gr. -1-k). bds. 9.99 (978-1-934650-39-4(0)) Just For Kids Pr., LLC.

Rissman, Rebecca. ABCs at the Park, 1 vol. 2012. (Everyday Alphabet Ser.). (ENG.). 32p. (gr. -1-k). pap. 9.95 (978-1-4109-4735-2(1)); lib. bdg. 25.32 (978-1-4109-4730-7(0)) Heinemann-Raintree.

—Counting at the Park, 1 vol. 2012. (I Can Count! Ser.). (ENG.). 24p. (gr. -1-k). pap. 9.95 (978-1-4329-6700-0(2)); lib. bdg. 25.32 (978-1-4329-6695-9(2)) Heinemann-Raintree.

—Eddie & Ellie's Opposites at the Park, 1 vol. 2013. (Eddie & Ellie's Opposites Ser.). (ENG.). 24p. (gr. -1-k). pap. 7.95 (978-1-4109-5347-6(5)); (Illus.). 22.65 (978-1-4109-5342-1(4)) Heinemann-Raintree. (NA-r).

—Going to a Park, 1 vol. 2012. (World of Field Trips Ser.). (ENG.). 24p. (gr. -1-1). lib. bdg. 22.65 (978-1-4329-6068-1(7), Acorn) Heinemann-Raintree.

—Parks, 1 vol. 2013. (Picture This! Ser.). (ENG.). 24p. (gr. -1-k). pap. 9.95 (978-1-4109-5259-2(2), NA-r) Heinemann-Raintree.

Ruffin, Frances E. Creating a City Park: Dividing Three-Digit Numbers by One-Digit Numbers Without Remainders. (PowerMath Ser.). (Illus.). 24p. 2009. (ENG.). (gr. 3-4). pap. 8.25 (978-0-8239-8926-3(7), PowerKids Pr.) 2004. (J). (gr. 5-9). lib. bdg. 22.50 (978-0-8239-8978-2(X)) Rosen Publishing Group, Inc., The.

—Creating a City Park: Dividing Three-digit Numbers by One-digit Numbers Without Remainders. 2009. (PowerMath: Intermediate Ser.). 24p. (gr. 3-4). 45.00 (978-1-60851-380-2(7), PowerKids Pr.) Rosen Publishing Group, Inc., The.

Stanos, Dimi, et al. Plants in the Park. 2007. (Windows on Literacy Ser.). (ENG., Illus.). 8p. (J). pap. 9.95 (978-0-7922-8463-5(1)) CENGAGE Learning.

Stillerman, Robbie. Amusement Park Stickers. 2004. (Dover Little Activity Books Stickers Ser.). (ENG., Illus.). 8p. (J). (gr. -1-5). pap. 1.50 (978-0-486-43305-9(6)) Dover Pubns., Inc.

Taylor, Trace & Sanchez, Lucia M. En el Parque: At the Park. 2011. (1-3Y ARC Press Comics Ser.). (SPA & ENG.). 16p. (J). pap. 5.99 (978-1-61541-454-3(1)) American Reading Co.

—En el parque (at the Park) 2011. (Lugares adonde voy Ser.). (SPA.). 12p. pap. 39.62 (978-1-61541-455-0(X)) American Reading Co.

Weekly Reader Editorial Staff. Things at the Park. 2006. (Things in My World Ser.). (Illus.). 16p. (gr. -1-2). lib. bdg. 19.00 (978-0-8368-6809-8(9), Weekly Reader Leveled Readers) Stevens, Gareth Publishing LLLP.

—Things at the Park (Las Cosas Del Parque) 2006. (Things in My World/ Las cosas de mi mundo Ser.). (ENG & SPA., Illus.). 16p. (gr. -1-2). pap. 5.30 (978-0-8368-7228-6(2), Weekly Reader Leveled Readers) Stevens, Gareth Publishing LLLP.

—Things at the Park/Las Cosas del Parque. 2006. (Things in My World/ Las cosas de mi mundo Ser.). (ENG & SPA., Illus.). 16p. (gr. -1-2). lib. bdg. 19.00 (978-0-8368-7221-7(5), Weekly Reader Leveled Readers) Stevens, Gareth Publishing LLLP.

Weekly Reader Editorial Staff, contrib. by. Things at the Park. 2006. (Things in My World Ser.). (Illus.). 16p. (gr. -1-2). pap. 5.30 (978-0-8368-6816-6(1), Weekly Reader Leveled Readers) Stevens, Gareth Publishing LLLP.

What Is a Park?, 6 Packs. (Discovery World Ser.). 16p. (gr. 1-2). 28.00 (978-0-7635-8453-5(3)) Rigby Education.

Williams, Colleen Madonna Flood. My Adventure at the Amusement Park. 2007. 44p. (J). 8.99 (978-1-59092-410-5(X)) Blue Forge Pr.

Wishinsky, Frieda. The Man Who Made Parks: The Story of Parkbuilder Frederick Law Olmsted. Zhang, Song Nan, illus. 2009. (ENG.). 32p. (J). (gr. k-12). pap. 10.95 (978-0-88776-902-3(0), Tundra Bks.) Tundra Bks. CAN. Dist: Penguin Random Hse. LLC.

Yoon, Salina. At the Park. 2011. (ENG., Illus.). 12p. (J). (gr. -1 — 1). bds. 5.99 (978-0-312-66298-1(X), 9780312662981) Feiwel & Friends.

PARKS—FICTION

Anderson, Mark A. Ma Ma, I'm Home, 1 vol. 2009. 48p. pap. 16.95 (978-1-4489-9077-1(7)) America Star Bks.

Baker, Keith. At the Park: A Mr. & Mrs. Green Adventure. 2016. (Green Light Readers Level 2 Ser.). (ENG., Illus.). 32p. (J). (gr. 1-4). pap. 3.99 (978-0-544-55556-3(2), HMH Books For Young Readers) Houghton Mifflin Harcourt Publishing Co.

—More Mr. & Mrs. Green, 1 vol. Baker, Keith, illus. 2007. (Mr. & Mrs. Green Ser.). (ENG., Illus.). 68p. (gr. 2-4). 27.07 (978-1-59961-302-4(6)) Spotlight.

Barkley, Callie. Amy on Park Patrol. Bishop, Tracy, illus. 2017. (Critter Club Ser.: 17). (ENG.). 128p. (J). (gr. k-3). pap. 5.99 **(978-1-4814-9432-8(5)**, Little Simon) Little Simon.

—Amy on Park Patrol. 2017. (Critter Club Ser.: 17). lib. bdg. 16.00 **(978-0-606-40208-8(X))** Turtleback Bks.

Bauer, Marion Dane. Little Dog, Lost. Bell, Jennifer A., illus. (ENG.). 208p. (J). (gr. 3-7). 2013. pap. 6.99 (978-1-4424-3424-0(4)) 2012. 16.99 (978-1-4424-3423-3(6)) Simon & Schuster Children's Publishing. (Atheneum Bks. for Young Readers).

Baumgarten, Josephine & Baumgarten, Michael. My Baby Monsters & I went to the Park. 2005. 32p. pap. 14.99 (978-1-4116-6348-0(9)) Lulu Pr., Inc.

Benenfeld, Rikki. Let's Go to the Park. 2015. (ENG., Illus.). 36p. (J). 10.95 (978-1-929628-82-7(X)) Hachai Publishing.

Benson, Glenda. The Adventures of Pepe & Gracie: Trouble in the Park. 2012. 20p. pap. 13.77 (978-1-4669-0840-6(8)) Trafford Publishing.

Bertrand, Diane Gonzalez. The Park Our Town Built. Bauerle, Tanja, illus. 2011. (ENG & SPA.). 32p. (gr. -1-3). lib. bdg. 16.95 (978-1-936299-14-0(3), Raven Tree Pr.,Csi) Continental Sales, Inc.

—The Park Our Town Built/El Parque Que Nuestro Pueblo Construyó. Bauerle, Tanja, illus. 2011. (ENG & SPA.). 32p. (gr. -1-3). lib. bdg. 16.95 (978-1-936299-12-6(7), Raven Tree Pr.,Csi) Continental Sales, Inc.

Bloomsbury USA. Lift & Look: at the Park. 2016. (ENG., Illus.). 12p. (J). (— 1). bds. 8.99 (978-1-61963-940-9(8), 9781619639409, Bloomsbury Activity Bks.) Bloomsbury Publishing USA.

Booking, Walt. Teddy's Tale. 2006. (Neighborhood Readers Ser.). (ENG.). 12p. (gr. 1-3). pap. 5.90 (978-1-4042-7054-1(X), Rosen Classroom) Rosen Publishing Group, Inc., The.

Bradford James Nolan. The Mouse Who Lived in Fenway Park. Jim Connelly, illus. 2009. 36p. pap. 19.99 (978-1-4389-4491-3(8)) AuthorHouse.

Bradley, A. M. Finnegan's Magic Sunglasses. 2013. 24p. pap. 24.95 (978-1-62709-814-4(3)) America Star Bks.

Butterworth, Nick. One Snowy Night. Butterworth, Nick, illus. 2008. (Tales from Percy's Park Ser.). (ENG., Illus.). 32p. (J). (gr. k-2). pap. 12.95 incl. audio compact disk (978-0-00-726024-9(5)) HarperCollins Pubs.

—One Snowy Night. Butterworth, Nick, illus. 2007. (ENG., Illus.). 32p. (J). 24.00 (978-0-00-725942-7(5)) HarperCollins Pubs. Ltd. GBR. Dist: Independent Pubs. Group.

Campbell, Rod. Buster's Park. 2003. (ENG., Illus.). 14p. (J). bds. 6.99 (978-0-333-76645-3(8)) Macmillan Pubs., Ltd. GBR. Dist: Trafalgar Square Publishing.

Carlson, Melody. Take Charge, 1 vol. 2016. (Faithgirlz / Girls of Harbor View Ser.). (ENG.). 272p. (J). (gr. 3-7). pap. 9.99 (978-0-310-75373-5(2)) Zonderkidz.

Carmen & Thane Johnson. Dogs Don't Wear Underwear. Bianca & Annie West, illus. 2009. 20p. pap. 12.99 (978-1-4389-4128-8(5)) AuthorHouse.

Carter, Larry. The Red Wallet. 2013. 28p. pap. 24.95 (978-1-4626-9667-3(8)) America Star Bks.

Cleveland, Marie. Jason's Giant Dilemma: A Storybook Land Adventure. 2007. 76p. per. 19.95 (978-1-4241-7811-7(8)) America Star Bks.

Cox, Phil Roxbee. Shark in the Park. Tyler, Jenny, ed. Cartwright, Stephen, illus. rev. ed. 2006. (Phonics Readers Ser.). 16p. (J). (gr. -1-k). pap. 6.99 (978-0-7945-1509-6(6), Usborne) EDC Publishing.

Cox, Phil Roxbee & Cartwright, Stephen. Shark in the Park. 2004. (Easy Words to Read Ser.). (Illus.). 16p. (J). (gr. 1-18). pap. 6.95 (978-0-7945-0171-6(0), Usborne) EDC Publishing.

Crow, Melinda Melton. Rocky & Daisy at the Park, 1 vol. Brownlow, Mike, illus. 2013. (My Two Dogs Ser.). (ENG.). 32p. (gr. 2-3). pap. 5.95 (978-1-4342-6118-2(2)); lib. bdg. 22.65 (978-1-4342-4163-4(7)) Stone Arch Bks.

Crowne, Alyssa. Green Princess Saves the Day. Alder, Charlotte, illus. 2010. (J). (Perfectly Princess Ser.: 3). (ENG.). 80p. (gr. 2-5). 4.99 (978-0-545-20848-2(3), Scholastic Paperbacks); 71p. (978-0-545-23414-6(X)) Scholastic, Inc.

Czubinski, Robert. The Many Adventures of Pig Batter: A Day at the Park, 1 vol. Czubinski, Amber, illus. 2009. 20p. pap. 24.95 (978-1-61546-495-1(6)) America Star Bks.

Dean, Sara. The Puppy Who Found a Boy, 1 vol. Hacker, Randy, illus. 2009. 13p. pap. 24.95 (978-1-61546-278-0(3)) America Star Bks.

DeMonte, Joe. Lucy & the Magic Factory. 2008. 79p. pap. 19.95 (978-1-60813-119-8(X)) America Star Bks.

Denice, Sonia. Chow-E-Chowz: Saved by a Whistle. 2011. 44p. pap. 18.46 (978-1-4567-1020-0(6)) AuthorHouse.

Disney Book Group Staff & Gold, Gina. Minnie a Walk in the Park, Level 1. Disney Storybook Artists Staff, illus. 2014. (World of Reading Ser.). (ENG.). 32p. (J). (gr. -1-k). pap. 3.99 (978-1-4847-0678-7(1)) Disney Pr.

Doyle, Helen. The Rainbow Pals. 2011. 96p. pap. 39.39 (978-1-4567-0169-7(X)) AuthorHouse.

Edwards, Nancy. Mom for Mayor. Chesworth, Michael D., illus. 2006. (ENG.). 96p. (J). (gr. 1-5). 16.95 (978-0-8126-2743-5(1)) Cricket Bks.

Feldman, Thea. Adventure in the Park. Ward, April, illus. 2006. 20p. (J). (978-0-696-23234-3(0)) Meredith Bks.

Finn, Rebecca, illus. Busy Park. 2016. (Busy Bks.). (ENG.). 10p. (J). (gr. -1). bds. 8.95 (978-1-4549-1943-8(4)) Sterling Publishing Co., Inc.

Forever Lost. 2011. (Hardy Boys (All New) Undercover Brothers Ser.: 36). (ENG.). 160p. (J). (gr. 3-7). pap. 6.99 (978-1-4424-0264-5(4), Aladdin) Simon & Schuster Children's Publishing.

Gallo, Tina. OLIVIA in the Park. Rose, Drew, illus. 2010. (Olivia TV Tie-In Ser.). (ENG.). 48p. (J). (gr. -1-1). 5.99 (978-1-4169-9887-7(X), Simon Scribbles) Simon Scribbles.

Geraldi, Michele J. Pennies at Piper Park. 2009. 24p. pap. 12.99 (978-1-4389-2829-6(7)) AuthorHouse.

Ghigna, Charles. Pick up the Park, 1 vol. Jatkowska, Ag, illus. 2012. (My Little Planet Ser.). (ENG.). 24p. (gr. -1 — 1). 6.95 (978-1-4048-7228-8(0)); lib. bdg. 22.65 (978-1-4048-6793-2(7)) Picture Window Bks. (My Little Planet).

Gilmore, Cathy. Fun at the Park with Ransom & Ripley. 2011. 20p. pap. 24.95 (978-1-4560-6643-7(9)) America Star Bks.

Going to the Park: Individual Title Six-Packs. (gr. -1-2). 23.00 (978-0-7635-9012-3(6)) Rigby Education.

Gordon, Amy. The Gorillas of Gill Park. 2003. (ENG., Illus.). 256p. (J). (gr. 4-6). tchr. ed. 16.95 (978-0-8234-1751-3(4)) Holiday Hse., Inc.

—Return to Gill Park. 2006. (ENG., Illus.). 240p. (J). (gr. 4-7). 16.95 (978-0-8234-1998-2(3)) Holiday Hse., Inc.

Harger, Teresa. Nicky & the Princess. 2010. 20p. pap. 12.79 (978-1-4520-6035-4(5)) AuthorHouse.

Haugaard, Kay. No Place. 2nd ed. 2007. (ENG., Illus.). 140p. (J). (gr. 2-8). per. 6.95 (978-1-57131-675-2(2)) Milkweed Editions.

Hensley, Sarah M. At the Park. Crowell, Knox, illus. l.t. ed. 2006. 10p. (J). (gr. -1-k). pap. 10.95 (978-1-57332-354-3(3), HighReach Learning, Incorporated) Carson-Dellosa Publishing, LLC.

Hill, Eric. Spot Goes to the Park. Hill, Eric, illus. 2005. (Spot Ser.). (ENG., Illus.). 24p. (J). (gr. -1 — 1). bds. 7.99 (978-0-399-24363-9(1), Warne) Penguin Young Readers Group.

Hinbest, Wendy. Frizzy Tizzy Goes to the Park. 2011. 20p. pap. 11.95 (978-1-4583-4346-8(4)) Lulu Pr., Inc.

Holub, Joan. Picnic! A Day in the Park. Terry, Will, illus. 2008. (Ant Hill Ser.). (ENG.). 24p. (J). (gr. -1-k). pap. 3.99 (978-1-4169-5133-9(4), Simon Spotlight) Simon Spotlight.

Hughes, John P. A Wish for Little Tommy Turtle. White, Tara B., illus. 2011. 48p. pap. 24.95 (978-1-4626-0011-3(5)) America Star Bks.

Huneke, Amanda. A Monster in the Park, 1 vol. Wolek, Guy, illus. 2013. (Monster on the Loose Ser.). (ENG.). 32p. (J). (gr. -1-4). 28.50 (978-1-61641-932-5(6)) Magic Wagon.

Hupf, Zetta & Hupf, Mitchell. Henry Goes to the Park, 1 vol. Hupf, Zetta, illus. 2009. (Illus.). 33p. pap. 24.95 (978-1-61546-279-7(1)) America Star Bks.

Ibeh, Chinwe. The Moment That Sandra Won. 2011. 28p. pap. 24.95 (978-1-4626-2938-1(5)) PublishAmerica, Inc.

Isaacs, Latricia. Mason & Baylee Learn to Count. 2011. 16p. (gr. -1). pap. 8.32 (978-1-4634-0442-0(5)) AuthorHouse.

Jeffs, Dixie. The Old Man. 2013. 20p. pap. 24.95 (978-1-62709-344-6(3)) America Star Bks.

Jenkins, Emily. Water in the Park: A Book about Water & the Times of the Day. Graegin, Stephanie, illus. 2013. (ENG.). 40p. (J). (gr. -1-2). 16.99 (978-0-375-87002-6(4), Schwartz & Wade Bks.) Random Hse. Children's Bks.

Jocelyn, Marthe. Over Under. Slaughter, Tom, illus. 2006. (ENG.). 16p. (J). (gr. k-k). bds. 7.95 (978-0-88776-790-6(7), Tundra Bks.) Tundra Bks. CAN. Dist: Penguin Random Hse. LLC.

Johnson, Angela. Lottie Paris Lives Here. Fischer, Scott M., illus. 2011. (ENG.). 32p. (J). (gr. k-4). 16.99 (978-0-689-87377-5(8), Simon & Schuster Bks. For Young Readers) Simon & Schuster Bks. For Young Readers.

Joyner, Andrew. Boris on the Move, Bk. 1. 2013. (Boris Ser.: 1). (ENG.). 80p. (J). (gr. k-2). pap. 4.99 (978-0-545-48443-5(X)) Scholastic, Inc.

—Boris on the Move. 2013. (Boris Ser.: 1). lib. bdg. 14.75 (978-0-606-31974-4(3), Turtleback) Turtleback Bks.

Kean, Edward. Howdy Doody in Funland. Seiden, Art, illus. 2011. 30p. 35.95 (978-1-258-02315-7(6)) Literary Licensing, LLC.

Kent, Lorna, illus. In the Park. 2004. 8p. (J). bds. 3.99 (978-1-85854-097-9(6)) Brimax Books Ltd. GBR. Dist: Byeway Bks.

Knudsen, Michelle. Carl the Complainer. Cocca-Leffler, Maryann, illus. 2005. (Social Studies Connects). 32p. (J). (gr. 1-3). pap. 5.95 (978-1-57565-157-6(2)) Kane Press, Inc.

Lane, Andy. Glendale: Nashville's Magical Park. Sloan, Michael, illus. 2009. 88p. (J). 22.95 (978-1-57736-408-5(2)) Providence Hse Pubs.

Little, Celeste. At the Park with Tommy & Scales. Motz, Mike, illus. 2012. 26p. (J). (-18). 12.95 (978-1-60131-139-9(7), Castlebridge Bks.) Big Tent Bks.

Lord, Cynthia. Monster Truck Mania! Anderson, Derek, illus. 2014. (ENG.). 40p. (J). (gr. -1-k). 16.99 (978-0-545-46261-7(4), Scholastic Pr.) Scholastic, Inc.

Lottie Paris Lives Here. 2014. (Classic Board Bks.). (ENG., Illus.). 34p. (J). (gr. -1-k). bds. 7.99 *(978-1-4814-0966-7(2)*, Little Simon) Little Simon.

Lotto, Lisa Marie. Oh How We Feel When We Are Sick with the Flu: Oh the Things We See When We Go to the Park. 2008. 28p. pap. 13.99 *(978-1-4343-6009-0(1))* AuthorHouse.

Lund, Wendy E. The Fly Away Balloon. 2010. 50p. pap. 16.50 *(978-1-60911-660-6(7)*, Eloquent Bks.) Strategic Book Publishing & Rights Agency (SBPRA).

Lyle-Soffe, Shari. Shoo Cat. Foster, Jack, illus. 2010. 16p. pap. 9.95 *(978-1-61633-033-0(3))* Guardian Angel Publishing, Inc.

Lynn, Cheryl. Kayla's Day at the Park. 2008. 16p. pap. 24.95 *(978-1-60813-169-3(6))* America Star Bks.

M. Ward. The Evergreens Go to the Park. 2009. (Illus.). 20p. pap. 11.49 *(978-1-4343-9761-4(0))* AuthorHouse.

Marie, Tamara. The Adventures of Madison. 2010. 32p. pap. 17.99 *(978-1-60957-972-2(0))* Salem Author Services.

Marino, Nan. Neil Armstrong Is My Uncle & Other Lies Muscle Man McGinty Told Me. 2009. (ENG.). 160p. (J). (gr. 3-7). 16.95 *(978-1-59643-499-8(6)*, 9781596434998) Roaring Brook Pr.

Mayer, Mercer. Going to the Sea Park. 2009. (Little Critter: I Can Read! Ser.). (J). lib. bdg. 13.55 *(978-0-606-06964-9(X)*, Turtleback) Turtleback Bks.

—Just Critters Who Care. Mayer, Mercer, illus. 2010. (My First I Can Read Ser.). (ENG., Illus.). 32p. (J). (gr. -1-3). 16.99 *(978-0-06-083560-6(5))*; pap. 3.99 *(978-0-06-083559-0(1))* HarperCollins Pubs.

Mcleod-Stecy, Tracey. The Stone Guardian. 2011. 144p. (gr. 4-6). pap. 11.95 *(978-1-4620-3954-8(5))* iUniverse, Inc.

Meachen Rau, Dana. At the Park. 2007. (Fun Time Ser.). (SPA., Illus.). 24p. (gr. k-1). lib. bdg. 15.95 *(978-0-7614-2613-4(2)*, Benchmark Bks.) Marshall Cavendish Corp.

—En el Parque. 2007. (¡A Divertirnos! Ser.). (SPA., Illus.). 24p. (gr. k-1). lib. bdg. 15.95 *(978-0-7614-2775-9(9)*, Benchmark Bks.) Marshall Cavendish Corp.

Meisel, Paul. See Me Run. Meisel, Paul, illus. (I Like to Read(r) Ser.). (ENG., Illus.). 24p. (J). (gr. -1-2). 2012. pap. 6.99 *(978-0-8234-2638-6(6))* 2011. 14.95 *(978-0-8234-2349-1(2))* Holiday Hse., Inc.

Messer, Celeste M. When Eagles Fly. Hoeffner, Deb, illus. 2004. 82-92p. 4.95 *(978-0-9702171-8-9(8))* AshleyAlan Enterprises.

Mumford, Carole. The Magnificent: Their Yellowstone Adventure, 1 vol. 2009. 73p. pap. 19.95 *(978-1-60813-595-0(0))* America Star Bks.

Muse, Ludi. My Day at the Park. 2007. 32p. per. 13.95 *(978-1-4259-6563-1(6))* AuthorHouse.

Nan, Carol. Nana the Baby Pine Tree. 2012. 24p. pap. 24.95 *(978-1-4626-8944-6(2))* America Star Bks.

Neil, Deanna. Lost in Yellowstone: The Land of Curiosities, 1872-1873, vol. 2. 2nd rev. ed. 2015. (J). reprint ed. 19.99 *(978-0-9798800-9-4(2))* EcoSeekers, The.

O'Donnell, Liam. Scout Hits the Trail. Huerta, Catherine, illus. (Pet Tales Ser.). (ENG.). 32p. (J). (gr. -1-3). 2008. 4.95 *(978-1-59249-740-9(3))* 2007. 9.95 *(978-1-59249-742-3(X))* Soundprints.

O'Donnell, Liam. Scout Hits the Trail. Huerta, Catherine, illus. 2007. (ENG.). 32p. (J). 2.95 *(978-1-59249-741-6(1))* Soundprints.

Oliver, Veronica A. The Rainbow Colors: Learning Primary & Secondary Colors. 2011. 20p. 11.59 *(978-1-4269-4805-3(0))* Trafford Publishing.

Parish, Herman. Amelia Bedelia Chapter Book #6: Amelia Bedelia Cleans Up (POB) Avril, Lynne, illus. 2015. (Amelia Bedelia Ser.). (ENG.). 160p. (J). (gr. 1-5). 9.99 *(978-0-06-233403-9(4)*, Greenwillow Bks.) HarperCollins Pubs.

—Amelia Bedelia Cleans Up. Avril, Lynne, illus. 2015. (Amelia Bedelia Ser.). (ENG.). 160p. (J). (gr. 1-5). pap. 4.99 *(978-0-06-233400-8(X)*, Greenwillow Bks.) HarperCollins Pubs.

Patricelli, Leslie. Faster! Faster! Patricelli, Leslie, illus. 2013. (Leslie Patricelli Board Bks.). (ENG., Illus.). 30p. (J). (-k). bds. 6.99 *(978-0-7636-6222-6(4))* Candlewick Pr.

—Faster! Faster!/Mas Rapido! Mas Rapido! Patricelli, Leslie, illus. 2013. (Leslie Patricelli Board Bks.). (ENG., Illus.). 30p. (J). (-k). bds. 6.99 *(978-0-7636-6611-8(4))* Candlewick Pr.

Peto, Judith E. & Talwar, Robert B. Jenny & Benny: Friends 2005. (Illus.). 28p. (J). (gr. -1-3). 16.95 *(978-0-9767511-0-6(0))* Lasting Bks. Publishing Co.

Priddy, Roger & Crimi-Trent, Ellen. My First Day at School. 2013. (Schoolies Ser.). (ENG., Illus.). 28p. (J). (gr. -1-1). 4.99 *(978-0-312-51612-3(6)*, 9780312516123, Priddy Bks.) St. Martin's Pr.

Random House. Thomas at the Animal Park (Thomas & Friends) Lapadula, Thomas, illus. 2014. (ENG.). 10p. (J). (— 1). 10.99 *(978-0-385-38469-8(6)*, Random Hse. Bks. for Young Readers) Random Hse. Children's Bks.

Reilly, Carmel. The Boy at the Park. Reynolds, Pat, illus. 2009. 24p. pap. 10.67 *(978-1-4190-5517-1(8))* Rigby Education.

Renek, Nava. Venice Is for Cats. 2013. (Illus.). pap. 20.00 *(978-0-923389-53-6(9))* Spuyten Duyvil Publishing.

Rey, H. A. Curious George at the Park. Meyer, Emily, ed. 2010. (Curious George Ser.). (ENG., Illus.). 10p. (J). (gr. -1 — 1). bds. 6.99 *(978-0-547-24300-9(6))* Houghton Mifflin Harcourt Publishing Co.

Reynolds, Peter H. I'm Here. Reynolds, Peter H., illus. 2011. (ENG., Illus.). 32p. (J). (gr. -1-3). 16.99 *(978-1-4169-9649-1(4)*, Atheneum Bks. for Young Readers) Simon & Schuster Children's Publishing.

Ricci, Christine. Dora's Picnic. Hall, Susan, illus. 2003. (Ready-to-Read Ser.: Vol. 1). (ENG.). 24p. (J). pap. 3.99 *(978-0-689-85238-1(X)*, Simon Spotlight/Nickelodeon) Simon Spotlight/Nickelodeon.

Richter, Bernd & Richter, Susan. Grandma & Grandpa Visit Denali. Drashner, Diane, illus. 2008. 48p. (J). pap. 9.95 *(978-1-931353-33-5(6))* Saddle Pal Creations, Inc.

Rigby Education Staff. Headline News. (Sails Literacy Ser.). (Illus.). 16p. (gr. 1-2). 27.00 *(978-0-7635-9930-0(1)*, 699301C99) Rigby Education.

Rowe, Jeannette. YoYo Goes to the Park. Rowe, Jeannette, illus. 2003. (Illus.). 12p. (J). pap. 5.95 *(978-1-58925-369-8(8))* Tiger Tales.

Roy, Ron. A Thief at the National Zoo. Bush, Timothy, illus. 2008. (Capital Mysteries Ser.: No. 9). 87p. (gr. k-3). 15.00 *(978-0-7569-8329-1(0))* Perfection Learning Corp.

Ruelle, Karen Gray. Bark Park, 1 vol. Ruelle, Karen Gray, illus. (ENG., Illus.). 32p. (J). (gr. -1-1). 2014. pap. 7.95 *(978-1-56145-773-1(6))* 2008. 15.95 *(978-1-56145-434-1(6))* Peachtree Pubs.

Schofield-Morrison, Connie. I Got the Rhythm. Morrison, Frank, illus. 2014. (ENG.). 32p. (J). (gr. -1-1). 16.99 *(978-1-61963-178-6(4)*, 9781619631786, Bloomsbury USA Childrens) Bloomsbury Publishing USA.

Scripture Teachers: Solomon & Friends Learn about Forgiveness. 2003. pap. *(978-0-9712894-1-3(7))* Lighthouse Christian Products Co.

Singleton, Linda Joy. Cash Kat, 1 vol. Wald, Christina, illus. 2016. (ENG & SPA.). 32p. (J). (gr. k-3). 17.95 *(978-1-62855-728-2(1))* Arbordale Publishing.

—Elena Efectivo, 1 vol. Wald, Christina, illus. 2016. (SPA.). 32p. (J). (gr. k-3). pap. 9.95 *(978-1-62855-742-8(7))* Arbordale Publishing.

Sivier, Janet. Charlotte & Jackson: The Butterfly. 2012. 28p. pap. 16.09 *(978-1-4669-4555-5(9))* Trafford Publishing.

Skidmore, Marlene. In Trouble Again! 2010. 24p. pap. 9.99 *(978-0-9845208-9-3(9))* Faithful Life Pubs.

Smith, Alex T. Claude at the Circus, 1 vol. Smith, Alex T., illus. 2013. (Claude Ser.). (ENG., Illus.). 96p. (J). (gr. 2-4). 12.95 *(978-1-56145-702-1(7))* Peachtree Pubs.

Snyder, Marilyn. A Second Chance for Tina. Shiffman, Lena, illus. 2003. (Hello Reader! Ser.). (J). *(978-0-439-44154-4(4))* Scholastic, Inc.

Springstubb, Tricia. Phoebe & Digger. Newman, Jeff, illus. (ENG.). 32p. (J). (gr. -1-2). 2016. 7.99 *(978-0-7636-8894-3(0))* 2013. 16.99 *(978-0-7636-5281-4(4))* Candlewick Pr.

Stefanescu, Estera. Megan's Great Day. 2009. 20p. pap. 15.99 *(978-1-4389-6318-1(1))* AuthorHouse.

Stine, R. L. Who's Your Mummy? 2009. (Goosebumps Horrorland Ser.: 6). (ENG.). 160p. (J). (gr. 3-7). 6.99 *(978-0-439-91874-9(X)*, Scholastic Paperbacks) Scholastic, Inc.

Stokely, Ted. Yaya & Uncle Ted Go Walk! 2010. 20p. 11.99 *(978-1-4520-9198-3(6))* AuthorHouse.

Svoboda, Linda Sue. The Little Brown Bird That Could. 2012. 20p. pap. 24.95 *(978-1-4626-8043-6(7))* America Star Bks.

Tesler, Ellen. Zeke in Central Park. 2010. 32p. pap. 12.99 *(978-1-4490-7211-7(9))* AuthorHouse.

The Book Company, ed. Park. (Sparkle Bks.). 10p. (J). bds. 4.99 *(978-1-74047-332-3(9))* Book Co. Publishing Pty, Ltd., The AUS. Dist: Penton Overseas, Inc.

Thurmond, Joey. Nojoe Makes New Friends. 2009. 16p. pap. 10.99 *(978-1-4490-4156-4(6))* AuthorHouse.

Tzingoker, Lilach. Sonny's Adventure in Mystery Park. 2010. 44p. pap. 19.95 *(978-1-60911-927-0(4)*, Eloquent Bks.) Strategic Book Publishing & Rights Agency (SBPRA).

A Walk in the Park. 2003. (J). per. *(978-1-57657-814-8(3))* Paradise Pr., Inc.

Walton, Rick. Girl & Gorilla. Berger, Joe, illus. 2016. 32p. (J). (gr. -1-3). 17.99 *(978-0-06-227891-3(6))* HarperCollins Pubs.

Ward, Kris A. Tony's Day in the Park. 2008. 42p. pap. 24.95 *(978-1-60813-351-2(6))* America Star Bks.

The Water Park. 2005. (Georgie Giraffe Set 1 Ser.). (J). 7.33 *(978-1-932570-38-0(1))* Pioneer Valley Bks.

Weiss, Ellen. Twins in the Park. Williams, Sam, illus. 2003. (Ready-To-Reads Ser.). (ENG.). 24p. (J). (gr. -1-k). pap. 3.99 *(978-0-689-85742-3(X)*, Simon Spotlight) Simon Spotlight.

West, C. The Adventures of Ice Cream & Honey Buns: A Day in the Park. 2012. 28p. pap. 16.09 *(978-1-4669-4700-9(4))* Trafford Publishing.

Winans, Carvin. Conrad Saves Pinger Park. Harrington, Leslie, illus. 2010. 32p. (J). (gr. -1-3). 8.95 *(978-1-60349-024-5(8)*, Marimba Bks.) Hudson Publishing Group, The.

Written By Kimberly M Sosnowski; Illustr. Ace's Wish for a Forever Home. Sosnowski, Tiffany, illus. 2011. 28p. pap. 24.95 *(978-1-4626-3031-6(6))* America Star Bks.

Young, Annemarie. At the Park, 1 vol. Redshaw, Louise, illus. 2013. (Start Reading Ser.). (ENG.). 24p. (gr. k-1). pap. 7.95 *(978-1-4765-3191-5(9))*; pap. 41.94 *(978-1-4765-3207-3(9))* Capstone Press of Coughlan Cos.

Zschock, Martha Day. Hello, Philadelphia! 2011. (Hello! Ser.). (ENG., Illus.). 16p. (J). (gr. -1-k). bds. 9.95 *(978-1-933212-64-7(0)*, Commonwealth Editions) Applewood Bks.

PARLIAMENTARY PRACTICE

Latchana Kenney, Karen. What Is a Parliamentary Government?, Vol. 1. 2014. (Understanding Political Systems Ser.). 48p. (YA). (gr. 6-8). 31.95 *(978-1-4824-0317-6(X))* Stevens, Gareth Publishing LLLP.

PARODIES

Ferrie, Chris. Goodnight Lab. 2017. (ENG.). 32p. (J). (-3). 17.99 ***(978-1-4926-5617-3(8)***, Sourcebooks Jabberwocky) Sourcebooks, Inc.

Hysom, Dennis Joe & Walker, Christine. Wooleycat's Musical Rhyme Time Theater. 2003. (Wooleycat's Favorite Nursery Rhymes Ser.). (Illus.). (J). pap. *(978-1-889910-26-0(0))* Tortuga Pr.

—Wooleycat's Musical Theater. Walker, Christine, illus. 2003. (Wooleycat's Favorite Nursery Rhymes Ser.). (Illus.). 32p. (J). (gr. -1-2). 18.95 incl. audio compact disk *(978-1-889910-25-3(2))* Tortuga Pr.

Vande Velde, Vivian. Tales from the Brothers Grimm & the Sisters Weird. Weinman, Brad, illus. 2005. (ENG.). 144p. (J). (gr. 5-7). reprint ed. pap. 6.99 *(978-0-15-205572-1(X))* Houghton Mifflin Harcourt Publishing Co.

PARROTS

About Parrots: A Guide for Children: a Guide for Children, 1 vol. 2014. (About... Ser.). (ENG., Illus.). 48p. (J). (gr. -1-2). 16.95 *(978-1-56145-795-3(7))* Peachtree Pubs.

Atlantic, Leonard. 95-Year-Old Parrots! 2016. (World's Longest-Living Animals Ser.). 00024p. (J). pap. 8.15 ***(978-1-4824-5616-5(8))*** Stevens, Gareth Publishing LLLP.

Barnes, Julia. Pet Parakeets. 2006. (Pet Pals Ser.). (Illus.). 32p. (gr. 2-6). lib. bdg. 26.00 *(978-0-8368-6780-0(7)*, Gareth Stevens Learning Library) Stevens, Gareth Publishing LLLP.

Bjorklund, Ruth. Parrots. 2012. (Nature's Children Ser.). (ENG.). 48p. (J). pap. 6.95 *(978-0-531-25481-3(X))*; lib. bdg. 28.00 *(978-0-531-26836-0(5))* Scholastic Library Publishing.

Bodden, Valerie. Parrots. (Amazing Animals Ser.). 24p. (J). 2011. (ENG.). (gr. 1-17). pap. 6.99 *(978-1-926722-24-5(8)*, Creative Paperbacks) 2010. (gr. -1-3). 16.95 *(978-1-58341-809-3(1)*, Creative Education) Creative Co., The.

Bowman, Chris. Parrots. 2015. (Animal Safari Ser.). (ENG., Illus.). 24p. (J). (gr. k-3). lib. bdg. 25.95 *(978-1-62617-165-7(3)*, Blastoff! Readers) Bellwether Media.

Bozzo, Linda. When Parrots Speak. 2017. (Animal Emotions Ser.). 32p. (J). (gr. 3-3). pap. 10.52 ***(978-0-7660-8864-1(2))***; lib. bdg. 25.27 ***(978-0-7660-8621-0(6))*** Enslow Pubs., Inc.

Calhoun, Kelly. Flashy Feathers: Macaw. 2015. (Guess What Ser.). (ENG., Illus.). 24p. (J). (gr. k-2). 28.50 *(978-1-63362-626-3(1)*, 206676) Cherry Lake Publishing.

Conure, Lunatico. Tico's Book. Durr, Carol Atkinson, illus. 2008. 36p. (J). 15.00 *(978-0-9717047-8-7(3))* Bay Media, Inc.

Dibble, Traci. Parrot Colors. 2016. (1-3Y Birds Ser.). (ENG., Illus.). 16p. (J). pap. 5.99 ***(978-1-63437-669-3(2))*** American Reading Co.

—The Parrot Family. 2017. (1-3Y Birds Ser.). (ENG.). 12p. pap. 5.99 ***(978-1-63437-843-7(1))*** American Reading Co.

Dubke, Karon. Pet Parrots up Close. (Pets up Close Ser.). (ENG.). 24p. (gr. k-1). 2015. pap. 6.95 *(978-1-4914-7763-2(6))* 2014. 26.65 *(978-1-4914-0581-9(3))* Capstone Press of Coughlan Cos. (Pebble Plus).

Fetty, Margaret. Parrots. 2006. (Smart Animals! Ser.). (Illus.). 32p. (J). (gr. 2-5). lib. bdg. 25.27 *(978-1-59716-163-3(2))* Bearport Publishing Co., Inc.

Frost, Helen. Parrots [Scholastic]. 2011. (Rain Forest Animals Ser.). 24p. pap. 0.50 *(978-1-4296-6313-7(8)*, Pebble Bks.) Capstone Press of Coughlan Cos.

Galeron, Henri. Parrots. Galeron, Henri, illus. 2012. (ENG., Illus.). 34p. (J). (gr. k-3). pap. 11.99 *(978-1-85103-370-6(X))* Moonlight Publishing, Ltd. GBR. Dist: Independent Pubs. Group.

Gallagher, Debbie. Parrots. 2009. (Zoo Animals 2 Ser.). 32p. (gr. 2). lib. bdg. 18.56 *(978-0-7614-4746-7(6))* Marshall Cavendish Corp.

Ganeri, Anita. Macaw, 1 vol. 2010. (Day in the Life: Rain Forest Animals Ser.). (ENG.). 24p. (gr. k-2). 23.32 *(978-1-4329-4105-5(4))*; pap. 6.79 *(978-1-4329-4116-1(X))* Heinemann-Raintree. (Heinemann Read & Learn).

Gareth Stevens Editorial Staff. Parrots. 2004. (All about Wild Animals Ser.). (Illus.). 32p. (gr. k-4). lib. bdg. 26.00 *(978-0-8368-4122-0(0)*, Gareth Stevens Learning Library) Stevens, Gareth Publishing LLLP.

Hanel, Rachael. Parrots. 2008. (Living Wild Ser.). (Illus.). 46p. (YA). (gr. 5-18). 22.95 *(978-1-58341-657-0(9)*, Creative Education) Creative Co., The.

Haney, Johannah. Parrots. 2008. (Great Pets Ser.). 48p. (gr. 3-18). lib. bdg. 29.93 *(978-0-7614-2998-2(0)*, Benchmark Bks.) Marshall Cavendish Corp.

Ho, Cammie. Parrot Parrot. 2016. (Life Cycle Bks.). (ENG., Illus.). 31p. (J). (gr. k-2). pap. 7.99 *(978-1-943241-04-0(X))* Phonic Monic.

Houston, Alecia. The Stories True of Gabby Cockatoo. Luna, Lauren, illus. 2010. 24p. pap. 11.25 *(978-1-60911-446-6(9)*, Strategic Bk. Publishing) Strategic Book Publishing & Rights Agency (SBPRA).

Howard, Fran. Parrots, 1 vol. 2012. (Birds Ser.). (ENG.). 24p. (gr. 1-2). lib. bdg. 25.32 *(978-1-4296-8685-3(5))* Capstone Press of Coughlan Cos.

Johnson, Jinny. Parrot. Woods, Michael, illus. 2007. (Zoo Animals in the Wild Ser.). 32p. (J). (gr. -1-3). lib. bdg. 28.50 *(978-1-58340-904-6(1))* Black Rabbit Bks.

Juaristi, Felipe & Felipe, Juaristi. El Loro de Haydn. 2004. (SPA.). 112p. (YA). 11.99 *(978-84-241-8667-8(2))* Everest Editora ESP. Dist: Lectorum Pubns., Inc.

Kalz, Jill. Parrots. 2006. (Wild World of Animals Ser.). (Illus.). 30p. (J). (gr. 3-5). 18.95 *(978-1-58341-434-7(7)*, Creative Education) Creative Co., The.

Kawa, Katie. Playful Parakeets. 2011. (Pet Corner Ser.). (Illus.). 24p. (gr. k-2). (J). pap. 8.15 *(978-1-4339-5611-9(X))*; (J). lib. bdg. 22.60 *(978-1-4339-5609-6(8))*; 69.20 *(978-1-4339-6884-6(3))* Stevens, Gareth Publishing LLLP.

—Playful Parakeets: Pericos Juguetones. 2011. (Pet Corner / RincÓN de Las Mascotas Ser.). (SPA & ENG., Illus.). 24p. (J). (gr. k-3). lib. bdg. 22.60 *(978-1-4339-5613-3(6))* Stevens, Gareth Publishing LLLP.

Klobuchar, Lisa. Cockatiels & Other Parrots. 2007. (World Book's Animals of the World Ser.). (Illus.). 64p. (J). *(978-0-7166-1327-5(1))* World Bk., Inc.

Kuskowski, Alex. Magnificent Macaws, 1 vol. Nobens, C. A., illus. 2013. (Unusual Pets Ser.). (ENG.). 24p. (J). (gr. -1-3). 24.21 *(978-1-61783-400-4(9))* ABDO Publishing Co.

LaRoche, Amelia. Care for a Pet Parrot. 2009. (How to Convince Your Parents You Can ... Ser.). (Illus.). 32p. (J). (gr. 1-4). lib. bdg. 25.70 *(978-1-58415-795-3(X))* Mitchell Lane Pubs., Inc.

Leon, Vicki. A Rainbow of Parrots. 2nd ed. 2006. (Jean-Michel Cousteau Presents Ser.). (ENG., Illus.). 48p. (J). (gr. 4). pap. 7.95 *(978-0-9766134-2-8(5))* London Town Pr.

Lya, Maria. The Wise Parrot & a Plan to Save the Forest: A Plan to Save the Forest. 2011. (Illus.). 28p. (gr. -1). pap. 20.16 *(978-1-4567-8106-4(5))* AuthorHouse.

Macken, JoAnn Early. Parakeets. 2003. (Weekly Reader Early Learning Library). (Illus.). 24p. (gr. k-3). pap. 8.15 *(978-0-8368-3847-3(5)*, Weekly Reader Leveled Readers) Stevens, Gareth Publishing LLLP.

Montgomery, Sy. Kakapo Rescue: Saving the World's Strangest Parrot. Bishop, Nic, illus. Bishop, Nic, photos by. 2010. (Scientists in the Field Ser.). (ENG.). 80p. (J). (gr. 5-7). 18.00 *(978-0-618-49417-0(0))* Houghton Mifflin Harcourt Publishing Co.

—Snowball: The Dancing Cockatoo. Oksner, Judith, illus. 2013. (ENG.). 64p. (J). pap. 15.00 *(978-0-87233-156-3(3))* Bauhan Publishing LLC.

Murray, Julie. Parrots, 1 vol. 2003. (Animal Kingdom Ser.). (ENG.). 24p. (gr. k-4). 25.65 *(978-1-57765-705-7(5)*, Buddy Bks.) ABDO Publishing Co.

National Geographic Kids Staff & Donohue, Moira Rose. Parrot Genius! And More True Stories of Amazing Animal Talents. 2014. (NGK Chapters Ser.). (ENG.). 112p. (J). (gr. 2-5). pap. 5.99 *(978-1-4263-1770-5(0))*; lib. bdg. 14.90 *(978-1-4263-1771-2(9))* National Geographic Society. (National Geographic Children's Bks.).

Nugent, Samantha. Parrot. 2015. (Illus.). 24p. (J). *(978-1-4896-4117-5(3))* Weigl Pubs., Inc.

Owen, Ruth. Parrots. 2011. (World's Smartest Animals Ser.). (ENG., Illus.). 32p. (J). (gr. k-5). pap. 11.75 *(978-1-61533-413-1(0))*; lib. bdg. 26.50 *(978-1-61533-375-2(4))* Windmill Bks.

Parrots. 2006. (Zooties Ser.). (J). 4.95 *(978-1-932396-20-1(9))* Wildlife Education, Ltd.

Parrots: Early Level Satellite, 6 Packs. (Sails Literacy Ser.). 16p. (gr. 1-2). 27.00 *(978-0-7578-3160-7(5))* Rigby Education.

Rockwood, Leigh. Parrots Are Smart! 2010. (Super Smart Animals Ser.). (Illus.). 24p. (J). pap. 8.25 *(978-1-4358-9844-8(3)*, PowerKids Pr.); (gr. 2-5). lib. bdg. 22.60 *(978-1-4358-9376-4(X))* Rosen Publishing Group, Inc., The.

Ryndak, Rob. Parrots. 2015. (Jungle Animals Ser.). (ENG., Illus.). 24p. (J). (gr. k-k). 22.60 *(978-1-4824-1756-2(1))* Stevens, Gareth Publishing LLLP.

Scheunemann, Pam. Parrots Talk!, 1 vol. 2011. (Animal Sounds Set 2 Ser.). (ENG., Illus.). 24p. (J). (gr. k-3). lib. bdg. 24.21 *(978-1-61613-574-4(3)*, SandCastle) ABDO Publishing Co.

Sexton, Colleen. Caring for Your Parakeet. 2010. (Pet Care Library). (ENG., Illus.). 24p. (J). (gr. 2-5). lib. bdg. 25.95 *(978-1-60014-470-7(5)*, Blastoff! Readers) Bellwether Media.

Smith, Catherine. Parakeet, Vol. 12. 2016. (Understanding & Caring for Your Pet Ser.: Vol. 12). (ENG., Illus.). 128p. (J). (gr. 5-8). 25.95 *(978-1-4222-3701-4(X))* Mason Crest.

Sonder, Ben. Parrots: A Portrait of the Animal World. 2012. (Portrait of the Animal World Ser.). (Illus.). 72p. 12.95 *(978-1-59764-270-5(3))* New Line Bks.

—Parrots - Pb: A Portrait of the Animal World. 2013. (Portrait of the Animal World Ser.). (Illus.). 72p. pap. 9.95 *(978-1-59764-330-6(0))* New Line Bks.

Spinner, Stephanie. Alex the Parrot: No Ordinary Bird. So, Meilo, illus. 2012. (ENG.). 48p. (J). (gr. 3-7). 17.99 *(978-0-375-86846-7(1)*, Knopf Bks. for Young Readers) Random Hse. Children's Bks.

Stevens, Kathryn. Parakeets. 2015. (Pet Care Ser.). (ENG.). 24p. (J). (gr. -1-2). 25.64 *(978-1-63143-730-4(5)*, 208549) Child's World, Inc., The.

PARROTS—FICTION

The adventures of officer Byrd. 2007. (J). 16.99 *(978-0-9787322-0-2(0))* Officer Byrd Publishing Co.

Agee, Jon. Terrific. 2017. (ENG., Illus.). 40p. (J). (gr. k-3). 17.99 ***(978-0-7352-2988-4(0)***, Dial Bks) Penguin Young Readers Group.

Anholt, Laurence. A Kiss Like This. Anholt, Catherine, illus. 2009. (ENG.). 32p. (J). (gr. -1-1). pap. 7.95 *(978-1-84507-862-1(4)*, Frances Lincoln) Quarto Publishing Group UK GBR. Dist: Hachette Bk. Group.

Barshaw, Ruth McNally. Best Friends Fur-Ever. Barshaw, Ruth McNally, illus. 2013. (Ellie Mcdoodle Diaries). (ENG., Illus.). 192p. (YA). (gr. 3-6). 12.99 *(978-1-61963-175-5(X)*, 9781619631755, Bloomsbury USA Childrens) Bloomsbury Publishing USA.

—Ellie McDoodle: Best Friends Fur-Ever. Barshaw, Ruth McNally, illus. 2011. (Ellie Mcdoodle Ser.). (ENG., Illus.). 192p. (YA). (gr. 3-6). pap. 7.99 *(978-1-59990-657-7(0)*, 9781599906577, Bloomsbury USA Childrens) Bloomsbury Publishing USA.

Bhandari, D. Growing Wings: Parrot's Day Out. 2010. 28p. 17.99 *(978-1-4520-1102-8(8))* AuthorHouse.

Blacklidge, Barbara. Lucky: My Story. 2010. 24p. (J). pap. 12.95 *(978-1-934449-64-6(4))* Legacy Publishing Services, Inc.

Borsky, Mary. Benny Bensky & the Parrot-Napper. Hendry, Linda, illus. 2008. (ENG.). 128p. (J). (gr. 4-7). pap. 9.95 *(978-0-88776-840-8(7)*, Tundra Bks.) Tundra Bks. CAN. Dist: Penguin Random Hse. LLC.

Boutros, Gladys. Bubba & the Sweet Pea. Balogh, Andras, illus. 2013. 86p. (J). pap. *(978-0-9873334-7-6(X))* Enlife Pty, Limited.

Brightwood, Laura. Knot for Singing Parrot. Pifer, Kimberly, ed. Brightwood, Laura, illus. 2012. (Illus.). (J). *(978-1-934409-23-7(5))* 3-C Institute for Social Development.

—Parrot's Winter Blues. Pifer, Kimberly, ed. Brightwood, Laura, illus. 2012. (Illus.). (J). *(978-1-934409-21-3(9))* 3-C Institute for Social Development.

Clawson, Kimberly. Fun O' Licious. Bellomy, Gail, illus. 2007. (ENG.). 56p. per. 16.95 *(978-1-4241-5556-9(8))* America Star Bks.

Coffey, M. Carol. Zoe Lucky: And the Green Gables' Mystery. 2008. 156p. pap. 12.95 *(978-1-4327-3190-8(4))* Outskirts Pr., Inc.

Coldon, Christine. Emmalynn: Home Tweet Home. 2011. 36p. (gr. -1). pap. 16.86 *(978-1-4567-3913-3(1))* AuthorHouse.

Colhoun, Sheelah. Elric's Florida Holiday. Cotton, Sue Lynn, illus. 2012. 20p. pap. 13.95 *(978-1-61493-110-2(0))* Peppertree Pr., The.

Connellan, Sue. Special Treasure. 2009. 40p. pap. 18.49 *(978-1-4343-7644-2(3))* AuthorHouse.

Cowley, Joy. Dan & the Parrot. 2009. pap. 8.25 *(978-1-60559-217-6(X))* Hameray Publishing Group, Inc.

Davey, Keith Peter. Squeaks Narrow Squeaks. Frost, Justine, illus. 2009. 32p. pap. 14.62 *(978-1-4120-4402-8(2))* Trafford Publishing.

DePalma, Mary Newell. The Perfect Gift. 2010. (J). pap. *(978-0-545-15403-1(0)*, Levine, Arthur A. Bks.) Scholastic, Inc.

Dicmas, Courtney. Harold Finds a Voice. Dicmas, Courtney, illus. 2013. (Child's Play Library). (ENG., Illus.). 32p. (J). *(978-1-84643-550-8(1))* Child's Play International Ltd.

Doudna, Kelly. Parrot Crackers, 1 vol. Haberstroh, Anne, illus. 2007. (Critter Chronicles Ser.). (ENG.). 24p. (J). (gr. k-3). lib. bdg. 24.21 *(978-1-59928-458-3(8)*, SandCastle) ABDO Publishing Co.

Douglas, Babette. Noreen: The Real King of the Jungle. Johnson, John, illus. 2006. (Kiss a Me Teacher Creature Stories Ser.). 20p. (J). (gr. -1-3). 9.99 *(978-1-890343-25-5(0))* Kiss A Me Productions, Inc.

Dubyn, Bj. The Thrilling & Dynamic Adventures of Barbara Ann, Her Kid Brother, Billy, Jr, & Manfred the Magnificent, Their Parrot. 2008. 104p. pap. 15.99 *(978-1-4363-2652-0(4))* Xlibris Corp.

PQR

Duckers, John. The Amazing Adventures of the Silly Six. 2013. (Illus.). 188p. pap. *(978-1-78148-626-9(3))* Grosvenor Hse. Publishing Ltd.

Dugan, Karen. Always Blue for Chicu. Dugan, Karen, illus. 2010. (ENG., Illus.). 32p. (J). (gr. k-2). 16.95 *(978-0-940719-09-5(6))* Gryphon Pr., The.

Erickson, John R. The Case of the Mysterious Voice. Holmes, Gerald L., illus. 2012. (Hank the Cowdog (Quality) Ser.: Vol. 58). (ENG.). 123p. (J). (gr. 3-6). pap. 5.99 *(978-1-59188-158-2(7))* Maverick Bks., Inc.

Feathers at Las Flores - Evaluation Guide: Evaluation Guide. 2006. (J). *(978-1-55942-405-9(2))* Witcher Productions.

Flambaum, Victor & Flambaum, Andrew. How to Make a Big Bang: A Cosmic Journey. 2012. (ENG.). 226p. (J). (gr. 7-10). pap. 14.95 *(978-1-936782-72-7(3))* Salem Author Services.

Flor Ada, Alma. Quiero Ayudar! Dominguez, Angela, illus. 2010.Tr. of Let Me Help! (ENG & SPA.). 32p. (J). (gr. -1-3). 16.95 *(978-0-89239-232-2(0))* Lee & Low Bks., Inc.

Fontanez, Edwin. En esta hermosa Isla. Fontanez, Edwin, illus. 2nd rev. ed. 2005. (SPA., Illus.). 32p. (J). 16.95 *(978-0-9640868-7-6(5))* Exit Studio.

Foreman, Michael. El Lorito Pelon. Diego, Rapi & Flores, Martha, illus. 2008. (SPA.). 30p. (J). (gr. 1-3). 15.99 *(978-1-930332-56-0(4))* Lectorum Pubns., Inc.

Friedman, Laurie. Love, Ruby Valentine. Cravath, Lynne Avril, illus. 2006. (ENG.). 32p. (J). (gr. k-3). lib. bdg. 16.95 *(978-1-57505-899-3(5),* Carolrhoda Bks.) Lerner Publishing Group.

—Ruby Valentine & the Sweet Surprise. Avril, Lynne, illus. 2014. (ENG.). 32p. (J). (gr. k-3). 16.95 *(978-0-7613-8873-9(7),* Carolrhoda Bks.) Lerner Publishing Group.

Futrell, Edgar Vernell. Twiddle de, the Talking Parrot. 2008. 28p. pap. 21.99 *(978-1-4363-0345-3(1))* Xlibris Corp.

Gilley, Jane. The Adventures of Solly Polly & Georgie Porgy. 2008. 24p. pap. *(978-1-906210-70-0(5))* Grosvenor Hse. Publishing Ltd.

Grace, Jaylen. Porridge the Two Faced Parrot. 2013. (Illus.). 72p. pap. *(978-1-78148-227-8(6))* Grosvenor Hse. Publishing Ltd.

Graham-Morgan, Ivet. Peter the Parrot Misses Home: Misses Home. 2011. 16p. 9.98 *(978-1-4343-9791-1(2))* AuthorHouse.

Hannaford, Linda S. Petie the Parrot's Amazing Adventures: P. D. Q., 1 vol. Lee, George T., illus. 2010. 16p. pap. 24.95 *(978-1-61582-767-1(6))* PublishAmerica, Inc.

Hapka, Catherine, pseud. Blu & Friends. 2011. (I Can Read Level 2 Ser.). (ENG.). 32p. (J). (gr. k-3). pap. 3.99 *(978-0-06-201487-0(0),* HarperFestival) HarperCollins Pubs.

—Rio - Learning to Fly. 2011. (I Can Read Level 2 Ser.). (ENG.). 32p. (J). (gr. k-3). pap. 3.99 *(978-0-06-201488-7(9),* HarperFestival) HarperCollins Pubs.

Harman, Michael. Parrot & the Fig Tree. 2nd ed. 2009. (Jataka Tales Ser.). (ENG., Illus.). 32p. (J). (gr. -1-3). pap. 8.95 *(978-0-89800-430-4(6))* Dharma Publishing.

Harmon, Victoria Marie. Say Hello to My Little Green Friend Tiki. 2013. 20p. pap. 24.95 *(978-1-63004-192-2(0))* America Star Bks.

Harper, Benjamin. Greetings from Rio! 2011. (Rio Ser.). (ENG.). 24p. (J). (gr. -1-2). pap. 3.99 *(978-0-06-202266-0(0),* HarperFestival) HarperCollins Pubs.

Harris, Patricia. Rowdy Racket in the Jungle. 2017. (Jungle Fun Ser.). 24p. (gr. 4-6). pap. 8.25 ***(978-1-5383-2128-7(9),*** PowerKids Pr.) Rosen Publishing Group, Inc., The.

Harris, Trudy. Say Something, Perico. RéBora, Cecilia, illus. 2011. (Millbrook Picture Books Ser.). (ENG.). 32p. (J). (gr. -1-2). lib. bdg. 16.95 *(978-0-7613-5231-0(7),* Millbrook Pr.) Lerner Publishing Group.

Haworth, Katie. Petunia Paris's Parrot. Williamson, Jo, illus. 2017. (ENG.). 40p. (J). (gr. -1-3). 17.99 *(978-1-4998-0437-9(7))* Little Bee Books Inc.

Hay, Sam. Flight of the Pummeled Parakeet. 2015. (Undead Pets Ser.: 6). lib. bdg. 16.00 *(978-0-606-38405-6(7))* Turtleback Bks.

Hirst, Daisy. The Girl with the Parrot on Her Head. Hirst, Daisy, illus. 2016. (ENG., Illus.). 40p. (J). (-k). 16.99 *(978-0-7636-7829-6(5))* Candlewick Pr.

Hoffman, Mary Ann. A Parrot for Pam. 2006. (Neighborhood Readers Ser.). (ENG.). 8p. (gr. -1-3). pap. 5.15 *(978-1-4042-5690-3(3),* Rosen Classroom) Rosen Publishing Group, Inc., The.

Holden, Pam. Stickybeak the Parrot, 6 pack. East, Jacqueline, illus. 2009. (Red Rocket Readers Ser.). (ENG.). 16p. (gr. -1-1). pap. *(978-1-877363-28-3(6),* Red Rocket Readers) Flying Start Bks.

Hornfray, Jenny. The Adventures of Parker the Parrot. 2008. 36p. pap. 15.49 *(978-1-4389-1229-5(3))* AuthorHouse.

Huelin, Jodi. The Movie Storybook. 2011. (Rio Ser.). (ENG.). 48p. (J). (gr. -1-2). pap. 8.99 *(978-0-06-202270-7(9),* HarperFestival) HarperCollins Pubs.

I Can: Individual Title Six-Packs. (Sails Literacy Ser.). 16p. (gr. k-18). 27.00 *(978-0-7635-4396-9(9))* Rigby Education.

Jafa, Manorama. The Parrot & the Mynah (English) 2013. (ENG.). 16p. pap. 4.95 *(978-93-5036-080-4(2))* Ratna, Sagar Pvt. Ltd. IND. Dist: Midpoint Trade Bks., Inc.

Jeune, Marie Carole. Rita & the Parrot. Saincilus, Larimer, illus. 2010. (HAT.). 32p. (J). pap. 16.95 *(978-1-60195-317-9(8))* International Step by Step Assn.

Judge, Lita. Good Morning to Me! Judge, Lita, illus. 2015. (ENG., Illus.). 40p. (J). (gr. -1-3). 17.99 *(978-1-4814-0369-6(9))* Simon & Schuster Children's Publishing.

Kargbo, Mariatu. Mr Byrd's Bird. 2011. 28p. pap. 24.95 *(978-1-4560-5435-9(X))* America Star Bks.

Kasten, Nancy, illus. First Feather 2003. 70p. (J). pap. 9.99 *(978-0-9744863-0-7(2))* Paulus Publishing.

Kauffman, Tracy. Gwendolyn's Wish. 2012. (-18). 24p. 24.95 *(978-1-62709-555-6(1));* 20p. pap. 24.95 *(978-1-4626-7207-3(8))* America Star Bks.

Kelley, Jane. The Desperate Adventures of Zeno & Alya. 2013. (ENG.). 208p. (J). (gr. 3-7). 15.99 *(978-1-250-02348-3(3),* 9781250023483) Feiwel & Friends.

Kennedy, Kim. Pirate Pete's Talk Like a Pirate. Kennedy, Doug, illus. 2007. (ENG.). 40p. (J). (gr. k-17). 16.95 *(978-0-8109-9348-8(1),* Abrams Bks. for Young Readers) Abrams, Inc.

Korman, Susan. Birds of a Feather. 2011. (Rio Ser.). (ENG.). 24p. (J). (gr. -1-2). pap. 3.99 *(978-0-06-202267-7(9),* HarperFestival) HarperCollins Pubs.

Korten, Gerri. The Parakeets & the Ginkgo Tree at Hide Park. I.t. ed. 2006. (Illus.). 36p. (J). 18.85 *(978-0-9785609-7-3(3))* New Global Publishing.

La Rue, Coco. A New Pig in Town. May, Kyla, illus. 2013. 127p. (J). pap. *(978-0-545-46607-3(5))* Scholastic, Inc.

Lerasle, Magdeleine. Songs from a Journey with a Parrot: Lullabies & Nursery Rhymes from Portugal & Brazil. Fronty, Aurélia, illus. 2013. (POR & ENG.). 52p. (J). (gr. -1-k). 16.95 *(978-2-923163-99-4(0))* La Montagne Secrete CAN. Dist: Independent Pubs. Group.

Ljungkvist, Laura. Pepi Sings a New Song. Ljungkvist, Laura, illus. 2010. (ENG., Illus.). 40p. (J). (gr. -1-3). 16.99 *(978-1-4169-9138-0(7),* Beach Lane Bks.) Beach Lane Bks.

Logue, Stephanie. Mango's Revenge. Murphy, Chris, illus. 2006. (J). pap. *(978-1-59336-769-5(4))* Mondo Publishing.

Lost: Individual Title, 6 Packs. (Story Steps Ser.). (gr. k-2). 23.00 *(978-0-7635-9817-4(8))* Rigby Education.

Manceau, Édouard. The Parrot Song. 2017. (ENG., Illus.). 32p. (J). (gr. -1-17). 12.95 *(978-1-84976-497-1(2))* Tate Publishing, Ltd. GBR. Dist: Hachette Bk. Group.

Martinez, Victor. Parrot in the Oven. Scott, Steve, illus. rev. ed. 2004. (ENG.). 240p. (YA). (gr. 8-18). pap. 8.99 *(978-0-06-447186-2(1),* Rayo) HarperCollins Pubs.

Massenot, Véronique. The Mermaid & the Parakeet: A Children's Book Inspired by Henri Matisse. Hié, Vanessa, illus. 2016. (ENG.). 32p. (J). (gr. -1-3). 14.95 *(978-3-7913-7265-5(3))* Prestel Verlag GmbH & Co KG. DEU. Dist: Penguin Random Hse. LLC.

Mcghee, Alison. Pablo & Birdy. Juan, Ana, illus. 2017. (ENG.). 304p. (J). (gr. 3-7). 17.99 ***(978-1-4814-7026-1(4),*** Atheneum/Caitlyn Dlouhy Books) Simon & Schuster Children's Publishing.

Meissner, David. The Missing Parrot: Set Of 6. 2010. (Early Connections Ser.). (J). pap. 39.00 net. *(978-1-4108-1552-1(8))* Benchmark Education Co.

Molesworth & Molesworth, Mary Louisa S. Peterkin. 2009. 128p. 23.95 *(978-1-60664-659-5(1))* Rodgers, Alan Bks.

Molesworth, Mary Louisa S. & Molesworth. Peterkin. 2009. 128p. pap. 10.95 *(978-1-60664-287-0(1))* Rodgers, Alan Bks.

Moore, S. D. The Adventures of Pj & Split Pea. Switzer, Bobbi, illus. 2008. 36p. per. 12.95 *(978-1-4327-1288-4(8))* Outskirts Pr., Inc.

—The Adventures of PJ & Split Pea Vol. II: Nothing but the Tooth. 2010. 37p. (J). pap. 12.95 *(978-1-4327-1289-1(6))* Outskirts Pr., Inc.

Mure, Nancy S. & Torre, Tom. The Pizza Man & the Parrots. 2014. (ENG., Illus.). 40p. (J). pap. 9.98 *(978-0-7443-2136-4(0))* SynergEbks.

Murguia, Bethanie Deeney. Cockatoo, Too. 2016. (ENG., Illus.). 40p. (J). (gr. -1-1). 17.99 *(978-1-4998-0102-6(5))* Little Bee Books Inc.

My Hat: Individual Title Six-Packs. (Sails Literacy Ser.). 16p. (gr. k-18). 27.00 *(978-0-7635-4436-2(1))* Rigby Education.

Nahal, Denise Abda. Hello Birdie! Tale of a Classroom Pet Based on a True Story. 2012. 16p. pap. 10.67 *(978-1-4669-6822-6(2))* Trafford Publishing.

Parakeet. 2004. (J). per. *(978-1-57657-398-3(2))* Paradise Pr., Inc.

Parish, John Lee. Cry Aloud: From Protest to Praise. 2007. (Illus.). 120p. per. 18.95 *(978-0-9758870-4-2(1))* Beverly Hills Publishing.

Parker, Emma & Renaud, Marguerite. Chatterbox Caz. 2010. (Illus.). 16p. pap. *(978-1-877561-77-1(0))* First Edition Ltd.

Parton, Paula. Room 17 'Where History Comes Alive!' Book Ii, Explorers. 2008. 120p. pap. 8.95 *(978-0-9794815-3-6(8))* Bellissima Publishing, LLC.

Pavanello, Roberto. The Dancing Vampire. Zeni, Marco, tr. from ITA. Pisapia, Blasco & Brughera, Pamela, illus. 2012. (Echo & the Bat Pack Ser.). (ENG.). 128p. (gr. 2-3). 25.32 *(978-1-4342-3837-5(7),* Echo & the Bat Pack) Stone Arch Bks.

Perry, Roseann. When Mama Says No. 2009. 36p. pap. 16.99 *(978-1-4389-1938-6(7))* AuthorHouse.

Pinkwater, Daniel M. Beautiful Yetta's Hanukkah Kitten. Pinkwater, Jill, illus. 2014. (ENG.). 32p. (J). (gr. -1-2). 17.99 *(978-0-312-62134-6(5),* 9780312621346) Feiwel & Friends.

Pippin, Sheila C. Katrina: Through Mango's Eyes. Pippin, Kristin A. & Pippin, Sheila C., illus. 2007. (J). (gr. -1-5). pap. 12.95 *(978-1-56167-956-0(9))* American Literary Pr.

Polly Parrot. 2006. (J). lib. bdg. 14.95 *(978-0-9774937-0-8(9))* Wood, Ella Sue.

Publications International Ltd. Staff. Look & Find Rio. 2011. 24p. (J). 7.98 *(978-1-4508-1382-2(8))* Publications International, Ltd.

—Rio Large Play As Ound. 2011. 24p. (J). 17.98 *(978-1-4508-0735-7(6))* Phoenix International Publications, Inc.

Punter, R. Stories of Pirates. 2004. (Young Reading Ser.: Vol. 1). 48p. (J). (gr. 2-18). pap. 5.99 *(978-0-7945-0583-7(X))* EDC Publishing.

Rawson, Katherine. If You Were a Parrot, 1 vol. Rogers, Sherry, illus. 2006. (ENG.). 32p. (J). (gr. -1-3). 15.95 *(978-0-9764943-9-3(6))* Arbordale Publishing.

Rey, Margret & Rey, H. A. Feeds the Animals, 1 vol. Vipah Interactive Staff, illus. 2005. (Read along Book & CD Ser.). (ENG.). 24p. (J). (gr. -1-3). audio compact disk 10.99 *(978-0-618-60387-9(5))* Houghton Mifflin Harcourt Publishing Co.

Reza, Connie. Leah Ann Adopta un Perico. 2006. (SPA., Illus.). 32p. (J). 19.99 incl. audio compact disk *(978-0-9714533-2-6(2))* Yo Puedo Publishing.

Roddie, Shen. The Gossipy Parrot. Terry, Michael, tr. Terry, Michael, illus. 2004. (ENG.). 32p. (J). (gr. k-2). 20.00 *(978-0-7475-6079-1(X))* Bloomsbury Publishing Plc GBR. Dist: Independent Pubs. Group.

—Gossipy Parrot Parrot. Terry, Michael, illus. 2003. (ENG.). 1p. (J). pap. 9.99 *(978-0-7475-6489-8(2))* Bloomsbury Publishing Plc GBR. Dist: Independent Pubs. Group.

Rogers, Jewels. The Princess & the Parakeet. 2011. 28p. pap. 12.50 *(978-1-4567-5170-8(0))* AuthorHouse.

Rushby, Pamela. Rosie & the Audition. Konye, Paul, illus. 2009. 24p. pap. 10.67 *(978-1-4190-5524-9(0))* Rigby Education.

—Rosie Goes Home. Konye, Paul, illus. 2009. (Rigby PM Stars Bridge Bks.). (ENG.). 24p. (gr. 2-3). pap. 8.70 *(978-1-4190-5529-4(1))* Rigby Education.

Sanchez, Juanita L. Pancho the Green Parrot Lays an Egg, 1 vol. Ramirez, Samuel, illus. 2009. 24p. pap. 24.95 *(978-1-61546-150-9(7))* America Star Bks.

Sandilands, Joyce. 3 on a Moonbeam. Padur, Simone, illus. 2004. 64p. *(978-0-9734383-1-4(2))* Whitlands Publishing, Ltd.

Scillian, Devin. Memoirs of a Parrot. Bowers, Tim, illus. 2016. (ENG.). 32p. (J). (gr. k-3). 16.99 *(978-1-58536-962-1(4),* 204036) Sleeping Bear Pr.

Scott, Janine. The Noisy Parrot. Rigby, Deborah, illus. 2009. (Treasure Chest Readers Ser.). 24p. (J). (gr. -1-2). pap. 8.15 *(978-1-60754-680-1(9));* lib. bdg. 22.60 *(978-1-60754-679-5(5))* Windmill Bks.

Small, Tanya. What You See Is What You Are. 2007. pap. 7.50 *(978-0-9705090-1-7(4))* MorningGlory Publishing.

Stine, R. L. Rotten School #15: Calling All Birdbrains. Park, Trip, illus. 4.99 *(978-0-06-123277-0(7))* HarperCollins Pubs.

Thompson, Chad J. Rhymes with Doug. Thompson, Chad J., illus. 2016. (ENG., Illus.). 40p. (J). (gr. -1-3). 16.99 *(978-1-4814-7095-7(7),* Aladdin) Simon & Schuster Children's Publishing.

True, J. J. Billy Brite: Africa & Beyond. 2011. (Illus.). 112p. pap. 14.03 *(978-1-4567-7281-9(3))* AuthorHouse.

Tweti, Mira. Here, There, & Everywhere: The Story of Sreeeeeeeet the Lorikeett. Brady, Lisa, illus. 2008. 47p. (J). (gr. 4-7). *(978-0-615-17122-7(2))* Parrot Pr.

Vaughn, J. D. Paula & the Parrot. Brisiane, Niche, illus. 2009. 16p. pap. 8.49 *(978-1-4389-8634-0(3))* AuthorHouse.

Ward, Erin & Weidmann, Pamela. Picasso Moves In. 2016. (ENG.). 60p. (J). (gr. 2). pap. 10.95 *(978-1-942603-35-1(5))* Heritage Builders, LLC.

Webb, Dirk. A Warm Summer's Day. 2010. 37p. 17.00 *(978-0-578-01867-6(5))* Webb, Dirk E.

What's New Cockatoo. 2005. (J). *(978-0-9767179-3-5(X))* ABC Development, Inc.

Williams, Brenda May. The Unusual Pet Shop. Williams, Raymond, illus. 2012. 24p. pap. 11.50 *(978-1-61897-798-4(9),* Strategic Bk. Publishing) Strategic Book Publishing & Rights Agency (SBPRA).

Williams, Fawn. The Adventures of Jj the Amazon Parrot. 2011. 32p. pap. 24.95 *(978-1-4626-4251-9(9))* America Star Bks.

Willis, Jeanne. Be Quiet, Parrot! Birchall, Mark, illus. 2005. (Picture Bks.). 32p. (J). (gr. k-2). 7.25 *(978-1-57505-492-6(2))* Lerner Publishing Group.

Witte, Anna. El Loro Tico Tango. Witte, Anna, illus. (SPA., Illus.). 24p. (J). 2011. (gr. -1-1). 9.99 *(978-1-84686-670-8(7))* 2005. pap. 6.99 *(978-1-84148-971-1(9))* Barefoot Bks., Inc.

—The Parrot Tico Tango. 2005. (ENG., Illus.). 24p. (J). (gr. -1-3). 6.99 *(978-1-905236-11-4(5))* Barefoot Bks., Inc.

—The Parrot Tico Tango. Witte, Anna, illus. 2005. (Illus.). 24p. (J). (gr. k-3). 15.99 *(978-1-84148-243-9(9))* Barefoot Bks., Inc.

Witte, Anna & Amador, Brian. The Parrot Tico Tango. Witte, Anna, illus. 2011. (ENG., Illus.). 24p. (J). (gr. -1-2). 9.99 *(978-1-84686-669-2(3))* Barefoot Bks., Inc.

PARTICLES (NUCLEAR PHYSICS)

Bortz, Alfred B. The Neutrino. 2004. (Library of Subatomic Particles Ser.). (Illus.). 64p. (gr. 7-12). lib. bdg. 31.95 *(978-0-8239-4529-0(4))* Rosen Publishing Group, Inc., The.

—The Neutron. 2004. (Library of Subatomic Particles Ser.). (Illus.). 64p. (gr. 7-12). lib. bdg. 31.95 *(978-0-8239-4530-6(8))* Rosen Publishing Group, Inc., The.

—The Proton. 2004. (Library of Subatomic Particles Ser.). (Illus.). 64p. (gr. 7-12). lib. bdg. 31.95 *(978-0-8239-4532-0(4))* Rosen Publishing Group, Inc., The.

Bortz, Fred. The Neutrino. 2009. (Library of Subatomic Particles Ser.). 64p. (gr. 6-6). 58.50 *(978-1-60853-879-9(6))* Rosen Publishing Group, Inc., The.

—The Neutron. 2009. (Library of Subatomic Particles Ser.). 64p. (gr. 6-6). 58.50 *(978-1-60853-880-5(X))* Rosen Publishing Group, Inc., The.

—The Proton. 2009. (Library of Subatomic Particles Ser.). 64p. (gr. 6-6). 58.50 *(978-1-60853-886-7(9))* Rosen Publishing Group, Inc., The.

—The Quark. (Library of Subatomic Particles Ser.). 64p. 2009. (gr. 6-6). 58.50 *(978-1-60853-889-8(3))* 2004. (Illus.). (gr. 7-12). lib. bdg. 31.95 *(978-0-8239-4533-7(2))* Rosen Publishing Group, Inc., The.

—Understanding Higgs Bosons. 2015. (Exploring the Subatomic World Ser.). (ENG., Illus.). 64p. (J). (gr. 8-8). lib. bdg. 34.21 *(978-1-5026-0550-4(3))* Cavendish Square Publishing.

Fields, B. H. & Bortz, Fred. Understanding Neutrons. 2015. (Exploring the Subatomic World Ser.). (ENG., Illus.). 64p. (J). (gr. 8-8). 34.21 *(978-1-5026-0542-9(2))* Cavendish Square Publishing.

—Understanding Quarks. 2015. (Exploring the Subatomic World Ser.). (ENG., Illus.). 64p. (J). (gr. 8-8). lib. bdg. 34.21 *(978-1-5026-0548-1(1))* Cavendish Square Publishing.

Latta, Sara. Smash! Exploring the Mysteries of the Universe with the Large Hadron Collider. Weigel, Jeff, illus. 2017. (Fiction — Young Adult Ser.). (ENG.). 72p. (YA). (gr. 8-12). 16.99 ***(978-1-5124-3594-8(5));*** 50.65 ***(978-1-5124-3593-1(7));*** 50.65 ***(978-1-5124-2701-1(2))*** Lerner Publishing Group. (Graphic Universe™).

Latta, Sara L. SMASH! Exploring the Mysteries of the Universe with the Large Hadron Collider. Weigel, Jeff, illus. 2017. (ENG.). 72p. (J). (gr. 8-12). 33.32 *(978-1-4677-8551-8(2))* Lerner Publishing Group.

Scientific American Staff. Beyond Extreme Physics. 2009. (Scientific American Cutting-Edge Science Ser.). 160p. (gr. 9-9). 63.90 *(978-1-60853-073-1(6))* Rosen Publishing Group, Inc., The.

Wells, Robert E. What's Smaller Than a Pygmy Shrew? 2012. (J). *(978-1-61913-158-3(7))* Weigl Pubs., Inc.

PARTIES

see also Entertaining

ABDO Publishing Company Staff. Cool Parties, 1 vol. 2012. (Cool Parties Ser.: 6). (ENG., Illus.). 32p. 171.00 *(978-1-61714-972-6(1),* Checkerboard Library) ABDO Publishing Co.

Adamson, Heather. Birthday Parties. 2010. (Special Days Ser.). 24p. (J). 25.65 *(978-1-60753-028-2(7))* Amicus Publishing.

Aretha, David. Ecstasy & Other Party Drugs: A MyReportLinks.com Book. 2005. (Drugs Ser.). (Illus.). 48p. (J). lib. bdg. 25.26 *(978-0-7660-5278-9(8),* MyReportLinks.com Bks.) Enslow Pubs., Inc.

Barker, Cicely Mary. How to Host a Flower Fairy Tea Party. 2004. (Flower Fairies Ser.). (ENG., Illus.). 48p. (J). (gr. -1-2). pap. 7.99 *(978-0-7232-5360-0(9),* Warne) Penguin Young Readers Group.

Barsocchini, Peter, creator. High School Musical 2 Party Planner. 2010. (Illus.). (J). pap. 4.99 *(978-0-7666-2846-5(9))* Modern Publishing.

Beery, Barbara. Barbara Beery's Pink Princess Party Cookbook. Williams, Zac, photos by. 2011. (ENG., Illus.). 64p. (J). (gr. 2-7). spiral bd. 15.99 *(978-1-4424-1231-6(3),* Simon & Schuster Bks. For Young Readers) Simon & Schuster Bks. For Young Readers.

Beker, Jeanne. The Big Night Out. Dion, Nathalie, illus. 2005. (ENG.). 80p. (J). (gr. 4-7). pap. 15.95 *(978-0-88776-719-7(2),* Tundra Bks.) Tundra Bks. CAN. Dist: Penguin Random Hse. LLC.

Bokram, Karen & Faithgirlz! and Girls' Life Magazine Editors. Best Party Book Ever! From Invites to Overnights & Everything in Between, 1 vol. 2014. (Faithgirlz Ser.). (ENG.). 160p. (J). pap. 14.99 *(978-0-310-74600-3(0))* Zonderkidz.

Bolte, Mari. Sleepover Girls. Franco, Paula, illus. 2014. (Sleepover Girls Crafts Ser.). (ENG.). 64p. (gr. 3-4). pap. 51.80 *(978-1-62370-201-4(1))* Capstone Young Readers of Coughlan Cos.

Braun, Eric. Plan a Holiday Party. 2014. (Party Time! Ser.). (ENG., Illus.). 32p. (gr. 4-8). lib. bdg. 26.60 *(978-1-4677-3834-7(4),* Lerner Pubns.) Lerner Publishing Group.

—Plan an Outdoor Party. 2014. (Party Time! Ser.). (ENG., Illus.). 32p. (gr. 4-8). lib. bdg. 26.60 *(978-1-4677-3833-0(6),* Lerner Pubns.) Lerner Publishing Group.

Canetti, Yanitzia. Party Colors/Colores Festivos: A World of Color. 2010. (ENG & SPA.). 24p. (J). pap. 6.99 *(978-1-59835-274-0(1),* BrickHouse Education) Cambridge BrickHouse, Inc.

Co-Ed Howling Noises Mystery Party Kit for 10 Players: Filled with Fun, Games & Laughter. 2004. (YA). 30.00 *(978-1-932839-38-8(0))* SimpliFun Studios.

Coan, Sharon. Mi Fiesta de Cumpleaños (My Birthday Party) 2016. (TIME for KIDS(r) Nonfiction Readers Ser.). (SPA., Illus.). 12p. (J). (gr. k-k). 4.99 *(978-1-4938-2972-9(6))* Teacher Created Materials, Inc.

—My Birthday Party. 2015. (TIME for KIDS(r) Nonfiction Readers Ser.). (ENG., Illus.). 12p. (gr. k-k). 4.99 *(978-1-4938-2063-4(X))* Teacher Created Materials, Inc.

Devore, Janna. Ballerina Cookbook. 2013. 94p. pap. *(978-1-4596-5916-2(3))* ReadHowYouWant.com, Ltd.

Dorling Kindersley Publishing Staff. Sleepover Party. 2016. (ENG., Illus.). 80p. (J). (gr. 2-4). 14.99 *(978-1-4654-5097-5(1),* DK Children) Dorling Kindersley Publishing, Inc.

Earle, Erin. Surprise Party! 2013. (Core Math Skills: Measurement & Geometry Ser.). 24p. (J). (gr. 1-2). 22.60 *(978-1-4777-2230-5(0));* (ENG.). pap. 8.25 *(978-1-4777-2103-2(7))* Rosen Publishing Group, Inc., The. (Rosen Classroom).

—Surprise Party! Shapes & Their Attributes. 2013. (Rosen Math Readers Ser.). (ENG.). 24p. (J). (gr. 1-2). pap. 49.50 *(978-1-4777-2104-9(5),* Rosen Classroom) Rosen Publishing Group, Inc., The.

Encarnacion, Elizabeth. The Girls' Guide to Campfire Activities. 2008. (ENG., Illus.). 124p. (J). (gr. 5-18). pap. 12.95 *(978-1-60433-003-8(1),* Applesauce Pr.) Cider Mill Pr. Bk. Pubs., LLC.

Everett, Reese. Class Parties, Yes or No. 2016. (Seeing Both Sides Ser.). (ENG.). 32p. (gr. 3-6). 32.79 *(978-1-68191-383-4(6))* Rourke Educational Media.

Freese, Joan. Vamos A Planear una Fiesta Con Matemáticas. Andersen, Gregg, photos by. 2008. (Matemáticas en Nuestro Mundo - Nivel 2 (Math in Our World - Level 2) Ser.). (SPA., Illus.). 24p. (gr. 1-4). lib. bdg. 22.00 *(978-0-8368-9021-1(3),* Weekly Reader Leveled Readers) Stevens, Gareth Publishing LLLP.

—Vamos a Planear una Fiesta con Matemáticas. 2008. (Las matemáticas en nuestro mundo - Nivel 2 (Math in Our World - Level 2) Ser.). (SPA.). 24p. (gr. 1-4). pap. 8.15 *(978-0-8368-9030-3(2),* Weekly Reader Leveled Readers) Stevens, Gareth Publishing LLLP.

Gamblin, Rose Tooley. The Birthday Party. 2007. (J). *(978-0-8127-0464-8(9))* Autumn Hse. Publishing Co.

Greenwald, Todd J., contrib. by. Wizards of Waverly Place Party Planner. 2009. (Wizards of Waverly Place Ser.). (Illus.). (J). pap. 4.99 *(978-0-7666-3302-5(0))* Modern Publishing.

Guidone, Lisa M. What Happens at a Museum? (¿Qué pasa en un Museo?) 2008. (Where People Work/Dónde Trabaja la Gente? Ser.). (SPA.). 24p. (gr. -1-3). pap. 8.15 *(978-0-8368-9381-6(6),* Weekly Reader Leveled Readers) Stevens, Gareth Publishing LLLP.

—What Happens at a Museum?/¿Qué Pasa en un Museo? 2008. (Where People Work/Dónde Trabaja la Gente? Ser.). (ENG & SPA.). 24p. (gr. -1-3). lib. bdg. 22.00 *(978-0-8368-9282-6(8),* Weekly Reader Leveled Readers) Stevens, Gareth Publishing LLLP.

Hall, Pamela. A Bully-Free Party, 1 vol. Ostrom, Bob, illus. 2012. (Bully-Free World Ser.). (ENG.). 24p. (J). (gr. -1-4). 27.07 *(978-1-61641-845-8(1))* Magic Wagon.

Hogenkamp, S. My Birthday: Learning the IR Sound. 2009. (PowerPhonics Ser.). 24p. (gr. 1-1). 39.90 *(978-1-60851-460-1(9),* PowerKids Pr.) Rosen Publishing Group, Inc., The.

Holden, Pam. Happy Birthday, 6 pack. Hawley, Kelvin, illus. 2009. (Red Rocket Readers Ser.). (ENG.). 16p. (gr. -1-1). pap. *(978-1-877363-03-0(0),* Red Rocket Readers) Flying Start Bks.

Hurley, Jo. Slumber-ific! Great Sleepover Ideas for You & Your Friends. Morley, Taia, illus. 2007. 63p. (J). *(978-0-439-02015-2(8))* Scholastic, Inc.

Hutchings, Amy & Nations, Susan. What Happens at a Party Store? 2008. (Where People Work Ser.). 24p. (J). (gr. -1-3).

lib. bdg. 22.00 *(978-0-8368-9277-2(1),* Weekly Reader Leveled Readers) Stevens, Gareth Publishing LLLP.
—What Happens at a Party Store?/¿Qué Pasa en una Tienda de Cosas para Fiestas} 2008. (Where People Work Ser.). 24p. (gr. -1-3). pap. 8.15 *(978-0-8368-9376-2(X));* (SPA.). pap. 8.15 *(978-0-8368-9382-3(4))* Stevens, Gareth Publishing LLLP. (Weekly Reader Leveled Readers).
—What Happens at a Party Store?/¿Qué Pasa en una Tienda de Cosas para Fiestas. 2008. (Where People Work/Dónde Trabaja la Gente? Ser.). (ENG & SPA.). 24p. (J). (gr. -1-3). lib. bdg. 22.00 *(978-0-8368-9283-3(6),* Weekly Reader Leveled Readers) Stevens, Gareth Publishing LLLP.
Jeffries, Joyce. Dinosaur Birthday Party. 2014. (Dinosaur School Ser.). 24p. (J). (gr. -1-1). 22.60 *(978-1-4824-0741-9(8))* Stevens, Gareth Publishing LLLP.
Jones, Jen. Accessory Parties: Planning a Party That Makes Your Friends Say Cool!, 1 vol. 2014. (Perfect Parties Ser.). (ENG.). 32p. (gr. 3-4). lib. bdg. 27.99 *(978-1-4765-4009-2(8),* Snap Bks.) Capstone Press of Coughlan Cos.
—Costume Parties: Planning a Party That Makes Your Friends Say Wow!, 1 vol. 2014. (Perfect Parties Ser.). (ENG.). 32p. (gr. 3-4). lib. bdg. 27.99 *(978-1-4765-4007-8(1),* Snap Bks.) Capstone Press of Coughlan Cos.
—Game Night Parties: Planning a Bash That Makes Your Friends Say Yeah!, 1 vol. 2014. (Perfect Parties Ser.). (ENG.). 32p. (gr. 3-4). lib. bdg. 27.99 *(978-1-4765-4006-1(3),* Snap Bks.) Capstone Press of Coughlan Cos.
—Pampering Parties: Planning a Party That Makes Your Friends Say Ahhh, 1 vol. 2014. (Perfect Parties Ser.). (ENG.). 32p. (gr. 3-4). lib. bdg. 27.99 *(978-1-4765-4008-5(X),* Snap Bks.) Capstone Press of Coughlan Cos.
—Perfect Parties, 1 vol. 2014. (Perfect Parties Ser.). (ENG.). 32p. (gr. 3-4). lib. bdg. 111.96 *(978-1-4765-4675-9(4),* Snap Bks.) Capstone Press of Coughlan Cos.
—Planning Perfect Parties: The Girls' Guide to Fun, Fresh, Unforgettable Events. 2014. (Craft It Yourself Ser.). (ENG.). 128p. (gr. 3-4). pap. 14.95 *(978-1-62370-063-8(9))* Capstone Young Readers of Coughlan Cos.
Jorgensen, Katrina. Food, Football, & Fun! Sports Illustrated Kids' Football Recipes. 2015. (Sports Illustrated Kids Ser.). (ENG., Illus.). 144p. (gr. 3-6). pap. 15.95 *(978-1-62370-230-4(5))* Capstone Press of Coughlan Cos.
—Football Party Recipes: Delicious Ideas for the Big Event. 2015. (Football Cookbooks Ser.). (ENG.). 48p. (gr. 3-6). lib. bdg. 31.32 *(978-1-4914-2136-9(3))* Capstone Press of Coughlan Cos.
—Football Tailgating Recipes: Tasty Treats for the Stadium Crowd. 2015. (Football Cookbooks Ser.). (ENG.). 48p. (gr. 3-6). lib. bdg. 31.32 *(978-1-4914-2137-6(1))* Capstone Press of Coughlan Cos.
Kalman, Bobbie. It Is My Birthday. 2010. (ENG., Illus.). 16p. (J). (gr. k-2). *(978-0-7787-9418-9(0));* pap. *(978-0-7787-9462-2(8))* Crabtree Publishing Co.
Kenney, Karen Latchana. Cool Family Parties: Perfect Party Planning for Kids, 1 vol. 2012. (Cool Parties Ser.). (ENG., Illus.). 32p. (J). (gr. 3-6). 28.50 *(978-1-61714-973-3(X))* ABDO Publishing Co.
—Cool Holiday Parties: Perfect Party Planning for Kids, 1 vol. 2012. (Cool Parties Ser.). (ENG., Illus.). 32p. (J). (gr. 3-6). 28.50 *(978-1-61714-974-0(8))* ABDO Publishing Co.
—Cool International Parties: Perfect Party Planning for Kids, 1 vol. 2012. (Cool Parties Ser.). (ENG., Illus.). 32p. (J). (gr. 3-6). 28.50 *(978-1-61714-975-7(6))* ABDO Publishing Co.
—Cool Slumber Parties: Perfect Party Planning for Kids, 1 vol. 2012. (Cool Parties Ser.). (ENG., Illus.). 32p. (J). (gr. 3-6). 28.50 *(978-1-61714-976-4(4))* ABDO Publishing Co.
—Cool Sports Parties: Perfect Party Planning for Kids, 1 vol. 2012. (Cool Parties Ser.). (ENG., Illus.). 32p. (J). (gr. 3-6). 28.50 *(978-1-61714-977-1(2))* ABDO Publishing Co.
—Cool Theme Parties: Perfect Party Planning for Kids, 1 vol. 2012. (Cool Parties Ser.). (ENG., Illus.). 32p. (J). (gr. 3-6). 28.50 *(978-1-61714-978-8(0))* ABDO Publishing Co.
Krulik, Nancy. Prom! The Complete Guide to a Truly Spectacular Night. Johnson, Kim, illus. 2003. 96p. (YA). 8.00 *(978-0-7567-9038-7(7))* DIANE Publishing Co.
Kruse, Nancy. Treasure Hunt: A Book of Clues for Parties. 2008. 116p. pap. 12.95 *(978-1-60145-565-9(8))* Booklocker.com, Inc.
Labat, Yancey C., illus. It's Party Time! 2006. 56p. (J). *(978-0-439-83227-4(6))* Scholastic, Inc.
Loh-Hagan, Virginia. Surprise Party. 2017. (D. I. Y. Make It Happen Ser.). (ENG., Illus.). 32p. (J). (gr. 4-8). lib. bdg. 29.93 *(978-1-63472-144-8(6),* 209148, 45th Parallel Press) Cherry Lake Publishing.
Lynette, Rachel. Let's Throw a Hanukkah Party! 2011. (J). 49.50 *(978-1-4488-2734-3(5));* 22.60 *(978-1-4488-2572-1(5));* pap. 8.25 *(978-1-4488-2733-6(7))* Rosen Publishing Group, Inc., The. (PowerKids Pr.).
Lyons, Shelly. If You Were a Question Mark [LTD Commodities]. Gray, Sara, illus. 2010. (Word Fun Ser.). 24p. pap. 3.50 *(978-1-4048-6253-1(6),* Nonfiction Picture Bks.) Picture Window Bks.
Maile, Ruby. Why Are You Having A Party? 2014. (Little Books of Answers: Level B Ser.). (Illus.). 16p. (gr. k-2). pap. 7.95 *(978-1-927136-10-2(5))* Three Crows Media NZL. Dist: RiverStream Publishing.
McKissick, Katherine. Fun & Games: Planning a Perfect Party: Division (Grade 3) 2017. (Mathematics Readers Ser.). (Illus.). 32p. (gr. 3-3). 8.99 ***(978-1-4807-5799-8(3))*** Teacher Created Materials, Inc.
Rober, Harold. Having a Sleepover. 2017. (Bumba Books (tm) — Fun Firsts Ser.). (ENG.). 24p. (J). (gr. -1-1). 12.99 ***(978-1-5124-3684-6(4))***; 38.65 ***(978-1-5124-2751-6(9))***; 38.65 ***(978-1-5124-3683-9(6))*** Lerner Publishing Group. (Lerner Pubns.).
Rober, Harold T. Having a Sleepover. 2017. (Bumba Books (tm) — Fun Firsts Ser.). (ENG., Illus.). 24p. (J). (gr. -1-1). 25.32 *(978-1-5124-2555-0(9))* Lerner Publishing Group.
Rosenberg, Carol & Rosenberg, Gary. Jon & Jayne's Guide to Throwing, Going To, & Surviving Parties: Advice & More from Your Average but Xtraordinary Friends. 2008. (Jon & Jayne Doe Ser.). (ENG., Illus.). 128p. (YA). (gr. 7-11). pap. 9.95 *(978-0-7573-0726-3(4))* Health Communications, Inc.
Salas, Laura Purdie. C Is for Cake! A Birthday Alphabet. 2010. (Alphabet Fun Ser.). (ENG.). 32p. (gr. 1-2). pap. 47.70 *(978-1-4296-5086-1(9));* lib. bdg. 27.32 *(978-1-4296-3914-9(8))* Capstone Press of Coughlan Cos. (Aplus Bks.).
Segarra, Mercedes. Fun Party Food: Little Chef Recipes. 2013. (Little Chef Ser.). 36p. (J). lib. bdg. 23.94 *(978-0-7660-4262-9(6));* pap. 7.95 *(978-1-4644-0467-2(4))* Enslow Pubs., Inc. (Enslow Elementary).
Smith, Thomasina. I Can Have a Party: Easy Decorations, Food & Games, Shown Step by Step. 2016. (ENG., Illus.). 48p. 7.99 *(978-1-86147-495-7(4),* Armadillo) Anness Publishing GBR. Dist: National Bk. Network.
Speechley, Greta. Birthday Crafts. 2010. (Creative Crafts for Kids Ser.). 32p. (J). (gr. 2-5). lib. bdg. 28.00 *(978-1-4339-3552-7(X));* (Illus.). pap. 10.50 *(978-1-4339-3553-4(8))* Stevens, Gareth Publishing LLLP. (Gareth Stevens Learning Library).
Speregen, Debra Newberger. Party Girl: How to Throw a Fab Fest. Tallardy, Laura, illus. 2008. 48p. pap. *(978-0-545-04093-8(0))* Scholastic, Inc.
Stardoll. Stardoll: Sticker Red Carpet Dress Up. 2013. (Stardoll Ser.). (ENG.). 24p. (J). (gr. 2-4). pap. 6.99 *(978-0-85751-178-2(5))* Transworld Publishers Ltd. GBR. Dist: Independent Pubs. Group.
Tan, Ming, et al. Getting Ready. 2007. (Windows on Literacy Ser.). (ENG., Illus.). 12p. pap. 10.95 *(978-0-7922-8456-7(9))* National Geographic School Publishing, Inc.
Thompson, Kim Mitzo. Birthday Party. 2011. (J). (gr. k-1). audio compact disk 4.99 *(978-1-59922-877-8(7))* Twin Sisters IP, LLC.
Torres, Laura. Rock Your Party. 2012. (Illus.). 32p. (gr. 3-5). pap. 8.95 *(978-1-926853-86-4(5))* Saunders Bk. Co. CAN. Dist: RiverStream Publishing.
Turnbull, Stephanie. Fun with Friends: Style Secrets for Girls. 2013. (Girl Talk Ser.). 32p. (gr. 4-7). 31.35 *(978-1-59920-946-3(2))* Black Rabbit Bks.
Ventura, Marne & Peschke, Marci. Kylie Jean Party Craft Queen, 1 vol. Mourning, Tuesday, illus. 2014. (Kylie Jean Craft Queen Ser.). (ENG.). 32p. (gr. 2-3). lib. bdg. 26.65 *(978-1-4795-2191-3(4))* Picture Window Bks.
Watson, Stephanie. Plan a Birthday Party. 2014. (Party Time! Ser.). (ENG., Illus.). 32p. (gr. 4-8). lib. bdg. 26.60 *(978-1-4677-3835-4(2),* Lerner Pubns.) Lerner Publishing Group.
—Plan a Sleepover Party. 2014. (Party Time! Ser.). (ENG., Illus.). 32p. (gr. 4-8). lib. bdg. 26.60 *(978-1-4677-3832-3(8),* Lerner Pubns.) Lerner Publishing Group.

PARTIES—FICTION

Adler, David A. Young Cam Jansen & the 100th Day of School, 15 vols. Natti, Susanna, illus. 2010. (Young Cam Jansen Ser.: 15). (ENG.). 32p. (J). (gr. 1-3). mass mkt. 3.99 *(978-0-14-241685-3(1),* Penguin Young Readers) Penguin Young Readers Group.
Aikins, Dave, illus. The Birthday Dance Party: Daisy's Fiesta de Quinceañera. 2006. (Dora the Explorer Ser.: 19). (ENG.). 24p. (J). (gr. -1-3). pap. 3.99 *(978-1-4169-1303-0(3),* Simon Spotlight/Nickelodeon) Simon Spotlight/Nickelodeon.
Alegria, Malin. Border Town #2: Quince Clash. 2012. (Border Town Ser.). (ENG.). 192p. (J). (gr. 7). pap. 5.99 *(978-0-545-40241-5(7),* Scholastic Paperbacks) Scholastic, Inc.
—Guerra de Quinceaneras (Quince Clash) 2013. (Border Town (Spanish) Ser.: 2). (SPA.). lib. bdg. 16.00 *(978-0-606-32401-4(1),* Turtleback) Turtleback Bks.
Allen, Francesca & Brooks, Felicity. Busy Truck. Crisp, Dan, illus. 2007. (Usborne Play Bks.). 10p. (J). (gr. -1-k). bds. 10.99 *(978-0-7945-1453-2(7),* Usborne) EDC Publishing.
Anfousse, Ginette. Polo et L'anniversaire. Sarrazin, Marisol, tr. 2003. (Polo Baby Board Bks.). (FRE., Illus.). 16p. (J). (— 1). bds. *(978-2-89021-656-3(X))* Diffusion du livre Mirabel (DLM).
Anna. The Magic Money Tree. 2009. (Illus.). 20p. pap. 15.49 *(978-1-4389-0472-6(X))* AuthorHouse.
Annie Starks-Johnson, Starks-Johnson & Annie Starks-Johnson. Dottie's Surprise Birthday Party. 2009. 24p. pap. 11.49 *(978-1-4389-4866-9(2))* AuthorHouse.
Arévalo, Josefina. Lo Que Paulito Olvidó. 2006. (SPA.). (J). *(978-1-59835-006-7(4))* Cambridge BrickHouse, Inc.
Arnold, Tedd. Big Family. Arnold, Tedd, illus. 2017. (Fly Guy Ser.: 17). (ENG., Illus.). 32p. (J). (gr. -1-3). 6.99 ***(978-0-545-66316-8(4))*** Scholastic, Inc.
Ashley, Sharon. I Wish I Could See. 2013. 24p. pap. 24.95 *(978-1-4626-9700-7(3))* America Star Bks.
Averill, Esther. Jenny's Birthday Book. Averill, Esther, illus. 2005. (New York Review Children's Collection). (ENG., Illus.). 44p. (J). (gr. -1-2). reprint ed. 15.95 *(978-1-59017-154-7(3),* NYR Children's Collection) New York Review of Bks., Inc., The.
Avraham, Kate Aver. What Will You Be, Sara Mee? O'Brien, Anne Sibley, illus. 2010. (ENG.). 32p. (J). (gr. -1-3). 16.95 *(978-1-58089-210-0(8));* pap. 7.95 *(978-1-58089-211-7(6))* Charlesbridge Publishing, Inc.
Awdry, Wilbert V. Halloween in Anopha. Courtney, Richard, illus. 2008. (Thomas in Town Ser.). (ENG.). 32p. (J). (gr. -1-2). 5.99 *(978-0-375-84413-3(9),* Random Hse. Bks. for Young Readers) Random Hse. Children's Bks.
Bach, Annie. Monster Party! 2014. (ENG., Illus.). 32p. (J). (gr. -1-k). 9.95 *(978-1-4549-1051-0(8))* Sterling Publishing Co., Inc.
Baena, Gloria. Invitacion a la Fiesta del Gran Gorila. Osorno, Laura, illus. 2003. (SPA.). 32p. (J). 8.95 *(978-958-04-7072-4(3))* Norma S.A. COL. Dist: Distribuidora Norma, Inc.
Bailey, Linda. Stanley's Party. Slavin, Bill, illus. 2004. (ENG.). 32p. (J). (gr. -1-2). pap. 8.99 *(978-1-55337-768-9(0))* Kids Can Pr., Ltd. CAN. Dist: Hachette Bk. Group.
Baltazar, Franco & Art Baltazar Comic Book Staff. Field Trippin, Vol. 5. 2011. (ENG., Illus.). 160p. (J). (gr. 2-5). pap. 12.99 *(978-1-4012-3173-6(X))* DC Comics.
Barchers, Suzanne I. Main Street Block Party, 1 vol. 2011. (Targeted Phonics Ser.). (ENG.). 16p. (J). (gr. k-2). pap. 5.99 *(978-1-4333-2923-4(9))* Teacher Created Materials, Inc.
Bardhan-Quallen, Sudipta. Duck, Duck, Moose! Jones, Noah Z., illus. 2014. (ENG.). 32p. (J). (gr. -1-k). 16.99 *(978-1-4231-7110-2(1))* Hyperion Bks. for Children.
Barn Party: Level M, 6 vols. 128p. (gr. 2-3). 49.95 *(978-0-7699-0983-7(3))* Shortland Pubns. (U. S. A.) Inc.
Basha, Irena Canaj. The Birthday Party, It Was Saturday... 2013. 16p. pap. 24.95 *(978-1-62709-182-4(3))* America Star Bks.
Bates, Angie. Hey Baby! 2010. (Sleepover Club Ser.). (ENG., Illus.). 144p. (J). (gr. 2-6). pap. 6.99 *(978-0-00-727704-9(0))* HarperCollins Pubs. Ltd. GBR. Dist: Independent Pubs. Group.
Bauer, Linda. Fruits & Flowers & Footprints OH MY!!! 2007. (Illus.). 29p. (J). 13.99 *(978-0-9798146-0-0(X))* Bauer, Linda.
Beck, Scott. Monster Sleepover! 2009. (ENG., Illus.). 32p. (J). (gr. k-2). 15.95 *(978-0-8109-4059-8(0),* Abrams Bks. for Young Readers) Abrams, Inc.
Benchmark Education Company, LLC Staff, compiled by. Celebrations. 2006. (J). 148.00 *(978-1-4108-7039-1(1))* Benchmark Education Co.
Benton, Lynne. Pirate Pete. Chapman, Neil, illus. 2008. (Tadpoles Ser.). (ENG.). 24p. (J). (gr. -1-3). pap. *(978-0-7787-3892-3(2))* Crabtree Publishing Co.
Berenstain, Jan & Berenstain, Mike. Berenstain Bears & the Forgiving Tree, 1 vol. 2011. (Berenstain Bears/Living Lights Ser.). (ENG.). 32p. (J). pap. 3.99 *(978-0-310-72084-3(2))* Zonderkidz.
Berenstain, Stan & Berenstain, Jan. The Berenstain Bears' Family Reunion. 2009. (Berenstain Bears — I Can Read Ser.). (J). lib. bdg. 13.55 *(978-0-606-04776-0(X),* Turtleback) Turtleback Bks.
Berlan, Kathryn. Andrew's Amazing Monsters. 2013. (ENG., Illus.). 32p. (J). (gr. -1-3). 16.99 *(978-1-4814-2160-7(3),* Atheneum Bks. for Young Readers) Simon & Schuster Children's Publishing.
Berrow, G. M. Pinkie Pie & the Rockin' Ponypalooza Party! 2013. (My Little Pony Chapter Bks.). (J). lib. bdg. 16.00 *(978-0-606-35299-4(6))* Turtleback Bks.
Bertrand, Diane Gonzales & Ventura, Gabriela Baeza. A Bean & Cheese Taco Birthday / un Cumpleaños con Tacos de Frijoles con Queso. Trujillo, Robert, illus. 2015. (SPA & ENG.). 32p. (J). (gr. k-3). 17.95 *(978-1-55885-812-1(1))* Arte Publico Pr.
—The Party for Papá Luis/La Fiesta para Papá Luis. Galindo, Alejandro, illus. 2010. (ENG.). 32p. (J). (gr. -1-3). 16.95 *(978-1-55885-532-8(7))* Arte Publico Pr.
Best, Cari. Three Cheers for Catherine the Great! Potter, Giselle, illus. 2003. (Catherine the Great Ser.). (ENG.). 32p. (J). (gr. -1-3). pap. 8.99 *(978-0-374-47551-2(2),* 9780374475512) Square Fish.
Bickel, Karla. Surprise Christmas Birthday Party. Bickel, Karla, illus. I.t. ed. 2004. (Illus.). 16p. (J). (gr. -1-6). pap. 5.00 *(978-1-891452-12-3(6),* 3) Heart Arbor Bks.
Birchall, Mark. Rabbit's Birthday Surprise. Birchall, Mark, illus. 2003. (Illus.). 32p. (J). (gr. -1-3). 15.95 *(978-0-87614-910-2(7),* Carolrhoda Bks.) Lerner Publishing Group.
Bird, Helen. Party Time. 2008. (Siti's Sisters Ser.). (ENG.). 36p. *(978-1-84167-726-2(4))* Ransom Publishing Ltd.
The Birthday Party. (Early Intervention Levels Ser.). 23.10 *(978-0-7362-0002-8(9))* CENGAGE Learning.
Birthday Vicious. 2014. (Ashley Project Ser.: 3). (ENG., Illus.). 304p. (J). (gr. 4-8). pap. 7.99 *(978-1-4424-9038-3(1),* Aladdin) Simon & Schuster Children's Publishing.
Black, Allyson. Crushed, Bk. 5. Spaziante, Patrick & Riley, Kellee, illus. 2011. (Scarlett & Crimson Ser.). (ENG.). 112p. (J). pap. 6.99 *(978-1-4169-9648-4(6),* Simon Spotlight) Simon Spotlight.
Blackburn, Sheila M. Stewie Scraps & the Giant Joggers. 2008. 76p. pap. *(978-1-903853-86-3(9))* Brilliant Pubns.
—Stewie Scraps & the Trolley Cart. 2008. 72p. pap. *(978-1-903853-88-7(5))* Brilliant Pubns.
Blackstone, Stella. Bear's Birthday. Harter, Debbie, illus. 2011.Tr. of El Cumpleanos de Oso. (ENG.). 24p. (J). (gr. -1-1). pap. 6.99 *(978-1-84686-515-2(8))* Barefoot Bks., Inc.
Blackwell-Burke, Melissa & Kunkel, Kristen. Rhyme Time Party. 2003. (J). spiral bd. 14.95 *(978-1-58605-955-2(6),* LeapFrog Schl. Hse.) LeapFrog Enterprises, Inc.
Blake, Jon. Crazy Party at the House of Fun. Roberts, David, illus. 2005. (ENG.). 128p. (J). (gr. 2-4). pap. 7.95 *(978-0-340-88460-7(6))* Hachette Children's Group GBR. Dist: Hachette Bk. Group.
Blanck, Cathy. A Party for Arty. 2004. (Illus.). 32p. (J). pap. *(978-0-9753059-0-4(5))* Red Barn Reading Inc.
Blankenship, Paula. We Both Read-Lulu's Wild Party. Reinhart, Larry, illus. 2009. (We Both Read Ser.). 44p. (J). 9.95 *(978-1-60115-231-2(0));* pap. 4.99 *(978-1-60115-232-9(9))* Treasure Bay, Inc.
Blevins, Wiley. Count on It. Kreloff, Elliott, illus. 2016. (Basic Concepts Ser.). (ENG.). 24p. (J). (gr. -1-1). lib. bdg. 14.99 *(978-1-63440-081-7(X))* Red Chair Pr.
Bluthenthal, Diana Cain. I'm Not Invited? Bluthenthal, Diana Cain, illus. 2008. (ENG., Illus.). 32p. (J). (gr. -1-2). 10.99 *(978-1-4169-7141-2(6),* Aladdin) Simon & Schuster Children's Publishing.
Bonwill, Ann. I Don't Want to Be a Pea! Rickerty, Simon, illus. 2012. (ENG.). 32p. (J). (gr. -1-1). 14.99 *(978-1-4424-3614-5(X),* Atheneum Bks. for Young Readers) Simon & Schuster Children's Publishing.
Border, Terry & Mack, Jeff. Happy Birthday, Cupcake! Border, Terry, illus. 2015. (ENG., Illus.). 32p. (J). (gr. k-3). bds. 17.99 *(978-0-399-17160-4(6),* Philomel Bks.) Penguin Young Readers Group.
Bowe, Julie. Birthday Glamour! 2015. (Victoria Torres, Unfortunately Average Ser.). (ENG.). 160p. (gr. 4-4). lib. bdg. 26.65 *(978-1-4965-0533-0(6))* Stone Arch Bks.
—Dance Fever. 2017. (Victoria Torres, Unfortunately Average Ser.). (ENG.). 160p. (gr. 4-4). lib. bdg. 26.65 *(978-1-4965-3819-2(6))* Stone Arch Bks.
Bower, Gary. There's a Party in Heaven! Bower, Jan, illus. 2007. 31p. (J). 11.99 *(978-0-9704621-8-3(2))* Storybook Meadow Publishing.
Bowman, Crystal. The Story of the Resurrection Eggs, 1 vol. Johnson, Richard G., illus. 2013. (ENG.). 40p. (J). 7.99 *(978-0-310-72595-4(X))* Zonderkidz.
Branning, Debe. The Adventures of Chickolet Pigolet: The Bribe of Frankenbeans. Knold, Nijlon, illus. 2008. 48p. pap. 7.95 *(978-1-935137-40-5(9))* Guardian Angel Publishing, Inc.
Brendler, Carol. Not Very Scary. Pizzoli, Greg, illus. 2014. (ENG.). 40p. (J). (gr. -1-1). 12.99 *(978-0-374-35547-0(9),* 9780374355470, Farrar, Straus & Giroux (BYR)) Farrar, Straus & Giroux.
Brian, Kate, pseud. Sweet 16. 2007. (ENG.). 288p. (YA). (gr. 7-12). pap. 9.99 *(978-1-4169-0033-7(0),* Simon & Schuster Bks. For Young Readers) Simon & Schuster Bks. For Young Readers.
—Vengeance. 2011. (Private Ser.). (ENG.). 240p. (YA). (gr. 9). pap. 9.99 *(978-1-4169-8473-3(9),* Simon & Schuster Bks. For Young Readers) Simon & Schuster Bks. For Young Readers.
Bridwell, Norman. Clifford's Birthday Party. Bridwell, Norman, illus. 50th anniv. ed. 2013. (Clifford Ser.). (ENG., Illus.). 32p. (J). (gr. -1-3). pap. 4.99 *(978-0-545-47956-1(8))* Scholastic, Inc.
Brown, Monica. Marisol McDonald & the Clash Bash/Marisol Mcdonald y la Fiesta Sin Igual. Palacios, Sara, illus. 2013. (Marisol Mcdonald Ser.). (ENG & SPA.). 40p. (J). 18.95 *(978-0-89239-273-5(8))* Lee & Low Bks., Inc.
Brown, Tameka Fryer. Around Our Way on Neighbors' Day. Riley-Webb, Charlotte, illus. 2010. (ENG.). 32p. (J). (gr. k-2). 16.95 *(978-0-8109-8971-9(9),* Abrams Bks. for Young Readers) Abrams, Inc.
Browne, Anthony. What If... ? Browne, Anthony, illus. 2014. (ENG., Illus.). 32p. (J). (gr. k-3). 16.99 *(978-0-7636-7419-9(2))* Candlewick Pr.
Brownlee, Sophia Grace & McClelland, Rosie. Tea Time with Sophia Grace & Rosie. McNicholas, Shelagh, illus. 2013. (J). (ENG.). 40p. (gr. -1-k). 17.99 *(978-0-545-50214-6(4));* pap. *(978-0-545-58534-7(1))* Scholastic, Inc. (Orchard Bks.).
Bruton, W., illus. The Dogs' Grand Dinner Party. 2011. (American Antiquarian Society Ser.). (ENG.). 16p. (gr. 1). 24.95 *(978-1-4290-9738-3(8))* Applewood Bks.
Bryant, Annie. Freaked Out. 2009. (Beacon Street Girls Ser.: 7). (ENG.). 272p. (J). (gr. 4-8). pap. 8.99 *(978-1-4169-6433-9(9),* Aladdin) Simon & Schuster Children's Publishing.
—Lucky Charm. 2009. (Beacon Street Girls Ser.: 8). (ENG.). 272p. (J). (gr. 4-8). pap. 9.99 *(978-1-4169-6434-6(7),* Aladdin) Simon & Schuster Children's Publishing.
Bryson, Theresa. Costume Party. 2011. (Early Connections Ser.). (J). *(978-1-61672-346-0(7))* Benchmark Education Co.
Buehner, Caralyn. Snowmen at Christmas. Buehner, Mark, illus. (ENG.). (J). (gr. -1-k). 2010. 28p. bds. 6.99 *(978-0-8037-3551-4(0))* 2005. 32p. 16.99 *(978-0-8037-2995-7(2))* Penguin Young Readers Group. (Dial Bks).
Bunting, Eve. Frog & Friends: Party at the Pond. 2011. (I am A Reader! Ser.). (ENG., Illus.). 40p. (gr. k-3). lib. bdg. 9.95 *(978-1-58536-549-4(1))* Sleeping Bear Pr.
Burkhart, Jessica. Masquerade. 2012. (Canterwood Crest Ser.: 16). lib. bdg. 18.40 *(978-0-606-26887-5(1),* Turtleback) Turtleback Bks.
Butler, Kristi T. A Big Surprise. Paparone, Pamela, illus. 2005. (Green Light Readers Level 1 Ser.). (ENG.). 24p. (J). (gr. -1-3). pap. 3.95 *(978-0-15-205141-9(4))* Houghton Mifflin Harcourt Publishing Co.
Byrd, Cari Grigsby. Where Did Pop Pop Go? 2013. 24p. pap. 24.95 *(978-1-62709-967-7(0))* America Star Bks.
Byrne, Marlene F. Ghost in the Graveyard. Graber, Jesse, illus. 2010. 57p. (J). pap. 9.99 *(978-0-9777135-4-7(7))* Celtic Marketing Inc.
Cabot, Meg. Party Princess. (ENG., (YA). 2006. (Princess Diaries: Vol. 7). Illus.). 304p. (gr. 7-12). 16.99 *(978-0-06-072453-5(6))* Vol. VII. 2008. (Princess Diaries: 7). 320p. (gr. 8). pap. 9.99 *(978-0-06-154374-6(8),* HarperTeen) HarperCollins Pubs.
Cabrera, Jane. One, Two, Buckle My Shoe. 2009. (ENG., Illus.). 32p. (J). (gr. -1-k). 16.95 *(978-0-8234-2230-2(5))* Holiday Hse., Inc.
Calford, Farley. The Complete Disaster, Rhonda's Birthday Party. 2009. 86p. pap. 9.95 *(978-1-60860-210-0(9),* Eloquent Bks.) Strategic Book Publishing & Rights Agency (SBPRA).
Callies, Debi. Frog Mill. 2008. 20p. pap. 24.95 *(978-1-60703-091-1(8))* America Star Bks.
Cammuso, Frank. Big Birthday Bash. 2014. (Misadventures of Salem Hyde Ser.). (ENG., Illus.). 96p. (J). (gr. 1-4). 14.95 *(978-1-4197-1025-4(7),* Amulet Bks.) Abrams, Inc.
Candau, Brittany. Cinderella. Godbey, Cory, illus. 2015. (ENG.). 40p. (J). (gr. -1-k). 16.99 *(978-1-4847-2360-9(0))* Disney Pr.
Captain Awesome Gets a Hole-In-One. 2014. (Captain Awesome Ser.: 12). (ENG., Illus.). 128p. (J). (gr. k-4). pap. 5.99 *(978-1-4814-1431-9(3),* Little Simon) Little Simon.
Carr, Lynn. Marty Likes to Party! 2011. 20p. pap. 11.99 *(978-1-4634-4418-1(4))* AuthorHouse.
Cecil, Lauren. Lalaloopsy: Cinder Slippers & the Grand Ball. Hill, Prescott, illus. 2013. (Lalaloopsy Ser.). (ENG.). 24p. (J). (gr. -1-3). pap. 3.99 *(978-0-545-47769-7(7))* Scholastic, Inc.
Cecil, Lauren & Scholastic, Inc. Staff. Party Time! Hill, Prescott, illus. 2011. (Lalaloopsy Ser.: 2). (ENG.). 24p. (J). (gr. -1-3). pap. 3.99 *(978-0-545-37998-4(9))* Scholastic, Inc.
Chan, Ruth. Where's the Party? 2016. (Georgie & Friends Ser.). (ENG., Illus.). 40p. (J). 17.99 *(978-1-62672-269-9(2),* 9781626722699) Roaring Brook Pr.
Chanda, J-P. Happy Birthday, SpongeBob! Martinez, Heather, illus. 2005. (SpongeBob SquarePants Ser.). (ENG.). 24p. (J). pap. 3.99 *(978-0-689-87674-5(2),* Simon Spotlight/Nickelodeon) Simon Spotlight/Nickelodeon.
Chase, Kit. Lulu's Party. Chase, Kit, illus. 2015. (ENG., Illus.). 32p. (J). (gr. -1-k). 16.99 *(978-0-399-25701-8(2),* G.P. Putnam's Sons Books for Young Readers) Penguin Young Readers Group.
Chef Jeff. Do Cows Eat Cake? 2008. 28p. pap. 13.99 *(978-1-4389-0494-8(0))* AuthorHouse.
Chloe Cow & the Party. 2004. (Play Pals Ser.). (Illus.). 12p. (J). bds. *(978-1-84229-644-8(2))* Top That! Publishing PLC.
Christopher, Matt. On Thin Ice. Koelsch, Michael, illus. 4th ed. 2004. (ENG.). 64p. (J). (gr. 1-4). pap. 13.99 *(978-0-316-73739-5(9))* Little, Brown Bks. for Young Readers.
Civardi, Anne. Going to a Party. Watt, Fiona, ed. Cartwright, Stephen, illus. 2007. (Usborne First Experiences Ser.). 16p. (J). (gr. -1-3). pap. 4.99 *(978-0-7945-1011-4(6),* Usborne) EDC Publishing.
Clar, David Austin & David Austin Clar Studio Staff, illus. Surprise Party. 2003. (Rainbow Fish & Friends Ser.). (ENG.).

PQR

24p. (J). (gr. -1-2). 9.95 *(978-1-59014-114-4(8))* North-South Bks., Inc.

Clark, Eleanor. Mary Elizabeth: Welcome to America. 2007. (Eleanor Ser.: Bk. 1). (Illus.). 187p. (J). (gr. 4-7). 14.99 *(978-0-9753036-7-2(8))* HonorNet.

Claus, Nancy. Santa's Prize. Ferchaud, Steve, illus. 2006. (J). *(978-0-9746747-5-9(3))* Cypress Bay Publishing.

Cohen, Jerianne. Max A. Million's Birthday Party. 2008. 193p. pap. 24.95 *(978-1-60672-844-4(X))* America Star Bks.

Cohen, Lee. The Surprise Party. Neuville, Loyal de, illus. 2010. (ENG.). 32p. (J). (gr. -1-12). lib. bdg. 16.95 *(978-1-934960-85-1(3),* Raven Tree Pr.,Csi) Continental Sales, Inc.

Cohn, Rachel. Kill All Happies. 2017. (ENG.). 288p. (YA). (gr. 9-17). 17.99 *(978-1-4231-5722-9(2))* Hyperion Pr.

Colfer, Chris. Trollbella Throws a Party: A Tale from the Land of Stories. Dorman, Brandon, illus. 2017. (ENG.). 32p. (J). (gr. -1-3). 17.99 *(978-0-316-38340-0(6))* Little Brown & Co.

Constantin, Pascale, illus. Little Monster. 2007. (I'm Going to Read(r) Ser.). (ENG.). 28p. (J). (gr. -1-k). pap. 3.95 *(978-1-4027-2078-9(5))* Sterling Publishing Co., Inc.

Cook, Tina H. Lindsey & the Yellow Masterpiece. 2011. 36p. pap. 15.99 *(978-1-4634-0306-5(2))* AuthorHouse.

Coombs, Kate & Austen, Jane. Goodnight Mr. Darcy: A Babylit Parody, 1 vol. 2014. (ENG., Illus.). 32p. (J). 16.99 *(978-1-4236-3670-0(8))* Gibbs Smith, Publisher.

Corderoy, Tracey. More! Warnes, Tim, illus. 2015. (ENG.). 32p. (J). (gr. -1-3). 16.99 *(978-1-58925-193-9(8))* Tiger Tales.

Coulton, Mia. Danny's Party. Coulton, Mia, photos by. 2004. (ENG., Illus.). (J). pap. 5.35 *(978-0-9746475-1-7(9))* Maryruth Bks., Inc.

Cousins, C. J. Bailey & Friends Have a Party. 2012. 16p. pap. 15.99 *(978-1-4772-7346-3(8))* AuthorHouse.

Cousins, Lucy. Maisy's Birthday Party Sticker Book. Cousins, Lucy, illus. 2015. (Maisy Ser.). (ENG., Illus.). 16p. (J). (gr. -1-2). pap. 7.99 *(978-0-7636-7735-0(3))* Candlewick Pr.

Cox, Judy. Happy Birthday, Mrs. Millie!, 0 vols. Mathieu, Joe, illus. 2012. (ENG.). 32p. (J). (gr. k-3). 16.99 *(978-0-7614-6126-5(4),* 9780761461265, Amazon Children's Publishing) Amazon Publishing.

Crawford, Shannon Joseph. Halloween War. 2011. 88p. pap. 19.95 *(978-1-61546-348-0(8))* America Star Bks.

Cross, Gillian & Quarto Generic Staff. The Roman Beanfeast. Asquith, Ros, illus. rev. ed. 2014. (ENG.). 88p. (J). (gr. 2-5). pap. 7.99 *(978-1-84780-488-4(8),* Frances Lincoln) Quarto Publishing Group UK GBR. Dist: Hachette Bk. Group.

Crow, Melinda Melton. Little Lizard's Big Party, 1 vol. Rowland, Andrew, illus. 2010. (Little Lizards Ser.). (ENG.). 32p. (gr. -1-1). lib. bdg. 22.65 *(978-1-4342-2007-3(9))* Stone Arch Bks.

—Little Lizard's Big Party. Rowland, Andrew & Rowlands, Andy, illus. 2010. (Little Lizards Ser.). (ENG.). 32p. (gr. -1-1). pap. 6.25 *(978-1-4342-2791-1(X))* Stone Arch Bks.

—Rocky & Daisy & the Birthday Party. Sassin, Eva, illus. 2013. (My Two Dogs Ser.). (ENG.). 32p. (gr. 1-3). pap. 29.70 *(978-1-4342-6296-7(0));* (gr. 2-3). pap. 5.95 *(978-1-4342-6205-9(7));* (gr. 2-3). lib. bdg. 22.65 *(978-1-4342-6011-6(9))* Stone Arch Bks.

Crowne, Alyssa. Pink Princess Rules the School. Alder, Charlotte, illus. 2009. 80p. (J). pap. *(978-0-545-16077-3(4))* Scholastic, Inc.

Czajak, Paul. Monster Needs a Party. Grieb, Wendy, illus. 2015. (Monster & Me Ser.). (ENG.). 32p. (J). (-k). 16.95 *(978-1-938063-55-8(4),* Mighty Media Kids) Mighty Media Pr.

Dale, Penny. Dinosaur Zoom! Dale, Penny, illus. (ENG., Illus.). (J). (-k). 2014. 24p. bds. 6.99 *(978-0-7636-7394-9(3))* 2013. 32p. 15.99 *(978-0-7636-6448-0(0))* Candlewick Pr. (Nosy Crow).

Darsana, Nam Aste. Guppie: God's Unified Perfect Plan Inspiring Everyone. 2011. 40p. pap. 21.99 *(978-1-4628-4535-4(5))* Xlibris Corp.

David Austin Clar Studio Staff, illus. Surprise Party. 2003. (Rainbow Fish & Friends Ser.). (ENG.). 24p. (J). (gr. -1). 3.99 *(978-1-59014-107-6(5))* North-South Bks., Inc.

Day, Alexandra. Carl's Snowy Afternoon. Day, Alexandra, illus. 2009. (Carl Ser.). (ENG., Illus.). 32p. (J). (gr. -1-1). 13.99 *(978-0-374-31086-8(6),* 9780374310868, Farrar, Straus & Giroux (BYR)) Farrar, Straus & Giroux.

De la Cruz, Melissa. Masquerade. 2008. (Blue Bloods Ser.). (ENG.). 336p. (J). (gr. 5-9). pap. 9.99 *(978-1-4231-0127-7(8))* Hyperion Pr.

Dean, Karen. Kitty Kate's Tea Party. Dean, Karen, illus. 2009. (ENG., Illus.). 48p. (J). *(978-1-934363-30-0(8))* Zoe Life Publishing.

deGroat, Diane. Happy Birthday to You, You Belong in a Zoo. deGroat, Diane, illus. 2007. (Gilbert & Friends Ser.). (ENG., Illus.). 32p. (J). (gr. -1-3). pap. 6.99 *(978-0-06-001029-4(0))* HarperCollins Pubs.

—Happy Birthday to You, You Belong in a Zoo. deGroat, Diane, illus. 2007. (Gilbert & Friends Ser.). (Illus.). (gr. -1-3). 17.00 *(978-0-7569-8108-2(5))* Perfection Learning Corp.

Deich, Cheri Bivin. The Messy Monkey Tea Party. Genth, Christina, illus. 2007. 32p. (J). (gr. -1-3). 15.95 *(978-1-60108-006-6(9))* Red Cygnet Pr.

Denton, P. J. Pony Party! Denos, Julia, illus. 5th ed. 2008. (Sleepover Squad Ser.: 5). (ENG.). 96p. (J). (gr. 1-4). pap. 4.99 *(978-1-4169-5931-1(9),* Aladdin) Simon & Schuster Children's Publishing.

dePaola, Tomie. Four Friends in Autumn. dePaola, Tomie, illus. 2004. (ENG., Illus.). 32p. (J). (gr. -1-3). 17.99 *(978-0-689-85980-9(5),* Simon & Schuster Bks. For Young Readers) Simon & Schuster Bks. For Young Readers.

Desbordes, Astrid. Edmond, the Moonlit Party. Boutavant, Marc, illus. 2015. (ENG.). 32p. (J). (gr. -1-3). 17.95 *(978-1-59270-174-2(4))* Enchanted Lion Bks., LLC.

Dewdney, Anna. Llama Llama - Birthday Party! Dewdney, Anna, illus. 2013. (Llama Llama Ser.). (ENG., Illus.). 16p. (J). (gr. -1-k). 6.99 *(978-0-448-45880-9(2),* Grosset & Dunlap) Penguin Young Readers Group.

Dey, Lorraine. The Rainforest Party / Fiesta en el bosque Tropical. 2012. (ENG.). 32p. 16.95 *(978-1-936299-28-7(3),* Raven Tree Pr.,Csi) Continental Sales, Inc.

Disney Book Group Staff. Haunted Clubhouse. 2010. (ENG., Illus.). 12p. (J). (gr. -1-k). bds. 6.99 *(978-1-4231-2832-8(X))* Disney Pr.

Disney Book Group Staff & Green, Rico. Cinderella: A Night at the Ball. Disney Storybook Art Team & Disney Book Group Staff, illus. 2015. (ENG.). 24p. (J). (gr. -1-k). pap. 3.99 *(978-1-4847-1111-8(4))* Disney Pr.

—Whisker Haven Tales: A Paw-Fect Party! Disney Storybook Art Team, illus. 2015. (ENG.). 48p. (J). (gr. -1-k). 12.99 *(978-1-4847-2995-3(1))* Disney Pr.

Disney Book Group Staff & Higginson, Sheila Sweeny. Henry Hugglemonster Pet Party. Disney Storybook Artists Staff & Disney Storybook Art Team, illus. 2014. (ENG.). 24p. (J). (gr. -1-k). pap. 4.99 *(978-1-4847-0263-5(8))* Disney Pr.

Disney Minnie Mouse Staff. Flutter Bow Fun. 2014. (ENG.). 14p. (J). (gr. -1-2). 14.99 *(978-0-7944-3025-2(2),* Reader's Digest Children's Bks.) Studio Fun International.

Disney Storybook Art Team, illus. Whisker Haven Tales - Halloween in Whisker Haven. 2016. (Read-Along Storybook & CD Ser.). (ENG.). 32p. (J). (gr. -1-k). pap. 6.99 *(978-1-4847-4707-0(0))* Disney Pr.

Donaldson, Babette. Emma Lea's First Tea Party. Van Dijk, Jerianne, illus. 2007. (ENG.). 32p. (J). 16.95 *(978-0-9792612-0-6(1))* Blue Gate Bks.

Donaldson, Joan. The Secret of the Red Shoes. Ettinger, Doris, illus. 2006. (ENG.). 32p. (J). (gr. -1-3). 8.95 *(978-0-8249-5522-9(6),* Ideal Pubns.) Worthy Publishing.

Doodler, Todd H. One Potato, Two Potato. Doodler, Todd H., illus. 2013. (ENG., Illus.). 32p. (J). (gr. -1-k). 14.99 *(978-1-4424-8517-4(5),* Little Simon) Little Simon.

Dooley, Norah. Everybody Brings Noodles. Thornton, Peter J., illus. 40p. (J). 2005. (ENG.). (gr. k-3). pap. 6.95 *(978-1-57505-916-7(9))* 2003. (gr. -1-3). 15.95 *(978-0-87614-455-8(5),* Carolrhoda Bks.) Lerner Publishing Group.

Dougherty, Brandi. The Valentine's Day Disaster. 2008. 204p. (J). pap. *(978-0-545-03168-4(0))* Scholastic, Inc.

Down, Reg. The Magic Knot: And other Tangles. 2007. (Illus.). 100p. (J). per. 14.95 *(978-0-9794452-0-0(5))* Lightly Pr.

Downing, Erin. A Funny Thing about Love: Dancing Queen; Prom Crashers; Drive Me Crazy. 2011. (ENG.). 656p. (YA). (gr. 7). pap. 9.99 *(978-1-4424-0645-2(3),* Simon Pulse) Simon Pulse.

Dyckman, Ame. Tea Party Rules. Campbell, K. G., illus. 2013. (ENG.). 36p. (J). (gr. -1-k). 16.99 *(978-0-670-78501-8(6),* Viking Books for Young Readers) Penguin Young Readers Group.

Easley, Terriana. Bubbles & Elle: A Party for Elle. 2011. 28p. pap. 24.95 *(978-1-4626-3635-8(7))* America Star Bks.

Eastman, P. D. Go, Dog. Go! 2015. (Big Bright & Early Board Book Ser.). (ENG., Illus.). 24p. (J). (gr. -1-2). bds. 6.99 *(978-0-553-52109-2(8),* Random Hse. Bks. for Young Readers) Random Hse. Children's Bks.

Eggleton, Jill. Clown's Party. Smith, Craig, illus. 2003. (Rigby Sails Early Ser.). (ENG.). 16p. (gr. 1-2). pap. 6.95 *(978-0-7578-8669-0(8))* Houghton Mifflin Harcourt Publishing Co.

Ehlert, Lois. Boo to You! Ehlert, Lois, illus. 2009. (ENG., Illus.). 42p. (J). (gr. -1-2). 17.99 *(978-1-4169-8625-6(1),* Beach Lane Bks.) Beach Lane Bks.

Elizabeth's Story 1848. 2014. (Secrets of the Manor Ser.: 3). (ENG., Illus.). 160p. (J). (gr. 3-7). pap. 6.99 *(978-1-4814-1840-9(8),* Simon Spotlight) Simon Spotlight.

Ellis, Kim. Bernard & His Dad. 2005. 49p. pap. 16.95 *(978-1-4137-7058-2(4))* America Star Bks.

Elrod, Julie. Splitting Hares. 2008. 36p. pap. 16.50 *(978-1-60693-484-5(8),* Eloquent Bks.) Strategic Book Publishing & Rights Agency (SBPRA).

Emanuel, Effie Ann. The Penguin Party, 1 vol. 2009. 32p. pap. 24.95 *(978-1-60813-544-8(6))* America Star Bks.

English, Karen. Birthday Blues. Freeman, Laura, illus. 2010. (ENG.). 96p. (J). (gr. 1-4). pap. 5.99 *(978-0-547-24893-6(8))* Houghton Mifflin Harcourt Publishing Co.

—Nikki & Deja. Freeman, Laura, illus. 2009. (ENG.). 80p. (J). (gr. -1-3). pap. 5.99 *(978-0-547-13362-1(6))* Houghton Mifflin Harcourt Publishing Co.

Eone, illus. Peppa's Halloween Party. 2016. (Peppa Pig Ser.). (ENG.). 24p. (J). (gr. -1-k). 4.99 *(978-0-545-92543-3(6))* Scholastic, Inc.

Epstein, Robin. First Pajama Party: Slumberrific Six. 2005. (Groovy Girls Ser.). (ENG., Illus.). 80p. (J). (gr. 2-5). 3.99 *(978-0-439-81431-7(6))* Scholastic, Inc.

Esbaum, Jill. If a T. Rex Crashes Your Birthday Party. Tolstikova, Daria & Tolstikova, Dasha, illus. 2016. (ENG.). 40p. (J). (gr. -1-2). 14.95 *(978-1-4549-1550-8(1))* Sterling Publishing Co., Inc.

Eubank, Patricia Reeder. Halloween 123s. Eubank, Patricia Reeder, illus. 2011. (Illus.). 22p. (J). bds. 6.99 *(978-0-8249-1868-2(1),* Ideal Pubns.) Worthy Publishing.

Evans, Cordelia. OLIVIA & the Fancy Party. Johnson, Shane L., illus. 2014. (Olivia TV Tie-In Ser.). (ENG.). 24p. (J). (gr. -1-2). pap. 3.99 *(978-1-4814-0364-1(8),* Simon Spotlight) Simon Spotlight.

—Olivia & the Fancy Party. 2014. (Olivia 8x8 Ser.). lib. bdg. 13.55 *(978-0-606-35762-3(9))* Turtleback Bks.

Evans, Rosemary R. The Little Princesses Magial Party. Taylor, Erin, illus. 2012. 40p. (J). 16.95 *(978-1-60743-759-8(7))* Wink Publishing.

Evans, Yvette Kemp. If I Take a Shower. 2008. 32p. pap. 24.95 *(978-1-4241-9953-2(0))* America Star Bks.

Facey, La-Toya S. Brielle-Elaine Tries to Fit In! 2011. 24p. pap. 14.99 *(978-1-4634-2353-7(5))* AuthorHouse.

Farrell, Connie. Sam's Harvest Party, 1 vol. Ellingsworth, Colleen, illus. 2009. 29p. pap. 24.95 *(978-1-60813-937-8(9))* America Star Bks.

Fazio, Maria R. Block Party! 2013. 28p. pap. 24.95 *(978-1-4241-2603-3(7))* America Star Bks.

Feldman, Thea. Princess Party. 2006. 3p. 5.99 *(978-1-932915-33-4(8))* Sandvik Publishing.

Fernandez, Joyce & Marsh, Laura. Eins und Zwei are One & Two. 2009. 22p. 15.95 *(978-0-578-00208-8(6))* My Second Language Publishing, USA.

—Un et Deux are One & Two. 2009. 22p. 15.95 *(978-0-615-26239-0(2))* My Second Language Publishing, USA.

—Un Is One. 2009. 21p. 15.95 *(978-0-615-26238-3(4))* My Second Language Publishing, USA.

—Uno Is One. 2009. 22p. 15.95 *(978-0-615-24460-0(2))* My Second Language Publishing, USA.

—Uno y Dos are One & Two. 2008. 22p. pap. 15.95 *(978-0-615-26150-8(7))* My Second Language Publishing, USA.

Figueroa, Juanita Kimberly. Kendra Gives a Birthday Party. 2012. 24p. pap. 24.95 *(978-1-4626-6009-4(6))* PublishAmerica, Inc.

Finzi, Ama. At Baba's House. 2011. 36p. pap. 16.46 *(978-1-4269-7095-5(1))* Trafford Publishing.

Fisch, Sholly & Age, Heroic. Happy Birthday, Superman!, 1 vol. Bone, J., illus. 2014. (DC Super Friends Ser.). (ENG.). 32p. (gr. 1-2). 22.60 *(978-1-4342-9222-3(3))* Stone Arch Bks.

Fisch, Sholly & Wolfram, Amy. Party, Party! 2015. (Teen Titans Go! Graphic Novels Ser.: 1). lib. bdg. 24.50 *(978-0-606-37251-0(2))* Turtleback Bks.

Fischer, Kelly. The Moon Throws a Birthday Party. Duckworth, Michelle, illus. 2011. (ENG.). 32p. (J). 19.50 *(978-1-58385-237-8(9))* ktf-writers-studio.

Fitzgerald, Caroline. Animal Kingdom Goes to New York. 2011. 48p. pap. 18.46 *(978-1-4520-9966-8(9))* AuthorHouse.

Fleischman, Sid. The Giant Rat of Sumatra. Hendrix, John, illus. 2005. 208p. (J). (gr. 5-18). 15.99 *(978-0-06-074238-6(0))* HarperCollins Pubs.

Flor Ada, Alma. Dear Peter Rabbit. Tryon, Leslie, illus. 2006. (Stories to Go! Ser.). (J). (gr. k-3). 12.65 *(978-0-7569-7322-3(8))* Perfection Learning Corp.

Flowerpot Press, contrib. by. Sockheadz: Party. 2013. (ENG., Illus.). 20p. (J). (gr. -1-k). 8.99 *(978-1-77093-617-1(3))* Flowerpot Children's Pr. Inc. CAN. Dist: Cardinal Pubs. Group.

Freedman, Claire. Dragon Jelly. Hendra, Sue, illus. 2015. (ENG.). 32p. (J). (gr. k-3). 14.99 *(978-1-61963-682-8(4),* 9781619636828, Bloomsbury USA Childrens) Bloomsbury Publishing USA.

French, Vivian. Emily Mouse's Birthday Party. Marshall, Mark, illus. 2016. (Early Reader Ser.). (ENG.). 64p. (J). (gr. k-3). 6.99 *(978-1-4440-1614-7(8),* Orion Children's Bks.) Hachette Children's Group GBR. Dist: Hachette Bk. Group.

Friedman, Laurie. Mallory's Super Sleepover. Kalis, Jennifer, illus. (Mallory Ser.: 16). (ENG.). 160p. (J). (gr. 2-5). 2012. pap. 5.95 *(978-1-4677-0209-6(9))*No. 16. 2011. 15.95 *(978-0-8225-8887-0(0))* Lerner Publishing Group. (Darby Creek).

—Ruby Valentine Saves the Day. Avril, Lynne, illus. 2010. (Carolrhoda Picture Bks.). (ENG.). 32p. (J). (gr. k-3). lib. bdg. 16.95 *(978-0-7613-4213-7(3))* Lerner Publishing Group.

Fronis, Aly. This Little Bunny. Rescek, Sanja, illus. 2016. (ENG.). 16p. (J). (gr. -1-1). bds. 5.99 *(978-1-4998-0105-7(X))* Little Bee Books Inc.

Furgang, Kathy. A Rainbow Party: Set Of 6. 2011. (Early Connections Ser.). (J). pap. 37.00 net. *(978-1-4108-1363-3(0))* Benchmark Education Co.

Gajewski, Lois. Benny, the Stubborn Bubble. 2011. 28p. (gr. 1-2). pap. 12.03 *(978-1-4567-4703-9(7))* AuthorHouse.

Gallagher, Diana G. Party! The Complicated Life of Claudia Cristina Cortez, 1 vol. Garvey, Brann, illus. 2008. (Claudia Cristina Cortez Ser.). (ENG.). 88p. (gr. 2-3). pap. 6.10 *(978-1-4342-0867-5(2));* lib. bdg. 26.65 *(978-1-4342-0771-5(4))* Stone Arch Bks. (Claudia Cristina Cortez).

Gallo, Tina. OLIVIA & the Christmas Party. Rose, Drew, illus. 2011. (Olivia TV Tie-In Ser.). (ENG.). 32p. (J). (gr. -1-1). 4.99 *(978-1-4424-3070-9(2),* Simon Scribbles) Simon Scribbles.

—Olivia Wishes on a Star. 2014. (Olivia 8x8 Ser.). lib. bdg. 13.55 *(978-0-606-36118-7(9))* Turtleback Bks.

Garratt, Irene Joyce. Happy Birthday: Two in One Stories. 2009. (Illus.). 12p. pap. 8.49 *(978-1-4389-4304-6(0))* AuthorHouse.

Gaston, Sharon D. Clean Your Own House & Misery Loves Company. 2009. 40p. pap. 18.50 *(978-1-4389-7831-4(6))* AuthorHouse.

Gates, Josephine Scribner. The live dolls' house Party. Keep, Virginia, illus. 2007. 104p. (J). lib. bdg. 59.00 *(978-1-60304-005-1(6))* Dollworks.

Gibbs, Lynne. Molly Mouse Is Shy: A Story of Shyness. Mitchell, Melanie, illus. 2009. (Let's Grow Together Ser.). 32p. (J). (gr. -1-2). pap. 10.55 *(978-1-60754-761-7(9));* lib. bdg. 22.60 *(978-1-60754-756-3(2))* Windmill Bks.

Gilson. Melusine Vol. 3: The Vampires' Ball. 2008. (Melusine Ser.: 3). (ENG., Illus.). 48p. (J). (gr. 4-7). pap. 11.95 *(978-1-905460-69-4(4))* CineBook GBR. Dist: National Bk. Network.

Glover, Dennis W. The Talking Flower. 2010. 32p. pap. 12.99 *(978-1-4490-5599-8(0))* AuthorHouse.

Godin, Thelma Lynne. Hula-Hoopin' Queen. Brantley-Newton, Vanessa, illus. 2014. (ENG.). 40p. (J). 18.95 *(978-1-60060-846-9(9))* Lee & Low Bks., Inc.

Godwin, Jane & Bell, Davina. Hattie Helps Out. Blackwood, Freya, illus. 2016. (ENG.). 32p. (J). (gr. -1-k). 19.99 *(978-1-74343-543-4(6))* Allen & Unwin AUS. Dist: Independent Pubs. Group.

Golden Books. Puppy Birthday to You! (Paw Patrol) Petrossi, Fabrizio, illus. 2015. (Little Golden Book Ser.). (ENG.). 24p. (J). (-k). 4.99 *(978-0-553-52277-8(9),* Golden Bks.) Random Hse. Children's Bks.

Golden Books Staff. Jumbo Coloring Party. Golden Books Staff, illus. 2010. (Jumbo Coloring Book Ser.). (ENG., Illus.). 224p. (J). (gr. -1-2). pap. 5.99 *(978-0-375-86352-3(4),* Golden Bks.) Random Hse. Children's Bks.

Gonzalez Bertrand, Diane. The Ruiz Street Kids (Los Muchachos de la Calle Ruiz) Ventura, Gabriela Baeza, tr. 2006. (ENG & SPA., Illus.). (J). pap. 9.95 *(978-1-55885-321-8(9),* Piñata Books) Arte Publico Pr.

Goodhart, Pippa. Hoppy Birthday, Jo-Jo! Birkett, Georgie, illus. 2005. (Green Bananas Ser.). (ENG.). 48p. (J). lib. bdg. *(978-0-7787-1025-7(4))* Crabtree Publishing Co.

Gownley, Jim. Amelia in Loosely in Disguise & Frightened: #3, 1 vol. Gownley, Jim, illus. 2011. (Amelia Rules! Ser.). (ENG., Illus.). 36p. 24.21 *(978-1-59961-789-3(7))* Spotlight.

Green, D. L. Zeke Meeks vs the Big Blah-Rific Birthday, 1 vol. Alves, Josh, illus. 2013. (Zeke Meeks Ser.). (ENG.). 128p. (gr. 2-2). 8.95 *(978-1-4048-8105-1(0));* lib. bdg. 22.65 *(978-1-4048-7637-8(5))* Picture Window Bks. (Zeke Meeks).

Gresh, Dannah. Secret Keeper Girl Pajama Party. 2014. (ENG.). 64p. (J). pap. 12.99 *(978-0-7369-6002-1(3))* Harvest Hse. Pubs.

Gritton, Steve. The Kandy Witch. 2007. (Illus.). (J). 18.95 *(978-0-9795361-0-6(3))* Bad Frog Art/SMG Bks.

Grosset & Dunlap. Ruby's Tea Party. 2016. (Penguin Young Readers Level 2 Ser.). lib. bdg. 13.55 *(978-0-606-38426-1(X))* Turtleback Bks.

Guest, Elissa Haden. Iris & Walter. Davenier, Christine, illus. 2006. (Iris & Walter Ser.). 43p. (gr. 1-4). 15.95 *(978-0-7569-7008-6(3))* Perfection Learning Corp.

—Iris & Walter & the Birthday Party. Davenier, Christine, illus. 2013. (Green Light Readers Level 3 Ser.). (ENG.). 44p. (J). (gr. 1-4). pap. 3.99 *(978-0-544-10498-3(6))* Houghton Mifflin Harcourt Publishing Co.

Gunnufson, Charlotte. Halloween Hustle, 0 vols. Atteberry, Kevan, illus. 2013. (ENG.). 32p. (J). (gr. -1-2). 16.99 *(978-1-4778-1723-0(9),* 9781477817230, Amazon Children's Publishing) Amazon Publishing.

Gutenberg, S. R. Abby Longbotham & the Quilt. 2008. 28p. pap. 24.95 *(978-1-4241-9428-5(8))* America Star Bks.

Guy, Ginger Foglesong. Fiesta! Moreno, Rene King, illus. 2007. (SPA.). 32p. (J). (gr. -1-3). 6.99 *(978-0-06-088226-6(3),* Greenwillow Bks.) HarperCollins Pubs.

Hacker, Erin. The Baker of Sweet City, 1 vol. 2010. 36p. pap. 24.95 *(978-1-4489-2550-6(9))* PublishAmerica, Inc.

Haesche, Richard, Sr. The Big Race. 2007. (ENG.). 222p. (J). per. 10.49 *(978-0-9798536-1-6(3))* Kreative X-Pressions Pubns.

Hale, Shannon & Hale, Dean. The Princess in Black & the Perfect Princess Party. Pham, LeUyen, illus. (Princess in Black Ser.). (ENG.). 96p. (J). (gr. k-3). 2016. pap. 6.99 *(978-0-7636-8758-8(8))* 2015. 14.99 *(978-0-7636-6511-1(8))* Candlewick Pr.

—The Princess in Black & the Perfect Princess Party. 2016. (Princess in Black Ser.: 2). lib. bdg. 17.20 *(978-0-606-37945-8(2))* Turtleback Bks.

Haley, Patty. Princess Pearl's Party (6 Pack) Woodford-Robinson, Rieko, illus. 2010. (ENG.). 12p. (gr. k-2). pap. *(978-1-61181-050-9(7),* Kaeden Bks.) Kaeden Corp.

Hall, Caroline V. Rhett & Abby: Abby's New Home. 2011. 40p. pap. 15.95 *(978-1-4497-1887-9(6),* WestBow Pr.) Author Solutions, Inc.

Hall, Kirsten. Birthday Beastie: All about Counting. Luedecke, Bev, illus. 2003. (Beastieville Ser.). 32p. (J). 19.50 *(978-0-516-22891-4(9),* Children's Pr.) Scholastic Library Publishing.

Hallinan, P. K. Happy Birthday! 2003. (J). (ENG., Illus.). 26p. bds. 7.95 *(978-0-8249-5453-6(X));* *(978-0-8249-6507-5(8))* Worthy Publishing. (Ideal Pubns.).

Hamilton, Tim. But! Hamilton, Tim, illus. 2014. (ENG., Illus.). 32p. (J). (gr. -1-2). 16.95 *(978-0-8234-3046-8(4))* Holiday Hse., Inc.

—Is That a Cat? 2015. (ENG., Illus.). 32p. (J). (gr. -1-3). 16.95 *(978-0-8234-3384-1(6))* Holiday Hse., Inc.

Hansen, Jeanne. Wow! an Upside down Cake Birthday Party! 2011. 24p. pap. 15.99 *(978-1-4653-6016-8(6))* Xlibris Corp.

Hanson, Warren. Bugtown Boogie. Johnson, Steve & Fancher, Lou, illus. 2008. 32p. (J). (gr. -1-3). 17.89 *(978-0-06-059938-6(3),* Geringer, Laura Book) HarperCollins Pubs.

Hapka, Catherine, pseud. Friends 4 Ever? 2008. (High School Musical Stories from East High Ser.). 124p. (J). (gr. 3-7). 12.65 *(978-0-7569-8820-3(9))* Perfection Learning Corp.

—Pony Scouts - Pony Party. Kennedy, Anne, illus. 2013. (I Can Read Level 2 Ser.). (ENG.). 32p. (J). (gr. -1-3). 16.99 *(978-0-06-208680-8(4));* pap. 3.99 *(978-0-06-208679-2(0))* HarperCollins Pubs.

Hardy, Sarah Frances. Puzzled by Pink. 2012. (ENG.). 32p. (J). (gr. -1-k). 16.99 *(978-0-670-01320-3(X),* Viking Books for Young Readers) Penguin Young Readers Group.

Hargreaves, Adam & Hargreaves, Roger. Mr. Birthday. Hargreaves, Adam, illus. 2007. (Mr. Men & Little Miss Ser.). (ENG., Illus.). 32p. (J). (gr. -1-2). mass mkt. 4.99 *(978-0-8431-2130-8(0),* Price Stern Sloan) Penguin Young Readers Group.

Harley, Bill. Bear's All-Night Party. Ferreira, Melissa, illus. 2005. (ENG.). 32p. (J). (gr. -1-2). 15.95 *(978-0-87483-572-4(0))* August Hse. Pubs., Inc.

Harrison, Hannah E. Bernice Gets Carried Away. 2015. (ENG., Illus.). 32p. (J). (gr. -1-k). 16.99 *(978-0-8037-3916-1(8),* Dial Bks) Penguin Young Readers Group.

Harrison, Jo. The Jewellery Box Fairies. 2013. (Illus.). 24p. pap. 19.82 *(978-1-4772-5112-6(X))* AuthorHouse.

Harrison, Lisi. Best Friends for Never. 2008. (Clique Novels Ser.). 197p. 20.00 *(978-1-60686-290-2(1))* Perfection Learning Corp.

Hartt-Sussman, Heather. Nana's Summer Surprise. Graham, Georgia, illus. 2013. (ENG.). 32p. (J). (gr. -1-1). 17.95 *(978-1-77049-324-7(7),* Tundra Bks.) Tundra Bks. CAN. Dist: Penguin Random Hse. LLC.

Harvey, Alex. Olivia & the Kite Party. Spaziante, Patrick, illus. 2012. (Olivia Ready-To-Read Level 1 Ser.). lib. bdg. 13.55 *(978-0-606-26360-3(8),* Turtleback) Turtleback Bks.

Harvey, Jacqueline. Clementine Rose & the Birthday Emergency. 2016. (Clementine Rose Ser.: 10). (ENG.). 160p. (J). (gr. 1-3). 8.99 *(978-0-85798-516-3(7))* Random Hse. Australia AUS. Dist: Independent Pubs. Group.

Hasbro. My Little Pony: Chapter Book Bind-Up. 2016. (ENG., Illus.). 416p. (J). (gr. 3-7). pap. 12.99 *(978-0-316-27259-9(0))* Little, Brown Bks. for Young Readers.

Hawa, Christine Elias. Joy the Girl How Never Smiled. 2011. 32p. pap. 16.19 *(978-1-4634-3636-0(X))* AuthorHouse.

Haworth, Margaret. When Daddy Goes Away: Rusty Books. Edwards, Paul, illus. l.t. ed. 2003. (Books That Help Ser.: Vol. 2). 34p. (J). (gr. -1-5). pap. 9.95 *(978-0-9740313-1-6(3))* Haworth, Margaret.

Hedgman, Janis. Party in the Garden. 2009. (Illus.). 52p. pap. *(978-1-84748-514-4(6))* Athena Pr.

Heible, Beverly. A Christmas Party on River Row. 2012. 98p. 22.95 *(978-1-62709-018-6(5))* America Star Bks.

Heim, Alastair. No Tooting at Tea. Not, Sara, illus. 2017. (ENG.). 40p. (J). (gr. -1-3). 16.99 *(978-0-544-77474-2(4),* Clarion Bks.) Houghton Mifflin Harcourt Trade & Reference Pubs.

Helms, Rhonda. Promposal. 2015. (ENG., Illus.). 224p. (YA). (gr. 7). pap. 9.99 *(978-1-4814-2231-4(6),* Simon Pulse) Simon Pulse.

Hill, Eric. Spot's Birthday Party. Hill, Eric, illus. 2007. (Spot Ser.). (ENG., Illus.). 24p. (J). (gr. -1 — 1). bds. 7.99 *(978-0-399-24770-5(X),* Warne) Penguin Young Readers Group.

Hinkler Books, ed. The Little Princess Tea Party. 2012. 40p. (J). 19.99 *(978-1-74308-402-1(1))* Hinkler Bks. Pty, Ltd. AUS. Dist: Ideals Pubns.

Hlad, Carole. Daisy's Dance Party: (from the Amanda's Cats Series) 2011. 24p. pap. 15.99 *(978-1-4628-8006-5(1))* Xlibris Corp.

Hodgson, Mona. The Princess Twins & the Tea Party, 1 vol. Olson, Julie, illus. 2016. (I Can Read! / Princess Twins Ser.). (ENG.). 32p. (J). pap. 3.99 *(978-0-310-75038-3(5))* Zonderkidz.

Hoffman, Mary Ann. Piñata Party. 2006. (Neighborhood Readers Ser.). (ENG.). 8p. (gr. -1-3). pap. 5.15 *(978-1-4042-5720-7(9),* Rosen Classroom) Rosen Publishing Group, Inc., The.

Holden, Pam. Pass It On, 6 pack. Hawley, Kelvin, illus. 2009. (Red Rocket Readers Ser.). (ENG.). 16p. (gr. 2-2). pap. *(978-1-877363-66-5(9),* Red Rocket Readers) Flying Start Bks.

—The Rainbow Party, 6 pack. Whimp, Pauline, illus. 2009. (Red Rocket Readers Ser.). (ENG.). 16p. pap. *(978-1-877363-82-5(0))* Flying Start Bks.

—Sally Snip Snap's Party, 6 pack. Storey, Jim, illus. 2009. (Red Rocket Readers Ser.). (ENG.). 16p. (gr. 2-1). pap. *(978-1-877363-57-3(X),* Red Rocket Readers) Flying Start Bks.

—The Surprise Visitor, 6 pack. Hoit, Richard, illus. 2009. (Red Rocket Readers Ser.). (ENG.). 16p. (gr. 2-2). pap. *(978-1-877363-85-6(5))* Flying Start Bks.

Holm, Jennifer L. & Holm, Matthew. Happy Birthday, Babymouse! Holm, Jennifer L. & Holm, Matthew, illus. 2014. (Babymouse Ser.: 18). (ENG., Illus.). 96p. (J). (gr. 2-5). 12.99 *(978-0-375-97097-9(5),* Random Hse. Bks. for Young Readers) Random Hse. Children's Bks.

—Happy Birthday, Babymouse. Holm, Jennifer L. & Holm, Matthew, illus. 2014. (Babymouse Ser.: 18). (ENG., Illus.). 96p. (J). (gr. 2-5). pap. 6.99 *(978-0-307-93161-0(7),* Random Hse. Bks. for Young Readers) Random Hse. Children's Bks.

—Happy Birthday, Babymouse. 2014. (Babymouse Ser.: 18). lib. bdg. 17.20 *(978-0-606-35567-4(7))* Turtleback Bks.

Holmes, Steve, illus. Animales Marinos: Mezcla y Diviertete. 2005. (Mezcla y Diviertete Ser.). (SPA.). 5p. (J). (gr. -1-7). *(978-970-718-291-2(1),* Silver Dolphin en Español) Advanced Marketing, S. de R. L. de C. V.

Holt, Kimberly Willis. Piper Reed Gets a Job. Davenier, Christine, illus. 2009. (Piper Reed Ser.: 3). (ENG.). 160p. (J). (gr. 3-6). 14.99 *(978-0-8050-8199-2(2),* 9780805081992, Holt, Henry & Co. Bks. For Young Readers) Holt, Henry & Co.

—Piper Reed, Party Planner. Davenier, Christine, illus. 2011. (Piper Reed Ser.: 3). (ENG.). 176p. (J). (gr. 3-6). pap. 7.99 *(978-0-312-61677-9(5),* 9780312616779) Square Fish.

Holub, Joan & Williams, Suzanne. Cinderella Stays Late. 2014. (Grimmtastic Girls Ser.: 1). lib. bdg. 16.00 *(978-0-606-35395-3(X))* Turtleback Bks.

Hook, Jacqueline A. You're Going to Be a Flower Girl. 2005. (J). per. *(978-0-9664783-3-4(9))* Jacqueline Beverly Hills.

Hooks, Gwendolyn. Pet Costume Party: A Pet Club Story, 1 vol. Byrne, Mike, illus. 2011. (Pet Club Ser.). (ENG.). 32p. (gr. 1-2). pap. 6.25 *(978-1-4342-3053-9(8))*; lib. bdg. 22.65 *(978-1-4342-2513-9(5))* Stone Arch Bks.

—Pets at the Party: A Pet Club Story, 1 vol. Byrne, Mike, illus. 2010. (Pet Club Ser.). (ENG & ABK.). 32p. (gr. 1-2). 22.65 *(978-1-4342-2054-7(0))*; pap. 6.25 *(978-1-4342-2796-6(0))* Stone Arch Bks.

Hordos, Sandra. Marissa Plans a Princess Tea Party. Allen, Joshua, illus. 2010. 28p. pap. 12.49 *(978-1-4520-2557-5(6))* AuthorHouse.

Horowitz, Dave. Twenty-Six Princesses. Horowitz, Dave, illus. 2008. (ENG., Illus.). 32p. (J). (gr. -1-k). 15.99 *(978-0-399-24607-4(X),* G.P. Putnam's Sons Books for Young Readers) Penguin Young Readers Group.

—Twenty-Six Princesses: An Alphabet Story. Horowitz, Dave, illus. 2011. (ENG., Illus.). 32p. (J). (gr. -1-k). pap. 6.99 *(978-0-14-241536-8(7),* Puffin Books) Penguin Young Readers Group.

Hosford, Kate. Big Birthday. Clifton-Brown, Holly, illus. 2012. (Carolrhoda Picture Bks.). (ENG.). 32p. (J). (gr. k-2). lib. bdg. 16.95 *(978-0-7613-5410-9(7))* Lerner Publishing Group.

Howe, James. Houndsley & Catina. Gay, Marie-Louise, illus. 2007. 36p. (J). (gr. k-2). lib. bdg. 12.65 *(978-0-7569-8141-9(7))* Perfection Learning Corp.

—Houndsley & Catina & the Birthday Surprise. Gay, Marie-Louise, illus. (ENG.). 48p. (J). (gr. k-4). 2013. (Candlewick Sparks Ser.). pap. 3.99 *(978-0-7636-6639-2(4))* 2006. (Houndsley & Catina Ser.: 2). 15.99 *(978-0-7636-2405-7(5))* Candlewick Pr.

—Houndsley & Catina & the Quiet Time. Gay, Marie-Louise, illus. 2013. (Candlewick Sparks Ser.). (ENG.). 48p. (J). (gr. k-4). pap. 3.99 *(978-0-7636-6863-1(X))* Candlewick Pr.

Huber, Mike. Evette's Invitation. Cowman, Joseph, illus. 2014. (ENG.). 32p. (gr. -1). 15.95 *(978-1-60554-212-6(1))* Redleaf Pr.

Hudgens, Melica, illus. Flim Flam & Other Such Gobbledygook. 2015. (J). 14.99 *(978-1-4621-1684-3(1))* Cedar Fort, Inc./CFI Distribution.

Hutchins, Hazel. Robyn's Party-in-the-Park. Cathcart, Yvonne, illus. 2005. 59p. (J). lib. bdg. 12.00 *(978-1-4242-1203-3(0))* Fitzgerald Bks.

—Robyn's Party-in-the-Park. Cathcart, Yvonne, illus. 2005. (Formac First Novels Ser.: 31). (ENG.). 64p. (J). (gr. 2-5). 14.95 *(978-0-88780-663-6(5),* 9780887806636) Formac Publishing Co., Ltd. CAN. Dist: Casemate Pubs. & Bk. Distributors, LLC.

—Robyn's Party in the Park, 1 vol. Cathcart, Yvonne, illus. 2005. (Formac First Novels Ser.: 31). (ENG.). 64p. (J). (gr. 2-5). 4.95 *(978-0-88780-662-9(7),* 9780887806629) Formac Publishing Co., Ltd. CAN. Dist: Casemate Pubs. & Bk. Distributors, LLC.

Hutchinson, Shaun David. Fml. 2013. (ENG.). 304p. (YA). (gr. 9). pap. 9.99 *(978-1-4424-3287-1(X))*; (Illus.). 17.99 *(978-1-4424-8318-7(0))* Simon Pulse. (Simon Pulse).

Idle, Molly. Tea Rex. 2013. (ENG., Illus.). 36p. (J). (gr. -1-k). 16.99 *(978-0-670-01430-9(3),* Viking Books for Young Readers) Penguin Young Readers Group.

Inches, Alison. La Quinceañera. Aikins, Dave, illus. 2006. (Dora la Exploradora Ser.). (SPA.). 24p. (J). (gr. -1-3). pap. 3.99 *(978-1-4169-2462-3(0),* Libros Para Ninos) Libros Para Ninos.

Iversen, Jeremy. Rush. 2011. (ENG.). 272p. (YA). (gr. 9). pap. 11.99 *(978-1-4424-2400-5(1),* Simon Pulse) Simon Pulse.

Izquierdo, Ana, tr. Caritas Felices: Winnie-the-Pooh. 2007. (Disney Winnie the Pooh (SilverDolphin) Ser.). (SPA., Illus.). 10p. (J). (gr. -1). bds. *(978-970-718-393-3(4),* Silver Dolphin en Español) Advanced Marketing, S. de R. L. de C. V.

Jackson, Armitra L. Eating Safe with Ace & Mace! 2007. 44p. per. 15.95 *(978-1-4327-1255-6(1))* Outskirts Pr., Inc.

Jakubowski, Michele. Party Pooper. Waters, Erica-Jane, illus. 2014. (Perfectly Poppy Ser.). (ENG.). 32p. (gr. k-2). lib. bdg. 22.65 *(978-1-4795-2282-8(1))* Picture Window Bks.

Jarman, Julia. Ants in Your Pants! Parker-Rees, Guy, illus. 2011. (ENG.). 32p. (J). (gr. -1-k). pap. 10.99 *(978-1-4083-0525-6(9))* Hodder & Stoughton GBR. Dist: Hachette Bk. Group.

Johnston, Annie Fellows. The Little Colonel's House Party. Meynell, Louis, illus. 2007. 176p. per. *(978-1-4065-3514-3(1))* Dodo Pr.

Johnston, Tony. Laugh-Out-Loud Baby. Gammell, Stephen, illus. 2012. (ENG.). 32p. (J). (gr. -1-3). 16.99 *(978-1-4424-1380-1(8),* Simon & Schuster Bks. For Young Readers) Simon & Schuster/Paula Wiseman Bks.

Jolliffe, Susan Rennick. Lady Ginny's Tea Parties, 1 vol. 2007. (ENG., Illus.). 32p. (J). (gr. -1-3). 18.95 *(978-1-55143-398-1(2))* Orca Bk. Pubs. USA.

JONAS #8: Prep School Party. 2010. 128p. pap. 4.99 *(978-1-4231-2673-7(4))* Disney Pr.

Judge, Chris. The Snow Beast. Judge, Chris, illus. 2015. (ENG., Illus.). 32p. (J). (gr. -1-3). 17.99 *(978-1-4677-9313-1(2))* Andersen Pr. GBR. Dist: Lerner Publishing Group.

Jules, Jacqueline. Abuela's Birthday. Smith, Kim, illus. 2015. (Sofia Martinez Ser.). (ENG.). 32p. (gr. k-2). lib. bdg. 21.32 *(978-1-4795-5775-2(7),* Sofia Martinez) Picture Window Bks.

Julius, Jessica. A New Reindeer Friend. 2015. lib. bdg. 13.55 *(978-0-606-36680-9(6))* Turtleback Bks.

Kann, Victoria. The Royal Tea Party. 2014. (Pinkalicious I Can Read Ser.). (J). lib. bdg. 13.55 *(978-0-606-35473-8(5))* Turtleback Bks.

Kargman, Jill & Karasyov, Carrie. Bittersweet Sixteen. 2006. (YA). (gr. 7-12). (ENG.). 240p. 15.99 *(978-0-06-077844-6(X))*; 230p. lib. bdg. 16.89 *(978-0-06-077845-3(8))* HarperCollins Pubs.

Kayler, Ralph. The Tea Party in the Tree Tops. 2009. 48p. pap. 19.49 *(978-1-4389-8000-3(0))* AuthorHouse.

Keene, Carolyn. Pool Party Puzzler. Francis, Peter, illus. 2015. (Nancy Drew Clue Book Ser.: 1). (ENG.). 96p. (J). (gr. 1-4). 16.99 *(978-1-4814-3896-4(4),* Aladdin) Simon & Schuster Children's Publishing.

Keithley, Laura Lee. Ellie's Big Day. Holliday, Holly, illus. 2008. 40p. pap. 24.95 *(978-1-60672-474-3(6))* America Star Bks.

Khan, Hana. Taylor's Birthday Party. Kemble, Mai S., illus. 2008. (J). *(978-1-60108-048-6(4))* Red Cygnet Pr.

Khan, Rukhsana. Big Red Lollipop. Blackall, Sophie, illus. 2010. (ENG.). 40p. (J). (gr. -1-3). 16.99 *(978-0-670-06287-4(1),* Viking Books for Young Readers) Penguin Young Readers Group.

Kimpton, Diana. A Surprise for Princess Ellie. Finlay, Lizzie, illus. 6th rev. ed. 2006. (ENG.). 96p. (gr. 1-4). pap. 3.99 *(978-0-7868-4875-1(8))* Hyperion Pr.

Kinra, Richa, illus. The Princess Panda Tea Party: A Cerebral Palsy Fairy Tale. 2014. 45p. (J). pap. 14.95 *(978-1-61599-219-5(7))* Loving Healing Pr., Inc.

Kirk, David. Happy Heartwood Day. 2005. (Illus.). (J). *(978-1-4156-3888-0(8),* Grosset & Dunlap) Penguin Publishing Group.

—Miss Spider's Tea Party. unabr. ed. 2008. (Scholastic Bookshelf Ser.). (ENG., Illus.). (J). (gr. -1-3). 18.95 *(978-0-545-02979-7(1))* Scholastic, Inc.

Kirk, David & Scholastic / LeapFrog. Miss Spider's Tea Party. 2008. (J). 13.99 *(978-1-59319-934-0(1))* LeapFrog Enterprises, Inc.

Kirkland, Kim M. Mi Mi's Mini Tea Party. Swope, Brenda, illus. 2011. 28p. pap. 24.95 *(978-1-4512-8099-9(8))* America Star Bks.

Klein, Abby. Halloween Parade. McKinley, John, illus. 2009. (Ready, Freddy! Reader List: No. 3). 32p. (J). *(978-0-545-14174-1(5))* Scholastic, Inc.

Klein, Adria F. Max y la Fiesta de Adopcion, 1 vol. Robledo, Sol, tr. from ENG. Gallagher-Cole, Mernie, illus. 2007. (Read-It! Readers en Español: la Vida de Max Ser.). (SPA.). 24p. (gr. -1-3). lib. bdg. 21.32 *(978-1-4048-3793-5(0),* Easy Readers) Picture Window Bks.

Kleinberg, Naomi. Abby's Pink Party. Brannon, Tom, illus. 2011. (ENG.). 12p. (J). (gr. k — 1). bds. 5.99 *(978-0-307-92956-3(6),* Random Hse. Bks. for Young Readers) Random Hse. Children's Bks.

—Elmo's Monster Mash. Moroney, Christopher, illus. 2010. (ENG.). 12p. (J). (gr. k — 1). 4.99 *(978-0-375-85804-8(0),* Random Hse. Bks. for Young Readers) Random Hse. Children's Bks.

Kline, Suzy & Wells, Rosemary. Horrible Harry & the Birthday Girl. Wummer, Amy, illus. 2016. (Horrible Harry Ser.: 34). (ENG.). 80p. (J). (gr. 2-5). bds. 14.99 *(978-0-451-47331-8(0),* Viking Books for Young Readers) Penguin Young Readers Group.

Kline, Trish & Donev, Mary. It's a Party! KA Reader 2. 2007. (Illus.). 32p. (J). per. 20.00 *(978-0-9717234-3-6(5))* Ghost Hunter Productions.

Knight, Chris. Piggy's Party. 2011. (Illus.). 36p. (gr. 1-2). pap. 17.07 *(978-1-4520-9585-1(X))* AuthorHouse.

Knight, Hilary. Eloise Throws a Party! Lyon, Tammie, illus. 2008. (Eloise Ser.). (ENG.). 32p. (J). (gr. -1-1). pap. 3.99 *(978-1-4169-6172-7(0),* Simon Spotlight) Simon Spotlight.

Kole MacLean, Christine. Mary Margaret Running Scared. 2010. 152p. pap. 14.98 *(978-0-557-24676-2(8))* Lulu Pr., Inc.

Kono, Erin Eitter. Caterina & the Perfect Party. 2013. (ENG., Illus.). 32p. (J). (gr. -1-k). 16.99 *(978-0-8037-3902-4(8),* Dial Bks) Penguin Young Readers Group.

Kosara, Victoria. Graduation Party. Durk, Jim, illus. 2010. (J). pap. *(978-0-545-23400-9(X))* Scholastic, Inc.

Krakower, Harold. Sugarland: Volume 2 Trouble in Sugarland. 2009. 28p. pap. 12.50 *(978-1-4490-1880-1(7))* AuthorHouse.

Krishnaswami, Uma. The Big Party. 2006. (Early Explorers Ser.). (J). pap. *(978-1-4108-6133-7(3))* Benchmark Education Co.

Kropf, Latifa Berry. It's Hanukkah Time! Cohen, Tod, photos by. 2004. (ENG., Illus.). 24p. (J). (gr. -1-1). 12.95 *(978-1-58013-120-9(4),* Kar-Ben Publishing) Lerner Publishing Group.

Ku, Grace. When Grace Was. 2009. 24p. pap. 12.99 *(978-1-4389-9945-6(3))* AuthorHouse.

Laird, Judie. Jane's Special Day. 2009. 16p. pap. 8.95 *(978-1-4490-1199-4(3))* AuthorHouse.

Landry, Leo. Trick or Treat. 2012. (ENG., Illus.). 32p. (J). (gr. -1-3). 12.99 *(978-0-547-24969-8(1))* Houghton Mifflin Harcourt Publishing Co.

Lansky, Bruce. Polar BRRR Delivers. Wummer, Amy, illus. 2010. 10p. (J). bds. 6.99 *(978-1-4169-9318-6(5))* Meadowbrook Pr.

LaRose, Melinda & Disney Book Group Staff. Birthday Bash! Disney Storybook Art Team, illus. 2014. (ENG.). 32p. (J). (gr. -1-k). pap. 4.99 *(978-1-4231-9935-9(9))* Disney Pr.

Larsen, Angela. Travel to Tomorrow: Book One of the Fifties Chix Series. 2011. (ENG.). 260p. 14.95 *(978-1-60746-817-2(4))* FastPrncil, Inc.

Lasota, Mary. Kitty Piper, Angel Cat, Book 3, A Surprise for Ashley. 2011. 48p. (gr. 1-2). pap. 11.66 *(978-1-4634-1031-5(X))* AuthorHouse.

Lawson, Jennifer. The Secret Tea Party at the Zoo. 2010. (Illus.). 34p. pap. 19.95 *(978-0-557-13707-7(1))* Lulu Pr., Inc.

Leedy, Loreen. Crazy Like a Fox. Leedy, Loreen, illus. 2009. (ENG., Illus.). 32p. (J). (gr. -1-3). 7.99 *(978-0-8234-2248-7(8))* Holiday Hse., Inc.

Lepp, Royden. Happy Birthday Barnabas, 1 vol. Lepp, Royden, illus. 2008. (I Can Read! / Barnabas Ser.). (ENG., Illus.). 32p. (J). (gr. -1-1). pap. 3.99 *(978-0-310-71586-3(5))* Zonderkidz.

Lester, Helen & Munsinger, Lynn. Happy Birdday, Tacky! Lester, Helen & Munsinger, Lynn, illus. 2013. (Tacky the Penguin Ser.). (ENG., Illus.). 32p. (J). (gr. -1-3). 16.99 *(978-0-547-91228-8(5))* Houghton Mifflin Harcourt Publishing Co.

Leveen, Tom. Party. 2011. (ENG.). 240p. (YA). (gr. 9). pap. 8.99 *(978-0-375-86392-9(3),* Ember) Random Hse. Children's Bks.

Lewis, J. Patrick, et al. First Dog's White House Christmas. Bowers, Tim, illus. 2010. (ENG.). 32p. (J). (gr. 1-4). 15.95 *(978-1-58536-503-6(3),* 202197) Sleeping Bear Pr.

Lindner, Brooke. Diego's Halloween Party. Mawhinney, Art, illus. 2008. (Go, Diego, Go! Ser.). (ENG.). 16p. (J). (gr. -1-k). bds. 5.99 *(978-1-4169-5497-2(X),* Simon Spotlight/Nickelodeon) Simon Spotlight/Nickelodeon.

Litwin, Eric. Dance Party Countdown. Lichtenheld, Tom, illus. 2017. (Groovy Joe Ser.: 2). (ENG.). 40p. (J). (gr. -1-k). 17.99 ***(978-0-545-88379-5(2),*** Orchard Bks.) Scholastic, Inc.

The live dolls' party Days. 2007. (Illus.). 160p. (J). lib. bdg. 59.00 *(978-1-60304-010-5(2))* Dollworks.

Loggia, Wendy. Aurora: The Perfect Party, 1 vol. Studio IBOIX, illus. 2012. (Disney Princesses Set 2 Ser.). (ENG.). 96p. (J). (gr. 2-6). lib. bdg. 24.21 *(978-1-59961-181-5(3))* Spotlight.

Lokaisingh, Jasmine. The Tales of Mme. Bovarie Vache & Mr. P. Huggins: In Huggsie's Birthday. 2011. 16p. 8.32 *(978-1-4520-4071-4(0))* AuthorHouse.

Lombardi, Kristine. It's a Surprise Playhouse Storybook. Mattel Inc. Staff, illus. 2010. (Storybook & Playset Ser.). (ENG.). 16p. (J). (gr. -1-2). bds. 15.99 *(978-0-7944-2005-5(2))* Reader's Digest Assn., Inc., The.

London, Jonathan & Wells, Rosemary. Froggy's Birthday Wish. Remkiewicz, Frank, illus. 2015. (Froggy Ser.). (ENG.). 32p. (J). (gr. -1-k). bds. 16.99 *(978-0-670-01572-6(5),* Viking Books for Young Readers) Penguin Young Readers Group.

Look, Lenore. Alvin Ho: Allergic to Birthday Parties, Science Projects, & Other Man-Made Catastrophes. Pham, LeUyen, illus. 2011. (Alvin Ho Ser.). (ENG.). 192p. (J). (gr. 1-4). 6.99 *(978-0-375-87369-0(4),* Yearling) Random Hse. Children's Bks.

Lord, Cynthia. Hot Rod Hamster & the Haunted Halloween Party. Anderson, Derek & Paprocki, Greg, illus. 2015. (Scholastic Reader, Level 2 Ser.). (ENG.). 32p. (J). (gr. k-2). pap. 3.99 *(978-0-545-81528-4(2),* Scholastic Pr.) Scholastic, Inc.

—Hot Rod Hamster & the Haunted Halloween Party! Anderson, Derek, illus. 2015. (ENG.). 32p. (J). (gr. -1-3). 16.99 *(978-0-545-81529-1(0),* Scholastic Pr.) Scholastic, Inc.

Lyles, Whitney. Party Games. 2012. (Romantic Comedies Ser.). (ENG.). 304p. (YA). (gr. 7). pap. 14.99 *(978-1-4424-6060-7(1),* Simon Pulse) Simon Pulse.

Lynn, Tammy. Happy Birthday Puppy: An I See Puppy Book. Stewart, Elaine, ed. Lynn, Tammy, illus. 2006. (Illus.). 12p. (J). bds. 6.99 *(978-0-9774277-0-3(6),* 0-9774277-0-6) I See Puppy, LLP.

Lytle, Robert A. Pirate Party. Williams, Bill, illus. 2006. (Mackinac Passage Ser.). 258p. (J). (gr. 4-7). pap. 9.95 *(978-0-9749412-5-7(5))* EDCO Publishing, Inc.

Machado, Ana Maria. What a Party!, 1 vol. Amado, Elisa, tr. from POR. Moreau, Hélène, illus. 2013. (ENG.). 32p. (J). (gr. -1-2). 18.95 *(978-1-55498-168-7(9))* Groundwood Bks. CAN. Dist: Publishers Group West (PGW).

Mack, Paulette. Cookout at Grandma's House: The Adventures of Mielle & Cheeky. 2006. (ENG., Illus.). 24p. per. 10.95 *(978-1-59800-998-9(2))* Outskirts Pr., Inc.

Mackall, Dandi Daley. Natalie & the Downside-Up Birthday, 1 vol. Blakeslee, Lys, illus. 2009. (That's Nat! Ser.). (ENG.). 96p. (J). (gr. 1-4). pap. 4.99 *(978-0-310-71569-6(5))* Zonderkidz.

Mackintosh, David. Marshall Armstrong Is New to Our School. 2011. (ENG., Illus.). 32p. (J). (gr. k-2). 17.95 *(978-1-4197-0036-1(7),* Abrams Bks. for Young Readers) Abrams, Inc.

Maed, Mary Ann Graziani. Filled to Capacity. 2008. 56p. pap. 24.50 *(978-0-615-16077-1(8))* Wishing Star Children's Bks.

Make Believe Ideas. Flower Friends Poppy's Shapes. 2013. (ENG.). 10p. (J). bds. 6.99 *(978-1-78235-603-5(7))* Make Believe Ideas GBR. Dist: Nelson, Thomas Inc.

Malone, Jen & Nall, Gail. You're Invited. 2015. (ENG., Illus.). 336p. (J). (gr. 4-8). 17.99 *(978-1-4814-3197-2(8),* Aladdin) Simon & Schuster Children's Publishing.

—You're Invited Too. 2016. (Mix Ser.). (ENG., Illus.). 304p. (J). (gr. 4-8). pap. 7.99 *(978-1-4814-3199-6(4),* Aladdin) Simon & Schuster Children's Publishing.

Man-Kong, Mary & Random House. A Surprise for a Friend (Barbie) 2015. (Pictureback(R) Ser.). (ENG., Illus.). 16p. (J). (gr. -1-2). 4.99 *(978-0-553-50942-7(X),* Random Hse. Bks. for Young Readers) Random Hse. Children's Bks.

Mandy, Stanley. Bella: The Birthday Party. Mandy, Stanley, illus. 2010. (ENG., Illus.). 32p. (J). (gr. -1-k). 9.95 *(978-1-58925-850-1(9))* Tiger Tales.

Mansfield, Katherine. The Garden Party. l.t. ed. 2006. pap. *(978-1-84702-354-4(1))* Echo Library.

—PARTIES AND PRESENTS: THREE SHORT STORIES LEVEL 2 ELEMENTARY/LOWER-INTERMEDIATE. 2010. (ENG., Illus.). 62p. pap. 12.00 *(978-84-8323-836-3(5))* Cambridge Univ. Pr.

—PARTIES AND PRESENTS THREE SHORT STORIES LEVEL 2 ELEMENTARY/LOWER-INTERMEDIATE WITH CD-ROM/AUDIO CD, 1 vol. 2010. (ENG., Illus.). 62p. pap. 14.25 incl. cd-rom *(978-84-8323-684-0(2))* Cambridge Univ. Pr.

Manushkin, Fran. Katie's Lucky Birthday, 1 vol. Lyon, Tammie, illus. 2011. (Katie Woo Ser.). (ENG.). 32p. (gr. k-2). pap. 5.95 *(978-1-4048-6612-6(4))*; lib. bdg. 21.32 *(978-1-4048-6514-3(4))* Picture Window Bks.

Marshall, Wendy. The O'Clocks: Mr. O'Clock Goes to A Party. 2008. 40p. pap. 18.49 *(978-1-4389-2403-8(8))* AuthorHouse.

Martin, David. Let's Have a Tree Party! Manders, Jeff & Manders, John, illus. 2012. (ENG.). 32p. (J). (gr. k-k). 15.99 *(978-0-7636-3704-0(1))* Candlewick Pr.

Masino, Brian. Cabbage Patch Kids: We Are All Best Friends. Karl, Linda, illus. 2006. (J). pap. *(978-0-439-76820-7(9))* Scholastic, Inc.

Mason, Jane B. & Stephens, Sarah Hines. Snowfall Surprise. 2009. (Candy Apple Ser.: 21). (ENG.). 144p. (J). (gr. 3-7). 5.99 *(978-0-545-10067-0(4),* Scholastic Paperbacks) Scholastic, Inc.

Maxson, H. A. & Young, Claudia H. Tea Party at Chestertown. Kosits, Andrew, illus. 2003. (Magical History Tours Ser.). 55p. (J). per. 8.95 *(978-0-9741713-0-2(1))* Bay Oak Pubs., Ltd.

McCafferty, Megan. The (Totally Not) Guaranteed Guide to Stressing, Obsessing & Second-Guessing. 2015. (Jessica Darling's It List Ser.: 3). (ENG.). 224p. (J). (gr. 3-7). 17.00 *(978-0-316-33324-5(7))* Little Brown & Co.

McClure, Wendy. The Princess & the Peanut Allergy. Lyon, Tammie, illus. 2012. (J). *(978-1-61913-127-9(7))* Weigl Pubs., Inc.

—The Princess & the Peanut Allergy, 1 vol. Lyon, Tammie, illus. 2009. (ENG.). 32p. (J). (gr. 1-3). 16.99 *(978-0-8075-6623-7(3))* Whitman, Albert & Co.

McConduit, Denise Walter. D. J. & the Debutante Ball, 1 vol. Henriquez, Emile F., illus. 2004. (D. J. Ser.). (ENG.). 32p. (J). (gr. k-3). 16.99 *(978-1-58980-173-8(3))* Pelican Publishing Co., Inc.

McCormick, Michelle. Priscilla Willa, Party Planner. 2013. (ENG.). 94p. (YA). pap. 9.95 *(978-1-4787-1444-6(1))* Outskirts Pr., Inc.

—Priscilla Willa, Party Planner: Night at the Haunted Hotel. 2013. (ENG.). 108p. (YA). pap. 9.95 *(978-1-4787-0890-2(5))* Outskirts Pr., Inc.

McCranie, Stephen. Belly Flop! Book 3. McCranie, Stephen, illus. 3rd ed. 2012. (Mal & Chad Ser.: 3). (ENG., Illus.). 240p. (J). (gr. 3-7). pap. 9.99 *(978-0-399-25658-5(X),* Philomel Bks.) Penguin Young Readers Group.

McDonald, Megan. Jessica Finch in Pig Trouble. Madrid, Erwin, illus. 2014. (Judy Moody Ser.: 1). (ENG.). 64p. (J). (gr. -1-1). 12.99 *(978-0-7636-5718-5(2))*; pap. 4.99 *(978-0-7636-7027-6(8))* Candlewick Pr.

—Jessica Finch in Pig Trouble. 2014. (Judy Moody & Friends Ser.). (Illus.). 60p. (J). lib. bdg. 14.75 *(978-0-606-35162-1(0))* Turtleback Bks.

McElroy, Jean & Childrens Books Staff. Let's Count 1 2 3! 2011. (ENG.). 12p. (J). (gr. -1 — 1). 4.99 *(978-1-4424-1198-2(8),* Little Simon) Little Simon.

McGee, Warner, illus. Monster Halloween Party. 2007. (Backyardigans Ser.). (ENG.). 14p. (J). (gr. -1-k). bds. 6.99 *(978-1-4169-3435-6(9),* Simon Spotlight/Nickelodeon) Simon Spotlight/Nickelodeon.

Mcgill, Leslie. Hero. 2015. (Cap Central Ser.: 6). (YA). lib. bdg. 20.80 *(978-0-606-37403-3(5))* Turtleback Bks.

McGrath, Barbara Barbieri. Birthday Counting. Tagel, Peggy, illus. 2017. (First Celebrations Ser.). (ENG.). 12p. (J). (— 1). bds. 6.99 *(978-1-58089-537-8(9))* Charlesbridge Publishing, Inc.

McLaughlin, Lauren. Mitzi Tulane, Preschool Detective, in What's That Smell? Ohi, Debbie Ridpath, illus. 2016. (ENG.). 32p. (J). (-k). 19.99 *(978-0-375-97176-1(9),* Random Hse. Bks. for Young Readers) Random Hse. Children's Bks.

McNair, Barbara. Tea Parties with Grandm. Hogan, Eric, illus. 2009. 48p. pap. 24.95 *(978-1-60749-617-5(8))* America Star Bks.

McNamara, Margaret. Sylva & the Fairy Ball. 2013. (Fairy Bell Sisters Ser.: 1). (J). lib. bdg. 14.75 *(978-0-606-31796-2(1),* Turtleback) Turtleback Bks.

Meadows, Daisy. Belle the Birthday Fairy. 2012. (Rainbow Magic Ser.). (ENG., Illus.). 176p. (J). (gr. 2-5). pap. 6.99 *(978-0-545-27054-0(5),* Scholastic Paperbacks) Scholastic, Inc.

—Belle the Birthday Fairy. 2012. (Rainbow Magic — Special Edition Ser.). lib. bdg. 17.20 *(978-0-606-23726-0(7),* Turtleback) Turtleback Bks.

—Eva the Enchanted Ball Fairy. 2012. (Rainbow Magic — the Princess Fairies Ser.: 7). lib. bdg. 14.75 *(978-0-606-26175-3(3),* Turtleback) Turtleback Bks.

—A Fairyland Costume Ball. 2012. (Scholastic Reader Level 2 Ser.). (ENG., Illus.). 32p. (J). (gr. 2-5). pap. 3.99 *(978-0-545-43389-1(4),* Scholastic Paperbacks) Scholastic, Inc.

—A Fairyland Costume Ball. 2012. (Rainbow Magic — Scholastic Reader Ser.). lib. bdg. 13.55 *(978-0-606-26235-4(0),* Turtleback) Turtleback Bks.

—Flora the Dress-Up Fairy. 2010. (Rainbow Magic Ser.). (ENG., Illus.). 192p. (J). (gr. 2-5). 6.99 *(978-0-545-22176-4(5),* Scholastic Paperbacks) Scholastic, Inc.

Meddaugh, Susan. Martha on the Case. 2010. (Martha Speaks Ser.). (ENG., Illus.). 112p. (J). (gr. 1-4). pap. 5.99 *(978-0-547-21055-1(8))* Houghton Mifflin Harcourt Publishing Co.
—Pool Party. 2011. (Martha Speaks Ser.). (ENG., Illus.). 24p. (J). (gr. -1-3). pap. 3.99 *(978-0-547-43882-5(6))* Houghton Mifflin Harcourt Publishing Co.
—Summer Fun, 3 bks. in 1. 2013. (Martha Speaks Ser.). (ENG., Illus.). 72p. (J). (gr. -1-3). pap. 7.99 *(978-0-547-97025-7(0))* Houghton Mifflin Harcourt Publishing Co.
Mei, Michael. The Goofy Gourmet: Let's Cook Today! 2008. (J). pap. 12.95 *(978-0-9800752-1-2(1))* Big Company, LLC, The.
Meister, Cari. Tiny the Birthday Dog. Davis, Rich, illus. 2013. (Tiny Ser.). (ENG.). 32p. (J). (gr. k-1). 14.99 *(978-0-670-01413-2(3))*; pap. 3.99 *(978-0-448-46478-7(0))* Penguin Young Readers Group. (Penguin Young Readers).
—Tiny the Birthday Dog. 2013. (Penguin Young Readers Level 1 Ser.). lib. bdg. 13.55 *(978-0-606-31706-1(6)*, Turtleback) Turtleback Bks.
Metzger, Steve. Princess Kitty. Okstad, Ella, illus. 2017. 32p. (J). (gr. -1-3). 17.99 *(978-0-06-230662-3(6))* HarperCollins Pubs.
Micinilio, Leanne Plein. Tia's Troubles: The First in a series of Tia's Adventures. 2011. 40p. pap. 16.99 *(978-1-4490-4695-8(9))* AuthorHouse.
Miles, Lisa. Best Friends: Over 1000 Reusable Stickers! 2014. (Little Hands Creative Sticker Play Ser.). (ENG.). 64p. (J). (gr. -1-2). pap. 9.99 *(978-1-4380-0390-0(0))* Barron's Educational Series, Inc.
Miller, Marie. Party Time. 2006. (Neighborhood Readers Ser.). (ENG.). 8p. (gr. -1-3). pap. 5.15 *(978-1-4042-6706-0(9)*, Rosen Classroom) Rosen Publishing Group, Inc., The.
Milway, Alex. Pigsticks & Harold & the Tuptown Thief. Milway, Alex, illus. 2015. (ENG., Illus.). 80p. (J). (gr. k-4). 12.99 *(978-0-7636-7809-8(0))* Candlewick Pr.
Mind Wave Inc. Strawberry Moshi's Activity Book. Mind Wave Inc., illus. 2012. (MoshiMoshiKawaii Ser.). (ENG., Illus.). 28p. (J). (gr. -1-2). pap. 4.99 *(978-0-7636-6236-3(4))* Candlewick Pr.
—Strawberry Princess Moshi's Activity Book. Mind Wave Inc., illus. 2012. (MoshiMoshiKawaii Ser.). (ENG., Illus.). 28p. (J). (gr. -1-2). pap., act. bk. ed. 4.99 *(978-0-7636-6237-0(2))* Candlewick Pr.
Mitchell, Pratima. Raju's Ride. Waterhouse, Stephen, illus. 2005. (ENG.). 24p. (J). lib. bdg. 23.65 *(978-1-59646-726-2(6))* Dingles & Co.
Miyakoshi, Akiko. The Tea Party in the Woods. Miyakoshi, Akiko, illus. 2015. (ENG., Illus.). 32p. (J). (gr. -1-2). 16.95 *(978-1-77138-107-9(8))* Kids Can Pr., Ltd. CAN. Dist: Hachette Bk. Group.
Monks, Lydia, illus. Mungo Monkey Has a Birthday Party. 2014. (ENG.). 14p. (J). (gr. -1). 12.99 *(978-1-4052-6866-0(2))* Egmont Bks., Ltd. GBR. Dist: Independent Pubs. Group.
Monroe, Chris. Bug on a Bike. Monroe, Chris, illus. 2014. (ENG., Illus.). 32p. (J). (gr. -1-2). 16.95 *(978-1-4677-2154-7(9)*, Carolrhoda Bks.) Lerner Publishing Group.
Moodie, Fiona. Noko's Surprise Party. 2008. (ENG., Illus.). 32p. (J). (gr. k-3). 16.95 *(978-1-84507-587-3(0)*, Frances Lincoln) Quarto Publishing Group UK GBR. Dist: Hachette Bk. Group.
Morgan, Anna & Turkienicz, Rachael. My (Worst) Best Sleepover Party, 1 vol. 2007. (ENG., Illus.). 128p. (J). (gr. 2-5). pap. 7.95 *(978-1-897187-20-3(3))* Second Story Pr. CAN. Dist: Orca Bk. Pubs. USA.
Morrow, Barbara Olenyik. Mr. Mosquito Put on His Tuxedo. Goembel, Ponder, illus. 2009. (ENG.). 32p. (J). (gr. -1-3). 16.95 *(978-0-8234-2072-8(8))* Holiday Hse., Inc.
Moulton, Mark K. A Royal Wedding. Good, Karen H., illus. 2007. (ENG.). 32p. (J). (gr. k-3). 14.99 *(978-0-8249-8677-3(6)*, Ideal Pubns.) Worthy Publishing.
Moulton, Mark Kimball. The Annual Snowman's Ball. Good, Karen Hillard, illus. 2007. (ENG.). 32p. (J). (gr. -1-3). 14.99 *(978-0-8249-5564-9(1)*, Ideal Pubns.) Worthy Publishing.
—One Enchanted Evening. Crouch, Karen Hillard, illus. 2003. 32p. (J). 14.95 *(978-0-8249-5480-2(7)*, Ideal Pubns.) Worthy Publishing.
Muecke, Anne & Moore, Clement C. The Dinosaurs' Night Before Christmas. Hale, Nathan, illus. 2008. (ENG.). 36p. (J). (gr. -1-3). 18.99 *(978-0-8118-6322-3(0))* Chronicle Bks. LLC.
Mullarkey, Lisa. TJ Zaps the New Kid: Stopping a Social Bully #1, 1 vol. LaCoste, Gary, illus. 2012. (TJ Trapper, Bully Zapper Ser.). (ENG.). 80p. (J). (gr. 2-5). lib. bdg. 27.07 *(978-1-61641-905-9(9)*, Calico Chapter Bks) Magic Wagon.
Munoz, Norma. Los Cuentos de la Casa del Arbol. Olson, John & Olson, Johan, illus. rev. ed. 2005. (Castillo de la Lectura Blanca Ser.). (SPA & ENG.). 72p. (J). (gr. -1-3). pap. 6.95 *(978-970-20-0124-9(2))* Castillo, Ediciones, S. A. de C. V. MEX. Dist: Macmillan.
Murray, Marjorie Dennis. Halloween Night. Dorman, Brandon, illus. (ENG.). 40p. (J). (gr. k-4). 2013. pap. 6.99 *(978-0-06-185773-7(4))* 2010. 9.99 *(978-0-06-201293-7(2))* HarperCollins Pubs. (Greenwillow Bks.).
Myracle, Lauren. Awesome Blossom. 2013. (Flower Power Ser.). (ENG.). 272p. (J). (gr. 4-8). 17.95 *(978-1-4197-0405-5(2)*, Amulet Bks.) Abrams, Inc.
—Awesome Blossom: A Flower Power Book. 2013. (Flower Power Ser.). (ENG.). 272p. (J). (gr. 3-7). pap. 7.95 *(978-1-4197-0791-9(4)*, Amulet Bks.) Abrams, Inc.
Neuschwander, Cindy. Sir Cumference & All the King's Tens. Geehan, Wayne, illus. 2009. (ENG.). 32p. (J). (gr. 3-7). 16.95 *(978-1-57091-727-1(2))* Charlesbridge Publishing, Inc.
Nickelodeon Staff. Party Time! 2013. (Spongebob Squarepants Step into Reading Ser.). lib. bdg. 13.55 *(978-0-606-32221-8(3)*, Turtleback) Turtleback Bks.
Night, P. J. Don't Drink the Punch! 2012. (You're Invited to a Creepover Ser.: 11). (ENG.). 160p. (J). (gr. 3-7). pap. 6.99 *(978-1-4424-5287-9(0)*, Simon Spotlight) Simon Spotlight.
—Don't Move a Muscle! 2016. (You're Invited to a Creepover Ser.: 21). (ENG., Illus.). 160p. (J). (gr. 3-7). pap. 6.99 *(978-1-4814-2922-1(1)*, Simon Spotlight) Simon Spotlight.
—The House Next Door. 2013. (You're Invited to a Creepover Ser.: 16). (ENG., Illus.). 160p. (J). (gr. 3-7). pap. 6.99 *(978-1-4424-8233-3(8)*, Simon Spotlight) Simon Spotlight.
—The House Next Door. 2013. (Creepover Ser.: 16). lib. bdg. 17.20 *(978-0-606-32323-9(6)*, Turtleback) Turtleback Bks.
—No Trick-Or-Treating!, 1 vol. 2013. (You're Invited to a Creepover Ser.). (ENG.). 192p. (J). (gr. 3-6). lib. bdg. 24.21 *(978-1-61479-061-7(2)*, Essential Library) ABDO Publishing Co.
—No Trick-Or-Treating! 2012. (Creepover Ser.: 9). lib. bdg. 17.20 *(978-0-606-26337-5(3)*, Turtleback) Turtleback Bks.
—Your Worst Nightmare. 2013. (Creepover Ser.: 17). lib. bdg. 17.20 *(978-0-606-32324-6(4)*, Turtleback) Turtleback Bks.
Nolen, Jerdine. Bradford Street Buddies: Block Party Surprise. Henninger, Michelle, illus. 2015. (Green Light Readers Level 3 Ser.). (ENG.). 48p. (J). (gr. 1-4). pap. 3.99 *(978-0-544-35863-8(5)*, HMH Books For Young Readers) Houghton Mifflin Harcourt Publishing Co.
North, Laura. Cinderella's Big Foot. 2014. (ENG., Illus.). 32p. (J). *(978-0-7787-0440-9(8))*; pap. *(978-0-7787-0448-5(3))* Crabtree Publishing Co.
Nosy Crow Staff. Violet Rose & the Surprise Party. Ho, Jannie, illus. 2016. (ENG.). (J). (gr. -1-3). 8.99 *(978-0-7636-8917-9(3)*, Nosy Crow) Candlewick Pr.
—Wickle Woo Has a Halloween Party. Ho, Jannie, illus. 2014. (ENG.). 8p. (J). (— 1). bds. 7.99 *(978-0-7636-7400-7(1)*, Nosy Crow) Candlewick Pr.
Novak, Matt. No Zombies Allowed. Novak, Matt, illus. 2014. (ENG., Illus.). 32p. (J). (gr. -1-1). 16.99 *(978-1-4814-2540-7(4)*, Atheneum Bks. for Young Readers) Simon & Schuster Children's Publishing.
Nurse, Lesley D. The Tale of Greedy Reeby. 2013. 82p. pap. 16.99 *(978-0-9797699-6-2(5))* Lion Prints Publishing.
Nyirenda, Vukani G. The Wise Old Tortoise & the Monkey. 2011. 24p. pap. 15.99 *(978-1-4568-9133-6(2))* Xlibris Corp.
Ochoa, Mary Lou. Andy's Arctic Party. 2009. 20p. pap. 9.14 *(978-1-4269-0943-6(8))* Trafford Publishing.
O'Connell, Rebecca. Baby Party. Poole, Susie, illus. (ENG.). 24p. (J). (gr. -1 — 1). 2017. bds. 7.99 ***(978-0-8075-0514-4(5))*** 2015. 15.99 *(978-0-8075-0512-0(9))* Whitman, Albert & Co.
O'Connor, Jane. Bonjour, Butterfly. Glasser, Robin Preiss, illus. (Fancy Nancy Ser.). (ENG.). 32p. (J). (gr. -1-2). 2012. 9.99 *(978-0-06-221053-1(X))* 2008. 17.99 *(978-0-06-123588-7(1))* HarperCollins Pubs.
—Fancy Day in Room 1-A. 2012. (Fancy Nancy - I Can Read! Ser.). (J). lib. bdg. 13.55 *(978-0-606-26259-0(8)*, Turtleback) Turtleback Bks.
—Fancy Nancy. Glasser, Robin Preiss, illus. 2009. (Fancy Nancy Ser.). (ENG.). 32p. (J). (gr. -1-3). pap. 24.99 *(978-0-06-171944-8(7)*, HarperFestival) HarperCollins Pubs.
—Fancy Nancy: Tea for Two. Glasser, Robin Preiss, illus. 2012. (Fancy Nancy Ser.). (ENG.). 24p. (J). (gr. -1-3). pap. 3.99 *(978-0-06-123597-9(0)*, HarperFestival) HarperCollins Pubs.
—Fancy Nancy - Super Secret Surprise Party. Glasser, Robin Preiss, illus. 2015. (I Can Read Level 1 Ser.). (ENG.). 32p. (J). (gr. -1-3). 16.99 *(978-0-06-226979-9(8))* HarperCollins Pubs.
—Fancy Nancy 10th Anniversary Edition. Glasser, Robin Preiss, illus. 2015. (Fancy Nancy Ser.). (ENG.). 40p. (J). (gr. -1-3). 17.99 *(978-0-06-235214-9(8))* HarperCollins Pubs.
—Fancy Nancy & the Fabulous Fashion Boutique. Glasser, Robin Preiss, illus. 2010. (Fancy Nancy Ser.). 32p. (J). (gr. -1-3). (ENG.). 17.99 *(978-0-06-123592-4(X))*; lib. bdg. 18.89 *(978-0-06-123593-1(8))* HarperCollins Pubs.
—Fancy Nancy Collector's Quintet. Glasser, Robin Preiss, illus. 2009. (I Can Read Level 1 Ser.). (J). (gr. k-3). pap. 16.99 *(978-0-06-171905-9(6))* HarperCollins Pubs.
—Nancy Clancy: My Secret Diary. Glasser, Robin Preiss, illus. 2015. (Fancy Nancy Ser.). (ENG.). 144p. (J). (gr. 1-5). pap. 11.99 *(978-0-06-234983-5(X))* HarperCollins Pubs.
—Super Secret Surprise Party. Glasser, Robin Preiss, illus. 2015. (I Can Read Level 1 Ser.). (ENG.). 32p. (J). (gr. -1-3). pap. 3.99 *(978-0-06-226978-2(X))* HarperCollins Pubs.
—Super Secret Surprise Party. 2015. (Fancy Nancy - I Can Read! Ser.). (J). lib. bdg. 13.55 *(978-0-606-36947-3(3))* Turtleback Bks.
—Tea for Two. Glasser, Robin Preiss, illus. 2012. (Fancy Nancy Picture Bks.). (J). lib. bdg. 13.55 *(978-0-606-23577-8(9)*, Turtleback) Turtleback Bks.
—Tea Parties. Glasser, Robin Preiss, illus. 2009. (Fancy Nancy Ser.). (ENG.). 40p. (J). (gr. -1-2). 12.99 *(978-0-06-180174-7(7))* HarperCollins Pubs.
Oliver, Charles Folkes. Little Willy & the Party Animals. 2011. (Illus.). 20p. (gr. -1). pap. 14.99 *(978-1-4567-5138-8(7))* AuthorHouse.
Olson, Nancy. Thanksgiving at Grandma's. Marino, Michael F., illus. 2009. 24p. pap. 10.95 *(978-1-4251-8909-9(1))* Trafford Publishing.
Orbach, Ruth. Apple Pigs. 2016. (ENG., Illus.). 32p. (J). (gr. k-2). 15.99 *(978-1-84365-302-8(8))* National Trust, Aylesbury GBR. Dist: Independent Pubs. Group.
Orman, Roscoe, illus. Ricky & Mobo. 2007. (J). 14.95 *(978-1-59299-255-3(2))* Inkwater Pr.
Orme, Helen. She's My Friend Now. 2008. (Siti's Sisters Ser.). (ENG., Illus.). 36p. pap. *(978-1-84167-740-8(X))* Ransom Publishing Ltd.
Osterhold, Jared, illus. Cooks up a Surprise. 2011. (Olivia TV Tie-In Ser.). (ENG.). 24p. (J). (gr. -1-2). pap. 3.99 *(978-1-4424-1384-9(0)*, Simon Spotlight) Simon Spotlight.
—OLIVIA Wishes on a Star. 2014. (Olivia TV Tie-In Ser.). (ENG.). 24p. (J). (gr. -1-2). pap. 3.99 *(978-1-4814-1769-3(X)*, Simon Spotlight) Simon Spotlight.
Oud, Pauline. Having a Party with Lily & Milo. Oud, Pauline, illus. 2012. (Clavis Toddler: Skills Ser.). (ENG., Illus.). 24p. (J). (— 1). 12.95 *(978-1-60537-129-0(7))* Cobblestone Publishing Co.
Pack, Sherri. Little Cat, 1 vol. 2009. 20p. pap. 24.95 *(978-1-60813-706-0(6))* America Star Bks.
Pankiw, Dr Mary & Pankiw, Mary. Misilla Mouse. 2011. 32p. pap. *(978-1-4269-5476-4(X))* Trafford Publishing (UK) Ltd.
Park, Barbara. Dumb Bunny. Brunkus, Denise, illus. 2009. (Junie B. Jones Ser.). (ENG.). 128p. (J). (gr. 1-4). 4.99 *(978-0-375-83810-1(4)*, Random Hse. Bks. for Young Readers) Random Hse. Children's Bks.
Park, Linda Sue. Xander's Panda Party. Phelan, Matt, illus. 2013. (ENG.). 40p. (J). (gr. -1-3). 16.99 *(978-0-547-55865-3(1))* Houghton Mifflin Harcourt Publishing Co.
Parker, Danny. Lola's Toy Box: Party at Cuddleton Castl. 2017. (Lola's Toy Box Ser.: 6). (ENG.). 96p. (J). (gr. k-2). pap. 6.99 ***(978-1-76012-685-8(3))*** Hardie Grant Egmont Pty. Ltd. AUS. Dist: Independent Pubs. Group.
Pascual, Dennis Mark. The Adventures of Dj the Butterfly & Friends Series Presents Dj's Birthday Party. 2012. 20p. pap. 10.15 *(978-1-105-35838-8(0))* Lulu Pr., Inc.
Patron, Susan. Lucky Breaks. Phelan, Matt, illus. 2009. (ENG.). 192p. (J). (gr. 3-7). 16.99 *(978-1-4169-3998-6(9)*, Atheneum Bks. for Young Readers) Simon & Schuster Children's Publishing.
Paul, Miranda. Blobfish Throws a Party. Caton, Maggie, illus. 2017. (ENG.). 32p. (J). (gr. -1-3). 16.99 ***(978-1-4998-0422-5(9))*** Little Bee Books Inc.
Peek, Merle & Giblin, James Cross. Mary Wore Her Red Dress & Henry Wore His Green Sneakers, 1 vol. 2006. (Read along Book & CD Ser.). (ENG., Illus.). 32p. (J). (gr. k — 1). audio compact disk 10.99 *(978-0-618-75249-2(8))* Houghton Mifflin Harcourt Publishing Co.
Peeler, Penny. The Adventures of Spike & Sally. 2011. 52p. pap. 15.99 *(978-1-4568-9981-3(3))* Xlibris Corp.
Perelman, Helen. The Sugar Ball. Waters, Erica-Jane, illus. 2013. (Candy Fairies Ser.: 6). (ENG.). 128p. (J). (gr. 2-5). 15.99 *(978-1-4424-6498-8(4)*, Simon & Schuster/Paula Wiseman Bks.) Simon & Schuster/Paula Wiseman Bks.
Perkins, T. J. In the Grand Scheme of Things: A Kim & Kelly Mystery. 2007. (Illus.). 151p. (YA). 10.99 *(978-0-9777538-4-0(0))* GumShoe Press.
Peschke, Marci. Party Queen, 1 vol. Mourning, Tuesday, illus. 2013. (Kylie Jean Ser.). (ENG.). 112p. (gr. 2-3). lib. bdg. 22.65 *(978-1-4048-7582-1(4)*, Kylie Jean) Picture Window Bks.
—Valentine Queen, 1 vol. Mourning, Tuesday, illus. 2014. (Kylie Jean Ser.). (ENG.). 112p. (gr. 2-3). 22.65 *(978-1-4795-2352-8(6)*, Kylie Jean) Picture Window Bks.
Pesson, Lauren. My Little Kappa Delta. 2006. (J). 15.00 *(978-0-9779594-0-2(6))* Lauren Elizabeth Design.
Phillips, Ruby Ann. Dream Birthday, 1 vol. Isik, Semur, illus. 2014. (Krystal Ball Ser.). (ENG.). 112p. (gr. 2-3). 25.32 *(978-1-4795-2178-4(7))* Picture Window Bks.
Pike, Christopher, pseud. Remember Me: Her Death Will Not Go Unpunished... 2010. (Remember Me Ser.: Vols. 1-3). (ENG., Illus.). 848p. (YA). (gr. 9). pap. 9.99 *(978-1-4424-0596-7(1)*, Simon Pulse) Simon Pulse.
—Until the End: The Party; the Dance; the Graduation. 2011. (ENG.). 896p. (YA). (gr. 9). pap. 9.99 *(978-1-4424-2252-0(1)*, Simon Pulse) Simon Pulse.
Pitchford, Dean. The Big One-Oh. 2009. (ENG.). 208p. (J). (gr. 3-7). 6.99 *(978-0-14-241292-3(9)*, Puffin Books) Penguin Young Readers Group.
Posner-Sanchez, Andrea. Three Royal Birthdays! (Disney Princess) Legramandi, Francesco & Matta, Gabriella, illus. 2015. (Pictureback(R) Ser.). (ENG.). 24p. (J). (gr. -1-2). 5.99 *(978-0-7364-3403-4(8)*, RH/Disney) Random Hse. Children's Bks.
Powell, Gail. The Adventures of Harold J. Kat. 2008. 40p. pap. 16.99 *(978-1-4259-6334-7(X))* AuthorHouse.
Powell-Tuck, Maudie. Pumpkin Party! Guile, Gill, illus. 2015. (ENG.). 22p. (J). (gr. -1-2). bds. 8.99 *(978-1-58925-206-6(3))* Tiger Tales.
The Presents: Individual Title Six-Packs. (Sails Literacy Ser.). 16p. (gr. k-18). 27.00 *(978-0-7635-4444-7(2))* Rigby Education.
Press, J. The Doodles of Sam Dibble. Kline, Michael, illus. 2013. (Doodles of Sam Dibble Ser.: 1). (ENG.). 128p. (J). (gr. 1-3). pap. 4.99 *(978-0-448-46107-6(2)*, Grosset & Dunlap) Penguin Young Readers Group.
—The Doodles of Sam Dibble. 2013. (Doodles of Sam Dibble Ser.: 1). lib. bdg. 14.75 *(978-0-606-29777-6(4)*, Turtleback) Turtleback Bks.
Pretty Princess- Royal Party. 2005. (J). bds. *(978-1-4194-0061-2(4))* Paradise Pr., Inc.
Priddy, Roger. Happy Birthday: A Touch-and-Feel Book. 2014. (Little Friends Ser.). (ENG.). 10p. (J). (gr. -1 — 1). bds. 6.99 *(978-0-312-51680-2(0)*, 9780312516802, Priddy Bks.) St. Martin's Pr.
Prieto, Anita C. Timothy Hubble & the King Cake Party, 1 vol. Howard, Virginia, illus. 2008. (ENG.). 32p. (J). (gr. k-3). 16.99 *(978-1-58980-584-2(4))* Pelican Publishing Co., Inc.
Prom Girl. 2nd ed. 2003. (J). pap. 8.95 *(978-0-9726917-0-3(7))* Prom Girl Publishing, Inc.
Publications International Ltd. Staff. Play A Sound Video Fifi's Painting Party. 2008. 24p. 19.98 *(978-1-4127-9435-0(8)*, PIL Kids) Publications International, Ltd.
Random House. Haunted House Party! (Bubble Guppies) MJ Illustrations, illus. 2015. (Hologramatic Sticker Book Ser.). (ENG.). 64p. (J). (gr. -1-2). pap. 4.99 *(978-0-385-38407-0(6)*, Golden Bks.) Random Hse. Children's Bks.
—Shape Patrol! (Paw Patrol) MJ Illustrations, illus. 2016. (ENG.). 24p. (J). (— 1). bds. 6.99 *(978-1-101-93695-5(9)*, Random Hse. Bks. for Young Readers) Random Hse. Children's Bks.
—Somebunny Loves You (Barbie) 2016. (Pictureback(R) Ser.). (ENG., Illus.). 16p. (J). (gr. -1-2). 4.99 *(978-1-101-93195-0(7)*, Random Hse. Bks. for Young Readers) Random Hse. Children's Bks.
Random House & Man-Kong, Mary. Happy Birthday, Barbie! Riley, Kellee, illus. 2014. (Pictureback(R) Ser.). (ENG.). 24p. (J). (gr. -1-2). 5.99 *(978-0-385-37320-3(1)*, Random Hse. Bks. for Young Readers) Random Hse. Children's Bks.
Raschka, Chris. New York Is English, Chattanooga Is Creek. Raschka, Chris, illus. 2005. (ENG., Illus.). 40p. (J). (gr. -1-2). 17.99 *(978-0-689-84600-7(2)*, Atheneum/Richard Jackson Bks.) Simon & Schuster Children's Publishing.
Raven, Margot Theis. America's White Table. Ellison, Chris & Benny, Mike, illus. 2005. (ENG.). 48p. (J). (gr. k-6). 16.95 *(978-1-58536-216-5(6))* Sleeping Bear Pr.
Ravin Lodding, Linda. The Queen Is Coming to Tea. von Kitzing, Constanze, illus. 2017. (ENG.). 32p. (J). (-4). 16.99 *(978-1-4926-0757-1(6)*, 9781492607571, Sourcebooks Jabberwocky) Sourcebooks, Inc.
Reichert, Amy. While Mama Had a Quick Little Chat. Boiger, Alexandra, illus. 2005. (ENG.). 40p. (J). (gr. -1-2). 16.99 *(978-0-689-85170-4(7)*, Atheneum/Richard Jackson Bks.) Simon & Schuster Children's Publishing.
Reisfeld, Randi. No Strings Attached: CC (Cape Cod): Partiers Preferred. 2013. (ENG., Illus.). 624p. (YA). (gr. 9). pap. 9.99 *(978-1-4424-5978-6(6)*, Simon Pulse) Simon Pulse.
Reisner, Molly. Dora's Princess Party. Aikins, Dave, illus. 2009. (Dora the Explorer Ser.). (ENG.). 12p. (J). (gr. -1-1). 6.99 *(978-1-4169-9045-1(3)*, Simon Spotlight/Nickelodeon) Simon Spotlight/Nickelodeon.
Rey, H. A. Happy Valentine's Day. Young, Mary O'Keefe, illus. 2011. (Curious George Ser.). (ENG.). 14p. (J). (gr. -1-3). 8.99 *(978-0-547-13107-8(0))* Houghton Mifflin Harcourt Publishing Co.
—Hooray for Halloween, Curious George. 2016. (Curious George Ser.). (ENG., Illus.). 24p. (J). (gr. -1-3). 9.99 *(978-0-544-69956-4(4)*, HMH Books For Young Readers) Houghton Mifflin Harcourt Publishing Co.
—Jorge el Curioso el Baile. 2013. (Curious George Ser.). (SPA & ENG., Illus.). 24p. (J). (gr. -1-3). pap. 3.99 *(978-0-547-96822-3(1))* Houghton Mifflin Harcourt Publishing Co.
—Jorge el Curioso Va a una Fiesta de Disfraces/Curious George Goes to a Costume Party (Bilingual) 2012. (Curious George Ser.). (ENG & SPA., Illus.). 24p. (J). (gr. -1-3). pap. 3.99 *(978-0-547-86575-1(9))* Houghton Mifflin Harcourt Publishing Co.
—Jorge el Curioso y la Pinata. 2009. (Curious George Ser.).Tr. of Curious George Pinata Party. (SPA & ENG., Illus.). 24p. (J). (gr. -1-3). pap. 3.99 *(978-0-547-23830-2(4))* Houghton Mifflin Harcourt Publishing Co.
—Pinata Party. 2009. (Curious George Ser.). (ENG., Illus.). 24p. (J). (gr. -1-3). pap. 3.99 *(978-0-547-11962-5(3))* Houghton Mifflin Harcourt Publishing Co.
Rey, H. A. & Rey, Margret. Curious George & the Pizza Party. 2013. (Curious George Ser.). (ENG., Illus.). 24p. (J). (gr. -1-3). pap. 4.99 *(978-0-544-10988-9(0))* Houghton Mifflin Harcourt Publishing Co.
—Curious George & the Pizza Party. Shalleck, Alan J., ed. 2010. (Curious George Ser.). (ENG., Illus.). 24p. (J). (gr. -1-3). 13.99 *(978-0-547-23211-9(X))* Houghton Mifflin Harcourt Publishing Co.
RH Disney. A Paw-Some Costume Party! (Disney Palace Pets Whisker Haven Tales) RH Disney, illus. 2017. (Little Golden Book Ser.). (ENG., Illus.). 24p. (J). (-k). 4.99 ***(978-0-7364-3723-3(1)***, Golden/Disney) Random Hse. Children's Bks.
Rickman, Jeanie Parker. The Rising Star Ball. Taylor, Jennifer, illus. 2006. 32p. per. 17.95 *(978-1-59858-201-7(1))* Dog Ear Publishing, LLC.
Rim, Sujean. Birdie's Big-Girl Dress. 2011. (Birdie Ser.). (ENG., Illus.). 40p. (J). (gr. -1-3). 16.99 *(978-0-316-13287-9(X))* Little Brown & Co.
Rinck, Maranke. The Prince Child. Linden, Martijn van der, illus. 2004. (ENG & GER.). 32p. (J). 16.95 *(978-1-932425-15-4(2)*, Lemniscaat) Boyds Mills Pr.
Rippin, Sally. The Best Party Ever. Spartels, Stephanie, illus. 2014. (ENG.). 48p. (J). pap. 4.99 *(978-1-61067-261-0(5))* Kane Miller.
—The Birthday Mix-Up. Fukuoka, Aki, illus. 2013. 43p. (J). *(978-1-61067-232-0(1))* Kane Miller.
—The Birthday Mix-Up: Billie B. Brown. Fukuoka, Aki, illus. 2014. (ENG.). 48p. (J). pap. 4.99 *(978-1-61067-182-8(1))* Kane Miller.
—The Robot Blues. Spartels, Stephanie, illus. 2014. (ENG.). 48p. (J). pap. 4.99 *(978-1-61067-124-8(4))* Kane Miller.
Rivas, Spelile. The Cucuy Stole My Cascarones / el Coco Me Robó Los Cascarones. Baeza Ventura, Gabriela, tr. Cervantes, Valeria, illus. 2013. (SPA & ENG.). 32p. (J). 17.95 *(978-1-55885-771-1(0)*, Piñata Books) Arte Publico Pr.
Roberts, LaDawna. The Haunted Birthday Party. 2007. 48p. per. 16.95 *(978-1-4241-8723-2(0))* America Star Bks.
Roberts, Scott. Patty Cake & Friends. 2006. (ENG., Illus.). 96p. pap. 12.95 *(978-1-59362-030-1(6)*, 9781593620301) Slave Labor Bks.
Robertson, Charmaine. The Burrito Party. 2016. (Rosen REAL Readers: Social Studies Nonfiction / Fiction: Family, Community, & the World Ser.). 8p. (gr. 1-k). pap. 5.46 *(978-1-5081-2497-9(3)*, Rosen Classroom) Rosen Publishing Group, Inc., The.
Robinson, Hilary. Ted's Party Bus. 2009. (ENG., Illus.). 24p. (J). pap. *(978-0-7787-3901-2(5))*; lib. bdg. *(978-0-7787-3870-1(1))* Crabtree Publishing Co.
Roddy-Worsham, Clara. Bear Baby's Birthday Gift. 2013. 24p. 24.95 *(978-1-4626-9940-7(5))* America Star Bks.
Roper, Robert, illus. Happy Birthday, Dora! 2010. (Dora the Explorer Ser.). (ENG.). 14p. (J). (gr. -1-k). bds. 6.99 *(978-1-4424-0333-8(0)*, Simon Spotlight/Nickelodeon) Simon Spotlight/Nickelodeon.
Rosa-Mendoza, Gladys. It's My Birthday!/Es Mi Cumpleanos! Simard, Remy, illus. 2006. (Englishspanish Foundations Ser.). (ENG & SPA.). 20p. (J). (gr. -1-k). bds. 6.95 *(978-1-931398-17-6(8))* Me+Mi Publishing.
Rosenberg, Madelyn. How to Behave at a Tea Party. Ross, Heather, illus. 2014. (ENG.). 32p. (J). (gr. -1-3). 17.99 *(978-0-06-227926-2(2)*, Tegen, Katherine Bks) HarperCollins Pubs.
Ross, Darien. The Carr House Cats at Christmas. 2012. 36p. pap. 18.41 *(978-1-4669-4794-8(2))* Trafford Publishing.
Ross, Tony. I Want a Party! Ross, Tony, illus. 2011. (Andersen Press Picture Books Ser.). (Illus.). (J). 16.95 *(978-0-7613-8089-4(2))* Andersen Pr. GBR. Dist: Lerner Publishing Group.
Rouillard, Wendy W. Barnaby's Tree House. 2005. (Illus.). 30p. (J). *(978-0-9651070-4-4(3))* Barnaby & Co.
Roza, Greg. The Peanut Butter Party. 2006. (Neighborhood Readers Ser.). (ENG., Illus.). 12p. (gr. 1-3). pap. 5.90 *(978-1-4042-6827-2(8)*, Rosen Classroom) Rosen Publishing Group, Inc., The.
Rubin, Adam. Fiesta Secreta de Pizza. Salmieri, Daniel, illus. 2015. (ENG & SPA.). 40p. (J). (gr. -1-k). 8.99 *(978-0-14-751560-5(2)*, Puffin Books) Penguin Young Readers Group.
—Secret Pizza Party. Salmieri, Daniel, illus. 2013. (ENG.). 36p. (J). (gr. -1-2). 17.99 *(978-0-8037-3947-5(8)*, Dial Bks) Penguin Young Readers Group.
Rudnick, Elizabeth. Cinderella. 2015. (ENG.). 176p. (J). (gr. 3-7). pap. 5.99 *(978-1-4847-1113-2(0))* Disney Pr.

Russell, Rachel Renée. Tales from a Not-So-Happy Heartbreaker. 2013. (Dork Diaries: 6). lib. bdg. 25.75 (978-0-606-32424-3(0), Turtleback) Turtleback Bks.

—Tales from a Not-So-Popular Party Girl. Russell, Rachel Renée, illus. 2010. (Dork Diaries: 2). (ENG., Illus.). 288p. (J). (gr. 4-8). 13.99 (978-1-4169-8008-7(3), Aladdin) Simon & Schuster Children's Publishing.

—Tales from a Not-So-Popular Party Girl. 2010. (Dork Diaries: 2). lib. bdg. 25.75 (978-0-606-32420-5(8), Turtleback) Turtleback Bks.

Russell, Rachel Renée, et al. Tales from a Not-So-Popular Party Girl. 2010. (ENG.). pap. (978-1-4424-4042-5(2), Aladdin Paperbacks) Simon & Schuster Children's Publishing.

Ryals, Lexi. Liv & Maddie: Double Trouble. 2015. (Liv & Maddie Junior Novel Ser.). (ENG.). 112p. (J). (gr. 3-7). pap. 5.99 (978-1-4847-1694-6(9)) Disney Pr.

Ryan, Pam Muñoz. Mice & Beans. Cepeda, Joe, illus. 2005. (gr. -1-3). lib. bdg. 17.00 (978-0-7569-5089-7(9)) Perfection Learning Corp.

Rylant, Cynthia. Annie & Snowball & the Dress-Up Birthday. Stevenson, Suçie, illus. (Annie & Snowball Ser.: 1). (ENG.). 40p. (J). (gr. k-2). 2008. pap. 3.99 (978-1-4169-1459-4(5)) 2007. 16.99 (978-1-4169-0938-5(9)) Simon Spotlight. (Simon Spotlight).

—Annie & Snowball & the Dress-Up Birthday. 2008. (Annie & Snowball Ready-To-Read Ser.). lib. bdg. 13.55 (978-1-4178-1126-7(9), Turtleback) Turtleback Bks.

—Brownie & Pearl Step Out. Biggs, Brian, illus. 2009. (Brownie & Pearl Ser.). (ENG.). 24p. (J). (gr. -1-3). 14.99 (978-1-4169-8632-4(4), Beach Lane Bks.) Beach Lane Bks.

—Brownie & Pearl Step Out. Biggs, Brian, illus. 2014. (Brownie & Pearl Ser.). (ENG.). 24p. (J). (gr. -1-k). 16.99 (978-1-4814-0314-6(1)); pap. 3.99 (978-1-4814-0313-9(3)) Simon Spotlight. (Simon Spotlight).

—Little Whistle's Dinner Party. Bowers, Tim, illus. 2007. (Little Whistle Ser.). 32p. (gr. -1-3). 24.21 (978-1-59961-255-3(0)) Spotlight.

Saldana, Rene. Dale, Dale, Dale / Hit It, Hit It, Hit It: Una Fiesta de Numeros / a Fiesta of Numbers. Flores, Carolyn Dee, illus. 2014. (ENG & SPA.). (J). 17.95 (978-1-55885-782-7(6), Piñata Books) Arte Publico Pr.

Salzano, Tammi. Truck Party. Wood, Hannah, illus. 2011. (ENG.). 20p. bds. 7.95 (978-1-58925-865-5(7)) Tiger Tales.

Salzmann, Mary Elizabeth. Leaping Lizards, 1 vol. Chawla, Neena, illus. 2007. (Critter Chronicles Ser.). (ENG.). 24p. (J). (gr. k-3). lib. bdg. 24.21 (978-1-59928-450-7(2), SandCastle) ABDO Publishing Co.

—Robin Hoods, 1 vol. Haberstroh, Anne, illus. 2007. (Critter Chronicles Ser.). (ENG.). 24p. (J). (gr. k-3). lib. bdg. 24.21 (978-1-59928-466-8(9), SandCastle) ABDO Publishing Co.

Sauer, Tammi. I Love Cake! Starring Rabbit, Porcupine, & Moose. Rozelaar, Angie, illus. 2016. 40p. (J). (gr. -1-3). 17.99 (978-0-06-227894-4(0), Tegen, Katherine Bks) HarperCollins Pubs.

Saunders, Karen. Suzy P. Forever Me. 2015. (Suzy P. Ser.). (ENG.). 352p. (J). (gr. 4-7). pap. 10.99 (978-1-78370-163-6(3)) Bonnier Publishing GBR. Dist: Independent Pubs. Group.

Scanlon, Liz Garton. Happy Birthday, Bunny! Graegin, Stephanie, illus. 2013. (ENG.). 32p. (J). (gr. -1-3). 16.99 (978-1-4424-0287-4(3), Beach Lane Bks.) Beach Lane Bks.

Schertle, Alice. Little Blue Truck's Halloween. McElmurry, Jill, illus. 2016. (Little Blue Truck Ser.). (ENG.). 16p. (J). (— 1). bds. 12.99 (978-0-544-77253-3(9), HMH Books For Young Readers) Houghton Mifflin Harcourt Publishing Co.

Scholastic, Inc. Staff & Hooks, Gwendolyn. The Mystery of the Missing Dog. Devard, Nancy, illus. 2004. (Just for You Ser.). (ENG.). 32p. (gr. k-3). pap. 3.99 (978-0-439-56864-7(1), Teaching Resources) Scholastic, Inc.

Schreiber, Ellen. Magic of the Moonlight. (Full Moon Ser.: 2). (ENG.). (YA). (gr. 8). 2012. 256p. pap. 9.99 (978-0-06-198656-7(9)) 2011. 240p. 17.99 (978-0-06-198657-4(7)) HarperCollins Pubs. (Tegen, Katherine Bks).

Schroeder, Lisa. Frosting & Friendship. 2013. (ENG., Illus.). 224p. (J). (gr. 3-7). 15.99 (978-1-4424-7396-6(7), Aladdin) Simon & Schuster Children's Publishing.

Scieszka, Jon. Pete's Party. Gordon, David et al, illus. 2008. (Jon Scieszka's Trucktown Ser.). (ENG.). 24p. (J). (gr. -1-k). lib. bdg. 13.89 (978-1-4169-4149-1(5), Simon Spotlight) Simon Spotlight.

Scieszka, Jon & Barnett, Mac. Battle Bunny. Myers, Matthew, illus. 2013. (ENG.). 32p. (J). (gr. k-4). 14.99 (978-1-4424-4673-1(0), Simon & Schuster Bks. For Young Readers) Simon & Schuster Bks. For Young Readers.

Scollon, William, et al. Minnie Be My Sparkly Valentine. Disney Storybook Art Team Staff, illus. 2014. (ENG.). 24p. (J). (gr. -1-k). pap. 5.99 (978-1-4231-6414-2(8)) Disney Pr.

Seibold, J. Otto. Count, Dagmar! 2011. (ENG.). 20p. (J). (gr. -1 — 1). 8.99 (978-0-8118-7773-2(6)) Chronicle Bks. LLC.

Sendak, Maurice. Bumble-Ardy. Sendak, Maurice, illus. 2011. (ENG., Illus.). 40p. (J). 17.95 (978-0-06-205198-1(9)) HarperCollins Pubs.

Shea, Therese. At the Luau. 2006. (Neighborhood Readers Ser.). (ENG.). 16p. (gr. 1-3). pap. 6.50 (978-1-4042-7002-2(7), Rosen Classroom) Rosen Publishing Group, Inc., The.

Shields, Carol Diggory. Saturday Night at the Dinosaur Stomp. Nash, Scott, illus. 2008. (ENG.). 32p. (J). (gr. -1-3). pap. 6.99 (978-0-7636-3887-0(0)) Candlewick Pr.

Siegal, Ida. Party Drama! (Emma Is on the Air #2) 2015. (Emma Is on the Air Ser.: 2). (ENG.). 128p. (J). (gr. 2-5). pap. 4.99 (978-0-545-68695-2(4), Scholastic Paperbacks) Scholastic, Inc.

Silverhardt, Lauryn. A Surprise Party. Yee, Josie, illus. 2003. (Dora the Explorer Ser.). (ENG.). 22p. (J). bds. 4.99 (978-0-689-85483-5(8), Simon Spotlight/Nickelodeon) Simon Spotlight/Nickelodeon.

Sloan, Brian. A Really Nice Prom Mess. 2008. (ENG., Illus.). 320p. (YA). (gr. 9-12). pap. 8.99 (978-1-4169-5389-0(2), Simon & Schuster Bks. For Young Readers) Simon & Schuster Bks. For Young Readers.

Smith, Adelene Keeler. Sophie Gets Curtains! 2010. 28p. (J). pap. 12.99 (978-1-4520-8943-0(4)) AuthorHouse.

Smith, Audrey. The Halloween Misfits. 2004. 23p. (J). pap. 9.95 incl. audio compact disk (978-0-9722673-4-2(4)) Audrey Productions.

Smith, J. D. The Best Mariachi in the World/El Mejor Mariachi del Mundo. de la Vega, Eida, tr. Jones, Dani, illus. 2008. (ENG & SPA.). 32p. (J). (gr. 4-7). lib. bdg. 16.95 (978-0-9770906-1-7(2), Raven Tree Pr.,Csi) Continental Sales, Inc.

Smith, Rosemary. Lizzie Goes to Tea. 2013. 32p. pap. 12.50 (978-1-62212-338-4(7), Strategic Bk. Publishing) Strategic Book Publishing & Rights Agency (SBPRA).

Soto, Gary. Chato & the Party Animals. Guevara, Susan, illus. (Chato Ser.). 25.95 incl. audio (978-1-59112-460-3(3)); 28.95 incl. audio compact disk (978-1-59112-920-2(6)); 25.95 incl. audio (978-1-59112-460-3(3)); pap. 37.95 incl. audio (978-1-59112-461-0(1)); pap. 39.95 incl. audio compact disk (978-1-59112-921-9(4)) Live Oak Media.

—Chato & the Party Animals. Guevara, Susan, illus. 2004. (Chato Ser.). (ENG.). 32p. (J). (gr. -1-3). reprint ed. pap. 7.99 (978-0-14-240032-6(7), Puffin Books) Penguin Young Readers Group.

—Chato & the Party Animals. Guevara, Susan, illus. 2004. (Chato Ser.). (gr. -1-3). 17.00 (978-0-7569-2921-3(0)) Perfection Learning Corp.

—Chato y los Amigos Pachangueros. Guevara, Susan, illus. 2004.Tr. of Chato & the Party Animals. (SPA & ENG.). 32p. (J). (gr. -1-3). reprint ed. pap. 7.99 (978-0-14-240033-3(5), Puffin Books) Penguin Young Readers Group.

Spaziante, Patrick, illus. OLIVIA & the Kite Party. 2012. (Olivia TV Tie-In Ser.). (ENG.). 24p. (J). (gr. -1-1). 16.99 (978-1-4424-4650-2(1), Simon Spotlight) Simon Spotlight.

—Olivia Plans a Tea Party: From the Fancy Keepsake Collection. 2011. (Olivia TV Tie-In Ser.). (ENG.). 28p. (J). (gr. -1-2). 6.99 (978-1-4423-3962-0(4), Simon Spotlight) Simon Spotlight.

Spohn, Kate. Turtle & Snake's Spooky Halloween. Spohn, Kate, illus. 2003. (Easy-to-Read Ser.). (Illus.). 32p. (J). (gr. -1-3). 11.65 (978-0-7569-1949-8(5)) Perfection Learning Corp.

Stanek, Robert, pseud. Have a Surprise Party. 2009. (Bugville Critters Ser.: No. 13). (ENG., Illus.). 52p. (J). 14.95 (978-1-57545-209-8(X), Reagent Pr. Bks. for Young Readers) RP Media.

Starr, Meg. Alicia's Happy Day, 1 vol. Van Wright, Cornelius & Hu, Ying-Hwa, illus. 2003. (ENG.). 32p. (J). pap. 5.95 (978-1-932065-06-0(7)) Star Bright Bks., Inc.

—Alicia's Happy Day, 1 vol. Hu, Ying-Hwa & Van Wright, Cornelius, illus. 2003. (ENG.). 32p. (J). (gr. -1-3). 15.95 (978-1-887734-85-1(6)) Star Bright Bks., Inc.

—Alicia's Happy Day (Spanish/English), 1 vol. Fiol, Maria, tr. from ENG. Van Wright, Cornelius & Hu, Ying-Hwa, illus. 2007. (SPA & ENG.). 32p. (J). (gr. k-3). pap. 6.95 (978-1-59572-116-7(9)) Star Bright Bks., Inc.

—Alicia's Happy Day (Spanish/English), 1 vol. Fiol, Maria, tr. Van Wright, Cornelius & Hu, Ying-Hwa, illus. 2007. (ENG.). 32p. (J). (gr. -1-3). 15.95 (978-1-59572-115-0(0)) Star Bright Bks., Inc.

Stern, A. J. Miss Fortune, 7 vols. Marts, Doreen Mulryan, illus. 2012. (Frankly, Frannie Ser.: 7). (ENG.). 128p. (J). (gr. 1-3). pap. 5.99 (978-0-448-45748-2(2), Grosset & Dunlap) Penguin Young Readers Group.

Sticker Dolly Dressing Parties (Revised) 2017. (Sticker Dolly Dressing Ser.). (ENG.). (J). pap. 9.99 **(978-0-7945-3784-5(7)**, Usborne) EDC Publishing.

Stine, R. L. The Birthday Party of No Return! 2012. (Goosebumps Hall of Horrors Ser.: 6). (ENG.). 160p. (J). (gr. 3-7). pap. 6.99 (978-0-545-28938-2(6), Scholastic Paperbacks) Scholastic, Inc.

—The Birthday Party of No Return. 2012. (Goosebumps HorrorLand: Hall of Horrors Ser.: 6). lib. bdg. 17.20 (978-0-606-23932-5(4), Turtleback) Turtleback Bks.

—Fear Street Super Thriller: Party Games & Don't Stay up Late. 2015. (Fear Street Ser.). (ENG.). 592p. (YA). (gr. 7-12). pap. 11.99 (978-1-250-07693-9(5), 9781250076939, St. Martin's Griffin) St. Martin's Pr.

—Slappy New Year! 2010. (Goosebumps Horrorland Ser.: 18). (ENG.). 160p. (J). (gr. 3-7). pap. 6.99 (978-0-545-16199-2(1), Scholastic Paperbacks) Scholastic, Inc.

Stockham, Jess, illus. Party! 2011. (Helping Hands Ser.). (ENG.). 24p. (J). (978-1-84643-413-6(0)) Child's Play International Ltd.

Stone, Kate. Happy Birthday, Mouse! (ENG.). 16p. (J). 2014. bds. 5.99 (978-1-4494-4387-0(7)) 2012. (Illus.). bds. 10.99 (978-1-4494-0838-1(9)) Andrews McMeel Publishing.

Stone, Kate & Accord Publishing Staff. Bunnies for Tea. 2013. (ENG., Illus.). 10p. (J). bds. 7.99 (978-1-4494-2887-7(8)) Andrews McMeel Publishing.

Studio Mouse Staff. Pooh & Roo. 2008. (ENG., Illus.). 36p. (J). (gr. -1). 7.99 (978-1-59069-420-6(1)) Studio Mouse LLC.

Sullivan, Kevin & Goldman, Leslie. Anne's Babysitting Blues. 2010. (Anne of Green Gables for Young Readers Ser.). (ENG.). 64p. (J). (gr. 2-4). pap. 4.95 (978-0-9736803-1-7(8)) Davenport Pr. CAN. Dist: Independent Pubs. Group.

Surplice, Holly. Guinea Pig Party. Surplice, Holly, illus. 2015. (ENG., Illus.). 24p. (J). (— 1). bds. 7.99 (978-0-7636-7604-9(7), Nosy Crow) Candlewick Pr.

Surprise Party. 2004. (Bella & Rosie Set 2 Ser.). (J). 7.67 (978-1-932570-21-2(7)) Pioneer Valley Bks.

Tada, Hiroshi. Who's There. Perry, Mia, tr. 2009. 24p. 11.95 (978-1-74126-350-3(6)) R.I.C. Pubns. AUS. Dist: SCB Distributors.

Taylor, Chloë. Dressed to Frill. Zhang, Nancy, illus. 2015. (Sew Zoey Ser.: 12). (ENG.). 160p. (J). (gr. 3-7). pap. 6.99 (978-1-4814-2930-6(2), Simon Spotlight) Simon Spotlight.

Tegen, Katherine. Dracula & Frankenstein Are Friends. Cushman, Doug, illus. 2003. 32p. (J). (gr. -1-3). 15.99 (978-0-06-000115-5(1)) HarperCollins Pubs.

Terry, Anne. Honest Bob, the Dog, Has a Tea Party. 2013. 30p. pap. 9.83 (978-1-62884-761-1(1)) Speedy Publishing LLC.

Thaler, Mike. Church Harvest Mess-Tivall, 1 vol. Lee, Jared, illus. 2010. (Tales from the Back Pew Ser.). (ENG.). 32p. (J). pap. 3.99 (978-0-310-71595-5(4)) Zonderkidz.

—The Spring Dance from the Black Lagoon. Lee, Jared, illus. 2009. 62p. (J). (978-0-545-07223-6(9)) Scholastic, Inc.

—The Spring Dance from the Black Lagoon, 1 vol. Lee, Jared, illus. 2012. (Black Lagoon Adventures Ser.: No. 2). (ENG.). 64p. (J). (gr. 2-5). 24.21 (978-1-59961-963-7(6)) Spotlight.

Thompson, Yvonne. Miss Tilly's Party. Krecskay, Stephen, illus. 2004. (J). per. (978-0-9749561-0-7(4)) My Sunshine Bks.

Trapani, Iza. Haunted Party. Trapani, Iza, illus. 2010. (ENG., Illus.). 28p. (J). (gr. -1-2). pap. 7.95 (978-1-58089-247-6(7)) Charlesbridge Publishing, Inc.

Trimble, Marcia. Liberty Cafe Is Open. Hayden, Jennifer, illus. 2006. (J). pap. 895.00 (978-1-891577-91-8(3)); 32p. lib. bdg. 15.95 (978-1-891577-90-1(5)) Images Pr.

Turner, Jill. Percival's Party. Townsend, Peter, illus. 2003. (J). pap. 12.95 (978-1-74047-235-7(7)) Book Co. Publishing Pty, Ltd., The AUS. Dist: Penton Overseas, Inc.

Tuttle, Mark. Lexi's Tea Party. Combs, Bradley, illus. 2011. 32p. pap. 24.95 (978-1-4560-9919-0(1)) America Star Bks.

Ure, Jean. Over the Moon. Donnelly, Karen, illus. 2006. (ENG.). 192p. (J). (gr. 4-7). per. 8.99 (978-0-00-716464-6(5), HarperCollins Children's Bks.) HarperCollins Pubs. Ltd. GBR. Dist: HarperCollins Pubs.

Valentin, Karen. Block Party. 2009. 32p. (J). (gr. -1-3). 6.95 (978-1-60349-017-7(5), Marimba Bks.) Hudson Publishing Group, The.

van Genechten, Guido. Big & Small. 2013. (Odd One Out Ser.). (ENG.). 18p. (J). (gr. -1-k). bds. 12.95 (978-1-60537-149-8(1)) Cobblestone Publishing Co.

—Ricky's Birthday. 2012. (ENG.). 24p. (J). (gr. -1-k). 16.95 (978-1-60537-119-1(X)) Cobblestone Publishing Co.

Volker, Kerstin. Lilly's Birthday Party. 2003. (Funny Friends Lift-and-Learn Bks.). (Illus.). 14p. (J). 5.99 (978-1-59384-022-8(5)) Parklane Publishing.

Vulliamy, Clara. Muffin & the Birthday Surprise. Vulliamy, Clara, illus. 2012. (ENG., Illus.). 32p. (J). (gr. -1-k). pap. 9.99 (978-1-4083-1245-2(X)) Hodder & Stoughton GBR. Dist: Hachette Bk. Group.

Wallace, Nancy Elizabeth. Tell-A-Bunny, 0 vols. Wallace, Nancy Elizabeth, illus. 2007. (ENG., Illus.). 36p. (J). (gr. -1-1). 7.99 (978-0-7614-5369-7(5), 9780761453697, Amazon Children's Publishing) Amazon Publishing.

Wallace, Nancy K. The Christmas Cats, 1 vol. Housley, Cathren, illus. 2011. (ENG.). 32p. (J). (gr. k-3). 16.99 (978-1-58980-979-6(3)) Pelican Publishing Co., Inc.

Walters, Eric. House Party, 1 vol. 2007. (Orca Soundings Ser.). (ENG.). (YA). (gr. 8-12). 112p. 14.95 (978-1-55143-743-9(0)); 128p. pap. 9.95 (978-1-55143-741-5(4)) Orca Bk. Pubs. USA.

Watt, Fiona. Complete Book of First Experiences. rev. ed. 2011. (First Experiences Ser.). 144p. (J). ring bd. 19.99 (978-0-7945-2948-2(8), Usborne) EDC Publishing.

Watt, Mélanie. Scaredy Squirrel Has a Birthday Party, 0 vols. Watt, Mélanie, illus. (ENG., Illus.). 32p. (J). (gr. -1-3). 2014. pap. 7.95 (978-1-55453-716-7(9)) 2011. 16.95 (978-1-55453-468-5(2)) Kids Can Pr., Ltd. CAN. Dist: Hachette Bk. Group.

Watts, Debra G. Carter Car & His Wild & Carazy Birthday. 2011. 40p. pap. 21.99 (978-1-4628-4864-5(8)) Xlibris Corp.

Weeks, Sarah. Oggie Cooder - Party Animal! 2011. (Oggie Cooder Ser.). (ENG.). 176p. (J). (gr. 2-5). pap. 6.99 (978-0-439-92796-3(X), Scholastic Paperbacks) Scholastic, Inc.

Weinberg, Jennifer Liberts. Happy Birthday, Mike! 2014. (Step into Reading Level 2 Ser.). lib. bdg. 13.55 (978-0-606-36006-7(9)) Turtleback Bks.

Weinert, Matthias. No Bath, No Cake! Polly's Pirate Party. 2013. (ENG., Illus.). 48p. (J). (gr. -1-3). 17.95 (978-0-7358-4112-3(8)) North-South Bks., Inc.

Wells, Carolyn. Patty at Home. 2007. (ENG.). 204p. per. 12.95 (978-1-4218-3321-7(2)) 1st World Publishing, Inc.

Wells, Rosemary. Bunny Party. 2003. (Max & Ruby Ser.). (ENG., Illus.). 32p. (J). (gr. -1-k). pap. 6.99 (978-0-14-250162-7(X), Puffin Books) Penguin Young Readers Group.

—Ten Kisses for Sophie! Wells, Rosemary, illus. 2016. (ENG., Illus.). 32p. (J). (— 1). 16.99 (978-0-670-01665-5(9), Viking Books for Young Readers) Penguin Young Readers Group.

West, C. The Adventures of Ice Cream & Honey Buns: It's a Party. 2012. 24p. pap. 14.93 (978-1-4669-4665-1(2)) Trafford Publishing.

Weston, Robert Paul. Prince Puggly of Spud & the Kingdom of Spiff. 2013. (ENG., Illus.). 224p. (J). (gr. 3-7). 15.99 (978-1-59514-567-3(2), Razorbill) Penguin Young Readers Group.

Weston Woods Staff, creator. Chato & the Party Animals. 2011. 38.75 (978-0-439-84581-6(5)) 2011. 18.95 (978-0-439-73984-9(5)) 2004. 29.95 (978-1-55592-703-5(3)) Weston Woods Studios, Inc.

—Three Cheers for Catherine the Great. 2011. 18.95 (978-0-439-80506-3(6)) Weston Woods Studios, Inc.

—Three Cheers for Catherine the Great! 2011. 38.75 (978-0-439-78620-1(7)) Weston Woods Studios, Inc.

Westover, Gail. Mrs Mouse's Garden Party in Giggleswick Village. Daly, Karen Anne, illus. 2012. 26p. pap. 9.95 (978-0-9821507-9-5(2)) Thistlewood Publishing.

Wheeler, Lisa. Boogie Knights. Siegel, Mark, illus. 2008. (ENG.). 40p. (J). (gr. -1-3). 16.99 (978-0-689-87639-4(4), Atheneum/Richard Jackson Bks.) Simon & Schuster Children's Publishing.

White, Toni. Ridge Street Prom. 2008. 182p. pap. 12.96 (978-1-4357-1966-8(2)) Lulu Pr., Inc.

Willems, Mo. Happy Pig Day! Willems, Mo, illus. 2011. (Elephant & Piggie Book Ser.). (ENG., Illus.). 64p. (J). (gr. -1-k). 9.99 (978-1-4231-4342-0(6)) Hyperion Pr.

—I Am Invited to a Party! Willems, Mo, illus. rev. ed. 2007. (Elephant & Piggie Book Ser.). (ENG., Illus.). 64p. (J). (gr. -1-k). 9.99 (978-1-4231-0687-6(3)) Hyperion Pr.

Willis, Jeanne. We're Going to a Party! Ross, Tony, illus. 2013. (ENG.). 16p. (J). (gr. -1-k). 12.99 (978-1-84939-122-1(X)) Andersen Pr. GBR. Dist: Independent Pubs. Group.

Wilson, Anna. Puppy Party, 1. unabr. ed. 2014. (ENG., Illus.). 256p. (J). (gr. 2-4). pap. 7.99 (978-0-330-51881-9(X)) Pan Macmillan GBR. Dist: Independent Pubs. Group.

Wilson, Karma. Bear Snores On. Chapman, Jane, illus. 2005. (Bear Bks.). (ENG.). 34p. (J). (gr. -1-k). bds. 7.99 (978-1-4169-0272-0(4), Little Simon) Little Simon.

Wilson, Wendy. Just Desserts. 2007. 53p. pap. 16.95 (978-1-4241-9285-4(4)) America Star Bks.

Wing, Natasha. The Night Before My Birthday. Wummer, Amy, illus. 2014. (Night Before Ser.). (ENG.). 32p. (J). (gr. -1-k). 4.99 (978-0-448-48000-8(X), Grosset & Dunlap) Penguin Young Readers Group.

—The Night Before My Birthday. 2014. (Night Before Ser.). lib. bdg. 14.75 (978-0-606-34133-2(1), Turtleback) Turtleback Bks.

Winkler, Henry & Oliver, Lin. Fake Snakes & Weird Wizards. Garrett, Scott, illus. 2015. (Here's Hank Ser.: No. 4). (ENG.). 128p. (J). (gr. 1-3). 5.99 (978-0-448-48252-1(5), Grosset & Dunlap) Penguin Young Readers Group.

Winnie the Pooh: Party in the Wood. 2011. 32p. pap. 4.99 (978-1-4231-5386-3(3)) Disney Pr.

Wolf, Elisabeth. Lulu in la la Land. 2013. (Lulu in la la Land Ser.: 1). (ENG.). 272p. (J). (gr. 3-6). pap. 6.99 (978-1-4022-8504-2(3), 9781402285042, Sourcebooks Jabberwocky) Sourcebooks, Inc.

Wood, Audrey. The Birthday Queen. Wood, Don, illus. 2013. (ENG.). 32p. (J). (gr. -1-3). 17.99 (978-0-545-41474-6(1), Blue Sky Pr., The) Scholastic, Inc.

Wood, Maryrose. The Mysterious Howling. Klassen, Jon, illus. (Incorrigible Children of Ashton Place Ser.: 1). (ENG.). (J). (gr. 3-7). 2015. 288p. pap. 6.99 (978-0-06-236693-1(9))Bk. I. 2010. 272p. 16.99 (978-0-06-179105-5(9)) HarperCollins Pubs.

Wright, Jason F. Penny's Christmas Jar Party. Sowards, Ben, illus. 2009. 32p. (J). 17.95 (978-1-60641-167-4(5), Shadow Mountain) Shadow Mountain Publishing.

Yasuda, Anita. The Crazy Clues, 1 vol. Harpster, Steve, illus. 2013. (Dino Detectives Ser.). (ENG.). 32p. (gr. 1-2). lib. bdg. 22.65 (978-1-4342-5971-4(4)) Stone Arch Bks.

—Crazy Clues. Harpster, Steve, illus. 2013. (Dino Detectives Ser.). (ENG.). 32p. (gr. 1-2). pap. 5.95 (978-1-4342-6200-4(6)) Stone Arch Bks.

Yasuda, Anita & Harpster, Steve. The Crazy Clues. 2013. (Dino Detectives Ser.). (ENG.). 32p. (gr. 1-2). pap. 29.70 (978-1-4342-6226-4(X)) Stone Arch Bks.

Yeoman, John. Mr. Nodd's Ark. Blake, Quentin, illus. 2016. (ENG.). 32p. (J). (-k). pap. 9.99 (978-1-78344-374-1(X)) Andersen Pr. GBR. Dist: Independent Pubs. Group.

Yolen, Jane. Come to the Fairies' Ball. Lippincott, Gary, illus. 2009. (ENG.). 32p. (J). (gr. 2-4). 17.95 (978-1-59078-464-8(2), Wordsong) Boyds Mills Pr.

—How Do Dinosaurs Say Happy Birthday? Teague, Mark, illus. 2011. (How Do Dinosaurs... Ser.). (ENG.). 12p. (J). (gr. -1-k). bds. 6.99 (978-0-545-15353-9(0), Blue Sky Pr., The) Scholastic, Inc.

Yorinks, Arthur. Flappy & Scrappy. Ivanov, Olga & Ivanov, Aleksey, illus. 2010. (I Can Read Level 2 Ser.). (ENG.). 48p. (J). (gr. k-3). 16.99 (978-0-06-205117-2(2)) HarperCollins Pubs.

—Flappy & Scrappy. Ivanov, Aleksey & Ivanov, Olga, illus. 2010. (I Can Read Level 2 Ser.). (ENG.). 48p. (J). (gr. k-3). pap. 3.99 (978-0-06-205913-0(0)) HarperCollins Pubs.

Zann, Tara. Wild Child: Forest's First Birthday Party. Belleza, Rhoda, ed. Widdowson, Dan, illus. 2017. (Wild Child Ser.: 3). (ENG.). 128p. (J). pap. 5.99 (978-1-250-10389-5(4), 9781250103895) Imprint IND. Dist: Macmillan.

PARTIES, POLITICAL

see Political Parties

PASSIONS

see Emotions

PASSIVE RESISTANCE

see also Boycotts; Nonviolence

Aronson, Marc & Budhos, Marina Tamar. Sugar Changed the World: A Story of Magic, Spice, Slavery, Freedom, & Science. 2010. (ENG., Illus.). 176p. (YA). (gr. 7-18). 21.99 (978-0-618-57492-6(1)) Houghton Mifflin Harcourt Publishing Co.

PASSOVER

Adler, David A. The Story of Passover. Weber, Jill, illus. (ENG.). 32p. (J). (gr. -1-3). 2015. 6.99 (978-0-8234-3304-9(8)) 2014. 15.95 (978-0-8234-2902-8(4)) Holiday Hse., Inc.

Aloian, Molly. Passover. 2009. (Celebrations in My World Ser.). (ENG., Illus.). 32p. (J). (gr. 1-3). pap. (978-0-7787-4311-8(X)) Crabtree Publishing Co.

Balsley, Tilda. ABC Passover Hunt. Poole, Helen, illus. 2016. (ENG.). 32p. (gr. -1-3). 17.99 (978-1-4677-7843-5(5), 1401803, Kar-Ben Publishing) Lerner Publishing Group.

—Lotsa Matzah. Gutierrez, Akemi, illus. 2013. (Passover Ser.). (ENG.). 12p. (J). (gr. -1-1). bds. 5.95 (978-0-7613-6629-4(6), Kar-Ben Publishing) Lerner Publishing Group.

Berger, Barry W. Passover Haggadah. Hall, Melanie W., illus. 2004. 36p. (978-0-9674319-3-2(X)) Messianic Perspectives.

Bullard, Lisa. Sarah's Passover. Basaluzzo, Constanza, illus. 2012. (Holidays & Special Days Ser.). 24p. (gr. k-2). (J). pap. 39.62 (978-0-7613-9245-3(9), Millbrook Pr.); (ENG.). pap. 6.95 (978-0-7613-8582-0(7), Millbrook Pr.); (ENG.). lib. bdg. 23.93 (978-0-7613-5081-1(0)) Lerner Publishing Group.

Cohen, Joan Freeman & Freeman, Jonathan M. In Every Generation: A Model Seder Haggadah. 2005. (J). (978-0-87441-731-9(7)) Behrman Hse., Inc.

Cohen, Tina. Pesach What & Why? 2005. 36p. 14.99 (978-1-4116-6454-8(X)) Lulu Pr., Inc.

dePaola, Tomie. My First Passover. dePaola, Tomie, illus. 2015. (ENG., Illus.). 14p. (J). (gr. -1-k). bds. 5.99 (978-0-448-44791-9(6), Grosset & Dunlap) Penguin Young Readers Group.

Dorling Kindersley Publishing Staff. Passover. 2004. (Ultimate Sticker Bks.). (ENG.). 16p. (J). (gr. k-3). pap. 6.99 (978-0-7566-0285-7(8), DK Children) Dorling Kindersley Publishing, Inc.

Fishman, Cathy Goldberg. Passover. Marshall, Ann & Reeves, Jeni, illus. 2006. (On My Own Holidays Ser.). (ENG.). 48p. (gr. 2-4). 25.26 (978-1-57505-656-2(9)) Lerner Publishing Group.

—Passover. Reeves, Jeni, illus. 2006. (On My Own Holidays Ser.). (ENG.). 48p. (gr. 2-4). per. 6.95 (978-1-57505-695-1(X), First Avenue Editions) Lerner Publishing Group.

Fishman, Cathy Goldberg & Hall, Melanie W. On Passover. 2003. (Illus.). 28p. (J). (gr. k-4). reprint ed. 16.00 (978-0-7567-6988-8(4)) DIANE Publishing Co.

Gillespie, Katie. Passover. 2015. (Let's Celebrate American Holidays Ser.). (ENG.). (J). lib. bdg. 27.13 *(978-1-4896-3629-4(3)*, AV2 by Weigl) Weigl Pubs., Inc.

Groner, Judyth Saypol & Wikler, Madeline. All about Passover. Kreiswirth, Kinny, illus. 2003. (ENG.). 32p. (J). (gr. -1-3). pap. 5.95 *(978-1-58013-060-8(7)*, Kar-Ben Publishing) Lerner Publishing Group.

Hayes, Amy. Celebrate Passover. 2015. (J). *(978-1-62713-478-1(6))* Cavendish Square Publishing.

Heiligman, Deborah. Celebrate Passover: With Matzah, Maror, & Memories. (Holidays Around the World Ser.). (ENG., Illus.). 32p. (J). (gr. 1-4). 2010. pap. 6.95 *(978-1-4263-0629-7(6))* 2007. 15.95 *(978-1-4263-0018-9(2))* 2007. lib. bdg. 23.90 *(978-1-4263-0019-6(0))* National Geographic Society. (National Geographic Children's Bks.).

—Holidays Around the World: Celebrate Passover: With Matzah, Maror, & Memories. 2017. (Holidays Around the World Ser.). (ENG., Illus.). 32p. (J). (gr. 1-4). pap. 7.99 *(978-1-4263-2745-2(5)*, National Geographic Children's Bks.) National Geographic Society.

Isaacs, Ronald H. & Rostoker-Gruber, Karen. The Family (and Frog!) Haggadah. Urbanovic, Jackie, illus. 2017. (J). *(978-0-87441-937-5(9))* Behrman Hse., Inc.

Kimmel, Eric A. Wonders & Miracles: A Passover Companion. Kimmel, Eric A., illus. 2004. (Wonders & Miracles Ser.). (ENG., Illus.). 144p. (J). 21.99 *(978-0-439-07175-8(5))* Scholastic, Inc.

Koffsky, Ann D. Frogs in the Bed: My Passover Seder Activity Book. 2014. (ENG & HEB., Illus.). 32p. (J). (gr. -1-3). pap. 7.95 *(978-0-87441-913-9(1))* Behrman Hse., Inc.

Korngold, Jamie. Seder in the Desert. Finkelstein, Jeff, photos by. 2014. (Passover Ser.). (ENG., Illus.). 32p. (J). (gr. -1-2). 7.95 *(978-0-7613-7502-9(3))*; 17.95 *(978-0-7613-7501-2(5))* Lerner Publishing Group. (Kar-Ben Publishing).

Kropf, Latifa Berry. It's Seder Time! Cohen, Tod, illus. Cohen, Tod, photos by. 2004. (ENG.). 24p. (J). (gr. -1-1). 12.95 *(978-1-58013-092-9(5)*, Kar-Ben Publishing) Lerner Publishing Group.

Lehman-Wilzig, Tami. Passover Around the World. Wolf, Elizabeth, illus. 2007. (Passover Ser.). (ENG.). 48p. (J). (gr. 3-5). lib. bdg. 15.95 *(978-1-58013-213-8(8))*; per. 7.95 *(978-1-58013-215-2(4))* Lerner Publishing Group. (Kar-Ben Publishing).

Leon, Carol Boyd. Dayenu! A Passover Haggadah for Families & Children. Connelly, Gwen, illus. 2008. 32p. (J). (gr. 1-3). 16.95 incl. audio compact disk *(978-1-60280-041-0(3))*; pap. 8.95 incl. audio compact disk *(978-1-60280-039-7(1))*; spiral bd. 16.95 incl. audio compact disk *(978-1-60280-040-3(5))*; bds. 24.95 incl. audio compact disk *(978-1-60280-042-7(1))* Ktav Publishing Hse., Inc.

Lewis, Anne Margaret. What Am I? Passover. Mills, Tom, illus. 2012. (ENG.). 24p. (J). (gr. -1 — 1). 9.99 *(978-0-8075-8971-7(3))* Whitman, Albert & Co.

Lupo, Tamar. Passover. 2006. (American Holidays Ser.). (Illus.). 24p. (J). (gr. 3-7). lib. bdg. 24.45 *(978-1-59036-462-8(7))*; per. 8.95 *(978-1-59036-465-9(1))* Weigl Pubs., Inc.

Murray, Julie. Passover, 1 vol. 2011. (Holidays Set 3 Ser.). (ENG., Illus.). 24p. (J). (gr. 1-4). 25.65 *(978-1-61783-040-2(2))* ABDO Publishing Co.

Pirotta, Saviour. Passover. 2007. (We Love Holidays Ser.). (Illus.). 24p. (J). (gr. 3-7). lib. bdg. 22.60 *(978-1-4042-3707-0(0)*, PowerKids Pr.) Rosen Publishing Group, Inc., The.

Polak, Monique. Passover: Festival of Freedom, 1 vol. 2016. (Orca Origins Ser.). (ENG., Illus.). 72p. (J). (gr. 3-7). 24.95 *(978-1-4598-0990-1(4))* Orca Bk. Pubs. USA.

Rossel, Seymour. The Storybook Haggadah. 2007. pap. 9.95 *(978-1-932687-59-0(9)*, Pitspopany Pr.) Simcha Media Group.

Schorr, Titus. We Celebrate Passover, 01 vols., 1. 2016. (Rosen REAL Readers: Social Studies Nonfiction / Fiction: Family, Community, & the World Ser.). (ENG.). 12p. (J). pap. 6.33 *(978-1-5081-1785-8(3)*, Rosen Classroom) Rosen Publishing Group, Inc., The.

Silberg, Francis Barry. The Story of Passover. Britt, Stephanie, illus. 2017. (J). *(978-0-8249-1652-7(2))* Worthy Publishing.

Story of Passover. 2004. pap. 6.95 *(978-0-8249-6277-7(X)*, Ideal Pubns.) Worthy Publishing.

Tabs, Judy & Steinberg, Barbara. Matzah Meals: A Passover Cookbook for Kids. Hauser, Bill, illus. 2004. (Passover Ser.). (ENG.). 64p. (J). (gr. 3-5). pap. 7.95 *(978-1-58013-086-8(0)*, Kar-Ben Publishing) Lerner Publishing Group.

Traditional Staff. Dayenu! A Favorite Passover Song. Latimer, Miriam, illus. 2012. (ENG.). 12p. (J). (gr. -1-k). bds. 7.99 *(978-0-545-31236-3(1)*, Cartwheel Bks.) Scholastic, Inc.

Webster, Christine. How to Draw Passover Symbols. 2009. (Kid's Guide to Drawing Ser.). 24p. (gr. 3-3). 47.90 *(978-1-61511-039-1(9)*, PowerKids Pr.) Rosen Publishing Group, Inc., The.

PASSOVER—FICTION

Akselrad, January & Young, Jennifer. Matzah & Miracles: A Passover Musical & Chapter Book. Palagonia, Peter, illus. 2012. (ENG.). 88p. (J). 15.00 *(978-0-9822134-8-3(4))* See The Wish.

Balsley, Tilda & Fischer, Ellen. Grover & Big Bird's Passover Celebration. Leigh, Tom, illus. 2013. (Passover Ser.). (ENG.). 24p. (J). (gr. -1-1). 6.95 *(978-0-7613-8492-2(8))*; lib. bdg. 16.95 *(978-0-7613-8491-5(X))* Lerner Publishing Group. (Kar-Ben Publishing).

Barash, Chris. Is It Passover Yet? Psacharopulo, Alessandra, illus. 2015. (ENG.). 32p. (J). (gr. -1-3). 16.99 *(978-0-8075-6330-4(7))* Whitman, Albert & Co.

Black, Joe. Afikomen Mambo. Prater, Linda, illus. 2011. (ENG.). 24p. (J). (gr. -1 — 1). pap. 8.95 *(978-0-7613-5639-4(8)*, Kar-Ben Publishing) Lerner Publishing Group.

—Afikomen Mambo. Brown, Richard E. & Prater, Linda, illus. 2011. (Passover Ser.). (ENG.). 24p. (J). (gr. -1 — 1). lib. bdg. 17.95 *(978-0-7613-5638-7(X)*, Kar-Ben Publishing) Lerner Publishing Group.

Clausman, Rachel. Miriam, Come Sit. 2011. 24p. pap. 11.32 *(978-1-4634-4812-7(0))* AuthorHouse.

Cohen, Deborah Bodin. Engineer Ari & the Passover Rush. Kober, Shahar, illus. 2015. (J). 6.99 *(978-1-4677-6201-4(6))*; (ENG.). 32p. lib. bdg. 17.95 *(978-1-4677-3470-7(5))* Lerner Publishing Group. (Kar-Ben Publishing).

Fireside, Bryna J. Private Joel & the Sewell Mountain Seder. Costello, Shawn, illus. 2008. (Passover Ser.). (J). (gr. 3-6). 47p. lib. bdg. 16.95 *(978-0-8225-7240-4(0))*; (ENG.). 48p. per. 6.95 *(978-0-8225-9050-7(6))* Lerner Publishing Group. (Kar-Ben Publishing).

Gehl, Laura. And Then Another Sheep Turned Up. Adele, Amy, illus. 2015. (J). 6.99 *(978-1-4677-1190-6(X))*; (ENG.). 32p. (gr. -1-3). lib. bdg. 17.95 *(978-1-4677-1188-3(8))* Lerner Publishing Group. (Kar-Ben Publishing).

Goldin, Barbara Diamond. The Passover Cowboy. Capaldi, Gina, illus. 2016. (J). *(978-1-68115-527-2(3))* Behrman Hse., Inc.

Hannigan, Lynne. Sam's Passover. 2004. (ENG., Illus.). 32p. pap. 5.95 *(978-0-7136-4084-7(7)*, 93342, A&C Black) Bloomsbury Publishing Plc GBR. Dist: Consortium Bk. Sales & Distribution.

Ho, Jannie. The Great Matzah Hunt. Ho, Jannie, illus. 2010. (ENG., Illus.). 12p. (J). (gr. -1-k). 6.99 *(978-0-8431-8969-8(X)*, Price Stern Sloan) Penguin Young Readers Group.

Jules, Jacqueline & Hechtkopf, Jacqueline. Going on a Hametz Hunt. Brown, Rick, illus. 2010. (Passover Ser.). (ENG.). 12p. (J). (gr. -1 — 1). 5.95 *(978-0-7613-5124-5(8)*, Kar-Ben Publishing) Lerner Publishing Group.

Kimmel, Eric A. Scarlett & Sam: Escape from Egypt. Stevanovic, Ivica, illus. 2015. (J). 6.99 *(978-1-4677-6207-6(5))*; (ENG.). 168p. (gr. 1-3). lib. bdg. 15.95 *(978-1-4677-3850-7(6))* Lerner Publishing Group. (Kar-Ben Publishing).

King, Emily. Clopper & the Lost Boy, 1 vol. Olson, Ed, illus. 2009. 32p. (J). 12.99 *(978-0-8254-2946-0(3))* Kregel Pubns.

Koffsky, Ann D., illus. Kayla & Kugel's Almost-Perfect Passover. 2016. (J). *(978-1-68115-508-1(7))* Behrman Hse., Inc.

Lanton, Sandy. The Littlest Levine. Keay, Claire, illus. 2014. (Passover Ser.). (ENG.). 24p. (J). (gr. -1-2). 7.95 *(978-0-7613-9046-6(4))*; 17.95 *(978-0-7613-9045-9(6))* Lerner Publishing Group. (Kar-Ben Publishing).

Leopold-Strauss, Linda. A Different Kind of Passover. Tugeau, Jeremy, illus. 2017. (ENG.). 32p. (gr. -1-3). 17.99 *(978-1-5124-0097-7(1))*; 23.99 ***(978-1-5124-2723-3(3))*** Lerner Publishing Group. (Kar-Ben Publishing).

Marshall, Linda Elovitz. The Passover Lamb. Mai-Wyss, Tatjana, illus. 2013. (ENG.). 32p. (J). (gr. 1-4). 17.99 *(978-0-307-93177-1(3)*, Random Hse. Bks. for Young Readers) Random Hse. Children's Bks.

Mermelstein, Yael. Izzy the Whiz & Passover McClean. Hartman, Carrie, illus. 2012. (Passover Ser.). (ENG.). 32p. (J). (gr. -1-2). lib. bdg. 17.95 *(978-0-7613-5653-0(3)*, Kar-Ben Publishing) Lerner Publishing Group.

—Izzy the Whiz & Passover Mcclean. Hartman, Carrie, illus. 2012. (Passover Ser.). (ENG.). 32p. (J). (gr. -1-2). pap. 7.95 *(978-0-7613-5654-7(1)*, Kar-Ben Publishing) Lerner Publishing Group.

Newman, Lesléa. A Sweet Passover. Slonim, David, illus. 2012. (ENG.). 40p. (J). (gr. k-2). 17.95 *(978-0-8109-9737-0(1)*, Abrams Bks. for Young Readers) Abrams, Inc.

Newman, Tracy. Passover Is Coming! Garófoli, Viviana, illus. 2016. (ENG.). 12p. (J). (gr. -1 — 1). 5.99 *(978-1-4677-5242-8(8)*, Kar-Ben Publishing) Lerner Publishing Group.

—Passover Is Coming! Garofoli, Viviana, illus. 2016. (ENG.). 12p. (gr. -1 — 1). 23.99 *(978-1-4677-9610-1(7)*, Kar-Ben Publishing) Lerner Publishing Group.

O'Connell, Rebecca. Penina Levine Is a Hard-boiled Egg. Lue Sue, Majella, illus. 2009. (ENG.). 192p. (J). (gr. 3-7). pap. 18.99 *(978-0-312-55026-4(X)*, 9780312550264) Square Fish.

Pearlman, Bobby. Passover Is Here! Desmoinaux, Christel, illus. 2005. (ENG.). 16p. (J). (gr. k-2). pap. 6.99 *(978-0-689-86587-9(2)*, Little Simon) Little Simon.

Peretz, I. L. & Goldin, Barbara Diamond. The Magician's Visit: A Passover Tale. Parker, Robert Andrew, illus. 2006. 28p. (J). (gr. 4-8). reprint ed. 15.00 *(978-1-4223-5408-7(3))*; pap. 5.00 *(978-1-4223-5400-1(8))* DIANE Publishing Co.

Portnoy, Mindy Avra. A Tale of Two Seders. Cis, Valeria, illus. 2010. (ENG.). 32p. (J). (gr. k-4). lib. bdg. 17.95 *(978-0-8225-9907-4(4))*; pap. 7.95 *(978-0-8225-9931-9(7))* Lerner Publishing Group. (Kar-Ben Publishing).

Rauchwerger, Diane Levin. Dinosaur on Passover. Wolff, Jason, illus. 2006. (ENG.). 24p. (J). (gr. -1-1). 15.95 *(978-1-58013-156-8(5))*; pap. 7.95 *(978-1-58013-161-2(1))* Lerner Publishing Group. (Kar-Ben Publishing).

Rothenberg, Joan. Matzah Ball Soup. Rothenberg, Joan, illus. 2005. (Illus.). 29p. (J). (gr. -1-2). reprint ed. 15.00 *(978-0-7567-8930-5(3))* DIANE Publishing Co.

Rouss, Sylvia. Sammy Spider's First Haggadah. Kahn, Katherine, illus. 2007. (Passover Ser.). (ENG.). 32p. (J). (gr. -1-3). per. 6.95 *(978-1-58013-230-5(8)*, Kar-Ben Publishing) Lerner Publishing Group.

Rouss, Sylvia A. A Sammy Spider Passover. Kahn, Katherine & Kahn, Katherine Janus, illus. 2017. (ENG.). 12p. (gr. -1 — 1). 5.99 *(978-1-4677-7970-8(9)*, Kar-Ben Publishing) Lerner Publishing Group.

Ruben, Kelly Easton. A Place for Elijah. Friar, Joanne H., illus. 2016. (ENG.). 32p. (J). (gr. k-4). 17.99 *(978-1-4677-7841-1(9)*, Kar-Ben Publishing) Lerner Publishing Group.

Schotter, Roni. Passover Magic, 0 vols. Hafner, Marylin, illus. 2011. (ENG.). 34p. (J). (gr. -1-3). pap. 7.99 *(978-0-7614-5842-5(5)*, 9780761458425, Amazon Children's Publishing) Amazon Publishing.

Shulman, Lisa. The Matzo Ball Boy. Litzinger, Rosanne, illus. 2007. (ENG.). 32p. (J). (gr. -1-2). pap. 6.99 *(978-0-14-240769-1(0)*, Puffin Books) Penguin Young Readers Group.

Silva, Shanna. Passover Scavenger Hunt. Sakamoto, Miki, illus. 2017. (ENG.). 24p. (gr. -1-3). 17.99 *(978-1-4677-8937-0(2)*, Kar-Ben Publishing) Lerner Publishing Group.

Sollish, Ari. Un Toque de Pesaj: A Touch of Passover. Becker, Boruch, illus. 2005.Tr. of Touch of Passover. (SPA.). 12p. (J). bds. 8.00 *(978-0-8266-0022-6(0))* Merkos L'Inyonei Chinuch.

—A Touch of Passover: A Touch & Feel Book. Becker, Boruch, illus. 2006. 12p. (J). bds. 7.95 *(978-0-8266-0021-9(2))* Merkos L'Inyonei Chinuch.

Strauss, Linda Leopold. The Elijah Door. Natchev, Alexi, illus. 2012. (ENG.). 32p. (J). 16.95 *(978-0-8234-1911-1(8))* Holiday Hse., Inc.

Wayland, April Halprin. More Than Enough. Kath, Katie, illus. 2016. (ENG.). 40p. (J). (-k). 16.99 *(978-0-8037-4126-3(X)*, Dial Bks) Penguin Young Readers Group.

Zucker, Jonny. Four Special Questions: A Passover Story. Cohen, Jan Barger, illus. 2003. (Festival Time Ser.). (ENG.). 24p. (J). (gr. -1-2). pap. 6.95 *(978-0-7641-2267-5(3))* Barron's Educational Series, Inc.

PASTEL DRAWING

Bolte, Mari. Paint It. 2013. (Paint It Ser.). (ENG.). 32p. (gr. 3-4). lib. bdg. 111.96 *(978-1-4765-3736-8(4)*, Snap Bks.) Capstone Press of Coughlan Cos.

—Paint It: The Art of Acrylics, Oils, Pastels, & Watercolors, 1 vol. Ice, D. C., illus. 2013. (Craft It Yourself Ser.). (ENG.). 144p. (gr. 3-4). pap. 14.95 *(978-1-62370-009-6(4))* Capstone Young Readers of Coughlan Cos.

—Pastels, 1 vol. Becker, Pamela, illus. 2013. (Paint It Ser.). (ENG.). 32p. (gr. 3-4). 27.99 *(978-1-4765-3111-3(0)*, Snap Bks.) Capstone Press of Coughlan Cos.

Merberg, Julie & Bober, Suzanne. Dancing with Degas. 2003. (Mini Masters Ser.: MINI). (ENG., Illus.). 22p. (J). (gr. -1-7). bds. 6.99 *(978-0-8118-4047-7(6))* Chronicle Bks. LLC.

PASTEL PAINTING

see Pastel Drawing

PASTELS

see Pastel Drawing

PASTEUR, LOUIS, 1822-1895

Ackerman, Jane. Louis Pasteur & the Founding of Microbiology. 2004. (Profiles in Science Ser.). (Illus.). 144p. (YA). (gr. 6-12). 26.95 *(978-1-931798-13-6(3))* Reynolds, Morgan Inc.

Alphin, Elaine Marie. Germ Hunter: A Story about Louis Pasteur. Verstraete, Elaine, illus. 2003. (Creative Minds Biography Ser.). 64p. (J). lib. bdg. 22.60 *(978-1-57505-179-6(6))*; (ENG.). (gr. 4-8). per. 8.95 *(978-0-87614-929-4(8))* Lerner Publishing Group. (Carolrhoda Bks.).

Ariel, A. D. Saving Lives the Story of Louis Pasteur. 2016. (Spring Forward Ser.). (J). (gr. 2). *(978-1-4900-9478-6(4))* Benchmark Education Co.

Dacquino, V. T. Louis Pasteur. 2011. (Early Connections Ser.). (J). *(978-1-61672-618-8(0))* Benchmark Education Co.

Dickmann, Nancy. Louis Pasteur: Germ Destroyer. 2015. (Superheroes of Science Ser.). (ENG., Illus.). 48p. (J). (gr. 6-6). pap. 14.05 *(978-1-4824-3141-4(6))* Stevens, Gareth Publishing LLLP.

Fandel, Jennifer. Louis Pasteur. 2003. (World Was Never the Same Ser.). (J). *(978-1-58417-266-6(5))* Lake Street Pubs.

Fandel, Jennifer, et al. Louis Pasteur & Pasteurization. Wilson, Keith, illus. 2007. (Inventions & Discovery Ser.). (ENG.). 32p. (gr. 3-4). pap. 8.10 *(978-0-7368-7896-8(3)*, Graphic Library) Capstone Press of Coughlan Cos.

—Louis Pasteur & Pasteurization, 1 vol. Wilson, Keith et al, illus. 2007. (Inventions & Discovery Ser.). (ENG.). 32p. (gr. 3-4). 30.65 *(978-0-7368-6844-0(5)*, Graphic Library) Capstone Press of Coughlan Cos.

Feinstein, Stephen. Louis Pasteur: The Father of Microbiology. 2008. (Inventors Who Changed the World Ser.). (Illus.). 128p. (J). (gr. 6-18). lib. bdg. 34.60 *(978-1-59845-078-1(6)*, MyReportLinks.com Bks.) Enslow Pubs., Inc.

Hunter, Nick. Louis Pasteur, 1 vol. 2014. (Science Biographies Ser.). (ENG.). 32p. (gr. 2-4). lib. bdg. 30.65 *(978-1-4109-6236-2(9)*, Raintree Perspectives) Heinemann-Raintree.

Kjelle, Marylou Morano. Louis Pasteur: Fighter Against Contagious Disease. 2005. (Uncharted, Unexplored, & Unexplained Ser.). (Illus.). 48p. (J). (gr. 4-8). lib. bdg. 29.95 *(978-1-58415-363-4(6)*, 1244912) Mitchell Lane Pubs., Inc.

Smith, Linda Wasmer. Louis Pasteur: Disease Fighter. rev. ed. 2007. (Great Minds of Science Ser.). (Illus.). 128p. (J). (gr. 4-10). lib. bdg. 33.27 *(978-0-7660-2792-3(9))* Enslow Pubs., Inc.

—Louis Pasteur: Genius Disease Fighter. 2015. (Genius Scientists & Their Genius Ideas Ser.). 96p. (J). (gr. 5-12). 27.94 *(978-0-7660-6575-8(8))*; pap. 10.95 *(978-0-7660-6576-5(6))* Enslow Pubs., Inc.

Vander Hook, Sue. Louis Pasteur: Groundbreaking Chemist & Biologist, 1 vol. 2011. (Essential Lives Set 6 Ser.). (ENG., Illus.). 112p. (J). (gr. 6-12). lib. bdg. 35.64 *(978-1-61714-783-8(4)*, Essential Library) ABDO Publishing Co.

Zamosky, Lisa. Louis Pasteur & the Fight Against Germs, 1 vol. 2007. (Science Readers Ser.). (SPA & ENG.). 32p. (J). (gr. 3-3). pap. 8.99 *(978-0-7439-0588-6(1))* Shell Educational Publishing.

PASTEUR, LOUIS, 1822-1895—FICTION

Malkus, Alida Sims. The Story of Louis Pasteur. Meadowcroft, Enid Lamonte, ed. Spier, Jo, illus. 2011. 190p. 42.95 *(978-1-258-05476-2(0))* Literary Licensing, LLC.

PASTIMES

see Amusements; Games; Recreation; Sports

PASTORS

see Clergy

PASTRY

Beery, Barbara. Pink Princess Cookbook, 1 vol. Snortum, Marty, photos by. 2006. (ENG., Illus.). 64p. (J). (gr. -1-3). spiral bd. 14.99 *(978-1-4236-0173-9(4))* Gibbs Smith, Publisher.

Patchett, Fiona, et al. Children's Book of Baking. Allman, Howard, photos by. 2007. (Children's Cooking Ser.). (ENG., Illus.). 96p. (J). 17.99 *(978-0-7945-1438-9(3)*, Usborne) EDC Publishing.

Price, Pamela S. Cool Pies & Tarts: Easy Recipes for Kids to Bake, 1 vol. 2010. (Cool Baking Ser.). (ENG.). 32p. (gr. 3-6). 28.50 *(978-1-60453-778-9(7)*, Checkerboard Library) ABDO Publishing Co.

PATHOLOGICAL PSYCHOLOGY

see Psychology, Pathological

PATHOLOGY

see also Bacteriology; Immunity; Medicine

Allman, Toney. The Medical Examiner. 2006. (Crime Scene Investigations Ser.). (ENG., Illus.). 128p. (gr. 7-12). lib. bdg. 40.40 *(978-1-59018-912-2(4)*, 1251556) Cengage Gale.

Brezina, Corona. Careers as a Medical Examiner. (Careers in Forensics Ser.). 64p. 2009. (gr. 5-5). 58.50 *(978-1-61511-799-4(7)*, Rosen Reference) 2008. (Illus.). (J). (gr. 3-7). lib. bdg. 31.95 *(978-1-4042-1347-0(3))* Rosen Publishing Group, Inc., The.

Goldsmith, Connie. Hepatitis. 2010. (USA TODAY Health Reports: Diseases & Disorders Ser.). (ENG., Illus.). 128p. (gr. 6-12). lib. bdg. 34.60 *(978-0-8225-6787-5(3))* Lerner Publishing Group.

Hyde, Natalie. What Is Germ Theory? 2010. (Shaping Modern Science Ser.). (ENG.). 64p. (J). (gr. 5-8). pap. *(978-0-7787-7208-8(X))* Crabtree Publishing Co.

Jeffrey, Gary. Autopsies: Pathologists at Work. 2009. (Graphic Forensic Science Ser.). (ENG.). 48p. (YA). (gr. 5-5). 58.50 *(978-1-61512-941-6(3)*, Rosen Reference) Rosen Publishing Group, Inc., The.

Langwith, Jacqueline. Hepatitis. 2009. (Perspectives on Diseases & Disorders Ser.). (ENG., Illus.). 144p. (gr. 10-12). 44.30 *(978-0-7377-4553-5(3)*, Greenhaven Pr., Inc.) Cengage Gale.

Moe, Barbara. Coping with PMS (Premenstrual Syndrome). 2009. (Coping Ser.). 192p. (gr. 7-12). 63.90 *(978-1-61512-007-9(6))* Rosen Publishing Group, Inc., The.

—Coping with Tourette's Syndrome & Other Tic Disorders. 2009. (Coping Ser.). 192p. (gr. 7-12). 63.90 *(978-1-61512-016-1(5))* Rosen Publishing Group, Inc., The.

Newman, Michael E. Soft Tissue Sarcomas. 2011. (Cancer & Modern Science Ser.). (J). lib. bdg. 31.95 *(978-1-4488-1307-0(7))* Rosen Publishing Group, Inc., The.

Ollhoff, Jim. What Are Germs?, 1 vol. 2009. (History of Germs Ser.). (ENG., Illus.). 32p. (YA). (gr. 5-9). 27.07 *(978-1-60453-502-0(4))* ABDO Publishing Co.

Roza, Greg. What Happens When I Throw Up? 2013. (My Body Does Strange Stuff! Ser.). (ENG., Illus.). 24p. (J). (gr. 1-3). pap. 8.15 *(978-1-4339-9353-4(8))*; lib. bdg. 22.60 *(978-1-4339-9352-7(X))* Stevens, Gareth Publishing LLLP.

Solway, Andrew. Human Body: Investigating an Unexplained Death. Stayte, James, illus. 2013. (Anatomy of an Investigation Ser.). (ENG.). 56p. (gr. 7-8). 34.65 *(978-1-4329-7604-0(4))*; pap. 9.95 *(978-1-4329-7610-1(9))* Heinemann-Raintree.

Stair, Nancy L. Choosing a Career in Mortuary Science & the Funeral Industry. 2009. (World of Work Ser.). 64p. (gr. 5-5). 58.50 *(978-1-60854-333-5(1))* Rosen Publishing Group, Inc., The.

Stefoff, Rebecca. Forensics & Medicine. 2010. (Forensic Science Investigated 2 Ser.). (Illus.). 80p. (J). (gr. 5). lib. bdg. 34.21 *(978-0-7614-4143-4(3))* Marshall Cavendish GBR. Dist: Marshall Cavendish Corp.

Walker, Maryalice. Pathology. Noziglia, Carla Miller & Siegel, Jay A., eds. 2013. (Solving Crimes with Science: Forensics Ser.: 12). (Illus.). 112p. (J). (gr. 7-18). 22.95 *(978-1-4222-2872-2(X))* Mason Crest.

What Happens When I Throw Up? 2013. (My Body Does Strange Stuff! Ser.). 24p. (J). (gr. 1-3). pap. 48.90 *(978-1-4339-9354-1(6))* Stevens, Gareth Publishing LLLP.

Williams, Linda D. Forensics & Medicine. 2008. (J). *(978-0-7614-3079-7(2))* Marshall Cavendish.

PATRICK, SAINT, 373?-463?

Bilinsky, Cornelia Mary. Patrick & the Fire: A Legend about Saint Patrick. Coburn, Maggie, illus. 2017. 25p. (J). pap. *(978-0-8198-6037-8(9))* Pauline Bks. & Media.

Driscoll, Christ. And God Blessed the Irish: The Story of Patrick. Kelley, Patrick, illus. 2007. 59p. (J). (gr. 3-7). 14.95 *(978-1-929039-40-1(9))* Ambassador Bks., Inc.

Freeman, Dorothy Rhodes. St. Patrick's Day. rev. ed. 2008. (Best Holiday Bks.). (Illus.). 48p. (J). (gr. 3-7). lib. bdg. 25.27 *(978-0-7660-3046-6(6))* Enslow Pubs., Inc.

Landau, Elaine. Celebrating St. Patrick's Day. 2012. (Celebrating Holidays Ser.). 48p. (J). (gr. 3-18). 25.27 *(978-0-7660-4035-9(6)*, Enslow Elementary) Enslow Pubs., Inc.

Simms, George Otto. Saint Patrick: Ireland's Patron Saint. Rooney, David, illus. 3rd rev. ed. 2004. (Exploring Ser.). (ENG.). 104p. pap. 8.95 *(978-0-86278-749-3(1))* O'Brien Pr., Ltd., The IRL. Dist: Dufour Editions, Inc.

PATRICK, SAINT, 373?-463?—FICTION

Smith, Sherry. The Wolf & the Shield: An Adventure with Saint Patrick. McNally, Nicholas, illus. 2016. 118p. (J). pap. *(978-0-8198-8356-8(5))* Pauline Bks. & Media.

Stengel, Joyce A. St. Patrick & the Three Brave Mice, 1 vol. Leonhard, Herb, illus. 2009. (ENG.). 32p. (J). (gr. k-3). 16.99 *(978-1-58980-663-4(8))* Pelican Publishing Co., Inc.

PATRIOTIC SONGS

see National Songs

PATRIOTISM

ABDO Publishing Company Staff & Scheunemann, Pam. United We Stand, Set. 2003. (United We Stand Ser.: 4). (ENG.). (J). (gr. k-3). lib. bdg. 96.84 *(978-1-57765-876-4(0)*, SandCastle) ABDO Publishing Co.

Amoroso, Cynthia. Patriotism. 2013. (Values to Live By Ser.). (ENG.). 24p. (J). (gr. -1-2). 25.64 *(978-1-62323-523-9(5)*, 206294) Child's World, Inc., The.

Jackson, Cody. Pint-Sized Patriots. 2012. (J). 24.95 *(978-1-937084-51-6(5)*, BQB Publishing) Boutique of Quality Books Publishing Co., Inc.

Kishel, Ann-Marie. U. S. Symbols. 2007. (First Step Nonfiction - Government Ser.). (ENG., Illus.). 24p. (gr. k-2). lib. bdg. 23.93 *(978-0-8225-6394-5(0)*, Lerner Pubns.) Lerner Publishing Group.

LaMachia, John. So What Is Patriotism Anyway? 2009. (Student's Guide to American Civics Ser.). 48p. (gr. 5-8). 53.00 *(978-1-61511-240-1(5)*, Rosen Reference) Rosen Publishing Group, Inc., The.

Manolis, Kay & Leslie, Tonya. Thomas Jefferson: A Life of Patriotism. 2007. (People of Character Ser.). (ENG., Illus.). 24p. (J). (gr. 2-5). lib. bdg. 25.95 *(978-1-60014-093-8(9))* Bellwether Media.

National Geographic Learning Staff. Celebrating Patriotic Holidays No. 4529: Honoring America. 2010. (ENG., Illus.). 16p. (C). (gr. -1-2). pap. 5.95 *(978-1-57471-574-3(7))* National Geographic School Publishing, Inc.

Peter, Val J. & Dowd, Tom. The Girls & Boys Town Book on Patriotism: Grades 7-12. 2004. 76p. pap. 25.95 *(978-1-889322-52-0(0)*, 48-318T) Boys Town Pr.

Scheunemann, Pam. Patriotism. 2003. (United We Stand Ser.). (ENG., Illus.). 24p. (J). (gr. k-3). lib. bdg. 24.21 (978-1-57765-880-1(9), SandCastle) ABDO Publishing Co.

Schuette, Sarah L. I Am Patriotic, 1 vol. 2004. (Character Values Ser.). (ENG., Illus.). 24p. (gr. k-1). 21.99 (978-0-7368-2571-9(1), Pebble Bks.) Capstone Press of Coughlan Cos.

Stone, Tanya Lee. A Is for America: A Patriotic Alphabet Book. Kelley, Gerald, illus. 2011. (ENG.). 24p. (J). (gr. -1-k). mass mkt. 4.99 (978-0-8431-9877-5(X), Price Stern Sloan) Penguin Young Readers Group.

Stout, Carol A. Proud to Be an American, 1. 2004. (Illus.). 168p. pap. 6.95 (978-1-886161-08-5(9)) Millennium Marketing & Publishing.

Warner, Roxie & Warner, Christian. Land of the Free, A to Z. Schartup, Adam, illus. 2014. (J). (978-1-62086-801-0(6)) Mascot Bks., Inc.

Webster, Christine. The Pledge of Allegiance. 2003. (Cornerstones of Freedom Ser.). (ENG., Illus.). 48p. (J). (gr. 4-6). 26.00 (978-0-516-22674-3(6), Children's Pr.) Scholastic Library Publishing.

PATRIOTISM—POETRY

Martin, Bill, Jr. & Sampson, Michael. I Pledge Allegiance. Raschka, Chris, illus. 2004. (ENG.). 40p. (J). (gr. 1-4). reprint ed. pap. 8.99 (978-0-7636-2527-6(2)) Candlewick Pr.

PATTON, GEORGE S. (GEORGE SMITH), 1885-1945

Gitlin, Martin. George S. Patton: World War II General & Military Innovator, 1 vol. 2010. (Military Heroes Ser.). (ENG.). 112p. (J). (gr. 6-12). lib. bdg. 35.64 (978-1-60453-964-6(X)) ABDO Publishing Co.

Stanley, George E. George S. Patton: War Hero. Henderson, Meryl, illus. 2007. (Childhood of Famous Americans Ser.). (ENG.). 192p. (J). (gr. 3-7). pap. 6.99 (978-1-4169-1547-8(8), Simon & Schuster/Paula Wiseman Bks.) Simon & Schuster/Paula Wiseman Bks.

Sutcliffe, Jane. George S. Patton JR. 2006. (History Maker Bios Ser.). (Illus.). 48p. (J). (gr. 3-7). lib. bdg. 26.60 (978-0-8225-2436-6(8), Lerner Pubns.) Lerner Publishing Group.

PAUL, THE APOSTLE, SAINT

Bower, Gary. The Frightening Philippi Jail. Chotiner, Barbara, illus. 2017. (Faith That God Built Book Ser.). (ENG.). 32p. 14.99 (978-1-4964-1750-3(X)) Tyndale Hse. Pubs.

Christian Focus Publications (CFP) Staff & MacKenzie, Carine. Jesus Is Alive: The Amazing Story. 2012. (Bible Wise Ser.). (ENG., Illus.). 32p. (J). (gr. k-3). pap. 3.99 (978-1-85792-344-5(8), c6b9724f-8c64-4ed3-9168-2af73f60ac83) Christian Focus Pubns. GBR. Dist: Bookmasters Distribution.

Dowley, Tim. Paul's Travels, 1 vol. 2010. (Candle Discovery Ser.). (Illus.). 28p. (J). (gr. 2-7). 14.99 (978-0-8254-7383-8(7), Candle Bks.) Lion Hudson PLC GBR. Dist: Kregel Pubns.

Fisher, Nancy. Take Your Students on a Cruise: Paul's Journeys Lesson Guide. Witte, Carol, ed. Hall, Beverly H., illus. 2004. 40p. (gr. 4-8). wbk. ed. 9.95 (978-1-890947-00-2(8), 308X) Rose Publishing.

Hill, Mary Lea. Saint Paul: The Thirteenth Apostle. Archambault, Matthew, illus. 2008. (Encounter the Saints Ser.: 22). 117p. (J). (gr. 3-7). per. 7.95 (978-0-8198-7102-2(8)) Pauline Bks. & Media.

Hovland, Stephenie. Lydia Believes. Dorenkamp Repa, Michelle, illus. 2014. (Arch Bks.). (ENG.). 16p. (J). (gr. k-4). pap. 2.49 (978-0-7586-4607-1(0)) Concordia Publishing Hse.

Jones, Rufus Matthew. St. Paul the Hero. 2007. (J). pap. (978-1-59731-350-6(5)) Perennis, Sophia.

The Journey's of Paul. Date not set. (J). stu. ed., act. bk. ed. 1.49 (978-0-88271-232-1(2), 1748) Regina Pr., Malhame & Co.

Lumsden, Colin, illus. People in the Life of Paul. 2003. (Bible Colour & Learn Ser.). 32p. pap. 2.50 (978-1-903087-50-3(3)) DayOne Pubns. GBR. Dist: Send The Light Distribution LLC.

—Story of Paul. 2003. (Bible Colour & Learn Ser.). 32p. pap. 2.50 (978-1-903087-46-6(5)) DayOne Pubns. GBR. Dist: Send The Light Distribution LLC.

Mackenzie, Carine. Paul: God's Traveller. 2014. (Bible Time Ser.). (ENG.). 32p. (J). pap. 3.99 (978-1-84550-382-6(1), d5fece0b-02c0-4ac4-a606-15b5d31ce48d) Christian Focus Pubns. GBR. Dist: Bookmasters Distribution.

Miles, David, illus. Paul Meets Jesus, 1 vol. 2016. (I Can Read! / Adventure Bible Ser.). (ENG.). 32p. (J). pap. 3.99 (978-0-310-75076-5(8)) Zonderkidz.

Moore, Alan & Tavner, Gill. Paul of Tarsus. Donnelly, Karen, illus. 2014. (New Testament Ser.). (ENG.). 64p. pap. 6.95 (978-1-906230-29-6(3)) Real Reads Ltd. GBR. Dist: Casemate Pubs. & Bk. Distributors, LLC.

Neeley, Deta Petersen & Neeley, Nathan Glen. Paul of Tarsus, V2: A Child's Story of the New Testament. 2011. 152p. 41.95 (978-1-258-07519-4(9)) Literary Licensing, LLC.

Sanders, Nancy I. Apostle Paul, 1 vol. 2014. (Get to Know Ser.). (ENG.). 128p. (J). pap. 7.99 (978-0-310-74473-3(3)) Zonderkidz.

Self, David. Saint Paul. Cockcroft, Jason, illus. 2009. (ENG.). 48p. (J). (gr. 2-7). 14.95 (978-0-7459-6097-5(9)) Lion Hudson PLC GBR. Dist: Independent Pubs. Group.

Selucky, Oldrich. Adventures of Saint Paul. Trouve, Marianne Lorraine, tr. from CZE. Krejcova, Zdenka, illus. 2008. Orig. Title: Pavel, dobrudruh Viry. 96p. (J). (gr. 1-3). pap. (978-0-8198-0786-1(9)) Pauline Bks. & Media.

Warner Press Kids, creator. Paul, a Servant of Jesus: Activity Book. 2008. 16p. (J). (gr. -1-3). pap. 11.34 (978-1-59317-327-2(X)) Warner Pr., Inc.

PAUL, THE APOSTLE, SAINT—FICTION

Colvin, Adele. The Donkey of Tarsus: His Tales about the Apostle Paul, 1 vol. Carmichael, Peyton, illus. 2010. (Donkey Tales Ser.). (ENG.). 32p. (J). (gr. k-3). 16.99 (978-1-58980-780-8(4)) Pelican Publishing Co., Inc.

Gormally, Eleanor. St Paul: The Man with the Letters. 2010. (ENG., Illus.). 32p. (J). pap. 16.95 (978-1-84730-177-2(0)) Veritas Pubns. IRL. Dist: Dufour Editions, Inc.

Hernandez, David. The Mighty Armor, 1 vol., Vol. 2. 2003. (Adventures of Toby Digz Ser.: 2). (ENG., Illus.). 96p. pap. 5.99 (978-1-4003-0196-6(3)) Nelson, Thomas Inc.

PAVLOVA, ANNA, 1885-1931

Allman, Barbara & Haas, Shelly O. Dance of the Swan: A Story about Anna Pavlova. 2006. (Creative Minds Biographies Ser.). (Illus.). 64p. (gr. 4-8). lib. bdg. 22.60 (978-1-57505-463-6(9)) Lerner Publishing Group.

Snyder, Laurel. Swan: The Life & Dance of Anna Pavlova. Morstad, Julie, illus. 2015. (ENG.). 52p. (J). (gr. 1-4). 17.99 (978-1-4521-1890-1(6)) Chronicle Bks. LLC.

PEACE

see also Disarmament; Security, International; War

Agnew, Kate, ed. War & Peace: A Collection of Classic Poetry & Prose. 2004. (ENG.). 176p. (J). (gr. 7). 9.95 (978-1-84046-570-9(0), Wizard Books) Icon Bks., Ltd. GBR. Dist: Publishers Group Canada.

Center for Learning Staff. Justice & Peace. 2007. (Religion Ser.). 124p. (YA). spiral bd. 18.95 (978-1-56077-795-3(8)) Center for Learning, The.

Darraj, Susan Muaddi. Mairead Corrigan & Betty Williams: Partners in Peace in Northern Ireland. 2006. (Modern Peacemakers Ser.). (Illus.). 106p. (J). (gr. 9-12). lib. bdg. 30.00 (978-0-7910-9001-5(9)) Facts On File, Inc.

Fish, Sandra Palmer. S E W for Peace. 2007. 48p. pap. 19.05 (978-0-9722839-7-7(8)) Just Write Bks.

Friedman-Brunt, Elyse. Conflict Resolution in American History, Gr. 8: Lessons from the Past, Lessons for Today. Chandler, Terrence, illus. 2003. 48p. (YA). pap., wbk. ed. 19.95 (978-1-878227-89-8(0)) Peace Education Foundation.

—Conflict Resolution in American History, Grade 8: Lessons from the Past, Lessons for Today. Chandler, Terrence, illus. 2003. 200p. pap., instr.'s training gde. ed. 29.95 (978-1-878227-88-1(2)) Peace Education Foundation.

Gottfried, Ted. The Fight for Peace: A History of Antiwar Movements in America. 2005. (People's History Ser.). (ENG., Illus.). 136p. (gr. 5-12). lib. bdg. 33.26 (978-0-7613-2932-9(3)) Lerner Publishing Group.

Haerens, Margaret. World Peace. 2015. (Opposing Viewpoints Ser.). (ENG., Illus.). 224p. (J). (gr. 10-12). 48.80 (978-0-7377-7304-0(9), Greenhaven Pr., Inc.) Cengage Gale.

Harcourt School Publishers Staff. Leaders for Peace. 3rd ed. 2003. (Horizons Ser.). (Illus.). (J). (gr. 3). pap. 5.50 (978-0-15-333278-4(6)) Harcourt Schl. Pubs.

Hess, Ingrid. Walk in Peace. 2009. (ENG.). 44p. (J). (gr. -1-k). pap. 13.99 (978-0-8361-9469-2(1)) Herald Pr.

Hoffman, Mary. Lines in the Sand: New Writing on War & Peace. Lassiter, Rhiannon, ed. 2003. (ENG., Illus.). 288p. (J). (gr. 2-18). pap. 8.95 (978-0-9729529-1-0(8)) Disinformation Co. Ltd., The.

Kerley, Barbara. A Little Peace. 2007. (Barbara Kerley Photo Inspirations Ser.). (ENG., Illus.). 32p. (J). (gr. -1-3). 16.95 (978-1-4263-0086-8(7)); 25.90 (978-1-4263-0087-5(5)) National Geographic Society. (National Geographic Children's Bks.).

Lampen, John. The Peace Kit. 2nd ed. 2007. (ENG., Illus.). 84p. per. (978-0-85245-372-8(8)) Quaker Books.

Ogden, Charlie. Peace & War. 2017. 32p. (J). (978-0-7787-3738-4(1)) Crabtree Publishing Co.

Promoting Peace - Puppet Scripts Manual. 2005. (J). spiral bd. (978-0-9768827-4-9(4)) Prevention Through Puppetry, Inc.

Promoting Peace - Student Workbook. 2005. (J). spiral bd. (978-0-9768827-3-2(6)) Prevention Through Puppetry, Inc.

Publishers, Chelsea House, creator. Modern Peacemakers Set, 12-Volumes. 2007. (Modern Peacemakers Ser.). (C). (gr. 9). 360.00 (978-0-7910-9701-4(3), Chelsea Hse.) Facts On File, Inc.

Radunsky, Vladimir. What Does Peace Feel Like? Radunsky, Vladimir, illus. 2004. (ENG., Illus.). 24p. (J). (gr. -1-3). 17.99 (978-0-689-86676-0(3), Atheneum Bks. for Young Readers) Simon & Schuster Children's Publishing.

Rivera, Sheila. Treaties & Resolutions. 2003. (World in Conflict-the Middle East Ser.). 32p. (gr. 4-8). 27.07 (978-1-59197-420-8(8), Abdo & Daughters) ABDO Publishing Co.

Scheunemann, Pam. Acting with Kindness, 1 vol. 2004. (Keeping the Peace Ser.). (ENG., Illus.). 24p. (J). (gr. k-3). lib. bdg. 24.21 (978-1-59197-557-1(3), SandCastle) ABDO Publishing Co.

—Being a Peacekeeper, 1 vol. 2004. (Keeping the Peace Ser.). (ENG., Illus.). 24p. (J). (gr. k-3). lib. bdg. 24.21 (978-1-59197-558-8(1), SandCastle) ABDO Publishing Co.

—Coping with Anger, 1 vol. 2004. (Keeping the Peace Ser.). (ENG., Illus.). 24p. (J). (gr. k-3). lib. bdg. 24.21 (978-1-59197-559-5(X), SandCastle) ABDO Publishing Co.

—Dealing with Bullies, 1 vol. 2004. (Keeping the Peace Ser.). (ENG., Illus.). 24p. (J). (gr. k-3). lib. bdg. 24.21 (978-1-59197-560-1(3), SandCastle) ABDO Publishing Co.

—Learning about Differences, 1 vol. 2004. (Keeping the Peace Ser.). (ENG., Illus.). 24p. (J). (gr. k-3). lib. bdg. 24.21 (978-1-59197-561-8(1), SandCastle) ABDO Publishing Co.

—Working Together, 1 vol. 2004. (Keeping the Peace Ser.). (ENG., Illus.). 24p. (J). (gr. k-3). lib. bdg. 24.21 (978-1-59197-562-5(X), SandCastle) ABDO Publishing Co.

Scheunemann, Pam & ABDO Publishing Company Staff. Keeping the Peace. 2004. (Keeping the Peace Ser.: 6). (ENG., Illus.). 24p. (J). (gr. k-3). lib. bdg. 145.26 (978-1-59197-556-4(5), SandCastle) ABDO Publishing Co.

Seiling, Rebecca. Plant a Seed of Peace. Rothshank, Brooke, illus. 2007. 115p. (J). (gr. 3-7). per. 15.99 (978-0-8361-9397-8(0)) Faith & Life Pr.

Short, Robyn & Williams, Nanon McKewn. Peace People. Bailey, Lindsey, illus. 2013. 38p. 18.95 (978-0-9911148-2-5(5)) Goodmedia Communications, LLC.

Skoor, Susan. The Lion & the Lamb. Shipley, Marie, illus. 2003. (ENG.). (J). pap. 12.95 (978-0-8309-1068-7(9)) Herald Publishing Hse.

Steele, Philip. Afghanistan: From War to Peace? 2012. (Our World Divided Ser.). (ENG., Illus.). 48p. (J). (gr. 5-8). 27.95 (978-1-4488-6030-2(X), Rosen Reference) Rosen Publishing Group, Inc., The.

Tor, Regina, et al. Growing Toward Peace. 2011. 90p. 38.95 (978-1-258-02528-1(0)) Literary Licensing, LLC.

Walker, Niki & Owlkids Books Inc. Staff. Why Do We Fight? Conflict, War, & Peace. 2013. (ENG., Illus.). 80p. (J). (gr. 6-9). 16.95 (978-1-926973-86-9(0), Owlkids) Owlkids Bks. Inc. CAN. Dist: Publishers Group West (PGW).

Walter, Virginia A. War & Peace: A Guide to Literature & New Media, Grades 4-8, 1 vol. 2006. (Children's & Young Adult Literature Reference Ser.). 288p. (C). pap. 45.00 (978-1-59158-271-7(7), LU2717, Libraries Unlimited) ABC-CLIO, LLC.

Wilson, Janet, illus. One Peace: True Stories of Young Activists, 1 vol. 2008. (ENG.). 52p. (J). (gr. 2-7). 19.95 (978-1-55143-892-4(5)) Orca Bk. Pubs. USA.

Winter, Jonah. Peaceful Heroes. Addy, Sean, illus. 2009. (J). pap. (978-0-439-62308-7(1), Levine, Arthur A. Bks.) Scholastic, Inc.

Winter, Jonah & Addy, Sean. Peaceful Heroes. 2009. (ENG., Illus.). 64p. (J). (gr. 4-7). 17.99 (978-0-439-62307-0(3), Levine, Arthur A. Bks.) Scholastic, Inc.

Yoder, Suzana E. Sensing Peace. 2010. (ENG., Illus.). 32p. (J). pap. 13.99 (978-0-8361-9515-6(9)) Herald Pr.

PEACE—FICTION

Abrams, Douglas Carlton & Tutu, Desmond. God's Dream. Pham, LeUyen, illus. 2010. (ENG.). 32p. (J). (— 1). bds. 7.99 (978-0-7636-4742-1(X)) Candlewick Pr.

Ashman, Linda. Peace, Baby! Lew-Vriethoff, Joanne, illus. 2013. (ENG.). 32p. (J). (gr. -1-k). 15.99 (978-1-4521-0613-7(4)) Chronicle Bks. LLC.

Avignone, June. A Peek into the Secret Little Ones of Turtle Back Island. My Wolf Dog, illus. 2004. 40p. (J). pap. (978-0-9654628-2-2(X)) Mill Street Forward, The.

Backer, Charles. Fireclaw. 2010. 288p. pap. 15.49 (978-1-4520-1229-2(6)) AuthorHouse.

Baskwill, Jane. If Peace Is... Carter, Stephanie, illus. 2003. (J). 23p. pap. 7.95 (978-1-59034-449-1(9)); 24p. (gr. 11-18). 15.95 (978-1-59034-448-4(0)) Mondo Publishing.

Berenstain, Mike. The Berenstain Bears Blessed Are the Peacemakers, 1 vol. 2014. (Berenstain Bears/Living Lights Ser.). (ENG.). 24p. (J). pap. 3.99 (978-0-310-73481-9(9)) Zonderkidz.

Carter, Cathy. You Are My Very Best Friend: The Adventures of Mike & Gabe (in English & Spanish) 2012. 26p. 24.95 (978-1-4626-7072-7(5)) America Star Bks.

Charters, Janet. The General. Foreman, Michael, illus. 2010. (ENG.). 48p. (J). (gr. k-12). 16.99 (978-0-7636-4875-6(2), Templar) Candlewick Pr.

Crawford, Quinton Douglass. Moochie the Soochie Visits the Peace People. 2007. 27p. 12.50 (978-0-615-14879-3(4)) Crawford, Quinton Douglass.

Damon, Matt. The Fall of General Custard, or the Overthrow of a Leftover. Kendall, Gideon, illus. 2016. (HumanKIND Project Ser.). (ENG.). 32p. (J). (gr. k-6). 17.95 (978-1-940468-33-4(7)) White Cloud Pr.

Doodler, Todd H. Peas on Earth. 2012. (ENG., Illus.). 20p. (J). (gr. k — 1). bds. 6.99 (978-0-307-93088-0(2), Robin Corey Bks.) Random Hse. Children's Bks.

Eshleman, Catherine, et al. Perry Passyflyer. 2012. 24p. pap. 17.99 (978-1-4685-9571-0(7)) AuthorHouse.

Hoffelt, Jane. We Share One World. Husted, Marty, illus. 2004. 32p. (J). per. 15.95 (978-0-9701907-8-9(6)) Illumination Arts Publishing Co., Inc.

Jacobson, John. The Quest: Adventure Story & Songs. Wilson, Roberta, illus. 2005. (ENG.). 48p. pap. 12.95 incl. audio compact disk (978-1-4234-0019-6(4), 1423400194) Leonard, Hal Corp.

Katz, Karen. Can You Say Peace? Katz, Karen, illus. 2006. (ENG., Illus.). 32p. (J). (gr. -1-2). 18.99 (978-0-8050-7893-0(2), 9780805078930, Holt, Henry & Co. Bks. For Young Readers) Holt, Henry & Co.

—Can You Say Peace? 2016. (J). lib. bdg. 18.40 (978-0-606-38444-5(8)) Turtleback Bks.

Krall, Dan. The Great Lollipop Caper. Krall, Dan, illus. 2013. (ENG., Illus.). 48p. (J). (gr. -1-3). 16.99 (978-1-4424-4460-7(6), Simon & Schuster Bks. For Young Readers) Simon & Schuster Bks. For Young Readers.

Kriescher, Jeanette "Netty". A Big Message from a Little Book: A Color-Blind World. 2008. 25p. pap. 24.95 (978-1-60563-376-3(3)) America Star Bks.

LeBox, Annette. Peace Is an Offering. Graegin, Stephanie, illus. 2015. (ENG.). 34p. (J). (gr. -1-k). 16.99 (978-0-8037-4091-4(3), Dial Bks) Penguin Young Readers Group.

Linden, Dianne. Shimmerdogs, 1 vol. 2008. (ENG.). 176p. (J). pap. 10.95 (978-1-897235-37-9(2)) Thistledown Pr., Ltd. CAN. Dist: Univ. of Toronto Pr.

McKee, David. Six Men. 2011. (ENG., Illus.). 44p. (J). (gr. -1-3). 16.95 (978-0-7358-4050-8(4)) North-South Bks., Inc.

Mulder, Michelle. Yeny & the Children for Peace, 1 vol. 2008. (Kids' Power Book Ser.). (ENG., Illus.). 104p. (J). (gr. 3-8). pap. 14.95 (978-1-897187-45-6(9)) Second Story Pr. CAN. Dist: Orca Bk. Pubs. USA.

Norsgaard, E. Jaediker. How Krokken & Poppen Made Peace. 2008. 31p. pap. 24.95 (978-1-60672-426-2(6)) America Star Bks.

Parr, Todd. The Peace Book. 2009. (ENG., Illus.). 32p. (J). (gr. -1-1). pap. 8.00 (978-0-316-04349-6(4)) Little Brown & Co.

—The Peace Book. (ENG.). 32p. (J). (gr. -1-1). 2005. 11.99 (978-0-316-05962-6(5)) 2004. (Illus.). 17.99 (978-0-316-83531-2(5)) Little, Brown Bks. for Young Readers. (Tingley, Megan Bks.).

Rodríguez-Nora, Tere. En busca de la Paz. Gordo, Aleix, illus. 2005. (SPA & ENG.). 32p. (J). (gr. 2-4). 13.95 (978-84-96046-51-1(6)) Ediciones Norte, Inc.

Skelton, Vonda Skinner. Bitsy & the Mystery at Amelia Island. 2005. (Bitsy Burroughs Mysteries Ser.). 183p. (J). (gr. 3-7). per. 8.95 (978-1-57072-307-0(9), Silver Dagger Mysteries) Overmountain Pr.

Stella, Pilar. Seeking Serenity. Cummings, Maris, illus. 2008. (ENG.). (J). (gr. -1-3). pap. 17.95 (978-1-60037-451-7(4)) Morgan James Publishing.

Syed, Jaweria T. Enchantment Realm's First Adventure. 2012. 94p. 24.99 (978-1-4771-1695-1(8)); pap. 15.99 (978-1-4771-1694-4(X)) Xlibris Corp.

Tutu, Desmond & Abrams, Douglas Carlton. God's Dream. Pham, LeUyen, illus. 2008. (ENG.). 40p. (J). (gr. k-12). 17.99 (978-0-7636-3388-2(7)) Candlewick Pr.

Williams, Sam. Talk Peace. Moriuchi, Mique, illus. 2005. 32p. (J). 16.95 (978-0-8234-1936-4(3)) Holiday Hse., Inc.

Woodson, Jacqueline. Peace, Locomotion. (ENG.). (J). 2010. 176p. (gr. 5-18). 8.99 (978-0-14-241512-2(X), Puffin Books) 2009. 144p. (gr. 4-7). 15.99 (978-0-399-24655-5(X), G.P. Putnam's Sons Books for Young Readers) Penguin Young Readers Group.

Young, Lena. Karma: Reaping What We Sow. Tsai, Dora, illus. 2005. 26p. (J). pap. (978-1-933554-00-6(2)) Primordia.

PEACE CORPS (U.S.)

Gallagher, Diane Shugrue, et al. Lives of Service: Stories from the Peace Corps. 2014. (Text Connections Ser.). (J). (gr. 6). (978-1-4900-1524-8(8)) Benchmark Education Co.

Suen, Anastasia. El Cuerpo de Paz. 2004. (Organizaciones de Ayuda (Helping Organizations) Ser.). (SPA & ENG., Illus.). 24p. (J). (gr. 2-4). lib. bdg. 22.60 (978-0-8239-6859-6(6)) Rosen Publishing Group, Inc., The.

—El Cuerpo de Paz (the Peace Corps) 2009. (Organizaciones de ayuda (Helping Organizations) Ser.). (SPA.). 24p. (gr. 2-2). 42.50 (978-1-60851-144-0(8), Editorial Buenas Letras) Rosen Publishing Group, Inc., The.

—The Peace Corps. 2009. (Helping Organizations Ser.). 24p. (gr. 2-2). 42.50 (978-1-61513-261-4(9), PowerKids Pr.) Rosen Publishing Group, Inc., The.

Vandegrift, Tom. 24 New Moons. 2003. 429p. (YA). pap. 20.95 (978-0-7414-1503-5(8)) Infinity Publishing.

Wimmer, Teresa. Peace Corps: Agents of Government. 2016. (Agents of Government Ser.). (ENG.). 48p. (J). (gr. 5-9). pap. 12.00 (978-1-62832-150-0(4), Creative Paperbacks) Creative Co., The.

PEACOCKS

Borgert-Spaniol, Megan. Peacocks. 2013. (Animal Safari Ser.). (ENG., Illus.). 24p. (J). (gr. k-3). lib. bdg. 25.95 (978-1-60014-914-6(6), Blastoff! Readers) Bellwether Media.

Buckingham, Suzanne. Meet the Peacock. 2009. (Scales & Tails Ser.). 24p. (gr. 2-3). 42.50 (978-1-60852-984-1(3)); (Illus.). (J). lib. bdg. 22.60 (978-1-4042-4503-7(0)) Rosen Publishing Group, Inc., The. (PowerKids Pr.).

Gish, Melissa. Peacocks. (Living Wild Ser.). (Illus.). 2017. (ENG.). 48p. (J). (gr. 4-7). pap. 12.00 (978-1-62832-303-0(5), Creative Paperbacks) 2016. 46p. (978-1-60818-707-2(1), Creative Education) Creative Co., The.

Lang, Elliott. Peafowls, Peacocks & Peahens Including Facts & Information about Blue, White, Indian & Green Peacocks Breeding, Owning, Keeping & Raising Pe. 2012. 140p. pap. (978-0-9566269-9-8(8)) IMB Publishing.

Marsico, Katie. A Peachick Grows Up. 2007. (Scholastic News Nonfiction Readers Ser.). (ENG., Illus.). 24p. (J). (gr. 1-2). pap. 6.95 (978-0-531-18699-2(7)) Scholastic Library Publishing.

Marx, Mandy R. Peacocks, 1 vol. 2011. (Colorful World of Animals Ser.). (ENG.). 24p. (gr. k-1). 26.65 (978-1-4296-6047-1(3), Pebble Plus) Capstone Press of Coughlan Cos.

Meister, Cari. Peacocks. 2015. (J). lib. bdg. 25.65 (978-1-62031-168-4(2), Bullfrog Bks.) Jump! Inc.

Pohl, Kathleen. Peacocks. 2007. (Animals I See at the Zoo Ser.). 24p. (gr. k-3). pap. 8.15 (978-0-8368-8228-5(8)); (Illus.). lib. bdg. 22.00 (978-0-8368-8221-6(0)) Stevens, Gareth Publishing LLLP. (Weekly Reader Leveled Readers).

—Peacocks (Pavos Reales) 2007. (Animals I See at the Zoo/ Animales que veo en el zoologico Ser.). (SPA.). 24p. (gr. k-3). pap. 8.15 (978-0-8368-8242-1(3), Weekly Reader Leveled Readers) Stevens, Gareth Publishing LLLP.

—Peacocks/Pavos Reales. 2007. (Animals I See at the Zoo/Animales que Veo en el Zoológico Ser.). (SPA & ENG., Illus.). 24p. (gr. k-3). lib. bdg. 22.00 (978-0-8368-8235-3(0), Weekly Reader Leveled Readers) Stevens, Gareth Publishing LLLP.

Underwood, Deborah. Colorful Peacocks. 2006. (Pull Ahead Bks.). (Illus.). 32p. (J). (gr. 3-7). lib. bdg. 22.60 (978-0-8225-5930-6(7), Lerner Pubns.) Lerner Publishing Group.

PEACOCKS—FICTION

Brightwell, Beverly. Pea Key & Sam. 2012. 20p. pap. 24.95 (978-1-62709-200-5(5)) America Star Bks.

—Pea Key & Sam Go to the State Fair. 2013. 24p. pap. 24.95 (978-1-62709-261-6(7)) America Star Bks.

Chand, Emlyn. Poppy the Proud: A Bird Brain Book. Shaw, Sarah, illus. ed. 2012. 3. (ENG.). 44p. (gr. k-3). 21.95 (978-1-62253-108-0(6)); pap. 10.95 (978-1-62253-120-2(5)) Evolved Publishing.

Curtis, Chary. Fancy & Brandy Peacock. 2005. (J). per. 9.99 (978-1-59879-030-6(7)) Lifevest Publishing, Inc.

Du Bois, Crystal L. God Made My Butt Big. 2012. 24p. pap. 14.93 (978-1-4669-0584-9(0)) Trafford Publishing.

Evans, Richard & Wilburg, Dale. Patunia Peacock: And Her Flair Weather Friend. 2013. 36p. pap. 15.49 (978-1-4669-9111-8(9)) Trafford Publishing.

Halverson, Barbara. Farm Friends Forever: Everyone Needs Friends. 2013. (ENG.). 27p. (J). pap. 13.95 (978-1-4787-1380-7(1)) Outskirts Pr., Inc.

Hodgkinson, Leigh. Limelight Larry. Hodgkinson, Leigh, illus. 2011. (ENG., Illus.). 32p. (J). (978-1-58925-102-1(4)) Tiger Tales.

Idle, Molly. Flora & the Peacocks. 2016. (ENG., Illus.). 40p. (J). (gr. -1-k). 17.99 (978-1-4521-3816-9(8)) Chronicle Bks. LLC.

Johnson, Gillian. Thora & the Incredible Crystals. 2007. (Illus.). 272p. (978-0-207-20017-5(3)) HarperCollins Pubs. Australia.

Jules, Jacqueline. Feathers for Peacock. Cann, Helen, illus. 2016. (ENG.). 28p. (J). (gr. -1-3). 16.95 (978-1-937786-53-3(6), Wisdom Tales) World Wisdom, Inc.

Laminack, Lester. Three Hens & a Peacock, 1 vol. Cole, Henry, illus. 2014. (ENG.). 32p. (J). (gr. -1-3). pap. 7.95 (978-1-56145-726-7(4)) Peachtree Pubs.

Long, Olivia. The Impossible Peacock. Long, Olivia, illus. Date not set. (Kaleidoscope Ser.). (Illus.). 32p. (J). (gr. -1-4). (978-1-880042-04-5(5)) Shelf-Life Bks.

Peet, Bill. The Spooky Tail of Prewitt Peacock. 2015. 32p. pap. 9.00 (978-1-61003-499-9(6)) Center for the Collaborative Classroom.

Weber, Roopa. Messy Penny. Szewczyk, Manda, illus. 2013. 38p. pap. 11.99 (978-0-9896966-2-3(6)) Karma Kollection LLC.

Woodson, Rick. Poodles & Thunderchicken. 2012. 40p. pap. 24.95 (978-1-4626-7531-9(X)) America Star Bks.

PEAFOWL

see Peacocks

PEANUTS

Bernard, Jan. Peanut Butter. 2016. (J). (978-1-4896-4537-1(3)) Weigl Pubs., Inc.

—Peanut Butter Before the Store. McGeehan, Dan, illus. 2012. (Before the Store Ser.). (ENG.). 32p. (J). (gr. 2-5). lib.

bdg. 29.93 *(978-1-60973-679-8(6)*, 201254) Child's World, Inc., The.

Best, B. J. Peanuts to Peanut Butter. 2016. (How It Is Made Ser.). 24p. (J). pap. 8.22 *(978-1-5026-2134-4(7))*; lib. bdg. 24.21 *(978-1-5026-2136-8(3))* Cavendish Square Publishing.

Della Casa, Chef Luca, contrib. by. No Peanuts, No Problem! Easy & Delecious Nut-Free Recipes for Kids with Allergies. 2016. (Allergy Aware Cookbooks Ser.). (ENG.). 32p. (gr. 3-4). lib. bdg. 27.99 *(978-1-4914-8054-0(8)*, Edge Bks.) Capstone Press of Coughlan Cos.

Driscoll, Laura. George Washington Carver: The Peanut Wizard. Weber, Jill, illus. 2003. (Smart about History Ser.). (ENG.). 32p. (J). (gr. k-4). mass mkt. 5.99 *(978-0-448-43243-4(9)*, Grosset & Dunlap) Penguin Young Readers Group.

Eudy, P. D. PB & J Delight. 2010. 32p. pap. 14.78 *(978-1-4520-0676-5(8))* AuthorHouse.

Heos, Bridget. From Peanuts to Peanut Butter: By Bridget Heos: Illustrated by Stephanie Fizer Coleman. Coleman, Stephanie Fizer, illus. 2017. (Who Made My Lunch? Ser.). (ENG.). 24p. (gr. 1-4). 20.95 ***(978-1-68151-123-8(1))*** Amicus Publishing.

McAneney, Caitlin. Peanut & Other Food Allergies, 1 vol. 2015. (ENG., Illus.). 24p. (J). pap. 8.25 *(978-1-4777-5807-6(0)*, PowerKids Pr.) Rosen Publishing Group, Inc., The.

McKissack, Patricia C. & McKissack, Fredrick L. George Washington Carver: Scientist & Inventor. 2013. (Famous African Americans Ser.). (Illus.). 24p. (J). (gr. k-18). lib. bdg. 22.60 *(978-0-7660-4102-8(6)*, Enslow Elementary) Enslow Pubs., Inc.

Micucci, Charles. Life & Times of the Peanut. 2014. 16.95 *(978-1-63419-716-8(X))* Perfection Learning Corp.

Nelson, Maria. I'm Allergic to Peanuts. 2014. (I'm Allergic Ser.). 24p. (J). (gr. 1-3). 22.60 *(978-1-4824-0974-1(7))*; pap. 8.15 *(978-1-4824-0975-8(5))* Stevens, Gareth Publishing LLLP.

Nelson, Robin. From Peanut to Peanut Butter. (Illus.). 24p. (gr. k-3). 2012. (Start to Finish, Second Series: Food Ser.: No. 2). (ENG.). (J). lib. bdg. 23.93 *(978-0-7613-9180-7(0)*, Lerner Pubns.) 2012. (Start to Finish, Second Series: Food Ser.: No. 2). (ENG., pap. 6.95 *(978-1-58013-969-4(8))* 2004. (Start to Finish Ser.). (J). 18.60 *(978-0-8225-0944-8(X)*, Lerner Pubns.) Lerner Publishing Group.

Nolan, Janet. PBandJ Hooray! 2016. (J). *(978-1-4896-3870-0(9))* Weigl Pubs., Inc.

—PB&J Hooray! Your Sandwich's Amazing Journey from Farm to Table. Patton, Julia, illus. 2014. (ENG.). 32p. (J). (gr. -1-3). 16.99 *(978-0-8075-6397-7(8))* Whitman, Albert & Co.

Sundance/Newbridge LLC Staff. From Peanuts to Peanut Butter. 2007. (Early Science Ser.). (gr. k-3). 18.95 *(978-1-4007-6170-8(0))*; pap. 6.10 *(978-1-4007-6166-1(2))* Sundance/Newbridge Educational Publishing.

PEANUTS—FICTION

Baron, Charlie & Gamson, Alyse. Peanut Butter & Jelly. 2013. 12p. pap. 10.97 *(978-1-62212-388-9(3)*, Strategic Bk. Publishing) Strategic Book Publishing & Rights Agency (SBPRA).

Blount-Jackson, Evetta. What? No Peanut Butter! 2011. 28p. pap. 14.50 *(978-1-4634-0230-3(9))* AuthorHouse.

Border, Terry. Peanut Butter's Yummy Numbers. Border, Terry, illus. 2016. (ENG., Illus.). 20p. (J). (— 1). bds. 6.99 *(978-0-399-54665-5(0)*, Philomel Bks.) Penguin Young Readers Group.

Borsky, Mary. Benny Bensky & the Parrot-Napper. Hendry, Linda, illus. 2008. (ENG.). 128p. (J). (gr. 4-7). pap. 9.95 *(978-0-88776-840-8(7)*, Tundra Bks.) Tundra Bks. CAN. Dist: Penguin Random Hse. LLC.

Fisher, Stacey & Paner, Amy, Illustrator. No Nuts for Nutty. 2008. 26p. 14.95 *(978-0-615-19778-4(7))* Fisher-Paner Publishing.

Frame, Andrew Graham. Ein Stein: The Chipmunk Who Became an Engineer. 2011. 32p. pap. 13.95 *(978-1-61204-009-7(8)*, Eloquent Bks.) Strategic Book Publishing & Rights Agency (SBPRA).

Golden Books. Snoopy & Friends. Golden Books, illus. 2015. (Little Golden Book Ser.). (ENG., Illus.). 24p. (J). (gr. -1-1). 4.99 *(978-1-101-93515-6(4)*, Golden Bks.) Random Hse. Children's Bks.

Graves, Mary. The Adventures of Peanut George. 2007. 72p. per. 19.95 *(978-1-4241-8274-9(3))* America Star Bks.

Howard, Marie. Punkin & the Peanut. 2012. 30p. 24.95 *(978-1-4626-7332-2(5))* America Star Bks.

Ketch, Ann. There Goes Peanut Butter! Totire, Valerie, illus. 2006. (ENG.). 12p. (gr. k-1). pap. 7.95 *(978-1-57874-036-9(3)*, 74-036-3, Kaeden Bks.) Kaeden Corp.

King, Rosemary. Peanut Brittle. 2011. 28p. pap. 13.59 *(978-1-4567-1444-4(9))* AuthorHouse.

Koster, Gloria. The Peanut-Free Café. Cocca-Leffler, Maryann, illus. 2012. (ENG.). 32p. (J). (gr. 1-3). pap. 7.99 *(978-0-8075-6387-8(0))* Whitman, Albert & Co.

Lewellyn, Natalie. Nutty to Meet You! Dr. Peanut Book #1. 2008. (Illus.). 32p. (J). 11.95 *(978-0-9777082-0-8(9))* One Monkey Bks.

Luper, Eric. Gumball's Summer Journal That He Definitely Finished All on His Own. Reed, Stephen, illus. 2015. (Amazing World of Gumball Ser.). (ENG.). 112p. (J). (gr. 3-7). 8.99 *(978-0-8431-8282-8(2)*, Cartoon Network Books) Penguin Young Readers Group.

McClure, Wendy. The Princess & the Peanut Allergy. Lyon, Tammie, illus. 2012. (J). *(978-1-61913-127-9(7))* Weigl Pubs., Inc.

Mehra, Heather & McManama, Kerry. Peanut-Free Tea for Three. Kline, Michael, illus. 2009. (J). *(978-0-9822150-1-2(0))* Parent Perks, Inc.

Middleton, Shawn. Sam & the Peanut Butter Crackers. 2009. 32p. pap. 12.99 *(978-1-4389-3400-6(9))* AuthorHouse.

Morrone Pedowitz, Laura. The Elephant Who Couldn't Eat Peanuts. 2009. 24p. pap. 11.49 *(978-1-4389-4760-0(7))* AuthorHouse.

Nazareth, Melanie. Can I Have Some Cake Too? Lehner-Rhoades, Shirley, illus. 2013. 32p. (J). pap. 14.95 *(978-1-935914-28-0(6))* River Sanctuary Publishing.

O'Connor, Jane. Peanut Butter & Jellyfish. 2015. (Fancy Nancy - I Can Read! Ser.). (J). lib. bdg. 13.55 *(978-0-606-36479-9(X))* Turtleback Bks.

One Pea, Two Pea, I Pee, You Pee. 2005. (J). bds. *(978-0-9761228-0-7(4))* World of Imagination.

Paner, Amy & Fisher, Stacey. Nutty Scurries to School. 2008. 25p. 14.95 *(978-0-615-23931-6(5))* Fisher-Paner Publishing.

Pangan, Catherine Hagerman. No Peanuts for Me! Warf, Gracie, illus. 2013. (ENG.). 30p. (J). (gr. -1-3). 14.95 *(978-1-62086-433-3(9))* Mascot Bks., Inc.

Schnitzlein, Danny. The Monster Who Ate My Peas, 1 vol. Faulkner, Matt, illus. 2010. (ENG.). 32p. (J). pap. 7.95 *(978-1-56145-533-1(4))* Peachtree Pubs.

Schulz, Charles M. Be Active. 2014. (ENG., Illus.). 72p. (J). (gr. -1-17). 7.95 *(978-0-7624-5336-8(2)*, Running Pr. Kids) Running Pr. Bk. Pubs.

—Be Unique: Peanuts Wisdom to Carry You Through. 2014. (ENG., Illus.). 72p. (J). (gr. -1-17). 7.95 *(978-0-7624-5337-5(0)*, Running Pr. Kids) Running Pr. Bk. Pubs.

Shultz, Charles M. Peanuts Ready-to-Reads, 8 vols., Set. Incl. It's a Home Run, Charlie Brown! Katschke, Judy. Lo Bianco, Nick, illus. lib. bdg. 24.21 *(978-1-59961-801-2(X))*; It's Time for School, Charlie Brown. Katschke, Judy. Lo Bianco, Nick, illus. lib. bdg. 24.21 *(978-1-59961-802-9(8))*; Kick the Football, Charlie Brown! Katschke, Judy. lib. bdg. 24.21 *(978-1-59961-803-6(6))*; Lose the Blanket, Linus! Bailer, Darice. Lo Bianco, Peter, illus. lib. bdg. 24.21 *(978-1-59961-804-3(4))*; Lucy's Advice. Katschke, Judy. Lo Bianco, Peter, illus. lib. bdg. 24.21 *(978-1-59961-805-0(2))*; Make a Trade, Charlie Brown! Bailer, Darice. Lo Bianco, Peter, illus. lib. bdg. 24.21 *(978-1-59961-806-7(0))*; Snoopy: Flying Ace to the Rescue. Bailer, Darice. Lo Bianco, Peter, illus. lib. bdg. 24.21 *(978-1-59961-807-4(9))*; Take a Hike, Snoopy. Katschke, Judy. lib. bdg. 24.21 *(978-1-59961-808-1(7))*; (gr. -1-2). (Peanuts Ready-To-Reads Ser.: 8). (ENG., Illus.). 32p. 2011. Set lib. bdg. 193.68 *(978-1-59961-800-5(1))* Spotlight.

Sofranac, Rodo. Polly & the Peanut Pull. 2013. (Illus.). 62p. pap. *(978-1-939625-24-3(6))* Inkwell Books LLC.

Stanley, Mary. Bruno, Peanut & Me. 2011. (Open Door Ser.). (ENG.). 66p. pap. 13.95 *(978-1-84840-103-7(5))* New Island Books IRL. Dist: Dufour Editions, Inc.

Strasser, Stephanie. Pink Peanut Butter. 2010. 28p. 12.49 *(978-1-4490-8383-0(8))* AuthorHouse.

Tait, Elena. The Day My Peanut Butter Lost Its Stick. Lee, Joe, illus. 2008. 24p. pap. 12.99 *(978-1-4389-1936-2(0))* AuthorHouse.

Talbot, Rose. The Adventures of Peanut, the Sugar Glider. 2007. 80p. per. 15.99 *(978-1-4257-9629-7(X))* Xlibris Corp.

Truscelli, John J. Can P B Find the Jelly? 2011. 24p. pap. 24.95 *(978-1-4626-2666-3(1))* America Star Bks.

Ureel, Jessica & Jacobs, Jessica. The Peanut Pickle: A Story about Peanut Allergy. Roslyn, Jacquelyn, illus. 2012. (ENG.). 48p. (J). (gr. -1-3). 14.95 *(978-1-61608-672-5(6)*, 608672, Sky Pony Pr.) Skyhorse Publishing Co., Inc.

Whelahan, Marlene. Once upon a Peanut: A true Story... Killian, Sue, illus. 2009. 24p. pap. 12.99 *(978-1-4389-5925-2(7))* AuthorHouse.

Wilson, Shannan. The Littlest Peanut: A Baby Book for the Teeny Tiny Ones. Cuniff, Joe, illus. 2011. 32p. 16.95 *(978-1-61254-023-8(6))* Brown Books Publishing Group.

PEARL HARBOR (HAWAII), ATTACK ON, 1941

Allen, Thomas B. Remember Pearl Harbor: American & Japanese Survivors Tell Their Stories. 2007. (Remember Ser.). (ENG., Illus.). 64p. (J). (gr. 5). 27.90 *(978-0-7922-3635-1(1)*, National Geographic Children's Bks.) National Geographic Society.

—Remember Pearl Harbor: Japanese & American Survivors Tell Their Stories. 2015. (ENG., Illus.). 64p. (J). (gr. 5). pap. 7.99 *(978-1-4263-2248-8(8)*, National Geographic Children's Bks.) National Geographic Society.

Anthony, Nathan & Gardner, Robert. The Attack on Pearl Harbor in United States History. 2014. (In United States History Ser.). (Illus.). 96p. (J). (gr. 5-12). 27.94 *(978-0-7660-5448-6(9))* Enslow Pubs., Inc.

Benoit, Peter. The Attack on Pearl Harbor. 2013. (Cornerstones of Freedom™, Third Ser.). (ENG., Illus.). 64p. (J). pap. 8.95 *(978-0-531-21959-1(3))*; lib. bdg. 30.00 *(978-0-531-23601-7(3))* Scholastic Library Publishing.

Bowman, Chris. The Attack on Pearl Harbor. 2014. (Disaster Stories Ser.). (ENG., Illus.). 24p. (J). (gr. 3-8). 29.95 *(978-1-62617-150-3(5)*, Black Sheep) Bellwether Media.

Darman, Peter, ed. Attack on Pearl Harbor: America Enters World War II. 2012. (World War II Ser.). (ENG., Illus.). 64p. (J). (gr. 7-12). lib. bdg. 31.95 *(978-1-4488-9233-4(3)*, Rosen Reference) Rosen Publishing Group, Inc., The.

Davenport, John C. The Attack on Pearl Harbor: The United States Enters World War II. 2008. (Milestones in American History Ser.). (Illus.). 128p. (YA). (gr. 7-12). 35.00 *(978-1-60413-010-2(5))* Facts On File, Inc.

Demuth, Patricia. What Was Pearl Harbor? 2013. (What Was... ? Ser.). lib. bdg. 16.00 *(978-0-606-31686-6(8)*, Turtleback) Turtleback Bks.

Demuth, Patricia Brennan. What Was Pearl Harbor? Mantha, John & Tomkinson, Tim, illus. 2013. (What Was? Ser.). (ENG.). 112p. (J). (gr. 3-7). pap. 5.99 *(978-0-448-46462-6(4)*, Grosset & Dunlap) Penguin Young Readers Group.

Dougherty, Steve. Attack on Pearl Harbor: World War II Strikes Home in the USA. 2011. (J). pap. *(978-0-545-32930-9(2))* Scholastic, Inc.

—Pearl Harbor: The U. S. Enters World War II. 2009. (24/7 Goes to War Ser.). (ENG.). 64p. (J). (gr. 6-12). lib. bdg. 29.00 *(978-0-531-25525-4(5)*, Children's Pr.) Scholastic Library Publishing.

Dougherty, Steven. Pearl Harbor: The U. S. Enters World War II. 2009. (24/7: Goes to War-NEW Ser.). (ENG.). 64p. (J). (gr. 6-12). pap. 7.95 *(978-0-531-25450-9(X)*, Watts, Franklin) Scholastic Library Publishing.

Dunn, Joe. The Bombing of Pearl Harbor, 1 vol. Wight, Joseph & Espinosa, Rod, illus. 2007. (Graphic History Ser.). (ENG.). 32p. (gr. 3-6). 28.50 *(978-1-60270-074-1(5)*, Graphic Planet-Nonfiction) ABDO Publishing Co.

Freed, Kira. Surviving Pearl Harbor. 2015. (Surviving Disaster Ser.). (ENG., Illus.). 48p. (J). (gr. 5-6). 30.25 *(978-1-4994-3649-5(1)*, Rosen Central) Rosen Publishing Group, Inc., The.

Garland, Sherry. Voices of Pearl Harbor, 1 vol. Johnson, Layne, illus. 2013. (ENG.). 40p. (J). (gr. 3-3). 17.99 *(978-1-4556-1609-1(5))* Pelican Publishing Co., Inc.

Goff, Elizabeth Hudson & Uschan, Michael V. The Bombing of Pearl Harbor. 2006. (Graphic Histories Ser.). (Illus.). 32p. (gr. 5-8). pap. 10.50 *(978-0-8368-6258-4(9))* Stevens, Gareth Publishing LLLP.

Hamen, Susan E. Pearl Harbor, 1 vol. 2009. (Essential Events Set 3 Ser.). (ENG., Illus.). 112p. (J). (gr. 6-12). lib. bdg. 35.64 *(978-1-60453-517-4(2))* ABDO Publishing Co.

Haugen, David M. The Attack on Pearl Harbor. Gale Editors, ed. 2011. (Perspectives on Modern World History Ser.). 224p. (YA). (gr. 10-12). 42.45 *(978-0-7377-5004-1(9)*, Greenhaven Pr., Inc.) Cengage Gale.

Johnson, Robin. Pearl Harbor. 2014. (ENG., Illus.). 48p. (J). *(978-0-7787-1367-8(9))* Crabtree Publishing Co.

Kaelberer, Angie Peterson & Fitzgerald, Stephanie. Pearl Harbor. 2017. (Eyewitness to World War II Ser.). (ENG.). 112p. (gr. 5-7). lib. bdg. 35.99 ***(978-0-7565-5582-5(5)***, CPB Grades 4-8) Compass Point Bks.

Krieg, Katherine. The Attack on Pearl Harbor: A History Perspectives Book. 2013. (Perspectives Library). (ENG., Illus.). 32p. (J). (gr. 4-8). 28.50 *(978-1-62431-413-1(9)*, 202772); pap. 14.21 *(978-1-62431-489-6(9)*, 202774) Cherry Lake Publishing.

Lassieur, Allison. The Attack on Pearl Harbor: An Interactive History Adventure. 2016. (You Choose: History Ser.). (ENG.). 112p. (gr. 3-4). pap. 6.95 *(978-1-5157-4260-9(1)*, You Choose Bks.) Capstone Press of Coughlan Cos.

—The Attack on Pearl Harbor [Scholastic]: An Interactive History Adventure. 2009. (You Choose: History Ser.). 112p. (gr. 3-4). pap. 0.86 *(978-1-4296-4046-6(4)*, You Choose Bks.) Capstone Press of Coughlan Cos.

Marshall Cavendish. The Attack on Pearl Harbor. 2011. (Perspectives on 3 Ser.). (Illus.). 112p. (J). (gr. 7). 39.93 *(978-1-60870-448-4(3))* Marshall Cavendish Corp.

McNeese, Tim. The Attack on Pearl Harbor: America Enters World War II. 2004. (First Battles Ser.). (Illus.). 112p. (YA). (gr. 6-12). 23.95 *(978-1-883846-78-7(1)*, First Biographies) Reynolds, Morgan Inc.

Otfinoski, Steven. Day of Infamy: The Story of the Attack on Pearl Harbor. 2015. (Tangled History Ser.). (ENG., Illus.). 112p. (gr. 3-4). pap. 6.95 *(978-1-4914-7082-4(8))* Capstone Press of Coughlan Cos.

Pierce, Alan. Bombing of Pearl Harbor, 1 vol. 2005. (American Moments Set Ii Ser.). (ENG., Illus.). 48p. (gr. 4-8). 27.07 *(978-1-59197-729-2(0)*, Abdo & Daughters) ABDO Publishing Co.

Rice, Dona Herweck. You Are There! Pearl Harbor, December 7, 1941. 2nd ed. 2016. (TIME for KIDS(r) Nonfiction Readers Ser.). (Illus.). 32p. (gr. 8-8). 8.99 ***(978-1-4938-3928-5(4))*** Teacher Created Materials, Inc.

Ross, Stewart & Woodward, Joe. Pearl Harbor. 2011. (Place in History Ser.). (Illus.). 48p. (YA). (gr. 5-9). lib. bdg. 34.25 *(978-1-84837-676-2(6))* Arcturus Publishing GBR. Dist: Black Rabbit Bks.

Salisbury, Graham. Under the Blood-Red Sun. 2014. (ENG.). 272p. (YA). (gr. 7-7). pap. 9.99 *(978-0-385-38655-5(9)*, Ember) Random Hse. Children's Bks.

Samuels, Charlie. The Attack on Pearl Harbor, Vol. 1. 2014. (Turning Points in US Military History Ser.). (ENG.). 48p. (J). (gr. 5-6). 31.95 *(978-1-4824-0409-8(5))* Stevens, Gareth Publishing LLLP.

Sutcliffe, Jane. The Attack on Pearl Harbor, 1 vol. Lentz, Bob, illus. 2006. (Disasters in History Ser.). (ENG.). 32p. (gr. 3-4). 30.65 *(978-0-7368-5477-1(0)*, Graphic Library) Capstone Press of Coughlan Cos.

Uschan, Michael V. The Bombing of Pearl Harbor. 2003. (Landmark Events in American History Ser.). (Illus.). 48p. (gr. 5-12). lib. bdg. 31.00 *(978-0-8368-5373-5(3)*, Gareth Stevens Secondary Library) Stevens, Gareth Publishing LLLP.

Uschan, Michael V. & Goff, Elizabeth Hudson. The Bombing of Pearl Harbor. Floor, Guus, illus. 2006. (Graphic Histories Ser.). 32p. (gr. 5-8). lib. bdg. 27.00 *(978-0-8368-6206-5(6))* Stevens, Gareth Publishing LLLP.

Wels, Susan. Pearl Harbor: America's Darkest Day. 2nd ed. 2006. (Illus.). 224p. 34.95 *(978-1-887656-78-8(2))* Tehabi Bks.

White, Steve. Pearl Harbor: A Day of Infamy. (Graphic Battles of World War II Ser.). (ENG.). 48p. 2009. (YA). (gr. 5-5). 58.50 *(978-1-61512-815-0(8)*, Rosen Reference) 2008. (Illus.). (gr. 3-8). pap. 14.05 *(978-1-4042-7428-0(6))* Rosen Publishing Group, Inc., The.

White, Steve D. Pearl Harbor: A Day of Infamy. Spahn, Jerrold, illus. 2007. (Graphic Battles of World War II Ser.). (ENG.). 48p. (YA). (gr. 4-7). lib. bdg. 31.95 *(978-1-4042-0785-1(6))* Rosen Publishing Group, Inc., The.

Whiting, Jim. The Story of the Attack on Pearl Harbor. 2005. (Monumental Milestones Ser.). (Illus.). 48p. (YA). (gr. 4-7). lib. bdg. 29.95 *(978-1-58415-397-9(0))* Mitchell Lane Pubs., Inc.

Woog, Adam. Pearl Harbor. 2013. (Illus.). 96p. (J). lib. bdg. *(978-1-60152-486-7(2))* ReferencePoint Pr., Inc.

Wukovits, John F. The Bombing of Pearl Harbor. 2011. (World History Ser.). (ENG.). 128p. (gr. 10-10). lib. bdg. 39.90 *(978-1-4205-0330-2(8)*, Lucent Bks.) Cengage Gale.

Yomtov, Nel. The Attack on Pearl Harbor: December 7 1941, 1 vol. 2014. (24-Hour History Ser.). (ENG.). 48p. (gr. 3-5). pap. 8.95 *(978-1-4329-9299-6(6))*; (Illus.). lib. bdg. 33.32 *(978-1-4329-9293-4(7))* Heinemann-Raintree. (NA-h).

Zullo, Allan. Heroes of Pearl Harbor. 2016. (Ten True Tales Ser.). (ENG., Illus.). 224p. (J). (gr. 3-7). pap. 5.99 *(978-0-545-87276-8(6))* Scholastic, Inc.

PEARL HARBOR (HAWAII), ATTACK ON, 1941—FICTION

Boyd, David. Pearl Harbor. Ng, Drew, illus. 2007. 48p. (J). lib. bdg. 23.08 *(978-1-4242-1640-6(0))* Fitzgerald Bks.

Earle, Joan Zuber, mem. The Children of Battleship Row: Pearl Harbor 1940-1941. 2004. 136p. pap. 16.95 *(978-1-57143-095-3(4))* RDR Bks.

Eaves, Victor Caleb. Vee's the Chapters of Expudict: Book One. 2008. 128p. pap. 12.00 *(978-1-4389-3385-6(1))* AuthorHouse.

Gutman, Dan. Ted & Me. 2012. (Baseball Card Adventures Ser.). (Illus.). 208p. (J). (gr. 5-9). (ENG.). 15.99 *(978-0-06-123487-3(7))*; lib. bdg. 16.89 *(978-0-06-123488-0(5))* HarperCollins Pubs.

Hamilton, Elizabeth L. Surprise at Pearl Harbor. 2004. (Character Mystery Ser.: No. 2). (Illus.). 144p. (J). per. 9.95 *(978-0-9754629-2-8(X)*, Character-in-Action) Quiet Impact, Inc.

Hudson Goff, Elizabeth & Uschan, Michael V. El Ataque a Pearl Harbor. 2007. (Historias Graficas (Graphic Histories) Ser.). (SPA.). 32p. (gr. 5-8). lib. bdg. 27.00 *(978-0-8368-7892-9(2))* Stevens, Gareth Publishing LLLP.

—El ataque a Pearl Harbor (the Bombing of Pearl Harbor) 2007. (Historias Graficas (Graphic Histories) Ser.). (SPA.). 32p. (gr. 5-8). pap. 10.50 *(978-0-8368-7899-8(X))* Stevens, Gareth Publishing LLLP.

Jenkins, Amanda. Mere Moments A Story of Pearl Harbor, the Day the Towers Fell. 2011. (Readers' & Writers' Genre Workshop Ser.). (J). pap. *(978-1-4509-3019-2(0))* Benchmark Education Co.

Lemke, Donald B. & Pattison, Ronda. Captured off Guard: The Attack on Pearl Harbor, 1 vol. St. Aubin, Claude, illus. 2008. (Historical Fiction Ser.). (ENG.). 56p. (gr. 2-3). pap. 6.25 *(978-1-4342-0493-6(6)*, Graphic Flash) Stone Arch Bks.

Mazer, Harry. A Boy at War: A Novel of Pearl Harbor. 2004. (Illus.). 104p. (gr. 5-9). 16.00 *(978-0-7569-4088-1(5))* Perfection Learning Corp.

Platt, Randall. Incommunicado. 2014. (ENG.). 336p. (J). (gr. 4-7). 14.95 *(978-1-62914-646-1(3)*, Sky Pony Pr.) Skyhorse Publishing Co., Inc.

Salisbury, Graham. Under the Blood Red Sun. 246p. (YA). 22.00 *(978-0-8446-7322-6(6))* Smith, Peter Pub., Inc.

Tarshis, Lauren. I Survived the Bombing of Pearl Harbor 1941. 2011. (I Survived Ser.: 4). (ENG.). 112p. (J). (gr. 2-5). pap. 4.99 *(978-0-545-20698-3(7)*, Scholastic Paperbacks) Scholastic, Inc.

—I Survived the Bombing of Pearl Harbor 1941. 2011. (I Survived ... Ser.: No. 4). lib. bdg. 14.75 *(978-0-606-23744-4(5)*, Turtleback) Turtleback Bks.

PEARLS

Machajewski, Sarah. Pearls. 2015. (Gems: Nature's Jewels Ser.). (ENG., Illus.). 24p. (J). (gr. 2-3). pap. 8.15 *(978-1-4824-2868-1(7))* Stevens, Gareth Publishing LLLP.

Petersen, Christine. Pearls, 1 vol. 2013. (Earth's Treasures Ser.). (ENG.). 32p. (J). (gr. 3-6). lib. bdg. 27.07 *(978-1-61783-873-6(X)*, Checkerboard Library) ABDO Publishing Co.

PEARLS—FICTION

Grandma Pearl: A Story about Inner Beauty. 2008. (Illus.). 32p. (J). 17.95 *(978-0-9799021-1-6(8))* Aspire Publishing.

Ihara, Shigekatsu. Pokémon: Diamond & Pearl Adventure!, Vol. 1. Ihara, Shigekatsu, illus. 2008. (ENG., Illus.). 208p. (J). (gr. k). pap. 9.99 *(978-1-4215-2286-9(1))* Viz Media.

—Pokémon: Diamond & Pearl Adventure!, Vol. 2. Ihara, Shigekatsu, illus. 2008. (ENG., Illus.). 192p. (J). (gr. 1). pap. 9.99 *(978-1-4215-2287-6(X))* Viz Media.

Johnson, Julia. The Pearl Diver. Stacey International Staff, ed. Al-Fakhri, Patricia, illus. 2003. (ARA & ENG.). 240p. (J). (gr. 3-6). *(978-1-900988-62-9(3)*, Stacey International) Stacey Publishing.

Kerven, Rosalind. Sparrow, the Crow & the Pearl. Williamson, Melanie, illus. 2005. (ENG.). 24p. (J). lib. bdg. 23.65 *(978-1-59646-754-5(1))* Dingles & Co.

Mau, Carol Demma. Wisdom from the Pearl Necklace. 2014. 138p. (J). pap. 11.99 *(978-1-4525-9012-7(5)*, Balboa Pr.) Author Solutions, Inc.

McKenny, Stephanie L. Pearls of My Own. 2012. 102p. pap. 10.00 *(978-0-9705008-5-4(8))* J & J Publishing Co.

O'Dell, Scott. The Black Pearl. 2009. 9.00 *(978-0-7848-3610-1(8)*, Everbind) Marco Bk. Co.

Saenz, Sandra C. Lot the Tot & the Beautiful Pearl. 2011. 16p. (gr. -1). 9.50 *(978-1-4567-5385-6(1))* AuthorHouse.

Stilton, Geronimo. The Enormouse Pearl Heist. 2012. (ENG.). 128p. (J). (gr. 2-5). pap. 7.99 *(978-0-545-34103-5(5)*, Scholastic Paperbacks) Scholastic, Inc.

—The Enormouse Pearl Heist. 2012. (Geronimo Stilton Ser.: 51). lib. bdg. 18.40 *(978-0-606-26756-4(5)*, Turtleback) Turtleback Bks.

Tozier, Christopher. Olivia Brophie & the Pearl of Tagelus. 2012. (ENG.). 208p. (J). pap. 12.95 *(978-1-56164-519-0(2))* Pineapple Pr., Inc.

Van Tassel, Mary A. Beach Ball's Discovery. 2013. 24p. pap. 24.95 *(978-1-4626-9698-7(8))* America Star Bks.

Wilson, Melissa Anne. Nalyn & the Indigo Pearl. 2008. (Illus.). 24p. (J). pap. 8.00 *(978-0-8059-7409-6(1))* Dorrance Publishing Co., Inc.

PEARY, ROBERT E. (ROBERT EDWIN), 1856-1920

Bedesky, Baron. Peary & Henson: The Race to the North Pole. 2006. (In the Footsteps of Explorers Ser.). (ENG., Illus.). 32p. (J). (gr. 4-7). lib. bdg. *(978-0-7787-2426-1(3))* Crabtree Publishing Co.

Petrie, Kristin. Robert Peary, 1 vol. 2007. (Explorers Set 2 Ser.). (ENG., Illus.). 32p. (gr. 4-5). 27.07 *(978-1-59679-746-8(0)*, Checkerboard Library) ABDO Publishing Co.

Warrick, Karen Clemens. The Race for the North Pole & Robert Peary in World History. 2003. (In World History Ser.). (Illus.). 128p. (J). (gr. 5-12). lib. bdg. 27.94 *(978-0-7660-1933-1(0))* Enslow Pubs., Inc.

PEASANT ART

see Art Industries and Trade; Folk Art

PEASANTS

see also Agricultural Laborers; Sociology, Rural

Hiller, Sandra J. The Life of a Colonial Blacksmith. 2013. (Jr. Graphic Colonial America Ser.). (ENG., Illus.). 24p. (J). (gr. 3-6). pap. 10.60 *(978-1-4777-1433-1(2))*; lib. bdg. 25.25 *(978-1-4777-1308-2(5))* Rosen Publishing Group, Inc., The. (PowerKids Pr.).

Hull, Robert. Peasant. 2009. (Illus.). 45p. (J). 32.80 *(978-1-59920-172-6(0))* Black Rabbit Bks.

Jeffrey, Gary. Rebellion & Revolt. 2014. (ENG., Illus.). 48p. (J). *(978-0-7787-0399-0(1))* Crabtree Publishing Co.

The Life of a Colonial Blacksmith. 2013. (Jr. Graphic Colonial America Ser.). 24p. (J). (gr. 3-6). pap. 63.60 *(978-1-4777-1434-8(0)*, PowerKids Pr.) Rosen Publishing Group, Inc., The.

PEBBLES

see Rocks

PECCARIES

George, Jean Craighead. Summer Moon. 2003. (J). (gr. 3-7). 20.75 *(978-0-8446-7243-4(2))* Smith, Peter Pub., Inc.

Person, Stephen. Collared Peccary: Cactus-Eater. 2012. (America's Hidden Animal Treasures Ser.). 32p. (J). (gr. 2-7).

lib. bdg. 26.60 *(978-1-61772-571-5(4))* Bearport Publishing Co., Inc.

Storad, Conrad J. Javelinas. 2008. (Early Bird Nature Bks.). (ENG., Illus.). 48p. (gr. 2-5). 26.60 *(978-0-8225-7890-1(5))* Lerner Publishing Group.

PECOS BILL (LEGENDARY CHARACTER)

Braun, Eric & Bowman, James Cloyd. Pecos Bill Tames a Colossal Cyclone, 1 vol. Weber, Lisa K., illus. 2014. (American Folk Legends Ser.). (ENG.). 32p. (gr. k-2). lib. bdg. 27.32 *(978-1-4795-5429-4(4))* Picture Window Bks.

Ferrell, David L. Pecos Bill. 2014. (Jr. Graphic American Legends Ser.). (Illus.). 24p. (J). (gr. 3-6). lib. bdg. 26.25 *(978-1-4777-7189-1(1),* PowerKids Pr.) Rosen Publishing Group, Inc., The.

Krensky, Stephen. Pecos Bill. 2008. pap. 40.95 *(978-0-8225-9296-9(7))* Lerner Publishing Group.

PEDAGOGY

see Education; Education—Study and Teaching; Teaching

PEDDLERS AND PEDDLING—FICTION

Chaconas, Dori. Pennies in a Jar, 1 vol. Lewin, Ted, illus. 2007. (ENG.). 32p. (J). (gr. 1-5). 16.95 *(978-1-56145-422-8(2))* Peachtree Pubs.

Derby, Sally & Derby. Two Fools & a Horse: An Orginal Tale, 1 vol. Rayevsky, Robert, illus. 2003. (ENG.). 32p. (J). (gr. k-3). 16.95 *(978-0-7614-5119-8(6))* Marshall Cavendish Corp.

Esphyr, Slobodkina & Slobodkina. Caps for Sale: A Tale of a Peddler, Some Monkeys & Their Monkey Business. 2014. (Reading Rainbow Bks). (ENG.). 48p. (J). 11.24 *(978-1-63245-155-2(7))* Lectorum Pubns., Inc.

Guest, Jacqueline & Leavey, Peggy Dymond. Growing up Ivy. 2010. (ENG.). 256p. (YA). (gr. 4-8). pap. 10.99 *(978-1-55488-723-1(2))* Dundurn CAN. Dist: Ingram Publisher Services.

Hunt, Mabel Leigh. The Peddler's Clock. Jones, Elizabeth Orton, illus. 2011. 30p. 35.95 *(978-1-258-09998-5(5))* Literary Licensing, LLC.

Merrill, Jean. The Pushcart War. Solbert, Ronni, illus. 50th anniv. ed. 2014. (ENG.). 232p. (J). (gr. 3-7). 15.95 *(978-1-59017-819-5(X),* NYR Children's Collection) New York Review of Bks., Inc., The.

—The Pushcart War. 2006. (J). 1.25 *(978-1-4193-8348-9(5))* Recorded Bks., Inc.

Slobodkina, Esphyr. Caps for Sale. Slobodkina, Esphyr, illus. 75th ed. 2015. (Reading Rainbow Bks.). (ENG., Illus.). 32p. (J). (gr. -1-3). bds. 8.99 *(978-0-06-147453-8(3),* HarperFestival) HarperCollins Pubs.

—Caps for Sale: A Tale of a Peddler, Some Monkeys & Their Monkey Business. Slobodkina, Esphyr, illus. 2008. (Young Scott Bks.). (Illus.). 48p. (J). (gr. -1-3). lib. bdg. 17.89 *(978-0-06-025778-1(4))* HarperCollins Pubs.

—Circus Caps for Sale. Slobodkina, Esphyr, illus. 2004. (Illus.). 40p. (J). (gr. -1-2). reprint ed. 17.00 *(978-0-7567-8345-7(3))* DIANE Publishing Co.

Slobodkina, Esphyr & Sayer, Ann Marie Mulhearn. Caps for Sale & the Mindful Monkeys. Slobodkina, Esphyr, illus. 2017. (Illus.). 48p. (J). (gr. -1-3). 17.99 ***(978-0-06-249988-2(2))*** HarperCollins Pubs.

Slobodkina, Esphyr & Sayer, Ann Marie Mulhearn. More Caps for Sale: Another Tale of Mischievous Monkeys. Slobodkina, Esphyr, illus. (Illus.). 40p. (J). (gr. -1-3). 2017. pap. 8.99 *(978-0-06-249957-8(2))* 2015. (ENG., 18.99 *(978-0-06-240545-6(4))* HarperCollins Pubs.

Slobodkina, Esphyr & Slobodkina. Caps for Sale: A Tale of a Peddler, Some Monkeys & Their Monkey Business. Slobodkina, Esphyr, illus. 2015. (Young Scott Bks.). (ENG., Illus.). 48p. (J). (gr. -1-3). 17.99 *(978-0-201-09147-2(X));* 75th ed. pap. 7.99 *(978-0-06-443143-9(6))* HarperCollins Pubs.

—Circus Caps for Sale. Slobodkina, Esphyr, illus. 2004. (ENG., Illus.). 48p. (J). (gr. -1-3). reprint ed. pap. 7.99 *(978-0-06-443793-6(0))* HarperCollins Pubs.

Slobodkina, Esphyr & Slobodkina, E. Caps for Sale. 2015. (J). (gr. k-3). 17.20 *(978-0-8085-2604-9(9),* Turtleback) Turtleback Bks.

Weston Woods Staff, creator. Caps for Sale. 2011. 38.75 *(978-0-439-72925-3(4));* 18.95 *(978-0-439-72924-6(6))* Weston Woods Studios, Inc.

PEDIATRICS

see Children—Diseases; Children—Health and Hygiene

PEDIGREES

see Heraldry

PEER PRESSURE

Auer, Jim. Standing up to Peer Pressure: A Guide to Being True to You. Alley, R. W., illus. 2003. 32p. (J). per. 7.95 *(978-0-87029-375-7(3))* Abbey Pr.

Burstein, John. I Said No! Refusal Skills. 2009. (Slim Goodbody's Life Skills 101 Ser.). (ENG., Illus.). 32p. (J). (gr. 3-6). pap. *(978-0-7787-4805-2(7),* 1302928); lib. bdg. *(978-0-7787-4789-5(1),* 1302928) Crabtree Publishing Co.

Etingoff, Kim. Handling Peer Pressure. 2013. (Junior Martial Arts Ser.: 9). 32p. (J). (gr. 4-18). 19.95 *(978-1-4222-2736-7(7))* Mason Crest.

Evans, Lesli. But All My Friends Smoke: Cigarettes & Peer Pressure. 2009. (Illus.). 112p. (J). pap. 26.95 *(978-1-4222-1327-8(7),* 1291217) Mason Crest.

Feller, Robyn M. Everything You Need to Know about Peer Pressure. 2009. (Need to Know Library). 64p. (gr. 5-5). 58.50 *(978-1-60854-081-5(2))* Rosen Publishing Group, Inc., The.

Ferguson, Addy. What to Do When Your Friends Are Bullies. 2014. (Stand up: Bullying Prevention Ser.). 24p. (J). (gr. k-3). lib. bdg. 23.60 *(978-1-4777-6877-8(7),* PowerKids Pr.) Rosen Publishing Group, Inc., The.

Human Relations Media, prod. Clued in! on Saying No. 2005. (ENG.). 32p. (J). pap. 4.95 *(978-1-55548-051-6(9),* 675) Human Relations Media.

Juzwiak, Richard. Frequently Asked Questions about Peer Pressure. 2008. (FAQ: Teen Life Ser.). (Illus.). 64p. (YA). (gr. 7-12). lib. bdg. 31.95 *(978-1-4042-1805-5(X))* Rosen Publishing Group, Inc., The.

Lites, B. James & Lites, James R. Lessons in Peer Pressure For Kids All over the World. 2nd ed. 2006. (J). per. 13.95 *(978-0-9787674-1-9(1))* Aztec Bk. Publishing.

Living with Peer Pressure & Bullying. 2010. (Teen's Guides). (Illus.). 176p. (gr. 6-12). pap. 14.95 *(978-0-8160-7915-5(3),* Checkmark Bks.) Facts On File, Inc.

Mototsune, Kat. Image: Deal with It from the Inside Out. Shannon, Ben, illus. (Lorimer Deal with It Ser.). (ENG.). 32p. (J). (gr. 4-9). 2017. lib. bdg. 22.65 ***(978-1-4594-1188-3(9),*** 9781459411883) 2007. pap. 12.95 *(978-1-55028-994-7(2),* 9781550289947) Lorimer, James & Co., Ltd., Pubs. CAN. Dist: Casemate Pubs. & Bk. Distributors, LLC.

Slavens, Elaine. Peer Pressure: Deal with It Without Losing Your Cool, 1 vol. Shannon, Ben, illus. 2004. (Lorimer Deal with It Ser.). (ENG.). 32p. (J). (gr. 4-6). 12.95 *(978-1-55028-815-5(6),* 9781550288155) Lorimer, James & Co., Ltd., Pubs. CAN. Dist: Casemate Pubs. & Bk. Distributors, LLC.

Sprague, Susan & Schwartz, S. Coping with Cliques: A Workbook to Help Girls Deal with Gossip, Put-Downs, Bullying & Other Mean Behavior. 2008. (Instant Help Ser.). (ENG.). 168p. (YA). (gr. 6-12). pap. 16.95 *(978-1-57224-613-3(8),* Instant Help Books) New Harbinger Pubns.

Stephens, Ronald, ed. Peer Pressure & Relationships. 2014. (Safety First Ser.: 11). 48p. (J). (gr. 5-18). 20.95 *(978-1-4222-3050-3(3))* Mason Crest.

Straight Talk about Peer Pressure. (YA). (gr. 6-8). 69.95 *(978-1-55942-199-7(1),* 9241V9) Witcher Productions.

Tarshis, Thomas Paul. Living with Peer Pressure & Bullying. 2010. (Teen's Guides). (Illus.). 176p. (gr. 6-12). 34.95 *(978-0-8160-7914-8(5))* Facts On File, Inc.

Webber, Diane. Your Space: Dealing with Friends & Peers. 2008. (Scholastic Choices Ser.). (ENG., Illus.). 112p. (YA). (gr. 8-12). pap. 8.95 *(978-0-531-14774-0(6),* Watts, Franklin) Scholastic Library Publishing.

World Book, Inc Staff, contrib. by. Bullied by Friends. 2013. (J). *(978-0-7166-2072-3(3))* World Bk., Inc.

—Bullied to Belong. 2013. 48p. (J). *(978-0-7166-2076-1(6))* World Bk., Inc.

PEER PRESSURE—FICTION

Anhalt, Ariela. Freefall. 2011. (ENG.). 252p. (YA). (gr. 9). pap. 14.99 *(978-0-547-55216-3(5))* Houghton Mifflin Harcourt Publishing Co.

Brewer, Heather. The Cemetery Boys. 2015. (ENG.). 288p. (YA). (gr. 8). 17.99 *(978-0-06-230788-0(6),* HarperTeen) HarperCollins Pubs.

Brightwood, Laura, illus. Left Out. Brightwood, Laura, . 2006. (J). *(978-0-9779290-7-8(8))* 3-C Institute for Social Development.

Cabot, Meg. Pants on Fire. (YA). 2008. (ENG.). 288p. (gr. 8). pap. 9.99 *(978-0-06-088017-0(1))* 2007. (ENG.). 272p. (gr. 7-10). 16.99 *(978-0-06-088015-6(5))* 2007. 260p. (gr. 7-10). lib. bdg. 17.89 *(978-0-06-088016-3(3))* HarperCollins Pubs. (HarperTeen).

Carlson, Melody. The Day the Circus Came to Town. Butterfield, Ned, illus. 2004. 31p. (gr. -1-3). 14.99 *(978-1-58134-158-4(X))* Crossway.

Christopher, Matt. Fairway Phenom. 2003. (ENG.). 144p. (J). (gr. 5-8). pap. 16.99 *(978-0-316-07551-0(5))* Little, Brown Bks. for Young Readers.

Cook, Julia. Peer Pressure Gauge. Dufalla, Anita, illus. 2013. (ENG.). 32p. (J). pap. 10.95 *(978-1-934490-48-8(2))* Boys Town Pr.

Cormier, Robert. The Chocolate War. 191p. (YA). (gr. 7-18). pap. 4.99 *(978-0-8072-1428-2(0),* Listening Library) Random Hse. Audio Publishing Group.

—The Chocolate War. 30th ed. 2004. (Readers Circle Ser.). (ENG.). 272p. (YA). (gr. 7-12). pap. 9.99 *(978-0-375-82987-1(3),* Ember) Random Hse. Children's Bks.

Crane, Cheri J. Moment of Truth: A Novel. 2005. 238p. (YA). *(978-1-59156-727-1(0))* Covenant Communications.

Daniels, Cheri & Nicewander, Carol. Shadow Tail Meets the Gang. 2008. 24p. pap. 11.49 *(978-1-4389-3259-0(6))* AuthorHouse.

Emerson, Kevin. Carlos Is Gonna Get It. 2008. (J). pap. *(978-0-439-93526-5(1),* Levine, Arthur A. Bks.) Scholastic, Inc.

Friedman, Laurie. Honestly, Mallory! 2009. pap. 34.95 *(978-0-7613-4788-0(7))* Lerner Publishing Group.

—Honestly, Mallory! Pollak, Barbara, illus. (Mallory Ser.: 8). (ENG.). 160p. (J). (gr. 2-5). 2008. pap. 5.95 *(978-1-58013-840-6(3),* First Avenue Editions) 2007. 15.95 *(978-0-8225-6193-4(X),* Carolrhoda Bks.) Lerner Publishing Group.

Geragotelis, Brittany. What the Spell. (Life's a Witch Ser.). (ENG., Illus.). (YA). (gr. 9). 2014. 352p. pap. 9.99 *(978-1-4424-6707-1(X))* 2013. 336p. 16.99 *(978-1-4424-6815-3(7))* Simon & Schuster Bks. For Young Readers. (Simon & Schuster Bks. For Young Readers).

Goobie, Beth. The Dream Where the Losers Go, 1 vol. 2006. (ENG.). 208p. (YA). (gr. 8-12). per. 8.95 *(978-1-55143-455-1(5))* Orca Bk. Pubs. USA.

Gownley, Jimmy. True Things: Adults Don't Want Kids to Know. Gownley, Jimmy, illus. 2010. (Amelia Rules! Ser.). (ENG., Illus.). 176p. (J). (gr. 2-7). 19.99 *(978-1-4169-8611-9(1));* pap. 11.99 *(978-1-4169-8609-6(X))* Simon & Schuster Children's Publishing. (Atheneum Bks. for Young Readers).

—The Tweenage Guide to Not Being Unpopular. Gownley, Jimmy, illus. 2010. (Amelia Rules! Ser.). (ENG., Illus.). 192p. (J). (gr. 2-7). pap. 12.99 *(978-1-4169-8608-9(1),* Atheneum Bks. for Young Readers) Simon & Schuster Children's Publishing.

Griffin, Adele. The Julian Game. 2011. (ENG.). 208p. (YA). (gr. 7-18). 7.99 *(978-0-14-241973-1(7),* Speak) Penguin Young Readers Group.

Hana's Year: Evaluation Guide. 2006. (J). *(978-1-55942-408-0(7))* Witcher Productions.

Hankins, M. Lil' Mikie Tells It Like It Is. 2007. 20p. per. 24.95 *(978-1-4137-0168-5(X))* America Star Bks.

Harrison, Lisi. P. S. I Loathe You. 2008. (Clique Novels Ser.). 208p. 20.00 *(978-1-60686-338-1(X))* Perfection Learning Corp.

Haworth-Attard, Barbara. My Life from Air-Bras to Zits. 2009. (ENG.). 288p. (YA). (gr. 7-10). pap. 9.95 *(978-0-7387-1483-7(6),* Flux) North Star Editions.

Hole, Stian & Bartlett, Don. Garmann's Street. 2010. (ENG.). 44p. (J). (gr. 1-5). 17.00 *(978-0-8028-5357-8(9),* Eerdmans Bks For Young Readers) Eerdmans, William B. Publishing Co.

Horrocks, Anita. What They Don't Know. braille ed. 2003. (J). (gr. 2). spiral bd. *(978-0-616-15267-6(1))* Canadian National Institute for the Blind/Institut National Canadien pour les Aveugles.

Juby, Susan. Getting the Girl: A Guide to Private Investigation, Surveillance, & Cookery. 2010. (ENG.). 352p. (YA). (gr. 8). pap. 8.99 *(978-0-06-076528-6(3),* HarperTeen) HarperCollins Pubs.

Koja, Kathe. Buddha Boy. 2004. (ENG.). 128p. (YA). (gr. 7-11). reprint ed. 6.99 *(978-0-14-240209-2(5),* Speak) Penguin Young Readers Group.

—Buddha Boy. 2004. 117p. (gr. 3-7). 16.00 *(978-0-7569-3117-9(7))* Perfection Learning Corp.

Kucharski, Linda. Sneak the Sneaker. 2010. 44p. pap. 15.50 *(978-1-60911-487-9(6),* Eloquent Bks.) Strategic Book Publishing & Rights Agency (SBPRA).

Kushner, Elisabeth. The Purim Superhero. Byrne, Mike, illus. 2013. (Purim Ser.). (ENG.). 32p. (J). (gr. -1-3). 7.95 *(978-0-7613-9062-6(6),* Kar-Ben Publishing) Lerner Publishing Group.

Larsen, Sharon G. The Parable of the Chocolate Chips. 2008. (J). *(978-1-59038-912-6(3))* Deseret Bk. Co.

Maloney, Brenna. Philomena's New Glasses. 2017. (ENG., Illus.). 40p. (J). (gr. -1-1). 16.99 ***(978-0-425-28814-6(5),*** Viking Books for Young Readers) Penguin Young Readers Group.

Margolis, Leslie. Fix. 2006. (ENG.). 256p. (YA). (gr. 9-12). pap. 7.99 *(978-1-4169-2456-2(6),* Simon Pulse) Simon Pulse.

Morgan, Amanda K. Secrets, Lies, & Scandals. (ENG.). (YA). (gr. 9). 2017. 368p. pap. 10.99 *(978-1-4814-4955-7(9))* 2016. (Illus.). 352p. 17.99 *(978-1-4814-4954-0(0))* Simon Pulse. (Simon Pulse).

Moss, Peggy, et al. Our Friendship Rules, 1 vol. Geis, Alissa Imre, illus. 2007. (ENG.). 32p. (gr. 2-6). 16.95 *(978-0-88448-291-8(X),* 884291) Tilbury Hse. Pubs.

Mullarkey, Lisa. Hair's Looking at You: Book 12, 1 vol. Harris, Phyllis, illus. 2012. (Katharine the Almost Great Ser.). (ENG.). 80p. (J). (gr. 1-4). 27.07 *(978-1-61641-833-5(8))* Magic Wagon.

Nash, Andy. Melinda & Her Mule: For Kids Blessed with a Strong Will. 2008. (J). *(978-0-8127-0453-2(3))* Autumn Hse. Publishing Co.

Nigro, D. M. The Wolfman, the Shrink & the Eighth-Grade Election. 2006. 116p. (J). pap. 13.50 *(978-1-931201-66-7(8))* Twilight Times Bks.

Northrop, Michael. Trapped. (ENG.). 240p. (J). 2012. (gr. 7). pap. 9.99 *(978-0-545-21013-3(5))* 2011. (gr. 9-10). 17.99 *(978-0-545-21012-6(7))* Scholastic, Inc. (Scholastic Pr.).

Penn, Tony. The Misadventures of Michael Mcmichaels: The Creepy Campers, vol. 3. Martin, Brian, illus. 2017. (Michael Mcmichaels Ser.: 3). (ENG.). 84p. (J). pap. 7.95 ***(978-1-944882-10-5(3))*** Boys Town Pr.

Plum-Ucci, Carol. The Body of Christopher Creed. 2008. (ENG., Illus.). 272p. (YA). (gr. 7). pap. 7.99 *(978-0-15-206386-3(2))* Houghton Mifflin Harcourt Publishing Co.

Polak, Monique. 121 Express, 1 vol. 2008. (Orca Currents Ser.). (ENG.). (J). (gr. 5-9). 144p. pap. 9.95 *(978-1-55143-976-1(X));* 112p. lib. bdg. 16.95 *(978-1-55143-978-5(6))* Orca Bk. Pubs. USA.

Rountree, Wendy. Lost Soul. 2003. 87p. (J). pap. 19.95 *(978-1-59129-975-2(6))* America Star Bks.

Rowleym'Lin. Knights of Right, BK 3: The Warrior's Guard. 2010. 80p. (J). pap. 6.99 *(978-1-60641-240-4(X),* Shadow Mountain) Shadow Mountain Publishing.

Rowold, Shirley. Big Bear. 2010. 42p. pap. 15.50 *(978-1-60860-851-5(4),* Eloquent Bks.) Strategic Book Publishing & Rights Agency (SBPRA).

Salm, Arthur. Anyway: A Story about Me with 138 Footnotes, 27 Exaggerations, & 1 Plate of Spaghetti. 2012. (ENG., Illus.). 192p. (J). (gr. 3-7). 15.99 *(978-1-4424-2930-7(5),* Simon & Schuster Bks. For Young Readers) Simon & Schuster Bks. For Young Readers.

—Anyway* *a Story about Me with 138 Footnotes, 27 Exaggerations, & 1 Plate of Spaghetti. 2013. (ENG., Illus.). 192p. (J). (gr. 3-7). pap. 7.99 *(978-1-4424-2931-4(3),* Simon & Schuster Bks. For Young Readers) Simon & Schuster Bks. For Young Readers.

Sauer, Tammi. Nugget & Fang. 2015. lib. bdg. 17.20 *(978-0-606-36825-4(6))* Turtleback Bks.

—Nugget & Fang: Friends Forever - Or Snack Time? Slack, Michael, illus. 2013. (ENG.). 40p. (J). (gr. -1-3). 16.99 *(978-0-547-85285-0(1))* Houghton Mifflin Harcourt Publishing Co.

Schmatz, Pat. Mousetraps. Hauser, Bill, illus. 2008. (ENG.). 192p. (YA). (gr. 7-12). 17.95 *(978-0-8225-8657-9(6),* Carolrhoda Bks.) Lerner Publishing Group.

Schraff, Anne. The Petition. 2008. (Passages Ser.). 103p. (J). (gr. 4-6). lib. bdg. 13.95 *(978-0-7569-8391-8(6))* Perfection Learning Corp.

Schultz Nicholson, Lorna. Northern Star, 1 vol. 2006. (Lorimer Sports Stories Ser.). (ENG.). 112p. (J). (gr. 4-8). 16.95 *(978-1-55028-911-4(X),* 9781550289114); 9.95 *(978-1-55028-910-7(1),* 9781550289107) Lorimer, James & Co., Ltd., Pubs. CAN. Dist: Casemate Pubs. & Bk. Distributors, LLC.

Spinelli, Jerry. Wringer. 2004. (ENG.). 256p. (J). (gr. 3-7). pap. 8.99 *(978-0-06-059282-0(6),* HarperTeen) HarperCollins Pubs.

Stampler, Ann Redisch. Where It Began. 2013. (ENG.). 384p. (YA). (gr. 9). pap. 9.99 *(978-1-4424-2322-0(6),* Simon Pulse) Simon Pulse.

Strasser, Todd. American Terrorist. 2017. (YA). pap. *(978-1-4814-6134-4(6),* Simon & Schuster Bks. For Young Readers) Simon & Schuster Bks. For Young Readers.

Wilde, Jerry. Peace in the Halls: Stories & Activities to Manage Anger & Prevent School Violence. 2003. 112p. (YA). (gr. 4-12). pap. 9.95 *(978-0-9657610-4-8(5))* LGR Publishing, Inc.

Wilson, Sarah. Hocus Focus. Wummer, Amy, tr. Wummer, Amy, illus. 2004. (Science Solves It! Ser.). 32p. (J). pap. 5.95 *(978-1-57565-136-1(X))* Kane Press, Inc.

PEGASUS (GREEK MYTHOLOGY)

Pearce, Q. L. Pegasus. 2008. (Monsters Ser.). (ENG., Illus.). 48p. (YA). (gr. 4-7). lib. bdg. 30.45 *(978-0-7377-4082-0(5),* LML02109-242877) Cengage Gale.

Rose, Simon. Pegasus: The Myth & Science. 2015. (J). *(978-1-5105-0020-4(0));* pap. *(978-1-5105-0269-7(6))* SmartBook Media, Inc.

PEKING (CHINA)

see Beijing (China)

PELE, 1940-

Brown, Monica. Pelé, King of Soccer (Pelé, el Rey del Fútbol) Gayesky, Fernando, tr. Gutierrez, Rudy, illus. 2008. (SPA & ENG.). 40p. (J). (gr. -1-3). 17.99 *(978-0-06-122779-0(X),* Rayo) HarperCollins Pubs.

Buckley, James, Jr. Pele: A Photographic Story of a Life. 2007. (DK Biography Ser.). (ENG., Illus.). 128p. (J). (gr. 5-12). pap. 6.99 *(978-0-7566-2987-8(X),* DK Children) Dorling Kindersley Publishing, Inc.

Cline-Ransome, Lesa. Young Pele: Soccer's First Star. Ransome, James E., illus. 2011. (ENG.). 40p. (J). (gr. -1-3). pap. 7.99 *(978-0-375-87156-6(X),* Dragonfly Bks.) Random Hse. Children's Bks.

Gagne, Tammy. What It's Like to Be Pele. de la Vega, Eida, tr. 2011. (What It's Like to Be... = Que Se Sienta Al Ser... Ser.). (ENG & SPA., Illus.). 32p. (J). (gr. -1-2). lib. bdg. 25.70 *(978-1-58415-993-3(6))* Mitchell Lane Pubs., Inc.

Hillstrom, Laurie Collier. Pele: Soccer Superstar. 2007. (Twentieth Century Most Influential Hispanics Ser.). (ENG., Illus.). 104p. (YA). (gr. 7-12). lib. bdg. 34.80 *(978-1-4205-0023-3(6))* Cengage Gale.

Riner, Dax. Pelé. 2010. (Sports Heroes & Legends Ser.). (ENG.). 120p. (gr. 5-12). lib. bdg. 30.60 *(978-0-7613-5368-3(2))* Lerner Publishing Group.

Trusdell, Brian. Pel: Soccer Star & Ambassador, 1 vol. 2014. (Legendary Athletes Set 2 Ser.). (ENG.). 112p. (gr. 5-12). lib. bdg. 34.22 *(978-1-62403-132-8(3),* SportsZone) ABDO Publishing Co.

PELICANS

Castro, Shirley. The Pelican Family Counting Book. Castro, Christopher, illus. 2006. (ENG.). (J). 15.00 *(978-0-9790307-0-3(6))* Castro, Shirley.

Cussen, Sarah. Those Peculiar Pelicans. Weaver, Steve, illus. Hammond, Roger, photos by. 2005. (Those Amazing Animals Ser.). (ENG.). 55p. (J). (gr. 3-7). per. 8.95 *(978-1-56164-340-0(8))* Pineapple Pr., Inc.

Cussen, Sarah R. Those Peculiar Pelicans. Weaver, Steve, illus. Hammond, Roger, photos by. 2006. (Those Amazing Animals Ser.). (ENG.). 55p. (J). (gr. 5-9). lib. bdg. 14.95 *(978-1-56164-358-5(0))* Pineapple Pr., Inc.

Dabritz, Evelyn. It's Not Easy Being a Pelican. Hoffman, Isobel, illus. 2012. 32p. (J). *(978-1-930401-87-7(6))* Central Coast Bks./Pr.

Gish, Melissa. Living Wild: Pelicans. 2017. (Living Wild Ser.). (ENG.). 48p. (J). (gr. 5-7). pap. 12.00 ***(978-1-62832-435-8(X),*** Creative Paperbacks) Creative Co., The.

—Pelicans. 2017. (J). ***(978-1-60818-832-1(9),*** Creative Education) Creative Co., The.

Harris, Tim. Pelicans. 2008. (Nature's Children Ser.). (Illus.). 52p. (J). *(978-0-7172-6241-0(3))* Grolier, Ltd.

Kingston, Anna. The Life Cycle of a Pelican. 2011. (Nature's Life Cycles Ser.). (Illus.). 24p. (J). (gr. 2-5). pap. 8.15 *(978-1-4339-4684-4(X));* lib. bdg. 22.60 *(978-1-4339-4683-7(1))* Stevens, Gareth Publishing LLLP. (Gareth Stevens Learning Library).

Picayo, Mario. Brown Pelicans. 2016. (J). pap. *(978-1-934370-61-2(4))* Editorial Campana.

Pohl, Kathleen. Pelicans. 2007. (Let's Read about Animals Ser.). (Illus.). 24p. (gr. k-3). pap. 8.15 *(978-0-8368-7826-4(4));* lib. bdg. 22.00 *(978-0-8368-7819-6(1))* Stevens, Gareth Publishing LLLP. (Weekly Reader Leveled Readers).

—Pelicans (Pelícanos) 2007. (Let's Read about Animals/ Conozcamos a los animales Ser.). (SPA., Illus.). 24p. (gr. k-3). pap. 8.15 *(978-0-8368-8015-1(3),* Weekly Reader Leveled Readers) Stevens, Gareth Publishing LLLP.

—Pelicans (Pelícanos) 2007. (Let's Read about Animals/ Conozcamos a los animales Ser.). (SPA., Illus.). 24p. (gr. k-3). lib. bdg. 22.00 *(978-0-8368-8008-3(0),* Weekly Reader Leveled Readers) Stevens, Gareth Publishing LLLP.

Stout, Frankie. Pelicans: Soaring the Seas. 2009. (Things with Wings Ser.). 24p. (gr. 2-3). 42.50 *(978-1-60854-354-0(4));* (Illus.). (J). lib. bdg. 22.60 *(978-1-4042-4497-9(2))* Rosen Publishing Group, Inc., The. (PowerKids Pr.).

Swan, Erin Pembrey. Pelicans, Cormorants, & Their Kin. 2003. (Animals in Order Ser.). (ENG., Illus.). 48p. (J). (gr. 4-6). pap. 6.95 *(978-0-531-16378-8(4),* Watts, Franklin) Scholastic Library Publishing.

PELICANS—FICTION

Casad, Mary Brooke. Bluebonnet at the Ocean Star Museum, 1 vol. Vincent, Benjamin, illus. 2012. (ENG.). 32p. (J). (gr. k-3). 16.99 *(978-1-4556-1721-0(0))* Pelican Publishing Co., Inc.

Castro, Shirley. The Pelican Family Series — Telly's Story. Castro, Christopher, illus. 2008. 36p. (J). 15.00 *(978-0-9790307-1-0(4))* Castro, Shirley.

Dahl, Roald. The Giraffe & the Pelly & Me. Blake, Quentin, illus. 2009. (ENG.). 96p. (Orig.). (J). (gr. 3-7). 7.99 *(978-0-14-241384-5(4),* Puffin Books) Penguin Young Readers Group.

Deutsch, Neil. Rose & the Pelican. 2013. 32p. pap. 19.99 *(978-1-4817-0947-7(X))* AuthorHouse.

Dixon, Virginia. What Happened to Willie? Thomas, Tim, illus. 2007. 32p. (J). 16.00 *(978-0-9795386-0-5(2))* Grand Productions.

Erickson, John R. The Case of the Dinosaur Birds. Holmes, Gerald L., illus. 2011. (Hank the Cowdog Ser.). (ENG.). 125p. (J). (gr. 3-6). pap. 5.99 *(978-1-59188-154-4(4))* Maverick Bks., Inc.

Fane, Judy B. Paddy the Pelican Survives the Storm. Alden, Carol, illus. 2010. 48p. pap. 16.50 *(978-1-60911-448-0(5),* Eloquent Bks.) Strategic Book Publishing & Rights Agency (SBPRA).

Froeber, Sarah & Mosher, Kim. Pelican & Pelicant. 2003. (Illus.). 36p. (J). 17.99 *(978-0-9744926-0-5(4))* Toucan Pr., Inc.

Glaze, Dave & Coteau Books Staff. Waiting for Pelly, 1 vol. 2003. (ENG., Illus.). 120p. (J). (gr. 3-6). pap. 7.95 *(978-1-55050-228-2(X))* Coteau Bks. CAN. Dist: Orca Bk. Pubs. USA.

P
Q
R

Gump, Granny. The Giraffe Who Went to School. 2011. 48p. pap. 21.99 *(978-1-4568-5805-6(X))* Xlibris Corp.

Halfmann, Janet. Pelican's Catch. Dacey, Bob & Bandelin, Debra, illus. (Smithsonian Oceanic Collection Ser.). (ENG.). 32p. (J). 2011. (gr. -1-3). 8.95 *(978-1-60727-657-9(7))* 2011. (gr. -1-3). 19.95 *(978-1-60727-656-2(9))* 2005. (gr. -1-2). 4.95 *(978-1-59249-286-2(X),* B4076) 2005. (gr. -1-2). 9.95 *(978-1-59249-311-1(4),* PB4076) 2005. (gr. -1-2). 19.95 *(978-1-59249-310-4(6),* BC4026) 2005. (gr. -1-2). 15.95 *(978-1-59249-287-9(8),* B4026) 2004. (gr. 2-7). 8.95 *(978-1-59249-309-8(2),* SC4026) 2004. (gr. -1-3). 6.95 *(978-1-59249-285-5(1),* S4026) Soundprints.

Harvey, Roland. On the River. 2016. (ENG.). 32p. (J). (gr. k-3). 17.99 *(978-1-76011-245-5(3))* Allen & Unwin AUS. Dist: Independent Pubs. Group.

Horender, Philip M. A Brave New Mouse: Ellis Island Approved Immigrant, 1 vol. Wolek, Guy, illus. 2013. (Maximilian P. Mouse, Time Traveler Ser.). (ENG.). 112p. (J). (gr. 3-6). lib. bdg. 27.07 *(978-1-61641-961-5(X),* Calico Chapter Bks) Magic Wagon.

Johnson, Rebecca. The Proud Pelican's Secret. Parish, Steve, illus. 2005. (Animal Storybooks Ser.). 24p. (gr. k-3). lib. bdg. 22.00 *(978-0-8368-5974-4(X),* Gareth Stevens Learning Library) Stevens, Gareth Publishing LLLP.

Keiser, Frances R. Annie the River Otter: The Adventures of Pelican Pete. Keiser, Hugh M., illus. l.t. ed. 2006. (ENG.). 34p. (J). 19.99 *(978-0-9668845-4-8(X))* Sagaponack Bks.

Lease, Janice. Pellina the Pelican. 2008. 48p. pap. 19.95 *(978-0-9800762-1-9(8))* Cinnamon Ridge Publishing.

Renaud, Andrea. Sammy the Surfing Pelican Meets Steve the Surf Guru. l.t. ed. 2003. (Illus.). 32p. (J). per. *(978-0-9717041-3-8(9))* A Happy Friend, Inc.

Ryan, Mike. Mayda Saves the Day. Ralph, Karin, illus. 2004. 60p. (J). (gr. 1-5). 14.95 *(978-0-9701319-3-5(3))* Temenos Pr.

Rylant, Cynthia. The Turtle. McDaniels, Preston, illus. 2006. (Lighthouse Family Ser.). 47p. (J). (gr. -1-3). 11.65 *(978-0-7569-6611-9(6))* Perfection Learning Corp.

—The Turtle. McDaniels, Preston, illus. 2005. (Lighthouse Family Ser.: 4). (ENG.). 48p. (J). (gr. 1-5). 15.99 *(978-0-689-86244-1(X),* Simon & Schuster Bks. For Young Readers) Simon & Schuster Bks. For Young Readers.

Sargent, Dave & Sargent, David, Jr. Petie Pelican: Be Proud of Yourself, 20 vols., Vol. 14. Lenoir, Jane, illus. 2nd ed. 2003. (Feather Tales Ser.: 14). 42p. (J). lib. bdg. 20.95 *(978-1-56763-745-8(0))* Ozark Publishing.

Scheunemann, Pam. Pelican's Pouch, 1 vol. 2007. (Critter Chronicles Ser.). (ENG., Illus.). 24p. (J). (gr. k-3). lib. bdg. 24.21 *(978-1-59928-462-0(6),* SandCastle) ABDO Publishing Co.

Sprecher, John. Tori & Cassandra & the Pelican in Peril. Forrest, James, illus. l.t. ed. Date not set. (Special Kids "Special Message" Book Ser.: Vol. 3). 32p. (J). (gr. k-4). pap. 10.00 *(978-1-892186-02-7(0))* Anythings Possible, Inc.

Zschock, Martha Day. Hello, New Orleans! 2011. (Hello! Ser.). (ENG., Illus.). 16p. (J). (gr. -1-k). bds. 9.95 *(978-1-933212-63-0(2),* Commonwealth Editions) Applewood Bks.

—Hello, San Francisco! 2012. (Hello! Ser.). (ENG., Illus.). 16p. (J). (gr. -1-k). bds. 9.95 *(978-1-933212-65-4(9),* Commonwealth Editions) Applewood Bks.

PELTS

see Hides and Skins

PEN AND INK DRAWING

see Pen Drawing

PEN DRAWING

Corfee, Stephanie. Girl Plus Pen: Doodle, Draw, Color, & Express Your Individual Style. Corfee, Stephanie, illus. 2016. (Craft It Yourself Ser.). (ENG., Illus.). 144p. (gr. 3-4). pap. 12.95 *(978-1-62370-596-1(7))* Capstone Young Readers of Coughlan Cos.

Peot, Margaret. Inkblot: Drip, Splat, & Squish Your Way to Creativity. Peot, Margaret, illus. 2011. (ENG., Illus.). 56p. (J). (gr. 6-18). 19.95 *(978-1-59078-720-5(X))* Boyds Mills Pr.

PENAL CODES

see Criminal Law

PENAL INSTITUTIONS

see Prisons

PENAL LAW

see Criminal Law

PENCIL DRAWING

Hosley, Maria. Airplanes, 1 vol. 2007. (First Drawings Ser.). (ENG., Illus.). 24p. (gr. -1-3). 25.65 *(978-1-59679-799-4(1),* Buddy Bks.) ABDO Publishing Co.

—Cars, 1 vol. 2007. (First Drawings Ser.). (ENG., Illus.). 24p. (J). (gr. -1-3). lib. bdg. 25.65 *(978-1-59679-800-7(9),* Buddy Bks.) ABDO Publishing Co.

—People, 1 vol. 2007. (First Drawings Ser.). (ENG., Illus.). 24p. (gr. -1-3). 25.65 *(978-1-59679-812-0(2),* Buddy Bks.) ABDO Publishing Co.

Levin, Freddie & Gordon, Freddie. 1-2-3 Draw Baby Animals. Levin, Freddie, illus. 2006. (ENG., Illus.). 64p. (J). pap. 8.99 *(978-0-939217-45-8(7))* Peel Productions, Inc.

Lynette, Rachel. Pencils Before the Store. McGeehan, Dan, illus. 2012. (Before the Store Ser.). (ENG.). 32p. (J). (gr. 2-5). lib. bdg. 29.93 *(978-1-60973-680-4(X),* 201255) Child's World, Inc., The.

Saltzberg, Barney. Andrew Drew & Drew. 2012. (ENG., Illus.). 40p. (J). (gr. -1-k). 16.95 *(978-1-4197-0377-5(3),* Abrams Appleseed) Abrams, Inc.

Top That! Kids, creator. Make Your Own Pencil Toppers. 2006. (Creative Studio Ser.). (Illus.). 48p. (J). (gr. -1-3). *(978-1-905359-86-8(1))* Top That! Publishing PLC.

PENGUINS

Adamson, Heather. Emperor Penguins. 2017. (Ocean Life up Close Ser.). (ENG., Illus.). 24p. (J). (gr. k-3). lib. bdg. 25.95 ***(978-1-62617-641-6(8),*** Blastoff! Readers) Bellwether Media.

Anderson, Jill. Emperor Penguins. 2007. (Wild Ones Ser.). (ENG., Illus.). 24p. (J). (gr. -1-1). 12.95 *(978-1-55971-972-8(9));* pap. 6.95 *(978-1-55971-973-5(7))* Cooper Square Publishing Llc.

Arlington, Jane & Langdon, Sharon. Penguins. 2006. (J). 7.99 *(978-1-59939-032-1(9))* Cornerstone Pr.

—Penguins. (Amazing Animals Ser.). 48p. 2009. (gr. 2-6). pap. 10.50 *(978-1-4339-2018-9(2),* Gareth Stevens Learning Library) 2008. (YA). (gr. 3-6). lib. bdg. 28.00 *(978-0-8368-9101-0(5))* Stevens, Gareth Publishing LLLP.

Arlon, Penelope. Penguins: Meet Teh Heroes of a Frozen World. 2012. (Scholastic Discover More Ser.). (ENG.). 80p. (J). (gr. 2-5). 12.99 *(978-0-545-33024-4(6),* Scholastic Reference) Scholastic, Inc.

Arlon, Penelope & Gordon-Harris, Tory. Penguins. 2012. (J). lib. bdg. *(978-0-531-22956-9(4))* Scholastic, Inc.

Arnold, Caroline. A Penguin's World, 1 vol. Arnold, Caroline, illus. 2006. (Caroline Arnold's Animals Ser.). (ENG., Illus.). 24p. (gr. k-2). 27.99 *(978-1-4048-1323-6(3),* 1253185) Picture Window Bks.

Baggott, Stella. Flip, Flap, Flop. 2008. (Bath Bks). 8p. (J). 14.99 *(978-0-7945-2177-6(0),* Usborne) EDC Publishing.

Barner, Bob. Penguins, Penguins, Everywhere! 2010. (ENG., Illus.). 20p. (J). (gr. -1 — 1). bds. 9.99 *(978-0-8118-7724-4(8))* Chronicle Bks. LLC.

Bell, Samantha. Penguins Are Awesome. 2018. (ENG.). 32p. (J). (gr. 3-6). 31.35 ***(978-1-63235-436-5(5),*** 12-Story Library) Pr. Room Editions LLC.

Berger, Melvin & Berger, Gilda. Penguins. 2010. (Illus.). 16p. (J). *(978-0-545-16080-3(4))* Scholastic, Inc.

Best, B. J. Penguins. 2016. (Migrating Animals Ser.). 24p. (J). pap. 8.22 *(978-1-5026-2106-1(1));* lib. bdg. 24.21 *(978-1-5026-2108-5(8))* Cavendish Square Publishing.

Bishop, Nic. Penguin Day. 2017. (ENG., Illus.). 32p. (J). (gr. -1-3). 16.99 *(978-0-545-20636-5(7),* Scholastic Pr.) Scholastic, Inc.

Bodden, Valerie. Amazing Animals - Penguins. 2010. (Amazing Animals Ser.). 24p. (J). (gr. -1-3). 16.95 *(978-1-58341-810-9(5),* Creative Education) Creative Co., The.

—Amazing Animals: Penguins. 2011. (Amazing Animals Ser.). (ENG.). 24p. (J). (gr. 1-3). pap. 8.99 *(978-0-89812-743-0(2),* Creative Paperbacks) Creative Co., The.

—Penguins. 2015. (J). pap. *(978-1-62832-258-3(6),* Creative Paperbacks) Creative Co., The.

Bone, Emily & Watt, Fiona. Penguins. 2010. (Beginner's Nature Ser.). 32p. (J). pap. 7.99 *(978-0-7945-2581-1(4),* Usborne) EDC Publishing.

Books Are Fun 8 Title Animal Lives Set: Penguins. 2006. (J). *(978-1-59566-310-8(X))* QEB Publishing Inc.

Boothroyd, Jennifer. From Egg to Penguin. 2016. (Start to Finish, Second Ser.). (ENG., Illus.). 24p. (J). (gr. k-3). 23.99 *(978-1-5124-1829-3(3))* Lerner Publishing Group.

Brannon, Cecelia H. Baby Penguins at the Zoo. 2016. (All about Baby Zoo Animals Ser.). (ENG.). 24p. (J). (gr. k-1). pap. 9.35 *(978-0-7660-7150-6(2));* (Illus.). lib. bdg. 22.60 *(978-0-7660-7152-0(9))* Enslow Pubs., Inc.

Bredeson, Carmen. Emperor Penguins up Close. 2006. (Zoom in on Animals! Ser.). (Illus.). 24p. (J). (gr. 1-3). lib. bdg. 22.60 *(978-0-7660-2497-7(0),* Enslow Elementary) Enslow Pubs., Inc.

Child's Play, creator. Penguin. 2005. (ENG., Illus.). 12p. (J). (gr. -1-k). bds. *(978-0-85953-680-6(7))* Child's Play International Ltd.

Clark, Willow. Penguins: Life in the Colony. 2011. (Animal Families Ser.). 24p. (J). (ENG.). pap. 8.25 *(978-1-4488-2606-3(3));* (Illus.). lib. bdg. 22.60 *(978-1-4488-2510-3(5))* Rosen Publishing Group, Inc., The. (PowerKids Pr.).

—Penguins: Pingüinos: Life in the Colony: Vida en la Colonia. 2011. (Animal Families / Familias de animales Ser.). (SPA & ENG., Illus.). 24p. lib. bdg. 22.60 *(978-1-4488-3124-1(5),* PowerKids Pr.) Rosen Publishing Group, Inc., The.

Cole, Carol A. The Penguin Lady, 1 vol. Rogers, Sherry, illus. 2012. 32p. (J). (gr. -1-3). (ENG.). 17.95 *(978-1-60718-527-7(X));* (ENG.). pap. 9.95 *(978-1-60718-536-9(9));* (SPA.). pap. 9.95 *(978-1-62855-420-5(7))* Arbordale Publishing.

Coleman, Miriam. Swimming with Penguins. 2009. (Flippers & Fins Ser.). (Illus.). 24p. (ENG.). (J). pap. 8.25 *(978-1-4358-3245-9(0),* 1300492, PowerKids Pr.); (YA). (gr. 1-3). lib. bdg. 22.60 *(978-1-4042-8094-6(4))* Rosen Publishing Group, Inc., The.

Cooper, Sharon Katz. When Penguins Cross the Ice: The Emperor Penguin Migration. Leonard, Tom, illus. 2015. (Extraordinary Migrations Ser.). (ENG.). 24p. (gr. 2-3). pap. 8.95 *(978-1-4795-6102-5(9))* Picture Window Bks.

—When Penguins Cross the Ice: The Emperor Penguin Migration. Leonard, Tom, illus. 2015. (Extraordinary Migrations Ser.). (ENG.). 24p. (gr. 2-3). lib. bdg. 26.65 *(978-1-4795-6078-3(2))* Picture Window Bks.

Costain, Meredith. Penguin. Hanna, Gary, illus. 2016. (Wild World Ser.). 00032p. (J). (gr. 1-2). pap. 10.00 *(978-1-4994-8223-2(X),* Windmill Bks.) Rosen Publishing Group, Inc., The.

Cussen, Sarah. Those Perky Penguins. 2011. (Those Amazing Animals Ser.). (ENG.). 56p. (J). 14.95 *(978-1-56164-504-6(4));* pap. 9.95 *(978-1-56164-505-3(2))* Pineapple Pr., Inc.

Daigle, Evelyne. The World of Penguins. Wright, Genevieve, tr. from FRE. Grenier, Daniel, illus. 2007. (ENG.). 48p. (J). (gr. 4-7). 18.95 *(978-0-88776-799-9(0),* Tundra Bks.) Tundra Bks. CAN. Dist: Penguin Random Hse. LLC.

—The World of Penguins. Wright, Genevieve, tr. from FRE. Grenier, Daniel, illus. 2008. (ENG.). 48p. (J). (gr. 4-7). pap. 12.95 *(978-0-88776-947-4(0),* Tundra Bks.) Tundra Bks. CAN. Dist: Penguin Random Hse. LLC.

De La Bedoyere C. Why Why Why Cant Penguins Fly. 2008. 32p. pap. *(978-1-84810-000-8(0))* Miles Kelly Publishing, Ltd.

de la Bédoyere, Camilla. Could a Penguin Ride a Bike? And Other Questions. Bitskoff, Aleksei, illus. 2015. (What If A Ser.). (ENG.). 24p. (J). (gr. -1-k). 15.95 *(978-1-60992-734-9(6))* QEB Publishing Inc.

De la Bédoyère, Camilla. Penguins. 2010. (Remarkable Man & Beast Ser.). (Illus.). 48p. (J). (gr. 3-18). lib. bdg. 19.95 *(978-1-4222-1972-0(0))* Mason Crest.

—Why Why Why... Can't Penguins Fly? 2010. (Why Why Why Ser.). 32p. (J). (gr. 1-3). lib. bdg. 18.95 *(978-1-4222-1573-9(3))* Mason Crest.

—The Wild Life of Penguins, 1 vol. 2015. (ENG.). 24p. (J). lib. bdg. 23.60 *(978-1-4777-5502-0(0),* Windmill Bks.) Rosen Publishing Group, Inc., The.

de le Bédoyère, Camilla. Egg to Penguin. 2010. (ENG., Illus.). 24p. (J). pap. *(978-1-84835-583-5(1))* QEB Publishing Inc.

Dickmann, Nancy. A Penguin's Life, 1 vol. 2010. (Watch It Grow Ser.). (ENG., Illus.). 24p. (gr. -1-1). 22.65 *(978-1-4329-4230-4(1));* pap. 6.29 *(978-1-4329-4233-5(6))* Heinemann-Raintree. (Acorn).

—La Vida del Pingüino. 2011. (¡Mira Cómo Crece! Ser.). (Illus.). 24p. (gr. -1-1). (SPA & ENG.). 22.65 *(978-1-4329-5279-2(X));* (ENG & SPA., pap. 6.29 *(978-1-4329-5291-4(9))* Heinemann-Raintree. (Bellota).

Dorling Kindersley Publishing Staff & Lock, Deborah. Emperor Penguins, Level 2. 2011. (DK Readers Ser.). (ENG.). 32p. (J). (gr. 1-3). pap. 3.99 *(978-0-7566-8923-0(6),* DK Children) Dorling Kindersley Publishing, Inc.

Durrie, Karen. I Am a Penguin. 2012. (J). *(978-1-61913-229-0(X));* pap. *(978-1-61913-230-6(3))* Weigl Pubs., Inc.

—Pingüino. 2013. (SPA.). (J). *(978-1-62127-573-2(6))* Weigl Pubs., Inc.

Edwards, Roberta. Emperor Penguins. Schwartz, Carol, illus. 2007. (Penguin Young Readers, Level 3 Ser.). (ENG.). 48p. (J). (gr. 1-3). mass mkt. 3.99 *(978-0-448-44664-6(2),* Penguin Young Readers) Penguin Young Readers Group.

Emily Rose Townsend. Penguins [Scholastic]. 2009. (Polar Animals Ser.). 24p. (gr. k-1). pap. 0.34 *(978-1-4296-4224-8(6),* Pebble Bks.) Capstone Press of Coughlan Cos.

Esbaum, Jill. Explore My World Penguins. 2014. (Explore My World Ser.). (ENG.). 32p. (J). (gr. -1-2). pap. 4.99 *(978-1-4263-1701-9(8),* National Geographic Children's Bks.) National Geographic Society.

Franks, Katie. Penguins. 2014. (Zoo's Who's Who Ser.). (Illus.). 24p. (J). (gr. k-2). pap. 49.50 *(978-1-4777-6577-7(8),* PowerKids Pr.) Rosen Publishing Group, Inc., The.

Gallagher, Debbie. Penguins. 2009. (Zoo Animals 2 Ser.). 32p. (gr. 2). lib. bdg. 18.56 *(978-0-7614-4747-4(4))* Marshall Cavendish Corp.

Galvin, Laura Gates. Baby Penguin Waddles. 2011. (ENG.). 16p. (J). *(978-1-60727-616-6(X))* Soundprints.

Gareth Stevens Publishing Staff, contrib. by. Penguins. 2004. (All about Wild Animals Ser.). (Illus.). 32p. (gr. k-4). lib. bdg. 26.00 *(978-0-8368-4186-2(7),* Gareth Stevens Learning Library) Stevens, Gareth Publishing LLLP.

Glaser, Rebecca Stromstad. Penguins Waddle. 2016. (ENG., Illus.). 16p. (J). (gr. -1 — 1). bds. 7.99 *(978-1-68152-070-4(2))* Amicus.

Goldish, Meish. Emperor Penguin: The World's Biggest Penguin. 2010. (More SuperSized! Ser.). (Illus.). 24p. (J). (gr. k-3). lib. bdg. 22.61 *(978-1-936087-29-7(4))* Bearport Publishing Co., Inc.

Gray, Susan H. Penguins Can't Fly. 2014. (Tell Me Why Library). (ENG., Illus.). 24p. (J). (gr. 2-5). 25.64 *(978-1-63188-010-0(1),* 205447) Cherry Lake Publishing.

Guiberson, Brenda Z. The Emperor Lays an Egg. Schonhorst, Elizabeth, ed. Paley, Joan, illus. rev. ed. 2004. (ENG.). 32p. (J). (gr. -1-3). pap. 8.99 *(978-0-8050-7636-3(0),* 9780805076363) Square Fish.

Hall, Katharine. Osos Polares y Pingüinos: Un Libro de Comparación y Contraste. 2014.Tr. of Polar Bears & Penguins: a Compare & Contrast Book. (SPA.). 32p. (J). (gr. -1-3). pap. 9.95 *(978-1-62855-227-0(1))* Arbordale Publishing.

Hall, Katherine. Polar Bears & Penguins: A Compare & Contrast Book, 1 vol. 2014. (Compare & Contrast Ser.). (ENG., Illus.). 32p. (J). (gr. -1-3). 17.95 *(978-1-62855-209-6(3))* Arbordale Publishing.

Hanel, Rachael. Penguins. 2008. (Living Wild Ser.). (Illus.). 46p. (J). (gr. 4-7). lib. bdg. 22.95 *(978-1-58341-658-7(7),* Creative Education) Creative Co., The.

Harris, Tim, ed. Penguins. 2012. (Animal Families Ser.). (ENG., Illus.). 32p. (gr. 2-5). 31.35 *(978-1-78121-005-5(5),* Brown Bear Bks.) Windmill Bks. Ltd. GBR. Dist: Black Rabbit Bks.

Hastings, Derek. Penguins - Pb: A Portrait of the Animal World. 2013. (Portrait of the Animal World Ser.). (Illus.). 72p. pap. 9.95 *(978-1-59764-325-2(4))* New Line Bks.

Hewett, Richard, illus. & photos by. A Penguin Chick Grows Up. Hewett, Richard, photos by. Hewett, Joan, photos by. 2004. (Baby Animals Ser.). 32p. (J). (gr. k-3). lib. bdg. 21.27 *(978-1-57505-200-7(8))* Lerner Publishing Group.

Hoff, Mary. Penguins. 2006. (Wild World of Animals Ser.). (Illus.). 31p. (J). 18.95 *(978-1-58341-435-4(5),* Creative Education) Creative Co., The.

Hoffman, Mary Ann. How Do Penguins Survive the Cold? 2009. (Real Life Readers Ser.). 24p. (gr. 3-4). pap. 8.25 *(978-1-4042-8007-6(3),* Rosen Classroom); 42.50 *(978-1-61511-214-2(6),* PowerKids Pr.) Rosen Publishing Group, Inc., The.

Hollenbeck, Kathleen. Penguins Family: The Story of a Humboldt Penguin. Stegos, Daniel, illus. 2005. (ENG.). 32p. (J). (gr. -1-2). 4.95 *(978-1-59249-348-7(3),* B4077); pap. 6.95 *(978-1-59249-347-0(5),* S4027) Soundprints.

Hollenbeck, Kathleen & Smithsonian Institution Staff. Penguin's Family (la familia del Pinguino) 2008. (MUL.). 16p. 14.95 *(978-1-59249-850-5(7))* Soundprints.

Hunt, Jilly. A Rookery of Penguins: And Other Bird Groups, 1 vol. 2012. (Animals in Groups Ser.). (ENG.). 48p. (gr. 4-6). pap. 9.95 *(978-1-4329-6491-7(7));* lib. bdg. 33.32 *(978-1-4329-6484-9(4))* Heinemann-Raintree. (Heinemann InfoSearch).

Jacquet, Luc. March of the Penguins: The Official Children's Book. Maison, Jerome, photos by. 2005. (ENG., Illus.). 32p. (J). (gr. 2-12). lib. bdg. 22.90 *(978-0-7922-6190-2(9));* per. 5.95 *(978-0-7922-6183-4(6))* National Geographic Society. (National Geographic Children's Bks.).

James, Helen Foster. Discover Penguins. 2015. (21st Century Basic Skills Library: Splash! Ser.). (ENG., Illus.). 24p. (J). (gr. 2-4). 24.21 *(978-1-63362-603-4(2),* 206596) Cherry Lake Publishing.

Jenkins, Martin. The Emperor's Egg. Chapman, Jane, illus. 2008. (Read, Listen, & Wonder Ser.). (ENG.). 32p. (J). (gr. -1-3). pap. 8.99 *(978-0-7636-3825-2(0))* Candlewick Pr.

—The Emperor's Egg Big Book: Read & Wonder Big Book. Chapman, Jane, illus. 2003. (Read & Wonder Ser.). (ENG.). 32p. (J). (gr. k-12). pap. 24.99 *(978-0-7636-2233-6(8))* Candlewick Pr.

Johnson, Robin. Les Manchots. 2012. (FRE.). 32p. (J). pap. 9.95 *(978-2-89579-442-4(1))* Bayard Canada CAN. Dist: Crabtree Publishing Co.

Jonas, Anne. Little Penguins. 2005. (Born to Be Wild Ser.). (Illus.). 24p. (gr. k-3). lib. bdg. 23.00 *(978-0-8368-4738-3(5),* Gareth Stevens Learning Library) Stevens, Gareth Publishing LLLP.

Kalman, Bobbie. Life Cycle of an Emperors. 2008. (FRE.). 32p. (J). pap. 9.95 *(978-2-89579-201-7(1))* Bayard Canada Livres CAN. Dist: Crabtree Publishing Co.

Kalman, Bobbie & Johnson, Robin. El Ciclo de Vida del Pinguino Emperador. 2007. (Ciclos de Vida Ser.). (SPA., Illus.). 32p. (J). (gr. 3-7). lib. bdg. *(978-0-7787-8672-6(2))* Crabtree Publishing Co.

—El Ciclo de Vida Del Pinguino Emperador. 2007. (Libro de Bobbie Kalman Ser.). (SPA., Illus.). 32p. (J). *(978-1-4287-3238-4(1))* Crabtree Publishing Co.

—El Ciclo de Vida del Pinguino Emperador. rev. ed. 2007. (Ciclos de Vida Ser.). (SPA., Illus.). 32p. (J). (gr. 3-7). pap. *(978-0-7787-8718-1(4))* Crabtree Publishing Co.

—Endangered Penguins. 2007. (Earth's Endangered Animals Ser.). (ENG., Illus.). 32p. (J). (gr. 3-7). lib. bdg. *(978-0-7787-1863-5(8));* (gr. -1-3). pap. *(978-0-7787-1909-0(X))* Crabtree Publishing Co.

—The Life Cycle of an Emperor Penguin. 2006. (Life Cycle Ser.). (ENG., Illus.). 32p. (J). (gr. -1-3). pap. *(978-0-7787-0704-2(0))* Crabtree Publishing Co.

Kawa, Katie. Baby Penguins. 2011. (Cute & Cuddly: Baby Animals Ser.). (Illus.). 24p. (J). (gr. k-2). (J). pap. 8.15 *(978-1-4339-5532-7(6));* (J). lib. bdg. 22.60 *(978-1-4339-5530-3(X));* 69.20 *(978-1-4339-6893-8(2))* Stevens, Gareth Publishing LLLP.

Kennington, Tammy. Penguins. 2014. (21st Century Skills Library: Exploring Our Oceans Ser.). (ENG., Illus.). 32p. (J). (gr. 3-6). 28.50 *(978-1-62431-605-0(0),* 203204) Cherry Lake Publishing.

Kolpin, Molly. Galapagos Penguins, 1 vol. 2012. (Endangered & Threatened Animals Ser.). (ENG., Illus.). 32p. (gr. 3-4). lib. bdg. 27.99 *(978-1-4296-8431-6(3),* Snap Bks.) Capstone Press of Coughlan Cos.

Kuskowski, Alex. Penguins, 1 vol. 2014. (Zoo Animals Ser.). (ENG.). 24p. (J). (gr. k-3). lib. bdg. 24.21 *(978-1-62403-274-5(5),* SandCastle) ABDO Publishing Co.

Landau, Elaine. Emperor Penguins. 2010. (Animals of the Snow & Ice Ser.). (Illus.). 32p. (J). (gr. 1-3). lib. bdg. 23.94 *(978-0-7660-3462-4(3))* Enslow Pubs., Inc.

Lar Rieu, Barry, text. Penguin Paradise. 2007. (Illus.). 62p. (YA). per. 16.00 *(978-0-9660373-1-9(6))* Gallant Hse. Publishing.

Leigh, Autumn. A Penguin Colony. 2013. (Animal Groups Ser.). (Illus.). 24p. (J). (gr. 1-3). pap. 8.15 *(978-1-4339-8210-1(2));* lib. bdg. 22.60 *(978-1-4339-8209-5(9))* Stevens, Gareth Publishing LLLP.

—A Penguin Colony / una Colonia de Pingüinos. 2013. (Animal Groups / Grupos de Animales Ser.). (ENG & SPA., Illus.). 24p. (gr. 1-3). 22.60 *(978-1-4339-8808-0(9))* Stevens, Gareth Publishing LLLP.

Lewis, Suzanne. A Penguin Named Patience: A Hurricane Katrina Rescue Story. Anchin, Lisa, illus. 2015. (ENG.). 24p. (J). (gr. 1-4). 15.95 *(978-1-58536-840-2(7),* 203732) Sleeping Bear Pr.

L'Heureux, J. J. Good Day Book. 2006. spiral bd. *(978-0-9785892-0-2(3))* BrainStream.

Lindeen, Mary. Penguins. 2013. (ENG., Illus.). 24p. (J). lib. bdg. 25.65 *(978-1-62031-066-3(X))* Jump! Inc.

Liu, Li. Penguins Have It All. 2016. (1-3Y Marine Life Ser.). (ENG., Illus.). 16p. (J). pap. 5.99 ***(978-1-63437-624-2(2))*** American Reading Co.

—What Penguins Need. 2016. (1-3Y Marine Life Ser.). (ENG., Illus.). 16p. (J). pap. 5.99 ***(978-1-63437-690-7(0))*** American Reading Co.

Lynch, Wayne. Penguins! The World's Coolest Birds. 2nd rev. ed. 2016. (ENG., Illus.). 80p. (J). (gr. 5-8). pap. 12.95 *(978-1-77085-858-9(X),* 9781770858589) Firefly Bks., Ltd.

Macken, JoAnn Early. Penguins/Los Pingüinos. 2003. (Weekly Reader Early Learning Library). (ENG & SPA., Illus.). 24p. (J). (gr. k-3). pap. 8.15 *(978-0-8368-4006-3(2),* Weekly Reader Leveled Readers) Stevens, Gareth Publishing LLLP.

Markle, Sandra. The Great Penguin Rescue: Saving the African Penguins. 2017. (ENG.). 48p. (J). (gr. 4-6). 30.65 ***(978-1-5124-1315-1(1),*** Millbrook Pr.) Lerner Publishing Group.

Markle, Sandra. A Mother's Journey. Marks, Alan, illus. (ENG.). 32p. (J). (gr. -1-3). 2006. pap. 7.95 *(978-1-57091-622-9(5))* 2005. 16.95 *(978-1-57091-621-2(7))* Charlesbridge Publishing, Inc.

—A Mother's Journey. Marks, Alan, illus. 2006. (gr. 4-7). 16.95 *(978-0-7569-6967-7(0))* Perfection Learning Corp.

Marsico, Katie. Emperor Penguin, 1 vol. 2011. (Day in the Life: Polar Animals Ser.). (ENG.). 24p. (J). (gr. k-2). pap. 6.79 *(978-1-4329-5334-8(6));* 23.32 *(978-1-4329-5327-0(3))* Heinemann-Raintree. (Heinemann Read & Learn).

Marzollo, Jean. Pierre the Penguin. Regan, Laura, illus. 2010. (ENG.). 32p. (J). (gr. -1-2). 15.95 *(978-1-58536-485-5(1))* Sleeping Bear Pr.

McLaughlin, Kari Massie. My Adventure with Penguins. 2009. (ENG.). 44p. (J). 8.99 *(978-1-59092-461-7(4))* Blue Forge Pr.

McNeil, Niki, et al. HOCPP 1123 Penguins. 2006. spiral bd. 16.00 *(978-1-60308-123-8(2))* In the Hands of a Child.

Meachen Rau, Dana. Adivina Quién Nada. 2008. (Adivina Quién Ser.). (SPA.). 32p. (gr. k-2). lib. bdg. 15.95 *(978-0-7614-3458-0(5),* Benchmark Bks.) Marshall Cavendish Corp.

Meinking, Mary. Shark vs. Penguin, 1 vol. 2011. (Predator vs. Prey Ser.). (ENG.). 32p. (gr. 1-2). pap. 8.29 *(978-1-4109-3946-3(4),* Read Me!) Heinemann-Raintree.

Mettler, René. Der Pinguin. 2005. (Meyers Klien Kinderbibliothek Ser.). (GER., Illus.). spiral bd. 14.25 *(978-3-411-09611-4(X),* MY611E) Langenscheidt Publishing Group.

Miller, Sara Swan. Emperor Penguins of the Antarctic. 2009. (Brrr! Polar Animals Ser.). (Illus.). 24p. (J). (gr. k-5). pap. 8.25 *(978-1-4358-3146-9(2),* 1291788, PowerKids Pr.); 24p. (gr. 2-3). 42.50 *(978-1-61511-748-2(2),* PowerKids Pr.); (YA). (gr. k-3). lib. bdg. 22.60 *(978-1-4358-2742-4(2))* Rosen Publishing Group, Inc., The.

Momatiuk, Yva. Face to Face with Penguins. Eastcott, John, photos by. 2009. (Face to Face with Animals Ser.). (ENG., Illus.). 32p. (J). (gr. 2-5). 25.90 *(978-1-4263-0562-7(1),*

National Geographic Children's Bks.) National Geographic Society.
Mornatiuk, Yva & National Geographic Kids Staff. Face to Face with Penguins. Eastcott, John, photos by. 2009. (Face to Face with Animals Ser.). (ENG., Illus.). 32p. (J). (gr. 2-5). 16.95 *(978-1-4263-0561-0(3)*, National Geographic Children's Bks.) National Geographic Society.
Morgan, Sally. Penguins. 2004. (QEB Animal Lives Ser.). (Illus.). 32p. (J). lib. bdg. 18.95 *(978-1-59566-037-4(2))* QEB Publishing Inc.
Morgan, Sally & Teacher Created Resources Staff. Penguins. 2006. (Animal Lives Ser.). (ENG., Illus.). 32p. pap. 7.99 *(978-1-4206-8163-5(X))* Teacher Created Resources, Inc.
Murray, Julie. Penguins, 1 vol. 2007. (Life Cycles Ser.). (ENG., Illus.). 24p. (gr. 4-7). 25.65 *(978-1-59928-709-6(9)*, Buddy Bks.) ABDO Publishing Co.
Murray, Laura K. Penguin. 2015. (Illus.). 32p. (J). *(978-1-60818-563-4(X)*, Creative Education) Creative Co., The.
—Penguin: Grow with Me. 2016. (Grow with Me Ser.). (ENG.). 32p. (J). (gr. 3-5). pap. 9.99 *(978-1-62832-164-7(4)*, Creative Paperbacks) Creative Co., The.
Niver, Heather Moore. 20 Fun Facts about Penguins. 2012. (Fun Fact File: Animals! Ser.). (ENG., Illus.). 32p. (J). (gr. 2-5). pap. 10.50 *(978-1-4339-6523-4(2))*; lib. bdg. 25.25 *(978-1-4339-6521-0(6))* Stevens, Gareth Publishing LLLP. (Gareth Stevens Learning Library).
O'Connell, Kim A. The Galapagos Penguin: A MyReportLinks.com Book. 2005. (Endangered & Threatened Animals Ser.). (Illus.). 48p. (J). lib. bdg. 26.60 *(978-0-7660-5063-1(7)*, MyReportLinks.com Bks.) Enslow Pubs., Inc.
Osborne, Mary Pope & Boyce, Natalie Pope. Penguins & Antarctica: A Nonfiction Companion to Eve of the Emperor Penguin. Murdocca, Sal, illus. 2008. (Magic Tree House - Fact Tracker Ser.: 18). (ENG.). 128p. (J). (gr. 2-5). 6.99 *(978-0-375-84664-9(6)*, Random Hse. Bks. for Young Readers) Random Hse. Children's Bks.
Owen, Ruth. Penguin Chicks. 2012. (Water Babies Ser.). 24p. (J). (gr. -1-3). lib. bdg. 21.32 *(978-1-61772-602-6(8))* Bearport Publishing Co., Inc.
Penguins. (Eyes on Nature Ser.). 32p. (J). (gr. 1). pap. *(978-1-882210-61-9(1))* Action Publishing, Inc.
Polinsky, Paige V. Emperor Penguin: Sensational Survivor. 2016. (ENG., Illus.). 24p. (J). 25.65 *(978-1-68078-148-9(0))* ABDO Publishing Co.
Priddy, Roger. Little Penguin. 2014. (Baby Touch & Feel Ser.). (ENG.). 12p. (J). (gr. -1 — 1). bds. 8.99 *(978-0-312-51716-2(1)*, 9780312517182, Priddy Bks.) St. Martin's Pr.
Pringle, Laurence. Penguins! Strange & Wonderful. Henderson, Meryl, illus. 2013. (Strange & Wonderful Ser.). (ENG.). 32p. (J). (gr. 3-5). pap. 7.95 *(978-1-62091-591-2(X))* Boyds Mills Pr.
—Penguins! Strange & Wonderful. Henderson, Meryl, illus. 2007. (Strange & Wonderful Ser.). (ENG.). 32p. (J). (gr. 2-8). 16.95 *(978-1-59078-090-9(6))* Boyds Mills Pr.
Raatma, Lucia. Penguins. 2012. (Nature's Children Ser.). (ENG., Illus.). 48p. (J). pap. 6.95 *(978-0-531-21081-9(2))*; (gr. 3-5). lib. bdg. 28.00 *(978-0-531-20906-6(7))* Scholastic Library Publishing. (Children's Pr.).
Rau, Dana Meachen. Guess Who Swims/Adivina Quién Nada. 2007. (Guess Who/Adivina Quién Ser.). (SPA & ENG.). 32p. (gr. k-2). 15.95 *(978-0-7614-3483-2(6))* Marshall Cavendish Corp.
Reher, Matt. Penguin Gets Away. 2016. (1G Marine Life Ser.). (ENG., Illus.). 28p. (J). pap. 5.99 ***(978-1-63437-615-0(3))*** American Reading Co.
Rettore. Penguin & Friends: A Soft & Fuzzy Book Just for Baby! 2017. (Friends Cloth Bks.). (ENG.). 8p. (J). (gr. -1 — 1). 9.99 *(978-1-4380-0976-6(3))* Barron's Educational Series, Inc.
Riggs, Kate. Penguins. 2012. (Seedlings Ser.). 24p. (J). (gr. -1-3). 15.95 *(978-1-60818-279-4(7)*, Creative Education) Creative Co., The.
—Seedlings: Penguins. 2013. (Seedlings Ser.). (ENG.). 24p. (J). (gr. -1-k). pap. 7.99 *(978-0-89812-786-7(6)*, Creative Paperbacks) Creative Co., The.
Rigo, L. Little Penguin. Rigo, L., illus. 2014. (Mini Look at Me Bks.). (ENG., Illus.). 10p. (J). (gr. -1 — 1). bds. 4.99 *(978-0-7641-6731-7(6))* Barron's Educational Series, Inc.
Rudolph, Jessica. Rockhopper Penguin. 2016. (Weird but Cute Ser.). (ENG., Illus.). 24p. (J). (gr. -1-3). lib. bdg. 17.95 *(978-1-62724-848-8(X))* Bearport Publishing Co., Inc.
Rustad, Martha E. H. A Baby Penguin Story. 2011. (Baby Animals Ser.). (ENG.). 24p. (gr. k-1). pap. 41.70 *(978-1-4296-7098-2(3)*, Pebble Plus) Capstone Press of Coughlan Cos.
—A Baby Penguin Story (La Historia de un Pingüino Bebé) Strictly Spanish Translation Services Staff, tr. 2012. (Animales Bebé/Baby Animals Ser.). (ENG, MUL & SPA., Illus.). 24p. (gr. k-1). lib. bdg. 26.65 *(978-1-4296-9221-2(9))* Capstone Press of Coughlan Cos.
—A Cool Caper. 2010. (Zoo Animal Mysteries Ser.). (ENG.). 24p. (gr. k-1). lib. bdg. 26.65 *(978-1-4296-4498-3(2)*, Pebble Plus) Capstone Press of Coughlan Cos.
Schafer, Kevin. Penguins 123. 2004. (Penguins Ser.). (ENG., Illus.). 32p. (J). (gr. -1 — 1). bds. 6.95 *(978-1-55971-906-3(0))* Cooper Square Publishing Llc.
—Penguins ABC. 2004. (Penguins Ser.). (ENG., Illus.). 32p. (J). (gr. -1 — 1). bds. 6.95 *(978-1-55971-905-6(2))* Cooper Square Publishing Llc.
Scholastic, Inc. Staff, contrib. by. Scholastic Discover More: Penguins Stickerbook. 2014. (Scholastic Discover More Ser.). (ENG.). 16p. (J). (gr. 2-5). 6.99 *(978-0-545-61231-9(4)*, Scholastic Paperbacks) Scholastic, Inc.
Schreiber, Anne. Penguins! 2009. (Readers Ser.). (ENG., Illus.). 32p. (J). (gr. k-3). lib. bdg. 13.90 *(978-1-4263-0427-9(7)*, National Geographic Children's Bks.) National Geographic Society.
—Penguins. 2009. (Readers Ser.). (ENG., Illus.). 32p. (J). (gr. k-3). 3.99 *(978-1-4263-0426-2(9)*, National Geographic Children's Bks.) National Geographic Society.
Schreiber, Anne, et al. National Geographic Readers: Cutest Animals Collection. 2014. (Readers Ser.). (ENG.). 128p. (J). (gr. k-3). pap. 7.99 *(978-1-4263-1522-0(8)*, National Geographic Children's Bks.) National Geographic Society.
Schuetz, Kari. Baby Penguins. 2013. (Super Cute! Ser.). (ENG., Illus.). 24p. (J). (gr. k-3). lib. bdg. 25.95 *(978-1-60014-931-3(6)*, Blastoff! Readers) Bellwether Media.
Schuh, Mari C. Penguins. 2017. (Black & White Animals Ser.). (ENG., Illus.). 24p. (gr. k-1). lib. bdg. 21.99 *(978-1-5157-3371-3(8))* Capstone Press of Coughlan Cos.
Schwartz, Carol & Edwards, Roberta. Emperor Penguins. Schwartz, Carol, illus. 2007. (All Aboard Science Reader Ser.). (Illus.). 48p. (gr. 1-3). 14.00 *(978-0-7569-8174-7(3))* Perfection Learning Corp.
Scott, Jonathan & Scott, Angela. Antarctica: Land of the Penguins. 2005. (Collins Big Cat Ser.). (ENG., Illus.). 32p. (J). (gr. 1-3). pap. 7.99 *(978-0-00-718640-2(1))* HarperCollins Pubs. Ltd. GBR. Dist: Independent Pubs. Group.
Sexton, Colleen. The Life Cycle of a Penguin. 2010. (Life Cycles Ser.). (ENG., Illus.). 24p. (J). (gr. k-3). lib. bdg. 25.95 *(978-1-60014-310-6(5)*, Blastoff! Readers) Bellwether Media.
Shively, Julie D. Baby Penguin. 2005. (Seaworld Animal Library: Vol. 2). (Illus.). 24p. (J). (gr. -1-k). bds. 6.95 *(978-0-8249-6616-4(3)*, Ideal Pubns.) Worthy Publishing.
Shulman, Lisa. How Penguins & Butterflies Grow, 6 vols., Set. 2004. (Phonics Readers Books 37-72 Ser.). (ENG.). 8p. (gr. k-1). pap. 35.70 *(978-0-7368-4053-8(2)*, Phonics Readers) Capstone Press of Coughlan Cos.
Sill, Cathryn. About Penguins: a Guide for Children: A Guide for Children, 1 vol. Sill, John, illus. 2nd rev. ed. 2013. (About ... Ser.). (ENG.). 48p. (J). (gr. -1-2). 7.95 *(978-1-56145-741-0(8))*; 16.95 *(978-1-56145-743-4(4))* Peachtree Pubs.
Sill, Cathryn P. About Penguins: A Guide for Children, 1 vol. Sill, John, illus. 2009. (ENG.). 48p. (J). (gr. -1-2). 15.95 *(978-1-56145-488-4(5))* Peachtree Pubs.
Simon, Seymour. Penguins. 2009. (ENG.). 32p. (J). (gr. k-4). pap. 6.99 *(978-0-06-446221-1(8))* HarperCollins Pubs.
—Penguins. 2009. (J). lib. bdg. 17.20 *(978-0-606-10540-8(9)*, Turtleback) Turtleback Bks.
Stefoff, Rebecca. Penguins. 2005. (Animalways Ser.). (Illus.). 112p. (J). (gr. 3-7). lib. bdg. *(978-0-7614-1743-9(5)*, Benchmark Bks.) Marshall Cavendish Corp.
Stevens, Kathryn. Positively Penguins! 2008. (Reading Rocks! Ser.). (ENG., Illus.). 32p. (J). (gr. 2-5). 28.50 *(978-1-60253-102-4(1)*, 200763) Child's World, Inc., The.
Stout, Frankie. Penguins: Nature's Coolest Birds. 2009. (Things with Wings Ser.). 24p. (gr. 2-3). 42.50 *(978-1-60854-355-7(2))*; (Illus.). (J). lib. bdg. 22.60 *(978-1-4042-4495-5(6))* Rosen Publishing Group, Inc., The. (PowerKids Pr.).
Swan, Erin Pembrey. Penguins: From Emperors to Macaronis. 2003. (Animals in Order Ser.). (ENG.). 48p. (gr. 4-6). pap. 6.95 *(978-0-531-16660-4(0)*, Watts, Franklin) Scholastic Library Publishing.
Swanson, Diane. Penguins. 2004. (Welcome to the World of Animals Ser.). (Illus.). 32p. (gr. 1-4). lib. bdg. 24.00 *(978-0-8368-4025-4(9)*, Gareth Stevens Learning Library) Stevens, Gareth Publishing LLLP.
Taylor, Barbara. Exploring Nature: Fantastic Penguins. 2014. (ENG., Illus.). 64p. (J). (gr. k-7). 12.99 *(978-1-84322-853-0(X)*, Armadillo) Anness Publishing GBR. Dist: National Bk. Network.
Taylor, Trace. Antarctic Penguins. 2008. (2G Marine Life Ser.). (ENG.). 12p. (J). (gr. k-2). pap. 5.99 *(978-1-59301-758-3(8))* American Reading Co.
Taylor, Trace & Sánchez, Lucía M. Pingüinos de la AntáRtida: Antarctic Penguins. 2010. (2G Animales Marinos Ser.). (ENG & SPA.). 12p. (J). (gr. k-2). pap. 6.99 *(978-1-61541-274-7(3))* American Reading Co.
Ticktock Media, Ltd. Staff. What Do Penguins Do? 2008. (What Do Animals Do? Ser.). (ENG.). 10p. (J). (gr. k — 1). bds. 4.95 *(978-1-84696-792-4(9)*, TickTock Books) Octopus Publishing Group GBR. Dist: Independent Pubs. Group.
Tourville, Amanda Doering. Penguin Pairs: Counting By 2s, 1 vol. Holm, Sharon Lane, illus. 2008. (Count the Critters Ser.). (ENG.). 24p. (J). (gr. k-3). 27.07 *(978-1-60270-265-3(9))* Magic Wagon.
Trattles, Patricia. Emperor Penguins. 2006. (Pull Ahead Bks.). (Illus.). 32p. (J). (gr. -1). 22.60 *(978-0-8225-3484-6(3)*, Lerner Pubns.) Lerner Publishing Group.
Twine, Alice. Penguins. (Baby Animals Ser.). 24p. 2009. (gr. 1-1). 42.50 *(978-1-61511-494-8(7)*, PowerKids Pr.) 2008. (Illus.). (J). (gr. 3-7). lib. bdg. 22.60 *(978-1-4042-4147-3(7))* Rosen Publishing Group, Inc., The.
—Penguins/Pingüinos. 2009. (Baby Animals/Animales bebé Ser.). (ENG & SPA.). 24p. (gr. 1-1). 42.50 *(978-1-61511-506-8(4)*, Editorial Buenas Letras) Rosen Publishing Group, Inc., The.
—Penguins/Pingüinos. Obregon, Jose Maria, tr. from ENG. 2008. (Baby Animals / Animales Bebé Ser.). (Illus.). 24p. (J). (gr. -1-3). lib. bdg. 22.60 *(978-1-4042-7686-4(6))* Rosen Publishing Group, Inc., The.
Ward, Finn. Penguins at the Zoo. 2015. (Zoo Animals Ser.). (ENG., Illus.). 24p. (J). (gr. k-k). pap. 8.15 *(978-1-4824-2605-2(6))* Stevens, Gareth Publishing LLLP.
—Pingüinos / Penguins at the Zoo. 2015. (Animales Del Zoológico / Zoo Animals Ser.). (ENG & SPA.). 24p. (J). (gr. k-k). lib. bdg. 22.60 *(978-1-4824-3235-0(8))* Stevens, Gareth Publishing LLLP.
Waters, Kate. Penguins. 2009. (Illus.). 32p. (J). *(978-0-545-07232-8(8))* Scholastic, Inc.
Watt, Fiona. Hide-and-Seek Penguins. 2008. (Touchy-Feely Flap Bks). 10p. (J). bds. 16.99 *(978-0-7945-2339-8(0)*, Usborne) EDC Publishing.
—Penguins Luxury Touchy-Feely Board Book. 2010. (Luxury Touchy-Feely Board Bks). 10p. (J). bds. 15.99 *(978-0-7945-2586-6(5)*, Usborne) EDC Publishing.
Waxman, Laura Hamilton. Emperor Penguins: Antarctic Diving Birds. 2016. (Comparing Animal Traits Ser.). (ENG., Illus.). 32p. (J). (gr. 2-4). 26.65 *(978-1-4677-9505-0(4)*, Lerner Pubns.) Lerner Publishing Group.
Wendorff, Anne. Penguins. 2008. (Oceans Alive Ser.). (ENG., Illus.). 24p. (J). (gr. k-3). lib. bdg. 25.95 *(978-1-60014-206-2(0))* Bellwether Media.
Westerskov, Kim, photos by. Penguins. 2004. (ENG., Illus.). 32p. (J). (gr. 4-4). pap. 7.47 net. *(978-0-7685-2111-5(4)*, Dominie Elementary) Pearson Schl.
Whitfield, David. Penguins. 2008. (Amazing Animals Ser.). (Illus.). 24p. (J). (gr. 2-4). pap. 8.95 *(978-1-59036-969-2(6))*; lib. bdg. 24.45 *(978-1-59036-968-5(8))* Weigl Pubs., Inc.
Wildlife Education. Penguins. 2007. (Illus.). 10p. (J). 5.99 *(978-1-932396-31-7(4)*, Critters Up Close) Wildlife Education, Ltd.
World Book, Inc. Staff, contrib. by. Bob the Penguin. 2017. (J). ***(978-0-7166-3527-7(5))*** World Bk., Inc.
Young, Louise O. Penguin Comes Home. Elmore, Larry, illus. 2005. (Soundprints' Amazing Animal Adventures! Ser.). (ENG.). 32p. (J). (gr. -1-2). 19.95 *(978-1-59249-327-2(0)*, BC7108) Soundprints.

PENGUINS—FICTION

Abraham, M. K. Piko the Penguinaut. Jan, R. R., illus. 2012. 112p. (J). 12.95 *(978-1-937489-00-7(0))* StoryRobin Co.
Ackerley, Sarah. Patrick the Somnambulist. Ackerley, Sarah, illus. 2008. (ENG., Illus.). 32p. (J). (gr. -1 — 1). 14.95 *(978-1-933831-07-7(3))* Blooming Tree Pr.
Anderson, Derek. Romeo & Lou Blast Off. Anderson, Derek, illus. 2014. (ENG., Illus.). 32p. (J). (gr. -1-3). 16.99 *(978-1-4814-1932-1(3)*, Simon & Schuster Bks. For Young Readers) Simon & Schuster Bks. For Young Readers.
Anderson, Laura Ellen. Evil Emperor Penguin. 2017. (ENG.). 64p. (J). (gr. 2-5). pap. 8.99 ***(978-1-338-13274-8(1))*** Scholastic, Inc.
Antony, Steve. I'll Wait, Mr. Panda. Antony, Steve, illus. 2016. (ENG., Illus.). 32p. (J). (gr. -1-k). 16.99 *(978-1-338-02836-2(7)*, Scholastic Pr.) Scholastic, Inc.
Armstrong, Kim. Petunia in Manhattan. 2009. 50p. pap. 12.99 *(978-1-935436-97-3(X))* Rodaian Pr.
Ashdown, Rebecca. Bob & Flo. 2015. (ENG., Illus.). 32p. (J). (gr. -1-3). 16.99 *(978-0-544-44430-0(2)*, HMH Books For Young Readers) Houghton Mifflin Harcourt Publishing Co.
—Bob & Flo & the Missing Bucket (Board Book) 2017. (ENG., Illus.). 26p. (J). (— 1). bds. 7.99 *(978-0-544-86711-6(4)*, HMH Books For Young Readers) Houghton Mifflin Harcourt Publishing Co.
—Bob & Flo Play Hide & Seek. 2016. (ENG., Illus.). 32p. (J). (gr. -1-3). 16.99 *(978-0-544-59631-3(5)*, HMH Books For Young Readers) Houghton Mifflin Harcourt Publishing Co.
—Bob & Flo Play Hide-And-Seek (Board Book) 2017. (ENG., Illus.). 26p. (J). (— 1). bds. 7.99 *(978-0-544-85959-3(6)*, HMH Books For Young Readers) Houghton Mifflin Harcourt Publishing Co.
Aspinall, Sarah. Penguins Love Colors. Aspinall, Sarah, illus. 2016. (ENG., Illus.). 40p. (J). (gr. -1-k). 17.99 *(978-0-545-87654-4(0)*, Blue Sky Pr., The) Scholastic, Inc.
Aspinall, Sarah. Penguins Love Their ABC's. Aspinall, Sarah, illus. 2017. (ENG., Illus.). 40p. (J). (gr. -1-k). 17.99 ***(978-1-338-13420-9(5)***, Blue Sky Pr., The) Scholastic, Inc.
Atwater, Richard. Mr. Popper's Penguins. 2009. 160p. pap. 6.99 *(978-0-316-10616-0(X))* Little, Brown Bks. for Young Readers.
Atwater, Richard & Atwater, Florence. Mr. Popper's Penguins. 2009. 9.00 *(978-0-7848-3295-0(1)*, Everbind) Marco Bk. Co.
Autrey, Nathan W. Purple Penguin Pumpkin Party. 2011. 42p. pap. 24.95 *(978-1-4560-8286-4(8))* America Star Bks.
Bailey, Ella, illus. One Day in Antarctica. 2016. (One Day on Our Blue Planet Ser.). (ENG.). 32p. (J). (gr. -1-2). 16.95 *(978-1-909263-67-3(2))* Flying Eye Bks. GBR. Dist: Consortium Bk. Sales & Distribution.
Bauer, Jutta. Madrechillona. 2nd ed. 2003. (Rosa y Manzana Ser.). (SPA., Illus.). 28p. (J). (gr. k-2). *(978-84-89804-36-4(2)*, LC30478) Lóguez Ediciones ESP. Dist: Lectorum Pubns., Inc.
Beggs, Melissa. Pompety-Pooh: Purplest Penguin in Zonkety Zoo. Laible, Steve William, ed. Almanstotter, Susanne, illus. 2013. 52p. pap. 12.95 *(978-0-9844784-9-1(3)*, Empire Holdings) Kodel Group, LLC, The.
Bennett, Eric. Noodles & Albie. Bannish, Liz, illus. 2014. (ENG.). (J). 17.95 *(978-1-937650-40-7(5))* Small Batch Bks.
Bentley, Tadgh. Little Penguin & the Lollipop. Bentley, Tadgh, illus. 2017. (Illus.). 40p. (J). (gr. -1-3). 17.99 ***(978-0-06-256078-0(6))*** HarperCollins Pubs.
—Little Penguin Gets the Hiccups. Bentley, Tadgh, illus. 2015. (ENG., Illus.). 40p. (J). (gr. -1-3). 17.99 *(978-0-06-233536-4(7))* HarperCollins Pubs.
—Little Penguin Gets the Hiccups Board Book. Bentley, Tadgh, illus. 2016. (Illus.). 34p. (J). (gr. -1 — 1). bds. 7.99 *(978-0-06-265224-9(9))* HarperCollins Pubs.
Berenstain, Stan, et al. Nothing Ever Happens at the South Pole. Berenstain, Jan & Berenstain, Mike, illus. 2012. (ENG.). 40p. (J). (gr. -1-3). 10.99 *(978-0-06-207532-1(2))* HarperCollins Pubs.
Berg & Holland. Tamino Pingüino y el Asunto Del Huevo. 2004. (SPA., Illus.). 202p. (J). 17.99 *(978-84-261-3301-4(0))* Juventud, Editorial ESP. Dist: Lectorum Pubns., Inc.
Bernstein, Laurie & Helm, Joanna. Penny the Penguin Has Pku. 2012. 24p. pap. 17.99 *(978-1-4772-7226-8(7))* AuthorHouse.
Bogan, Paulette. Virgil & Owen. 2015. (ENG., Illus.). 32p. (J). (gr. k-3). 16.99 *(978-1-61963-372-8(8)*, 9781619633728, Bloomsbury USA Childrens) Bloomsbury Publishing USA.
—Virgil & Owen Stick Together. Bogan, Paulette, illus. 2016. (ENG., Illus.). 32p. (J). 16.99 *(978-1-61963-373-5(6)*, 9781619633735, Bloomsbury USA Childrens) Bloomsbury Publishing USA.
Bollinger, Georgia G. The Penguins' Perilous Picnic. 2011. 32p. pap. 14.50 *(978-1-4634-2200-4(8))* AuthorHouse.
Book Buddy: Penguin with Story Book. Orig. Title: Child's Play. (Illus.). 10p. (J). (gr. -1-3). reprint ed. *(978-1-881469-45-2(X))* Safari, Ltd.
Bowser, Ken. Homesick Penguin: Empathy/Caring for Others. Bowser, Ken, illus. 2014. (Funny Bone Readers: Being a Friend Ser.). (Illus.). 24p. (gr. -1-1). pap. 4.99 *(978-1-939656-03-2(6))* Red Chair Pr.
Boynton, Sandra. Your Personal Penguin. 2006. (ENG., Illus.). 24p. (J). (gr. k — 1). bds. 6.95 *(978-0-7611-4372-7(6)*, 14372) Workman Publishing Co., Inc.
Brooks, Erik. Polar Opposites, 0 vols. 2010. (ENG., Illus.). 32p. (J). (gr. -1-3). 16.99 *(978-0-7614-5685-8(6)*, 9780761456858, Amazon Children's Publishing) Amazon Publishing.
Budge, Donald. Where Is My Butt? Parton, Daron, illus. 2016. (ENG.). 32p. (J). (gr. -1-2). 14.95 *(978-1-4549-1697-0(4))* Sterling Publishing Co., Inc.
Burks, James. Bird & Squirrel on Ice. 2014. (Bird & Squirrel Ser.). (ENG.). 128p. (J). (gr. 2-5). pap. 8.99 *(978-0-545-56318-5(6)*, Graphix) Scholastic, Inc.
Burns, John. The Many Adventures of Pengey Penguin. Coles, James, illus. 2005. 207p. (J). per. 17.95 *(978-0-9774227-0-8(4))* San Francisco Story Works.
Buzzeo, Toni. One Cool Friend. 2014. (KOR.). 32p. (J). (gr. k-3). *(978-89-7938-087-3(9))* Dasan Publishing Hse.
—One Cool Friend. Small, David, illus. 2012. (ENG.). 32p. (J). (gr. k-3). 17.99 *(978-0-8037-3413-5(1)*, Dial Bks) Penguin Young Readers Group.
—One Cool Friend. Small, David, illus. 2015. DVD 59.95 *(978-0-545-67553-6(7))* Scholastic, Inc.
Caines-Floyd, Eydi. The Story of Wanton Desire. 2009. 64p. (J). pap. 26.49 *(978-1-4389-3156-2(5))* AuthorHouse.
Callahan, Susan. Always Right. 2012. 20p. pap. 15.99 *(978-1-4772-0424-5(5))* AuthorHouse.
Carr, Paul C. The Adventures of Three Cousins. 2006. 24.00 *(978-0-8059-9032-4(1))* Dorrance Publishing Co., Inc.
Chand, Emlyn. Courtney Saves Christmas. Giffin, Noelle, illus. 2012. 60p. 21.95 *(978-1-62253-114-1(0))* Evolved Publishing.
Chartier, Doris E. Ben's Desert Journey. 2009. 32p. pap. 14.49 *(978-1-4389-7756-0(5))* AuthorHouse.
Clayton, Dallas. Lily the Unicorn. Clayton, Dallas, illus. 2014. (ENG., Illus.). 48p. (J). (gr. -1-3). 17.99 *(978-0-06-211668-0(1))* HarperCollins Pubs.
Clough, Lisa. Petal & Poppy & the Penguin. Briant, Ed, illus. 2014. (Green Light Readers Level 2 Ser.). (ENG.). 32p. (J). (gr. -1-3). 12.99 *(978-0-544-13770-7(1))*; pap. 3.99 *(978-0-544-13330-3(7))* Houghton Mifflin Harcourt Publishing Co. (HMH Books For Young Readers).
Cobb, Amelia. The Puzzled Penguin. 2016. (Zoe's Rescue Zoo Ser.: 2). (ENG.). 128p. (J). (gr. 2-5). pap. 4.99 *(978-0-545-84222-8(0)*, Scholastic Paperbacks) Scholastic, Inc.
Colby, Carolyn. Penny Penguin: A Baby Penguin's Adventures on the Ice & Snow. Warren, Leonard, illus. 2011. 50p. 35.95 *(978-1-258-09986-2(1))* Literary Licensing, LLC.
Cole, Carol A. La Dama de Los Pingüinos, 1 vol. Rogers, Sherry, illus. 2012. (SPA & ENG.). 32p. (J). (gr. -1-3). 17.95 *(978-1-60718-697-7(7))* Arbordale Publishing.
Corderoy, Tracey. Lost Little Penguin, 1 vol. Scott, Gavin, illus. 2014. (ENG.). 32p. (J). (gr. -1-2). 14.95 *(978-1-62370-116-1(3))* Capstone Young Readers of Coughlan Cos.
—Magical Snow Garden. Chapman, Jane, illus. 2014. (ENG.). 32p. (J). (gr. -1-3). 16.99 *(978-1-58925-162-5(8))* Tiger Tales.
Cosson, Kip. Ned Visits New York. 2006. (ENG., Illus.). 40p. (J). 16.95 *(978-0-9789384-0-6(2))* Kip Kids of New York.
Coudray, Jean-Luc. A Goofy Guide to Penguins: TOON Level 1. Coudray, Philippe, illus. 2016. (ENG.). 40p. (J). (gr. k). 12.95 *(978-1-935179-96-2(9))* TOON Books / RAW Junior, LLC.
Courtenay, L. A. Space Penguins Cosmic Crash! Davies, James, illus. 2015. (Space Penguins Ser.). (ENG.). 112p. (gr. 2-3). lib. bdg. 22.65 *(978-1-4342-9785-3(3))* Stone Arch Bks.
—Space Penguins Galaxy Race! Davies, James, illus. 2015. (Space Penguins Ser.). (ENG.). 112p. (gr. 2-3). lib. bdg. 22.65 *(978-1-4342-9783-9(7))* Stone Arch Bks.
—Space Penguins Meteor Madness! Davies, James, illus. 2015. (Space Penguins Ser.). (ENG.). 112p. (gr. 2-3). lib. bdg. 22.65 *(978-1-4342-9782-2(9))* Stone Arch Bks.
—Space Penguins Star Attack! Davies, James, illus. 2015. (Space Penguins Ser.). (ENG.). 112p. (gr. 2-3). lib. bdg. 22.65 *(978-1-4342-9784-6(5))* Stone Arch Bks.
Courtenay, Lucy. Space Penguins. Davies, James, illus. 2015. (Space Penguins Ser.). (ENG.). 112p. (gr. 2-3). 90.60 *(978-1-4965-0255-1(8)*, Space Penguins) Stone Arch Bks.
Creek, Silent. All the Ice of Afric. 2009. 160p. 22.95 *(978-1-4401-2118-0(4))* iUniverse, Inc.
Cuyler, Margery. Please Say Please! Penguin's Guide to Manners. Hillenbrand, Will, illus. 2005. (J). *(978-0-439-67874-2(9))* Scholastic, Inc.
Dahl, Michael. Penguin Misses Mom. Vidal, Oriol, illus. 2016. (Hello Genius Ser.). (ENG.). 20p. (gr. 1-2). bds. 7.99 *(978-1-4795-8739-1(7))* Picture Window Bks.
—Penguin Says Please, 1 vol. Vidal, Oriol, illus. 2011. (Hello Genius Ser.). (ENG.). 20p. (gr. 1-2). bds. 7.99 *(978-1-4048-6788-8(0))* Picture Window Bks.
Davies, Gill. I Won't Do That Today: A Story of Stubbornness. O'Neill, Rachael, illus. 2009. (Let's Grow Together Ser.). 32p. (J). (gr. -1-2). pap. 10.55 *(978-1-60754-765-5(1))*; lib. bdg. 22.60 *(978-1-60754-758-7(9))* Windmill Bks.
Dombey, Elizabeth & Muldrow, Diane. How Do Penguins Play? Walker, David, illus. 2011. (Little Golden Book Ser.). (ENG.). 24p. (J). (gr. -1-k). 4.99 *(978-0-375-86501-5(2)*, Golden Bks.) Random Hse. Children's Bks.
Doudna, Kelly. Penguin Suit, 1 vol. Chawla, Neena, illus. 2006. (Animal Tales Ser.). 24p. (J). (gr. k-3). (ENG.). lib. bdg. 24.21 *(978-1-59679-957-8(9)*, SandCastle); pap. 48.42 *(978-1-59679-958-5(7))* ABDO Publishing Co.
Dunbar, Polly. Penguin. Dunbar, Polly, illus. 2010. (ENG., Illus.). 40p. (J). (gr. -1-3). pap. 6.99 *(978-0-7636-4972-2(4))* Candlewick Pr.
Duracell and the National Center for Missing & Exploited Children (NCMEC), creator. The Great Tomato Adventure: A Story about Smart Safety Choices. 2007. 0.00 *(978-0-9795307-0-8(9))* Duracell & the National Ctr. for Missing & Exploited Children (NCMEC).
Dyer, Heather. Tina & the Penguin. Levert, Mireille, illus. 2004. (ENG.). 32p. (J). (gr. -1-3). pap. 5.95 *(978-1-55337-767-2(2))* Kids Can Pr., Ltd. CAN. Dist: Hachette Bk. Group.
Eaton, Maxwell, III. The Flying Beaver Brothers & the Evil Penguin Plan. 2012. (Flying Beaver Brothers Ser.). (ENG.). 96p. (J). (gr. 1-4). pap. 7.99 *(978-0-375-86447-6(4)*, Knopf Bks. for Young Readers) Random Hse. Children's Bks.
—The Flying Beaver Brothers & the Evil Penguin Plan. 2012. (Flying Beaver Brothers Ser.: 1). lib. bdg. 17.20 *(978-0-606-23869-4(7)*, Turtleback) Turtleback Bks.
Edquist, Patrick. Zombie Penguins of the Antarctic. 2011. 40p. pap. 16.99 *(978-1-4567-6291-9(5))* AuthorHouse.
Emanuel, Effie Ann. The Penguin Party, 1 vol. 2009. 32p. pap. 24.95 *(978-1-60813-544-8(6))* America Star Bks.
Esposito, Tony. The Vagabond Penguin. 2010. 44p. 24.20 *(978-1-4269-4081-1(5))* Trafford Publishing.
Evans, Courtney. Percy the Penguin, 1 vol. 2010. 26p. pap. 24.95 *(978-1-4489-4881-9(9))* PublishAmerica, Inc.
Fenstermacher, Mary Wisham. Pablo Visits the Ocean. 2011. 60p. pap. 23.88 *(978-1-4634-6035-8(X))* AuthorHouse.

Ford, Emily. Ten Playful Penguins. Julian, Russell, illus. 2015. (ENG.). 22p. (J). (gr. -1 — 1). bds. 12.99 (978-0-545-79439-8(0), Cartwheel Bks.) Scholastic, Inc.

Friesen, Ray. A Cheese Related Mishap & Other Stories. 2005. (Lookit! Ser.). (ENG., Illus.). 100p. per. 8.95 (978-0-9728177-6-9(X)) Don't Eat Any Bugs Productions.

—Lookit!, Vol. 2. 2004. (YA). per. 4.95 (978-0-9728177-3-8(5)) Don't Eat Any Bugs Prodns.

Fromental, Jean-Luc. 365 Penguins. Jolivet, Joëlle, illus. 2006. (ENG.). 48p. (J). (gr. -1-3). 19.95 (978-0-8109-4460-2(X), Abrams Bks. for Young Readers) Abrams, Inc.

Garbowska, Agata, et al. Gandy & Parker Escape the Zoo: An Illustrated Adventure. Garbowska, Agata, illus. 2013. (Illus.). 97p. pap. (978-1-897472-82-8(X)) Golden Meteorite Pr.].

Garden, Randa Sue. Penny the Penguin. 2003. 48p. per. 7.95 (978-0-615-12322-6(8)) Garden, Randa.

Gevry, Claudine, illus. One Little Penguin & His Friends: A Pushing, Turning, Counting Book. 2012. (ENG.). 10p. (J). bds. (978-1-84956-027-6(7)) Top That! Publishing PLC.

Gliori, Debi. Dragon's Extraordinary Egg. 2014. (ENG., Illus.). 32p. (J). (gr. -1-3). 17.99 (978-0-8027-3759-5(5), 9780802737595, Bloomsbury USA Childrens) Bloomsbury Publishing USA.

Glover, Clair. Fairy Penguin - the Penguin Who Loves to Play. 2013. 26p. pap. (978-1-78222-119-7(0)) Paragon Publishing, Rothersthorpe.

Golub, Osu. Penguins Go for the Gold. 2009. 16p. pap. 10.00 (978-1-4490-3907-3(3)) AuthorHouse.

Gough, Simon. I Can'T Fly & I Can'T Swim. 2011. (Illus.). 24p. pap. 11.44 (978-1-4567-8063-0(8)) AuthorHouse.

Grant, Sharon. Mr. Special Visits Mrs. Precious' Class. 2004. (J). per. 9.95 (978-1-59427-032-1(5)) Aglob Publishing.

Greenberg, Nicki. The Naughtiest Reindeer Goes South. 2017. (Naughtiest Reindeer Ser.: 3). (ENG.). 32p. (J). (gr. -1-1). 12.99 **(978-1-76029-311-6(3))** Allen & Unwin AUS. Dist: Independent Pubs. Group.

Greene, Kristy. How Penguins Lost Their Flight. 2012. 20p. pap. 24.95 (978-1-4626-7697-2(9)) America Star Bks.

Griffin, Esther M. Alex, the Lonely, Black-Footed Penguin. 2012. pap. 11.95 (978-0-7414-7832-0(3)) Infinity Publishing.

Guion, Melissa. Baby Penguins Everywhere! Guion, Melissa, illus. (ENG., Illus.). (J). (gr. -1-k). 2013. 28p. bds. 6.99 (978-0-399-16516-0(9)) 2012. 32p. 16.99 (978-0-399-25535-9(4)) Penguin Young Readers Group. (Philomel Bks.).

—Baby Penguins Love Their Mama. Guion, Melissa, illus. 2014. (ENG., Illus.). 32p. (J). (gr. -1-k). 16.99 (978-0-399-16365-4(4), Philomel Bks.) Penguin Young Readers Group.

Hale, Bruce. Key Lardo: A Chet Gecko Mystery. Hale, Bruce, illus. 2007. (Chet Gecko Ser.: 12). (ENG., Illus.). 128p. (J). (gr. 2-5). pap. 5.99 (978-0-15-205235-5(6)) Houghton Mifflin Harcourt Publishing Co.

Hancocks, Helen. Penguin in Peril. Hancocks, Helen, illus. 2014. (ENG., Illus.). 32p. (J). (gr. -1-2). 15.99 (978-0-7636-7159-4(2), Templar) Candlewick Pr.

Hinojosa, Francisco. Yanka, Yanka. Hinojosa, Francisco, illus. 2003. (SPA., Illus.). 44p. (J). (gr. k-3). pap. 10.95 (978-968-19-0440-1(0)) Santillana USA Publishing Co., Inc.

Hollenbeck, Kathleen M. Penguin's Family: The Story of the a Humboldt Penguin. Stegos, Daniel J., illus. 2008. (ENG.). 32p. (J). (gr. -1-3). 19.95 (978-1-59249-765-2(9)) Soundprints.

Hooper, Meredith & Quarto Generic Staff. Ponko & the South Pole. Ormerod, Jan, illus. 2012. (ENG.). 32p. (J). (gr. -1-1). pap. 8.99 (978-1-84780-403-7(9), Frances Lincoln) Quarto Publishing Group UK GBR. Dist: Hachette Bk. Group.

Horácek, Petr. Blue Penguin. Horácek, Petr, illus. 2016. (ENG., Illus.). 32p. (J). (gr. -1-2). 15.99 (978-0-7636-9251-3(4)) Candlewick Pr.

Hub, Ulrich. Be at the Ark by Eight. Mühle, Jörg, illus. 2012. (ENG.). 68p. (J). 12.00 (978-0-8028-5410-0(9), Eerdmans Bks For Young Readers) Eerdmans, William B. Publishing Co.

Humphreys, Neil. Picking up a Penguin's Egg Really Got Me into Trouble. Cheng, Puay Koon, illus. 2014. (Abbie Rose & the Magic Suitcase Ser.). (ENG.). 24p. (J). (gr. -1-3). pap. 9.90 (978-981-4484-18-3(0)) Marshall Cavendish International (Asia) Private Ltd. SGP. Dist: National Bk. Network.

Hunt, Peter. The Fairy Penguin's Lesson & Other Tales. 2012. 44p. pap. 32.70 (978-1-4797-4712-2(2)) Xlibris Corp.

Idle, Molly. Flora & the Penguin. 2014. (ENG., Illus.). 40p. (J). (gr. -1-k). 16.99 (978-1-4521-2891-7(X)) Chronicle Bks. LLC.

Inkpen, Mick. Penguin Small. 2016. (ENG., Illus.). 32p. (J). (gr. -1-k). pap. 7.99 (978-1-4449-1821-2(4)) Hachette Children's Group GBR. Dist: Hachette Bk. Group.

Innovative Kids Staff, creator. Playful Penguins. 2012. (ENG.). 6p. (J). (gr. -1 — 1). 14.99 (978-1-60169-266-5(8)) Innovative Kids.

Iwasa, Megumi. Yours Sincerely, Giraffe. Takabatake, Jun, illus. 2017. (ENG.). 104p. (gr. k-3). 16.99 (978-1-927271-88-9(6)); 9.99 **(978-1-77657-114-7(2))** Gecko Pr. NZL. Dist: Lerner Publishing Group.

Jadoul, Èmile. All by Myself! 2012. (ENG.). 26p. (J). 14.00 (978-0-8028-5411-7(7), Eerdmans Bks For Young Readers) Eerdmans, William B. Publishing Co.

Jamaldinian, Joe. Bob Winging It. Jamaldinian, Joe, illus. 2005. (Illus.). 32p. (J). 14.00 (978-0-9766657-0-0(0)) Jamaldinian, Yousef.

Jeffers, Oliver. Lost & Found. Jeffers, Oliver, illus. 2005. (ENG., Illus.). 32p. (J). (gr. -1-2). 17.99 (978-0-399-24503-9(0), Philomel Bks.) Penguin Young Readers Group.

—Up & Down. Jeffers, Oliver, illus. 2010. (ENG., Illus.). 40p. (J). (gr. -1-2). 17.99 (978-0-399-25545-8(1), Philomel Bks.) Penguin Young Readers Group.

John, Jory. Penguin Problems. Smith, Lane, illus. 2016. (ENG.). 32p. (J). (gr. -1-2). lib. bdg. 20.99 (978-0-375-97465-6(2), Random Hse. Bks. for Young Readers) Random Hse. Children's Bks.

John Taylor, Jeannie St. Penguin's Special Christmas Tree. l.t. ed. 2012. 36p. (J). pap. (978-1-4596-3452-7(7)) ReadHowYouWant.com, Ltd.

Johnson, Lori. The Prodigal Penguin. 2010. 20p. 13.95 (978-1-4497-0252-6(X)) iUniverse, Inc.

Johnston, Johanna. Penguin's Way. Weisgard, Leonard, illus. 2015. (ENG.). 48p. 20.00 (978-1-85124-427-0(1)) Bodleian Library GBR. Dist: Chicago Distribution Ctr.

Jonell, Bob. Penny the Chinstrap Penguin, 1 vol. Prince, Brian, illus. 2010. 22p. 24.95 (978-1-4489-5334-9(0)) PublishAmerica, Inc.

Joyce, Melanie. Fly, Freddy, Fly. Seal, Julia, illus. 2014. (J). (978-1-4351-5806-1(7)) Barnes & Noble, Inc.

Judge, Lita. Flight School. Judge, Lita, illus. 2014. (ENG., Illus.). 40p. (J). (gr. -1-3). 17.99 (978-1-4424-8177-0(3), Atheneum Bks. for Young Readers) Simon & Schuster Children's Publishing.

Kemp, Dane. Imaginary Tales. 2011. 186p. pap. 24.95 (978-1-4560-4686-6(1)) America Star Bks.

Kimmel, Elizabeth Cody. Mi Pinguino Oliver. Lewis, H. B., illus. 2004. Tr. of My Penguin Osbert. (SPA.). (J). 15.99 (978-84-88342-68-3(3)) S.A. Kokinos ESP. Dist: Lectorum Pubns., Inc.

—My Penguin Osbert. Lewis, H. B., illus. (ENG.). 40p. (J). (gr. -1-3). 2011. pap. 6.99 (978-0-7636-5730-7(1)) 2008. 7.99 (978-0-7636-3692-0(4)) 2004. 16.99 (978-0-7636-1699-1(0)) Candlewick Pr.

—My Penguin Osbert in Love. Lewis, H. B., illus. 2010. (ENG.). 48p. (J). (gr. -1-3). 7.99 (978-0-7636-5001-8(3)) Candlewick Pr.

Kimmel, Elizabeth Cody & Buck, Lewis. My Penguin Osbert in Love, Set. Lewis, H. B., illus. 2008. (ENG.). 48p. (J). (gr. -1-3). 16.99 (978-0-7636-3032-4(2)) Candlewick Pr.

Klein, Judith Anne. Tuxedo Flyer. 2009. 28p. pap. 14.65 (978-1-4490-0635-8(3)) AuthorHouse.

Krupinski, Tiffany J. Pangi the Penguin. 2011. 20p. pap. 24.95 (978-1-4560-6074-9(0)) America Star Bks.

Lammers, Elizabeth A. & McKinney, Dan. The Tale of the Black Igloo: Another Adventure of Pepe & Pierre, 1 vol. Epstein, Gabriela, illus. 2010. 26p. pap. 24.95 (978-1-60610-433-0(0)) PublishAmerica, Inc.

Latimer, Àlex, illus. Penguin's Hidden Talent, 1 vol. 2012. (ENG.). 32p. (J). 15.95 (978-1-56145-629-1(2)) Peachtree Pubs.

Lawton, Diana. Paulie the Penguin Meets Sammy the Seal. 2012. 30p. 24.95 (978-1-4626-6782-6(1)) America Star Bks.

Lenton, Steven. Five Christmas Penguins. 2016. (ENG., Illus.). 12p. (J). (gr. -1). bds. 9.99 (978-1-62686-822-9(0), Silver Dolphin Bks.) Readerlink Distribution Services, LLC.

Lenz Mulligan Rights and Co. Staff, et al. Little Penguin. 2008. (Little Finger Puppet Board Bks.: FING). (ENG., Illus.). 12p. (J). (gr. -1 — 1). bds. 6.99 (978-0-8118-6355-1(7)) Chronicle Bks. LLC.

Lesley, Sharon. The Red Scarf & Other Stories. 2010. 165p. pap. 14.95 (978-1-4457-6720-8(1)) Lulu Pr., Inc.

Lester, Helen. Tacky & the Haunted Igloo. Munsinger, Lynn, illus. 2015. (Tacky the Penguin Ser.). (ENG.). 32p. (J). 16.99 (978-0-544-33994-1(0), HMH Books For Young Readers) Houghton Mifflin Harcourt Publishing Co.

—Tacky & the Winter Games. Munsinger, Lynn, illus. 2007. (Tacky the Penguin Ser.). (ENG.). 32p. (J). (gr. -1-3). 6.95 (978-0-618-95674-6(3)) Houghton Mifflin Harcourt Publishing Co.

—Tacky Goes to Camp. Munsinger, Lynn, illus. 2009. (Tacky the Penguin Ser.). (ENG.). 32p. (J). (gr. -1-3). 16.00 (978-0-618-98812-9(2)) Houghton Mifflin Harcourt Publishing Co.

—Tacky Goes to Camp. 2012. (Tacky the Penguin Ser.). lib. bdg. 17.20 (978-0-606-23992-9(8), Turtleback) Turtleback Bks.

—Tacky the Penguin. Munsinger, Lynn, illus. (Tacky the Penguin Ser.). (ENG.). 32p. (J). (gr. -1-3). 2008. bds. 7.99 (978-0-547-13344-7(8)) 2006. audio compact disk 10.99 (978-0-618-73754-3(5)) Houghton Mifflin Harcourt Publishing Co.

—Tackylocks & the Three Bears. Munsinger, Lynn, illus. 2004. (Tacky the Penguin Ser.). (ENG.). 32p. (J). (gr. -1-3). 6.99 (978-0-618-43953-9(6)) Houghton Mifflin Harcourt Publishing Co.

Lester, Helen & Munsinger, Lynn. Happy Birdday, Tacky! Lester, Helen & Munsinger, Lynn, illus. 2013. (Tacky the Penguin Ser.). (ENG., Illus.). 32p. (J). (gr. -1-3). 16.99 (978-0-547-91228-8(5)) Houghton Mifflin Harcourt Publishing Co.

Lewis, Jill. A Mom in a Million. Gulbis, Stephen, illus. 2005. 32p. (J). (978-1-84458-368-3(6), Pavilion Children's Books) Pavilion Bks.

Little Penguin & Friends. (Flocked Soft-to-Touch Board Ser.). 5p. bds. (978-1-4054-9446-5(8)) Parragon, Inc.

Logan, Christopher. Daphne. 2008. 145p. pap. 18.95 (978-1-4357-5038-8(1)) Lulu Pr., Inc.

London, Jonathan. Little Penguin: The Emperor of Antarctica, 0 vols. Olson, Julie, illus. 2011. (ENG.). 36p. (J). (gr. -1-3). 17.99 (978-0-7614-5954-5(5), 9780761459545, Amazon Children's Publishing) Amazon Publishing.

Lukachko, Mary Louise. Peter the Blue Penguin. 2012. 28p. pap. 24.95 (978-1-4626-8186-0(7)) America Star Bks.

Lumry, Amanda & Hurwitz, Laura. South Pole Penguins. 2007. (Adventures of Riley Ser.). (Illus.). 36p. (J). (gr. -1-3). 15.95 (978-0-9748411-5-1(3)); lib. bdg. 18.95 (978-0-9748411-8-2(8)) Eaglemont Pr.

Mackey, Stephen. Miki, Set. Mackey, Stephen, illus. 2012. (ENG., Illus.). 48p. (J). (gr. -1-k). 16.99 (978-1-4449-0651-6(8)) Hodder & Stoughton GBR. Dist: Hachette Bk. Group.

Martin, Mairead S. The Forgotten Little Penguin. 2013. 34p. pap. (978-0-9576676-0-0(4)) Dream Cloud Bks.

Mattassi, Ezio. Pepito the Penguin, 1 vol. Mattassi, Ezio, illus. 2009. (Illus.). 15p. pap. 24.95 (978-1-61582-731-2(5)) PublishAmerica, Inc.

Matthews, Alex. Penguins of Madagascar, Vol. 1. Fereyra, Lucas, illus. 2015. (ENG.). 64p. (J). (gr. 1-4). pap. 6.99 (978-1-78276-251-5(5)) Titan Bks. Ltd. GBR. Dist: Penguin Random Hse. LLC.

Mayfield, Sue. I Can, You Can, Toucan! 2006. (Green Bananas Ser.). (ENG., Illus.). 48p. (J). (gr. -1-3). lib. bdg. (978-0-7787-1032-5(7)) Crabtree Publishing Co.

—I Can, You Can, Toucan! Padua, Rochelle, illus. 2005. (Green Bananas Ser.). (ENG.). 48p. (J). (gr. k-2). pap. 5.99 (978-1-4052-1793-4(6)) Egmont Bks., Ltd. GBR. Dist: Independent Pubs. Group.

Maynor, Megan. Ella & Penguin: a Perfect Match. Bonnet, Rosalinde, illus. 2017. 32p. (J). (gr. -1-3). 17.99 (978-0-06-233089-5(6)) HarperCollins Pubs.

—Ella & Penguin Stick Together. Bonnet, Rosalinde, illus. 2016. 32p. (J). (gr. -1-3). 17.99 (978-0-06-233088-8(8)) HarperCollins Pubs.

McAuliffe, Nichola. Attila, Loolagax & the Eagle. Collins, Ross, tr. Collins, Ross, illus. 2003. (ENG.). 128p. (J). pap. 10.99 (978-0-7475-6499-7(X)) Bloomsbury Publishing Plc GBR. Dist: Independent Pubs. Group.

McGuinness, Jeff. Paddy the Penguin's Adventure. Starr, Lisa, illus. l.t. ed. 2006. 33p. (J). 27.95 (978-1-59879-231-7(8)); (gr. -1-3). per. 15.95 (978-1-59879-229-4(6)) Lifevest Publishing, Inc.

McNamee, Kevin. My Brother the Frog. Morris, Alexander, illus. 2011. 24p. 19.95 (978-1-61633-167-2(4)); pap. 10.95 (978-1-61633-159-7(3)) Guardian Angel Publishing, Inc.

McPhail, David. Peter Loves Penguin. 2014. (David Mcphail's Love Ser.). (ENG., Illus.). 22p. (J). (gr. -1 — 1). bds. 8.95 (978-1-4197-1337-8(X), Abrams Appleseed) Abrams, Inc.

Meadows, Daisy. Pia the Penguin Fairy. 2011. (Illus.). 63p. (J). (978-0-545-28873-6(8)) Scholastic, Inc.

Meschenmoser, Sebastian. Gordon & Tapir. 2016. (ENG., Illus.). 60p. (J). 18.95 (978-0-7358-4253-3(1)) North-South Bks., Inc.

Messer, Claire. Grumpy Pants. Messer, Claire, illus. 2016. (ENG., Illus.). 32p. (J). (gr. -1-3). 16.99 (978-0-8075-3075-7(1)) Whitman, Albert & Co.

Metzger, Steve. Five Little Penguins Slipping on the Ice. Bryant, Laura, illus. 2008. (ENG.). (J). (gr. -1-3). 18.95 (978-0-545-07408-7(8)) Scholastic, Inc.

Milbourne, Anna. How Big Is a Million? Riglietti, Serena, illus. 2008. (J). (978-0-545-11519-3(1)) Scholastic, Inc.

—How Big Was a Dinosaur? 2011. (Picture Books Ser.). 24p. (J). ring bd. 10.99 (978-0-7945-3002-0(8), Usborne) EDC Publishing.

—How Deep Is the Sea? Riglietti, Serena, illus. 2010. (Picture Bks). 24p. (J). 10.99 (978-0-7945-2311-4(0)) EDC Publishing.

—How High Is the Sky? Riglietti, Serena, illus. 2009. (Picture Bks). 24p. (J). (gr. -1). 10.99 (978-0-7945-2273-5(4), Usborne) EDC Publishing.

Milne, J. E. The Adventures of Haole the Penguin: The Inner Game of Surfing. 2011. 264p. 25.95 (978-1-4327-7160-7(4)); pap. 13.95 (978-1-4327-7142-3(6)) Outskirts Pr., Inc.

Minor, Florence F. If You Were a Penguin. Minor, Wendell, illus. 2009. 32p. (J). (gr. -1-2). lib. bdg. 18.89 (978-0-06-113098-4(2)) HarperCollins Pubs.

Minor, Wendell & Minor, Florence F. If You Were a Penguin. Minor, Wendell, illus. 2008. (ENG., Illus.). 32p. (J). (gr. -1-2). 17.99 (978-0-06-113097-7(4), Tegen, Katherine Bks) HarperCollins Pubs.

Mitchell, Lance B. The Penguin Adventures of Ping & Pong. 2008. 32p. pap. 24.95 (978-1-60474-124-7(4)) America Star Bks.

Mitter, Matt. Penny Penguin. Brown, Jo, illus. 2010. (Snappy Fun Ser.). (ENG.). 10p. (J). bds. 7.99 (978-0-7944-2014-7(1)) Reader's Digest Assn., Inc., The.

Monsell, Mary Elise. A Fish Named Yum Vol. IV: MR. PIN. 2007. 72p. (gr. 1-4). per. 8.95 (978-0-595-47246-8(X), Backinprint.com) iUniverse, Inc.

—Mr Pin: The Chocolate Files. 2007. 68p. (gr. -1-3). per. 8.95 (978-0-595-47318-2(0), Backinprint.com) iUniverse, Inc.

—The Mysterious Cases of Mr. Pin, Vol. I. 2007. 68p. (gr. -1-3). per. 8.95 (978-0-595-47247-5(8), Backinprint.com) iUniverse, Inc.

—The Spy Who Came North from the Pole. 2007. 68p. (gr. -1-3). per. 8.95 (978-0-595-47248-2(6), Backinprint.com) iUniverse, Inc.

Murphy, Mary. I Like It When... Campoy, F. Isabel & Flor Ada, Alma, trs. from ENG. 2008. (ENG., Illus.). 22p. (J). (gr. k — 1). bds. 6.95 (978-0-15-206045-9(6)) Houghton Mifflin Harcourt Publishing Co.

—I Like It When... 2005. (ENG., Illus.). 22p. (J). (gr. k — 1). bds. 6.95 (978-0-15-205649-0(1)) Houghton Mifflin Harcourt Publishing Co.

—Let's Go! 2005. (ENG., Illus.). 16p. (J). bds. 14.99 (978-1-4052-1115-4(6)) Egmont Bks., Ltd. GBR. Dist: Trafalgar Square Publishing.

My First Story Coll Twinkle, Itsy Bitsy & Ten Little Penguins. 2009. 26p. pap. (978-1-84879-204-3(2)) Make Believe Ideas.

One Cool Friend. 2014. pap. 16.99 (978-0-545-67554-3(5)) Scholastic, Inc.

Osborne, Mary Pope. Eve of the Emperor Penguin. Murdocca, Sal, illus. 2008. (Magic Tree House Merlin Mission Ser.: No. 12). (ENG.). 128p. (J). (gr. 2-5). 11.99 (978-0-375-83733-3(7), Random Hse. Bks. for Young Readers) Random Hse. Children's Bks.

Ostermeyer, Tim. Snowball's Antarctic Adventures. 2011. (Illus.). 46p. (J). (gr. -1-3). 18.95 (978-0-9794228-3-6(3)) Ostermeyer Photography.

Oxley, Jennifer & Aronson, Billy. Peg + Cat: The Penguin Problem. 2016. (Peg + Cat Ser.). (ENG.). 32p. (J). (gr. -1-2). 12.99 (978-0-7636-9073-1(2), Candlewick Entertainment) Candlewick Pr.

Panpan, Alice. Antarctic Wings. 2011. 36p. pap. 21.99 (978-1-4568-6210-7(3)) Xlibris Corp.

Parnell, Declan. Make Way for Penguins, 01 vols., 1. 2016. (Rosen REAL Readers: Social Studies Nonfiction / Fiction: Family, Community, & the World Ser.). (ENG.). 8p. (J). pap. 5.46 (978-1-5081-1884-8(1), Rosen Classroom) Rosen Publishing Group, Inc., The.

Pendergrass, Daphne. Meet the Penguins! Style Guide, Style, illus. 2014. (Penguins of Madagascar Ser.). (ENG.). 24p. (J). (gr. -1-3). pap. 3.99 (978-1-4814-3734-9(8), Simon Spotlight) Simon Spotlight.

The Penguin Who Wanted to Sparkle. (Glitter Books... Ser.). 24p. (978-1-4054-9472-4(7)) Parragon, Inc.

Perlman, Janet. The Penguin & the Pea. Perlman, Janet, illus. 2006. (ENG., Illus.). 32p. (J). (gr. -1-2). 7.95 (978-1-55337-983-6(7)) Kids Can Pr., Ltd. CAN. Dist: Hachette Bk. Group.

Pfister, Marcus. Penguin Pete. 2013. (Penguin Pete Ser.). (ENG., Illus.). 32p. (J). (gr. -1-3). 14.95 (978-0-7358-4118-5(7)) North-South Bks., Inc.

—Penguin Pete & Pat. 2014. (Penguin Pete Ser.). (ENG., Illus.). 32p. (J). (gr. k-3). 14.95 (978-0-7358-4155-0(1)) North-South Bks., Inc.

Pichon, Liz. Penguins. 2008. (J). (978-0-545-08292-1(7), Orchard Bks.) Scholastic, Inc.

Pilkey, Dav. Ricky Ricotta's Mighty Robot vs. the Unpleasant Penguins from Pluto. Santat, Dan, illus. 2016. (Ricky Ricotta's Mighty Robot Ser.: 9). (ENG.). 128p. (J). (gr. -1-3). 15.99 (978-0-545-63016-0(9)) Scholastic, Inc.

Pimot, Karen Hutchins. The Blue Penguin. Klanot, Makenna Karen, illus. 2008. 44p. pap. 14.95 (978-1-934246-79-5(4)) Peppertree Pr., The.

Portis, Antoinette. A Penguin Story. Portis, Antoinette, illus. 2008. (ENG., Illus.). 40p. (J). (gr. -1-3). 17.99 (978-0-06-145688-6(8)) HarperCollins Pubs.

Priddy, Roger. Pip the Little Penguin. 2016. (Alphaprints Ser.). (ENG.). 32p. (J). 16.99 (978-0-312-52139-4(1), 9780312521394, Priddy Bks.) St. Martin's Pr.

Proimos, James. Waddle! Waddle! Proimos, James, illus. 2015. (ENG., Illus.). 32p. (J). (gr. -1-3). 17.99 (978-0-545-41846-1(1), Scholastic Pr.) Scholastic, Inc.

Publications International Ltd. Staff, ed. Look & Find Surfs Up. 2007. (Illus.). 24p. (J). 7.10 (978-1-4127-6836-8(5), PIL Kids) Publications International, Ltd.

Punter, Russell. Chilly Little Penguin. 2009. (First Reading Level 2 Ser.). 32p. (J). 6.99 (978-0-7945-2424-1(9), Usborne) EDC Publishing.

Randall, Ronne. Snuggle up, Little Penguin! Church, Caroline Jayne, illus. 2003. (Little Friends Ser.). 14p. (J). 12.95 (978-1-57145-919-0(7), Silver Dolphin Bks.) Readerlink Distribution Services, LLC.

Rash, Andy. Archie the Daredevil Penguin. Rash, Andy, illus. 2015. (ENG., Illus.). 34p. (J). (gr. -1-3). 16.99 (978-0-451-47123-9(7), Viking Books for Young Readers) Penguin Young Readers Group.

Rees, Douglas. Uncle Pirate. Auth, Tony, illus. (ENG.). 112p. (J). (gr. 2-5). 2009. pap. 6.99 (978-1-4169-4763-9(9)) 2008. 15.99 (978-1-4169-4762-2(0)) McElderry, Margaret K. Bks. (McElderry, Margaret K. Bks.).

—Uncle Pirate to the Rescue. Auth, Tony, illus. 2010. (ENG.). 112p. (J). (gr. 2-5). pap. 6.99 (978-1-4169-7505-2(5), McElderry, Margaret K. Bks.) McElderry, Margaret K. Bks.

Renert, Gerry. Nathan & the Really Big Bully. Bradshaw, Carrie, illus. 2012. (ENG.). 32p. 16.95 (978-1-62167-072-8(4), Raven Tree Pr.,Csi) Continental Sales, Inc.

Reyes, Nikki. An Unexpected Guest: It Started with a fish. It ended with a Friend. 2009. 48p. pap. 17.49 (978-1-4363-9133-7(4)) Xlibris Corp.

Richardson, Justin & Parnell, Peter. And Tango Makes Three. Cole, Henry, illus. 2005. (ENG.). 32p. (J). (gr. -1-3). 17.99 (978-0-689-87845-9(1), Simon & Schuster Bks. For Young Readers) Simon & Schuster Bks. For Young Readers.

—And Tango Makes Three: 10th Anniversary Edition. Cole, Henry, illus. 10th ed. 2015. (ENG.). 40p. (J). (gr. -1-3). 17.99 (978-1-4814-4884-0(6), Simon & Schuster Bks. For Young Readers) Simon & Schuster Bks. For Young Readers.

Rigo, L., illus. Little Penguin. 2010. (Look at Me Bks.). (ENG.). 10p. (J). (gr. -1-k). bds. 8.99 (978-0-7641-6353-1(1)) Barron's Educational Series, Inc.

Roberts, Daniel. The Penguin & the Polar Bear. 2009. 32p. pap. 14.95 (978-1-4389-2845-6(9)) AuthorHouse.

Rosario, Joann. The PenguinThat Boom- Booms to a Ferret That Zoom- Zoomed. Rosario, Joann, illus. 2004. (Illus.). 28p. (J). (gr. -1-5). pap. 10.00 (978-0-9758746-4-6(0), 1246169) J.G.R. Enterprises.

Ross, Melissa. Today I Am a Penguin. Ross, Melissa, illus. 2012. (Illus.). 24p. pap. 10.95 (978-1-61633-306-5(5)) Guardian Angel Publishing, Inc.

Rossell, Judith. Oliver. Rossell, Judith, illus. 2012. (ENG., Illus.). 32p. (J). (gr. -1-2). 16.99 (978-0-06-202210-3(5)) HarperCollins Pubs.

Ryan, Pam Muñoz. Tony Baloney. Fotheringham, Edwin, illus. 2011. (ENG.). 40p. (J). (gr. -1-k). 17.99 (978-0-545-23135-0(3), Scholastic Pr.) Scholastic, Inc.

—Tony Baloney: Buddy Trouble. Fotheringham, Edwin, illus. 2014. (ENG.). 40p. (J). (gr. k-2). 6.99 (978-0-545-48169-4(4), Scholastic Pr.) Scholastic, Inc.

—Tony Baloney: Buddy Trouble. Fotheringham, Ed, illus. 2013. 38p. (J). pap. (978-0-545-48170-0(8)) Scholastic, Inc.

—Tony Baloney: Pen Pal. Fotheringham, Ed, illus. 2014. 39p. (J). pap. (978-0-545-69227-4(X), Scholastic Pr.) Scholastic, Inc.

—Tony Baloney: School Rules. Fotheringham, Edwin, illus. (J). (gr. k-2). 2013. (ENG.). 40p. 6.99 (978-0-545-48166-3(X)) 2012. pap. (978-0-545-48167-0(8)) Scholastic, Inc.

—Tony Baloney: Pen Pal. Fotheringham, Edwin, illus. 2015. (Tony Baloney Ser.). (ENG.). 40p. (J). (gr. k-2). 6.99 (978-0-545-65037-3(2), Scholastic Pr.) Scholastic, Inc.

Rylant, Cynthia. Little Penguins. Robinson, Christian, illus. 2016. (ENG.). 40p. (J). (gr. -1-2). 17.99 (978-0-553-50770-6(2), Schwartz & Wade Bks.) Random Hse. Children's Bks.

Salzano, Tammi. One Snowy Day. Wood, Hannah, illus. 2010. (ENG.). 24p. (J). (gr. -1-k). bds. 8.95 (978-1-58925-857-0(6)) Tiger Tales.

Samoun, Abigail. How Penguin Says Please! Watts, Sarah, illus. 2015. (Little Traveler Ser.). (ENG & MUL.). 24p. (J). (gr. -1-k). bds. 6.95 (978-1-4549-1496-9(3)) Sterling Publishing Co., Inc.

Sang, Franchesca Ho, compiled by. Wisdom of Penguins. 2006. (Illus.). 128p. (J). (978-1-59258-254-9(0)) Hylas Publishing.

Sansone, V. K. A Daunting Quest for Quincy & Quigley. 2009. 32p. pap. 8.98 (978-0-557-03594-6(5)) Lulu Pr., Inc.

Savage, Stephen. Where's Walrus? & Penguin? 2015. (ENG., Illus.). 32p. (J). (gr. -1-k). 16.99 (978-0-545-40295-8(6), Scholastic Pr.) Scholastic, Inc.

Scott, Cavan, et al. Penguins of Madagascar Vol. 2: Operation Heist. Bartolini, Egle, illus. 2015. (ENG.). 64p. (J). (gr. 1-4). pap. 6.99 (978-1-78276-252-2(3)) Titan Bks. Ltd. GBR. Dist: Penguin Random Hse. LLC.

Scraper, Katherine. Pen Pal Penguin. Callen, Liz, illus. 2012. 8p. (J). (978-0-7367-2639-9(X)) Zaner-Bloser, Inc.

—Save the Fairy Penguins. 2005. (J). pap. (978-1-4108-4214-5(2)) Benchmark Education Co.

Server, David & Lanzing, Jackson. Penguins of Madagascar, Vol. 2. 2011. (ENG.). 52p. (J). pap. 6.95 *(978-1-936340-30-9(5),* 9781936340309) Ape Entertainment.
Smith, Sarah, illus. Where's My Mommy? 2009. (J). *(978-0-7607-8404-4(3))* Barnes & Noble, Inc.
Sonnebom, Scott. Meet the South Police. Lozano, Omar, illus. 2015. (North Police Ser.). (ENG.). 32p. (gr. k-2). lib. bdg. 21.32 *(978-1-4795-6486-6(9))* Picture Window Bks.
St-Laurent, Christina. Macaroni's Midnight Madness. 2011. 28p. pap. 15.99 *(978-1-4628-5427-1(3))* Xlibris Corp.
Stephens, Sarah. Pooches of Power!, 1 vol. Baltazar, Art, illus. 2011. (DC Super-Pets Ser.). (ENG.). 56p. (gr. 2-2). pap. 4.95 *(978-1-4048-6620-1(5));* lib. bdg. 23.99 *(978-1-4048-6306-4(0))* Picture Window Bks. (DC Super-Pets).
Stepp, Shirley. Pongo Penguin's Whale of a Tale. 2012. 24p. 24.95 *(978-1-4626-5478-9(9))* America Star Bks.
Straub-Martin, Susan M. Legends, Loves & Great Lakes. 2013. 28p. pap. 15.00 *(978-0-9830321-6-8(5))* Strauberry Studios.
Teckentrup, Britta. Up & Down. Teckentrup, Britta, illus. 2014. (ENG., Illus.). 28p. (J). (-k). 17.99 *(978-0-7636-7129-7(0),* Templar) Candlewick Pr.
Ted in a Red Bed Kid Kit. 2004. (Kid Kits Ser.). (Illus.). 10p. (J). bds. 9.95 *(978-1-58086-404-6(X))* EDC Publishing.
Tickle, Jack. Fish on a Dish! Tickle, Jack, illus. 2015. (ENG., Illus.). 24p. (J). (gr. -1-3). 16.99 *(978-1-58925-191-5(1))* Tiger Tales.
Toenies, Claudia. A Very Special Penguin. 2007. 36p. per. 16.99 *(978-1-4343-3074-1(5))* AuthorHouse.
Tomlinson, Jill. The Penguin Who Wanted to Find Out. Howard, Paul, illus. 2014. (ENG.). 96p. (J). (gr. -1-2). pap. 10.99 *(978-1-4052-7191-2(4))* Egmont Bks., Ltd. GBR. Dist: Independent Pubs. Group.
Tomorrow, Tom. The Very Silly Mayor. 2009. (ENG., Illus.). 36p. (J). (gr. -1-3). 16.99 *(978-1-935439-01-1(4))* Ig Publishing, Inc.
Toms, K. 10 Little Penguins. 2009. (Kate Toms Ser.). 26p. bds. 7.99 *(978-1-84610-980-5(9))* Make Believe Ideas GBR. Dist: Nelson, Thomas Inc.
—10 Little Penguins Mini Book & Plush. 2009. 26p. pap. *(978-1-84879-065-0(1))* Make Believe Ideas.
Top That Publishing Staff, ed. One Little Penguin & His Friends: A Pushing, Turning, Counting Book. Gévry, Claudine, illus. 2007. 10p. (J). (gr. -1-3). bds. *(978-1-84666-268-3(0),* Tide Mill Pr.) Top That! Publishing PLC.
Top That!, creator. Shapes with Penny the Penguin. 2012. (Learn with Magnets Ser.). (ENG., Illus.). 10p. (J). (gr. -1). *(978-1-84956-671-1(2))* Top That! Publishing PLC.
Trussell-Cullen, Alan. The Lonely Penguin's Blog, 1 vol. 2013. (Fiction Readers Ser.). (ENG., Illus.). 28p. (J). (gr. 2-2). pap. 6.99 *(978-1-4333-5559-2(0))* Shell Educational Publishing.
Ullrich, Hortense. La Aventura de Lorenzo. (SPA.). (J). 7.95 *(978-958-04-7447-0(8))* Norma S.A. COL. Dist: Distribuidora Norma, Inc.
—La Prueba de Valor de Lorenzo. (SPA.). (J). 7.95 *(978-958-04-7069-4(3))* Norma S.A. COL. Dist: Distribuidora Norma, Inc.
van Genechten, Guido. No Ghost under My Bed. 2010. (ENG.). 30p. (J). (gr. -1-k). 17.95 *(978-1-60537-069-9(X))* Cobblestone Publishing Co.
Watt, Fiona. That's Not My Penguin. Wells, Rachel, illus. 2007. (Usborne Touchy-Feely Board Bks.). 8p. (gr. -1-k). bds. 7.99 *(978-0-7945-1810-3(9),* Usborne) EDC Publishing.
Watt, Mélanie. Augustine. Watt, Mélanie, illus. 2008. (ENG., Illus.). 32p. (J). (gr. -1-2). pap. 7.95 *(978-1-55453-268-1(X))* Kids Can Pr., Ltd. CAN. Dist: Hachette Bk. Group.
Weeks, Sarah. Without You. Duranceau, Suzanne, illus. 40p. (J). (gr. -1-2). 2007. (ENG.). pap. 6.99 *(978-0-06-113998-7(X))* 2003. 16.99 *(978-0-06-027816-8(1),* Geringer, Laura Book) HarperCollins Pubs.
West, Tracey, adapted by. Penguins of Madagascar Movie Novelization. 2014. (Penguins of Madagascar Ser.). (ENG., Illus.). 144p. (J). (gr. 3-7). pap. 6.99 *(978-1-4814-3728-8(3),* Simon Spotlight) Simon Spotlight.
What I Learned from a Penguin. 2005. (YA). lib. bdg. 19.95 *(978-1-886565-42-5(2))* MindWorks Pr.
Willis, Jeanne. Penguin Pandemonium. 2013. (Awesome Animals Ser.). (ENG., Illus.). 192p. (J). (gr. 2-7). pap. 6.99 *(978-1-4380-0301-6(3))* Barron's Educational Series, Inc.
—Penguin Pandemonium: the Rescue. 2013. (Awesome Animals Ser.). (ENG., Illus.). 176p. (J). (gr. 2-6). pap. 6.99 *(978-1-4380-0306-1(4))* Barron's Educational Series, Inc.
—Take Turns, Penguin! Birchall, Mark, illus. 2003. (Picture Bks.). 32p. (J). (gr. -1-3). 7.95 *(978-1-57505-493-3(0),* Carolrhoda Bks.) Lerner Publishing Group.
Wilson, Karma. Don't Be Afraid, Little Pip. Chapman, Jane, illus. 2009. (ENG.). 40p. (J). (gr. -1-2). 16.99 *(978-0-689-85987-8(2),* McElderry, Margaret K. Bks.) McElderry, Margaret K. Bks.
—What's in the Egg, Little Pip? Chapman, Jane, illus. 2010. (ENG.). 40p. (J). (gr. -1-3). 17.99 *(978-1-4169-4204-7(1),* McElderry, Margaret K. Bks.) McElderry, Margaret K. Bks.
—Where Is Home, Little Pip? Chapman, Jane, illus. 2008. (ENG.). 40p. (J). (gr. -1-3). 17.99 *(978-0-689-85983-0(X),* McElderry, Margaret K. Bks.) McElderry, Margaret K. Bks.
Wilson, Rosalee. Elijah the Penguin. 2007. 60p. pap. 16.95 *(978-0-9798154-8-5(7))* Living Waters Publishing Co.
Wisham Fenstermacher, Mary. Pablo Visits the Desert. 2010. 52p. pap. 22.49 *(978-1-4490-5180-8(4))* AuthorHouse.
Yoon, Salina. Penguin & Pinecone. Yoon, Salina, illus. (Penguin Ser.). (ENG., Illus.). (J). (gr. -1-1). 2014. 32p. bds. 7.99 *(978-0-8027-3731-1(5),* 9780802737311) 2012. 40p. 14.99 *(978-0-8027-2843-2(X),* 9780802728432) Bloomsbury Publishing USA. (Bloomsbury USA Childrens).
—Penguin & Pumpkin. 2014. (Penguin Ser.). (ENG., Illus.). 40p. (J). (gr. -1-1). 14.99 *(978-0-8027-3732-8(3),* 9780802737328, Bloomsbury USA Childrens) Bloomsbury Publishing USA.
—Penguin & Pumpkin. 2014. (Illus.). (J). *(978-0-8027-3770-0(6))* Walker & Co.
—Penguin Gets Dressed! Yoon, Salina, illus. 2010. (Illus.). 10p. bds. 7.95 *(978-1-60747-750-1(5),* Pickwick Pr.) Phoenix Bks., Inc.
—Penguin Gets Ready for Bed! Yoon, Salina, illus. 2010. (Illus.). 10p. bds. 7.95 *(978-1-60747-751-8(3),* Pickwick Pr.) Phoenix Bks., Inc.
—Penguin Goes to the Farm! Yoon, Salina, illus. 2010. (Illus.). 10p. bds. 7.95 *(978-1-60747-752-5(1),* Pickwick Pr.) Phoenix Bks., Inc.
—Penguin in Love. Yoon, Salina, illus. (Penguin Ser.). (ENG., Illus.). (J). (gr. -1-1). 2014. 34p. bds. 7.99 *(978-0-8027-3758-8(7),* 9780802737588) 2013. 40p. 14.99 *(978-0-8027-3600-0(9),* 9780802736000) Bloomsbury Publishing USA. (Bloomsbury USA Childrens).
—Penguin on Vacation. Yoon, Salina, illus. (Penguin Ser.). (ENG., Illus.). (J). (gr. -1-1). 2015. 34p. bds. 7.99 *(978-0-8027-3837-0(0),* 9780802738370) 2013. 40p. 14.99 *(978-0-8027-3397-9(2),* 9780802733979) Bloomsbury Publishing USA. (Bloomsbury USA Childrens).
—Penguin's Big Adventure. 2015. (Penguin Ser.). (ENG., Illus.). 40p. (J). (gr. -1-1). 14.99 *(978-0-8027-3828-8(1),* 9780802738288, Bloomsbury USA Childrens) Bloomsbury Publishing USA.
—Penguin's Christmas Wish. (Penguin Ser.). (ENG.). (J). 2017. 32p. bds. 7.99 ***(978-1-68119-573-5(9),*** 9781681195735) 2016. 40p. 14.99 *(978-1-68119-155-3(5),* 9781681191553) Bloomsbury Publishing USA. (Bloomsbury USA Childrens).
—Pingüino Enamorado. 2017. 36p. (J). (gr. k). 20.99 ***(978-84-8470-545-1(5))*** Corimbo, Editorial S.L. ESP. Dist: Lectorum Pubns., Inc.
Young, Louise. Penguin Comes Home. Elmore, Larry, illus. 2005. (Soundprints' Amazing Animal Adventures! Ser.). (ENG.). 32p. (J). (gr. -1-2). 9.95 *(978-1-59249-329-6(7),* PS7158) Soundprints.
Young, Louise O. Penguin Comes Home. Elmore, Larry, illus. (Amazing Animal Adventures Ser.). (ENG.). 36p. (J). (gr. -1-2). 2005. 2.95 *(978-1-59249-325-8(4),* S7158) 2005. 15.95 *(978-1-59249-324-1(6),* B7108) 2004. pap. 6.95 *(978-1-59249-326-5(2),* S7108) Soundprints.
Young, Louise O. & Elmore, Larry. Penguin Comes Home. 2005. (Soundprints' Amazing Animal Adventures! Ser.). (ENG., Illus.). 32p. (J). (gr. -1-3). 8.95 *(978-1-59249-328-9(9),* SC7108) Soundprints.
Young, Timothy. The Angry Little Puffin, 1 vol. 2014. (ENG., Illus.). 40p. (J). (gr. 5-8). 16.99 *(978-0-7643-4805-1(1),* 9780764348051) Schiffer Publishing, Ltd.

PENICILLIN

Adams, Jonathan S. Antibiotics. 2017. ***(978-1-5026-2873-2(2))*** Cavendish Square Publishing.
De la Bédoyère, Guy & De la Bédoyère, Camilla. The Discovery of Penicillin. 2005. (Milestones in Modern Science Ser.). (Illus.). 48p. (gr. 6-12). lib. bdg. 31.00 *(978-0-8368-5852-5(2),* Gareth Stevens Secondary Library) Stevens, Gareth Publishing LLLP.
Rooney, Anne. Alexander Fleming & the Discovery of Penicillin. 2012. (Miracle Makers Ser.). (ENG., Illus.). 48p. (YA). (gr. 5-8). 27.95 *(978-1-4488-6035-7(0),* Rosen Reference) Rosen Publishing Group, Inc., The.

PENINSULAR WAR, 1807-1814—FICTION

Fortescue, W. J. The Drummer's Coat. 2007. 120p. 94.99 *(978-1-4280-7656-3(5));* per. 88.99 *(978-1-4280-7658-7(1))* IndyPublish.com.
Henty, George Alfred. The Young Buglers: A Tale of the Peninsular War. 2007. (ENG.). 270p. pap. 21.99 *(978-1-4264-3587-4(8));* 334p. pap. 24.99 *(978-1-4264-3638-3(6))* Creative Media Partners, LLC.
Styles, Showell. The Flying Ensign: Greencoats Against Napoleon. 2003. (Budget Bks.). Orig. Title: Greencoat Against Napoleon. 297p. (YA). pap. 14.95 *(978-1-883937-70-6(1))* Bethlehem Bks.

PENITENTIARIES

see Prisons

PENN, WILLIAM, 1644-1718

Boothroyd, Jennifer. William Penn. 2009. pap. 6.95 *(978-0-8225-6431-7(9))* Lerner Publishing Group.
—William Penn: A Life of Tolerance. 2006. (Pull Ahead Bks.). (Illus.). 32p. (J). (gr. 3-7). lib. bdg. 22.60 *(978-0-8225-6387-7(8),* Lerner Pubns.) Lerner Publishing Group.
Figley, Marty Rhodes. Who Was William Penn? And Other Questions about the Founding of Pennsylvania. 2012. (Six Questions of American History Ser.). (ENG.). 48p. (gr. 4-6). pap. 56.72 *(978-0-7613-9241-5(6));* pap. 9.95 *(978-0-7613-8571-4(1));* (Illus.). lib. bdg. 30.60 *(978-0-7613-5328-7(3))* Lerner Publishing Group.
Foster, Genevieve. The World of William Penn. 2008. (Illus.). 192p. (J). pap. *(978-1-893103-30-6(7))* Beautiful Feet Bks.
Hinman, Bonnie. The Life & Times of William Penn. 2006. (Profiles in American History Ser.). (Illus.). 48p. (J). (gr. 4-8). lib. bdg. 29.95 *(978-1-58415-433-4(0),* 1259521) Mitchell Lane Pubs., Inc.
Jacobson, Ryan. William Penn: Founder of Pennsylvania. Stiles, Tim, illus. 2006. (Graphic Biographies Ser.). (ENG.). 32p. (gr. 3-4). 30.65 *(978-0-7368-6501-2(2),* Graphic Library) Capstone Press of Coughlan Cos.
Levy, Janey. William Penn: Shaping a Nation. 2009. (Real Life Readers Ser.). 32p. (ENG., Illus.). (J). (gr. 5-6). pap. 10.00 *(978-1-4358-0195-0(4),* 1291824); (gr. 5-5). 47.90 *(978-1-61511-376-7(2));* (J). (gr. 4-6). lib. bdg. 25.25 *(978-1-4358-3016-5(4));* (Illus.). (J). 60.00 *(978-1-4358-0196-7(2),* 1291824) Rosen Publishing Group, Inc., The. (PowerKids Pr.).
Marsh, Carole. William Penn. 2003. 12p. (gr. k-4). 2.95 *(978-0-635-02358-2(X))* Gallopade International.
Mountjoy, Shane. Philadelphia. 2007. (Colonial Settlements in America Ser.). (Illus.). 100p. (YA). (gr. 5-9). lib. bdg. 30.00 *(978-0-7910-9336-8(0))* Facts On File, Inc.
Swain, Gwenyth. Freedom Seeker: A Story about William Penn. Harvey, Lisa, illus. 2003. (Creative Minds Biographies Ser.). 64p. (J). 22.60 *(978-1-57505-176-5(1));* (ENG.). (gr. 4-8). pap. 8.95 *(978-0-87614-931-7(X))* Lerner Publishing Group. (Carolrhoda Bks.).
William Penn's Peaceable Kingdom (NCHS) 52p. (J). (gr. 5-8). spiral bd., tchr.'s planning gde. ed. 11.50 *(978-0-382-40930-1(2))* Cobblestone Publishing Co.

PENNSYLVANIA

Bobek, Joanne R. A Day at Pond Snow. 2011. 16p. 8.47 *(978-1-4567-1706-3(5))* AuthorHouse.
Bodden, Valerie. Pennsylvania. 2010. (Let's Explore America Ser.). 24p. (J). (gr. k-2). 19.95 *(978-1-58341-836-9(9))* Creative Co., The.
Derkins, Susie. The Meltdown at Three Mile Island. 2009. (When Disaster Strikes! Ser.). 48p. (gr. 5-8). 53.00 *(978-1-60854-781-4(7),* Rosen Reference) Rosen Publishing Group, Inc., The.
Hammer, Maxwell. Sidney Crosby: NHL MVP & Champion. 2015. (Today's MVPs & Champions Ser.). (ENG.). 24p. (J). (gr. 2-5). 27.07 *(978-1-63143-740-3(2),* 208575) Child's World, Inc., The.
Hasan, Heather. Pennsylvania: Past & Present. 2009. (Illus.). 48p. (J). 70.50 *(978-1-4358-5581-6(7));* pap. 11.75 *(978-1-4358-5580-9(9));* (ENG., lib. bdg. 29.25 *(978-1-4358-5291-4(5))* Rosen Publishing Group, Inc., The. (Rosen Reference).
Jerome, Kate Boehm. Pennsylvania: What's So Great about This State?, 100 vols. 2011. (Arcadia Kids Ser.). (ENG.). 32p. (J). pap. 7.99 *(978-1-58973-021-2(6))* Arcadia Publishing.
Kane, Kristen. K Is for Keystone: A Pennsylvania Alphabet. Knorr, Laura, illus. 2003. (Discover America State by State Ser.). (ENG.). 40p. (J). 17.95 *(978-1-58536-104-5(6))* Sleeping Bear Pr.
Lusted, Marcia Amidon. Pennsylvania: The Keystone State. 2010. (Illus.). 24p. (J). pap. 8.25 *(978-1-4358-3374-6(0),* 1300536, PowerKids Pr.) Rosen Publishing Group, Inc., The.
Maine, Tyler. Pennsylvania. 2016. (States Ser.). (ENG., Illus.). 32p. (gr. 3-4). lib. bdg. 27.32 *(978-1-5157-0425-6(4))* Next Page Pr., The.
Marsh, Carole. My First Book about Pennsylvania. 2004. (Pennsylvania Experience! Ser.). (Illus.). 32p. (J). (gr. k-4). pap. 7.95 *(978-0-7933-9587-3(9))* Gallopade International.
—Pennsylvania Current Events Projects: 30 Cool, Activities, Crafts, Experiments & More for Kids to Do to Learn about Your State! 2003. (Pennsylvania Experience Ser.). 32p. (gr. k-8). pap. 5.95 *(978-0-635-02057-4(2),* Marsh, Carole Bks.) Gallopade International.
—Pennsylvania Geography Projects: 30 Cool, Activities, Crafts, Experiments & More for Kids to Do to Learn about Your State! 2003. (Pennsylvania Experience Ser.). 32p. (gr. k-5). pap. 5.95 *(978-0-635-01857-1(8),* Marsh, Carole Bks.) Gallopade International.
—Pennsylvania Government Projects: 30 Cool, Activities, Crafts, Experiments & More for Kids to Do to Learn about Your State! 2003. (Pennsylvania Experience Ser.). 32p. (gr. k-5). pap. 5.95 *(978-0-635-01957-8(4),* Marsh, Carole Bks.) Gallopade International.
—Pennsylvania Jeopardy! Answers & Questions about Our State! 2004. (Pennsylvania Experience! Ser.). (Illus.). 32p. (J). (gr. 3-8). pap. 7.95 *(978-0-7933-9588-0(7))* Gallopade International.
—Pennsylvania "Jography" A Fun Run Thru Our State! 2004. (Pennsylvania Experience! Ser.). (Illus.). 32p. (J). (gr. 3-8). pap. 7.95 *(978-0-7933-9589-7(5))* Gallopade International.
—Pennsylvania People Projects: 30 Cool, Activities, Crafts, Experiments & More for Kids to Do to Learn about Your State! 2003. (Pennsylvania Experience Ser.). 32p. (gr. k-5). pap. 5.95 *(978-0-635-02007-9(6),* Marsh, Carole Bks.) Gallopade International.
—Pennsylvania Symbols & Facts Projects: 30 Cool, Activities, Crafts, Experiments & More for Kids to Do to Learn about Your State! 2003. (Pennsylvania Experience Ser.). 32p. (gr. k-5). pap. 5.95 *(978-0-635-01907-3(8),* Marsh, Carole Bks.) Gallopade International.
—Pennsylvania's Big Activity Book. 2004. (Pennsylvania Experience! Ser.). (Illus.). 96p. (J). (gr. 2-6). pap. 9.95 *(978-0-7933-9590-3(9))* Gallopade International.
—The Proud Pennsylvania Coloring Book. 2004. (Pennsylvania Experience! Ser.). (Illus.). 32p. (J). (gr. k-2). pap. 3.95 *(978-0-7933-9591-0(7))* Gallopade International.
McNamara, Connie. My First University of Pittsburgh Words. 2004. (ENG.). (J). 11.95 *(978-0-9759703-2-4(1))* Shamrock Publishing, Inc.
Mercer, Henry C., et al. Color Me Pennsylvania: Our Heritage. 2007. (Illus.). 22p. (J). pap. 12.00 *(978-1-4223-1491-3(X))* DIANE Publishing Co.
El Meson en Belen (The Bethlehem Inn) (SPA.). (J). *(978-0-7899-0876-6(X),* 496235) Editorial Unilit.
Mis, M. S. How to Draw Pennsylvania's Sights & Symbols. 2009. (Kid's Guide to Drawing America Ser.). 32p. (gr. k-k). 50.50 *(978-1-61511-091-9(7),* PowerKids Pr.) Rosen Publishing Group, Inc., The.
Murray, Julie. Pennsylvania, 1 vol. 2006. (United States Ser.). (ENG., Illus.). 32p. (gr. 2-4). 27.07 *(978-1-59197-697-4(9),* Buddy Bks.) ABDO Publishing Co.
Noble, Trinka Hakes. One for All: A Pennsylvania Number Book. Papp, Lisa, illus. 2005. (Count Your Way Across the USA Ser.). (ENG.). 40p. (J). (gr. k-5). 16.95 *(978-1-58536-200-4(X))* Sleeping Bear Pr.
—Pennsylvania Reader. Darnell, K. L., illus. rev. ed. 2007. (State Readers Ser.). (ENG.). 96p. (J). (gr. 1-5). 12.95 *(978-1-58536-320-9(0))* Sleeping Bear Pr.
O'Connell, Kim A. Pennsylvania: A MyReportLinks. Com Book. 2003. (States Ser.). (Illus.). 48p. (J). lib. bdg. 25.26 *(978-0-7660-5153-9(6),* MyReportLinks.com Bks.) Enslow Pubs., Inc.
Peters, Stephen & Hart, Joyce. Pennsylvania. 2nd rev. ed. 2008. (Celebrate the States Ser.). 144p. (gr. 6-18). lib. bdg. 42.79 *(978-0-7614-3403-0(8),* Benchmark Bks.) Marshall Cavendish Corp.
Polley, J. Patrick & Polley, JoAnn. My Trip to Gettysburg, 1 vol. Shekerow, Mark D., ed. Hanstick, Kevin R., illus. 2007. (My Trip Ser.). (ENG.). 80p. (J). spiral bd. 14.95 *(978-1-58980-456-2(2))* Pelican Publishing Co., Inc.
Somervill, Barbara A. Pennsylvannia. 2003. (From Sea to Shining Sea Ser.: 2). (ENG., Illus.). 80p. (J). 30.50 *(978-0-516-22388-9(7),* Children's Pr.) Scholastic Library Publishing.
Swain, Gwenyth. Pennsylvania. (J). 2012. lib. bdg. 25.26 *(978-0-7613-4553-4(1),* Lerner Pubns.) 2nd exp. rev. ed. 2003. (Illus.). 84p. (gr. 3-6). pap. 6.95 *(978-0-8225-4147-9(5))* Lerner Publishing Group.
Treasure Maps of Clarion County. 2004. per. 19.95 *(978-0-9743881-1-3(4))* Hufnagel Software.
Way, Jennifer. Pennsylvania/Pensilvania. Brusca, Maria Cristina, tr. from ENG. 2006. (Bilingual Library of the United States of America Ser.: Set 2). (ENG & SPA., Illus.). 32p. (J). (gr. 3-6). lib. bdg. 25.25 *(978-1-4042-3103-0(X))* Rosen Publishing Group, Inc., The.

PENNSYLVANIA—FICTION

Abbott, E. F. Mary Jemison: Native American Captive. 2016. (Based on a True Story Ser.). (ENG., Illus.). 224p. (J). 15.99 *(978-1-250-06838-5(X),* 9781250068385) Feiwel & Friends.
Alender, Katie. The Dead Girls of Hysteria Hall. (ENG.). 336p. (J). (gr. 7). 2016. pap. 9.99 *(978-1-338-03239-0(9))* 2015. 18.99 *(978-0-545-63999-6(9))* Scholastic, Inc.
—The Dead Girls of Hysteria Hall. 2016. (ENG.). 329p. (YA). (gr. 7). 20.85 *(978-0-606-39121-4(5))* Turtleback Bks.
Alexander, Yvonne. Adventure in Autou. 2012. 230p. pap. 15.99 *(978-1-62230-262-8(1))* Salem Author Services.
Alger, Horatio. Joe the Hotel Boy. 2006. pap. *(978-1-4065-0712-6(1))* Dodo Pr.
—Joe the Hotel Boy: Or: Winning Out by Pluck. 2007. 164p. pap. 19.99 *(978-1-4346-5069-6(3));* 172p. pap. 21.99 *(978-1-4346-5070-2(7))* Creative Media Partners, LLC.
Altsheler, Joseph A. The Scouts of the Valley. (Young Trailers Ser.: Vol. 7). reprint ed. 2008. 272p. pap. 11.95 *(978-1-60597-237-4(1))* 2007. 276p. per. 14.95 *(978-1-60424-040-5(7))* Standard Pubns., Inc. (Book Jungle).
—The Scouts of the Valley: A Story of Wyoming & the Chemung. 2005. (Young Trailers Ser.: Vol. 7). (J). reprint ed. 29.95 *(978-1-4218-1054-6(9));* 344p. pap. 14.95 *(978-1-4218-1154-3(5))* 1st World Publishing, Inc. (1st World Library - Literary Society).
—The Scouts of the Valley: A Story of Wyoming & the Chemung. 2007. (Young Trailers Ser.: Vol. 7). (ENG.). 284p. (J). reprint ed. pap. 21.99 *(978-1-4346-0327-2(X))* Creative Media Partners, LLC.
—The Scouts of the Valley: A Story of Wyoming & the Chemung. 2006. (Young Trailers Ser.: Vol. 7). (J). reprint ed. pap. *(978-1-4065-0821-5(7))* Dodo Pr.
—The Scouts of the Valley: A Story of Wyoming & the Chemung. 2007. (Young Trailers Ser.: Vol. 7). 208p. (J). reprint ed. per. *(978-1-4068-1685-3(X))* Echo Library.
—The Scouts of the Valley: A Story of Wyoming & the Chemung. 2004. (Young Trailers Ser.: Vol. 7). (J). reprint ed. pap. 27.95 *(978-1-4191-8163-4(7));* pap. 1.99 *(978-1-4192-8163-1(1))* Kessinger Publishing, LLC.
—The Scouts of the Valley (Webster's French Thesaurus Edition) 2008. (Young Trailers Ser.: Vol. 7). (FRE & ENG.). 360p. pap. 28.95 *(978-0-497-97888-4(1))* Icon Group International, Inc.
Anderson, Laurie Halse. Forge. 2012. 18.00 *(978-1-61383-316-2(4))* Perfection Learning Corp.
—Forge. (Seeds of America Trilogy Ser.). (ENG., Illus.). (J). (gr. 5-9). 2012. 320p. pap. 8.99 *(978-1-4169-6145-1(3))* 2010. 304p. 18.99 *(978-1-4169-6144-4(5))* Simon & Schuster Children's Publishing. (Atheneum Bks. for Young Readers).
—Forge. 2012. (Seeds of America Trilogy Ser.: 2). lib. bdg. 18.40 *(978-0-606-23680-5(5),* Turtleback) Turtleback Bks.
—Prom. 2006. (ENG.). 240p. (YA). (gr. 7-18). reprint ed. 8.99 *(978-0-14-240570-3(1),* Speak) Penguin Young Readers Group.
—Prom. 2006. (YA). 1.25 *(978-1-4193-5096-2(X))* Recorded Bks., Inc.
Andrews, Jesse. Me & Earl & the Dying Girl. (ENG.). 304p. (YA). (gr. 9-17). 2012. 17.95 *(978-1-4197-0176-4(2),* Amulet Bks.) 2015. 17.95 *(978-1-4197-2027-7(9))* 2015. 17.95 *(978-1-4197-2013-0(9),* Amulet Bks.) 2015. pap. 9.95 *(978-1-4197-1960-8(2),* Amulet Bks.) Abrams, Inc.
—Me & Earl & the Dying Girl. 2015. (CHI.). 320p. (YA). (gr. 9-17). pap. *(978-986-344-282-0(8))* Rye Field Publishing, Co.
—Me & Earl & the Dying Girl. 2015. lib. bdg. 20.80 *(978-0-606-37113-1(3))* Turtleback Bks.
Armstrong, Cara. Moxie: The Dachshund of Fallingwater. 2010. (ENG.). 32p. (J). 19.95 *(978-1-933979-70-0(4),* 10cb4a3a-e256-4798-b1d9-ce1ed88e1459) Bright Sky Pr.
Ayres, Katherine. Macaroni Boy. 2004. (ENG.). 192p. (J). (gr. 3-7). per. 6.99 *(978-0-440-41884-9(4),* Yearling) Random Hse. Children's Bks.
—Voices at Whisper Bend. 2009. (Mysteries Through Time Ser.). 176p. (YA). (gr. 4-8). 31.95 *(978-1-60754-182-0(3));* pap. 15.25 *(978-1-60754-183-7(1))* Windmill Bks.
Barrett, Judi. The Complete Cloudy with a Chance of Meatballs: Cloudy with a Chance of Meatballs; Pickles to Pittsburgh. Barrett, Ronald, illus. 2009. (ENG.). 64p. (J). (gr. -1-3). 19.99 *(978-1-4424-0199-0(0),* Atheneum Bks. for Young Readers) Simon & Schuster Children's Publishing.
Bender, Carrie. Hemlock Hill Hideaway: Whispering Brook Series #4. 2007. (Illus.). 168p. pap. 8.99 *(978-1-60126-022-2(9))* Masthof Pr.
—Timber Lane Cove. 2003. (ENG.). 144p. (YA). pap. 8.99 *(978-0-8361-9202-5(8))* Herald Pr.
Benyo, Richard. The South Street Gang vs. the Coalcracker Cyclops. 2010. (ENG.). 151p. pap. 8.00 *(978-1-58966-208-7(3))* Univ. of Scranton Pr.
Bryant, Jen. The Fortune of Carmen Navarro. 2011. (ENG.). 240p. (YA). (gr. 7). pap. 8.99 *(978-0-375-85097-4(X),* Ember) Random Hse. Children's Bks.
Carlson, J. Kelley. Freeing Golden Eagle. 2007. 140p. 19.95 *(978-1-4327-0315-8(3));* per. 10.95 *(978-1-4327-0302-8(1))* Outskirts Pr., Inc.
Carvell, Marlene. Sweetgrass Basket. 2005. (ENG.). 256p. (J). (gr. 5-6). 16.99 *(978-0-525-47547-7(8),* Dutton Books for Young Readers) Penguin Young Readers Group.
Cassidy, Colette. DIVCO, the Little Milk Truck. 2007. (Illus.). 28p. (J). pap. 7.99 *(978-0-615-17346-7(2))* Redcay Publishing.
Church, Lorraine. Pencilvani. 2009. (Illus.). 32p. pap. 12.99 *(978-1-4389-2072-6(5))* AuthorHouse.
Cody, Matthew. Powerless. 2011. (Supers of Noble's Green Ser.). (ENG.). 288p. (J). (gr. 3-7). 7.99 *(978-0-375-84489-8(9),* Yearling) Random Hse. Children's Bks.
—Super. (Supers of Noble's Green Ser.). (ENG.). 304p. (J). (gr. 3-7). 2014. 7.99 *(978-0-375-87291-4(4),* Yearling) 2012. 16.99 *(978-0-375-86894-8(1),* Knopf Bks. for Young Readers) Random Hse. Children's Bks.

P Q R

Collins, Nafessa. Mrs. Precious & the Possum. 2012. 56p. (gr. -1). pap. 8.95 *(978-1-4759-1273-9(0))* iUniverse, Inc.
Connelly, Neil. The Miracle Stealer. 2010. (ENG.). 240p. (J). (gr. 9-18). 17.99 *(978-0-545-13195-7(2)*, Levine, Arthur A. Bks.) Scholastic, Inc.
Connelly, Neil O. The Miracle Stealer. 2012. (ENG.). 240p. (J). (gr. 9-9). pap. 9.99 *(978-0-545-13312-8(2)*, Levine, Arthur A. Bks.) Scholastic, Inc.
Connolly, Brian A. Hawk. 2007. 156p. 20.95 *(978-1-60264-030-6(0))*; 160p. per. 13.95 *(978-1-60264-029-0(7))* Virtualbookworm.com Publishing, Inc.
Cook, Kajsa. Discoveries in the Shriver Family Attic: How a Woman & Her Children Dealt with the Battle of Gettysburg. 2009. (Illus.). 122p. (J). (gr. 4-8). pap. 8.95 *(978-1-57249-398-8(4)*, White Mane Kids) White Mane Publishing Co., Inc.
Corbett, Sue. The Last Newspaper Boy in America. 2010. (ENG.). 208p. (J). (gr. 5-18). 6.99 *(978-0-14-241696-9(7)*, Puffin Books) Penguin Young Readers Group.
Curtis, Vanessa. The Baking Life of Amelie Day. Eccles, Jane, illus. 2015. (Middle-Grade Novels Ser.). (ENG.). 176p. (gr. 4-7). lib. bdg. 25.27 *(978-1-4965-2216-0(8))* Stone Arch Bks.
Czerw, Nancy Carpenter. Itty & Bitty - On the Road. Berlin, Rose Mary, illus. 2008. (Itty & Bitty Ser.: 3). (ENG.). 32p. (J). (gr. -1-3). 16.95 *(978-0-9755618-4-3(7))* McWitty Pr., Inc.
Dana Kittendorf. Trail of Dreams. 2009. 136p. 21.95 *(978-1-4401-7787-3(2))* iUniverse, Inc.
Darlington, Edgar B. P. The Circus Boys Across the Continent. 2005. 27.95 *(978-1-4218-1020-1(4))*; 212p. pap. 12.95 *(978-1-4218-1120-8(0))* 1st World Publishing, Inc. (1st World Library - Literary Society).
Dellasega, Cheryl. Nugr90, 0 vols. LaPierre, Karina, illus. 2007. (Bloggrls Ser.: 1). (ENG.). 192p. (YA). (gr. 7-11). pap. 9.99 *(978-0-7614-5396-3(2)*, 9780761453963, Amazon Children's Publishing) Amazon Publishing.
Douglas, Ryke Leigh. The Big Wheel. 2010. (Illus.). 21p. (J). pap. 15.95 *(978-1-4327-4495-3(X))* Outskirts Pr., Inc.
—Sam's Surprise. 2008. 28p. per. 12.95 *(978-1-4327-0850-4(3))* Outskirts Pr., Inc.
Dreistadt, Jessica R. Ashley & Tiana. 2009. 96p. pap. 10.00 *(978-0-578-02239-0(7))* Dreistadt, Jessica R.
Dudek, Mike. The Fairytale of the Morley Dog. 2007. (Illus.). 40p. (YA). spiral bd. 2.49 *(978-0-9740380-1-8(6))* Dudek, Mike.
Earl, Cheri Pray & Williams, Carol Lynch. Secret in Pennsylvania. 2009. (J). *(978-1-56145-477-8(X)*, Peachtree Junior) Peachtree Pubs.
Erskine, Kathryn. The Absolute Value of Mike. 2012. (ENG.). 272p. (J). (gr. 5-18). pap. 7.99 *(978-0-14-242101-7(4)*, Puffin Books) Penguin Young Readers Group.
—Quaking. 2010. (ENG.). 256p. (YA). (gr. 7-18). 7.99 *(978-0-14-241476-7(X)*, Speak) Penguin Young Readers Group.
Faigen, Anne G. New World Waiting. 2006. iii, 188p. (J). pap. *(978-0-9744715-5-6(0))* Local History Co., The.
Fantaskey, Beth. Jekel Loves Hyde. 2011. (ENG.). 288p. (YA). (gr. 9). pap. 8.99 *(978-0-547-55027-5(8))* Houghton Mifflin Harcourt Publishing Co.
—Jessica's Guide to Dating on the Dark Side. 2010. (ENG., Illus.). 384p. (YA). (gr. 9-18). pap. 8.99 *(978-0-547-25940-6(9))* Houghton Mifflin Harcourt Publishing Co.
Federle, Tim. Better Nate Than Ever. 2014. (ENG., Illus.). 296p. (J). (gr. 4-8). pap. 7.99 *(978-1-4424-4691-5(9)*, Simon & Schuster Bks. For Young Readers) Simon & Schuster Bks. For Young Readers.
—Better Nate Than Ever. 2014. lib. bdg. 18.40 *(978-0-606-35430-1(1))* Turtleback Bks.
Ficklin, Jonene H. The Garden Gate. 2005. (YA). 14.95 *(978-0-9761188-2-4(3))* Victor's Crown Publishing.
Finneyfrock, Karen. The Sweet Revenge of Celia Door. 2014. (ENG.). 288p. (YA). (gr. 7). pap. 9.99 *(978-0-14-750995-6(5)*, Speak) Penguin Young Readers Group.
Franckowiak, Jon. When I Grow up I Want to be a Nittany Lion. 2008. 32p. pap. 9.95 *(978-0-9715415-0-4(7))* Franckowiak, Jon.
Freeman, Martha. Effie Starr Zook Has One More Question. 2017. (ENG., Illus.). 224p. (J). (gr. 3-7). 16.99 *(978-1-4814-7264-7(X)*, Simon & Schuster/Paula Wiseman Bks.) Simon & Schuster/Paula Wiseman Bks.
—Who Stole New Year's Eve? 2013. (Chickadee Court Mystery Ser.). (ENG.). 224p. (J). (gr. 2-7). 16.95 *(978-0-8234-2750-5(1))* Holiday Hse., Inc.
—Who Stole Uncle Sam? 2008. (Chickadee Court Mystery Ser.). (ENG., Illus.). 128p. (J). (gr. 3-7). 16.95 *(978-0-8234-2091-9(4))* Holiday Hse., Inc.
Galante, Cecilia. The World from up Here. (ENG.). 320p. (J). (gr. 3-7). 2017. pap. 6.99 ***(978-0-545-84846-6(6))*** 2016. 16.99 *(978-0-545-84845-9(8)*, Scholastic Pr.) Scholastic, Inc.
Gamble, Adam & Jasper, Mark. Good Night Pittsburgh. Palmer, Ruth, illus. 2012. (Good Night Our World Ser.). (ENG.). 20p. (J). (gr. k — 1). bds. 9.95 *(978-1-60219-073-3(9))* Good Night Bks.
Gantos, Jack. Dead End in Norvelt. 2011. (Norvelt Ser.: 1). (ENG., Illus.). 352p. (J). (gr. 5-9). 15.99 *(978-0-374-37993-3(9)*, 9780374379933, Farrar, Straus & Giroux (BYR)) Farrar, Straus & Giroux.
—Dead End in Norvelt. 2013. (Norvelt Ser.: 1). (ENG., Illus.). 384p. (J). (gr. 5-9). pap. 8.99 *(978-1-250-01023-0(3)*, 9781250010230) Square Fish.
—Dead End in Norvelt. 2013. (J). lib. bdg. 18.40 *(978-0-606-31901-0(8)*, Turtleback) Turtleback Bks.
—From Norvelt to Nowhere. 2013. (Norvelt Ser.: 2). (ENG.). 288p. (J). (gr. 5-9). 16.99 *(978-0-374-37994-0(7)*, 9780374379940, Farrar, Straus & Giroux (BYR)) Farrar, Straus & Giroux.
—From Norvelt to Nowhere. 2015. (J). lib. bdg. 18.40 *(978-0-606-37280-0(6))* Turtleback Bks.
Garland, Sherry. Voices of Gettysburg, 1 vol. Hierstein, Judith, illus. 2010. (Voices of History Ser.). (ENG.). 40p. (J). (gr. 3-3). 17.99 *(978-1-58980-653-5(0))* Pelican Publishing Co., Inc.
Gilbert, Joan. Mule Boy. Burke, Kathryn Schaar, illus. 2004. 248p. (YA). per. 12.95 *(978-0-930973-30-8(5))* Moore, Hugh Historical Park & Museums, Inc.
Glover, Dennis W. The Goat Farm. 2009. 32p. pap. 12.99 *(978-1-4490-1532-9(8))* AuthorHouse.
Grandpa Dennis, as told by. George Washington's Smallest Army: The Miracle Before Trenton. 2009. 216p. (J). pap. 17.49 *(978-1-4389-3147-0(6))* AuthorHouse.
Gregory, Kristiana. The Winter of Red Snow. 2010. (Dear America Ser.). (ENG.). 192p. (J). (gr. 3-7). 12.99 *(978-0-545-23802-1(1)*, Scholastic Pr.) Scholastic, Inc.
Gurevich, Margaret. Gina's Balance. 2016. (What's Your Dream? Ser.). (ENG., Illus.). 96p. (gr. 3-4). lib. bdg. 25.32 *(978-1-4965-3443-9(3))* Capstone Press of Coughlan Cos.
Haas, Jessie. Chase. 2007. 256p. (J). (gr. 5-9). lib. bdg. 17.89 *(978-0-06-112851-6(1))* HarperCollins Pubs.
Hershenhorn, Esther. Fancy That. Lloyd, Megan, illus. 2003. (ENG.). 32p. (J). (gr. k-3). tchr. ed. 16.95 *(978-0-8234-1605-9(4))* Holiday Hse., Inc.
Higgins, Joanna. Waiting for the Queen: A Novel of Early America. 2013. (ENG.). 256p. (J). (gr. 4-10). 16.95 *(978-1-57131-700-1(7))* Milkweed Editions.
Hope, Laura Lee. Six Little Bunkers at Grandpa Ford's. 2007. (ENG.). 138p. pap. 18.99 *(978-1-4346-1214-4(7))*; 156p. pap. 21.99 *(978-1-4346-1285-4(6))* Creative Media Partners, LLC.
—Six Little Bunkers at Mammy June S. 2007. (ENG.). 140p. pap. 18.99 *(978-1-4264-9315-7(0))* Creative Media Partners, LLC.
—Six Little Bunkers at Mammy Junes. l.t. ed. 2007. (ENG.). 156p. pap. 21.99 *(978-1-4264-9696-7(6))* Creative Media Partners, LLC.
Hubler, Marsha. Southern Belle's Special Gift, 1 vol. 2009. (Keystone Stables Ser.). (ENG.). 128p. (J). pap. 7.99 *(978-0-310-71794-2(9))* Zonderkidz.
—Summer Camp Adventure, 1 vol. 2009. (Keystone Stables Ser.). (ENG.). 128p. (J). pap. 7.99 *(978-0-310-71795-9(7))* Zonderkidz.
Huffman, Nancy E. The Misadventures of Taylor R. Bailey. 2010. 112p. 23.99 *(978-1-4490-5791-6(8))*; pap. 13.99 *(978-1-4490-5790-9(X))* AuthorHouse.
Irwin, John P. The Cubby Files; Tales of a Pennsylvania Black Bear Growing Up. 2009. 96p. pap. 15.99 *(978-1-4415-0209-4(2))* Xlibris Corp.
Jacobs, Lily. The Littlest Bunny in Pennsylvania: An Easter Adventure. Dunn, Robert, illus. 2015. (ENG.). 32p. (J). (-3). 9.99 *(978-1-4926-1177-6(8)*, Sourcebooks Jabberwocky) Sourcebooks, Inc.
—The Littlest Bunny in Pittsburgh: An Easter Adventure. Dunn, Robert, illus. 2015. (ENG.). 32p. (J). (-3). 9.99 *(978-1-4926-1183-7(2)*, Sourcebooks Jabberwocky) Sourcebooks, Inc.
James, Eric. A Halloween Scare in Pennsylvania. Le Ray, Marina, illus. 2014. (ENG.). 32p. (J). (-5). 9.99 *(978-1-4926-0627-7(8)*, 9781492606277, Sourcebooks Jabberwocky) Sourcebooks, Inc.
—A Halloween Scare in Pittsburgh. Le Ray, Marina, illus. 2015. (ENG.). 32p. (J). (-5). 9.99 *(978-1-4926-2396-0(2)*, 9781492623960, Sourcebooks Jabberwocky) Sourcebooks, Inc.
—Santa's Sleigh Is on Its Way to Pennsylvania. Dunn, Robert, illus. 2015. (ENG.). 32p. (J). (-2). 12.99 *(978-1-4926-2745-6(3)*, Sourcebooks Jabberwocky) Sourcebooks, Inc.
—Santa's Sleigh Is on Its Way to Pittsburgh: A Christmas Adventure. Dunn, Robert, illus. 2016. (ENG.). 32p. (J). (-2). 12.99 *(978-1-4926-4351-7(3)*, 9781492643517, Sourcebooks Jabberwocky) Sourcebooks, Inc.
Jeffers, Sunni. Eyes on the Prize. 2009. (Tales from Grace Chapel Inn Ser.). (ENG.). 328p. pap. 13.99 *(978-0-8249-4787-3(8)*, Ideal Pubns.) Worthy Publishing.
Kay, Alan. Breaking the Rules. 2007. (Young Heroes of History Ser.: 7). 149p. (J). pap. 7.95 *(978-1-57249-389-6(5)*, White Mane Kids) White Mane Publishing Co., Inc.
Kay, Alan N. Crossroads at Gettysburg. 2005. (Young Heroes of History Ser.: 6). (Illus.). 166p. (J). (gr. 3-7). per. 7.95 *(978-1-57249-359-9(3)*, White Mane Kids) White Mane Publishing Co., Inc.
Keay, Ben. Perfect Solution. Hsu, Florence, illus. 2009. (YA). *(978-1-933791-09-8(8))* Finial Publishing.
Kelaita, Lynda. Some Houses Are White. 2009. 32p. pap. 10.95 *(978-1-935125-44-0(3))* Robertson Publishing.
Knopp, Sue, creator. Study Guide for Wolf Journal: A Novel. 2005. 60p. per. 7.95 *(978-1-58939-827-6(0))* Virtualbookworm.com Publishing, Inc.
Koraido, Beth S. Summers with Grampa Gus. 2008. 63p. pap. 19.95 *(978-1-60703-384-4(4))* America Star Bks.
Leavitt, Lindsey. Sean Griswold's Head. (ENG.). (YA). (gr. 7-12). 2012. 304p. pap. 9.99 *(978-1-59990-911-0(1)*, 9781599909110) 2011. 288p. 16.99 *(978-1-59990-498-6(5)*, 9781599904986) Bloomsbury Publishing USA. (Bloomsbury USA Childrens).
Lewis, Beverly. SummerHill Secrets. 2007. (Summerhill Secrets Ser.: Vols. 1-5). (ENG.). Vol. 1. 560p. (gr. 6-9). pap. 17.00 *(978-0-7642-0445-6(9))* Vol. 2. (Illus.). 544p. (gr. 11-12). pap. 17.00 *(978-0-7642-0452-4(1))* Bethany Hse. Pubs.
Little Farm down the Lane, Bk. III. 2005. pap. 10.99 *(978-1-59781-702-8(3))* Salem Author Services.
Lois, Lowry. Crow Call. 2011. (J). (gr. -1-2). 29.95 incl. audio compact disk *(978-0-545-29674-8(9))* Weston Woods Studios, Inc.
Lokko, CNN. Adventures of Elizabeth Sam. 2012. 280p. pap. *(978-9964-70-151-2(9))* Afram Pubns. Ghana, Ltd.
Lubar, David. Sleeping Freshmen Never Lie. 2007. (ENG.). 288p. (YA). (gr. 7-18). 10.99 *(978-0-14-240780-6(1)*, Speak) Penguin Young Readers Group.
—Sophomores & Other Oxymorons. 2015. (ENG.). 432p. (YA). (gr. 7). 17.99 *(978-0-525-42970-8(0)*, Dutton Books for Young Readers) Penguin Young Readers Group.
Lupica, Mike. The Underdogs. (ENG.). (J). (gr. 5-18). 2012. 304p. pap. 7.99 *(978-0-14-242139-0(1)*, Puffin Books) 2011. 288p. 17.99 *(978-0-399-25001-9(8)*, Philomel Bks.) Penguin Young Readers Group.
Macor, Jim. Frazier Fir, A Christmas Fable. Macor, Jim, illus. 2007. (Illus.). 32p. (J). 17.95 *(978-0-9785551-3-9(9))* Zuber Publishing.
Magnin, Joyce. Carrying Mason, 1 vol. 2013. (ENG.). 176p. (J). pap. 6.99 *(978-0-310-72682-1(4))* Zonderkidz.
Marsh, Carole. The Mystery in Chocolate Town: Hershey, Pennsylvania. (Real Kids, Real Places Ser.). (Illus.). (J). 2009. 143p. lib. bdg. 18.99 *(978-0-635-07025-8(1)*, Marsh, Carole Mysteries) 2007. 145p. (gr. 2-8). 14.95 *(978-0-635-06389-2(1))* Gallopade International.
—The Mystery in Chocolate Town Hershey, Pennsylvania. 2007. (Real Kids, Real Places Ser.). (Illus.). 145p. (J). (gr. 2-8). per. 7.99 *(978-0-635-06333-5(6))* Gallopade International.
Martin, Joanna F. Betsey's Wishes. 2010. (Illus.). 255p. (J). (gr. 3-6). 9.80 *(978-0-7399-2424-2(9))* Rod & Staff Pubs., Inc.
Matson, Morgan. Second Chance Summer. (ENG.). (YA). (gr. 7). 2013. 496p. pap. 10.99 *(978-1-4169-9068-0(2))* 2012. 480p. 19.99 *(978-1-4169-9067-3(4))* Simon & Schuster Bks. For Young Readers. (Simon & Schuster Bks. For Young Readers).
Mazeroski, Kelly. Maz, You're Up! Lauso, Judith, illus. 2010. 24p. (J). pap. 12.95 *(978-0-936340-18-0(5))* Historical Society of Western Pennsylvania.
McGough, Michael R. The Lincoln Inn. 2004. (Illus.). 108p. (YA). per. 14.95 *(978-1-57747-108-0(3))* Thomas Pubns.
McKain, Susan & Swann, Sandy. Tugger & Mini-Mew. 2011. 32p. pap. 15.95 *(978-1-4634-4920-9(8))* AuthorHouse.
Morgan, Melissa J. Alex's Challenge. 2005. (Camp Confidential Ser.: 4). (ENG.). 160p. (J). (gr. 3-7). mass mkt. 4.99 *(978-0-448-43876-4(3)*, Grosset & Dunlap) Penguin Young Readers Group.
—Grace's Twist. 2005. (Camp Confidential Ser.: 3). (ENG.). 160p. (J). (gr. 3-7). mass mkt. 4.99 *(978-0-448-43875-7(5)*, Grosset & Dunlap) Penguin Young Readers Group.
—Natalie's Secret. 2005. (Camp Confidential Ser.: 1). (ENG.). 160p. (J). (gr. 3-7). 4.99 *(978-0-448-43737-8(6)*, Grosset & Dunlap) Penguin Young Readers Group.
Mostoller, Marcia. Emma's Summer Camp Dilemm. 2011. 64p. pap. 19.95 *(978-1-4626-2814-8(1))* America Star Bks.
Mullarkey, John & Mullarkey, Lisa. Johnstown Flood: An Up2U Historical Fiction Adventure, 1 vol. Martin, Dana, illus. 2013. (Up2U Adventures Ser.). (ENG.). 80p. (J). (gr. 2-5). lib. bdg. 27.07 *(978-1-61641-967-7(9)*, Calico Chapter Bks) Magic Wagon.
Osborne, Mary Pope. Standing in the Light: The Diary of Catharine Carey Logan, Delaware Valley, Pennsylvania, 1763. 2011. (Dear America Ser.). (ENG.). 176p. (J). (gr. 5-9). 12.99 *(978-0-545-26687-1(4))* Scholastic, Inc.
Otis, James. Stephen of Philadelphi: A Story of Penn's Colony. 2007. 144p. per. 9.95 *(978-0-9790876-5-3(1))* Living Bks. Pr.
Paulsen, Gary. Woods Runner. 2011. (ENG.). 176p. (YA). (gr. 7). pap. 7.99 *(978-0-375-85908-3(X)*, Lamb, Wendy Bks.) Random Hse. Children's Bks.
Peaslee Levine, Martha. The Twelve Days of Christmas in Pennsylvania. Dougherty, Rachel, illus. 2014. (Twelve Days of Christmas in America Ser.). (ENG.). 40p. (J). (gr. k). 12.95 *(978-1-4549-0889-0(0))* Sterling Publishing Co., Inc.
Price, Bc. Mabel & Her Litter Of. 2008. 132p. pap. 12.00 *(978-0-615-20692-9(1))* BCP Pubns.
Quick, Matthew. Boy21. 2013. (ENG.). 272p. (YA). (gr. 7-17). pap. 10.99 *(978-0-316-12796-7(5))* Little, Brown Bks. for Young Readers.
Richards, Jame. Three Rivers Rising. 2011. (ENG.). 306p. (YA). (gr. 7). pap. 8.99 *(978-0-375-85369-2(3)*, Ember) Random Hse. Children's Bks.
Richter, Conrad. The Light in the Forest. Chappell, Warren, illus. 2005. (Everyman's Library Children's Classics Ser.). (ENG.). 176p. (J). (gr. 5-7). 15.95 *(978-1-4000-4426-9(X)*, Everyman's Library) Knopf Doubleday Publishing Group.
Ruby, Lois. Rebel Spirits. 2013. 292p. (YA). *(978-0-545-55282-0(6))* Scholastic, Inc.
Ryan, Pam Muñoz. Echo. 2015. (ENG., Illus.). 512p. (J). (gr. 5-9). 19.99 *(978-0-439-87402-1(5)*, Scholastic Pr.) Scholastic, Inc.
Salerni, Dianne K. The Caged Graves. 2014. (ENG.). 336p. (YA). (gr. 7). pap. 8.99 *(978-0-544-33622-3(4)*, HMH Books For Young Readers) Houghton Mifflin Harcourt Publishing Co.
Schlitz, Laura Amy. The Hired Girl. 2015. (ENG., Illus.). 400p. (J). (gr. 7-10). 17.99 *(978-0-7636-7818-0(X))* Candlewick Pr.
—The Hired Girl. 2018. lib. bdg. 22.10 ***(978-0-606-40389-4(2))*** Turtleback Bks.
Serrano, Tina. The Catfish Caper. 2011. 54p. pap. 16.95 *(978-1-4560-6590-4(4))* America Star Bks.
Seyfert, Ella Mae. Amish Moving Day. Jones, Henrietta, illus. 2011. 132p. 40.95 *(978-1-258-01315-8(0))* Literary Licensing, LLC.
Shepard, Sara. Killer. 2010. (Pretty Little Liars Ser.: 6). (YA). lib. bdg. 20.85 *(978-0-606-12278-8(8)*, Turtleback) Turtleback Bks.
—Pretty Little Liars Bind-Up #1: Pretty Little Liars & Flawless. 2014. (Pretty Little Liars Ser.). (ENG.). 656p. (YA). (gr. 9). pap. 10.99 *(978-0-06-232292-0(3)*, HarperTeen) HarperCollins Pubs.
—Wicked. 5th ed. 2008. (Pretty Little Liars Ser.: 5). (ENG.). 320p. (YA). (gr. 9). 17.99 *(978-0-06-156607-3(1)*, HarperTeen) HarperCollins Pubs.
Siegrist, Bonnie. Little Farm down the Lane -Book IV. 2007. pap. 10.99 *(978-1-60034-912-6(9))* Salem Author Services.
Siegrist, Bonnie Bedi. Little Farm down the Lane Book V. 2008. 124p. pap. 11.99 *(978-1-60647-848-6(6))* Salem Author Services.
Silvano, Wendi. Love Is All Around Pennsylvania. Czernichowska, Joanna, illus. 2016. (ENG.). 32p. (J). (-6). 12.99 *(978-1-4926-2954-2(5)*, Sourcebooks Jabberwocky) Sourcebooks, Inc.
—Love Is All Around Pittsburgh. Czernichowska, Joanna, illus. 2016. (ENG.). 32p. (J). (-6). 12.99 *(978-1-4926-2956-6(1)*, Sourcebooks Jabberwocky) Sourcebooks, Inc.
Skurzynski, Gloria. Good-Bye, Billy Radish. 2013. (ENG., Illus.). 152p. (J). (gr. 3-7). pap. 13.99 *(978-1-4814-0158-6(0)*, Simon & Schuster Bks. For Young Readers) Simon & Schuster Bks. For Young Readers.
Smallman, Steve. Santa Is Coming to Pittsburgh. Dunn, Robert, illus. 2013. (ENG.). 32p. (J). (-3). 9.99 *(978-1-4022-8982-8(0)*, Sourcebooks Jabberwocky) Sourcebooks, Inc.
Smith-Ready, Jeri. This Side of Salvation. 2014. (ENG., Illus.). 384p. (YA). (gr. 9). 17.99 *(978-1-4424-3948-1(3)*, Simon Pulse) Simon Pulse.
Smith, William D. Becoming a Superhero: Adventures of an American Superhero. 2008. 128p. per. 13.95 *(978-1-4327-2071-1(6))* Outskirts Pr., Inc.
Sonnenblick, Jordan. Curveball: The Year I Lost My Grip. 304p. 2014. (ENG.). (J). (gr. 7). pap. 9.99 *(978-0-545-32070-2(4)*, Scholastic Paperbacks) 2012. pap. 17.99 *(978-0-545-39311-9(6))* Scholastic, Inc.
—Zen & the Art of Faking It. (ENG.). 272p. (J). (gr. 7-12). 2010. 9.99 *(978-0-439-83709-5(X)*, Scholastic Paperbacks) 2007. 16.99 *(978-0-439-83707-1(3)*, Scholastic Pr.) Scholastic, Inc.
Spinelli, Jerry. Love, Stargirl. 2009. (ENG.). 288p. (YA). (gr. 7). pap. 9.99 *(978-0-375-85644-0(7)*, Ember) Random Hse. Children's Bks.
Stauffer, Sharon. Cornfield Baby: And Other Nature Surprises. 2003. (Illus.). 179p. 8.40 *(978-0-7399-2314-6(5)*, 2344) Rod & Staff Pubs., Inc.
Stef. Be Careful What You Wish For. 2008. 380p. 29.99 *(978-1-4363-5233-8(9))*; pap. 19.99 *(978-1-4363-5232-1(0))* Xlibris Corp.
Sullivan, Paul. Breaker at Dawn. 2010. (J). pap. *(978-0-88092-705-5(4))* Royal Fireworks Publishing Co.
Sully, Katherine. Night-Night Pennsylvania. Kolanovic, Dubravka & Poole, Helen, illus. 2016. (ENG.). 20p. (J). (-1). bds. 9.99 *(978-1-4926-4219-0(3)*, 9781492642190, Sourcebooks Jabberwocky) Sourcebooks, Inc.
Taschek, Karen. The Risen Horse. 2010. (ENG.). 248p. (YA). (gr. 7-18). pap. 15.95 *(978-0-8263-4837-1(8))* Univ. of New Mexico Pr.
Thomas, Kara. The Darkest Corners. (ENG.). (YA). (gr. 9). 2017. 352p. pap. 9.99 ***(978-0-553-52148-1(9)**, Ember)* 2016. 336p. 17.99 *(978-0-553-52145-0(4)*, Delacorte Pr.) Random Hse. Children's Bks.
Vinsh, Aara J. Ben, the Miracle Horse, 1 vol. 2010. 193p. pap. 24.95 *(978-1-4489-7591-4(3))* America Star Bks.
Wagner, Lloyd S. Ghosts at Gettysburg: An Oliver Family Adventure. 2007. 144p. 21.95 *(978-0-595-70995-3(8))*; per. 11.95 *(978-0-595-46877-5(2))* iUniverse, Inc.
Walkup, Jennifer. Second Verse. 2013. 270p. pap. 15.95 *(978-1-935462-87-3(3))*; (ENG.). 200p. (YA). (gr. 7-12). pap. 11.95 *(978-1-935462-85-9(7))* Luminis Bks., Inc.
Weeks, Sarah. Pie. 2013. (ENG.). 192p. (J). (gr. 3-7). pap. 6.99 *(978-0-545-27012-0(X)*, Scholastic Paperbacks) Scholastic, Inc.
Welch, Sheila Kelly. The Shadowed Unicorn. 2011. 192p. (gr. -1). pap. 12.95 *(978-1-4502-6991-9(5))* iUniverse, Inc.
Weston Woods Staff, creator. Crow Call. 2011. 38.75 *(978-0-545-37494-1(4))*; 18.95 *(978-0-545-37493-4(6))* Weston Woods Studios, Inc.
Williams, Carol Lynch & Earl, Cheri Pray. Sweet Secrets in Pennsylvania. Oliphant, Manelle, illus. 2013. (Just in Time Ser.: 2). (ENG.). 152p. (J). (gr. 3-7). pap. 9.95 *(978-1-938301-76-6(5))* Familius LLC.
Wolk, Lauren. Wolf Hollow. 2016. (ENG.). 304p. (J). (gr. 5-7). 16.99 *(978-1-101-99482-5(7)*, Dutton Books for Young Readers) Penguin Young Readers Group.

PENNSYLVANIA—HISTORY

Ammon, Richard. Valley Forge. Farnsworth, Bill, illus. 2004. (ENG.). 32p. (J). (gr. 4-6). tchr. ed. 17.95 *(978-0-8234-1746-9(8))* Holiday Hse., Inc.
Boehm Jerome, Kate. Pittsburgh & the State of Pennsylvania: Cool Stuff Every Kid Should Know. 2011. (Arcadia Kids Ser.). (ENG., Illus.). 48p. (J). (gr. 3-6). pap. 9.99 *(978-1-4396-0095-5(3))* Arcadia Publishing.
Boothroyd, Jennifer. William Penn. 2009. pap. 6.95 *(978-0-8225-6431-7(9))* Lerner Publishing Group.
—William Penn: A Life of Tolerance. 2006. (Pull Ahead Bks.). (Illus.). 32p. (J). (gr. 3-7). lib. bdg. 22.60 *(978-0-8225-6387-7(8)*, Lerner Pubns.) Lerner Publishing Group.
Epstein, Brad M. Pittsburgh Steelers 101. 2010. (ENG., Illus.). 24p. (J). bds. *(978-1-60730-124-0(5)*, 101 Bk.) Michaelson Entertainment.
Evdokimoff, Natasha. Pennsylvania. 2011. (Guide to American States Ser.). (Illus.). 48p. (YA). (gr. 3-6). 29.99 *(978-1-61690-810-2(6))* Weigl Pubs., Inc.
—Pennsylvania: The Keystone State. 2016. (J). *(978-1-4896-4929-4(8))* Weigl Pubs., Inc.
Ferut, Michael. Gettysburg. 2014. (Scariest Places on Earth Ser.). (ENG., Illus.). 24p. (J). (gr. 3-7). lib. bdg. 25.95 *(978-1-60014-995-5(2)*, Torque Bks.) Bellwether Media.
Figley, Marty Rhodes. Who Was William Penn? And Other Questions about the Founding of Pennsylvania. 2012. (Six Questions of American History Ser.). (ENG.). 48p. (gr. 4-6). pap. 56.72 *(978-0-7613-9241-5(6))*; pap. 9.95 *(978-0-7613-8571-4(1))*; (Illus.). lib. bdg. 30.60 *(978-0-7613-5328-7(3))* Lerner Publishing Group.
Fox, Arthur B. Pittsburgh During the American Civil War 1860-1865. 2004. (Illus.). 236p. pap. 29.95 *(978-0-9760563-0-0(5)*, 7526S) Mechling Bookbindery.
Friesen, Helen Lepp. Pennsylvania: The Keystone State. 2012. (J). *(978-1-61913-395-2(4))*; pap. *(978-1-61913-396-9(2))* Weigl Pubs., Inc.
Galchefski, Christina, compiled by. Coloring the Pieces of Luzerne County 2003. (Illus.). 36p. (J). 4.00 *(978-0-937537-12-1(8))* Wyoming Historical & Geological Society.
Gamble, Adam & Jasper, Mark. Good Night Pennsylvania. 2013. (Good Night Our World Ser.). (ENG., Illus.). 20p. (J). (— 1). bds. 9.95 *(978-1-60219-074-0(7))* Good Night Bks.
Gow, Mary. Johnstown Flood: The Day the Dam Burst. 2003. (American Disasters Ser.). (Illus.). 48p. (J). (gr. 4-10). lib. bdg. 25.27 *(978-0-7660-2109-9(2))* Enslow Pubs., Inc.
Grey, Rochelle, text. My RiverPlace on the Schuylkill Coloring Book. 2006. (Illus.). 12p. (J). *(978-0-9785538-0-7(2))* RiverPlace Development Corp.
Gunderson, Jessica. Pennsylvania. 2009. (This Land Called America Ser.). 32p. (YA). (gr. 3-6). 19.95 *(978-1-58341-791-1(5))* Creative Co., The.
Hart, Joyce & Hantula, Richard. Pennsylvania. 2nd rev. ed. 2010. (It's My State! Ser.). 80p. (gr. 3-18). lib. bdg. 31.36 *(978-0-76870-058-5(5))* Marshall Cavendish Corp.
Hengel, Katherine. Rupert & the Liberty Bell: A Story about Pennsylvania, 1 vol. Doucet, Bob, illus. 2010. (Fact & Fable: State Stories Set 2 Ser.). (ENG.). 24p. (J). (gr. -1-3). 25.65 *(978-1-60453-926-4(7))* ABDO Publishing Co.
Hinman, Bonnie. Pennsylvania: William Penn & the City of Brotherly Love. 2006. (Building America Ser.). (Illus.). 48p. (J). (gr. 3-7). lib. bdg. 29.95 *(978-1-58415-463-1(2))* Mitchell Lane Pubs., Inc.

Jacobson, Ryan. William Penn: Founder of Pennsylvania. Stiles, Tim, illus. 2006. (Graphic Biographies Ser.). (ENG.). 32p. (gr. 3-4). 30.65 *(978-0-7368-6501-2(2),* Graphic Library) Capstone Press of Coughlan Cos.

Jeffrey, Gary. George Washington & the Winter at Valley Forge. 2011. (Graphic Heroes of the American Revolution Ser.). 24p. (J). (gr. 3-8). pap. 8.15 *(978-1-4339-6014-7(1),* Gareth Stevens Learning Library); (Illus.). lib. bdg. 23.95 *(978-1-4339-6174-8(1))* Stevens, Gareth Publishing LLLP.

Jerome, Kate B. Lucky to Live in Pennsylvania. 2017. (Arcadia Kids Ser.). (ENG., Illus.). 32p. (J). 16.99 ***(978-0-7385-2772-7(6))*** Arcadia Publishing.

—The Wise Animal Handbook Pennsylvania. 2017. (Arcadia Kids Ser.). (ENG., Illus.). 32p. (J). 16.99 ***(978-0-7385-2840-3(4))*** Arcadia Publishing.

Kurtz, Jane. Celebrating Pennsylvania: 50 States to Celebrate. Canga, C. B., illus. 2015. (Green Light Readers Level 3 Ser.). (ENG.). 40p. (J). (gr. 1-4). 12.99 *(978-0-544-41972-8(3),* HMH Books For Young Readers) Houghton Mifflin Harcourt Publishing Co.

Leathers, Daniel. The Johnstown Flood 1889. 2007. (Natural Disasters Ser.). (Illus.). 32p. (J). (gr. 1-4). lib. bdg. 25.70 *(978-1-58415-570-6(1))* Mitchell Lane Pubs., Inc.

Levy, Janey. William Penn: Shaping a Nation. 2009. (Real Life Readers Ser.). 32p. (ENG., Illus.). (J). (gr. 5-6). pap. 10.00 *(978-1-4358-0195-0(4),* 1291824); (gr. 5-5). 47.90 *(978-1-61511-376-7(2));* (J). (gr. 4-6). lib. bdg. 25.25 *(978-1-4358-3016-5(4));* (Illus.). (J). 60.00 *(978-1-4358-0196-7(2),* 1291824) Rosen Publishing Group, Inc., The. (PowerKids Pr.).

Lusted, Marcia Amidon. Pennsylvania: The Keystone State. 2009. (Our Amazing States Ser.). (Illus.). 24p. (J). lib. bdg. 22.60 *(978-1-4042-8124-0(X),* 1300536, PowerKids Pr.) Rosen Publishing Group, Inc., The.

—The Three Mile Island Nuclear Disaster, 1 vol. 2012. (Essential Events Set 8 Ser.). (ENG.). 112p. (J). (gr. 6-12). lib. bdg. 35.64 *(978-1-61783-311-3(8))* ABDO Publishing Co.

Marciniak, Kristin. What's Great about Pennsylvania? 2014. (Our Great States Ser.). (Illus.). 32p. (gr. 2-5). (J). lib. bdg. 26.60 *(978-1-4677-3334-2(2),* Lerner Pubns.); (ENG., pap. 7.95 *(978-1-4677-4526-0(X))* Lerner Publishing Group.

Marsh, Carole. Exploring Pennsylvania Through Project-Based Learning: Geography, History, Government, Economics & More. 2016. (Pennsylvania Experience Ser.). (ENG.). (J). pap. 9.99 *(978-0-635-12362-6(2))* Gallopade International.

—Pennsylvania History Projects: 30 Cool, Activities, Crafts, Experiments & More for Kids to Do to Learn about Your State! 2003. (Pennsylvania Experience Ser.). 32p. (gr. k-5). pap. 5.95 *(978-0-635-01807-6(1),* Marsh, Carole Bks.) Gallopade International.

Martin, Iain C. Gettysburg: The True Account of Two Young Heroes in the Greatest Battle of the Civil War. 2013. (ENG., Illus.). 208p. (YA). (gr. 6-12). 16.95 *(978-1-62087-532-2(2),* 620532, Sky Pony Pr.) Skyhorse Publishing Co., Inc.

McHugh, Erin. Pennsylvania. Schrier, Alfred, illus. 2010. (ENG.). 52p. (J). (gr. -1-17). 9.95 *(978-1-57912-821-0(1),* 81821, Black Dog & Leventhal Pubs. Inc.) Hachette Bks.

Meachen Rau, Dana & Brown, Jonatha A. Pennsylvania. 2005. (Portraits of the States Ser.). (Illus.). 32p. (gr. 2-6). pap. 10.50 *(978-0-8368-4652-2(4));* lib. bdg. 26.00 *(978-0-8368-4633-1(8))* Stevens, Gareth Publishing LLLP. (Gareth Stevens Learning Library).

Micklos, John, Jr. Exploring the Pennsylvania Colony. 2016. (Exploring the 13 Colonies Ser.). (ENG., Illus.). 48p. (gr. 3-4). lib. bdg. 31.99 *(978-1-5157-2232-8(5))* Capstone Press of Coughlan Cos.

Micklos, John. Washington's Crossing the Delaware & the Winter at Valley Forge—Through Primary Sources. 2013. (American Revolution Through Primary Sources Ser.). 48p. (J). (gr. 4-10). pap. 8.95 *(978-1-4644-0190-9(X))* Enslow Pubs., Inc.

Mis, Melody S. The Colony of Pennsylvania: A Primary Source History. (Primary Source Library of the Thirteen Colonies & the Lost Colony Ser.). 24p. (gr. 3-4). 2009. 42.50 *(978-1-60854-153-9(3))* 2006. (Illus.). (J). lib. bdg. 22.60 *(978-1-4042-3437-6(3))* Rosen Publishing Group, Inc., The. (PowerKids Pr.).

Moore, Noreen. Reaching Tidewater: Life on the Delaware Canal. 2004. (Illus.). v, 92p. (J). pap. 5.95 *(978-1-57249-358-2(5),* White Mane Kids) White Mane Publishing Co., Inc.

Mountjoy, Shane. Philadelphia. 2007. (Colonial Settlements in America Ser.). (Illus.). 100p. (YA). (gr. 5-9). lib. bdg. 30.00 *(978-0-7910-9336-8(0))* Facts On File, Inc.

Murphy, Jim. An American Plague: The True & Terrifying Story of the Yellow Fever Epidemic Of 1793. 2003. (ENG., Illus.). 176p. (J). (gr. 5-7). tchr. ed. 21.99 *(978-0-395-77608-7(2))* Houghton Mifflin Harcourt Publishing Co.

Noble, Trinka Hakes. Little Pennsylvania Board Book. Brett, Jeannie, illus. 2010. (My Little State Ser.). (ENG.). 22p. (J). 9.95 *(978-1-58536-506-7(8))* Sleeping Bear Pr.

Prentzas, G. S. The Colony of Pennsylvania. 2006. (Primary Sources of the Thirteen Colonies & the Lost Colony Ser.). (ENG., Illus.). 64p. (gr. 4-8). per. 12.95 *(978-1-4042-0673-1(6))* Rosen Publishing Group, Inc., The.

—A Primary Source History of the Colony of Pennsylvania. (Primary Sources of the Thirteen Colonies & the Lost Colony Ser.). 64p. 2009. (gr. 5-8). 58.50 *(978-1-60851-887-6(6))* 2006. (Illus.). (YA). (gr. 4-7). lib. bdg. 31.95 *(978-1-4042-0433-1(4))* Rosen Publishing Group, Inc., The.

Rajczak, Michael. Haunted! Gettysburg. 2013. 32p. (J). (gr. 3-6). 26.60 *(978-1-4339-9248-3(5));* pap. 63.00 *(978-1-4339-9250-6(7));* pap. 10.50 *(978-1-4339-9249-0(3))* Stevens, Gareth Publishing LLLP.

Richards, Marlee. The Johnstown Flood: Core Events of Deadly Disaster, 1 vol. 2014. (What Went Wrong? Ser.). (ENG.). 32p. (gr. 3-4). pap. 7.95 *(978-1-4765-5131-9(6));* lib. bdg. 27.32 *(978-1-4765-4182-2(5))* Capstone Press of Coughlan Cos. (Fact Finders).

Robinson, Hilda & Kunkel, Jeff. Didn't We Have Fun! Robinson, Hilda, illus. 2012. (Illus.). 48p. (J). 19.95 *(978-1-933987-17-0(0),* Crickhollow Bks.) Great Lakes Literary, LLC.

Robinson, Tom. Pittsburgh Steelers, 1 vol. 2010. (Inside the NFL Ser.). (ENG.). 48p. (YA). (gr. 3-6). lib. bdg. 32.79 *(978-1-61714-025-9(2))* ABDO Publishing Co.

Schiel, Katy. The Whiskey Rebellion: An Early Challenge to America's New Government. (Life in the New American Nation Ser.). 32p. 2009. (gr. 4-4). 47.90 *(978-1-61514-289-7(4))* 2004. (ENG., Illus.). (gr. 5-8). pap. 10.00 *(978-0-8239-4262-6(7))* Rosen Publishing Group, Inc., The.

Somervill, Barbara A. Pennsylvania (Revised Edition) 2014. (America the Beautiful, Third Ser. (Revised Edition) Ser.). (ENG., Illus.). 144p. (J). lib. bdg. 40.00 *(978-0-531-28289-2(9))* Scholastic Library Publishing.

Spinelli, Jerry. Knots in My Yo-Yo Strong. Gentieu, Penny, photos by. 2014. (Illus.). 158p. pap. 11.00 *(978-1-61003-375-6(2))* Center for the Collaborative Classroom.

Swain, Gwenyth. Freedom Seeker: A Story about William Penn. Harvey, Lisa, illus. 2003. (Creative Minds Biographies Ser.). 64p. (J). 22.60 *(978-1-57505-176-5(1));* (ENG.). (gr. 4-8). pap. 8.95 *(978-0-87614-931-7(X))* Lerner Publishing Group. (Carolrhoda Bks.).

Tieck, Sarah. Pennsylvania, 1 vol. 2012. (Explore the United States Ser.). (ENG.). 32p. (J). (gr. 2-5). lib. bdg. 28.50 *(978-1-61783-376-2(2),* Big Buddy Bks.) ABDO Publishing Co.

Trumbauer, Lisa. Pennsylvania, 1620-1776. 2005. (National Geographic Voices from ColonialAmerica Ser.). (ENG., Illus.). 112p. (J). (gr. 5-9). 21.95 *(978-0-7922-6596-2(3),* National Geographic Children's Bks.) National Geographic Society.

Trumbauer, Lisa. Pennsylvania, 1620-1776. 2006. (National Geographic Voices from ColonialAmerica Ser.). (ENG., Illus.). 112p. (J). (gr. 5-9). 32.90 *(978-0-7922-6854-3(7),* National Geographic Children's Bks.) National Geographic Society.

Varonka, Steve. Hard Coal Times Vol. 3: Early Coal Transportation. 2004. (Illus.). 24p. (YA). 4.72 *(978-0-9709630-5-5(X))* Coal Hole Productions.

Waring, Kerry Jones, et al. Pennsylvania. 2015. lib. bdg. *(978-1-62712-766-0(6));* (ENG., Illus.). 80p. (J). (gr. 4-4). 34.21 *(978-1-5026-0015-8(3))* Cavendish Square Publishing.

Way, Jennifer. Pennsylvania. 2009. (Bilingual Library of the United States of America Ser.). (ENG & SPA.). 32p. (gr. 2-2). 47.90 *(978-1-60853-382-4(4),* Editorial Buenas Letras) Rosen Publishing Group, Inc., The.

Wheeler, Jill C. Pennsylvania, 1 vol. 2009. (United States Ser.). (ENG., Illus.). 48p. (YA). (gr. 2-5). 27.07 *(978-1-60453-673-7(X))* ABDO Publishing Co.

Ziff, John. Northeast: New Jersey, New York, Pennsylvania, Vol. 19. 2015. (Let's Explore the States Ser.). (Illus.). 64p. (J). (gr. 5). 23.95 *(978-1-4222-3329-0(4))* Mason Crest.

PENNSYLVANIA DUTCH

Williamson, Chet. Pennsylvania Dutch Alphabet, 1 vol. Stacy, Alan, illus. 2007. (ENG.). 32p. (J). (gr. k-3). 16.99 *(978-1-58980-496-8(1))* Pelican Publishing Co., Inc.

PENNSYLVANIA GERMANS

see Pennsylvania Dutch

PENOLOGY

see Prisons

PEOPLE WITH DISABILITIES

see also People with Mental Disabilities; Sick

Adams, Colleen. The Courage of Helen Keller. 2009. (Reading Room Collection 2 Ser.). 24p. (gr. 3-4). 42.50 *(978-1-60851-992-7(9),* PowerKids Pr.) Rosen Publishing Group, Inc., The.

Adler, David A. Helen Keller. Wallner, John C. & Wallner, John, illus. 2003. (ENG.). 32p. (J). (gr. k-3). tchr. ed. 14.95 *(978-0-8234-1606-6(2))* Holiday Hse., Inc.

Andrysek, Jan & Mihailidis, Alex. New Hands, New Life: Robots, Prostheses & Innovation. 2017. (ENG., Illus.). 64p. (J). (gr. 4-7). 19.95 ***(978-1-77085-969-2(1),*** 9781770859692); pap. 9.95 ***(978-1-77085-991-3(8),*** 9781770859913) Firefly Bks., Ltd.

Apel, Melanie Ann. Let's Talk about Being in a Wheelchair. 2009. (Let's Talk Library). 24p. (gr. 2-3). 42.50 *(978-1-60853-438-8(3),* PowerKids Pr.) Rosen Publishing Group, Inc., The.

Barasch, Lynne. Knockin' on Wood: Starring Peg Leg Bates. 2004. (ENG., Illus.). 32p. (J). 16.95 *(978-1-58430-170-7(8))* Lee & Low Bks., Inc.

Basinger, Carol. Everything You Need to Know about Deafness. 2005. (Need to Know Library). (Illus.). 64p. (J). (gr. 7-12). lib. bdg. 31.95 *(978-0-8239-3165-1(X),* NTDEAF) Rosen Publishing Group, Inc., The.

Beale, Brian A. My Name Is Colin: ... & this Is Who I Am. 2010. 24p. 17.95 *(978-1-4520-3298-6(X))* AuthorHouse.

Bender, Lionel. Explaining Blindness. 2009. (Explaining... Ser.). 48p. (gr. 7-12). 37.10 *(978-1-59920-310-2(3))* Black Rabbit Bks.

Beyer, Mark. Stevie Wonder. 2009. (Rock & Roll Hall of Famers Ser.). 112p. (gr. 5-8). 63.90 *(978-1-60852-475-4(2),* Rosen Reference) Rosen Publishing Group, Inc., The.

Borrelli, Kristin K. Sometimes I Make Noises. 2012. 24p. (-18). pap. 24.95 *(978-1-4626-9527-0(2))* America Star Bks.

Brocker, Susan. Vision Without Sight: Human Capabilities. 2007. (Shockwave: Life Science & Medicine Ser.). (ENG., Illus.). 36p. (J). (gr. 4-6). lib. bdg. 25.00 *(978-0-531-17769-3(6),* Children's Pr.) Scholastic Library Publishing.

Burcaw, Shane. Laughing at My Nightmare. 2014. (ENG., Illus.). 256p. (YA). (gr. 9). 17.99 *(978-1-62672-007-7(X),* 9781626720077) Roaring Brook Pr.

Busic, Valerie. Jason's First Day. OI Foundation, ed. Meyers, Jeff, illus. Lt. ed. 2004. 48p. per. 8.50 *(978-0-9642189-4-9(1))* Osteogenesis Imperfecta Foundation.

Butler, Darren J. Helen Keller: Leader Without Sight or Sound. 2012. (Illus.). 108p. (J). pap. *(978-1-59421-083-9(7))* Seacoast Publishing, Inc.

Carillo, Christina Martin. Come Smile with Me. 2011. 40p. pap. 24.95 *(978-1-4560-8297-0(3))* America Star Bks.

Carolina Canines for Service & Nowak, Pat. A Job for Arabella. Baumgardner, Mary Alice, illus. 2007. 56p. (J). per. *(978-0-9800070-0-8(3))* Carolina Canines for Service Inc.

Derke, Connie Butterfield. Mommy Has 1 Foot: Learning about Numbers - Learning about People. Smith, Tracy, illus. 2003. (Kayla's Learning Books). 24p. (J). (gr. 1-6). pap. 5.95 *(978-0-9747063-0-6(2))* Derke, Connie.

Devillier, Christy. Helen Keller, 1 vol. 2004. (First Biographies Set Iv Ser.). (ENG., Illus.). 32p. (gr. k-4). 27.07 *(978-1-59197-514-4(X),* Buddy Bks.) ABDO Publishing Co.

Dwight, Laura. Brothers & Sisters, 1 vol. (ENG., Illus.). 32p. (J). 2012. pap. 7.95 *(978-1-59572-364-2(1))* 2005. (gr. -1-3). 15.95 *(978-1-887734-80-6(5))* Star Bright Bks., Inc.

Esherick, Joan. Breaking down Barriers: Youth with Physical Challenges. 2003. (Youth with Special Needs Ser.). (Illus.). 127p. (YA). (gr. 7). pap. 14.95 *(978-1-4222-0420-7(0))* Mason Crest.

—Guaranteed Rights: The Legislation That Protects Youths with Special Needs. 2003. (Youth with Special Needs Ser.). (Illus.). 127p. (YA). (gr. 7). pap. 14.95 *(978-1-4222-0423-8(5))* Mason Crest.

—The Journey Toward Recovery: Youth with Brain Injury. 2003. (Youth with Special Needs Ser.). (Illus.). 127p. (YA). (gr. 7). pap. 14.95 *(978-1-4222-0425-2(1))* Mason Crest.

—The Laws That Protect Youth with Special Needs. Albers, Lisa et al, eds. 2014. (Living with a Special Need Ser.: 16). 128p. (J). (gr. 7-18). 25.95 *(978-1-4222-3039-8(2))* Mason Crest.

—Physical Challenges. Albers, Lisa et al, eds. 2014. (Living with a Special Need Ser.: 16). 128p. (J). (gr. 7-18). 25.95 *(978-1-4222-3041-1(4))* Mason Crest.

Flath, Camden. Kids with Special Needs: IDEA (Individuals with Disabilities Education Act), 11 vols., Set. Incl. Finding My Voice: Kids with Speech Impairment. Stewart, Sheila. (Illus.). (gr. 5-18). lib. bdg. 19.95 *(978-1-4222-1722-1(1));* Hidden Child: Kids with Autism. Stewart, Sheila. (Illus.). (gr. 5-18). lib. bdg. 19.95 *(978-1-4222-1724-5(8));* I Can Do It! Kids with Physical Challenges. Stewart, Sheila. (Illus.). (gr. 5-18). lib. bdg. 19.95 *(978-1-4222-1723-8(X));* Listening with Your Eyes: Kids Who Are Deaf & Hard of Hearing. Stewart, Sheila. (gr. 5-18). lib. bdg. 19.95 *(978-1-4222-1717-7(5));* My Name Is Not Slow: Kids with Intellectual Disabilities. Stewart, Sheila. (gr. 5-18). lib. bdg. 19.95 *(978-1-4222-1718-4(3));* Seeing with Your Fingers: Kids with Blindness & Visual Impairment. Stewart, Sheila. (Illus.). (gr. 7-18). lib. bdg. 19.95 *(978-1-4222-1716-0(7));* Sick All the Time: Kids with Chronic Illness. Chastain, Zachary. (gr. 5-18). lib. bdg. 19.95 *(978-1-4222-1719-1(1));* Speed Racer: Kids with Attention-Deficit/Hyperactivity Disorder. Stewart, Sheila. (gr. 5-18). lib. bdg. 19.95 *(978-1-4222-1721-4(3));* What's Wrong with My Brain? Kids with Brain Injury. Stewart, Sheila. (gr. 5-18). lib. bdg. 19.95 *(978-1-4222-1725-2(6));* Why Can't I Learn Like Everyone Else? Kids with Learning Disabilities. Stewart, Sheila. (gr. 5-18). lib. bdg. 19.95 *(978-1-4222-1726-9(4));* (YA). 2010. (Illus.). 48p. 2011. Set lib. bdg. 219.45 *(978-1-4222-1727-6(2))* Mason Crest.

Fukumoto, Jan. It's Hard Not to Stare: Helping Children Understand Disabilities. Huff, Tim, illus. 2013. 38p. pap. *(978-1-927355-28-2(1))* BayRidge Bks.

Gibson, Karen Bush. Ways to Help Children with Disabilities: A Guide to Giving Back. 2010. (How to Help Ser.). (Illus.). 48p. (J). (gr. 4-8). lib. bdg. 29.95 *(978-1-58415-916-2(2))* Mitchell Lane Pubs., Inc.

Gold, Susan Dudley. Americans with Disabilities ACT. 2010. (Landmark Legislation Ser.). 128p. (YA). (gr. 7-12). 39.93 *(978-1-60870-039-4(9))* Marshall Cavendish Corp.

Goldish, Meish. Everything You Need to Know about Dyslexia. 2009. (Need to Know Library). 64p. (gr. 5-5). 58.50 *(978-1-60854-066-2(9))* Rosen Publishing Group, Inc., The.

—Surf Dog Miracles. 2012. (Dog Heroes Ser.). 32p. (J). (gr. 2-7). lib. bdg. 25.27 *(978-1-61772-577-7(3))* Bearport Publishing Co., Inc.

Green, Joanne. The Story of Thumper the Cleft-Affected Bunny. 2008. 56p. pap. *(978-1-897512-14-2(7))* Saga Bks.

Hale, Natalie. Oh, Brother! Growing up with a Special Needs Sibling. Sternberg, Kate, tr. Sternberg, Kate, illus. 2004. 48p. (J). 14.95 *(978-1-59147-060-1(9));* pap. 9.95 *(978-1-59147-061-8(7))* American Psychological Assn. (Magination Pr.).

Haugen, David M. Disabilities. Greenhaven Press Editors & Gale Editors, eds. 2014. (Teen Rights & Freedoms Ser.). (ENG., Illus.). 176p. (gr. 10-12). lib. bdg. 42.00 *(978-0-7377-6995-1(5),* Greenhaven Pr., Inc.) Cengage Gale.

Haugen, Hayley Mitchell. People with Disabilities. 2011. (Social Issues Firsthand Ser.). 192p. (J). lib. bdg. 33.75 *(978-0-7377-4798-0(6),* Greenhaven Pr., Inc.) Cengage Gale.

Hayes, Amy. Disability Rights Movement. 2016. (Civic Participation: Working for Civil Rights Ser.). 00032p. (J). (gr. 5-5). 26.25 *(978-1-4994-2850-6(2));* pap. 10.00 *(978-1-4994-2679-3(8))* Rosen Publishing Group, Inc., The. (PowerKids Pr.).

Health Physically Challenged. (J). *(978-0-8136-9354-5(3))* Modern Curriculum Pr.

Hoge, Robert. Ugly. Robinson, Keith, illus. 2016. (ENG.). 208p. (J). (gr. 3-7). 16.99 *(978-0-425-28775-0(0),* Viking Books for Young Readers) Penguin Young Readers Group.

Horan, Mark, et al. Disabilities & Disorders in Literature for Youth: A Selective Annotated Bibliography for K-12. 2009. (Literature for Youth Ser.: 12). (ENG.). 400p. 95.00 *(978-0-8108-5977-7(7))* Scarecrow Pr., Inc.

Hucks, Doris, I Am a Shining Star. 2011. 36p. pap. 18.00 *(978-1-4634-1916-5(3))* AuthorHouse.

Jeffrey, Laura S. All about Braille: Reading by Touch. 2004. (Transportation & Communication Ser.). (Illus.). 48p. (J). lib. bdg. 25.27 *(978-0-7660-2184-6(X))* Enslow Pubs., Inc.

Johnson, Nerissa & Parra, Angelo. Teen Reflections, Then & Now. 2011. (Readers' & Writers' Genre Workshop Ser.). (YA). pap. *(978-1-4509-3025-3(5))* Benchmark Education Co.

Jones, Phill. Disability Rights. 2012. (J). *(978-1-61753-042-5(5),* Chelsea Hse.) Facts On File, Inc.

Kennedy, Leola. There's a Reason. 2012. 82p. pap. *(978-1-77069-445-3(5))* Word Alive Pr.

Klein, Steve. The Power of Early Speed. 2005. (Elements of Handicapping Ser.). (ENG., Illus.). 144p. per. 14.95 *(978-1-932910-98-8(0))* Daily Racing Form.

Kluth, Paula & Schwarz, Patrick. Pedro's Whale, 1 vol. 2010. (ENG., Illus.). 32p. (J). 18.95 *(978-1-59857-160-8(5))* Brookes Publishing.

Kovatch, Sarah. Special Helpers. 2005. (Illus.). 16p. (J). *(978-0-7367-2854-6(6))* Zaner-Bloser, Inc.

Kurtz Kingsley, Linda. Blue Skies for Lupe. 2015. (ENG., Illus.). 32p. (J). pap. *(978-1-60613-271-5(7))* Woodbine Hse.

Larabie, Gayle. Is My Dad Still My Dad? 2005. (Illus.). 32p. (J). *(978-1-55306-873-0(4))* Essence Publishing.

Leavitt, Amie Jane. Helping People with Disabilities & Special Needs Through Service Learning, 1 vol. 2015. (ENG., Illus.). 80p. (J). 34.60 *(978-1-4777-7965-1(5),* Rosen Young Adult) Rosen Publishing Group, Inc., The.

Levete, Sarah. Explaining Deafness. 2009. (Explaining... Ser.). 48p. (gr. 7-12). 37.10 *(978-1-59920-313-3(8))* Black Rabbit Bks.

Lewis, Wendy. Sabrina, the Girl with a Hole in Her Heart. 2011. 16.95 *(978-0-615-47819-7(0))* Two Dolphins Publishing Group.

Libal, Autumn. My Name Isn't Slow: Youth with Mental Retardation. 2003. (Youth with Special Needs Ser.). (Illus.). 127p. (YA). (gr. 7). pap. 14.95 *(978-1-4222-0426-9(X))* Mason Crest.

—The Ocean Inside: Youth Who Are Deaf & Hard of Hearing. 2003. (Youth with Special Needs Ser.). (Illus.). 127p. (YA). (gr. -1). pap. 14.95 *(978-1-4222-0427-6(8))* Mason Crest.

Libal, Joyce. Finding My Voice: Youth with Speech Impairment. 2003. (Youth with Special Needs Ser.). (Illus.). 127p. (YA). pap. 14.95 *(978-1-4222-0422-1(7))* Mason Crest.

Like Me Like You. 2005. (Like Me Like You Ser.). (Illus.). 32p. (gr. 2-4). 69.00 *(978-0-7910-8462-5(0),* Chelsea Hse.) Facts On File, Inc.

MacRae, Sloan. Respecting the Contributions of Disabled Americans. 2012. (Stop Bullying Now! Ser.). (ENG., Illus.). 24p. (J). (gr. 3-6). pap. 8.25 *(978-1-4488-7518-4(8));* lib. bdg. 22.60 *(978-1-4488-7445-3(9))* Rosen Publishing Group, Inc., The. (PowerKids Pr.).

Manson, Ainslie. Boy in Motion: Rick Hansen's Story. Benoit, Renné, illus. 2009. (ENG.). 48p. (J). (gr. k-3). pap. 12.00 *(978-1-55365-427-8(7))* Greystone Books Ltd. CAN. Dist: Publishers Group West (PGW).

Marks, Elizabeth. Growing Together Across the Autism Spectrum: A Kid's Guide to Living with, Learning from, & Loving a Parent with Autism Spectrum Disorder. Marks, Elizabeth, illus. 2015. (ENG., Illus.). 47p. (J). pap. 19.95 *(978-1-942197-08-9(X))* Autism Asperger Publishing Co.

Martin, Mabel. Talking with Hands. Witmer, Ruth, illus. 2007. (Little Jewel Book Ser.). 24p. (J). (gr. 2). pap. 2.70 *(978-0-7399-2394-8(3))* Rod & Staff Pubs., Inc.

Mcclelland, Grace. The Gift of Grace. 2012. (ENG.). (J). pap. 20.00 *(978-1-4507-2003-8(X))* Independent Pub.

McCurry, Chris & Waddington, Emma. Why Are People Different Colors? Big Issues for Little People Around Identity & Diversity. Thomas, Louis, illus. 2016. (Life & Soul Library). (ENG.). 32p. (J). (gr. -1-3). 12.99 *(978-1-84780-864-6(6),* Frances Lincoln Children's Bks.) Quarto Publishing Group UK GBR. Dist: Hachette Bk. Group.

McIntosh, Kenneth & Walker, Ida. Youth with Cultural/Language Differences: Interpreting an Alien World. 2009. (Helping Youth with Mental, Physical, & Social Challenges Ser.). (Illus.). 128p. (YA). (gr. 7-18). lib. bdg. 24.95 *(978-1-4222-0141-1(4))* Mason Crest.

McNeese, Tim. Disability Rights Movement, 1 vol. 2013. (Essential Library of Social Change Ser.). (ENG.). 112p. (J). (gr. 6-12). lib. bdg. 35.64 *(978-1-61783-886-6(1),* Essential Library) ABDO Publishing Co.

Mecum, Shelly & Chun, Peggy. Watercolor Cat. 2007. 48p. 14.95 *(978-1-56647-838-0(3))* Mutual Publishing LLC.

Meyer, D J. Sibling Slam Book. 2005. (ENG., Illus.). 152p. pap. 15.95 *(978-1-890627-52-2(6))* Woodbine Hse.

Meyer, Donald J. & Vadasy, Patricia. Living with a Brother or Sister with Special Needs: A Book for Sibs. 2nd exp. rev. ed. 2003. (ENG., Illus.). 144p. (C). (gr. -1-18). pap. 24.95 *(978-0-295-97547-4(4))* Univ. of Washington Pr.

Mikayla. Our Friend Mikayla. Resh, Kimberly, ed. 2007. (Illus.). 48p. (J). (gr. k-3). 14.95 *(978-1-4243-0734-0(1))* Independent Publisher Services.

Miller, Vivian. Grandma's Mercedes. 2010. 36p. pap. 15.49 *(978-1-4520-1710-5(7))* AuthorHouse.

Moore-Mallinos, Jennifer & Roca, Nuria. My Brother Is Autistic. Fabrega, Marta, illus. 2008. (Let's Talk about It Bks.). (ENG.). 32p. (J). (gr. -1-2). pap. 7.99 *(978-0-7641-4044-0(2))* Barron's Educational Series, Inc.

—My Friend Has down Syndrome. Fabrega, Marta, illus. 2008. (Let's Talk about It Ser.). (ENG.). 32p. (J). (gr. -1-2). pap. 7.99 *(978-0-7641-4076-1(0))* Barron's Educational Series, Inc.

Moss, Wendy L. & Taddonio, Susan A. The Survival Guide for Kids with Physical Disabilities & Challenges. 2015. (ENG., Illus.). 128p. (J). (gr. 3-8). pap. 14.99 *(978-1-63198-033-6(5))* Free Spirit Publishing, Inc.

Nelid, Piper. No One Is Like Sarah, 01 vols., 1. 2016. (Rosen REAL Readers: Social Studies Nonfiction / Fiction: Family, Community, & the World Ser.). (ENG.). 8p. (J). pap. 5.46 *(978-1-5081-1665-3(2),* Rosen Classroom) Rosen Publishing Group, Inc., The.

Nichols, Susan. Confronting Ableism. 2017. (J). pap. ***(978-1-5383-8160-1(5))*** Rosen Publishing Group, Inc., The.

Olin, Nicki. God Made Me Special, Just Like You! 2012. 28p. pap. 12.95 *(978-1-61244-061-3(4))* Halo Publishing International.

Parker, Vic. Overcoming Personal Challenges, 1 vol. 2012. (Kids Making a Difference Ser.). (ENG.). 48p. (gr. 3-5). lib. bdg. 32.65 *(978-1-4329-6503-7(4),* NA-h) Heinemann-Raintree.

Perron, Brigitte. I'm a Champ. 2010. 32p. 14.95 *(978-1-4269-1176-7(9))* Trafford Publishing.

—Je suis Grand. 2010. (FRE.). 36p. 16.95 *(978-1-4269-1173-6(4))* Trafford Publishing.

—Je Suis un Vainqueur. 2010. (FRE.). 32p. pap. 14.95 *(978-1-4269-1153-8(X))* Trafford Publishing.

Phillips, Karen, ed. What about You? 2009. (ENG., Illus.). 50p. (J). (gr. 3). 16.95 *(978-1-59174-612-6(4))* Klutz.

Poole, H. W. Disability & Families, Vol. 12. 2016. (Families Today Ser.). (Illus.). 48p. (J). (gr. 5). 20.95 *(978-1-4222-3614-7(5))* Mason Crest.

Pope, Ellen Dittman. Friends with a Difference. Dixon, Carol, illus. 2009. (J). *(978-0-929915-92-0(5))* Headline Bks., Inc.

Ratto, Linda Lee. (dis) Ability. 2004. (YA). per. 16.95 *(978-0-9748508-2-5(9))* Power Pr.

Rouss, Sylvia A. A Circle of Smiles: A Story about Beit Issie Shapiro, Israel's Leading Organization in the Field of Disability. 2010. (J). pap. *(978-0-9829273-1-1(2))* IGI Pr.

Rue, Nancy N. Lucy Out of Bounds, 1 vol. 2016. (Faithgirlz / a Lucy Novel Ser.). (ENG.). 224p. (J). pap. 7.99 *(978-0-310-75505-0(0))* Zonderkidz.

Sabin, Ellen. The Special Needs Acceptance Book: Being a Friend to Someone with Special Needs. 2007. (Illus.). 64p. (J). 17.95 *(978-0-9759868-5-1(6))* Watering Can.

Sabin, Ellen & Driscoll, Patricia. The Healing Heroes Book: Braving the Changes When Someone You Love Is Wounded in Service. 2012. (ENG., Illus.). 64p. (J). spiral bd. 19.95 *(978-0-9826416-0-6(5))* Watering Can.

Santomauro, Josie. You Are Special Too: A Book for Brothers & Sisters of Children Diagnosed with Asperger Syndrome. Marino, Carla, illus. 2009. (ENG.). 32p. (C). pap. 9.95 *(978-1-84310-656-2(6),* 4742) Kingsley, Jessica Pubs. GBR. Dist: Macmillan Distribution Ltd.

Schaefer, Lola M. Some Kids Are Blind. Saunders-Smith, Gail, ed. rev. ed. 2008. (Understanding Differences Ser.). (ENG., Illus.). 24p. (gr. k-1). pap. 6.29 *(978-1-4296-1774-1(8),* Pebble Bks.) Capstone Press of Coughlan Cos.

—Some Kids Use Wheelchairs. Saunders-Smith, Gail, ed. rev. ed. 2008. (Understanding Differences Ser.). (ENG., Illus.). 24p. (gr. k-1). per. 6.29 *(978-1-4296-1776-5(4),* Pebble Bks.) Capstone Press of Coughlan Cos.

—Some Kids Wear Leg Braces. Saunders-Smith, Gail, ed. rev. ed. 2008. (Understanding Differences Ser.). (ENG., Illus.). 24p. (gr. k-1). pap. 6.29 *(978-1-4296-1777-2(2),* Pebble Bks.) Capstone Press of Coughlan Cos.

Schultz Nicholson, Lorna. Fighting for Gold: The Story of Canada's Sledge Hockey Paralympic Gold, 1 vol. 2009. (Lorimer Recordbooks Ser.). (ENG., Illus.). 128p. (gr. 8-12). 9.95 *(978-1-55277-030-6(3),* 9781552770306); (YA). 16.95 *(978-1-55277-031-3(1))* Lorimer, James & Co., Ltd., Pubs. CAN. Dist: Casemate Pubs. & Bk. Distributors, LLC.

Souder, Patricia. Blindness & Vision Impairment. Albers, Lisa et al, eds. 2014. (Living with a Special Need Ser.: 16). 128p. (J). (gr. 7-18). 25.95 *(978-1-4222-3030-5(9))* Mason Crest.

Souder, Patti. A Different Way of Seeing: Youth with Visual Impairments & Blindness. 2003. (Youth with Special Needs Ser.). (Illus.). 127p. (YA). (gr. 7). pap. 14.95 *(978-1-4222-0418-4(9))* Mason Crest.

Steininger-Moore, Cheryl A. Blue Tooth Sleuth. Schafer, Holden J., illus. 2013. 26p. 16.50 *(978-1-61314-141-0(6));* (J). pap. 9.99 *(978-1-61314-142-7(4),* Innovo Pr.) Innovo Publishing, LLC.

Stewart, Gail B. Alexandra Scott: Champion for Cancer Research. 2006. (Young Heroes Ser.). (ENG., Illus.). 64p. (J). (gr. 4-7). lib. bdg. 28.75 *(978-0-7377-3613-7(5),* Kidhaven) Cengage Gale.

Stewart, Nancy. Katrina & Winter: Partners in Courage. 2012. 24p. 19.95 *(978-1-61633-242-6(5));* pap. 11.95 *(978-1-61633-243-3(3))* Guardian Angel Publishing, Inc.

Stewart, Sheila. Finding My Voice: Kids with Speech Impairment. 2009. (Kids with Special Needs Ser.). 48p. (YA). (gr. 5-18). pap. 7.95 *(978-1-4222-1925-6(9))* Mason Crest.

—I Can Do It! Kids with Physical Challenges. 2009. (Kids with Special Needs Ser.). 48p. (YA). (gr. 5-18). pap. 7.95 *(978-1-4222-1926-3(7))* Mason Crest.

—Listening with Your Eyes: Kids Who Are Deaf & Hard of Hearing. 2009. (Kids with Special Needs Ser.). 48p. (YA). (gr. 5-18). pap. 7.95 *(978-1-4222-1920-1(8))* Mason Crest.

—My Name Is Not Slow: Kids with Intellectual Disabilities. 2009. (Kids with Special Needs Ser.). 48p. (YA). (gr. 5-18). pap. 7.95 *(978-1-4222-1921-8(6))* Mason Crest.

Stewart, Sheila & Flath, Camden. I Can Do It! Kids with Physical Challenges. 2010. (Kids with Special Needs Ser.). (Illus.). 48p. (YA). (gr. 5-18). lib. bdg. 19.95 *(978-1-4222-1723-8(X))* Mason Crest.

Sundquist, Josh. We Should Hang Out Sometime: Embarrassingly, a True Story. 2016. (ENG.). 352p. (YA). (gr. 7-17). pap. 10.99 *(978-0-316-25100-6(3))* Little, Brown Bks. for Young Readers.

Thornton, Denise. Physical Disabilities: The Ultimate Teen Guide. 2007. (It Happened to Me Ser.: 17). (ENG., Illus.). 176p. (gr. 8-12). 55.00 *(978-0-8108-5300-3(0))* Scarecrow Pr., Inc.

Tourville, Amanda Doering. Friends with Disabilities, 4 vols., Set. Sorra, Kristin, illus. Incl. My Friend Has ADHD. Flaherty, Terry. lib. bdg. 25.99 *(978-1-4048-5749-0(4));* My Friend Has Autism. lib. bdg. 25.99 *(978-1-4048-5750-6(8));* My Friend Has down Syndrome. lib. bdg. 25.99 *(978-1-4048-5751-3(6));* My Friend Has Dyslexia. lib. bdg. 25.99 *(978-1-4048-5752-0(4));* (Illus.). (gr. k-3). (Friends with Disabilities Ser.). (ENG.). 24p. 2010. Set lib. bdg. 103.96 *(978-1-4048-6004-9(5))* Picture Window Bks.

—Helen Keller: Courageous Learner & Leader, 1 vol. 2013. (Beginner Biographies Set 2 Ser.). (ENG., Illus.). 32p. (J). (gr. -1-4). 28.50 *(978-1-61641-938-7(5))* Magic Wagon.

Whelahan, Marlene Verno. My Best Friend's Sister... A True Story. 2010. 20p. 12.99 *(978-1-4389-8729-3(3))* AuthorHouse.

PEOPLE WITH DISABILITIES—BIOGRAPHY

Adams, Colleen. The Courage of Helen Keller. 2003. (Reading Room Collection 2 Ser.). (Illus.). 24p. (J). lib. bdg. 22.60 *(978-0-8239-3710-3(0))* Rosen Publishing Group, Inc., The.

All about Me: Growing up with Turner Syndrome & Nonverbal Learning Disabilities. 2004. (J). lib. bdg. 14.95 *(978-0-9759850-0-7(0));* per. *(978-0-9759850-1-4(9))* Maple Leaf Ctr.

Currie-McGhee, Leanne K. Emmanuel Osofu Yeboah: Champion for Ghana's Disabled. 2006. (Young Heroes Ser.). (ENG., Illus.). 64p. (gr. 4-8). lib. bdg. 35.70 *(978-0-7377-3614-4(3),* Kidhaven) Cengage Gale.

Delano, Marfe Ferguson. Helen's Eyes: A Photobiography of Annie Sullivan, Helen Keller's Teacher. 2008. (Photobiographies Ser.). (ENG., Illus.). 64p. (J). (gr. 5). 27.90 *(978-1-4263-0210-7(X));* 17.95 *(978-1-4263-0209-1(6))* National Geographic Society. (National Geographic Children's Bks.).

Donaldson, Madeline. Louis Braille. 2008. pap. 52.95 *(978-0-8225-9393-5(9))* Lerner Publishing Group.

Edwards, Karen. Christopher Reeve: A Real-Life Superhero. 2005. (Illus.). 32p. (J). *(978-0-669-51411-7(X))* Great Source Education Group, Inc.

Eggleton, Jill. Up to the Challenge. 2007. (Connectors Ser.). (gr. 2-5). pap. *(978-1-877453-21-2(8))* Global Education Systems Ltd.

Feinstein, Stephen. Read about Helen Keller. 2004. (I Like Biographies! Ser.). (Illus.). 24p. (J). lib. bdg. 22.60 *(978-0-7660-2299-7(4))* Enslow Pubs., Inc.

Hollingsworth, Tamara. Helen Keller: A New Vision, 1 vol. 2nd rev. ed. 2013. (Nonfiction Readers Ser.). (ENG., Illus.). 48p. (J). (gr. 4-4). pap. 29.96 *(978-1-4807-1115-0(2))* Shell Educational Publishing.

Lauren, Jill. That's Like Me!, 1 vol. 2009. (ENG.). 32p. (J). (gr. k-3). 17.95 *(978-1-59572-207-2(6))* Star Bright Bks., Inc.

Lobb, Nancy. 16 Extraordinary Americans with Disabilities. 2nd ed. 2007. (16 Extraordinary Ser.). (Illus.). 139p. (J). (gr. 3-7). tchr. ed., per. 25.00 *(978-0-8251-6278-7(5))* Walch Education.

Manson, Ainslie. Roll On: Rick Hansen Wheels Around the World, 1 vol. Lightburn, Ron, illus. 2013. (ENG.). 40p. (J). (gr. k-5). pap. 10.95 *(978-1-77100-268-4(9))* Greystone Books Ltd. CAN. Dist: Publishers Group West (PGW).

Mills, Nathan & Peck, Audrey. Helen Keller: Miracle Child. 2012. (Rosen Readers Ser.). (ENG., Illus.). 24p. (J). (gr. 1-2). pap. 8.25 *(978-1-4488-8824-5(7),* Rosen Classroom) Rosen Publishing Group, Inc., The.

Moore, Sherry. Jason's #16 Dream. 2005. 48p. pap. 16.95 *(978-1-4137-6878-7(4))* America Star Bks.

Mueller, Pamela Bauer. Aloha Crossing. 2008. (Aloha Set Ser.: 2). (ENG., Illus.). 176p. (J). (gr. 3-7). pap. 8.99 *(978-0-9685097-9-1(7))* Pinata Publishing CAN. Dist: Midpoint Trade Bks., Inc.

Ninteau, Sherrie. Rick's Story-the Story of Rick Hoyt. 2009. (J). 14.95 *(978-1-934878-87-3(1))* Mascot Bks., Inc.

O'Brien, John A. Who Was Helen Keller? Harrison, Nancy, illus. 2003. (Who Was...? Ser.). 107p. (J). (gr. 3-7). 12.65 *(978-0-7569-1596-4(1))* Perfection Learning Corp.

Packard, Mary. Beating the Odds: A Chapter Book. 2004. (True Tales Ser.). (ENG.). (J). 22.50 *(978-0-516-23731-2(4),* Children's Pr.) Scholastic Library Publishing.

Peck, Audrey. Helen Keller: Miracle Child. 2012. (Beginning Biographies Ser.). (ENG., Illus.). 24p. (J). (gr. 1-3). 22.60 *(978-1-4488-8593-0(0),* PowerKids Pr.) Rosen Publishing Group, Inc., The.

Powers, J. L. Colors of the Wind: The Story of Blind Artist & Champion Runner George Mendoza. Mendoza, George, illus. 2014. (J). 18.95 *(978-1-930900-73-8(2))* Purple Hse. Pr.

Quinlan, Don. Rick Hansen: Larger Than Life, 1 vol. 2013. (ENG.). 64p. (J). *(978-1-55455-195-8(1))* Fitzhenry & Whiteside, Ltd.

Sandler, Michael. Jean Driscoll: Dream Big, Work Hard! 2006. (Defining Moments Ser.). (Illus.). 32p. (J). (gr. 2-5). lib. bdg. 25.27 *(978-1-59716-268-5(X))* Bearport Publishing Co., Inc.

Senker, Cath. Stephen Hawking. 2015. (Against the Odds Biographies Ser.). (ENG., Illus.). 48p. (gr. 3-6). 33.32 *(978-1-4846-2466-1(1))* Heinemann-Raintree.

Senker, Cath & Throp, Claire. Against the Odds Biographies. 2015. (Against the Odds Biographies Ser.). (ENG.). 48p. (gr. 3-6). lib. bdg. 133.28 *(978-1-4846-2468-5(8),* Heinemann InfoSearch) Heinemann-Raintree.

Stout, Glenn. Able to Play: Overcoming Physical Challenges. 2012. (Good Sports Ser.). (ENG., Illus.). 112p. (J). (gr. 5-7). pap. 5.99 *(978-0-547-41733-2(0))* Houghton Mifflin Harcourt Publishing Co.

Sullivan, George. Helen Keller: Her Life in Pictures. 2007. (Helen Keller Ser.). (ENG., Illus.). 80p. (J). (gr. 2-5). 17.99 *(978-0-439-91815-2(4),* Scholastic Nonfiction) Scholastic, Inc.

Sutcliffe, Jane. Helen Keller. 2009. (History Maker Biographies Ser.). (gr. k-2). 27.93 *(978-0-7613-4223-6(0),* Lerner Pubns.) Lerner Publishing Group.

Thompson, Laurie Ann. Emmanuel's Dream: The True Story of Emmanuel Ofosu Yeboah. Qualls, Sean, illus. 2015. (ENG.). 40p. (J). (gr. -1-3). 17.99 *(978-0-449-81744-5(X),* Schwartz & Wade Bks.) Random Hse. Children's Bks.

PEOPLE WITH DISABILITIES—EDUCATION

Bryant, John E. Taking Speech Disorders to School. Schader, Karen, ed. Dineen, Tom, illus. 2004. (Special Kids in School Ser.: Sixteenth). (J). per. 11.95 *(978-1-891383-24-3(8),* 70016) JayJo Bks., LLC.

Comprendiendo las Diferencias. 2010. (Comprendiendo Las Diferencias/Understanding Differences Ser.).Tr. of Understanding Differences. (MUL & ENG.). 24p. lib. bdg. 65.97 *(978-1-4296-4607-9(1))* Capstone Press of Coughlan Cos.

Duckworth, Katie. Education. 2004. (Children's Rights Ser.). (J). lib. bdg. 27.10 *(978-1-58340-419-5(8))* Black Rabbit Bks.

O'Brien, John A. Who Was Helen Keller? Harrison, Nancy, illus. 2003. (Who Was...? Ser.). 107p. (J). (gr. 3-7). 12.65 *(978-0-7569-1596-4(1))* Perfection Learning Corp.

Spencer, Leslie. Social Stories for Children with Disabilities. 2011. 28p. pap. 24.95 *(978-1-4560-2202-0(4))* America Star Bks.

PEOPLE WITH DISABILITIES—FICTION

Abdullah, Shaila & Abdullah, Aanyah. My Friend Suhana: A Story of Friendship & Cerebral Palsy. 2014. 30p. pap. 14.95 *(978-1-61599-211-9(1))* Loving Healing Pr., Inc.

Akbarpour, Ahmad. Good Night, Commander, 1 vol. Eskandani, Shadi & Mixter, Helen, trs. from PER. Zahedi, Morteza, illus. 2010. (ENG.). 24p. (J). (gr. 1). 17.95 *(978-0-88899-989-4(5))* Groundwood Bks. CAN. Dist: Publishers Group West (PGW).

Alborghetti, Marci. The Miracle of the Myrrh. Blondon, Herve, illus. 2003. (J). 16.95 *(978-0-87946-249-9(3),* 708) ACTA Pubns.

Alpert, Mark. The Six. 2015. (Six Ser.: 1). (ENG.). 368p. (J). (gr. 6-12). 16.99 *(978-1-4926-1529-3(3),* 9781492615293) Sourcebooks, Inc.

Armstrong, Gregory D. The Day Buddy Flew. 2013. 42p. (J). 21.99 *(978-0-578-12191-8(3))* Armstrong, Greg.

—Don't Laugh at Me. 2013. 32p. 21.99 *(978-0-578-12368-4(1))* Armstrong, Greg.

Arnold, David. Kids of Appetite. (ENG.). (YA). (gr. 9). 2017. 368p. pap. 10.99 ***(978-0-14-751366-3(9),*** Speak) 2016. 352p. 18.99 *(978-0-451-47078-2(8),* Viking Books for Young Readers) Penguin Young Readers Group.

—Kids of Appetite. 2017. lib. bdg. 22.10 ***(978-0-606-40491-4(0))*** Turtleback Bks.

Asare, Meshack. Sosu's Call. Asare, Meshack, illus. 2006. (ENG., Illus.). 40p. (J). (gr. k-4). 11.99 *(978-1-929132-21-8(2))* Kane Miller.

Atkins, Ben. The Breakaway Kid. Woods, Vanessa, illus. 2nd rev. ed. 2005. (ENG.). 32p. (J). per. 8.00 *(978-0-9768653-0-8(0))* Summer Day Publishing, LLC.

Auch, M. J. One-Handed Catch. 2009. (ENG.). 272p. (J). (gr. 5-9). pap. 6.99 *(978-0-312-53575-9(9),* 9780312535759) Square Fish.

Auch, Mary Jane. One-Handed Catch. 2009. 272p. (J). (gr. 5-9). pap. 6.99 *(978-0-312-58002-5(9))* Square Fish.

Avi. Prairie School. Farnsworth, Bill, illus. 2003. (I Can Read Level 4 Ser.). (ENG.). 48p. (J). (gr. 3-4). pap. 3.99 *(978-0-06-051318-4(7))* HarperCollins Pubs.

—Prairie School. Farnsworth, Bill, illus. 2003. (I Can Read Bks.). 47p. (gr. 3-7). 14.00 *(978-0-7569-1452-3(3))* Perfection Learning Corp.

Balardo, Sharon. I Am Abel. 2012. 24p. pap. 17.99 *(978-1-4772-7798-0(6))* AuthorHouse.

Balliett, Blue. The Danger Box. 2012. (ENG.). 320p. (J). (gr. 3-7). pap. 7.99 *(978-0-439-85210-4(2),* Scholastic Paperbacks) Scholastic, Inc.

Banister, Katie Rodriguez & Banister, Steve. Aunt Katie's Visit: A Child's First Book on Disabilities. Whitfield, Eric T., illus. 2003. (J). 16.99 *(978-0-9744908-0-9(6))* Access-4-All, Inc.

Baratz-Logsted, Lauren. Crazy Beautiful. 2011. (ENG.). 204p. (YA). (gr. 7). pap. 12.95 *(978-0-547-40310-6(0))* Houghton Mifflin Harcourt Publishing Co.

Barchers, Suzanne I. Kate & Gail, 1 vol. 2011. (Targeted Phonics Ser.). (ENG., Illus.). 16p. (J). (gr. k-2). pap. 5.99 *(978-1-4333-2907-4(7))* Teacher Created Materials, Inc.

—On a Walk with Ren, 1 vol. 2011. (Targeted Phonics Ser.). (ENG., Illus.). 16p. (J). (gr. k-2). pap. 5.99 *(978-1-4333-2417-8(2))* Teacher Created Materials, Inc.

Barnes, Bobbie Jo. The Message. 2012. 24p. pap. 24.95 *(978-1-4626-9047-3(5))* America Star Bks.

Barrett, Granny Rita. The Adventures on Granny's Fun-Ee Farm: Book 1. 2012. 20p. pap. 14.00 *(978-1-4772-8356-1(0))* AuthorHouse.

Barta, Jeralyn. Rolling with Life. 2010. 24p. pap. 15.99 *(978-1-4490-6862-2(6))* AuthorHouse.

Bauer, Marion Dane. The Double-Digit Club. 2004. (ENG.). 126p. (J). (gr. 4-6). tchr. ed. 16.95 *(978-0-8234-1805-3(7))* Holiday Hse., Inc.

Bee, Stevie J. Cross Your Heart. 2009. 216p. 25.50 *(978-1-60860-133-2(1),* Eloquent Bks.) Strategic Book Publishing & Rights Agency (SBPRA).

Benjamin, Irwin H. The Legend of Toad Torrington. 2011. 24p. pap. 12.79 *(978-1-4634-3746-6(3))* AuthorHouse.

Berk, Josh. The Dark Days of Hamburger Halpin. 2011. (ENG.). 258p. (YA). (gr. 7). pap. 8.99 *(978-0-375-84625-0(5),* Ember) Random Hse. Children's Bks.

Best, Cari. My Three Best Friends & Me, Zulay. Brantley-Newton, Vanessa, illus. 2015. (ENG.). 40p. (J). (gr. -1-3). 17.99 *(978-0-374-38819-5(9),* 9780374388195, Farrar, Straus & Giroux (BYR)) Farrar, Straus & Giroux.

Bevins, Rose. Coming to Terms. 2004. (Cover-To-Cover Books). (Illus.). 64p. pap. 9.00 *(978-0-7891-6018-8(8));* 56p. (J). (gr. 1-4). lib. bdg. 16.95 *(978-0-7569-1371-7(3))* Perfection Learning Corp.

Bingham, Kelly. Formerly Shark Girl. (ENG.). 352p. (YA). (gr. 7). 2015. pap. 8.99 *(978-0-7636-7673-5(X))* 2013. 16.99 *(978-0-7636-5362-0(4))* Candlewick Pr.

—Shark Girl. (ENG., Illus.). 288p. (YA). (gr. 7). 2010. pap. 8.99 *(978-0-7636-4627-1(X))* 2007. 16.99 *(978-0-7636-3207-6(4))* Candlewick Pr.

Black, Chuck. Rise of the Fallen: Wars of the Realm, Book 2. 2015. (Wars of the Realm Ser.). (ENG.). 320p. (YA). (gr. 7). pap. 11.99 *(978-1-60142-504-1(X),* Multnomah Bks.) Crown Publishing Group.

Bloor, Edward. Tangerine. (ENG.). 320p. (J). (gr. 5-7). 2007. 18.00 *(978-0-15-201246-5(X))* 2006. (Illus.). pap. 8.99 *(978-0-15-205780-0(3))* Houghton Mifflin Harcourt Publishing Co.

—Tangerine Spanish Edition. de la Vega, Pablo, tr. 2014. (ENG.). 384p. (J). (gr. 5-7). 16.99 *(978-0-544-33611-7(9),* HMH Books For Young Readers) Houghton Mifflin Harcourt Publishing Co.

Blos, Joan W. Brothers of the Heart: A Story of the Old Northwest, 1837-1838. 2008. (ENG.). 176p. (J). (gr. 3-7). pap. 5.99 *(978-1-4169-7561-8(6),* Simon & Schuster/Paula Wiseman Bks.) Simon & Schuster/Paula Wiseman Bks.

Boles, Jennifer. Bonnie Butterfly. 2010. 20p. pap. 11.99 *(978-1-4490-4913-3(3))* AuthorHouse.

Boles, Jim. Ivan the Invacar Helps Big Dog. Cunningham, Bob, illus. 2012. 56p. pap. 19.95 *(978-0-9845983-5-9(9))* People Ink Pr.

Boles, S. Ivan the Invacar Saves the Wobbly Hubcap. Cunningham, Bob, illus. 2014. (J). pap. 7.95 *(978-0-9893267-3-5(X))* People Ink Pr.

Borrelli, Theresa "Terrie". Why Is Jamie Different? 2012. 24p. pap. 24.95 *(978-1-4137-9883-8(7))* America Star Bks.

Bowen, Julie. Sometimes I Can't Talk Well. 2013. 32p. pap. 13.99 *(978-1-4624-0575-6(4),* Inspiring Voices) Author Solutions, Inc.

Bradley, Kimberly Brubaker. The War That Saved My Life. (ENG.). (J). (gr. 4-7). 2016. 336p. 8.99 *(978-0-14-751048-8(1),* Puffin Books) 2015. 320p. 17.99 *(978-0-8037-4081-5(6),* Dial Bks) Penguin Young Readers Group.

—The War That Saved My Life. 2016. (J). lib. bdg. 19.65 *(978-0-606-38843-6(5))* Turtleback Bks.

Bray, Libba. Going Bovine. 2010. (ENG.). 496p. (YA). (gr. 9). pap. 10.99 *(978-0-385-73398-4(4),* Ember) Random Hse. Children's Bks.

Brenna, Beverley. Something to Hang on To. 2009. (ENG.). 176p. (J). pap. 12.95 *(978-1-897235-57-7(7))* Thistledown Pr., Ltd. CAN. Dist: Univ. of Toronto Pr.

Brouwer, Sigmund. Counterattack. 2009. (Robot Wars Ser.: 4). (ENG.). 304p. (YA). pap. 6.99 *(978-1-4143-2312-1(3),* Tyndale Kids) Tyndale Hse. Pubs.

—Final Battle. 2009. (Robot Wars Ser.: 5). (ENG.). 320p. (YA). pap. 7.99 *(978-1-4143-2313-8(1),* Tyndale Kids) Tyndale Hse. Pubs.

Brown, Donna. Crippled Like Me. 2009. 36p. pap. 14.75 *(978-1-60693-986-4(6),* Eloquent Bks.) Strategic Book Publishing & Rights Agency (SBPRA).

Brown, Irene Bennett. Before the Lark. 2011. (ENG.). 208p. (J). (gr. 4-7). pap. 18.95 *(978-0-89672-727-4(0))* Texas Tech Univ. Pr.

Brudos, Susan E. & Rubino, Alisa A., illus. Wayne's Trail. 2004. (J). pap. *(978-0-932991-62-1(9))* Place In The Woods, The.

Bryant, Louella. Two Tracks in the Snow. Fargo, Todd, illus. Lt. ed. 2004. (Turtle Bks.). 32p. (J). lib. bdg. 15.95 *(978-0-944727-46-1(8));* per. 9.95 *(978-0-944727-45-4(X))* Jason & Nordic Pubs. (Turtle Bks.).

Bundschuh, Rick. Burned, 1 vol. 2014. (Faithgirlz / Soul Surfer Ser.). (ENG.). 128p. (J). pap. 7.99 *(978-0-310-74555-6(1))* Zonderkidz.

—Clash, 1 vol. 2014. (Faithgirlz / Soul Surfer Ser.). (ENG.). 128p. (J). pap. 7.99 *(978-0-310-74582-2(9))* Zonderkidz.

Bundy, Tamara. Walking with Miss Millie. 2017. (ENG.). 240p. (J). (gr. 5). 16.99 ***(978-0-399-54456-9(9),*** Nancy Paulsen Books) Penguin Young Readers Group.

Bunker, Lisa. Felix Yz. 2017. (ENG.). 288p. (J). (gr. 5-9). 16.99 *(978-0-425-28850-4(1),* Viking Books for Young Readers) Penguin Young Readers Group.

Burnett, Frances Hodgson. The Secret Garden. 2012. (Illus.). 304p. *(978-1-4351-4212-1(8))* Barnes & Noble, Inc.

—The Secret Garden. Robinson, Charles, illus. 2011. 304p. (J). *(978-1-4351-3344-0(7))* Barnes & Noble, Inc.

—The Secret Garden. Moore, Inga, illus. 2008. (ENG.). 272p. (J). (gr. 1-4). 22.99 *(978-0-7636-3161-1(2))* Candlewick Pr.

—The Secret Garden. 2003. (ENG., Illus.). 288p. (gr. 12-18). mass mkt. 5.95 *(978-0-451-52883-4(2),* Signet) Penguin Publishing Group.

—The Secret Garden. Lawrie, Robin, illus. 2008. (Puffin Classics Ser.). (ENG.). 368p. (J). (gr. 3-7). 5.99 *(978-0-14-132106-6(7),* Puffin Books) Penguin Young Readers Group.

—The Secret Garden. 2003. (Modern Library Classics Ser.). (ENG.). 288p. (J). (gr. 3-7). pap. 7.95 *(978-0-8129-6998-6(7),* Modern Library) Random House Publishing Group.

—The Secret Garden. 2013. (ENG.). 384p. (J). (gr. 4-7). pap. 11.99 *(978-0-09-957295-4(8))* Random Hse. GBR. Dist: Independent Pubs. Group.

—The Secret Garden. Ingpen, Robert R., illus. 2011. (Sterling Illustrated Classics Ser.). (ENG.). 240p. (J). (gr. 5-18). 19.95 *(978-1-4027-7872-8(4))* Sterling Publishing Co., Inc.

—The Secret Garden. Moore, Inga, illus. 2010. (ENG.). 272p. (J). (gr. 1-4). pap. 16.99 *(978-0-7636-4732-2(2))* Candlewick Pr.

—The Secret Garden, 1 vol. Simon, Ute, illus. 2011. (Calico Illustrated Classics Ser.: No. 3). (ENG.). 112p. (J). (gr. 3-6). 27.07 *(978-1-61641-108-4(2))* Magic Wagon.

—The Secret Garden. Corvino, Lucy, illus. 2005. (Classic Starts(tm) Ser.). (ENG.). 160p. (J). (gr. 2-4). 6.95 *(978-1-4027-1319-4(3))* Sterling Publishing Co., Inc.

—The Secret Garden. Tudor, Tasha, illus. 100th anniv. ed. 2010. (Trophy Bk.). (ENG.). 384p. (J). (gr. 4-18). reprint ed. pap. 6.99 *(978-0-06-440188-3(X))* HarperCollins Pubs.

—The Secret Garden: A Young Reader's Edition of the Classic Story. 2005. 332p. 29.95 *(978-1-4218-0619-8(3),* 1st World Library - Literary Society) 1st World Publishing, Inc.

—The Secret Garden: A Young Reader's Edition of the Classic Story. (J). 22.95 *(978-0-8488-0692-7(1))* Amereon Ltd.

—The Secret Garden: A Young Reader's Edition of the Classic Story. 2004. (Illus.). (J). (gr. 1-4). spiral bd. *(978-0-616-14565-4(9));* spiral bd. *(978-0-616-14566-1(7))* Canadian National Institute for the Blind/Institut National Canadien pour les Aveugles.

—The Secret Garden: A Young Reader's Edition of the Classic Story. 2005. 132p. per. 5.95 *(978-1-4209-2229-5(7))* Digireads.com Publishing.

—The Secret Garden: A Young Reader's Edition of the Classic Story. 2004. reprint ed. pap. 1.99 *(978-1-4192-8193-8(3));* pap. 28.95 *(978-1-4179-2544-5(2))* Kessinger Publishing, LLC.

—The Secret Garden: A Young Reader's Edition of the Classic Story. (English As a Second Language Bk.). (Illus.). 92p. pap. 4.46 net. *(978-0-582-53417-9(8))* Longman Publishing Group.

—The Secret Garden: A Young Reader's Edition of the Classic Story. 2005. (ENG.). 24.95 *(978-1-55742-519-5(1));* pap. 15.95 *(978-1-55742-524-9(8))* Wildside Pr., LLC.

—The Secret Garden: With a Discussion of Compassion. Lauter, Richard, illus. 2003. (Values in Action Illustrated Classics Ser.). 191p. (J). *(978-1-59203-037-8(8))* Learning Challenge, Inc.

Burnett, Frances Hodgson & Naxos of America Staff. The Secret Garden. 3rd ed. 2008. (Hear It Read It Classics Ser.: 0). (ENG., Illus.). 144p. (J). (gr. 2-4). 9.95 *(978-1-4022-1244-4(5),* Sourcebooks Jabberwocky) Sourcebooks, Inc.

Busby, Cylin. Blink Once. 2012. (ENG.). 304p. (YA). (gr. 7-12). 17.99 *(978-1-59990-818-2(2),* 9781599908182, Bloomsbury USA Childrens) Bloomsbury Publishing USA.

Carillo, Christina. Life Can Be A Smile. 2010. 30p. pap. 21.99 *(978-1-4500-2848-6(9))* Xlibris Corp.

Carl, Dave. Super Cyclist. Mack, Kathryn, illus. 2010. (ENG.). (J). pap. 12.00 *(978-0-9785160-8-6(7))* Etcetera Pr. LLC.

Carlson, Nancy & Isaak, Armond. Armond Goes to a Party: A Book about Asperger's & Friendship. 2014. (ENG., Illus.). 32p. (J). 15.99 *(978-1-57542-466-8(5))* Free Spirit Publishing, Inc.

Carol Hersh. Handy Sandy. Baker, David, illus. 2011. 28p. pap. 24.95 *(978-1-4560-8991-7(9))* America Star Bks.

Carrier, Therese & Carrier, Stephen. Josiah's School Fun Day. Hatfield, Tommy, illus. 2007. 29p. (J). 16.95 *(978-0-9797648-0-6(7))* Carrier, Therese.

Carter, Jimmy. The Little Baby Snoogle- Fleejer. Carter, Amy, illus. 2014. (ENG.). 24p. (J). 19.95 *(978-1-55728-671-0(X))* Univ. of Arkansas Pr.

Cassidy, Yvonne. How Many Letters Are in Goodbye? 2016. (ENG.). 432p. (YA). pap. 11.99 *(978-0-7387-4745-3(9),* Flux) North Star Editions.

Castan, Mike. Fighting for Dontae. 2012. (ENG.). 144p. (YA). 16.95 *(978-0-8234-2348-4(4))* Holiday Hse., Inc.

Cate, Shari. The Dreams of King Neb. 2013. 16p. pap. 7.95 *(978-1-4497-9970-0(1),* WestBow Pr.) Author Solutions, Inc.

Chaconas, Dori. Dancing with Katya, 1 vol. Bergum, Constance R., illus. 2006. (ENG.). 32p. (J). (gr. k-3). 16.95 *(978-1-56145-376-4(5))* Peachtree Pubs.

Chillemi, Stacey. My Daddy Has Epilepsy. 2007. (ENG., Illus.). 64p. (J). per. 34.50 *(978-1-4303-0220-9(8))* Lulu Pr., Inc.

Christopher, Matt. The Great Quarterback Switch. 2008. (New Matt Christopher Sports Library). 144p. (J). (gr. 4-6). lib. bdg. 26.60 (978-1-59953-216-5(6)) Norwood Hse. Pr.

Clements, Andrew. Things Not Seen. 2004. (ENG.). 256p. (J). (gr. 5-18). reprint ed. pap. 6.99 (978-0-14-240076-0(9), Speak) Penguin Young Readers Group.

—Things Not Seen. 2004. 251p. (gr. 5-9). 17.00 (978-0-7569-2599-4(1)) Perfection Learning Corp.

—Things Not Seen. 2004. 256p. (J). (gr. 4-7). pap. 38.00 incl. audio (978-1-4000-9014-3(8), Listening Library) Random Hse. Audio Publishing Group.

Cocca-Leffler, Maryann. Janine & the Field Day Finish. Cocca-Leffler, Maryann, illus. 2016. (ENG., Illus.). 32p. (J). (gr. -1-3). 16.99 (978-0-8075-3756-5(X)) Whitman, Albert & Co.

Coolidge, Susan. What Katy Did. 2013. (ENG., Illus.). 200p. (J). 15.00 (978-1-84135-843-7(6)) Award Pubns. Ltd. GBR. Dist: Parkwest Pubns., Inc.

—What Katy Did. Ledyard, Addie, illus. 2013. 132p. pap. (978-1-909735-03-3(5)) Aziloth Bks.

—What Katy Did. 2012. 246p. pap. (978-1-78139-262-1(5)) Benediction Classics.

—What Katy Did. Hellard, Susan, illus. 2016. (ENG.). 246p. (J). pap. 9.99 **(978-1-84749-607-2(5)**, 9781847496072, Alma Classics) Bloomsbury Publishing USA.

—What Katy Did. 2017. (ENG., Illus.). (J). (gr. 4-6). pap. 9.90 **(978-1-366-50696-2(0))** Blurb, Inc.

—What Katy Did. 2015. (ENG., Illus.). (J). (gr. 2-4). 25.95 **(978-1-297-62709-5(1))** 2012. 300p. pap. 29.75 (978-1-286-00091-5(2)) 2012. 302p. pap. 29.75 (978-1-286-07372-8(3)) 2011. 290p. (gr. 3-7). pap. 28.75 (978-1-179-65265-8(7)) 2010. (ENG.). 300p. pap. 29.75 (978-1-178-00783-1(9)) 2010. (ENG.). 282p. (gr. 3-7). pap. 28.75 (978-1-177-27477-7(9)) 2010. 302p. pap. 29.75 (978-1-145-74830-9(9)) 2008. 164p. (gr. 4-7). 25.99 (978-0-554-28634-1(3)) 2008. 164p. (gr. 4-7). 22.99 (978-0-554-37937-1(6)) 2007. (ENG.). 144p. pap. 18.99 (978-1-4346-5943-9(7)) 2007. (ENG.). 160p. pap. 21.99 (978-1-4346-5944-6(5)) Creative Media Partners, LLC.

—What Katy Did. 2007. (ENG.). 148p. per. (978-1-4065-1527-5(2)) Dodo Pr.

—What Katy Did. 2006. (Dover Children's Classics Ser.). (ENG., Illus.). 160p. (J). (gr. 3-8). per. 6.95 (978-0-486-44760-5(X)) Dover Pubns., Inc.

—What Katy Did. 2007. (ENG.). 104p. per. (978-1-4068-4855-7(7)) Echo Library.

—What Katy Did. 2010. (Illus.). 92p. (gr. 3-7). pap. 19.99 (978-1-153-74507-9(0)) 2009. 104p. pap. 6.40 (978-0-217-53637-0(9)) General Bks. LLC.

—What Katy Did. 2010. 132p. pap. (978-1-4076-5115-6(3)) HardPr.

—What Katy Did. Ledyard, Addie, illus. 284p. 2010. 35.16 (978-1-163-85079-4(9)) 2010. pap. 23.16 (978-1-163-77965-1(2)) 2007. 43.95 (978-0-548-53870-8(0)) 2007. per. 28.95 (978-0-548-48700-6(6)) Kessinger Publishing, LLC.

—What Katy Did. 2010. (Puffin Classics Ser.). (ENG., Illus.). 240p. (J). (gr. 5-7). pap. 5.99 (978-0-14-132671-9(9), Puffin Books) Penguin Young Readers Group.

—What Katy Did. 2013. (ENG., Illus.). 256p. (J). (gr. 4-7). pap. 12.99 (978-0-09-957312-8(1)) Random Hse. GBR. Dist: Independent Pubs. Group.

—What Katy Did. 2007. (ENG.). 192p. pap. 12.45 (978-1-60424-403-8(8), Book Jungle) Standard Pubns., Inc.

—What Katy Did. 2011. 162p. (gr. 3-7). pap. (978-3-8424-6664-7(1)) Tredition GmbH.

—What Katy Did. 2010. 144p. pap. 4.99 (978-1-61720-100-4(6)) Wilder Pubns., Corp.

Coolidge, Susan & Ledyard, Addie. What Katy Did. 2010. (ENG.). 292p. pap. 28.75 (978-1-172-34659-2(3)) Creative Media Partners, LLC.

Cormier, Robert. Heroes. 2006. (York Notes Ser.). (ENG., Illus.). 112p. pap. (978-1-4058-3559-6(1)) Pearson Education, Ltd.

Coy, John. Gap Life. 2016. (ENG.). 224p. (YA). 17.99 (978-1-250-08895-6(X), 9781250088956) Feiwel & Friends.

Cozzo, Karole. How to Keep Rolling after a Fall. 2016. (ENG.). 272p. (YA). pap. 9.99 (978-1-250-07928-2(4), 9781250079282) Feiwel & Friends.

Craik, Maria Dinah. The Little Lame Prince. 2008. 120p. 24.99 (978-0-554-21709-3(0)) 2006. 124p. pap. 18.99 (978-1-4264-0755-0(6)) 2006. 118p. pap. 19.99 (978-1-4264-0739-0(4)) Creative Media Partners, LLC.

—The Little Lame Prince. 2007. 128p. pap. 9.95 (978-1-60424-390-1(2), Book Jungle) Standard Pubns., Inc.

Crawford, Brittany. I Sit in a Wheelchair but I Will Be Okay! 2010. 26p. pap. 12.50 (978-1-60911-200-4(8), Eloquent Bks.) Strategic Book Publishing & Rights Agency (SBPRA).

Creech, Sharon. Granny Torrelli Makes Soup. Raschka, Chris, illus. 2012. (ENG.). 160p. (J). (gr. 3-7). reprint ed. pap. 6.99 (978-0-06-440960-5(0)) HarperCollins Pubs.

—Granny Torrelli Makes Soup. Raschka, Chris, illus. 2004. (Joanna Cotler Bks.). 141p. (gr. 3-7). 17.00 (978-0-7569-4604-3(2)) Perfection Learning Corp.

Crockett-Blassingame, Linda, illus. See the Ocean. 2006. 32p. (J). 14.95 (978-0-9778143-0-5(0)) Inclusive Books LLC.

Cummings, Priscilla. Blindsided. (ENG.). (J). (gr. 5-18). 2011. 256p. 7.99 (978-0-14-241902-1(8), Puffin Books) 2010. 240p. 16.99 (978-0-525-42161-0(0), Dutton Books for Young Readers) Penguin Young Readers Group.

Cunningham, Julia. Burnish Me Bright. 2008. (J). (gr. 3-7). 23.75 (978-0-8446-6252-7(6)) Smith, Peter Pub., Inc.

Curtis, Marci Lyn. The One Thing. 2015. (ENG., Illus.). 336p. (YA). (gr. 7-12). 17.99 (978-1-4847-0902-3(0)) Hyperion Bks. for Children.

Cushman, Karen. Alchemy & Meggy Swann. 2011. (ENG.). 176p. (J). (gr. 5-7). pap. 7.99 (978-0-547-57712-8(5)) Houghton Mifflin Harcourt Publishing Co.

Daines, Julie. Unraveled: A Tale of True Love. 2014. 192p. (J). pap. 14.99 (978-1-62108-627-7(5)) Covenant Communications, Inc.

Danneberg, Julie. Family Reminders. Shelley, John, illus. 2009. (ENG.). 112p. (J). (gr. 3-7). 14.95 (978-1-58089-320-6(1)) Charlesbridge Publishing, Inc.

De felice, Cynthia. The Light on Hogback Hill. 2008. (ENG.). 128p. (J). (gr. 4-6). pap. 7.99 (978-1-4169-8691-1(X), Simon & Schuster/Paula Wiseman Bks.) Simon & Schuster/Paula Wiseman Bks.

DeBear, Kirsten. Toby & Tutter Therapy Dogs. Dwight, Laura, photos by. 2012. (ENG., Illus.). 32p. (J). 17.95 (978-0-9847812-0-1(X)) Toby & Tutter Publishing.

DeGross, Monalisa. Donavan's Double Trouble. Bates, Amy, illus. 192p. (J). (gr. 2-5). 2008. lib. bdg. 16.89 (978-0-06-077294-9(8)) 2007. (ENG.). 16.99 (978-0-06-077293-2(X)) HarperCollins Pubs. (Amistad).

DeHart, Leslie Marie. Paloma: The Lilly Fairy, 1 vol. 2010. 50p. pap. 16.95 (978-1-4489-6818-3(6)) America Star Bks.

Demetrios, Heather. I'll Meet You There. 2015. (ENG.). 400p. (YA). (gr. 9). 17.99 (978-0-8050-9795-5(3), 9780805097955, Holt, Henry & Co. Bks. For Young Readers) Holt, Henry & Co.

Demonia, Lori. Leah's Voice. Turchan, Monique, illus. 2012. 28p. pap. 12.95 (978-1-61244-089-7(4)) Halo Publishing International.

Denman, K. L. Spiral, 1 vol. 2008. (Orca Soundings Ser.). (ENG.). (YA). (gr. 8-12). 112p. 16.95 (978-1-55143-932-7(8)); 128p. pap. 9.95 (978-1-55143-930-3(1)) Orca Bk. Pubs. USA.

DeWoskin, Rachel. Blind. 2014. (ENG.). 416p. (YA). (gr. 7). 17.99 (978-0-670-78522-3(9), Viking Books for Young Readers) Penguin Young Readers Group.

Dewoskin, Rachel. Blind. 2016. (ENG.). 416p. (YA). (gr. 7). pap. 10.99 (978-0-14-242455-1(2), Speak) Penguin Young Readers Group.

Di Fiore, Mariangela. Elephant Man. Hedger, Rosie, tr. from NOR. Hodnefjeld, Hilde, illus. 2015. (ENG.). 52p. (J). (gr. 3-6). 19.95 (978-1-55451-778-7(8), 9781554517787) Annick Pr., Ltd. CAN. Dist: Publishers Group West (PGW).

Dion. Chess with Butterflies. 2006. (Illus.). 65p. (J). (gr. 4). pap. 4.95 (978-1-881929-43-7(4)) Oxton Hse., Pubs.

—Fishing with Balloons. 2004. (Illus.). 57p. (J). pap. 4.95 (978-1-881929-34-5(5)) Oxton Hse., Pubs.

Dodson, Merilee. Kids from Critter Cove. Gregor, Terril, illus. 2007. 48p. per. 24.95 (978-1-4137-2644-2(5)) America Star Bks.

Dorris, Michael. Sees Behind Trees. 104p. (J). (gr. 4-6). pap. 4.95 (978-0-8072-1516-6(3), Listening Library) Random Hse. Audio Publishing Group.

Doti, James. Jimmy Finds His Voice. Mertins, Lisa, illus. 2013. (J). 14.95 (978-1-935204-47-3(5)) Salem Author Services.

Doyle, Marissa. Courtship & Curses. 2013. (ENG.). 368p. (YA). (gr. 9-13). pap. 10.99 (978-1-250-02744-3(6)) Square Fish.

Draper, Sharon M. Out of My Mind. 2009. 9.00 (978-0-7848-3780-1(5), Everbind) Marco Bk. Co.

—Out of My Mind. (ENG., Illus.). (J). (gr. 5). 2012. 320p. pap. 9.99 (978-1-4169-7171-9(8)) 2010. 304p. 18.99 (978-1-4169-7170-2(X)) Simon & Schuster Children's Publishing. (Atheneum Bks. for Young Readers).

—Out of My Mind. 2012. lib. bdg. 20.85 (978-0-606-25672-8(5), Turtleback) Turtleback Bks.

Duey, Kathleen & Bale, Karen A. Swamp: Louisiana 1851. 2016. (Survivors Ser.). (ENG., Illus.). 160p. (J). (gr. 3-7). pap. 6.99 (978-1-4814-2783-8(0), Aladdin) Simon & Schuster Children's Publishing.

Duff, Justin. Wishing Well. 2012. 32p. pap. 21.99 (978-1-4771-2099-6(8)) Xlibris Corp.

Dungy, Tony & Dungy, Lauren. You Can Be a Friend. Mazellan, Ron, illus. 2011. (ENG.). 32p. (J). (gr. -1-2). 16.99 (978-1-4169-9771-9(7), Little Simon Inspirations) Little Simon Inspirations.

Durfee, Jody Wind. Hadley-Hadley Benson. 2013. (ENG.). 144p. (J). pap. 11.99 (978-1-62108-151-7(6)) Covenant Communications, Inc.

Dwight, Laura. We Can Do It!, 1 vol. Dwight, Laura, photos by. 2005. (ENG., Illus.). 32p. (J). pap. 5.95 (978-1-59572-033-7(2)) Star Bright Bks., Inc.

Eames, Brian. The Dagger Quick. (Dagger Chronicles Ser.). (ENG., (J). (gr. 3-7). 2013. Illus.). 352p. pap. 6.99 (978-1-4424-8368-2(7)) 2011. 336p. 15.99 (978-1-4424-2311-4(0)) Simon & Schuster/Paula Wiseman Bks. (Simon & Schuster/Paula Wiseman Bks.).

—The Dagger X. 2013. (Dagger Chronicles Ser.). (ENG.). 368p. (J). (gr. 3-7). 15.99 (978-1-4424-6855-9(6), Simon & Schuster Bks. For Young Readers) Simon & Schuster Bks. For Young Readers.

—The Dagger X. 2013. (Dagger Chronicles Ser.). (ENG., Illus.). 368p. (J). (gr. 3-7). pap. 6.99 (978-1-4424-6856-6(4), Simon & Schuster/Paula Wiseman Bks.) Simon & Schuster/Paula Wiseman Bks.

Eareckson Tada, Joni & Jensen, Steve. The Meanest Teacher. 2005. (Darcy & Friends Ser.). 144p. (gr. 3-6). pap. 5.99 (978-1-58134-256-7(X), Crossway Bibles) Crossway.

—The Mission Adventure. 2005. (Darcy & Friends Ser.). 143p. (gr. 3-6). pap. 5.99 (978-1-58134-257-4(8), Crossway Bibles) Crossway.

Edward, J. P. The Outsider. 2012. 24p. pap. 24.95 (978-1-4626-7213-4(2)) America Star Bks.

Edwards, Janet. Earth Girl. 2013. (ENG.). 350p. (YA). (gr. 7). 17.99 (978-1-61614-765-5(2), Pyr Bks.) Prometheus Bks., Pubs.

Eggleton, Jill. Tony's Dad. Hawley, Kelvin, illus. 2003. (Rigby Sails Sailing Solo Ser.). (ENG.). 24p. (gr. 1-2). pap. 9.05 (978-0-7578-3975-7(4)) Rigby Education.

Elkeles, Simone. Leaving Paradise. 2007. 20.80 (978-1-4177-8393-9(1), Turtleback) Turtleback Bks.

—Return to Paradise. 2010. (Leaving Paradise Novel Ser.: 2). (ENG.). 312p. (YA). (gr. 8-18). pap. 9.95 (978-0-7387-1868-2(8), Flux) North Star Editions.

—Return to Paradise. 2010. lib. bdg. 20.80 (978-0-606-14994-5(5), Turtleback) Turtleback Bks.

Elliott, Rebecca. Just Because. (ENG., Illus.). (J). (gr. k-2). 2014. 12p. bds. 7.99 (978-0-7459-6460-7(5)) 2012. 32p. pap. 8.99 (978-0-7459-6235-1(1)) Lion Hudson PLC GBR. Dist: Independent Pubs. Group.

—Just Because. Elliott, Rebecca, illus. 2011. (ENG., Illus.). 32p. (J). (gr. -1-2). 14.99 (978-0-7459-6267-2(X)) Lion Hudson PLC GBR. Dist: Independent Pubs. Group.

—Sometimes. Elliott, Rebecca, illus. 2014. (ENG., Illus.). 32p. (J). (gr. k-2). pap. 8.99 (978-0-7459-6269-6(6)) Lion Hudson PLC GBR. Dist: Independent Pubs. Group.

English, James. Galia's Dad Is in a Wheelchair. 2017. (ENG., Illus.). 20p. (gr. 1). pap. 6.95 **(978-0-87565-649-6(8))** Texas Christian Univ. Pr.

Ferris, Jean. Of Sound Mind. 2004. (ENG.). 224p. (YA). (gr. 7). reprint ed. pap. 10.99 (978-0-374-45584-2(8), 9780374455842, Farrar, Straus & Giroux (BYR)) Farrar, Straus & Giroux.

—Of Sound Mind. 2004. 215p. (YA). (gr. 7). 14.60 (978-0-7569-2970-1(9)) Perfection Learning Corp.

Field, Jenepher. The Cloth Covered Notebook: That Was My Mother's Story. 2010. (ENG., Illus.). 97p. pap. 11.99 (978-0-9826781-6-9(9)) Etcetera Pr. LLC.

Fiona Fox Staff, ed. The Secret Garden. 2012. (ENG., Illus.). 64p. 15.00 (978-1-84135-837-6(1)) Award Pubns. Ltd. GBR. Dist: Parkwest Pubns., Inc.

Fitzpatrick, Huntley. What I Thought Was True. 2014. (ENG.). 416p. (YA). (gr. 9). 17.99 (978-0-8037-3909-3(5), Dial Bks) Penguin Young Readers Group.

Flake, Sharon G. Pinned. (ENG.). 240p. (J). 2014. (gr. 9). pap. 9.99 (978-0-545-05733-2(7)) 2012. (gr. 8-9). 17.99 (978-0-545-05718-9(3)) Scholastic, Inc. (Scholastic Pr.).

Fleming, Bryn. Jasper & Willie: Wildfire. 2015. (Range Riders Ser.). (ENG.). 130p. (J). 28.99 (978-1-941821-92-3(8)); pap. 9.99 (978-1-941821-71-8(5)) Graphic Arts Ctr. Publishing Co. (West Winds Pr.).

Foreman, Michael. Seal Surfer. Foreman, Michael, illus. 2007. (ENG., Illus.). 36p. (J). (gr. k-4). pap. 12.99 (978-1-84270-578-0(4)) Andersen Pr. GBR. Dist: Independent Pubs. Group.

Fournier, Kevin Mark. Sandbag Shuffle. 2007. (ENG.). 240p. (gr. 8-13). per. 12.95 (978-1-897235-22-5(4)) Thistledown Pr., Ltd. CAN. Dist: Univ. of Toronto Pr.

Fox, Nita. Captain Benjamin Dale. Wallace, Andrea, illus. 2008. 32p. (J). (gr. -1-3). pap. 5.99 (978-0-9816107-0-2(6)) Fox's Den Publishing.

Franco, Karen. Just Hold My Hand. 2013. 48p. pap. (978-1-4602-0616-4(9)) FriesenPress.

Franklin, Miriam Spitzer. Extraordinary. 2015. (ENG.). 256p. (J). (gr. 2-7). 14.99 (978-1-63220-402-8(9), Sky Pony Pr.) Skyhorse Publishing Co., Inc.

Frizzell, Colin. Chill, 1 vol. 2006. (Orca Soundings Ser.). (ENG.). 128p. (YA). (gr. 8-12). per. 9.95 (978-1-55143-507-7(1)) Orca Bk. Pubs. USA.

Fudge, Benjamin. Enrique Speaks with His Hands. Edmonson, Tim, illus. 2008. (ENG.). 32p. (J). (gr. -1-3). 16.95 (978-0-9800649-3-3(7)) Hilton Publishing Co.

Fussell, Sandy. Owl Ninja. James, Rhian Nest, illus. 2011. (Samurai Kids Ser.: 2). (ENG.). 272p. (J). (gr. 4-7). 15.99 (978-0-7636-5003-2(X)) Candlewick Pr.

—Shaolin Tiger. James, Rhian Nest, illus. 2011. (Samurai Kids Ser.: 3). (ENG.). 272p. (J). (gr. 4-7). pap. 6.99 (978-0-7636-5702-4(6)) Candlewick Pr.

—White Crane. James, Rhian Nest, illus. 2010. (Samurai Kids Ser.: 1). (ENG.). 256p. (J). (gr. 4-7). 15.99 (978-0-7636-4503-8(6)) Candlewick Pr.

Gaffney, Ellen. Wings for a Flower. Gaffney, Ellen, illus. 2013. (Illus.). 32p. 16.95 (978-0-9882212-6-0(8)) Three Bean Pr.

Gallo, Donald R., ed. Owning It: Stories about Teens with Disabilities. (ENG., Illus.). 224p. (YA). (gr. 7). 2010. mass mkt. 6.99 (978-0-7636-4661-5(X)) 2008. 17.99 (978-0-7636-3255-7(4)) Candlewick Pr.

Gantos, Jack. What Would Joey Do? 2004. (Joey Pigza Ser.). 229p. (J). (gr. 5-9). 13.65 (978-0-7569-2597-0(5)) Perfection Learning Corp.

—What Would Joey Do? 2014. (Joey Pigza Ser.: 3). (ENG.). 256p. (J). (gr. 5-9). pap. 7.99 (978-1-250-06169-0(5), 9781250061690) Square Fish.

Gehret, Jeanne. The Don't-Give-Up Kid: And Learning Disabilities. LaDuca, Michael, illus. 4th ed. 2009. (Coping Ser.). (ENG.). 32p. (J). (gr. 1-3). 17.95 (978-0-9821982-0-9(5)) Verbal Images Pr.

Gellman, Ellie. Jeremy's Dreidel. Mola, Maria, illus. 2012. (Hanukkah Ser.). 32p. (J). (gr. k-3). (ENG.). lib. bdg. 17.95 (978-0-7613-7507-4(4)); (SPA & ENG.). 7.95 (978-0-7613-7508-1(2)) Lerner Publishing Group. (Kar-Ben Publishing).

Geraldine Anderson. Bev's Amazing Adventures: The Kitten. 2012. 28p. pap. 24.95 (978-1-4626-7386-5(4)) America Star Bks.

Getzinger, Donna. Special. 2004. 108p. (J). pap. 7.95 (978-0-87714-530-1(X)) i-5 Publishing LLC.

Gianferrari, Maria. Hello Goodbye Dog. Barton, Patrice, illus. 2017. (ENG.). 40p. (J). 16.99 (978-1-62672-177-7(7), 9781626721777) Roaring Brook Pr.

Giff, Patricia Reilly. All the Way Home. 2003. (ENG., Illus.). 176p. (J). (gr. 3-7). pap. 7.99 (978-0-440-41182-6(3), Yearling) Random Hse. Children's Bks.

Gillmore, Inez Haynes. Maida's Little Shop. 2007. (ENG.). 158p. pap. 19.99 (978-1-4346-1156-7(6)); 172p. pap. 21.99 (978-1-4346-1227-4(9)) Creative Media Partners, LLC.

Goldin, Barbara Diamond. Cakes & Miracles: A Purim Tale, 0 vols. Zollars, Jaime, illus. 2010. (ENG.). 32p. (J). (gr. k-3). 17.99 (978-0-7614-5701-5(1), 9780761457015, Amazon Children's Publishing) Amazon Publishing.

Gordon, Kathy L. I'm not sick, I have a Handicap. 2011. 24p. (gr. 1-2). pap. 11.32 (978-1-4567-5660-4(5)) AuthorHouse.

Grabenstein, Chris. I Funny: A Middle School Story. Patterson, James, ed. Park, Laura, illus. 2012. 303p. (J). 11.99 (978-0-316-22638-7(6), 1351607) Little Brown & Co.

Green, Amy. Escape from Riddler's Pass, Vol. 2. 2011. (ENG., Illus.). 176p. (J). pap. 7.99 (978-1-59317-433-0(0)) Warner Pr., Inc.

Green, Tim. Lost Boy. (J). (gr. 3-7). 2016. 320p. pap. 6.99 (978-0-06-231709-4(1)) 2015. (ENG.). 304p. 16.99 (978-0-06-231708-7(3)) HarperCollins Pubs.

Greene, Janice. No Way to Run, 1 vol. unabr. ed. 2010. (Q Reads Ser.). (ENG.). 32p. (YA). (gr. 9-12). pap. 6.95 (978-1-61651-184-5(2)) Saddleback Educational Publishing, Inc.

Greene, Joanne. Lippy the Lion. 2006. (ENG.). 64p. per. (978-1-894936-67-5(1)) Saga Bks.

Griffin, Paul. The Orange Houses. 2011. (ENG.). 176p. (YA). (gr. 9-18). 8.99 (978-0-14-241982-3(6), Speak) Penguin Young Readers Group.

Griswold, Melissa. Friends, Like You. Fisher, Cynthia, illus. abr. ed. 2007. 32p. (J). 15.00 (978-0-9797287-3-0(8)) Mainstream Ctr., Schl. for the Deaf, The.

—Friends, Like You: Children's Activity Book. Fisher, Cynthia, illus. 2007. 16p. (J). (978-0-9797287-4-7(6)) Mainstream Ctr., Schl. for the Deaf, The.

Gutman, Dan. The Million Dollar Putt. 2007. 69p. (J). (gr. 3-7). 13.65 (978-0-7569-8281-2(2)) Perfection Learning Corp.

Hagman, Harvey Dixon. Majesty from Assateague, 1 vol. Aiken, David, illus. 2009. (ENG.). 80p. (J). pap. 8.95 (978-0-87033-552-5(9), 9780870335525, Cornell Maritime Pr./Tidewater Pubs.) Schiffer Publishing, Ltd.

Hale, Marian. The Truth about Sparrows. 2007. (ENG.). 288p. (YA). (gr. 7-12). per. 9.99 (978-0-312-37133-3(0), 9780312371333) Square Fish.

Hale, Shannon. Dangerous. (ENG.). 416p. (YA). (gr. 7). 2015. pap. 9.99 (978-1-61963-819-8(3), 9781619638198) 2014. 17.99 (978-1-59990-168-8(4), 9781599901688) Bloomsbury Publishing USA. (Bloomsbury USA Childrens).

Halliday, John. Shooting Monarchs. 2007. (ENG.). 144p. (YA). (gr. 8). pap. 8.95 (978-1-4169-5559-7(3), McElderry, Margaret K. Bks.) McElderry, Margaret K. Bks.

Hambrick, Sharon. Tommy's Race. Manning, Maurie J., illus. 2004. (Fig Street Kids Ser.). 95p. (J). (gr. 1-2). 7.49 (978-1-59166-286-0(9)) BJU Pr.

Harkness, Karen. Coralee's Best Run Yet. 2007. (Illus.). 40p. (J). per. 7.99 net. (978-0-9800934-0-7(6)) H&W Publishing Inc.

Harris, Donna. Ruff Life. 2011. 240p. pap. 17.99 (978-1-4567-5081-7(X)) AuthorHouse.

Harris, Loretta. The Inside Struggle. 2007. 30p. (YA). 1.99 (978-0-9786681-3-6(8)) Triumphant Living Enterprises, Inc.

Hartman, Carrie. Child of Mine. 2007. (ENG., Illus.). 32p. (J). lib. bdg. 11.99 (978-1-934277-12-6(6)) Mam Green Publishing, Inc.

Hartry, Nancy. Watching Jimmy. 2009. (ENG.). 160p. (YA). (gr. 4-7). 16.95 (978-0-88776-871-2(7), Tundra Bks.) Tundra Bks. CAN. Dist: Penguin Random Hse. LLC.

Haskell, Merrie. Handbook for Dragon Slayers. 2013. (ENG.). 336p. (J). (gr. 3-7). 16.99 (978-0-06-200816-9(1)) HarperCollins Pubs.

Hayward, Mark Brauner. I See Without My Eyes. Hartman, Nancy Lee, illus. 2009. 32p. pap. 12.99 (978-1-4343-3823-5(1)) AuthorHouse.

Hebron, Yvette C. Ross. Cherry Blossom Kids & the Three-legged Dog. 2007. (Illus.). 48p. (J). 18.95 (978-0-9774982-0-8(4)) Steveedee Publishing Co.

Hege, Lynnita Rae. Dan & God's Gifts. Hackman, Evelyn, illus. 2016. 109p. (J). **(978-0-7399-2520-1(2))** Rod & Staff Pubs., Inc.

Henry, April. Count All Her Bones. 2017. (Girl, Stolen Ser.). (ENG.). 240p. (YA). 17.99 (978-1-62779-591-3(X), 9781627795913, Holt, Henry & Co. Bks. For Young Readers) Holt, Henry & Co.

—Girl, Stolen. 2010. (Girl, Stolen Ser.). (ENG.). 224p. (YA). (gr. 7-12). 18.99 (978-0-8050-9005-5(3), 9780805090055, Holt, Henry & Co. Bks. For Young Readers) Holt, Henry & Co.

Henry, Heather French. Las Zapatas Magicas de Claire. 2007. (Claire's Everyday Adventures Ser Ser.). (SPA & ENG., Illus.). 32p. (J). (gr. k-4). pap. 9.95 (978-1-932824-03-2(0)) Cubbie Blue Publishing.

Herbauts, Anne, creator. What Color Is the Wind? 2016. (ENG., Illus.). 48p. (J). (gr. k). pap. 19.95 (978-1-59270-221-3(X)) Enchanted Lion Bks., LLC.

Herrera, Juan Felipe. SkateFate. 2015. 128p. (YA). (gr. 8). pap. 9.99 (978-0-06-143289-7(X), HarperTeen) HarperCollins Pubs.

Herrera, Juan Felipe & Cuevas, Ernesto, illus. Featherless. 2013.Tr. of Desplumado. (SPA & ENG.). 32p. (J). pap. 8.95 (978-0-89239-303-9(3)) Lee & Low Bks., Inc.

Hervey, Cheston & Doane, Darren. Kill the Dragon, Get the Girl. 2017. (J). pap. **(978-1-59128-188-7(1))** Canon Pr.

Holman, Nedra. Beautiful Queen. Velitchenko, Olga, illus. 2008. 40p. (J). (978-1-4363-5461-5(7)) Xlibris Corp.

Hostetter, Joyce Moyer. Comfort. 2011. (ENG.). 312p. (J). (gr. 5-12). pap. 7.95 (978-1-59078-895-0(8), Calkins Creek) Boyds Mills Pr.

Hubler, Marsha. Leading the Way, 1 vol. 2010. (Keystone Stables Ser.). (ENG.). 128p. (J). pap. 7.99 (978-0-310-71796-6(5)) Zonderkidz.

—The Long Ride Home, 1 vol. 2010. (Keystone Stables Ser.). (ENG.). 144p. (J). pap. 7.99 (978-0-310-71692-1(6)) Zonderkidz.

—Summer Camp Adventure, 1 vol. 2009. (Keystone Stables Ser.). (ENG.). 128p. (J). pap. 7.99 (978-0-310-71795-9(7)) Zonderkidz.

Hughes, Jack. Dachy's Deaf. 2014. (Dinosaur Friends Ser.). (Illus.). 32p. (J). (gr. k-3). lib. bdg. 26.25 (978-1-4777-9222-3(8)) Windmill Bks.

Hugo, Victor. The Hunchback of Notre-Dame. Corvino, Lucy, illus. 2008. (Classic Starts(tm) Ser.). (ENG.). 160p. (J). (gr. 2-4). 6.95 (978-1-4027-4575-1(3)) Sterling Publishing Co., Inc.

—The Hunchback of Notre Dame: Illusrtrated Edition, 1 vol. 2012. (Calico Illustrated Classics Ser.: No. 4). (ENG., Illus.). 112p. (J). (gr. 3-6). 27.07 (978-1-61641-614-0(9)) Magic Wagon.

The Hunchback of Notre Dame. (Read-Along Ser.). (J). 7.99 incl. audio (978-1-55723-992-1(4)) Walt Disney Records.

Ikuwa, Robert Lono. The Face of Her King. 2007.Tr. of Ke Alo o Kona Moi. (ENG & HAW.). (J). lib. bdg. (978-0-9773495-3-1(5)) Na Kamalei Koolauloa Early Education Program.

Irick, Angela. Ashley Wins the First Day of School. 2012. 16p. pap. 15.99 (978-1-4772-7182-7(1)) AuthorHouse.

Jackson, Alisha. Noah's Fire Engine. 2011. 16p. 9.00 (978-1-4567-2977-6(2)) AuthorHouse.

Jasnoch, Dorothy. Frankie the Bunny: Newfound Friends. Korzeniowski, Samson O., ed. Jasnoch, Dorothy, illus. 2013. (Illus.). 28p. 17.99 (978-1-937752-15-6(1)) Owl About Bks. Pub., Inc.

Jin-Ho, Jung. Look Up! Jin-Ho, Jung, illus. 2016. (ENG., Illus.). 32p. (J). (gr. -1-1). 16.95 (978-0-8234-3652-1(7)) Holiday Hse., Inc.

John, Antony. Five Flavors of Dumb. 2011. (ENG.). 368p. (YA). (gr. 7-18). 8.99 (978-0-14-241943-4(5), Speak) Penguin Young Readers Group.

John, Louise. My Chair. Elkerton, Andy, illus. 2013. (Start Reading Ser.). (ENG.). 24p. (gr. k-1). pap. 41.94 (978-1-4765-3225-7(7)); pap. 7.95 (978-1-4765-3200-4(1)) Capstone Press of Coughlan Cos.

Johnson, Harriet McBryde. Accidents of Nature. rev. ed. 2006. (ENG.). 240p. (YA). (gr. 7-12). 19.99 (978-0-8050-7634-9(4),

Holt, Henry & Co. Bks. For Young Readers) Holt, Henry & Co.

—Accidents of Nature. rev. l.t. ed. 2007. (Thorndike Literacy Bridge Ser.). 273p. (YA). (gr. 7-12). 22.95 (978-0-7862-9182-3(6)) Thorndike Pr.

Johnson, Lois Walfrid. Mystery of the Missing Map. 2009. (J). 8.99 (978-0-88062-283-7(0)) Mott Media.

Johnston, Julie. Hero of Lesser Causes. pap. 6.95 (978-0-7737-5850-6(X)) Stoddart Kids CAN. Dist: Fitzhenry & Whiteside, Ltd.

—Hero of Lesser Causes. 2003. (ENG.). 232p. (J). (gr. 5). pap. 10.95 (978-0-88776-649-7(8), Tundra Bks.) Tundra Bks. CAN. Dist: Penguin Random Hse. LLC.

Jones, Patrick & Chartier, Brent. Collateral Damage. 2015. (ENG.). 128p. (YA). (gr. 6-12). pap. 7.99 (978-1-4677-8091-9(X)) Lerner Publishing Group.

Jordan, Sherryl. The Raging Quiet. l.t. ed. 2005. 416p. 22.95 (978-0-7862-7313-3(5), Large Print Pr.) Thorndike Pr.

Kamata, Suzanne. Gadget Girl: The Art of Being Invisible. 2013. (ENG., Illus.). 256p. (YA). pap. 14.95 (978-1-936846-38-2(1)) GemmaMedia.

Kats, Jewel. Cinderella's Magical Wheelchair: An Empowering Fairy Tale. Kinra, Richa, illus. 2012. (J). 24p. 29.95 (978-1-61599-113-6(1)); 20p. pap. 16.95 (978-1-61599-112-9(3)) Loving Healing Pr., Inc.

—Miss Popular Steals the Show: Girls in Wheelchairs Rule! Stenton, Murray, illus. 2014. 37p. (J). pap. 14.95 (978-1-61599-236-2(7)) Loving Healing Pr., Inc.

Kaufman, Sashi. Wired Man & Other Freaks of Nature. 2016. (ENG.). 264p. (YA). (gr. 9-12). 17.99 (978-1-4677-8563-1(6), Carolrhoda Bks.) Lerner Publishing Group.

Kennedy, J. Aday. Buster Bear & Uncle B. Movshina, Marina, illus. 2012. 20p. pap. 10.95 (978-1-61633-235-8(2)) Guardian Angel Publishing, Inc.

Kent, Renee Holmes. Robyn Flies Home, Vol. 4. 2004. (Adventures in Misty Falls Ser.: Vol. 4). (Illus.). 100p. (gr. 4-7). pap. 4.99 (978-1-56309-764-5(8), N007106) New Hope Pubs.

Kent, Rose. Rocky Road. 2012. (ENG.). 304p. (J). (gr. 3-7). 7.99 (978-0-375-86345-5(1), Yearling) Random Hse. Children's Bks.

Keplinger, Kody. Run. (ENG.). 304p. (gr. 9). 2017. (J). pap. 10.99 **(978-0-545-83114-7(8)**, Scholastic Paperbacks) 2016. (YA). 17.99 (978-0-545-83113-0(X), Scholastic Pr.) Scholastic, Inc.

Ketchen, Susan. Born That Way. 2009. (ENG.). 176p. (YA). (gr. 7-10). pap. 12.95 (978-0-88982-254-2(9)) Oolichan Bks. CAN. Dist: Univ. of Toronto Pr.

Keyes, Daniel. Flores para Algernon. 2003. (SPA.). 224p. (J). (978-84-483-0262-7(1)) Acento Editorial.

Khan, Rukhsana. King for a Day, 1 vol. Krömer, Christiane, illus. 2014. (ENG.). 32p. (J). 17.95 (978-1-60060-659-5(8)) Lee & Low Bks., Inc.

Kim, YeShil. My Best Buddy. Tanco, Miguel, illus. 2014. (MySELF Bookshelf Ser.). (ENG.). 32p. (J). (gr. k-2). pap. 11.94 (978-1-60357-693-2(2)); lib. bdg. 25.27 (978-1-59953-658-3(7)) Norwood Hse. Pr.

Kingsley, Linda Kurtz. Bringing up Sophie. Kingsley, Linda Kurtz, illus. 2010. (Illus.). 32p. (J). lib. bdg. 15.95 (978-0-944727-25-6(5), Turtle Bks.) Jason & Nordic Pubs.

—Bringing up Sophie. 2009. (Illus.). 32p. (J). pap. 9.95 (978-0-944727-24-9(7), Turtle Bks.) Jason & Nordic Pubs.

—Signs of Jays. Kingsley, Linda Kurtz, illus. 2008. (Illus.). 32p. (J). (ENG.). lib. bdg. 15.95 (978-0-944727-23-2(9)); pap. 9.95 (978-0-944727-22-5(0)) Jason & Nordic Pubs. (Turtle Bks.).

Kinra, Richa, illus. The Princess Panda Tea Party: A Cerebral Palsy Fairy Tale. 2014. 45p. (J). pap. 14.95 (978-1-61599-219-5(7)) Loving Healing Pr., Inc.

Kinsella, Audrey. Dingle: The Helpful Ice Cream Cone Delivery Dog. 2010. 24p. 14.49 (978-1-4490-8362-5(5)) AuthorHouse.

Kinsey-Warnock, Natalie. Lumber Camp Library. Bernardin, James, illus. 2003. (ENG.). 96p. (J). (gr. 2-5). pap. 4.99 (978-0-06-444292-3(6)) HarperCollins Pubs.

Klein, Adria F. Max's Fun Day, 1 vol. Gallagher-Cole, Mernie, illus. 2007. (Read-It! Readers: the Life of Max Ser.). (ENG.). 24p. (gr. -1-2). lib. bdg. 21.32 (978-1-4048-3150-6(9), 1265797, Easy Readers) Picture Window Bks.

Klimo, Kate. Dog Diaries #10: Rolf. Jessell, Tim, illus. 2017. (Dog Diaries). (ENG.). 160p. (J). (gr. 2-5). pap. 7.99 (978-0-399-55128-4(X), Random Hse. Bks. for Young Readers) Random Hse. Children's Bks.

Klise, Kate. Stand Straight, Ella Kate: The True Story of a Real Giant. Klise, M. Sarah, illus. 2010. (ENG.). 32p. (J). (gr. 1-3). 16.99 (978-0-8037-3404-3(2), Dial Bks) Penguin Young Readers Group.

Knox, Dahk. Zander, Friend of the Se. 2008. 32p. pap. 7.95 (978-1-58275-229-7(X)) Black Forest Pr.

Kobliner Shaw, Beth & Shaw, Jacob. Jacob's Eye Patch. Feiffer, Jules, illus. 2013. (ENG.). 32p. 17.00 (978-1-4767-3732-4(0)) Simon & Schuster.

Koertge, Ron. Now Playing: Stoner & Spaz II. 2011. (ENG., Illus.). 224p. (YA). (gr. 9-18). 16.99 (978-0-7636-5081-0(1)) Candlewick Pr.

—Stoner & Spaz. 2011. (ENG., Illus.). 192p. (YA). (gr. 9). pap. 7.99 (978-0-7636-5757-4(3)) Candlewick Pr.

Konigsburg, E. L. The View from Saturday. 280p. (YA). (gr. 5-18). pap. 4.95 (978-0-8072-1511-1(2), Listening Library) Random Hse. Audio Publishing Group.

Kositchek, Gloria. Dream Prom, 1 vol. 2009. 174p. pap. 24.95 (978-1-4489-9632-2(5)) America Star Bks.

Kraemer, Lillian Rosa. The Wheelchair Adventures of Jeannie & the Wallpaper Children. Drown, Eleanor J., illus. 2011. 150p. 40.95 (978-1-258-08936-8(X)) Literary Licensing, LLC.

Kravitz, Danny. Tommy Mcknight & the Great Election. 2016. (Presidential Politics Ser.). (ENG.). 96p. (gr. 3-4). lib. bdg. 26.65 (978-1-4965-2585-7(X), Connect) Stone Arch Bks.

Kuhns, Jennifer. Hailey's Dream. Sneed, Patty, illus. 2013. 32p. pap. 13.95 (978-0-9846811-8-1(3)) Shalako Pr.

Kumin, Maxine. Lizzie! 2014. (ENG., Illus.). 162p. (J). (gr. 4-7). 21.95 (978-1-60980-518-0(6), Triangle Square) Seven Stories Pr.

Kupfer, Wendy. Let's Hear It for Almigal. Lyon, Tammie, illus. 2012. (ENG.). 32p. (J). (gr. k-2). 16.99 (978-0-9838294-0-9(3)) Handfinger Pr.

L. A. Goal Members, contrib. by. Disabled Fables: Aesop's Fables Retold & Illustrated by Artists with Developmental Disabilities, 1 vol. 2005. (ENG., Illus.). 32p. (J). (gr. 1-18). 19.95 (978-1-932065-97-8(0)) Star Bright Bks., Inc.

Laird, Elizabeth. Red Sky in the Morning. 2012. (ENG.). 192p. (gr. 3-10). pap. 12.95 (978-1-60846-153-0(X)) Haymarket Bks.

Laird, Elizabeth & Davison, Roz. Jungle School. Sim, David, illus. 2006. (Green Bananas Ser.). (ENG.). 48p. (J). (gr. -1-3). (978-0-7787-1042-4(4)) Crabtree Publishing Co.

Langston, Laura. Stepping Out, 1 vol. 2016. (Orca Limelights Ser.). (ENG.). 144p. (J). (gr. 6-9). pap. 9.95 (978-1-4598-0895-9(9)) Orca Bk. Pubs. USA.

Larson, Kirby. Liberty. 2016. (Dogs of World War II Ser.). (ENG.). 240p. (J). (gr. 3-7). 16.99 (978-0-545-84071-2(6), Scholastic Pr.) Scholastic, Inc.

Levin, Betty. The Unmaking of Duncan Veerick. 2007. (ENG.). 212p. (J). (gr. 9-12). 16.95 (978-1-932425-96-3(9), Front Street) Boyds Mills Pr.

Lewis, Beverly. In Jesse's Shoes: Appreciating Kids with Special Needs. Nikiel, Laura Gibbons, illus. 2007. (ENG.). 32p. (J). (gr. -1-4). 11.99 (978-0-7642-0313-8(4)) Bethany Hse. Pubs.

Limb, Lisa. The Wishing Wheelchair. 2009. 40p. pap. 16.99 (978-1-4389-4205-6(2)) AuthorHouse.

Lindstrom, Eric. Not If I See You First. 2015. (ENG.). 320p. (YA). (gr. 10-17). 18.00 (978-0-316-25985-9(3)) Little Brown & Co.

Liu, Carol & Caldarone, Marybeth Sidoti. Arlene on the Scene. 2010. 206p. (J). (gr. 3-5). pap. 7.95 (978-1-934572-54-2(3)) Emerald Bk. Co.

Loewen, Ann E. Fast for My Feet. 2013. 176p. (978-1-4602-3384-9(0)) FriesenPress.

Lois, Lowry. Gathering Blue. (Giver Quartet Ser.: 2). (ENG.). 256p. (YA). (gr. 7). 2013. pap. 9.99 (978-0-547-90414-6(2)) 2012. 17.99 (978-0-547-99568-7(7)) Houghton Mifflin Harcourt Publishing Co.

—Gathering Blue. unabr. ed. 2004. (Middle Grade Cassette Librariestm Ser.). 224p. (J). (gr. 5-9). pap. 38.00 incl. audio (978-0-8072-0989-9(9), S YA 250 SP, Listening Library) Random Hse. Audio Publishing Group.

—Gathering Blue. 2013. (Giver Quartet Ser.: 2). lib. bdg. 20.85 (978-0-606-31673-6(6), Turtleback) Turtleback Bks.

Long, Susan Hill. The Magic Mirror: Concerning a Lonely Princess, a Foundling Girl, a Scheming King & a Pickpocket Squirrel. 2016. (ENG., Illus.). 320p. (J). (gr. 3-7). 16.99 (978-0-553-51134-5(3), Knopf Bks. for Young Readers) Random Hse. Children's Bks.

Look, Lenore. Ruby Lu, Empress of Everything. Wilsdorf, Anne, illus. 2007. 164p. (gr. 1-5). 16.00 (978-0-7569-8113-6(1)) Perfection Learning Corp.

—Ruby Lu, Empress of Everything. Wilsdorf, Anne, illus. 2006. (ENG.). 176p. (J). (gr. 1-5). 16.99 (978-0-689-86460-5(4), Atheneum Bks. for Young Readers) Simon & Schuster Children's Publishing.

Lord, Cynthia. Rules. 2009. 8.44 (978-0-7848-2921-9(7), Everbind) Marco Bk. Co.

—Rules. 2008. (Illus.). 200p. (gr. 4-7). 17.00 (978-0-7569-8283-6(9)) Perfection Learning Corp.

—Rules. (J). 2008. 77.49 (978-1-4361-5837-4(0)) 2007. 220.75 (978-1-4281-5209-0(1)) 2007. 74.75 (978-1-4281-5208-3(3)) 2007. 87.75 (978-1-4281-5214-4(8)) 2007. 89.75 (978-1-4281-5212-0(1)) 2007. (SPA.). 72.75 (978-1-4281-5210-6(5)) Recorded Bks., Inc.

—Rules. (ENG.). (J). (gr. 3-7). 2008. 224p. pap. 7.99 (978-0-439-44383-8(0), Scholastic Paperbacks) 2006. 208p. 15.99 (978-0-439-44382-1(2), Scholastic Pr.) Scholastic, Inc.

—Rules. rev. l.t. ed. 2007. (Literacy Bridge Middle Reader Ser.). 191p. (J). (gr. 4-7). 23.95 (978-0-7862-9559-3(7)) Thorndike Pr.

—Rules. 2008. lib. bdg. 17.20 (978-1-4178-2956-9(7)) Turtleback Bks.

Lovelace, Eloise. Elvin's Friends. 2012. 20p. pap. 17.99 (978-1-4685-7615-3(1)) AuthorHouse.

Luning, Barbara. The Quilted Zoo. 2008. 28p. pap. 15.99 (978-1-4363-1778-8(9)) Xlibris Corp.

Lupica, Mike. Million-Dollar Throw. 2010. (ENG.). 272p. (J). (gr. 5-18). 7.99 (978-0-14-241558-0(8), Puffin Books) Penguin Young Readers Group.

—Million-Dollar Throw. 2010. (Million Dollar Sports Ser.). lib. bdg. 18.40 (978-0-606-25316-1(5), Turtleback) Turtleback Bks.

Macri, Rebecca. Pip: A Very Special Little Caterpillar. 2010. 32p. (J). 16.95 (978-1-886057-61-6(3)) Warren Publishing, Inc.

Madden, Kerry. Gentle's Holler. 2007. (Maggie Valley Ser.). 237p. (gr. 4-7). 17.00 (978-0-7569-8090-0(9)) Perfection Learning Corp.

Maguire, Gregory. Missing Sisters. 2009. 192p. (J). 16.99 (978-0-06-123204-6(1)); (ENG.). (gr. 3-7). pap. 6.99 (978-0-06-123203-9(3)) HarperCollins Pubs.

Mahony, Mary. School is Not for Me, Jeremy James Conor McGee. Frederick, Sarah, illus. 2009. (J). pap. 7.95 (978-0-9658879-4-6(4)) Redding Pr.

Martelli, Dawn. Like Me. Wharton, Jennifer Heyd, illus. 2004. (J). (978-1-893516-01-4(6)) Our Child Pr.

Martin, Rafe. Birdwing. 2007. (ENG.). 384p. (J). (gr. 7-12). pap. 7.99 (978-0-439-21168-0(9), Levine, Arthur A. Bks.) Scholastic, Inc.

Martone, Ginny. Trouble at Big Bear Falls. 2011. 90p. pap. 19.95 (978-1-4626-2558-1(4)) America Star Bks.

Massey, David. Taken. 2014. (ENG.). 320p. (J). (gr. 9). 18.99 (978-0-545-66128-7(5), Chicken Hse., The) Scholastic, Inc.

Matlin, Marlee & Cooney, Doug. Nobody's Perfect. 2006. (ENG., Illus.). 240p. (J). (gr. 3-7). 15.95 (978-0-689-86986-0(X), Simon & Schuster Bks. For Young Readers) Simon & Schuster Bks. For Young Readers.

McBay, Bruce & Heneghan, James. Waiting for Sarah. 2004. 170p. (gr. 7). 17.95 (978-0-7569-4567-1(4)) Perfection Learning Corp.

Mcelfresh, Lynn. Strong Deaf. 2012. 130p. 18.95 (978-1-60898-126-7(6)); pap. 9.95 (978-1-60898-127-4(4)) namelos llc.

McGovern, Cammie. Say What You Will. (ENG.). (YA). (gr. 9). 2015. 368p. pap. 9.99 (978-0-06-227111-2(3)) 2014. 352p. 17.99 (978-0-06-227110-5(5)) HarperCollins Pubs. (HarperTeen).

—A Step Toward Falling. (YA). (gr. 9). 2016. 384p. pap. 9.99 (978-0-06-227114-3(8)) 2015. (ENG.). 368p. 17.99 (978-0-06-227113-6(X)) HarperCollins Pubs. (HarperTeen).

—A Step Toward Falling. 2016. (YA). lib. bdg. 20.85 (978-0-606-39483-3(4)) Turtleback Bks.

McKinnon, Hannah Roberts. The Properties of Water. 2010. (ENG.). 176p. (YA). (gr. 5-9). 27.99 (978-0-374-36145-7(2), 9780374361457, Farrar, Straus & Giroux (BYR)) Farrar, Straus & Giroux.

Messer, Celeste M. The Gift. 2004. (Adventures of Andi O'Malley Ser.). (Illus.). 82-92p. (J). (gr. 4-7). 4.95 (978-0-9702171-3-4(7)) AshleyAlan Enterprises.

Meyers, Ann Marie. Up in the Air. 2013. 244p. (J). 22.99 (978-1-939967-03-9(1), Jolly Fish Pr.) North Star Editions.

Michelinie, David, et al. Freemind - The Origin. 2003. (Freemind Ser.). (Illus.). 112p. 14.95 (978-0-9744225-0-3(9)) Future Comics.

Mikaelsen, Ben. Petey. 2010. (ENG.). 256p. (J). (gr. 3-7). pap. 6.99 (978-1-4231-3174-8(6)) Hyperion Pr.

—Petey. 2011. 8.32 (978-0-7848-3604-0(3), Everbind) Marco Bk. Co.

—Stranded. 2010. (ENG.). 288p. (J). (gr. 3-7). pap. 5.99 (978-1-4231-3362-9(5)) Hyperion Pr.

Miles, Ellen. Honey. 2009. 75p. (J). (978-1-60744-367-4(8)) Scholastic, Inc.

Miller-Lachmann, Lyn. Gringolandia. 2009. (ENG.). 288p. (YA). (gr. 9-18). 18.95 (978-1-931896-49-8(6)) Curbstone Pr.

Miller, Sarah. Miss Spitfire: Reaching Helen Keller. (ENG.). (J). (gr. 5-7). 2010. 256p. pap. 7.99 (978-1-4424-0851-7(0)) 2007. 240p. 17.99 (978-1-4169-2542-2(2)) Simon & Schuster Children's Publishing. (Atheneum Bks. for Young Readers).

Miranda, Conchita. Yago's Heartbeat. 2011. (Light (Cuento de Luz) Ser.). (ENG., Illus.). 42p. (J). (gr. 1-4). (978-84-938240-3-7(8)) D P & G Military Pubs.

Modesto, Michelle. Revenge & the Wild. 2016. 384p. (YA). (gr. 9). 17.99 (978-0-06-236615-3(7)) HarperCollins Pubs.

Montgomery, L. M. Kilmeny of the Orchard. 2010. 146p. pap. 16.95 (978-1-60444-108-6(9)) IndoEuropeanPublishing.com.

Moore, Genevieve. Catherine's Story. Littlewood, Karin, illus. 2010. (ENG.). 32p. (J). (gr. k-3). 17.95 (978-1-84507-655-9(9), Frances Lincoln) Quarto Publishing Group UK GBR. Dist: Hachette Bk. Group.

Moore-Mallinos, Jennifer, et al. It's Called Dyslexia. Fabrega, Marta, illus. 2007. (Live & Learn Ser.). (ENG.). 32p. (J). (gr. -1-2). pap. 7.99 (978-0-7641-3794-5(8)) Barron's Educational Series, Inc.

Moskowitz, Hannah. Invincible Summer. 2011. (ENG.). 288p. (YA). (gr. 9-18). pap. 9.99 (978-1-4424-0751-0(4), Simon Pulse) Simon Pulse.

Murillo, Vinicio. Roderick Roach. 2013. 50p. pap. 10.95 (978-1-62516-018-8(6), Strategic Bk. Publishing) Strategic Book Publishing & Rights Agency (SBPRA).

My Uncle Has Wheels. 2005. (J). 8.00 (978-0-9767077-1-4(3)) Carson, Tracy.

Nichol, Tim. Stephen Harris in Trouble: A Dyspraxic Drama in Several Clumsy Acts. 2003. (ENG.). 144p. (J). pap. 19.95 (978-1-84310-134-5(3), 4267) Kingsley, Jessica Pubs. GBR. Dist: Macmillan Distribution Ltd.

North, Sharon Rae. My Brand New Leg. 2003. (Illus.). 40p. (J). per. 11.95 (978-0-9741544-0-4(7), Baby Faye Bks.) Northstar Entertainment Group, LLC.

Oakes, Stephanie. The Sacred Lies of Minnow Bly. 2015. (ENG.). 400p. (YA). (gr. 9). 17.99 (978-0-8037-4070-9(0), Dial Bks) Penguin Young Readers Group.

O'Donnell, Liam. Ginger Leads the Way. Diefendorf, Cathy, illus. (Pet Tales Ser.). (ENG.). 32p. (J). (gr. -1-2). 2005. 2.95 (978-1-59249-359-3(9), 1B024) 2005. 4.95 (978-1-59249-358-6(0), 1B023) 2004. 9.95 (978-1-59249-360-9(2), 1B025) Soundprints.

Oelschlager, Vanita. My Grampy Can't Walk. Hegan, Robin & Blackwood, Kristin, illus. 2008. (ENG.). 36p. (J). (gr. -1-3). 9.95 (978-0-9800162-0-8(7)) VanitaBooks.

O'Guilin, Peadar. The Call. 2016. (ENG.). 320p. (YA). (gr. 9). 18.99 (978-1-338-04561-1(X)) Scholastic, Inc.

Oliveira, Luis. Children of Hope 2. 2008. 74p. pap. 15.95 (978-0-615-19723-4(X)) Desktop Prepress Services.

O'Neill, Kaney. Dream & Reach. 2003. (Illus.). 29p. (J). pap. (978-0-9747797-0-6(9)) ONeill, Gene & Assoc.

Palacio, R. J. Auggie & Me: Three Wonder Stories. 2015. (ENG.). 320p. (J). (gr. 3-7). 16.99 (978-1-101-93485-2(9), Knopf Bks. for Young Readers) Random Hse. Children's Bks.

—We're All Wonders. 2017. (ENG.). 32p. (J). (gr. -1-3). 18.99 **(978-1-5247-6649-8(6))**; (Illus.). lib. bdg. 21.99 **(978-1-5247-6650-4(X))** Random Hse. Children's Bks. (Knopf Bks. for Young Readers).

Palacio, R. J. Wonder. 2015. (JPN.). 420p. (J). (978-4-593-53495-1(X)) Holp Shuppan, Publishing.

—Wonder. 2015. (SPA.). 160p. (J). (gr. 3-7). pap. 9.95 (978-607-31-3242-8(5)) Penguin Random House Grupo Editorial, S.A. de C.V. MEX. Dist: Two Rivers Distribution.

—Wonder. (ENG.). (J). (gr. 3-7). 2015. 176p. 12.99 (978-0-553-49907-0(6)) 2012. 320p. 16.99 (978-0-375-86902-0(6)) 2012. 320p. lib. bdg. 19.99 (978-0-375-96902-7(0)) Random Hse. Children's Bks. (Knopf Bks. for Young Readers).

—Wonder. l.t. ed. 2013. (ENG.). 482p. 23.99 (978-1-4104-5741-7(9)) Thorndike Pr.

—Wonder. 2012. lib. bdg. 29.40 (978-0-606-36646-5(6)) Turtleback Bks.

Patterson, James. House of Robots: Robot Revolution. Neufeld, Juliana, illus. 2017. (House of Robots Ser.: 3). (ENG.). 336p. (J). (gr. 3-7). 13.99 (978-0-316-34958-1(5), Jimmy Patterson) Little Brown & Co.

Patterson, James & Grabenstein, Chris. I Even Funnier: A Middle School Story. Park, Laura, illus. 2013. (I Funny Ser.: 2). (ENG.). 368p. (J). (gr. 3-7). 13.99 (978-0-316-20697-6(0), Jimmy Patterson) Little Brown & Co.

—I Funny: A Middle School Story. Park, Laura, illus. (I Funny Ser.: 1). (ENG.). 320p. (J). (gr. 3-7). 2015. pap. 8.00 (978-0-316-20692-1(X)) 2013. 13.99 (978-0-316-32200-3(8)) Little Brown & Co. (Jimmy Patterson).

—I Funny TV: A Middle School Story. Park, Laura, illus. 2015. (I Funny Ser.: 4). (ENG.). 336p. (J). (gr. 3-7). 13.99 (978-0-316-30109-1(4), Jimmy Patterson) Little Brown & Co.

—I Totally Funniest: A Middle School Story. Park, Laura, illus. 2015. (J). 320p. (978-0-316-26161-6(0)); (ENG.). 336p. (gr. 3-7). 13.99 (978-0-316-40593-5(0), Jimmy Patterson) Little Brown & Co.

Pellegrin, Leeann. Hey I'm Alex. Rolf, Heidi, illus. 2012. 26p. pap. 12.95 (978-1-61244-049-1(5)) Halo Publishing International.

Pemberton, Teresa. Trissy's New Shoes. 2013. 32p. pap. 13.95 (978-1-4497-9337-1(1), WestBow Pr.) Author Solutions, Inc.

Perez, Annette. My Brain Won't Float Away / Mi cerebro no va a salir Flotando. Herranz Brooks, Jacqueline, tr. Fundora, Yolanda V., illus. 2007. (ENG & SPA.). 32p. (J). 19.95 (978-0-9725611-2-9(9), Campanita Bks.) Editorial Campana.

Perry, Jolene. The Summer I Found You. 2014. (ENG.). 256p. (YA). (gr. 8-12). 16.99 (978-0-8075-8369-2(3)) Whitman, Albert & Co.

Petrillo, Genevieve & Lyon, Lea. Keep Your Ear on the Ball, 1 vol. Lyon, Lea, illus. 2007. (ENG., Illus.). 32p. (J). (gr. -1-3). 16.95 (978-0-88448-296-3(0)) Tilbury Hse. Pubs.

Phyllarry (Rittmueller), Kathryn. Beauregart the Bear. 2009. (ENG., Illus.). 64p. (J). 12.95 (978-0-943972-80-0(9)) Homestead Publishing.

Piper, Deb. From A— to Zulinski. 2008. (J). pap. (978-0-88092-713-0(5)); lib. bdg. (978-0-88092-712-3(7)) Royal Fireworks Publishing Co.

Pitzer, Marjorie W. I Like Berries, Do You? Pitzer, Marjorie W., photos by. 2013. (ENG., Illus.). 14p. (J). 11.95 (978-1-60613-183-1(4)) Woodbine Hse.

Platt, Chris. Willow King, 1 vol. 2010. (ENG.). 192p. (J). (gr. 3-7). pap. 6.95 (978-1-56145-549-2(0)) Peachtree Pubs.

Polacco, Patricia. The Junkyard Wonders. Polacco, Patricia, illus. 2010. (ENG., Illus.). 48p. (J). (gr. 1-4). 17.99 (978-0-399-25078-1(6), Philomel Bks.) Penguin Young Readers Group.

Porter, Pamela. The Crazy Man, 1 vol. 2006. (ENG.). 176p. (J). (gr. 3-7). pap. 8.95 (978-0-88899-695-4(0)) Groundwood Bks. CAN. Dist: Publishers Group West (PGW).

Portman, Frank. Andromeda Klein. 2010. (ENG.). 432p. (YA). (gr. 9). pap. 9.99 (978-0-385-73526-1(X), Delacorte Bks. for Young Readers) Random Hse. Children's Bks.

Potter, Noel Gyro. A Wheel Life Lesson, 1 vol. Cannon, Joseph, illus. 2008. (Adventures of Marshall & Art Ser.). (ENG.). 32p. (gr. -1-4). 28.50 (978-1-60270-202-8(0), Looking Glass Library) ABDO Publishing Co.

Powell, Randy. Tribute to Another Dead Rock Star. 2003. (ENG.). 224p. (YA). (gr. 7-12). pap. 14.99 (978-0-374-47968-8(2), Sunburst) Farrar, Straus & Giroux.

Prince-Stokes, Cathy. The Story of Peabo, 1 vol. Edsall, Steven, illus. 2009. 35p. pap. 24.95 (978-1-61582-732-9(3)) America Star Bks.

Purkapile, Susan & Peck, Amy. Mumbles the Bumble Bee: The Bee Who Couldn't Buzz. Ducommun, Barbara, illus. 2008. (J). (978-1-930596-87-0(1)) Amherst Pr.

Reagan, Marianne & Reagan, John. It's Okay to Be Me. 2013. 28p. pap. 24.95 (978-1-63004-045-1(2)) America Star Bks.

Reichert, Paul. The Lemonade Ripple: A Sweet Story of Kindness & Charity. 2012. (ENG., Illus.). 40p. (J). (gr. -1-k). 12.95 (978-1-61608-701-2(3), 608701, Sky Pony Pr.) Skyhorse Publishing Co., Inc.

Reynolds, Jason. As Brave As You. (ENG.). 432p. (J). (gr. 5). 2017. pap. 7.99 (978-1-4814-1591-0(3), Atheneum Bks. for Young Readers) 2016. (Illus.). 16.99 (978-1-4814-1590-3(5), Atheneum/Caitlyn Dlouhy Books) Simon & Schuster Children's Publishing.

Rice, Linda. Rhino's Special Ears, 1 vol. 2010. 30p. pap. 24.95 (978-1-61582-178-5(3)) PublishAmerica, Inc.

Richardson, Faith. Tree Root & River Rat. 2003. (Illus.). 248p. (J). 21.95 (978-0-9744989-4-2(7)); pap. 12.95 (978-0-9744989-5-9(5)) Fox Song Bks.

Ridling, Carole. The Homerun Kid. 2011. 24p. pap. 11.32 (978-1-4567-4998-9(6)) AuthorHouse.

Rivera, Lassen. Mi Silla de Ruedas. Alvarez, Mrinali, illus. 2006. (SPA.). 28p. 8.95 (978-0-8477-1568-8(X)) Univ. of Puerto Rico Pr.

Robinson, Gary. Tribal Journey. 2013. (YA). 111p. (978-1-939053-87-9(0)); (ENG.). 120p. pap. 9.95 (978-1-939053-01-5(3), 7th Generation) Book Publishing Co.

Rocklin, Joanne. Fleabrain Loves Franny. (ENG.). 288p. (J). (gr. 3-7). 2015. pap. 8.95 (978-1-4197-1676-8(X)) 2014. 16.95 (978-1-4197-1068-1(0)) Abrams, Inc. (Amulet Bks.).

Roos, Stephen. The Gypsies Never Came. Liepke, Peter, photos by. 2010. (ENG., Illus.). 128p. (J). (gr. 3-7). pap. 7.99 (978-1-4424-2940-6(2), Simon & Schuster Bks. For Young Readers) Simon & Schuster Bks. For Young Readers.

Rose, Marilyn C. Kylie Gets a Cochlear Implant. 2013. 32p. pap. 13.00 (978-1-62516-170-3(0), Strategic Bk. Publishing) Strategic Book Publishing & Rights Agency (SBPRA).

Roth, Judith L. & Rothshank, Brooke, illus. Julia's Words. 2008. (J). (gr. -1-3). pap. 12.99 (978-0-8361-9417-3(9)) Herald Pr.

Sachar, Louis. The Cardturner. 2011. (ENG.). 352p. (YA). (gr. 7). pap. 9.99 (978-0-385-73663-3(0), Ember) Random Hse. Children's Bks.

—The Cardturner. 2011. lib. bdg. 20.85 (978-0-606-23428-3(4), Turtleback) Turtleback Bks.

—Small Steps. 2008. (Readers Circle Ser.). 257p. (gr. 5-9). 20.00 (978-0-7569-9130-2(7)) Perfection Learning Corp.

—Small Steps. 2008. (ENG.). 288p. (YA). (gr. 7-9). pap. 9.99 (978-0-385-73315-1(1), Ember) Random Hse. Children's Bks.

—Small Steps. rev. l.t. ed. 2006. 339p. 23.95 (978-0-7862-8297-5(5)) Thorndike Pr.

Salisbury, Linda G. The Mysterious Jamestown Suitcase: A Bailey Fish Adventure. Grotke, Christopher A., illus. 2006. (Bailey Fish Adventures Ser.). 191p. (J). (gr. 3-7). per. 8.95 (978-1-881539-43-8(1)) Tabby Hse. Bks.

Sanford, Agnes. Melissa & the Little Red Book. Heinen, Sandy, illus. (J). (gr. 1-6). pap. 3.95 (978-0-910924-81-8(3)) Macalester Park Publishing Co., Inc.

Savage, J. Scott. Land Keep. 2009. (Farworld Ser.: Bk. 2). 432p. (YA). (gr. 5-18). 18.95 (978-1-60641-164-3(0), Shadow Mountain) Shadow Mountain Publishing.

Schnee, Silke. Prince Noah & the School Pirates. Sistig, Heike, illus. 2016. (Prince Noah Book Ser.). (ENG.). 32p. (J). 16.00 (978-0-87486-765-7(7)) Plough Publishing Hse.

Schneider, Maxwell. Do You Hear Me? Laughs for the Hard of Hearing by the Hard of Hearing, 1. 2003. (Illus.). 138p. per. 8.95 *(978-0-9727520-0-8(5)*, B555) Harris Communications, Inc.

Schneider, Robyn. The Beginning of Everything. (ENG.). 352p. (YA). (gr. 8). 2014. pap. 9.99 *(978-0-06-221714-1(3)*, Tegen, Katherine Bks) 2013. 17.99 *(978-0-06-221713-4(5))* HarperCollins Pubs.

Scott, Rosanna. Peter & Friends at Camp. Fargo, Todd, illus. l.t. ed. 2006. (Turtle Books). 32p. (J). (gr. k-4). pap. 9.95 *(978-0-944727-51-5(4))*; lib. bdg. 15.95 *(978-0-944727-52-2(2))* Jason & Nordic Pubs. (Turtle Bks.).

Sedgwick, Marcus. She Is Not Invisible. 2014. (ENG.). 224p. (YA). (gr. 7). 16.99 *(978-1-59643-801-9(0)*, 9781596438019) Roaring Brook Pr.

—She Is Not Invisible. 2015. (ENG.). 240p. (YA). (gr. 7). pap. 9.99 *(978-1-250-05698-6(5)*, 9781250056986) Square Fish.

Seki, Sunny. Yuko-Chan & the Daruma Doll: The Adventures of a Blind Japanese Girl Who Saves Her Village. 2012. (ENG., Illus.). 32p. (J). (gr. -1-3). 15.95 *(978-4-8053-1187-5(8))* Tuttle Publishing.

Selznick, Brian. Wonderstruck. Selznick, Brian, illus. 2011. (ENG., Illus.). 640p. (J). (gr. 4-7). 29.99 *(978-0-545-02789-2(6)*, Scholastic Pr.); 300.00 *(978-0-545-38985-3(2))* Scholastic, Inc.

Shonka, Maria. The Snail with Two Slippers. Sanchez, Evan, illus. 2011. 40p. pap. 24.95 *(978-1-60836-786-3(X))* America Star Bks.

Smith-Armand, Kristie. Diamond in the Rough: More Fun Adventures with Abby Diamond. 2010. 256p. pap. 16.95 *(978-1-4502-4618-7(4))* iUniverse, Inc.

Smith, D. James. It Was September When We Ran Away the First Time. 2012. (ENG.). 240p. (J). (gr. 3-7). pap. 11.99 *(978-1-4169-3810-1(9)*, Atheneum Bks. for Young Readers) Simon & Schuster Children's Publishing.

—Probably the World's Best Story about a Dog & the Girl Who Loved Me. 2011. (ENG.). 256p. (J). pap. 5.99 *(978-1-4169-9652-1(4)*, Atheneum Bks. for Young Readers) Simon & Schuster Children's Publishing.

—Probably the World's Best Story about a Dog & The Girl Who Loved Me. 2010. (ENG.). 240p. (J). (gr. 4-7). pap. 11.99 *(978-1-4424-2194-3(0)*, Atheneum Bks. for Young Readers) Simon & Schuster Children's Publishing.

Smith, Yolonda L. Differently Able Me. 2011. 24p. pap. 15.99 *(978-1-4568-4650-3(7))* Xlibris Corp.

Souliere, Lisa. Toasters Are Easy, School Not So Much. Rockwell, Joanna, illus. 2012. 20p. pap. 10.95 *(978-1-60976-654-2(7)*, Strategic Bk. Publishing) Strategic Book Publishing & Rights Agency (SBPRA).

Sovern, Megan Jean. The Meaning of Maggie. 2015. (ENG.). 232p. (J). (gr. 3-7). pap. 6.99 *(978-1-4521-2876-4(6))* Chronicle Bks. LLC.

Spencer, Leslie. Social Stories for Children with Disabilities, 1 vol. 2010. 46p. 24.95 *(978-1-4512-0917-4(7))* PublishAmerica, Inc.

Spitz, Clarita. Enrique Tiene Cinco Anos. 2014. (SPA.). 48p. (J). (gr. 2-3). pap. 14.99 *(978-958-30-4161-7(0))* Panamericana Editorial COL. Dist: Lectorum Pubns., Inc.

Spurlock, Cathy. Toby, the Two-Toed Tiger. 2008. 24p. pap. 24.95 *(978-1-60563-108-0(6))* America Star Bks.

Stahler, David, Jr. The Seer. 2008. 320p. (J). pap. 6.99 *(978-0-06-052290-2(9)*, Eos) HarperCollins Pubs.

Stamm, Linda J. Lilly & Zander: A Children's Story about Equine-Assisted Activities. Whitaker, Suzanne, illus. 2014. (J). pap. *(978-1-938313-03-5(8))* Graphite Pr.

Stenton, Murray, illus. My Brother Is Special: A Sibling with Cerebral Palsy. 2016. (J). pap. ***(978-1-61599-309-3(6))*** Loving Healing Pr., Inc.

Stevens, Eric & Fuentes, Benny. Skateboard Sonar, 1 vol. Sandoval, Gerardo, illus. 2010. (Sports Illustrated Kids Graphic Novels Ser.). (ENG.). 56p. (gr. 2-3). pap. 7.19 *(978-1-4342-2295-4(0))*; 26.65 *(978-1-4342-1910-7(0))* Stone Arch Bks.

Stevenson, Robin. A Thousand Shades of Blue, 1 vol. 2008. (ENG.). 240p. (YA). (gr. 7-12). pap. 12.95 *(978-1-55143-921-1(2))* Orca Bk. Pubs. USA.

Stinson, Kathy. What Happened to Ivy, 1 vol. 2012. (ENG.). 256p. (YA). (gr. 6-9). pap. 11.95 *(978-1-926920-81-8(3))* Second Story Pr. CAN. Dist: Orca Bk. Pubs. USA.

Stratton-Porter, Gene. Freckles. (J). reprint ed. lib. bdg. 24.95 *(978-0-89190-949-1(4)*, Rivercity Pr.) Amereon Ltd.

—Freckles. l.t. ed. 2007. (ENG.). 248p. pap. 22.99 *(978-1-4264-5654-1(9))* Creative Media Partners, LLC.

—Freckles. 2006. 236p. (YA). 19.95 *(978-1-934169-32-2(3))*; pap. 8.95 *(978-1-934169-33-9(1))* Norilana Bks.

—Wonder, Hope, Love, & Loss: The Selected Novels of Gene Stratton-Porter. 2015. (ENG.). 784p. (gr. 6). pap. 17.99 *(978-1-63220-320-5(0)*, Sky Pony Pr.) Skyhorse Publishing Co., Inc.

Stuve-Bodeen, Stephanie. Babu's Song. Boyd, Aaron, illus. 2003. (ENG.). 32p. (J). 16.95 *(978-1-58430-058-8(2))* Lee & Low Bks., Inc.

Suen, Anastasia. Helping Sophia, 1 vol. Ebbeler, Jeffrey, illus. 2007. (Main Street School - Kids with Character Ser.). (ENG.). 32p. (gr. -1-4). 28.50 *(978-1-60270-030-7(3)*, Looking Glass Library) ABDO Publishing Co.

Sundquist, Josh. Love & First Sight. 2017. (ENG.). 288p. (YA). (gr. 7-17). 17.99 *(978-0-316-30535-8(9))* Little Brown & Co.

Swaney, Kathleen M. William's in a Wheelchair. Wysong, Ryan, illus. 2008. 24p. pap. 24.95 *(978-1-60703-447-6(6))* America Star Bks.

Tashjian, Janet. My Life As a Cartoonist. Tashjian, Jake, illus. 2013. (My Life Ser.: 3). (ENG.). 272p. (J). (gr. 4-7). 13.99 *(978-0-8050-9609-5(4)*, 9780805096095, Holt, Henry & Co. Bks. For Young Readers) Holt, Henry & Co.

—Tru Confessions. 2007. (ENG., Illus.). 176p. (J). (gr. 4-7). per. 15.99 *(978-0-312-37273-6(6)*, 9780312372736) Square Fish.

Taylor, Theodore. Timothy of the Cay. 2007. (ENG., Illus.). 176p. (J). (gr. 5-7). pap. 6.99 *(978-0-15-206320-7(X))* Houghton Mifflin Harcourt Publishing Co.

—The Weirdo. 2006. (Illus.). 292p. (gr. 7-12). 18.00 *(978-0-7569-6752-9(X))* Perfection Learning Corp.

Taylor, Theodore & Taylor, Theodore. The Weirdo. 2006. (ENG., Illus.). 304p. (YA). (gr. 7-12). pap. 8.99 *(978-0-15-205666-7(1))* Houghton Mifflin Harcourt Publishing Co.

Terry, Trueman & Trueman. Stuck in Neutral. 2014. (ENG.). 128p. (J). (gr. 8-12). 13.24 *(978-1-63245-299-3(5))* Lectorum Pubns., Inc.

Thomas, Leah. Because You'll Never Meet Me. 2015. (ENG.). 352p. (YA). (gr. 9-12). 17.99 *(978-1-61963-590-6(9)*, 9781619635906, Bloomsbury USA Childrens) Bloomsbury Publishing USA.

—Nowhere near You. 2017. (ENG.). 400p. (YA). 17.99 *(978-1-68119-178-2(4)*, 9781681191782, Bloomsbury USA Childrens) Bloomsbury Publishing USA.

Tolley, Diane Stringham & Tolley, Diane Stringam. Carving Angels. 2011. 121p. (J). 12.99 *(978-1-59955-944-5(7)*, Bonneville Bks.) Cedar Fort, Inc./CFI Distribution.

Tomos, Angharad. Y Llipryn Llwyd. 2005. (WEL., Illus.). 48p. pap. *(978-0-86243-095-5(X))* Y Lolfa.

Tooke, Wes. King of the Mound: My Summer with Satchel Paige. (ENG.). 160p. (J). (gr. 3-7). 2013. pap. 7.99 *(978-1-4424-3347-2(7))* 2012. (Illus.). 17.99 *(978-1-4424-3346-5(9))* Simon & Schuster Bks. For Young Readers. (Simon & Schuster Bks. For Young Readers).

Trueman, Terry. Life Happens Next. 2012. (Stuck in Neutral Ser.: 3). (ENG.). 144p. (YA). (gr. 9). 17.99 *(978-0-06-202803-7(0)*, HarperTeen) HarperCollins Pubs.

Trueman, Terry & Trueman. Stuck in Neutral. 2012. (Stuck in Neutral Ser.: 1). (ENG.). 144p. (YA). (gr. 8-18). pap. 9.99 *(978-0-06-447213-5(2)*, HarperTeen) HarperCollins Pubs.

Trufant, Robert & Mullins, Tinnesha. Angel Fingers Series: Na'dyd Goes to School. 2004. (Angel Fingers Ser.). (Illus.). 19p. (J). (gr. -1-2). 14.95 *(978-0-9760160-0-7(1))* Mullins Pubns. & Apparel, LLC.

Uhlberg, Myron. The Printer, 1 vol. Sørensen, Henri, illus. 2009. (ENG.). 32p. (J). (gr. -1-3). pap. 8.95 *(978-1-56145-483-9(4))* Peachtree Pubs.

—The Printer, 1 vol. Sorensen, Henri, tr. Sorensen, Henri, illus. 2003. (ENG.). 32p. (J). (gr. k-3). 16.95 *(978-1-56145-221-7(1))* Peachtree Pubs.

Van Draanen, Wendelin. The Running Dream. 2011. (ENG.). 352p. (YA). (gr. 7-18). 16.99 *(978-0-375-86667-8(1)*, Knopf Bks. for Young Readers) Random Hse. Children's Bks.

Vaught, Susan. Super Max & the Mystery of Thornwood's Revenge. 2017. (ENG., Illus.). 352p. (J). (gr. 3-7). 16.99 ***(978-1-4814-8683-5(7)***, Simon & Schuster/Paula Wiseman Bks.) Simon & Schuster/Paula Wiseman Bks.

Veenendall, Jennifer. Arnie & His School Tools: Simple Sensory Solutions That Build Success. 2008. (ENG., Illus.). 47p. (J). (gr. 1-7). 18.95 *(978-1-934575-15-4(1))* Autism Asperger Publishing Co.

—Why Does Izzy Cover Her Ears? Dealing with Sensory Overload. 2009. (Illus.). 39p. (J). 18.95 *(978-1-934575-46-8(1))* Autism Asperger Publishing Co.

Venkatraman, Padma. A Time to Dance. (ENG.). (YA). (gr. 7). 2015. 336p. pap. 9.99 *(978-0-14-751440-0(1)*, Speak) 2014. 320p. 17.99 *(978-0-399-25710-0(1)*, Nancy Paulsen Books) Penguin Young Readers Group.

Villasenor, Victor. The Stranger & the Red Rooster: El Forastero y el Gallo Rojo. Ventura, Gabriela Baeza, tr. Jara, Jose, illus. 2005. (ENG & SPA.). 26p. (J). (gr. -1-2). 16.95 *(978-1-55885-420-8(7)*, Piñata Books) Arte Publico Pr.

Vision, Mutiya Sahar. Disabilities. Alcantara, Ignacio, illus. 2009. 32p. 17.00 *(978-0-9659538-9-4(0))* Von Curtis Publishing.

Vogelaar, Alie. One Day at a Time, Margreet. VanBrugge, Jeanne, tr. from DUT. Kramer, Jaap, illus. 2004. Orig. Title: Elke Dag Genoeg, Margreet. 124p. *(978-0-9670728-6-9(7))* Early Foundations Pubs.

Voigt, Cynthia. Izzy, Willy-Nilly. 2005. (ENG.). 336p. (YA). (gr. 7). mass mkt. 8.99 *(978-1-4169-0339-0(9)*, Simon Pulse) Simon Pulse.

Vrabel, Beth. A Blind Guide to Normal. 2016. (ENG.). 272p. (J). (gr. 2-7). 16.99 *(978-1-5107-0228-8(8)*, Sky Pony Pr.) Skyhorse Publishing Co., Inc.

—A Blind Guide to Stinkville. 2015. (ENG.). 264p. (J). (gr. 2-7). 16.99 *(978-1-63450-157-6(8)*, Sky Pony Pr.) Skyhorse Publishing Co., Inc.

Wait, Lea. Wintering Well. 2006. (ENG., Illus.). 192p. (J). (gr. 3-7). pap. 6.99 *(978-0-689-85647-1(4)*, McElderry, Margaret K. Bks.) McElderry, Margaret K. Bks.

Walker, D. S. Delightfully Different. 2010. 160p. (gr. -1). 22.95 *(978-1-4502-6051-0(9))*; pap. 12.95 *(978-1-4502-6050-3(0))* iUniverse, Inc.

Wallace, Bill. The Legend of Thunderfoot. 2007. (ENG.). 160p. (J). (gr. 3-7). pap. 5.99 *(978-1-4169-0692-6(4)*, Simon & Schuster/Paula Wiseman Bks.) Simon & Schuster/Paula Wiseman Bks.

Walsh, Patrick M., Jr. Who Says Timmy Can't Play: The Derby: A Timmy Wallings Story. McGriff, Aaron, ed. WFM Services, illus. 2011. 135p. (J). *(978-0-9842929-3-6(4))* Daddy Bean Bks.

Walters, Eric. My Name Is Blessing. Fernandes, Eugenie, illus. 2013. (ENG.). 32p. (J). (gr. 1-4). 17.95 *(978-1-77049-301-8(8)*, Tundra Bks.) Tundra Bks. CAN. Dist: Penguin Random Hse. LLC.

Waters, Terrance D. I f I Y: A Novel Based on a True Story. 2008. 148p. 26.00 *(978-1-4251-3496-9(3))* Trafford Publishing.

Watson, Carrie Gordon. Ascending the Boneyard. 2017. (ENG.). 272p. (YA). (gr. 9). pap. 10.99 *(978-1-4814-3185-9(4)*, Simon Pulse) Simon Pulse.

Watson, Cristy. On Cue, 1 vol. 2016. (Orca Currents Ser.). (ENG.). 144p. (J). (gr. 5-9). pap. 9.95 *(978-1-4598-1105-8(4))* Orca Bk. Pubs. USA.

Werlin, Nancy. Are You Alone on Purpose? 2007. (ENG.). 208p. (YA). (gr. 7-18). 7.99 *(978-0-14-240777-6(1)*, Speak) Penguin Young Readers Group.

Wess, Robert, illus. & photos by. Friends at Work & Play. Wess, Robert, photos by. Bunnett, Rochelle, photos by. 2003. 32p. (J). 14.95 *(978-0-9660884-2-7(5))*; pap. *(978-0-9660884-1-0(7))* Our Kids Pr.

Whelan, Gloria. Forgive the River, Forgive the Sky. 2004. 96p. (J). pap. 8.00 *(978-0-8028-5256-4(4))* Eerdmans, William B. Publishing Co.

White, Andrea. Window Boy. 2008. (ENG.). 256p. (J). (gr. 4-7). 17.95 *(978-1-933979-14-4(3)*, 9781933979144) Bright Sky Pr.

Willard, Elizabeth Kimmel. Mary Ingalls on Her Own. 2007. (Little House Sequel Ser.). (ENG.). 192p. (J). (gr. 3-7). 16.99 *(978-0-06-000905-2(5))* HarperCollins Pubs.

Winkelmann, Mary. Wheels. 2012. 66p. (gr. 10-12). pap. 10.43 *(978-1-4669-5560-8(0))* Trafford Publishing.

Withers, Pam. Daredevil Club, 1 vol. 2006. (Orca Currents Ser.). (ENG.). 112p. (J). (gr. 5-9). per. 9.95 *(978-1-55143-614-2(0))* Orca Bk. Pubs. USA.

Wonder, 2 vols., Set. 2014. (ENG.). 432p. (J). (gr. 3-7). 31.98 *(978-0-553-49906-3(8)*, Knopf Bks. for Young Readers) Random Hse. Children's Bks.

Wood, Gail. Lizzie & the Big Lake Mystery. 2015. (Illus.). ix, 93p. (J). pap. *(978-1-57249-416-9(6)*, White Mane Kids) White Mane Publishing Co., Inc.

Yoo, Paula. Good Enough. 2012. (ENG.). 336p. (YA). (gr. 8). pap. 7.99 *(978-0-06-079090-5(3)*, HarperTeen) HarperCollins Pubs.

Young, Suzanne. All in Pieces. 2016. (ENG., Illus.). 272p. (YA). (gr. 9). 17.99 *(978-1-4814-1883-6(1)*, Simon Pulse) Simon Pulse.

Zajac, Kristen K. Ebeneezer's Cousin. Houdeshell, Jennifer Thomas, illus. 2013. 24p. 19.95 *(978-1-61633-440-6(1))* Guardian Angel Publishing, Inc.

PEOPLE WITH DISABILITIES—REHABILITATION

Wright, Rebecca. Ups & Downs: Elementary Monologues That Explore Emotions. 2016. (ENG.). 192p. (J). pap. 15.95 *(978-1-56608-209-9(9)*, Meriwether Publishing) Meriwether Publishing, Ltd.

PEOPLE WITH MENTAL DISABILITIES

see also Mental Illness; Mentally Ill

Bowman-Kruhm, Mary. Everything You Need to Know about down Syndrome. 2009. (Need to Know Library). 64p. (gr. 5-5). 58.50 *(978-1-60854-065-5(0))* Rosen Publishing Group, Inc., The.

Greenhaven Press Editors. Mental Illness. 2016. (Opposing Viewpoints Ser.). (ENG.). 224p. (J). (gr. 10-12). pap. 33.80 *(978-0-7377-7513-6(0)*, Greenhaven Pr., Inc.) Cengage Gale.

Greenhaven Press Staff. Mental Illness. 2016. (Opposing Viewpoints Ser.). (ENG.). 224p. (J). (gr. 10-12). 48.80 *(978-0-7377-7512-9(2)*, Greenhaven Pr., Inc.) Cengage Gale.

Hoopmann, Kathy. All Cats Have Asperger Syndrome. 2006. (ENG., Illus.). 72p. (gr. 3-7). pap. 14.95 *(978-1-84310-481-0(4)*, 4467) Kingsley, Jessica Pubs. GBR. Dist: Macmillan Distribution Ltd.

Lauren, Jill. That's Like Me!, 1 vol. 2009. (ENG.). 32p. (J). (gr. k-3). pap. 7.95 *(978-1-59572-208-9(4))* Star Bright Bks., Inc.

Libal, Autumn. Intellectual Disabilities. Albers, Lisa et al, eds. 2014. (Living with a Special Need Ser.: 16). 128p. (J). (gr. 7-18). 25.95 *(978-1-4222-3037-4(6))* Mason Crest.

Martin, Michael J. Teen Depression. 2004. (Illus.). 96p. (YA). (gr. 7-12). per. 32.45 *(978-1-59018-502-5(1)*, Lucent Bks.) Cengage Gale.

McIntosh, Kenneth & Livingston, Phyllis. Youth with Conduct Disorder: In Trouble with the World. 2007. (Helping Youth with Mental, Physical, & Social Disabilities Ser.). (Illus.). 128p. (YA). pap. 14.95 *(978-1-4222-0440-5(5))* Mason Crest.

Parent, Lauren. I'm Different but I'm Special. Parent, Lauren, illus. l.t. ed. 2006. (Illus.). 21p. (J). (gr. -1-3). per. 10.99 *(978-1-59879-259-1(8))* Lifevest Publishing, Inc.

Rosenberg, Marsha Sarah. Coping When a Brother or Sister Is Autistic. (Coping Ser.). 192p. (gr. 7-12). 2009. 63.90 *(978-1-61511-986-8(8))* 2005. (Illus.). (YA). lib. bdg. 34.60 *(978-0-8239-3194-1(3))* Rosen Publishing Group, Inc., The.

—Everything You Need to Know When a Brother or Sister Is Autistic. 2005. (Need to Know Library). (Illus.). 64p. (YA). (gr. 7-12). lib. bdg. 31.95 *(978-0-8239-3123-1(4)*, NTAUTI) Rosen Publishing Group, Inc., The.

Skotko, Brian & Levine, Susan P. Fasten Your Seatbelt: A Crash Course on Down Syndrome for Brothers & Sisters. 2008. (ENG.). 192p. (YA). (gr. 4-9). pap. 18.95 *(978-1-890627-86-7(0))* Woodbine Hse.

Stewart, Sheila & Flath, Camden. My Name Is Not Slow: Kids with Intellectual Disabilities. 2010. (Kids with Special Needs Ser.). 48p. (YA). (gr. 5-18). lib. bdg. 19.95 *(978-1-4222-1718-4(3))* Mason Crest.

Whelahan, Marlene Verno. My Best Friend's Sister... A True Story. 2010. 20p. 12.99 *(978-1-4389-8729-3(3))* AuthorHouse.

Yoshida, Yuko. How to Be Yourself in a World That's Different: An Asperger Syndrome Study Guide for Adolescents. Wing, Lorna, ed. Sanders, Esther, tr. from JPN. 2006. (ENG., Illus.). 112p. pap. 15.95 *(978-1-84310-504-6(7)*, 7484) Kingsley, Jessica Pubs. GBR. Dist: Macmillan Distribution Ltd.

PEOPLE WITH MENTAL DISABILITIES—EDUCATION

Ronay, Laura. Kids Like Me... Learn ABCs. Kishimoto, Jon Wayne, illus. 2008. (ENG.). 32p. (J). (gr. -1-1). 12.95 *(978-1-60613-000-1(5))* Woodbine Hse.

—Kids Like Me... Learn Colors. Kishimoto, Jon Wayne, illus. 2008. (ENG.). 16p. (J). (gr. -1-1). 11.95 *(978-1-60613-001-8(3))* Woodbine Hse.

PEOPLE WITH MENTAL DISABILITIES—FICTION

Acorn, Alesa. Diary of the Beloved Book One: The Hidden. 2011. 512p. 31.95 *(978-1-4634-0276-1(7))*; pap. 21.95 *(978-1-4634-0274-7(0))* AuthorHouse.

Bowen, Fred. Perfect Game, 1 vol. 2013. (Fred Bowen Sports Stories Ser.). (ENG.). 144p. (J). (gr. 2-6). 14.95 *(978-1-56145-701-4(9))*; pap. 5.95 *(978-1-56145-625-3(X))* Peachtree Pubs.

Byars, Betsy. The Summer of the Swans. 2004. (Puffin Modern Classics Ser.). (ENG.). 144p. (J). (gr. 3-7). pap. 6.99 *(978-0-14-240114-9(5)*, Puffin Books) Penguin Young Readers Group.

—The Summer of the Swans. 2008. (Puffin Modern Classics Ser.). (Illus.). 129p. (gr. 4). 16.00 *(978-0-7569-8944-6(2))* Perfection Learning Corp.

Byrd, Lee Merrill. Treasure on Gold Street/El Tesoro de la Calle D'Oro: A Neighborhood Story in Spanish & English. Castro L., Antonio, illus. 2003. (ENG & SPA.). 40p. (J). (gr. 4-6). 16.95 *(978-0-938317-75-3(X))* Cinco Puntos Pr.

—El Ttesoro en la Calle Oro: A Neighborhood Story in English & Spanish. Franco, Sharon, tr. Castro L., Antonio, illus. 2007.Tr. of Treasure on Gold Street. (SPA & ENG.). 40p. (J). (gr. 4-6). pap. 8.95 *(978-1-933693-11-8(8))* Cinco Puntos Pr.

Castan, Mike. Fighting for Dontae. 2012. (ENG.). 144p. (YA). 16.95 *(978-0-8234-2348-4(4))* Holiday Hse., Inc.

Centre for Addiction and Mental Health Staff. Can I Catch It Like a Cold? Coping with a Parent's Depression. Weissmann, Joe, illus. 2009. (Coping Ser.). (ENG.). 32p. (J). (gr. k-3). 17.95 *(978-0-88776-956-6(X)*, Tundra Bks.) Tundra Bks. CAN. Dist: Penguin Random Hse. LLC.

Chase, L. P. Today Is Tuesday. 2006. (J). pap. 9.00 *(978-0-87426-069-4(8))* Whitmore Publishing Co.

Cocca-Leffler, Maryann. Janine. Cocca-Leffler, Maryann, illus. 2015. (ENG., Illus.). 32p. (J). (gr. -1-3). 16.99 *(978-0-8075-3754-1(3))* Whitman, Albert & Co.

Curtis, Christopher Paul. Bucking the Sarge. 2006. (Readers Circle Ser.). (ENG.). 288p. (YA). (gr. 7-7). reprint ed. mass mkt. 6.99 *(978-0-440-41331-8(1)*, Laurel Leaf) Random Hse. Children's Bks.

Fontes, Justine. Benito Runs. 2011. (Surviving Southside Ser.). (ENG.). 104p. (YA). (gr. 6-12). lib. bdg. 27.93 *(978-0-7613-6151-0(0))* Lerner Publishing Group.

Gallo, Donald R., ed. Owning It: Stories about Teens with Disabilities. 2008. (ENG., Illus.). 224p. (YA). (gr. 7-13). 17.99 *(978-0-7636-3255-7(4))* Candlewick Pr.

Gamache, Line. Hello, Me Pretty. Cochrane, KerryAnn, tr. from FRE. 2007. (ENG., Illus.). 64p. per. *(978-1-894994-23-1(X))* Conundrum Pr.

Gehret, Jeanne. The Don't-Give-Up Kid: And Learning Differences. DePauw, Sandra A., illus. 3rd rev. ed. 2003. 40p. (J). (gr. 1-5). pap. 9.95 *(978-1-884281-10-5(9))* Verbal Images Pr.

Green, Jack. The Microchip Kid. 2011. 52p. pap. 16.95 *(978-1-4560-8494-3(1))* America Star Bks.

Haines, Lise. Girl in the Arena. (ENG.). 336p. (YA). (gr. 9-13). 2010. pap. 9.99 *(978-1-59990-521-1(3)*, 9781599905211) 2009. 16.99 *(978-1-59990-372-9(5)*, 9781599903729) Bloomsbury Publishing USA. (Bloomsbury USA Childrens).

Hamilton, Kersten. Tyger Tyger. 2011. (ENG.). 336p. (YA). (gr. 7). pap. 18.99 *(978-0-547-57732-6(X))* Houghton Mifflin Harcourt Publishing Co.

—When the Stars Threw down Their Spears. (ENG.). 400p. (YA). (gr. 7). 2014. pap. 8.99 *(978-0-544-22771-2(9)*, HMH Books For Young Readers) 2013. 16.99 *(978-0-547-73964-9(8))* Houghton Mifflin Harcourt Publishing Co.

Hesse, Karen. Wish on a Unicorn. 2009. (ENG.). 128p. (J). (gr. 3-7). pap. 16.99 *(978-0-312-37611-6(1)*, 9780312376116) Square Fish.

Hill, Genita. My Very Special Brother. McCall, William L., illus. 2007. 40p. per. 24.95 *(978-1-4241-8852-9(0))* America Star Bks.

Holt, Kimberly Willis. My Louisiana Sky. 208p. (YA). (gr. 5-18). 4.99 *(978-0-8072-8291-5(X)*, Listening Library) Random Hse. Audio Publishing Group.

—My Louisiana Sky. 2011. (ENG.). 224p. (J). (gr. 4-7). pap. 7.99 *(978-0-312-66095-6(2)*, 9780312660956) Square Fish.

Hubler, Marsha. Blue Ribbon Champ, 1 vol. rev. ed. 2010. (Keystone Stables Ser.). (ENG.). 112p. (J). pap. 7.99 *(978-0-310-71797-3(3))* Zonderkidz.

Hyde, Catherine Ryan. The Year of My Miraculous Reappearance. 2009. (ENG.). 240p. (YA). (gr. 7). pap. 8.99 *(978-0-375-83261-1(0)*, Knopf Bks. for Young Readers) Random Hse. Children's Bks.

Kats, Jewel. Hansel & Gretel: A Fairy Tale with a Down Syndrome Twist. Lenart, Claudia, illus. 2014. 37p. (J). *(978-1-61599-251-5(0))* Loving Healing Pr., Inc.

Krukar, Jeff, et al. Melting Down: A Comic for Kids with Asperger's Disorder & Challenging Behavior (the Orp Library) 2013. 74p. pap. 12.99 *(978-1-939418-20-3(8))* Writer of the Round Table Pr.

Lange, Erin Jade. Dead Ends. 2013. (ENG.). 336p. (YA). (gr. 9). 17.99 *(978-1-61963-080-2(X)*, 9781619630802, Bloomsbury USA Childrens); 288p. pap. 17.99 *(978-1-61963-081-9(8))* Bloomsbury Publishing USA.

Lean, Sarah. A Dog Called Homeless. 2012. (ENG.). 208p. (J). (gr. 3-7). 16.99 *(978-0-06-212220-9(7)*, Tegen, Katherine Bks) HarperCollins Pubs.

Lewis, Beverly. In Jesse's Shoes: Appreciating Kids with Special Needs. Nikiel, Laura Gibbons, illus. 2007. (ENG.). 32p. (J). (gr. -1-4). 11.99 *(978-0-7642-0313-8(4))* Bethany Hse. Pubs.

Long, Tyler. Wires, 1 vol. Fleming, Christopher, illus. 2009. 28p. pap. 24.95 *(978-1-60836-217-2(5))* America Star Bks.

Lytton, Deborah. Silence. 2015. (ENG.). 320p. (YA). (gr. 7). 17.99 *(978-1-60907-945-1(0)*, Shadow Mountain) Shadow Mountain Publishing.

Mackall, Dandi Daley. The Silence of Murder. (ENG.). 336p. (YA). (gr. 9). 2012. pap. 9.99 *(978-0-375-87293-8(0)*, Ember) 2011. 16.99 *(978-0-375-86896-2(8)*, Knopf Bks. for Young Readers) Random Hse. Children's Bks.

Magnin, Joyce. Carrying Mason, 1 vol. 2013. (ENG.). 176p. (J). pap. 6.99 *(978-0-310-72682-1(4))* Zonderkidz.

McGill, Justin. Friends Forever, Signed Jeremy E. 2007. 48p. per. 16.95 *(978-1-4241-8794-2(X))* America Star Bks.

Morpurgo, Michael. Private Peaceful. 2006. 18.00 *(978-0-7569-6630-0(2))* Perfection Learning Corp.

—Private Peaceful. 2006. (YA). 1.25 *(978-1-4193-2976-0(6))* Recorded Bks., Inc.

—Private Peaceful. 2006. (After Words Ser.). (ENG., Illus.). 224p. (J). (gr. 7-12). per. 7.99 *(978-0-439-63653-7(1)*, Scholastic Paperbacks) Scholastic, Inc.

Morton, Clay & Morton, Gail. Why Johnny Doesn't Flap: NT Is OK. Merry, Alex, illus. 2015. (ENG.). 32p. (J). 16.95 *(978-1-84905-721-9(4)*, 8100) Kingsley, Jessica Pubs. GBR. Dist: Macmillan Distribution Ltd.

Nelson, Suzanne. Serendipity's Footsteps. 2015. (ENG.). 368p. (YA). (gr. 7). 17.99 *(978-0-385-39212-9(5)*, Knopf Bks. for Young Readers) Random Hse. Children's Bks.

Nolan, Han. A Face in Every Window. 2008. (ENG., Illus.). 276p. (YA). (gr. 7). pap. 15.95 *(978-0-15-206418-1(4))* Houghton Mifflin Harcourt Publishing Co.

Nuzum, K. A. A Small White Scar. 2008. (ENG.). 208p. (J). (gr. 5). pap. 8.99 *(978-0-06-075641-3(1))* HarperCollins Pubs.

Schnee, Silke. Prince Noah & the School Pirates. Sistig, Heike, illus. 2016. (Prince Noah Book Ser.). (ENG.). 32p. (J). 16.00 *(978-0-87486-765-7(7))* Plough Publishing Hse.

—The Prince Who Was Just Himself. Sistig, Heike, illus. 2015. (Prince Noah Book Ser.). (ENG.). 32p. (J). (gr. -1-4). 16.00 *(978-0-87486-682-7(0))* Plough Publishing Hse.

Sheldon, Kaylene Kauwila. A Day with Makana. 2007.Tr. of I Kekahi la me Makana. (ENG & HAW.). (J). lib. bdg.

(978-0-9773495-2-4(7)) Na Kamalei Koolauloa Early Education Program.

Sommer, Bill & Tilghman, Natalie. A 52-Hertz Whale. 2015. (ENG.). 200p. (YA). (gr. 8-12). 18.99 (978-1-4677-7917-3(2)) Lerner Publishing Group.

Sommer, Bill & Tilghman, Natalie Haney. A 52-Hertz Whale. 2015. (ENG.). 200p. (YA). (gr. 8-12). 18.99 (978-1-4677-8811-3(2), Carolrhoda Lab™) Lerner Publishing Group.

Spain, Susan. The Deep Cut, 0 vols. 2014. (ENG.). 228p. pap. 9.99 (978-1-4778-4768-8(5), 9781477847688, Amazon Children's Publishing) Amazon Publishing.

Spain, Susan Rosson. The Deep Cut, 1 vol. 2006. (ENG., Illus.). 224p. (J). (gr. 5-9). 16.99 (978-0-7614-5316-1(4)) Marshall Cavendish Corp.

Tashjian, Janet. Tru Confessions. 2007. (ENG., Illus.). 176p. (J). (gr. 4-7). per. 15.99 (978-0-312-37273-6(6), 9780312372736) Square Fish.

Vazquez, Tiziana & Llano, Gabriella. In My World: Down Syndrome. 2013. 108p. 23.99 (978-1-4772-9274-7(8)); pap. 14.95 (978-1-4772-9188-7(1)) AuthorHouse.

Venter, Liezl & Niekerk, Clarabelle Van. Understanding Sam & Asperger Syndrome. 2008. (ENG., Illus.). 48p. (J). (gr. k-2). 17.95 (978-0-9747217-1-2(9)) Skeezel Pr.

Williams, Michael. Now Is the Time for Running. 2013. (ENG.). 240p. (YA). (gr. 7-17). pap. 10.99 (978-0-316-07788-0(7)) Little, Brown Bks. for Young Readers.

Wood, June Rae. The Man Who Loved Clowns. 2005. (ENG.). 224p. (J). (gr. 3-7). 6.99 (978-0-14-240422-5(5), Puffin Books) Penguin Young Readers Group.

—The Man Who Loved Clowns. 2005. 224p. (gr. 3-7). 16.00 (978-0-7569-5516-8(5)) Perfection Learning Corp.

Wright, Betty Ren. The Dollhouse Murders. 2008. (ENG.). 149p. (J). (gr. 4-7). pap. 7.99 (978-0-8234-2172-5(4)) Holiday Hse., Inc.

Yates, Alma J. Sammy's Song: A Novel. 2005. 272p. (J). (978-1-59156-945-9(1)) Covenant Communications.

PEOPLE'S DEMOCRACIES

see Communist Countries

PEOPLE'S REPUBLIC OF CHINA

see China

PEPYS, SAMUEL, 1633-1703

Howell, Izzi. Samuel Pepys. 2016. (Fact Cat: History Ser.). (ENG., Illus.). 24p. (J). (gr. k-2). 14.99 (978-1-5263-0097-3(4), Wayland) Hachette Children's Group GBR. Dist: Hachette Bk. Group.

PERCEPTION

see also Self-perception

Aikins, Dave, et al. Baby Sees: A First Book of Faces. Aikins, Dave, illus. 2013. (Sassy Ser.). (ENG., Illus.). 12p. (J). (gr. -1 — 1). bds. 6.99 (978-0-448-47787-9(4), Grosset & Dunlap) Penguin Young Readers Group.

Alaina, Maria. Patterns in Nature, 1 vol. (Wonder Readers Next Steps: Math Ser.). (ENG.). (gr. -1-1). 2013. 20p. lib. bdg. 22.65 (978-1-4765-0034-8(7)) 2011. 16p. pap. 35.94 (978-1-4296-8138-4(1)) 2011. 32p. pap. 5.99 (978-1-4296-7815-5(1)) Capstone Press of Coughlan Cos. (Wonder Readers).

Alexander, Emmett. Sort It by Size. 2015. (Sort It Out! Ser.). (ENG., Illus.). 24p. (J). (gr. k-1). pap. 8.15 (978-1-4824-2573-4(4)) Stevens, Gareth Publishing LLLP.

Apel, Melanie Ann. Let's Talk about Feeling Confused. 2009. (Let's Talk Library). 24p. (gr. 2-3). 42.50 (978-1-60853-439-5(1), PowerKids Pr.) Rosen Publishing Group, Inc., The.

Bartowski, Amy. Shapes at the Store: Identify & Describe Shapes. 2013. (InfoMax Math Readers Ser.). (ENG.). 16p. (J). (gr. k-1). pap. 42.00 (978-1-4777-1974-9(1)); (Illus.). pap. 7.00 (978-1-4777-1973-2(3)) Rosen Publishing Group, Inc., The. (Rosen Classroom).

Bluemel Oldfield, Dawn. Patterns at the Seashore. 2014. (Math Blast!: Seeing Patterns All Around Ser.). (ENG.). 32p. (J). (gr. -1-3). lib. bdg. 26.60 (978-1-62724-335-3(6)) Bearport Publishing Co., Inc.

Burstein, John. Patterns: What's on the Wall? Destiny Images Staff, illus. 2003. (Math Monsters Ser.). 24p. (J). (gr. k-4). lib. bdg. 21.00 (978-0-8368-3816-9(5), Weekly Reader Leveled Readers) Stevens, Gareth Publishing LLLP.

Burton, Margie, et al. Looking Down. 2011. (Early Connections Ser.). (J). (978-1-61672-260-9(6)) Benchmark Education Co.

Capote, Lori. Monster Knows Patterns, 1 vol. Wass, Chip, illus. 2013. (Monster Knows Math Ser.). (ENG.). 24p. (gr. 3-4). lib. bdg. 24.65 (978-1-4048-7949-2(8)) Picture Window Bks.

Carlton Books, ed. Eye Twisters: Boggle, Baffle & Blow Your Mind! 2014. (ENG., Illus.). 96p. (J). (gr. 2). pap. 7.95 (978-1-78312-033-8(9)) Carlton Bks., Ltd. GBR. Dist: Sterling Publishing Co., Inc.

Carr, Aaron. Animal Patterns. 2011. (J). (978-1-61690-590-3(5)); (978-1-61690-945-1(5)) Weigl Pubs., Inc.

—Diseños de Animales. 2012. (SPA.). (J). (978-1-61913-204-7(4)) Weigl Pubs., Inc.

—Diseños de Las Plantas. 2012. (SPA.). (J). (978-1-61913-207-8(9)) Weigl Pubs., Inc.

Clark Sawyer, J. Patterns in the Snow. 2015. (J). lib. bdg. (978-1-62724-340-7(2)) Bearport Publishing Co., Inc.

Cleary, Brian P. A-B-a-B-A: A Book of Pattern Play. Gable, Brian, illus. 2010. (Math Is CATegorical (r) Ser.). (ENG.). 32p. (J). (gr. k-3). lib. bdg. 16.95 (978-0-8225-7880-2(8)) Lerner Publishing Group.

Coan, Sharon. Message Received!, 1 vol. (Science Readers: Content & Literacy Ser.). (ENG., Illus.). 24p. (gr. 1-1). 2015. (J). 22.96 (978-1-4938-1152-6(5)) 2014. pap. 8.99 (978-1-4807-4565-0(0)) Teacher Created Materials, Inc.

Cobb, Vicki. On Stage. 2008. pap. 52.95 (978-0-8225-9450-5(1)) Lerner Publishing Group.

Corcorane, Ann. Patterns Everywhere! 2011. (Wonder Readers Emergent Level Ser.). (ENG.). 32p. (gr. -1-1). pap. 5.99 (978-1-4296-7869-8(0), Wonder Readers) Capstone Press of Coughlan Cos.

—Patterns Everywhere. 2011. (Wonder Readers Emergent Level Ser.). (ENG.). 16p. (gr. -1-1). pap. 35.94 (978-1-4296-8137-7(3), Wonder Readers) Capstone Press of Coughlan Cos.

Davies, Ann. Fun Size. (Illus.). 40p. (J). 19.95 (978-1-85479-230-3(X)) O'Mara, Michael Bks., Ltd. GBR. Dist: Trans-Atlantic Pubns., Inc.

Deen, Marilyn. Finding Patterns, 1 vol. 2011. (Wonder Readers: Mathematics Ser.). (ENG.). (gr. -1-2). 20p. lib. bdg. 22.65 (978-1-4296-8632-7(4)); 32p. pap. 5.99 (978-1-4296-7919-0(0)) Capstone Press of Coughlan Cos. (Wonder Readers).

Domiano, Gloria. Ship Shapes: Identify & Describe Shapes. 2013. (Rosen Math Readers Ser.). (ENG.). 16p. (J). (gr. k-1). pap. 42.00 (978-1-4777-1666-3(1)); (Illus.). pap. 7.00 (978-1-4777-1665-6(3)) Rosen Publishing Group, Inc., The. (Rosen Classroom).

Dorling Kindersley Publishing Staff. Optical Illusions 2. 2017. (ENG.). 32p. (J). (gr. 3-7). 19.99 **(978-1-4654-6324-1(0)**, DK Children) Dorling Kindersley Publishing, Inc.

Dorling Kindersley Publishing Staff. SENSEational Illusions. 2015. (ENG., Illus.). 32p. (J). (gr. 3-7). 19.99 (978-1-4654-3829-4(7), DK Children) Dorling Kindersley Publishing, Inc.

Dubuc, Marianne. In Front of My House. Ghione, Yvette, tr. from FRE. Dubuc, Marianne, illus. 2010. (ENG., Illus.). 120p. (J). (gr. -1-2). 18.95 (978-1-55453-641-2(3)) Kids Can Pr., Ltd. CAN. Dist: Hachette Bk. Group.

Felix, Rebecca. Patterns at the Zoo. 2015. (21st Century Basic Skills Library: Patterns All Around Ser.). (ENG., Illus.). 24p. (J). (gr. k-3). pap. 12.79 (978-1-63188-935-6(4), 206001) Cherry Lake Publishing.

—Patterns in Food. 2015. (21st Century Basic Skills Library: Patterns All Around Ser.). (ENG., Illus.). 24p. (J). (gr. k-3). pap. 12.79 (978-1-63188-936-3(2), 206005) Cherry Lake Publishing.

—Patterns in Sports. 2015. (21st Century Basic Skills Library: Patterns All Around Ser.). (ENG., Illus.). 24p. (J). (gr. k-3). 24.21 (978-1-63188-921-9(4), 206008) Cherry Lake Publishing.

—Patterns in the City. 2015. (21st Century Basic Skills Library: Patterns All Around Ser.). (ENG.). 24p. (J). (gr. k-3). pap. 12.79 (978-1-63188-938-7(9), 206013) Cherry Lake Publishing.

—Patterns on the Farm. 2015. (21st Century Basic Skills Library: Patterns All Around Ser.). (ENG., Illus.). 24p. (J). (gr. k-3). pap. 12.79 (978-1-63188-939-4(7), 206017) Cherry Lake Publishing.

Freese, Joan. Un Desfile de Patrones. 2007. (Las matimaticas en nuestro mundo (Spanish- Math in Our World) Ser.). (SPA.). 24p. (gr. 1-2). pap. 8.15 (978-0-8368-8500-2(7), Weekly Reader Leveled Readers) Stevens, Gareth Publishing LLLP.

—Un Desfile de Patrones. McKinley, Kay, photos by. 2007. (Matimáticas en Nuestro Mundo (Math in Our World) Ser.). (SPA., Illus.). 24p. (gr. 1-2). lib. bdg. 22.00 (978-0-8368-8491-3(4), Weekly Reader Leveled Readers) Stevens, Gareth Publishing LLLP.

—Patterns on Parade. McKinley, Kay, photos by. 2007. (Math in Our World Ser.). (Illus.). 24p. (gr. 1-2). lib. bdg. 22.00 (978-0-8368-8473-9(6), Weekly Reader Leveled Readers) Stevens, Gareth Publishing LLLP.

Frisch-Schmoll, Joy. Exploring Opposites. 2013. (Exploring Opposites Ser.). (ENG.). 24p. (gr. k-1). pap. 27.80 (978-1-62065-903-8(4)); pap. 166.80 (978-1-62065-904-5(2)); lib. bdg. 106.60 (978-1-62065-120-9(3)) Capstone Press of Coughlan Cos. (Pebble Plus).

—In & Out. 2013. (Exploring Opposites Ser.). (ENG.). 24p. (gr. k-1). pap. 41.70 (978-1-62065-898-7(4)); (Illus.). pap. 7.29 (978-1-62065-897-0(6)); (Illus.). lib. bdg. 26.65 (978-1-62065-119-3(X)) Capstone Press of Coughlan Cos. (Pebble Plus).

—Near & Far. 2013. (Exploring Opposites Ser.). (ENG.). 24p. (gr. k-1). pap. 41.70 (978-1-62065-900-7(X)); (Illus.). pap. 7.29 (978-1-62065-899-4(2)); (Illus.). lib. bdg. 26.65 (978-1-62065-117-9(3)) Capstone Press of Coughlan Cos. (Pebble Plus).

—Top & Bottom. 2013. (Exploring Opposites Ser.). (ENG.). 24p. (gr. k-1). pap. 41.70 (978-1-62065-902-1(6)); (Illus.). pap. 7.29 (978-1-62065-901-4(8)); (Illus.). lib. bdg. 26.65 (978-1-62065-116-2(5)) Capstone Press of Coughlan Cos. (Pebble Plus).

Gifford, Clive. Eye Benders: The Science of Seeing & Believing. 2014. (ENG.). 64p. (J). (gr. 5-9). pap. 9.99 (978-1-4380-0366-5(8)) Barron's Educational Series, Inc.

Goldstone, Bruce. I See a Pattern Here. Goldstone, Bruce, illus. 2015. (ENG., Illus.). 32p. (J). (gr. 2-5). 17.99 (978-0-8050-9209-7(9), 9780805092097, Holt, Henry & Co. Bks. For Young Readers) Holt, Henry & Co.

Gordon, Sharon. Up Down (Arriba Abajo) 2006. (Bookworms Ser.). (ENG & SPA., Illus.). 24p. (gr. k-1). lib. bdg. 15.95 (978-0-7614-2449-9(0)) Marshall Cavendish Corp.

Gunderson, Jessica. How Big? Wacky Ways to Compare Size, 1 vol. Keino, illus. 2013. (Wacky Comparisons Ser.). (ENG.). 24p. (gr. -1-2). 27.99 (978-1-4048-8325-3(8)); pap. 8.95 (978-1-4795-1915-6(4)) Picture Window Bks.

Hoban, Tana. Black & White. Hoban, Tana, illus. 2007. (ENG., Illus.). 16p. (J). (gr. -1 — 1). bds. 7.99 (978-0-06-117211-3(1), Greenwillow Bks.) HarperCollins Pubs.

—Black White. Hoban, Tana, illus. 2017. (Illus.). 36p. (J). (gr. -1 — 1). pap. 8.99 (978-0-06-265690-2(2), Greenwillow Bks.) HarperCollins Pubs.

Jeffries, Joyce. Big & Small. 2013. (Dinosaur School Ser.). (Illus.). 24p. (J). (gr. -1-1). pap. 8.15 (978-1-4339-8084-8(3)); lib. bdg. 22.60 (978-1-4339-8083-1(5)) Stevens, Gareth Publishing LLLP.

—Near & Far. 2013. (Dinosaur School Ser.). (Illus.). 24p. (gr. -1-1). 22.60 (978-1-4339-8099-2(1)); pap. 8.15 (978-1-4339-8100-5(9)) Stevens, Gareth Publishing LLLP.

—Shapes at School: Identify & Describe Shapes. 2013. (Rosen Math Readers Ser.). (ENG.). 16p. (J). (gr. k-1). pap. 42.00 (978-1-4777-1588-8(6)); (Illus.). pap. 7.00 (978-1-4777-1587-1(8)) Rosen Publishing Group, Inc., The. (Rosen Classroom).

—Which Is Different? 2013. (Dinosaur School Ser.). (Illus.). 24p. (gr. -1-1). 22.60 (978-1-4339-8103-6(3)); pap. 8.15 (978-1-4339-8104-3(1)) Stevens, Gareth Publishing LLLP.

Johnson, Tami. Cerca y Lejos. 2010. (Palabras para Adónde/Where Words Ser.).Tr. of Near & Far. (SPA, ENG & MUL.). 32p. (gr. 1-2). lib. bdg. 27.32 (978-1-4296-5337-4(X), A+ Bilingue/Bilingual) Capstone Press of Coughlan Cos.

—Encima y Debajo. 2010. (Palabras para Adónde/Where Words Ser.).Tr. of Above & Below. (SPA, ENG & MUL.). 32p. (gr. 1-2). lib. bdg. 27.32 (978-1-4296-5335-0(3), A+ Bilingue/Bilingual) Capstone Press of Coughlan Cos.

Kalman, Bobbie. How Are They the Same? 2011. (ENG.). 16p. (J). pap. (978-0-7787-9581-0(0)) Crabtree Publishing Co.

—¿Qué Aspecto Tiene? 2008. (SPA.). 24p. (J). lib. bdg. (978-0-7787-8723-5(0)) Crabtree Publishing Co.

—¿Qué Sigue? 2008. (SPA.). 24p. (J). lib. bdg. (978-0-7787-8727-3(3)) Crabtree Publishing Co.

—What Comes Next? 2007. (Looking at Nature Ser.). (ENG., Illus.). 24p. (J). (gr. -1-2). pap. (978-0-7787-3339-3(4)) Crabtree Publishing Co.

Look at Mealtime. (Look at Me Ser.). (Illus.). (J). bds. 5.95 (978-0-590-24863-1(4)) Scholastic, Inc.

Lowery, Lawrence F. Look & See. 2nd ed. 2004. (J). per. (978-0-9762724-9-6(0)) Educational Research & Applications, LLC.

Markovics, Joyce L. Patterns in the Jungle. 2014. (Math Blast!: Seeing Patterns All Around Ser.). (ENG.). 32p. (J). (gr. -1-3). lib. bdg. 26.60 (978-1-62724-338-4(0)) Bearport Publishing Co., Inc.

McGrath, Barbara Barbieri. Teddy Bear Patterns. Nihoff, Tim, illus. 2013. (McGrath Math Ser.). (ENG.). 32p. (J). (gr. -1-3). pap. 7.95 (978-1-58089-423-4(2)); lib. bdg. 16.95 (978-1-58089-422-7(4)) Charlesbridge Publishing, Inc.

Mealtime. 2003. (J). per. (978-1-57657-893-3(3)) Paradise Pr., Inc.

Mineo, Tyrone. Near & Far with Birds. 2011. (Animal Math Ser.). (Illus.). 24p. (J). (gr. 1-3). pap. 8.15 (978-1-4339-5668-3(3)); lib. bdg. 22.60 (978-1-4339-5666-9(7)) Stevens, Gareth Publishing LLLP.

Mitten, Luana K. Arriba y abajo (under & Over) 2009. (Conceptos (Concepts) Ser.). (ENG & SPA., Illus.). 24p. (J). (gr. k-2). lib. bdg. 22.79 (978-1-60694-572-8(6)) Rourke Educational Media.

—Dentro y fuera (in & Out) 2009. (Conceptos (Concepts) Ser.). (ENG & SPA., Illus.). 24p. (J). (gr. k-2). lib. bdg. 22.79 (978-1-60694-573-5(4)) Rourke Educational Media.

Moore, Gareth. Seeing Is Believing. 2015. (Brain Benders Ser.). (ENG., Illus.). 32p. (J). (gr. 3-6). pap. 7.99 (978-1-4677-7201-3(1), Lerner Pubns.) Lerner Publishing Group.

National Geographic Kids Staff. Match! 2011. (ENG., Illus.). 24p. (J). (gr. k-k). bds. 6.99 (978-1-4263-0871-0(X), National Geographic Children's Bks.) National Geographic Society.

—What in the World? 2014. (ENG., Illus.). 48p. (J). (gr. 3-7). 16.99 (978-1-4263-1517-6(1), National Geographic Children's Bks.) National Geographic Society.

Penn, M. W. It's a Pattern!, 1 vol. 2011. (Pebble Math Ser.). (ENG.). 24p. (gr. k-1). pap. 6.29 (978-1-4296-7067-8(3)); pap. 35.70 (978-1-4296-7071-5(1)); lib. bdg. 21.99 (978-1-4296-6037-2(6)) Capstone Press of Coughlan Cos. (Pebble Bks.).

Picthall, Chez, des. Flowers. 2015. (ENG., Illus.). 10p. (J). 9.99 (978-1-907604-76-8(6)) Award Pubns. Ltd. GBR. Dist: Parkwest Pubns., Inc.

—Spots & Dots. 2015. (ENG., Illus.). 10p. (J). 9.99 (978-1-909763-02-9(0)) Award Pubns. Ltd. GBR. Dist: Parkwest Pubns., Inc.

Pistoia, Sara. Patterns. 2013. (Simply Math Ser.). (ENG.). 24p. (J). (gr. -1-2). 27.07 (978-1-62323-533-8(2), 206339) Child's World, Inc., The.

Randolph, Joanne. What I Look Like When I Am Confused. (Let's Look at Feelings Ser.).Tr. of What I Look Like When I am Confused. 24p. 2009. (gr. k-1). 42.50 (978-1-61514-239-2(8)) 2004. (Illus.). (gr. -1-1). 22.60 (978-1-4042-2510-7(2)) Rosen Publishing Group, Inc., The. (PowerKids Pr.).

—What I Look Like When I am Confused / Cómo me veo cuando estoy Confundido. 2009. (Let's Look at Feelings / un vistazo a los sentimientos Ser.). (ENG & SPA.). 24p. (gr. k-1). 42.50 (978-1-61514-246-0(0), Editorial Buenas Letras) Rosen Publishing Group, Inc., The.

Rauen, Amy. Vamos a Encontrar lo Más Corto y lo Más Largo. 2008. (Matemáticas para empezar (Getting Started with Math) Ser.). (SPA.). 16p. (gr. -1-2). pap. 5.30 (978-0-8368-8997-0(5), Weekly Reader Leveled Readers) Stevens, Gareth Publishing LLLP.

—Vamos a Encontrar lo Mas Corto y lo Más Largo. 2008. (Matemáticas para Empezar (Getting Started with Math) Ser.). (SPA., Illus.). 16p. (gr. -1-2). lib. bdg. 19.00 (978-0-8368-8992-5(4), Weekly Reader Leveled Readers) Stevens, Gareth Publishing LLLP.

Rivera, Sheila. In & Out. 2004. (First Step Nonfiction Ser.). (J). pap. 3.95 (978-0-8225-5353-3(8), Lerner Pubns.) Lerner Publishing Group.

—Near & Far. 2004. (First Step Nonfiction Ser.). (J). pap. 3.95 (978-0-8225-5354-0(6), Lerner Pubns.) Lerner Publishing Group.

—Over & Under. 2004. (First Step Nonfiction Ser.). (J). pap. 3.95 (978-0-8225-5350-2(3), Lerner Pubns.) Lerner Publishing Group.

Scholastic, Inc. Staff. Preschool Basic Skills: Visual Perception & Drawing Activities. 2003. (Preschool Basic Skills Ser.). (ENG.). 48p. 6.99 (978-0-439-50026-5(5), Teaching Resources) Scholastic, Inc.

Shea, Bobby Kennedy. Patterns with Pandas. 2013. (Animal Math Ser.). 24p. (J). (gr. 1-3). pap. 48.90 (978-1-4339-9320-6(1)); (ENG., Illus.). lib. bdg. 22.60 (978-1-4339-9318-3(X)) Stevens, Gareth Publishing LLLP.

Shea, Bobby Kennedy & Kennedy Shea, Bobby. Patterns with Pandas. 2013. 24p. (J). (gr. 1-3). pap. 8.15 (978-1-4339-9319-0(8)) Stevens, Gareth Publishing LLLP.

Smallwood, Sally & Jones, Bryony. Circle. Fox, Rebecca, illus. 2011. (Shapes Are Fun Ser.). (ENG.). 24p. (J). (gr. k — 1). bds. (978-1-84089-610-7(8)) Zero to Ten, Ltd.

—Rectangle. Fox, Rebecca, illus. 2011. (Shapes Are Fun Ser.). (ENG.). 14p. (J). (gr. k — 1). bds. (978-1-84089-613-8(2)) Zero to Ten, Ltd.

—Square. Fox, Rebecca, illus. 2011. (Shapes Are Fun Ser.). (ENG.). 14p. (J). (gr. k — 1). bds. (978-1-84089-612-1(4)) Zero to Ten, Ltd.

Smith, A. G. Visual Illusions Stained Glass Coloring Book. 2008. (Dover Design Stained Glass Coloring Book Ser.). (ENG., Illus.). 32p. (gr. 3-8). pap. 6.99 (978-0-486-46563-0(2)) Dover Pubns., Inc.

Sohn, Emily & Townsend, Laura. Patterns & Textures: Who Took the Pets? 2011. (IScience Readers Ser.). 32p. (J). (gr. 3-4). lib. bdg. 22.60 (978-1-59953-414-5(2)) Norwood Hse. Pr.

Steffora, Tracey. Patterns at the Museum, 1 vol. 2011. (Math Around Us Ser.). (ENG.). 24p. (gr. -1-1). 22.65 (978-1-4329-4923-5(3)); pap. 6.29 (978-1-4329-4931-0(4)) Heinemann-Raintree. (Acorn).

Stiles, Dan. Baby's First Bloox: Colors, Shapes, & Patterns. 2014. (ENG., Illus.). 22p. (J). (— 1). bds. 16.95 (978-1-57687-684-8(5), powerHouse Bks.) powerHouse Cultural Entertainment, Inc.

Tuxworth, Nicola. Patterns: Learn-a-Word Book. 2016. (ENG., Illus.). 20p. bds. 6.99 (978-1-86147-462-9(8), Armadillo) Anness Publishing GBR. Dist: National Bk. Network.

Wilcox, Charlotte. The Iroquois. 2006. (Native American Histories Ser.). (ENG., Illus.). 56p. (gr. 3-6). lib. bdg. 27.93 (978-0-8225-2637-7(9), Lerner Pubns.) Lerner Publishing Group.

World Book, Inc Staff, contrib. by. Nature's Patterns. 2010. (J). (978-0-7166-7740-6(7)) World Bk., Inc.

PERCEPTION—FICTION

Condon, Bill. The Simple Things. Norling, Beth, illus. 2015. 168p. (J). (gr. 3-5). 9.99 (978-1-74331-724-2(7)) Allen & Unwin AUS. Dist: Independent Pubs. Group.

Cook, Julia. I Just Want to Do It My Way! My Story about Staying on Task & Asking for Help! De Weerd, Kelsey, illus. 2013. (ENG.). 32p. (J). 10.95 (978-1-934490-43-3(1)) Boys Town Pr.

Diggle, David Mark. Bella: Shares Her Sticky Plan. Preuss, Sarah Louise, illus. 2011. 24p. (J). pap. (978-0-9871658-9-3(5)) Diggle de Doo Productions Pty, Ltd.

Harris, Elissa. M. I. N. D. 2016. (ENG.). 272p. (YA). pap. 10.95 (978-1-929345-26-7(7)) Poisoned Pen Pr.

Holden, Pam. Dinosaur Hunters, 6 pack. Storey, Jim & Hawley, Kelvin, illus. 2009. (Red Rocket Readers Ser.). (ENG.). 16p. (gr. 2-2). pap. (978-1-877363-59-7(6), Red Rocket Readers) Flying Start Bks.

Javaherbin, Mina & Jalal al-Din Rumi. Elephant in the Dark. Yelchin, Eugene, illus. 2015. (ENG.). 40p. (J). (gr. -1-3). 17.99 (978-0-545-63670-4(1), Scholastic Pr.) Scholastic, Inc.

Knudsen, Michelle. Big Mean Mike. Magoon, Scott, illus. 2012. (ENG.). 40p. (J). (gr. -1-3). 15.99 (978-0-7636-4990-6(2)) Candlewick Pr.

Margulies, Paul. What Julianna Could See. Zonneveld, Famke, illus. 2004. 32p. (J). pap. 11.95 (978-0-88010-515-6(1)) SteinerBooks, Inc.

Moss, Marissa. Amelia's Boredom Survival Guide. Moss, Marissa, illus. 2013. (Amelia Ser.). (ENG., Illus.). 64p. (J). (gr. 2-5). pap. 6.99 (978-1-4424-8369-9(5), Simon & Schuster/Paula Wiseman Bks.) Simon & Schuster/Paula Wiseman Bks.

Norac, Carl. My Daddy Is a Giant: For Everyone Who Has the Best Daddy in the World. Godon, Ingrid, illus. 2004. 32p. (J). (ENG & TWI.). pap. (978-1-84444-376-5(0)); (ENG & TGL.). pap. (978-1-84444-373-4(6)); (ENG & URD.). pap. (978-1-84444-377-2(9)); (ENG & VIE.). pap. (978-1-84444-378-9(7)); (YOR & ENG.). pap. (978-1-84444-379-6(5)); (ENG & KOR.). pap. (978-1-84444-300-0(0)); (ALB & ENG.). pap. (978-1-84444-351-2(5)); (ENG & BEN.). pap. (978-1-84444-353-6(1)); (ENG & BUL.). pap. (978-1-84444-354-3(X)); (ENG & CHI.). pap. (978-1-84444-355-0(8)); (SPA & ENG.). pap. (978-1-84444-372-7(8)); (SOM & ENG.). pap. (978-1-84444-371-0(X)); (ENG & SNA.). pap. (978-1-84444-370-3(1)); (ENG & RUS.). pap. (978-1-84444-369-7(8)); (ENG & PAN.). pap. (978-1-84444-366-6(3)); (ENG & KUR.). pap. (978-1-84444-365-9(5)); (ENG & JPN.). pap. (978-1-84444-364-2(7)); (ITA & ENG.). pap. (978-1-84444-363-5(9)); (FRE & ENG.). pap. (978-1-84444-359-8(0)); (ENG & HRV.). pap. (978-1-84444-357-4(4)); (ENG & CHI.). pap. (978-1-84444-356-7(6)) Mantra Lingua.

Norac, Carl & Gordon, Ingrid. My Daddy Is a Giant: For Everyone Who Has the Best Daddy in the World. 2004. (Illus.). 32p. (J). (ENG & ARA.). pap. (978-1-84444-352-9(3)); (ENG & PER., pap. (978-1-84444-358-1(2)); (GER & ENG., pap. (978-1-84444-360-4(4)); (ENG & GUJ., pap. (978-1-84444-361-1(2)); (ENG & HIN., pap. (978-1-84444-362-8(0)); (POL & ENG., pap. (978-1-84444-367-3(1)); (POR & ENG., pap. (978-1-84444-368-0(X)); (ENG & TAM., pap. (978-1-84444-374-1(4)); (TUR & ENG., pap. (978-1-84444-375-8(2)) Mantra Lingua.

Pham, LeUyen. There's No Such Thing As Little. 2015. (ENG., Illus.). 48p. (J). (gr. -1-2). 17.99 (978-0-385-39150-4(1), Knopf Bks. for Young Readers) Random Hse. Children's Bks.

Rizvi, Sobia. Zebra Stripes. 2011. 24p. pap. 15.99 (978-1-4653-4618-6(X)) Xlibris Corp.

Rogers, Alan. En Forme de Bateau. 2003. (Little Giants Ser.). (FRE., Illus.). 16p. (J). (gr. -1-k). 5.95 (978-1-58728-177-8(5), Two-Can Publishing) T&N Children's Publishing.

Shannon, George. White Is for Blueberry. Dronzek, Laura, illus. 2005. 40p. (J). (gr. -1). lib. bdg. 17.89 (978-0-06-029276-8(8)) HarperCollins Pubs.

Shannon, George & Shannon. White Is for Blueberry. Dronzek, Laura, illus. 2005. (ENG.). 40p. (J). (gr. -1-3). 17.99 (978-0-06-029275-1(X), Greenwillow Bks.) HarperCollins Pubs.

Shively, Julie. What Belongs? Kurtz, John, illus. 2004. (Baby Looney Toons Ser.). (ENG.). 16p. (J). 6.95 (978-0-8249-6561-7(2), Ideal Pubns.) Worthy Publishing.

PERCUSSION INSTRUMENTS

see also names of percussion instruments, e.g. Drums

Appice, Carmine. Realistic Rock for Kids (My 1st Rock & Roll Drum Method) Drum Beats Made Simple!, Book, 2 CDs & DVD. 2012. (ENG.). 32p. pap. 27.99 (978-0-7390-8917-0(X)) Alfred Publishing Co., Inc.

Fyffe, Daniel. Indoor Percussion Ensembles & Drum Corps. 2009. (Team Spirit! Ser.). 64p. (gr. 6-6). 53.00 (978-1-60853-270-4(4)) Rosen Publishing Group, Inc., The.

Ganeri, Anita. Drums & Percussion Instruments. 2011. (ENG., Illus.). 32p. (J). pap. 10.95 *(978-1-77092-030-9(7))* Saunders Bk. Co. CAN. Dist: RiverStream Publishing.

Landau, Elaine. Are the Drums for You? 2010. (Ready to Make Music Ser.). (ENG.). 40p. (gr. 4-6). lib. bdg. 27.93 *(978-0-7613-5426-0(3)*, Lerner Pubns.) Lerner Publishing Group.

Nunn, Daniel. Percussion, 1 vol. 2011. (Instruments & Music Ser.). (ENG.). 24p. (gr. -1-1). pap. 6.29 *(978-1-4329-5067-5(3))*; 22.65 *(978-1-4329-5060-6(6))* Heinemann-Raintree. (Acorn).

PERFORMING ARTS

see also Theater

also art forms performed on stage or screen, e.g. Ballet

All the World's a Stage! Individual Title Six-Packs. (Action Packs Ser.). 104p. (gr. 3-5). 44.00 *(978-0-7635-8406-1(1))* Rigby Education.

Backstage Pass, 6 Packs. (Bookweb Ser.). 32p. (gr. 4-18). 34.00 *(978-0-7635-3737-1(3))* Rigby Education.

Beall, Pamela Conn & Nipp, Susan Hagen. Wee Sing & Move. Guida, Liisa Chauncy & Klein, Nancy, illus. 2009. (Wee Sing Ser.). (ENG.). 64p. (J). (gr. -1-2). 10.99 *(978-0-8431-8959-9(2)*, Price Stern Sloan) Penguin Young Readers Group.

The Britannica Guide to the Visual & Performing Arts. 2015. (Britannica Guide to the Visual & Performing Arts Ser.). (ENG.). 128p. (YA). (gr. 9-10). 720.00 *(978-1-68048-199-0(1)*, Britannica Educational Publishing) Rosen Publishing Group, Inc., The.

Cohn, Jessica. On the Job in the Theater. Scheuer, Lauren, illus. 2016. (Core Content Social Studies — on the Job Ser.). (ENG.). 32p. (J). (gr. 2-5). lib. bdg. 26.65 *(978-1-63440-113-5(1))* Red Chair Pr.

Colson, Mary. Being a Makeup Artist. 2012. (On the Radar: Awesome Jobs Ser.). (ENG., Illus.). 32p. (J). (gr. 4-8). lib. bdg. 26.60 *(978-0-7613-7777-1(8)*, Lerner Pubns.) Lerner Publishing Group.

Dowd, Olympia. A Young Dancer's Apprenticeship. 2003. (Illus.). 128p. (J). (gr. 7-18). pap. 14.95 *(978-0-7613-1898-9(4)*, Twenty-First Century Bks.) Lerner Publishing Group.

Emmer, Rae. Drama Club: Club de Teatro. 2004. (School Activities / Actividades Escolares Ser.). (SPA & ENG., Illus.). 24p. (J). lib. bdg. 22.60 *(978-0-8239-6898-5(7)*, Editorial Buenas Letras) Rosen Publishing Group, Inc., The.

Encyclopaedia Britannica, Inc. Staff, compiled by. The Arts. 2003. (Britannica Learning Library). (Illus.). (gr. 2-5). 14.95 *(978-1-59339-004-4(1)*, 049905-EN-REF) Encyclopaedia Britannica, Inc.

Facts on File, Inc. Staff. Performing Arts. 2012. (Discovering Careers Ser.). (Illus.). 121p. (gr. 4-9). 24.95 *(978-0-8160-8059-5(3)*, Ferguson Publishing Co.) Facts On File, Inc.

Fraser, Fil. Alberta's Camelot Vol. 1: Culture & the Arts in the Lougheed Years, 1 vol. rev. ed. 2003. (ENG., Illus.). 240p. (gr. 4). pap. 21.95 *(978-1-55105-393-6(4)*, 1551053934) Lone Pine Publishing USA.

Hill, Z. B. Performing Arts. 2014. (Art Today! Ser.: 10). 64p. (J). (gr. 7-18). 23.95 *(978-1-4222-3174-6(7))* Mason Crest.

Hobbs, Mike. Entertainment. 2013. (Young Entrepreneurs' Club Ser.). 48p. (gr. 5-11). 37.10 *(978-1-59920-921-0(7))* Black Rabbit Bks.

Kallen, Stuart A. Careers in Entertainment. 2017. (Exploring Careers Ser.). (ENG.). 80p. (YA). (gr. 5-12). ***(978-1-68282-198-5(6))*** ReferencePoint Pr., Inc.

Lusted, Marcia Amidon. Entertainment, 1 vol. 2011. (Inside the Industry Ser.). (ENG., Illus.). 112p. (J). (gr. 6-12). lib. bdg. 35.64 *(978-1-61714-799-9(0)*, Essential Library) ABDO Publishing Co.

Mason, Antony. Performing Arts. 2004. (Culture Encyclopedia Ser.). (Illus.). 40p. (YA). (gr. 5-18). lib. bdg. 19.95 *(978-1-59084-481-6(5))* Mason Crest.

Meyer, Susan. Performing & Creating Speeches, Demonstrations, & Collaborative Learning Experiences with Cool New Digital Tools. 2013. (Way Beyond PowerPoint: Making 21st Century Presentations Ser.). 48p. (J). (gr. 5-8). 29.95 *(978-1-4777-1837-7(0))*; pap. 11.75 *(978-1-4777-1851-3(6))* Rosen Publishing Group, Inc., The. (Rosen Reference).

Performing & Creating Speeches, Demonstrations, & Collaborative Learning Experiences with Cool New Digital Tools. 2013. (Way Beyond PowerPoint: Making 21st Century Presentations Ser.). 48p. (J). (gr. 5-8). pap. 70.50 *(978-1-4777-1852-0(4)*, Rosen Reference) Rosen Publishing Group, Inc., The.

Performing Arts. 2010. (Career Launcher Ser.). 168p. (J). (gr. 9-18). 34.95 *(978-0-8160-7953-7(6)*, Ferguson Publishing Co.); pap. 14.95 *(978-0-8160-7975-9(7)*, Checkmark Bks.) Facts On File, Inc.

Pinky & the Brain in Bubba Bo Bob Brain. (Illus.). 32p. (J). (gr. -1-18). pap. 7.89 incl. audio *(978-1-56826-759-3(2)*, KR2) Rhino Entertainment Co, A Warner Music Group Co.

Schubert, Leda. Monsieur Marceau: Actor Without Words. DuBois, Gérard, illus. 2012. (ENG.). 40p. (J). (gr. -1-3). 17.99 *(978-1-59643-529-2(1)*, 9781596435292) Roaring Brook Pr.

Sylvester, Kevin. Showtime: Meet the People Behind the Scenes. 2013. (ENG., Illus.). 88p. (J). (gr. 5-7). 21.95 *(978-1-55451-487-8(8)*, 9781554514878); pap. 12.95 *(978-1-55451-486-1(X)*, 9781554514861) Annick Pr., Ltd. CAN. Dist: Publishers Group West (PGW).

PERFORMING ARTS—BIOGRAPHY

Abbey, Cherie D., ed. Biography Today: Profiles of People of Interest to Young Readers. (Biography Today Subject Ser.: 10). 2005. 200p. lib. bdg. 44.00 *(978-0-7808-0712-9(X))* 2004. 200p. lib. bdg. 44.00 *(978-0-7808-0751-8(0))* 2004. (Illus.). 248p. (gr. 3-18). lib. bdg. 44.00 *(978-0-7808-0709-9(X))* 2003. 248p. lib. bdg. 44.00 *(978-0-7808-0647-4(6))* Omnigraphics, Inc.

Levinson, Cynthia. Watch Out for Flying Kids!, 1 vol. 2015. (ENG., Illus.). 216p. (J). (gr. 5-9). 22.95 *(978-1-56145-821-9(X))* Peachtree Pubs.

Triumph Books Staff. Austin Mahone: Startin' Something Spectacular. 2013. (ENG.). 112p. (J). (gr. 4-7). pap. 12.95 *(978-1-60078-915-1(3))* Triumph Bks.

PERFORMING ARTS—FICTION

Charon Aldredge. Kiddie Rhythms the Show. 2010. 16p. pap. 15.00 *(978-1-4269-1970-1(0))* Trafford Publishing.

Cowley, Joy. Smarty Pants & the Talent Show. 2009. pap. 8.25 *(978-1-60559-241-1(2))* Hameray Publishing Group, Inc.

deRubertis, Barbara. Alexander Anteater's Amazing Act. Alley, R. W., illus. 2010. (Animal Antics A to Z Ser.). 32p. (J). (ENG.). (gr. -1-3). pap. 7.95 *(978-1-57565-300-6(1))*; (gr. k-1). lib. bdg. 22.60 *(978-1-57565-304-4(4))* Kane Press, Inc.

Eulberg, Elizabeth. Take a Bow. 2013. (ENG.). 288p. (J). (gr. 7). pap. 9.99 *(978-0-545-33476-1(4)*, Scholastic Paperbacks) 2012. (ENG.). 288p. (J). (gr. 7). 17.99 *(978-0-545-33474-7(8))* 2012. 280p. (YA). pap. *(978-0-545-43982-4(5))* Scholastic, Inc.

Harris, Lee. Carla & the Great Talent Show. 2009. 80p. pap. 10.00 *(978-1-60860-515-6(9)*, Strategic Bk. Publishing) Strategic Book Publishing & Rights Agency (SBPRA).

Henkes, Kevin. Wemberly Worried. 2003. (Illus.). (J). (gr. -1-2). audio compact disk 28.95 *(978-1-59112-360-6(7))* Live Oak Media.

Hodgkinson, Jo. The Talent Show. Hodgkinson, Jo, illus. 2011. (ENG., Illus.). 32p. (J). (gr. -1-3). 16.95 *(978-0-7613-7487-9(6))* Lerner Publishing Group.

Holabird, Katharine. A Day at Miss Lilly's. Craig, Helen, illus. 2007. (Angelina Ballerina Ser.). (ENG.). 24p. (J). (gr. -1-1). pap. 4.99 *(978-0-448-44548-9(4)*, Grosset & Dunlap) Penguin Publishing Group.

Kain, P. G. Dramatic Pause. 2012. (Commercial Breaks Ser.: 3). (ENG.). 288p. (J). (gr. 4-9). pap. 6.99 *(978-1-4169-9788-7(1)*, Aladdin) Simon & Schuster Children's Publishing.

Ketchum, Liza. The Life Fantastic. 2017. (ENG.). 256p. (YA). 17.99 *(978-1-4405-9876-0(2)*, Simon Pulse) Simon Pulse.

Kline, Suzy. Horrible Harry & the Missing Diamond. Wummer, Amy, illus. 2013. (Horrible Harry Ser.: 30). (ENG.). 80p. (J). (gr. 2-4). 14.99 *(978-0-670-01426-2(5)*, Viking Books for Young Readers) Penguin Young Readers Group.

LaMarche, Una. You in Five Acts. 2016. (ENG.). 352p. (YA). (gr. 7). 17.99 *(978-1-101-99893-9(8)*, Razorbill) Penguin Young Readers Group.

Margolis, Leslie. One Tough Chick. 2013. (Annabelle Unleashed Ser.). (ENG.). 176p. (YA). (gr. 3-6). 15.99 *(978-1-59990-961-5(8)*, 9781599909615, Bloomsbury USA Childrens) Bloomsbury Publishing USA.

Moskowitz, Hannah. Not Otherwise Specified: A Novel. 2015. (ENG., Illus.). 304p. (YA). (gr. 9). pap. 11.99 *(978-1-4814-0595-9(0)*, Simon Pulse) Simon Pulse.

Noël, Alyson. Unrivaled. (Beautiful Idols Ser.: 1). (YA). (gr. 9). 2017. 448p. pap. 9.99 *(978-0-06-232453-5(5))* 2016. 432p. 17.99 *(978-0-06-232452-8(7))* HarperCollins Pubs. (Tegen, Katherine Bks).

—Unrivaled: A Beautiful Idols Novel. 2016. 420p. (YA). *(978-0-06-245840-7(X))* HarperCollins Pubs.

Perelman, Helen. The Chocolate Rose. Waters, Erica-Jane, illus. 2013. (Candy Fairies Ser.: 11). (ENG.). 128p. (J). (gr. 2-5). pap. 5.99 *(978-1-4424-5299-2(4)*, Aladdin) Simon & Schuster Children's Publishing.

—The Chocolate Rose. Waters, Erica-Jane, illus. 2013. (Candy Fairies Ser.: 11). (ENG.). 128p. (J). (gr. 2-5). 15.99 *(978-1-4424-6499-5(2)*, Simon & Schuster/Paula Wiseman Bks.) Simon & Schuster/Paula Wiseman Bks.

Reisfeld, Randi. All Access. rev. ed. 2007. (ENG.). 288p. (gr. 7-12). pap. 8.99 *(978-1-4231-0503-9(6))* Hyperion Pr.

Rennison, Louise. A Midsummer Tights Dream. 2013. (Misadventures of Tallulah Casey Ser.: 2). (ENG.). 272p. (YA). (gr. 8). pap. 9.99 *(978-0-06-179938-9(6)*, HarperTeen) HarperCollins Pubs.

—Withering Tights. (Misadventures of Tallulah Casey Ser.: 1). (ENG.). (YA). (gr. 8). 2012. 304p. pap. 8.99 *(978-0-06-179933-4(5))* 2011. 288p. 16.99 *(978-0-06-179931-0(9))* HarperCollins Pubs. (HarperTeen).

Robinson, Craig & Mansbach, Adam. Jake the Fake Keeps It Real. Knight, Keith, illus. 2017. (Jake the Fake Ser.: 1). (ENG.). 144p. (J). (gr. 3-7). 13.99 *(978-0-553-52351-5(1)*, Crown Books For Young Readers) Random Hse. Children's Bks.

Ross, Dev. We Both Read-Oh No! We're Doing a Show! Johnson, Meredith, illus. 2011. 44p. (J). 9.95 *(978-1-60115-255-8(8))*; pap. 4.99 *(978-1-60115-256-5(6))* Treasure Bay, Inc.

Rushton, Rosie. I Think I'll Just Curl up & Die. 2005. 176p. (J). pap. 5.99 *(978-0-7868-5188-1(0))* Hyperion Bks. for Children.

Snowflake Day! 2014. (Daniel Tiger's Neighborhood Ser.). (ENG., Illus.). 14p. (J). (gr. -1-k). bds. 5.99 *(978-1-4814-1771-6(1)*, Simon Spotlight) Simon Spotlight.

Thaler, Mike. The Three Wise Guys, 1 vol. Lee, Jared, illus. 2010. (Tales from the Back Pew Ser.). (ENG.). 32p. (J). (gr. 1-4). pap. 3.99 *(978-0-310-71593-1(8))* Zonderkidz.

Weston Woods Staff, creator. The Clown of God. 2011. 29.95 *(978-0-545-08638-7(8))*; 18.95 *(978-0-545-08632-5(9))* Weston Woods Studios, Inc.

—Scrambled States of America Talent Show. 2011. 38.75 *(978-0-545-34954-3(0))*; 18.95 *(978-0-545-34618-4(5))* Weston Woods Studios, Inc.

Whittemore, Jo. D Is for Drama. 2012. (Mix Ser.). (ENG.). 272p. (J). (gr. 4-8). pap. 6.99 *(978-1-4424-4152-1(6)*, Aladdin) Simon & Schuster Children's Publishing.

Wiles, Deborah. The Aurora County All-Stars. 2009. (ENG., Illus.). 256p. (J). (gr. 2-5). pap. 7.99 *(978-0-15-206626-0(8))* Houghton Mifflin Harcourt Publishing Co.

PERFUMES

Loh-Hagan, Virginia. Odor Tester. 2015. 32p. (J). pap. *(978-1-63470-053-5(8))* Cherry Lake Publishing.

PERIODIC LAW

Adair, Rick. Beryllium. (Understanding the Elements of the Periodic Table Ser.). 48p. 2009. (gr. 6-6). 53.00 *(978-1-60854-634-3(9)*, Rosen Reference) 2007. (Illus.). (YA). (gr. 5-9). lib. bdg. 29.25 *(978-1-4042-1003-5(2))* Rosen Publishing Group, Inc., The.

Basher, Simon & Dingle, Adrian. The Periodic Table: Elements with Style! Basher, Simon, illus. 2010. (Basher Science Ser.). (ENG., Illus.). 128p. (J). (gr. 5-9). 14.99 *(978-0-7534-6613-1(9)*, 9780753466131, Kingfisher) Roaring Brook Pr.

Belval, Brian. Gold. 2007. (Understanding the Elements of the Periodic Table Ser.). (ENG., Illus.). 48p. (YA). lib. bdg. 29.25 *(978-1-4042-0708-0(2))* Rosen Publishing Group, Inc., The.

—Silver. 2009. (Understanding the Elements of the Periodic Table Ser.). 48p. (gr. 6-6). 53.00 *(978-1-60854-682-4(9)*, Rosen Reference) Rosen Publishing Group, Inc., The.

Crabtree Publishing Company Staff & Jackson, Tom. Introducing the Periodic Table. 2012. (ENG., Illus.). 32p. (J). *(978-0-7787-4230-2(X))*; pap. *(978-0-7787-4234-0(2))* Crabtree Publishing Co.

Dingle, Adrian & Basher, Simon. The Periodic Table: Elements with Style! Basher, Simon, illus. 2007. (Basher Science Ser.). (ENG., Illus.). 128p. (J). (gr. 5-9). pap. 8.99 *(978-0-7534-6085-6(8)*, 9780753460856, Kingfisher) Roaring Brook Pr.

Dingle, Adrian, et al. Basher Science: the Complete Periodic Table: All the Elements with Style! Basher, Simon, illus. 2015. (Basher Science Ser.). (ENG.). 192p. (J). (gr. 5-9). pap. 11.99 *(978-0-7534-7197-5(3)*, 9780753471975, Kingfisher) Roaring Brook Pr.

—Basher Science: the Complete Periodic Table: All the Elements with Style. Basher, Simon, illus. 2015. (Basher Science Ser.). (ENG.). 192p. (J). (gr. 5-9). 16.99 *(978-0-7534-7196-8(5)*, 9780753471968, Kingfisher) Roaring Brook Pr.

Gray, Leon. The Basics of the Periodic Table. 2013. (Core Concepts Ser.). 96p. (YA). (gr. 7-12). 34.60 *(978-1-4777-2712-6(4))* Rosen Publishing Group, Inc., The.

Green, Joey. The Electric Pickle: 50 Experiments from the Periodic Table, from Aluminum to Zinc. 2017. (ENG.). 272p. pap. 19.99 ***(978-1-61373-959-4(1))*** Chicago Review Pr., Inc.

Halka, Monica & Nordstrom, Brian. Periodic Table of the Elements, 6 vols., Set. 2011. (Periodic Table of the Elements Ser.). (C). (gr. 9). 240.00 *(978-0-8160-8299-5(5))* Facts On File, Inc.

Ham, Becky. The Periodic Table. 2008. (Essential Chemistry Ser.). 114p. (YA). (gr. 7-12). 35.00 *(978-0-7910-9533-1(9))* Facts On File, Inc.

Hasan, Heather. Aluminum. 2009. (Understanding the Elements of the Periodic Table Ser.). 48p. (gr. 6-6). 53.00 *(978-1-60854-629-9(2)*, Rosen Reference) Rosen Publishing Group, Inc., The.

—Fluorine. 2007. (Understanding the Elements of the Periodic Table Ser.). (Illus.). 48p. (YA). (gr. 5-9). lib. bdg. 29.25 *(978-1-4042-1005-9(9))* Rosen Publishing Group, Inc., The.

—Iron. (Understanding the Elements of the Periodic Table Ser.). 48p. 2009. (gr. 6-6). 53.00 *(978-1-60854-658-9(6)*, Rosen Reference) 2005. (Illus.). (J). (gr. 5-8). lib. bdg. 29.25 *(978-1-4042-0157-6(2))* Rosen Publishing Group, Inc., The.

—Nitrogen. (Understanding the Elements of the Periodic Table Ser.). 48p. 2009. (gr. 6-6). 53.00 *(978-1-60854-673-2(X)*, Rosen Reference) 2005. (Illus.). (J). (gr. 5-8). lib. bdg. 29.25 *(978-1-4042-0158-3(0))* Rosen Publishing Group, Inc., The.

Holt, Rinehart and Winston Staff. Holt Science & Technology Chapter 12: Physical Science: Periodic Table. 5th ed. 2004. (Illus.). pap. 12.86 *(978-0-03-030404-0(0))* Holt McDougal.

Johanson, Paula. Lithium. 2009. (Understanding the Elements of the Periodic Table Ser.). 48p. (gr. 6-6). 53.00 *(978-1-60854-661-9(6)*, Rosen Reference) Rosen Publishing Group, Inc., The.

Lew, Kristi. Argon. (Understanding the Elements of the Periodic Table Ser.). 48p. 2009. (gr. 6-6). 53.00 *(978-1-60854-632-9(2)*, Rosen Reference) 2008. (Illus.). (YA). (gr. 5-9). lib. bdg. 29.25 *(978-1-4042-1409-5(7))* Rosen Publishing Group, Inc., The.

Mullins, Matt. The Elements. 2011. (True Bk Ser.). (ENG., Illus.). 48p. (J). pap. 6.95 *(978-0-531-26585-7(4))*; lib. bdg. 29.00 *(978-0-531-26323-5(1))* Scholastic Library Publishing. (Children's Pr.).

Roza, Greg. Arsenic. 2009. (Understanding the Elements of the Periodic Table Ser.). 48p. (gr. 6-6). 53.00 *(978-1-60854-633-6(0)*, Rosen Reference) Rosen Publishing Group, Inc., The.

—Calcium. (Understanding the Elements of the Periodic Table Ser.). 48p. 2009. (gr. 6-6). 53.00 *(978-1-60854-641-1(1)*, Rosen Reference) 2007. (Illus.). (YA). (gr. 5-9). lib. bdg. 29.25 *(978-1-4042-1963-2(3))* Rosen Publishing Group, Inc., The.

—Chromium. 2009. (Understanding the Elements of the Periodic Table Ser.). 48p. (gr. 6-6). 53.00 *(978-1-60854-644-2(6)*, Rosen Reference) Rosen Publishing Group, Inc., The.

—Potassium. (Understanding the Elements of the Periodic Table Ser.). 48p. 2009. (gr. 6-6). 53.00 *(978-1-60854-678-7(0)*, Rosen Reference) 2007. (Illus.). (YA). (gr. 5-9). lib. bdg. 29.25 *(978-1-4042-1964-9(1))* Rosen Publishing Group, Inc., The.

—Titanium. (Understanding the Elements of the Periodic Table Ser.). 48p. 2009. (gr. 6-6). 53.00 *(978-1-60854-688-6(8)*, Rosen Reference) 2008. (Illus.). (YA). (gr. 5-9). lib. bdg. 29.25 *(978-1-4042-1412-5(7))* Rosen Publishing Group, Inc., The.

—Zirconium. 2009. (Understanding the Elements of the Periodic Table Ser.). 48p. (gr. 6-6). 53.00 *(978-1-60854-690-9(X)*, Rosen Reference); (YA). (gr. 5-9). lib. bdg. 29.25 *(978-1-4358-5070-5(X))* Rosen Publishing Group, Inc., The.

Saucerman, Linda. Carbon. 2009. (Understanding the Elements of the Periodic Table Ser.). 48p. (gr. 6-6). 53.00 *(978-1-60854-642-8(X)*, Rosen Reference) Rosen Publishing Group, Inc., The.

—Chlorine. (Understanding the Elements of the Periodic Table Ser.). 48p. 2009. (gr. 6-6). 53.00 *(978-1-60854-643-5(8)*, Rosen Reference) 2007. (Illus.). (YA). (gr. 5-9). lib. bdg. 29.25 *(978-1-4042-1962-5(5))* Rosen Publishing Group, Inc., The.

—Hydrogen. 2009. (Understanding the Elements of the Periodic Table Ser.). 48p. (gr. 6-6). 53.00 *(978-1-60854-656-5(X)*, Rosen Reference) Rosen Publishing Group, Inc., The.

—Hydrogen: The Fuel for Life. 2005. (Understanding the Elements of the Periodic Table Ser.). (Illus.). 48p. (J). (gr. 5-8). lib. bdg. 29.25 *(978-1-4042-0156-9(4))* Rosen Publishing Group, Inc., The.

Slade, Suzanne. Elements & the Periodic Table. (Library of Physical Science Ser.). 24p. (gr. 4-4). 2009. 42.50 *(978-1-60853-781-5(1)*, PowerKids Pr.) 2007. (ENG., Illus.). pap. 7.05 *(978-1-4042-2165-9(4)*, PowerKids Pr.) 2006. (Illus.). (YA). lib. bdg. 22.60 *(978-1-4042-3418-5(7))* Rosen Publishing Group, Inc., The.

Stefoff, Rebecca. The Four Elements & the Periodic Table. 2014. 48p. pap. 29.93 *(978-1-62712-518-5(3))* Cavendish Square Publishing.

Thomas, Michele. Oxygen. (Understanding the Elements of the Periodic Table Ser.). 48p. 2009. (gr. 6-6). 53.00 *(978-1-60854-674-9(8)*, Rosen Reference) 2005. (Illus.). (J). (gr. 5-8). lib. bdg. 29.25 *(978-1-4042-0159-0(9))* Rosen Publishing Group, Inc., The.

—Sodium. 2009. (Understanding the Elements of the Periodic Table Ser.). 48p. (gr. 6-6). 53.00 *(978-1-60854-685-5(3)*, Rosen Reference) Rosen Publishing Group, Inc., The.

Understanding the Elements of the Periodic Table. 2005. (Illus.). 48p. (gr. 5-8). lib. bdg. 159.00 *(978-1-4042-0348-8(6))* Rosen Publishing Group, Inc., The.

Understanding the Elements of the Periodic Table, 6 bks., Set 3. Incl. Beryllium. Adair, Rick. (gr. 5-9). lib. bdg. 29.25 *(978-1-4042-1003-5(2))*; Boron. Adair, Rick. (gr. 5-9). lib. bdg. 29.25 *(978-1-4042-1004-2(0))*; Fluorine. Hasan, Heather. (gr. 5-9). lib. bdg. 29.25 *(978-1-4042-1005-9(9))*; Lithium. Johanson, Paula. (gr. 5-9). lib. bdg. 29.25 *(978-1-4042-0940-4(9))*; Magnesium. Willett, Edward. (gr. 5-9). lib. bdg. 29.25 *(978-1-4042-1007-3(5))*; Neon. Willett, Edward. (gr. 3-7). lib. bdg. 29.25 *(978-1-4042-1008-0(3))*; (Illus.). 48p. (YA). 2007. 2007. Set lib. bdg. 159.00 *(978-1-4042-1043-1(1))* Rosen Publishing Group, Inc., The.

Wiker, Benjamin. The Mystery of the Periodic Table. Bendick, Jeanne, illus. 2003. (Living History Library). 170p. (YA). pap. 14.95 *(978-1-883937-71-3(X))* Bethlehem Bks.

Willett, Edward. Magnesium. 2009. (Understanding the Elements of the Periodic Table Ser.). 48p. (gr. 6-6). 53.00 *(978-1-60854-664-0(0)*, Rosen Reference) Rosen Publishing Group, Inc., The.

Wu, Ronald W. Carbon. 2005. (Understanding the Elements of the Periodic Table Ser.). (Illus.). 48p. (YA). (gr. 5-9). lib. bdg. 29.25 *(978-1-4042-0155-2(6))* Rosen Publishing Group, Inc., The.

Zannos, Susan. Dmitri Mendeleyev & the Periodic Table. 2004. (Uncharted, Unexplored, & Unexplained Ser.). (Illus.). 48p. (J). (gr. 4-8). lib. bdg. 29.95 *(978-1-58415-267-5(2))* Mitchell Lane Pubs., Inc.

PERIODIC TABLE OF ELEMENTS

see Periodic Law

PERIODICALS

see also Newspapers

Bodden, Valerie. Print & Subscription Sources. 2012. (Research for Writing Ser.). 48p. (gr. 5-12). 23.95 *(978-1-60818-205-3(3)*, Creative Education) Creative Co., The.

Guidone, Lisa M. What Happens at a Magazine? 2008. (Where People Work Ser.). 24p. (J). (gr. -1-3). lib. bdg. 22.00 *(978-0-8368-9275-8(5)*, Weekly Reader Leveled Readers) Stevens, Gareth Publishing LLLP.

—What Happens at a Magazine?/¿Qué Pasa en la Editorial de una Revista? 2008. (Where People Work Ser.). 24p. (gr. -1-3). pap. 8.15 *(978-0-8368-9374-8(3)*, Weekly Reader Leveled Readers) Stevens, Gareth Publishing LLLP.

Guidone, Lisa M. & Nations, Susan. What Happens at a Magazine?/¿Qué Pasa en la Editorial de una Revista? 2008. (Where People Work/Dónde Trabaja la Gente? Ser.). (SPA.). 24p. (gr. -1-3). pap. 8.15 *(978-0-8368-9380-9(8)*, Weekly Reader Leveled Readers) Stevens, Gareth Publishing LLLP.

—What Happens at a Magazine?/¿Qué Pasa en la Editorial de Una Revista? 2008. (Where People Work/Dónde Trabaja la Gente? Ser.). (ENG & SPA.). 24p. (J). (gr. -1-3). lib. bdg. 22.00 *(978-0-8368-9281-9(X)*, Weekly Reader Leveled Readers) Stevens, Gareth Publishing LLLP.

Hamilton, John. Magazines, 1 vol. 2005. (Straight to the Source Ser.). (ENG., Illus.). 32p. (gr. k-6). 27.07 *(978-1-59197-546-5(8)*, Checkerboard Library) ABDO Publishing Co.

In the News, 6 vols., Set 5. Incl. Biofuels: Sustainable Energy in the 21st Century. Johanson, Paula. lib. bdg. 31.95 *(978-1-4358-3584-9(0))*; Election of Barack Obama: Race & Politics in America. Porterfield, Jason. lib. bdg. 31.95 *(978-1-4358-3586-3(7))*; Illegal Immigration & Amnesty: Open Borders & National Security. Levy, Janey. lib. bdg. 31.95 *(978-1-4358-3583-2(2))*; Same-Sex Marriage: The Debate. Nagle, Jeanne. lib. bdg. 31.95 *(978-1-4358-3582-5(4))*; Superbugs: The Rise of Drug-Resistant Germs. Watson, Stephanie. lib. bdg. 31.95 *(978-1-4358-3585-6(9))*; U. S. Economic Crisis. Freedman, Jeri. lib. bdg. 31.95 *(978-1-4358-3587-0(5))*; (YA). (gr. 7-12). 2010. (Illus.). 64p. 2010. Set lib. bdg. 175.50 *(978-1-4358-3612-9(X))* Rosen Publishing Group, Inc., The.

Petley, Julian. Newspapers & Magazines. 2003. (Media Wise Ser.). (Illus.). 64p. (J). lib. bdg. 28.50 *(978-1-58340-258-0(6))* Black Rabbit Bks.

Rocha, Toni L. Careers in Magazine Publishing. 2009. (Career Resource Library). 192p. (gr. 7-12). 63.90 *(978-1-60853-399-2(9))* Rosen Publishing Group, Inc., The.

PERRY, MATTHEW CALBRAITH, 1794-1858

Blumberg, Rhoda. Commodore Perry in the Land of the Shogun. 2003. (ENG., Illus.). 144p. (J). (gr. 3-18). pap. 9.99 *(978-0-06-008625-1(4))* HarperCollins Pubs.

—Commodore Perry in the Land of the Shogun. 2003. (Illus.). 144p. (gr. 3-7). 20.00 *(978-0-7569-1440-0(X))* Perfection Learning Corp.

McNeese, Tim. The Perry Expedition & the Opening of Japan. 2012. (J). 35.00 *(978-1-60413-924-2(2)*, Chelsea Hse.) Facts On File, Inc.

Wittner, David G. Commodore Matthew Perry & the Perry Expedition to Japan. 2009. (Library of American Lives & Times Ser.). 112p. (gr. 5-5). 69.20 *(978-1-60853-474-6(X))* Rosen Publishing Group, Inc., The.

PERSEUS (GREEK MYTHOLOGY)

Harkins, Susan Sales & Harkins, William H. Perseus. 2007. (Profiles in Greek & Roman Mythology Ser.). (Illus.). 48p. (YA). (gr. 4-7). lib. bdg. 29.95 *(978-1-58415-558-4(2))* Mitchell Lane Pubs., Inc.

Hepplewhite, Peter & Salariya, David. The Adventures of Perseus. Bergin, Mark, illus. 2013. 32p. (J). *(978-1-4351-5119-2(4))* Barnes & Noble, Inc.

Jeffrey, Gary. Perseus Slays the Gorgon Medusa. 2012. (Graphic Mythical Heroes Ser.). (Illus.). 24p. (J). (gr. 3-5). 23.95 *(978-1-4339-7523-3(8))*; pap. 8.15 *(978-1-4339-7524-0(6))* Stevens, Gareth Publishing LLLP.

McCaughrean, Geraldine. Perseus. 2005. (Heroes Ser.). (ENG., Illus.). 160p. (J). (gr. -1-7). 17.95 *(978-0-8126-2735-0(0))* Cricket Bks.

Roesser, Blanche. The Story of Perseus. 2015. (Stories in the Stars Ser.). (ENG., Illus.). 24p. (J). (gr. 1-2). 22.60 *(978-1-4824-2683-0(8))* Stevens, Gareth Publishing LLLP.

Storrie, Paul D. Perseus: The Hunt for Medusa's Head. Yeates, Thomas, illus. 2008. (Graphic Myths & Legends Ser.). (ENG.). 48p. (gr. 4-8). lib. bdg. 27.93 *(978-0-8225-7528-3(0))* Lerner Publishing Group.

—Perseus: The Hunt for Medusa's Head [a Greek Myth]. Yeates, Thomas, illus. 2015. (Graphic Myths & Legends Ser.). (ENG.). 48p. (gr. 4-8). 21.32 *(978-1-4677-5984-7(8)*, Lerner Digital) Lerner Publishing Group.

Weiss, Lynne. Perseus & Medusa, 1 vol., 1. 2014. (Jr. Graphic Myths: Greek Heroes Ser.). (ENG.). 24p. (J). (gr. 3-6). 26.25 *(978-1-4777-6232-5(9)*, PowerKids Pr.) Rosen Publishing Group, Inc., The.

PERSIAN GULF WAR, 1991

Calvert, John. The Arabian Peninsula in the Age of Oil. 2009. (Making of the Middle East Ser.). (Illus.). 88p. (YA). (gr. 3-7). lib. bdg. 22.95 *(978-1-4222-0172-5(4))* Mason Crest.

Cooke, Tim. The Gulf War on the Front Lines, 1 vol. 2014. (Life on the Front Lines Ser.). (ENG., Illus.). 32p. (gr. 3-4). 27.99 *(978-1-4914-0847-6(2)*, Edge Bks.) Capstone Press of Coughlan Cos.

Dongweck, James. The Goblin's Story. Bixby, Sean, illus. 2013. (J). *(978-0-9719632-2-1(3))* Golden Monkey Publishing, LLC.

George, Enzo. The Persian Gulf War: War Against Iraqi Aggression. 2014. (Voices of War Ser.). 48p. (J). (gr. 4-6). 31.36 *(978-1-62712-876-6(X))* Cavendish Square Publishing.

Gitlin, Martin. Operation Desert Storm, 1 vol. 2009. (Essential Events Set 3 Ser.). (ENG., Illus.). 112p. (J). (gr. 6-12). lib. bdg. 35.64 *(978-1-60453-516-7(4))* ABDO Publishing Co.

Gunderson, Cory Gideon. U. N. Weapons Inspectors. 2003. (World in Conflict-the Middle East Ser.). 32p. (gr. 4-8). 27.07 *(978-1-59197-414-7(3)*, Abdo & Daughters) ABDO Publishing Co.

Hillstrom, Laurie Collier. War in the Persian Gulf: From Operation Desert Storm to Operation Iraqi Freedom Reference Library, 3 vols. Incl. War in the Persian Gulf: Biographies. Hillstrom, Kevin. 320p. (J). 106.00 *(978-0-7876-6564-7(9))*; War in the Persian Gulf Almanac: From Operation Desert Storm to Operation Iraqi Freedom. Carnagie, Julie, ed. 224p. 106.00 *(978-0-7876-6563-0(0))*; (War in the Persian Gulf Reference Library). (ENG., Illus.). 208p. 2004. 286.00 *(978-0-7876-6562-3(2)*, GML10504-182625, UXL) Cengage Gale.

Holden, Henry M. The Persian Gulf War: A MyReportLinks.com Book. 2003. (U.S. Wars Ser.). (Illus.). 48p. (J). (gr. 4-10). lib. bdg. 26.60 *(978-0-7660-5109-6(9))* Enslow Pubs., Inc.

Lowery, Zoe. Key Figures of the Wars in Iraq & Afghanistan. 2015. (Biographies of War Ser.). (ENG., Illus.). 112p. (J). (gr. 7-8). 32.90 *(978-1-68048-066-5(9)*, Britannica Educational Publishing) Rosen Publishing Group, Inc., The.

Martin, Michael. The Persian Gulf War: Saddam's Failed Invasion. 2004. (History's Great Defeats Ser.). (ENG.). (J). (gr. 7-10). 30.85 *(978-1-59018-428-9(X)*, Lucent Bks.) Cengage Gale.

McArthur, Debra. Desert Storm — the First Persian Gulf War in American History. 2004. (In American History Ser.). (Illus.). 128p. (J). lib. bdg. 26.60 *(978-0-7660-2149-5(1))* Enslow Pubs., Inc.

Murdico, Suzanne J. The Gulf War. (War & Conflict in the Middle East Ser.). 64p. 2009. (gr. 5-5). 58.50 *(978-1-60854-737-1(X))* 2004. (Illus.). (gr. 7-12). lib. bdg. 31.95 *(978-0-8239-4551-1(0))* Rosen Publishing Group, Inc., The.

Perritano, John. Desert Storm. 2010. (America at War Ser.). 32p. (J). 27.00 *(978-0-531-23210-1(7)*, Watts, Franklin) Scholastic Library Publishing.

Peterson, J. E. Tensions in the Gulf, 1978-1991. 2007. (Making of the Middle East Ser.). (Illus.). 88p. (J). (gr. 3-7). lib. bdg. 22.95 *(978-1-4222-0175-6(9))* Mason Crest.

Rice, Earle. Overview of the Persian Gulf War 1990. 2008. (Monumental Milestones Ser.). (Illus.). 48p. (YA). (gr. 4-7). lib. bdg. 29.95 *(978-1-58415-696-3(1))* Mitchell Lane Pubs., Inc.

Yasuda, Anita. The Gulf War. 2015. (Wars in U. S. History Ser.). (ENG.). 32p. (J). (gr. 2-5). 28.50 *(978-1-63143-713-7(5)*, 208537) Child's World, Inc., The.

Zeinert, Karen & Miller, Mary. The Brave Women of the Gulf Wars: Operation Desert Storm & Operation Iraqi Freedom. 2005. (Women at War Ser.). (ENG., Illus.). 96p. (gr. 7-12). 30.60 *(978-0-7613-2705-9(3)*, Millbrook Pr.) Lerner Publishing Group.

Zwier, Lawrence J. & Weltig, Matthew S. The Persian Gulf & Iraqi Wars. 2005. (Chronicle of America's Wars Ser.). (Illus.). 96p. (J). (gr. 3-7). lib. bdg. 27.93 *(978-0-8225-0848-9(6))* Lerner Publishing Group.

PERSONAL APPEARANCE

see Beauty, Personal

PERSONAL DEVELOPMENT

see Personality; Success

PERSONAL FINANCE

see Finance, Personal

PERSONAL GROOMING

see Beauty, Personal

PERSONAL IDENTITY

see Identity (Psychology); Personality

PERSONAL LIBERTY

see Liberty

PERSONALITY

see also Identity (Psychology); Individuality

Allman, Toney. Understanding Personality. 2017. (ENG.). 80p. (J). (gr. 5-12). ***(978-1-68282-277-7(X))*** ReferencePoint Pr., Inc.

Berry, Joy. Help Me Be Good Being Selfish. Bartholomew, illus. 2010. (Help Me Be Good Ser.). (ENG.). 32p. (J). (gr. -1-2). pap. 4.99 *(978-1-60577-133-5(3))* Berry, Joy Enterprises.

Brownlie, Marion. Spirit of Self. 2013. 36p. pap. *(978-0-9875551-5-1(4))* Aurora House.

Dolphin, Colleen. Adventurous to Zealous: All about Me from A to Z, 1 vol. 2009. (Let's Learn A to Z Ser.). (ENG., Illus.). 32p. (J). (gr. -1-2). 27.07 *(978-1-60453-490-0(7)*, 1293204) ABDO Publishing Co.

Dorling Kindersley Publishing Staff. How to Be a Genius. 2013. (ENG.). 192p. (J). (gr. 5-12). pap. 12.99 *(978-1-4654-1424-3(X)*, DK Children) Dorling Kindersley Publishing, Inc.

Greenspon, Thomas S. What to Do When Good Enough Isn't Good Enough: The Real Deal on Perfectionism: A Guide for Kids. 2007. (ENG., Illus.). 128p. (YA). (gr. 4-8). pap. 10.99 *(978-1-57542-234-3(4))* Free Spirit Publishing, Inc.

Jones, Steven. Journey to Excellence: An Introduction to E4. 2003. 75p. (YA). per. 19.99 *(978-0-9729798-0-1(8))* Keytochange Publishing, Inc.

Kalman, Bobbie. Today Is a Great Day! 2010. (My World Ser.). (ENG.). 16p. (J). (gr. k-3). *(978-0-7787-9506-3(3))*; pap. *(978-0-7787-9531-5(4))* Crabtree Publishing Co.

Klutz Editors. Rule the World: 119 Shortcuts to Total World Domination. 2011. (ENG.). 120p. (J). (gr. 3-7). 16.99 *(978-1-59174-849-6(6))* Klutz.

Lewis, Barbara A. What Do You Stand For? - For Kids: A Guide to Building Character. Lisovskis, Marjorie, ed. 2005. (ENG., Illus.). 176p. (J). (gr. 3-7). pap. 14.99 *(978-1-57542-174-2(7))* Free Spirit Publishing, Inc.

Meiners, Cheri J. Bounce Back! Allen, Elizabeth, illus. 2014. (Being the Best Me Ser.). (ENG.). 40p. (J). (gr. -1-3). 14.99 *(978-1-57542-457-6(6))* Free Spirit Publishing, Inc.

Miller, Reagan. Step Forward with Optimism. 2016. (Step Forward! Ser.). (ENG., Illus.). 24p. (J). (gr. 2-5). *(978-0-7787-2780-4(7))* Crabtree Publishing Co.

Nelms, Davis Kenyon. Inner-Fire Kindling: Simple Exercises for the Permanent Establishment of Fulfilling Thoughts. 2004. (Illus.). 128p. per. 19.95 *(978-0-9654169-7-9(6))* Billings Worldwide Brain.

Obregón, José María. Lionel Messi. 2009. (World Soccer Stars / Estrellas del fútbol mundial Ser.). (ENG & SPA.). 24p. (gr. 2-2). 42.50 *(978-1-60854-848-4(1)*, Editorial Buenas Letras) Rosen Publishing Group, Inc., The.

Potts, Francesca. What's Your Personality? Facts, Trivia, & Quizzes. 2017. (Mind Games Ser.). (ENG., Illus.). (J). (gr. 2-5). lib. bdg. 27.99 ***(978-1-5124-3413-2(2))*** Lerner Publishing Group.

Rosen, Michael J. & Carlson, Daniel. Just My Type: Understanding Personality Profiles. 2016. (Nonfiction - Young Adult Ser.). (ENG., Illus.). 80p. (YA). (gr. 7-12). 34.65 *(978-1-4677-8010-0(3))*; 51.99 *(978-1-4677-9579-1(8))* Lerner Publishing Group. (Twenty-First Century Bks.).

Shepherd, Jodie. Optimism: Sunny-Side Up! 2015. (Rookie Talk about It(tm) Ser.). (ENG.). 32p. (J). pap. 5.95 *(978-0-531-21383-4(8)*, Children's Pr.) Scholastic Library Publishing.

Thomas, Pat. I Can Do It! A First Look at Not Giving Up. Harker, Lesley, illus. 2010. (First Look At... Ser.). (ENG.). 32p. (J). (gr. -1-3). pap. 6.99 *(978-0-7641-4515-5(0))* Barron's Educational Series, Inc.

Welbourn, Shannon. Step Forward with Grit. 2016. (Step Forward! Ser.). (ENG., Illus.). 24p. (J). (gr. 2-5). *(978-0-7787-2767-5(X))* Crabtree Publishing Co.

Williams, Jane A. A Bluestocking Guide - Building a Personal Model for Success: Companion Workbook to Richard J. Maybury's Uncle Eric Talks about Personal, Career, & Financial Security. Daniels, Kathryn, ed. 2004. (Bluestocking Guide Ser.). (ENG.). 47p. (YA). pap. 10.95 *(978-0-942617-39-9(8))* Bluestocking Pr.

PERSONALITY—FICTION

Alafaci, Marie. Zelda's Big Adventure. McG, Shane, illus. 2017. (ENG.). 32p. (J). (gr. -1-3). 16.99 ***(978-1-328-66081-7(8)***, Clarion Bks.) Houghton Mifflin Harcourt Trade & Reference Pubs.

Allen, Teresa R. The Tale of the Teeny, Tiny Black Ant: Helping Children Learn Persistence. Seroya, Tea, illus. 2011. (Let's Talk Ser.). (ENG.). 48p. (J). (gr. -1-2). pap. 9.95 *(978-0-88282-351-5(5))* New Horizon Pr. Pubs., Inc.

Atkinson, Elizabeth. I, Emma Freke. 2010. (Exceptional Reading & Language Arts Titles for Intermediate Grades Ser.). (ENG.). 240p. (J). (gr. 4-7). 16.95 *(978-0-7613-5604-2(5)*, Carolrhoda Bks.) Lerner Publishing Group.

Bogan, Paulette. Bossy Flossy. Bogan, Paulette, illus. 2016. (ENG., Illus.). 32p. (J). 16.99 *(978-1-62779-358-2(5)*, 9781627793582, Holt, Henry & Co. Bks. For Young Readers) Holt, Henry & Co.

Bowen, Fred. The Final Cut, 1 vol. 2009. (All-Star Sports Story Ser.). (ENG., Illus.). 112p. (J). pap. 6.95 *(978-1-56145-510-2(5))* Peachtree Pubs.

—Soccer Team Upset, 1 vol. 2009. (Fred Bowen Sports Story Ser.). (ENG.). 128p. (J). (gr. 2-7). pap. 6.95 *(978-1-56145-495-2(8))* Peachtree Pubs.

—T. J. 's Secret Pitch, 1 vol. 2009. (All-Star Sports Story Ser.). (ENG., Illus.). 112p. (J). pap. 5.95 *(978-1-56145-504-1(0))* Peachtree Pubs.

Cameron, Sharon. The Dark Unwinding. 2013. (ENG.). 336p. (J). (gr. 7). pap. 9.99 *(978-0-545-32787-9(3)*, Scholastic Paperbacks) Scholastic, Inc.

Chaconas, Dori & Bader, Bonnie. Spring Cleaning. McCue, Lisa, illus. 2015. (Cork & Fuzz Ser.: 10). (ENG.). 32p. (J). (gr. 1-3). 14.99 *(978-0-670-01686-0(1)*, Penguin Young Readers) Penguin Young Readers Group.

Crouch, Cheryl. Troo Makes a Big Splash, 1 vol. Zimmer, Kevin, illus. 2011. (I Can Read! / Rainforest Friends Ser.). (ENG.). 32p. (J). (gr. -1-2). pap. 3.99 *(978-0-310-71810-9(4))* Zonderkidz.

Dane Rehagen. How Katie Got Her Meow. 2010. 42p. pap. 15.00 *(978-1-4251-8664-7(5))* Trafford Publishing.

Delessert, Etienne. Spartacus the Spider. 2010. (ENG., Illus.). 32p. (J). (gr. 1-3). 17.95 *(978-1-56846-213-4(1)*, Creative Editions) Creative Co., The.

Denise, Susan Denise. The Little Lazy Lizard. 2008. 16p. pap. 24.95 *(978-1-60474-502-3(9))* America Star Bks.

Ephron, Delia. The Girl with the Mermaid Hair. 2010. (ENG.). 320p. (YA). (gr. 8-18). 16.99 *(978-0-06-154260-2(1)*, HarperTeen) HarperCollins Pubs.

Errico, Daniel. The Journey of the Noble Gnarble. Turrill, Tiffany, illus. 2013. (ENG.). 32p. (J). (gr. -1-k). 16.95 *(978-1-62087-732-6(5)*, 620732, Sky Pony Pr.) Skyhorse Publishing Co., Inc.

Gold, Rachel. Being Emily. 2012. (ENG.). 264p. (gr. 9). pap. 15.95 *(978-1-59493-283-0(2))* Bella Bks., Inc.

Goldberg, Whoopi. Perfectly Prima. No. 3. Roos, Maryn, illus. 2010. (ENG.). 160p. (J). (gr. 1-17). pap. 4.99 *(978-0-7868-5262-8(3)*, Jump at the Sun) Hyperion Bks. for Children.

Gutman, Dan. The Million Dollar Strike. 2006. 176p. (J). (gr. 3-7). 13.65 *(978-0-7569-7023-9(7))* Perfection Learning Corp.

Halvorson, Marilyn. Blue Moon. 2004. (Orca Soundings Ser.). 109p. (gr. 4-7). 19.95 *(978-0-7569-4285-4(3))* Perfection Learning Corp.

Hart, Christine. Best Laid Plans, 1 vol. 2009. (Lorimer SideStreets Ser.). (ENG.). 152p. (YA). (gr. 9-12). 16.95 *(978-1-55277-447-2(3)*, 9781552774472); 9.95 *(978-1-55277-446-5(5)*, 9781552774465) Lorimer, James & Co., Ltd., Pubs. CAN. Dist: Casemate Pubs. & Bk. Distributors, LLC.

Hyatt, Patricia Rusch. The Quite Contrary Man: A True American Tale. Brown, Kathryn, illus. 2011. (ENG.). 32p. (J). (gr. 1-4). 16.95 *(978-0-8109-4065-9(5)*, Abrams Bks. for Young Readers) Abrams, Inc.

Jones, Christianne C. The Messy One, 1 vol. Martinez-Neal, Juana, illus. 2012. (Little Boost Ser.). (ENG.). 32p. (gr. k-3). 7.95 *(978-1-4048-7417-6(8)*, Little Boost) Picture Window Bks.

Keller, Elinoar & Peleg-Segal, Naama. Just Like I Wanted. Gordon-Noy, Aya, illus. 2015. (ENG.). 26p. (J). 17.00 *(978-0-8028-5453-7(2)*, Eerdmans Bks For Young Readers) Eerdmans, William B. Publishing Co.

Kimmel, Elizabeth Cody. The Reinvention of Moxie Roosevelt. 2011. (ENG.). 256p. (J). (gr. 5-18). 6.99 *(978-0-14-241870-3(6)*, Puffin Books) Penguin Young Readers Group.

Krosoczka, Jarrett J. It's Tough to Lose Your Balloon. 2015. (ENG., Illus.). 40p. (J). (gr. -1-2). lib. bdg. 20.99 *(978-0-385-75480-4(9)*, Knopf Bks. for Young Readers) Random Hse. Children's Bks.

Law, Felicia. Benjamin the Bear: A Tale of Selfishness. Spoor, Mike, illus. 2010. (Animal Fair Values Ser.). (ENG.). 32p. (J). (gr. -1-3). pap. 10.55 *(978-1-60754-915-4(8))*; lib. bdg. 22.60 *(978-1-60754-905-5(0))* Windmill Bks.

Legrand, Claire. The Cavendish Home for Boys & Girls. Watts, Sarah, illus. 2012. (ENG.). 352p. (J). (gr. 5). 16.99 *(978-1-4424-4291-7(3)*, Simon & Schuster Bks. For Young Readers) Simon & Schuster Bks. For Young Readers.

Levine, Rhoda. Three Ladies Beside the Sea. Gorey, Edward, illus. 2010. (ENG.). 40p. (J). (gr. k-4). 14.95 *(978-1-59017-354-1(6)*, NYR Children's Collection) New York Review of Bks., Inc., The.

Lewis-Cook, Ashley. Beautiful Me! 2012. (Illus.). 16p. pap. 15.99 *(978-1-4772-1291-2(4))* AuthorHouse.

Parker, David & Lyon, Tammie. ¡Soy Optimista! Lyon, Tammie, illus. 2011. (SPA., Illus.). (J). *(978-0-545-27356-5(0))* Scholastic, Inc.

Paul, Chris. Long Shot: Never Too Small to Dream Big. Morrison, Frank, illus. 2009. (ENG.). 32p. (J). (gr. -1-3). 17.99 *(978-1-4169-5079-0(6)*, Simon & Schuster Bks. For Young Readers) Simon & Schuster Bks. For Young Readers.

Potter, Ellen. Olivia Kidney & the Secret Beneath the City. 2009. (ENG.). 336p. (J). (gr. 3-7). 9.99 *(978-0-14-241263-3(5)*, Puffin Books) Penguin Young Readers Group.

Rodgers, Mary. Freaky Friday. 2003. (ENG.). 176p. (J). (gr. 5-18). pap. 6.99 *(978-0-06-057010-1(5)*, HarperTeen) HarperCollins Pubs.

—Freaky Friday. 2003. (J). (gr. 7-12). 17.20 *(978-0-613-68424-8(9)*, Turtleback) Turtleback Bks.

Rodgers, Mary, ed. Freaky Friday. 145p. (J). (gr. 4-6). pap. 4.95 *(978-0-8072-1390-2(X)*, Listening Library) Random Hse. Audio Publishing Group.

Rodriguez, Alex. Out of the Ballpark. Morrison, Frank, illus. 2012. (ENG.). 32p. (J). (gr. -1-3). pap. 6.99 *(978-0-06-115196-5(3))* HarperCollins Pubs.

Salm, Arthur. Anyway* *a Story about Me with 138 Footnotes, 27 Exaggerations, & 1 Plate of Spaghetti. 2013. (ENG., Illus.). 192p. (J). (gr. 3-7). pap. 7.99 *(978-1-4424-2931-4(3)*, Simon & Schuster Bks. For Young Readers) Simon & Schuster Bks. For Young Readers.

Schirmer, Jodi L. Dear Deer Friend. 2008. 24p. pap. 11.95 *(978-1-4327-2540-2(8))* Outskirts Pr., Inc.

Scraper, Katherine. Remember the Rules. 2006. (Early Explorers Ser.). (J). pap. *(978-1-4108-6031-6(0))* Benchmark Education Co.

Skye, obert. Choke. 2010. (Pillage Ser.: 2). (ENG., Illus.). 336p. (YA). (gr. 7). 17.99 *(978-1-60641-653-2(7)*, Shadow Mountain) Shadow Mountain Publishing.

Tarter, Mildred. Rexis! Where Are You! 2010. 24p. pap. 16.49 *(978-1-4389-6874-2(4))* AuthorHouse.

Wilhelm, Hans. Pelican & Pelican't. 2007. (Illus.). (J). *(978-0-545-00910-2(3))* Scholastic, Inc.

Zackery, Gary D. & Borgstedt, John. Stephen. 2011. 108p. 22.45 *(978-1-4567-2712-3(5))*; pap. 16.00 *(978-1-4567-2711-6(7))* AuthorHouse.

PERSONNEL MANAGEMENT—VOCATIONAL GUIDANCE

Freedman, Jeri. Careers in Human Resources. 2013. (Essential Careers Ser.). 80p. (YA). (gr. 7-12). 33.25 *(978-1-4777-1791-2(9))* Rosen Publishing Group, Inc., The.

PERSONNEL SERVICE IN EDUCATION

see Educational Counseling

PERSPECTIVE

see also Drawing

Burmeister, AimeeLeigh. Perspective for Kids Volume One Introduction to Perspective. 2010. 40p. pap. 26.00 *(978-0-557-68821-0(3))* Lulu Pr., Inc.

Levy, Janey. Renaissance Paintings: Using Perspective to Represent Three-Dimensional Objects. (PowerMath Ser.). 32p. 2009. (ENG., Illus.). (gr. 5-6). pap. 10.00 *(978-1-4042-5115-1(4))* 2009. (gr. 4-5). 47.90 *(978-1-60851-416-8(1)*, PowerKids Pr.) 2005. (Illus.). (J). (gr. 3-6). lib. bdg. 25.25 *(978-1-4042-2926-6(4)*, PowerKids Pr.) Rosen Publishing Group, Inc., The.

PERSUASION (RHETORIC)

see Public Speaking; Rhetoric

PERU

Annabelle Alpaca Travels to Peru. 2005. (J). per. 7.99 *(978-0-9746409-1-4(3))* O'Neill, Jan.

Brewer, Paul. The Lima Embassy Siege & Latin American Terrorism. 2006. (Terrorism in Today's World Ser.). (Illus.). 48p. (gr. 5-12). pap. 14.05 *(978-0-8368-6564-6(2))*; lib. bdg. 31.00 *(978-0-8368-6557-8(X))* Stevens, Gareth Publishing LLLP. (Gareth Stevens Secondary Library).

Crespi, Jess. Exploring Peru with the Five Themes of Geography. (Library of the Western Hemisphere Ser.). 24p. 2009. (gr. 4-4). 42.50 *(978-1-60853-929-1(6)*, PowerKids Pr.) 2005. (Illus.). (J). (gr. 5-7). lib. bdg. 22.60 *(978-1-4042-2676-0(1)*, PowerKids Pr.) 2005. (ENG., Illus.). (gr. 3-8). pap. 8.25 *(978-0-8239-4636-5(3))* Rosen Publishing Group, Inc., The.

Croy, Anita. Peru. 2007. (Countries of the World Ser.). (ENG., Illus.). 64p. (J). (gr. 5-5). lib. bdg. 27.90 *(978-1-4263-0031-8(X)*, National Geographic Children's Bks.) National Geographic Society.

—Peru - National Geographic. 2009. (Countries of the World Ser.). (ENG., Illus.). 64p. (J). (gr. 5). pap. 12.95 *(978-1-4263-0570-2(2)*, National Geographic Children's Bks.) National Geographic Society.

Falconer, Kieran & Quek, Lynette. Peru. 2nd rev. ed. 2006. (Cultures of the World Ser.). (Illus.). 144p. (J). (gr. 6-7). lib. bdg. 42.79 *(978-0-7614-2068-2(1)*, Benchmark Bks.) Marshall Cavendish Corp.

Falconer, Kieran, et al. Peru. 2016. (Cultures of the World (r) Ser.). (ENG., Illus.). 144p. (J). (gr. 5-5). lib. bdg. 47.07 *(978-1-5026-1843-6(5))* Cavendish Square Publishing.

Fazzi, Cindy. How to Draw Peru's Sights & Symbols. 2009. (Kid's Guide to Drawing the Countries of the World Ser.). 48p. (gr. 4-4). 53.00 *(978-1-61511-121-3(2)*, PowerKids Pr.) Rosen Publishing Group, Inc., The.

Gritzner, Charles & Gritzner, Yvonne. Peru. 2004. (Modern World Nations Ser.). (Illus.). 120p. (gr. 6-12). 35.00 *(978-0-7910-7478-7(1)*, Chelsea Hse.) Facts On File, Inc.

Johnson, Robin & Kalman, Bobbie. Spotlight on Peru. 2008. (Spotlight on my Country Ser.). (ENG., Illus.). 32p. (J). (gr. 3-7). pap. *(978-0-7787-3482-6(X))* Crabtree Publishing Co.

Levy, Janey. 20 Fun Facts about Machu Picchu, Vol. 1. 2014. (Fun Fact File: World Wonders! Ser.). 32p. (J). (gr. 2-3). (ENG.). pap. 10.50 *(978-1-4824-0455-5(9))*; 25.25 *(978-1-4824-0452-4(4))* Stevens, Gareth Publishing LLLP.

Lewin, Ted. Lost City: The Discovery of Machu Picchu. Lewin, Ted, illus. 2012. (ENG., Illus.). 48p. (J). (gr. 2-5). pap. 8.99 *(978-0-14-242580-0(X)*, Puffin Books) Penguin Young Readers Group.

Mann, Elizabeth. Machu Picchu: The Story of the Amazing Inkas & Their City in the Clouds. Crehore, Amy, illus. 2006. (Wonders of the World Book Ser.). (ENG.). 48p. (J). (gr. 4-8). pap. 12.95 *(978-1-931414-10-4(6)*, 9781931414104) Mikaya Pr.

Markovics, Joyce L. Peru. 2016. (Countries We Come From Ser.). (ENG.). 32p. (J). (gr. -1-3). lib. bdg. 19.95 *(978-1-944102-73-9(6))* Bearport Publishing Co., Inc.

Márquez, Herón. Peru in Pictures. 2nd rev. expurg. ed. 2004. (Visual Geography Series, Second Ser.). (ENG., Illus.). 80p. (gr. 5-12). 31.93 *(978-0-8225-1999-7(2))* Lerner Publishing Group.

National Geographic Traveler - Peru. 2nd rev. ed. 2015. (National Geographic Traveler Ser.). (ENG., Illus.). 320p. pap. 25.95 *(978-1-4262-1362-5(X))* National Geographic Society.

Raum, Elizabeth. Machu Picchu. 2015. (Ancient Wonders Ser.). (Illus.). 32p. (J). 28.50 *(978-1-60753-468-6(1))* Amicus Publishing.

Sheen, Barbara. Peru. 2010. (Taste of Culture Ser.). 64p. lib. bdg. 30.45 *(978-0-7377-5346-2(3)*, Kidhaven) Cengage Gale.

Shields, Charles J. Peru. (South America Today Ser.). 64p. 2009. (Illus.). (J). (gr. 4-7). 21.95 *(978-1-4222-0639-3(4))* 2007. (YA). (gr. 7-18). pap. 9.95 *(978-1-4222-0706-2(4))* Mason Crest.

PERU—ANTIQUITIES

Garbe, Suzanne. Secrets of Machu Picchu: Lost City of the Incas, 1 vol. 2014. (Archaeological Mysteries Ser.). (ENG.). 32p. (gr. 3-4). lib. bdg. 27.99 *(978-1-4765-9919-9(X))* Capstone Press of Coughlan Cos.

Leaf, Christina. Machu Picchu: The Lost Civilization. 2017. (Abandoned Places Ser.). (ENG., Illus.). 24p. (J). (gr. 3-7). lib. bdg. 25.95 ***(978-1-62617-696-6(5)***, Torque Bks.) Bellwether Media.

Nagelhout, Ryan. Ancient Inca Technology. 2016. (Spotlight on the Maya, Aztec, & Inca Civilizations Ser.). (Illus.). 32p. (J). (gr. 6-4). pap. 11.75 *(978-1-4994-1953-5(8)*, PowerKids Pr.) Rosen Publishing Group, Inc., The.

Peterson, Sheryl. Machu Picchu. 2005. (Ancient Wonders of the World Ser.). (Illus.). 32p. (J). (gr. 4-7). lib. bdg. 18.95 *(978-1-58341-357-9(X)*, Creative Education) Creative Co., The.

Richardson, Gillian & Kissock, Heather. Machu Picchu. 2012. (J). 27.13 *(978-1-61913-250-4(8))*; pap. 12.95 *(978-1-61913-256-6(7))* Weigl Pubs., Inc.

Riggs, Kate. Machu Picchu. 2009. (Places of Old Ser.). 24p. (J). (gr. 1-5). lib. bdg. 24.25 *(978-1-58341-709-6(5)*, Creative Education) Creative Co., The.

PERU—FICTION

Anderson, Geraldine. Bev's Amazing Adventures Book Ii: The Girl from Peru. 2013. 20p. pap. 24.95 *(978-1-62709-129-9(7))* America Star Bks.

Booher, Brock. The Charity Chip. 2015. pap. 16.99 *(978-1-4621-1669-0(8))* Cedar Fort, Inc./CFI Distribution.

Brown, Monica. Lola Levine & the Vacation Dream. 2017. (Lola Levine Ser.: 5). (J). lib. bdg. 16.00 ***(978-0-606-40222-4(5))*** Turtleback Bks.

Carson, John E. & Carson, Marlene R. The Wire Forest of Peru. 2007. (Ramblin' Rose Ser.). 205p. (YA). (gr. 8-12). per. 8.99 *(978-0-9776043-9-5(X))* Aspirations Media, Inc.

Chen, Justina. A Blind Spot for Boys. 2014. (ENG.). 336p. (YA). (gr. 7-17). 18.00 *(978-0-316-10253-7(9))* Little, Brown Bks. for Young Readers.

Church, Anna. Hug-A-Bug Travels to Peru. Church, Anna & Taylor, Nicole, illus. 2013. 44p. pap. 12.00 *(978-0-9831449-4-6(X))* Mighty Lion Ventures.

Diaz, Katacha. Carolina's Gift: A Story of Peru. Landolt, Gredna, illus. 2003. (ENG.). 32p. (J). (gr. k-3). 15.95 *(978-1-56899-695-0(0)*, B8005) Soundprints.

Eby, Wes. Jungle Jeopardy. 2006. 56p. 7.75 *(978-0-8341-2228-4(6))* Beacon Hill Pr. of Kansas City.

Evans, Richard. Michael Vey Books One & Two: The Prisoner of Cell 25; Rise of the Elgen. 2014. (Michael Vey Ser.). (ENG., Illus.). 720p. (YA). (gr. 7). pap. 13.99 *(978-1-4814-2034-1(8)*, Simon Pulse/Mercury Ink) Simon Pulse/Mercury Ink.

—Rise of the Elgen. (Michael Vey Ser.: 2). (ENG., Illus.). 352p. (YA). (gr. 7). 2013. pap. 11.99 *(978-1-4424-7510-6(2))* 2012. 17.99 *(978-1-4424-5414-9(8))* Simon Pulse/Mercury Ink. (Simon Pulse/Mercury Ink).

Finnish, V. K. The Society's Traitor. Oshida, Tim, illus. 2012. (The Discoveries of Arthur Grey ser.: 1). (ENG.). 298p. (J). (gr. 4-8). 27.99 *(978-0-9852202-0-4(1))* Panama Hat Publishing, Ltd.

Frith, Nicholas John. Hector & Hummingbird. Frith, Nicholas John, illus. 2016. (ENG., Illus.). 32p. (J). (gr. -1-3). 17.99 *(978-0-545-85701-7(5))* Scholastic, Inc.

Garcia, Randolph. The Steamer Trunk Adventures #2: The Ghosts of Machu Picchu. 2006. (ENG.). 88p. per. 16.95 *(978-1-4241-1843-4(3))* PublishAmerica, Inc.

Hamilton, Martha & Weiss, Mitch. The Stolen Smell. Wrenn, Tom, illus. 2007. (Story Cove Ser.). (ENG.). 32p. (J). (gr. -1-3). 3.95 *(978-0-87483-838-1(X))* August Hse. Pubs., Inc.

Henty, George Alfred. The Treasure of the Incas: The Treasure of the Incas. 2007. (ENG.). 308p. pap. 23.99 *(978-1-4264-4045-8(6))* Creative Media Partners, LLC.

Hergé. Prisoners of the Sun. 2014. (Adventures of Tintin: Young Readers Edition Ser.). (ENG., Illus.). 96p. (J). (gr. 3-17). pap. 9.00 *(978-0-316-40917-9(0))* Little, Brown Bks. for Young Readers.

Horowitz, Anthony. Evil Star. 2007. (Gatekeepers Ser.: 2). 318p. lib. bdg. 19.65 *(978-1-4177-7663-4(3)*, Turtleback) Turtleback Bks.

Jendresen, Erik & Villoldo, Alberto. The First Story Ever Told. Yoshi, illus. 2008. (ENG.). 36p. (J). (gr. -1-2). 12.99 *(978-1-4169-8961-5(7)*, Simon & Schuster Bks. For Young Readers) Simon & Schuster Bks. For Young Readers.

Jensen, Kathryn. Splash! 2012. 194p. 29.95 *(978-1-4489-6574-8(8))* America Star Bks.

Kain, Wallace M. The Red Column: A Young Woman's Capture, Imprisonment & Escape in the Amazon Jungle. 2006. (YA). per. 12.95 *(978-0-9742148-1-8(7))* Inkberry Pr.

Lacey, Josh. Island of Thieves. 2013. (ENG.). 240p. (J). (gr. 5-7). pap. 7.99 *(978-0-544-10485-3(4))* Houghton Mifflin Harcourt Publishing Co.

Lacey, Josh & Pakenham, Sarah. Island of Thieves. 2012. (ENG.). 240p. (J). (gr. 5-7). 15.99 *(978-0-547-76327-9(1))* Houghton Mifflin Harcourt Publishing Co.

mercedes cecilia. Kusikiy A Child from Taquile, Peru. mercedes cecilia & mercedes cecilia, illus. 2011. (Illus.). (J). pap. 24.99 *(978-0-9844079-9-6(5))* Keepers of Wisdom and Peace Bks.

Mitchell, Sara. Carlos & Diego: A Tale from Peru. Vasquez, Natalia, illus. 2016. 24p. (J). pap. *(978-1-927244-57-9(9))* Flying Start Bks.

—Carlos & Diego (Big Book Edition) A Tale from Peru. Vasquez, Natalia, illus. 2016. 24p. (J). pap. *(978-1-927244-67-8(6))* Flying Start Bks.

O'Dell, Scott. The Seven Serpents Trilogy. 2009. (ENG.). 560p. (J). (gr. 4-6). pap. 19.99 *(978-1-4022-1836-1(2)*, Sourcebooks Jabberwocky) Sourcebooks, Inc.

Oshida, Tim, illus. The Society's Traitor. 2nd ed. 2015. (The Discoveries of Arthur Grey ser.: 1). (ENG.). 304p. (J). (gr. 4-8). 27.99 *(978-1-943317-00-4(3))* Panama Hat Publishing, Ltd.

Packard, Albert. Cavern of Babel. Boyles, Shawn, illus. 2006. (J). per. 14.95 *(978-0-9790652-0-0(8))* Diamond Triple C Ranch.

Paris, Harper. The Mystery Across the Secret Bridge. Calo, Marcos, illus. 2015. (Greetings from Somewhere Ser.: 7). (ENG.). 128p. (J). (gr. k-4). pap. 5.99 *(978-1-4814-2367-0(3)*, Little Simon) Little Simon.

Russell, Elaine. Martin Mcmillan & the Lost Inca City. Cornell du Houx, Emily M. D., illus. 2005. 128p. (gr. 5-18). pap. 10.00 *(978-1-882190-86-7(6))* Polar Bear & Co.

Simpson, Joe & Bembibre, Cecilia. Tocando el Vacío. 2014. (SPA., Illus.). 64p. pap., stu. ed. 13.75 incl. audio compact disk *(978-84-9848-133-4(3))* Edinumen, Editorial ESP. Dist: Cambridge Univ. Pr.

Stilton, Thea. Thea Stilton & the Secret City. 2010. (Thea Stilton Ser.: 4). (ENG.). 176p. (J). (gr. 2-5). 8.99 *(978-0-545-15061-3(2)*, Scholastic Paperbacks) Scholastic, Inc.

PERU—HISTORY

Baer, Suzie. Peru's MRTA: Tupac Amaru Revolutionary Movement. 2005. (Inside the World's Most Infamous Terrorist Organizations Ser.). (Illus.). 64p. (YA). (gr. 7-12). lib. bdg. 31.95 *(978-0-8239-3824-7(7))* Rosen Publishing Group, Inc., The.

Baicker, Karen. Conquistador: Francisco Pizarro Ravages the Inca Empire. 2011. (J). pap. *(978-0-545-32940-8(X))* Scholastic, Inc.

Benge, Janet & Benge, Geoff. Klaus-Dieter John: Hope in the Land of the Incas. 2014. (Illus.). 216p. (J). pap. 9.99 *(978-1-57658-755-3(X))* YWAM Publishing.

Burling, Alexis. The Destruction of the Inca Civilization. 2017. (J). ***(978-1-5081-7738-8(4)***, Rosen Young Adult) Rosen Publishing Group, Inc., The.

Byers, Helen. Peru. 2007. (Nonfiction Reading & Writing Workshops Ser.). (ENG., Illus.). 24p. (J). pap. 14.95 *(978-0-7922-4538-4(5))* CENGAGE Learning.

Cavallo, Anna. Peru. 2011. (Country Explorers Ser.). (ENG., Illus.). 48p. (gr. 2-4). lib. bdg. 29.27 *(978-0-7613-6416-0(1))* Lerner Publishing Group.

DiConsiglio, John. Francisco Pizarro: Destroyer of the Inca Empire. 2008. (Wicked History Ser.). (ENG., Illus.). 128p. (J). 31.00 *(978-0-531-18551-3(6)*, Watts, Franklin) Scholastic Library Publishing.

Hinman, Bonnie. We Visit Peru. 2010. (Your Land & My Land Ser.). (Illus.). 64p. (J). (gr. 3-6). lib. bdg. 33.95 *(978-1-58415-886-8(7))* Mitchell Lane Pubs., Inc.

Hoogenboom, Lynn. Francisco Pizarro. 2009. (Primary Source Library of Famous Explorers Ser.). 24p. (gr. 4-4). 42.50 *(978-1-60854-121-8(5)*, PowerKids Pr.) Rosen Publishing Group, Inc., The.

—Francisco Pizarro: A Primary Source Biography. 2006. (Primary Source Library of Famous Explorers Ser.). (Illus.). 24p. (YA). (gr. 2-5). lib. bdg. 22.60 *(978-1-4042-3038-5(6))* Rosen Publishing Group, Inc., The.

Hoyle, R. L. Peru. (SPA., Illus.). 260p. pap. 39.95 *(978-84-261-1080-0(0)*, JV800) Juventud, Editorial ESP. Dist: Continental Bk. Co., Inc.

Hunefeldt, Christine. Peru. 2nd rev. ed. 2010. (Brief History Ser.). (Illus.). 352p. (J). (gr. 9). 49.50 *(978-0-8160-8144-8(1))* Facts On File, Inc.

Johnson, Robin & Kalman, Bobbie. Conoce Perú. 2009. (SPA.). 32p. (J). *(978-0-7787-8194-3(1))*; (gr. 2-5). pap. *(978-0-7787-8214-8(X))* Crabtree Publishing Co.

Kachurek, Sandra J. Francisco Pizarro: Explorer of South America. 2004. (Explorers! Ser.). (Illus.). 48p. (J). lib. bdg. 23.93 *(978-0-7660-2178-5(5))* Enslow Pubs., Inc.

Kaspar, Anna. A Look at Pluto & Other Dwarf Planets. 2007. (Astronomy Now! Ser.). (Illus.). 24p. (YA). (gr. 2-5). lib. bdg. 22.60 *(978-1-4042-3824-4(7))* Rosen Publishing Group, Inc., The.

Leaf, Christina. Machu Picchu: The Lost Civilization. 2017. (Abandoned Places Ser.). (ENG., Illus.). 24p. (J). (gr. 3-7). lib. bdg. 25.95 ***(978-1-62617-696-6(5)***, Torque Bks.) Bellwether Media.

Meinking, Mary. Machu Picchu, 1 vol. 2014. (Digging up the Past Ser.). (ENG., Illus.). 112p. (J). (gr. 6-12). lib. bdg. 35.64 *(978-1-62403-234-9(6)*, Essential Library) ABDO Publishing Co.

Morlock, Theresa. Ancient Inca Geography. 2016. (Spotlight on the Maya, Aztec, & Inca Civilizations Ser.). 32p. (J). (gr. 6-4). pap. 11.75 *(978-1-4994-1943-6(0)*, PowerKids Pr.) Rosen Publishing Group, Inc., The.

Mountjoy, Shane. Francisco Pizarro & the Conquest of the Inca. Goetzmann, William H., ed. 2005. (Explorers of New Lands Ser.). (Illus.). 100p. (gr. 5-8). 30.00 *(978-0-7910-8614-8(3)*, Chelsea Hse.) Facts On File, Inc.

O'Brien, Cynthia. Explore with Francisco Pizarro. 2015. (Travel with the Great Explorers Ser.). (ENG., Illus.). 32p. (J). (gr. 3-6). *(978-0-7787-1700-3(3))* Crabtree Publishing Co.

Owings, Lisa. Peru. 2011. (Exploring Countries Ser.). (ENG., Illus.). 32p. (J). (gr. 3-7). lib. bdg. 26.95 *(978-1-60014-621-3(X))* Bellwether Media.

Ramen, Fred. Francisco Pizarro: The Exploration of Peru & the Conquest of the Inca. 2009. (Library of Explorers & Exploration Ser.). 112p. (gr. 5-8). 66.50 *(978-1-60853-603-0(3)*, Rosen Reference) Rosen Publishing Group, Inc., The.

Saunders, Nicholas J. & Saunders, Nick. The Inca City of Cuzco. 2005. (Places in History Ser.). (Illus.). 48p. (gr. 5-12). lib. bdg. 31.00 *(978-0-8368-5812-9(3)*, World Almanac Library) Stevens, Gareth Publishing LLLP.

Schmidt, Gary D. Martin de Porres: The Rose in the Desert. Diaz, David, illus. 2012. (ENG.). 32p. (J). (gr. 1-4). lib. bdg. 16.99 *(978-0-547-61218-8(4))* Houghton Mifflin Harcourt Publishing Co.

Shields, Charles J. Peru, Vol. 13. Henderson, James D., ed. 2015. (Discovering South America: History, Politics, & Culture Ser.). (Illus.). 64p. (J). (gr. 7). lib. bdg. 22.95 *(978-1-4222-3302-3(2))* Mason Crest.

Somervill, Barbara A. Francisco Pizarro: Conqueror of the Incas, 1 vol. 2005. (Signature Lives: Renaissance Era Ser.). (ENG., Illus.). 112p. (gr. 6-7). 35.32 *(978-0-7565-0815-9(0)*, 1240121, Signature Lives) Compass Point Bks.

Sonneborn, Liz. Pizarro: Conqueror of the Mighty Incas. 2010. (Great Explorers of the World Ser.). (Illus.). 112p. (J). (gr. 7-12). 33.27 *(978-1-59845-128-3(6))* Enslow Pubs., Inc.

Thomas, Emma. The Inca Tomb. 2011. (History Detectives Ser.). (ENG.). 32p. (J). (gr. 4-7). spiral bd. 9.95 *(978-1-84898-187-4(2)*, TickTock Books) Octopus Publishing Group GBR. Dist: Independent Pubs. Group.

Waldron, Melanie. Geography Matters in the Inca Empire. 2015. (Geography Matters in Ancient Civilizations Ser.). (ENG., Illus.). 48p. (gr. 3-6). 33.32 *(978-1-4846-0965-1(4)*, Heinemann InfoSearch) Heinemann-Raintree.

Wood, Alix. Uncovering the Culture of Ancient Peru, 01 vols., 1. 2016. (Archaeology & Ancient Cultures Ser.). (ENG.). 32p. (J). pap. 10.00 *(978-1-5081-4667-4(5)*, PowerKids Pr.) Rosen Publishing Group, Inc., The.

World Book, Inc Staff, contrib. by. The Enduring Mystery of Machu Picchu. 2015. (Illus.). 48p. (J). *(978-0-7166-2675-6(6))* World Bk., Inc.

—The Mysteries in the Nazca Desert. 2015. (Illus.). 48p. (J). *(978-0-7166-2676-3(4))* World Bk., Inc.

Zronik, John Paul & Zronik, John. Francisco Pizarro: Journeys Through Peru & South America. 2005. (In the Footsteps of Explorers Ser.). (ENG., Illus.). 32p. (J). (gr. -1-9). pap. *(978-0-7787-2447-6(6))* Crabtree Publishing Co.

PESTICIDE POLLUTION

see Pesticides—Environmental Aspects

PESTICIDES—ENVIRONMENTAL ASPECTS

Hile, Lori. Rachel Carson: Environmental Pioneer, 1 vol. 2014. (Women in Conservation Ser.). (ENG., Illus.). 48p. (gr. 3-6). 33.32 *(978-1-4846-0471-7(7))*; pap. 8.99 *(978-1-4846-0476-2(8))* Heinemann-Raintree. (Heinemann InfoSearch).

Landau, Jennifer. Pesticides & Your Body. 2012. (Incredibly Disgusting Environments Ser.). (ENG., Illus.). 48p. (J). (gr. 5-8). pap. 11.75 *(978-1-4488-8422-3(5))*; lib. bdg. 29.25 *(978-1-4488-8413-1(6))* Rosen Publishing Group, Inc., The. (Rosen Reference).

PESTS

see Fungi; Insect Pests; Parasites; Zoology, Economic

PETER, THE APOSTLE, SAINT

Bahamon, Claire. Peter Fished the Springs of Galilee. Sampson, Anne, ed. Cinelli, Lisa, illus. 2015. (ENG.). 32p. (J). pap. 7.99 *(978-0-9961139-0-8(8))* Donkey's Quest Pr.

Brennan, Gerald T. The Man Who Never Died: The Life & Adventures of St. Peter, the First Pope. 2005. (Illus.). 87p. (J). (gr. 3-7). per. 11.95 *(978-1-933184-09-8(4))* Sophia Institute Pr.

Holder, Jennifer. Peter Said Yes! 2014. (Happy Day Ser.). (ENG.). 16p. (J). pap. 2.49 *(978-1-4143-9525-8(6)*, Happy Day) Tyndale Hse. Pubs.

Lumsden, Colin, illus. Story of Peter. 2003. (Bible Colour & Learn Ser.). 32p. pap. 2.50 *(978-1-903087-45-9(7))* DayOne Pubns. GBR. Dist: Send The Light Distribution LLC.

MacKenzie, Carine. Peter: The Apostle. McLaren, Duncan, illus. 2014. (Bible Time Ser.). (ENG.). 32p. (J). (gr. -1-2). pap. 3.99 *(978-1-84550-170-9(5)*, d221e48d-3015-44b8-b919-078a770c5b42) Christian Focus Pubns. GBR. Dist: Bookmasters Distribution.

—Peter: The Fisherman. McLaren, Duncan, illus. 2014. (Bible Time Ser.). (ENG.). 32p. (J). (gr. -1-2). pap. 3.99 *(978-1-84550-171-6(3)*, df59357e-a2a3-4d70-96e4-8ff92835271b) Christian Focus Pubns. GBR. Dist: Bookmasters Distribution.

Moore, Alan & Tavner, Gill. Simon Peter. Donnelly, Karen, illus. 2014. (New Testament Ser.). (ENG.). 64p. pap. 6.95 *(978-1-906230-26-5(9))* Real Reads Ltd. GBR. Dist: Casemate Pubs. & Bk. Distributors, LLC.

Willoughby, R. Peter Goes Feet First! Buckley, Joel, illus. 2004. 64p. pap. *(978-1-85999-766-6(X))* Scripture Union.

—Peter Strides Out. Buckley, Joel, illus. 2004. 64p. pap. *(978-1-84427-022-4(X))* Scripture Union.

PETER PAN (FICTITIOUS CHARACTER)—FICTION

BARRIE / LEFFLER. Peter Pan. 2016. (ENG., Illus.). 176p. 25.00 *(978-0-7358-4259-5(0))* North-South Bks., Inc.

Barrie, J. M. The Complete Adventures of Peter Pan Includes: The Little White Bird, Peter Pan in Kensington Gardens(Illustrated) & Peter. Rackham, Arthur & Bedford, F. D., illus. 2013. 326p. *(978-1-78139-361-1(3))* Benediction Classics.

—Peter & Wendy. 2013. (Cambridge Library Collection - Fiction & Poetry Ser.). (ENG., Illus.). 302p. 72.00 *(978-1-108-06034-9(X))* Cambridge Univ. Pr.

—Peter Pan. 2008. 124p. (gr. 5-18). 23.95 *(978-1-60664-889-6(6))*; pap. 10.95 *(978-1-60664-007-4(0))* Aegypan.

—Peter Pan. (SPA.). 191p. 15.95 *(978-84-206-3689-4(4))* Alianza Editorial, S. A. ESP. Dist: Distribooks, Inc.

—Peter Pan. Press, Jenny, illus. 2013. (Storyteller Book Ser.). (ENG.). 48p. (J). (gr. k-5). pap. 7.99 *(978-1-84322-884-4(X)*, Armadillo) Anness Publishing GBR. Dist: National Bk. Network.

—Peter Pan. 2005. 112p. per. 6.95 *(978-1-933652-07-8(1))* Bed Bks.

—Peter Pan. Date not set. (C). pap. *(978-0-7593-9877-1(1)*, Cengage Learning) CENGAGE Learning.

—Peter Pan. Cowley, Joy, ed. Jang, Yeong-seon, illus. 2015. (World Classics Ser.). (ENG.). 32p. (gr. k-4). 26.65 *(978-1-925246-45-2(0))*; 7.99 *(978-1-925246-71-1(X))*; 26.65 *(978-1-925246-19-3(1))* ChoiceMaker Pty. Ltd., The AUS. (Big and SMALL). Dist: Lerner Publishing Group.

—Peter Pan. 2005. 96p. per. 4.95 *(978-1-4209-2538-8(5))* Digireads.com Publishing.

—Peter Pan. 2006. pap. *(978-1-4065-0949-6(3))* Dodo Pr.

—Peter Pan. 2009. 276p. (gr. 3-7). pap. *(978-1-4068-9291-8(2))* Echo Library.

—Peter Pan. Bustelo, Gabriela, tr. Vicente, Fernando, illus. 2006. (Alfaguara Infantil y Juvenil Ser.). 229p. (J). (gr. 4-7). pap. *(978-970-770-677-4(5))* Ediciones Alfaguara.

—Peter Pan. pap. 16.95 *(978-2-07-051627-8(X))* Gallimard, Editions FRA. Dist: Distribooks, Inc.

—Peter Pan. Minalima Staff, illus. 2015. (ENG.). 256p. 27.99 *(978-0-06-236222-3(4)*, Collins Design) HarperCollins Pubs.

—Peter Pan. (J). pap. *(978-0-340-71498-0(0))* Hodder & Stoughton.

—Peter Pan. Cowley, Joy, ed. Jang, Yeong-seon, illus. 2015. (World Classics Ser.). (ENG.). 32p. (J). (gr. k-4). 26.65 *(978-1-925186-71-0(7))*; pap. 7.99 *(978-1-925186-65-9(2))* Lerner Publishing Group.

—Peter Pan, 1 vol. Mullarkey, Lisa, illus. 2010. (Calico Illustrated Classics Ser.: No. 1). (ENG.). 112p. (J). (gr. 3-6). 27.07 *(978-1-60270-710-8(3))* Magic Wagon.

—Peter Pan. Barrie, J. M., ed. Bedford, F. D. & Rackham, Arthur, illus. 2009. (ENG.). 287p. *(978-1-905716-40-1(0)*, Collector's Library, The) Pan Macmillan.

—Peter Pan. 160p. pap. *(978-1-85471-231-8(4))* Penguin Bks., Ltd.

—Peter Pan. (Puffin Chalk Ser.). (ENG.). (J). 2013. 224p. (gr. 3-7). pap. 7.99 *(978-0-14-750865-2(7))* 2009. (Illus.). 240p. (gr. 5-7). 5.99 *(978-0-14-132257-5(8))* Penguin Young Readers Group. (Puffin Books).

—Peter Pan. 2013. (ENG., Illus.). 256p. (J). (gr. 4-7). pap. 10.99 *(978-0-09-957304-3(0))* Random Hse. GBR. Dist: Independent Pubs. Group.

—Peter Pan. 2010. (ENG., Illus.). (J). 14.99 ***(978-1-61382-749-9(0))*** Simon & Brown.

—Peter Pan. 2003. (Aladdin Classics Ser.). (ENG.). 256p. (J). (gr. 3-7). pap. 7.99 *(978-0-689-86691-3(7)*, Aladdin) Simon & Schuster Children's Publishing.

—Peter Pan. McKowen, Scott, illus. 2008. (Sterling Unabridged Classics Ser.). (ENG.). 160p. (J). 9.95 *(978-1-4027-5426-5(4))* Sterling Publishing Co., Inc.

—Peter Pan. Bedford, F. D., illus. 2004. (Modern Library Classics Ser.). (ENG.). 192p. (J). (gr. 3-7). pap. 10.00 *(978-0-8129-7297-9(X)*, Modern Library) Random House Publishing Group.

—Peter Pan. Andreasen, Dan, illus. 2009. (Classic Starts(tm) Ser.). (ENG.). 160p. (J). (gr. 2-4). 6.95 *(978-1-4027-5421-0(3))* Sterling Publishing Co., Inc.

—Peter Pan. Bedford, F. D., illus. 2005. (Barnes & Noble Classics Ser.). (ENG.). 208p. per. 7.95 *(978-1-59308-213-0(4))* Barnes & Noble, Inc.

—Peter Pan. l.t. ed. 2003. (Perennial Bestsellers Ser.). (ENG.). 248p. (J). 29.95 *(978-0-7862-5263-3(4))* Thorndike Pr.

—Peter Pan. 2003. (Aladdin Classics Ser.). 228p. (gr. 3-7). lib. bdg. 18.40 *(978-0-613-86964-5(8)*, Turtleback) Turtleback Bks.

—Peter Pan: A Bed Book First Edition Classic. 2005. 112p. 12.95 *(978-1-933652-30-6(6))* Bed Bks.

—Peter Pan: An Illustrated Classic for Kids & Young Readers (Excellent for Bedtime & Young Readers) eMusic, Tom, ed. Friday, Arthur, illus. 2013. 38p. pap. 6.99 *(978-1-62321-067-0(4))* Tommye-music Corp. DBA Tom eMusic.

—Peter Pan: Complete & Unabridged. Barrie, J. M., illus. 2005. (Illus.). 176p. reprint ed. pap. 17.00 *(978-0-7567-9445-3(5))* DIANE Publishing Co.

—Peter Pan: From the Story by J. M. Barrie. Costa, Patricia Castelao et al, illus. 2009. (ENG.). 48p. (J). (gr. 3-7). 12.95 *(978-0-7624-3543-2(7)*, Running Pr. Kids) Running Pr. Bk. Pubs.

—Peter Pan: Peter & Wendy & Peter Pan in Kensington Gardens. 2004. (ENG., Illus.). 352p. (gr. 12-18). 11.00 *(978-0-14-243793-3(X)*, Penguin Classics) Penguin Publishing Group.

—Peter Pan: The Original Tale of Neverland. Jaramillo, Raquel, illus. Jaramillo, Raquel, photos by. unabr. ed. 2003. 135p. (YA). (gr. 5-8). reprint ed. 25.00 *(978-0-7567-6883-6(7))* DIANE Publishing Co.

—Peter Pan - the Original Classic Edition. 2011. pap. *(978-1-74244-781-0(3)*, Tebbo) Emereo Pty Ltd.

—Peter Pan & Wendy. 2013. (ENG.). 172p. (YA). 14.95 *(978-1-940849-05-8(5))* Ancient Wisdom Pubns.

—Peter Pan & Wendy. 2010. 224p. pap. 19.95 *(978-0-557-36915-7(0))* Lulu Pr., Inc.

—Peter Pan & Wendy. Foreman, Michael, illus. 2003. (Chrysalis Childrens Classics Ser.). 176p. (YA). pap. *(978-1-84365-039-3(8)*, Pavilion Children's Books) Pavilion Bks.

—Peter Pan & Wendy. Foreman, Michael, illus. 2010. (ENG.). 160p. (J). (gr. 2-7). 19.99 *(978-1-84365-136-9(X)*, Pavilion Children's Books) Pavilion Bks. GBR. Dist: Independent Pubs. Group.

—Peter Pan & Wendy: Centenary Edition. Ingpen, Robert R., illus. 2004. (ENG.). 216p. (J). *(978-1-897035-12-2(8)*, Blue Heron Bks.) Raincoast Bk. Distribution.

—Peter Pan & Wendy: Centenary Edition. Ingpen, Robert R., illus. 2010. (Sterling Illustrated Classics Ser.). (ENG.). 216p. (J). (gr. 5-18). 19.95 *(978-1-4027-2868-6(9))* Sterling Publishing Co., Inc.

—Peter Pan, by J. M. Barrie - the Original Classic Edition. 2011. mass mkt. *(978-1-74244-961-6(1)*, Tebbo) Emereo Pty Ltd.

—Peter Pan in Kensington Gardens. (J). 18.95 *(978-0-8488-0427-5(9))* Amereon Ltd.

—Peter Pan in Kensington Gardens. 2013. 123p. reprint ed. lthr. 69.00 *(978-0-7426-2518-1(4))* Classic Bks.

—Peter Pan in Kensington Gardens. 2006. pap. *(978-1-4065-0950-2(7))* Dodo Pr.

—Peter Pan in Kensington Gardens. unabr. ed. 2012. (Illus.). 147p. 39.99 *(978-1-4622-8152-7(4))* Repressed Publishing LLC.

—Peter Pan in Kensington Gardens. 2009. 108p. (gr. -1-18). pap. 9.95 *(978-1-60664-381-5(9))* Rodgers, Alan Bks.

—Peter Pan in Kensington Gardens & Peter & Wendy. 2009. 120p. pap. 7.99 *(978-1-4209-3191-4(1))* Digireads.com Publishing.

—Tommy & Grizel. 2006. (Illus.). pap. *(978-1-4065-0954-0(X))* Dodo Pr.

Barrie, J. M. & Bedford, F. D. Peter Pan. 2012. (Illus.). 200p. *(978-1-4351-4201-5(2))* Barnes & Noble, Inc.

Barrie, J. M. & Edens, Cooper. Peter Pan. (SPA.). 174p. 26.95 *(978-84-666-0760-5(9))* Ediciones B ESP. Dist: Spanish Pubs., LLC.

Barrie, J. M. & Lindner, Brooke. Peter Pan. Bedford, Francis Donkin & Rackham, Arthur, illus. 2015. (Word Cloud Classics Ser.). (ENG.). 272p. pap. 14.99 *(978-1-62686-392-7(X)*, Thunder Bay Pr.) Readerlink Distribution Services, LLC.

Barrie, J. M. & Random House Disney Staff. Peter Pan. Walt Disney Studios Staff & Dempster, Al, illus. 2007. (Little Golden Book Ser.). (ENG.). 24p. (J). (gr. -1-2). 4.99 *(978-0-7364-0238-5(1)*, Golden/Disney) Random Hse. Children's Bks.

Barrie, J. M. & Sterne, Laurence. The Life & Opinions of Tristram Shandy, Gentleman. 2015. (Vintage Classics Ser.). (ENG.). 762p. pap. 13.95 *(978-0-09-951915-7(1))* Random Hse. GBR. Dist: Independent Pubs. Group.

Barrie, J. M., et al. Peter Pan. Wilkinson, Annie, illus. 2015. (Ladybird Classics Ser.). (ENG.). 72p. (J). (gr. k-3). 8.99 *(978-1-4093-1222-2(4))* Penguin Bks., Ltd. GBR. Dist: Independent Pubs. Group.

—Peter Pan. Tentler-Krylov, Victoria, illus. 2017. (ENG.). 28p. (J). (gr. -1-1). 17.95 ***(978-1-63322-222-9(5)***, Moondance) Quarto Publishing Group USA.

Barton, Zoe. Always Neverland. 2011. (ENG.). 320p. (J). (gr. 3-7). 16.99 *(978-0-06-196325-4(9))* HarperCollins Pubs.

Disney Book Group Staff. Peter Pan Read-Along Storybook & CD. Disney Storybook Art Team, illus. 2013. (Read-Along Storybook & CD Ser.). (ENG.). 32p. (J). (gr. -1-k). pap. 6.99 *(978-1-4231-8034-0(8))* Disney Pr.

Hoena, B. A. & Barrie, J. M. Peter Pan. Cano, Fernando, illus. 2015. (Graphic Revolve: Common Core Editions Ser.). (ENG.). 72p. (gr. 2-3). lib. bdg. 27.99 *(978-1-4965-0372-5(4))* Stone Arch Bks.

Jenny Press Staff. Peter Pan. 2016. (ENG., Illus.). 24p. pap. 7.99 *(978-1-86147-815-3(1)*, Armadillo) Anness Publishing GBR. Dist: National Bk. Network.

McCaughrean, Geraldine. Peter Pan de Rojo Escarlata. Gonzalez-Gallarza, Isabel, tr. Wyatt, David, illus. 2006. 296p. (J). (gr. 5-8). 17.95 *(978-958-704-467-6(3))* Ediciones Alfaguara ESP. Dist: Santillana USA Publishing Co., Inc.

—Peter Pan in Scarlet. Fischer, Scott M., illus. (ENG.). 320p. (J). (gr. 4-9). 2008. pap. 6.99 *(978-1-4169-1809-7(4))* 2006. 19.99 *(978-1-4169-1808-0(6))* McElderry, Margaret K. Bks. (McElderry, Margaret K. Bks.).

O'Connor, Daniel & Barrie, J. M. The Peter Pan Picture Book. Woodward, Alice B., illus. 2015. (ENG.). 96p. (J). (gr. k-3). pap. 12.99 *(978-0-486-79430-3(X))* Dover Pubns., Inc.

Pearson, Ridley & Barry, Dave. Peter & the Secret of Rundoon. Call, Greg, illus. rev. ed. 2009. (Peter & the Starcatchers Ser.: Bk. 3). (ENG.). 496p. (J). (gr. 5-9). pap. 9.99 *(978-1-4231-2326-2(3))* Hyperion Pr.

Peter Pantm. 2003. (J). 173.68 *(978-0-06-056911-2(5))* HarperCollins Pubs.

Publications International Ltd. Staff, ed. Peter Pan. 2007. (SPA.). (J). 3.98 *(978-1-4127-8878-6(1))* Publications International, Ltd.

Randolph, Grace. Muppet Peter Pan. Mebberson, Amy, illus. 2010. (Muppet Show Ser.). (ENG.). 112p. (J). pap. 9.99 *(978-1-60886-507-9(X))* Boom! Studios.

Randolph, Grace & Barks, Carl. Muppet Peter Pan. Mebberson, Amy, illus. 2010. (Muppet Show Ser.). (ENG.). 112p. (J). 24.99 *(978-1-60886-531-4(2))* Boom! Studios.

Random House Disney Staff. Peter Pan Step into Reading (Disney Peter Pan) Random House Disney Staff, illus. 2013. (Step into Reading Ser.). (ENG., Illus.). 32p. (J). (gr. -1-1). 3.99 *(978-0-7364-3114-9(4),* RH/Disney) Random Hse. Children's Bks.

Random House Editors. Disney Peter Pan. 2013. (Step into Reading Level 1 Ser.). lib. bdg. 13.55 *(978-0-606-26973-5(8),* Turtleback) Turtleback Bks.

Sabuda, Robert, illus. Peter Pan: A Pop-Up Adaptation of J. M. Barrie's Original Tale. 2008. (ENG.). 16p. (J). 39.99 *(978-0-689-85364-7(5),* Little Simon) Little Simon.

PETER RABBIT (FICTITIOUS CHARACTER)—FICTION

Berry, Ron. Can You Make Peter Rabbit Giggle? Sharp, Chris, illus. 2012. 10p. (J). bds. 10.99 *(978-0-8249-1418-9(X),* Ideal Pubns.) Worthy Publishing.

Burgess, Thornton W. Mother West Wind 'How' Stories. 2008. 108p. (gr. -1-3). 22.95 *(978-1-60664-893-3(4));* pap. 9.95 *(978-1-60664-012-8(7))* Aegypan.

—Mrs Peter Rabbit. 2006. 120p. (gr. -1-3). 22.95 *(978-1-59818-464-8(4))* Aegypan.

Calumus, Bic-. The Tale of Peter Rabbit, the Original Latin Version, C 777 B C Faithfully Translated by Bic-Calamus. 2009. 48p. pap. 9.95 *(978-1-60693-626-9(3),* Eloquent Bks.) Strategic Book Publishing & Rights Agency (SBPRA).

Dorling Kindersley Publishing Staff & Hallinan, Camilla. The Ultimate Peter Rabbit. 2016. (ENG., Illus.). 128p. (J). (gr. 5). 19.99 *(978-1-4654-5976-3(6),* DK Children) Dorling Kindersley Publishing, Inc.

Flor Ada, Alma. Dear Peter Rabbit. Tryon, Leslie, illus. 2006. (Stories to Go! Ser.). (J). (gr. k-3). 12.65 *(978-0-7569-7322-3(8))* Perfection Learning Corp.

Jeremy Fisher Rocks Out. 2015. (Illus.). (J). *(978-1-4844-5560-9(6),* Warne, Frederick Pubs.) Penguin Bks., Ltd.

Potter, Beatrix. Hello, Peter! 2012. (Peter Rabbit Ser.). (ENG.). 10p. (J). (gr. -1-k). bds. 6.99 *(978-0-7232-6744-7(8),* Warne) Penguin Young Readers Group.

—The Miniature World of Peter Rabbit, 12 vols. 2007. (Peter Rabbit Ser.). (ENG., Illus.). 780p. (J). (gr. -1-2). 16.99 *(978-0-7232-5785-1(X),* Warne) Penguin Young Readers Group.

—Munch! 2009. (Peter Rabbit Naturally Better Ser.). (ENG.). 10p. (J). (gr. -1 — 1). bds. 7.99 *(978-0-7232-6390-6(6),* Warne) Penguin Young Readers Group.

—Peekaboo! 2009. (Peter Rabbit Naturally Better Ser.). (ENG.). 10p. (J). (gr. -1 — 1). bds. 6.99 *(978-0-7232-6350-0(7),* Warne) Penguin Young Readers Group.

—Peter Rabbit. 2008. (Peter Rabbit Ser.). (ENG., Illus.). 12p. (J). (gr. -1 — 1). bds. 8.99 *(978-0-7232-5956-5(9),* Warne) Penguin Young Readers Group.

—The Peter Rabbit & Friends Treasury. Potter, Beatrix, illus. 2006. (Illus.). 240p. (J). (gr. k-4). reprint ed. 20.00 *(978-1-4223-5452-0(0))* DIANE Publishing Co.

—Peter Rabbit & the Pumpkin Patch. Palmer, Ruth, illus. 2013. (Peter Rabbit Ser.). (ENG.). 32p. (J). (gr. -1-2). pap. 3.99 *(978-0-7232-7124-6(0),* Warne) Penguin Young Readers Group.

—Peter Rabbit Book & Toy. 2006. (Peter Rabbit Ser.). (ENG., Illus.). 70p. (J). (gr. -1 — 1). 16.99 *(978-0-7232-5356-3(0),* Warne) Penguin Young Readers Group.

—Peter Rabbit Finger Puppet Book. 2011. (Peter Rabbit Ser.). (ENG., Illus.). 14p. (J). (gr. -1-k). bds. 12.99 *(978-0-7232-6639-6(5),* Warne) Penguin Young Readers Group.

—The Peter Rabbit Gift Set: Including a Classic Board Book & Peter Rabbit Plush. Santore, Charles, illus. 2017. (ENG.). 8p. (J). bds. 16.95 *(978-1-60433-685-6(4),* Applesauce Pr.) Cider Mill Pr. Bk. Pubs., LLC.

—Peter Rabbit Rainbow Shapes & Colors. Potter, Beatrix, illus. 2006. (Peter Rabbit Seedlings Ser.). (ENG., Illus.). 10p. (J). (gr. k-18). bds. 5.99 *(978-0-7232-5722-6(1),* Puffin) Penguin Publishing Group.

—Sgeulachd Pheadair Rabaid. MacDonald, James, 1st, tr. from ENG. Potter, Beatrix, illus. 2008.Tr. of Tale of Peter Rabbit. (GAE., Illus.). 84p. *(978-0-9552326-3-3(5))* Grace Note Pubns.

—Show Me Your Ears. 2010. (Peter Rabbit Ser.). (ENG.). 12p. (J). (gr. -1-k). 9.99 *(978-0-7232-6433-0(3),* Warne) Penguin Young Readers Group.

—The Story of Peter Rabbit. McCue, Lisa, illus. 2005. (Easter Ornament Bks.). (ENG.). 20p. (J). (gr. -1-1). 10.99 *(978-0-7944-0527-4(4),* Reader's Digest Children's Bks.) Studio Fun International.

—The Tale of Peter Rabbit. 2013. (Children's Classics Ser.). (ENG., Illus.). 46p. pap. 9.99 *(978-1-909676-49-7(7),* Sovereign) Bollinger, Max GBR. Dist: Lightning Source UK, Ltd.

—The Tale of Peter Rabbit. Hague, Michael, illus. 2003. 29p. (J). (gr. 2-5). reprint ed. 16.00 *(978-0-7567-6968-0(X))* DIANE Publishing Co.

—The Tale of Peter Rabbit. (Peter Rabbit Naturally Better Ser.). (ENG.). (J). (gr. -1-2). 2009. 72p. 6.99 *(978-0-7232-6392-0(2))* 2007. (Illus.). 24p. bds. 7.99 *(978-0-7232-5793-6(0))* Penguin Young Readers Group. (Warne).

—The Tale of Peter Rabbit. Vining, Alex, illus. 2004. (Peter Rabbit Ser.). (ENG.). 32p. (J). (gr. -1-k). mass mkt. 3.99 *(978-0-448-43521-3(7),* Warne) Penguin Young Readers Group.

—The Tale of Peter Rabbit. McPhail, David, illus. 2014. (ENG.). 28p. (J). (gr. -1 — 1). bds. 6.99 *(978-0-545-65096-0(8),* Cartwheel Bks.) Scholastic, Inc.

—The Tale of Peter Rabbit. (Illus.). 12p. 4.95 *(978-1-58989-271-2(2));* 6p. (J). bds. 3.95 *(978-1-58989-201-9(1))* Thurman Hse., LLC.

—The Tale of Peter Rabbit: A Sound Story Book. 2013. (Peter Rabbit Ser.). (ENG., Illus.). 10p. (J). (gr. -1-2). 12.99 *(978-0-7232-6856-7(8),* Warne) Penguin Young Readers Group.

—The Tale of Peter Rabbit: Commemorative Edition. movie tie-in ed. 2006. (Peter Rabbit Ser.: 1). (ENG., Illus.). 80p. (J). (gr. -1-2). 6.99 *(978-0-7232-5873-5(2),* Warne) Penguin Young Readers Group.

—Touch & Feel. 2005. (Peter Rabbit Ser.). (ENG., Illus.). 12p. (J). (gr. -1-k). bds. 12.99 *(978-0-7232-5578-9(4),* Warne) Penguin Young Readers Group.

—Treehouse Rescue! 2013. (Peter Rabbit Animation Ser.). (ENG., Illus.). 32p. (J). (gr. -1-k). 3.99 *(978-0-7232-8040-8(1),* Warne) Penguin Young Readers Group.

—Where's Peter? 2011. (Peter Rabbit Ser.). (ENG.). 12p. (J). (gr. -1-k). bds. 10.99 *(978-0-7232-6636-5(0),* Warne) Penguin Young Readers Group.

—The World of Peter Rabbit, 23 vols., Set. 2006. (Peter Rabbit Ser.). (ENG., Illus.). 1388p. (J). (gr. -1-2). 160.00 *(978-0-7232-5763-9(9),* Warne) Penguin Young Readers Group.

Potter, Beatrix & Penguin Young Readers Group Staff. The Tale of Peter Rabbit, Set. gif. ed. 2010. (Peter Rabbit Ser.). (ENG.). 64p. (J). (gr. -1 — 1). 12.99 *(978-0-7232-6546-7(1),* Warne) Penguin Young Readers Group.

Potter, Beatrix & Taylor, Judy. My First Year. 2006. (Peter Rabbit Ser.). (ENG.). 48p. (gr. k-12). 12.99 *(978-0-7232-5683-0(7),* Warne) Penguin Young Readers Group.

Santore, Charles & Potter, Beatrix. Peter Rabbit Board Book. Encarnacion, Elizabeth, ed. 2014. (ENG., Illus.). 22p. (J). bds. 8.95 *(978-1-60433-511-8(4),* Applesauce Pr.) Cider Mill Pr. Bk. Pubs., LLC.

Thompson, Emma. The Christmas Tale of Peter Rabbit. Taylor, Eleanor, illus. 2013. (Peter Rabbit Ser.). (ENG.). 72p. (J). (gr. -1-2). 20.00 *(978-0-7232-7694-4(3),* Warne) Penguin Young Readers Group.

—The Further Tale of Peter Rabbit. Taylor, Eleanor, illus. 2012. (Peter Rabbit Ser.). (ENG.). 72p. (J). (gr. -1-2). 20.00 *(978-0-7232-6910-6(6),* Warne) Penguin Young Readers Group.

Thompson, Emma, et al. Sgeulachd Eile Mu Pheader Rabaid. Taylor, Eleonor, illus. 2012.Tr. of Further Tale of Peter Rabbit. (GLA.). 80p. (J). *(978-1-907676-12-3(0))* Grace Note Pubns.

Warne. Be My Friend. 2014. (Peter Rabbit Animation Ser.). (ENG.). 32p. (J). (gr. -1-k). 3.99 *(978-0-14-135506-1(9),* Warne) Penguin Young Readers Group.

—Merry Christmas, Peter! 2014. (Peter Rabbit Animation Ser.). (ENG.). 32p. (J). (gr. -1-k). 9.99 *(978-0-14-135173-5(X),* Warne) Penguin Young Readers Group.

—My Father's Flying Machine. 2015. (Peter Rabbit Animation Ser.). (ENG., Illus.). 32p. (J). (gr. -1-k). 3.99 *(978-0-7232-9564-8(6),* Warne) Penguin Young Readers Group.

—A Present for Mom. 2015. (Peter Rabbit Animation Ser.). (ENG., Illus.). 32p. (J). (gr. -1-k). 3.99 *(978-0-7232-9568-6(9),* Warne) Penguin Young Readers Group.

Warne, Frederick & Potter, Beatrix. The Complete Adventures of Peter Rabbit. 2007. (Peter Rabbit Ser.). (ENG., Illus.). 96p. (J). (gr. -1-2). 16.99 *(978-0-7232-5916-9(X),* Warne) Penguin Young Readers Group.

PETROLEUM

see also Gasoline

Benoit, Peter. The BP Oil Spill. 2011. (J). pap. *(978-0-531-29029-3(8))* Children's Pr., Ltd.

—The BP Oil Spill. 2011. (True Bks.). 48p. (J). (gr. 3-5). lib. bdg. 29.00 *(978-0-531-20630-0(0),* Children's Pr.) Scholastic Library Publishing.

Bethea, Nikole Brooks. Oil & Coal. 2013. (J). *(978-1-61080-972-6(6));* (ENG.). 32p. (gr. 4-8). 28.50 *(978-1-61080-897-2(5),* 202567); (ENG.). 32p. (gr. 4-8). pap. 14.21 *(978-1-61080-922-1(X),* 202569) Cherry Lake Publishing.

Bredeson, Carmen. The Spindletop Gusher: The Story of the Texas Oil Boom. 2010. (ENG., Illus.). 64p. (gr. 4-7). pap. 9.95 *(978-1-933979-66-3(6),* c91933b9-871a-41d6-aa3c-dc2e578fd946) Bright Sky Pr.

Brevard, Katherine McLean & Miller, Davis Worth. The Story of Oil: How It Changed the World, 1 vol. 2010. (World Transformed Ser.). (ENG.). 64p. (gr. 6-7). lib. bdg. 33.99 *(978-0-7565-4314-3(2),* CPB Grades 4-8) Compass Point Bks.

Centore, Michael. Oil & Gas in the Arctic. 2017. (Exploring the Polar Regions Today Ser.: Vol. 8). (ENG.). (YA). (gr. 7-12). 23.95 ***(978-1-4222-3869-1(5))*** Mason Crest.

Cunningham, Kevin. Gasoline. 2008. (21st Century Skills Library: Global Products Ser.). (ENG.). 32p. (gr. 4-8). lib. bdg. 28.50 *(978-1-60279-121-3(X),* 200097) Cherry Lake Publishing.

Ditchfield, Christin. Oil. 2003. (True Bks.). (ENG., Illus.). 48p. (J). (gr. 3-5). pap. 6.95 *(978-0-516-29367-7(2),* Children's Pr.) Scholastic Library Publishing.

Doeden, Matt. Finding Out about Coal, Oil, & Natural Gas. 2014. (Searchlight Books — What Are Energy Sources? Ser.). (Illus.). 40p. (gr. 3-4). (J). lib. bdg. 27.93 *(978-1-4677-3654-1(6),* Lerner Pubns.); pap. 8.95 *(978-1-4677-4553-6(7))* Lerner Publishing Group.

Edwards, Ron, et al. Oil & Gas. 2004. (Rocks, Minerals, & Resources Ser.). (ENG., Illus.). 32p. (J). pap. *(978-0-7787-1444-6(6));* lib. bdg. *(978-0-7787-1412-5(8))* Crabtree Publishing Co.

Friedman, Lauri S. The BP Oil Spill. Greenhaven Press Editors, ed. 2011. (Writing the Critical Essay Ser.). (ENG., Illus.). 128p. (gr. 6-10). 38.30 *(978-0-7377-5833-7(3))* Cengage Gale.

Goldish, Meish. Oil Spill: Deepwater Horizon. 2017. (Eco-Disasters Ser.). (ENG.). 32p. (J). (gr. 2-7). 19.95 ***(978-1-68402-226-7(6))*** Bearport Publishing Co., Inc.

Goldstein, Margaret J. Fuel under Fire: Petroleum & Its Perils. 2015. (ENG., Illus.). 104p. (gr. 7-12). (J). lib. bdg. 34.65 *(978-1-4677-3831-6(X));* 34.65 *(978-1-4677-8802-1(3))* Lerner Publishing Group. (Twenty-First Century Bks.).

Graham, Ian. From Crude Oil to Fast Food Snacks: An Energy Journey Through the World of Heat. 2015. (Energy Journeys Ser.). (ENG., Illus.). 48p. (gr. 3-6). 33.32 *(978-1-4846-0885-2(2),* Heinemann InfoSearch) Heinemann-Raintree.

Haerens, Margaret. Offshore Drilling. 2010. (Opposing Viewpoints Ser.). (ENG.). 240p. (J). 42.95 *(978-0-7377-4779-9(X));* pap. 29.45 *(978-0-7377-4780-5(3))* Cengage Gale. (Greenhaven Pr., Inc.).

—Oil. 2010. (Global Viewpoints Ser.). (Illus.). 224p. (J). 40.45 *(978-0-7377-4719-5(6));* pap. 27.95 *(978-0-7377-4720-1(X))* Cengage Gale. (Greenhaven Pr., Inc.).

hal, marcovitz. Is Offshore Oil Drilling Worth the Risks? 2011. (YA). lib. bdg. *(978-1-60152-143-9(X))* ReferencePoint Pr., Inc.

Haugen, David M. The BP Oil Spill. 2011. (At Issue Ser.). (ENG.). 128p. (gr. 10-12). pap. 27.80 *(978-0-7377-5569-5(5),* Greenhaven Pr., Inc.) Cengage Gale.

—Drilling in the Gulf of Mexico. 2011. (At Issue Ser.). (ENG.). 128p. (gr. 10-12). 39.40 *(978-0-7377-5568-8(7))* Cengage Gale.

Hicks, Terry Allan. The Pros & Cons of Oil. 2014. (Economics of Energy Ser.). 80p. (YA). (gr. 7-10). lib. bdg. 35.64 *(978-1-62712-927-5(8))* Cavendish Square Publishing.

Horn, Geoffrey M., et al. Coal, Oil, & Natural Gas. 2010. (Energy Today Ser.). 48p. (J). (gr. 3-6). 30.00 *(978-1-60413-785-9(1))* Facts On File, Inc.

Manatt, Kathleen. Searching for Oil. 2007. (21st Century Skills Library: Power Up! Ser.). (ENG.). 32p. (gr. 4-8). pap. 14.21 *(978-1-60279-100-8(7),* 200661) Cherry Lake Publishing.

Manatt, Kathleen G. Searching for Oil. 2007. (21st Century Skills Library: Power Up! Ser.). (ENG., Illus.). 32p. (gr. 4-8). lib. bdg. 28.50 *(978-1-60279-043-8(4),* 200057) Cherry Lake Publishing.

marcovitz, hal. How Serious a Threat Is Climate Change? 2011. (Illus.). 96p. (YA). lib. bdg. *(978-1-60152-142-2(1))* ReferencePoint Pr., Inc.

Metcalf, Tom. Oil. Des Chenes, Elizabeth & McCage, Crystal D., eds. 2006. (Fueling the Future Ser.). (ENG., Illus.). 120p. (gr. 10-12). lib. bdg. 44.60 *(978-0-7377-3588-8(0),* 1256646, Greenhaven Pr., Inc.) Cengage Gale.

Mooney, Carla. Oil Spills & Offshore Drilling. 2011. (Compact Research Ser.). 96p. (YA). (gr. 5-18). lib. bdg. *(978-1-60152-141-5(3))* ReferencePoint Pr., Inc.

Nelson, Drew. Life on an Oil Rig. 2013. (Extreme Jobs in Extreme Places Ser.). (Illus.). 32p. (gr. 3-6). 26.60 *(978-1-4339-8497-6(0));* pap. 10.50 *(978-1-4339-8498-3(9))* Stevens, Gareth Publishing LLLP. (Gareth Stevens Learning Library).

Parker, Steve. Oil, Vol. 12. 2015. (North American Natural Resources Ser.). (Illus.). 64p. (J). (gr. 7). 23.95 *(978-1-4222-3386-3(3))* Mason Crest.

—Oil & Gas. 2004. (Science Files Ser.). (Illus.). 32p. (gr. 2-6). lib. bdg. 26.00 *(978-0-8368-4031-5(3),* Gareth Stevens Learning Library) Stevens, Gareth Publishing LLLP.

Pipe, Jim. Oil. 2010. (J). 28.50 *(978-1-59604-211-7(7))* Black Rabbit Bks.

Rae, Alison. Oil, Plastics, & Power. 2010. (Development Without Damage Ser.). (YA). (gr. 5-9). 34.25 *(978-1-59920-251-8(4))* Black Rabbit Bks.

Rajczak Nelson, Kristen. How Oil Is Formed. 2016. (From the Earth: How Resources Are Made Ser.). 32p. (J). (gr. 4-3). pap. 10.50 *(978-1-4824-4721-7(5))* Stevens, Gareth Publishing LLLP.

Redmond, Jim. Oil Makes Gasoline Power. 2003. (From Resource to Energy Source Ser.). (J). *(978-1-58417-292-5(4));* pap. *(978-1-58417-293-2(2))* Lake Street Pubs.

Scherer, Lauri S., ed. Oil. 2013. (Introducing Issues with Opposing Viewpoints Ser.). (ENG., Illus.). 144p. (gr. 7-10). lib. bdg. 36.95 *(978-0-7377-6279-2(9),* Greenhaven Pr., Inc.) Cengage Gale.

Schuh, Mari. Sugars & Fats. 2012. (What's on Myplate? Ser.). (ENG.). 24p. (gr. k-1). pap. 41.70 *(978-1-4296-9423-0(8),* Pebble Plus) Capstone Press of Coughlan Cos.

Wyler, Rose & McSpadden, Warren W. Oil Comes to Us. Luykx, Th. D., illus. 2011. 32p. pap. 35.95 *(978-1-258-10512-9(8))* Literary Licensing, LLC.

Zemlicka, Shannon. Del Petróleo a la Gasolina. 2006. (De Principio a Fin Ser.). (SPA., Illus.). 24p. (J). (gr. 3-7). lib. bdg. 18.60 *(978-0-8225-6496-6(3),* Ediciones Lerner) Lerner Publishing Group.

—Del petróleo a la gasolina (from Oil to Gas) 2006. (De Principio a Fin (Start to Finish) Ser.). (Illus.). 24p. (J). (gr. -1-3). per. 5.95 *(978-0-8225-6633-5(8),* Ediciones Lerner) Lerner Publishing Group.

—From Oil to Gas. (Start to Finish, Second Series: Everyday Products Ser.). (Illus.). 24p. (gr. k-3). 2013. (ENG.). lib. bdg. 23.93 *(978-0-7613-9185-2(1))* 2003. (J). 18.60 *(978-0-8225-0718-5(8))* Lerner Publishing Group. (Lerner Pubns.).

PETROLEUM—FICTION

Bottoms, Bud. Davey & the GOM Giant Oil Monster. 2008. (Illus.). 39p. (J). (gr. -1-5). per. 14.95 *(978-0-9795444-1-5(6))* Summerland Publishing.

PETROLEUM—HISTORY

Gardner, Timothy. Oil. 2009. (Diminishing Resources Ser.). (Illus.). 111p. (J). lib. bdg. 28.95 *(978-1-59935-117-9(X))* Reynolds, Morgan Inc.

Marrin, Albert. Black Gold: The Story of Oil in Our Lives. 2013. (ENG.). 192p. (YA). (gr. 7). pap. 15.99 *(978-0-375-85968-7(3),* Knopf Bks. for Young Readers) Random Hse. Children's Bks.

PETROLEUM AS FUEL

Bickerstaff, Linda. Oil Power of the Future: New Ways of Turning Petroleum into Energy. 2009. (Library of Future Energy Ser.). 64p. (gr. 5-5). 58.50 *(978-1-60853-628-3(9))* Rosen Publishing Group, Inc., The.

Graham, Ian. From Crude Oil to Fast Food Snacks: An Energy Journey Through the World of Heat. 2015. (Energy Journeys Ser.). (ENG., Illus.). 48p. (gr. 3-6). 33.32 *(978-1-4846-0885-2(2),* Heinemann InfoSearch) Heinemann-Raintree.

Knight, M. J. Why Should I Walk More Often? 2009. (One Small Step Ser.). (YA). (gr. 2-5). 28.50 *(978-1-59920-268-6(9))* Black Rabbit Bks.

Murray, Julie. Oil to Gas, 1 vol. 2006. (Beginning to End Set 1 - 8 Titles Ser.). (ENG.). 24p. (gr. k-4). 25.65 *(978-1-59679-913-4(7),* Buddy Bks.) ABDO Publishing Co.

PETROLEUM ENGINES

see Internal Combustion Engines

PETROLEUM INDUSTRY AND TRADE

Bolden, Tonya. Searching for Sarah Rector: The Richest Black Girl in America. 2014. (ENG., Illus.). 80p. (J). (gr. 3-7). 21.95 *(978-1-4197-0846-6(5),* Abrams Bks. for Young Readers) Abrams, Inc.

Bowman, Chris. Oil Field Worker. 2014. (Dangerous Jobs Ser.). (ENG., Illus.). 24p. (J). (gr. 3-7). lib. bdg. 25.95 *(978-1-62617-111-4(4),* Torque Bks.) Bellwether Media.

Bright, Michael. From Oil Rig to Gas Pump. 2016. (Source to Resource Ser.). (ENG., Illus.). 32p. (J). (gr. 3-6). *(978-0-7787-2706-4(8))* Crabtree Publishing Co.

Calvert, John. The Arabian Peninsula in the Age of Oil. 2009. (Making of the Middle East Ser.). (Illus.). 88p. (YA). (gr. 3-7). lib. bdg. 22.95 *(978-1-4222-0172-5(4))* Mason Crest.

Centore, Michael. Oil & Gas in the Arctic. 2017. (Exploring the Polar Regions Today Ser.: Vol. 8). (ENG.). (YA). (gr. 7-12). 23.95 ***(978-1-4222-3869-1(5))*** Mason Crest.

Dalton, Anna. Examining Oil Spills. 2015. (ENG., Illus.). 48p. (J). lib. bdg. 24.95 net. *(978-1-934545-65-2(1))* Oliver Pr., Inc.

Gardner, Timothy. Oil. 2009. (Diminishing Resources Ser.). (Illus.). 111p. (J). lib. bdg. 28.95 *(978-1-59935-117-9(X))* Reynolds, Morgan Inc.

Gunderson, Cory Gideon. The Need for Oil. 2003. (World in Conflict-the Middle East Ser.). 32p. (gr. 4-8). 27.07 *(978-1-59197-417-8(8),* Abdo & Daughters) ABDO Publishing Co.

Hicks, Terry Allan. The Pros & Cons of Oil. 2014. (Economics of Energy Ser.). 80p. (YA). (gr. 7-10). lib. bdg. 35.64 *(978-1-62712-927-5(8))* Cavendish Square Publishing.

Jarrow, Jesse. Oil, Steel, & Railroads: America's Big Businesses in the Late 1800s. (America's Industrial Society in the 19th Century Ser.). 32p. 2009. (gr. 4-4). 47.90 *(978-1-61511-337-8(1))* 2004. (ENG., Illus.). (gr. 5-8). pap. 10.00 *(978-0-8239-4276-3(7))* Rosen Publishing Group, Inc., The.

Lankford, Ronnie D., ed. Foreign Oil Dependence. 2012. (At Issue Ser.). (ENG.). 128p. (gr. 10-12). lib. bdg. 39.40 *(978-0-7377-6177-1(6),* Greenhaven Pr., Inc.) Cengage Gale.

Marcovitz, Hal. Energy Security, 1 vol. 2011. (Essential Issues Set 2 Ser.). (ENG., Illus.). 112p. (J). (gr. 6-12). lib. bdg. 35.64 *(978-1-61714-771-5(0),* Essential Library) ABDO Publishing Co.

Miller, Debra A. Oil. Gale Editors, ed. 2010. (Current Controversies Ser.). (ENG.). 224p. (gr. 10-12). 46.40 *(978-0-7377-4919-9(9));* pap. 32.00 *(978-0-7377-4920-5(2))* Cengage Gale. (Greenhaven Pr., Inc.).

Pipe, Jim. Oil. 2010. (J). 28.50 *(978-1-59604-211-7(7))* Black Rabbit Bks.

Rajczak Nelson, Kristen. How Oil Is Formed. 2016. (From the Earth: How Resources Are Made Ser.). 32p. (J). (gr. 4-3). pap. 10.50 *(978-1-4824-4721-7(5))* Stevens, Gareth Publishing LLLP.

Spilsbury, Richard & Spilsbury, Louise. The Oil Industry. 2011. (Development or Destruction? Ser.). (ENG.). 48p. (YA). (gr. 5-8). pap. 11.75 *(978-1-4488-6998-5(6));* lib. bdg. 29.25 *(978-1-4488-6991-6(9))* Rosen Publishing Group, Inc., The.

Stone, Adam. The Deepwater Horizon Oil Spill. 2014. (Disaster Stories Ser.). (ENG., Illus.). 24p. (J). (gr. 3-8). 29.95 *(978-1-62617-152-7(1),* Black Sheep) Bellwether Media.

Thomas, William. Oil Rig Worker. 2010. (Benchmark Rockets: Dirty & Dangerous Jobs Ser.). 32p. (J). (gr. 3-6). 28.50 *(978-1-60870-173-5(5))* Marshall Cavendish Corp.

Wagner, Heather Lehr, et al. The Organization of the Petroleum Exporting Countries. 2008. (Global Organizations Ser.). (Illus.). 112p. (YA). (gr. 7-12). 35.00 *(978-1-60413-102-4(0))* Facts On File, Inc.

PETROLEUM INDUSTRY AND TRADE—FICTION

Dixon, Franklin W. Running on Fumes. 2005. 150p. (J). lib. bdg. 16.92 *(978-1-4242-0384-0(8))* Fitzgerald Bks.

William MacLeod Raine. Gunsight Pass. l.t. ed. 2007. (ENG.). 280p. pap. 23.99 *(978-1-4264-8104-8(7))* Creative Media Partners, LLC.

Winfield, Arthur M. Rover Boys in the Land of Luck or Stirri. 2006. pap. 30.95 *(978-1-4286-4101-3(7))* Kessinger Publishing, LLC.

PETROLEUM INDUSTRY AND TRADE—VOCATIONAL GUIDANCE

Horn, Geoffrey M. Oil Rig Roughneck. 2008. (Cool Careers: Adventure Careers Ser.). (Illus.). 32p. (gr. 5-8). pap. 10.50 *(978-0-8368-8890-4(1));* lib. bdg. 26.00 *(978-0-8368-8883-6(9))* Stevens, Gareth Publishing LLLP.

PETS

see also Domestic Animals

also names of animals, e.g. Cats; Dogs

Abbott, Simon. Pop & Play: Pets. 2014. (ENG., Illus.). 10p. (J). (gr. -1-k). bds. 7.99 *(978-0-7534-7156-2(6),* 9780753471562, Kingfisher) Roaring Brook Pr.

ABDO Publishing Company Staff. Unusual Pets, 1 vol. 2013. (Unusual Pets Ser.: 6). (ENG.). 24p. (J). (gr. -1-3). lib. bdg. 145.26 *(978-1-61783-396-0(7),* SandCastle) ABDO Publishing Co.

—Xtreme Pets. 2013. (Xtreme Pets Ser.: 6). 32p. (gr. 3-9). lib. bdg. 162.42 *(978-1-61783-969-6(8),* Abdo & Daughters) ABDO Publishing Co.

About Pets Staff. Hamsters. 2003. (Illus.). 64p. pap. 4.95 *(978-0-7434-4542-9(2))* ibooks, Inc.

—Tropical Fish. 2003. (Illus.). 64p. pap. 4.95 *(978-0-7434-4543-6(0))* ibooks, Inc.

Accord Publishing Staff, et al. Stick to It - Pets: A Magnetic Puzzle Book. 2010. (ENG.). 14p. (J). (gr. -1). bds. 16.99 *(978-0-7407-9726-2(3))* Andrews McMeel Publishing.

Ackland, Nick. What Noise Does a Cat Make? Bee, Bella, illus. 2016. (What Noise Does A... . Ser.). (ENG.). 10p. (J). (gr. -1 — 1). bds. 6.99 *(978-0-7641-6842-0(8))* Barron's Educational Series, Inc.

Adelman, Beth. Dogs & Cats: Saving Our Precious Pets. 2017. (Protecting the Earth's Animals Ser.: Vol. 8). (ENG.). (YA). (gr. 5-8). 23.95 ***(978-1-4222-3875-2(X))*** Mason Crest.

Adelman, Heidi. Weird Pets. 2007. (Reading Rocks! Ser.). (ENG., Illus.). 32p. (J). (gr. 2-5). 28.50 *(978-1-59296-862-6(7),* 200752) Child's World, Inc., The.

Agusta, Autum. Rita & Rascal. 2013. 116p. (gr. 2-4). 22.25 *(978-1-4669-6973-5(3));* pap. 12.25 *(978-1-4669-6971-1(7))* Trafford Publishing.

Algeo, Matthew. Abe & Fido: Lincoln's Love of Animals & the Touching Story of His Favorite Canine Companion. 2015.

(ENG., Illus.). 176p. 22.95 *(978-1-55652-222-2(3))* Chicago Review Pr., Inc.

All about Pets. 2016. (All about Pets Ser.). 24p. (gr. 1-k). pap. 56.10 *(978-0-7660-7963-2(5))*; lib. bdg. 135.60 *(978-0-7660-7488-0(9))* Enslow Pubs., Inc.

All My Pets. (Girls' World Ser.). 16p. (J). *(978-2-7643-0142-5(1))* Phidal Publishing, Inc./Editions Phidal, Inc.

All My Pets: What's New? (Girls' Activity Kit Ser.). (J). *(978-2-7643-0213-2(4))* Phidal Publishing, Inc./Editions Phidal, Inc.

Alligators Are Not Pets! 2013. (When Pets Attack! Ser.). 32p. (J). (gr. 3-6). pap. 63.00 *(978-1-4339-9280-3(9))* Stevens, Gareth Publishing LLLP.

Antol, Jenna. "Do" The Once Forgotten Little Bunny Who Grew to Become a World Record Holder. 2012. (ENG.). 36p. (J). pap. 14.95 *(978-1-4787-1593-1(6))* Outskirts Pr., Inc.

Armadillo. Let's Look & See: Pets. 2014. (ENG., Illus.). 24p. (J). (gr. k-2). bds. 6.99 *(978-1-86147-378-3(8)*, Armadillo) Anness Publishing GBR. Dist: National Bk. Network.

Aronson, Virginia & Szejko, Allyn. Iguana Invasion! Exotic Pets Gone Wild in Florida. 2010. (ENG.). 69p. (YA). (gr. 7-18). 16.95 *(978-1-56164-468-1(4))*; pap. 12.95 *(978-1-56164-469-8(2))* Pineapple Pr., Inc.

Atlantic, Leonard. We Play with Pets! 2017. (Ways to Play Ser.). 24p. (gr. k-k). pap. 8.15 ***(978-1-4824-6357-6(1))*** Stevens, Gareth Publishing LLLP.

Autrey, Jacquelyn & Yeager, Alice. U.S. Presidents & Their Animal Friends. Passarella, Jennie, illus. 2004. 32p. (J). *(978-1-59421-005-1(5))* Seacoast Publishing, Inc.

Bailey, Debbie. Mi Animalito. Huszar, Susan, photos by. 2003. (Hablemos Ser.).Tr. of My Pet. (SPA., Illus.). 16p. (J). (gr. -1 — 1). bds. 5.95 *(978-1-55037-826-9(0)*, 9781550378269) Annick Pr., Ltd. CAN. Dist: Publishers Group West (PGW).

—My Pet. Huszar, Susan, photos by. 3rd ed. 2003. (Talk-About-Bks.: 18). (ENG., Illus.). 16p. (J). (gr. -1 — 1). bds. 6.95 *(978-1-55037-816-0(3)*, 9781550378160) Annick Pr., Ltd. CAN. Dist: Publishers Group West (PGW).

Baker, Charles F., ed. Pets: Cats, Dogs, Horses, & Camels, Too! 2005. (ENG., Illus.). 32p. (J). (gr. 1-5). 17.95 *(978-0-8126-7925-0(3))* Cobblestone Publishing Co.

Barry, Holly M. Helen Keller's Best Friend Belle. Thermes, Jennifer, illus. 2013. (ENG.). 32p. (J). (gr. -1-3). 16.99 *(978-0-8075-3198-3(7))* Whitman, Albert & Co.

Basic Domestic Pet Library. 2005. (Basic Domestic Pet Library). (gr. 6-12). 82.50 *(978-0-7910-9191-3(0)*, Chelsea Hse.) Facts On File, Inc.

Beck, Angela. Guinea Pigs: Keeping & Caring for Your Pet. 2013. (Keeping & Caring for Your Pet Ser.). 72p. (J). lib. bdg. 29.27 *(978-0-7660-4184-4(0))* Enslow Pubs., Inc.

Beck, Isabel L., et al. Trophies Kindergarten: Pet Day. 2003. (Trophies Ser.). (gr. k-6). 13.80 *(978-0-15-329519-5(8))* Harcourt Schl. Pubs.

Bennett, Mia. Ferrets. 2017. (Our Weird Pets Ser.). 24p. (J). (gr. 7-8). 23.60 ***(978-1-5081-5416-7(3)***, PowerKids Pr.) Rosen Publishing Group, Inc., The.

Berman, Gina Dalpra. Remembering Pets: A Book for Children Who Have Lost a Special Friend. Schneider, Barbara Hoss, illus. 2010. (ENG.). 30p. (gr. -1-3). 14.95 *(978-1-885003-68-3(4))* Reed, Robert D. Pubs.

Berman, Ruth. My Pet Dog. Hustace, Billy, photos by. 2005. (All about Pets Ser.). (Illus.). 64p. (gr. 2-6). lib. bdg. 22.60 *(978-0-8225-2259-1(4))* Lerner Publishing Group.

Beylon, Cathy. At the Pet Shop. 2004. (Dover Coloring Bks.). (ENG., Illus.). 32p. (J). (gr. -1-2). pap. 3.95 *(978-0-486-43644-9(6))* Dover Pubns., Inc.

—Favorite Pets. 2007. (Dover Nature Coloring Book Ser.). (ENG., Illus.). 32p. (J). (gr. -1-8). 2.95 *(978-0-486-45641-6(2))* Dover Pubns., Inc.

—I Love Pets Coloring Book. 2014. (ENG.). 64p. (J). (gr. -1-3). pap. 3.99 *(978-0-486-77964-5(5))* Dover Pubns., Inc.

Bicknell, Joanna. Carry-Me Pets. 2008. (Carry-Me Ser.). (Illus.). 12p. (gr. -1-k). 6.99 *(978-1-84610-720-7(2))* Make Believe Ideas GBR. Dist: Nelson, Thomas Inc.

—Googlies: Pet Pals. 2006. (Illus.). 12p. (gr. -1). per. *(978-1-84610-296-7(0))* Make Believe Ideas.

—Googlies: Pet Pals. 2007. (Googlies Ser.). (Illus.). 14p. (gr. -1). bds. 6.95 *(978-1-84610-478-7(5))* Make Believe Ideas GBR. Dist: Nelson, Thomas Inc.

Big Cats Are Not Pets! 2013. (When Pets Attack! Ser.). 32p. (J). (gr. 3-6). pap. 63.00 *(978-1-4339-9275-9(2))* Stevens, Gareth Publishing LLLP.

Biniok, Janice. Adopting a Pet. 2011. (J). 34.95 *(978-1-932904-73-4(5))* Eldorado Ink.

—Guinea Pigs. 2009. (Illus.). 112p. (J). 14.95 *(978-1-932904-37-6(9))* Eldorado Ink.

—Rabbits. 2009. (Illus.). 112p. (J). 14.95 *(978-1-932904-40-6(9))* Eldorado Ink.

Binns, Tristan Boyer. Hermit Crabs, 1 vol. 2nd ed. 2010. (Keeping Unusual Pets Ser.). (ENG.). 48p. (gr. 3-6). 32.65 *(978-1-4329-3854-3(1)*, NA-h) Heinemann-Raintree.

Birney, Betty G. Humphrey's World of Pets. 2013. (Humphrey Ser.). (ENG.). 224p. (J). (gr. 3-7). 10.99 *(978-0-14-750953-6(X)*, Puffin Books) Penguin Young Readers Group.

Bjorklund, Ruth. Lizards. 2008. (Great Pets Ser.). 48p. (gr. 3-18). lib. bdg. 29.93 *(978-0-7614-2997-5(2)*, Benchmark Bks.) Marshall Cavendish Corp.

Blackie. Mels -A-Bob. 2012. 20p. pap. 17.99 *(978-1-4685-9661-8(6))* AuthorHouse.

Bodden, Valerie. Guinea Pigs. 2009. (My First Look at: Pets Ser.). (J). (gr. 1-5). 24.25 *(978-1-58341-723-2(0)*, Creative Education) Creative Co., The.

Boone, Eugene. The Big Book of Pet Names: More Than 10,000 Pet Names - Includes Celebrity Pet Names - the Most Complete Guide to Pet Names & Meanings. 2004. (Illus.). 412p. pap. 15.95 *(978-0-930865-54-2(5))* RSVP Pr.

Boothroyd, Jennifer. How I Care for My Pet. 2014. (First Step Nonfiction - Responsibility in Action Ser.). (ENG., Illus.). 24p. (gr. k-2). lib. bdg. 23.93 *(978-1-4677-3632-9(5)*, Lerner Pubns.) Lerner Publishing Group.

Bozzo, Linda. Mi Primera Mascota Pequeña. 2008. (My First Pet Bilingual Library from the American Humane Association Ser.).Tr. of My First Guinea Pig & Other Small Pets. (ENG & SPA., Illus.). 32p. (J). (gr. 1-3). lib. bdg. 23.94 *(978-0-7660-3037-4(7))* Enslow Pubs., Inc.

—My First Guinea Pig & Other Small Pets. 2007. (My First Pet Library from the American Humane Association Ser.). (Illus.). 32p. (J). (gr. 1-2). lib. bdg. 23.94 *(978-0-7660-2752-7(X)*, Enslow Elementary) Enslow Pubs., Inc.

Brett, Flora. Pet Perspectives. 2015. (Pet Perspectives Ser.). (ENG.). 24p. (gr. 1-2). 101.28 *(978-1-4914-6911-8(0)*, First Facts) Capstone Press of Coughlan Cos.

Britton, Tamara L. Rottweilers, 1 vol. 2013. (Dogs Set 10 Ser.). (ENG.). 24p. (J). (gr. 3-6). lib. bdg. 25.65 *(978-1-61783-591-9(9)*, Checkerboard Library) ABDO Publishing Co.

Brownlee, Christen. Beware of (Prairie) Dog! A Pet Swap Goes Viral. 2011. (J). pap. *(978-0-545-32805-0(5))* Scholastic, Inc.

—Cute, Furry, & Deadly: Diseases You Can Catch from Your Pet! 2007. (24/7: Science Behind the Scenes Ser.). (ENG., Illus.). 64p. (J). (gr. 9-12). pap. 7.95 *(978-0-531-18737-1(3)*, Watts, Franklin) Scholastic Library Publishing.

Burke Battistini, Maryanne. Lacey's Story: A Little Tale That Wags. 2009. 72p. pap. 24.99 *(978-1-4389-8874-0(5))* AuthorHouse.

Burton, Margie, et al. Caring for Our Pets. 2011. (Early Connections Ser.). (J). *(978-1-61672-251-7(7))* Benchmark Education Co.

Cammarata, Jan. Karli's Kritters. 2009. 20p. pap. 12.00 *(978-1-4389-6726-4(8))* AuthorHouse.

Cantor, Don & Cantor, Michael. The Perfect Pet: Finding a pet that is dear to your Heart. Martin, McDonald, illus. 2010. 30p. (J). pap. 9.95 *(978-0-9823906-6-5(1))* Wiggles Pr.

Carr, Aaron. Ferret. 2014. (Illus.). 24p. (J). *(978-1-62127-292-3(3))* Weigl Pubs., Inc.

—Frog. 2014. (Illus.). 24p. (J). *(978-1-62127-293-9(1))* Weigl Pubs., Inc.

—Guinea Pig. 2014. (Illus.). 24p. (J). *(978-1-62127-294-6(X))* Weigl Pubs., Inc.

—Hamster. 2011. (J). *(978-1-61690-923-9(4))*; *(978-1-61690-569-9(7))* Weigl Pubs., Inc.

—Hermit Crab. 2014. (J). *(978-1-4896-3098-8(8))* Weigl Pubs., Inc.

—Iguana. 2014. (Illus.). 24p. (J). *(978-1-62127-295-3(8))* Weigl Pubs., Inc.

—Rat. 2014. (J). *(978-1-4896-3102-2(X))* Weigl Pubs., Inc.

—Salamander. 2014. (J). *(978-1-4896-3106-0(2))* Weigl Pubs., Inc.

Carraway, Rose. Fun Frogs. 2012. (Pet Corner Ser.). (ENG.). 24p. (J). (gr. k-2). pap. 8.15 *(978-1-4339-6287-5(X))*; lib. bdg. 22.60 *(978-1-4339-6285-1(3))* Stevens, Gareth Publishing LLLP.

—Fun Frogs: Ranas Saltarinas. 2012. (Pet Corner / RincóN de Las Mascotas Ser.). (SPA & ENG.). 24p. (J). (gr. k-3). lib. bdg. 22.60 *(978-1-4339-6637-8(9))* Stevens, Gareth Publishing LLLP.

—Marvelous Mice. 2012. (Pet Corner Ser.). (ENG.). 24p. (J). (gr. k-2). pap. 8.15 *(978-1-4339-6299-8(3))*; lib. bdg. 22.60 *(978-1-4339-6297-4(7))* Stevens, Gareth Publishing LLLP.

—Marvelous Mice: Ratones Maravillosos. 2012. (Pet Corner / RincóN de Las Mascotas Ser.). (SPA & ENG., Illus.). 24p. (J). (gr. k-3). lib. bdg. 22.60 *(978-1-4339-6643-9(3))* Stevens, Gareth Publishing LLLP.

—Slithering Snakes. 2012. (Pet Corner Ser.). (ENG., Illus.). 24p. (J). (gr. k-2). pap. 8.15 *(978-1-4339-6303-2(5))*; lib. bdg. 22.60 *(978-1-4339-6301-8(9))* Stevens, Gareth Publishing LLLP.

—Slithering Snakes: Serpientes Resbaladizas. 2012. (Pet Corner / RincóN de Las Mascotas Ser.). (SPA & ENG.). 24p. (J). (gr. k-3). lib. bdg. 22.60 *(978-1-4339-6645-3(X))* Stevens, Gareth Publishing LLLP.

—Terrific Turtles. 2012. (Pet Corner Ser.). (ENG., Illus.). 24p. (J). (gr. k-2). pap. 8.15 *(978-1-4339-6311-7(6))*; lib. bdg. 22.60 *(978-1-4339-6309-4(4))* Stevens, Gareth Publishing LLLP.

—Terrific Turtles: Tortugas Asombrosas. 2012. (Pet Corner / RincóN de Las Mascotas Ser.). (SPA & ENG.). 24p. (J). (gr. k-3). lib. bdg. 22.60 *(978-1-4339-6647-7(6))* Stevens, Gareth Publishing LLLP.

Casado, Dami. Los Ruidos de Las Mascotas. 2005. (SPA.). 12p. 7.99 *(978-84-272-8293-3(1))* Molino, Editorial ESP. Dist: Santillana USA Publishing Co., Inc.

Chapman, J. Pet Pals: Learning the P Sound. 2009. (PowerPhonics Ser.). 24p. (gr. 1-1). 39.90 *(978-1-60851-467-0(6)*, PowerKids Pr.) Rosen Publishing Group, Inc., The.

Chin, Amanda. Pet's Playground: Playing Safe in a Dog-And-Cat World. Feldman, Luke, illus. 2009. 104p. (J). pap. 11.95 *(978-1-58326-115-6(X))* American Animal Hospital Assn. Pr.

Coates, Jennifer. Lizards. 2009. (Illus.). 112p. (J). 14.95 *(978-1-932904-39-0(5))* Eldorado Ink.

—Snakes. 2009. (Illus.). 112p. (J). 14.95 *(978-1-932904-41-3(7))* Eldorado Ink.

Collard, Sneed B., III. Insects: The Most Fun Bug Book Ever. 2017. (ENG., Illus.). 48p. (J). (gr. 4-7). lib. bdg. 17.99 *(978-1-58089-642-9(1))* Charlesbridge Publishing, Inc.

Collard, Sneed B. Sneed B. Collard III's Most Fun Book Ever about Lizards. 2012. (ENM & ENG., Illus.). 48p. (J). (gr. 4-7). pap. 7.95 *(978-1-58089-325-1(2))* Charlesbridge Publishing, Inc.

Color All About: A Giant Coloring Book about Loving Our Pets: Pets. 2004. (Illus.). 36p. (J). *(978-1-59949-002-1(1))* Food Marketing Consultants, Inc.

Colson, Mary. Pets Undercover! 2017. (Pets Undercover! Ser.). (ENG.). 32p. (gr. 2-4). 119.96 *(978-1-4109-8621-4(7)*, Read Me!) Heinemann-Raintree.

Colson, Rob. Ferret. 2017. (Pet to Get Ser.). (ENG., Illus.). 32p. (J). (gr. 4-6). pap. 12.99 *(978-0-7502-8958-0(9)*, Wayland) Hachette Children's Group GBR. Dist: Hachette Bk. Group.

—Lizard. 2017. (Pet to Get Ser.). (ENG., Illus.). 32p. (J). (gr. 4-6). pap. 12.99 *(978-0-7502-8930-6(9)*, Wayland) Hachette Children's Group GBR. Dist: Hachette Bk. Group.

—Rat. 2017. (Pet to Get Ser.). (ENG., Illus.). 32p. (J). (gr. 4-6). pap. 12.99 ***(978-0-7502-8929-0(5)***, Wayland) Hachette Children's Group GBR. Dist: Hachette Bk. Group.

—Snake. 2017. (Pet to Get Ser.). (ENG., Illus.). 32p. (J). (gr. 4-6). pap. 12.99 ***(978-0-7502-8933-7(3)***, Wayland) Hachette Children's Group GBR. Dist: Hachette Bk. Group.

Connolly, Randy, et al. Poison Ivy, Pets & People: Scratching the Poison Ivy, Oak & Sumac Itch. 2005. (10thingstoknow about ... Ser.). (Illus.). 104p. pap. 9.95 *(978-0-9722400-1-7(2))* 2Lakes Publishing.

Connors, Kathleen. What's It Like to Be the President's Pet? 2014. (White House Insiders Ser.). 24p. (J). (gr. 2-5). 22.60 *(978-1-4824-1105-8(9))* Stevens, Gareth Publishing LLLP.

Coppendale, Jane. The Ultimate Pet Guide. 2007. (J). spiral bd. *(978-1-59566-500-3(5))* QEB Publishing Inc.

Coppendale, Jean. Puppy. 2004. (QEB You & Your Pet Ser.). (Illus.). 32p. (J). lib. bdg. 15.95 *(978-1-59566-051-0(8))* QEB Publishing Inc.

Craats, Rennay. Caring for Your Frog. 2005. (Caring for Your Pet Ser.). (Illus.). 32p. (J). (gr. 4-7). per. 9.95 *(978-1-59036-218-1(7))*; lib. bdg. 26.00 *(978-1-59036-198-6(9))* Weigl Pubs., Inc.

—Caring for Your Gecko. (Caring for Your Pet Ser.). (Illus.). 32p. (J). 2005. (gr. -1-3). lib. bdg. 26.00 *(978-1-59036-119-1(9))* 2004. per. 9.95 *(978-1-59036-154-2(7))* Weigl Pubs., Inc.

—Caring for Your Snake. (Caring for Your Pet Ser.). (Illus.). 32p. (J). 2005. (gr. 4-7). per. 9.95 *(978-1-59036-216-7(0))* 2004. lib. bdg. 26.00 *(978-1-59036-196-2(2))* Weigl Pubs., Inc.

—Gecko. 2009. (My Pet Ser.). (Illus.). 32p. (J). (gr. 3-5). pap. 9.95 *(978-1-60596-099-9(3))*; lib. bdg. 26.00 *(978-1-60596-098-2(5))* Weigl Pubs., Inc.

Craats, Rennay & Gillespie, Katie. Gecko. 2015. (J). *(978-1-4896-2958-6(0))* Weigl Pubs., Inc.

Cryan, Mary Beth. BFF - Pets: Easy-to-Make Models to Share with Your Best Friend! 2013. (Dover Children's Activity Bks.). (ENG.). 16p. (J). (gr. 1-5). pap. 9.99 *(978-0-486-49113-4(7))* Dover Pubns., Inc.

Cunningham, Alan Blain, compiled by. Goodbye My Good Friend: Memories of Lost Animal Companions & Loved Ones. 2007. (ENG., Illus.). 112p. per. 15.95 *(978-0-9777072-2-5(5))* Agreka Bks., LLC.

Day, Trevor. Pets Parents Hate! [Scholastic]: Animal Life Cycles. 2011. (Extreme! Ser.). 32p. pap. 1.00 *(978-1-4296-6487-5(8)*, Fact Finders) Capstone Press of Coughlan Cos.

de Lambilly-Bresson, Elisabeth. Animales de la Casa. 2007. (Los animales nos cuentan su vida (Animal Show & Tell) Ser.). (SPA., Illus.). 16p. (gr. -1-3). lib. bdg. 19.00 *(978-0-8368-8102-8(8)*, Gareth Stevens Learning Library) Stevens, Gareth Publishing LLLP.

Denzer, Barbara. The Kids Guide to Petiquette: The Inside Scoop on Pet Behavior. 2007. (J). 7.95 *(978-0-9744749-2-2(4))* Crazy Pet Pr., The.

Denzer, Barbara & Denzer, Missy. The Crazy Kids Guide to Cooking for Your Pet: Recipes, Jokes, Pet Care Tips & Fun Things to Do with Your Pet Featuring the Back Bones of Character. Rodriguez, Manny, illus. 2004. 64p. (J). (gr. k-7). 12.95 *(978-0-9744749-0-8(8))* Crazy Pet Pr., The.

Deverell, Christine. Pop-up Pets. Deverell, Richard & King, Chris, illus. 2005. 12p. (J). (gr. k-4). reprint ed. 20.00 *(978-0-7567-8776-9(9))* DIANE Publishing Co.

Dils, Tracey E. My Pet & Me, 1,2,3: A Pets Counting Book. 2015. (1, 2, 3... Count with Me Ser.). (ENG., Illus.). 24p. (J). (gr. k-2). 19.95 *(978-1-60753-716-8(8))* Amicus Publishing.

Dobson, Starr. My Goat Gertrude, 1 vol. Dodwell, Dayle, illus. 2012. (ENG.). 32p. (J). (gr. -1-3). 18.95 *(978-1-55109-861-6(X))* Nimbus Publishing, Ltd. CAN. Dist: Orca Bk. Pubs. USA.

Domnauer, Teresa. Peculiar Pets. 2006. (Extreme Readers: Level 1 Ser.). (Illus.). 32p. (J). (gr. -1-3). 11.60 *(978-0-7569-6838-0(0))* Perfection Learning Corp.

Donner, Andrea, ed. What Pets Teach Us: Life's Lessons Learned from Our Best Friends. 2006. (ENG., Illus.). 32p. (J). (gr. -1-1). 12.95 *(978-1-59543-393-0(7))* Willow Creek Pr., Inc.

Dorling Kindersley Publishing Staff. Baby Pets! 2010. (ENG.). 16p. (J). (gr. -1 — 1). bds. 6.99 *(978-0-7566-7134-1(5)*, DK Children) Dorling Kindersley Publishing, Inc.

—Little Hide & Seek Pets. 2014. (ENG.). 16p. (J). (gr. -1 — 1). bds. 7.99 *(978-1-4654-2460-0(1)*, DK Children) Dorling Kindersley Publishing, Inc.

—My First Pets. 2016. (ENG., Illus.). 36p. (J). (— 1). bds. 5.99 *(978-1-4654-4489-9(0)*, DK Children) Dorling Kindersley Publishing, Inc.

—Noisy Pets Peekaboo! 2016. (ENG., Illus.). 12p. (J). (— 1). bds. 12.99 *(978-1-4654-4407-3(6)*, DK Children) Dorling Kindersley Publishing, Inc.

—Pet Party! 2016. (Ultimate Sticker Collections). (ENG.). 96p. (J). (gr. k-4). pap. 12.99 *(978-1-4654-5130-9(7)*, DK Children) Dorling Kindersley Publishing, Inc.

—Touch & Feel Pets. 2012. (Touch & Feel Ser.). (ENG.). 12p. (J). (gr. -1-k). bds. 6.99 *(978-0-7566-8990-2(2)*, DK Children) Dorling Kindersley Publishing, Inc.

—Ultimate Sticker Book: Pets. 2017. (Ultimate Sticker Bks.). (ENG.). 32p. (J). (gr. k-2). pap. 6.99 *(978-1-4654-6200-8(7)*, DK Children) Dorling Kindersley Publishing, Inc.

Doudna, Kelly. Bashful Ball Pythons, 1 vol. Nobens, C. A., illus. 2013. (Unusual Pets Ser.). (ENG.). 24p. (J). (gr. -1-3). 24.21 *(978-1-61783-397-7(5))* ABDO Publishing Co.

—Hilarious Hedgehogs, 1 vol. Nobens, C. A., illus. 2013. (Unusual Pets Ser.). (ENG.). 24p. (J). (gr. -1-3). 24.21 *(978-1-61783-399-1(1))* ABDO Publishing Co.

Dubke, Karon, et al. Pets up Close. 2014. (Pets up Close Ser.). (ENG.). 24p. (gr. k-1). 106.60 *(978-1-4914-0664-9(X)*, Pebble Plus) Capstone Press of Coughlan Cos.

Eck, Kristin. Animals in My House. 2004. (Look-And-Learn Books). (J). lib. bdg. 8.95 *(978-1-4042-2701-9(6)*, PowerKids Pr.) Rosen Publishing Group, Inc., The.

Ede, Lara. Press-Out & Play Pampered Pets. 2013. (ENG.). 18p. (J). pap. 4.99 *(978-1-78235-564-9(2))* Make Believe Ideas GBR. Dist: Nelson, Thomas Inc.

Editors of Silver Dolphin Books. Peek-A-Boo Sliders: Pets. Choux, Nathalie, illus. 2017. (Peek-A-Boo Sliders Ser.). (ENG.). 10p. (J). bds. 8.99 *(978-1-62686-768-0(2)*, Silver Dolphin Bks.) Readerlink Distribution Services, LLC.

Edwards, Nicola. A Pet. 2003. (Saying Goodbye to Ser.). (Illus.). 32p. (J). (gr. -1-2). lib. bdg. 16.95 *(978-1-932333-19-0(3))* Chrysalis Education.

Ellis, Carol. Hamsters & Gerbils. 2008. (Great Pets Ser.). 48p. (gr. 3-18). lib. bdg. 29.93 *(978-0-7614-2999-9(9)*, Benchmark Bks.) Marshall Cavendish Corp.

Feldman, Thea. ASPCA Mix & Match Pets: A Colors & Counting Book. 2015. (Mix & Match Ser.: 1). (ENG.). 12p. (J). (gr. -1-k). 8.99 *(978-0-7944-3299-7(9)*, Reader's Digest Children's Bks.) Studio Fun International.

Ferguson, Jennifer. Unwanted Litter. 2010. 68p. pap. 37.37 *(978-1-4535-3471-7(7))* Xlibris Corp.

Ferri, Francesca. Peek-a-Boo Pets. Ferri, Francesca, illus. 2009. (ENG., Illus.). 8p. (J). (gr. -1-k). 8.99 *(978-0-7641-6971-7(8))* Barron's Educational Series, Inc.

Ferry, April. All Sorts of Pets. 2016. (1-3Y Animals Ser.). (ENG., Illus.). 16p. (J). pap. 5.99 ***(978-1-63437-598-6(X))*** American Reading Co.

Fiorella, Christina. My Boy Kyle. 2010. 20p. 13.99 *(978-1-4520-6519-9(5))* AuthorHouse.

Fleury, Rick & Staehr, Linda. Rainbows for Buckerou. 2013. 24p. pap. 10.95 *(978-1-4497-8775-2(4)*, WestBow Pr.) Author Solutions, Inc.

Foran, Jill. Caring for Your Dog. Marshall, Diana & Nault, Jennifer, eds. 2003. (Caring for Your Pet Ser.). (Illus.). 32p. (J). pap. 9.95 *(978-1-59036-063-7(X))* Weigl Pubs., Inc.

—Caring for Your Guinea Pig. 2004. (Caring for Your Pet Ser.). (Illus.). 32p. (J). per. 9.95 *(978-1-59036-151-1(2))*; lib. bdg. 26.00 *(978-1-59036-116-0(4))* Weigl Pubs., Inc.

—Caring for Your Hamster. Marshall, Diana & Nault, Jennifer, eds. 2003. (Caring for Your Pet Ser.). (Illus.). 32p. (J). pap. 9.95 *(978-1-59036-066-8(4))* Weigl Pubs., Inc.

—Caring for Your Rabbit. Marshall, Diana & Nault, Jennifer, eds. 2003. (Caring for Your Pet Ser.). (Illus.). 32p. (J). pap. 9.95 *(978-1-59036-064-4(8))* Weigl Pubs., Inc.

Foran, Jill & Gillespie, Katie. Guinea Pig. 2015. (J). *(978-1-4896-2962-3(9))* Weigl Pubs., Inc.

Fortuna, Lois. Caring for a Pet. 2016. (We Can Do It! Ser.). (ENG., Illus.). 24p. (J). (gr. k-k). pap. 8.15 *(978-1-4824-3795-9(3))* Stevens, Gareth Publishing LLLP.

Frattini, Stephane. Face-to-Face with the Cat. Klein, Jean-Louis & Hubert, Marie-Luce, illus. 2004. (Face to Face Ser.). 28p. (J). 9.95 *(978-1-57091-454-6(0))* Charlesbridge Publishing, Inc.

Fretland VanVoorst, Jenny. Therapy Cats, Dogs, & Rabbits. 2013. (We Work! Animals with Jobs Ser.). 24p. (J). (gr. -1-3). lib. bdg. 21.32 *(978-1-61772-895-2(0))* Bearport Publishing Co., Inc.

Funny Faces: Wacky Pets. (J). *(978-1-86091-113-2(7)*, 91) Standard International Media.

Gagne, Tammy. Care for a Pet Hedgehog. 2009. (How to Convince Your Parents You Can ... Ser.). 32p. (J). (gr. 1-4). 25.70 *(978-1-58415-798-4(4))* Mitchell Lane Pubs., Inc.

—Care for a Wolfdog. 2009. (How to Convince Your Parents You Can ... Ser.). 32p. (J). (gr. 1-4). 25.70 *(978-1-58415-796-0(8))* Mitchell Lane Pubs., Inc.

Gaines, Ann. Kids Top 10 Pet Reptiles & Amphibians. 2015. (American Humane Association Top 10 Pets for Kids Ser.). 48p. (J). (gr. 3-4). 25.27 *(978-0-7660-6645-8(2)* Enslow Pubs., Inc.

—Kids Top 10 Small Mammal Pets. 2015. (American Humane Association Top 10 Pets for Kids Ser.). 48p. (J). (gr. 3-4). 25.27 *(978-0-7660-6650-2(9))* Enslow Pubs., Inc.

Gaines, Ann Graham. Kids Top 10 Pet Reptiles & Amphibians. 2015. (American Humane Association Top 10 Pets for Kids Ser.). 48p. (J). (gr. 3-4). pap. 8.95 *(978-0-7660-6646-5(0)*, Enslow Elementary) Enslow Pubs., Inc.

—Kids Top 10 Small Mammal Pets. 2015. (American Humane Association Top 10 Pets for Kids Ser.). 48p. (J). (gr. 3-4). pap. 8.95 *(978-0-7660-6651-9(7)*, Enslow Elementary) Enslow Pubs., Inc.

—Top 10 Small Mammals for Kids. 2008. (Top Pets for Kids with American Humane Ser.). (Illus.). 48p. (J). (gr. 3-4). lib. bdg. 25.27 *(978-0-7660-3075-6(X)*, Enslow Elementary) Enslow Pubs., Inc.

Galvin, Laura & McCune, Jamie. I Love My Pet. 2011. (ENG.). 16p. (J). 6.95 *(978-1-60727-286-1(5))* Soundprints.

Ganeri, Anita. Nibble's Guide to Caring for Your Hamster, 1 vol. Peterson, Rick, illus. 2013. (Pets' Guides). (ENG.). 32p. (gr. 1-3). pap. 8.29 *(978-1-4329-7140-3(9))*; lib. bdg. 27.32 *(978-1-4329-7133-5(6))* Heinemann-Raintree. (Heinemann First Library).

Ganeri, Anita & Peterson, Rick. Pets' Guides. 2013. (Pets' Guides). (ENG.). 32p. (gr. 1-3). pap. 47.94 *(978-1-4329-7143-4(3))*; lib. bdg. 163.92 *(978-1-4329-7136-6(0))* Heinemann-Raintree. (Heinemann First Library).

Gardeski, Christina Mia. Hamsters: Questions & Answers. 2016. (Pet Questions & Answers Ser.). (ENG., Illus.). 24p. (gr. k-1). lib. bdg. 26.65 *(978-1-5157-0352-5(5)*, Pebble Plus) Capstone Press of Coughlan Cos.

—Pet Questions & Answers. 2016. (Pet Questions & Answers Ser.). (ENG.). 24p. (gr. k-1). 159.90 *(978-1-5157-0713-4(X)*, Pebble Plus) Capstone Press of Coughlan Cos.

—Pet Rabbits: Questions & Answers. 2016. (Pet Questions & Answers Ser.). (ENG., Illus.). 24p. (gr. k-1). lib. bdg. 26.65 *(978-1-5157-0342-6(8)*, Pebble Plus) Capstone Press of Coughlan Cos.

Garwood, Mary. Pawprints upon My Heart II: The Journey Continues. 2004. 132p. (J). per. 11.95 *(978-0-9714086-3-0(7))* Tarbutton Pr.

George, Chris. Pets Are Fun. 2017. (Early Concepts Ser.). 24p. (gr. 4-6). pap. 8.25 ***(978-1-5081-6221-6(2)***, PowerKids Pr.) Rosen Publishing Group, Inc., The.

Gintrac, Brigitte. Let's Play with Lou. 2010. 24p. pap. 15.95 *(978-1-4389-5243-7(0))* AuthorHouse.

Glaser, Rebecca. Bunnies Hop. 2017. (Amicus Ink Board Bks.). (ENG., Illus.). 14p. (J). (gr. -1 — 1). bds. 7.99 ***(978-1-68152-199-2(7))*** Amicus.

—Fish Swim. 2017. (Amicus Ink Board Bks.). (ENG., Illus.). 14p. (J). (gr. -1 — 1). bds. 7.99 ***(978-1-68152-198-5(9))*** Amicus.

—Kittens Pounce. 2017. (Amicus Ink Board Bks.). (ENG., Illus.). 14p. (J). (gr. -1 — 1). bds. 7.99 ***(978-1-68152-197-8(0))*** Amicus.

—Puppies Chase. 2017. (Amicus Ink Board Bks.). (ENG., Illus.). 14p. (J). (gr. -1 — 1). bds. 7.99 ***(978-1-68152-196-1(2))*** Amicus.

Graubart, Norman D. Mi Hmster / My Hamster, 1 vol., 1. Green, Christina, ed. 2014. (¡Las Mascotas Son Geniales! / Pets Are Awesome! Ser.). (SPA & BYN.). 24p. (J). (gr. k-2). 23.60 *(978-1-4777-3313-4(2)*, PowerKids Pr.) Rosen Publishing Group, Inc., The.

—Mi Tortuga / My Turtle, 1 vol., 1. Green, Christina, ed. 2014. (¡Las Mascotas Son Geniales! / Pets Are Awesome! Ser.).

P
Q
R

(SPA & BYN.). 24p. (J). (gr. k-2). 23.60 (978-1-4777-3316-5(7), PowerKids Pr.) Rosen Publishing Group, Inc., The.

—My Hamster, 1 vol., 1. 2014. (Pets Are Awesome! Ser.). (ENG.). 24p. (J). (gr. k-2). 23.60 (978-1-4777-2868-0(6), PowerKids Pr.) Rosen Publishing Group, Inc., The.

—My Turtle, 1 vol., 1. 2014. (Pets Are Awesome! Ser.). (ENG.). 24p. (J). (gr. k-2). 23.60 (978-1-4777-2869-7(4), PowerKids Pr.) Rosen Publishing Group, Inc., The.

Gray, Elizabeth. A Giraffe for a Pet, 1 vol. Valente, Christa, illus. 2010. 16p. 24.95 (978-1-4489-6515-1(2)) PublishAmerica, Inc.

Graziano, John, illus. Woof! Funny Pet Stories. 2012. 96p. (J). pap. (978-0-545-38687-6(X)) Ripley Entertainment, Inc.

Great Pets, 5 bks., Set. Incl. Hamsters & Gerbils. Ellis, Carol. lib. bdg. 29.93 (978-0-7614-2999-9(9)); Lizards. Bjorklund, Ruth. lib. bdg. 29.93 (978-0-7614-2997-5(2)); Parrots. Haney, Johannah. lib. bdg. 29.93 (978-0-7614-2998-2(0)); Small Dogs. Hart, Joyce. (YA). lib. bdg. 29.93 (978-0-7614-2995-1(6)); Snakes. Hart, Joyce. lib. bdg. 29.93 (978-0-7614-2996-8(4)); 48p. (gr. 3-18). 2008. Set lib. bdg. 149.64 (978-0-7614-2994-4(8)); Set lib. bdg. 149.64 (978-0-7614-2706-3(6)) Marshall Cavendish Corp. (Benchmark Bks.).

Green, Gail. The Kids' Guide to Projects for Your Pet, 1 vol. 2012. (Kids' Guides). (ENG.). 32p. (gr. 3-4). lib. bdg. 27.99 (978-1-4296-7662-5(0), Edge Bks.) Capstone Press of Coughlan Cos.

Greenwell, Jessica. Pets Sticker Book. 2011. (First Sticker Books Ser.). 16p. (J). pap. 6.99 (978-0-7945-2995-6(X), Usborne) EDC Publishing.

Greve, Meg & Sturm, Jeanne. Mi Mascota: Pet Tricks. 2008. (ENG & SPA., Illus.). 24p. (J). 19.44 (978-1-60472-507-0(9)) Rourke Educational Media.

Grossi, Craig. Craig & Fred: the True Story of a Marine & His Dog. 2017. 256p. (J). (gr. 3). 16.99 **(978-0-06-269335-8(2))** HarperCollins Pubs.

Gunderson, Megan M. Australian Shepherds, 1 vol. 2013. (Dogs Set 10 Ser.). (ENG.). 24p. (J). (gr. 3-6). lib. bdg. 25.65 (978-1-61783-588-9(9), Checkerboard Library) ABDO Publishing Co.

—Scottish Deerhounds, 1 vol. 2013. (Dogs Set 10 Ser.). (ENG.). 24p. (J). (gr. 3-6). lib. bdg. 25.65 (978-1-61783-592-6(7), Checkerboard Library) ABDO Publishing Co.

—Whippets, 1 vol. 2013. (Dogs Set 10 Ser.). (ENG.). 24p. (J). (gr. 3-6). lib. bdg. 25.65 (978-1-61783-593-3(5), Checkerboard Library) ABDO Publishing Co.

Gunzi, Christane. Pets. 2nd rev. ed. 2015. (ENG., Illus.). 34p. (J). 7.99 (978-1-906572-13-6(5)) Award Pubns. Ltd. GBR. Dist: Parkwest Pubns., Inc.

Gunzi, Christiane. Friendly Pets. 2007. (Feels Real Ser.). (ENG., Illus.). 10p. (J). (gr. -1-k). bds. 5.99 (978-0-7641-6024-0(9)) Barron's Educational Series, Inc.

Hamilton, Lynn. Caring for Your Bird. 2003. (Caring for Your Pet Ser.). (Illus.). 32p. (J). (gr. -1-3). lib. bdg. 26.00 (978-1-59036-037-8(0)) Weigl Pubs., Inc.

—Caring for Your Ferret. (Caring for Your Pet Ser.). (Illus.). 32p. (J). 2007. per. 9.95 (978-1-59036-150-4(4)) 2004. lib. bdg. 26.00 (978-1-59036-115-3(6)) Weigl Pubs., Inc.

—Caring for Your Fish. 2005. (Caring for Your Pet Ser.). (Illus.). 32p. (J). (gr. 4-7). lib. bdg. 26.00 (978-1-59036-035-4(4)) Weigl Pubs., Inc.

—Caring for Your Turtle. 2004. (Caring for Your Pet Ser.). (Illus.). 32p. (J). per. 9.95 (978-1-59036-153-5(9)) Weigl Pubs., Inc.

—Ferret. 2009. (My Pet Ser.). (Illus.). 32p. (J). (gr. 3-5). pap. 9.95 (978-1-60596-097-5(7)); lib. bdg. 26.00 (978-1-60596-096-8(9)) Weigl Pubs., Inc.

—Turtle. 2009. (My Pet Ser.). (Illus.). 32p. (J). (gr. 3-5). lib. bdg. 26.00 (978-1-60596-088-3(8)) Weigl Pubs., Inc.

—Turtle: My Pet. 2009. (Illus.). 32p. (J). pap. 9.95 (978-1-60596-089-0(6)) Weigl Pubs., Inc.

Hamilton, Lynn & Gillespie, Katie. Ferret. 2015. (J). (978-1-4896-2954-8(8)) Weigl Pubs., Inc.

—Turtle. 2015. (J). (978-1-4896-2974-6(2)) Weigl Pubs., Inc.

Hamilton, Lynn A. Caring for Your Bird. Marshall, Diana & Nault, Jennifer, eds. 2003. (Caring for Your Pet Ser.). (Illus.). 32p. (J). pap. 9.95 (978-1-59036-067-5(2)) Weigl Pubs., Inc.

—Caring for Your Fish. Kissock, Heather & Marshall, Diana, eds. 2003. (Caring for Your Pet Ser.). (Illus.). 32p. (J). pap. 9.95 (978-1-59036-065-1(6)) Weigl Pubs., Inc.

—Caring for Your Turtle. 2005. (Caring for Your Pet Ser.). (Illus.). 32p. (J). (gr. -1-3). lib. bdg. 26.00 (978-1-59036-118-4(0)) Weigl Pubs., Inc.

Hamilton, S. L. Bugs. 2013. (Xtreme Pets Ser.). (Illus.). 32p. (J). (gr. 3-9). lib. bdg. 27.07 (978-1-61783-970-2(1), Abdo & Daughters) ABDO Publishing Co.

—Cats. 2013. (Xtreme Pets Ser.). (Illus.). 32p. (J). (gr. 3-9). lib. bdg. 27.07 (978-1-61783-971-9(X), Abdo & Daughters) ABDO Publishing Co.

—Dogs. 2013. (Xtreme Pets Ser.). (Illus.). 32p. (J). (gr. 3-9). lib. bdg. 27.07 (978-1-61783-972-6(8), Abdo & Daughters) ABDO Publishing Co.

—Fish. 2013. (Xtreme Pets Ser.). (Illus.). 32p. (J). (gr. 3-9). lib. bdg. 27.07 (978-1-61783-973-3(6), Abdo & Daughters) ABDO Publishing Co.

—Reptiles. 2013. (Xtreme Pets Ser.). (Illus.). 32p. (J). (gr. 3-9). lib. bdg. 27.07 (978-1-61783-974-0(4), Abdo & Daughters) ABDO Publishing Co.

—Spiders. 2013. (Xtreme Pets Ser.). (Illus.). 32p. (J). (gr. 3-9). lib. bdg. 27.07 (978-1-61783-975-7(2), Abdo & Daughters) ABDO Publishing Co.

Hammond, Charmaine. Toby, the Pet Therapy Dog, & His Hospital Friends. Prevac, Rose Anne, illus. 2011. (ENG.). 36p. (J). pap. 12.99 (978-0-9836045-0-1(9), Kendahl Hse. Pr.) Youngs, Bettie Bks.

—Toby, the Pet Therapy Dog, Says Be a Buddy, Not a Bully. 2013. (ENG., Illus.). 34p. (J). pap. 12.99 (978-0-9836045-4-9(1)) Youngs, Bettie Bks.

—Toby, the Pet Therapy Dog, Says Be a Buddy Not a Bully. Prevec, Rose Anne, illus. 2013. (ENG.). (J). pap. 12.95 (978-0-9836045-5-6(X), Kendahl Hse. Pr.) Youngs, Bettie Bks.

Haney, Johannah. Ferrets. 2009. (Great Pets 3 Ser.). 48p. (gr. 3). lib. bdg. 29.93 (978-0-7614-4153-3(0)) Marshall Cavendish Corp.

Harasymiw, Mark. Alligators Are Not Pets! 2013. (When Pets Attack! Ser.). 32p. (J). (gr. 3-6). pap. 10.50 (978-1-4339-9279-7(5)) Stevens, Gareth Publishing LLLP.

Harasymiw, Mark & Harasymiw, Mark J. Alligators Are Not Pets! 2013. 32p. (J). (gr. 3-6). 26.60 (978-1-4339-9278-0(7)) Stevens, Gareth Publishing LLLP.

Harpan, Gaile. True Puppy Tails. 2010. 24p. pap. 12.95 (978-1-936343-26-3(6)) Peppertree Pr., The.

Harrington, Jane. Extreme Pets. 2007. (ENG., Illus.). 164p. (J). (gr. 2-5). pap., instr.'s hndbk. ed. 12.99 (978-0-439-82948-9(8)) Scholastic, Inc.

Harrison, Megan Bernadette. Fears, Tears, & Laughter: The Adventures of Kitty Tom & Blossom Book Two, 1 vol. 2010. 48p. pap. 24.95 (978-1-4489-9314-7(8)) PublishAmerica, Inc.

Harrison, Paul. My Pet. 2011. (Window on the World Ser.). (Illus.). 32p. (978-1-84089-662-6(0)) Zero to Ten, Ltd.

Hart, Joyce. Snakes. 2008. (Great Pets Ser.). 48p. (gr. 3-18). lib. bdg. 29.93 (978-0-7614-2996-8(4), Benchmark Bks.) Marshall Cavendish Corp.

Harte, May. Hide-and-Seek Pets. 2004. (Hide-And-Seek Books). (J). lib. bdg. 21.25 (978-1-4042-2815-3(2), PowerKids Pr.) Rosen Publishing Group, Inc., The.

—Hide & Seek Pets. 2009. (Tough Toddler Bks). 16p. (gr. k-k). 42.50 (978-1-60854-572-8(5), PowerKids Pr.) Rosen Publishing Group, Inc., The.

Head, Honor. Cats & Kittens. 2007. (QEB Know Your Pet Ser.). (Illus.). 32p. lib. bdg. 19.95 (978-1-59566-217-0(0)) QEB Publishing Inc.

—Horses & Ponies. 2007. (QEB Know Your Pet Ser.). (Illus.). 32p. (J). lib. bdg. 19.95 (978-1-59566-219-4(7)) QEB Publishing Inc.

Healing Your Heart When Your Animal Friend Is Gone: A Children's Pet Bereavement Workbook. 2004. (J). 14.95 (978-0-9748512-0-4(5)) Bree's Gift Publishing.

Heathcote, Peter. Lizards, 1 vol. 2nd ed. 2010. (Keeping Unusual Pets Ser.). (ENG., Illus.). 48p. (gr. 3-6). 32.65 (978-1-4329-3853-6(3), NA-h) Heinemann-Raintree.

Heighton, Mary Beth & Laskey, Andrew. What I Do When You're Not Home, 1 vol. 2009. 38p. pap. 24.95 (978-1-60813-167-9(X)) America Star Bks.

Heinemann Educational Ltd. Publishing Staff. The Wild Side of Pets Package. 2004. pap. 243.00 (978-1-4109-1387-6(2)) Harcourt Schl. Pubs.

Heneghan, Judith. Love Your Hamster. 2013. (Your Perfect Pet Ser.). (ENG., Illus.). 32p. (gr. k-5). 25.25 (978-1-4777-0186-7(9)); pap. 10.00 (978-1-4777-0200-0(8)) Windmill Bks.

Heos, Bridget. Do You Really Want a Guinea Pig? Longhi, Katya, illus. 2015. (Do You Really Want a Pet? Ser.). (ENG.). 24p. (J). (gr. 1-3). 19.95 (978-1-60753-749-6(4)) Amicus Publishing.

—Do You Really Want a Lizard? Longhi, Katya, illus. 2015. (Do You Really Want a Pet? Ser.). (ENG.). 24p. (J). (gr. 1-3). 19.95 (978-1-60753-750-2(8)) Amicus Publishing.

—Do You Really Want a Turtle? Longhi, Katya, illus. 2015. (Do You Really Want a Pet? Ser.). (ENG.). 24p. (J). (gr. 1-3). 19.95 (978-1-60753-752-6(4)) Amicus Publishing.

Herglotz, Pam Herglotz. Ichabod & the Chipmunks. 2010. 40p. pap. 17.91 (978-0-557-19218-2(8)) Lulu Pr., Inc.

Hernandez-Divers, Sonia. Geckos, 1 vol. 2nd ed. 2010. (Keeping Unusual Pets Ser.). (ENG., Illus.). 48p. (gr. 3-6). 32.65 (978-1-4329-3849-9(5), NA-h) Heinemann-Raintree.

—Snakes, 1 vol. 2nd ed. 2010. (Keeping Unusual Pets Ser.). (ENG., Illus.). 48p. (gr. 3-6). 32.65 (978-1-4329-3851-2(7), NA-h) Heinemann-Raintree.

Herriot, James. James Herriot's Treasury for Children: Warm & Joyful Tales by the Author of All Creatures Great & Small. Brown, Ruth & Barrett, Peter, illus. 2014. (ENG.). 272p. (J). (gr. -1-3). 24.99 (978-1-250-05813-3(9), 9781250058133, St. Martin's Griffin) St. Martin's Pr.

Hibbert, Clare. Hamster. 2004. (Illus.). 32p. (J). lib. bdg. 27.10 (978-1-58340-433-1(3)) Black Rabbit Bks.

Highlights for Children, compiled by. Playful Pets. 2009. (Hidden Pictures Playground Ser.). (ENG., Illus.). 32p. (J). (gr. -1-1). pap. 5.49 (978-0-87534-318-1(X)) Highlights for Children.

Highlights for Children Editorial Staff, compiled by. All about Pets. 2016. (All about Activity Bks.). (ENG.). 32p. (J). (gr. -1-k). pap. 4.99 (978-1-62979-541-6(0), Highlights) Boyds Mills Pr.

Hile, Lori. Animal Survival. 2011. (Extreme Survival Ser.). (ENG.). 56p. (gr. 5-5). pap. 9.49 (978-1-4109-3980-7(4), Raintree Freestyle) Heinemann-Raintree.

Hodge, Susie. Artists & Their Pets: True Stories of Famous Artists & Their Animal Friends. Lemay, Violet, illus. 2017. (ENG.). 192p. (J). (gr. 2-5). 14.95 **(978-1-946064-01-1(7))** Duo Pr. LLC.

Holden, Pam. Look after Pets. 2015. (ENG., Illus.). 16p. (-1). pap. (978-1-77654-115-7(4), Red Rocket Readers) Flying Start Bks.

HOP, LLC. Hooked on Animals Pets Super Activity Kit. 2006. (J). (gr. -1). 9.99 (978-1-933863-20-7(X)) HOP, LLC.

How to Choose a Pet: Individual Title Six-Packs. (Discovery World Ser.). 24p. (gr. 1-2). 33.00 (978-0-7635-8475-7(4)) Rigby Education.

Hunt, James. I Have a New Puppy! Now What? A Puppy Survival Guide for Kids. Dickens, Christina, illus. 2007. (Fireman James & Flame Ser.). 40p. (J). (gr. 1-3). 14.99 (978-0-9769401-0-4(8)) Hunt, J. L. Publishing.

Hutmacher, Kimberly M. I Want a Pet. 2012. (I Want a Pet Ser.). (ENG.). 24p. (gr. k-1). lib. bdg. 106.60 (978-1-4296-8116-2(0), Pebble Plus) Capstone Press of Coughlan Cos.

Hyland, Tony & Scarborough, Kate. Killer Pets. 2012. (Fast Facts Ser.). 32p. (gr. 4-6). pap. 28.50 (978-1-59771-327-6(9)) Sea-To-Sea Pubns.

Ikids Staff & Francis, Guy. Pets. 2009. (ENG., Illus.). 10p. (J). (gr. -1-1). 15.99 (978-1-58476-940-8(8)) Innovative Kids.

Ipcizade, Catherine. BIG Pets. 2010. (Big Ser.). (ENG.). 24p. (gr. k-1). lib. bdg. 26.65 (978-1-4296-3997-2(0), Pebble Plus) Capstone Press of Coughlan Cos.

Jeffrey, Laura S. Birds: How to Choose & Care for a Bird. 2004. (American Humane Pet Care Library). (Illus.). 48p. (J). (gr. 3-4). lib. bdg. 25.27 (978-0-7660-2515-8(2)) Enslow Pubs., Inc.

—Cats: How to Choose & Care for a Cat. 2004. (American Humane Pet Care Library). (Illus.). 48p. (J). lib. bdg. 25.27 (978-0-7660-2516-5(0)) Enslow Pubs., Inc.

—Choosing a Hamster, Gerbil, Guinea Pig, Rabbit, Ferret, Mouse, or Rat: How to Choose & Care for a Small Mammal. 2013. (American Humane Association Pet Care Ser.). 48p. (J). (gr. 3-18). lib. bdg. 25.27 (978-0-7660-4082-3(8)); pap. 8.95 (978-1-4644-0217-3(5), Enslow Elementary) Enslow Pubs., Inc.

—Dogs: How to Choose & Care for a Dog. 2004. (American Humane Pet Care Library). (Illus.). 48p. (J). lib. bdg. 25.27 (978-0-7660-2520-2(9)) Enslow Pubs., Inc.

—Fish: How to Choose & Care for a Fish. 2004. (American Humane Pet Care Library). (Illus.). 48p. (J). lib. bdg. 25.27 (978-0-7660-2517-2(9)) Enslow Pubs., Inc.

—Hamsters, Gerbils, Guinea Pigs, Rabbits, Ferrets, Mice, & Rats: How to Choose & Care for a Small Mammal. 2004. (American Humane Pet Care Library). (Illus.). 48p. (J). lib. bdg. 25.27 (978-0-7660-2518-9(7)) Enslow Pubs., Inc.

—Horses: How to Choose & Care for a Horse. 2004. (American Humane Pet Care Library). (Illus.). 48p. (J). lib. bdg. 25.27 (978-0-7660-2519-6(5)) Enslow Pubs., Inc.

Johnson, J. Angelique. Getting a Pet, Step by Step, 1 vol. 2011. (Step-By-Step Stories Ser.). (ENG.). 32p. (gr. 1-2). lib. bdg. 27.32 (978-1-4296-6024-2(4), Aplus Bks.) Capstone Press of Coughlan Cos.

Johnson, Jinny. Guinea Pig. 2014. (My New Pet Ser.). 24p. (gr. k-3). lib. bdg. 28.50 (978-1-62588-029-1(4)) Black Rabbit Bks.

—Hamster & Gerbil. 2014. (My New Pet Ser.). 24p. (gr. k-3). lib. bdg. 28.50 (978-1-62588-030-7(8)) Black Rabbit Bks.

Jojo. Landon Wants a Puppy. 2009. 68p. pap. 26.99 (978-1-4389-4656-6(2)) AuthorHouse.

Jones, Tammy. Big Pet, Little Pet. 2009. (Sight Word Readers Set A Ser.). (J). 3.49 net. (978-1-60719-153-7(9)) Newmark Learning LLC.

—My Pet. 2009. (Sight Word Readers Set A Ser.). (J). 3.49 net. (978-1-60719-145-2(8)) Newmark Learning LLC.

Kadylak, Shirley. Cody's New Pet. 2012. 32p. pap. 15.95 (978-1-4497-5986-5(6), WestBow Pr.) Author Solutions, Inc.

Kain, Kathleen. All about Pets. Miyake, Yoshi, illus. 2004. (Treasure Tree Ser.). 32p. (J). (978-0-7166-1626-9(2)) World Bk., Inc.

Kaleta, Don. Puppy Scents: The Kids' Guide to Puppy Care. Habel, Helen, illus. 2010. (ENG.). 72p. (J). pap. 17.95 (978-0-615-39881-5(2)) Kaleta Publishing, LLC.

Kalman, Bobbie. Baby Pets. 2012. (ENG., Illus.). 24p. (J). (978-0-7787-4075-9(7)); pap. (978-0-7787-4080-3(3)) Crabtree Publishing Co.

—My Big & Small Pets. 2010. (My World Ser.). (ENG., Illus.). 16p. (J). (gr. k-2). (978-0-7787-9426-4(1)); pap. (978-0-7787-9470-7(9)) Crabtree Publishing Co.

Kalman, Bobbie & MacAulay, Kelley. Les Cochons D'Inde. 2011. (FRE., Illus.). 32p. (J). pap. 9.95 (978-2-89579-391-5(3)) Bayard Canada CAN. Dist: Crabtree Publishing Co.

—Guinea Pigs. Crabtree, Marc, illus. Crabtree, Marc, photos by. 2003. (Pet Care Ser.). (ENG.). 32p. (J). lib. bdg. (978-0-7787-1755-3(0)) Crabtree Publishing Co.

Karwoski, Gail Langer. Terriers: Loyal Hunting Companions, 1 vol. 2013. (Hunting Dogs Ser.). (ENG.). 32p. (gr. 3-4). lib. bdg. 27.99 (978-1-4296-9989-1(2), Edge Bks.) Capstone Press of Coughlan Cos.

Kawa, Katie. Furry Hamsters. 2011. (Pet Corner Ser.). (Illus.). 24p. (J). (gr. k-2). pap. 8.15 (978-1-4339-5605-8(5)); lib. bdg. 22.60 (978-1-4339-5603-4(9)) Stevens, Gareth Publishing LLLP.

—Furry Hamsters: Hámsteres Peludos. 2011. (Pet Corner / RincóN de Las Mascotas Ser.). (SPA., Illus.). 24p. (J). (gr. k-3). lib. bdg. 22.60 (978-1-4339-5607-2(1)) Stevens, Gareth Publishing LLLP.

Kennedy, Marge. Pets at the White House. 2009. (Scholastic News Nonfiction Readers Ser.). (ENG.). 24p. (J). (gr. 1-2). pap. 6.95 (978-0-531-22433-5(3)) Scholastic Library Publishing.

Khan, Sarah. Pets Lift-the-Flap. 2005. (Luxury Lift-the-Flap Learners Ser.). 16p. (J). (gr. 1-18). 11.95 (978-0-7945-0914-9(2), Usborne) EDC Publishing.

Kingfisher Editors, ed. Animal Babies Around the House. 2005. (Animal Babies Ser.). (ENG., Illus.). 24p. (J). (gr. -1-k). bds. 6.99 (978-0-7534-5840-2(3), 9780753458402, Kingfisher) Roaring Brook Pr.

Korte, Steve. DC Super-Pets Character Encyclopedia, 1 vol. Baltazar, Art, illus. 2013. (DC Super-Pets Ser.). (ENG.). 128p. (gr. 1-3). 26.60 (978-1-4795-2030-5(6), DC Super-Pets) Picture Window Bks.

Kramer, Nash. How Many Pets Do You Have? 2014. (Little Books of Answers: Level C Ser.). (Illus.). 16p. (gr. k-2). pap. 7.95 (978-1-927136-20-1(2)) Three Crows Media NZL. Dist: RiverStream Publishing.

Kulka, Joe, illus. My Crocodile Does Not Bite. 2013. (ENG.). 32p. (J). (gr. k-3). lib. bdg. 16.95 (978-0-7613-8937-8(7), Carolrhoda Bks.) Lerner Publishing Group.

Kuskowski, Alex. Portly Potbellied Pigs, 1 vol. Nobens, C. A., illus. 2013. (Unusual Pets Ser.). (ENG.). 24p. (J). (gr. -1-3). 24.21 (978-1-61783-401-1(7)) ABDO Publishing Co.

—Super Simple Pet Critter Crafts: Fun & Easy Animal Crafts. 2016. (ENG., Illus.). 32p. (J). (978-1-68078-163-2(4)) ABDO Publishing Co.

—Tricky Tarantulas, 1 vol. Nobens, C. A., illus. 2013. (Unusual Pets Ser.). (ENG.). 24p. (J). (gr. -1-3). 24.21 (978-1-61783-402-8(5)) ABDO Publishing Co.

Ladybird. Favourite Pets. 2016. (Read It Yourself with Ladybird Ser.). (ENG.). 32p. (J). 5.99 (978-0-241-23734-2(3)) Penguin Bks., Ltd. GBR. Dist: Independent Pubs. Group.

—Favourite Pets, Level 1. 2016. (Read It Yourself with Ladybird Ser.). (ENG.). 32p. (J). (gr. 2-4). pap. 9.99 (978-0-241-23732-8(7)) Penguin Bks., Ltd. GBR. Dist: Independent Pubs. Group.

Lawrence-Loughlin, Amy. For the Love of Gus: A True Rescue to Riches Tale. 2012. 36p. pap. 15.49 (978-1-4669-5371-0(3)) Trafford Publishing.

Leavitt, Amie Jane. Care for a Pet Sugar Glider. 2009. (How to Convince Your Parents You Can ... Ser.). (Illus.). 32p. (J). (gr. 1-4). lib. bdg. 25.70 (978-1-58415-800-4(X)) Mitchell Lane Pubs., Inc.

Lee, Lynne. Bramble'S Story. 2009. 60p. pap. 19.99 (978-1-60693-427-2(9), Eloquent Bks.) Strategic Book Publishing & Rights Agency (SBPRA).

Let's Get a Pet! 2017. (Let's Get a Pet! Ser.). 24p. (gr. 1-2). pap. 48.90 **(978-1-5382-0201-2(8))**; lib. bdg. 135.60 **(978-1-5382-0200-5(X))** Stevens, Gareth Publishing LLLP.

Lim, Annalees. Pet Crafts, 01 vols., 1. 2016. (Creating Creature Crafts Ser.). (ENG., Illus.). 24p. (J). pap. 10.60 (978-1-5081-9109-4(3), 1397691, Windmill Bks.) Rosen Publishing Group, Inc., The.

Linde, Barbara M. Snakes Are Not Pets! 2013. (When Pets Attack! Ser.). 32p. (J). (gr. 3-6). 26.60 (978-1-4339-9298-8(1)); pap. 63.00 (978-1-4339-9300-8(7)) Stevens, Gareth Publishing LLLP.

Liss-Levinson, Nechama & Baskette, Molly Phinney. Remembering My Pet: A Kid's Own Spiritual Workbook for When a Pet Dies. 2007. (ENG., Illus.). 48p. (gr. 3-7). wbk. ed. 30.99 (978-1-59473-221-8(3), 9781594732218, Skylight Paths Publishing) LongHill Partners, Inc.

Lloyd, Camilla. Pets. 2017. (Photo Word Book Ser.). (ENG., Illus.). 24p. (J). (gr. -1-k). pap. 6.99 (978-0-7502-8899-6(X), Wayland) Hachette Children's Group GBR. Dist: Hachette Bk. Group.

Lodien, Jennie, des. Cat Tales. 2004. (Illus.). 48p. (YA). ring bd. 16.95 (978-0-9746341-8-0(2)) Chin & A Pr.

—A Doggie Diary: The story of our Dog. 2003. (Illus.). 48p. (YA). ring bd. 16.95 (978-0-9746341-7-3(4)) Chin & A Pr.

—Life on a Leash: My Dog's Story. 2003. (Illus.). 48p. (YA). ring bd. 16.95 (978-0-9746341-6-6(6)) Chin & A Pr.

Loh-Hagan, Virginia. Pet Food Tester. 2016. (Odd Jobs Ser.). (ENG., Illus.). 32p. (J). (gr. 4-8). 29.93 (978-1-63471-096-1(7), 208495, 45th Parallel Press) Cherry Lake Publishing.

Lollis, Sylvia & Hogan, Joyce W. Should We Have Pets? A Persuasive Text. 2003. (Illus.). 32p. (J). pap. 6.00 (978-1-59034-044-8(2)) Mondo Publishing.

Lomberg, Michelle. Caring for Your Horse. 2004. (Caring for Your Pet Ser.). (Illus.). 32p. (J). (gr. 4-7). per. 9.95 (978-1-59036-152-8(0)); lib. bdg. 26.00 (978-1-59036-117-7(2)) Weigl Pubs., Inc.

—Caring for Your Spider. 2004. (Caring for Your Pet Ser.). (Illus.). 32p. (J). (gr. 4-7). per. 9.95 (978-1-59036-155-9(5)); lib. bdg. 26.00 (978-1-59036-120-7(2)) Weigl Pubs., Inc.

—Horse. 2009. (My Pet Ser.). (Illus.). 32p. (J). (gr. 3-5). pap. 9.95 (978-1-60596-093-7(4)); lib. bdg. 26.00 (978-1-60596-092-0(6)) Weigl Pubs., Inc.

—Spider. 2009. (My Pet Ser.). (Illus.). 32p. (J). (gr. 3-5). pap. 9.95 (978-1-60596-095-1(0)); lib. bdg. 26.00 (978-1-60596-094-4(2)) Weigl Pubs., Inc.

Lomberg, Michelle & Gillespie, Katie. Spider. 2015. (J). (978-1-4896-2970-8(X)) Weigl Pubs., Inc.

Love, Ann & Drake, Jane. Talking Tails: The Incredible Connection Between People & Their Pets. Slavin, Bill, illus. (ENG.). 80p. (J). (gr. 4-7). 2012. pap. 9.95 (978-1-77049-359-9(X)) 2010. 22.95 (978-0-88776-884-2(9)) Tundra Bks. CAN. (Tundra Bks.). Dist: Penguin Random Hse. LLC.

Lunis, Natalie. Furry Ferrets. 2009. (Peculiar Pets Ser.). (Illus.). 24p. (YA). (gr. 2-5). lib. bdg. 22.61 (978-1-59716-860-1(2)) Bearport Publishing Co., Inc.

—Green Iguanas. 2009. (Peculiar Pets Ser.). (Illus.). 24p. (YA). (gr. 2-5). lib. bdg. 22.61 (978-1-59716-863-2(7)) Bearport Publishing Co., Inc.

MacAulay, Kelley, et al. Les Lapins. 2011. (Petit Monde Vivant (Small Living World) Ser.: No. 78). (FRE., Illus.). 32p. (J). pap. 9.95 (978-2-89579-372-4(7)) Bayard Canada Livres CAN. Dist: Crabtree Publishing Co.

Macken, JoAnn Early. Kittens. 2003. (Weekly Reader Early Learning Library). (Illus.). 24p. (gr. k-3). pap. 8.15 (978-0-8368-3846-6(7), Weekly Reader Leveled Readers) Stevens, Gareth Publishing LLLP.

—Parakeets. 2003. (Weekly Reader Early Learning Library). (Illus.). 24p. (gr. k-3). pap. 8.15 (978-0-8368-3847-3(5), Weekly Reader Leveled Readers) Stevens, Gareth Publishing LLLP.

—Puppies. 2003. (Weekly Reader Early Learning Library). (Illus.). 24p. (gr. k-3). pap. 8.15 (978-0-8368-3848-0(3), Weekly Reader Leveled Readers) Stevens, Gareth Publishing LLLP.

Maher, Jack. Animal Instincts. 2011. (J). pap. (978-0-531-22560-8(7)) Scholastic, Inc.

Make Believe Ideas, Ltd., creator. Pets & Puppies Pack. 2007. (Touch & Sparkle Ser.). (Illus.). (gr. -1-k). per., bds. (978-1-84610-692-7(3)) Make Believe Ideas.

Make Your Own Pom Pom Pets. 2004. (Fun Kits Ser.). (Illus.). 48p. (J). (978-1-84229-861-9(5)) Top That! Publishing PLC.

Mansfield, Carol M. Jake & Jebadiah Visit the Veterinarian, 1 vol. 2010. 22p. pap. 24.95 (978-1-4489-2548-3(7)) PublishAmerica, Inc.

Markle, Sandra. Animal Heroes: True Rescue Stories. 2008. (ENG., Illus.). 64p. (gr. 3-8). 29.27 (978-0-8225-7884-0(0), Millbrook Pr.) Lerner Publishing Group.

Marzolf, Julie. Big Cats Are Not Pets! 2013. 32p. (J). (gr. 3-6). 26.60 (978-1-4339-9273-5(6)); pap. 10.50 (978-1-4339-9274-2(4)) Stevens, Gareth Publishing LLLP.

—Gross Things about Your Pets. 2012. (That's Gross! Ser.). (Illus.). 24p. (J). (gr. 2-5). 22.60 (978-1-4339-7119-8(4)); pap. 8.15 (978-1-4339-7120-4(8)) Stevens, Gareth Publishing LLLP. (Gareth Stevens Learning Library).

Mascotas. 2005. (Collection Abre Tus Ojos, Collection Eye Openers Ser.).Tr. of Pets. (SPA.). (J). (gr. k-2). 6.95 (978-950-11-0899-6(6)) Sigmar ARG. Dist: Iaconi, Mariuccia Bk. Imports.

Mason, Paul. Caring for Critters. 2011. (ENG.). 24p. (J). pap. (978-0-7787-7870-7(3)); (gr. 3-6). (978-0-7787-7848-6(7)) Crabtree Publishing Co.

Matthews, Derek. Escucha y Aprende - Mascotas. 2005. (Escucha y Aprende Ser.). (SPA., Illus.). 10p. (J). (gr. -1-k). (978-970-718-299-8(7), Silver Dolphin en Español) Advanced Marketing, S. de R. L. de C. V.

McBride, Anne. Hamsters, Vol. 12. 2016. (Understanding & Caring for Your Pet Ser.). (Illus.). 128p. (J). (gr. 5). 25.95 (978-1-4222-3699-4(4)) Mason Crest.

McDonnell, Patrick. The Mutts Diaries. 2014. (Mutts Kids Ser.: 1). (ENG., Illus.). 224p. (J). pap. 9.99 (978-1-4494-5870-6(X)) Andrews McMeel Publishing.

McKenzie, Rosemarie. Cupcakes for Penny. 2011. 28p. pap. 15.99 (978-1-4568-2335-1(3)) Xlibris Corp.

McNicholas, June. Ferrets, 1 vol. 2nd ed. 2010. (Keeping Unusual Pets Ser.). (ENG., Illus.). 48p. (gr. 3-6). 32.65 (978-1-4329-3848-2(7), NA-h) Heinemann-Raintree.

Mead, Wendy. Kids Top 10 Pet Birds. 2015. (American Humane Association Top 10 Pets for Kids Ser.). 48p. (J). (gr. 3-4). 25.27 (978-0-7660-6625-0(8)); pap. 8.95 (978-0-7660-6626-7(6), Enslow Elementary) Enslow Pubs., Inc.

Meister, Cari. Birds. 2014. (Illus.). 24p. (J). lib. bdg. 25.65 (978-1-62031-120-2(8), Bullfrog Bks.) Jump! Inc.

—Cats. 2014. (Illus.). 24p. (J). lib. bdg. 25.65 (978-1-62031-121-9(6), Bullfrog Bks.) Jump! Inc.

—Dogs. 2014. (Illus.). 24p. (J). lib. bdg. 25.65 (978-1-62031-122-6(4), Bullfrog Bks.) Jump! Inc.

—Fish. 2014. (Illus.). 24p. (J). lib. bdg. 25.65 (978-1-62031-123-3(2), Bullfrog Bks.) Jump! Inc.

—Guinea Pigs. 2014. (Illus.). 24p. (J). lib. bdg. 25.65 (978-1-62031-127-1(5), Bullfrog Bks.) Jump! Inc.

—Hamsters. 2014. (Illus.). 24p. (J). lib. bdg. 25.65 (978-1-62031-124-0(0), Bullfrog Bks.) Jump! Inc.

—Rabbits. 2014. (Illus.). 24p. (J). lib. bdg. 25.65 (978-1-62031-125-7(9), Bullfrog Bks.) Jump! Inc.

—Turtles. 2014. (Illus.). 24p. (J). lib. bdg. 25.65 (978-1-62031-126-4(7), Bullfrog Bks.) Jump! Inc.

Melanie Z. Kato the True Story of a Siamese Cat. 2012. 28p. 24.95 (978-1-4626-6919-6(0)) America Star Bks.

Mellion, Nicole. Liam's Pets. Filipina, Monika, illus. 2017. (Text Connections Guided Close Reading Ser.). (J). (gr. 1). (978-1-4900-1802-7(6)) Benchmark Education Co.

Mi. Mi's Pets. 2012. 20p. pap. 13.77 (978-1-4669-4019-2(0)) Trafford Publishing.

Miles, Ellen. Guide to Puppies. 2013. (Puppy Place Ser.). lib. bdg. 16.00 (978-0-606-31503-6(9), Turtleback) Turtleback Bks.

—Kitty Corner: Guide to Kittens. 2013. (Kitty Corner Ser.). lib. bdg. 16.00 (978-0-606-31502-9(0), Turtleback) Turtleback Bks.

Miles, Lisa. Origami Pets. 2013. (Amazing Origami Ser.). 32p. (J). (gr. 2-5). pap. 63.00 (978-1-4339-9658-0(8)); pap. 10.50 (978-1-4339-9657-3(X)); (ENG., Illus.). lib. bdg. 26.60 (978-1-4339-9656-6(1)) Stevens, Gareth Publishing LLLP.

Miller, Pat. A Pet for Every Person. 2007. (Illus.). 24p. (J). (978-1-60213-016-6(7), Upstart Bks.) Highsmith Inc.

Mills, Nathan & Jamison, Linc. Caring for My Pet. 2012. (Rosen Readers Ser.). (ENG., Illus.). 16p. (J). (gr. k-1). pap. 7.00 (978-1-4488-8710-1(0), Rosen Classroom) Rosen Publishing Group, Inc., The.

Mitchell Lane Publishers Inc. Staff. How to Convince Your Parents You Can..., 10 vols., Set. 2009. (J). (gr. 1-4). lib. bdg. 257.00 (978-1-58415-664-2(3)) Mitchell Lane Pubs., Inc.

Moberg, Julia. Presidential Pets: The Weird, Wacky, Little, Big, Scary, Strange Animals That Have Lived in the White House. 2012. 96p. pap. 14.95 (978-1-60734-471-1(8)) Charlesbridge Publishing, Inc.

—Presidential Pets: the Weird, Wacky, Little, Big, Scary, Strange Animals That Have Lived in the White House. Jeff Albrecht Studios, Jeff Albrecht, illus. 2016. (ENG.). 96p. (J). (gr. 3-7). pap. 9.95 (978-1-62354-086-9(0)) Charlesbridge Publishing, Inc.

Moore, Elizabeth. Taking Care of a Pet. 2011. (Wonder Readers Emergent Level Ser.). (ENG.). (gr. -1-1). 8p. pap. 35.94 (978-1-4296-8234-3(5)); 32p. pap. 5.99 (978-1-4296-7847-6(X)) Capstone Press of Coughlan Cos. (Wonder Readers).

Mumme, Sarah. Guess Who's My Pet. Samuel, Janet, illus. 2015. (Guess Who's... Bks.). (ENG.). 10p. (J). (gr. -1 — 1). 5.99 (978-0-7641-6800-0(2)) Barron's Educational Series, Inc.

Murray, Julie. Mutts, 1 vol. 2003. (Animal Kingdom Ser.). (ENG.). 24p. (gr. k-4). 25.65 (978-1-57765-641-8(5), Buddy Bks.) ABDO Publishing Co.

National Geographic. National Geographic Kids: 125 True Stories of Amazing Pets. 2014. lib. bdg. 24.50 (978-0-606-35574-2(X)) Turtleback Bks.

National Geographic Kids Staff. 125 True Stories of Amazing Pets: Inspiring Tales of Animal Friendship & Four-Legged Heroes, Plus Crazy Animal Antics. 2014. (ENG., Illus.). 112p. (J). (gr. 3-7). pap. 12.99 (978-1-4263-1459-9(0), National Geographic Children's Bks.) National Geographic Society.

National Geographic Kids Staff & Donohue, Moira Rose. Kangaroo to the Rescue! And More True Stories of Amazing Animal Heroes. 2015. (NGK Chapters Ser.). (ENG.). 112p. (J). (gr. 2-5). pap. 5.99 (978-1-4263-1913-6(4)); lib. bdg. 14.90 (978-1-4263-1915-0(0)) National Geographic Society. (National Geographic Children's Bks.).

Nelson, Maria. I'm Allergic to Pets. 2014. (I'm Allergic Ser.). 24p. (J). (gr. 1-3). 22.60 (978-1-4824-0979-6(8)) Stevens, Gareth Publishing LLLP.

Nelson, Robin. Pet Frog. 2003. (First Step Nonfiction). (Illus.). 24p. (J). (gr. k-2). lib. bdg. 18.60 (978-0-8225-1271-4(8)) Lerner Publishing Group.

—Pet Hamster. 2003. (First Step Nonfiction). (Illus.). 24p. (J). (gr. k-2). lib. bdg. 18.60 (978-0-8225-1269-1(6)) Lerner Publishing Group.

Niven, Felicia Lowenstein. Learning to Care for Small Mammals. 2010. (Beginning Pet Care with American Humane Ser.). 48p. (J). 25.27 (978-0-7660-3195-1(0), Enslow Elementary) Enslow Pubs., Inc.

Niven, Felicia Lowenstein & Library Association Staff. Learning to Care for Reptiles & Amphibians. 2010. (Beginning Pet Care with American Humane Ser.). 48p. (J). 25.27 (978-0-7660-3194-4(2), Enslow Elementary) Enslow Pubs., Inc.

Niver, Heather Moore. Ostriches Are Not Pets! 2013. (When Pets Attack! Ser.). 32p. (J). (gr. 3-6). pap. 10.50 (978-1-4339-9284-1(1)) Stevens, Gareth Publishing LLLP.

Niver, Heather Moore & Moore Niver, Heather. Ostriches Are Not Pets! 2013. 32p. (J). (gr. 3-6). 26.60 (978-1-4339-9283-4(3)) Stevens, Gareth Publishing LLLP.

Olsson, Elizabeth. The Tiny Pink House. 2010. 24p. 19.95 (978-1-4520-1203-2(2)) AuthorHouse.

Orcutt, Cherie. A Beautiful Husky Needs a Home. Frongia, Daniela, illus. 2012. 32p. pap. 21.00 (978-1-4685-7156-1(7)) AuthorHouse.

Ormiston, Rickey. My Dog Wiggles. 2010. 20p. 11.49 (978-1-4490-9824-7(X)) AuthorHouse.

Ostriches Are Not Pets! 2013. (When Pets Attack! Ser.). 32p. (J). (gr. 3-6). pap. 63.00 (978-1-4339-9285-8(X)) Stevens, Gareth Publishing LLLP.

O'Sullivan, Elizabeth. Sugar Gliders. 2008. (Early Bird Nature Bks.). (ENG.). 48p. (gr. 2-5). 26.60 (978-0-8225-7891-8(3)) Lerner Publishing Group.

Our Weird Pets. 2017. (Our Weird Pets Ser.). 24p. (gr. 7-8). 141.60 **(978-1-4994-3496-5(0))**; pap. 49.50 **(978-1-5081-5433-4(3))** Rosen Publishing Group, Inc., The. (PowerKids Pr.).

Owen, Ruth. Icky House Invaders. 2011. (Up Close & Gross Ser.). 24p. (YA). (gr. 2-5). lib. bdg. 22.61 (978-1-61772-124-3(7)) Bearport Publishing Co., Inc.

Page, Claire. Carry-Me Pets. 2008. (Carry-Me Ser.). (Illus.). 10p. (J). (gr. -1). bds. (978-1-84610-878-5(0)) Make Believe Ideas.

Pearce, Sue & Quin, Caroline. Pets. 2004. (Activities for 3-5 Year Olds Ser.). (Illus.). 32p. pap. 11.00 (978-1-897675-38-0(0)) Brilliant Pubns. GBR. Dist: Parkwest Pubns., Inc.

Perfect Pets, 1 vol., Set. Incl. Brilliant Birds. Salzmann, Mary Elizabeth. lib. bdg. 24.21 (978-1-59928-744-7(7)); Cuddly Cats. Hanson, Anders. lib. bdg. 24.21 (978-1-59928-745-4(5)); Dandy Dogs. Salzmann, Mary Elizabeth. lib. bdg. 24.21 (978-1-59928-746-1(3)); Flashy Fish. Salzmann, Mary Elizabeth. Craig, Diane, ed. lib. bdg. 24.21 (978-1-59928-747-8(1)); Frisky Ferrets. Doudna, Kelly. Craig, Diane, ed. lib. bdg. 24.21 (978-1-59928-748-5(X)); Goofy Guinea Pigs. Salzmann, Mary Elizabeth. Craig, Diane, ed. lib. bdg. 24.21 (978-1-59928-749-2(8)); Handsome Horses. Hanson, Anders. lib. bdg. 24.21 (978-1-59928-750-8(1)); Hidden Hermit Crabs. Doudna, Kelly. lib. bdg. 24.21 (978-1-59928-751-5(X)); Lively Lizards. Hanson, Anders. lib. bdg. 24.21 (978-1-59928-752-2(8)); Rascally Rabbits. Doudna, Kelly. lib. bdg. 24.21 (978-1-59928-753-9(6)); Running Rats. Doudna, Kelly. lib. bdg. 24.21 (978-1-59928-754-6(4)); Terrific Turtles. Hanson, Anders. lib. bdg. 24.21 (978-1-59928-755-3(2)); (Illus.). (J). (gr. k-3). (Perfect Pets Ser.: 12). (ENG.). 24p. 2007. Set lib. bdg. 290.52 (978-1-59928-743-0(9), SandCastle) ABDO Publishing Co.

Perry, Sondra. The Most Unusual Pet Ever, Henry Our Great Blue Heron & His Adventures 2nd Edition. Byer, Janice, illus. 2014. 18.95 (978-1-62652-432-3(7)) Salem Author Services.

Pet Day: Individual Title Six-Packs. (gr. k-1). 23.00 (978-0-7635-8826-7(1)) Rigby Education.

Pet Day at School, 6 Packs. (Story Steps Ser.). (gr. k-2). 32.00 (978-0-7635-9606-4(X)) Rigby Education.

Pet Dictionary: An a to Z of Animal Companions. 2005. (Illus.). 64p. (J). pap. (978-0-439-75459-0(3)) Scholastic, Inc.

Pet Project. (Bratz Fiction Totally Awesome Tales Ser.). 128p. pap. (978-1-4054-8738-2(0)) Parragon, Inc.

Peters, Gregory N. Real Animal Heroes, 1 vol. 2014. (Real World Adventures Ser.). (ENG.). 48p. (gr. 4-12). 31.99 (978-1-4765-8532-1(6)) Capstone Press of Coughlan Cos.

Petersen, Christine. The Smart Kid's Guide to Losing a Pet. Rooney, Ronnie, illus. 2014. (Smart Kid's Guide to Everyday Life Ser.). (ENG.). 32p. (J). (gr. 2-5). 28.50 (978-1-62687-346-9(1), 207186) Child's World, Inc., The.

Petrie, Kristin. Chameleons, 1 vol. 2012. (Unique Pets Ser.). (ENG.). 24p. (J). (gr. 3-6). lib. bdg. 25.65 (978-1-61783-439-4(4), Checkerboard Library) ABDO Publishing Co.

—Potbellied Pigs, 1 vol. 2012. (Unique Pets Ser.). (ENG.). 24p. (J). (gr. 3-6). lib. bdg. 25.65 (978-1-61783-442-4(4), Checkerboard Library) ABDO Publishing Co.

—Sugar Gliders, 1 vol. 2012. (Unique Pets Ser.). (ENG.). 24p. (J). (gr. 3-6). lib. bdg. 25.65 (978-1-61783-443-1(2), Checkerboard Library) ABDO Publishing Co.

—Tarantulas, 1 vol. 2012. (Unique Pets Ser.). (ENG.). 24p. (J). (gr. 3-6). lib. bdg. 25.65 (978-1-61783-444-8(0), Checkerboard Library) ABDO Publishing Co.

Pets: Individual Title Six-Packs. (Literatura 2000 Ser.). (gr. k-1). 28.00 (978-0-7635-0062-7(3)) Rigby Education.

Pickett, Robert & Pickett, Justine, illus. Cat. Pickett, Robert & Pickett, Justine, photos by. 2004. 32p. (J). lib. bdg. 27.10 (978-1-58340-431-7(7)) Black Rabbit Bks.

—Dog. Pickett, Robert & Pickett, Justine, photos by. 2004. 32p. (J). lib. bdg. 27.10 (978-1-58340-430-0(9)) Black Rabbit Bks.

Piney Grove Elementary School (Kernsville, N.C.) Staff & Scholastic, Inc. Staff, contrib. by. A Kid for Jack: A True Story. 2012. (Illus.). 28p. (978-0-545-51574-0(2)) Scholastic, Inc.

Playful Pets. (Flip Flap Fun Book Ser.). 10p. (J). bds. (978-2-7643-0182-1(0)) Phidal Publishing, Inc./Editions Phidal, Inc.

Pomerance, Diane. Animal Companions: Your Friends, Teachers & Guides. Mier, Vanessa, illus. 2003. 9.95 (978-0-9708500-2-7(6)) Polaire Pubns.

Priddy, Roger. My Carry-Along Sound Book: Perfect Pets. 2014. (My Carry-Along Sound Bks.). (ENG.). 10p. (J). (— 1). bds. 9.99 (978-0-312-51720-5(3), 9780312517205, Priddy Bks.) St. Martin's Pr.

—Perfect Pets. 2006. (Bright Baby Touch & Feel Ser.). (ENG., Illus.). 10p. (J). (gr. -1 — 1). bds. 4.95 (978-0-312-49860-3(8), 9780312498603, Priddy Bks.) St. Martin's Pr.

—Simple First Sounds Noisy Pets. 2012. (ENG., Illus.). 10p. (J). (gr. -1-k). bds. 9.99 (978-0-312-51381-8(X), 9780312513818, Priddy Bks.) St. Martin's Pr.

—Vampire Pets. 2014. (Funny Faces Ser.). (ENG.). 10p. (J). (gr. -1-1). bds. 8.99 (978-0-312-51721-2(1), 9780312517212, Priddy Bks.) St. Martin's Pr.

Puchalski, Robin. Foo Foo the Shih Poo: My First Day Home. 2012. 20p. pap. 24.95 (978-1-4626-6625-6(6)) America Star Bks.

Purple Walrus & Other Perfect Pets: 6 Each of 1 Anthology, 6 vols. (Wildcats Ser.). 32p. (gr. 2-8). (978-0-322-00575-4(2)) Wright Group/McGraw-Hill.

Rabe, Tish. Oh, the Pets You Can Get! All about Our Animal Friends. Ruiz, Aristides & Mathieu, Joe, illus. 2005. (Cat in the Hat's Learning Library). (ENG.). 48p. (J). (gr. -1-3). 9.99 (978-0-375-82278-0(X), Random Hse. Bks. for Young Readers) Random Hse. Children's Bks.

Rajczak, Kristen. Sequential Words with Your Pets. 2013. (Write Right! Ser.). 24p. (J). (gr. 2-5). pap. 8.15 (978-1-4339-9078-6(4)); (ENG., Illus.). lib. bdg. 22.60 (978-1-4339-9077-9(6)) Stevens, Gareth Publishing LLLP.

Rake, Jody Sullivan. Why Rabbits Eat Poop & Other Gross Facts about Pets, 1 vol. 2012. (Gross Me Out Ser.). (ENG.). 24p. (gr. 1-2). pap. 7.29 (978-1-4296-7956-5(5)); pap. 41.70 (978-1-4296-8378-4(3)); lib. bdg. 25.32 (978-1-4296-7609-0(4)) Capstone Press of Coughlan Cos. (First Facts).

Randolph, Joanne. Classroom Pets, 6 bks., Set. Incl. Fish. lib. bdg. 22.60 (978-1-4042-3681-3(3), 1266091); Guinea Pigs. lib. bdg. 22.60 (978-1-4042-3676-9(7)); Rabbits. lib. bdg. 22.60 (978-1-4042-3680-6(5)); Snakes. lib. bdg. 22.60 (978-1-4042-3679-0(1)); Tarantulas. lib. bdg. 22.60 (978-1-4042-3678-3(3)); Turtles. lib. bdg. 22.60 (978-1-4042-3677-6(5), 1266096); (Illus.). 24p. (J). (gr. 3-7). 2007. 2007. Set lib. bdg. 127.50 (978-1-4042-3608-0(2), PowerKids Pr.) Rosen Publishing Group, Inc., The.

Rayner, Matthew. I Am Your Pet, 2 vols., Set. Sawyer, Darren, photos by. Incl. Guinea Pig. lib. bdg. 26.00 (978-0-8368-8385-5(3)); Rat. lib. bdg. 26.00 (978-0-8368-8386-2(1)); (Illus.). 32p. (gr. k-4). 2007., Gareth Stevens Learning Library 2007. Set lib. bdg. 47.86 o.p. (978-0-8368-8384-8(5)) Stevens, Gareth Publishing LLLP.

Rayner, Matthew & BVetMed MRCVS Staff. Cat. Burton, Jane & Greenaway, Frank, photos by. 2004. (I Am Your Pet Ser.). (Illus.). 32p. (gr. k-4). lib. bdg. 26.00 (978-0-8368-4102-2(6), Gareth Stevens Learning Library) Stevens, Gareth Publishing LLLP.

—Dog. Burton, Jane & Greenaway, Frank, photos by. 2004. (I Am Your Pet Ser.). (Illus.). 32p. (gr. k-4). lib. bdg. 26.00 (978-0-8368-4103-9(4), Gareth Stevens Learning Library) Stevens, Gareth Publishing LLLP.

—Hamster. Greenaway, Frank & Burton, Jane, photos by. 2004. (I Am Your Pet Ser.). (Illus.). 32p. (gr. k-4). lib. bdg. 26.00 (978-0-8368-4104-6(2), Gareth Stevens Learning Library) Stevens, Gareth Publishing LLLP.

—I Am Your Pet, 4 bks. Greenaway, Frank & Burton, Jane, photos by. Incl. Cat. lib. bdg. 26.00 (978-0-8368-4102-2(6)); Dog. lib. bdg. 26.00 (978-0-8368-4103-9(4)); Hamster. lib. bdg. 26.00 (978-0-8368-4104-6(2)); Rabbit. lib. bdg. 26.00 (978-0-8368-4105-3(0)); 32p. (gr. k-4)., Gareth Stevens Learning Library (Illus.). 2004. Set lib. bdg. 93.32 o.p. (978-0-8368-4101-5(8)) Stevens, Gareth Publishing LLLP.

—Rabbit. Burton, Jane & Greenaway, Frank, photos by. 2004. (I Am Your Pet Ser.). (Illus.). 32p. (gr. k-4). lib. bdg. 26.00 (978-0-8368-4105-3(0), Gareth Stevens Learning Library) Stevens, Gareth Publishing LLLP.

Reher, Matt & Fonzone, Taylor. Is a Bird a Good Pet? 2016. (1G Science Ser.). (ENG., Illus.). 28p. (J). pap. 5.99 **(978-1-63437-681-5(1))** American Reading Co.

Reid, Siuna A. Reptiles Are Cool- Understanding My Tortoise. Lodge, Vivienne E., ed. 2013. (Illus.). 76p. pap. (978-0-9576568-2-6(3)) Siuna A Reid.

Reilly, Cherie Brooks. Feathered & Furry Friends at the Farm. 2012. 108p. (gr. -1). pap. 11.92 (978-1-4669-4095-6(6)) Trafford Publishing.

Ring, Susan. Caring for Your Cat. Kissock, Heather & Marshall, Diana, eds. 2003. (Caring for Your Pet Ser.). (Illus.). 32p. (J). pap. 9.95 (978-1-59036-062-0(1)) Weigl Pubs., Inc.

Ripley's Inc. Staff. Woof! Graziano, John, illus. 2012. (Ripley's Shout Outs Ser.: 3). (ENG.). 96p. (J). (gr. 2-5). pap. 4.99 (978-0-545-38077-5(4)) Scholastic, Inc.

Rissman, Rebecca. Should Wendy Walk the Dog? Taking Care of Your Pets, 1 vol. 2013. (What Would You Do? Ser.). (ENG., Illus.). 24p. (gr. -1-1). pap. 6.29 (978-1-4329-7243-1(X)); lib. bdg. 22.65 (978-1-4329-7237-0(5)) Heinemann-Raintree. (Acorn).

Rizzi, Kathleen. Who Lives Here?, 1 vol. 2012. (ENG., Illus.). 32p. (J). bds. 5.95 (978-1-59572-264-5(5)) Star Bright Bks., Inc.

—Who Lives Here? (Arabic/English) 2012. (ARA & ENG., Illus.). 24p. (J). bds. 5.95 (978-1-59572-351-2(X)) Star Bright Bks., Inc.

—Who Lives Here? (Hmong/English), 1 vol. 2012. (HMN & ENG., Illus.). 24p. (J). 5.95 (978-1-59572-352-9(8)) Star Bright Bks., Inc.

—Who Lives Here? (Portuguese/English), 1 vol. 2012. (POR & ENG., Illus.). 24p. (J). 5.95 (978-1-59572-353-6(6)) Star Bright Bks., Inc.

—Who Lives Here? (Spanish/English), 1 vol. 2012. (SPA & ENG., Illus.). 32p. (J). bds. 5.95 (978-1-59572-349-9(8)) Star Bright Bks., Inc.

Rober, Harold. Getting a Pet. 2017. (Bumba Books (tm) — Fun Firsts Ser.). (ENG.). 24p. (J). (gr. -1-1). 12.99 **(978-1-5124-3675-4(5))**; 38.65 **(978-1-5124-3674-7(7))**; 38.65 **(978-1-5124-2749-3(7))** Lerner Publishing Group. (Lerner Pubns.).

Rober, Harold. I Love Hermit Crabs. 2016. (Bumba Books (tm) — Pets Are the Best Ser.). (ENG.). 24p. (J). (gr. -1-1). lib. bdg. 25.32 (978-1-5124-1418-9(2)) Lerner Publishing Group.

Rober, Harold T. Getting a Pet. 2017. (Bumba Books (tm) — Fun Firsts Ser.). (ENG., Illus.). 24p. (J). (gr. -1-1). 25.32 (978-1-5124-2553-6(2)) Lerner Publishing Group.

Roberts, Heulwen. Anifeiliaid Anwes. 2005. (WEL., Illus.). 16p. pap. (978-1-85644-778-2(2)) CAA.

Robinson, Joanna Jarc. Phillip & Penny Learn about Pronouns. Hu, Caroline, illus. 2014. (Language Builders Ser.). (ENG.). 32p. (J). (gr. 2-4). lib. bdg. 25.27 (978-1-59953-670-5(6)) Norwood Hse. Pr.

Romaine, Claire. Matemáticas con Mascotas / Math with Pets. de la Vega, Eida, tr. 2016. (¡Matemáticas en Todas Partes! / Math Is Everywhere! Ser.). (ENG & SPA.). 24p. (gr. k-k). lib. bdg. 22.60 (978-1-4824-5216-7(2)) Stevens, Gareth Publishing LLLP.

Rooney, Anne. So You Want a Pet? 2015. (Collins Big Cat Ser.). (ENG.). 24p. (J). (gr. 2-2). pap. 7.95 (978-0-00-759116-9(0)) HarperCollins Pubs. Ltd. GBR. Dist: Independent Pubs. Group.

Ross, Daisy. Peter's Pets. 2012. (InfoMax Readers Ser.). (ENG., Illus.). 16 pp.p. (J). (gr. k-1). pap. 7.00 (978-1-4488-8929-7(4), Rosen Classroom) Rosen Publishing Group, Inc., The.

Ross, Michael Elsohn. Indoor Zoo. Seeley, Tim, illus. 2003. (You Are the Scientist Ser.). 48p. (J). (gr. 3-6). lib. bdg. 23.93 (978-0-87614-621-7(3)) Lerner Publishing Group.

Ross, Tony. Mascotas. 2006. (Little Princess Ser.).Tr. of Pets. (SPA.). (J). (gr. -1-k). bds. 7.95 (978-968-19-1485-1(6), AT33279) Lectorum Pubns., Inc.

—Mascotas: La Pequena Princesa. 2006. (SPA., Illus.). 14p. (gr. -1-k). bds. (978-84-372-2400-8(4)) Altea, Ediciones, S.A. - Grupo Santillana.

Roswell, Jackie. Gerbils. 2017. (Illus.). 128p. (J). (978-1-4222-3691-8(9)) Mason Crest.

Rowe, Brooke. What Pet Should You Get? 2015. (Illus.). 32p. (J). (978-1-63470-034-4(1)) Cherry Lake Publishing.

Rudy, Maggie. I Wish I Had a Pet. Rudy, Maggie, illus. 2014. (ENG., Illus.). 40p. (J). (gr. -1-3). 15.99 (978-1-4424-5332-6(X), Beach Lane Bks.) Beach Lane Bks.

Ryan, Victoria. When Your Pet Dies: A Healing Handbook for Kids. Ryan, Victoria & Alley, R. W., illus. 2003. (Elf-Help Books for Kids). 32p. (J). per. 7.95 (978-0-87029-376-4(1)) Abbey Pr.

Salzano, Tammi J., et al. Animal Friends. 2009. (Illus.). 32p. (J). (978-0-545-13901-4(5)) Scholastic, Inc.

Salzmann, Mary Elizabeth. Ant Farm to Zebra Fish: Pets from A to Z, 1 vol. 2009. (Let's Learn A to Z Ser.). (ENG., Illus.). 32p. (J). (gr. -1-2). 27.07 (978-1-60453-494-8(X)) ABDO Publishing Co.

Schafer, Susan. Invasive Mammals. 2016. (Invasive Species Ser.). (ENG.). 48p. (J). (gr. 4-4). 31.36 (978-1-5026-1832-0(X)) Cavendish Square Publishing.

Schuette, Sarah L. Pets All Around: A Spot-It Challenge, 1 vol. 2012. (Spot It Ser.). (ENG.). 32p. (gr. 1-2). lib. bdg. 27.32 (978-1-4296-8713-3(4)) Capstone Press of Coughlan Cos.

Sequential Words with Your Pets. 2013. (Write Right! Ser.). 24p. (J). (gr. 2-5). pap. 48.90 (978-1-4339-9079-3(2)) Stevens, Gareth Publishing LLLP.

Sexton, Colleen. Caring for Your Turtle. 2010. (Pet Care Library). (ENG., Illus.). 24p. (J). (gr. 2-5). lib. bdg. 25.95 (978-1-60014-472-1(1), Blastoff! Readers) Bellwether Media.

Sigurdsson, Rev. Rupert. A Lifetime of Pets, 1 vol. 2010. 63p. pap. 19.95 (978-1-4489-5803-0(2)) America Star Bks.

Silverstein, Alvin, et al. Beautiful Birds. 2003. (What a Pet! Ser.). (Illus.). 48p. (gr. 5-8). lib. bdg. 23.90 (978-0-7613-2513-0(1), Millbrook Pr.) Lerner Publishing Group.

—Boas & Pythons: Cool Pets! Kelley, Gerald, illus. 2012. (Far-Out & Unusual Pets Ser.). 48p. (J). (gr. 3-4). pap. 8.95 (978-1-4644-0129-9(2)); 25.27 (978-0-7660-3878-3(5)) Enslow Pubs., Inc. (Enslow Elementary).

—Creepy Crawlies. 2003. (What a Pet! Ser.). (ENG., Illus.). 48p. (gr. 3-6). lib. bdg. 23.93 (978-0-7613-2511-6(5), Millbrook Pr.) Lerner Publishing Group.

—Curious Cats. 2003. (What a Pet! Ser.). (ENG., Illus.). 48p. (gr. 3-6). lib. bdg. 23.93 (978-0-7613-2512-3(3), Millbrook Pr.) Lerner Publishing Group.

—Hairless Dogs: Cool Pets! 2012. (Far-Out & Unusual Pets Ser.). (Illus.). 48p. (J). (gr. 3-4). pap. 8.95 (978-1-4644-0124-4(1), Enslow Elementary) Enslow Pubs., Inc.

—Hermit Crabs: Cool Pets! Kelley, Gerald, illus. 2011. (Far-Out & Unusual Pets Ser.). 48p. (J). (gr. 2-5). lib. bdg. 25.27 (978-0-7660-3684-0(7)) Enslow Pubs., Inc.

—Poison Dart Frogs: Cool Pets! Kelley, Gerald, illus. 2012. (Far-Out & Unusual Pets Ser.). 48p. (J). (gr. 3-4). pap. 8.95 (978-1-4644-0126-8(8)); 25.27 (978-0-7660-3881-3(5)) Enslow Pubs., Inc. (Enslow Elementary).

—Rats: Cool Pets! Kelley, Gerald, illus. 2012. (Far-Out & Unusual Pets Ser.). 48p. (J). (gr. 3-4). pap. 8.95 (978-1-4644-0127-5(6), Enslow Elementary) Enslow Pubs., Inc.

—Tarantulas: Cool Pets! Kelley, Gerald, illus. 2012. (Far-Out & Unusual Pets Ser.). 48p. (J). (gr. 3-4). pap. 8.95 (978-1-4644-0128-2(4)); 25.27 (978-0-7660-3883-7(1)) Enslow Pubs., Inc. (Enslow Elementary).

Siminovich, Lorena, illus. You Are My Baby: Pets. 2014. (ENG.). 10p. (J). (gr. -1 — 1). bds. 8.99 (978-1-4521-3430-7(8)) Chronicle Bks. LLC.

Simon, Elizabeth. Caring for Your Iguana. 2005. (Caring for Your Pet Ser.). (Illus.). 32p. (J). per. 9.95 (978-1-59036-215-0(2)); (gr. 4-7). lib. bdg. 26.00 (978-1-59036-195-5(4)) Weigl Pubs., Inc.

—Caring for Your Rat. (Caring for Your Pet Ser.). (Illus.). 32p. (J). 2005. (gr. 4-7). per. 9.95 (978-1-59036-217-4(9)) 2004. lib. bdg. 26.00 (978-1-59036-197-9(0)) Weigl Pubs., Inc.

Simonds, Lucy. People & Pets. 2007. (Trackers-Math Ser.). (gr. 2-5). pap. 5.00 (978-1-59055-920-8(7)) Pacific Learning, Inc.

Sjonger, Rebecca & Kalman, Bobbie. Gerbils. Crabtree, Marc, illus. Crabtree, Marc, photos by. 2003. (Pet Care Ser.). (ENG.). 32p. (J). lib. bdg. (978-0-7787-1752-2(6)) Crabtree Publishing Co.

—Hamsters. Crabtree, Marc, illus. Crabtree, Marc, photos by. 2003. (Pet Care Ser.). (ENG.). 32p. (J). lib. bdg. (978-0-7787-1753-9(4)) Crabtree Publishing Co.

—Mice. Crabtree, Marc, illus. Crabtree, Marc, photos by. 2003. (Pet Care Ser.). (ENG.). 32p. (J). pap. (978-0-7787-1786-7(0)); lib. bdg. (978-0-7787-1754-6(2)) Crabtree Publishing Co.

—Puppies. 2003. (Pet Care Ser.). (ENG., Illus.). 32p. (J). lib. bdg. (978-0-7787-1751-5(8)) Crabtree Publishing Co.

Sjonger, Rebecca, et al. Les Souris. 2011. (Petit Monde Vivant (Small Living World) Ser.: No. 77). (FRE., Illus.). 32p. (J). pap. 9.95 (978-2-89579-371-7(9)) Bayard Canada Livres CAN. Dist: Crabtree Publishing Co.

Smalley, Carol Parenzan. Care for a Pet Hamster. 2009. (How to Convince Your Parents You Can ... Ser.). 32p. (J). (gr. 1-4). 25.70 (978-1-58415-804-2(2)) Mitchell Lane Pubs., Inc.

Sparling, Rebecca. Gerbils. 2009. (Illus.). 112p. (J). 14.95 (978-1-932904-36-9(0)) Eldorado Ink.

Starosta, Paul. Face-to-Face with the Hamster. 2004. (Illus.). 25p. (J). 9.95 (978-1-57091-456-0(7)) Charlesbridge Publishing, Inc.

Stevenson, Sharry. Gibby's Story. 2012. 36p. pap. 18.41 (978-1-4669-3322-4(4)) Trafford Publishing.

Steward, Martha. Darby's Story: The Life of an Adopted Dog. 2009. 36p. pap. 15.95 (978-1-4490-2775-9(X)) AuthorHouse.

Stock, Lisa & Dorling Kindersley Publishing Staff. Friends Perfect Pets, Level 2. 2014. (DK Readers Ser.). (ENG.). 32p. (J). (gr. k-4). pap. 3.99 (978-1-4654-1984-2(5), DK Children) Dorling Kindersley Publishing, Inc.

Stoltman, Joan. My First Bird. 2017. (Let's Get a Pet! Ser.). 24p. (J). (gr. 1-2). pap. 8.15 ***(978-1-4824-6437-5(3))*** Stevens, Gareth Publishing LLLP.

—My First Cat. 2017. (Let's Get a Pet! Ser.). 24p. (gr. 1-2). pap. 8.15 ***(978-1-4824-6445-0(4))*** Stevens, Gareth Publishing LLLP.

—My First Dog. 2017. (Let's Get a Pet! Ser.). 24p. (gr. 1-2). pap. 8.15 ***(978-1-4824-6449-8(7))*** Stevens, Gareth Publishing LLLP.

Stone, Kelly P. What Do Pets Do When They Go up to Heaven?, 1 vol. Stone, Kelly P. & Stone, Joyce M., illus. 2009. 13p. pap. 24.95 *(978-1-61546-212-4(0))* America Star Bks.

Sullivant, Holly. Hamsters. 2009. (Illus.). 112p. (J). 14.95 *(978-1-932904-38-3(7))* Eldorado Ink.

Tattam, Mark. Pets. 2005. (Lift Stick & Learn Ser.). (Illus.). 12p. (J). (gr. -1-3). *(978-1-905051-70-0(0))* Make Believe Ideas.

Terry, Paul. Top 10 for Kids Pets. 2015. (ENG., Illus.). 96p. (J). (gr. 3-6). pap. 9.95 *(978-1-77085-527-4(0)*, 9781770855274) Firefly Bks., Ltd.

Thomas, Isabel. Pet Projects. 2015. (Pet Projects Ser.). (ENG.). 32p. (gr. 3-5). lib. bdg. 111.96 *(978-1-4109-8068-7(5)*, Snap Bks.) Capstone Press of Coughlan Cos.

—Pets' Guides, 1 vol. 2014. (Pets' Guides). (ENG.). 32p. (gr. 1-3). 163.92 *(978-1-4846-0265-2(X)*, Heinemann First Library) Heinemann-Raintree.

—Slinky's Guide to Caring for Your Snake, 1 vol. Peterson, Rick, illus. 2014. (Pets' Guides). (ENG.). 32p. (gr. 1-3). pap. 8.29 *(978-1-4846-0270-6(6))*; 27.32 *(978-1-4846-0263-8(3))* Heinemann-Raintree. (Heinemann First Library).

—Squeak's Guide to Caring for Your Pet Rats or Mice, 1 vol. Peterson, Rick, illus. 2014. (Pets' Guides). (ENG.). 32p. (gr. 1-3). pap. 8.29 *(978-1-4846-0271-3(4))*; 27.32 *(978-1-4846-0264-5(1))* Heinemann-Raintree. (Heinemann First Library).

Thomas Nelson. Touch & Sparkle Pets. 2016. (ENG.). 12p. (gr. -1). bds. *(978-1-78598-131-9(5))* Make Believe Ideas.

Thomas, Pat. I Miss My Pet: A First Look at When a Pet Dies. Harker, Lesley, illus. 2012. (First Look At... Ser.). (ENG.). 32p. (J). (gr. -1-3). pap. 7.99 *(978-1-4380-0188-3(6))* Barron's Educational Series, Inc.

Toliver, Marilyn. Marcellus Really Wants a Pet. 2012. 28p. pap. 16.09 *(978-1-4669-0090-5(3))* Trafford Publishing.

Tracy, Kathleen. The Frog in Our Class. 2011. (Randy's Corner Ser.). (Illus.). 32p. (J). (gr. -1-2). lib. bdg. 25.70 *(978-1-58415-977-3(4))* Mitchell Lane Pubs., Inc.

Tuxworth, Nicola. Pets. 2015. (ENG., Illus.). 20p. bds. 6.99 *(978-1-86147-647-0(7)*, Armadillo) Anness Publishing GBR. Dist: National Bk. Network.

U. S. National Geographic Society Staff & Spears, James. National Geographic Kids Everything Pets: Furry Facts, Photos, & Fun-Unleashed! 2013. (National Geographic Kids Everything Ser.). (ENG.). 64p. (J). (gr. 3-7). lib. bdg. 21.90 *(978-1-4263-1363-9(2)*, National Geographic Children's Bks.) National Geographic Society.

U. S. National Geographic Society Staff, et al. Pets: Furry Facts, Photos, & Fun-Unleashed! 2013. (National Geographic Kids Everything Ser.). (ENG., Illus.). 64p. (J). (gr. 3-7). pap. 12.95 *(978-1-4263-1362-2(4)*, National Geographic Children's Bks.) National Geographic Society.

Van Der Linden, Elly. The Little Hamster. Lavreys, Debbie, illus. 2007. 12p. (gr. -1-k). *(978-0-86315-605-2(3))* Floris Bks.

Velasquez, Maria. Pet Parade. Mooney, Alyssa, illus. 2007. (J). pap. 21.00 *(978-0-15-379895-5(5))* Houghton Mifflin Harcourt School Pubs.

Verdick, Elizabeth. Tails Are Not for Pulling. Heinlen, Marieka, illus. 2005. (Best Behavior Ser.). (ENG.). (J). 40p. (gr. 4-7). pap. 11.95 *(978-1-57542-181-0(X))*; 24p. (gr. 3-7). 7.95 *(978-1-57542-180-3(1))* Free Spirit Publishing, Inc.

Vincenti, Catherine, ed. & illus. Pet Pals Grades 3-4: A Spanish-English Workbook. Vincenti, Catherine, illus. 2003.Tr. of Mascotas Companeros. (SPA.). 34p. wbk. ed. 3.00 *(978-0-941246-21-7(3)*, Humane Society Pr.) National Assn. for Humane & Environmental Education.

—Pet Pals Grades 5-6: A Spanish-English Workbook. Vincenti, Catherine, illus. 2003.Tr. of Mascotas Companeros. (SPA.). 34p. wbk. ed. 3.00 *(978-0-941246-22-4(1)*, Humane Society Pr.) National Assn. for Humane & Environmental Education.

—Pet Pals Grades K-2: A Spanish-English Workbook. Vincenti, Catherine, illus. 2003.Tr. of Mascotas Companeros. (SPA.). 34p. (J). wbk. ed. 3.00 *(978-0-941246-20-0(5)*, Humane Society Pr.) National Assn. for Humane & Environmental Education.

Walker, Niki & Kalman, Bobbie. Kittens. 2003. (Pet Care Ser.). (ENG., Illus.). 32p. (J). pap. *(978-0-7787-1782-9(8))* Crabtree Publishing Co.

Walker, Rob. Pet Animals. 2009. (Chunkie Hunkies Ser.). (ENG.). 18p. (J). (gr. -1). bds. 4.99 *(978-0-7641-6213-8(6))* Barron's Educational Series, Inc.

Wallace, Bruce & Make Believe Ideas Staff. Pets. 2005. (Touch & Sparkle Ser.). (Illus.). 12p. (gr. -1-k). bds. *(978-1-905051-01-4(8))* Make Believe Ideas.

Walter Foster Creative Team. Sticker Pictures - Pets: Stick, Color & Create One Sticker at a Time! 2017. (Sticker & Color-By-Number Ser.). (ENG., Illus.). 48p. (J). (gr. k-3). pap. 9.95 *(978-1-63322-278-6(0)*, Walter Foster Jr) Quarto Publishing Group USA.

Walter Foster Creative Team, ed. All about Drawing Horses & Pets. 2008. (All about Drawing Ser.). (ENG., Illus.). 80p. (J). (gr. 1-3). pap. 9.95 *(978-1-60058-580-7(9)*, 1600585809) Quarto Publishing Group USA.

Webb, Cheryl Renee. Do Pets & Other Animals Go to Heaven? How to Recover from the Loss of an Animal Friend. 2003. (Illus.). 108p. per. 15.95 *(978-0-9726363-0-8(7))* Brite Bks.

West, David. Animals in the Home. 2013. (Nora the Naturalist's Animals Ser.). 24p. (gr. k-3). 28.50 *(978-1-62588-005-5(7))* Black Rabbit Bks.

—Pets in the Home. West, David, illus. 2014. (Nora the Naturalist's Animals Ser.). (Illus.). 24p. (J). (gr. k-3). pap. 8.95 *(978-1-62588-052-9(9))* Black Rabbit Bks.

Wheeler, Jill C. Goldendoodles, 1 vol. 2008. (Dogs Set 7:Designer Dogs Ser.). (ENG., Illus.). 24p. (J). (gr. 2-5). 25.65 *(978-1-59928-963-2(6))* ABDO Publishing Co.

When Pets Attack! 2013. (When Pets Attack! Ser.). 32p. (J). (gr. 3-6). 159.60 *(978-1-4339-9677-1(4))*; pap. 63.00 *(978-1-4339-9741-9(X))*; pap. 378.00 *(978-1-4339-9742-6(8))* Stevens, Gareth Publishing LLLP.

Where Is My Pet?, 6 Packs. (Chiquilibros Ser.). (gr. k-1). 23.00 *(978-0-7635-0438-0(6))* Rigby Education.

William H. Sadlier Staff. Good Pets: Big Book, Vol. 3. 2005. (Emergent Library: Vol. 1). (gr. -1-1). 24.00 net. *(978-0-8215-8910-6(5))* Sadlier, William H. Inc.

Wittrock, Jeni. Pet Hermit Crabs up Close. 2015. (Pets up Close Ser.). (ENG.). 24p. (gr. k-1). lib. bdg. 26.65 *(978-1-4914-2109-3(6)*, Pebble Plus) Capstone Press of Coughlan Cos.

—Pets up Close. 2015. (Pets up Close Ser.). (ENG.). 24p. (gr. k-1). lib. bdg. 53.30 *(978-1-4914-2601-2(2)*, Pebble Plus) Capstone Press of Coughlan Cos.

World Book, Inc Staff, contrib. by. Green Anoles & Other Pet Lizards. 2009. (J). *(978-0-7166-1368-8(9))* World Bk., Inc.

—Hamsters & Other Pet Rodents. 2009. (J). *(978-0-7166-1370-1(0))* World Bk., Inc.

—World of Pets. 2010. (J). *(978-0-7166-7745-1(8))* World Bk., Inc.

Yoyo Books, creator. Pets. 2011. (ENG., Illus.). 10p. (gr. -1-k). bds. *(978-94-6151-208-6(2))* YoYo Bks.

Zondervan Staff. Cats, Dogs, Hamsters, & Horses, 1 vol. 2010. (I Can Read! / Made by God Ser.). (ENG., Illus.). 32p. (J). (gr. -1-2). pap. 3.99 *(978-0-310-72009-6(5))* Zonderkidz.

Zullo, Allan. Bad Pets Save Christmas! 2012. 139p. (J). pap. *(978-0-545-61229-6(2))* Scholastic, Inc.

—Miracle Pets: True Tales of Courage & Survival. 2011. 122p. *(978-0-545-25507-3(4))* Scholastic, Inc.

PETS—FICTION

Abbott, Rosalind. A Pet for Me. Seltzer, Jerry, illus. 2013. 24p. (J). 16.95 *(978-1-60131-155-9(9)*, Castlebridge Bks.) Big Tent Bks.

Abbott, Simon, illus. Happy Street: Pet Shop. 2014. (Happy Street Ser.). (ENG.). 10p. (J). (gr. -1-k). 9.99 *(978-1-4052-6864-6(6))* Egmont Bks., Ltd. GBR. Dist: Independent Pubs. Group.

Adams, Jean Ekman. When Dogs Dream. 2013. 32p. (J). 15.95 *(978-1-933855-84-4(3)*, Rio Nuevo Pubs.) Rio Nuevo Pubs.

Adamson, Ged. Shark Dog! Adamson, Ged, illus. 2017. (Illus.). 40p. (J). (gr. -1-3). 17.99 *(978-0-06-245713-4(6))* HarperCollins Pubs.

Albee, Sarah. Off to Bed. Ebert, Len, illus. 2006. (Step-By-Step Readers Ser.). (J). pap. *(978-1-59939-060-4(4)*, Reader's Digest Young Families, Inc.) Studio Fun International.

Alexander, Lori. Backhoe Joe. Cameron, Craig, illus. 2014. (ENG.). 40p. (J). (gr. -1-3). 15.99 *(978-0-06-225015-5(9))* HarperCollins Pubs.

Alvarez, Jennifer Lynn. The Pet Washer. 2nd ed. 2012. (ENG.). 171p. (J). (gr. 3-7). pap. 8.99 *(978-0-9848484-5-4(2))* Dreamcatcher Bks.

Amateau, Gigi. Chancey of the Maury River. 2010. (ENG., Illus.). 256p. (J). (gr. 4-7). pap. 6.99 *(978-0-7636-4523-6(0))* Candlewick Pr.

Amdahl Elco, Anita & Weikert Stelmach, Katherine. Who Is in That Shell? Patch, Michael, illus. 2012. 130p. (J). pap. 13.50 *(978-0-9883568-0-1(5))* Inkwell Books LLC.

Anderson, Laurie Halse. New Beginnings #13, 13 vols. 2012. (Vet Volunteers Ser.: 13). (ENG.). 192p. (J). (gr. 3-7). 6.99 *(978-0-14-241675-4(4)*, Puffin Books) Penguin Young Readers Group.

—Treading Water. 2014. (Vet Volunteers Ser.: 16). (ENG.). 192p. (J). (gr. 3-7). pap. 6.99 *(978-0-14-241678-5(9)*, Puffin Books) Penguin Young Readers Group.

Arguello, John. Ophelia & the Pet Peeve. 2009. 24p. pap. 12.99 *(978-1-4389-9197-9(5))* AuthorHouse.

Arnold, Tedd. Fly Guy's Ninja Christmas. Arnold, Tedd, illus. 2016. (Fly Guy Ser.: 16). (ENG., Illus.). 32p. (J). (gr. -1-3). 6.99 *(978-0-545-66277-2(X))* Scholastic, Inc.

—A Pet for Fly Guy. Arnold, Tedd, illus. 2014. (Fly Guy Ser.). (ENG., Illus.). 32p. (J). (gr. -1-3). 16.99 *(978-0-545-31615-6(4)*, Orchard Bks.) Scholastic, Inc.

—There Was an Old Lady Who Swallowed Fly Guy. Arnold, Tedd, illus. 2007. (Fly Guy Ser.: 4). (ENG., Illus.). 32p. (J). (gr. -1-3). 6.99 *(978-0-439-63906-4(9))* Scholastic, Inc.

Arruzza, Rick. No Descanso Para Sparky. Newton, Pilar, illus. 2004. (SPA.). 24p. (J). mass mkt. 7.95 *(978-0-9744509-3-3(6))* Three Spots Productions.

—No Rest for Sparky. Newton, Pilar, illus. 2004. 24p. (J). mass mkt. 7.95 *(978-0-9744509-2-6(8))* Three Spots Productions.

Arsenault, Isabelle. Colette's Lost Pet. 2017. (ENG., Illus.). 48p. (J). (gr. -1-2). 17.99 ***(978-0-553-53659-1(1))***; lib. bdg. 20.99 ***(978-0-553-53660-7(5))*** Random Hse. Children's Bks. (Random Hse. Bks. for Young Readers).

Asch, Frank. The Ghost of P. S. 42. Kanzler, John, illus. 2014. (Class Pets Ser.). (ENG.). 96p. (J). (gr. 2-5). pap. 13.99 *(978-1-4814-3624-3(4)*, Simon & Schuster/Paula Wiseman Bks.) Simon & Schuster/Paula Wiseman Bks.

Auch, Mary Jane. I Was a Third Grade Bodyguard. Auch, Herm, illus. 2003. (ENG.). 73p. (J). (gr. 4-6). tchr. ed. 16.95 *(978-0-8234-1775-9(1))* Holiday Hse., Inc.

Auerbach, Annie. Meet Boulder the Construction-Bot. 2013. (Transformers Passport to Reading Ser.). (J). lib. bdg. 13.55 *(978-0-606-32274-4(4)*, Turtleback) Turtleback Bks.

Aulbach, Kathy. Flower Sprouts: Let's have a Fest! 2009. 29p. 15.95 *(978-0-615-21683-6(8))* Flower Sprouts.

AZ Books Staff. My Pets. Yaroshevich, Angelica, ed. 2012. (Open the Book-I Am Alive Ser.). (ENG.). 8p. (J). (— 1). bds. 5.95 *(978-1-61889-045-0(X))* AZ Bks. LLC.

Baby Pets: Chunky photo Book. 2006. (J). bds. 3.99 *(978-1-934004-01-2(4))* Byeway Bks.

Baglio, Ben M. Come Back, Buddy! 2004. (Illus.). 118p. (J). pap. *(978-0-439-68883-3(3))* Scholastic, Inc.

—Help Find Honey! 2006. (Pet Finders Club Ser.: Vol. 10). (Illus.). 157p. (J). *(978-0-439-87143-3(3))* Scholastic, Inc.

—Max Is Missing. 2005. (Pet Finders Club Ser.: Vol. 2). (Illus.). 126p. (J). pap. *(978-0-439-68884-0(1))* Scholastic, Inc.

Baker, Courtney. The Perfect Pet. Snider, Jackie, illus. 2003. (Hello Reader! Ser.). (J). pap. *(978-0-439-47111-4(7))* Scholastic, Inc.

Bakos, Lisa M. Too Many Moose! Chambers, Mark, illus. 2016. (ENG.). 40p. (J). (-4). 16.99 *(978-1-4926-0935-3(8)*, 9781492609353, Sourcebooks Jabberwocky) Sourcebooks, Inc.

Baltazar, Art & Aureliani, Franco. Super-Pets!, 1 vol. Baltazar, Art, illus. 2013. (Superman Family Adventures Ser.). (ENG., Illus.). 32p. (gr. 1-2). 22.60 *(978-1-4342-4792-6(9))* Stone Arch Bks.

Banerjee, Anjali. Seaglass Summer. 2011. (ENG., Illus.). 176p. (J). (gr. 3-7). pap. 7.99 *(978-0-375-84399-0(X)*, Yearling) Random Hse. Children's Bks.

Barkley, Callie. Ellie the Flower Girl. Bishop, Tracy, illus. 2016. (Critter Club Ser.: 14). (ENG.). 128p. (J). (gr. k-4). pap. 5.99 *(978-1-4814-6718-6(2)*, Little Simon) Little Simon.

Barkley, Callie. Marion & the Secret Letter. 2017. (Critter Club Ser.: 16). lib. bdg. 16.00 ***(978-0-606-39739-1(6))*** Turtleback Bks.

Barroux, Stephane, illus. My Goldfish. 2009. 36p. (J). (gr. -1-2). 15.00 *(978-0-8028-5334-9(X)*, Eerdmans Bks For Young Readers) Eerdmans, William B. Publishing Co.

Barshaw, Ruth McNally. Best Friends Fur-Ever. Barshaw, Ruth McNally, illus. 2013. (Ellie Mcdoodle Diaries). (ENG., Illus.). 192p. (YA). (gr. 3-6). 12.99 *(978-1-61963-175-5(X)*, 9781619631755, Bloomsbury USA Childrens) Bloomsbury Publishing USA.

—Ellie McDoodle: Best Friends Fur-Ever. Barshaw, Ruth McNally, illus. 2011. (Ellie Mcdoodle Ser.). (ENG., Illus.). 192p. (YA). (gr. 3-6). pap. 7.99 *(978-1-59990-657-7(0)*, 9781599906577, Bloomsbury USA Childrens) Bloomsbury Publishing USA.

Bartoletti, Susan Campbell. Nobody's Diggier Than a Dog. Giacobbe, Beppe, illus. 2005. (ENG.). 40p. (gr. -1-17). 15.99 *(978-0-7868-1824-2(7))* Hyperion Pr.

Barton, Byron. My Bus Board Book. Barton, Byron, illus. 2015. (ENG., Illus.). 38p. (J). (gr. -1 — 1). bds. 7.99 *(978-0-06-228738-0(9)*, Greenwillow Bks.) HarperCollins Pubs.

Battersea Dogs and Cats Home Staff & Red Fox Staff. Rusty's Story. 2010. (ENG., Illus.). 112p. (J). pap. 8.99 *(978-1-84941-124-0(7)*, Red Fox) Random House Children's Books GBR. Dist: Independent Pubs. Group.

Battersea Dogs Home Staff & Red Fox Staff. Chester's Story. 2010. (ENG., Illus.). 128p. (J). pap. 8.99 *(978-1-84941-123-3(9)*, Red Fox) Random House Children's Books GBR. Dist: Independent Pubs. Group.

Beck, Carolyn. Wellington's Rainy Day, 1 vol. Kerrigan, Brooke, illus. 2011. (ENG.). 32p. (J). (gr. -1-3). 19.95 *(978-1-55469-284-2(9))* Orca Bk. Pubs. USA.

Beck, Sharon. The Fish in Our Class. 2011. (Randy's Corner Ser.). (Illus.). 32p. (J). (gr. -1-2). lib. bdg. 25.70 *(978-1-58415-978-0(2))* Mitchell Lane Pubs., Inc.

Beck, W. H. Malcolm at Midnight. Lies, Brian, illus. (ENG.). 272p. (J). (gr. 2-5). 2015. pap. 7.99 *(978-0-544-33666-7(6)*, HMH Books For Young Readers) 2012. 16.99 *(978-0-547-68100-9(3))* Houghton Mifflin Harcourt Publishing Co.

—Malcolm under the Stars. Lies, Brian, illus. (ENG.). 272p. (J). (gr. 2-5). 2016. pap. 7.99 *(978-0-544-81312-0(X))* 2015. 16.99 *(978-0-544-39267-0(1))* Houghton Mifflin Harcourt Publishing Co. (HMH Books For Young Readers).

Bell, Samantha. The Perfect Pet, 1 vol. 2013. (SPA.). 32p. (J). (gr. -1-3). pap. 9.95 *(978-1-60718-701-1(9))* Arbordale Publishing.

Bennett, Kelly. No a Norman: La Historia de un Pececito Dorado. Jones, Noah Z., illus. 2016. (ENG & SPA.). 32p. (J). 6.99 *(978-0-7636-8906-3(8))* Candlewick Pr.

—Not Norman: A Goldfish Story. Jones, Noah Z., illus. 2008. (ENG.). 32p. (J). (gr. -1-3). pap. 6.99 *(978-0-7636-2763-8(1))* Candlewick Pr.

Bentley, Catherine & Bentley, Dawn. Hoppy Goes to School. Huerta, Catherine, illus. 2006. (Pet Tales Ser.). (ENG.). 32p. (J). 2.95 *(978-1-59249-558-0(3))* Soundprints.

Bentley, Dawn. Hoppy Goes to School. Huerta, Catherine, illus. 2006. (ENG.). 32p. (J). pap. 9.95 *(978-1-59249-559-7(1))*; (gr. -1-3). 4.95 *(978-1-59249-556-6(7))* Soundprints.

Berenstain, Jan & Berenstain, Mike. The Berenstain Bears' Really Big Pet Show. Berenstain, Jan & Berenstain, Mike, illus. 2008. (Berenstain Bears Ser.). (Illus.). 32p. (J). (gr. -1-2). 8.99 *(978-0-06-057406-2(2))*; (ENG., pap. 3.99 *(978-0-06-057390-4(2))* HarperCollins Pubs. (HarperFestival).

Berenstain, Stan & Berenstain, Jan. The Berenstain Bears' Pet Show. 2014. (ENG.). 32p. (J). (-3). 9.99 *(978-1-4022-9090-9(X)*, Sourcebooks Jabberwocky) Sourcebooks, Inc.

Berry, Lynne. Pig & Pug. Correll, Gemma, illus. 2015. (ENG.). 40p. (J). (gr. -1-3). 16.99 *(978-1-4814-2131-7(X)*, Simon & Schuster Bks. For Young Readers) Simon & Schuster Bks. For Young Readers.

Best, Cari. Ava & the Real Lucille, 1 vol. Valentine, Madeline, illus. 2012. (ENG.). 32p. (J). (gr. -1-3). 16.99 *(978-0-374-39903-0(4)*, 9780374399030, Farrar, Straus & Giroux (BYR)) Farrar, Straus & Giroux.

Beyers, Kathryn. Babe's Vacation. 2012. 32p. pap. 17.49 *(978-1-4771-5671-1(2))* Xlibris Corp.

Biedrzycki, David. Me & My Dragon. Biedrzycki, David, illus. 2011. (ENG., Illus.). 40p. (J). (gr. -1-3). 17.95 *(978-1-58089-278-0(7))* Charlesbridge Publishing, Inc.

—Me & My Dragon: Christmas Spirit. Biedrzycki, David, illus. 2015. (ENG., Illus.). 40p. (J). (gr. -1-3). lib. bdg. 17.95 *(978-1-58089-622-1(7))* Charlesbridge Publishing, Inc.

—Me & My Dragon: Scared of Halloween. Biedrzycki, David, illus. 2013. (ENG., Illus.). 32p. (J). (gr. -1-3). pap. 7.95 *(978-1-58089-659-7(6))* Charlesbridge Publishing, Inc.

Biedrzycki, David & Canetti, Yanitzia. Mi Dragón y Yo. Biedrzycki, David, illus. 2014. (SPA., Illus.). 32p. (J). (gr. -1-3). pap. 7.95 *(978-1-58089-574-3(3))*; lib. bdg. 17.95 *(978-1-58089-693-1(6))* Charlesbridge Publishing, Inc.

Bird, Benjamin. Supergirl's Pet Problem! Levins, Tim, illus. 2015. (Amazing Adventures of Superman! Ser.). (ENG.). 32p. (gr. k-2). pap. 3.95 *(978-1-4795-6523-8(7)*, DC Super Heroes) Stone Arch Bks.

Birney, Betty G. Humphrey's School Fair Surprise. Burris, Priscilla, illus. 2016. (Humphrey's Tiny Tales Ser.: 4). (ENG.). 112p. (J). (gr. k-3). 14.99 *(978-0-399-17229-8(7)*, G.P. Putnam's Sons Books for Young Readers) Penguin Young Readers Group.

—Humphrey's Treasure Hunt Trouble. Burris, Priscilla, illus. 2017. (Humphrey's Tiny Tales Ser.: 6). (ENG.). 96p. (J). (gr. k-3). 4.99 ***(978-0-14-751462-2(2)***, Puffin Books); 14.99 ***(978-0-399-17231-1(9)***, G.P. Putnam's Sons Books for Young Readers) Penguin Young Readers Group.

Birney, Betty G. Secrets According to Humphrey. 2014. (Humphrey Ser.: 10). (ENG.). 144p. (J). (gr. 3-7). 15.99 *(978-0-399-25796-4(9)*, G.P. Putnam's Sons Books for Young Readers) Penguin Young Readers Group.

—Secrets According to Humphrey. 2015. (According to Humphrey Ser.: 10). lib. bdg. 16.00 *(978-0-606-36600-7(8))* Turtleback Bks.

Black, Angie. Adopting Jake. Lucas, Diane, illus. 2010. 32p. pap. 12.95 *(978-1-935268-47-5(3))* Halo Publishing International.

Blacklidge, Barbara. Lucky: My Story. 2010. 24p. (J). pap. 12.95 *(978-1-934449-64-6(4))* Legacy Publishing Services, Inc.

Blake, Linda. My Pet Rabbit. 2012. 24p. 24.95 *(978-1-4626-6187-9(4))* America Star Bks.

Blake, Quentin. Loveykins. Blake, Quentin, illus. 2003. (Illus.). 32p. (J). (gr. k-3). 15.95 *(978-1-56145-282-8(3))* Peachtree Pubs.

Blake, Quentin & Blake, Quentin. Loveykins. 2016. (ENG., Illus.). 32p. (J). (gr. -1-3). pap. 7.95 *(978-1-56145-760-1(4))* Peachtree Pubs.

Blance, Ellen & Cook, Tony. Monster Buys a Pet. Date not set. (Illus.). 40p. pap. 129.15 *(978-0-582-19311-6(7))* Addison-Wesley Longman, Ltd. GBR. Dist: Trans-Atlantic Pubns., Inc.

Blevins, Wiley. Max Has a Fish. Clanton, Ben, illus. 2012. (Penguin Young Readers, Level 1 Ser.). (ENG.). 32p. (J). (gr. k-1). pap. 3.99 *(978-0-448-46158-8(7)*, Penguin Young Readers) Penguin Young Readers Group.

—Max Has a Fish. 2012. (Penguin Young Readers Level 1 Ser.). lib. bdg. 13.55 *(978-0-606-26640-6(2)*, Turtleback) Turtleback Bks.

Blume, Erma Hill. Tattle-Tale Pete. 2012. 28p. pap. 24.95 *(978-1-62709-097-1(5))* America Star Bks.

Boelts, Maribeth. Before You Were Mine. Walker, David, illus. 2007. (ENG.). 32p. (J). (gr. -1-3). 15.99 *(978-0-399-24526-8(X)*, G.P. Putnam's Sons Books for Young Readers) Penguin Young Readers Group.

—Before You Were Mine. Walker, David, illus. 2008. (J). (gr. -1-3). 27.95 incl. audio *(978-0-8045-6961-3(4))*; 29.95 incl. audio compact disk *(978-0-8045-4184-8(1))* Spoken Arts, Inc.

Boland, Janice. Zippers. Pfeiffer, Judith, illus. 2003. (Books for Young Learners). (ENG.). 8p. (J). pap. 15.00 *(978-1-57274-700-5(5)*, BB2220, Bks. for Young Learners) Owen, Richard C. Pubs., Inc.

Bolton, Robin. Sunny Goes Out to Play. 2011. 28p. pap. 12.03 *(978-1-4634-2530-2(9))* AuthorHouse.

Bonnell, Kris. Pets for Us. 2007. (J). pap. 5.95 *(978-1-933727-50-9(0))* Reading Reading Bks., LLC.

—We Love Pets. 2007. (J). pap. 5.95 *(978-1-933727-56-1(X))* Reading Reading Bks., LLC.

Bove, Candace Scobie. Calypso: A Day in the Life of a Puppy. 2012. 24p. 24.95 *(978-1-4626-4122-2(9))* America Star Bks.

Bowen, Anne. I Know an Old Teacher. Gammell, Stephen, illus. 2008. (ENG.). 32p. (J). (gr. k-3). 16.95 *(978-0-8225-7984-7(7)*, Carolrhoda Bks.) Lerner Publishing Group.

Bradmon, Karen. Goldie: A Fishtale of Adventure. 2008. 22p. pap. 24.95 *(978-1-60672-472-9(X))* America Star Bks.

Bremauntz, M. The Adventures of Marcela & Little Joey: Little Joey Loves Bugs. 2010. 32p. 17.25 *(978-1-4269-4417-8(9))* Trafford Publishing.

Brett, Jan. Annie & the Wild Animals. 2012. (ENG., Illus.). 32p. (J). (gr. -1-3). audio compact disk 10.99 *(978-0-547-85082-5(4))* Houghton Mifflin Harcourt Publishing Co.

—Annie & the Wild Animals. Brett, Jan, illus. 2012. (ENG., Illus.). 32p. (J). (gr. -1-k). 17.99 *(978-0-399-16104-9(X)*, G.P. Putnam's Sons Books for Young Readers) Penguin Young Readers Group.

—Annie & the Wild Animals Send-A-Story. 2011. (Send a Story Ser.). (ENG., Illus.). 32p. (J). (gr. -1-3). pap. 4.99 *(978-0-547-56692-4(1))* Houghton Mifflin Harcourt Publishing Co.

Brewer, Elly. Jerry & the Jannans. 2006. (ENG.). 320p. (J). (gr. 4-7). pap. 11.99 *(978-0-7475-8213-7(0))* Bloomsbury Publishing Plc GBR. Dist: Independent Pubs. Group.

Brezinova, Ivona. To Have a Dog. Deisadze, Zaur, illus. 2007. (POL & ENG.). 32p. (J). pap. 12.95 *(978-1-60195-106-9(X))* International Step by Step Assn.

Bright, J. E. Heroes of the High Seas, 1 vol. Baltazar, Art, illus. 2011. (DC Super-Pets Ser.). (ENG.). 56p. (gr. 2-2). 23.99 *(978-1-4048-6263-0(3))*; pap. 4.95 *(978-1-4048-6621-8(3))* Picture Window Bks. (DC Super-Pets).

Bright, Phoebe. Lucky Stars #2: Wish upon a Pet. 2012. (Lucky Stars Ser.). (ENG.). 96p. (J). (gr. 2-5). 5.99 *(978-0-545-41999-4(9)*, Scholastic Paperbacks) Scholastic, Inc.

Brodsky, Kathy. Just Sniffing Around. Bennett, Cameron, illus. 2009. (ENG.). 40p. 19.99 *(978-0-578-03620-5(7))* Helpingwords.

Brown, Marc. Arthur & the School Pet. 2005. (Step into Reading Sticker Bks.). (Illus.). 24p. 14.00 *(978-0-7569-5571-7(8))* Perfection Learning Corp.

—Arthur & the School Pet. 2003. (Step into Reading Ser.). (ENG., Illus.). 24p. (J). (gr. k-3). pap. 3.99 *(978-0-375-81001-5(3)*, Random Hse. Bks. for Young Readers) Random Hse. Children's Bks.

—Arthur & the School Pet. 2003. (Arthur Step into Reading Ser.). (gr. -1-2). lib. bdg. 13.55 *(978-0-613-57492-1(3)*, Turtleback) Turtleback Bks.

—Arthur's New Puppy. (Arthur Adventure Ser.). (J). (gr. k-3). 7.98 incl. audio NewSound, LLC.

—Arthur's Pet Business. Brown, Marc, illus. rev. ed. 2007. (ENG., Illus.). 32p. (J). (gr. -1-3). pap. 10.99 *(978-0-316-11863-7(X))* Little, Brown Bks. for Young Readers.

Brown, Peter. Children Make Terrible Pets. 2010. (Starring Lucille Beatrice Bear Ser.). (ENG., Illus.). 40p. (J). (gr. -1-3). 17.99 *(978-0-316-01548-6(2))* Little, Brown Bks. for Young Readers.

Bruel, Nick. Bad Kitty School Daze. 2013. (Bad Kitty Ser.). (ENG., Illus.). 160p. (J). (gr. 2-5). 13.99 *(978-1-59643-670-1(0)*, 9781596436701) Roaring Brook Pr.

—Bad Kitty School Daze. 2014. (Bad Kitty Ser.). (ENG., Illus.). 176p. (J). (gr. 2-5). pap. 6.99 (978-1-250-03947-7(9), 9781250039477) Square Fish.

—Bad Kitty Storytime Set. unabr. ed. 2014. (ENG.). (J). 12.99 (978-1-4272-3178-9(8), 9781427231789) Macmillan Audio.

Buckeridge, Anthony. Jennings' Little Hut. 2008. (Jennings Ser.: 3). (ENG.). 210p. (J). (gr. -1-12). pap. 12.95 (978-0-7551-1367-5(5)) House of Stratus, Inc. GBR. Dist: Gardners Bks. Ltd.

Buggs, Michael A. Tabard. Buggs, Michael A., illus. (Illus.). 64p. (Orig.). (J). (gr. 2-6). pap. 15.00 (978-0-9657723-0-3(6)) Mogul Comics.

Burchette, Ruby J. The Dog Went to School, 1 vol. 2010. 48p. pap. 16.95 (978-1-4489-4962-5(9)) America Star Bks.

Burkhart, Jessica. Bella's Birthday Unicorn. Ying, Victoria, illus. 2014. (Unicorn Magic Ser.: 1). (ENG.). 144p. (J). (gr. 1-4). 15.99 (978-1-4814-1105-9(5)); pap. 5.99 (978-1-4424-9822-8(6)) Simon & Schuster Children's Publishing. (Aladdin).

—The Hidden Treasure. Ying, Victoria, illus. 2015. (Unicorn Magic Ser.: 4). (ENG.). 112p. (J). (gr. 1-4). pap. 5.99 (978-1-4424-9829-7(3), Aladdin) Simon & Schuster Children's Publishing.

—Where's Glimmer? Ying, Victoria, illus. 2014. (Unicorn Magic Ser.: 2). (ENG.). 144p. (J). (gr. 1-4). pap. 5.99 (978-1-4424-9824-2(2), Aladdin) Simon & Schuster Children's Publishing.

Burlingham, Abi. Best Friends. Everitt-Stewart, Andy, illus. 2009. (Stories to Grow with Ser.). 24p. (J). (gr. -1-2). 22.60 (978-1-60754-475-3(X)); pap. 8.15 (978-1-60754-476-0(8)) Windmill Bks.

Cabral, Jeane. Bad Dog Ben. 2009. (Jeane Cabral Bks.). (Illus.). (J). bds. 12.99 (978-1-934650-05-9(6)) Just For Kids Pr., LLC.

Calmenson, Stephanie. May I Pet Your Dog? The How-to Guide for Kids Meeting Dogs (and Dogs Meeting Kids) Ormerod, Jan, illus. 2007. (ENG.). 32p. (J). (gr. -1-3). 13.99 (978-0-618-51034-4(6), Clarion Bks.) Houghton Mifflin Harcourt Trade & Reference Pubs.

Camacho, Norma I. Mikey/Jackster. 2011. 48p. (gr. 4-6). pap. 9.89 (978-1-4669-0155-1(1)) Trafford Publishing.

Cameron, Ann. Spunky Tells All. Castillo, Lauren, illus. 2011. (ENG.). 112p. (J). (gr. 3-6). 16.99 (978-0-374-38000-7(7), 9780374380007, Farrar, Straus & Giroux (BYR)) Farrar, Straus & Giroux.

Campbell, Rod. Dear Zoo. Campbell, Rod, illus. 2005. (Dear Zoo & Friends Ser.). (ENG., Illus.). 20p. (J). (gr. -1-k). 14.99 (978-0-689-87751-3(X), Little Simon) Little Simon.

—Dear Zoo. Campbell, Rod, illus. 2004. (RUS & ENG., Illus.). 16p. (J). bds. (978-1-84444-178-5(4)) Mantra Lingua.

—Dear Zoo. 2004. (BEN & ENG., Illus.). 16p. (J). bds. (978-1-84444-169-3(5)) Mantra Lingua.

—Dear Zoo. Campbell, Rod, illus. 2004. (Illus.). 16p. (J). (VIE & ENG.). bds. (978-1-84444-183-9(0)); (CHI & ENG., bds. (978-1-84444-171-6(7)); (ENG & HIN., bds. (978-1-84444-175-4(X)); (ENG & PAN., bds. (978-1-84444-176-1(8)); (ENG & POR., bds. (978-1-84444-177-8(6)); (ENG & SPA., bds. (978-1-84444-179-2(2)); (ENG & SOM., bds. (978-1-84444-180-8(6)); (ENG & TUR., bds. (978-1-84444-181-5(4)); (URD & ENG., bds. (978-1-84444-182-2(2)); (ENG & GUJ., bds. (978-1-84444-174-7(1)); (ENG & FRE., bds. (978-1-84444-173-0(3)); (CHI & ENG., bds. (978-1-84444-170-9(9)); (ENG & PER., bds. (978-1-84444-172-3(5)); (ENG & ARA., bds. (978-1-84444-168-6(7)); (ENG & ALB., bds. (978-1-84444-167-9(9)) Mantra Lingua.

—Dear Zoo: From the Zoo. Campbell, Rod, illus. 25th ed. 2007. (ENG., Illus.). 18p. (J). (gr. -1 — 1). bds. 6.99 (978-1-4169-4737-0(X), Little Simon) Little Simon.

Candlewick Press Staff. Peppa Pig & the Great Vacation. 2014. (Peppa Pig Ser.). (ENG.). 32p. (J). (-k). 12.99 (978-0-7636-6986-7(5), Candlewick Entertainment) Candlewick Pr.

Capucilli, Alyssa Satin. Biscuit's Pet & Play Christmas. Schories, Pat & Young, Mary O'Keefe, illus. 2006. (Biscuit Ser.). (ENG.). 12p. (J). (gr. -1-1). bds. 7.99 (978-0-06-009470-6(2), HarperFestival) HarperCollins Pubs.

Carbone, Courtney. Palace Pets: Snuggle Buddies. 2014. (Step into Reading Level 2 Ser.). lib. bdg. 13.55 (978-0-606-35193-5(0)) Turtleback Bks.

—Pet Friends Forever! 2014. (Pictureback(R) Ser.). (ENG., Illus.). 24p. (J). (gr. -1-2). 5.99 (978-0-385-38786-6(5), RH/Disney) Random Hse. Children's Bks.

—Snuggle Buddies. Random House Disney Staff, illus. 2014. (Step into Reading Ser.). (ENG.). 32p. (J). (gr. -1-1). 3.99 (978-0-7364-3155-2(1)); lib. bdg. 12.99 (978-0-7364-8158-8(3)) Random Hse. Children's Bks. (RH/Disney).

Carlisle, Samantha. The Day Sam Lost Lucky. 2009. (Illus.). 52p. pap. 13.95 (978-1-4327-2412-2(6)) Outskirts Pr., Inc.

Carney, Larry, adapted by. Silly Farm. 2010. (ENG., Illus.). 24p. (J). pap. 6.95 (978-1-60072-156-4(7)) PC Treasures, Inc.

Carson, Jeanelle. Lexi Lou Meets Jadie Bear. 2010. 36p. pap. 15.49 (978-1-4520-9449-6(7)) AuthorHouse.

Carter, Tammy. My Friend, Dinner. 2013. 28p. pap. 24.95 (978-1-4241-0629-5(X)) America Star Bks.

Carvajal, Victor. Chipana. (SPA.). (YA). (gr. 5-8). pap. 7.95 (978-958-04-5044-3(7), NR3753) Norma S.A. COL. Dist: Distribuidora Norma, Inc., Lectorum Pubns., Inc.

Ceville, Laura. My Dog, Jack. 2013. 24p. pap. 8.99 (978-1-938768-25-5(6)) Gypsy Pubns.

Chall, Marsha Wilson. Pick a Pup. Henry, Jed, illus. 2011. (ENG.). 32p. (J). (gr. -1-k). 16.99 (978-1-4169-7961-6(1), McElderry, Margaret K. Bks.) McElderry, Margaret K. Bks.

Charlesworth, Liza. The Best Pet: An Animal Friends Reader. Smith, Ian, illus. 2015. 16p. (J). **(978-0-545-85961-5(1))** Scholastic, Inc.

Chicatelli, Joy. Bailey's Heartstrings. Rottinger, Amy, illus. 2011. 28p. pap. 12.95 (978-1-935268-96-3(1)) Halo Publishing International.

Chichester Clark, Emma. Plenty of Love to Go Around. Chichester Clark, Emma, illus. 2016. (ENG., Illus.). 32p. (J). (-k). 17.99 (978-0-399-54666-2(9), Nancy Paulsen Books) Penguin Young Readers Group.

Chimenti, Maureen. The Day My Pet Went to Heaven. 2008. 44p. pap. 17.99 (978-1-4389-3271-2(5)) AuthorHouse.

Christopher, Matt. You Lucky Dog. Vasconcellos, Daniel, illus. 8th ed. 2003. (ENG.). 64p. (J). (gr. 1-4). pap. 13.99 (978-0-316-73805-7(0)) Little, Brown Bks. for Young Readers.

—You Lucky Dog. Vasconcellos, Daniel, illus. 2003. (Soccer Cats Ser.: Bk. 8). 49p. (J). (gr. 2-4). 12.65 (978-0-7569-3907-6(0)) Perfection Learning Corp.

Cibos, Lindsay. Peach Fuzz, 1 vol., Vol. 1. Hodges, Jared, illus. 2009. (Tokyopop Ser.). (ENG.). 160p. (gr. 2-6). 25.65 (978-1-59961-571-4(1)) Spotlight.

—Peach Fuzz Vol. 2: Show & Tell, 1 vol. Hodges, Jared, illus. 2009. (Tokyopop Ser.). (ENG.). 176p. (gr. 2-6). 25.65 (978-1-59961-572-1(X)) Spotlight.

—Peach Fuzz Vol. 3: Prince Edwin, 1 vol. Hodges, Jared, illus. 2009. (Tokyopop Ser.). (ENG.). 176p. (gr. 2-6). 25.65 (978-1-59961-573-8(8)) Spotlight.

Clara Mulholland. Naughty Miss Bunny. 2007. 128p. per. 10.95 (978-1-4218-3938-7(5), 1st World Library - Literary Society) 1st World Publishing, Inc.

Clark, Sandra. My Tears Count Too. 2009. 84p. pap. 28.99 (978-1-4389-8357-8(3)) AuthorHouse.

Climo, Liz. Rory the Dinosaur Wants a Pet. 2016. (ENG., Illus.). 40p. (J). (gr. -1-3). 16.99 (978-0-316-27729-7(0)) Little Brown & Co.

Coe, Victoria J. Fenway & Hattie & the Evil Bunny Gang. 2017. (Fenway & Hattie Ser.). (ENG.). 192p. (J). (gr. 3-7). 16.99 (978-1-101-99633-1(1), G.P. Putnam's Sons Books for Young Readers) Penguin Young Readers Group.

Cohen, Lettie. Lila's New Pet. 2013. 20p. pap. 17.99 (978-1-4817-0109-9(6)) AuthorHouse.

Collins, Ellen M. My Book: Fun Favorite Stories. 2010. 68p. pap. 26.99 (978-1-4490-5236-2(3)) AuthorHouse.

Cooney, Doug. The Beloved Dearly. DiTerlizzi, Tony, illus. 2003. (ENG.). 192p. (J). (gr. 3-7). pap. 7.99 (978-0-689-86354-7(3), Simon & Schuster Bks. For Young Readers) Simon & Schuster Bks. For Young Readers.

Coons, Anita. Graze, Gaze & Saddle Days. 2005. (Illus.). 144p. (J). per. 10.95 (978-1-59713-003-5(6)) Goose River Pr.

Cooper, D. C. Rascal the Baby Squirrel. 2013. 32p. (978-1-4602-2658-2(5)) FriesenPress.

Cordone Warner, Debra. Henry's Daily Walk. 2010. 56p. pap. 24.99 (978-0-557-60667-2(5)) Lulu Pr., Inc.

Corlyn, Ron. The House That Grew. 2013. 24p. pap. 24.95 (978-1-63000-118-6(X)) America Star Bks.

Costain, Meredith. Stella & the Pet Parade. McGowan, Shane, illus. 2015. (Legends in Their Own Lunchbox Ser.). (ENG.). 48p. (gr. 1-2). pap. 7.99 (978-1-4966-0243-5(9), Legends in Their Own Lunchbox) Capstone Classroom.

Coven, Wanda. Heidi Heckelbeck & the Tie-Dyed Bunny. 2014. (Heidi Heckelbeck Ser.: 10). lib. bdg. 16.00 (978-0-606-35429-5(8)) Turtleback Bks.

Coville, Bruce. Jeremy Thatcher, Dragon Hatcher: A Magic Shop Book. Lippincott, Gary A., illus. 20th ed. 2007. (Magic Shop Book Ser.: 2). (ENG.). 176p. (J). (gr. 5-7). pap. 7.99 (978-0-15-206252-1(1)) Houghton Mifflin Harcourt Publishing Co.

Coxon, Michele. Have You Fed the Cat? (Spanish/English) Coxon, Michele, illus. 2004. (SPA & ENG., Illus.). 32p. (J). 15.95 (978-1-59572-001-6(4)); pap. 5.95 (978-1-59572-002-3(2)) Star Bright Bks., Inc.

Crossno, Frances M. Cole's Perfect Puppy, Perfect Puppies Book One. 2016. (ENG., Illus.). 98p. (J). pap. 14.95 (978-1-5069-0168-8(9)) First Edition Design eBook Publishing.

Crouse, Livingstone. Kisses for Kindergarten. Pamintuan, Macky, illus. 2017. (ENG.). 40p. (J). (gr. -1). 17.99 (978-1-62686-703-1(8), Silver Dolphin Bks.) Readerlink Distribution Services, LLC.

Crow, Melinda Melton. Little Lizard's New Pet, 1 vol. Rowland, Andrew, illus. 2011. (Little Lizards Ser.). (ENG.). 32p. (gr. -1-1). pap. 6.25 (978-1-4342-3049-2(X)); lib. bdg. 22.65 (978-1-4342-2508-5(9)) Stone Arch Bks.

Cynthia, Rylant. Every Living Thing. 2014. (ENG.). 96p. (J). (gr. 5-9). 10.24 (978-1-63245-336-5(3)) Lectorum Pubns., Inc.

Dadey, Debbie. The Secret Sea Horse. Avakyan, Tatevik, illus. 2013. (Mermaid Tales Ser.: 6). (ENG.). 112p. (J). (gr. 1-4). 15.99 (978-1-4424-8261-6(3)); pap. 5.99 (978-1-4424-8260-9(5)) Simon & Schuster Children's Publishing. (Aladdin).

Dahl, Michael. Animal Etiquette. Persico, Zoe, illus. 2016. (Me & My Pet Ser.). (ENG.). 24p. (gr. 1-2). 45.30 (978-1-5158-0255-6(8), Fiction Picture Bks.) Picture Window Bks.

Dale, Jay. My Pets, 1 vol. Richards, Kirsten, illus. 2012. (Wonder Words Ser.). (ENG.). 32p. (gr. k-2). pap. 5.99 (978-1-4296-8886-4(6), Engage Literacy) Capstone Press of Coughlan Cos.

Daly, Cathleen. Prudence Wants a Pet. King, Stephen Michael, illus. 2011. (ENG.). 32p. (J). (gr. -1-2). 17.99 (978-1-59643-468-4(6), 9781596434684) Roaring Brook Pr.

Darling, Nina. Pet Shop Talk: A Grooming for Max, 1 vol. 2009. 27p. pap. 24.95 (978-1-60813-646-9(9)) America Star Bks.

Davies, Katie. The Great Rabbit Rescue. Shaw, Hannah, illus. 2011. (Great Critter Capers Ser.). (ENG.). 224p. (J). (gr. 3-7). 12.99 (978-1-4424-2064-9(2), Beach Lane Bks.) Beach Lane Bks.

Davis, Jim. Garfield Caution - Wide Load. 2013. (Garfield Ser.: 56). (ENG., Illus.). 96p. pap. 14.00 (978-0-345-52596-3(5), Ballantine Bks.) Random House Publishing Group.

—Garfield Gets in a Pickle. 2012. (Garfield Ser.: 54). lib. bdg. 25.75 (978-0-606-26835-6(9), Turtleback) Turtleback Bks.

Dawson, Brianog Brady. Danny's Pesky Pet. Connor, Michael, tr. Connor, Michael, illus. 2003. (Pandas Ser.: 25). (ENG.). 64p. (J). pap. 9.95 (978-0-86278-803-2(X)) O'Brien Pr., Ltd., The IRL. Dist: Dufour Editions, Inc.

de Brunhoff, Laurent. Babar & the Wully-Wully. 2012. (ENG., Illus.). 40p. (J). (gr. k-2). 15.95 (978-1-4197-0381-2(1), Abrams Bks. for Young Readers) Abrams, Inc.

de Rham, Mickey. Hey Bossie, You're a Spokescow! Gusterson, Leigh, illus. 2004. 24p. (J). 9.95 (978-0-9755216-0-1(8)) Plaidswede Publishing.

Dean, James. Pete the Cat & the Tip-Top Tree House. Dean, James, illus. 2017. (My First I Can Read Ser.). (Illus.). 32p. (J). (gr. -1-3). pap. 3.99 (978-0-06-240431-2(8)) HarperCollins Pubs.

Dean, James & Dean, Kimberly. A Pet for Pete. Dean, James, illus. 2014. (My First I Can Read Ser.). (ENG., Illus.). 32p. (J). (gr. -1-3). pap. 3.99 (978-0-06-230379-0(1)) HarperCollins Pubs.

Delaney, Michael. Obi, Gerbil on the Loose! 2008. (ENG.). 208p. (J). (gr. 5-18). 16.99 (978-0-525-47890-4(6), Dutton Books for Young Readers) Penguin Young Readers Group.

dePaola, Tomie. Little Grunt & the Big Egg: A Prehistoric Fairy Tale. dePaola, Tomie, illus. 2008. (ENG., Illus.). 32p. (J). (gr. -1-3). pap. 6.99 (978-0-14-241143-8(4), Puffin Books) Penguin Young Readers Group.

—Little Grunt & the Big Egg: A Prehistoric Fairy Tale. 2007. 29.95 incl. audio compact disk (978-0-8045-4158-9(2)); 27.95 incl. audio (978-0-8045-6944-6(4)) Spoken Arts, Inc.

Diamond, Lorraine. I Want a Camel for a Pet, 1 vol. 2009. 13p. pap. 24.95 (978-1-61546-425-8(5)) America Star Bks.

Diamond, Shendl, illus. & text. The True Story of Critter Angels by Yani. Diamond, Shendl, text. 2005. (J). 15.95 (978-0-9764724-3-8(0)) LikeMinds Pr.

Dipucchio, Kelly. Gilbert Goldfish Wants a Pet. Shea, Bob, illus. 2011. (ENG.). 32p. (J). (gr. -1-k). 16.99 (978-0-8037-3394-7(1), Dial Bks) Penguin Young Readers Group.

Disney Book Group. Doc Mcstuffins Pet Vet. Disney Storybook Art Team, illus. 2015. (ENG.). 24p. (J). (gr. -1-k). pap. 4.99 (978-1-4847-1557-4(8)) Disney Pr.

—Whisker Haven Tales Petite's Great Feats (Storybook Plus Collectible Toy) Disney Storybook Art Team, illus. 2016. (ENG.). 128p. (J). (gr. 1-3). 14.99 (978-1-4847-5243-2(0)) Disney Pr.

—Whisker Haven Tales with the Palace Pets: Nuzzles & the Easter Egg Mix-Up: Read-along Storybook & CD. Disney Storybook Art Team, illus. 2016. (Read-Along Storybook & CD Ser.). (ENG.). 32p. (J). (gr. -1-k). pap. 6.99 (978-1-4847-8695-6(5)) Disney Pr.

Disney Book Group Staff. Palace Pets: Summer the Kitten for Rapunzel. 2014. (ENG.). 10p. (J). (gr. -1-k). bds. 9.99 (978-1-4847-1184-2(X)) Disney Pr.

—Palace Pets: Teacup the Pup for Belle. 2014. (ENG., Illus.). 10p. (J). (gr. -1-k). bds. 9.99 (978-1-4847-1183-5(1)) Disney Pr.

—Royal Kittens: A Palace Pets Book & Magnetic Play Set. 2015. (ENG.). 32p. (J). (gr. -1-k). 14.99 (978-1-4847-0512-4(2)) Disney Pr.

—5- Minute Palace Pets Stories. 2015. (5-Minute Stories Ser.). (ENG.). 192p. (J). (gr. -1-k). 12.99 (978-1-4847-0463-9(0)) Disney Pr.

Disney Book Group Staff & Higginson, Sheila Sweeny. Henry Hugglemonster Pet Party. Disney Storybook Artists Staff & Disney Storybook Art Team, illus. 2014. (ENG.). 24p. (J). (gr. -1-k). pap. 4.99 (978-1-4847-0263-5(8)) Disney Pr.

Disney Book Group Staff & Scollon, Bill. Sofia the First: a Royal Mouse in the House. Lee, Grace, illus. 2015. (ENG.). 40p. (J). (gr. -1-k). 8.99 (978-1-4847-0643-5(9)) Disney Pr.

Disney Minnie Mouse Staff. Disney Minnie. 2013. (Carry along Play Book Ser.: 1). (ENG.). 14p. (J). (gr. -1-2). 14.99 (978-0-7944-2897-6(5), Reader's Digest Children's Bks.) Studio Fun International.

Disney Storybook Art Team. Whisker Haven Tales with the Palace Pets: Winter in Whisker Haven: Read-Along Storybook & CD. 2016. (ENG.). 32p. (J). (gr. -1-k). pap. 6.99 (978-1-4847-4709-4(7)) Disney Pr.

DiTerlizzi, Angela. Some Pets. Wenzel, Brendan, illus. 2016. (ENG.). 32p. (J). (gr. -1-3). 17.99 (978-1-4814-4402-6(6), Beach Lane Bks.) Beach Lane Bks.

Dmaples. Big Dog, Little Puppy. 2012. 28p. pap. 19.99 (978-1-4685-6064-0(6)) AuthorHouse.

Dominguez, Angela. María Tenía una Llamita. Dominguez, Angela, illus. 2013.Tr. of Maria Had a Little Llama. (SPA & ENG., Illus.). 32p. (J). (gr. -1-2). 17.99 (978-0-8050-9333-9(8), 9780805093339, Holt, Henry & Co. Bks. For Young Readers) Holt, Henry & Co.

Dorling Kindersley Publishing Staff. Pets. 2010. (Baby Touch & Feel Ser.). (ENG., Illus.). 14p. (J). (gr. -1 — 1). bds. 5.99 (978-0-7566-6684-2(8), DK Children) Dorling Kindersley Publishing, Inc.

Downie, David. David & Jacko. Tatsi, Andreanna, tr. Seroya, Tea, illus. 2012. 52p. pap. (978-1-922159-24-3(7)); pap. (978-1-922159-15-1(8)) Blue Peg Publishing.

—David & Jacko. Ivanova, Kalina, tr. Seroya, Tea, illus. 2012. 52p. pap. (978-1-922159-01-4(8)) Blue Peg Publishing.

—David & Jacko. Seroya, Tea, illus. 2012. 52p. pap. (978-1-922159-99-1(9)) Blue Peg Publishing.

Drescher, Henrik. Love the Beastie: A Spin-and-Play Book. 2011. (ENG., Illus.). 11p. (J). (gr. -1-3). 12.95 (978-0-7611-6109-7(0), 16109) Workman Publishing Co., Inc.

Dubois, Rikki Marie-José Grenier. Muffy Was Fluffy. 2012. 28p. pap. 24.95 (978-1-62709-167-1(X)) America Star Bks.

Duchene-Marshall, Michele A. Shirley's Red Satin Shoes. Marshall, Alan David, ed. Ousley, Clayton Gerard, photos by. l.t. ed. 2003. (Illus.). 17p. (J). spiral bd. 10.00 (978-0-9761675-1-8(4)) Storybook Acres.

Dullaart, Alberta M. Snowy Black & White. 2010. 20p. 10.49 (978-1-4520-1385-5(3)) AuthorHouse.

Duncan-Pauley, Chadney. A Bull's Paradise. 2009. 32p. pap. 15.60 (978-0-557-17660-1(3)) Lulu Pr., Inc.

Dunn, Judy. The Little Rabbit. Dunn, Phoebe, photos by. 2016. (Step into Reading Ser.). (ENG., Illus.). 32p. (J). (gr. -1-1). pap. 3.99 (978-0-553-53354-5(1), Random Hse. Bks. for Young Readers) Random Hse. Children's Bks.

Dvok, Eduard & Dvorák, Eduard. Bobek, the Cat with a Pompon Tail. Dvorák, Jaroslav, illus. 2010. 52p. pap. 17.00 (978-1-60911-734-4(4), Eloquent Bks.) Strategic Book Publishing & Rights Agency (SBPRA).

Dyckman, Ame. You Don't Want a Unicorn! Climo, Liz, illus. 2017. (ENG.). 40p. (J). (gr. -1-3). 16.99 (978-0-316-34347-3(1)) Little Brown & Co.

Earhart, Kristin. Puppy Powers #2: Wag, You're It! 2014. (Puppy Powers Ser.: 2). (ENG., Illus.). 96p. (J). (gr. 2-5). pap. 4.99 (978-0-545-61760-4(X), Scholastic Paperbacks) Scholastic, Inc.

—Puppy Powers #3: Take a Bow-Wow. 2014. (Puppy Powers Ser.: 3). (ENG.). 96p. (J). (gr. 2-5). pap. 4.99 (978-0-545-61761-1(8), Scholastic Paperbacks) Scholastic, Inc.

Easton, Marilyn. New Girl in Town. 2013. (LEGO Friends Chapter Bks.: 1). lib. bdg. 14.75 (978-0-606-31548-7(9), Turtleback) Turtleback Bks.

Eaton, Jason Carter. How to Train a Train. Rocco, John, illus. (ENG.). (J). 2016. 28p. (-k). bds. 7.99 (978-0-7636-8899-8(1)) 2013. 48p. (gr. -1-3). 16.99 (978-0-7636-6307-0(7)) Candlewick Pr.

Edgin, Brenda. Little Winston & His Big Adventures in Natchez: New Home near the Woods. 2011. 16p. 12.99 (978-1-4567-3639-2(6)) AuthorHouse.

Edwards, Sal A. A Forever Family: Living in the Big House. 2012. 42p. (-18). pap. 17.45 (978-1-4624-0329-5(8), Inspiring Voices) Author Solutions, Inc.

Edwards, Sonia. Noson y Llygaid Llachar. 2005. (WEL., Illus.). 88p. pap. 4.99 (978-1-84323-400-5(9)) Gomer Pr. GBR. Dist: Gomer Pr.

Egea, Marcelo. Sobe, the Cat That Thinks He's a Dog. 2012. 24p. pap. 15.99 (978-1-4691-5925-6(2)) Xlibris Corp.

Elliott, David. This Orq. (He #1!) Nichols, Lori, illus. 2016. (ENG.). 40p. (J). (gr. -1-2). 16.95 (978-1-62979-336-8(1)) Boyds Mills Pr.

—This Orq. (He Say UGH!) Nichols, Lori, illus. 2015. (ENG.). 40p. (J). (gr. -1-3). 16.95 (978-1-62091-789-3(0)) Boyds Mills Pr.

Elliott, Rebecca. Baxter Is Missing - A Branches Book. Elliott, Rebecca, illus. 2017. (Owl Diaries: 6). (ENG., Illus.). 80p. (J). (gr. k-2). pap. 4.99 **(978-1-338-04284-9(X))** Scholastic, Inc.

Elliott, Rebecca. Missing Jack. Elliott, Rebecca, illus. 2015. (ENG., Illus.). 32p. (J). (gr. -1-k). 16.99 (978-0-7459-6502-4(4)) Lion Hudson PLC GBR. Dist: Independent Pubs. Group.

Emerson, Carl. Monster Boy & the Classroom Pet, 1 vol. Levin, Lon, illus. 2008. (Monster Boy Ser.). (ENG.). 32p. (gr. -1-4). 28.50 (978-1-60270-234-9(9), Looking Glass Library) ABDO Publishing Co.

Emma Treehouse Ltd. My Pets. Davis, Caroline, illus. 2007. (Easy Flaps Ser.). 10p. (J). (gr. -1). bds. 6.95 (978-1-58925-824-2(X)) Tiger Tales.

Erickson, Carol. Not a Used Dog, at All. 2009. 32p. pap. 14.49 (978-1-4389-5204-8(X)) AuthorHouse.

Estes, Allison & Stark, Dan. Izzy & Oscar. Dockray, Tracy, illus. 2015. (ENG.). 40p. (J). (-2). 16.99 (978-1-4926-0150-0(0), 9781492601500, Sourcebooks Jabberwocky) Sourcebooks, Inc.

Evans, Cathy. Halo & the Rainbows. 2013. 36p. pap. 16.95 (978-1-4624-0704-0(8), Inspiring Voices) Author Solutions, Inc.

Ewart, Franzeska G. & Quarto Generic Staff. Sita, Snake-Queen of Speed. Bate, Helen, illus. 2012. (ENG.). 96p. (J). (gr. 3-6). pap. 8.99 (978-1-84780-330-6(X), Frances Lincoln) Quarto Publishing Group UK GBR. Dist: Hachette Bk. Group.

Exelby, Kathy. My Dog Harpo: The Biggest Kid I Know. Wall Darby, Colleen, illus. 2007. (J). per. 20.00 (978-1-932583-39-7(4)) digital@batesjackson llc.

Faciana, Michelle. Snickers' Day Out. 2010. 16p. 9.99 (978-1-4490-5216-4(9)) AuthorHouse.

Farnsley, Kathleen. This Little Piggy Named Pony. 2008. 24p. pap. 12.99 (978-1-4389-2659-9(6)) AuthorHouse.

Fay, Nancy Cartnick. I Wanted a Puppy - Not Fish! 2012. 24p. pap. 15.99 (978-1-4691-7535-5(5)) Xlibris Corp.

Feiffer, Jules. A Room with a Zoo. Feiffer, Jules, illus. 2007. (ENG., Illus.). 192p. (gr. 2-7). per. 7.99 (978-0-7868-3703-8(9), di Capua, Michael Bks.) Hyperion Bks. for Children.

Feldman, Thea. ASPCA Pet Rescue Club - Too Big to Run. 2015. (ENG.). 128p. (J). (gr. 1-3). lib. bdg. 16.99 (978-0-7944-3513-4(0), Reader's Digest Children's Bks.) Studio Fun International.

—Disney Palace Pets: Adventure Tales. 2015. (Hidden Stories Ser.). (ENG.). 10p. (J). (gr. -1-1). 15.99 (978-0-7944-3504-2(1), Reader's Digest Children's Bks.) Studio Fun International.

—Hooray for Palace Pets! Disney Storybook Artists Staff, illus. 2015. (ENG.). 12p. (J). (gr. -1-k). bds. 10.99 (978-0-7944-3389-5(8), Reader's Digest Children's Bks.) Studio Fun International.

Ferry, Beth. Land Shark. Mantle, Ben, illus. 2015. (ENG.). 36p. (J). (gr. -1-k). 16.99 (978-1-4521-2458-2(2)) Chronicle Bks. LLC.

Finch, Kate. A Big Surprise. 2013. (Pet Hotel Ser.: 2). lib. bdg. 14.75 (978-0-606-31985-0(9), Turtleback) Turtleback Bks.

—On with the Show! Gurney, John Steven, illus. 2014. 76p. (J). (978-1-4242-5954-0(1)) Scholastic, Inc.

—On with the Show! 2014. (Pet Hotel Ser.: 4). lib. bdg. 14.75 (978-0-606-35201-7(5)) Turtleback Bks.

—Pet Hotel #4: on with the Show! Gurney, John Steven & Jessell, Tim, illus. 2014. (Pet Hotel Ser.: 4). (ENG.). 96p. (J). (gr. 2-5). pap. 4.99 (978-0-545-50184-2(9), Scholastic Paperbacks) Scholastic, Inc.

Fine, Dvm. Too Many Pets & Not Enough Homes! 2012. 24p. pap. 12.56 (978-1-4669-0248-0(5)) Trafford Publishing.

Finkbeiner, Betty Ladley. Pepper's Forever Home. 2013. 24p. pap. 15.99 (978-1-4797-6982-7(7)) Xlibris Corp.

Finzi, Arna. At Baba's House. 2011. 36p. pap. 16.46 (978-1-4269-7095-5(1)) Trafford Publishing.

Fisher, C. R. The Adventures of Sam Fisher: It's Ruff to Be A Puppy. 2008. 64p. pap. 19.49 (978-1-4389-2040-5(7)) AuthorHouse.

Flamburis, Georgia M. How Karis' Kitten Got Its Name. 2012. 34p. pap. 9.99 (978-0-615-47908-8(1)) Flamburis, Georgia.

Flor Ada, Alma. Daniel's Pet. Karas, G. Brian, illus. 2010. (Rise & Shine Ser.). (ENG.). 24p. (C). (gr. -1-3). pap. 6.95 (978-0-15-204865-5(0)) National Geographic School Publishing, Inc.

—Daniel's Pet. 2003. (Green Light Readers — Level 1 Ser.). (gr. -1-2). 13.50 (978-0-613-64481-5(6), Turtleback) Turtleback Bks.

Forde, Catherine. Slippy. 2012. (Stoke Books Titles Ser.). 72p. (J). (gr. 5-8). pap. 7.95 (978-1-78112-032-3(3)); pap. 45.32 (978-0-7613-9223-1(8)); lib. bdg. 22.60 (978-1-78112-031-6(5)) Stoke Bks.

Foreman, Michael. El Lorito Pelon. Diego, Rapi & Flores, Martha, illus. 2008. (SPA.). 30p. (J). (gr. 1-3). 15.99 (978-1-930332-56-0(4)) Lectorum Pubns., Inc.

Fox, Paula. La Habitacion de Mauricio. 2003.Tr. of Maurice's Room. (SPA., Illus.). 96p. (J). (gr. 3-5). (978-84-279-3457-3(2), NG4695) Noguer y Caralt Editores, S. A. ESP. Dist: Lectorum Pubns., Inc.

Franciosi, Pete. Dusty Wants A Kitty. 2011. 23p. 14.95 (978-1-4327-7596-4(0)) Outskirts Pr., Inc.

Fraser, Ian. Life with Mammoth, 0 vols. Fraser, Mary Ann, illus. (Ogg & Bob Ser.). (ENG.). 64p. (J). (gr. k-3). 2013. pap. 9.99 (978-1-4778-1615-8(1), 9781477816158) 2010. 14.99 (978-0-7614-5722-0(4), 9780761457220) Amazon Publishing. (Amazon Children's Publishing).

—Meet Mammoth, 0 vols. Fraser, Mary Ann, illus. 2013. (Ogg & Bob Ser.). (ENG.). 64p. (J). (gr. 1-3). pap. 9.99 (978-1-4778-1617-2(8), 9781477816172, Amazon Children's Publishing) Amazon Publishing.

Fraser, Mary Ann. Pet Shop Follies. 2010. (ENG.). 32p. (J). (gr. -1-1). 16.95 (978-1-59078-619-2(X)) Boyds Mills Pr.

—Pet Shop Lullaby. Fraser, Mary Ann, illus. 2009. (ENG., Illus.). 32p. (J). (gr. -1-1). 16.95 (978-1-59078-618-5(1)) Boyds Mills Pr.

Frazer, Rebecca. Barbie Loves Pets. An, Jiyoung, illus. 2007. (Pictureback(R) Ser.). (ENG.). 16p. (J). (gr. -1-2). pap. 3.99 (978-0-375-84797-4(9), Golden Bks.) Random Hse. Children's Bks.

Freeman, Martha. The Case of the Bug on the Run. 2014. (First Kids Mystery Ser.: 6). (ENG.). 144p. (J). (gr. 2-7). pap. 6.99 (978-0-8234-3188-5(6)) Holiday Hse., Inc.

—The Case of the Bug on the Run: First Kids Mystery #6. 2013. (First Kids Mystery Ser.: 6). (ENG.). 144p. (J). (gr. 2-7). 16.95 (978-0-8234-2872-4(9)) Holiday Hse., Inc.

Freytag, Lorna. My Humongous Hamster Goes to School. Freytag, Lorna, illus. 2015. (My Humongous Hamster Ser.). (ENG., Illus.). 32p. (J). (gr. -1-3). 16.99 (978-1-62779-140-3(X), 9781627791403, Holt, Henry & Co. Bks. For Young Readers) Holt, Henry & Co.

Friedman, Laurie. Mallory vs. Max. Schmitz, Tamara, illus. 2006. (Mallory Ser.: 3). (ENG.). 160p. (J). (gr. 2-5). per. 5.95 (978-1-57505-863-4(4), First Avenue Editions) Lerner Publishing Group.

—Ruby Valentine & the Sweet Surprise. Avril, Lynne, illus. 2014. (ENG.). 32p. (J). (gr. k-3). 16.95 (978-0-7613-8873-9(7), Carolrhoda Bks.) Lerner Publishing Group.

Froeb, Lori. I Am Daisy, Level 2. Lemay, Violet, illus. 2015. (Rescue Readers Ser.: 2). (ENG.). 32p. (J). (gr. k-3). lib. bdg. 16.99 (978-0-7944-3350-5(2)) Reader's Digest Assn., Inc., The.

—I Am McKinley, Level 2. Sakamoto, Miki, illus. 2015. (Rescue Readers Ser.: 1). (ENG.). 32p. (J). (gr. k-3). lib. bdg. 16.99 (978-0-7944-3349-9(9)) Reader's Digest Assn., Inc., The.

Gallagher, Diana G. A No-Sneeze Pet, 1 vol. Juarez, Adriana & Puglisi, Adriana, illus. 2013. (Pet Friends Forever Ser.). (ENG.). 88p. (gr. 1-3). pap. 5.95 (978-1-4795-1862-3(X)); lib. bdg. 25.32 (978-1-4048-7499-2(2)) Picture Window Bks.

—Pet Friends Forever, 1 vol. 2014. (Pet Friends Forever Ser.). (ENG.). 88p. (gr. 1-3). 151.92 (978-1-4795-4433-2(7)) Picture Window Bks.

—The Pet Store Pet Show, 1 vol. Puglisi, Adriana, illus. 2014. (Pet Friends Forever Ser.). (ENG.). 88p. (gr. 1-3). 25.32 (978-1-4795-2177-7(9)) Picture Window Bks.

Galvin, Laura Gates. My First Pet. Schwaeber, Barbie Heit & Halpenny, Karen, eds. 2008. (ENG., Illus.). 24p. (J). (gr. -1). 4.99 (978-1-59069-654-5(9)) Studio Mouse LLC.

Ganz, Yaffa. Raise a Rabbit, Grow a Goose. Klineman, Harvey, illus. 2008. 30p. 14.99 (978-1-59826-235-3(1)) Feldheim Pubs.

Gardiner, C. Pirate Betty of Wigan. 2013. 12p. pap. 10.60 (978-1-291-30672-9(2)) Lulu Pr., Inc.

Gee, Randi. Everybody Has a Cat Named Molly. 2010. 32p. pap. 15.50 (978-0-557-27671-4(3)) Lulu Pr., Inc.

George, Jean Craighead. Crowbar, the Smartest Bird in the World. Minor, Wendell, illus. 2015. (J). (978-0-06-000257-2(3)) HarperCollins Pubs.

George, Kallie. The Enchanted Egg. Boiger, Alexandra, illus. 2015. (Magical Animal Adoption Agency Ser.). (ENG.). 138p. (J). (gr. 3-7). 14.99 (978-1-4231-8383-9(5)) Disney Pr.

—The Enchanted Egg. Boiger, Alexandra, illus. 2016. (Magical Animal Adoption Agency Ser.). (ENG.). 160p. (J). (gr. 2-5). pap. 5.99 (978-1-4847-0146-1(1)) Hyperion Bks. for Children.

George, Kallie & Boiger, Alexandra. The Missing Magic. Boiger, Alexandra, illus. 2016. (Magical Animal Adoption Agency Ser.). (ENG., Illus.). 144p. (J). (gr. 2-5). 14.99 (978-1-4231-8384-6(3)) Hyperion Bks. for Children.

Gerrard, K. A. My Family Is a Zoo. Dodd, Emma, illus. 2016. (ENG.). 32p. (J). 16.99 (978-1-61963-851-8(7), 9781619638518, Bloomsbury USA Childrens) Bloomsbury Publishing USA.

Giancamilli, Vanessa. Patches Finds a Home. Hatala, Dan, illus. 2006. (Pet Tales Ser.). (ENG.). 32p. (J). (gr. -1-3). 4.95 (978-1-59249-639-6(3)); pap. 2.95 (978-1-59249-640-2(7)) Soundprints.

Gilbert, Frances. I Love Pink! Unten, Eren, illus. 2017. (Step into Reading Ser.). (ENG.). 32p. (J). (gr. -1-1). 3.99 (978-1-101-93737-2(8), Random Hse. Bks. for Young Readers) Random Hse. Children's Bks.

—I Love Pink. Unten, Eren, illus. 2017. (Step into Reading Ser.). (ENG.). 32p. (J). (gr. -1-1). lib. bdg. 12.99 (978-1-101-93738-9(6), Random Hse. Bks. for Young Readers) Random Hse. Children's Bks.

Gilman, Grace. Dixie & the Best Day Ever. Rogers, Jacqueline, illus. 2014. (I Can Read Level 1 Ser.). (ENG.). 32p. (J). (gr. -1-3). pap. 3.99 (978-0-06-208659-4(6)) HarperCollins Pubs.

Giuliani, Al. New Nanny. 2013. (Jessie Junior Novel Ser.). (ENG.). 128p. (J). (gr. 3-7). pap. 5.99 (978-1-4231-8369-3(X)) Disney Pr.

Glazer, Maryann. The Adventures of Teddy Bark-Lee: Teddy Goes to the Doctor. 2009. 28p. pap. 13.99 (978-1-4490-2836-7(5)) AuthorHouse.

Glesener, Loretta. Bringing Back Dinner Time. 2011. 40p. pap. 24.95 (978-1-4560-4221-9(1)) America Star Bks.

Golden Books. Race Against Time (Mr. Peabody & Sherman) Fransisco, Tina, illus. 2014. (Super Color with Stickers Ser.). (ENG.). 96p. (J). (gr. -1-2). pap. 3.99 (978-0-385-37151-3(9), Golden Bks.) Random Hse. Children's Bks.

Golden Books Staff & Shealy, Dennis R. Secret Life of Pets. Kellman, Craig, illus. 2016. (Little Golden Book Ser.). (ENG.). 24p. (J). (gr. -1-2). 4.99 (978-0-399-55481-0(5), Golden Bks.) Random Hse. Children's Bks.

Gomes, Linda Nunes. Special Words: A Story about Multicultural Families & Their Pets. Levine, Lenora D., illus. 2007. (YA). per. 12.99 (978-1-934400-02-9(5)) Rock Village Publishing.

Good Dog... Not So Good Dog. 2007. (J). (978-0-9793568-1-0(4)) Merlin, Debbi.

Gorbachev, Valeri. The Best Cat. Gorbachev, Valeri, illus. 2010. (ENG., Illus.). 32p. (J). (gr. -1-2). 15.99 (978-0-7636-3675-3(4)) Candlewick Pr.

—Cats Are Cats. Gorbachev, Valeri, illus. 2014. (ENG., Illus.). 32p. (J). (gr. -1-3). 16.95 (978-0-8234-3052-9(9)) Holiday Hse., Inc.

Gotsch, Connie. Belle's Star. Cogan, John, illus. 2009. 134p. (J). pap. 8.99 (978-1-932926-01-9(1), Kinkajou Pr.) Artemesia Publishing, LLC.

—Belle's Trial. Cogan, John, illus. 2010. (ENG & ABK.). 150p. (J). pap. 8.99 (978-1-932926-12-5(7), Kinkajou Pr.) Artemesia Publishing, LLC.

Gott, Barry, illus. Class Pets. 2005. (I'm Going to Read(r) Ser.). (ENG.). 48p. (J). (gr. 2-3). pap. 3.95 (978-1-4027-2709-2(7)) Sterling Publishing Co., Inc.

Granger, Barbara. Down to Earth with a Bump. 2009. (Illus.). 40p. pap. 16.99 (978-1-4389-1211-0(0)) AuthorHouse.

Graves, Keith. Puppy! 2016. (ENG., Illus.). 32p. (J). 16.99 (978-1-62672-225-5(0), 9781626722255) Roaring Brook Pr.

Green, D. L. Zeke Meeks vs the Pain-In-the-Neck Pets, 1 vol. Alves, Josh, illus. 2014. (Zeke Meeks Ser.). (ENG.). 128p. (gr. 2-2). 22.65 (978-1-4795-2166-1(3), Zeke Meeks) Picture Window Bks.

Greenwood, Grace. History of My Pets by Grace Greenwood [Pseud.], with Engravings from Designs by Billings. 2006. 128p. per. 16.99 (978-1-4255-0870-8(7)) Michigan Publishing.

Griffis, Molly. The Buffalo in the Mall. Doner, Kim, illus. 32p. 8.95 (978-1-57168-635-0(5)) Eakin Pr.

Grindley, Sally. Captain Pepper's Pets. Parkins, David, illus. 2004. 48p. (J). pap. (978-0-7534-1042-4(7), Kingfisher) Roaring Brook Pr.

Griner, Jack. Archibald My Pet Pig. Knudson, Dana, illus. 2011. pap. 8.95 (978-0-9836081-1-0(3)) Canoed Sun Publishing, LLC.

Grubman, Bonnie. How Do You Get a Mouse to Smile?, 1 vol. Van Wright, Cornelius, illus. 2009. (ENG.). 32p. (J). (gr. -1-3). pap. 6.50 (978-1-59572-167-9(3)) Star Bright Bks., Inc.

Gulliver, Amanda, illus. Pets. 2011. (Baby Rattle Bks.). 12p. (J). (gr. -1-k). 6.99 (978-0-7641-6392-0(2)) Barron's Educational Series, Inc.

Gutierrez-Haley, Lisa. The New Pet: Adventures of Hayden & Jace. 2011. 20p. pap. 24.95 (978-1-4626-1872-9(3)) America Star Bks.

Gutman, Dan. My Weird School: Class Pet Mess! Paillot, Jim, illus. 2017. (I Can Read Level 2 Ser.). 32p. (J). (gr. -1-3). pap. 3.99 (978-0-06-236746-4(3)) HarperCollins Pubs.

Hahn. Brian. It's Not the Yellow Fever. 2013. 20p. pap. 24.95 (978-1-62709-969-1(7)) America Star Bks.

Hale, Rachael. Baby's Best Friend. 2011. (ENG.). 20p. (J). (gr. -1 — 1). bds. 6.99 (978-0-316-12962-6(3)) Little, Brown Bks. for Young Readers.

Hall, Kirsten. Slider's Pet: All about Nature. Luedecke, Bev, illus. 2004. (Beastieville Ser.). (J). 19.50 (978-0-516-22898-3(6), Children's Pr.) Scholastic Library Publishing.

Hamilton, Patricia D. Peaches the Private Eye Poodle: Finding Dipsey Doodle. 2008. 32p. pap. 13.50 (978-1-60693-276-6(4), Eloquent Bks.) Strategic Book Publishing & Rights Agency (SBPRA).

—Peaches the Private Eye Poodle: Finding Foster a Home. 2010. 36p. (gr. -1-3). pap. 13.50 (978-1-60911-108-3(7), Eloquent Bks.) Strategic Book Publishing & Rights Agency (SBPRA).

Hanning, Jacob. Mommy's Little Helper: That's Me. 2012. 28p. pap. 24.95 (978-1-4626-5649-3(8)) America Star Bks.

Hano, Patricia. Tyler Meets the Moon. 2010. 28p. pap. 11.99 (978-1-60911-189-2(3), Eloquent Bks.) Strategic Book Publishing & Rights Agency (SBPRA).

Hanson, Sandy. A Camel's Story, I Met the Lamb. 2012. 62p. 24.99 (978-1-61996-615-4(8)); pap. 14.99 (978-1-61996-614-7(X)) Salem Author Services.

Hanson, Shelley. K9 Crew Beginnings. 2004. 160p. (J). per. 9.99 (978-0-9752887-0-2(9)) Tail Wagging Productions.

Hapka, Catherine, pseud. ASPCA Pet Rescue Club: the Lonely Pony. 2015. (Pet Rescue Club Ser.: 3). (ENG., Illus.). 128p. (J). (gr. 1-3). lib. bdg. 16.99 (978-0-7944-3454-0(1)) Reader's Digest Assn., Inc., The.

—No Time for Hallie. Regan, Dana, illus. 2015. (Pet Rescue Club Ser.: 2). (ENG.). 128p. (J). (gr. 1-3). lib. bdg. 16.99 (978-0-7944-3352-9(9)) Reader's Digest Assn., Inc., The.

—No Time for Hallie. Regan, Dana, illus. 2015. (Pet Rescue Club Ser.: 2). (ENG.). 128p. (J). (gr. 1-3). pap. 5.99 (978-0-7944-3313-0(8)) Studio Fun International.

—Too Big to Run. 2015. (Pet Rescue Club Ser.: 4). (ENG.). 128p. (J). (gr. 1-3). pap. 5.99 (978-0-7944-3453-3(3), Reader's Digest Children's Bks.) Studio Fun International.

Hapka, Cathy, pseud. ASPCA Pet Rescue Club Collection, Bks. 1-3. Regan, Dana, illus. 2016. (Pet Rescue Club Ser.: 5). (ENG.). 384p. (J). (gr. 1-3). pap. 8.99 (978-0-7944-3572-1(6), Reader's Digest Children's Bks.) Studio Fun International.

Harley, Stephen. The Christmastime Dog Rescue. 2013. 24p. pap. 10.95 (978-1-4624-0774-3(9), Inspiring Voices) Author Solutions, Inc.

Harmon, Minnie. Golden's Routine. 2010. 28p. pap. 15.99 (978-1-4500-3321-3(0)) Xlibris Corp.

Harper, Aimee. Crystal. 2010. (Dream Dogs Ser.: Bk. 4). (ENG., Illus.). 112p. (J). (gr. -1-3). 5.99 (978-0-00-732037-0(X)) HarperCollins Pubs. Ltd. GBR. Dist: Independent Pubs. Group.

—Dream Dogs - Nugget. 2010. (Dream Dogs Ser.: Bk. 3). (ENG., Illus.). 112p. (J). (gr. -1-3). 6.99 (978-0-00-732036-3(1)) HarperCollins Pubs. Ltd. GBR. Dist: Independent Pubs. Group.

Harrington, Claudia. Book 1: Otis the Very Large Dog. 2016. (Hank the Pet Sitter Ser.). (ENG.). (gr. -1-3). lib. bdg. 27.07 (978-1-62402-187-9(5)) ABDO Publishing Co.

—Book 4: Elmer the Very Sneaky Sheep. 2016. (Hank the Pet Sitter Ser.). (ENG.). (gr. -1-3). lib. bdg. 27.07 (978-1-62402-190-9(5)) ABDO Publishing Co.

Harrington, Jenna. Katie Mcginty Wants a Pet! Simpson, Finn, illus. 2015. (ENG.). 32p. (J). (gr. -1-3). 16.99 (978-1-58925-192-2(X)) Tiger Tales.

Harris, Robie H. Goodbye Mousie. Ormerod, Jan, illus. 2004. (ENG.). 32p. (J). (gr. -1-3). reprint ed. 16.99 (978-0-689-87134-4(1), Aladdin) Simon & Schuster Children's Publishing.

Harrison, Megan Bernadette. The Adventures of Kitty Tom & Blossom: Book One. 2009. 36p. pap. 24.95 (978-1-60749-257-3(1)) America Star Bks.

Hasbro & O'Ryan, Ellie. Littlest Pet Shop: Project FUN-Way: Starring Russell Ferguson! 2015. (ENG.). 160p. (J). (gr. 3-7). pap. 5.99 (978-0-316-30138-1(8)) Little, Brown Bks. for Young Readers.

Hay, Sam. Flight of the Pummeled Parakeet. 2015. (Undead Pets Ser.: 6). lib. bdg. 16.00 (978-0-606-38405-6(7)) Turtleback Bks.

—Gasp of the Ghoulish Guinea Pig. 2016. (Undead Pets Ser.: 7). lib. bdg. 16.00 (978-0-606-38406-3(5)) Turtleback Bks.

—Goldfish from Beyond the Grave. 2015. (Undead Pets Ser.: 4). lib. bdg. 16.00 (978-0-606-36220-7(7)) Turtleback Bks.

—Night of the Howling Hound, No. 3. Cooper, Simon, illus. 2014. (Undead Pets Ser.: 3). (ENG.). 112p. (J). (gr. 1-3). 5.99 (978-0-448-47797-8(1), Grosset & Dunlap) Penguin Young Readers Group.

—Rise of the Zombie Rabbit #5. Cooper, Simon, illus. 2015. (Undead Pets Ser.: 5). (ENG.). 112p. (J). (gr. 1-3). 5.99 (978-0-448-47799-2(8), Grosset & Dunlap) Penguin Young Readers Group.

Hays, Anna Jane. The Pup Speaks Up. Petrone, Valeria, illus. 2003. (Step into Reading Ser.). 32p. (gr. -1-1). 14.00 (978-0-7569-1696-1(8)) Perfection Learning Corp.

—The Pup Speaks Up. Petrone, Valeria, illus. 2003. (Step into Reading Ser.). (ENG.). 32p. (J). (gr. -1-1). pap. 3.99 (978-0-375-81232-3(6), Random Hse. Bks. for Young Readers) Random Hse. Children's Bks.

HB Staff. The Perfect Pet. 97th ed. 2003. (First-Place Reading Ser.). (gr. 1-18). pap. 16.50 (978-0-15-308133-0(3)) Harcourt Schl. Pubs.

Heide, Florence Parry. A Promise Is a Promise. Auth, Tony, illus. 2007. (ENG.). 40p. (J). (gr. k-4). 15.99 (978-0-7636-2285-5(0)) Candlewick Pr.

Heilbroner, Joan. A Pet Named Sneaker. Lemaître, Pascal, illus. 2013. (Beginner Books Ser.). (ENG.). 48p. (J). (gr. k-3). 8.99 (978-0-307-97580-5(0), Random Hse. Bks. for Young Readers) Random Hse. Children's Bks.

Heiligman, Deborah. Fun Dog, Sun Dog, 0 vols. Bowers, Tim, illus. 2011. (ENG.). 34p. (J). (gr. -1-2). pap. 7.99 (978-0-7614-5836-4(0), 9780761458364, Amazon Children's Publishing) Amazon Publishing.

Helakoski, Leslie. Doggone Feet! Helakoski, Leslie, illus. 2013. (ENG., Illus.). 40p. (J). (gr. -1-2). 16.95 (978-1-59078-933-9(4)) Boyds Mills Pr.

Here Kitty. 2005. 32p. (J). 12.99 (978-0-9758709-3-8(9), A.W.A. Gang) Journey Stone Creations, LLC.

Hermes, Patricia. Emma Dilemma & the New Nanny, 0 vols. Carter, Abby, illus. 2010. (Emma Dilemma Ser.: 1). (ENG.). 114p. (J). (gr. 3-6). pap. 6.99 (978-0-7614-5619-3(8), 9780761456193, Amazon Children's Publishing) Amazon Publishing.

—Emma Dilemma, the Nanny, & the Secret Ferret, 0 vols. Carter, Abby, illus. 2010. (Emma Dilemma Ser.: 5). (ENG.). 112p. (J). (gr. 3-6). 15.99 (978-0-7614-5650-6(3), 9780761456506, Amazon Children's Publishing) Amazon Publishing.

Herrera, Juan Felipe & Cuevas, Ernesto, illus. Featherless. 2013.Tr. of Desplumado. (SPA & ENG.). 32p. (J). pap. 8.95 (978-0-89239-303-9(3)) Lee & Low Bks., Inc.

Hicks, Kelli. Maddie's Pet Peeve. 2015. (ENG.). 48p. (gr. k-3). 27.07 (978-1-63430-372-9(5)) Rourke Educational Media.

Hietpas, Polly. Hello Rosie Cat. 2009. 16p. pap. 8.49 (978-1-4490-0283-1(8)) AuthorHouse.

Hileman, Jane & Pitt, Marilyn. Come with Me. Bianchi, John, illus. 2010. (1G Potato Chip Bks.). (ENG.). 12p. (J). (gr. k-1). pap. 5.99 (978-1-61541-162-7(3)) American Reading Co.

Hill, Meggan. Nico & Lola: Kindness shared between a boy & a dog. 2009. 32p. (J). (978-0-615-23040-5(7)) Genuine Prints, LLC.

—Nico & Lola: Kindness Shared Between a Boy & a Dog. Graunke, Susan M., illus. 2010. (ENG.). 40p. (J). (gr. -1-3). 16.99 (978-0-06-199043-4(4)) HarperCollins Pubs.

Hillert, Margaret. Dear Dragon Gets a Pet. Pullan, Jack, illus. 2015. (BeginningtoRead Ser.). (ENG.). 32p. (J). (gr. k-2). pap. 11.94 (978-1-60357-791-5(2)); lib. bdg. 22.60 (978-1-59953-706-1(0)) Norwood Hse. Pr.

Hobbie, Holly. A Cat Named Swan. 2017. (ENG., Illus.). 32p. (J). (gr. -1-2). 17.99 (978-0-553-53744-4(X), Random Hse. Bks. for Young Readers) Random Hse. Children's Bks.

Hobbs, Constance. Bugsy's Special Event. 2008. 64p. pap. 10.50 (978-0-9556783-7-0(4)) Hobbs, Constance GBR. Dist: Lulu Pr., Inc.

Hock, Dan. The Afternoon Auction: An Iggy & Igor Mystery. 2004. (Illus.). 48p. (J). per. 4.99 (978-0-9754046-0-7(1)) Anticipation Pr.

Hodge, A. D. Bubbles & Boundaries. 2013. 32p. (978-1-4602-2858-6(8)) FriesenPress.

Hoena, Blake A. Ack's New Pet, 1 vol. Harpster, Steve, illus. 2014. (Eek & Ack Early Chapter Bks.). (ENG.). 32p. (gr. k-2). lib. bdg. 22.65 (978-1-4342-6406-0(8)) Stone Arch Bks.

Hoffman, Mary Ann. A Parrot for Pam. 2006. (Neighborhood Readers Ser.). (ENG.). 8p. (gr. -1-3). pap. 5.15 (978-1-4042-5690-3(3), Rosen Classroom) Rosen Publishing Group, Inc., The.

Holland, Frances. Ryan's Praying Mantis, 1 vol. 2009. 19p. pap. 24.95 (978-1-60749-432-4(9)) PublishAmerica, Inc.

Homberg, Ruth. The Best Ball (Disney Palace Pets: Whisker Haven Tales) RH Disney, illus. 2017. (Step into Reading Ser.). (ENG.). 24p. (J). (gr. -1-1). pap. 4.99 (978-0-7364-3596-3(4), RH/Disney) Random Hse. Children's Bks.

Hooks, Gwendolyn. The Best Trick: A Pet Club Story, 1 vol. Byrne, Mike, illus. 2010. (Pet Club Ser.). (ENG.). 32p. (gr. 1-2). 22.65 (978-1-4342-2052-3(4)); pap. 6.25 (978-1-4342-2794-2(4)) Stone Arch Bks.

—The Cat Food Mystery: A Pet Club Story, 1 vol. Byrne, Mike, illus. 2011. (Pet Club Ser.). (ENG.). 32p. (gr. 1-2). pap. 6.25 (978-1-4342-3051-5(1)); lib. bdg. 22.65 (978-1-4342-2511-5(9)) Stone Arch Bks.

—Find the Cat! A Pet Club Story. Byrne, Mike, illus. 2010. (Pet Club Ser.). (ENG.). 32p. (gr. 1-2). pap. 6.25 (978-1-4342-2795-9(2)) Stone Arch Bks.

—The Lucky Charm: A Pet Club Story, 1 vol. Byrne, Mike, illus. 2011. (Pet Club Ser.). (ENG.). 32p. (gr. 1-2). pap. 6.25 (978-1-4342-3052-2(X)) Stone Arch Bks.

—The Noisy Night: A Pet Club Story, 1 vol. Byrne, Mike, illus. 2010. (Pet Club Ser.). (ENG.). 32p. (gr. 1-2). 22.65 (978-1-4342-2049-3(4)); pap. 6.25 (978-1-4342-2793-5(6)) Stone Arch Bks.

—Pet Club. Byrne, Mike, illus. 2013. (Pet Club Ser.). (ENG.). 32p. (gr. -1-1). 135.90 (978-1-4342-8841-7(2)) Stone Arch Bks.

—Pet Costume Party: A Pet Club Story, 1 vol. Byrne, Mike, illus. 2011. (Pet Club Ser.). (ENG.). 32p. (gr. 1-2). pap. 6.25 (978-1-4342-3053-9(8)); lib. bdg. 22.65 (978-1-4342-2513-9(5)) Stone Arch Bks.

—The Pet Wash: A Pet Club Story, 1 vol. Byrne, Mike, illus. 2011. (Pet Club Ser.). (ENG.). 32p. (gr. 1-2). pap. 6.25 (978-1-4342-3054-6(6)); lib. bdg. 22.65 (978-1-4342-2514-6(3)) Stone Arch Bks.

—Pets at the Party: A Pet Club Story, 1 vol. Byrne, Mike, illus. 2010. (Pet Club Ser.). (ENG & ABK.). 32p. (gr. 1-2). 22.65 (978-1-4342-2054-7(0)); pap. 6.25 (978-1-4342-2796-6(0)) Stone Arch Bks.

Hope, Laura Lee. Bunny Brown & His Sister Sue. 2005. 188p. pap. 11.95 (978-1-4218-1165-9(0), 1st World Library - Literary Society) 1st World Publishing, Inc.

Housel, Debra. Charlotte's Web: An Instructional Guide for Literature. rev. ed. 2015. (Great Works). (ENG., Illus.). 72p. (gr. 3-5). pap. 9.99 (978-1-4807-6995-3(9)) Shell Educational Publishing.

Howe, James. Bunnicula Meets Edgar Allan Crow. Fortune, Eric, illus. (Bunnicula & Friends Ser.). (ENG.). 160p. (J). (gr. 3-7). 2008. pap. 6.99 (978-1-4169-1473-0(0)) 2006. 15.95 (978-1-4169-1458-7(7)) Simon & Schuster Children's Publishing. (Atheneum Bks. for Young Readers).

Howland, Naomi. The Better-Than-Best Purim, 0 vols. 2012. (ENG.). 32p. (J). (gr. -1-2). 16.99 (978-0-7614-6203-3(1), 9780761462033, Amazon Children's Publishing) Amazon Publishing.

Hubbard, Sharron/Y. Link & Rosie's Pets. Schleihs, Kristin, illus. 2007. (J). bds. (978-0-9762434-3-4(1)) Link & Rosie Pr.

Hughes, Emily C. My Little Pony: Ponies Love Pets! 2014. (Passport to Reading Level 1 Ser.). (ENG., Illus.). 32p. (J). (gr. -1-3). pap. 3.99 (978-0-316-36885-8(7)) Little, Brown Bks. for Young Readers.

—Ponies Love Pets! 2014. (Passport to Reading Level 1 Ser.). (J). lib. bdg. 13.55 (978-0-606-35298-7(8)) Turtleback Bks.

Hughes, Shirley. Alfie & the Birthday Surprise. Hughes, Shirley, illus. 2009. (Alfie Ser.). (ENG., Illus.). 32p. (J). (gr. -1-k). pap. 12.99 (978-1-86230-787-2(3), Red Fox) Random House Children's Books GBR. Dist: Independent Pubs. Group.

Hull, Rod. Dr. Potts, My Pets Have Spots! PB. 2017. (Illus.). 32p. (J). (gr. -1-2). 8.99 (978-1-78285-324-4(3)) Barefoot Bks., Inc.

Huneck, Stephen. Sally Goes to Heaven. 2014. (ENG., Illus.). 48p. (J). (gr. k-2). 18.95 (978-1-4197-0969-2(0), Abrams Bks. for Young Readers) Abrams, Inc.

Hurst, Christine. Symphony Smythe Wants a Pet. 2013. (Illus.). 50p. pap. (978-0-473-26322-5(X)) Prickly Cat Publishing.

Hurwitz, Johanna. Amazing Monty. McGrory, Anik, illus. 2013. (Monty Ser.). (ENG.). 112p. (J). (gr. k-4). pap. 5.99 (978-0-7636-6561-6(4)) Candlewick Pr.

Husband Haddow, Barbara. One More Than Enough. 2011. 34p. pap. (978-1-77067-260-4(5)) FriesenPress.

Hutton, John. Pets: Baby Unplugged. Kang, Andrea, illus. 2011. (Baby Unplugged Ser.). (ENG.). 14p. (J). (— 1). bds. 7.99 (978-1-936669-02-8(1)) Blue Manatee Press.

Ignato, Shirley. Wing ding my Chameleon. 2011. 20p. (gr. -1). pap. 12.74 (978-1-4634-1342-2(4)) AuthorHouse.

Impey, Rose & Dhami, Narinder. Mega Sleepover Club, No. 2. 2010. (Sleepover Club Ser.). (ENG.). 280p. (J). (gr. 2-4). pap., pap., pap. 9.99 (978-0-00-710903-6(2)) HarperCollins Pubs. Ltd. GBR. Dist: HarperCollins Pubs.

Ishida, Sanae. Chibi Samurai Wants a Pet: An Adventure with Little Kunoichi the Ninja Girl. 2017. (Little Kunoichi, the Ninja Girl Ser.). (ENG.). 32p. (J). (gr. -1-2). 16.99 (978-1-63217-117-7(1), Little Bigfoot) Sasquatch Bks.

J, Granny. Pinky Gets a New Puppy: Pinky Frink's Adventures. 2012. 38p. pap. 17.99 (978-1-105-86479-7(0)) Lulu Pr., Inc.

Jamieson, Victoria. The Great Art Caper. Jamieson, Victoria, illus. 2017. (Pets on the Loose! Ser.). (ENG., Illus.). 64p. (J). 15.99 (978-1-62779-118-2(3), 9781627791182, Holt, Henry & Co. Bks. For Young Readers) Holt, Henry & Co.

—The Great Pet Escape. Jamieson, Victoria, illus. 2016. (Pets on the Loose! Ser.). (ENG., Illus.). 64p. (J). 15.99 (978-1-62779-105-2(1), 9781627791052, Holt, Henry & Co. Bks. For Young Readers) Holt, Henry & Co.

Jane, Pamela. Winky Blue Goes Wild! Tilley, Debbie, illus. 2003. 64p. (J). 13.95 (978-1-59034-588-7(6)); pap. (978-1-59034-589-4(4)) Mondo Publishing.

Janovitz, Marilyn. Go Baby Go. 2011. (ENG., Illus.). 24p. (J). bds. 7.99 (978-1-4022-5937-1(9), Sourcebooks Jabberwocky) Sourcebooks, Inc.

Javernick, Ellen. The Birthday Pet, 0 vols. O'Malley, Kevin, illus. 2012. (ENG.). 34p. (J). (gr. k-3). pap. 7.99 (978-0-7614-6238-5(4), 9780761462385, Amazon Children's Publishing) Amazon Publishing.

Jeffers, Oliver. This Moose Belongs to Me. Jeffers, Oliver, illus. 2012. (ENG., Illus.). 32p. (J). (gr. -1-2). 17.99 (978-0-399-16103-2(1), Philomel Bks.) Penguin Young Readers Group.

Jenkins, Amanda. George & Grace Find an Egg. Zolotic, Aleksander, illus. 2017. (Text Connections Guided Close Reading Ser.). (J). (gr. 2). (978-1-4900-1846-1(8)) Benchmark Education Co.

Jenkins, Emily. Cinco Criaturas. Cortes, Eunice, tr. Bogacki, Tomek, illus. 2003. (Picture Bks.).Tr. of Five Creatures. (SPA.). (J). (978-970-690-648-9(7)) Planeta Mexicana Editorial S. A. de C. V.

Jenkins, Jerry B. & Fabry, Chris. Hollywood Holdup. 2006. (Red Rock Mysteries Ser.: 12). (ENG.). 224p. (YA). (gr.

8-12). per. 6.99 (978-1-4143-0151-8(0), Tyndale Kids) Tyndale Hse. Pubs.

Jennings, Patrick. We Can't All Be Rattlesnakes. (J). 2011. (ENG.). 144p. (gr. 3-7). pap. 5.99 (978-0-06-082117-3(5)) 2009. 121p. lib. bdg. 16.89 (978-0-06-082116-6(7)) HarperCollins Pubs.

Joey & Scout. 2004. (Illus.). (J). 7.95 (978-0-9753704-0-7(5)) MYHRECO.

Johnson, Angela. Julius. Pilkey, Dav, illus. 2015. 32p. pap. 7.00 (978-1-61003-548-4(8)) Center for the Collaborative Classroom.

Johnson, Myrna. I Still Want a Pet. 2016. (ENG., Illus.). (gr. k-6). pap. 12.00 **(978-1-62288-157-4(5))** Austin, Stephen F. State Univ. Pr.

Johnson, Sandi. Harold the Hopping Hamster. Johnson, Britt, ed. Sturgeon, Bobbi, illus. l.t. ed. 2003. (ENG.). 34p. (J). (gr. k-5). pap. 12.99 (978-1-929063-91-8(1), 322) Moons & Stars Publishing For Children.

Jones, Molly. Something in the Air. Welch, Sheila Kelly, illus. 2005. (J). (978-1-893516-03-8(2)) Our Child Pr.

Juan, Ana. The Pet Shop Revolution. 2011. (J). pap. (978-0-545-12811-7(0), Levine, Arthur A. Bks.) Scholastic, Inc.

Julie, Aunt. Paddleduck! Julie, A Little Girl from Texas. 2011. 56p. (gr. 2-4). pap. 8.95 (978-1-4269-2584-9(0)) Trafford Publishing.

Kagiliery, Theodore. Angelo & Peter. 2012. 32p. pap. 19.99 (978-1-4772-2893-7(4)) AuthorHouse.

Kalomas, Alice & Kerr, Lenora. Sir Wrinkles Goes to School. Utomo, Gabhor, illus. 2005. (J). 16.95 (978-0-9766639-1-1(0)) Sir Wrinkles Pr.

Kankey, Andrew T. Penelope & Mrs Grace: A Swine Mystery. 2011. 80p. 17.95 (978-1-4575-0531-7(2)) Dog Ear Publishing, LLC.

Kats, Jewel. Jenny & Her Dog Both Fight Cancer: A Tale of Chemotherapy & Caring. 2015. (J). pap. (978-1-61599-279-9(0)) Loving Healing Pr., Inc.

Katz, Karen. Where Is Baby's Puppy? Katz, Karen, illus. 2011. (ENG., Illus.). 14p. (J). (gr. -1 — 1). bds. 6.99 (978-1-4169-8684-3(7), Little Simon) Little Simon.

Kawai, Ritsuko. Hamtaro Postcard Book. Kawai, Ritsuko, illus. 2003. (Hamtaro Ser.). (ENG., Illus.). 24p. (J). pap. 7.95 (978-1-56931-845-4(X)) Viz Media.

Keane, Dave. Who Wants a Tortoise? Campbell, K. G., illus. 2016. (ENG.). 40p. (J). (gr. k-3). 17.99 (978-0-385-75417-0(5), Knopf Bks. for Young Readers) Random Hse. Children's Bks.

Kear, Nicole C. The Fix-It Friends: Wish You Were Here. Dockray, Tracy, illus. 2017. (Fix-It Friends Ser.: 4). (ENG.). 160p. (J). pap. 5.99 **(978-1-250-08670-9(1)**, 9781250086709) Imprint IND. Dist: Macmillan.

Keats, Ezra Jack. Pet Show! (J). (gr. -1-3). pap. 12.95 incl. audio Weston Woods Studios, Inc.

Keene, Carolyn. Pets on Parade. Francis, Peter, illus. 2016. (Nancy Drew Clue Book Ser.: 6). (ENG.). 96p. (J). (gr. 1-4). pap. 5.99 (978-1-4814-5823-8(X), Aladdin) Simon & Schuster Children's Publishing.

Kellogg, Steven. The Mysterious Tadpole. Kellogg, Steven, illus. 25th anniv. ed. 2004. (ENG., Illus.). 40p. (J). (gr. k-3). reprint ed. pap. 6.99 (978-0-14-240140-8(4), Puffin Books) Penguin Young Readers Group.

Kennedy Center Staff. Unleashed: The Lives of White House Pets. Hoyt, Ard, illus. 2011. (ENG.). 112p. (J). (gr. 2-5). pap. 5.99 (978-1-4169-4862-9(7), Simon & Schuster Bks. For Young Readers) Simon & Schuster Bks. For Young Readers.

Kent, Derek Taylor. El Perro con Sombrero: A Bilingual Doggy Tale. Henry, Jed, illus. 2015. (ENG & SPA.). 40p. (J). (gr. -1-2). 17.99 (978-0-8050-9989-8(1), 9780805099898, Holt, Henry & Co. Bks. For Young Readers) Holt, Henry & Co.

Kerr, Mike. Mike & a Lynx Named Kitty. Vitt, Karren, illus. 2nd rev. ed. 2006. 112p. per. 13.50 (978-1-931195-36-2(6)) KiwE Publishing, Ltd.

Kessler, Kathryn. Marvin Discovers Snow. 2010. 36p. (J). pap. 15.77 (978-1-4520-0590-4(7)) AuthorHouse.

Kimmel, Eric A. Hiss-S-S-S! 2012. (ENG.). 208p. (J). 17.95 (978-0-8234-2415-3(4)) Holiday Hse., Inc.

King, Zelda. The Class Surprise. 2006. (Neighborhood Readers Ser.). (ENG.). 16p. (gr. 1-3). pap. 6.50 (978-1-4042-6994-1(0), Rosen Classroom) Rosen Publishing Group, Inc., The.

Klein, Abby. Stop That Hamster! McKinley, John, illus. 2008. (Ready, Freddy! Ser.: Bk. 12). 95p. (gr. -1-3). 16.00 (978-0-7569-8300-0(2)) Perfection Learning Corp.

Koeppel, Ruth. Nick Jr. Wonder Pets Adventures: Book & Magnetic Playset. 2009. 16p. (J). bds. 14.99 (978-0-7944-1769-7(8)) Reader's Digest Assn., Inc., The.

Koster, Amy Sky. Cuddly Princess Pals. 2014. lib. bdg. 13.55 (978-0-606-35552-0(9)) Turtleback Bks.

Krinsky, Ed. Pip, Veronica & the Harmonica. Evans, Casey, illus. 2013. 32p. pap. 13.00 (978-1-62516-945-7(0), Strategic Bk. Publishing) Strategic Book Publishing & Rights Agency (SBPRA).

Kruse, Anne. Takota's Dream. 2010. pap. 16.99 (978-0-578-05291-5(1)) Sisterhaus Publishing.

Kruse, Donald W. Gorilla Soup! 2012. 48p. pap. 12.95 (978-1-59663-862-4(1), Castle Keep Pr.) Rock, James A. & Co. Pubs.

La Rue, Coco. The Dog Rules. May, Kyla, illus. 2011. (ENG.). 128p. (J). (gr. 2-5). pap. 4.99 (978-0-545-28261-1(6), Scholastic Paperbacks) Scholastic, Inc.

—A New Pig in Town. May, Kyla, illus. 2013. 127p. (J). pap. (978-0-545-46607-3(5)) Scholastic, Inc.

Lagonegro, Melissa. The Cookie Boogie (Disney Palace Pets: Whisker Haven Tales) RH Disney, illus. 2016. (Step into Reading Ser.). (ENG.). 24p. (J). (gr. -1-1). 4.99 (978-0-7364-3623-6(5), RH/Disney) Random Hse. Children's Bks.

Laird, Lisa J. I'm the Only One Who Loves Cliff the Goat. 2009. 48p. pap. 19.49 (978-1-4389-5660-2(6)) AuthorHouse.

Lambert, George J. 8 Boys & 8 Beasts, 1 vol. Lambert, Celeste, illus. 2010. 24p. 24.95 (978-1-4489-5901-3(2)) PublishAmerica, Inc.

Lane, Nickel. The Ferret Crusaders: Quest of the Wish A Pod. 2nd ed. 2004. 73p. (J). per. 8.49 (978-1-4116-0459-9(8)) Lulu Pr., Inc.

Lawson, Sue. Ferret Boy. (Illus.). 256p. pap. (978-0-7344-0465-7(4), Lothian Children's Bks.) Hachette Australia.

Lee, Tonya Lewis & Lee, Spike. Please, Puppy, Please. Nelson, Kadir, illus. 2005. (ENG.). 32p. (J). (gr. -1-3). 17.99 (978-0-689-86804-7(9), Simon & Schuster Bks. For Young Readers) Simon & Schuster Bks. For Young Readers.

Lehman, Seth. The Color Pets. 2006. (Illus.). 52p. (J). 7.00 net. (978-0-9787986-0-4(0)) 4All Ages LLC.

Lennon, Margie. Snowball's Sheepdog Adventures: Summer. 2012. 24p. pap. 14.99 (978-1-4685-4655-2(4)) AuthorHouse.

Lewman, David. Secret Life of Pets. Random House, illus. 2016. (Deluxe Junior Novel Ser.). (ENG.). 144p. (J). (gr. 2-5). 9.99 (978-0-399-55490-2(4), Random Hse. Bks. for Young Readers) Random Hse. Children's Bks.

—Secret Life of Pets. Golden Books Staff & Kellman, Craig, illus. 2016. (Big Golden Book Ser.). (ENG.). 32p. (J). (gr. -1-2). 9.99 (978-0-399-55477-3(7), Golden Bks.) Random Hse. Children's Bks.

Light, Steven. Have You Seen My Monster? Light, Steve, illus. 2015. (ENG.). 48p. (J). (-k). 16.99 (978-0-7636-7513-4(X)) Candlewick Pr.

Lindgren, Barbro. Julia Wants a Pet. Dyssegaard, Elisabeth Kallick, tr. Eriksson, Eva, illus. 2003. 32p. (J). (gr. -1 — 1). 15.00 (978-91-29-65940-5(X)) R & S Bks. SWE. Dist: Macmillan.

Little Airplane Productions & Fogarty, Alexandria, illus. Baby Beaver Rescue. 2009. (Wonder Pets! Ser.). (ENG.). 24p. (J). (gr. -1-2). pap. 3.99 (978-1-4169-8499-3(2), Simon Spotlight/Nickelodeon) Simon Spotlight/Nickelodeon.

Little, Celeste. Scales. Motz, Mike, illus. 2012. 24p. (J). 12.95 (978-1-60131-116-0(8)) Big Tent Bks.

Little, Jean. Emma's Strange Pet. Plecas, Jennifer, illus. (I Can Read Level 3 Ser.). 64p. (J). (gr. k-3). 2004. (ENG.). pap. 3.99 (978-0-06-444259-6(4)) 2003. 15.99 (978-0-06-028350-6(5)) HarperCollins Pubs.

Llewellyn, Claire. New Pet. East, Jacqueline, illus. 2013. (Start Reading Ser.). (ENG.). 24p. (gr. k-1). pap. 7.95 (978-1-4765-4123-5(X)) Capstone Press of Coughlan Cos.

Lockard, Donna Lee. Sasha the Tortoise's Summer Vacation. 2013. (ENG.). 36p. (J). pap. 19.95 (978-1-4787-0938-1(3)) Outskirts Pr., Inc.

Lodge, Jo. Pets. 2014. (Touch & Feel Buggy Buddies Ser.). (ENG., Illus.). 12p. (J). (— 1). bds. 7.99 (978-1-4472-6801-7(6)) Pan Macmillan GBR. Dist: Independent Pubs. Group.

Loewen, Nancy. Good-Bye, Jeepers: What to Expect When Your Pet Dies, 1 vol. Lyles, Christopher, illus. 2011. (Life's Challenges Ser.). (ENG.). 24p. (gr. 2-3). lib. bdg. 25.99 (978-1-4048-6680-5(9)) Picture Window Bks.

Loftus, Tracy. Lucky Pup & Miss Millie Go Home. 2012. 28p. pap. 19.99 (978-1-4772-6922-0(3)) AuthorHouse.

Loggins, Kenny. Moose N' Me. Nash, Joshua, illus. 2013. (ENG.). 32p. (J). (gr. -1-3). 14.95 (978-0-578-07552-5(0)) Charlesbridge Publishing, Inc.

Lombardi, Kristine A. The Grumpy Pets. 2016. (ENG., Illus.). 32p. (J). (gr. k-2). 14.95 (978-1-4197-1888-5(6), Abrams Bks. for Young Readers) Abrams, Inc.

London, Olivia. My Little Pony: Meet the Ponies of Ponyville. 2013. (Passport to Reading Level 1 Ser.). (ENG., Illus.). 32p. (J). (gr. -1-3). 4.99 (978-0-316-22815-2(X)) Little, Brown Bks. for Young Readers.

Long, Ethan. Me & My Big Mouse, 0 vols. 2014. (ENG.). 32p. (J). (gr. -1-k). 16.99 (978-1-4778-4728-2(6), 9781477847282, Amazon Children's Publishing) Amazon Publishing.

Long, Olivia. The Boy & the Dog. Long, Olivia, illus. Date not set. (Pets & Their People Ser.). (Illus.). 32p. (J). (gr. k-5). (978-1-880042-07-6(X)) Shelf-Life Bks.

—Diary of a Dog. Long, Olivia, illus. Date not set. (Pets & Their People Ser.). (Illus.). 32p. (J). (gr. -1-4). 9.95 (978-1-880042-06-9(1), SL12456) Shelf-Life Bks.

—Too Many Kittens. Long, Olivia, illus. Date not set. (Pets & Their People Ser.). (Illus.). 32p. (J). (gr. -1-4). (978-1-880042-09-0(6)) Shelf-Life Bks.

Lopresti, Tony. My Cat. Johnson, Deborah C., illus. 2012. 24p. pap. 13.99 (978-0-9838018-6-3(X)) 4RV Publishing, LLC.

Lord, Cynthia. Jelly Bean. McGuire, Erin, illus. 2014. (Shelter Pet Squad Ser.: 1). (ENG.). 128p. (J). (gr. 1-3). 16.99 (978-0-545-63596-7(9)); (gr. 2-5). pap. 5.99 (978-0-545-63597-4(7)) Scholastic, Inc. (Scholastic Pr.).

—Jelly Bean. 2014. (Shelter Pet Squad Ser.: 1). lib. bdg. 16.00 (978-0-606-36063-0(8)) Turtleback Bks.

—Merlin. McGuire, Erin, illus. 2015. (Shelter Pet Squad Ser.: 2). (ENG.). 128p. (J). (gr. 2-5). 16.99 (978-0-545-63599-8(3)) Scholastic, Inc.

Lucero, Len & Tracy, Kristina. Woo-Hoo ... Chris P. Is 2! Weber, Penny, illus. 2015. (ENG.). 32p. 14.99 (978-1-4019-4441-4(8), Hay Hse. Lifestyles) Hay Hse., Inc.

Luke, Melinda. The Green Dog. Manning, Jane K., illus. 2006. (Science Solves It Ser.). 32p. (J). pap. 7.99 (978-0-15-356581-6(0)) Houghton Mifflin Harcourt School Pubs.

Luthardt, Kevin. Peep!, 1 vol. Luthardt, Kevin, illus. (ENG., Illus.). 36p. (J). 2013. (gr. -1-1). 7.95 (978-1-56145-682-6(9)) 2003. (gr. k-1). 15.95 (978-1-56145-046-6(4)) Peachtree Pubs.

Lyle-Soffe, Shari. Shoo Cat. Foster, Jack, illus. 2010. 16p. pap. 9.95 (978-1-61633-033-0(3)) Guardian Angel Publishing, Inc.

MacDonald, Maryann. The Christmas Cat. Bates, Amy June, illus. 2013. (ENG.). 32p. (J). (gr. -1-k). 16.99 (978-0-8037-3498-2(0), Dial Bks) Penguin Young Readers Group.

Mack, Phillip. Missy Finds a Home. 2005. v, 93p. pap. 14.00 (978-1-4120-6681-5(6)) Trafford Publishing.

Magee, Wes. Blue, Where Are You? Suggs, Margaret, illus. 2007. (Flyers Ser.: 16). (ENG.). 64p. (J). pap. 9.95 (978-1-84717-009-5(9)) O'Brien Pr., Ltd., The IRL. Dist: Dufour Editions, Inc.

Maithya, Susan M. Struffel Cares: Struffel's New Pet. 2012. 40p. pap. 20.99 (978-1-4772-3323-8(7)) AuthorHouse.

Man-Kong, Mary. I Can Be a Pet Vet. An, Jiyoung, illus. 2010. (Step into Reading Ser.). (ENG.). 32p. (J). (gr. -1-1). pap. 3.99 (978-0-375-86581-7(0), Random Hse. Bks. for Young Readers) Random Hse. Children's Bks.

Mantchev, Lisa. Strictly No Elephants. Yoo, Taeeun, illus. 2015. (ENG.). 32p. (J). (gr. -1-3). 17.99 (978-1-4814-1647-4(2), Simon & Schuster Bks. For Young Readers) Simon & Schuster Bks. For Young Readers.

Marino, Gianna. Splotch. 2017. (ENG., Illus.). 40p. (J). (gr. -1-1). 17.99 (978-0-451-46957-1(7), Viking Books for Young Readers) Penguin Young Readers Group.

Marinsky, Jane. Just Perfect. 2012. (Illus.). 32p. (J). (gr. k). 16.95 (978-1-56792-428-2(X)) Godine, David R. Pub.

Marsoli, Lisa Ann. Dinos are Big Babies & Dylan's Pets. Smitherton, Jeb, illus. 2005. (J). bds. 19.99 (978-0-9767325-7-0(2)) Toy Quest.

—Dylan's Pets from A to Z. Santat, Dan, illus. 2005. (J). bds. 14.99 (978-0-9767325-1-8(3)) Toy Quest.

Martin, Stephen W. Charlotte & the Rock. Cotterill, Samantha, illus. 2017. (ENG.). 32p. (J). (-k). 16.99 (978-1-101-99389-7(8), Dial Bks) Penguin Young Readers Group.

Massey, Jane, illus. Mascotas. (Coloca y Siente). (SPA.). 10p. (J). (gr. k-2). bds. (978-968-5308-66-3(7), Silver Dolphin en Español) Advanced Marketing, S. de R. L. de C. V.

Mather, David. A Frog in the House. 2011. 32p. (gr. 1-2). 16.95 (978-0-9819307-9-4(4)); pap. 9.95 (978-0-9819307-8-7(6)) Raven Productions, Inc.

Mathews, Madge. Amelia Asks May I Have A Pet. Cook, Laurie, illus. 2008. 24p. (J). 3.99 (978-0-9796536-1-2(4), EPI Kid Bks.) EPI Bks.

Matson, Erik. Robobattlepets - Home Invasion. 2012. 144p. pap. 7.99 (978-0-9841187-6-2(4)) Asteroid Publishing.

Mayer, Mercer. Just One More Pet. Mayer, Mercer, illus. 2013. (Little Critter Ser.). (ENG., Illus.). 24p. (J). (gr. -1-2). pap. 3.99 (978-0-06-147807-9(5), HarperFestival) HarperCollins Pubs.

—Just One More Pet. 2013. (Little Critter Ser.). (J). lib. bdg. 13.55 (978-0-606-31791-7(0), Turtleback) Turtleback Bks.

—Too Many Dinosaurs. Mayer, Mercer, illus. 2012. (ENG., Illus.). 40p. (J). (gr. -1-2). pap. 6.99 (978-0-8234-2543-3(6)) Holiday Hse., Inc.

McCann, Jesse L., et al. Crisis of Infinite Kryptos, 1 vol. 2014. (Krypto the Superdog Ser.). (ENG., Illus.). 32p. (gr. 1-2). 22.60 (978-1-4342-6471-8(8)) Stone Arch Bks.

McCardie, Amanda. Our Very Own Dog. Rubbino, Salvatore, illus. 2017. (ENG.). 32p. (J). (gr. -1-2). 15.99 (978-0-7636-8948-3(3)) Candlewick Pr.

McCarty, Peter. Hondo & Fabian. McCarty, Peter, illus. 2007. (ENG., Illus.). 40p. (J). (gr. -1-1). per. 8.99 (978-0-312-36747-3(3), 9780312367473) Square Fish.

McCombie, Karen. My Big (Strange) Happy Family. Monks, Lydia, illus. 2009. (J). pap. (978-0-385-73597-1(9), Yearling) Random Hse. Children's Bks.

McDonald, Brenda. How Do You Love A Big Dog? 2007. 18.00 (978-0-8059-7314-3(1)) Dorrance Publishing Co., Inc.

McDonald, Megan. Triple Pet Trouble. Madrid, Erwin, illus. 2015. (Judy Moody Ser.: 6). (ENG.). 64p. (J). (gr. -1-1). 12.99 (978-0-7636-7443-4(5)) Candlewick Pr.

—Triple Pet Trouble. 2015. (Judy Moody & Friends Ser.). lib. bdg. 14.75 (978-0-606-36872-8(8)) Turtleback Bks.

McDonnell, Patrick. The Mutts Diaries. 2016. (ENG., Illus.). 226p. (J). (gr. 3-7). 29.99 (978-1-4494-7380-8(6)) Andrews McMeel Publishing.

—Year of Yesh. 2016. lib. bdg. 33.05 (978-0-606-39185-6(1)) Turtleback Bks.

McGhee, Holly M. Matylda, Bright & Tender. 2017. (ENG.). 224p. (J). (gr. 3-7). 16.99 (978-0-7636-8951-3(3)) Candlewick Pr.

McGill, Erin. I Do Not Like Al's Hat. McGill, Erin, illus. 2017. (Illus.). 32p. (J). (gr. -1-3). 17.99 (978-0-06-245576-5(1), Greenwillow Bks.) HarperCollins Pubs.

McGreal, Sue. Jimmy Fox's Great Pet Adventure. 2013. 68p. pap. (978-1-78299-607-1(9)) FeedARead.com.

McKay, Hilary. Lulu & the Rabbit Next Door. Lamont, Priscilla, illus. 2014. (Lulu Ser.: Book 4). (ENG.). 112p. (J). (gr. 1-5). 13.99 (978-0-8075-4816-5(2)) Whitman, Albert & Co.

McKenna, Martin. The Octopuppy. 2015. (ENG., Illus.). 32p. (J). (gr. -1-k). 16.99 (978-0-545-75140-7(3), Scholastic Pr.) Scholastic, Inc.

McKinlay, Meg. Duck for a Day. Rudge, Leila, illus. 2012. (ENG.). 96p. (J). (gr. 2-4). 12.99 (978-0-7636-5784-0(0)) Candlewick Pr.

McLean, Claire. Bo & the Ghosts of the White House Pets. 2012. 88p. pap. 17.95 (978-1-4626-7416-9(X)) America Star Bks.

McNeely Schultz, Geri. Kristie's Excellent Adventures: A Visit to the Fridge. Bertolami, Vince, illus. 2013. (ENG.). 40p. (J). pap. 9.99 (978-1-935766-88-9(0)) Windy City Pubs.

McOmber, Rachel B., ed. McOmber Phonics Storybooks: Ben Has a Pet. rev. ed. (Illus.). (J). (978-0-944991-26-8(2)) Swift Learning Resources.

MCP Staff. Ben's Pets, Level 3, Bk. 31. (J). (gr. -1-3). 24.50 (978-0-8136-1963-7(7)) Modern Curriculum Pr.

McPhail, David. Crash! the Cat. McPhail, David, illus. 2016. (ENG., Illus.). 32p. (J). (gr. -1-2). 16.95 (978-0-8234-3649-1(7)) Holiday Hse., Inc.

—Dot & Bob. 2008. (Green Light Readers Level 1 Ser.). (ENG., Illus.). 24p. (J). (gr. -1-1). pap. 3.95 (978-0-15-206541-6(5)) Houghton Mifflin Harcourt Publishing Co.

McQuinn, Anna. Lola Gets a Cat. Beardshaw, Rosalind, illus. 2017. (ENG.). 28p. (J). (-k). lib. bdg. 15.99 (978-1-58089-736-5(3)) Charlesbridge Publishing, Inc.

Meadows, Daisy. Bella the Bunny Fairy. Ripper, Georgie, illus. 2008. (Pet Fairies Ser.: 2). (ENG.). 80p. (J). (gr. -1-3). 4.99 (978-0-545-04185-0(6), Scholastic Paperbacks) Scholastic, Inc.

—Bella the Bunny Fairy. Ripper, Georgie, illus. 2008. (Rainbow Magic — the Pet Fairies Ser.). 65p. (gr. 7). lib. bdg. 14.75 (978-1-4178-2996-5(6), Turtleback) Turtleback Bks.

—Georgia the Guinea Pig Fairy. Ripper, Georgie, illus. 2008. (Pet Fairies Ser.: 3). (ENG.). 80p. (J). (gr. -1-3). 4.99 (978-0-545-04186-7(4), Scholastic Paperbacks) Scholastic, Inc.

—Georgia the Guinea Pig Fairy. Ripper, Georgie, illus. 2008. (Rainbow Magic — the Pet Fairies Ser.). 65p. (gr. 3). lib. bdg. 14.75 (978-1-4178-2997-2(4), Turtleback) Turtleback Bks.

—Harriet the Hamster Fairy. Ripper, Georgie, illus. 2008. (Rainbow Magic — the Pet Fairies Ser.). 67p. (gr. -1-3). lib. bdg. 14.75 (978-1-4178-3007-7(7), Turtleback) Turtleback Bks.

—Katie the Kitten Fairy. Ripper, Georgie, illus. 2008. (J). (Pet Fairies Ser.: 1). (ENG.). 80p. (gr. -1-3). pap. 4.99 (978-0-545-02816-5(7), Scholastic Paperbacks); 65p. pap. (978-0-545-13320-3(3)) Scholastic, Inc.

—Katie the Kitten Fairy. Ripper, Georgie, illus. 2008. (Rainbow Magic — the Pet Fairies Ser.). 65p. (gr. 1-4). lib. bdg. 14.75 (978-1-4178-2999-6(0), Turtleback) Turtleback Bks.

—Lauren the Puppy Fairy. Ripper, Georgie, illus. 2008. (Pet Fairies Ser.: 4). (ENG.). 80p. (J). (gr. -1-3). pap. 4.99 (978-0-545-04187-4(2), Scholastic Paperbacks) Scholastic, Inc.

—Molly the Goldfish Fairy. Ripper, Georgie, illus. 2008. (Pet Fairies Ser.: 6). (ENG.). 80p. (J). (gr. -1-3). pap. 4.99 (978-0-545-04189-8(9), Scholastic Paperbacks) Scholastic, Inc.

—Molly the Goldfish Fairy. Ripper, Georgie, illus. 2008. (Rainbow Magic — the Pet Fairies Ser.). 68p. (gr. -1-3). lib. bdg. 14.75 (978-1-4178-3001-5(8), Turtleback) Turtleback Bks.

—Penny the Pony Fairy. 2008. (Rainbow Magic — the Pet Fairies Ser.). lib. bdg. 14.75 (978-1-4178-3008-4(5), Turtleback) Turtleback Bks.

—Pet Fairies to the Rescue! 2013. (Rainbow Magic — Scholastic Reader Ser.). lib. bdg. 13.55 (978-0-606-31510-4(1), Turtleback) Turtleback Bks.

Meagher, Ed. D. Zach & His Dog: A Story of Bonding, Love, & Loss for Children & Adults to Share Together. 2009. 56p. pap. 23.99 (978-1-4389-4228-5(1)) AuthorHouse.

Messner, Kate. Marty McGuire Has Too Many Pets! 2015. (Marty Mcguire Ser.: 3). lib. bdg. 16.00 (978-0-606-37021-9(8)) Turtleback Bks.

Miles, Ellen. Maggie & Max. 2008. (Puppy Place Ser.: 10). (ENG.). 96p. (J). (gr. 2-5). 4.99 (978-0-545-03456-2(6), Scholastic Paperbacks) Scholastic, Inc.

—Molly. 2013. (Puppy Place Ser.: 31). lib. bdg. 14.75 (978-0-606-32385-7(6), Turtleback) Turtleback Bks.

—Pugsley. 2008. 81p. (J). (978-0-545-09948-6(X)) Scholastic, Inc.

Mills, Claudia. Cody Harmon, King of Pets. Shepperson, Rob, illus. 2016. (Franklin School Friends Ser.: 5). (ENG.). 144p. (J). 15.99 (978-0-374-30223-8(5), 9780374302238, Farrar, Straus & Giroux (BYR)) Farrar, Straus & Giroux.

—Pet Disasters. Francis, Guy, illus. 2012. (Mason Dixon Ser.). (ENG.). 176p. (J). (gr. 4-7). 6.99 (978-0-375-87274-7(4), Yearling) Random Hse. Children's Bks.

Milo, Margaret D. Matthew Pet Adventure. 2012. 24p. 24.95 (978-1-4626-6850-2(X)) America Star Bks.

Moncure, Jane Belk. A Wish-For Dinosaur: A Just-for-Fun Book. Regan, Dana, illus. 2013. (Magic Castle Readers Ser.). (ENG.). 32p. (J). (gr. -1-2). 25.64 (978-1-62323-576-5(6), 206308) Child's World, Inc., The.

Monstrata, Nessi. Monster High Diaries: Frankie Stein & the New Ghoul in School. 2015. (Monster High Diaries: 2). (ENG., Illus.). 160p. (J). (gr. 3-7). 9.99 (978-0-316-30094-0(2)) Little, Brown Bks. for Young Readers.

Montgomery, Lewis B. The Case of the Amazing Zelda. Wummer, Amy, illus. 2009. (Milo & Jazz Mysteries Ser.). 96p. (J). (ENG.). (gr. -1-2). pap. 6.95 (978-1-57565-296-2(X)); Vol. 4. (gr. k-3). 22.60 (978-1-57565-298-6(6)) Kane Press, Inc.

—The Case of the Amazing Zelda. Wummer, Amy, illus. 2012. (Milo & Jazz Mysteries Ser.: Vol. 4). (ENG.). (J). (gr. 2-4). pap. 20.95 incl. audio compact disk (978-1-4301-1209-9(3)) Live Oak Media.

—The Case of the Poisoned Pig. Montgomery, Lewis B., illus. 2009. (Milo & Jazz Mysteries Ser.). (Illus.). 96p. (J). (gr. 2-5). 22.60 (978-1-57565-289-4(7)) Kane Press, Inc.

—The Case of the Poisoned Pig. Wummer, Amy, illus. 2009. (Milo & Jazz Mysteries Ser.). (ENG.). 96p. (J). (gr. 2-6). pap. 6.95 (978-1-57565-286-3(2)) Kane Press, Inc.

Morningforest, Chris & Raymond, Rebecca. Taking Care of Funny Pets. 2006. 36p. (J). pap. 15.43 (978-1-4116-7710-4(2)) Lulu Pr., Inc.

Morris, Kyle. Watching the Puppy Grow. 2017. (Text Connections Guided Close Reading Ser.). (J). (gr. 1). (978-1-4900-1805-8(0)) Benchmark Education Co.

Morrison, Cathy. I Want a Pet. 2012. (ENG.). 32p. (J). (978-1-58925-113-7(X)) Tiger Tales.

Mortensen, Lori. The Cat That Disappeared, 1 vol. Simard, Remy, illus. 2010. (My First Graphic Novel Ser.). (ENG.). 32p. (gr. k-2). pap. 6.25 (978-1-4342-2282-4(9)); lib. bdg. 24.65 (978-1-4342-1887-2(2)) Stone Arch Bks. (My First Graphic Novel).

—The Class Pet. 2016. (Spring Forward Ser.). (J). (gr. 1). (978-1-4900-2228-4(7)) Benchmark Education Co.

Moyer, Anna B. Her Name Is Sophi. 2013. 28p. pap. 16.09 (978-1-4669-7275-9(0)) Trafford Publishing.

Mubiru, Betha. Muzinge the Bird. 2004. (Illus.). 16p. pap. (978-9970-02-447-6(7)) Fountain Pubs. Ltd. UGA. Dist: Michigan State Univ. Pr.

Muench-Williams, Heather. I Want a Pet. Teeple, Jackie, illus. l.t. ed. 2006. 12p. (J). (gr. -1-k). pap. 10.95 (978-1-57332-353-6(5), HighReach Learning, Incorporated) Carson-Dellosa Publishing, LLC.

Mulholland, Clara. Naughty Miss Bunny. 2007. 128p. 25.95 (978-1-4218-3838-0(9), 1st World Library - Literary Society) 1st World Publishing, Inc.

Mullican, Judy. Taking Care of Pets. Ruminski, Jeff, illus. l.t. ed. 2004. (HRL Big Book Ser.). 8p. (J). (gr. -1-1). pap. 10.95 (978-1-57332-278-2(4)); pap. 10.95 (978-1-57332-279-9(2)) Carson-Dellosa Publishing, LLC. (HighReach Learning, Incorporated).

Murphy, Nancy K. Rv Adventures by Sweetie, Miss Bell, Pierce & Sadie: By Sweetie Miss Bell, Pierce & Sad. 2011. 50p. pap. 15.99 (978-1-4653-4158-7(7)) Xlibris Corp.

Murray, Caryn Eve. Philomena's Homecoming: The (mostly) true story of a New York prairie dog's search for a Family. 2010. 48p. pap. 8.95 (978-1-4502-2769-8(4)) iUniverse, Inc.

Murray, Diana. Grimelda & the Spooktacular Pet Show. Ross, Heather, illus. 2017. 40p. (J). (gr. -1-3). 16.99 **(978-0-06-226449-7(4)**, Tegen, Katherine Bks) HarperCollins Pubs.

Murray, Martine. Henrietta: There's No One Better. 2010. (Henrietta Ser.). (ENG., Illus.). 96p. (J). (gr. k-2). pap. 10.99 (978-1-74114-718-6(2)) Allen & Unwin AUS. Dist: Independent Pubs. Group.

—Henrietta: There's No One Better. 2006. (Illus.). 88p. (J). 9.99 *(978-0-439-80749-4(2),* Levine, Arthur A. Bks.) Scholastic, Inc.

Muthu, Antony M. Athim. 2008. 48p. pap. 19.49 *(978-1-4389-3074-9(7))* AuthorHouse.

Myers, Don. My Life with Roger. 2009. (Illus.). 49p. (J). pap. 12.95 *(978-1-4327-3873-0(9))* Outskirts Pr., Inc.

Myers, Martha. Nibbles, the Mostly Mischievous Monkey. 2003. (Julius & Friends Ser.: Vol. 10). (Illus.). 91p. (J). 6.99 *(978-0-8163-1947-3(2))* Pacific Pr. Publishing Assn.

Myracle, Lauren. Friends of a Feather. Henry, Jed, illus. 2015. (Life of Ty Ser.: 3). (ENG.). 144p. (J). (gr. 1-4). 5.99 *(978-0-14-242320-2(3),* Puffin Books); 12.99 *(978-0-525-42288-4(9),* Dutton Books for Young Readers) Penguin Young Readers Group.

Namm, Diane. Pick a Pet. Suarez, Maribel, tr. Suarez, Maribel, illus. 2004. (My First Reader Ser.). (ENG.). 31p. (J). 18.50 *(978-0-516-24417-4(5),* Children's Pr.) Scholastic Library Publishing.

Nash, Andy. Marcus & His Monkey: For Kids Blessed with Popularity. 2010. (J). *(978-0-8127-0452-5(5))* Autumn Hse. Publishing Co.

—Tatum & Her Tiger: For Kids Blessed with Passion. 2007. (Illus.). (J). 9.99 *(978-0-8127-0451-8(7))* Autumn Hse. Publishing Co.

Naylor, Phyllis Reynolds. Patches & Scratches, 0 vols. Ramsey, Marcy, illus. 2010. (Simply Sarah Ser.: 0). (ENG.). 80p. (J). (gr. 2-6). pap. 6.99 *(978-0-7614-5731-2(3),* 9780761457312, Amazon Children's Publishing) Amazon Publishing.

Nees, Susan. Class Pets. 2013. (Missy's Super Duper Royal Deluxe Ser.: 2). (ENG., Illus.). 80p. (J). (gr. k-2). pap. 4.99 *(978-0-545-43852-0(7))* Scholastic, Inc.

—Class Pets. 2013. (Missy's Super Duper Royal Deluxe Ser.: 2). lib. bdg. 14.75 *(978-0-606-31980-5(8),* Turtleback) Turtleback Bks.

Neumeyer, P. & Gorey, E. The Donald Boxed Set. 2012. 48p. (J). *(978-0-7649-6130-4(6))* Pomegranate Communications, Inc.

Nicklaus, Terry. Schweppe. 2012. 24p. pap. 15.99 *(978-1-4771-4565-4(6))* Xlibris Corp.

Niemann, Christoph. The Pet Dragon: A Story about Adventure, Friendship, & Chinese Characters. Niemann, Christoph, illus. 2008. (ENG., Illus.). 40p. (J). (gr. -1-3). 16.99 *(978-0-06-157776-5(6),* Greenwillow Bks.) HarperCollins Pubs.

No Trouble at All! Individual Title Six-Packs. (Action Packs Ser.). 120p. (gr. 3-5). 44.00 *(978-0-7635-8397-2(9))* Rigby Education.

Norris II, Charles H. Fat Little Ugly Friend. 2008. 12p. per. 24.95 *(978-1-4241-9222-9(6))* America Star Bks.

Noyes, William H., Jr. Mittens. 2008. 36p. pap. 24.95 *(978-1-4241-9440-7(7))* America Star Bks.

Numan, Aisha. The Chameleon Pet. 2003. (Illus.). 52p. (gr. -1-3). pap. *(978-9966-46-682-2(7))* Heinemann Kenya, Limited (East African Educational Publishers Ltd E.A.E.P.) KEN. Dist: Michigan State Univ. Pr.

O'Connor, George. If I Had a Triceratops. O'Connor, George, illus. 2015. (ENG., Illus.). 32p. (J). (gr. -1-2). 15.99 *(978-0-7636-6013-0(2))* Candlewick Pr.

O'Donnell, Liam. Winston in the City. (ENG., Illus.). 32p. (J). (gr. -1-2). 9.95 *(978-1-59249-449-1(8),* 1B033) Soundprints.

—Winston in the City. Hatala, Dan, illus. 2005. (Pet Tales Ser.). (ENG.). 32p. (J). (gr. -1-2). pap. 2.95 *(978-1-59249-448-4(X),* 1B032) Soundprints.

—Winston in the City. Hatala, Dan, illus. 2005. (Pet Tales Ser.). (ENG.). 32p. (J). (gr. -1 — 1). 4.95 *(978-1-59249-447-7(1),* 1B031) Soundprints.

Offill, Jenny. Sparky! Appelhans, Chris, illus. 2014. (ENG.). 40p. (J). (gr. -1-3). 16.99 *(978-0-375-87023-1(7),* Schwartz & Wade Bks.) Random Hse. Children's Bks.

Ogden, Charles. Nod's Limbs. Carton, Rick, illus. 2007. (Edgar & Ellen Ser.: 6). (ENG.). 224p. (J). (gr. 3-7). 24.99 *(978-1-4169-1501-0(X),* Simon & Schuster/Paula Wiseman Bks.) Simon & Schuster/Paula Wiseman Bks.

—Pet's Revenge. Carton, Rick, illus. 2006. (Edgar & Ellen Ser.: 4). (ENG.). 192p. (J). (gr. 3-7). 23.99 *(978-1-4169-1408-2(0),* Simon & Schuster/Paula Wiseman Bks.) Simon & Schuster/Paula Wiseman Bks.

O'Grady, Patricia. The Naughty Ones. 2010. 24p. pap. 12.99 *(978-1-4520-2502-5(9))* AuthorHouse.

Old Cat & the Kitten. 2014. (ENG., Illus.). 128p. (J). (gr. 3-7). pap. 6.99 *(978-1-4814-1938-3(2),* Aladdin) Simon & Schuster Children's Publishing.

Oliveto, Michelle. My Dog the Faker. 2012. 24p. 24.95 *(978-1-4560-2194-8(X))* America Star Bks.

O'Neal, Shaquille. Little Shaq. Taylor, Theodore, III, illus. 2016. (ENG.). 80p. (J). 9.99 *(978-1-61963-879-2(7),* 9781619638792, Bloomsbury USA Childrens) Bloomsbury Publishing USA.

Orback, Craig, illus. Paul Bunyan. 2007. (On My Own Folklore Ser.). (ENG.). 48p. (gr. 2-4). per. 6.95 *(978-0-8225-6479-9(3),* First Avenue Editions) Lerner Publishing Group.

O'Reilly, Sean. My Missing Monster, 1 vol. 2010. (Mighty Mighty Monsters Ser.). (ENG.). 48p. (gr. 2-3). lib. bdg. 23.99 *(978-1-4342-2153-7(9))* Stone Arch Bks.

Orloff, Karen Kaufman. I Wanna Iguana. Catrow, David, illus. 2004. (ENG.). 32p. (J). (gr. -1-3). 16.99 *(978-0-399-23717-1(8),* G.P. Putnam's Sons Books for Young Readers) Penguin Young Readers Group.

Orr, Wendy. Missing! - A Cat Called Buster. Boase, Susan, illus. 2011. (Rainbow Street Shelter Ser.: 2). (ENG.). 128p. (J). (gr. 2-5). 15.99 *(978-0-8050-8932-5(2),* 9780805089325, Holt, Henry & Co. Bks. For Young Readers) Holt, Henry & Co.

Owens, Connie S. Missing Maggie: The Death of a Pet. 2003. (J). pap. 5.99 *(978-1-59317-007-3(6))* Warner Pr., Inc.

Palatini, Margie. The Perfect Pet. Whatley, Bruce, illus. 2003. 32p. (J). (gr. -1-2). 16.99 *(978-0-06-000108-7(9))* HarperCollins Pubs.

Paraskevas, Betty. Peter Pepper's Pet Spectacular. Paraskevas, Michael, illus. 2007. 32p. (J). (gr. 2-6). pap. 14.95 *(978-1-60095-257-9(7))* Carson-Dellosa Publishing, LLC.

Parish, Peggy. No More Monsters for Me! 2003. 22.95 *(978-0-673-75926-9(1))* Celebration Pr.

Parker, Emma. Pet Day. 2010. (Illus.). pap. *(978-1-877561-28-3(2))* First Edition Ltd.

Patchett, Mary Elwyn. Ajax: Golden Dog of the Australian Bush. Tansley, Eric, illus. 2011. 172p. 42.95 *(978-1-258-01103-1(4))* Literary Licensing, LLC.

Patton, Julia. Drat That Fat Cat! Patton, Julia, illus. 2016. (ENG., Illus.). 32p. (J). (gr. -1-3). 16.99 *(978-0-8075-1713-0(5))* Whitman, Albert & Co.

Pearl, B. B. Poerava's Heaven. 2011. (Illus.). 88p. pap. 12.85 *(978-1-4567-8985-5(6))* AuthorHouse.

Peet, Joy. Sophia's Flutterfly. 2008. 19p. pap. 24.95 *(978-1-60610-806-2(9))* America Star Bks.

Pennypacker, Sara. Pax. Klassen, Jon, illus. 2016. (ENG.). (J). (gr. 3-3). 16.99 ***(978-0-06-245703-5(9))*** Blackstone Audio, Inc.

—Pax. Klassen, Jon, illus. 2016. 288p. (J). (gr. 3-7). 16.99 *(978-0-06-237701-2(9))* HarperCollins Pubs.

—Pax. 2017. (SPA.). lib. bdg. 29.35 ***(978-0-606-40010-7(9))*** Turtleback Bks.

—PAX: UNA HISTORIA DE PAZ Y AMISTAD. 2017. (SPA.). 304p. (gr. -1-2). pap. 16.95 ***(978-84-15594-95-6(X),*** Nube De Tinta) Penguin Random House Grupo Editorial ESP. Dist: Two Rivers Distribution.

Perret, Delphine. The Big Bad Wolf & Me. 2006. (ENG., Illus.). 64p. (J). (gr. -1-3). 9.95 *(978-1-4027-3725-1(4))* Sterling Publishing Co., Inc.

Pet Stories Set 2 800888, 3 vols. 2005. (J). pap. *(978-1-59794-063-4(1))* Environments, Inc.

Pet Stories Set 800887, 3 vols. 2005. (J). pap. *(978-1-59794-062-7(3))* Environments, Inc.

Pet Tales! 2017. (Pet Tales! Ser.). 24p. (gr. 4-6). 94.40 ***(978-1-5081-5794-6(4));*** pap. 33.00 ***(978-1-5081-5771-7(5))*** Rosen Publishing Group, Inc., The. (PowerKids Pr.).

Peters, Kathryn. A Pet for Elizabeth Rose. Peters, Kathryn, illus. Lt. ed. 2005. (Illus.). 42p. (J). 8.99 *(978-0-9752647-9-9(6))* Proton Arts.

Petrucha, Stefan & Pendleton, Thomas. Prey. 2008. (Wicked Dead Ser.). (ENG.). 208p. (J). (gr. 7-18). pap. 9.99 *(978-0-06-113853-9(3),* HarperTeen) HarperCollins Pubs.

The Pets: Individual Title Six-Packs. (Sails Literacy Ser.). 16p. (gr. k-18). 27.00 *(978-0-7635-4420-1(5))* Rigby Education.

Pets Board Book Set 800792, 6. 2005. (J). bds. *(978-1-59794-022-1(4))* Environments, Inc.

Pett, Mark. Lizard from the Park. Pett, Mark, illus. 2015. (ENG., Illus.). 40p. (J). (gr. -1-3). 17.99 *(978-1-4424-8321-7(0),* Simon & Schuster Bks. For Young Readers) Simon & Schuster Bks. For Young Readers.

Philip, Simon. I Don't Know What to Call My Cat. Bailey, Ella, illus. 2017. (ENG.). 32p. (J). (gr. -1-3). 16.99 *(978-0-544-97143-1(4),* HMH Books For Young Readers) Houghton Mifflin Harcourt Publishing Co.

Picayo, Mario. A Very Smart Cat: Una Gata Muy Inteligente. Fundora, Yolanda V., illus. 2008. (SPA & ENG.). 32p. (J). *(978-1-934370-00-1(2))* Editorial Campana.

Pinson, Mignon L. My Two Best Friends Are Hamsters. 2010. 24p. 12.99 *(978-1-4520-3309-9(9))* AuthorHouse.

Pintozzi, Nick. Bentley & the Great Fire. Pintozzi, Nick et al, illus. 2004. 16.95 *(978-0-9749465-2-8(4))* BentDaiSha, LLC.

Pitt, Marilyn & Hileman, Jane. Get Up. Bianchi, John, illus. 2010. (1G Potato Chip Bks.). (ENG.). 12p. (J). (gr. k-1). pap. 5.99 *(978-1-61541-069-9(4))* American Reading Co.

—Let Me In. Bianchi, John, illus. 2010. (1G Potato Chip Bks.). (ENG.). 12p. (J). (gr. k-1). pap. 5.99 *(978-1-61541-168-9(2))* American Reading Co.

—The Storm. Bianchi, John, illus. 2010. (1G Potato Chip Bks.). (ENG.). 12p. (J). (gr. k-1). pap. 5.99 *(978-1-61541-232-7(8))* American Reading Co.

Pitt, Marilyn & Sánchez, Lucía M. ¡Arriba! Bianchi, John, illus. 2010. (1G Libros Papas Fritas Ser.).Tr. of Get Up. (SPA & ENG.). 12p. (J). (gr. k-1). pap. 6.99 *(978-1-61541-084-2(8))* American Reading Co.

Pittar, Gill. Milly, Molly & the Ferryman. Morrell, Cris, illus. 2004. 28p. pap. *(978-1-86972-004-9(0))* Milly Molly Bks.

Polak, Monique. Finding Elmo, 1 vol. 2007. (Orca Currents Ser.). (ENG.). 112p. (gr. 5-9). 112p. lib. bdg. 14.95 *(978-1-55143-688-3(4));* 128p. per. 9.95 *(978-1-55143-686-9(8))* Orca Bk. Pubs. USA.

—Forensics Squad Unleashed, 1 vol. 2016. (ENG.). 208p. (J). (gr. 3-6). pap. 9.95 *(978-1-4598-0979-6(3))* Orca Bk. Pubs. USA.

Porter, Gary. Duffy: The Tale of a Terrier. 2011. (Illus.). 256p. (J). 22.95 *(978-1-59298-369-8(3))* Beaver's Pond Pr., Inc.

Porter, Lisa. Billy & Froggy. 2011. 24p. pap. 12.79 *(978-1-4634-3528-8(2))* AuthorHouse.

Posner-Sanchez, Andrea. Cuddly Princess Pals. Random House Disney Staff, illus. 2014. (Pictureback(R) Ser.). (ENG.). 24p. (J). (gr. -1-2). 3.99 *(978-0-7364-3135-4(7),* RH/Disney) Random Hse. Children's Bks.

—The Hugglefish (Disney Junior: Henry Hugglemonster). Laguna, Fabio & Gallego, James, illus. 2015. (Little Golden Book Ser.). (ENG.). 24p. (J). (-k). 4.99 *(978-0-7364-3360-0(0),* Golden/Disney) Random Hse. Children's Bks.

—A Royal Pet Problem. RH Disney Staff, illus. 2015. (Little Golden Book Ser.). (ENG.). 24p. (J). (-k). 4.99 *(978-0-7364-3308-2(2),* Golden/Disney) Random Hse. Children's Bks.

Posner-Sanchez, Andrea, illus. Dog Days. 2016. 22p. (J). ***(978-1-5182-3229-9(9))*** Random Hse., Inc.

Potash, Mildred. Millie & Cupcake. 2013. (ENG.). 24p. (J). pap. 10.95 *(978-1-4787-0997-8(9))* Outskirts Pr., Inc.

Poydar, Nancy. Fish School. 2009. (ENG., Illus.). 32p. (J). (gr. -1-3). 16.95 *(978-0-8234-2140-4(6))* Holiday Hse., Inc.

Preller, James. Swamp Monster. Bruno, Iacopo, illus. 2015. (Scary Tales Ser.: 6). (ENG.). 96p. (J). (gr. 2-5). 15.99 *(978-1-250-04097-8(3),* 9781250040978) Feiwel & Friends.

Procter, Diann. It Happened in the Goldfish Bowl. Procter, Bill, illus. 2007. 28p. pap. 24.95 *(978-1-4241-8357-9(X))* America Star Bks.

Provencher, Rose-Marie. Slithery Jake. Carter, Abby, illus. 2004. (ENG.). 32p. (J). 15.99 *(978-0-06-623820-3(X))* HarperCollins Pubs.

Provensen, Alice. A Day in the Life of Murphy. Provensen, Alice, illus. 2003. (ENG., Illus.). 40p. (J). (gr. -1-3). 17.99 *(978-0-689-84884-1(6),* Simon & Schuster Bks. For Young Readers) Simon & Schuster Bks. For Young Readers.

Publications International Ltd. Staff. First Look & Find Wonder Pets. 2008. 16p. (J). bds. 9.98 *(978-1-4127-9394-0(7),* PIL Kids) Publications International, Ltd.

Publications International Ltd. Staff, ed. Disney(r) Princess First Look & Find(r)Palace Pets. 2015. 16p. (J). bds. *(978-1-4508-8634-5(5),* 1450886345) Publications International, Ltd.

—Disney(r) Princess Palace Pets: Little Pop-Up Songbook. 2014. 10p. (J). bds. *(978-1-4508-8635-2(3),* 1450886353) Publications International, Ltd.

—Handy Manny. 2008. 16p. (J). bds. 9.98 *(978-1-4127-9373-5(4),* PIL Kids) Publications International, Ltd.

—Wonder Pets: Save the Baby Kitten. 2008. (J). bds. 10.98 *(978-1-4127-9198-4(7))* Publications International, Ltd.

Punnett, Dick. Name Patty's Pets: A Talk-along Book. Punnett, Yvonne, ed. 2nd ed. 2005. (Talk-Along Bks.). (Illus.). 32p. (J). pap. 6.99 *(978-0-9657211-5-8(9))* Tomoka Pr.

Ralston, Carole. Light in the Forest. 2012. 24p. 24.95 *(978-1-4626-6263-8(8))* America Star Bks.

Rand, Emily. A Dog Day. 2015. (ENG., Illus.). 32p. (gr. -1 — 1). 18.95 *(978-1-84976-290-8(2))* Tate Publishing, Ltd. GBR. Dist: Abrams, Inc.

Random House. Duke's Tale. Random House, illus. 2016. (Pictureback(R) Ser.). (ENG., Illus.). 24p. (J). (gr. -1-2). 4.99 *(978-0-399-55495-7(5),* Random Hse. Bks. for Young Readers) Random Hse. Children's Bks.

—Meet the Pets. Random House, illus. 2016. (Step into Reading Ser.). (ENG., Illus.). 32p. (J). (gr. -1-2). 4.99 *(978-0-399-55483-4(1),* Random Hse. Bks. for Young Readers) Random Hse. Children's Bks.

—My First Pet (Barbie) 2016. (Pictureback(R) Ser.). (ENG., Illus.). 16p. (J). (gr. -1-2). 4.99 *(978-1-101-93729-7(7),* Random Hse. Bks. for Young Readers) Random Hse. Children's Bks.

Random House & Man-Kong, Mary. Meet the Pets. Random House, illus. 2016. (Step into Reading Ser.). (ENG., Illus.). 32p. (J). (gr. -1-2). 12.99 *(978-0-399-55484-1(X),* Random Hse. Bks. for Young Readers) Random Hse. Children's Bks.

Random House Disney Staff. Secret Life of Pets. Random House Disney Staff, illus. 2016. (Pictureback(R) Ser.). (ENG., Illus.). 16p. (J). (gr. -1-2). 4.99 *(978-0-399-55486-5(6),* Random Hse. Bks. for Young Readers) Random Hse. Children's Bks.

Random House Editors & RH Disney Staff. Aurora & the Helpful Dragon/Tiana & Her Furry Friend. Disney Storybook Artists Staff & Studio Iboix Staff, illus. 2011. (Pictureback(R) Ser.). (ENG.). 32p. (J). (gr. -1-2). pap. 4.99 *(978-0-7364-2757-9(0),* RH/Disney) Random Hse. Children's Bks.

Rankine-Van Wassenhoven, Jacqueline. A Little Honey for Serge. 2009. 16p. pap. 9.00 *(978-1-4490-0810-9(0))* AuthorHouse.

Rasheed, Winona. Smiles & Frowns Through Animal Town's Storybook. 2008. 55p. pap. 13.70 *(978-1-4357-4617-6(1))* Lulu Pr., Inc.

Ray Charles Lockamy, Inez Eason. The Adventures of Tracks & Cookout. 2010. 40p. pap. *(978-1-4269-2159-9(4))* Trafford Publishing (UK) Ltd.

Rebal, Tara. Sarah Sue Smith: A Crooked Wharf Adventure. 2010. 52p. pap. 22.49 *(978-1-4520-7165-7(9))* AuthorHouse.

Redbank, Tennant. The Pet Pawlympics (Disney Palace Pets: Whisker Haven Tales) RH Disney et al, illus. 2016. (Disney Chapters Ser.). (ENG.). 64p. (J). (gr. 1-4). 5.99 *(978-0-7364-3513-0(1),* RH/Disney) Random Hse. Children's Bks.

Reed, Tom. Pookus & Buckie: A Children's Book Based on a True Story. Carter, Sandy Lewis, illus. I.t. ed. 2005. 36p. (J). per. 11.95 *(978-0-9749725-4-1(1),* 10000, Lonestar Abilene Publishing) LoneStar Abilene Publishing, LLC.

Reiche, Dietlof & Brownjohn, John. Freddy in Peril: Book Two in the Golden Hamster Saga. Cepeda, Joe, illus. 2004. 202p. (J). pap. *(978-0-439-64984-1(6))* Scholastic, Inc.

Rennich, Lori. When Cooper Got to Heaven. 2011. 28p. pap. 21.99 *(978-1-4568-6199-5(9))* Xlibris Corp.

Resnicoff, Stan. Stanley, the Seal of Approval. 2012. (ENG.). (J). pap. *(978-1-4675-1535-1(3))* Independent Pub.

Reynolds, Judy. A Blue Jay's Choice. 2010. 72p. pap. 10.49 *(978-1-4520-6455-0(5))* AuthorHouse.

RH Disney. High-Flying Tea (Disney Palace Pets: Whisker Haven Tales) RH Disney, illus. 2016. (Pictureback Ser.). (ENG., Illus.). 24p. (J). (gr. -1-2). pap. 4.99 *(978-0-7364-3551-2(4),* Random Hse. Bks. for Young Readers) Random Hse. Children's Bks.

—The Royal Derby (Disney Palace Pets: Whisker Haven Tales) RH Disney, illus. 2016. (Pictureback Ser.). (ENG., Illus.). 24p. (J). (gr. -1-2). 4.99 *(978-0-7364-3496-6(8),* Random Hse. Bks. for Young Readers) Random Hse. Children's Bks.

—Tutu Terrific! (Disney Palace Pets: Whisker Haven Tales) Wu, Vivien, illus. 2016. (Little Golden Book Ser.). (ENG.). 24p. (J). (-k). 4.99 *(978-0-7364-3504-8(2),* Golden/Disney) Random Hse. Children's Bks.

RH Disney Staff. The Cake-Tillion (Disney Palace Pets: Whisker Haven Tales) RH Disney Staff, illus. 2016. (Pictureback Ser.). (ENG., Illus.). 16p. (J). (gr. -1-2). 5.99 *(978-0-7364-3387-7(2),* RH/Disney) Random Hse. Children's Bks.

—Furry, Fluffy & Fabulous! (Disney Princess: Palace Pets) Disney Storybook Artists Staff, illus. 2014. (Big Golden Book Ser.). (ENG.). 64p. (J). (gr. -1-2). 9.99 *(978-0-7364-3263-4(9),* Golden/Disney) Random Hse. Children's Bks.

—Welcome to Whisker Haven (Disney Palace Pets: Whisker Haven Tales) RH Disney Staff, illus. 2016. (Big Golden Book Ser.). (ENG., Illus.). 32p. (J). (gr. -1-2). 9.99 *(978-0-7364-3474-4(7),* Golden/Disney) Random Hse. Children's Bks.

Rice, Dona Herweck & Thompson, Chad. Old Mother Hubbard, 1 vol. 2009. (Early Childhood Themes Ser.). (ENG., Illus.). 16p. (J). (gr. -1-2). pap. 19.99 *(978-1-4333-1478-0(9))* Shell Educational Publishing.

Richardson, Lin Douglas. The Meaning of Me. 2011. 28p. pap. 24.95 *(978-1-4626-2891-9(5))* America Star Bks.

Ries, Lori. Good Dog, Aggie. Dormer, Frank W., illus. (ENG.). 48p. (J). (gr. -1-3). 2012. pap. 5.95 *(978-1-57091-646-5(2))* 2009. 12.95 *(978-1-57091-645-8(4))* Charlesbridge Publishing, Inc.

Ries, Lori, et al. Tita y Ben: Tres Cuentos. Dormer, Frank W., illus. 2010. (SPA.). 48p. (J). (gr. -1-3). 13.95 *(978-1-57091-934-3(8));* pap. 5.95 *(978-1-57091-935-0(6))* Charlesbridge Publishing, Inc.

Rieser, Karen. A Cat with Three Tales. 2013. 48p. pap. 8.95 *(978-1-937260-93-4(3))* Sleepytown Pr.

Rippin, Sally. The New Friend: Hey Jack! Spartels, Stephanie, illus. 2014. (ENG.). 48p. (J). pap. 4.99 *(978-1-61067-125-5(2))* Kane Miller.

Rissi, Anica Mrose. The Teacher's Pet. OHora, Zachariah, illus. 2017. (ENG.). 40p. (J). (gr. -1-k). 17.99 *(978-1-4847-4364-5(4))* Disney Pr.

Ritz, C. Tiger's World: Growing Up. 2013. 72p. pap. *(978-1-77097-596-5(9))* FriesenPress.

Robare, Jay, illus. Pets in Heaven Activity Book: Children's Companion Book to: Do Pets & Other Animals Go to Heaven? 2003. 86p. (J). per. 12.95 *(978-0-9726363-1-5(5),* 6315) Brite Bks.

Robbins, Jacqui. The New Girl... & Me. Phelan, Matt, illus. 2006. (ENG.). 32p. (J). (gr. -1-2). 17.99 *(978-0-689-86468-1(X),* Atheneum/Richard Jackson Bks.) Simon & Schuster Children's Publishing.

Roberton, Fiona. A Tale of Two Beasts. Roberton, Fiona, illus. 2015. (ENG., Illus.). 32p. (J). pap. 12.99 *(978-1-61067-361-7(1))* Kane Miller.

Roberts, Victoria. Best Pet Ever. Allwright, Deborah, illus. 2011. (ENG.). 32p. pap. 7.95 *(978-1-58925-432-9(5))* Tiger Tales.

Roddy, Lee. The City Bear's Adventures. 2008. (D. J. Dillon Adventure Ser.: No. 2). (J). 7.99 *(978-0-88062-266-0(0))* Mott Media.

Rogers, Jewels. The Princess & the Rabbit. 2011. 28p. pap. 12.50 *(978-1-4567-5171-5(9))* AuthorHouse.

Roland, Timothy. Monkey Me & the Pet Show. 2014. (Monkey Me Ser.: 2). (ENG.). 96p. (J). (gr. 1-3). 15.99 *(978-0-545-55981-2(2))* Scholastic, Inc.

—Monkey Me & the Pet Show. 2014. (Monkey Me Ser.: 2). lib. bdg. 14.75 *(978-0-606-35359-5(3))* Turtleback Bks.

Rose, Dorothy. I Wish That I Could Have a Pet. 2014. (ENG., Illus.). 24p. (J). (gr. -1-3). pap. 13.99 *(978-1-4814-2649-7(4),* Little Simon) Little Simon.

Rosen, Lev Ac & Rosen, Ellis J. Woundabout. Rosen, Lev Ac & Rosen, Ellis J., illus. 2015. (ENG., Illus.). 288p. (J). (gr. 3-7). 17.00 *(978-0-316-37078-3(9))* Little Brown & Co.

Ross, Tony. I Want a Cat! Ross, Tony, illus. 2008. (ENG., Illus.). 32p. (J). (gr. -1-k). pap. 12.99 *(978-1-84270-691-6(8))* Andersen Pr. GBR. Dist: Independent Pubs. Group.

Ross, Tony, illus. Rita's Rhino. 2015. (J). 17.32 *(978-1-4677-6319-6(5))* Lerner Publishing Group.

Rosseter, Patrick W. Grampa Pat's Little Animal Tales. 2008. 88p. pap. 10.99 *(978-1-60647-466-2(9))* Salem Author Services.

Rostoker-Gruber, Karen. Ferret Fun, 0 vols. De Tagyos, Paul Rátz, illus. 2011. (ENG.). 32p. (J). (gr. k-3). 17.99 *(978-0-7614-5817-3(4),* 9780761458173, Amazon Children's Publishing) Amazon Publishing.

Roundtree, Beth. Wilhamina Constance Winston Churchill Ingersol & the Cat. 2012. 24p. pap. 10.99 *(978-1-4624-0389-9(1),* Inspiring Voices) Author Solutions, Inc.

Rowe, Helen, illus. Fun with Pets: A Pop-Up Book. 2016. (ENG.). 12p. (J). (gr. -1 — 1). bds. 8.99 *(978-1-4998-0300-6(1))* Little Bee Books Inc.

Rowe, W. W. Jerry's Mastery. 2017. (ENG.). 103p. (YA). (gr. 8-17). pap. 8.95 ***(978-1-936012-80-0(4))*** Larson Pubns.

Roy, Ron. A to Z Mysteries Collection, No. 1. Gurney, John Steven, illus. 2010. (to Z Mysteries Ser.: Nos. 1-4). (ENG.). 384p. (J). (gr. 1-4). 9.99 *(978-0-375-85946-5(2),* Random Hse. Bks. for Young Readers) Random Hse. Children's Bks.

—The Canary Caper. Gurney, John Steven, illus. unabr. ed. 2004. (A to Z Mysteries Ser.: No. 3). 80p. (J). (gr. k-3). pap. 17.00 incl. audio *(978-0-8072-1705-4(0),* S FTR 271 SP, Listening Library) Random Hse. Audio Publishing Group.

Russell, Bill. Bruno the Red Ear Slider. 2013. 24p. pap. 24.95 *(978-1-62709-547-1(0))* America Star Bks.

Russell, Rachel Renée. Tales from a Not-So-Perfect Pet Sitter. Russell, Rachel Renée, illus. 2015. (Dork Diaries: 10). (ENG., Illus.). 320p. (J). (gr. 4-8). 13.99 *(978-1-4814-5704-0(7),* Aladdin) Simon & Schuster Children's Publishing.

—Tales from a Not-So-Perfect Pet Sitter. Russell, Rachel Renée, illus. 2015. (Dork Diaries: 10). (ENG., Illus.). 320p. (J). (gr. 4-8). lib. bdg. 25.75 *(978-0-606-37923-6(1))* Turtleback Bks.

Rylant, Cynthia. Annie & Snowball & the Pink Surprise. Stevenson, Suçie, illus. (Annie & Snowball Ser.: 4). (ENG.). 40p. (J). (gr. k-2). 2010. pap. 3.99 *(978-1-4169-1462-4(5))* 2008. 16.99 *(978-1-4169-0941-5(9))* Simon Spotlight. (Simon Spotlight).

—Annie & Snowball & the Wintry Freeze. Stevenson, Suçie, illus. (Annie & Snowball Ser.: 8). (ENG.). 40p. (J). (gr. k-2). 2011. pap. 3.99 *(978-1-4169-7206-8(4))* 2010. 16.99 *(978-1-4169-7205-1(6))* Simon Spotlight. (Simon Spotlight).

—Henry & Mudge & the Funny Lunch. Bracken, Carolyn, illus. 2005. (Henry & Mudge Ser.: 24). (ENG.). 40p. (J). (gr. k-2). pap. 3.99 *(978-0-689-83444-8(6),* Simon Spotlight) Simon Spotlight.

Salamoff, Paul J. Bo Obama: The White House Tails. 2010. (ENG.). 40p. pap. 6.99 *(978-1-61623-925-1(5))* Bluewater Productions, Inc.

Sands, Kathryn Ann. How Chili Willie Got His Name. 2013. 24p. pap. 17.99 *(978-1-4817-0641-4(1))* AuthorHouse.

Sandstrom, Heather. Brenda Badbroom & the Very Best Pet Yet. 2008. 28p. pap. 14.99 *(978-1-4389-0324-8(3))* AuthorHouse.

Santat, Dan. Sidekicks. 2011. (ENG., Illus.). 224p. (J). (gr. 3-7). pap. 12.99 *(978-0-439-29819-3(9),* Levine, Arthur A. Bks.) Scholastic, Inc.

Santillo, LuAnn. Steve & Pete. Santillo, LuAnn, ed. 2003. (Half-Pint Kids Readers Ser.). (Illus.). 7p. (J). (gr. -1-1). pap. 1.00 *(978-1-59256-103-2(9))* Half-Pint Kids, Inc.

—The Vet. Santillo, LuAnn, ed. 2003. (Half-Pint Kids Readers Ser.). (Illus.). 7p. (J). (gr. -1-1). pap. 1.00 *(978-1-59256-123-0(3))* Half-Pint Kids, Inc.

Sarah's Pet: Level L, 6 vols. 128p. (gr. 2-3). 41.95 *(978-0-7699-0990-5(6))* Shortland Pubns. (U. S. A.) Inc.

Sargent, Dave & Sargent, Pat. A Puppy for Bobby/un cachorro para Robertito, 10 vols. Robinson, Laura, illus. 2004. (Learn to Read Ser.: 10). (ENG & SPA.). 18p. (J). pap. 10.95 *(978-1-56763-982-7(8))* Ozark Publishing.

—Puppy for Bobby/un cachorro para Robertito, 10, 11. Robinson, Laura, illus. 2004. (Learn to Read Ser.: 10). (ENG & SPA.). 18p. (J). lib. bdg. 19.95 *(978-1-56763-981-0(X))* Ozark Publishing.

Satchwell, Sm. Len Stories. 2012. (Illus.). 24p. pap. 19.82 *(978-1-4685-0478-1(9))* AuthorHouse.

Sathre, Vivian. J. B. Wigglebottom & the Parade of Pets: True Ringside Tales, BBQ, & down-Home Recipies. O'Neill, Catharine, illus. 2013. (ENG.). 96p. (J). (gr. 2-5). pap. 13.99 *(978-1-4814-2159-1(X)*, Atheneum Bks. for Young Readers) Simon & Schuster Children's Publishing.

Sauer, Tammi. Me Want Pet! Shea, Bob, illus. 2012. (ENG.). 40p. (J). (gr. -1-3). 17.99 *(978-1-4424-0810-4(3)*, Simon & Schuster/Paula Wiseman Bks.) Simon & Schuster/Paula Wiseman Bks.

Saumier, Chantelle. Vinnie! Star of the Show. 2013. 40p. *(978-1-4602-3098-5(1))*; pap. *(978-1-4602-1741-2(1))* FriesenPress.

Sayles, Kristi. Jacob's Monkey-the Trouble with Lying. 2005. 38p. (J). pap. 10.29 *(978-1-4116-6429-6(9))* Lulu Pr., Inc.

Sazaklis, John. Deep-Sea Duel, 1 vol. Baltazar, Art, illus. 2012. (DC Super-Pets Ser.). (ENG.). 56p. (gr. 2-2). pap. 4.95 *(978-1-4048-7662-0(6))*; lib. bdg. 23.99 *(978-1-4048-6489-4(X))* Picture Window Bks. (DC Super-Pets).

Scanlon, Michael. How We Met! Little Airplane Productions Staff, illus. 2010. (Wonder Pets! Ser.). (ENG.). 24p. (J). pap. 3.99 *(978-1-4424-0654-4(2)*, Simon Spotlight/Nickelodeon) Simon Spotlight/Nickelodeon.

Schlangen, DVM, Mary. Zoe's Good-Bye. 2005. (Illus.). 32p. (J). 17.95 *(978-1-59298-110-6(0))* Beaver's Pond Pr., Inc.

Schnitt, Deborah. Petey's Angel. 2012. 25.95 *(978-0-7414-7845-0(5))*; pap. 18.95 *(978-0-7414-7844-3(7))* Infinity Publishing.

Scholastic, Inc. Staff. Dear Mrs. Larue. 2005. (ENG.). (J). pap. 550.00 *(978-0-439-70787-9(0)*, Sidekicks TM) Scholastic, Inc.

Scollon, William. Minnie's Pet Salon. 2013. (Mickey & Friends World of Reading Ser.). (J). lib. bdg. 13.55 *(978-0-606-32290-4(6)*, Turtleback) Turtleback Bks.

Scott, Brandon James, illus. The Big Pet Story. 2013. (Justin Time Ser.). (ENG.). 36p. (J). (gr. -1-3). 15.95 *(978-1-59702-041-1(9))* Immedium.

Seagreaves, Kelly E. The Best Pet. Zoller, Jayson D., illus. l.t. ed. 2004. 29p. (J). lib. bdg. 14.95 *(978-1-932338-56-0(X))*; per. 8.99 *(978-1-932338-53-9(5))* Lifevest Publishing, Inc.

Sebring, Ruthie. Charlie, Itty's Guinea Pig, 1 vol. 2010. 30p. 24.95 *(978-1-4489-4391-3(4))* PublishAmerica, Inc.

Seignobosc, Francoise. Springtime for Jeanne-Marie. 2004. (Illus.). (J). mass mkt. 9.99 *(978-0-9740599-3-8(5))* Omnibus Publishing.

Selig, Josh. Go, Wonder Pets! Little Airplane Productions, illus. 2008. (Wonder Pets! Ser.). (ENG.). 26p. (J). bds. 5.99 *(978-1-4169-4723-3(X)*, Simon Spotlight/Nickelodeon) Simon Spotlight/Nickelodeon.

Seuling, Barbara. Robert & the Attack of the Giant Tarantula. Brewer, Paul, illus. 2003. (Oh No, It's Robert Ser.). (ENG.). 64p. (J). pap. 3.99 *(978-0-439-23545-7(6)*, Scholastic Paperbacks) Scholastic, Inc.

Seuss, Dr. What Pet Should I Get? 2015. (Classic Seuss Ser.). (ENG., Illus.). 48p. (J). (gr. -1-2). 17.99 *(978-0-553-52426-0(7))*; lib. bdg. 20.99 *(978-0-553-52427-7(5))* Random Hse. Children's Bks. (Random Hse. Bks. for Young Readers).

—What Pet Should I Get? 2015. 48p. (J). lib. bdg. 30.60 *(978-0-606-37381-4(0))* Turtleback Bks.

Sexton, Bethany. Big Dog, Little Dog, Fish. Briggs Johnson, Chloe, illus. 2015. (ENG.). 17.95 *(978-1-59298-862-4(8))* Beaver's Pond Pr., Inc.

S.H., Addan. Guardabosque Del Ano 3000: Canis Familiaris Evolucion. 2004. (SPA., Illus.). 340p. pap. *(978-1-84401-133-9(X))* Athena Pr.

Shadow. 2006. (J). *(978-1-933343-17-4(6))* Stabenfeldt Inc.

Shah, Yasmin. Abby & the Feather Quest. 2010. (Illus.). 48p. pap. 10.49 *(978-1-4343-9839-0(0))* AuthorHouse.

Shan Shan, Kathryn. Everyday Circus. Wilson, Lynda Farrington, illus. 2013. 48p. pap. 10.97 *(978-1-939896-01-8(0))* Levity Pr.

Shaw, Ellie. Together Again. 2012. 24p. pap. 24.95 *(978-1-4626-6427-6(X))* America Star Bks.

Shea, Lisa. Littlest Pet Shop: a New Attitude: Starring Sunil Nevla. 2017. (ENG.). 144p. (J). (gr. 3-7). pap. 5.99 *(978-0-316-39525-0(0))* Little, Brown Bks. for Young Readers.

—Littlest Pet Shop: Sugar & Spice: Starring Pepper Clark. 2016. (ENG.). 144p. (J). (gr. 3-7). pap. 5.99 *(978-0-316-39523-6(4))* Little, Brown Bks. for Young Readers.

Shephard, H. Ferebee. Jonathan & Roscoe. 2011. 24p. pap. 14.39 *(978-1-4634-4881-3(3))* AuthorHouse.

Shepherd, Donna J. & Foster, Jack. Where Is Salami. 2011. (Illus.). 16p. pap. 9.95 *(978-1-61633-147-4(X))* Guardian Angel Publishing, Inc.

Shields, Gillian. DogFish. Taylor, Dan, illus. 2008. (ENG.). 32p. (J). (gr. -1-2). 16.99 *(978-1-4169-7127-6(0)*, Atheneum Bks. for Young Readers) Simon & Schuster Children's Publishing.

Shyba, Jessica. Bathtime with Theo & Beau. 2016. (ENG., Illus.). 40p. (J). 16.99 *(978-1-250-05907-9(0)*, 9781250059079) Feiwel & Friends.

—Naptime with Theo & Beau. 2015. (ENG., Illus.). 40p. (J). (gr. -1-k). 16.99 *(978-1-250-05906-2(2)*, 9781250059062) Feiwel & Friends.

Siegel, Randy. My Snake Blake. Bloch, Serge, illus. 2012. (ENG.). 32p. (J). (gr. -1-1). 16.99 *(978-1-59643-584-1(4)*, 9781596435841) Roaring Brook Pr.

Siems, Thomas F. The Dangerous Pet. 2009. 48p. pap. 21.99 *(978-1-4415-3454-5(7))* Xlibris Corp.

Silverstein, Shel. Who Wants a Cheap Rhinoceros? Silverstein, Shel, illus. 50th anniv. ed. 2014. (ENG., Illus.). 64p. (J). (gr. -1-3). 17.99 *(978-1-4814-1593-4(X)*, Simon & Schuster Bks. For Young Readers) Simon & Schuster Bks. For Young Readers.

Simmons, Lynn Sheffield. Bo, the Famous Retriever, 1 vol. Hampton, Lin, illus. 2003. (Bo Ser.). (ENG.). 128p. (J). (gr. 3-6). 10.95 *(978-1-58980-217-9(9))* Pelican Publishing Co., Inc.

Singleton, Linda Joy. A Cat Is Better. Martin, Jorge, illus. 2017. (ENG.). 32p. (J). (gr. -1-3). 16.99 *(978-1-4998-0278-8(1))* Little Bee Books Inc.

Sky Koster, Amy. Cute, Sweet, & Petite! (Disney Princess: Palace Pets) Random House Disney Staff, illus. 2015. (Big Golden Book Ser.). (ENG.). 64p. (J). (gr. -1-2). 9.99 *(978-0-7364-3412-6(7)*, Golden/Disney) Random Hse. Children's Bks.

Sky Koster, Amy & Tillworth, Mary. The Knight Night Guard. Random House Disney Staff, illus. 2016. (Step into Reading Ser.). (ENG.). 24p. (J). (gr. -1-1). 4.99 *(978-0-7364-3450-8(X)*, RH/Disney) Random Hse. Children's Bks.

Smith, Sindy. Ervin & Alma's Little Mouse House. 2013. 38p. 24.95 *(978-1-63004-209-7(9))*; 40p. pap. 24.95 *(978-1-62709-189-3(0))* America Star Bks.

Snyder, Sandy. There's Only One I in Charlie. Ferrenburg, Susie, illus. 2011. 48p. pap. 24.95 *(978-1-4626-4086-7(9))* America Star Bks.

Snyder, Sharon J. Zeus Comes Home. 2012. 20p. pap. 24.95 *(978-1-4626-5860-2(1))* America Star Bks.

Sommer, Carl. Tied up in Knots Read-along 2003. (Another Sommer-Time Story Ser.). (Illus.). 48p. (J). lib. bdg. 23.95 incl. audio *(978-1-57537-753-7(5))* Advance Publishing, Inc.

—Tied up in Knots Read-along. Budwine, Greg, illus. 2003. (Another Sommer-Time Story Ser.). (ENG.). 48p. (J). lib. bdg. 23.95 incl. audio compact disk *(978-1-57537-703-2(9))* Advance Publishing, Inc.

Spellmeyer, William. Ick-n-Pog: How it all Began Book 1. 2010. 104p. pap. 12.99 *(978-1-4251-9236-5(X))* Trafford Publishing.

Spiegelman, Nadja. Zig & Wikki in Something Ate My Homework. Loeffler, Trade, illus. 2013. (ENG.). 40p. (J). (gr. -1-3). pap. 6.99 *(978-1-935179-38-2(1))* TOON Books / RAW Junior, LLC.

—Zig & Wikki in Something Ate My Homework. Mouly, Francoise, ed. Loeffler, Trade, illus. 2010. (ENG.). 40p. (J). (gr. -1-3). 12.95 *(978-1-935179-02-3(0))* TOON Books / RAW Junior, LLC.

Spiegelman, Nadja & Loeffler, Trade. Zig & Wikki in Something Ate My Homework, 1 vol. 2013. (Toon Bks). (ENG.). 40p. (J). (gr. 2-3). lib. bdg. 27.07 *(978-1-61479-157-7(0))* Spotlight.

—Zig & Wikki in Something Ate My Homework. 2013. (Toon Books Level 3 Ser.). lib. bdg. 14.75 *(978-0-606-32252-2(3)*, Turtleback) Turtleback Bks.

Spitz, Eleanor. Phoenix the Rising Star. 2013. 26p. pap. 11.95 *(978-1-61244-223-5(4))* Halo Publishing International.

Spitz, Mary Y. Mint's Christmas Message. Pierce, Joanne Y., illus. 2003. 32p. 14.95 *(978-0-9724570-0-2(3))* Mother Moose Pr.

Spooky Pet, 6 vols., Set D,Pack. (Smart Start Ser.). (gr. k-1). 23.00 *(978-0-7635-0455-7(6))* Rigby Education.

Staake, Bob. My Pet Book. 2014. (ENG., Illus.). 40p. (J). (gr. -1-2). lib. bdg. 20.99 *(978-0-375-97195-2(5)*, Random Hse. Bks. for Young Readers) Random Hse. Children's Bks.

Staniszewski, Anna. Dogosaurus Rex. Hawkes, Kevin, illus. 2017. (ENG.). 40p. (J). 17.99 *(978-0-8050-9706-1(6)*, 9780805097061, Holt, Henry & Co. Bks. For Young Readers) Holt, Henry & Co.

Starling, Landa. If You Sleep with a Cat on Your Head. Formelio, Lorri, illus. 2008. 27p. pap. 24.95 *(978-1-60703-318-9(6))* America Star Bks.

Staunton, Ted. Morgan's Pet Plot, 1 vol. Slavin, Bill & Shannon, Ben, illus. 2003. (Formac First Novels Ser.: 24). (ENG.). 64p. (J). (gr. 1-5). 4.95 *(978-0-88780-587-5(6)*, 9780887805875) Formac Publishing Co., Ltd. CAN. Dist: Casemate Pubs. & Bk. Distributors, LLC.

—Morgan's Pet Plot. Slavin, Bill, illus. 2003. (Formac First Novels Ser.: 24). (ENG.). 64p. (J). (gr. 1-5). 14.95 *(978-0-88780-588-2(4)*, 9780887805882) Formac Publishing Co., Ltd. CAN. Dist: Casemate Pubs. & Bk. Distributors, LLC.

Stephens, Kat. Where Did Gypsy Go? 2010. 32p. (gr. -1). 15.50 *(978-1-4490-8008-2(1))* AuthorHouse.

Stern, A. J. Doggy Day Care, 2 vols. Marts, Doreen Mulryan, illus. 2010. (Frankly, Frannie Ser.: 2). (ENG.). 128p. (J). (gr. 1-3). pap. 4.99 *(978-0-448-45350-7(9)*, Grosset & Dunlap) Penguin Young Readers Group.

Stine, R. L. Claws! 2011. (Goosebumps Hall of Horrors Ser.: 1). (ENG.). 160p. (J). (gr. 3-7). pap. 6.99 *(978-0-545-28933-7(5)*, Scholastic Paperbacks) Scholastic, Inc.

—The Great Smelling Bee, 1 vol. Park, Trip, illus. 2011. (Rotten School Ser.: No. 2). (ENG.). 128p. (gr. 2-5). 24.21 *(978-1-59961-826-5(5))* Spotlight.

—Little Shop of Hamsters. 2010. (Goosebumps Horrorland Ser.: 14). (ENG.). 160p. (J). (gr. 3-7). 6.99 *(978-0-545-16195-4(9)*, Scholastic Paperbacks) Scholastic, Inc.

—Little Shop of Hamsters. 2010. (Goosebumps HorrorLand Ser.: 14). lib. bdg. 17.20 *(978-0-606-10559-0(X)*, Turtleback) Turtleback Bks.

Stock, Lisa. Perfect Pets. 2014. (DK Reader Level 2 Ser.). lib. bdg. 13.55 *(978-0-606-35731-9(9))* Turtleback Bks.

Stower, Adam. Silly Doggy! Stower, Adam, illus. 2012. (ENG., Illus.). 40p. (J). (gr. -1-k). 16.99 *(978-0-545-37323-4(9)*, Orchard Bks.) Scholastic, Inc.

Studio Mouse Staff. Pet Friends. rev. ed. 2008. (ENG.). 12p. (J). 12.99 *(978-1-59069-611-8(5))* Studio Mouse LLC.

Sullivan, Mary. Ball. 2015. (ENG., Illus.). 32p. (J). (— 1). bds. 7.99 *(978-0-544-31361-5(3)*, HMH Books For Young Readers) Houghton Mifflin Harcourt Publishing Co.

Summers, Darien. The Mischievous Hare. 2009. (Illus.). 48p. pap. 9.95 *(978-1-4327-4602-5(2))* Outskirts Pr., Inc.

Summers, Terry. Peter Wanted a Pet. Kai, illus. 2012. 26p. 24.95 *(978-1-4626-6120-6(3))* America Star Bks.

Surovec, Yasmine. My Pet Human. 2017. (My Pet Human Ser.). (ENG., Illus.). 112p. (J). 12.99 *(978-1-62672-074-9(6)*, 9781626720749) Roaring Brook Pr.

—My Pet Human. 2016. (ENG.). 108p. (J). (gr. 1-5). 16.00 *(978-0-606-39282-2(3))* Turtleback Bks.

Swain, Cynthia. Can We Have a Pet? 2006. (Early Explorers Ser.). (J). pap. *(978-1-4108-6037-8(X))* Benchmark Education Co.

Swann, Sandy & McKain, Susan. Tugger: The Pretzel Pup. 2010. (Illus.). 36p. pap. 16.99 *(978-1-4490-8499-8(0))* AuthorHouse.

Taeschner, Jacquelin. Boss. 2005. pap. 32.50 *(978-1-4208-7369-6(5))* AuthorHouse.

Taylor, Thomas. The Pets You Get. Reynolds, Adrian, illus. 2013. 32p. (gr. -1-3). 16.95 *(978-1-4677-1143-2(8))* Andersen Pr. GBR. Dist: Lerner Publishing Group.

Tennapel, Doug. Tommysaurus Rex. 2013. (ENG., Illus.). 144p. (J). (gr. 4-7). pap. 10.99 *(978-0-545-48383-4(2)*, Graphix) Scholastic, Inc.

TenNapel, Doug. Tommysaurus Rex. 2013. (ENG., Illus.). 144p. (J). (gr. 3-7). 19.99 *(978-0-545-48382-7(4)*, Graphix) Scholastic, Inc.

Tesler, Ellen. Maggie Adopts a Rescue Dog. 2013. 24p. pap. 17.99 *(978-1-4817-0570-7(9))* AuthorHouse.

The Guide Dog, Thelma. For the Love of My Pet. Hartley, Joshua, illus. 2012. (ENG.). 26p. (gr. k-5). pap. 14.95 *(978-1-61448-338-0(8))* Morgan James Publishing.

Things That Go! (Flip Flap Fun Book Ser.). 10p. (J). bds. *(978-2-89393-933-9(3))* Phidal Publishing, Inc./Editions Phidal, Inc.

Thorpe, Kiki. Into the Waves. Christy, Jana, illus. 2016. (Never Girls Ser.: 11). (ENG.). 128p. (J). (gr. 1-4). 5.99 *(978-0-7364-3525-3(5)*, RH/Disney) Random Hse. Children's Bks.

Thyroff, Brad. Albert & Freddie. Gillen, Rosemarie, illus. 2013. 24p. pap. 9.99 *(978-1-61286-190-6(3))* Avid Readers Publishing Group.

Tidd, Louise Vitellaro. La Mejor Mascota. Handelman, Dorothy, photos by. 2007. (Lecturas para niños de verdad - Nivel 2 (Real Kids Readers - Level 2) Ser.).Tr. of Best Pet Yet. (SPA., Illus.). 32p. (J). (gr. -1-3). per. 5.95 *(978-0-8225-7804-8(2)*, Ediciones Lerner) Lerner Publishing Group.

Tortorich, Vinnie. Monty: A Friendship Can Lead to a Miracle 2004. (Illus.). 36p. (J). 16.95 *(978-0-9762854-0-3(1)*, 2500) National Horseman Publishing Inc., The.

Tracy, Kathleen. The Hamster in Our Class. 2011. (Randy's Corner Ser.). (Illus.). 32p. (J). (gr. -1-2). lib. bdg. 25.70 *(978-1-58415-980-3(4))* Mitchell Lane Pubs., Inc.

—The Turtle in Our Class. 2011. (Randy's Corner Ser.). (Illus.). (J). (gr. -1-2). lib. bdg. 25.70 *(978-1-58415-979-7(0))* Mitchell Lane Pubs., Inc.

Truesdell, Charlotte White. Steinway Kitty. 2010. 16p. 8.49 *(978-1-4490-5922-4(8))* AuthorHouse.

Ulrich, George. Mrs. Picasso's Polliwog: A Mystery. Ulrich, George, illus. 2003. (Illus.). 32p. pap. 7.95 *(978-1-891577-84-0(0))*; (J). (gr. -1-7). lib. bdg. 15.95 *(978-1-891577-83-3(2))* Images Pr.

Urbanovic, Jackie. Duck & Cover. Urbanovic, Jackie, illus. 2009. (Max the Duck Ser.: 3). (ENG., Illus.). 32p. (J). (gr. -1-2). 17.99 *(978-0-06-121444-8(2))* HarperCollins Pubs.

Uy, Katherine Nepomuceno. Teeny Tiny People & Pets. 2012. 60p. pap. 31.99 *(978-1-4691-5710-8(1))* Xlibris Corp.

Van Allsburg, Chris. The Misadventures of Sweetie Pie. 2014. (ENG., Illus.). 32p. (J). (gr. -1-3). 18.99 *(978-0-547-31582-9(1)*, HMH Books For Young Readers) Houghton Mifflin Harcourt Publishing Co.

van de Vendel, Edward. The Dog That Nino Didn't Have. Van Hertbruggen, Anton, illus. 2015. (ENG.). 34p. (J). 17.00 *(978-0-8028-5451-3(6)*, Eerdmans Bks For Young Readers) Eerdmans, William B. Publishing Co.

Venable, Colleen A. F. Raining Cats & Detectives. Yue, Stephanie, illus. 2012. (Guinea Pig, Pet Shop Private Eye Ser.: 5). lib. bdg. 17.15 *(978-0-606-26631-4(3)*, Turtleback) Turtleback Bks.

Vernick, Audrey. I Won a What? Neubecker, Robert, illus. 2016. (ENG.). 40p. (J). (gr. -1-2). 17.99 *(978-0-553-50993-9(4)*, Knopf Bks. for Young Readers) Random Hse. Children's Bks.

Verrett, Michael. It Followed Me Home Can I Keep It? 2010. 35p. pap. 10.00 *(978-0-557-28827-4(4))* Lulu Pr., Inc.

—It Followed Me Home Can I Keep It? (full Color) 2010. 35p. pap. 19.00 *(978-0-557-29796-2(6))* Lulu Pr., Inc.

Victoria, Roberts. The Best Pet Ever. Deborah, Allwright, illus. 2010. (ENG.). 32p. (J). (gr. -1-2). 15.95 *(978-1-58925-089-5(3))* Tiger Tales.

Viorst, Judith. Lulu & the Brontosaurus. Smith, Lane, illus. (ENG.). 128p. (J). (gr. 1-5). 2012. pap. 7.99 *(978-1-4169-9962-1(0))* 2010. 17.99 *(978-1-4169-9961-4(2))* Simon & Schuster Children's Publishing. (Atheneum Bks. for Young Readers).

—Lulu & the Brontosaurus. 2012. (Lulu Ser.: 1). lib. bdg. 18.40 *(978-0-606-23676-8(7)*, Turtleback) Turtleback Bks.

Viselman, Kenn. Li'l Pet Hospital: The Great Race. 2003. 32p. pap. 3.99 *(978-0-06-054840-7(1)*, Harper Entertainment) HarperCollins Pubs.

Voake, Charlotte. Melissa's Octopus & Other Unsuitable Pets. Voake, Charlotte, illus. 2015. (ENG., Illus.). 32p. (J). (gr. -1-2). 16.99 *(978-0-7636-7481-6(8))* Candlewick Pr.

Wallace, Bill. Goosed! Rogers, Jacqueline, illus. 2004. (ENG.). 128p. (J). (gr. 2-4). pap. 6.99 *(978-0-689-86681-4(X)*, Aladdin) Simon & Schuster Children's Publishing.

—No Dogs Allowed! 2004. (ENG.). 214p. (J). (gr. 4-6). tchr. ed. 16.95 *(978-0-8234-1818-3(9))* Holiday Hse., Inc.

Wallace, Carol. One Nosy Pup. Björkman, Steve, illus. 2004. (ENG.). 40p. (J). 15.95 *(978-0-8234-1917-3(7))* Holiday Hse., Inc.

Walthers, Joanie. The Fish Smuggler. Walthers, Don, illus. 2013. (ENG.). 24p. (J). 19.95 *(978-1-4787-1167-4(1))* Outskirts Pr., Inc.

Watkins, Constance L. Happy Was His Name. 2011. 24p. (gr. 1-2). pap. 11.75 *(978-1-4634-0421-5(2))* AuthorHouse.

Watson, Jane Werner. Pets for Peter Book & Puzzle. Battaglia, Aurelius, illus. 2017. (Little Golden Book Ser.). (ENG.). 22p. (J). (gr. -1-2). 5.99 *(978-0-399-55363-9(0)*, Golden Bks.) Random Hse. Children's Bks.

Webb, Holly. Kitten Nobody Wanted. Williams, Sophy, illus. 2015. (Pet Rescue Adventures Ser.). (ENG.). 128p. (J). (gr. 2-6). lib. bdg. 19.99 *(978-1-58925-182-3(2))* Tiger Tales.

—Leo All Alone. Williams, Sophy, illus. 2016. (Pet Rescue Adventures Ser.). (ENG.). 128p. (J). (gr. 2-6). 4.99 *(978-1-58925-482-4(1))* Tiger Tales.

—The Lost Puppy. Williams, Sophy, illus. 2016. (Pet Rescue Adventures Ser.). (ENG.). 128p. (J). (gr. 2-6). pap. 4.99 *(978-1-58925-491-6(0))* Tiger Tales.

—The Missing Kitten. Williams, Sophy, illus. 2016. (Pet Rescue Adventures Ser.). (ENG.). 128p. (J). (gr. 2-6). pap. 4.99 *(978-1-58925-488-6(0))* Tiger Tales.

—The Scruffy Puppy. Williams, Sophy, illus. 2016. (Pet Rescue Adventures Ser.). (ENG.). 128p. (J). (gr. 2-6). pap. 4.99 *(978-1-58925-490-9(2))* Tiger Tales.

Webb, Ryan. Buddy: Dog of the Smoky Mountains. 2013. (Illus.). 34p. (J). pap. 12.00 *(978-0-9847836-3-2(6))* Celtic Cat Publishing.

Weir, Patricia. My Kitty & Me. 2008. 20p. per. 24.95 *(978-1-60441-908-5(3))* America Star Bks.

Wells, Rosemary. Ivy Takes Care. LaMarche, Jim, illus. 2015. (ENG.). 208p. (J). (gr. 3-7). pap. 6.99 *(978-0-7636-7660-5(8))* Candlewick Pr.

Wendling, Nathalie & Glatzmayer, Thomas. Melanie & Tommy Have Two Pet Rats & One Syndrome. 2010. 48p. pap. *(978-1-926582-67-2(5))* Insomniac Pr.

Wensley, Walter F. Yorkie. 2011. 44p. pap. 19.50 *(978-1-4634-3185-3(6))* AuthorHouse.

Weston Woods Staff, creator. Children Make Terrible Pets. 2011. 29.95 *(978-0-545-40221-7(2))* Weston Woods Studios, Inc.

—Corduroy. 2011. 29.95 *(978-0-545-14916-7(9))*; 18.95 *(978-0-545-14078-2(1))*; 38.75 *(978-0-545-14080-5(3))* Weston Woods Studios, Inc.

—Crictor. 2011. 18.95 *(978-0-545-23360-6(7))*; 38.75 *(978-0-545-23361-3(5))* Weston Woods Studios, Inc.

—Hondo & Fabian. 2011. 18.95 *(978-0-545-14958-7(4))*; 38.75 *(978-0-545-14959-4(2))* Weston Woods Studios, Inc.

—Millions of Cats Weston Woods. 2011. 18.95 *(978-0-439-72840-9(1))*; 38.75 *(978-0-439-72842-3(8))*; 29.95 *(978-0-439-73496-7(7))* Weston Woods Studios, Inc.

—Pet Show! 2011. 38.75 *(978-0-439-72866-9(5))*; 18.95 *(978-0-439-72865-2(7))*; 29.95 *(978-0-439-73506-3(8))* Weston Woods Studios, Inc.

Wheeler, Lisa. The Pet Project: Cute & Cuddly Vicious Verses. OHora, Zachariah, illus. 2013. (ENG.). 40p. (J). (gr. -1-3). 16.99 *(978-1-4169-7595-3(0)*, Atheneum Bks. for Young Readers) Simon & Schuster Children's Publishing.

Wheeler, Mary A. Over the Edge. 2010. 373p. pap. 16.95 *(978-1-4327-5994-0(9))* Outskirts Pr., Inc.

Which Pet Measures Up? 2003. (J). per. *(978-1-932524-02-4(9))* Region IV Education Service Ctr.

Whimsy. Benny's Pets. Meadow, Amy, illus. 2005. 32p. (J). 15.95 *(978-0-9702675-0-4(9))* World of Whimsy Productions, LLC.

Whiteside, Andy. Valentino Finds a Home, 1 vol. Hnatov, Catherine, illus. 2012. (ENG.). (J). 32p. 15.95 *(978-1-59572-284-3(X))*; 24p. pap. 5.95 *(978-1-59572-286-7(6))* Star Bright Bks., Inc.

Wiebe, Trina. Lizards Don't Wear Lip Gloss. Sarrazin, Marisol, illus. 2004. (Abby & Tess Pet-Sitters Ser.). 91p. 15.95 *(978-0-7569-3425-5(7))* Perfection Learning Corp.

Willems, Mo. The Pigeon Wants a Puppy! Willems, Mo, illus. 2008. (Pigeon Ser.). (ENG., Illus.). 40p. (J). (gr. -1-k). 16.99 *(978-1-4231-0960-0(0))* Hyperion Pr.

Williams, Eula. Loving Danger. Branch Jr., Robert F., illus. 2012. 20p. pap. 24.95 *(978-1-4626-6954-7(9))* America Star Bks.

Williams, Rozanne Lanczak. How Can I Get a Pet? Reid, Mick, illus. 2006. (Learn to Write Ser.). 8p. (J). (gr. k-2). pap. *(978-1-59198-290-6(1)*, 6184) Creative Teaching Pr., Inc.

—How Can I Get a Pet? Maio, Barbara & Faulkner, Stacey, eds. Reid, Mick, illus. 2006. (J). per. 6.99 *(978-1-59198-363-7(0))* Creative Teaching Pr., Inc.

Williams, T. E. Fluffy!! 2011. 24p. 16.25 *(978-1-4520-3743-1(4))* AuthorHouse.

Willis, Jeanne. The Pet Person. Ross, Tony, illus. 2015. (ENG.). 32p. (J). (-k). pap. 9.99 *(978-1-78344-242-3(5))* Andersen Pr. GBR. Dist: Independent Pubs. Group.

Wing, Natasha. The Night Before the New Pet. 2016. (Night Before Ser.). lib. bdg. 14.75 *(978-0-606-38418-6(9))* Turtleback Bks.

Winkler, Henry & Oliver, Lin. Day of the Iguana. 2004. (Hank Zipzer Ser.: No. 3). 160p. (J). (gr. 2-6). pap. 29.00 incl. audio *(978-1-4000-9008-2(3)*, Listening Library) Random Hse. Audio Publishing Group.

—A Short Tale about a Long Dog. Garrett, Scott, illus. 2014. (Here's Hank Ser.: 2). (ENG.). 128p. (J). (gr. 1-3). 14.99 *(978-0-448-48240-8(1))*;No. 2. 5.99 *(978-0-448-47998-9(2))* Penguin Young Readers Group. (Grosset & Dunlap).

—A Short Tale about a Long Dog. 2014. (Here's Hank Ser.: 2). lib. bdg. 16.00 *(978-0-606-34143-1(9)*, Turtleback) Turtleback Bks.

—Stop That Frog! Garrett, Scott, illus. 2014. (Here's Hank Ser.: 3). (ENG.). 128p. (J). (gr. 1-3). 5.99 *(978-0-448-48152-4(9))*; 14.99 *(978-0-448-48241-5(X))* Penguin Young Readers Group. (Grosset & Dunlap).

—Stop That Frog! 2014. (Here's Hank Ser.: 3). lib. bdg. 16.00 *(978-0-606-36161-3(8))* Turtleback Bks.

Wise, William. Christopher Mouse: The Tale of a Small Traveler. Benson, Patrick, illus. 2006. (ENG.). 160p. (YA). (gr. 2-5). per. 7.99 *(978-1-58234-708-0(5)*, 9781582347080, Bloomsbury USA Childrens) Bloomsbury Publishing USA.

—Christopher Mouse: The Tale of a Small Traveler. Benson, Patrick, tr. Benson, Patrick, illus. 2004. (ENG.). 160p. (YA). (gr. 3-6). 15.95 *(978-1-58234-878-0(2)*, 9781582348780, Bloomsbury USA Childrens) Bloomsbury Publishing USA.

Wolczyk, Deborah R. Maisie - the Dress up Cat. 2010. 76p. pap. 24.99 *(978-1-4520-7681-2(2))* AuthorHouse.

Wolf, Carol A. Foggy Dog Discovers Christmas. 2012. 40p. pap. 16.46 *(978-1-4669-6253-8(4))* Trafford Publishing.

Wrecks, Billy. Super-Pets! Golden Books Staff & Beavers, Ethen, illus. 2016. (Little Golden Book Ser.). (ENG.). 24p. (J). (gr. -1-k). 4.99 *(978-0-553-53923-3(X)*, Golden Bks.) Random Hse. Children's Bks.

Yaccarino, Dan. Journey to the Center of Town. 2017. (Class Pet Squad Ser.: 1). (J). lib. bdg. 17.20 ***(978-0-606-39943-2(7))*** Turtleback Bks.

Yaccarino, Dan. New Pet. Yaccarino, Dan, illus. 2003. (ENG., Illus.). 40p. (J). (gr. -1-2). pap. 4.99 *(978-0-7868-1429-9(2))* Hyperion Pr.

PQR

Yager, Jan. The Reading Rabbit. Lyman, Mitzi, illus. 32p. (J). 2014. (ENG.). 25.95 (978-1-938998-00-3(6)) 2013. pap. 17.95 (978-1-938998-01-0(4)) Hannacroix Creek Bks., Inc.

Yolen, Jane. How Do Dinosaurs Choose Their Pets? Teague, Mark, illus. 2016. (ENG.). 40p. (J). (gr. -1-k). 16.99 (978-1-338-03278-9(X), Blue Sky Pr., The) Scholastic, Inc.

Young, Amy. A Unicorn Named Sparkle. Young, Amy, illus. 2016. (ENG., Illus.). 40p. (J). 16.99 (978-0-374-30185-9(9), 9780374301859, Farrar, Straus & Giroux (BYR)) Farrar, Straus & Giroux.

Young, Jessica. Pet-Rified. Secheret, Jessica, illus. 2017. (Finley Flowers Ser.). (ENG.). 128p. (gr. 2-3). lib. bdg. 25.32 (978-1-4795-9805-2(4), Finley Flowers) Picture Window Bks.

Young, Judy. A Pet for Miss Wright. Wesson, Andrea, illus. 2011. (ENG.). 40p. (J). (gr. 1-4). lib. bdg. 15.95 (978-1-58536-509-8(2), 202202) Sleeping Bear Pr.

Youngs, Kendahl Brooke. Kendahl Gets a Puppy. 2012. (ENG.). (J). pap. 13.95 (978-0-9836045-8-7(4), Kendahl Hse. Pr.) Youngs, Bettie Bks.

Zambak Çucok Publishing Staff, ed. The Rainbow: Niloya 1. 2016. (J). pap. 4.99 (978-1-4621-1862-5(3), Horizon Pubs.) Cedar Fort, Inc./CFI Distribution.

Zeltser, David. Stinker. Patton, Julia, illus. 2017. (ENG.). 32p. (gr. -1-3). 17.99 (978-1-5124-1792-0(0), Carolrhoda Bks.) Lerner Publishing Group.

Zsikai-Spiker, Lisa Marie. Buster & Snoopy. Schimmelman, Alex, illus. 2012. 24p. 24.95 (978-1-4626-7112-0(8)) America Star Bks.

Zullo, Allan. Bad Pets: On the Loose! 2012. 125p. (J). pap. (978-0-545-46041-5(7)) Scholastic, Inc.

PHANTOM OF THE OPERA (FICTITIOUS CHARACTER)—FICTION

Behling, Steve. Iron Man: Invasion of the Space Phantoms. 2016. (Mighty Marvel Chapter Bks.). (J). lib. bdg. 16.00 (978-0-606-38305-9(0)) Turtleback Bks.

Coker, Lauren. The Phantom's Lullaby: A Novel. 2008. 332p. pap. 19.95 (978-0-595-47695-4(3)) iUniverse, Inc.

Francis, Pauline, retold by. The Phantom of the Opera. 2010. (Essential Classics - Horror Ser.). (Illus.). 56p. pap. (978-0-237-54095-1(9)) Evans Brothers, Ltd.

Knighton, Kate, retold by. Phantom of the Opera. 2008. (Young Reading Series 2 Gift Bks). 64p. (J). 8.99 (978-0-7945-2082-3(0), Usborne) EDC Publishing.

PHANTOMS

see Apparitions; Ghosts

PHARMACEUTICAL CHEMISTRY

see also Drugs; Materia Medica; Pharmacy; Poisons

Field, Jon Eben. Medicine Cabinet Chemistry. 2011. (Chemtastrophe! Ser.). (ENG.). 32p. (J). (gr. 5-8). pap. (978-0-7787-5304-9(2)); lib. bdg. (978-0-7787-5287-5(9)) Crabtree Publishing Co.

Kendrick, Karolyn. Chemistry in Medicine: Set Of 6. 2010. (Navigators Ser.). (J). pap. 48.00 net. (978-1-4108-6233-4(X)) Benchmark Education Co.

—Chemistry in Medicine: Text Pairs. 2008. (Bridges/Navigators Ser.). (J). (gr. 5). 81.00 (978-1-4108-8410-7(4)) Benchmark Education Co.

Romero, Libby. Medical Chemistry. 2006. (J). pap. (978-1-4108-6499-4(5)) Benchmark Education Co.

PHARMACOPOEIAS

see Materia Medica

PHARMACY

see also Botany, Medical; Drugs; Materia Medica; Pharmaceutical Chemistry

Carroll, Jamuna. The Pharmaceutical Industry. 2008. (Opposing Viewpoints Ser.). (ENG., Illus.). 212p. (YA). (gr. 10-12). 27.50 (978-0-7377-4239-8(9), LML02109-243153); pap. 39.70 (978-0-7377-4238-1(0), LML02109-243118) Cengage Gale. (Greenhaven Pr., Inc.).

Chambers, Catherine. Living Forever: The Pharmaceutical Industry. 2012. (Big-Buck Business Ser.). (Illus.). 48p. (J). (gr. 6-8). 31.95 (978-1-4339-7755-8(9)); pap. 14.05 (978-1-4339-7756-5(7)) Stevens, Gareth Publishing LLLP. (Gareth Stevens Secondary Library).

Gill, Monica K. Biopharmaceuticals. 2015. (Biotechnology Revolution Ser.). (ENG., Illus.). 128p. (J). (gr. 10-10). lib. bdg. 38.75 (978-1-62275-582-0(0), Britannica Educational Publishing) Rosen Publishing Group, Inc., The.

Miller, Malinda. The Pharmaceutical Industry: Better Medicine for the 21st Century. 2010. (New Careers for the 21st Century Ser.). 64p. (YA). (gr. 7-18). lib. bdg. 22.95 (978-1-4222-1819-8(8)) Mason Crest.

Ruschmann, Paul. Prescription & Non-Prescription Drugs. 2007. (Point/Counterpoint Ser.). (Illus.). 120p. (YA). (gr. 9-12). lib. bdg. 35.00 (978-0-7910-9552-2(5)) Facts On File, Inc.

Sayler, Mary Harwell. Prescription Pain Relievers. 2010. (Understanding Drugs Ser.). (Illus.). 112p. (YA). (gr. 9-12). 34.95 (978-1-60413-549-7(2)) Facts On File, Inc.

Walker, Ida. Sedatives & Hypnotics: Deadly Downers. 2012. (J). pap. (978-1-4222-2459-5(7)) Mason Crest.

—Sedatives & Hypnotics: Deadly Downers. Henningfield, Jack E., ed. 2012. (Illicit & Misused Drugs Ser.). 128p. (J). (gr. 7). 24.95 (978-1-4222-2440-3(6)) Mason Crest.

PHARMACY—VOCATIONAL GUIDANCE

Miller, Malinda. The Pharmaceutical Industry: Better Medicine for the 21st Century. 2010. (New Careers for the 21st Century Ser.). 64p. (YA). (gr. 7-18). pap. 9.95 (978-1-4222-2040-5(0)) Mason Crest.

PHEASANTS—FICTION

Meierhenry, Mark & Volk, David. The Mystery of the Pheasants. Turnbull, Susan, illus. 2012. 44p. (J). 14.95 (978-0-9845041-9-0(2)) South Dakota State Historical Society Pr.

PHELPS, MICHAEL, 1985-

Fishman, Jon M. Michael Phelps. 2017. (Sports All-Stars Ser.). (ENG.). 32p. (J). (gr. 2-5). 12.99 (978-1-5124-5400-0(1), Lerner Pubns.); 39.99 (978-1-5124-5397-3(8), Lerner Pubns.); 39.99 (978-1-5124-5398-0(6), Lerner Pubns.); (Illus.). pap. 8.99 (978-1-5124-5401-7(X)); (Illus.). lib. bdg. 26.65 (978-1-5124-5396-6(X)) Lerner Publishing Group.

Goldish, Meish. Michael Phelps: Anything Is Possible! 2009. (Defining Moments Ser.). (Illus.). 32p. (YA). (gr. 2-5). lib. bdg. 25.27 (978-1-59716-855-7(6)) Bearport Publishing Co., Inc.

Kennedy, Mike. Michael Phelps. 2009. (People We Should Know Ser.). (ENG.). 48p. (J). (gr. 3-5). pap. 10.50 (978-1-4339-2151-3(0)); lib. bdg. 31.00 (978-1-4339-1950-3(8)) Stevens, Gareth Publishing LLLP. (Gareth Stevens Learning Library).

Markovics, Joyce L. Michael Phelps. 2017. (Amazing Americans: Olympians Ser.). (ENG.). 24p. (J). (gr. -1-3). 17.95 (978-1-68402-239-7(8)) Bearport Publishing Co., Inc.

McDowell, Pamela. Michael Phelps. 2014. (Illus.). 24p. (J). (978-1-62127-391-2(1)) Weigl Pubs., Inc.

Michael Phelps. rev. ed. 2009. (Amazing Athletes Ser.). (gr. 2-5). pap. 6.95 (978-0-7613-4138-3(2), First Avenue Editions) Lerner Publishing Group.

Nagelhout, Ryan. Michael Phelps: Greatest Swimmer of All Time. 2017. (Breakout Biographies Ser.). 32p. (J). (gr. 9-10). pap. 10.00 (978-1-5081-6066-3(X), PowerKids Pr.) Rosen Publishing Group, Inc., The.

Phelps, Michael & Abrahamson, Alan. How to Train with a T. Rex & Win 8 Gold Medals. Jenkins, Ward, illus. 2009. (ENG.). 32p. (J). (gr. -1-3). 17.99 (978-1-4169-8669-0(3), Simon & Schuster Bks. For Young Readers) Simon & Schuster Bks. For Young Readers.

Sheen, Barbara, ed. Michael Phelps. 2010. (People in the News Ser.). (ENG.). 96p. (YA). (gr. 7-12). 33.95 (978-1-4205-0282-4(4)) Cengage Gale.

Tieck, Sarah. Michael Phelps: Olympic Champion, 1 vol. 2009. (Big Buddy Biographies Set 2 Ser.). (ENG., Illus.). 32p. (J). (gr. 2-5). 28.50 (978-1-60453-550-1(4)) ABDO Publishing Co.

—Michael Phelps: The Greatest Olympian, 1 vol. 2013. (Big Buddy Biographies Set 9 Ser.). (ENG.). 32p. (J). (gr. 2-5). lib. bdg. 28.50 (978-1-61783-753-1(9), Big Buddy Bks.) ABDO Publishing Co.

Torsiello, David P. Michael Phelps: Swimming for Olympic Gold. 2009. (Hot Celebrity Biographies Ser.). (Illus.). 48p. (J). (gr. 5-9). lib. bdg. 25.27 (978-0-7660-3591-1(3)); pap. 8.95 (978-0-7660-3630-7(8)) Enslow Pubs., Inc.

Zuehlke, Jeffrey. Michael Phelps. (First Step Nonfiction Ser.). 32p. 2005. (Illus.). (J). (gr. 2-5). per. 5.95 (978-0-8225-2631-5(X)) 2005. (Illus.). (J). (gr. 3-7). lib. bdg. 23.93 (978-0-8225-2431-1(7)) 2009. (ENG.). (gr. 2-5). 25.26 (978-0-7613-4055-3(6)) Lerner Publishing Group.

—Michael Phelps (Revised Edition) 2009. pap. 40.95 (978-0-7613-4777-4(1)) Lerner Publishing Group.

PHILADELPHIA (PA.)

Ashley, Susan. The Liberty Bell. 2004. (Weekly Reader Early Learning Library). (Illus.). 24p. (YA). (gr. 1-4). lib. bdg. 22.00 (978-0-8368-4141-1(7), Weekly Reader Leveled Readers) Stevens, Gareth Publishing LLLP.

Douglas, Lloyd G. The Liberty Bell. 2003. (Welcome Bks.). (Illus.). 24p. (J). 19.00 (978-0-516-25852-2(4)); (ENG., (gr. -1-2). pap. 4.95 (978-0-516-27875-9(4)) Scholastic Library Publishing. (Children's Pr.).

Eldridge, Alison & Eldridge, Stephen. The Liberty Bell: An American Symbol. 2012. (All about American Symbols Ser.). 24p. (J). (gr. -1-16). 22.60 (978-0-7660-4059-5(3), Enslow Elementary) Enslow Pubs., Inc.

Gamble, Adam. Good Night Philadelphia. Kelly, Cooper, illus. 2006. (Good Night Our World Ser.). (ENG.). 20p. (J). (gr. k — 1). bds. 9.95 (978-0-9777979-4-3(5)) Good Night Bks.

James, Lincoln. Making History: The Liberty Bell. 2006. (Tony Stead Nonfiction Independent Reading Collection). (ENG.). 24p. (gr. 3-6). pap. 8.85 (978-1-4042-5587-6(7)) Rosen Publishing Group, Inc., The.

Jango-Cohen, Judith. The Liberty Bell. 2003. (Pull Ahead Books-American Symbols Ser.). (ENG.). 32p. (gr. k-3). pap. 7.95 (978-0-8225-3754-0(0)); (Illus.). lib. bdg. 22.60 (978-0-8225-3803-5(2)) Lerner Publishing Group.

Magaziner, Henry Jonas. Our Liberty Bell. O'Brien, John A., illus. 2007. (ENG.). 32p. (J). (gr. 1-5). 15.95 (978-0-8234-1892-3(8)) Holiday Hse., Inc.

—Our Liberty Bell. O'Brien, John, illus. 2007. (ENG.). 32p. (J). (gr. 1-5). 5.95 (978-0-8234-2081-0(7)) Holiday Hse., Inc.

Silate, Jennifer. The Liberty Bell. 2006. (Primary Sources of American Symbols Ser.). (Illus.). 24p. (J). (gr. -1-3). lib. bdg. 22.60 (978-1-4042-2687-6(7)) Rosen Publishing Group, Inc., The.

PHILADELPHIA (PA.)—FICTION

Anderson, Laurie Halse. Fever 1793. 2014. (ENG.). 272p. (J). 12.24 (978-1-63245-124-8(7)) Lectorum Pubns., Inc.

Brown, Philip. Franky Franklyn's Philadelphia Adventure. 2011. 108p. 21.99 (978-1-4567-5423-5(8)); pap. 10.99 (978-1-4567-1269-3(1)) AuthorHouse.

Cox, Judy. Mrs. Millie Goes to Philly!, 0 vols. Mathieu, Joe, illus. 2013. (ENG.). 32p. (J). (gr. -1-2). pap. 9.99 (978-1-4778-1680-6(1), 9781477816806, Amazon Children's Publishing) Amazon Publishing.

Davis, Anthony C. I Ain't Lying. 2008. 112p. pap. 19.95 (978-1-60474-087-5(6)) America Star Bks.

De Laurentiis, Giada, et al. Philadelphia! #8. Gambatesa, Francesca, illus. 2016. (Recipe for Adventure Ser.: 8). (ENG.). 160p. (J). (gr. 2-4). bds. 6.99 (978-0-448-48395-5(5), Grosset & Dunlap) Penguin Young Readers Group.

Edgeworth, Maria. Rosamond: With Other Tales. by Maria Edgeworth. 2006. 388p. per. 26.99 (978-1-4255-4076-0(7)) Michigan Publishing.

Extreme Danger. 2007. 15.00 (978-0-7569-7603-3(0)) Perfection Learning Corp.

Griffin, Wiley Chase. Chase the Shark: Flies Like a Bird. 2010. 28p. pap. 12.50 (978-1-4520-5173-4(9)) AuthorHouse.

Grocki, Jennifer. From A to Zamboni, the Alphabet Hockey Style! Flyers Edition. Lendway, Andy, illus. 2007. 32p. (J). 16.95 (978-0-9793833-0-4(7)) Team Kidz, Inc.

Halley, Marilyn. Apple-Green Eyes. 2005. pap. 8.00 (978-0-8059-6681-7(1)) Dorrance Publishing Co., Inc.

Holm, Jennifer L. The Creek. 2003. 240p. (J). (gr. 7-18). 15.99 (978-0-06-000133-9(X)); 16.89 (978-0-06-000134-6(8)) HarperCollins Pubs.

Horender, Philip M. Yankee Mouse: Gettysburg Address Observer, 1 vol. Wolek, Guy, illus. 2013. (Maximilian P. Mouse, Time Traveler Ser.). (ENG.). 112p. (J). (gr. 3-6). lib. bdg. 27.07 (978-1-61641-958-5(X), Calico Chapter Bks) Magic Wagon.

Jacobs, Lily. The Littlest Bunny in Philadelphia: An Easter Adventure. Dunn, Robert, illus. 2015. (ENG.). 32p. (J). (-3). 9.99 (978-1-4926-1180-6(8), Sourcebooks Jabberwocky) Sourcebooks, Inc.

James, Eric. A Halloween Scare in Philadelphia. Le Ray, Marina, illus. 2015. (ENG.). 32p. (J). (-5). 9.99 (978-1-4926-2395-3(4), 9781492623953, Sourcebooks Jabberwocky) Sourcebooks, Inc.

—Santa's Sleigh Is on Its Way to Philadelphia: A Christmas Adventure. Dunn, Robert, illus. 2016. (ENG.). 32p. (J). (-2). 12.99 (978-1-4926-4350-0(5), 9781492643500, Sourcebooks Jabberwocky) Sourcebooks, Inc.

Johnson, Maureen. The Key to the Golden Firebird. 2004. (ENG.). 304p. (J). (gr. 7-18). 15.99 (978-0-06-054138-5(5)) HarperCollins Pubs.

Kelly, David A. The Philly Fake. Meyers, Mark, illus. 2014. (Ballpark Mysteries Ser.: Bk. 9). (ENG.). 112p. (J). (gr. 1-4). 4.99 (978-0-307-97785-4(4), Random Hse. Bks. for Young Readers) Random Hse. Children's Bks.

—The Philly Fake. 2014. (Ballpark Mysteries Ser.: Bk. 9). lib. bdg. 14.75 (978-0-606-35566-7(9)) Turtleback Bks.

Kientz, Chris & Hockensmith, Steve. Claws & Effect. Nielsen, Lee, illus. 2016. (Secret Smithsonian Adventures Ser.: 2). (ENG.). 64p. (gr. 4-7). pap. 10.95 (978-1-58834-567-7(X), Smithsonian Bks.) Smithsonian Institution Scholarly Pr.

Mark, Jessica & Mark, Rebecca. Sky the Fly Explores Philadelphia. 2013. 28p. pap. 11.00 (978-1-4349-3272-3(9), RoseDog Bks.) Dorrance Publishing Co., Inc.

Marsh, Carole. The Mystery on the Underground Railroad. 2009. (Real Kids, Real Places Ser.). (Illus.). 146p. (J). lib. bdg. 18.99 (978-0-635-06991-7(1), Marsh, Carole Mysteries) Gallopade International.

—The Mystery on the Underground Railroad (Hardcover) 2003. 160p. (gr. 2-8). 14.95 (978-0-635-02110-6(2)) Gallopade International.

Mohsenian, Javad. 9/11 Children. 2006. (ENG.). 128p. per. 10.95 (978-0-7414-3218-6(8)) Infinity Publishing.

Mulubah, Sr. Denise's Pet Dove. 2009. 36p. pap. 16.99 (978-1-4389-7536-8(8)) AuthorHouse.

Neri, G. Ghetto Cowboy. Watson, Jesse Joshua, illus. 2013. (ENG.). 224p. (J). (gr. 5). pap. 6.99 (978-0-7636-6453-4(7)) Candlewick Pr.

Ostow, Micol. GoldenGirl. 2009. (Bradford Ser.). (ENG.). 224p. (YA). (gr. 9-18). pap. 9.99 (978-1-4169-6118-5(6), Simon Pulse) Simon Pulse.

Rinaldi, Ann. Finishing Becca: A Story about Peggy Shippen & Benedict Arnold. 2004. (Great Episodes Ser.). (ENG.). 384p. (YA). (gr. 7-8). pap. 17.95 (978-0-15-205079-5(5)) Houghton Mifflin Harcourt Publishing Co.

Rubin, Sarah. The Impossible Clue. 2017. (J). pap. (978-0-545-94272-0(1), Chicken Hse., The) Scholastic, Inc.

Silvano, Wendi. Love Is All Around Philadelphia. Czemichowska, Joanna, illus. 2016. (ENG.). 32p. (J). (-6). 12.99 (978-1-4926-2955-9(3), Sourcebooks Jabberwocky) Sourcebooks, Inc.

Skewes, John & Mullin, Michael. Larry Gets Lost in Philadelphia. Skewes, John, illus. 2013. (Larry Gets Lost Ser.). (ENG., Illus.). 32p. (J). (gr. -1-2). 17.99 (978-1-57061-792-8(9), Little Bigfoot) Sasquatch Bks.

Smallman, Steve. Santa Is Coming to Philadelphia. Dunn, Robert, illus. 2012. (ENG.). 32p. (J). (-3). 9.99 (978-1-4022-7518-0(8), Sourcebooks Jabberwocky) Sourcebooks, Inc.

Smith, Roland. Independence Hall. (I, Q Ser.: Bk. 1). (ENG., 312p. (gr. 5-9). 2009. Illus.). (J). 15.95 (978-1-58536-468-8(1)) 2008. (YA). pap. 8.95 (978-1-58536-325-4(1)) Sleeping Bear Pr.

Spinelli, Jerry. Eggs. 2008. (ENG., Illus.). 240p. (J). (gr. 3-7). pap. 8.99 (978-0-316-16647-8(2)) Little, Brown Bks. for Young Readers.

Vivian, Siobhan. Same Difference. 2014. (ENG.). 304p. (J). pap. 9.99 (978-0-545-75802-4(5)) Scholastic, Inc.

Zschock, Martha Day. Hello, Philadelphia! 2011. (Hello! Ser.). (ENG., Illus.). 16p. (J). (gr. -1-k). bds. 9.95 (978-1-933212-64-7(0), Commonwealth Editions) Applewood Bks.

PHILADELPHIA (PA.)—HISTORY

ABC Travel Guides for Kids-Philadelphia. 2004. (J). per. 12.95 (978-0-9760047-0-7(4)) Rosenberger, Matthew.

Boehm Jerome, Kate. Philadelphia & the State of Pennsylvania: Cool Stuff Every Kid Should Know. 2011. (Arcadia Kids Ser.). (ENG., Illus.). 48p. (J). (gr. 3-6). pap. 9.99 (978-1-4396-0094-8(5)) Arcadia Publishing.

Burt, Barbara & Schifini, Alfredo. Colonial Life. 2007. (Avenues Ser.). (ENG., Illus.). 40p. (J). pap. 19.95 (978-0-7922-8678-3(2)) CENGAGE Learning.

Cheung, Shu Pui, et al. Walking on Solid Ground. Wei, Deborah & Kodish, Debora, eds. Chau, Ming, photos by. 2004. (ENG & CHI., Illus.). 64p. (J). pap. 12.95 (978-0-9644937-4-2(8), 09644937-4-8) Philadelphia Folklore Project.

Epstein, Brad. Philadelphia Eagles 101. 2010. (Illus.). 24p. (J). bds. (978-1-60730-123-3(7), 101 Bk.) Michaelson Entertainment.

Figley, Marty Rhodes. Prisoner for Liberty. Orback, Craig, illus. (On My Own History Ser.). (ENG.). 48p. (gr. 2-4). 2009. pap. 6.95 (978-0-8225-9022-4(0), First Avenue Editions) 2008. lib. bdg. 25.26 (978-0-8225-7280-0(X), Millbrook Pr.) Lerner Publishing Group.

—Salvar a la Campana de la Libertad. Lepp, Kevin, illus. 2005. (Yo Solo - Historia (on My Own - History) Ser.). (SPA.). 48p. (J). (gr. 3-7). lib. bdg. 25.26 (978-0-8225-3094-7(5), Ediciones Lerner); (gr. 2-5). per. 6.95 (978-0-8225-3095-4(3)) Lerner Publishing Group.

—Salvar a la Campana de la Libertad; Saving the Liberty Bell. 2008. pap. 40.95 (978-0-7613-3933-5(7)) Lerner Publishing Group.

—Saving the Liberty Bell. Lepp, Kevin, illus. 2005. (On My Own History Ser.). (ENG.). 48p. (gr. 2-4). pap. 6.95 (978-1-57505-696-8(8)) Lerner Publishing Group.

Figley, Mary Rhodes. Prisoner for Liberty. 2009. pap. 40.95 (978-0-7613-4796-5(8)) Lerner Publishing Group.

Hess, Deborah. The Liberty Bell. 2007. (J). pap. 6.99 (978-0-7614-3391-0(0)) Marshall Cavendish Corp.

Hopper, Whitney. I Visit the Liberty Bell. 2016. (Symbols of Our Country Ser.). 00024p. (J). (gr. 1-1). pap. 8.25 (978-1-4994-2732-5(8), PowerKids Pr.) Rosen Publishing Group, Inc., The.

Kelly, Elaine A. & Carl, Jean R. Among the Buildings That Touch the Sky: Philadelphia. Noone, Cathleen L., illus. 2009. (978-0-578-06873-2(7)) U. S. ISBN Agency.

Kopp, Megan. Liberty Bell with Code. 2012. (AV2 American Icons Ser.). (ENG., Illus.). 24p. (J). pap. 12.95 (978-1-61913-301-3(6)); lib. bdg. 27.13 (978-1-61913-078-4(5)) Weigl Pubs., Inc. (AV2 by Weigl).

Lloyd, Sandra Mackenzie, ed. Patriots, Pirates, Heroes & Spies: Stories from Historic Philadelphia. 2012. (ENG., Illus.). 192p. 11.95 (978-0-9855319-0-4(8)) Historic Philadelphia, Inc.

McDonald, Megan. Saving the Liberty Bell. Carrington, Marsha Gray, illus. 2005. (ENG.). 32p. (J). (gr. k-3). 17.99 (978-0-689-85167-4(7), Atheneum/Richard Jackson Bks.) Simon & Schuster Children's Publishing.

Mountjoy, Shane. Philadelphia. 2007. (Colonial Settlements in America Ser.). (Illus.). 100p. (YA). (gr. 5-9). lib. bdg. 30.00 (978-0-7910-9336-8(0)) Facts On File, Inc.

Nelson, Deb. Philadelphia. 2016. (Dropping in On Ser.). (ENG., Illus.). 32p. (gr. 2-4). 32.79 (978-1-68191-409-1(3)) Rourke Educational Media.

Orr, Tamra B. The Liberty Bell: Introducing Primary Sources. 2016. (Introducing Primary Sources Ser.). (ENG., Illus.). 32p. (gr. 1-2). lib. bdg. 27.99 (978-1-4914-8224-7(9)) Capstone Press of Coughlan Cos.

Randolph, Ryan. Betsy Ross: The American Flag, & Life in a Young America. 2009. (Library of American Lives & Times Ser.). 112p. (gr. 5-5). 69.20 (978-1-60853-473-9(1)) Rosen Publishing Group, Inc., The.

Reed, Cristie. Liberty Bell. 2014. (ENG.). 32p. (gr. 3-6). 32.79 (978-1-62717-738-2(8)) Rourke Educational Media.

Roberts, Russell. Philadelphia. 2009. (Class Trip Ser.). (Illus.). 48p. (J). (gr. 2-5). lib. bdg. 29.95 (978-1-58415-807-3(7)) Mitchell Lane Pubs., Inc.

Rustad, Martha. Can We Ring the Liberty Bell? Poling, Kyle, illus. 2014. (Cloverleaf Books — Our American Symbols Ser.). 24p. (gr. k-2). pap. 6.95 (978-1-4677-4467-6(0), Millbrook Pr.) Lerner Publishing Group.

Sedlacek, Jan Gill. Colors of a City: Philadelphia. Oudinot, Wanda & Baum, Kipley, photos by. 2012. (Illus.). 46p. (J). pap. 14.00 (978-0-9836878-7-0(0)) Aperture Pr., LLC.

Smith, Robin Wayne. If You Got It, a Truck Brought It. Smith, Robin Wayne, illus. 2012. (Illus.). 20p. pap. 6.00 (978-0-615-63721-1(3)) Bright Tyke Creations LLC.

Warrick, Karen Clemens. Independence National Historical Park: A MyReportLinks.com Book. 2005. (Virtual Field Trips Ser.). (Illus.). 48p. (J). (gr. 4-10). lib. bdg. 26.60 (978-0-7660-5224-6(9), MyReportLinks.com Bks.) Enslow Pubs., Inc.

Wyner, Zach. Philadelphia 76ers. 2013. (On the Hardwood Ser.). (ENG., Illus.). 48p. (gr. 3-8). pap. 8.95 (978-1-61570-831-4(6)) Scobre Pr. Corp.

Zschock, Martha Day. Journey Around Philadelphia from A to Z. 2006. (Journeys Ser.). (ENG., Illus.). 32p. (J). (gr. 1-6). 17.95 (978-1-933212-28-9(4), Commonwealth Editions) Applewood Bks.

PHILADELPHIA (PA.)—HISTORY—FICTION

Alger, Horatio. Jack's Ward. 2005. 28.95 (978-1-4218-1454-4(4)); 260p. pap. 13.95 (978-1-4218-1554-1(0)) 1st World Publishing, Inc. (1st World Library - Literary Society).

—Jack's Ward. 2006. pap. (978-1-4065-0711-9(3)) Dodo Pr.

—Jack's Ward: Or, The Boy Guardian. 2006. 176p. pap. 19.99 (978-1-4264-0882-3(X)); (ENG.). 168p. pap. 21.99 (978-1-4264-0863-2(3)) Creative Media Partners, LLC.

—Timothy Crump's Ward. 2005. 27.95 (978-1-4218-1451-3(X)); 220p. pap. 12.95 (978-1-4218-1551-0(6)) 1st World Publishing, Inc. (1st World Library - Literary Society).

Bender, Albert C. More 'Kids in the Alley' Tales. 2011. (Illus.). 200p. pap. 16.95 (978-1-4327-7174-4(4)) Outskirts Pr., Inc.

Blackwood, Gary. Curiosity. 2015. (ENG.). 336p. (J). (gr. 4-7). 8.99 (978-0-14-242448-3(X), Puffin Books) Penguin Young Readers Group.

Coleman, Evelyn. Shadows on Society Hill. 2007. (American Girl Mysteries Ser.). (ENG., Illus.). 192p. (J). (gr. 4-7). 10.95 (978-1-59369-163-9(7), American Girl) American Girl Publishing, Inc.

Dennard, Susan. Something Strange & Deadly. (Something Strange & Deadly Trilogy Ser.: 1). (ENG.). (YA). (gr. 9). 2013. 416p. pap. 9.99 (978-0-06-208327-2(9)) 2012. 400p. 17.99 (978-0-06-208326-5(0)) HarperCollins Pubs. (HarperTeen).

Haislip, Phyllis Hall. Lili's Gift: A Civil War Healer's Story. 2008. (ENG., Illus.). 204p. (J). pap. 8.95 (978-1-57249-392-6(5), White Mane Kids) White Mane Publishing Co., Inc.

Noble, Trinka Hakes. The Scarlet Stockings Spy. Papp, Robert, illus. 2004. (Tales of Young Americans Ser.). (ENG.). 48p. (J). (gr. 1-7). 16.95 (978-1-58536-230-1(1)) Sleeping Bear Pr.

PHILADELPHIA (PA.)—INDEPENDENCE HALL

see Independence Hall (Philadelphia, Pa.)

PHILADELPHIA PHILLIES (BASEBALL TEAM)

Connery-Boyd, Peg. Philadelphia Phillies. 2016. (Hawk's Nest Activity Bks.: 0). (ENG.). 64p. (J). (gr. k-3). pap., act. bk. ed. 8.99 (978-1-4926-3368-6(2)) Sourcebooks, Inc.

Frisch, Aaron. Philadelphia Phillies. 2009. (World Series Champions Ser.). (Illus.). 23p. (J). (gr. 2-3). 24.25 (978-1-58341-693-8(5), Creative Education) Creative Co., The.

Gilbert, Sara. Philadelphia Phillies. 2013. (Illus.). 24p. (J). 25.65 (978-1-60818-270-1(3), Creative Education) Creative Co., The.

—World Series Champs: Philadelphia Phillies. 2013. (World Series Champions Ser.). (ENG.). 24p. (J). (gr. 1-3). pap. 7.99 (978-0-89812-821-5(8), Creative Paperbacks) Creative Co., The.

Goodman, Michael E. The Story of the Philadelphia Phillies. 2011. (J). 35.65 (978-1-60818-051-6(4), Creative Education) 2007. (Illus.). 48p. (YA). (gr. 4-7). lib. bdg. 32.80 (978-1-58341-497-2(5)) Creative Co., The.

Jackson, Dave. Philadelphia Phillies, 1 vol. (Inside MLB Ser.). (ENG., Illus.). 48p. (gr. 3-6). 2011. (YA). lib. bdg. 32.79 (978-1-61714-054-9(6)) 2014. (J). lib. bdg. 32.79 (978-1-62403-480-0(2), SportsZone) ABDO Publishing Co.

Kelley, K. C. Philadelphia Phillies. 2014. (Favorite Baseball Teams Ser.). (ENG.). 32p. (J). (gr. 1-4). 28.50 (978-1-62323-977-0(X), 206754) Child's World, Inc., The.

—Philadelphia Phillies. 2016. (J). (978-1-4896-5944-6(7), AV2 by Weigl) Weigl Pubs., Inc.

MacRae, Sloan. The Philadelphia Phillies. 2012. 24p. (J). 49.50 *(978-1-4488-5150-8(5))*; pap. 8.25 *(978-1-4488-5149-2(1))*; lib. bdg. 22.60 *(978-1-4488-5008-2(8))* Rosen Publishing Group, Inc., The. (PowerKids Pr.).

Savage, Jeff. Ryan Howard. 2008. (Amazing Athletes Ser.). (Illus.). 32p. (J). (gr. 3-7). lib. bdg. 23.93 *(978-0-8225-8833-7(1)*, Lerner Pubns.) Lerner Publishing Group.

Stewart, Mark. The Philadelphia Phillies. 2012. (Team Spirit Ser.). 48p. (J). (gr. 3-6). lib. bdg. 29.27 *(978-1-59953-492-3(4))* Norwood Hse. Pr.

Tometich, Annabelle. Superstars of the Philadelphia Phillies. 2014. (Pro Sports Superstars Ser.). 24p. (J). 27.10 *(978-1-60753-595-9(5))* Amicus Publishing.

PHILANTHROPISTS

Basen, Ryan. Dwight Howard: Gifted & Giving Basketball Star. 2010. (Sports Stars Who Give Back Ser.). (Illus.). 128p. (YA). (gr. 5-9). 33.27 *(978-0-7660-3586-7(7))* Enslow Pubs., Inc.

—Kyle Busch: Gifted & Giving Racing Star. 2010. (Sports Stars Who Give Back Ser.). (Illus.). 128p. (J). (gr. 5-9). 33.27 *(978-0-7660-3589-8(1))* Enslow Pubs., Inc.

Belmonte, Kevin. A Journey Through the Life of William Wilberforce: The Abolitionist Who Changed the Face of a Nation. 2007. (Illus.). 122p. *(978-0-89221-671-0(9))* New Leaf Pub. Group.

Benge, Janet & Benge, Geoff. William Wilberforce: Take up the Fight. 2015. (ENG.). 201p. (YA). pap. 9.99 *(978-1-62486-057-7(5))* Emerald Bks.

De Capua, Sarah. Andrew Carnegie. 2007. (21st Century Skills Library: Life Skills Biographies Ser.). (ENG., Illus.). 48p. (gr. 4-8). lib. bdg. 31.36 *(978-1-60279-067-4(1)*, 200038) Cherry Lake Publishing.

De Lorenzo, Dawn. Peanut Butter & Jelly Possibilities: Youthful Inspirations. 2004. 96p. (J). (gr. 5-18). per. 12.95 *(978-0-9745190-0-5(6))* Crysalis Publishing, Inc.

Edge, Laura Bufano. Andrew Carnegie. 2004. (Lerner Biographies Ser.). (Illus.). 128p. (J). (gr. 6-12). lib. bdg. 27.93 *(978-0-8225-4965-9(4))* Lerner Publishing Group.

Gillam, Scott. Andrew Carnegie: Industrial Giant & Philanthropist, 1 vol. 2009. (Essential Lives Set 3 Ser.). (ENG., Illus.). 112p. (J). (gr. 6-12). lib. bdg. 35.64 *(978-1-60453-521-1(0))* ABDO Publishing Co.

Gitlin, Martin. David Wright: Gifted & Giving Baseball Star. 2010. (Sports Stars Who Give Back Ser.). (Illus.). 128p. (J). (gr. 5-9). 33.27 *(978-0-7660-3588-1(3))* Enslow Pubs., Inc.

Kent, Zachary. Andrew Carnegie: Industrialist & Philanthropist. 2015. (Legendary American Biographies Ser.). 96p. (J). (gr. 6-12). pap. 10.95 *(978-0-7660-6436-2(0))* Enslow Pubs., Inc.

Larsen, Andrew. Andrew Carnegie: The Man Who Loved Libraries. Maurey, Katty, illus. 2017. (ENG.). 32p. (J). (gr. 1-5). 16.95 ***(978-1-77147-267-8(7))*** Owlkids Bks. Inc. CAN. Dist: Publishers Group West (PGW).

Parker, Lewis K. Andrew Carnegie & the Steel Industry. 2009. (American Tycoons Ser.). 24p. (gr. 3-3). 42.50 *(978-1-61511-388-0(6)*, PowerKids Pr.) Rosen Publishing Group, Inc., The.

Rajczak Nelson, Kristen. Andrew Carnegie & the Steel Industry. 2016. (Great Entrepreneurs in U. S. History Ser.). (Illus.). 32p. (J). (gr. 5-5). pap. 11.75 *(978-1-4994-2115-6(X)*, PowerKids Pr.) Rosen Publishing Group, Inc., The.

Rappoport, Ken. Dale Earnhardt, Jr: A Car Racer Who Cares. 2011. (Sports Stars Who Care Ser.). (Illus.). 48p. (J). (gr. 3-18). pap. 8.95 *(978-1-59845-228-0(2)*, Enslow Elementary); (gr. 2-5). lib. bdg. 25.27 *(978-0-7660-3777-9(0))* Enslow Pubs., Inc.

—David Wright: A Baseball Star Who Cares. 2011. (Sports Stars Who Care Ser.). (Illus.). 48p. (J). (gr. 3-18). pap. 8.95 *(978-1-59845-229-7(0)*, Enslow Elementary); (gr. 2-5). lib. bdg. 25.27 *(978-0-7660-3775-5(4))* Enslow Pubs., Inc.

Robinson, Tom. Ben Roethlisberger: Gifted & Giving Football Star. 2010. (Sports Stars Who Give Back Ser.). (Illus.). 128p. (J). (gr. 5-9). lib. bdg. 33.27 *(978-0-7660-3590-4(5))* Enslow Pubs., Inc.

Roselius, J. Chris. David Beckham: Gifted & Giving Soccer Star. 2010. (Sports Stars Who Give Back Ser.). (Illus.). 128p. (J). (gr. 5-9). lib. bdg. 33.27 *(978-0-7660-3587-4(5))* Enslow Pubs., Inc.

Small, Cathleen. Melinda Gates: Philanthropist & Education Advocate. 2017. (J). ***(978-1-5026-2707-0(8))*** Cavendish Square Publishing.

Takase, Naoko, illus. Helen Keller: From Darkness to Light. 2011. (Biographical Comic Ser.). (ENG.). 152p. (J). (gr. 2-6). 18.99 *(978-1-4215-4238-6(2))*; pap. 9.99 *(978-1-4215-4239-3(0))* Shogakukan JPN. Dist: Simon & Schuster, Inc.

Torres, John Albert. Shaun White: A Snowboarder & Skateboarder Who Cares. 2013. (Sports Stars Who Care Ser.). 48p. (J). lib. bdg. 25.27 *(978-0-7660-4295-7(2))*; (gr. 3-4). pap. 8.95 *(978-1-4644-0535-8(2))* Enslow Pubs., Inc. (Enslow Elementary).

Wade, Mary Dodson. Henrietta King: Loving the Land. Farnsworth, Bill, illus. 2011. (ENG.). 24p. 16.95 *(978-1-933979-64-9(X)*, dcf39346-020e-471d-9505-349b26473e11) Bright Sky Pr.

Waxman, Laura Hamilton. W. K. Kellogg. 2006. (History Maker Biographies Ser.). (Illus.). 48p. (J). (gr. 3-7). lib. bdg. 26.60 *(978-0-8225-6578-9(1)*, Lerner Pubns.) Lerner Publishing Group.

Wilner, Barry. Peyton Manning: A Football Star Who Cares. 2011. (Sports Stars Who Care Ser.). (Illus.). 48p. (J). (gr. 3-18). pap. 8.95 *(978-1-59845-232-7(0)*, Enslow Elementary); (gr. 2-5). lib. bdg. 25.27 *(978-0-7660-3774-8(6))* Enslow Pubs., Inc.

—Tom Brady: A Football Star Who Cares. 2011. (Sports Stars Who Care Ser.). (Illus.). 48p. (J). (gr. 3-18). pap. 8.95 *(978-1-59845-233-4(9)*, Enslow Elementary); (gr. 2-5). lib. bdg. 25.27 *(978-0-7660-3773-1(8))* Enslow Pubs., Inc.

Yasuda, Anita. Hannah Taylor. 2011. 24p. (YA). (gr. 2-4). *(978-1-77071-646-9(7))*; pap. *(978-1-77071-650-6(5))* Weigl Educational Pubs. Ltd.

—Hannah Taylor: Ma Vie. Karvonen, Tanjah, tr. from ENG. 2011. (FRE., Illus.). 24p. (YA). (gr. 2-4). *(978-1-77071-434-2(0))* Weigl Educational Pubs. Ltd.

PHILANTHROPY

see Gifts; Social Service

PHILIP II, KING OF SPAIN, 1527-1598

Hilliam, David. Philip II: King of Spain & Leader of the Counter-Reformation. 2009. (Rulers, Scholars, & Artists of the Renaissance Ser.). 112p. (gr. 5-8). 66.50 *(978-1-60852-944-5(4)*, Rosen Reference) Rosen Publishing Group, Inc., The.

PHILIPPINE ISLANDS

see Philippines

PHILIPPINES

Burgan, Michael. Philippines, 1 vol. 2012. (Countries Around the World Ser.). (ENG.). 48p. (gr. 3-6). pap. 9.95 *(978-1-4329-6134-3(9)*, NA-h) Heinemann-Raintree.

Corrigan, Jim. Filipino Immigration. 2005. (Changing Face of North America Ser.). (Illus.). 112p. (YA). lib. bdg. 24.95 *(978-1-59084-684-1(2))* Mason Crest.

Dandan-Albano, Corazon & Jimenez, Gidget Roceles. All about the Philippines: Stories, Songs, Crafts & Games for Kids. 2017. (ENG., Illus.). 64p. (J). (gr. 3-6). 14.95 *(978-0-8048-4848-0(3))* Tuttle Publishing.

Enderlein, Cheryl L. Christmas in the Philippines, 1 vol. 2013. (Christmas Around the World Ser.). (ENG.). 24p. (gr. 1-2). lib. bdg. 25.32 *(978-1-62065-139-1(4))* Capstone Press of Coughlan Cos.

Fazzi, Cindy. How to Draw the Philippines's Sights & Symbols. 2009. (Kid's Guide to Drawing the Countries of the World Ser.). 48p. (gr. 4-4). 53.00 *(978-1-61511-128-2(X)*, PowerKids Pr.) Rosen Publishing Group, Inc., The.

Fishman, Jon M. Manny Pacquiao. 2016. (Amazing Athletes Ser.). (ENG., Illus.). 32p. (J). (gr. 2-5). 26.65 *(978-1-4677-9387-2(6))* Lerner Publishing Group.

Franchino, Vicky. Philippines. 2010. (Explorer Library: Social Studies Explorer Ser.). (ENG.). 48p. (gr. 4-8). lib. bdg. 31.36 *(978-1-60279-834-2(6)*, 200534) Cherry Lake Publishing.

Goldsworthy, Steve. Philippines. 2014. (J). *(978-1-4896-3062-9(7))* Weigl Pubs., Inc.

Gray, Shirley W. The Philippines. 2003. (True Bks.). (ENG.). 48p. (J). (gr. 3-5). pap. 6.95 *(978-0-516-27775-2(8)*, Children's Pr.) Scholastic Library Publishing.

Gray, Shirley Wimbish. The Philippines. 2003. (True Bks.). (ENG., Illus.). 48p. (J). 25.00 *(978-0-516-24212-5(1)*, Children's Pr.) Scholastic Library Publishing.

Jimenez, Gidget Roceles. All about the Philippines: Stories, Songs & Crafts for Kids. Dandan-Albano, Corazon, illus. 2015. (ENG.). 64p. (J). (gr. 3-6). 16.95 *(978-0-8048-4072-9(5))* Tuttle Publishing.

Kalman, Bobbie. Spotlight on the Philippines. 2011. (Spotlight on My Country Ser.: No. 18). (ENG.). 32p. (J). (gr. k-3). pap. *(978-0-7787-3489-5(7))* Crabtree Publishing Co.

Kemper, Bitsy. The Philippines. 2015. (One World, Many Countries Ser.). (ENG.). 32p. (J). (gr. 1-4). 28.50 *(978-1-63407-054-6(2)*, 208893) Child's World, Inc., The.

Laurel, Jaime M. & Romulo, Liana. My First Book of Tagalog Words: Filipino Rhymes & Verses. 2007. (ENG., Illus.). 28p. (J). (gr. -1-3). 12.95 *(978-0-8048-3819-1(4))* Tuttle Publishing.

Lieurance, Suzanne. The Philippines: A MyReportLinks. com Book. 2004. (Top Ten Countries of Recent Immigrants Ser.). (Illus.). 48p. (J). lib. bdg. 26.60 *(978-0-7660-5175-1(7)*, MyReportLinks.com Bks.) Enslow Pubs., Inc.

Longworth, Holly. The Philippines. 2015. (Countries We Come From Ser.). (ENG., Illus.). 32p. (J). (gr. k-3). lib. bdg. 26.60 *(978-1-62724-855-6(2))* Bearport Publishing Co., Inc.

Mildenstein, Tammy. Philippines. 2004. (Modern World Nations Ser.). (Illus.). 120p. (gr. 6-12). 35.00 *(978-0-7910-8024-5(2)*, Chelsea Hse.) Facts On File, Inc.

Otfinoski, Steven. World War II Infantrymen: An Interactive History Adventure. 2013. (You Choose: World War II Ser.). (ENG., 112p. (gr. 3-4). Illus.). pap. 6.95 *(978-1-62065-716-4(3))*; lib. bdg. 31.99 *(978-1-4296-9964-8(7))* Capstone Press of Coughlan Cos. (You Choose Bks.).

The Philippines. 2014. (ENG.). 144p. (J). lib. bdg. 40.00 *(978-0-531-20790-1(0))* Scholastic Library Publishing.

Romulo, Liana. Filipino Celebrations: A Treasury of Feasts & Festivals. Dandan-Albano, Corazon, illus. 2012. (ENG.). 48p. (J). (gr. k-4). 16.95 *(978-0-8048-3821-4(6))* Tuttle Publishing.

Schraff, Anne. Philippines. 2009. pap. 52.95 *(978-0-7613-4731-6(3))* Lerner Publishing Group.

Schraff, Anne E. Philippines. 2009. (Country Explorers Ser.). (ENG.). 48p. (gr. 2-4). 29.27 *(978-1-58013-596-2(X))* Lerner Publishing Group.

Sexton, Colleen A. Philippines in Pictures. 2006. (Visual Geography Series, Second Ser.). (ENG., Illus.). 80p. (gr. 5-12). 31.93 *(978-0-8225-2677-3(8))* Lerner Publishing Group.

PHILIPPINES—FICTION

Blaine, John. The Golden Skull: Rick Brant Science Adventure Story. 2011. 224p. 44.95 *(978-1-258-09873-5(3))* Literary Licensing, LLC.

Dandan-Albano, Corazon & Romulo, Liana. Filipino Friends. 2006. (ENG., Illus.). 32p. (J). (gr. 1-3). 15.95 *(978-0-8048-3822-1(4))* Tuttle Publishing.

de la Paz, Myrna J. Abadeha: The Philippine Cinderella. Tang, Youshan, illus. 2014. (ENG.). 32p. (J). pap. 8.95 *(978-1-885008-44-2(9)*, Shen's Bks.) Lee & Low Bks., Inc.

Galang, M. Evelina. Angel de la Luna & the 5th Glorious Mystery. 2013. (ENG.). 304p. (J). (gr. 6). pap. 12.00 *(978-1-56689-333-6(X))* Coffee Hse. Pr.

Gourlay, Candy. Tall Story. 2012. (ENG.). 304p. (J). (gr. 5). 6.99 *(978-0-385-75233-6(4)*, Yearling) Random Hse. Children's Bks.

The Jesus Jeepney. 2007. 32p. pap. 4.50 *(978-0-8341-2276-5(6)*, 083-412-2766) Beacon Hill Pr. of Kansas City.

Koehler, Hanne Lore & Laraya-Coutts, Corie. A Tale of a Malipayon Warrior. 2010. 128p. 21.95 *(978-1-4502-1344-8(8))*; pap. 11.95 *(978-1-4502-1346-2(4))* iUniverse, Inc.

Lazo Gilmore, Dorina K. Cora Cooks Pancit. Valiant, Kristi, illus. 2014. (ENG.). 32p. (J). pap. 9.95 *(978-1-885008-48-0(1))*; (gr. -1-3). 17.95 *(978-1-885008-35-0(X))* Lee & Low Bks., Inc. (Shen's Bks.).

Lennon, Andrew J. & Lennon, Jeffrey L. Things Can Get Better. 2010. 20p. 12.95 *(978-1-4490-9454-6(6))* AuthorHouse.

Polacco, Patricia. Tucky Jo & Little Heart. Polacco, Patricia, illus. 2015. (ENG., Illus.). 48p. (J). (gr. -1-3). 17.99 *(978-1-4814-1584-2(0)*, Simon & Schuster Bks. For Young Readers) Simon & Schuster Bks. For Young Readers.

Ralphson, G. Harvey. Boy Scouts in the Philippines. 2007. 112p. per. *(978-1-4068-3729-2(6))* Echo Library.

—Boy Scouts in the Philippines: Or the Key to the Treaty Box. 2007. (ENG.). 146p. pap. 18.99 *(978-1-4346-3798-7(0))*; 164p. pap. 21.99 *(978-1-4346-3799-4(9))* Creative Media Partners, LLC.

Ray, Keri. The Saving Journey. 2009. 48p. pap. 10.49 *(978-1-4389-5008-2(X))* AuthorHouse.

Romeu, Emma. Naufragio en las Filipinas. 2003.Tr. of Shipwrecked in the Philippines. (SPA., Illus.). 162p. (J). (gr. 5-8). pap. 9.95 *(978-968-19-0555-2(5))* Santillana USA Publishing Co., Inc.

Salisbury, Graham. Hunt for the Bamboo Rat. 2014. (ENG., Illus.). 336p. (YA). (gr. 7). 16.99 *(978-0-375-84266-5(7)*, Lamb, Wendy Bks.) Random Hse. Children's Bks.

Schraff, Anne. Something Dreadful down Below, 1 vol. unabr. ed. 2010. (Q Reads Ser.). (ENG.). 32p. (YA). (gr. 9-12). pap. 6.95 *(978-1-61651-205-7(9))* Saddleback Educational Publishing, Inc.

Sia, Cress. The Bamboo Dance. Butler, Lisa, illus. 2011. (ENG.). 32p. (J). (gr. -1-3). 12.99 *(978-0-615-48984-1(2))* Hartlyn Kids Media, LLC.

Spradlin, Michael P. Prisoner of War. 2017. (ENG.). 272p. (J). (gr. 7). 17.99 ***(978-0-545-85783-3(X)***, Scholastic Pr.) Scholastic, Inc.

PHILOLOGY

see Language and Languages

PHILOSOPHERS

Abboud, Tony. Al Kindi: The Father of Arab Philosophy. 2009. (Great Muslim Philosophers & Scientists of the Middle Ages Ser.). 112p. (gr. 6-6). 66.50 *(978-1-61513-176-1(0)*, Rosen Reference) Rosen Publishing Group, Inc., The.

Anderson, Margaret J. & Stephenson, Karen F. Aristotle: Genius Philosopher & Scientist. 2015. (Genius Scientists & Their Genius Ideas Ser.). 96p. (J). (gr. 5-12). 27.94 *(978-0-7660-6535-2(9))*; pap. 10.95 *(978-0-7660-6536-9(7))* Enslow Pubs., Inc.

—Aristotle: Philosopher & Scientist. 2004. (Great Minds of Science Ser.). (Illus.). 112p. (J). lib. bdg. 27.94 *(978-0-7660-2096-2(7))* Enslow Pubs., Inc.

Bowen, Richard. Socrates: Greek Philosopher. 2013. (People of Importance Ser.: 21). (Illus.). 32p. (J). (gr. 4-18). 19.95 *(978-1-4222-2857-9(6))* Mason Crest.

Cam, Philip. Philosophy Park: A Beginner's Guide to Great Philosophers & Their Ideas. 2013. 112p. pap. 24.95 *(978-1-74286-191-3(1))* ACER Pr. AUS. Dist: ISBS Publisher Services.

Carew-Miller, Anna. Confucius: Great Chinese Philosopher. 2004. (Great Names Ser.). (Illus.). 32p. (J). (gr. 3-18). lib. bdg. 19.95 *(978-1-59084-149-5(2))* Mason Crest.

Cates, David. Karl Marx: Philosopher & Revolutionary, 1 vol. 2011. (Essential Lives Set 7 Ser.). (ENG., Illus.). 112p. (J). (gr. 6-12). lib. bdg. 35.64 *(978-1-61783-005-1(4))* ABDO Publishing Co.

Coakley, Louis C. & Karamanides, Dimitra. Pythagoras: Mathematician & Mystic. 2015. (Greatest Greek Philosophers Ser.). (ENG., Illus.). 112p. (J). (gr. 7-8). 35.60 *(978-1-4994-6132-9(1)*, Rosen Young Adult) Rosen Publishing Group, Inc., The.

Coddington, Andrew. Henry David Thoreau: Writer of the Transcendentalist Movement. 2016. (Great American Thinkers Ser.). 128p. (J). (gr. 9-9). 45.64 *(978-1-5026-1928-0(8))* Cavendish Square Publishing.

Conklin, Wendy & Lee, Gisela. Confucius: Chinese Philosopher, 1 vol. 2007. (Primary Source Readers Ser.). (ENG.). 32p. (J). (gr. 4-4). pap. 8.99 *(978-0-7439-0437-7(0))* Shell Educational Publishing.

Crompton, Samuel Willard. Emanuel Swedenborg. 2004. (Spiritual Leaders & Thinkers Ser.). (Illus.). 120p. (J). (gr. 9-13). 30.00 *(978-0-7910-8102-0(8)*, Chelsea Hse.) Facts On File, Inc.

Demi & Muhammad, Henry. Al-Ghazali. 2015. (ENG., Illus.). 48p. pap. 19.95 *(978-1-941610-12-1(9))* Fons Vitae of Kentucky, Inc.

Dhillon, Natasha C. & Lim, Jun. Socrates: The Father of Ethics & Inquiry. 2015. (Greatest Greek Philosophers Ser.). (ENG.). 112p. (J). (gr. 7-8). 35.60 *(978-1-4994-6134-3(8)*, Rosen Young Adult) Rosen Publishing Group, Inc., The.

Dorling Kindersley Publishing Staff. Children's Book of Philosophy. 2015. (ENG., Illus.). 144p. (J). (gr. 3-7). 19.99 *(978-1-4654-2923-0(9)*, DK Children) Dorling Kindersley Publishing, Inc.

Duignan, Brian, ed. The Britannica Guide to the World's Most Influential People (Print/eBook Combo Set), 8 vols., Set. Incl. 100 Most Influential Philosophers of All Time. 368p. (YA). (gr. 9-12). 2009. E-Book 106.00 *(978-1-61530-072-3(4))*; (Britannica Guide to the World's Most Influential People Ser.). 384p. 2009. Set E-Book 848.00 *(978-1-61530-165-2(8))* Rosen Publishing Group, Inc., The.

Escalera, Manuel Silva. Cassandrita y Los Sabios: De Los 10 Mandamientos y Filosofia. 2012. (SPA.). 108p. (gr. -1). pap. 14.95 *(978-1-4772-0516-7(0))* AuthorHouse.

Gordon, Susan. Montesquieu: The French Philosopher Who Shaped Modern Government. 2009. (Philosophers of the Enlightenment Ser.). 112p. (gr. 5-8). 66.50 *(978-1-60851-166-2(9)*, Rosen Reference) Rosen Publishing Group, Inc., The.

Gow, Mary. The Great Philosopher: Plato & His Pursuit of Knowledge. 2010. (Great Minds of Ancient Science & Math Ser.). 128p. (J). (gr. 4-7). 33.27 *(978-0-7660-3119-7(5))* Enslow Pubs., Inc.

—The Great Thinker: Aristotle & the Foundations of Science. 2010. (Great Minds of Ancient Science & Math Ser.). 128p. (J). (gr. 4-7). 33.27 *(978-0-7660-3121-0(7))* Enslow Pubs., Inc.

Hall, Derek, ed. Philosophy, Invention, & Engineering. 2009. (FAYFT: Great Scientists Ser.). 64p. (gr. 4-10). 39.95 *(978-1-933834-48-1(X))* Brown Bear Bks.

Harkins, Susan Sales & Harkins, William H. The Life & Times of Pythagoras. 2007. (Biography from Ancient Civilizations Ser.). (Illus.). 48p. (J). (gr. 4-8). lib. bdg. 29.95 *(978-1-58415-545-4(0))* Mitchell Lane Pubs., Inc.

Isle, Mick. Aristotle: Pioneering Philosopher & Founder of the Lyceum. 2009. (Library of Greek Philosophers Ser.). 112p. (gr. 6-6). 66.50 *(978-1-60853-658-0(0)*, Rosen Reference) Rosen Publishing Group, Inc., The.

Jones, Viola & Hasan, Heather. Archimedes: Innovative Mathematician, Engineer, & Inventor. 2015. (Greatest Greek Philosophers Ser.). (ENG., Illus.). 112p. (J). (gr. 7-8). 35.60 *(978-1-4994-6124-4(0)*, Rosen Young Adult) Rosen Publishing Group, Inc., The.

Klepeis, Alicia. Pythagoras. 2017. (Junior Biography From Ancient Civilization Ser.). (gr. 4-6). 29.95 *(978-1-68020-032-4(1))* Mitchell Lane Pubs., Inc.

Lim, Bridget & Viegas, Jennifer. Al-Kindi. 2016. (Physicians, Scientists, & Mathematicians of the Islamic World Ser.). 112p. (J). (gr. 6-6). 37.10 *(978-1-5081-7138-6(6))* Rosen Publishing Group, Inc., The.

Love, D. Anne. Of Numbers & Stars: The Story of Hypatia. Paparone, Pamela & Paparone, Pam, illus. 2006. (ENG.). 32p. (J). (gr. 4-8). 16.95 *(978-0-8234-1621-9(6))* Holiday Hse., Inc.

Lusted, Marcia. Plato. 2017. (Junior Biography From Ancient Civilization Ser.). (gr. 4-6). 29.95 *(978-1-68020-026-3(7))* Mitchell Lane Pubs., Inc.

Martin. Dietrich Bonhoeffer. 2011. (Champion of Freedom Ser.). (gr. 7-12). 28.95 *(978-1-59935-169-8(2))* Reynolds, Morgan Inc.

Miller, Anna Carew & Carew-Miller, Anna. Confucius: Great Chinese Philosopher. 2013. (People of Importance Ser.: 21). (Illus.). 32p. (J). (gr. 4-18). 19.95 *(978-1-4222-2845-6(2))* Mason Crest.

Nagle, Jeanne, ed. Top 101 Philosophers, 1 vol., 1. 2014. (People You Should Know Ser.). (ENG.). 152p. (YA). (gr. 7-12). 35.25 *(978-1-62275-132-7(9))* Rosen Publishing Group, Inc., The.

Philosophers of the Enlightenment. (Illus.). (YA). (gr. 5-8). 191.70 *(978-1-4042-0620-5(5)*, Rosen Reference) Rosen Publishing Group, Inc., The.

Rodríguez, Ricardo. Walter Benjamin -Salida de Emergencia. 2005. (SPA.). 116p. (YA). *(978-958-30-1598-4(9))* Panamericana Editorial.

Roscoe, Kelly & Isle, Mick. Aristotle: The Father of Logic. 2015. (Greatest Greek Philosophers Ser.). (ENG.). 112p. (J). (gr. 7-8). 35.60 *(978-1-4994-6126-8(7)*, Rosen Young Adult) Rosen Publishing Group, Inc., The.

Rosenberg, Aaron. Thomas Hobbes: An English Philosopher in the Age of Reason. (Philosophers of the Enlightenment Ser.). 112p. 2009. (gr. 5-8). 66.50 *(978-1-60851-167-9(7)*, Rosen Reference) 2005. (Illus.). (J). (gr. 3-7). lib. bdg. 34.60 *(978-1-4042-0419-5(9))* Rosen Publishing Group, Inc., The.

Rössig, Wolfgang. Karl Marx. 2009. (Profiles in Economics Ser.). 112p. (YA). lib. bdg. 28.95 *(978-1-59935-132-2(3))* Reynolds, Morgan Inc.

Santillian, Beatriz & Randall, Bernard. Solon: Athenian Statesman & Poet. 2017. (Leaders of the Ancient World Ser.). 112p. (J). (gr. 12-11). 37.10 ***(978-1-5081-7493-6(8)***, Rosen Young Adult) Rosen Publishing Group, Inc., The.

Sharafeddine, Fatima. The Amazing Discoveries of Ibn Sina, 1 vol. Ali, Intelaq Mohammed, illus. 2015. (ENG.). 32p. (J). (gr. 1-6). 17.95 *(978-1-55498-710-8(5))* Groundwood Bks. CAN. Dist: Publishers Group West (PGW).

Sherman, Patrice. John Locke: Philosopher of the Enlightenment, 1 vol. 2012. (Primary Source Readers Ser.). (ENG.). 32p. (J). (gr. 4-4). pap. 8.99 *(978-1-4333-5014-6(9))* Teacher Created Materials, Inc.

Tent, M. B. W., ed. Gottfried Wilhelm Leibniz: The Polymath Who Brought Us Calculus. 2011. (ENG., Illus.). 260p. (C). 36.95 *(978-1-4398-9222-0(9)*, K14134) AK Peters, Ltd.

Tracy, Kathleen. The Life & Times of Confucius. 2004. (Biography from Ancient Civilizations Ser.). (Illus.). 48p. (J). (gr. 4-8). lib. bdg. 29.95 *(978-1-58415-246-0(X))* Mitchell Lane Pubs., Inc.

Trouvé, Marianne Lorraine. Saint Thomas Aquinas: Missionary of Truth. Morrison, Cathy, illus. 2015. 137p. (J). pap. 8.95 *(978-0-8198-9026-9(X))* Pauline Bks. & Media.

Urbina, Manuel Iván. Sören Kierkegaard -la conciencia de un Desesperado. 2005. (SPA.). 128p. (YA). *(978-958-30-1701-8(9))* Panamericana Editorial.

Viegas, Jennifer. William James: American Philosopher, Psychologist, & Theologian. 2009. (Library of American Thinkers Ser.). 112p. (gr. 6-6). 66.50 *(978-1-60853-517-0(7)*, Rosen Reference) Rosen Publishing Group, Inc., The.

Whiting, Jim. The Life & Times of Plato. 2006. (Biography from Ancient Civilizations Ser.). (Illus.). 48p. (J). (gr. 3-7). lib. bdg. 29.95 *(978-1-58415-507-2(8)*, 1259591) Mitchell Lane Pubs., Inc.

PHILOSOPHERS' STONE

see Alchemy

PHILOSOPHY

see also Belief and Doubt; Ethics; God; Good and Evil; Humanism; Knowledge, Theory of; Logic; Mind and Body; Psychology; Universe

also general subjects with the subdivision Philosophy, e.g. History—Philosophy, etc.

Cam, Philip. Philosophy Park: A Beginner's Guide to Great Philosophers & Their Ideas. 2013. 112p. pap. 24.95 *(978-1-74286-191-3(1))* ACER Pr. AUS. Dist: ISBS Publisher Services.

Carr, Aaron. Opuestos. 2013. (Ninos y la Ciencia Ser.). (SPA., Illus.). 24p. (J). (gr. -1-3). lib. bdg. 27.13 *(978-1-62127-611-1(2)*, AV2 by Weigl) Weigl Pubs., Inc.

Cowcher, Helen. Desert Elephants, 1 vol. Cowcher, Helen, illus. 2011. (ENG., Illus.). 40p. (J). (gr. k-3). 16.99 *(978-0-374-31774-4(7)*, 9780374317744, Farrar, Straus & Giroux (BYR)) Farrar, Straus & Giroux.

Dayton, Connor. Water. 2014. (Four Elements Ser.). (Illus.). 32p. (J). (gr. k-3). pap. 60.00 *(978-1-4777-9265-0(1))* Windmill Bks.

Dorling Kindersley Publishing Staff. Children's Book of Philosophy. 2015. (ENG., Illus.). 144p. (J). (gr. 3-7). 19.99 *(978-1-4654-2923-0(9)*, DK Children) Dorling Kindersley Publishing, Inc.

Earth. 2014. (Four Elements Ser.). 32p. (J). (gr. k-3). pap. 10.00 *(978-1-4777-9273-5(2))* Windmill Bks.

Enz, Tammy & Biskup, Agnieszka. Science Behind Superman. 2017. (Science Behind Superman Ser.). (ENG.). 24p. (gr. 1-2). pap. 27.80 *(978-1-5157-5117-5(1)*, DC Super Heroes) Stone Arch Bks.

Espejo, Roman. Culture of Beauty. 2009. (Opposing Viewpoints Ser.). (ENG., Illus.). 240p. (J). 29.45 *(978-0-7377-4509-2(6))*; pap. 42.95 *(978-0-7377-4508-5(8))* Cengage Gale.

Fire. 2014. (Four Elements Ser.). (Illus.). 32p. (J). (gr. k-3). pap. 60.00 *(978-1-4777-9269-8(4))* Windmill Bks.

Franco, Eloise. The Young Look. 2003. (Illus.). 168p. (gr. 3-7). 5.95 *(978-0-87516-294-2(0)*, Devorss Pubns.) DeVorss & Co.

Gunderson, Jessica. How Big? Wacky Ways to Compare Size, 1 vol. Keino, illus. 2013. (Wacky Comparisons Ser.). (ENG.). 24p. (gr. -1-2). 27.99 *(978-1-4048-8325-3(8))*; pap. 8.95 *(978-1-4795-1915-6(4))* Picture Window Bks.

—How Long? Wacky Ways to Compare Length, 1 vol. Sinkovec, Igor, illus. 2013. (Wacky Comparisons Ser.). (ENG.). 24p. (gr. -1-2). 27.99 *(978-1-4048-8324-6(X))*; pap. 8.95 *(978-1-4795-1914-9(6))* Picture Window Bks.

Gunderson, Jessica & Weakland, Mark. Wacky Comparisons. 2013. (Wacky Comparisons Ser.). (ENG.). 24p. (gr. -1-2). pap. 31.80 *(978-1-4795-1970-5(7))*; lib. bdg. 111.96 *(978-1-4048-8145-7(X))* Picture Window Bks.

Hill, Z. B. Optimism & Self-Confidence. Croft, Cindy, ed. 2014. (Causes & Effects of Emotions Ser.: 13). 64p. (J). (gr. 7-18). 23.95 *(978-1-4222-3076-3(7))* Mason Crest.

Houk, Katherine. The Little Book of Sticky Isms. 2011. 36p. pap. 15.00 *(978-0-557-67022-2(5))* Lulu Pr., Inc.

Krishnamurti, J. Que Estas Haciendo con Tu Vida: Comentarios Sobre el Vivir para Jovenes. 2003. (Teen Bks. on Living: Vol. 1). (SPA., Illus.). 240p. *(978-84-7556-277-3(9)*, 1500) Oceano Difusion Editorial, S. A.

Lightner, Laura. FirstFires. Messina, Linda, illus. 2008. 27p. (J). 31.99 *(978-1-4363-4542-2(1))* Xlibris Corp.

Markowitz-Meredith, Susan. What Is Form? 2009. (Get Art Smart Ser.). (ENG., Illus.). 24p. (J). (gr. k-3). pap. *(978-0-7787-5138-0(4))*; lib. bdg. *(978-0-7787-5124-3(4))* Crabtree Publishing Co.

McCurrach, Moriah. Kids Without Limits: You can be anything you want to Be! 2007. 52p. per. 9.95 *(978-0-595-46425-8(4))* iUniverse, Inc.

Morrison, Matthew. Big Questions: Incredible Adventures in Thinking. Chalk, Gary, illus. 2007. (ENG.). 204p. (J). (gr. 4-8). pap. 7.95 *(978-1-84046-670-6(7))* Icon Bks., Ltd. GBR. Dist: Publishers Group Canada.

Nelson, S. D., illus. Greet the Dawn: The Lakota Way. 2012. (J). 18.95 *(978-0-9845041-6-9(8)*, South Dakota State Historical Society Pr.) South Dakota State Historical Society Pr.

Phelan, J. W. Philosophy: Themes & Thinkers. 2005. (Cambridge International Examinations Ser.). (ENG., Illus.). 354p. (gr. 8-12). pap. 40.31 *(978-0-521-53742-1(8))* Cambridge Univ. Pr.

Philosophie: Scholastik, Logik, Metaphysik: Einblick in Modelle und Schulen der Philosophie. (Duden-Schuelerduden Ser.). (GER.). 492p. (YA). 27.95 *(978-3-411-02206-9(X))* Bibliographisches Institut & F. A. Brockhaus AG DEU. Dist: Continental Bk. Co., Inc.

Playing with Plato: The Republic as a Lens into Popular Culture. 2004. (YA). per. *(978-1-932948-05-9(8))* Student Pr. Initiative.

Ruggiero, Adriane, ed. Confucianism. 2005. (Religions & Religious Movements Ser.). (ENG.). 224p. (gr. 10-12). lib. bdg. 46.40 *(978-0-7377-2567-4(2)*, Greenhaven Pr., Inc.) Cengage Gale.

Seidman, David. What If I'm an Atheist? A Teen's Guide to Exploring a Life Without Religion. 2015. (ENG., Illus.). 256p. (YA). (gr. 7). pap. 12.99 *(978-1-58270-406-7(6))* Simon Pulse/Beyond Words.

Simpson, Deb. Pink Place Paperback. 2010. 32p. pap. 18.50 *(978-0-557-47673-2(9))* Lulu Pr., Inc.

Tatarsky, Daniel. Cool Philosophy: Filled with Facts for Kids of All Ages. 2015. (ENG., Illus.). 112p. (J). (gr. 5). 14.99 *(978-1-909396-77-7(X)*, Pavilion) Pavilion Bks. GBR. Dist: Independent Pubs. Group.

Teague Meyer, Terry. Optimism. 2013. (7 Character Strengths of Highly Successful Students Ser.). 64p. (J). (gr. 5-8). 31.95 *(978-1-4488-9545-8(6))*; pap. 77.70 *(978-1-4488-9562-5(6))*; pap. 12.95 *(978-1-4488-9561-8(8))* Rosen Publishing Group, Inc., The.

Walker, Robert. Live It: Optimism. 2009. (ENG., Illus.). 32p. (J). (gr. 3-6). lib. bdg. *(978-0-7787-4887-8(1))* Crabtree Publishing Co.

Weakland, Mark. Football Opposites, 1 vol. 2013. (SI Kids Rookie Bks.). (ENG.). 32p. (gr. 1-2). lib. bdg. 27.32 *(978-1-4296-9960-0(4))* Capstone Press of Coughlan Cos.

—How Heavy? Wacky Ways to Compare Weight, 1 vol. Bolton, Bill, illus. 2013. (Wacky Comparisons Ser.). (ENG.). 24p. (gr. -1-2). 27.99 *(978-1-4048-8322-2(3))*; pap. 8.95 *(978-1-4795-1912-5(X))* Picture Window Bks.

—How Tall? Wacky Ways to Compare Height, 1 vol. Sinkovec, Igor, illus. 2013. (Wacky Comparisons Ser.). (ENG.). 24p. (gr. -1-2). 27.99 *(978-1-4048-8323-9(1))*; pap. 8.95 *(978-1-4795-1913-2(8))* Picture Window Bks.

PHILOSOPHY, ANCIENT

Roscoe, Kelly & Isle, Mick. Aristotle: The Father of Logic. 2015. (Greatest Greek Philosophers Ser.). (ENG.). 112p. (J). (gr. 7-8). 35.60 *(978-1-4994-6126-8(7)*, Rosen Young Adult) Rosen Publishing Group, Inc., The.

PHILOSOPHY, GREEK

see Philosophy, Ancient

PHILOSOPHY, MORAL

see Ethics

PHILOSOPHY, ROMAN

see Philosophy, Ancient

PHILOSOPHY OF RELIGION

see Religion—Philosophy

PHOENICIA

Fine, Jil. Writing in Ancient Phoenicia. 2003. (Writing in the Ancient World Ser.). (Illus.). 24p. (J). lib. bdg. 22.60 *(978-0-8239-6507-6(4)*, PowerKids Pr.) Rosen Publishing Group, Inc., The.

Reece, Katherine E. The Phoenicians: The Mysterious Sea People. 2004. (Ancient Civilizations Ser.). (Illus.). 48p. (gr. 4-8). lib. bdg. *(978-1-59515-236-7(9))* Rourke Educational Media.

PHONETICS

see also Speech; Voice

ABDO Publishing Company Staff & Salzmann, Mary Elizabeth. First Sounds: Set Of 47. 2005. (First Sounds Ser.: 47). (ENG.). 24p. (J). (gr. k-3). lib. bdg. 1137.87 *(978-1-59679-120-6(9)*, SandCastle) ABDO Publishing Co.

Acorn's Gold Mine. 2004. (J). cd-rom 39.00 *(978-1-890265-12-0(8))* Janelle Pubns., Inc.

Activity Worksheets. 2004. (J). spiral bd. 29.95 *(978-1-886441-64-4(2))* Zoo-phonics, Inc.

The Adventures of Tutankhamen: Level T. Group 2, 6 vols. (Sunshine Ser.). 48p. 44.95 *(978-0-7802-4175-6(4))* Wright Group/McGraw-Hill.

Akers, Martin & Benchmark Education Co., LLC Staff. Fran Grabs It. 2015. (BuildUp Ser.). (J). (gr. 1). *(978-1-4900-0719-9(9))* Benchmark Education Co.

—A Night Hunt for Food. 2015. (BuildUp Ser.). (J). (gr. 1). *(978-1-4900-0735-9(0))* Benchmark Education Co.

Al Circo, Al Circo! 2003. 35.50 *(978-0-8136-8083-5(2))*; stu. ed. 35.50 *(978-0-8136-8081-1(6))* Modern Curriculum Pr.

Alfarrimas Phonics Kit. (J). (gr. k). 767.22 *(978-0-7362-2629-5(X))* CENGAGE Learning.

Alliteration Configuration. 2006. (Illus.). 60p. (J). 24.99 *(978-0-9790434-0-6(9))* Jamiram Publishing.

Alphabet & Phonemic Awareness Activity Cards (OCR) 2004. (J). 14.95 *(978-1-56911-192-5(8))* Learning Resources, Inc.

Alphasnaps & Snapphonics: Snapphonics Big Book: Eek! Squeak! A Leak! 2003. 36.95 *(978-0-673-60206-0(0))* Celebration Pr.

Alphasnaps & Snapphonics: Snapphonics Big Book: Scat the Cat. 2003. 36.95 *(978-0-673-60207-7(9))* Celebration Pr.

Alphasnaps & Snapphonics: Snapphonics Package With 4 Big Books. 2003. 499.95 *(978-0-673-59265-1(0))* Celebration Pr.

Ancient Man of the Ice: Level T. Group 2, 6 vols. (Sunshine Ser.). 48p. 44.95 *(978-0-7802-4182-4(7))* Wright Group/McGraw-Hill.

Anin, Ravi & Benchmark Education Co., LLC Staff. In Our Town. 2015. (BuildUp Ser.). (J). (gr. 1). *(978-1-4900-0737-3(7))* Benchmark Education Co.

Anin, Ravi, et al. In Our Town - Ray Makes a Choice - a Room for Moose: BuildUp Unit 9 Lap Book. Anderson, Nicola, illus. 2015. (Build up Core Phonics Ser.). (J). (gr. 1). *(978-1-4900-2608-4(8))* Benchmark Education Co.

The Ants & the Grasshopper: R-Controlled Review: Level C, 6 vols. (Wright Skills Ser.). 16p. (gr. k-3). 26.50 *(978-0-322-01501-2(4))* Wright Group/McGraw-Hill.

Arita, Vera. Animals Sing Aloha. Louie, Ron, illus. 2009. (ENG.). 20p. (J). (gr. -1-1). bds. 7.95 *(978-1-933067-29-2(2))* Beachhouse Publishing, LLC.

Astroword: Complete CD-ROM & Lab Pack Sets. 2003. 499.95 *(978-0-7652-0907-8(1))*; 1849.95 *(978-0-7652-0909-2(8))* Modern Curriculum Pr.

Astroword: Module 1-Phonemic Awareness (K-1) 2003. *(978-0-7652-0577-3(7))* Modern Curriculum Pr.

Astroword: Module 10-Vowel Digraphs & Diphthongs (1-3) 2003. 166.95 net. *(978-0-7652-0831-6(8))* Modern Curriculum Pr.

Astroword: Module 12-Base Words & Endings (2-6) 2003. 55.50 net. *(978-0-7652-0589-6(0))* Modern Curriculum Pr.

Astroword: Module 13-Compound Words (2-6) 2003. 55.50 net. *(978-0-7652-0590-2(4))* Modern Curriculum Pr.

Astroword: Module 14-Suffixes (2-6) 2003. 158.95 net. *(978-0-7652-0835-4(0))*; 55.50 net. *(978-0-7652-0591-9(2))* Modern Curriculum Pr.

Astroword: Module 15-Prefixes (2-6) 2003. 158.95 net. *(978-0-7652-0836-1(9))*; 55.50 net. *(978-0-7652-0592-6(0))* Modern Curriculum Pr.

Astroword: Module 6-Consonant Blends & Digraphs (1-2) 2003. 166.95 net. *(978-0-7652-0825-5(3))* Modern Curriculum Pr.

Astroword: Module 7-Long Vowels A, I (1-3) 2003. 166.95 net. *(978-0-7652-0826-2(1))* Modern Curriculum Pr.

Astroword: Module 8-Long Vowels I, O (1-3) 2003. 166.95 net. *(978-0-7652-0828-6(8))* Modern Curriculum Pr.

Astroword: Module 9-Long Vowels E, U (1-3) 2003. 166.95 net. *(978-0-7652-0829-3(6))* Modern Curriculum Pr.

Baron, L. A Day with My Dad: Learning the D Sound. 2009. (PowerPhonics Ser.). 24p. (gr. 1-1). 39.90 *(978-1-60851-429-8(3)*, PowerKids Pr.) Rosen Publishing Group, Inc., The.

Battiston, I. My Red Rose: Learning the R Sound. 2009. (PowerPhonics Ser.). 24p. (gr. 1-1). 39.90 *(978-1-60851-462-5(5)*, PowerKids Pr.) Rosen Publishing Group, Inc., The.

The Battle of Bowling Street: Level 4, 6 vols. (Fluency Strand Ser.). (gr. 4-8). 45.00 *(978-1-4045-1224-5(1))* Wright Group/McGraw-Hill.

Beginning Consonants (Gr. K-1) 2003. (J). *(978-1-58232-037-3(3))* ECS Learning Systems, Inc.

Benchmark Education Company, LLC Staff, compiled by. BuildUp Phonics Skill Bag Set. 2006. (Phonics Ser.). (J). 2169.00 *(978-1-4108-6365-2(4))* Benchmark Education Co.

—Phonics Poetry Posters. 2008. (Phonics Ser.). (J). (gr. k-1). 289.00 *(978-1-4108-8450-3(3))* Benchmark Education Co.

—Phonological Awareness. 2005. pap. 47.00 *(978-1-4108-5064-5(1))* Benchmark Education Co.

—SpiralUp Phonics Lesson Resources. 2005. (Phonics Ser.). spiral bd. 470.00 *(978-1-4108-5832-0(4))* Benchmark Education Co.

—SpiralUp Phonics Skill Bag Set. 2006. (Phonics Ser.). (J). spiral bd. 825.00 *(978-1-4108-6366-9(2))* Benchmark Education Co.

—SpiralUp Phonics Support Tools. 2005. (Phonics Ser.). spiral bd. 180.00 *(978-1-4108-5833-7(2))* Benchmark Education Co.

—Start up Phonics Readers Add to Pack: Set Of 26. 2004. (Phonics Ser.). (J). pap. 98.00 *(978-1-4108-1500-2(5))* Benchmark Education Co.

—Start up Phonics Readers Set. ed. 2004. (Phonics Ser.). (J). spiral bd., instr.'s gde. ed. 575.00 *(978-1-4108-1489-0(0))* Benchmark Education Co.

Benjamin, Joseph, et al. Ten Red Hens - Get up, Meg! - Dan & Ed: StartUp Unit 6 Lap Book. Pike, Carol et al, illus. 2015. (Start up Core Phonics Ser.). (J). (gr. k). *(978-1-4900-2595-7(2))* Benchmark Education Co.

Bennett, Liza & Benchmark Education Co., LLC Staff. I Am Sam. 2015. (StartUp Ser.). (J). (gr. k). *(978-1-4900-0686-4(9))* Benchmark Education Co.

—I See. 2015. (StartUp Ser.). (J). (gr. k). *(978-1-4900-0687-1(7))* Benchmark Education Co.

Bennett, Liza & Ling, Lei. I Am Sam - I See - I See Nat: StartUp Unit 2 Lap Book. Palacios, Sara et al, illus. 2015. (Start up Core Phonics Ser.). (J). (gr. k). *(978-1-4900-2591-9(X))* Benchmark Education Co.

Bentley, Linda M. & Bentley, Linda. The Big Book of Quick & Easy Art Activities: More Than 75 Creative Activities with Curriculum Connections That Keep Kids Creating & Learning All Year Long! 2007. (ENG., Illus.). 208p. pap. 26.99 *(978-0-439-58060-1(9)*, Teaching Resources) Scholastic, Inc.

Benton, Celia & Benchmark Education Co., LLC Staff. Use It to Pull. 2015. (StartUp Ser.). (J). (gr. k). *(978-1-4900-0711-3(3))* Benchmark Education Co.

Bergen, Lara Rice. Phonics Comics: the Fearless Four - Level 2. Semple, Dave, illus. 2007. (ENG.). 24p. (J). (gr. 1-17). per. 3.99 *(978-1-58476-564-6(X))* Innovative Kids.

Blends & Digraphs (Gr. 1-2) 2003. (J). *(978-1-58232-109-7(4))* ECS Learning Systems, Inc.

Blevins, Wiley. Can You See It?, 6 vols., Set. 2003. (Phonics Readers 1-36 Ser.). (ENG.). 8p. (gr. k-1). pap. 29.70 *(978-0-7368-3191-8(6)*, Phonics Readers) Capstone Press of Coughlan Cos.

—Is It Hot? Is It Not?, 6 vols., Set. 2003. (Phonics Readers 1-36 Ser.). (ENG.). 8p. (gr. k-1). pap. 29.70 *(978-0-7368-3186-4(X)*, Phonics Readers) Capstone Press of Coughlan Cos.

—Mapping the World, 6 vols., Set. 2004. (Phonics Readers Books 37-72 Ser.). (ENG.). 8p. (gr. k-1). pap. 35.70 *(978-0-7368-4075-0(3)*, Phonics Readers) Capstone Press of Coughlan Cos.

—Maps, 6 vols., Set. 2003. (Phonics Readers 1-36 Ser.). (ENG.). 8p. (gr. k-1). pap. 29.70 *(978-0-7368-3213-7(0)*, Phonics Readers) Capstone Press of Coughlan Cos.

—Meat-Eating Plants, 6 vols., Set. 2004. (Phonics Readers Books 37-72 Ser.). (ENG.). 8p. (gr. k-1). pap. 35.70 *(978-0-7368-4065-1(6)*, Phonics Readers) Capstone Press of Coughlan Cos.

—Phonics from A to Z. 2nd ed. 2006. (Scholastic Teaching Strategies Ser.). (ENG., Illus.). 240p. (gr. k-3). pap., instr.'s gde. ed. 25.99 *(978-0-439-84511-3(4)*, Teaching Resources) Scholastic, Inc.

Blue Collection. (Elefonetica Ser.). (SPA.). (gr. 1-2). 373.22 *(978-0-7362-0795-9(3))* CENGAGE Learning.

Bradshaw, Georgine & Wrighton, Charlene. Basic Kit - Kindergarten. Clark, Irene, illus. 2005. Orig. Title: Basic Kit II. (J). 249.95 *(978-1-886441-31-6(6))* Zoo-phonics, Inc.

—Kindergarten Zoo-per Kit. Clark, Irene, illus. 2005. (J). 499.95 *(978-1-886441-37-7(0)*, ZOP4219) Zoo-phonics, Inc.

—Preschool Zoo-per Kit. Clark, Irene, illus. 2005. (J). 449.95 *(978-1-886441-32-3(4)*, ZOP4218) Zoo-phonics, Inc.

Buitres En La Playa: Little Books, Level 4, Vol. 19. 2003. (Fonolibros Ser.). (SPA.). 25.50 *(978-0-7652-0096-9(1))* Modern Curriculum Pr.

Callella, Kim. Build-a-Skill Instant Books Short & Long Vowels. Shiotsu, Vicky & Faulkner, Stacey, eds. Campbell, Jenny & Tom, Darcy, illus. 2007. (J). 4.99 *(978-1-59198-412-2(2))* Creative Teaching Pr., Inc.

Campbell, Barbara. Lets Build Something: A Story Book/Coloring Book/Workbook. 2009. 64p. pap. 14.95 *(978-0-692-00349-7(5))* Mumford Institute.

Un Canguro en la Cocina! Little Books, Level 10, Vol. 2. 2003. (Fonolibros Ser.). (SPA.). 25.50 *(978-0-7652-0111-9(9))* Modern Curriculum Pr.

Carson-Dellosa Publishing Staff. Phonics. 2006. (ENG., Illus.). 54p. (gr. -1-2). 2.99 *(978-0-7696-4749-4(9)*, Brighter Child) Carson-Dellosa Publishing, LLC.

—Phonics for First Grade. 2010. (Home Workbooks Ser.). (ENG.). 64p. (gr. 1-1). pap. 4.49 *(978-1-60418-785-4(9))* Carson-Dellosa Publishing, LLC.

—Phonics for Kindergarten, Grade K. 2010. (Home Workbooks Ser.). (ENG.). 64p. (gr. k-k). pap. 4.49 *(978-1-60418-774-8(3))* Carson-Dellosa Publishing, LLC.

Carson, J. Visiting the Vet: Learning the V Sound. 2009. (PowerPhonics Ser.). 24p. (gr. 1-1). 39.90 *(978-1-60851-476-2(5)*, PowerKids Pr.) Rosen Publishing Group, Inc., The.

Cartwright, Stephen. Usborne Phonics Flashcards: Dog. Cartwright, Stephen, illus. 2007. (Usborne Flashcards Ser.). (Illus.). 48p. (J). (gr. -1-k). 9.99 *(978-0-7945-1516-4(9)*, Usborne) EDC Publishing.

La Casa de Abuelito. 2003. (SPA., Illus.). 35.50 *(978-0-8136-8526-7(5))* Modern Curriculum Pr.

Cernak, Kim. Build-a-Skill Instant Books Consonant Blends & Digraphs. Shiotsu, Vicky & Faulkner, Stacey, eds. Campbell, Jenny & Tom, Darcy, illus. 2007. (J). 4.99 *(978-1-59198-410-8(6))* Creative Teaching Pr., Inc.

Chapman, Sherill, et al, adapted by. More Phonics. 2004. (Kids Can Learn with Franklin Ser.). (ENG., Illus.). 32p. (J). (gr. 1-3). 3.95 *(978-1-55337-599-9(8))* Kids Can Pr., Ltd. CAN. Dist: Hachette Bk. Group.

Charlesworth, Liza. Animal Phonics Readers: A Big Collection of Exciting Informational Books That Target & Teach Key Phonics Skills. 2014. (ENG.). (-2). 129.99 *(978-0-545-57814-1(0)*, Teaching Resources) Scholastic, Inc.

Classification (Gr. 1-2) 2003. (J). *(978-1-58232-040-3(3))* ECS Learning Systems, Inc.

Cleary, Brian P. The Bug in the Jug Wants a Hug. Miskimins, Jason, illus. 2009. (Sounds Like Reading (r) Ser.: 1). (ENG.). (gr. -1-2). pap. 39.62 *(978-0-7613-4700-2(3))* Lerner Publishing Group.

—Chips & Cheese & Nana's Knees: What Is Alliteration? Goneau, Martin, illus. 2015. (Words Are CATegorical (r) Ser.). (ENG.). 32p. (gr. 2-5). lib. bdg. 17.95 *(978-1-4677-2649-8(4)*, Millbrook Pr.) Lerner Publishing Group.

—The Clown in the Gown Drives the Car with the Star. Miskimins, Jason, illus. 2009. (Sounds Like Reading (r) Ser.: 8). (ENG.). (gr. -1-2). pap. 39.62 *(978-0-7613-4707-1(0))* Lerner Publishing Group.

—The Frail Snail on the Trail. Miskimins, Jason, illus. 2009. (Sounds Like Reading (r) Ser.: 4). (ENG.). (gr. -1-2). pap. 39.62 *(978-0-7613-4703-3(8))* Lerner Publishing Group.

—The Nice Mice in the Rice. Miskimins, Jason, illus. 2009. (Sounds Like Reading (r) Ser.: 3). (ENG.). (gr. -1-2). pap. 39.62 *(978-0-7613-4702-6(X))* Lerner Publishing Group.

—Stop, Drop, & Flop in the Slop. Miskimins, Jason, illus. 2009. (Sounds Like Reading (r) Ser.: 2). (ENG.). (gr. -1-2). pap. 39.62 *(978-0-7613-4701-9(1))* Lerner Publishing Group.

—The Thing on the Wing Can Sing. Miskimins, Jason, illus. 2009. (Sounds Like Reading (r) Ser.: 5). (ENG.). (gr. -1-2). pap. 39.62 *(978-0-7613-4704-0(6))* Lerner Publishing Group.

—Whose Shoes Would You Choose. Miskimins, Jason, illus. 2009. (Sounds Like Reading (r) Ser.: 6). (ENG.). (gr. -1-2). pap. 39.62 *(978-0-7613-4705-7(4))* Lerner Publishing Group.

Cochran, Kate & Benchmark Education Co., LLC Staff. A Room for Moose. 2015. (BuildUp Ser.). (J). (gr. 1). *(978-1-4900-0739-7(3))* Benchmark Education Co.

Cochran, Kate, et al. Why Kittens Hide - Pete Mule's Hat - a Snail in May: BuildUp Unit 6 Lap Book. Piwowarski, Marcin et al, illus. 2015. (Build up Core Phonics Ser.). (J). (gr. 1). *(978-1-4900-2605-3(3))* Benchmark Education Co.

Coleccion A, Level A. (De Canciones A Cuentos Ser.). (SPA.). (gr. k-18). 444.07 *(978-1-56334-873-0(X))* CENGAGE Learning.

Coleccion B, Level B. (De Canciones A Cuentos Ser.). (SPA.). (gr. 1-18). 434.56 *(978-1-56334-991-1(4))* CENGAGE Learning.

Coleccion C, Level C. (De Canciones A Cuentos Ser.). (SPA.). (gr. 2-18). 406.81 *(978-0-7362-0440-8(7))* CENGAGE Learning.

Cole's Notes: Long Vowel o, CVCe Pattern: Level B, 6 vols. (Wright Skills Ser.). 16p. (gr. k-3). 17.95 *(978-0-322-03101-2(X))* Wright Group/McGraw-Hill.

Collins Easy Learning, Collins Easy. Phonics Quick Quizzes Ages 5-7. 2017. (Collins Easy Learning KS1 Ser.). (ENG., Illus.). 32p. (J). (gr. k-2). pap. 6.99 ***(978-0-00-821244-5(9))*** HarperCollins Pubs. Ltd. GBR. Dist: Independent Pubs. Group.

Come & Get It: Consonant l: Level A, 6 vols. (Wright Skills Ser.). 12p. (gr. k-3). 17.95 *(978-0-322-03116-6(8))* Wright Group/McGraw-Hill.

Come on, Dot: Short Vowel o: Level A, 6 vols. (Wright Skills Ser.). 12p. (gr. k-3). 17.95 *(978-0-322-03112-8(5))* Wright Group/McGraw-Hill.

Complete Phonics Readers Program. (Phonics Readers Ser.). (gr. k-2). 1322.95 *(978-0-7368-4098-9(2))* Red Brick Learning.

Complete Program, Set D. 2004. (Phonics Readers Books 37-72 Ser.). (ENG.). 8p. (gr. k-1). pap. 428.40 *(978-0-7368-4090-3(7)*, Phonics Readers) Capstone Press of Coughlan Cos.

Consonants (Gr. K-1) 2003. (J). *(978-1-58232-108-0(6))* ECS Learning Systems, Inc.

Corner Store. (J). 21.95 *(978-0-8136-4337-3(6))* Modern Curriculum Pr.

Crane, Kathy Dickerson. Phonics - The Gerbil Plays Guitar on the Girafee, Bk. 3. Klistoff, Lorin & Coan, Sharon, eds. McMahon, Kelly, illus. 2004. (Phonics (Teacher Created Resources) Ser.). (ENG.). 176p. pap. 17.99 *(978-0-7439-3017-8(7))* Teacher Created Resources, Inc.

Cuando Seamos Grandes: Little Books, Level 12, Vol. 4. 2003. (Fonolibros Ser.). 35.50 *(978-0-7652-0113-3(5))* Modern Curriculum Pr.

Cuentos de la Luna: Little Books, Level 20, Vol. 12. 2003. (Fonolibros Ser.). 34.95 *(978-0-7652-0122-5(4))* Modern Curriculum Pr.

Dan & the Fan: Consonants d, f, n, p; Short Vowel a word families: Level A, 6 vols. (Wright Skills Ser.). 12p. (gr. k-3). 17.95 *(978-0-322-01446-6(8))* Wright Group/McGraw-Hill.

D'Avanzo, Maria. Turn & Talk Vocalic R: Bk341. 2007. (J). spiral bd. 27.95 *(978-1-58650-708-4(7))* Super Duper Pubns.

Davies, Aysha & Benchmark Education Co., LLC Staff. Lunch for Patch. 2015. (BuildUp Ser.). (J). (gr. 1). *(978-1-4900-0723-6(7))* Benchmark Education Co.

de Diaz, Rosario Ahumada. Juguemos a Leer: Libro de Lectura. (SPA.). (J). 6.95 *(978-968-24-1220-2(X)*, TRM391) Trillas Editorial, S. A. MEX. Dist: Continental Bk. Co., Inc.

Delgado, Ben & Benchmark Education Co., LLC Staff. Big Bus. 2015. (BuildUp Ser.). (J). (gr. 1). *(978-1-4900-0717-5(2))* Benchmark Education Co.

Den of Thieves: Level 6, 6 vols. (Fluency Strand Ser.). (gr. 4-8). 45.00 *(978-1-4045-1238-2(1))* Wright Group/McGraw-Hill.

Un Desastre Monumental Vol. 12: Little Books, Level 4. 2003. (Fonolibros Ser.). 25.50 *(978-0-7652-0089-1(9))* Modern Curriculum Pr.

Did You Know? Big Book: Level L. Group 1. (Sunshine Ser.). 24p. 36.50 *(978-0-322-00334-7(2))* Wright Group/McGraw-Hill.

Diego, John & Benchmark Education Co., LLC Staff. Go Slow, Go Fast. 2015. (BuildUp Ser.). (J). (gr. 1). *(978-1-4900-0731-1(8))* Benchmark Education Co.

—Grace & Ace. 2015. (BuildUp Ser.). (J). (gr. 1). *(978-1-4900-0727-4(X))* Benchmark Education Co.

Diego, John, et al. Go Slow, Go Fast - Read a USA Time Line - High in the Sky: BuildUp Unit 7 Lap Book. 2015. (Build up Core Phonics Ser.). (J). (gr. 1). *(978-1-4900-2606-0(1))* Benchmark Education Co.

Discovering Phonics. 2005. (ENG., Illus.). (J). *(978-0-9774310-7-6(X))* Educational Tools, Inc.

DK Spanish Staff. DK Workbooks: Spelling, First Grade: Spelling, First Grade. 2015. (ENG.). 60p. (J). (gr. k-4). pap. 6.99 *(978-1-4654-2910-0(7)*, DK Children) Dorling Kindersley Publishing, Inc.

Donde Viven? Little Books, Level 8, Vol. 14. 2003. (Fonolibros Ser.). 25.50 *(978-0-7652-0091-4(0))* Modern Curriculum Pr.

Don't Scratch, Max! (Consonant x), Level K. 2003. ("Plaid" Phonics & Stories Libraries). (gr. k-1). 34.95 *(978-0-8136-9126-8(5))* Modern Curriculum Pr.

Dorling Kindersley Publishing Staff. DK Workbooks: Spelling, Kindergarten: Spelling, Kindergarten. 2015. (ENG.). 60p. (J). (gr. -1-1). pap. 6.99 *(978-1-4654-2915-5(8)*, DK Children) Dorling Kindersley Publishing, Inc.

—DK Workbooks: Spelling, Pre-K: Spelling, Pre-K. 2015. (ENG.). 60p. (J). (gr. -1-k). pap. 6.99 *(978-1-4654-2917-9(4)*, DK Children) Dorling Kindersley Publishing, Inc.

—DK Workbooks: Spelling, Second Grade: Spelling, Second Grade. 2015. (ENG.). 60p. (J). (gr. 1-3). pap. 6.99 *(978-1-4654-2912-4(3),* DK Children) Dorling Kindersley Publishing, Inc.

—DK Workbooks: Spelling, Third Grade: Spelling, Third Grade. 2015. (ENG.). 60p. (J). (gr. 2-4). pap. 6.99 *(978-1-4654-2913-1(1),* DK Children) Dorling Kindersley Publishing, Inc.

—10 Minutes a Day - Phonics, Grade K. 2013. (ENG., Illus.). 80p. (J). (gr. -1-1). pap. 9.99 *(978-1-4654-1713-8(3),* DK Children) Dorling Kindersley Publishing, Inc.

Douglas, Vincent & Blevins, Wiley. Money, 6, Set. 2004. (Phonics Readers Books 37-72 Ser.). (ENG.). 8p. (gr. k-1). pap. 35.70 *(978-0-7368-4052-1(4),* Phonics Readers) Capstone Press of Coughlan Cos.

Dr Awkward: Level 6, 6 vols. (Fluency Strand Ser.). (gr. 4-8). 45.00 *(978-1-4045-1239-9(X))* Wright Group/McGraw-Hill.

En Busca de Bravo: Little Books, Level 12, Vol. 27. 2003. (Fonolibros Ser.). 35.50 *(978-0-7652-0106-5(2))* Modern Curriculum Pr.

En el Bano, 6, Pack. (Chiquilibros Ser.). (SPA.). (gr. k-1). 23.00 *(978-0-7635-8616-4(1))* Rigby Education.

En el Supermercado, 6, Pack. (Chiquilibros Ser.). (SPA.). (gr. k-1). 23.00 *(978-0-7635-8617-1(X))* Rigby Education.

En la Playa, 6, Pack. (Chiquilibros Ser.). (SPA.). (gr. k-1). 23.00 *(978-0-7635-8618-8(8))* Rigby Education.

Esa Mosca! Little Books, Level 3, Vol. 15. 2003. (Fonolibros Ser.). 25.50 *(978-0-7652-0092-1(9))* Modern Curriculum Pr.

Esparza, Thomas, Jr., prod. Esther's Playhouse, Disk C. 2004. (Illus.). (J). cd-rom *(978-1-879817-44-9(6),* Children) Star Light Pr.

Evan-Moor. Basic Phonics Skills, Level A: Grades PreK-K. 2004. (ENG.). 288p. (J). pap. 29.99 *(978-1-55799-966-5(X))* Evan-Moor Educational Pubs.

—Basic Phonics Skills, Level B: Grades K-1. 2004. (ENG.). 288p. (J). pap. 29.99 *(978-1-55799-967-2(8),* EMC 3319) Evan-Moor Educational Pubs.

—Basic Phonics Skills, Level C: Grades 1-2. 2004. (ENG.). 288p. (J). pap. 29.99 *(978-1-55799-968-9(6),* EMC 3320) Evan-Moor Educational Pubs.

—Basic Phonics Skills, Level D: Grades 2-3. 2004. (ENG.). 288p. (J). pap. 29.99 *(978-1-55799-969-6(4),* EMC 3321) Evan-Moor Educational Pubs.

—Phonics Centers Level A, Grades PreK-K. 2004. (ENG., Illus.). 192p. (J). (gr. -1-k). pap. 21.99 *(978-1-55799-980-1(5),* EMC 3327) Evan-Moor Educational Pubs.

—Phonics Centers Level B, Grades K-1. 2004. (ENG., Illus.). 192p. (J). (gr. k-1). pap. 21.99 *(978-1-55799-981-8(3),* EMC 3328) Evan-Moor Educational Pubs.

—Phonics Centers, Level C, Grades 1-2. 2004. (ENG., Illus.). 192p. (J). (gr. 1-2). pap. 21.99 *(978-1-55799-982-5(1),* EMC 3329) Evan-Moor Educational Pubs.

—Phonics Centers, Level D, Grades 2-3. 2004. (ENG., Illus.). 192p. (J). (gr. 2-3). pap. 21.99 *(978-1-55799-983-2(X),* EMC 3330) Evan-Moor Educational Pubs.

The Farm: Individual Title Six-Packs. (Chiquilibros Ser.). (gr. k-1). 23.00 *(978-0-7635-0413-7(0))* Rigby Education.

The Farm: Individual Title Two-Packs. (Chiquilibros Ser.). (gr. -1-1). 12.00 *(978-0-7635-8529-7(7))* Rigby Education.

Fast Forward! 2003. (Fast Forward! Ser.). Level C. (J). (gr. 1-18). stu. ed., per. 7.95 *(978-1-58830-779-8(4))*Level D. (J). (gr. 2-18). stu. ed., per. 7.95 *(978-1-58830-780-4(8))*Level D. (J). (gr. 2-18). stu. ed., per. 67.95 *(978-1-58830-334-9(9))*Level A. tchr. ed., per., tchr.'s training gde. ed. 39.95 *(978-1-58830-783-5(2))*Level A. (J). (gr. 1-18). stu. ed., per. 7.95 *(978-1-58830-777-4(8))*Level B. tchr. ed., per., tchr.'s training gde. ed. 39.95 *(978-1-58830-784-2(0))*Level B. (J). (gr. 1-18). stu. ed., per. 7.95 *(978-1-58830-778-1(6))*Level E. (J). (gr. 1-18). stu. ed., per. 7.95 *(978-1-58830-781-1(6))*Level E. (J). (gr. 2-18). stu. ed., per. 67.95 *(978-1-58830-335-6(7))*Level F. (J). (gr. 2-18). stu. ed., per. 67.95 *(978-1-58830-336-3(5))*Level F. (J). (gr. 2-18). stu. ed., per. 7.95 *(978-1-58830-782-8(4))* Metropolitan Teaching & Learning Co.

Feldman, Jean. Dr Jean Variety Pack. 2007. (J). (gr. -1-3). pap. 56.87 incl. audio compact disk *(978-1-59198-719-2(9))* Creative Teaching Pr., Inc.

Feldman, Jean R. & Karapetkova, Holly. Deck the Room (Tune, Deck the Halls) Lap Book. 2010. (ENG., Illus.). 12p. (gr. -1-k). 9.95 *(978-1-61590-184-5(1))* Rourke Educational Media.

Fenner, M. On My Block: Learning the BL Sound. 2009. (PowerPhonics Ser.). 24p. (gr. 1-1). 39.90 *(978-1-60851-464-9(1),* PowerKids Pr.) Rosen Publishing Group, Inc., The.

Flash Kids Editors, ed. Phonics Blends: Grade 1 (Flash Skills) 2010. (Flash Skills Ser.). (ENG.). 64p. (J). pap. 3.95 *(978-1-4114-3444-8(7),* Spark Publishing Group) Sterling Publishing Co., Inc.

—Phonics Vowels: Grade 1 (Flash Skills) 2010. (Flash Skills Ser.). (ENG.). 64p. (J). pap. 3.95 *(978-1-4114-3445-5(5),* Spark Publishing Group) Sterling Publishing Co., Inc.

Flip, Flap, & Fluff: Family Blends: Level B, 6 vols. (Wright Skills Ser.). 16p. (gr. k-3). 17.95 *(978-0-322-01459-6(X))* Wright Group/McGraw-Hill.

Flynn, Cam & Benchmark Education Co., LLC Staff. Mark Sees the Stars. 2015. (BuildUp Ser.). (J). (gr. 1). *(978-1-4900-0734-2(2))* Benchmark Education Co.

—Paul Takes a Walk. 2015. (BuildUp Ser.). (J). (gr. 1). *(978-1-4900-0741-0(5))* Benchmark Education Co.

Flynn, Cam, et al. Mark Sees the Stars - a Night Hunt for Food - Red Bird Chirps: BuildUp Unit 8 Lap Book. Filipina, Monika et al, illus. 2015. (Build up Core Phonics Ser.). (J). (gr. 1). *(978-1-4900-2607-7(X))* Benchmark Education Co.

Fonolibros Series: Complete Stage One. 2003. (SPA.). 1230.95 *(978-0-7652-1052-4(5))* Modern Curriculum Pr.

Fonolibros Series: Complete Stage Two. 2003. (SPA.). 895.50 *(978-0-7652-1053-1(3))* Modern Curriculum Pr.

Fowler, Allan. Sound-a-Likes: Homonyms & Phonics, 4 bks., Set. Cafferata, Sue, illus. (J). (gr. k-4). lib. bdg. 73.80 *(978-1-56674-901-5(8))* Forest Hse. Publishing Co., Inc.

The Fox: Consonants q, x, z; -ack, -ick, -ill word families: Level A, 6 vols. (Wright Skills Ser.). 12p. (gr. k-3). 17.95 *(978-0-322-01456-5(5))* Wright Group/McGraw-Hill.

Funny Faces & Funny Places. (Little Book Practice Reader Ser.). (J). *(978-0-8136-0687-3(X))* Modern Curriculum Pr.

Gale, John E. Speedyread: A Phonics-Based Reading & Spelling Program. 2005. 353p. ring bd. 275.00 *(978-0-9777683-0-1(9))* Mirror Pond Publishing.

Gallagher, Carole M. Little ABC Phonics Workbook. 2006. 283p. (J). 14.50 *(978-0-9702197-1-8(7))* Gallagher, Carole M.

El Gato Que Rompio las Reglas: Little Books, Level 18, Vol. 7. 2003. (Fonolibros Ser.). 35.50 *(978-0-7652-0117-1(8))* Modern Curriculum Pr.

Gaydos, Nora. Clever Critters. Sullivan, Mary & Gray, Steve, illus. 2008. (NIR! Leveled Readers Ser.). (ENG.). 128p. (J). (gr. -1-3). 16.99 *(978-1-58476-666-7(2),* Now I'm Reading!) Random Hse. Children's Bks.

—Now I'm Reading! Slide, See & Say Flashcards - 50 Short Vowel Words! 2011. (ENG., Illus.). 25p. (J). (gr. -1-2). 9.99 *(978-1-60169-074-6(6))* Innovative Kids.

—Phonics Comics: Pony Tales - Level 1. Hamilton, Pamela, illus. 2007. (ENG.). 24p. (J). (gr. 1-17). per. 3.99 *(978-1-58476-553-0(4))* Innovative Kids.

Gifford, Myrna. Talking & Walking: A Read-and-Sing Book. Cooper, Frances, illus. 2005. 12p. (J). 9.95 *(978-0-9720763-9-5(5))* Action Factor, Inc.

—Two Little Letters: A Read-and-Sing Book. Cooper, Frances, illus. 2005. 12p. (J). 9.95 *(978-0-9720763-8-8(7))* Action Factor, Inc.

—What's That Sound? A Read-and-Sing Book. Cooper, Frances, illus. 2003. 12p. (J). 9.95 *(978-0-9720763-3-3(6))* Action Factor, Inc.

Gifford, Myrna Ross. Outlaws: A Read-and-Sing Book. Cooper, Frances, illus. 2005. 12p. (J). 9.95 *(978-0-9754618-1-5(8))* Action Factor, Inc.

—Silent E: A Read-and-Sing Book. Cooper, Frances, illus. 2005. 12p. (J). 9.95 *(978-0-9754618-0-8(X))* Action Factor, Inc.

Giglio, Judy. Dreaming of Great Ideas, 6 vols., Set. 2004. (Phonics Readers Books 37-72 Ser.). (ENG.). 8p. (gr. k-1). pap. 35.70 *(978-0-7368-4064-4(8),* Phonics Readers) Capstone Press of Coughlan Cos.

—Sounds & How We Hear Them, 6 vols., Set. 2004. (Phonics Readers Books 37-72 Ser.). (ENG.). 8p. (gr. k-1). pap. 35.70 *(978-0-7368-4069-9(9),* Phonics Readers) Capstone Press of Coughlan Cos.

Goldish. Lights, Camera, Action: Small Books X6 (Discovery Phonics), Level B. 2003. ("Plaid" Phonics & Stories Libraries). (gr. 2-3). 38.50 *(978-0-8136-9147-3(8))* Modern Curriculum Pr.

Gomez, Sonia & Benchmark Education Co., LLC Staff. It Can Fit! 2015. (StartUp Ser.). (J). (gr. k). *(978-1-4900-0690-1(7))* Benchmark Education Co.

Gordon, Lynn. The Big Collection of Phonics Flipbooks: 200 Reproducible Flipbooks That Target the Phonics & Word Study Skills Every Primary Student Needs to Know. 2009. (ENG.). 240p. (gr. k-3). pap. 24.99 *(978-0-545-07418-6(5),* Teaching Resources) Scholastic, Inc.

Green Collection. (Elefonetica Ser.). (SPA.). (gr. 1-2). 324.85 *(978-0-7362-0784-3(8))* CENGAGE Learning.

Green, Lila & Benchmark Education Co., LLC Staff. Mr. Dan Has a Plan. 2015. (BuildUp Ser.). (J). (gr. 1). *(978-1-4900-0713-7(X))* Benchmark Education Co.

Green, Lila, et al. Mr. Dan Has a Plan - We Can Fix It! - a Big Job: BuildUp Unit 1 Lap Book. Chambers, Nick, illus. 2015. (Build up Core Phonics Ser.). (J). (gr. 1). *(978-1-4900-2600-8(2))* Benchmark Education Co.

Grizzly & the Bumble-bee: Big Book: Level K. Group 1. (Sunshine Ser.). 16p. 36.50 *(978-0-7802-5789-4(8))* Wright Group/McGraw-Hill.

Group/McGraw-Hill, Wright. Phonics & Word Study Complete Kits: Phonics & Word Study: Level A. (gr. k-3). 339.95 *(978-0-322-03871-4(5))* Wright Group/McGraw-Hill.

—Phonics & Word Study Complete Kits: Phonics & Word Study: Level B. (gr. k-3). 429.50 *(978-0-322-03872-1(3))* Wright Group/McGraw-Hill.

—Sunshine: Early Emergent - Group 3: 1 Each of 4 Student Books: Level A. (Sunshine Ser.). 16.95 *(978-0-322-03707-6(7))* Wright Group/McGraw-Hill.

—Sunshine: Early Emergent - Group 3: 1 Each of 4 Student Books: Level C. (Sunshine Ser.). 16.95 *(978-0-322-03709-0(3))* Wright Group/McGraw-Hill.

—Sunshine: Early Emergent - Group 3:1 Each of 4 Student Books: Level B. (Sunshine Ser.). 16.95 *(978-0-322-03708-3(5))* Wright Group/McGraw-Hill.

—The Wright Skills: Level A Sets - 1 Each of 40 Titles (includes Short Vowels) (Wright Skills Ser.). (gr. k-3). *(978-0-322-03873-8(1))* Wright Group/McGraw-Hill.

—The Wright Skills: Level A Sets - 6 Each of 40 Titles (includes Short Vowels) (Wright Skills Ser.). (gr. k-3). 730.50 *(978-0-322-03874-5(X))* Wright Group/McGraw-Hill.

—The Wright Skills: Level A Sets - Short Vowels only: 1 Each of 19 Titles. (Wright Skills Ser.). (gr. k-3). 56.95 *(978-0-322-06473-7(2))* Wright Group/McGraw-Hill.

—The Wright Skills: Level A Sets - Short Vowels only: 6 Each of 19 Titles. (Wright Skills Ser.). (gr. k-3). 122.95 *(978-0-322-06474-4(0))* Wright Group/McGraw-Hill.

—The Wright Skills: Level B Sets - 1 Each of 40 Titles (includes long Vowels) (Wright Skills Ser.). (gr. k-3). 143.95 *(978-0-322-03878-3(2))* Wright Group/McGraw-Hill.

—The Wright Skills: Level B Sets - 6 Each of 40 Titles (includes long Vowels) (gr. k-3). 860.50 *(978-0-322-03880-6(4))* Wright Group/McGraw-Hill.

Guardians of the Garden: Level 3, 6 vols. (Fluency Strand Ser.). (gr. 4-8). 45.00 *(978-1-4045-1218-4(7))* Wright Group/McGraw-Hill.

Hands on Consonant Sounds (Gr. K-1) 2003. (J). *(978-1-58232-115-8(9))* ECS Learning Systems, Inc.

Hands on Sight Words (Gr. 1-2) 2003. (J). *(978-1-58232-118-9(3))* ECS Learning Systems, Inc.

Hands on Vowel Sounds (Gr. 1-2) 2003. (J). *(978-1-58232-116-5(7))* ECS Learning Systems, Inc.

Hap & the Hat: Consonant h: Level A, 6 vols. (Wright Skills Ser.). 12p. (gr. k-3). 17.95 *(978-0-322-03110-4(9))* Wright Group/McGraw-Hill.

Harcourt School Publishers Staff. Collections: Phonics Activity Book. 2003. (First-Place Reading Ser.). (Illus.). (gr. k-6). 6.90 *(978-0-15-313423-4(2))* Harcourt Schl. Pubs.

—Decodable Book, Bk. 17. 3rd ed. 2003. (Trophies Ser.). pap. 7.00 *(978-0-15-326764-2(X))* Harcourt Schl. Pubs.

HarperCollins UK. Phonics & Spelling. 2011. (Collins Practice Ser.). (ENG.). 96p. (J). pap. 11.99 *(978-0-00-745235-4(7))* HarperCollins Pubs. Ltd. GBR. Dist: Independent Pubs. Group.

Hasbrouck, Ph.D., Jan, contrib. by. Quick Phonics Assessment. 2007. spiral bd. 200.00 *(978-1-4108-6802-2(8))* Benchmark Education Co.

Hassan, Miriam & Benchmark Education Co., LLC Staff. Gabe, Kate, Dave. 2015. (StartUp Ser.). (J). (gr. k). *(978-1-4900-0708-3(3))* Benchmark Education Co.

—Go up, up, Up. 2015. (StartUp Ser.). (J). (gr. k). *(978-1-4900-0696-3(6))* Benchmark Education Co.

—Win, Win, Win! 2015. (StartUp Ser.). (J). (gr. k). *(978-1-4900-0701-4(6))* Benchmark Education Co.

Hassan, Miriam, et al. Win, Win, Win! - I Am Lin - Jim & Jan: StartUp Unit 7 Lap Book. Palacios, Sara, illus. 2015. (Start up Core Phonics Ser.). (J). (gr. k). *(978-1-4900-2596-4(0))* Benchmark Education Co.

HB Staff. Fantastic Phonics Practice!, 40 bks., Set. 97th ed. 2003. (Harcourt Title I Reading Programs Ser.). (gr. 1-18). pap. 130.20 *(978-0-15-309070-7(7))* Harcourt Schl. Pubs.

Headway Level D Real Phonics Workbook A. (J). (gr. 2). *(978-0-89688-294-2(2),* 88-294) SRA/McGraw-Hill.

Headway Level F Real Phonic Workbook. (J). (gr. 3). *(978-0-89688-295-9(0),* 88-295) SRA/McGraw-Hill.

Hidden Pictures Phonics (Gr. 1-2) 2003. (J). *(978-1-58232-064-9(0))* ECS Learning Systems, Inc.

Hiebert, Elfrieda H. & Juel, Connie. Can a Cow Hop? (Little Book Practice Reader Ser.). (J). *(978-0-8136-0796-2(5))* Modern Curriculum Pr.

—Pat's Perfect Pizza, Level 3, Bk. 14. (J). (gr. -1-3). 24.50 *(978-0-8136-1945-3(9))* Modern Curriculum Pr.

—Pop Pops the Popcorn. (J). *(978-0-8136-2008-4(2))* Modern Curriculum Pr.

Hinkler Books Staff, ed. Phonics. 2009. (ENG.). 24p. (J). 9.99 *(978-0-8249-1400-4(7),* Ideal Pubns.) Worthy Publishing.

Hirsh, Mia & Benchmark Education Co., LLC Staff. Cat in a Cap. 2015. (StartUp Ser.). (J). (gr. k). *(978-1-4900-0693-2(1))* Benchmark Education Co.

—Val Is a Vet. 2015. (StartUp Ser.). (J). (gr. k). *(978-1-4900-0706-9(7))* Benchmark Education Co.

Hogenkamp, S. My Birthday: Learning the IR Sound. 2009. (PowerPhonics Ser.). 24p. (gr. 1-1). 39.90 *(978-1-60851-460-1(9),* PowerKids Pr.) Rosen Publishing Group, Inc., The.

Hollander, Cass. Keeping Fit, 6 vols., Set. 2004. (Phonics Readers Books 37-72 Ser.). (ENG.). 8p. (gr. k-1). pap. 35.70 *(978-0-7368-4058-3(3),* Phonics Readers) Capstone Press of Coughlan Cos.

Hooked on Phonics - Get Ready to Read - Letter Names. 2005. (J). (gr. -1-18). 99.99 *(978-1-931020-46-6(9))* HOP, LLC.

Hooked on Phonics - Get Ready to Read - Letter Sounds. 2005. (J). (gr. -1-18). 99.99 *(978-1-931020-47-3(7))* HOP, LLC.

HOP, LLC. Hooked on Phonics Beginning Reading with Bible Stories. 2006. 29.99 *(978-1-931020-80-0(9))* HOP, LLC.

—Hooked on Phonics Learn to Read (Kindergarten & First Grade) 2006. 139.99 *(978-1-931020-95-4(7))* HOP, LLC.

—Hooked on Phonics Reading Comprehension. 2006. 64p. 3.79 *(978-1-933863-94-8(3))* HOP, LLC.

—Hooked on Phonics Word Games. 2006. 64p. 3.79 *(978-1-933863-93-1(5))* HOP, LLC.

HOP LLC Staff. Hooked on Phonics - Learn to Read Kindergarten. 2005. (J). (gr. k-18). 69.99 *(978-1-931020-29-9(9))* HOP, LLC.

—Hooked on Phonics - Learn to Read Second Grade. 2005. (J). (gr. 2-18). 69.99 *(978-1-931020-31-2(0))* HOP, LLC.

HOP LLC Staff, ed. Hooked on Phonics - Learn to Read First Grade. 2005. (J). (gr. 1-18). 69.99 *(978-1-931020-30-5(2))* HOP, LLC.

La Hora de Comer, 6 Packs. (Chiquilibros Ser.). (SPA.). (gr. k-1). 23.00 *(978-0-7635-8590-7(4))* Rigby Education.

Hsu, Kim & Benchmark Education Co., LLC Staff. Read a USA Time Line. 2015. (BuildUp Ser.). (J). (gr. 1). *(978-1-4900-0732-8(6))* Benchmark Education Co.

Huggles Can Jungle: Level A. Group 1. (Sunshine Ser.). 8p. 20.95 *(978-0-7802-5707-8(3))* Wright Group/McGraw-Hill.

I Can Say S. (Illus.). 160p. 19.95 *(978-0-937857-88-5(2),* 1478) Speech Bin, Inc., The.

I Can Swim. (J). 14.15 *(978-0-8136-2035-0(X))* Modern Curriculum Pr.

I'm Learning My Phonics. 2004. (Flash Card + Music CD Learning Kits Ser.). (Illus.). 20p. 18.99 *(978-1-894677-61-5(7))* Kidzup Productions.

J My Name Is Jess: Take-Home Book. 2005. (Emergent Library: Vol. 2). (YA). (gr. -1-1). 12.60 *(978-0-8215-7265-8(2))* Sadlier, William H. Inc.

Jake's Big Day: Long Vowel a, CVCe Pattern: Level B, 6 vols. (Wright Skills Ser.). 16p. (gr. k-3). 17.95 *(978-0-322-01465-7(4))* Wright Group/McGraw-Hill.

Joe's Toe: Long o Digraphs: Level B, 6 vols. (Wright Skills Ser.). 16p. (gr. k-3). 26.50 *(978-0-322-01480-0(8))* Wright Group/McGraw-Hill.

Jog to the Dam: Consonants g, h, j; Short Vowel o word families: Level A, 6 vols. (Wright Skills Ser.). 12p. (gr. k-3). 17.95 *(978-0-322-01448-0(4))* Wright Group/McGraw-Hill.

Johnson, Bruce. We Read Phonics-A Day at the Zoo. Johnson, Meredith, illus. 2012. 32p. (J). 9.95 *(978-1-60115-349-4(X));* pap. 4.99 *(978-1-60115-350-0(3))* Treasure Bay, Inc.

Johnson, Tiffany & Benchmark Education Co., LLC Staff. I. 2015. (StartUp Ser.). (J). (gr. k). *(978-1-4900-0684-0(2))* Benchmark Education Co.

—Kids Have Fun. 2015. (StartUp Ser.). (J). (gr. k). *(978-1-4900-0704-5(0))* Benchmark Education Co.

Johnson, Tiffany, et al. Kids Have Fun - Yes, Cubs! - Val Is a Vet: StartUp Unit 8 Lap Book. Leonidou, Niki, illus. 2015. (Start up Core Phonics Ser.). (J). (gr. k). *(978-1-4900-2597-1(9))* Benchmark Education Co.

Jones, Shelley V. & Gunn, Barbara. Read Well Magazine Unit 20: Slanted Text. 2003. (Read Well Level K Ser.). (Illus.). 8p. (J). *(978-1-59318-104-8(3))* Cambium Education, Inc.

—Shells on the Shore: Read Well Level K Unit 14 Storybook. Jerde, Susan, illus. 2003. (Read Well Level K Ser.). 20p. (J). *(978-1-57035-685-8(8),* 55546) Cambium Education, Inc.

Jones, Tambor & Benchmark Education Co., LLC Staff. Cole & Rose. 2015. (BuildUp Ser.). (J). (gr. 1). *(978-1-4900-0726-7(1))* Benchmark Education Co.

Jordan, Sara & Brudzynski, Jack. Funky Phonics Learn to Read. 2004. (Funky Phonics Learn to Read Ser.: 2). (ENG., Illus.). 64p. (J). 15.95 *(978-1-55386-011-2(X),* 155386011X) Jordan, Sara Publishing.

Kalar, Bonnie. At Dawn. Spreen, Kathe, illus. Date not set. 8p. (J). (gr. -1-2). pap. *(978-1-891619-24-3(1))* Corona Pr.

—At the Lake. Spreen, Kathe, illus. Date not set. 12p. (J). (gr. -1-2). pap. *(978-1-891619-34-2(9))* Corona Pr.

—At the Pond. Spreen, Kathe, illus. Date not set. 8p. (J). (gr. -1-2). pap. *(978-1-891619-07-6(1))* Corona Pr.

—At the Zoo. Spreen, Kathe, illus. Date not set. 8p. (J). (gr. -1-2). pap. *(978-1-891619-18-2(7))* Corona Pr.

—Beth & Thad. Spreen, Kathe, illus. Date not set. 12p. (J). (gr. -1-2). pap. *(978-1-891619-17-5(9))* Corona Pr.

—The Bird & the Shirt. Spreen, Kathe, illus. Date not set. 12p. (J). (gr. -1-2). pap. *(978-1-891619-30-4(6))* Corona Pr.

—Burt. Spreen, Kathe, illus. Date not set. 8p. (J). (gr. -1-2). pap. *(978-1-891619-31-1(4))* Corona Pr.

—Chuck & the Chick. Spreen, Kathe, illus. Date not set. 8p. (J). (gr. -1-2). pap. *(978-1-891619-16-8(0))* Corona Pr.

—The Clown. Spreen, Kathe, illus. Date not set. 12p. (J). (gr. -1-2). pap. *(978-1-891619-22-9(5))* Corona Pr.

—The Cook & the Crook. Spreen, Kathe, illus. Date not set. 12p. (J). (gr. -1-2). pap. *(978-1-891619-29-8(2))* Corona Pr.

—The Crows. Spreen, Kathe, illus. Date not set. 8p. (J). (gr. -1-2). pap. *(978-1-891619-28-1(4))* Corona Pr.

—A Dream. Spreen, Kathe, illus. Date not set. 12p. (J). (gr. -1-2). pap. *(978-1-891619-23-6(3))* Corona Pr.

—Early Phonetic Readers - Set A, 5 bks., Set. Spreen, Kathe, illus. Incl. Bob. pap. *(978-1-891619-01-4(2));* Cat & the Ant. pap. *(978-1-891619-02-1(0));* Gus on the Bus. pap. *(978-1-891619-03-8(9));* Hen & the Jet. pap. *(978-1-891619-05-2(5));* Tim & Kim. pap. *(978-1-891619-04-5(7));* 8p. (J). (gr. -1-2). 1998. (Illus.). 8.25 *(978-1-891619-00-7(4))* Corona Pr.

—Early Phonetic Readers - Set B, 5 bks., Set. Spreen, Kathe, illus. Incl. At the Pond. pap. *(978-1-891619-07-6(1));* Fran & the Doll. pap. *(978-1-891619-09-0(8));* Fred. pap. *(978-1-891619-10-6(1));* Stan & His Sled. pap. *(978-1-891619-08-3(X));* Trip. pap. *(978-1-891619-11-3(X));* 8p. (J). (gr. -1-2). (Illus.). 8.25 *(978-1-891619-06-9(3))* Corona Pr.

—Early Phonetic Readers - Set C, 20 bks., Set. Spreen, Kathe, illus. Incl. At Dawn. 8p. pap. *(978-1-891619-24-3(1));* At the Zoo. 8p. pap. *(978-1-891619-18-2(7));* Beth & Thad. 12p. pap. *(978-1-891619-17-5(9));* Bird & the Shirt. 12p. pap. *(978-1-891619-30-4(6));* Bright Light. 8p. 5.25 hd *(978-1-891619-32-8(2));* Burt. 8p. pap. *(978-1-891619-31-1(4));* Chuck & the Chick. 8p. pap. *(978-1-891619-16-8(0));* Clown. 12p. pap. *(978-1-891619-22-9(5));* Cook & the Crook. 12p. pap. *(978-1-891619-29-8(2));* Crows. 8p. pap. *(978-1-891619-28-1(4));* Dream. 12p. pap. *(978-1-891619-23-6(3));* Gail Sails. 12p. pap. *(978-1-891619-20-5(9));* Gay & Jay Play. 8p. pap. *(978-1-891619-19-9(5));* Jack. 12p. pap. *(978-1-891619-13-7(6));* Joan's Coat. 12p. pap. *(978-1-891619-21-2(7));* Josh & the Fish. 8p. pap. *(978-1-891619-14-4(4));* Lew & His New Cap. 8p. pap. *(978-1-891619-27-4(6));* Mark at the Farm. 12p. pap. *(978-1-891619-25-0(X));* Scouts. 8p. pap. *(978-1-891619-26-7(8));* Sheep & the Bee. 8p. pap. *(978-1-891619-15-1(2));* (J). (gr. -1-2). (Illus.). 38.50 *(978-1-891619-12-0(8))* Corona Pr.

—Early Phonetic Readers - Set D, 3 bks., Set. Spreen, Kathe, illus. Incl. At the Lake. 12p. pap. *(978-1-891619-34-2(9));* Mike. 8p. pap. *(978-1-891619-35-9(7));* Rose & the Mole. 12p. pap. *(978-1-891619-36-6(5));* (J). (gr. -1-2). (Illus.). 6.25 *(978-1-891619-33-5(0))* Corona Pr.

—Early Phonetic Readers - Set E, 7 bks., Set. Spreen, Kathe, illus. Incl. Ann Paints & Plays. pap. *(978-1-891619-40-3(3));* Clair at Home. pap. *(978-1-891619-44-1(6));* Good Day. pap. *(978-1-891619-41-0(1));* Kirk & the Deer. pap. *(978-1-891619-43-4(8));* Miss Lane's Class. pap. *(978-1-891619-38-0(1));* Neal Camps Out. pap. *(978-1-891619-39-7(X));* Trip to the Beach. pap. *(978-1-891619-42-7(X));* 12p. (J). (gr. -1-2). (Illus.). Set pap. 14.50 *(978-1-891619-37-3(3))* Corona Pr.

—Fran & the Doll. Spreen, Kathe, illus. Date not set. 8p. (J). (gr. -1-2). pap. *(978-1-891619-09-0(8))* Corona Pr.

—Fred. Spreen, Kathe, illus. Date not set. 8p. (J). (gr. -1-2). pap. *(978-1-891619-10-6(1))* Corona Pr.

—Gail Sails. Spreen, Kathe, illus. Date not set. 12p. (J). (gr. -1-2). pap. *(978-1-891619-20-5(9))* Corona Pr.

—Gay & Jay Play. Spreen, Kathe, illus. Date not set. 8p. (J). (gr. -1-2). pap. *(978-1-891619-19-9(5))* Corona Pr.

—Joan's Coat. Spreen, Kathe, illus. Date not set. 12p. (J). (gr. -1-2). pap. *(978-1-891619-21-2(7))* Corona Pr.

—Lew & His New Cap. Spreen, Kathe, illus. Date not set. 8p. (J). (gr. -1-2). pap. *(978-1-891619-27-4(6))* Corona Pr.

—Mark at the Farm. Spreen, Kathe, illus. Date not set. 12p. (J). (gr. -1-2). pap. *(978-1-891619-25-0(X))* Corona Pr.

—Mike. Spreen, Kathe, illus. Date not set. 8p. (J). (gr. -1-2). pap. *(978-1-891619-35-9(7))* Corona Pr.

—Rose & the Mole. Spreen, Kathe, illus. Date not set. 12p. (J). (gr. -1-2). pap. *(978-1-891619-36-6(5))* Corona Pr.

—The Sheep & the Bee. Spreen, Kathe, illus. Date not set. 8p. (J). (gr. -1-2). pap. *(978-1-891619-15-1(2))* Corona Pr.

—Stan & His Sled. Spreen, Kathe, illus. Date not set. 8p. (J). (gr. -1-2). pap. *(978-1-891619-08-3(X))* Corona Pr.

—The Trip. Spreen, Kathe, illus. Date not set. 8p. (J). (gr. -1-2). pap. *(978-1-891619-11-3(X))* Corona Pr.

Katschke, Judy. Phonics Comics. Baumann, Marty, illus. 2006. (ENG.). 24p. (J). (gr. 1-17). per. 3.99 *(978-1-58476-411-3(2),* IKIDS) Innovative Kids.

Kertell, Lynn Maslen. Bob Books: First Stories. Sullivan, Dana, illus. 2015. (ENG.). (J). (gr. k-2). pap. 16.99 *(978-0-545-73409-7(6))* Scholastic, Inc.

Khatri, Meeta. Can You Sound Out with Me? 2012. (ENG.). 35p. (J). pap. 14.95 *(978-1-4327-8618-2(0))* Outskirts Pr., Inc.

Kids Can Press Staff. First Phonics. 2003. (Kids Can Learn with Franklin Ser.). (ENG., Illus.). 32p. (J). (gr. k-2). 3.95

PQR

(978-1-55337-594-4(7)) Kids Can Pr., Ltd. CAN. Dist: Hachette Bk. Group.

Kindergarten Review 1.1: Take-Home Version. 2004. (Scott Foresman Reading Ser.). (gr. 1-18). stu. ed. 48.00 (978-0-328-02543-5(7)) Addison-Wesley Educational Pubs., Inc.

Kozyrev, Joann Rishel. Sound Bites: Pronunciation Activities. 2004. (ENG.). 256p. (C). pap. 40.95 (978-0-618-25972-4(4), 330538) Thomson ELT.

Kratky, Lada. A Avenues Level: Alphachant Phonics Kit. 2003. (Summer School Ser.). (ENG.). (C). (gr. -1-k). pap. 1405.95 (978-0-7362-2020-0(8)) CENGAGE Learning.

Kratky, Lada, et al. Add-on Components. 2003. (Summer School Ser.). (ENG.). (C). (gr. -1-k). pap. 18.95 (978-0-7362-2007-1(0)) CENGAGE Learning.

Kumon Editors, ed. My Book of Rhyming Words Long Vowels. 2007. (Kumon Workbooks Ser.). (ENG., Illus.). 82p. pap. 7.95 (978-1-933241-37-1(3)) Kumon Publishing North America, Inc.

LaCoste, Gary, illus. First Word Search: Phonics Word Search. 2011. (First Word Search Ser.). (ENG.). 64p. (J). (gr. -1-1). pap. 4.95 (978-1-4027-7801-8(5)) Sterling Publishing Co., Inc.

—Phonics Fun. 2011. (First Word Search Ser.). (ENG.). 64p. (J). (gr. -1-1). pap. 4.95 (978-1-4027-8391-3(4)) Sterling Publishing Co., Inc.

Ladybird. Ladybird I'm Ready for Phonics: Say the Sounds. 2016. (Ladybird I'm Ready Ser.). (ENG., Illus.). 48p. (J). (gr. -1-1). pap. 11.99 **(978-0-241-21598-2(6))** Penguin Bks., Ltd. GBR. Dist: Independent Pubs. Group.

Lane, Tracy & Benchmark Education Co., LLC Staff. A Snail in May. 2015. (BuildUp Ser.). (J). (gr. 1). (978-1-4900-0730-4(X)) Benchmark Education Co.

Lane, Tracy, et al. Shade Lake - Cole & Rose - Grace & Ace: BuildUp Unit 5 Lap Book. Chambers, Nick & Battuz, Christine, illus. 2015. (Build up Core Phonics Ser.). (J). (gr. 1). (978-1-4900-2604-6(5)) Benchmark Education Co.

LaRosa, Paula & Benchmark Education Co., LLC Staff. I Am Pat. 2015. (StartUp Ser.). (J). (gr. k). (978-1-4900-0691-8(5)) Benchmark Education Co.

—Time to Tug. 2015. (StartUp Ser.). (J). (gr. k). (978-1-4900-0710-6(5)) Benchmark Education Co.

LaRosa, Paula, et al. Time to Tug - Use a Mule - Can He See Me? StartUp Unit 10 Lap Book. 2015. (Start up Core Phonics Ser.). (J). (gr. k). (978-1-4900-2599-5(5)) Benchmark Education Co.

Las Estaciones: Individual Title Two-Packs. (Chiquilibros Ser.). (SPA.). (gr. -1-1). 12.00 (978-0-7635-8563-1(7)) Rigby Education.

Laurence, Jo. How to Be a Wizard at Phonics. 48p. (J). (gr. 1-4). pap. (978-1-875739-64-6(5)) Wizard Bks.

Leber, Nancy. Sounds All Around Us, 6 vols., Set. 2003. (Phonics Readers 1-36 Ser.). (ENG.). 8p. (gr. k-1). pap. 29.70 (978-0-7368-3217-5(3), Phonics Readers) Capstone Press of Coughlan Cos.

Lectura en Familia: Spanish Phonics Grade 1 Combo. (SPA.). (gr. 1-18). 200.04 (978-0-7362-1490-2(9)) CENGAGE Learning.

Lectura en Familia: Spanish Phonics Grade 2 Combo. (SPA.). (gr. 2-18). 114.18 (978-0-7362-1491-9(7)) CENGAGE Learning.

Lee, Etrulia R. Phonics Is My Way Series, 21 bks. Incl. Blake the Duck. 24p. (gr. -1-2). 1994. pap. (978-1-884876-09-7(9)); Dill. 20p. (gr. -1-2). 1995. pap. (978-1-884876-03-5(X)); Footprints in the Sand. 32p. (gr. k-2). 1994. pap. (978-1-884876-19-6(6)); Horse on a Porch. 36p. (gr. k-2). 1994. pap. (978-1-884876-15-8(3)); I Can Jump. 16p. (gr. -1-2). 1994. pap. (978-1-884876-01-1(3)); I Like to Dream. 32p. (gr. k-2). 1994. pap. (978-1-884876-11-0(0)); Jam, Ham & Yams. 20p. (gr. -1-2). 1994. pap. (978-1-884876-02-8(1)); Mel. 20p. (gr. -1-2). 1994. pap. (978-1-884876-07-3(2)); Mel Is Back. 32p. (gr. k-2). 1994. pap. (978-1-884876-13-4(7)); Mel's Store. 36p. (gr. k-2). 1994. pap. (978-1-884876-21-9(8)); Red Beans & Rice. 32p. (gr. k-2). 1994. pap. (978-1-884876-20-2(X)); Skates & Grapes. 24p. (gr. k-2). 1994. pap. (978-1-884876-12-7(9)); Space Trip. 24p. (gr. k-2). 1994. pap. (978-1-884876-18-9(8)); Stuff. 20p. (gr. k-2). 1994. pap. (978-1-884876-17-2(X)); Team. 24p. (gr. -1-2). 1994. pap. (978-1-884876-08-0(0)); Tiff & His Bone. 28p. (gr. -1-2). 1994. pap. (978-1-884876-04-2(8)); Train Ride. 20p. (gr. -1-2). 1994. pap. (978-1-884876-10-3(2)); Wake up Time. 20p. (gr. -1-2). 1994. pap. What Would You Say? 24p. (gr. k-2). 1994. pap. (978-1-884876-14-1(5)); Zip-a-Zap Zing. 32p. (gr. k-2). 1994. pap. (978-1-884876-16-5(1)); (Illus.). (J). 149.95 (978-1-884876-00-4(5)) Chamike Pubs.

Lee, Kim & Benchmark Education Co., LLC Staff. Pop! Pop! Pop! 2015. (StartUp Ser.). (J). (gr. k). (978-1-4900-0692-5(3)) Benchmark Education Co.

Lee, Kim, et al. Pop! Pop! Pop! - Cat in a Cap - Hot, Hot, Hot: StartUp Unit 4 Lap Book. Filipina, Monika et al, illus. 2015. (Start up Core Phonics Ser.). (J). (gr. k). (978-1-4900-2593-3(6)) Benchmark Education Co.

Lee, Quinlan B. Star Wars Phonics Boxed Set #2 (Star Wars) 2015. (Star Wars Ser.). (ENG.). (J). (gr. -1-k). pap. 12.99 (978-0-545-84045-3(7)) Scholastic, Inc.

Lee, Wan & Benchmark Education Co., LLC Staff. A Fish Wish. 2015. (BuildUp Ser.). (J). (gr. 1). (978-1-4900-0722-9(9)) Benchmark Education Co.

El Leon Ruge: Little Books, Level 12, 28. 2003. (Fonolibros Ser.). 35.50 (978-0-7652-0107-2(0)) Modern Curriculum Pr.

Let's Read — Letter Sounds. 2003. 16p. (J). 3.79 (978-1-58792-050-9(6)) Trend Enterprises, Inc.

Let's Read Big Book, 3 bks., Set, Level B. (Phonics & Friends Ser.). (gr. -1-2). 14.76 (978-0-7362-1064-5(4)) CENGAGE Learning.

Letters & Sounds, Level A. Incl. Headway Level A Thinking Book. (978-0-89688-280-5(2), 88-280); Level A. suppl. ed. (978-0-89688-774-9(X), 88-774); Level A. suppl. ed. (J). (gr. k-6). pap., stu. ed., act. bk. ed. (978-0-89688-274-4(8), 88-274) Open Court Publishing Co.

Level a Big Book Program. (Phonics & Friends Ser.). (gr. -1-2). 651.23 (978-0-7362-0355-5(9)) CENGAGE Learning.

Level E Classroom Set. (Phonics & Friends Ser.). (gr. -1-2). 682.59 (978-0-7362-0601-3(9)) CENGAGE Learning.

Level E Let's Read Little Book Set. (Phonics & Friends Ser.). (gr. -1-2). 14.76 (978-0-7362-1068-3(7)) CENGAGE Learning.

Level F Classroom Set. (Phonics & Friends Ser.). (gr. -1-2). 682.59 (978-0-7362-0644-0(2)) CENGAGE Learning.

Level F Let's Read Little Book Set. (Phonics & Friends Ser.). (gr. -1-2). 14.76 (978-0-7362-1069-0(5)) CENGAGE Learning.

Levels E-F Super Classroom Set. (Phonics & Friends Ser.). (gr. -1-2). 1204.58 (978-0-7362-0596-2(9)) CENGAGE Learning.

Lewis, Samantha & Benchmark Education Co., LLC Staff. I Am Lib. 2015. (StartUp Ser.). (J). (gr. k). (978-1-4900-0702-1(4)) Benchmark Education Co.

Ling, Lei & Benchmark Education Co., LLC Staff. A Home for Moles. 2015. (StartUp Ser.). (J). (gr. k). (978-1-4900-0709-0(1)) Benchmark Education Co.

—I See Nat. 2015. (StartUp Ser.). (J). (gr. k). (978-1-4900-0688-8(5)) Benchmark Education Co.

Lloyd, Sue. Letter Sound Strips, 30 vols. Stephen, Lib, illus. 2012. (Jolly Phonics Ser.). (ENG.). (J). (gr. k-2). 13.50 (978-1-84414-030-5(X), Jolly Phonics) Jolly Learning, Ltd. GBR. Dist: American International Distribution Corp.

Lloyd, Sue & Wernham, Sara. Stories: Join Our Adventures & Learn Your Sounds. Stephen, Lib, illus. 2008. (ENG.). 80p. (J). 29.50 (978-1-84414-081-7(4), Jolly Learning) Jolly Learning, Ltd. GBR. Dist: American International Distribution Corp.

Lluch, Alex A. Let's Leap Ahead Phonics. 2012. (ENG.). 80p. (J). (gr. -1). spiral bd. 9.95 (978-1-936061-74-7(0)) WS Publishing.

—Let's Leap Ahead: Phonics, Colors & More Play & Learn! 2013. (ENG., Illus.). 126p. (J). (gr. -1). pap. 7.95 (978-1-61351-071-1(3)) WS Publishing.

Long Vowels (Gr. 1-2) 2003. (J). (978-1-58232-111-0(6)) ECS Learning Systems, Inc.

Los animales se Acostaron: Individual Title-Six Packs. (Chiquilibros Ser.). (SPA.). (gr. k-1). 23.00 (978-0-7635-8623-2(4)) Rigby Education.

Los Tres Deseos: Little Books, Level 20, Vol. 8. 2003. (Fonolibros Ser.). 34.95 (978-0-7652-0118-8(6)) Modern Curriculum Pr.

Lucia Kemp, Henry. Now I Know My Alphabet & Phonics. 2014. (Now I Know My Ser.). (ENG.). 224p. (gr. -1-1). pap. 8.99 (978-0-545-77684-4(8), Teaching Resources) Scholastic, Inc.

MacDonald, Kimber. The Misfits, Level 3. Swain, Wilson, illus. 2006. (ENG.). 24p. (J). (gr. 1-17). per. 3.99 (978-1-58476-421-2(X), IKIDS) Innovative Kids.

Mackinnon, Mairi. Phonics Workbook 3. 2013. (Very First Reading Workbooks Ser.). 32p. (J). pap. 7.99 (978-0-7945-3191-1(1), Usborne) EDC Publishing.

—Phonics Workbook 4. 2013. (Very First Reading Workbooks Ser.). 32p. (J). pap. 7.99 (978-0-7945-3192-8(X), Usborne) EDC Publishing.

Madu, Abraham. The Road to take to School Is the Phonics Way: Companion Book for Students. 2003. 98p. pap. 11.95 (978-0-595-27748-3(9)) iUniverse, Inc.

Mairi, Mackinnon. Phonics Workbook 1. 2012. (Very First Reading Workbooks Ser.). 36p. (J). pap. 7.99 (978-0-7945-3115-7(6), Usborne) EDC Publishing.

—Phonics Workbook 2. 2012. (Very First Reading Workbooks Ser.). 36p. (J). pap. 7.99 (978-0-7945-3116-4(4), Usborne) EDC Publishing.

Major, Sarah. C Collection. 2012. pap. 112.95 incl. cd-rom (978-1-936981-39-7(4)) Child1st Pubns., LLC.

Make Believe Ideas. I Love to Learn Phonics Letter Sounds. 2013. (ENG.). 40p. (J). pap. 4.99 (978-1-78235-204-4(X)) Make Believe Ideas GBR. Dist: Nelson, Thomas Inc.

—I Love to Learn Phonics Read & Spell. 2013. (ENG.). 40p. (J). pap. 4.99 (978-1-78235-205-1(8)) Make Believe Ideas GBR. Dist: Nelson, Thomas Inc.

La Manana: Individual Title Two-Packs. (Chiquilibros Ser.). (SPA.). (gr. -1-1). 12.00 (978-0-7635-8551-8(3)) Rigby Education.

Mann, Elsa & Benchmark Education Co., LLC Staff. Hot, Hot, Hot. 2015. (StartUp Ser.). (J). (gr. k). (978-1-4900-0694-9(X)) Benchmark Education Co.

—Jim & Jan. 2015. (StartUp Ser.). (J). (gr. k). (978-1-4900-0703-8(2)) Benchmark Education Co.

Mapaches Y Mapachitos: Little Books, Level 14, Vol. 22. 2003. (Fonolibros Ser.). 34.95 (978-0-7652-0100-3(3)) Modern Curriculum Pr.

Marcel Meringue: Level 2, 6 vols. (Fluency Strand Ser.). (gr. 4-8). 45.00 (978-1-4045-1212-2(8)) Wright Group/McGraw-Hill.

Marks, Melanie. Phonics Comics: Spooky Sara - Level 3, Level 3. Ball, Victoria, illus. 2006. (ENG.). 24p. (J). (gr. 1-17). per. 3.99 (978-1-58476-473-1(2), IKIDS) Innovative Kids.

—Phonics Comics: Super Sam - Level 3: Issue 1. Collins, Daryll, illus. 2006. (ENG.). 24p. (J). (gr. 1-17). per. 3.99 (978-1-58476-420-5(1), IKIDS) Innovative Kids.

Marrow, Lesley Mandel & Vacca, Richard T. Sadlier Phonics: Level A. 2001st rev. ed. 2004. (Sadlier Phonics Reading Program). (Illus.). 344p. (gr. 1-18). pap., stu. ed. 9.00 net. (978-0-8215-7001-2(3)) Sadlier, William H. Inc.

—Sadlier Phonics: Level B Grade 2. 2004. (Phonics Pre K-C(3) & Word Study D(4)-F(6) Ser.: Vol. 4). (Illus.). 336p. (gr. 2-18). pap., tchr. ed. 64.00 net. (978-0-8215-7012-8(9)) Sadlier, William H. Inc.

—Sadlier Phonics: Level C Grade 3. 2001st ed. 2004. (Sadlier Phonics Reading Program). (Illus.). 336p. (gr. 3-18). pap., tchr. ed. 64.00 net. (978-0-8215-7013-5(7)) Sadlier, William H. Inc.

—Sadlier Phonics: Level K. 2004. (Sadlier Phonics (Pre K-Level C) Ser.). (Illus.). 232p. (gr. k-18). pap., stu. ed. 9.00 net. (978-0-8215-7000-5(5)) Sadlier, William H. Inc.

—Sadlier Phonics/Reading: Level B. 2004. (Phonics Pre K-C(3) & Word Study D(4)-F(6) Ser.: Vol. 4). (Illus.). 240p. (gr. 2-18). pap., stu. ed. 9.00 net. (978-0-8215-7002-9(1)) Sadlier, William H. Inc.

—Sadlier Phonics/Reading: Level C. 2001st rev. ed. 2004. (Sadlier Phonics Reading Program). (Illus.). 224p. (gr. 3-18). pap., stu. ed. 9.00 net. (978-0-8215-7003-6(X)) Sadlier, William H. Inc.

Martinez, Jerry. A Walk in the Park. 2011. 32p. pap. 21.99 (978-1-4568-5229-0(9)) Xlibris Corp.

Martyn, Marilyn. Phonics for Kids. 2012. 180p. pap. 24.19 (978-1-4691-3259-4(1)) Xlibris Corp.

Max Is Sick: Consonants q, x, z; -ack, -ick, -ill word families: Level A, 6 vols. (Wright Skills Ser.). 12p. (gr. k-3). 17.95 (978-0-322-01457-2(3)) Wright Group/McGraw-Hill.

McAdams Moore, Carol. Phonics Comics: Cave Dave - Level 1. Dammer, Mike, illus. 2007. (ENG.). 24p. (J). (gr. 1-17). per. 3.99 (978-1-58476-552-3(6)) Innovative Kids.

McConnell, S. Let's Bring Mom Breakfast: Learning the BR Sound. 2009. (PowerPhonics Ser.). 24p. (gr. 1-1). 39.90 (978-1-60851-455-7(2), PowerKids Pr.) Rosen Publishing Group, Inc., The.

McConochie, Jennifer. Shape & Say. 2009. 172p. pap. 29.99 (978-1-4269-1401-0(6)) Trafford Publishing.

McCutcheon, Randall, et al. Glencoe Speech. 3rd ed. 2004. (Ntc: Speech Comm Matters Ser.). (ENG., Illus.). 605p. (gr. 9-12). stu. ed. 104.56 (978-0-07-861618-1(2), 0078616182) McGraw-Hill Higher Education.

McGraw-Hill Staff. Listen!Listen!Letter Sounds in Rhymes Complt Set. (gr. k-1). 210.95 (978-0-322-02636-0(9)) Wright Group/McGraw-Hill.

McKay, Sindy. We Read Phonics-I Want to Be a Cowboy! Raglin, Tim, illus. 2012. 32p. (J). 9.95 (978-1-60115-351-7(1)); pap. 4.99 (978-1-60115-352-4(X)) Treasure Bay, Inc.

MCP Phonics & Stories Library, 20 bks. 2003. (J). Level C. instr.'s training gde. ed. 52.95 (978-0-7652-0542-1(4))Level A. instr.'s training gde. ed. 52.95 (978-0-7652-0532-2(7))Level B. instr.'s training gde. ed. 52.95 (978-0-7652-0537-7(8)) Modern Curriculum Pr.

MCP Staff. Baby Bear's Ride, Level A, Bk. 1. (J). (gr. -1-3). 24.50 (978-0-8136-1931-6(9)) Modern Curriculum Pr.

—By the Tree, Level 4, Bk. 22. (J). (gr. -1-3). 24.50 (978-0-8136-0693-4(4)) Modern Curriculum Pr.

—Can a Cow Hop?, Level 4, Bk. 27. (J). (gr. -1-3). 24.50 (978-0-8136-0795-5(7)) Modern Curriculum Pr.

—The Cat Came Back (Consonant c), Level 2, Bk. 19. 2003. ("Plaid" Phonics & Stories Libraries). (gr. -1-3). 24.50 (978-0-8136-5418-8(1)) Modern Curriculum Pr.

—Cat Chat, 6 bks., set, Level 10, Bk. 35. 2003. (J). (gr. -1-3). 24.50 (978-0-8136-2067-1(8)) Modern Curriculum Pr.

—Dive In!, 6 bks., set, Level 10, Bk. 44. 2003. (J). (gr. -1-3). 33.50 (978-0-8136-2083-1(X)) Modern Curriculum Pr.

—Dragon's Lunch, 6 bks., set, Level 10, Bk. 39. 2003. (J). (gr. -1-3). 33.50 (978-0-8136-2073-2(2)) Modern Curriculum Pr.

—Fast As a Fox, Level 4, Bk. 29. (J). (gr. -1-3). 24.50 (978-0-8136-1961-3(0)) Modern Curriculum Pr.

—Good Girl! (Consonant g), Level K. 2003. ("Plaid" Phonics & Stories Libraries). (gr. -1-3). 24.50 (978-0-8136-5416-4(5)) Modern Curriculum Pr.

—How to Make a Hen House (Consonant h), Level K. 2003. ("Plaid" Phonics & Stories Libraries). (gr. -1-3). 24.50 (978-0-8136-5425-6(4)) Modern Curriculum Pr.

—Jan Can Juggle (Consonant j), Level K. 2003. ("Plaid" Phonics & Stories Libraries). (gr. -1-3). 24.50 (978-0-8136-5427-0(0)) Modern Curriculum Pr.

—Keys (Consonant k), Level K. 2003. ("Plaid" Phonics & Stories Libraries). (gr. -1-3). 24.50 (978-0-8136-5434-8(3)) Modern Curriculum Pr.

—Let's Move!, Level 2, Bk. 18. (J). (gr. -1-3). 24.50 (978-0-8136-0684-2(5)) Modern Curriculum Pr.

—Look Closer (Consonant l), Level K. 2003. ("Plaid" Phonics & Stories Libraries). (gr. -1-3). 24.50 (978-0-8136-5429-4(7)) Modern Curriculum Pr.

—A Mess, Level 4, Bk. 3. (J). (gr. -1-3). 21.95 (978-0-8136-1935-4(1)) Modern Curriculum Pr.

—My Cat, Level 4, Bk. 13. 2003. (J). (gr. -1-3). 24.50 (978-0-8136-0679-8(9)) Modern Curriculum Pr.

—My Monster & Me, Level 2, Bk. 6. (J). (gr. -1-3). 24.50 (978-0-8136-0675-0(6)) Modern Curriculum Pr.

—One Bee Got on the Bus, Level 3, Bk. 9. (J). (gr. -1-3). 21.95 (978-0-8136-0739-9(6)) Modern Curriculum Pr.

—The Party, Level 4, Bk. 4. (J). (gr. -1-3). 24.50 (978-0-8136-1937-8(8)) Modern Curriculum Pr.

—Shell Shopping, 6 bks., set, Level A. 2003. (J). (gr. -1-3). 33.50 (978-0-8136-0797-9(3)) Modern Curriculum Pr.

—Six Go By, Level A. 2003. (J). (gr. -1-3). 21.95 (978-0-8136-0672-9(1)) Modern Curriculum Pr.

—Socks: Consonant N, Level K. 2003. ("Plaid" Phonics & Stories Libraries). (gr. -1-3). 24.50 (978-0-8136-5411-9(4)) Modern Curriculum Pr.

—Ted's Red Sled, Level 4, Bk. 40. (J). (gr. -1-3). 24.50 (978-0-8136-1969-9(6)) Modern Curriculum Pr.

—Too High!, Level 4, Bk. 37. 2003. (J). (gr. -1-3). 24.50 (978-0-8136-0774-0(4)) Modern Curriculum Pr.

—Two Turtles (Consonant t), Level 1, Bk. 15. 2003. ("Plaid" Phonics & Stories Libraries). (gr. -1-3). 24.50 (978-0-8136-5414-0(9)) Modern Curriculum Pr.

—Very Big, Level 4, Bk. 45. 2003. (J). (gr. -1-3). 24.50 (978-0-8136-1447-2(3)) Modern Curriculum Pr.

—Vulture on Vacation, Level 3, Bk. 5. (J). (gr. -1-3). 24.50 (978-0-8136-1939-2(4)) Modern Curriculum Pr.

—Whale Watch (Consonant w), Level K. 2003. ("Plaid" Phonics & Stories Libraries). (gr. -1-3). 24.50 (978-0-8136-5493-5(9)) Modern Curriculum Pr.

—What Rhymes with Cat?, Level A, Bk. 2. (J). (978-0-8136-1933-0(5)) Modern Curriculum Pr.

—Where Do They Live?, Level 3, Bk. 17. (J). (gr. -1-3). 24.50 (978-0-8136-1949-1(1)) Modern Curriculum Pr.

—Yes I Can! Consonants j, f, g, l, d, Level 4, Bk. 26. 2003. (J). (gr. -1-3). 24.50 (978-0-8136-0766-5(3)) Modern Curriculum Pr.

—Zebra's Yellow Van (Consonant v), Level K. 2003. ("Plaid" Phonics & Stories Libraries). (gr. -1-3). 24.50 (978-0-8136-5439-3(4)) Modern Curriculum Pr.

Medias, 6 vols., Pack. (Chiquilibros Ser.). (SPA.). (gr. k-1). 23.00 (978-0-7635-8595-2(5)) Rigby Education.

Meow-Meow Gets Out: Diphthongs ou, ow: Level B, 6 vols. (Wright Skills Ser.). 16p. (gr. k-3). 26.50 (978-0-322-01484-8(0)) Wright Group/McGraw-Hill.

Metz, L. On the Job: Learning the O Sound. 2009. (PowerPhonics Ser.). 24p. (gr. 1-1). 39.90 (978-1-60851-466-3(8), PowerKids Pr.) Rosen Publishing Group, Inc., The.

Mi Casa: Individual Title Six-Packs. (Literatura 2000 Ser.). (SPA.). (gr. 1-2). 28.00 (978-0-7635-1071-8(8)) Rigby Education.

Mischel, Jenny Ann. Animal Alphabet. Bell-Myers, Darcy, illus. 2006. (J). bds. (978-0-9769239-0-9(4)) Perfect 4 Preschool.

Modern Staff. Day at Our Dairy Farm. (J). (gr. k-1). 38.95 (978-0-8136-1358-1(2)) Modern Curriculum Pr.

Monaghan, Jennifer. The Illustrated Phonics Booklet. 2012. (ENG.). (J). pap. (978-1-4675-2946-4(X)) Independent Pub.

Un Monstruo Debajo de la Cama: Little Books, Level 28. 2003. (Fonolibros Ser.: Vol. 9). 39.50 (978-0-7652-0119-5(4)) Modern Curriculum Pr.

Moore, M. Meet My Mom: Learning the M Sound. 2009. (PowerPhonics Ser.). 24p. (gr. 1-1). 39.90 (978-1-60851-459-5(5), PowerKids Pr.) Rosen Publishing Group, Inc., The.

Moreau, Maryellen Rooney & Welch, Brian Scott. Talk to Write, Write to Learn Manual: A Teachers' Manual for Differentiated Instruction & Tiered Intervention. 2007. pap. 65.00 (978-0-9761393-9-3(1)) Mindwing Concepts, Inc.

Mortimer, Susan. Alphabet Island Phonics 2B. 2004. (J). pap. 7.99 (978-1-931292-06-1(X)) Eagle's Wings Educational Materials.

Moskal, G. Family Fun: Learning the F Sound. 2009. (PowerPhonics Ser.). 24p. (gr. 1-1). 39.90 (978-1-60851-441-0(2), PowerKids Pr.) Rosen Publishing Group, Inc., The.

—I Like Winter: Learning the ER Sound. 2009. (PowerPhonics Ser.). 24p. (gr. 1-1). 39.90 (978-1-60851-451-9(X), PowerKids Pr.) Rosen Publishing Group, Inc., The.

Mr Hoot's Room: Variant Vowel Review: Level C, 6 vols. (Wright Skills Ser.). 16p. (gr. k-3). 26.50 (978-0-322-01504-3(9)) Wright Group/McGraw-Hill.

Mrs Patches & Her Fudge: Silent Consonants: Level C, 6 vols. (Wright Skills Ser.). 16p. (gr. k-3). 26.50 (978-0-322-01503-6(0)) Wright Group/McGraw-Hill.

Mrs. Sheep's Garden (18), Vol. 18. (Early Intervention Levels Ser.). 5.31 (978-0-7362-0607-5(8)) CENGAGE Learning.

My First Sight Words (Gr. K-1) 2003. (J). (978-1-58232-090-8(X)) ECS Learning Systems, Inc.

Nickelodeon Staff, ed. Phonics - Spongebob Squarepants. 2010. (Write, Slide & Learn Ser.). 14p. (J). (gr. -1-1). 9.99 (978-1-74184-520-4(3), Ideal Pubns.) Worthy Publishing.

Night Mare Trip: Level 5, 6 vols. (Fluency Strand Ser.). (gr. 4-8). 45.00 (978-1-4045-1230-6(6)) Wright Group/McGraw-Hill.

No Sweat! Short e Digraph: Level B, 6 vols. (Wright Skills Ser.). 16p. (gr. k-3). 26.50 (978-0-322-01477-0(8)) Wright Group/McGraw-Hill.

Novelli, Joan. Phonics: 30 Instant Centers with Reproducible Templates & Activities That Help Kids Practice Important Literacy Skills-Independently! 2006. (Shoe Box Learning Centers Ser.). (ENG.). 80p. (J). pap. 12.99 (978-0-439-53796-4(7), Teaching Resources) Scholastic, Inc.

Nutria, Nutria: Student Book. 2003. 33.95 (978-0-8136-8075-0(1)) Modern Curriculum Pr.

Ocho Amigos en Total: Little Books, Level 4, Vol. 2525. 2003. (Fonolibros Ser.). 25.50 (978-0-7652-0104-1(6)) Modern Curriculum Pr.

Ochoa, Louisa & Benchmark Education Co., LLC Staff. Know about Storms. 2015. (BuildUp Ser.). (J). (gr. 1). (978-1-4900-0740-3(7)) Benchmark Education Co.

Ochoa, Louisa, et al. Know about Storms - Paul Takes a Walk - City Lights: BuildUp Unit 10 Lap Book. Jennings, Sarah, illus. 2015. (Build up Core Phonics Ser.). (J). (gr. 1). (978-1-4900-2609-1(6)) Benchmark Education Co.

Olo: Level 6, 6 vols. (Fluency Strand Ser.). (gr. 4-8). 45.00 (978-1-4045-1237-5(3)) Wright Group/McGraw-Hill.

Once, Twice, Boom: Level 7, 6 vols. (Fluency Strand Ser.). (gr. 4-8). 45.00 (978-1-4045-1240-5(3)) Wright Group/McGraw-Hill.

Orange Collection. (Elefonetica Ser.). (SPA.). (gr. 1-2). 296.76 (978-0-7362-0790-4(2)) CENGAGE Learning.

Orphan Train: Medial Digraphs: Level C, 6 vols. (Wright Skills Ser.). 16p. (gr. k-3). 26.50 (978-0-322-01498-5(0)) Wright Group/McGraw-Hill.

Orshoski, Paul. We Read Phonics-Who Took the Cookbook? Light, Kelly, illus. 2012. 32p. (J). 9.95 (978-1-60115-347-0(3)); pap. 4.99 (978-1-60115-348-7(1)) Treasure Bay, Inc.

Out of the Computer: Level 6, 6 vols. (Fluency Strand Ser.). (gr. 4-8). 45.00 (978-1-4045-1235-1(7)) Wright Group/McGraw-Hill.

Out of the Sunless Land: Level T. Group 2, 6 vols. (Sunshine Ser.). 48p. 44.95 (978-0-7802-4186-2(X)) Wright Group/McGraw-Hill.

Padilla, Mara & Benchmark Education Co., LLC Staff. High in the Sky. 2015. (BuildUp Ser.). (J). (gr. 1). (978-1-4900-0733-5(4)) Benchmark Education Co.

—A Sled Club. 2015. (BuildUp Ser.). (J). (gr. 1). (978-1-4900-0718-2(0)) Benchmark Education Co.

La Paleteria: Individual Title Two-Packs. (Chiquilibros Ser.). (SPA.). (gr. -1-1). 12.00 (978-0-7635-8554-9(8)) Rigby Education.

Papil: Level T. Group 1, 6 vols. (Sunshine Ser.). 48p. 44.95 (978-0-7802-5600-2(X)) Wright Group/McGraw-Hill.

Parker, Helen. Wipe Clean Phonics. 2007. (Wipe Clean Ser.). (Illus.). 12p. (J). bds. (978-1-84610-583-8(8)) Make Believe Ideas.

El Pastel de Javier: Little Books, Level 16, Vol. 3. 2003. (Fonolibros Ser.). 25.50 (978-0-7652-0112-6(7)) Modern Curriculum Pr.

El Pato Atascado: Little Books, Level 10, Vol. 20. 2003. (Fonolibros Ser.). 25.50 (978-0-7652-0098-3(8)) Modern Curriculum Pr.

Paws, Jaws, & Claws: Variant Vowels al, au, aw: Level B, 6 vols. (Wright Skills Ser.). 16p. (gr. k-3). 26.50 (978-0-322-01482-4(4)) Wright Group/McGraw-Hill.

Phonemic Awareness, Level 1. 2003. (Illus.). (J). spiral bd. (978-1-58605-822-7(3), LeapFrog Schl. Hse.) LeapFrog Enterprises, Inc.

Phonemic Awareness Pack. (Phonemic Awareness Pack Ser.). (gr. -1-k). 523.57 incl. audio compact disk (978-0-7362-0899-4(2)) CENGAGE Learning.

Phonemic Awareness Pack with Tapes. (Phonemic Awareness Pack Ser.). (gr. -1-k). 538.88 (978-0-7362-0900-7(X)) CENGAGE Learning.

Phonics. 2004. (Scott Foresman Reading Ser.). (gr. k-18). suppl. ed., wbk. ed. 1.95 (978-0-328-02433-9(3)); (gr. k-6).

tchr. ed., wbk. ed. 48.00 *(978-0-673-61433-9(6))*; (gr. k-6). wbk. ed. 5.25 *(978-0-673-61428-5(X))*; (gr. 1-18). suppl. ed., wbk. ed. 48.00 *(978-0-673-61430-8(1))*; (gr. 2-18). suppl. ed., wbk. ed. 48.00 *(978-0-673-61431-5(X))*; (gr. 3-18). tchr. ed., wbk. ed. 48.00 *(978-0-673-61432-2(8))* Addison-Wesley Educational Pubs., Inc.

Phonics. 2004. (Help with Homework Ser.). 32p. (J). (gr. k-2). wbk. ed. 3.99 *(978-1-904586-15-9(5))* Byeway Bks.

Phonics 3-4. 2003. (Gold Stars Workbook Ser.). (Illus.). 32p. (J). 2.98 *(978-1-4054-1192-9(9))* Parragon, Inc.

Phonics 4-5. 2003. (Illus.). 32p. (J). 2.98 *(978-1-4054-1193-6(7))* Parragon, Inc.

Phonics 5-6. 2003. (Gold Stars Workbook Ser.). (Illus.). 32p. (J). 2.98 *(978-1-4054-1194-3(5))* Parragon, Inc.

Phonics 6-7. 2003. (Gold Stars Workbook Ser.). (Illus.). 32p. (J). 2.98 *(978-1-4054-1195-0(3))* Parragon, Inc.

Phonics & Word Study Complete Kits: Phonics & Word Study: Level C. (gr. k-3). 333.95 *(978-0-322-01644-6(4))* Wright Group/McGraw-Hill.

Phonics & Word Study Core Kits: Phonics & Word Study: Level A. (gr. k-3). 153.50 *(978-0-322-01641-5(X))* Wright Group/McGraw-Hill.

Phonics & Word Study Core Kits: Phonics & Word Study: Level B. (gr. k-3). 185.50 *(978-0-322-01643-9(6))* Wright Group/McGraw-Hill.

Phonics & Word Study Core Kits: Phonics & Word Study: Level C. (gr. k-3). 153.50 *(978-0-322-01645-3(2))* Wright Group/McGraw-Hill.

Phonics Decodable Reader 1. 2004. (Scott Foresman Reading Ser.). (gr. 1-18). suppl. ed. 3.35 *(978-0-673-65172-3(X))* Addison-Wesley Educational Pubs., Inc.

Phonics Decodable Reader 2. 2004. (Scott Foresman Reading Ser.). (gr. 1-18). suppl. ed. 3.35 *(978-0-673-65173-0(8))* Addison-Wesley Educational Pubs., Inc.

Phonics Decodable Reader 3. 2004. (Scott Foresman Reading Ser.). (gr. 1-18). suppl. ed. 3.35 *(978-0-673-65174-7(6))* Addison-Wesley Educational Pubs., Inc.

Phonics Decodable Reader 33-41. 2004. (Scott Foresman Reading Ser.). (gr. 1-18). suppl. ed. 7.75 *(978-0-673-65180-8(0))* Addison-Wesley Educational Pubs., Inc.

Phonics Decodable Reader 42-50. 2004. (Scott Foresman Reading Ser.). (gr. 1-18). suppl. ed. 7.75 *(978-0-673-65181-5(9))* Addison-Wesley Educational Pubs., Inc.

Phonics Decodable Reader 5. 2004. (Scott Foresman Reading Ser.). (gr. 1-18). suppl. ed. 3.35 *(978-0-673-65176-1(2))* Addison-Wesley Educational Pubs., Inc.

Phonics Plus Staff. Phonics Plus. 2nd ed. Bk. D. (J). 9.55 *(978-0-8136-0394-0(3))*Bk. E. tchr. ed. 9.55 *(978-0-8136-0395-7(1))*Bk. F. (J). 9.55 *(978-0-8136-0396-4(X))* Modern Curriculum Pr.

Phonics Practice Book. (De Canciones A Cuentos Ser.). (SPA.). (gr. 1-18). 9.13 *(978-1-56334-895-2(0))* CENGAGE Learning.

Phonics Puzzles (Gr. 1) 2003. (J). *(978-1-58232-047-2(0))* ECS Learning Systems, Inc.

Phonics Readers. (Phonics Readers 1-36 Ser.). (ENG.). 8p. (gr. k-1). Bks. 1-36, Set C. 2003. pap. 356.40 *(978-0-7368-3225-0(4))*Set E. 2004. pap. 428.40 *(978-0-7368-4092-7(3))*Set F. 2004. pap. 428.40 *(978-0-7368-4094-1(X))* Capstone Press of Coughlan Cos. (Phonics Readers).

Phonics Readers Big Books. 2005. (J). pap. 95.00 *(978-1-58970-687-3(0))* Lakeshore Learning Materials.

Phonics Readers Bks. 1-36, Set: A Complete Program. 2003. (Phonics Readers 1-36 Ser.). (ENG.). 8p. (gr. k-1). pap. 387.35 *(978-0-7368-3221-2(1)*, Phonics Readers) Capstone Press of Coughlan Cos.

Phonics Readers Bookshelf Collection, 36 bks., Set. 2004. (gr. 1-18). 594.00 *(978-0-328-00401-0(4))*; (gr. 2-18). 495.00 *(978-0-328-00402-7(2))*; (gr. 3-18). 495.00 *(978-0-328-00403-4(0))* Addison-Wesley Educational Pubs., Inc.

Phonics Readers Student Books. 2005. (J). pap. 29.95 *(978-1-58970-685-9(4))* Lakeshore Learning Materials.

Phonics Songs & Rhymes Flip Chart. 2004. (gr. 1-18). suppl. ed. 109.15 *(978-0-673-59716-8(4))* Addison-Wesley Educational Pubs., Inc.

Phonics Take-Home Readers. 2004. (Scott Foresman Reading Ser.). (gr. 3-18). 48.00 *(978-0-673-61260-1(0))* Addison-Wesley Educational Pubs., Inc.

Pigs & Dogs Play Ball: Consonants b, w; Short Vowel i word families: Level A, 6 vols. (Wright Skills Ser.). 12p. (gr. k-3). 17.95 *(978-0-322-01450-3(6))* Wright Group/McGraw-Hill.

The Pink Tent: Final Blends -nd, -nk, -nt: Level B, 6 vols. (Wright Skills Ser.). 16p. (gr. k-3). 17.95 *(978-0-322-01462-6(X))* Wright Group/McGraw-Hill.

La Pizzeria, 2 Packs. (Chiquilibros Ser.). (SPA.). (gr. -1-1). 12.00 *(978-0-7635-8555-6(6))* Rigby Education.

Places to Visit, Places to See: Take-Home Book. 2005. (Lee Bennett Hopkins Worlds of Poetry Classroom Library). (YA). (gr. k-3). 13.50 *(978-0-8215-0568-7(8))* Sadlier, William H. Inc.

Powell, Marie. Dan Can! Cartwright, Amy, illus. 2016. (Word Families Ser.). (ENG.). 16p. (J). (gr. k-3). 17.95 *(978-1-60753-924-7(1))* Amicus Publishing.

—Go to Bed, Ted! Cartwright, Amy, illus. 2016. (Word Families Ser.). (ENG.). 16p. (gr. k-3). 17.95 *(978-1-60753-927-8(6))* Amicus Publishing.

—The Map Trap. Cartwright, Amy, illus. 2016. (Word Families Ser.). (ENG.). 16p. (J). (gr. k-3). 17.95 *(978-1-60753-928-5(4))* Amicus Publishing.

—Stop, Pop! Cartwright, Amy, illus. 2016. (Word Families Ser.). (ENG.). 16p. (gr. k-3). 17.95 *(978-1-60753-925-4(X))* Amicus Publishing.

—What Good Is an A? 2015. (Vowels Ser.). (ENG., Illus.). 16p. (J). (gr. k-2). 17.95 *(978-1-60753-708-3(7))* Amicus Publishing.

—When, Jen? Cartwright, Amy, illus. 2016. (Word Families Ser.). (ENG.). 16p. (J). (gr. k-3). 17.95 *(978-1-60753-926-1(8))* Amicus Publishing.

—Win, Min! By Marie Powell: Illustrated by Amy Cartwright. Cartwright, Amy, illus. 2016. (Word Families Ser.). (ENG.). 16p. (J). (gr. k-3). 17.95 *(978-1-60753-929-2(2))* Amicus Publishing.

Publications International Ltd. Staff, ed. Kindergarten Boot Camp. 2010. (J). 20.98 *(978-1-4508-0069-3(6))* Publications International, Ltd.

—My First Phonics Dictionary. 2011. (Illus.). 96p. (J). 8.98 *(978-1-4508-1480-5(8))* Phoenix International Publications, Inc.

Puedes Subir: Little Books, Level 3, 8. 2003. (Fonolibros Ser.). 25.50 *(978-0-7652-0085-3(6))* Modern Curriculum Pr.

Puedo Salir? Student Book. 2003. 35.50 *(978-0-8136-8099-6(9))* Modern Curriculum Pr.

Pulse Fun with Phonics. 2006. cd-rom 4.99 *(978-1-60245-039-4(0))* GDL Multimedia, LLC.

Quake: Level 4, 6 vols. (Fluency Strand Ser.). (gr. 4-8). 45.00 *(978-1-4045-1226-9(8))* Wright Group/McGraw-Hill.

Que Es Eso? Little Books, Level 3, Vol. 26. 2003. (Fonolibros Ser.). 25.50 *(978-0-7652-0105-8(4))* Modern Curriculum Pr.

Que Es Una Linea? Little Books, Level 6, 3. 2003. 25.50 *(978-0-7652-0079-2(1))* Modern Curriculum Pr.

Que Gato! Little Books, Level 16, Vol. 5. 2003. (Fonolibros Ser.). 35.50 *(978-0-7652-0114-0(3))* Modern Curriculum Pr.

Que quiere Beto? Individual Title-Six Packs. (Chiquilibros Ser.). (SPA.). (gr. k-1). 23.00 *(978-0-7635-8610-2(2))* Rigby Education.

Que Soy? Little Books, Level 4, 9. 2003. (Fonolibros Ser.). 25.50 *(978-0-7652-0086-0(4))* Modern Curriculum Pr.

Queen Jelly Bean: Vowel Digraph Review: Level C, 6 vols. (Wright Skills Ser.). 16p. (gr. k-3). 26.50 *(978-0-322-01499-2(9))* Wright Group/McGraw-Hill.

Queen on a Quilt (Consonant q), Level K. 2003. ("Plaid" Phonics & Stories Libraries). (gr. -1-3). 24.50 *(978-0-8136-5437-9(8))* Modern Curriculum Pr.

Quit It! Consonant q: Level A, 6 vols. (Wright Skills Ser.). 12p. (gr. k-3). 17.95 *(978-0-322-03122-7(2))* Wright Group/McGraw-Hill.

Rasinski, Timothy V. 100 Reproducible Word Study Lessons That Help Kids Boost Reading, Vocabulary, Spelling & Phonics Skills - Independently! 2005. (Daily Word Ladders Ser.). (ENG., Illus.). 112p. (gr. 4-6). pap. 15.99 *(978-0-439-77345-4(8)*, Teaching Resources) Scholastic, Inc.

Read & Spell with Zoo-phonics. 2004. (J). cd-rom 29.95 *(978-1-886441-46-0(4))* Zoo-phonics, Inc.

Read & Spell with Zoo=Phonics Guide for CD-ROM. 2004. (J). 14.95 *(978-1-886441-45-3(6))* Zoo-phonics, Inc.

Reading at Home: Phonics Grade 1 Combo. (gr. 1-18). 517.92 *(978-0-7362-1401-8(1))* CENGAGE Learning.

Reading at Home: Phonics Grade 2 Combo. (gr. 2-18). 368.64 *(978-0-7362-1402-5(X))* CENGAGE Learning.

Reading Rods Phonemic Awareness Activity Book. 2003. (J). pap. 4.95 *(978-1-56911-117-8(0))* Learning Resources, Inc.

Reading Rods Phonemic Awareness Activity Cards, Set 2. 2003. (J). 19.95 *(978-1-56911-113-0(8))* Learning Resources, Inc.

Reading Rods Readers: Phonics Foundation 1 Classpack. 2003. (J). per. 249.95 *(978-1-56911-575-6(3))* Learning Resources, Inc.

Reading Rods Readers: Phonics Foundation 2 Classpack. 2003. (J). per. 249.95 *(978-1-56911-576-3(1))* Learning Resources, Inc.

Reading Rods Readers: Phonics Foundation Set 1. 2003. (J). pap. 44.95 *(978-1-56911-121-5(9))* Learning Resources, Inc.

Reading Rods Readers: Phonics Foundation Set 2. 2003. (J). pap. 44.95 *(978-1-56911-122-2(7))* Learning Resources, Inc.

Ready Reader Staff. At the Track, 6 bks., set, Level 8, Bk. 29. 2003. (J). (gr. -1-3). pap. 30.95 *(978-0-8136-2063-3(5))* Modern Curriculum Pr.

—Little Frog's Monster Story, 6 bks., set, Level 6, Bk. 12. 2003. (J). (gr. -1-3). pap. 33.50 *(978-0-8136-0806-8(6))* Modern Curriculum Pr.

—Something to Munch, 6 bks., set, Level 8, Bk. 38. 2003. (J). (gr. -1-3). pap. 33.50 *(978-0-8136-2071-8(6))* Modern Curriculum Pr.

Rhodes, Immacula A. Write-N-Seek: Phonics: Motivating Practice Pages to Help Kids Master Phonics Skills. 2017. (Write-N-Seek: Ser.). (ENG.). 64p. (gr. -1-2). pap. 10.99 ***(978-1-338-18021-3(5))*** Scholastic, Inc.

El Rio Crece: Little Books, Level 16. 2003. (Fonolibros Ser.). 35.50 *(978-0-7652-0110-2(0))* Modern Curriculum Pr.

Ristuccia, Christine & Ristuccia, James. The Entire World of S & Z Instructional Workbook: A Comprehensive Approach to Remediate Frontal & Lateral Lisps. I.t. ed. 2003. (Illus.). 208p. (J). per. 34.99 *(978-0-9723457-4-3(4))* Say It Right.

Robinson, Lisa & Benchmark Education Co., LLC Staff. Can He See Me? 2015. (StartUp Ser.). (J). (gr. k). *(978-1-4900-0712-0(1))* Benchmark Education Co.

—I Zip to My Job. 2015. (StartUp Ser.). (J). (gr. k). *(978-1-4900-0707-6(5))* Benchmark Education Co.

Robinson, Lisa, et al. Mr. Max - Gabe, Kate, & Dave - a Home for Moles: StartUp Unit 9 Lap Book. Czernichowska, Joanna, illus. 2015. (Start up Core Phonics Ser.). (J). (gr. k). *(978-1-4900-2598-8(7))* Benchmark Education Co.

Rogers, Jane & Benchmark Education Co., LLC Staff. Get Well, Red Hen! 2015. (BuildUp Ser.). (J). (gr. 1). *(978-1-4900-0716-8(4))* Benchmark Education Co.

Rogers, Jane, et al. Get Well, Red Hen! - Big Bus - a Sled Club: BuildUp Unit 2 Lap Book. Anderson, Nicola & Greenhead, Bill, illus. 2015. (Build up Core Phonics Ser.). (J). (gr. 1). *(978-1-4900-2601-5(0))* Benchmark Education Co.

Roman, Douglas T. How to Learn Phonics: Students' Workbook with More Than 3,000 Words to Make Good Readers. 2013. 160p. pap. 54.35 *(978-1-4669-8556-8(9))* Trafford Publishing.

Rooney Moreau, Maryellen & Welch, Brian Scott. Talk to Write, Write to Learn Kit. 2007. pap. 199.95 *(978-0-9769527-5-6(0))* Mindwing Concepts, Inc.

Rosario, Sherwin, illus. Meet the Vowels. 2005. 12p. (J). bds. 7.99 *(978-0-9767008-2-1(4))* Preschool Prep Co.

Rose, Emma. Energy Every Day, 6 vols., Set. 2004. (Phonics Readers Books 37-72 Ser.). (ENG.). 8p. (gr. k-1). pap. 35.70 *(978-0-7368-4086-6(9)*, Phonics Readers) Capstone Press of Coughlan Cos.

Rosen, Rachel, et al. Sit, Sit, Sit - I Can Fit! - I Am Pat: StartUp Unit 3 Lap Book. 2015. (Start up Core Phonics Ser.). (J). (gr. k). *(978-1-4900-2592-6(8))* Benchmark Education Co.

Russo, Gina & Benchmark Education Co., LLC Staff. A Big Job. 2015. (BuildUp Ser.). (J). (gr. 1). *(978-1-4900-0715-1(6))* Benchmark Education Co.

A Saludar Y A Celebrar: Little Books, Level 4, Vol. 23. 2003. (Fonolibros Ser.). (SPA.). 25.50 *(978-0-7652-0101-0(1))* Modern Curriculum Pr.

Sandviks HOP, Inc. Staff. Discover Reading: Baby Edition. 2007. 39.99 *(978-1-60143-760-0(9))* HOP, LLC.

—Discover Reading Toddler Edition. 2007. 39.99 *(978-1-60143-765-5(X))* HOP, LLC.

—Hooked on English. 2007. 199.99 *(978-1-60143-752-5(8))* HOP, LLC.

—Hooked on First Grade. 2007. 39.99 *(978-1-60143-750-1(1))* HOP, LLC.

Sandviks HOP, Inc. Staff, contrib. by. Hooked on Second Grade Super Workbook. 2007. 320p. (J). pap. 12.99 *(978-1-60143-468-5(5))* HOP, LLC.

Santillo, LuAnn. Fun with Phonemes. Santillo, LuAnn, ed. 2004. (Half-Pint Readers Ser.). (Illus.). 36p. (J). (gr. -1-1). pap. 11.95 *(978-1-59256-129-2(2))* Half-Pint Kids, Inc.

—Lots More Fun with Phonemes. Santillo, LuAnn, ed. 2004. (Half-Pint Readers Ser.). (Illus.). 36p. (J). (gr. -1-1). pap. 11.95 *(978-1-59256-131-5(4))* Half-Pint Kids, Inc.

—More Fun with Phonemes. Santillo, LuAnn, ed. 2004. (Half-Pint Readers Ser.). (Illus.). 36p. (J). (gr. -1-1). pap. 11.95 *(978-1-59256-130-8(6))* Half-Pint Kids, Inc.

Santos, D. Friends: Learning the FR Sound. 2009. (PowerPhonics Ser.). 24p. (gr. 1-1). 39.90 *(978-1-60851-442-7(0)*, PowerKids Pr.) Rosen Publishing Group, Inc., The.

—I Can Draw: Learning the DR Sound. 2009. (PowerPhonics Ser.). 24p. (gr. 1-1). 39.90 *(978-1-60851-446-5(3)*, PowerKids Pr.) Rosen Publishing Group, Inc., The.

—My New Glasses: Learning the GL Sound. 2009. (PowerPhonics Ser.). 24p. (gr. 1-1). 39.90 *(978-1-60851-461-8(7)*, PowerKids Pr.) Rosen Publishing Group, Inc., The.

Sarkisian, K. You Need Your Nose: Learning the N Sound. 2009. (PowerPhonics Ser.). 24p. (gr. 1-1). 39.90 *(978-1-60851-482-3(X)*, PowerKids Pr.) Rosen Publishing Group, Inc., The.

Saxton, Brenda, illus. Reading Pals: Alphabet Recognition Gr. Pre K-K. 2007. (J). per. 6.99 *(978-1-59198-435-1(1))* Creative Teaching Pr., Inc.

Scat! Said the Cat: Big Book: Level D. Group 1. (Sunshine Ser.). 8p. 20.95 *(978-0-7802-5734-4(0))* Wright Group/McGraw-Hill.

Schmauss, Judy Kentor, et al. Reader's Clubhouse Long Vowels Level 2 Valu-Pak, 6 vols. 2006. (Reader's Clubhouse Ser.). (ENG., Illus.). 120p. (J). (gr. -1-1). pap. 15.96 *(978-0-7641-7969-3(1))* Barron's Educational Series, Inc.

schneider, Sandra. Secrets of the Symbols: Advanced Phonics Book including 54 skill Cards. Hoppe, Gail, ed. schneider, Sandra, illus. 2008. (Illus.). 76p. (J). 18.00 *(978-0-9761987-5-8(4))* Magic Penny Reading.

Scholastic, Inc. Staff, contrib. by. Turn-to-Learn Wheels in Color - Phonics: 25 Ready-to-Go Manipulative Wheels That Help Children Practice & Master Key Phonics Skills to Become Successful Readers. 2010. (ENG.). 112p. (gr. k-2). 20.99 *(978-0-545-22400-0(4)*, Teaching Resources) Scholastic, Inc.

Scholastic, Inc. Staff & Chapman, Cindy. Baby Animals, 6 vols., Set. 2003. (Phonics Readers 1-36 Ser.). (ENG.). 8p. (gr. k-1). pap. 29.70 *(978-0-7368-3188-8(6)*, Phonics Readers) Capstone Press of Coughlan Cos.

School Zone Interactive Staff. Phonics Review. rev. ed. 2003. (On-Track Software Ser.). (ENG.). 64p. (J). (gr. 1-2). 15.99 *(978-1-58947-844-2(4))* School Zone Publishing Co.

School Zone Publishing. Phonics. 2003. (ENG.). (J). (gr. 2-3). cd-rom 19.99 *(978-1-58947-935-7(1))* School Zone Publishing Co.

School Zone Publishing Company Staff. Los Sonidos para Empezar Beginning Sounds. 2007. (ENG.). 64p. (J). pap. 2.69 *(978-1-58947-974-6(2))* School Zone Publishing Co.

—Phonics Review. (Illus.). (J). 19.99 incl. audio compact disk *(978-0-88743-967-4(5))* School Zone Publishing Co.

Scott Foresman Reading: Phonics. 2004. (gr. 1-18). *(978-0-328-07405-1(5))*; *(978-0-328-05637-8(5))*; *(978-0-328-07389-4(X))*; *(978-0-328-05636-1(7))*; *(978-0-328-05638-5(3))*; *(978-0-328-05645-3(6))*; *(978-0-328-05643-9(X))*; *(978-0-328-05642-2(1))*; *(978-0-328-05641-5(3))*; *(978-0-328-05640-8(5))*; *(978-0-328-05639-2(1))* Addison-Wesley Educational Pubs., Inc. (Scott Foresman).

Set B Complete Program. 2003. (Phonics Readers 1-36 Ser.). (ENG.). 8p. (gr. k-1). pap. 356.40 *(978-0-7368-3223-6(8)*, Phonics Readers) Capstone Press of Coughlan Cos.

Shaskan, Trisha Speed. If You Were Alliteration. Gray, Sara, illus. 2008. (Word Fun Ser.). (ENG.). 24p. (gr. 2-4). lib. bdg. 27.99 *(978-1-4048-4097-3(4))* Picture Window Bks.

Sheffield, S. A Train on the Track: Learning the TR Sound. 2009. (PowerPhonics Ser.). 24p. (gr. 1-1). 39.90 *(978-1-60851-430-4(7)*, PowerKids Pr.) Rosen Publishing Group, Inc., The.

Shelly's Shell: Digraph sh: Level B, 6 vols. (Wright Skills Ser.). 16p. (gr. k-3). 17.95 *(978-0-322-01471-8(9))* Wright Group/McGraw-Hill.

Shems, Ed, illus. First Word Search: Phonics, Phonics, Phonics! 2011. (First Word Search Ser.). (ENG.). 64p. (J). (gr. -1-1). pap. 4.95 *(978-1-4027-7805-6(8))* Sterling Publishing Co., Inc.

Shiotsu, Vicky. Build-a-Skill Instant Books Beginning & Ending Consonant Sounds. Faulkner, Stacey, ed. Campbell, Jenny & Tom, Darcy, illus. 2007. (J). 4.99 *(978-1-59198-416-0(5))* Creative Teaching Pr., Inc.

Shopping: Big Book: Level A. (Sunshine Ser.). 8p. 20.95 *(978-0-7802-5710-8(3))* Wright Group/McGraw-Hill.

Short & Long Vowels (Gr. 1-2) 2003. (J). *(978-1-58232-038-0(1))* ECS Learning Systems, Inc.

Short, Deborah J., et al. Avenues Level B. 2003. (Avenues Ser.). (ENG.). (C). (gr. 1-18). pap. 2485.95 *(978-0-7362-2542-7(0))* CENGAGE Learning.

—Avenues Level C. 2003. (Avenues Ser.). (ENG.). (C). (gr. 2-18). pap. 2171.95 *(978-0-7362-2543-4(9))* CENGAGE Learning.

—Avenues PreK Level. 2004. (Avenues Ser.). (ENG.). (C). pap. 1919.95 *(978-0-7362-2540-3(4))* CENGAGE Learning.

—Read-Alone Phonics Stories. 2003. (Avenues Ser.). (ENG.). (C). (gr. 1-2). pap. 18.95 *(978-0-7362-1656-2(1))* CENGAGE Learning.

Short Vowels (Gr. 1-2) 2003. (J). *(978-1-58232-110-3(8))* ECS Learning Systems, Inc.

Sicinski-Skeans, Sharon & Baron, Lindamichelle. The Write Direction: Hardcover Student Book. 2003. (Illus.). (J). (gr. 4). stu. ed. 18.95 *(978-0-7652-0751-7(6))*; (gr. 5). stu. ed. 18.95 *(978-0-7652-0752-4(4))* Modern Curriculum Pr.

The Silly Supper: Medial Consonants: Level C, 6 vols. (Wright Skills Ser.). 16p. (gr. k-3). 26.50 *(978-0-322-01491-6(3))* Wright Group/McGraw-Hill.

Singer, Beth & Benchmark Education Co., LLC Staff. We Can Fix It! 2015. (BuildUp Ser.). (J). (gr. 1). *(978-1-4900-0714-4(8))* Benchmark Education Co.

SIPPS Beginning Hand-held Sound Cards. 2004. *(978-1-57621-455-8(9))* Center for the Collaborative Classroom.

SIPPS Beginning Package of Little Books. 2004. *(978-1-57621-458-9(3))* Center for the Collaborative Classroom.

SIPPS Beginning Reproducible Book. 2004. *(978-1-57621-459-6(1))* Center for the Collaborative Classroom.

SIPPS Beginning Sound Wall Cards. 2004. *(978-1-57621-454-1(0))* Center for the Collaborative Classroom.

SIPPS Extension Sound Wall Cards. 2004. *(978-1-57621-461-9(3))* Center for the Collaborative Classroom.

Sloppy Tiger Bedtime: Big Book: Level M. Group 1. (Sunshine Ser.). 24p. 36.50 *(978-0-7802-5791-7(X))* Wright Group/McGraw-Hill.

Smith, K. Be Safe on the Bus: Learning the B Sound. 2009. (PowerPhonics Ser.). 24p. (gr. 1-1). 39.90 *(978-1-60851-434-2(X)*, PowerKids Pr.) Rosen Publishing Group, Inc., The.

Snake at the Lake: Long Vowel Review: Level C, 6 vols. (Wright Skills Ser.). 16p. (gr. k-3). 26.50 *(978-0-322-01496-1(4))* Wright Group/McGraw-Hill.

Somerville, Louisa. Phonics, Ages 6-7. Tulip, Jenny, illus. 2016. (ENG.). 32p. (J). (gr. -1-12). pap. 6.99 *(978-1-86147-684-5(1)*, Armadillo) Anness Publishing GBR. Dist: National Bk. Network.

Something Is Strange about Paula's New Friends: Variant Vowels au, aw, oo; s-Blends; Digraphs sh, ck, Level B. 2003. ("Plaid" Phonics & Stories Libraries). (gr. 2-3). 38.50 *(978-0-8136-9148-0(6))* Modern Curriculum Pr.

Soto, Luisa & Benchmark Education Co., LLC Staff. Bob, Tab, & I. 2015. (StartUp Ser.). (J). (gr. k). *(978-1-4900-0695-6(8))* Benchmark Education Co.

—Yes, Cubs! 2015. (StartUp Ser.). (J). (gr. k). *(978-1-4900-0705-2(9))* Benchmark Education Co.

Soto, Luisa, et al. Bob, Tab, & I - Go up, up, up - Rob, Ron, & I: StartUp Unit 5 Lap Book. Leone, Fabio & Lopez, Michelle, illus. 2015. (Start up Core Phonics Ser.). (J). (gr. k). *(978-1-4900-2594-0(4))* Benchmark Education Co.

Sounding Out the Alphabet. 2004. (J). cd-rom, audio compact disk 9.95 *(978-1-930006-62-1(4)*, Reading Co., The) Rhoades & Assocs.

Sounds & Lettersb Set: Level A. (Sing-along Songs Ser.). (gr. -1-2). audio compact disk 66.18 *(978-0-7362-0419-4(9))* CENGAGE Learning.

Splink & Splank: 3-letter blends str, scr, spr, spl: Level B, 6 vols. (Wright Skills Ser.). 16p. (gr. k-3). 17.95 *(978-0-322-01464-0(6))* Wright Group/McGraw-Hill.

Sprick, Marilyn, et al. Read Well Magazine Unit 13: Plain Text. 2004. (Read Well Level K Ser.). (Illus.). 8p. (J). *(978-1-57035-743-5(9))* Cambium Education, Inc.

—Read Well Magazine Unit 13: Slanted Text. 2004. (Read Well Level K Ser.). (Illus.). 8p. (J). *(978-1-57035-769-5(2))* Cambium Education, Inc.

—Read Well Magazine Unit 14: Slanted Text. 2004. (Read Well Level K Ser.). (Illus.). 8p. (J). *(978-1-57035-698-8(X))* Cambium Education, Inc.

—Read Well Magazine Unit 16: Plain Text. 2004. (Read Well Level K Ser.). (Illus.). 8p. (J). *(978-1-57035-746-6(3))* Cambium Education, Inc.

—Read Well Magazine Unit 17: Plain Text. 2003. (Read Well Level K Ser.). (Illus.). 8p. (J). *(978-1-57035-747-3(1))* Cambium Education, Inc.

—Read Well Magazine Unit 18: Plain Text. 2004. (Read Well Level K Ser.). (Illus.). 8p. (J). *(978-1-57035-748-0(X))* Cambium Education, Inc.

—Read Well Magazine Unit 18: Slanted Text. 2003. (Read Well Level K Ser.). (Illus.). 8p. (J). *(978-1-59318-102-4(7))* Cambium Education, Inc.

—Read Well Magazine Unit 19: Plain Text. 2003. (Read Well Level K Ser.). (Illus.). 8p. (J). *(978-1-57035-749-7(8))* Cambium Education, Inc.

—Read Well Magazine Unit 19: Slanted Text. 2003. (Read Well Level K Ser.). (Illus.). 8p. (J). *(978-1-59318-103-1(5))* Cambium Education, Inc.

—Read Well Magazine Unit 2: Plain Text. 2003. (Read Well Level K Ser.). (Illus.). 8p. (J). *(978-1-57035-733-6(1))* Cambium Education, Inc.

—Read Well Magazine Unit 2: Slanted Text. 2003. (Read Well Level K Ser.). (Illus.). 8p. (J). *(978-1-57035-783-1(8))* Cambium Education, Inc.

—Read Well Magazine Unit 20: Plain Text. 2003. (Read Well Level K Ser.). (Illus.). 8p. (J). *(978-1-57035-775-6(7))* Cambium Education, Inc.

—Read Well Magazine Unit 3: Plain Text. 2003. (Read Well Level K Ser.). (Illus.). 8p. (J). *(978-1-57035-734-3(X))* Cambium Education, Inc.

—Read Well Magazine Unit 3: Slanted Text. 2003. (Read Well Level K Ser.). (Illus.). 8p. (J). *(978-1-57035-784-8(6))* Cambium Education, Inc.

—Read Well Magazine Unit 4: Plain Text. 2003. (Read Well Level K Ser.). (Illus.). 8p. (J). *(978-1-57035-732-9(3))* Cambium Education, Inc.

P
Q
R

—Read Well Magazine Unit 4: Slanted Text. 2003. (Read Well Level K Ser.). (Illus.). 8p. (J). *(978-1-57035-785-5(4))* Cambium Education, Inc.
—Read Well Magazine Unit 5: Plain Text. 2003. (Read Well Level K Ser.). (Illus.). 8p. (J). *(978-1-57035-736-7(6))* Cambium Education, Inc.
—Read Well Magazine Unit 5: Slanted Text. 2004. (Read Well Level K Ser.). (Illus.). 6p. (J). *(978-1-57035-786-2(2))* Cambium Education, Inc.
—Read Well Magazine Unit 6: Plain Text. 2003. (Read Well Level K Ser.). (Illus.). 8p. (J). *(978-1-57035-737-4(4))* Cambium Education, Inc.
—Read Well Magazine Unit 6: Slanted Text. 2003. (Read Well Level K Ser.). (Illus.). 8p. (J). *(978-1-57035-787-9(0))* Cambium Education, Inc.
—Read Well Magazine Unit 7: Plain Text. 2003. (Read Well Level K Ser.). (Illus.). 8p. (J). *(978-1-57035-738-1(2))* Cambium Education, Inc.
—Read Well Magazine Unit 8: Plain Text. 2003. (Read Well Level K Ser.). (Illus.). 8p. (J). *(978-1-57035-726-8(9))* Cambium Education, Inc.
—Read Well Magazine Unit 8: Slanted Text. 2003. (Read Well Level K Ser.). (Illus.). 8p. (J). *(978-1-57035-789-3(7))* Cambium Education, Inc.
—Read Well Magazine Unit 9: Plain Text. 2003. (Read Well Level K Ser.). (Illus.). 8p. (J). *(978-1-57035-739-8(0))* Cambium Education, Inc.
—Read Well Magazine Unit 9: Slanted Text. 2003. (Read Well Level K Ser.). (Illus.). 8p. (J). *(978-1-57035-790-9(0))* Cambium Education, Inc.
—Rescue Workers: Read Well Level K Unit 11 Storybook. Zilis, Tom, illus. 2003. (Read Well Level K Ser.). 20p. (J). *(978-1-57035-682-7(3), 55511)* Cambium Education, Inc.
—Spiders: Read Well Level K Unit 1 Storybook. Shupe, Bobbi & Crum, Anna-Maria, illus. 2003. (Read Well Level K Ser.). 20p. (J). *(978-1-57035-673-5(4))* Cambium Education, Inc.
—Spiders: Unit 1 Read Well Level K Teacher's Storybook. Shupe, Bobbi & Crum, Anna-Maria, illus. 2003. (Read Well Level K Ser.). 20p. (J). *(978-1-57035-696-4(3))* Cambium Education, Inc.
—Student Workbook 1 (Plain Text) Units 1-9 Plus Review Unit. 2003. (Read Well Level K Ser.). (Illus.). 104p. (J). *(978-1-59318-166-6(3))* Cambium Education, Inc.
—Student Workbook 1 (Slant Text) Units 1-9 Plus Review Unit. 2003. (Read Well Level K Ser.). (Illus.). 104p. (J). *(978-1-59318-169-7(8))* Cambium Education, Inc.
—Student Workbook 2 (Plain Text) Units 10-18 Plus Review Unit. 2003. (Read Well Level K Ser.). (Illus.). 104p. (J). *(978-1-59318-167-3(1))* Cambium Education, Inc.
—Student Workbook 2 (Slant Text) Units 10-18 Plus Review Unit. 2003. (Read Well Level K Ser.). (Illus.). 104p. (J). *(978-1-59318-170-3(1))* Cambium Education, Inc.
Starfall Education. The Big Hit. Starfall Education, ed. 2004. (ENG., Illus.). 8p. (J). pap. *(978-1-59577-003-5(8))* Starfall Education.
—Zac the Rat. Starfall Education, ed. 2004. (ENG., Illus.). 8p. (J). pap. *(978-1-59577-001-1(1))* Starfall Education.
Steck-Vaughn Staff. Core Skills - At Home with Phonics. 2003. (At Home with Phonics Ser.). (ENG.). 144p. (gr. k-k). pap. 14.99 *(978-0-7398-7955-9(3))*; (gr. 1-1). pap. 14.99 *(978-0-7398-7956-6(1))*; (gr. 2-2). pap. 14.99 *(978-0-7398-7957-3(X))* Houghton Mifflin Harcourt Publishing Co.
—Core Skills, Grade 3: At Home with Phonics. 2003. (At Home with Phonics Ser.). (ENG.). 144p. (gr. 3-3). pap. 14.99 *(978-0-7398-7958-0(8))* Houghton Mifflin Harcourt Publishing Co.
—Phonics: Sounds, Words, & Meanings. 2004. (Phonics+ Ser.). (ENG., Illus.). 160p. (gr. 1-1). pap. 14.99 *(978-0-7398-8861-2(7))* Houghton Mifflin Harcourt Publishing Co.
—Phonics Decoding Skills Handbook. 2004. (Phonics+ Handbook Ser.). (ENG., Illus.). 160p. (gr. 3-6). pap. 14.99 *(978-0-7398-8863-6(3))* Houghton Mifflin Harcourt Publishing Co.
—Phonics+Sounds, Words, & Meanings. 2004. (Phonics+ Ser.). (ENG., Illus.). 160p. (gr. k-k). pap. 14.99 *(978-0-7398-8860-5(9))* Houghton Mifflin Harcourt Publishing Co.
Sterling-Orth, Angela. Sound Reading: Literature Lists for Phonology & Articulation. 2005. (Illus.). (J). pap. 10.95 *(978-1-932054-28-6(6))* Super Duper Pubns.
A Stormy Story: R-Controlled o: Level B, 6 vols. (Wright Skills Ser.). 16p. (gr. k-3). 26.50 *(978-0-322-01487-9(5))* Wright Group/McGraw-Hill.
The Story of Cat & Rat: Benchmark Assessment Book for Level B: Level B, 6 vols. (Wright Skills Ser.). 16p. (gr. k-3). 26.50 *(978-0-322-03099-2(4))* Wright Group/McGraw-Hill.
Story Time Staff. Vowel Sounds: Rapping, Word Mapping & Rhyming. Doyle, Alfreda C., ed. 2005. (Illus.). 20p. (gr. 4-8). wbk. ed., tchr.'s training gde. ed. 25.95 *(978-1-56820-128-3(1))* Story Time Stories That Rhyme.
Strange Days: Level 7, 6 vols. (Fluency Strand Ser.). (gr. 4-8). 45.00 *(978-1-4045-1241-2(1))* Wright Group/McGraw-Hill.
Stribling, Anne & Benchmark Education Co., LLC Staff. Get up, Meg! 2015. (StartUp Ser.). (J). (gr. k). *(978-1-4900-0699-4(0))* Benchmark Education Co.
Student Pack. (Cuentacuentos Ser.). (SPA.). (gr. k-18). 83.31 *(978-1-56334-798-6(9))* CENGAGE Learning.
Sunshine: Early Emergent - 1 Each of 4 Big Books: Level A-D. (Sunshine Ser.). 82.95 *(978-0-7802-6772-5(9))* Wright Group/McGraw-Hill.
Sunshine: Early Emergent - Group 1: 1 Each of 8 Student Books: Level A. (Sunshine Ser.). 33.50 *(978-0-7802-7118-0(1))* Wright Group/McGraw-Hill.
Sunshine: Early Emergent - Group 1:1 Each of 8 Student Books: Level C. (Sunshine Ser.). 33.50 *(978-0-7802-7122-7(X))* Wright Group/McGraw-Hill.
Sunshine: Early Emergent - Group 2: 1 Each of 8 Student Books: Level A. (Sunshine Ser.). 33.50 *(978-0-7802-7119-7(X))* Wright Group/McGraw-Hill.
Sunshine: Early Emergent - Group 2:1 Each of 8 Student Books: Level B. (Sunshine Ser.). 33.50 *(978-0-7802-7121-0(1))* Wright Group/McGraw-Hill.
Sunshine: Early Emergent - Group 2:1 Each of 8 Student Books: Level C. (Sunshine Ser.). 33.50 *(978-0-7802-7123-4(8))* Wright Group/McGraw-Hill.
Sunshine: Early Emergent - Nonfiction 1: 1 Each of 4 Student Books: Level A. (Sunshine Ser.). 16.95 *(978-0-7802-3763-6(3))* Wright Group/McGraw-Hill.
Sunshine: Early Emergent - Nonfiction:1 Each of 4 Student Books: Level A. 16.95 *(978-0-7802-3772-8(2))* Wright Group/McGraw-Hill.
Sunshine: Early Emergent: 1 Each of 8 Student Books: Level B. (Sunshine Ser.). 24.95 *(978-0-7802-7120-3(3))* Wright Group/McGraw-Hill.
Super Classroom Set. (Elefonetica Ser.). (SPA.). (gr. 1-2). 939.56 *(978-0-7362-0782-9(1))* CENGAGE Learning.
Tanner, S. Clouds: Learning the CL Sound. 2009. (PowerPhonics Ser.). 24p. (gr. 1-1). 39.90 *(978-1-60851-439-7(0),* PowerKids Pr.) Rosen Publishing Group, Inc., The.
Tat Is Sad: Consonant d: Level A, 6 vols. (Wright Skills Ser.). 12p. (gr. k-3). 17.95 *(978-0-322-03105-0(2))* Wright Group/McGraw-Hill.
Teaching Resources Staff. Phonics Tales! Interactive E-Storybooks: 25 e-Books with Engaging Interactive Whiteboard Activities That Teach Key Phonics Skills. 2013. (ENG., Illus.). 136p. (gr. k-2). 129.99 *(978-0-545-54447-4(5),* Teaching Resources) Scholastic, Inc.
Terror Bear Canyon: Level 5, 6 vols. (Fluency Strand Ser.). (gr. 4-8). 45.00 *(978-1-4045-1225-2(X))* Wright Group/McGraw-Hill.
TestSMART Plus Phonics, Short Vowels Level K-1. 2004. (J). *(978-1-57022-502-4(8))* ECS Learning Systems, Inc.
Thomas, M. Summer at the Beach: Learning the EA Sound. 2009. (PowerPhonics Ser.). 24p. (gr. 1-1). 39.90 *(978-1-60851-472-4(2),* PowerKids Pr.) Rosen Publishing Group, Inc., The.
Thompson, Kim & Carder, Ken. Phonics. Billman, Dave et al, illus. 2009. 96p. (J). (gr. -1-3). pap. 10.99 incl. audio compact disk *(978-1-57583-820-5(6))* Twin Sisters IP, LLC.
Thrills at the Fair: 3-letter blends: Level C, 6 vols. (Wright Skills Ser.). 16p. (gr. k-3). 26.50 *(978-0-322-01494-7(8))* Wright Group/McGraw-Hill.
Thud! Thump! Thud! Digraph th: Level B, 6 vols. (Wright Skills Ser.). 16p. (gr. k-3). 17.95 *(978-0-322-01473-2(5))* Wright Group/McGraw-Hill.
La Tienda: Individual Title Two-Packs. (Chiquilibros Ser.). (SPA.). (gr. -1-1). 12.00 *(978-0-7635-8559-4(9))* Rigby Education.
Time for Lunch (Consonant f), Level K. 2003. ("Plaid" Phonics & Stories Libraries). (gr. -1-3). 24.50 *(978-0-8136-5420-1(3))* Modern Curriculum Pr.
Time Warp: Level T. Group 1, 6 vols. (Sunshine Ser.). 48p. 44.95 *(978-0-7802-5602-6(6))* Wright Group/McGraw-Hill.
To Catch a Thief: Level 3, 6 vols. (Fluency Strand Ser.). (gr. 4-8). 45.00 *(978-1-4045-1219-1(5))* Wright Group/McGraw-Hill.
To the Moon & Beyond: Level T. Group 3, 6 vols. (Sunshine Ser.). 48p. 44.95 *(978-0-322-01835-8(8))* Wright Group/McGraw-Hill.
Together, 6 vols. (Sunshinetm Ser.). 16p. (gr. k-18). 29.50 *(978-0-7802-5426-8(0))* Wright Group/McGraw-Hill.
Tomato: Level 4, 6 vols. (Fluency Strand Ser.). (gr. 4-8). 45.00 *(978-1-4045-1223-8(3))* Wright Group/McGraw-Hill.
Too Many Graphs: Digraph ph: Level B, 6 vols. (Wright Skills Ser.). 16p. (gr. k-3). 17.95 *(978-0-322-01475-6(1))* Wright Group/McGraw-Hill.
Trevia, Rick & Benchmark Education Co., LLC Staff. City Lights. 2015. (BuildUp Ser.). (J). (gr. 1). *(978-1-4900-0742-7(3))* Benchmark Education Co.
Unccor: Level 5, 6 vols. (Fluency Strand Ser.). (gr. 4-8). 45.00 *(978-1-4045-1231-3(4))* Wright Group/McGraw-Hill.
Up in a Tree: Level D. Group 1. (Sunshine Ser.). 8p. 20.95 *(978-0-7802-5736-8(7))* Wright Group/McGraw-Hill.
Upper Emergent Skills Guide. (Sunshine Skills Guides). 25.95 *(978-0-7802-9810-1(1))* Wright Group/McGraw-Hill.
Uss, John & Benchmark Education Co., LLC Staff. Dan & Ed. 2015. (StartUp Ser.). (J). (gr. k). *(978-1-4900-0700-7(8))* Benchmark Education Co.
A Van in the Mud: Consonant v: Level A, 6 vols. (Wright Skills Ser.). 12p. (gr. k-3). 17.95 *(978-0-322-03118-0(4))* Wright Group/McGraw-Hill.
VanLeeuwen. Phonics Connection Grade 3. 2003. (Phonics Connection Ser.). 160p. (gr. 3-18). 8.95 *(978-1-932210-25-5(3))* Rainbow Bridge Publishing.
Variant Sounds, Diphthongs, Suffixes & Prefixes Big Book & CD Set: Level F. (Sing-along Songs Ser.). (gr. -1-2). 48.46 incl. audio compact disk *(978-0-7362-0678-5(7))* CENGAGE Learning.
Vastola, P. Rain: Learning the AI Sound. 2009. (PowerPhonics Ser.). 24p. (gr. 1-1). 39.90 *(978-1-60851-469-4(2),* PowerKids Pr.) Rosen Publishing Group, Inc., The.
—What I Think: Learning the TH Sound. 2009. (PowerPhonics Ser.). 24p. (gr. 1-1). 39.90 *(978-1-60851-479-3(X),* PowerKids Pr.) Rosen Publishing Group, Inc., The.
Un Verano en el Lago Zafiro: Little Books, Level 24, Vol. 10. 2003. (Fonolibros Ser.). 34.95 *(978-0-7652-0120-1(8))* Modern Curriculum Pr.
Verdadero O Falso? Little Books, Level 16, Vol. 11. 2003. (Fonolibros Ser.). 34.95 *(978-0-7652-0121-8(6))* Modern Curriculum Pr.
A Very Fine Time: Long Vowel i, CVCe Pattern: Level B, 6 vols. (Wright Skills Ser.). 16p. (gr. k-3). 17.95 *(978-0-322-01467-1(0))* Wright Group/McGraw-Hill.
Wait for Me: Take-Home Book. 2005. (Emergent Library: Vol. 2). (YA). (gr. -1-1). 12.60 *(978-0-8215-7261-0(X))* Sadlier, William H. Inc.
Wake Up! Long Vowel a, CVCe Pattern: Level B, 6 vols. (Wright Skills Ser.). 16p. (gr. k-3). 17.95 *(978-0-322-03129-6(X))* Wright Group/McGraw-Hill.
Wax, Wendy. Phonics Comics: Clara the Klutz - Level 2. Sullivan, Mary, illus. 2007. (ENG.). 24p. (J). (gr. 1-17). per. 3.99 *(978-1-58476-565-3(8))* Innovative Kids.
We Can! Level A: Consonant W. (Wright Skills Ser.). 12p. (gr. k-3). 17.95 *(978-0-322-03114-2(1))* Wright Group/McGraw-Hill.
Weil, Ann. Ice Skating. Fletcher, Rusty, illus. 2004. (Elements of Reading: Phonics Ser.). 16p. pap. 40.00 *(978-0-7398-9010-3(7))* Houghton Mifflin Harcourt Supplemental Pubs.
Weiss, Bobbi Jg & Weiss, David Cody. Phonic Comics - Hiro Dragon Warrior: Fight or Flight Level 2, Issue 3. 2011. (ENG., Illus.). 24p. (J). (gr. 1-17). pap. 3.99 *(978-1-60169-111-8(4))* Innovative Kids.
Wernham, Sara & Lloyd, Sue. Jolly Phonics Activity Book 4: Ai, J, Oa, Ie, Ee, Or, 7 vols. Stephen, Lib, illus. 2010. (ENG.). 7p. (J). pap. *(978-1-84414-156-2(X))* Jolly Learning, Ltd.
When the Alligator Came to Class: Short a; Consonants c, p; Blends cl, cr, scr, pl, spl, Level A. 2003. ("Plaid" Phonics & Stories Libraries). (gr. 1-2). 38.50 *(978-0-8136-9141-1(9))* Modern Curriculum Pr.
Wilkens, Karen & Benchmark Education Co., LLC Staff. ABC. 2015. (StartUp Ser.). (J). (gr. k). *(978-1-4900-0683-3(4))* Benchmark Education Co.
—I Like. 2015. (StartUp Ser.). (J). (gr. k). *(978-1-4900-0685-7(0))* Benchmark Education Co.
William H. Sadlier Staff. J My Name Is Jess. 2005. (Emergent Library: Vol. 2). (gr. -1-1). 24.00 net. *(978-0-8215-8935-9(0))* Sadlier, William H. Inc.
—Looking at Lizards: Big Book, Vol. 2. 2005. (Emergent Library: Vol. 1). (gr. -1-1). 24.00 net. *(978-0-8215-8906-9(7))* Sadlier, William H. Inc.
—Wait for Me. 2005. (Emergent Library: Vol. 2). (gr. -1-1). 24.00 net. *(978-0-8215-8931-1(8))* Sadlier, William H. Inc.
—Wake up, Sleepyheads!, Vol. 2. 2005. (Early Library). (gr. k-2). 24.00 net. *(978-0-8215-8955-7(5))* Sadlier, William H. Inc.
Williams, Richie. There's a Bear with a Pear! 2006. (Illus.). 32p. (J). 19.50 *(978-0-9777100-0-3(9))* Geoscience Information Services.
Winget, Kerry. Differential Processing Training Program Acoustic Linguistic Tasks. 2007. per. 32.95 *(978-0-7606-0723-7(0))* LinguiSystems, Inc.
—Differential Processing Training Program Acoustic Tasks. 2007. per. 32.95 *(978-0-7606-0722-0(2))* LinguiSystems, Inc.
—Differential Processing Training Program Linguistic Tasks. 2007. per. 32.95 *(978-0-7606-0724-4(9))* LinguiSystems, Inc.
Word Families. 2005. (J). *(978-1-60015-010-4(1))* Steps To Literacy, LLC.
Word Wall Words. 2004. (gr. k-18). suppl. ed. 39.70 *(978-0-673-62182-5(0))*; (gr. 1-18). suppl. ed. 220.50 *(978-0-673-62183-2(9))*; (gr. 2-18). suppl. ed. 220.50 *(978-0-673-62184-9(7))*; (gr. 3-18). suppl. ed. 220.50 *(978-0-673-62185-6(5))* Addison-Wesley Educational Pubs., Inc.
A World Worth Keeping: Level T. Group 1, 6 vols. (Sunshine Ser.). 48p. 44.95 *(978-0-7802-6092-4(9))* Wright Group/McGraw-Hill.
The Wrecks: Level T. Group 2, 6 vols. (Sunshine Ser.). 48p. 44.95 *(978-0-7802-4177-0(0))* Wright Group/McGraw-Hill.
Wrestle Mania: Magazine Anthology: Level 5, 6 vols. (Comprehension Strand Ser.). (gr. 4-8). 54.00 *(978-0-322-06036-4(2))* Wright Group/McGraw-Hill.
The Wright Skills: Level B Sets - Long vowels only: 1 Each of 6 Titles. (gr. k-3). 17.95 *(978-0-322-01934-8(6))* Wright Group/McGraw-Hill.
The Wright Skills: Level B Sets - Long vowels only: 6 Each of 6 Titles. (gr. k-3). 109.50 *(978-0-322-01935-5(4))* Wright Group/McGraw-Hill.
The Wright Skills: Level C Sets - 1 Each of 16 Titles. (gr. k-3). 69.95 *(978-0-322-00734-5(8))* Wright Group/McGraw-Hill.
The Wright Skills: Level C Sets - 6 Each of 16 Titles. (gr. k-3). 322.95 *(978-0-322-00813-7(1))* Wright Group/McGraw-Hill.
Wrighton, Charlene & Bradshaw, Georgine. Basic Kit - Preschool. Clark, Irene, illus. 2005. Orig. Title: Basis Kit I. (J). 249.95 *(978-1-886441-30-9(8))* Zoo-phonics, Inc.
Yamile Y Yo Vol. 21: Little Books, Level 12. 2003. (Fonolibros Ser.). 34.95 *(978-0-7652-0099-0(6))* Modern Curriculum Pr.
Yip & Yap: Consonant y: Level A, 6 vols. (Wright Skills Ser.). 12p. (gr. k-3). 17.95 *(978-0-322-03120-3(6))* Wright Group/McGraw-Hill.
Yo Se Nadar! Little Books, Level 2, Vol. 18. 2003. (Fonolibros Ser.). 25.50 *(978-0-7652-0095-2(3))* Modern Curriculum Pr.
York. Phonics, Level A. 2004. (Steck-Vaughn Phonics Ser.). (ENG.). 416p. (gr. 1-1). tchr. ed., spiral bd. 64.50 *(978-0-7398-9140-7(5))* Houghton Mifflin Harcourt Publishing Co.
Zoboomafoo: Beginning Phonics. 2003. 32p. pap., wbk. ed. 14.95 incl. cd-rom *(978-1-57791-020-6(6))*; pap., wbk. ed. 14.95 incl. cd-rom *(978-1-57791-021-3(4))* Brighter Minds Children's Publishing.
Zone Zoomers: Level 2, 6 vols. (Fluency Strand Ser.). (gr. 4-8). 45.00 *(978-1-4045-1213-9(6))* Wright Group/McGraw-Hill.
Zoo-phonics Quick Tests for the Classroom. 2004. cd-rom *(978-1-886441-41-5(3))* Zoo-phonics, Inc.

PHONICS

see Phonetics

PHONOGRAPH

see also Sound—Recording and Reproducing

Doak, Robin S. The Phonograph. 2005. (Great Inventions Ser.). (Illus.). 48p. (gr. 5-12). lib. bdg. 31.00 *(978-0-8368-5877-8(8),* Gareth Stevens Secondary Library) Stevens, Gareth Publishing LLLP.
Kuskowski, Alex. Super Simple Phonograph Projects: Inspiring & Educational Science Activities, 1 vol. 2016. (ENG., Illus.). 32p. (J). *(978-1-62403-731-3(3))* ABDO Publishing Co.
National Geographic Learning Staff. Thomas Edison, Level 3 - World Windows. 2011. (World Windows Ser.). (ENG., Illus.). 16p. (J). stu. ed. 9.95 *(978-1-133-49279-5(7))* Cengage Heinle.
Salzmann, Mary Elizabeth. Phonograph, 1 vol. 2016. (ENG., Illus.). 24p. (J). *(978-1-62403-710-8(0))* ABDO Publishing Co.
Top That. Fun Kits Play the REC. 2008. *(978-1-84666-594-3(9))* Top That! Publishing PLC.

PHONOLOGY

see Phonetics

PHOTOGRAPHERS

Acker, Kerry. Dorothea Lange. 2003. (Women in the Arts Ser.). (Illus.). 112p. (gr. 6-12). 30.00 *(978-0-7910-7460-2(9),* Chelsea Hse.) Facts On File, Inc.
Anderson, Christopher C. L. Margaret Bourke-White: Adventurous Photographer. 2005. (Great Life Stories Ser.). (ENG., Illus.). 127p. (J). (gr. 6-8). 30.50 *(978-0-531-12405-5(3),* Watts, Franklin) Scholastic Library Publishing.
Anderson, William. Les Kelly. Kelly, Leslie A., illus. Date not set. (J). (gr. 3-7). Vol. 1. 9.99 *(978-0-06-440851-6(5))* Vol. 2. 9.99 *(978-0-06-440850-9(7))* HarperCollins Pubs.
Armstrong, Jennifer. Photo by Brady: A Picture of the Civil War. 2005. (ENG., Illus.). 160p. (J). (gr. 4-9). 22.99 *(978-0-689-85785-0(3),* Atheneum Bks. for Young Readers) Simon & Schuster Children's Publishing.
—Photo by Brady: A Picture of the Civil War. 2013. (ENG., Illus.). 128p. (J). pap. 11.95 *(978-0-689-85786-7(1),* Simon & Schuster/Paula Wiseman Bks.) Simon & Schuster/Paula Wiseman Bks.
Baxter, Kathleen & McConnell, Robert L., contrib. by. Civil War Witness: Mathew Brady's Photos Reveal the Horrors of War, 1 vol. 2013. (Captured History Ser.). (ENG.). 64p. (gr. 5-7). 34.65 *(978-0-7565-4693-9(1),* CPB Grades 4-8) Compass Point Bks.
Braun, Marta. Muybridge & the Riddle of Locomotion. 2013. (ENG., Illus.). 24p. (J). (gr. 4-12). 19.95 *(978-1-77085-229-7(8),* 9781770852297) Firefly Bks., Ltd.
Bueno, Julián David. Henry Cartier - Bresson- el azar y el Instante. 2005. (SPA.). 132p. (YA). *(978-958-30-1704-9(3))* Panamericana Editorial.
Burgan, Michael. Shadow Catcher: How Edward S. Curtis Documented American Indian Dignity & Beauty. 2015. (Captured History Ser.). (ENG., Illus.). 64p. (gr. 5-7). pap. 9.10 *(978-0-7565-4998-5(1))* Compass Point Bks.
Cerullo, Mary M. Journey to Shark Island: A Shark Photographer's Close Encounters, 1 vol. Rotman, Jeffrey L., illus. Rotman, Jeffrey L., photos by. 2014. (Shark Expedition Ser.). (ENG.). 40p. (gr. 5-7). lib. bdg. 31.99 *(978-0-7565-4887-2(X))* Compass Point Bks.
—Searching for Great White Sharks: A Shark Diver's Quest for Mr. Big, 1 vol. Rotman, Jeffrey L., photos by. 2014. (Shark Expedition Ser.). (ENG., Illus.). 40p. (gr. 5-7). lib. bdg. 31.99 *(978-0-7565-4884-1(5))* Compass Point Bks.
—Shark Expedition: A Shark Photographer's Close Encounters. Rotman, Jeffrey L., photos by. 2015. (ENG., Illus.). 144p. (gr. 5-7). pap. 12.95 *(978-1-62370-156-7(2))* Capstone Press of Coughlan Cos.
—Sharks of the Deep: A Shark Photographer's Search for Sharks at the Bottom of the Sea, 1 vol. Rotman, Jeffrey L., illus. Rotman, Jeffrey L., photos by. 2014. (Shark Expedition Ser.). (ENG.). 40p. (gr. 5-7). lib. bdg. 31.99 *(978-0-7565-4886-5(1))* Compass Point Bks.
Crabtree, Marc. Meet My Neighbor, the Photographer. 2013. (ENG., Illus.). 24p. (J). *(978-0-7787-0873-5(X))*; pap. *(978-0-7787-0877-3(2))* Crabtree Publishing Co.
Dallas, Justin & Rissman, Rebecca. Fashion Photographer: The Coolest Jobs on the Planet, 1 vol. 2014. (Coolest Jobs on the Planet Ser.). (ENG., Illus.). 48p. (gr. 6-6). 32.65 *(978-1-4109-6641-4(0))*; pap. 8.99 *(978-1-4109-6647-6(X))* Heinemann-Raintree.
Goodall, Lian. Photographing Greatness: The Story of Karsh. Thompson, Samantha, illus. 2007. (Stories of Canada Ser.: 11). (ENG.). 96p. (J). 21.99 *(978-1-894917-34-6(0),* Napoleon & Co.) Dundurn CAN. Dist: Ingram Publisher Services.
Hollihan, Kerrie Logan. Reporting under Fire: 16 Daring Women War Correspondents & Photojournalists. 2014. (Women of Action Ser.). (ENG., Illus.). 256p. (YA). (gr. 7). 19.95 *(978-1-61374-710-0(1))* Chicago Review Pr., Inc.
Jenson-Elliott, Cindy. Ansty Ansel: Ansel Adams, a Life in Nature. Hale, Christy, illus. 2016. (ENG.). 32p. (J). 17.99 *(978-1-62779-082-6(9),* 9781627790826, Holt, Henry & Co. Bks. For Young Readers) Holt, Henry & Co.
King, David C. Dorothea Lange: Photographer of the People. 2009. (ENG., Illus.). 88p. (C). (gr. 6-18). lib. bdg. 158.00 *(978-0-7656-8154-6(4),* Y181941) Routledge.
Litwin, Laura Baskes. Dorothea Lange: A Life in Pictures. 2007. (People to Know Today Ser.). (Illus.). 128p. (J). (gr. 3-7). lib. bdg. 33.27 *(978-0-7660-2697-1(3))* Enslow Pubs., Inc.
Martin, Jacqueline Briggs. Snowflake Bentley. Azarian, Mary, illus. 2009. (ENG.). 32p. (J). (gr. -1-3). pap. 7.99 *(978-0-547-24829-5(6))* Houghton Mifflin Harcourt Publishing Co.
McConnell, Robert L., contrib. by. Civil War Witness: Mathew Brady's Photos Reveal the Horrors of War, 1 vol. 2013. (Captured History Ser.). (ENG.). 64p. (gr. 5-7). pap. 9.10 *(978-0-7565-4699-1(0),* CPB Grades 4-8) Compass Point Bks.
Murray, Stuart A. P. Mathew Brady: Photographer of Our Nation. 2009. (ENG., Illus.). 83p. (gr. 6-18). lib. bdg. 158.00 *(978-0-7656-8151-5(X),* Y182957) Routledge.
Nardo, Don. Mathew Brady: The Camera Is the Eye of History. 2008. (Americans—the Spirit of a Nation Ser.). (Illus.). 128p. (J). (gr. k-5). lib. bdg. 33.27 *(978-0-7660-3023-7(7))* Enslow Pubs., Inc.
Plain, Nancy. Light on the Prairie: Solomon D. Butcher, Photographer of Nebraska's Pioneer Days. 2012. (ENG., Illus.). 128p. (YA). pap. 16.95 *(978-0-8032-3520-5(8),* Bison Bks.) Univ. of Nebraska Pr.
Quintero, Isabel & Iturbide, Graciela. Photographic: The Life of Graciela Iturbide. Peña, Zeke, illus. 2017. (J). **(978-1-60606-557-0(2),** J. Paul Getty Museum) Getty Pubns.
Rosenstock, Barb. Dorothea's Eyes: Dorothea Lange Photographs the Truth. DuBois, Gerard, illus. 2016. (ENG.). 40p. (J). (gr. 2-7). 16.95 *(978-1-62979-208-8(X),* Calkins Creek) Boyds Mills Pr.
Rubiano, Roberto. Robert Capa -Imágenes de Guerra. 2005. (SPA.). 168p. (YA). *(978-958-30-1905-0(4))* Panamericana Editorial.
Rubin, Susan Goldman. Stand There! She Shouted: The Invincible Photographer Julia Margaret Cameron. Ibatoulline, Bagram, illus. 2014. (ENG.). 80p. (J). (gr. 3-7). 18.99 *(978-0-7636-5753-6(0))* Candlewick Pr.
Schuike, Flip & Schudel, Matt. Witness to Our Times: My Life As a Photojournalist. 2003. (ENG., Illus.). 160p. (J). (gr. 7-18). 19.95 *(978-0-8126-2682-7(6))* Cricket Bks.
Show Me America, 5 vols., Set. Incl. Dorothea Lange: Photographer of the People. King, David C. 88p. (C). 2009. lib. bdg. 158.00 *(978-0-7656-8154-6(4),* Y181941); George Catlin: Painter of Indian Life. Worth, Richard. 80p. (C). 2009. lib. bdg. 158.00 *(978-0-7656-8152-2(8),* Y182314); John Trumbull: Painter of the Revolutionary War. Murray, Stuart A. P. 83p. (C). 2008. lib. bdg. 158.00 *(978-0-7656-8150-8(1),*

Y182501); Lewis Hine: Photographer of Americans at Work. Worth, Richard. 83p. (C). 2009. lib. bdg. 158.00 (978-0-7656-8153-9(6), Y182862); Mathew Brady: Photographer of Our Nation. Murray, Stuart A. P. 83p. 2009. lib. bdg. 158.00 (978-0-7656-8151-5(X), Y182957); (Illus.). (gr. 6-18). (ENG.). 2009. Set lib. bdg. 140.00 (978-0-7656-8149-2(8), Y183560) Routledge.

Sills, Leslie. In Real Life: Stories about Women Photographers. 2005. (J). (978-0-7868-2077-1(2)) Hyperion Pr.

Somervill, Barbara A. Wildlife Photographer. (21st Century Skills Library: Cool STEAM Careers Ser.). (ENG.). 32p. (gr. 4-7). 2015. (J). 29.93 (978-1-63362-569-3(9), 206460) 2008. (Illus.). lib. bdg. 28.50 (978-1-60279-300-2(X), 200139) Cherry Lake Publishing.

Tanaka, Kazumi. Kazumi Tanaka: Words & Works. 2003. (Illus.). 104p. 14.95 (978-1-878607-84-3(7)) Kent Gallery.

Thomas, Isabel. Being a Photographer. 2012. (On the Radar: Awesome Jobs Ser.). (ENG., Illus.). 32p. (J). (gr. 4-8). lib. bdg. 26.60 (978-0-7613-7779-5(4), Lerner Pubns.) Lerner Publishing Group.

Thomas, William David. Wildlife Photographer. 2008. (Cool Careers: Adventure Careers Ser.). (Illus.). 32p. (gr. 5-8). pap. 10.50 (978-0-8368-8892-8(8)); lib. bdg. 26.00 (978-0-8368-8885-0(5)) Stevens, Gareth Publishing LLLP.

Weatherford, Carole Boston. Gordon Parks: How the Photographer Captured Black & White America. Christoph, Jamey, illus. 2015. (ENG.). 32p. (J). (gr. k-3). 16.99 (978-0-8075-3017-7(4)) Whitman, Albert & Co.

West, Krista. Ansel Adams. 2011. (Conservation Heroes Ser.). (Illus.). 128p. (YA). (gr. 6-12). 35.00 (978-1-60413-946-4(3), Chelsea Hse.) Facts On File, Inc.

Weston Woods Staff, creator. Snowflake Bentley. 2011. 18.95 (978-0-545-31414-5(3)); 38.75 (978-0-545-31415-2(1)) Weston Woods Studios, Inc.

Worth, Richard. Lewis Hine: Photographer of Americans at Work. 2009. (ENG., Illus.). 83p. (C). (gr. 6-18). lib. bdg. 158.00 (978-0-7656-8153-9(6), Y182862) Routledge.

PHOTOGRAPHY

see also Cameras; Nature Study

About Face: Portraits of Activism. 2004. (YA). per. (978-1-932948-06-6(6)) Student Pr. Initiative.

Bankston, John. Louis Daguerre & the Story of the Daguerreotype. 2004. (Uncharted, Unexplored, & Unexplained Ser.). (Illus.). 48p. (J). (gr. 4-8). lib. bdg. 29.95 (978-1-58415-247-7(8)) Mitchell Lane Pubs., Inc.

Bartlett, Karen T. A Kid's Guide to Chicago. Brown, Don, illus. 2010. 64p. pap. 16.95 (978-1-934907-03-0(0)) Twin Lights Pubs., Inc.

Baxter, Kathleen & Sandmann, Alexa L. Captured History, 4 vols., Set. Incl. Birmingham 1963: How a Photograph Rallied Civil Rights Support. Tougas, Shelley. lib. bdg. 34.65 (978-0-7565-4398-3(3)); Migrant Mother: How a Photograph Defined the Great Depression. Nardo, Don. lib. bdg. 34.65 (978-0-7565-4397-6(5)); Raising the Flag: How a Photograph Gave a Nation Hope in Wartime. Burgan, Michael. lib. bdg. 34.65 (978-0-7565-4395-2(9)); (gr. 5-7). CPB Grades 4-8 (Captured History Ser.). (ENG.). 64p. 2011. Set lib. bdg. 103.95 (978-0-7565-4399-0(1)) Compass Point Bks.

Beardsley, Kurt. Under Saharan Skies. 2004. (Illus.). 96p. per. 25.00 (978-0-9761103-0-9(X), 1000) International Vaquero Productions.

Bodden, Valerie. Photography. 2008. (Media Sources Ser.). (J). pap. 9.95 (978-0-89812-531-3(6)); (Illus.). 24p. lib. bdg. 24.25 (978-1-58341-558-0(0)) Creative Co., The. (Creative Education).

Bohn, Klaus. Healthy Me: I Love Fruit, I Love Veggies. Bohn, Klaus, illus. 2012. (ENG., Illus.). 44p. (J). pap. (978-1-77143-034-0(6), CCB Publishing) CCB Publishing.

Buckley, Annie & Buckley, James, Jr. Inside Photography. 2007. (Reading Rocks! Ser.). (ENG., Illus.). 32p. (J). (gr. 2-5). 28.50 (978-1-59296-867-1(8), 200744) Child's World, Inc., The.

Burgan, Michael. Exposing Hidden Worlds: How Jacob Riis' Photos Became Tools for Social Reform. 2017. (Captured History Ser.). (ENG.). 64p. (gr. 5-7). lib. bdg. 34.65 **(978-0-7565-5618-1(X)**, CPB Grades 4-8) Compass Point Bks.

Burgan, Michael. The Hindenburg in Flames: How a Photograph Marked the End of the Airship. 2016. (Captured World History Ser.). (ENG.). 64p. (gr. 5-7). lib. bdg. 34.65 (978-0-7565-5441-5(1), CPB Grades 4-8) Compass Point Bks.

Cerullo, Mary M. Shark Expedition, 1 vol. Rotman, Jeffrey L., photos by. 2014. (Shark Expedition Ser.). (ENG., Illus.). 40p. (gr. 5-7). 127.96 (978-0-7565-4888-9(8), CPB Grades 4-8) Compass Point Bks.

—Shark Expedition: A Shark Photographer's Close Encounters. Rotman, Jeffrey L., photos by. 2015. (ENG., Illus.). 144p. (gr. 5-7). pap. 12.95 (978-1-62370-156-7(2)) Capstone Press of Coughlan Cos.

Chapel, Jamie Moore & Eberhardt, Nancy Chapel. ¿Qué Es Diferente ... ¿Qué Es lo Mismo? 2013. 34p. pap. 10.00 (978-1-939054-14-2(1)) Rowe Publishing and Design.

Coll-Seck, Jayden. My Mom Shows Me Old Photos, 01 vols., 1. 2016. (Rosen REAL Readers: Social Studies Nonfiction / Fiction: Family, Community, & the World Ser.). (ENG.). 8p. (J). pap. 5.46 (978-1-5081-1689-9(X), Rosen Classroom) Rosen Publishing Group, Inc., The.

Crabtree, Marc. Meet My Neighbor, the Photographer. 2013. (ENG., Illus.). 24p. (J). (978-0-7787-0873-5(X)); pap. (978-0-7787-0877-3(2)) Crabtree Publishing Co.

Dallas, Justin & Rissman, Rebecca. Fashion Photographer: The Coolest Jobs on the Planet, 1 vol. 2014. (Coolest Jobs on the Planet Ser.). (ENG., Illus.). 48p. (gr. 6-6). 32.65 (978-1-4109-6641-4(0)); pap. 8.99 (978-1-4109-6647-6(X)) Heinemann-Raintree.

Davis, John. The Camera Book. 2015. (ENG., Illus.). 128p. (gr. 3-6). pap. 15.99 (978-0-7112-3644-8(5), Frances Lincoln) Quarto Publishing Group UK GBR. Dist: Hachette Bk. Group.

Dell, Pamela. Man on the Moon: How a Photograph Made Anything Seem Possible, 1 vol. 2011. (Captured History Ser.). (ENG.). 64p. (gr. 5-7). pap. 9.10 (978-0-7565-4447-8(5), CPB Grades 4-8) Compass Point Bks.

Digital Photo Activity Kit Deluxe Vivitar 3700 series Lab-10. 2005. (J). cd-rom 1790.00 (978-1-933229-02-7(0)) APTE, Inc.

Digital Photo Activity Kit Deluxe Vivitar 3700 series Lab-15. 2005. (J). cd-rom 2610.00 (978-1-933229-03-4(9)) APTE, Inc.

Digital Photo Activity Kit Deluxe Vivitar 3700 series Lab-20. 2005. (J). 3260.00 (978-1-933229-04-1(7)) APTE, Inc.

Digital Photo Activity Kit Deluxe Vivitar 3700 series Lab-25. 2005. (J). 3924.00 (978-1-933229-05-8(5)) APTE, Inc.

Digital Photo Activity Kit Deluxe Vivitar 3700 series Lab-30. 2005. (J). 4585.00 (978-1-933229-06-5(3)) APTE, Inc.

Digital Photo Activity Kit Deluxe Vivitar 3700 series Lab-35. 2005. (J). 5239.00 (978-1-933229-07-2(1)) APTE, Inc.

Digital Photo Activity Kit Deluxe Vivitar 3700 series Lab-5. 2005. (J). cd-rom 648.95 (978-1-933229-01-0(2)) APTE, Inc.

Digital Photo Activity Kit Deluxe Vivitar 3700 Series school Version. 2005. (J). cd-rom 133.95 (978-1-933229-00-3(4)) APTE, Inc.

Digital Photo Activity Kit Deluxe Vivitar 5300 series Lab- 2005. (J). 1759.95 (978-1-933229-09-6(8)) APTE, Inc.

Digital Photo Activity Kit Deluxe Vivitar 5300 series Lab-10. 2005. (J). 3469.99 (978-1-933229-10-2(1)) APTE, Inc.

Digital Photo Activity Kit Deluxe Vivitar 5300 series Lab-15. 2005. (J). 5129.95 (978-1-933229-11-9(X)) APTE, Inc.

Digital Photo Activity Kit Deluxe Vivitar 5300 series Lab-25. 2005. (J). 8123.90 (978-1-933229-12-6(8)) APTE, Inc.

Digital Photo Activity Kit Deluxe Vivitar 5300 series Lab-30. 2005. (J). 9624.95 (978-1-933229-14-0(4)) APTE, Inc.

Digital Photo Activity Kit Deluxe Vivitar 5300 series Lab-35. 2005. (J). 11119.95 (978-1-933229-15-7(2)) APTE, Inc.

Digital Photo Activity Kit Deluxe Vivitar 5300 series Single. 2005. (J). 359.99 (978-1-933229-08-9(X)) APTE, Inc.

Dutcher, Jim & Dutcher, Jamie. Living with Wolves! True Stories of Adventures with Animals. 2016. (NGK Chapters Ser.). (ENG., Illus.). 112p. (J). (gr. 2-5). pap. 5.99 (978-1-4263-2563-2(0), National Geographic Children's Bks.) National Geographic Society.

Dyan, Penelope. By the Sea — -A Kid's Guide to Valletta, Malt. Weigand, John D., photos by. 2011. (Illus.). 36p. pap. 11.95 (978-1-935630-55-5(5)) Bellissima Publishing, LLC.

—High on a Hill! a Kid's Guide to Innsbruck, Austr. Weigand, John D., photos by. 2011. (Illus.). 40p. pap. 12.95 (978-1-935630-76-0(8)) Bellissima Publishing, LLC.

—Steam Train! All the Way to Canterbury, England. Weigand, John D., photos by. 2011. (Illus.). 40p. pap. 11.95 (978-1-935630-75-3(X)) Bellissima Publishing, LLC.

Elton, Candice & Elton, Richard. My Family Album. 2003. (Illus.). 32p. (J). 19.95 (978-1-58685-323-5(6)) Gibbs Smith, Publisher.

—My Vacation Album: Includes: Reusable Camera, Film, Batteries & Glue Stick. Lee, Fran, illus. 2003. 28p. (J). spiral bd. 19.95 (978-1-58685-280-1(9)) Gibbs Smith, Publisher.

Essential Photography. 2004. (I-Quest Ser.). (Illus.). 48p. (J). per. (978-1-84229-744-5(9)) Top That! Publishing PLC.

Fandel, Jennifer. Picture Yourself Writing Nonfiction: Using Photos to Inspire Writing. 2011. (See It, Write It Ser.). (ENG.). 32p. (gr. 3-4). pap. 47.70 (978-1-4296-7208-5(0), Fact Finders) Capstone Press of Coughlan Cos.

Fast, Suellen M. America's Daughters. Fast, Suellen M., photos by. (Illus.). 100p. (Orig.). (J). (gr. k-18). pap. 19.00 (978-0-935281-13-2(4)) Daughter Culture Pubns.

Fretland VanVoorst, Jenny. Photography. 2016. (Artist's Studio Ser.). 24p. (J). (gr. k-2). lib. bdg. 25.65 (978-1-62031-283-4(2), Bullfrog Bks.) Jump! Inc.

Furgang, Adam. Snap & Share: Exploring the Potential of Instagram & Other Photo & Video Apps, 1 vol. 2015. (ENG.). 48p. (YA). 30.25 (978-1-4777-7934-7(5), Rosen Reference) Rosen Publishing Group, Inc., The.

Gardner, Jane P. Photo Science, Vol. 11. Lewin, Russ, ed. 2015. (Science 24/7 Ser.). (Illus.). 48p. (J). (gr. 5). 20.95 (978-1-4222-3413-6(4)) Mason Crest.

Gelber, Lisa & Roberts, Jody. P Is for Peanut: A Photographic A-B-C. 2007. (ENG., Illus.). 58p. (J). (gr. -1-3). 9.95 (978-0-89236-878-5(0)) Oxford Univ. Pr., Inc.

Gerard, James H. The Blue Marble: How a Photograph Revealed Earth's Fragile Beauty, 1 vol. 2014. (Captured World History Ser.). (ENG., Illus.). 64p. (gr. 5-7). pap. 8.95 (978-0-7565-4788-2(1), CPB Grades 4-8) Compass Point Bks.

Greenagel, Frank L., photos by. Think Like a Photographer! How to Take Better Pictures Than Anyone in Your Family. 2006. (Illus.). (J). (978-1-59336-766-4(X)) Mondo Publishing.

Handler, Daniel. Girls Standing on Lawns. Kalman, Maira, illus. 2014. (ENG.). 64p. (gr. 3-7). 14.95 (978-0-87070-908-1(9)) Museum of Modern Art.

Honovich, Nancy & Griffiths, Annie. National Geographic Kids Guide to Photography: Tips & Tricks on How to Be a Great Photographer from the Pros & Your Pals at My Shot. 2015. (ENG., Illus.). 160p. (J). (gr. 3-7). pap. 14.99 (978-1-4263-2066-8(3), National Geographic Children's Bks.) National Geographic Society.

Horne, Ronald William. Forgotten Faces: A Window into Our Immigrant Past (5x8-Clr-BW) 2004. (Illus.). 120p. per. 24.95 (978-0-9747395-1-9(0), FF5x8ClrBW) Personal Genesis Publishing.

Houblon, Marie. A World of Colors: Seeing Colors in a New Way. 2009. (ENG., Illus.). 48p. (J). (gr. -1-2). 25.90 (978-1-4263-0559-7(1)); 16.95 (978-1-4263-0556-6(7)) National Geographic Society. (National Geographic Children's Bks.).

Janovich, Leah. Patty's Pictures. Billin-Frye, Paige, illus. 2010. 16p. (J). (978-0-545-24820-4(5)) Scholastic, Inc.

Kallen, Stuart A. Photography. 2007. (Eye on Art Ser.). (ENG., Illus.). 112p. (J). (gr. 4-7). lib. bdg. 34.80 (978-1-59018-986-3(8), Lucent Bks.) Cengage Gale.

Kulling, Monica. It's a Snap! George Eastman's First Photograph. Slavin, Bill, illus. 2009. (Great Idea Ser.). (ENG.). 32p. (J). (gr. k-3). 17.95 (978-0-88776-881-1(4), Tundra Bks.) Tundra Bks. CAN. Dist: Penguin Random Hse. LLC.

Lightning Bolt Books: Famous Places, 18 vols., Set. Incl. Alamo. Nelson, Kristin L. 2010. lib. bdg. 26.60 (978-0-7613-6017-9(4)); Capitol Building. Piehl, Janet. 2009. 26.60 (978-1-57505-966-2(5)); Empire State Building. Bullard, Lisa. 2009. 26.60 (978-0-8225-9404-8(8)); Erie Canal. Bullard, Lisa. 2009. 26.60 (978-0-8225-9405-5(6)); Everglades. Bullard, Lisa. 2010. lib. bdg. 26.60 (978-0-7613-4453-7(5)); Gateway Arch. Bullard, Lisa. 2009. 26.60 (978-0-8225-9406-2(4)); Golden Gate Bridge. Zuehlke, Jeffrey. (Illus.). (J). 2009. 26.60 (978-0-8225-9407-9(2), 1299390); Grand Canyon. Zuehlke, Jeffrey. 2010. lib. bdg. 26.60 (978-0-7613-4261-8(3)); Great Lakes. Piehl, Janet. 2010. lib. bdg. 26.60 (978-0-7613-4456-8(X)); Hoover Dam. Zuehlke, Jeffrey. 2009. 26.60 (978-0-8225-9408-6(0)); Lincoln Memorial. Nelson, Kristin L. (Illus.). (J). 2010. lib. bdg. 25.26 (978-0-7613-6018-6(2)); Mount Rushmore. Jango-Cohen, Judith. (Illus.). (J). 2010. lib. bdg. 25.26 (978-0-7613-6021-6(2)); Redwood Forests. Bullard, Lisa. 2010. lib. bdg. 26.60 (978-0-7613-4452-0(7)); Rocky Mountains. Zuehlke, Jeffrey. 2010. lib. bdg. 26.60 (978-0-7613-4454-4(3)); Statue of Liberty. Braithwaite, Jill. (Illus.). 2010. lib. bdg. 26.60 (978-0-7613-6020-9(4)); Washington Monument. Nelson, Kristin L. (Illus.). (J). 2010. lib. bdg. 25.26 (978-0-7613-6019-3(0)); White House. Braithwaite, Jill. 2010. lib. bdg. 26.60 (978-0-7613-6016-2(6)); Yellowstone National Park. Piehl, Janet. 2010. lib. bdg. 26.60 (978-0-7613-4455-1(1)); 32p. (gr. k-2). 2009. Set lib. bdg. 454.68 (978-0-8225-9403-1(X), Lerner Pubns.) Lerner Publishing Group.

Lüsted, Marcia Amidon. For People Who Are Good with a Camera. 2016. (Cool Careers Without College Ser.). 00104p. (J). (gr. 7-7). 38.45 (978-1-5081-7276-5(5)) Rosen Publishing Group, Inc., The.

Mauro, Paul & Melton, H. Keith. Crime Scene & Surveillance Photography. 2004. (Detective Academy Ser.). (Illus.). 48p. (J). (978-0-439-57182-1(0)) Scholastic, Inc.

McDougall, Carol & LaRamee-Jones, Shanda. Baby Look, 1 vol. 2013. (Baby Steps Ser.). (ENG., Illus.). 16p. (J). (gr. -1-k). bds. 8.95 (978-1-55109-937-8(3)) Nimbus Publishing, Ltd. CAN. Dist: Orca Bk. Pubs. USA.

Mosley, Kim, text. Workbook for Black & White Photography, 1 vol. 3rd ed. 2005. (ENG.). 48p. (C). (978-0-9663215-1-7(0)) Mosley, Kim.

Murphy, Patricia J. Discovering Underwater Secrets with a Nature Photographer. 2007. (I Like Science! Ser.). (Illus.). 24p. (J). (gr. 1-3). lib. bdg. 22.60 (978-0-7660-2816-6(X), Enslow Elementary) Enslow Pubs., Inc.

My Cool World in Photos. 2008. (Best Friends Club Ser.). 32p. (978-1-4075-1615-8(9)) Parragon, Inc.

Omoth, Tyler. Busting Boredom with Technology. 2017. (Boredom Busters Ser.). (ENG., Illus.). 32p. (gr. 3-4). lib. bdg. 27.99 (978-1-5157-4705-5(0)) Capstone Press of Coughlan Cos.

Oxlade, Chris. Cameras: With 9 Easy-to-Do Experiments & 230 Exciting Pictures. 2016. (ENG., Illus.). 64p. 12.99 (978-1-86147-663-0(9), Armadillo) Anness Publishing GBR. Dist: National Bk. Network.

Pelusey, Michael & Pelusey, Jane. Photography. 2005. (Media Ser.). (Illus.). 32p. (gr. 5-8). lib. bdg. 21.95 (978-0-7910-8805-0(7), Chelsea Hse.) Facts On File, Inc.

Photography. (Make it Work Ser.). 42p. (J). (gr. 4-8). pap. (978-1-882210-43-5(3)) Action Publishing, Inc.

Publications International Ltd. Staff, ed. Itsy Bitsy Spider. 2010. 12p. (J). bds. 3.98 (978-1-60553-147-2(2)) Publications International, Ltd.

Rabbat, Suzy. Post It! Sharing Photos with Friends & Family. 2012. (Explorer Junior Library: Information Explorer Junior Ser.). (ENG.). 24p. (gr. 1-4). 28.50 (978-1-61080-485-1(6), 202095); pap. 12.79 (978-1-61080-659-6(X), 202269) Cherry Lake Publishing.

—Super Smart Information Strategies: Using Digital Images. 2010. (Explorer Library: Information Explorer Ser.). (ENG.). 32p. (gr. 4-8). lib. bdg. 28.50 (978-1-60279-954-7(7), 200633) Cherry Lake Publishing.

Rausch, Monica L. George Eastman & the Camera. 2007. (Inventors & Their Discoveries Ser.). (Illus.). 24p. (gr. 1-4). pap. 8.15 (978-0-8368-7730-4(6)); lib. bdg. 22.00 (978-0-8368-7499-0(4)) Stevens, Gareth Publishing LLLP. (Weekly Reader Leveled Readers).

Rissman, Rebecca. Picture This! 2013. (Picture This! Ser.). (ENG.). 24p. (gr. -1-k). pap. 35.80 (978-1-4109-5261-5(4), NA-r) Heinemann-Raintree.

Sanderson, Krystyna. Light at Ground Zero: St. Paul's Chapel After 9/11. Bustard, Ned, ed. 2003. (Illus.). 120p. per. 11.99 (978-0-9658798-4-2(4)) Square Halo Bks.

Sandler, Martin W. The Dust Bowl Through the Lens: How Photography Revealed & Helped Remedy a National Disaster. 2009. (Through the Lens Ser.). (ENG., Illus.). 96p. (J). (gr. 5-9). 22.99 (978-0-8027-9547-2(1), 9780802795472, Bloomsbury USA Childrens) Bloomsbury Publishing USA.

Schaub, Stephen, photos by. Through a Glass Darkly: Photographs by Stephen M. Schaub. 2004. (ENG & FRE., Illus.). 60p. 65.00 (978-0-9669079-1-9(4)) Indian Hill Gallery of Fine Photography.

Senior, Kathryn, et al. Photography. (Make It Work! Ser.). (Illus.). 48p. (J). pap. 7.99 (978-0-590-24913-3(4)); pap. 16.99 (978-0-590-24912-6(6)) Scholastic, Inc.

Skerry, Brian. The Whale Who Stole Hearts: And More True Stories of Amazing Animal Adventures. 2014. (NGK Chapters Ser.). (ENG., Illus.). 112p. (J). (gr. 2-5). pap. 5.99 (978-1-4263-1520-6(1), National Geographic Children's Bks.) National Geographic Society.

Skerry, Brian & Zoehfeld, Kathleen Weidner. The Whale Who Won Hearts. 2014. (NGK Chapters Ser.). (ENG., Illus.). 112p. (J). (gr. 2-5). lib. bdg. 14.90 (978-1-4263-1521-3(X), National Geographic Children's Bks.) National Geographic Society.

Skog, Jason. Taking the Shot. 2012. (Photography for Teens Ser.). (ENG.). 48p. (gr. 5-7). lib. bdg. 29.32 (978-0-7565-4490-4(4), CPB Grades 4-8) Compass Point Bks.

Skog, Jason & Kalz, Jill. Displaying the Shot. 2012. (Photography for Teens Ser.). (ENG.). 48p. (gr. 5-7). 29.32 (978-0-7565-4491-1(2), CPB Grades 4-8) Compass Point Bks.

Smith-Llera, Danielle. Serena vs. Venus: How a Photograph Spotlighted the Fight for Equality. 2017. (Captured History Sports Ser.). (ENG., Illus.). 64p. (gr. 5-7). lib. bdg. 34.65 (978-0-7565-5529-0(9), CPB Grades 4-8) Compass Point Bks.

Smith-Llera, Danielle & Burgan, Michael. Captured History Sports. 2017. (Captured History Sports Ser.). (ENG.). 64p. (gr. 5-7). 277.20 (978-0-7565-5550-4(7), CPB Grades 4-8) Compass Point Bks.

Spence, Kelly. Maker Projects for Kids Who Love Photography. 2016. (Be a Maker! Ser.). (ENG.). 32p. (J). (gr. 5-8). (978-0-7787-2578-7(2)) Crabtree Publishing Co.

Spencer, Jeffrey. Building for the Ages: Omaha's Architectural Landmarks. 2003. (Illus.). 208p. (YA). lib. bdg. 39.95 (978-0-9745410-1-3(X)) Omaha Bks.

Stanton, Brandon. Little Humans. Stanton, Brandon, photos by. 2014. (ENG., Illus.). 40p. (J). (gr. -1-1). 17.99 (978-0-374-37456-3(2), 9780374374563, Farrar, Straus & Giroux (BYR)) Farrar, Straus & Giroux.

Stewart, Gail B. The Crime Scene Photographer. 2008. (Crime Scene Investigations Ser.). (ENG., Illus.). 128p. (gr. 7-10). lib. bdg. 40.40 (978-1-4205-0036-3(8), LML02109-240023, Lucent Bks.) Cengage Gale.

Stuckey, Rachel. Get into Photography. 2016. (Get-Into-It Guides). (ENG.). 32p. (J). (gr. 3-6). (978-0-7787-2643-2(6)) Crabtree Publishing Co.

Sullivan, George. Click! Click! Click! Photography for Children. 2011. (ENG., Illus.). 96p. (J). (gr. 3-7). 14.95 (978-3-7913-7079-8(0)) Prestel Verlag GmbH & Co KG. DEU. Dist: Penguin Random Hse. LLC.

Thomas, Isabel. Being a Photographer. 2012. (On the Radar: Awesome Jobs Ser.). (ENG., Illus.). 32p. (J). (gr. 4-8). lib. bdg. 26.60 (978-0-7613-7779-5(4), Lerner Pubns.) Lerner Publishing Group.

—Photographs, 1 vol. 2011. (Start with Art Ser.). (ENG.). 24p. (gr. k-2). 23.32 (978-1-4329-5021-7(5), Heinemann Read & Learn) Heinemann-Raintree.

Thompson, Gary. Digital Photography & Your PC: A Guide to Using Your PC to Create Your Own Personalized Photo Albums. 2003. (Illus.). 166p. (YA). spiral bd. 29.95 (978-0-9749763-0-3(X)) Guiding Horizons.

Thomson, Ruth. Photos Framed: A Fresh Look at the World's Most Memorable Photographs. 2014. (ENG., Illus.). 64p. (J). (gr. 5). 18.99 (978-0-7636-7154-9(1)) Candlewick Pr.

Tress, Arthur, photos by. Facing Up: Tress: Facing Up. ltd. ed. 2004. (ENG & FRE., Illus.). 1250.00 (978-0-9761396-7-6(7), Tress-LE1) Top Choice Pr., LLC.

Turnbull, Stephanie. Cool Stuff to Photograph. 2015. (ENG., Illus.). 32p. (J). pap. 9.95 (978-1-77092-224-2(5)) RiverStream Publishing.

—Photography. 2015. (Try This! Ser.). (ENG., Illus.). 24p. (gr. 2-6). 27.10 (978-1-62588-374-2(9)) Black Rabbit Bks.

Turnbull, Stephaniel. Cool Stuff to Photograph. 2014. (Cool Stuff Ser.). 32p. (gr. 2-5). 31.35 (978-1-62588-190-8(8)) Black Rabbit Bks.

VanVoorst, Jenny Fretland. La Fotografía. 2016. (El Estudio del Artista (Artist's Studio)).Tr. of Photography. (SPA.). 24p. (J). lib. bdg. 25.65 (978-1-62031-324-4(3), Bullfrog Bks.) Jump! Inc.

Ventura, Marne. The 12 Most Influential Photographs of All Time. 2018. (ENG.). 32p. (gr. 3-6). 31.35 **(978-1-63235-412-9(8)**, 12-Story Library) Pr. Room Editions LLC.

Walters, John. Sportswriting & Sports Photography, Vol. 10. Ferrer, Al, ed. 2015. (Careers off the Field Ser.). (Illus.). 64p. (J). (gr. 7). lib. bdg. 23.95 (978-1-4222-3273-6(5)) Mason Crest.

Wanless, Harold R. Book of Aerial Stereo Photographs, 10 bks., Set. (Illus.). (J). (gr. 7-12). spiral bd. 13.50 (978-0-8331-1703-8(3), 589) Hubbard Scientific, Inc.

We are Photogirls Staff. DIY Fashion Shoot Book. 2014. (ENG., Illus.). 144p. 17.95 (978-1-78067-299-1(3)) King, Laurence Publishing GBR. Dist: Hachette Bk. Group.

Weatherford, Carole Boston. Dorothea Lange. Green, Sarah, illus. 2017. (ENG.). 32p. (J). (gr. -1-3). 16.99 (978-0-8075-1699-7(6)) Whitman, Albert & Co.

Webber, Diane. Shot & Framed: Photographers at the Crime Scene. 2007. (24/7: Science Behind the Scenes Ser.). (ENG., Illus.). 64p. (YA). (gr. 9-12). 29.00 (978-0-531-12063-7(5), Watts, Franklin) Scholastic Library Publishing.

Wyatt, Valerie. Welcome to the World. Newell, Lennette, illus. 2011. (ENG.). 24p. (J). (gr. -1 — 1). 14.95 (978-1-55453-593-4(X)) Kids Can Pr., Ltd. CAN. Dist: Hachette Bk. Group.

PHOTOGRAPHY, AERIAL

see Aerial Photography

PHOTOGRAPHY—AESTHETICS

see Photography, Artistic

PHOTOGRAPHY, ARTISTIC

Bower, John. Lingering Spirit: A Photographic Tribute to Indiana's Fading, Forlorn, & Forgotten Places. 2003. (Illus.). 144p. per. 22.00 (978-0-9745186-0-2(3)) Studio Indiana.

Burkhard, Balthasar. Click, Said the Camera. 2006. (Illus.). 42p. pap. 30.00 (978-3-907044-56-8(8)) Lars Muller Pubs. CHE. Dist: Springer.

Burnett, Craig. Jeff Wall. 2006. (ENG., Illus.). 128p. (gr. 8-17). pap. 24.95 (978-1-85437-611-4(X)) Tate Publishing, Ltd. GBR. Dist: Hachette Bk. Group.

Finger, Brad. 13 Photos Children Should Know. 2011. (ENG., Illus.). 48p. (J). (gr. 3-7). 14.95 (978-3-7913-7047-7(2)) Prestel Verlag GmbH & Co KG. DEU. Dist: Penguin Random Hse. LLC.

Kallas, Randi & Dougherty, Mike, eds. Rochester, Minnesota: A Visual & Historic Journey. 2003. (Illus.). 136p. pap. 24.95 (978-0-9659875-3-0(1)) Riggott, Dean Photography.

Lynch, Marietta & Perry, Patricia. No More Monkeys: A Photographic Version of the Children's Finger Game. (Orig.). (J). (gr. -1-3). pap. 2.95 (978-0-9610962-0-5(9)) Lynch, Marietta & Patricia Perry.

Quintero, Isabel & Iturbide, Graciela. Photographic: The Life of Graciela Iturbide. Peña, Zeke, illus. 2017. (J). **(978-1-60606-557-0(2)**, J. Paul Getty Museum) Getty Pubns.

PHOTOGRAPHY—FICTION

Alphin, Elaine Marie. Picture Perfect. 2003. (ENG., Illus.). 256p. (YA). (gr. 5-12). 15.95 (978-0-8225-0535-8(5)) Lerner Publishing Group.

Archer, Jennifer. Through Her Eyes. 2012. (ENG.). 400p. (YA). (gr. 8). pap. 9.99 (978-0-06-183459-2(9), HarperTeen) HarperCollins Pubs.

Avi. The Seer of Shadows. 2009. (ENG.). 224p. (J). (gr. 4-7). pap. 6.99 (978-0-06-000017-2(1)) HarperCollins Pubs.

Bailer, Darice. Railroad!, Level 3: A Story of the Transcontinental Railroad. Farnsworth, Bill, illus. 3rd ed. 2004. (Soundprints' Read-and-Discover Ser.). (ENG.). 48p. (J). (gr. 1-4). pap. 3.95 (978-1-59249-017-2(4), S2007) Soundprints.

Bauer, Joan. Thwonk. 2005. (ENG.). 224p. (YA). (gr. 7-7). pap. 7.99 (978-0-14-240429-4(2), Speak) Penguin Young Readers Group.

—Thwonk. 2005. 215p. (gr. 7-12). 18.00 (978-0-7569-5782-7(6)) Perfection Learning Corp.

Bentley, Sue. Picture Perfect #13. Swan, Angela & Farley, Andrew, illus. 2014. (Magic Kitten Ser.: 13). (ENG.). 128p. (J). (gr. 1-3). 4.99 (978-0-448-46796-2(8), Grosset & Dunlap) Penguin Young Readers Group.

Bernard, Janice. The Gum. 2011. 40p. pap. 21.99 (978-1-4568-6487-3(4)) Xlibris Corp.

Bick, Ilsa J. The Sin-Eater's Confession. Elyum Studio, illus. 2014. (ENG.). 296p. (YA). (gr. 9-12). pap. 9.95 (978-1-4677-3705-0(4), Carolrhoda Lab™) Lerner Publishing Group.

—The Sin-Eater's Confession. 2013. (ENG.). 296p. (YA). (gr. 9-12). 17.95 (978-0-7613-5687-5(8)) Lerner Publishing Group.

Breisacher, Cathy. Petunia Pepper's Picture Day. Elden, Christian, illus. 2010. 32p. (J). 14.99 (978-1-59317-397-5(0)) Warner Pr., Inc.

Cangilla-McAdam, Claudia. Maria's Mysterious Mission. Crum, Anna-Maria, illus. 2007. 32p. (J). (gr. 3-7). 12.95 (978-1-56579-588-4(1)) Fielder, John Publishing.

Chatel, Kim. A Talent for Quiet. Chatel, Kim, photos by. 2009. (Illus.). 32p. pap. 10.95 (978-1-935137-56-6(5)) Guardian Angel Publishing, Inc.

Cheese, Please! Individual Title Six-Packs. (Story Steps Ser.). (gr. k-2). 29.00 (978-0-7635-9589-0(6)) Rigby Education.

Chen, Justina. A Blind Spot for Boys. 2014. (ENG.). 336p. (YA). (gr. 7-17). 18.00 (978-0-316-10253-7(9)) Little, Brown Bks. for Young Readers.

Cunliffe, John. Postman Pat Takes a Photo. (Illus.). 20p. (J). 11.99 (978-0-340-73712-5(3)) Hodder & Stoughton GBR. Dist: Trafalgar Square Publishing.

Da Costa, Deborah. Hanukkah Moon. Mosz, Gosia, illus. 2007. (Hanukkah Ser.). 32p. (J). (gr. -1-3). 17.95 (978-1-58013-244-2(8), Kar-Ben Publishing) Lerner Publishing Group.

—Hanukkah Moon. Mosz, Gosia, illus. 2007. (Hanukkah Ser.). (ENG.). 32p. (J). (gr. 1-4). 10.95 (978-1-58013-245-9(6), Kar-Ben Publishing) Lerner Publishing Group.

Devlin, Calla. Right Where You Left Me. 2017. (ENG., Illus.). 256p. (YA). (gr. 9). 17.99 **(978-1-4814-8699-6(3)**, Atheneum Bks. for Young Readers) Simon & Schuster Children's Publishing.

Doudna, Kelly. Goat Cheese, 1 vol. Haberstroh, Anne, illus. 2006. (Animal Tales Ser.). 24p. (J). (gr. k-3). (ENG.). lib. bdg. 24.21 (978-1-59679-937-0(4), SandCastle); pap. 48.42 (978-1-59679-938-7(2)) ABDO Publishing Co.

Dower, Laura. They Came from Planet Q. Schlafman, Dave, illus. 2010. (Monster Squad Ser.: 4). (ENG.). 144p. (J). (gr. 2-4). pap. 5.99 (978-0-448-44915-9(3), Grosset & Dunlap) Penguin Young Readers Group.

Dwyer, Cynthia. Can You See Me Now? Schuepbach, Lynnette, illus. 2006. 24p. (J). 12.95 (978-0-9677685-8-8(6)) Grannie Annie Family Story Celebration, The.

Echols, Jennifer. Perfect Couple. 2015. (Superlatives Ser.). (ENG., Illus.). 336p. (YA). (gr. 9). pap. 10.99 (978-1-4424-7448-2(3), Simon Pulse) Simon Pulse.

Enderle, Dotti. Tell No One!, 1 vol. McWilliam, Howard, illus. 2010. (Ghost Detectors Ser.: No. 1). (ENG.). 80p. (J). (gr. 2-5). 27.07 (978-1-60270-692-7(1)) Magic Wagon.

Enderle, Judith Ross & Gordon, Stephanie Jacob. Smile, Principessa! Curmi, Serena, illus. 2012. (ENG.). 40p. (J). (gr. -1-1). 16.99 (978-1-4424-3096-9(6), McElderry, Margaret K. Bks.) McElderry, Margaret K. Bks.

Fields, Jan. Chase the Chupacabra, 1 vol. Brundage, Scott, illus. 2014. (Monster Hunters Ser.). (ENG.). 80p. (J). (gr. 8-12). 27.07 (978-1-62402-044-5(5)) Magic Wagon.

—Hunt for Sewer Gators, 1 vol. Brundage, Scott, illus. 2014. (Monster Hunters Ser.). (ENG.). 80p. (J). (gr. 8-12). 27.07 (978-1-62402-045-2(3)) Magic Wagon.

—Search for Bigfoot, 1 vol. Brundage, Scott, illus. 2014. (Monster Hunters Ser.). (ENG.). 80p. (J). (gr. 8-12). 27.07 (978-1-62402-046-9(1)) Magic Wagon.

—Tame Tahoe Tessie, 1 vol. Brundage, Scott, illus. 2014. (Monster Hunters Ser.). (ENG.). 80p. (J). (gr. 8-12). 27.07 (978-1-62402-047-6(X)) Magic Wagon.

—Track the Turtle Lake Monster, 1 vol. Brundage, Scott, illus. 2016. (ENG.). 80p. (J). lib. bdg. (978-1-62402-155-8(7)) Magic Wagon.

Geras, Adèle. Cecily's Portrait. 2009. (Historical House Ser.). 169p. (YA). (gr. 5-18). pap. 5.99 (978-0-7945-2334-3(X), Usborne) EDC Publishing.

Gibaldi, Lauren. Autofocus. 2016. 352p. (YA). (gr. 9). 17.99 (978-0-06-230223-6(X), HarperTeen) HarperCollins Pubs.

Giles, Lamar. Endangered. 2015. (ENG.). 288p. (YA). (gr. 9). 17.99 (978-0-06-229756-3(2), HarperTeen) HarperCollins Pubs.

Gregory, Kristiana & Campbell, Mary Exa Atkins. Earthquake at Dawn. 2003. (Great Episodes Ser.). (ENG., Illus.). 224p. (J). (gr. 5-7). pap. 13.95 (978-0-15-204681-1(X)) Houghton Mifflin Harcourt Publishing Co.

Gutknecht, Allison. Never Wear Red Lipstick on Picture Day: And Other Lessons I've Learned. Lewis, Stevie, illus. 2014. (ENG.). 176p. (J). (gr. 2-5). 16.99 (978-1-4814-2959-7(0), Aladdin) Simon & Schuster Children's Publishing.

Gutman, Dan. The Lincoln Project. 2016. (Flashback Four Ser.: 1). 240p. (J). (gr. 3-7). 16.99 (978-0-06-237441-7(9)) HarperCollins Pubs.

—Ms. Joni Is a Phony! Paillot, Jim, illus. 2017. (My Weirdest School Ser.: 7). 112p. (J). (gr. 1-5). pap. 4.99 (978-0-06-242929-2(9)) HarperCollins Pubs.

Hidier, Tanuja Desai. Born Confused. 2014. (ENG.). 512p. (J). (gr. 9). pap. 10.99 (978-0-545-66451-6(9), PUSH) Scholastic, Inc.

Honeyman, Kay. Interference. 2016. (ENG.). 352p. (YA). (gr. 7). 17.99 (978-0-545-81232-0(1), Levine, Arthur A. Bks.) Scholastic, Inc.

Jaden, Denise. Never Enough. 2012. (ENG.). 400p. (YA). (gr. 9). pap. 9.99 (978-1-4424-2907-9(0), Simon Pulse) Simon Pulse.

Jordan, Apple & RH Disney Staff. Barbie: On Your Toes. Wolcott, Karen, illus. 2005. (Step into Reading Ser.: No. 1). (ENG.). 32p. (J). (gr. -1-1). pap. 3.99 (978-0-375-83142-3(8), Random Hse. Bks. for Young Readers) Random Hse. Children's Bks.

Kernan, Elizabeth. Patty's Pictures. 2006. (Neighborhood Readers Ser.). (ENG.). 12p. (gr. -1-3). pap. 5.90 (978-1-4042-6471-7(X), Rosen Classroom) Rosen Publishing Group, Inc., The.

King, A. S. Glory O'Brien's History of the Future. 2014. (ENG.). 320p. (YA). (gr. 10-17). 18.00 (978-0-316-22272-3(0)) Little, Brown Bks. for Young Readers.

Knudsen, Shannon. Testing the Truth. 2015. (ENG.). 104p. (YA). (gr. 6-12). 27.99 (978-1-4677-5708-9(X)) Lerner Publishing Group.

Larson, Kirby. The Fences Between Us: The Diary of Piper Davis. 2010. (Dear America Ser.). (J). (ENG.). 320p. (gr. 3-7). 12.99 (978-0-545-22418-5(7)); (Illus.). 313p. pap. (978-0-545-27094-6(4)) Scholastic, Inc.

Lemke, Donald B. & Pattison, Ronda. Captured off Guard: The Attack on Pearl Harbor, 1 vol. St. Aubin, Claude, illus. 2008. (Historical Fiction Ser.). (ENG.). 56p. (gr. 2-3). pap. 6.25 (978-1-4342-0493-6(6), Graphic Flash) Stone Arch Bks.

Lord, Cynthia. Half a Chance. 2014. (ENG.). 224p. (J). (gr. 3-7). 16.99 (978-0-545-03533-0(3), Scholastic Pr.) Scholastic, Inc.

Maas, Susan Thogerson. Picture Imperfect. 2015. 228p. (J). pap. (978-1-941720-10-3(2)) Ashberry Lane.

Marcus, Kimberly. Exposed. 2012. (ENG.). 272p. (YA). (gr. 9). pap. 8.99 (978-0-375-86591-6(8), Ember) Random Hse. Children's Bks.

McBride, Kristina. The Tension of Opposites. 2011. (ENG.). 288p. (J). (gr. 9). pap. 8.99 (978-1-60684-213-3(7), Carolrhoda Lab™) Lerner Publishing Group.

McIntosh, Kenneth. Close-Up: Forensic Photography. 2009. (J). pap. 24.95 (978-1-4222-1455-8(9)) Mason Crest.

—Close-Up: Forensic Photography, 5 vols. Sanborn, Casey, illus. 2007. (Crime Scene Club Ser.: Bk. 5). 144p. (YA). (gr. 9-12). lib. bdg. 24.95 (978-1-4222-0251-7(8)) Mason Crest.

McNamara, Margaret. Class Picture Day. Gordon, Mike, illus. 2011. (Robin Hill School Ser.). (ENG.). 32p. (J). (gr. -1-1). pap. 3.99 (978-1-4169-9173-1(5), Simon Spotlight) Simon Spotlight.

Menchin, Scott. Goodnight Selfie. Collet-Derby, Pierre, illus. 2015. (ENG.). 32p. (J). (gr. -1-3). 14.99 (978-0-7636-3182-6(5)) Candlewick Pr.

Meyer, Carolyn. Girl with a Camera. 2017. (ENG.). 352p. (J). (gr. 4-9). 17.95 (978-1-62979-584-3(4), Calkins Creek) Boyds Mills Pr.

Mills, Charles. The Bandit of Benson Park. 2003. (Honors Club Story Ser.: Vol. 1). 127p. (J). (978-0-8163-1977-0(4)) Pacific Pr. Pubns.

Nees, Susan. Picture Day. 2013. (Missy's Super Duper Royal Deluxe Ser.: 1). (ENG., Illus.). 80p. (J). (gr. k-2). 15.99 (978-0-545-49609-4(8)); pap. 4.99 (978-0-545-43851-3(9)) Scholastic, Inc.

—Picture Day. 2013. (Missy's Super Duper Royal Deluxe Ser.: 1). lib. bdg. 14.75 (978-0-606-31979-9(4), Turtleback) Turtleback Bks.

Nelson, Suzanne. Hot Cocoa Hearts: a Wish Novel. 2016. (ENG.). 256p. (J). (gr. 4-7). pap. 6.99 (978-0-545-92889-2(3), Scholastic Paperbacks) Scholastic, Inc.

Perini, Mark & Cross, Julie. Halfway Perfect. 2015. (ENG.). 384p. (YA). (gr. 8-12). pap. 9.99 (978-1-4022-9719-9(X), 9781402297199) Sourcebooks, Inc.

Perkins, Lynne Rae. Pictures from Our Vacation. Perkins, Lynne Rae, illus. 2007. (Illus.). 32p. (J). (gr. k-3). 17.89 (978-0-06-085098-2(1), Greenwillow Bks.) HarperCollins Pubs.

Perkins, Lynne Rae & Perkins, Lynne R. Pictures from Our Vacation. Perkins, Lynne Rae, illus. 2007. (ENG., Illus.). 32p. (J). (gr. k-3). 17.99 (978-0-06-085097-5(3), Greenwillow Bks.) HarperCollins Pubs.

Rao, Sirish. Monkey Photo. Chitrakar, Swarna, illus. 2010. (ENG.). 32p. (J). (gr. -1-1). (978-81-907546-2-0(9)) Tara Publishing.

Rey, H. A. Dinosaur Tracks. 2011. (Curious George Ser.). (ENG., Illus.). 24p. (J). (gr. -1-3). pap. 3.99 (978-0-547-43888-7(5)) Houghton Mifflin Harcourt Publishing Co.

—Jorge el Curioso Huellas de Dinosaurio. 2011. (Curious George Ser.). (ENG & SPA., Illus.). 24p. (J). (gr. -1-3). pap. 3.99 (978-0-547-55798-4(1)) Houghton Mifflin Harcourt Publishing Co.

Romano, Juliana. Summer in the Invisible City. 2016. (ENG.). 320p. (YA). (gr. 9). 17.99 (978-0-525-42917-3(4), Dial Bks) Penguin Young Readers Group.

Schroeder, Lisa. Charmed Life #2: Mia's Golden Bird. 2014. (Charmed Life Ser.: 2). (ENG.). 192p. (J). (gr. 3-7). pap. 5.99 (978-0-545-60377-5(3)) Scholastic, Inc.

—Mia's Golden Bird. 2014. (Charmed Life Ser.: 2). lib. bdg. 16.00 (978-0-606-35850-7(1)) Turtleback Bks.

Scotton, Rob. Russell & the Lost Treasure. Scotton, Rob, illus. 2006. (ENG., Illus.). 32p. (J). (gr. -1-2). 15.99 (978-0-06-059851-8(4)) HarperCollins Pubs.

Shea, Therese. Carmen's Photo Album. 2006. (Neighborhood Readers Ser.). (ENG.). 12p. (gr. 1-3). pap. 5.90 (978-1-4042-6795-4(6), Rosen Classroom) Rosen Publishing Group, Inc., The.

Sher, Emil. Young Man with Camera. Wyman, David, photos by. 2015. (ENG., Illus.). 240p. (J). (gr. 7). 17.99 (978-0-545-54131-2(X), Levine, Arthur A. Bks.) Scholastic, Inc.

Shutter. 2015. (ENG.). 384p. (YA). (gr. 8-12). 17.99 (978-1-250-04467-9(7)) Feiwel & Friends.

Snyder, Karen. Safari Smooches. LaGrange, Tiffany, illus. 2011. 24p. pap. 12.95 (978-1-936343-95-9(9)) Peppertree Pr., The.

Sonnenblick, Jordan. Curveball: The Year I Lost My Grip. 304p. 2014. (ENG.). (J). (gr. 7). pap. 9.99 (978-0-545-32070-2(4), Scholastic Paperbacks) 2012. pap. 17.99 (978-0-545-39311-9(6)) Scholastic, Inc.

Stolarz, Laurie Faria. Shutter. 2016. (ENG.). 352p. (YA). (gr. 9-17). 17.99 (978-1-4847-2790-4(8)) Hyperion Pr.

Tatulli, Mark. Desmond Pucket & the Mountain Full of Monsters. 2014. (Desmond Pucket Ser.: 2). (ENG.). 240p. (J). 13.99 (978-1-4494-3549-3(1)) Andrews McMeel Publishing.

Toliver, K. S. Pam Brown Is Picture Perfect!! 2008. 28p. pap. 12.95 (978-1-4327-2058-2(9)) Outskirts Pr., Inc.

Townley, Roderick. The Red Thread: A Novel in Three Incarnations. 2012. (ENG.). 304p. (YA). (gr. 7). pap. 14.99 (978-1-4169-0895-1(1), Atheneum Bks. for Young Readers) Simon & Schuster Children's Publishing.

Tracy, Kristen. Project (un)Popular Book #1. (Project (un)Popular Ser.). (ENG.). 336p. (J). (gr. 5). 2017. 7.99 **(978-0-553-51051-5(7)**, Yearling) 2016. 16.99 (978-0-553-51048-5(7), Delacorte Bks. for Young Readers) Random Hse. Children's Bks.

Turner, Amber McRee. Circa Now. 2014. (ENG., Illus.). 288p. (J). (gr. 3-7). 16.99 (978-1-4231-7639-8(1)) Hyperion Bks. for Children.

Vivian, Siobhan. A Little Friendly Advice. 2015. (ENG.). 256p. (J). (gr. 7). pap. 9.99 (978-0-545-75801-7(7), PUSH) Scholastic, Inc.

Wheeler, Elizabeth. Asher's Fault. 2013. (ENG.). 264p. (gr. 7). pap. 11.95 (978-1-60282-982-4(9)) Bold Strokes Bks.

—Asher's Out. 2015. (ENG.). 264p. (J). (gr. 7). pap. 11.95 (978-1-62639-411-7(3)) Bold Strokes Bks.

Ylvisaker, Anne. The Luck of the Buttons. 2012. (ENG., Illus.). 240p. (J). (gr. 3-7). pap. 6.99 (978-0-7636-6061-1(2)) Candlewick Pr.

PHOTOGRAPHY—HISTORY

Aller, Susan Bivin. George Eastman. 2003. (History Maker Biographies Ser.). (ENG., Illus.). 48p. (gr. 3-6). lib. bdg. 27.93 (978-0-8225-0200-5(3)) Lerner Publishing Group.

Bankston, John. Louis Daguerre & the Story of the Daguerreotype. 2004. (Uncharted, Unexplored, & Unexplained Ser.). (Illus.). 48p. (J). (gr. 4-8). lib. bdg. 29.95 (978-1-58415-247-7(8)) Mitchell Lane Pubs., Inc.

Buckley, Annie. Photography. 2008. (21st Century Skills Innovation Library: Innovation in Entertainment Ser.). (ENG., Illus.). 32p. (gr. 4-8). lib. bdg. 28.50 (978-1-60279-221-0(6), 200152) Cherry Lake Publishing.

Burgan, Michael. Breaker Boys: How a Photograph Helped End Child Labor, 1 vol. 2011. (Captured History Ser.). (ENG.). 64p. (gr. 5-7). pap. 9.10 (978-0-7565-4510-9(2), CPB Grades 4-8) Compass Point Bks.

Ford, Carin T. George Eastman: The Kodak Camera Man. 2004. (Famous Inventors Ser.). (Illus.). 32p. (J). lib. bdg. 22.60 (978-0-7660-2247-8(1)) Enslow Pubs., Inc.

James, Sara. Photography. 2014. (Art Today! Ser.: 10). 64p. (J). (gr. 7-18). 23.95 (978-1-4222-3175-3(5)) Mason Crest.

Kuskowski, Alex & Craig, Diane. Super Simple Camera Projects: Inspiring & Educational Science Activities, 1 vol. 2016. (ENG., Illus.). 32p. (J). (978-1-62403-730-6(5)) ABDO Publishing Co.

Mattern, Joanne. George Eastman & Photographic Film. 2004. (Uncharted, Unexplored, & Unexplained Ser.). (Illus.). 48p. (J). (gr. 4-8). lib. bdg. 29.95 (978-1-58415-258-3(3)) Mitchell Lane Pubs., Inc.

Murray, Stuart A. P. Mathew Brady: Photographer of Our Nation. 2009. (ENG., Illus.). 83p. (gr. 6-18). lib. bdg. 158.00 (978-0-7656-8151-5(X), Y182957) Routledge.

Nagelhout, Ryan. The Problem with Early Cameras. 2015. (Bloopers of Invention Ser.). (ENG., Illus.). 24p. (J). (gr. 2-3). pap. 8.15 (978-1-4824-2756-1(7)) Stevens, Gareth Publishing LLLP.

Oxlade, Chris & Ganeri, Anita. The Camera, 1 vol. 2010. (Tales of Invention Ser.). (ENG.). 32p. (gr. 3-5). 30.65 (978-1-4329-3828-4(2), NA-h) Heinemann-Raintree.

Pobst, Sandy. The Camera. 2005. (Great Inventions Ser.). (Illus.). 48p. (gr. 5-12). lib. bdg. 31.00 (978-0-8368-5801-3(8), Gareth Stevens Secondary Library) Stevens, Gareth Publishing LLLP.

Steffoff, Rebecca. The Camera. 2007. (Great Inventions Ser.). (Illus.). 128p. (gr. 8-18). lib. bdg. 29.95 (978-0-7614-2596-0(9), Benchmark Bks.) Marshall Cavendish Corp.

Vallencourt, Margaret. The History of Photography. 2015. (Britannica Guide to the Visual & Performing Arts Ser.). (ENG.). 128p. (J). (gr. 9-10). 45.00 (978-1-68048-073-3(1), Britannica Educational Publishing) Rosen Publishing Group, Inc., The.

PHOTOGRAPHY, JOURNALISTIC

see Photojournalism

PHOTOGRAPHY—VOCATIONAL GUIDANCE

Somervill, Barbara A. Wildlife Photographer. 2015. (21st Century Skills Library: Cool STEAM Careers Ser.). (ENG.). 32p. (J). (gr. 4-7). 29.93 (978-1-63362-569-3(9), 206460) Cherry Lake Publishing.

Sommers, Michael A. Wildlife Photographers: Life Through a Lens. 2005. (Extreme Careers Ser.). (Illus.). 64p. (YA). (gr. 5-8). 31.95 (978-0-8239-3638-0(4)) Rosen Publishing Group, Inc., The.

PHOTOGRAPHY OF ANIMALS

see also Animal Painting and Illustration

Burkhard, Balthasar. Click, Said the Camera. 2006. (Illus.). 42p. pap. 30.00 (978-3-907044-56-8(8)) Lars Muller Pubs. CHE. Dist: Springer.

Cerullo, Mary M. Searching for Great White Sharks: A Shark Diver's Quest for Mr. Big, 1 vol. Rotman, Jeffrey L., photos by. 2014. (Shark Expedition Ser.). (ENG., Illus.). 40p. (gr. 5-7). lib. bdg. 31.99 (978-0-7565-4884-1(5)) Compass Point Bks.

—Seeking Giant Sharks: A Shark Diver's Quest for Whale Sharks, Basking Sharks, & Manta Rays, 1 vol. Rotman, Jeffrey L., illus. Rotman, Jeffrey L., photos by. 2014. (Shark Expedition Ser.). (ENG.). 40p. (gr. 5-7). lib. bdg. 31.99 (978-0-7565-4885-8(3)) Compass Point Bks.

—Sharks of the Deep: A Shark Photographer's Search for Sharks at the Bottom of the Sea, 1 vol. Rotman, Jeffrey L., illus. Rotman, Jeffrey L., photos by. 2014. (Shark Expedition Ser.). (ENG.). 40p. (gr. 5-7). lib. bdg. 31.99 (978-0-7565-4886-5(1)) Compass Point Bks.

Earhart, Kristin, ed. Life-Size Zoo: From Tiny Rodents to Gigantic Elephants, an Actual Size Animal Encyclopedia. Fukuda, Toyofumi, photos by. 2009. (ENG., Illus.). 48p. (gr. -1). 17.95 (978-1-934734-20-9(9)) Seven Footer Pr.

Kalman, Bobbie. It Looks Like a Dog. 2011. (ENG.). 16p. (J). lib. bdg. (978-0-7787-9546-9(2)); pap. (978-0-7787-9571-1(3)) Crabtree Publishing Co.

Leach, Michael & Lland, Meriel. Wildlife Watcher Guide: Animal Tracking - Photography Skills - Fieldcraft - Safety - Footprint Indentification - Camera Traps - Making a Blind - Night-TimeTracking. 2016. (ENG., Illus.). 96p. (J). (gr. 5-8). pap. 9.95 (978-1-77085-742-1(7), 9781770857421) Firefly Bks., Ltd.

L'Heureux, J. J. Good Day Book. 2006. spiral bd. (978-0-9785892-0-2(3)) BrainStream.

Momatiuk, Yva. Face to Face with Wild Horses. Eastcott, John, photos by. 2009. (Face to Face with Animals Ser.). (ENG., Illus.). 32p. (J). (gr. 2-5). 16.95 (978-1-4263-0466-8(8), National Geographic Children's Bks.) National Geographic Society.

Somervill, Barbara A. Wildlife Photographer. 2008. (21st Century Skills Library: Cool Careers Ser.). (ENG., Illus.). 32p. (gr. 4-8). lib. bdg. 28.50 (978-1-60279-300-2(X), 200139) Cherry Lake Publishing.

Sommers, Michael. Wildlife Photographers: Life Through a Lens. 2009. (Extreme Careers Ser.). 64p. (gr. 5-5). 58.50 (978-1-61512-421-3(7), Rosen Reference) Rosen Publishing Group, Inc., The.

Thomas, William David. Wildlife Photographer. 2008. (Cool Careers: Adventure Careers Ser.). (Illus.). 32p. (gr. 5-8). pap. 10.50 (978-0-8368-8892-8(8)); lib. bdg. 26.00 (978-0-8368-8885-0(5)) Stevens, Gareth Publishing LLLP.

Vyn, Gerrit. Wildlife Photographer: The Coolest Jobs on the Planet, 1 vol. 2013. (Coolest Jobs on the Planet Ser.). (ENG.). 48p. (gr. 5-8). 32.65 (978-1-4109-5485-5(4)); pap. 8.99 (978-1-4109-5490-9(0)) Heinemann-Raintree.

Watts, Gillian. Creatures Close Up. Martin, Philippe, photos by. 2016. (ENG., Illus.). 64p. (J). (gr. 3-7). pap. 9.95 (978-1-77085-782-7(6), 9781770857827) Firefly Bks., Ltd.

PHOTOGRAPHY OF NATURE

see Nature Photography

PHOTOJOURNALISM

Burgan, Michael. Ali's Knockout Punch: How a Photograph Stunned the Boxing World. 2017. (Captured History Sports Ser.). (ENG., Illus.). 64p. (gr. 5-7). lib. bdg. 34.65 (978-0-7565-5527-6(2), CPB Grades 4-8) Compass Point Bks.

—Olympic Gold 1936: How the Image of Jesse Owens Crushed Hitler's Evil Myth. 2017. (Captured History Sports Ser.). (ENG., Illus.). 64p. (gr. 5-7). lib. bdg. 34.65 (978-0-7565-5528-3(0), CPB Grades 4-8) Compass Point Bks.

Koh, Frederick. The 10 Most Compelling News Images. 2008. (J). 14.99 (978-1-55448-533-8(9)) Scholastic Library Publishing.

Linde, Barbara & Benchmark Education Co. Staff. Opinions about Matthew Brady. 2014. (Text Connections Ser.). (J). (gr. 5). (978-1-4900-1380-0(6)) Benchmark Education Co.

PHOTOPLAYS

see Motion Picture Plays

PHOTOSYNTHESIS

Andersen, Jill. Plants Need Light. 2016. (Rosen REAL Readers: STEM & STEAM Collection). 8p. (gr. 1-k). pap. 5.46 (978-1-5081-2386-6(1), Rosen Classroom) Rosen Publishing Group, Inc., The.

Bang, Molly & Chisholm, Penny. Living Sunlight: How Plants Bring the Earth to Life. Bang, Molly, illus. 2009. (ENG., Illus.). 40p. (J). (gr. -1-3). 18.99 (978-0-545-04422-6(7), Blue Sky Pr., The) Scholastic, Inc.

Famighetti, Robert, et al. How Do Plants Get Food? 2009. (Science in the Real World Ser.). (Illus.). 32p. (gr. 4-6). 28.00 (978-1-60413-468-1(2), Chelsea Clubhouse) Facts On File, Inc.

Goldsworthy, Kaite. Producers. 2016. (J). **(978-1-4896-5779-4(7))** 2011. (J). (gr. 4-6). pap. 12.95 (978-1-61690-716-7(9), AV2 by Weigl) 2011. (Illus.). 24p. (YA). (gr. 2-5). 27.13 (978-1-61690-710-5(X)) Weigl Pubs., Inc.

Haelle, Tara. Edible Sunlight. 2016. (Let's Explore Science Ser.). (ENG., Illus.). 48p. (gr. 5-8). 35.64 (978-1-68191-399-5(2)) Rourke Educational Media.

Higgins, Nadia. Experiment with Photosynthesis. 2015. (Lightning Bolt Books (tm) — Plant Experiments Ser.). (ENG., Illus.). 32p. (gr. k-2). 26.65 (978-1-4677-5732-4(2)); pap. 8.99 (978-1-4677-6075-1(7)) Lerner Publishing Group. (Lerner Pubns.).

Hopkins, William G. Photosynthesis & Respiration. 2006. (Green World Ser.). (Illus.). 168p. (gr. 6-12). lib. bdg. 37.50 (978-0-7910-8561-5(9)) Facts On File, Inc.

Juettner, Bonnie. Photosynthesis. 2005. (KidHaven Science Library). (ENG., Illus.). 48p. (J). (gr. 3-7). lib. bdg. 27.50 (978-0-7377-2350-2(5), Greenhaven Pr., Inc.) Cengage Gale.

Kalman, Bobbie. La Fotosíntesis: De la Luz Del Sol Al Alimento. 2006. (Cambios Que Suceden en la Naturaleza Ser.). (SPA., Illus.). 32p. (J). (gr. 3-7). pap. (978-0-7787-8386-2(3)) Crabtree Publishing Co.

—La Fotosíntesis: De la Luz del Sol al Alimento. 2006. (Cambios Que Suceden en la Naturaleza Ser.). (SPA., Illus.). 32p. (J). (gr. 3-7). lib. bdg. (978-0-7787-8372-5(3)) Crabtree Publishing Co.

—How Do Living Things Find Food? 2010. (Introducing Living Things Ser.). (ENG.). 24p. (J). (gr. 1-4). pap. (978-0-7787-3258-7(4)); lib. bdg. (978-0-7787-3234-1(7)) Crabtree Publishing Co.

—Photosynthesis: Changing Sunlight into Food. (ENG.). 32p. (J). 2008. (978-0-7787-7717-5(0)) 2005. (Illus.). (gr. -1-3). pap. (978-0-7787-2308-0(9)) Crabtree Publishing Co.

Kalman, Bobbie & Sjonger, Rebecca. Photosynthesis: Changing Sunlight into Food. 2008. (ENG.). 32p. (J). (978-0-7787-7716-8(2)) Crabtree Publishing Co.

Latham, Donna. Respiration & Photosynthesis. 2016. (Sci-Hi: Life Science Ser.). (ENG.). 48p. (gr. 4-4). pap. 8.99 (978-1-4109-8632-0(2), Sci-Hi) Heinemann-Raintree.

Lawrence, Ellen. Cooking with Sunshine: How Plants Make Food. 2012. (Science Slam: Plant-Ology Ser.). 24p. (J). (gr. -1-3). lib. bdg. 23.93 (978-1-61772-586-9(2)) Bearport Publishing Co., Inc.

—How Plants Clean the Air. 2014. (Science Slam: Plant-Ology Ser.). (ENG.). 24p. (J). (gr. -1-3). lib. bdg. 23.93 *(978-1-62724-305-6(4))* Bearport Publishing Co., Inc.

Maloof, Torrey. Photosynthesis, 1 vol. 2015. (Science Readers: Content & Literacy Ser.). (ENG., Illus.). 32p. (gr. 3-3). pap. 8.99 *(978-1-4807-4640-4(1))* Teacher Created Materials, Inc.

O'Donnell, Liam. Understanding Photosynthesis with Max Axiom, Super Scientist, 1 vol. Dominguez, Richard & Barnett, Charles, III, illus. 2007. (Graphic Science Ser.). (ENG.). 32p. (gr. 3-4). per. 8.10 *(978-0-7368-7893-7(9),* 1264938, Graphic Library) Capstone Press of Coughlan Cos.

O'Donnell, Liam & Barnett, Charles, III. Cómo Comprender la Fotosíntesis con Max Axiom, Supercientífico. Dominguez, Richard, illus. 2013. (Ciencia Gráfica Ser.). (SPA.). 32p. (gr. 3-4). pap. 8.10 *(978-1-62065-984-7(0));* lib. bdg. 30.65 *(978-1-62065-180-3(7))* Capstone Press of Coughlan Cos.

O'Donnell, Liam & Barnett III, Charles. Understanding Photosynthesis with Max Axiom, Super Scientist, 1 vol. Dominguez, Richard et al, illus. 2007. (Graphic Science Ser.). (ENG.). 32p. (gr. 3-4). 30.65 *(978-0-7368-6841-9(0),* 1264938, Graphic Library) Capstone Press of Coughlan Cos.

Silverstein, Alvin, et al. Photosynthesis. 2007. (Science Concepts, Second Ser.). (Illus.). 80p. (YA). (gr. 5-9). lib. bdg. 31.93 *(978-0-8225-6798-1(9))* Lerner Publishing Group.

Spiro, Ruth & Chan, Irene. Baby Loves Thermodynamics! 2017. (ENG., Illus.). 20p. (J). (— 1). bds. 8.99 ***(978-1-58089-768-6(1))*** Charlesbridge Publishing, Inc.

Staub, Frank. Photosynthesis. 2003. (World of Wonder Ser.). (Illus.). 32p. (J). lib. bdg. *(978-1-58341-265-7(4),* Creative Education) Creative Co., The.

Waldron, Melanie. Leaves, 1 vol. 2014. (Plant Parts Ser.). (ENG.). 32p. (gr. 2-4). lib. bdg. 30.65 *(978-1-4109-5421-3(8),* Raintree Perspectives) Heinemann-Raintree.

Wells, Robert E. Why Do Elephants Need the Sun? 2012. (J). 34.28 *(978-1-61913-142-2(0))* Weigl Pubs., Inc.

—Why Do Elephants Need the Sun? Wells, Robert E., illus. 2012. (Wells of Knowledge Science Ser.). (ENG., Illus.). 32p. (J). (gr. -1-3). pap. 7.99 *(978-0-8075-9082-9(7))* Whitman, Albert & Co.

PHYSICAL CHEMISTRY

see Chemistry, Physical and Theoretical

PHYSICAL CULTURE

see Physical Education and Training

PHYSICAL EDUCATION AND TRAINING

see also Athletics; Coaching (Athletics); Exercise; Games; Gymnastics; Health Education; Physical Fitness; Sports

also names of kinds of exercises, e.g. Fencing; Judo

Abramovitz, Melissa. Skiing. Lucent Books, ed. 2014. (Science Behind Sports Ser.). (ENG., Illus.). 128p. (gr. 7-10). lib. bdg. 39.40 *(978-1-4205-1155-0(6),* Lucent Bks.) Cengage Gale.

Becker, Helaine. Skateboarding Science. 2008. (Sports Science Ser.). (ENG., Illus.). 32p. (J). (gr. 4-6). pap. *(978-0-7787-4553-2(8));* lib. bdg. *(978-0-7787-4536-5(8))* Crabtree Publishing Co.

Biskup, Agnieszka. Hockey: How It Works. 2010. (Science of Sports (Sports Illustrated for Kids) Ser.). (ENG.). 48p. (gr. 3-4). pap. 59.70 *(978-1-4296-5109-7(1))* Capstone Press of Coughlan Cos.

Bloom, Paul. Rules in the Gym. 2015. (School Rules Ser.). (ENG., Illus.). 24p. (J). (gr. k-k). pap. 8.15 *(978-1-4824-2645-8(5))* Stevens, Gareth Publishing LLLP.

Boudreau, Hélène. Swimming Science. 2008. (Sports Science Ser.). (ENG., Illus.). 32p. (J). (gr. 4-6). pap. *(978-0-7787-4555-6(4));* lib. bdg. *(978-0-7787-4538-9(4))* Crabtree Publishing Co.

Bow, James. Baseball Science. 2008. (Sports Science Ser.). (ENG., Illus.). 32p. (J). (gr. 4-6). pap. *(978-0-7787-4551-8(1))* Crabtree Publishing Co.

—Cycling Science. 2008. (Sports Science Ser.). (ENG., Illus.). 32p. (J). (gr. 4-6). pap. *(978-0-7787-4552-5(X));* lib. bdg. *(978-0-7787-4535-8(X))* Crabtree Publishing Co.

Bow, Patricia. Tennis Science. 2008. (Sports Science Ser.). (ENG., Illus.). 32p. (J). (gr. 4-6). pap. *(978-0-7787-4556-3(2));* lib. bdg. *(978-0-7787-4539-6(2))* Crabtree Publishing Co.

Brezina, Corona. What Happens to Your Body When You Are Weight Training. 2009. (How & Why of Exercise Ser.). (Illus.). 48p. (YA). (gr. 5-9). 29.25 *(978-1-4358-5307-2(5))* Rosen Publishing Group, Inc., The.

Chaline, Eric. Martial Arts for Athletic Conditioning. 2003. (Martial & Fighting Arts Ser.). (Illus.). 96p. (J). (gr. 7-18). lib. bdg. *(978-1-59084-397-0(5))* Mason Crest.

Compton, Leanne, et al. Jump Start 7 & 8: Health & Physical Education. 2007. 336p. pap. 41.00 incl. cd-rom *(978-0-521-70156-3(2))* Cambridge Univ. Pr.

Davis, Barbara. 404 Deskside Activities for Energetic Kids. 2006. (SmartFun Activity Bks.). (ENG., Illus.). 168p. (gr. -1-5). pap. 14.95 *(978-0-89793-467-1(9),* Hunter Hse.) Turner Publishing Co.

Dintiman, George Blough. Speed Improvement for Young Athletes: How to Sprint Faster in Your Sport in 30 Workouts. rev. ed. 2006. (Illus.). 153p. pap. 17.95 *(978-0-938074-26-7(1))* National Assn. of Speed & Explosion.

DiPrimio, Pete. The World of CrossFit. 2014. 48p. (gr. 4-8). 29.95 *(978-1-61228-552-8(X))* Mitchell Lane Pubs., Inc.

Entrenamiento Deportivo Series, 6 bks., Set. 2003. (Entrenamiento Deportivo Ser.). (SPA & ENG., Illus.). (J). 103.50 *(978-0-8239-6913-5(4),* Editorial Buenas Letras) Rosen Publishing Group, Inc., The.

Ferguson. Coaches & Fitness Professionals. 2nd rev. ed. 2008. (Careers in Focus Ser.). 188p. (gr. 6-12). 32.95 *(978-0-8160-7284-2(1),* Ferguson Publishing Co.) Facts On File, Inc.

Fridell, Ron. Sports Technology. 2009. pap. 52.95 *(978-0-7613-4785-9(2))* Lerner Publishing Group.

Gallagher, R., et al. Addysg Gorfforol Trwy Ddiagramau: Llawlyfr Adolygu TGAU. 2005. (WEL., Illus.). 92p. pap. *(978-1-85644-562-7(3))* CAA.

Gardner, Robert, et al. Ace Your Sports Science Project: Great Science Fair Ideas. 2009. (Ace Your Physics Science Project Ser.). (Illus.). 128p. (J). (gr. 5-18). lib. bdg. 33.27 *(978-0-7660-3229-3(9))* Enslow Pubs., Inc.

Gigliotti, Jim. STEM in Sports. 2015. (STEM in Sports Ser.). (Illus.). 64p. (J). (gr. 7). 23.95 *(978-1-4222-3233-0(6))* Mason Crest.

Glass, Maya. The Marching Book. 2004. (Let's Get Moving Ser.). (Illus.). 24p. (J). (gr. k-1). lib. bdg. 22.60 *(978-1-4042-2516-9(1),* PowerKids Pr.) Rosen Publishing Group, Inc., The.

Goodstein, Madeline. Sports Science Fair Projects. 2015. (Prize-Winning Science Fair Projects Ser.). (ENG.). 128p. (J). (gr. 7-7). lib. bdg. 37.27 *(978-0-7660-7026-4(3))* Enslow Pubs., Inc.

Harcourt School Publishers Staff. Harcourt Physical Education Posters, Grades 3-6. 3rd ed. 2003. (Illus.). 55.20 *(978-0-15-339102-6(2))* Harcourt Schl. Pubs.

Hardman, Lizabeth. Baseball. 2010. (Science Behind Sports Ser.). (ENG., Illus.). 128p. (gr. 7-10). 39.40 *(978-1-4205-0262-6(X))* Cengage Gale.

Hyde, Natalie. Soccer Science. 2008. (Sports Science Ser.). (ENG., Illus.). 32p. (J). (gr. 4-6). pap. *(978-0-7787-4554-9(6))* Crabtree Publishing Co.

James, Rob. AS/A Level Physical Education: Skills Acquisition & Sports Psychology. 2010. 204p. pap. 13.95 *(978-1-4441-1545-1(6))* Hodder Education Group GBR. Dist: Trans-Atlantic Pubns., Inc.

Kortemeier, Todd. 12 Ways to Improve Athletic Performance. 2017. (Healthy Living Ser.). (ENG., Illus.). 32p. (J). (gr. 3-6). 21.95 *(978-1-63235-369-6(5))* Pr. Room Editions LLC.

Lasslett, Sally, et al. Jump Start 9 & 10: Health & Physical Education. 2007. pap. 32.95 incl. cd-rom *(978-0-521-70167-9(8))* Cambridge Univ. Pr.

Mason, Paul. Improving Speed. 2011. (Training for Sports Ser.). (Illus.). 32p. (YA). (gr. 5-9). 26.50 *(978-1-4488-3302-3(7))* Rosen Publishing Group, Inc., The.

—Improving Strength & Power. 2011. (Training for Sports Ser.). (Illus.). 32p. (YA). (gr. 5-9). 26.50 *(978-1-4488-3301-6(9))* Rosen Publishing Group, Inc., The.

Massad, Diane Patterson. Hang On! The Kidskills International Training Series. 2004. (Kidskills America Training Ser.). (ENG., Illus.). (YA). spiral bd. 12.95 *(978-0-9710641-9-5(9))* Kidskills International.

—Making Muscles! The Kidskills America Training Series. 2004. (Kidskills America Training Ser.). (Illus.). 75p. (J). spiral bd. 12.95 *(978-0-9710641-6-4(4))* Kidskills International.

—Up & Over! The Kidskills America Training Series. 2004. (Kidskills America Training Ser.). (Illus.). 75p. (J). spiral bd. 12.95 *(978-0-9710641-5-7(6),* Kidskills America) Kidskills International.

McLean, Linda, et al. National 4 & 5 Physical Education. 2014. (ENG.). 16p. (YA). (gr. 9-11). pap. 23.99 *(978-0-00-750477-0(2))* HarperCollins Pubs. Ltd. GBR. Dist: Independent Pubs. Group.

Middlewood, G. & Debenham, A. 43 Team-Building Activities. 2007. 64p. per. *(978-1-903853-57-3(5))* Brilliant Pubns.

Morris, Ann. That's Our Gym Teacher! Linenthal, Peter, illus. Linenthal, Peter, photos by. 2003. (That's Our School Ser.). (ENG.). 32p. (gr. k-3). lib. bdg. 22.60 *(978-0-7613-2403-4(8),* Millbrook Pr.) Lerner Publishing Group.

Smibert, Angie. 12 Ways to Improve Athletic Performance. 2016. (Healthy Living Ser.). (ENG., Illus.). 32p. (J). pap. 9.95 *(978-1-63235-387-0(3),* 12-Story Library) Pr. Room Editions LLC.

Sports. 2010. (Experimenting with Everyday Science Ser.). (Illus.). 160p. (gr. 6-12). 35.00 *(978-1-60413-170-3(5),* Chelsea Hse.) Facts On File, Inc.

Stille, Darlene R. The Science of Gym Class: More Than Just Dodgeball & Sweatpants, 1 vol. 2011. (Everyday Science Ser.). (ENG.). 64p. (gr. 5-7). pap. 9.10 *(978-0-7565-4504-8(8),* CPB Grades 4-8) Compass Point Bks.

Thompson, Graham. Physical Education: Anatomy & Exercise Physiology. 2010. 204p. pap. 13.95 *(978-1-4441-1540-6(5))* Hodder Education Group GBR. Dist: Trans-Atlantic Pubns., Inc.

Verdick, Elizabeth & Lisovskis, Marjorie. Reach. 2013. (Happy Healthy Baby(r) Ser.). (ENG., Illus.). 22p. (J). bds. 6.99 *(978-1-57542-424-8(X))* Free Spirit Publishing, Inc.

Wiggins-James, Nesta. AS/A-Level Physical Education: Historical Factors & Contemporary Issues. 2010. 204p. pap. 13.95 *(978-1-4441-1544-4(8))* Hodder Education Group GBR. Dist: Trans-Atlantic Pubns., Inc.

Yancey, Diane. Basketball. 2011. (Science Behind Sports Ser.). 128p. (YA). (gr. 7-12). 34.45 *(978-1-4205-0293-0(X))* Cengage Gale.

PHYSICAL FITNESS

Abdo Publishing. Move Your Body: A Kid's Guide to Fitness, 1 vol. 2013. (Move Your Body Ser.: 6). (ENG.). 32p. (J). (gr. 2-5). lib. bdg. 162.42 *(978-1-61783-559-9(5),* Buddy Bks.) ABDO Publishing Co.

—Super Simple Body, 1 vol. 2013. (Super Simple Your Body Ser.: 6). (ENG.). 32p. (J). (gr. k-4). lib. bdg. 162.42 *(978-1-61783-608-4(7),* Super SandCastle) ABDO Publishing Co.

Aliotti, Johnny. Johnny's Simple Dumbbell Workout. 2004. spiral bd. 14.95 *(978-0-9740600-1-9(1));* (Illus.). 102p. per. 13.95 *(978-0-9740600-0-2(3))* ProTips(TM) Media.

Bailey, Megan. Fit & Fun. 2013. (Healthy Kids Ser.). (ENG.). 24p. (J). (gr. 1-4). 28.50 *(978-1-62323-543-7(X),* 206268) Child's World, Inc., The.

Berger, Melvin & Berger, Gilda. Kicking, Running, & Stretching. 2007. (Illus.). 32p. (J). pap. *(978-0-439-02449-5(8))* Scholastic, Inc.

Berton, Judy & Guimond, Rick. Do a Dance Picture Book. 2006. (Illus.). (J). spiral bd. 8.95 *(978-0-9761051-1-4(X))* Kidrich Corp.

Blackwell, Amy Hackney. Personal Care Services, Fitness & Education. 2008. (Great Careers with a High School Diploma Ser.). 114p. (C). (gr. 9). 32.95 *(978-0-8160-7045-9(8),* Ferguson Publishing Co.) Facts On File, Inc.

Bodden, Valerie. Being Fit. 2015. (J). *(978-1-60818-506-1(0),* Creative Education) Creative Co., The.

—Healthy Plates: Being Fit. 2015. (Healthy Plates Ser.). (ENG.). 24p. (J). (gr. 1-3). pap. 9.99 *(978-1-62832-106-7(7),* Creative Paperbacks) Creative Co., The.

Borgert-Spaniol, Megan. Keeping Fit. 2012. (Eating Right with Myplate Ser.). (ENG., Illus.). 24p. (J). (gr. k-3). lib. bdg. 25.95 *(978-1-60014-758-6(5),* Blastoff! Readers) Bellwether Media.

Brezina, Corona. What Happens to Your Body When You Are Weight Training. 2009. (How & Why of Exercise Ser.). (Illus.). 48p. (YA). (gr. 5-9). 29.25 *(978-1-4358-5307-2(5))* Rosen Publishing Group, Inc., The.

Burgan, Michael. Health Careers in Sports, Vol. 10. Ferrer, Al, ed. 2015. (Careers off the Field Ser.). (Illus.). 64p. (J). (gr. 7). lib. bdg. 23.95 *(978-1-4222-3268-2(9))* Mason Crest.

Burkhead, Frank, Jr. Sports Ministry for Christ. 2005. 49p. (YA). per. 10.25 *(978-0-9770043-5-5(X))* New Global Publishing.

Burton, Margie, et al. Your Body. 2011. (Early Connections Ser.). (J). *(978-1-61672-549-5(4))* Benchmark Education Co.

Canino, Kate. Maintaining a Healthy Weight. 2010. (Healthy Habits Ser.). (Illus.). 64p. (YA). (gr. 5-8). pap. 12.95 *(978-1-4488-0609-6(7));* lib. bdg. 31.95 *(978-1-4358-9439-6(1))* Rosen Publishing Group, Inc., The. (Rosen Reference).

Carle, Eric. De la Cabeza a los Pies, 1 vol. Carle, Eric, illus. 2007.Tr. of From Head to Toe. (SPA., Illus.). 32p. (J). (gr. -1-3). pap. 6.99 *(978-0-06-051313-9(6))* HarperCollins Pubs.

—From Head to Toe. Carle, Eric, illus. 2007. (ENG., Illus.). 32p. (J). (gr. -1-k). pap. 24.99 *(978-0-06-111972-9(5),* HarperFestival) HarperCollins Pubs.

Carleton, Kate. What Happens to Your Body When You Cycle. 2009. (How & Why of Exercise Ser.). (Illus.). 48p. (YA). (gr. 5-9). 29.25 *(978-1-4358-5308-9(3))* Rosen Publishing Group, Inc., The.

Cleland, Jo. Get Moving. 2012. (ENG., Illus.). 24p. (gr. k-2). pap. 8.95 *(978-1-61810-216-4(8))* Rourke Educational Media.

Coan, Sharon. Good for Me: Play & Exercise. 2015. (TIME for KIDS(r) Nonfiction Readers Ser.). (ENG., Illus.). 12p. (gr. k-k). 4.99 *(978-1-4938-2152-5(0))* Teacher Created Materials, Inc.

Crockett, Kyle A. Nutrition for Achievement in Sports & Academics. Borus, Joshua, ed. 2013. (Understanding Nutrition: a Gateway to Physical & Mental Health Ser.). (Illus.). 48p. (J). (gr. 5-18). pap. 9.95 *(978-1-4222-2990-3(4));* 19.95 *(978-1-4222-2884-5(3))* Mason Crest.

Dahn Healer School. Home Massage Therapy Book 1: Heal Yourself & Your Loved Ones, 2 vols. 2004. (Dahnhak, the Way to Perfect Health Ser.: Vol. 2). (Illus.). 142p. per. 17.95 *(978-0-9720282-9-5(3))* Healing Society, Inc.

Dee, Janet. A Practical Guide to Everyday Health & Well Being. 2005. (J). 9.95 *(978-0-9768403-1-2(6))* Wings Above.

DiPrimio, Pete. The World of CrossFit. 2014. 48p. (gr. 4-8). 29.95 *(978-1-61228-552-8(X))* Mitchell Lane Pubs., Inc.

Doeden, Matt. Stay Fit! How You Can Get in Shape. 2009. pap. 52.95 *(978-0-7613-4687-6(2))* Lerner Publishing Group.

—Stay Fit! How You Can Get in Shape. Desrocher, Jack, illus. 2008. (Health Zone Ser.). 64p. (YA). (gr. 4-7). lib. bdg. 30.60 *(978-0-8225-7553-5(1))* Lerner Publishing Group.

Dru Tecco, Betsy. Food for Fuel: The Connection Between Food & Physical Activity. 2008. (Library of Nutrition Ser.). (Illus.). 48p. (YA). (gr. 8-12). lib. bdg. 29.25 *(978-1-4042-1871-0(8),* Rosen Reference) Rosen Publishing Group, Inc., The.

El-Hewie, Mohamed F. Essentials of Weightlifting & Strength Training. 2nd rev. exp. ed. 2005. (Illus.). 700p. lib. bdg. 85.00 *(978-0-9719581-9-7(X))* Shaymaa Publishing Corp.

Evans, Lynette. Move Your Bones. 2007. (Shockwave: the Human Experience Ser.). (ENG., Illus.). 36p. (J). (gr. 3-5). 25.00 *(978-0-531-17761-7(0),* Children's Pr.) Scholastic Library Publishing.

Fisher, Beverly. Mental Toughness for Personal Fitness: Workbook for Life 2004. (Illus.). 64p. pap. 10.99 *(978-0-9745066-0-9(5))* Sports In Mind.

Furgang, Kathy. Having Healthful Habits & Tener hábitos Sanos: 6 English, 6 Spanish Adaptations. 2011. (ENG & SPA.). (J). 97.00 net. *(978-1-4108-5710-1(7))* Benchmark Education Co.

Gagne, Tammy. African Dance Trends. 2014. (Illus.). 48p. (J). (gr. 4-8). 29.95 *(978-1-61228-557-3(0))* Mitchell Lane Pubs., Inc.

Gifford, Clive. Sports. 2010. (Healthy Lifestyles Ser.). 48p. (J). 35.65 *(978-1-60753-088-6(0))* Amicus Publishing.

Gilliam, Thomas & Neill, Jane. Move It. Lose It. Live Healthy: Achieve a Healthier Workplace One Employee at a Time! 2004. (J). per. 19.95 *(978-0-9762703-0-0(7))* Gilliam, T. & Associates, LLC.

Gogerly, Liz. Exercise. Gordon, Mike, illus. 2008. (Looking after Me Ser.). (ENG.). 32p. (J). (gr. -1-3). pap. *(978-0-7787-4118-3(4))* Crabtree Publishing Co.

Goodbody, Slim & Burstein, John. A Million Moves: Keeping Fit. 2008. (Slim Goodbody's Lighten Up! Ser.). (ENG., Illus.). 32p. (J). (gr. 3-7). pap. *(978-0-7787-3930-2(9));* lib. bdg. *(978-0-7787-3912-8(0))* Crabtree Publishing Co.

Greathouse, Lisa. Find Your Sport, 1 vol. 2011. (Science Readers: a Closer Look Ser.). (ENG., Illus.). 32p. (J). (gr. 2-2). pap. 8.99 *(978-1-4333-3090-2(3))* Teacher Created Materials, Inc.

—Get Moving, 1 vol. 2011. (Science Readers: a Closer Look Ser.). (ENG.). 32p. (J). (gr. 3-3). pap. 8.99 *(978-1-4333-3089-6(X))* Teacher Created Materials, Inc.

—Healthy Habits, Healthy You, 1 vol. 2011. (Science Readers: a Closer Look Ser.). (ENG., Illus.). 32p. (J). (gr. 3-3). pap. 8.99 *(978-1-4333-3091-9(1))* Teacher Created Materials, Inc.

Green, Emily K. Keeping Fit. 2006. (Blastoff! Readers Ser.). (ENG., Illus.). 24p. (J). (gr. k-3). lib. bdg. 24.95 *(978-1-60014-006-8(8))* Bellwether Media.

—Keeping Fit. 2011. (Blastoff! Readers: New Food Guide Pyramid Ser.). (Illus.). 24p. (J). pap. 5.95 *(978-0-531-25853-8(X),* Children's Pr.) Scholastic Library Publishing.

Hallinan, P. K. Let's Be Fit. 2007. (ENG., Illus.). 32p. (J). (gr. 3-7). 8.99 *(978-0-8249-5528-1(5),* Ideal Pubns.) Worthy Publishing.

Harcourt School Publishers Staff. Be Active! Cardiovascular Flipchart. 2nd ed. 2003. (Illus.). (J). (gr. 1-6). 9.20 *(978-0-15-340983-7(5))* Harcourt Schl. Pubs.

—Be Active! Flexibility Flipchart. 2nd ed. 2003. (Illus.). (J). (gr. 1-6). 9.20 *(978-0-15-340981-3(9))* Harcourt Schl. Pubs.

—Be Active! Movement Flipchart. 2nd ed. 2003. (Illus.). (J). 9.20 *(978-0-15-340982-0(7))* Harcourt Schl. Pubs.

—Be Active! Strength Flipchart. 2nd ed. 2003. (Illus.). (J). (gr. 1-6). 9.20 *(978-0-15-340980-6(0))* Harcourt Schl. Pubs.

—Be Active! Program: Health & Fitness. 4th ed. 2004. (Illus.). (gr. k-2). 311.60 *(978-0-15-341407-7(3));* (gr. 3-6). 314.90 *(978-0-15-341408-4(1))* Harcourt Schl. Pubs.

—Health & Fitness: Activity Book. 4th ed. 2003. (gr. -1). pap., act. bk. ed. 4.80 *(978-0-15-341170-0(8))* Harcourt Schl. Pubs.

—Health & Fitness: Resources for Spanish Speakers. 4th ed. 2004. (SPA.). (gr. 1). pap. 20.00 *(978-0-15-341180-9(5));* (gr. 2). pap. 20.00 *(978-0-15-341181-6(3));* (gr. 3). pap. 25.40 *(978-0-15-341182-3(1));* (gr. 4). pap. 25.40 *(978-0-15-341183-0(X));* (gr. 5). pap. 25.40 *(978-0-15-341184-7(8));* (gr. 6). pap. 25.40 *(978-0-15-341185-4(6))* Harcourt Schl. Pubs.

—Health & Fitness 5-Pack: Activity Book. 4th ed. 2003. (gr. -1). act. bk. ed. 23.70 *(978-0-15-341171-7(6))* Harcourt Schl. Pubs.

—Health & Fitness, Grade 3-6. 4th ed. 2003. pap., tchr. ed. 88.20 *(978-0-15-341101-4(5))* Harcourt Schl. Pubs.

—Health & Fitness, Grade K-2. 4th ed. 2003. pap., tchr. ed. 84.80 *(978-0-15-341100-7(7))* Harcourt Schl. Pubs.

Hau, Stephanie. I Can Live To 100! Secrets Just for Kids. Hau, Joseph, illus. 2005. 60p. (J). per. 9.95 *(978-0-9767324-0-2(8),* Kids Can) Proactive Publishing.

Head, Honor. Keeping Fit. 2013. (Let's Read & Talk about Ser.). (Illus.). 32p. (J). (gr. 2-5). 28.50 *(978-1-59771-396-2(1))* Sea-To-Sea Pubns.

Heart E Heart & Friends Activity Book: Have Fun the Healthy Way. 2004. (J). per. 11.95 *(978-0-9762703-2-4(3))* Gilliam, T. & Associates, LLC.

Heart E Heart & Friends Storybook for Children Ages 2 to 4 Years Old: A Children's Way to a Healthy Lifestyle. 2004. (J). per. 5.95 *(978-0-9762703-1-7(5))* Gilliam, T. & Associates, LLC.

Heling, Kathryn & Hembrook, Deborah. I Wish I Was Strong Like Manuel/Quisiera Ser Fuerte Como Manuel. Vega, Eida de la, tr. Adamson, Bonnie, illus. 2008. (I Wish Ser.). (ENG & SPA.). 32p. (J). (gr. -1-3). pap. 7.95 *(978-0-9770906-8-6(X),* Raven Tree Pr.,Csi) Continental Sales, Inc.

—I Wish I Was Tall Like Willie/Quisiera Ser Tan Alto Como Willie. Adamson, Bonnie, illus. 2008. (I Wish Ser.). (ENG & SPA.). 32p. (J). (gr. 4-7). 16.95 *(978-0-9794462-0-7(1),* Raven Tree Pr.,Csi) Continental Sales, Inc.

Heron, Jackie. Get Moving in the City, 1 vol. Avakyan, Tatevik, illus. 2012. (Move & Get Healthy Ser.). (ENG.). 32p. (J). (gr. k-3). 28.50 *(978-1-61641-859-5(1))* Magic Wagon.

—Let's Move in the Outdoors, 1 vol. Avakyan, Tatevik, illus. 2012. (Move & Get Healthy Ser.). (ENG.). 32p. (J). (gr. k-3). 28.50 *(978-1-61641-862-5(1))* Magic Wagon.

Hewitt, Sally. Keeping Healthy. 2015. (ENG.). 24p. (gr. -1-2). 23.99 *(978-1-939581-82-2(6))* QEB Publishing Inc.

Higgins, Nadia. Get Moving with Friends & Family, 1 vol. Avakyan, Tatevik, illus. 2012. (Move & Get Healthy Ser.). (ENG.). 32p. (J). (gr. k-3). 28.50 *(978-1-61641-860-1(5))* Magic Wagon.

Hill, Z. B. Endurance & Cardio Training. Hart, Diane H., ed. 2014. (Integrated Life of Fitness Ser.). 64p. (J). (gr. 7-18). pap. 11.95 *(978-1-4222-3198-2(4));* 23.95 *(978-1-4222-3160-9(7))* Mason Crest.

Hoeft, Jen. FUNdamental Fitness: Playground Exercises for Grownups, 1. 2004. 144p. per. 19.95 *(978-0-9762868-0-6(7))* Read Publishing.

Hopwood, Lolly & Kusters, YoYo. Move! Shea, Bob & Flowers, Luke, illus. 2016. (ENG.). 32p. (J). (gr. -1-1). bds. 12.95 *(978-0-7611-8733-2(2))* Workman Publishing Co., Inc.

Hovius, Christopher. Fitness & Nutrition. McDonnell, Mary Ann & Forman, Sara, eds. 2013. (Young Adult's Guide to the Science of Health Ser.: 15). 128p. (J). (gr. 7-18). 24.95 *(978-1-4222-2809-8(6))* Mason Crest.

Hunt, Charles. The Perfect Diet: The Ultimate Weight Solution for Every Body. 2004. *(978-0-9630377-2-5(2))* Hunt Thompson Media.

Hunt, Jamie. Getting Stronger, Getting Fit: The Importance of Exercise. 2010. (Kids & Obesity Ser.). (Illus.). 48p. (YA). lib. bdg. 19.95 *(978-1-4222-1709-2(4))* Mason Crest.

Hunt, Sara. Stay Fit: Your Guide to Staying Active. 2011. (Healthy Me Ser.). (ENG.). 32p. (gr. 3-4). pap. 47.70 *(978-1-4296-7294-8(3),* Snap Bks.) Capstone Press of Coughlan Cos.

Hurst, Brooklynn. Fitness for Teens: Getting you Motivated for Life by Providing Principles for Healthy Living. 2nd exp. l.t. ed. 2004. (ENG., Illus.). 108p. (YA). spiral bd. 20.00 *(978-0-9746262-3-9(6))* Achieving Corporate Excellence, Inc.

James, Sara. Flexibility & Agility. Hart, Diane H., ed. 2014. (Integrated Life of Fitness Ser.). 64p. (J). (gr. 7-18). pap. 11.95 *(978-1-4222-3200-2(X));* 23.95 *(978-1-4222-3162-3(3))* Mason Crest.

—Yoga & Pilates. Hart, Diane H., ed. 2014. (Integrated Life of Fitness Ser.). (Illus.). 64p. (J). (gr. 7-18). pap. 11.95 *(978-1-4222-3204-0(2));* 23.95 *(978-1-4222-3166-1(6))* Mason Crest.

Jorgensen, Katrina. Football Fuel: Recipes for Before, During, & after the Big Game. 2015. (Football Cookbooks Ser.). (ENG.). 48p. (gr. 3-6). lib. bdg. 31.32 *(978-1-4914-2135-2(5))* Capstone Press of Coughlan Cos.

Kallio, Jamie. 12 Ways to Stay Active & Fit. 2017. (J). *(978-1-62143-513-6(X))* Pr. Room Editions LLC.

Kallio, Jamie & Hand, Carol. 12 Ways to Stay Active & Fit. 2016. (Healthy Living Ser.). (ENG., Illus.). 32p. (J). pap. 9.95 *(978-1-63235-389-4(X))* Pr. Room Editions LLC.

Kawa, Katie. Staying Fit with Sports! 2013. (Rosen Readers Ser.). (ENG.). 24p. (J). (gr. 3-4). pap. 49.50 *(978-1-4777-2592-4(X));* pap. 8.25 *(978-1-4777-2590-0(3))* Rosen Publishing Group, Inc., The. (Rosen Classroom).

Kray, Peter. The Monster. 2003. 91p. per. 12.95 *(978-0-9715715-1-8(1))* Greenleaf Book Group.

Kreisman, Rachelle. Start Sweating! A Kids' Guide to Being Active. Haggerty, Tim, illus. 2014. (Start Smart: Health Ser.). 32p. (J). (gr. 1-3). pap. 7.95 *(978-1-937529-64-2(9))* Red Chair Pr.

Labrecque, Ellen. Stamina: Get Stronger & Play Longer!, 1 vol. 2012. (Exercise! Ser.). (ENG.). 32p. (gr. 1-3). 27.32 *(978-1-4329-6733-8(9),* Heinemann First Library) Heinemann-Raintree.

Lee, Ilchi. Meridian Exercise for Self-Healing Book 1: Classfied by Common Symptoms, 2 vols. 2003. (Dahnhak, the Way to

Perfect Health Ser.: Vol. 1). (Illus.). 151p. per. 17.95 *(978-0-9720282-7-1(7))* Healing Society, Inc.

—Meridian Exercise for Self-Healing Book 2: Classified by Common Symptoms, 2 vols., Vol. 2. 2003. (Dahnhak, the Way to Perfect Health Ser.: 2). (Illus.). 193p. per. 17.95 *(978-0-9720282-8-8(5))* Healing Society, Inc.

Lewis, Alexandra. The Ultimate Jump Rope Book. 2010. (ENG., Illus.). 80p. (J). pap. 12.95 *(978-1-60433-102-8(X))* Cider Mill Pr. Bk. Pubs., LLC.

Libal, Autumn. Exercise for Fitness & Weight Loss. Garcia, Victor, ed. 2014. (Understanding Obesity Ser.: 10). (Illus.). 104p. (J). (gr. 7-18). lib. bdg. 24.95 *(978-1-4222-3060-2(0))* Mason Crest.

Lockspeiser, Nancy Flanders. Flexible You: 21 Stretches a Day for a 9-Lives Body: a Cat's Quick Guide to Stretching & Self-Massage. Lockspeiser, Nancy Flanders, illus. 2004. (Illus.). 48p. spiral bd. 14.94 *(978-0-9752922-0-4(X))* Catamount Publishing LLC.

Madison, Lynda. Food & You: Eat Right, Being Strong & Feeling Great. 2008. (ENG.). 64p. (YA). (gr. 3-18). spiral bd. 8.95 *(978-1-59369-415-9(6))* American Girl Publishing, Inc.

Marsico, Katie. Fitness Math. 2015. (ENG., Illus.). 32p. (J). (gr. 3-4). 26.65 *(978-1-4677-8578-5(4))* Lerner Publishing Group.

Mason, Paul. Improving Flexibility. 2017. (Training for Sport Ser.). (ENG., Illus.). 32p. (J). (gr. 4-6). pap. 11.99 *(978-0-7502-9763-9(8)*, Wayland) Hachette Children's Group GBR. Dist: Hachette Bk. Group.

—Improving Strength & Power. 2017. (Training for Sport Ser.). (ENG., Illus.). 32p. (J). (gr. 4-6). pap. 11.99 *(978-0-7502-9764-6(6)*, Wayland) Hachette Children's Group GBR. Dist: Hachette Bk. Group.

—Improving Strength & Power. 2011. (Training for Sports Ser.). (Illus.). 32p. (YA). (gr. 5-9). 26.50 *(978-1-4488-3301-6(9))* Rosen Publishing Group, Inc., The.

Massad, Diane. Go! STOP Go! Vol. 3: The Kidskills America Training Series. 2004. (Kidskills America Training Ser.: Three). (Illus.). 75p. (J). spiral bd. 12.95 *(978-0-9710641-3-3(X))* Kidskills International.

Massad, Diane P. Moving Right Along! The Kidskills America Training Series. 2004. (Kidskills America Training Ser.: 2). (Illus.). 71p. (J). spiral bd. 12.95 *(978-0-9710641-2-6(1)*, Kidskills America) Kidskills International.

McIntosh, J. S. Elite Forces Selection. 2010. (Special Forces Ser.). 64p. (YA). (gr. 7-18). lib. bdg. 22.95 *(978-1-4222-1839-6(2))* Mason Crest.

McKay, Sindy. We Both Read-Happy & Healthy. 2003. 44p. (J). (gr. 1-2). 7.99 *(978-1-891327-47-6(X))* Treasure Bay, Inc.

Meiners, Cheri J. & Allen, Elizabeth. Grow Strong! A Book about Healthy Habits. 2016. (Being the Best Me Ser.). (ENG., Illus.). 40p. (J). (gr. -1-2). pap. 9.99 *(978-1-63198-085-5(8))* Free Spirit Publishing, Inc.

Meter, Pete O. & Meter, Pete. Walk the Walk: The Kid's Book of Pedometer Challenges. 2008. (ENG., Illus.). 56p. (J). (gr. 4). spiral bd. 12.95 *(978-1-60433-048-9(1)*, Applesauce Pr.) Cider Mill Pr. Bk. Pubs., LLC.

Nagle, Jeanne. What Happens to Your Body When You Swim. 2009. (How & Why of Exercise Ser.). (Illus.). 48p. (YA). (gr. 5-9). 29.25 *(978-1-4358-5309-6(1))* Rosen Publishing Group, Inc., The.

Pappas, Diane H., et al. Why I Need Exercise. Estrada, Ric, illus. 2007. (J). pap. *(978-0-545-01428-1(X))* Scholastic, Inc.

Payment, Simone. What Happens to Your Body When You Run. 2009. (How & Why of Exercise Ser.). (Illus.). 48p. (YA). (gr. 5-9). 29.25 *(978-1-4358-5306-5(7))* Rosen Publishing Group, Inc., The.

Peters, Celeste A. Health. 2016. (J). ***(978-1-5105-2237-4(9))*** SmartBook Media, Inc.

Phillips, Georgina. Ouch! Extreme Feats of Human Endurance, 1. unabr. ed. 2010. (Science Of... Ser.). (ENG., Illus.). 96p. (J). (gr. 2-6). pap. 5.99 *(978-0-330-45405-6(6))* Macmillan Pubs., Ltd. GBR. Dist: Independent Pubs. Group.

Potts, Sue. Get Fit with Video Workouts. 2014. (ENG., Illus.). 48p. (J). (gr. 4-8). 29.95 *(978-1-61228-550-4(3))* Mitchell Lane Pubs., Inc.

Rainey, Don L., et al. Foundations of Personal Fitness. 2005. (Ntc: Found of Personal Fitness Ser.). (ENG., Illus.). 432p. (gr. 8-12). stu. ed. 80.36 *(978-0-07-845127-0(2)*, 0078451272) McGraw-Hill Education.

Rice, Dona Herweck. Keeping Fit with Sports, 1 vol. 2nd rev. ed. 2014. (TIME for KIDS(r) Nonfiction Readers Ser.). (ENG., Illus.). 20p. (J). (gr. 1-1). pap. 19.96 *(978-1-4807-1029-0(6))* Shell Educational Publishing.

—Keeping Fit with Sports, 1 vol. 2nd rev. ed. 2011. (TIME for KIDS(r) Nonfiction Readers Ser.). (ENG.). 20p. (J). (gr. 1-1). 4.99 *(978-1-4333-3596-9(4))* Teacher Created Materials, Inc.

—Manteniense en Forma con Deportes, 1 vol. 2nd rev. ed. 2012. (Nonfiction Readers Ser.). (SPA.). 20p. (J). (gr. 1-1). pap. 4.99 *(978-1-4333-4429-9(7))* Teacher Created Materials, Inc.

—Mantenerse Sano, 1 vol. 2nd rev. ed. 2012. (Nonfiction Readers Ser.).Tr. of Staying Healthy. (SPA., Illus.). 20p. (J). (gr. 1-1). pap. 4.99 *(978-1-4333-4428-2(9))* Teacher Created Materials, Inc.

—Physical Feats & Failures, 1 vol. 2nd rev. ed. 2012. (TIME for KIDS(r) Nonfiction Readers Ser.). (ENG.). 48p. (J). (gr. 4-4). pap. 9.99 *(978-1-4333-4870-9(5))* Teacher Created Materials, Inc.

—Staying Healthy, 1 vol. 2nd rev. ed. 2011. (Nonfiction Readers Ser.). (ENG.). 20p. (J). (gr. 1-1). pap. 4.99 *(978-1-4333-3595-2(6))* Teacher Created Materials, Inc.

Rissman, Rebecca. Fit Girl: Yoga for Fitness & Flexibility. 2015. (Yoga for You Ser.). (ENG.). 64p. (gr. 4-5). lib. bdg. 34.65 *(978-1-4914-2120-8(7))* Capstone Press of Coughlan Cos.

Rissman, Rebecca & Smith, Sian. Getting Exercise, 1 vol. 2012. (Take Care of Yourself! Ser.). (ENG.). 24p. (gr. -1-1). 22.65 *(978-1-4329-6710-9(X))*; pap. 6.29 *(978-1-4329-6717-8(7))* Heinemann-Raintree. (Acorn).

Rodomista, Kim. 101 Cool Pool Games for Children: Fun & Fitness for Swimmers of All Levels. Patterson, Robin, illus. 2006. (SmartFun Activity Bks.). (ENG.). 160p. spiral bd. 19.95 *(978-0-89793-484-8(9))*; (gr. -1). per. 14.95 *(978-0-89793-483-1(0))* Turner Publishing Co. (Hunter Hse.).

Rosen Publishing Staff. Fitness for the Mind & Body, 1 vol. 2015. (Fitness for the Mind & Body Ser.). (ENG.). 192p. (YA). 153.00 *(978-1-4777-8170-8(6)*, Rosen Young Adult) Rosen Publishing Group, Inc., The.

Royston, Angela. Why Do I Run? 2012. (My Body Ser.). (ENG., Illus.). 24p. (gr. k-4). pap. 7.95 *(978-1-77092-000-2(5))* Saunders Bk. Co. CAN. Dist: RiverStream Publishing.

Rustad, Martha E. H. I Stay Active. 2017. (Healthy Me Ser.). (ENG., Illus.). 24p. (gr. k-1). lib. bdg. 21.99 *(978-1-5157-3982-1(1))* Capstone Press of Coughlan Cos.

Salzmann, Mary Elizabeth. Run! Jump! Play! Healthy Active Habits, 1 vol. 2014. (Healthy Habits Ser.). (ENG.). 24p. (J). (gr. -1-3). 24.21 *(978-1-62403-530-2(2))* ABDO Publishing Co.

Schaefer, Adam. Mantenerse Sano, 1 vol. 2010. (Salud y el Estado Fisico Ser.). (SPA.). 32p. (gr. 1-3). 27.32 *(978-1-4329-4445-2(2))*; pap. 8.29 *(978-1-4329-4450-6(9))* Heinemann-Raintree.

Schmidt, Debra. Careers in Sports & Fitness. 2016. (Exploring Careers Ser.). (ENG., Illus.). 80p. (J). (gr. 5-12). 38.60 *(978-1-60152-814-8(0))* ReferencePoint Pr., Inc.

Schuh, Mari. Get Moving!, 1 vol. 2012. (What's on Myplate? Ser.). (ENG., Illus.). 24p. (gr. k-1). pap. 7.29 *(978-1-4296-9414-8(9)*, Pebble Plus) Capstone Press of Coughlan Cos.

Schuh, Mari C. Get Moving!, 1 vol. 2012. (What's on Myplate? Ser.). (ENG., Illus.). 24p. (gr. k-1). lib. bdg. 26.65 *(978-1-4296-8747-8(9)*, Pebble Plus) Capstone Press of Coughlan Cos.

—¡Muévete! Strictly Spanish LLC. Staff, tr. from ENG. 2013. (¿Qué Hay en Miplato?/What's on My Plate? Ser.).Tr. of Get Moving! (SPA, ENG & MUL.). 24p. (gr. k-1). lib. bdg. 26.65 *(978-1-62065-944-1(1))* Capstone Press of Coughlan Cos.

Scott, Celicia. Sports & Fitness. Hart, Diane H., ed. 2014. (Integrated Life of Fitness Ser.). 64p. (J). (gr. 7-18). pap. 11.95 *(978-1-4222-3201-9(8))*; 23.95 *(978-1-4222-3163-0(1))* Mason Crest.

—Weight Lifting & Strength Building. Hart, Diane H., ed. 2014. (Integrated Life of Fitness Ser.). 64p. (J). (gr. 7-18). pap. 11.95 *(978-1-4222-3203-3(4))*; 23.95 *(978-1-4222-3165-4(8))* Mason Crest.

Selwyn, Josephine. How Can I Get Fit? 2014. (Little Books of Answers: Level e Ser.). (Illus.). 16p. (gr. k-2). pap. 7.95 *(978-1-927136-43-0(1))* Three Crows Media NZL. Dist: RiverStream Publishing.

Senker, Cath. Exercise & Play. 2008. (Healthy Choices Ser.). (Illus.). 24p. (J). (gr. 3-7). lib. bdg. 22.60 *(978-1-4042-4305-7(4)*, PowerKids Pr.) Rosen Publishing Group, Inc., The.

Shryer, Donna & Forschmiedt, Jodi. Peak Performance: Sports Nutrition. 2009. (Benchmark Rockets Ser.). 32p. (gr. 5-18). 28.50 *(978-0-7614-4366-7(5))* Marshall Cavendish Corp.

Sjonger, Rebecca. Do Your Bit to Be Physically Fit! 2015. (ENG., Illus.). 24p. (J). *(978-0-7787-1879-6(4))* Crabtree Publishing Co.

—Hop, Throw, & Play: Build Your Skills Every Day! 2016. (ENG., Illus.). 24p. (J). *(978-0-7787-2349-3(6))* Crabtree Publishing Co.

Smithyman, Kathryn & Kalman, Bobbie. Active Kids: Fun Ways to Be Active. 2003. (Kid Power Ser.). (ENG., Illus.). 32p. (J). (gr. 3). pap. *(978-0-7787-1275-6(3))*; lib. bdg. *(978-0-7787-1253-4(2))* Crabtree Publishing Co.

Spilsbury, Louise. Get Active! 2010. (Crabtree Connections Ser.). (ENG.). 24p. (J). (gr. 3-6). *(978-0-7787-9941-2(7))*; pap. *(978-0-7787-9963-4(8))* Crabtree Publishing Co.

Sports & Fitness (Gr. PreK-5) 2003. (J). *(978-1-58232-026-7(8))* ECS Learning Systems, Inc.

Steck-Vaughn Company, creator. Fitness. 2009. (Fact Matters: Healthy Bodies Ser.). (Illus.). 32p. pap. 8.67 *(978-1-4190-5469-3(4))* Heinemann-Raintree.

Strauss, Greg. Eleven Minute Workout: Total Fitness in 11 Minutes a Day. 2003. (Illus.). 124p. per. 11.00 *(978-0-9744568-0-5(2)*, EMW:0974456802) Motion Fitness LLC.

Tecco, Betsy Dru. Food for Fuel: The Connection Between Food & Physical Activity. (Library of Nutrition Ser.). 48p. 2009. (gr. 5-8). 53.00 *(978-1-60853-766-2(8)*, Rosen Reference) 2008. (ENG., Illus.). (gr. 5-8). per. 11.75 *(978-1-4042-1635-8(9))* 2004. (Illus.). (J). lib. bdg. 26.50 *(978-1-4042-0303-7(6))* Rosen Publishing Group, Inc., The.

Tieck, Sarah. Stay Fit, 1 vol. 2012. (ENG.). 32p. 27.07 *(978-1-61783-236-9(7)*, Buddy Bks.) ABDO Publishing Co.

Tourville, Amanda Doering. Get up & Go: Being Active, 1 vol. Rooney, Ronnie, illus. 2008. (How to Be Healthy! Ser.). (ENG.). 24p. (gr. k-2). 26.65 *(978-1-4048-4811-5(8))* Picture Window Bks.

—Muévete. Rooney, Ronnie, illus. 2011. (Cómo Mantenernos Saludables/How to Be Healthy Ser.).Tr. of Get up & Go. (ENG, SPA & MUL.). 24p. (gr. k-2). 26.65 *(978-1-4048-6893-9(3))* Picture Window Bks.

Tuminelly, Nancy. Super Simple Bend & Stretch: Healthy & Fun Activities to Move Your Body, 1 vol. 2011. (Super Simple Exercise Ser.). (ENG., Illus.). 32p. (J). (gr. k-3). 27.07 *(978-1-61714-959-7(4))* ABDO Publishing Co.

—Super Simple Hop & Jump: Healthy & Fun Activities to Move Your Body, 1 vol. 2011. (Super Simple Exercise Ser.). (ENG., Illus.). 32p. (J). (gr. k-3). 27.07 *(978-1-61714-960-3(8))* ABDO Publishing Co.

—Super Simple Move & Shake: Healthy & Fun Activities to Move Your Body, 1 vol. 2011. (Super Simple Exercise Ser.). (ENG., Illus.). 32p. (J). (gr. k-3). 27.07 *(978-1-61714-961-0(6))* ABDO Publishing Co.

—Super Simple Punch & Kick: Healthy & Fun Activities to Move Your Body, 1 vol. 2011. (Super Simple Exercise Ser.). (ENG., Illus.). 32p. (J). (gr. k-3). 27.07 *(978-1-61714-962-7(4))* ABDO Publishing Co.

—Super Simple Throw & Catch: Healthy & Fun Activities to Move Your Body, 1 vol. 2011. (Super Simple Exercise Ser.). (ENG., Illus.). 32p. (J). (gr. k-3). 27.07 *(978-1-61714-963-4(2))* ABDO Publishing Co.

—Super Simple Walk & Run: Healthy & Fun Activities to Move Your Body, 1 vol. 2011. (Super Simple Exercise Ser.). (ENG., Illus.). 32p. (J). (gr. k-3). 27.07 *(978-1-61714-964-1(0))* ABDO Publishing Co.

Vogel, Elizabeth. A Hacer Ejercicio! 2004. (Limpieza y Salud Todo el Dia Ser.). (SPA & ENG., Illus.). 24p. (J). (gr. 1-2). lib. bdg. 18.75 *(978-0-8239-6614-1(3)*, Editorial Buenas Letras) Rosen Publishing Group, Inc., The.

—Let's Exercise = a Hacer Ejercicio. 2004. (Limpieza y salud todo el Día Ser.). (ENG & SPA., Illus.). 24p. (J). lib. bdg. 18.75 *(978-0-8239-6615-8(1)*, Editorial Buenas Letras) Rosen Publishing Group, Inc., The.

—Let's Exercise / ¡A hacer Ejercicio! 2009. (Clean & Healthy All Day Long / Limpieza y salud todo el día Ser.). (SPA.). 24p. (gr. 1-1). 37.50 *(978-1-61511-871-7(3)*, Editorial Buenas Letras) Rosen Publishing Group, Inc., The.

West, Dorothy F. Nutrition, Food, & Fitness. 3rd ed. 2006. (ENG., Illus.). 510p. (gr. 9-12). 62.64 *(978-1-59070-527-8(0))* Goodheart-Willcox Pub.

White, Andrea & Mimi, Vance. Tummies on the Run. Shepperson, Rob, illus. 2012. 32p. pap. 11.95 *(978-1-60898-134-2(7))* namelos llc.

Willis, Laurie. Exercise & Fitness. 2013. (Issues That Concern You Ser.). (ENG., Illus.). 144p. (gr. 7-10). lib. bdg. 42.00 *(978-0-7377-6293-8(4))* Cengage Gale.

Winkler, Peter, et al. Keeping Fit. 2006. (Nonfiction Reading & Writing Workshops Ser.). (ENG., Illus.). 32p. (J). pap. 17.95 *(978-0-7922-8863-3(7))* CENGAGE Learning.

PHYSICAL GEOGRAPHY

see also Climate; Earth (Planet); Earthquakes; Geophysics; Glaciers; Ice; Icebergs; Lakes; Meteorology; Mountains; Ocean; Rivers; Tides; Volcanoes; Winds

ABDO Publishing Company Staff. Continents. 2003. (Continents Ser.). (ENG.). 32p. (gr. k-4). *(978-1-57765-957-0(0)*, Buddy Bks.) ABDO Publishing Co.

Anderson, Sheila. Plateaus. 2008. (First Step Nonfiction - Landforms Ser.). (ENG., Illus.). 24p. (gr. k-2). lib. bdg. 23.93 *(978-0-8225-8592-3(8)*, Lerner Pubns.) Lerner Publishing Group.

—Valleys. 2008. (First Step Nonfiction - Landforms Ser.). (ENG., Illus.). 24p. (gr. k-2). lib. bdg. 23.93 *(978-0-8225-8591-6(X)*, Lerner Pubns.) Lerner Publishing Group.

Benchmark Education Co., LLC. Physical & Human Geography. 2014. (PRIME Ser.). (J). (gr. 6-8). pap. *(978-1-4509-9502-3(0))* Benchmark Education Co.

Benchmark Education Company, LLC Staff, compiled by. Cactus & Canyons & Regions. 2005. spiral bd. 225.00 *(978-1-4108-5805-4(7))* Benchmark Education Co.

Brennan, Linda Crotta. U. S. Landforms: What You Need to Know. 2017. (Fact Files Ser.). (ENG.). 24p. (gr. 1-2). lib. bdg. 25.32 ***(978-1-5157-8112-7(7)***, First Facts) Capstone Press of Coughlan Cos.

Britannica, Learning Library. Planet Earth. 2003. (Illus.). 64p. 14.95 *(978-1-59339-032-7(7))* Encyclopaedia Britannica, Inc.

Coote, Roger. Earth. 2003. (Knowledge Masters Ser.). (Illus.). 32p. (YA). pap. incl. cd-rom *(978-1-903954-11-9(8)*, Pavilion Children's Books) Pavilion Bks.

Dayton, Connor. Rock Formations. 2009. (Rocks & Minerals Ser.). 24p. (gr. 2-3). 42.50 *(978-1-60852-502-7(3)*, PowerKids Pr.) Rosen Publishing Group, Inc., The.

DeCristofano, Carolyn. National Geographic Kids Ultimate Space Atlas. 2017. (ENG.). 160p. (J). (gr. 3-7). lib. bdg. 22.90 ***(978-1-4263-2803-9(6))***; (Illus.). pap. 12.99 ***(978-1-4263-2802-2(8))*** National Geographic Society. (National Geographic Children's Bks.).

Gall, Susan B., ed. Junior Worldmark Encyclopedia of Physical Geography, 5 vols. 2003. (Illus.). (J). *(978-0-7876-6266-0(6))*; *(978-0-7876-6267-7(4))*; *(978-0-7876-6633-0(5))*; *(978-0-7876-6269-1(0))*; *(978-0-7876-6268-4(2))* Cengage Gale. (UXL).

Ganeri, Anita. Canyon Hunters, 1 vol. 2011. (Landform Adventurers Ser.). (ENG.). 32p. (gr. 1-2). pap. 8.29 *(978-1-4109-4146-6(9))*; 29.99 *(978-1-4109-4139-8(6))* Heinemann-Raintree. (Read Me!).

Green, Emily K. Forests. 2006. (Learning about the Earth Ser.). (ENG., Illus.). 24p. (J). (gr. k-3). lib. bdg. 25.95 *(978-1-60014-036-5(X))* Bellwether Media.

Green, Jen. Barron's Amazing Fact-Packed, Fold-Out Atlas of the World: With Awesome Pop-Up Map! Engel, Christiane, illus. 2014. (ENG.). 56p. (J). (gr. 3-6). 18.99 *(978-0-7641-6746-1(4))* Barron's Educational Series, Inc.

Griffin, Mary. Los Lugares Más Altos de la Tierra (Earth's Highest Places) 2015. (Lugares Extremos de la Tierra (Earth's Most Extreme Places) Ser.). (SPA.). 24p. (J). (gr. 2-3). 22.60 *(978-1-4824-1917-7(3))* Stevens, Gareth Publishing LLLP.

Grucella, Cali. A Look at Landforms. 2009. (Real Life Readers Ser.). 8p. (gr. k-1). pap. 5.15 *(978-1-4042-7983-4(0)*, Rosen Classroom) Rosen Publishing Group, Inc., The.

Harcourt School Publishers Staff. Horizons: States & Regions. 3rd ed. 2003. (Harcourt School Publishers Horizons Ser.). (ENG., Illus.). 584p. (gr. 3-4). pupil's gde. ed. 83.95 *(978-0-15-320942-0(9))* Harcourt Schl. Pubs.

—Horizons 2003 Vol. 1: States & Regions. 3rd ed. 2003. (Harcourt School Publishers Horizons Ser.). (ENG.). 600p. (gr. 3-4). tchr. ed. 161.50 *(978-0-15-320944-4(5))* Harcourt Schl. Pubs.

Holt, Rinehart and Winston Staff. Holt Science & Technology Chapter 2: Earth Science: Maps & Models of the Earth. 5th ed. 2004. (Illus.). pap. 12.86 *(978-0-03-030271-8(4))* Holt McDougal.

Junior Worldmark Encyclopedia of Physical Geography, 5 vols. 2003. (ENG., Illus.). 832p. (J). 458.00 *(978-0-7876-6265-3(8)*, UXL) Cengage Gale.

Kalman, Bobbie. ¿Qué le Da Forma a la Tierra? 2009. (SPA.). 32p. (J). *(978-0-7787-8240-7(9))*; pap. *(978-0-7787-8257-5(3))* Crabtree Publishing Co.

Kusky, Timothy. The Coast. 2008. (Hazardous Earth Ser.). 155p. (gr. 6-12). 39.50 *(978-0-8160-6467-0(9))* Facts On File, Inc.

Lerner Publishing Group Staff, ed. Time Nature's Wonders: The Science & Splendor of Earth's Most Fascinating Places. 2008. (Time Inc. Home Entertainment Library-Bound Titles Ser.). (ENG.). 128p. (gr. 5-12). lib. bdg. 39.93 *(978-0-7613-4228-1(1)*, Twenty-First Century Bks.) Lerner Publishing Group.

Lewis, J. Patrick. Earth & You - A Closer View: Nature's Features. Canyon, Christopher, illus. 2004. (Sharing Nature with Children Book Ser.). 36p. (J). (gr. -1-3). 16.95 *(978-1-58469-016-0(X))*; (gr. 4-7). pap. 7.95 *(978-1-58469-015-3(1))* Dawn Pubns.

Looye, Juliette, text. I Live on an Island. 2004. (Illus.). 16p. (J). pap. *(978-0-7367-1936-0(9))* Zaner-Bloser, Inc.

Marsico, Katie. The Highest & the Lowest. 2015. (True Book(tm), a — Extreme Places Ser.). (ENG., Illus.). 48p. (J). lib. bdg. 31.00 *(978-0-531-21723-8(X)*, Children's Pr.) Scholastic Library Publishing.

Mattern, Joanne. Sand, Silt, & Mud & the Rock Cycle. 2009. (Illus.). 24p. (J). (gr. 3-6). pap. 8.25 *(978-1-4358-3263-3(9)*, PowerKids Pr.) Rosen Publishing Group, Inc., The.

Meachen Rau, Dana. Land. 2008. (Earth Matters Ser.). 32p. (gr. 1-2). lib. bdg. 15.95 *(978-0-7614-3043-8(1)*, Benchmark Bks.) Marshall Cavendish Corp.

—Land/La Tierra. 2008. (Earth Matters/El Planeta Es Importante Ser.). (SPA & ENG.). 32p. (gr. k-1). lib. bdg. 15.95 *(978-0-7614-3490-0(9)*, Benchmark Bks.) Marshall Cavendish Corp.

—La Tierra. 2008. (Planeta Es Importante Ser.). (SPA.). 32p. (gr. 1-2). lib. bdg. 15.95 *(978-0-7614-3465-8(8)*, Benchmark Bks.) Marshall Cavendish Corp.

Moignot, Daniel. Atlas of the Earth. 2012. (ENG., Illus.). 36p. (J). (gr. -1-k). spiral bd. 14.99 *(978-1-85103-406-2(4))* Moonlight Publishing, Ltd. GBR. Dist: Independent Pubs. Group.

Nadeau, Isaac. Peninsulas. 2006. (Library of Landforms Ser.). (Illus.). 24p. (J). (gr. 3-7). lib. bdg. 22.60 *(978-1-4042-3125-2(0)*, PowerKids Pr.) Rosen Publishing Group, Inc., The.

Nagel, Rob. UXL Encyclopedia of Landforms & Other Geologic Features, 3 vols. 2003. (Illus.). xxviii, 314p. (J). *(978-0-7876-7672-8(1))*; *(978-0-7876-7671-1(3))*; *(978-0-7876-7670-4(5))* Cengage Gale. (UXL).

Richards, Jon. Planet Earth. Simkins, Ed, illus. 2013. (World in Infographics Ser.). (ENG.). 32p. (J). (gr. 3-7). 15.95 *(978-1-926973-75-3(5))* Owlkids Bks. Inc. CAN. Dist: Publishers Group West (PGW).

Ripley's Believe It Or Not! Staff, et al. Extreme Earth: Fun, Facts, & Earth-Shattering Stories... 2010. (Twist Ser.: 7). (ENG., Illus.). 48p. (J). 12.95 *(978-1-893951-78-5(2))* Ripley Entertainment, Inc.

Rustad, Martha E. H. The Highest Places on Earth. 2010. (Extreme Planet Ser.). (ENG.). 24p. (gr. 1-2). lib. bdg. 25.32 *(978-1-4296-3963-7(6)*, First Facts) Capstone Press of Coughlan Cos.

—The Lowest Places on Earth. 2010. (Extreme Planet Ser.). (ENG.). 24p. (gr. 1-2). lib. bdg. 25.32 *(978-1-4296-3965-1(2)*, First Facts) Capstone Press of Coughlan Cos.

S. P. C. K. Stories from the History of Sweden. 2006. pap. 29.50 *(978-1-4101-0922-4(4))* Fredonia Bks.

Samuels, Charlie. Mapping the Physical World. 2017. (Mapping in the Modern World Ser.). (ENG.). 32p. (J). ***(978-0-7787-3236-5(3))***; pap. ***(978-0-7787-3242-6(8))*** Crabtree Publishing Co.

Slade, Suzanne. The Rock Cycle. 2009. (Planet Earth Ser.). 24p. (gr. 5-8). pap. 8.25 *(978-1-4358-2673-1(6)*, Rosen Classroom) Rosen Publishing Group, Inc., The.

Soll, Karen. Highest Places on the Planet. 2016. (Extreme Earth Ser.). (ENG., Illus.). 24p. (gr. k-1). lib. bdg. 26.65 *(978-1-4914-8342-8(3)*, Pebble Plus) Capstone Press of Coughlan Cos.

—Lowest Places on the Planet. 2016. (Extreme Earth Ser.). (ENG.). 24p. (gr. k-1). lib. bdg. 26.65 *(978-1-4914-8343-5(1)*, Pebble Plus) Capstone Press of Coughlan Cos.

Taylor, Barbara. Understanding Landforms. 2007. (Geography Skills/Watts Ser.). (Illus.). 46p. (J). (gr. 4-7). lib. bdg. 32.80 *(978-1-59920-049-1(X))* Black Rabbit Bks.

Tull, Mary. Plains. 2007. (Nonfiction Reading & Writing Workshops Ser.). (ENG., Illus.). 32p. (J). pap. 17.95 *(978-0-7922-4564-3(4))* CENGAGE Learning.

Tull, Mary & National Geographic Learning Staff. Coasts. 2007. (Nonfiction Reading & Writing Workshops Ser.). (ENG., Illus.). 32p. (J). pap. 17.95 *(978-0-7922-4563-6(6))* CENGAGE Learning.

Twist, Clint. Extreme Earth. 2010. (Ripley Twists Ser.). (Illus.). 48p. (J). (gr. 3-18). lib. bdg. 19.95 *(978-1-4222-1829-7(5)*, 1318258) Mason Crest.

Twist, Clint, et al. Extreme Earth. 2009. (Ripley Twists Ser.). (Illus.). 48p. (J). (gr. 3-18). pap. 8.95 *(978-1-4222-2067-2(2)*, 1318258) Mason Crest.

Van Gorp, Lynn. Investigating Landforms, 1 vol. 2007. (Science Readers Ser.). (ENG., Illus.). 32p. (J). (gr. 4-4). pap. 8.99 *(978-0-7439-0557-2(1))* Shell Educational Publishing.

World Book, Inc Staff, contrib. by. Earth's Features. 2010. (J). *(978-0-7166-7738-3(5))* World Bk., Inc.

Zuravicky, Orli. Map Math: Learning about Latitude & Longitude Using Coordinate Systems. 2009. (PowerMath Ser.). (ENG.). 32p. (gr. 5-6). pap. 10.00 *(978-1-4042-5133-5(2)*, PowerKids Pr.) Rosen Publishing Group, Inc., The.

PHYSICAL GEOGRAPHY—NORTH AMERICA

Harcourt School Publishers Staff. Horizons: Texas Edition. 3rd ed. 2003. (Illus.). (gr. 4). 70.10 *(978-0-15-320181-3(9))* Harcourt Schl. Pubs.

—Horizons: US History. 3rd ed. 2003. (Harcourt School Publishers Horizons Ser.). (ENG., Illus.). 826p. (gr. 5-5). pupil's gde. ed. 93.85 *(978-0-15-320182-0(7))* Harcourt Schl. Pubs.

PHYSICAL STAMINA

see Physical Fitness

PHYSICAL THERAPY—VOCATIONAL GUIDANCE

Amidon Lusted, Marcia. Jump-Starting a Career in Physical Therapy & Rehabilitation. 2013. (Health Care Careers in 2 Years Ser.). 80p. (YA). (gr. 7-12). 33.25 *(978-1-4777-1695-3(5))* Rosen Publishing Group, Inc., The.

Flath, Camden. Therapy Jobs in Educational Settings: Speech, Physical, Occupational & Audiology. 2010. (New Careers for the 21st Century Ser.). (Illus.). 64p. (YA). (gr. 7-18). pap. 9.95 *(978-1-4222-2047-4(8))* Mason Crest.

Kassnoff, David. Working As a Physical Therapist in Your Community. 2015. (Careers in Your Community Ser.). (ENG., Illus.). 80p. (J). (gr. 7-8). 34.25 *(978-1-4994-6109-1(7)*, Rosen Young Adult) Rosen Publishing Group, Inc., The.

PHYSICAL TRAINING

see Physical Education and Training

PHYSICALLY CHALLENGED PEOPLE

see People with Disabilities

PHYSICALLY DISABLED PEOPLE

see People with Disabilities

PHYSICALLY HANDICAPPED

see People with Disabilities

PHYSICIANS

see also Women Physicians
also names of specialists, e.g. Surgeons

Anderson, Catherine Corley. John F. Kennedy. 2005. (Just the Facts Biographies Ser.). (ENG., Illus.). 112p. (gr. 5-12). lib. bdg. 27.93 *(978-0-8225-2643-8(3)*, Lerner Pubns.) Lerner Publishing Group.

Askew, Amanda & Crowson, Andrew. Doctor. 2012. (Illus.). 24p. (gr. 1-3). pap. 7.95 *(978-1-926853-47-5(4))* Saunders Bk. Co. CAN. Dist: RiverStream Publishing.

Bailey, Diane. Physics. 2017. (Illus.). 64p. (J). *(978-1-4222-3554-6(8))* Mason Crest.

Bankston, John. Joseph Lister & the Story of Antiseptics. 2004. (Uncharted, Unexplored, & Unexplained Ser.). (Illus.). 48p. (J). (gr. 4-8). lib. bdg. 29.95 *(978-1-58415-262-0(1))* Mitchell Lane Pubs., Inc.

Bell, Samantha. Sports Medicine Doctor. 2015. (21st Century Skills Library: Cool STEAM Careers Ser.). (ENG., Illus.). 32p. (J). (gr. 4-7). pap. 14.21 *(978-1-63362-654-6(7)*, 206441) Cherry Lake Publishing.

Bellamy, Adam. This Is My Doctor. 2016. (All about My World Ser.). (Illus.). 24p. (J). pap. 9.35 *(978-0-7660-8098-0(6))* Enslow Pubs., Inc.

Benge, Janet & Benge, Geoff. Klaus-Dieter John: Hope in the Land of the Incas. 2014. (Illus.). 216p. (J). pap. 9.99 *(978-1-57658-755-3(X))* YWAM Publishing.

Bennett, Howard J. Lions Aren't Scared of Shots: A Story for Children about Visiting the Doctor. Weber, M. S., illus. 2006. 32p. (J). (gr. -1-3). 14.95 *(978-1-59147-473-9(6)*, 441A473); per. 9.95 *(978-1-59147-474-6(4)*, 441A474) American Psychological Assn. (Magination Pr.).

BENSON, Mary Rubec. Follow the Warrior's Path: Life Story of Ohiyesa Better Known As Dr. Eastman. 2003. (YA). pap. 14.95 *(978-0-89992-155-6(8))* Council for Indian Education.

Boyd, Nicole. A Doctor's Busy Day. 2009. (Reading Room Collection 2 Ser.). 24p. (gr. 3-4). 42.50 *(978-1-60851-952-1(X)*, PowerKids Pr.) Rosen Publishing Group, Inc., The.

Brill, Marlene Targ. Doctors. (Pull Ahead Bks.). (Illus.). 32p. (J). 2005. lib. bdg. 22.60 *(978-0-8225-1689-7(6))* 2004. pap. 5.95 *(978-0-8225-2531-8(3)*, Lerner Pubns.) Lerner Publishing Group.

Brooks, Felicity. Daisy Doctor. Litchfield, Jo, illus. 2005. 24p. (J). pap. 6.95 *(978-0-7945-0724-4(7)*, Usborne) EDC Publishing.

Bryant, Jennifer. A River of Words: The Story of William Carlos Williams. Sweet, Melissa, illus. 2008. (ENG.). 34p. (J). (gr. 4-7). 17.50 *(978-0-8028-5302-8(1)*, Eerdmans Bks For Young Readers) Eerdmans, William B. Publishing Co.

Buckley, James, Jr. A Day with a Doctor. 2007. (Reading Rocks! Ser.). (ENG., Illus.). 32p. (J). (gr. 2-5). 28.50 *(978-1-59296-866-4(X)*, 200739) Child's World, Inc., The.

Charles, Audrey. I Can Be a Doctor. 2017. (I Can Be Anything! Ser.). 24p. (gr. k-k). pap. 8.15 ***(978-1-4824-6317-0(2))*** Stevens, Gareth Publishing LLLP.

Christy, Lee Louis. I Go to Work as a Doctor. 2003. (I Go to Work As Ser.). (Illus.). (J). *(978-1-58417-042-6(5))*; pap. *(978-1-58417-107-2(3))* Lake Street Pubs.

Civardi, Anne. Going to the Doctor. rev. ed. 2005. 16p. (J). pap. 4.95 *(978-0-7945-1004-6(3)*, Usborne) EDC Publishing.

Clark, Sarah Kartchner. Doctors Then & Now, 1 vol. 2006. (Primary Source Readers Ser.). (ENG.). 32p. (J). (gr. 2-2). pap. 8.99 *(978-0-7439-9373-9(X))* Shell Educational Publishing.

Coan, Sharon. Trabajadores Que Me Cuidan (Workers Who Take Care of Me) 2016. (TIME for KIDS(r) Nonfiction Readers Ser.). (SPA.). 12p. (J). (gr. k-k). 4.99 *(978-1-4938-3028-2(7))* Teacher Created Materials, Inc.

Crabtree, Marc. Meet My Neighbor, the Doctor. 2013. (ENG., Illus.). 24p. (J). *(978-0-7787-0871-1(3))*; pap. *(978-0-7787-0875-9(6))* Crabtree Publishing Co.

Dawson, Patricia. A Doctor's Job. 2014. (Community Workers Ser.). 24p. (J). (gr. k-2). pap. 8.22 *(978-1-62712-991-6(X))*; lib. bdg. 24.21 *(978-1-62712-990-9(1))* Cavendish Square Publishing.

La Doctora, 2 Pack. (Chiquilibros Ser.). (SPA.). (gr. -1-1). 12.00 *(978-0-7635-8564-8(5))* Rigby Education.

Dyan, Penelope. The Place of Tales — a Kid's Guide to Canterbury, Kent, England. Weigand, John, photos by. 2011. (Illus.). 40p. pap. 12.95 *(978-1-935630-66-1(0))* Bellissima Publishing, LLC.

Elford, Jole Shack. William Harvey & the Mechanics of the Heart. 2005. (Illus.). 141p. (YA). (gr. 6-10). reprint ed. 28.00 *(978-0-7567-9712-6(8))* DIANE Publishing Co.

Farndon, John. Quacks & con Artists: The Dubious History of Doctors. Dean, Venitia, illus. 2017. (Sickening History of Medicine Ser.). (ENG.). 32p. (J). (gr. 3-6). 26.65 *(978-1-5124-1560-5(X))*; 19.99 ***(978-1-5124-3636-5(4))***; 30.65 ***(978-1-5124-2712-7(8))***; 30.65 ***(978-1-5124-3635-8(6))*** Lerner Publishing Group.

Ferguson Publishing Staff, contrib. by. Physicians. 3rd rev. ed. 2010. (Careers in Focus Ser.). (Illus.). 229p. (gr. 6-12). 32.95 *(978-0-8160-8027-4(5)*, Ferguson Publishing Co.) Facts On File, Inc.

Flor Ada, Alma & Campoy, F. Isabel, contrib. by. Voces. (Literature Collection of Puertas Al Sol Ser.).Tr. of Voices. (SPA.). 32p. (J). (gr. k-6). pap. 13.95 *(978-1-59437-707-5(3))* Santillana USA Publishing Co., Inc.

Foy, Debbie. Medical Pioneers. 2011. (20th Century Lives Ser.). (ENG.). 32p. (YA). (gr. 3-6). lib. bdg. 26.50 *(978-1-4488-3293-4(4))* Rosen Publishing Group, Inc., The.

Gogerly, Liz. Doctors & Nurses. 2016. (Play the Part Ser.). (ENG., Illus.). 24p. (J). (gr. k-2). pap. 10.99 *(978-0-7502-9705-9(0)*, Wayland) Hachette Children's Group GBR. Dist: Hachette Bk. Group.

Goldish, Meish. Doctors to the Rescue. 2011. (Work of Heroes: First Responders in Action Ser.). 32p. (YA). (gr. 1-4). lib. bdg. 25.27 *(978-1-61772-285-1(5))* Bearport Publishing Co., Inc.

Gorman, Jacqueline Laks. Doctors. 2010. (People in My Community Ser.). (ENG.). 24p. (J). (gr. k-3). pap. 8.15 *(978-1-4339-3804-7(9))*; lib. bdg. 22.60 *(978-1-4339-3803-0(0))* Stevens, Gareth Publishing LLLP.

Gow, Mary. The Greatest Doctor of Ancient Times: Hippocrates & His Oath. 2009. (Great Minds of Ancient Science & Math Ser.). (Illus.). 128p. (J). (gr. 4-7). lib. bdg. 33.27 *(978-0-7660-3118-0(7))* Enslow Pubs., Inc.

Gregory, Josh. Sports Medicine: Science, Technology, & Engineering. 2016. (Calling All Innovators: a Career for You Ser.). (ENG., Illus.). 64p. (J). lib. bdg. 32.00 *(978-0-531-23004-6(X)*, Children's Pr.) Scholastic Library Publishing.

—What Do They Do? Doctors. 2010. (Community Connections: What Do They Do? Ser.). (ENG.). 24p. (gr. 2-5). lib. bdg. 25.64 *(978-1-60279-805-2(2)*, 200500) Cherry Lake Publishing.

Griffin, Lydia. Susan Anderson: Colorado's Doc Susie. 2010. (ENG., Illus.). 72p. (J). pap. 8.95 *(978-0-86541-108-1(5))* Filter Pr., LLC.

Hapka, Cathy, pseud. My Little Doctor Bag Book. Sharp, Paul, illus. 2005. (J). *(978-1-57151-754-8(5))* Playhouse Publishing.

Harcourt School Publishers Staff. Your Health Reader: The Doctor. 3rd ed. 2003. (Illus.). pap. 9.40 *(978-0-15-338776-0(9))* Harcourt Schl. Pubs.

Harness, Cheryl. Mary Walker Wears the Pants: The True Story of the Doctor, Reformer, & Civil War Hero. Molinari, Carlo, illus. 2013. (ENG.). 32p. (J). (gr. 1-3). 16.99 *(978-0-8075-4990-2(8))* Whitman, Albert & Co.

Harrison, Lorraine. Doctors on the Job. 2017. (Jobs in Our Community Ser.). 24p. (J). (gr. k-k). pap. 49.50 *(978-1-5345-2138-4(0))*; (gr. 1-1). 24.60 *(978-1-5345-2139-1(9))*; (gr. 1-1). pap. 8.25 *(978-1-5345-2137-7(2))* Cengage Gale.

Heath, Erin. Doctors in Our Community. 2009. (On the Job Ser.). (ENG.). 24p. (J). pap. 8.25 *(978-1-4358-2454-6(7))*; (Illus.). lib. bdg. 22.60 *(978-1-4042-8070-0(7)*, 1300565) Rosen Publishing Group, Inc., The. (PowerKids Pr.).

Heos, Bridget. Let's Meet a Doctor. Moran, Mike, illus. 2013. (Cloverleaf Books — Community Helpers Ser.). (ENG.). 24p. (gr. k-2). pap. 6.95 *(978-1-4677-0801-2(1))*; lib. bdg. 23.93 *(978-0-7613-9028-2(6))* Lerner Publishing Group. (Millbrook Pr.).

Herweck, Diana. All in a Day's Work: ER Doctor, 1 vol. 2nd rev. ed. 2013. (Nonfiction Readers Ser.). (ENG., Illus.). 64p. (J). (gr. 5-5). pap. 31.96 *(978-1-4333-7429-6(3))* Teacher Created Materials, Inc.

—ER Doctor, 1 vol. 2nd rev. ed. 2013. (Nonfiction Readers Ser.). (ENG.). 64p. (J). (gr. 5-5). pap. 10.99 *(978-1-4333-4906-5(X))* Teacher Created Materials, Inc.

Hunsaker, Jennifer. Physical Therapists. 2017. (Careers in Healthcare Ser.: Vol. 13). (ENG.). (YA). (gr. 7-12). 23.95 ***(978-1-4222-3803-5(2))*** Mason Crest.

James, Emily. Elizabeth Blackwell. 2017. (Great Scientists & Inventors Ser.). (ENG., Illus.). 24p. (gr. k-1). lib. bdg. 26.65 *(978-1-5157-3882-4(5))* Capstone Press of Coughlan Cos.

Jankowski, Connie. Hippocrates: Making the Way for Medicine, 1 vol. 2007. (Science Readers Ser.). (ENG.). 32p. (J). (gr. 3-3). pap. 8.99 *(978-0-7439-0596-1(2))* Shell Educational Publishing.

Juarez, Christine. Hector P. Garcia. 2016. (Great Hispanic & Latino Americans Ser.). (ENG.). 24p. (gr. k-1). lib. bdg. 21.99 *(978-1-5157-1891-8(3)*, Pebble Bks.) Capstone Press of Coughlan Cos.

Kenan, Tessa. Hooray for Dentists! 2017. (Bumba Books (tm) — Hooray for Community Helpers! Ser.). (ENG.). 24p. (J). (gr. -1-1). 25.32 ***(978-1-5124-3351-7(9))*** Lerner Publishing Group.

—Hooray for Doctors! 2017. (Bumba Books (tm) — Hooray for Community Helpers! Ser.). (ENG.). 24p. (J). (gr. -1-1). pap. 6.99 ***(978-1-5124-5550-2(4))***; (Illus.). 25.32 ***(978-1-5124-3350-0(0)***, Lerner Pubns.) Lerner Publishing Group.

Kidder, Tracy. Mountains Beyond Mountains (Adapted for Young People) The Quest of Dr. Paul Farmer, a Man Who Would Cure the World. 2014. (ENG.). (YA). (gr. 7). lib. bdg. 19.60 ***(978-1-68065-029-7(7))*** Perfection Learning Corp.

Kidder, Tracy & French, Michael. Mountains Beyond Mountains (Adapted for Young People) The Quest of Dr. Paul Farmer, a Man Who Would Cure the World. 2014. (ENG.). 288p. (YA). (gr. 7). pap. 9.99 *(978-0-385-74319-8(X)*, Ember) Random Hse. Children's Bks.

King, Aven. A Doctor's Tools. 2015. (Community Helpers & Their Tools Ser.). (ENG., Illus.). 24p. (J). (gr. 2-3). pap. 8.25 *(978-1-4994-0838-6(2)*, PowerKids Pr.) Rosen Publishing Group, Inc., The.

Klar, Jeremy & Lily, Henrietta M. Josef Mengele, 01 vols., 1. 2016. (Holocaust Ser.). (ENG., Illus.). 112p. (J). 35.60 *(978-1-5081-7047-1(9)*, Rosen Young Adult) Rosen Publishing Group, Inc., The.

Kummer, Patricia K. Sports Medicine Doctor. 2008. (21st Century Skills Library: Cool Careers Ser.). (ENG.). 32p. (gr. 4-8). lib. bdg. 28.50 *(978-1-60279-302-6(6)*, 200141) Cherry Lake Publishing.

Lim, Bridget & Ramen, Fred. Albucasis: The Father of Modern Surgery. 2016. (Physicians, Scientists, & Mathematicians of the Islamic World Ser.). 112p. (gr. 6-6). 37.10 *(978-1-5081-7140-9(8))* Rosen Publishing Group, Inc., The.

Louie, Ai-Ling. Yo-Yo & Yeou-Cheng Ma, Finding Their Way: Amazing Asian Americans. Peng, Cathy, illus. 2012. (Biographies of Amazing Asian Americans Ser.: 2). (ENG.). 48p. (J). pap. 16.99 *(978-0-9787465-0-6(3))* Dragoneagle Pr.

Lowenstein, Felicia. What Does a Doctor Do? 2005. (What Does a Community Helper Do? Ser.). (Illus.). 24p. (J). (gr. 1-3). lib. bdg. 22.60 *(978-0-7660-2542-4(X)*, Enslow Elementary) Enslow Pubs., Inc.

Lusted, Marcia. Hippocrates. 2017. (Junior Biography From Ancient Civilization Ser.). (gr. 4-6). 29.95 *(978-1-68020-030-0(5))* Mitchell Lane Pubs., Inc.

Marsico, Katie. The Doctor. 2011. (Colonial People 2 Ser.). 48p. (gr. 3). 29.93 *(978-1-60870-412-5(2))* Marshall Cavendish Corp.

Martin, Oscar, Jr., creator. Doctors I.t. ed. 2003. (Illus.). 25p. (J). E-Book 19.95 incl. cd-rom *(978-0-9748416-5-6(X))* Build Your Story.

Mattern, Joanne. I Use Math at the Doctor's. 2005. (Daily Math Ser.). (Illus.). 24p. (gr. k-3). pap. 8.15 *(978-0-8368-4861-8(6))*; lib. bdg. 22.00 *(978-0-8368-4854-0(3))* Stevens, Gareth Publishing LLLP. (Weekly Reader Leveled Readers).

Meachen Rau, Dana. Doctors. 2007. (Tools We Use Ser.). (Illus.). 32p. (gr. k-2). lib. bdg. 15.95 *(978-0-7614-2659-2(0)*, Benchmark Bks.) Marshall Cavendish Corp.

—Doctors/Los Doctores. 2007. (Tools We Use/Instrumentos de Trabajo Ser.). (SPA & ENG., Illus.). 32p. (gr. k-2). lib. bdg. 15.95 *(978-0-7614-2824-4(0)*, Benchmark Bks.) Marshall Cavendish Corp.

—Los Doctores. 2007. (Instrumentos de Trabajo Ser.). (SPA & ENG., Illus.). 32p. (gr. k-2). lib. bdg. 15.95 *(978-0-7614-2799-5(6)*, Benchmark Bks.) Marshall Cavendish Corp.

Miller, Connie Colwell. I'll Be a Doctor. Baroncelli, Silvia, illus. 2016. (When I Grow Up Ser.). (ENG.). 24p. (J). (gr. k-3). 20.95 *(978-1-60753-760-1(5))* Amicus Publishing.

Murray, Julie. Doctors, 1 vol. 2015. (ENG., Illus.). 24p. (J). 27.07 *(978-1-62970-912-3(3))* ABDO Publishing Co.

—Medicos. 2016. (Trabajos en Mi Comunidad Ser.). (SPA.). 24p. (J). (gr. k-5). pap. 7.95 *(978-1-4966-0717-1(1))* Capstone Classroom.

Niven, Felicia Lowenstein. Lo Que Hacen los Doctores. 2007. (What Does a Community Helper Do? Bilingual Ser.).Tr. of What Doctors Do. (ENG & SPA., Illus.). 24p. (J). (gr. 1-3). lib. bdg. 22.60 *(978-0-7660-2824-1(0)*, Enslow Elementary) Enslow Pubs., Inc.

Oelschlager, Vanita. Bonyo Bonyo. Blackwood, Kristin & Blanc, Mike, illus. 2010. (ENG.). 42p. (J). (gr. -1-3). pap. 8.95 *(978-0-9819714-4-5(X))*; 15.95 *(978-0-9819714-3-8(1))* VanitaBooks.

Owen, Ann & Picture Window Books Staff. Keeping You Healthy: A Book about Doctors, 1 vol. Thomas, Eric, illus. 2003. (Community Workers Ser.). (ENG.). 24p. (gr. -1-3). per. 8.95 *(978-1-4048-0479-1(X))* Picture Window Bks.

Parks, Peggy J. Doctor. 2003. (Exploring Careers Ser.). (ENG., Illus.). 48p. (J). (gr. 3-5). 27.50 *(978-0-7377-1484-5(0)*, Kidhaven) Cengage Gale.

Phillips, Hannah. Doctor. 2016. (Here to Help Ser.). (ENG., Illus.). 24p. (J). (gr. k-2). 16.99 *(978-1-4451-3991-3(X)*, Franklin Watts) Hachette Children's Group GBR. Dist: Hachette Bk. Group.

QEB Start Reading & Talking National Book Stores Edition: First Experiences: Going to the Doctor. 2006. (J). per. *(978-1-59566-253-8(7))* QEB Publishing Inc.

Raines, Christie. My Trip to the Hospital. 2012. (ENG.). 24p. (J). pap. 15.95 *(978-1-4327-9423-1(X))* Outskirts Pr., Inc.

Rameck, Hunt, et al. We Beat the Street: How a Friendship Pact Led to Success. 2014. (ENG.). 208p. (J). 12.24 *(978-1-63245-093-7(3))* Lectorum Pubns., Inc.

Ramen, Fred. Albucasis (Abu al-Qasim Al-Zahrawi) Renowned Muslim Surgeon of the Tenth Century. 2009. (Great Muslim Philosophers & Scientists of the Middle Ages Ser.). 112p. (gr. 6-6). 66.50 *(978-1-61513-178-5(7)*, Rosen Reference) Rosen Publishing Group, Inc., The.

Rau, Dana Meachen. Doctors. 2007. (J). pap. 6.99 *(978-0-7614-3291-3(4))* Marshall Cavendish Corp.

Ready, Dee. Dentists Help. 2013. (Our Community Helpers Ser.). (ENG.). 24p. (gr. k-1). pap. 35.70 *(978-1-62065-842-0(9))*; pap. 6.29 *(978-1-62065-841-3(0))*; lib. bdg. 21.99 *(978-1-62065-081-3(9))* Capstone Press of Coughlan Cos. (Pebble Bks.).

—Doctors Help, 1 vol. 2013. (Our Community Helpers Ser.). (ENG.). 24p. (gr. k-1). pap. 6.29 *(978-1-62065-843-7(7))*; pap. 35.70 *(978-1-62065-844-4(5))*; lib. bdg. 21.99 *(978-1-62065-078-3(9))* Capstone Press of Coughlan Cos. (Pebble Bks.).

Rich, Mari. Medicine, Vol. 10. Gilmore, Malinda & Pouson, Mel, eds. 2016. (Black Achievement in Science Ser.). (Illus.). 64p. (J). (gr. 7). 23.95 *(978-1-4222-3561-4(0))* Mason Crest.

Rissman, Rebecca. Going to the Doctor: Comparing Past & Present, 1 vol. 2014. (Comparing Past & Present Ser.). (ENG., Illus.). 24p. (gr. -1-1). lib. bdg. 22.65 *(978-1-4329-8992-7(8)*, Acorn) Heinemann-Raintree.

Rivera, Sheila. Doctor. 2005. (First Step Nonfiction - Work People Do Ser.). (ENG.). 8p. (gr. -1-1). pap. 4.95 *(978-0-8225-5357-1(0)*, Lerner Pubns.) Lerner Publishing Group.

Rivera, Sheila & Kishel, Ann-Marie. Elizabeth Blackwell: A Life of Diligence. 2007. (Pull Ahead Books-Biographies Ser.). (ENG.). 32p. (gr. k-3). pap. 7.95 *(978-0-8225-6453-9(X))* Lerner Publishing Group.

Rodríguez, Ana María. Edward Jenner: Conqueror of Smallpox. 2006. (Great Minds of Science Ser.). (Illus.). 128p. (J). (gr. 4-10). lib. bdg. 33.27 *(978-0-7660-2504-2(7))* Enslow Pubs., Inc.

Rogers, Amy B. Que Hacen Los Doctores? / What Do Doctors Do? 2015. (Ayudantes de la Comunidad / Helping the Community Ser.). (ENG & SPA.). 24p. (J). (gr. 1-1). 23.60 *(978-1-4994-0620-7(7)*, PowerKids Pr.) Rosen Publishing Group, Inc., The.

—What Do Doctors Do? 2015. (Helping the Community Ser.). (ENG., Illus.). 24p. (J). (gr. 1-1). pap. 8.25 *(978-1-4994-0617-7(7)*, PowerKids Pr.) Rosen Publishing Group, Inc., The.

Scholastic, Inc. Staff, contrib. by. If I Were a Doctor. 2015. (Rookie Toddler(tm) Ser.). (ENG., Illus.). 12p. (J). bds. 6.95 *(978-0-531-21264-6(5)*, Children's Pr.) Scholastic Library Publishing.

Schraff, Anne. Charles Drew: Pioneer in Medicine. 2003. (Famous Inventors Ser.). (Illus.). 32p. (J). (gr. 1-4). lib. bdg. 22.60 *(978-0-7660-2008-5(8))* Enslow Pubs., Inc.

Sharafeddine, Fatima. The Amazing Discoveries of Ibn Sina, 1 vol. Ali, Intelaq Mohammed, illus. 2015. (ENG.). 32p. (J). (gr. 1-6). 17.95 *(978-1-55498-710-8(5))* Groundwood Bks. CAN. Dist: Publishers Group West (PGW).

Shepherd, Jodie. A Day with Doctors. 2012. (Rookie Read-About Community Ser.). (ENG., Illus.). 32p. (J). pap. 5.95 *(978-0-531-29250-1(9))*; lib. bdg. 23.00 *(978-0-531-28950-1(8))* Scholastic Library Publishing.

Siemens, Jared. Doctors. 2016. (J). ***(978-1-5105-2103-2(8))*** SmartBook Media, Inc.

—Doctors. 2015. (Illus.). 24p. (J). *(978-1-4896-3641-6(2))* Weigl Pubs., Inc.

Simon, Samantha. Physician Assistants. 2017. (Careers in Healthcare Ser.: Vol. 13). (ENG.). (YA). (gr. 7-12). 23.95 ***(978-1-4222-3804-2(0))*** Mason Crest.

Smith, Ian. Going to the Doctor. 2015. (ENG.). 24p. (gr. -1-2). 23.99 *(978-1-939581-81-5(8))* QEB Publishing Inc.

Spielman, Gloria. Janusz Korczak's Children. Archambault, Matthew, illus. 2007. (Kar-Ben for Older Readers Ser.). 40p. (J). (gr. 3-7). lib. bdg. 17.95 *(978-1-58013-255-8(3))*; (ENG.). pap. 7.95 *(978-0-8225-7050-9(5))* Lerner Publishing Group. (Kar-Ben Publishing).

Stefoff, Rebecca. Forensics & Medicine. 2010. (Forensic Science Investigated 2 Ser.). (Illus.). 80p. (J). (gr. 5). lib. bdg. 34.21 *(978-0-7614-4143-4(3))* Marshall Cavendish GBR. Dist: Marshall Cavendish Corp.

Suen, Anastasia. Doctors Without Borders. 2009. (Helping Organizations Ser.). 24p. (gr. 2-2). 42.50 *(978-1-61513-258-4(9)*, PowerKids Pr.) Rosen Publishing Group, Inc., The.

—Médicos sin Fronteras (Doctors Without Borders) 2009. (Organizaciones de ayuda (Helping Organizations) Ser.). (SPA.). 24p. (gr. 2-2). 42.50 *(978-1-60851-147-1(2)*, Editorial Buenas Letras) Rosen Publishing Group, Inc., The.

Thalhamer, Ellen Viola. Let's Play Doctor: I Love to Pretend! 2010. 36p. pap. 15.99 *(978-1-4490-7487-6(1))* AuthorHouse.

Tourville, Amanda Doering. Whose Gadgets Are These?, 1 vol. 2011. (Community Helper Mysteries Ser.). (ENG.). 24p. (gr. k-1). lib. bdg. 26.65 *(978-1-4296-6082-2(1)*, Pebble Plus) Capstone Press of Coughlan Cos.

—Whose Tools Are These?, 1 vol. 2011. (Community Helper Mysteries Ser.). (ENG.). 24p. (gr. k-1). lib. bdg. 26.65 *(978-1-4296-6081-5(3)*, Pebble Plus) Capstone Press of Coughlan Cos.

Venezia, Mike. Daniel Hale Williams: Surgeon Who Opened Hearts & Minds. 2010. (Getting to Know the World's Greatest Inventors & Scientists Ser.). 32p. (J). (gr. 3-4). pap. 6.95 *(978-0-531-22350-5(7)*, Children's Pr.) Scholastic Library Publishing.

Wheeler, Jill C. E. R. Doctors, 1 vol. 2003. (Everyday Heroes Ser.). (ENG., Illus.). 32p. (gr. k-6). 27.07 *(978-1-57765-859-7(0)*, Checkerboard Library) ABDO Publishing Co.

Whiting, Jim. The Life & Times of Hippocrates. 2006. (Biography from Ancient Civilizations Ser.). (Illus.). 48p. (J). (gr. 3-7). lib. bdg. 29.95 *(978-1-58415-512-6(4)*, 1259600) Mitchell Lane Pubs., Inc.

Wood, Alix. Mystery in the Morgue: Be a Pathologist. 2017. (Crime Solvers Ser.). 48p. (gr. 6-6). pap. 84.30 ***(978-1-5382-0621-8(8))*** Stevens, Gareth Publishing LLLP.

Yomtov, Nel. Epidemiologist. 2013. (21st Century Skills Library: Cool STEM Careers Ser.). (ENG.). 32p. (gr. 4-8). 28.50 *(978-1-62431-007-2(9)*, 202479); pap. 14.21 *(978-1-62431-031-7(1)*, 202481) Cherry Lake Publishing.

Yount, Lisa. William Harvey: Discoverer of How Blood Circulates. 2008. (Great Minds of Science Ser.). (Illus.). 128p. (J). (gr. 4-10). lib. bdg. 33.27 *(978-0-7660-3010-7(5))* Enslow Pubs., Inc.

—William Harvey: Genius Discoverer of Blood Circulation. 2015. (Genius Scientists & Their Genius Ideas Ser.). 96p. (J). (gr. 5-12). 27.94 *(978-0-7660-6585-7(5))*; pap. 10.95 *(978-0-7660-6586-4(3))* Enslow Pubs., Inc.

PHYSICIANS—FICTION

Abbott, Simon, illus. Doctor: With a Pop-Out Surgery & Play Pieces! 2014. (Happy Street Ser.). (ENG.). 10p. (J). (gr. -1-k). bds. 9.99 *(978-1-4052-7058-8(6))* Egmont Bks., Ltd. GBR. Dist: Independent Pubs. Group.

Aguirre, Ann. Vanguard. 2017. (Razorland Trilogy Ser.). (ENG.). 368p. (J). 17.99 *(978-1-250-08982-3(4)*, 9781250089823) Feiwel & Friends.

Alcott, Louisa May. Les Quatre Filles du Docteur March.Tr. of Little Women. (FRE.). (J). pap. 19.95 *(978-2-07-051516-5(8))* Gallimard, Editions FRA. Dist: Distribooks, Inc.

Anderson, Laurie Halse. Manatee Blues, No. 4. 2008. (Vet Volunteers Ser.: 4). (ENG.). 144p. (J). (gr. 3-7). 7.99 *(978-0-14-241084-4(5)*, Puffin Books) Penguin Young Readers Group.

Aryal, Aimee. Hello, Doc! 2008. (J). 14.95 *(978-1-934878-47-7(2))* Mascot Bks., Inc.

Bacon, Joy. Oliver Bean, Doctors Aren't Mean! Edward J Russell Elementary School Students, illus. 2007. (ENG.). 32p. (J). (gr. 4-7). pap. 8.95 *(978-0-9792371-1-9(4))* Keene Publishing.

Bailey, Leslie J. Jacub's Journey. DeBroeck, Sarah, illus. 2011. 28p. pap. 24.95 *(978-1-4560-9951-0(5))* America Star Bks.

Banks, Steven. Spongebob Goes to the Doctor. Saunders, Zina, illus. 2005. 22p. (J). lib. bdg. 15.00 *(978-1-4242-0976-7(5))* Fitzgerald Bks.

Banner, Angela. Ant & Bee & the Doctor. 2014. (Ant & Bee Ser.). (ENG., Illus.). 88p. (J). (gr. -1-k). 7.99 *(978-1-4052-7073-1(X))* Egmont Bks., Ltd. GBR. Dist: Independent Pubs. Group.

Barchers, Suzanne I. Kip Gets Sick, 1 vol. 2011. (Targeted Phonics Ser.). (ENG., Illus.). 16p. (J). (gr. k-2). pap. 5.99 *(978-1-4333-2422-2(9))* Teacher Created Materials, Inc.

Beaty, Andrea. Doctor Ted. Lemaître, Pascal, illus. 2008. (ENG.). 32p. (J). (gr. -1-3). 17.99 *(978-1-4169-2820-1(0)*, McElderry, Margaret K. Bks.) McElderry, Margaret K. Bks.

Beinstein, Phoebe & A and J Studios Staff. Di "Aaaa"! Dora Va al Médico. 2008. (Dora la Exploradora Ser.). (SPA & ENG., Illus.). 24p. (J). (gr. -1-2). pap. 3.99 *(978-1-4169-5492-7(9)*, Libros Para Ninos) Libros Para Ninos.

—Say Ahhh! Dora Goes to the Doctor. 2008. (Dora the Explorer Ser.: 26). (ENG., Illus.). 24p. (J). (gr. -1-2). pap. 3.99 *(978-1-4169-5430-9(9)*, Simon Spotlight/Nickelodeon) Simon Spotlight/Nickelodeon.

Bender, Carol. The Doctor's Little Stowaway. 2009. 28p. pap. 13.99 *(978-1-4490-3711-6(9))* AuthorHouse.

Benenfeld, Rikki. I Go to the Doctor. Benenfeld, Rikki, illus. 2004. (Toddler Experience Ser.). (Illus.). (J). lib. bdg. 10.95 *(978-1-929628-15-5(3))* Hachai Publishing.

Beobi & the Magic Coloring Book A Visit to the Doctor. 2005. (J). 3.99 *(978-0-9743847-3-3(9))* Cohn, Tricia.

Brewer, Jo Ann. The Little Girl No One Wanted. 2011. 48p. pap. 15.99 *(978-1-4568-6581-8(1))* Xlibris Corp.

Bridwell, Norman. Clifford Va al Doctor. Bridwell, Norman, illus. 2011. (Scholastic Reader Level 1 Ser.).Tr. of Clifford Goes to the Doctor. (SPA., Illus.). 32p. (J). (gr. -1-3). pap. 3.99 *(978-0-545-34118-9(3)*, Scholastic en Espanol) Scholastic, Inc.

Brooks, Felicity. Daisy the Doctor. Litchfield, Jo, illus. 2008. (Jobs People Do Ser.). 23p. (J). (gr. k-3). pap. 6.99 *(978-0-7945-2214-8(9)*, Usborne) EDC Publishing.

Brown, Mary. An Ear for Graci. 2011. 16p. 8.99 *(978-1-4520-9702-2(X))* AuthorHouse.

P Q R

Bryant, Cathy. The Doctor Said I Have Leukemi. Bunker, Thomas, illus. 2012. 24p. pap. 24.95 *(978-1-4560-6929-2(2))* America Star Bks.
By Kaleena Ma. Glasses for Me? Oh No! Dawn Phillips, illus. 2009. 40p. pap. 18.49 *(978-1-4389-5418-9(2))* AuthorHouse.
Capucilli, Alyssa Satin. Biscuit Visits the Doctor. Berlin, Rose Mary & Schories, Pat, illus. 2008. (Biscuit Ser.). (ENG.). 24p. (J). (gr. -1-1). pap. 3.99 *(978-0-06-112843-1(0),* HarperFestival) HarperCollins Pubs.
Chambers, Cindy. Beamer Learns the Signs of a Stroke & How to Help. 2013. 28p. pap. 14.95 *(978-1-4575-1725-9(6))* Dog Ear Publishing, LLC.
Chase, L. P. Today Is Tuesday. 2006. (J). pap. 9.00 *(978-0-87426-069-4(8))* Whitmore Publishing Co.
Chwast, Seymour & Lofting, Hugh. Dr. Dolittle. Chwast, Seymour, illus. 2015. (ENG., Illus.). 40p. (J). (gr. 4-7). 18.99 *(978-1-56846-258-5(1),* Creative Editions) Creative Co., The.
Civardi, Anna. Going to the Doctor Sticker Book. 2009. (First Experiences Sticker Book Ser.). 16p. (J). pap. 6.99 *(978-0-7945-2572-9(5),* Usborne) EDC Publishing.
Civardi, Anne. Going to the Hospital. 2009. (First Experiences Sticker Bks). 18p. (J). pap. 6.99 *(978-0-7945-2431-9(1),* Usborne) EDC Publishing.
—Going to the Hospital. Bates, Michelle, ed. Cartwright, Stephen, illus. rev. ed. 2005. (Usborne First Experiences Ser.). 16p. (J). (gr. -1-3). per. 4.99 *(978-0-7945-1006-0(X),* Usborne) EDC Publishing.
Cole, Joanna. My Friend the Doctor. Chambliss, Maxie, illus. 2005. (ENG.). 32p. (J). (gr. -1 — 1). 6.99 *(978-0-06-050500-4(1),* HarperFestival) HarperCollins Pubs.
Compestine, Ying Chang. Revolution Is Not a Dinner Party. 2009. (ENG.). 272p. (J). (gr. 5-9). pap. 9.99 *(978-0-312-58149-7(1),* 9780312581497) Square Fish.
Cousineau, Craig S. Skippy & Oaf Explore the Battles of the Immune System. 2010. (ENG., Illus.). 180p. (J). (gr. 2-4). pap. 9.95 *(978-1-933255-56-9(0))* DNA Pr.
Cousins, Lucy. Maisy, Charley, & the Wobbly Tooth. Cousins, Lucy, illus. 2009. (Maisy Ser.). (ENG., Illus.). 32p. (J). (gr. k-k). pap. 6.99 *(978-0-7636-4369-0(6))* Candlewick Pr.
Cowley, Joy. Poor Sore Hungry Giant. 2009. pap. 8.25 *(978-1-60559-237-4(4))* Hameray Publishing Group, Inc.
Cushman, Karen. Matilda Bone. 2014. (ENG.). 176p. (J). (gr. 5-7). pap. 6.99 *(978-0-547-72242-9(7),* HMH Books For Young Readers) Houghton Mifflin Harcourt Publishing Co.
—Matilda Bone. unabr. ed. 2004. (Middle Grade Cassette Librariestm Ser.). 176p. (J). (gr. 5-9). pap. 36.00 incl. audio *(978-0-8072-1725-2(5),* S YA 252 SP, Listening Library) Random Hse. Audio Publishing Group.
Davis, David Denton. Polly's Promise: A Story about Thriving Rather Than Simply Surviving... Turning Apparent Disability into Gifted Ability. 2013. 80p. pap. 21.95 *(978-1-4787-0275-7(3))* Outskirts Pr., Inc.
DeFelice, Cynthia C. The Apprenticeship of Lucas Whitaker. 2007. (ENG.). 160p. (J). (gr. 5-9). per. 9.99 *(978-0-374-40014-9(8),* 9780374400149) Square Fish.
Depken, Kristen L. I Can Be a Baby Doctor. 2013. (Barbie Step into Reading Level 2 Ser.). lib. bdg. 13.55 *(978-0-606-26968-1(1),* Turtleback) Turtleback Bks.
—I Can Be... a Baby Doctor (Barbie) Das Grup, illus. 2013. (Step into Reading Ser.). (ENG.). 32p. (J). (gr. -1-1). pap. 3.99 *(978-0-307-98112-7(6),* Random Hse. Bks. for Young Readers) Random Hse. Children's Bks.
Derubertis, Barbara. Izzy Impala's Imaginary Illnesses. 2010. pap. 45.32 *(978-0-7613-6511-2(7))* Kane Press, Inc.
deRubertis, Barbara. Izzy Impala's Imaginary Illnesses. Alley, R. W., illus. 2010. (Animal Antics A to Z Ser.). 32p. (J). (gr. -1-3). pap. 7.95 *(978-1-57565-313-6(3));* lib. bdg. 22.60 *(978-1-57565-320-4(6))* Kane Press, Inc.
deRubertis, Barbara & DeRubertis, Barbara. Izzy Impala's Imaginary Illnesses. Alley, R. W., illus. 2012. (Animal Antics A to Z Ser.). 32p. (J). (gr. 2 — 1). cd-rom 7.95 *(978-1-57565-402-7(4))* Kane Press, Inc.
Disney Book Group. Doc McStuffins: Awesome Guy to the Rescue! - Bella's Big Break, 2 bks. in 1. Disney Storybook Art Team, illus. 2015. (ENG.). 48p. (J). (gr. -1-k). pap. 5.99 *(978-1-4847-0695-4(1))* Disney Pr.
—Doc Mcstuffins Cuddle Me, Lambie. Disney Storybook Art Team, illus. 2015. (ENG.). 40p. (J). (gr. -1-k). 8.99 *(978-1-4847-1420-1(2))* Disney Pr.
Disney Book Group Staff. Doc Mcstuffins Dad's Favorite Toy. Disney Storybook Art Team, illus. 2015. (ENG.). 24p. (J). (gr. -1-k). pap. 4.99 *(978-1-4847-2164-3(0))* Disney Pr.
—Doc Mcstuffins Helping Hands. Disney Storybook Artists Staff & Disney Storybook Art Team, illus. 2014. (Sneak-A-Peek Ser.). (ENG.). 14p. (J). (gr. -1-k). bds. 8.99 *(978-1-4847-0766-1(4))* Disney Pr.
—Doc on Call. Disney Storybook Art Team, illus. 2015. (ENG.). 40p. (J). (gr. -1-k). 10.99 *(978-1-4847-2187-2(X))* Disney Pr.
Disney Book Group Staff & Higginson, Sheila Sweeny. Doc Mcstuffins Doc's Big Book of Boo-Boos. Disney Storybook Artists Staff, illus. 2014. (ENG.). 64p. (J). (gr. -1-k). 10.99 *(978-1-4231-8483-6(1))* Disney Pr.
—Doc Mcstuffins Doctor's Helper: Purchase Includes Disney EBook! Disney Storybook Artists Staff, illus. 2014. (ENG.). 40p. (J). (gr. -1-k). 16.99 *(978-1-4231-8390-7(8))* Disney Pr.
Disney Book Group Staff & Weinberg, Jennifer Liberts. World of Reading: Doc Mcstuffins Blame It on the Rain: Level 1. Disney Storybook Artists Staff & Disney Storybook Art Team, illus. 2014. (World of Reading Ser.). (ENG.). 32p. (J). (gr. -1-k). pap. 3.99 *(978-1-4847-0676-3(5))* Disney Pr.
Disney Book Group Staff, et al. Doc Mcstuffins Boo to You! Disney Storybook Artists Staff, illus. 2014. (ENG.). 12p. (J). (gr. -1-k). bds. 7.99 *(978-1-4231-8388-4(6))* Disney Pr.
Disney Junior Staff. Disney Doc Mcstuffins Guess Who, Doc! 2014. (Guess Who Ser.: 1). (ENG.). 10p. (J). (gr. -1-k). 10.99 *(978-0-7944-3005-4(8),* Reader's Digest Children's Bks.) Studio Fun International.
Disney Staff. Disney Doc Mcstuffins Happy to Be Healthy! 2014. (Dress-Up Ser.: 4). (ENG.). 24p. (J). (gr. -1-1). 11.99 *(978-0-7944-3019-1(8),* Reader's Digest Children's Bks.) Studio Fun International.
Draper, Sharon M. November Blues. 2009. (Jericho Trilogy Ser.). (ENG.). 400p. (YA). (gr. 7). mass mkt. 8.99 *(978-1-4169-0699-5(1),* Simon Pulse) Simon Pulse.
Dumas, Kim Foster. Gator Gets a Nose Bleed. 2012. 24p. 24.95 *(978-1-4626-4239-7(X))* America Star Bks.
Elchgar, Yasmin. Noonoo the Doctor. 2013. 20p. pap. 13.77 *(978-1-4907-1037-2(X))* Trafford Publishing.
Electra, Agnes. Medical School for Children: Part I. 2011. 46p. pap. 18.00 *(978-0-60911-756-6(5),* Eloquent Bks.) Strategic Book Publishing & Rights Agency (SBPRA).
Evans, Jan. Repetitive Rhonda. 2007. (Illus.). 29p. (J). 18.95 *(978-0-9720176-7-1(4))* Breath & Shadows Productions.
Faulkerson, President & CEO Jeffery, Founder. IT's GOOD to BE GOLDEN: Golden Innovations. 2008. 30p. 14.95 *(978-0-615-19351-9(X))* PRACTICAL SOLUTIONS Writing, Editing, Consulting.
—IT's GOOD to BE GOLDEN: the Story of Henry the Heart. 2008. 19p. 14.95 *(978-0-615-19350-2(1))* PRACTICAL SOLUTIONS Writing, Editing, Consulting.
Freeman, Don. Corduroy Goes to the Doctor. McCue, Lisa, illus. 2005. (Corduroy Ser.). (ENG.). 14p. (J). (gr. -1 — 1). bds. 5.99 *(978-0-670-06031-3(3),* Viking Books for Young Readers) Penguin Young Readers Group.
Ganz, Yaffa. The Travels & Tales of Dr. Emanuel J. Mitzva. 2003. (J). 15.99 *(978-1-58330-581-2(5))* Feldheim Pubs.
Gay, Michel. Bibunde. 2003. (SPA.). 40p. *(978-84-8470-043-2(7))* Corimbo, Editorial S.L.
—Doctor Bibunde. 2003. (SPA.). 134p. *(978-84-8470-045-6(3))* Corimbo, Editorial S.L.
Gaydos, Nora. Now I'm Growing! - A Visit to the Doctor. Gutierrez, Akemi, illus. 2011. (ENG.). 30p. (J). (gr. -1-17). 8.99 *(978-1-60169-153-8(X))* Innovative Kids.
Going to the Doctor: Individual Title Six-Packs. (gr. -1-2). 27.00 *(978-0-7635-9450-3(4))* Rigby Education.
Golden Books. The Doctor Is In! Unten, Eren, illus. 2012. (Little Golden Book Ser.). (ENG.). 24p. (J). (gr. k-k). 4.99 *(978-0-307-97588-1(6),* Golden Bks.) Random Hse. Children's Bks.
Gorbachev, Valeri. Doctor Nice. (ENG.). 32p. (J). (gr. -1-3). 2016. 6.99 *(978-0-8234-3690-3(X))* 2015. (Illus.). 16.95 *(978-0-8234-3203-5(3))* Holiday Hse., Inc.
Greene, Kathi. Betty Gets Ready for the Doctor. 2009. 28p. pap. 15.00 *(978-1-4389-4936-9(7))* AuthorHouse.
Greensill, Rowina Anne. James Goes to Play School. 2010. (Illus.). 28p. pap. 12.49 *(978-1-4490-7039-7(6))* AuthorHouse.
Griffith, Christina. Why Jubilee & Ashanti go to the Doctor? 2011. 28p. pap. 13.54 *(978-1-4269-7069-6(2))* Trafford Publishing.
Guerra, S. F. Billy the Kid Is Not Crazy, 0 vols. 2013. (ENG.). 224p. (J). (gr. 4-6). 16.99 *(978-1-4778-1732-2(8),* 9781477817322, Amazon Children's Publishing) Amazon Publishing.
Hands, Nikki. Lilly Bunny Goes to the Doctor. 2011. 28p. pap. 24.95 *(978-1-4626-3638-9(1))* America Star Bks.
Hansell, Donna. The Adventures of Kirbey the Kidney. 2012. 20p. pap. 11.59 *(978-1-4669-4527-2(3))* Trafford Publishing.
Hewitt, Franz. Monster Doctor, M. D. 2010. 40p. pap. 18.49 *(978-0-557-53188-2(8))* Lulu Pr., Inc.
Higginson, Sheila Sweeny & Disney Book Group Staff. Brontosaurus Breath. Disney Storybook Art Team, illus. 2013. (World of Reading Ser.). (ENG.). 32p. (J). (gr. -1-k). pap. 3.99 *(978-1-4231-6894-2(1))* Disney Pr.
—The Mermaid Dives In. Disney Storybook Art Team, illus. 2013. (ENG.). 24p. (J). (gr. -1-k). pap. 4.99 *(978-1-4231-7132-4(2))* Disney Pr.
Horne, Jay. Published Youth Volume Two. 2010. 61p. pap. 10.99 *(978-0-557-30674-9(4))* Lulu Pr., Inc.
Howard, Cheryl Lynne. Captured by Love: A Wild Horse Story Based on Psalm 139. 2011. 48p. pap. 11.00 *(978-1-4567-1822-0(3))* AuthorHouse.
Hurley, Crystal. The Witch with an Itch. 2008. 24p. pap. 24.95 *(978-1-60703-339-4(9))* America Star Bks.
Hutchings, Paul. Halloween Tails. 2012. 24p. pap. 24.95 *(978-1-4626-7106-9(3))* America Star Bks.
Jansson, Tove. Moomin & the Golden Tail. 2014. (Moomin Ser.). (ENG., Illus.). 56p. (J). (gr. 4-7). pap. 9.95 *(978-1-77046-133-8(7),* 9781770461338) Drawn & Quarterly Pubns. CAN. Dist: Macmillan.
Jenisch, Betty. Rennie. 2007. 9.00 *(978-0-8059-8947-2(1))* Dorrance Publishing Co., Inc.
Jensen, Patricia. I Am Sick. Hantel, Johanna, illus. (My First Reader Ser.). (ENG.). 32p. (J). (gr. k-1). 2006. per. 3.95 *(978-0-516-24970-4(3))* 2005. lib. bdg. 18.50 *(978-0-516-24878-3(2))* Scholastic Library Publishing. (Children's Pr.).
Jones, Wendy Lou. Bastian - Defender of Golden Downs. 2013. 234p. pap. 10.95 *(978-0-9777110-3-1(X))* Royal Knight Inc.
Katschke, Judy. Karate Kangaroos (Disney Junior: Doc Mcstuffins) Random House Disney Staff & Martinez, Heather, illus. 2016. (Little Golden Book Ser.). (ENG.). 24p. (J). (gr. -1-k). 4.99 *(978-0-7364-3382-2(1),* Golden/Disney) Random Hse. Children's Bks.
Katz, Alan. Let's Get a Checkup! Lemaître, Pascal, illus. 2010. (ENG.). 16p. (J). (gr. -1-1). bds. 7.99 *(978-1-4169-8992-9(7),* Little Simon) Little Simon.
Kelman, Marcy. Doc Mcstuffins Doc's Mobile Clinic. Disney Storybook Artists Staff, illus. 2014. (ENG.). 12p. (J). (gr. -1-k). bds. 7.99 *(978-1-4231-9420-0(9))* Disney Pr.
Kelman, Marcy & Disney Book Group Staff. Out of the Box. Disney Storybook Art Team, illus. 2014. (Flap 'n Tab Ser.). (ENG.). 10p. (J). (gr. -1-k). bds. 6.99 *(978-1-4231-8092-0(5))* Disney Pr.
Klein, Adria F. Max Goes to the Doctor, 1 vol. Gallagher-Cole, Mernie, illus. 2007. (Read-It! Readers: the Life of Max Ser.). (ENG.). 24p. (gr. -1-2). lib. bdg. 21.32 *(978-1-4048-3680-8(2));* per. 3.95 *(978-1-4048-3686-0(1),* 1274408) Picture Window Bks. (Easy Readers).
—Max Va Al Doctor. Lozano, Clara, tr. from ENG. Gallagher-Cole, Mernie, illus. 2008. (Read-It! Readers en Español: la Vida de Max Ser.). (SPA.). 24p. (gr. -1-3). per. 3.95 *(978-1-4048-4584-8(4),* Easy Readers) Picture Window Bks.
Kramer, Paul M. Are You Afraid of the Doctor? 2016. (ENG.). 32p. 15.95 *(978-0-9819745-3-8(8))* Aloha Wellness Pubs.
Kristen, Mantooth. Danny Goes to the Doctor. Kristen, Mantooth, illus. 2007. (Illus.). 24p. (J). 10.00 *(978-0-9800580-0-0(7))* Ballyhoo Printing.
Krumrey, Melanie. Bagels, Buddy, & Me: A Story about Gluten Intolerance & Celiac Disease. 2007. (Illus.). 40p. (J). per. 14.95 *(978-0-9797703-0-2(0))* Mustard Seed Pr.
Lange, Willem. Favor Johnson: A Christmas Story. Dodson, Bert, illus. 2009. (ENG.). 32p. (J). (gr. 1-3). 16.95 *(978-1-59373-082-6(9))* Bunker Hill Publishing, Inc.
Lee, Jared D., illus. The Dentist from the Black Lagoon, 1 vol. 2014. (ENG.). 32p. (J). 24.21 *(978-1-61479-197-3(X))* Spotlight.
Lewellyn, Natalie. Nutty to Meet You! Dr. Peanut Book #1. 2008. (Illus.). 32p. (J). 11.95 *(978-0-9777082-0-8(9))* One Monkey Bks.
Lofting, Hugh. The Story of Doctor Dolittle: Animal Talk. Kanzler, John, illus. 2008. (Easy Reader Classics Ser.). (ENG.). 32p. (gr. 3-7). lib. bdg. 24.21 *(978-1-59961-338-3(7))* Spotlight.
—The Story of Doctor Dolittle: The Circus Crocodile. Kanzler, John, illus. 2008. (Easy Reader Classics Ser.). (ENG.). 32p. (gr. 3-7). lib. bdg. 24.21 *(978-1-59961-339-0(5))* Spotlight.
London, Jonathan. Froggy Goes to the Doctor. 2004. (Illus.). (J). (gr. k-3). spiral bd. *(978-0-616-14586-9(1));* spiral bd. *(978-0-616-14585-2(3))* Canadian National Institute for the Blind/Institut National Canadien pour les Aveugles.
—Froggy Goes to the Doctor. Remkiewicz, Frank, illus. 2004. (Froggy Ser.). (ENG.). 32p. (J). (gr. -1-k). pap. 6.99 *(978-0-14-240193-4(5),* Puffin Books) Penguin Young Readers Group.
—Froggy Goes to the Doctor. 2004. (Froggy Ser.). (J). (gr. -1-18). 1.25 *(978-1-4025-3420-1(5))* Recorded Bks., Inc.
—Here Comes Doctor Hippo: A Little Hippo Story. Eduar, Gilles, illus. 2012. (Little Hippo Ser.). (ENG.). 32p. (J). (gr. -1-k). 15.95 *(978-1-59078-851-6(6))* Boyds Mills Pr.
Lynch, Chris. Prime Evil. 2010. (Cyberia Ser.: 3). (ENG.). 160p. (J). (gr. 3-7). 16.99 *(978-0-545-02795-3(0),* Scholastic Pr.) Scholastic, Inc.
MacDonald George. Gutta Percha Willie: The Working Genius. l.t. ed. 2007. (ENG.). 262p. pap. 23.99 *(978-1-4264-3992-6(X));* 142p. pap. 18.99 *(978-1-4264-3934-6(2))* Creative Media Partners, LLC.
MacDonald, George. The History of Gutta-Percha Willie. 2006. 116p. per. 9.95 *(978-1-59818-578-2(0))* Aegypan.
Marie, Jill Jana. Balloon Blessing. Zamboni, David, illus. 2008. 28p. pap. 12.95 *(978-0-9820479-7-2(5))* Peppertree Pr., The.
Marsh, Carole. The Adventure Diaries of Dharma, the Dedicated Doctor!, 3 vols. 2003. 48p. (J). (gr. 1-4). pap. 5.95 *(978-0-635-01157-2(3))* Gallopade International.
Marvel & Busse, R. R. Strange Tales & Talismans. 2016. (ENG., Illus.). 96p. (J). (gr. 3-7). 9.99 *(978-0-316-27156-1(X))* Little, Brown Bks. for Young Readers.
McDonald, Megan. Doctora Judy Moody. Reynolds, Peter H., illus. 2005. (SPA.). 74p. (J). (gr. 3-5). per. 7.95 *(978-1-59820-034-8(8))* Ediciones Alfaguara ESP. Dist: Two Rivers Distribution.
McGinnis, Mindy. A Madness So Discreet. 2015. (ENG.). 384p. (YA). (gr. 9). 17.99 *(978-0-06-232086-5(6))* HarperCollins Pubs.
Meister, Cari. The Shivery Shark, 1 vol. Harpster, Steve, illus. 2011. (Ocean Tales Ser.). (ENG.). 32p. (gr. 2-3). pap. 6.25 *(978-1-4342-3391-2(X));* lib. bdg. 22.65 *(978-1-4342-3200-7(X))* Stone Arch Bks.
Middleton Gray, Family Np. Maddie Goes to the Nurse Practitioner. 2008. 32p. pap. 13.50 *(978-1-4389-0220-3(4))* AuthorHouse.
Miles, Talaythea L. Fly, My Lupus Butterfly, Fly. 2012. 24p. pap. 14.93 *(978-1-4669-1504-6(8))* Trafford Publishing.
Morgan, Nicola. Fleshmarket. 2003. (ENG.). 272p. (J). (gr. 7-17). pap. 9.99 *(978-0-340-85557-7(6))* Hodder & Stoughton GBR. Dist: Hachette Bk. Group.
Nakagawa, Masafumi. Dr. Mouse's Mission. Perry, Mia Lynn, tr. Yamawaki, Yuriko, illus. 2007. (R. I. C. Story Chest Ser.). 27p. (J). (gr. -1-1). 14.95 incl. audio compact disk *(978-1-74126-051-9(5))* R.I.C. Pubns. AUS. Dist: SCB Distributors.
Oxenbury, Helen. Con el Medico (At the Doctor's) (SPA.). 24p. (J). 7.95 *(978-84-261-1998-8(0))* Juventud, Editorial ESP. Dist: AIMS International Bks., Inc.
Palmer, Robin. Girl vs. Superstar, Bk. 1. 2010. (Yours Truly, Lucy B. Parker Ser.: 1). (ENG.). 224p. (J). (gr. 5-18). 6.99 *(978-0-14-241500-9(6),* Puffin Books) Penguin Young Readers Group.
Parkinson, Curtis. Death in Kingsport. 2007. (ENG.). 224p. (YA). (gr. 5-9). per. 11.95 *(978-0-88776-827-9(X),* Tundra Bks.) Tundra Bks. CAN. Dist: Penguin Random Hse. LLC.
Pasternak, Boris Leonidovich. Doktor Zivago. 32.95 *(978-5-04-004105-3(5))* Dksmo-Press, Izdatel'skaja firma RUS. Dist: Distribooks, Inc.
Patrick, Wellman. Mr. Duz Goes to the Doctor. Sam, Kagan, illus. 2007. 24p. (J). 5.95 *(978-0-9796226-6-3(2))* MrDuz.com.
Pinkwater, Daniel M. Mrs. Noodlekugel & Four Blind Mice. Stower, Adam, illus. 2013. (Mrs. Noodlekugel Ser.). (ENG.). 96p. (J). (gr. k-4). 14.99 *(978-0-7636-5054-4(4))* Candlewick Pr.
Posner-Sanchez, Andrea. Boomer Gets His Bounce Back (Disney Junior: Doc Mcstuffins) RH Disney Staff, illus. 2013. (Little Golden Book Ser.). (ENG.). 24p. (J). (-k). 4.99 *(978-0-7364-3143-9(8),* Golden/Disney) Random Hse. Children's Bks.
—Shake Your Tail Feathers (Disney Junior: Doc Mcstuffins) Random House Disney Staff, illus. 2015. (Little Golden Book Ser.). (ENG.). 24p. (J). (-k). 3.99 *(978-0-7364-3274-0(4),* Golden/Disney) Random Hse. Children's Bks.
Pressler, Mirjam. Malka. Murdoch, Brian, tr. 2005. 280p. (YA). (gr. 7-12). 13.65 *(978-0-7569-5217-4(4))* Perfection Learning Corp.
Publications International Ltd. Staff, ed. Disney(r) Doc McStuffinsOh Doc, What Can the Matter Be? 2015. 12p. (J). bds. *(978-1-4508-9350-3(3),* 1450893503) Publications International, Ltd.
—Elmo Goes to the Doctor. 2010. 14p. (J). bds. 16.98 *(978-1-4127-4609-0(4))* Phoenix International Publications, Inc.
Quiller-Couch, Mabel. Kitty Trenire. 2006. (ENG.). 210p. pap. 20.99 *(978-1-4264-7475-0(X))* 2007. 230p. pap. 22.99 *(978-1-4264-7552-8(7))* Creative Media Partners, LLC.
Rader, Jared. Sandy's Dream. Meyers, Sarah, illus. 2007. 16p. (J). (gr. -1-3). 10.99 *(978-1-59879-398-7(5))* Lifevest Publishing, Inc.
Rahnama, Seyed Javad. Minty Ear. 2011. (Illus.). 20p. pap. 14.11 *(978-1-4567-8188-0(X))* AuthorHouse.
Random House Staff & Roper, Robert. Dora Goes to the Doctor/Dora Goes to the Dentist (Dora the Explorer) Random House Staff, illus. 2013. (Pictureback(R) Ser.). (ENG., Illus.). 32p. (J). (gr. -1-2). 4.99 *(978-0-449-81771-1(7),* Random Hse. Bks. for Young Readers) Random Hse. Children's Bks.
Rebello, Gleeson & Harisiades, Jamie. Darebone's Big Break. 2013. (Illus.). 38p. (J). pap. 14.95 *(978-0-9829256-7-6(0))* SDP Publishing.
—Darebone's Big Break (Hardcover) 2013. (Illus.). 38p. (J). 19.95 *(978-0-9889381-4-4(6))* SDP Publishing.
Reuterstrand, Siri. Ellis Goes to the Doctor. Wik, Jenny, illus. 2012. (ENG.). 24p. (J). (gr. -1-k). 12.95 *(978-1-61608-662-6(9),* 608662, Sky Pony Pr.) Skyhorse Publishing Co., Inc.
Rigby Education Staff, ed. Going to the Doctor. (Illus.). 8p. (J). bds. 3.95 *(978-0-7635-6427-8(3),* 764273C99) Rigby Education.
Rinaldi, Ann. An Acquaintance with Darkness. 2005. (Great Episodes Ser.). (ENG.). 384p. (YA). (gr. 7-8). pap. 9.99 *(978-0-15-205387-1(5))* Houghton Mifflin Harcourt Publishing Co.
—An Acquaintance with Darkness. 2005. (Great Episodes Ser.). 374p. (gr. 7-12). 18.00 *(978-0-7569-5040-8(6))* Perfection Learning Corp.
Rocheleau, Nicole. Ollie Ollie in Come Free! 2006. 76p. pap. 16.95 *(978-1-4241-0433-8(5))* PublishAmerica, Inc.
Rohrer, Kim. The Adventures of Little Dooey: The Doctor. 2012. 24p. pap. 9.95 *(978-0-9848050-7-5(9),* Little Creek Bks.) Jan-Carol Publishing, INC.
Roper, Robert. Dora Goes to the Doctor. 2013. (Dora the Explorer 8X8 Ser.). lib. bdg. 14.75 *(978-0-606-32216-4(7),* Turtleback) Turtleback Bks.
Rose, Marilyn C. Kylie Gets a Cochlear Implant. 2013. 32p. pap. 13.00 *(978-1-62516-170-3(0),* Strategic Bk. Publishing) Strategic Book Publishing & Rights Agency (SBPRA).
Rose, Mary. Doctor, Doctor. 2010. (ENG., Illus.). 20p. 4.81 *(978-0-19-440075-6(1))* Oxford Univ. Pr., Inc.
Salenas, Bobbi. Cinderella Latina - Cinicienta Latina. La Madrid, Enriquee, tr. Salenas, Bobbi, illus. 2003. (SPA., Illus.). (YA). (gr. 3-12). 19.95 *(978-0-934925-06-8(2))* Pinata Pubns.
Sanschagrin, Joceline. Caillou at the Doctor. Brignaud, Pierre, illus. 3rd ed. 2013. (Step by Step Ser.). (ENG.). 24p. (J). (gr. -1-k). bds. 5.99 *(978-2-89718-058-4(7))* Caillouet, Gerry.
Sargent, Dave & Sargent, Pat. Gus: (Slate Grullo) Be Thankful, 30 vols., Vol. 32. Lenoir, Jane, illus. 2003. (Saddle up Ser.; Vol. 32). 42p. (J). lib. bdg. 23.60 *(978-1-56763-693-2(4));* pap. 10.95 *(978-1-56763-694-9(2))* Ozark Publishing.
Sateren, Shelley Swanson. Max & Zoe at the Doctor, 1 vol. Sullivan, Mary, illus. 2013. (Max & Zoe Ser.). (ENG.). 32p. (gr. k-2). pap. 5.19 *(978-1-4048-8060-3(7),* Max & Zoe) Picture Window Bks.
Scarry, Richard. Richard Scarry's Nicky Goes to the Doctor. 2014. lib. bdg. 14.75 *(978-0-606-35561-2(8))* Turtleback Bks.
Scarry, Richard & Golden Books Staff. Nicky Goes to the Doctor. 2014. (Pictureback(R) Ser.). (ENG., Illus.). 24p. (J). (gr. -1-2). pap. 4.99 *(978-0-307-11842-4(8),* Random Hse. Bks. for Young Readers) Random Hse. Children's Bks.
Schauer, M. RIP, M. D. Vosburg, M., illus. 2010. (ENG.). 88p. pap. 12.99 *(978-1-60699-369-9(0),* 699369) Fantagraphics Bks.
Scotton, Rob. Splat the Cat Goes to the Doctor. Scotton, Rob, illus. 2014. (Splat the Cat Ser.). (ENG., Illus.). 24p. (J). (gr. -1-3). pap. 4.99 *(978-0-06-211588-1(X),* HarperFestival) HarperCollins Pubs.
Shaw, Helen. Five Cents Worth, 1 vol. rev. ed. 2013. (Fiction Readers Ser.). (ENG., Illus.). 32p. (J). (gr. 3-3). pap. 8.99 *(978-1-4333-5642-1(2))* Shell Educational Publishing.
Smith, Leone. Jasmine Finds a Doctor. Smith, Marcelle, illus. 2011. 30p. pap. 12.50 *(978-1-61204-042-4(X),* Strategic Bk. Publishing) Strategic Book Publishing & Rights Agency (SBPRA).
Steig, William. Doctor de Soto. Steig, William, illus. 2010. (ENG., Illus.). 32p. (J). (gr. -1-3). pap. 7.99 *(978-0-312-61189-7(7),* 9780312611897) Square Fish.
—Doctor de Soto Book & CD Storytime Set, 1 vol. Steig, William, illus. unabr. ed. 2012. (ENG., Illus.). (J). (gr. k-3). 12.99 *(978-1-4272-3219-9(9),* 9781427232199) Macmillan Audio.
Stevenson, Robert Louis. Dr. Jekyll & Mr. Hyde. 2008. (Bring the Classics to Life Ser.). (ENG., Illus.). 72p. (gr. 4-12). pap., act. bk. ed. 10.95 *(978-0-931334-50-4(0),* EDCTR-402B) EDCON Publishing Group.
—Dr. Jekyll & Mr. Hyde, 1 vol. 2010. (Illustrated Classics Ser.). (ENG., Illus.). 64p. (YA). (gr. 9-12). per. 9.95 *(978-1-56254-894-0(8))* Saddleback Educational Publishing, Inc.
—The Strange Case of Dr. Jekyll & Mr. Hyde. (Classics Illustrated Ser.). (Illus.). 52p. (YA). pap. 4.95 *(978-1-57209-008-8(1))* Classics International Entertainment, Inc.
—The Strange Case of Dr. Jekyll & Mr. Hyde. Andrews, Gary, illus. 2008. (Fast Track Classics Ser.). (ENG.). 48p. pap. 10.00 *(978-1-4190-5082-4(6))* Steck-Vaughn.
—The Strange Case of Dr. Jekyll & Mr. Hyde. McKowen, Scott, illus. 2011. (Sterling Unabridged Classics Ser.). (ENG.). 96p. (J). 9.95 *(978-1-4027-8402-6(3))* Sterling Publishing Co., Inc.
—The Strange Case of Dr. Jekyll & Mr. Hyde. Akib, Jamel, illus. 2006. (Classic Starts(tm) Ser.). (ENG.). 160p. (J). (gr. 2-4). 6.95 *(978-1-4027-2667-5(8),* 1252057) Sterling Publishing Co., Inc.
—Strange Case of Dr. Jekyll & Mr. Hyde. Kennedy, Cam, illus. 2008. (ENG.). 48p. (YA). (gr. 5). pap. 11.95 *(978-0-88776-882-8(2),* Tundra Bks.) Tundra Bks. CAN. Dist: Penguin Random Hse. LLC.
—The Strange Case of Dr. Jekyll & Mr. Hyde (Quality Library Classics) 2008. (YA). pap. 14.95 *(978-1-57545-703-1(2))* RP Media.
Stevenson, Robert Louis & Venable, Alan. The Strange Case of Dr. Jekyll & Mr. Hyde. 2005. (Classic Literature Ser.). 108p. pap. 9.95 *(978-1-4105-0119-6(1));* pap., E-Book 69.00 incl. audio compact disk *(978-1-4105-0117-2(5))* Johnston, Don Inc.

Stewart, Paul & Riddell, Chris. Barnaby Grimes: Curse of the Night Wolf. 2012. (Barnaby Grimes Ser.). (ENG.). 224p. (J). (gr. 3-7). 6.99 *(978-0-385-73697-8(5)*, Yearling) Random Hse. Children's Bks.
Stine, R. L. The Five Masks of Dr. Scream. 2011. (Goosebumps Hall of Horrors Ser.: 3). (ENG.). 192p. (J). (gr. 3-7). pap. 7.99 *(978-0-545-28936-8(X)*, Scholastic Paperbacks) Scholastic, Inc.
Stockham, Jessica, illus. Doctor. 2011. (First Time Ser.). (ENG.). 24p. (J). (gr. 2-2). pap. *(978-1-84643-334-4(7))* Child's Play International Ltd.
Van Wyk, Tasja. Twins: Meet the Doctor. 2011. (Illus.). 28p. pap. 13.78 *(978-1-4567-7813-2(7))* AuthorHouse.
Venkatraman, Padma. Climbing the Stairs. 2010. (ENG., Illus.). 272p. (YA). (gr. 7-18). 9.99 *(978-0-14-241490-3(5)*, Speak) Penguin Young Readers Group.
Verne, Jules. The Field of Ice: Part II of the Adventures of Captain Hatteras. 2007. (ENG.). 154p. pap. 19.99 *(978-1-4264-3591-1(6))*; 170p. pap. 21.99 *(978-1-4264-3642-0(4))* Creative Media Partners, LLC.
Vernon, Louise A. Key to the Prison. Eitzen, Allan, illus. 2nd ed. 2003. (Louise A. Vernon Ser.). (ENG.). 146p. (YA). (gr. 4-9). pap. 8.99 *(978-0-8361-1698-4(4))* Herald Pr.
Walden, Pamela Charlene. Puff Bear Goes to the Hospital. 2013. 44p. pap. 9.99 *(978-1-62839-470-2(6))* Salem Author Services.
Walley, Keith. An Angel to Guide Me. 2012. 62p. pap. 12.99 *(978-1-105-68254-4(4))* Lulu Pr., Inc.
Ward, C. L. Portia the Porcupine Visits the Doctor. 2010. 36p. pap. 16.95 *(978-1-4490-9230-6(6))* AuthorHouse.
Warwick, J. M. An Open Vein. 2007. (YA). per. 12.95 *(978-1-933963-96-9(4))* Grove Creek Publishing, LLC.
Watt, Fiona. Complete Book of First Experiences. rev. ed. 2011. (First Experiences Ser.). 144p. (J). ring bd. 19.99 *(978-0-7945-2948-2(8)*, Usborne) EDC Publishing.
Weinberg, Jennifer Liberts. Doc Mcstuffins: Blame It on the Rain. 2014. (World of Reading Ser.). (J). lib. bdg. 13.55 *(978-0-606-35909-2(5))* Turtleback Bks.
Wells, Rosemary. A Visit to Dr. Duck. Wells, Rosemary, illus. 2014. (ENG., Illus.). 30p. (J). (-k). bds. 7.99 *(978-0-7636-7229-4(7))* Candlewick Pr.
Weston Woods Staff, creator. Doctor de Soto. 2011. (SPA.). 29.95 *(978-0-439-73624-4(2))*; 38.75 *(978-0-439-78365-1(8))* Weston Woods Studios, Inc.
Whelan, Gloria. Listening for Lions. 2006. (ENG.). 208p. (J). (gr. 5-9). pap. 6.99 *(978-0-06-058176-3(X))* HarperCollins Pubs.
—Listening for Lions. 2007. 194p. (gr. 5-9). 16.00 *(978-0-7569-7800-6(9))* Perfection Learning Corp.
White, Paul. Jungle Doctor & the Whirlwind. 2015. (Flamingo Fiction 9-13s Ser.). (ENG., Illus.). 176p. (J). (gr. 5-7). pap. 8.99 *(978-1-84550-296-6(5)*, 635eeceb-43fd-433d-9826-6b2bf5273d01) Christian Focus Pubns. GBR. Dist: Bookmasters Distribution.
—Jungle Doctor in Slippery Places. 2011. (Flamingo Fiction 9-13s Ser.). (ENG., Illus.). 160p. (J). (gr. 4-7). pap. 8.99 *(978-1-84550-298-0(1)*, ad8bbad9-6595-4aeb-8c4f-f089b189b088) Christian Focus Pubns. GBR. Dist: Bookmasters Distribution.
—Jungle Doctor Meets a Lion. 2011. (Flamingo Fiction 9-13s Ser.). (ENG., Illus.). 176p. (J). 8.99 *(978-1-84550-392-5(9)*, 9781845503925) Christian Focus Pubns. GBR. Dist: Bookmasters Distribution.
—Jungle Doctor on Safari. 2011. (Flamingo Fiction 9-13s Ser.). (ENG., Illus.). 144p. (J). 8.99 *(978-1-84550-391-8(0)*, 9781845503918) Christian Focus Pubns. GBR. Dist: Bookmasters Distribution.
—Jungle Doctor on the Hop. 2015. (Flamingo Fiction 9-13s Ser.). (ENG., Illus.). 160p. (J). (gr. 4-7). per. 8.99 *(978-1-84550-297-3(3)*, 941c8ee3-121e-4dda-84ae-b6809a4d4b39) Christian Focus Pubns. GBR. Dist: Bookmasters Distribution.
—Jungle Doctor Pulls a Leg. 2008. (Flamingo Fiction 9-13s Ser.). (ENG., Illus.). 176p. (J). 8.99 *(978-1-84550-389-5(9)*, f2e81c42-c4a7-4d63-91eb-64573f61d40a) Christian Focus Pubns. GBR. Dist: Bookmasters Distribution.
—Jungle Doctor Spots a Leopard. 2008. (Flamingo Fiction 9-13s Ser.). (ENG., Illus.). 176p. (J). (gr. 5-7). per. 8.99 *(978-1-84550-301-7(5)*, 6c36bf51-d79e-4a21-bb4f-54dc3b30085b) Christian Focus Pubns. GBR. Dist: Bookmasters Distribution.
—Jungle Doctor Stings a Scorpion. 2008. (Flamingo Fiction 9-13s Ser.). (ENG., Illus.). 160p. (J). 8.99 *(978-1-84550-390-1(2)*, 21dc615c-019a-4cfe-b2da-d2c676461510) Christian Focus Pubns. GBR. Dist: Bookmasters Distribution.
—Jungle Doctor's Crooked Dealings. 2011. (Flamingo Fiction 9-13s Ser.). (ENG., Illus.). 144p. (J). (gr. 5-7). pap. 8.99 *(978-1-84550-299-7(X)*, 9b21af6e-da89-4bc5-b0d9-5ce6419b0795) Christian Focus Pubns. GBR. Dist: Bookmasters Distribution.
—Jungle Doctor's Enemies. 2011. (Flamingo Fiction 9-13s Ser.). (ENG., Illus.). 160p. (J). (gr. 5-7). pap. 8.99 *(978-1-84550-300-0(7)*, c2552503-49be-450c-84cc-9ec522751da8) Christian Focus Pubns. GBR. Dist: Bookmasters Distribution.
Whitney, A. D. T. Patience Strong's Outings by Mrs a D T Whitney. 2006. 236p. per. 20.99 *(978-1-4255-2007-6(3))* Michigan Publishing.
Wiggins, D. L. Where Dreams Are Born. Carter, Kelly, illus. 2012. 26p. (J). 16.95 *(978-1-60131-128-3(1)*, Castlebridge Bks.) Big Tent Bks.
Winslow, Justin, illus. El Perro y el Gato. Winslow, Justin, . 2010.Tr. of Perro y el Gato: la Nieve. (SPA.). 28p. 3.99 *(978-0-9828167-3-8(1))* Home Box Office, Inc.
Wolfe, Bradley W. Upside Downside Up. 2009. 144p. 27.99 *(978-0-557-11670-6(8))* Lulu Pr., Inc.
Wright, Unasue Sellers. Dr. Chubby. 2013. 32p. pap. 13.95 *(978-1-4497-8931-2(5)*, WestBow Pr.) Author Solutions, Inc.
Young, Judy. Digger & Daisy Go to the Doctor. Sullivan, Dana, illus. 2014. (I AM a READER!: Digger & Daisy Ser.). (ENG.). 32p. (J). (gr. k-2). 9.99 *(978-1-58536-845-7(8)*, 203674); pap. 4.99 *(978-1-58536-846-4(6)*, 203728) Sleeping Bear Pr.
—Digger et Daisy Vont Au Docteur (Digger & Daisy Go to the Doctor) Sullivan, Dana, illus. 2016. (I AM a READER: Digger & Daisy Ser.). (FRE & ENG.). 32p. (J). (gr. k-2). 12.95 *(978-1-62753-949-4(2)*, 204172) Sleeping Bear Pr.
—Digger y Daisy Van Al Médico (Digger & Daisy Go to the Doctor) Sullivan, Dana, illus. 2016. (I AM a READER: Digger & Daisy Ser.). (SPA & ENG.). 32p. (J). (gr. k-2). 9.99 *(978-1-62753-953-1(0)*, 204176) Sleeping Bear Pr.
12 Doctors, 12 Stories, 13 vols. gif. ed. 2014. (ENG.). 592p. (YA). pap. 24.99 *(978-0-14-135971-7(4)*, 9780141359717) Penguin Bks., Ltd. GBR. Dist: Diamond Comic Distributors, Inc.

PHYSICISTS

Allman, Toney. J. Robert Oppenheimer: Theoretical Physicist, Atomic Pioneer. 2005. (Giants of Science Ser.). (ENG., Illus.). 64p. (J). (gr. 3-7). lib. bdg. 28.35 *(978-1-56711-889-6(5)*, Blackbirch Pr., Inc.) Cengage Gale.
Anderson, Jennifer Joline. Albert Einstein: Revolutionary Physicist, 1 vol. 2014. (Great Minds of Science Ser.). (ENG., Illus.). 48p. (J). (gr. 8-12). lib. bdg. 32.79 *(978-1-62403-379-7(2))* ABDO Publishing Co.
Anderson, Margaret J. Isaac Newton: Greatest Genius of Science. 2015. (Genius Scientists & Their Genius Ideas Ser.). 96p. (J). (gr. 5-12). 27.94 *(978-0-7660-6570-3(7))*; pap. 10.95 *(978-0-7660-6571-0(5))* Enslow Pubs., Inc.
Anderson, Margaret Jean. Isaac Newton: The Greatest Scientist of All Time. 2008. (Great Minds of Science Ser.). (Illus.). 128p. (J). (gr. 3-7). lib. bdg. 33.27 *(978-0-7660-2793-0(7))* Enslow Pubs., Inc.
Bankston, John. Stephen Hawking: Breaking the Boundaries of Time & Space. 2005. (Great Minds of Science Ser.). (Illus.). 128p. (J). lib. bdg. 27.94 *(978-0-7660-2281-2(1))* Enslow Pubs., Inc.
Barnham, Kay. Isaac Newton, 1 vol. 2014. (Science Biographies Ser.). (ENG.). 32p. (gr. 2-4). lib. bdg. 30.65 *(978-1-4109-6235-5(0)*, Raintree Perspectives) Heinemann-Raintree.
Berne, Jennifer. On a Beam of Light: A Story of Albert Einstein. Radunsky, Vladimir, illus. (ENG.). 56p. (J). 2016. (gr. k-3). 7.99 *(978-1-4521-5211-0(X))* 2013. (gr. 1-4). 17.99 *(978-0-8118-7235-5(1))* Chronicle Bks. LLC.
Bingham, Derick. Michael Faraday: Spiritual Dynamo. 2010. (Trailblazers Ser.). (ENG.). 176p. (J). pap. 8.99 *(978-1-84550-156-3(X)*, 6da8f6db-c74f-4245-818d-6fca339103d3) Christian Focus Pubns. GBR. Dist: Bookmasters Distribution.
Bingham, Hettie. Brian Cox. 2016. (Real-Life Stories Ser.). (ENG., Illus.). 32p. (J). (gr. 4-6). pap. 11.99 *(978-0-7502-8954-2(6)*, Wayland) Hachette Children's Group GBR. Dist: Hachette Bk. Group.
Bodden, Valerie. Nuclear Physicist Chien-Shiung Wu. 2016. (STEM Trailblazer Bios Ser.). (ENG., Illus.). 32p. (J). (gr. 2-5). 26.65 *(978-1-5124-0786-0(0))* Lerner Publishing Group.
Bortz, Fred. Laws of Motion & Isaac Newton. 2013. (Revolutionary Discoveries of Scientific Pioneers Ser.). (Illus.). 80p. (J). (gr. 7-12). 33.25 *(978-1-4777-1808-7(7))* Rosen Publishing Group, Inc., The.
Borzendowski, Janice. Marie Curie: Mother of Modern Physics. 2009. (Sterling Biographies(r) Ser.). (ENG., Illus.). 128p. (J). (gr. 5-18). pap. 5.95 *(978-1-4027-5318-3(7))* Sterling Publishing Co., Inc.
Brallier, Jess M. Who Was Albert Einstein? Parker, Robert Andrew, illus. 2003. (Who Was... ? Ser.). 105p. (gr. 4-7). 15.00 *(978-0-7569-1586-5(4))* Perfection Learning Corp.
Brezina, Corona. Galileo Galilei. 2017. (Leaders of the Scientific Revolution Ser.). 112p. (J). (gr. 12-13). 37.10 ***(978-1-5081-7468-4(7)***, Rosen Young Adult) Rosen Publishing Group, Inc., The.
Brown, Don. Odd Boy Out: Young Albert Einstein. 2008. (ENG., Illus.). 32p. (J). (gr. -1-3). pap. 7.99 *(978-0-547-01435-7(X))* Houghton Mifflin Harcourt Publishing Co.
Christensen, Bonnie. I, Galileo. 2012. (ENG., Illus.). 40p. (J). (gr. 3-7). 20.99 *(978-0-375-96753-5(2))*; 17.99 *(978-0-375-86753-8(8))* Random Hse. Children's Bks. (Knopf Bks. for Young Readers).
Cooperman, Stephanie. Chien-Shiung Wu: Pioneering Physicist & Atomic Researcher. 2004. (Women Hall of Famers in Mathematics & Science Ser.). (Illus.). 112p. (gr. 5-8). lib. bdg. 34.60 *(978-0-8239-3875-9(1)*, Rosen Reference) Rosen Publishing Group, Inc., The.
Cooperman, Stephanie H. Chien-Shiung Wu: Pioneering Physicist & Atomic Researcher. 2009. (Women Hall of Famers in Mathematics & Science Ser.). 112p. (gr. 5-8). 63.90 *(978-1-60854-810-1(4)*, Rosen Reference) Rosen Publishing Group, Inc., The.
Cornell, Kari. Theoretical Physicist Stephen Hawking. 2016. (STEM Trailblazer Bios Ser.). (ENG., Illus.). 32p. (J). (gr. 2-5). 26.65 *(978-1-4677-9528-9(3)*, Lerner Pubns.) Lerner Publishing Group.
Culp, Jennifer. Neil DeGrasse Tyson. 2014. (Great Science Writers Ser.). (Illus.). 112p. (J). (gr. 7-12). 35.60 *(978-1-4777-7691-9(5))* Rosen Publishing Group, Inc., The.
Dakers, Diane. Albert Einstein: Forging the Path of Modern Physics. 2013. (ENG., Illus.). 112p. (J). *(978-0-7787-1188-9(9))*; pap. *(978-0-7787-1190-2(0))* Crabtree Publishing Co.
Delano, Marfe Ferguson. Genius. 2008. (Photobiographies Ser.). (ENG., Illus.). 64p. (J). (gr. 5). 7.95 *(978-1-4263-0294-7(0)*, National Geographic Children's Bks.) National Geographic Society.
Delano, Marfe Ferguson & National Geographic Kids Staff. Genius: A Photobiography of Albert Einstein. 2015. (Photobiographies Ser.). (ENG.). 64p. (J). (gr. 5). pap. 7.99 *(978-1-4263-2219-8(4)*, National Geographic Children's Bks.) National Geographic Society.
Demuth, Patricia Brennan. Who Was Galileo? 2015. (Who Was... ? Ser.). lib. bdg. 16.00 *(978-0-606-36594-9(X))* Turtleback Bks.
Demuth, Patricia Brennan & dePaola, Tomie. Who Was Galileo? O'Brien, John & Harrison, Nancy, illus. 2015. (Who Was? Ser.). (ENG.). 112p. (J). (gr. 3-7). 5.99 *(978-0-448-47985-9(0)*, Grosset & Dunlap) Penguin Young Readers Group.
DiPrimio, Peter. Neil Degrasse Tyson. 2015. (ENG., Illus.). 32p. (J). 26.50 *(978-1-62469-090-7(4))* Purple Toad Publishing, Inc.
Doeden, Matt. Theoretical Physicist Brian Greene. 2015. (STEM Trailblazer Bios Ser.). (ENG.). 32p. (gr. 2-5). pap. 7.95 *(978-1-4677-6115-4(X))*; lib. bdg. 26.60 *(978-1-4677-5790-4(X))* Lerner Publishing Group. (Lerner Pubns.).
Ferry, Joseph. Maria Goeppert Mayer. 2003. (Women in Science Ser.). (Illus.). 112p. (gr. 6-12). 30.00 *(978-0-7910-7247-9(9)*, Chelsea Hse.) Facts On File, Inc.
Forman, Lillian E. Albert Einstein: Physicist & Genius, 1 vol. 2009. (Essential Lives Set 3 Ser.). (ENG., Illus.). 112p. (J). (gr. 6-12). lib. bdg. 35.64 *(978-1-60453-524-2(5))* ABDO Publishing Co.
Frisch, Aaron. Albert Einstein. 2005. (Genius Ser.). (Illus.). 48p. (J). (gr. 5-9). lib. bdg. 21.95 *(978-1-58341-328-9(6)*, Creative Education) Creative Co., The.
Gianopoulos, Andrea & Barnett, Charles, III. Isaac Newton & the Laws of Motion, 1 vol. Miller, Phil, illus. 2007. (Inventions & Discovery Ser.). (ENG.). 32p. (gr. 3-4). pap. 8.10 *(978-0-7368-7899-9(8)*, 1264949, Graphic Library) Capstone Press of Coughlan Cos.
Gianopoulos, Andrea & Barnett III, Charles. Isaac Newton & the Laws of Motion [Scholastic]. Miller, Phil, illus. 2010. (Inventions & Discovery Ser.). 32p. pap. 0.45 *(978-1-4296-5969-7(6)*, Capstone Interactive Library) Capstone Digital.
Goldenstern, Joyce. Albert Einstein: Genius of the Theory of Relativity. 2015. (Genius Scientists & Their Genius Ideas Ser.). 96p. (J). (gr. 5-12). 27.94 *(978-0-7660-6515-4(4))*; pap. 10.95 *(978-0-7660-6516-1(2))* Enslow Pubs., Inc.
—Albert Einstein: Physicist & Genius. rev. ed. 2007. (Great Minds of Science Ser.). (Illus.). 128p. (J). (gr. 4-10). lib. bdg. 33.27 *(978-0-7660-2838-8(0))* Enslow Pubs., Inc.
Gomez, Rebecca. Albert Einstein, 1 vol. 2003. (First Biographies Ser.). (ENG., Illus.). 32p. (J). (gr. 1-4). 27.07 *(978-1-57765-946-4(5))* ABDO Publishing Co.
Gordon, Fernando. Albert Einstein, 1 vol. 2016. (ENG., Illus.). 24p. (J). *(978-1-68078-155-7(3))* ABDO Publishing Co.
—Anders Celsius, 1 vol. 2016. (ENG., Illus.). 24p. (J). *(978-1-68078-153-3(7))* ABDO Publishing Co.
—Sir Isaac Newton, 1 vol. 2016. (ENG., Illus.). 24p. (J). *(978-1-68078-158-8(8))* ABDO Publishing Co.
Graham, Ian. You Wouldn't Want to Be Sir Isaac Newton! A Lonely Life You'd Rather Not Lead. Antram, David, illus. 2013. (You Wouldn't Want to... Ser.). (ENG.). 32p. (J). 29.00 *(978-0-531-25943-6(9))*; pap. 9.95 *(978-0-531-23040-4(6))* Scholastic Library Publishing. (Watts, Franklin).
—You Wouldn't Want to Be Sir Isaac Newton! A Lonely Life You'd Rather Not Lead. 2013. (You Wouldn't Want To... Ser.). lib. bdg. 20.80 *(978-0-606-31632-3(9)*, Turtleback) Turtleback Bks.
Graubart, Norman D. Neil DeGrasse Tyson: Spokesperson for Science. 2015. (Exceptional African Americans Ser.). (ENG.). 24p. (J). (gr. 3-4). pap. 9.35 *(978-0-7660-6666-3(5))* Enslow Pubs., Inc.
Graubart, Norman D. & Tyson, Neil deGrasse. Neil DeGrasse Tyson: Spokesperson for Science. 2015. (Exceptional African Americans Ser.). (ENG., Illus.). 24p. (J). (gr. 3-4). 22.60 *(978-0-7660-6668-7(1))* Enslow Pubs., Inc.
Hanson-Harding, Alexandra. Albert Einstein, 01 vols., 1. 2016. (Britannica Beginner Bios Ser.). (ENG., Illus.). 32p. (J). pap. 12.90 *(978-1-5081-0060-7(8)*, Britannica Educational Publishing) Rosen Publishing Group, Inc., The.
Hasday, Judy L. Albert Einstein: The Giant of 20th Century Science. 2004. (Nobel Prize-Winning Scientists Ser.). (Illus.). 128p. (J). lib. bdg. 26.60 *(978-0-7660-2185-3(8))* Enslow Pubs., Inc.
Haynie, Rachel. First, You Explore: The Story of Young Charles Townes. Cook, Trahern, illus. 2014. (Young Palmetto Bks.). (ENG.). 40p. (J). 29.95 *(978-1-61117-343-7(4))* Univ. of South Carolina Pr.
Henderson, Harry. The Curie Family. 2012. (Trailblazers in Science & Technology Ser.). 136p. (gr. 6-12). 35.00 *(978-1-60413-675-3(8)*, Chelsea Hse.) Facts On File, Inc.
Hightower, Paul. Galileo: Astronomer & Physicist. rev. ed. 2008. (Great Minds of Science Ser.). (Illus.). 128p. (J). (gr. k-5). lib. bdg. 33.27 *(978-0-7660-3008-4(3))* Enslow Pubs., Inc.
Hightower, Paul W. Galileo: Genius Astronomer. 2015. (Genius Scientists & Their Genius Ideas Ser.). 96p. (J). (gr. 5-12). 27.94 *(978-0-7660-6560-4(X))*; pap. 10.95 *(978-0-7660-6561-1(8))* Enslow Pubs., Inc.
Hilliam, Rachel. Galileo Galilei: Father of Modern Science. (Rulers, Scholars, & Artists of the Renaissance Ser.). 112p. 2009. (gr. 5-8). 66.50 *(978-1-60852-941-4(X)*, Rosen Reference) 2004. (Illus.). (J). lib. bdg. 34.60 *(978-1-4042-0314-3(1))* Rosen Publishing Group, Inc., The.
Hollihan, Kerrie Logan. Isaac Newton & Physics for Kids: His Life & Ideas with 21 Activities. 2009. (For Kids Ser.). (ENG., Illus.). 144p. (J). (gr. 4-7). pap. 16.95 *(978-1-55652-778-4(0))* Chicago Review Pr., Inc.
Indovino, Shaina. Women in Physics. Lee-Karlon, Ann, ed. 2013. (Major Women in Science Ser.: 10). 64p. (J). (gr. 7-18). 22.95 *(978-1-4222-2930-9(0))* Mason Crest.
Isaac Newton: Organizing the Universe. 2004. (Great Scientists Ser.). (Illus.). 144p. (YA). (gr. 6-12). 26.95 *(978-1-931798-01-3(X))* Reynolds, Morgan Inc.
James, Emily. Albert Einstein. 2017. (Great Scientists & Inventors Ser.). (ENG., Illus.). 24p. (gr. k-1). lib. bdg. 26.65 *(978-1-5157-3884-8(1)*, Pebble Plus) Capstone Press of Coughlan Cos.
Kamberg, Mary-Lane. Stephen Hawking. 2014. (Great Science Writers Ser.). (Illus.). 112p. (J). (gr. 7-12). 35.60 *(978-1-4777-7683-4(4))* Rosen Publishing Group, Inc., The.
Kenney, Karen Latchana. Stephen Hawking: Extraordinary Theoretical Physicist, 1 vol. 2014. (Great Minds of Science Ser.). (ENG.). 48p. (gr. 8-12). lib. bdg. 32.79 *(978-1-62403-381-0(4))* ABDO Publishing Co.
Kleiner, Mariela. Meet Einstein. Garofoli, Viviana, illus. 2011. 28p. (J). (gr. -1-1). lib. bdg. *(978-0-615-31579-9(8))* Meet Bks., LLC.
Krull, Kathleen. Albert Einstein. Kulikov, Boris, illus. 2015. (Giants of Science Ser.). (ENG.). 144p. (J). (gr. 3-7). 7.99 *(978-0-14-751464-6(9)*, Puffin Books) Penguin Young Readers Group.
—Isaac Newton. Kulikov, Boris, illus. 2008. (Giants of Science Ser.). (ENG.). 128p. (J). (gr. 3-7). 7.99 *(978-0-14-240820-9(4)*, Puffin Books) Penguin Young Readers Group.
Lakin, Patricia. Albert Einstein: Genius of the Twentieth Century. Daniel, Alan & Daniel, Lea, illus. 2005. (Ready-To-read SOFA Ser.). (ENG.). 48p. (J). (gr. 1-3). pap. 3.99 *(978-0-689-87034-7(5)*, Simon Spotlight) Simon Spotlight.
Lassieur, Allison. Albert Einstein: Genius of the Twentieth Century. 2005. (Great Life Stories Ser.). (ENG., Illus.). 127p. (J). (gr. 6-8). 30.50 *(978-0-531-12401-7(0)*, Watts, Franklin) Scholastic Library Publishing.
Lee, T. S. The Stephen Hawking Story: The First Stephen Hawking Comic Biography. 2010. 179p. (J). pap. 14.95 *(978-0-9819542-9-5(4))* DASANBOOKS.
LeVine, Harry, III. The Great Explainer: The Story of Richard Feynman. 2009. (Profiles in Science Ser.). 144p. (YA). (gr. 7-10). 28.95 *(978-1-59935-113-1(7))* Reynolds, Morgan Inc.
Lin, Yoming S. Isaac Newton & Gravity. 2012. (Eureka! Ser.). (Illus.). 24p. (YA). (gr. 3-6). lib. bdg. 22.60 *(978-1-4488-5032-7(0))* Rosen Publishing Group, Inc., The.
MacLeod, Elizabeth. Albert Einstein: A Life of Genius. 2003. (Snapshots: Images of People & Places in History Ser.). (ENG., Illus.). 32p. (J). (gr. 3-7). 6.95 *(978-1-55337-397-1(9))* Kids Can Pr., Ltd. CAN. Dist: Hachette Bk. Group.
—Marie Curie. Mantha, John, illus. 2009. (Kids Can Read Ser.). (ENG.). 32p. (J). (gr. 1-3). 3.95 *(978-1-55453-297-1(3))*; 14.95 *(978-1-55453-296-4(5))* Kids Can Pr., Ltd. CAN. Dist: Hachette Bk. Group.
Marsh, Carole. Albert Einstein. 2003. 12p. (gr. k-4). 2.95 *(978-0-635-02352-0(0))* Gallopade International.
Marsico, Katie. Genius Physicist Albert Einstein. 2017. (STEM Trailblazer Bios Ser.). (ENG.). 32p. (J). (gr. 2-5). pap. 8.99 ***(978-1-5124-5629-5(2))***; (Illus.). 26.65 ***(978-1-5124-3451-4(5)***, Lerner Pubns.) Lerner Publishing Group.
Mattern, Joanne & Santrey, Laurence. Albert Einstein, Creative Genius. Beier, Ellen, illus. 2005. 45p. (J). pap. *(978-0-439-80152-2(4))* Scholastic, Inc.
May, Andrew. Albert Einstein: Scientist. 2016. (History Makers Ser.). 144p. (J). 45.64 *(978-1-5026-2441-3(9))* Cavendish Square Publishing.
McLeese, Don. Albert Einstein. 2005. (Inventores Famosos Ser.). (SPA & ENG., Illus.). 24p. (J). 22.79 *(978-1-59515-673-0(9))* Rourke Educational Media.
McPherson, Stephanie Sammartino. Albert Einstein. 2004. (History Maker Bios Ser.). (Illus.). 48p. (J). (gr. 3-5). lib. bdg. 26.60 *(978-0-8225-0350-7(6))* Lerner Publishing Group.
Meltzer, Brad. I Am Albert Einstein. Eliopoulos, Christopher, illus. 2014. (Ordinary People Change the World Ser.). (ENG.). 40p. (J). (gr. k-3). 14.99 *(978-0-8037-4084-6(0)*, Dial Bks) Penguin Young Readers Group.
Meltzer, Milton. Albert Einstein: A Biography. 2007. (ENG., Illus.). 48p. (J). (gr. 1-5). 16.95 *(978-0-8234-1966-1(5))* Holiday Hse., Inc.
Meyer, Susan. Isaac Newton. 2017. (Leaders of the Scientific Revolution Ser.). 112p. (J). (gr. 12-13). 37.10 ***(978-1-5081-7470-7(9)***, Rosen Young Adult) Rosen Publishing Group, Inc., The.
Miklowitz, Gloria D. Albert Einstein. 2004. (ENG., Illus.). 32p. (J). (gr. 2-5). pap. 5.97 net. *(978-0-7685-1212-0(3)*, Dominie Elementary) Pearson Schl.
Mooney, Carla. Isaac Newton: Genius Mathematician & Physicist, 1 vol. 2014. (Great Minds of Science Ser.). (ENG.). 48p. (gr. 8-12). lib. bdg. 32.79 *(978-1-62403-382-7(2))* ABDO Publishing Co.
Newland, Sonya. Stephen Hawking: Pioneering Scientist. 2016. (Inspirational Lives Ser.). (ENG., Illus.). 32p. (J). (gr. 4-6). pap. 11.99 *(978-0-7502-9209-2(1)*, Wayland) Hachette Children's Group GBR. Dist: Hachette Bk. Group.
Novelli, Luca. Einstein & the Time Machine. 2017. (Flashes of Genius Ser.). (ENG., Illus.). 112p. (J). (gr. 3). pap. 9.99 ***(978-1-61373-865-8(X))*** Chicago Review Pr., Inc.
—Newton & the Antigravity Formula. 2017. (Flashes of Genius Ser.). (ENG., Illus.). 112p. (J). (gr. 2). pap. 9.99 ***(978-1-61373-861-0(7))*** Chicago Review Pr., Inc.
O'Donnell, Kerri. Galileo: Man of Science. 2009. (Reading Room Collection 2 Ser.). 24p. (gr. 3-4). 42.50 *(978-1-60851-964-4(3)*, PowerKids Pr.) Rosen Publishing Group, Inc., The.
—Sir Isaac Newton: Using the Laws of Motion to Solve Problems. (Math for the Real World Ser.). 32p. 2009. (ENG., Illus.). (gr. 6-7). pap. 10.00 *(978-1-4042-6079-5(X))* 2009. (gr. 5-5). 47.90 *(978-1-60851-366-6(1)*, PowerKids Pr.) 2006. (Illus.). (YA). (gr. 5-9). lib. bdg. 25.25 *(978-1-4042-3363-8(6))* Rosen Publishing Group, Inc., The.
Panchyk, Richard. Galileo for Kids: His Life & Ideas, 25 Activities. 2005. (For Kids Ser.). (ENG., Illus.). 184p. (J). (gr. 4). pap. 18.95 *(978-1-55652-566-7(4))* Chicago Review Pr., Inc.
Pasachoff, Naomi E. Ernest Rutherford: Father of Nuclear Science. 2005. (Great Minds of Science Ser.). (Illus.). 128p. (J). lib. bdg. 26.60 *(978-0-7660-2441-0(5))* Enslow Pubs., Inc.
—Niels Bohr: Physicist & Humanitarian. 2003. (Great Minds of Science Ser.). (Illus.). 128p. (J). (gr. 4-10). lib. bdg. 27.94 *(978-0-7660-1997-3(7))* Enslow Pubs., Inc.
Pascal, Janet. Who Was Isaac Newton? Foley, Tim & Harrison, Nancy, illus. 2014. (Who Was? Ser.). (ENG.). 112p. (J). (gr. 3-7). pap. 5.99 *(978-0-448-47913-2(3)*, Grosset & Dunlap) Penguin Young Readers Group.
Pohlen, Jerome. Albert Einstein & Relativity for Kids: His Life & Ideas with 21 Activities & Thought Experiments. 2012. (For Kids Ser.). (ENG., Illus.). 144p. (J). (gr. 4). pap. 16.95 *(978-1-61374-028-6(X))* Chicago Review Pr., Inc.
Riddolls, Tom. Sally Ride: The First American Woman in Space. 2010. (Crabtree Groundbreaker Biographies Ser.). (ENG., Illus.). 112p. (J). pap. *(978-0-7787-2550-3(2))*; (gr. 5-8). lib. bdg. *(978-0-7787-2541-1(3))* Crabtree Publishing Co.
Romero, Libby & National Geographic Kids Staff. Albert Einstein. 2016. (Readers Bios Ser.). (ENG., Illus.). 48p. (J). (gr. 1-4). pap. 3.99 *(978-1-4263-2536-6(3)*, National Geographic Children's Bks.) National Geographic Society.
Salas, Laura Purdie. Discovering Nature's Laws: A Story about Isaac Newton. Reynolds, Emily C. S., tr. Reynolds, Emily C. S., illus. 2003. (Creative Minds Biographies Ser.). (ENG.). 64p. (gr. 4-8). pap. 8.95 *(978-1-57505-606-7(2))*; lib. bdg. 22.60 *(978-1-57505-183-3(4))* Lerner Publishing Group.
Sally Ride: Life on a Mission. 2014. (Real-Life Story Ser.). (ENG., Illus.). 160p. (J). (gr. 3-7). 18.99

P
Q
R

(978-1-4424-8854-0(9), Aladdin) Simon & Schuster Children's Publishing.

Salzmann, Mary Elizabeth. Michael Faraday, 1 vol. 2016. (ENG., Illus.). 24p. (J). (978-1-68078-156-4(1)) ABDO Publishing Co.

Santrey, Laurence & Mattern, Joanne. Un Genio Creativo. Beier, Ellen, illus. 2007.Tr. of Albert Einstein. (SPA & ENG.). 48p. (J). (gr. k-2). pap. 4.99 (978-0-439-87479-3(3), Scholastic en Espanol) Scholastic, Inc.

Scherer, Glenn & Fletcher, Marty. J. Robert Oppenheimer: The Brain Behind the Bomb. 2007. (Inventors Who Changed the World Ser.). (Illus.). 128p. (J). (gr. 5-9). lib. bdg. 34.60 (978-1-59845-050-7(6), MyReportLinks.com Bks.) Enslow Pubs., Inc.

Senker, Cath. Stephen Hawking. 2015. (Against the Odds Biographies Ser.). (ENG., Illus.). 48p. (gr. 3-6). 33.32 (978-1-4846-2466-1(1)) Heinemann-Raintree.

Sherman, Josepha. J. J. Thomson & the Discovery of Electrons. 2005. (Uncharted, Unexplored, & Unexplained Ser.). (Illus.). 48p. (J). (gr. 4-8). lib. bdg. 29.95 (978-1-58415-370-2(9)) Mitchell Lane Pubs., Inc.

Slade, Suzanne. Albert Einstein: Scientist & Genius. Schultz, Jolene, illus. 2007. (Biographies Ser.). (ENG.). 24p. (gr. k-3). 25.99 (978-1-4048-3730-0(2), Nonfiction Picture Bks.) Picture Window Bks.

Snedden, Robert. Stephen Hawking: Master of the Cosmos. 2015. (Superheroes of Science Ser.). (ENG., Illus.). 48p. (J). (gr. 6-6). pap. 14.05 (978-1-4824-3157-5(2)) Stevens, Gareth Publishing LLLP.

Spangenburg, Ray, et al. Chien-Shiung Wu: The Elegance of Experiment. 2009. (Makers of Modern Science Ser.). (Illus.). 144p. (gr. 6-12). 35.00 (978-0-8160-6177-8(7), Chelsea Hse.) Facts On File, Inc.

—Richard Feynman: Quarks, Bombs, & Bongos. 2010. (Makers of Modern Science Ser.). (Illus.). 192p. (gr. 6-12). 35.00 (978-0-8160-6176-1(9), Chelsea Hse.) Facts On File, Inc.

Sprunger, Reed. Albert Einstein: Brilliant Scientist, 1 vol. 2013. (Beginner Biographies Set 2 Ser.). (ENG.). 32p. (J). (gr. -1-4). lib. bdg. 28.50 (978-1-61641-937-0(7), Looking Glass Library) Magic Wagon.

Steele, Philip. Isaac Newton: Mi Mejor Amigo Es la Verdad. 2007. (SPA., Illus.). 416p. (J). (gr. 4-8). pap. 14.99 (978-970-58-0222-5(X)) Altea, Ediciones, S.A. - Grupo Santillana ESP. Dist: Two Rivers Distribution.

Stiefel, Chana. Sky High. 2011. (J). (978-0-531-22558-5(5)) Scholastic, Inc.

Stine, Megan. Who Was Sally Ride? 2013. (Who Was? Ser.). (ENG.). 112p. (J). (gr. 3-7). pap. 5.99 (978-0-448-46687-3(2), Grosset & Dunlap) Penguin Young Readers Group.

—Who Was Sally Ride? 2013. (Who Was... ? Ser.). lib. bdg. 16.00 (978-0-606-31683-5(3), Turtleback) Turtleback Bks.

Stux, Erica. Enrico Fermi: Trailblazer in Nuclear Physics. 2004. (Nobel Prize-Winning Scientists Ser.). (Illus.). 128p. (J). lib. bdg. 27.94 (978-0-7660-2177-8(7)) Enslow Pubs., Inc.

Sullivan, Anne Marie. Sir Isaac Newton: Famous English Scientist. (Illus.). 32p. (J). 2013. (People of Importance Ser.: 21). (gr. 4-18). 19.95 (978-1-4222-2856-2(8)) 2004. (Great Names Ser.). (gr. 3-18). lib. bdg. 19.95 (978-1-59084-139-6(5)) Mason Crest.

Venezia, Mike. Albert Einstein: Universal Genius. Venezia, Mike, illus. (Getting to Know the World's Greatest Inventors & Scientists Ser.). (ENG., Illus.). 32p. (J). 2009. (gr. 3-4). pap. 6.95 (978-0-531-22206-5(3), Children's Pr.) 2008. (gr. 2-5). 28.00 (978-0-531-14975-1(7)) Scholastic Library Publishing.

—Lise Meitner: Had the Right Vision about Nuclear Fission. Venezia, Mike, illus. (Getting to Know the World's Greatest Inventors & Scientists Ser.). (ENG., Illus.). 32p. (J). 2010. (gr. 3-4). pap. 6.95 (978-0-531-20776-5(5), Children's Pr.) 2009. (gr. 2-5). 28.00 (978-0-531-23702-1(8)) Scholastic Library Publishing.

—Luis Alvarez: Wild Idea Man. Venezia, Mike, illus. (Getting to Know the World's Greatest Inventors & Scientists Ser.). (ENG., Illus.). 32p. (J). 2010. (gr. 3-4). pap. 6.95 (978-0-531-20777-2(3), Children's Pr.) 2009. (gr. 2-5). 28.00 (978-0-531-23703-8(6)) Scholastic Library Publishing.

—Stephen Hawking: Cosmologist Who Gets a Big Bang Out of the Universe. Venezia, Mike, illus. 2009. (Getting to Know the World's Greatest Inventors & Scientists Ser.). (ENG., Illus.). 32p. (J). (gr. 3-4). pap. 6.95 (978-0-531-21337-7(4), Children's Pr.); (gr. 2-5). 28.00 (978-0-531-23728-1(1)) Scholastic Library Publishing.

Wade McCormick, Lisa. Albert Einstein. 2014. (Great Science Writers Ser.). (Illus.). 112p. (J). (gr. 7-12). 35.60 (978-1-4777-7687-2(7)) Rosen Publishing Group, Inc., The.

Weir, Jane. Max Planck: Uncovering the World of Matter, 1 vol. 2007. (Science Readers Ser.). (ENG.). 32p. (J). (gr. 3-3). pap. 8.99 (978-0-7439-0568-8(7)) Shell Educational Publishing.

Wheeler, Jill C. Chien-Shiung Wu: Phenomenal Physicist, 1 vol. 2012. (Women in Science Ser.). (ENG., Illus.). 32p. (J). (gr. 3-6). lib. bdg. 27.07 (978-1-61783-451-6(3), Checkerboard Library) ABDO Publishing Co.

Wyckoff, Edwin Brit. The Man Who Invented the Laser: The Genius of Theodore H. Maiman. 2013. (Genius Inventors & Their Great Ideas Ser.). 48p. (J). (gr. 3-4). pap. 8.95 (978-1-4644-0208-1(6)); (Illus.). 25.27 (978-0-7660-4138-7(7)) Enslow Pubs., Inc. (Enslow Elementary).

Yasuda, Anita. Albert Einstein. 2013. (J). (978-1-62127-305-9(9)); pap. (978-1-62127-311-0(3)) Weigl Pubs., Inc.

Yeatts, Tabatha. Albert Einstein: The Miracle Mind. 2007. (Sterling Biographies(r) Ser.). (ENG., Illus.). 128p. (J). (gr. 5-9). pap. 5.95 (978-1-4027-3228-7(7)) Sterling Publishing Co., Inc.

Yount, Lisa. Edward Pickering & His Women Computers. 2012. (Trailblazers in Science & Technology Ser.). 150p. (gr. 6-12). 35.00 (978-1-60413-664-7(2), Chelsea Hse.) Facts On File, Inc.

Zannos, Susan. Michael Faraday & the Discovery of Electromagnetism. 2004. (Uncharted, Unexplored, & Unexplained Ser.). (Illus.). 48p. (J). (gr. 4-8). lib. bdg. 29.95 (978-1-58415-307-8(5)) Mitchell Lane Pubs., Inc.

PHYSICISTS—FICTION

Avery, Ben & Rogers, Bud. Berlin Breakout, 1 vol. Gaudiamo, Adi Darda, illus. 2008. (Z Graphic Novels / TimeFlyz Ser.). (ENG.). 160p. (J). (gr. 4-7). pap. 6.99 (978-0-310-71363-0(3)) Zondervan.

AZ Books, creator. Little Physicist. 2012. (Millions of Inventions Ser.). (ENG., Illus.). 16p. (J). (gr. 1-3). pap. 5.95 (978-1-61889-303-1(3)) AZ Bks. LLC.

Jacobs, Edgar P. Atlantis Mystery. 2012. (Blake & Mortimer Ser.: 12). (ENG., Illus.). 72p. (J). (gr. 5-12). pap. 15.95 (978-1-84918-107-5(1)) CineBook GBR. Dist: National Bk. Network.

—Blake & Mortimer Vol. 17: the Secret of the Swordfish Part 3. 2014. (Blake & Mortimer Ser.: 17). (ENG., Illus.). 64p. pap. 15.95 (978-1-84918-174-7(8)) CineBook GBR. Dist: National Bk. Network.

—The Mystery of the Great Pyramid. (Blake & Mortimer Ser.: 2). (ENG., Illus.). Pt. 1. 2007. 72p. pap. 15.95 (978-1-905460-37-3(6))Pt. 2. 2008. 56p. pap. 15.95 (978-1-905460-38-0(4)) CineBook GBR. Dist: National Bk. Network.

—S. O. S. Meteors. 2009. (Blake & Mortimer Ser.: 6). (ENG., Illus.). 64p. pap. 15.95 (978-1-905460-97-7(X)) CineBook GBR. Dist: National Bk. Network.

—The Secret of the Swordfish. 2013. (Blake & Mortimer Ser.: 16). (ENG., Illus.). 64p. pap. 15.95 (978-1-84918-161-7(6)) CineBook GBR. Dist: National Bk. Network.

Sente, Yves. The Sarcophagi of the Sixth Coninent, Pt. 1, Vol. 9. Juillard, André, illus. 2011. (Blake & Mortimer Ser.: 9). (ENG.). 64p. (gr. 5-17). pap. 15.95 (978-1-84918-067-2(9)) CineBook GBR. Dist: National Bk. Network.

Sente, Yves & Juillard, Andre. The Gondwana Shrine. 2012. (Blake & Mortimer Ser.: 11). (ENG., Illus.). 64p. pap. 15.95 (978-1-84918-094-8(6)) CineBook GBR. Dist: National Bk. Network.

—The Oath of the Five Swords, Vol. 18. 2014. (Blake & Mortimer Ser.: 18). (ENG., Illus.). 72p. pap. 15.95 (978-1-84918-191-4(8)) CineBook GBR. Dist: National Bk. Network.

—The Sarcophagi of the Sixth Continent, Pt. 2. 2011. (Blake & Mortimer Ser.: 10). (ENG., Illus.). 64p. pap. 15.95 (978-1-84918-077-1(6)) CineBook GBR. Dist: National Bk. Network.

Tourville, Jacqueline. Albie's First Word: A Tale Inspired by Albert Einstein's Childhood. Evans, Wynne, illus. 2014. (ENG.). 40p. (J). (gr. -1-3). 17.99 (978-0-307-97893-6(1), Schwartz & Wade Bks.) Random Hse. Children's Bks.

PHYSICS

see also Astrophysics; Chemistry, Physical and Theoretical; Dynamics; Electricity; Electronics; Geophysics; Gravitation; Hydrostatics; Light; Liquids; Magnetism; Matter; Mechanics; Music—Acoustics and Physics; Nuclear Physics; Optics; Quantum Theory; Radiation; Radioactivity; Relativity (Physics); Sound; Thermodynamics

Alaina, Maria. Estimating. 2011. (Wonder Readers Early Level Ser.). (ENG.). 16p. (gr. -1-1). pap. 35.94 (978-1-4296-8085-1(7), Wonder Readers) Capstone Press of Coughlan Cos.

Bailey, Gerry & Law, Felicia. Energy & Movement. 2015. (Stone Age Science Ser.). (ENG., Illus.). 32p. (J). (gr. 3-7). lib. bdg. (978-0-7787-1888-8(3)) Crabtree Publishing Co.

Barkan, Joanne. Rookie Read-About Science: Physical Science, 6 bks., Set. Incl. What Is Density? (Illus.). 32p. (J). (gr. 1-2). 2006. lib. bdg. 20.50 (978-0-516-23618-6(0)); 2006. 117.00 o.p. (978-0-516-25417-3(0), Children's Pr.) Scholastic Library Publishing.

Barr, George. Sports Science for Young People. 2011. (Dover Children's Science Bks.). (ENG., Illus.). 176p. (J). (gr. 3-8). pap. 11.95 (978-0-486-26527-8(7), 26527-7) Dover Pubns., Inc.

Basher, Simon. Basher Science: Extreme Physics. Basher, Simon, illus. 2013. (Basher Science Ser.). (ENG., Illus.). 64p. (J). (gr. 5-9). pap. 7.99 (978-0-7534-6956-9(1), 9780753469569, Kingfisher) Roaring Brook Pr.

Basher, Simon & Green, Dan. Physics: Why Matter Matters! Basher, Simon, illus. 2008. (Basher Science Ser.). (ENG., Illus.). 128p. (J). (gr. 5-9). pap. 8.99 (978-0-7534-6214-0(1), 9780753462140, Kingfisher) Roaring Brook Pr.

Basiswissen Mathematik zur Physik. (Duden Abiturhilfen Ser.). (GER.). 96p. (YA). (gr. 11-13). (978-3-411-04841-0(7)) Bibliographisches Institut & F. A. Brockhaus AG DEU. Dist: International Bk. Import Service, Inc.

Bateman, Graham, ed. Electricity & Electronics. 2011. (FAYFT: Introducing Physics Ser.). 64p. (gr. 4-10). lib. bdg. 39.95 (978-1-936333-09-7(0)) Brown Bear Bks.

Benchmark Education Company, LLC Staff, compiled by. Physical Science. 2006. spiral bd. 115.00 (978-1-4108-6922-7(9)) 2006. spiral bd. 140.00 (978-1-4108-6936-4(9)) 2006. spiral bd. 145.00 (978-1-4108-6945-6(8)) 2006. spiral bd. 170.00 (978-1-4108-6930-2(X)) 2005. spiral bd. 385.00 (978-1-4108-5868-9(5)) 2005. spiral bd. 145.00 (978-1-4108-5869-6(3)) 2005. spiral bd. 385.00 (978-1-4108-5439-1(6)) 2005. spiral bd. 750.00 (978-1-4108-5438-4(8)) 2005. spiral bd. 400.00 (978-1-4108-4517-7(6)) 2005. spiral bd. 140.00 (978-1-4108-3917-6(6)) 2005. spiral bd. 280.00 (978-1-4108-3916-9(8)) 2005. spiral bd. 50.00 (978-1-4108-3871-1(4)) 2005. spiral bd. 110.00 (978-1-4108-3864-3(1)) 2005. spiral bd. 180.00 (978-1-4108-3845-2(5)) 2005. spiral bd. 335.00 (978-1-4108-3844-5(7)) Benchmark Education Co.

—Science Theme: Physical Science. 2005. spiral bd. 220.00 (978-1-4108-5310-3(1)) Benchmark Education Co.

Bingaman, Jay. Physical Science Student Lab Manual. Matthews, Douglas L., ed. 2003. (Illus.). stu. ed., per., wbk. ed. (978-1-931680-30-1(2), Expert Systems for Teachers) Teaching Point, Inc.

Boothroyd, Jennifer. Give It a Push! Give It a Pull! A Look at Forces. 2010. (Lightning Bolt Books (tm) — Exploring Physical Science Ser.). (ENG.). 32p. (gr. k-2). pap. 7.95 (978-0-7613-6056-8(5)) Lerner Publishing Group.

—What Is a Solid? 2007. (First Step Nonfiction - States of Matter Ser.). (ENG., Illus.). 24p. (gr. k-2). lib. bdg. 23.93 (978-0-8225-6836-0(5), Lerner Pubns.) Lerner Publishing Group.

Brezina, Corona. Discovering Relativity, 1 vol. 2015. (ENG.). 112p. (J). 35.60 (978-1-4777-8006-0(8), Rosen Young Adult) Rosen Publishing Group, Inc., The.

Brown, Jordan D. The Innings & Outs of Baseball. Kennedy, Kelly & Downey, Dagney, illus. 2015. (Science of Fun Stuff Ser.). (ENG.). 48p. (J). (gr. 1-3). 16.99 (978-1-4814-2862-0(4)); pap. 3.99 (978-1-4814-2861-3(6)) Simon Spotlight. (Simon Spotlight).

—The Thrills & Chills of Amusement Parks. Borgions, Mark, illus. 2015. (Science of Fun Stuff Ser.). (ENG.). 48p. (J). (gr. 1-3). pap. 3.99 (978-1-4814-2858-3(6), Simon Spotlight) Simon Spotlight.

Burton, Margie, et al. What Floats? What Sinks? 2011. (Early Connections Ser.). (J). (978-1-61672-547-1(8)) Benchmark Education Co.

—What Pushes? What Pulls? 2011. (Early Connections Ser.). (J). (978-1-61672-548-8(6)) Benchmark Education Co.

Cientificos! 8: Ciencias Fisicas. (SPA.). (J). 55.00 (978-958-04-6347-4(6)) Norma S.A. COL. Dist: Distribuidora Norma, Inc.

Cleary, Brian P. On the Scale, a Weighty Tale. Gable, Brian, illus. 2010. (Math Is CATegorical (r) Ser.). (ENG.). 32p. (gr. k-3). pap. 6.95 (978-1-58013-845-1(4), First Avenue Editions) Lerner Publishing Group.

—On the Scale, A Weighty Tale. 2010. pap. 39.62 (978-0-7613-6997-4(X)) Lerner Publishing Group.

Contemporary Discourse in the Field of Physics, 6 bks., Set. 2006. (YA). lib. bdg. 183.60 (978-1-4042-0630-4(2)) Rosen Publishing Group, Inc., The.

Cooke, Andy & Martin, Jean. Spectrum Physics Class Book. 2004. (Spectrum Key Stage 3 Science Ser.). (ENG., Illus.). 182p. pap. 27.50 (978-0-521-54923-3(X)) Cambridge Univ. Pr.

Core Concepts: Set 3: Physics. 2014. (Core Concepts Ser.). 96p. (YA). (gr. 7-12). 356.00 (978-1-4777-7772-5(5)) Rosen Publishing Group, Inc., The.

Curran, Greg. Physics. 2005. (Illus.). 1p. (gr. 9-12). pap. 15.99 (978-1-56414-768-4(1)) Career Pr., Inc.

Curry, Don L. What Is Mass? 2005. (Rookie Read-About Science Ser.). (ENG., Illus.). 32p. (J). (gr. 1-2). pap. 4.95 (978-0-516-24666-6(6), Children's Pr.) Scholastic Library Publishing.

Cutnell, John D. Test Bank to Accompany Physics. 6th ed. 2004. 516p. (YA). (978-0-471-23124-0(X)) Wiley, John & Sons, Inc.

Diagram Group Staff. Physics: An Illustrated Guide to Science. 2006. (Science Visual Resources Ser.). (Illus.). 208p. (gr. 6-12). 49.50 (978-0-8160-6167-9(X)) Facts On File, Inc.

Earth & Moon, 6 vols. (Sunshinetm Science Ser.). 24p. (gr. 1-2). 31.50 (978-0-7802-0293-1(7)); 36.95 (978-0-7802-0544-4(8)) Wright Group/McGraw-Hill.

Ehrlich, Robert, et al. Physics Matters: An Introduction to Conceptual Physics. 2004. (ENG., Illus.). 176p. (C). pap., lab manual ed. 43.95 (978-0-471-26154-4(8), Wiley) Wiley, John & Sons, Inc.

Fakhruddin, Hasan. Physics Demos & Hands-ons. 2006. 188p. pap. 23.30 (978-1-4116-8162-0(2)) Lulu Pr., Inc.

Farndon, John & Graham, Ian. Discovering Science. 2010. (Science Library). 40p. (J). (gr. 3-18). lib. bdg. 19.95 (978-1-4222-1548-7(2)) Mason Crest.

Ferrie, Chris. General Relativity for Babies. 2017. (Baby University Ser.: 0). (ENG., Illus.). 24p. (J). bds. 9.99 **(978-1-4926-5626-5(7)**, Sourcebooks Jabberwocky) Sourcebooks, Inc.

—Newtonian Physics for Babies. 2017. (Baby University Ser.: 0). (ENG., Illus.). 24p. (J). bds. 9.99 **(978-1-4926-5620-3(8)**, Sourcebooks Jabberwocky) Sourcebooks, Inc.

Field, Andrea R., ed. The Science of Physics. 2011. (Introduction to Physics Ser.). (ENG.). 80p. (YA). (gr. 7-12). lib. bdg. 31.70 (978-1-61530-676-3(5)) Rosen Publishing Group, Inc., The.

Gardner, Jane P. Physics: Investigate the Forces of Nature. Carbaugh, Samuel, illus. 2014. (Inquire & Investigate Ser.). (ENG.). 128p. (J). (gr. 6-10). 21.95 (978-1-61930-227-3(6)) Open City Bks.

Gardner, Robert. Solids, Liquids, & Gases Experiments Using Water, Air, Marbles, & More: One Hour or Less Science Experiments. 2012. (Last-Minute Science Projects Ser.). (Illus.). 48p. (J). (gr. 5-18). 25.27 (978-0-7660-3962-9(5)) Enslow Pubs., Inc.

Gardner, Robert, et al. Ace Your Sports Science Project: Great Science Fair Ideas. 2009. (Ace Your Physics Science Project Ser.). (Illus.). 128p. (J). (gr. 5-18). lib. bdg. 33.27 (978-0-7660-3229-3(9)) Enslow Pubs., Inc.

Glencoe McGraw-Hill Staff. Physical Science. 2004. (Physical Science Ser.). (ENG.). (gr. 8-8). pap., stu. ed., pupil's gde. ed. 7.72 (978-0-07-866091-7(2), 0078660912) McGraw-Hill Education.

—Waves, Sound, & Light. 2nd ed. 2004. (GLEN SCI: SOUND & LIGHT Ser.). (ENG., Illus.). 192p. (gr. 6-8). stu. ed. 32.40 (978-0-07-861776-8(6), 0078617766) McGraw-Hill Higher Education.

Glencoe McGraw-Hill Staff & McGraw-Hill Education Staff. Physical Science. 2004. (Physical Science Ser.). (ENG., Illus.). 448p. (gr. 8-8). stu. ed., per., wbk. ed. 22.08 (978-0-07-866089-4(0), 0078660890) McGraw-Hill Education.

Goodstein, Madeline. Sports Science Fair Projects. 2015. (Prize-Winning Science Fair Projects Ser.). (ENG.). 128p. (J). (gr. 7-7). lib. bdg. 37.27 (978-0-7660-7026-4(3)) Enslow Pubs., Inc.

Hammond, Richard. Can You Feel the Force? 2015. (Big Questions Ser.). (ENG., Illus.). 96p. (J). (gr. 3-7). pap. 9.99 (978-1-4654-3904-8(8), DK Children) Dorling Kindersley Publishing, Inc.

Hantula, Richard. Science at Work in Auto Racing. 2011. (Benchmark Rockets: Sports Science Ser.). 32p. (gr. 4). 28.50 (978-1-60870-586-3(2)) Marshall Cavendish GBR. Dist: Marshall Cavendish Corp.

—Science at Work in Baseball. 2011. (Benchmark Rockets: Sports Science Ser.). (Illus.). 32p. (J). (gr. 4). 28.50 (978-1-60870-587-0(0)) Marshall Cavendish GBR. Dist: Marshall Cavendish Corp.

—Science at Work in Basketball. 2011. (Benchmark Rockets: Sports Science Ser.). 32p. (gr. 4). 28.50 (978-1-60870-588-7(9)) Marshall Cavendish GBR. Dist: Marshall Cavendish Corp.

—Science at Work in Football. 2011. (Benchmark Rockets: Sports Science Ser.). 32p. (gr. 4). 28.50 (978-1-60870-589-4(7)) Marshall Cavendish Corp.

—Science at Work in Snowboarding. 2011. (Benchmark Rockets: Sports Science Ser.). (Illus.). 32p. (J). (gr. 4). 28.50 (978-1-60870-590-0(0)) Marshall Cavendish Corp.

—Science at Work in Soccer. 2011. (Benchmark Rockets: Sports Science Ser.). (Illus.). 32p. (J). (gr. 4). 28.50 (978-1-60870-591-7(9)) Marshall Cavendish Corp.

Harris, Tim. Physical Science. 2015. (Science Q & A Ser.). (ENG., Illus.). 32p. (J). (gr. 5-5). pap. 10.58 (978-1-5026-0624-2(0)) Cavendish Square Publishing.

Hoffmann, Sara. Solids. 2012. (First Step Nonfiction - Kinds of Matter Ser.). (ENG., Illus.). 8p. (gr. -1-1). pap. 4.95 (978-1-4677-0517-2(9)) Lerner Publishing Group.

—Staying Still. 2012. (First Step Nonfiction - Balance & Motion Ser.). (ENG., Illus.). 8p. (gr. -1-1). pap. 4.95 (978-1-4677-0515-8(2), Lerner Pubns.) Lerner Publishing Group.

Holics, László. 300 Creative Physics Problems with Solutions. 2010. (ENG., Illus.). 538p. 115.00 (978-1-84331-869-9(5), 1843318695) Anthem Pr. GBR. Dist: Books International, Inc.

Holman. Science Spectacular: Physics: Enhanced Online Edition. 4th ed. 2004. 17.26 (978-0-03-037157-8(0)) Holt McDougal.

—Science Spectacular: Physics: Online Edition Upgrade. 4th ed. 2004. 31.93 (978-0-03-037177-6(5)) Holt McDougal.

Holt, Rinehart and Winston Staff. Holt Physics: Premier Online Edition. 6th ed. 2005. 19.93 (978-0-03-040089-6(9)) Holt McDougal.

—Holt Science & Technology. 4th ed. 2004. (Holt Science & Technology Ser.). (ENG., Illus.). 816p. (gr. 8-8). 92.70 (978-0-03-073168-6(2)) Houghton Mifflin Harcourt Publishing Co.

—Holt Science & Technology: Physical Science. 5th ed. 2004. tchr. ed. 128.80 (978-0-03-066482-3(9)) Holt McDougal.

—Holt Science & Technology: Physical Science: Enhanced Online Edition. 4th ed. 2004. 17.26 (978-0-03-037152-3(X)) Holt McDougal.

—Holt Science & Technology Chapter 1: Physical Science: The World of Physical Science. 5th ed. 2004. (Illus.). pap. 12.86 (978-0-03-030356-2(7)) Holt McDougal.

—Holt Science & Technology Chapter 7: Physical Science: Forces in Fluids. 5th ed. 2004. (Illus.). pap. 12.86 (978-0-03-030386-9(9)) Holt McDougal.

—Holt Science & Technology Chapter 8: Physical Science: Work & Machines. 5th ed. 2004. (Illus.). pap. 12.86 (978-0-03-030391-3(5)) Holt McDougal.

—Holt Science & Technology Online Edition. 5th ed. 2004. 15.93 (978-0-03-030599-3(3)); 15.93 (978-0-03-030601-3(9)); 15.93 (978-0-03-030602-0(7)); 15.93 (978-0-03-030603-7(5)); 15.93 (978-0-03-030604-4(3)); 15.93 (978-0-03-030606-8(X)); 15.93 (978-0-03-030583-2(7)); 15.93 (978-0-03-030586-3(1)); 15.93 (978-0-03-030591-7(8)); 15.93 (978-0-03-030594-8(2)); 15.93 (978-0-03-030596-2(9)); 15.93 (978-0-03-030597-9(7)); 15.93 (978-0-03-030598-6(5)); 15.93 (978-0-03-030581-8(0)); 15.93 (978-0-03-030582-5(9)) Holt McDougal.

—Holt Science Spectrum: A Physical Approach - Spanish Study Guide. 4th ed. Date not set. pap. 11.20 (978-0-03-068273-5(8)) Holt McDougal.

—Holt Science Spectrum Chptr. 7: Solutions. 4th ed. Date not set. (Illus.). pap. 11.20 (978-0-03-068584-2(2)) Holt McDougal.

—Holt Science Spectrum Chptr. 11: Forces. 4th ed. Date not set. pap. 11.20 (978-0-03-068583-5(4)) Holt McDougal.

—Physics: Premier Online Edition. 6th ed. Date not set. 83.93 (978-0-03-036843-1(X)) Holt McDougal.

—Physics: Science Special - Assessments. 4th ed. 2004. (SPA.). pap. 11.20 (978-0-03-068333-6(5)) Holt McDougal.

—Science Spectrum: Physics Math Skills. 4th ed. 2004. pap., wbk. ed. 11.13 (978-0-03-067084-8(5)) Holt McDougal.

Hughes, Susan. Is It Heavy or Light? 2012. (ENG., Illus.). 24p. (J). (978-0-7787-2048-5(9)); pap. (978-0-7787-2055-3(1)) Crabtree Publishing Co.

Hunter, Nick. Is Time Travel Possible? 2016. (Top Secret! Ser.). (ENG., Illus.). 48p. (gr. 4-6). lib. bdg. 33.32 (978-1-4109-8162-2(2)) Heinemann-Raintree.

Integrated Physics & Chemistry, Chapter 1, Activities. 2005. (Illus.). 22p. (YA). pap. 5.00 (978-1-59476-173-7(6)) Paradigm Accelerated Curriculum.

Integrated Physics & Chemistry Chapter 1, Text. 2005. Orig. Title: (Key Topics. (Illus.). 34p. (YA). pap. 7.00 (978-1-59476-161-4(2)) Paradigm Accelerated Curriculum.

Integrated Physics & Chemistry, Chapter 10, Activities. 2005. (Illus.). 32p. (YA). pap. 5.00 (978-1-59476-182-9(5)) Paradigm Accelerated Curriculum.

Integrated Physics & Chemistry, Chapter 10, Text. 2005. (Illus.). 68p. (YA). pap. 7.00 (978-1-59476-170-6(1)) Paradigm Accelerated Curriculum.

Integrated Physics & Chemistry, Chapter 11, Activities. 2005. (Illus.). 40p. (YA). pap. 5.00 (978-1-59476-183-6(3)) Paradigm Accelerated Curriculum.

Integrated Physics & Chemistry, Chapter 11, Text. 2005. (Illus.). 64p. (YA). pap. 7.00 (978-1-59476-171-3(X)) Paradigm Accelerated Curriculum.

Integrated Physics & Chemistry, Chapter 12, Activities. 2005. (Illus.). 32p. (YA). pap. 5.00 (978-1-59476-184-3(1)) Paradigm Accelerated Curriculum.

Integrated Physics & Chemistry, Chapter 12, Text. 2005. (Illus.). 66p. (YA). pap. 7.00 (978-1-59476-172-0(8)) Paradigm Accelerated Curriculum.

Integrated Physics & Chemistry, Chapter 2, Activities. 2005. (Illus.). 42p. (YA). pap. 5.00 (978-1-59476-174-4(4)) Paradigm Accelerated Curriculum.

Integrated Physics & Chemistry, Chapter 2, Text. 2005. (Illus.). 66p. (YA). pap. 7.00 (978-1-59476-162-1(0)) Paradigm Accelerated Curriculum.

Integrated Physics & Chemistry, Chapter 3 Activities. 2005. (Illus.). 32p. (YA). pap. 5.00 (978-1-59476-175-1(2)) Paradigm Accelerated Curriculum.

Integrated Physics & Chemistry, Chapter 3, Text. 2005. (Illus.). 66p. (YA). pap. 7.00 (978-1-59476-163-8(9)) Paradigm Accelerated Curriculum.

Integrated Physics & Chemistry, Chapter 4, Text. 2005. (Illus.). 64p. (YA). pap. 7.00 (978-1-59476-164-5(7)) Paradigm Accelerated Curriculum.

Integrated Physics & Chemistry, Chapter 5, Activities. 2005. (Illus.). 32p. (YA). pap. 5.00 *(978-1-59476-177-5(9))* Paradigm Accelerated Curriculum.
Integrated Physics & Chemistry, Chapter 5, Text. 2005. (Illus.). 64p. (YA). pap. 7.00 *(978-1-59476-165-2(5))* Paradigm Accelerated Curriculum.
Integrated Physics & Chemistry, Chapter 6, Activities. 2005. (Illus.). 32p. (YA). pap. 5.00 *(978-1-59476-178-2(7))* Paradigm Accelerated Curriculum.
Integrated Physics & Chemistry, Chapter 6, Text. 2005. (Illus.). 64p. (YA). pap. 7.00 *(978-1-59476-166-9(3))* Paradigm Accelerated Curriculum.
Integrated Physics & Chemistry, Chapter 7, Activities. 2005. (Illus.). 32p. (YA). pap. 5.00 *(978-1-59476-179-9(5))* Paradigm Accelerated Curriculum.
Integrated Physics & Chemistry, Chapter 7, Text. 2005. (Illus.). 66p. (YA). pap. 7.00 *(978-1-59476-167-6(1))* Paradigm Accelerated Curriculum.
Integrated Physics & Chemistry, Chapter 8, Activities. 2005. (Illus.). 32p. (YA). pap. 5.00 *(978-1-59476-180-5(9))* Paradigm Accelerated Curriculum.
Integrated Physics & Chemistry, Chapter 8, Text. 2005. (Illus.). 64p. (YA). pap. 7.00 *(978-1-59476-168-3(X))* Paradigm Accelerated Curriculum.
Integrated Physics & Chemistry, Chapter 9, Activities. 2005. (Illus.). 32p. (YA). pap. 5.00 *(978-1-59476-181-2(7))* Paradigm Accelerated Curriculum.
Integrated Physics & Chemistry, Chapter 9, Text. 2005. (Illus.). 68p. (YA). pap. 7.00 *(978-1-59476-169-0(8))* Paradigm Accelerated Curriculum.
Integrated Physics & Chemistry, Full Course Kit, 25 bks. 2005. (Illus.). 7969p. (YA). 169.00 *(978-1-59476-187-4(6))* Paradigm Accelerated Curriculum.
Integrated Physics & Chemistry, Teacher's Resource Kit with CD. 2005. (Illus.). 439p. (YA). pap. 25.00 *(978-1-59476-185-0(X))* Paradigm Accelerated Curriculum.
Johnson, Rose. Discoveries in Physics That Changed the World, 1 vol. 2015. (ENG.). 48p. (J). 30.25 *(978-1-4777-8603-1(1)*, Rosen Reference) Rosen Publishing Group, Inc., The.
Keller, R W. Physics Level I Laboratory Workbook. 2005. (Real Science-4-Kids Ser.). (Illus.). 56p. (J). (gr. 3-7). per. 23.95 *(978-0-9749149-5-4(9))* Gravitas Pubns., Inc.
Keller, Rebecca W. Physics Level I. 2005. (Real Science-4-Kids Ser.). (Illus.). 65p. (J). (gr. 3-6). 24.95 *(978-0-9749149-4-7(0))* Gravitas Pubns., Inc.
—Pre-Level I Physics Laboratory Workbook. 2009. 126p. pap. 23.95 *(978-0-9823163-2-0(1))* Gravitas Pubns., Inc.
Kelly, Lynne. Simple Concepts in Physics: Sound & Light. (Illus.). 88p. (J). (gr. 5-6). pap. *(978-1-875739-69-1(6))* Wizard Bks.
Kenney, Karen Latchana. States of Matter Investigations. 2017. (Key Questions in Physical Science Ser.). (ENG.). 32p. (J). (gr. 3-6). 27.99 ***(978-1-5124-4006-5(X))*** Lerner Publishing Group.
Kenney, Karen Latchana. Stephen Hawking: Extraordinary Theoretical Physicist, 1 vol. 2014. (Great Minds of Science Ser.). (ENG.). 48p. (gr. 8-12). lib. bdg. 32.79 *(978-1-62403-381-0(4))* ABDO Publishing Co.
Kukla, Lauren. Mass at Work, 1 vol. 2016. (ENG., Illus.). 24p. (J). *(978-1-68078-143-4(X))* ABDO Publishing Co.
Lancaster, Juliana. PBIS- Lift, Spin, Drop & Fall. 2005. pap., stu. ed. 8.00 *(978-1-58591-564-4(5))* It's About Time, Herff Jones Education Div.
Lawrence, Ellen. Water. 2013. (Science Slam: FUN-Damental Experiments Ser.). (Illus.). 24p. (J). (gr. -1-3). lib. bdg. 23.93 *(978-1-61772-736-8(9))* Bearport Publishing Co., Inc.
Leavitt, Amie Jane. Physical Computing & Makerspaces. 2014. (Digital & Information Literacy Ser.). (Illus.). 48p. (J). (gr. 5-8). 30.25 *(978-1-4777-7659-9(1)*, Rosen Reference) Rosen Publishing Group, Inc., The.
Lee, Cora. The Great Motion Mission: A Surprising Story of Physics in Everyday Life. Rolston, Steve, illus. 2009. (ENG.). 120p. (J). (gr. 4-6). 24.95 *(978-1-55451-185-3(2)*, 9781554511853); pap. 14.95 *(978-1-55451-184-6(4)*, 9781554511846) Annick Pr., Ltd. CAN. Dist: Publishers Group West (PGW).
Lerner Publishing Group Staff. Lightning Bolt Books: Exploring Physical Science, 6 vols., Set. 2011. (J). (gr. k-2). lib. bdg. 151.56 *(978-0-7613-7482-4(5))* Lerner Publishing Group.
LernerClassroom Editors. Early Bird Physics Teaching Guide. 2009. pap. 7.95 *(978-0-8225-5540-7(9))* Lerner Publishing Group.
LernerClassroom Editors, ed. Teaching Guide for Lbb / Exploring Physical Science. 2010. pap. 5.95 *(978-0-7613-6693-5(8))* Lerner Publishing Group.
The Library of Physics, 6 bk. set. 2005. (YA). (gr. 7-12). lib. bdg. 151.50 *(978-1-4042-0381-5(8))* Rosen Publishing Group, Inc., The.
Lindeen, Mary. Color & Shape. 2017. (BeginningtoRead Ser.). (ENG.). 32p. (J). (-2). 22.60 ***(978-1-59953-882-2(2))***; pap. 11.94 ***(978-1-68404-101-5(5))*** Norwood Hse. Pr.
Lord, Roberta. Reflections: English Version. 2003. 200p. 9.95 net. *(978-1-931934-23-7(1))* Back Yard Pub.
Manolis, Kay. Density. 2008. (First Science Ser.). (ENG., Illus.). 24p. (J). (gr. 2-5). lib. bdg. 25.95 *(978-1-60014-224-6(9))* Bellwether Media.
Mastering Physics. 2015. (Mastering Physics Ser.). (ENG.). 48p. (J). (gr. 7-7). 188.16 *(978-1-5026-0300-5(4))* Cavendish Square Publishing.
McDougal-Littell Publishing Staff. Electricity & Magnetism 2005. 2004. (McDougal Littell Middle School Science Ser.). (ENG., Illus.). 64p. (gr. 6-8). lib. bdg., stu. ed. 21.80 *(978-0-618-33440-7(8)*, 2-01027) Great Source Education Group, Inc.
—Matter & Energy. 2004. (McDougal Littell Middle School Science Ser.). (ENG., Illus.). 64p. (gr. 6-8). lib. bdg. 21.80 *(978-0-618-33444-5(0)*, 2-01031) Great Source Education Group, Inc.
—Modules: Physical Science. 2004. (McDougal Littell Science Ser.). (ENG.). 48p. (gr. 6-8). pap., lab manual ed. 15.30 *(978-0-618-43729-0(0)*, 2-01222) Great Source Education Group, Inc.
—Modules: Physical Science - Motion & Forces PE. 2004. (McDougal Littell Science Ser.). (ENG.). 64p. (gr. 6-8). pap., lab manual ed. 15.30 *(978-0-618-43733-7(9)*, 2-01226) Great Source Education Group, Inc.
—Modules: Physical Science, Matter & Energy. 2004. (McDougal Littell Science Ser.). (ENG.). 48p. (gr. 6-8). pap., lab manual ed. 15.30 *(978-0-618-43732-0(0)*, 2-01225) Great Source Education Group, Inc.
—Waves, Sound & Light. 2004. (McDougal Littell Science Ser.). (ENG.). 64p. (gr. 6-8). pap., lab manual ed. 15.30 *(978-0-618-43736-8(3)*, 2-01229) Great Source Education Group, Inc.
—Waves, Sound, & Light. 2004. (McDougal Littell Middle School Science Ser.). (ENG., Illus.). 64p. (gr. 6-8). lib. bdg. 21.80 *(978-0-618-33446-9(7)*, 2-01033) Great Source Education Group, Inc.
McDougal-Littell Publishing Staff, creator. Motion & Forces. 2005. (McDougal Littell Science Ser.). (Illus.). 176p. (gr. 6-12). lib. bdg. *(978-0-618-33442-1(4)*, 2-01029) Holt McDougal.
McGraw-Hill Staff, creator. Physical Science. 2nd ed. 2004. (Physical Science Ser.). (ENG., Illus.). 920p. (gr. 8-8). stu. ed. 115.76 *(978-0-07-860051-7(0)*, 0078600510) McGraw-Hill Higher Education.
—Waves, Sound, & Light Laboratory Activites Manual. 2004. (GLEN SCI: SOUND & LIGHT Ser.). (ENG., Illus.). 26p. (gr. 6-8). pap., stu. ed., lab manual ed. 5.96 *(978-0-07-867322-1(4)*, 0078673224) McGraw-Hill Higher Education.
McPartland, Randall. Understanding Quantum Physics. 2015. (J). lib. bdg. *(978-1-62713-433-0(6))* Cavendish Square Publishing.
Moore, Rob. Why Do Balls Bounce? 2010. (Solving Science Mysteries Ser.). 24p. (ENG.). (J). pap. 8.25 *(978-1-61531-910-7(7)*, PowerKids Pr.); (Illus.). (J). 49.50 *(978-1-61531-911-4(5)*, 1307162, PowerKids Pr.); (Illus.). (YA). (gr. 3-6). lib. bdg. 22.60 *(978-1-61531-889-6(5))* Rosen Publishing Group, Inc., The.
Moreau, Nancy. Physics: Physical Setting STARReview. 2003. (ENG., Illus.). 397p. (YA). per. 15.95 *(978-0-935487-76-3(X)*, STAReviews) N&N Publishing Co., Inc.
Murphy, John, ed. Physics: Understanding the Properties of Matter & Energy. 2014. (Study of Science Ser.). (Illus.). 160p. (J). (gr. 7-12). 35.25 *(978-1-62275-418-2(2))* Rosen Publishing Group, Inc., The.
Nagelhout, Ryan. The Science of Football. 2015. (Sports Science Ser.). (ENG.). 32p. (J). (gr. 4-5). pap. 10.00 *(978-1-4994-1066-2(2)*, PowerKids Pr.) Rosen Publishing Group, Inc., The.
Nelson, Beth. Science Spectacular Physics: Enhanced Online Edition. 6th ed. Date not set. cd-rom 87.33 *(978-0-03-040014-8(7))* Holt McDougal.
Newland, Sonya. Doodle Yourself Smart... Physics. 2012. (Doodle Bks.). (ENG., Illus.). 128p. pap. 12.95 *(978-1-60710-439-1(3)*, Thunder Bay Pr.) Readerlink Distribution Services, LLC.
Nikolo, Martin. Physics for the Rest of Us. 2003. (Illus.). 280p. pap. 79.95 *(978-0-9741638-0-2(5))* Copernicus Pr.
Nsrc. Science & Technology for Children Books: Ecosystems. 2004. (Illus.). 64p. (J). *(978-1-933008-05-9(9))* Smithsonian Science Education Ctr. (SSEC).
—Science & Technology for Children Books: Floating & Sinking. 2004. (Illus.). 64p. (J). *(978-1-933008-07-3(5))* Smithsonian Science Education Ctr. (SSEC).
—Science & Technology for Children Books: Magnets & Motors. 2004. (Illus.). 64p. (J). *(978-1-933008-10-3(5))* Smithsonian Science Education Ctr. (SSEC).
O'Connell, Diane. Strong Force: The Story of Physicist Shirley Ann Jackson. 2006. (ENG., Illus.). 128p. per. 19.95 *(978-0-309-09553-2(0)*, Joseph Henry Pr.) National Academies Pr.
Oxlade, Chris. Calentar, 1 vol. 2010. (Materiales Cambiantes Ser.). (SPA.). 32p. (gr. 1-3). 27.32 *(978-1-4329-4429-2(0))*; pap. 8.95 *(978-1-4329-4434-6(7))* Heinemann-Raintree.
—Enfriar, 1 vol. 2010. (Materiales Cambiantes Ser.).Tr. of Cooling. (SPA.). 32p. (gr. 1-3). 27.32 *(978-1-4329-4430-8(4))*; pap. 8.95 *(978-1-4329-4435-3(5))* Heinemann-Raintree.
—Heating, 1 vol. 2012. (How Does My Home Work? Ser.). (ENG.). 24p. (gr. k-1). lib. bdg. 23.32 *(978-1-4329-6564-8(6)*, Heinemann Read & Learn) Heinemann-Raintree.
—Solids: An Investigation. 2008. (Science Investigations Ser.). (Illus.). 32p. (YA). (gr. 4-7). lib. bdg. 26.50 *(978-1-4042-4284-5(8))* Rosen Publishing Group, Inc., The.
Oxlade, Chris, et al, eds. The Usborne Illustrated Dictionary of Physics. 2nd rev. ed. 2004. (Illustrated Dictionaries Ser.). (ENG., Illus.). 1p. (YA). (gr. 7-18). pap. 12.95 *(978-0-7460-3796-6(1))* EDC Publishing.
Paris, Stephanie. Vroom! Speed & Acceleration, 1 vol. 2nd rev. ed. 2013. (Nonfiction Readers Ser.). (ENG., Illus.). 64p. (J). (gr. 5-5). pap. 31.96 *(978-1-4333-7437-1(4))* Teacher Created Materials, Inc.
Peterson, Megan Cooley. Scooby-Doo! a Science of Electricity Mystery: The Mutant Crocodile. Cornia, Christian, illus. 2017. (Scooby-Doo Solves It with S. T. E. M. Ser.). (ENG.). 32p. (gr. 3-4). pap. 7.95 *(978-1-5157-3702-5(0))* Capstone Press of Coughlan Cos.
Phelan, Glen. What Is Matter? 2007. (Language, Literacy, & Vocabulary - Reading Expeditions Ser.). (ENG., Illus.). 36p. (J). pap. 18.95 *(978-0-7922-5442-3(2))* CENGAGE Learning.
Randolph, Joanne. Liquids in My World. 2006. (My World of Science Ser.). (Illus.). 24p. (J). (gr. 3-7). lib. bdg. 18.75 *(978-1-4042-3285-3(0)*, PowerKids Pr.) Rosen Publishing Group, Inc., The.
—Solids in My World. (Journeys Ser.). 24p. 2007. (ENG.). (gr. k-8). pap. 7.05 *(978-1-4042-8422-7(2)*, Rosen Classroom) 2006. (Illus.). (J). (gr. 3-7). lib. bdg. 18.75 *(978-1-4042-3283-9(4)*, PowerKids Pr.) Rosen Publishing Group, Inc., The.
—Solids in My World: Los Sólidos en Mi Mundo. 2006. (My World of Science/ Mi mundo y la Ciencia Ser.). (ENG & SPA., Illus.). 24p. (J). (gr. k-3). 16.00 *(978-1-4042-3314-0(8))* Rosen Publishing Group, Inc., The.
Regan, Lisa. Physics Is Out of This World. 2016. (Amazing World of Science & Math Ser.). 48p. (gr. 5-5). pap. 14.05 *(978-1-4824-4982-2(X))* Stevens, Gareth Publishing LLLP.
Reinke, Beth Bence. Measuring Volume. Petelinsek, Kathleen, illus. 2014. (Explorer Junior Library: Math Explorer Junior Ser.). (ENG.). 24p. (J). (gr. 1-4). 28.50 *(978-1-62431-651-7(4)*, 203116) Cherry Lake Publishing.
Richards, Roy. En Movimiento. (Coleccion 101 Trucos Cientificos). (SPA., Illus.). (J). (gr. 3-5). pap. *(978-950-724-176-5(0)*, LMA8753) Lumen ARG. Dist: Lectorum Pubns., Inc.
Riley, Peter D. Checkpoint Physics. 2005. (Illus.). 192p. pap. 47.50 *(978-0-7195-8069-7(2))* Hodder Education Group GBR. Dist: Trans-Atlantic Pubns., Inc.
Rivera, Sheila. Is It Heavy or Light? 2005. (First Step Nonfiction - Properties of Matter Ser.). (ENG.). 8p. (gr. -1-1). pap. 4.95 *(978-0-8225-5408-0(9)*, Lerner Pubns.) Lerner Publishing Group.
Rosen Publishing Staff. The Scientist's Guide to Physics: Set 2, 1 vol. 2015. (Scientist's Guide to Physics Ser.). (ENG.). 112p. (YA). 142.40 *(978-1-4777-8059-6(9)*, Rosen Young Adult) Rosen Publishing Group, Inc., The.
Rosinsky, Natalie M. & Picture Window Books Staff. Imanes: Atraen y Rechazan, 1 vol. Robledo, Sol, tr. from ENG. Boyd, Sheree, illus. 2007. (Ciencia Asombrosa Ser.).Tr. of Magnets: Pulling Together & Pushing Apart. (SPA.). 24p. (gr. k-4). 26.65 *(978-1-4048-3220-6(3))* Picture Window Bks.
Royston, Angela, et al. Essential Physical Science. 2013. (Essential Physical Science Ser.). (ENG.). 48p. (gr. 4-6). lib. bdg. 133.28 *(978-1-4329-8147-1(1)*, Heinemann InfoSearch) Heinemann-Raintree.
Ryan, Lawrie, et al. Physics. 2003. (ENG., Illus.). 80p. pap. *(978-0-7487-6801-1(7))* Nelson Thornes Ltd.
Science & Technology for Children Books, Ecosystems Set, 8 vols. 2004. (Illus.). (J). *(978-1-933008-17-2(2))* Smithsonian Science Education Ctr. (SSEC).
Science & Technology for Children Books, Floating & Sinking Set, 8 vols. 2004. (Illus.). 64p. (J). *(978-1-933008-19-6(9))* Smithsonian Science Education Ctr. (SSEC).
Science & Technology for Children Books, Magnets & Motors Set, 8 vols. 2004. (Illus.). 64p. (J). *(978-1-933008-22-6(9))* Smithsonian Science Education Ctr. (SSEC).
The Science of Energy. 2016. (Illus.). 48p. (J). *(978-1-4222-3513-3(0))* Mason Crest.
Sian revision gears at Work. 2004. (Science in A Nutshell Ser.). (J). *(978-1-59242-037-7(0))* Delta Education, LLC.
Sian revision pulley Power. 2004. (J). *(978-1-59242-061-2(3))* Delta Education, LLC.
Sian Solids. 2004. (J). *(978-1-59242-073-5(7))* Delta Education, LLC.
Smith, Ben. Why Does This Float? 2014. (Little Books of Answers: Level d Ser.). (Illus.). 16p. (gr. k-2). pap. 7.95 *(978-1-927136-39-3(3))* Three Crows Media NZL. Dist: RiverStream Publishing.
Solway, Andrew. Energy & Matter. 2010. (CC: 21st Century Science Ser.). 112p. (gr. 6-12). 42.80 *(978-1-933834-72-6(2))* Brown Bear Bks.
Somervill, Barbara A. Mass & Weight, 1 vol. 2010. (Measure It! Ser.). (ENG., Illus.). 32p. (gr. 3-6). 33.32 *(978-1-4329-3765-2(0))*; pap. 8.29 *(978-1-4329-3771-3(5))* Heinemann-Raintree. (Heinemann InfoSearch).
Sonneborn, Liz. Forces in Nature: Understanding Gravitational, Electrical, & Magnetic Force. 2005. (Library of Physics Ser.). (ENG., Illus.). 48p. (YA). lib. bdg. 29.25 *(978-1-4042-0332-7(X))* Rosen Publishing Group, Inc., The.
Sootin, Harry. Experiments with MacHines & Matter. Aloise, Frank, illus. 2012. 96p. 38.95 *(978-1-258-23744-8(X))*; pap. 23.95 *(978-1-258-24341-8(5))* Literary Licensing, LLC.
Spiro, Ruth & Chan, Irene. Baby Loves Quantum Physics! 2017. (ENG., Illus.). 20p. (J). (— 1). bds. 8.99 ***(978-1-58089-769-3(X))*** Charlesbridge Publishing, Inc.
Spyglass Books-Physical Science Complete Set. (Spyglass Books-Physical Science Ser.). (gr. 1-2). 119.58 *(978-0-7565-0785-5(5))* Compass Point Bks.
Stewart, Melissa. Energy in Motion. 2006. (Rookie Read-About Science Ser.). (ENG., Illus.). 32p. (J). (gr. 1-2). pap. 4.95 *(978-0-516-23736-7(5)*, Children's Pr.) Scholastic Library Publishing.
Stockley, Corinne, et al. Illustrated Dictionary of Physics. Johnson, Fiona, illus. 2007. (Illustrated Dictionaries Ser.). 128p. (J). (gr. 4-7). pap. 12.99 *(978-0-7945-1561-4(4)*, Usborne) EDC Publishing.
Strauss, Michael J. Investigating the Natural World of Chemistry with Kids: Experiments, Writing, & Drawing Activities for Learning Science. 2012. 226p. pap. 25.95 *(978-1-61233-155-3(6))* Universal Pubs.
Usborne Books Staff, ed. Illustrated Dictionary of Physics. rev. ed. 2004. (Illustrated Dictionaries Ser.). (Illus.). 128p. (J). (gr. 7-18). lib. bdg. 20.95 *(978-1-58086-283-7(7))* EDC Publishing.
VanCleave, Janice Pratt. Even More of Janice Vancleave's Wild, Wacky, & Weird Physics Experiments. 2017. (Janice VanCleave's Wild, Wacky, & Weird Science Experiments Ser.). 64p. (gr. 10-10). 34.45 ***(978-1-4994-6690-4(0)***, Rosen Central) Rosen Publishing Group, Inc., The.
VanVoorst, Jenny Fretland. Bicycles. 2016. (Early Physics Fun). 24p. (J). (gr. 2-5). lib. bdg. 25.65 *(978-1-62031-314-5(6)*, Pogo) Jump! Inc.
—Boomerangs. 2016. (Early Physics Fun). 24p. (J). (gr. 2-5). lib. bdg. 25.65 *(978-1-62031-315-2(4)*, Pogo) Jump! Inc.
—Hula Hoops. 2016. (Early Physics Fun). 24p. (J). (gr. 2-5). lib. bdg. 25.65 *(978-1-62031-316-9(2)*, Pogo) Jump! Inc.
—Paper Airplanes. 2016. (Early Physics Fun). 24p. (J). (gr. 2-5). lib. bdg. 25.65 *(978-1-62031-317-6(0)*, Pogo) Jump! Inc.
—Slides. 2016. 24p. (J). (gr. 2-5). lib. bdg. 25.65 *(978-1-62031-318-3(9)*, Pogo) Jump! Inc.
—Trampolines. 2016. (Early Physics Fun). 24p. (J). (gr. 2-5). lib. bdg. 25.65 *(978-1-62031-319-0(7)*, Pogo) Jump! Inc.
Walker, Sally M. Investigating Matter. 2011. (Searchlight Books How Does Energy Work Ser.). (ENG., Illus.). (gr. 3-6). pap. 51.01 *(978-0-7613-8409-0(X))*; 40p. 27.93 *(978-0-7613-5776-6(9))*; 40p. pap. 8.95 *(978-0-7613-7875-4(8))* Lerner Publishing Group.
—Libros de Energia para Madrugadores; Early Bird Energy: Complete Set. 2008. pap. 316.95 *(978-1-58013-301-2(0))* Lerner Publishing Group.
—Sound. King, Andy, photos by. 2005. (Early Bird Energy Ser.). (Illus.). 48p. (J). (gr. 3-7). lib. bdg. 25.26 *(978-0-8225-2634-6(4)*, Lerner Pubns.) Lerner Publishing Group.
Weir, Jane. Isaac Newton & the Laws of the Universe, 1 vol. 2007. (Science Readers Ser.). (ENG.). 32p. (J). (gr. 3-3). pap. 8.99 *(978-0-7439-0574-9(1))* Shell Educational Publishing.
Weir, Kirsten & Brent, Lynnette. States of Matter. 2008. (Why Chemistry Matters Ser.). (ENG., Illus.). 32p. (J). (gr. 3-7). pap. *(978-0-7787-4251-7(2))* Crabtree Publishing Co.
What Floats? Big Book: Level C. 8p. 20.95 *(978-0-322-00370-5(9))* Wright Group/McGraw-Hill.
Whiteley, Peter & Bassarath, Haydn. Physics. 2nd rev. ed. 2007. (ENG.). 126p. pap. 9.50 *(978-0-521-69294-6(6))* Cambridge Univ. Pr.
Willett, Edward. The Basics of Quantum Physics: Understanding the Photoelectric Effect & Line Spectra. 2004. (Library of Physics Ser.). (Illus.). 48p. (YA). lib. bdg. 29.25 *(978-1-4042-0334-1(6))* Rosen Publishing Group, Inc., The.
Williams, Gareth, et al. New Physics for You. 2nd ed. 2006. (ENG., Illus.). 400p. (YA). pap., stu. ed. 54.50 *(978-0-7487-8328-1(8))* Nelson Thornes Ltd. GBR. Dist: Trans-Atlantic Pubns., Inc.
World Book, Inc Staff, contrib. by. Encyclopedia of Matter & Energy. 2013. (Illus.). 245p. (J). *(978-0-7166-7521-1(8))* World Bk., Inc.
Yamamoto, Lani. Albert 2. Yamamoto, Lani, illus. 2005. (ENG., Illus.). 32p. (J). (gr. k-6). 10.95 *(978-1-58536-265-3(4))* Sleeping Bear Pr.
Zuchora-Walske, Christine. We're the Center of the Universe! Science's Biggest Mistakes about Astronomy & Physics. 2014. (Science Gets It Wrong Ser.). (Illus.). 32p. (gr. 4-6). pap. 7.95 *(978-1-4677-4552-9(9))*; (ENG., lib. bdg. 26.60 *(978-1-4677-3663-3(5)*, Lerner Pubns.) Lerner Publishing Group.

PHYSICS, ASTRONOMICAL

see Astrophysics

PHYSICS—EXPERIMENTS

Ace Academics, ed. Physics: A Whole Course in a Box! 2007. (Exambusters Ser.). 384p. (gr. 7-18). 12.95 *(978-1-881374-87-9(4)*, Exambusters) Ace Academics, Inc.
Almukahhal, Raja. Physics Laboratory Experiments for the Gifted: Middle & High School. 2005. (Illus.). 90p. *(978-0-910609-51-7(9))* Gifted Education Pr.
Bobrowsky, Matthew, et al. Using Physics Gadgets & Gizmos, Grades 9-12: Phenomenon-Based Learning. 2014. (ENG., Illus.). 169p. (J). pap. 31.95 *(978-1-936959-36-5(4))* National Science Teachers Assn.
Bonnet, Robert L. & Keen, Dan. Home Run! Science Projects with Baseball & Softball. 2009. (Score! Sports Science Projects Ser.). (Illus.). 104p. (J). (gr. 5-9). lib. bdg. 33.27 *(978-0-7660-3365-8(1))* Enslow Pubs., Inc.
Braun, Eric. Joe-Joe the Wizard Brews up Solids, Liquids, & Gases, 1 vol. Boyden, Robin, illus. 2012. (In the Science Lab Ser.). (ENG.). 24p. (gr. 2-3). pap. 9.95 *(978-1-4048-7238-7(8))* Picture Window Bks.
Brown, Jordan D. Science Stunts: Fun Feats of Physics. Owsley, Anthony, illus. 2016. (ENG.). 80p. (J). (gr. 3-7). 16.95 *(978-1-62354-064-7(X))* Charlesbridge Publishing, Inc.
Cobb, Vicki. I Fall Down. Gorton, Julia, illus. 2004. (Science Play Ser.). (ENG.). 40p. (J). (gr. -1-3). 17.99 *(978-0-688-17842-0(1))* HarperCollins Pubs.
Davies, Kate. What's Physics All About? 2010. (Science Stories Ser.). 96p. (YA). (gr. 3-18). pap. 10.99 *(978-0-7945-2118-9(5)*, Usborne) EDC Publishing.
Ebner, Aviva. Engineering Science Experiments. 2011. (Experiments for Future Scientists Ser.). (Illus.). 164p. (J). (gr. 5-8). 35.00 *(978-1-60413-852-8(1))* Facts On File, Inc.
Farndon, John. Experimenting with Physics. 2008. (Experimenting with Science Ser.). 112p. (YA). (gr. 4-18). lib. bdg. 35.64 *(978-0-7614-3929-5(3)*, Benchmark Bks.) Marshall Cavendish Corp.
Gardner, Robert. Bicycle Science Projects: Physics on Wheels. 2004. (Science Fair Success Ser.). (Illus.). 112p. (J). lib. bdg. 27.94 *(978-0-7660-1630-9(7))* Enslow Pubs., Inc.
—Heavy-Duty Science Projects with Weight: How Much Does It Weigh? 2003. (Sensational Science Experiments Ser.). (Illus.). 48p. (J). (gr. 1-4). lib. bdg. 23.93 *(978-0-7660-2013-9(4))* Enslow Pubs., Inc.
—Physics Experiments in Your Own Light Box. 2015. (Design, Build, Experiment Ser.). (ENG., Illus.). 128p. (J). (gr. 7-7). lib. bdg. 37.27 *(978-0-7660-6958-9(3))* Enslow Pubs., Inc.
—Physics Projects with a Light Box You Can Build. 2007. (Build-A-Lab! Science Experiments Ser.). (Illus.). 128p. (J). (gr. 3-7). lib. bdg. 33.27 *(978-0-7660-2810-4(0))* Enslow Pubs., Inc.
Gardner, Robert & Conklin, Joshua. Experiments for Future Engineers. 2016. (Experiments for Future STEM Professionals Ser.). 128p. (J). (gr. 6-6). 37.27 *(978-0-7660-7853-6(1))* Enslow Pubs., Inc.
—Experiments for Future Physicists. 2016. (Experiments for Future STEM Professionals Ser.). 128p. (J). (gr. 6-6). 37.27 *(978-0-7660-7855-0(8))* Enslow Pubs., Inc.
Gardner, Robert & Shortelle, Dennis. Slam Dunk! Science Projects with Basketball. 2009. (Score! Sports Science Projects Ser.). (Illus.). 104p. (J). (gr. 5-9). lib. bdg. 33.27 *(978-0-7660-3366-5(X))* Enslow Pubs., Inc.
Gardner, Robert, et al. Ace Your Physical Science Project: Great Science Fair Ideas. 2009. (Ace Your Physics Science Project Ser.). (Illus.). 128p. (J). (gr. 5-18). lib. bdg. 33.27 *(978-0-7660-3225-5(6))* Enslow Pubs., Inc.
Glencoe McGraw-Hill Staff. Glencoe Physical Science. 2004. (Physical Science Ser.). (ENG., Illus.). 200p. (gr. 8-8). stu. ed., per., lab manual ed. 7.72 *(978-0-07-866084-9(X)*, 007866084X) McGraw-Hill Education.
Goodstein, Madeline P. Goal! Science Projects with Soccer. 2009. (Score! Sports Science Projects Ser.). (Illus.). 104p. (J). (gr. 5-9). lib. bdg. 33.27 *(978-0-7660-3106-7(3))* Enslow Pubs., Inc.
—Wheels! Science Projects with Bicycles, Skateboards, & Skates. 2009. (Score! Sports Science Projects Ser.). (Illus.). 104p. (J). (gr. 5-9). lib. bdg. 33.27 *(978-0-7660-3107-4(1))* Enslow Pubs., Inc.
Hollihan, Kerrie Logan. Isaac Newton & Physics for Kids: His Life & Ideas with 21 Activities. 2009. (For Kids Ser.). (ENG., Illus.). 144p. (J). (gr. 4-7). pap. 16.95 *(978-1-55652-778-4(0))* Chicago Review Pr., Inc.
Hopwood, James. Cool Gravity Activities: Fun Science Projects about Balance, 1 vol. 2008. (Cool Science Ser.). (ENG.). 32p. (YA). (gr. 2-5). 28.50 *(978-1-59928-908-3(3))* ABDO Publishing Co.

Low, A. M. Popular Scientific Recreations - Science. 2006. 292p. per. *(978-1-4067-9717-6(0),* Hesperides Pr.) Read Bks.

Mercer, Bobby. Junk Drawer Physics: 50 Awesome Experiments That Don't Cost a Thing. 2014. (Junk Drawer Science Ser.). (ENG., Illus.). 208p. (J). (gr. 4). pap. 14.95 *(978-1-61374-920-3(1))* Chicago Review Pr., Inc.

Merrill, Amy French. Everyday Physical Science Experiments with Solids. 2009. (Science Surprises Ser.). 24p. (gr. 3-3). 42.50 *(978-1-60853-064-9(7),* PowerKids Pr.) Rosen Publishing Group, Inc., The.

Oxlade, Chris. Hands-on Science Projects: Physics. 2008. (ENG., Illus.). 64p. (J). (gr. 4-7). pap. 7.99 *(978-1-84476-620-8(9))* Anness Publishing GBR. Dist: National Bk. Network.

Slade, Suzanne. Cool Physics Activities for Girls, 1 vol. 2012. (Girls Science Club Ser.). (ENG.). 32p. (gr. 3-4). pap. 8.19 *(978-1-4296-8022-6(9));* pap. 47.70 *(978-1-4296-8520-7(4))* Capstone Press of Coughlan Cos. (Snap Bks.).

Taylor-Butler, Christine. Think Like a Scientist in the Gym. 2011. (Explorer Junior Library: Science Explorer Junior Ser.). (ENG.). 32p. (gr. 4-8). lib. bdg. 28.50 *(978-1-61080-163-8(6),* 201096) Cherry Lake Publishing.

VanCleave, Janice. More of Janice VanCleave's Wild, Wacky, & Weird Physics Experiments. 2016. (Janice VanCleave's Wild, Wacky, & Weird Science Experiments Ser.). 00064p. (J). (gr. 5-5). pap. 12.95 *(978-1-4994-6553-2(X),* Rosen Young Adult) Rosen Publishing Group, Inc., The.

VanCleave, Janice Pratt. Janice VanCleave's Wild, Wacky, & Weird Physics Experiments. 2016. (Janice VanCleave's Wild, Wacky, & Weird Science Experiments Ser.). 64p. (J). (gr. 5-5). pap. 12.95 *(978-1-4777-8977-3(4),* Rosen Reference) Rosen Publishing Group, Inc., The.

VanCleave, Janice Pratt. Many More of Janice VanCleave's Wild, Wacky, & Weird Physics Experiments. 2017. (J). ***(978-1-4994-3955-7(5))*** Rosen Publishing Group, Inc., The.

Williams, Zella. Experiments with Physical Science. (Do-It-Yourself Science Ser.). 24p. (gr. 2-3). 2009. 47.90 *(978-1-61512-189-2(7),* PowerKids Pr.) 2007. (Illus.). (J). lib. bdg. 25.25 *(978-1-4042-3659-2(7))* Rosen Publishing Group, Inc., The.

PHYSICS—HISTORY

Atkinson, Mary. The Earth Is Flat! 2007. (Shockwave: Science in Practice Ser.). (ENG., Illus.). 36p. (J). (gr. 3-5). 25.00 *(978-0-531-17580-4(4),* Children's Pr.) Scholastic Library Publishing.

Bendick, Jeanne. Archimedes & the Door of Science: Immortals of Science. 2011. 154p. (gr. 5-8). 41.95 *(978-1-258-01488-9(2))* Literary Licensing, LLC.

Bodden, Valerie. Nuclear Physicist Chien-Shiung Wu. 2016. (STEM Trailblazer Bios Ser.). (ENG., Illus.). 32p. (J). (gr. 2-5). 26.65 *(978-1-5124-0786-0(0))* Lerner Publishing Group.

Gordon, Fernando. Sir Isaac Newton, 1 vol. 2016. (ENG., Illus.). 24p. (J). *(978-1-68078-158-8(8))* ABDO Publishing Co.

Graham, Ian. You Wouldn't Want to Be Sir Isaac Newton! A Lonely Life You'd Rather Not Lead. Antram, David, illus. 2013. (You Wouldn't Want to... Ser.). (ENG.). 32p. (J). 29.00 *(978-0-531-25943-6(9));* pap. 9.95 *(978-0-531-23040-4(6))* Scholastic Library Publishing. (Watts, Franklin).

—You Wouldn't Want to Be Sir Isaac Newton! A Lonely Life You'd Rather Not Lead. 2013. (You Wouldn't Want To... Ser.). lib. bdg. 20.80 *(978-0-606-31632-3(9),* Turtleback) Turtleback Bks.

Hall, Derek. Physical Sciences. 2009. (FAYFT: Great Scientists Ser.). 64p. (gr. 4-10). 39.95 *(978-1-933834-46-7(3))* Brown Bear Bks.

Hunter, Nick. Gravity. 2017. (Great Scientific Theories Ser.). (ENG.). 32p. (gr. 4-6). lib. bdg. 30.65 ***(978-1-4109-8729-7(9),*** Raintree Perspectives) Heinemann-Raintree.

Meyer, Susan. Isaac Newton. 2017. (Leaders of the Scientific Revolution Ser.). 112p. (J). (gr. 12-13). 37.10 ***(978-1-5081-7470-7(9),*** Rosen Young Adult) Rosen Publishing Group, Inc., The.

Oxlade, Chris. Hands-on Science Projects: Physics. 2008. (ENG., Illus.). 64p. (J). (gr. 4-7). pap. 7.99 *(978-1-84476-620-8(9))* Anness Publishing GBR. Dist: National Bk. Network.

Renn, Jürgen, ed. Einstein's Annalen Papers (Annalen der Physik) The Complete Collection, 1901-1922. 2005. (ENG & GER., Illus.). 590p. 176.00 *(978-3-527-40564-0(X),* Wiley-VCH) Wiley, John & Sons, Inc.

PHYSICS, TERRESTRIAL

see Geophysics

PHYSICS—VOCATIONAL GUIDANCE

Ferguson. Careers in Focus: Mathematics & Physics. 2nd rev. ed. 2008. (Careers in Focus Ser.). 202p. (gr. 6-12). 32.95 *(978-0-8160-7274-3(4),* Ferguson Publishing Co.) Facts On File, Inc.

Indovino, Shaina. Women in Physics. Lee-Karlon, Ann, ed. 2013. (Major Women in Science Ser.: 10). 64p. (J). (gr. 7-18). 22.95 *(978-1-4222-2930-9(0))* Mason Crest.

PHYSIOGRAPHY

see Physical Geography

PHYSIOLOGICAL CHEMISTRY

see Biochemistry

PHYSIOLOGISTS

Bosarge, Jerusha. Inventing Ott: The Legacy of Arthur C. Guyton. 2005. (Illus.). 120p. (J). (gr. 3-7). 10.95 *(978-1-893062-78-8(3))* Quail Ridge Pr., Inc.

Elford, Jole Shack. William Harvey & the Mechanics of the Heart. 2005. (Illus.). 141p. (YA). (gr. 6-10). reprint ed. 28.00 *(978-0-7567-9712-6(8))* DIANE Publishing Co.

Saunders, Barbara R. Ivan Pavlov: Exploring the Mysteries of Behavior. 2006. (Great Minds of Science Ser.). (Illus.). 112p. (J). (gr. 4-7). lib. bdg. 33.27 *(978-0-7660-2506-6(3))* Enslow Pubs., Inc.

Tracy, Kathleen. Friedrich Miescher & the Story of Nucleic Acid. 2005. (Uncharted, Unexplored, & Unexplained Ser.). (Illus.). 48p. (J). (gr. 4-8). lib. bdg. 29.95 *(978-1-58415-369-6(5))* Mitchell Lane Pubs., Inc.

Yount, Lisa. William Harvey: Discoverer of How Blood Circulates. 2008. (Great Minds of Science Ser.). (Illus.). 128p. (J). (gr. 4-10). lib. bdg. 33.27 *(978-0-7660-3010-7(5))* Enslow Pubs., Inc.

—William Harvey: Genius Discoverer of Blood Circulation. 2015. (Genius Scientists & Their Genius Ideas Ser.). 96p. (J). (gr. 5-12). pap. 10.95 *(978-0-7660-6586-4(3))* Enslow Pubs., Inc.

PHYSIOLOGY

see also Anatomy; Blood; Body Temperature; Bones; Cells; Digestion; Growth; Nervous System; Nutrition; Old Age; Reproduction; Respiration; Senses and Sensation

also names of organs, e.g. Heart

Andrews, Barbara. The Respiratory System. 2006. (J). pap. *(978-1-4108-6511-3(8))* Benchmark Education Co.

Arbuthnott, Gill. What Makes Your Body Work? Mones, Marc, illus. 2016. (ENG.). 64p. (J). *(978-0-7787-2241-0(4))* Crabtree Publishing Co.

Bailey, Gerry & Way, Steve. Body & Health. 2009. (Simply Science Ser.). (Illus.). 32p. (YA). (gr. 3-6). lib. bdg. 26.00 *(978-1-4339-0030-3(0))* Stevens, Gareth Publishing LLLP.

Bailey, Jacqui. What Happens When Your Heart Beats? 2008. (How Your Body Works Ser.). (Illus.). 30p. (J). lib. bdg. 26.50 *(978-1-4042-4430-6(1),* PowerKids Pr.) Rosen Publishing Group, Inc., The.

Ballard, Carol. How Your Body Moves. 2010. (Your Body at Work Ser.). (ENG.). 32p. (YA). (gr. 2-5). lib. bdg. 26.60 *(978-1-4339-4100-9(7))* Stevens, Gareth Publishing LLLP.

—How Your Brain Works. 2010. (Your Body at Work Ser.). (ENG.). 32p. (YA). (gr. 2-5). lib. bdg. 26.60 *(978-1-4339-4103-0(1))* Stevens, Gareth Publishing LLLP.

—The Skeleton & Muscles. 2005. (Exploring the Human Body Ser.). (ENG., Illus.). 32p. (J). (gr. 3-6). lib. bdg. 27.80 *(978-0-7377-3022-7(6),* Greenhaven Pr., Inc.) Cengage Gale.

Benbow, Ann & Mably, Colin. Sensational Human Body Science Projects. LaBaff, Tom, illus. 2009. (Real Life Science Experiments Ser.). 48p. (J). (gr. 2-5). lib. bdg. 25.27 *(978-0-7660-3149-4(7))* Enslow Pubs., Inc.

Bethune, Helen. Why Does My Heart Pump? 2010. (Solving Science Mysteries Ser.). (Illus.). 24p. (J). pap. 8.25 *(978-1-4488-0404-7(3),* PowerKids Pr.); (YA). (gr. 3-6). 22.60 *(978-1-4488-0403-0(5))* Rosen Publishing Group, Inc., The.

Biskup, Agnieszka. Stopping Runaway Trains: Superman & the Science of Strength. 2016. (Superman Science Ser.). (ENG., Illus.). 32p. (gr. 3-4). lib. bdg. 27.32 *(978-1-5157-0914-5(0),* DC Super Heroes) Stone Arch Bks.

Brett, Flora. Your Body Systems. 2015. (Your Body Systems Ser.). (ENG.). 24p. (gr. 1-2). lib. bdg. 151.92 *(978-1-4914-2516-9(4),* First Facts) Capstone Press of Coughlan Cos.

—Your Circulatory System Works! 2015. (Your Body Systems Ser.). (ENG.). 24p. (gr. 1-2). lib. bdg. 25.32 *(978-1-4914-2063-8(4))* Capstone Press of Coughlan Cos.

—Your Digestive System Works! 2015. (Your Body Systems Ser.). (ENG.). 24p. (gr. 1-2). lib. bdg. 25.32 *(978-1-4914-2064-5(2))* Capstone Press of Coughlan Cos.

—Your Muscular System Works! 2015. (Your Body Systems Ser.). (ENG.). 24p. (gr. 1-2). lib. bdg. 25.32 *(978-1-4914-2065-2(0))* Capstone Press of Coughlan Cos.

—Your Nervous System Works! 2015. (Your Body Systems Ser.). (ENG.). 24p. (gr. 1-2). lib. bdg. 25.32 *(978-1-4914-2066-9(9))* Capstone Press of Coughlan Cos.

—Your Respiratory System Works! 2015. (Your Body Systems Ser.). (ENG.). 24p. (gr. 1-2). lib. bdg. 25.32 *(978-1-4914-2067-6(7))* Capstone Press of Coughlan Cos.

—Your Skeletal System Works! 2015. (Your Body Systems Ser.). (ENG.). 24p. (gr. 1-2). lib. bdg. 25.32 *(978-1-4914-2068-3(5))* Capstone Press of Coughlan Cos.

Buchanan, Shelly. Animal Senses. 2015. (Science Readers: Content & Literacy Ser.). (ENG.). 32p. (J). (gr. 4-4). pap. 8.99 *(978-1-4807-4678-7(9))* Teacher Created Materials, Inc.

Burstein, John. The Mighty Muscular & Skeletal Systems: How Do My Bones & Muscles Work? 2009. (Slim Goodbody's Body Buddies Ser.). (ENG., Illus.). 32p. (J). (gr. 3-5). lib. bdg. *(978-0-7787-4419-1(1))* Crabtree Publishing Co.

Calabresi, Linda. Human Body. 2008. (Insiders Ser.). (ENG., Illus.). 64p. (J). (gr. 3-7). 17.99 *(978-1-4169-3861-3(3),* Simon & Schuster Bks. For Young Readers) Simon & Schuster Bks. For Young Readers.

Capicola, Anthony. Spit & Phlegm. 2017. (Your Body at Its Grossest Ser.). 24p. (gr. 1-2). pap. 48.90 ***(978-1-4824-6473-3(X))*** Stevens, Gareth Publishing LLLP.

Centore, Michael. Water. 2017. (J). ***(978-1-4222-3746-5(X))*** Mason Crest.

Chambers, Catherine. See for Yourself: Body Science. 2010. (Crabtree Connections Ser.). (ENG.). 24p. (J). (gr. 3-6). *(978-0-7787-9950-4(6));* pap. *(978-0-7787-9972-6(7))* Crabtree Publishing Co.

Chang, Heidi. The Skin on Your Body, 1 vol. 2015. (ENG.). 32p. (J). 23.45 *(978-1-62275-644-5(4),* Britannica Educational Publishing) Rosen Publishing Group, Inc., The.

Claybourne, Anna. Smelly Farts & Other Body Horrors. 2014. (ENG.). 32p. (J). *(978-0-7787-1404-0(7))* Crabtree Publishing Co.

Cohen, Robert Z. The Stomach & Intestines in Your Body, 1 vol. 2015. (ENG.). 32p. (J). 23.45 *(978-1-62275-632-2(0),* Britannica Educational Publishing) Rosen Publishing Group, Inc., The.

Creative Media Applications Staff, contrib. by. The Human Body & the Environment: How Our Surroundings Affect Our Health, 4 vols. 2003. (Middle School Reference Ser.). (Illus.). 576p. (C). (gr. 6-8). 195.00 *(978-0-313-32558-8(8),* MS2558, Greenwood) ABC-CLIO, LLC.

Crispin, Sam. Vomit! 2017. (Your Body at Its Grossest Ser.). 24p. (gr. 1-2). pap. 48.90 ***(978-1-4824-6481-8(0))*** Stevens, Gareth Publishing LLLP.

Daniels, Patricia, et al. Ultimate Bodypedia: An Amazing Inside-Out Tour of the Human Body. 2014. (ENG.). 272p. (J). (gr. 2-5). lib. bdg. 33.90 *(978-1-4263-1722-4(0),* National Geographic Children's Bks.) National Geographic Society.

Daynes, Katie & King, Colin. Tu Cuerpo: Conoce Por Dentro. 2007. (Titles in Spanish Ser.). (Illus.). 15p. (J). (gr. -1). bds. 12.99 *(978-0-7460-8386-4(6),* Usborne) EDC Publishing.

deMarin, Layne. Everybody Moves. 2011. (Wonder Readers Fluent Level Ser.). (ENG.). 16p. (gr. -1-2). pap. 35.94 *(978-1-4296-8086-8(5),* Wonder Readers) Capstone Press of Coughlan Cos.

Dorling Kindersley Publishing Staff. Human Body! 2017. (ENG.). 208p. (J). (gr. 4-7). 24.99 ***(978-1-4654-6239-8(2),*** DK Children) Dorling Kindersley Publishing, Inc.

Dorling Kindersley Publishing Staff. Pocket Genius: Human Body. 2016. (Pocket Genius Ser.). (ENG., Illus.). 160p. (J). (gr. 3-7). pap. 4.99 *(978-1-4654-4588-9(9),* DK Children) Dorling Kindersley Publishing, Inc.

Dorling Kindersley Publishing Staff, creator. My First Spanish Body Board Book/Mi Primer Libro del Cuerpo. 2005. (My First Bks.). (SPA & ENG., Illus.). 36p. (J). (gr. -1 — 1). bds. 5.99 *(978-0-7566-1501-7(1),* DK Children) Dorling Kindersley Publishing, Inc.

Editors of Kingfisher. Incredible Human Body. 2016. (Fast Facts Ser.). (ENG., Illus.). 32p. (J). pap. 6.99 *(978-0-7534-7301-6(1),* 9780753473016, Kingfisher) Roaring Brook Pr.

Emerson, Charles P. & Betts, George Herbert. Living at Our Best, Book: Habits of Right Living Series. 2011. 338p. 50.95 *(978-1-258-08164-5(4))* Literary Licensing, LLC.

Enslow, Brian. My Body. 2010. (All about My Body Ser.). (Illus.). 24p. (J). 22.60 *(978-0-7660-3811-0(4));* pap. 7.95 *(978-1-59845-172-6(3))* Enslow Pubs., Inc. (Enslow Elementary).

Farnsworth, Vesta J. The House We Live in or the Making of the Body. 2004. reprint ed. pap. 24.95 *(978-1-4179-2036-5(X))* Kessinger Publishing, LLC.

Felix, Rebecca. Keeping Cool in Summer. 2014. (21st Century Basic Skills Library: Let's Look at Summer Ser.). (ENG.). 24p. (J). (gr. k-3). 22.79 *(978-1-63137-597-2(0),* 205171) Cherry Lake Publishing.

Furgang, Kathy. My Brain. 2009. (My Body Ser.). 24p. (gr. 3-3). 42.50 *(978-1-61514-686-4(5),* PowerKids Pr.) Rosen Publishing Group, Inc., The.

Galvin, Laura Gates. Human Body A to Z. MacDonald, Judy, illus. 2012. (ENG.). 40p. 9.95 *(978-1-60727-296-0(2))* Soundprints.

Ganeri, Anita. Human Body. 2013. (Kingfisher Readers Ser.). (ENG., Illus.). 32p. (J). (gr. k-3). 12.99 *(978-0-7534-6962-0(6),* 9780753469620, Kingfisher) Roaring Brook Pr.

Glass, Maya. The Jumping Book. 2009. (Let's Get Moving Ser.). 24p. (gr. k-k). 42.50 *(978-1-61514-228-6(2),* PowerKids Pr.) Rosen Publishing Group, Inc., The.

—The Jumping Book / Saltar. 2009. (Let's Get Moving / Diviértete en movimiento Ser.). (ENG & SPA.). 24p. (gr. k-1). 42.50 *(978-1-61514-234-7(7),* Editorial Buenas Letras) Rosen Publishing Group, Inc., The.

Goddard, Jolyon. Inside the Human Body. 2010. (Invisible Worlds Ser.). 48p. (gr. 4). 28.50 *(978-0-7614-4190-8(5))* Marshall Cavendish Corp.

Goldsmith, Mike. In One End & Out the Other. Watson, Richard, illus. 2014. (Flip Flap Journeys Ser.). (ENG.). 14p. (J). (gr. k-2). 12.99 *(978-1-4052-6830-1(1))* Egmont Bks., Ltd. GBR. Dist: Independent Pubs. Group.

Gomdori Co. Staff & Han, Hyun-dong. Survive! Inside the Human Body, Vol. 1: The Digestive System. 2013. (ENG., Illus.). 184p. (gr. 2). pap. 17.95 *(978-1-59327-471-9(8))* No Starch Pr., Inc.

—Survive! Inside the Human Body, Vol. 2: The Circulatory System. 2013. (ENG., Illus.). 180p. (gr. 2). pap. 17.95 *(978-1-59327-472-6(6))* No Starch Pr., Inc.

—Survive! Inside the Human Body, Vol. 3: The Nervous System. 2013. (ENG., Illus.). 184p. (gr. 2). pap. 17.95 *(978-1-59327-473-3(4))* No Starch Pr., Inc.

Green, Jen. Inside Animals. 2010. (Invisible Worlds Ser.). 48p. (gr. 4). 28.50 *(978-0-7614-4195-3(6))* Marshall Cavendish Corp.

Guerber, Hélène Adeline. Yourself & Your House Wonderful. 2012. 330p. pap. 13.50 *(978-1-936639-24-3(6))* St. Augustine Academy Pr.

Gunzi, Christiane. My Body. Murrell, Deborah, ed. 2015. (ENG., Illus.). 34p. (J). 7.99 *(978-1-906572-22-8(4))* Award Pubns. Ltd. GBR. Dist: Parkwest Pubns., Inc.

Halvorson, Karin. Inside Your Germs, 1 vol. 2016. (Super Simple Body Set 2 Ser.). (ENG., Illus.). 32p. (J). (gr. k-4). 27.07 *(978-1-62403-944-7(8))* ABDO Publishing Co.

Haslam, Andrew, et al. Body. (Make It Work! Ser.). (Illus.). 48p. (J). pap. 7.99 *(978-0-590-24614-9(3));* pap. 15.95 *(978-0-590-24333-9(0))* Scholastic, Inc.

Holden, Arianne. It's Fun to Learn about My Body: A Busy Picture Book Full of Fabulous Facts & Things to Do! 2016. (ENG., Illus.). 32p. (J). (gr. -1-12). pap. 9.99 *(978-1-86147-730-9(9))* Anness Publishing, Inc.

Holden, Pam. Going Up, 6 pack. Hawley, Kelvin, illus. 2009. (Red Rocket Readers Ser.). (ENG.). 16p. (gr. -1-1). pap. *(978-1-877363-18-4(9),* Red Rocket Readers) Flying Start Bks.

Human Body. 2014. (DK Eyewitness Bks.). (ENG.). 72p. (J). (gr. 3-7). lib. bdg. 19.99 *(978-1-4654-2620-8(5),* DK Children) Dorling Kindersley Publishing, Inc.

Hyde, Natalie. Human Body Mysteries Revealed. 2010. (ENG., Illus.). 32p. (J). pap. *(978-0-7787-7430-3(9));* (gr. 4-7). lib. bdg. *(978-0-7787-7415-0(5))* Crabtree Publishing Co.

Ipcizade, Catherine. The Slowest Animals, 1 vol. 2010. (Extreme Animals Ser.). (ENG.). 24p. (gr. k-1). lib. bdg. 26.65 *(978-1-4296-5310-7(8),* Pebble Plus) Capstone Press of Coughlan Cos.

Jennings, Ken. The Human Body. Lowery, Mike, illus. 2015. (Ken Jennings' Junior Genius Guides). (ENG.). 160p. (J). (gr. 3-5). pap. 7.99 *(978-1-4814-0173-9(4),* Little Simon) Little Simon.

Johnson, Rebecca L. Ultra-Organized Cell Systems. 2008. pap. 52.95 *(978-0-8225-9384-3(X))* Lerner Publishing Group.

—Ultra-Organized Cell Systems. Desrocher, Jack & Fairman, Jennifer, illus. 2007. (Microquests Ser.). (ENG.). 48p. (gr. 3-5). lib. bdg. 29.27 *(978-0-8225-7138-4(2),* Millbrook Pr.) Lerner Publishing Group.

Jones, Peter. The Complete Guide to the Human Body. 2015. (Illus.). 144p. (J). *(978-1-4351-6167-2(X))* Barnes & Noble, Inc.

Kalman, Bobbie. Warm-Blooded or Cold-Blooded? 2008. (Big Science Ideas Ser.). (ENG., Illus.). 32p. (J). (gr. 1-4). pap. *(978-0-7787-3301-0(7))* Crabtree Publishing Co.

Kirk, Bill. The Ins & Outs of Air: The Sum of Our Parts Series. 2013. (GER., Illus.). 24p. pap. 10.95 *(978-1-61633-391-1(X))* Guardian Angel Publishing, Inc.

Kolpin, Molly. Why Do I Burp? 2015. (My Silly Body Ser.). (ENG.). 24p. (gr. k-1). lib. bdg. 26.65 *(978-1-4914-2105-5(3),* Pebble Plus) Capstone Press of Coughlan Cos.

—Why Do I Hiccup? 2015. (My Silly Body Ser.). (ENG.). 24p. (gr. k-1). lib. bdg. 26.65 *(978-1-4914-2106-2(1),* Pebble Plus) Capstone Press of Coughlan Cos.

—Why Do I Sneeze? 2015. (My Silly Body Ser.). (ENG.). 24p. (gr. k-1). lib. bdg. 26.65 *(978-1-4914-2108-6(8),* Pebble Plus) Capstone Press of Coughlan Cos.

—Why Do I Yawn? 2015. (My Silly Body Ser.). (ENG.). 24p. (gr. k-1). lib. bdg. 26.65 *(978-1-4914-2107-9(X),* Pebble Plus) Capstone Press of Coughlan Cos.

Korb, Rena B. & Weinhaus, Anthony J. My Brain, 1 vol. Simard, Remy, illus. 2010. (My Body Ser.). (ENG.). 32p. (J). (gr. k-3). 28.50 *(978-1-60270-805-1(3))* Magic Wagon.

Lawrence, Ellen. Wet, Blue, & Good for You. 2016. (Drip, Drip, Drop: Earth's Water Ser.). (ENG., Illus.). 24p. (J). (gr. -1-3). 17.95 *(978-1-943553-25-9(4))* Bearport Publishing Co., Inc.

Lew, Kristi. Farts, Vomit, & Other Functions That Help Your Body. 2011. (Nasty (but Useful!) Science Ser.). (ENG.). 32p. (gr. 3-4). pap. 8.10 *(978-1-4296-6345-8(6));* pap. 47.70 *(978-1-4296-6471-4(1))* Capstone Press of Coughlan Cos. (Fact Finders).

Libra, Anna. Why Does My Head Hurt? An Inside Look at the Nervous System. 2003. (J). pap. *(978-1-58417-065-5(4))* Lake Street Pubs.

—Why Does My Stomach Ache? An Inside Look at the Digestive System. 2003. (J). lib. bdg. *(978-1-58417-005-1(0))* Lake Street Pubs.

Macaulay, David. The Way We Work: Getting to Know the Amazing Human Body. 2008. (ENG., Illus.). 336p. (J). (gr. 5-7). 35.00 *(978-0-618-23378-6(4))* Houghton Mifflin Harcourt Publishing Co.

Margulies, Sheldon. The Fascinating Body: How It Works. 2004. (ENG., Illus.). 424p. (J). pap. 43.95 *(978-1-57886-076-0(8))* Scarecrow Pr., Inc.

Marsico, Katie. I Burp. 2015. (Tell Me Why Library). (ENG., Illus.). 24p. (J). (gr. 2-5). 27.07 *(978-1-63188-992-9(3),* 205880) Cherry Lake Publishing.

Martin, Ruth. Little Explorers: My Amazing Body. Sanders, Allan, illus. 2015. (Little Explorers Ser.). (ENG.). 18p. (J). (gr. -1-3). 9.99 *(978-1-4998-0040-1(1))* Little Bee Books Inc.

Mason, Paul. Your Growling Guts & Dynamic Digestive System. 2015. (Your Brilliant Body! Ser.). (ENG., Illus.). 32p. (J). (gr. 3-7). lib. bdg. *(978-0-7787-2197-0(3))* Crabtree Publishing Co.

Mattern, Joanne. I Have the Hiccups. 2016. (Rookie Read-About Health Ser.). (ENG., Illus.). 32p. (J). pap. 5.95 *(978-0-531-22582-0(8),* Children's Pr.) Scholastic Library Publishing.

Maynard, Christopher, et al. How Your Body Works. 2004. (Knowledge Masters Plus Ser.). (Illus.). 32p. (YA). pap. incl. cd-rom *(978-1-903954-44-7(4),* Pavilion Children's Books) Pavilion Bks.

Meister, Cari. Totally Wacky Facts about the Human Body. 2016. (Mind Benders Ser.). (ENG.). 112p. (gr. 1-3). lib. bdg. 23.32 *(978-1-4914-8359-6(8))* Capstone Press of Coughlan Cos.

—Totally Wacky Facts about YOU! 2016. (Mind Benders Ser.). (ENG., Illus.). 240p. (gr. 1-3). pap. 7.95 *(978-1-4914-8376-3(8))* Capstone Press of Coughlan Cos.

Morgan, Philip & Martineau, Susan. Moving Your Body. 2011. (Positive Steps Ser.). 32p. (gr. 2-5). lib. bdg. 31.35 *(978-1-59920-493-2(2))* Black Rabbit Bks.

Murray, Julie. The Body, 1 vol. 2009. (That's Gross!:A Look at Science Ser.). (ENG., Illus.). 32p. (J). (gr. 2-5). 28.50 *(978-1-60453-554-9(7))* ABDO Publishing Co.

—Slowest Animals, 1 vol. 2010. (That's Wild!: A Look at Animals Ser.). (ENG.). 32p. (J). (gr. 2-5). 28.50 *(978-1-60453-979-0(8))* ABDO Publishing Co.

—Strongest Animals, 1 vol. 2010. (That's Wild!: A Look at Animals Ser.). (ENG.). 32p. (J). (gr. 2-5). 28.50 *(978-1-60453-981-3(X))* ABDO Publishing Co.

My Body Does Strange Stuff! 2013. (My Body Does Strange Stuff! Ser.). 24p. (J). (gr. 1-3). 135.60 *(978-1-4339-9673-3(1));* pap. 293.40 *(978-1-4339-9764-8(9));* pap. 48.90 *(978-1-4339-9763-1(0))* Stevens, Gareth Publishing LLLP.

Nagelhout, Ryan. The Heart & Blood in Your Body, 1 vol. 2015. (ENG.). 32p. (J). 23.45 *(978-1-62275-640-7(1),* Britannica Educational Publishing) Rosen Publishing Group, Inc., The.

—How Pigeons & Other Animals Sense Magnetic Fields. 2015. (Superior Animal Senses Ser.). (ENG., Illus.). 24p. (J). (gr. 3-4). pap. 8.25 *(978-1-4994-0992-5(3),* PowerKids Pr.) Rosen Publishing Group, Inc., The.

Newquist, H. P. & Wells, Rosemary. The Human Body. 2015. (Smithsonian: Invention & Impact Ser.: 1). (ENG., Illus.). 112p. (J). (gr. 3-7). bds. 18.99 *(978-0-451-47643-2(3),* Viking Books for Young Readers) Penguin Young Readers Group.

Parker, Steve. Human Body. 2013. (Illus.). 48p. (J). *(978-1-4351-5091-1(0))* Barnes & Noble, Inc.

—What about the Human Body. 2008. 40p. pap. *(978-1-84810-070-1(1))* Miles Kelly Publishing, Ltd.

Perish, Patrick. Disgusting Bodily Functions. 2014. (Totally Disgusting Ser.). (ENG.). 24p. (J). (gr. 3-7). 25.95 *(978-1-62617-129-9(7),* Epic Bks.) Bellwether Media.

Pimentel, Annette Bay. My Stomach. Alberini, Teresa, illus. 2015. (Inside My Body Ser.). (ENG.). 24p. (J). (gr. 1-3). 19.95 *(978-1-60753-758-8(3))* Amicus Publishing.

Pipe, Jim. You Wouldn't Want to Live Without Sleep! Bergin, Mark, illus. 2016. (You Wouldn't Want to Live Without... Ser.). (ENG.). 32p. (J). lib. bdg. 29.00 *(978-0-531-21492-3(3))* Scholastic Library Publishing.

Podesto, Martine. The Body. 2008. (My Science Notebook Ser.). (Illus.). 104p. (YA). (gr. 5-9). lib. bdg. 31.00 *(978-0-8368-9212-3(7))* Stevens, Gareth Publishing LLLP.

Rake, Jody Sullivan. Speed, Strength, & Stealth: Animal Weapons & Defenses, 1 vol. 2012. (Animal Weapons & Defenses Ser.). (ENG.). 32p. (gr. 1-2). 26.65 *(978-1-4296-6507-0(6));* pap. 8.10 *(978-1-4296-8010-3(5));* pap. 47.70 *(978-1-4296-8503-0(4))* Capstone Press of Coughlan Cos. (Blazers).

Rice, Christopher. My First Body Book. (Illus.). (J). pap. 22.99 *(978-0-590-24611-8(9))* Scholastic, Inc.

Riehecky, Janet. Teeth, Claws, & Jaws: Animal Weapons & Defenses, 1 vol. 2012. (Animal Weapons & Defenses Ser.). (ENG.). 32p. (gr. 1-2). 26.65 *(978-1-4296-6506-3(8));* pap.

8.10 *(978-1-4296-8012-7(1))* Capstone Press of Coughlan Cos. (Blazers).
Riley, Ange Belle Chandler. The House in Which You Live. 2005. reprint ed. pap. 24.95 *(978-1-4191-3533-0(3))* Kessinger Publishing, LLC.
Rinder, Lenore. Bones & Skin. Oszkay, Zulay, tr. Date not set. Tr. of Huesos y Piel. (J). (gr. -1-7). pap. 5.00 *(978-0-9678778-1-5(4),* 002) Child Scope Productions.
Ripley's Believe It or Not Editors & Ripley's Believe It Or Not! Staff. Ripley Twists: Human Body PORTRAIT EDN. 2014. (Twist Ser.). (ENG.). 48p. (J). 12.95 *(978-1-893951-84-6(7))* Ripley Entertainment, Inc.
Rockett, Paul. 100 Trillion Good Bacteria Living in the Human Body. Ruffle, Mark, illus. 2015. (Big Countdown Ser.). (ENG.). 32p. (gr. 3-5). 29.99 *(978-1-4109-6877-7(4),* Raintree Perspectives) Heinemann-Raintree.
Rushworth, Gary. Body Systems: Human Cells: Text Pairs. 2008. (Bridges/Navigators Ser.). (J). (gr. 5). 81.00 *(978-1-4108-8406-0(6))* Benchmark Education Co.
—Body Systems: Skeletal & Muscular: Text Pairs. 2008. (Bridges/Navigators Ser.). (J). (gr. 5). 81.00 *(978-1-4108-8408-4(2))* Benchmark Education Co.
Saddleback, creator. Human Body. 2008. (Factoscope Ser.). (Illus.). 64p. (YA). (gr. 8-12). per. 10.95 *(978-1-59905-234-2(2))* Saddleback Educational Publishing, Inc.
Samuels, Charlie. Astonishing Bodies. 2012. (ENG.). 32p. (J). *(978-0-7787-8006-9(6));* pap. *(978-0-7787-8011-3(2))* Crabtree Publishing Co.
Scherrer, David L. & Klepacki, Linda M. Celebrating Changes: Everything You Always Wanted to Know about Sex in Middle School. 2004. (Worth Waiting for Ser.). 176p. (YA). (gr. 11-18). 19.99 *(978-0-7814-4077-6(7),* 0781440777) Cook, David C.
Seidlitz, Lauri. Human Body. 2007. (Life Science (Weigl Hardcover) Ser.). (Illus.). 32p. (J). (gr. 4-7). lib. bdg. 26.00 *(978-1-59036-705-6(7));* per. 9.95 *(978-1-59036-706-3(5))* Weigl Pubs., Inc.
Shaffer, Jody Jensen. My Heart. Alberini, Teresa, illus. 2015. (Inside My Body Ser.). (ENG.). 24p. (J). (gr. 1-3). 19.95 *(978-1-60753-755-7(9))* Amicus Publishing.
—My Lungs. Alberini, Teresa, illus. 2015. (Inside My Body Ser.). (ENG.). 24p. (J). (gr. 1-3). 19.95 *(978-1-60753-756-4(7))* Amicus Publishing.
—My Muscles. Alberini, Teresa, illus. 2015. (Inside My Body Ser.). (ENG.). 24p. (J). (gr. 1-3). 19.95 *(978-1-60753-757-1(5))* Amicus Publishing.
Shier, David N., et al. Hole's Essentials of Human Anatomy & Physiology with OLC bind-In Card. 8th rev. ed. 2003. 640p. (J). (gr. 6-12). 123.75 *(978-0-07-293224-9(4),* 9780072932249) Glencoe/McGraw-Hill.
Silver, Donald M. & Wynne, Patricia J. The Body Book: Easy-To-Make Hands-on Models That Teach. 2008. (ENG.). 128p. (gr. 3-6). pap. 18.99 *(978-0-545-04873-6(7),* Teaching Resources) Scholastic, Inc.
Silverstein, Alvin, et al. Snot, Poop, Vomit, & More: The Yucky Body Book. Kelley, Gerald, illus. 2010. (Yucky Science Ser.). 48p. (J). (gr. 5-9). 25.27 *(978-0-7660-3318-4(X))* Enslow Pubs., Inc.
Slack, Michael H., illus. Gross Body Science, 5 vols., Set. Incl. Clot & Scab: Gross Stuff about Your Scrapes, Bumps, & Bruises. Lew, Kristi. lib. bdg. 29.27 *(978-0-8225-8965-5(6));* Crust & Spray: Gross Stuff in Your Eyes, Ears, Nose, & Throat. Larsen, C. S. lib. bdg. 29.27 *(978-0-8225-8964-8(8));* Hawk & Drool: Gross Stuff in Your Mouth. Donovan, Sandy. lib. bdg. 29.27 *(978-0-8225-8966-2(4));* Itch & Ooze: Gross Stuff on Your Skin. Lew, Kristi & Lewandowski, Laura C. lib. bdg. 29.27 *(978-0-8225-8963-1(X));* Rumble & Spew: Gross Stuff in Your Stomach & Intestines. Donovan, Sandy. lib. bdg. 29.27 *(978-0-8225-8899-3(4));* (Illus.). 48p. (gr. 3-5). 2009. Set lib. bdg. 146.35 *(978-0-8225-8898-6(6),* Millbrook Pr.) Lerner Publishing Group.
Smith, Sian & Guillain, Charlotte. How Does My Body Work?, 1 vol. 2011. (ENG.). 24p. (gr. -1-1). 25.99 *(978-1-4329-5349-2(4),* Acorn Read-Aloud) Heinemann-Raintree.
Sohn, Emily & Sharp, Katie. Human Body: Train it Right. 2011. (iScience Readers Ser.). 32p. (J). (gr. 3-4). lib. bdg. 22.60 *(978-1-59953-413-8(4))* Norwood Hse. Pr.
Spilsbury, Louise. Head-to-Toe Body Questions. 2010. (Crabtree Connections Ser.). (ENG.). 24p. (J). (gr. 3-6). *(978-0-7787-9954-2(9));* pap. *(978-0-7787-9976-4(X))* Crabtree Publishing Co.
—What Is the Structure of an Animal?, 1 vol., 1. 2014. (Let's Find Out! Ser.). (ENG.). 32p. (gr. 3-6). 23.45 *(978-1-62275-246-1(5))* Rosen Publishing Group, Inc., The.
Spilsbury, Louise & Spilsbury, Richard. Life Processes, 1 vol. (Essential Life Science Ser.). (ENG., Illus.). 48p. (gr. 4-6). 2014. lib. bdg. 33.32 *(978-1-4329-7810-5(1))* 2013. pap. 9.95 *(978-1-4329-7841-9(1))* Heinemann-Raintree. (Heinemann InfoSearch).
Steele, Philip. My Body. 2009. (Now We Know About... Ser.). (ENG., Illus.). 24p. (J). (gr. k-3). pap. *(978-0-7787-4738-3(7))* Crabtree Publishing Co.
Steele, Philip & Goldsmith, Mike. My Body. 2009. (ENG., Illus.). 24p. (J). (gr. k-4). lib. bdg. *(978-0-7787-4721-5(2))* Crabtree Publishing Co.
Stewart, Melissa. How Is My Brain Like a Supercomputer? And Other Questions about ... the Human Body. Bull, Peter, illus. 2014. (Good Question! Ser.). (ENG.). 40p. (J). (gr. 1). 12.95 *(978-1-4549-0680-3(4))* Sterling Publishing Co., Inc.
—How Is My Brain Like a Supercomputer? And Other Questions about the Human Body. Bull, Peter, illus. 2014. (Good Question! Ser.). (ENG.). 32p. (J). (gr. 1). pap. 5.95 *(978-1-4549-0681-0(2))* Sterling Publishing Co., Inc.
Stewart, Melissa & American Museum of Natural History Staff. World's Fastest Animals, Level 2. 2014. (Amer Museum of Nat History Easy Readers Ser.: 1). (ENG., Illus.). 32p. (J). (gr. k-1). pap. 3.95 *(978-1-4027-7793-6(0))* Sterling Publishing Co., Inc.
Stout, Frankie. Nature's Strongest Animals. (Extreme Animals Ser.). 24p. 2009. (gr. 2-3). 42.50 *(978-1-61512-382-7(2))* 2008. (Illus.). (J). (gr. 3-7). lib. bdg. 22.60 *(978-1-4042-4158-9(2))* Rosen Publishing Group, Inc., The. (PowerKids Pr.).
Swanson, Diane. You Are Weird: Your Body's Peculiar Parts & Funny Functions. Boake, Kathy, illus. 2009. (ENG.). 40p. (J). (gr. 3-7). 16.95 *(978-1-55453-282-7(5));* pap. 7.95 *(978-1-55453-283-4(3))* Kids Can Pr., Ltd. CAN. Dist: Hachette Bk. Group.
Swanson, Jennifer. Building with Poop. 2017. (J). pap. ***(978-0-7660-9108-5(2))*** Enslow Pubs., Inc.
Taylor, Julia V. The Body Image Workbook for Teens: Activities to Help Girls Develop a Healthy Body Image in an Image-Obsessed World. 2014. (ENG.). 200p. (YA). (gr. 6-12). pap. 16.95 *(978-1-62625-018-5(9))* New Harbinger Pubns.
Troupe, Thomas Kingsley. You Call That a Nose? Learning about Human Senses with the Garbage Gang. Toye, Derek, illus. 2015. (Garbage Gang's Super Science Questions Ser.). (ENG.). 24p. (gr. k-2). lib. bdg. 26.65 *(978-1-4795-7058-4(3))* Picture Window Bks.
Walker, Denise. Cells & Life Processes. 2007. (Basic Biology Ser.). (Illus.). 48p. (YA). (gr. 5-9). lib. bdg. 34.25 *(978-1-58340-988-6(2))* Black Rabbit Bks.
Walker, Richard. Human Body. 2006. (Kingfisher Knowledge Ser.). (Illus.). 64p. (J). *(978-0-7534-1317-3(5),* Kingfisher) Roaring Brook Pr.
Way, Jennifer. The Hopping Book / Brincar en un Pie. 2009. (Let's Get Moving / Diviértete en movimiento Ser.). (SPA.). 24p. (gr. k-1). 42.50 *(978-1-61514-233-0(9),* Editorial Buenas Letras) Rosen Publishing Group, Inc., The.
Way, Jennifer. The Hopping Book. 2009. (Let's Get Moving Ser.). 24p. (gr. k-k). 42.50 *(978-1-61514-227-9(4),* PowerKids Pr.) Rosen Publishing Group, Inc., The.
Winburn, William B., illus. Knees & Toes. 2009. (Rookie Toddler: Sing along Toddler Ser.). (ENG.). 12p. (J). (gr. -1). bds. 6.95 *(978-0-531-24546-0(2))* Scholastic Library Publishing.
World Book, Inc Staff, contrib. by. The Digestive & Urinary Systems. 2013. (J). *(978-0-7166-1843-0(5))* World Bk., Inc.
—Explore & Learn-Me & My Body. 2008. (J). *(978-0-7166-3021-0(4))* World Bk., Inc.
—My Body. 2007. (J). *(978-0-7166-7727-7(X))* World Bk., Inc.
—The Respiratory System. 2013. (Illus.). 32p. (J). *(978-0-7166-1847-8(8))* World Bk., Inc.
Wynne, Patricia J. & Silver, Donald M. My First Human Body Book. 2009. (Dover Children's Science Bks.). (ENG., Illus.). 32p. (J). (gr. 1-5). pap. 3.99 *(978-0-486-46821-1(6))* Dover Pubns., Inc.
Zelinger, Laurie & Zelinger, Jordan. Please Explain Anxiety to Me! Simple Biology & Solutions for Children & Parents. Sabella, Elisa, illus. 2010. 38p. 32.95 *(978-1-61599-051-1(8));* 40p. pap. 21.95 *(978-1-61599-029-0(1))* Loving Healing Pr., Inc.

PHYSIOLOGY, COMPARATIVE

Adamson, Heather. Animals with Speed. 2010. (Our Animal World Ser.). 24p. (J). 25.65 *(978-1-60753-007-7(4))* Amicus Publishing.
De la Bédoyère, Camilla. Fastest & Slowest. 2010. (Animal Opposites Ser.). (ENG., Illus.). 32p. (J). (gr. -1-3). pap. 5.95 *(978-1-55407-809-7(1),* 9781554078097) Firefly Bks., Ltd.

PHYSIOLOGY OF PLANTS

see Plant Physiology

PHYTOGEOGRAPHY

see Plant Distribution

PIANISTS

Batten, Jack. Oscar Peterson: The Man & His Jazz. 2012. (ENG., Illus.). 192p. (YA). (gr. 5). 19.95 *(978-1-77049-269-1(0),* Tundra Bks.) Tundra Bks. CAN. Dist: Penguin Random Hse. LLC.
Gordon, Stewart. Planning Your Piano Success: A Blueprint for Aspiring Musicians. 2014. (ENG.). 192p. pap. 21.95 *(978-0-19-994244-2(7))* Oxford Univ. Pr., Inc.
Harrah, Madge. Blind Boone: Piano Prodigy. 2004. (Trailblazers Biographies Ser.). (Illus.). 112p. (J). (gr. 5-9). lib. bdg. 30.60 *(978-1-57505-057-7(9))* Lerner Publishing Group.
Kaufmann, Anne. Glenn Gould: Sketches of Solitude. Koci, Rudin, illus. 2013. *(978-0-9868657-9-4(6))* Brownridge Publishing.
Lang, Lang. Lang Lang - Playing with Flying Keys. 2010. (ENG.). 256p. (J). (gr. 3-7). mass mkt. 7.99 *(978-0-440-42284-6(1),* Laurel Leaf) Random Hse. Children's Bks.
Rusch, Elizabeth. For the Love of Music: The Remarkable Story of Maria Anna Mozart. Fancher, Lou & Johnson, Steve, illus. 2011. (ENG.). 32p. (J). (gr. k-3). 16.99 *(978-1-58246-326-1(3),* Tricycle Pr.) Random Hse. Children's Bks.
Shichtman, Sandra H. & Indenbaum, Dorothy. The Joy of Creation: The Story of Clara Schumann. 2011. (Classical Composers Ser.). (Illus.). 159p. lib. bdg. 28.95 *(978-1-59935-123-0(4))* Reynolds, Morgan Inc.

PIANISTS—FICTION

Beard, Sarah. Porcelain Keys. 2014. pap. 15.99 *(978-1-4621-1396-5(6),* Horizon Pubs.) Cedar Fort, Inc./CFI Distribution.
Cheng, Andrea. Where Do You Stay? 2011. (ENG.). 136p. (J). (gr. 5-7). 17.95 *(978-1-59078-707-6(2))* Boyds Mills Pr.
Coveleskie, Sally, et al. Henry the Steinway & the Piano Recital. Friedman, Laura, illus. 2003. (Henry the Steinway Ser.: Vol. 1). 32p. (J). (gr. k-3). *(978-1-931721-05-9(X))* Bright Sky Pr.
de Brunhoff, Laurent. Babar Raconte le Pianiste. (Babar Ser.). (FRE., Illus.). 48p. (J). (gr. -1-3). 19.95 *(978-0-7859-8822-9(X))* French & European Pubns., Inc.
Hunt, Julie. KidGlovz. Newman, Dale, illus. 2017. (ENG.). 288p. (J). (gr. 3-7). 19.99 ***(978-1-74237-852-7(8))*** Allen & Unwin AUS. Dist: Independent Pubs. Group.
Perdue, Gillian. Conor's Concert. Connor, Michael, illus. 2003. (Pandas Ser.: 26). (ENG.). 64p. (J). pap. 9.95 *(978-0-86278-847-6(1))* O'Brien Pr., Ltd., The IRL. Dist: Dufour Editions, Inc.
Richmond, Peter. Always a Catch. 2014. (ENG.). 288p. (YA). (gr. 7). 17.99 *(978-0-399-25055-2(7),* Philomel Bks.) Penguin Young Readers Group.
Scattergood, Augusta. The Way to Stay in Destiny. 2015. (ENG.). 192p. (J). (gr. 3-7). 16.99 *(978-0-545-53824-4(6),* Scholastic Pr.) Scholastic, Inc.
Weston, Rhonda. Playing to Distraction. 2011. 48p. pap. 16.95 *(978-1-4560-4076-5(6))* America Star Bks.
Zarr, Sara. The Lucy Variations. 2014. (ENG.). 336p. (YA). (gr. 7-17). pap. 10.00 *(978-0-316-20500-9(1))* Little, Brown Bks. for Young Readers.

PIANO

Amoroso, Cynthia & Noyed, Robert B. Pianos. 2010. (Music Makers Ser.). (ENG.). 24p. (J). (gr. -1-2). 27.07 *(978-1-60253-355-4(5),* 200506) Child's World, Inc., The.
Barden, Christine H., et al. Music for Little Mozarts Little Mozarts Perform the Nutcracker: 8 Favorites form Tchaikovsky's Nutcracker Suite. 2007. (Music for Little Mozarts Ser.). (ENG.). 24p. (J). pap. 7.95 *(978-0-7390-4822-1(8))* Alfred Publishing Co., Inc.
Congratulations: Grade 2 Piano. 9.95 *(978-1-85909-813-4(4),* Warner Bros. Pubns.) Alfred Publishing Co., Inc.
Dvorak, Antonin. Dances for Solo Piano. Buechner, Sara Davis, ed. 2013. (ENG.). 208p. pap. 19.95 *(978-0-486-49730-3(5))* Dover Pubns., Inc.
Ganeri, Anita. Pianos & Keyboards. 2011. (ENG., Illus.). 32p. (J). 10.95 *(978-1-77092-031-6(5))* Saunders Bk. Co. CAN. Dist: RiverStream Publishing.
Green, Dan & Harrod, Elisa. How to Improve at Playing Piano. 2010. (ENG.). 48p. (J). pap. *(978-0-7787-3601-1(6));* lib. bdg. *(978-0-7787-3579-3(6))* Crabtree Publishing Co.
Healy, Nick. The Piano. 2005. (What in the World Ser.). (Illus.). 48p. (J). (gr. 5-9). lib. bdg. 21.95 *(978-1-58341-376-0(6),* Creative Education) Creative Co., The.
Liszt, Franz. Danse Macabre & Other Piano Transcriptions. Glover, Daniel, ed. 2013. (ENG.). 208p. pap. 16.95 *(978-0-486-49731-0(3))* Dover Pubns., Inc.
Phoenix Books Staff, illus. Thomas' Piano Book. 2014. 14p. (J). bds. 12.98 *(978-1-4508-6584-5(4),* 1450865844) Phoenix International Publications, Inc.
Piano Accompaniment. 2003. (Share the Music Ser.). (gr. k-18). *(978-0-02-295579-3(8));* (gr. 1-18). *(978-0-02-295580-9(1));* (gr. 2-18). *(978-0-02-295581-6(X));* (gr. 3-18). *(978-0-02-295582-3(8));* (gr. 4-18). *(978-0-02-295583-0(6));* (gr. 5-18). *(978-0-02-295584-7(4));* (gr. 6-18). *(978-0-02-295585-4(2))* Macmillan/McGraw-Hill Schl. Div.
Riggs, Kate. Making Music: Piano. 2014. (Making Music Ser.). (ENG.). 24p. (J). (gr. 1-3). pap. 9.99 *(978-0-89812-948-9(6),* Creative Paperbacks) Creative Co., The.
Rusch, Elizabeth. The Music of Life: Bartolomeo Cristofori & the Invention of the Piano. Priceman, Marjorie, illus. 2017. (ENG.). 48p. (J). (gr. -1-3). 17.99 *(978-1-4814-4484-2(0))* Simon & Schuster Children's Publishing.
Salzmann, Mary Elizabeth. What in the World Is a Piano?, 1 vol. 2012. (ENG.). 24p. 25.65 *(978-1-61783-207-9(3),* Super SandCastle) ABDO Publishing Co.
Sebba, Jane. Abracadabra Piano 3 Vol. 3: Graded Pieces for the Young Pianist. 2004. (ENG., Illus.). 48p. pap. 7.95 *(978-0-7136-3726-7(9),* 93115, A&C Black) Bloomsbury Publishing Plc GBR. Dist: Consortium Bk. Sales & Distribution.

PIANO—INSTRUCTION AND STUDY

Alexander, Dennis, et al. Alfred's Premier Piano Course: Lesson 3. 2007. (Premier Piano Course Ser.: Bk 3). (ENG., Illus.). 48p. pap. 8.99 *(978-0-7390-4639-5(X))* Alfred Publishing Co., Inc.
—Alfred's Premier Piano Course: Performance 3. Manus, Morton, ed. 2007. (Alfred's Premier Piano Course Ser.). (Illus.). 32p. pap. 6.95 *(978-0-7390-4743-9(4))* Alfred Publishing Co., Inc.
—Alfred's Premier Piano Course - Theory 3. Manus, Morton, ed. 2007. (Premier Piano Course Ser.: Bk 3). (ENG., Illus.). 32p. pap. 7.99 *(978-0-7390-4750-7(7))* Alfred Publishing Co., Inc.
—Alfred's Premier Piano Course Assignment Book: Level 1A-6. Manus, Morton, ed. 2007. (Premier Piano Course Ser.). (ENG.). 80p. pap. 6.95 *(978-0-7390-4877-1(5))* Alfred Publishing Co., Inc.
—Premier Piano Course, Technique, Bk. 1A. Manus, Morton, ed. 2008. (Premier Piano Course Ser.: Bk 1A). (ENG., Illus.). 32p. pap. 7.99 *(978-0-7390-4543-5(1))* Alfred Publishing Co., Inc.
Barden, Christine H., et al, contrib. by. Alfred's Kid's Piano Course Notespeller, Bk 1 And 2: Music Reading Activities That Make Learning Even Easier! 2012. (Alfred's Kid's Piano Course Ser.: Bk 1 & 2). (ENG.). 48p. pap. 8.99 *(978-0-7390-9245-3(6))* Alfred Publishing Co., Inc.
Barden, Christine H., et al. Alfred's Kid's Piano Course, Bk 2: The Easiest Piano Method Ever!, Book, CD & DVD. 2013. (Alfred's Kid's Piano Course Ser.: Bk 2). (ENG.). pap. 19.95 *(978-0-7390-9666-6(4))* Alfred Publishing Co., Inc.
Burnam, Edna Mae. Step by Step Piano Course - Book 6. 2005. (ENG.). 64p. pap. 7.99 *(978-1-4234-3591-4(5),* 1423435915) Willis Music Co.
—Write It Right Bk. 5: With Step by Step. 2005. (ENG., Illus.). 24p. pap. 5.99 *(978-1-4234-3603-4(2),* 1423436032) Willis Music Co.
Celik, Vladislav. You Too Can Play Piano & Organ Without Teacher, Vol. 1. (Music Instructional Ser.). (Illus.). 96p. (J). pap. 12.95 incl. audio *(978-0-9624062-1-8(X))* Music Institute of California.
Dyke, Sylvie. Piano Music Made Easy. 2012. (Illus.). 28p. pap. *(978-1-78148-794-5(4))* Grosvenor Hse. Publishing Ltd.
Elliot, K. & Gimmell, K. Piano Course Book 1. rev. ed. 2008. (Music Ser.). 32p. (J). pap. 7.99 *(978-0-7945-1539-3(8),* Usborne) EDC Publishing.
Kowalchyk, Gayle, et al. My First Pop Songs, Book 1: Eleven Favorite Pop Songs for the Beginning Pianist. 2008. (My First... Ser.: Bk 1). (ENG., Illus.). 24p. pap. 7.95 *(978-0-7390-5101-6(6))* Alfred Publishing Co., Inc.
—My First Pop Songs, Book 2: Eleven Favorite Pop Songs for the Beginning Pianist. 2008. (My First... Ser.: Bk 2). (ENG., Illus.). 24p. pap. 7.95 *(978-0-7390-5102-3(4))* Alfred Publishing Co., Inc.
Marks, Anthony. Easy Piano Classics. Rogers, Kirsteen, ed. Whatmore, Candice, illus. 2007. (Easy Piano Classics Ser.). 64p. (J). 18.99 *(978-0-7945-1273-6(9),* Usborne) EDC Publishing.
Marshall, Karen & Hammond, Heather. Get Set! Piano Pieces Book 2. 2014. (Get Set! Ser.). (ENG., Illus.). 24p. (J). pap. 11.95 ***(978-1-4081-9278-8(0))*** HarperCollins Pubs. Ltd. GBR. Dist: Independent Pubs. Group.
—Get Set! Piano Tutor Book 2. 2014. (Get Set! Ser.). (ENG., Illus.). 48p. (J). pap. 12.95 ***(978-1-4081-9307-5(8))*** HarperCollins Pubs. Ltd. GBR. Dist: Independent Pubs. Group.
Matz, Carol. Learn to Play Piano with Strawberry Shortcake: Early Elementary. 2007. (ENG., Illus.). 24p. (J). (gr. -1-3). pap. 7.95 *(978-0-7390-4958-7(5))* Alfred Publishing Co., Inc.
Musgrave, Paul Christopher & Musgrave, Machiko Yamane. Doctor Mozart Music Theory Workbook Level 3 - in-Depth Piano Theory Fun for Children's Music Lessons & Home Schooling - Highly Effective for Beginn. 2012. (Illus.). 48p. pap. *(978-0-9881688-0-0(4))* April Avenue Media.
Patrick Green, Ann. Piano Music for Little Fingers: Book 2. 2nd ed. 2012. (Dover Music for Piano Ser.). (ENG.). 48p. (J). (gr. -1-4). pap. 7.95 *(978-0-486-48825-7(X))* Dover Pubns., Inc.
Philipp, Lillie H. Piano Technique: Tone, Touch, Phrasing & Dynamics. 2010. (Dover Books on Music Ser.). (ENG., Illus.). 96p. (gr. 7-18). reprint ed. pap. 10.95 *(978-0-486-24272-9(2))* Dover Pubns., Inc.
Rejino, Mona. Just for Kids: HLSPL Composer Showcase NFMC 2014-2016 Selection Elementary Level. 2011. (ENG.). 24p. pap. 7.99 *(978-1-61774-200-2(7),* 1617742007) Leonard, Hal Corp.
Rodwell, A. The Juvenile Pianist (1836) 2014. (Classic Texts in Music Education Ser.: Volume 31). (ENG., Illus.). 200p. pap. 25.95 *(978-1-84383-984-2(9))* Boydell & Brewer, Inc.
Sebba, Jane. Abracadabra Piano, Bk. 1. Edwards, Gunvor & Felstead, Cathie, illus. (ENG.). 48p. (J). pap. *(978-0-7136-3724-3(2),* 93113, A&C Black) Bloomsbury Publishing Plc.
Sembos, Evangelos C. Solo Piano for Children. 2008. 48p. pap. 16.95 *(978-1-4357-1537-0(3))* Lulu Pr., Inc.
Tornquist, Carol. Creativity - Level 5: Music in Me - A Piano Method for Young Christian Students. 2007. (ENG.). 48p. pap. 8.95 *(978-1-4234-1887-0(5),* 1423418875) Leonard, Hal Corp.
—Hymns & Holidays - Solos to Play, Level 4: Music in Me - A Piano Method for Young Christian Students. 2007. (ENG.). 32p. pap. 8.95 *(978-1-4234-3374-3(2),* 1423433742) Leonard, Hal Corp.
—Lesson - Level 4: Reading Music: Music in Me - A Piano Method for Young Christian Students. 2007. (ENG.). 48p. pap. 8.95 *(978-1-4234-1885-6(9),* 1423418859) Leonard, Hal Corp.
—Theory & Technique - Level 4: Music in Me - A Piano Method for Young Christian Students. 2007. (ENG.). 48p. pap. 8.95 *(978-1-4234-3375-0(0),* 1423433750) Leonard, Hal Corp.
—Theory & Technique - Level 5: Music in Me - A Piano Method for Young Christian Students. 2007. (ENG.). 48p. pap. 8.95 *(978-1-4234-4952-2(5),* 1423449525) Leonard, Hal Corp.
Tunstall, Tricia. Note by Note: A Celebration of the Piano Lesson. 2009. (ENG.). 224p. pap. 15.99 *(978-1-4165-4051-9(2))* Simon & Schuster.
Wedgwood, Pam. More Up-Grade Piano. 2003. (Faber Edition: up-Grade! Ser.). (ENG.). 24p. (gr. k-1). pap. 12.25 *(978-0-571-51956-9(3))* Faber & Faber, Ltd. GBR. Dist: Alfred Publishing Co., Inc.
Wedgwood, Pamela. Up-Grade! Piano. 2003. (Faber Edition: up-Grade! Ser.). (ENG.). 24p. (gr. k-1). pap. 12.25 *(978-0-571-51737-4(4))* Faber & Faber, Ltd. GBR. Dist: Alfred Publishing Co., Inc.

PIANO MUSIC

Adolphe, Bruce. Piano Puzzlers: Thirty Popular Melodies & Folk Tunes in the Styles of Famous Composers. 2004. 42p. 21.95 *(978-0-9701249-2-0(9))* PollyRhythm Productions.
Alfred Publishing Staff & Turner, Barrie Carson. Classic FM — Classics for Children. 2011. (Faber Edition: Classic FM Ser.). (ENG.). pap., pap. 13.80 *(978-0-571-53578-1(X))* Faber Music, Ltd. GBR. Dist: Alfred Publishing Co., Inc.
Baker, Ed. Blues Riffs for Piano. Date not set. 30p. (YA). pap. 14.95 incl. audio *(978-0-89524-928-9(6))* Cherry Lane Music Co.
Bergerac. A First Book of Classical Music for the Beginning Pianist: With Downloadable MP3s. 2014. (ENG.). 48p. pap. 6.95 *(978-0-486-78009-2(0))* Dover Pubns., Inc.
Faber, Nancy, et al. BigTime Kids' Songs: Level 4. 2012. (ENG.). 40p. pap. 7.99 *(978-1-61677-629-9(3),* 1616776293) Faber Piano Adventures(r).
Feldstein, Sandy & Clark, Larry. Arietta - Clarinet/Bass Clarinet Solo w/ Piano Acc. w/ CD. 2005. (YA). pap. 9.95 *(978-1-932895-18-6(3))* PlayinTime Productions, Inc.
—Arietta - Flute/Oboe Solo w/ Pianio Acc & CD. 2005. (YA). pap. 9.95 *(978-1-932895-17-9(5))* PlayinTime Productions, Inc.
—Arietta - Trombone/Bariton/Bassoon Solo w/ Piano Acc. W/CD. 2005. (YA). pap. 9.95 *(978-1-932895-23-0(X))* PlayinTime Productions, Inc.
—Arietta - Trumpet/Baritone Solo w/ Piano Acc. W/CD. 2005. (YA). pap. 9.95 *(978-1-932895-21-6(3))* PlayinTime Productions, Inc.
—Arietta - Tuba Solo w/Piano Acc. w/ CD. 2005. (YA). pap. 9.95 *(978-1-932895-24-7(8))* PlayinTime Productions, Inc.
—Arietta- Keyboard Percussion Solo w/Piano Acc. W/CD. 2005. (YA). pap. *(978-1-932895-25-4(6))* PlayinTime Productions, Inc.
—Arietta - Alto Sax/Bari Sax Solo w/ Piano Acc. w/ CD. 2005. (YA). pap. 9.95 *(978-1-932895-19-3(1))* PlayinTime Productions, Inc.
—Bacarolle - Flute/Oboe Solo with Piano Acc. W/CD. 2005. (YA). pap. *(978-1-932895-87-2(6))* PlayinTime Productions, Inc.
—Bacarolle - Tenor Sax Solo with Piano Acc. W/CD. 2005. (YA). pap. 10.95 *(978-1-932895-90-2(6))* PlayinTime Productions, Inc.
—Barbara Allen - Alto Sax/Bari. Sax Solo with Piano Acc. W/CD. 2005. (YA). pap. 9.95 *(978-1-932895-59-9(0))* PlayinTime Productions, Inc.
—Barbara Allen - Clarinet/Bass Clarinet Solo with Piano Acc. W/CD. 2005. (YA). pap. 9.95 *(978-1-932895-58-2(2))* PlayinTime Productions, Inc.
—Barbara Allen - Flute/Oboe Solo with Piano Acc. W/CD. 2005. (YA). pap. 9.95 *(978-1-932895-57-5(4))* PlayinTime Productions, Inc.
—Barbara Allen - Horn in F Solo with Piano Acc. W/CD. 2005. (YA). pap. 9.95 *(978-1-932895-62-9(0))* PlayinTime Productions, Inc.

—Barbara Allen - Keyboard Percussion Solo with Piano Acc. W/CD. 2005. (YA). pap. 9.95 *(978-1-932895-65-0(5))* PlayinTime Productions, Inc.
—Barbara Allen - Tenor Sax Solo with Piano Acc. W/CD. 2005. (YA). pap. 9.95 *(978-1-932895-60-5(4))*; pap. 9.95 *(978-1-932895-61-2(2))* PlayinTime Productions, Inc.
—Barbara Allen - Trombone/Baritone/Bassoon Solo with Piano Acc. W/CD. 2005. (YA). pap. 9.95 *(978-1-932895-63-6(9))* PlayinTime Productions, Inc.
—Barbara Allen - Tuba Solo with Piano Acc. W/CD. 2005. (YA). pap. 9.95 *(978-1-932895-64-3(7))* PlayinTime Productions, Inc.
—Barcarolle - Alto Sax. /Bari. Sax Solo with Piano Acc. 2005. (YA). pap. 10.95 incl. audio compact disk *(978-1-932895-89-6(2))* PlayinTime Productions, Inc.
—Barcarolle - Clarinet/Bass Clarinet Solo with Piano Acc. 2005. (YA). pap. 10.95 incl. audio compact disk *(978-1-932895-88-9(4))* PlayinTime Productions, Inc.
—Barcarolle - Keyboard Percussion Solo with Piano Acc. 2005. (YA). pap. 10.95 incl. audio compact disk *(978-1-932895-95-7(7))* PlayinTime Productions, Inc.
—Barcarolle - Snare Drum Solo with Piano Acc. 2005. (YA). pap. 10.95 *(978-1-932895-96-4(5))* PlayinTime Productions, Inc.
—Barcarolle - Tuba Solo with Piano Acc. 2005. (YA). pap. 10.95 incl. audio compact disk *(978-1-932895-94-0(9))* PlayinTime Productions, Inc.
—Barcarolle -Trombone/Baritone/Bassoon Solo with Piano Acc. 2005. (YA). pap. 10.95 incl. audio compact disk *(978-1-932895-93-3(0))* PlayinTime Productions, Inc.
—Barcarolle-Trumpet/Baritone Solo with Piano Acc. 2005. (YA). pap. 10.95 incl. audio compact disk *(978-1-932895-91-9(4))* PlayinTime Productions, Inc.
—Fafare Minuet - Keyboard Percussion Solo with Piano Acc. W/CD. 2005. (YA). pap. 9.95 *(978-1-932895-55-1(8))* PlayinTime Productions, Inc.
—Fanfare & Minuet -Flute/Oboe Solo with Piano Acc. W/CD. 2005. (YA). pap. 9.95 *(978-1-932895-47-6(7))* PlayinTime Productions, Inc.
—Fanfare Minuet - Alto Sax/Bari. Sax Solo with Piano Acc. W/CD. 2005. (YA). pap. 9.95 *(978-1-932895-49-0(3))* PlayinTime Productions, Inc.
—Fanfare Minuet - Clarinet/Bass Clarinet Solo with Piano Acc. 2005. (YA). pap. 9.95 incl. audio compact disk *(978-1-932895-48-3(5))* PlayinTime Productions, Inc.
—Fanfare Minuet - Horn in F Solo with Piano Acc. 2005. (YA). pap. 9.95 incl. audio compact disk *(978-1-932895-52-0(3))* PlayinTime Productions, Inc.
—Fanfare Minuet - Snare Drim Solo with Piano Acc. 2005. (YA). pap. incl. audio compact disk *(978-1-932895-56-8(6))* PlayinTime Productions, Inc.
—Fanfare Minuet - Tenor Sax Solo with Piano Acc. 2005. (YA). pap. 9.95 incl. audio compact disk *(978-1-932895-50-6(7))* PlayinTime Productions, Inc.
—Fanfare Minuet - Tuba Solo with Piano Acc. W/CD. 2005. (YA). pap. 9.95 *(978-1-932895-54-4(X))* PlayinTime Productions, Inc.
—The Fifers - Alto Sax. /Bari. Sax Solo with Piano Acc. 2005. (YA). pap. 10.95 incl. audio compact disk *(978-1-932895-79-7(5))* PlayinTime Productions, Inc.
—The Fifers - Clarinet/Bass Clarinet Solo with Piano Acc. W/CD. 2005. (YA). pap. 10.95 *(978-1-932895-78-0(7))* PlayinTime Productions, Inc.
—The Fifers - Flute/Oboe Solo with Piano Acc. 2005. (YA). pap. 10.95 incl. audio compact disk *(978-1-932895-77-3(9))* PlayinTime Productions, Inc.
—The Fifers - Horn in F Solo with Piano Acc. 2005. (YA). pap. 10.95 incl. audio compact disk *(978-1-932895-82-7(5))* PlayinTime Productions, Inc.
—The Fifers - Keyboard Percussion Solo with Piano Acc. 2005. (YA). pap. 10.95 incl. audio compact disk *(978-1-932895-85-8(X))* PlayinTime Productions, Inc.
—The Fifers - Snare Drum Solo with Piano Acc. W/CD. 2005. (YA). pap. 10.95 *(978-1-932895-86-5(8))* PlayinTime Productions, Inc.
—The Fifers - Tenor Sax. Solo with Piano Acc. 2005. (YA). pap. 10.95 incl. audio compact disk *(978-1-932895-80-3(9))* PlayinTime Productions, Inc.
—The Fifers - Trombone/Baritone/Bassoon Solo with Piano Acc. 2005. (YA). pap. 10.95 incl. audio compact disk *(978-1-932895-83-4(3))* PlayinTime Productions, Inc.
—The Fifers - Tuba Solo with Piano Acc. 2005. (YA). pap. 10.95 incl. audio compact disk *(978-1-932895-84-1(1))* PlayinTime Productions, Inc.
—Horn in F Solo with Piano Acc. 2005. (YA). pap. 10.95 incl. audio compact disk *(978-1-932895-92-6(2))* PlayinTime Productions, Inc.
—Scherzando - Flute Solo with Piano Acc. w/CD. 2005. (YA). pap. 9.95 *(978-1-932895-26-1(4))* PlayinTime Productions, Inc.
—Scherzando -Horn in F Solo with Piano Acc. W/CD. 2005. (YA). pap. 9.95 *(978-1-932895-31-5(0))* PlayinTime Productions, Inc.
—Schezando - Clarinet/Bass Clarinet Solo with Piano acc. W/CD. 2005. (YA). pap. 9.95 *(978-1-932895-27-8(2))* PlayinTime Productions, Inc.
—Sensational Snare - Snare Drum Solo with Piano Acc. W/cd. 2005. (YA). pap. 9.95 *(978-1-932895-36-0(1))* PlayinTime Productions, Inc.
—Snarendipity - Snare Drum Solo with Piano Acc. W/CD. 2005. (YA). pap. 9.95 *(978-1-932895-66-7(3))* PlayinTime Productions, Inc.
—Sonatina - Alto Sax/Bari. Sax Solo with Piano Acc. W/CD. 2005. (YA). pap. 10.95 *(978-1-932895-69-8(8))* PlayinTime Productions, Inc.
—Sonatina - Clarinet/Bass Clarinet Solo with Piano Acc. W/CD. 2005. (YA). pap. 10.95 *(978-1-932895-68-1(X))* PlayinTime Productions, Inc.
—Sonatina - Flute/Oboe Solo with Piano Acc. W/CD. 2005. (YA). pap. *(978-1-932895-67-4(1))* PlayinTime Productions, Inc.
—Sonatina - Horn in F Solo with Piano Acc. W/CD. 2005. (YA). pap. 10.95 *(978-1-932895-72-8(8))* PlayinTime Productions, Inc.
—Sonatina - Keyboard Percussion Solo with Piano Acc. W/CD. 2005. (YA). pap. 10.95 *(978-1-932895-75-9(2))* PlayinTime Productions, Inc.
—Sonatina - Snare Drum Solo with Piano Acc. W/CD. 2005. (YA). pap. 10.95 *(978-1-932895-76-6(0))* PlayinTime Productions, Inc.
—Sonatina - Tenor Sax Solo with Piano Acc. W/CD. 2005. (YA). pap. 10.95 *(978-1-932895-70-4(1))* PlayinTime Productions, Inc.
—Sonatina - Trombone/Baritone/Bassoon Solo with Piano Acc. W/CD. 2005. (YA). pap. 10.95 *(978-1-932895-73-5(6))* PlayinTime Productions, Inc.
—Sonatina - Trumpet/Baritone Solo with Piano Acc. W/CD. 2005. (YA). pap. 10.95 *(978-1-932895-71-1(X))* PlayinTime Productions, Inc.
—Sonatina - Tuba Solo with Piano Acc. W/CD. 2005. (YA). pap. 10.95 *(978-1-932895-74-2(4))* PlayinTime Productions, Inc.
—Variations on a Theme by Greig -Flute Solo w/Piano Acc. W/CD. 2005. (YA). pap. 9.95 *(978-1-932895-37-7(X))* PlayinTime Productions, Inc.
—Variations on a Theme by Grieg - Alto Sax/Bari. Sax Solo with Piano Acc. W/CD. 2005. (YA). pap. 9.95 *(978-1-932895-39-1(6))* PlayinTime Productions, Inc.
—Variations on a Theme by Grieg - Clarinet/Bass Clarinet Solo with Piano Acc. W/CD. 2005. (YA). pap. 9.95 *(978-1-932895-38-4(8))* PlayinTime Productions, Inc.
—Variations on a Theme by Greig - Keyboard Percussion Solo with Piano Acc. W/CD. 2005. (YA). pap. 9.95 *(978-1-932895-45-2(0))* PlayinTime Productions, Inc.
—Variations on a Theme by Grieg - Snare Drum Solo with Piano Acc. W/CD. 2005. (YA). pap. 9.95 *(978-1-932895-46-9(9))* PlayinTime Productions, Inc.
—Variations on a Theme by Greig - Trombone/Baritone/Basson Solo with Piano Acc. W/CD. 2005. (YA). pap. 9.95 *(978-1-932895-43-8(4))* PlayinTime Productions, Inc.
—Variations on a Theme by Greig - Trumpet/Baritone Solo with Piano Acc. W/CD. 2005. (YA). pap. 9.95 *(978-1-932895-41-4(8))* PlayinTime Productions, Inc.
—Variations on a Theme by Greig - Tuba Solo with Piano Acc. W/CD. 2005. (YA). pap. 9.95 *(978-1-932895-44-5(2))* PlayinTime Productions, Inc.
—Variations on the theme by Greig - Horn in F Solo with Piano Acc. W/CD. 2005. (YA). pap. 9.95 *(978-1-932895-42-1(6))* PlayinTime Productions, Inc.
—Variatons on a theme by Grieg- Tenor Sax Solo with Piano Acc. W/CD. 2005. (YA). pap. 9.95 *(978-1-932895-40-7(X))* PlayinTime Productions, Inc.
Finn, Cheryl. Beanstalk's Basics for Piano, Vol. Prep B. 2005. (ENG.). 40p. pap. 10.99 *(978-0-87718-044-9(X)*, 087718044X) Willis Music Co.
Finn, Cheryl, et al. Beanstalk's Basics for Piano Bk. A: Lesson Book Preparatory. 2005. (ENG.). 48p. pap. 12.99 *(978-0-87718-037-1(7)*, 0877180377) Willis Music Co.
—Beanstalk's Basics for Piano Bk. B: Lesson Book Preparatory Book. 2005. (ENG.). 48p. pap. 12.99 *(978-0-87718-038-8(5)*, 0877180385) Willis Music Co.
Hal Leonard Corp. Staff, creator. Teaching Little Fingers to Play More Broadway Songs: Mid to Later Elementary Level. 2012. (ENG.). 32p. pap. 12.99 incl. audio compact disk *(978-1-4584-1768-8(9)*, 1458417689) Willis Music Co.
Ingkavet, Andrew. Play Piano for Kids: Penguins Don't Play Piano, but You Can! 2012. (ENG.). pap. *(978-1-4675-3174-0(X))* Independent Pub.
Jones, Edward Huws, ed. Unbeaten Tracks: 8 Contemporary Pieces for Trumpet & Piano. 2003. (Faber Edition: Unbeaten Tracks Ser.). (ENG.). 32p. (gr. 4-7). pap. 13.80 *(978-0-571-52005-3(7))* Faber & Faber, Ltd. GBR. Dist: Alfred Publishing Co., Inc.
Lowe, Marilyn & Gordon, Edwin. Music Moves for Piano. 2004. (J). Bk. 1. 56p. 17.95 *(978-1-57999-343-6(5)*, G-6439)Bk. 2. 55p. 17.95 *(978-1-57999-345-0(1)*, G-6441) G I A Pubns., Inc.
—Music Moves for Piano Preparatory Book. 2004. 36p. (J). 14.95 *(978-1-57999-341-2(9)*, G-6437) G I A Pubns., Inc.
Lowe, Marilyn, et al. Music Moves for Piano Boogies & Blues. 2004. 30p. (J). 7.95 *(978-1-57999-349-8(4)*, G-6445) G I A Pubns., Inc.
Marks, A. Easy Piano Tunes. 2004. (Easy Tunes Ser.). (Illus.). 32p. (J). pap. 8.95 *(978-0-7945-0474-8(4))* EDC Publishing.
—Piano Tunes for Children. 2004. (Easy Tunes Ser.). (Illus.). 32p. (J). pap. 8.95 *(978-0-7945-0459-5(0))* EDC Publishing.
Marshall, Karen & Hammond, Heather. Get Set! Piano Pieces Book 2. 2014. (Get Set! Ser.). (ENG., Illus.). 24p. (J). pap. 11.95 ***(978-1-4081-9278-8(0))*** HarperCollins Pubs. Ltd. GBR. Dist: Independent Pubs. Group.
—Get Set! Piano Tutor Book 2. 2014. (Get Set! Ser.). (ENG., Illus.). 48p. (J). pap. 12.95 ***(978-1-4081-9307-5(8))*** HarperCollins Pubs. Ltd. GBR. Dist: Independent Pubs. Group.
More What Else Can I Play: Piano Grade 1. (gr. 1). 6.95 *(978-1-85909-523-2(2)*, Warner Bros. Pubns.) Alfred Publishing Co., Inc.
More What Else Can I Play: Piano Grade 2. (gr. 2). 6.95 *(978-1-85909-524-9(0)*, Warner Bros. Pubns.) Alfred Publishing Co., Inc.
Music. Gr 6 Stm Te/Piano Accomp. 2003. (Share the Music Ser.). (gr. 6-18). *(978-0-02-295593-9(3))* Macmillan/McGraw-Hill Schl. Div.
Okun, Milton, ed. Christmas Carols for Piano Duet. 63p. (YA). pap. 14.95 *(978-0-89524-948-7(0)*, 02505651) Cherry Lane Music Co.
—From a Distance & Twenty-Four Other Easy Listening Favorites for Easy Piano. 119p. (Orig.). (YA). pap. 12.95 *(978-0-89524-871-8(9)*, 02505508) Cherry Lane Music Co.
Patrick Green, Ann. Piano Music for Little Fingers: Book 1. 2012. (Dover Music for Piano Ser.). (ENG.). 64p. (J). (gr. -1-4). pap. 6.95 *(978-0-486-48824-0(1))* Dover Pubns., Inc.
—Piano Music for Little Fingers: Primer. 2012. (Dover Music for Piano Ser.). (ENG.). 64p. (gr. -1-3). pap. 8.95 *(978-0-486-48823-3(3))* Dover Pubns., Inc.
Phoenix International Staff, illus. Baby Einstein: Little Piano Book. 2014. 12p. (J). bds. 12.98 *(978-1-4508-7546-2(7)*, 1450875467) Publications International, Ltd.
—Thomas & Friends(r) - Thomas' Piano Book. deluxe ed. 2014. 12p. (J). bds. 17.98 *(978-1-4127-4552-9(7)*, 1412745527) Phoenix International Publications, Inc.
Pollock, Malcolm, et al. Abracadabra Flute Piano Accompaniments: The Way to Learn Through Songs & Tunes. 2003. (ENG., Illus.). 80p. (J). (gr. 1-3). pap. 24.95 ***(978-0-7136-6624-3(2))*** HarperCollins Pubs. Ltd. GBR. Dist: Independent Pubs. Group.
Publications International Ltd. Staff, ed. Disney Princess: Royal Recital. 2011. 14p. (J). bds. 17.98 *(978-1-4508-1006-7(3))* Phoenix International Publications, Inc.
—Minnie Mouse: Pretty Piano Play-Along: Piano Book. 2013. (Illus.). 14p. (J). (gr. k-3). bds. 18.98 *(978-1-4508-6770-2(7)*, a4f2852b-3a90-4b10-ac4c-e802ee4cfa50) Phoenix International Publications, Inc.
—Nickelodeon Dora the Explorer: Follow the Music. 2011. 14p. (J). 18.98 *(978-1-4508-0712-8(7))* Phoenix International Publications, Inc.
—Nickelodeon Dora the Explorer: Follow the Music: Piano Book. 2013. 14p. (J). bds. 16.98 *(978-1-4508-6380-3(9)*, 355bc6ba-2b76-413c-bb3d-3975072deb9b) Phoenix International Publications, Inc.
—Princess Songs Play & Learn. 2010. 24p. (J). 12.98 *(978-1-4508-0113-3(7))* Phoenix International Publications, Inc.
Rocherolle, Eugenie. Eugenie Rocherolle Keyboard Capers. 2004. (Composer Spotlight Ser.). (ENG., Illus.). 28p. pap. 7.00 *(978-0-7579-1897-1(2))* Alfred Publishing Co., Inc.
Spivak, Samuel. Children's Cowboy Songs for Piano. Barbelle, illus. 2011. 28p. 35.95 *(978-1-258-06408-2(1))* Literary Licensing, LLC.
Tansman, Alexandre. Alexandre Tansman: Je Joue Pour Papa: Douze Morceaux Tres Faciles et en Grosses Notes. 2007. (ENG.). 28p. pap. 16.95 *(978-1-4234-2730-8(0)*, 1423427300) Leonard, Hal Corp.
Tokarjewa, Viktorija. Der Pianist: Erzaehlungen. (GER.). 176p. *(978-3-257-06139-0(0))* Diogenes Verlag AG CHE. Dist: International Bk. Import Service, Inc.
Tornquist, Carol. Music in Me: A Piano Method for Young Christian Students. 2006. (ENG.). 32p. pap. 8.95 *(978-1-4234-1876-4(X)*, 142341876X); 32p. pap. 8.95 *(978-1-4234-1881-8(6)*, 1423418816); 32p. pap. 8.95 *(978-1-4234-1878-8(6)*, 1423418786); 40p. pap. 8.95 *(978-1-4234-1888-7(3)*, 1423418883); 32p. pap. 8.95 *(978-1-4234-1889-4(1)*, 1423418891); 32p. pap. 8.95 *(978-1-4234-1890-0(5)*, 1423418905); 32p. pap. 8.95 *(978-1-4234-1880-1(8)*, 1423418808); 40p. pap. 8.95 *(978-1-4234-1877-1(8)*, 1423418778); 32p. pap. 8.95 *(978-1-4234-1896-2(4)*, 1423418964); 32p. pap. 8.95 *(978-1-4234-1895-5(6)*, 1423418956); 32p. pap. 8.95 *(978-1-4234-1894-8(8)*, 1423418948); 32p. pap. 8.95 *(978-1-4234-1891-7(3)*, 1423418913); 32p. pap. 8.95 *(978-1-4234-1892-4(1)*, 1423418921); 40p. pap. 8.95 *(978-1-4234-1893-1(X)*, 142341893X); 32p. pap. 8.95 *(978-1-4234-1879-5(4)*, 1423418794) Leonard, Hal Corp.
Turner, Gary. Piano Method for Young Beginners, Book 1. Stewart, James, illus. 2006. (Young Beginner Giant Coloring Bks.). 44p. pap. incl. audio compact disk *(978-1-86469-098-9(4))* LearnToPlayMusic.com Pty Ltd.
Twelsiek, Monika, ed. Animals: 30 Easy Piano Pieces for Children. 2009. (ENG.). 48p. pap. 12.99 *(978-3-7957-5874-5(2)*, 3795758742) Schott Music Corp.
Unknown. More Little Peppers. 2004. (Faber Edition: Little Peppers Ser.). (ENG.). 24p. pap. 11.25 *(978-0-571-52314-6(5))* Faber & Faber, Ltd. GBR. Dist: Alfred Publishing Co., Inc.

PICASSO, PABLO, 1881-1973

Bailer, Darice. Pablo Picasso. Morrow, J. T., illus. 2014. (World's Greatest Artists Ser.). (ENG.). 24p. (J). (gr. 2-5). 28.50 *(978-1-62687-353-7(4)*, 207193) Child's World, Inc., The.
Bernier-Grand, Carmen T. Picasso: I the King, Yo el Rey, 0 vols. Diaz, David, illus. 2012. (ENG.). 64p. (J). (gr. 5-10). 19.99 *(978-0-7614-6177-7(9)*, 9780761461777, Amazon Children's Publishing) Amazon Publishing.
Fandel, Jennifer. Pablo Picasso. (Illus.). (J). 2016. 80p. *(978-1-60818-720-1(9))* 2005. 48p. (gr. 5-9). lib. bdg. 21.95 *(978-1-58341-331-9(6))* Creative Co., The. (Creative Education).
Flor Ada, Alma & Campoy, F. Isabel, contrib. by. Sonrisas. (Literature Collection of Puertas Al Sol Ser.). (SPA.). 32p. (J). (gr. k-6). pap. 13.95 *(978-1-59437-701-3(4))* Santillana USA Publishing Co., Inc.
Geis, Patricia. Pablo Picasso. 2014. (Meet the Artist Ser.). (ENG., Illus.). 18p. (J). (gr. 2-7). 24.95 *(978-1-61689-251-7(X))* Princeton Architectural Pr.
Hodge, Susie & Picasso, P. Pablo Picasso. 2004. (Lives of the Artists Ser.). (Illus.). 48p. (gr. 5-12). pap. 14.05 *(978-0-8368-5606-4(6))*; lib. bdg. 31.00 *(978-0-8368-5601-9(5))* Stevens, Gareth Publishing LLLP. (Gareth Stevens Secondary Library).
Hyde, Margaret, ed. Picasso for Kids, 1 vol. 2nd rev. ed. 2008. (Great Art for Kids Ser.). (ENG., Illus.). 14p. (J). (gr. k-k). bds. 8.95 *(978-1-58980-659-7(X))* Pelican Publishing Co., Inc.
Hyde, Margaret E., ed. Picasso for Kids, 1 vol. 2004. (Great Art for Kids Ser.). (ENG., Illus.). 12p. (J). 8.95 *(978-1-58980-205-6(5))* Pelican Publishing Co., Inc.
Jacobson, Rick. Picasso: Soul on Fire. Jacobson, Rick & Fernandez, Laura, illus. (ENG.). 32p. (J). (gr. 5-18). 2011. pap. 8.95 *(978-1-77049-263-9(1))* 2004. 15.95 *(978-0-88776-599-5(8))* Tundra Bks. CAN. (Tundra Bks.). Dist: Penguin Random Hse. LLC.
Kelley, True. Quién Fue Pablo Picasso? Kelley, True & Harrison, Nancy, illus. 2012. (Who Was? Ser.). (ENG & SPA.). 112p. (J). (gr. 3-7). pap. 7.99 *(978-0-448-46175-5(7)*, Grosset & Dunlap) Penguin Young Readers Group.
—Who Was Pablo Picasso? Kelley, True & Harrison, Nancy, illus. 2009. (Who Was? Ser.). (ENG.). 112p. (J). (gr. 3-7). pap. 5.99 *(978-0-448-44987-6(0)*, Grosset & Dunlap) Penguin Young Readers Group.
Klein, Adam G. Pablo Picasso, 1 vol. 2007. (Great Artists Set 2 Ser.). (ENG., Illus.). 32p. (gr. -1-3). 27.07 *(978-1-59679-733-8(9)*, Checkerboard Library) ABDO Publishing Co.
Lebscky, Ibi. Pablito. Cardoni, Paolo, illus. (Coleccion Seran Famosos).Tr. of Little Pablo Picasso. (SPA.). 28p. (J). (gr. 2-4). 14.95 *(978-84-233-1265-8(8))* Ediciones Destino ESP. Dist: AIMS International Bks., Inc.
Lemay, Violet, illus. 100 Pablo Picassos. 2015. (ENG.). 32p. (J). (gr. k-5). 14.99 *(978-1-938093-32-6(1)*, 1388806) Duo Pr. LLC.
Lomberg, Michelle. Pablo Picasso. 2016. (J). *(978-1-4896-4625-5(6))* Weigl Pubs., Inc.
Lowery, Linda. Pablo Picasso. 2006. (Yo Solo Biografías Ser.). (SPA., Illus.). 48p. (J). (gr. 3-7). lib. bdg. 23.93 *(978-0-8225-6259-7(6)*, Ediciones Lerner) Lerner Publishing Group.
Mason, Antony. El Arte Moderno: En los Tiempos de Picasso. 2005. (Arte Alrededor del Mundo Ser.). (Illus.). 48p. (J). (gr. 4-7). pap. 9.95 *(978-85-7416-240-9(X))* Callis Editora Ltda BRA. Dist: Independent Pubs. Group.
Nichols, Catherine. Pablo Picasso. (Primary Source Library of Famous Artists Ser.). 32p. (gr. 3-4). 2009. 42.50 *(978-1-60854-103-4(7))* 2006. (Illus.). (J). lib. bdg. 23.95 *(978-1-4042-2764-4(4))* Rosen Publishing Group, Inc., The. (PowerKids Pr.).
Pablo Picasso. 2006. (J). pap. 6.95 *(978-0-8225-6624-3(9)*, Ediciones Lerner) Lerner Publishing Group.
Penrose, Antony & Picasso, Pablo. The Boy Who Bit Picasso. 2011. (ENG., Illus.). 48p. (J). (gr. k-2). 17.95 *(978-0-8109-9728-8(2)*, Abrams Bks. for Young Readers) Abrams, Inc.
Richardson, Adele & Fandel, Jennifer. Pablo Picasso. 2017. (Odysseys in Artistry Ser.). (ENG., Illus.). 80p. (J). (gr. 7-11). pap. 14.99 *(978-1-62832-316-0(7)*, Creative Paperbacks) Creative Co., The.
Rollyson, Carl. Pablo Picasso: A Biography for Beginners. 2009. 88p. pap. 9.95 *(978-1-4401-3247-6(X))* iUniverse, Inc.
Spence, David. Picasso. 2010. (Great Artists & Their World Ser.). 48p. 32.80 *(978-1-84898-315-1(8))* Black Rabbit Bks.
—Picasso: Una Revolucion en el Arte. (Coleccion Grandes Artistas).Tr. of Picasso: Breaking the Rules of Art. (SPA.). 226p. (YA). (gr. 5-8). 12.76 *(978-84-8211-134-6(5))* Celeste Ediciones, S.A. ESP. Dist: Lectorum Pubns., Inc.
Stephens, Pamela Geiger. Dropping in on Picasso. McNeill, Jim, illus. 2004. 32p. (J). 15.95 *(978-1-56290-325-1(X))* Crystal Productions.
Venezia, Mike. Pablo Picasso. Venezia, Mike, illus. 2014. (Getting to Know the World's Greatest Artists Ser.). (ENG., Illus.). 40p. (J). pap. 7.95 *(978-0-531-22537-0(2))*; lib. bdg. 29.00 *(978-0-531-21976-8(3))* Scholastic Library Publishing.
Vila, Carmen. Tracy Knows Picasso: Children's Art History Read-Along Book. (Illus.). 24p. (J). (gr. 1-6). incl. audio *(978-0-9635047-0-8(3))* VILA Group, Inc., The.

PICASSO, PABLO, 1881-1973—FICTION

Anholt, Laurence. Picasso & the Girl with a Ponytail. 2007. (Anholt's Artists Books for Children Ser.). (ENG., Illus.). 32p. (J). (gr. -1-3). pap. 8.99 *(978-0-7641-3853-9(7))* Barron's Educational Series, Inc.
Picasso, Pablo. Birds & Other Animals with Pablo Picasso. 2017. (First Concepts with Fine Artists Ser.). (ENG.). 30p. (J). (gr. -1 — 1). bds. 9.95 ***(978-0-7148-7418-0(3))*** Phaidon Pr., Inc.
Ploss, Skip. If Picasso Were a Fish. Ploss, Skip, illus. 2006. (Illus.). 40p. (J). (gr. k-2). 15.99 *(978-1-4116-9220-6(9))* Lulu Pr., Inc.
Scott, Elaine. Secrets of the Cirque Medrano. 2008. (ENG., Illus.). 216p. (J). (gr. 5-9). 15.95 *(978-1-57091-712-7(4))* Charlesbridge Publishing, Inc.
—The Spanish Web: An Encounter with Picasso. 2004. (Art Encounters Ser.). (J). 15.95 *(978-0-8230-0410-2(4))*; pap. 6.99 *(978-0-8230-0413-3(9))* Watson-Guptill Pubns., Inc.

PICKETT, BILL, APPROXIMATELY 1860-1932

Landau, Elaine. Bill Pickett: Wild West Cowboy. 2004. (Best of the West Biographies Ser.). (Illus.). 48p. (J). lib. bdg. 25.27 *(978-0-7660-2215-7(3))* Enslow Pubs., Inc.
Sanford, William R. & Green, Carl R. Bill Pickett: Courageous African-American Cowboy. 2012. (Courageous Heroes of the American West Ser.). (Illus.). 48p. (J). (gr. 5-18). 22.60 *(978-0-7660-4001-4(1))* Enslow Pubs., Inc.

PICKLING

see Canning and Preserving

PICNICKING

At the Lake: KinderReaders Individual Title Six-Packs. (Kinderstarters Ser.). 8p. (gr. -1-1). 21.00 *(978-0-7635-8663-8(3))* Rigby Education.
Benjamin, Tina. Let's Have a Picnic. 2015. (Let's Go Outdoors! Ser.). (ENG., Illus.). 24p. (J). (gr. k-k). pap. 8.15 *(978-1-4824-2625-0(0))* Stevens, Gareth Publishing LLLP.
La Excursion (The Picnic) (Granja Oso de Miel Ser.). (SPA., Illus.). (J). bds. 4.99 *(978-0-7899-0608-3(2)*, 495050) Editorial Unilit.
Meachen Rau, Dana. At a Picnic. 2007. (Fun Time Ser.). (SPA., Illus.). 24p. (gr. k-1). lib. bdg. 15.95 *(978-0-7614-2607-3(8)*, Benchmark Bks.) Marshall Cavendish Corp.
—En el Picnic. 2007. (¡A Divertimos! Ser.). (SPA., Illus.). 24p. (gr. k-1). lib. bdg. 15.95 *(978-0-7614-2779-7(1)*, Benchmark Bks.) Marshall Cavendish Corp.
The Special Ride: Individual Title Six-Packs. 16p. (gr. 2-18). 35.00 *(978-0-7635-9377-3(X))* Rigby Education.

PICNICKING—FICTION

Adeney, Anne. Five Teddy Bears. Shimmen, Cathy, illus. 2008. (Tadpoles Ser.). (ENG.). 24p. (J). (gr. -1-k). pap. *(978-0-7787-3884-8(1))*; lib. bdg. *(978-0-7787-3853-4(1))* Crabtree Publishing Co.
Agha-Khan, Aliyar. Cyrus & Kaleo Go Rock Hunting. 2012. 32p. pap. 12.99 *(978-1-4634-1567-9(2))* AuthorHouse.
Bagnoli, Christine. Miguel's Family Picnic. 2006. (Neighborhood Readers Ser.). (ENG.). 16p. (gr. 1-3). pap. 6.50 *(978-1-4042-7006-0(X)*, Rosen Classroom) Rosen Publishing Group, Inc., The.
Beckford, Lois. The Interesting Pen Pal. 2010. 44p. pap. 21.99 *(978-1-4415-0878-2(3))* Xlibris Corp.
Bell, Rebecca. Rebekah Armstronge. 2012. 48p. pap. 21.99 *(978-1-4772-2136-5(0))* AuthorHouse.
Bollinger, Georgia G. The Penguins' Perilous Picnic. 2011. 32p. pap. 14.50 *(978-1-4634-2200-4(8))* AuthorHouse.
Bond, Rebecca. Pig & Goose & the First Day of Spring. Bond, Rebecca, illus. 2017. (ENG., Illus.). 48p. (J). (gr. k-3). lib. bdg. 12.99 *(978-1-58089-594-1(8))* Charlesbridge Publishing, Inc.
Brendler, Carol. The Pickwicks' Picnic: A Counting Adventure. Kurilla, Renée, illus. 2017. (ENG.). 40p. (J). (gr. -1-3). 16.99 ***(978-0-544-83958-8(7))***, Clarion Bks.) Houghton Mifflin Harcourt Trade & Reference Pubs.
Brooke, Samantha. Best Friends Forever. 2011. (Strawberry Shortcake Ser.). (ENG.). 24p. (J). (gr. -1-k). pap. 4.99

(978-0-448-45721-5(0), Grosset & Dunlap) Penguin Young Readers Group.

Bunting, Eve. A Picnic in October. Carpenter, Nancy, illus. 2010. (Rise & Shine Ser.). (ENG.). 32p. (C). (gr. -1-3). reprint ed. pap. 12.95 (978-0-15-205065-8(5)) National Geographic School Publishing, Inc.

Burningham, John. Picnic. Burningham, John, illus. 2014. (ENG., Illus.). 32p. (J). (-k). 16.99 (978-0-7636-6945-4(8)) Candlewick Pr.

Cabot, Meg. Blast from the Past. 2010. (Allie Finkle's Rules for Girls Ser.: 6). (ENG.). 240p. (J). (gr. 3-7). 15.99 (978-0-545-04048-8(5), Scholastic Pr.) Scholastic, Inc.

Carr, Elias. Ava y el Picnic Raquitico. Garton, Michael, illus. 2016. (SPA.). (J). **(978-1-5064-2095-0(8))** Augsburg Fortress, Pubs.

Cleveland, Marie. Jason's Giant Dilemma: A Storybook Land Adventure. 2007. 76p. per. 19.95 (978-1-4241-7811-7(8)) America Star Bks.

Condon, Bill. Planet Puzzle, 1 vol. 2013. (Fiction Readers Ser.). (ENG., Illus.). 28p. (J). (gr. 2-2). pap. 6.99 (978-1-4333-5562-2(0)) Shell Educational Publishing.

Cowan, Charlotte. Moose with Loose Poops. Neal, Penelope, illus. 2008. (Dr. Hippo Ser.). (ENG.). 32p. (J). (gr. -1-2). 17.95 (978-0-9753516-5-9(6)) Hippocratic Pr., The.

Cronin, Doreen. Click, Clack, Quackity-Quack: A Typing Adventure. Lewin, Betsy, illus. 2008. (Click, Clack Book Ser.). (ENG.). 14p. (J). (gr. -1-k). 14.99 (978-1-4169-5517-7(8), Little Simon) Little Simon.

—Click, Clack, Quackity-Quack: An Alphabetical Adventure. Lewin, Betsy, illus. 2005. (Click, Clack Book Ser.). (ENG.). 24p. (J). (gr. -1-3). 17.99 (978-0-689-87715-5(3), Atheneum Bks. for Young Readers) Simon & Schuster Children's Publishing.

Cronin, Doreen & Lewin, Betsy. Click, Clack, Quackity-Quack: An Alphabetical Adventure. 2006. (Doreen Cronin: Click-Clack & More Ser.). (ENG.). (gr. -1-3). lib. bdg. 24.21 (978-1-59961-089-4(2)) Spotlight.

Davis, Catherine. Abby & Alex Feel Their Hearts' Little. 2006. 57p. pap. 16.95 (978-1-4241-4586-7(4)) PublishAmerica, Inc.

DiTerlizzi, Tony & DiTerlizzi, Angela. Yummy Trip! DiTerlizzi, Tony, illus. 2010. (Adventure of Meno Ser.: 3). (ENG., Illus.). 48p. (J). (gr. -1-k). 9.99 (978-1-4169-7150-4(5), Simon & Schuster Bks. For Young Readers) Simon & Schuster Bks. For Young Readers.

Dotlich, Rebecca Kai. Peanut & Pearl's Picnic Adventure. Alley, R. W., illus. 2008. (My First I Can Read Ser.). (ENG.). 32p. (J). (gr. -1 — 1). pap. 3.99 (978-0-06-054922-0(X)) HarperCollins Pubs.

Elder, Elizabeth. When I'm with You. Mansmann, Leslie, illus. 2003. (ENG.). 32p. (J). 15.95 (978-0-9671662-8-5(4)) Islandport Pr., Inc.

Etting, Tali. Max's Amazing Adventure. 2011. (Illus.). 32p. 14.09 (978-1-4567-7251-2(1)) AuthorHouse.

Fellure, Kathy Boyd. Mr Snowman Ate Our Picnic Lunch. 2011. 36p. pap. 16.95 (978-0-557-79684-7(9)) Lulu Pr., Inc.

Flor Ada, Alma. Celebrate Fourth of July with Champ, the Scamp. Mazali, Gustavo, illus. 2006. (Cuentos para Celebrar / Stories to Celebrate Ser.). 30p. (gr. k-6). per. 11.95 (978-1-59820-131-4(X)) Santillana USA Publishing Co., Inc.

Flowerpot Press, contrib. by. Sockheadz: Picnic. 2013. (ENG., Illus.). 20p. (J). (gr. -1-k). 8.99 (978-1-77093-616-4(5)) Flowerpot Children's Pr. Inc. CAN. Dist: Cardinal Pubs. Group.

Froeb, Lori. A Sister's Love: Storybook & Necklace. 2016. (ENG.). 32p. (J). (gr. -1-k). 14.99 (978-0-7944-3574-5(2), Reader's Digest Children's Bks.) Studio Fun International.

Gallo, Lisa. A Picnic Adventure. Thomas, Laura, illus. 2010. (Strawberry Shortcake Ser.). (ENG.). 32p. (J). (gr. 1-3). mass mkt. 3.99 (978-0-448-45345-3(2), Penguin Young Readers) Penguin Young Readers Group.

Geraldi, Michele J. Pennies at Piper Park. 2009. 24p. pap. 12.99 (978-1-4389-2829-6(7)) AuthorHouse.

Giurco, Diane. The Adventures of Willy & Nilly. 2008. (Illus.). 32p. pap. 14.49 (978-1-4389-1134-2(3)) AuthorHouse.

Glass, Graeme. A Bee's Kiss. Trone, Jo, illus. 2012. 60p. pap. 21.50 (978-1-61897-383-2(5), Strategic Bk. Publishing) Strategic Book Publishing & Rights Agency (SBPRA).

Glennon, Michelle. My Big Green Teacher: Taking the Green Road. Glennon, Michelle, illus. 2008. (Illus.). 32p. (J). 19.95 (978-0-9796625-7-7(5)) GDG Publishing.

Goode, Diane. The Most Perfect Spot. Goode, Diane, illus. 2006. (ENG., Illus.). 32p. (J). (gr. -1-3). 16.99 (978-0-06-072697-3(0)) HarperCollins Pubs.

Goodrich, C. C. Barnabee: At the Picnic. 2009. (Illus.). 32p. pap. 13.99 (978-1-4389-8388-2(3)) AuthorHouse.

Gupta, Jennifer. Silly Turtle! That's Not on the Menu! 2008. 28p. pap. 13.99 (978-1-4343-9183-4(3)) AuthorHouse.

Harris, Robie H. What's So Yummy? All about Eating Well & Feeling Good. Westcott, Nadine Bernard, illus. 2014. (Let's Talk about You & Me Ser.). (ENG.). 40p. (J). (-k). 15.99 (978-0-7636-3632-6(0)) Candlewick Pr.

Holden, Pam. A Quick Picnic, 6 pack. Ross, Christine, illus. 2009. (Red Rocket Readers Ser.). (ENG.). 16p. (gr. -1-1). pap. (978-1-877363-22-1(7), Red Rocket Readers) Flying Start Bks.

Holub, Joan. Picnic! A Day in the Park. Terry, Will, illus. 2008. (Ant Hill Ser.). (ENG.). 24p. (J). (gr. -1-k). pap. 3.99 (978-1-4169-5133-9(4), Simon Spotlight) Simon Spotlight.

Honigsberg, Peter John. Too Much Picnic. Jones, Ryan, illus. 2006. 32p. (J). 16.95 (978-1-57143-154-7(3)) RDR Bks.

Jacqueline, Thomas. Birthday Picnic. 2010. 24p. pap. 9.99 (978-0-88144-493-3(6)) Yorkshire Publishing Group.

Jennings, Sharon, et al, adapted by. Franklin's Picnic. 2006. (Kids Can Read Ser.). (ENG., Illus.). 32p. (J). (gr. 1-2). 14.95 (978-1-55337-714-6(1)) Kids Can Pr., Ltd. CAN. Dist: Hachette Bk. Group.

Judson, Clara Ingram. Mary Jane: Her Book. 2007. 88p. per. (978-1-4065-4677-4(1)) Dodo Pr.

Jumbo & the Stranger. 2004. (J). per. 15.99 (978-0-9744205-5-4(7)) Golden Eagle Publishing Hse., Inc.

Katzler, Eva. Florentine & Pig. Mikhail, Jess, illus. 2012. (ENG.). 32p. (J). 17.89 (978-1-59990-949-3(9), 9781599909493); (gr. -1-6). 16.99 (978-1-59990-847-2(6), 9781599908472) Bloomsbury Publishing USA. (Bloomsbury USA Childrens).

Kennedy, Anne Vittur. The Farmer's Away! Baa! Neigh! Kennedy, Anne Vittur, illus. 2014. (ENG., Illus.). 32p. (J). (-k). 15.99 (978-0-7636-6679-8(3)) Candlewick Pr.

Kennedy, Jimmy. The Teddy Bears' Picnic. Day, Alexandra, illus. 2015. (Classic Board Bks.). (ENG.). 34p. (J). (gr. -1-k). bds. 7.99 (978-1-4814-2274-1(X), Little Simon) Little Simon.

Khing, T. T. Where Is the Cake? 2010. (ENG & DUT., Illus.). 32p. (J). (gr. -1-3). pap. 7.95 (978-0-8109-8924-5(7)) UK Abrams Bks. for Young Readers.

Kids Can Press Staff. Franklin's Picnic. 2006. (Kids Can Read Ser.). (ENG., Illus.). 32p. (J). (gr. 1-2). 3.95 (978-1-55337-715-3(X)) Kids Can Pr., Ltd. CAN. Dist: Hachette Bk. Group.

Klein, Adria F. Max Come Al Aire Libre, 1 vol. Robledo, Sol, tr. from ENG. Gallagher-Cole, Mernie, illus. 2007. (Read-It! Readers en Español: la Vida de Max Ser.). (SPA.). 24p. (gr. -1-3). lib. bdg. 21.32 (978-1-4048-3795-9(7), Easy Readers) Picture Window Bks.

Krishnaswami, Uma. The Ants Have a Picnic. 2006. (Early Explorers Ser.). (J). pap. (978-1-4108-6115-3(5)) Benchmark Education Co.

Kruusval, Catarina. Franny's Friends. Sandin, Joan, tr. from SWE. 2008. (Illus.). 32p. (J). (gr. -1-1). 16.00 (978-91-29-66836-0(0)) R & S Bks. SWE. Dist: Macmillan.

Levy, Janey. The Piggles Picnic. 2006. (Neighborhood Readers Ser.). (ENG.). 12p. (gr. -1-3). pap. 5.90 (978-1-4042-6455-7(8), Rosen Classroom) Rosen Publishing Group, Inc., The.

Lies, Brian. Bats at the Beach. (Bat Book Ser.). (ENG., Illus.). 32p. (J). (gr. -1 — 1). 2011. bds. 11.99 (978-0-547-55437-2(0)) 2006. 17.99 (978-0-618-55744-8(X)) Houghton Mifflin Harcourt Publishing Co.

Lovell, H. N. Wootie's Delightful Picnic. 2006. (J). pap. 12.95 (978-0-9761182-4-4(6)) Alpha Run Pr., LLC.

Lucy's Picnic. 2006. (J). (978-0-9764719-3-6(0)) MiceWorks.

Mack, Jeff, illus. Good News, Bad News. 2012. (ENG.). 40p. (J). (gr. -1-1). 16.99 (978-1-4521-0110-1(8)) Chronicle Bks. LLC.

McCully, Emily Arnold. Picnic. McCully, Emily Arnold, illus. 2003. (Illus.). 32p. (J). (gr. -1-k). 16.89 (978-0-06-623855-5(2)); (ENG., 17.99 (978-0-06-623854-8(4)) HarperCollins Pubs.

Mello, Alondra. Alanora's Magic Tree: Alanora's Spirit Journey. 2007. 48p. per. 12.97 (978-1-932344-77-6(2)) Thornton Publishing, Inc.

Mendicino, Ellen, et al. Zuko the Zany Dog. 2013. 70p. pap. 9.99 (978-0-9890288-0-6(1)) Mindstir Media.

Michaels, Evan. Tressa & Dan's Picnic at the Zoo. 2010. (Illus.). 34p. (J). pap. 19.95 (978-0-9826865-0-8(1)) Win Publishing, LLC.

Michiko Florence, Debbi. The Disappearing Picnic. Roe, Monika, illus. 2016. (Dorothy & Toto Ser.). (ENG.). 40p. (gr. k-2). lib. bdg. 21.32 (978-1-4795-8704-9(4)) Capstone Press of Coughlan Cos.

Miles, Ryan. The Picnic Nightmare. 2012. 24p. pap. 24.95 (978-1-4512-7153-9(0)) America Star Bks.

Murphy, Mary. Panda Foo & the New Friend. Murphy, Mary, illus. 2007. (ENG., Illus.). 32p. (J). (gr. k-k). 15.99 (978-0-7636-3405-6(0)) Candlewick Pr.

Murphy, Stuart J. Freda Organiza una Merienda. 2011. (I See I Learn Ser.). (SPA & ENG., Illus.). 32p. (J). (-k). 14.95 (978-1-58089-488-3(7)); pap. 6.95 (978-1-58089-489-0(5)) Charlesbridge Publishing, Inc.

—Freda Plans a Picnic. 2010. (I See I Learn Ser.). (ENG., Illus.). 32p. (J). (gr. -1-k). 14.95 (978-1-58089-456-2(9)); pap. 6.95 (978-1-58089-457-9(7)) Charlesbridge Publishing, Inc.

Myott, Lanita. RJ Saves the Day. 2003. 19p. 11.16 (978-1-4116-0354-7(0)) Lulu Pr., Inc.

Nash, Andy. Tatum & Her Tiger: For Kids Blessed with Passion. 2007. (Illus.). (J). 9.99 (978-0-8127-0451-8(7)) Autumn Hse. Publishing Co.

Naylor, Phyllis Reynolds. Please Do Feed the Bears. Escriva, Ana Lopez, illus. 2007. (ENG.). 40p. (J). (gr. -1-2). 11.99 (978-1-4169-6750-7(8), Simon & Schuster/Paula Wiseman Bks.) Simon & Schuster/Paula Wiseman Bks.

Nelson, Jim. Crosstown Crush. 2005. 82p. Vol. 1, Bk. 1. (YA). pap. 9.00 (978-1-4116-5266-8(5)) Vol. 1,Bk. 2. pap. 9.00 (978-1-4116-6654-2(2)) Lulu Pr., Inc.

Paterson, Brian. The Picnic: Board Book. 2006. (ENG., Illus.). 16p. (J). (gr. -1). bds. 6.99 (978-0-00-717421-8(7), HarperCollins Children's Bks.) HarperCollins Pubs. Ltd. GBR. Dist: Trafalgar Square Publishing.

Patty & Pop's Picnic: Take-Home Book. 2005. (Emergent Library: Vol. 2). (YA). (gr. -1-1). 12.60 (978-0-8215-7262-7(8)) Sadlier, William H. Inc.

Phillipps, J. C. The Simples Love a Picnic. 2014. (ENG., Illus.). 32p. (J). (gr. -1-3). 16.99 (978-0-544-16667-7(1), HMH Books For Young Readers) Houghton Mifflin Harcourt Publishing Co.

The Picnic, 6 Packs. (gr. k-1). 23.00 (978-0-7635-8836-6(9)) Rigby Education.

Piggy Toes Press Staff. All the Way's I Love You Mini. Downing, Julie, illus. 2005. (ENG.). 10p. (J). 4.95 (978-1-58117-437-3(3), Intervisual/Piggy Toes) Bendon, Inc.

Pittar, Gill. Milly, Molly & the Picnic. Morrell, Cris, illus. 2005. 28p. (gr. -1). pap. (978-1-86972-045-2(8)) Milly Molly Bks.

Polacco, Patricia. Picnic at Mudsock Meadow. 2009. (ENG.). 32p. (J). (gr. k-3). pap. 7.99 (978-0-14-241392-0(5), Puffin Books) Penguin Young Readers Group.

Rathmann, Peggy. The Day the Babies Crawled Away. Rathmann, Peggy, illus. 2003. (ENG., Illus.). 40p. (J). (gr. -1-k). 17.99 (978-0-399-23196-4(X), G.P. Putnam's Sons Books for Young Readers) Penguin Young Readers Group.

Reid, Hunter. Let's Have a Picnic! Hinton, Stephanie, illus. 2016. (Fluorescent Pop! Ser.). (ENG.). 14p. (J). (gr. -1-k). bds. 5.99 (978-1-4998-0220-7(X)) Little Bee Books Inc.

Ricci, Christine. Dora's Picnic. Hall, Susan, illus. 2003. (Ready-to-Read Ser.: Vol. 1). (ENG.). 24p. (J). pap. 3.99 (978-0-689-85238-1(X), Simon Spotlight/Nickelodeon) Simon Spotlight/Nickelodeon.

Rigby Education Staff. Headline News. (Sails Literacy Ser.). (Illus.). 16p. (gr. 1-2). 27.00 (978-0-7635-9930-0(1), 699301C99) Rigby Education.

Ritchey, Kate. A Perfect Picnic. 2013. (Mickey & Friends World of Reading Ser.). (J). lib. bdg. 13.55 (978-0-606-31753-5(8), Turtleback) Turtleback Bks.

Rosenthal, Betsy R. Porcupine's Picnic: Who Eats What? Capizzi, Giusi, illus. 2017. (ENG.). 32p. (gr. -1-2). 19.99 (978-1-4677-9519-7(4)); 30.65 **(978-1-5124-2840-7(X))** Lerner Publishing Group. (Millbrook Pr.).

Santillo, LuAnn. The Picnic. Santillo, LuAnn, ed. 2003. (Half-Pint Kids Readers Ser.). (Illus.). 7p. (J). (gr. -1-1). pap. (978-1-59256-090-5(3)) Half-Pint Kids, Inc.

—The Trip. Santillo, LuAnn, ed. 2003. (Half-Pint Kids Readers Ser.). (Illus.). 7p. (J). (gr. -1-1). pap. 1.00 (978-1-59256-057-8(1)) Half-Pint Kids, Inc.

Sargent-Barker, Erika. Living with a Legend. 2012. 32p. pap. 16.95 (978-1-4626-9618-5(X)) America Star Bks.

Shakespeare, Nancy. Benjamin the Bear Goes on a Picnic. Clouette, Katie, illus. 2013. (Benjamin the Bear Ser.). (ENG.). (J). (gr. -1-3). 14.95 (978-1-62086-314-5(6)) Mascot Bks., Inc.

Simont, Marc. The Stray Dog. Simont, Marc, illus. 2003. (ENG., Illus.). 32p. (J). (gr. -1-3). pap. 6.99 (978-0-06-443669-4(1)) HarperCollins Pubs.

Smith, B. M. My Very Own Picnic Basket: An Evan & Cassie Adventure. 2012. 28p. pap. 24.95 (978-1-4626-7551-7(4)) America Star Bks.

Smythe, Katie. The Summer Picnic. 2015. (Rosen REAL Readers: STEM & STEAM Collection). (ENG.). 8p. pap. 5.46 (978-1-4994-9557-7(9), Rosen Classroom) Rosen Publishing Group, Inc., The.

Snowden, Gary. The Lost Treasure of Hawkins Cave. Pierce Clark, Donna, illus. 2013. 112p. pap. 7.99 (978-1-938768-10-1(8)) Gypsy Pubns.

Spencer, Hannah. With All Best Wishes, Mrs Butterbean. 2008. 28p. pap. 13.50 (978-1-60693-138-7(5), Eloquent Bks.) Strategic Book Publishing & Rights Agency (SBPRA).

Squires, Ricky. Lily & Ike, 1 vol. 2010. 32p. 24.95 (978-1-4512-9308-1(9)) PublishAmerica, Inc.

Stanek, Robert, pseud. Have a Backyard Picnic. 2009. (Bugville Critters Ser.: No. 14). (ENG., Illus.). 52p. (J). 14.95 (978-1-57545-210-4(3), Reagent Pr. Bks. for Young Readers) RP Media.

Stone, Jessica J. Picnic at the Zoo. 2011. 24p. 11.32 (978-1-4567-4386-4(4)) AuthorHouse.

Studio Mouse Staff. Pooh & Piglet. 2008. (ENG., Illus.). 36p. (J). (gr. -1). 7.99 (978-1-59069-419-0(8)) Studio Mouse LLC.

Su, Lucy. Make a Picnic. Su, Lucy, illus. 2003. (Kitten & Baby Kitten Ser.). (Illus.). 32p. (YA). (978-1-85602-445-7(8), Pavilion Children's Books) Pavilion Bks.

Thompson, Lauren. Mouse's First Summer. Erdogan, Buket, illus. 2013. (Classic Board Bks.). (ENG.). 34p. (J). (gr. -1 — 1). bds. 7.99 (978-1-4424-5842-0(9), Little Simon) Little Simon.

—Mouse's First Summer. Erdogan, Buket, illus. 2014. (J). (978-1-4351-5506-0(8)) Simon & Schuster.

Twin Sisters(r) Staff. Five Little Skunks. 2010. (J). (gr. k-2). pap. 4.99 (978-1-59922-509-8(3)) Twin Sisters IP, LLC.

Underwood, Barbara J. Paula's Pickle Picnic. Pfeiffer, Judith, illus. 2006. (ENG.). 20p. (gr. 1-3). pap. 8.95 (978-1-57874-293-6(5), Kaeden Bks.) Kaeden Corp.

—Paula's Pickle Picnic (6 Pack) Pfeiffer, Judith, illus. 2006. (ENG.). 20p. (gr. 1-3). pap. (978-1-57874-294-3(3), Kaeden Bks.) Kaeden Corp.

Ungerer, Tomi. The Mellops Strike Oil. 2011. (ENG., Illus.). 32p. (gr. -1-2). 12.95 (978-0-7148-6249-1(5)) Phaidon Pr., Inc.

Van Stockum, Hilda. A Day on Skates: The Story of a Dutch Picnic. Van Stockum, Hilda, illus. 2007. (Illus.). 40p. (J). (gr. 1). 19.95 (978-1-932350-18-0(7)) Bethlehem Bks.

Wax, Wendy. Picnic Day! Artful Doodlers, illus. 2006. 24p. (J). lib. bdg. 15.00 (978-1-4242-0952-1(8)) Fitzgerald Bks.

Weinberger, Kimberly. Spring Is Here, Hello Kitty! (Hello Kitty) Hino, Sachiho, illus. 2016. (Hello Kitty Ser.). (ENG.). 32p. (J). (gr. k-2). pap. 3.99 (978-1-338-11364-8(X)) Scholastic, Inc.

Wells, Bridget & Wells, Alexis. Mason & Molly: Picnic. 2010. 12p. 13.00 (978-1-4269-3469-8(6)) Trafford Publishing.

Wells, Rosemary. Bunny Mail. Wells, Rosemary, illus. 2004. (Max & Ruby Ser.). (ENG., Illus.). 32p. (J). (gr. -1-k). 15.99 (978-0-670-03630-1(7), Viking Books for Young Readers) Penguin Young Readers Group.

William H. Sadlier Staff. Patty & Pop's Picnic. 2005. (Emergent Library: Vol. 2). (gr. -1-1). 24.00 net. (978-0-8215-8932-8(6)) Sadlier, William H. Inc.

Williams, David K. The Picnic. Ovresat, Laura, illus. 2006. (Green Light Readers Level 1 Ser.). (gr. -1-1). 13.95 (978-0-7569-7209-7(4)) Perfection Learning Corp.

Williams, David K. & Williams, David. The Picnic. Ovresat, Laura, illus. 2006. (Green Light Readers Level 1 Ser.). (ENG.). 24p. (J). (gr. -1-3). pap. 3.95 (978-0-15-205782-4(X)) Houghton Mifflin Harcourt Publishing Co.

Willis, Lisa M. The Bug's Picnic. 2008. 28p. pap. 24.95 (978-1-60563-389-3(5)) America Star Bks.

Yeoman, John. The Bear's Water Picnic. Blake, Quentin, illus. 2011. (ENG.). 40p. (J). (gr. k-k). pap. 12.99 (978-1-84939-004-0(5)) Andersen Pr. GBR. Dist: Independent Pubs. Group.

Young, Lauren. Ally M. & Ally G. Rooney, Sandra, illus. 2006. 20p. (J). 9.95 (978-1-4120-8518-2(7)) Trafford Publishing.

Young, Polly G. Pokey Pig's Picnic. Raymond, Janet Y., illus. 2007. (J). pap. 15.00 (978-0-8059-7298-6(6)) Dorrance Publishing Co., Inc.

PICTOGRAPHS

see Picture-Writing

PICTORIAL WORKS

see Pictures

PICTURE BOOKS

see also Stories without Words

Abadzis, Nick. Pigs Might Fly. Dye, Jerel, illus. 2017. (Pigs Might Fly Ser.). (ENG.). 208p. (J). pap. 15.99 (978-1-62672-086-2(X), 9781626720862, First Second Bks.) Roaring Brook Pr.

Abnett, Dan & Lanning, Andy. Penguins of Madagscar: The Great Drain Robbery. 2015. (ENG., Illus.). 112p. (J). (gr. 1-4). pap. 14.99 (978-1-78276-695-7(2)) Titan Bks. Ltd. GBR. Dist: Penguin Random Hse. LLC.

Abnett, Dan, et al. Dreamworks Classics, Shrek & Madagascar, Game On, Vol. 3. Gallant, S., illus. 2016. (ENG.). 64p. (J). (gr. 3-7). pap. 6.99 (978-1-78276-248-5(5)) Titan Bks. Ltd. GBR. Dist: Penguin Random Hse. LLC.

—Shrek & Madagascar, Vol. 1. 2015. (ENG., Illus.). 64p. (J). (gr. 1-4). pap. 6.99 (978-1-78276-246-1(9)) Titan Bks. Ltd. GBR. Dist: Penguin Random Hse. LLC.

Abrams, Pam. Now I Eat My ABC's. Wolf, Bruce, illus. 2004. (ENG.). 8p. (J). (gr. k — 1). bds. 7.99 (978-0-439-64942-1(0), Cartwheel Bks.) Scholastic, Inc.

Abramson, Beverley. Off We Go! 2006. (ENG., Illus.). 24p. (J). (gr. -1-k). 15.95 (978-0-88776-728-9(1), Tundra Bks.) Tundra Bks. CAN. Dist: Penguin Random Hse. LLC.

Accord Publishing Staff. Where Does Love Come From? Kirkova, Milena, illus. 2012. (ENG.). 18p. (J). bds. 5.99 (978-1-4494-2884-6(3)) Andrews McMeel Publishing.

Acreman, Hayley. Found You Rabbit! Acreman, Hayley, illus. 2011. (ENG., Illus.). 34p. (J). (gr. k-2). pap. 9.95 (978-1-905762-87-3(9)) Parthian Bks. GBR. Dist: Independent Pubs. Group.

Adam, Guillain & Guillain, Charlotte. Treats for a T. Rex. Wildish, Lee, illus. 2nd ed. 2016. (George's Amazing Adventures Ser.). (ENG.). 32p. (J). (gr. -1-k). pap. 10.99 (978-1-4052-7362-6(3)) Egmont Bks., Ltd. GBR. Dist: Independent Pubs. Group.

Adams, Ben. Chico Plays Hide & Seek. Cameron, Craig, illus. 2013. (Googly Eyes Ser.). (ENG.). 12p. (J). (gr. -1-k). bds. 6.99 (978-1-84322-280-4(9), Armadillo) Anness Publishing GBR. Dist: National Bk. Network.

—The Pig with the Curliest Tail. Cameron, Craig, illus. 2013. (Googly Eyes Ser.). (ENG.). 12p. (J). (gr. -1-k). bds. 6.99 (978-1-84322-618-5(9), Armadillo) Anness Publishing GBR. Dist: National Bk. Network.

—Polly the Farm Puppy. Cameron, Craig, illus. 2013. (Googly Eyes Ser.). (ENG.). 12p. (J). (gr. -1-k). bds. 6.99 (978-1-84322-319-1(8), Armadillo) Anness Publishing GBR. Dist: National Bk. Network.

Adams, Chris. Dan the Biggest Dump Truck, Vol. Briggs-Greenberg, Ruthie, illus. 2017. (ENG.). 40p. (J). (gr. -1-2). 15.95 (978-1-63076-056-4(0)) Muddy Boots Pr.

Adams, Jennifer. Alice in Wonderland: A Colors Primer, 1 vol. Oliver, Alison, illus. 2012. (ENG.). 22p. (J). (gr. k-1). bds. 9.99 (978-1-4236-2477-6(7)) Gibbs Smith, Publisher.

—A Christmas Carol: A Babylit Colors Primer, 1 vol. Oliver, Alison, illus. 2012. (ENG.). 22p. (J). (gr. k-1). bds. 9.99 (978-1-4236-2575-9(7)) Gibbs Smith, Publisher.

—Dracula, 1 vol. Oliver, Alison, illus. 2012. (ENG.). 22p. (J). (gr. k-1). bds. 9.99 (978-1-4236-2480-6(7)) Gibbs Smith, Publisher.

—Edgar & the Tattle-Tale Heart Board Book, 1 vol. Stucki, Ron, illus. 2015. (ENG.). 34p. (J). bds. 9.99 (978-1-4236-4176-6(0)) Gibbs Smith, Publisher.

—Edgar Gets Ready for Bed, 1 vol. Stucki, Ron, illus. 2014. (ENG.). 32p. (J). 16.99 (978-1-4236-3528-4(0)) Gibbs Smith, Publisher.

—Edgar Gets Ready for Bed Board Book, 1 vol. Stucki, Ron, illus. 2015. (ENG.). 22p. (J). bds. 9.99 (978-1-4236-4175-9(2)) Gibbs Smith, Publisher.

—Jane Eyre: A Counting Primer, 1 vol. Oliver, Alison, illus. 2012. (ENG.). 22p. (J). (gr. k-1). bds. 9.99 (978-1-4236-2474-5(2)) Gibbs Smith, Publisher.

—A Midsummer Night's Dream: A Babylit Fairies Primer, 1 vol. Oliver, Alison, illus. 2016. (ENG.). 22p. (J). bds. 9.99 (978-1-4236-4181-0(7)) Gibbs Smith, Publisher.

—Moby-Dick, 1 vol. Oliver, Alison, illus. 2013. (ENG.). 22p. (J). (gr. k-1). bds., bds. 9.99 (978-1-4236-3204-7(4)) Gibbs Smith, Publisher.

—Pride & Prejudice: A Counting Primer, 1 vol. Oliver, Alison, illus. 2011. (ENG.). 22p. (J). (gr. k-1). bds. 9.99 (978-1-4236-2202-4(2)) Gibbs Smith, Publisher.

—Sense & Sensibility: An Opposites Primer, 1 vol. Oliver, Alison, illus. 2013. (ENG.). 22p. (J). (gr. k-1). bds., bds. 9.99 (978-1-4236-3170-5(6)) Gibbs Smith, Publisher.

—Wuthering Heights: A Weather Primer, 1 vol. Oliver, Alison, illus. 2013. (ENG.). 22p. (J). (gr. k-1). bds., bds. 9.99 (978-1-4236-3173-6(0)) Gibbs Smith, Publisher.

Adams, Pam, illus. The Farmer in the Dell. 2013. (Classic Books with Holes 8x8 with CD Ser.). (ENG.). 16p. (J). (gr. -1). pap. incl. audio compact disk (978-1-84643-624-6(9)) Child's Play International Ltd.

Adams, Sarah. Gary & Ray. 2012. (Illus.). 36p. (J). pap. (978-1-84780-260-6(5), Frances Lincoln) Quarto Publishing Group UK.

Adams, Wayne. Laci the Ladybug. Kern, Shelly, illus. 2012. 16p. pap. 24.95 (978-1-4626-7615-6(4)) America Star Bks.

Adams, William J. Hate That Thunder/Odio Ese Trueno, 1 vol. Stiglich, Tom, illus. 2007. (Mandy & Andy Bks.). (ENG & SPA.). 49p. (J). (gr. k-2). per. 10.95 (978-0-9772757-1-7(X)) Mandy & Andy Bks., Inc.

Adamson, Jean. Topsy & Tim: First Sleepover. 2016. (Topsy & Tim Ser.). (ENG., Illus.). 32p. (J). (gr. -1-k). pap. 9.99 **(978-0-241-18970-2(5))** Penguin Bks., Ltd. GBR. Dist: Independent Pubs. Group.

—Topsy & Tim Go for Gold. Worsley, Belinda & Adamson, Gareth, illus. 2016. (Topsy & Tim Ser.). (ENG.). 32p. (J). (gr. -1-1). pap. 9.99 **(978-1-4093-0946-8(0))** Penguin Bks., Ltd. GBR. Dist: Independent Pubs. Group.

Adewoyin, Beverly. Inside the Mommie Pond. 2013. (ENG.). 28p. (J). pap. 11.95 (978-1-4327-9703-4(4)) Outskirts Pr., Inc.

Adler, David A. Money Madness. Miller, Edward, illus. 2009. (ENG.). 32p. (J). (gr. -1-3). pap. 7.99 (978-0-8234-2272-2(0)) Holiday Hse., Inc.

—A Picture Book of Patrick Henry. Wallner, John et al, illus. 2005. (ENG.). 32p. (J). (gr. k-3). pap. 6.95 (978-0-8234-1678-3(X)) Holiday Hse., Inc.

Adler, David A. & Adler, Michael S. A Picture Book of Cesar Chavez. Olofsdotter, Marie, illus. 2011. (ENG.). 32p. (J). pap. 7.99 (978-0-8234-2383-5(2)) Holiday Hse., Inc.

—A Picture Book of Harry Houdini. Matt, Collins, illus. 2010. (ENG.). 32p. (J). (gr. -1-3). pap. 7.99 (978-0-8234-2302-6(6)) Holiday Hse., Inc.

Agee, Jon. Little Santa. 2015. (ENG., Illus.). 34p. (J). (— 1). bds. 7.99 (978-0-525-42940-1(9), Dial Bks) Penguin Young Readers Group.

Aguirre, Zuriñe. Sardines of Love. Aguirre, Zuriñe, illus. 2015. (Child's Play Library). (ENG., Illus.). 36p. (J). (978-1-84643-726-7(1)) Child's Play International Ltd.

Ajmera, Maya & Derstine, Elise Hofer. Music Everywhere! Pon, Cynthia, illus. 2014. (ENG.). 32p. (J). (gr. -1-3). pap. 7.95 (978-1-57091-937-4(2)) Charlesbridge Publishing, Inc.

Akiona, Micalynn. My Mom Can Do Anything. 2011. 28p. pap. 15.99 (978-1-4568-2006-0(0)) Xlibris Corp.

Albee, Sarah. The Bunny Hop (Sesame Street) 2015. (Little Golden Book Ser.). (ENG., Illus.). 24p. (J). (-k). 4.99 (978-0-553-50798-0(2), Golden Bks.) Random Hse. Children's Bks.

—Elmo's 12 Days of Christmas. Swanson, Maggie, illus. 2015. (Little Golden Book Ser.). (ENG.). 24p. (J). (-k). 4.99 (978-0-553-52430-7(5), Golden Bks.) Random Hse. Children's Bks.

—Halloween ABC. Woolf, Julia, illus. 2015. (Little Golden Board Book Ser.). (ENG.). 26p. (J). (-k). bds. 7.99 (978-0-553-52422-2(4), Random Hse. Bks. for Young Readers) Random Hse. Children's Bks.

—The Monsters on the Bus (Sesame Street) Ewers, Joe, illus. 2013. (Little Golden Book Ser.). (ENG.). 24p. (J). (-k). 4.99 (978-0-307-98058-8(8), Golden Bks.) Random Hse. Children's Bks.

Albers, Josef. Squares & Other Shapes: With Josef Albers. 2016. (ENG., Illus.). 30p. (gr. -1 — 1). bds. 9.95 (978-0-7148-7256-8(3)) Phaidon Pr., Inc.

Albers, Joseph. Squares & Other Shapes: With Josef Albers. 2016. (ENG., Illus.). 30p. bds. 9.95 (978-0-7148-7255-1(5)) Phaidon Pr., Inc.

Albon, Lucie, illus. Little Ballerina: A Children's Book Inspired by Edgar Degas. 2011. (ENG.). 32p. (J). (gr. -1-3). 14.95 (978-3-7913-7081-1(2)) Prestel Verlag GmbH & Co KG. DEU. Dist: Penguin Random Hse. LLC.

Alborozo. The Acrobat. 2013. (Child's Play Library). (ENG., Illus.). 32p. (J). pap. (978-1-84643-633-8(8)) Child's Play International Ltd.

Alborozo, Gabriel. The Colour Thief. 2015. (ENG., Illus.). 32p. (J). (gr. -1-1). 18.99 (978-1-4088-4753-4(1), 9781408847534, Bloomsbury USA Childrens) Bloomsbury Publishing USA.

Album, Jenny. Bea Gives up Her Dummy: The Book That Makes Children Want to Move on from Dummies! Keay, Claire, illus. 2015. (ENG.). 50p. (J). pap. (978-0-9926167-3-1(5)) Little Boo Publishing.

Alemagna, Beatrice. The Bug Next Door. David, Annette, tr. from FRE. 2012. (ENG., Illus.). 40p. (gr. -1-4). 12.95 (978-0-7148-6356-6(4)) Phaidon Pr., Inc.

—The Misfits. 2017. (ENG., Illus.). 40p. (J). (gr. -1-k). 18.99 (978-1-84780-637-6(6), Frances Lincoln) Quarto Publishing Group UK GBR. Dist: Hachette Bk. Group.

Alemagna, Beatrice. On a Magical Do-Nothing Day. Alemagna, Beatrice, illus. 2017. (Illus.). 48p. (J). (gr. -1-3). 17.99 **(978-0-06-265760-2(7))** HarperCollins Pubs.

Alemanno, Andrea. A Surprise for Lady Lily. 2014. (ENG., Illus.). 36p. 16.99 (978-88-97737-30-8(7)) Officina Libraria srl ITA. Dist: National Bk. Network.

Alexander, Christian. The Granimal. Fenton, Tanya, illus. 2016. (ENG.). 155p. (J). (gr. -1-3). pap. 11.99 (978-1-907432-22-4(1)) Hogs Back Bks. GBR. Dist: Independent Pubs. Group.

Alexander, Claire. Millie Shares. 2014. (ENG., Illus.). 32p. (J). (gr. -1-k). pap. 9.99 (978-1-4052-6409-9(8)) Egmont Bks., Ltd. GBR. Dist: Independent Pubs. Group.

Alexander, Liza. Splish-Splash Spring! (Sesame Street) Ewers, Joe, illus. 2016. (Pictureback Ser.). (ENG.). 24p. (J). (gr. -1-3). 4.99 (978-1-101-93429-6(8), Random Hse. Bks. for Young Readers) Random Hse. Children's Bks.

Alkhayyat, Mithaa. My Own Special Way. Sharafeddini, Fatima, tr. Fidawi, Maya, illus. 2012. (ENG.). 64p. (J). (gr. -1-k). pap. 7.99 (978-1-4440-0320-8(8), Orion Children's Bks.) Hachette Children's Group GBR. Dist: Hachette Bk. Group.

Alko, Selina, illus. My Fathers World. 2006. 36p. (J). 14.99 (978-0-7847-1440-9(1), 04075) Standard Publishing.

Allabach, P. R. Dragon & Captain. Tumbloom, Lucas, illus. 2015. (ENG.). 32p. (J). (gr. k-2). 17.95 (978-1-936261-33-8(2)) Flashlight Pr.

Allan, Jo. Hungry Hettie, 1 vol. 2010. (ENG., Illus.). 24p. (J). (gr. -1-1). 11.95 (978-0-86315-779-0(3)) Floris Bks. GBR. Dist: SteinerBooks, Inc.

Allan, Nicholas. The Royal Nappy. Allan, Nicholas, illus. 2013. (ENG., Illus.). 32p. (J). pap. 10.99 (978-1-78295-025-7(7), Red Fox) Random House Children's Books GBR. Dist: Independent Pubs. Group.

Allen, Constance. My Name Is Elmo (Sesame Street) Swanson, Maggie, illus. 2016. (Little Golden Board Book Ser.). (ENG.). 26p. (J). (— 1). bds. 7.99 (978-1-101-93746-4(7), Golden Bks.) Random Hse. Children's Bks.

—Peekaboo, Elmo! (Sesame Street) Prebenna, David, illus. 2014. (Big Bird's Favorites Board Bks.). (ENG.). 24p. (J). (— 1). bds. 4.99 (978-0-449-81483-3(1), Random Hse. Bks. for Young Readers) Random Hse. Children's Bks.

Allen, Debbie. Dancing in the Wings. Nelson, Kadir, illus. 2003. (ENG.). 32p. (J). (gr. -1-3). 7.99 (978-0-14-250141-2(7), Puffin Books) Penguin Young Readers Group.

Allen, Elaine Ann. Olly Explores 7 Wonders of the Chesapeake Bay, 1 vol. Nash, Kelli, illus. 2015. (ENG.). 32p. (J). 16.99 (978-0-7643-4938-6(4), 9780764349386) Schiffer Publishing, Ltd.

Allen, Kathryn Madeline. A Kiss Means I Love You. Futran, Eric, photos by. 2016. (ENG., Illus.). 16p. (J). (gr. -1 — 1). bds. 7.99 (978-0-8075-4189-0(3)) Whitman, Albert & Co.

Allen, Pat. The Field by the Sea. 2010. 20p. 21.50 (978-1-4457-3405-7(2)) Lulu Pr., Inc.

Allen, Traudi. The Squeaky Door. 2012. 40p. pap. 16.95 (978-1-4525-0826-9(7)) Balboa Pr.

Alphablocks. P's Popping Party. 2015. (Alphablocks Ser.). (ENG., Illus.). 24p. (J). (gr. k-2). pap. 8.99 (978-1-4052-7834-8(X)) Egmont Bks., Ltd. GBR. Dist: Independent Pubs. Group.

Altes, Marta. No! 2011. (Child's Play Library). (ENG., Illus.). 32p. (J). (978-1-84643-417-4(3)) Child's Play International Ltd.

Alvarez, Lourdes M. My First Book Alphabet. Brooks, David, illus. 2005. (My First Book Ser.). 9p. (J). (gr. -1-17). bds. 3.95 (978-1-933050-08-9(X)) Sweetwater Pr.

—My First Book Colors. Brooks, David, illus. 2005. (My First Book Ser.). 9p. (J). (gr. -1-1). bds. 3.95 (978-1-933050-07-2(1)) Sweetwater Pr.

—My First Book Numbers. Brooks, David, illus. 2005. (My First Book Ser.). 9p. (J). (gr. -1-1). bds. 3.95 (978-1-933050-06-5(3)) Sweetwater Pr.

—My First Book Shapes. Brooks, David, illus. 2005. (My First Book Ser.). 9p. (J). (gr. -1-1). bds. 3.95 (978-1-933050-11-9(X)) Sweetwater Pr.

The Amazing Body - The Five Senses, 5 vols. 2005. (Amazing Body: the Five Senses Ser.). (ENG., Illus.). 24p. (J). (gr. k-3). 53.30 (978-1-4048-1000-6(5)) Picture Window Bks.

Ambatchew, Daniel. Mimi Mystery. 2012. (Illus.). 39p. pap. 10.95 (978-9988-647-83-4(2)) Sub-Saharan Pubs. & Traders GHA. Dist: African Bks. Collective, Ltd.

American Museum of Natural History. ABC Birds. 2016. (AMNH ABC Board Bks.). (ENG., Illus.). 18p. (J). (gr. -1-k). bds. 7.95 (978-1-4549-1986-5(8)) Sterling Publishing Co., Inc.

—ABC Rainforest. 2016. (AMNH ABC Board Bks.). (ENG., Illus.). 18p. (J). (gr. -1-k). bds. 7.95 (978-1-4549-1746-5(6)) Sterling Publishing Co., Inc.

—ABC Universe. 2015. (AMNH ABC Board Bks.). (ENG., Illus.). 18p. (J). (gr. -1-k). bds. 7.95 (978-1-4549-1409-9(2)) Sterling Publishing Co., Inc.

—Baby Dolphin's First Swim. 2017. (First Discoveries Ser.). (ENG., Illus.). 32p. (J). (gr. -1). 14.95 **(978-1-4549-2236-0(2))** Sterling Publishing Co., Inc.

—Camouflage. 2016. (Science for Toddlers Ser.). (ENG., Illus.). 18p. (J). (gr. -1). bds. 7.95 (978-1-4549-2079-3(3)) Sterling Publishing Co., Inc.

American Museum of Natural History. Sharks. 2017. (Science for Toddlers Ser.). (ENG., Illus.). 26p. (J). (gr. -1). bds. 7.95 **(978-1-4549-2128-8(5))** Sterling Publishing Co., Inc.

American Museum of Natural History & Lach, Will. I Am NOT a Dinosaur! Lambert, Jonny, illus. 2016. (ENG.). 40p. (J). (gr. -1-2). 14.95 (978-1-4549-1491-4(2)) Sterling Publishing Co., Inc.

Amery, H. & Cartwright, S. Three Little Pigs. 2004. (First Stories Ser.). 16p. (J). pap. 4.99 (978-0-7945-0609-4(7)) EDC Publishing.

Amery, Heather. Three Little Pigs. Tyler, Jenny, ed. 2004. (Usborne First Stories Ser.). (Illus.). 16p. (J). (gr. -1). lib. bdg. 12.95 (978-1-58086-623-1(9), Usborne) EDC Publishing.

Amnesty International Staff. Dreams of Freedom: In Words & Pictures. 2015. (ENG., Illus.). 48p. (J). (gr. 1-4). 18.99 (978-1-84780-453-2(5), Frances Lincoln) Quarto Publishing Group UK GBR. Dist: Hachette Bk. Group.

—We Are All Born Free: The Universal Declaration of Human Rights in Pictures. 2016. (ENG., Illus.). 72p. (J). (gr. 1-4). pap. 8.99 (978-1-84780-663-5(5), Frances Lincoln) Quarto Publishing Group UK GBR. Dist: Littlehampton Bk Services, Ltd.

Andersen, Hans Christian. The Little Christmas Tree: With an Advent Calendar Just for You! Downer, Maggie, illus. 2015. (ENG.). 10p. (J). (gr. k-3). bds. 7.99 (978-1-86147-291-5(9), Armadillo) Anness Publishing GBR. Dist: National Bk. Network.

Anderson, Airlie. Cat's Colours. Anderson, Airlie, illus. 2016. (Child's Play Library). (ENG., Illus.). 32p. (J). pap. (978-1-84643-760-1(1)) Child's Play International Ltd.

Anderson, Airlie, illus. Ten Little Ducks. 2008. (Activity Bks.). (ENG.). 24p. (J). (gr. -1-1). (978-1-84643-182-1(4)) Child's Play International Ltd.

Anderson, Doug. Hadley & the Bean. 2004. (Illus.). (J). 16.95 (978-1-59404-038-2(9)) Peanut Butter Publishing.

Anderson, M. T. Me, All Alone, at the End of the World. Hawkes, Kevin, illus. 2017. (ENG.). 48p. (J). (gr. 1-4). 14.99 (978-0-7636-8902-5(5)) Candlewick Pr.

Anderson, Richard. A Home Run for Bunny. Purnell, Gerald, illus. 2013. (ENG.). (J). (gr. -1-3). 16.95 (978-0-9855417-2-9(5)) Inspire Every Child dba Illumination Arts.

Anderson, Ted, et al. My Little Pony: Pony Tales Volume 2: Pony Tales Volume 2. Mebberson, Amy, illus. 2014. (My Little Pony Ser.). (ENG.). 104p. pap. 17.99 (978-1-61377-873-9(2), 9781613778739) Idea & Design Works, LLC.

Anderson, William T. Almanzo Picture Book Biography. Date not set. (Illus.). 40p. (J). (gr. -1-3). 15.99 (978-0-06-028975-1(9)); pap. 5.99 (978-0-06-443684-7(5)); lib. bdg. 16.89 (978-0-06-028976-8(7)) HarperCollins Pubs.

Andreae, Giles. I Love My Daddy. Dodd, Emma, illus. 2014. (ENG.). 26p. (J). (gr. -1 — 1). bds. 6.99 (978-1-4231-9970-0(7)) Hyperion Bks. for Children.

—I Love You Father Christmas. Dodd, Emma, illus. 2016. (ENG.). 24p. (J). (gr. -1 — 1). bds. 8.99 (978-1-4083-3806-7(4), Orchard Bks.) Hachette Children's Group GBR. Dist: Hachette Bk. Group.

—Mad about Mega Beasts! Wojtowycz, David, illus. 2015. (ENG.). 32p. (J). (gr. -1-k). pap. 9.99 (978-1-4083-2936-8(0)) Hodder & Stoughton GBR. Dist: Hachette Bk. Group.

—Morris the Mankiest Monster. McIntyre, Sarah, illus. 2011. (ENG.). 32p. (J). (gr. -1-k). pap. 14.95 (978-0-552-55935-5(0)) Transworld Publishers Ltd. GBR. Dist: Independent Pubs. Group.

—My Little World of Happy, 9 vols. Cronin, Janet, illus. 2013. (World of Happy Ser.). (ENG.). 90p. (J). (— 1). bds. 15.99 (978-1-4052-6082-4(3)) Egmont Bks., Ltd. GBR. Dist: Independent Pubs. Group.

Andrews, Alexa. At the Beach. Keimig, Candice, illus. 2013. (Penguin Young Readers, Level 1 Ser.). (ENG.). 32p. (J). (gr. k-1). 14.99 (978-0-448-46570-8(1)); pap. 3.99 (978-0-448-46471-8(3)) Penguin Young Readers Group. (Penguin Young Readers).

Andrews, Jackie. Great Big Enormous Turnip. Taylor, Lawrie, illus. 2012. (ENG.). 32p. (J). pap. 6.50 (978-1-84135-192-6(X)) Award Pubns. Ltd. GBR. Dist: Parkwest Pubns., Inc.

Andrews, Julie & Hamilton, Emma Walton. A Fairy Merry Christmas. 2012. (Passport to Reading Level 1 Ser.). (J). lib. bdg. 14.75 (978-0-606-26692-5(5), Turtleback) Turtleback Bks.

Andrews, Julie & Walton Hamilton, Emma. The Very Fairy Princess: Valentines from the Heart. Davenier, Christine, illus. 2015. (ENG.). 32p. (J). (gr. -1-3). pap. 5.99 (978-0-316-28324-3(X)) Little, Brown Bks. for Young Readers.

—The Very Fairy Princess - A Winter Wonderland Surprise. Davenier, Christine, illus. 2015. (ENG.). 32p. (J). (gr. -1-3). pap. 5.99 (978-0-316-28306-9(1)) Little, Brown Bks. for Young Readers.

Andrews McMeel Publishing, LLC Staff. Hop, Pop, & Play. 2014. (ENG.). 12p. (J). bds. 5.99 (978-1-4494-6053-2(4)) Andrews McMeel Publishing.

Anfousse, Ginette & Sarrazin, Marisol. Polo et le Garde-Manger. 2003. (Polo Ser.). (FRE., Illus.). 32p. (J). (gr. -1-3). bds. (978-2-89021-601-3(2)) Diffusion du livre Mirabel (DLM).

Anholt, Catherine & Anholt, Laurence. First Words & Pictures. 2014. (ENG., Illus.). 32p. (J). (gr. -1-k). pap. 8.99 (978-1-84780-473-0(X), Frances Lincoln) Quarto Publishing Group UK GBR. Dist: Hachette Bk. Group.

Anholt, Laurence. Babies, Babies, Babies! Anholt, Catherine, illus. 2013. (ENG.). 32p. (J). (gr. -1-k). pap. 9.99 (978-1-4083-1436-4(3)) Hodder & Stoughton GBR. Dist: Hachette Bk. Group.

—The Big Book of Love. Anholt, Catherine, illus. 2017. (ENG.). 32p. (J). (gr. -1-k). pap. 9.99 (978-1-4083-3598-7(0), Orchard Bks.) Hachette Children's Group GBR. Dist: Hachette Bk. Group.

—The Big Book of Love. Anholt, Catherine, illus. 2015. (ENG.). 32p. (J). (gr. -1-k). 13.99 (978-1-4083-3597-0(2)) Hodder & Stoughton GBR. Dist: Hachette Bk. Group.

—Billy & the Big New School. Anholt, Catherine, illus. 2015. (Kipper Ser.). (ENG.). 32p. (J). (gr. -1-k). pap. 10.99 (978-1-4083-3979-4(X)) Hodder & Stoughton GBR. Dist: Hachette Bk. Group.

—Frida Kahlo. 2016. (ENG., Illus.). 32p. (J). 19.99 (978-1-84780-666-6(X), Frances Lincoln Children's Bks.) Quarto Publishing Group UK GBR. Dist: Littlehampton Bk Services, Ltd.

—The Magical Garden of Claude Monet. 2007. (Anholt's Artists Books for Children Ser.). (ENG., Illus.). 32p. (J). (gr. -1-3). (978-0-7641-3855-3(3)) Barron's Educational Series, Inc.

—Tell Us a Story, Papa Chagall. 2015. (ENG., Illus.). 32p. (J). (gr. -1-3). pap. 10.99 (978-1-84780-658-1(9), Frances Lincoln Children's Bks.) Quarto Publishing Group UK GBR. Dist: Hachette Bk. Group.

—Two Nests. Coplestone, Jim, illus. 2013. (ENG.). 32p. (J). (gr. -1-1). 17.99 (978-1-84780-323-8(7), Frances Lincoln) Quarto Publishing Group UK GBR. Dist: Hachette Bk. Group.

—We Love Bears. Anholt, Catherine, illus. 2012. (ENG.). 32p. (J). (gr. -1-k). pap. 10.99 (978-1-4083-1169-1(0)) Hodder & Stoughton GBR. Dist: Hachette Bk. Group.

Anness Publishing Ltd. Let's Look & See: Vehicles. 2014. (ENG., Illus.). 24p. (J). (gr. -1-k). bds. 6.99 (978-1-86147-375-2(3), Armadillo) Anness Publishing GBR. Dist: National Bk. Network.

Anónimo. Juguemos en el Bosque. Bergna, Monica, illus. 2004. (SPA.). 28p. (J). (gr. k-18). pap. 6.50 (978-980-257-282-3(9)) Ekare, Ediciones VEN. Dist: Iaconi, Mariuccia Bk. Imports.

Anthony, Michelle. The Big God Story, 1 vol. Godbey, Cory, illus. 2010. (ENG.). 36p. (J). 12.99 (978-1-4347-6454-6(0)) Cook, David C.

Anthony, Ross. Please Don't Step on the Ants. Anthony, Ross, illus. 2006. (ENG, CHI, SPA & JPN., Illus.). (J). per. (978-0-9727894-4-8(8)) Arizona Blueberry Studios.

Antony, Steve. Green Lizards vs. Red Rectangles. Antony, Steve, illus. 2015. (ENG., Illus.). 32p. (J). (gr. -1-k). 16.99 (978-0-545-84902-9(0), Scholastic Pr.) Scholastic, Inc.

Appel, Dee. The Friends in My Garden. Francour, Kathleen, photos by. Date not set. (Tiny Times Board Book Ser.). (Illus.). 10p. (J). bds. 5.99 (978-0-7369-0564-0(2)) Harvest Hse. Pubs.

—Let's Play Dress Up. Francour, Kathleen, photos by. Date not set. (Tiny Times Board Book Ser.). (Illus.). 10p. (J). bds. 5.99 (978-0-7369-0563-3(4)) Harvest Hse. Pubs.

Apple, Sam. The Saddest Toilet in the World. Ricks, Sam, illus. 2016. (ENG.). 32p. (J). (gr. -1-2). 17.99 (978-1-4814-5122-2(7), Aladdin) Simon & Schuster Children's Publishing.

Archer, Claire. Wolf Spiders, 1 vol. 2014. (Spiders Ser.). (ENG.). 24p. (J). (gr. 4-8). lib. bdg. 28.50 (978-1-62970-076-2(2)) ABDO Publishing Co.

Arcturus Publishing Staff. Santa's Sleigh. 2013. (ENG., Illus.). 10p. (J). bds. 9.95 (978-1-78212-186-2(2)) Arcturus Publishing GBR. Dist: Bookmasters Distribution.

Ardizzone, Edward. Tim All Alone. 2015. (Little Tim Ser.). (ENG., Illus.). 56p. (J). (gr. k-3). 18.99 (978-1-84780-628-4(7), Frances Lincoln) Quarto Publishing Group UK GBR. Dist: Hachette Bk. Group.

—Tim to the Rescue. 2015. (Little Tim Ser.). (ENG., Illus.). 56p. (J). (gr. k-3). 18.99 (978-1-84780-630-7(9), Frances Lincoln) Quarto Publishing Group UK GBR. Dist: Hachette Bk. Group.

—Tim's Friend Towser. 2015. (Little Tim Ser.). (ENG., Illus.). 56p. (J). (gr. -1-2). 18.99 (978-1-84780-631-4(7), Frances Lincoln) Quarto Publishing Group UK GBR. Dist: Hachette Bk. Group.

Ardwin, Juanita. Remember When, 1 vol. 2009. 40p. pap. 19.95 (978-1-4489-2008-2(6)) PublishAmerica, Inc.

Armadillo. Let's Count 123: A Very First Number Book. 2015. (ENG., Illus.). 48p. bds. 9.99 (978-1-86147-659-3(0), Armadillo) Anness Publishing GBR. Dist: National Bk. Network.

—Let's Look & See: Animals. 2014. (ENG., Illus.). 24p. (J). (gr. k-2). bds. 6.99 (978-1-86147-376-9(1), Armadillo) Anness Publishing GBR. Dist: National Bk. Network.

—Let's Look & See: Pets. 2014. (ENG., Illus.). 24p. (J). (gr. k-2). bds. 6.99 (978-1-86147-378-3(8), Armadillo) Anness Publishing GBR. Dist: National Bk. Network.

—Things That Go! Tractors Trucks Trains Planes Helicopters Balloons Ships Ferries Boats Bicycles Motorcycles Cars. 2016. (ENG., Illus.). 48p. (J). (gr. -1-12). bds. 9.99 (978-1-86147-693-7(0), Armadillo) Anness Publishing GBR. Dist: National Bk. Network.

Armadillo Press Staff. My Book of Baby Animals: A Fun-Packed Picture & Puzzle Book for Little Ones. 2016. (ENG., Illus.). 48p. bds. 9.99 (978-1-86147-662-3(0), Armadillo) Anness Publishing GBR. Dist: National Bk. Network.

Armadillo Publishing Staff. Words - Let's Look & See. 2015. (ENG., Illus.). 24p. bds. 6.99 (978-1-86147-485-8(7), Armadillo) Anness Publishing GBR. Dist: National Bk. Network.

Armitage, Ronda. The Pirates. Robins, Arthur, illus. 2013. (ENG.). 32p. (J). (gr. -1-k). pap. 10.99 (978-1-4083-1274-2(3)) Hodder & Stoughton GBR. Dist: Hachette Bk. Group.

—Wave the Flag & Blow the Whistle: A Railway Adventure. Gordon, Andrew, illus. 2012. (ENG.). 32p. (J). (gr. -1-k). 17.99 (978-1-4052-5339-0(8)) Egmont Bks., Ltd. GBR. Dist: Independent Pubs. Group.

Armstrong, Ashley Sage-Taylor. The Adventures of Starlight & Sunny: Building a Dream , How to Focus & Make Your Dreams Come to Life, with Positive Conscious Morals. Picture Boo. 2013. 52p. pap. (978-1-927863-04-6(X)) Armstrong, Ashley.

—The Adventures of Starlight & Sunny: I Am Me ! Who Are You?, How to Find Good Quality Friends & Stand up for One Another, with Positive Morals, Pi. 2013. 52p. pap. (978-1-927863-00-8(7)) Armstrong, Ashley.

—The Adventures of Starlight & Sunny: The Secret Valley , Book 2, How to Be Happy, to Find Inner Beauty & Peace, with Positive Conscious Morals, P. 2013. 52p. pap. (978-0-9919517-9-6(4)) Armstrong, Ashley.

Armstrong, Jeannette C. Dancing with the Cranes. Hall, Ron, illus. 2nd rev. ed. 2009. (ENG.). 24p. pap. 10.95 (978-1-894778-70-1(7)) Theytus Bks., Ltd. CAN. Dist: Univ. of Toronto Pr.

Arnold, Caroline. A Panda's World. Arnold, Caroline, illus. 2015. (Caroline Arnold's Black & White Animals Ser.). (ENG., Illus.). 20p. (gr. -1-2). bds. 7.99 (978-1-4795-6354-8(4)) Picture Window Bks.

Arnold, Nick, et al. Sticker Activity Atlas. (Illus.). 8p. (J). pap. 9.99 (978-0-590-24921-8(5)) Scholastic, Inc.

Arps, Melissa & Lagonegro, Melissa. Beauty & the Beast Big Golden Book (Disney Beauty & the Beast) RH Disney, illus. 2017. (Big Golden Book Ser.). (ENG.). 48p. (J). (gr. -1-2). 9.99 (978-0-7364-3575-8(1), Golden/Disney) Random Hse. Children's Bks.

—Belle's Story. RH Disney, illus. 2017. (Pictureback(R) Ser.). (ENG.). 24p. (J). (gr. -1-1). pap. 4.99 (978-0-7364-3592-5(1), RH/Disney) Random Hse. Children's Bks.

Arruzza, Rick. El Paseo de Sparky. Newton, Pilar, illus. 2003. (SPA.). 24p. mass mkt. 7.95 (978-0-9744509-1-9(X)) Three Spots Productions.

—Sparky's Walk. Newton, Pilar, illus. 2003. 24p. (J). mass mkt. 7.95 (978-0-9744509-0-2(1)) Three Spots Productions.

Arsenault, Moira. Bubbles. 2011. 28p. pap. 15.99 (978-1-4568-5057-9(1)) Xlibris Corp.

Arthur, Clint. Bleep Blop Bloop, 1. Schedeen, Minnie, illus. 2006. 24p. (J). per. 8.99 net. (978-1-4276-0218-3(2)) Aardvark Global Publishing.

Arthur, Jenny. Little Witch. Arthur, Jenny, illus. 2012. (Spooky Sounds Ser.). (ENG., Illus.). 10p. (J). (gr. k — 1). 7.99 (978-0-230-74487-5(7)) Macmillan Pubs., Ltd. GBR. Dist: Independent Pubs. Group.

Asch, Frank. Mr. Maxwell's Mouse, 0 vols. Asch, Devin, illus. 2014. (ENG.). 32p. (J). (gr. k-4). pap. 8.95 (978-1-77138-117-8(5)) Kids Can Pr., Ltd. CAN. Dist: Hachette Bk. Group.

Ashdown, Rebecca. Bob & Flo & the Missing Bucket (Board Book) 2017. (ENG., Illus.). 26p. (J). (— 1). bds. 7.99 (978-0-544-86711-6(4), HMH Books For Young Readers) Houghton Mifflin Harcourt Publishing Co.

Ashman, Linda. Ella WHO? Sanchez, Sara, illus. 2017. (ENG.). 32p. (J). (gr. -1). 14.95 (978-1-4549-1904-9(3)) Sterling Publishing Co., Inc.

—Hey, Coach! Smith, Kim, illus. 2016. (ENG.). 32p. (J). (gr. -1). 14.95 (978-1-4549-1607-9(9)) Sterling Publishing Co., Inc.

—Just Another Morning. Muñoz, Claudio, illus. 2004. (ENG.). 32p. (J). (gr. -1-3). 15.99 (978-0-06-029053-5(6)) HarperCollins Pubs.

Asim, Jabari. Boy of Mine. Pham, LeUyen, illus. 2010. (ENG.). 20p. (J). (gr. -1 — 1). bds. 6.99 (978-0-316-73577-3(9)) Little, Brown Bks. for Young Readers.

—Girl of Mine. Pham, LeUyen, illus. 2010. (ENG.). 20p. (J). (gr. -1 — 1). bds. 6.99 (978-0-316-73578-0(7)) Little, Brown Bks. for Young Readers.

Asquith, Ros & Quarto Generic Staff. It's Not Fairy. 2013. (ENG., Illus.). 32p. (J). (gr. -1-3). 17.99 (978-1-84780-236-1(2), Frances Lincoln) Quarto Publishing Group UK GBR. Dist: Hachette Bk. Group.

Assorted. Once upon a Time ... 2014. (Storytale Treasuries Ser.). (ENG., Illus.). 144p. (J). (gr. -1-k). 14.99 **(978-1-78445-159-2(2))** Top That! Publishing PLC GBR. Dist: Independent Pubs. Group.

—Treasury of Adventure Stories. 2014. (Storytale Treasuries Ser.). (ENG., Illus.). 144p. (J). (gr. -1-k). 14.99 **(978-1-78445-035-9(9))** Top That! Publishing PLC GBR. Dist: Independent Pubs. Group.

Aston, Dianna Hutts. A Rock Is Lively. Long, Sylvia, illus. 2015. (ENG.). 40p. (J). (gr. k-3). 7.99 (978-1-4521-4555-6(5)) Chronicle Bks. LLC.

Atherton, Isabel. Smelly Ghost. Straker, Bethany, illus. 2013. (ENG.). 32p. (J). (gr. -1-k). 14.95 (978-1-62087-989-4(1), 620989, Sky Pony Pr.) Skyhorse Publishing Co., Inc.

Atinuke. Baby Goes to Market. Brooksbank, Angela, illus. 2017. (ENG.). 32p. (J). (gr. -1-2). 16.99 **(978-0-7636-9570-5(X))** Candlewick Pr.

Atkins, Jill. Toad Swims for his Life! Mostyn, David, illus. 2004. (ENG.). 24p. (J). lib. bdg. 23.65 (978-1-59646-712-5(6)) Dingles & Co.

—Tortoise Races Home. Blake, Beccy, illus. 2009. (Tadpoles Ser.). (ENG.). 24p. (J). (gr. -1-2). pap. (978-0-7787-3902-9(3)) Crabtree Publishing Co.

Atkinson, Cale. Where Oliver Fits. 2017. (ENG., Illus.). 40p. (J). (gr. -1-2). 17.99 **(978-1-101-91907-1(8)**, Tundra Bks.) Tundra Bks. CAN. Dist: Penguin Random Hse. LLC.

Atwood, Frederick D. Rocks & Minerals - Pb: A Portrait of the Natural World. 2013. (Portrait of the Natural World Ser.). (Illus.). 72p. pap. 9.95 (978-1-59764-332-0(7)) New Line Bks.

Atwood, Margaret. Up in the Tree, 1 vol. 2010. (ENG., Illus.). 32p. (J). (gr. k-k). 19.95 (978-1-55498-080-2(1)) Groundwood Bks. CAN. Dist: Publishers Group West (PGW).

Auerbach, Annie. Attack of the Boggans. 2013. (Epic Ser.). (ENG., Illus.). 24p. (J). (gr. -1-3). pap. 3.99 *(978-0-06-220989-4(2),* HarperFestival) HarperCollins Pubs.
—Welcome to Moonhaven. 2013. (Epic Ser.). (ENG., Illus.). 24p. (J). (gr. -1-3). pap. 3.99 *(978-0-06-220987-0(6),* HarperFestival) HarperCollins Pubs.
Auerbach, Annie & PopCap Games Staff. The Three Little Pigs Fight Back. Grosvenor, Charles & Roberts, Jeremy, illus. 2013. (Plants vs. Zombies Ser.). (ENG.). 24p. (J). (gr. -1-3). pap. 4.99 *(978-0-06-222838-3(2),* HarperFestival) HarperCollins Pubs.
Aulenback, Stephany. If I Wrote a Book about You. Holmes, Denise, illus. 2014. (ENG.). 32p. (J). (gr. -1-3). 16.95 *(978-1-927018-46-0(3),* 9781927018460) Simply Read Bks. CAN. Dist: Ingram Publisher Services.
Austin, Mike. Monsters Love School. Austin, Mike, illus. 2014. (ENG., Illus.). 40p. (J). (gr. -1-3). 15.99 *(978-0-06-228618-5(8))* HarperCollins Pubs.
Author, Oxford. Oxford Picture Dictionary Content Area for Kids. 2nd ed. 2012. (ENG & SPA., Illus.). 208p. pap. 26.19 *(978-0-19-401777-0(X))* Oxford Univ. Pr., Inc.
—Oxford Picture Dictionary Content Areas for Kids Pack: Reproducibles Collection. 2nd ed. 2012. (ENG.). pap. 290.06 *(978-0-19-401784-8(2))* Oxford Univ. Pr., Inc.
Avery, Emmajane. The Wallace Collection Children's Art Book. 2009. (Wallace Collection). (Illus.). 48p. pap. 20.00 *(978-0-900785-90-0(X))* Holberton, Paul Publishing GBR. Dist: Casemate Pubs. & Bk. Distributors, LLC.
Award, Anna. The Story of Goldilocks. 2012. (ENG.). 24p. (J). pap. 9.95 *(978-1-84135-517-7(8))* Award Pubns. Ltd. GBR. Dist: Parkwest Pubns., Inc.
Award Publications Limited Staff, creator. My First Bumper Colouring Fun: ABC & 1 2 3. 2013. (ENG., Illus.). 32p. (J). (gr. -1-3). pap. 6.50 *(978-1-84135-997-7(1))* Award Pubns. Ltd. GBR. Dist: Parkwest Pubns., Inc.
Away in a Manger Coloring Book. 16p. (J). 1.89 *(978-0-7847-1260-3(3))* Standard Publishing.
Awdry, W. Dinos & Discoveries / Emily Saves the World. 2015. (Thomas & Friends 8X8 Ser.). lib. bdg. 14.75 *(978-0-606-36403-4(X))* Turtleback Bks.
Awdry, Wilbert V. Thomas in Charge/Sodor's Steamworks. Random House Staff, illus. 2012. (Pictureback(R) Ser.). (ENG.). 32p. (J). (gr. -1-2). pap. 4.99 *(978-0-307-93119-1(6),* Random Hse. Bks. for Young Readers) Random Hse. Children's Bks.
Axworthy, Anni. The Dragon Who Couldn't Do Dragony Things. 2008. (Little Dragon Ser.). (ENG., Illus.). 32p. (J). (gr. -1-k). pap. *(978-1-84089-344-1(3))* Zero to Ten, Ltd.
AZ Books, creator. What Shape? 2012. (Smarty Ser.). (ENG., Illus.). 10p. (J). (gr. -1 — 1). 9.95 *(978-1-61889-247-8(9))* AZ Bks. LLC.
Azadi, Azita. Thank You Sun. 2009. 32p. pap. 16.50 *(978-1-4269-2197-1(7))* Trafford Publishing.
Azore, Barbara. Wanda & the Frogs. Graham, Georgia, illus. 2012. (ENG.). 32p. (J). (gr. -1-1). pap. 7.95 *(978-1-77049-307-0(7),* Tundra Bks.) Tundra Bks. CAN. Dist: Penguin Random Hse. LLC.
—Wanda & the Wild Hair. Graham, Georgia, illus. 2012. (ENG.). 32p. (J). (gr. -1-2). pap. 7.95 *(978-1-77049-306-3(9),* Tundra Bks.) Tundra Bks. CAN. Dist: Penguin Random Hse. LLC.
—Wanda's Freckles. Graham, Georgia, illus. 2012. (ENG.). 24p. (J). (gr. -1-2). pap. 7.95 *(978-1-77049-308-7(5),* Tundra Bks.) Tundra Bks. CAN. Dist: Penguin Random Hse. LLC.
Babsky, Irene. Playing with Words. 2009. (ENG.). 64p. (J). (gr. -1-3). pap. 7.99 *(978-1-84476-621-5(7))* Anness Publishing GBR. Dist: National Bk. Network.
Baby Shakespeare. (Illus.). 28p. (J). (gr. -1). pap. 21.95 incl. VHS *(978-1-892309-18-1(1))* Baby Einstein Co., LLC, The.
Bach, Annie. Monster Park! 2016. (ENG., Illus.). 32p. (J). (gr. -1-k). 9.95 *(978-1-4549-1547-8(1))* Sterling Publishing Co., Inc.
—Monster Party! (ENG., Illus.). (J). 2017. 22p. (— 1). bds. 6.95 *(978-1-4549-2136-3(6))* 2014. 32p. (gr. -1-k). 9.95 *(978-1-4549-1051-0(8))* Sterling Publishing Co., Inc.
Bach, Nancy. Cristoforo Colombo e la Pasta Al Pomodoro - Christopher Columbus & the Pasta with Tomato Sauce: A Bilingual Picture Book (Italian-English Text) Lätti, Leo, illus. 2013. 30p. pap. *(978-1-938712-06-7(4))* Roxby Media Ltd.
—Galileo Galilei e la Torre Di Pisa - Galileo Galilei & the Pisa Tower: A Bilingual Picture Book about the Italian Astronomer (Italian-English Text) Lätti, Leo, illus. 2013. 26p. pap. *(978-1-938712-07-4(2))* Roxby Media Ltd.
Bad Bat. 2012. (Collins Big Cat Ser.). (ENG.). 16p. (J). pap., wbk. ed. 4.99 *(978-0-00-747282-6(X))* HarperCollins Pubs. Ltd. GBR. Dist: Independent Pubs. Group.
Baer, Edith. This Is the Way We Go to School. 2014. 17.00 *(978-1-63419-734-2(8))* Perfection Learning Corp.
Baeten, Lieve. Up & Away with the Little Witch. 2011. (ENG., Illus.). 32p. (J). (gr. -1-2). 16.95 *(978-0-7358-4004-1(0))* North-South Bks., Inc.
Baggott, Stella. Baby's Very First Bath Book. 2011. (Baby's Very First Ser.). 10p. (J). 9.99 *(978-0-7945-2972-7(0),* Usborne) EDC Publishing.
—Baby's Very First Touchy-Feely Book. 2010. (Baby's Very First Board Bks). 10p. (J). bds. 9.99 *(978-0-7945-2647-4(0),* Usborne) EDC Publishing.
Bailey, Catherine. Hypnosis Harry. Rich, Sarita, illus. 2016. (ENG.). 40p. (J). (gr. -1-k). 16.99 *(978-1-63450-171-2(3),* Sky Pony Pr.) Skyhorse Publishing Co., Inc.
Bailey, Linda. If Kids Ruled the World. Jorisch, Stéphane & Huyck, David, illus. 2014. (ENG.). 32p. (J). (gr. -1-2). 16.95 *(978-1-55453-591-0(3))* Kids Can Pr., Ltd. CAN. Dist: Hachette Bk. Group.
—If You Happen to Have a Dinosaur. Jack, Colin, illus. (ENG.). (J). 2017. 30p. (— 1). bds. 8.99 *(978-1-101-91891-3(8))* 2014. 40p. (gr. -1-2). 17.99 *(978-1-77049-568-5(1))* Tundra Bks. CAN. (Tundra Bks.). Dist: Penguin Random Hse. LLC.
—Stanley's Beauty Contest. Slavin, Bill, illus. 2009. (ENG.). 32p. (J). (gr. -1-2). 17.95 *(978-1-55453-318-3(X))* Kids Can Pr., Ltd. CAN. Dist: Hachette Bk. Group.
—Stanleys Wild Ride. Slavin, Bill, illus. 2008. (ENG.). 32p. (J). (gr. -1-2). pap. 7.95 *(978-1-55453-254-4(X))* Kids Can Pr., Ltd. CAN. Dist: Hachette Bk. Group.
Bailey, Linda & Masse, Josée. Goodnight, Sweet Pig. Masse, Josée, illus. 2007. (ENG., Illus.). 32p. (J). (gr. -1-k). 18.95 *(978-1-55337-844-0(X))* Kids Can Pr., Ltd. CAN. Dist: Hachette Bk. Group.
Baines, Becky. National Geographic Kids Funny Fill-In: My Backyard Adventure. 2014. (NG Kids Funny Fill In Ser.). (ENG.). 48p. (J). (gr. 3-7). pap. 4.99 *(978-1-4263-1738-5(7),* National Geographic Children's Bks.) National Geographic Society.
Bajtlik, Jan. Alphadoodler: The Activity Book That Brings Letters to Life. 2016. (ENG., Illus.). 160p. (J). (gr. k-2). pap. 16.95 *(978-1-84976-405-6(0))* Tate Publishing, Ltd. GBR. Dist: Abrams, Inc.
Bak, Jenny. Ten Gifts from Santa Claus: A Counting Book. Harding, Niall, illus. 2011. (ENG.). 22p. (J). (gr. -1-k). 14.99 *(978-1-4052-5127-3(1))* Egmont Bks., Ltd. GBR. Dist: Independent Pubs. Group.
Baker, Adam. Maury C. Moose & the Forest Noel. 2014. (ENG., Illus.). 96p. (gr. 1-6). pap. 10.95 *(978-1-63047-054-8(6))* Morgan James Publishing.
Baker, Liza. Harold & the Purple Crayon: Under the Sea. 2003. (Festival Reader Ser.). (ENG., Illus.). 32p. (J). (gr. -1-2). pap. 3.99 *(978-0-06-000178-0(X),* HarperFestival) HarperCollins Pubs.
Baker-Smith, Grahame. The Twelve Days of Christmas: Panorama Pops. Baker-Smith, Grahame, illus. 2017. (Panorama Pops Ser.). (ENG., Illus.). 30p. (J). (gr. k-4). 8.99 ***(978-0-7636-9485-2(1))*** Candlewick Pr.
Baker, Stacy. Sammy's Secret. 2005. (J). lib. bdg. 19.95 *(978-1-933732-03-9(2))* Big Ransom Studio.
Baldwin, Christy. Remembering Wilma. Barnes, Sarah, illus. I.t. ed. 2005. 22p. (J). per. 9.95 *(978-0-9765072-0-8(X))* Tribute Bks.
Balet, Jan. Amos & the Moon. 2016. (ENG., Illus.). 24p. (J). 17.95 *(978-1-62326-052-1(3))* AMMO Bks., LLC.
—The Five Rollatinis. 2016. (ENG., Illus.). 24p. (J). 17.95 *(978-1-62326-053-8(1))* AMMO Bks., LLC.
Balla, Trace. Rockhopping. 2016. (ENG., Illus.). 80p. (J). (gr. 3-6). 18.99 *(978-1-76011-234-9(8))* Allen & Unwin AUS. Dist: Independent Pubs. Group.
Balsley, Tilda. Crabbing. Wyrick, Monica, illus. 2016. (Young Palmetto Bks.). (ENG.). 32p. (J). 18.99 *(978-1-61117-640-7(9))* Univ. of South Carolina Pr.
Baltazar, Art. Aw Yeah Comics! Vol. 2: Time for... Adventure! Baltazar, Franco, illus. 2015. (ENG.). 168p. (J). (gr. 3-7). pap. 12.99 *(978-1-61655-689-1(7))* Dark Horse Comics.
Bancroft, Bronwyn. Why I Love Australia. Bancroft, Bronwyn, illus. 2016. (ENG., Illus.). 32p. (J). (gr. -1-k). 11.99 *(978-1-76012-512-7(1))* Little Hare Bks. AUS. Dist: Independent Pubs. Group.
Banner, Angela. Ant & Bee. 2014. (Ant & Bee Ser.: 1). (ENG., Illus.). 112p. (Orig.). (J). (gr. -1-k). 7.99 *(978-1-4052-6671-0(6))* Egmont Bks., Ltd. GBR. Dist: Independent Pubs. Group.
—Ant & Bee & Kind Dog. 2014. (Ant & Bee Ser.). (ENG., Illus.). 112p. (J). (gr. -1-k). 7.99 *(978-1-4052-7075-5(6))* Egmont Bks., Ltd. GBR. Dist: Independent Pubs. Group.
—Ant & Bee & the ABC. 2014. (Ant & Bee Ser.). (ENG., Illus.). 96p. (J). (gr. -1-k). 7.99 *(978-1-4052-7074-8(8))* Egmont Bks., Ltd. GBR. Dist: Independent Pubs. Group.
—Ant & Bee & the Doctor. 2014. (Ant & Bee Ser.). (ENG., Illus.). 88p. (J). (gr. -1-k). 7.99 *(978-1-4052-7073-1(X))* Egmont Bks., Ltd. GBR. Dist: Independent Pubs. Group.
—Ant & Bee & the Rainbow. 2014. (Ant & Bee Ser.). (ENG., Illus.). 96p. (J). (gr. -1-k). 7.99 *(978-1-4052-6674-1(0))* Egmont Bks., Ltd. GBR. Dist: Independent Pubs. Group.
—Ant & Bee Count 123. 2015. (Ant & Bee Ser.). (ENG., Illus.). 96p. (J). (gr. -1-k). 7.99 *(978-1-4052-7513-2(8))* Egmont Bks., Ltd. GBR. Dist: Independent Pubs. Group.
—Ant & Bee Go Shopping. 2015. (Ant & Bee Ser.). (ENG., Illus.). 84p. (J). (gr. -1-k). 7.99 *(978-1-4052-7514-9(6))* Egmont Bks., Ltd. GBR. Dist: Independent Pubs. Group.
—Ant & Bee Three Story Collection. 2016. (Ant & Bee Ser.). (ENG., Illus.). 336p. (J). (gr. -1-k). 15.99 *(978-1-4052-7932-1(X))* Egmont Bks., Ltd. GBR. Dist: Independent Pubs. Group.
—Ant & Bee Time. 2015. (Ant & Bee Ser.). (ENG., Illus.). 96p. (J). (gr. -1-k). 7.99 *(978-1-4052-7516-3(2))* Egmont Bks., Ltd. GBR. Dist: Independent Pubs. Group.
—Around the World with Ant & Bee. 2014. (Ant & Bee Ser.). (ENG., Illus.). 96p. (J). (gr. -1-k). 7.99 *(978-1-4052-6676-5(7))* Egmont Bks., Ltd. GBR. Dist: Independent Pubs. Group.
—Happy Birthday with Ant & Bee. 2014. (Ant & Bee Ser.). (ENG., Illus.). 96p. (J). (gr. -1-k). 7.99 *(978-1-4052-6675-8(9))* Egmont Bks., Ltd. GBR. Dist: Independent Pubs. Group.
—Left & Right with Ant & Bee. 2016. (Ant & Bee Ser.). (ENG., Illus.). 96p. (J). (gr. -1-k). 7.99 *(978-1-4052-7929-1(X))* Egmont Bks., Ltd. GBR. Dist: Independent Pubs. Group.
—Make a Million with Ant & Bee. 2016. (Ant & Bee Ser.). (ENG., Illus.). 96p. (J). (gr. -1-k). 7.99 *(978-1-4052-7930-7(3))* Egmont Bks., Ltd. GBR. Dist: Independent Pubs. Group.
—More Ant & Bee. 2014. (Ant & Bee Ser.: 2). (ENG., Illus.). 112p. (J). (gr. -1-k). 7.99 *(978-1-4052-6672-7(4))* Egmont Bks., Ltd. GBR. Dist: Independent Pubs. Group.
Banyard, Antonia & Ayer, Paula. Water Wow! A Visual Exploration. Wuthrich, Belle, illus. 2016. (Visual Exploration Ser.). (ENG.). 64p. (J). (gr. 3-7). pap. 12.95 *(978-1-55451-821-0(0))* Annick Pr., Ltd. CAN. Dist: Publishers Group West (PGW).
Bar-el, Dan. Dream Boats. Wakelin, Kirsti Anne, illus. 2013. (ENG.). 44p. (J). (gr. -1-3). 17.95 *(978-1-897476-87-1(6))* Simply Read Bks. CAN. Dist: Ingram Publisher Services.
—A Fish Named Glub, 0 vols. Bisaillon, Josee, illus. 2014. (ENG.). 32p. (J). (gr. -1-3). 16.95 *(978-1-55453-812-6(2))* Kids Can Pr., Ltd. CAN. Dist: Hachette Bk. Group.
Bar-El, Dan. It's Great Being a Dad. Perry, Gina, illus. 2017. (ENG.). 32p. (J). (gr. -1-3). 16.99 *(978-1-77049-605-7(X),* Tundra Bks.) Tundra Bks. CAN. Dist: Penguin Random Hse. LLC.
Bar-el, Dan. Nine Words Max. Huyck, David, illus. 2014. (ENG.). 32p. (J). (gr. k-4). 17.99 *(978-1-77049-562-3(2),* Tundra Bks.) Tundra Bks. CAN. Dist: Penguin Random Hse. LLC.
Barasch, Lynne. First Come the Zebra, 1 vol. Barasch, Lynne, illus. 2005. (ENG., Illus.). 40p. (J). pap. 10.95 *(978-1-62014-029-1(2))* Lee & Low Bks., Inc.
Barber, Elke & Barber, Alex. Is Daddy Coming Back in a Minute? Explaining Sudden Death to Very Young Children in Words They Can Understand. 2016. (ENG., Illus.). 40p. (J). 18.95 *(978-1-78592-106-3(1),* 8555) Kingsley, Jessica Pubs. GBR. Dist: Macmillan Distribution Ltd.
—What Happened to Daddy's Body? Explaining What Happens after Death in Words Very Young Children Can Understand. 2016. (ENG., Illus.). 40p. (J). 18.95 *(978-1-78592-107-0(X),* 8559) Kingsley, Jessica Pubs. GBR. Dist: Macmillan Distribution Ltd.
Barber, Tom & Chapman, Lynne. Open Wide! 2004. (Illus.). 32p. 14.95 *(978-1-84458-241-9(8))* Avalon Publishing Group.
Barberi, Gladys. Pink Fire Trucks. Safar, Lina, illus. 2013.Tr. of Los Camiones de Bomberos de Color Rosado. 30p. (J). 16.95 *(978-1-60131-145-0(1))* Big Tent Bks.
Barefoot Books Staff & Amador Family Staff. The Wheels on the Bus. Williamson, Melanie, illus. 2014. 24p. (J). (gr. -1-2). 9.99 *(978-1-84686-788-0(6))* Barefoot Bks., Inc.
Barker, Cordell. The Cat Came Back. 2017. (ENG., Illus.). 48p. (J). (gr. k-3). 19.95 ***(978-1-77085-929-6(2),*** 9781770859296) Firefly Bks., Ltd.
Barklem, Jill. Adventures in Brambly Hedge. 2014. (ENG., Illus.). 128p. (J). 29.99 *(978-0-00-746145-5(3),* HarperCollins Children's Bks.) HarperCollins Pubs. Ltd. GBR. Dist: HarperCollins Pubs.
Barklem, Jill. A Year in Brambly Hedge. Barklem, Jill, illus. 2017. (ENG., Illus.). 128p. (J). 29.99 ***(978-0-00-824117-9(1),*** HarperCollins Children's Bks.) HarperCollins Pubs. Ltd. GBR. Dist: HarperCollins Pubs.
Barman, Adrienne. Creaturepedia. 2015. (Creaturepedia Ser.). (ENG., Illus.). 216p. (J). 22.99 *(978-1-84780-634-5(1),* Wide Eyed Editions) Quarto Publishing Group UK GBR. Dist: Littlehampton Bk Services, Ltd.
Barnes, Lesley. Jill & Dragon. 2016. (ENG., Illus.). 32p. (J). (gr. k-2). 17.95 *(978-1-84976-340-0(2))* Tate Publishing, Ltd. GBR. Dist: Abrams, Inc.
—Jill & Lion. 2017. (ENG., Illus.). 32p. (J). (gr. -1-2). 17.95 *(978-1-84976-437-7(9))* Tate Publishing, Ltd. GBR. Dist: Abrams, Inc.
Barnes, Lesley, illus. Flyaway. 2016. (ENG.). 18p. (J). (gr. -1-2). 15.99 *(978-1-84780-645-1(7),* Frances Lincoln Children's Bks.) Quarto Publishing Group UK GBR. Dist: Hachette Bk. Group.
Barnes, Steven John. Hector. 2012. (ENG., Illus.). 36p. (J). (gr. -1-5). 16.99 *(978-1-60887-070-7(7),* Earth Aware Editions) Mandala Publishing.
Barnett, Mac. Noisy Night. Biggs, Brian, illus. 2017. (ENG.). 32p. (J). 16.99 *(978-1-59643-967-2(X),* 9781596439672) Roaring Brook Pr.
Barnett, Mac, et al. The Clock Without a Face. Teplin, Scott & Rex, Adam, illus. 2010. (ENG.). 30p. (gr. 2-18). bds. 19.95 *(978-1-934781-71-5(1))* McSweeney's Publishing.
Barrett Browning, Elizabeth & Browning, Elizabeth Barrett. How Do I Love Thee? McDonough, Mati, illus. 2016. (ENG.). 32p. (J). (gr. -1-3). 16.95 *(978-1-937359-83-6(2))* Cameron & Co., Inc.
Barrett, Phillip, illus. Where's Larry? 2016. (ENG.). 32p. (J). pap. 15.00 *(978-1-84717-276-1(8))* O'Brien Pr., Ltd., The IRL. Dist: Dufour Editions, Inc.
Barrie, J. M. Peter Pan. Press, Jenny, illus. 2013. (Storyteller Book Ser.). (ENG.). 48p. (J). (gr. k-5). pap. 7.99 *(978-1-84322-884-4(X),* Armadillo) Anness Publishing GBR. Dist: National Bk. Network.
Barroux, Stephane-Yves. Mr Leon's Paris. 2013. (ENG., Illus.). 32p. (J). (gr. k-2). 17.99 *(978-1-907912-07-8(X))* Phoenix Yard Bks. GBR. Dist: Independent Pubs. Group.
Bartlett, Alison. Erice the Reindeer. (Illus.). 32p. (J). *(978-0-340-65598-6(4))* Hodder & Stoughton.
Barton, Bethany. Give Bees a Chance. Barton, Bethany, illus. 2017. (ENG., Illus.). 40p. (J). (gr. -1-3). 16.99 *(978-0-670-01694-5(2),* Viking Books for Young Readers) Penguin Young Readers Group.
Barton, Byron. My Bike Lap Book. Barton, Byron, illus. 2016. (Illus.). 40p. (J). (gr. -1-3). pap. 12.99 *(978-0-06-233702-3(5),* Greenwillow Bks.) HarperCollins Pubs.
—My Bus. Barton, Byron, illus. 2014. (ENG., Illus.). 40p. (J). (gr. -1-3). 16.99 *(978-0-06-228736-6(2),* Greenwillow Bks.) HarperCollins Pubs.
—My Car. Barton, Byron, illus. (ENG., Illus.). (J). (gr. -1-3). 2003. 36p. bds. 7.99 *(978-0-06-056045-4(2))* 2004. 40p. reprint ed. pap. 6.99 *(978-0-06-058940-0(X))* HarperCollins Pubs. (Greenwillow Bks.).
Barton, Sally. Fairy House. Barton, Sally, illus. 2016. (ENG., Illus.). 24p. (J). (gr. -1-1). pap. 9.99 *(978-1-907432-19-4(1))* Hogs Back Bks. GBR. Dist: Independent Pubs. Group.
Baruzzi, Agnese. Opposites: A Cut-Paper Book. Baruzzi, Agnese, illus. 2013. (ENG., Illus.). 10p. (J). (— 1). 15.99 *(978-1-85707-803-9(9))* Tango Bks. GBR. Dist: Independent Pubs. Group.
Bash, Sarah E. My Daddy Is Strong, Handsome, & Tall. 2009. 32p. pap. 12.99 *(978-1-4389-5470-7(0))* AuthorHouse.
Bass, Saul, illus. Henri's Walk to Paris. 2012. (ENG.). 48p. (J). (gr. -1-4). 19.95 *(978-0-7893-2263-0(3))* Universe Publishing.
Bastianich, Lidia Matticchio. Lidia's Egg-Citing Farm Adventure. Graef, Renee, illus. 2015. (ENG.). 60p. (J). (gr. -1-17). 16.95 *(978-0-7624-5126-5(2),* Running Pr. Kids) Running Pr. Bk. Pubs.
—Nonna Tell Me a Story: Lidia's Christmas Kitchen. Logan, Laura, illus. 2010. (ENG.). 56p. (J). (gr. -1-3). 15.95 *(978-0-7624-3692-7(1))* Running Pr. Bk. Pubs.
Batt, Tanya Robyn & Barefoot Books. Faery's Gift. Ceccoli, Nicoletta, illus. 2015. 32p. (J). (gr. -1-2). 10.99 *(978-1-78285-145-5(3))* Barefoot Bks., Inc.
Battut, Éric. Little Mouse's Big Secret. 2017. (ENG., Illus.). 22p. (J). (— 1). bds. 6.95 *(978-1-4549-2154-7(4))* Sterling Publishing Co., Inc.
Bauman, Amy. Farm Animal Sounds. 2010. 12p. (J). (gr. -1). 9.95 *(978-1-60747-708-2(4),* Pickwick Pr.) Phoenix Bks., Inc.
Baxter, Nicola. Head, Shoulders, Knees & Toes & Other Action Rhymes. Buckingham, Gabriella, illus. 2013. (ENG.). 16p. (J). (gr. -1-6). bds. 7.99 *(978-1-84322-829-5(7),* Armadillo) Anness Publishing GBR. Dist: National Bk. Network.
—Kaleidoscope Book: My First Book of Learning. Elliott, Rebecca, illus. 2013. (ENG.). 16p. bds. 16.99 *(978-1-84322-930-8(7),* Armadillo) Anness Publishing GBR. Dist: National Bk. Network.
—Learn to Count. Elliott, Rebecca, illus. 2013. (ENG.). 16p. (J). (gr. -1-2). bds. 17.99 *(978-1-84322-984-1(6),* Armadillo) Anness Publishing GBR. Dist: National Bk. Network.
—Learn to Tell Time: With Magnets to Use Again & Again! Elliott, Rebecca, illus. 2013. (ENG.). 16p. (J). (gr. -1-12). bds. 17.99 *(978-1-84322-638-3(3),* Armadillo) Anness Publishing GBR. Dist: National Bk. Network.
—The Mermaid & the Star. Rigby, Deborah, illus. 2025. 14p. (J). bds. *(978-1-84322-907-0(2),* Armadillo) Anness Publishing.
—My Ballet Theatre: Peek Inside the 3-D Windows. Chaffey, Samantha, illus. 2014. (ENG.). 24p. (J). (gr. -1-12). 16.99 *(978-1-84322-949-0(8),* Armadillo) Anness Publishing GBR. Dist: National Bk. Network.
—My First 200 Words: Learning Is Fun with Teddy the Bear! Lacome, Susie, illus. 2016. (ENG.). 24p. (J). (gr. -1-12). pap. 7.99 *(978-1-86147-759-0(7),* Armadillo) Anness Publishing GBR. Dist: National Bk. Network.
—My First Fairy Tales: Eight Exciting Picture Stories for Little Ones. Parry, Jo, illus. 2013. (ENG.). 16p. (J). (gr. -1-2). bds. 13.99 *(978-1-84322-991-9(9),* Armadillo) Anness Publishing GBR. Dist: National Bk. Network.
—My First Farmyard Tales: Eight Exciting Picture Stories for Little Ones. Lodge, Ali, illus. 2013. (ENG.). 16p. (J). (gr. -1-2). bds. 13.99 *(978-1-84322-990-2(0),* Armadillo) Anness Publishing GBR. Dist: National Bk. Network.
—My First Words: At Home. Lacome, Susie, illus. 2016. (ENG.). 24p. (J). (gr. -1-12). pap. 7.99 *(978-1-86147-769-9(4),* Armadillo) Anness Publishing GBR. Dist: National Bk. Network.
—My First Words: Nature. Lacome, Susie, illus. 2016. (ENG.). 24p. (J). (gr. -1-12). pap. 7.99 *(978-1-86147-770-5(8),* Armadillo) Anness Publishing GBR. Dist: National Bk. Network.
—My First Words: Out & about (Giant Size) Lacome, Susie, illus. 2016. (ENG.). 24p. (J). (gr. -1-12). pap. 7.99 *(978-1-86147-777-4(5),* Armadillo) Anness Publishing GBR. Dist: National Bk. Network.
—My Perfect Doll's House: Peek Inside the 3D Windows. Chaffey, Samantha, illus. 2013. (ENG.). 12p. (J). (gr. k-4). 16.99 *(978-1-84322-924-7(2),* Armadillo) Anness Publishing GBR. Dist: National Bk. Network.
—Pull the Lever: Who's at Nursery? Lawson, Peter, illus. 2014. (ENG.). 8p. (J). (gr. -1-1). bds. 6.99 *(978-1-86147-393-6(1),* Armadillo) Anness Publishing GBR. Dist: National Bk. Network.
—Rhymes for Playtime Fun. Shuttleworth, Cathie, illus. 2013. (ENG.). 80p. (J). (gr. -1-k). pap. 9.99 *(978-1-84322-921-6(8))* Anness Publishing GBR. Dist: National Bk. Network.
—Sing-Along Songs for Children: Join in with Your Free CD. Finn, Rebecca, illus. 2014. (ENG.). 12p. (J). (gr. -1-k). bds. 14.99 *(978-1-84322-892-9(0),* Armadillo) Anness Publishing GBR. Dist: National Bk. Network.
—The Starlight Ballerina. Jones, Deborah, illus. 2025. 14p. (J). bds. *(978-1-84322-885-1(8))* Anness Publishing.
—Tales from the Toy Box. Press, Jenny, illus. 2012. (ENG.). 80p. (J). (gr. k-4). pap. 9.99 *(978-1-84322-951-3(X))* Anness Publishing GBR. Dist: National Bk. Network.
—Trouble on the Ice: First Reading Books for 3-5 Year Olds. Ball, Geoff, illus. 2014. (ENG.). 24p. (J). (gr. -1-k). 5.99 *(978-1-86147-323-3(0),* Armadillo) Anness Publishing GBR. Dist: National Bk. Network.
—The Trouble with Tippers. Ball, Geoff, illus. 2012. (ENG.). 24p. (J). (gr. -1-k). pap. 6.99 *(978-1-84322-783-0(5),* Armadillo) Anness Publishing GBR. Dist: National Bk. Network.
—The Trouble with Tractors. Ball, Geoff, illus. 2012. (ENG.). 24p. pap. 6.99 *(978-1-84322-784-7(3),* Armadillo) Anness Publishing GBR. Dist: National Bk. Network.
—The Trouble with Trains. Ball, Geoff, illus. 2012. (ENG.). 24p. (J). (gr. -1-k). pap. 6.99 *(978-1-84322-785-4(1),* Armadillo) Anness Publishing GBR. Dist: National Bk. Network.
—The Trouble with Trucks. Ball, Geoff, illus. 2012. (ENG.). 24p. (J). (gr. -1-k). pap. 6.99 *(978-1-84322-786-1(X),* Armadillo) Anness Publishing GBR. Dist: National Bk. Network.
—We Love Animals on the Farm. Henson, Gaby, illus. 2013. (ENG.). 12p. (J). (gr. -1-12). 9.99 *(978-1-84322-693-2(6),* Armadillo) Anness Publishing GBR. Dist: National Bk. Network.
—3-Minute Animal Stories. Everitt-Stewart, Andy, illus. 2013. (ENG.). 80p. (J). (gr. -1-k). pap. 9.99 *(978-1-84322-978-0(1),* Armadillo) Anness Publishing GBR. Dist: National Bk. Network.
Baxter, Nicola & Adams, Ben. Freddie the Fish, Star of the Show. Cameron, Craig, illus. 2013. (Googly Eyes Ser.). (ENG.). 12p. (J). (gr. -1-k). bds. 6.99 *(978-1-84322-621-5(9),* Armadillo) Anness Publishing GBR. Dist: National Bk. Network.
Baxter, Nicola & Birkinshaw, Marie. A Treasury for Little Ones: Hours of Fun for Babies & Toddlers - Stories & Rhymes, Puzzles to Solve, & Things to Make & Do. Endersby, Frank, illus. 2014. (ENG.). 80p. (J). (gr. -1-6). 14.99 *(978-1-86147-368-4(0),* Armadillo) Anness Publishing GBR. Dist: National Bk. Network.
Baxter, Nicola & Ladybird Books Staff. Goldilocks & the Three Bears. 2015. (First Favourite Tales Ser.). (ENG., Illus.). 32p. (J). (-k). 7.99 *(978-1-4093-0629-0(1))* Penguin Bks., Ltd. GBR. Dist: Independent Pubs. Group.
Bazaldua, Barbara & Bergen, Lara. Rapunzel & the Golden Rule/Jasmine & the Two Tigers (Disney Princess) Studio IBOIX & Disney Storybook Artists Staff, illus. 2011. (Pictureback(R) Ser.). (ENG.). 32p. (J). (gr. -1-2). pap. 4.99 *(978-0-7364-2829-3(1),* RH/Disney) Random Hse. Children's Bks.
Beale, Madeline. Sarah's Happy Holidays. Goh, Douglas, illus. 2017. (ENG.). 24p. 10.00 *(978-981-4751-88-9(X))* Marshall Cavendish International (Asia) Private Ltd. SGP. Dist: National Bk. Network.
Beard, Lauren, illus. The Fairytale Hairdresser & Father Christmas. 2014. (Fairytale Hairdresser Ser.: 5). (ENG.). 32p. (J). (-k). pap. 9.99 *(978-0-552-57052-7(4))* Transworld Publishers Ltd. GBR. Dist: Independent Pubs. Group.
Bears for Kids: Amazing Pictures & Fun Fact Children Book. 2013. 32p. pap. 12.97 *(978-1-63022-034-1(5))* Speedy Publishing LLC.

P
Q
R

Beaty, Andrea. Iggy Peck, Architect. Roberts, David, illus. 2010. (ENG.). 32p. (J). (gr. k-17). pap. 7.95 (978-0-8109-8928-3(X)) UK Abrams Bks. for Young Readers.

Beavington, Ruth. Edward Bear. 2012. (Illus.). 112p. (gr. 1-2). 19.95 (978-1-84624-721-7(7)) Book Guild, Ltd. GBR. Dist: Trans-Atlantic Pubns., Inc.

Beck, Ian. The Christmas Story. 2005. (ENG., Illus.). 32p. (J). pap. 13.99 (978-0-552-54937-0(1)) Transworld Publishers Ltd. GBR. Dist: Independent Pubs. Group.

Becker, Helaine. Juba This, Juba That. Lightburn, Ron, illus. 2011. (ENG.). 24p. (J). (gr. k-k). 17.95 (978-0-88776-975-7(6), Tundra Bks.) Tundra Bks. CAN. Dist: Penguin Random Hse. LLC.

Becker, Shelly. Even Superheroes Have Bad Days. Kaban, Eda, illus. 2016. (ENG.). 40p. (J). (gr. -1-4). 14.95 (978-1-4549-1394-8(0)) Sterling Publishing Co., Inc.

Beckford, Lois. The Interesting Pen Pal. 2010. 44p. pap. 21.99 (978-1-4415-0878-2(3)) Xlibris Corp.

Beckler, Bruce. My Daddy Is A Deputy Sheriff. Finney, Simone, illus. l.t. ed. 2004. 14p. (J). per. 5.59 (978-0-9745210-4-6(3)) Myers Publishing Co.

—My Daddy Is A Fire Fighter: My Daddy Is A Fireman. Peek, Jeannette, illus. l.t. ed. 2004. 16p. (J). 5.59 (978-0-9745210-8-4(6)) Myers Publishing Co.

—My Daddy Is a Police Officer: My Daddy Wears a Star. Finney, Simone, illus. l.t. ed. 2004. 14p. (J). per. 5.59 (978-0-9745210-3-9(5)) Myers Publishing Co.

—My Daddy Is A Police Officer: Wears A Badge, 8 bks. Finney, Simone, illus. l.t. ed. 2004. 14p. (J). per. 5.59 (978-0-9745210-2-2(7)) Myers Publishing Co.

—My Mommy Is A Deputy Sheriff. Finney, Simone, illus. l.t. ed. 2004. 14p. (J). 5.59 (978-0-9745210-7-7(8)) Myers Publishing Co.

—My Mommy Is A Nurse. Peek, Jeannette, illus. l.t. ed. 2004. 20p. (J). 5.59 (978-0-9745210-9-1(4)) Myers Publishing Co.

—My Mommy Is A Police Officer: My Mommy Wears A Badge. Finney, Simone, illus. l.t. ed. 2004. 14p. (J). per. 5.59 (978-0-9745210-5-3(1)) Myers Publishing Co.

—My Mommy Is A Police Officer: My Mommy Wears A Star. Finney, Simone, illus. l.t. ed. 2004. 14p. (J). 5.59 (978-0-9745210-6-0(X)) Myers Publishing Co.

Bedford, David. The Three Ninja Pigs. Moor, Becka, illus. 2016. (ENG.). 32p. (J). pap. 10.99 (978-1-4711-2191-3(7), Simon & Schuster Children's) Simon & Schuster, Ltd. GBR. Dist: Simon & Schuster, Inc.

Bednar, Martin. Sandy's Vision. 2006. (J). lib. bdg. 19.95 (978-1-933732-15-2(6)) Big Ransom Studio.

Bee, William. And the Cars Go... Bee, William, illus. 2013. (ENG., Illus.). 32p. (J). (-k). 15.99 (978-0-7636-6580-7(0)) Candlewick Pr.

—Migloo's Day. Bee, William, illus. 2015. (ENG., Illus.). (J). (gr. -1-2). 14.99 (978-0-7636-7374-1(9)) Candlewick Pr.

—Stanley the Mailman, 1 vol. Bee, William, illus. 2016. (Stanley Ser.). (ENG., Illus.). 32p. (J). (gr. -1-2). 14.95 (978-1-56145-867-7(8)) Peachtree Pubs.

—Stanley's Diner, 1 vol. Bee, William, illus. 2015. (Stanley Ser.). (ENG., Illus.). 32p. (J). (gr. -1-2). 14.95 (978-1-56145-802-8(3)) Peachtree Pubs.

—Stanley's Store, 1 vol. Bee, William, illus. 2017. (Stanley Ser.). (ENG., Illus.). 32p. (J). (gr. -1-2). 14.95 (978-1-56145-868-4(6)) Peachtree Pubs.

Behling, Steve. Spider-Man Retro. Panosian, Dan, illus. 2017. (ENG.). 48p. (J). (gr. 1-3). 10.99 (978-1-4847-4928-9(6), Marvel Pr.) Disney Publishing Worldwide.

Beiser, Tim. Bradley McGogg: The Very Fine Frog. Berman, Rachel, illus. (ENG.). 24p. (J). (gr. k-k). 2011. pap. 7.95 (978-1-77049-276-9(3)) 2009. 17.95 (978-0-88776-864-4(4)) Tundra Bks. CAN. (Tundra Bks.). Dist: Penguin Random Hse. LLC.

—Little Chicken Duck. Slavin, Bill, illus. 2013. (ENG.). 24p. (J). (gr. -1-2). 17.95 (978-1-77049-392-6(1), Tundra Bks.) Tundra Bks. CAN. Dist: Penguin Random Hse. LLC.

Bell, Cece. Bee-Wigged. Bell, Cece, illus. 2017. (ENG., Illus.). 40p. (J). (gr. -1-3). 6.99 (978-0-7636-9312-1(X)) Candlewick Pr.

—Sock Monkey Takes a Bath. Bell, Cece, illus. 2015. (ENG., Illus.). 32p. (J). (gr. -1-3). 14.00 (978-0-7636-7759-6(0)) Candlewick Pr.

Belshaw, Yvonne & Sheldon, Tamia. Toby the Flying Cat. 2013. 24p. pap. 9.99 (978-1-62395-495-6(9)) Xist Publishing.

BELTEI, Nadia. Emily's BOOKS: Coloring & Activity book, age Level: 2-3. 2010. 39p. pap. 19.99 (978-0-557-32843-7(8)) Lulu Pr., Inc.

Benaglia, Fred, illus. Hug This Book! 2016. (ENG.). 32p. (gr. -1-k). 16.95 (978-0-7148-7284-1(9)) Phaidon Pr., Inc.

Bennett, Jeffrey. Max Goes to Mars: A Science Adventure with Max the Dog. Okamoto, Alan, illus. 2015. (Science Adventures with Max the Dog Ser.). (ENG.). 32p. (J). (gr. 2-4). 15.00 (978-1-937548-44-5(9)) Big Kid Science.

—Max Goes to the Space Station: A Science Adventure with Max the Dog. Carroll, Michael, illus. 2013. (Science Adventures with Max the Dog Ser.). (ENG.). 32p. (J). (gr. 2-4). 15.00 (978-1-937548-28-5(7)) Big Kid Science.

Bennett, Leonie. Locket Out. Adams, Arlene, illus. 2004. (ENG.). 24p. (J). lib. bdg. 23.65 (978-1-59646-688-3(X)) Dingles & Co.

—No Problem! Brown, Judy, illus. 2004. (ENG.). 16p. (J). lib. bdg. 23.65 (978-1-59646-680-7(4)) Dingles & Co.

Benoit-Renard, Anne. Navani from Delhi. Rigaudie, Mylène, illus. 2014. (AV2 Fiction Readalong Ser.: Vol. 133). (ENG.). 32p. (J). (gr. -1-3). lib. bdg. 34.28 (978-1-4896-2271-6(3), AV2 by Weigl) Weigl Pubs., Inc.

Benson, Cindy. Chloe & Hairy Go to School. 2012. 32p. pap. 12.99 (978-0-9855202-9-8(9)) Kids At Heart Publishing, LLC.

Bentley, Dawn. Gingerbread Man. 2005. (Holiday Sparklers Book Ser.). (ENG., Illus.). 10p. (J). 4.95 (978-1-58117-163-1(3), Intervisual/Piggy Toes) Bendon, Inc.

Bentley, Jools. The Hippopandamouse. 2016. (ENG., Illus.). 32p. (J). (gr. -1-k). 18.99 (978-1-4472-8889-3(0)) Pan Macmillan GBR. Dist: Independent Pubs. Group.

Bentley, Sue. Picture Perfect. 2014. (Magic Kitten Ser.: 13). lib. bdg. 14.75 (978-0-606-35683-1(5)) Turtleback Bks.

Bently, Peter. Dustbin Dad. Ayto, Russell, illus. 2013. (ENG.). 32p. (J). pap. 8.99 (978-1-84738-874-2(4), Simon & Schuster Children's) Simon & Schuster, Ltd. GBR. Dist: Simon & Schuster, Inc.

—A Lark in the Ark. Chapman, Lynne, illus. 2015. (ENG.). 24p. (J). (gr. -1-k). pap. 12.99 (978-1-4052-7508-8(1)) Egmont Bks., Ltd. GBR. Dist: Independent Pubs. Group.

—Rich Witch, Poor Witch. Field, Jim, illus. 2014. (ENG.). 32p. (J). (gr. -1-k). pap. 8.99 (978-1-4472-2018-3(8)) Pan Macmillan GBR. Dist: Independent Pubs. Group.

—Royal Visit. 2017. (Tooth Fairy Ser.). (ENG., Illus.). 32p. (J). (gr. -1-k). 17.99 (978-1-4449-2853-2(8)) Hachette Children's Group GBR. Dist: Hachette Bk. Group.

Berenstain, Mike. Berenstain Bears/Living Lights: The Berenstain Bears' Harvest Festival, 1 vol. 2015. (Berenstain Bears/Living Lights Ser.). (ENG., Illus.). 24p. (J). pap. 3.99 (978-0-310-74865-6(8)) Zonderkidz.

Berenstain, Stan & Berenstain, Jan. The Berenstain Bears Go to School. deluxe ed. 2016. (First Time Books(R) Ser.). (ENG., Illus.). 32p. (J). (gr. -1-2). pap. 6.99 (978-0-399-55589-3(7), Random Hse. Bks. for Young Readers) Random Hse. Children's Bks.

Beresford, Elisabeth. Deep Space Womble. (Illus.). 15p. (J). (gr. k-6). pap. (978-0-340-74671-4(8)) Hodder & Stoughton.

—The Ghost of Wimbledon Common. (Illus.). 15p. (J). (gr. k-6). pap. (978-0-340-73579-4(1)) Hodder & Stoughton.

—The Snow Womble. Price, Nick, illus. 2013. (Wombles Ser.). (ENG.). 32p. (J). pap. 12.99 (978-1-4088-3424-4(3), 9781408834244, Bloomsbury USA Childrens) Bloomsbury Publishing USA.

—Tomsk to the Rescue. (Illus.). 15p. (J). (gr. k-6). pap. (978-0-340-73581-7(3)) Hodder & Stoughton.

—The Wombles: Chaos on the Common. (Illus.). 16p. (J). (gr. k-6). pap. (978-0-340-74674-5(2)) Hodder & Stoughton.

—Wombles Camping & Cloudberries. (Illus.). 15p. (J). (gr. k-6). pap. (978-0-340-73584-8(8)) Hodder & Stoughton.

Berg, Brook. What Marion Taught Willis. Alberg, Nathan, illus. 2005. (J). 16.95 (978-1-932146-31-8(8), 1242215) Highsmith Inc.

Berg, Jean Horton. The Playful Little Dog. Robertson, Maurice, illus. 2016. (G&d Vintage Ser.). (ENG.). 24p. (J). (-k). 7.99 (978-0-448-48218-7(5), Grosset & Dunlap) Penguin Young Readers Group.

Berger, Samantha. A Crankenstein Valentine. Santat, Dan, illus. 2014. (ENG.). 40p. (J). (gr. -1-3). 17.99 (978-0-316-37638-9(8)) Little, Brown Bks. for Young Readers.

Bergman, Mara. Glitter Kitty. Monks, Lydia, illus. 2014. (ENG.). 32p. (J). 8.99 (978-1-4711-2216-3(6), Simon & Schuster Children's) Simon & Schuster, Ltd. GBR. Dist: Simon & Schuster, Inc.

Berkes, Marianne. Over in the Ocean: In a Coral Reef, 1 vol. Canyon, Jeanette, illus. 2004. 36p. (J). (gr. -1-2). (ENG.). 16.95 (978-1-58469-063-4(1)); pap. 8.95 (978-1-58469-062-7(3)) Dawn Pubns.

Berne, Jennifer. Manfish: The Story of Jacques Cousteau. Puybaret, Éric, illus. 2015. (ENG.). 38p. (J). (gr. k-3). 9.99 (978-1-4521-4123-7(1)) Chronicle Bks. LLC.

Berning, Terri J. Grace Alone Is Enough, 1 vol. Arling, Jackie L., illus. 2010. 34p. 24.95 (978-1-4512-9045-5(4)) PublishAmerica, Inc.

Berrios, Frank. Football with Dad. Biggs, Brian, illus. 2015. (Little Golden Book Ser.). (ENG.). 24p. (J). (-k). 4.99 (978-0-385-37925-0(0), Golden Bks.) Random Hse. Children's Bks.

—Lights Out!; Tow Truck Trouble. RH Disney Staff, illus. 2010. (Pictureback(R) Ser.). (ENG.). 32p. (J). (gr. -1-2). pap. 4.99 (978-0-7364-2713-5(9), RH/Disney) Random Hse. Children's Bks.

Bertrand, Diane Gonzales. My Pal, Victor/Mi Amigo, Victor. de La Vega, Eida, tr. 2008. (ENG., Illus.). 32p. (J). (gr. -1-3). per. 7.95 (978-1-932748-72-7(5), Raven Tree Pr.,Csi) Continental Sales, Inc.

Beskow, Elsa. The Land of Long Ago. 2010. (ENG., Illus.). 32p. (J). (gr. -1-1). 17.95 (978-0-86315-771-4(8)) Floris Bks. GBR. Dist: SteinerBooks, Inc.

Bethel, Ellie. Michael Recycle Saves Christmas. Colombo, Alexandra, illus. 2010. (Michael Recycle Ser.). (ENG.). 32p. (J). (gr. 2-5). 15.99 (978-1-60010-843-3(1), 9781600108433) Idea & Design Works, LLC.

Bethel, Ellie & Patterson, Ellie. Michael Recycle Meets Bootleg Peg. Colombo, Alexandra, illus. 2014. (Michael Recycle Ser.). (ENG.). 28p. (J). (gr. 2-5). 17.99 (978-1-61377-708-4(6), 9781613777084) Idea & Design Works, LLC.

Bevan, Clare. Catkin the Fairy Kitten. Johnson-Isaacs, Cally, illus. 2015. (Mimi's Magical Fairy Friends Ser.: 1). (ENG.). 32p. (J). (gr. -1-2). pap. 10.99 **(978-1-4472-7701-9(5))** Pan Macmillan GBR. Dist: Independent Pubs. Group.

—Comet the Fairy Unicorn. Johnson-Isaacs, Cally, illus. 2015. (Mimi's Magical Fairy Friends Ser.: 3). (ENG.). 32p. (J). (gr. -1-2). pap. 10.99 **(978-1-4472-9424-5(6))** Pan Macmillan GBR. Dist: Independent Pubs. Group.

—Moonbeam the Fairy Dragon. Johnson-Isaacs, Cally, illus. 2016. (Mimi's Magical Fairy Friends Ser.: 4). (ENG.). 32p. (J). (gr. -1-2). pap. 10.99 **(978-1-4472-9543-3(9))** Pan Macmillan GBR. Dist: Independent Pubs. Group.

Bevans, Ph. D. Don't Do That, Harry! The Balloon Story. 2009. 20p. pap. 10.49 (978-1-4490-2926-5(4)) AuthorHouse.

Beveridge, Dorothy. Counting Belize Frogs & Toads. Beveridge, Jim, photos by. 2012. (Illus.). 26p. pap. (978-976-8142-47-4(2)) Producciones de la Hamaca.

Biedrzycki, David. Ace Lacewing: Bad Bugs Are My Business. Biedrzycki, David, illus. 2011. (ENG., Illus.). 44p. (J). (gr. k-4). pap. 8.95 (978-1-57091-693-9(4)) Charlesbridge Publishing, Inc.

—Ace Lacewing Bug Detective: The Big Swat. Biedrzycki, David, illus. 2012. (ENG., Illus.). 44p. (J). (gr. k-4). pap. 8.95 (978-1-57091-748-6(5)) Charlesbridge Publishing, Inc.

—Me & My Dragon. Biedrzycki, David, illus. 2011. (ENG., Illus.). 40p. (J). (gr. -1-3). pap. 7.95 (978-1-58089-279-7(5)) Charlesbridge Publishing, Inc.

Big Blue Bubble Inc., Big Blue. My Singing Monsters Search & Find. 2015. (My Singing Monsters Ser.). (ENG., Illus.). 24p. (J). (gr. 1). pap. 11.99 (978-1-4052-7686-3(X)) Egmont Bks., Ltd. GBR. Dist: Independent Pubs. Group.

The Big Picture. 2010. (Big Picture Ser.). (ENG.). 24p. (gr. 1-2). pap. 333.60 (978-1-4296-5829-4(0), First Facts) Capstone Press of Coughlan Cos.

The Big Race, Level 2. 2016. (Ladybird Readers Ser.). (ENG.). 16p. (J). pap., act. bk. ed. 5.99 (978-0-241-25456-1(6)) Penguin Bks., Ltd. GBR. Dist: Independent Pubs. Group.

Biggs, Brian. Tinyville Town: I'm a Librarian. 2017. (Tinyville Town Ser.). (ENG., Illus.). 22p. (J). (gr. -1 — 1). bds. 7.95 (978-1-4197-2322-3(7), Abrams Appleseed) Abrams, Inc.

Big's Big Baby. (Looney Tunes Song & Sound Bks.). (Illus.). 16p. (J). (gr. -1-k). 7.98 (978-0-7853-1608-4(6), PI10) Publications International, Ltd.

Bilik-Franklin, MidiAna & Griffith, Indigo, photos by. The Carseat Tourist. 2006. (Illus.). (J). bds. 7.95 (978-0-9772825-0-0(3)) Critter Camp Inc.

Billet, Marion. My First London Bus. Billet, Marion, illus. 2015. (Whizzy Wheels Ser.). (ENG., Illus.). 10p. (J). (-k). bds. 9.99 (978-0-230-76057-8(0)) Pan Macmillan GBR. Dist: Independent Pubs. Group.

—My First London Taxi. Billet, Marion, illus. 2015. (Whizzy Wheels Ser.). (ENG., Illus.). 10p. (J). (-k). bds. 11.99 (978-0-230-76103-2(8)) Pan Macmillan GBR. Dist: Independent Pubs. Group.

—My First Train. Billet, Marion, illus. 2015. (Whizzy Wheels Ser.). (ENG., Illus.). 10p. (J). (gr. -1-k). bds. 11.99 (978-1-4472-7697-5(3)) Pan Macmillan GBR. Dist: Independent Pubs. Group.

Billet, Marion, illus. Hello! London. 2014. (Hello! Ser.). (ENG.). 10p. (J). (-k). bds. 15.99 (978-1-4472-4682-4(9)) Pan Macmillan GBR. Dist: Independent Pubs. Group.

—My First London Sticker Book. 2015. (ENG.). 32p. (J). (gr. k-3). pap. 10.99 (978-1-4472-7617-3(5)) Pan Macmillan GBR. Dist: Independent Pubs. Group.

Billings, David. Louie the Buoy. 2010. 36p. pap. 16.99 (978-1-4520-3010-4(3)) AuthorHouse.

Birdsong, Michelle. Sneasy the Greasy Babysits Abigail. 2009. 20p. pap. 7.32 (978-1-4120-7205-2(0)) Trafford Publishing.

Birkett, Georgie. Peekaboo! - Who Are You? Birkett, Georgie, illus. 2014. (Felty Flaps Ser.). (ENG., Illus.). 10p. (J). (gr. -1). bds. 9.99 (978-1-4472-6098-1(8)) Pan Macmillan GBR. Dist: Independent Pubs. Group.

—Red, Blue, Peekaboo! Birkett, Georgie, illus. 2015. (Felty Flaps Ser.). (ENG., Illus.). 10p. (J). (— 1). bds. 9.99 (978-1-4472-6099-8(6)) Pan Macmillan GBR. Dist: Independent Pubs. Group.

Biro, Val. Gumdrop Finds a Ghost. (Illus.). 27p. (J). (978-0-340-71062-3(4)); pap. (978-0-340-71063-0(2)) Hodder & Stoughton.

—Gumdrop Makes a Start. (Illus.). 27p. (J). (978-0-340-71058-6(6)); pap. (978-0-340-71059-3(4)) Hodder & Stoughton.

—Gumdrop's Merry Christmas. (Illus.). 26p. (J). (978-0-340-71060-9(8)) Hodder & Stoughton.

Bixley, Donovan, illus. Pussycat, Pussycat: Purrfect Nursery Rhymes. 2016. (ENG.). 24p. (J). (— 1). pap. 9.99 (978-1-927262-28-3(3)) Upstart Pr. NZL. Dist: Independent Pubs. Group.

Blackstone, Stella. Bear Takes a Trip (Oso Se Va de Viaje) Harter, Debbie, illus. 2013. (ENG & SPA.). 24p. (J). (gr. k-1). 6.99 (978-1-84686-945-7(5)) Barefoot Bks., Inc.

—Bear's Birthday (L'Anniversaire de l'Ours) Harter, Debbie, illus. 2013. (ENG & FRE.). 24p. (J). (gr. k-1). pap. 6.99 (978-1-84686-944-0(7)) Barefoot Bks., Inc.

—Bear's Birthday/El Cumpleanos de Oso. Harter, Debbie, illus. 2013. (ENG & SPA.). 24p. (J). (gr. k-1). 6.99 (978-1-84686-943-3(9)) Barefoot Bks., Inc.

—Cleo & Caspar. Mockford, Caroline, illus. 2013. (ENG.). 24p. (J). 6.99 (978-1-78285-053-3(8)) Barefoot Bks., Inc.

—Cleo in the Snow. Mockford, Caroline, illus. 2013. (ENG.). 24p. (J). 6.99 (978-1-78285-054-0(6)); 6.99 (978-1-78285-055-7(4)) Barefoot Bks., Inc.

—Cleo on the Move. Mockford, Caroline, illus. 2013. (ENG.). 24p. (J). 6.99 (978-1-78285-056-4(2)); (gr. -1-k). pap. 6.99 (978-1-78285-057-1(0)) Barefoot Bks., Inc.

—Cleo the Cat. Mockford, Caroline, illus. 2013. (ENG.). 24p. (J). (gr. -1-k). pap. 6.99 (978-1-78285-051-9(1)) Barefoot Bks., Inc.

—Hip Shapes. Bell, Siobhan, illus. 2012. (ENG.). 24p. (J). (gr. -1-k). 6.99 (978-1-84686-762-0(2)) Barefoot Bks., Inc.

—Who Are You, Baby Kangaroo? Beaton, Clare, illus. 2005. (ENG.). 24p. (J). (gr. -1-2). bds. 6.99 (978-1-905236-19-0(0)) Barefoot Bks., Inc.

—You & Me. Manna, Giovanni, illus. 2009. (ENG.). 32p. (J). 14.99 (978-1-84686-336-3(8)) Barefoot Bks., Inc.

Blackstone, Stella & Barefoot Books Staff. Bear's School Day. Harter, Debbie, illus. 2014. 24p. (J). (gr. -1-1). 6.99 (978-1-78285-085-4(6)) Barefoot Bks., Inc.

Blackstone, Stella & Bauer, Stephanie. Octopus Opposites. Bauer, Stephanie, illus. 2011. (ENG., Illus.). 32p. (J). (gr. -1-k). 8.99 (978-1-84686-591-6(3)) Barefoot Bks., Inc.

Blackstone, Stella & Scribens, Sunny. Baby's First Words. 2017. (Illus.). 30p. (J). (gr. -1-k). 14.99 **(978-1-78285-321-3(9))** Barefoot Bks., Inc.

Blackstone, Stella, et al. Walking Through the Jungle. 2011. (ENG., Illus.). 32p. (J). (gr. -1-2). 9.99 (978-1-84686-660-9(X)) Barefoot Bks., Inc.

Blackwell, Archie. Secrets of the Dinosaur World: Jurassic Giants & Other Prehistoric Creatures. 2014. (ENG., Illus.). 80p. (J). (gr. 3). pap. 16.95 (978-1-78097-285-5(7)) Carlton Bks., Ltd. GBR. Dist: Sterling Publishing Co., Inc.

Blair, Rachael. Maya's Gossamer: A Gentle Guide on How to Manifest Virtues in Children. 2014. 80p. pap. 27.99 (978-1-4525-8684-7(5), Balboa Pr.) Author Solutions, Inc.

Blake, Michel. Out to Play. Candlewick Press Staff, illus. 2005. (Easy Open Board Book Ser.). (ENG.). 16p. (J). (— 1). bds. 5.99 (978-0-7636-2767-6(4)) Candlewick Pr.

Blake, Quentin. Jack & Nancy. 2013. (ENG., Illus.). 32p. (J). (gr. -1-k). pap. 14.99 (978-1-84941-689-4(3), Red Fox) Random House Children's Books GBR. Dist: Independent Pubs. Group.

Blake, Quentin. Three Little Monkeys. Chichester Clark, Emma, illus. 2017. 40p. (J). (gr. -1-3). 18.99 **(978-0-06-267067-0(0))** HarperCollins Pubs.

Blake, Stephanie. Poop-Di-Doop! 2015. (ENG., Illus.). 40p. (J). 15.95 (978-0-7358-4204-5(3)) North-South Bks., Inc.

Bland, Nick. Some Moms. 2017. (ENG., Illus.). 24p. (J). (gr. -1-1). 9.95 (978-0-7624-6200-1(0), Running Pr.) Running Pr. Bk. Pubs.

Blazin' Hot: Picture Book (English) NL 9x9 with Snipe. 2007. (J). 5.99 (978-1-933934-46-4(8)) Mighty Kids Media.

Bledsoe, Amanda. Chores, S'mores!, 1 vol. Perry, Jodi, ed. 2009. 28p. pap. 24.95 (978-1-60703-605-0(3)) PublishAmerica, Inc.

—Chores S'mores, 1 vol. 2010. 26p. 24.95 (978-1-4512-1507-6(X)) PublishAmerica, Inc.

Bleu, Kennedy. Cotter Otter in Treasure Water. Goembel, Ponder, illus. 2014. (ENG.). 24p. (J). pap. 24.95 (978-1-63004-814-3(3)) America Star Bks.

Blight, Peter. The Lonely Giraffe. Terry, Michael, illus. 2006. (Bloomsbury Paperbacks Ser.). (ENG.). 32p. (J). (gr. -1-3). pap. 12.99 (978-0-7475-7144-5(9)) Bloomsbury Publishing Plc GBR. Dist: Trafalgar Square Publishing.

Bloch, Serge. The Big Adventure of a Little Line. 2016. (ENG., Illus.). 88p. (J). (gr. 1-3). 19.95 (978-0-500-65058-5(6), 565058) Thames & Hudson.

—Sam & His Dad. Bloch, Serge, illus. 2012. (ENG., Illus.). 40p. (J). (gr. -1-3). 24.95 (978-0-9806070-8-6(6)) Wilkins Farago Pty, Ltd. AUS. Dist: Independent Pubs. Group.

Blossom, Maggie. Wizard of Oz. Pearse, Asha, illus. 2014. (ENG.). 16p. (J). (gr. -1-4). 7.99 (978-1-4867-0009-7(8)) Flowerpot Children's Pr. Inc. CAN. Dist: Cardinal Pubs. Group.

Bluemle, Elizabeth. Dogs on the Bed. Wilsdorf, Anne, illus. 2013. (ENG.). 32p. (J). (gr. -1-2). pap. 6.99 (978-0-7636-6736-8(6)) Candlewick Pr.

Blume, Judy. The One in the Middle Is the Green Kangaroo. 39p. (J). (gr. k-3). pap. 3.99 (978-0-8072-1337-7(3), Listening Library) Random Hse. Audio Publishing Group.

Blyton, Enid. Stories Jesus Told. 2012. (ENG.). 24p. (J). pap. 9.95 (978-1-84135-745-4(6)) Award Pubns. Ltd. GBR. Dist: Parkwest Pubns., Inc.

—Story of Jesus. 2012. (ENG.). 24p. (J). pap. 9.95 (978-1-84135-744-7(8)) Award Pubns. Ltd. GBR. Dist: Parkwest Pubns., Inc.

Boam, Jon, illus. Colour Me Menagerie. 2012. (Colour Me Ser.). (ENG.). 24p. (J). (gr. -1-k). 6.00 (978-1-907704-09-3(4)) Nobrow Ltd. GBR. Dist: Consortium Bk. Sales & Distribution.

Boddy, Gary. Giraffe's Holiday in Sydney. 2007. 23p. 19.95 (978-1-84799-919-1(0)) Lulu Pr., Inc.

—This Cow These Cows. 2007. 31p. 21.00 (978-1-84799-960-3(3)) Lulu Pr., Inc.

Bodecker, N. M. The Mushroom Center Disaster. Blegvad, Erik & Starr, Branka, illus. 2004. (ENG.). 48p. (J). reprint ed. (978-1-931561-98-3(2)) MacAdam/Cage Publishing, Inc.

—Quimble Wood. Starr, Branka, illus. 2004. (ENG.). 32p. (J). reprint ed. (978-1-931561-97-6(4)) MacAdam/Cage Publishing, Inc.

Boehne, Jacob A. Two Long Ears, 1 vol. 2016. (ENG., Illus.). 24p. (J). bds. 9.99 (978-0-7643-5039-9(0), 9780764350399) Schiffer Publishing, Ltd.

Boelts, Maribeth. A Bike Like Sergio's. Jones, Noah Z., illus. 2016. (ENG.). 40p. (J). (gr. k-3). 15.99 (978-0-7636-6649-1(1)) Candlewick Pr.

Bogart, Jo Ellen. Big & Small, Room for All. Newland, Gillian, illus. 2017. (ENG.). 30p. (J). (— 1). bds. 7.99 **(978-0-14-319893-2(9)**, Tundra Bks.) Tundra Bks. CAN. Dist: Penguin Random Hse. LLC.

Bogart, Jo Ellen. Count Your Chickens. Smith, Lori Joy, illus. 2017. (ENG.). 32p. (J). (-k). 16.99 (978-1-77049-792-4(7), Tundra Bks.) Tundra Bks. CAN. Dist: Penguin Random Hse. LLC.

Bolam, Emily. In the Jungle. 2013. (ENG., Illus.). 10p. (J). bds. (978-0-230-76713-3(3)) Barron's Educational Series, Inc.

Bolden, Tonya. Beautiful Moon: A Child's Prayer. Velasquez, Eric, illus. 2014. (ENG.). 32p. (J). (gr. k-2). 16.95 (978-1-4197-0792-6(2), Abrams Bks. for Young Readers) Abrams, Inc.

Boldt, Claudia. Melvin: The Luckiest Monkey in the World. 2013. (ENG., Illus.). 32p. (J). (gr. -1-k). 14.95 (978-1-84976-086-7(1)) Tate Publishing, Ltd. GBR. Dist: Abrams, Inc.

—Odd Dog. 2012. (ENG., Illus.). 32p. (J). (gr. -1-1). 16.95 (978-0-7358-4068-3(7)) North-South Bks., Inc.

—Outfoxed. 2016. (ENG., Illus.). 32p. (J). (gr. k-2). 16.95 (978-1-84976-313-4(5)) Tate Publishing, Ltd. GBR. Dist: Abrams, Inc.

Boldt, Mike. 123 Versus ABC. Boldt, Mike, illus. 2013. (ENG., Illus.). 32p. (J). (gr. -1-3). 17.99 (978-0-06-210299-7(0)) HarperCollins Pubs.

Bond, Felicia. The Halloween Play. Bond, Felicia, illus. 2003. Orig. Title: The Halloween Performance. (Illus.). 32p. (J). (gr. -1-18). 6.99 (978-0-06-054443-0(0)) HarperCollins Pubs.

Bond, Michael. The Paddington Treasury. Alley, R. W., illus. 2014. (Paddington Ser.). (ENG.). 160p. (J). (gr. -1-3). 21.99 (978-0-06-231242-6(1)) HarperCollins Pubs.

Bonfield, Chloe. The Perfect Tree. 2016. (ENG., Illus.). 32p. (J). (gr. -1-17). 16.95 (978-0-7624-5586-7(1), Running Pr. Kids) Running Pr. Bk. Pubs.

Bonnet, Rosalinde. Very First Words Christmas. 2011. (Very First Words Board Book Ser.). 24p. (J). ring bd. 6.99 (978-0-7945-2937-6(2), Usborne) EDC Publishing.

Bonnet, Rosalinde, illus. Alphabet Picture Book. 2011. (Alphabet Picture Book Ser.). 26p. (J). ring bd. 11.99 (978-0-7945-2954-3(2), Usborne) EDC Publishing.

Bonnice, Lindsey. Libby & Pearl: The Best of Friends. Bonnice, Lindsey, illus. 2016. (Illus.). 32p. (J). (gr. -1-3). 14.99 (978-0-06-245927-5(9)) HarperCollins Pubs.

Bonwill, Ann. Naughty Toes. Murfin, Teresa, illus. 2011. (ENG.). 32p. 15.95 (978-1-58925-103-8(2)); pap. 7.95 (978-1-58925-430-5(9)) Tiger Tales.

Boon, Fiona, ed. The Great Fairy Baking Competition. Ede, Lara, illus. Snaith, Andy, photos by. 2013. (ENG.). 64p. (J). 12.99 (978-1-78235-591-5(X)) Make Believe Ideas GBR. Dist: Nelson, Thomas Inc.

Borando, Silvia. Black Cat, White Cat. 2015. (Minibombo Ser.). (ENG., Illus.). 48p. (J). (-k). 14.00 (978-0-7636-8106-7(7)) Candlewick Pr.

—The Cat Book: A Minibombo Book. Borando, Silvia, illus. 2017. (Minibombo Ser.). (ENG., Illus.). 32p. (J). (-k). 9.99 (978-0-7636-9472-2(X)) Candlewick Pr.

Borando, Silvia, et al. The White Book. 2015. (Minibombo Ser.). (ENG., Illus.). 48p. (J). (gr. -1-k). 14.00 (978-0-7636-8107-4(5)) Candlewick Pr.

Bosak, Susan V. Dream: A Tale of Wonder, Wisdom & Wishes. Dillon, Leo et al, illus. 2004. 40p. (J). (978-1-896232-04-1(3), TCP Pr.) Communication Project, The.

—A Little Something. McGaw, Laurie, illus. 2008. 32p. (J). (978-1-896232-06-5(X), TCP Pr.) Communication Project, The.

Bourke, Nike & Danalis, Stella. What the Sky Knows. 2005. (Illus.). 32p. (J). (978-0-7022-3501-6(6)) Univ. of Queensland Pr.

Bowie, C. W. Busy Fingers. Willingham, Fred, illus. 2004. (ENG.). 28p. (J). (gr. -1 — 1). bds. 7.95 (978-1-58089-048-9(2)) Charlesbridge Publishing, Inc.

Bowie, Sarah. Let's See Ireland! Bowie, Sarah, illus. 2016. (ENG., Illus.). 32p. (J). 18.00 (978-1-84717-731-5(X)) O'Brien Pr., Ltd., The IRL. Dist: Dufour Editions, Inc.

Bowles, Paula. Little Lou & the Woolly Mammoth. 2015. (ENG., Illus.). 32p. (J). (gr. -1-1). 18.99 (978-1-4088-3965-2(2), 9781408839652, Bloomsbury USA Childrens) Bloomsbury Publishing USA.

Bowman, Crystal. My Christmas Stocking: Filled with God's Love, 1 vol. Gevry, Claudine, illus. 2015. (ENG.). 14p. (J). bds. 6.99 (978-0-310-73823-7(7)) Zonderkidz.

Bowness, Kim. The Brave Engineers. 2007. (Illus.). 30p. (J). lib. bdg. 19.95 (978-1-933732-36-7(9)) Big Ransom Studio.

Box, Su. Baby Jesus. 2014. (Bible Dial-A-Picture Bks.). (ENG., Illus.). 8p. (J). (gr. -1-k). bds. 6.99 (978-0-7641-6694-5(8)) Barron's Educational Series, Inc.

—Noah's Ark. East, Jacqueline, illus. 2014. (Bible Dial-A-Picture Bks.). (ENG.). 8p. (J). (gr. -1-k). bds. 6.99 (978-0-7641-6695-2(6)) Barron's Educational Series, Inc.

Boyd, Lizi. I Love Grandma. Boyd, Lizi, illus. 2009. (Super Sturdy Picture Bks.). (ENG., Illus.). 24p. (J). (gr. -1-k). 8.99 (978-0-7636-3728-6(9)) Candlewick Pr.

Boyer, Mitch. Vivian the Dog Moves to the City. Boyer, Mitch, illus. 2017. (Illus.). 40p. (J). (gr. -1-3). 17.99 **(978-0-06-267327-5(0))** HarperCollins Pubs.

Boyle, Joanna. The Tip-Tap Dancing Cat. 2014. (ENG., Illus.). 32p. (J). (gr. -1-1). pap. 8.99 (978-1-84365-275-5(7), Pavilion) Pavilion Bks. GBR. Dist: Independent Pubs. Group.

Boynton, Sandra. Buenas Noches a Todos. Boynton, Sandra, illus. 2004.Tr. of Going to Bed Book. (SPA., Illus.). 14p. (J). (gr. -1 — 1). bds. 5.99 (978-0-689-86652-4(6), Libros Para Ninos) Libros Para Ninos.

—Christmas Parade. Boynton, Sandra, illus. 2012. (ENG., Illus.). 32p. (J). (gr. -1-1). 14.99 (978-1-4424-6813-9(0), Little Simon) Little Simon.

—Perritos: Un Libro para Contar y Ladrar. Boynton, Sandra, illus. 2004.Tr. of Doggies. (SPA., Illus.). 14p. (J). (gr. -1 — 1). bds. 5.99 (978-0-689-86303-5(9), Libros Para Ninos) Libros Para Ninos.

Bradman, Tony. Flora the Fairy. Carlow, Emma, illus. 2nd ed. 2016. (Reading Ladder Ser.). (ENG.). 48p. (J). (gr. k-2). pap. 7.99 (978-1-4052-8225-3(8)) Egmont Bks., Ltd. GBR. Dist: Independent Pubs. Group.

—Mr. Wolf Bounces Back, 1 vol. Warburton, Sarah, illus. 2013. (After Happily Ever After Ser.). (ENG.). 56p. (gr. 2-3). pap. 5.05 (978-1-4342-6414-5(9), After Happily Ever After) Stone Arch Bks.

—Red Riding Hood Takes Charge, 1 vol. Warburton, Sarah, illus. 2013. (After Happily Ever After Ser.). (ENG.). 56p. (gr. 2-3). pap. 5.05 (978-1-4342-6413-8(0), After Happily Ever After) Stone Arch Bks.

—Through My Window: Celebrating 30 Years of a Children's Classic. Browne, Eileen, illus. 30th rev. ed. 2016. (ENG.). 32p. (J). (gr. -1-2). pap. 10.99 (978-1-84780-756-4(9), Frances Lincoln Children's Bks.) Quarto Publishing Group UK GBR. Dist: Hachette Bk. Group.

Bradman, Tony & Quarto Generic Staff. Wait & See. Browne, Eileen, illus. rev. ed. 2012. (ENG.). 32p. (J). (gr. -1-1). pap. 8.99 (978-1-84780-181-4(1), Frances Lincoln) Quarto Publishing Group UK GBR. Dist: Hachette Bk. Group.

Bradshaw, Lauren. Henry's Bright Idea. Kirwan, Wednesday, illus. 2016. (Walnut Animal Society Ser.). (ENG.). 32p. (J). (-k). 17.95 (978-1-937359-94-2(8)) Cameron & Co., Inc.

Bramsen, Carin. Just a Duck? 2015. (ENG., Illus.). 40p. (J). (gr. -1-2). lib. bdg. 20.99 (978-0-375-97344-4(3), Random Hse. Bks. for Young Readers) Random Hse. Children's Bks.

Brandenburg, Jim & National Geographic Kids Staff. Face to Face with Wolves. 2010. (Face to Face with Animals Ser.). (ENG., Illus.). 32p. (J). (gr. 2-5). pap. 6.95 (978-1-4263-0698-3(9), National Geographic Children's Bks.) National Geographic Society.

Brandt, Lois. Maddi's Fridge. Vogel, Vin, illus. 2014. (ENG.). 32p. (J). (gr. k-3). 17.95 (978-1-936261-29-1(4)) Flashlight Pr.

Brandy. CAN & CAN't Believe in Themselves: Big Life Lessons for Little Kids. 2017. (ENG., Illus.). 40p. (J). (gr. -1-3). 10.00 **(978-981-4771-29-0(5))** Marshall Cavendish International (Asia) Private Ltd. SGP. Dist: National Bk. Network.

—COULD & COULDN't Are Not Afraid of the Dark: Big Life Lessons for Little Kids. 2017. (ENG., Illus.). 40p. 10.00 **(978-981-4771-30-6(9))** Marshall Cavendish International (Asia) Private Ltd. SGP. Dist: National Bk. Network.

—DID & DIDN't Learn When to Study & When to Play: Big Life Lessons for Little Kids. 2017. (ENG., Illus.). 40p. 10.00 **(978-981-4771-31-3(7))** Marshall Cavendish International (Asia) Private Ltd. SGP. Dist: National Bk. Network.

—WAS & WASN't Learn That It's Good to Win, but Its Ok to Lose: Big Life Lessons for Little Kids. 2017. (ENG., Illus.). 40p. 10.00 **(978-981-4771-32-0(5))** Marshall Cavendish International (Asia) Private Ltd. SGP. Dist: National Bk. Network.

—WILL & WON't Learn to Share: Big Life Lessons for Little Kids. 2017. (ENG., Illus.). 40p. 10.00 **(978-981-4771-33-7(3))** Marshall Cavendish International (Asia) Private Ltd. SGP. Dist: National Bk. Network.

Brannon, Pat. Has a Donkey Ever Brought You Breakfast in Bed? Demming, Karen, illus. 2012. 38p. pap. 10.00 (978-1-938634-90-1(X)) Freedom of Speech Publishing, Inc.

Braud, Alexis. Parade, 1 vol. 2016. (ENG., Illus.). 32p. (J). (gr. -1-3). 16.99 (978-1-4556-2148-4(X)) Pelican Publishing Co., Inc.

Braun, Eric, et al. Encounter: Narrative Nonfiction Picture Books. 2017. (Encounter: Narrative Nonfiction Picture Bks.). (ENG.). 40p. (gr. 3-5). pap. 47.70 (978-1-4914-8051-9(3)) Encounter Bks.

Braun, Sebastien, illus. Santa's Noisy House. 2013. (ENG.). 12p. (J). (gr. -1-k). 17.99 (978-0-230-76411-8(8)) Pan Macmillan GBR. Dist: Independent Pubs. Group.

Bray, Darrell. I Remember Pop's General Store. 2013. 24p. pap. 24.95 (978-1-63004-679-8(5)) America Star Bks.

Bredehoft, Linda. Oh, Where Is My Ducky?, 1 vol. 2005. (Big Idea Bks.). (ENG., Illus.). 12p. (J). (gr. -1-1). bds. 6.99 (978-0-310-70746-2(3)) Zonderkidz.

Brennan, Sarah. The Tale of Temujin. Harrison, Harry, illus. 2012. (ENG.). 32p. (J). (978-1-937160-23-4(8)) Auspicious Times.

Brett, Jan. Armadillo Rodeo. Brett, Jan, illus. 2004. (ENG., Illus.). 32p. (J). (gr. -1-3). pap. 6.99 (978-0-14-240125-5(0), Puffin Books) Penguin Young Readers Group.

—Fritz & the Beautiful Horses. Brett, Jan, illus. 2016. (ENG., Illus.). 32p. (J). (-k). 17.99 (978-0-399-17458-2(3), G.P. Putnam's Sons Books for Young Readers) Penguin Young Readers Group.

—The Mitten. Brett, Jan, illus. 20th anniv. ed. 2009. (ENG., Illus.). 32p. (J). (gr. -1-k). 17.99 (978-0-399-25296-9(7), G.P. Putnam's Sons Books for Young Readers) Penguin Young Readers Group.

Brewster, Benjamin & dePaola, Tomie. The Baby Elephant. Burchard, Peter, illus. 2015. (G&d Vintage Ser.). (ENG.). 32p. (J). (-k). bds. 7.99 (978-0-448-48448-8(X), Grosset & Dunlap) Penguin Young Readers Group.

Brian, Janeen. I'm a Dirty Dinosaur. James, Ann, illus. 2014. (ENG.). 22p. (J). 11.99 (978-1-61067-296-2(8)) Kane Miller.

Bridge, Chris Helene. Read to Me! Bilingual. 2016. (ENG., Illus.). 32p. (J). pap. 9.95 (978-1-942945-36-9(1), 9781942945369) Bright Sky Pr.

Bridwell, Norman. Clifford's Family. Bridwell, Norman, illus. 2010. (Clifford 8x8 Ser.). (ENG., Illus.). 32p. (J). (gr. -1-3). pap. 3.99 (978-0-545-21585-5(4), Cartwheel Bks.) Scholastic, Inc.

Brière-haquet, Alice & Csil. Mrs. Eiffel: The Love Story Behind the Eiffel Tower. 2015. (ENG., Illus.). 32p. (J). (gr. -1-3). 19.95 (978-3-89955-755-8(7)) Die Gestalten Verlag DEU. Dist: Penguin Random Hse. LLC.

Briers, Erica. Little Lamb to the Rescue. Boey, Stephanie, illus. 2004. (ENG.). 24p. (J). (978-1-55168-257-0(5)) Fenn, H. B. & Co., Ltd.

Bright, Rachel. Benjamin & the Super Spectacles. 2013. (Wonderful World of Walter & Winnie Ser.). (ENG., Illus.). 32p. (J). pap. 9.99 (978-0-00-744550-9(4), HarperCollins Children's Bks.) HarperCollins Pubs. Ltd. GBR. Dist: HarperCollins Pubs.

British Museum of Natural History Staff, contrib. by. What Do Animals Eat Colouring Book. (Illus.). 8p. (J). (gr. -1-6). pap. 2.95 (978-0-565-00808-6(0)) Natural History Museum Pubns. GBR. Dist: Parkwest Pubns., Inc.

Britland, Jan. The Adventures of Rodger Dodger Dog. Swaim, Michael, illus. 2009. 40p. pap. 15.95 (978-1-936051-23-6(0)) Peppertree Pr., The.

Brocoli, Steffie & Bidet, Catherine. Through the Forest. 2016. (ENG., Illus.). 30p. (J). (gr. k-2). 19.95 (978-0-500-65076-9(4), 565076) Thames & Hudson.

Brooke, L. Leslie. Johnny Crow's Picture Book. 2015. (ENG., Illus.). 192p. (J). (gr. k-3). pap. 14.99 (978-0-486-79598-0(5)) Dover Pubns., Inc.

—Ring o' Roses, a Nursery Rhyme Picture Book. Brooke, L. Leslie, illus. 2012. (Illus.). 102p. pap. 9.99 (978-1-61720-438-8(2)) Wilder Pubns., Corp.

Brooks, David, illus. Animals. 2005. (My First Book Ser.). 9p. (J). (gr. -1-1). bds. 3.95 (978-1-933050-09-6(8)) Sweetwater Pr.

Brooks, F. & Litchfield, J. Picture Dictionary: A First Alphabetical Word Book. 2004. (Picture Dictionaries Ser.). 96p. (J). lib. bdg. 24.95 (978-1-58086-437-4(6)) EDC Publishing.

Brooks, Felicity. Brush Your Teeth, Max & Millie. 2011. (Toddler Bks). 24p. (J). ring bd. 7.99 (978-0-7945-2998-7(4), Usborne) EDC Publishing.

—Build a Picture Tractors Sticker Book. Lovell, Katie, illus. 2013. (Build a Picture Sticker Bks). 24p. (J). pap. 6.99 (978-0-7945-3319-9(1), Usborne) EDC Publishing.

—Take Turns, Max & Millie. 2011. (Toddler Bks). 24p. (J). ring bd. 7.99 (978-0-7945-3000-6(1), Usborne) EDC Publishing.

—Time for Bed, Max & Millie. 2011. (Toddler Bks). 24p. (J). ring bd. 7.99 (978-0-7945-3068-6(0), Usborne) EDC Publishing.

—Very First Animals Board Book. 2010. (Very First Words Board Bks). 10p. (J). bds. 6.99 (978-0-7945-2479-1(6), Usborne) EDC Publishing.

—Very First Numbers. 2009. (First Words Board Bks). 18p. (J). bds. 6.99 (978-0-7945-2354-1(4), Usborne) EDC Publishing.

Brooks, Felicity & Fearn, Katrina. First Dot-To-Dot Animals. 2013. (First Dot-To-Dot Ser.). 16p. (J). pap. 5.99 (978-0-7945-3198-0(9), Usborne) EDC Publishing.

Brooks, Susie. Five Silly Monkeys. Tarbett, Debbie, illus. 2009. (ENG.). 14p. (J). (gr. k — 1). bds. 9.99 (978-0-545-10222-3(7), Cartwheel Bks.) Scholastic, Inc.

Brosnan, Paris. Billy Bee - Sugarplums & Honey. 2017. (ENG., Illus.). 27p. (J). pap. 13.95 **(978-1-78710-075-6(8)**, 4d1efa56-0d47-487a-bc8e-b11fdf88ec5d) Austin, Stan AUS. Dist: Bookmasters Distribution.

Brothers Grimm. Snow White & Rose Red. Vivanco, Kelly, illus. 2014. (ENG.). 40p. (J). (gr. -1-4). 17.95 (978-1-927018-34-7(X)) Simply Read Bks. CAN. Dist: Ingram Publisher Services.

Broutin & Stehr. Baldomero Va A la Escuela. (SPA.). 26p. (978-84-95150-47-9(6)) Corimbo, Editorial S.L.

Brown, Alison. Eddie & Dog, 1 vol. 2014. (ENG.). 32p. (gr. -1-2). 14.95 (978-1-62370-114-7(7)) Capstone Young Readers of Coughlan Cos.

Brown, Carron. Space Station. Johnson, Bee, illus. 2016. (ENG.). 36p. (J). 12.99 (978-1-61067-411-9(1)) Kane Miller.

Brown, Heather & Accord Publishing Staff. Chomp! 2012. (ENG., Illus.). 12p. (J). bds. 7.99 (978-1-4494-1016-2(2)) Andrews McMeel Publishing.

Brown, James. Archie & George & the New Bikes. 2016. (Early Reader Ser.). (ENG., Illus.). 64p. (J). (gr. k-3). pap. 6.99 (978-1-4440-1529-4(X), Orion Children's Bks.) Hachette Children's Group GBR. Dist: Hachette Bk. Group.

Brown, Janet. Jack & the Beanstalk: My First Reading Book. Morton, Ken, illus. 2015. (ENG.). 24p. pap. 6.99 (978-1-86147-474-2(1), Armadillo) Anness Publishing GBR. Dist: National Bk. Network.

—Pinocchio: My First Reading Book. Morton, Ken, illus. 2015. (ENG.). 24p. pap. 6.99 (978-1-86147-475-9(X), Armadillo) Anness Publishing GBR. Dist: National Bk. Network.

Brown, Marc. Arthur's Perfect Christmas. 2004. (ENG., Illus.). 40p. (J). (gr. -1-1). pap. 6.99 (978-0-316-00130-4(9), Tingley, Megan Bks.) Little, Brown Bks. for Young Readers.

Brown, Margaret Wise. The Golden Egg Book. Weisgard, Leonard, illus. 2015. (Little Golden Book Ser.). (ENG.). 24p. (J). (-k). 4.99 (978-0-385-38476-6(9), Golden Bks.) Random Hse. Children's Bks.

—Goodnight Moon. Hurd, Clement, illus. 60th anniv. ed. 2007. (ENG.). (J). (gr. -1 — 1). 34p. bds. 8.99 (978-0-694-00361-7(1), HarperFestival); 32p. pap. 8.99 (978-0-06-443017-3(0)) HarperCollins Pubs.

—Goodnight Moon. Hurd, Clement, illus. (J). pap. 32.75 incl. audio. (gr. -1-3). 24.95 incl. audio Weston Woods Studios, Inc.

—Home for a Bunny. Williams, Garth, illus. 2012. (Little Golden Book Ser.). (ENG.). 24p. (J). (gr. k-k). 4.99 (978-0-307-93009-5(2), Golden Bks.) Random Hse. Children's Bks.

Brown, Mick. From Round about Midnight until about Five! 2012. 60p. pap. 27.45 (978-1-4772-2701-5(6)) AuthorHouse.

Brown, Peter. Chowder. 2012. (Chowder Book Ser.). (ENG., Illus.). 32p. (J). (gr. -1-3). pap. 7.99 (978-0-316-20088-2(3)) Little, Brown Bks. for Young Readers.

Brown, Ruth. The Big Sneeze. 2011. (ENG., Illus.). 32p. (J). (gr. k-k). pap. 9.99 (978-1-84939-052-1(5)) Andersen Pr. GBR. Dist: Independent Pubs. Group.

—Greyfriars Bobby. Brown, Ruth, illus. 2013. (ENG., Illus.). 32p. (J). (gr. -1-k). pap. 12.99 (978-1-84939-632-5(9)) Andersen Pr. GBR. Dist: Independent Pubs. Group.

—Snail Trail. Brown, Ruth, illus. 2013. (ENG., Illus.). 24p. (J). (gr. -1-k). 12.99 (978-1-84939-252-5(8)) Andersen Pr. GBR. Dist: Independent Pubs. Group.

—Ten Seeds. 2013. (ENG., Illus.). 24p. (J). (gr. -1-k). 10.99 (978-1-84939-251-8(X)) Andersen Pr. GBR. Dist: Independent Pubs. Group.

Brown, Ruth, illus. The Christmas Mouse. 2013. (J). (978-1-4351-5021-8(X)) Barnes & Noble, Inc.

Brown, Ruth & Brown, Ken. Lion in the Long Grass. 2013. (Silver Tales Ser.). (ENG., Illus.). (J). (gr. -1-2). pap. (978-1-74352-445-9(5)) Hinkler Bks. Pty, Ltd.

Browne, Christopher. Marlo. Browne, Christopher, illus. 2017. (Illus.). 40p. (J). (gr. -1-3). 17.99 (978-0-06-244113-3(2)) HarperCollins Pubs.

Browne, Susan Chalker. Freddy's Hockey Hero, 1 vol. Rose, Hilda, illus. 2010. (ENG.). 32p. (J). (gr. k-3). 10.95 (978-1-897174-62-3(4), Tuckamore Bks) Creative Bk. Publishing CAN. Dist: Orca Bk. Pubs. USA.

Brownjohn, Emma. Yes I Can! Be Healthy. Brownjohn, Emma, illus. 2011. (Yes I Can! Ser.). (ENG., Illus.). 18p. (J). (gr. -1-k). 12.99 (978-1-85707-734-6(2)) Tango Bks. GBR. Dist: Independent Pubs. Group.

Brownlow, Mike. Ten Little Dinosaurs. Rickerty, Simon, illus. 2016. (Ten Little Ser.). (ENG.). 32p. (J). (gr. -1-k). pap. **(978-1-4083-3401-0(1)**, Orchard Bks.) Hachette Children's Group GBR. Dist: Hachette Bk. Group.

Brownlow, Mike, illus. Dinosaurs of Doom! 2011. (Time Pirates Ser.). (ENG.). 12p. (J). (gr. k-2). bds. 24.99 (978-0-230-74179-9(7)) Macmillan Pubs., Ltd. GBR. Dist: Independent Pubs. Group.

Bruna, Dick. The Apple. 2013. (ENG., Illus.). 28p. (J). (gr. -1-1). 7.95 (978-1-84976-214-4(7)) Tate Publishing, Ltd. GBR. Dist: Abrams, Inc.

—Farmer John's Seeds. 2004. (Illus.). 12p. pap. 5.99 (978-1-59226-191-8(4)) Big Tent Entertainment, Inc.

—I Can Count. 2012. (ENG., Illus.). 28p. 7.95 (978-1-84976-076-8(4)) Tate Publishing, Ltd. GBR. Dist: Abrams, Inc.

—My Vest Is White. 2012. (ENG., Illus.). 28p. 7.95 (978-1-84976-075-1(6)) Tate Publishing, Ltd. GBR. Dist: Abrams, Inc.

—On My Scooter. 2013. (ENG., Illus.). 28p. (J). (gr. -1-1). 7.95 (978-1-84976-216-8(3)) Tate Publishing, Ltd. GBR. Dist: Abrams, Inc.

—Round, Square, Triangle. 2012. (ENG., Illus.). 28p. 7.95 (978-1-84976-077-5(2)) Tate Publishing, Ltd. GBR. Dist: Abrams, Inc.

—The School. 2013. (ENG., Illus.). 28p. (J). (gr. -1 — 1). 7.95 (978-1-84976-215-1(5)) Tate Publishing, Ltd. GBR. Dist: Abrams, Inc.

Brundin, Anders & Dranger, Joanna Rubin. Dudley the Daydreamer. Perry, Frank, tr. from SWE. 2008. (ENG., Illus.). 32p. (J). (gr. k-2). pap. 12.95 (978-1-905341-10-8(5)) WingedChariot Pr. GBR. Dist: Independent Pubs. Group.

Bruzzone, Catherine. Spanish-English Picture Dictionary. 2011. (First Bilingual Picture Dictionaries Ser.). (SPA & ENG., Illus.). 48p. (J). (gr. -1-3). pap. 7.99 (978-0-7641-4661-9(0)) Barron's Educational Series, Inc.

Bryan, Jennifer Liu. Hilda, A Very Loyal Goat. 2009. 40p. (J). 15.95 (978-0-9816265-1-2(3)) Next Chapter Pr.

Bryant, Ann. Tag. 2009. (ENG., Illus.). 24p. (J). pap. (978-0-7787-3900-5(7)); lib. bdg. (978-0-7787-3869-5(8)) Crabtree Publishing Co.

Buble, Brandee. O'Shae the Octopus. Liska, Eliska, illus. 2014. (ENG.). 32p. (J). (gr. -1-3). 15.95 (978-1-927018-56-9(0)) Simply Read Bks. CAN. Dist: Ingram Publisher Services.

Buchwald, Claire. Are You Ready for Me? Hansen, Amelia, illus. 2009. (Sit! Stay! Read! Ser.). (ENG.). 24p. (J). (gr. k-1). pap. 7.95 (978-0-940719-08-8(8)) Gryphon Pr., The.

Buckingham, Gabriella, illus. The Wheels on the Bus & Other Action Rhymes. 2013. (ENG.). 16p. (J). (gr. -1-12). bds. 7.99 (978-1-84322-830-1(0), Armadillo) Anness Publishing GBR. Dist: National Bk. Network.

Buckley, Elizabeth & Keyes, Joan Ross. Oxford Picture Dictionary Content Area for Kids. 2nd ed. 2012. (ENG., Illus.). 184p. pap., wbk. ed. 17.00 (978-0-19-401779-4(6)) Oxford Univ. Pr., Inc.

Buehner, Caralyn. Snowmen at Work. Buehner, Mark, illus. 2012. (ENG.). 32p. (J). (gr. -1-2). 16.99 (978-0-8037-3579-8(0), Dial Bks) Penguin Young Readers Group.

Buffalo, Tom And Tracey. Loganæs Big Night Out. 2008. 24p. pap. 11.99 (978-1-4389-1893-8(3)) AuthorHouse.

Bulla, Clyde Robert. A Tree Is a Plant. Schuett, Stacey, illus. 2016. (Let's-Read-And-Find-Out Science 1 Ser.). 40p. (J). (gr. -1-3). pap. 6.99 (978-0-06-238210-8(1)) HarperCollins Pubs.

Bunn, Cullen. Terrible Lizard. 2015. (ENG., Illus.). 136p. (J). pap. 19.99 (978-1-62010-236-7(6), 9781620102367) Oni Pr., Inc.

Bunting, Eve. Emma's Turtle. Winborn, Marsha, illus. 2014. (ENG.). 32p. (J). (gr. -1-2). pap. 6.95 (978-1-62091-735-0(1)) Boyds Mills Pr.

—Hurry! Hurry! Mack, Jeff, illus. 2014. (ENG.). 40p. (J). (gr. -1 — 1). pap. 6.99 (978-0-544-22733-0(6), HMH Books For Young Readers) Houghton Mifflin Harcourt Publishing Co.

—My Special Day at Third Street School. Bloom, Suzanne, illus. 2009. (ENG.). 32p. (J). (gr. k-2). pap. 10.95 (978-1-59078-745-8(5)) Boyds Mills Pr.

—Peepers. Ransome, James E., illus. 2017. (ENG.). 32p. (J). (gr. -1-3). pap. 7.99 **(978-1-328-74047-2(1)**, HMH Books For Young Readers) Houghton Mifflin Harcourt Publishing Co.

—Scary, Scary Halloween Gift Edition. Brett, Jan, illus. 2017. (ENG.). 40p. (J). (gr. -1-3). 8.99 (978-0-544-88034-4(X), HMH Books For Young Readers) Houghton Mifflin Harcourt Publishing Co.

—Yard Sale. Castillo, Lauren, illus. (ENG.). 32p. (J). (gr. -1-2). 2017. 6.99 (978-0-7636-9305-3(7)) 2015. 15.99 (978-0-7636-6542-5(8)) Candlewick Pr.

Burach, Ross. I Am Not a Chair! Burach, Ross, illus. 2017. (Illus.). 40p. (J). (gr. -1-3). 17.99 (978-0-06-236016-8(7)) HarperCollins Pubs.

Burgess, Matthew. Enormous Smallness: The Story of e. e. Cummings. Di Giacomo, Kris, illus. 2015. (ENG.). 64p. (J). (gr. -1-3). 17.95 (978-1-59270-171-1(X)) Enchanted Lion Bks., LLC.

Burks, James. Gabby & Gator. 2015. (ENG., Illus.). 192p. (J). (gr. 1-17). pap. 10.00 (978-0-316-25935-4(7), Yen Pr.) Orbit.

Burnham, Janet Hayward. The Dragoness Mess. 2003. (Illus.). 32p. (J). (gr. k-1). pap. 12.95 (978-0-9740743-1-3(4)) My Little Jessie Pr.

Burningham, John. Mr. Gumpy's Outing. Date not set. (Illus.). (J). bds. 6.95 (978-0-8050-7373-7(6), Holt, Henry & Co. Bks. For Young Readers) Holt, Henry & Co.

—Picnic. Burningham, John, illus. 2014. (ENG., Illus.). 32p. (J). (-k). 16.99 (978-0-7636-6945-4(8)) Candlewick Pr.

Burns, Joanne. What Is Heaven Like? 2005. 35p. (J). 10.99 (978-1-4116-3360-5(1)) Lulu Pr., Inc.

Burow, Ginger. The Night That Was Christmas, 1 vol. 2009. 21p. pap. 24.95 (978-1-4489-9842-5(5)) America Star Bks.

Burslem, Tobe. Bermendani. 2011. 28p. pap. 21.99 (978-1-4628-5490-5(7)) Xlibris Corp.

Burton, Robert. Wally A. Bow 21st Century Abow. 2010. 48p. 19.49 (978-1-4520-8046-8(1)) AuthorHouse.

Bush, Emilie P. Steamduck Learns to Fly! Petty, William Kevin, illus. 2012. 36p. pap. 11.95 (978-0-9849028-1-1(3)) Coal City Stories.

Bustos, Eduardo & Rodríguez, Lucho. Going Ape! 2012. (ENG., Illus.). 24p. (J). (gr. k-3). 9.95 (978-1-77049-282-0(8), Tundra Bks.) Tundra Bks. CAN. Dist: Penguin Random Hse. LLC.

Butchart, Pamela. Yikes, Ticklysaurus! Lloyd, Sam, illus. 2015. (ENG.). 32p. (J). (gr. -1-1). 18.99 (978-1-4088-3969-0(5), 9781408839690, Bloomsbury USA Childrens) Bloomsbury Publishing USA.

Butlin, Ron. Here Come the Trolls! Hutcheson, Jim, illus. 2016. (ENG.). 32p. (J). (gr. -1-2). pap. (978-1-78027-295-5(2)) Birlinn, Ltd.

Butterfield, Moira. Muddypaws. Mendez, Simon, illus. 2008. (Picture Books... Ser.). 32p. (J). (978-1-4075-1840-4(2)) Parragon, Inc.

Butterworth, Nick. The Whisperer. Butterworth, Nick, illus. 2005. (ENG., Illus.). 32p. (J). (gr. k-3). pap. 15.95 (978-0-00-712018-5(4), HarperCollins Children's Bks.) HarperCollins Pubs. Ltd. GBR. Dist: HarperCollins Pubs.

Buzzeo, Toni. But I Read It on the Internet! Yoshikawa, Sachiko, illus. 2013. 32p. (J). 17.95 (978-1-60213-062-3(0), Upstart Bks.) Highsmith Inc.

Byeway Books, creator. Colors. 2011. (My First Picture Fun Bks.). (ENG., Illus.). 24p. (gr. -1-k). bds. 5.99 (978-1-60176-021-0(3)) Byeway Bks.

—Rhymes. 2011. (My First Picture Fun Bks.). (ENG., Illus.). 24p. (J). (gr. -1). bds. 5.99 (978-1-60176-022-7(1)) Byeway Bks.

Byrne, John Patrick. Donald & Benoit. Byrne, John Patrick, illus. 2011. (ENG., Illus.). 64p. (J). (gr. 2-5). 17.95 (978-0-7893-2084-1(3)) Universe Publishing.

Byrne, Richard. I Want to Go First! Byrne, Richard, illus. 2017. (ENG., Illus.). 32p. (J). 16.99 **(978-1-250-12771-6(8)**, 9781250127716, Holt, Henry & Co. Bks. For Young Readers) Holt, Henry & Co.

Cabrera, Jane. Mommy, Carry Me Please! Cabrera, Jane, illus. 2006. (ENG., Illus.). 32p. (J). (gr. 3-6). 16.95 (978-0-8234-1935-7(5)) Holiday Hse., Inc.

—Row, Row, Row Your Boat. Cabrera, Jane, illus. 2016. (ENG., Illus.). 24p. (J). bds. 7.99 (978-0-8234-3632-3(2)) Holiday Hse., Inc.

Cache, Dee. Captain Tugalong, 1 vol. Burns, Howard M., illus. 2009. (ENG.). 30p. (J). (gr. -1-3). 12.95 (978-0-87033-515-0(4), 9780870335150, Cornell Maritime Pr./Tidewater Pubs.) Schiffer Publishing, Ltd.

Cafaro, Phyllis. The Legend of Captain McFinn & Friends. 2012. (ENG., Illus.). 24p. pap. 19.99 (978-0-9799283-1-4(1), 9780979928314) Cold River Pubns.

Cain, Marie Mowery. A Message for You. 2013. (Big Books, Blue Ser.). (ENG & SPA., Illus.). 16p. pap. 33.00 (978-1-59246-013-7(5)) Big Books, by George!

Calì, Davide. The Enemy. Bloch, Serge, illus. 2013. Orig. Title: L' Ennemi. (ENG.). 64p. (J). (gr. 4-7). 24.99 (978-0-9585571-8-4(7)) Wilkins Farago Pty, Ltd. AUS. Dist: Independent Pubs. Group.

Calì, Davide. The Tiny Tale of Little Pea. Mourrain, Sébastien, illus. 2017. (ENG.). 40p. (J). (gr. -1-2). 17.99 **(978-1-77138-843-6(9))** Kids Can Pr., Ltd. CAN. Dist: Hachette Bk. Group.

Campagne, Michelle & Gallant, Dany. Fabuleuse Melodie De. 2013. (FRE., Illus.). 44p. (J). (gr. -1-k). 16.95 (978-2-923163-30-7(3)) La Montagne Secrete CAN. Dist: Independent Pubs. Group.

Campbell, K. G. Lester's Dreadful Sweaters. Campbell, K. G., illus. 2012. (ENG., Illus.). 32p. (J). (gr. -1-3). 16.95 (978-1-55453-770-9(3)) Kids Can Pr., Ltd. CAN. Dist: Hachette Bk. Group.

Campbell, Wanda Gail. Little Buckets Full of Big Love. 2008. (Illus.). 48p. pap. 19.49 *(978-1-4389-0688-1(9))* AuthorHouse.

Camping Caper: Picture Book (English) 8x8. 2007. (Illus.). (J). 5.99 *(978-1-933934-64-8(6))* Mighty Kids Media.

Campos, Maria de Fatima. Victoria's Day. 2015. (ENG., Illus.). 32p. (J). (gr. -1-1). pap. 10.99 *(978-1-84780-424-2(1)*, Frances Lincoln) Quarto Publishing Group UK GBR. Dist: Hachette Bk. Group.

Candlewick Press, Candlewick. Peppa Pig & the Busy Day at School. Candlewick Press, Candlewick & Ladybird Books Staff, illus. 2013. (Peppa Pig Ser.). (ENG.). 32p. (J). (-k). 12.99 *(978-0-7636-6525-8(8)*, Candlewick Entertainment) Candlewick Pr.

—Peppa Pig & the I Love You Game. 2015. (Peppa Pig Ser.). (ENG.). 32p. (J). (-k). 12.99 *(978-0-7636-8126-5(1)*, Candlewick Entertainment) Candlewick Pr.

Candy Cane Press, creator. Safe at Home! Indoor Safety. 2005. (ENG., Illus.). 14p. (J). (gr. -1-k). bds. 12.95 *(978-0-8249-6592-1(2)*, Ideal Pubns.) Worthy Publishing.

—Safe at Play: Outdoor Safety. 2005. (ENG., Illus.). 14p. (J). (gr. -1-k). bds. 12.95 *(978-0-8249-6593-8(0)*, Ideal Pubns.) Worthy Publishing.

Cane, Ella. My World. 2013. (My World Ser.). (ENG.). 24p. (gr. k-1). pap. 35.70 *(978-1-4765-3683-5(X))*; lib. bdg. 131.94 *(978-1-4765-3682-8(1))* Capstone Press of Coughlan Cos. (Pebble Bks.).

Canetti, Yanitzia. Colores escolares/School Colors: A World of Color. 2010. (ENG & SPA.). 24p. (J). pap. 6.99 *(978-1-59835-272-6(5)*, BrickHouse Education) Cambridge BrickHouse, Inc.

—Colorful Shapes/Figuras de Colores: A World of Color. 2010. (SPA & ENG.). 24p. (J). pap. 6.99 *(978-1-59835-278-8(4)*, BrickHouse Education) Cambridge BrickHouse, Inc.

—Colorful Sights Paisajes de Colores: A World of Color. 2010. (SPA & ENG.). 24p. (J). pap. 6.99 *(978-1-59835-280-1(6)*, BrickHouse Education) Cambridge BrickHouse, Inc.

—Colors on Colors/Colores Sobre Colores: A World of Color. 2010. (SPA & ENG.). 24p. (J). pap. 6.99 *(978-1-59835-276-4(8)*, BrickHouse Education) Cambridge BrickHouse, Inc.

—Tasty Colors/Colores de Sabores: A World of Color. 2010. (SPA & ENG.). 24p. (J). pap. 6.99 *(978-1-59835-270-2(9)*, BrickHouse Education) Cambridge BrickHouse, Inc.

Capote, Lori. Monster Knows Math. Wass, Chip, illus. 2013. (Monster Knows Math Ser.). (ENG.). 24p. (gr. 3-4). lib. bdg. 98.60 *(978-1-4048-7950-8(1))* Picture Window Bks.

Caravan, Jill. Pandas: A Portrait of the Animal World. 2nd rev. ed. 2012. (Portrait of the Animal World Ser.). (Illus.). 72p. 12.95 *(978-1-59764-230-9(4))* New Line Bks.

Carbonell-Matela, Anna. Whitaker Farm. 2012. 24p. pap. 15.99 *(978-1-4691-6352-9(7))* Xlibris Corp.

Carey, Anna. The Making of Mollie. 2017. (ENG.). 304p. (J). pap. 13.00 ***(978-1-84717-847-3(2))*** O'Brien Pr., Ltd., The IRL. Dist: Dufour Editions, Inc.

Carle, Eric. Eric Carle Classics: The Tiny Seed - Pancakes, Pancakes! - Walter the Baker. Carle, Eric, illus. 2011. (World of Eric Carle Ser.). (ENG., Illus.). 112p. (J). (gr. -1-2). 19.99 *(978-1-4424-3988-7(2)*, Simon & Schuster Bks. For Young Readers) Simon & Schuster Bks. For Young Readers.

—Have You Seen My Cat? 2012. (Eric Carle Ready-To-Read Ser.). lib. bdg. 13.55 *(978-0-606-26356-6(X)*, Turtleback) Turtleback Bks.

—A House for Hermit Crab. Carle, Eric, illus. 2004. (World of Eric Carle Ser.). (ENG., Illus.). 32p. (J). (gr. k-3). bds. 8.99 *(978-0-689-87064-4(7)*, Little Simon) Little Simon.

—My Very First Book of Shapes. Carle, Eric, illus. 2005. (ENG., Illus.). 20p. (J). (gr. -1 — 1). bds. 5.99 *(978-0-399-24387-5(9)*, Philomel Bks.) Penguin Young Readers Group.

—Pancakes, Pancakes! Carle, Eric, illus. 2004. (World of Eric Carle Ser.). (ENG., Illus.). 32p. (J). (gr. -1-3). bds. 8.99 *(978-0-689-87148-1(1)*, Little Simon) Little Simon.

—The Tiny Seed. Carle, Eric, illus. 2005. (World of Eric Carle Ser.). (ENG., Illus.). 34p. (J). (gr. -1-k). bds. 8.99 *(978-0-689-87149-8(X)*, Little Simon) Little Simon.

Carlin, Laura. A World of Your Own. 2014. (ENG., Illus.). 48p. (gr. -1-2). 19.95 *(978-0-7148-6362-7(9))* Phaidon Pr., Inc.

Carlisle, Emma. Bears at the Beach. 2016. (ENG., Illus.). 32p. (J). (gr. -1-2). 18.99 ***(978-1-4472-5744-8(8))*** Pan Macmillan GBR. Dist: Independent Pubs. Group.

Carlisle, Emma. Lion Practice. 2015. (ENG., Illus.). 32p. (J). (gr. -1-k). 18.99 *(978-1-4472-5742-4(1))* Pan Macmillan GBR. Dist: Independent Pubs. Group.

Carlson, Nancy. Think Big! 2005. (Illus.). 28p. (J). (gr. -1-3). 15.95 *(978-1-57505-622-7(4)*, Carolrhoda Bks.) Lerner Publishing Group.

Carlton, Glenis. Four Snails & an Umbrella. 2016. (ENG., Illus.). 22p. (J). pap. 13.95 *(978-1-78612-331-2(2)*, 5af02be0-d843-45e8-8626-a4101b34ada6) Austin, Stan AUS. Dist: Bookmasters Distribution.

Carney, Charles. A Day Just for Daddies. 2011. (Illus.). 24p. (J). 15.99 *(978-1-60010-439-8(8))* Idea & Design Works, LLC.

Carpenter, Tad. I Say, You Say Colors! 2014. (ENG., Illus.). 18p. (J). (gr. -1 — 1). bds. 6.99 *(978-0-316-20072-1(7))* Little, Brown Bks. for Young Readers.

—I Say, You Say Feelings! 2014. (ENG., Illus.). 18p. (J). (gr. -1 — 1). bds. 6.99 *(978-0-316-20074-5(3))* Little, Brown Bks. for Young Readers.

Carr, Jan. Greedy Apostrophe: A Cautionary Tale. Long, Ethan, illus. 2009. (ENG.). 32p. (J). (gr. 1-3). pap. 7.95 *(978-0-8234-2205-0(4))* Holiday Hse., Inc.

Carrington, Leonora. Leche Del Sueno. 2013. (SPA.). 46.95 *(978-607-16-1217-5(9))* Fondo de Cultura Economica USA.

—The Milk of Dreams. 2017. (ENG., Illus.). 48p. (J). (gr. 1-4). 15.95 *(978-1-68137-094-1(8)*, NYR Children's Collection) New York Review of Bks., Inc., The.

Carson-Dellosa Publishing Staff. Hidden Pictures, Grades PK - 1. 2010. (Home Workbooks Ser.). (ENG.). 64p. (gr. -1-1). pap. 4.49 *(978-1-60418-770-0(0))* Carson-Dellosa Publishing, LLC.

Carter, Amy. The Not So Wicked, Wicked Witch! 2009. 24p. pap. 15.95 *(978-1-4327-3781-8(3))* Outskirts Pr., Inc.

Carter, Anne Laurel. Under a Prairie Sky, 1 vol. Daniel, Alan & Daniel, Lea, illus. 2004. (ENG.). 32p. (J). (gr. -1-3). pap. 7.95 *(978-1-55143-282-3(X))* Orca Bk. Pubs. USA.

Carter, David A. Bugs at the Beach. Carter, David A., illus. 2016. (David Carter's Bugs Ser.). (ENG., Illus.). 24p. (J). (gr. -1-1). pap. 3.99 *(978-1-4814-4050-9(0)*, Simon Spotlight) Simon Spotlight.

—One Red Dot: A Pop-Up Book for Children of All Ages. Carter, David A., illus. 2005. (ENG., Illus.). 18p. (J). (gr. -1-3). 29.99 *(978-0-689-87769-8(2)*, Little Simon) Little Simon.

Carter, Pete. Our Dog Benji. Henderson, James, illus. 2017. (ENG.). 32p. (J). (gr. -1-3). 17.99 *(978-1-925335-33-0(X)*, EK Bks.) Exisle Publishing Pty Ltd. AUS. Dist: Hachette Bk. Group.

Casale, Roberto, illus. El Osito Binky. 2017.Tr. of Little Binky Bear. (J). 7.99 ***(978-0-9986498-0-1(5))*** Show n' Tell Publishing.

Casey, Dawn. A Lullaby for Little One. Fuge, Charles, illus. 2015. (ENG.). 32p. (J). (-k). 12.99 *(978-0-7636-7608-7(X)*, Nosy Crow) Candlewick Pr.

Cash, John Carter. The Cat in the Rhinestone Suit. Nash, Scott, illus. 2012. (ENG.). 32p. (J). (gr. -1-3). 17.99 *(978-1-4169-7483-3(0)*, Little Simon Inspirations) Little Simon Inspirations.

Caston, Jane. Will You Help Doug Find His Dog? Saldaña, Carmen, illus. 2017. 36p. (J). (gr. -1-1). 14.99 ***(978-1-78285-320-6(0))*** Barefoot Bks., Inc.

Castor, Daniel & Castor, Harriet. Wondaglop Plot. (Illus.). 61p. (J). pap. 6.99 *(978-0-340-63442-4(1))* Hodder & Stoughton GBR. Dist: Trafalgar Square Publishing.

Castro, Shirley. The Pelican Family Series — Stelly & the Sticky, Gooey Taffy. Castro, Christopher, illus. 2011. 36p. (J). 15.00 *(978-0-9790307-3-4(0))* Castro, Shirley.

Cate, Annette LeBlanc. The Magic Rabbit. 2013. lib. bdg. 17.20 *(978-0-606-31601-9(9)*, Turtleback) Turtleback Bks.

Catlow, Nikalas, et al. The Funny Fingers Are Going on Holiday. 2015. (Funny Fingers Ser.: 3). (ENG., Illus.). 32p. (J). (gr. -1-k). pap. 10.99 *(978-1-4052-7366-4(6))* Egmont Bks., Ltd. GBR. Dist: Independent Pubs. Group.

Caudle, Ruth. Yvette, Annette & Renette. 2007. (Illus.). 32p. (J). 16.99 *(978-0-9793039-0-6(7))* Haiti World.

Caughill, Jeff. The Good Old Hockey Game. 2012. 28p. pap. *(978-1-105-58056-7(3))* Lulu.com.

Cave, Kathryn & Riddell, Chris. Counting Sheep: A Bedtime Adventure! Riddell, Chris, illus. 2014. (ENG., Illus.). 32p. (J). (gr. -1-2). pap. 8.99 *(978-1-84780-480-8(2)*, Frances Lincoln) Quarto Publishing Group UK GBR. Dist: Hachette Bk. Group.

Caviezel, Giovanni. Ballerina. Mesturini, C., illus. 2011. (Mini People Shape Bks.). (ENG.). 10p. (J). bds. 5.99 *(978-0-7641-6436-1(8))* Barron's Educational Series, Inc.

—Builder. Mesturini, C., illus. 2011. (Mini People Shape Bks.). (ENG.). 10p. (J). bds. 5.99 *(978-0-7641-6437-8(6))* Barron's Educational Series, Inc.

—Cowboy. Mesturini, C., illus. 2011. (Mini People Shape Bks.). (ENG.). 10p. (J). bds. 5.99 *(978-0-7641-6438-5(4))* Barron's Educational Series, Inc.

—Fairy. Mesturini, Cristina, illus. 2009. (Mini People Shape Bks.). (ENG.). 12p. (J). (gr. -1-2). bds. 5.99 *(978-0-7641-6218-3(7))* Barron's Educational Series, Inc.

—Farmer. Mesturini, C., illus. 2011. (Mini People Shape Bks.). (ENG.). 10p. (J). bds. 5.99 *(978-0-7641-6439-2(2))* Barron's Educational Series, Inc.

—Police Officer. Mesturini, Cristina, illus. 2009. (Mini People Shape Bks.). (ENG.). 12p. (J). (gr. -1-2). bds. 5.99 *(978-0-7641-6221-3(7))* Barron's Educational Series, Inc.

—Policeman's Safety Hints. 2013. (ENG.). 12p. (J). (gr. -1-2). bds. 8.99 *(978-0-7641-6721-8(9))* Barron's Educational Series, Inc.

Caviezel, Giovanni, illus. Little Bee. 2014. (Mini-Creatures Ser.). (ENG.). 8p. (J). (gr. -1 — 1). bds. 4.99 *(978-0-7641-6713-3(8))* Barron's Educational Series, Inc.

—Little Crab. 2014. (Mini-Creatures Ser.). (ENG.). 8p. (J). (gr. -1 — 1). bds. 4.99 *(978-0-7641-6714-0(6))* Barron's Educational Series, Inc.

—Little Snail. 2014. (Mini-Creatures Ser.). (ENG.). 8p. (J). (gr. -1 — 1). bds. 4.99 *(978-0-7641-6715-7(4))* Barron's Educational Series, Inc.

Caviezel, Giovanni & Mesturini, Cristina. Fireman. 2009. (Mini People Shape Bks.). (ENG., Illus.). 10p. (J). (gr. -1-2). bds. 5.99 *(978-0-7641-6220-6(9))* Barron's Educational Series, Inc.

Cech, John. The Nutcracker. Puybaret, Eric, illus. 2016. (ENG.). 40p. (J). (gr. -1-2). pap. 6.95 *(978-1-4549-2116-5(1))* Sterling Publishing Co., Inc.

Cecil, Randy. Lucy. Cecil, Randy, illus. 2016. (ENG., Illus.). 144p. (J). (gr. k-3). 19.99 *(978-0-7636-6808-2(7))* Candlewick Pr.

Centre for Addiction and Mental Health Staff. Can I Catch It Like a Cold? Coping with a Parent's Depression. Weissmann, Joe, illus. 2009. (Coping Ser.). (ENG.). 32p. (J). (gr. k-3). 17.95 *(978-0-88776-956-6(X)*, Tundra Bks.) Tundra Bks. CAN. Dist: Penguin Random Hse. LLC.

Cerulli, Claudia. Ottavia e I Gatti Di Roma - Octavia & the Cats of Rome: A Bilingual Picture Book in Italian & English. Lätti, Leo, illus. 2013. 40p. pap. *(978-1-938712-11-1(0))* Roxby Media Ltd.

Cervone, Shannon. The Black Suitcase. Vene, Alessandro, illus. 2013. (ENG.). 32p. (J). 15.99 *(978-1-938501-08-1(X))* Turn the Page Publishing.

Chaban, Liz. Jules of the World: The California Caper. 2012. 42p. pap. 18.99 *(978-1-105-92248-0(0))* Lulu Pr., Inc.

Chadwick, Anita. Rosebuds Puppies. 2012. 20p. pap. 13.77 *(978-1-4669-1632-6(X))* Trafford Publishing.

Challoner, Jack & Walshaw, Rodney. Rocks & Minerals: Crystals; Erosion; Geology; Fossils. 2015. (ENG., Illus.). 64p. 12.99 *(978-1-86147-465-0(2)*, Armadillo) Anness Publishing GBR. Dist: National Bk. Network.

Chan, Marty. True Story. Bennett, Lorna, illus. 2009. (ENG.). 32p. (J). 9.95 *(978-0-9810449-0-3(5))* Ink Jockey, Inc. CAN. Dist: Univ. of Toronto Pr.

Chand, Emlyn. Ricky the Runt: A Bird Brain Book. Giffin, Noelle, illus. l.t. ed. 2013. 8. (ENG.). 52p. (gr. k-3). pap. 10.95 *(978-1-62253-125-7(6))* Evolved Publishing.

—Vicky Finds a Valentine: Bird Brain Books. Giffin, Noelle, illus. ed. 2013. (ENG.). 50p. (gr. k-1). pap. 10.95 *(978-1-62253-116-5(7))* Evolved Publishing.

Chandler, Pauline. Mr. Rabbit the Farmer. Smith, Eric, illus. 2005. (ENG.). 24p. (J). lib. bdg. 23.65 *(978-1-59646-736-1(3))* Dingles & Co.

Chapman, Lynne. Baby Goes Baaaaa! Chapman, Lynne, illus. 2013. (ENG., Illus.). 24p. (J). (— 1). 7.99 *(978-1-4052-5830-2(6))* Egmont Bks., Ltd. GBR. Dist: Independent Pubs. Group.

Chapman, Pat. The Best Mum in the World. Chapman, Cat, illus. 2017. (ENG.). 32p. (J). (gr. -1-k). 14.99 ***(978-1-927262-80-1(1))*** Upstart Pr. NZL. Dist: Independent Pubs. Group.

Chappell, Billie-Jean & Williams, Frederick C. Happiness Colouring Book. Williams, Frederick C., illus. 2012. (Illus.). 36p. pap. *(978-0-9566564-2-1(0))* Dreamality Bks.

Charles, Faustin. The Selfish Crocodile Book of Colours. Terry, Michael, illus. 2013. (Selfish Crocodile Ser.). (ENG.). 14p. (J). bds. 10.99 *(978-1-4088-1449-9(8)*, 9781408814499, Bloomsbury USA Childrens) Bloomsbury Publishing USA.

—The Selfish Crocodile Book of Sounds. Terry, Michael, illus. 2012. (Selfish Crocodile Ser.). (ENG.). 14p. (J). (gr. -1-3). bds. 10.99 *(978-1-4088-1450-5(1)*, 9781408814505, Bloomsbury USA Childrens) Bloomsbury Publishing USA.

Charles, Faustin & Beynon-Davies, Paul. The Selfish Crocodile Book of Numbers. Terry, Michael, illus. 2012. (Selfish Crocodile Ser.). (ENG.). 12p. (J). (gr. -1-k). bds. 10.99 *(978-1-4088-1451-2(X)*, 9781408814512, Bloomsbury USA Childrens) Bloomsbury Publishing USA.

Charon Aldredge. Kiddie Rhythms the Show. 2010. 16p. pap. 15.00 *(978-1-4269-1970-1(0))* Trafford Publishing.

Chedekel, Evelyn. The Fake Doughnut. Le, Loanne, illus. 2013. 24p. 16.95 *(978-0-9888974-0-3(7))* BugaBk. llc.

Cheetham, Stephen, illus. Off to the Park! 2014. (Tactile Bks.). (ENG.). 12p. (J). *(978-1-84643-502-7(1))* Child's Play International Ltd.

Chernesky, Felicia Sanzari. The Boy Who Said Nonsense. Anderson, Nicola, illus. 2016. (ENG.). 32p. (J). (gr. -1-3). 16.99 *(978-0-8075-5742-6(0))* Whitman, Albert & Co.

Chichester Clark, Emma. Bears Don't Read! Chichester Clark, Emma, illus. 2016. (Illus.). 32p. (J). 12.99 *(978-1-61067-366-2(2))* Kane Miller.

—Come to School Too, Blue Kangaroo! Chichester Clark, Emma, illus. 2013. (ENG., Illus.). 32p. (J). pap. 9.99 *(978-0-00-725868-0(2)*, HarperCollins Children's Bks.) HarperCollins Pubs. Ltd. GBR. Dist: HarperCollins Pubs.

—Lulu & the Treasure Hunt! Chichester Clark, Emma, illus. 2013. (Wagtail Town Ser.). (ENG., Illus.). 32p. (J). pap. 9.99 *(978-0-00-742517-4(1)*, HarperCollins Children's Bks.) HarperCollins Pubs. Ltd. GBR. Dist: HarperCollins Pubs.

—Plum & Rabbit & Me, Bk. 3. Chichester Clark, Emma, illus. 2010. (Humber & Plum Ser.: 3). (ENG., Illus.). 32p. (J). (gr. -1-k). pap. 9.99 *(978-0-00-727325-6(8)*, HarperCollins Children's Bks.) HarperCollins Pubs. Ltd. GBR. Dist: HarperCollins Pubs.

Chiew, Suzanne. Friends to the Rescue. Pedler, Caroline, illus. 2016. (ENG.). 32p. (J). (gr. -1-2). 16.99 *(978-1-68010-007-5(6))* Tiger Tales.

Child, Lauren. Beware of the Storybook Wolves. Child, Lauren, illus. 2012. (ENG., Illus.). 32p. (J). (gr. -1-k). pap. 9.99 *(978-1-4083-1480-7(0))* Hodder & Stoughton GBR. Dist: Hachette Bk. Group.

—I Can't Stop Hiccuping! 2010. (Charlie & Lola Ser.). lib. bdg. 13.55 *(978-0-606-10629-0(4)*, Turtleback) Turtleback Bks.

Child's Play Staff. Spring. Busby, Ailie, illus. 2015. (Seasons Ser.: 4). (ENG.). 12p. (J). (gr. 1-1). bds. *(978-1-84643-741-0(5))* Child's Play International Ltd.

—Summer. Busby, Ailie, illus. 2015. (Seasons Ser.: 4). (ENG.). 12p. (J). (gr. 1-1). bds. *(978-1-84643-742-7(3))* Child's Play International Ltd.

—What's That Noise? CHOO! CHOO! Guess the Vehicle! Cocoretto, illus. 2015. (What's That Noise? Ser.: 4). (ENG.). 12p. (J). bds. *(978-1-84643-746-5(6))* Child's Play International Ltd.

—What's That Noise? SNAP! SNAP! Guess the Animal! Cocoretto, illus. 2015. (What's That Noise? Ser.: 4). (ENG.). 12p. (J). bds. *(978-1-84643-748-9(2))* Child's Play International Ltd.

—What's That Noise? TAP! TAP! Guess the Toy! Cocoretto, illus. 2015. (What's That Noise? Ser.: 4). (ENG.). 12p. (J). bds. *(978-1-84643-747-2(4))* Child's Play International Ltd.

—What's That Noise? TOOT! TOOT! Guess the Instrument! Cocoretto, illus. 2015. (What's That Noise? Ser.: 4). (ENG.). 12p. (J). bds. *(978-1-84643-749-6(0))* Child's Play International Ltd.

—Winter. Busby, Ailie, illus. 2015. (Seasons Ser.: 4). (ENG.). 12p. (J). (gr. 1-1). bds. *(978-1-84643-745-8(8))* Child's Play International Ltd.

Chin, Jason. Redwoods. Chin, Jason, illus. 2009. (ENG., Illus.). 40p. (J). (gr. -1-3). 18.99 *(978-1-59643-430-1(9)*, 9781596434301) Roaring Brook Pr.

Chissick, Michael. Seahorse's Magical Sun Sequences: How All Children (And Sea Creatures) Can Use Yoga to Feel Positive, Confident & Completely Included. Peacock, Sarah, illus. 2015. (ENG.). 48p. (J). 19.95 *(978-1-84819-283-6(5)*, 8079, Singing Dragon) Kingsley, Jessica Pubs. GBR. Dist: Macmillan Distribution Ltd.

Chorkung, illus. Sea Creatures. 2017. (First Explorers Ser.). (ENG.). 10p. (J). (— 1). bds. 8.95 ***(978-1-4549-2658-0(9))*** Sterling Publishing Co., Inc.

Christelow, Eileen. Cinco Monitos Colección de Oro. 2012. (Five Little Monkeys Story Ser.). (ENG & SPA., Illus.). 192p. (J). (gr. -1-3). 11.99 *(978-0-547-74593-0(1))* Houghton Mifflin Harcourt Publishing Co.

—Five Little Monkeys Trick-Or-Treat. 2015. (Five Little Monkeys Story Ser.). (ENG., Illus.). 36p. (J). (— 1). bds. 7.99 *(978-0-544-43062-4(X)*, HMH Books For Young Readers) Houghton Mifflin Harcourt Publishing Co.

Christmas Stable, 1 vol. 2014. (Candle Tiny Tots Ser.). (ENG., Illus.). 16p. (J). 11.99 *(978-1-78128-122-2(X)*, Candle Bks.) Lion Hudson PLC GBR. Dist: Kregel Pubns.

Church, Caroline Jayne. I Love My Bunny. 2015. (Love Meez Ser.: 3). (ENG., Illus.). 10p. (J). (— 1). bds. 7.99 *(978-0-545-83596-1(8)*, Cartwheel Bks.) Scholastic, Inc.

—I Love My Robot. Church, Caroline Jayne, illus. 2015. (Love Meez Ser.: 4). (ENG., Illus.). 10p. (J). (— 1). bds. 7.99 *(978-0-545-83593-0(3)*, Cartwheel Bks.) Scholastic, Inc.

Chwast, Seymour. Get Dressed! 2012. (ENG., Illus.). 18p. (J). (gr. -1 — 1). 14.95 *(978-1-4197-0107-8(X)*, Abrams Appleseed) Abrams, Inc.

Cioffi, Dom, illus. Digby & the Lake Monster. l.t. ed. 2006. 36p. (J). per. *(978-0-9745931-0-4(9))* Vermont Bookworks.

Clanton, Ben. Boo Who? Clanton, Ben, illus. 2017. (ENG., Illus.). 32p. (J). (gr. -1-2). 15.99 ***(978-0-7636-8824-0(X))*** Candlewick Pr.

Clanton, Ben. Mo's Mustache. 2013. (ENG., Illus.). 32p. (J). (gr. -1-2). 16.99 *(978-1-77049-538-8(X)*, Tundra Bks.) Tundra Bks. CAN. Dist: Penguin Random Hse. LLC.

Clarke, Isabel. My Big Book of Words. Tulip, Jenny, illus. 2014. (ENG.). 40p. (J). (gr. -1-k). 12.99 *(978-1-86147-325-7(7)*, Armadillo) Anness Publishing GBR. Dist: National Bk. Network.

Clarke, Jane. How to Bathe Your Little Dino. Birkett, Georgie, illus. 2017. 16p. (J). bds. 8.99 *(978-1-61067-495-9(2))* Kane Miller.

—I'm Not Wearing That! Mostyn, David, illus. 2005. (ENG.). 24p. (J). lib. bdg. 23.65 *(978-1-59646-716-3(9))* Dingles & Co.

—Prince Albert's Birthday. Chatterton, Martin, illus. 2005. 24p. (J). lib. bdg. 23.65 *(978-1-59646-748-4(7))* Dingles & Co.

Clarke, Justine & Baysting, Arthur. Gobbledygook Is Eating a Book. 2016. (ENG.). 32p. (J). (gr. -1-2). 13.99 ***(978-0-14-350693-5(5))*** Random Hse. Australia AUS. Dist: Independent Pubs. Group.

Clarke, Lyndia A. Tidy up Tommy. Clarke, Lyndia A., illus. 2005. (Illus.). (J). 1700.00 *(978-0-9762898-6-9(5))* LightHouse Pr.

Clarkson, Kelly. River Rose & the Magical Christmas. Fleming, Lucy, illus. 2017. (ENG.). 32p. (J). (gr. -1-3). 19.99 ***(978-0-06-269764-6(1))*** HarperCollins Pubs.

Clarkson, Stephanie. Let's Get Moving with Wenlock & Mandeville! 2012. (London 2012 Ser.). (ENG., Illus.). 32p. (J). (gr. -1-k). pap. 10.99 *(978-1-84732-645-4(5))* Carlton Bks., Ltd. GBR. Dist: Independent Pubs. Group.

Class 1-208. Pizza Place Ghost, 1 vol. 2013. (Scooby-Doo! Picture Clue Bks.). (ENG.). 24p. (J). (gr. -1-1). lib. bdg. 24.21 *(978-1-61479-038-9(8)*, Essential Library) ABDO Publishing Co.

Claybourne, Anna. Animal Atlas. Gwinn, Saskia, ed. Wald, Christina, illus. 2014. (ENG.). 64p. (J). (gr. -1-3). 17.99 *(978-1-4088-4218-8(1)*, 9781408842188, Bloomsbury USA Childrens) Bloomsbury Publishing USA.

Clayton, Dallas. An Awesome Book of Thanks!, 0 vols. unabr. ed. 2010. (ENG.). 86p. (gr. 4-6). 17.95 *(978-1-935597-37-7(X)*, 9781935597377, Two Lions) Amazon Publishing.

Cleave, Andrew. Snakes & Reptiles - Pb: A Portrait of the Animal World. 2013. (Portrait of the Animal World Ser.). (Illus.). 80p. pap. 9.95 *(978-1-59764-318-4(1))* New Line Bks.

Clement, Debbie. Red, White, & Blue. 2010. 19.95 *(978-0-578-06631-8(9))* Rainbows Within Reach.

Clement, Gary. The Great Poochini. 2004. (J). (gr. 1-4). spiral bd. *(978-0-616-03027-1(4))* Canadian National Institute for the Blind/Institut National Canadien pour les Aveugles.

Clement, Loic. A Thousand Billion Things (and Some Sheep) Montel, Anne, illus. 2017. (ENG.). 32p. (J). (gr. -1-2). 17.95 ***(978-1-910277-42-3(8)***, Words & Pictures) Quarto Publishing Group UK GBR. Dist: Hachette Bk. Group.

Clerici, Lorenzo. The Dog Book: A Minibombo Book. Clerici, Lorenzo, illus. 2017. (Minibombo Ser.). (ENG., Illus.). 32p. (J). (-k). 9.99 *(978-0-7636-9487-6(8))* Candlewick Pr.

Climo, Liz. Rory the Dinosaur: Me & My Dad. 2015. (Illus.). 48p. (J). pap. *(978-0-316-26391-7(5))* Little Brown & Co.

Coats, Lucy. Bear's Best Friend. Dyer, Sarah, illus. 2014. (ENG.). 32p. (J). (gr. -1-k). 21.00 *(978-1-4088-2725-3(5)*, 9781408827253, Bloomsbury USA Childrens) Bloomsbury Publishing USA.

Cocca-Leffler, Maryann. Rain Brings Frogs: A Little Book of Hope. Cocca-Leffler, Maryann, illus. 2011. (ENG., Illus.). 32p. (J). (gr. -1-2). 9.99 *(978-0-06-196106-9(X))* HarperCollins Pubs.

Cochran, Bruce. First Birthday Bear. 10p. (J). *(978-1-886386-35-8(8))* Trisar, Inc.

—First Pony: Blue. 10p. (J). *(978-1-886386-34-1(X))* Trisar, Inc.

—First Pony: Pink. 10p. (J). *(978-1-886386-33-4(1))* Trisar, Inc.

—It's the Big 1: Blue. 10p. (J). *(978-1-886386-37-2(4))* Trisar, Inc.

—It's the Big 1: Pink. 10p. (J). *(978-1-886386-36-5(6))* Trisar, Inc.

Cocoretto, illus. In the Ocean. 2016. (Peekaboo! Ser.: 4). (ENG.). 12p. (J). bds. *(978-1-84643-867-7(5))* Child's Play International Ltd.

Coelho, Rogério. Boat of Dreams, 1 vol. 2017. (ENG., Illus.). 80p. (gr. 2-17). 22.95 *(978-0-88448-528-5(5)*, 884528) Tilbury Hse. Pubs.

Cofer, Amadeus. Friendship Rules: How to Make & Keep Friends, 1. l.t. ed. 2004. (Illus.). 36p. (J). 14.00 *(978-1-932957-00-6(6))* Legacy Pubs.

Coh, Smiljana. The Seven Princesses. 2016. (ENG., Illus.). 40p. (J). (gr. -1-17). 16.95 *(978-0-7624-5587-4(X)*, Running Pr. Kids) Running Pr. Bk. Pubs.

Cohen, Jeff. Eva & Sadie & the Worst Haircut EVER! Allen, Elanna, illus. 2014. (ENG.). 32p. (J). (gr. -1-3). 17.99 *(978-0-06-224906-7(1))* HarperCollins Pubs.

Cole, Barbara H. Anna & Natalie, 1 vol. Himler, Ronald, illus. 2010. (ENG.). 32p. (J). pap. 6.95 *(978-1-59572-211-9(4))* Star Bright Bks., Inc.

Cole, Joanne & Cole, Michael. Bod & Breakfast. 2016. (Bod Ser.). (ENG., Illus.). 32p. (J). (gr. -1-1). 9.99 *(978-1-4052-8057-0(3))* Egmont Bks., Ltd. GBR. Dist: Independent Pubs. Group.

—Bod & the Cake. 2016. (Bod Ser.). (ENG., Illus.). 32p. (J). (gr. -1-1). 9.99 *(978-1-4052-8056-3(5))* Egmont Bks., Ltd. GBR. Dist: Independent Pubs. Group.

—Bod & the Cherry Tree. 2015. (Bod Ser.). (ENG., Illus.). 32p. (J). (gr. -1-1). 9.99 *(978-1-4052-7753-2(X))* Egmont Bks., Ltd. GBR. Dist: Independent Pubs. Group.

—Bod's Apple. 2015. (Bod Ser.). (ENG., Illus.). 32p. (J). (gr. -1-1). 9.99 *(978-1-4052-7587-3(1))* Egmont Bks., Ltd. GBR. Dist: Independent Pubs. Group.

—Bod's Dream. 2016. (Bod Ser.). (ENG., Illus.). 32p. (J). (gr. -1-1). 9.99 *(978-1-4052-7588-0(X))* Egmont Bks., Ltd. GBR. Dist: Independent Pubs. Group.

—Bod's Present. 2016. (Bod Ser.). (ENG., Illus.). 32p. (J). (gr. -1-1). 9.99 *(978-1-4052-7754-9(8))* Egmont Bks., Ltd. GBR. Dist: Independent Pubs. Group.

Cole, Michael. Bod in the Park. Cole, Joanne, illus. 2017. (Bod Ser.). (ENG.). 32p. (J). (gr. -1-1). 9.99

(978-1-4052-8059-4(X)) Egmont Bks., Ltd. GBR. Dist: Independent Pubs. Group.
—Bod on the Beach. Cole, Joanne, illus. 2017. (Bod Ser.). (ENG.). 32p. (J). (gr. -1-1). 9.99 (978-1-4052-8060-0(3)) Egmont Bks., Ltd. GBR. Dist: Independent Pubs. Group.
Collier, Kelly. A Horse Named Steve. Collier, Kelly, illus. 2017. (ENG., Illus.). 32p. (J). (gr. -1-3). 16.95 (978-1-77138-736-1(X)) Kids Can Pr., Ltd. CAN. Dist: Hachette Bk. Group.
Collins, Billy. Voyage. Romagna, Karen, illus. 2014. (ENG.). 32p. (J). (gr. 1-2). 16.95 (978-1-59373-154-0(X)) Bunker Hill Publishing, Inc.
Collins Easy Learning, Collins Easy. Times Tables Quick Quizzes Ages 5-7. 2017. (Collins Easy Learning KS1 Ser.). (ENG., Illus.). 32p. (J). (gr. k-3). pap. 6.95 (978-0-00-821249-0(X)) HarperCollins Pubs. Ltd. GBR. Dist: Independent Pubs. Group.
Collins, Pat Lowery. I Am a Dancer. Graham, Mark, illus. 2008. (Millbrook Picture Books Ser.). 30p. (J). (gr. 3-7). 22.60 (978-0-8225-6369-3(X), Millbrook Pr.) Lerner Publishing Group.
Collins, Peggy. In the Garden. Collins, Peggy, illus. 2009. (ENG., Illus.). 40p. (J). 14.95 (978-1-60433-026-7(0), Applesauce Pr.) Cider Mill Pr. Bk. Pubs., LLC.
Collins, Ross. My Amazing Dad. 2014. (ENG., Illus.). 32p. (J). pap. 8.99 (978-1-4711-2258-3(1), Simon & Schuster Children's) Simon & Schuster, Ltd. GBR. Dist: Simon & Schuster, Inc.
Colman, Michelle Sinclair. Not That Tutu! Nakata, Hiroe, illus. 2013. (ENG.). 20p. (J). (— 1). bds. 7.99 (978-0-307-97698-7(X), Robin Corey Bks.) Random Hse. Children's Bks.
Colorful Cars. 2017. (Colorful Cars Ser.). 24p. (gr. 4-6). pap. 24.75 (978-1-5081-6178-3(X), PowerKids Pr.) Rosen Publishing Group, Inc., The.
Colton, Nicola. A Dublin Fairytale. 2016. (ENG., Illus.). 32p. (J). 18.00 (978-1-84717-774-2(3)) O'Brien Pr., Ltd., The IRL. Dist: Dufour Editions, Inc.
Combes, Mélanie, illus. Hello! Farm. 2016. (Hello! Ser.). (ENG.). 10p. (J). (gr. -1-k). bds. 16.99 (978-1-4472-7719-4(8)) Pan Macmillan GBR. Dist: Independent Pubs. Group.
Conkling, Fleur & dePaola, Tomie. The Bingity-Bangity School Bus. Wood, Ruth, illus. 2015. (G&d Vintage Ser.). (ENG.). 24p. (J). (gr. -1-k). bds. 7.99 (978-0-448-48763-2(2), Grosset & Dunlap) Penguin Young Readers Group.
Cook, David C. Publishing Staff & Tangvald, Christine. Josiah, the Boy King. 2004. (Pencil Fun Bks.: Vol. 10). 16p. (J). (gr. 1-4). pap. 9.90 (978-1-55513-918-6(3), 1555139183) Cook, David C.
Cook, Julia. Sorry, I Forgot to Ask! My Story about Asking Permission & Making an Apology! De Weerd, Kelsey, illus. 2012. (ENG.). 32p. 16.95 (978-1-934490-29-7(6)); pap. 10.95 (978-1-934490-28-0(8)) Boys Town Pr.
—Table Talk: A Book about Table Manners. DuFalla, Anita, illus. 2016. (Building Relationships Ser.: Vol. 7). (ENG.). 32p. (J). pap. 10.95 (978-1-934490-97-6(0)) Boys Town Pr.
Cook, Katie. My Little Pony: Friendship Is Magic Part 2: Friendship Is Magic Part 2. Price, Andy, illus. 2014. (My Little Pony Ser.). (ENG.). 52p. (J). (gr. 2-5). pap. 6.99 (978-1-61377-860-9(0), 9781613778609) Idea & Design Works, LLC.
—My Little Pony: Friendship Is Magic Volume 3: Friendship Is Magic Volume 3. Price, Andy, illus. 2014. (My Little Pony Ser.). (ENG.). 104p. pap. 17.99 (978-1-61377-854-8(6), 9781613778548) Idea & Design Works, LLC.
Cool by the Pool: Picture Book (English) 8x8. 2007. (J). 5.99 (978-1-933934-37-2(9)) Mighty Kids Media.
Cool by the Pool: Picture Book (English) NL 9x9 with Snipe. 2007. (J). 5.99 (978-1-933934-47-1(6)) Mighty Kids Media.
Coombs, Kate. Goodnight Mr. Darcy Board Book, 1 vol. Arnold, Alli, illus. 2015. (ENG.). 22p. (J). bds. 9.99 (978-1-4236-4177-3(9)) Gibbs Smith, Publisher.
Cooper, Jenny, illus. Do Your Ears Hang Low? 2017. (ENG.). 40p. (J). (gr. -1). 12.95 (978-1-4549-1614-7(1)) Sterling Publishing Co., Inc.
Cordell, Matthew. Wish. Cordell, Matthew, illus. 2015. (ENG., Illus.). 48p. (J). (gr. -1-k). 16.99 (978-1-4847-0875-0(X)) Hyperion Bks. for Children.
Corderoy, Tracey. Flower in the Snow. Allsopp, Sophie, illus. 2012. (ENG.). 32p. (J). (-3). 16.99 (978-1-4022-7740-5(7), 1350490, Sourcebooks Jabberwocky) Sourcebooks, Inc.
—The Grunt & the Grouch. 2013. (Grunt & the Grouch Ser.). (ENG.). 112p. (gr. 1-3). 50.64 (978-1-4342-4851-0(8)) Stone Arch Bks.
Corr, Christopher. Deep in the Woods. 2017. (ENG., Illus.). 32p. (J). (gr. -1-1). 17.99 (978-1-84780-726-7(7), Frances Lincoln Children's Bks.) Quarto Publishing Group UK GBR. Dist: Hachette Bk. Group.
Corrigan, Kathleen. ABC, 1 vol. 2014. (Canadian Board Bks.). (ENG & FRE.). 20p. bds. 7.99 (978-1-62370-223-6(2)) Capstone Young Readers of Coughlan Cos.
—123, 1 vol. 2014. (Canadian Board Bks.). (ENG & FRE.). 20p. bds. 7.99 (978-1-62370-224-3(0)) Capstone Young Readers of Coughlan Cos.
Cortez, Tammy. AbbeyLoo & Gus the Talking Toad. Landry, Noemie Gionet, illus. 2015. (ENG.). 32p. (J). pap. 9.95 (978-1-943274-38-3(X), 9781943274383) Waldorf Publishing.
Cosgrove, Stephen. Button Breaker. 2016. (Treasure Trolls Ser.). (ENG., Illus.). 32p. (J). (gr. k-4). pap. 7.95 (978-1-941437-79-7(6)) Heritage Builders, LLC.
—Snicker Doodle. 2016. (Treasure Trolls Ser.). (ENG., Illus.). 32p. (J). (gr. k-4). pap. 7.95 (978-1-941437-82-7(6)) Heritage Builders, LLC.
—Sparkles. 2016. (Treasure Trolls Ser.). (ENG., Illus.). 32p. (J). (gr. k-4). pap. 7.95 (978-1-941437-81-0(8)) Heritage Builders, LLC.
—Tizzy. 2016. (Treasure Trolls Ser.). (ENG., Illus.). 32p. (J). (gr. k-4). pap. 7.95 (978-1-941437-83-4(4)) Heritage Builders, LLC.
Cossons, Malcolm & Stevens, Neil. Dot to Dot... 2013. (ENG., Illus.). 32p. (J). (gr. -1-k). 15.95 (978-0-500-65015-8(2), 565015) Thames & Hudson.
Côté, Geneviève. Me & You. Côté, Geneviève, illus. 2009. (Piggy & Bunny Ser.). (ENG., Illus.). 32p. (J). (gr. -1-k). 16.95 (978-1-55453-446-3(1)) Kids Can Pr., Ltd. CAN. Dist: Hachette Bk. Group.
Côté, Geneviève. Bob's Hungry Ghost. 2014. (ENG., Illus.). 32p. (J). (gr. -1-2). 17.99 (978-1-77049-713-9(7), Tundra Bks.) Tundra Bks. CAN. Dist: Penguin Random Hse. LLC.
—Mr. King's Castle. Côté, Geneviève, illus. 2013. (Mr. King Ser.). (ENG., Illus.). 32p. (J). (gr. -1-2). 16.95 (978-1-55453-972-7(2)) Kids Can Pr., Ltd. CAN. Dist: Hachette Bk. Group.
—Mr. King's Things. Côté, Geneviève, illus. 2012. (Mr. King Ser.). (ENG., Illus.). 32p. (J). (gr. -1-2). 16.95 (978-1-55453-700-6(2)) Kids Can Pr., Ltd. CAN. Dist: Hachette Bk. Group.
—Without You. Côté, Geneviève, illus. 2011. (Piggy & Bunny Ser.). (ENG., Illus.). 32p. (J). (gr. -1-k). 16.95 (978-1-55453-620-7(0)) Kids Can Pr., Ltd. CAN. Dist: Hachette Bk. Group.
Cotter, Bill. Don't Push the Button! 2013. (ENG., Illus.). 32p. (J). (-3). 16.99 (978-1-4022-8746-6(1), Sourcebooks Jabberwocky) Sourcebooks, Inc.
—Don't Touch This Book! 2016. (ENG., Illus.). 28p. (J). bds. 6.99 (978-1-4926-4804-8(3), 9781492648048, Sourcebooks Jabberwocky) Sourcebooks, Inc.
Cotton, Katie. The Road Home. Jacoby, Sarah, illus. 2017. (ENG.). 32p. (J). (gr. k-2). 15.95 (978-1-4197-2374-2(X), Abrams Bks. for Young Readers) Abrams, Inc.
Cottringer, Anne. Hot Dog. Walker, Katherine, illus. 2005. (ENG.). 24p. (J). lib. bdg. 23.65 (978-1-59646-738-5(X)) Dingles & Co.
Cottswold, Wooley. Rose & the Bald-Headed Elephant. 2009. (Illus.). 28p. (J). 16.95 (978-0-9779064-0-6(X)) Archie Publishing.
Coudrille, Jonathon. Farmer Fisher's Russian Christmas. 2013. 42p. pap. (978-1-908867-20-9(5)) FootSteps Pr.
Courgeon, Rémi. Toothpick. 2017. (ENG., Illus.). 36p. (J). (gr. k-4). 17.95 (978-1-59270-210-7(4)) Enchanted Lion Bks., LLC.
Courtney-Tickle, Jessica. The Unexpected Visitor. 2017. (ENG., Illus.). 32p. (J). (gr. -1-k). pap. 9.99 (978-1-4052-8365-6(3)) Egmont Bks., Ltd. GBR. Dist: Independent Pubs. Group.
Cousins, Lucy. Beep, Beep, Maisy! Cousins, Lucy, illus. 2017. (Maisy Ser.). (ENG., Illus.). 16p. (J). (-k). bds. 12.99 (978-0-7636-9407-4(X)) Candlewick Pr.
—Maisy's Plane. Cousins, Lucy, illus. 2015. (Maisy Ser.). (ENG., Illus.). 18p. (J). (— 1). bds. 5.99 (978-0-7636-7304-8(8)) Candlewick Pr.
—Noah's Ark. Cousins, Lucy, illus. 2004. (ENG., Illus.). 22p. (J). (gr. k-k). bds. 6.99 (978-0-7636-2446-0(2)) Candlewick Pr.
—Peck, Peck, Peck. Cousins, Lucy, illus. 2013. (ENG., Illus.). 32p. (J). (-k). 15.99 (978-0-7636-6621-7(1)) Candlewick Pr.
—Treasury of Nursery Rhymes. 2015. (ENG., Illus.). 22p. (J). (-k). 15.99 (978-1-4472-7724-8(4)) Pan Macmillan GBR. Dist: Independent Pubs. Group.
Covello, Paul. Toronto ABC. 2014. (ENG., Illus.). 15p. (J). bds. 10.50 (978-1-4434-3144-6(3), Harper Trophy) HarperCollins Pubs.
Covington, Jean. Nanny Planted Love. (J). 2006. per. 11.99 (978-1-933732-12-1(1)) 2005. lib. bdg. 19.95 (978-0-9754728-9-7(5)) Big Ransom Studio.
Cowell, Cressida. The Thing. Layton, Neal, illus. 2015. (Emily Brown Ser.). (ENG.). 32p. (J). (gr. -1-k). pap. 10.99 (978-1-4449-2340-7(4)) Hodder & Stoughton GBR. Dist: Hachette Bk. Group.
Cowell, Cressida & Layton, Neal. Cheer up Your Teddy Bear. 2015. (Emily Brown Ser.). (ENG., Illus.). 32p. (J). (gr. -1-k). pap. 10.99 (978-1-4449-2342-1(0)) Hodder & Stoughton GBR. Dist: Hachette Bk. Group.
Cowell, Cressida & Mayhew, James. Emily Brown: Emily Brown & the Elephant Emergency. Layton, Neal, illus. 2015. (Emily Brown Ser.). (ENG.). 32p. (J). (gr. -1-k). pap. 10.99 (978-1-4449-2343-8(9)) Hodder & Stoughton GBR. Dist: Hachette Bk. Group.
Cowling, Douglas. Vivaldi's Ring of Mystery. Fernandez, Laura & Jacobson, Rick, illus. 2004. (ENG.). 44p. (J). (978-0-439-96904-8(2), North Winds Pr) Scholastic Canada, Ltd.
Cox, Phil Roxbee, ed. Find the Duck. Cartwright, Stephen, illus. 2004. (Find It Board Bks.). (ENG.). 1p. (J). (gr. -1-18). bds. 3.95 (978-0-7460-3821-5(6)) EDC Publishing.
Cox, Tracey M. Arachnabet- an Alphabet of Spiders. 2013. 20p. pap. 9.95 (978-1-61633-362-1(6)) Guardian Angel Publishing, Inc.
Coxall, Darcy. Where Is My Bear? Wittebrood, Menno, illus. 2015. (ENG.). 32p. (J). (gr. -1-1). pap. 8.99 (978-1-907432-09-5(4)) Hogs Back Bks. GBR. Dist: Independent Pubs. Group.
Coyle, Carmela Lavigna. Do Princesses Boogie? Gordon, Mike, illus. 2016. (ENG.). 26p. (J). (gr. -1-2). bds. 7.95 (978-1-63076-159-2(1)) Taylor Trade Publishing.
Craig, Jenny. I Believe in Genevieve. Edelson, Wendy, illus. 2013. (ENG.). 40p. (J). (gr. -1-3). 16.95 (978-1-62157-085-1(1), Regnery Kids) Regnery Publishing, Inc., An Eagle Publishing Co.
Craig, Lindsey. Farmyard Beat. Brown, Marc, illus. 2012. (ENG.). 32p. (J). (gr. k-k). bds. 6.99 (978-0-307-93082-8(3), Knopf Bks. for Young Readers) Random Hse. Children's Bks.
Crawford, Georgina. Archie-Parchie-Piddley-Poo. 2009. (Illus.). 24p. pap. 12.99 (978-1-4389-7307-4(1)) AuthorHouse.
Cree, Tahara, text. Bonnie the Bee. 2012. (ENG., Illus.). 13p. pap. 5.00 (978-0-9824964-3-5(5)) Creative Education & Publishing.
Creek, Lorie. Who Is This Jesus? A Hidden Picture Book. Creek, Chris, illus. 2012. (J). 18.99 (978-1-60908-909-2(X)) Deseret Bk. Co.
Crews, Donald. Freight Train. Crews, Donald, illus. (Illus.). (J). (gr. -1 — 1). 2016. 32p. bds. 7.99 (978-0-06-245708-0(X)) 2008. (SPA & ENG., 24p. pap. 7.99 (978-0-06-056204-5(8)) 2003. (SPA & ENG., 24p. 16.99 (978-0-06-056202-1(1)) HarperCollins Pubs. (Greenwillow Bks.).
Croft, Malcolm. One Direction in 3D: Unofficial & Unauthorised. 2015. (ENG., Illus.). 48p. (J). (gr. 4). 12.95 (978-1-78097-564-1(3)) Carlton Bks., Ltd. GBR. Dist: Sterling Publishing Co., Inc.
Cronin, Doreen. A Barnyard Collection: Click, Clack, Moo & More. Lewin, Betsy, illus. 2010. (Click, Clack Book Ser.). (ENG.). 128p. (J). (gr. -1-3). 19.99 (978-1-4424-1263-7(1), Atheneum Bks. for Young Readers) Simon & Schuster Children's Publishing.
—Boom Snot Twitty This Way That Way. Liwska, Renata, illus. 2015. (ENG.). 32p. (J). (-k). 16.99 (978-0-670-78577-3(6), Viking Books for Young Readers) Penguin Young Readers Group.
—Click, Clack, Moo. 2016. (Simon & Schuster Ready-To-Read Level 2 Ser.). (Illus.). (J). lib. bdg. 13.55 (978-0-606-39751-3(5)) Turtleback Bks.
—Click, Clack, Moo: Cows That Type. braille ed. 2004. (Illus.). (J). (gr. k-3). spiral bd. (978-0-616-07227-1(9)) Canadian National Institute for the Blind/Institut National Canadien pour les Aveugles.
—Click, Clack, Moo: Cows That Type, Set. Lewin, Betsy, illus. 2009. (Click, Clack Book Ser.). (ENG.). 16p. (J). (gr. -1-k). bds. 14.99 (978-1-4169-5516-0(X), Little Simon) Little Simon.
—Click, Clack, Surprise! Lewin, Betsy, illus. 2016. (Click, Clack Book Ser.). (ENG.). 40p. (J). (gr. -1-3). 17.99 (978-1-4814-7031-5(0), Atheneum/Caitlyn Dlouhy Books) Simon & Schuster Children's Publishing.
—Diary of a Worm: Nat the Gnat. Bliss, Harry, illus. 2014. (I Can Read Level 1 Ser.). (ENG.). 32p. (J). (gr. -1-3). pap. 3.99 (978-0-06-208707-2(X)) HarperCollins Pubs.
—Duck for President. Lewin, Betsy, illus. 2004. (Click, Clack Book Ser.). (ENG.). 32p. (J). (gr. -1-3). 17.99 (978-0-689-86377-6(2), Atheneum Bks. for Young Readers) Simon & Schuster Children's Publishing.
Cronin, Doreen & Simon and Schuster/LeapFrog Staff. Click, Clack, Moo: Cows That Type. Lewin, Betsy, illus. 2008. (J). 13.99 (978-1-59319-936-4(8)) LeapFrog Enterprises, Inc.
Cross, Gillian. Sam Sorts It Out. Mier, Colin, illus. 2005. (ENG.). 24p. (J). lib. bdg. 23.65 (978-1-59646-702-6(9)) Dingles & Co.
Cross, Ken. Who Is Pat Dump? 2009. 48p. pap. 21.99 (978-1-4363-9568-7(2)) Xlibris Corp.
Cross, Mandy & Ross, Mandy. The Sly Fox & the Little Red Hen. 2015. (First Favourite Tales Ser.). (ENG., Illus.). 32p. (J). (-k). 7.99 (978-1-4093-0955-0(X)) Penguin Bks., Ltd. GBR. Dist: Independent Pubs. Group.
Crossley-Holland, Kevin. The Riddlemaster, 1 vol. Jorisch, Stéphane, illus. 2016. (ENG.). 32p. (J). (gr. 2-5). 16.95 (978-1-926890-11-6(3)) Tradewind Bks. CAN. Dist: Orca Bk. Pubs. USA.
Crossley, Kimball. When I Am with Dad. Gamb, Katie, illus. 2016. (ENG.). 32p. (J). (gr. -1-3). 17.95 (978-0-9912935-7-5(6)) Two Little Birds Bks.
Crow, Melinda Melton. Truck Buddies, 1 vol. Rooney, Ronnie, illus. 2009. (Truck Buddies Ser.). (ENG.). 32p. (gr. -1-1). pap. 6.25 (978-1-4342-1756-1(6)) Stone Arch Bks.
Crowther, Robert. The Most Amazing Hide-and-Seek Numbers Book. Crowther, Robert, illus. 2010. (ENG., Illus.). 12p. (J). (gr. -1-2). pap. 12.99 (978-0-7636-5029-2(3)) Candlewick Pr.
Crum, Shutta. Mine! Barton, Patrice, illus. 2011. (ENG.). 32p. (J). (gr. -1-2). 16.99 (978-0-375-86711-8(2), Knopf Bks. for Young Readers) Random Hse. Children's Bks.
—Uh-Oh! Barton, Patrice, illus. 2015. (ENG.). 32p. (J). (-k). 16.99 (978-0-385-75268-8(7), Knopf Bks. for Young Readers) Random Hse. Children's Bks.
Cullimore, Stan. Alien Swap. Schon, Nick, illus. 2005. (ENG.). 24p. (J). lib. bdg. 23.65 (978-1-59646-744-6(4)) Dingles & Co.
Cumming, Hannah. The Cloud. Cumming, Hannah, illus. 2010. (Child's Play Library). (ENG., Illus.). 32p. (J). (gr. 1-2). pap. (978-1-84643-343-6(6)) Child's Play International Ltd.
—The Lost Stars. Cumming, Hannah, illus. 2011. (Child's Play Library). (ENG., Illus.). 32p. (J). (978-1-84643-416-7(5)) Child's Play International Ltd.
Cummings, Troy. The Eensy Weensy Spider Freaks Out! (Big-Time!) Cummings, Troy, illus. 2015. (ENG., Illus.). 40p. (J). (gr. -1-2). 7.99 (978-0-553-49672-7(7), Dragonfly Bks.) Random Hse. Children's Bks.
Cummings, W. T. The Girl in the White Hat. 2017. (ENG., Illus.). 32p. (J). 14.95 (978-0-486-81586-2(2)) Dover Pubns., Inc.
Cunliffe, John. Postman Pat & the Goat's Supper. (Illus.). 20p. (J). (978-0-340-71437-9(9)) Hodder & Stoughton.
—Postman Pat Mends a Clock. (Illus.). 20p. (J). pap. 11.99 (978-0-340-73718-7(2)) Hodder & Stoughton GBR. Dist: Trafalgar Square Publishing.
—Postman Pat Surprise Breakfast. (Illus.). 24p. (J). (978-0-340-71433-1(6)) Hodder & Stoughton.
—Postman Pats Special Delivery Bind. (Illus.). 94p. (J). 22.99 (978-0-340-71055-5(1)) Hodder & Stoughton GBR. Dist: Trafalgar Square Publishing.
Cunningham, S. C. Ginormous Joe's Broken Bark. 2009. 48p. pap. 21.90 (978-1-4490-3116-9(1)) AuthorHouse.
Currie, Robin. Baby Bible 123. 2005. (Baby Bible Ser.). (Illus.). 48p. (J). bds. 12.99 (978-0-7814-3906-0(X), 078143906X) Cook, David C.
Curry, Casey. I Remember You Today: An Interactive Picturebook for Children Dealing with the Loss of a Sibling or Parent. 2003. (Illus.). 24p. (J). wbk. ed. (978-1-884878-15-2(6)) Annapolis Publishing Co.
Curtis, Joan Scott. The Number Fairy. 2012. (ENG.). (J). pap. 18.00 (978-1-4675-5219-6(4)) Independent Pub.
Curto Family, The & Fischer, Rusty. One Little Christmas Tree. 2012. 26p. pap. 9.99 (978-0-9840338-1-2(5)) Good Times at Home LLC.
Custer, Jason. Everyday Monsters. 2005. (J). lib. bdg. 19.95 (978-0-9754728-3-5(6)) Big Ransom Studio.
Cutbill, Andy, illus. Albie & the Big Race. 2004. (ENG.). 32p. (J). pap. 9.99 (978-0-00-712212-7(8)) HarperCollins Pubs. Ltd. GBR. Dist: Trafalgar Square Publishing.
Czekaj, Jef. Dog Rules. Czekaj, Jef, illus. 2016. (Illus.). 32p. (J). (gr. -1-3). 17.99 (978-0-06-228018-3(X)) HarperCollins Pubs.
Daddo, Andrew. When I Grow Up. Bentley, Jonathan, illus. 2017. 32p. 17.99 (978-0-7333-3341-5(9)) ABC Bks. AUS. Dist: HarperCollins Pubs.
Dahimène, Adelheid. Donkeys. Stollinger, Heide, illus. 2014. (ENG.). 48p. (J). (gr. k-3). 17.95 (978-0-7358-4160-4(8)) North-South Bks., Inc.
Dahl, Michael. Animal Etiquette. Persico, Zoe, illus. 2016. (Me & My Pet Ser.). (ENG.). 24p. (gr. 1-2). 45.30 (978-1-5158-0255-6(8), Fiction Picture Bks.) Picture Window Bks.
—Be a Star, Wonder Woman! Lozano, Omar, illus. 2017. (DC Super Heroes Ser.). (ENG.). 32p. (gr. -1-2). 15.95 (978-1-62370-875-7(3), DC Super Heroes) Stone Arch Bks.
Dahl, Michael. Monster Street, Set. Ornia-Blanco, Miguel, illus. Incl. Cold Feet. lib. bdg. 23.99 (978-1-4048-6070-4(3)); In One Ear, Out the Other. lib. bdg. 23.99 (978-1-4048-6068-1(1)); Two Heads Are Better Than One. lib. bdg. 23.99 (978-1-4048-6067-4(3)); (gr. 1-2). (Monster Street Ser.). (ENG., Illus.). 32p. 2010. Set lib. bdg. 71.97 (978-1-4048-6352-1(4), Monster Street) Picture Window Bks.
Dahle, Stefanie. Lily, the Little Elf Princess. 2015. (ENG., Illus.). 32p. (J). 17.95 (978-0-7358-4177-2(2)) North-South Bks., Inc.
Dale, Elizabeth. Off to Market. Pal, Erika, illus. 2013. (ENG.). 32p. (J). (gr. -1-3). 17.99 (978-1-84780-338-2(5), Frances Lincoln) Quarto Publishing Group UK GBR. Dist: Hachette Bk. Group.
Daley, Lashon. Mr. Okra Sells Fresh Fruits & Vegetables, 1 vol. Henriquez, Emile, illus. 2016. (ENG.). 32p. (J). (gr. k-3). 16.99 (978-1-4556-2112-5(9)) Pelican Publishing Co., Inc.
Daley, Michael J. Beach Socks, 1 vol. Corke, Estelle, illus. 2013. (ENG.). 10p. (J). bds. 6.99 (978-1-59572-637-7(3)) Star Bright Bks., Inc.
Daly, Jude. Seb & Hamish. Daly, Niki, illus. 2014. (ENG.). 32p. (J). (gr. -1-1). 17.99 (978-1-84780-412-9(8), Frances Lincoln Children's Bks.) Quarto Publishing Group UK GBR. Dist: Hachette Bk. Group.
Daly, Kathleen N. Jingle Bells. Miller, J. P., illus. 2015. (Little Golden Book Ser.). (ENG.). 24p. (J). (-k). 4.99 (978-0-553-51112-3(2), Golden Bks.) Random Hse. Children's Bks.
Daly, Niki. A Song for Jamela. Daly, Niki, illus. 2014. (ENG., Illus.). 36p. (J). (gr. -1-2). pap. 8.99 (978-1-84780-429-7(2), Frances Lincoln) Quarto Publishing Group UK GBR. Dist: Hachette Bk. Group.
Daly, Niki & Quarto Generic Staff. No More Kisses for Bernard! 2012. (ENG., Illus.). 32p. (J). (gr. -1-1). 17.99 (978-1-84780-105-0(6), Frances Lincoln) Quarto Publishing Group UK GBR. Dist: Hachette Bk. Group.
Damm, Antje. Waiting for Goliath. Damm, Antje, illus. 2017. (ENG., Illus.). 32p. (J). (gr. -1-3). 16.99 (978-1-77657-141-3(X)) Gecko Pr. NZL. Dist: Lerner Publishing Group.
Damschroder, Scott. The Crazy Carnival Clown We Call Croc. 2006. (Illus.). 40p. (J). lib. bdg. 19.95 (978-0-9754728-1-1(X)) Big Ransom Studio.
Dane Rehagen. How Katie Got Her Meow. 2010. 42p. pap. 15.00 (978-1-4251-8664-7(5)) Trafford Publishing.
Danger Alert: Picture Book (English) 2006. (Illus.). 47p. (J). 5.99 (978-1-933934-03-7(4)) Mighty Kids Media.
Danger Alert: Picture Book (English) 8x8. 2007. (J). 5.99 (978-1-933934-39-6(5)) Mighty Kids Media.
Danger Alert: Picture Book (English) 9x9 with Snipe. 2007. (J). 5.99 (978-1-933934-49-5(2)) Mighty Kids Media.
Danielsdottir, Sigrun. Your Body Is Awesome: Body Respect for Children. Bjarkadottir, Björk, illus. 2014. (ENG.). 36p. (J). 17.95 (978-1-84819-228-7(2), 2674, Singing Dragon) Kingsley, Jessica Pubs. GBR. Dist: Macmillan Distribution Ltd.
—Your Body Is Brilliant: Body Respect for Children. Bjarkadottir, Bjork, illus. 2014. (ENG.). 36p. (J). 17.95 (978-1-84819-221-8(5), 2672, Singing Dragon) Kingsley, Jessica Pubs. GBR. Dist: Macmillan Distribution Ltd.
Darlison, Aleesah. Ellabeth's Light Cancelled. Brailsford, Jill, illus. 2017. (Unicorn Riders Ser.). (ENG.). 112p. (gr. 3-5). lib. bdg. 22.65 (978-1-4795-6551-1(2)) Picture Window Bks.
—Krystal's Charge Cancelled. Brailsford, Jill, illus. 2017. (Unicorn Riders Ser.). (ENG.). 112p. (gr. 3-5). lib. bdg. 22.65 (978-1-4795-6550-4(4)) Picture Window Bks.
Das, Amrita, illus. Hope Is a Girl Selling Fruit. 2014. (ENG.). 28p. 16.95 (978-93-83145-02-7(1)) Tara Books Agency IND. Dist: Publishers Group West (PGW).
Davenport, Andrew. Here Come the Teletubbies. 2004. (Illus.). (J). (gr. -1-2). spiral bd. (978-0-616-03029-5(0)); spiral bd. (978-0-616-04551-0(4)) Canadian National Institute for the Blind/Institut National Canadien pour les Aveugles.
Davey, Owen, illus. Foxly's Feast. 2014. (ENG.). 32p. (J). (-k). 14.95 (978-1-62914-608-9(0), Sky Pony Pr.) Skyhorse Publishing Co., Inc.
David, Juliet. All Aboard with Noah: Pop-Up, 1 vol. Canuso, Julie & Canuso, Jackie, illus. 2016. (ENG.). 12p. (J). 14.99 (978-1-78128-249-6(8), Candle Bks.) Lion Hudson PLC GBR. Dist: Kregel Pubns.
—The Christmas Story, 1 vol. Ellis, Elina, illus. 2016. (ENG.). 24p. (J). 8.99 (978-1-78128-282-3(X), Candle Bks.) Lion Hudson PLC GBR. Dist: Kregel Pubns.
—The Easter Story, 1 vol. Parry, Jo, illus. 2015. (ENG.). 12p. (J). bds. 3.99 (978-1-85985-992-6(5), Candle Bks.) Lion Hudson PLC GBR. Dist: Kregel Pubns.
—The Great Flood, 1 vol. Parry, Jo, illus. 2014. (ENG.). 12p. (J). bds. 3.99 (978-1-85985-991-9(7), Candle Bks.) Lion Hudson PLC GBR. Dist: Kregel Pubns.
—My Friend Jesus, 1 vol. Prole, Helen, illus. 2016. (Candle Bible for Toddlers Ser.). (ENG.). 32p. (J). pap. 4.99 (978-1-78128-280-9(3), Candle Bks.) Lion Hudson PLC GBR. Dist: Kregel Pubns.
—My Very First Christmas Story, 1 vol. Siewert, Pauline, illus. 2015. 14p. (J). 7.99 (978-1-78128-231-1(5), Candle Bks.) Lion Hudson PLC GBR. Dist: Kregel Pubns.
—My Very First Easter, 1 vol. Prole, Helen, illus. 2016. (ENG.). 24p. (J). pap. 4.99 (978-1-78128-244-1(7), Candle Bks.) Lion Hudson PLC GBR. Dist: Kregel Pubns.
—My Very First Story of Christmas, 1 vol. Prole, Helen, illus. 2016. (Candle Bible for Toddlers Ser.). (ENG.). 24p. (J). pap. 4.99 (978-1-78128-285-4(4), Candle Bks.) Lion Hudson PLC GBR. Dist: Kregel Pubns.
—Prayers for Little Girls, 1 vol. Clay, Julie, illus. 2014. 64p. (J). 12.99 (978-1-85985-990-2(9), Candle Bks.) Lion Hudson PLC GBR. Dist: Kregel Pubns.
David, Juliet & Embleton-Hall, Chris. Noah's Amazing Ark: A Lift-The-Flap Adventure, 1 vol. 2017. (ENG., Illus.). 14p. (J). 9.99 (978-1-78128-317-2(6), Candle Bks.) Lion Hudson PLC GBR. Dist: Kregel Pubns.

Davidson, Michael. Ready, Teddy, Go! Davidson, Michael, illus. 2013. (ENG., Illus.). 32p. (J). (gr. -1-k). 18.99 *(978-1-4083-2023-5(1))* Hodder & Stoughton GBR. Dist: Hachette Bk. Group.

Davidson, Susanna. Animalium Poster Book. Scott, Katie, illus. 2017. (ENG.). 56p. (J). (gr. 2-4). pap. 22.00 *(978-0-7636-9318-3(9)*, Big Picture Press) Candlewick Pr.

—Christmas Carol (Picture Book) 2007. (Picture Book Classics Ser.). 24p. (J). 9.99 *(978-0-7945-1894-3(X)*, Usborne) EDC Publishing.

—Cinderella Picture Book. 2015. (Picture Bks.). (ENG.). 24p. (J). 9.99 *(978-0-7945-3423-3(6)*, Usborne) EDC Publishing.

—Nutcracker with Music. 2012. (Picture Books with Music Ser.). 24p. (J). bds. 18.99 *(978-0-7945-2646-7(2)*, Usborne) EDC Publishing.

—Swan Lake with Music. 2012. (Picture Books with Music Ser.). 24p. (J). bds. 18.99 *(978-0-7945-3301-4(9)*, Usborne) EDC Publishing.

Davies, Becky. Peekaboo Pals Opposites. Lucas, Gareth, illus. 2016. (Peekaboo Pals Ser.). (ENG.). 20p. (J). (gr. -1). bds. 14.95 *(978-1-62686-522-8(1)*, Silver Dolphin Bks.) Readerlink Distribution Services, LLC.

Davies, Nicola. Deadly! The Truth about the Most Dangerous Creatures on Earth. Layton, Neal, illus. 2015. (Animal Science Ser.). (ENG.). 64p. (J). (gr. 3-7). pap. 7.99 *(978-0-7636-7971-2(2))* Candlewick Pr.

—The Promise. Carlin, Laura, illus. (ENG.). 40p. (J). (gr. k-4). 2017. 8.99 *(978-0-7636-9303-9(0))* 2014. 16.99 *(978-0-7636-6633-0(5))* Candlewick Pr.

Davies, Stephen. All Aboard for the Bobo Road. Corr, Christopher, illus. 2016. (ENG.). 32p. (J). (gr. -1-3). 17.99 *(978-1-5124-1598-8(7))* Andersen Pr. GBR. Dist: Lerner Publishing Group.

Davies, Stephen & Corr, Christopher. The Goggle-Eyed Goats. 2013. (ENG., Illus.). 32p. (J). (gr. -1-k). pap. 12.99 *(978-1-84939-312-6(5))* Andersen Pr. GBR. Dist: Independent Pubs. Group.

Dávila, Claudia. Super Red Riding Hood. Dávila, Claudia, illus. 2014. (ENG., Illus.). 32p. (J). (gr. -1-2). 16.95 *(978-1-77138-020-1(9))* Kids Can Pr., Ltd. CAN. Dist: Hachette Bk. Group.

Davis, Anne. No Dogs Allowed!, No. 1. Davis, Anne, illus. 2011. (ENG., Illus.). 32p. (J). (gr. -1-3). 16.99 *(978-0-06-075353-5(6))* HarperCollins Pubs.

Davis, Caroline. Animals in the Water. 2009. (My First Noisy Bath Bks.). (ENG.). 8p. (J). (gr. -1). 4.99 *(978-0-7641-9591-4(3))* Barron's Educational Series, Inc.

—Diggers. Davis, Caroline, illus. 2010. (ENG., Illus.). 20p. (J). bds. *(978-1-4083-0785-4(5)*, Orchard Bks.) Hachette Children's Group GBR. Dist: Hachette Bk. Group.

—First Abc. 2012. (ENG., Illus.). 10p. (J). (gr. k-1). bds. 7.99 *(978-1-84322-772-4(X))* Anness Publishing GBR. Dist: National Bk. Network.

—First Opposites. 2012. (ENG., Illus.). 10p. (J). (gr. -1-1). bds. 7.99 *(978-1-84322-844-8(0)*, Armadillo) Anness Publishing GBR. Dist: National Bk. Network.

—First Pictures. 2012. (ENG., Illus.). 196p. bds. 7.99 *(978-1-84322-774-8(6)*, Armadillo) Anness Publishing GBR. Dist: National Bk. Network.

—First Words. 2012. (ENG., Illus.). 196p. bds. 7.99 *(978-1-84322-842-4(4)*, Armadillo) Anness Publishing GBR. Dist: National Bk. Network.

Davis, Jacky. Ladybug Girl Ready for Snow. Soman, David, illus. 2014. (Ladybug Girl Ser.). (ENG.). 12p. (J). (gr. -1 — 1). bds. 5.99 *(978-0-8037-4137-9(5)*, Dial Bks) Penguin Young Readers Group.

Davis, Jacky & Bader, Bonnie. I Love You, Bingo. Soman, David, illus. 2015. (Ladybug Girl Ser.). (ENG.). 32p. (J). (gr. 1-2). 3.99 *(978-0-448-48756-4(X)*, Penguin Young Readers) Penguin Young Readers Group.

Davis, Jim & Michiels, Cedric. Unfair Weather. Dargaud Media Staff & Ellipsanime Staff, illus. 2013. (Garfield Show Ser.). (ENG.). 64p. (J). (gr. 1-5). pap. 7.99 *(978-1-59707-422-3(5)*, 9781597074223) Papercutz.

Davis, Robin & Starr, Lara. Wookiee Pies, Clone Scones, & Other Galactic Goodies. 2012. (ENG., Illus.). 64p. (J). (gr. -1-17). 22.99 *(978-1-4521-0466-9(2))* Chronicle Bks. LLC.

Davison, Max & Cooper, Chris. Cat about Town. Bartolini, Egle & Alvarez, Dave, illus. 2016. (ENG.). 64p. (J). (gr. 1-4). pap. 6.99 *(978-1-78585-332-6(5))* Titan Bks. Ltd. GBR. Dist: Penguin Random Hse. LLC.

Davison, Roz & Laird, Elizabeth. Jungle School. Sims, David, illus. 2nd ed. 2016. (Reading Ladder Ser.). (ENG.). 48p. (J). (gr. k-2). pap. 7.99 *(978-1-4052-8226-0(6))* Egmont Bks., Ltd. GBR. Dist: Independent Pubs. Group.

Dawnay, Gabby. London Calls. Barrow, Alex, illus. 2015. (ENG.). 32p. (gr. k-3). 13.95 *(978-1-84976-230-4(9))* Tate Publishing, Ltd. GBR. Dist: Abrams, Inc.

Dawnay, Gabby & Barrow, Alex. If I Had a Dinosaur. 2017. (ENG., Illus.). 32p. (gr. -1-2). 14.95 *(978-0-500-65099-8(3)*, 565099) Thames & Hudson.

Dawson, Eugene T. Little Valerie Wants to Grow Taller. 2009. 24p. pap. 14.95 *(978-1-4389-7002-8(1))* AuthorHouse.

Day, Alexandra. Carl & the Sick Puppy. 2012. (My Readers: Level 1 Ser.). (J). lib. bdg. 13.55 *(978-0-606-26121-0(4)*, Turtleback) Turtleback Bks.

de Beer, Hans, pseud. Kleiner eisbar wohin fahrst Du. pap. 17.95 *(978-3-423-07954-9(1))* Deutscher Taschenbuch Verlag GmbH & Co KG DEU. Dist: Distribooks, Inc.

—The Little Polar Bear Lars & the Husky Pup. 2012. (Little Polar Bear Ser.). (ENG., Illus.). 32p. (J). (gr. -1-2). pap. 7.95 *(978-0-7358-4078-2(4))* North-South Bks., Inc.

—Nugget on Top of the World. 2015. (ENG & DUT., Illus.). 32p. (J). 17.95 *(978-0-7358-4242-7(6))* North-South Bks., Inc.

de Brunhoff, Jean. The Babar Collection: Five Classic Stories. 2017. (ENG., Illus.). 240p. (J). (gr. -1-k). pap. 22.99 **(978-1-4052-7989-5(3))** Egmont Bks., Ltd. GBR. Dist: Independent Pubs. Group.

de Brunhoff, Jean. Classic Tales of Babar. 2014. (ENG., Illus.). 112p. (J). (gr. -1-1). 19.99 *(978-1-4052-6420-4(9))* Egmont Bks., Ltd. GBR. Dist: Independent Pubs. Group.

de Brunhoff, Laurent. Babar Visits Another Planet. rev. ed. 2012. (ENG., Illus.). 40p. (J). (gr. k-2). 16.95 *(978-1-4197-0342-3(0)*, Abrams Bks. for Young Readers) Abrams, Inc.

—Babar's Counting Book. rev. ed. 2012. (ENG., Illus.). 40p. (J). (gr. k-2). 16.95 *(978-1-4197-0341-6(2)*, Abrams Bks. for Young Readers) Abrams, Inc.

—Babar's Little Girl. rev. ed. 2012. (ENG., Illus.). 40p. (J). (gr. k-2). 16.95 *(978-1-4197-0340-9(4)*, Abrams Bks. for Young Readers) Abrams, Inc.

De La Barre De Nanteuil, Andrea. Mademoiselle Oiseau & the Letter from Her Past. 2015. (ENG., Illus.). 144p. (J). (gr. 3-7). 24.95 *(978-3-89955-757-2(3))* Die Gestalten Verlag DEU. Dist: Penguin Random Hse. LLC.

de Maeyer, Gregie. Juul. 2003. (SPA., Illus.). 204p. *(978-84-85334-90-2(6))* Lóguez Ediciones ESP. Dist: Lectorum Pubns., Inc.

De Roma, Giuseppino. Francis of Assisi. (Illus.). 31p. 7.95 *(978-1-875570-64-5(0))* St Pauls Pubns. AUS. Dist: St Pauls/Alba Hse. Pubs.

De Smet, Marian & Meijer, Marja. Encerrada: Anna's Tight Squeeze. Pacheco, Laura Emilia, tr. Uitgeverij, Clavis, illus. 2004. 28p. (J). 14.95 *(978-970-29-0665-0(2))* Santillana USA Publishing Co., Inc.

Dean, James. Twinkle, Twinkle, Little Star. Dean, James, illus. 2014. (Pete the Cat Ser.). (ENG., Illus.). 32p. (J). (gr. -1-3). 9.99 *(978-0-06-230416-2(X))* HarperCollins Pubs.

DeGarmo, John & DeGarmo, Kelly. A Different Home: A New Foster Child's Story. Trammell, Norma Jeanne, illus. 2014. (ENG.). 48p. (J). 14.95 *(978-1-84905-987-9(X)*, 2757) Kingsley, Jessica Pubs. GBR. Dist: Macmillan Distribution Ltd.

Degen, Bruce. Degen Picture Book. Date not set. (Illus.). 32p. (J). (gr. -1-1). 5.99 *(978-0-06-443579-6(2))* HarperCollins Pubs.

Delacre, Lulu. How Far Do You Love Me?, 1 vol. Delacre, Lulu, illus. 2013. (ENG., Illus.). 32p. (J). 11.95 *(978-1-60060-882-7(5))* Lee & Low Bks., Inc.

DeLand, M. Maitland. The Great Katie Kate Discusses Diabetes. 2010. (Illus.). 32p. 14.95 *(978-1-60832-039-4(1)*, Greenleaf Book Group Pr.) Greenleaf Book Group.

—The Great Katie Kate Offers Answers about Asthma. 2011. (Illus.). 32p. 14.95 *(978-1-60832-074-5(X))* Greenleaf Book Group.

DeLand, M. Maitland. Baby Santa & the Lost Letters. 2011. (Illus.). 36p. (J). 14.95 *(978-1-60832-194-0(0))* Greenleaf Book Group.

Delaporte, Bérengère & Leroy, Jean. Superfab Saves the Day. 2014. (ENG., Illus.). 40p. (J). (gr. -1-3). 16.95 *(978-1-77147-076-6(3)*, Owlkids) Owlkids Bks. Inc. CAN. Dist: Publishers Group West (PGW).

Delaronde, Deborah L. Duck's Bay. Dawson, Sheldon, illus. 2004. 48p. (J). pap. *(978-1-894717-24-3(4)*, Spotlight Poets) Pemmican Pubns., Inc.

DeLong, Lucianne. Mrs. Mumford's Missing. Richoll, Stephanie, illus. 2013. (Saloman Sawdust's Snappy Stories Ser.). (ENG.). 24p. (J). 4.99 *(978-0-9833237-5-4(5))* Krullstone Publishing, LLC.

Demarest, Chris L. Bus. 2017. (ENG., Illus.). 16p. (J). (— 1). bds. 6.99 *(978-0-544-87087-1(5)*, HMH Books For Young Readers) Houghton Mifflin Harcourt Publishing Co.

—Train. 2017. (ENG., Illus.). 16p. (J). (— 1). bds. 6.99 *(978-0-544-87608-8(3)*, HMH Books For Young Readers) Houghton Mifflin Harcourt Publishing Co.

Demarest, Jeannie. My Best Friend Troubles. 2009. 28p. pap. 21.99 *(978-1-4415-3236-7(6))* Xlibris Corp.

Demers, Dominique. Today, Maybe, 1 vol. Grimard, Gabrielle, illus. 2011. (ENG.). 32p. (J). (gr. -1-3). 19.95 *(978-1-55469-400-6(0))* Orca Bk. Pubs. USA.

Dencer, Christine. Misty. Meserve, Jessica, illus. 2015. (Stanley & Me Ser.: 1). (ENG.). 34p. (J). 12.95 *(978-1-927018-59-0(5))* Simply Read Bks. CAN. Dist: Ingram Publisher Services.

Denchfield, Nick. Charlie Chick, 1. Parker, Ant, illus. 2014. (Charlie Chick Ser.). (ENG.). 14p. (J). 12.99 *(978-1-4472-5764-6(2))* Pan Macmillan GBR. Dist: Independent Pubs. Group.

—Charlie Chick Learns to Fly. Parker, Ant, illus. 2016. (Charlie Chick Ser.: 3). (ENG.). 16p. (J). (gr. -1-k). 12.99 *(978-1-5098-0712-3(8))* Pan Macmillan GBR. Dist: Independent Pubs. Group.

—Frankie the Frog. Parker, Ant, illus. 2016. (Charlie Chick Ser.: 4). (ENG.). 16p. (J). (gr. -1-k). bds. 12.99 *(978-1-5098-1767-2(0))* Pan Macmillan GBR. Dist: Independent Pubs. Group.

Denis, Toni. How Do the Children Pray? Olds, Irene, illus. 2010. 16p. 10.99 *(978-1-4490-5164-8(2))* AuthorHouse.

Dennis, Sarah, illus. Cinderella: A Cut-Paper Book. 2015. (ENG.). 52p. (J). (gr. -1-k). 19.99 *(978-1-85707-843-5(8))* Tango Bks. GBR. Dist: Independent Pubs. Group.

Denver, John. Ancient Rhymes, a Dolphin Lullaby: With Audio CD & Score, 1 vol. Canyon, Christopher, illus. 2004. (Sharing Nature with Children Book Ser.). (ENG.). 36p. (J). (gr. -1-6). 19.95 *(978-1-58469-064-1(X))* Dawn Pubns.

dePaola, Tomie. Nana Upstairs & Nana Downstairs. unabr. ed. 2006. (J). (gr. k-3). pap. 17.95 incl. audio *(978-0-8045-6943-9(6))*; pap. 19.95 incl. audio compact disk *(978-0-8045-4157-2(4))* Spoken Arts, Inc.

Depisco, Dorothea. Beetle Bugs Party: A Counting Book. Parry, Jo, illus. 2005. 10p. (J). (gr. -1-3). 10.95 *(978-1-58117-415-1(2)*, Intervisual/Piggy Toes) Bendon, Inc.

Dergachov, Oleg. The Yellow Elves. Andryczyk, Mark, tr. from UKR. 2004. (Illus.). 14p. (J). pap. *(978-0-9735003-0-1(1))* StudioNib Publishing.

Desai, Naina. Fun Jungle. 2009. 28p. pap. 13.99 *(978-1-4490-2058-3(5))* AuthorHouse.

Deuchars, Marion. Bob the Artist. 2016. (ENG., Illus.). 32p. (J). (gr. -1-k). 15.95 *(978-1-78067-767-5(7))* King, Laurence Publishing GBR. Dist: Hachette Bk. Group.

deVet, L. J. Teddy's Christmas Wish. Zabarylo-Duma, Ewa, illus. 2013. (ENG.). 48p. (J). *(978-0-9873686-0-7(5))*; pap. *(978-0-9873686-1-4(3))* Print-Rite Publishers.

Devine, Monica. Kayak Girl. Dwyer, Mindy, illus. 2012. 32p. (J). pap. 12.95 *(978-1-60223-188-7(5))* Univ. of Alaska Pr.

Dewdney, Anna. Llama Llama Easter Egg. Dewdney, Anna, illus. 2015. (Llama Llama Ser.). (ENG., Illus.). 14p. (J). (— 1). bds. 5.99 *(978-0-451-46982-3(8)*, Viking Books for Young Readers) Penguin Publishing Group.

—Llama Llama Mad at Mama. 2009. (Illus.). (J). *(978-0-545-15933-3(4))* Scholastic, Inc.

Dhami, Narinder. Monster under the Stairs. Spoor, Mike, illus. 2005. (ENG.). 24p. (J). lib. bdg. 23.65 *(978-1-59646-718-7(5))* Dingles & Co.

—Samosa Thief. Blundell, Tony, illus. 2005. (ENG.). 24p. (J). lib. bdg. 23.65 *(978-1-59646-708-8(8))* Dingles & Co.

Diane, Rachel And Rebecca Sall. Mother Earth's Message. 2009. 28p. pap. 15.99 *(978-1-4363-8613-5(6))* Xlibris Corp.

Diaper Days Songs. (Baby Looney Tunes Song Bks.). (Illus.). 16p. (J). (gr. -1). 7.98 *(978-0-7853-1612-1(4)*, PI112) Publications International, Ltd.

Diaz, James & Diaz, Francesca. Making Shapes: A Pop-Up Book. 2013. (ENG., Illus.). 10p. 19.95 *(978-1-85707-827-5(6))* Tango Bks. GBR. Dist: Independent Pubs. Group.

DiCamillo, Kate. Great Joy. Ibatoulline, Bagram, illus. 2010. (ENG.). 32p. (J). (gr. -1-3). 8.99 *(978-0-7636-4996-8(1))* Candlewick Pr.

—Louise, the Adventures of a Chicken. Bliss, Harry, illus. 2009. (J). (gr. -1-2). 29.95 incl. audio compact disk *(978-1-4301-0688-3(3))* Live Oak Media.

DiCicco, Sue. Peek-a-Boo Baby. 2010. 12p. (J). (gr. -1). 9.95 *(978-1-60747-709-9(2)*, Pickwick Pr.) Phoenix Bks., Inc.

Dickens, Frank. Fly Away Peter. 2017. (ENG., Illus.). 32p. (J). (gr. k-2). pap. 9.99 **(978-1-84365-321-9(4)**, Pavilion) Pavilion Bks. GBR. Dist: Independent Pubs. Group.

Dicmas, Courtney. Wild Bath Time! 2014. (Wild! Ser.: 4). (ENG., Illus.). 14p. (J). (gr. k-k). bds. *(978-1-84643-686-4(9))* Child's Play International Ltd.

—Wild Bedtime! 2014. (Wild! Ser.: 4). (ENG., Illus.). 14p. (J). (gr. k-k). bds. *(978-1-84643-687-1(7))* Child's Play International Ltd.

—Wild Mealtime! 2014. (Wild! Ser.: 4). (ENG., Illus.). 14p. (J). (gr. k-k). bds. *(978-1-84643-684-0(2))* Child's Play International Ltd.

—Wild Playtime! 2014. (Wild! Ser.: 4). (ENG., Illus.). 14p. (J). (gr. k-k). bds. *(978-1-84643-685-7(0))* Child's Play International Ltd.

Dinosaurs. (Illus.). (J). (gr. -1-6). pap. 2.95 *(978-0-565-01078-2(6))* Natural History Museum Pubns. GBR. Dist: Parkwest Pubns., Inc.

Dipucchio, Kelly. Grace for President. Pham, LeUyen, illus. 2012. (ENG.). 40p. (J). (gr. 1-3). 16.99 *(978-1-4231-3999-7(2))* Hyperion Pr.

Discovery Education. 2013. (Discovery Education Ser.). 32p. (J). (gr. 3-6). 1035.25 *(978-1-4777-1555-0(X))*; pap. 2460.00 *(978-1-4777-2737-9(X))*; pap. 410.00 *(978-1-4777-2736-2(1))* Rosen Publishing Group, Inc., The. (PowerKids Pr.).

Dismondy, Maria & Tulloch, Stephen. The Little Linebacker: A Story of Determination, bks. 2, vol. 2. Heyworth, Heather, illus. 2016. (ENG.). 32p. (J). (gr. k-2). pap. 10.95 *(978-0-9848558-4-1(X))* Dismondy, Maria Inc.

Disney Book Group. The Jungle Book Movie Picture Book. 2016. (ENG.). 40p. (J). (gr. -1-k). 16.99 *(978-1-4847-2578-8(6))* Disney Pr.

—Pete's Dragon Junior Novel: With 8 Pages of Photos from the Movie! 2016. (ENG.). 144p. (J). (gr. 3-7). pap. 5.99 *(978-1-4847-4992-0(8))* Disney Pr.

—Zootopia Picture Book: A Day in the Life of Judy Hopps. 2016. (ENG.). 40p. (J). (gr. -1-k). 16.99 *(978-1-4847-2102-5(0))* Disney Pr.

Disney Book Group & Hurley, Kalikolehua. The Mighty Maui Makes a Friend. Disney Storybook Art Team & Isvandi, Mehrdad, illus. 2017. (ENG.). 32p. (J). (gr. 1-3). 16.99 *(978-1-4847-8292-7(5))* Disney Pr.

Disney Book Group & Knowles, Heather. Moana Ocean Picture Book. Marnat, Annette, illus. 2016. (ENG.). 40p. (J). (gr. -1-k). 16.99 *(978-1-4847-4360-7(1))* Disney Pr.

Disney Book Group, et al. Pirates of the Caribbean. Disney Storybook Art Team & Wall, Mike, illus. 2017. (Disney Parks Presents Ser.). (ENG.). 32p. (J). (gr. -1-k). 17.99 *(978-1-4847-2786-7(X))* Disney Pr.

Disney Book Group Staff. Part of Their World. Disney Storybook Artists Staff, illus. 2013. (ENG.). 40p. (J). (gr. -1-17). 15.99 *(978-1-4231-6757-0(0))* Disney Pr.

Disney Book Group Staff & Hicks, Barbara Jean. Frozen an Amazing Snowman. Disney Storybook Artists Staff & Mosqueda, Olga, illus. 2014. (ENG.). 40p. (J). (gr. -1-k). 16.99 *(978-1-4231-8514-7(5))* Disney Pr.

Disney Book Group Staff & Marsoli, Lisa Ann. Frozen Sing-Along Storybook. Disney Storybook Artists Staff, illus. 2014. (ENG.). 128p. (J). (gr. 1-3). 17.99 *(978-1-4847-2035-6(0))* Disney Pr.

Disney Book Group Staff, et al. It's a Small World. Chou, Joey, illus. 2011. (Disney Parks Presents Ser.). (ENG.). 32p. (J). (gr. -1 — 1). 16.99 *(978-1-4231-4689-6(1))* Disney Pr.

Disney Editors. Olaf Loves... Everything! 2016. (Frozen 8X8 Ser.). lib. bdg. 14.75 **(978-0-606-39858-9(9))** Turtleback Bks.

Dixon, Andy. Star Quest. Brooks, Felicity, ed. Harris, Nick, illus. 2006. (Usborne Fantasy Puzzle Bks.). 32p. (YA). (gr. 7). lib. bdg. 15.99 *(978-1-58086-906-5(8)*, Usborne) EDC Publishing.

Dixon, Pamela. A Windy Day Walk. Homer, Maree, illus. 2016. (ENG.). 32p. (J). (gr. 1-4). *(978-0-473-34486-3(6))* Lizzy Web Bks.

Dobbins, Jan. A Farmer's Life for Me. Huliska-Beith, Laura, illus. 2013. (ENG.). 24p. (J). (gr. k-3). pap. 6.99 *(978-1-84686-939-6(0))* Barefoot Bks., Inc.

Dobell, Darcy. The Oyster Who Looked at the Sky. 2008. (ENG., Illus.). 32p. 16.95 *(978-0-88982-250-4(6))* Oolichan Bks. CAN. Dist: Univ. of Toronto Pr.

Dodd, Emma. Counting. 2017. (ENG., Illus.). 12p. (J). (gr. -1-12). bds. 9.99 **(978-1-86147-839-9(9)**, Armadillo) Anness Publishing GBR. Dist: National Bk. Network.

—On the Farm. 2017. (ENG., Illus.). 12p. (J). (gr. -1-12). bds. 9.99 **(978-1-86147-838-2(0)**, Armadillo) Anness Publishing GBR. Dist: National Bk. Network.

Dodd, Emma, illus. Dog & Friends: Birthday. 2017. (ENG.). 12p. (J). (gr. -1-12). bds. 9.99 **(978-1-86147-836-8(4)**, Armadillo) Anness Publishing GBR. Dist: National Bk. Network.

—Dog & Friends: Busy Day. 2017. (ENG.). 12p. (J). (gr. -1-12). bds. 9.99 **(978-1-86147-835-1(6)**, Armadillo) Anness Publishing GBR. Dist: National Bk. Network.

—Dog's 123: A Canine Counting Adventure! 2016. (ENG.). 14p. bds. 14.99 *(978-1-86147-698-2(1)*, Armadillo) Anness Publishing GBR. Dist: National Bk. Network.

—Dog's ABC: An Alphabet Adventure! 2016. (ENG.). 14p. bds. 14.99 *(978-1-86147-699-9(X)*, Armadillo) Anness Publishing GBR. Dist: National Bk. Network.

—Dog's Farmyard Friends: A Touch & Tickle Book - with Fun-To-Feel Flocking! 2016. (ENG.). 12p. (J). (gr. -1-12). bds. 14.99 *(978-1-86147-719-4(8)*, Armadillo) Anness Publishing GBR. Dist: National Bk. Network.

Dodd, Sarah J. Legs. Capizzi, Giusi, illus. 2015. (ENG.). 32p. (J). (gr. -1-k). 16.99 *(978-0-7459-6597-0(0))* Lion Hudson PLC GBR. Dist: Independent Pubs. Group.

Doherty, Gillian. 1001 Animales Que Buscar. 2004. (1001 Things to Spot Ser.).Tr. of 1001 Animals to Spot. (SPA., Illus.). (J). pap. 6.95 *(978-0-7460-5081-1(X))* EDC Publishing.

—1001 Things to Spot Long Ago. 2010. (1001 Things to Spot Ser.). 32p. (J). 9.99 *(978-0-7945-2731-0(0)*, Usborne) EDC Publishing.

Doi, Kaya, illus. Chirri & Chirra. 2016. (ENG.). 40p. (J). (gr. -1-3). 15.95 *(978-1-59270-199-5(X))* Enchanted Lion Bks., LLC.

Dolan, Elys. The Mystery of the Haunted Farm. Dolan, Elys, illus. 2016. (ENG., Illus.). (J). (gr. -1-3). 17.99 *(978-0-7636-8658-1(1)*, Nosy Crow) Candlewick Pr.

—Nuts in Space. Dolan, Elys, illus. 2015. (ENG., Illus.). 32p. (J). (gr. k-3). 17.99 *(978-0-7636-7609-4(8)*, Nosy Crow) Candlewick Pr.

Don, Lari, et al. Little Red Riding Hood. Chauffrey, Celia, illus. 2012. (ENG.). 32p. (J). (gr. -1-3). 9.99 *(978-1-84686-768-2(1))* Barefoot Bks., Inc.

Donaldson, Connie & Polinko, Les. The Ganorch under the Porch. Polinko, Les, illus. 2013. (Illus.). 36p. pap. 9.95 *(978-0-9836682-3-7(X))* Hearthstone Rose.

Donaldson, Julia. Animal Music. Sharratt, Nick, illus. 2014. (ENG.). 24p. (J). (— 1). pap. 9.99 *(978-1-4472-1095-5(6))* Pan Macmillan GBR. Dist: Independent Pubs. Group.

—Chocolate Mousse for Greedy Goose. Sharratt, Nick, illus. 2015. (ENG.). 18p. (J). (-k). bds. 9.99 *(978-1-4472-8788-9(6))* Pan Macmillan GBR. Dist: Independent Pubs. Group.

—The Flying Bath. Roberts, David, illus. (ENG.). (J). (gr. -1-k). 2016. 32p. pap. 9.99 *(978-1-4472-7711-8(2))* 2014. 400p. 19.99 *(978-0-230-74260-4(2))* Pan Macmillan GBR. Dist: Independent Pubs. Group.

—Freddie & the Fairy, 7. George, Karen, illus. 4th ed. 2012. (ENG.). 32p. (J). (gr. -1-k). 9.99 *(978-0-330-51118-6(1))* Pan Macmillan GBR. Dist: Independent Pubs. Group.

—Goat Goes to Playgroup. Sharratt, Nick, illus. (ENG.). (J). 2014. 26p. bds. 9.99 *(978-1-4472-5484-3(8))*8. 2013. 32p. (gr. -1-k). pap. 9.99 *(978-1-4472-1094-8(8))* Pan Macmillan GBR. Dist: Independent Pubs. Group.

—Jack & the Flumflum Tree. Roberts, David, illus. 2016. (ENG.). 30p. (J). (gr. -1-k). bds. 9.99 *(978-1-4472-8549-6(2))* Pan Macmillan GBR. Dist: Independent Pubs. Group.

—Night Monkey, Day Monkey. Richards, Lucy, illus. 2016. (ENG.). 26p. (J). (gr. -1-k). bds. 10.99 *(978-1-4052-8334-2(3))* Egmont Bks., Ltd. GBR. Dist: Independent Pubs. Group.

—One Mole Digging A Hole. Sharratt, Nick, illus. 2015. (ENG.). 22p. (J). (-k). bds. 9.99 *(978-1-4472-8790-2(8))* Pan Macmillan GBR. Dist: Independent Pubs. Group.

—One Ted Falls Out of Bed. Currey, Anna, illus. (ENG.). (J). 2014. 12p. (gr. -1 — 1). bds. 8.99 *(978-1-4472-0995-9(8))* 2015. 32p. (— 1). pap. 7.99 *(978-1-4472-6614-3(5))* Pan Macmillan GBR. Dist: Independent Pubs. Group.

—The Reiver Rat: The Highway Rat in Scots. Robertson, James, tr. from ENG. Scheffler, Axel, illus. 2015. (ENG.). 32p. (J). (-k). pap. 10.99 *(978-1-84502-996-8(8))* Black and White Publishing Ltd. GBR. Dist: Independent Pubs. Group.

—Room on the Broom Board Book. Sheffler, Axel, illus. 2012. (ENG.). 24p. (J). (— 1). bds. 6.99 *(978-0-8037-3841-6(2)*, Dial Bks) Penguin Young Readers Group.

—Rosie's Hat. Currey, Anna, illus. 2015. (ENG.). 32p. (J). (-k). pap. 9.99 *(978-1-4472-6612-9(9))* Pan Macmillan GBR. Dist: Independent Pubs. Group.

—Spinderella. Braun, Sebastian, illus. 2017. (ENG.). 32p. (J). (gr. -1-k). pap. 9.99 **(978-1-4052-8272-7(X))** Egmont Bks., Ltd. GBR. Dist: Independent Pubs. Group.

—Toddle Waddle. Sharratt, Nick, illus. 2012. (ENG.). 32p. (J). (— 1). bds. 8.99 *(978-0-230-75751-6(0))* Pan Macmillan GBR. Dist: Independent Pubs. Group.

—What the Jackdaw Saw: Book & CD Pack, 2 vols. Sharratt, Nick, illus. 2015. (ENG.). 32p. (J). (gr. -1-k). 14.99 *(978-1-5098-0622-5(9))* Pan Macmillan GBR. Dist: Independent Pubs. Group.

—Whit the Clockleddy Heard. Robertson, James, tr. from ENG. Monks, Lydia, illus. 2015. (ENG.). 32p. (J). (-k). pap. 10.99 *(978-1-84502-957-9(7))* Black and White Publishing Ltd. GBR. Dist: Independent Pubs. Group.

Donaldson, Julia & Robertson, James. Room on the Broom in Scots. Scheffler, Axel, illus. 2014. (ENG.). 32p. (J). (-k). pap. 10.99 *(978-1-84502-753-7(1))* Black and White Publishing Ltd. GBR. Dist: Independent Pubs. Group.

Doney, Meryl. The Very Worried Sparrow. Hansen, Gaby, illus. 3rd ed. 2015. (ENG.). 32p. (J). (gr. -1-k). pap. 8.99 *(978-0-7459-6580-2(6))* Lion Hudson PLC GBR. Dist: Independent Pubs. Group.

Donofrio, Beverly. Mary & the Mouse, the Mouse & Mary. McClintock, Barbara, illus. 2014. (Mary & the Mouse Ser.). (ENG.). 32p. (J). (gr. -1-2). 7.99 *(978-0-385-38872-6(1)*, Dragonfly Bks.) Random Hse. Children's Bks.

Doodlemum & Smith, Justine. My Mummy Says. Stevens, Angie, illus. 2014. (Families & Friends Ser.). (ENG.). 16p. (J). (-k). bds. 9.99 *(978-1-4472-6097-4(X))* Pan Macmillan GBR. Dist: Independent Pubs. Group.

Doodler, Todd H. Peas on Earth. 2012. (ENG., Illus.). 20p. (J). (gr. k — 1). bds. 6.99 *(978-0-307-93088-0(2)*, Robin Corey Bks.) Random Hse. Children's Bks.

Doolittle, Sara. Lillie's Smile. Locke, Margo, illus. 2011. 32p. (J). pap. 18.99 *(978-0-9827611-6-8(3)*, Catch the Spirit of Appalachia) Ammons Communications, Ltd.

Dopffer, Guillaume & Nicola, Baxter. My First 200 Words in French: Learning Is Fun with Teddy the Bear! Lacome, Susie, illus. 2016. (ENG & FRE.). 24p. (J). (gr. -1-12). pap. 7.99 *(978-1-86147-760-6(0)*, Armadillo) Anness Publishing GBR. Dist: National Bk. Network.

Dorfman, Craig. I Knew You Could! A Book for All the Stops in Your Life. Ong, Cristina, illus. 2003. (Little Engine That Could

Ser.). (ENG.). 32p. (J). (gr. -1-2). 11.99 (978-0-448-43148-2(3), Grosset & Dunlap) Penguin Young Readers Group.

Dorling Kindersley Publishing Staff. Baby Faces. 2016. (ENG., Illus.). 14p. (J). (— 1). bds. 5.99 (978-1-4654-4466-0(1), DK Children) Dorling Kindersley Publishing, Inc.

—Baby Night-Night. 2016. (ENG., Illus.). 14p. (J). (— 1). bds. 5.99 (978-1-4654-4389-2(4), DK Children) Dorling Kindersley Publishing, Inc.

—Baby Talk: 6 Giant Flasp for Baby to Flip. 2005. (Fun Flaps Ser.). (ENG., Illus.). 14p. (J). (gr. -1-k). bds. 4.99 (978-0-7566-0986-3(0), DK Children) Dorling Kindersley Publishing, Inc.

—Baby Touch & Feel: Halloween. 2017. (Baby Touch & Feel Ser.). (ENG., Illus.). 14p. (J). (— 1). bds. 5.99 **(978-1-4654-6235-0(X)**, DK Children) Dorling Kindersley Publishing, Inc.

—Big Busy Book - Words. 2013. (ENG.). 14p. (J). (gr. -1 — 1). bds. 9.99 (978-1-4654-0926-3(2), DK Children) Dorling Kindersley Publishing, Inc.

—Boys' Potty Time. 2010. (ENG., Illus.). 14p. (J). (gr. -1-k). bds. 7.99 (978-0-7566-5884-7(5), DK Children) Dorling Kindersley Publishing, Inc.

—Dinosaur. 2016. (ENG., Illus.). 36p. (J). bds. (978-0-241-23758-8(0)) Dorling Kindersley Publishing, Inc.

—Disney Frozen: Ultimate Sticker Collection. 2015. (Ultimate Sticker Collections). (ENG.). 96p. (J). (gr. 1-4). pap. 12.99 (978-1-4654-4080-8(1), DK Children) Dorling Kindersley Publishing, Inc.

—Farm. 2013. (ENG.). 12p. (J). (gr. -1 — 1). bds. 9.99 (978-1-4654-0924-9(6), DK Children) Dorling Kindersley Publishing, Inc.

—Fire Truck. 2003. (Wheelie Bks.). (ENG., Illus.). 12p. (J). (gr. -1-k). bds. 6.99 (978-0-7894-9712-3(3), DK Children) Dorling Kindersley Publishing, Inc.

—Follow the Trail: Farm. 2016. (Follow the Trail Ser.). (ENG., Illus.). 14p. (J). (-k). bds. 9.99 (978-1-4654-4480-6(7), DK Children) Dorling Kindersley Publishing, Inc.

—Hide & Seek: Things That Go. 2013. (ENG., Illus.). 48p. (J). (gr. -1 — 1). 12.99 (978-1-4654-0931-7(9), DK Children) Dorling Kindersley Publishing, Inc.

—My First Dinosaur. 2016. (ENG., Illus.). 36p. (J). (— 1). bds. 5.99 (978-1-4654-4491-2(2), DK Children) Dorling Kindersley Publishing, Inc.

—My First Pets. 2016. (ENG., Illus.). 36p. (J). (— 1). bds. 5.99 (978-1-4654-4489-9(0), DK Children) Dorling Kindersley Publishing, Inc.

—My First Things That Go. 2016. (ENG., Illus.). 36p. (J). (— 1). bds. 5.99 (978-1-4654-4490-5(4), DK Children) Dorling Kindersley Publishing, Inc.

—My First Trucks. 2015. (My First Bks.). (ENG.). 36p. (J). (gr. -1 — 1). bds. 5.99 (978-1-4654-2904-9(2), DK Children) Dorling Kindersley Publishing, Inc.

—My World: Miles from Tomorrowland. 2016. (ENG., Illus.). 40p. (J). (-k). 9.99 (978-1-4654-4463-9(7), DK Children) Dorling Kindersley Publishing, Inc.

—My World: Doc Mcstuffins. 2016. (ENG., Illus.). 40p. (J). (-k). 9.99 (978-1-4654-4462-2(9), DK Children) Dorling Kindersley Publishing, Inc.

—Peekaboo Sophie! 2013. (ENG.). 12p. (J). (gr. -1 — 1). bds. 6.99 (978-1-4654-0960-7(2), DK Children) Dorling Kindersley Publishing, Inc.

—Playtime. 2012. (Touch & Feel Ser.). (ENG.). 12p. (J). (gr. -1-k). bds. 6.99 (978-1-4654-0166-3(0), DK Children) Dorling Kindersley Publishing, Inc.

—Sophie la Girafe: Hide & Seek. 2016. (ENG., Illus.). 16p. (J). (— 1). bds. 6.99 (978-1-4654-4461-5(0), DK Children) Dorling Kindersley Publishing, Inc.

—Sophie la Girafe: on the Move. 2016. (Baby Touch & Feel Ser.). (ENG., Illus.). 14p. (J). (— 1). bds. 5.99 (978-1-4654-4395-3(9), DK Children) Dorling Kindersley Publishing, Inc.

—Sophie la Girafe: Sophie's Big First Word Book. 2016. (ENG., Illus.). 18p. (J). (gr. -1 — 1). bds. 9.99 (978-1-4654-4494-3(7), DK Children) Dorling Kindersley Publishing, Inc.

—Sophie la Girafe: Sophie's Pull the Tab Play Book. 2016. (ENG., Illus.). 10p. (J). (gr. -1 — 1). bds. 6.99 (978-1-4654-4467-7(X), DK Children) Dorling Kindersley Publishing, Inc.

Dorling Kindersley Publishing Staff, ed. Buenas Noches, Bebe! / Good Night, Baby! 2004. (Soft-To-Touch Bks.). (SPA & ENG., Illus.). 18p. (J). (gr. -1-k). bds. 5.99 (978-0-7566-0438-7(9), DK Children) Dorling Kindersley Publishing, Inc.

—Buenos Dias, Bebe! 2004. (Soft-To-Touch Bks.).Tr. of Good Morning, Baby! (SPA & ENG., Illus.). 18p. (J). (gr. -1 — 1). bds. 5.99 (978-0-7566-0437-0(0), DK Children) Dorling Kindersley Publishing, Inc.

Dotlich, Rebecca Kai. One Day, the End: Short, Very Short, Shorter-Than-Ever Stories. Koehler, Fred, illus. 2015. (ENG.). 32p. (J). (gr. -1-3). 16.95 (978-1-62091-451-9(4), 1396728) Boyds Mills Pr.

Douglas, Rachel. "You're a Meany!" Drewes, Dan, illus. 2011. 13p. pap. 10.19 (978-1-4567-8643-4(1)) AuthorHouse.

Dover, Ilana. The Talking MacHine: The Story of Alexander Graham Bell. 2012. 36p. pap. 17.49 (978-1-4691-8328-2(5)) Xlibris Corp.

Dowley, Tim. Would You Like to Know the Story of Christmas?, 1 vol. Reeves, Eira, illus. 2015. (ENG.). 28p. (J). pap. 2.99 (978-1-78128-197-0(1), Candle Bks.) Lion Hudson PLC GBR. Dist: Kregel Pubns.

—Would You Like to Know the Story of Easter?, 1 vol. Reeves, Eira, illus. 2016. (ENG.). 28p. (J). pap. 2.99 (978-1-78128-198-7(X), Candle Bks.) Lion Hudson PLC GBR. Dist: Kregel Pubns.

Dowley, Tim & Jefferson, Graham. Would You Like to Know God?, 1 vol. Reeves, Eira, illus. 2016. (ENG.). 28p. (J). pap. 2.99 (978-1-78128-275-5(7), Candle Bks.) Lion Hudson PLC GBR. Dist: Kregel Pubns.

Dowley, Tim, et al. The Complete Collection, 1 vol. Reeves, Eira, illus. 2017. (ENG.). 168p. (J). pap. 12.99 (978-1-78128-327-1(3), Candle Bks.) Lion Hudson PLC GBR. Dist: Kregel Pubns.

Dowling, Paul. The Night Journey. 2003. 12p. (J). 9.95 (978-1-57717-290-1(6)) New Line Bks.

Downer, Maggie, illus. Noah: My First Storybook. 2016. (ENG.). 48p. (J). (gr. -1-12). bds. 9.99 (978-1-86147-776-7(7), Armadillo) Anness Publishing GBR. Dist: National Bk. Network.

Doyle, Malachy. King Donal's Secret. Watson, Richard, illus. 2005. (ENG.). 24p. (J). lib. bdg. 23.65 (978-1-59646-740-8(1)) Dingles & Co.

—Rory's Lost His Voice. Semple, David, illus. 2005. (ENG.). 24p. (J). lib. bdg. 23.65 (978-1-59646-714-9(2)) Dingles & Co.

Drake, Jennifer & Feltham, Sarah. Scotty's Postcards from Rome. 2012. (ENG., Illus.). 27p. (J). pap. 10.95 (978-0-578-10548-2(9)) Drake Feltham Publishing.

Drehsen, Britta. Flip-O-Saurus. Ball, Sara, illus. 2010. (ENG.). 22p. (J). (gr. -1-k). bds. 15.95 (978-0-7892-1061-6(4), Abbeville Kids) Abbeville Pr., Inc.

Drescher, Daniela. Little Fairy's Christmas, 1 vol. 2010. (ENG., Illus.). 24p. (J). (gr. -1-1). 16.95 (978-0-86315-773-8(4)) Floris Bks. GBR. Dist: SteinerBooks, Inc.

—What's Hiding in There? 2008. Orig. Title: Was Raschelt Denn Da? (ENG., Illus.). 16p. (J). (978-0-86315-634-2(7)) Floris Bks.

Driscoll, Laura & Disney Book Group Staff. I Love You, My Bunnies. Tyminski, Lori et al, illus. 2008. (ENG.). 24p. (J). (gr. -1-k). pap. 3.99 (978-1-4231-2095-7(7)) Disney Pr.

Drops of Water. Date not set. 9.95 (978-0-89868-291-5(6)); pap. 3.95 (978-0-89868-290-8(8)) ARO Publishing Co.

Drummond, Ree. Charlie the Ranch Dog: Where's the Bacon? deGroat, Diane, illus. 2013. (I Can Read Level 1 Ser.). (ENG.). 32p. (J). (gr. -1-3). 16.99 (978-0-06-221909-1(X)); pap. 3.99 (978-0-06-221908-4(1)) HarperCollins Pubs.

Druvert, Hélène. Mary Poppins: Up, up & Away. 2017. (ENG., Illus.). 36p. (gr. k-4). 24.95 (978-0-500-65104-9(3), 565104) Thames & Hudson.

—Paris up, up & Away. 2016. (ENG., Illus.). 34p. (J). (gr. -1-1). 24.95 (978-0-500-65059-2(4), 565059) Thames & Hudson.

Du Bois, Crystal L. God Made My Butt Big. 2012. 24p. pap. 14.93 (978-1-4669-0584-9(0)) Trafford Publishing.

DuBois, Juli. The Happiness of Being Me: An A-Z Owners Manual, 1 vol. Zitnak, Alison Day, illus. 2009. 47p. pap. 24.95 (978-1-60749-613-7(5)) America Star Bks.

Dubuc, Marianne. In Front of My House. Ghione, Yvette, tr. from FRE. Dubuc, Marianne, illus. 2010. (ENG., Illus.). 120p. (J). (gr. -1-2). 18.95 (978-1-55453-641-2(3)) Kids Can Pr., Ltd. CAN. Dist: Hachette Bk. Group.

Dudar, Judy. I Spy a Bunny, 1 vol. Rudnicki, Richard, illus. 2009. (ENG.). 32p. (J). (gr. -1-2). 17.95 (978-1-55109-700-8(1)) Nimbus Publishing, Ltd. CAN. Dist: Orca Bk. Pubs. USA.

Dufek, Holly. Busy on the Farm: With Casey & Friends. Nunn, Paul E. & Kasun, Mike, illus. 2017. (ENG.). 32p. (J). 14.99 (978-1-937747-79-4(4)) Octane Pr.

Dugan, Joanne. ABC Nyc: A Book about Seeing New York City. 2005. (ENG., Illus.). 56p. (J). (gr. -1-1). 17.95 (978-0-8109-5854-8(6)) Abrams, Inc.

Dumont, Claire. Noel: An Unforgettable Night! 2017. (ENG., Illus.). 32p. (J). 14.95 **(978-0-8091-6780-7(8))** Paulist Pr.

Dunbar, Joyce. Do Dare Duck. Massey, Jane, illus. 2015. (ENG.). 32p. (J). (-k). pap. 9.99 (978-1-78008-024-6(7)) Transworld Publishers Ltd. GBR. Dist: Independent Pubs. Group.

Dunbar, Joyce & Varley, Susan. The Spring Rabbit. 2015. (ENG., Illus.). 32p. (J). (gr. -1-k). pap. 13.99 (978-1-78344-078-8(3)) Andersen Pr. GBR. Dist: Independent Pubs. Group.

Dunlap, Cirocco. This Book Will Not Be Fun. Tallec, Olivier, illus. 2017. (ENG.). 32p. (J). (gr. -1-2). 17.99 **(978-0-399-55061-4(5))**; lib. bdg. 20.99 **(978-0-399-55062-1(3))** Random Hse. Children's Bks. (Random Hse. Bks. for Young Readers).

Dunn, James & Quarto Generic Staff. ABC London. Slater, Kate, illus. rev. ed. 2014. (ENG.). 40p. (J). (gr. k-3). pap. 8.99 (978-1-84780-495-2(0), Frances Lincoln) Quarto Publishing Group UK GBR. Dist: Hachette Bk. Group.

Dunn, Jill. Littering Is for Losers. Hill, Bodhi, illus. 2012. 64p. (J). 21.99 (978-0-9852146-2-3(7)) AM Ink Publishing.

Dunn, Phoebe. The Little Kitten. 2015. (ENG., Illus.). 14p. (J). (— 1). bds. 6.99 (978-0-553-51138-3(6), Random Hse. Bks. for Young Readers) Random Hse. Children's Bks.

Dunrea, Olivier. Jasper & Joop: A Perfect Pair: One Tidy, One Messy. 2014. (Gossie & Friends Ser.). (ENG., Illus.). 32p. (J). (— 1). bds. 6.99 (978-0-544-17320-0(1), HMH Books For Young Readers) Houghton Mifflin Harcourt Publishing Co.

Dunston, Marc. The Magic of Giving, 1 vol. Cantrell, Katie, illus. 2010. (ENG.). 32p. (J). (gr. k-3). 16.99 (978-1-58980-805-8(3)) Pelican Publishing Co., Inc.

duopress labs, et al. 1000 Totally Epic, True & Wacky Soccer Stories. 2017. (ENG., Illus.). 156p. (J). (gr. 3-7). pap. 12.95 (978-1-938093-81-4(X), Duo Pr. LLC (US)) Duo Pr. LLC.

Duopress Labs Staff. Hello, Ocean Friends. 2015. (ENG., Illus.). 20p. (J). (-k). bds. 7.95 (978-1-938093-41-8(0)) Duo Pr. LLC.

Duren, Sheila Gregory. Pepper's Great Move! 2011. 28p. pap. 15.99 (978-1-4568-6766-9(0)) Xlibris Corp.

Duvoisin, Roger. The House of Four Seasons. 2017. (ENG., Illus.). 40p. (J). (gr. -1-1). 16.95 (978-1-68137-098-9(0), NYR Children's Collection) New York Review of Bks., Inc., The.

—Petunia, Beware! Duvoisin, Roger, illus. 2011. (ENG., Illus.). 40p. (J). (gr. -1-2). reprint ed. pap. 7.99 (978-0-679-80334-8(3), Dragonfly Bks.) Random Hse. Children's Bks.

—Veronica. 2nd ed. 2016. (ENG., Illus.). 32p. 20.00 (978-1-85124-245-0(7)) Bodleian Library GBR. Dist: Chicago Distribution Ctr.

Dwyer, Judy. Storybook Starters. (Illus.). (J). (gr. k-3). pap. (978-1-876367-01-5(6)) Wizard Bks.

Dyan, Penelope. Some Bunny Loves You! 2013. 34p. pap. 11.95 (978-1-61477-068-8(9)) Bellissima Publishing, LLC.

Dyer, Saje, et al. Good-Bye, Bumps! Talking to What's Bugging You. 2014. (ENG., Illus.). 28p. 14.95 (978-1-4019-4585-5(6)) Hay Hse., Inc.

Dynamo. Googly Eyes: Flipper the Seal Makes a Discovery! 2014. (ENG., Illus.). 12p. (J). (gr. -1-2). bds. 6.99 (978-1-84322-905-6(6), Armadillo) Anness Publishing GBR. Dist: National Bk. Network.

—Googly Eyes: Goodnight, Benjy Bunny! 2014. (ENG., Illus.). 12p. (J). (gr. -1-12). bds. 6.99 (978-1-84322-879-0(3), Armadillo) Anness Publishing GBR. Dist: National Bk. Network.

Dyson, Nikki, illus. 1,000 Things to Eat. 2015. (1,000 Pictures Ser.). (ENG.). 34p. (J). (gr. k-5). 14.99 (978-0-7945-3406-6(6), Usborne) EDC Publishing.

Eakle, Janice. 3 A's & 3 B's All the Way to Z, 1 vol. Eakle, Tayah, illus. 2009. 36p. pap. 24.95 (978-1-60813-739-8(2)) America Star Bks.

Earth Picture Book. 2009. 64p. 8.99 (978-1-4231-2204-3(6)) Disney Pr.

Eastman, P. D. Ve, Perro, Ve! Perdomo, Adolfo Perez, tr. 2003. (Bright & Early Board Books(TM) Ser.).Tr. of Go, Dog, Go! (SPA & ENG., Illus.). 24p. (J). (— 1). bds. 4.99 (978-0-375-82361-9(1), Random House Para Ninos) Random Hse. Children's Bks.

Easton, Marilyn. Eris to the Rescue. 2013. (LEGO Legends of Chima: Comic Reader Ser.: 3). lib. bdg. 13.55 (978-0-606-32398-7(8), Turtleback) Turtleback Bks.

Eaton, Jason Carter. Great, Now We've Got Barbarians! Fearing, Mark, illus. 2017. (ENG.). 40p. (J). (gr. -1-3). 15.99 (978-0-7636-6827-3(3)) Candlewick Pr.

—How to Track a Truck. Rocco, John, illus. 2016. (ENG.). 32p. (J). (gr. -1-3). 16.99 (978-0-7636-8065-7(6)) Candlewick Pr.

—How to Train a Train. Rocco, John, illus. 2016. (ENG.). 28p. (J). (-k). bds. 7.99 (978-0-7636-8899-8(1)) Candlewick Pr.

Eddy, Olympia. Mysterious View. 2010. 20p. pap. 13.99 (978-1-60844-423-6(6)) Dog Ear Publishing, LLC.

Edens, Cooper. Edens Picture Book, No. 3. Day, Alexandra, illus. Date not set. (J). 14.99 (978-0-06-205153-0(9)) HarperCollins Pubs.

Edgson, Alison, illus. The Magician's Apprentice. 2011. (Flip-Up Fairy Tales Ser.). (ENG.). 24p. (J). (gr. 2-2). (978-1-84643-370-2(3)) Child's Play International Ltd.

Edgson, Alison & Stockham, Jessica. Hansel & Gretel. Petrlik, Andrea, illus. 2006. (Flip-Up Fairy Tales Ser.). (ENG.). 24p. (J). (gr. 1-2). (978-1-904550-73-0(8)) Child's Play International Ltd.

Educational Adventures, creator. Blazin' Hot: Picture Book (Spanish) 9x9. 2006. (SPA., Illus.). (J). 5.99 (978-0-9770455-4-9(4)) Mighty Kids Media.

—Cool by the Pool: Picture Book (Spanish) 9x9. 2007. (Illus.). (J). per. 5.99 (978-1-933934-72-3(7)) Mighty Kids Media.

—Danger Alert: Picture Book (Spanish) 9x9. 2006. (Illus.). (J). 5.99 (978-1-933934-04-4(2)) Mighty Kids Media.

—Free Wheelin' Picture Book (Spanish) w/ Snipe. 2006. (Illus.). (J). 5.99 (978-0-9770455-6-3(0)) Mighty Kids Media.

—Poison Patrol: Picture Book (Spanish) 9x9. 2006. (Illus.). (J). 5.99 (978-1-933934-00-6(X)) Mighty Kids Media.

—Street Smarts: Picture Book (Spanish) 9x9. 2007. (Illus.). (J). per. 5.99 (978-1-933934-77-8(8)) Mighty Kids Media.

Edward, Justine. Shine. 2013. 28p. pap. 13.95 (978-1-4525-7531-5(2), Balboa Pr.) Author Solutions, Inc.

Edwards, Caroline. Who Took Poppy's Skates? 2010. (ENG., Illus.). 24p. pap. (978-1-84876-392-0(1)) Troubador Publishing Ltd.

Edwards, Josh. Christmas, 1 vol. Embleton-Hall, Chris, illus. 2014. (ENG.). 10p. (J). bds. 11.99 **(978-1-85985-999-5(2)**, Lion Children's) Lion Hudson PLC GBR. Dist: Kregel Pubns.

Edwards, Josh. Pull-Out David & Goliath, 1 vol. Embleton Hall, Chris, illus. 2014. (ENG.). 10p. (J). bds. 11.99 (978-1-85985-997-1(6), Candle Bks.) Lion Hudson PLC GBR. Dist: Kregel Pubns.

Edwards, Josh & David, Juliet. The Helpful Donkey, 1 vol. Barnard, Lucy, illus. 2015. (Bible Animals Ser.). (ENG.). 14p. (J). bds. 9.99 (978-1-78128-180-2(7), Candle Bks.) Lion Hudson PLC GBR. Dist: Kregel Pubns.

—Little Lost Sheep, 1 vol. Barnard, Lucy, illus. 2015. (Bible Animals Ser.). (ENG.). 14p. (J). bds. 9.99 (978-1-78128-179-6(3), Candle Bks.) Lion Hudson PLC GBR. Dist: Kregel Pubns.

Edwards, Pamela Duncan. Dinosaur Sleepover. Allwright, Deborah, illus. 2014. (Let's Read! Ser.). (ENG.). 32p. (J). (gr. k-2). pap. 7.99 (978-1-4472-4530-8(X)) Pan Macmillan GBR. Dist: Independent Pubs. Group.

Edwards, Wallace. The Painted Circus: P. T. Vermin Presents a Mesmerizing Menagerie of Trickery & Illusion Guaranteed to Beguile & Bamboozle the Beholder. Edwards, Wallace, illus. 2007. (ENG., Illus.). 32p. (J). (gr. 1-4). 17.95 (978-1-55337-720-7(6)) Kids Can Pr., Ltd. CAN. Dist: Hachette Bk. Group.

Eeles, Alex. Bedtime on the Farm Red Band. Ortu, Davide, illus. 2016. (Cambridge Reading Adventures Ser.). (ENG.). 16p. pap. 6.56 (978-1-316-50081-1(0)) Cambridge Univ. Pr.

Egmont UK, Egmont. Peekaboo! Sea. 2014. (Animaru Ser.). (ENG., Illus.). 12p. (J). (— 1). bds. 9.99 (978-1-4052-6778-6(X)) Egmont Bks., Ltd. GBR. Dist: Independent Pubs. Group.

Ehlert, Lois. Growing Vegetable Soup. 2004. (ENG., Illus.). 32p. (J). (gr. k — 1). bds. 6.95 (978-0-15-205055-9(8)) Houghton Mifflin Harcourt Publishing Co.

Eisenberg, Rebecca & Kjesbo, Rynette. Cool in School Communication Game: Gb362. Lefebvre, Patrick, photos by. 2011. (Illus.). (J). 64.95 net. (978-1-58650-994-1(2)) Super Duper Pubns.

Eisner, Fern. Saba's Room. 2009. 28p. pap. 15.99 (978-1-4415-1843-9(6)) Xlibris Corp.

Eliot, T. S. Macavity: The Mystery Cat. Robins, Arthur, illus. 75th ed. 2016. (Old Possum Picture Bks.). (ENG.). 32p. (J). (-k). pap. 9.95 (978-0-571-30813-2(9)) Faber & Faber, Inc.

Eliot, T. S., et al. Macavity's Not There! A Lift-the-Flap Book. Robins, Arthur, illus. 2017. (Old Possum Picture Bks.). (ENG.). 16p. (-k). 14.95 (978-0-571-32863-5(6)) Faber & Faber, Inc.

Elliott, David. On the Wing. Stadtlander, Becca, illus. (ENG.). 32p. (J). (gr. -1-2). 2017. 6.99 (978-0-7636-9302-2(2)) 2014. 16.99 (978-0-7636-5324-8(X)) Candlewick Pr.

Elliott, George. The Boy Who Loved Bananas. Krystoforski, Andrej, illus. 2005. 32p. (J). (gr. -1-2). 15.95 (978-1-55337-744-3(3)) Kids Can Pr., Ltd. CAN. Dist: Hachette Bk. Group.

Elliott, Odette. Sammy Goes Flying. McIntyre, Georgina, illus. 2011. (ENG.). 32p. (J). (gr. -1-k). pap. 9.99 (978-1-84853-050-8(1)) Transworld Publishers Ltd. GBR. Dist: Independent Pubs. Group.

Elliott, Rebecca. Dalmatian in a Digger. 2017. (Fiction Picture Bks.). (ENG.). 32p. (gr. k-2). lib. bdg. 27.99 (978-1-5158-0684-4(7), Fiction Picture Bks.) Picture Window Bks.

—Just Because. 2012. (ENG., Illus.). 32p. (J). (gr. k-2). pap. 8.99 (978-0-7459-6235-1(1)) Lion Hudson PLC GBR. Dist: Independent Pubs. Group.

—Just Because. Elliott, Rebecca, illus. 2011. (ENG., Illus.). 32p. (J). (gr. -1-2). 14.99 (978-0-7459-6267-2(X)) Lion Hudson PLC GBR. Dist: Independent Pubs. Group.

—The Last Tiger. Elliott, Rebecca, illus. 2013. (ENG., Illus.). 32p. (J). (gr. k-2). pap. 8.99 (978-0-7459-6349-5(8)) Lion Hudson PLC GBR. Dist: Independent Pubs. Group.

—Missing Jack. Elliott, Rebecca, illus. 2015. (ENG., Illus.). 32p. (J). (gr. -1-k). 16.99 (978-0-7459-6502-4(4)) Lion Hudson PLC GBR. Dist: Independent Pubs. Group.

—Noah's Noisy Animals. Elliott, Rebecca, illus. 2016. (ENG., Illus.). 5p. (J). (— 1). bds. 7.99 (978-0-7459-6561-1(X)) Lion Hudson PLC GBR. Dist: Independent Pubs. Group.

—Not So Silent Night! Elliott, Rebecca, illus. 2016. (ENG., Illus.). 5p. (J). (— 1). bds. 7.99 (978-0-7459-6560-4(1)) Lion Hudson PLC GBR. Dist: Independent Pubs. Group.

—Sometimes. Elliott, Rebecca, illus. 2014. (ENG., Illus.). 32p. (J). (gr. k-2). pap. 8.99 (978-0-7459-6269-6(6)) Lion Hudson PLC GBR. Dist: Independent Pubs. Group.

—Zoo Girl. Elliott, Rebecca, illus. 2013. (ENG., Illus.). 32p. (J). (gr. k-2). pap. 8.99 (978-0-7459-6270-2(X)) Lion Hudson PLC GBR. Dist: Independent Pubs. Group.

Ellis, Carson. Du Iz Tak? Ellis, Carson, illus. 2016. (ENG., Illus.). 48p. (J). (gr. -1-3). 16.99 (978-0-7636-6530-2(4)) Candlewick Pr.

Ellis, Elina. The Big Adventure. 2015. (ENG., Illus.). 32p. (J). (gr. -1-3). 16.99 (978-1-4998-0109-5(2)) Little Bee Books Inc.

Elmquist, Laurie. Beach Baby, 1 vol. MacKay, Elly, illus. 2016. (ENG.). 24p. (J). (gr. -1-k). bds. 9.95 (978-1-4598-0954-3(8)) Orca Bk. Pubs. USA.

Elschner, Géraldine. The Little Hippo: A Children's Book Inspired by Egyptian Art. Klauss, Anja, illus. 2014. (ENG.). 32p. (J). (gr. -1-3). 14.95 (978-3-7913-7167-2(3)) Prestel Verlag GmbH & Co KG. DEU. Dist: Penguin Random Hse. LLC.

—Where Is the Frog? A Children's Book Inspired by Claude Monet. Girel, Stephane, illus. 2013. (ENG.). 32p. (J). (gr. -1-3). 14.95 (978-3-7913-7139-9(8)) Prestel Verlag GmbH & Co KG. DEU. Dist: Penguin Random Hse. LLC.

Elschner, Géraldine & Nille, Peggy. The Cat & the Bird: A Children's Book Inspired by Paul Klee. 2012. (ENG., Illus.). 32p. (J). (gr. -1-3). 14.95 (978-3-7913-7099-6(5)) Prestel Verlag GmbH & Co KG. DEU. Dist: Penguin Random Hse. LLC.

Elsohn Ross, Michael. Mama's Milk / Mamá Me Alimenta. Wolff, Ashley, illus. 2016. (ENG & SPA.). 24p. (J). (-k). bds. 7.99 (978-0-553-53874-8(8), Tricycle Pr.) Random Hse. Children's Bks.

Elwick, Elissa. The Princess & the Sleep Stealer. Elwick, Elissa, illus. 2012. (ENG., Illus.). 32p. (J). (gr. -1-k). pap. 9.99 (978-0-230-75068-5(0)) Macmillan Pubs., Ltd. GBR. Dist: Independent Pubs. Group.

Emberley, Barbara. One Wide River to Cross. Emberley, Barbara, ed. 2015. (ENG., Illus.). 32p. 17.95 (978-1-62326-059-0(0)) AMMO Bks., LLC.

—The Story of Paul Bunyan. Emberley, Ed, illus. 2015. (ENG.). 32p. 17.95 (978-1-62326-062-0(0)) AMMO Bks., LLC.

Emberley, Ed. The Wing on a Flea. 2015. (ENG., Illus.). 48p. 17.95 (978-1-62326-058-3(2)) AMMO Bks., LLC.

Emberley, Rebecca & Emberley, Ed. Mice on Ice. 2013. (I Like to Read(r) Ser.). (ENG.). 24p. (J). (gr. -1-3). pap. 6.99 (978-0-8234-2908-0(3)) Holiday Hse., Inc.

Emmett, Jonathan. Foxes in the Snow, 11. Harry, Rebecca, illus. 3rd ed. 2012. (ENG.). 32p. (J). (gr. -1-k). pap. 9.99 (978-0-230-71229-4(0)) Pan Macmillan GBR. Dist: Independent Pubs. Group.

—The Treasure of Captain Claw. Cox, Steve, illus. 2012. (ENG.). 32p. (J). (gr. -1-k). pap. 9.99 (978-1-84616-741-6(8)) Hodder & Stoughton GBR. Dist: Hachette Bk. Group.

Empson, Jo. Never Ever. Empson, Jo, illus. 2013. (Child's Play Library). (ENG., Illus.). 32p. (J). (978-1-84643-552-2(8)) Child's Play International Ltd.

—Rabbityness. Empson, Jo, illus. 2012. (Child's Play Library). (ENG., Illus.). 32p. (J). (978-1-84643-482-2(3)) Child's Play International Ltd.

Encounter: Narrative Nonfiction Picture Books. (Encounter: Narrative Nonfiction Picture Bks.). (ENG.). 2016. 113.27 (978-1-4914-8050-2(5)) 2015. 46.85 (978-1-62370-595-4(9)) Encounter Bks.

Enderle, Judith Ross & Gordon, Stephanie Jacob. Smile, Principessa! Curmi, Serena, illus. 2012. (ENG.). 40p. (J). (gr. -1-1). 16.99 (978-1-4424-3096-9(6), McElderry, Margaret K. Bks.) McElderry, Margaret K. Bks.

Engel, Christiane. We Are Moving: Louis & Bobo. Engel, Christiane, illus. 2007. (ENG., Illus.). 28p. (J). (gr. k-2). pap. 7.99 (978-1-84458-375-1(9)) Pavilion Bks. GBR. Dist: Independent Pubs. Group.

Engelbreit, Mary. A Night of Great Joy, 1 vol. 2016. (ENG., Illus.). 32p. (J). 16.99 (978-0-310-74354-5(0)) Zonderkidz.

Engledow, Dave. The Little Girl Who Didn't Want to Go to Bed. Engledow, Dave, illus. 2017. (Illus.). 40p. (J). (gr. -1-3). 17.99 **(978-0-06-242537-9(4))** HarperCollins Pubs.

Ennis, Garth. ERF. 2013. (ENG., Illus.). 48p. (J). 14.99 (978-0-615-62967-4(9), 9780615629674, Dynamite Entertainment) Dynamic Forces, Inc.

Eone, illus. George Catches a Cold (Peppa Pig) 2017. (Peppa Pig Ser.). (ENG.). 24p. (J). (gr. -1-k). pap. 3.99 (978-1-338-05419-4(8)) Scholastic, Inc.

Esbaum, Jill, et al. Adorable Animals Collection. 2017. (Explore My World Ser.). (ENG., Illus.). 96p. (J). (gr. -1-2). pap. 9.99 **(978-1-4263-2949-4(0)**, National Geographic Children's Bks.) National Geographic Society.

Esberger, Trudi. The Boy Who Lost His Bumble. Esberger, Trudi, illus. 2014. (Child's Play Library). (ENG., Illus.). 32p. (J). (978-1-84643-661-1(3)) Child's Play International Ltd.

Esmaili, Roza. Zagros & Nature Force: Coloring Book. Sun Rise Illustration and Computer Animation Staff, illus. Date not set. 74p. (J). (gr. k-8). pap. 2.49 (978-0-9656185-1-9(X)) Esmaili, Inc.

Evans, Jane. How Are You Feeling Today Baby Bear? Exploring Big Feelings after Living in a Stormy Home. Jackson, Laurence, illus. 2014. (ENG.). 32p. (J). 15.95

P
Q
R

(978-1-84905-424-9(X), 3151) Kingsley, Jessica Pubs. GBR. Dist: Macmillan Distribution Ltd.

Evans, Michael. Poggle & the Birthday Present. Evans, Michael, illus. 2011. (Poggle Ser.). (ENG., Illus.). 32p. (J). (gr. k — 1). pap. 8.99 (978-1-4052-5359-8(2)) Egmont Bks., Ltd. GBR. Dist: Independent Pubs. Group.

Evanson, Ashley. London: A Book of Opposites. Evanson, Ashley, illus. 2015. (Hello, World Ser.). (ENG., Illus.). 14p. (J). (— 1). bds. 6.99 (978-0-448-48916-2(3), Grosset & Dunlap) Penguin Young Readers Group.

Ewashen, Julie. Life in the Arctic with Nina & Nikita. 2013. 56p. pap. (978-1-4602-2727-5(1)) FriesenPress.

Exactly Like Me. 2003. (J). per. 8.95 (978-0-9746151-0-3(2)) Alta Retreat Ctr.

Eystad, Janet Lynn. What I Got into Last Summer. 2012. 28p. 24.95 (978-1-4626-5316-4(2)) America Star Bks.

Eyuboglu, Melisa, illus. Angel in a Bubble. Eyuboglu, Melisa, . 2007. 28p. (J). 10.95 (978-1-933090-48-1(0)) Guardian Angel Publishing, Inc.

Fabrikant, Amy. When Kayla Was Kyle. Levine, Jennifer, illus. 2013. 32p. pap. 8.95 (978-1-61286-154-8(7)) Avid Readers Publishing Group.

Faces. Date not set. (Illus.). 40p. (J). 3.98 (978-1-4054-0174-6(5)) Parragon, Inc.

Fagan, Cary. Ella May & the Wishing Stone. Cote, Genevieve, illus. 2014. (ENG.). 32p. (J). (gr. -1-1). pap. 8.99 (978-1-77049-410-7(3), Tundra Bks.) Tundra Bks. CAN. Dist: Penguin Random Hse. LLC.

—Little Blue Chair. Young, Cybèle & Kloepper, Madeline, illus. 2017. (ENG.). 40p. (J). (gr. -1-2). 16.99 (978-1-77049-755-9(2), Tundra Bks.) Tundra Bks. CAN. Dist: Penguin Random Hse. LLC.

Fajerman, Deborah. How to Speak Moo! 2014. (ENG.). 32p. (J). (gr. -1-k). bds. 7.99 (978-0-7641-6752-2(9)) Barron's Educational Series, Inc.

Fakhouri, Shoua. Omar's First Day at School Pink B Band. Pérez, Moni, illus. 2016. (Cambridge Reading Adventures Ser.). (ENG.). 16p. pap. 6.56 (978-1-316-60811-1(5)) Cambridge Univ. Pr.

Falconer, Ian. Olivia. Falconer, Ian, illus. unabr. ed. 2004. (Classic Board Bks.). (ENG., Illus.). 34p. (J). (gr. -1-k). bds. 7.99 (978-0-689-87472-7(3), Atheneum Bks. for Young Readers) Simon & Schuster Children's Publishing.

—Olivia the Spy. Falconer, Ian, illus. 2017. (ENG., Illus.). 40p. (J). (gr. -1-3). 17.99 (978-1-4814-5795-8(0), Atheneum/Caitlyn Dlouhy Books) Simon & Schuster Children's Publishing.

Falconer, Ian, et al. Olivia & Her Great Adventures. Osterhold, Jared & Johnson, Shane L., illus. 2012. (J). (978-1-4351-4316-6(7), Simon Spotlight) Simon Spotlight.

Falsetto, Rita. A Cat's Furry Tale. 2011. 60p. pap. 31.99 (978-1-4568-4802-6(X)) Xlibris Corp.

Falwell, Cathryn. Feast For 10. 2017. (ENG., Illus.). 32p. (J). (gr. -1-3). 26.99 (978-0-544-93030-8(4), HMH Books For Young Readers) Houghton Mifflin Harcourt Publishing Co.

—Rainbow Stew, 1 vol. Falwell, Cathryn, illus. 2013. (ENG., Illus.). 32p. (J). 17.95 (978-1-60060-847-6(7)) Lee & Low Bks., Inc.

Familius Staff & Miles, David. Slide-N-Seek: Earth. 2017. (ENG., Illus.). 10p. (J). 15.95 (978-1-944822-45-3(3)) Familius LLC.

Fantasia, Kathryn. Pass It On. Flanagan, Jeff, illus. 2009. 28p. pap. 18.65 (978-1-4415-5446-8(7)) Xlibris Corp.

Farah, Mo, et al. Ready Steady Mo! 2017. (ENG., Illus.). 32p. (J). (gr. -1-k). pap. 8.99 **(978-1-4449-3407-6(4))** Hachette Children's Group GBR. Dist: Hachette Bk. Group.

Fardell, John. Jeremiah Jellyfish Flies High! Fardell, John, illus. 2011. (ENG., Illus.). 32p. (J). (gr. -1-k). pap. 13.99 (978-1-84939-147-4(5)) Andersen Pr. GBR. Dist: Independent Pubs. Group.

Farley, Robin. Mia: The Sweetest Valentine. 2012. (J). lib. bdg. 14.75 (978-0-606-26872-1(3), Turtleback) Turtleback Bks.

—Mia & the Big Sister Ballet. 2012. (Mia I Can Read Bks.). (J). lib. bdg. 13.55 (978-0-606-26282-8(2), Turtleback) Turtleback Bks.

Farnsworth, Bill, illus. The Great Stone Face. 2005. 32p. (J). pap. 8.00 (978-0-8028-5292-2(0)) Eerdmans, William B. Publishing Co.

Farquharson, Jerome. Playtime to Bedtime: Memories That Last Forever... 2011. (Illus.). 24p. (J). pap. 10.95 (978-0-615-45886-1(6)) JFAR Bks.

Faulkner, Nicholas. A Visual History of Ships & Navigation. 2016. (Visual History of the World Ser.). 00096p. (J). (gr. 8-8). 37.10 (978-1-4994-6594-5(7)) Rosen Publishing Group, Inc., The.

Faust, Lauren. The Magic Begins, Vol. 1. 2013. (My Little Pony Ser.). (ENG., Illus.). 112p. (J). (gr. 2-5). pap. 7.99 (978-1-61377-754-1(X), 9781613777541) Idea & Design Works, LLC.

Favorite, Deborah. The Tush People. Arinsberg, Norman, illus. (J). 11.95 (978-0-9722514-0-2(5)) Tush People, The.

Favorite Little Golden Books for Springtime, 5 vols. 2013. (ENG., Illus.). 24p. (J). (-k). 19.95 (978-0-307-98061-8(8), Golden Bks.) Random Hse. Children's Bks.

Fawcett, Sally. What Could It Be? Exploring the Imaginative World of Shapes. 2016. (ENG., Illus.). 32p. (J). (gr. -1-2). 17.99 (978-1-925335-02-6(X), EK Bks.) Exisle Publishing Pty Ltd. AUS. Dist: Hachette Bk. Group.

Fearnley, Jan. Flying Like Flittermouse. 2013. (Bottlenose Bay Ser.: 2). (ENG., Illus.). 32p. (J). (gr. -1). pap. 10.99 (978-1-4052-6536-2(1)) Egmont Bks., Ltd. GBR. Dist: Independent Pubs. Group.

Feelings. Date not set. 5.95 (978-0-89868-345-5(9)) ARO Publishing Co.

Feeney, Tatyana. Little Owl's Orange Scarf. 2015. (ENG.). 28p. (J). (— 1). bds. 6.99 (978-0-553-49673-4(5), Knopf Bks. for Young Readers) Random Hse. Children's Bks.

—Small Bunny's Blue Blanket. 2013. (ENG.). 24p. (J). (— 1). bds. 6.99 (978-0-385-75363-0(2), Knopf Bks. for Young Readers) Random Hse. Children's Bks.

Fergus, Maureen. Buddy & Earl Go Exploring, 1 vol. Sookocheff, Carey, illus. 2016. (Buddy & Earl Ser.: 2). (ENG.). 32p. (J). (gr. k-2). 16.95 (978-1-55498-714-6(8)) Groundwood Bks. CAN. Dist: Publishers Group West (PGW).

—The Day Santa Stopped Believing in Harold. Atkinson, Cale, illus. 2016. (ENG.). 32p. (J). (gr. -1-3). 16.99 (978-1-77049-824-2(9), Tundra Bks.) Tundra Bks. CAN. Dist: Penguin Random Hse. LLC.

Fernandez, Joyce. Little Bird - Pajarito. 2010. 31p. 15.95 (978-0-615-23709-1(6)) My Second Language Publishing, USA.

Ferrell, Sean. I Don't Like Koala. Santoso, Charles, illus. 2015. (ENG.). 40p. (J). (gr. -1-3). 17.99 (978-1-4814-0068-8(1), Atheneum Bks. for Young Readers) Simon & Schuster Children's Publishing.

Ferri, Francesca, illus. Peek-A-Boo. 2005. (ENG.). 10p. (J). 8.99 (978-0-7641-5851-3(1)) Barron's Educational Series, Inc.

Ferri, Jean-Yves. Asterix & the Picts. Conrad, Didier, illus. 2013. (ENG.). 48p. (J). (gr. 4-7). 17.99 (978-1-4440-1167-8(7), Orion) Orion Publishing Group, Ltd. GBR. Dist: Hachette Bk. Group.

Ferrie, Chris. Quantum Physics for Babies. 2017. (Baby University Ser.: 0). (ENG., Illus.). 24p. (J). bds. 9.99 **(978-1-4926-5622-7(4)**, Sourcebooks Jabberwocky) Sourcebooks, Inc.

Feuchter, Anke. Felix from Berlin. Durand, Élodie, illus. 2014. (AV2 Fiction Readalong Ser.: Vol. 126). (ENG.). 32p. (J). (gr. -1-3). lib. bdg. 34.28 (978-1-4896-2277-8(2), AV2 by Weigl) Weigl Pubs., Inc.

Fiedler, Heidi. Bugs: A Close-Up Photographic Look Inside Your World. 2017. (Up Close Ser.). (ENG., Illus.). (J). (gr. k-6). lib. bdg. 27.99 **(978-1-942875-36-9(3)**, Walter Foster Jr) Quarto Publishing Group USA.

—Butterflies: A Close-Up Photographic Look Inside Your World. 2017. (Up Close Ser.). (ENG., Illus.). (J). (gr. k-6). lib. bdg. 27.99 **(978-1-942875-37-6(1)**, Walter Foster Jr) Quarto Publishing Group USA.

—Sea Swimmers: A Close-Up Photographic Look Inside Your World. 2017. (Up Close Ser.). (ENG., Illus.). (J). (gr. k-6). lib. bdg. 27.99 **(978-1-942875-34-5(7)**, Walter Foster Jr) Quarto Publishing Group USA.

Fienberg, Anna & Fienberg, Barbara. Once Tashi Met a Dragon. Gamble, Kim, illus. 2014. (Tashi Ser.). (ENG.). 34p. (J). (gr. k-2). 16.99 (978-1-74175-887-0(4)) Allen & Unwin AUS. Dist: Independent Pubs. Group.

Fierstein, Harvey. The Sissy Duckling. Cole, Henry, illus. 2014. (ENG.). 40p. (J). (gr. -1-3). pap. 9.99 (978-1-4424-9817-4(X), Little Simon) Little Simon.

Filippis, Dina De. Mrs Nguyen's Garden. 2011. 28p. pap. 15.99 (978-1-4568-3337-4(5)) Xlibris Corp.

Finch, Mary. Three Billy Goats Gruff PB W CD. 2016. (ENG., Illus.). 32p. (J). (gr. -1-1). 9.99 (978-1-78285-305-3(7)) Barefoot Bks., Inc.

Finch, Mary & Messing, Debra. The Little Red Hen. Slater, Kate, illus. 2013. (ENG.). 32p. (J). pap. 7.99 (978-1-78285-041-0(4)); (gr. -1-2). 16.99 (978-1-84686-575-6(1)); (gr. -1-2). 9.99 (978-1-84686-751-4(7)) Barefoot Bks., Inc.

Fine, Anne. Ruggles. Brown, Ruth, illus. 2011. (ENG.). 32p. (J). (gr. k-k). pap. 8.99 (978-1-84939-206-8(4)) Andersen Pr. GBR. Dist: Independent Pubs. Group.

Finn, Rebecca. Rudy Learns to Fly, 6. 2012. (Sparkly Christmas Ser.). (ENG., Illus.). 12p. (J). (gr. -1-k). bds. 5.99 (978-0-230-75386-0(8)) Macmillan Pubs., Ltd. GBR. Dist: Independent Pubs. Group.

—Sammy the Snowman! 2013. (Sparkly Christmas Ser.). (ENG., Illus.). 12p. (J). (gr. -1-k). bds. 5.99 (978-0-230-76062-2(7)) Pan Macmillan GBR. Dist: Independent Pubs. Group.

Finnan, Kristie. Mommy's High Heel Shoes. Achilles, Pat, illus. 2008. 32p. (J). 16.99 (978-0-9817565-2-3(2)) Mommy Workshop Bks.

Firefly Books Staff. Bedtime. (ENG., Illus.). 10p. bds. (978-1-55209-358-0(1)) Firefly Bks., Ltd.

Fisher, Dorothy Canfield. Understood Betsy - Illustrated. Williamson, Ada C., illus. 2013. 112p. pap. 3.97 (978-1-60386-582-1(9), Merchant Bks.) Rough Draft Printing.

Fisher, Henry. When I Dream of ABC. 2014. (Illus.). (J). (978-1-4351-5469-8(X)) Barnes & Noble, Inc.

Fisher, Martin & Davison, Max. Home, Vol. 1. 2015. (ENG., Illus.). 64p. (J). (gr. 1-4). pap. 6.99 (978-1-78276-228-7(0)) Titan Bks. Ltd. GBR. Dist: Penguin Random Hse. LLC.

Fisher, Teresa. Croc on the Rock. 2012. 20p. pap. 13.77 (978-1-4669-1936-5(1)) Trafford Publishing.

Fisher, Valorie. Ellsworth's Extraordinary Electric Ears: And Other Amazing Alphabet Anecdotes. Fisher, Valorie, illus. 2009. (ENG., Illus.). 36p. (J). (gr. -1-3). 10.99 (978-1-4424-0658-2(5), Atheneum Bks. for Young Readers) Simon & Schuster Children's Publishing.

Fitzgerald, D. M. The True Story of the Big Red Onion. Cudd, Savannah, illus. 2013. 36p. 18.99 (978-0-9890288-7-5(9)); pap. 10.99 (978-0-9890288-5-1(2)) Mindstir Media.

Fitzpatrick, Joe. I Am So Awesome. Kummer, Mark, illus. 2014. (ENG.). 32p. (J). (gr. k-4). 7.99 (978-1-4867-0005-9(5)) Flowerpot Children's Pr. Inc. CAN. Dist: Cardinal Pubs. Group.

Fitzpatrick, Marie-Louise. Owl Bat Bat Owl. Fitzpatrick, Marie-Louise, illus. 2017. (ENG., Illus.). 32p. (J). (gr. -1-2). 15.99 (978-0-7636-9161-5(5)) Candlewick Pr.

Fleabite. 2004. (J). 14.95 (978-0-9746710-0-0(2)) Terra Linda Publishing.

Fleming, Denise. The Everything Book. Fleming, Denise, illus. rev. ed. 2004. (ENG., Illus.). 26p. (J). (— 1). bds. 7.95 (978-0-8050-7709-4(X), 9780805077094, Holt, Henry & Co. Bks. For Young Readers) Holt, Henry & Co.

Fletcher, Steffi. The Lone Ranger. Dreany, E. Joseph, illus. 2013. (Little Golden Book Ser.). (ENG.). 24p. (J). (-k). 4.99 (978-0-449-81793-3(8), Golden Bks.) Random Hse. Children's Bks.

Fletcher, Tom. There's a Monster in Your Book, 4 vols. 2017. (ENG.). (J). 71.96 **(978-0-525-50216-6(5)**, Random Hse. Bks. for Young Readers) Random Hse. Children's Bks.

—There's a Monster in Your Book. Abbott, Greg, illus. 2017. (ENG.). 32p. (J). (gr. -1-2). 17.99 **(978-1-5247-6456-2(6)**, Random Hse. Bks. for Young Readers) Random Hse. Children's Bks.

Fletcher, Tom & Poynter, Dougie. The Dinosaur That Pooped a Planet! Parsons, Garry, illus. 2017. (Dinosaur That Ser.). (ENG.). 32p. (J). (gr. -1-3). 15.99 **(978-1-4814-9866-1(5)**, Aladdin) Simon & Schuster Children's Publishing.

Fliess, Sue. Bella's New Baby. 2016. (Little Golden Book Ser.). (ENG., Illus.). 24p. (J). (gr. -1-k). 4.99 (978-0-553-51064-5(9), Golden Bks.) Random Hse. Children's Bks.

—From Here to There. Engel, Christiane, illus. 2016. (ENG.). 32p. (J). (gr. -1-3). 16.99 (978-0-8075-2622-4(3)) Whitman, Albert & Co.

—How to Be a Pirate. Dyson, Nikki, illus. 2014. (Little Golden Book Ser.). (ENG.). 24p. (J). (-k). 4.99 (978-0-449-81309-6(6), Golden Bks.) Random Hse. Children's Bks.

—I'm a Ballerina! Chou, Joey, illus. 2015. (Little Golden Book Ser.). (ENG.). 24p. (J). (-k). 4.99 (978-0-553-49758-8(8), Golden Bks.) Random Hse. Children's Bks.

—We're Getting a Pet! Christy, Jana, illus. 2015. (Little Golden Book Ser.). (ENG.). 24p. (J). (-k). 4.99 (978-0-385-37554-2(9), Golden Bks.) Random Hse. Children's Bks.

Florian, Douglas. Once I Was a Pollywog. Bakos, Barbara, illus. 2016. (Animals Play Ser.). (ENG.). 18p. (J). (gr. -1-1). bds. 6.99 (978-1-4998-0141-5(6)) Little Bee Books Inc.

—The Wonderful Habits of Rabbits. Sanchez, Sonia, illus. 2016. (ENG.). 32p. (J). (gr. -1-3). 16.99 (978-1-4998-0104-0(1)) Little Bee Books Inc.

Flowerpot Press Staff, contrib. by. Sockheadz: Counting. 2013. (ENG., Illus.). 20p. (J). (gr. -1-k). 6.99 (978-1-77093-594-5(0)) Flowerpot Children's Pr. Inc. CAN. Dist: Cardinal Pubs. Group.

—Sockheadz: First Words. 2013. (ENG., Illus.). 20p. (J). (gr. -1-k). 6.99 (978-1-77093-595-2(9)) Flowerpot Children's Pr. Inc. CAN. Dist: Cardinal Pubs. Group.

Fluent Stage 3. 2005. (Little Celebrations Picture/Text & Literacy Cards Ser.). (J). (gr. k-3). 128.50 (978-0-673-77359-3(0)) Celebration Pr.

Foce, Natalia, tr. from ENG. Daniel, el Príncipe que Oraba Apps, Fred, illus. l.t. ed. 2009. (SPA & ENG.). 32p. (J). 3.49 (978-1-932789-19-5(7)) Editorial Sendas Antiguas, LLC.

—La Historia de Pablo — Viajes de Aventura, 1. Apps, Fred, illus. l.t. ed. 2009. Orig. Title: Journeys of Adventure — the Story of Paul. (SPA & ENG.). 32p. (J). 3.49 (978-1-932789-23-2(5)) Editorial Sendas Antiguas, LLC.

—Jesus el Milagroso. Anderson, Jeff, illus. l.t. ed. 2009. Orig. Title: Jesus the Miracle Worker. (SPA & ENG.). 24p. (J). 3.49 (978-1-932789-28-7(6)) Editorial Sendas Antiguas, LLC.

—Jesus Maestro. Anderson, Jeff, illus. l.t. ed. 2009. Orig. Title: Jesus the Teacher. (SPA & ENG.). 24p. (J). 3.49 (978-1-932789-26-3(X)) Editorial Sendas Antiguas, LLC.

—Jesus Narrador. Anderson, Jeff, illus. l.t. ed. 2009. Orig. Title: Jesus the Storyteller. (SPA & ENG.). 24p. (J). 3.49 (978-1-932789-25-6(1)) Editorial Sendas Antiguas, LLC.

—Jesus Niño. Anderson, Jeff, illus. l.t. ed. 2009. Orig. Title: Jesus the Child. (SPA & ENG.). 24p. (J). 3.49 (978-1-932789-24-9(3)) Editorial Sendas Antiguas, LLC.

—Jesus Salvador. Anderson, Jeff, illus. l.t. ed. 2009. Orig. Title: Jesus the Saviour. (SPA & ENG.). 24p. (J). 3.49 (978-1-932789-29-4(4)) Editorial Sendas Antiguas, LLC.

—Jesus Sanador. Anderson, Jeff, illus. l.t. ed. 2009. Orig. Title: Jesus the Healer. (SPA & ENG.). 24p. (J). 3.49 (978-1-932789-27-0(8)) Editorial Sendas Antiguas, LLC.

—El Nacimiento de Jesús: El Niño Prometido, 1. Apps, Fred, illus. l.t. ed. 2009. Orig. Title: The Birth of Jesus — the Promised Child. (SPA & ENG.). 32p. (J). 3.49 (978-1-932789-20-1(0)) Editorial Sendas Antiguas, LLC.

—El Plan de Rescate: La Historia de Noe, 1. Apps, Fred, illus. l.t. ed. 2009. Orig. Title: The Rescue Plan. (SPA & ENG.). 32p. (J). 3.49 (978-1-932789-15-7(4)) Editorial Sendas Antiguas, LLC.

—La Resurrección: Jesús Está Vivo, 1. Apps, Fred, illus. l.t. ed. 2009. Orig. Title: The Resurrection — Jesus Is Alive. (SPA & ENG.). 32p. (J). 3.49 (978-1-932789-21-8(9)) Editorial Sendas Antiguas, LLC.

—Samuel, el Niño que Escuchaba. Apps, Fred, illus. l.t. ed. 2009. (SPA & ENG.). 32p. (J). 3.49 (978-1-932789-17-1(0)) Editorial Sendas Antiguas, LLC.

—Saúl — el Milagro en el Camino, 1. Apps, Fred, illus. l.t. ed. 2009. Orig. Title: Saul — the Miracle on the Road. (SPA & ENG.). 32p. (J). 3.49 (978-1-932789-22-5(7)) Editorial Sendas Antiguas, LLC.

Foley, Greg. Thank You Bear Board Book. Foley, Greg, illus. 2012. (ENG., Illus.). 28p. (J). (gr. -1-k). bds. 6.99 (978-0-670-78507-0(5), Viking Books for Young Readers) Penguin Young Readers Group.

Foreman, Michael. The Little Bookshop & the Origami Army! Foreman, Michael, illus. 2015. (Origami Girl Ser.). (ENG., Illus.). 32p. (J). (gr. -1-k). 16.99 (978-1-78344-120-4(8)) Andersen Pr. GBR. Dist: Independent Pubs. Group.

—Moose. Foreman, Michael, illus. 2015. (ENG., Illus.). 32p. (J). (gr. -1-k). pap. 9.99 (978-1-78344-101-3(1)) Andersen Pr. GBR. Dist: Independent Pubs. Group.

—Newspaper Boy & Origami Girl! Foreman, Michael, illus. 2013. (Origami Girl Ser.). (ENG., Illus.). 32p. (J). (gr. -1-k). 16.99 (978-1-84939-451-2(2)) Andersen Pr. GBR. Dist: Independent Pubs. Group.

—One World. 2012. (ENG., Illus.). 32p. (J). (gr. -1-k). pap. 12.99 (978-1-84939-304-1(4)) Andersen Pr. GBR. Dist: Independent Pubs. Group.

—Superfrog & the Big Stink! Foreman, Michael, illus. 2014. (ENG., Illus.). 32p. (J). (gr. -1-k). pap. 9.99 (978-1-78344-030-6(9)) Andersen Pr. GBR. Dist: Independent Pubs. Group.

Fosberry, Jennifer. Isabella: Star of the Story. Litwin, Mike, illus. 2013. (ENG.). 32p. (J). (-3). 16.99 (978-1-4022-7936-2(1), 9781402279362, Sourcebooks Jabberwocky) Sourcebooks, Inc.

Fox, Diane. Rain or Shine. Fox, Christyan, illus. 2013. (ENG.). 20p. (J). (gr. -1-k). pap. 9.99 (978-1-4083-1613-9(7)) Hodder & Stoughton GBR. Dist: Hachette Bk. Group.

Foxe, Steve. The Big Book of the Alola Region. Golden Books, illus. 2017. (Big Golden Book Ser.). (ENG.). 48p. (J). (gr. -1-2). 10.99 **(978-1-5247-7009-9(4)**, Golden Bks.) Random Hse. Children's Bks.

Foy, Debbie. Bubbles, Tub, Have a Scrub! 2016. (All by Myself Ser.). (ENG., Illus.). 20p. (J). (gr. -1-k). pap. 6.99 (978-0-7502-9615-1(1), Wayland) Hachette Children's Group GBR. Dist: Hachette Bk. Group.

—Pants, Vest, Getting Dressed! 2017. (All by Myself Ser.). (ENG., Illus.). 20p. (J). (gr. -1-k). pap. 6.99 (978-0-7502-9620-5(8), Wayland) Hachette Children's Group GBR. Dist: Hachette Bk. Group.

—Spoon, Cup, Dinner's Up! 2017. (All by Myself Ser.). (ENG., Illus.). 20p. (J). (gr. -1-k). pap. 6.99 (978-0-7502-9621-2(6), Wayland) Hachette Children's Group GBR. Dist: Hachette Bk. Group.

—Toys, Play, Tidy Away! 2016. (All by Myself Ser.). (ENG., Illus.). 20p. (J). (gr. -1-k). pap. 6.99 (978-0-7502-9616-8(X), Wayland) Hachette Children's Group GBR. Dist: Hachette Bk. Group.

Franco, Betsy. Summer Beat. Middleton, Charlotte, illus. 2011. (ENG.). 36p. (J). (gr. -1-1). 14.99 (978-1-4424-4339-6(1), McElderry, Margaret K. Bks.) McElderry, Margaret K. Bks.

Francois, Saragine. The White Gorilla & the Three Chimpanzees a Day from the Zoo. 2011. 28p. pap. 14.99 (978-1-4520-3190-3(8)) AuthorHouse.

Frank, Janet & Golden Books Staff. Daddies. Gergely, Tibor, illus. 2011. (Little Golden Book Ser.). (ENG.). 24p. (J). (gr. -1-2). 4.99 (978-0-375-86130-7(0), Golden Bks.) Random Hse. Children's Bks.

Franks, Alison. On My Feet! 2013. 24p. pap. 28.03 (978-1-4797-6958-2(4)) Xlibris Corp.

Frasconi, Antonio. The House That Jack Built: A Picture Book in Two Languages. 2017. (ENG & FRE., Illus.). 32p. 14.95 **(978-0-486-81646-3(X))** Dover Pubns., Inc.

Fraser, Frank. The Bible Amigos: Five Loaves, Two Fish, & One Big Hat. 2014. (ENG., Illus.). 48p. (J). 7.99 (978-1-62416-888-8(4)) Barbour Publishing, Inc.

—The Bible Amigos: Jonah & the Bear. 2014. (ENG., Illus.). 48p. (J). 7.99 (978-1-62416-887-1(6)) Barbour Publishing, Inc.

Fredrickson, Anne. The Baseball Brothers. 2008. lib. bdg. 12.95 (978-0-615-20146-7(6)) Fredrickson, Anne.

Fredrickson, Lane. Monster Trouble. Robertson, Michael, illus. 2015. (ENG.). 32p. (J). (gr. -1-2). 14.95 (978-1-4549-1345-0(2)) Sterling Publishing Co., Inc.

Free Wheelin' Picture Book (English) NL 9x9 with Snipe. 2007. (J). 5.99 (978-1-933934-48-8(4)) Mighty Kids Media.

Freedman, Claire. Where Snowflakes Fall. Macnaughton, Tina, illus. 2012. 24p. (J). (978-1-4351-4321-0(3)) Barnes & Noble, Inc.

Freedman, Claire & Scott, Gavin. Cuddle Bear. 2013. (ENG.). (J). 26.99 (978-1-61067-193-4(7)) Kane Miller.

Freeman, Anna Harber. Love You More Than Anything. Henry, Jed, illus. 2016. (Snuggle Time Stories Ser.). (ENG.). 24p. (J). (— 1). bds. 6.95 (978-1-4549-1490-7(4)) Sterling Publishing Co., Inc.

Freeman, Don. Corduroy. 2014. (Corduroy Ser.). (ENG., Illus.). 32p. (J). (gr. -1 — 1). bds. 7.99 (978-0-451-47079-9(6), Viking Books for Young Readers) Penguin Young Readers Group.

—A Pocket for Corduroy. 2015. (Corduroy Ser.). (ENG.). 32p. (J). (— 1). bds. 7.99 (978-0-451-47113-0(X), Viking Books for Young Readers) Penguin Young Readers Group.

Freeman, Tor. Benji Bear's Busy Day. Freeman, Tor, illus. 2015. (ENG., Illus.). 18p. (J). (-k). bds. 17.99 (978-1-5098-0111-4(1)) Pan Macmillan GBR. Dist: Independent Pubs. Group.

—Olive & the Big Secret. Freeman, Tor, illus. 2012. (ENG., Illus.). 32p. (J). (gr. -1-3). 15.99 (978-0-7636-6149-6(X), Templar) Candlewick Pr.

French, Jess. Tickly Minibeast Adventures. Woodward, Jonathan, illus. 2016. (ENG.). 32p. (J). (gr. -1-k). 10.99 (978-1-4052-7756-3(4)) Egmont Bks., Ltd. GBR. Dist: Independent Pubs. Group.

French, Vivian. Cave-Baby & the Mammoth. Williams, Lisa, illus. 2010. 32p. pap. (978-1-84089-635-0(3)) Zero to Ten, Ltd.

Friester, Paul & Goossens, Philippe. Owl Howls Again! 2015. (ENG., Illus.). 32p. (J). 15.95 (978-0-7358-4129-1(2)) North-South Bks., Inc.

Fritz, Jean & dePaola, Tomie. Bunny Hopwell's First Spring. Dixon, Rachel, illus. 2015. (G&d Vintage Ser.). (ENG.). 32p. (J). (gr. -1-k). bds. 7.99 (978-0-448-48463-1(3), Grosset & Dunlap) Penguin Young Readers Group.

Frohlich, Anja. Animals in the Outhouse. Kiss, Gergely, illus. 2012. (ENG.). 28p. (J). (gr. k-3). 16.95 (978-1-61608-659-6(9), 608659, Sky Pony Pr.) Skyhorse Publishing Co., Inc.

Fromental, Jean-Luc. Rapido's Next Stop. Jolivet, Joëlle, illus. 2012. (ENG.). 20p. (J). (gr. k-2). 17.95 (978-1-4197-0195-5(9), Abrams Bks. for Young Readers) Abrams, Inc.

Frosty the Snowman: Songs of the Season: 5-Button Song Book. (Illus.). 10p. (J). (gr. -1-2). 7.98 (978-0-7853-2067-8(9), PI27) Publications International, Ltd.

Fuggle, Debbie. The Two Little Fir Trees. 2012. 28p. pap. 32.70 (978-1-4691-3253-2(2)) Xlibris Corp.

Fujii, Hideaki. LBX Vol. 1: New Dawn Raisers. 2014. (ENG., Illus.). 192p. (J). pap. 9.99 (978-1-4215-7695-4(3)) Viz Media.

Fuller, Rachel, illus. Look at Me! 2009. (New Baby Ser.). (ENG.). 12p. (J). (gr. -1). bds. (978-1-84643-278-1(2)) Child's Play International Ltd.

Funk, Josh. The Case of the Stinky Stench. Kearny, Brendan, illus. 2017. (Lady Pancake & Sir French Toast Ser.). (ENG.). 40p. (J). (gr. k-3). 16.95 **(978-1-4549-1960-5(4))** Sterling Publishing Co., Inc.

Furie, Matt. The Night Riders. 2012. (ENG., Illus.). 48p. 17.95 (978-1-936365-56-2(1)) McSweeney's Publishing.

Furie, Matt, illus. The Night Riders. 2013. (ENG.). 48p. (J). (gr. -1-3). 8.95 (978-1-938073-72-4(X)) McSweeney's Publishing.

Furman, Simon. Kung Fu Panda Collection - Ready, Set Po!, Vol. 1. Robinson, Lee et al, illus. 2016. (ENG.). 112p. (J). (gr. 1-4). pap. 12.99 (978-1-78276-697-1(9)) Titan Bks. Ltd. GBR. Dist: Penguin Random Hse. LLC.

Fusek Peters, Andrew. The Ant & the Big Bad Bully Goat. Wadham, Anna, illus. 2010. (Traditional Tales with a Twist Ser.). (ENG.). 32p. (J). (gr. -1-2). audio compact disk (978-1-84643-348-1(7)) Child's Play International Ltd.

—The Talkative Tortoise. 2011. (Traditional Tales with a Twist Ser.). (ENG., Illus.). 32p. (J). (978-1-84643-418-1(1)) Child's Play International Ltd.

G., Ashley. Critter Colors. G., Ashley, illus. 2015. (ENG., Illus.). 28p. (J). (gr. -1-k). bds. 7.99 (978-1-4814-4218-3(X), Little Simon) Little Simon.

Gaiman, NEil. Chu's Day at the Beach Board Book. Rex, Adam, illus. 2016. 36p. (J). (gr. -1 — 1). bds. 7.99 *(978-0-06-238124-8(5),* HarperFestival) HarperCollins Pubs.
Galbraith, Kathryn O. Arbor Day Square, 1 vol. Moore, Cyd, illus. 2016. (ENG.). 32p. (J). (gr. -1-3). pap. 7.95 *(978-1-56145-922-3(4))* Peachtree Pubs.
Galdone, Paul. Cinderella. 2013. (Folk Tale Classics Ser.). (ENG., Illus.). 48p. (J). (gr. -1-3). 8.99 *(978-0-547-98867-2(2))* Houghton Mifflin Harcourt Publishing Co.
Gale, Emily. Just Josie & the Number 7. Byrne, Mike, illus. 2010. (Picture Books Ser.). 25p. (J). (gr. -1-1). *(978-1-4075-9505-4(9))* Parragon, Inc.
—Just Josie & the Perfect Day. Byrne, Mike, illus. 2010. (Picture Books Ser.). 25p. (J). (gr. -1-1). *(978-1-4075-9506-1(7))* Parragon, Inc.
Galindo, Renata. The Cherry Thief. Galindo, Renata, illus. 2014. (Child's Play Library). (ENG., Illus.). 32p. (J). *(978-1-84643-652-9(4)); (978-1-84643-651-2(6))* Child's Play International Ltd.
Gall, Chris. Dinotrux. 2012. (Dinotrux Ser.: 1). (ENG., Illus.). 32p. (J). (gr. -1-3). pap. 7.99 *(978-0-316-13392-0(2))* Little, Brown Bks. for Young Readers.
—Dinotrux Dig the Beach. 2017. (Dinotrux Ser.: 3). (ENG., Illus.). 32p. (J). (gr. -1-3). 7.99 *(978-0-316-46381-2(7))* Little, Brown Bks. for Young Readers.
—Revenge of the Dinotrux. 2015. (Dinotrux Ser.: 2). (ENG., Illus.). 28p. (J). (gr. -1 — 1). bds. 6.99 *(978-0-316-40635-2(X))* Little, Brown Bks. for Young Readers.
Gallardo, Yuri, ed. Houses & Apartments under 1000 Square Feet. 2013. (ENG., Illus.). 256p. pap. 24.95 *(978-1-77085-214-3(X),* 9781770852143) Firefly Bks., Ltd.
Galvin, Laura Gates. Baby Duck Gets Lost. 2007. (Baby Animals Ser.). (ENG., Illus.). 16p. (gr. -1-k). 6.95 *(978-1-59249-747-8(0))* Soundprints.
Gamble, Adam & Jasper, Mark. Good Night Austin. Palmer, Ruth & Veno, Joe, illus. 2015. (Good Night Our World Ser.). (ENG.). 20p. (J). (— 1). bds. 9.95 *(978-1-60219-233-1(2))* Good Night Bks.
—Good Night Boats. Veno, Joe, illus. 2016. (Good Night Our World Ser.). (ENG.). 20p. (J). (— 1). bds. 9.95 *(978-1-60219-500-4(5))* Good Night Bks.
—Good Night Grand Canyon. Kelly, Cooper, illus. 2016. (Good Night Our World Ser.). (ENG.). 20p. (J). (— 1). bds. 9.95 *(978-1-60219-503-5(X))* Good Night Bks.
—Good Night Grandma. Kelly, Cooper, illus. 2016. (ENG.). 20p. (J). (— 1). bds. 9.95 *(978-1-60219-409-0(2))* Good Night Bks.
—Good Night Little Brother. Kelly, Cooper, illus. 2016. (Good Night Our World Ser.). (ENG.). 20p. (J). (— 1). bds. 9.95 *(978-1-60219-505-9(6))* Good Night Bks.
—Good Night Little Monsters. Kelly, Cooper, illus. 2017. (Good Night Our World Ser.). (ENG.). 20p. (J). (gr. -1 — 1). bds. 9.95 ***(978-1-60219-489-2(0))*** Good Night Bks.
—Good Night Little Sister. Kelly, Cooper, illus. 2016. (Good Night Our World Ser.). (ENG.). 20p. (J). (— 1). bds. 9.95 *(978-1-60219-506-6(4))* Good Night Bks.
—Good Night Mommy. Kelly, Cooper, illus. 2015. (Good Night Our World Ser.). (ENG.). 20p. (J). (— 1). bds. 9.95 *(978-1-60219-230-0(8))* Good Night Bks.
—Good Night Nebraska. 2015. (Good Night Our World Ser.). (ENG., Illus.). 20p. (J). (— 1). bds. 9.95 *(978-1-60219-087-0(9))* Good Night Bks.
—Good Night New Mexico. Palmer, Ruth, illus. 2014. (Good Night Our World Ser.). (ENG.). 20p. (J). (— 1). bds. 9.95 *(978-1-60219-088-7(7))* Good Night Bks.
—Good Night Snow. 2016. (Good Night Our World Ser.). (ENG., Illus.). 20p. (J). (— 1). bds. 9.95 *(978-1-60219-412-0(2))* Good Night Bks.
—Good Night Summer. Blackmore, Katherine, illus. 2017. (Good Night Our World Ser.). (ENG.). 20p. (J). (— 1). bds. 9.95 *(978-1-60219-440-3(8))* Good Night Bks.
Gamonal, Dulce. Diego from Madrid. Audouin, Laurent, illus. 2014. (AV2 Fiction Readalong Ser.: Vol. 124). (ENG.). 32p. (J). (gr. -1-3). lib. bdg. 34.28 *(978-1-4896-2280-8(2),* AV2 by Weigl) Weigl Pubs., Inc.
Ganeri, Anita. Lifesize: Ocean. Jackson-Carter, Stuart, illus. 2014. (ENG.). 32p. (J). (gr. k-4). 16.99 *(978-0-7534-7096-1(9),* 9780753470961, Kingfisher) Roaring Brook Pr.
Gangloff, Sylviane, illus. Ping & Pong. 2015. (Talking Back Ser.). (ENG.). 36p. (J). (gr. -1-2). 7.95 *(978-0-7892-1244-3(7),* Abbeville Kids) Abbeville Pr., Inc.
—Rainier the Reindeer. 2015. (Talking Back Ser.). (ENG.). 36p. (J). (gr. -1-2). 7.95 *(978-0-7892-1243-6(9),* Abbeville Kids) Abbeville Pr., Inc.
Gardner, Louise, illus. Old MacDonald. 2004. 24p. (J). bds. 6.99 *(978-1-85854-901-9(9))* Brimax Books Ltd. GBR. Dist: Byeway Bks.
Gardner, Sally. Book of Princesses. (Illus.). 96p. (J). 19.95 *(978-1-85881-350-9(6),* Orion) Orion Publishing Group, Ltd. GBR. Dist: Trafalgar Square Publishing.
—The Little Nut Tree. Gardner, Sally, illus. 2014. (ENG., Illus.). 64p. (J). (gr. -1-k). pap. 7.99 *(978-1-4440-1027-5(1),* Orion Children's Bks.) Hachette Children's Group GBR. Dist: Hachette Bk. Group.
Garland, Sarah. Azzi in Between. 2016. (ENG., Illus.). 40p. (J). (gr. 2-6). pap. 9.99 *(978-1-84780-651-2(1),* Frances Lincoln) Quarto Publishing Group UK GBR. Dist: Littlehampton Bk Services, Ltd.
—Eddie's Kitchen. 2014. (ENG., Illus.). 40p. (J). (gr. -1-2). pap. 8.99 *(978-1-84780-003-9(3),* Frances Lincoln) Quarto Publishing Group UK GBR. Dist: Hachette Bk. Group.
—Eddie's Tent: And How to Go Camping. 2015. (ENG., Illus.). 40p. (J). (gr. -1-2). 17.99 *(978-1-84780-408-2(X),* Frances Lincoln) Quarto Publishing Group UK GBR. Dist: Hachette Bk. Group.
Garland, Sarah, illus. Eddie's Toolbox: And How to Make & Mend Things. 2011. (ENG.). 40p. (J). (gr. -1-2). *(978-1-84780-053-4(X))* Rough Guides, Ltd.
Garnett, Sandy, creator. The Rainbow Riders. 2011. (Rainbow Riders Ser.). (ENG., Illus.). 36p. 18.00 *(978-0-9822348-5-3(6),* Chelsea Pr.) Chelsea Multimedia.
Garza, Armando N. Itty Bitty Saves the Day. 2007. (Illus.). 22p. (J). (gr. -1-3). 21.99 *(978-1-59879-482-3(5))* Lifevest Publishing, Inc.
Gassman, Julie A. You Get What You Get, 1 vol. Horne, Sarah, illus. 2013. (Little Boost Ser.). (ENG.). 32p. (gr. k-3). 14.95 *(978-1-4795-2157-9(4),* Little Boost) Picture Window Bks.
Gates, Susan. Mole Who was Scared of the Dark. Breakespeare, Andrew, illus. 2005. (ENG.). 24p. (J). lib. bdg. 23.65 *(978-1-59646-710-1(X))* Dingles & Co.
Gauch, Patricia Lee. Christina Katerina & the Box. 2012. (ENG.). 32p. (J). (gr. -1-3). 7.95 *(978-1-59078-915-5(6))* Boyds Mills Pr.
Gauthier, Elizabeth. A Bald Chimpanzee: An Adventure in ABCs. Gauthier, Elizabeth & Bonney, Joan, illus. 2012. (ENG.). 40p. (J). pap. 12.99 *(978-0-9833593-5-7(0),* Frog Legs Ink) Gauthier Pubns. Inc.
Gaven, Jim. Friends Find Fun for Food: All about Alliterations. 2013. 28p. pap. 24.95 *(978-1-63000-140-7(6))* America Star Bks.
Gavin, Ciara. Room for Bear. 2015. (ENG., Illus.). 32p. (J). (gr. -1-2). 16.99 *(978-0-385-75473-6(6),* Knopf Bks. for Young Readers) Random Hse. Children's Bks.
Gehl, Laura. Peep & Egg: I'm Not Trick-Or-Treating. Wan, Joyce, illus. 2017. (Peep & Egg Ser.). (ENG.). 32p. (J). bds. 7.99 *(978-0-374-30543-7(9),* 9780374305437, Farrar, Straus & Giroux (BYR)) Farrar, Straus & Giroux.
Geisert, Arthur, creator. Thunderstorm. (ENG., Illus.). (J). 2015. 34p. (gr. k). 60.00 *(978-1-59270-170-4(1))* 2013. 32p. (gr. -1). 17.95 *(978-1-59270-133-9(7))* Enchanted Lion Bks., LLC.
George, Boy, illus. I Hear... 2013. (ENG.). 36p. (J). (gr. -1-k). 12.99 *(978-1-908473-07-3(X))* PatrickGeorge GBR. Dist: Independent Pubs. Group.
George, Joshua. Animals: Sticker Book Fun for Little Ones! 2017. (My First Sticker Book Ser.). (ENG.). 36p. (J). (gr. -1-k). pap. 8.99 ***(978-1-78700-068-1(0))*** Top That! Publishing PLC GBR. Dist: Independent Pubs. Group.
—Fame-Mouse. Bakos, Barbara, illus. 2017. (ENG.). 32p. (J). (gr. -1-k). pap. 9.99 ***(978-1-78445-704-4(3))*** Top That! Publishing PLC GBR. Dist: Independent Pubs. Group.
George, Joshua. Tiny Whale. Pinillos, Puy, illus. 2015. (ENG.). 32p. (J). (gr. -1-1). pap. 10.99 *(978-1-78445-287-2(4))* Top That! Publishing PLC GBR. Dist: Independent Pubs. Group.
George, Kallie. The Melancholic Mermaid. Halpin, Abigail, illus. 2011. (ENG.). 64p. (J). (gr. k-4). 16.95 *(978-1-897476-53-6(1))* Simply Read Bks. CAN. Dist: Ingram Publisher Services.
George, Lynn. The Leaf Pile. 2006. (Neighborhood Readers Ser.). (ENG.). 16p. (gr. 1-3). pap. 6.50 *(978-1-4042-7120-3(1),* Rosen Classroom) Rosen Publishing Group, Inc., The.
George, Patrick. I Smell... 2013. (ENG., Illus.). 36p. (J). (gr. -1-k). 12.99 *(978-1-908473-05-9(3))* PatrickGeorge GBR. Dist: Independent Pubs. Group.
—I Taste... George, Patrick, illus. 2013. (ENG., Illus.). 36p. (J). (gr. -1-k). 12.99 *(978-1-908473-06-6(1))* PatrickGeorge GBR. Dist: Independent Pubs. Group.
—I Touch .. George, Patrick, illus. 2013. (ENG., Illus.). 36p. (J). (gr. -1-k). 12.99 *(978-1-908473-08-0(8))* PatrickGeorge GBR. Dist: Independent Pubs. Group.
George, Sandy. Anika's Travel Diaries: The Lava Island Trip. 2012. 28p. pap. 17.99 *(978-1-4772-9297-6(7))* AuthorHouse.
Geraghty, Paul. Help Me! Geraghty, Paul, illus. 2011. (ENG., Illus.). 32p. (J). (gr. -1-k). pap. 8.99 *(978-1-84939-027-9(4))* Andersen Pr. GBR. Dist: Independent Pubs. Group.
—Hoppameleon. Geraghty, Paul, illus. 2014. (ENG., Illus.). 32p. (J). (gr. -1-k). pap. 9.99 *(978-1-84939-773-5(2))* Andersen Pr. GBR. Dist: Independent Pubs. Group.
—The Hunter. Geraghty, Paul, illus. 2012. (ENG., Illus.). 32p. (J). (gr. k-2). pap. 12.99 *(978-1-84939-376-8(1))* Andersen Pr. GBR. Dist: Independent Pubs. Group.
—Rotten & Rascal: The Two Terrible Pterosaur Twins. 2013. (ENG., Illus.). 32p. (J). (gr. k-2). pap. 9.99 *(978-1-84939-563-2(2))* Andersen Pr. GBR. Dist: Independent Pubs. Group.
—Tortuga. 2013. (ENG., Illus.). 32p. (J). (gr. k-2). pap. 9.99 *(978-1-84939-557-1(8))* Andersen Pr. GBR. Dist: Independent Pubs. Group.
Geras, Adèle. My Ballet Dream. McNicholas, Shelagh, illus. 2012. (ENG.). 32p. (J). (gr. -1-k). pap. 10.99 *(978-1-4083-0980-3(7))* Hodder & Stoughton GBR. Dist: Hachette Bk. Group.
Gerlings, Rebecca. Enormouse! Gerlings, Rebecca, illus. 2011. (ENG., Illus.). 32p. (J). (gr. -1-k). pap. 8.99 *(978-1-4052-4832-7(7))* Egmont Bks., Ltd. GBR. Dist: Independent Pubs. Group.
—Ho-Ho-Hopeless Santa. Jennings, Sarah, illus. 2016. (ENG.). 32p. (J). 8.99 *(978-1-4711-4600-8(6),* Simon & Schuster Children's) Simon & Schuster, Ltd. GBR. Dist: Simon & Schuster, Inc.
Gerra, Laurent. Tying the Knot, Vol. 45. 2014. (Lucky Luke Ser.: 45). (ENG., Illus.). 48p. pap. 11.95 *(978-1-84918-188-4(8))* CineBook GBR. Dist: National Bk. Network.
Gershman, Regina. Animals from My Window. 2011. 24p. pap. 16.44 *(978-1-4634-2094-9(3))* AuthorHouse.
Gerstein, Mordicai. Mountains of Tibet. Gerstein, Mordicai, illus. 2013. (ENG., Illus.). 32p. (J). (gr. k-5). 14.99 *(978-1-78285-047-2(3))* Barefoot Bks., Inc.
Gestalten. My Body: The Human Body in Illustrations. Section Graphics Golden Staff, illus. 2016. (ENG.). 48p. (J). (gr. 3-7). 24.95 *(978-3-89955-712-1(3))* Die Gestalten Verlag DEU. Dist: Penguin Random Hse. LLC.
Ghigna, Charles. Hail to Spring! Watson, Laura, illus. 2015. (Springtime Weather Wonders Ser.). (ENG.). 20p. (gr. -1-2). bds. 7.99 *(978-1-4795-6041-7(3))* Picture Window Bks.
—Sunshine Brightens Springtime. Watson, Laura, illus. 2015. (Springtime Weather Wonders Ser.). (ENG.). 20p. (gr. -1-2). bds. 7.99 *(978-1-4795-6043-1(X))* Picture Window Bks.
The Ghost Ship. 2013. (Illus.). (J). *(978-1-4351-4725-6(1))* Barnes & Noble, Inc.
Gibbons, Gail. Ice Cream: The Full Scoop. 2008. (ENG., Illus.). 32p. (J). (gr. 4-8). 7.99 *(978-0-8234-2155-8(4))* Holiday Hse., Inc.
Gibbons, Gail, et al. The Moon Book. Gibbons, Gail, illus. 2003. (Avenues Ser.). (ENG., Illus.). 32p. (C). (gr. k-3). 12.95 *(978-0-8234-1364-5(0))* National Geographic School Publishing, Inc.
Gibbs, Edward. I Spy under the Sea. Gibbs, Edward, illus. 2012. (ENG., Illus.). 32p. (J). (gr. k-k). 14.99 *(978-0-7636-5952-3(5),* Templar) Candlewick Pr.
Gidali, Orit. Nora the Mind Reader. Gordon-Noy, Aya, illus. 2012. (ENG.). 32p. (J). (gr. -1-3). 15.95 *(978-1-59270-120-9(5))* Enchanted Lion Bks., LLC.
Giesler, Dagmar & Geisler, Dagmar. Max juega en la Arena. 2004. (Coleccion Max Max Ser.). (SPA.). (J). bds. 11.95 *(978-84-261-3295-6(2))* Juventud, Editorial ESP. Dist: Distribooks, Inc.
Giles, Sophie, et al. My First Picture Dictionary. Burton, Terry & Hicks, Angela, illus. 2014. (ENG.). 125p. 17.50 *(978-1-84135-873-4(8))* Award Pubns. Ltd. GBR. Dist: Parkwest Pubns., Inc.
Gilleland, Linda. I Love You, Baby Deer. Irish, Leigh Ann, illus. 2012. 56p. 19.99 *(978-1-61254-025-2(2))* Brown Books Publishing Group.
Gillingham, Sara. In My Barn. Siminovich, Lorena, illus. 2012. (ENG.). 12p. (J). (gr. -1 — 1). bds. 8.99 *(978-1-4521-0641-0(X))* Chronicle Bks. LLC.
Gilman, Phoebe. The Balloon Tree. 2004. (J). (gr. k-3). spiral bd. *(978-0-616-01650-3(6))* Canadian National Institute for the Blind/Institut National Canadien pour les Aveugles.
Gilmore, Dorina Lazo. A Stone in the Soup. Hires, Josh, illus. 2006. 39p. per. 15.00 *(978-0-938911-29-6(5))* Individualized Education Systems/Poppy Lane Publishing.
Gilmore, Rachna. The Flute, 1 vol. Biswas, Pulak, illus. 2012. (ENG.). 32p. (J). (gr. -1-2). 16.95 *(978-1-896580-57-9(2))* Tradewind Bks. CAN. Dist: Orca Bk. Pubs. USA.
Gingras, Charlotte. L' Ecuyere. DuBois, Gérard, illus. 2004. (Picture Bks.). (FRE.). 32p. (J). (gr. -1). *(978-2-89021-666-2(7)); pap. (978-2-89021-665-5(9))* Diffusion du livre Mirabel (DLM).
Gingrich, Callista. Christmas in America. Arciero, Susan, illus. 2015. (Ellis the Elephant Ser.). (ENG.). 40p. (J). (gr. -1-3). 16.99 *(978-1-62157-345-6(1),* Regnery Kids) Regnery Publishing, Inc., An Eagle Publishing Co.
Girel, Stephane, illus. A Bird in Winter: A Children's Book Inspired by Pieter Breugel. 2011. (ENG.). 32p. (J). (gr. -1-3). 14.95 *(978-3-7913-7080-4(4))* Prestel Verlag GmbH & Co KG. DEU. Dist: Penguin Random Hse. LLC.
Giuliani, Alfred. Zootopia. Wu, Vivien, illus. 2016. (J). *(978-1-4806-9720-1(6),* Golden Bks.) Random Hse. Children's Bks.
Giusti, Katiuscia. The Clean-Up Contest. 2014. (AV2 Animated Storytime Ser.: Vol. 29). (ENG., Illus.). 32p. (J). (gr. -1-3). lib. bdg. 29.99 *(978-1-4896-2299-0(3),* AV2 by Weigl) Weigl Pubs., Inc.
Given, Cate. Cartwheeling. Hill-Peterson, Jodi, illus. 2006. (J). *(978-0-9790057-1-8(X))* Paws In the Sand Publishing.
Glass, Eleri. The Red Shoes. Spires, Ashley, illus. 2017. (ENG.). 40p. (J). (gr. -1-3). 8.99 *(978-1-927018-85-9(4))* Simply Read Bks. CAN. Dist: Ingram Publisher Services.
Gliori, Debi. Alfie in the Bath. 2015. (ENG., Illus.). 24p. (J). (gr. -1-1). 18.99 *(978-1-4088-5351-1(5),* 9781408853511, Bloomsbury USA Childrens) Bloomsbury Publishing USA.
—Babysits. 2015. (ENG., Illus.). 32p. (J). (gr. -1-k). pap. 10.99 *(978-1-4083-3635-9(9))* Hodder & Stoughton GBR. Dist: Hachette Bk. Group.
—The Tobermory Cat. 2015. (ENG., Illus.). 32p. (J). (gr. -1-k). pap. *(978-1-78027-131-6(X))* Birlinn, Ltd.
—Tobermory Cat 1, 2, 3. 2015. (ENG., Illus.). 32p. (J). (gr. -1-k). *(978-1-78027-199-6(9))* Birlinn, Ltd.
Golden Books. Barbie Dreamtopia Big Golden Book (Barbie Dreamtopia) 2017. (Big Golden Book Ser.). (ENG., Illus.). 48p. (J). (gr. -1-2). 9.99 *(978-1-5247-0117-8(3),* Golden Bks.) Random Hse. Children's Bks.
—The Epic Trolls. Golden Books, illus. 2016. (4 Color Plus 1,000 Stickers Ser.). (ENG., Illus.). 64p. (J). (gr. -1-2). pap. 12.99 *(978-0-399-55901-3(9),* Golden Bks.) Random Hse. Children's Bks.
—Marshall to the Rescue! (Paw Patrol) Golden Books & Jackson, Mike, illus. 2016. (Big Golden Book Ser.). (ENG.). 32p. (J). (gr. -1-2). 9.99 *(978-1-101-93847-8(1),* Golden Bks.) Random Hse. Children's Bks.
—Pat the Pet (Pat the Bunny) Vilela, Luiz, illus. 2014. (Lift-The-Flap Ser.). (ENG.). 16p. (J). (— 1). 14.99 *(978-0-385-37673-0(1),* Golden Bks.) Random Hse. Children's Bks.
—The Poky Little Puppy's Playtime. DiCicco, Sue, illus. 2017. (Tabbed Board Book Ser.). (ENG.). 16p. (J). (— 1). bds. 8.99 ***(978-0-399-55289-2(8),*** Golden Bks.) Random Hse. Children's Bks.
—Power up! 2017. (Hologramatic Sticker Book Ser.). (ENG.). 64p. (J). (gr. -1-2). pap. 4.99 *(978-0-399-55697-5(4),* Golden Bks.) Random Hse. Children's Bks.
—The Princess & the Pea. Christy, Jana, illus. 2013. (Little Golden Book Ser.). (ENG.). 24p. (J). (-k). 4.99 *(978-0-307-97951-3(2),* Golden Bks.) Random Hse. Children's Bks.
Golden Books & Williams, Garth. Bunnies' ABC. Williams, Garth, illus. 2015. (Little Golden Book Ser.). (ENG., Illus.). 24p. (J). (-k). 4.99 *(978-0-385-39128-3(5),* Golden Bks.) Random Hse. Children's Bks.
Golden Books, et al. Albert: The Little Tree with Big Dreams. Martinez, Heather, illus. 2016. (Big Golden Book Ser.). (ENG.). 32p. (J). (gr. -1-2). 9.99 *(978-0-399-55120-8(4),* Golden Bks.) Random Hse. Children's Bks.
Golden Books Staff. Bunny's Garden. Golden Books Staff, illus. 2010. (Shaped Board Book Ser.). (ENG., Illus.). 12p. (J). (gr. -1 — 1). bds. 7.99 *(978-0-375-85788-1(5),* Golden Bks.) Random Hse. Children's Bks.
—Trainloads of Fun. Golden Books Staff, illus. 2010. (Jumbo Coloring Book Ser.). (ENG., Illus.). 224p. (J). (gr. -1-2). pap. 5.99 *(978-0-375-86363-9(X),* Golden Bks.) Random Hse. Children's Bks.
Goldie, Sonia. Ghosts. Boutavant, Marc, illus. 2013. (ENG.). 40p. (J). (gr. -1-3). 16.95 *(978-1-59270-142-1(6))* Enchanted Lion Bks., LLC.
Goldman, Marcia, photos by. Lola Goes to School. 2016. (Lola Ser.). (ENG., Illus.). 32p. (J). (gr. -1-k). 16.95 *(978-1-939547-27-9(X))* Creston Bks.
Goldman Marshall, Lauren. My Beautiful Bow: An Adoption Story. Marschell, Hannah, illus. 2010. 36p. pap. 14.95 *(978-1-60844-395-6(7))* Dog Ear Publishing, LLC.
Goldsmith, Mike. The Airport. Daubney, Kate, illus. 2015. (I Explore Ser.). (ENG.). 12p. (J). (gr. -1-k). bds. 6.95 *(978-1-4549-1495-2(5))* Sterling Publishing Co., Inc.
—Digging for Dinosaurs. Daubney, Kate, illus. 2015. (I Explore Ser.). (ENG.). 12p. (J). (gr. -1-k). bds. 6.95 *(978-1-4549-1501-0(3))* Sterling Publishing Co., Inc.
—Discover Science: Materials. 2012. (Discover Science Ser.). (ENG., Illus.). 56p. (J). (gr. -1-3). 9.99 *(978-0-7534-6781-7(X),* 9780753467817, Kingfisher) Roaring Brook Pr.
Gomez, Yuliana. UmiCar's Big Race/la Gran Carrera de UmiCar (Team Umizoomi) Random House, illus. 2014. (Pictureback Ser.). (ENG.). 24p. (J). (gr. -1-2). 3.99 *(978-0-385-38437-7(8),* Random Hse. Bks. for Young Readers) Random Hse. Children's Bks.
Gomi, Taro. I Know Numbers! 2017. (ENG., Illus.). 40p. (J). (gr. -1-k). 15.99 ***(978-1-4521-5918-8(1))*** Chronicle Bks. LLC.
Gonyea, Mark. Monkey Suit. 2015. (ENG., Illus.). 28p. (J). (-k). bds. 10.95 *(978-1-57687-772-2(8),* powerHouse Bks.) powerHouse Cultural Entertainment, Inc.
The Good Samaritan. 2014. (Illus.). 24p. (J). *(978-1-84898-934-4(2),* TickTock Books) Octopus Publishing Group.
Goodhart, Pippa. House that Jack Built. Parker, Andy, illus. 2004. (ENG.). 24p. (J). lib. bdg. 23.65 *(978-1-59646-700-2(2))* Dingles & Co.
—Just Imagine. Sharrat, Nick, illus. 2014. 32p. (J). 12.99 *(978-1-61067-343-3(3))* Kane Miller.
Goodings, Christina. Guess Who? Noah's Ark: A Flip-The-Flap Book. Muss, Angela, illus. 2014. (ENG.). 6p. (J). (— 1). bds. 9.99 *(978-0-7459-6496-6(6))* Lion Hudson PLC GBR. Dist: Independent Pubs. Group.
Goodspeed, Judy. Saddle Up. 2007. (Illus.). 24p. (J). (ENG.). 14.99 *(978-0-9794660-7-6(5));* 24.99 *(978-0-9794660-0-7(8));* per. 12.99 *(978-0-9794660-1-4(6))* Dragonfly Publishing, Inc.
Gooly & Campbell Books Staff. Happy Families. Hyun, Kim, illus. 2015. (Chat About Ser.). (ENG.). 22p. (J). (— 1). bds. 9.99 ***(978-1-4472-7729-3(5))*** Pan Macmillan GBR. Dist: Independent Pubs. Group.
Gooly, Gooly, et al. Best Friends. Hyun, Kim, illus. 2015. (Chat About Ser.). (ENG.). 22p. (J). (— 1). bds. 9.99 ***(978-1-4472-7730-9(9))*** Pan Macmillan GBR. Dist: Independent Pubs. Group.
Gorbachev, Valeri. Big Little Hippo. 2017. (ENG., Illus.). 40p. (J). (gr. -1). 14.95 *(978-1-4549-1906-3(X))* Sterling Publishing Co., Inc.
—Two Little Chicks Go to School. 2011. (ENG., Illus.). 28p. (J). (gr. -1-3). 6.95 *(978-0-7358-4027-0(X))* North-South Bks., Inc.
Gorbachev, Valeri, illus. Goldilocks & the Three Bears. 2015. (ENG.). 40p. (J). 15.95 *(978-0-7358-4211-3(6))* North-South Bks., Inc.
Gordon, Gordon Coyle. Do Princesses Wear Hiking Boots? 2016. (ENG., Illus.). 32p. (J). (gr. -1-1). bds. 7.95 *(978-1-63076-164-6(8))* Taylor Trade Publishing.
Gordon, Lynn, et al. Circus Fantastico. 2010. (ENG., Illus.). 38p. (J). (gr. k-3). 16.99 *(978-0-7407-9199-4(0))* Andrews McMeel Publishing.
Gorey, Jill & Haller, Nancy. Pups of the Spirit, 1 vol. Melmon, Deborah, illus. 2015. (ENG.). 22p. (J). bds. 9.99 *(978-0-310-74798-7(8))* Zonderkidz.
Gorgas, Paula Blais. The Perfect Purple Present. l.t. ed. 2007. (Illus.). 24p. (J). 24.99 *(978-0-9794660-4-5(0));* per. 12.99 *(978-0-9794660-5-2(9))* Dragonfly Publishing, Inc.
Goscinny, René & Sempé, Jean-Jacques. Nicholas in Trouble. Bell, Anthea, tr. from FRE. 2013. (ENG., Illus.). 128p. pap. *(978-0-7148-6686-4(5))* Phaidon Pr., Inc.
Goss, Shelia M. & Hughes, Vi. Once upon a Bathtime, 1 vol. Shefrin, Sima Elizabeth, illus. 2011. (ENG.). 32p. (J). (gr. -1-k). 17.95 *(978-1-896580-54-8(8))* Tradewind Bks. CAN. Dist: Orca Bk. Pubs. USA.
Gottlieb, Suzanne. What Is Red? Bobri, Vladimir, illus. 2016. (ENG.). 24p. (J). 20.00 *(978-1-85124-458-4(1))* Bodleian Library GBR. Dist: Chicago Distribution Ctr.
Graffito Books Staff & Helm, Zebedee. Dogs of the World: Ultimate Guide Books to Everything! Helm, Zebedee, illus. 2012. (ENG., Illus.). 32p. (J). (gr. k-2). 14.99 *(978-0-9560284-3-3(8))* Korero Books LLP GBR. Dist: Independent Pubs. Group.
Graham, Alistair. Full Moon Soup. Graham, Alistair, illus. 2003. (Full Moon Soup & Full Moon Afloat Ser.). (Illus.). 32p. (YA). pap. *(978-1-85602-071-8(1),* Pavilion Children's Books) Pavilion Bks.
Graham, Bob. A Bus Called Heaven. Graham, Bob, illus. 2012. (ENG., Illus.). 40p. (J). (gr. -1-2). 16.99 *(978-0-7636-5893-9(6))* Candlewick Pr.
—The Silver Button. Graham, Bob, illus. 2013. (ENG., Illus.). 32p. (J). (gr. -1-1). 16.99 *(978-0-7636-6437-4(5))* Candlewick Pr.
Graham, Cenesha. I Want to Help. 2011. 24p. pap. 14.56 *(978-1-4634-1803-8(5))* AuthorHouse.
Graham, Elspeth. Sandwich that Jack Made. Mould, Chris, illus. 2004. (ENG.). 24p. (J). lib. bdg. 23.65 *(978-1-59646-698-2(7))* Dingles & Co.
Graham, Judith A. The Didley-Doo's Go on an Adventure, 1 vol. 2009. 33p. pap. 24.95 *(978-1-60749-897-1(9))* America Star Bks.
Graham, Mark. Hello, I Am Fiona from Scotland. Sofilas, Mark, illus. 2014. (AV2 Fiction Readalong Ser.: Vol. 128). (ENG.). 32p. (J). (gr. -1-3). lib. bdg. 34.28 *(978-1-4896-2253-2(5),* AV2 by Weigl) Weigl Pubs., Inc.
Grahame, Kenneth & Williams, Nicholas. An Gwyns I'n Helyk. Shepard, Ernest H., illus. 2013. (COR.). 202p. pap. *(978-1-78201-029-6(7))* Evertype.
Grambling, Lois G. Can I Bring Woolly to the Library, Ms. Reeder? Love, Judy, illus. 2012. (Prehistoric Pets Ser.). (ENG.). 32p. (J). (gr. k-3). pap. 7.95 *(978-1-58089-282-7(5))* Charlesbridge Publishing, Inc.
Granfield, Linda. What Am I? Herbert, Jennifer, illus. 2007. (ENG.). 32p. (J). (gr. k-k). 15.95 *(978-0-88776-812-5(1),* Tundra Bks.) Tundra Bks. CAN. Dist: Penguin Random Hse. LLC.
Grant, Carolyn E. Maggie's Neighborhood. 2009. 24p. pap. 11.99 *(978-1-4389-7230-5(X))* AuthorHouse.

Grant, Carrie and David. Elephant's Birthday Bells: Jump up & Join In. Busby, Ailie, illus. 2013. 32p. (J). pap. 7.99 (978-1-61067-181-1(3)) Kane Miller.
—Lion's Speedy Sauce: Jump up & Join In. Busby, Ailie, illus. 2013. 32p. (J). pap. 7.99 (978-1-61067-180-4(5)) Kane Miller.
Grant, Jacob. Scaredy Kate. 2014. (ENG., Illus.). 32p. (J). (gr. -1-k). pap. 7.99 (978-1-4380-0364-1(1)) Barron's Educational Series, Inc.
Gravett, Emily. Dogs. Gravett, Emily, illus. 2010. (ENG., Illus.). 32p. (J). (gr. -1-1). 15.99 (978-1-4169-8703-1(7), Simon & Schuster Bks. For Young Readers) Simon & Schuster Bks. For Young Readers.
Gray, Kes. Daisy Yuk! Sharratt, Nick, illus. 2016. (Daisy Picture Bks.: 4). (ENG.). 32p. (J). (gr. -1-k). pap. 11.99 **(978-1-78295-647-1(6)**, Red Fox) Random House Children's Books GBR. Dist: Independent Pubs. Group.
—Get Well Friends: Momo Goes Flying! McQuillan, Mary, illus. 2015. (Get Well Friends Ser.). (ENG.). 32p. (J). (gr. -1-k). pap. 9.99 (978-1-4449-0029-3(3)) Hodder & Stoughton GBR. Dist: Hachette Bk. Group.
—Nuddy Ned. Parsons, Garry, illus. 2014. (ENG.). 32p. (J). (gr. -1-k). 13.99 (978-1-4088-3659-0(9), 9781408836590, Bloomsbury USA Childrens) Bloomsbury Publishing USA.
—Tiger Ways. Sharratt, Nick, illus. 2016. (Daisy Picture Bks.: 6). (ENG.). 32p. (J). (gr. -1-k). pap. 11.99 **(978-1-78295-649-5(2)**, Red Fox) Random House Children's Books GBR. Dist: Independent Pubs. Group.
—Zippo the Super Hippo. Dyson, Nikki, illus. 2015. (ENG.). 32p. (J). (gr. -1-2). 16.99 **(978-1-4472-7990-7(5))** Pan Macmillan GBR. Dist: Independent Pubs. Group.
Gray, Kes & Sharratt, Nick. Daisy - Really, Really. 2016. (Daisy Picture Bks.: 2). (ENG., Illus.). 32p. (J). (gr. -1-k). pap. 11.99 **(978-1-78295-646-4(8)**, Red Fox) Random House Children's Books GBR. Dist: Independent Pubs. Group.
Gray, Libba Moore. Is There Room on the Feather Bed? 2004. (Illus.). (J). (gr. -1-2). spiral bd. (978-0-616-04555-8(7)); spiral bd. (978-0-616-03037-0(1)) Canadian National Institute for the Blind/Institut National Canadien pour les Aveugles.
Greaves, Margaret. The Mice of Nibbling Village. Pinkney, Jane, illus. 2011. (ENG.). 32p. (J). (gr. -1-k). 14.99 (978-1-84365-189-5(0)) National Trust, Aylesbury GBR. Dist: Independent Pubs. Group.
Green, Alison. The Fox in the Dark. Allwright, Deborah, illus. 2012. (ENG.). 32p. (J). (gr. -1-1). pap. 7.95 (978-1-58925-437-4(6)) Tiger Tales.
Green, Jen. Big Fantastic Earth. 2016. (Illus.). 96p. (J). (978-1-5182-1730-2(3)) Dorling Kindersley Publishing, Inc.
Green, Katie May. Seen & Not Heard. Green, Katie May, illus. 2015. (ENG., Illus.). 32p. (J). (gr. k-3). 15.99 (978-0-7636-7612-4(8)) Candlewick Pr.
Green, Ruth, illus. Stanley's Plan. 2015. (ENG.). 32p. (J). (gr. -1-3). 16.95 (978-1-84976-305-9(4)) Tate Publishing, Ltd. GBR. Dist: Abrams, Inc.
Greenberg, Carmel. Who Stole Pop Pop's Underwear? Jennings, Randy, illus. 2009. (ENG.). 46p. 16.99 (978-0-615-20924-1(6), d1f87490-1e8c-4369-845e-33a85fc9fd96) Kicks and Giggles Today.
Greenberg, David E. The Ugly Brown Pear. 2010. 40p. pap. 12.96 (978-0-557-28055-1(9)) Lulu Pr., Inc.
Greenberg, Nicki. My Dog Dash. 2016. (ENG.). 32p. (J). (gr. -1-1). 19.99 **(978-1-76011-067-3(1))** Allen & Unwin AUS. Dist: Independent Pubs. Group.
—The Naughtiest Reindeer. Greenberg, Nicki, illus. 2014. (ENG., Illus.). 32p. (J). (gr. -1-k). 14.99 (978-1-74331-304-6(7)) Allen & Unwin AUS. Dist: Independent Pubs. Group.
Greenberg, Nicki. The Naughtiest Reindeer Goes South. 2017. (Naughtiest Reindeer Ser.: 3). (ENG.). 32p. (J). (gr. -1-1). 12.99 **(978-1-76029-311-6(3))** Allen & Unwin AUS. Dist: Independent Pubs. Group.
Greenleaf, E. Who Wants to Nap? (Illus.). 32p. (J). (gr. 2-3). lib. bdg. 9.95 (978-0-87783-050-4(9)) Oddo Publishing, Inc.
Gresham, Xanthe. The Princess & the Pea. Clara, Miss, illus. 2013. (ENG.). 40p. (J). 17.99 (978-1-84686-905-1(6)) Barefoot Bks., Inc.
Grey, Mini. Traction Man Is Here! 2012. lib. bdg. 18.40 (978-0-606-26385-6(3), Turtleback) Turtleback Bks.
Griffith, Linda Hill, illus. Best Ever Ring Bearer. 2010. (ENG.). 24p. 10.99 (978-1-4022-3818-5(5)) Sourcebooks, Inc.
—Most Special Flower Girl. 2010. (ENG.). 24p. 10.99 (978-1-4022-3817-8(7)) Sourcebooks, Inc.
Grill, William, illus. Shackleton's Journey. 2014. (ENG.). 80p. (J). (gr. -1-2). 24.00 (978-1-909263-10-9(9)) Flying Eye Bks. GBR. Dist: Consortium Bk. Sales & Distribution.
Grillo, Trine. I'm Not Afraid of That. 2011. (Illus.). 44p. (J). pap. 18.99 (978-1-59092-761-8(3)) Blue Forge Pr.
Grimm, J. & W. Sleeping Beauty. Dusikova, Maja, illus. 2012. (ENG.). 32p. (J). (gr. -1-3). 17.95 (978-0-7358-4087-4(3)) North-South Bks., Inc.
—The Three Little Pigs. Watts, Edith M B. B., Bernadette, illus. 2012. (ENG.). 32p. (J). 16.95 (978-0-7358-4058-4(X)) North-South Bks., Inc.
Grimm, Jacob & Grimm, Wilhelm. Little Red Riding Hood. Sourdais, Clémentine, illus. 2014. (ENG.). 28p. (J). (gr. -1-3). 16.95 (978-3-89955-723-7(9)) Die Gestalten Verlag DEU. Dist: Penguin Random Hse. LLC.
Grimm, Jacob & Grimm, Wilhelm K. Snow White. Garcia, Camille Rose, illus. 2012. (ENG.). 80p. 14.99 (978-0-06-206446-2(0), Collins Design) HarperCollins Pubs.
Grimm, Jacob, et al. Hansel & Gretel. Rowe, Louise, illus. 2nd ed. 2014. (Fairytale Pop-Ups Ser.). (ENG.). 16p. (J). (gr. k-2). 27.99 (978-1-85707-858-9(6)) Tango Bks. GBR. Dist: Independent Pubs. Group.
Grimm, Jeanette. Living with Grandma & Grandpa. 2010. 24p. pap. 15.99 (978-1-4535-5573-6(0)) Xlibris Corp.
Grindley, Sally. Help! Utton, Peter, illus. 2015. (Kipper Ser.). (ENG.). 32p. (J). (gr. -1-k). 14.99 (978-1-4449-2473-2(7)) Hodder & Stoughton GBR. Dist: Hachette Bk. Group.
—Keep Out! Bears About! 2015. (ENG., Illus.). 32p. (J). (gr. -1-k). pap. 12.99 (978-1-4449-1416-0(2)) Hodder & Stoughton GBR. Dist: Hachette Bk. Group.
Grindley, Sally & Foreman, Michael. La Playa de Pedro. 2003.Tr. of Peter's Place. (SPA., Illus.). 32p. (J). (gr. 1-3). 19.99 (978-84-261-3314-4(2)) Juventud, Editorial ESP. Dist: Lectorum Pubns., Inc.

Grossman, Linda Sky & Toronto Child Abuse Centre Staff. I'M a Great Little Kid, Set. (ENG., Illus.). 1p. 79.95 (978-1-896764-75-7(4)) Second Story Pr. CAN. Dist: Orca Bk. Pubs. USA.
—I'm a Great Little Kid, Set. (ENG., Illus.). 1p. pap. 39.95 (978-1-896764-74-0(6)) Second Story Pr. CAN. Dist: Orca Bk. Pubs. USA.
Groves, Julia, illus. Animal Babies in the Forest! 2016. (Animal Babies Ser.: 4). (ENG.). 14p. (J). bds. (978-1-84643-878-3(0)) Child's Play International Ltd.
Grylls, Pinny. The Very Hopeless Sheepdog. Wellesley, Rosie, illus. 2014. (ENG.). 32p. (J). (gr. -1-1). pap. 11.99 (978-1-84365-219-9(6), Pavilion) Pavilion Bks. GBR. Dist: Independent Pubs. Group.
Guarnaccia, Steven. Cinderella: A Fashionable Tale. 2013. (ENG., Illus.). 32p. (J). (gr. k-2). 19.95 (978-1-4197-0986-9(0), Abrams Bks. for Young Readers) Abrams, Inc.
Guerras, Safia. Lou Lou. 2012. (Illus.). 40p. (978-1-78132-021-1(7)); pap. (978-1-78132-019-8(5)) SilverWood Bks.
Guess Who? Christmas: A Flip-The-Flap Book. 2015. (ENG., Illus.). 6p. (J). (— 1). bds. 9.99 (978-0-7459-6408-9(7)) Lion Hudson PLC GBR. Dist: Independent Pubs. Group.
Guettier, Bénédicte. At the Circus. 2011. (Funny Faces Ser.). (Illus.). 14p. bds. (978-1-84089-678-7(7)) Zero to Ten, Ltd.
—Dinosaur Dinners. 2011. (Funny Faces Ser.). (Illus.). 14p. bds. (978-1-84089-677-0(9)) Zero to Ten, Ltd.
Gugler, Laurel Dee. There's a Billy Goat in the Garden. Beaton, Clare, illus. 2003. 32p. (J). (gr. -1-2). 14.99 (978-1-84148-089-3(4)) Barefoot Bks., Inc.
Guibert, Emmanuel. Thunder Horse. 2013. (Ariol Graphic Novels Ser.). (ENG., Illus.). 124p. (J). (gr. 1-5). pap. 12.99 (978-1-59707-412-4(8), 9781597074124) Papercutz.
Guillain, Adam. Marshmallows for Martians. Guillain, Charlotte & Wildish, Lee, illus. 2nd ed. 2014. (George's Amazing Adventures Ser.). (ENG.). 32p. (J). (-k). pap. 11.99 (978-1-4052-6681-9(3)) Egmont Bks., Ltd. GBR. Dist: Independent Pubs. Group.
Guillain, Adam & Guillain, Charlotte. Doughnuts for a Dragon. Wildish, Lee, illus. 2nd ed. 2015. (George's Amazing Adventures Ser.). (ENG.). 32p. (J). (gr. -1-k). pap. 10.99 (978-1-4052-7054-0(3)) Egmont Bks., Ltd. GBR. Dist: Independent Pubs. Group.
—School Gremlins. Chatterton, Chris, illus. 2017. (ENG.). 18p. (J). (gr. -1-k). pap. 10.99 **(978-1-4052-7714-3(9))** Egmont Bks., Ltd. GBR. Dist: Independent Pubs. Group.
Guillain, Adam & Guillain, Charlotte. Socks for Santa. Wildish, Lee, illus. 2nd ed. 2016. (George's Amazing Adventures Ser.). (ENG.). 32p. (J). (gr. -1-k). pap. 10.99 (978-1-4052-7055-7(1)) Egmont Bks., Ltd. GBR. Dist: Independent Pubs. Group.
Guillain, Charlotte & Guillain, Adam. Muffins for Mummies. Wildish, Lee, illus. 2017. (George's Amazing Adventures Ser.). (ENG.). 32p. (J). (gr. -1-k). pap. 10.99 **(978-1-4052-7363-3(1))** Egmont Bks., Ltd. GBR. Dist: Independent Pubs. Group.
Guillain, Charlotte & Guillain, Adam. Spaghetti with the Yeti. Wildish, Lee, illus. 2nd ed. 2014. (George's Amazing Adventures Ser.). (ENG.). 32p. (J). (gr. -1-k). pap. 10.99 (978-1-4052-6351-1(2)) Egmont Bks., Ltd. GBR. Dist: Independent Pubs. Group.
Gulliver, Amanda, illus. Pets. 2011. (Baby Rattle Bks.). 12p. (J). (gr. -1-k). 6.99 (978-0-7641-6392-0(2)) Barron's Educational Series, Inc.
—Underwater. 2011. (Baby Rattle Bks.). 12p. (J). (gr. -1-k). 6.99 (978-0-7641-6393-7(0)) Barron's Educational Series, Inc.
—Zoo. 2011. (Baby Rattle Bks.). 12p. (J). (gr. -1-k). 6.99 (978-0-7641-6394-4(9)) Barron's Educational Series, Inc.
Gunzi, Christiane. Colours. 2nd rev. ed. 2015. (ENG., Illus.). 34p. (J). 7.99 (978-1-906572-20-4(8)) Award Pubns. Ltd. GBR. Dist: Parkwest Pubns., Inc.
—Farm. 2nd rev. ed. 2015. (ENG., Illus.). 34p. (J). 7.95 (978-1-906572-28-0(3)) Award Pubns. Ltd. GBR. Dist: Parkwest Pubns., Inc.
—My Body. Murrell, Deborah, ed. 2015. (ENG., Illus.). 34p. (J). 7.99 (978-1-906572-22-8(4)) Award Pubns. Ltd. GBR. Dist: Parkwest Pubns., Inc.
—My Favourite Things. 2013. (ENG., Illus.). 6p. (J). bds. 7.95 (978-1-907604-37-9(5)) Award Pubns. Ltd. GBR. Dist: Parkwest Pubns., Inc.
—My Lovely Day. 2013. (ENG., Illus.). 6p. (J). bds. 7.95 (978-1-907604-36-2(7)) Award Pubns. Ltd. GBR. Dist: Parkwest Pubns., Inc.
—Opposites. Murrell, Deborah, ed. 2nd rev. ed. 2015. (ENG., Illus.). 34p. (J). 7.99 (978-1-906572-21-1(6)) Award Pubns. Ltd. GBR. Dist: Parkwest Pubns., Inc.
—Pets. 2nd rev. ed. 2015. (ENG., Illus.). 34p. (J). 7.99 (978-1-906572-13-6(5)) Award Pubns. Ltd. GBR. Dist: Parkwest Pubns., Inc.
—Zoo. Zwemmer, Dominic, ed. 2015. (ENG., Illus.). 34p. (J). 7.95 (978-1-906572-30-3(5)) Award Pubns. Ltd. GBR. Dist: Parkwest Pubns., Inc.
—1 2 3. 2015. (ENG., Illus.). 34p. (J). 7.99 (978-1-906572-18-1(6)) Award Pubns. Ltd. GBR. Dist: Parkwest Pubns., Inc.
Gunzi, Christiane. Colours. 2015. (ENG., Illus.). 6p. (J). 7.99 (978-1-907604-95-9(2)) Award Pubns. Ltd. GBR. Dist: Parkwest Pubns., Inc.
—Fluffy Babies. 2006. (Feels Real Bks.). (ENG., Illus.). 10p. (J). (gr. -1). bds. 6.99 (978-0-7641-5948-0(8)) Barron's Educational Series, Inc.
—Little Ponies: A Feels Real Book to Touch & Share. 2015. (ENG., Illus.). 8p. (J). 9.99 (978-1-909763-10-4(1)) Award Pubns. Ltd. GBR. Dist: Parkwest Pubns., Inc.
—Numbers. 2015. (ENG., Illus.). 6p. (J). 7.99 (978-1-907604-94-2(4)) Award Pubns. Ltd. GBR. Dist: Parkwest Pubns., Inc.
—On the Farm. 2015. (ENG., Illus.). 8p. (J). 9.99 (978-1-909763-09-8(8)) Award Pubns. Ltd. GBR. Dist: Parkwest Pubns., Inc.
—On the Farm. 2005. (Feels Real Bks.). (ENG., Illus.). 10p. (J). bds. 6.99 (978-0-7641-5856-8(2)) Barron's Educational Series, Inc.

—Under the Sea. 2006. (Feels Real Bks.). (ENG., Illus.). 10p. (J). (gr. -1). bds. 6.99 (978-0-7641-5951-0(8)) Barron's Educational Series, Inc.
Gurney, Stella. Not so Silly Sausage. Million, Liz, illus. 2011. 32p. pap. (978-1-84089-707-4(4)) Zero to Ten, Ltd.
Gürth, Per-Henrik. Canada in Colours. Gürth, Per-Henrik, illus. 2013. (ENG., Illus.). 24p. (J). (gr. -1 — 1). pap. 7.95 (978-1-55453-760-0(6)) Kids Can Pr., Ltd. CAN. Dist: Hachette Bk. Group.
—Snowy Sports: Ready, Set, Play! Gürth, Per-Henrik, illus. 2009. (ENG., Illus.). 24p. (J). (gr. -1-2). 14.95 (978-1-55337-367-4(7)) Kids Can Pr., Ltd. CAN. Dist: Hachette Bk. Group.
Guthrie, Woody. Enviarme a Ti, Level 2. Flor Ada, Alma, tr. Rosenberry, Vera, illus. 2003. (Dejame Leer Ser.). (SPA.). 8p. (J). (gr. -1-1). 6.50 (978-0-673-36301-5(5), Good Year Bks.) Celebration Pr.
Gutiérrez, Elisa & Owlkids Books Inc. Staff. Letter Lunch, 0 vols. 2014. (ENG., Illus.). 32p. (J). (gr. -1-2). 16.95 (978-1-77147-000-1(3), Owlkids) Owlkids Bks. Inc. CAN. Dist: Publishers Group West (PGW).
Guttiere, Benedicte. When Christmas Comes. 2011. (Funny Faces Ser.). (Illus.). 14p. bds. (978-1-84089-710-4(4)) Zero to Ten, Ltd.
Gyatso, Geshe Kelsang. What Is Buddhism? Buddhism for Children Level 3. 2013. (Buddhism for Children Ser.). (ENG., Illus.). 32p. (J). (gr. 4-6). 8.95 (978-1-61606-023-7(9)) Tharpa Pubns. GBR. Dist: Ingram Publisher Services.
Hachler, Bruno & Muller, Birte. Farley Farts. 2014. (ENG., Illus.). 32p. (J). (gr. k-3). 14.95 (978-0-7358-4165-9(9)) North-South Bks., Inc.
Hader, Berta and Elmer. Mother Goose Picture Book. 2014. (ENG., Illus.). 160p. (J). (gr. -1). 25.00 (978-1-60660-054-2(0)) Dover Pubns., Inc.
Hadithi, Mwenye. Sleepy Cheetah. 2017. (African Animal Tales Ser.). (ENG., Illus.). 32p. (J). (gr. -1-k). pap. 7.99 (978-1-4449-2620-0(9)) Hachette Children's Group GBR. Dist: Hachette Bk. Group.
Haft, Sheryl. I Love You, Blankie. Massey, Jane, illus. 2015. (ENG.). 22p. (J). (gr. -1 — 1). bds. 8.99 (978-0-316-28356-4(8)) Little, Brown Bks. for Young Readers.
Hagin, Karen. Jeremy, the Giraffe Who Was Afraid of Heights. 2005. (J). lib. bdg. 19.95 (978-0-9754728-8-0(7)) Big Ransom Studio.
Hahm, Ji-seul. Prokofiev's Peter & the Wolf. Lupton, David, illus. 2016. (Music Storybooks Ser.). (ENG.). 44p. (gr. 3-6). 26.65 (978-1-925247-39-8(2), Big and SMALL) ChoiceMaker Pty. Ltd., The AUS. Dist: Lerner Publishing Group.
Hahn, Daniel. Happiness Is a Watermelon on Your Head. Dreis, Stella, illus. 2013. (ENG.). 40p. (J). (gr. k-2). pap. 9.99 (978-1-907912-05-4(3)) Phoenix Yard Bks. GBR. Dist: Independent Pubs. Group.
Hailes, Ronald. The Pink Rabbit. 2009. 24p. pap. 10.96 (978-1-4269-1456-0(3)) Trafford Publishing.
Hale, Rachael. Hugs & Kisses. 2012. (ENG., Illus.). 20p. (J). (gr. -1 — 1). bds. 6.99 (978-0-316-13063-9(X)) Little, Brown Bks. for Young Readers.
Hallowell, George & Holub, Joan. Wagons Ho! Avril, Lynne, illus. 2014. (AV2 Fiction Readalong Ser.: Vol. 153). (ENG.). 32p. (J). (gr. -1-3). lib. bdg. 34.28 (978-1-4896-2389-8(2), AV2 by Weigl) Weigl Pubs., Inc.
Hamernik, Cathy. What Do You See? 2008. 24p. pap. 16.50 (978-1-60693-388-6(4), Strategic Bk. Publishing) Strategic Book Publishing & Rights Agency (SBPRA).
Hamilton, Benny. The Goat in the Coat. 2010. 36p. (J). pap. 21.95 (978-1-4327-4884-5(X)) Outskirts Pr., Inc.
Hamilton, Kersten. Blue Boat. Petrone, Valeria, illus. 2016. (ENG.). 26p. (J). (-k). bds. 7.99 (978-1-101-99853-3(9), Viking Books for Young Readers) Penguin Young Readers Group.
—Red Truck. Petrone, Valeria, illus. 2012. (ENG.). 24p. (J). (gr. -1-k). bds. 6.99 (978-0-670-01467-5(2), Viking Books for Young Readers) Penguin Young Readers Group.
Hamilton, Virginia. The People Could Fly: The Picture Book. Dillon, Leo & Dillon, Diane, illus. 2015. (ENG.). 32p. (J). (gr. k-12). 7.99 (978-0-553-50780-5(X), Dragonfly Bks.) Random Hse. Children's Bks.
—The People Could Fly: The Picture Book. 2015. lib. bdg. 18.40 (978-0-606-36377-8(7)) Turtleback Bks.
—The People Could Fly: The Picture Book. Dillon, Leo & Dillon, Diane, illus. movie tie-in ed. 2004. (ENG.). 32p. (J). (gr. k-12). 16.95 (978-0-375-82405-0(7), Knopf Bks. for Young Readers) Random Hse. Children's Bks.
Hammond, Charmaine. Toby, the Pet Therapy Dog, & His Hospital Friends. Prevac, Rose Anne, illus. 2011. (ENG.). 36p. (J). pap. 12.99 (978-0-9836045-0-1(9), Kendahl Hse. Pr.) Youngs, Bettie Bks.
Hancocks, Helen. Penguin in Peril. Hancocks, Helen, illus. 2014. (ENG., Illus.). 32p. (J). (gr. -1-2). 15.99 (978-0-7636-7159-4(2), Templar) Candlewick Pr.
Handford, Martin. Where's Waldo? the Incredible Paper Chase. 2011. (Where's Waldo? Ser.). (ENG., Illus.). 24p. (J). (gr. k-4). pap. 7.99 (978-0-7636-4725-4(X)) Candlewick Pr.
Hannah, Vickie. There's A Schnoozle in My Closet. 2004. (J). lib. bdg. 19.95 (978-0-9754728-4-2(4)) Big Ransom Studio.
Hansen, Doug & Aesop. Aesop in California. 2013. (J). 16.95 (978-1-59714-235-9(2)) Heyday.
Hansen, Nichole. Kids Count. Hansen, Tevin, illus. 2015. 44p. (J). pap. 9.49 (978-1-941429-18-1(1)) Handersen Publishing.
Hansen, Tevin & Hansen, Nichole. The Thumb Book. Hansen, Tevin, illus. 2015. (ENG., Illus.). 48p. pap. 9.99 (978-1-941429-21-1(1)) Handersen Publishing.
Hanson, Faye. Cinderella's Secret Diary. Hanson, Faye, illus. 2013. (ENG., Illus.). 24p. (J). (gr. 1-3). 19.99 (978-0-230-74204-8(1)) Pan Macmillan GBR. Dist: Independent Pubs. Group.
Hanson, P. H. My Granny's Purse. 2013. (ENG., Illus.). 16p. (J). (gr. -1-1). bds. 14.95 (978-0-7611-7742-5(6), 17742) Workman Publishing Co., Inc.
Harcourt School Publishers Staff. Horizons Big Book Collection. 2nd ed. 2003. (Illus.). (gr. 1). pap. 840.00 (978-0-15-337573-6(6)); (gr. 2). pap. 840.00 (978-0-15-337581-1(7)) Harcourt Schl. Pubs.

—Horizons Big Book Collection Unit 1. 2nd ed. 2003. (Illus.). pap. 140.00 (978-0-15-337574-3(4)); pap. 140.00 (978-0-15-337812-6(3)) Harcourt Schl. Pubs.
—Horizons Big Book Collection Unit 2. 2nd ed. 2003. (Illus.). pap. 140.00 (978-0-15-337813-3(1)); pap. 140.00 (978-0-15-337575-0(2)) Harcourt Schl. Pubs.
—Horizons Big Book Collection Unit 3. 2nd ed. 2003. (Illus.). pap. 140.00 (978-0-15-337577-4(9)); pap. 140.00 (978-0-15-337814-0(X)) Harcourt Schl. Pubs.
—Horizons Big Book Collection Unit 4. 2nd ed. 2003. (Illus.). pap. 140.00 (978-0-15-337578-1(7)); pap. 140.00 (978-0-15-337815-7(8)) Harcourt Schl. Pubs.
—Horizons Big Book Collection Unit 5. 2nd ed. 2003. (Illus.). pap. 140.00 (978-0-15-337579-8(5)); (J). pap. 140.00 (978-0-15-337816-4(6)) Harcourt Schl. Pubs.
—Horizons Big Book Collection Unit 6. 2nd ed. 2003. (Illus.). pap. 140.00 (978-0-15-337580-4(9)); pap. 140.00 (978-0-15-337817-1(4)) Harcourt Schl. Pubs.
Hargreaves, Roger. Mr. Muddle. 2010. (Mr. Men & Little Miss Ser.). (ENG.). 32p. (J). (gr. -1-2). mass mkt. 3.99 (978-0-8431-9958-1(X), Price Stern Sloan) Penguin Young Readers Group.
Harker, Jillian. I Wish... McLean, Gill, illus. 2010. (Picture Books Ser.). (J). (gr. -1-k). bds. (978-1-4075-9462-0(1)) Parragon, Inc.
Harman, Jax. A Big Fat Naughty Cat. 2016. (ENG.). 22p. (J). pap. 14.95 (978-1-78612-470-8(X), cfa1b37e-ba05-40bd-aae8-4168ad431174) Austin, Stan AUS. Dist: Bookmasters Distribution.
Harper, Charise Mericle. Cupcake. Harper, Charise Mericle, illus. 2010. (ENG., Illus.). 32p. (J). (gr. -1-1). 14.99 (978-1-4231-1897-8(9)) Hyperion Pr.
—Go! Go! Go! Stop! 2015. (ENG.). 32p. (J). (-k). bds. 7.99 (978-0-553-53391-0(6), Knopf Bks. for Young Readers) Random Hse. Children's Bks.
Harper, Jamie. Miss Mingo Weathers the Storm. Harper, Jamie, illus. (ENG., Illus.). 40p. (J). (gr. -1-3). 2017. 6.99 **(978-0-7636-9514-9(9))** 2012. 15.99 (978-0-7636-4931-9(7)) Candlewick Pr.
Harriman, Marinell & Harriman, Robert. A Myriad of Minstrels. Harriman, Marinell & Harriman, Robert, illus. (Illus.). 32p. (Orig.). (J). (gr. 5-7). pap. 3.50 (978-0-940920-00-2(X)) Drollery Pr.
Harris, Amber. Bingo Did It! Hoyt, Ard, illus. 2016. (Wisteria Jane Book Ser.). (ENG.). 32p. (J). (gr. -1-3). 16.95 (978-1-60554-491-5(4)) Redleaf Pr.
Harrison, Paul. Billy on the Ball. Raga, Silvia, illus. 2010. 32p. pap. (978-1-84089-634-3(5)) Zero to Ten, Ltd.
—Elephant Rides Again. Million, Liz, illus. 2009. (Get Ready (Windmill Books) Ser.). 32p. (J). (gr. k-2). lib. bdg. 22.60 (978-1-60754-259-9(5)) Windmill Bks.
—Undersea Adventure. Nascimbeni, Barbara, illus. 2011. 32p. pap. (978-1-84089-638-1(8)) Zero to Ten, Ltd.
Harrod-Eagles, Cynthia. I Love You to the Moon. Poh, Jennie, illus. 2014. (ENG.). 22p. (J). (gr. -1). bds. 8.95 (978-1-58925-642-2(5)) Tiger Tales.
—It's Spring Time! Baccala, Gladys, illus. 2013. (ENG.). 16p. (gr. -1). bds. 8.95 (978-1-58925-639-2(5)) Tiger Tales.
Hart, Caryl. Catch That Rat. McLaughlin, Tom, illus. 2013. (ENG.). 32p. (J). pap. 8.99 (978-1-84738-931-2(7), Simon & Schuster Children's) Simon & Schuster, Ltd. GBR. Dist: Simon & Schuster, Inc.
—Don't Put Your Pants on Your Head, Fred! Hodgkinson, Leigh, illus. 2012. (ENG.). 32p. (J). (gr. -1-k). pap. 9.99 (978-1-4083-0917-9(3)) Hodder & Stoughton GBR. Dist: Hachette Bk. Group.
—How to Catch a Dragon. Eaves, Ed, illus. 2014. (ENG.). 32p. pap. 8.99 (978-0-85707-959-6(X), Simon & Schuster Children's) Simon & Schuster, Ltd. GBR. Dist: Simon & Schuster, Inc.
—The Princess & the Presents. Warburton, Sarah, illus. 2014. (ENG.). 32p. (J). (gr. -1-2). 16.99 (978-0-7636-7398-7(6), Nosy Crow) Candlewick Pr.
—Whiffy Wilson: The Wolf Who Wouldn't Wash. Lord, Leonie, illus. 2012. (ENG.). 32p. (J). (gr. -1-k). pap. 10.99 (978-1-4083-0919-3(X)) Hodder & Stoughton GBR. Dist: Hachette Bk. Group.
Hartman, Bob. The Sheep in Wolf's Clothing. Raglin, Tim, illus. 2014. (ENG.). 28p. (J). (gr. k-2). 16.99 (978-0-7459-6515-4(6)) Lion Hudson PLC GBR. Dist: Independent Pubs. Group.
Hartmann, Annabelle. As Big As a Mountain. 2003. (Illus.). 32p. (YA). (978-1-84365-001-0(0), Pavilion Children's Books) Pavilion Bks.
Hartt-Sussman, Heather. Noni Speaks Up. Côté, Geneviève, illus. 2016. (ENG.). 24p. (J). (gr. -1-2). 16.99 (978-1-77049-839-6(7), Tundra Bks.) Tundra Bks. CAN. Dist: Penguin Random Hse. LLC.
Harvey, Damian. Mr. Fox's Socks. Rescek, Sanja, illus. 2004. (ENG.). 16p. (J). lib. bdg. 23.65 (978-1-59646-678-4(2)) Dingles & Co.
—Snail's Legs. Paul, Korky, illus. 2015. (ENG.). 32p. (J). (gr. -1-2). pap. 8.99 (978-1-84780-712-0(7), Frances Lincoln) Quarto Publishing Group UK GBR. Dist: Hachette Bk. Group.
Harwood, Beth. One Snowy Night. Ronchi, Susanna, illus. 2005. 12p. (J). (978-1-84011-627-4(7)) Templar Publishing.
Haskamp, Steven, illus. Five Silly Monkeys. 2006. (ENG.). 12p. (J). (gr. -1-k). 12.95 (978-1-58117-460-1(8), Intervisual/Piggy Toes) Bendon, Inc.
Hasselius, Michelle M. & Tucker, Rosalyn. Presidential Biographies, 1 vol. 2014. (Presidential Biographies Ser.). (ENG.). 24p. (gr. k-1). lib. bdg. 79.95 (978-1-4765-9623-5(9), Pebble Plus) Capstone Press of Coughlan Cos.
Hastings, Derek. Penguins - Pb: A Portrait of the Animal World. 2013. (Portrait of the Animal World Ser.). (Illus.). 72p. pap. 9.95 (978-1-59764-325-2(4)) New Line Bks.
Hatkoff, Juliana, et al. Winter's Tail: How One Little Dolphin Learned to Swim Again. 2011. (ENG.). 40p. (J). (gr. -1-3). pap. 6.99 (978-0-545-34830-0(7), Scholastic Paperbacks) Scholastic, Inc.
Haugen, Matt. I Wanna Be a Dinosaur! Mirocha, Stephanie, illus. 2015. (ENG.). 32p. (J). (— 1). 16.95 (978-1-57999-999-5(9)) G I A Pubns., Inc.
Haughom, Lisa, illus. People, Places & Things. 2010. (J). (978-1-58865-541-7(5)) Kidsbooks, LLC.

Hawcock, David. Dinosaurs! Pop-Up Paper Designs. Hawcock, David, illus. 2015. (ENG., Illus.). 16p. (J). (gr. -1-k). 14.99 *(978-1-85707-804-6(7))* Tango Bks. GBR. Dist: Independent Pubs. Group.

—0-20. Hawcock, David, illus. 2015. (ENG., Illus.). 52p. (J). (gr. -1-k). 14.99 *(978-1-85707-898-5(5))* Tango Bks. GBR. Dist: Independent Pubs. Group.

Hawes, Alison. A Hot Day Pink a Band. Lee, Maxine, illus. 2016. (Cambridge Reading Adventures Ser.). (ENG.). 16p. pap. 6.56 *(978-1-316-60069-6(6))* Cambridge Univ. Pr.

—School Trip. Mould, Chris, illus. 2004. (ENG.). 24p. (J). lib. bdg. 23.65 *(978-1-59646-694-4(4))* Dingles & Co.

Hawes, Carlin. Abigail's Bunny. 2012. 16p. pap. 12.68 *(978-1-4669-5601-8(1))* Trafford Publishing.

Hawkins, Colin & Hawkins, Jacqui. Witch Pigs. 2006. (Illus.). 32p. (J). (gr. 1-2). 19.99 *(978-0-224-06467-5(3),* Jonathan Cape) Random Hse. GBR. Dist: Trafalgar Square Publishing.

Hawkins, Emily. Atlas of Miniature Adventures: A Pocket-Sized Collection of Small-scale Wonders - Because Bigger Isn't Always Better. Letherland, Lucy, illus. 2016. (Atlas Of Ser.). (ENG.). 64p. (J). 9.99 *(978-1-84780-909-4(X),* Wide Eyed Editions) Quarto Publishing Group UK GBR. Dist: Littlehampton Bk Services, Ltd.

—Good Night, Little Bunny: A Changing-Picture Book. Butler, John, illus. 2011. (ENG.). 14p. (J). (gr. -1-2). 12.99 *(978-0-7636-5263-0(6),* Templar) Candlewick Pr.

Haworth, Katie. Terrible Tim! Hughes, Laura, illus. 2016. (ENG.). 32p. (J). (gr. -1-3). 16.99 *(978-1-4998-0137-8(8))* Little Bee Books Inc.

Hayes, Felix. Doctor Monkey. Broadway, Hannah, illus. 2013. (Monkey & Robot Ser.). (ENG.). 32p. (J). (gr. -1-k). pap. 10.99 *(978-1-4088-0654-8(1),* 9781408806548, Bloomsbury USA Childrens) Bloomsbury Publishing USA.

—In the Snow. Broadway, Hannah, illus. 2014. (Monkey & Robot Ser.). (ENG.). 32p. (J). (gr. -1-k). pap. 10.99 *(978-1-4088-0656-2(8),* 9781408806562, Bloomsbury USA Childrens) Bloomsbury Publishing USA.

Hayes, Karel. The Autumn Visitors. 2015. (ENG., Illus.). 32p. (J). (gr. -1-3). 16.95 *(978-1-60893-454-6(3))* Down East Bks.

Hays, Anna Jane. Ready, Set, Preschool! Kelley, True, illus. 2016. (ENG.). 40p. (J). (gr. -1-2). 7.99 *(978-1-101-94024-2(7),* Dragonfly Bks.) Random Hse. Children's Bks.

Heapy, Teresa. Very Little Red Riding Hood. Heap, Sue, illus. 2014. (Very Little Ser.). (ENG.). 32p. (J). (gr. -1-3). 16.99 *(978-0-544-28000-7(8),* HMH Books For Young Readers) Houghton Mifflin Harcourt Publishing Co.

Heart, Sandra. Pemanna & Yerbo, the Toe-Tamals Family & Friends. 2011. 44p. pap. 21.99 *(978-1-4568-3296-4(4))* Xlibris Corp.

Hedderwick, Mairi. Island Stories. Hedderwick, Mairi, illus. 2010. (Katie Morag Ser.: 12). (ENG., Illus.). 32p. (J). (gr. k-2). pap. 19.99 *(978-1-84941-088-5(7),* Red Fox) Random House Children's Books GBR. Dist: Independent Pubs. Group.

—Katie Morag & the Big Boy Cousins. Hedderwick, Mairi, illus. 2010. (Katie Morag Ser.: 5). (ENG., Illus.). 32p. (J). (gr. k-2). pap. 12.99 *(978-1-84941-089-2(5),* Red Fox) Random House Children's Books GBR. Dist: Independent Pubs. Group.

Hegarty, Patricia. The River. Clulow, Hanako, illus. 2016. (J). 12.99 *(978-1-61067-468-3(5))* Kane Miller.

Heidecker, Samie. Who's Looking at Whom? Christmas, 1 vol. 2010. 38p. 24.95 *(978-1-4489-4855-0(X))* PublishAmerica, Inc.

Heiligman, Deborah. From Caterpillar to Butterfly. Weissman, Bari, illus. 2015. (Let's-Read-And-Find-Out Science 1 Ser.). (ENG.). 32p. (J). (gr. -1-3). pap. 6.99 *(978-0-06-238183-5(0))* HarperCollins Pubs.

Heiman, Laura. My Favorite Michael. Keen, Sophie, illus. 2009. (J). (gr. -1-2). 32p. 15.95 *(978-1-58925-086-4(9));* 24p. pap. 7.95 *(978-1-58925-419-0(8))* Tiger Tales.

Heinrichs, Cynthia. Mermaids. Lee, Jumin, illus. 2011. (ENG.). 32p. (J). (gr. -1-3). 16.95 *(978-1-897476-37-6(X))* Simply Read Bks. CAN. Dist: Ingram Publisher Services.

Helakoski, Leslie. Hoot & Honk Can't Sleep. 2017. (ENG., Illus.). 40p. (J). (gr. -1-k). 14.95 *(978-1-4549-2125-7(0))* Sterling Publishing Co., Inc.

Heling, Kathryn & Hembrook, Deborah. Clothesline Clues to Jobs People Do. Davies, Andy Robert, illus. 2014. (ENG.). 40p. (J). (gr. -1-2). pap. 7.95 *(978-1-58089-252-0(3))* Charlesbridge Publishing, Inc.

Hellen, N. Touch & Peek with Teddy & Me. 2003. (ENG., Illus.). 18p. (J). 9.99 *(978-1-85292-184-2(6),* Campbell Bks.) Pan Macmillan GBR. Dist: Trafalgar Square Publishing.

Hellsing, Lennart & Strøyer, Poul. The Cantankerous Crow. 2016. (ENG., Illus.). 28p. (J). (gr. k-1). 19.95 *(978-0-500-65079-0(9),* 565079) Thames & Hudson.

Helman, Andrea. 1, 2, 3 Moose. Wolfe, Art, photos by. 2016. (ENG., Illus.). 20p. (J). (— 1). bds. 9.99 *(978-1-63217-032-5(9),* Little Bigfoot) Sasquatch Bks.

Helmore, Jim & Wall, Karen. Stripy Horse - Off We Go! 2014. (Stripy Horse Ser.). (ENG., Illus.). 12p. (J). (gr. -1-k). bds. 7.99 *(978-1-4052-5746-6(6))* Egmont Bks., Ltd. GBR. Dist: Independent Pubs. Group.

Hemingway, Edward. Bad Apple: A Tale of Friendship. Hemingway, Edward, illus. 2015. (ENG., Illus.). 32p. (J). (gr. -1-k). 8.99 *(978-0-14-751748-7(6),* Puffin Books) Penguin Young Readers Group.

Hendra, Sue. Double Dave. 2016. (My Freaky Family Ser.). (ENG., Illus.). 32p. (J). (gr. -1-k). pap. 7.99 *(978-1-4449-2556-2(3))* Hachette Children's Group GBR. Dist: Hachette Bk. Group.

Hendricks, Brenda K. What's the Buzz, Bumbly Bee? Hendricks, Brenda K., illus. 2013. (Illus.). 30p. pap. 9.99 *(978-0-9826582-3-9(0))* Two Small Fish Pubns.

Heneghan, Judith. Brandon's So Bossy! Hughes, Jack, illus. 2016. (Dragon School Ser.). (ENG.). 32p. (J). (gr. -1-k). pap. ***(978-0-7502-8357-1(2),*** Wayland) Hachette Children's Group GBR. Dist: Hachette Bk. Group.

—Ruby's So Rude! Hughes, Jack, illus. 2016. (Dragon School Ser.). (ENG.). 32p. (J). (gr. -1-k). pap. ***(978-0-7502-8356-4(4),*** Wayland) Hachette Children's Group GBR. Dist: Hachette Bk. Group.

Henkes, Kevin. Birds Board Book. Dronzek, Laura, illus. 2017. 32p. (J). (gr. -1 — 1). bds. 7.99 *(978-0-06-257305-6(5),* Greenwillow Bks.) HarperCollins Pubs.

—A Box of Treats: Five Little Picture Books about Lilly & Her Friends. Henkes, Kevin, illus. 2004. (ENG., Illus.). (J). (gr. -1-k). pap. 14.99 *(978-0-06-073211-0(3),* Greenwillow Bks.) HarperCollins Pubs.

Herder, Ronald. Great Works for Piano Four Hands. Herder, Ronald, ed. 2012. (Dover Music for Piano Ser.). (ENG.). 224p. pap. 22.95 *(978-0-486-40173-7(1))* Dover Pubns., Inc.

Herz, Henry, et al. Mabel & the Queen of Dreams, 1 vol. Woods, Lisa, illus. 2016. (ENG.). 32p. (J). 16.99 *(978-0-7643-5137-2(0),* 9780764351372) Schiffer Publishing, Ltd.

Hest, Amy. Are You Sure, Mother Bear? Tobia, Lauren, illus. 2016. (ENG.). 32p. (J). (-k). 15.99 *(978-0-7636-7207-2(6))* Candlewick Pr.

—Charley's First Night. Oxenbury, Helen, illus. 2012. (ENG.). 32p. (J). (gr. -1-2). 15.99 *(978-0-7636-4055-2(7))* Candlewick Pr.

Hibbs, Gillian. Tilly's at Home Holiday. Hibbs, Gillian, illus. 2014. (Child's Play Library). (ENG., Illus.). 32p. (J). *(978-1-84643-601-7(X))* Child's Play International Ltd.

Hibbs, Linda. My First Book of Indonesian Words: An ABC Rhyming Book of Indonesian Language & Culture. Laud, Julia, illus. 2016. (ENG & IND.). 32p. (J). (gr. -1-3). 12.95 *(978-0-8048-4557-1(3))* Tuttle Publishing.

Hickox, Rebecca. Per & the Dala Horse. Gilbert, Yvonne, illus. 2003. 32p. (J). pap. 8.95 *(978-1-57534-034-0(8))* Skandisk, Inc.

Hicks, Barbara Jean. I Like Black & White. Prap, Lila, illus. 2006. 24p. (J). (gr. -1-3). 9.95 *(978-1-58925-056-7(7))* Tiger Tales.

Hicks, Barbara Jean & Disney Book Group Staff. A Sister More Like Me. Disney Storybook Artists Staff et al, illus. 2013. (ENG.). 32p. (J). (gr. 1-3). 15.99 *(978-1-4231-7014-3(8))* Disney Pr.

Hicks, Kelli. I Can Prove It! Investigating Science. 2012. (ENG.). 24p. (J). (gr. 4-5). pap. 8.95 *(978-1-61810-244-7(3))* Rourke Educational Media.

Hicks, Linda Ashman. Just Another Amazing Morning. Date not set. 32p. (J). (gr. -1-3). pap. 5.99 *(978-0-06-443712-7(4))* HarperCollins Pubs.

Hicks, Robert Z. Tommie Turtle's Secret. Rolseth, Ruthie, illus. 2007. (ENG.). 40p. (J). 16.95 *(978-0-9792031-0-7(4))* R.Z. Enterprises of Florida.

Higginbotham, Anastasia, illus. Death Is Stupid. 2016. (Ordinary Terrible Things Ser.). (ENG.). 66p. (J). (gr. -1-3). pap. 16.95 *(978-1-55861-925-8(9))* Feminist Pr. at The City Univ. of New York.

Higginson, Sheila Sweeny. Drip, Drop! the Rain Won't Stop! Your Turn, My Turn Reader. Yee, Josie, illus. 2010. (Playskool Ser.). (ENG.). 24p. (J). (gr. -1-k). pap. 3.99 *(978-1-4169-9046-8(1),* Simon Spotlight) Simon Spotlight.

Highlights for Children Editorial Staff, creator. Farm Time. 2016. (Highlights(tm) Find & Color Hidden Pictures(r) Ser.). (ENG.). 32p. (J). (gr. -1-k). pap. 5.99 *(978-1-62979-715-1(4),* Highlights) Boyds Mills Pr.

Hill, Cheryl E. R Is for Reading Books. Pierce, Dave G., illus. 2012. 56p. pap. 17.99 *(978-0-9859770-0-9(0))* N.O.A.H Bks.

Hill, Eric. Spot Says Please. Hill, Eric, illus. 2013. (Spot Ser.). (ENG., Illus.). 14p. (J). (gr. -1-k). bds. 5.99 *(978-0-7232-7832-0(6),* Warne) Penguin Young Readers Group.

—Spot's Christmas. Hill, Eric, illus. 2004. (Spot Ser.). (ENG., Illus.). 12p. (J). (gr. -1 — 1). bds. 5.99 *(978-0-399-24320-2(8),* Warne) Penguin Young Readers Group.

Hill, Monica. Rin Tin Tin & the Lost Indian. Greene, Hamilton, illus. 2011. 28p. pap. 35.95 *(978-1-258-00567-2(0))* Literary Licensing, LLC.

Hillenbrand, Will. Spring Is Here. Hillenbrand, Will, illus. 2012. (ENG., Illus.). 32p. (J). pap. 7.99 *(978-0-8234-2431-3(6))* Holiday Hse., Inc.

Hillenburg, Stephen. SpongeBob Comics: Book 1: Silly Sea Stories. 2017. (SpongeBob Comics Ser.). (ENG., Illus.). 112p. (J). (gr. 3-7). pap. 10.95 ***(978-1-4197-2319-3(7),*** Amulet Bks.) Abrams, Inc.

—SpongeBob Comics: Book 2: Aquatic Adventurers, Unite! 2017. (SpongeBob Comics Ser.). (ENG., Illus.). 112p. (J). (gr. 3-7). pap. 10.95 ***(978-1-4197-2320-9(0),*** Amulet Bks.) Abrams, Inc.

Hills, Tad. Rocket's Mighty Words. 2013. (ENG.). 22p. (J). (-k). bds. 10.99 *(978-0-385-37233-6(7),* Schwartz & Wade Bks.) Random Hse. Children's Bks.

Hindley, Judy. Eyes, Nose, Fingers, & Toes: A First Book All about You. Granström, Brita, illus. 2004. (ENG.). 24p. (J). (gr. k-k). bds. 6.99 *(978-0-7636-2383-8(0))* Candlewick Pr.

Hineman, Jonathan. Goodbye, Santa. Cruz, Cheryl, illus. 2013. 26p. (J). 16.95 *(978-1-60131-172-6(9))* Big Tent Bks.

Hines, Bethany. That's Not Funny, Bunny! Hines, Bethany, illus. 2017. (ENG., Illus.). 32p. (J). (gr. -1-k). pap. 9.99 ***(978-1-78445-104-2(5))*** Top That! Publishing PLC GBR. Dist: Independent Pubs. Group.

Hirschi, Ron. Ocean Seasons, 1 vol. Carlson, Kirsten, illus. 2007. (ENG.). 32p. (J). (gr. k-4). pap. 9.95 *(978-1-60718-863-6(5))* Arbordale Publishing.

Hirst, Daisy. The Girl with the Parrot on Her Head. Hirst, Daisy, illus. 2016. (ENG., Illus.). 40p. (J). (-k). 16.99 *(978-0-7636-7829-6(5))* Candlewick Pr.

Hirst, Daisy. Hilda & the Runaway Baby. Hirst, Daisy, illus. 2017. (ENG., Illus.). 32p. (J). (-k). 16.99 ***(978-0-7636-9490-6(8))*** Candlewick Pr.

Hiscock, Bruce. The Big Caribou Herd: Life in the Arctic National Wildlife Refuge. Hiscock, Bruce, illus. 2003. (ENG., Illus.). 32p. (J). (gr. 2-4). 16.95 *(978-1-59078-010-7(8))* Boyds Mills Pr.

History Speaks: Picture Books Plus Reader's Theater, 12 vols., Set. Incl. Alice Ray & the Salem Witch Trials. Knudsen, Shannon. Palmer, Ruth, illus. 2011. 27.93 *(978-0-7613-5879-4(X));* Annie Shapiro & the Clothing Workers' Strike. Brill, Marlene Targ. Akib, Jamel, illus. 2010. lib. bdg. 27.93 *(978-1-58013-672-3(9));* Benjamin Brown & the Great Steamboat Race. Jordan, Shirley. Chayka, Doug & Kemly, Kathleen, illus. 2011. lib. bdg. 27.93 *(978-1-58013-674-7(5));* Clara Morgan & the Oregon Trail Journey. Figley, Marthy Rhodes. Orback, Craig, illus. 2011. 27.93 *(978-0-7613-5878-7(1));* Ellen Craft's Escape from Slavery. Moore, Cathy. Braught, Mark, illus. 2010. lib. bdg. 27.93 *(978-0-7613-5875-6(7));* Enrique Esparza & the Battle of the Alamo. Brown, Susan Taylor. Reeves, Jeni, illus. 2010. lib. bdg. 27.93 *(978-0-8225-8566-4(9));* George Washington & the Story of the U. S. Constitution. Ransom, Candice. Reeves, Jeni, illus. 2011. 27.93 *(978-0-7613-5877-0(3));* John Greenwood's Journey to Bunker Hill. Figley, Marty Rhodes. Orback, Craig, illus. 2010. lib. bdg. 27.93 *(978-1-58013-673-0(7));* Johnny Moore & the Wright Brothers' Flying Machine. Schulz, Walter A. Bowles, Doug, illus. 2011. lib. bdg. 27.93 *(978-0-7613-5876-3(5));* Little Rock Nine Stand up for Their Rights. Lucas, Eileen. Gustavson, Adam, illus. 2011. lib. bdg. 27.93 *(978-0-7613-5874-9(9));* Lizzie Newton & the San Francisco Earthquake. Krensky, Stephen. Tugeau, Jeremy, illus. 2010. lib. bdg. 27.93 *(978-0-8225-9031-6(X));* 48p. (gr. 2-4)., Millbrook Pr. 2011. Set lib. bdg. 335.16 *(978-0-7613-5100-9(0))* Lerner Publishing Group.

Ho, Cammie. Butterfly Butterfly. 2016. (Life Cycle Bks.). (ENG., Illus.). 27p. (J). (gr. k-2). pap. 7.99 *(978-1-943241-03-3(1))* Phonic Monic.

—Duckling Duckling. 2016. (Life Cycle Bks.). (ENG., Illus.). 33p. (J). (gr. k-2). pap. 7.99 *(978-1-943241-00-2(7))* Phonic Monic.

—Ladybug Ladybug. 2016. (Life Cycle Bks.). (ENG., Illus.). 29p. (J). (gr. k-2). pap. 7.99 *(978-1-943241-02-6(3))* Phonic Monic.

—Parrot Parrot. 2016. (Life Cycle Bks.). (ENG., Illus.). 31p. (J). (gr. k-2). pap. 7.99 *(978-1-943241-04-0(X))* Phonic Monic.

—Tadpole Tadpole. 2016. (Life Cycle Bks.). (ENG., Illus.). 31p. (J). (gr. k-2). pap. 7.99 *(978-1-943241-01-9(5))* Phonic Monic.

Hobbie, Holly. Gem. 2012. (ENG., Illus.). 32p. (J). (gr. -1-3). 16.99 *(978-0-316-20334-0(3))* Little, Brown Bks. for Young Readers.

Hoberman, Mary Ann. You Read to Me, I'll Read to You: Very Short Fables to Read Together. Emberley, Michael, illus. 2013. (You Read to Me, I'll Read to You Ser.). (ENG.). 32p. (J). (gr. -1-3). 7.00 *(978-0-316-21847-4(2))* Little, Brown Bks. for Young Readers.

Hoberman, Mary Ann & Emberley, Michael. You Read to Me, I'll Read to You No. 2: Very Short Scary Tales to Read Together. Emberley, Michael, illus. 2009. (ENG., Illus.). 32p. (J). (gr. -1-3). pap. 7.99 *(978-0-316-04351-9(6))* Little Brown & Co.

Hodakov, Levi. I Go to the Ohel. Rosenfeld, D. L. & Leverton, Yossi, eds. Benenfeld, Rikki, illus. 2011. (Toddler Experience Ser.). 32p. (J). 10.95 *(978-1-929628-61-2(7))* Hachai Publishing.

Hodge, Deborah. Bear's Winter Party, 1 vol. Cinar, Lisa, illus. 2016. (ENG.). 32p. (J). (gr. -1-2). 16.95 *(978-1-55498-853-2(5))* Groundwood Bks. CAN. Dist: Publishers Group West (PGW).

Hodgkinson, Leigh. Goldilocks & Just One Bear. Hodgkinson, Leigh, illus. 2012. (ENG., Illus.). 32p. (J). (gr. -1-2). 15.99 *(978-0-7636-6172-4(4),* Nosy Crow) Candlewick Pr.

—Troll Swap. Hodgkinson, Leigh, illus. 2014. (ENG., Illus.). 32p. (J). (gr. -1-2). 15.99 *(978-0-7636-7101-3(0),* Nosy Crow) Candlewick Pr.

Hodgson, Jesse. Pongo. 2013. (ENG., Illus.). 32p. (J). (gr. -1-2). 16.95 *(978-1-909263-09-3(5))* Flying Eye Bks. GBR. Dist: Consortium Bk. Sales & Distribution.

Hodgson, Karen J. Hugh's Blue Day. Collins, Ross, illus. 2010. (ENG.). 32p. (J). (gr. -1-k). pap. 9.99 *(978-1-907432-00-2(0))* Hogs Back Bks. GBR. Dist: Independent Pubs. Group.

—The Robot Who Couldn't Cry. Dina, Madalina, illus. 2010. (ENG.). 32p. (J). (gr. -1-2). pap. 9.99 *(978-1-907432-01-9(9))* Hogs Back Bks. GBR. Dist: Independent Pubs. Group.

—The Teeny-Weeny Walking Stick. Lambert, Sally Anne, illus. 2010. (ENG.). 32p. (J). (gr. -1-2). pap. 9.99 *(978-1-907432-02-6(7))* Hogs Back Bks. GBR. Dist: Independent Pubs. Group.

Hoffman, Don. Abigail Is a Big Girl. Dakins, Todd, illus. 2nd ed. 2016. (Billy & Abby Ser.). (ENG.). 28p. (J). (gr. -1-k). pap. 3.99 *(978-1-943154-03-6(1))* Peek-A-Boo Publishing.

—Billy Is a Big Boy. Dakins, Todd, illus. 2nd ed. 2016. (Billy & Abby Ser.). (ENG.). 28p. (J). (gr. -1-k). pap. 3.99 *(978-1-943154-02-9(3))* Peek-A-Boo Publishing.

—A Counting Book with Billy & Abigail. Dakins, Todd, illus. 2nd ed. 2016. (Billy & Abby Ser.). (ENG.). 24p. (J). (gr. -1-k). pap. 3.99 *(978-1-943154-08-1(2))* Peek-A-Boo Publishing.

—Good Morning, Good Night Billy & Abigail. Dakins, Todd, illus. 2nd ed. 2016. (Billy & Abby Ser.). (ENG.). 24p. (J). (gr. -1-k). pap. 3.99 *(978-1-943154-09-8(0))* Peek-A-Boo Publishing.

—A Very Special Snowflake. Dakins, Todd, illus. 2nd ed. 2016. (ENG.). 28p. (J). (gr. -1-k). pap. 3.99 *(978-1-943154-01-2(5))* Peek-A-Boo Publishing.

Hoffman, Don & Palmer, Priscilla. Turbo & Tuxedo. Nadler, Anna, illus. 2016. (ENG.). 32p. (J). (gr. -1-k). pap. 3.99 *(978-1-943154-04-3(X))* Peek-A-Boo Publishing.

Hoffmann, E. T. A. The Nutcracker. Innocenti, Roberto, illus. 2017. (ENG.). 136p. (J). (gr. 3-5). 29.99 ***(978-1-56846-313-1(8),*** Creative Editions) Creative Co., The.

—The Nutcracker. Zwerger, Lisbeth, illus. 2016. (ENG.). 40p. 19.95 *(978-0-7358-4270-0(1))* North-South Bks., Inc.

Hoffmann, Heinrich. Struwwelpeter: Or Pretty Stories & Funny Pictures. Hoffmann, Heinrich, illus. 2010. (ENG., Illus.). 48p. (J). (gr. 2-7). 15.99 *(978-1-84365-153-6(X),* Pavilion Children's Books) Pavilion Bks. GBR. Dist: Independent Pubs. Group.

Hofmann-Maniyar, Ariane, illus. Ice in the Jungle. 2015. (Child's Play Library). (ENG.). 32p. (J). pap. *(978-1-84643-730-4(X))* Child's Play International Ltd.

Hofmeyr, Dianne. Zeraffa Giraffa. Ray, Jane, illus. 2015. (ENG.). 40p. (J). pap. 9.99 *(978-1-84780-661-1(9),* Frances Lincoln Children's Bks.) Quarto Publishing Group UK GBR. Dist: Littlehampton Bk Services, Ltd.

Holcomb, Carrie E., ed. Buggin' with Ruud. 2007. (Illus.). 48p. (J). per. 6.99 *(978-0-696-23690-7(7))* Meredith Bks.

Holden, Arianne. It's Fun to Learn about Colors: A Busy Picture Book Full of Fabulous Facts & Things to Do! 2016. (ENG., Illus.). 32p. 9.99 *(978-1-86147-710-1(4),* Armadillo) Anness Publishing GBR. Dist: National Bk. Network.

—It's Fun to Learn about My Body: A Busy Picture Book Full of Fabulous Facts & Things to Do! 2016. (ENG., Illus.). 32p. (J). (gr. -1-12). pap. 9.99 *(978-1-86147-730-9(9))* Anness Publishing, Inc.

Holden, Robert. The Pied Piper of Hamelin. Zak, Drahos, illus. 2004. 28p. (J). (gr. k-4). reprint ed. 15.00 *(978-0-7567-7686-2(4))* DIANE Publishing Co.

Holl, Adelaide & Duvoisin, Roger. The Rain Puddle. 2017. (ENG., Illus.). 36p. (J). 20.00 *(978-1-85124-469-0(7))* Bodleian Library GBR. Dist: Chicago Distribution Ctr.

Holmes, Andy. If You Give a Boy a Bible. 2004. 32p. (J). 10.99 *(978-0-8254-5513-1(8))* Kregel Pubns.

Holtz, Monica Stauber. Behind the Zoo: Find Out What the Animals Eat & Do at Irvine Park Zoo, Chippewa Falls, Wisconsin. Opatz, Shane, illus. Opatz, Shane, photos by. 2011. (J). *(978-0-9837617-1-6(X))* Holtz Creative Enterprises.

Holub, Joan & Williams, Suzanne. Goldilocks Breaks In. 2015. (Grimmtastic Girls Ser.: 6). (ENG.). 192p. (J). (gr. 3-7). pap. 5.99 *(978-0-545-78394-1(1),* Scholastic Paperbacks) Scholastic, Inc.

Holzwarth, Werner. The Story of the Little Mole Who Knew It Was None of His Business. Erlbruch, Wolf, illus. 2012. (ENG.). 24p. (J). (gr. -1-2). bds. 17.99 *(978-1-84365-132-1(7),* Pavilion Children's Books) Pavilion Bks. GBR. Dist: Independent Pubs. Group.

Hong, Seonna. Animus. 2015. (ENG., Illus.). 100p. (J). (gr. -1-7). pap. 25.00 *(978-0-9729388-5-3(0))* Baby Tattoo Bks.

Hood, Karen Jean Matsko. Angels, Angels Way up High. Whispering Pine Press International, ed. Alexandra Dzhiganskaya, illus. 2017. (Hood Picture Book Ser.). (J). bk. 2. pap. 15.95 *(978-1-930948-09-9(3))* Vol. 2. 24.95 *(978-1-930948-81-5(6))* Whispering Pine Pr. International, Inc.

Hood, Susan. Mission: New Baby. Lundquist, Mary, illus. 2015. (ENG.). 32p. (J). (gr. -1-2). 16.99 *(978-0-385-37672-3(3),* Random Hse. Bks. for Young Readers) Random Hse. Children's Bks.

—The Tooth Mouse. Nadeau, Janice, illus. 2012. (ENG.). 32p. (J). (gr. -1-2). 16.95 *(978-1-55453-565-1(4))* Kids Can Pr., Ltd. CAN. Dist: Hachette Bk. Group.

Hooks, Bell. Skin Again. Raschka, Chris, illus. 2017. (ENG.). 40p. (J). (gr. -1-k). 12.99 ***(978-1-4847-9923-9(2),*** Jump at the Sun) Hyperion Bks. for Children.

Hooper, Meredith & Quarto Generic Staff. Ponko & the South Pole. Ormerod, Jan, illus. 2012. (ENG.). 32p. (J). (gr. -1-1). pap. 8.99 *(978-1-84780-403-7(9),* Frances Lincoln) Quarto Publishing Group UK GBR. Dist: Hachette Bk. Group.

Hoopmann, Kathy. Blue Bottle Mystery - the Graphic Novel: An Asperger Adventure. 2015. (Asperger Adventures Ser.). (ENG., Illus.). 64p. (J). 18.95 *(978-1-84905-650-2(1),* 7952) Kingsley, Jessica Pubs. GBR. Dist: Macmillan Distribution Ltd.

Hopgood, Tim. Little Answer. 2015. (ENG., Illus.). 32p. (J). (gr. -1-k). pap. 11.99 *(978-0-552-56778-7(7))* Transworld Publishers Ltd. GBR. Dist: Independent Pubs. Group.

—UnpOppable. 2013. (ENG., Illus.). 32p. (J). (gr. -1-k). pap. 8.99 *(978-0-330-51740-9(6))* Pan Macmillan GBR. Dist: Independent Pubs. Group.

—Walter's Wonderful Web. 2016. (ENG., Illus.). 32p. (J). 16.99 *(978-0-374-30352-5(5),* 9780374303525, Farrar, Straus & Giroux (BYR)) Farrar, Straus & Giroux.

Hopkins, Douglas. Princess June & the Shadow Pirates, 1 vol. 2007. (ENG., Illus.). 32p. (J). (gr. -1-2). per. 8.95 *(978-1-894294-88-1(2),* Tuckamore Bks) Creative Bk. Publishing CAN. Dist: Orca Bk. Pubs. USA.

Hopman, Philip. Valentine & His Violin. 2012. (ENG., Illus.). 32p. (J). (gr. -1). 17.95 *(978-1-935954-17-0(2),* 9781935954170) Lemniscaat USA.

Horácek, Petr. Blue Penguin. Horácek, Petr, illus. 2016. (ENG., Illus.). 32p. (J). (gr. -1-2). 15.99 *(978-0-7636-9251-3(4))* Candlewick Pr.

—The Fly. Horácek, Petr, illus. 2015. (ENG., Illus.). 32p. (J). (gr. -1-2). 14.99 *(978-0-7636-7480-9(X))* Candlewick Pr.

—Jonathan & Martha. 2012. (ENG., Illus.). 40p. (gr. -1-1). 14.95 *(978-0-7148-6351-1(3))* Phaidon Pr., Inc.

—The Mouse Who Reached the Sky. Horácek, Petr, illus. 2016. (ENG., Illus.). 32p. (J). (-k). 16.99 *(978-0-7636-7916-3(X))* Candlewick Pr.

Horvath, James. Build, Dogs, Build: A Tall Tail. Horvath, James, illus. 2016. (I Can Read Level 1 Ser.). (Illus.). 32p. (J). (gr. -1-3). pap. 3.99 *(978-0-06-235705-2(0))* HarperCollins Pubs.

—Dig, Dogs, Dig: A Construction Tail. Horvath, James, illus. 2013. (ENG., Illus.). 40p. (J). (gr. -1-3). 15.99 *(978-0-06-218964-6(6))* HarperCollins Pubs.

Hoshino, Ryuichi. Finding Nemo. 2016. (ENG., Illus.). 176p. (J). 15.99 *(978-1-4278-5658-6(3),* 9781427856586) TOKYOPOP, Inc.

Houghton Mifflin Harcourt Children's Group Staff & Rey, H. A. Family Storybook Treasury: Tales of Laughter, Curiosity, & Fun. 2011. (ENG., Illus.). 304p. (J). (gr. -1-3). 18.99 *(978-0-547-61221-8(4))* Houghton Mifflin Harcourt Publishing Co.

Houran, Lori Haskins. A Dozen Cousins. Usher, Sam, illus. 2015. (ENG.). 32p. (J). (gr. k-1). 14.95 *(978-1-4549-1062-6(3))* Sterling Publishing Co., Inc.

Howard, Paul. I Went to the Supermarket. 2017. (ENG., Illus.). 32p. (J). 20.99 *(978-1-4088-4468-7(0),* 9781408844687, Bloomsbury USA Childrens) Bloomsbury Publishing USA.

Howarth, Heidi. The Otter Who Loved to Hold Hands. Howarth, Daniel, illus. 2014. (J). *(978-1-4351-5537-4(8))* Barnes & Noble, Inc.

Howarth, Naomi. The Crow's Tale. 2015. (ENG., Illus.). 32p. (J). (gr. -1-2). 18.99 *(978-1-84780-614-7(7),* Frances Lincoln) Quarto Publishing Group UK GBR. Dist: Littlehampton Bk Services, Ltd.

Howe, James. Big Bob, Little Bob. Anderson, Laura Ellen, illus. 2016. (ENG.). 32p. (J). (gr. -1-1). 15.99 *(978-0-7636-4436-9(6))* Candlewick Pr.

Howell, Gill. Selkie Child. Keen, Sophie, illus. 2005. (ENG.). 24p. (J). lib. bdg. 23.65 *(978-1-59646-750-7(9))* Dingles & Co.

—Snow King. Cann, Helen, illus. 2005. (ENG.). 24p. (J). lib. bdg. 23.65 *(978-1-59646-742-2(8))* Dingles & Co.

—Tortoise & the Baboon. Woody, illus. 2004. (ENG.). 16p. (J). lib. bdg. 23.65 *(978-1-59646-686-9(3))* Dingles & Co.

Hoyle, Alice. Pretend Friends: A Story about Schizophrenia & Other Illnesses That Can Cause Hallucinations. Reis, Lauren, illus. 2015. (ENG.). 36p. 14.95

P
Q
R

(978-1-84905-624-3(2), 7689) Kingsley, Jessica Pubs. GBR. Dist: Macmillan Distribution Ltd.

Hoyt, Charlene. Where the Leprechauns Hide. Fischer, Sandi, illus. 2007. (ENG.). 40p. per. 12.99 (978-0-9792258-9-5(2)) Bezalel Bks.

Hsu, Yi Ling. Typhoon Holidays: Taiwan. Cowley, Joy, ed. Kwag, Jin-yeong, illus. 2015. (Global Kids Storybooks Ser.). (ENG.). 32p. (gr. 1-4). 26.65 (978-1-925246-04-9(3)); 7.99 (978-1-925246-56-8(6)); 26.65 (978-1-925246-30-8(2)) ChoiceMaker Pty. Ltd., The AUS. (Big and SMALL). Dist: Lerner Publishing Group.

Hu, Vicky. The Muses: Greek Mythology (Mitologia Griega) 2009. 44p. pap. 21.99 (978-1-4415-3415-6(6)) Xlibris Corp.

Hubbard, Ben & Langley, Andrew. Adventures in Space. 2015. (Adventures in Space Ser.). (ENG.). 48p. (gr. 4-6). lib. bdg. 133.28 (978-1-4846-2518-7(8), Heinemann InfoSearch) Heinemann-Raintree.

Hubbell, Patricia. Cars: Rushing! Honking! Zooming!, 0 vols. Halsey, Megan & Addy, Sean, illus. 2010. (ENG.). 32p. (J). (gr. -1-1). pap. 6.99 (978-0-7614-5616-2(3), 9780761456162, Amazon Children's Publishing) Amazon Publishing.

Huber, Mike. The Amazing Erik. Cowman, Joseph, illus. 2014. (ENG.). 32p. (gr. -1). 15.95 (978-1-60554-209-6(1)) Redleaf Pr.

—Evette's Invitation. Cowman, Joseph, illus. 2014. (ENG.). 32p. (gr. -1). 15.95 (978-1-60554-212-6(1)) Redleaf Pr.

Huber, Raymond. Flight of the Honey Bee. Lovelock, Brian, illus. 2015. (Read & Wonder Ser.). (ENG.). 32p. (J). (gr. -1-2). 6.99 (978-0-7636-7648-3(9)) Candlewick Pr.

Hudson, Cheryl Willis. Hands Can. Bourke, John-Francis, photos by. 2012. (ENG., Illus.). 32p. (J). (gr. k-k). pap. 24.99 (978-0-7636-5819-9(7)) Candlewick Pr.

Hudson, Ella. Hudson Hates School. 2014. (ENG., Illus.). 32p. (J). (gr. k-3). pap. 8.99 (978-1-84780-375-7(X), Frances Lincoln) Quarto Publishing Group UK GBR. Dist: Hachette Bk. Group.

Hudson, Lynne. Sniff. Hudson, Lynne, illus. 2016. (ENG., Illus.). 24p. (J). (gr. -1-1). pap. 9.99 (978-1-907432-18-7(3)) Hogs Back Bks. GBR. Dist: Independent Pubs. Group.

Hudson, Sue. I Love You. Watanabe, Kaori, illus. 2004. (My First Taggies Book Ser.). (ENG.). 3p. (J). (gr. k — 1). 12.99 (978-0-439-64947-6(1), Cartwheel Bks.) Scholastic, Inc.

Huggins, Peter. Trosclair & the Alligator, 1 vol. Gardiner, Lindsey, illus. 2013. (ENG.). 32p. (J). pap. 7.95 (978-1-59572-640-7(3)) Star Bright Bks., Inc.

Hughes, Emily, illus. Wild. 2013. (ENG.). 32p. (J). (gr. -1-2). 16.95 (978-1-909263-08-6(7)) Flying Eye Bks. GBR. Dist: Consortium Bk. Sales & Distribution.

Hughes, Emma. Striker, Slow Down! A Calming Book for Children Who Are Always on the Go. Smisson, John, illus. 2016. (ENG.). 40p. (J). 16.95 (978-1-84819-327-7(0), 8680, Singing Dragon) Kingsley, Jessica Pubs. GBR. Dist: Macmillan Distribution Ltd.

Hughes, John Ceiriog. All Through the Night. Boulton, Harold, tr. from WEL. Alizadeh, Kate, illus. 2013. (ENG.). 24p. (J). (gr. -1-2). bds. 12.95 (978-1-927018-09-5(9)) Simply Read Bks. CAN. Dist: Ingram Publisher Services.

Hughes, Marghanita. Toffee at Home on the Farm. (Illus.). 20p. 13.95 (978-1-899827-50-3(1)) Scottish Children's Pr. GBR. Dist: Wilson & Assocs.

Hughes, Mónica. Little Mouse Deer & the Crocodile. Moricuchi, Mique, illus. 2004. 24p. (J). lib. bdg. 23.65 (978-1-59646-684-5(7)) Dingles & Co.

—More Little Mouse Deer Tales. Clemenston, John, illus. 2005. 24p. (J). lib. bdg. 23.65 (978-1-59646-730-9(4)) Dingles & Co.

Hughes-Odgers, Kyle. One Thousand Trees. 2017. (ENG.). 32p. (J). (gr. -1-3). 14.99 **(978-1-925164-72-5(1))** Fremantle Pr. AUS. Dist: Independent Pubs. Group.

Hughes, Sarah Anne. Reptiles & Amphibians. Peterson, Roger Tory, ed. Hughes, Sarah Anne, illus. 2nd ed. 2013. (Peterson Field Guide Color-In Bks.). (ENG., Illus.). 64p. (J). 8.95 (978-0-544-02695-7(0)) Houghton Mifflin Harcourt Publishing Co.

Hughes, Shirley. Alfie & His Very Best Friend. 2016. (Alfie Ser.). (ENG., Illus.). 32p. (J). (gr. -1-k). 19.99 **(978-1-78230-061-8(9))** Random Hse. GBR. Dist: Independent Pubs. Group.

—Alfie & Mum. 2017. (Alfie Ser.). (ENG., Illus.). 32p. (J). (gr. -1-k). pap. 11.99 **(978-1-78295-645-7(X)**, Red Fox) Random House Children's Books GBR. Dist: Independent Pubs. Group.

—Alfie Outdoors. 2016. (Alfie Ser.). (ENG., Illus.). 32p. (J). (-k). pap. 9.99 (978-1-78295-265-7(9), Red Fox) Random House Children's Books GBR. Dist: Independent Pubs. Group.

—Alfie's Christmas. 2016. (Alfie Ser.). (ENG., Illus.). 32p. (J). (gr. -1-k). 12.99 **(978-1-78230-064-9(3))** Random Hse. GBR. Dist: Independent Pubs. Group.

—Alphie's Numbers. 2015. (Alfie Ser.). (ENG., Illus.). 32p. (J). (gr. -1-k). pap. 9.99 (978-1-84941-846-1(2), Red Fox) Random House Children's Books GBR. Dist: Independent Pubs. Group.

—Jonadab & Rita. Hughes, Shirley, illus. 2010. (Alfie Ser.). (ENG., Illus.). 32p. (J). (gr. -1-k). pap. 11.99 (978-1-86230-313-3(4), Red Fox) Random House Children's Books GBR. Dist: Independent Pubs. Group.

—Lucy & Tom at the Seaside. 2016. (ENG., Illus.). 32p. (J). (-k). pap. 12.99 (978-1-78295-516-0(X), Red Fox) Random House Children's Books GBR. Dist: Independent Pubs. Group.

Hughes, Susan. Earth to Audrey. Poulin, Stéphane, illus. 2007. (ENG.). 32p. (J). (gr. k-3). 6.95 (978-1-55453-165-3(9)) Kids Can Pr., Ltd. CAN. Dist: Hachette Bk. Group.

Hulin, Rachel, photos by. Flying Henry. 2013. (ENG., Illus.). 40p. (J). (-k). 12.95 (978-1-57687-626-8(8), powerHouse Bks.) powerHouse Cultural Entertainment, Inc.

Hull, Maureen. Rainy Days with Bear. l.t. ed. 2012. 51p. (J). pap. (978-1-4596-3453-4(5)) ReadHowYouWant.com, Ltd.

Humphreys, Audrey. The Dragon Princess. 2012. 24p. pap. 24.99 (978-1-4691-6554-7(6)) Xlibris Corp.

Humphreys, Neil. I Trapped a Dolphin but It Really Wasn't My Fault. Cheng, Puay Koon, illus. 2013. (Abbie Rose & the Magic Suitcase Ser.). (ENG.). 24p. (J). (gr. -1-3). pap. 9.90 (978-981-4408-51-6(4)) Marshall Cavendish International (Asia) Private Ltd. SGP. Dist: National Bk. Network.

—Picking up a Penguin's Egg Really Got Me into Trouble. Cheng, Puay Koon, illus. 2014. (Abbie Rose & the Magic Suitcase Ser.). (ENG.). 24p. (J). (gr. -1-3). pap. 9.90 (978-981-4484-18-3(0)) Marshall Cavendish International (Asia) Private Ltd. SGP. Dist: National Bk. Network.

Huneck, Stephen. Sally in the Snow. 2014. (Sally Board Bks.). (ENG., Illus.). 20p. (J). (gr. -1 — 1). bds. 7.95 (978-1-4197-1227-2(6), Abrams Appleseed) Abrams, Inc.

Hunnicutt, M. E. The Wedding Wonderful. 2013. 24p. pap. 24.95 (978-1-62709-035-3(5)) America Star Bks.

Hurd, Thacher, illus. The Pea Patch Jig. rev. ed. 2015. (ENG.). 40p. (J). (gr. -1). 16.95 (978-1-939547-21-7(0)) Creston Bks.

Hurd, Thacher & Hurd, Thacher. Mystery on the Docks. Hurd, Thacher, illus. 25th anniv. ed. 2008. (Trophy Picture Bks.). (ENG., Illus.). 32p. (J). (gr. -1-3). pap. 8.99 (978-0-06-443058-6(8)) HarperCollins Pubs.

Hurry, Helen. Peepo! Boo! Who Are You? 2014. (ENG., Illus.). 12p. (J). 17.00 (978-0-85707-679-3(5), Simon & Schuster Children's) Simon & Schuster, Ltd. GBR. Dist: Simon & Schuster, Inc.

Hurst, Carol Otis. Picture Books in the Classroom: Addressing Concepts & Skills throughout the Curriculum Through Literature Kindergarten through Grade 2 2004. (Illus.). 285p. cd-rom 29.95 (978-0-9748509-1-7(8)) Hurst, Carol Consultants.

Hurtado, Ernest R. Freddy the Unfixer. 2011. 28p. (J). pap. 21.99 (978-1-4568-0995-9(4)) Xlibris Corp.

Husar, Jaco & Husar, Stephane. Hello, I Am Lily from New York City. Rigaudie, Mylène, illus. 2014. (AV2 Fiction Readalong Ser.: Vol. 129). (ENG.). 32p. (J). (gr. -1-3). lib. bdg. 34.28 (978-1-4896-2259-4(4), AV2 by Weigl) Weigl Pubs., Inc.

Husar, Stephane. Hello, I Am Charlie from London. Robert, Yannick, illus. 2014. (AV2 Fiction Readalong Ser.: Vol. 127). (ENG.). 32p. (J). (gr. -1-3). lib. bdg. 34.28 (978-1-4896-2256-3(X), AV2 by Weigl) Weigl Pubs., Inc.

—Hello, I Am Max from Sydney. Sofilas, Mark, illus. 2014. (AV2 Fiction Readalong Ser.: Vol. 130). (ENG.). 32p. (J). (gr. -1-3). lib. bdg. 34.28 (978-1-4896-2250-1(0), AV2 by Weigl) Weigl Pubs., Inc.

—Paolo from Rome. Le Grand, Claire, illus. 2014. (AV2 Fiction Readalong Ser.: Vol. 134). (ENG.). 32p. (J). (gr. -1-3). lib. bdg. 34.28 (978-1-4896-2274-7(8), AV2 by Weigl) Weigl Pubs., Inc.

Hutchins, Pat. Rosie's Walk. 2009. 9.00 (978-0-7848-2915-8(2), Everbind) Marco Bk. Co.

Hutt, Sarah. Animals Are Delicious. Ladd, Dave & Anderson, Stephanie, illus. 2016. (ENG.). 48p. (gr. -1 — 1). 17.95 (978-0-7148-7144-8(3)) Phaidon Pr., Inc.

Huusmann, Thomas-Bo & Fables, Aesops. The Lion & the Mouse. 2013. 26p. pap. (978-87-995724-4-1(3)) Huusmann, Thomas-Bo.

Hvass & Hannibal. Technicolor Treasure Hunt: Learn to Count with Nature. 2016. (ENG.). 14p. (J). (gr. -1-k). bds. 12.99 (978-1-84780-780-9(1), Wide Eyed Editions) Quarto Publishing Group UK GBR. Dist: Hachette Bk. Group.

Hvass, Nan Na & Hannibal, Sofie, illus. Technicolour Treasure Hunt: Learn to Count with Nature. 2016. (ENG.). 14p. (J). bds. 12.99 (978-1-84780-744-1(5), Wide Eyed Editions) Quarto Publishing Group UK GBR. Dist: Littlehampton Bk Services, Ltd.

Hyde, Margaret E. Mo Smells Sweet Dreams: A Scentsational Journey. Chaudhary, Aman, illus. 2012. (Mo's Nose Ser.). (ENG.). 24p. (J). (-k). 17.95 (978-0-9816255-8-4(4)) Mo's Nose, LLC.

Hyde, Margaret E., ed. Cassatt for Kids, 1 vol. 2003. (Great Art for Kids Ser.). (ENG., Illus.). 10p. (J). (gr. k-k). bds. 8.95 (978-1-58980-202-5(0)) Pelican Publishing Co., Inc.

Hyman, Zachary. The Bambino & Me. Pullen, Zachary, illus. 2014. (ENG.). 48p. (J). (gr. 1-4). 17.99 (978-1-77049-627-9(0), Tundra Bks.) Tundra Bks. CAN. Dist: Penguin Random Hse. LLC.

Hyun, Kim. Getting Dressed: A Book about Dressing, with Tabs for Older Babies. 2016. (Chat About Ser.). (ENG., Illus.). 22p. (J). bds. 9.99 **(978-1-5098-0457-3(9))** Pan Macmillan GBR. Dist: Independent Pubs. Group.

Icilda. God Made Me Perfect & Wonderful: To Do What? 2009. 28p. pap. 13.99 (978-1-4490-4545-6(6)) AuthorHouse.

Ikids Staff. Ibaby - Goodnight, Baby: Tuck All the Babies into Their Beds. Larranaga, Ana Martin, illus. 2006. (ENG.). 12p. (J). (gr. -1 — 1). 9.99 (978-1-58476-482-3(1), IKIDS) Innovative Kids.

Imperato, Teresa. Colors All Around: A Turn & Pop Book. Petrone, Valeria, illus. 2005. (Turn & Pop Book Ser.). 10p. (J). bds. 5.95 (978-1-58117-277-5(X), Intervisual/Piggy Toes) Bendon, Inc.

—Good Morning, Good Night! Mitchell, Melanie, illus. 2006. (ENG.). 12p. (J). (gr. -1-18). 9.95 (978-1-58117-279-9(6), Intervisual/Piggy Toes) Bendon, Inc.

—How Many Ducks in a Row? A Turn & Pop Book. Petrone, Valeria, illus. 2005. 10p. (J). bds. 5.95 (978-1-58117-278-2(8), Intervisual/Piggy Toes) Bendon, Inc.

Inches, Alison. Dora Loves Boots (Dora the Explorer) Random House Beginners Books Staff & MJ Illustrations Staff, illus. 2013. (Pictureback(R) Ser.). (ENG.). 16p. (J). (gr. -1-2). 4.99 (978-0-385-37345-6(7), Random Hse. Bks. for Young Readers) Random Hse. Children's Bks.

Ingham, Anne. The Ball Book. 2012. 28p. pap. 21.99 (978-1-4691-8747-1(7)) Xlibris Corp.

Inglese, Judith. I Have a Friend. Inglese, Judith, illus. 2014. (ENG., Illus.). 40p. (J). 17.95 (978-1-935874-22-5(5)) Satya Hse. Pubns.

Inkpen, Chloë & Inkpen, Mick. Hello Ladybird! 2014. (Zoe & Beans Ser.). (ENG., Illus.). 12p. (J). (— 1). bds. 9.99 (978-0-230-76655-6(2)) Pan Macmillan GBR. Dist: Independent Pubs. Group.

—The Magic Hoop! 2015. (Zoe & Beans Ser.). (ENG., Illus.). 32p. (J). (-k). pap. 9.99 (978-0-330-51840-6(2)) Pan Macmillan GBR. Dist: Independent Pubs. Group.

—Pirate Treasure! 2015. (Zoe & Beans Ser.). (ENG., Illus.). 32p. (J). (-k). pap. 9.99 (978-1-4472-4327-4(7)) Pan Macmillan GBR. Dist: Independent Pubs. Group.

Inkpen, Chloe & Inkpen, Mick. We're Not Scared! 2015. (Zoe & Beans Ser.). (ENG., Illus.). 12p. (J). (— 1). bds. 9.99 (978-0-230-76656-3(0)) Pan Macmillan GBR. Dist: Independent Pubs. Group.

Inkpen, Chloë & Inkpen, Mick. Zoe & Beans/Pirate Treasure! 2014. (Zoe & Beans Ser.). (ENG., Illus.). 24p. (J). (-k). 17.99 (978-0-230-77285-4(4)) Pan Macmillan GBR. Dist: Independent Pubs. Group.

Inkpen, Mick. Beachmoles & Bellvine. MC, ed. 2006. (Blue Nose Island Ser.: Bk. 2). (Illus.). 34p. (J). (gr. -1). 13.95 (978-1-84456-225-1(5)) Hodder & Stoughton GBR. Dist: Trafalgar Square Publishing.

—Beachmoles & Bellvine. 2004. (ENG., Illus.). 32p. (J). (gr. -1-k). 16.99 (978-0-340-87865-1(7)) Hodder & Stoughton GBR. Dist: Hachette Bk. Group.

—Hide Me, Kipper. 2016. (Kipper Ser.). (ENG., Illus.). 32p. (J). (gr. -1-k). 7.99 (978-1-4449-2977-5(1)) Hachette Children's Group GBR. Dist: Hachette Bk. Group.

—Kipper: Kipper's Christmas Eve. 2016. (Kipper Ser.). (ENG., Illus.). 26p. (J). (gr. -1-k). bds. 8.99 (978-1-4449-3029-0(X)) Hachette Children's Group GBR. Dist: Hachette Bk. Group.

—Kipper's Beach Ball. 2016. (Kipper Ser.). (ENG., Illus.). 32p. (J). (gr. -1-k). pap. 7.99 (978-1-4449-2402-2(8)) Hachette Children's Group GBR. Dist: Hachette Bk. Group.

—Kipper's Birthday. 2014. (ENG., Illus.). 32p. (J). (gr. -1-k). pap. 10.99 **(978-1-4449-1817-5(0))** Hachette Children's Group GBR. Dist: Hachette Bk. Group.

—Kipper's Monster. 2016. (Get Well Friends Ser.). (ENG., Illus.). 32p. (J). (gr. -1-k). pap. 7.99 (978-1-4449-2383-4(8)) Hachette Children's Group GBR. Dist: Hachette Bk. Group.

—Kipper's New Pet. 2016. (Kipper Ser.). (ENG., Illus.). 32p. (J). (gr. -1-k). pap. 7.99 (978-1-4449-3048-1(6)) Hachette Children's Group GBR. Dist: Hachette Bk. Group.

—Kipper's Snowy Day. 2015. (Kipper Ser.). (ENG., Illus.). 32p. (J). (gr. -1-k). pap. 10.99 (978-1-4449-2409-1(5)) Hodder & Stoughton GBR. Dist: Hachette Bk. Group.

—One Year with Kipper. 2015. (ENG., Illus.). 32p. (J). (gr. -1-k). pap. 10.99 (978-1-4449-1820-5(6)) Hodder & Stoughton GBR. Dist: Hachette Bk. Group.

—Penguin Small. 2016. (ENG., Illus.). 32p. (J). (gr. -1-k). pap. 7.99 (978-1-4449-1821-2(4)) Hachette Children's Group GBR. Dist: Hachette Bk. Group.

—A Royal Lullabyhullaballoo! 2017. (ENG., Illus.). 40p. (J). (gr. -1-k). pap. 10.99 **(978-1-4449-3051-1(6))** Hachette Children's Group GBR. Dist: Hachette Bk. Group.

—Silly Big Bear. 2017. (Wibbly Pig Ser.). (ENG., Illus.). 32p. (J). (gr. -1-k). pap. 8.99 **(978-1-4449-3125-9(3))** Hachette Children's Group GBR. Dist: Hachette Bk. Group.

—This Is My Book. Inkpen, Mick, illus. 2010. (ENG., Illus.). 32p. (J). (gr. -1-k). pap. 8.99 (978-0-340-98963-0(7)) Hodder & Stoughton GBR. Dist: Hachette Bk. Group.

—Threadbear. 2016. (ENG., Illus.). 32p. (J). (gr. -1-k). pap. 8.99 (978-1-4449-2405-3(2)) Hachette Children's Group GBR. Dist: Hachette Bk. Group.

—Ticky Christmas. 2016. (Wibbly Pig Ser.). (ENG., Illus.). 32p. (J). (gr. -1-k). pap. 8.99 (978-1-4449-2410-7(9)) Hachette Children's Group GBR. Dist: Hachette Bk. Group.

Inkpen, Mick & Layton, Neal. Kipper's Toybox. 2015. (Kipper Ser.). (ENG., Illus.). 32p. (J). (gr. -1-k). pap. 10.99 (978-1-4449-2377-3(3)) Hodder & Stoughton GBR. Dist: Hachette Bk. Group.

Innovative Kids Staff, creator. Soft Shapes Photo Books: Tropical Fish. 2012. (ENG., Illus.). 8p. (J). (gr. -1 — 1). 10.99 (978-1-60169-225-2(0)) Innovative Kids.

—Vehicles. 2012. (ENG., Illus.). 1p. (J). (gr. -1 — 1). 10.99 (978-1-60169-224-5(2)) Innovative Kids.

Ipcar, Dahlov, illus. Black & White. 2015. (Dahlov Ipcar Collection). (ENG.). 40p. (J). (gr. -1-2). 17.95 (978-1-909263-44-4(3)) Flying Eye Bks. GBR. Dist: Consortium Bk. Sales & Distribution.

—The Wonderful Egg. 2014. (Dahlov Ipcar Collection). (ENG.). 48p. (J). (gr. -1-2). 19.95 (978-1-909263-28-4(1)) Flying Eye Bks. GBR. Dist: Consortium Bk. Sales & Distribution.

Ipcizade, Catherine. 'Twas the Day Before Zoo Day, 1 vol. Hodson, Ben, illus. 2008. (Basic Math Operations Ser.). (ENG.). 32p. (J). (gr. -1-2). 17.95 (978-1-60718-585-7(7)) Arbordale Publishing.

Irving Ed.D., Harry R. Un Image-Word D'Enfants et Livre Simple de Phrase: Version Francaise Catégories Primaires. 2010. 192p. pap. 51.53 (978-1-4251-6396-9(3)) Trafford Publishing.

Isadora, Rachel. Say Hello! Isadora, Rachel, illus. 2010. (ENG., Illus.). 32p. (J). (-k). 16.99 (978-0-399-25230-3(4), G.P. Putnam's Sons Books for Young Readers) Penguin Young Readers Group.

Isis, Watalia. Ronald's Adventures Throught Time & Imagination. 2013. (Illus.). 40p. pap. (978-0-9575371-8-7(2)) Starflower Pr.

Israel, Susan E. Be Just Me. 2012. 26p. pap. (978-0-9827449-6-3(X)) Roxby Media Ltd.

Ives, Burl. Sailing on a Very Fine Day. Myers, Bernice & Myers, Lou, illus. 2011. 32p. pap. 35.95 (978-1-258-04002-4(6)) Literary Licensing, LLC.

Ives, Penny. Rabbit Pie. Ives, Penny, illus. 2012. (Child's Play Library). (ENG., Illus.). 22p. (J). (gr. 1-1). bds. (978-1-84643-513-3(7)) Child's Play International Ltd.

Iwamura, Kazuo. Bedtime in the Forest. 2010. (ENG., Illus.). 32p. (J). (gr. -1-3). 16.95 (978-0-7358-2310-5(3)) North-South Bks., Inc.

—Hooray for Summer! 2010. (ENG., Illus.). 32p. (J). (gr. -1-k). 16.95 (978-0-7358-2285-6(9)) North-South Bks., Inc.

Iwamura, Kazuo & Yamashita, Haruo. Seven Little Mice Go to School. 2011. (ENG., Illus.). 32p. (J). (gr. -1-k). 17.95 (978-0-7358-4012-6(1)) North-South Bks., Inc.

—Seven Little Mice Go to the Beach. 2012. (ENG., Illus.). 32p. (J). (gr. -1-1). 16.95 (978-0-7358-4073-7(3)) North-South Bks., Inc.

Izumo, Rebecca. Colorful Race Cars. 2017. (Wonderful World of Colors Ser.). 24p. (gr. 4-6). pap. 8.25 **(978-1-5383-2095-2(9)**, PowerKids Pr.) Rosen Publishing Group, Inc., The.

Jackson, Antonia. The Easter Story. Ferri, Giuliano, illus. 2015. (ENG.). 32p. (J). (gr. k-4). 14.99 (978-0-7459-6508-6(3)) Lion Hudson PLC GBR. Dist: Independent Pubs. Group.

Jackson, Antonia & Nagy, Krisztina Kallai. My Advent Calendar Christmas Book. 2014. (ENG., Illus.). 32p. (J). (-2). 9.99 (978-0-7459-6392-1(7)) Lion Hudson PLC GBR. Dist: Independent Pubs. Group.

Jackson, Ellen & Barden, Amy-Clare. Picky Eaters. 2017. (ENG., Illus.). 16p. (J). (gr. -1-2). bds. 7.95 (978-1-4549-1901-8(9)) Sterling Publishing Co., Inc.

Jackson, Kate. Santa's Special Helper: A Spot-the-Difference Christmas Adventure! 2016. (ENG.). 18p. (J). bds. 7.99 (978-1-4926-4175-9(8), 9781492641759, Sourcebooks Jabberwocky) Sourcebooks, Inc.

Jacobson, Ryan. Super Animal Powers. Tekiela, Stan, photos by. 2016. (Wildlife Picture Bks.). (ENG., Illus.). 32p. (J). (gr. -1-3). 12.95 (978-1-59193-648-0(9)) Adventure Pubns.

Jacobson, Ryan. What Eats That? Tekiela, Stan, photos by. 2017. (Wildlife Picture Bks.). (ENG., Illus.). 32p. (J). (gr. -1-3). 14.95 **(978-1-59193-749-4(3))** Adventure Pubns.

Jahn, Benny. Ah-Choo - God Bless You. Scott, Chelsey, illus. 2009. 24p. pap. 11.95 (978-1-60844-178-5(4)) Dog Ear Publishing, LLC.

James, Ann. Bird & Bear. James, Ann, illus. 2015. (ENG., Illus.). 40p. (J). (gr. -1-2). 16.99 (978-1-4998-0037-1(1)) Little Bee Books Inc.

James, Diane. Here We Go. 2004. (Jigsaw Rhymes Ser.). (Illus.). 12p. (J). (gr. -1-k). 9.95 (978-1-58728-024-5(8), Two-Can Publishing) T&N Children's Publishing.

James, Simon. Baby Brains. James, Simon, illus. 2016. (ENG., Illus.). 32p. (J). (gr. -1-3). 9.99 (978-0-7636-8177-7(6)) Candlewick Pr.

Jamieson, Tom. The Big Bad Mood. Rozelaar, Angie & Demidova, Olga, illus. 2017. (ENG.). 32p. (J). 16.99 **(978-1-4088-3919-5(9)**, 9781408839195, Bloomsbury USA Childrens) Bloomsbury Publishing USA.

—Sproutzilla vs. Christmas. Byrne, Mike, illus. 2016. (ENG.). 32p. (J). (gr. -1-1). pap. 10.99 **(978-1-5098-2278-2(X))** Pan Macmillan GBR. Dist: Independent Pubs. Group.

Janisch, Heinz. The King & the Sea. 2015.Tr. of Der Koenig und das Meer. (Illus.). 48p. (J). (gr. 2-4). 16.99 (978-1-877579-94-3(7)) Gecko Pr. NZL. Dist: Lerner Publishing Group.

Janousky, Peggy Robbins. Move It, Miss Macintosh! Lands, Meghan, illus. 2016. (ENG.). 32p. (J). (gr. -1-2). 17.95 (978-1-55451-863-0(6)) Annick Pr., Ltd. CAN. Dist: Publishers Group West (PGW).

—Move It, Miss Macintosh! Lands, Meghan, illus. 2016. (ENG.). 32p. (J). (gr. -1-2). 9.95 (978-1-55451-862-3(8)) Annick Pr., Ltd. CAN. Dist: Publishers Group West (PGW).

Janry, Tome, illus. Spirou & Fantasio in Moscow, Vol. 6. 2014. (Spirou & Fantasio Ser.: 6). (ENG.). 48p. pap. 11.95 (978-1-84918-193-8(4)) CineBook GBR. Dist: National Bk. Network.

Jarman, Julia. The Best Kiss. Waters, Erica-Jane, illus. 2014. (ENG.). 32p. (J). (gr. -1-k). pap. 8.99 (978-1-4449-2091-8(X)) Hodder & Stoughton GBR. Dist: Hachette Bk. Group.

—Molly & the Giant. Sholto, Walker, illus. 2005. (ENG.). 24p. (J). lib. bdg. 23.65 (978-1-59646-746-0(0)) Dingles & Co.

Jarman, Julia & Sutcliffe, Mandy. Big Bouncy Bed. Reynolds, Adrian, illus. 2015. (ENG.). 32p. (J). (gr. -1-k). pap. 10.99 (978-1-4083-0544-7(5)) Hodder & Stoughton GBR. Dist: Hachette Bk. Group.

Jarvis. Who Is Happy? 2016. (ENG.). 22p. (J). (gr. -1-k). 16.99 (978-1-84780-842-4(5), Frances Lincoln Children's Bks.) Quarto Publishing Group UK GBR. Dist: Hachette Bk. Group.

Jarvis, illus. Who Is Happy? 2016. (ENG.). 22p. (J). 16.99 (978-1-84780-722-9(4), Frances Lincoln Children's Bks.) Quarto Publishing Group UK GBR. Dist: Littlehampton Bk Services, Ltd.

Jatkowska, Ag, illus. The Christmas Treasure Hunt. 2014. (ENG.). 10p. (J). (gr. -1-k). 15.99 (978-0-230-76863-5(6)) Pan Macmillan GBR. Dist: Independent Pubs. Group.

Jay, Alison. Bee & Me. Jay, Alison, illus. 2017. (ENG., Illus.). 32p. (J). (-k). 15.99 (978-0-7636-9010-6(4)) Candlewick Pr.

Jay, Alison & Gershator, Phillis. Listen, Listen. 2008. (ENG., Illus.). 32p. (J). (gr. -1-k). 14.99 (978-1-84686-201-4(9)) Barefoot Bks., Inc.

Jay, Larsen. What If Cows Could...? 2005. (J). lib. bdg. 19.95 (978-1-933732-01-5(6)) Big Ransom Studio.

Jefferies, Rosie & Naish, Sarah. Callum Kindly & the Very Weird Child: A Story about Sharing Your Home with a Different Child. Evens, Megan, illus. 2017. (Therapeutic Parenting Bks.). (ENG.). 32p. (J). pap. 14.95 **(978-1-78592-300-5(5)**, 9228) Kingsley, Jessica Pubs. GBR. Dist: Macmillan Distribution Ltd.

Jeffers, Oliver. Once upon an Alphabet: Short Stories for All the Letters. Jeffers, Oliver, illus. 2014. (ENG., Illus.). 112p. (J). (gr. -1-k). 26.99 (978-0-399-16791-1(9), Philomel Bks.) Penguin Publishing Group.

—Once upon an Alphabet: Short Stories for All the Letters. Jeffers, Oliver, illus. 2017. (ENG., Illus.). 26p. (J). (— 1). bds. 8.99 (978-0-399-54542-9(5), Philomel Bks.) Penguin Young Readers Group.

Jenkins, Martin. Exploring Space: from Galileo to the Mars Rover & Beyond. Biesty, Stephen, illus. 2017. (ENG.). 64p. (J). (gr. 3-7). 17.99 (978-0-7636-8931-5(9)) Candlewick Pr.

Jenkyns, Brenda. Ever After. 2012. pap. 11.95 (978-0-7414-7620-3(7)) Infinity Publishing.

Jenn, Lady. Talking Flower Garden: A Series of Ricky's Secret Friends, 6, vol. 5. Jenn, Lady, illus. 2016. (Ricky's Secret Friends Picturebook Ser.). (ENG & CHI., Illus.). (gr. 1-4). 29.95 (978-0-9787591-1-7(7)) Direct World Publishing.

Jennings, Linda. Duna y Dan. Chapman, Jane, illus. (SPA.). 28p. (J). (gr. k-1). (978-84-8418-027-2(1), ZZ4481) Zendrera Zariquiey, Editorial ESP. Dist: Lectorum Pubns., Inc.

Jennings, Sharon. Bearcub & Mama. Watt, Mélanie, illus. 2007. (ENG.). 32p. (J). (gr. -1-2). 6.95 (978-1-55453-162-2(4)) Kids Can Pr., Ltd. CAN. Dist: Hachette Bk. Group.

Jennings, Sharon, et al, adapted by. Franklin's Picnic. 2006. (Kids Can Read Ser.). (ENG., Illus.). 32p. (J). (gr. 1-2). 14.95 (978-1-55337-714-6(1)) Kids Can Pr., Ltd. CAN. Dist: Hachette Bk. Group.

Jennings, Sharon, et al. Franklin the Detective. Gagnon, Céleste, illus. 2004. 32p. (J). pap. (978-0-439-41822-5(4)) Scholastic, Inc.

Jenny Press Staff. Peter Pan. 2016. (ENG., Illus.). 24p. pap. 7.99 (978-1-86147-815-3(1), Armadillo) Anness Publishing GBR. Dist: National Bk. Network.

Jenny Press Staff, illus. Sleeping Beauty. 2016. (ENG.). 24p. pap. 7.99 (978-1-86147-816-0(X), Armadillo) Anness Publishing GBR. Dist: National Bk. Network.

Jensen, Bonnie Rickner. A Very Merry Christmas Prayer, 1 vol. 2015. (ENG., Illus.). 24p. (J). bds. 8.99 (978-0-7180-3053-7(2)) Nelson, Thomas Inc.

Jensen, Peder Skytte. Anton & Rosita: All Roads Lead to Rome. 2011. (Illus.). 40p. (gr. 1-2). pap. 20.38 (978-1-4567-8077-7(8)) AuthorHouse.

Jeremies, Christian & Jeremies, Fabian. The Big Penguin Party. 2015. (ENG., Illus.). 32p. (J). (-3). 16.99 (978-1-4926-2334-2(2), Sourcebooks Jabberwocky) Sourcebooks, Inc.

Jian, Li. The Horse & the Mysterious Drawing: A Story in English & Chinese. 2013. (ENG., Illus.). 42p. (J). (gr. -1-3). 16.95 (978-1-60220-984-8(7)) BetterLink Pr., Inc.

—Ming's Adventure with the Terracotta Army. Wert, Yijin, tr. 2013. (ENG & CHI., Illus.). 42p. (J). (gr. -1-3). 16.95 (978-1-60220-983-1(9)) BetterLink Pr., Inc.

—The Snake Goddess Colors the World: A Chinese Tale Told in English & Chinese. 2013. (ENG & CHI., Illus.). 42p. (J). (gr. -1-3). 16.95 (978-1-60220-982-4(0)) BetterLink Pr., Inc.

—The Water Dragon: A Chinese Legend. 2012. (ENG., Illus.). 42p. (J). (gr. -1-3). 16.95 (978-1-60220-978-7(2)) BetterLink Pr., Inc.

Jin, Nayoung. Shooting Star Rider. Cote, Genevieve, illus. 2017. (ENG.). 36p. (J). (gr. -1-3). 16.95 (978-1-77229-020-2(3)) Simply Read Bks. CAN. Dist: Ingram Publisher Services.

Job. Yakari & Nanabozo. Derib, illus. 2014. (Yakari Ser.: 11). (ENG.). 48p. pap. 11.95 (978-1-84918-177-8(2)) CineBook GBR. Dist: National Bk. Network.

Jocelyn, Marthe. Over Under. Slaughter, Tom, illus. 2005. (ENG.). 24p. (J). (gr. k-k). 15.95 (978-0-88776-708-1(7), Tundra Bks.) Tundra Bks. CAN. Dist: Penguin Random Hse. LLC.

Jocelyn, Marthe, illus. Sam Sorts. 2017. (ENG.). 32p. (J). (gr. -1-2). 16.99 (978-1-101-91805-0(5), Tundra Bks.) Tundra Bks. CAN. Dist: Penguin Random Hse. LLC.

John, Louise. I Can Hear!, 1 vol. Elkerton, Andy, illus. 2013. (Start Reading Ser.). (ENG.). 24p. (gr. k-1). pap. 7.95 (978-1-4765-3199-1(4)); pap. 41.94 (978-1-4765-3219-6(2)) Capstone Press of Coughlan Cos.

—My Chair, 1 vol. Elkerton, Andy, illus. 2013. (Start Reading Ser.). (ENG.). 24p. (gr. k-1). pap. 7.95 (978-1-4765-3200-4(1)); pap. 41.94 (978-1-4765-3225-7(7)) Capstone Press of Coughlan Cos.

John Taylor, Jeannie St. Penguin's Special Christmas Tree. l.t. ed. 2012. 36p. (J). pap. (978-1-4596-3452-7(7)) ReadHowYouWant.com, Ltd.

Johnson, Crockett. Magic Beach. 2005. (ENG., Illus.). 64p. (J). (gr. -1-3). 18.95 (978-1-932425-27-7(6), Lemniscaat) Boyds Mills Pr.

—Time for Spring. Johnson, Crockett, illus. 2016. (Illus.). 40p. (J). (gr. -1-3). 14.99 (978-0-06-243033-5(5)) HarperCollins Pubs.

Johnson, D. B. Henry Hikes to Fitchburg. 2006. (ENG., Illus.). 32p. (J). (gr. -1-3). reprint ed. 7.99 (978-0-618-73749-9(9)) Houghton Mifflin Harcourt Publishing Co.

Johnson, Dennis. The Tree That Went Sailing. 2009. (J). pap. (978-1-61623-539-0(X)) Independent Pub.

Johnson, Florence. The Christmas ABC. Wilkin, Eloise, illus. 2015. (Big Golden Board Book Ser.). (ENG.). 24p. (J). (-k). bds. 10.99 (978-0-553-52225-9(6), Golden Bks.) Random Hse. Children's Bks.

Johnson, Julia & Styles, Emily. A Is for Arabia. 2012. (ENG., Illus.). 32p. (gr. -1-3). pap. 8.50 (978-1-900988-93-3(3), Stacey International) Stacey Publishing GBR. Dist: Casemate Pubs. & Bk. Distributors, LLC.

Johnson, Michael. Iroquois: People of the Longhouse. 2013. (ENG., Illus.). 160p. 35.00 (978-1-77085-218-1(2), 9781770852181) Firefly Bks., Ltd.

Johnson, Myrna. Cool Cats Carry Canes. 2014. (ENG., Illus.). 32p. (gr. -1-3). pap. 12.00 (978-1-62288-088-1(9)) Austin, Stephen F. State Univ. Pr.

Johnston, Jan. Amélie the Most Amazing Butterfly: I Do So Love Being a Butterfly ... 2013. (Illus.). 24p. pap. 17.99 (978-1-4817-8018-6(2)) AuthorHouse.

—Lisa Finds a Playful Tree Elf: No! I Am Not a Fairy! 2013. (Illus.). 24p. pap. 17.99 (978-1-4817-8020-9(4)) AuthorHouse.

Johnston, Johanna. Whale's Way. Weisgard, Leonard, illus. 2015. (ENG.). 48p. 20.00 (978-1-85124-428-7(X)) Bodleian Library GBR. Dist: Chicago Distribution Ctr.

Johnston, Tony. Desert Song, 1 vol. Young, Ed, illus. 2010. (ENG.). 32p. (J). (gr. 3-4). pap. 7.99 (978-1-57805-171-7(1)) Sierra Club Bks. for Children.

Jonas, Debbie Sue. The Key Lime Candies Clubt in Two Turtles' Tales. 2012. 44p. pap. 17.49 (978-1-4691-5283-7(5)) Xlibris Corp.

Jones, Birdy. Mister Cool. Lynch, Tara, illus. 2015. (ENG.). 34p. (J). (gr. 1-4). 16.95 (978-1-57687-719-7(1), powerHouse Bks.) powerHouse Cultural Entertainment, Inc.

Jones, Bryony. Very Tasty Vegetables. 2011. (ENG., Illus.). 14p. (J). (gr. -1-k). bds. (978-1-84089-615-2(9)) Zero to Ten, Ltd.

—Where's Santa? Whelon, Chuck, illus. 2015. (ENG.). 32p. (J). (gr. k-3). 12.99 (978-1-4814-0619-2(1), Aladdin) Simon & Schuster Children's Publishing.

Jones, Christianne C. Lacey Walker, Nonstop Talker, 1 vol. Watson, Richard, illus. 2013. (Little Boost Ser.). (ENG.). 32p. (gr. k-3). 14.95 (978-1-4795-2156-2(6), Little Boost) Picture Window Bks.

Jones, Elisabeth & Jones, Lis. A Walk in the Wild Woods. Coplestone, Jim, illus. 2010. (ENG.). 32p. (J). (gr. -1-1). 16.95 (978-1-84507-956-7(6), Frances Lincoln) Quarto Publishing Group UK GBR. Dist: Hachette Bk. Group.

Jones, Frankie. In the Wild. 2015. (What Can You Spot? Ser.). (ENG., Illus.). 18p. (J). (gr. -1 — 1). bds. 6.99 (978-1-4998-0055-5(X)) Little Bee Books Inc.

Jones, Janey Louise. The Sleepover. 2016. (Princess Poppy Picture Bks.). (ENG., Illus.). 32p. (J). (gr. -1-k). pap. 11.99 **(978-0-552-57069-5(9))** Transworld Publishers Ltd. GBR. Dist: Independent Pubs. Group.

Jones, Lara. All Aboard! 2015. (Poppy Cat Ser.). (ENG., Illus.). 18p. (J). (gr. -1-k). bds. 7.99 (978-0-230-75400-3(7)) Pan Macmillan GBR. Dist: Independent Pubs. Group.

—Blast Off! 2015. (Poppy Cat Ser.). (ENG., Illus.). 18p. (J). (gr. -1-k). bds. 7.99 (978-0-230-75399-0(X)) Pan Macmillan GBR. Dist: Independent Pubs. Group.

Jones, Nicholas. Pandora's Feather. 2017. (ENG., Illus.). 20p. (J). pap. 14.95 **(978-1-78554-790-4(9)**, de3aac81-0dee-412b-83d2-c5f05b43b521) Austin, Stan AUS. Dist: Bookmasters Distribution.

Jones, Sonia. Yoga Poga Shmoga! Dakins, Todd, illus. 2016. (ENG.). 36p. (J). (gr. k-2). pap. 3.99 (978-1-943154-32-6(5), See-Saw Publishing) Peek-A-Boo Publishing.

—Yoga Poga Shmoga! Dakins, Todd, illus. 2016. (ENG.). 36p. (J). (gr. k-2). 7.95 (978-1-943154-33-3(3), See-Saw Publishing) Peek-A-Boo Publishing.

Jones, Tammy. My Pet. 2009. (Sight Word Readers Set A Ser.). (J). 3.49 net. (978-1-60719-145-2(8)) Newmark Learning LLC.

—My Town. 2009. (Sight Word Readers Set A Ser.). (J). (978-1-60719-147-6(4)) Newmark Learning LLC.

—We Go to School. 2009. (Sight Word Readers Set A Ser.). (J). 3.49 net. (978-1-60719-146-9(6)) Newmark Learning LLC.

—We Have Fruit. 2009. (Sight Word Readers Set A Ser.). (J). (978-1-60719-136-0(9)) Newmark Learning LLC.

—We Like Birthdays. 2009. (Sight Word Readers Set A Ser.). (J). 3.49 net. (978-1-60719-149-0(0)) Newmark Learning LLC.

—What Has Stripes? 2009. (Sight Word Readers Set A Ser.). (J). 3.49 net. (978-1-60719-151-3(2)) Newmark Learning LLC.

Jordan, Meredith & Abramson, Andra Serlin. Kids Meet the Snakes. 2013. (Kids Meet Ser.: 1). (ENG., Illus.). 96p. (J). spiral bd. 12.95 (978-1-60433-303-9(0), Applesauce Pr.) Cider Mill Pr. Bk. Pubs., LLC.

Josiah, Iris. Tiny Bird. 2012. (Illus.). 28p. (J). pap. (978-0-9572728-4-2(7)) Tiny Island Pr.

—Tiny Goat. 2012. (Illus.). 28p. (J). pap. (978-0-9572728-2-8(0)) Tiny Island Pr.

—Tiny Goat's Alphabet Book. 2015. (Illus.). 40p. (J). pap. (978-0-9572728-7-3(1)) Tiny Island Pr.

—Tiny Hen. 2012. (Illus.). 28p. (J). pap. (978-0-9572728-3-5(9)) Tiny Island Pr.

—Tiny Hen's Alphabet Book. 2015. (Illus.). 40p. (J). pap. (978-0-9572728-8-0(X)) Tiny Island Pr.

—Tiny Pig. 2012. (Illus.). 28p. (J). pap. (978-0-9572728-1-1(2)) Tiny Island Pr.

—Tiny Pig's Alphabet Book. 2015. (Illus.). 40p. (J). pap. (978-0-9572728-6-6(3)) Tiny Island Pr.

—Tiny Rabbit. 2012. (Illus.). 28p. (J). pap. (978-0-9572728-0-4(4)) Tiny Island Pr.

—Tiny Rabbit's Alphabet Book. 2015. (Illus.). 40p. (J). pap. (978-0-9572728-5-9(5)) Tiny Island Pr.

Joslin, Mary. Saint Francis: The Good Man of Assisi. Wisenfeld, Alison, illus. 2015. (ENG.). 32p. (J). (gr. k-4). 9.99 (978-0-7459-6492-8(3)) Lion Hudson PLC GBR. Dist: Independent Pubs. Group.

Joubert, Beverly & Joubert, Dereck. African Animal Alphabet. 2011. (ENG., Illus.). 48p. (J). (gr. -1-k). 16.95 (978-1-4263-0781-2(0), National Geographic Children's Bks.) National Geographic Society.

Jovanovic, Katarina. The King Has Goat Ears, 1 vol. Beha, Philippe, illus. 2008. (ENG.). 32p. (J). (gr. k-2). 16.95 (978-1-896580-22-7(X)) Tradewind Bks. CAN. Dist: Orca Bk. Pubs. USA.

Joyce, William. The Sandman. Joyce, William, illus. 2012. (Guardians of Childhood Ser.). (ENG., Illus.). 48p. (J). (gr. -1-3). 17.99 (978-1-4424-3042-6(7), Atheneum Bks. for Young Readers) Simon & Schuster Children's Publishing.

Judge, Chris. The Brave Beast. 2013. (ENG., Illus.). 32p. (J). (gr. -1-k). pap. 12.99 (978-1-84939-561-8(6)) Andersen Pr. GBR. Dist: Independent Pubs. Group.

—Brian & the Vikings. 2015. (ENG., Illus.). 32p. (J). pap. 13.00 (978-1-84717-687-5(9)) O'Brien Pr., Ltd., The IRL. Dist: Dufour Editions, Inc.

—The Great Explorer. 2012. (ENG., Illus.). 32p. (J). (gr. -1-2). pap. 13.99 (978-1-84939-401-7(6)) Andersen Pr. GBR. Dist: Independent Pubs. Group.

Jugran, Jan. Baby Dolphins. Larranaga, Ana Martin, illus. 2006. (ENG.). 6p. (J). (gr. -1 — 1). 14.99 (978-1-58476-490-8(2), IKIDS) Innovative Kids.

Julian, Sean. The Great Big Sleep. 2016. (ENG., Illus.). 32p. (J). (gr. -1-k). pap. 12.99 **(978-1-84941-988-8(4)**, Red Fox) Random House Children's Books GBR. Dist: Independent Pubs. Group.

Jullien, Jean. This Is Not a Book. 2016. (ENG., Illus.). 32p. (gr. -1 — 1). bds. 12.95 (978-0-7148-7112-7(5)) Phaidon Pr., Inc.

Just One More Swim. 2008. (Picture Books... Ser.). 32p. (978-1-4075-1842-8(9)) Parragon, Inc.

Kaiser, Lori. George Washington. Kaiser, Lori, illus. 2012. (Illus.). 26p. pap. (978-0-9836651-7-5(6)) Roxby Media Ltd.

Kala & Kol. Where Your Love Is: For Peace Is in This Place. 2012. 60p. pap. 31.99 (978-1-4691-5926-3(0)) Xlibris Corp.

Kaldor, Connie. A Duck in New York City. Fil and Julie Staff, illus. 2005. (ENG.). 36p. (J). (gr. -1-2). 16.95 (978-2-923163-02-4(8)) La Montagne Secrete CAN. Dist: Independent Pubs. Group.

—A Poodle in Paris. Fil and Julie Staff, illus. 2006. (ENG.). 36p. (J). (gr. -1-2). 16.95 (978-2-923163-12-3(5)) La Montagne Secrete CAN. Dist: Independent Pubs. Group.

Kallevig, Christine P. Nature Fold-along Stories: Quick & Easy Origami Tales about Plants & Animals. 2009. (ENG., Illus.). 80p. (Orig.). (J). (gr. k-8). pap. 11.95 (978-0-9628769-2-9(5)) Storytime Ink International.

Kalomas, Alice & Kerr, Lenora. Sir Wrinkles. Utomo, Gabhor, illus. 2005. (J). 14.95 (978-0-9766639-0-4(2)) Sir Wrinkles Pr.

Kalz, Jill. No Snow for Christmas, 1 vol. Erkocak, Sahin, illus. 2013. (Pfeffernut County Ser.). (ENG.). 32p. (gr. 3-4). 8.99 (978-1-4795-2158-6(2), Fiction Picture Bks.) Picture Window Bks.

—Pretty Princess Party: Hidden Picture Puzzles, 1 vol. Epstein, Len & Pullan, Jack, illus. 2013. (Seek It Out Ser.). (ENG.). 32p. (gr. 1-2). 26.65 (978-1-4048-7943-0(9)) Picture Window Bks.

Kamke, Bridget. The Story of the Infinipede. Ospital, Geneveive, illus. 2003. (J). 19.95 (978-0-9744306-0-7(9)) You Can Do It! Productions.

Kane, Kim. Esther's Rainbow. Acton, Sara, illus. 2015. (ENG.). 32p. (J). (gr. -1-k). 16.99 (978-1-925266-28-3(1)) Allen & Unwin AUS. Dist: Independent Pubs. Group.

Kaneko, Yuki. Into the Snow. Saito, Masamitsu, illus. 2016. (ENG.). 32p. (J). (gr. -1-2). 16.95 (978-1-59270-188-9(4)) Enchanted Lion Bks., LLC.

Kangaroo at the Zoo IR. 2017. (Phonics Readers Ser.). (ENG.). (J). pap. 6.99 **(978-0-7945-3716-6(2)**, Usborne) EDC Publishing.

Kann, Victoria. Flower Girl. Kann, Victoria, illus. 2013. (Pinkalicious Ser.). (ENG., Illus.). 24p. (J). (gr. -1-3). pap. 3.99 (978-0-06-218766-6(X), HarperFestival) HarperCollins Pubs.

—Pinkalicious: Pinkie Promise. Kann, Victoria, illus. 2011. (I Can Read Level 1 Ser.). (ENG., Illus.). 32p. (J). (gr. -1-3). pap. 3.99 (978-0-06-192887-1(9)) HarperCollins Pubs.

—Pinkalicious & the New Teacher. Kann, Victoria, illus. 2014. (Pinkalicious Ser.). (ENG., Illus.). 24p. (J). (gr. -1-3). pap. 6.99 (978-0-06-218913-4(1), HarperFestival) HarperCollins Pubs.

—Pinkalicious: Apples, Apples, Apples! Kann, Victoria, illus. 2016. (Pinkalicious Ser.). (Illus.). 24p. (J). (gr. -1-3). pap. 4.99 (978-0-06-241079-5(2), HarperFestival) HarperCollins Pubs.

—Pinkie Promise. Kann, Victoria, illus. 2011. (I Can Read Level 1 Ser.). (ENG., Illus.). 32p. (J). (gr. -1-3). 16.99 (978-0-06-192888-8(7)) HarperCollins Pubs.

Kao, Sleepless. Duet. 2015. (ENG., Illus.). 34p. (J). (gr. -1-3). 16.95 (978-1-897476-76-5(0)) Simply Read Bks. CAN. Dist: Ingram Publisher Services.

Kaplan, Michael B. Betty Bunny Loves Easter. Jorisch, Stéphane, illus. 2015. (Betty Bunny Ser.). (ENG.). 32p. (J). (gr. -1-k). 16.99 (978-0-8037-4061-7(1), Dial Bks) Penguin Young Readers Group.

Kartinyeri, Doris. Bush Games & Knucklebones. McInerney, Kunyi June-Anne, illus. 2003. 32p. (J). pap. (978-1-875641-81-9(5)) Magabala Bks.

Kate Smith Designs, illus. Who's Playing on the Farm? 2011. (Magic Bath Bks.). (ENG.). 8p. (J). (gr. -1-3). 5.99 (978-1-4380-7179-4(5)) Barron's Educational Series, Inc.

—Who's Playing Outdoors? 2011. (Magic Bath Bks.). (ENG.). 8p. (J). (gr. -1-3). 5.99 (978-1-4380-7178-7(7)) Barron's Educational Series, Inc.

Katirgis, Jane. Baby Forest Animals. 2010. (All about Baby Animals Ser.). (Illus.). 24p. (J). pap. 7.95 (978-1-59845-161-0(8), Enslow Elementary) Enslow Pubs., Inc.

Katschke, Judy. Shrek the Third. 2007. (Illus.). (J). (978-0-696-23947-2(7)) Meredith Bks.

Katz, Karen. Princess Baby. Katz, Karen, illus. 2012. (Princess Baby Ser.). (ENG., Illus.). 30p. (J). (gr. k-k). bds. 7.99 (978-0-307-93146-7(3), Schwartz & Wade Bks.) Random Hse. Children's Bks.

—Princess Baby, Night-Night. Katz, Karen, illus. 2014. (Princess Baby Ser.). (ENG., Illus.). 28p. (J). (— 1). bds. 7.99 (978-0-385-37848-2(3), Schwartz & Wade Bks.) Random Hse. Children's Bks.

—Where Is Baby's Belly Button? Katz, Karen, illus. anniv. ed. 2009. (ENG., Illus.). 14p. (J). (gr. -1 — 1). bds. 12.99 (978-1-4169-8733-8(9), Little Simon) Little Simon.

—Where Is Baby's Belly Button? 2005. (CHI.). 12p. (J). 6.95 (978-986-7517-72-2(5)) Shan Jen Publishing Co., Ltd. TWN. Dist: Chinasprout, Inc.

Kaufman, Elliott, photos by. Numbers Everywhere. 2013. (ENG., Illus.). 32p. (J). (gr. -1). 12.95 (978-0-7892-1157-6(2), Abbeville Kids) Abbeville Pr., Inc.

Kean, Edward. Howdy Doody's Lucky Trip. McNaught, Harry, illus. 2011. 30p. 35.95 (978-1-258-02772-8(0)) Literary Licensing, LLC.

Kebbe, Jonathan. Shredder. Nayler, Sarah, illus. 2014. (ENG.). 80p. (J). (gr. k-2). pap. 7.99 (978-0-552-56898-2(8)) Transworld Publishers Ltd. GBR. Dist: Independent Pubs. Group.

Kellerhals-Stewart, Heather. Skookum Sal, Birling Gal. Blaine, Janice, illus. unabr. ed. 2003. (ENG.). 32p. (J). pap. 18.95 (978-1-55017-285-0(9)) Harbour Publishing Co., Ltd. CAN. Dist: Midpoint Trade Bks., Inc.

Kelley, Marty. Almost Everybody Farts. 2017. (ENG., Illus.). 32p. (J). (gr. -1). 12.95 (978-1-4549-1954-4(X)) Sterling Publishing Co., Inc.

Kellogg, Steven. The Missing Mitten Mystery. Kellogg, Steven, illus. 2004. (Picture Puffins Ser.). (Illus.). (gr. -1-3). 17.00 (978-0-7569-2581-9(9)) Perfection Learning Corp.

Kelly, John. The Beastly Pirates. 2015. (ENG., Illus.). 32p. (J). (gr. -1-1). 18.99 (978-1-4088-4983-5(6), 9781408849835, Bloomsbury USA Childrens) Bloomsbury Publishing USA.

—Sir Scaly Pants the Dragon Knight. Kelly, John, illus. 2015. (ENG., Illus.). 32p. (J). (gr. -1-1). 18.99 (978-1-4088-5602-4(6), 9781408856024, Bloomsbury USA Childrens) Bloomsbury Publishing USA.

Kelly, Sharon L. C. M. Coco's Vineyard Vacation: Double Fun on Martha's Vineyard. Galbraith, Alison L., illus. 2005. 40p. (J). 16.95 (978-0-9766283-0-9(9)) Secret Garden Bookworks.

Keltie, Helen. The Mysterious Lake: Otriana. 2013. 68p. pap. 8.99 (978-1-4525-0949-5(2), Balboa Pr.) Author Solutions, Inc.

Kempter, Christa & Weldin, Frauke. Wally & Mae. 2010. (ENG., Illus.). 32p. (J). (gr. -1-k). pap. 7.95 (978-0-7358-2290-0(5)) North-South Bks., Inc.

Kendall, Jane. Tennessee Rose. 2012. (Horse Diaries: 9). lib. bdg. 18.40 (978-0-606-26554-6(6), Turtleback) Turtleback Bks.

Kendall, Penny. Sleepy Baby. 2011. (Illus.). 14p. bds. (978-1-84089-609-1(4)) Zero to Ten, Ltd.

—Socks. 2011. (Illus.). 14p. bds. (978-1-84089-608-4(6)) Zero to Ten, Ltd.

Kennedy, Anne Vittur. The Farmer's Away! Baa! Neigh! Kennedy, Anne Vittur, illus. 2014. (ENG., Illus.). 32p. (J). (-k). 15.99 (978-0-7636-6679-8(3)) Candlewick Pr.

—One Spring Lamb, 1 vol. 2016. (ENG., Illus.). 20p. (J). bds. 8.99 (978-0-7180-8782-1(8)) Nelson, Thomas Inc.

Kennedy, Kim. Pirate Pete. Kennedy, Doug & Kennedy, Roy D., illus. 2010. (ENG.). 40p. (J). (gr. 1-4). pap. 8.95 (978-0-8109-8923-8(9)) Abrams, Inc.

Kenney, Cindy. Veggie Tales I Can! And So Can You!, 1 vol. 2004. (Big Idea Books / VeggieTales Ser.). (ENG., Illus.). (J). bds. 12.99 (978-0-310-70893-3(1)) Zonderkidz.

Kent, Allegra. Ballerina Swan. McCully, Emily Arnold, illus. 2013. (ENG.). 32p. (J). (gr. -1-3). pap. 6.99 (978-0-8234-2906-6(7)) Holiday Hse., Inc.

Kent, Lorna, illus. At the Beach. 2004. 8p. (J). bds. 3.99 (978-1-85854-087-0(9)) Brimax Books Ltd. GBR. Dist: Byeway Bks.

Kerley, Barbara. Portland Baby. Cleland, Josh, illus. 2017. (Local Baby Ser.). (ENG.). 22p. (J). (gr. -1-k). bds. 8.95 **(978-1-946064-05-9(X))** Duo Pr. LLC.

Kerr, Judith. The Crocodile under the Bed. 2014. (ENG., Illus.). 32p. (J). 17.99 (978-0-00-758675-2(2), HarperCollins Children's Bks.) HarperCollins Pubs. Ltd. GBR. Dist: HarperCollins Pubs.

—Goose in a Hole. Kerr, Judith, illus. 2006. (ENG., Illus.). 40p. (J). (gr. k-2). pap. 9.99 (978-0-00-720794-7(8), HarperCollins Children's Bks.) HarperCollins Pubs. Ltd. GBR. Dist: Independent Pubs. Group.

—Goose in a Hole. 2005. (ENG., Illus.). 100p. (J). (gr. k-2). 15.99 (978-0-00-720793-0(X)) HarperCollins Pubs. Ltd. GBR. Dist: Independent Pubs. Group.

—The Tiger Who Came to Tea. 2006. pap. (978-0-06-052468-5(5)) HarperCollins Canada, Ltd.

Kerven, Rosalind. Sparrow, the Crow & the Pearl. Williamson, Melanie, illus. 2005. (ENG.). 24p. (J). lib. bdg. 23.65 (978-1-59646-754-5(1)) Dingles & Co.

Kessler, Leonard P. Mr. Pine's Purple House. Kessler, Leonard P., illus. 40th anniv. ed. 2005. (Illus.). 64p. (J). 16.00 (978-1-930900-32-5(5)) Purple Hse. Pr.

Khan, Aliyah. The Adventures of Solomon Spider: Solomon Sees the City. 2011. 28p. (gr. -1 — 1). pap. 14.09 (978-1-4490-1546-6(8)) AuthorHouse.

Khan, Hena. Golden Domes & Silver Lanterns: A Muslim Book of Colors. Amini, Mehrdokht, illus. 2015. (ENG.). 32p. (J). (gr. -1-k). 7.99 (978-1-4521-4121-3(5)) Chronicle Bks. LLC.

Khing, T. T. Where Is the Cake? 2010. (ENG & DUT., Illus.). 32p. (J). (gr. -1-3). pap. 7.95 (978-0-8109-8924-5(7)) UK Abrams Bks. for Young Readers.

Khzouz, Medlaine. Suzie Time. 2011. 24p. pap. 15.99 (978-1-4568-7454-4(3)) Xlibris Corp.

Kickliy. Musnet: The Mouse of Monet. 2016. (Musnet Ser.: 1). (ENG., Illus.). 56p. (J). (gr. 2). 19.95 (978-1-941250-09-9(2), odod bks.) Uncivilized Bks.

A Kid's Guide to the Classification of Living Things. (Illus.). (J). (gr. k-5). 127.50 (978-0-8239-7257-9(7)) Rosen Publishing Group, Inc., The.

Kilgras, Heidi. The Tickle Book. 2017. (Little Golden Book Ser.). (ENG., Illus.). 24p. (J). (-k). 4.99 **(978-0-399-55529-9(3)**, Golden Bks.) Random Hse. Children's Bks.

Kilgus, Walter C. Bess Takes a Ride. 2008. 36p. pap. 17.49 (978-1-4257-8807-0(6)) Xlibris Corp.

Killen, Nicola. I Got a Crocodile. 2013. (ENG., Illus.). 32p. (J). 15.99 (978-0-85707-577-2(2)) Simon & Schuster, Ltd. GBR. Dist: Simon & Schuster, Inc.

Kim, Byung-Gyu & Hao, K. T. The 100th Customer. Ferri, Giuliano, illus. 2005. (ENG.). 32p. (J). (gr. -1-17). 15.95 (978-1-933327-03-7(0)) Purple Bear Bks., Inc.

Kim, Cecil. I Can't Sleep: Imagination - Bedtime. Cowley, Joy, ed. Bisaillon, Josee, illus. 2015. (Step up - Creative Thinking Ser.). (ENG.). 32p. (gr. -1-2). 26.65 (978-1-925246-13-1(2)); 26.65 (978-1-925246-39-1(6)); 7.99 (978-1-925246-65-0(5)) ChoiceMaker Pty. Ltd., The AUS. (Big and SMALL). Dist: Lerner Publishing Group.

—One Little Bean: Observation - Life Cycle. Cowley, Joy, ed. Dattola, Chiara, illus. 2015. (Step up - Creative Thinking Ser.). (ENG.). 32p. (gr. -1-2). 26.65 (978-1-925246-12-4(4)); 26.65 (978-1-925246-38-4(8)); 7.99 (978-1-925246-64-3(7)) ChoiceMaker Pty. Ltd., The AUS. (Big and SMALL). Dist: Lerner Publishing Group.

Kim, Soo-hyeon. There It Is! Observation - Objects. Cowley, Joy, ed. Lee, Hyeon-joo, illus. 2015. (Step up - Creative Thinking Ser.). (ENG.). 32p. (gr. -1-2). 26.65 (978-1-925246-09-4(4)); 26.65 (978-1-925246-35-3(3)); 7.99 (978-1-925246-61-2(2)) ChoiceMaker Pty. Ltd., The AUS. (Big and SMALL). Dist: Lerner Publishing Group.

—What Does the Bee See? Observation - Parts & Whole. Cowley, Joy, ed. Jo, Eun-hwa, illus. 2015. (Step up - Creative Thinking Ser.). (ENG.). 32p. (gr. -1-2). 26.65 (978-1-925246-34-6(5)); 7.99 (978-1-925246-60-5(4)); 26.65 (978-1-925246-08-7(6)) ChoiceMaker Pty. Ltd., The AUS. (Big and SMALL). Dist: Lerner Publishing Group.

—What Does the Bee See? Observation - Parts & Whole. Cowley, Joy, ed. Jo, Eun-hwa, illus. 2015. (Step up - Creative Thinking Ser.). (ENG.). 32p. (J). (gr. -1-2). 7.99 (978-1-925186-54-3(7)) Lerner Publishing Group.

Kimmel, Eric A. Even Higher! A Rosh Hashanah Story by I. L. Peretz. Weber, Jill, illus. 2010. (ENG.). 32p. (J). (gr. -1-3). pap. 6.95 (978-0-8234-2298-2(4)) Holiday Hse., Inc.

—Joha Makes a Wish: A Middle Eastern Tale, 0 vols. Rayyan, Omar, illus. 2013. (ENG.). 40p. (J). (gr. k-3). pap. 7.99 (978-1-4778-1687-5(9), 9781477816875, Amazon Children's Publishing) Amazon Publishing.

—Los Tres Cabritos, 0 vols. Gilpin, Stephen, illus. 2012. (SPA & ENG.). 32p. (J). (gr. k-3). pap. 9.99 (978-0-7614-5961-3(8), 9780761459613, Amazon Children's Publishing) Amazon Publishing.

Kimmelman, Leslie. Everybody Bonjours! McMenemy, Sarah, illus. 2015. (ENG.). 40p. (J). (gr. -1-2). pap. 7.99 (978-0-553-50782-9(6), Dragonfly Bks.) Random Hse. Children's Bks.

Kimura, Yuichi. On the Seesaw Bridge. Hata, Kowshiro, illus. 2011. (ENG.). 36p. (J). (gr. -1-3). 14.95 (978-1-935654-18-6(7), Vertical) Vertical, Inc.

Kinast, Susan. Play from A to Z. 2006. (J). lib. bdg. 19.95 (978-1-933732-11-4(3)) Big Ransom Studio.

King, Anthea. Where Do Butterflies Go ... ?? 2013. 32p. pap. (978-1-4602-1743-6(8)) FriesenPress.

King, Corinne & Fenton, Corinne. Queenie: One Elephant's Story. Gouldthorpe, Peter, illus. 2013. (ENG.). 24p. (J). (gr. k-3). 16.99 (978-0-7636-6375-9(1)) Candlewick Pr.

Kinkade, Thomas, illus. Away in a Manger. 2005. 32p. (J). 16.99 (978-0-06-078730-1(9)) Zonderkidz.

Kipling, Rudyard. The Jungle Book. Thorne, Jenny, illus. 2014. (ENG.). 48p. (J). (gr. k-5). pap. 7.99 (978-1-84322-882-0(3), Armadillo) Anness Publishing GBR. Dist: National Bk. Network.

Kirk, Bill. The Ins & Outs of Air: The Sum of Our Parts Series. 2013. (GER., Illus.). 24p. pap. 10.95 (978-1-61633-391-1(X)) Guardian Angel Publishing, Inc.

Kirk, Daniel. Library Mouse. 2010. (ENG., Illus.). 32p. (J). (gr. 1-4). pap. 7.95 (978-0-8109-8929-0(8)) UK Abrams Bks. for Young Readers.

—Library Mouse: A Museum Adventure. 2012. (ENG., Illus.). 32p. (J). (gr. k-2). 17.95 *(978-1-4197-0173-3(8),* Abrams Bks. for Young Readers) Abrams, Inc.

—Library Mouse No. 2: A Friend's Tale. 2010. (ENG., Illus.). 32p. (J). (gr. 1-4). pap. 7.95 *(978-0-8109-8930-6(1))* UK Abrams Bks. for Young Readers.

Kirkby, Joanne & Cooper, Sharon, illus. Mosaic Picture Sticker Book. 2015. (Mosaic Sticker Bks.). (ENG.). 24+12p. (J). (gr. k-5). pap. 10.99 *(978-0-7945-3015-0(X),* Usborne) EDC Publishing.

Kirkland, Kim M. Car Cars Go Zoom Zoom Zoom. 2012. 24p. pap. 24.95 *(978-1-4626-6926-4(3))* America Star Bks.

Kirschner, Jason. Mr. Particular. 2016. (ENG., Illus.). 40p. (J). (gr. -1). 14.95 *(978-1-4549-1818-9(7))* Sterling Publishing Co., Inc.

Kitamura, Satoshi. Pot-San's Tabletop Tales. Kitamura, Satoshi, illus. 2013. (ENG., Illus.). 32p. (J). (gr. -1-k). 22.99 *(978-1-84939-378-2(8))* Andersen Pr. GBR. Dist: Independent Pubs. Group.

—When Sheep Can't Sleep (Cuando los Borregos no Pueden Dormir) (SPA.). (J). (gr. 1-6). 19.95 *(978-84-372-6605-3(X))* Santillana USA Publishing Co., Inc.

Kitten. (Buggy Buddies Ser.). (Illus.). (J). (gr. -1). bds. *(978-1-56021-350-5(7),* 201) W.J. Fantasy, Inc.

Kizer, Linda M. Plug, the Lonely Little Fire Hydrant. 2009. 60p. pap. 26.99 *(978-1-4490-2873-2(X))* AuthorHouse.

Kleinberg, Naomi. Elmo's Christmas Snowman (Sesame Street) Brannon, Tom, illus. 2013. (ENG.). 12p. (J). (— 1). bds. 6.99 *(978-0-449-81257-0(X),* Random Hse. Bks. for Young Readers) Random Hse. Children's Bks.

Kleven, Elisa. Sun Bread. 2004. (ENG., Illus.). 32p. (J). (gr. -1-k). reprint ed. pap. 6.99 *(978-0-14-240073-9(4),* Puffin Books) Penguin Young Readers Group.

Klutz Editors, contrib. by. Shrinky Dinks Refill, Pack. (ENG.). 8p. 8.95 *(978-1-57054-585-6(5))* Klutz.

Knapman, Timothy. Let's Read! - Little Ogre's Surprise Supper. Cort, Ben, illus. 2014. (Let's Read! Ser.). (ENG.). 32p. (J). (gr. k-2). pap. 7.99 *(978-1-4472-4531-5(8))* Pan Macmillan GBR. Dist: Independent Pubs. Group.

—A Moster Moved In! Schauer, Loretta, illus. 2015. (ENG.). 32p. (J). 16.99 *(978-1-58925-176-2(8))* Tiger Tales.

—The New Royal Baby. East, Nick, illus. 2015. (ENG.). 32p. (J). (gr. -1-k). pap. 10.99 *(978-1-4052-7828-7(5))* Egmont Bks., Ltd. GBR. Dist: Independent Pubs. Group.

—Superhero Dad. Berger, Joe, illus. 2016. (ENG.). (J). (gr. -1-2). 15.99 *(978-0-7636-8657-4(3),* Nosy Crow) Candlewick Pr.

Knapp, Andrew. Let's Find Momo! A Hide-And-Seek Board Book. 2017. (Find Momo Ser.). (ENG., Illus.). 24p. (J). (-k). bds. 9.99 *(978-1-59474-958-2(2))* Quirk Bks.

Knoll, Linda L. Patient for Pumpkins. 2014. (ENG., Illus.). 32p. (J). (gr. -1-3). 15.95 *(978-1-58394-708-1(6))* North Atlantic Bks.

Knudsen, Michelle. Marilyn's Monster. Phelan, Matt, illus. 2015. (ENG.). 40p. (J). (gr. -1-3). 16.99 *(978-0-7636-6011-6(6))* Candlewick Pr.

—Marilyn's Monster. Phelan, Matt, illus. 2017. (ENG.). (J). (gr. -1-3). lib. bdg. 17.20 ***(978-0-606-39844-2(9))*** Turtleback Bks.

Koch, Joann. Annie's World. 2009. 20p. (J). pap. 9.95 *(978-1-4327-4063-4(6))* Outskirts Pr., Inc.

Koehler, Lana & Adams, Gloria. Ah-Choo! Min, Ken, illus. 2016. (ENG.). 40p. (J). (gr. k-2). 14.95 *(978-1-4549-1415-0(7))* Sterling Publishing Co., Inc.

Kohara, Kazuno. Here Comes Jack Frost. Kohara, Kazuno, illus. 2011. (ENG., Illus.). 32p. (J). (gr. -1-1). pap. 7.99 *(978-0-312-60446-2(7),* 9780312604462) Square Fish.

Komalasari, Arie. Kiki the Orangutan: The Big Banana Festival. 2013. (ENG., Illus.). 32p. (J). (gr. -1-3). 14.95 *(978-0-8048-4324-9(4))* Tuttle Publishing.

Konishi, Noriyuki. Yo-kai Watch. (Yo-Kai Watch Ser.: 6). (ENG., Illus.). 192p. (J). Vol. 6. 2016. pap. 9.99 *(978-1-4215-9217-6(7))* Vol. 7. 2017. pap. 9.99 *(978-1-4215-9218-3(5))* Viz Media.

Koniver, Laura. From the Ground Up. Koniver, Laura, illus. 2012. (Illus.). 44p. (J). pap. 16.99 *(978-1-937848-03-3(5))* Do Life Right, Inc.

Kooser, Ted. The Bell in the Bridge. Root, Barry, illus. 2016. (ENG.). 32p. (J). (gr. 1-4). 16.99 *(978-0-7636-6481-7(2))* Candlewick Pr.

Koralek, Jenny. The Coat of Many Colors. Baynes, Pauline, illus. 2004. 32p. (J). 16.00 *(978-0-8028-5277-9(7))* Eerdmans, William B. Publishing Co.

Koren, Robert. The Moon in the Man. 2010. 28p. pap. 15.99 *(978-1-4535-3946-0(8))* Xlibris Corp.

Korr, Mary. Winston the water Dog: Portuguese water dog tales book One. 2009. 40p. pap. 17.49 *(978-1-4415-8406-9(4))* Xlibris Corp.

Kove, Torill. My Grandmother Ironed the King's Shirts. 2017. (ENG., Illus.). 32p. (J). (gr. 2-5). 16.95 ***(978-1-77085-967-8(5),*** 9781770859678) Firefly Bks., Ltd.

Kovecses, Anna. One Thousand Things. 2015. (Learn with Little Mouse Ser.). (ENG.). 80p. (J). (gr. -1 — 1). 16.99 *(978-1-84780-702-1(X),* Wide Eyed Editions) Quarto Publishing Group UK GBR. Dist: Hachette Bk. Group.

—One Thousand Things: Learn to Say Your First Words with Little Mouse. 2015. (Learn with Little Mouse Ser.). (ENG., Illus.). 80p. (J). 16.99 *(978-1-84780-607-9(4),* Wide Eyed Editions) Quarto Publishing Group UK GBR. Dist: Littlehampton Bk Services, Ltd.

Kralapp, Karl E. Fish Food. Kralapp, Karl E., illus. 2013. (Illus.). 28p. pap. 9.99 *(978-1-937165-62-8(0))* Orange Hat Publishing.

Kranowitz, Asher. Absolutely No Dogs Allowed. Abrams, Annette, illus. 2016. (ENG.). 32p. (J). pap. 14.95 *(978-1-935567-58-5(6))* Sensory Resources.

Kranz, Linda. Where I Belong. 2016. (ENG., Illus.). 32p. (J). (gr. -1-1). 12.95 *(978-1-63076-066-3(8))* Taylor Trade Publishing.

Kratt, Chris & Kratt, Martin. Wild in Africa! (Wild Kratts) Fruchter, Jason, illus. 2016. (Little Golden Book Ser.). (ENG.). 24p. (J). (-k). 4.99 *(978-1-101-93862-1(5),* Golden Bks.) Random Hse. Children's Bks.

Kraulis, Julie. An Armadillo in New York. 2016. (ENG., Illus.). 32p. (J). (gr. k-4). 16.99 *(978-1-77049-891-4(5),* Tundra Bks.) Tundra Bks. CAN. Dist: Penguin Random Hse. LLC.

—An Armadillo in Paris. 2014. (ENG., Illus.). 32p. (J). (gr. k-4). 17.99 *(978-1-77049-526-5(6),* Tundra Bks.) Tundra Bks. CAN. Dist: Penguin Random Hse. LLC.

—Whimsy's Heavy Things. Kraulis, Julie, illus. 2013. (ENG., Illus.). 32p. (J). (gr. -1-1). 17.95 *(978-1-77049-403-9(0),* Tundra Bks.) Tundra Bks. CAN. Dist: Penguin Random Hse. LLC.

Krause, Ute. Oscar & the Very Hungry Dragon. Krause, Ute, illus. 2015. (ENG., Illus.). 40p. (J). 8.95 *(978-0-7358-4230-4(2))* North-South Bks., Inc.

Krauss, Ruth. Bears. Sendak, Maurice, illus. 2005. (ENG.). 24p. (J). 21.99 *(978-0-06-027994-3(X))* HarperCollins Pubs.

—The Carrot Seed. Johnson, Crockett, illus. 60th anniv. ed. 2004. 32p. (J). (gr. -1-3). lib. bdg. 17.89 *(978-0-06-023351-8(6))* HarperCollins Pubs.

Krawczyk, Sabine & Delafosse, Claude. Let's Look at Insects. Krawczyk, Sabine, illus. 2012. (ENG., Illus.). 38p. (J). (gr. k-3). pap. 11.99 *(978-1-85103-279-2(7))* Moonlight Publishing, Ltd. GBR. Dist: Independent Pubs. Group.

Krebs, Laurie. Riding on a Caravan: A Silk Road Adventure. 2017. (ENG., Illus.). 32p. (J). (gr. -1-4). 8.99 ***(978-1-78285-344-2(8))*** Barefoot Bks., Inc.

Kredensor, Diane. Ollie & Moon in New York City. Meskin, Mike, photos by. 2017. (Pictureback(R) Ser.). (ENG., Illus.). 32p. (J). (gr. -1-2). pap. 5.99 ***(978-1-5247-1574-8(3),*** Random Hse. Bks. for Young Readers) Random Hse. Children's Bks.

—Ollie & Moon in Paris. Kress, Sandra, photos by. 2017. (Pictureback(R) Ser.). (ENG., Illus.). 32p. (J). (gr. -1-2). pap. 5.99 ***(978-1-5247-1575-5(1),*** Random Hse. Bks. for Young Readers) Random Hse. Children's Bks.

Krishna, McArthur. What Would It Be Like? Dasgupta, Ishaan & Sadr, Ayeshe, illus. 2016. (ENG.). 34p. (J). (gr. 3-4). 17.99 *(978-0-692-58721-8(7),* Little Adventures) Amberjack Publishing Co.

Kronheim, Joseph Martin. My First Picture Book. 2007. (Illus.). 56p. per. *(978-1-4065-3654-6(7))* Dodo Pr.

Kropp, Joseph P. Nathan Meets His Monsters. Johnston, Phillip, illus. 2012. 34p. 16.95 *(978-1-890905-59-0(3))*; pap. 9.95 *(978-1-890905-58-3(5))* Day to Day Enterprises.

Krosoczka, Jarrett J. Punk Farm on Tour. 2015. (ENG., Illus.). 40p. (J). (gr. -1-2). 7.99 *(978-0-553-50778-2(8),* Dragonfly Bks.) Random Hse. Children's Bks.

Krudwig, Vickie L., creator. Silly Circles Sketch Pad. 2004. (Illus.). 50p. (J). spiral bd. *(978-0-9700127-2-2(1))* Sweet Success Pr.

Krulik, Nancy. Ice-Cream Dreams. Martinez, Heather, illus. 2004. 22p. (J). lib. bdg. 15.00 *(978-1-4242-0975-0(7))* Fitzgerald Bks.

Kruse, Donald W. Gorilla Soup! 2012. 48p. pap. 12.95 *(978-1-59663-862-4(1),* Castle Keep Pr.) Rock, James A. & Co. Pubs.

Krusinski, Anna. Farm Friends: A Visit to the Local Farm. 2016. (Kubu Ser.). (ENG., Illus.). 34p. (J). (gr. -1-2). pap. 5.99 *(978-1-57826-475-9(8),* Hatherleigh Pr.) Hatherleigh Co., Ltd., The.

Kubler, Annie. Itsy, Bitsy Spider. 2005. (Sign & Singalong Ser.). (ENG., Illus.). 12p. (J). (gr. k-k). bds. *(978-1-904550-43-3(6))* Child's Play International Ltd.

Kubler, Annie, illus. Dress Up! 2012. (Mix & Match Babies Ser.). (ENG.). 12p. (J). bds. *(978-1-84643-485-3(8))* Child's Play International Ltd.

—Teddy Bear, Teddy Bear. 2005. (Sign & Singalong Ser.). (ENG.). 12p. (J). (gr. k-1). bds. *(978-1-904550-40-2(1))* Child's Play International Ltd.

—Twinkle, Twinkle, Little Star. 2005. (Sign & Singalong Ser.). (ENG.). 12p. (J). (gr. k-k). bds. *(978-1-904550-42-6(8))* Child's Play International Ltd.

Kubler, Annie & Adams, Pam. Down by the Station. 2005. 16p. (J). bds. *(978-0-85953-457-4(X))* Child's Play International Ltd.

Kuenzler, Lou. Eat Your People! Wojtowycz, David, illus. (ENG.). 32p. (J). (gr. -1-k). 2017. pap. 7.99 *(978-1-4083-3034-0(2))* 2016. 17.99 *(978-1-4083-3033-3(4))* Hachette Children's Group GBR. (Orchard Bks.). Dist: Hachette Bk. Group.

Kulling, Monica. Merci Mister Dash! Melo, Esperanca, illus. 2011. (ENG.). 32p. (J). (gr. -1-2). 17.95 *(978-0-88776-964-1(0),* Tundra Bks.) Tundra Bks. CAN. Dist: Penguin Random Hse. LLC.

Kumon Publishing, ed. My Book of Amazing Tracing. 2012. (Illus.). 80p. (J). pap. 7.95 *(978-4-7743-0007-8(1))* Kumon Publishing North America, Inc.

Kunhardt, Dorothy. Now Open the Box. Kunhardt, Dorothy, illus. 2013. (ENG., Illus.). 72p. (J). (gr. -1-2). 16.95 *(978-1-59017-708-2(8),* NYR Children's Collection) New York Review of Bks., Inc., The.

Kuo, Julia. Everyone Eats. Kuo, Julia, illus. 2012. (ENG., Illus.). 22p. (J). (gr. -1). 9.95 *(978-1-897476-74-1(4))* Simply Read Bks. CAN. Dist: Ingram Publisher Services.

Kusama, Yayoi & Andersen, Hans Christian. The Little Mermaid. 2016. (ENG., Illus.). 96p. 45.00 *(978-87-92877-59-8(1))* Louisana DNK. Dist: D.A.P./Distributed Art Pubs.

Kushner, Tony. Brundibar. Sendak, Maurice, illus. 2003. (ENG.). 56p. (J). (gr. -1-17). 24.99 *(978-0-7868-0904-2(3),* di Capua, Michael Bks.) Hyperion Bks. for Children.

Kuskin, Karla. Roar & More. 2004. (ENG., Illus.). 48p. (J). (gr. -1-3). 11.95 *(978-1-59078-249-1(6))* Boyds Mills Pr.

Kusugak, Michael. The Littlest Sled Dog, 1 vol. Krykorka, Vladyana, illus. 2010. (ENG.). 32p. (J). (gr. -1-3). pap. 10.95 *(978-1-55469-174-6(5))* Orca Bk. Pubs. USA.

Kutschbach, Doris. Art Detective: Spot the Difference! 2013. (ENG., Illus.). 48p. (J). (gr. 3-7). 14.95 *(978-3-7913-7104-7(5))* Prestel Verlag GmbH & Co KG. DEU. Dist: Penguin Random Hse. LLC.

Lacey, Minna. Big Book of Big Machines. 2010. (Big Book of Big Machines Ser.). 14p. (J). 13.99 *(978-0-7945-2764-8(7),* Usborne) EDC Publishing.

Ladybird. I'm Ready... for School! 2016. (Ladybird I'm Ready Ser.). (ENG., Illus.). 48p. (J). (— 1). pap. 11.99 ***(978-0-241-21597-5(8))*** Penguin Bks., Ltd. GBR. Dist: Independent Pubs. Group.

Ladybird. On the Farm. 2016. (Read It Yourself with Ladybird Ser.). (ENG., Illus.). 32p. (J). (gr. 2-4). 5.99 *(978-0-241-23731-1(9))* Penguin Bks., Ltd. GBR. Dist: Independent Pubs. Group.

Ladybird Books Staff. Have Their Eyes Tested. 2017. (Topsy & Tim Ser.). (ENG., Illus.). 32p. (J). (gr. -1-1). pap. 9.99 ***(978-0-241-28254-0(3))*** Penguin Bks., Ltd. GBR. Dist: Independent Pubs. Group.

Ladybird Christmas Time. 2016. (ENG., Illus.). 72p. (J). (gr. 2-4). 16.99 *(978-0-241-26302-0(6))* Penguin Bks., Ltd. GBR. Dist: Independent Pubs. Group.

Lafortune, Claude. The Wonderful Story of Christmas. gif. ed. 2003. (Illus.). 24p. *(978-2-89507-438-0(0))* Novalis Publishing.

Lagonegro, Melissa. Beauty & the Beast Deluxe Step into Reading (Disney Beauty & the Beast) RH Disney, illus. 2017. (Step into Reading Ser.). (ENG.). 24p. (J). (gr. -1-1). pap. 4.99 *(978-0-7364-3594-9(8),* RH/Disney) Random Hse. Children's Bks.

Lagrange, Tiffany. My Abc Blue Book. LaGrange, Tiffany, illus. 2008. 32p. pap. 12.95 *(978-1-934246-38-2(7))* Peppertree Pr., The.

Lallemand, Orianne. Blue Bird?'s Palace. 2016. (ENG., Illus.). 32p. (J). (gr. 1-5). 16.99 *(978-1-84686-885-6(8))* Barefoot Bks., Inc.

Lambe, Mona. Yintin Tales. 2013. (Illus.). 60p. pap. *(978-0-9576015-0-5(6))* Moyin Bks.

Lamont, Priscilla. Nursery Rhyme Crimes: Little Bo Peep. 2012. (Illus.). 24p. (J). pap. *(978-1-84780-354-2(7),* Frances Lincoln) Quarto Publishing Group UK.

—Tom, Tom, the Piper's Son. 2012. (ENG., Illus.). 24p. (J). (gr. k-3). 15.99 *(978-1-84780-155-5(2),* Frances Lincoln) Quarto Publishing Group UK GBR. Dist: Hachette Bk. Group.

Lang, Heather. Fearless Flyer: Ruth Law & Her Flying Machine. Colón, Raúl, illus. 2016. (ENG.). 40p. (J). (gr. k-3). 16.95 *(978-1-62091-650-6(9))* Boyds Mills Pr.

Langen, Annette. Felix Travels Back in Time. Droop, Constanza, illus. 2004. 40p. (J). 14.99 *(978-1-59384-032-7(2))* Parklane Publishing.

Langford, Jane. Hero. Vince, Dawn, illus. 2005. (ENG.). 24p. (J). lib. bdg. 23.65 *(978-1-59646-720-0(7))* Dingles & Co.

—An Old Red Hat. Axworthy, Anni, illus. 2004. (ENG.). 24p. (J). lib. bdg. 23.65 *(978-1-59646-676-0(6))* Dingles & Co.

Lanning, Andrea J. The Imposturous Egg. Lanning, Andrea J., illus. Corcacas, Maria, photos by. 2012. (Illus.). 32p. *(978-0-9571677-0-4(9))*; pap. *(978-0-9571677-4-2(1))* Ginnal Creatives Ltd.

Lansky, Bruce. Early Birdy Gets the Worm. Wummer, Amy, illus. 2010. 10p. (J). bds. 6.99 *(978-1-4169-9316-2(9))* Meadowbrook Pr.

—Monkey See, Monkey Do at the Zoo. Wummer, Amy, illus. 2010. 10p. (J). bds. 6.99 *(978-1-4169-9317-9(7))* Meadowbrook Pr.

—Polar BRRR Delivers. Wummer, Amy, illus. 2010. 10p. (J). bds. 6.99 *(978-1-4169-9318-6(5))* Meadowbrook Pr.

Larranaga, Ana M. Pull & Play - Opposites. Martín, Ana I., illus. 2013. (Pull & Play Ser.). (ENG.). 10p. (J). (— 1). bds. 7.99 *(978-0-230-75040-1(0))* Pan Macmillan GBR. Dist: Independent Pubs. Group.

Larry, V. & Mark, K. Larry Bendeco Johannes Von Sloop. Meyers, Stephanie, illus. 2014. (ENG.). 32p. (J). (gr. k-5). 7.99 *(978-1-4867-0000-4(4))* Flowerpot Children's Pr. Inc. CAN. Dist: Cardinal Pubs. Group.

Larsen, Andrew. The Imaginary Garden. Luxbacher, Irene, illus. 2009. (ENG.). 32p. (J). (gr. -1-2). 16.95 *(978-1-55453-279-7(5))* Kids Can Pr., Ltd. CAN. Dist: Hachette Bk. Group.

—In the Tree House. Petricic, Dusan, illus. 2013. (ENG.). 32p. (J). (gr. -1-2). 16.95 *(978-1-55453-635-1(9))* Kids Can Pr., Ltd. CAN. Dist: Hachette Bk. Group.

Larsen, Kirsten. It's Sharing Day! Zalme, Ron, illus. 2007. (SPA & ENG.). (J). pap. *(978-0-439-92237-1(2),* Scholastic) Scholastic, Inc.

Larsen, Mylisa & Raff, Anna. If I Were a Kangaroo. 2017. (ENG., Illus.). 32p. (J). (— 1). 17.99 *(978-0-451-46958-8(5),* Viking Books for Young Readers) Penguin Young Readers Group.

Larson, Hope. Knife's Edge: A Graphic Novel. Mock, Rebecca, illus. 2017. (Four Points Ser.: 2). (ENG.). 224p. (J). 19.99 *(978-0-374-30044-9(5),* 9780374300449, Farrar, Straus & Giroux (BYR)) Farrar, Straus & Giroux.

Larson, Mitch & McCarthy, Meghan. When Cutie Calls. 2014. (My Little Pony Ser.). (ENG., Illus.). 128p. (J). (gr. 2-5). pap. 7.99 *(978-1-61377-830-2(9),* 9781613778302) Idea & Design Works, LLC.

Lasky, Kathryn. Untitled Historical #1: Picturebook Series. 2005. 32p. (J). 15.49 *(978-0-7868-2436-6(0))*; (ENG.). 14.99 *(978-0-7868-0503-7(X))* Hyperion Pr.

—Untitled Historical #2: Picturebook Series. 2005. 32p. (J). 15.49 *(978-0-7868-2437-3(9))*; (ENG.). 14.99 *(978-0-7868-0504-4(8))* Hyperion Pr.

—Untitled Historical #3: Picturebook Series. 2005. 32p. (J). 15.49 *(978-0-7868-2438-0(7))*; (ENG.). 14.99 *(978-0-7868-0505-1(6))* Hyperion Pr.

Lathey, Nicola & Blake, Tracey. Small Talk/Going to the Park Board Book: A First Experience Book for Babies. Busby, Ailie, illus. 2016. (ENG.). 24p. (J). (— 1). bds. 10.99 ***(978-1-4472-7693-7(0))*** Pan Macmillan GBR. Dist: Independent Pubs. Group.

—Small Talk/It's Bedtime Board Book. Busby, Ailie, illus. 2016. (ENG.). 24p. (J). bds., bds. 11.99 ***(978-1-4472-7692-0(2))*** Pan Macmillan GBR. Dist: Independent Pubs. Group.

Latimer, Miriam. Dear Panda. 2014. (ENG., Illus.). 32p. (J). (gr. -1-3). 17.95 *(978-1-77147-078-0(X),* Owlkids) Owlkids Bks. Inc. CAN. Dist: Publishers Group West (PGW).

Laufer, Tiffany A. The Porch Dream. 2009. (Bellaboo & Friends Ser.). (Illus.). 32p. 15.99 *(978-0-9820088-2-9(1))* Bellaboozle Books, Inc.

Laughing Elephant Staff, compiled by. By the Sea. 2013. (Shape Bks.). (ENG., Illus.). 16p. pap. 9.95 *(978-1-59583-702-8(7))* Laughing Elephant.

Laverde, Arlene. Alaska's Three Little Pigs. Dwyer, Mindy, illus. 2015. (Paws IV Ser.). (ENG.). 20p. (J). (— 1). bds. 8.99 *(978-1-57061-974-8(3),* Little Bigfoot) Sasquatch Bks.

Lavie, Oren. The Bear Who Wasn't There & the Fabulous Forest. Erlbruch, Wolf, illus. 2016. (ENG.). 48p. (J). (gr. -1-2). 17.95 *(978-1-61775-490-6(0),* Black Sheep) Akashic Bks.

Law, Daisy. Secret, Secret. 2016. (ENG., Illus.). 40p. 15.95 *(978-1-78592-042-4(1),* 8368) Kingsley, Jessica Pubs. GBR. Dist: Macmillan Distribution Ltd.

Law, Jessica. A Hole in the Bottom of the Sea. McDonald, Jill, illus. 2013. (ENG.). 24p. (J). (gr. k-3). pap. 6.99 *(978-1-84686-948-8(X))* Barefoot Bks., Inc.

Lawrence, Donna. The Miracle of Susie the Puppy That Changed the Law. Coble, Lynn Bemer, ed. Cappoen, Jennifer Tipton, illus. 2012. 54p. 24.95 *(978-0-9846724-2-4(7))* Paws and Claws Publishing, LLC.

—Susie's Tale Hand with Paw We Changed the Law. Coble, Lynn Bemer, ed. Cappoen, Jennifer Tipton, illus. 2012. 64p. 24.95 *(978-0-9846724-1-7(9))* Paws and Claws Publishing, LLC.

Lawson, JonArno. Leap! Bisaillon, Josée, illus. 2017. (ENG.). 32p. (J). (gr. -1-2). 16.99 ***(978-1-77138-678-4(9))*** Kids Can Pr., Ltd. CAN. Dist: Hachette Bk. Group.

Lawson, Julia & Goodman, Polly. Weather. 2011. (Little Steps Ser.). (ENG., Illus.). 14p. (J). (gr. -1-k). bds. *(978-1-84089-591-9(8))* Zero to Ten, Ltd.

Lazar, Tara. Normal Norman. Britton, Stephen, illus. 2016. (ENG.). 40p. (J). (gr. -1). 14.95 *(978-1-4549-1321-4(5))* Sterling Publishing Co., Inc.

Lazo, Dorina. Children of the San Joaquin Valley. Hires, Josh, photos by. 2005. (Illus.). 35p. (YA). (gr. 7-12). pap. 15.00 *(978-0-938911-28-9(7))* Individualized Education Systems/Poppy Lane Publishing.

Le Jars, David. Uno, Dos, Hola y Adios. 2004. (Hablemos Ser.).Tr. of One, Two, Hello & Goodbye to You. (SPA., Illus.). 24p. (J). (gr. -1-k). 9.95 *(978-1-58728-948-4(2),* Two-Can Publishing) T&N Children's Publishing.

Learning Fun, Early & Priddy, Roger. Things That Go. 2010. (ENG., Illus.). 20p. (J). bds. *(978-1-84915-141-2(5),* Priddy Bks.) St. Martin's Pr.

Lebihan, Kara & Allwright, Deborah. Mrs Vickers' Knickers. Allwright, Deborah, illus. 2013. (ENG., Illus.). 32p. (J). (gr. -1). pap. 10.99 *(978-1-4052-5395-6(9))* Egmont Bks., Ltd. GBR. Dist: Independent Pubs. Group.

Leblanc, André. The Red Piano. Werner, Justine, tr. from FRE. Barroux, illus. 2010.Tr. of Piano Rouge. (ENG.). 40p. (J). (gr. 2-4). 16.99 *(978-0-9806070-1-7(9))* Wilkins Farago Pty, Ltd. AUS. Dist: Independent Pubs. Group.

Leblond, Michaël & Bertrand, Frédérique. Pyjamarama: Carnival. 2017. (ENG., Illus.). 22p. (gr. k-4). pap. 16.95 ***(978-0-500-65125-4(6),*** 565125) Thames & Hudson.

Lebost, Diana. Mr. Kite & the Perilous Flight: Izzy & Daisy. Ersoz, Sahin, illus. 2013. 88p. pap. 18.95 *(978-0-9912023-5-5(X))* Pep & Olie Publishing.

Lee, Edith. Romeo & Julie Square. 2012. 28p. pap. *(978-0-9881235-0-2(9))* Bound Publishing.

Lee, G. I Want My Kitty Cat Tv! Scott, E., illus. 2012. 24p. pap. 24.95 *(978-1-4626-6610-2(8))* America Star Bks.

Lee, Gia. Hurricane Hound. Davis, Jason, illus. 2011. 40p. pap. 24.95 *(978-1-4560-9743-1(1))* America Star Bks.

Lee, Ji-yeong. Tchaikovsky's Swan Lake. Pacheco, Gabriel, illus. 2016. (Music Storybooks Ser.). (ENG.). 44p. (gr. 3-6). pap. 9.99 *(978-1-925247-11-4(2),* Big and SMALL) ChoiceMaker Pty. Ltd., The AUS. Dist: Lerner Publishing Group.

Lee, Mark. Twenty Big Trucks in the Middle of the Street. Cyrus, Kurt, illus. 2013. (ENG.). 32p. (J). (gr. -1-2). 15.99 *(978-0-7636-5809-0(X))* Candlewick Pr.

Lee, Mary R. Island Dog Books. 2009. 32p. (J). 20.99 *(978-1-4363-0351-4(6))* Xlibris Corp.

Lee, Maxine, illus. Zebra's Sneeze. 2015. (Pardon Me! Ser.: 4). (ENG.). 14p. (J). *(978-1-84643-753-3(9))* Child's Play International Ltd.

Lee, Yiting. Mr White. 2013. (ENG., Illus.). 32p. (J). (gr. -1-k). pap. 7.99 *(978-1-907432-13-2(2))* Hogs Back Bks. GBR. Dist: Independent Pubs. Group.

Leese, Vickie. When God Created Little Girls... 2011. 22p. pap. 17.99 *(978-1-61379-521-7(1))* Salem Author Services.

Lefebvre, Jason. Too Much Glue. Retz, Zac, illus. 2013. (ENG.). 32p. (J). (gr. k-2). 16.95 *(978-1-936261-27-7(8))* Flashlight Pr.

Leighton, Noreen. Mr Tilly & the Christmas Lights. Wilson, Lorna, illus. 2013. 38p. pap. *(978-0-9573315-7-0(6))* Tatterdemalion Blue.

—Mr Tilly & the Halloween Mystery. Wilson, Lorna, illus. 2013. 42p. pap. *(978-0-9573315-6-3(8))* Tatterdemalion Blue.

Leist, Christina, illus. Jack the Bear. 2009. (ENG.). 40p. (J). (gr. -1-3). 16.95 *(978-1-894965-97-2(3))* Simply Read Bks. CAN. Dist: Ingram Publisher Services.

Lemay, Violet. Southern Baby. Lemay, Violet, illus. 2015. (ENG., Illus.). 22p. (gr. k — 1). bds. 8.95 *(978-1-938093-45-6(3),* Duo Pr. Llc (US)) Duo Pr. LLC.

Lemke, Donald. Justice League Classic: the Mightiest Magic. Spaziante, Patrick, illus. 2015. (ENG.). 24p. (J). (gr. -1-3). pap. 3.99 *(978-0-06-234490-8(0),* HarperFestival) HarperCollins Pubs.

Lemke, Horst, illus. Places & Faces. 32p. (J). (gr. -1). 14.95 *(978-0-87592-041-2(1))* Scroll Pr., Inc.

Leng, Qin, illus. Not Just Another Princess Story. 2015. (ENG.). 62p. (J). 16.95 *(978-1-927018-57-6(9))* Simply Read Bks. CAN. Dist: Ingram Publisher Services.

Lennon, Liz. I Keep Clean. 2017. (Little Stars,Sea-To-Sea Ser.). (ENG., Illus.). 24p. (J). (gr. -1-k). pap. 6.99 *(978-1-4451-4761-1(0),* Franklin Watts) Hachette Children's Group GBR. Dist: Hachette Bk. Group.

—My Behaviour - I Am Kind. 2017. (Little Stars,Sea-To-Sea Ser.). (ENG., Illus.). 24p. (J). (gr. -1-k). pap. 6.99 *(978-1-4451-4762-8(9),* Franklin Watts) Hachette Children's Group GBR. Dist: Hachette Bk. Group.

—My Behaviour - I Can Help. 2017. (Little Stars,Sea-To-Sea Ser.). (ENG., Illus.). 24p. (J). (gr. -1-k). pap. 6.99 *(978-1-4451-4764-2(5),* Franklin Watts) Hachette Children's Group GBR. Dist: Hachette Bk. Group.

—My Behaviour - I Don't Hit. 2017. (Little Stars,Sea-To-Sea Ser.). (ENG., Illus.). 24p. (J). (gr. -1-k). pap. 6.99 *(978-1-4451-4763-5(7),* Franklin Watts) Hachette Children's Group GBR. Dist: Hachette Bk. Group.

—What I Like: Holidays. 2017. (Little Stars Ser.). (ENG., Illus.). 24p. (J). (gr. -1-k). pap. 6.99 *(978-1-4451-4766-6(1),* Franklin Watts) Hachette Children's Group GBR. Dist: Hachette Bk. Group.

—What I Like: The Seaside. 2017. (Little Stars Ser.). (ENG., Illus.). 24p. (J). (gr. -1-k). pap. 6.99 *(978-1-4451-4767-3(X),* Franklin Watts) Hachette Children's Group GBR. Dist: Hachette Bk. Group.

—What I Like - My Food. 2017. (Little Stars Ser.). (ENG., Illus.). 24p. (J). (gr. -1-k). pap. 6.99 *(978-1-4451-4768-0(8)*, Franklin Watts) Hachette Children's Group GBR. Dist: Hachette Bk. Group.
—What I Like - Where I Live. 2017. (Little Stars Ser.). (ENG., Illus.). 24p. (J). (gr. -1-k). pap. 6.99 *(978-1-4451-4769-7(6)*, Franklin Watts) Hachette Children's Group GBR. Dist: Hachette Bk. Group.
Lenski, Lois. The Little Airplane. 2015. (ENG., Illus.). 32p. (J). (-k). bds. 6.99 *(978-0-385-39208-2(7)*, Random Hse. Bks. for Young Readers) Random Hse. Children's Bks.
Leprince de Beaumont, Jeanne-Marie. Beauty & the Beast. Pignataro, Anna, illus. 2016. (Once upon a Timeless Tale Ser.). (ENG.). 32p. (J). (gr. k-2). 9.99 *(978-1-921894-88-6(1))* Little Hare Bks. AUS. Dist: Independent Pubs. Group.
Lerner Publishing Group Staff. History Speaks: Picture Books Plus Reader's Theater, 6 vols., Set. 2011. (J). (gr. 2-4). lib. bdg. 167.58 *(978-0-7613-7483-1(3))* Lerner Publishing Group.
Lester, Sharon. The Boy Who Wouldn't Sit Still!, Vol. 2. Smith, Jeff, illus. 2nd ed. 2011. 40p. (J). 15.95 *(978-0-9802302-2-2(5))* Privileged Communications, LLC.
Lesynski, Loris. Boy Soup. Martchenko, Michael, illus. 2nd ed. 2008. (ENG.). 32p. (J). (gr. -1-2). 18.95 *(978-1-55451-143-3(7)*, 9781554511433); pap. 6.95 *(978-1-55451-142-6(9)*, 9781554511426) Annick Pr., Ltd. CAN. Dist: Publishers Group West (PGW).
Let's Say Our Numbers. 2007. (Simple First Words Ser.). (Illus.). 14p. (J). *(978-1-84332-520-8(9))* Priddy Bks.
Letscher, Lance. The Perfect Machine. 2010. (ENG., Illus.). 56p. (J). 19.95 *(978-0-292-72338-2(5))* Univ. of Texas Pr.
Leung, Peyton. The Pirate Girl's Treasure. Leung, Hilary, illus. 2012. (ENG.). 32p. (J). (gr. -1-3). 16.95 *(978-1-55453-660-3(X))* Kids Can Pr., Ltd. CAN. Dist: Hachette Bk. Group.
Levandowski, Barbara. The Adventures of Muffin & Alexander: The Please & Thank You Tea Party. 2012. 36p. pap. 18.41 *(978-1-4669-6246-0(1))* Trafford Publishing.
LeVerrier, Renee. The Four Friends. 2011. (Illus.). 44p. (J). pap. 18.99 *(978-1-59092-762-5(1))* Blue Forge Pr.
Levin, Jack E. & Levin, Norma R. My Dog Spot. Levin, Jack E. & Levin, Norma R., illus. 2016. (ENG., Illus.). 40p. (J). (gr. -1-3). 17.99 *(978-1-4814-6907-4(X)*, Aladdin) Simon & Schuster Children's Publishing.
Levine, Arthur A. & Kath, Katie. What a Beautiful Morning. 2016. (ENG., Illus.). 40p. (J). (gr. -1-17). 16.95 *(978-0-7624-5906-3(9)*, Running Pr. Kids) Running Pr. Bk. Pubs.
Levine, Gail Carson. Betsy Who Cried Wolf. Nash, Scott, illus. 2005. (ENG.). 40p. (J). (gr. -1-3). reprint ed. pap. 6.99 *(978-0-06-443640-3(3))* HarperCollins Pubs.
Levison, Jesse. U Is for Underwear. 2014. (ENG., Illus.). 28p. (J). (-k). bds. 9.95 *(978-1-57687-690-9(X)*, powerHouse Bks.) powerHouse Cultural Entertainment, Inc.
Lewellyn, Claire. Ladybug. Mendez, Simon, illus. 2004. (Starting Life Ser.). (ENG.). 24p. (J). (gr. k-3). 16.95 *(978-1-55971-892-9(7))* Cooper Square Publishing Llc.
Lewin, Ted. I See & See. Lewin, Ted, illus. 2016. (I Like to Read(r) Ser.). (ENG., Illus.). 24p. (J). (gr. -1-3). 6.99 *(978-0-8234-3545-6(8))* Holiday Hse., Inc.
Lewis, Anne Margaret. Tears of Mother Bear. Fritz, Kathleen Cheney, illus. 2012. (ENG.). 32p. (J). (gr. -1-3). pap. 8.95 *(978-1-934133-62-0(0)*, Mackinac Island Press, Inc.) Charlesbridge Publishing, Inc.
Lewis, Brandt. Fingers for Halloween. Doerrfeld, Cori, illus. 2017. (ENG.). 12p. (J). (gr. -1 — 1). bds. 7.99 ***(978-0-316-37800-0(3))*** Little, Brown Bks. for Young Readers.
Lewis, Emma. The Museum of Me. 2016. (ENG., Illus.). 48p. (J). (gr. -1-17). 17.95 *(978-1-84976-414-8(X))* Tate Publishing, Ltd. GBR. Dist: Abrams, Inc.
Lewis, Jan. Baby's First Book of Prayers. 2013. (ENG., Illus.). 24p. (J). (gr. -1-12). bds. 6.99 *(978-1-86147-340-0(0)*, Armadillo) Anness Publishing GBR. Dist: National Bk. Network.
—Baby's First Stories of Jesus. 2015. (ENG., Illus.). 24p. (J). (gr. -1-2). bds. 6.99 *(978-1-86147-415-5(6)*, Armadillo) Anness Publishing GBR. Dist: National Bk. Network.
—Farm. 2015. (ENG., Illus.). 24p. bds. 6.99 *(978-1-86147-635-7(3)*, Armadillo) Anness Publishing GBR. Dist: National Bk. Network.
—First Fairy Tales: Puss in Boots. 2015. (ENG., Illus.). 24p. bds. 6.99 *(978-1-86147-626-5(4)*, Armadillo) Anness Publishing GBR. Dist: National Bk. Network.
—First Fairy Tales Aladdin & the Lamp. 2013. (ENG., Illus.). 24p. (J). (gr. -1-12). bds. 6.99 *(978-1-86147-337-0(0)*, Armadillo) Anness Publishing GBR. Dist: National Bk. Network.
—First Fairy Tales Goldilocks & the Three Bears. 2013. (ENG., Illus.). 24p. (J). (gr. -1-12). bds. 6.99 *(978-1-86147-332-5(X)*, Armadillo) Anness Publishing GBR. Dist: National Bk. Network.
—First Fairy Tales Little Red Riding Hood. 2013. (ENG., Illus.). 24p. (J). (gr. -1-12). bds. 6.99 *(978-1-86147-336-3(2)*, Armadillo) Anness Publishing GBR. Dist: National Bk. Network.
—First Fairy Tales Snow White. 2013. (ENG., Illus.). 24p. (J). (gr. -1-12). bds. 6.99 *(978-1-86147-335-6(4)*, Armadillo) Anness Publishing GBR. Dist: National Bk. Network.
—Look & Learn with Little Dino: Colour Fun. Lewis, Jan, illus. 2014. (ENG., Illus.). 24p. (J). (gr. -1-2). bds. 6.99 *(978-1-86147-380-6(X)*, Armadillo) Anness Publishing GBR. Dist: National Bk. Network.
—My First Words. 2015. (ENG., Illus.). 24p. bds. 6.99 *(978-1-86147-498-8(9)*, Armadillo) Anness Publishing GBR. Dist: National Bk. Network.
Lewis, Jan, illus. ABC: Turn the Wheels; Find the Words. 2016. (ENG.). 10p. bds. 14.99 *(978-1-86147-712-5(0)*, Armadillo) Anness Publishing GBR. Dist: National Bk. Network.
—Ask Me about Colours: Lift the Flaps & Find the Answers! 2016. (ENG.). 14p. (J). (gr. -1-12). 10.99 *(978-1-86147-775-0(9)*, Armadillo) Anness Publishing GBR. Dist: National Bk. Network.
—Fairy Palace: You Are Invited to a Party in the Fairy Palace! 2015. (ENG.). 10p. (J): (gr. k-3). bds. 7.99 *(978-1-86147-315-8(X)*, Armadillo) Anness Publishing GBR. Dist: National Bk. Network.
—First Fairy Tales: Cinderella. 2013. (ENG.). 24p. (J). (gr. -1-k). bds. 6.99 *(978-1-86147-334-9(6)*, Armadillo) Anness Publishing GBR. Dist: National Bk. Network.
—First Fairy Tales: Sleeping Beauty. 2013. (ENG.). 24p. (J). (gr. -1-k). bds. 6.99 *(978-1-86147-338-7(9)*, Armadillo) Anness Publishing GBR. Dist: National Bk. Network.
—Look & Learn with Little Dino: Action Words. 2014. (ENG.). 24p. (J). (gr. k-2). bds. 6.99 *(978-1-86147-382-0(6)*, Armadillo) Anness Publishing GBR. Dist: National Bk. Network.
—Look & Learn with Little Dino: Busy Day. 2014. (ENG.). 24p. (J). (gr. k-2). bds. 6.99 *(978-1-86147-379-0(6)*, Armadillo) Anness Publishing GBR. Dist: National Bk. Network.
—Look & Learn with Little Dino: Count 123. 2014. (ENG.). 24p. (J). (gr. -1-1). bds. 6.99 *(978-1-86147-381-3(8)*, Armadillo) Anness Publishing GBR. Dist: National Bk. Network.
—My First 123. 2014. (ENG.). 24p. (J). (gr. -1-k). bds. 6.99 *(978-1-86147-371-4(0)*, Armadillo) Anness Publishing GBR. Dist: National Bk. Network.
—My First 123: Learn to Count from 1 To 100! 2015. (ENG.). 48p. pap. 9.99 *(978-1-86147-425-4(3)*, Armadillo) Anness Publishing GBR. Dist: National Bk. Network.
—My First ABC. 2014. (ENG.). 24p. (J). (gr. -1-k). bds. 6.99 *(978-1-86147-372-1(9)*, Armadillo) Anness Publishing GBR. Dist: National Bk. Network.
—My First ABC: Learn the Alphabet with 300 Words & Pictures. 2016. (ENG.). 48p. (J). (gr. -1-12). pap. 9.99 *(978-1-86147-728-6(7)*, Armadillo) Anness Publishing GBR. Dist: National Bk. Network.
—My First Animals. 2014. (ENG.). 24p. (J). (gr. -1-k). bds. 6.99 *(978-1-86147-373-8(7)*, Armadillo) Anness Publishing GBR. Dist: National Bk. Network.
—My First Bible Stories: Adam & Eve, Noah's Ark, Moses, Joseph, David & Goliath, Jesus. 2016. (ENG.). 48p. (J). (gr. -1-12). bds. 9.99 *(978-1-86147-737-8(6)*, Armadillo) Anness Publishing GBR. Dist: National Bk. Network.
—My First Colours. 2014. (ENG.). 24p. (J). (gr. -1-k). bds. 6.99 *(978-1-86147-374-5(5)*, Armadillo) Anness Publishing GBR. Dist: National Bk. Network.
—My First Learning Library: 3 Great Books: First Abc First 123 First Words, 3 vols. 2014. (ENG.). 72p. (J). (gr. -1-1). bds., bds., bds. 9.99 *(978-1-86147-387-5(7)*, Armadillo) Anness Publishing GBR. Dist: National Bk. Network.
—Performance. 2012. (First Time Ser.). (ENG.). 24p. (J). *(978-1-84643-487-7(4))* Child's Play International Ltd.
—Santa's Christmas Box of Books: A Festive Box of Fun Picture Books. 2017. (ENG.). 1p. bds. 14.99 *(978-1-86147-738-5(4)*, Armadillo) Anness Publishing GBR. Dist: National Bk. Network.
—Santa's Workshop: The Inside Story! 2015. (ENG.). 10p. (J). (gr. k-4). bds. 7.99 *(978-1-86147-314-1(1)*, Armadillo) Anness Publishing GBR. Dist: National Bk. Network.
—The Princess & the Pea. 2015. (ENG.). 24p. bds. 6.99 *(978-1-86147-467-4(9)*, Armadillo) Anness Publishing GBR. Dist: National Bk. Network.
—Words: Turn the Wheels, Find the Pictures. 2015. (ENG.). 10p. bds. 14.99 *(978-1-86147-660-9(4)*, Armadillo) Anness Publishing GBR. Dist: National Bk. Network.
—123: Turn the Wheels - Learn to Count! 2015. (ENG.). 10p. (J). (gr. -1-12). bds. 14.99 *(978-1-86147-661-6(2)*, Armadillo) Anness Publishing GBR. Dist: National Bk. Network.
Lewis, Jill. Something Delicious. Pye, Ali, illus. 2014. (Little Somethings Ser.: 1). (ENG.). 32p. (J). (gr. -1-k). pap. 9.99 *(978-1-4052-6238-5(9))* Egmont Bks., Ltd. GBR. Dist: Independent Pubs. Group.
—Ug-a-Lug: Four Cavemen & a Prehistoric Pencil. Rickerty, Simon, illus. 2014. (ENG.). 32p. (J). 16.99 *(978-1-4711-1728-2(6))* Simon & Schuster, Ltd. GBR. Dist: Simon & Schuster, Inc.
Lewis, Jill & Allwright, Debbie. Hooray for Frilly Knickers. Allwright, Deborah, illus. 2016. (ENG.). 32p. (J). (gr. -1-k). pap. 10.99 *(978-1-4052-7821-8(8))* Egmont Bks., Ltd. GBR. Dist: Independent Pubs. Group.
Lewis, K. s. & Lewis, K. S. Happiness: A Charlie Travel Adventure Story. 2009. 28p. pap. 21.20 *(978-0-557-12094-9(2))* Lulu Pr., Inc.
Li, Maggie. The Amazing Human Body Detectives: Facts, Myths & Quirks of the Body. 2016. (ENG., Illus.). 32p. (J). (gr. k-3). 15.99 *(978-1-84365-297-7(8)*, Pavilion) Pavilion Bks. GBR. Dist: Independent Pubs. Group.
Li-Qiong, Yu. A New Year's Reunion: A Chinese Story. Cheng-Liang, Zhu, illus. 2013. (ENG.). 40p. (J). (gr. -1-2). 6.99 *(978-0-7636-6748-1(X))* Candlewick Pr.
Lickens, Alice V. Dance to the Boogaloo? 2014. (ENG., Illus.). 32p. (J). (gr. -1-k). pap. 9.99 *(978-1-84365-229-8(3)*, Pavilion) Pavilion Bks. GBR. Dist: Independent Pubs. Group.
Lie, Bjø Rune. Slush Mountain. 2016. (ENG., Illus.). 32p. (J). (gr. -1-3). 16.95 *(978-1-927018-82-8(X))* Simply Read Bks. CAN. Dist: Ingram Publisher Services.
Light, John. The Flower. Evans, Lisa, illus. 2011. (Child's Play Library). (ENG.). 32p. (J). *(978-1-84643-070-1(4))* Child's Play International Ltd.
Light, Steve. The Bunny Burrow Buyer's Book: A Tale of Rabbit Real Estate. 2016. (ENG., Illus.). 16p. (J). (gr. -1-3). 19.95 *(978-1-57687-752-4(3)*, powerHouse Bks.) powerHouse Cultural Entertainment, Inc.
Lightburn, Ron. Frankenstink! A Cautionary Tale. 2015. (ENG., Illus.). 32p. (J). (gr. -1-3). 17.99 *(978-1-77049-694-1(7)*, Tundra Bks.) Tundra Bks. CAN. Dist: Penguin Random Hse. LLC.
Lightburn, Sandra. Pumpkin People, 1 vol. Lightburn, Ron, illus. 2009. (ENG.). 32p. (J). (gr. -1-5). 17.95 *(978-1-55109-681-0(1))* Nimbus Publishing, Ltd. CAN. Dist: Orca Bk. Pubs. USA.
Lin, Kelly Jenkins. Mr. Astley's Blueberries. Fiddy, Samantha Lane, illus. 2012. 36p. pap. 12.95 *(978-0-615-67849-8(1))* Three Flower Farm Pr.
Linden, Joanne. Ben & Zip: Two Short Friends. Goldsmith, Tom, illus. 2014. (ENG.). 32p. (J). (gr. -1-k). 16.95 *(978-1-936261-28-4(6))* Flashlight Pr.
Lindgren, Astrid. A Calf for Christmas, 1 vol. Lawson, Polly, tr. from SWE. Törnqvist, Marit, illus. 2010. (ENG.). 36p. (J). (gr. -1-2). 17.95 *(978-0-86315-785-1(8))* Floris Bks. GBR. Dist: SteinerBooks, Inc.
Lindsay, Courtney B. ABC Scream, It's Halloween! 2010. 48p. 17.99 *(978-1-4520-3889-6(9))* AuthorHouse.
Lindstrom, Eva. My Dog Mouse. Lindstrom, Eva, illus. 2017. (ENG., Illus.). 32p. (J). (gr. -1-1). 16.99 ***(978-1-77657-148-2(7))*** Gecko Pr. NZL. Dist: Lerner Publishing Group.
Linenthal, Peter. Look at the Animals! 2006. (ENG., Illus.). 18p. (J). (gr. -1 — 1). bds. 6.99 *(978-0-525-47582-8(6)*, Dutton Books for Young Readers) Penguin Young Readers Group.
Ling, Nancy Tupper. Double Happiness. Chau, Alina, illus. 2015. (ENG.). 48p. (J). (gr. k-3). 16.99 *(978-1-4521-2918-1(5))* Chronicle Bks. LLC.
Linn, Susie. Alice in Wonderland. Ball, Alexandra, illus. 2017. (ENG.). 32p. (J). (gr. -1-k). pap. 9.99 ***(978-1-78445-246-9(7))*** Top That! Publishing PLC GBR. Dist: Independent Pubs. Group.
—Princesses. 2016. (My First Sticker Book Ser.). (ENG.). (J). pap. ***(978-1-78445-768-6(X))*** Top That! Publishing PLC.
—Princesses. Ellis, Lauren, illus. 2017. (Magnetic Play Ser.). (ENG.). 12p. (J). (gr. -1-1). 12.99 ***(978-1-78700-247-0(0))*** Top That! Publishing PLC GBR. Dist: Independent Pubs. Group.
Lionni, Leo. The Greentail Mouse. 2013. (ENG., Illus.). 32p. (J). (gr. -1-2). pap. 7.99 *(978-0-307-98151-6(7)*, Dragonfly Bks.) Random Hse. Children's Bks.
—Pezzettino. 2012. (ENG., Illus.). 40p. (J). (gr. -1-3). pap. 6.99 *(978-0-307-92999-0(X)*, Dragonfly Bks.) Random Hse. Children's Bks.
—Swimmy. 2017. (ENG.). 32p. (J). (gr. -1-2). 7.99 *(978-0-399-55550-3(1)*, Dragonfly Bks.) Random Hse. Children's Bks.
—What? 2014. (ENG., Illus.). 16p. (J). (— 1). bds. 5.99 *(978-0-385-75406-4(X)*, Knopf Bks. for Young Readers) Random Hse. Children's Bks.
—Where? 2014. (ENG., Illus.). 16p. (J). (— 1). bds. 5.99 *(978-0-385-75407-1(8)*, Knopf Bks. for Young Readers) Random Hse. Children's Bks.
—Who? 2014. (ENG., Illus.). 16p. (J). (— 1). bds. 5.99 *(978-0-385-75405-7(1)*, Knopf Bks. for Young Readers) Random Hse. Children's Bks.
Lippman, Peter & Gikow, Louise. The Land of Dinosaurs. 2012. (ENG., Illus.). 11p. 10.95 *(978-0-7611-6598-9(3)*, 16598) Workman Publishing Co., Inc.
Litchfield, Jo. Bit-Bot & the Blob. 2013. (ENG., Illus.). 40p. (J). (gr. -1-k). pap. 10.99 *(978-1-4052-5513-4(7))* Egmont Bks., Ltd. GBR. Dist: Independent Pubs. Group.
Litchfield, Jo, illus. First Picture 123. 2005. (First Picture Board Books Ser.). 16p. (J). 11.95 *(978-0-7945-0939-2(8)*, Usborne) EDC Publishing.
Little Bear, Shena. How the lone wolf got her Name. 2008. 80p. pap. 9.95 *(978-0-578-00171-5(3))* Stone Castle Publishing.
Little Golden Book Christmas Stories. 2015. (Little Golden Book Treasury Ser.). (ENG., Illus.). 224p. (J). (-k). 12.99 *(978-0-553-52227-3(2)*, Golden Bks.) Random Hse. Children's Bks.
Little Mole Boxed Book & Toy Set. 2013. (ENG., Illus.). 24p. (J). (gr. -1-2). 22.99 *(978-1-84365-217-5(X)*, Pavilion) Pavilion Bks. GBR. Dist: Independent Pubs. Group.
Little Red Riding Hood. 2017. (Picture Bks.). (ENG.). (J). 9.99 ***(978-0-7945-3723-4(5)***, Usborne) EDC Publishing.
Little Red Riding Pooh: A Fairy Tale Friend a Board Book & Plush Figure. 2004. (Pooh's Fairy Tale Theater Ser.). 12p. (J). 6.99 *(978-0-7364-2239-0(0)*, RH/Disney) Random Hse. Children's Bks.
Litton, Jonathan. Snip Snap: Pop-Up Fun. Nowowiejska, Kasia, illus. 2015. (Little Snappers Ser.). (ENG.). 10p. (J). 9.99 *(978-1-58925-548-7(8))* Tiger Tales.
The Lizard Library. (Illus.). (J). (gr. k-5). 112.50 *(978-0-8239-7274-6(7))* Rosen Publishing Group, Inc., The.
Llewellyn, Claire. It's Fun to Learn about Sizes: A Busy Picture Book Full of Fabulous Facts & Things to Do! 2016. (ENG., Illus.). 32p. (J). (gr. -1-12). 9.99 *(978-1-86147-761-3(9)*, Armadillo) Anness Publishing GBR. Dist: National Bk. Network.
—It's Fun to Learn about Sums: A Busy Picture Book Full of Fabulous Facts & Things to Do! 2016. (ENG., Illus.). 32p. (J). (gr. -1-12). 9.99 *(978-1-86147-762-0(7)*, Armadillo) Anness Publishing GBR. Dist: National Bk. Network.
—It's Fun to Learn about Words: A Busy Picture Book Full of Fabulous Facts & Things to Do! 2016. (ENG., Illus.). 32p. (J). (gr. -1-12). 9.99 *(978-1-86147-743-9(0)*, Armadillo) Anness Publishing GBR. Dist: National Bk. Network.
Lloyd, Camilla. Pets. 2017. (Photo Word Book Ser.). (ENG., Illus.). 24p. (J). (gr. -1-k). pap. 6.99 *(978-0-7502-8899-6(X)*, Wayland) Hachette Children's Group GBR. Dist: Hachette Bk. Group.
Lloyd, Jennifer. The Best Thing about Kindergarten. Leng, Qin, illus. 2013. (ENG.). 36p. (J). (gr. -1-1). 16.95 *(978-1-897476-82-6(5))* Simply Read Bks. CAN. Dist: Ingram Publisher Services.
—Murilla Gorilla & the Hammock Problem. Lee, Jacqui, illus. 2014. (Murilla Gorilla Ser.: 3). (ENG.). 42p. (J). (gr. -1-3). 9.95 *(978-1-927018-47-7(1))* Simply Read Bks. CAN. Dist: Ingram Publisher Services.
—Murilla Gorilla & the Lost Parasol. Lee, Jacqui, illus. 2013. (Murilla Gorilla Ser.: 2). (ENG.). 42p. (J). (gr. -1-3). 9.95 *(978-1-927018-23-1(4))* Simply Read Bks. CAN. Dist: Ingram Publisher Services.
Lloyd-Jones, Sally. Song of the Stars, 1 vol. Jay, Alison, illus. 2015. (ENG.). 32p. (J). bds. 7.99 *(978-0-310-73630-1(7))* Zonderkidz.
Lloyd, Sam. Grumpy Gertie. 2013. (ENG., Illus.). 24p. (J). (gr. -1-k). 12.99 *(978-1-84365-228-1(5)*, Pavilion) Pavilion Bks. GBR. Dist: Independent Pubs. Group.
—Shape Sorters - Numbers, 2. Lloyd, Sam, illus. 2011. (Shape Sorters Ser.). (ENG., Illus.). 12p. (J). (gr. k-k). bds. 7.99 *(978-0-230-70962-1(1))* Macmillan Pubs., Ltd. GBR. Dist: Independent Pubs. Group.
Lo Monaco, Gérard. A Sea Voyage. 2016. (ENG., Illus.). 8p. (J). (gr. k-2). 29.95 *(978-0-500-65088-2(8)*, 565088) Thames & Hudson.
Lobel, Anita. Potatoes, Potatoes. 2004. 40p. (J). 16.89 *(978-0-06-051818-9(9))*; 15.99 *(978-0-06-023927-5(1))*; lib. bdg. 16.89 *(978-0-06-023928-2(X))* HarperCollins Pubs.
Lock, Deborah. Wild Baby Animals. 2016. (Illus.). 48p. (J). *(978-1-5182-1132-4(1))* Dorling Kindersley Publishing, Inc.
Lodge, Jo. Baby's Very First Book: Faces: A Rag/cloth Book about Faces with Mirror, Crinkly Pages & High-Contrast Images. 2016. (ENG., Illus.). 8p. (J). 10.99 ***(978-1-5098-0705-5(5))*** Pan Macmillan GBR. Dist: Independent Pubs. Group.
—Cosy Cuddlers: Zebra. 2004. (Cosy Cuddlers Ser.). (ENG., Illus.). 8p. (J). (gr. -1-k). pap. 7.99 *(978-1-4050-3456-2(4)*, Campbell Bks.) Pan Macmillan GBR. Dist: Independent Pubs. Group.
—Flip Flap, Mr Croc: A Mix & Match Book. 2014. (ENG., Illus.). 14p. (J). (gr. -1-k). 8.99 *(978-1-4449-0992-0(4))* Hodder & Stoughton GBR. Dist: Hachette Bk. Group.
—Little Roar's Red Boots. 2013. (ENG., Illus.). 20p. (J). (gr. -1-k). 8.99 *(978-1-4449-0482-6(5))* Hodder & Stoughton GBR. Dist: Hachette Bk. Group.
—Little Roar's Round Balloon. 2013. (ENG., Illus.). 20p. (J). (gr. -1-k). 5.99 *(978-1-4449-0483-3(3))* Hodder & Stoughton GBR. Dist: Hachette Bk. Group.
—Peekaboo Little Roar. 2013. (ENG., Illus.). 12p. (J). (gr. -1-k). 10.99 *(978-1-4449-0478-9(7))* Hodder & Stoughton GBR. Dist: Hachette Bk. Group.
Lodge, Jo, illus. Pounce! Little Kitten. 2017. (Little Movers Ser.). (ENG.). 10p. (J). (gr. -1-k). bds. 9.99 ***(978-1-5098-0669-0(5))*** Pan Macmillan GBR. Dist: Independent Pubs. Group.
Lodge, Katherine. Let's Find Mimi: Around the World. 2014. (ENG., Illus.). 32p. (J). (gr. -1-k). 10.99 *(978-1-4449-1292-0(5))* Hodder & Stoughton GBR. Dist: Hachette Bk. Group.
Loeb, Lisa. Lisa Loeb's Silly Sing-Along: The Disappointing Pancake & Other Zany Songs. O'Rourke, Ryan, illus. 2011. (ENG.). 24p. (J). (gr. -1-2). 14.95 *(978-1-4027-6915-3(6))* Sterling Publishing Co., Inc.
Loewen, Nancy. Baby Wants Mama, 0 vols. Melmon, Deborah, illus. 2013. (ENG.). 24p. (J). (gr. -1-k). 14.99 *(978-1-4778-1651-6(8)*, 9781477816516, Amazon Children's Publishing) Amazon Publishing.
—The Other Side of the Story. Bernardini, Cristian & Guerlais, Gérald, illus. 2013. (Other Side of the Story Ser.). (ENG.). 24p. (gr. 2-3). pap. 13.90 *(978-1-4048-8087-0(9))* Picture Window Bks.
—The Other Side of the Story. Guerlais, Gérald & Bernardini, Cristian, illus. 2013. (Other Side of the Story Ser.). (ENG.). 24p. (gr. 2-3). pap. 41.70 *(978-1-4048-8088-7(7))* Picture Window Bks.
—The Other Side of the Story. Bernardini, Cristian & Guerlais, Gérald, illus. 2013. (Other Side of the Story Ser.). (ENG.). 24p. (gr. 2-3). lib. bdg. 163.92 *(978-1-4048-7939-3(0))* Picture Window Bks.
Loewen, Nancy & Speed Shaskan, Trisha. The Other Side of the Story. Jatkowska, Ag et al, illus. 2013. (Other Side of the Story Ser.). (ENG.). 24p. (gr. 2-3). lib. bdg. 54.64 *(978-1-4048-7255-4(8))* Picture Window Bks.
Loggins, Kenny. Moose N' Me. Nash, Joshua, illus. 2013. (ENG.). 32p. (J). (gr. -1-3). 14.95 *(978-0-578-07552-5(0))* Charlesbridge Publishing, Inc.
Lolley, Sarah. Emilie & the Mighty Om. Kao, Sleepless, illus. 2014. (ENG.). 40p. (J). (gr. -1-3). 16.95 *(978-1-897476-35-2(3))* Simply Read Bks. CAN. Dist: Ingram Publisher Services.
London, Jonathan. Froggy Builds a Tree House. 2013. (Froggy Ser.). (ENG.). 32p. (J). (-k). pap. 6.99 *(978-0-14-242533-6(8)*, Puffin Books) Penguin Young Readers Group.
—Froggy Builds a Tree House. 2013. (Froggy Ser.). lib. bdg. 17.20 *(978-0-606-30518-1(1)*, Turtleback) Turtleback Bks.
—Froggy's Birthday Wish. Remkiewicz, Frank, illus. 2016. (Froggy Ser.). (ENG.). 32p. (J). (-k). 6.99 *(978-0-14-751799-9(0)*, Puffin Books) Penguin Young Readers Group.
—Froggy's Worst Playdate. Remkiewicz, Frank, illus. 2015. (Froggy Ser.). (ENG.). 32p. (J). (gr. -1-k). pap. 6.99 *(978-0-14-242229-8(0)*, Puffin Books) Penguin Young Readers Group.
—Here Comes Doctor Hippo: A Little Hippo Story. Eduar, Gilles, illus. (Little Hippo Ser.). (ENG.). 32p. (J). (gr. -1-k). 2013. pap. 6.95 *(978-1-62091-595-0(2))* 2012. 15.95 *(978-1-59078-851-6(6))* Boyds Mills Pr.
—Otters Love to Play. So, Meilo, illus. 2016. (ENG.). 32p. (J). (gr. k-3). 16.99 *(978-0-7636-6913-3(X))* Candlewick Pr.
Long, Ethan. Big Cat. Long, Ethan, illus. 2016. (I Like to Read(r) Ser.). (ENG., Illus.). 24p. (J). (gr. -1-3). 6.99 *(978-0-8234-3539-5(3))* Holiday Hse., Inc.
—Me & My Big Mouse, 0 vols. 2014. (ENG.). 32p. (J). (gr. -1-k). 16.99 *(978-1-4778-4728-2(6)*, 9781477847282, Amazon Children's Publishing) Amazon Publishing.
Long, Loren. Otis's Busy Day. Long, Loren, illus. 2014. (Otis Ser.). (ENG., Illus.). 32p. (J). (gr. k-1). pap. 3.99 *(978-0-448-48130-2(8)*, Penguin Young Readers) Penguin Young Readers Group.
Longstaff, Abie. And How Rapunzel Got Her Prince! Beard, Lauren, illus. 2014. (Fairytale Hairdresser Ser.: 1). (ENG.). 32p. (J). (-k). pap. 9.99 *(978-0-552-56186-0(X))* Transworld Publishers Ltd. GBR. Dist: Independent Pubs. Group.
—The Fairytale Hairdresser & Cinderella. Beard, Lauren, illus. 2014. (Fairytale Hairdresser Ser.: 2). (ENG.). 32p. (J). (-k). pap. 13.99 *(978-0-552-56535-6(0))* Transworld Publishers Ltd. GBR. Dist: Independent Pubs. Group.
—The Fairytale Hairdresser & Sleeping Beauty. Beard, Lauren, illus. 2014. (Fairytale Hairdresser Ser.: 3). (ENG.). 32p. (J). (-k). pap. 12.99 *(978-0-552-56755-8(8))* Transworld Publishers Ltd. GBR. Dist: Independent Pubs. Group.
—The Fairytale Hairdresser & Snow White. Beard, Lauren, illus. 2015. (Fairytale Hairdresser Ser.: 4). (ENG.). 32p. (J). (-k). pap. 9.99 *(978-0-552-56777-0(9))* Transworld Publishers Ltd. GBR. Dist: Independent Pubs. Group.
—The Fairytale Hairdresser & the Little Mermaid. Beard, Lauren, illus. 2015. (Fairytale Hairdresser Ser.). (ENG.). 32p. (J). (-k). pap. 10.99 *(978-0-552-57054-1(0))* Transworld Publishers Ltd. GBR. Dist: Independent Pubs. Group.
Longworth, Holly. The Philippines. 2015. (Countries We Come From Ser.). (ENG., Illus.). 32p. (J). (gr. k-3). lib. bdg. 26.60 *(978-1-62724-855-6(2))* Bearport Publishing Co., Inc.
Looney Tunes Talk Back to the Movies. (Looney Tunes Song & Sound Bks.). (Illus.). 24p. (J). (gr. -1-6). 14.98 *(978-0-7853-1253-6(6)*, PI5) Publications International, Ltd.
Lore, Erin, illus. Timmy the Dragon. I.t. ed. 2007. 32p. (J). 8.95 *(978-0-9741562-7-9(2))* Yarrow Pr.
Lorenz Books Staff, creator. Patterns, 12 vols. 2006. (Learn-A-Word Picture Bks.). (ENG., Illus.). 12p. (J). (gr.

PQR

-1-k). bds. 6.99 *(978-0-7548-1460-3(2))* Anness Publishing GBR. Dist: National Bk. Network.

Lorenzo, Rose, et al. A Dog's Life. 2007. (Windows on Literacy Ser.). (ENG., Illus.). 8p. (J). pap. 9.95 *(978-0-7922-8480-2(1))* National Geographic School Publishing, Inc.

Lorton, Barbara. Sidney Seagull Marks Lighthouses & Buoys of the Chesapeake. 2013. (Illus.). 28p. pap. 16.99 *(978-1-4582-1055-5(3)*, Abbott Pr.) Author Solutions, Inc.

Loth, Sebastian. Clementine. 2011. (ENG., Illus.). 32p. (J). (gr. -1-3). 14.95 *(978-0-7358-4009-6(1))* North-South Bks., Inc.

—Remembering Crystal. 2010. (ENG., Illus.). 64p. (J). (gr. -1-3). 14.95 *(978-0-7358-2300-6(6))* North-South Bks., Inc.

Lovasik, Lawrence G. Los Angeles. (Illus.). (J). 1.50 *(978-0-89942-465-1(1))* Catholic Bk. Publishing Corp.

Love, Pamela. A Cub Explores. Sykes, Shannon, illus. 2004. (ENG.). 32p. (J). (gr. -1-17). 15.95 *(978-0-89272-593-9(1))* Down East Bks.

Lovvorn, Ann R. Chocolate Puddles. Reece, James A., illus. 2010. 36p. pap. 15.49 *(978-1-4520-5158-1(5))* AuthorHouse.

Low, J. H. The Hyena & the Monster. Low, J. H., illus. 2016. (ENG., Illus.). 32p. 10.00 *(978-981-4721-69-1(7))* Marshall Cavendish International (Asia) Private Ltd. SGP. Dist: National Bk. Network.

—The Lazy Hyena. Low, J. H., illus. 2016. (ENG., Illus.). 32p. 10.00 *(978-981-4721-70-7(0))* Marshall Cavendish International (Asia) Private Ltd. SGP. Dist: National Bk. Network.

—Lost in the Gardens. Low, J. H., illus. 2015. (ENG., Illus.). 48p. 10.00 *(978-981-4677-10-3(8))* Marshall Cavendish International (Asia) Private Ltd. SGP. Dist: National Bk. Network.

—There Is Nothing Buried Here. Low, J. H., illus. 2016. (ENG., Illus.). 32p. 10.00 *(978-981-4721-67-7(0))* Marshall Cavendish International (Asia) Private Ltd. SGP. Dist: National Bk. Network.

—A Thief in the Night. Low, J. H., illus. 2016. (ENG., Illus.). 32p. 10.00 *(978-981-4721-68-4(9))* Marshall Cavendish International (Asia) Private Ltd. SGP. Dist: National Bk. Network.

Lowell, Susan. Josefina Javelina: A Hairy Tale. MacPherson, Bruce, illus. 2005. (ENG.). 32p. (J). (gr. -1-3). 15.95 *(978-0-87358-790-7(1))* Cooper Square Publishing Llc.

—The Tortoise & the Jackrabbit: La Tortuga y la Liebre. Harris, Jim, illus. 2004. (New Bilingual Picture Book Ser.). (ENG, SPA & MUL.). 32p. (J). (gr. -1-3). pap. 7.95 *(978-0-87358-869-0(X))* Cooper Square Publishing Llc.

Lowrey, Janette Sebring. The Poky Little Puppy. Tenggren, Gustaf, illus. 2011. (Little Golden Book Ser.). (ENG.). 24p. (J). (— 1). bds. 6.99 *(978-0-375-86129-1(7)*, Golden Bks.) Random Hse. Children's Bks.

—Where Is the Poky Little Puppy? Tenggren, Gustaf, illus. 2015. (Little Golden Book Ser.). (ENG.). 24p. (J). (-k). 4.99 *(978-0-375-84750-9(2)*, Golden Bks.) Random Hse. Children's Bks.

Loyie, Larry & Brissenden, Constance. The Gathering Tree. 2nd ed. 2006. (Larry Loyie Ser.). (ENG., Illus.). 48p. pap. 18.95 *(978-1-894778-42-8(1))* Theytus Bks., Ltd. CAN. Dist: Univ. of Toronto Pr.

LUCAS, David. Christmas at the Toy Museum. LUCAS, David, illus. 2012. (ENG., Illus.). 32p. (J). (gr. -1-2). 15.99 *(978-0-7636-5868-7(5))* Candlewick Pr.

Lucas, David. A Letter for Bear. 2013. (ENG., Illus.). 32p. (J). (gr. -1-2). 14.95 *(978-1-909263-13-0(3))* Flying Eye Bks. GBR. Dist: Consortium Bk. Sales & Distribution.

Lucero, Len & Tracy, Kristina. How to Roll Like Chris P. Bacon. 2nd ed. 2014. (ENG., Illus.). 36p. 14.99 *(978-1-4019-4440-7(X)*, Hay Hse. Lifestyles) Hay Hse., Inc.

Ludwig, Trudy. My Secret Bully. Marble, Abigail, illus. 2015. (ENG.). 32p. (J). (gr. 1-4). 7.99 *(978-0-553-50940-3(3)*, Dragonfly Bks.) Random Hse. Children's Bks.

Lüftner, Kai. Lily Loves. Drews, Judith, illus. 2012. (ENG.). 32p. (J). (gr. -1-3). pap. 16.95 *(978-1-897476-94-9(9))* Simply Read Bks. CAN. Dist: Ingram Publisher Services.

Luna, Pilar P. Hello, Sunny Day! 2012. 40p. pap. 20.99 *(978-1-4490-0244-2(7))* AuthorHouse.

Lund, Deb. Monsters on Machines. Neubecker, Robert, illus. 2017. (ENG.). 40p. (J). (gr. -1-3). pap. 6.99 *(978-0-544-92783-4(4)*, HMH Books For Young Readers) Houghton Mifflin Harcourt Publishing Co.

Lund, Evelyn. It Happened on Alphabet Street. 2003. (ENG., Illus.). 32p. (J). pap. 12.95 *(978-1-878044-50-1(8)*, Wild Rose) Mayhaven Publishing, Inc.

Lunn, Carolyn. Tomas & the Galapagos Adventure. Rades, Ashley, illus. 2016. (ENG.). 28p. (J). (gr. 3-4). 15.99 *(978-0-692-58289-3(4)*, Little Adventures) Amberjack Publishing Co.

Luongo, Ruth E. Beautiful, Big & Bright: The Journey of Sunny Sunflower Seed. 2005. 48p. pap. 16.99 *(978-1-4116-1161-0(6))* Lulu Pr., Inc.

Lutz, Barbara. My Cat. 2011. 28p. pap. 15.99 *(978-1-4628-4512-5(6))* Xlibris Corp.

Lyon, George Ella. What Forest Knows. 2014. (ENG., Illus.). 40p. (J). (gr. -1-3). 17.99 *(978-1-4424-6775-0(4)*, Atheneum Bks. for Young Readers) Simon & Schuster Children's Publishing.

Macalino, Damien. What If an Alligator Ate an Avalanche. Paj, Eduardo, illus. 2013. 32p. pap. 10.00 *(978-0-9836303-8-8(0))* Crystal Mosaic Bks.

Macaulay, David & Keenan, Sheila. Castle: How It Works. 2015. (ENG., Illus.). 32p. (J). (gr. 1-4). 17.99 *(978-1-62672-208-8(0)*, 9781626722088, Macaulay, David Studio) Roaring Brook Pr.

—Jet Plane: How It Works. 2015. (ENG., Illus.). 32p. (J). (gr. -1-k). 17.99 *(978-1-62672-210-1(2)*, 9781626722101, Macaulay, David Studio) Roaring Brook Pr.

MacCarthy, Patricia. Moon Forest. 2013. (ENG., Illus.). 32p. (J). (gr. -1-1). 17.99 *(978-1-84780-283-5(4)*, Frances Lincoln) *Quarto Publishing Group UK* GBR. Dist: Hachette Bk. Group.

MacDonald, Alan. The Magic Porridge Pot. 2015. (First Favourite Tales Ser.). (ENG., Illus.). 32p. (J). (-k). 7.99 *(978-1-4093-0954-3(1))* Penguin Bks., Ltd. GBR. Dist: Independent Pubs. Group.

Macdonald, Fiona. Inca Town. Mark, Bergin, illus. 2017. (Time Traveler's Guide Ser.). 48p. (gr. 3-7). 37.10 ***(978-1-911242-01-7(6))*** Book Hse. GBR. Dist: Black Rabbit Bks.

MacGregor, Roy. The Highest Number in the World. Despres, Genevieve, illus. 2014. (ENG.). 32p. (J). (gr. 1-4). 17.99 *(978-1-77049-575-3(4)*, Tundra Bks.) Tundra Bks. CAN. Dist: Penguin Random Hse. LLC.

Mack, Jeff. Hush Little Polar Bear. Mack, Jeff, illus. 2013. (ENG., Illus.). 36p. (J). (gr. -1-1). bds. 7.99 *(978-1-59643-945-0(9)*, 9781596439450) Roaring Brook Pr.

Mackall, Dandi Daley. The Legend of the Easter Robin: An Easter Story of Compassion & Faith, 1 vol. Cowdrey, Richard, illus. 2016. (ENG.). 30p. (J). 16.99 *(978-0-310-74964-6(6))* Zonderkidz.

Mackenzie, Carine. Sara y Abraham: La maravillosa Promesa. Foce, Natalia C., tr. from ENG. Apps, Fred, illus. 2009. (Biblewise Ser.). Orig. Title: Sarah & Abraham - the Wonderful Promise. (SPA & ENG.). 32p. (J). 3.49 *(978-1-932789-14-0(6))* Editorial Sendas Antiguas, LLC.

MacKenzie, Emily. There's Broccoli in My Ice Cream! MacKenzie, Emily, illus. 2017. (ENG., Illus.). 32p. (J). 9.99 ***(978-1-4088-7330-4(3)***, 9781408873304, Bloomsbury USA Childrens) Bloomsbury Publishing USA.

MacKey, Esther L. Meet Mickey. 2012. 28p. pap. 7.95 *(978-1-937260-18-7(6))* Sleepytown Pr.

Mackey, Stephen. Pushka. 2013. (ENG., Illus.). 240p. (J). (gr. -1-k). pap. 8.99 *(978-1-4449-0135-1(4))* Hodder & Stoughton GBR. Dist: Hachette Bk. Group.

Mackintosh, David. What's up Mumu? Mackintosh, David, illus. 2015. (ENG., Illus.). 32p. (J). 17.99 *(978-0-00-812469-4(8)*, HarperCollins Children's Bks.) HarperCollins Pubs. Ltd. GBR. Dist: HarperCollins Pubs.

Maclear, Kyo. The Fog. Pak, Kenard, illus. 2017. (ENG.). 48p. (J). (gr. -1-3). 16.99 *(978-1-77049-492-3(8)*, Tundra Bks.) Tundra Bks. CAN. Dist: Penguin Random Hse. LLC.

—Julia, Child. Morstad, Julie, illus. 2014. (ENG.). 32p. (J). (gr. k-12). 17.99 *(978-1-77049-449-7(9)*, Tundra Bks.) Tundra Bks. CAN. Dist: Penguin Random Hse. LLC.

—The Liszts. Sardà, Júlia, illus. 2016. (ENG.). 40p. (J). (gr. k-4). 16.99 *(978-1-77049-496-1(0)*, Tundra Bks.) Tundra Bks. CAN. Dist: Penguin Random Hse. LLC.

—Virginia Wolf. Arsenault, Isabelle, illus. 2012. (ENG.). 32p. (J). (gr. -1-3). 16.95 *(978-1-55453-649-8(9))* Kids Can Pr., Ltd. CAN. Dist: Hachette Bk. Group.

Maclear, Kyo. Yak & Dove. Shapiro, Esmé, illus. 2017. (ENG.). 24p. (J). (gr. -1-3). 18.99 ***(978-1-77049-494-7(4)***, Tundra Bks.) Tundra Bks. CAN. Dist: Penguin Random Hse. LLC.

Maclear, Kyo & Arsenault, Isabelle. Spork. Arsenault, Isabelle, illus. 2010. (ENG., Illus.). 32p. (J). (gr. -1-2). 16.95 *(978-1-55337-736-8(2))* Kids Can Pr., Ltd. CAN. Dist: Hachette Bk. Group.

MacLeod, Elizabeth. I Heard a Little Baa. Phillips, Louise, illus. 2007. (ENG.). 30p. (J). (gr. -1 — 1). bds. 7.95 *(978-1-55453-179-0(9))* Kids Can Pr., Ltd. CAN. Dist: Hachette Bk. Group.

Macleod, Robert. Vikingworld: The Age of Seafarers & Sagas. 2014. (ENG., Illus.). 80p. (J). (gr. 3). 19.95 *(978-1-78312-046-8(0))* Carlton Bks., Ltd. GBR. Dist: Sterling Publishing Co., Inc.

Macnair, Patricia. Sensational Senses. Watson, Richard, illus. 2016. (ENG.). 14p. (J). (gr. k-2). 14.99 *(978-1-4052-7163-9(9))* Egmont Bks., Ltd. GBR. Dist: Independent Pubs. Group.

Macomber, Debbie & Carney, Mary Lou. The Truly Terribly Horrible Sweater... That Grandma Knit. Nguyen, Vincent, illus. 2009. (ENG.). 32p. (J). (gr. -1-2). 16.99 *(978-0-06-165093-2(5))* HarperCollins Pubs.

MacPherson, Elizabeth. A Tale of Tails. Williams, Garth, illus. 2016. (Little Golden Book Ser.). (ENG.). 24p. (J). (gr. -1-k). 4.99 *(978-0-385-37863-5(7)*, Golden Bks.) Random Hse. Children's Bks.

Madden, Colleen, illus. Happy Birthday to You! 2017. (ENG.). 26p. (J). (gr. -1-5). 12.95 *(978-1-63322-243-4(8)*, Moondance) Quarto Publishing Group USA.

Maddern, Eric. The Fire Children: A West African Folk Tale. Lessac, Frané, illus. 2015. (ENG.). 32p. (J). (gr. -1-2). pap. 9.99 *(978-1-84780-652-9(X)*, Frances Lincoln) Quarto Publishing Group UK GBR. Dist: Hachette Bk. Group.

Mader, C. Roger. Tiptop Cat. Mader, C. Roger, illus. 2014. (ENG., Illus.). 40p. (J). (gr. -1-3). 17.99 *(978-0-544-14799-7(5)*, HMH Books For Young Readers) Houghton Mifflin Harcourt Publishing Co.

Madhu, Kailash. The Wise Tree & Meu: Mind & Spirit. 2012. 108p. pap. 40.81 *(978-1-4669-2744-5(5))* Trafford Publishing.

Magabala Books Staff. Australian Babies. 2005. (Illus.). 10p. (J). bds. *(978-1-875641-92-5(0))* Magabala Bks.

Magee, Wes. Little Dragon. Warburton, Sarah, illus. 2004. (ENG.). 24p. (J). lib. bdg. 23.65 *(978-1-59646-690-6(1))* Dingles & Co.

Magsamen, Sandra. Baa, Moo, I Love You! A Book of Animal Sounds. 2014. (I Love Learning Ser.). (ENG., Illus.). 14p. (J). (gr. -1 — 1). bds. 7.99 *(978-0-316-13358-6(2))* Little, Brown Bks. for Young Readers.

—Beecause I Love You. 2014. (ENG., Illus.). 14p. (J). (gr. -1 — 1). bds. 7.99 *(978-0-316-25519-6(X))* Little, Brown Bks. for Young Readers.

—I Love Shapes! 2014. (I Love Learning Ser.). (ENG., Illus.). 14p. (J). (gr. -1 — 1). bds. 7.99 *(978-0-316-13357-9(4))* Little, Brown Bks. for Young Readers.

—I Love You Snow Much. Magsamen, Sandra, illus. 2015. (ENG., Illus.). 10p. (J). (gr. -1 — 1). bds. 7.99 *(978-0-316-37876-5(3))* Little, Brown Bks. for Young Readers.

—Peep, Peep, I Love You! 2012. (Padded Cloth Covers with Lift-The-Flaps Ser.). (ENG., Illus.). 10p. (J). (gr. -1-17). bds. 7.99 *(978-0-316-07006-5(8))* Little, Brown Bks. for Young Readers.

Main, Mackinnon. Phonics Workbook 1. 2012. (Very First Reading Workbooks Ser.). 36p. (J). pap. 7.99 *(978-0-7945-3115-7(6)*, Usborne) EDC Publishing.

—Phonics Workbook 2. 2012. (Very First Reading Workbooks Ser.). 36p. (J). pap. 7.99 *(978-0-7945-3116-4(4)*, Usborne) EDC Publishing.

Make Believe Ideas. Little Red Riding Hood. 2015. (ENG.). 24p. (J). bds. 7.99 *(978-1-78393-536-9(7))* Make Believe Ideas GBR. Dist: Nelson, Thomas Inc.

Malam, John. Greek Town. Antram, David, illus. 2017. (Time Traveler's Guide Ser.). 48p. (gr. 3-7). 37.10 ***(978-1-911242-00-0(8))*** Book Hse. GBR. Dist: Black Rabbit Bks.

Malnor, Carol L. On Kiki's Reef, 1 vol. Hunner, Trina L., illus. 2014. (ENG.). 32p. (J). (gr. k-4). 16.95 *(978-1-58469-476-2(9))* Dawn Pubns.

Malone, Peter & Prokofiev, Sergei. Sergei Prokofiev's Peter & the Wolf: With a Fully-Orchestrated & Narrated CD. Malone, Peter, illus. 2004. (ENG., Illus.). 40p. (J). (gr. -1-2). 19.99 *(978-0-375-82430-2(8)*, Knopf Bks. for Young Readers) Random Hse. Children's Bks.

Malouf, Ranya. Blue Fish's Secret Wish. 2011. 32p. pap. *(978-9963-610-72-3(2))* Rimal Pubns.

Mamada, Mineko. Which Is Round? Which Is Bigger? Mamada, Mineko, illus. 2013. (ENG., Illus.). 24p. (J). (gr. -1-1). 16.95 *(978-1-55453-973-4(0))* Kids Can Pr., Ltd. CAN. Dist: Hachette Bk. Group.

Man-Kong, Mary. Frosty the Snowman Pictureback (Frosty the Snowman) Random House, illus. 2014. (Pictureback(R) Ser.). (ENG.). 24p. (J). (gr. -1-2). 3.99 *(978-0-385-38724-8(5)*, Random Hse. Bks. for Young Readers) Random Hse. Children's Bks.

—Here Comes Peter Cottontail. Random House, illus. 2015. (Pictureback(R) Ser.). (ENG.). 16p. (J). (gr. -1-2). 4.99 *(978-0-553-50821-5(0)*, Random Hse. Bks. for Young Readers) Random Hse. Children's Bks.

—Magical Mermaid Adventure. 2014. (Pictureback(R) Ser.). (ENG., Illus.). 16p. (J). (gr. -1-2). 3.99 *(978-0-385-37308-1(2)*, Random Hse. Bks. for Young Readers) Random Hse. Children's Bks.

—My First Visit to the Doctor. Riley, Kellee, illus. 2017. (Pictureback(R) Ser.). (ENG.). 16p. (J). (gr. -1-2). pap. 4.99 *(978-0-399-55810-8(1)*, Random Hse. Bks. for Young Readers) Random Hse. Children's Bks.

Manceau, Édouard. The Race, 0 vols. Owlkids Books Inc. Staff & Quinn, Sarah, trs. from FRE. 2014. (ENG & FRE., Illus.). 64p. (J). (gr. -1-4). 17.95 *(978-1-77147-055-1(0)*, Owlkids) Owlkids Bks. Inc. CAN. Dist: Publishers Group West (PGW).

Mandell, B. B. Samanthasaurus Rex. Kaufman, Suzanne, illus. 2016. 32p. (J). (gr. -1-3). 17.99 *(978-0-06-234873-9(6))* HarperCollins Pubs.

Manderly, Lorin. Lilith Celebrates Lammas. Drewes, Dan, illus. 2010. 36p. pap. 15.50 *(978-1-4520-2689-3(0))* AuthorHouse.

Mandracchia, Charles, creator. A Wacky Wonder World. l.t. ed. 2005. (Illus.). 24p. (J). 13.95 *(978-0-9721957-1-3(8))* Mandracchia, Charles.

Manning, Maurie J. The Aunts Go Marching. 2003. (ENG., Illus.). 32p. (J). (gr. -1-18). 15.95 *(978-1-59078-026-8(4))* Boyds Mills Pr.

Manning, Mick. Woolly Mammoth. Granstrom, Brita, illus. 2015. (ENG.). 32p. (J). (gr. -1-2). pap. 9.99 *(978-1-84780-664-2(3)*, Frances Lincoln) Quarto Publishing Group UK GBR. Dist: Hachette Bk. Group.

Manning, Mick & Granström, Brita. Dino-Dinners. Manning, Mick & Granström, Brita, illus. 2015. (ENG., Illus.). 32p. (J). (gr. -1-1). pap. 9.99 *(978-1-84780-665-9(1)*, Frances Lincoln) Quarto Publishing Group UK GBR. Dist: Hachette Bk. Group.

Manolessou, Katherina. Mummy & Me. 2017. (ENG., Illus.). 24p. (J). (— 1). bds. 10.99 ***(978-1-4472-8877-0(7))*** Pan Macmillan GBR. Dist: Independent Pubs. Group.

Manolessou, Katherina. Zoom Zoom Zoom. (ENG., Illus.). (J). (gr. -1-k). 2016. 30p. bds. 10.99 *(978-1-4472-8871-8(8))* 2014. 32p. 19.99 *(978-0-230-76378-4(2))* Pan Macmillan GBR. Dist: Independent Pubs. Group.

Manson, Beverlie, illus. The Little Mermaid. 2017. (ENG.). 24p. (J). (gr. -1-12). pap. 7.99 ***(978-1-86147-828-3(3)***, Armadillo) Anness Publishing GBR. Dist: National Bk. Network.

Manuel Reeves, Emily. Fiona Flamingo Has Lost Her Pink. 2013. 20p. pap. 10.00 *(978-0-9821506-1-0(X))* Reeves, Emily.

Manushkin, Fran. Happy in Our Skin. Tobia, Lauren, illus. 2015. (ENG.). 32p. (J). (-k). 15.99 *(978-0-7636-7002-3(2))* Candlewick Pr.

—Katie Woo: Star Writer. Lyon, Tammie, illus. 2013. (Katie Woo: Star Writer Ser.). (ENG.). 32p. (gr. k-2). pap. 35.70 *(978-1-4795-1991-0(X))*; lib. bdg. 123.90 *(978-1-4048-8082-5(8))* Picture Window Bks.

—Katie Woo's Super Stylish Activity Book, 1 vol. Alder, Charlie, illus. 2013. (Katie Woo Ser.). (ENG.). 64p. (gr. k-2). pap. 4.95 *(978-1-4795-2047-3(0))* Picture Window Bks.

Maraja, illus. Alice in Wonderland Picture Book. 2013. (Shape Bks.). (ENG.). 16p. (J). pap. 9.95 *(978-1-59583-701-1(9))* Laughing Elephant.

Marchus, Linda. The Gorilla Who Wanted to Dance. Marchus, Linda, illus. 2003. (Illus.). 32p. (J). lib. bdg. 15.95 *(978-0-9723122-1-9(8))* Wee Read Publishing.

Marcus, Leonard S. Ways of Telling: Conversations on the Art of the Picture Book. 2005. (Illus.). 247p. reprint ed. 30.00 *(978-0-7567-9704-1(7))* DIANE Publishing Co.

Marie, Lynne. Hedgehog Goes to Kindergarten. Kennedy, Anne, illus. 2011. (J). pap. *(978-0-545-29874-2(1))* Scholastic, Inc.

Marinaro, Stacy. Nap Time. 2009. 34p. pap. 16.50 *(978-0-557-06881-4(9))* Lulu Pr., Inc.

Marino, Gianna. Night Animals. Marino, Gianna, illus. 2015. (ENG., Illus.). 32p. (J). (gr. -1-k). 16.99 *(978-0-451-46954-0(2)*, Viking Books for Young Readers) Penguin Young Readers Group.

Marley, Cedella & Marley, Bob. One Love: Based on the Song by Bob Marley. Newton, Vanessa, illus. 2011. (ENG.). 32p. (J). (gr. -1-1). 16.99 *(978-1-4521-0224-5(4))* Chronicle Bks. LLC.

Marovic, Mason A. Divorce & Me. 2009. 44p. pap. 21.99 *(978-1-4363-9171-9(7))* Xlibris Corp.

Marsh, Carole. The Mystery at Grizzly Graveyard. 2014. (Real Kids, Real Places Ser.: Vol. 3). (ENG., Illus.). 158p. (J). (gr. 3-5). pap. 7.99 *(978-0-635-11187-6(X)*, Marsh, Carole Mysteries) Gallopade International.

—The Mystery at Rattlesnake Ridge. 2014. (Wildlife Mysteries Ser.). (ENG., Illus.). 158p. (J). (gr. 2-9). pap. 7.99 *(978-0-635-11188-3(8)*, Marsh, Carole Bks.) Gallopade International.

Marshall, Natalie. Millie-Mae: In Winter. 2014. (Illus.). (J). *(978-1-4351-5613-5(7))* Barnes & Noble, Inc.

Martell, Hazel Mary. Roman Town. Mark, Bergin, illus. 2017. (Time Traveler's Guide Ser.). 48p. (gr. 3-7). 37.10 ***(978-1-911242-02-4(4))*** Book Hse. GBR. Dist: Black Rabbit Bks.

Martin, David. Let's Have a Tree Party! Manders, Jeff & Manders, John, illus. 2012. (ENG.). 32p. (J). (gr. k-k). 15.99 *(978-0-7636-3704-0(1))* Candlewick Pr.

Martin, Susi. Animal 123. 2014. (ENG., Illus.). 32p. (J). (gr. -1-2). 9.95 *(978-1-77085-454-3(1)*, 9781770854543) Firefly Bks., Ltd.

—Animal ABC. 2014. (ENG., Illus.). 32p. (J). (gr. -1-2). 9.95 *(978-1-77085-456-7(8)*, 9781770854567) Firefly Bks., Ltd.

Martins, Isabel Minhós. Coming & Going. Carvalho, Bernardo, illus. 2014. (ENG.). 48p. (gr. -1-3). 16.95 *(978-1-84976-161-1(2))* Tate Publishing, Ltd. GBR. Dist: Abrams, Inc.

—When I Was Born. Matoso, Madalena, illus. 2011. (ENG.). 32p. (gr. -1-3). 12.95 *(978-1-85437-958-0(5))* Tate Publishing, Ltd. GBR. Dist: Abrams, Inc.

Martins, Isabel Minhós & Matoso, Madalena. Where Do We Go When We Disappear? 2013. (ENG., Illus.). 44p. (J). (gr. -1-1). 14.95 *(978-1-84976-160-4(4))* Tate Publishing, Ltd. GBR. Dist: Abrams, Inc.

Marzo, Bridget, illus. Tiz & Ott's Big Draw. 2015. (ENG.). 32p. (J). (gr. -1-3). 15.95 *(978-1-84976-310-3(0))* Tate Publishing, Ltd. GBR. Dist: Abrams, Inc.

Marzollo, Jean. Funny Frog. 2012. (I Spy — Scholastic Ser.). lib. bdg. 13.55 *(978-0-606-23969-1(3)*, Turtleback) Turtleback Bks.

—Mama Mama - Papa Papa. Regan, Laura, illus. 2003. (Flip Boardbks.). (ENG.). 32p. (J). (gr. -1 — 1). bds. 7.99 *(978-0-06-051915-5(0)*, HarperFestival) HarperCollins Pubs.

Maskell, Hazell. Very First Words. 2009. (First Words Board Bks). 18p. (J). bds. 6.99 *(978-0-7945-2052-6(9)*, Usborne) EDC Publishing.

Mason, Margaret H. These Hands. Cooper, Floyd, illus. 2015. (ENG.). 32p. (J). (gr. -1-3). 7.99 *(978-0-544-55546-4(5)*, HMH Books For Young Readers) Houghton Mifflin Harcourt Publishing Co.

Massenot, Véronique. The Dreaming Giant: A Children's Book Inspired by Wassily Kandinsky. Nille, Peggy, illus. 2017. (ENG.). 32p. (J). (gr. -1-3). 14.95 ***(978-3-7913-7279-2(3))*** Prestel Verlag GmbH & Co KG. DEU. Dist: Penguin Random Hse. LLC.

—The Great Wave: A Children's Book Inspired by Hokusai. Pilorget, Bruno, illus. 2011. (ENG.). 32p. (J). (gr. -1-3). 14.95 *(978-3-7913-7058-3(8))* Prestel Verlag GmbH & Co KG. DEU. Dist: Penguin Random Hse. LLC.

—Journey on the Clouds: A Children's Book Inspired by Marc Chagall. Pilorget, Bruno, illus. 2011. (ENG.). 32p. (J). (gr. -1-3). 14.95 *(978-3-7913-7057-6(X))* Prestel Verlag GmbH & Co KG. DEU. Dist: Penguin Random Hse. LLC.

Massenot, Véronique & Hie, Vanessa. The Three Musicians: A Children's Book Inspired by Pablo Picasso. 2013. (ENG., Illus.). 32p. (J). (gr. -1-3). 14.95 *(978-3-7913-7151-1(7))* Prestel Verlag GmbH & Co KG. DEU. Dist: Penguin Random Hse. LLC.

Massie, Felix. Terry Perkins & His Upside down Frown. 2018. (ENG., Illus.). 32p. (J). 17.99 *(978-1-84780-620-8(1)*, Frances Lincoln Children's Bks.) Quarto Publishing Group UK GBR. Dist: Littlehampton Bk Services, Ltd.

Masterson, Madeleine Ann. An Egyptian Tale. 2017. (ENG.). 25p. (J). pap. 11.95 ***(978-1-78629-977-2(1)***, c20bd08d-45ad-4764-95e9-07207fb527f9) Austin, Stan AUS. Dist: Bookmasters Distribution.

Matheson, Anne. I Love to Sing. Cutting, David A., illus. 2014. (ENG.). 32p. (J). (gr. 1-5). 7.99 *(978-1-4867-0001-1(2))* Flowerpot Children's Pr. Inc. CAN. Dist: Cardinal Pubs. Group.

Mathias, Irene. The Short Straw. Uhren, Anja, illus. 2017. (ENG.). 30p. (J). (gr. -1-4). 14.99 ***(978-1-941429-77-8(7))*** Handersen Publishing.

Matisse, Henri & Phaidon Editors. Blue & Other Colours: With Henri Matisse. 2016. (ENG., Illus.). 30p. bds. 9.95 *(978-0-7148-7132-5(X))* Phaidon Pr., Inc.

Matthews, Caitlín & Barefoot Books. Fireside Stories: Tales for a Winter's Eve. Cann, Helen, illus. 2015. 96p. (J). (gr. 2-6). 19.99 *(978-1-78285-251-3(4))* Barefoot Bks., Inc.

Maurer, Ashley, illus. Jennie Jenkins. 2015. (First Steps in Music Ser.). (ENG.). 32p. (J). (— 1). 16.95 *(978-1-62277-139-4(7))* G I A Pubns., Inc.

Mauss, Doug, ed. The Action Bible: God's Redemptive Story. Cariello, Sergio, illus. 2010. (Action Bible Ser.). (ENG.). 752p. (J). (gr. -1-2). 27.99 *(978-0-7814-4499-6(3))* Cook, David C.

Mavrikis, Peter. Classic Warships. 2014. (Illus.). 48p. (J). *(978-1-4351-5368-4(5))* Barnes & Noble, Inc.

Mawhinney, Art & Johnson, Shane L., illus. OLIVIA Meets Olivia. 2011. (Olivia TV Tie-In Ser.). (ENG.). 24p. (J). (gr. -1-2). pap. 3.99 *(978-1-4424-4707-3(9)*, Simon Spotlight) Simon Spotlight.

Mayaprua, Alejandro Taish. Nantu & Auju: How the Moon & the Potoo Bird Came to Be. Youth of the Achuar Tribe of Ecuador, illus. 2005. (J). 15.95 *(978-0-9745477-0-1(0))* Arutam Pr.

Mayer, Kirsten. Attack of the Evil Minions! Miller, Ed, illus. 2013. (ENG.). 32p. (J). (gr. -1-3). 12.99 *(978-0-316-23444-3(3))* Little, Brown Bks. for Young Readers.

Mayer, Mercer. All That I Can Be. 2017. (Pictureback(R) Ser.). (ENG., Illus.). 48p. (J). (gr. -1-2). 5.99 ***(978-0-399-55377-6(0)***, Random Hse. Bks. for Young Readers) Random Hse. Children's Bks.

—Fair Play. 2012. (Big Little Critter Ser.: 1). (ENG., Illus.). 98p. (J). 12.95 *(978-1-60746-763-2(1)*, Premiere) FastPrncil, Inc.

—Helping Out. 2012. (Big Little Critter Ser.: 2). (ENG., Illus.). 96p. (J). 12.95 *(978-1-60746-071-8(8)*, Premiere) FastPrncil, Inc.

—Just a Special Thanksgiving. Mayer, Mercer, illus. 2015. (Little Critter Ser.). (ENG., Illus.). 24p. (J). (gr. -1-2). pap. 4.99 *(978-0-06-147811-6(3)*, HarperFestival) HarperCollins Pubs.

—Just Me & My Mom/Just Me & My Dad (Mercer Mayer's Little Critter) Mayer, Mercer, illus. 2014. (Pictureback(R) Ser.). (ENG., Illus.). 48p. (J). (gr. -1-2). 4.99 *(978-0-385-37175-9(6)*, Random Hse. Bks. for Young Readers) Random Hse. Children's Bks.

—Just My Brother, Sister, & Me. 2016. (Pictureback(R) Ser.). (ENG., Illus.). 48p. (J). (gr. -1-2). 5.99

(978-0-553-53987-5(6), Random Hse. Bks. for Young Readers) Random Hse. Children's Bks.
—Just My Lost Treasure. Mayer, Mercer, illus. 2014. (Little Critter Ser.). (ENG., Illus.). 24p. (J). (gr. -1-3). pap. 3.99 (978-0-06-147806-2(7), HarperFestival) HarperCollins Pubs.
Mayfield, Dan. Jasper & the Magpie: Enjoying Special Interests Together. Merry, Alex, illus. 2014. (ENG.). 36p. (J). 15.95 (978-1-84905-579-6(3), 6080) Kingsley, Jessica Pubs. GBR. Dist: Macmillan Distribution Ltd.
Mayfield, Sue. I Can, You Can, Toucan! Padua, Rochelle, illus. 2005. (Green Bananas Ser.). (ENG.). 48p. (J). (gr. k-2). pap. 5.99 (978-1-4052-1793-4(6)) Egmont Bks., Ltd. GBR. Dist: Independent Pubs. Group.
Mayhew, James. Boy. Mayhew, James, illus. 2011. (ENG., Illus.). 32p. (J). (gr. -1-k). pap. 8.99 (978-1-4083-1409-8(6)) Hodder & Stoughton GBR. Dist: Hachette Bk. Group.
—Katie & the Bathers. 2016. (Katie Ser.). (ENG., Illus.). 32p. (J). (gr. k-17). pap. 9.99 (978-1-4083-3189-7(6), Orchard Bks.) Hachette Children's Group GBR. Dist: Hachette Bk. Group.
—Katie & the Dinosaurs. Mayhew, James, illus. 2014. (ENG., Illus.). 32p. (J). (gr. -1-k). 9.99 (978-1-4083-3191-0(8)) Hodder & Stoughton GBR. Dist: Hachette Bk. Group.
—Katie & the Mona Lisa. 2016. (Katie Ser.). (ENG., Illus.). 32p. (J). (gr. -1-k). pap. 10.99 (978-1-4083-3194-1(2), Orchard Bks.) Hachette Children's Group GBR. Dist: Hachette Bk. Group.
—Katie & the Spanish Princess. 2015. (Katie Ser.). (ENG., Illus.). 32p. (J). (gr. -1-k). pap. 11.99 (978-1-4083-3242-9(6)) Hodder & Stoughton GBR. Dist: Hachette Bk. Group.
—Katie & the Starry Night. Mayhew, James, illus. 2013. (ENG., Illus.). 32p. (J). (gr. -1-k). pap. 9.99 (978-1-4083-0466-2(X)) Hodder & Stoughton GBR. Dist: Hachette Bk. Group.
—Katie & the Waterlily Pond. Mayhew, James, illus. 2015. (Katie Ser.). (ENG., Illus.). 32p. (J). (gr. -1-k). pap. 10.99 (978-1-4083-3245-0(0)) Hodder & Stoughton GBR. Dist: Hachette Bk. Group.
—Katie's London Christmas. 2016. (Katie Ser.). (ENG., Illus.). 32p. (J). (gr. -1-k). pap. 10.99 (978-1-4083-2642-8(6), Orchard Bks.) Hachette Children's Group GBR. Dist: Hachette Bk. Group.
—Katie's Picture Show. Mayhew, James, illus. 2014. (ENG., Illus.). 32p. (J). (gr. -1-k). 16.99 (978-1-4083-3605-2(7)) Hodder & Stoughton GBR. Dist: Hachette Bk. Group.
—Nutcracker. 2012. (Ella Bella Ballerina Ser.). (ENG., Illus.). 32p. (J). (gr. 1-3). 14.99 (978-0-7641-6581-8(X)) Barron's Educational Series, Inc.
—Starlight Sailor. Morris, Jackie, illus. 2013. (ENG.). 24p. (J). (gr. -1-1). 14.99 (978-1-84686-936-5(6)) Barefoot Bks., Inc.
Mayhew, James & McQuillan, Mary. Katie & the British Artists. Mayhew, James, illus. 2015. (Katie Ser.). (ENG., Illus.). 32p. (J). (gr. -1-k). 9.99 (978-1-4083-3190-3(X)) Hodder & Stoughton GBR. Dist: Hachette Bk. Group.
Mayhew, James & Wildish, Lee. Katie & the Starry Night. Mayhew, James, illus. 2015. (Katie Ser.). (ENG., Illus.). 32p. (J). (gr. -1-k). pap. 9.99 (978-1-4083-3243-6(4)) Hodder & Stoughton GBR. Dist: Hachette Bk. Group.
Mayo, Margaret. Choo Choo Clickety-Clack! Ayliffe, Alex, illus. 2005. (ENG.). 32p. (J). (gr. k-3). 16.95 (978-1-57505-819-1(7)) Lerner Publishing Group.
Mazur, Gabrielle. Boppy & Me. Collins, Linda, illus. 2013. 38p. 14.97 (978-1-4507-3897-2(4)) Bush Publishing Inc.
—Boppy & Me. Collins, Linda, illus. 2013. 38p. pap. 12.95 (978-1-4507-3906-1(7)) Bush Publishing Inc.
McAllister, Margaret. Emily & the Lamb. Vince, Dawn, illus. 2005. (ENG.). 24p. (J). lib. bdg. 23.65 (978-1-59646-756-9(8)) Dingles & Co.
—15 Things Not to Do with a Granny. Sterling, Holly, illus. 2016. (15 Things Not to Do Ser.). (ENG.). 32p. (J). 17.99 (978-1-84780-852-3(2), Frances Lincoln Children's Bks.) Quarto Publishing Group UK GBR. Dist: Littlehampton Bk Services, Ltd.
McBratney, Sam. Guess How Much I Love You in the Winter: Deluxe Cut Paper Edition. Jeram, Anita, illus. 2016. (Guess How Much I Love You Ser.). (ENG.). 12p. (J). (-k). 18.99 (978-0-7636-9057-1(0)) Candlewick Pr.
McCarthy, Laura. My Daddy Can Too!!! 2011. 24p. pap. 28.03 (978-1-4568-3778-5(8)) Xlibris Corp.
McCarthy, Michael. The Story of Daniel in the Lions' Den. Ferri, Giuliano, illus. 2003. 32p. (J). (gr. 1-3). 16.99 (978-1-84148-209-5(9)) Barefoot Bks., Inc.
McCartney, Tania. A New York Year: Twelve Months in the Life of New York's Kids. Snerling, Tina, illus. 2016. (Kids' Year Ser.). (ENG.). 32p. (J). (gr. -1-3). 17.99 (978-1-925335-07-1(0), EK Bks.) Exisle Publishing Pty Ltd. AUS. Dist: Hachette Bk. Group.
—Peas in a Pod. Snerling, Tina, illus. (ENG.). 32p. (J). (gr. -1-2). 2016. pap. 9.99 (978-1-925335-28-6(3), EK Bks.) 2015. 17.95 (978-1-921966-71-2(8)) Exisle Publishing Pty Ltd. AUS. Dist: Hachette Bk. Group.
—Smile Cry: Happy or Sad, Wailing or Glad - How Do You Feel Today? Rackiyeft, Jess, illus. 2017. (ENG.). 32p. (J). (gr. -1-k). 12.99 (978-1-925335-37-8(2), EK Bks.) Exisle Publishing Pty Ltd. AUS. Dist: Hachette Bk. Group.
—Smile/Cry: Happy or Sad, Wailing or Glad - How Do You Feel Today? Rackiyeft, Jess, illus. 2016. (ENG.). 32p. (J). (gr. -1-1). 16.95 (978-1-921966-98-9(X), EK Bks.) Exisle Publishing Pty Ltd. AUS. Dist: Hachette Bk. Group.
McClintock. Little Princess Picture Book. Date not set. (Illus.). 40p. (J). (gr. -1-3). pap. 4.99 (978-0-06-443539-0(3)) HarperCollins Pubs.
McCloud, Carol, et al. Bucket Filling from a to Z: The Key to Being Happy. Zimmer, Glenn, illus. 2017. (ENG.). 32p. (J). (gr. -1-4). pap. 9.95 (978-0-9974864-3-8(0)) Bucket Fillers, Inc.
McConnell, Lynn. Grandma's Tree. 2009. 24p. pap. 11.49 (978-1-4389-8069-0(8)) AuthorHouse.
McCool, Ben, et al. Grumpy Cat & Pokey, Vol. 3. 2017. (ENG., Illus.). 104p. (J). 12.99 (978-1-5241-0246-3(6), 9781524102463, Dynamite Entertainment) Dynamic Forces, Inc.
McCorkle, Brent & Parker, Amy. Firebird: He Lived for the Sunshine. Corley, Rob & Vollmer, Chuck, illus. 2017. (ENG.). 32p. (J). (gr. -1-1). pap. 3.99 (**978-1-4627-4518-0(0)**, B&H Kids) B&H Publishing Group.
McCranie, Stephen. Belly Flop! Book 3. McCranie, Stephen, illus. 3rd ed. 2012. (Mal & Chad Ser.: 3). (ENG., Illus.). 240p. (J). (gr. 3-7). pap. 9.99 (978-0-399-25658-5(X), Philomel Bks.) Penguin Young Readers Group.
McCue, Lisa. HideAway Husky. 2016. (HideAway Pets Bks.). (ENG., Illus.). 32p. (J). (gr. -1-2). 9.95 (978-1-4549-1812-7(8)) Sterling Publishing Co., Inc.
—Quiet Bunny & Noisy Puppy. 2015. (ENG., Illus.). 40p. (J). (gr. -1-1). pap. 6.95 (978-1-4549-1681-9(8)) Sterling Publishing Co., Inc.
—Quiet Bunny's Many Colors. 2016. (ENG., Illus.). 40p. (J). (gr. -1-1). pap. 6.95 (978-1-4549-1911-7(6)) Sterling Publishing Co., Inc.
McCully, Emily Arnold. First Snow. McCully, Emily Arnold, illus. 2003. (ENG., Illus.). 32p. (J). (gr. -1-3). 17.99 (978-0-06-623852-4(8)) HarperCollins Pubs.
McCurry, Kristen. Eye-Look Picture Games. 2012. (Eye-Look Picture Games Ser.). (ENG.). 32p. (J). (gr. 1-2). lib. bdg. 81.96 (978-1-4296-8103-2(9), Aplus Bks.) Capstone Press of Coughlan Cos.
—Pick a Picture, Write a Poem!, 1 vol. 2014. (Little Scribe Ser.). (ENG.). 32p. (gr. 1-2). lib. bdg. 27.32 (978-1-4765-4237-9(6), Aplus Bks.) Capstone Press of Coughlan Cos.
—Pick a Picture, Write a Report!, 1 vol. 2014. (Little Scribe Ser.). (ENG.). 32p. (gr. 1-2). lib. bdg. 27.32 (978-1-4765-4239-3(2), Aplus Bks.) Capstone Press of Coughlan Cos.
—Pick a Picture, Write a Story!, 1 vol. 2014. (Little Scribe Ser.). (ENG.). 32p. (gr. 1-2). lib. bdg. 27.32 (978-1-4765-4238-6(4), Aplus Bks.) Capstone Press of Coughlan Cos.
—Pick a Picture, Write an Opinion!, 1 vol. 2014. (Little Scribe Ser.). (ENG.). 32p. (gr. 1-2). lib. bdg. 27.32 (978-1-4765-4240-9(6), Aplus Bks.) Capstone Press of Coughlan Cos.
McDermid, Val. My Granny Is a Pirate. Robins, Arthur, illus. 2012. (ENG.). 32p. (J). (gr. -1-k). pap. 9.99 (978-1-4083-0927-8(0)) Hodder & Stoughton GBR. Dist: Hachette Bk. Group.
McDermott, Mustafa Yusuf. Muslim Nursery Rhymes. rev. ed. 2015. (ENG., Illus.). 30p. (J). 14.95 (978-0-86037-563-0(3)) Kube Publishing Ltd. GBR. Dist: Consortium Bk. Sales & Distribution.
McDonald, Jill. Hello, World! Solar System. 2016. (ENG., Illus.). 26p. (J). (— 1). bds. 7.99 (978-0-553-52103-0(9), Doubleday Bks. for Young Readers) Random Hse. Children's Bks.
—Hello, World! Weather. 2016. (ENG., Illus.). 26p. (J). (— 1). bds. 7.99 (978-0-553-52101-6(2), Doubleday Bks. for Young Readers) Random Hse. Children's Bks.
McDoogle, Farrah. Olivia the Ballerina. Spaziante, Patrick, illus. 2013. (Olivia TV Tie-In Ser.). (ENG.). 24p. (J). (gr. -1-1). 16.99 (978-1-4424-8515-0(9), Simon Spotlight) Simon Spotlight.
McElligott, Matthew. Even Monsters Need Haircuts. McElligott, Matthew, illus. 2015. (ENG., Illus.). 30p. (J). (gr. -1-2). bds. 6.99 (978-0-8027-3839-4(7), 9780802738394, Bloomsbury USA Childrens) Bloomsbury Publishing USA.
McGinley, Phyllis, et al. Little Golden Book Farm Favorites. Rojankovsky, Feodor & Gergely, Tibor, illus. 2012. (Little Golden Book Favorites Ser.). (ENG.). 80p. (J). (gr. k-k). 7.99 (978-0-307-93020-0(3), Golden Bks.) Random Hse. Children's Bks.
McGrath, Barbara Barbieri. Teddy Bear Addition. Nihoff, Tim, illus. 2014. (McGrath Math Ser.). (ENG.). 32p. (J). (gr. -1-3). pap. 7.95 (978-1-58089-425-8(9)) Charlesbridge Publishing, Inc.
McGraw, Royal, et al. Grumpy Cat, Vol. 1. 2016. (ENG., Illus.). 104p. (J). 12.99 (978-1-60690-796-2(4), 9781606907962, Dynamite Entertainment) Dynamic Forces, Inc.
McGreevy, Anne Kelly. Liliana Loretta Larue. Desrochers, Fache, illus. 2017. (ENG.). 28p. (J). pap. 8.95 (978-1-68350-069-8(5)) Morgan James Publishing.
McGrellis, Barbara. Love Never Fails. 2013. 24p. pap. 10.99 (978-1-4624-0745-3(5), Inspiring Voices) Author Solutions, Inc.
McGuire Woods, Molly. Puppy Chase. 2016. (Barbie Chapters Ser.). (ENG.). 64p. (J). (gr. 1-4). lib. bdg. 12.99 (978-0-399-55137-6(9), Random Hse. Bks. for Young Readers) Random Hse. Children's Bks.
McKain, Kelly. The Haunted Shipwreck. Johansson, Cecilia, illus. 2004. (Mermaid Rock Ser.). 48p. (J). (978-0-439-62647-7(1)) Scholastic, Inc.
McKee, Brett. Monsters Don't Cry! Burfoot, Ella, illus. 2012. (ENG.). 32p. (J). (gr. -1-k). 19.99 (978-1-84939-291-4(9)) Andersen Pr. GBR. Dist: Independent Pubs. Group.
McKee, Brett. Sir Ned & the Nasties. McKee, David, illus. 2017. (ENG.). 32p. (J). (-k). 19.99 (**978-1-78344-534-9(3)**) Andersen Pr. GBR. Dist: Independent Pubs. Group.
McKee, David. The Adventures of King Rollo. 2016. (ENG., Illus.). 32p. (J). (-k). 19.99 (978-1-78344-468-7(1)) Andersen Pr. GBR. Dist: Independent Pubs. Group.
—Denver. McKee, David, illus. 2012. (ENG., Illus.). 32p. (J). (gr. -1-k). pap. 9.99 (978-1-84939-389-8(3)) Andersen Pr. GBR. Dist: Independent Pubs. Group.
—Elmer & Aunt Zelda. McKee, David, illus. 2017. (ENG., Illus.). 32p. (J). (gr. -1-3). 17.99 (978-1-5124-3945-8(2)) Andersen Pr. GBR. Dist: Lerner Publishing Group.
—Elmer & the Flood. McKee, David, illus. 2015. (ENG., Illus.). 32p. (J). (gr. -1-3). 17.99 (978-1-4677-9314-8(0)) Lerner Publishing Group.
—Elmer & the Race. McKee, David, illus. 2016. (ENG., Illus.). 32p. (J). (gr. -1-3). 17.99 (978-1-5124-1624-4(X)) Andersen Pr. GBR. Dist: Lerner Publishing Group.
—Elmer & the Rainbow. 2016. (Elmer Ser.). (ENG., Illus.). 30p. (J). (-k). ring bd. 9.99 (978-1-78344-424-3(X)) Andersen Pr. GBR. Dist: Independent Pubs. Group.
—Elmer's Colours (English-Polish) 2010. (Elmer Ser.). (POL & ENG., Illus.). 16p. (J). (gr. k — 1). bds. 8.95 (978-1-84059-531-4(0)) Milet Publishing.
—Elmer's Day. 2010. (Elmer Ser.). (ENG & POL., Illus.). 16p. (J). (gr. k — 1). 8.95 (978-1-84059-532-1(9)) Milet Publishing.
—Elmer's New Friend. 2003. (ENG., Illus.). 11p. (J). 8.99 (978-1-84270-034-1(0)) Andersen Pr. GBR. Dist: Trafalgar Square Publishing.
—The Extraordinary Adventures of Mr Benn Diver. 2015. (Mr. Benn Ser.). (ENG., Illus.). 32p. (J). (gr. -1-k). pap. 9.99 (978-1-4449-2204-2(1)) Hodder & Stoughton GBR. Dist: Hachette Bk. Group.
—The Hill & the Rock. McKee, David, illus. 2012. (ENG., Illus.). 32p. (J). (gr. -1-k). pap. 12.99 (978-1-84939-305-8(2)) Andersen Pr. GBR. Dist: Independent Pubs. Group.
—Isabel's Noisy Tummy. McKee, David, illus. 2013. (ENG., Illus.). 32p. (J). (gr. -1-k). pap. 9.99 (978-1-84939-689-9(2)) Andersen Pr. GBR. Dist: Independent Pubs. Group.
—Melric: The Magician Who Lost His Magic. McKee, David, illus. 2013. (Melric Ser.). (ENG., Illus.). 32p. (J). (gr. -1-k). 16.99 (978-1-84939-439-0(3)) Andersen Pr. GBR. Dist: Independent Pubs. Group.
—Melric & the Crown. 2016. (Melric Ser.). (ENG., Illus.). 32p. (J). (-k). 22.99 (978-1-78344-411-3(8)) Andersen Pr. GBR. Dist: Independent Pubs. Group.
—Melric & the Dragon. McKee, David, illus. 2016. (Melric Ser.: 4). (ENG., Illus.). 32p. (J). (-k). pap. 9.99 (978-1-78344-210-2(7)); (gr. -1-k). 16.99 (978-1-78344-162-4(3)) Andersen Pr. GBR. Dist: Independent Pubs. Group.
—Melric & the Petnapping. McKee, David, illus. 2014. (Melric Ser.). (ENG., Illus.). 32p. (J). (gr. -1-k). 16.99 (978-1-78344-008-5(2)) Andersen Pr. GBR. Dist: Independent Pubs. Group.
—Melric the Magician Who Lost His Magic. McKee, David, illus. 2013. (Melric Ser.). (ENG., Illus.). 32p. (J). (gr. -1-k). pap. 12.99 (978-1-84939-525-0(X)) Andersen Pr. GBR. Dist: Independent Pubs. Group.
Mckee, David. Mr Benn: Spaceman. 2015. (Mr. Benn Ser.). (ENG., Illus.). 32p. (J). (gr. -1-k). pap. 9.99 (978-1-4449-2206-6(8)) Hodder & Stoughton GBR. Dist: Hachette Bk. Group.
McKee, David. Not Now, Bernard. 2015. (ENG., Illus.). 32p. (J). (gr. -1-k). pap. 10.99 (978-1-78344-290-4(5)) Andersen Pr. GBR. Dist: Independent Pubs. Group.
McKee, David. Two Can Toucan. 40th ed. 2017. (ENG., Illus.). 32p. (J). (-k). 14.99 (**978-1-78344-480-9(0)**) Andersen Pr. GBR. Dist: Independent Pubs. Group.
McKendry, Sam. Are You Ticklish? Mitchell, Melanie, illus. 2006. (ENG.). 12p. (J). (gr. -1-18). bds. 10.95 (978-1-58117-376-5(8), Intervisual/Piggy Toes) Bendon, Inc.
McKernan, Wendy. The Thing I Say I Saw Last Night: A Christmas Story. Bzymek, Izabela, illus. 2011. 32p. (J). (978-0-9866204-0-9(8)); pap. (978-0-9866204-1-6(6)) Little Dragon Publishing.
McKittrick, Erin. My Coyote Nose & Ptarmigan Toes: An Almost-True Alaskan Adventure. Higman, Valisa, illus. 2016. (Paws IV Ser.). (ENG.). 32p. (J). (gr. -1-2). 17.99 (978-1-63217-052-1(3), Little Bigfoot) Sasquatch Bks.
McLaughlin, Julie. Hungry Mr. Gator. McKay, Ann Marie, illus. 2005. (J). 15.99 (978-0-933101-24-1(4)) Legacy Pubns.
McLaughlin, Tom. The Cloudspotter. McLaughlin, Tom, illus. 2015. (ENG., Illus.). 32p. (J). (gr. -1-1). 18.99 (978-1-4088-5496-9(1), 9781408854969, Bloomsbury USA Childrens) Bloomsbury Publishing USA.
—The Story Machine. 2015. (ENG., Illus.). 32p. (J). (gr. -1-1). 12.99 (978-1-4088-3934-8(2), 9781408839348, Bloomsbury USA Childrens) Bloomsbury Publishing USA.
McLean, Wendy & Book Company Staff. Follow an Elf. Worthington, Leonie, illus. 2003. (Sparkle Bks.). 10p. (J). bds. 8.95 (978-1-74047-314-9(0)) Book Co. Publishing Pty, Ltd., The AUS. Dist: Penton Overseas, Inc.
McLellan, Stephanie Simpson. Leon's Song. Bonder, Dianna, illus. 2004. (ENG.). 32p. (J). (gr. -1-3). (978-1-55041-813-2(0)) Fitzhenry & Whiteside, Ltd.
McLelland, Kate. Blackbird Blackbird What Do You Do? 2016. (ENG., Illus.). 32p. (J). (gr. -1-k). 17.99 (978-1-4449-2121-2(5)) Hachette Children's Group GBR. Dist: Hachette Bk. Group.
—Blackbird, Blackbird, What Do You Do? 2017. (ENG., Illus.). 32p. (J). (gr. -1-k). pap. 7.99 (978-1-4449-2122-9(3)) Hachette Children's Group GBR. Dist: Hachette Bk. Group.
McLoughlin Brothers, creator. Snowflake Stories. 2011. (American Antiquarian Society Ser.). (ENG., Illus.). 16p. (gr. 1). 24.95 (978-1-4290-9735-2(3)) Applewood Bks.
McMullan, Kate. The Amazing Adventures of Supercat! Making the World Safe for Blankies. Lemaître, Pascal, illus. 2011. (ENG.). 40p. (J). (gr. k — 1). 7.95 (978-0-7611-6320-6(4), 16320) Workman Publishing Co., Inc.
—I'm Cool! McMullan, Jim, illus. 2015. 40p. (J). (gr. -1-3). 17.99 (978-0-06-230629-6(4)) HarperCollins Pubs.
McNamee, Kevin. If I Could Be Anything. Movshina, Marina, illus. 2009. 16p. pap. 9.95 (978-1-61633-011-8(2)) Guardian Angel Publishing, Inc.
—Just for Today. Movshina, Marina, illus. 2012. 16p. pap. 9.95 (978-1-61633-314-0(6)) Guardian Angel Publishing, Inc.
McNaughton, Janet. Brave Jack & the Unicorn. Tooke, Susan, illus. 2005. (ENG.). 32p. (J). (gr. k-3). 15.95 (978-0-88776-677-0(3), Tundra Bks.) Tundra Bks. CAN. Dist: Penguin Random Hse. LLC.
MCP Staff. Zelda's Zipper. 2003. (J). 38.95 (978-0-8136-1323-9(X)) Modern Curriculum Pr.
McPhail, David. The Blue Door. Ellis, Sarah, ed. O'Connor, John, illus. 2003. (ENG.). 32p. pap. (978-1-55041-802-6(5)) Fitzhenry & Whiteside, Ltd.
—Hermanos Brothers. Calvo, Carlos, tr. 2017. (ENG & SPA., Illus.). 28p. (J). (— 1). bds. 4.99 (978-0-544-91586-2(0), HMH Books For Young Readers) Houghton Mifflin Harcourt Publishing Co.
—Pig Pig Meets the Lion. McPhail, David, illus. 2012. (Illus.). pap. 15.95 (978-1-60734-080-5(1)); (ENG., 32p. (J). (gr. -1-3). 15.95 (978-1-58089-358-9(9)) Charlesbridge Publishing, Inc.
McQuinn, Anna. My Friend Mei Jing. Frey, Ben, illus. Cheung, Irvin, photos by. 2009. (ENG.). 32p. (J). (gr. -1-1). 17.95 (978-1-55451-153-2(4), 9781554511532) Annick Pr., Ltd. CAN. Dist: Publishers Group West (PGW).
Mead, Purnima. Bibia Meets Gripper. 2013. 24p. pap. 12.45 (978-1-4497-9751-5(2), WestBow Pr.) Author Solutions, Inc.
Meadows, Daisy. Natalie the Christmas Stocking Fairy. 2014. (Rainbow Magic — Special Edition Ser.). lib. bdg. 17.20 (978-0-606-36055-5(7)) Turtleback Bks.
Meddaugh, Susan. Martha Says It with Flowers. 2010. (Martha Speaks Ser.). (ENG., Illus.). 32p. (J). (gr. -1-3). 12.99 (978-0-547-21058-2(2)) Houghton Mifflin Harcourt Publishing Co.
Medina, Andre, illus. Meet the Monsters. 2015. (Hotel Transylvania 2 Ser.). (ENG.). 16p. (J). (gr. -1-3). pap. 5.99 (978-1-4814-4802-4(1), Simon Spotlight) Simon Spotlight.
Medina, Meg. Mango, Abuela, & Me. Dominguez, Angela, illus. 2015. (ENG.). 32p. (J). (gr. k-3). 15.99 (978-0-7636-6900-3(8)) Candlewick Pr.
Medina, Tony & Watson, Jesse Joshua. I & I Bob Marley, 1 vol. 2009. (ENG., Illus.). 48p. (J). pap. 10.95 (978-1-62014-030-7(6)) Lee & Low Bks., Inc.
Meeuwissen, Tony. Remarkable Animals: Mix & Match to Create 100 Crazy Creatures. Meeuwissen, Tony, illus. rev. ed. 2016. (ENG., Illus.). 24p. (J). (gr. -1-k). 7.99 (978-1-84780-762-5(3), Frances Lincoln Children's Bks.) Quarto Publishing Group UK GBR. Dist: Hachette Bk. Group.
Meister, Cari. What Can I Be? 2004. (Rookie Reader Skill Set Ser.). (ENG.). 24p. (J). (gr. k-2). pap. 4.95 (978-0-516-27810-0(X), Children's Pr.) Scholastic Library Publishing.
Mellen, Wynette. What Do You See? Rasmussen, Jennifer, illus. 2012. 42p. (J). pap. 9.95 (978-0-9839957-4-6(5)) Freundship Pr., LLC.
Melling, David. Colour with Splosh! 2017. (Splosh Ser.). (ENG., Illus.). 32p. (J). (gr. -1-k). pap. 7.99 (**978-1-4449-3181-5(4)**) Hachette Children's Group GBR. Dist: Hachette Bk. Group.
—How to Hug with Hugless Douglas. 2016. (Hugless Douglas Ser.). (ENG., Illus.). 14p. (J). (gr. -1-k). 9.99 (978-1-4449-2408-4(7)) Hachette Children's Group GBR. Dist: Hachette Bk. Group.
—Hugless Douglas & the Big Sleepover. 2013. (ENG., Illus.). 32p. (J). (978-1-58925-116-8(4)) Tiger Tales.
—Splosh! 2017. (Splosh Ser.). (ENG., Illus.). 32p. (J). (gr. -1-k). pap. 7.99 (**978-1-4449-0847-3(2)**) Hachette Children's Group GBR. Dist: Hachette Bk. Group.
Melling, David. The Star-Faced Crocodile. 2016. (ENG., Illus.). 32p. (J). (gr. -1-k). pap. 7.99 (978-1-4449-2078-9(2)) Hodder & Stoughton GBR. Dist: Hachette Bk. Group.
Melton, Lexi. Buck Toothed Charlie & Other Stories. 2010. 72p. pap. 34.99 (978-1-4490-6183-8(4)) AuthorHouse.
Meltzer, Lynn. The Construction Crew. Eko-Burgess, Carrie, illus. 2017. (ENG.). 32p. (J). bds. 7.99 (978-1-250-11267-5(2), 9781250112675, Holt, Henry & Co. Bks. For Young Readers) Holt, Henry & Co.
Meneely, Starr. What a Lovely Sound! 2013. (Illus.). 32p. pap. (978-0-9575371-3-2(1)) Starflower Pr.
Meng, Cece. World Pizza. Shi, Ellen, illus. 2017. (ENG.). 32p. (J). (gr. -1). 14.95 (978-1-4549-1946-9(9)) Sterling Publishing Co., Inc.
Mercer, Graham. The Secret Cave. 2009. 52p. pap. 10.50 (978-1-4092-9055-1(7)) Lulu Pr., Inc.
Meredith, Samantha. Flip & Find Builders. 2016. (Flip & Find Ser.). (ENG., Illus.). 10p. (J). (— 1). bds. 7.99 (978-1-4472-7714-9(7)) Pan Macmillan GBR. Dist: Independent Pubs. Group.
—Flip & Find Farmers Board Book. 2016. (Flip & Find Ser.). (ENG., Illus.). 10p. (J). (— 1). bds. 7.99 (978-1-4472-7715-6(5)) Pan Macmillan GBR. Dist: Independent Pubs. Group.
—Flip & Find Pilots: A Guess Who/Where Flap Book about a Pilot. Meredith, Samantha, illus. 2016. (Flip & Find Ser.). (ENG., Illus.). 12p. (J). (— 1). bds. 7.99 (978-1-4472-7717-0(1)) Pan Macmillan GBR. Dist: Independent Pubs. Group.
Merrie Melodies. (Looney Tunes Song & Sound Bks.). (Illus.). 24p. (J). (gr. -1-5). 14.98 (978-0-7853-1249-9(8), PI4) Publications International, Ltd.
Merritt, Kate, illus. Indestructibles: Baby Babble. 2012. (Indestructibles Ser.). (ENG.). 12p. (J). (gr. k — 1). pap. 5.95 (978-0-7611-6880-5(X), 16880) Workman Publishing Co., Inc.
—Indestructibles: Baby Faces. 2012. (Indestructibles Ser.). (ENG.). 12p. (J). (gr. k — 1). pap. 5.95 (978-0-7611-6881-2(8), 16881) Workman Publishing Co., Inc.
Merry, Margaret. The Lonely Digger. 2009. 72p. pap. 21.50 (978-1-60860-144-8(7), Strategic Bk. Publishing) Strategic Book Publishing & Rights Agency (SBPRA).
Meschenmoser, Sebastian. Mr. Squirrel & the Moon. 2015. (ENG., Illus.). 48p. (J). 18.95 (978-0-7358-4156-7(X)) North-South Bks., Inc.
—3 Wishes for Pugman. Meschenmoser, Sebastian, illus. 2012. (ENG., Illus.). 44p. (J). (gr. k-2). 22.99 (978-0-9806070-9-3(4)) Wilkins Farago Pty, Ltd. AUS. Dist: Independent Pubs. Group.
Messaoudi, Michele. My Mum Is a Wonder. Peckham, Ruth, illus. 2016. (ENG.). 24p. (J). (gr. -1). 8.95 (978-0-86037-298-1(7)) Kube Publishing Ltd. GBR. Dist: Consortium Bk. Sales & Distribution.
Metcalf, Paula. My Mummy. Barnard, Lucy, illus. 2015. (ENG.). 24p. (J). (-1). bds. 9.99 (978-1-4472-7699-9(X)) Pan Macmillan GBR. Dist: Independent Pubs. Group.
—Rabbits Don't Lay Eggs! Johnson-Isaacs, Cally, illus. 2016. (ENG.). 24p. (J). (gr. -1-k). bds. 9.99 (978-1-4472-8277-8(9)) Pan Macmillan GBR. Dist: Independent Pubs. Group.
Metsola, Aino-Maija. Colours: With Lift-Flap Surprises on Every Page. 2015. (Learning Garden Ser.). (ENG., Illus.). 14p. (J). bds. 9.99 (978-1-84780-609-3(0), Wide Eyed Editions) Quarto Publishing Group UK GBR. Dist: Littlehampton Bk Services, Ltd.
—Counting. 2015. (Learning Garden Ser.). (ENG., Illus.). 14p. (J). bds. 9.99 (978-1-84780-610-9(4), Wide Eyed Editions) Quarto Publishing Group UK GBR. Dist: Littlehampton Bk Services, Ltd.
—Traffic Jam: Puzzle Book. 2016. (Learning Garden Ser.). (ENG., Illus.). 14p. (J). bds. 14.99 (978-1-84780-746-5(1), Wide Eyed Editions) Quarto Publishing Group UK GBR. Dist: Littlehampton Bk Services, Ltd.
Metzger, Steve. I Love You All Year Long. Keay, Claire, illus. 2009. 20p. (J). (gr. -1-k). 8.95 (978-1-58925-847-1(9)) Tiger Tales.
Meunier, Henri. A Beary Merry Christmas. Choux, Nathalie, illus. 2017. (Super-Duper Duo Ser.). (ENG.). 32p. (J). (gr. -1-3). 8.99 (**978-1-328-76678-6(0)**, HMH Books For Young Readers) Houghton Mifflin Harcourt Publishing Co.
Meyers, Carly J. J. Michael's Superheroes. Bruner, Garth, illus. 2013. 28p. (J). pap. (978-0-8425-2845-0(8), BYU Creative Works) Brigham Young Univ.

PQR

Miceli, Mary Anne. Confessor's Animal Wartime Blues. 2009. 56p. pap. 31.99 *(978-1-4415-2867-4(9))* Xlibris Corp.

Michael. Bedwin, 1 vol. David, Amanda, illus. 2009. (ENG.). 46p. 24.95 *(978-1-60813-258-4(7))* America Star Bks.

Michalak, Jamie. Fizzy's Lunch Lab: Escape from Greasy World. Lunch Lab, LLC., Llc., illus. 2015. (Fizzy's Lunch Lab Ser.). (ENG.). 48p. (J). (gr. 1-4). pap. 5.99 *(978-0-7636-7546-2(6)*, Candlewick Entertainment) Candlewick Pr.

Miedzybrodzka, Wiktoria. Jungle. Fretczak-Rodak, Monika, illus. 2014. (Mommy & Me Bath Bks.). (ENG.). 6p. (J). (gr. -1 — 1). 4.99 *(978-1-4380-7485-6(9))* Barron's Educational Series, Inc.

Migliardo, Emiliano, illus. Seek & Find Christmas. 2017. (ENG.). 24p. (J). pap. 4.99 ***(978-1-68119-542-1(9)***, 9781681195421, Bloomsbury Activity Bks.) Bloomsbury Publishing USA.

Milbourne, Anna. Sunny Day (Picture Book) 2008. (Picture Bks). 24p. (J). 9.99 *(978-0-7945-2117-2(7)*, Usborne) EDC Publishing.

—Under the Sea. Shimmen, Cathy, illus. 2007. (Picture Bks). 32p. (J). 9.99 *(978-0-7945-1801-1(X)*, Usborne) EDC Publishing.

—Where Do Baby Animals Come From? 2012. (Picture Bks). 24p. (J). bds. 10.99 *(978-0-7945-3284-0(5)*, Usborne) EDC Publishing.

Miles, David. The Book. Hoopes, Natalie, illus. 2015. (ENG.). 32p. (J). 16.95 *(978-1-939629-65-4(9))* Familius LLC.

Milet Publishing Staff. Clothes. 2014. (My First Bilingual Book Ser.). (Illus.). 20p. (J). (— 1). (ENG & KOR.). bds. 7.99 *(978-1-84059-865-0(4))*; (SPA & ENG., bds. 7.99 *(978-1-84059-870-4(0))* Milet Publishing.

—Clothes - My First Bilingual Book. 2014. (My First Bilingual Book Ser.). (Illus.). 20p. (J). (— 1). (POR & ENG.). bds. 7.99 *(978-1-84059-867-4(0))*; (ENG & VIE., bds. 7.99 *(978-1-84059-873-5(5))*; (ENG & CHI., bds. 7.99 *(978-1-84059-860-5(3))*; (ENG & ITA., bds. 7.99 *(978-1-84059-864-3(6))* Milet Publishing.

—Colors. 2010. (My First Bilingual Book Ser.). (SPA & ENG., Illus.). 24p. (J). (gr. k — 1). bds. 7.99 *(978-1-84059-539-0(6))* Milet Publishing.

—Colours. 2010. (My First Bilingual Book Ser.). (Illus.). 24p. (J). (gr. k — 1). (ENG & JPN.). bds. 7.99 *(978-1-84059-563-5(9))*; (KOR & ENG., bds. 7.99 *(978-1-84059-564-2(7))* Milet Publishing.

—Colours - My First Bilingual Book. 2010. (My First Bilingual Book Ser.). (Illus.). 24p. (J). (gr. k — 1). (ENG & ITA.). bds. 8.99 *(978-1-84059-537-6(X))*; (POR & ENG., bds. 7.99 *(978-1-84059-565-9(5))*; (RUS & ENG., bds. 7.99 *(978-1-84059-566-6(3))*; (ENG & POL., bds. 8.99 *(978-1-84059-538-3(8))* Milet Publishing.

—Jobs Empregos. 2012. (My First Bilingual Book Ser.). (ENG & POR., Illus.). 24p. (J). (gr. k — 1). bds. 7.99 *(978-1-84059-709-7(7))* Milet Publishing.

—Music. 2012. (My First Bilingual Book Ser.). (ENG, POL & POR., Illus.). 24p. (J). (gr. k — 1). bds. 7.99 *(978-1-84059-724-0(0))* Milet Publishing.

—Music - My First Bilingual Book. 2012. (My First Bilingual Book Ser.). (ENG & POR., Illus.). 24p. (J). (gr. k — 1). bds. 7.99 *(978-1-84059-725-7(9))* Milet Publishing.

—My Bilingual Book - Sight. 2014. (My Bilingual Book Ser.). (ENG & TUR., Illus.). 28p. (J). (gr. -1-k). 9.95 *(978-1-84059-801-8(8))* Milet Publishing.

—My Bilingual Book - Smell. 2014. (My Bilingual Book Ser.). (ENG & CHI., Illus.). 28p. (J). (gr. -1-k). 9.95 *(978-1-84059-806-3(9))* Milet Publishing.

—My Bilingual Book-Hearing. 2014. (My Bilingual Book Ser.). (ENG & TUR., Illus.). 28p. (J). (gr. -1-k). 9.95 *(978-1-84059-785-1(2))*; 9.95 *(978-1-84059-779-0(8))*; 9.95 *(978-1-84059-774-5(7))* Milet Publishing.

—My Bilingual Book-Hearing (English-Arabic) 2014. (My Bilingual Book Ser.). (ENG & ARA., Illus.). 28p. (J). (gr. -1-k). 9.95 *(978-1-84059-772-1(0))* Milet Publishing.

—My Bilingual Book-Hearing (English-Bengali) 2014. (My Bilingual Book Ser.). (ENG & BEN., Illus.). 28p. (J). (gr. -1-k). 9.95 *(978-1-84059-773-8(9))* Milet Publishing.

—My Bilingual Book-Hearing (English-Farsi) 2014. (My Bilingual Book Ser.). (ENG & PER., Illus.). 28p. (J). (gr. -1-k). 9.95 *(978-1-84059-775-2(5))* Milet Publishing.

—My Bilingual Book-Hearing (English-French) 2014. (My Bilingual Book Ser.). (ENG & FRE., Illus.). 28p. (J). (gr. -1-k). 9.95 *(978-1-84059-776-9(3))* Milet Publishing.

—My Bilingual Book-Hearing (English-German) 2014. (My Bilingual Book Ser.). (ENG & GER., Illus.). 28p. (J). (gr. -1-k). 9.95 *(978-1-84059-777-6(1))* Milet Publishing.

—My Bilingual Book-Hearing (English-Italian) 2014. (My Bilingual Book Ser.). (ENG & ITA., Illus.). 28p. (J). (gr. -1-k). 9.95 *(978-1-84059-778-3(X))* Milet Publishing.

—My Bilingual Book-Hearing (English-Polish) 2014. (My Bilingual Book Ser.). (ENG, POL & POR., Illus.). 28p. (J). (gr. -1-k). 9.95 *(978-1-84059-780-6(1))* Milet Publishing.

—My Bilingual Book-Hearing (English-Portuguese) 2014. (My Bilingual Book Ser.). (ENG & POR., Illus.). 28p. (J). (gr. -1-k). 9.95 *(978-1-84059-781-3(X))* Milet Publishing.

—My Bilingual Book-Hearing (English-Russian) 2014. (My Bilingual Book Ser.). (ENG & RUS., Illus.). 28p. (J). (gr. -1-k). 9.95 *(978-1-84059-782-0(8))* Milet Publishing.

—My Bilingual Book-Hearing (English-Somali) 2014. (My Bilingual Book Ser.). (ENG & SOM., Illus.). 28p. (J). (gr. -1-k). 9.95 *(978-1-84059-783-7(6))* Milet Publishing.

—My Bilingual Book-Hearing (English-Urdu) 2014. (My Bilingual Book Ser.). (ENG & URD., Illus.). 28p. (J). (gr. -1-k). 9.95 *(978-1-84059-786-8(0))* Milet Publishing.

—My Bilingual Book-Hearing (English-Vietnamese) 2014. (My Bilingual Book Ser.). (ENG & VIE., Illus.). 28p. (J). (gr. -1-k). 9.95 *(978-1-84059-787-5(9))* Milet Publishing.

—My Bilingual Book-Sight. 2014. (My Bilingual Book Ser.). *(ENG & KOR., Illus.). 28p. (J). (gr. -1-k).* 9.95 *(978-1-84059-795-0(X))* Milet Publishing.

—My Bilingual Book-Sight (English-Bengali) 2014. (My Bilingual Book Ser.). (ENG & BEN., Illus.). 28p. (J). (gr. -1-k). 9.95 *(978-1-84059-789-9(5))* Milet Publishing.

—My Bilingual Book-Sight (English-Chinese) 2014. (My Bilingual Book Ser.). (ENG & CHI., Illus.). 28p. (J). (gr. -1-k). 9.95 *(978-1-84059-790-5(9))* Milet Publishing.

—My Bilingual Book-Sight (English-Farsi) 2014. (My Bilingual Book Ser.). (ENG & PER., Illus.). 28p. (J). (gr. -1-k). 9.95 *(978-1-84059-791-2(7))* Milet Publishing.

—My Bilingual Book-Sight (English-French) 2014. (My Bilingual Book Ser.). (ENG & FRE., Illus.). 28p. (J). (gr. -1-k). 9.95 *(978-1-84059-792-9(5))* Milet Publishing.

—My Bilingual Book-Sight (English-German) 2014. (My Bilingual Book Ser.). (ENG & GER., Illus.). 28p. (J). (gr. -1-k). 9.95 *(978-1-84059-793-6(3))* Milet Publishing.

—My Bilingual Book-Sight (English-Italian) 2014. (My Bilingual Book Ser.). (ENG & ITA., Illus.). 28p. (J). (gr. -1-k). 9.95 *(978-1-84059-794-3(1))* Milet Publishing.

—My Bilingual Book-Sight (English-Polish) 2014. (My Bilingual Book Ser.). (ENG, POL & POR., Illus.). 28p. (J). (gr. -1-k). 9.95 *(978-1-84059-796-7(8))* Milet Publishing.

—My Bilingual Book-Sight (English-Portuguese) 2014. (My Bilingual Book Ser.). (ENG & POR., Illus.). 28p. (J). (gr. -1-k). 9.95 *(978-1-84059-797-4(6))* Milet Publishing.

—My Bilingual Book-Sight (English-Russian) 2014. (My Bilingual Book Ser.). (ENG & RUS., Illus.). 28p. (J). (gr. -1-k). 9.95 *(978-1-84059-798-1(4))* Milet Publishing.

—My Bilingual Book-Sight (English-Somali) 2014. (My Bilingual Book Ser.). (ENG & SOM., Illus.). 28p. (J). (gr. -1-k). 9.95 *(978-1-84059-799-8(2))* Milet Publishing.

—My Bilingual Book-Sight (English-Spanish) 2014. (My Bilingual Book Ser.). (ENG & SPA., Illus.). 28p. (J). (gr. -1-k). 9.95 *(978-1-84059-800-1(X))* Milet Publishing.

—My Bilingual Book-Sight (English-Urdu) 2014. (My Bilingual Book Ser.). (ENG & URD., Illus.). 28p. (J). (gr. -1-k). 9.95 *(978-1-84059-802-5(6))* Milet Publishing.

—My Bilingual Book-Sight (English-Vietnamese) 2014. (My Bilingual Book Ser.). (ENG & VIE., Illus.). 28p. (J). (gr. -1-k). 9.95 *(978-1-84059-803-2(4))* Milet Publishing.

—My Bilingual Book-Smell. 2014. (My Bilingual Book Ser.). (ENG & KOR., Illus.). 28p. (J). (gr. -1-k). 9.95 *(978-1-84059-811-7(5))* Milet Publishing.

—My Bilingual Book-Smell (English-Arabic) 2014. (My Bilingual Book Ser.). (ENG & ARA., Illus.). 28p. (J). (gr. -1-k). 9.95 *(978-1-84059-804-9(2))* Milet Publishing.

—My Bilingual Book-Smell (English-Bengali) 2014. (My Bilingual Book Ser.). (ENG & BEN., Illus.). 28p. (J). (gr. -1-k). 9.95 *(978-1-84059-805-6(0))* Milet Publishing.

—My Bilingual Book-Smell (English-Farsi) 2014. (My Bilingual Book Ser.). (ENG & PER., Illus.). 28p. (J). (gr. -1-k). 9.95 *(978-1-84059-807-0(7))* Milet Publishing.

—My Bilingual Book-Smell (English-Italian) 2014. (My Bilingual Book Ser.). (ENG & ITA., Illus.). 28p. (J). (gr. -1-k). 9.95 *(978-1-84059-810-0(7))* Milet Publishing.

—My Bilingual Book-Smell (English-Urdu) 2014. (My Bilingual Book Ser.). (ENG & URD., Illus.). 28p. (J). (gr. -1-k). 9.95 *(978-1-84059-818-6(2))* Milet Publishing.

—My First Bilingual Book - Clothes. 2014. (My First Bilingual Book Ser.). (Illus.). 20p. (J). (— 1). (ENG & RUS.). bds. 7.99 *(978-1-84059-868-1(9))*; (FRE & ENG., bds. 7.99 *(978-1-84059-862-9(X))*; (ENG & TUR., bds. 7.99 *(978-1-84059-871-1(9))*; (ENG & URD., bds. 7.99 *(978-1-84059-872-8(7))*; (ENG, POL & POR., bds. 7.99 *(978-1-84059-866-7(2))*; (ENG & BEN., bds. 7.99 *(978-1-84059-859-9(X))*; (ENG & PER., bds. 7.99 *(978-1-84059-861-2(1))*; (ENG & GER., bds. 7.99 *(978-1-84059-863-6(8))*; (ENG & SOM., bds. 7.99 *(978-1-84059-869-8(7))*; (ENG & ARA., bds. 7.99 *(978-1-84059-858-2(1))* Milet Publishing.

—My First Bilingual Book - Numbers. 2010. (My First Bilingual Book Ser.). (Illus.). 24p. (J). (gr. k — 1). (ENG & GER.). bds. 7.99 *(978-1-84059-542-0(6))*; (SPA & ENG., bds. 8.99 *(978-1-84059-545-1(0))*; (ENG & TUR., bds. 7.99 *(978-1-84059-546-8(9))* Milet Publishing.

—My First Bilingual Book - Plants. 2014. (My First Bilingual Book Ser.). (Illus.). 20p. (J). (— 1). (ENG & SOM.). bds. 7.99 *(978-1-84059-885-8(9))*; (ENG & TUR., bds. 7.99 *(978-1-84059-887-2(5))*; (ENG & CHI., bds. 7.99 *(978-1-84059-876-6(X))*; (ENG & ARA., bds. 7.99 *(978-1-84059-874-2(3))*; (POR & ENG., bds. 7.99 *(978-1-84059-883-4(2))* Milet Publishing.

—My First Bilingual Book - Plants (English-Farsi) 2014. (My First Bilingual Book Ser.). (ENG & PER., Illus.). 20p. (J). (— 1). bds. 7.99 *(978-1-84059-877-3(8))* Milet Publishing.

—My First Bilingual Book - Plants (English-Korean) 2014. (My First Bilingual Book Ser.). (ENG & KOR., Illus.). 20p. (J). (— 1). bds. 7.99 *(978-1-84059-881-0(6))* Milet Publishing.

—My First Bilingual Book - School. 2014. (My First Bilingual Book Ser.). (Illus.). 20p. (J). (— 1). (ENG & PER.). bds. 7.99 *(978-1-84059-893-3(X))*; (ENG & CHI., bds. 7.99 *(978-1-84059-892-6(1))*; (ENG & GER., bds. 7.99 *(978-1-84059-895-7(6))*; (FRE & ENG., bds. 7.99 *(978-1-84059-894-0(8))*; (ENG & BEN., bds. 7.99 *(978-1-84059-891-9(3))*; (POR & ENG., bds. 7.99 *(978-1-84059-899-5(9))*; (ENG & VIE., bds. 7.99 *(978-1-84059-905-3(7))*; (ENG & TUR., bds. 7.99 *(978-1-84059-903-9(0))* Milet Publishing.

—My First Bilingual Book - School (English-Korean) 2014. (My First Bilingual Book Ser.). (ENG & KOR., Illus.). 20p. (J). (— 1). bds. 7.99 *(978-1-84059-897-1(2))* Milet Publishing.

—My First Bilingual Book - School (English-Somali) 2014. (My First Bilingual Book Ser.). (ENG & SOM., Illus.). 20p. (J). (— 1). bds. 7.99 *(978-1-84059-901-5(4))* Milet Publishing.

—My First Bilingual Book - Tools. 2014. (My First Bilingual Book Ser.). (Illus.). 20p. (J). (— 1). (ENG, POL & POR.). bds. 7.99 *(978-1-84059-914-5(6))*; (ENG & GER., bds. 7.99 *(978-1-84059-911-4(1))*; (ENG & URD., bds. 7.99 *(978-1-84059-920-6(0))*; (ENG & BEN., bds. 7.99 *(978-1-84059-907-7(3))*; (SPA & ENG., bds. 7.99 *(978-1-84059-918-3(9))*; (ENG & ARA., bds. 7.99 *(978-1-84059-906-0(5))*; (ENG & RUS., bds. 7.99 *(978-1-84059-916-9(2))*; (ENG & TUR., bds. 7.99 *(978-1-84059-919-0(7))* Milet Publishing.

—My First Bilingual Book - Tools - English. 2014. (My First Bilingual Book Ser.). (ENG & VIE., Illus.). 20p. (J). (— 1). bds. 7.99 *(978-1-84059-921-3(9))* Milet Publishing.

—My First Bilingual Book - Tools - Ferramentas. 2014. (My First Bilingual Book Ser.). (POR & ENG., Illus.). 20p. (J). (— 1). bds. 7.99 *(978-1-84059-915-2(4))* Milet Publishing.

—My First Bilingual Book - Tools (English-Somali) 2014. (My First Bilingual Book Ser.). (ENG & SOM., Illus.). 20p. (J). (— 1). bds. 7.99 *(978-1-84059-917-6(0))* Milet Publishing.

—My First Bilingual Book - Vehicles. 2014. (My First Bilingual Book Ser.). (ENG & SOM., Illus.). 20p. (J). (— 1). bds. 7.99 *(978-1-84059-933-6(2))*; bds. 7.99 *(978-1-84059-937-4(5))*; bds. 7.99 *(978-1-84059-924-4(3))*; bds. 7.99 *(978-1-84059-935-0(9))*; bds. 7.99 *(978-1-84059-925-1(1))*; bds. 7.99 *(978-1-84059-929-9(4))* Milet Publishing.

—My First Bilingual Book - Vehicles (English-Russian) 2014. (My First Bilingual Book Ser.). (ENG & RUS., Illus.). 20p. (J). (— 1). bds. 7.99 *(978-1-84059-932-9(4))* Milet Publishing.

—My First Bilingual Book-Music (English-Russian) 2012. (My First Bilingual Book Ser.). (ENG & RUS., Illus.). 24p. (J). (gr. k — 1). bds. 7.99 *(978-1-84059-726-4(7))* Milet Publishing.

—My First Bilingual Book-Music (English-Somali) 2012. (My First Bilingual Book Ser.). (ENG & SOM., Illus.). 24p. (J). (gr. k — 1). bds. 7.99 *(978-1-84059-727-1(5))* Milet Publishing.

—My First Bilingual Book-Opposites. 2012. (My First Bilingual Book Ser.). (ENG & CHI., Illus.). 24p. (J). (gr. k — 1). bds. 7.99 *(978-1-84059-734-9(8))* Milet Publishing.

—Numbers - My First Bilingual Book. 2010. (My First Bilingual Book Ser.). (Illus.). 24p. (J). (gr. k — 1). (FRE & ENG.). bds. 7.99 *(978-1-84059-541-3(8))*; (ENG & ITA., bds. 7.99 *(978-1-84059-543-7(4))*; (ENG & POL., bds. 8.99 *(978-1-84059-544-4(2))* Milet Publishing.

—Opposites. 2012. (My First Bilingual Book Ser.). (ENG & PER., Illus.). 24p. (J). (gr. k — 1). bds. 7.99 *(978-1-84059-735-6(6))* Milet Publishing.

—Plants - My First Bilingual Book. 2014. (My First Bilingual Book Ser.). (Illus.). 20p. (J). (— 1). (FRE & ENG.). bds. 7.99 *(978-1-84059-878-0(6))*; (ENG & VIE., bds. 7.99 *(978-1-84059-889-6(1))*; (ENG & RUS., bds. 7.99 *(978-1-84059-884-1(0))*; (SPA & ENG., bds. 7.99 *(978-1-84059-886-5(7))*; (ENG & URD., bds. 7.99 *(978-1-84059-888-9(3))*; (ENG & ITA., bds. 7.99 *(978-1-84059-880-3(8))*; (ENG & BEN., bds. 7.99 *(978-1-84059-875-9(1))*; (ENG, POL & POR., bds. 7.99 *(978-1-84059-882-7(4))* Milet Publishing.

—School. 2014. (My First Bilingual Book Ser.). (ENG & ITA., Illus.). 20p. (J). (— 1). bds. 7.99 *(978-1-84059-896-4(4))* Milet Publishing.

—School - My First Bilingual Book. 2014. (My First Bilingual Book Ser.). (Illus.). 20p. (J). (— 1). (SPA & ENG.). bds. 7.99 *(978-1-84059-902-2(2))*; (ENG & RUS., bds. 7.99 *(978-1-84059-900-8(6))*; (ENG & URD., bds. 7.99 *(978-1-84059-904-6(9))*; (ENG & ARA., bds. 7.99 *(978-1-84059-890-2(5))* Milet Publishing.

—School - My First Bilingual Book (Szkola) 2014. (My First Bilingual Book Ser.). (ENG, POL & POR., Illus.). 20p. (J). (— 1). bds. 7.99 *(978-1-84059-898-8(0))* Milet Publishing.

—Sight - English-Arabic. 2014. (My Bilingual Book Ser.). (ENG & ARA., Illus.). 28p. (J). (gr. -1-k). 9.95 *(978-1-84059-788-2(7))* Milet Publishing.

—Smell / Das Riechen. 2014. (My Bilingual Book Ser.). (ENG & GER., Illus.). 28p. (J). (gr. -1-k). 9.95 *(978-1-84059-809-4(3))* Milet Publishing.

—Smell (English-French) 2014. (My Bilingual Book Ser.). (ENG & FRE., Illus.). 28p. (J). (gr. -1-k). 9.95 *(978-1-84059-808-7(5))* Milet Publishing.

—Tools. 2014. (My First Bilingual Book Ser.). (ENG & ITA., Illus.). 20p. (J). (— 1). bds. 7.99 *(978-1-84059-912-1(X))* Milet Publishing.

—Tools - My First Bilingual Book. 2014. (My First Bilingual Book Ser.). (ENG & PER., Illus.). 20p. (J). (— 1). bds. 7.99 *(978-1-84059-909-1(X))*; bds. 7.99 *(978-1-84059-913-8(8))*; bds. 7.99 *(978-1-84059-908-4(1))* Milet Publishing.

—Tools (English-French) 2014. (My First Bilingual Book Ser.). (FRE & ENG., Illus.). 20p. (J). (— 1). bds. 7.99 *(978-1-84059-910-7(3))* Milet Publishing.

—Vehicles. 2014. (My First Bilingual Book Ser.). (Illus.). 20p. (J). (— 1). (ENG & ITA.). bds. 7.99 *(978-1-84059-928-2(6))*; (ENG & ARA., bds. 7.99 *(978-1-84059-922-0(7))*; (SPA & ENG., bds. 7.99 *(978-1-84059-934-3(0))* Milet Publishing.

—Vehicles - My First Bilingual Book. 2014. (My First Bilingual Book Ser.). (Illus.). 20p. (J). (— 1). (POR & ENG.). bds. 7.99 *(978-1-84059-931-2(6))*; (ENG, POL & POR., bds. 7.99 *(978-1-84059-930-5(8))*; (ENG & URD., bds. 7.99 *(978-1-84059-936-7(7))*; (FRE & ENG., bds. 7.99 *(978-1-84059-926-8(X))*; (ENG & BEN., bds. 7.99 *(978-1-84059-923-7(5))* Milet Publishing.

—Vehicles (English-German) 2014. (My First Bilingual Book Ser.). (ENG & GER., Illus.). 20p. (J). (— 1). bds. 7.99 *(978-1-84059-927-5(8))* Milet Publishing.

Milford, Diana Viola. Fuzzum & Wuzzum, 1 vol. 2010. 34p. pap. 24.95 *(978-1-4489-9168-6(4))* PublishAmerica, Inc.

Milgrim, David. Moo Bird. 2016. (Illus.). 32p. (J). ***(978-1-5182-0400-5(7))*** Scholastic, Inc.

—Moo Bird. Milgrim, David, illus. 2015. (Scholastic Reader, Level 1 Ser.). (ENG., Illus.). 32p. (J). (gr. -1-1). pap. 3.99 *(978-0-545-82502-3(4))* Scholastic, Inc.

Miller, Arthur. Jane's Blanket. Parker, Al, illus. 2017. (ENG.). 64p. (J). (gr. -1-3). 24.95 ***(978-3-89955-786-2(7))*** Die Gestalten Verlag DEU. Dist: Penguin Random Hse. LLC.

—Jane's Blanket. Al, Parker, illus. 2015. (ENG.). 64p. pap. 9.99 *(978-0-486-79682-6(5))* Dover Pubns., Inc.

Miller, J. Philip & Greene, Sheppard M. We All Sing with the Same Voice. Meisel, Paul, illus. 2005. (ENG.). 32p. (J). (gr. -1-2). reprint ed. pap. 6.99 *(978-0-06-073900-3(2))* HarperCollins Pubs.

Miller, Janet. DuckDumB. 2010. 32p. pap. 21.95 *(978-0-557-57669-2(5))* Lulu Pr., Inc.

Miller, Kerri. My Twin & Me - Fun with Twin Brothers & Sisters. 2013. (Illus.). 20p. pap. *(978-0-9576753-0-8(5))* Hot Tub Publishing, Ltd.

Miller, Mona. Hero of the Month! Random House, illus. 2017. (Pictureback(R) Ser.). (ENG.). 16p. (J). (gr. -1-2). pap. 5.99 ***(978-1-5247-6604-7(6)***, Random Hse. Bks. for Young Readers) Random Hse. Children's Bks.

—Poppy & Branch's Big Adventure. 2017. (Illus.). 32p. (J). ***(978-1-5182-3647-1(2))*** Random Hse., Inc.

Miller, Pat Zietlow. Wherever You Go. 2015. (ENG., Illus.). 32p. (J). (gr. -1-3). 17.00 *(978-0-316-40002-2(5))* Little, Brown Bks. for Young Readers.

Millett, Peter. The Great Escape White Band. Belli, Alfredo, illus. 2016. (Cambridge Reading Adventures Ser.). (ENG.). 24p. pap. 7.19 *(978-1-107-55158-9(7))* Cambridge Univ. Pr.

Milligan, Bryce. Brigid's Cloak: An Ancient Irish Story. Cann, Helen, illus. 2005. (ENG.). 32p. (J). (gr. k-17). 9.00 *(978-0-8028-5297-7(1)*, Eerdmans Bks For Young Readers) Eerdmans, William B. Publishing Co.

Millsaps, Grace & Murphy, Ryan. You Wouldn't Like Me Without My Coffee. Marin, Danny, illus. 2014. (ENG.). 40p. (J). (gr. k-2). 17.95 *(978-0-9904093-0-4(9))* Millfree Mursaps Media.

Milne, Sarah. The Lost Hat. 2017. (ENG., Illus.). 20p. (J). pap. 13.95 ***(978-1-78823-017-9(5)***, eac97656-e34d-421d-a45e-6759a4392813) Austin, Stan AUS. Dist: Bookmasters Distribution.

Minchin, Adele. The Caravan Club. 2003. 224p. pap. 12.00 *(978-0-7043-4978-0(7))* Women's Pr., Ltd., The GBR. Dist: Trafalgar Square Publishing.

Minhós Martins, Isabel. The World in a Second. Carvalho, Bernardo, illus. 2015. (ENG.). 56p. (J). (gr. -1-3). 18.95 *(978-1-59270-157-5(4))* Enchanted Lion Bks., LLC.

Mini My First Picture Dictiona. 2004. (Early Learning Ser.). 18p. (J). bds. 2.99 *(978-1-85854-832-6(2))* Brimax Books Ltd. GBR. Dist: Byeway Bks.

Mitchell, Melanie, illus. Good Morning, Good Night Bilingual: Buenos Dias! Buenas Noches! 2005. (ENG & SPA.). 12p. (J). 9.95 *(978-1-58117-389-5(X)*, Intervisual/Piggy Toes) Bendon, Inc.

Mitchell, Pratima. Raju's Ride. Waterhouse, Stephen, illus. 2005. (ENG.). 24p. (J). lib. bdg. 23.65 *(978-1-59646-726-2(6))* Dingles & Co.

Mitchell, Robin. Snowy & Chinook. Steedman, Judith, illus. 2005. (ENG.). 22p. (J). (gr. -1-3). 15.95 *(978-0-9688768-9-3(7))* Simply Read Bks. CAN. Dist: Ingram Publisher Services.

Mitton, Tony. Twist & Hop, Minibeast Bop. Parker-Rees, Guy, illus. 2017. (ENG.). 32p. (J). (gr. -1-k). pap. 7.99 *(978-1-4083-3687-8(1)*, Orchard Bks.) Hachette Children's Group GBR. Dist: Hachette Bk. Group.

Miyares, Daniel. Pardon Me! Miyares, Daniel, illus. 2014. (ENG., Illus.). 40p. (J). (gr. -1-3). 16.99 *(978-1-4424-8997-4(9)*, Simon & Schuster Bks. For Young Readers) Simon & Schuster Bks. For Young Readers.

Miyazaki, Hayao. Howls Moving Castle Picture Book. Miyazaki, Hayao, illus. 2005. (ENG., Illus.). 184p. 19.99 *(978-1-4215-0090-4(6))* Viz Media.

MJ Illustrations (Group) Staff, contrib. by. Marshall to the Rescue! 2016. (Illus.). (J). ***(978-1-4806-9669-3(2)***, Golden Bks.) Random Hse. Children's Bks.

Moerbeek, Kees. Cinderella. 2011. (My Secret Scrapbook Diary Ser.). (ENG., Illus.). 10p. (J). *(978-1-84643-450-1(5))* Child's Play International Ltd.

—Little Red Riding Hood. 2011. (My Secret Scrapbook Diary Ser.). (ENG., Illus.). 10p. (J). *(978-1-84643-447-1(5))* Child's Play International Ltd.

—Puss in Boots. 2014. (My Secret Scrapbook Diary Ser.). (ENG., Illus.). 10p. (J). *(978-1-84643-592-8(7))* Child's Play International Ltd.

—The Ugly Duckling. 2014. (My Secret Scrapbook Diary Ser.). (ENG., Illus.). 10p. (J). *(978-1-84643-593-5(5))* Child's Play International Ltd.

Mole in a Hole IR. 2017. (Phonics Readers Ser.). (ENG.). (J). pap. 6.99 ***(978-0-7945-3715-9(4)***, Usborne) EDC Publishing.

Molk, Laurel. Eeny, Meeny, Miney, Mo, & Flo. Molk, Laurel, illus. 2015. (ENG., Illus.). 32p. (J). (gr. -1-k). 16.99 *(978-0-670-01538-2(5)*, Viking Books for Young Readers) Penguin Young Readers Group.

Moller, Jonathan R. Bath Time: Picture Book. l.t. ed. 2003. (Illus.). 71p. pap. 19.95 *(978-0-9740169-0-0(X))* Lemonflavor Productions.

Molloy, Tom. Everything but the Beach: A Slice of Manchester Life. 2012. (Illus.). 192p. (J). pap. 9.60 *(978-1-291-15817-5(0))* Lulu Pr., Inc.

Momenceau, Amandine. Mrs Fox. 2016. (ENG., Illus.). 48p. (J). (gr. -1-2). 19.95 *(978-0-500-65089-9(6)*, 565089) Thames & Hudson.

A Monarch Universe CD: Children's Picture Book. 2007. (J). cd-rom 22.95 *(978-0-9800222-2-3(3))* UPfirst.com Bks.

Monfreid, Dorothée de. A Day with Dogs. 2017. (ENG., Illus.). 64p. (gr. -1-1). 19.99 ***(978-1-77657-098-0(7))*** Gecko Pr. NZL. Dist: Lerner Publishing Group.

Moniz, Michael. The Boy & the Whale. 2013. (ENG., Illus.). 36p. (J). (gr. -1-3). 16.95 *(978-1-927018-14-9(5))* Simply Read Bks. CAN. Dist: Ingram Publisher Services.

—The Cardinal & the Crow. Moniz, Michael, illus. 2015. (ENG., Illus.). 235p. (J). 16.95 *(978-1-927018-58-3(7))* Simply Read Bks. CAN. Dist: Ingram Publisher Services.

Monks, Julie. Let's Read! Marcello Mouse & the Masked Ball, 7. 2014. (Let's Read! Ser.). (ENG., Illus.). 32p. (J). (gr. k-2). pap. 7.99 *(978-1-4472-3695-5(5))* Pan Macmillan GBR. Dist: Independent Pubs. Group.

Monks, Lydia. Eeeek, Mouse! 2015. (ENG., Illus.). 32p. (J). (gr. -1-k). pap. 10.99 *(978-1-4052-7692-4(4))* Egmont Bks., Ltd. GBR. Dist: Independent Pubs. Group.

—Go, Go, Gorilla! 2017. (ENG., Illus.). 32p. (J). (gr. -1-k). pap. 9.99 *(978-1-4052-7815-7(3))* Egmont Bks., Ltd. GBR. Dist: Independent Pubs. Group.

—Mungo Monkey Goes to School. 2014. (ENG., Illus.). 14p. (J). (gr. -1-k). 13.99 *(978-1-4052-6909-4(X))* Egmont Bks., Ltd. GBR. Dist: Independent Pubs. Group.

—Mungo Monkey to the Rescue. 2016. (ENG., Illus.). 14p. (J). (gr. -1-k). 10.99 *(978-1-4052-7818-8(8))* Egmont Bks., Ltd. GBR. Dist: Independent Pubs. Group.

Montana, Hannah. Live from London. 2010. (Hannah Montana on Tour Ser.: No. 4). 80p. (gr. 2-5). pap. 3.99 *(978-1-4231-1815-2(4))* Disney Pr.

Montardre, Hélène. The Cat & the Dog. 2003. (Illus.). 8p. (J). bds. 7.95 *(978-1-58728-483-0(9)*, Two-Can Publishing) T&N Children's Publishing.

—Night & Day. 2003. (Illus.). 8p. (J). bds. 7.95 *(978-1-58728-481-6(2)*, Two-Can Publishing) T&N Children's Publishing.

Montejo, Victor. Blanca Flor: Una Princessa Maya, 1 vol. Yockteng, Rafael, illus. 2005. (SPA.). 36p. (J). (gr. 1). 16.95 *(978-0-88899-600-8(4))* Groundwood Bks. CAN. Dist: Publishers Group West (PGW).

Montgomery, Margaret, illus. The Adventures of Anna Banana Shoeshine: Anna Banana Takes a Bath. 2006. 40p. (J). *(978-1-930401-49-5(3))* Central Coast Bks./Pr.

Montgomery, Ross. The Building Boy. Litchfield, David, illus. 2017. (ENG.). 32p. 16.95 ***(978-0-571-31409-6(0))*** Faber & Faber, Inc.

Moodie, Fiona. Noko's Surprise Party. 2008. (ENG., Illus.). 32p. (J). (gr. k-3). 16.95 *(978-1-84507-587-3(0),* Frances Lincoln) Quarto Publishing Group UK GBR. Dist: Hachette Bk. Group.

Moon, Jo, illus. In the Pond. 2014. (ENG.). 8p. (J). (— 1). 11.99 *(978-0-230-76660-0(9))* Pan Macmillan GBR. Dist: Independent Pubs. Group.

—Under the Sea. 2014. (ENG.). 8p. (J). (— 1). 10.99 *(978-0-230-76659-4(5))* Pan Macmillan GBR. Dist: Independent Pubs. Group.

Moore, Brian L. The Story Behind Santa Sacks. Mulligan, Todd, illus. 2004. 32p. *(978-0-9732651-0-1(8))* Hills-n-Hollows Publishing.

Moore, David. Expl on Your Own the Island /Formed in 1 Day. 2009. (Explore on Your Own Ser.). (ENG., Illus.). 12p. (J). pap. 7.95 *(978-0-7362-5522-6(2))* National Geographic School Publishing, Inc.

Mora, Pat. Agua Agua Agua, Level 2. Flor Ada, Alma, tr. Ortega, Jose, illus. 3rd ed. 2003. (Dejame Leer Ser.). (SPA.). 16p. (J). (gr. -1-1). 6.50 *(978-0-673-36292-6(2),* Good Year Bks.) Celebration Pr.

—Book Fiesta! Celebrate Children's Day/Book Day; Celebremos el Dia de Los Ninos/el Dia de Los Libros. López, Rafael, illus. 2016. 40p. (J). (gr. -1-1). pap. 6.99 *(978-0-06-128878-4(0))* HarperCollins Pubs.

Moreillon, Judi. Vamos a Leer. Mercado, Mary M., tr. from ENG. Teis, Kyra, illus.Tr. of Read to Me. (SPA.). 12p. (J). 2005. bds. 6.95 *(978-1-59572-015-3(4))* 2004. 6.95 *(978-1-932065-50-3(4))* Star Bright Bks., Inc.

Morgan, Angie. Shouty Arthur. 2016. (Shouty Arthur Ser.: 1). (ENG., Illus.). 32p. (J). (gr. -1-k). pap. 9.99 *(978-1-4052-6677-2(5))* Egmont Bks., Ltd. GBR. Dist: Independent Pubs. Group.

Morgan, Michaela. Band of Friends. Price, Nick, illus. 2005. (ENG.). 24p. (J). lib. bdg. 23.65 *(978-1-59646-734-7(7))* Dingles & Co.

—Mouse with No Name. Mikhail, Jess, illus. 2004. (ENG.). 24p. (J). lib. bdg. 23.65 *(978-1-59646-682-1(0))* Dingles & Co.

—Never Shake a Rattlesnake. Sharratt, Nick, illus. (ENG.). 32p. (J). (gr. -1-k). 2016. pap. 8.99 *(978-1-5098-1704-7(2))*1. 2012. pap. 8.99 *(978-0-330-51229-9(3))* Pan Macmillan GBR. Dist: Independent Pubs. Group.

—Shy Shark. Gomez, Elena, illus. 2005. (ENG.). 24p. (J). lib. bdg. 23.65 *(978-1-59646-722-4(3))* Dingles & Co.

Morgan, Ruth. Big Liam, Little Liam. Archbold, Tim, illus. 2005. (ENG.). 24p. (J). lib. bdg. 23.65 *(978-1-59646-728-6(2))* Dingles & Co.

—Jess & the Bean Root. Vagnozzi, Barbara, illus. 2005. (ENG.). 24p. (J). lib. bdg. 23.65 *(978-1-59646-732-3(0))* Dingles & Co.

Morgand, Virginie. Achoo! 2016. (ENG., Illus.). 36p. (J). (gr. -1 — 1). 16.95 *(978-1-84976-376-9(3))* Tate Publishing, Ltd. GBR. Dist: Abrams, Inc.

—What Do Grown-Ups Do All Day? Morgand, Virginie, illus. 2016. (ENG., Illus.). 64p. (J). 22.99 *(978-1-84780-809-7(3),* Wide Eyed Editions) Quarto Publishing Group UK GBR. Dist: Littlehampton Bk Services, Ltd.

Morning, Carey. The Shepherd Girl of Bethlehem: A Nativity Story. Marks, Alan, illus. 2016. (ENG.). 32p. (J). (gr. -1-k). pap. 8.99 *(978-0-7459-6232-0(7))* Lion Hudson PLC GBR. Dist: Independent Pubs. Group.

Morris, Jackie. Little Evie in the Wild Wood. Hyde, Catherine, illus. 2013. (ENG.). 40p. (J). (gr. -1-2). 18.99 *(978-1-84780-371-9(7),* Frances Lincoln) Quarto Publishing Group UK GBR. Dist: Hachette Bk. Group.

—Song of the Golden Hare. 2013. (ENG., Illus.). 40p. (J). (gr. k-3). 18.99 *(978-1-84780-450-1(0),* Frances Lincoln) Quarto Publishing Group UK GBR. Dist: Hachette Bk. Group.

Morris, Jackie. Tell Me a Dragon. 2017. (ENG., Illus.). 40p. (J). (gr. -1-k). 17.99 ***(978-1-84780-242-2(7),*** Frances Lincoln) Quarto Publishing Group UK GBR. Dist: Hachette Bk. Group.

Morris, Jackie & Quarto Generic Staff. I Am Cat. 2013. (ENG., Illus.). 32p. (J). (gr. k-3). 17.99 *(978-1-84780-135-7(8),* Frances Lincoln) Quarto Publishing Group UK GBR. Dist: Hachette Bk. Group.

Morris, Kim Ely. Through the Eyes of Love. 2009. (Illus.). 24p. pap. 14.99 *(978-1-4389-6756-1(X))* AuthorHouse.

Morris, Richard T. This Is a Moose. 2014. (ENG., Illus.). 48p. (J). (gr. -1-3). 18.00 *(978-0-316-21360-8(8))* Little, Brown Bks. for Young Readers.

Morris, Tony, illus. Papa Panov's Special Day. 2017. (ENG.). 32p. (J). (gr. k-2). 7.99 ***(978-0-7459-6562-8(8))*** Lion Hudson PLC GBR. Dist: Independent Pubs. Group.

Morstad, Julie. How To. Morstad, Julie, illus. 2013. (ENG., Illus.). 36p. (J). (gr. -1-3). 16.95 *(978-1-897476-57-4(4))* Simply Read Bks. CAN. Dist: Ingram Publisher Services.

Mortimer, Rachael. Red Riding Hood & the Sweet Little Wolf. Pichon, Liz, illus. 2013. (ENG.). 32p. 12.95 *(978-1-58925-117-5(2))* Tiger Tales.

—The Three Billy Goats Fluff. Pichon, Liz, illus. 2013. (ENG.). 32p. (J). (gr. -1-2). pap. 7.95 *(978-1-58925-439-8(2))* Tiger Tales.

Mortmain, Beatrice. I Help at Grandpa's House. Aguilera, Aurora, illus. 2017. (Ways I Help Ser.). 24p. (J). (gr. 4-6). pap. 8.25 ***(978-1-5081-5677-2(8),*** PowerKids Pr.) Rosen Publishing Group, Inc., The.

Morton, Ken, illus. Cinderella. 2012. (ENG.). 24p. (J). (gr. -1-12). 5.99 *(978-1-84322-803-5(3))* Anness Publishing GBR. Dist: National Bk. Network.

Moses, Anne E. Gatos Musikos: A Secret Told by the Moon. 2013. (Illus.). 58p. 24.95 *(978-1-4575-2189-8(X))* Dog Ear Publishing, LLC.

Moses, Brian. The Frog Olympics. Husband, Amy, illus. 2017. (ENG.). 32p. (J). (gr. -1-k). pap. 9.99 ***(978-0-7502-9683-0(6),*** Wayland) Hachette Children's Group GBR. Dist: Hachette Bk. Group.

Moshier, Joe & Sonnenburg, Chris. Go, Pea, Go! 2015. (ENG., Illus.). 32p. (J). (gr. -1-17). 14.95 *(978-0-7624-5678-9(7),* Running Pr. Kids) Running Pr. Bk. Pubs.

Moss, Marissa. Amelia's Cross-My-Heart, Hope-to-Die Guide to the Real, True You! Moss, Marissa, illus. 2010. (Amelia Ser.). (ENG., Illus.). 64p. (J). (gr. 5-8). 9.99 *(978-1-4169-8710-9(X),* Simon & Schuster/Paula Wiseman Bks.) Simon & Schuster/Paula Wiseman Bks.

Moss, Miriam. Matty in a Mess! Simmons, Jane, illus. 2010. (Matty & Milly Ser.). (ENG.). 32p. (J). (gr. k-k). pap. 9.99 *(978-1-84270-946-7(1))* Andersen Pr. GBR. Dist: Independent Pubs. Group.

—Matty Takes Off! Simmons, Jane, illus. 2008. (Matty & Milly Ser.). (ENG.). 32p. (J). (gr. -1-k). 19.95 *(978-1-84270-701-2(9))* Andersen Pr. GBR. Dist: Independent Pubs. Group.

Moss, Patricia Crocker. Dillie's Encounter with the Bucket Man. 2010. 36p. pap. 21.99 *(978-1-4535-4460-0(7))* Xlibris Corp.

Mostoller, Marcia. Poor William Dill. 2011. 28p. pap. 24.95 *(978-1-4626-0835-5(3))* America Star Bks.

Mother Goose Programs, prod. What's the BIG Idea? Shapes & Spaces Librarian Manual. 2008. 70p. pap. *(978-0-9753985-9-3(8))* Mother Goose Programs.

Mountbatten-Windsor, Sarah & York, Sarah. Tea for Ruby. 2012. lib. bdg. 18.40 *(978-0-606-26884-4(7),* Turtleback) Turtleback Bks.

Muir, Nicola. Baba Didi & the Godwits Fly, 1 vol. Hayward, Annie, illus. 2013. (ENG.). 32p. (J). (gr. k-4). 8.95 *(978-1-78026-130-0(6))* New Internationalist Pubns., Ltd. GBR. Dist: Consortium Bk. Sales & Distribution.

Mullen, Amy. Colors of New England. 2017. (Naturally Local Ser.). (ENG., Illus.). 20p. (J). (gr. -1-k). bds. 8.95 ***(978-1-938093-99-9(2))*** Duo Pr. LLC.

Muller, Carrie & Halsey, Jacqueline. The Terrible, Horrible, Smelly Pirate, 1 vol. Orchard, Eric, illus. 2008. (ENG.). 32p. (J). (gr. k-3). pap. 11.95 *(978-1-55109-655-1(2))* Nimbus Publishing, Ltd. CAN. Dist: Orca Bk. Pubs. USA.

Mullin, Rene. Albitir. 2014. (ENG., Illus.). 40p. (J). 13.95 *(978-0-85640-917-2(0))* Blackstaff Pr., Ltd. GBR. Dist: Dufour Editions, Inc.

Mumford, Martha. The Royal Baby's Big Red Bus Tour of London. Grey, Ada, illus. 2017. (ENG.). 32p. (J). 12.99 *(978-1-4088-6896-6(2),* 9781408868966, Bloomsbury USA Childrens) Bloomsbury Publishing USA.

Munsch, Robert. Angela's Airplane. Martchenko, Michael, illus. 2016. (ENG.). 24p. (J). (-k). bds. 7.99 *(978-1-55451-829-6(6))* Annick Pr., Ltd. CAN. Dist: Publishers Group West (PGW).

—L' Anniversaire. Martchenko, Michael, illus. 2003. (Droles D'Histories Ser.).Tr. of Moira's Birthday. (FRE.). 24p. (J). (gr. k-18). pap. *(978-2-89021-114-8(2))* Diffusion du livre Mirabel (DLM).

—Le Dodo. Martchenko, Michael, illus. 2003. (Droles D'Histories Ser.).Tr. of Mortimer. (FRE.). 24p. (J). (gr. k-18). pap. *(978-2-89021-055-4(3))* Diffusion du livre Mirabel (DLM).

—The Fire Station. Martchenko, Michael, illus. 5th ed. 2012. (ENG.). 24p. (J). (gr. -1-k). bds. 7.99 *(978-1-55451-423-6(1),* 9781554514236) Annick Pr., Ltd. CAN. Dist: Publishers Group West (PGW).

—Love You Forever Pop-Up Edition. McGraw, Sheila, illus. 2017. (ENG.). 14p. (J). (gr. -1-1). 24.95 ***(978-1-77085-965-4(9),*** 9781770859654) Firefly Bks., Ltd.

—Mud Puddle. Petricic, Dusan, illus. 4th ed. 2012. (Munsch for Kids Ser.). (ENG.). 32p. (J). (gr. -1-2). 9.95 *(978-1-55451-426-7(6),* 9781554514267) Annick Pr., Ltd. CAN. Dist: Publishers Group West (PGW).

—The Paper Bag Princess: The Story Behind the Story. Martchenko, Michael, illus. 3rd anniv. ed. 2005. (ENG.). 64p. (J). (gr. -1-12). 19.95 *(978-1-55037-915-0(1),* 9781550379150) Annick Pr., Ltd. CAN. Dist: Publishers Group West (PGW).

—Pigs. Martchenko, Michael, illus. 2014. (ENG.). 26p. (J). (gr. -1-k). bds. 7.99 *(978-1-55451-628-5(5),* 9781554516285) Annick Pr., Ltd. CAN. Dist: Publishers Group West (PGW).

—50 below Zero. Martchenko, Michael, illus. 3rd ed. 2013. (Munsch for Kids Ser.). (ENG.). 22p. (J). (gr. -1-k). bds. 7.99 *(978-1-55451-532-5(7),* 9781554515325) Annick Pr., Ltd. CAN. Dist: Publishers Group West (PGW).

Muntean, Michaela. Elmo Can... Taste! Touch! Smell! See! Hear! (Sesame Street) Swanson, Maggie, illus. 2013. (Big Bird's Favorites Board Bks.). (ENG.). 24p. (J). (— 1). bds. 4.99 *(978-0-307-98078-6(2),* Random Hse. Bks. for Young Readers) Random Hse. Children's Bks.

Murphy, Julie. Gilly's Treasure. Fontano, Jay, illus. 2016. (ENG.). 14.99 *(978-1-4621-1845-8(3),* Sweetwater Bks.) Cedar Fort, Inc./CFI Distribution.

Murphy, Lorna. Maisie's Mountain. 2013. (Illus.). 40p. pap. *(978-0-9568666-2-2(X))* Bluebudgie Publishing.

Murphy, Mary. Say Hello Like This. Murphy, Mary, illus. 2014. (ENG., Illus.). 32p. (J). (-k). 12.99 *(978-0-7636-6951-5(2))* Candlewick Pr.

Murphy, Stuart J. Emma's Friendwich. 2010. (I See I Learn Ser.). (ENG., Illus.). 32p. (J). (gr. -1-k). pap. 6.95 *(978-1-58089-451-7(8))* Charlesbridge Publishing, Inc.

—Freda Plans a Picnic. 2010. (I See I Learn Ser.). (ENG., Illus.). 32p. (J). (gr. -1-k). pap. 6.95 *(978-1-58089-457-9(7))* Charlesbridge Publishing, Inc.

—Percy Plays It Safe. 2010. (I See I Learn Ser.). (ENG., Illus.). 32p. (J). (gr. -1-k). pap. 6.95 *(978-1-58089-453-1(4))* Charlesbridge Publishing, Inc.

Murray, Alison. Hare & Tortoise. Murray, Alison, illus. 2016. (ENG., Illus.). 32p. (J). (-k). 16.99 *(978-0-7636-8721-2(9))* Candlewick Pr.

Murray, Diana. Doris the Bookasaurus. Chen, Yuyi, illus. 2017. (ENG.). 40p. (J). 17.99 *(978-1-250-11676-5(7),* 9781250116765) Imprint IND. Dist: Macmillan.

—Groggle's Monster Valentine. Langley, Bats, illus. 2017. (ENG.). 32p. (J). (gr. -1-k). 9.99 *(978-1-5107-0508-1(2),* Sky Pony Pr.) Skyhorse Publishing Co., Inc.

Murray, Stuart. Submarines. 2014. (Illus.). 48p. (J). *(978-1-4351-5371-4(5))* Barnes & Noble, Inc.

Murray, Tamsyn. Snug as a Bug. Abbot, Judi, illus. 2013. (ENG.). 32p. (J). *(978-0-85707-108-8(4))* Barnes & Noble, Inc.

—Snug as a Bug. Abbot, Judi, illus. 2014. (ENG.). 32p. (J). (gr. -1). pap. 8.99 *(978-0-85707-109-5(2))* Simon & Schuster, Ltd. GBR. Dist: Simon & Schuster, Inc.

—Snug As a Bug. Abbot, Judi & Gaviraghi, Giuditta, illus. 2013. 30p. (J). *(978-1-4351-4731-7(6))* Barnes & Noble, Inc.

Musselwhite, Helen. Little Houses: A Counting Book. 2015. (ENG., Illus.). 32p. (J). (gr. -1-k). 15.95 *(978-1-78067-613-5(1))* King, Laurence Publishing GBR. Dist: Hachette Bk. Group.

Muszynski, Julie. Henley in Hollywood. 2015. (ENG., Illus.). 56p. 20.00 *(978-0-9905320-0-2(3))* Glitterati, Inc.

My First 100 Words in Spanish/English. 2003. 32p. (J). 11.95 *(978-0-7525-7769-2(7))* Parragon, Inc.

My First Book of Trucks. 2004. (Illus.). 18p. (J). bds. 5.99 *(978-1-85854-431-1(9))* Brimax Books Ltd. GBR. Dist: Byeway Bks.

My Little Story of Christmas, 1 vol. 2015. (ENG., Illus.). 20p. (J). pap. 3.99 *(978-1-78128-151-2(3),* Candle Bks.) Lion Hudson PLC GBR. Dist: Kregel Pubns.

Na, Il Sung. Welcome Home, Bear: A Book of Animal Habitats. 2015. (ENG., Illus.). 32p. (J). (— 1). 16.99 *(978-0-385-75375-3(6),* Knopf Bks. for Young Readers) Random Hse. Children's Bks.

Na, Il Sung, illus. Welcome Home, Bear: A Book of Animal Habitats. 2015. (ENG.). 32p. (J). (— 1). lib. bdg. 19.99 *(978-0-385-75376-0(4),* Knopf Bks. for Young Readers) Random Hse. Children's Bks.

Nadel, Carolina. Daddy's Home. Nadel, Carolina, illus. 2012. (Illus.). 32p. 19.95 *(978-0-9792761-4-9(4))* Mookind Pr.

Nagara, Innosanto. A de Activista. 2014. (SPA.). (J). *(978-1-60980-570-8(4))* Seven Stories Pr.

— A Is for Activist. Nagara, Innosanto, illus. 2012. (ENG., Illus.). 28p. bds. 15.00 *(978-0-9883448-9-1(0))* Kupu Kupu Pr.

Nanji, Shenaaz. An Alien in My House, 1 vol. McLeod, Chum, illus. 2003. (ENG.). 24p. (J). (gr. -1-3). 15.95 *(978-1-896764-77-1(0))* Second Story Pr. CAN. Dist: Orca Bk. Pubs. USA.

Naoshi. Ice Cream Work. Naoshi, illus. 2015. (ENG & JPN., Illus.). 40p. (J). 14.99 *(978-0-9834917-3-6(9))* Overcup Pr.

Nastanlieva, Vanya. Mo & Beau. 2015. (ENG., Illus.). 36p. (J). (gr. -1-3). 15.95 *(978-1-927018-63-7(3))* Simply Read Bks. CAN. Dist: Ingram Publisher Services.

—The New Arrival. 2017. (ENG., Illus.). 1p. (J). (gr. -1-3). 8.99 *(978-1-77229-009-7(2))* Simply Read Bks. CAN. Dist: Ingram Publisher Services.

—The New Arrival. Nastanlieva, Vanya, illus. 2013. (ENG., Illus.). 32p. (J). (gr. -1-3). 16.95 *(978-1-927018-13-2(7))* Simply Read Bks. CAN. Dist: Ingram Publisher Services.

National Geographic Kids Staff. Animals, Dinosaurs, Why? - National Geographic Kids, Set. 2014. (National Geographic Little Kids First Big Bks.). (ENG.). 384p. (J). (gr. -1-3). pap. 44.85 *(978-1-4263-2010-1(8),* National Geographic Children's Bks.) National Geographic Society.

—Match! 2011. (ENG., Illus.). 24p. (J). (gr. k-k). bds. 6.99 *(978-1-4263-0871-0(X),* National Geographic Children's Bks.) National Geographic Society.

National Geographic Staff. Count! No. 1,2,3. 2011. (ENG., Illus.). 24p. (J). (gr. k-k). bds. 6.99 *(978-1-4263-0891-8(4),* National Geographic Children's Bks.) National Geographic Society.

Natural History. (Illus.). (J). (gr. -1-6). pap., act. bk. ed. 2.95 *(978-0-565-00857-4(9))* Natural History Museum Pubns. GBR. Dist: Parkwest Pubns., Inc.

Natus, Uwe. The Creation of the World. Geisler, Dagmar, illus. 2016. (ENG.). 28p. (J). (gr. -1-3). 14.99 *(978-1-5064-0883-5(4),* Sparkhouse Family) Augsburg Fortress, Pubs.

Nayar, Nandini. What Could It Be? Manetti, Francesco, illus. 2013. (ENG.). 28p. (J). (gr. -1). 11.95 *(978-81-8190-285-6(8))* Karadi Tales Co. Pvt, Ltd. IND. Dist: Consortium Bk. Sales & Distribution.

Nazeer, Tasnim & Publishing, Greenbirdbooks Childrens. Allah's Gifts. Frongia, Daniela, illus. 2012. 26p. pap. *(978-0-9562141-7-1(7))* Greenbird Bks.

Nazran, Govinder, illus. Aladdin. (ENG.). 2017. 24p. pap. 7.99 *(978-1-86147-819-1(4))* 2014. 48p. (J). (gr. 2-5). pap. 7.99 *(978-1-84322-790-8(8))* Anness Publishing GBR. (Armadillo). Dist: National Bk. Network.

Neasi, Barbara J. Como Yo. Hantel, Johanna, illus. 2003. (Rookie Reader Español Ser.).Tr. of Just Like Me. (SPA.). 32p. (J). (gr. k-2). pap. 4.95 *(978-0-516-27795-0(2),* Children's Pr.) Scholastic Library Publishing.

Nedelcu, Ovi. Just Like Daddy. 2015. (ENG., Illus.). 32p. (J). (gr. -1-2). 17.95 *(978-1-57687-756-2(6),* powerHouse Bks.) powerHouse Cultural Entertainment, Inc.

Nelid, Piper. My Father Teaches Overseas, 01 vols., 1. 2016. (Rosen REAL Readers: Social Studies Nonfiction / Fiction: Family, Community, & the World Ser.). (ENG.). 12p. (J). pap. 6.33 *(978-1-5081-1734-6(9),* Rosen Classroom) Rosen Publishing Group, Inc., The.

Nelson, Dianne Elizabeth. By Here. 2009. 32p. pap. 14.49 *(978-1-4490-0366-1(4))* AuthorHouse.

Nelson, Marilyn. Ostrich & Lark. Artists of the Kuru Art Project in Botswana, San, illus. 2012. (ENG.). 32p. (J). (gr. k-4). 16.95 *(978-1-59078-702-1(1))* Boyds Mills Pr.

—Snook Alone. Ering, Timothy Basil, illus. 2012. (ENG.). 48p. (J). (gr. -1-3). pap. 7.99 *(978-0-7636-6120-5(1))* Candlewick Pr.

Nelson, Scott. Mulch the Lawnmower. 2006. (Illus.). 32p. 15.98 *(978-0-9745715-4-6(7))* KRBY Creations, LLC.

—My Tummy Disaster. 2015. (Embarrassing to the Max Ser.). (ENG., Illus.). 32p. (gr. k-3). pap. 9.95 *(978-1-941437-54-4(0))* Heritage Builders, LLC.

Nesbitt, Kenn. More Bears! Cummings, Troy, illus. 2010. (ENG.). 32p. (J). (gr. k-3). 14.99 *(978-1-4022-3835-2(5),* Sourcebooks Jabberwocky) Sourcebooks, Inc.

Newby-Tynes, Claudia. His Love Flows. 2012. 28p. pap. 24.95 *(978-1-4626-8270-6(7))* America Star Bks.

Newcome, Zita. This Royal Baby. Newcome, Zita, illus. 2013. (ENG., Illus.). 12p. (J). (— 1). bds. 14.99 *(978-0-230-77284-7(6))* Pan Macmillan GBR. Dist: Independent Pubs. Group.

Newell, Peter. Rocket Book. 2016. (Peter Newell Children's Bks.). (ENG., Illus.). 52p. (J). (gr. 2-6). 9.95 *(978-0-8048-4742-1(8))* Tuttle Publishing.

Newman, Marlene. Myron's Magic Cow. 2005. (Illus.). 40p. (J). 16.99 *(978-1-84148-495-2(4))* Barefoot Bks., Inc.

Newman, Nanette. Ben's Book. Birkett, Georgie, illus. 2011. (ENG.). 32p. (J). (gr. -1-k). pap. 9.99 *(978-1-84365-193-2(9),* Pavilion Children's Books) Pavilion Bks. GBR. Dist: Independent Pubs. Group.

Newman, Robin. Hildie Bitterpickles Needs Her Sleep. Ewald, Chris, illus. 2016. (ENG.). 32p. (J). (gr. -1-3). 16.99 *(978-1-939547-23-1(7))* Creston Bks.

Newmark Learning, compiled by. Sight Word Readers 12 copy set with Rack Set A. 2009. (Sight Word Readers Set A Ser.). (J). 1095.12 net. *(978-1-60719-159-9(8))* Newmark Learning LLC.

Newton, Jill. Don't Wake Mr Bear! Newton, Jill, illus. 2011. (ENG., Illus.). 32p. (J). (gr. -1). pap. 9.99 *(978-1-4052-4966-9(8))* Egmont Bks., Ltd. GBR. Dist: Independent Pubs. Group.

Nicholson, Melissa. Prissy & Pop Deck the Halls. Nicholson, Melissa, illus. 2016. (Illus.). 32p. (J). (gr. -1-3). 17.99 *(978-0-06-243996-3(0))* HarperCollins Pubs.

Nicholson, William. Clever Bill. 2016. (ENG., Illus.). 32p. (J). (gr. -1-k). 15.99 *(978-1-4052-8332-8(7))* Egmont Bks., Ltd. GBR. Dist: Independent Pubs. Group.

Nick, Barbara. Bella the Dragon. Steckler, Elaine, illus. 2013. 36p. pap. 11.75 *(978-1-938078-05-7(5))* Catto Creations, LLC.

Nickelodeon Staff, ed. Words - Dora the Explorer. 2010. (Write, Slide & Learn Ser.). 14p. (J). (gr. -1-1). 9.99 *(978-1-74184-519-8(X),* Ideal Pubns.) Worthy Publishing.

Nicklin, Flip, et al. Face to Face with Whales. 2010. (Face to Face with Animals Ser.). (ENG., Illus.). 32p. (J). (gr. 2-5). pap. 6.95 *(978-1-4263-0697-6(0),* National Geographic Children's Bks.) National Geographic Society.

Nicol, Scott Thomas. Dr. Jim & the Special Stethoscope. Youngblood, David W., illus. 2010. (Adventures of Dr. Jim Ser.). 32p. (J). pap. 12.95 *(978-0-9830355-7-2(1),* Creative Hse. Kids Pr.) Bourgeois Media & Consulting.

Nicoll, David. Bean at the Fair. 2012. 24p. pap. 15.99 *(978-1-4691-4706-2(8))* Xlibris Corp.

—Bean on the Farm. 2012. 24p. pap. 15.99 *(978-1-4691-7837-0(0))* Xlibris Corp.

Niehaus, Rebecca. The Birth of a Kitten. 2011. 48p. pap. 19.99 *(978-1-4567-6556-9(6))* AuthorHouse.

Nielsen, Gwyn English. Torey the Turkey Goes Skiing. 2003. (Illus.). 24p. (Orig.). (J). (gr. -1-4). pap. 5.99 *(978-0-9660726-0-0(X))* C.G.S. Pr.

Nilsen, Anna. Bella's Butterfly Ball. Partis, Joanne, illus. 2012. (ENG.). 20p. (J). (gr. -1-1). pap. 9.99 *(978-1-84365-194-9(7),* Pavilion Children's Books) Pavilion Bks. GBR. Dist: Independent Pubs. Group.

—Bella's Midsummer Secret. Partis, Joanne, illus. 2005. (ENG.). 18p. (J). (gr. -1-1). pap. 9.99 *(978-1-84458-338-6(4),* Pavilion Children's Books) Pavilion Bks. GBR. Dist: Independent Pubs. Group.

—My Mum's Best. Dodd, Emma, illus. 2011. 24p. bds. *(978-1-84089-679-4(5))* Zero to Ten, Ltd.

Nimmo, Jenny. The Beasties. Millward, Gwen, illus. 2012. (ENG.). 32p. (J). (gr. -1-k). pap. 8.99 *(978-1-4052-4335-3(X))* Egmont Bks., Ltd. GBR. Dist: Independent Pubs. Group.

Nippert-Eng, Christena E. Gorillas up Close. 2016. (ENG., Illus.). 176p. (J). (gr. 3-7). 19.99 *(978-1-62779-091-8(8),* 9781627790918, Holt, Henry & Co. Bks. For Young Readers) Holt, Henry & Co.

No Laughing Matter. 2003. (Illus.). pap. 7.60 *(978-0-7398-7531-5(0))* Steck-Vaughn.

No Laughing Matter, 6 vols. (Ragged Island Mysteriestm Ser.). 161p. (gr. 5-7). 42.50 *(978-0-322-01653-8(3))* Wright Group/McGraw-Hill.

Noensie, Pamela & Lamore, Garretta. Tari: the Little Balinese Dancer. 2017. (ENG., Illus.). 32p. (J). (gr. k-3). 8.99 *(978-0-8048-4898-5(X))* Tuttle Publishing.

Nolte, Nancy. Richard Scarry's the Gingerbread Man. Scarry, Richard, illus. 2015. (Little Golden Book Ser.). (ENG.). 24p. (J). (-k). 4.99 *(978-0-385-37619-8(7),* Golden Bks.) Random Hse. Children's Bks.

Nordqvist, Sven. The Birthday Cake: The Adventures of Pettson & Findus. 2015. (Adventures of Pettson & Findus Ser.). (ENG., Illus.). 32p. (J). 17.95 *(978-0-7358-4203-8(5))* North-South Bks., Inc.

—Findus Plants Meatballs. Large, Nathan, tr. from SWE. Nordqvist, Sven, illus. 2013. (ENG., Illus.). 28p. (J). (gr. -1-3). *(978-1-907359-29-3(X))* Hawthorn Pr.

—The Fox Chase: The Adventures of Findus & Pettson. Nordqvist, Sven, illus. 2015. (Adventures of Pettson & Findus Ser.). (ENG., Illus.). 32p. (J). 17.95 *(978-0-7358-4215-1(9))* North-South Bks., Inc.

Norman, Kim. Ten on the Sled. Woodruff, Liza, illus. (ENG.). (J). 2015. 32p. (gr. -1). pap. 6.95 *(978-1-4549-1683-3(4))* 2014. 24p. (— 1). bds. 6.95 *(978-1-4549-1191-3(3))* Sterling Publishing Co., Inc.

North, Merry. My Grandma & Me: A Picture, Play & Tote Book. 2004. 10p. (J). (gr. -1-18). bds. 5.99 *(978-1-57151-724-1(3))* Playhouse Publishing.

Norton, Tamra. Bearubs & Flutterberries. 2008. (Bearubs Ser.). pap. 3.99 *(978-0-9796008-1-4(2))* Lindsley, David Studio.

—Bearubs Clydes New Job. 2008. (Bearubs Ser.). 32p. pap. 3.99 *(978-0-9796008-2-1(0))* Lindsley, David Studio.

—Meet Bearubs. 2008. (Bearubs Ser.). 32p. pap. 3.99 *(978-0-9796008-0-7(4))* Lindsley, David Studio.

Nosy Crow Staff. Get Out of My Bath! Teckentrup, Britta, illus. 2015. (ENG.). 24p. (J). (gr. -1-2). 15.99 *(978-0-7636-8006-0(0),* Nosy Crow) Candlewick Pr.

—Noodle Loves the Beach. Billet, Marion, illus. 2012. (Noodle Ser.). (ENG.). 10p. (J). (gr. k — 1). bds. 8.99 *(978-0-7636-5898-4(7),* Nosy Crow) Candlewick Pr.

—Old MacDonald Had a Farm: Sing along with Me! Huang, Yu-Hsuan, illus. 2016. (Sing along with Me! Ser.). (ENG.). (J). (-k). bds. 8.99 *(978-0-7636-8652-9(2),* Nosy Crow) Candlewick Pr.

—The Three Little Pigs: A Nosy Crow Fairy Tale. Bryan, Ed, illus. 2016. (ENG.). (J). (gr. -1-2). 9.99 *(978-0-7636-8655-0(7),* Nosy Crow) Candlewick Pr.

Novesky, Amy. Love Is a Tutu. Gillingham, Sara, illus. 2016. (Love Is Ser.). (ENG.). 24p. (J). (-k). 12.95 *(978-1-937359-81-2(6))* Cameron & Co., Inc.

—Me, Frida. Diaz, David, illus. 2015. (ENG.). 32p. (J). (gr. k-2). 9.95 *(978-1-4197-1516-7(X),* Abrams Bks. for Young Readers) Abrams, Inc.

Novick, Mary. The Big Book of Animals & Bugs. Hale, Jenny, illus. (Double Delights Ser.). 32p. (J). pap. *(978-1-877003-38-7(7))* Little Hare Bks. AUS. Dist: HarperCollins Pubs. Australia.

Novotny-Hunter, Jana. A Bear Hug at Bedtime. Widdowson, Kay, illus. 2017. (Child's Play Library). (ENG.). 32p. (J). pap. ***(978-1-84643-988-9(4))*** Child's Play International Ltd.

Nuhfer, Heather. Friendship Is Magic. Mebberson, Amy, illus. 2013. (My Little Pony Ser.). (ENG.). 104p. pap. 17.99 (978-1-61377-760-2(4), 9781613777602) Idea & Design Works, LLC.

Nunn, Daniel. Eddie & Ellie's Opposites. 2013. (Eddie & Ellie's Opposites Ser.). (ENG.). 24p. (gr. -1-k). pap. 27.80 (978-1-4109-5349-0(1)); lib. bdg. 90.60 (978-1-4109-5344-5(0)) Heinemann-Raintree. (NA-r).

Nutkis, Phyllis. When the World Was Quiet. Argoff, Patti, illus. 2003. (J). pap. 10.95 (978-1-929628-14-8(5)) Hachai Publishing.

Nye, Naomi Shihab. Baby Radar. Carpenter, Nancy, illus. 2003. 32p. (J). lib. bdg. 16.89 (978-0-688-15949-8(4)) HarperCollins Pubs.

Oaks, Kristen M. My Home Can Be a Holy Place. Burr, Dan, illus. 2015. (J). 18.99 (978-1-62972-099-9(2)) Deseret Bk. Co.

Oaks, Kristen M. & Phillips, JoAnn. The Testimony Glove. Burr, Dan, illus. 2010. (J). (gr. -1-4). 17.99 (978-1-60641-151-3(9)) Deseret Bk. Co.

Obed, Ellen Bryan. Twelve Kinds of Ice. McClintock, Barbara, illus. 2015. (ENG.). 64p. (J). (gr. 1-4). 6.99 (978-0-544-55554-9(6), HMH Books For Young Readers) Houghton Mifflin Harcourt Publishing Co.

Oberman, Sheldon. The Wind That Wanted to Rest. Waldman, Neil, illus. 2012. (ENG.). 32p. (J). (gr. k-2). 17.95 (978-1-59078-858-5(3)) Boyds Mills Pr.

O'Brien, Eileen. This Little Piggy. Tyler, Jenny, ed. Edward, Linda, illus. 2004. (Carry-Me Bks.). 16p. (J). 5.95 (978-0-7945-0125-9(7), Usborne) EDC Publishing.

O'Brien, Melanie. Pat Them Gently. Runnells, Treesha, illus. 2006. (ENG.). 10p. (J). (gr. -1-3). bds. 8.95 (978-1-58117-462-5(4), Intervisual/Piggy Toes) Bendon, Inc.

O'Connor, Jane. Apples Galore! Glasser, Robin Preiss, illus. 2013. (I Can Read Level 1 Ser.). (ENG.). 32p. (J). (gr. -1-3). 16.99 (978-0-06-208311-1(2)) HarperCollins Pubs.

—Budding Ballerina. 2013. (Fancy Nancy Picture Bks.). (J). lib. bdg. 13.55 (978-0-606-32158-7(6), Turtleback) Turtleback Bks.

—Fanciest Doll in the Universe. Glasser, Robin Preiss, illus. 2013. (Fancy Nancy Ser.). 32p. (J). (gr. -1-3). (ENG.). 17.99 (978-0-06-170384-3(2)); lib. bdg. 18.89 (978-0-06-170385-0(0)) HarperCollins Pubs.

—Fancy Nancy - Apples Galore! Glasser, Robin Preiss, illus. 2013. (I Can Read Level 1 Ser.). (ENG.). 32p. (J). (gr. -1-3). pap. 3.99 (978-0-06-208310-4(4)) HarperCollins Pubs.

—Fancy Nancy - Budding Ballerina. Glasser, Robin Preiss, illus. 2013. (Fancy Nancy Ser.). (ENG.). 24p. (J). (gr. -1-3). pap. 3.99 (978-0-06-208628-0(6), HarperFestival) HarperCollins Pubs.

—Fancy Nancy & the Fall Foliage. Glasser, Robin Preiss, illus. 2014. (Fancy Nancy Ser.). (ENG.). 24p. (J). (gr. -1-3). pap. 4.99 (978-0-06-208630-3(8), HarperFestival) HarperCollins Pubs.

—Fancy Nancy: Nancy Clancy Sees the Future, 3 vols. Glasser, Robin Preiss, illus. 2013. (Fancy Nancy Ser.). (ENG.). 112p. (J). (gr. 1-5). 9.99 (978-0-06-208297-8(3)) HarperCollins Pubs.

—Fancy Nancy Storybook Treasury. Glasser, Robin Preiss, illus. 2013. (Fancy Nancy Ser.). (ENG.). 192p. (J). (gr. -1-3). 11.99 (978-0-06-211978-0(8)) HarperCollins Pubs.

—Fancy Nancy's Elegant Easter. Bracken, Carolyn & Glasser, Robin Preiss, illus. 2009. (Fancy Nancy Ser.). (ENG.). 16p. (J). (gr. -1-3). pap. 6.99 (978-0-06-170379-9(6), HarperFestival) HarperCollins Pubs.

—Fancy Nancy's Perfectly Posh Paper Doll Book. Glasser, Robin Preiss & Bracken, Carolyn, illus. 2009. (Fancy Nancy Ser.). (ENG.). 16p. (J). (gr. -1-3). pap. 6.99 (978-0-06-187328-7(4), HarperFestival) HarperCollins Pubs.

—Puppy Party. Glasser, Robin Preiss, illus. 2013. (Fancy Nancy Ser.). (ENG.). 24p. (J). (gr. -1-3). pap. 3.99 (978-0-06-208627-3(8), HarperFestival) HarperCollins Pubs.

Ohi, Ruth. Chicken, Pig, Cow. Ohi, Ruth, illus. 2008. (ENG., Illus.). 32p. (J). (gr. -1-k). 2nd ed. 19.95 (978-1-55451-157-0(7), 9781554511570) 6th ed. pap. 6.95 (978-1-55451-156-3(9), 9781554511563) Annick Pr., Ltd. CAN. Dist: Publishers Group West (PGW).

—Me & My Brother. Ohi, Ruth, illus. 2007. (ENG., Illus.). 24p. (J). (gr. -1-k). 19.95 (978-1-55451-092-4(9), 9781554510924); pap. 6.95 (978-1-55451-091-7(0), 9781554510917) Annick Pr., Ltd. CAN. Dist: Publishers Group West (PGW).

Okido Staff. What's Inside? See-Through Pages & Magic Surprises! 2013. (ENG., Illus.). 96p. (J). (gr. -1-3). 19.95 (978-0-500-65019-6(5), 565019) Thames & Hudson.

Old MacDonald. (J). 46.95 (978-0-8136-8807-7(8)) Modern Curriculum Pr.

Old MacDonald. (J). (gr. k-3). (978-0-663-46485-2(4), MD7225) Silver, Burdett & Ginn, Inc.

O'Leary, John. Goldilocks: A Pop-Up Book. O'Leary, John, illus. 2015. (ENG., Illus.). 16p. (J). (gr. -1-k). 19.99 (978-1-85707-888-6(8)) Tango Bks. GBR. Dist: Independent Pubs. Group.

O'Leary, Sara. This Is Sadie. Morstad, Julie, illus. 2015. (Sadie Mac Ser.). (ENG.). 32p. (J). (gr. -1-2). 17.99 (978-1-77049-532-6(0), Tundra Bks.) Tundra Bks. CAN. Dist: Penguin Random Hse. LLC.

—When I Was Small. Morstad, Julie, illus. 2012. (ENG.). 32p. (J). (gr. -1-3). 16.95 (978-1-897476-38-3(8)) Simply Read Bks. CAN. Dist: Ingram Publisher Services.

—When You Were Small. Morstad, Julie, illus. 2017. (ENG.). 40p. (J). (gr. -1-3). 8.99 (978-1-77229-008-0(4)) Simply Read Bks. CAN. Dist: Ingram Publisher Services.

Oliver, Martin. Off with Their Heads! Pinder, Andrew, illus. 2017. (Buster Reference Ser.). (ENG.). 128p. (J). (gr. 3-7). pap. 8.99 **(978-1-78055-465-5(6))** O'Mara, Michael Bks., Ltd. GBR. Dist: Independent Pubs. Group.

Oliver, Narelle. Tide Pool Secrets. Oliver, Narelle, illus. 2017. (ENG., Illus.). 32p. (J). (gr. -1-2). 18.99 (978-0-7636-9159-2(3)) Candlewick Pr.

Olsen, Jan Z. Mat Man on the Go. Delaney, Molly, illus. 2010. (ENG.). stu. ed. 13.75 (978-1-934825-39-6(5)) Handwriting Without Tears.

Omary, Rachel, illus. Animals in Dari. l.t. ed. 2003. 4p. (J). spiral bd. 10.95 (978-0-9740535-3-0(8)) Knight Publishing.

—Animals in Farsi. l.t. ed. 2003. 4p. (J). spiral bd. 10.95 (978-0-9740535-4-7(6)) Knight Publishing.

—Animals in Pashto. l.t. ed. 2003. 4p. (J). spiral bd. 10.95 (978-0-9740535-5-4(4)) Knight Publishing.

One Cool Friend. 2014. pap. 16.99 (978-0-545-67554-3(5)) Scholastic, Inc.

O'Neal, Jayce. Crazy Circus World. 2009. (Illus.). 40p. (978-1-55452-372-6(9)) Essence Publishing.

O'Neill, Elizabeth & McPherson, Missie. Alfred Visits New York City. 2003. (Illus.). 24p. (J). pap. 12.00 (978-1-4120-1338-3(0)) Funny Bone Bks.

O'Neill, Michael Patrick. Fishy Friends: A Journey Through the Coral Kingdom. O'Neill, Michael Patrick, photos by. 2003. (Illus.). 64p. (J). 19.95 (978-0-9728653-0-2(6)) Batfish Bks.

Onyefulu, Ifeoma. Grandma Comes to Stay. Onyefulu, Ifeoma, photos by. (First Experiences Ser.). (ENG., Illus.). 32p. (J). (gr. -1-2). 2015. pap. 9.99 (978-1-84780-251-4(6)) 2010. 17.99 (978-1-84507-865-2(9)) Quarto Publishing Group UK GBR. (Frances Lincoln). Dist: Hachette Bk. Group.

—New Shoes for Helen. Onyefulu, Ifeoma, photos by. 2011. (First Experiences Ser.). (ENG., Illus.). 32p. (J). (gr. -1-2). 17.95 (978-1-84780-128-9(5), Frances Lincoln) Quarto Publishing Group UK GBR. Dist: Hachette Bk. Group.

Opal, Paola. Bitsy. 2012. (Simply Small Ser.). (ENG., Illus.). 76p. (J). (gr. k — 1). bds. 7.95 (978-1-897476-65-9(5)) Simply Read Bks. CAN. Dist: Ingram Publisher Services.

—Dotty. 2010. (Simply Small Ser.). (ENG., Illus.). 24p. (J). (gr. -1 — 1). bds. 7.95 (978-1-897476-54-3(X)) Simply Read Bks. CAN. Dist: Ingram Publisher Services.

—Pippy. 2013. (Simply Small Ser.: 12). (ENG., Illus.). 24p. (J). bds. 7.95 (978-1-897476-92-5(2)) Simply Read Bks. CAN. Dist: Ingram Publisher Services.

Oram, Hiawyn. Beetle & Bug & the Grissel Hunt. Kitamura, Satoshi, illus. 2015. (ENG.). 36p. (J). (gr. -1-k). pap. 9.99 (978-1-78344-042-9(2)) Andersen Pr. GBR. Dist: Independent Pubs. Group.

—In the Attic. Kitamura, Satoshi, illus. 2012. (ENG.). 32p. (J). (gr. -1-k). pap. 13.99 (978-1-84939-298-3(6)) Andersen Pr. GBR. Dist: Independent Pubs. Group.

Orloff, Karen Kaufman. Miles of Smiles. Lozano, Luciano, illus. 2016. (ENG.). 32p. (J). (gr. -1-1). 14.95 (978-1-4549-1699-4(0)) Sterling Publishing Co., Inc.

Oroma Alikor-Adele. The Lonely Bugerfly. 2010. 28p. pap. 21.99 (978-1-4535-6225-3(7)) Xlibris Corp.

Orsolini, Laura. Maddalena. 2016. (ENG., Illus.). 36p. (J). (gr. -1-3). 16.95 (978-1-77229-007-3(6)) Simply Read Bks. CAN. Dist: Ingram Publisher Services.

Ortner, Nick & Taylor, Alison. The Big Book of Hugs: A Baxter the Bear Story. Polizzi, Michelle, illus. 2016. (ENG.). 32p. 16.99 (978-1-4019-5172-6(4)) Hay Hse., Inc.

Oskarsson, Bardur. The Flat Rabbit. 2014. (ENG., Illus.). 40p. (J). (gr. -1-4). 16.95 (978-1-77147-059-9(3), Owlkids) Owlkids Bks. Inc. CAN. Dist: Publishers Group West (PGW).

Oswald, Helen. Cat & Dog. Waring, Zoe, illus. 2016. (ENG.). 32p. (J). (gr. -1-1). pap. 8.99 (978-1-78445-286-5(6)) Top That! Publishing PLC GBR. Dist: Independent Pubs. Group.

O'Toole, Janet. On the Farm: Lift the Flaps to Find Out about Farms! Adams, Ben, illus. 2013. (ENG.). 16p. bds. 6.99 (978-1-84322-794-6(0), Armadillo) Anness Publishing GBR. Dist: National Bk. Network.

O'Toole, Janet & Anness Publishing Staff. First Words: Lift the Flaps to Find Out about Words! Adams, Ben, illus. 2013. (ENG.). 16p. bds. 6.99 (978-1-84322-795-3(9), Armadillo) Anness Publishing GBR. Dist: National Bk. Network.

—Vehicles: Lift the Flaps to Find Out about Vehicles! Adams, Ben, illus. 2013. (ENG.). 16p. bds. 6.99 (978-1-84322-728-1(2), Armadillo) Anness Publishing GBR. Dist: National Bk. Network.

O'Toole, Patrick. Alphabetimals Picture Dictionary. 2014. (ENG.). 144p. (J). (gr. -1). pap. 6.99 (978-0-486-49180-6(3)) Dover Pubns., Inc.

Ottersley, Martha T. Dora & the Winter Games (Dora the Explorer) Hall, Susan, illus. 2013. (Pictureback(R) Ser.). (ENG.). 24p. (J). (gr. -1-2). 3.99 (978-0-385-37930-4(7), Random Hse. Bks. for Young Readers) Random Hse. Children's Bks.

Over in the Meadow. (J). (gr. 1). stu. ed. 23.50 (978-0-8136-0271-4(8)) Modern Curriculum Pr.

Owens, Katherine. Tree Seasons Ball, 1 bk. l.t. ed. 2004. (Illus.). 40p. (J). per. 19.99 (978-0-9760419-0-0(1), TREESEASONSBALL) ThatsMyLife Co.

Oxford Picture Dictionary Content Area for Kids English Dictionary Student Pack. 2012. pap. 31.80 (978-0-19-401787-9(7)) Oxford Univ. Pr., Inc.

Oxford Picture Dictionary Content Area for Kids English-Spanish Dictionary Student Pack. 2012. pap. 31.80 (978-0-19-401788-6(5)) Oxford Univ. Pr., Inc.

Oxford Picture Dictionary for Kids 2e Ebook Pack. 2nd ed. 2013. (ENG.). 12.44 (978-0-19-401795-4(8)) Oxford Univ. Pr., Inc.

Pachek, Mary C. Isabella & the Merry Mouse House: A Christmas Story Coloring Book. Noad, Jordan, illus. 2009. 34p. pap. 14.49 (978-1-4389-8467-4(7)) AuthorHouse.

Pacovská, Kveta. The Sun Is Yellow. 2012. (ENG., Illus.). 32p. (J). 24.95 (978-1-84976-064-5(0)) Tate Publishing, Ltd. GBR. Dist: Abrams, Inc.

Pagnoni, Roberta & Rigo, Laura, illus. My Easter Basket. 2016. (ENG.). 10p. (J). (gr. -1 — 1). bds. 6.99 (978-0-7641-6822-2(3)) Barron's Educational Series, Inc.

Painted Daisies Inc. Staff & Borgatti, Katherine. Shermit's Adventure to Sprinkle Island. Painted Daisies Inc. Staff, illus. 2010. (ENG., Illus.). 32p. (J). 15.95 (978-0-615-34491-1(7)) Painted Daisies Inc.

Paiva, Johannah Gilman. Is There a Monster in My Closet? Long, Paulette Rich, illus. 2014. (ENG.). 32p. (J). (gr. -1-3). 7.99 (978-1-4867-0002-8(0)) Flowerpot Children's Pr. Inc. CAN. Dist: Cardinal Pubs. Group.

Paiva, Johannah Gilman, ed. Zoo Friends. 2013. (Illus.). 20p. (J). bds. 8.99 (978-1-77093-629-4(7)) Flowerpot Children's Pr. Inc. CAN. Dist: Cardinal Pubs. Group.

Palatini, Margie. Untitled Picture Book. 2005. 32p. (J). 14.99 (978-0-7868-0323-1(1)) Hyperion Pr.

Palmer, Priscilla & Hoffman, Don. Tony the Ferry Riding Pigeon. Goldberger, Dylan, illus. 2016. (ENG.). 32p. (J). (gr. k-2). pap. 3.99 (978-1-943154-05-0(8)) Peek-A-Boo Publishing.

Pan, Hui-Mei. Piggy in My Pocket. 2004. (Illus.). 14p. (J). bds. 5.95 (978-1-887734-96-7(1)) Star Bright Bks., Inc.

—Piggy in My Pocket (Spanish/English), 1 vol. del Risco, Eida, tr. Pan, Hui-Mei, illus. 2004. (ENG & SPA., Illus.). 32p. (J). bds. 5.95 (978-1-932065-11-4(3)) Star Bright Bks., Inc.

—What's in Grandma's Grocery Bag?, 1 vol. 2004. (ENG., Illus.). 32p. (J). bds. 6.25 (978-1-887734-97-4(X)) Star Bright Bks., Inc.

Pandell, Karen. I Love You, Baby, from Head to Toe! Cowen-Fletcher, Jane, illus. 2010. (ENG.). 16p. (J). (— 1). bds. 8.99 (978-0-7636-5089-6(7)) Candlewick Pr.

Panpan, Alice. Antarctic Wings. 2011. 36p. pap. 21.99 (978-1-4568-6210-7(3)) Xlibris Corp.

Paratore, Coleen Murtagh. Big. O'Malley, Judy, ed. Fennell, Clare, illus. 2012. (ENG.). 32p. (J). (gr. -1-2). 18.95 (978-0-9829938-5-9(4)) March 4th, Inc.

Parker, Amy & Walsh, Sarah. Tiny Blessings: for Bedtime. Running Press Staff, ed. 2016. (ENG., Illus.). 10p. (J). (gr. -1-17). bds. 7.95 (978-0-7624-5990-2(5), Running Pr. Kids) Running Pr. Bk. Pubs.

—Tiny Blessings: for Giving Thanks. Running Press Staff, ed. 2016. (ENG., Illus.). 10p. (J). (gr. -1-17). bds. 7.95 (978-0-7624-5989-6(1), Running Pr. Kids) Running Pr. Bk. Pubs.

Parker, Danny. Perfect. Blackwood, Freya, illus. 2017. (ENG.). 32p. (J). (— 1). 16.99 (978-1-921894-84-8(9)) Little Hare Bks. AUS. Dist: Independent Pubs. Group.

Parker, Emma. At the Circus. 2010. (Illus.). 20p. pap. (978-1-877561-52-8(5)) First Edition Ltd.

—At the Farm. 2010. (Illus.). pap. (978-1-877547-94-2(8)) First Edition Ltd.

—Bath Time. 2010. (Illus.). pap. (978-1-877547-83-6(2)) First Edition Ltd.

—Blah the Bacteria. 2010. (Illus.). pap. (978-1-877547-46-1(8)) First Edition Ltd.

—The Butterfly on the Subway. 2010. (Illus.). pap. (978-1-877547-81-2(6)) First Edition Ltd.

—Can Your Dog? 2010. (Illus.). pap. (978-1-877547-96-6(4)) First Edition Ltd.

—Captain Gold. 2010. (Illus.). pap. (978-1-877561-26-9(6)) First Edition Ltd.

—The Carousel. 2010. (Illus.). 16p. pap. (978-1-877561-73-3(8)) First Edition Ltd.

—Cat on the High Seas. 2010. (Illus.). 16p. pap. (978-1-877561-75-7(4)) First Edition Ltd.

—Cecil the Caterpillar. 2010. (Illus.). pap. (978-1-877547-95-9(6)) First Edition Ltd.

—Chuck the Chilli. 2010. (Illus.). pap. (978-1-877547-92-8(1)) First Edition Ltd.

—Dancing Class. 2010. (Illus.). pap. (978-1-877561-05-4(3)) First Edition Ltd.

—Davey Dory. 2010. (Illus.). 20p. pap. (978-1-877561-58-0(4)) First Edition Ltd.

—Delia Dynamite. 2010. (Illus.). 24p. pap. (978-1-877561-35-1(5)) First Edition Ltd.

—The Fluffiest Chicken. 2010. (Illus.). pap. (978-1-877561-13-9(4)) First Edition Ltd.

—The Frog That Did Not Like Water. 2010. (Illus.). pap. (978-1-877547-93-5(X)) First Edition Ltd.

—The Fruity Girls. 2010. (Illus.). pap. (978-1-877561-11-5(8)) First Edition Ltd.

—Granny Odd Legs. 2010. (Illus.). pap. (978-1-877547-86-7(7)) First Edition Ltd.

—Groat & the Coat. 2010. (Illus.). pap. (978-1-877547-99-7(9)) First Edition Ltd.

—How Many Fish? 2010. (Illus.). pap. (978-1-877561-10-8(X)) First Edition Ltd.

—How Shall I Get to School Today? 2010. (Illus.). pap. (978-1-877547-84-3(0)) First Edition Ltd.

—Jack & the Beanstalk. 2010. (Illus.). 24p. pap. (978-1-877561-49-8(5)) First Edition Ltd.

—Karaoke Colin. 2010. (Illus.). 20p. pap. (978-1-877561-34-4(7)) First Edition Ltd.

—The Lightning Game. 2010. (Illus.). 24p. pap. (978-1-877561-55-9(X)) First Edition Ltd.

—The Lucky Pearl. 2010. (Illus.). 20p. pap. (978-1-877561-18-4(5)) First Edition Ltd.

—Lulu & the Seed. 2010. (Illus.). pap. (978-1-877547-82-9(4)) First Edition Ltd.

—The Magic Show. 2010. (Illus.). pap. (978-1-877561-23-8(1)) First Edition Ltd.

—The Magic Snow Globe. 2010. (Illus.). pap. (978-1-877561-30-6(4)) First Edition Ltd.

—Missy Hip Hoppo. 2010. (Illus.). 16p. pap. (978-1-877561-56-6(8)) First Edition Ltd.

—The Monkey in the Tree. 2010. (Illus.). pap. (978-1-877547-91-1(3)) First Edition Ltd.

—Mr Grumpy Bunny. 2010. (Illus.). pap. (978-1-877561-22-1(3)) First Edition Ltd.

—The Naughty Puppy. 2010. (Illus.). pap. (978-1-877547-89-8(1)) First Edition Ltd.

—The Not So Scary Scarecrow. 2010. (Illus.). pap. (978-1-877547-88-1(3)) First Edition Ltd.

—One Leg Ned. 2010. (Illus.). pap. (978-1-877561-12-2(6)) First Edition Ltd.

—Pet Day. 2010. (Illus.). pap. (978-1-877561-28-3(2)) First Edition Ltd.

—Robot Tim. 2010. (Illus.). 20p. pap. (978-1-877561-54-2(1)) First Edition Ltd.

—Safari Adventure. 2010. (Illus.). pap. (978-1-877561-29-0(0)) First Edition Ltd.

—Sam the Traveling Snail. 2010. (Illus.). pap. (978-1-877561-19-1(3)) First Edition Ltd.

—Sebastian the Ant. 2010. (Illus.). pap. (978-1-877561-14-6(2)) First Edition Ltd.

—Skipping Sally. 2010. (Illus.). pap. (978-1-877561-24-5(X)) First Edition Ltd.

—Snafu & the Shoes. 2010. (Illus.). pap. (978-1-877561-00-9(2)) First Edition Ltd.

—The Snowman Olympics. 2010. (Illus.). 20p. pap. (978-1-877561-36-8(3)) First Edition Ltd.

—Sooty the Stink Bomb. 2010. (Illus.). pap. (978-1-877561-15-3(0)) First Edition Ltd.

—The Space Rocket. 2010. (Illus.). pap. (978-1-877547-87-4(5)) First Edition Ltd.

—The Spaghetti Tree. 2010. (Illus.). pap. (978-1-877561-02-3(9)) First Edition Ltd.

—Splat & the Hat. 2010. (Illus.). pap. (978-1-877561-04-7(5)) First Edition Ltd.

—Square Sidney. 2010. 16p. pap. (978-1-877561-31-3(2)) First Edition Ltd.

—Summer Camp. 2010. (Illus.). pap. (978-1-877561-27-6(4)) First Edition Ltd.

—The Wedding Day. 2010. (Illus.). 16p. pap. (978-1-877561-51-1(7)) First Edition Ltd.

—What a Hullabaloo. 2010. 20p. pap. (978-1-877561-32-0(0)) First Edition Ltd.

—The Wickedest Witch. 2010. (Illus.). pap. (978-1-877561-17-7(7)) First Edition Ltd.

Parker, Emma & Renaud, Marguerite. Chatterbox Caz. 2010. (Illus.). 16p. pap. (978-1-877561-77-1(0)) First Edition Ltd.

—Dragon Bowling. 2010. (Illus.). 24p. pap. (978-1-877561-82-5(7)) First Edition Ltd.

—Hedgehogs. 2010. (Illus.). 16p. pap. (978-1-877561-80-1(0)) First Edition Ltd.

—The Honey Bee Race. 2010. (Illus.). 16p. pap. (978-1-877561-78-8(9)) First Edition Ltd.

Parker, Marjorie Blain. Psst! I Love You. Hanson, Sydney, illus. 2017. (Snuggle Time Stories Ser.). (ENG.). 32p. (J). (gr. -1-k). 9.95 (978-1-4549-1721-2(0)) Sterling Publishing Co., Inc.

Parker-Rees, Guy. Party Time with Littlebob & Plum: Lots of Lift-the-Flap Fun. Parker-Rees, Guy, illus. 2012. (ENG., Illus.). 20p. (J). (gr. k-2). 12.99 (978-1-4083-0443-3(0)) Hodder & Stoughton GBR. Dist: Hachette Bk. Group.

—Tom & Millie: Whizzy Busy People. 2014. (ENG., Illus.). 32p. (J). (gr. -1-k). pap. 10.99 (978-1-4083-1552-1(1)) Hodder & Stoughton GBR. Dist: Hachette Bk. Group.

Parker, Sandy. What Day Is Today? Hofher, Cathy, illus. l.t. ed. 2003. 24p. (gr. k-1). 13.95 (978-0-9643462-3-9(0), 10, Just Think Bks.) Canary Connect Pubns.

Parnell, Declan. Mr. Wilson Is Our Crossing Guard, 01 vols., 1. 2016. (Rosen REAL Readers: Social Studies Nonfiction / Fiction: Family, Community, & the World Ser.). (ENG.). 8p. (J). pap. 5.46 (978-1-5081-1704-9(7), Rosen Classroom) Rosen Publishing Group, Inc., The.

Parr, Todd. Be Who You Are! 2016. (ENG., Illus.). 32p. (J). (gr. -1-1). 17.99 (978-0-316-26523-2(3)) Little, Brown Bks. for Young Readers.

—The Daddy Book. 2015. (ENG., Illus.). 20p. (J). (gr. -1 — 1). bds. 6.99 (978-0-316-25784-8(2)) Little, Brown Bks. for Young Readers.

—The Mommy Book. 2016. (ENG., Illus.). 20p. (J). (gr. -1 — 1). bds. 6.99 (978-0-316-33774-8(9)) Little, Brown Bks. for Young Readers.

—Otto Goes to School. 2013. (Passport to Reading Level 1 Ser.). (ENG., Illus.). 32p. (J). (gr. -1-1). 4.99 (978-0-316-22931-9(8)) Little, Brown Bks. for Young Readers.

Parry, Alan & Parry, Linda. The Herald Angels. 2003. (Illus.). 16p. 9.99 (978-1-85608-253-2(9)) Hunt, John Publishing Ltd. GBR. Dist: Send The Light Distribution LLC.

—Look for the Rainbow: Look Through the Telescope, Lift the Flaps, Work the Puzzles, See the Pop-Ups, & Enjoy Hours of Fun with Noah. 2003. (Illus.). 14p. 12.99 (978-1-85608-212-9(1)) Hunt, John Publishing Ltd. GBR. Dist: Send The Light Distribution LLC.

Partis, Joanne. Look at Me! Partis, Joanne, illus. 2007. (Baby Bks.). (ENG., Illus.). 10p. (J). (gr. k — 1). 4.99 (978-1-84458-365-2(1)) Pavilion Bks. GBR. Dist: Independent Pubs. Group.

Pasquali, Elena. The Animals' Christmas. Ferri, Giuliano, illus. 2016. (ENG.). 32p. (J). (gr. 2-4). 8.99 (978-0-7459-6249-8(1)) Lion Hudson PLC GBR. Dist: Independent Pubs. Group.

—Santa's Midnight Sleighride. Vagnozzi, Barbara, illus. 2013. (Finger-Trail Animal Tales Ser.). (ENG.). 10p. (J). (gr. -1-k). bds. 9.99 (978-0-7459-6242-9(4)) Lion Hudson PLC GBR. Dist: Independent Pubs. Group.

—Two-Minute Bedtime Stories. Smee, Nicola, illus. 2010. (Two-Minute Stories Ser.). (ENG.). 48p. (J). (gr. -1-k). 12.99 (978-0-7459-6079-1(0)) Lion Hudson PLC GBR. Dist: Independent Pubs. Group.

Patel, Sanjay & Haynes, Emily. Ganesha's Sweet Tooth. 2015. (ENG., Illus.). 40p. (J). (gr. -1-3). 7.99 (978-1-4521-4556-3(3)) Chronicle Bks. LLC.

Paterson Jr., John B. & Paterson Sr, John B. Roberto's Trip to the Top. Alarcao, Renato, illus. 2010. (ENG.). 40p. (J). (gr. -1-3). pap. 6.99 (978-0-7636-4755-1(1)) Candlewick Pr.

Patricelli, Leslie. Binky. Patricelli, Leslie, illus. 2005. (Leslie Patricelli Board Bks.). (ENG., Illus.). 24p. (J). (— 1). bds. 6.99 (978-0-7636-2364-7(4)) Candlewick Pr.

—Blankie. Patricelli, Leslie, illus. 2005. (Leslie Patricelli Board Bks.). (ENG., Illus.). 24p. (J). (— 1). bds. 6.99 (978-0-7636-2363-0(6)) Candlewick Pr.

—Higher! Higher! Patricelli, Leslie, illus. 2010. (Leslie Patricelli Board Bks.). (ENG., Illus.). 30p. (J). (-k). bds. 6.99 (978-0-7636-4433-8(1)) Candlewick Pr.

Patrick, Denise Lewis. MaDear's Old Green House. Sadler, Sonia Lynn, illus. 2004. 32p. (J). (gr. k-3). 16.95 (978-0-940975-55-2(6), Sankofa Bks.) Just Us Bks., Inc.

PatrickGeorge Staff. I See... 2013. (ENG., Illus.). 36p. (J). (gr. -1-k). 12.99 (978-1-908473-04-2(5)) PatrickGeorge GBR. Dist: Independent Pubs. Group.

Patterson, C. Marie. Little Dinky's Love for Basketball. 2009. 24p. pap. 15.99 (978-1-4415-1255-0(1)) Xlibris Corp.

Patterson, Rebecca. Nightbear. 2014. (ENG., Illus.). 32p. (J). (-k). pap. 11.99 (978-1-78008-008-6(5)) Transworld Publishers Ltd. GBR. Dist: Independent Pubs. Group.

Pattullo, Alice. An Animal ABC. 2017. (ENG., Illus.). 64p. (J). (gr. -1-1). 17.99 **(978-1-84365-313-4(3)**, Pavilion) Pavilion Bks. GBR. Dist: Independent Pubs. Group.

Paul, Alison. The Plan. Lehman, Barbara, illus. 2015. (ENG.). 32p. (J). (gr. -1-3). 17.99 (978-0-544-28333-6(3), HMH Books For Young Readers) Houghton Mifflin Harcourt Publishing Co.

Paul, Ann Whitford. Fiesta Fiasco. Long, Ethan, illus. 2012. pap. 18.95 (978-1-4301-1099-6(6)) Live Oak Media.

Paul Frank Industries. Only in Dreams. 2011. (ENG., Illus.). 24p. (J). (gr. -1 — 1). bds. 6.99 (978-0-8118-7867-8(8)) Chronicle Bks. LLC.

Paula, Cristina De. Sweet Pomchu. 2011. 28p. pap. 15.99 (978-1-4568-5816-2(5)) Xlibris Corp.

Paye, Won-Ldy & Lippert, Margaret H. Mrs. Chicken & the Hungry Crocodile. Paschkis, Julie, illus. 2014. (ENG.). 32p.

(J). (gr. -1-2). pap. 7.99 *(978-1-250-04673-4(4),* 9781250046734) Square Fish.

Peanuts Picture Books. 2013. (Peanuts Picture Bks.: 5). (ENG.). 24-48p. (J). (gr. -1-4). lib. bdg. 121.05 *(978-1-61479-028-0(0))* ABDO Publishing Co.

Pearce, Philippa. Amy's Three Best Things. Craig, Helen, illus. 2013. (ENG.). 40p. (J). (gr. -1-3). 15.99 *(978-0-7636-6314-8(X))* Candlewick Pr.

Pellegrini, Isabelle. Eva from Stockholm. Picard, Charline, illus. 2014. (AV2 Fiction Readalong Ser.: Vol. 125). (ENG.). 32p. (J). (gr. -1-3). lib. bdg. 34.28 *(978-1-4896-2265-5(9),* AV2 by Weigl) Weigl Pubs., Inc.

Penado, Martha. Eggstinkt. 2008. 32p. pap. 24.95 *(978-1-60610-906-9(5))* America Star Bks.

Pendziwol, Jean E. No Dragons for Tea. 2004. (Illus.). (J). (gr. k-3). spiral bd. *(978-0-616-01755-5(3))*; spiral bd. *(978-0-616-01756-2(1))* Canadian National Institute for the Blind/Institut National Canadien pour les Aveugles.

Penn, Mw. Sidney the Silly Who Only Eats 6. Tommer, Sarah, illus. 2013. 36p. pap. 13.95 *(978-0-9840425-7-9(1))* MathWord Pr., LLC.

Penrose, Antony. Miró's Magic Animals. 2016. (ENG., Illus.). 48p. (J). (gr. -1-2). 14.95 *(978-0-500-65066-0(7),* 565066) Thames & Hudson.

People. Date not set. (I Can Draw Ser.). 32p. (J). 4.98 *(978-1-4054-0020-6(X))* Parragon, Inc.

Percival, Tom. Jack's Amazing Shadow. Percival, Tom, illus. 2013. (ENG., Illus.). 32p. (J). (gr. -1-k). pap. 9.99 *(978-1-84365-220-5(X),* Pavilion) Pavilion Bks. GBR. Dist: Independent Pubs. Group.

Perez-Martinez, Irella. Suyensita & Her Adventures. 2011. 48p. pap. 21.99 *(978-1-4568-5767-7(3))* Xlibris Corp.

Pericoli, Matteo. London for Children. 2014. (ENG., Illus.). 64p. (J). (gr. -1). 16.99 *(978-1-4472-1313-0(0))* Pan Macmillan GBR. Dist: Independent Pubs. Group.

Perkins, Myrna. What Makes Honey? Perkins, William C. & Perkins, Lori L., illus. 32p. (Orig.). (J). (gr. -1-3). pap. 3.95 *(978-0-937729-03-8(5))* Markins Enterprises.

Perkins, T. J. Four Little Witches, 1 vol. Pinero, Eimi, illus. 2015. (ENG.). 40p. (J). 12.99 *(978-0-7643-4943-0(0),* 9780764349430) Schiffer Publishing, Ltd.

Perl, Erica S. Chicken Butt's Back! Cole, Henry, illus. 2011. (ENG.). 32p. (J). (gr. -1-k). 13.95 *(978-0-8109-9729-5(0),* Abrams Bks. for Young Readers) Abrams, Inc.

Perlman, Janet. The Penguin & the Pea. Perlman, Janet, illus. 2006. (ENG., Illus.). 32p. (J). (gr. -1-2). 7.95 *(978-1-55337-983-6(7))* Kids Can Pr., Ltd. CAN. Dist: Hachette Bk. Group.

Perrault, Charles. A Storyteller Book: Cinderella. Spenceley, Annabel, illus. 2014. (ENG.). 48p. (J). (gr. k-5). pap. 7.99 *(978-1-84322-883-7(1))* Anness Publishing GBR. Dist: National Bk. Network.

Perry, Robert. Down at the Seaweed Cafe. Guzek, Greta, illus. unabr. ed. 2010. (ENG.). 32p. (J). pap. 9.95 *(978-0-88971-246-1(8))* Nightwood Editions CAN. Dist: Midpoint Trade Bks., Inc.

Pessin-Whedbee, Brook. Who Are You? The Kid's Guide to Gender & Identity. Bardoff, Naomi, illus. 2016. (ENG.). 40p. (J). 18.95 *(978-1-78592-728-7(0),* 8673) Kingsley, Jessica Pubs. GBR. Dist: Macmillan Distribution Ltd.

Petek-Markic, Zdenka. Birds. 2012. 52p. pap. 19.97 *(978-1-61897-694-9(X),* Strategic Bk. Publishing) Strategic Book Publishing & Rights Agency (SBPRA).

Peters, Andrew. Bear & Turtle & the Great Lake Race. Edgson, Alison, illus. 2010. (Traditional Tales with a Twist Ser.). (ENG.). 32p. (J). (gr. -1-2). audio compact disk *(978-1-84643-347-4(9))* Child's Play International Ltd.

Peterson, Mary. Snail Has Lunch. Peterson, Mary, illus. 2016. (Pix Ser.). (ENG., Illus.). 64p. (J). (gr. 1-4). 12.99 *(978-1-4814-5302-8(5),* Aladdin) Simon & Schuster Children's Publishing.

Peterson, Megan Cooley & Rustad, Martha E. H. Show Me Reptiles: My First Picture Encyclopedia, 1 vol. 2012. (My First Picture Encyclopedias Ser.). (ENG., Illus.). 32p. (gr. 1-2). lib. bdg. 27.32 *(978-1-4296-8571-9(9))* Capstone Press of Coughlan Cos.

Petrlik, Andrea, illus. Shoo, Fly! 2008. (J). *(978-0-545-03046-5(3))* Scholastic, Inc.

Petrone, Epp. Anna's Teeth. Maiste, Piia, illus. 2013. 94p. pap. *(978-9949-511-27-3(5))* Petrone Print.

Peyo & Delporte, Yvan. The Smurfs Anthology. 2013. (Smurfs Anthology Ser.). (ENG., Illus.). 192p. (J). (gr. 6-5). 19.99 *(978-1-59707-417-9(9),* 9781597074179) Papercutz.

Pfeffer, Wendy. From Seed to Pumpkin. Hale, James Graham, illus. 2015. (Let's-Read-And-Find-Out Science 1 Ser.). (ENG.). 40p. (J). (gr. -1-3). pap. 6.99 *(978-0-06-238185-9(7))* HarperCollins Pubs.

—From Tadpole to Frog. Keller, Holly, illus. 2015. (Let's-Read-And-Find-Out Science 1 Ser.). (ENG.). 32p. (J). (gr. -1-3). pap. 6.99 *(978-0-06-238186-6(5))* HarperCollins Pubs.

—Light Is All Around Us. Meisel, Paul, illus. (Let's-Read-And-Find-Out Science 2 Ser.). (ENG.). 40p. (J). (gr. -1-3). 2015. pap. 6.99 *(978-0-06-238190-3(3))* 2014. 17.99 *(978-0-06-029121-1(4))* HarperCollins Pubs.

—What's It Like to Be a Fish? Keller, Holly, illus. 2015. (Let's-Read-And-Find-Out Science 1 Ser.). (ENG.). 32p. (J). (gr. -1-3). pap. 6.99 *(978-0-06-238199-6(7))* HarperCollins Pubs.

Pfister, Marcus. Ava's Poppy. 2012. (ENG., Illus.). 32p. (J). (gr. -1-3). 16.95 *(978-0-7358-4057-7(1))* North-South Bks., Inc.

—Good Night, Little Rainbow Fish. 2017. (Rainbow Fish Ser.: 1). (ENG., Illus.). 12p. (J). (gr. -1-k). bds. 9.95 ***(978-0-7358-4285-4(X))*** North-South Bks., Inc.

—Milo & the Mysterious Island. 2014. (Milo Ser.). (ENG., Illus.). 32p. (J). (gr. k-3). 17.95 *(978-0-7358-4173-4(X))* North-South Bks., Inc.

—Penguin Pete & Pat. 2014. (Penguin Pete Ser.). (ENG., Illus.). 32p. (J). (gr. k-3). 14.95 *(978-0-7358-4155-0(1))* North-South Bks., Inc.

—Rainbow Fish / Perz Arco Iris. 2015. (Rainbow Fish Ser.). (ENG & SPA., Illus.). 32p. (J). 9.95 *(978-0-7358-4197-0(7))* North-South Bks., Inc.

—Rainbow Fish & the Sea Monsters' Cave. 2015. (Rainbow Fish Ser.). (ENG., Illus.). 32p. (J). pap. 9.95 *(978-3-314-01733-9(2))* North-South Bks., Inc.

—The Rainbow Fish Anniversary Edition. 2017. (ENG., Illus.). 32p. (J). (gr. -1-3). 25.00 ***(978-0-7358-4284-7(1))*** North-South Bks., Inc.

—Rainbow Fish Opposites. 2013. (Rainbow Fish Ser.). (ENG., Illus.). 12p. (J). (gr. 1-1). bds. 7.95 *(978-0-7358-4146-8(2))* North-South Bks., Inc.

—Rainbow Fish to the Rescue! 2015. (Rainbow Fish Ser.).Tr. of Regenbogenfisch, Komm Hilf Mir! (ENG., Illus.). 32p. (J). pap. 9.95 *(978-3-314-01574-8(7))* North-South Bks., Inc.

Pfister, Marcus. You Can't Win Them All, Rainbow Fish. 2017. (ENG., Illus.). 32p. (J). (gr. -1-3). 18.95 ***(978-0-7358-4287-8(6))*** North-South Bks., Inc.

Phaidon Editors & Matisse, Henri. Blue & Other Colors. 2016. (ENG., Illus.). 30p. (gr. -1 — 1). bds. 9.95 *(978-0-7148-7142-4(7))* Phaidon Pr., Inc.

Philip, Simon. You Must Bring a Hat! Hindley, Kate, illus. 2017. (ENG.). 40p. (J). (gr. -1). 16.95 ***(978-1-4549-2688-7(0))*** Sterling Publishing Co., Inc.

Phillips, Clifton C. We Are Children of Eden. 2011. 28p. pap. 9.99 *(978-1-61286-010-7(9))* Avid Readers Publishing Group.

Phillips, Gina & Martin, Stuart. Ants & Caterpillars. 2003. (Busy Bugs Ser.). 12p. (J). bds. 14.95 *(978-1-74047-240-1(3))* Book Co. Publishing Pty, Ltd., The AUS. Dist: Penton Overseas, Inc.

Phillips, Jillian. The World Around Us! Hearing. 2010. (Dover Coloring Bks.). (ENG., Illus.). 32p. (J). (gr. k-3). pap. 4.99 *(978-0-486-47730-5(4))* Dover Pubns., Inc.

—The World Around Us! Seeing. 2010. (Dover Coloring Bks.). (ENG., Illus.). 32p. (J). (gr. k-3). pap. 4.99 *(978-0-486-47731-2(2))* Dover Pubns., Inc.

Phoenix International Staff, illus. Write-and-Erase Look & Find(r) Disney: Packed with 'Find 'Ems & Picture Puzzles! Look, Circle, Wipe Clean, & Play Again! 2014. 20p. (J). bds. *(978-1-4508-8033-6(9),* 1450880339) Phoenix International Publications, Inc.

Pichon, Liz. Black Bill. Pichon, Liz, illus. 2006. (Illus.). 32p. (J). (gr. -1-3). 15.95 *(978-1-58925-053-6(2))* Tiger Tales.

Pickford, Sue. When Angus Met Alvin. 2014. (ENG., Illus.). 32p. (J). (gr. -1-3). 17.99 *(978-1-84780-304-7(0),* Frances Lincoln) Quarto Publishing Group UK GBR. Dist: Hachette Bk. Group.

Picthall & Gunzi Ltd, creator. In the Jungle. 2006. (Feels Real Bks.). (ENG., Illus.). 10p. (J). (gr. -1). bds. 6.99 *(978-0-7641-5949-7(6))* Barron's Educational Series, Inc.

Picthall, Chez. Baby Animals. 2015. (ENG., Illus.). 10p. (J). 7.99 *(978-1-906572-07-5(0))* Award Pubns. Ltd. GBR. Dist: Parkwest Pubns., Inc.

—Bedtime. Hewett, Angela, illus. 2015. (ENG.). 10p. (J). 11.99 *(978-1-909763-43-2(8))* Award Pubns. Ltd. GBR. Dist: Parkwest Pubns., Inc.

—Flip Flaps Zoo. 2015. (ENG., Illus.). 18p. (J). 9.99 *(978-1-907604-53-9(7))* Award Pubns. Ltd. GBR. Dist: Parkwest Pubns., Inc.

—Racers. Gunzi, Christiane, ed. 2015. (ENG., Illus.). 12p. (J). pap. 7.99 *(978-1-907604-80-5(4))* Award Pubns. Ltd. GBR. Dist: Parkwest Pubns., Inc.

Picthall, Chez, creator. Flip Flap Colours: A Turn-the-Flap Book! 2014. (ENG., Illus.). 36p. pap. 10.00 *(978-1-906572-79-2(8))* Award Pubns. Ltd. GBR. Dist: Parkwest Pubns., Inc.

—Flip Flaps Shapes. 2014. (ENG., Illus.). 32p. bds. 10.00 *(978-1-906572-80-8(1))* Award Pubns. Ltd. GBR. Dist: Parkwest Pubns., Inc.

Picthall, Chez, des. Flowers. 2015. (ENG., Illus.). 10p. (J). 9.99 *(978-1-907604-76-8(6))* Award Pubns. Ltd. GBR. Dist: Parkwest Pubns., Inc.

—Spots & Dots. 2015. (ENG., Illus.). 10p. (J). 9.99 *(978-1-909763-02-9(0))* Award Pubns. Ltd. GBR. Dist: Parkwest Pubns., Inc.

Picture, Play & Tote Counter Diaplay. (J). *(978-1-57151-726-5(X))* Playhouse Publishing.

Piers, Helen. Long Neck & Thunder Foot. Foreman, Michael, illus. 2013. (ENG.). 32p. (J). (gr. -1-k). pap. 8.99 *(978-1-84939-482-6(2))* Andersen Pr. GBR. Dist: Independent Pubs. Group.

Pilkey, Dav. The Paperboy. 2015. 32p. pap. 7.00 *(978-1-61003-556-9(9))* Center for the Collaborative Classroom.

Pinfold, Levi. Black Dog. Pinfold, Levi, illus. 2012. (ENG., Illus.). 32p. (J). (gr. -1-3). 15.99 *(978-0-7636-6097-0(3),* Templar) Candlewick Pr.

—The Django. Pinfold, Levi, illus. 2010. (ENG., Illus.). 40p. (J). (gr. k-4). 16.99 *(978-0-7636-4788-9(8),* Templar) Candlewick Pr.

Pinky & the Brain. (Look & Find Bks.). (Illus.). 24p. (J). (gr. k-5). 7.98 *(978-0-7853-1607-7(8),* PI11) Publications International, Ltd.

Pinnington, Andrea. The Pirate Creativity Book. 2011. (Creativity Bks.). (ENG.). 80p. (J). (gr. 1-4). pap. 12.99 *(978-0-7641-4778-4(1))* Barron's Educational Series, Inc.

—The Princess Creativity Book: Includes Stickers, Fold-Out Scene, Stencils, & Pretty Paper. 2011. (Creativity Bks.). 96p. (J). (gr. 1-4). pap. 12.99 *(978-0-7641-4675-6(0))* Barron's Educational Series, Inc.

Piper, Sophie. The Lion Book of Nursery Fables. Kolanovic, Dubravka, illus. 2014. (ENG.). 128p. (J). (gr. -1 — 1). 17.99 *(978-0-7459-6466-9(4))* Lion Hudson PLC GBR. Dist: Independent Pubs. Group.

Piper, Watty & dePaola, Tomie. The Little Engine That Could. Hauman, George and Doris & Hauman, Doris, illus. 2015. (Little Engine That Could Ser.). (ENG.). 26p. (J). (gr. -1 — 1). bds. 11.99 *(978-0-448-48731-1(4),* Grosset & Dunlap) Penguin Young Readers Group.

Pirc, Jerri J. Kate & Caboodle. Smith, Jane, illus. 2015. pap. *(978-0-473-32583-1(7))* Pirc, Jerri J.

Pittar, Gill. Milly, Molly & Alf. 2005. 28p. *(978-1-86972-018-6(0))* Milly Molly Bks.

—Milly, Molly & Aunt Maude. 2004. 28p. *(978-1-86972-014-8(8))* Milly Molly Bks.

—Milly, Molly & Different Dads. 2004. 28p. *(978-1-86972-019-3(9))* Milly Molly Bks.

—Milly, Molly & Sock Heaven. 2004. 28p. *(978-1-86972-015-5(6))* Milly Molly Bks.

—Milly, Molly & Special Friends. 2004. 28p. *(978-1-86972-017-9(2))* Milly Molly Bks.

Piven, Hanoch. My Dog Is As Smelly As Dirty Socks: And Other Funny Family Portraits. Piven, Hanoch, illus. 2012. (ENG., Illus.). 40p. (J). (gr. -1-3). pap. 7.99 *(978-0-307-93089-7(0),* Dragonfly Bks.) Random Hse. Children's Bks.

Platt, Richard & Biesty, Stephen. Man-of-War. (Illus.). (J). pap. 21.95 *(978-0-590-74610-6(3))* Scholastic, Inc.

Player, Micah, illus. Lately Lily: The Adventures of a Travelling Girl. 2014. (ENG.). 32p. (J). (gr. -1-k). 16.99 *(978-1-4521-1525-2(7))* Chronicle Bks. LLC.

Podd, Gloria. A Royal Runt. 2013. 20p. pap. 24.95 *(978-1-63004-012-3(6))* America Star Bks.

Poison Patrol: Picture Book 8x8. 2007. (J). 5.99 *(978-1-933934-40-2(9))* Mighty Kids Media.

Poison Patrol: Picture Book (English) 9x9 with Snipe. 2007. (J). 5.99 *(978-1-933934-50-1(6))* Mighty Kids Media.

Pollard, Mary Jean. Octrina the Octopus. 2011. 28p. pap. 15.99 *(978-1-4568-4778-4(3))* Xlibris Corp.

Pomranz, Craig. Made by Raffi. Chamberlain, Margaret, illus. 2016. (ENG.). 40p. (J). (gr. 1-4). pap. 9.99 *(978-1-84780-596-6(5),* Frances Lincoln) Quarto Publishing Group UK GBR. Dist: Hachette Bk. Group.

Ponti, Claude. En El Coche. 2003. (SPA.). 32p. 15.95 *(978-84-95150-08-0(5))* Corimbo, Editorial S.L. ESP. Dist: Distribooks, Inc.

Ponzi, Emiliano. The Journey of the Penguin. 2015. (ENG., Illus.). 96p. (gr. k-12). 18.00 *(978-0-14-310785-9(2),* Penguin Books) Penguin Publishing Group.

Poole, Helen. Clara's Crazy Curls, 1 vol. Poole, Helen, illus. 2014. (ENG., Illus.). 40p. (J). (gr. -1-3). 14.95 *(978-1-62370-043-0(4))* Capstone Young Readers of Coughlan Cos.

Poole, Susie. A Christmas Journey. Poole, Susie, illus. 2014. (ENG., Illus.). 48p. (gr. -1-3). 12.99 *(978-1-4336-8343-5(1),* B&H Kids) B&H Publishing Group.

Pop up Picture Books: Hurry, Santa, Hurry! 2007. 6p. *(978-1-4054-9475-5(1))* Parragon, Inc.

Popper, Garry. Ali in Egypt. Johnson, Andi, illus. 2004. 36p. (gr. -1-7). 4.00 *(978-1-84161-078-8(X))* Ravette Publishing, Ltd. GBR. Dist: Parkwest Pubns., Inc.

—Billy Joe in the U. S. A. Johnson, Andi, illus. 2004. 36p. (gr. -1-7). 4.00 *(978-1-84161-053-5(4))* Ravette Publishing, Ltd. GBR. Dist: Parkwest Pubns., Inc.

—James & Jemma in Great Britain. Johnson, Andi, illus. 2004. 36p. (gr. -1-7). 4.00 *(978-1-84161-054-2(2))* Ravette Publishing, Ltd. GBR. Dist: Parkwest Pubns., Inc.

—Keito in Japan. Johnson, Andi, illus. 2004. 36p. (gr. -1-7). 4.00 *(978-1-84161-058-0(5))* Ravette Publishing, Ltd. GBR. Dist: Parkwest Pubns., Inc.

—Kez in Australia. Johnson, Andi, illus. 2004. 36p. (gr. -1-7). 4.00 *(978-1-84161-055-9(0))* Ravette Publishing, Ltd. GBR. Dist: Parkwest Pubns., Inc.

—Lena & Peter in Germany. Johnson, Andi, illus. 2004. 36p. (gr. -1-7). 4.00 *(978-1-84161-060-3(7))* Ravette Publishing, Ltd. GBR. Dist: Parkwest Pubns., Inc.

—Li & Lilly May in China. Johnson, Andi, illus. 2004. 36p. (gr. -1-7). 4.00 *(978-1-84161-057-3(7))* Ravette Publishing, Ltd. GBR. Dist: Parkwest Pubns., Inc.

—Mario in Italy. Johnson, Andi, illus. 2004. 36p. (gr. -1-7). 4.00 *(978-1-84161-059-7(3))* Ravette Publishing, Ltd. GBR. Dist: Parkwest Pubns., Inc.

—Mina in India. Johnson, Andi, illus. 2004. 36p. (gr. -1-7). 4.00 *(978-1-84161-079-5(8))* Ravette Publishing, Ltd. GBR. Dist: Parkwest Pubns., Inc.

—Paul in France. Johnson, Andi, illus. 2004. 36p. (gr. -1-7). 4.00 *(978-1-84161-056-6(9))* Ravette Publishing, Ltd. GBR. Dist: Parkwest Pubns., Inc.

Porter, Matthew. Tails Chasing Tails. 2013. (ENG., Illus.). 20p. (J). (— 1). bds. 9.99 *(978-1-57061-852-9(6),* Little Bigfoot) Sasquatch Bks.

Posada, Jorge. Sí, Puedes. Colón, Raúl, illus. 2010.Tr. of Play Ball! (SPA.). 32p. (J). (gr. 1-5). 6.99 *(978-1-4169-9826-6(8),* Simon & Schuster/Paula Wiseman Bks.) Simon & Schuster/Paula Wiseman Bks.

Posner-Sanchez, Andrea. Happy PEEPS-Oween! (Peeps) Massironi, Daniela, illus. 2017. (Pictureback(R) Ser.). (ENG.). 16p. (J). (-k). pap. 4.99 ***(978-1-5247-6507-1(4),*** Random Hse. Bks. for Young Readers) Random Hse. Children's Bks.

Posner-Sanchez, Andrea. Meet Maui. The Disney Storybook Art Team, illus. 2017. (Pictureback(R) Ser.). (ENG.). 24p. (J). (gr. -1-2). pap. 4.99 *(978-0-7364-3738-7(X),* RH/Disney) Random Hse. Children's Bks.

Potter, Beatrix. Peter Rabbit 1 2 3. 2013. (Peter Rabbit Ser.). (ENG., Illus.). 24p. (J). (gr. -1-k). bds. 6.99 *(978-0-7232-6867-3(3),* Warne) Penguin Young Readers Group.

—Peter Rabbit A B C: With Giant Fold-Out Pages. 2013. (Peter Rabbit Ser.). (ENG., Illus.). 16p. (J). (gr. -1-k). bds. 6.99 *(978-0-7232-6864-2(9),* Warne) Penguin Young Readers Group.

—The Tailor of Gloucester, 5 vols. 110th ed. 2012. (Peter Rabbit Ser.: 3). (ENG., Illus.). 64p. (J). (gr. -1-2). 6.99 *(978-0-7232-6771-3(5),* Warne) Penguin Young Readers Group.

—The Tale of Benjamin Bunny, 5 vols. 110th ed. 2012. (Peter Rabbit Ser.: 4). (ENG., Illus.). 64p. (J). (gr. -1-2). 6.99 *(978-0-7232-6773-7(1),* Warne) Penguin Young Readers Group.

—The Tale of Jemima Puddle-Duck. 2012. (Peter Rabbit Ser.: 9). (ENG., Illus.). 64p. (J). (gr. -1-2). 6.99 *(978-0-7232-6778-2(2),* Warne) Penguin Young Readers Group.

—The Tale of Mr. Jeremy Fisher. 2012. (Peter Rabbit Ser.: 7). (ENG., Illus.). 64p. (J). (gr. -1-2). 6.99 *(978-0-7232-6776-8(6),* Warne) Penguin Young Readers Group.

—The Tale of Mrs. Tittlemouse. 2012. (Peter Rabbit Ser.: 11). (ENG., Illus.). 64p. (J). (gr. -1-2). 6.99 *(978-0-7232-6780-5(4),* Warne) Penguin Young Readers Group.

—The Tale of Peter Rabbit. 2013. (Children's Classics Ser.). (ENG., Illus.). 46p. pap. 9.99 *(978-1-909676-49-7(7),* Sovereign) Bollinger, Max GBR. Dist: Lightning Source UK, Ltd.

—The Tale of Peter Rabbit, 5 vols. 110th ed. 2012. (Peter Rabbit Ser.). (ENG., Illus.). 72p. (J). (gr. -1-2). 6.99 *(978-0-7232-6769-0(3),* Warne) Penguin Young Readers Group.

—The Tale of Squirrel Nutkin. 2013. (Children's Classics Ser.). (ENG., Illus.). 46p. pap. 9.99 *(978-1-909676-06-0(3),* Sovereign) Bollinger, Max GBR. Dist: Lightning Source UK, Ltd.

—The Tale of Squirrel Nutkin, 5 vols. 110th ed. 2012. (Peter Rabbit Ser.: 2). (ENG., Illus.). 64p. (J). (gr. -1-2). 6.99 *(978-0-7232-6770-6(7),* Warne) Penguin Young Readers Group.

—The Tale of the Flopsy Bunnies. 2012. (Peter Rabbit Ser.). (ENG., Illus.). 64p. (J). (gr. -1-2). 6.99 *(978-0-7232-6779-9(0),* Warne) Penguin Young Readers Group.

—The Tale of Timmy Tiptoes. 110th ed. 2012. (Peter Rabbit Ser.: 12). (ENG., Illus.). 64p. (J). (gr. -1-2). 6.99 *(978-0-7232-6781-2(2),* Warne) Penguin Young Readers Group.

—The Tale of Tom Kitten. 2012. (Peter Rabbit Ser.: 8). (ENG., Illus.). 64p. (J). (gr. -1-2). 6.99 *(978-0-7232-6777-5(4),* Warne) Penguin Young Readers Group.

—The Tale of Two Bad Mice, 5 vols. 110th ed. 2012. (Peter Rabbit Ser.: 5). (ENG., Illus.). 64p. (J). (gr. -1-2). 6.99 *(978-0-7232-6774-4(X),* Warne) Penguin Young Readers Group.

—Treehouse Rescue! 2013. (Peter Rabbit Animation Ser.). (ENG., Illus.). 32p. (J). (gr. -1-k). 3.99 *(978-0-7232-8040-8(1),* Warne) Penguin Young Readers Group.

Potter, Giselle. Tell Me What to Dream About. 2015. (ENG., Illus.). 40p. (J). (gr. -1-2). 17.99 *(978-0-385-37423-1(2),* Schwartz & Wade Bks.) Random Hse. Children's Bks.

Powell, Amy. Hope Music. Farley, Katherine, illus. 2006. 32p. (J). (gr. -1-3). per. 12.00 *(978-0-9773608-4-0(9))* Shiny Red Ball Publishing.

Powell, Debbie. Make It Grow. 2016. (ENG., Illus.). 16p. (J). (gr. -1-2). 14.99 *(978-1-84780-789-2(5),* Frances Lincoln Children's Bks.) Quarto Publishing Group UK GBR. Dist: Hachette Bk. Group.

—Trucks. Powell, Debbie, illus. 2012. (ENG., Illus.). 16p. (J). (gr. -1 — 1). bds. 5.99 *(978-0-7636-5934-9(7))* Candlewick Pr.

Powell, Jillian. Dance Just Like Me, 1 vol. Gulliver, Amanda, illus. 2013. (Start Reading Ser.). (ENG.). 24p. (gr. k-1). pap. 7.95 *(978-1-4765-3188-5(9))*; pap. 41.94 *(978-1-4765-3209-7(5))* Capstone Press of Coughlan Cos.

Prasadam-halls, Smriti. Have You Seen Duck? Berg, Michelle, illus. 2012. (ENG.). 12p. (J). (gr. -1-k). 7.99 *(978-1-4083-1500-2(9))* Hodder & Stoughton GBR. Dist: Hachette Bk. Group.

Prasadam-Halls, Smriti. In the Garden. Scobie, Lorna, illus. 2017. (Pairs Ser.). (ENG.). 12p. (J). (gr. -1-k). bds. 9.99 *(978-1-84780-883-7(2),* Frances Lincoln Children's Bks.) Quarto Publishing Group UK GBR. Dist: Hachette Bk. Group.

Prasadam-halls, Smriti. Noisy Farm. Scheffler, Axel, illus. 2014. (ENG.). 10p. (J). (gr. -1-k). 19.99 *(978-0-230-76680-8(3))* Pan Macmillan GBR. Dist: Independent Pubs. Group.

Pratt, Pierre. Marcel et Andre. 2003. (Picture Bks.). (FRE., Illus.). 32p. (J). (gr. -1). *(978-2-89021-633-4(0))* Diffusion du livre Mirabel (DLM).

Press Out Sticker: Camilla the Cupcake Fairy. 2015. (ENG.). 36p. (J). (gr. -1-7). pap. *(978-1-78393-779-0(3))* Make Believe Ideas.

Preston-Gannon, Frann. Deep Deep Sea. 2015. (ENG., Illus.). 14p. (J). (— 1). bds. 7.99 *(978-1-84365-268-7(4),* Pavilion) Pavilion Bks. GBR. Dist: Independent Pubs. Group.

—Sloth Slept On. 2015. (ENG., Illus.). 32p. (J). (gr. -1 — 1). 14.95 *(978-1-4549-1611-6(7))* Sterling Publishing Co., Inc.

Price, Jesse. Dad. 2008. 28p. pap. 15.99 *(978-1-4363-1489-3(5))* Xlibris Corp.

Price, M. J. Momot. Grandma & Grandpa Are Retiring. 2013. 32p. pap. 24.95 *(978-1-63000-966-3(0))* America Star Bks.

Prichard, Diana. The Cow in Patrick O'Shanahan's Kitchen. Knopf, Heather, illus. 2013. (ENG.). 32p. (J). (gr. -1-3). 17.95 *(978-1-939775-01-6(9))* March 4th, Inc.

Priddy Books Staff. Kids Can Time. 2003. (J). bds. *(978-0-312-49171-0(9),* Priddy Bks.) St. Martin's Pr.

Priddy, Roger. Baby Basics Animals. 2013. (Baby Basics Ser.). (ENG., Illus.). 10p. (J). (gr. -1 — 1). bds. 4.99 *(978-0-312-51553-9(7),* 9780312515539, Priddy Bks.) St. Martin's Pr.

—Baby Touch & Feel: Hugs. 2013. (Baby Touch & Feel Ser.). (ENG.). 10p. (J). (gr. -1 — 1). bds. 8.99 *(978-0-312-51649-9(5),* 9780312516499, Priddy Bks.) St. Martin's Pr.

—Bright Baby Touch & Feel Easter. 2012. (Bright Baby Touch & Feel Ser.). (ENG., Illus.). 12p. (J). (gr. -1 — 1). bds. 4.95 *(978-0-312-51375-7(5),* 9780312513757, Priddy Bks.) St. Martin's Pr.

—Christmas Treasure Hunt. 2014. (ENG., Illus.). 16p. (J). (— 1). bds. 9.99 *(978-0-312-51735-9(1),* 9780312517359, Priddy Bks.) St. Martin's Pr.

—Farm Friends. 2013. (My Carry-Along Sound Bks.). (ENG.). 10p. (J). (gr. -1 — 1). bds. 9.99 *(978-0-312-51645-1(2),* 9780312516451, Priddy Bks.) St. Martin's Pr.

—Lift-The-Flap Tab: on the Go. 2014. (Lift-The-Flap Tab Bks.). (ENG., Illus.). 16p. (J). (gr. -1 — 1). bds. 8.99 *(978-0-312-51731-1(9),* 9780312517311, Priddy Bks.) St. Martin's Pr.

—Lift the Tab: Christmas. 2016. (Lift-The-Flap Tab Bks.). (ENG.). 16p. (J). bds. 8.99 *(978-0-312-52071-7(9),* 9780312520717, Priddy Bks.) St. Martin's Pr.

—On the Go. 2013. (Hello Baby Ser.). (ENG., Illus.). 16p. (J). (gr. -1 — 1). bds. 4.99 *(978-0-312-51599-7(5),* 9780312515997, Priddy Bks.) St. Martin's Pr.

—Pen Control. 2012. (Wipe Clean Ser.). (ENG., Illus.). 24p. (J). (gr. -1-1). bds. 8.95 *(978-0-312-51395-5(X),* 9780312513955, Priddy Bks.) St. Martin's Pr.

—Pip the Little Penguin. 2016. (Alphaprints Ser.). (ENG.). 32p. (J). 16.99 *(978-0-312-52139-4(1),* 9780312521394, Priddy Bks.) St. Martin's Pr.

—Rudolph the Red-Nosed Reindeer Slide & Find. 2014. (Slide & Find Ser.). (ENG., Illus.). 10p. (J). (gr. -1 — 1). bds. 7.99 *(978-0-312-51750-2(5),* 9780312517502, Priddy Bks.) St. Martin's Pr.

P
Q
R

—Sticker Doodle Do. 2013. (Sticker Doodle Ser.). (ENG., Illus.). 128p. (J). (gr. -1-3). pap. 6.99 (978-0-312-51591-1(X), 9780312515911, Priddy Bks.) St. Martin's Pr.
—Sticker Doodle You. 2013. (Sticker Doodle Ser.). (ENG., Illus.). 128p. (J). (gr. -1-3). pap. 6.99 (978-0-312-51589-8(8), 9780312515898, Priddy Bks.) St. Martin's Pr.
—T Is for Truck. 2014. (ABC Bks.). (ENG.). 24p. (J). (gr. -1 — 1). bds. 12.99 (978-0-312-51734-2(3), 9780312517342, Priddy Bks.) St. Martin's Pr.
—The Talent Show. Crimi-Trent, Ellen, illus. 2014. (Schoolies Ser.). (ENG.). 28p. (J). (gr. -1-1). 4.99 (978-0-312-51664-2(9), 9780312516642, Priddy Bks.) St. Martin's Pr.
—Treasure Hunt for Boys. 2010. (ENG.). 22p. (J). (gr. k-3). bds. 9.99 (978-0-312-50818-0(2), 9780312508180, Priddy Bks.) St. Martin's Pr.
—Treasure Hunt for Girls. 2010. (ENG.). 22p. (J). (gr. k-3). bds. 9.99 (978-0-312-50817-3(4), 9780312508173, Priddy Bks.) St. Martin's Pr.
—Wiggle & the Whale: A Book of Funny Friends. 2016. (Alphaprints Ser.). (ENG.). 32p. (J). 16.99 (978-0-312-52136-3(7), 9780312521363, Priddy Bks.) St. Martin's Pr.
—1000 Animal Stickers. 2010. (ENG., Illus.). 128p. (J). (gr. -1-2). pap. 9.99 (978-0-312-50941-5(3), 9780312509415, Priddy Bks.) St. Martin's Pr.
The Princess & the Magic Locket. (My Tooth Is Loose!). (Illus.). 32p. (J). (978-1-4054-1022-9(1)) Parragon, Inc.
Pringle, Laurence. Octopuses! Strange & Wonderful. Henderson, Meryl, illus. 2015. (ENG.). 32p. (J). (gr. 1-4). 16.95 (978-1-59078-928-5(8)) Boyds Mills Pr.
Pritchard, Gabby. Omar in Trouble Orange Band. Pérez, Moni, illus. 2016. (Cambridge Reading Adventures Ser.). (ENG.). 16p. pap. 6.56 (978-1-316-50329-4(1)) Cambridge Univ. Pr.
Pritchard, Louise & Gunzi, Christiane. Mega Tractors: Amazing Tractors & Other Tough Farm Machines. 2016. (Mega Vehicles Ser.). (ENG.). 32p. (J). (gr. -1-2). pap. 6.99 (978-1-4380-0917-9(8)) Barron's Educational Series, Inc.
Pritchett, Susan & Wetterwald, Florence. Sardine Goes Fishing (a Blabla Book) 2017. (ENG., Illus.). 24p. (J). (— 1). bds. 7.99 **(978-0-553-52052-1(0)**, Random Hse. Bks. for Young Readers) Random Hse. Children's Bks.
Propes, Chrysti Carol. I Am Here. Bostrom, Laura, illus. 3rd ed. 2013. 32p. 24.95 (978-0-9790791-9-1(5)) Fig & The Vine, LLC, The.
Proysen, Alf. Mrs Pepperpot & the Treasure: A Classic Story with a Touch of Magic. Offen, Hilda, illus. 2013. (ENG.). 32p. (J). (gr. k-2). pap. 10.99 (978-1-84941-866-9(7), Red Fox) Random House Children's Books GBR. Dist: Independent Pubs. Group.
—Mrs Pepperpot Minds the Baby: A Classic Story with a Touch of Magic. Offen, Hilda, illus. 2013. (ENG.). 32p. (J). (gr. k-2). pap. 10.99 (978-1-84941-864-5(0), Red Fox) Random House Children's Books GBR. Dist: Independent Pubs. Group.
Publications International Ltd. Staff. Frozen - Anna's Friends. 2013. (Illus.). 10p. (J). (gr. k-3). bds. 10.99 (978-1-4508-6819-8(3), 48412b6e-ab38-47b0-836d-0f0ef6217ed1) Phoenix International Publications, Inc.
—My 1St Libraries Winnie the Pooh. 2011. 10p. (J). bds. 13.98 (978-1-4508-0870-5(0)) Phoenix International Publications, Inc.
Publications International Ltd. Staff, ed. Disney Pixar Picture Puzzle. 2010. 128p. (J). spiral bd. 12.98 (978-1-60553-132-8(4)) Phoenix International Publications, Inc.
—Disney Princess Picture Puzzles. 2010. 128p. (J). pap. 13.98 (978-1-60553-131-1(6)) Phoenix International Publications, Inc.
—I Can Be a Princess: Picture Book. 2014. 22p. (J). bds. 4.98 (978-1-4508-8582-9(9), 1450885829) Publications International, Ltd.
—Look & Find - Captain America: The First Avenger. 2011. 24p. (J). 3.75 net. (978-1-4508-1877-3(3)) Phoenix International Publications, Inc.
—Mickey Mouse Clubhouse. 2010. 128p. (J). pap. 12.98 (978-1-60553-129-8(4), PIL Kids) Publications International, Ltd.
Puchner, Willy. The ABC of Fabulous Princesses. 2014. (ENG., Illus.). 64p. (J). (gr. k-3). 19.95 (978-0-7358-4113-0(6)) North-South Bks., Inc.
—The ABC of Fantastic Princes. 2015. (ENG., Illus.). 64p. (J). 19.95 (978-0-7358-4198-7(5)) North-South Bks., Inc.
Puck. Babies Around the World. Lemay, Violet, illus. 2017. (ENG.). 20p. (J). (gr. -1 — 1). bds. 7.95 (978-1-938093-87-6(9), Duo Pr. Llc (US)) Duo Pr. LLC.
—One to Ten L. A. Puck, illus. 2016. (ENG., Illus.). 22p. (J). (gr. k-k). bds. 9.95 (978-1-938093-49-4(6), Duo Pr. Llc (US)) Duo Pr. LLC.
Pulley, Kelly. The Cycling Wangdoos. Pulley, Kelly, illus. 2011. (Illus.). 32p. (J). (gr. -1-3). 16.95 (978-0-9820812-1-1(9), Frog Legs Ink) Gauthier Pubns. Inc.
—The Cycling Wangdoos, 1 vol. 2017. (ENG.). 32p. (J). 16.99 **(978-0-7643-5406-9(X)**, 9780764354069) Schiffer Publishing, Ltd.
Punter, Russell. Pirate Stories for Little Children. 2015. (Stories for Little Children Gift Bks.). (ENG.). 176p. (J). 19.99 (978-0-7945-2260-5(2), Usborne) EDC Publishing.
Puttock, Simon & Bartlett, Alison. Pig's Prize. 2004. (ENG., Illus.). 28p. (J). (gr. -1-k). 17.99 (978-1-4052-0538-2(5)) Egmont Bks., Ltd. GBR. Dist: Independent Pubs. Group.
Pyle, Robert Michael & Peterson, Roger Tory. Butterflies. Peterson, Roger Tory, ed. Hughes, Sarah Anne, illus. 2nd ed. 2013. (Peterson Field Guide Color-In Bks.). (ENG.). 64p. (J). 8.95 (978-0-544-03339-9(6)) Houghton Mifflin Harcourt Publishing Co.
Quansah, Carol-Ann. The Garden. 2010. 40p. pap. 22.65 (978-1-4535-1345-3(0)) Xlibris Corp.
Quarto Generic Staff. My Bear Griz. McGinness, Suzanne, illus. 2011. (ENG.). 32p. (J). (gr. -1-1). 17.95 (978-1-84780-113-5(7), Frances Lincoln) Quarto Publishing Group UK GBR. Dist: Hachette Bk. Group.
Quattlebaum, Mary. Jo MacDonald Had a Garden. Bryant, Laura J., illus. 2013. (ENG.). 26p. (J). (gr. -1 — 1). bds. 7.95 (978-1-58469-225-6(1)) Dawn Pubns.
—Jo MacDonald Saw a Pond. Bryant, Laura J., illus. 2013. (ENG.). 26p. (J). (gr. -1 — 1). bds. 7.95 (978-1-58469-224-9(3)) Dawn Pubns.
Quayle, Susan. Mouse's Best Day Ever: Children's Reflexology to Soothe Sore Teeth & Tums. Muldoon, Melissa, illus. 2016. (ENG.). 44p. 16.95 (978-1-84819-315-4(7), 8437, Singing Dragon) Kingsley, Jessica Pubs. GBR. Dist: Macmillan Distribution Ltd.
Rabe, Tish. I Love the Nightlife! Ruiz, Aristides & Mathieu, Joe, illus. 2010. (Pictureback Ser.). (ENG.). 16p. (J). (gr. -1-2). pap. 3.99 (978-0-375-86354-7(0), Random Hse. Bks. for Young Readers) Random Hse. Children's Bks.
—I Love You, Grandma! Hitch, David, illus. 2016. (Little Golden Book Ser.). (ENG.). 24p. (J). (-k). 4.99 (978-1-101-93455-5(7), Golden Bks.) Random Hse. Children's Bks.
—Night Lights (Dr. Seuss/Cat in the Hat) Ruiz, Aristides & Mathieu, Joe, illus. 2014. (Pictureback(R) Ser.). (ENG.). 16p. (J). (gr. -1-2). pap. 4.99 (978-0-385-37116-2(0), Random Hse. Bks. for Young Readers) Random Hse. Children's Bks.
—Trick-or-Treat!/Aye-Aye! Ruiz, Aristides & Mathieu, Joe, illus. 2012. (Pictureback(R) Ser.). (ENG.). 32p. (J). (gr. -1-2). pap. 4.99 (978-0-307-93056-9(4), Random Hse. Bks. for Young Readers) Random Hse. Children's Bks.
Rabei, Carolina. Crunch! Rabei, Carolina, illus. 2015. (Child's Play Library). (ENG., Illus.). 36p. (J). pap. (978-1-84643-732-8(6)) Child's Play International Ltd.
Radford, James & Wooders, Dave. Adventures on the Queen Mary: ... tales of a Teenage Crew Member! 2015. (ENG., Illus.). 274p. pap. 25.00 (978-0-692-54554-6(9)) Perfect Page, The.
Radford, Sheri. Penelope & the Humongous Burp. l.t. ed. 2012. 64p. (J). pap. (978-1-4596-3451-0(9)) ReadHowYouWant.com, Ltd.
Radford, Tracey. Animal Fun! Touch & Feel: Stroke the Animals! 2016. (ENG., Illus.). 10p. (J). (gr. 1-4). 6.95 (978-1-78249-401-0(4), 1782494014, CICO Books) Ryland Peters & Small GBR. Dist: WIPRO.
—Animal Fun Where Do I Live? 2016. (ENG., Illus.). 10p. (J). (gr. 1-4). 6.95 (978-1-78249-399-0(9), 1782493999, CICO Books) Ryland Peters & Small GBR. Dist: WIPRO.
Raeside, Adrian. The Rainbow Bridge: A Visit to Pet Paradise. 2012. (ENG., Illus.). 32p. (J). 9.95 (978-1-55017-584-4(X)) Harbour Publishing Co., Ltd. CAN. Dist: Midpoint Trade Bks., Inc.
Rahim, Yasmeen. Hassan & Aneesa Go to Masjid. Burgess, Omar, illus. 2016. (Hassan & Aneesa Ser.). (ENG.). 20p. (J). pap. 5.99 (978-0-86037-521-0(8)) Kube Publishing Ltd. GBR. Dist: Consortium Bk. Sales & Distribution.
—Hassan & Aneesah Go to Madrasa. Burgess, Omar, illus. 2016. (Hassan & Aneesa Ser.). (ENG.). 28p. (J). pap. 5.99 (978-0-86037-459-6(9)) Kube Publishing Ltd. GBR. Dist: Consortium Bk. Sales & Distribution.
Rainville, Doris I., creator. The Girl Who Never Let Her Mother Brush Her Hair. l.t. ed. 2003. (Illus.). 24p. (J). per. 7.95 (978-0-9744879-0-8(2)) Magical Creations.
—The Power of Love. l.t. ed. 2003. (Illus.). 24p. (J). per. 7.95 (978-0-9744879-1-5(0)) Magical Creations.
Raisinghani, Jaya. I Will Always Know. 2013. 16p. pap. 17.00 (978-1-4669-3491-7(3)) Trafford Publishing.
Raisner Glass, Beth. Blue-Ribbon Dad. Moore, Margie, illus. 2011. (ENG.). 32p. (J). (gr. k-2). 15.95 (978-0-8109-9727-1(4), Abrams Bks. for Young Readers) Abrams, Inc.
Ramadier, Cédric. Help! the Wolf Is Coming! Burgess, Linda, tr. from FRE. Bourgeau, Vincent, illus. 2015.Tr. of Au Secours, Voila le Loup! (ENG.). 22p. (J). (gr. -1 — 1). bds. 14.99 (978-1-927271-84-1(3)) Gecko Pr. NZL. Dist: Lerner Publishing Group.
Ramsay, Betsy. Cecil Centipede's Career. Christman, Therese, illus. 2005. 25p. (J). per. 19.99 (978-1-4208-7870-7(0)) AuthorHouse.
Randall, Ronne. The Little Red Hen. 2015. (First Favourite Tales Ser.). (ENG., Illus.). 32p. (J). (-k). 7.99 (978-1-4093-0958-1(4)) Penguin Bks., Ltd. GBR. Dist: Independent Pubs. Group.
Random House. Abraca-Genie! Random House & Aikins, Dave, illus. 2017. (Pictureback(R) Ser.). (ENG.). 24p. (J). (gr. -1-2). pap. 5.99 (978-1-5247-1784-1(3), Random Hse. Bks. for Young Readers) Random Hse. Children's Bks.
—Barbie Dreamtopia Pictureback (Barbie) 2017. (Pictureback(R) Ser.). (ENG., Illus.). 24p. (J). (gr. -1-2). pap. 4.99 **(978-1-5247-1646-2(4)**, Random Hse. Bks. for Young Readers) Random Hse. Children's Bks.
—Barbie Summer 2016 Movie Pictureback (Barbie) 2016. (Pictureback(R) Ser.). (ENG., Illus.). 24p. (J). (gr. -1-2). 4.99 (978-1-101-93750-1(5), Random Hse. Bks. for Young Readers) Random Hse. Children's Bks.
—Beware of Bebop & Rocksteady! (Teenage Mutant Ninja Turtles) Spaziante, Patrick, illus. 2016. (Book & CD Ser.). (ENG.). 24p. (J). (gr. -1-2). pap. 6.99 (978-0-399-55468-1(8), Random Hse. Bks. for Young Readers) Random Hse. Children's Bks.
—The Fearsome Footprints/Thomas the Brave (Thomas & Friends) Stubbs, Tommy, illus. 2014. (Pictureback(R) Ser.). (ENG.). 24p. (J). (gr. -1-2). 4.99 (978-0-385-37392-0(9), Random Hse. Bks. for Young Readers) Random Hse. Children's Bks.
—Great Island Adventure. 2016. (Pictureback(R) Ser.). (ENG., Illus.). 24p. (J). (gr. -1-2). 4.99 (978-0-399-55098-0(4), Random Hse. Bks. for Young Readers) Random Hse. Children's Bks.
—Happy Troll-O-ween! Random House, illus. 2017. (Pictureback(R) Ser.). (ENG., Illus.). 16p. (J). (gr. -1-2). pap. 4.99 **(978-1-5247-6958-1(4)**, Random Hse. Bks. for Young Readers) Random Hse. Children's Bks.
—Ice Team (Paw Patrol) Jackson, Mike, illus. 2015. (Glitter Picturebook Ser.). (ENG.). 16p. (J). (gr. -1-2). 5.99 (978-0-553-52281-5(7), Random Hse. Bks. for Young Readers) Random Hse. Children's Bks.
—Nickelodeon Pictureback Collection (Nickelodeon) Random House, illus. 2017. (Pictureback Favorites Ser.). (ENG., Illus.). 96p. (J). (gr. -1-2). 9.99 (978-1-5247-0067-6(3), Random Hse. Bks. for Young Readers) Random Hse. Children's Bks.
—Saved by the Shell! (Teenage Mutant Ninja Turtles) Random House, illus. 2017. (Pictureback(R) Ser.). (ENG., Illus.). 24p. (J). (gr. -1-2). pap. 5.99 **(978-1-5247-6984-0(3)**, Random Hse. Bks. for Young Readers) Random Hse. Children's Bks.
—Speed Lights! (Blaze & the Monster Machines) Random House & Dynamo Limited Staff, illus. 2016. (Step into Reading Ser.). (ENG.). 24p. (J). (gr. -1-1). pap. 4.99 (978-0-399-55692-0(3), Random Hse. Bks. for Young Readers) Random Hse. Children's Bks.
—SpongeBob's Slap Shot (SpongeBob SquarePants) Random House, illus. 2014. (Pictureback(R) Ser.). (ENG., Illus.). 24p. (J). (gr. -1-2). 3.99 (978-0-385-37852-9(1), Random Hse. Bks. for Young Readers) Random Hse. Children's Bks.
Random House & Chlebowski, Rachel. Dance! Hug! Sing! Random House, illus. 2016. (Pictureback(R) Ser.). (ENG., Illus.). 16p. (J). (gr. -1-2). pap. 4.99 (978-0-399-55897-9(7), Random Hse. Bks. for Young Readers) Random Hse. Children's Bks.
Random House Disney Staff. Big Trouble in Little Rodentia. Random House Disney Staff, illus. 2016. (Pictureback(R) Ser.). (ENG., Illus.). 24p. (J). (gr. -1-2). 4.99 (978-0-7364-3531-4(X), RH/Disney) Random Hse. Children's Bks.
—A Dino Named Arlo/a Boy Named Spot, 2 bks. in 1. Random House Disney Staff, illus. 2015. (Pictureback(R) Ser.). (ENG., Illus.). 24p. (J). (gr. -1-2). 4.99 (978-0-7364-3083-8(0), RH/Disney) Random Hse. Children's Bks.
—Out of Branch's Bunker. Random House Disney Staff et al, illus. 2016. (Pictureback(R) Ser.). (ENG.). 24p. (J). (gr. -1-2). pap. 4.99 (978-0-399-55899-3(3), Random Hse. Bks. for Young Readers) Random Hse. Children's Bks.
Random House Disney Staff & Scollon, Bill. The Big Case. Random House Disney Staff & Disney Storybook Art Team, illus. 2016. (Step into Reading Ser.). (ENG.). 32p. (J). (gr. -1-1). 4.99 (978-0-7364-3456-0(9), RH/Disney) Random Hse. Children's Bks.
Random House Staff. An Egg-Stra Special Easter! (Barbie) Duarte, Pamela, illus. 2014. (Color Plus Card Stock Ser.). (ENG.). 48p. (J). (gr. -1-2). pap. 3.99 (978-0-385-37319-7(8), Random Hse. Bks. for Young Readers) Random Hse. Children's Bks.
Rankin, Heather & Rankin, Heather. All It Takes Is One Friend. 2012. 46p. pap. (978-0-9878945-0-2(1)) Our Farm Bks.
Ransom, Jeanie Franz. What Really Happened to Humpty? From the Files of a Hard-Boiled Detective. Axelsen, Stephen, illus. 2010. (Nursery-Rhyme Mysteries Ser.). (ENG.). 40p. (J). (gr. 1-4). pap. 7.95 (978-1-58089-391-6(0)) Charlesbridge Publishing, Inc.
Raposo, Joe. Sing. Lichtenheld, Tom, illus. 2016. (ENG.). 32p. (J). bds. 8.99 (978-1-62779-502-9(2), 9781627795029, Holt, Henry & Co. Bks. For Young Readers) Holt, Henry & Co.
Rassi, Lee. Capital Heroes. 2008. (Illus.). 56p. pap. 23.99 (978-1-4343-8208-5(7)) AuthorHouse.
Ray, Cindy & Kids Write On, creators. The Stapler Caper: You Write the Story. 2008. (ENG., Illus.). 28p. (J). 16.95 (978-0-615-23574-5(3)) Kids Write On, LLC.
Ray, Jane. Cinderella. Ray, Jane, illus. 2012. (ENG., Illus.). 12p. (J). (gr. k-4). 19.99 (978-0-7636-6175-5(9)) Candlewick Pr.
Ray, Mary Lyn. Go to Sleep, Little Farm. Neal, Christopher Silas, illus. 2015. (ENG.). 38p. (J). (— 1). bds. 8.99 (978-0-544-57916-3(X), HMH Books For Young Readers) Houghton Mifflin Harcourt Publishing Co.
Rayner, Catherine. Smelly Louie. Rayner, Catherine, illus. (ENG., Illus.). (J). (gr. -1-k). 2016. 24p. bds. 10.99 (978-1-5098-0344-6(0)) 2014. 32p. 19.99 (978-0-230-74250-5(5)) Pan Macmillan GBR. Dist: Independent Pubs. Group.
Read-It! Readers - Gus the Hedgehog. 2005. (Read-It! Readers: Gus the Hedgehog Ser.). (ENG., Illus.). 32p. (gr. k-3). 79.96 (978-1-4048-0995-6(3)) Picture Window Bks.
Read It! Readers: Folk Tales, 6 vols. 2005. (Read-It! Readers: Folk Tales Ser.). (ENG., Illus.). 32p. (gr. k-3). 59.97 (978-1-4048-0999-4(6)) Picture Window Bks.
Reader, Gwendolin. The Life Cycle of A Snowman. 2010. 24p. pap. 12.50 (978-1-4520-7686-7(3)) AuthorHouse.
Ready Reader Staff. What Do We Have to Get?, 6 bks., set, Level 6, Bk. 13. 2003. (J). (gr. -1-3). pap. 33.50 (978-0-8136-2021-3(X)) Modern Curriculum Pr.
—Where Does the Rabbit Hop?, 6 bks., set, Level 8, Bk. 30. 2003. (J). (gr. -1-3). 33.50 (978-0-8136-0793-1(0)) Modern Curriculum Pr.
Recob, Amy. The BugaBees: Friends with Food Allergies. 2009. (Illus.). 32p. (J). (978-1-59298-279-0(4)) Beaver's Pond Pr., Inc.
Redford, Ali & Stickleberry, Plum. The Boy Who Built a Wall Around Himself. Simpson, Kara, illus. 2015. (ENG.). 32p. (J). 15.95 (978-1-84905-683-0(8), 8121) Kingsley, Jessica Pubs. GBR. Dist: Macmillan Distribution Ltd.
Reece, Colleen L. & DeMarco, Julie Reece. God Loves You Whoever You Are. Snider, K. C., illus. 2011. 20p. pap. 10.95 (978-1-61633-183-2(6)) Guardian Angel Publishing, Inc.
Reeve, Rosie. Rory & the Monstersitter. 2015. (ENG., Illus.). 32p. (J). (gr. -1-1). 18.99 (978-1-4088-4550-9(4), 9781408845509, Bloomsbury USA Childrens) Bloomsbury Publishing USA.
Regan, Dian. Space Boy & His Dog. Neubecker, Robert, illus. 2015. (Space Boy Ser.). (ENG.). 32p. (J). (gr. k-5). 16.95 (978-1-59078-955-1(5)) Boyds Mills Pr.
Regan, Patrick. The Nutcracker. Kuricheva, Natasha, illus. 2016. (ENG.). 26p. (J). bds. 9.99 (978-1-4494-5586-6(7)) Andrews McMeel Publishing.
Regordosa, Adria. Dustrats. 2017. (ENG., Illus.). 32p. (J). (gr. -1-2). 16.99 (978-1-57687-821-7(X), powerHouse Bks.) powerHouse Cultural Entertainment, Inc.
Reich, J. J. Deer Dad: Kampp Tales Outdoor Adventures. Johnathan, Kuehl, illus. 2006. (BAT.). 32p. (J). (978-0-9762971-0-9(8)) Outdoor Originals LLC.
Reid, Aimee. Mama's Day with Little Gray. 2014. (ENG., Illus.). 32p. (J). (-k). 16.99 (978-0-449-81083-5(6), Random Hse. Bks. for Young Readers) Random Hse. Children's Bks.
Reid, Camilla. Lulu Loves Numbers. Busby, Ailie, illus. 2015. (ENG.). 12p. (J). (gr. -1-1). bds. 8.99 (978-1-4088-4957-6(7), 9781408849576, Bloomsbury USA Childrens) Bloomsbury Publishing USA.
—Lulu Loves Shapes. Busby, Ailie, illus. 2015. (ENG.). 12p. (J). (gr. -1-1). bds. 8.99 (978-1-4088-4958-3(5), 9781408849583, Bloomsbury USA Childrens) Bloomsbury Publishing USA.
Reidy, Hannah. Crazy Creature Capers. Mackie, Clare, illus. 2003. (Crazy Creatures Ser.). 26p. (J). pap. (978-1-84089-222-2(6)) Zero to Ten, Ltd.
Reilly, Michael. Monster Sandwich. 2009. 50p. (J). pap. 31.99 (978-1-4415-0056-4(1)) Xlibris Corp.
Renyi Bilingual Picture Dictionaries, 12 vols., Set. Date not set. (Illus.). 2304p. 244.40 (978-1-56674-937-4(9)) Forest Hse. Publishing Co., Inc.
Rescek, Sanja. Buggy Buddies Fairy Moonbeam. Rescek, Sanja, illus. 2015. (Buggy Buddies Ser.). (ENG., Illus.). 8p. (J). (-k). bds. 8.99 (978-1-4472-7614-2(0)) Pan Macmillan GBR. Dist: Independent Pubs. Group.
—Buggy Buddies Fairy Sunshine. Rescek, Sanja, illus. 2015. (Buggy Buddies Ser.). (ENG., Illus.). 8p. (J). (-k). bds. 8.99 (978-1-4472-7612-8(4)) Pan Macmillan GBR. Dist: Independent Pubs. Group.
Revenge of the Tune Squad. Date not set. (Space Jam Eye Illusion Bks.). (Illus.). 24p. (J). (gr. 1-6). pap. 2.95 (978-1-56144-889-0(3), SJMO32) Modern Publishing.
Rey, H. A. Builds a Home. 2011. (Curious George Ser.). (ENG., Illus.). 24p. (J). (gr. -1-3). 6.99 (978-0-547-59410-1(0)) Houghton Mifflin Harcourt Publishing Co.
—Curious George Discovers Germs (Science Storybook) 2015. (Curious George Ser.). (ENG., Illus.). 32p. (J). (gr. -1-3). 6.99 (978-0-544-43066-2(2), HMH Books For Young Readers) Houghton Mifflin Harcourt Publishing Co.
—Curious George Discovers the Ocean (Science Storybook) 2015. (Curious George Ser.). (ENG., Illus.). 32p. (J). (gr. -1-3). 6.99 (978-0-544-43065-5(4), HMH Books For Young Readers) Houghton Mifflin Harcourt Publishing Co.
—Curious George Discovers the Rainbow (Science Storybook) 2015. (Curious George Ser.). (ENG., Illus.). 32p. (J). (gr. -1-3). 6.99 (978-0-544-43068-6(9), HMH Books For Young Readers) Houghton Mifflin Harcourt Publishing Co.
—Curious George Discovers the Senses. 2015. (Curious George Ser.). (ENG., Illus.). 32p. (J). (gr. -1-3). 6.99 (978-0-544-50023-5(7), HMH Books For Young Readers) Houghton Mifflin Harcourt Publishing Co.
—Curious George Discovers the Sun (Science Storybook) 2015. (Curious George Ser.). (ENG., Illus.). 32p. (J). (gr. -1-3). 6.99 (978-0-544-43067-9(0), HMH Books For Young Readers) Houghton Mifflin Harcourt Publishing Co.
—Get Well, Curious George. 2017. (Curious George Ser.). (ENG., Illus.). 24p. (J). (gr. -1-3). 14.99 **(978-0-544-97750-1(5)**, HMH Books For Young Readers) Houghton Mifflin Harcourt Publishing Co.
—Sweet Dreams, Curious George. 2016. (Curious George Ser.). (ENG., Illus.). 24p. (J). (gr. -1-3). 4.99 (978-0-544-50321-2(X), HMH Books For Young Readers) Houghton Mifflin Harcourt Publishing Co.
—Where Is Curious George? Around the Town: A Look-And-Find Book. 2015. (Curious George Ser.). (ENG., Illus.). 32p. (J). (gr. -1-3). 9.99 (978-0-544-38072-1(X), HMH Books For Young Readers) Houghton Mifflin Harcourt Publishing Co.
Rey, H. A. & Hapka, Catherine. Merry Christmas, Curious George (with Stickers) Young, Mary O'Keefe, illus. 2017. (Curious George Ser.). (ENG.). 24p. (J). (gr. -1-3). pap. 5.99 **(978-1-328-69558-1(1)**, HMH Books For Young Readers) Houghton Mifflin Harcourt Publishing Co.
Rey, H. A. & Rey, Margret. Goes to the Beach. 2014. (Curious George Ser.). (ENG., Illus.). 24p. (J). (gr. -1-3). pap. 4.99 (978-0-544-25001-7(X), HMH Books For Young Readers) Houghton Mifflin Harcourt Publishing Co.
Rey, H. A. & Young, Mary OKeefe. Ready for School. 2017. (Curious George Ser.). (ENG., Illus.). 14p. (J). (— 1). bds. 7.99 (978-0-544-93120-6(3), HMH Books For Young Readers) Houghton Mifflin Harcourt Publishing Co.
Reynolds, Peter H. Peter Reynolds Creatrilogy Box Set (Dot, Ish, Sky Color) 2012. (ENG.). (J). (gr. k-4). 40.00 (978-0-7636-6327-8(1)) Candlewick Pr.
RH Disney. Finding Dory Padded Board Book (Disney/Pixar Finding Dory) RH Disney, illus. 2016. (Padded Board Book Ser.). (ENG., Illus.). 30p. (J). (— 1). bds. 11.99 (978-0-7364-3558-1(1), RH/Disney) Random Hse. Children's Bks.
—Where Monsters Live. RH Disney, illus. 2016. (Pictureback(R) Ser.). (ENG., Illus.). 24p. (J). (gr. -1-2). 4.99 (978-0-7364-3649-6(9), RH/Disney) Random Hse. Children's Bks.
RH Disney Staff. Ariel's Royal Wedding/Aurora's Royal Wedding (Disney Princess) RH Disney Staff, illus. 2014. (Pictureback(R) Ser.). (ENG., Illus.). 32p. (J). (gr. -1-2). 4.99 (978-0-7364-3167-5(5), RH/Disney) Random Hse. Children's Bks.
Rhodes, Julie & Quarto Generic Staff. The Very Noisy House. Paul, Korky, illus. 2014. (ENG.). 32p. (J). (gr. -1-k). 17.99 (978-1-84507-983-3(3), Frances Lincoln) Quarto Publishing Group UK GBR. Dist: Hachette Bk. Group.
Rhymes, Wriggly. No Place Like Home. 2013. (Illus.). 40p. pap. 11.00 (978-1-78035-602-0(1), Fastprint Publishing) Upfront Publishing Ltd. GBR. Dist: Printondemand-worldwide.com.
Rice, Inez & Bobri, Vladimir. The March Wind. 2017. (ENG., Illus.). 32p. (J). 20.00 (978-1-85124-461-4(1)) Bodleian Library GBR. Dist: Chicago Distribution Ctr.
Rice, Tim & Webber, Andrew Lloyd. Joseph & the Amazing Technicolor Dreamcoat. Blake, Quentin, illus. 2012. (ENG.). 48p. (J). (gr. 2-4). 16.99 (978-1-84365-103-1(3), Pavilion Children's Books) Pavilion Bks. GBR. Dist: Independent Pubs. Group.
Richards, Dan. The Problem with Not Being Scared of Monsters. Neubecker, Robert, illus. 2014. (ENG.). 32p. (J). (gr. -1-3). 15.95 (978-1-62091-024-5(1)) Boyds Mills Pr.
Richards, Josie Aleardi. Grandma's Just Not Herself. Rowland, Lauri, illus. 2010. 36p. pap. 13.95 (978-1-60911-236-3(9), Eloquent Bks.) Strategic Book Publishing & Rights Agency (SBPRA).
Richardson, Bill. The Aunts Come Marching. Nugent, Cynthia, illus. 2007. (ENG.). 32p. (J). (gr. -1-3). 15.95 (978-1-55192-990-3(2)) Raincoast Bk. Distribution CAN. Dist: Publishers Group West (PGW).
Richardson, Deborra. Treasures at the Museum. 2011. (Illus.). 64p. (J). pap. 5.99 (978-0-9824945-1-6(3)) Elevator Group, The.

Riddell, Chris. The Emperor of Absurdia. 2016. (ENG., Illus.). 32p. (J). (gr. -1-2). 11.99 (978-1-5098-1373-5(X)) Pan Macmillan GBR. Dist: Independent Pubs. Group.

—Mr Underbed. Riddell, Chris, illus. 2012. (ENG., Illus.). 32p. (J). (gr. -1-k). pap. 10.99 (978-1-84270-942-9(9)) Andersen Pr. GBR. Dist: Independent Pubs. Group.

—Wendel & the Robot. 2016. (ENG., Illus.). 32p. (J). (gr. -1-2). 9.99 (978-1-5098-1374-2(8)) Pan Macmillan GBR. Dist: Independent Pubs. Group.

Rider, Cynthia. Chatterbox Turtle. Petrlik, Andrea, illus. 2004. (ENG.). 24p. (J). lib. bdg. 23.65 (978-1-59646-696-8(0)) Dingles & Co.

—Our Snowman. Evans, Nicola, illus. 2013. (Start Reading Ser.). (ENG.). 24p. (gr. k-1). pap. 41.94 (978-1-4765-3229-5(X)); pap. 7.95 (978-1-4765-3196-0(X)) Capstone Press of Coughlan Cos.

—Pirate Treasure, 1 vol. Aguilar, Sandra, illus. 2013. (Start Reading Ser.). (ENG.). 24p. (gr. k-1). pap. 7.95 (978-1-4765-4129-7(9)) Capstone Press of Coughlan Cos.

—What a Windy Day!, 1 vol. Evans, Nicola, illus. 2013. (Start Reading Ser.). (ENG.). 24p. (gr. k-1). pap. 7.95 (978-1-4765-3198-4(6)); pap. 41.94 (978-1-4765-3234-9(6)) Capstone Press of Coughlan Cos.

Ries, Lori. Aggie the Brave. Dormer, Frank W., illus. 2012. (ENG.). 48p. (J). (gr. -1-3). pap. 5.95 (978-1-57091-636-6(5)) Charlesbridge Publishing, Inc.

Rigo, L. Little Owl. 2011. (Look at Me Bks.). (ENG., Illus.). 10p. (J). bds. 8.99 (978-0-7641-6447-7(3)) Barron's Educational Series, Inc.

—Little Pony. 2011. (Look at Me Bks.). (ENG., Illus.). 10p. (J). bds. 8.99 (978-0-7641-6448-4(1)) Barron's Educational Series, Inc.

—Little Reindeer. 2011. (Look at Me Bks.). (ENG., Illus.). 10p. (J). bds. 7.99 (978-0-7641-6450-7(3)) Barron's Educational Series, Inc.

Rigo, L., illus. Little Duckling. 2011. (Look at Me Bks.). 10p. (J). bds. 7.99 (978-0-7641-6425-5(2)) Barron's Educational Series, Inc.

—Little Elephant. 2011. (Look at Me Bks.). 10p. (J). bds. 8.99 (978-0-7641-6426-2(0)) Barron's Educational Series, Inc.

—Little Lamb. 2011. (Look at Me Bks.). 10p. (J). (gr. -1). bds. 7.99 (978-0-7641-6427-9(9)) Barron's Educational Series, Inc.

Rikkers, Doris Wynbeek. Little Jesus, Little Me, 1 vol. 2017. (ENG., Illus.). 14p. (J). bds. 6.99 (978-0-310-76177-8(8)) Zonderkidz.

Rinaldo, Luana. Beep Beep Stories. 2016. (ENG., Illus.). 12p. (J). bds. 12.99 (978-1-5098-0899-1(X)) Pan Macmillan GBR. Dist: Independent Pubs. Group.

—Farm Stories. 2016. (ENG., Illus.). 12p. (J). bds. 12.99 (978-1-5098-0900-4(7)) Pan Macmillan GBR. Dist: Independent Pubs. Group.

Rinaldo, Luana & Prasadam-halls, Smriti. Who Am I? This Is My Tail. 2012. (ENG., Illus.). 12p. (J). (gr. -1-k). 7.99 (978-1-4083-1510-1(6)) Hodder & Stoughton GBR. Dist: Hachette Bk. Group.

Ringbom, Antonia & Wiklund, Alison. The Hiding Hyena. 2nd ed. 2007. (YA). (978-0-9789617-1-8(4)) H.B.P., Inc.

Risom, Ole. I Am a Bunny. Scarry, Richard, illus. 2004. (Golden Sturdy Book Ser.). (ENG.). 26p. (J). (gr. k — 1). bds. 7.99 (978-0-375-82778-5(1), Golden Bks.) Random Hse. Children's Bks.

Rissman, Rebecca. Parks, 1 vol. 2013. (Picture This! Ser.). (ENG.). 24p. (gr. -1-k). pap. 9.95 (978-1-4109-5259-2(2), NA-r) Heinemann-Raintree.

—Simple Machines: Real Size Science, 1 vol. 2013. (Real Size Science Ser.). (ENG.). 24p. (gr. -1-1). 22.65 (978-1-4329-7877-8(2)); pap. 6.95 (978-1-4329-7884-6(5)) Heinemann-Raintree. (Acorn).

Ritchie, Alison. The Tortoise & the Hare. Noj, Nahta, illus. 2015. (ENG.). 32p. (J). (-k). 15.99 (978-0-7636-7601-8(2), Templar) Candlewick Pr.

Rivas, H. J. Word Sag: A Bedtime Story. 2012. 24p. pap. 15.99 (978-1-4691-5661-3(X)) Xlibris Corp.

Rivett, Rachel. Are You Sad, Little Bear? A Book about Learning to Say Goodbye. Macnaughton, Tina, illus. (ENG.). (J). (-k). 2013. 32p. 9.99 (978-0-7459-6430-0(3)) 2010. 28p. 12.99 (978-0-7459-6137-8(1)) Lion Hudson PLC GBR. Dist: Independent Pubs. Group.

Rizzi, Kathleen. What's in My Dresser?, 1 vol. Riggs, Jenna, illus. 2013. (ENG.). 32p. (J). bds. 7.99 (978-1-59572-165-5(7)) Star Bright Bks., Inc.

Rml. An Interesting Crew. 2012. 16p. (-18). pap. 15.99 (978-1-4772-8699-9(3)) AuthorHouse.

Robbins, Becky. Creature Teacher. 2016. (ENG., Illus.). 25p. (J). pap. 10.95 (978-1-78612-354-1(1), 9b9495a8-cc78-438c-ac17-3ade2a4a0aac) Austin, Stan AUS. Dist: Bookmasters Distribution.

Robbins, Heather Roan. Talulla Bear's Bedtime Book: A Sleepytime Tale. 2016. (ENG., Illus.). 32p. (J). (gr. 8-2). 14.95 (978-1-78249-379-2(4), 1782493794, CICO Books) Ryland Peters & Small GBR. Dist: WIPRO.

Robert, Na'ima B. Ramadan Moon. Adl, Shirin, illus. 2015. (ENG.). 32p. (J). (gr. -1-2). pap. 7.95 (978-1-84780-206-4(0), Frances Lincoln) Quarto Publishing Group UK GBR. Dist: Hachette Bk. Group.

Roberts, Ceri. Refugees & Migrants. Kai, Hanane, illus. 2017. (Children in Our World Ser.). (ENG.). 32p. (J). (gr. 1-4). 9.99 (978-1-4380-5020-1(8)) Barron's Educational Series, Inc.

Roberts, Daniel. The Ghost of Froggy's Swamp. 2012. 36p. pap. 18.99 (978-1-4772-0316-3(8)) AuthorHouse.

—The Good Night Book: A Book of Animal Sounds. 2009. 36p. pap. 16.99 (978-1-4389-8278-6(X)) AuthorHouse.

—Mouse & His Balloon. 2011. 32p. pap. 14.95 (978-1-4634-2090-1(0)) AuthorHouse.

—The Naughty Dog. 2010. 32p. 14.95 (978-1-4490-8344-1(7)) AuthorHouse.

—Young Pep Squad Mysteries. 2011. 36p. pap. 16.99 (978-1-4567-9640-2(2)) AuthorHouse.

Roberts, Lynn. Cinderella: an Art Deco Fairy Tale. 2017. (ENG., Illus.). 40p. (J). (gr. -1-3). pap. 9.99 (978-1-84365-319-6(2), Pavilion) Pavilion Bks. GBR. Dist: Independent Pubs. Group.

—Rapunzel: a Groovy 1970's Fairy Tale. 2017. (ENG., Illus.). 40p. (J). (gr. k-2). pap. 9.99 (978-1-84365-318-9(4), Pavilion) Pavilion Bks. GBR. Dist: Independent Pubs. Group.

Roberts, Lynn & Roberts, David. Sleeping Beauty. 2017. (ENG., Illus.). 32p. (J). (gr. -1-1). 17.99 (978-1-84365-291-5(9), Pavilion) Pavilion Bks. GBR. Dist: Independent Pubs. Group.

Roberts, Melva J. Mrs Moon's Pond. 2011. 28p. pap. 21.99 (978-1-4628-4613-9(0)) Xlibris Corp.

Roberts, Phyllis. Teeny Tiny Star. 2007. (Illus.). 30p. (J). lib. bdg. 19.95 (978-1-933732-40-4(7)) Big Ransom Studio.

Roberts, Tony. Turquie the Turkey. 2011. 28p. pap. 15.99 (978-1-4568-5969-5(2)) Xlibris Corp.

Robertson, David A. When We Were Alone, 1 vol. Flett, Julie, illus. 2017. (ENG.). 24p. (J). (gr. k-3). 18.95 (978-1-55379-673-2(X), HighWater Pr.) Portage & Main Pr. CAN. Dist: Orca Bk. Pubs. USA.

Robertson, James. Katie's A tae Z: An Alphabet for Wee Folk. Sutherland, Karen, illus. 2014. (ENG.). 20p. (J). (-k). bds. 12.99 (978-1-84502-754-4(X)) Black and White Publishing Ltd. GBR. Dist: Independent Pubs. Group.

Robertson, M. P., et al. Dare to Care: Pet Dragon. 2016. (ENG., Illus.). 32p. (J). (gr. 1-4). 17.99 (978-1-84780-589-8(2), Frances Lincoln Children's Bks.) Quarto Publishing Group UK GBR. Dist: Hachette Bk. Group.

Robinson, Hilary. Beauty & the Pea. Sanfilippo, Simona, illus. 2013. (ENG.). 32p. (J). pap. (978-0-7787-1159-9(5)) Crabtree Publishing Co.

—Cinderella & the Beanstalk. Sanfilippo, Simona, illus. 2013. (ENG.). 32p. (J). pap. (978-0-7787-1161-2(7)) Crabtree Publishing Co.

—Hansel, Gretel, & the Ugly Duckling. Sanfilippo, Simona, illus. 2013. (ENG.). 32p. (J). pap. (978-0-7787-1166-7(8)) Crabtree Publishing Co.

—Rapunzel & the Billy Goats. Sanfilippo, Simona, illus. 2013. (ENG.). 32p. (J). pap. (978-0-7787-1158-2(7)) Crabtree Publishing Co.

—Ted's Party Bus. 2009. (ENG., Illus.). 24p. (J). pap. (978-0-7787-3901-2(5)); lib. bdg. (978-0-7787-3870-1(1)) Crabtree Publishing Co.

Robinson, Mark. Vile: A Cautionary Tale for Little Monsters. Home, Sarah, illus. 2011. (ENG.). 32p. (J). (gr. k-2). 14.99 (978-0-7459-6254-2(8)) Lion Hudson PLC GBR. Dist: Independent Pubs. Group.

Robinson, Michelle. Elephant's Pyjamas. Fox, Emily, illus. 2016. (ENG.). 32p. (J). 17.99 (978-0-00-816479-9(7), HarperCollins Children's Bks.) HarperCollins Pubs. Ltd. GBR. Dist: HarperCollins Pubs.

—How to Find a Fruit Bat. Tobia, Lauren, illus. (ENG.). 32p. (J). (gr. -1-k). 2013. pap. 10.99 (978-1-4083-0855-4(X)) 2012. 14.99 (978-1-4083-0854-7(1)) Hodder & Stoughton GBR. Dist: Hachette Bk. Group.

Robinson, Nicola. The Monster Machine. Robinson, Nicola, illus. 2013. (ENG., Illus.). 32p. (J). (gr. -1-k). pap. 8.99 (978-1-84365-200-7(5), Pavilion) Pavilion Bks. GBR. Dist: Independent Pubs. Group.

Robson, Kirsteen. Mosaic Sticker Flowers. 2015. (Mosaic Sticker Bks.). (ENG.). 20+10p. (J). (gr. k-5). pap. 9.99 (978-0-7945-3545-2(3), Usborne) EDC Publishing.

Roca, Nuria. Fall. 2004. (Seasons Ser.). (ENG., Illus.). 36p. (J). pap. 6.95 (978-0-7641-2729-8(2)) Barron's Educational Series, Inc.

Roche, Jackie, illus. The Derby Ram. 2010. (First Steps in Music Ser.). (ENG.). 32p. (J). (gr. -1-k). 16.95 (978-1-57999-783-0(X)) G I A Pubns., Inc.

Roche, Maite. My First Pictures of Jesus. 2012. 14p. 6.99 (978-1-58617-651-8(X)) Ignatius Pr.

Rock, Lois. A Gift for Baby's Christening. Rescek, Sanja, illus. 2014. (ENG.). 48p. (J). (— 1). 9.99 (978-0-7459-6490-4(7)) Lion Hudson PLC GBR. Dist: Independent Pubs. Group.

—A Gift for Baby's Dedication. Rescek, Sanja, illus. 2014. (ENG.). 48p. (J). (— 1). 9.99 (978-0-7459-6491-1(5)) Lion Hudson PLC GBR. Dist: Independent Pubs. Group.

—Look Inside Noah's Ark. Coloji, Livia, illus. 2016. (ENG.). 6p. (J). (gr. k-2). bds. 12.99 (978-0-7459-7612-9(3)) Lion Hudson PLC GBR. Dist: Independent Pubs. Group.

—My Very First Nativity Story. Ayliffe, Alex, illus. 2015. (My Very First Ser.). (ENG.). 48p. (J). (gr. -1-k). 7.99 (978-0-7459-6911-4(9)) Lion Hudson PLC GBR. Dist: Independent Pubs. Group.

—Noah's Ark. Allsopp, Sophie, illus. 2014. (ENG.). 32p. (J). (gr. k-2). 6.99 (978-0-7459-6321-1(8)) Lion Hudson PLC GBR. Dist: Independent Pubs. Group.

—On That Christmas Night. Jay, Alison, illus. 2016. (ENG.). 32p. (J). (gr. k-4). 16.99 (978-0-7459-6588-8(1)) Lion Hudson PLC GBR. Dist: Independent Pubs. Group.

Rockwell, Anne. Bugs Are Insects. Jenkins, Steve, illus. 2015. (Let's-Read-And-Find-Out Science 1 Ser.). (ENG.). 40p. (J). (gr. -1-3). pap. 6.99 (978-0-06-238182-8(2)) HarperCollins Pubs.

Rodriguez, Rachel Victoria. Building on Nature: The Life of Antoni Gaudi. Paschkis, Julie, illus. 2009. (ENG.). 32p. (J). (gr. k-3). 19.99 (978-0-8050-8745-1(1), 9780805087451, Holt, Henry & Co. Bks. For Young Readers) Holt, Henry & Co.

—Through Georgia's Eyes. Paschkis, Julie, illus. rev. ed. 2006. (ENG.). 32p. (J). (gr. k-3). 18.99 (978-0-8050-7740-7(5), 9780805077407, Holt, Henry & Co. Bks. For Young Readers) Holt, Henry & Co.

Roffey, M. First Words Indoors. 2003. (Illus.). 12p. (J). 3.99 (978-1-85292-227-6(3), Campbell Bks.) Pan Macmillan GBR. Dist: Trafalgar Square Publishing.

Rogers, Alan. Le Vent Tourne! 2003. (Little Giants Ser.). (FRE., Illus.). 16p. (J). (gr. -1-k). 5.95 (978-1-58728-179-2(1), Two-Can Publishing) T&N Children's Publishing.

Rogers, Andy. The Puppy Brothers Adventures with Forest Friends - Children's Picture Book for Ages 3 To 8. 2013. 38p. pap. 10.00 (978-1-63022-036-5(1)) Speedy Publishing LLC.

Rohmann, Eric. A Kitten Tale. (ENG., 32p. (J). (gr. -1-2). 2015. Illus.). bds. 6.99 (978-0-553-49831-8(2), Knopf Bks. for Young Readers) 2012. pap. 7.99 (978-0-307-97774-8(9), Dragonfly Bks.) Random Hse. Children's Bks.

Rohner, Dorothia, illus. Effie's Image. 2006. 32p. (J). (gr. -1-3). 17.95 (978-0-9759829-5-2(8)) Praireland Pr.

Rooks, Elizabeth. Where Does Santa Go on Vacation after Christmas? 2012. 24p. pap. 17.99 (978-1-4772-6535-2(X)) AuthorHouse.

Rooney, Rachel. A Patch of Black, 8. Allwright, Deborah, illus. 2014. (ENG.). 32p. (J). (-k). pap. 9.99 (978-0-230-71443-4(9)) Pan Macmillan GBR. Dist: Independent Pubs. Group.

Roop, Connie, et al. Our Solar System. 2016. (Science for Toddlers Ser.: 1). (ENG., Illus.). 26p. (J). (gr. -1 — 1). bds. 7.95 (978-1-4549-1418-1(1), 1404673) Sterling Publishing Co., Inc.

Root, Andrew. Hamsters Don't Fight Fires! Olien, Jessica, illus. 2017. 40p. (J). (gr. -1-3). 17.99 (978-0-06-245294-8(0)) HarperCollins Pubs.

Root, Phyllis. Creak! Said the Bed. Dunnick, Regan, illus. 2015. (ENG.). 32p. (J). (gr. -1-3). 6.99 (978-0-7636-7969-9(0)) Candlewick Pr.

—Rattletrap Car Big Book. Barton, Jill, illus. 2009. (ENG.). 40p. (J). (gr. -1-3). pap. 24.99 (978-0-7636-4139-9(1)) Candlewick Pr.

Rosa-Mendoza, Gladys. Animals at the Farm/Animales de la Granja. Wolff, Jason, illus. 2004. (English-Spanish Foundations Ser.). (SPA & ENG.). 20p. (J). (gr. -1). bds. 6.95 (978-1-931398-13-8(5)) Me+Mi Publishing.

—Cars, Trucks & Planes/Carros, Camiones y Aviones. Tugeau, Jeremy, illus. 2004. (English-Spanish Foundations Ser.). (SPA & ENG.). 20p. (J). (gr. -1). bds. 6.95 (978-1-931398-14-5(3)) Me+Mi Publishing.

—Lupe Lupita, Where Are You?/Lupe Lupita, Donde Estas? Ochoa, Ana, illus. 2005. (English-Spanish Foundations Ser.). (SPA & ENG.). 20p. (J). (gr. -1). bds. 6.95 (978-1-931398-16-9(X)) Me+Mi Publishing.

Roscoe, Charlie. The Red Prince. Cole, Tom Clohosy, illus. 2016. (ENG.). 32p. (J). (-k). 16.99 (978-0-7636-8912-4(2), Templar) Candlewick Pr.

Rose, Nancy. The Secret Life of Squirrels: A Love Story. 2014. (ENG., Illus.). 32p. (J). (gr. -1-3). 17.00 (978-0-316-37027-1(4)) Little, Brown Bks. for Young Readers.

Rosebrough, Ellen. Dora's Chilly Day (Dora the Explorer) Mcgee, Warner & MJ Illustrations Staff, illus. 2013. (Pictureback Ser.). (ENG.). 16p. (J). (gr. -1-2). 3.99 (978-0-449-81950-0(7), Random Hse. Bks. for Young Readers) Random Hse. Children's Bks.

Rosen, Lucy. M. K. Saves the Day. 2013. (I Can Read Level 2 Ser.). (ENG., Illus.). 32p. (J). (gr. -1-3). pap. 3.99 (978-0-06-220991-7(4)) HarperCollins Pubs.

—Meet the Leafmen. 2013. (I Can Read Level 2 Ser.). (ENG., Illus.). 32p. (J). (gr. -1-3). pap. 3.99 (978-0-06-220993-1(0)) HarperCollins Pubs.

Rosen, Michael. Aesop's Fables, 1 vol. Hacikyan, Talleen, illus. 2013. (ENG.). 32p. (J). (gr. -1-2). 16.95 (978-1-896580-81-4(5)) Tradewind Bks. CAN. Dist: Orca Bk. Pubs. USA.

—Burping Bertha. Ross, Tony, illus. 2012. (ENG.). 64p. (J). (gr. -1-2). pap. 8.99 (978-1-84939-406-2(7)) Andersen Pr. GBR. Dist: Independent Pubs. Group.

—Send for a Superhero! McEwen, Katharine, illus. 2014. (ENG.). 40p. (J). (gr. -1-2). 16.99 (978-0-7636-6438-1(3)) Candlewick Pr.

Rosenberg, Natascha & Kempter, Christa. When Mama Can't Sleep. 2011. (ENG., Illus.). 24p. (J). (gr. -1 — 1). 6.95 (978-0-7358-4015-7(6)) North-South Bks., Inc.

Rosenthal, Amy Krouse. I Wish You More. Lichtenheld, Tom, illus. 2015. (ENG.). 40p. (J). (gr. k-3). 14.99 (978-1-4521-2699-9(2)) Chronicle Bks. LLC.

—Little Pea. Corace, Jen, illus. 2015. (ENG.). 32p. (J). (gr. -1-k). bds. 7.99 (978-1-4521-4289-0(0)) Chronicle Bks. LLC.

—Wumbers. Lichtenheld, Tom, illus. 2015. (ENG.). 40p. (J). (gr. k-3). 7.99 (978-1-4521-4122-0(3)) Chronicle Bks. LLC.

Ross, Mandy & Ladybird Books Staff. Little Red Riding Hood. 2015. (First Favourite Tales Ser.). (ENG., Illus.). 32p. (J). (-k). 7.99 (978-1-4093-0631-3(3)) Penguin Bks., Ltd. GBR. Dist: Independent Pubs. Group.

Ross, Melanie H. & Willis, Jeanne. Mayfly Day. Ross, Tony, illus. 2012. (ENG.). 32p. (J). (gr. -1-k). pap. 10.99 (978-1-84270-606-0(3)) Andersen Pr. GBR. Dist: Independent Pubs. Group.

Ross, Thea. Lucy Loves Winter. 2004. 16p. (J). bds. 4.99 (978-1-59384-077-8(2)) Parklane Publishing.

Ross, Tony. Goldilocks & the Three Bears. 2016. (ENG., Illus.). 10p. (J). (-k). ring bd. 9.99 (978-1-78344-409-0(6)) Andersen Pr. GBR. Dist: Independent Pubs. Group.

Ross, Tony & Ross, Tony. Goldilocks & the Three Bears. 40th ed. 2017. (ENG., Illus.). 32p. (J). (-k). 14.99 (978-1-78344-469-4(X)) Andersen Pr. GBR. Dist: Independent Pubs. Group.

Rosselson, Leon. Tom the Whistling Wonder. Haslam, John, illus. 2005. (ENG.). 24p. (J). lib. bdg. 23.65 (978-1-59646-758-3(4)) Dingles & Co.

Roth, Anthony H. Little Anthony Doesn't Want to Eat His Dinner. 2012. 26p. 24.95 (978-1-4626-5776-6(1)) America Star Bks.

Roth, Carol. Five Little Ducklings Go to School. Julian, Sean, illus. 2015. (ENG.). 32p. (J). (gr. -1-2). 17.95 (978-0-7358-4132-1(2)) North-South Bks., Inc.

—The Little School Bus. Paparone, Pamela, illus. 2004. (ENG.). 32p. (J). (gr. k-1). pap. 7.95 (978-0-7358-1905-4(X)) North-South Bks., Inc.

—Where's My Mommy? Julian, Sean, illus. 2012. (ENG.). 32p. (J). 17.95 (978-0-7358-4032-4(6)) North-South Bks., Inc.

Roth, Carol & Julian, Sean. Five Little Ducklings Go to Bed. 2013. (Illus.). 32p. (J). pap. (978-0-7358-4153-6(5)) North-South Bks., Inc.

Roth, Jurgen Philip Philip Philip Kevin Kevin P Geneen Philip Philip Philip Marie, Carol. Little Bunny's Sleepless Night. Gorbachev, Valeri, illus. 2013. (ENG.). 40p. (J). (gr. -1-2). 17.95 (978-0-7358-4123-9(3)) North-South Bks., Inc.

Roth, Sarra J. Not the Quitting Kind. Bishop, Tracy, illus. 2014. 32p. pap. 16.99 (978-1-4413-1415-4(6)) Peter Pauper Pr. Inc.

Rowand, Phyllis. It Is Night. Dronzek, Laura, illus. 2014. (ENG.). 32p. (J). (gr. -1-3). 16.99 (978-0-06-225024-7(8), Greenwillow Bks.) HarperCollins Pubs.

Rowe, Thereza. Hearts. Rowe, Thereza, illus. 2014. (ENG., Illus.). 32p. (J). (gr. -1-3). 12.95 (978-1-935179-59-7(4)) TOON Books / RAW Junior, LLC.

Rowland, Lucy. The Birthday Invitation. Hughes, Laura, illus. 2017. (ENG.). 32p. (J). 16.99 (978-1-4088-6298-8(0), 9781408862988, Bloomsbury USA Childrens) Bloomsbury Publishing USA.

—Pirate Pete & His Smelly Feet. Chambers, Mark, illus. 2017. (ENG.). 32p. (J). (gr. -1-1). 16.99 (978-1-5098-1776-4(X)) Pan Macmillan GBR. Dist: Independent Pubs. Group.

Roy, Philip. Jellybean Mouse. Torrey Balsara, Andrea, illus. 2014. (ENG.). 32p. 11.95 (978-1-55380-344-7(2)) Ronsdale Pr. CAN. Dist: SPD-Small Pr. Distribution.

Roy, Ronald. Turkey Trouble on the National Mall. 2012. (Capital Mysteries Ser.: 14). lib. bdg. 14.75 (978-0-606-26809-7(X), Turtleback) Turtleback Bks.

Rozelaar, Angie, illus. Hello School. 2016. (Hello! Ser.). (ENG.). 10p. (J). (gr. -1-k). 15.99 (978-1-4472-6693-8(5)) Pan Macmillan GBR. Dist: Independent Pubs. Group.

Rubin, Adam. Big Bad Bubble. Salmieri, Daniel, illus. 2017. (ENG.). 40p. (J). (gr. -1-3). pap. 7.99 (978-0-544-92782-7(6), HMH Books For Young Readers) Houghton Mifflin Harcourt Publishing Co.

—Big Bad Bubble. Salmieri, Daniel, illus. 2017. (ENG.). (J). (gr. -1-3). lib. bdg. 18.40 (978-0-606-39829-9(5)) Turtleback Bks.

Rubin, Adam. Those Darn Squirrels Fly South. Salmieri, Daniel, illus. 2015. (ENG.). 32p. (J). (gr. -1-3). 7.99 (978-0-544-55545-7(7), HMH Books For Young Readers) Houghton Mifflin Harcourt Publishing Co.

Rubino, Michael. Bang! How We Came to Be. 2011. (ENG.). 69p. (J). (gr. 4-7). pap. 17.00 (978-1-61614-472-2(6)) Prometheus Bks., Pubs.

Rubow, Carol. God Loves You. 2010. (Illus.). 32p. (J). (gr. -1). 12.99 (978-0-7586-1855-9(7)) Concordia Publishing Hse.

—God Loves You Mini Book. 2010. 32p. (J). (gr. -1). pap. 2.49 (978-0-7586-1856-6(5)) Concordia Publishing Hse.

Rue, Leonard Lee. Wolves - Pb: A Portrait of the Animal World. 2013. (Portrait of the Animal World Ser.). (Illus.). 80p. pap. 9.95 (978-1-59764-326-9(2)) New Line Bks.

Ruiz, John. The Squirrel, the Eagle & the Red Hawk. 2012. 32p. pap. 21.99 (978-1-4691-7970-4(9)) Xlibris Corp.

Rumi. Two Parrots. Rashin, illus. 2014. (ENG.). 32p. (J). (gr. k-3). 17.95 (978-0-7358-4171-0(3), 9780735841710) North-South Bks., Inc.

Runnells, Treesha. Forest Friends: A Fold-Out Fun Book. Runnells, Treesha, illus. 2005. (Fold-Out Fun Ser.). (Illus.). 10p. (J). 4.95 (978-1-58117-275-1(3), Intervisual/Piggy Toes) Bendon, Inc.

—Safari Friends: Fold-Out Fun. Runnells, Treesha, illus. 2005. (Fold-Out Fun Ser.). (Illus.). 10p. (J). 4.95 (978-1-58117-276-8(1), Intervisual/Piggy Toes) Bendon, Inc.

Russell, Natalie. Donkey's Busy Day. Russell, Natalie, illus. 2009. (ENG., Illus.). 32p. (J). (gr. k-k). pap. 11.95 (978-0-7475-9547-2(X)) Bloomsbury Publishing Plc GBR. Dist: Independent Pubs. Group.

—Home Sweet Hamish. 2008. (Bloomsbury Paperbacks Ser.). (ENG., Illus.). 32p. (J). (gr. -1-2). pap. 10.95 (978-0-7475-8319-6(6)) Bloomsbury Publishing Plc GBR. Dist: Independent Pubs. Group.

Russo, Marisabina. The Bunnies Are Not in Their Beds. Russo, Marisabina, illus. 2013. (ENG., Illus.). 40p. (J). (gr. -1-2). pap. 7.99 (978-0-307-98126-4(6), Dragonfly Bks.) Random Hse. Children's Bks.

—Little Bird Takes a Bath. 2015. (ENG., Illus.). 40p. (J). (gr. -1-2). 16.99 (978-0-385-37014-1(8), Schwartz & Wade Bks.) Random Hse. Children's Bks.

Rustrian, Edvin E. The Adventures of Timmy & Jay. 2010. 24p. pap. 15.99 (978-1-4535-3792-3(9)) Xlibris Corp.

Ryan, Darlene & Manchester, Peter. Kisses, Kisses, Kisses. 2004. (Illus.). 24p. (J). (978-1-55131-092-3(9)) Univ. of New Brunswick, Dept. of Graphic Services.

Ryder, Joanne. Won't You Be My Kissaroo? Sweet, Melissa, illus. 2015. (ENG.). 40p. (J). (gr. -1 — 1). pap. 6.99 (978-0-15-205820-3(6), HMH Books For Young Readers) Houghton Mifflin Harcourt Publishing Co.

Rylant, Cynthia. Let's Go Home: The Wonderful Things about a House. Halperin, Wendy Anderson, illus. 2005. (ENG.). 32p. (J). (gr. -1-3). 7.99 (978-1-4169-0839-5(0), Simon & Schuster Bks. For Young Readers) Simon & Schuster Bks. For Young Readers.

—The Stars Will Still Shine. Beeke, Tiphanie, illus. 2005. (ENG.). 40p. (J). (gr. -1-3). 17.99 (978-0-06-054639-7(5)) HarperCollins Pubs.

Ryski, Dawid. My Four Seasons. 2017. (ENG., Illus.). 32p. (J). (gr. -1-3). 19.95 (978-3-89955-784-8(0)) Die Gestalten Verlag DEU. Dist: Penguin Random Hse. LLC.

Sabatier-Morel, Francoise & Pellegrini, Isabelle. Marie from Paris. Camcam, Princesse, illus. 2014. (AV2 Fiction Readalong Ser.: Vol. 131). (ENG.). 32p. (J). (gr. -1-3). lib. bdg. 34.28 (978-1-4896-2262-4(4), AV2 by Weigl) Weigl Pubs., Inc.

SACHS, Andrew. Teddybear Tales. 2013. (ENG., Illus.). 32p. (J). (gr. -1-1). 5.99 (978-1-84322-811-0(4), Armadillo) Anness Publishing GBR. Dist: National Bk. Network.

Sadler, Marilyn. Ten Eggs in a Nest. Fleming, Michael, illus. 2014. (Bright & Early Books(R) Ser.). (ENG.). 48p. (J). (gr. -1-2). 9.99 (978-0-449-81082-8(8)); lib. bdg. 13.99 (978-0-375-97151-8(3)) Random Hse. Children's Bks. (Random Hse. Bks. for Young Readers).

Sadler, Marilyn & Comstock, Eric. Charlie Piechart & the Case of the Missing Hat. Comstock, Eric, illus. 2016. (Charlie Piechart Ser.). (Illus.). 40p. (J). (gr. -1-3). 17.99 (978-0-06-237056-3(1), Tegen, Katherine Bks) HarperCollins Pubs.

Safran, Sheri. Let's Dress! Fuller, Rachel, illus. 2011. (ENG.). 20p. (J). (gr. -1-2). 18.99 (978-1-85707-725-4(3)) Tango Bks. GBR. Dist: Independent Pubs. Group.

Sage, Molly. At the Beach. Sage, Molly, illus. 2007. (ENG., Illus.). 6p. (J). (gr. k — 1). 6.99 (978-1-85602-497-6(0)) Pavilion Bks. GBR. Dist: Independent Pubs. Group.

Saillard, Remi, illus. Funny Machines for George the Sheep: A Children's Book Inspired by Leonardo Da Vinci. 2014. (ENG.). 32p. (J). (gr. -1-3). 14.95 (978-3-7913-7166-5(5)) Prestel Verlag GmbH & Co KG. DEU. Dist: Penguin Random Hse. LLC.

Sakai, Komako. Emily's Balloon. 2015. (ENG., Illus.). 44p. (J). (gr. -1-7). pap. 7.99 (978-1-4521-4567-9(9)) Chronicle Bks. LLC.

Sakmar-Sullivan, Eva M. Willie the Taxi Cat, 1 vol. 2013. (ENG., Illus.). 32p. (J). 16.99 (978-0-7643-4436-7(6), 9780764344367) Schiffer Publishing, Ltd.

Sala, Laurenne. You Made Me a Mother. Glasser, Robin Preiss, illus. 2016. 32p. (J). (gr. -1-3). 15.99 (978-0-06-235886-8(3)) HarperCollins Pubs.

Salisbury, Mark. Walt Disney's Alice in Wonderland: An Illustrated Journey Through Time. 2016. (Disney Editions Deluxe Ser.). (ENG., Illus.). 176p. pap. 29.99 (978-1-4847-3769-9(5), Disney Editions) Disney Pr.

Saltzberg, Barney. Tea with Grandpa. Saltzberg, Barney, illus. 2014. (ENG., Illus.). 40p. (J). (gr. -1-2). 15.99 (978-1-59643-894-1(0), 9781596438941) Roaring Brook Pr.

Salwi, Dilip. Meet the Four Elements (English) 2nd ed. 2013. (ENG.). 64p. (J). (gr. 4-6). pap. 6.95 (978-81-8332-876-0(8)) Ratna, Sagar Pvt. Ltd. IND. Dist: Midpoint Trade Bks., Inc.

—Meet the Four Elements (Hindi) 2nd ed. 2013. (ENG.). 64p. (J). (gr. 4-6). pap. 6.95 (978-81-8332-878-4(4)) Ratna, Sagar Pvt. Ltd. IND. Dist: Midpoint Trade Bks., Inc.

—Meet the Four Elements (Marathi) 2nd ed. 2013. (ENG.). 64p. pap. 6.95 (978-93-5036-121-4(3)) Ratna, Sagar Pvt. Ltd. IND. Dist: Midpoint Trade Bks., Inc.

Salzano, Tammi. One Little Blueberry. Whelan, Kat, illus. 2011. (ENG.). 22p. (J). (gr. -1-k). 12.95 (978-1-58925-859-4(2)) Tiger Tales.

—One Rainy Day. Wood, Hannah, illus. 2011. (ENG.). 24p. (J). (gr. -1-k). bds. 8.95 (978-1-58925-860-0(6)) Tiger Tales.

Sammarco, Teresa "T". The What If Book. Curley, Carol, illus. 2013. (J). lib. bdg. 16.95 (978-1-59598-236-0(1)) HenschelHAUS Publishing.

Samoun, Abigail. How Iguana Says I Love You! Watts, Sarah, illus. 2016. (Little Traveler Ser.). (ENG & MUL.). 22p. (J). (gr. -1-k). bds. 6.95 (978-1-4549-1813-4(6)) Sterling Publishing Co., Inc.

—How Monkey Says My Name Is! Watts, Sarah, illus. 2016. (Little Traveler Ser.). (ENG & MUL.). 22p. (J). (gr. -1-k). bds. 6.95 (978-1-4549-1814-1(4)) Sterling Publishing Co., Inc.

Sams, Carl R., II & Stoick, Jean, photos by. Lost in the Woods: A Photographic Fantasy. 2004. (ENG., Illus.). 48p. (J). 19.95 (978-0-9671748-8-4(0)) Sams, II, Carl R. Photography, Inc.

Samuil, Marshak. Baggage. 2012. (ENG., Illus.). 12p. 12.95 (978-0-87070-842-8(2)) Museum of Modern Art.

Sancton, Sylvaine. Some Birds ..., 1 vol. Sancton, Sylvaine, photos by. 2013. (ENG., Illus.). 40p. (J). (gr. k-3). pap. 14.99 (978-1-4556-1863-7(2)) Pelican Publishing Co., Inc.

Sandall, Ellie. Daisy Plays Hide-and-Seek. Sandall, Ellie, illus. (ENG., Illus.). 32p. (J). (gr. -1-k). 2012. pap. 8.99 (978-1-4052-5457-1(2)) 2011. 17.99 (978-1-4052-5419-9(X)) Egmont Bks., Ltd. GBR. Dist: Independent Pubs. Group.

Sandburg, Carl. The Wedding Procession of the Rag Doll & the Broom Handle & Who Was in It. Pincus, Harriet, illus. 2017. (ENG.). 32p. 16.95 (978-0-486-81585-5(4)) Dover Pubns., Inc.

Sandu, Anca. The Astonishing Case of the Stolen Stories. 2015. (ENG., Illus.). 32p. (J). (-k). pap. 9.99 (978-1-78008-034-5(4)) Transworld Publishers Ltd. GBR. Dist: Independent Pubs. Group.

Santamaria, Jenni Currie & Keyes, Joan Ross. Content Areas for Kids: Accelerates Academic Language Development. 2nd ed. 2012. (ENG., Illus.). 200p. pap. 26.19 (978-0-19-401775-6(3)) Oxford Univ. Pr., Inc.

Santamaria, Jenni Currie, et al. Oxford Picture Dictionary Content Areas for Kids. 2nd ed. 2012. (ENG., Illus.). 376p. tchr. ed., spiral bd. 64.31 (978-0-19-401780-0(X)) Oxford Univ. Pr., Inc.

Santore, Charles. A Stowaway on Noah's Ark. 2015. (ENG., Illus.). 56p. (J). (gr. -1). 17.95 (978-1-60433-543-9(2), Applesauce Pr.) Cider Mill Pr. Bk. Pubs., LLC.

—William the Curious: Knight of the Water Lilies. Santore, Charles, illus. 2014. (ENG., Illus.). 44p. (J). (gr. -1). 16.95 (978-1-60433-474-6(6)) Cider Mill Pr. Bk. Pubs., LLC.

Sassi, Laura. Goodnight, Ark, 1 vol. Chapman, Jane, illus. 2015. (ENG.). 24p. (J). bds. 8.99 (978-0-310-74938-7(7)) Zonderkidz.

—Goodnight, Manger, 1 vol. Chapman, Jane, illus. 2015. (ENG.). 32p. (J). 16.99 (978-0-310-74556-3(X)) Zonderkidz.

Sattler, Jennifer. My Friend Moe. 2017. (ENG., Illus.). 22p. (J). (gr. -1 — 1). bds. 7.99 **(978-0-7641-6897-0(5))** Barron's Educational Series, Inc.

Sauer, Cat. Gwendolyn the Ghost. Jankowski, Daniel, illus. l.t. ed. 2006. (Brown Bag Bedtime Bks.: 1). 29p. (J). (gr. -1-2). 16.95 incl. audio compact disk (978-0-9704460-9-1(8)) Writer's Ink. Studios, Inc.

Sauer, Tammi. Caring for Your Lion. Cummings, Troy, illus. 2017. (ENG.). 32p. (J). (gr. -1). 16.95 **(978-1-4549-1609-3(5))** Sterling Publishing Co., Inc.

—Me Want Pet! Shea, Bob, illus. 2012. (ENG.). 40p. (J). (gr. -1-3). 17.99 (978-1-4424-0810-4(3), Simon & Schuster/Paula Wiseman Bks.) Simon & Schuster/Paula Wiseman Bks.

—Your Alien Returns. Fujita, Goro, illus. 2016. (ENG.). 40p. (J). (gr. -1). 14.95 (978-1-4549-1130-2(1)) Sterling Publishing Co., Inc.

Savage, Sarah. Are You a Boy or Are You a Girl? Fisher, Fox, illus. 2017. (ENG.). 32p. (J). 16.95 **(978-1-78592-267-1(X)**, 9045) Kingsley, Jessica Pubs. GBR. Dist: Macmillan Distribution Ltd.

Savage, Stephen. Little Tug. Savage, Stephen, illus. 2015. (ENG., Illus.). 34p. (J). (gr. -1-1). bds. 7.99 (978-1-62672-124-1(6), 9781626721241) Roaring Brook Pr.

Savary, Fabien. Caillou: Que Falta? Tipeo, illus. 2004. (Caillou Ser.).Tr. of What's Missing? (SPA & ENG.). 12p. (J). (gr. -1-17). bds. 4.95 (978-1-58728-349-9(2)) Cooper Square Publishing Llc.

Savary, Fabien & Vadeboncoeur, Isabelle. Caillou: Los Contrarios. Tipeo, illus. 2004. (Caillou Ser.).Tr. of What's the Difference? (SPA & ENG.). 12p. (J). (gr. -1-17). bds. 4.95 (978-1-58728-348-2(4)) Cooper Square Publishing Llc.

Saxby, Claire. Emu. Byrne, Graham, illus. 2015. (ENG.). 32p. (J). (gr. k-3). 16.99 (978-0-7636-7479-3(6)) Candlewick Pr.

Saxon, Victoria. Big Trouble in Little Rodentia. 2016. (Illus.). (J). **(978-1-5182-0883-6(5))** Random House Children's Books.

Sayres, David. Flatland. Emberley, Rebecca, ed. Emberley, Rebecca, illus. 2014. (ENG.). 32p. 18.95 (978-0-9912935-0-6(9)) Two Little Birds Bks.

Scarry, Patsy. Richard Scarry's the Bunny Book. Scarry, Richard, illus. 2015. (Big Golden Book Ser.). (ENG.). 32p. (J). (-k). 9.99 (978-0-385-39090-3(4), Golden Bks.) Random Hse. Children's Bks.

Scarry, Richard. Busy, Busy World. Scarry, Richard, illus. 2015. (ENG., Illus.). 96p. (J). (gr. -1-2). 15.99 (978-0-385-38480-3(7), Golden Bks.) Random Hse. Children's Bks.

—Richard Scarry's Best Bunny Book Ever! Scarry, Richard, illus. 2014. (Little Golden Book Favorites Ser.). (ENG., Illus.). 80p. (J). (-k). 7.99 (978-0-385-38467-4(X), Golden Bks.) Random Hse. Children's Bks.

—Richard Scarry's Best Nursery Tales Ever. 2014. (ENG., Illus.). 72p. (J). (gr. -1-2). 15.99 (978-0-385-37533-7(6), Golden Bks.) Random Hse. Children's Bks.

—Richard Scarry's Cars. 2015. (ENG., Illus.). 24p. (J). (— 1). bds. 4.99 (978-0-385-38926-6(4), Golden Bks.) Random Hse. Children's Bks.

—Richard Scarry's Let's Count with Lowly. 2013. (Richard Scarry's Concept Bks.). (ENG.). 18p. (J). (gr. -1 — 1). bds. 7.99 (978-0-7641-6600-6(X)) Barron's Educational Series, Inc.

—Richard Scarry's Nicky Goes to the Doctor. 2014. lib. bdg. 14.75 (978-0-606-35561-2(8)) Turtleback Bks.

—Richard Scarry's What Do People Do All Day? 2015. (ENG., Illus.). 96p. (J). (gr. -1-2). 15.99 (978-0-553-52059-0(8), Golden Bks.) Random Hse. Children's Bks.

Schaefer, Lola M. An Island Grows. Felstead, Cathie, illus. 2006. (ENG.). 40p. (J). (gr. -1-3). 17.99 (978-0-06-623930-9(3), Greenwillow Bks.) HarperCollins Pubs.

Scharer, Kathrin. All Aboard with Joanna! 2013. (ENG., Illus.). 34p. 16.99 (978-88-97737-09-4(9)) Officina Libraria srl ITA. Dist: National Bk. Network.

Scheffler, Axel, illus. Lizzy the Lamb. 2015. (Buggy Buddies Ser.). (ENG.). 12p. (J). (— 1). bds. 7.99 (978-0-230-75616-8(6)) Pan Macmillan GBR. Dist: Independent Pubs. Group.

—Pip the Puppy. 2015. (Buggy Buddies Ser.). (ENG.). 12p. (J). (— 1). bds. 7.99 (978-0-230-75617-5(4)) Pan Macmillan GBR. Dist: Independent Pubs. Group.

Schertle, Alice. Little Blue Truck Leads the Way. McElmurry, Jill, illus. 2009. (Little Blue Truck Ser.). (ENG.). 40p. (J). (gr. -1-3). 17.99 (978-0-15-206389-4(7)) Houghton Mifflin Harcourt Publishing Co.

—Very Hairy Bear. Phelan, Matt, illus. 2012. lib. bdg. 17.20 (978-0-606-26605-5(4), Turtleback) Turtleback Bks.

Scheyder, S. Jane. One More Thing. Scheyder, Jacob P., illus. 2013. (ENG.). 42p. (J). pap. 7.99 (978-0-9830318-6-4(X)) Andres & Blanton.

Schick-Jacobowitz, Jeannie, et al. A Bit of Applause for Mrs. Claus. 2012. (ENG.). 32p. (J). (-3). 15.99 (978-1-4022-7085-7(2), Sourcebooks Jabberwocky) Sourcebooks, Inc.

Schmidt, Jacqueline. Patchwork Goes under Cover. 2014. (Patchwork Adventures Ser.). (ENG., Illus.). 32p. (J). (gr. -1-2). 17.95 (978-1-57687-717-3(5), powerHouse Bks.) powerHouse Cultural Entertainment, Inc.

Schnee-Bosch, Penny. Mommy Always Comes Back. Bosch, David, illus. 2013. 40p. pap. 13.95 (978-0-9727993-6-2(2)) Athanata Arts, Ltd.

Schneider, Judy. But Not Quite. Weeks, Mary, illus. 2004. (J). 19.95 (978-1-59404-005-4(2)) Peanut Butter Publishing.

Scholastic, Inc. Staff, contrib. by. The World of Harry Potter: Harry Potter Poster Book. 2011. (Illus.). 125p. (J). pap. (978-0-545-31482-4(8)) Scholastic, Inc.

Schomer-Wendel, Gretchen & Schomer, Adam Anthony. All Around Town. 2009. (Becka & the Big Bubble Ser.). (Illus.). 32p. (J). (gr. -1-3). pap. 10.55 (978-1-60754-105-9(X)) Windmill Bks.

School Zone Staff. Big Hidden Pictures & More. 2009. 320p. (J). pap. 12.99 (978-1-60159-258-3(2)) School Zone Publishing Co.

—My First Dot-To-Dots. 2009. (J). pap. 1.50 net. (978-1-60159-246-0(9)) School Zone Publishing Co.

—My First Hidden Pictures. 2009. (J). pap. 2.99 (978-1-60159-251-4(5)) School Zone Publishing Co.

Schotter, Roni. Hanukkah! Hafner, Marylin, illus. 2014. (ENG.). 32p. (J). (gr. -1-3). pap. 7.99 (978-0-316-37028-8(2)) Little, Brown Bks. for Young Readers.

Schuette, Sarah L. Pets All Around: A Spot-It Challenge, 1 vol. 2012. (Spot It Ser.). (ENG.). 32p. (gr. 1-2). lib. bdg. 27.32 (978-1-4296-8713-3(4)) Capstone Press of Coughlan Cos.

—Spot It, Learn It!, 1 vol. 2014. (Spot It, Learn It! Ser.). (ENG.). 32p. (gr. 1-2). lib. bdg. 109.28 (978-1-4765-7920-7(2), Aplus Bks.) Capstone Press of Coughlan Cos.

Schuh, Mari C. Show Me Transportation: My First Picture Encyclopedia, 1 vol. 2012. (My First Picture Encyclopedias Ser.). (ENG., Illus.). 32p. (gr. 1-2). lib. bdg. 27.32 (978-1-4296-8570-2(0)) Capstone Press of Coughlan Cos.

Schulz, Charles. A Charlie Brown Christmas. Running Press Staff, ed. 2010. (ENG., Illus.). 10p. (J). (gr. -1-3). 22.95 (978-0-7624-4004-7(X)) Running Pr. Bk. Pubs.

Schwartz, Joanne. Our Corner Grocery Store. Beingessner, Laura, illus. 2009. (ENG.). 32p. (J). (gr. -1-2). 19.95 (978-0-88776-868-2(7), Tundra Bks.) Tundra Bks. CAN. Dist: Penguin Random Hse. LLC.

Schwarz, Viviane. Counting with Tiny Cat. Schwarz, Viviane, illus. 2017. (ENG., Illus.). 32p. (J). (-k). 14.99 **(978-0-7636-9462-3(2))** Candlewick Pr.

Scieszka, Jon. Math Curse. Smith, Lane, illus. 2011. (J). (gr. 1-4). 29.95 (978-0-545-13458-3(7)) Weston Woods Studios, Inc.

—The True Story of the 3 Little Pigs! Smith, Lane, illus. 25th anniv. ed. 2014. (ENG.). 32p. (J). (gr. k-3). 17.99 (978-0-451-47195-6(4), Viking Books for Young Readers) Penguin Young Readers Group.

Scollon, Bill. The Big Case. 2016. (Step into Reading Level 3 Ser.). lib. bdg. 14.75 (978-0-606-38488-9(X)) Turtleback Bks.

—Disney*Pixar Finding Dory Movie Theater Storybook & Movie Projector. 2016. (Movie Theater Ser.: 1). (ENG.). 32p. (J). (gr. -1-2). 19.99 (978-0-7944-3668-1(4), Reader's Digest Children's Bks.) Studio Fun International.

Scott-Dixon, Valerie. My Fuzzy Wuzzy Hair. 2012. 32p. pap. 24.95 (978-1-4626-6426-9(1)) America Star Bks.

Scott, Foresman and Company Staff. Work & Play, Big & Little, You & Me. (J). 18.82 (978-0-673-21373-0(0), Scott Foresman) Addison Wesley Schl.

Scott, MaryJo. Corduroy's Colors. McCue, Lisa, illus. 2016. (Corduroy Ser.). (ENG.). 14p. (J). (— 1). bds. 5.99 (978-0-451-47247-2(0), Viking Books for Young Readers) Penguin Young Readers Group.

—Corduroy's Shapes. McCue, Lisa, illus. 2016. (Corduroy Ser.). (ENG.). 14p. (J). (— 1). bds. 5.99 (978-0-451-47250-2(0), Viking Books for Young Readers) Penguin Young Readers Group.

Scotton, Rob. Oopsie-Daisy. Scotton, Rob, illus. 2014. (Splat the Cat Ser.). (ENG., Illus.). 24p. (J). (gr. -1-3). pap. 4.99 (978-0-06-211585-0(5), HarperFestival) HarperCollins Pubs.

—Splat the Cat & the Big Secret. Farley, Rick & Eberz, Robert, illus. 2016. (J). **(978-1-4844-8600-9(5))** Publishers Quality Library Service.

—Splat the Cat & the Quick Chicks. Eberz, Robert, illus. 2016. 30p. (J). **(978-1-4844-7139-5(3))** Harper & Row Ltd.

Scotton, Rob. Splat the Cat Takes the Cake. 2012. (Splat the Cat: I Can Read Ser.). (J). lib. bdg. 13.55 (978-0-606-23582-2(5), Turtleback) Turtleback Bks.

Scribens, Sunny, et al. Space Song Rocket Ride. Sim, David, illus. 2014. 32p. (J). (gr. -1-2). 9.99 (978-1-78285-098-4(8)) Barefoot Bks., Inc.

Seabag-Montefiore, Mary. Black Beauty (Picture Book) Marks, Alan, illus. 2008. (Picture Book Classics Ser.). 24p. (J). 9.99 (978-0-7945-2250-6(5), Usborne) EDC Publishing.

Seaworthy, Oscar. Port Side Pirates. 2008. (ENG., Illus.). 32p. (J). 6.99 (978-1-84686-205-2(1)); 9.99 (978-1-84686-153-6(5)) Barefoot Bks., Inc.

Sebe, Masayuki. Let's Count to 100! Sebe, Masayuki, illus. 2011. (ENG., Illus.). 24p. (J). (gr. -1-2). 16.95 (978-1-55453-661-0(8)) Kids Can Pr., Ltd. CAN. Dist: Hachette Bk. Group.

—Let's Count To 100! Sebe, Masayuki, illus. 2014. (ENG., Illus.). 24p. (J). (gr. -1-2). 7.95 (978-1-55453-813-3(0)) Kids Can Pr., Ltd. CAN. Dist: Hachette Bk. Group.

Seder, Rufus Butler. ABC Animals!: a Scanimation Picture Book. 2016. (Scanimation Ser.). (ENG., Illus.). 16p. (J). 16.95 (978-0-7611-7782-1(5)) Workman Publishing Co., Inc.

—Santa! A Scanimation Picture Book. 2013. (Scanimation Ser.). (ENG., Illus.). 24p. (J). (gr. k-12). 14.95 (978-0-7611-7725-8(6), 17725) Workman Publishing Co., Inc.

Segel, Robert G. Machine Gun Inventors: A Military History Coloring Book. Pajot, Lauren, illus. 2016. 16p. 4.95 (978-0-9823918-2-2(X)) Chipotle Publishing, LLC.

Sendak, Maurice. Donde Viven los Monstruos. 2003. (SPA., Illus.). 40p. (J). (gr. k-3). 12.95 (978-84-372-2185-4(4)) Altea, Ediciones, S.A. - Grupo Santillana ESP. Dist: Santillana USA Publishing Co., Inc.

—In the Night Kitchen. 2009. (Illus.). 19.00 (978-0-7569-9298-9(2)) Perfection Learning Corp.

—Where the Wild Things Are. Sendak, Maurice, illus. 25th anniv. ed. 2012. (ENG., Illus.). 48p. (J). (gr. -1-3). 18.95 (978-0-06-025492-6(0)); pap. 8.95 (978-0-06-443178-1(9)) HarperCollins Pubs.

Senior, Olive. Anna Carries Water, 1 vol. James, Laura, illus. 2014. (ENG.). 40p. (J). (gr. k-3). 18.95 (978-1-896580-60-9(2)) Tradewind Bks. CAN. Dist: Orca Bk. Pubs. USA.

Sergeyeva, Marina. Nikki & Nick Are Great Friends to Pick. Sergeyeva, Marina, illus. 2012. (Illus.). 34p. 19.95 (978-0-9834735-4-1(4)) Leo Publishing.

Sermons, Faye. No Ordinary Cat. Becket, Nancy, illus. 2009. 40p. pap. 16.99 (978-1-4389-6242-9(6)) AuthorHouse.

Server, Lee. Lions - Pb: A Portrait of the Animal World. 2013. (Portrait of the Animal World Ser.). (Illus.). 72p. pap. 9.95 (978-1-59764-331-3(9)) New Line Bks.

—Tigers - Pb: A Portrait of the Animal World. 2013. (Portrait of the Animal World Ser.). (Illus.). 72p. pap. 9.95 (978-1-59764-319-1(X)) New Line Bks.

Sesame Workshop, Sesame & McQuillan, Susan. Sesame Street Let's Cook! 2015. (Sesame Street Ser.). (ENG., Illus.). 128p. (gr. -1-k). spiral bd. 17.99 (978-0-544-45436-1(7)) Houghton Mifflin Harcourt Publishing Co.

Seuss, Gerald Mcboing Boing. Crawford, Mel, illus. 2017. (Classic Seuss Ser.). (ENG.). 40p. (J). (gr. k-4). 16.99 **(978-1-5247-1635-6(9))**; lib. bdg. 19.99 **(978-1-5247-1757-5(6))** Random Hse. Children's Bks. (Random Hse. Bks. for Young Readers).

Seuss, Dr. The Cat in the Hat. 2012. (Beginner Books(R) Ser.). (ENG.). 72p. (J). (gr. k-3). 17.99 (978-0-449-81086-6(0), Random Hse. Bks. for Young Readers) Random Hse. Children's Bks.

—The Cat in the Hat Book & Hat. 2012. (Beginner Books Ser.). (ENG.). 72p. (J). (gr. k-3). 24.99 (978-0-307-93044-6(0), Random Hse. Bks. for Young Readers) Random Hse. Children's Bks.

—Gerald McBoing Boing. Seuss, Dr., illus. 2004. (Little Golden Book Ser.). (ENG., Illus.). 24p. (J). (gr. -1-2). 4.99 (978-0-375-82721-1(8), Golden Bks.) Random Hse. Children's Bks.

—Happy Birthday, Baby! Gerardi, Jan, illus. 2009. (Dr. Seuss Nursery Collection). (ENG.). 12p. (J). (— 1). 11.99 (978-0-375-84621-2(2), Random Hse. Bks. for Young Readers) Random Hse. Children's Bks.

—If I Ran the Zoo. 2014. (Classic Seuss Ser.). (ENG., Illus.). 64p. (J). (gr. k-4). 17.99 (978-0-385-37905-2(6), Random Hse. Bks. for Young Readers) Random Hse. Children's Bks.

—The Many Mice of Mr. Brice. McKie, Roy, illus. 2015. (Big Bright & Early Board Book Ser.). (ENG.). 24p. (J). (— 1). bds. 6.99 (978-0-553-49733-5(2), Random Hse. Bks. for Young Readers) Random Hse. Children's Bks.

—Who's Who in the Dr. Seuss Crew, 5 vols., Set. 2013. (ENG.). (J). (gr. k-4). 74.85 (978-0-385-37620-4(0), Random Hse. Bks. for Young Readers) Random Hse. Children's Bks.

—Would You Rather Be a Bullfrog? 2014. (Big Bright & Early Board Book Ser.). (ENG., Illus.). 24p. (J). (— 1). bds. 6.99 (978-0-385-37515-3(8), Random Hse. Bks. for Young Readers) Random Hse. Children's Bks.

Seven, John & Christy, Jana. Happy Punks 1 2 3: A Counting Story. 2013. (ENG., Illus.). 32p. (gr. -1). bds. 15.95 (978-1-933149-67-7(1)) Manic D Pr.

Seyderhelm, Amanda. Isaac & the Red Jumper. Scott, Ann, illus. 2013. 26p. pap. (978-0-9572146-1-3(8)) HARK Pubns.

Shah, Sapna Jaiswal. Sapna Aunty's Hindi Book of Colors: Rang. 2004. (HIN.). (J). 8.00 (978-0-9741686-0-9(2)) 3N Media Group.

Shand, Jennifer. Why Do Tractors Have Such Big Tires? Paiva, Johannah Gilman, ed. Fabbri, Daniele, illus. 2014. (ENG.). 20p. (J). (gr. k-4). 8.99 (978-1-4867-0382-1(8)) Flowerpot Children's Pr. Inc. CAN. Dist: Cardinal Pubs. Group.

Shannon, George. Hands Say Love. Yoo, Taeeun, illus. 2014. (ENG.). 32p. (J). (gr. -1-1). 17.00 (978-0-316-08479-6(4)) Little, Brown Bks. for Young Readers.

Shapur, Mira. Singer & the Paint. Shapur, Fredun, illus. 2017. (ENG.). 32p. (J). 16.95 (978-1-84976-475-9(1)) Tate Publishing, Ltd. GBR. Dist: Abrams, Inc.

Sharpe, Jemima, illus. Mr Moon Wakes Up. 2016. (Child's Play Library). (ENG.). 32p. (J). pap. (978-1-84643-693-2(1)) Child's Play International Ltd.

Sharpe, Katie & Sharpe, Tony. Wake up Sun. 2008. (ENG.). 28p. 14.99 (978-1-4389-2897-5(1)) AuthorHouse.

Sharratt, Nick & Goodhart, Pippa. Little Monster's Day Out with Dad. Sharratt, Nick, illus. 2017. (Little Monster Ser.). (ENG., Illus.). 16p. (J). (gr. -1-k). 9.99 **(978-1-4052-7644-3(4))** Egmont Bks., Ltd. GBR. Dist: Independent Pubs. Group.

Sharratt, Nick & Tucker, Stephen. The Three Little Pigs, 2 vols. Sharratt, Nick, illus. 2016. (Lift-The-Flap Fairy Tales Ser.). (ENG., Illus.). 24p. (J). (gr. -1-k). bds. 11.99 (978-1-5098-1713-9(1)) Pan Macmillan GBR. Dist: Independent Pubs. Group.

Shattil, Wendy, et al, photos by. Sierra Babies. 2013. (Illus.). 26p. (J). 8.95 (978-1-56037-557-9(4)) Farcountry Pr.

Shava, Ryder. Mr. Ramirez Is My Teacher, 01 vols., 1. 2016. (Rosen REAL Readers: Social Studies Nonfiction / Fiction: Family, Community, & the World Ser.). (ENG.). 8p. (J). pap. 5.46 (978-1-5081-1710-0(1), Rosen Classroom) Rosen Publishing Group, Inc., The.

Shaw, Mary. Brady Brady & the Cleanup Hitters. Temple, Chuck, illus. 2008. 32p. (J). pap. (978-1-897169-11-7(6)) Brady Brady, Inc.

Shaw, Nancy E. Sheep in a Shop (board Book) Apple, Margot, illus. 2017. (ENG.). 28p. (J). (— 1). bds. 7.99 **(978-1-328-70286-9(3)**, HMH Books For Young Readers) Houghton Mifflin Harcourt Publishing Co.

Shea, Bob. Dinosaur vs. Bedtime. Shea, Bob, illus. 2011. (Dinosaur vs. Book Ser.). (ENG., Illus.). 30p. (J). (gr. -1-k). bds. 6.99 (978-1-4231-3788-7(4)) Hyperion Pr.

—Dinosaur vs. Santa. Shea, Bob, illus. 2014. (Dinosaur vs. Book Ser.). (ENG., Illus.). 30p. (J). (gr. -1-k). bds. 7.99 (978-1-4231-6824-9(0)) Hyperion Bks. for Children.

Shealy, Dennis. I'm a Bulldozer. 2015. (Little Golden Book Ser.). (ENG., Illus.). 24p. (J). (-k). 3.99 (978-0-553-49683-3(2), Golden Bks.) Random Hse. Children's Bks.

Shealy, Dennis. My Little Golden Book about Dinosaurs. Laberis, Steph, illus. 2017. (Little Golden Book Ser.). (ENG.). 24p. (J). (-k). 4.99 **(978-0-385-37861-1(0)**, Golden Bks.) Random Hse. Children's Bks.

Shealy, Dennis & Little Golden Books Staff. I'm a Monster Truck. Staake, Bob, illus. 2011. (Little Golden Book Ser.). (ENG.). 24p. (J). (gr. -1-2). 4.99 (978-0-375-86132-1(7), Golden Bks.) Random Hse. Children's Bks.

Sheckels, Astrid, illus. Nic & Nellie, 1 vol. 2013. (ENG.). 32p. (J). (gr. 1-4). 17.95 (978-1-934031-52-0(6), 9781934031520) Islandport Pr., Inc.

Sheehan, Peter. Willy Wagtail grows Up. 2010. 32p. pap. 19.99 (978-1-4461-3281-4(1)) Lulu Pr., Inc.

Shepherd, Donna J. Sully's Topsy Tale. Collier, Kevin Scott, illus. 2010. 20p. pap. 10.95 (978-1-61633-047-7(3)) Guardian Angel Publishing, Inc.

Shepherd, Jessica. Grandma. 2014. (Child's Play Library). (ENG., Illus.). 32p. (J). (978-1-84643-602-4(8)) Child's Play International Ltd.

Sheth, Kashmira. Tiger in My Soup, 1 vol. Ebbeler, Jefferey, illus. 2015. (ENG.). 32p. (J). (gr. -1-3). pap. 7.95 (978-1-56145-890-5(2)) Peachtree Pubs.

Shields, Gillian. Cinderella's (Not So) Ugly Sisters: The True Fairy Tale! Delaporte, Bérengère, illus. 2016. (ENG.). 32p. (J). (gr. -1-k). pap. 9.99 (978-1-4050-2162-3(4)) Pan Macmillan GBR. Dist: Independent Pubs. Group.

—When the World Was Waiting for You Baby Book. Currey, Anna, illus. 2013. (ENG.). 32p. (J). (gr. -1-1). 22.99 (978-1-4088-4213-3(0), 9781408842133, Bloomsbury USA Childrens) Bloomsbury Publishing USA.

Shipton, Paul. Clown School. Blake, Beccy, illus. 2005. (ENG.). 24p. (J). lib. bdg. 23.65 (978-1-59646-752-1(5)) Dingles & Co.

Shirin Yim, Bridges. Ruby's Wish. Blackall, Sophie, illus. 2015. (ENG.). 36p. (J). (gr. 3-7). 7.99 (978-1-4521-4569-3(5)) Chronicle Bks. LLC.

Shirley, Alice. The Gentle Lion & the Little Owlet. Shirley, Alice, illus. 2013. Orig. Title: Owlet & Pussycat. (ENG., Illus.). 32p. (J). (gr. -1-k). pap. 8.99 (978-1-84365-199-4(8), Pavilion) Pavilion Bks. GBR. Dist: Independent Pubs. Group.

Shorrock, Claire. Magnus. 2015. (ENG., Illus.). 32p. (J). (gr. -1-k). 16.99 (978-0-7459-6572-7(5)) Lion Hudson PLC GBR. Dist: Independent Pubs. Group.

Short, Robyn & Williams, Nanon McKewn. Peace People. Bailey, Lindsey, illus. 2013. 38p. 18.95 (978-0-9911148-2-5(5)) Goodmedia Communications, LLC.

Shoshan, Beth. That's When I'm Happy. East, Jacqueline, illus. 2011. (978-1-4351-3618-2(7)) Barnes & Noble, Inc.

Shraya, Vivek. The Boy & the Bindi. Perera, Rajni, illus. 2016. (ENG.). 38p. (J). (gr. -1-3). 17.95 (978-1-55152-668-3(9)) Arsenal Pulp Pr. CAN. Dist: Consortium Bk. Sales & Distribution.

Shyba, Jessica. Bathtime with Theo & Beau. 2016. (ENG., Illus.). 40p. (J). 16.99 (978-1-250-05907-9(0), 9781250059079) Feiwel & Friends.

Siddals, Mary McKenna. Compost Stew: An a to Z Recipe for the Earth. Wolff, Ashley, illus. 2014. (ENG.). 40p. (J). (gr. -1-2). 7.99 (978-0-385-75538-2(4), Dragonfly Bks.) Random Hse. Children's Bks.

Sierra, Judy. Mind Your Manners, B. B. Wolf. Seibold, J. Otto, illus. 2012. (ENG.). 40p. (J). (gr. -1-2). pap. 7.99 (978-0-307-93101-6(3), Dragonfly Bks.) Random Hse. Children's Bks.

—Mind Your Manners, B. B. Wolf. 2012. lib. bdg. 18.40 (978-0-606-26784-7(0), Turtleback) Turtleback Bks.

—Suppose You Meet a Dinosaur: a First Book of Manners. Bowers, Tim, illus. 2016. (ENG.). 40p. (J). (gr. -1-2). 7.99 (978-1-101-93250-6(3), Dragonfly Bks.) Random Hse. Children's Bks.

—We Love Our School! Davick, Linda, illus. 2016. (ENG.). 24p. (J). (gr. -1-2). 6.99 (978-1-101-94025-9(5), Dragonfly Bks.) Random Hse. Children's Bks.

Sif, Birgitta. Oliver. Sif, Birgitta, illus. 2012. (ENG., Illus.). 40p. (J). (gr. -1-3). 16.99 *(978-0-7636-6247-9(X))* Candlewick Pr.
Sillett, Devon. The Leaky Story. Tortop, Anil, illus. 2017. (ENG.). 32p. (J). (gr. -1-3). 17.99 *(978-1-925335-39-2(9))*, EK Bks.) Exisle Publishing Pty Ltd. AUS. Dist: Hachette Bk. Group.
Silver Dolphin en Español Editors. Tesoro de Libros de Calcomanías Princesas. 2004. (Disney Calcomanías Ser.). (SPA., Illus.). 72p. (J). pap. *(978-970-718-106-9(0))*, Silver Dolphin en Español) Advanced Marketing, S. de R. L. de C. V.
Silver, Gail. Peace, Bugs, & Understanding: An Adventure in Sibling Harmony. Ly, Youme Nguyen, illus. 2014. (ENG.). 48p. (J). (gr. -1-3). 16.95 *(978-1-937006-63-1(8))*, Plum Blossom Bks.) Parallax Pr.
Silverstein, Shel. Lafcadio, the Lion Who Shot Back. Silverstein, Shel, illus. 2013. (ENG., Illus.). 112p. (J). (gr. -1-3). 16.99 *(978-0-06-025675-3(3))* HarperCollins Pubs.
—Lafcadio, the Lion Who Shot Back. 2009. (CHI., Illus.). (J). *(978-7-5442-4521-0(7))* Nanhai Publishing Co.
Sim, Stephanie. Copycat. 2016. (ENG., Illus.). 32p. (J). (gr. -1-2). 16.95 *(978-1-927018-76-7(5))* Simply Read Bks. CAN. Dist: Ingram Publisher Services.
Simard, Danielle. Little Word Catcher, 1 vol. Côté, Geneviève & Second Story Press Staff, illus. 2008. (ENG.). 32p. (J). (gr. 1-3). 14.95 *(978-1-897187-44-9(0))* Second Story Pr. CAN. Dist: Orca Bk. Pubs. USA.
Simee. Giggles Feel Good, 1 vol. 2010. 18p. pap. 24.95 *(978-1-4489-4878-9(9))* PublishAmerica, Inc.
Simmonds, Posy. Baker Cat. Simmonds, Posy, illus. 2015. (ENG., Illus.). 32p. (J). (gr. -1-k). pap. 11.99 *(978-1-78344-105-1(4))* Andersen Pr. GBR. Dist: Independent Pubs. Group.
—Fred. 2014. (ENG., Illus.). 32p. (J). (-k). pap. 9.99 *(978-1-78344-029-0(5))* Andersen Pr. GBR. Dist: Independent Pubs. Group.
Simms, Albert Clint. My Values & Morales Treasury. 2011. 114p. 32.50 *(978-1-257-16162-1(8))* Lulu Pr., Inc.
Simon, Annette. Robot Zombie Frankenstein! Simon, Annette, illus. 2012. (ENG., Illus.). 40p. (J). (gr. -1-3). 16.99 *(978-0-7636-5124-4(9))* Candlewick Pr.
Simon, Francesca. Gold Medal Games. Ross, Tony, illus. 2017. (Horrid Henry Ser.). (ENG.). 24p. (J). (gr. 1-3). pap. 8.99 ***(978-1-5101-0127-2(6)***, Orion Children's Bks.) Hachette Children's Group GBR. Dist: Hachette Bk. Group.
Simon, Seymour. Water. 2017. 40p. (J). (gr. 1-5). pap. 6.99 ***(978-0-06-247054-6(X))*** HarperCollins Pubs.
Simont, Marc. The Stray Dog. Simont, Marc, illus. 2003. (ENG., Illus.). 32p. (J). (gr. -1-3). pap. 6.99 *(978-0-06-443669-4(1))* HarperCollins Pubs.
Simpson, Caroll. The First Beaver, 1 vol. Simpson, Caroll, illus. 2015. (Coastal Spirit Tales Ser.). (ENG., Illus.). 32p. (J). (gr. k-3). pap. 12.95 ***(978-1-77203-062-4(7))*** Heritage Hse. CAN. Dist: Orca Bk. Pubs. USA.
Sims, Lesley & Sims, Lesley. Stories from Around the World for Children. 2013. (Picture Bks). 128p. (J). ring bd. 18.99 *(978-0-7945-3210-9(1))*, Usborne) EDC Publishing.
Singh, Lee. ABC & Do. Wall, Karen, illus. 2013. (ENG.). 24p. (J). (gr. -1-k). 19.99 *(978-1-4052-6532-4(9))* Egmont Bks., Ltd. GBR. Dist: Independent Pubs. Group.
Sís, Peter. Fire Truck. Sís, Peter, illus. 2004. (ENG., Illus.). 28p. (J). (gr. -1-1). bds. 6.99 *(978-0-06-056259-5(5))*, Greenwillow Bks.) HarperCollins Pubs.
Sisler, Celeste. Legend of the NeverBeast - Fawn's Field Guide: A Reusable Sticker Book. 2015. (ENG., Illus.). 12p. (J). (gr. -1-3). pap. 6.99 *(978-0-316-28355-7(X))* Little, Brown Bks. for Young Readers.
Sitzenstock, Gabriele. Raising Puppy. 2006. (J). spiral bd. 12.95 *(978-1-59872-721-0(4))* Instant Pub.
Sixtus, Albert. Rabbit School: A Light-Hearted Tale. Freischlad, Roland, tr. from GER. Koch-Gotha, Fritz, illus. 2009. (ENG.). 32p. (J). (gr. -1-2). 14.95 *(978-1-56792-383-4(6))* Godine, David R. Pub.
Skewes, John. Larry Loves Boston! 2016. (Larry Gets Lost Ser.). (ENG., Illus.). 20p. (J). (— 1). pap. 9.99 *(978-1-63217-047-7(7))*, Little Bigfoot) Sasquatch Bks.
—Larry Loves Washington, DC! 2016. (Larry Gets Lost Ser.). (ENG., Illus.). 20p. (J). (— 1). pap. 9.99 *(978-1-63217-048-4(5))*, Little Bigfoot) Sasquatch Bks.
Skewes, John & Fox, Andrew. Larry Gets Lost in Prehistoric Times: From Dinosaurs to the Stone Age. Skewes, John, illus. 2013. (Larry Gets Lost Ser.). (ENG., Illus.). 32p. (J). (gr. -1-2). 16.99 *(978-1-57061-862-8(3))*, Little Bigfoot) Sasquatch Bks.
Skorpen, Liesel Moak. Outside My Window. Mayer, Mercer, illus. 2004. 32p. (J). (gr. -1-3). 16.89 *(978-0-06-050775-6(6))* HarperCollins Pubs.
Slade, Suzanne. The House That George Built. Bond, Rebecca, illus. 2015. (ENG.). 32p. (J). (gr. 1-4). pap. 7.95 *(978-1-58089-263-6(9))* Charlesbridge Publishing, Inc.
Slate, Joseph. Miss Bindergarten Stays Home from Kindergarten. Wolff, Ashley, illus. 2004. (ENG.). 48p. (J). (gr. -1-k). reprint ed. pap. 6.99 *(978-0-14-230127-2(2))*, Puffin Books) Penguin Young Readers Group.
Slater, Kate. Magpie's Treasure. Slater, Kate, illus. 2012. (ENG., Illus.). 32p. (J). (gr. -1 — 1). pap. 10.99 *(978-1-84939-075-0(4))* Andersen Pr. GBR. Dist: Independent Pubs. Group.
Slavin, Bill. Who Broke the Teapot?! 2016. (ENG., Illus.). 32p. (J). (gr. -1-2). 16.99 *(978-1-77049-833-4(8))*, Tundra Bks.) Tundra Bks. CAN. Dist: Penguin Random Hse. LLC.
Slegers, Liesbet. Happy Halloween! Slegers, Liesbet, illus. 2011. (ENG., Illus.). 32p. (J). (gr. -1-k). 15.95 *(978-1-60537-101-6(7))* Cobblestone Publishing Co.
Slobodkin, Louis & Slobodkin, Florence. Too Many Mittens / a Good Place to Hide / the Little Mermaid Who Could Not Sing. 2017. (Dover Children's Classics Ser.). (ENG., Illus.). 112p. (J). pap. 14.99 *(978-0-486-81588-6(9))* Dover Pubns., Inc.
Smale, Denise L. What If the Sun Didn't Rise. Smale, Denise L. & Blowars, Ryan, illus. 2011. 32p. pap. 24.95 *(978-1-4560-5032-0(X))* America Star Bks.
Smallman, Steve. Bear's Big Bottom, 1 vol. Yarlett, Emma, illus. 2014. (ENG.). 32p. (gr. -1-2). 14.95 *(978-1-62370-118-5(X))* Capstone Young Readers of Coughlan Cos.
Smart, Jamie. Where's the Doctor? 2017. (ENG., Illus.). 40p. (YA). pap. 9.99 *(978-1-4059-0904-4(8))*, 9781405909044) Penguin Bks., Ltd. GBR. Dist: Diamond Comic Distributors, Inc.
Smith, A. J. Even Monsters... 2014. (ENG., Illus.). 32p. (J). (-3). 16.99 *(978-1-4022-8652-0(X))*, 9781402286520, Sourcebooks Jabberwocky) Sourcebooks, Inc.
Smith, Alex T. Claude All at Sea. 2017. (Claude Ser.). (ENG., Illus.). 32p. (J). (gr. -1-k). pap. 6.99 ***(978-1-4449-0368-3(3))*** Hachette Children's Group GBR. Dist: Hachette Bk. Group.
Smith, Brendan Powell. The Christmas Story: The Brick Bible for Kids. 2012. (ENG., Illus.). 32p. (J). (gr. -1-k). 12.95 *(978-1-62087-173-7(4))*, 620173, Sky Pony Pr.) Skyhorse Publishing Co., Inc.
Smith Bresciani, Cathleen & Eldredge, Richard. Sassafrass Jones & the Search for a Forever Home. 2013. 54p. 24.99 *(978-0-578-12084-3(4))* Misfit Mouse.
Smith, Lane. Abe Lincoln's Dream. Smith, Lane, illus. 2012. (ENG., Illus.). 32p. (J). (gr. k-4). 16.99 *(978-1-59643-608-4(5))*, 9781596436084) Roaring Brook Pr.
Smith, Lesley, et al. Brer Rabbit & the Great Race. 2014. (ENG., Illus.). 24p. (J). pap. 6.95 *(978-1-84135-963-2(7))* Award Pubns. Ltd. GBR. Dist: Parkwest Pubns., Inc.
Smith, Linda. Smith Picture Book. Date not set. (Illus.). 32p. (J). (gr. -1-3). 5.99 *(978-0-06-443621-2(7))* HarperCollins Pubs.
Smith, Lori Joy. The Good Morning Book. 2017. (ENG., Illus.). 24p. (J). (gr. -1-k). 12.95 *(978-1-77229-004-2(1))* Simply Read Bks. CAN. Dist: Ingram Publisher Services.
—The Goodnight Book. 2014. (ENG., Illus.). 24p. (J). (gr. -1-k). 12.95 *(978-1-927018-42-2(0))*, 9781927018422) Simply Read Bks. CAN. Dist: Ingram Publisher Services.
Smith, Mike. Catch the Cuddle. 2015. (ENG., Illus.). 18p. (J). (gr. -1-k). pap. 11.99 *(978-1-4052-7190-5(6))* Egmont Bks., Ltd. GBR. Dist: Independent Pubs. Group.
Smith, Nikki. Five Little Speckled Frogs Activity Guide. 2010. 66p. pap. 10.00 *(978-0-557-36823-5(5))* Lulu Pr., Inc.
Smith, Sarah. The Butterfly House. 2014. (ENG., Illus.). 32p. (gr. -1-3). 19.95 *(978-1-84976-205-2(8))* Tate Publishing, Ltd. GBR. Dist: Abrams, Inc.
—Home & Dry. Smith, Sarah, illus. 2016. (Child's Play Library). (ENG., Illus.). 32p. (J). pap. *(978-1-84643-756-4(3))* Child's Play International Ltd.
Smith, Sherri. Where's the Baby??? 2012. (ENG.). 39p. pap. 11.95 *(978-1-4327-9609-9(7))* Outskirts Pr., Inc.
Smith, Suzanne & Taylor, Lindsay. Doodle Girl & the Monkey Mystery. Mauri, Marnie, illus. 2016. (ENG.). 32p. (J). pap. 9.99 *(978-1-4711-2318-4(9))*, Simon & Schuster Children's) Simon & Schuster, Ltd. GBR. Dist: Simon & Schuster, Inc.
Smothers, Ethel Footman. Auntee Edna. Clay, Wil, illus. 2004. 32p. (J). pap. 8.00 *(978-0-8028-5246-5(7))*; 16.00 *(978-0-8028-5154-3(1))* Eerdmans, William B. Publishing Co.
Snow White & Rose Red. 2016. (Ladybird Tales Ser.). (ENG., Illus.). 48p. (J). (gr. k-2). 9.99 *(978-0-7232-9447-4(X))* Penguin Bks., Ltd. GBR. Dist: Independent Pubs. Group.
Sobel, June. The Goodnight Train (lap Board Book) Huliska-Beith, Laura, illus. 2017. (ENG.). 30p. (J). (— 1). bds. 12.99 ***(978-1-328-76438-6(9)***, HMH Books For Young Readers) Houghton Mifflin Harcourt Publishing Co.
Sobrino, Javier. Me Gusta. Villamuza, Noemí, tr. Villamuza, Noemí, illus. (SPA.). 28p. 20.99 *(978-84-88342-35-5(7))* S.A. Kokinos ESP. Dist: Lectorum Pubns., Inc.
Sofer, Barbara. Ilan Ramon: Israel's First Astronaut. 2004. (General Jewish Interest Ser.). (J). pap. 6.95 *(978-0-929371-49-8(6))* Lerner Publishing Group.
—Shabbat Shalom: Israel's First Astronaut. 2004. (Illus.). 12p. (J). 16.95 *(978-0-930494-91-9(1))*, Kar-Ben Publishing) Lerner Publishing Group.
Sollinger, Emily. Dinotrux to the Rescue! 2016. (Dinotrux Passport Reading Level 1 Ser.). (J). lib. bdg. 13.55 *(978-0-606-38320-2(4))* Turtleback Bks.
—Dinotrux: Where Is the Water? 2017. (Passport to Reading Level 1 Ser.). (ENG., Illus.). 32p. (J). (gr. -1-3). pap. 4.99 *(978-0-316-26090-9(8))* Little, Brown Bks. for Young Readers.
Sommer, Carl. Can You Help Me Find My Smile? Budwine, Greg, illus. 2003. (Another Sommer-Time Story Ser.). (ENG.). 48p. (J). (gr. 1-4). 16.95 incl. audio compact disk *(978-1-57537-507-6(9))* Advance Publishing, Inc.
—I Am a Lion! 2003. (Another Sommer-Time Story Ser.). (Illus.). 48p. (J). (gr. k-4). lib. bdg. 23.95 incl. audio *(978-1-57537-759-9(4))* Advance Publishing, Inc.
—I Am a Lion! Budwine, Greg, illus. 2003. (Another Sommer-Time Story Ser.). (ENG.). 48p. (J). (gr. k-4). lib. bdg. 23.95 incl. audio compact disk *(978-1-57537-709-4(8))* Advance Publishing, Inc.
—I Am a Lion! 2003. (Another Sommer-Time Story Ser.). (Illus.). 48p. (J). (gr. 1-4). 16.95 incl. audio *(978-1-57537-558-8(3))* Advance Publishing, Inc.
—I Am a Lion! Budwine, Greg, illus. 2003. (Another Sommer-Time Story Ser.). (ENG.). 48p. (J). (gr. 1-4). 16.95 incl. audio compact disk *(978-1-57537-509-0(5))* Advance Publishing, Inc.
—If Only I Were... 2003. (Another Sommer-Time Story Ser.). (Illus.). 48p. (J). (gr. 1-4). 16.95 incl. audio *(978-1-57537-551-9(6))* Advance Publishing, Inc.
—If Only I Were... James, Kennon, illus. 2003. (Another Sommer-Time Story Ser.). (ENG.). 48p. (J). 16.95 incl. audio compact disk *(978-1-57537-502-1(8))* Advance Publishing, Inc.
—King of the Pond. 2003. (Another Sommer-Time Story Ser.). (Illus.). 48p. (J). (gr. k-4). lib. bdg. 23.95 incl. audio *(978-1-57537-766-7(7))*; (gr. 1-4). 16.95 incl. audio *(978-1-57537-565-6(6))* Advance Publishing, Inc.
—King of the Pond. Budwine, Greg, illus. 2003. (Another Sommer-Time Story Ser.). (ENG.). 48p. (J). (gr. k-4). lib. bdg. 23.95 incl. audio compact disk *(978-1-57537-716-2(0))*; (gr. 1-4). 16.95 incl. audio compact disk *(978-1-57537-516-8(8))* Advance Publishing, Inc.
—Light Your Candle. 2003. (Another Sommer-Time Story Ser.). (Illus.). 48p. (J). (gr. k-4). lib. bdg. 23.95 incl. audio compact disk *(978-1-57537-768-1(3))*; 16.95 incl. audio *(978-1-57537-567-0(2))* Advance Publishing, Inc.
—Light Your Candle. James, Kennon, illus. 2003. (Another Sommer-Time Story Ser.). 48p. (J). (ENG.). 16.95 incl. audio compact disk *(978-1-57537-518-2(4))*; lib. bdg. 23.95 incl. audio compact disk *(978-1-57537-718-6(7))* Advance Publishing, Inc.
—The Little Red Train. 2003. (Another Sommer-Time Story Ser.). (Illus.). 48p. (J). (gr. k-4). lib. bdg. 23.95 incl. audio *(978-1-57537-764-3(0))* Advance Publishing, Inc.
—The Little Red Train. James, Kennon, illus. 2003. (Another Sommer-Time Story Ser.). (ENG.). 48p. (J). (gr. k-3). 16.95 incl. audio compact disk *(978-1-57537-014-9(X))*; lib. bdg. 23.95 incl. audio compact disk *(978-1-57537-714-8(4))* Advance Publishing, Inc.
—The Little Red Train. 2003. (Another Sommer-Time Story Ser.). (Illus.). 48p. (J). (gr. 1-4). 16.95 incl. audio compact disk *(978-1-57537-514-4(1))*; 16.95 incl. audio *(978-1-57537-563-2(X))* Advance Publishing, Inc.
—Mayor for a Day. 2003. (Another Sommer-Time Story Ser.). (Illus.). 48p. (J). (gr. 1-4). 16.95 incl. audio *(978-1-57537-562-5(1))* Advance Publishing, Inc.
—Mayor for a Day. Westbrook, Dick, illus. 2003. (Another Sommer-Time Story Ser.). (ENG.). 48p. (J). (gr. k-4). lib. bdg. 23.95 incl. audio compact disk *(978-1-57537-713-1(6))*; (gr. 1-4). 16.95 incl. audio compact disk *(978-1-57537-513-7(3))* Advance Publishing, Inc.
—No Longer a Dilly Dally, 1 bk. 2003. (Another Sommer-Time Story Ser.). (Illus.). 48p. (J). 16.95 incl. audio *(978-1-57537-550-2(8))* Advance Publishing, Inc.
—No Longer a Dilly Dally, 11 vols. James, Kennon, illus. 2003. (Another Sommer-Time Story Ser.). (ENG.). 48p. (J). (gr. 1-4). 16.95 incl. audio compact disk *(978-1-57537-501-4(X))* Advance Publishing, Inc.
—No One Will Ever Know. Westbrook, Dick, illus. 2003. (Another Sommer-Time Story Ser.). (ENG.). 48p. (J). (gr. 1-4). 16.95 incl. audio compact disk *(978-1-57537-506-9(0))* Advance Publishing, Inc.
—The Sly Fox & the Chicks. 2003. (Another Sommer-Time Story Ser.). (Illus.). 48p. (J). (gr. 1-4). 16.95 incl. audio *(978-1-57537-553-3(2))* Advance Publishing, Inc.
—The Sly Fox & the Chicks. James, Kennon, illus. 2003. (Another Sommer-Time Story Ser.). (ENG.). 48p. (J). 16.95 incl. audio compact disk *(978-1-57537-504-5(4))* Advance Publishing, Inc.
—Tied up in Knots. Budwine, Greg, illus. 2003. (Another Sommer-Time Story Ser.). (ENG.). 48p. (J). 16.95 incl. audio compact disk *(978-1-57537-503-8(6))* Advance Publishing, Inc.
—Tied up in Knots. 2003. (Another Sommer-Time Story Ser.). (Illus.). 48p. (J). (gr. 1-4). 16.95 incl. audio *(978-1-57537-552-6(4))* Advance Publishing, Inc.
—The Ugly Caterpillar. 2003. (Another Sommer-Time Story Ser.). (Illus.). 48p. (J). (gr. 1-4). 16.95 incl. audio *(978-1-57537-564-9(8))* Advance Publishing, Inc.
—The Ugly Caterpillar. Budwine, Greg, illus. 2003. (Another Sommer-Time Story Ser.). 48p. (J). (gr. 1-4). 16.95 incl. audio compact disk *(978-1-57537-515-1(X))* Advance Publishing, Inc.
—You Move You Lose. 2003. (Another Sommer-Time Story Ser.). (Illus.). 48p. (J). (gr. 1-4). 16.95 incl. audio *(978-1-57537-554-0(0))* Advance Publishing, Inc.
—You Move You Lose. James, Kennon, illus. 2003. (Another Sommer-Time Story Ser.). (ENG.). 48p. (J). (gr. 1-4). 16.95 incl. audio compact disk *(978-1-57537-505-2(2))* Advance Publishing, Inc.
—Your Job Is Easy. James, Kennon, illus. 2003. (Another Sommer-Time Story Ser.). (ENG.). 48p. (J). (gr. -1-4). 9.95 *(978-1-57537-018-7(2))*; (gr. 1-4). 16.95 incl. audio compact disk *(978-1-57537-517-5(6))*; (gr. 2-4). lib. bdg. 16.95 *(978-1-57537-067-5(0))* Advance Publishing, Inc.
—Your Job Is Easy. 2003. (Another Sommer-Time Story Ser.). (Illus.). 48p. (J). (gr. 1-4). 16.95 incl. audio *(978-1-57537-566-3(4))* Advance Publishing, Inc.
Sonder, Ben. Parrots: A Portrait of the Animal World. 2012. (Portrait of the Animal World Ser.). (Illus.). 72p. 12.95 *(978-1-59764-270-5(3))* New Line Bks.
—Parrots - Pb: A Portrait of the Animal World. 2013. (Portrait of the Animal World Ser.). (Illus.). 72p. pap. 9.95 *(978-1-59764-330-6(0))* New Line Bks.
Sookocheff, Carey. Solutions for Cold Feet. 2016. (ENG., Illus.). 48p. (J). (gr. -1-3). 16.99 *(978-1-77049-873-0(7))*, Tundra Bks.) Tundra Bks. CAN. Dist: Penguin Random Hse. LLC.
Sornson, Bob. The Juice Box Bully: Empowering Kids to Stand up for Others. 2010. (ENG., Illus.). 32p. (J). (gr. k-5). pap. 10.95 *(978-1-933916-72-9(9))* Early Learning Foundation, LLC.
Space Firsts. (Illus.). (J). (gr. k-5). 119.70 *(978-0-8239-7268-5(2))* Rosen Publishing Group, Inc., The.
Space Missions. (Illus.). (J). (gr. k-5). 119.70 *(978-0-8239-7142-8(2))* Rosen Publishing Group, Inc., The.
Spalding, Andrea. Dance Baby Dance, 1 vol. 2009. (ENG.). 24p. (J). (gr. -1 — 1). bds. 9.95 *(978-1-55469-079-4(X))* Orca Bk. Pubs. USA.
Spalding, Andrea & Scow, Alfred. Secret of the Dance, 1 vol. Gait, Darlene, illus. 2009. (ENG.). 32p. (J). (gr. -1-3). 9.95 *(978-1-55469-129-6(X))* Orca Bk. Pubs. USA.
Spanyol, Jessica. Clive & His Art. Spanyol, Jessica, illus. 2016. (All about Clive Ser.: 4). (ENG., Illus.). 14p. (J). bds. *(978-1-84643-883-7(7))* Child's Play International Ltd.
—Clive & His Babies. Spanyol, Jessica, illus. 2016. (All about Clive Ser.). (ENG., Illus.). 14p. (J). bds. *(978-1-84643-882-0(9))* Child's Play International Ltd.
—Clive & His Bags. Spanyol, Jessica, illus. 2016. (All about Clive Ser.). (ENG., Illus.). 14p. (J). bds. *(978-1-84643-884-4(5))* Child's Play International Ltd.
—Clive & His Hats. Spanyol, Jessica, illus. 2016. (All about Clive Ser.). (ENG., Illus.). 14p. (J). bds. *(978-1-84643-885-1(3))* Child's Play International Ltd.
—Clive Is a Librarian. Spanyol, Jessica, illus. 2017. (Clive's Jobs Ser.: 4). (ENG., Illus.). 14p. (J). bds. ***(978-1-84643-989-6(2))*** Child's Play International Ltd.
—Clive Is a Nurse. Spanyol, Jessica, illus. 2017. (Clive's Jobs Ser.: 4). (ENG., Illus.). 14p. (J). bds. ***(978-1-84643-991-9(4))*** Child's Play International Ltd.
—Clive Is a Teacher. Spanyol, Jessica, illus. 2017. (Clive's Jobs Ser.: 4). (ENG., Illus.). 14p. (J). bds. ***(978-1-84643-990-2(6))*** Child's Play International Ltd.
—Clive Is a Waiter. Spanyol, Jessica, illus. 2017. (Clive's Jobs Ser.: 4). (ENG., Illus.). 14p. (J). bds. ***(978-1-84643-992-6(2))*** Child's Play International Ltd.
Sparkes, Amy. Ellie's Magical Wellies. East, Nick, illus. 2017. (ENG.). 32p. (J). (gr. -1-k). pap. 10.99 ***(978-1-4052-7379-4(8))*** Egmont Bks., Ltd. GBR. Dist: Independent Pubs. Group.
—Once upon a Wish. Ogilvie, Sara, illus. 2017. (ENG.). 32p. (J). (gr. -1-k). pap. 9.99 ***(978-1-84941-661-0(3)***, Red Fox) Random House Children's Books GBR. Dist: Independent Pubs. Group.
Speight, Peter. Wally the Whale Says: To Be Safe on a Bike. 2015. (ENG., Illus.). 18p. (J). pap. *(978-1-78222-438-9(6))* Paragon Publishing, Rothersthorpe.
Spenceley, Annabel, illus. Beauty & the Beast. (ENG.). 2017. 24p. pap. 7.99 *(978-1-86147-817-7(8))* 2013. 48p. (J). (gr. -1-4). pap. 7.99 *(978-1-84322-789-2(4))* Anness Publishing GBR. (Armadillo). Dist: National Bk. Network.
—Cinderella. 2016. (ENG.). 24p. pap. 7.99 *(978-1-86147-813-9(5))*, Armadillo) Anness Publishing GBR. Dist: National Bk. Network.
Sper, Emily. Follow the Yarn: A Book of Colors. Sper, Emily, illus. 2016. (ENG., Illus.). 24p. (J). (gr. -1 — 1). bds. 7.99 *(978-0-9754902-8-0(1))*, 9780975490280) Jump Pr.
Spergel, Heather. Cloud City: A Child's Journey Through Bereavement. Stylou, Georgia, illus. 2013. (ENG.). 40p. (J). 15.95 *(978-1-938501-45-6(4))* Turn the Page Publishing.
—Gabi Babaroni on Broadway. Vene, Alessandro, illus. 2013. (ENG.). 32p. (J). 18.99 *(978-1-938501-29-6(2))* Turn the Page Publishing.
—NiNi Spergelini: Guitar-Ific! Perla, Brian, illus. 2013. (NiNi Spergelini Ser.: 1). (ENG.). 32p. (J). 18.99 *(978-0-9832148-5-4(9))* Turn the Page Publishing.
Sperring, Mark. Dino-Daddy. Lloyd, Sam, illus. 2015. (ENG.). 32p. (J). (gr. -1-1). 18.99 *(978-1-4088-4969-0(0))*, 9781408849699, Bloomsbury USA Childrens) Bloomsbury Publishing USA.
Sperring, Mark. The Naughty Naughty Baddies. Tazzyman, David, illus. 2017. (ENG.). 32p. (J). 9.99 ***(978-1-4088-4973-6(9)***, 9781408849736, Bloomsbury USA Childrens) Bloomsbury Publishing USA.
Spigarelli, Jane, et al. Oxford Picture Dictionary: Low Beginning. 3rd ed. 2017. (ENG.). 272p. pap., wbk. ed. 22.00 ***(978-0-19-451124-7(3))*** Oxford Univ. Pr., Inc.
Spilsbury, Louise. Poverty & Hunger. Kai, Hanane, illus. 2017. (Children in Our World Ser.). (ENG.). 32p. (J). (gr. 1-4). 9.99 ***(978-1-4380-5019-5(4))*** Barron's Educational Series, Inc.
Spinelli, Eileen. Cold Snap. Priceman, Marjorie, illus. 2015. (ENG.). 40p. (J). (gr. k-3). 7.99 *(978-0-375-84626-7(3))*, Dragonfly Bks.) Random Hse. Children's Bks.
—Now It Is Winter. DePalma, Mary Newell, illus. 2004. 32p. (J). 16.00 *(978-0-8028-5244-1(0))* Eerdmans, William B. Publishing Co.
Spires, Ashley. Edie's Ensembles. 2014. (ENG., Illus.). 32p. (J). (gr. -1-3). 17.99 *(978-1-77049-490-9(1))*, Tundra Bks.) Tundra Bks. CAN. Dist: Penguin Random Hse. LLC.
—Larf. Spires, Ashley, illus. (ENG., Illus.). 32p. (J). (gr. -1-2). 2014. 8.95 *(978-1-55453-902-4(1))* 2012. 16.95 *(978-1-55453-701-3(0))* Kids Can Pr., Ltd. CAN. Dist: Hachette Bk. Group.
—The Most Magnificent Thing, 0 vols. Spires, Ashley, illus. 2014. (ENG., Illus.). 32p. (J). (gr. -1-2). 16.95 *(978-1-55453-704-4(5))* Kids Can Pr., Ltd. CAN. Dist: Hachette Bk. Group.
—Over-Scheduled Andrew. 2016. (ENG., Illus.). 32p. (J). (gr. -1-3). 16.99 *(978-1-77049-484-8(7))*, Tundra Bks.) Tundra Bks. CAN. Dist: Penguin Random Hse. LLC.
—Penguin & the Cupcake. 2nd ed. 2014. (ENG., Illus.). 32p. (J). (gr. -1-3). 16.95 *(978-1-927018-45-3(5))* Simply Read Bks. CAN. Dist: Ingram Publisher Services.
Spizzirri, Linda, ed. Cats of the Wild. (Illus.). 32p. (J). (gr. 1-8). pap. 4.98 incl. audio *(978-0-86545-045-5(5))* Spizzirri Pr., Inc.
—Endangered Species. (Illus.). 32p. (J). (gr. 1-8). pap. 4.98 incl. audio *(978-0-86545-041-7(2))* Spizzirri Pr., Inc.
Springstubb, Tricia. Phoebe & Digger. Newman, Jeff, illus. 2013. (ENG.). 32p. (J). (gr. -1-2). 16.99 *(978-0-7636-5281-4(4))* Candlewick Pr.
Squires, Patricia. Enter Here. 2008. 62p. (J). 41.99 *(978-1-4257-7867-5(4))* Xlibris Corp.
Sretaw. Homonym Hunt. 2010. 24p. pap. 28.03 *(978-1-4500-5228-3(2))* Xlibris Corp.
Srinivasan, Divya. Little Owl's Colors. Srinivasan, Divya, illus. 2015. (ENG., Illus.). 18p. (J). (— 1). 5.99 *(978-0-451-47456-8(2))*, Viking Books for Young Readers) Penguin Young Readers Group.
Staller, Mary J. Meet Sandy Gull. 2013. 20p. pap. 10.00 *(978-1-4251-3171-5(9))* Trafford Publishing.
Stanek, Gerald. Sarah 'n' Dippity. Stanek, Joyce Huntington, illus. 2004. (ENG.). 28p. (J). 14.95 *(978-0-9747417-0-3(1))* Shiver Hill Bks.
Stanké, Claudie. Les Bisous. Malépart, Céline, illus. 2004. (Picture Bks.). (FRE.). 32p. (J). (gr. -1). *(978-2-89021-694-5(2))*; pap. *(978-2-89021-693-8(4))* Diffusion du livre Mirabel (DLM).
Starishevsky, Jill. My Body Belongs to Me: A Book about Body Safety. Padrón, Angela, illus. 2014. (ENG.). 32p. (J). (gr. -1-3). 12.99 *(978-1-57542-461-3(4))* Free Spirit Publishing, Inc.
Starr, Ringo, pseud. Octopus's Garden. Cort, Ben, illus. 2014. (ENG.). 32p. (J). (gr. -1-3). 17.99 *(978-1-4814-0362-7(1))*, Aladdin) Simon & Schuster Children's Publishing.
Staunton, Ted. Harry & Clare's Super Staycation. Song, Mika, illus. 2017. (ENG.). 32p. (J). (gr. -1-3). 16.99 *(978-1-77049-827-3(3))*, Tundra Bks.) Tundra Bks. CAN. Dist: Penguin Random Hse. LLC.
Steel, Danielle. Pretty Minnie in Paris. Valiant, Kristi, illus. 2014. (ENG.). 32p. (J). (gr. -1-2). 17.99 *(978-0-385-37000-4(8))*, Doubleday Bks. for Young Readers) Random Hse. Children's Bks.
Steers, Billy. Tractor Mac Harvest Time. 2017. (Tractor Mac Ser.). (ENG., Illus.). 24p. (J). pap. 4.99 *(978-0-374-30600-7(1))*, 9780374306007, Farrar, Straus & Giroux (BYR)) Farrar, Straus & Giroux.
Steers, Billy. Tractor Mac Plane Jane's Journey. Steers, Billy, illus. 2017. (Tractor Mac Ser.). (ENG., Illus.). 16p. (J). bds. 5.99 ***(978-0-374-30634-2(6)***, 9780374306342, Farrar, Straus & Giroux (BYR)) Farrar, Straus & Giroux.
Steggall, Susan. Following the Tractor. 2015. (ENG., Illus.). 32p. (J). pap. 8.99 *(978-1-84780-657-4(0))*, Frances Lincoln)

Quarto Publishing Group UK GBR. Dist: Littlehampton Bk Services, Ltd.
Stein, David Ezra. Dinosaur Kisses. Stein, David Ezra, illus. 2014. (ENG., Illus.). 34p. (J). (-k). bds. 6.99 *(978-0-7636-7389-5(7))* Candlewick Pr.
—Ice Boy. Stein, David Ezra, illus. 2017. (ENG., Illus.). 40p. (J). (gr. -1-2). 15.99 *(978-0-7636-8203-3(9))* Candlewick Pr.
Stein, Joshua David. Can I Eat That? 2016. (ENG., Illus.). 40p. 16.95 *(978-0-7148-7110-3(9))* Phaidon Pr., Inc.
Steiner, Nancy. On This Night: The Steps of the Seder in Rhyme. Leff, Tova, illus. 2013. 32p. (J). 10.95 *(978-1-929628-51-3(X))* Hachai Publishing.
Stephens, Helen. Betsy Goes to the Doctor. 2015. (Betsy First Experiences Ser.). (ENG., Illus.). 32p. (J). (gr. -1-k). 10.99 *(978-1-4052-6824-0(7))* Egmont Bks., Ltd. GBR. Dist: Independent Pubs. Group.
—The Big Adventure of the Smalls. Stephens, Helen, illus. 2012. (ENG., Illus.). 32p. (J). (gr. -1-3). 15.99 *(978-1-4424-5058-5(4)*, Aladdin) Simon & Schuster Children's Publishing.
Stephens, Helen, illus. Betsy Makes a Splash. 2014. (Betsy First Experiences Ser.). (ENG.). 32p. (J). 11.99 *(978-1-4052-6822-6(0))* Egmont Bks., Ltd. GBR. Dist: Independent Pubs. Group.
Stephenson, Kristina. Sir Charlie Stinky Socks & the Really Big Adventure. 2015. (Sir Charlie Stinky Socks Ser.). (ENG., Illus.). 32p. (J). (gr. -1-k). pap. 12.99 *(978-1-4052-7768-6(8))* Egmont Bks., Ltd. GBR. Dist: Independent Pubs. Group.
—Sir Charlie Stinky Socks & the Really Dreadful Spell. 2015. (Sir Charlie Stinky Socks Ser.). (ENG., Illus.). 32p. (J). (gr. -1-k). pap. 12.99 *(978-1-4052-7770-9(X))* Egmont Bks., Ltd. GBR. Dist: Independent Pubs. Group.
—Sir Charlie Stinky Socks & the Really Frightful Night. 2015. (Sir Charlie Stinky Socks Ser.). (ENG., Illus.). 32p. (J). (gr. -1-k). pap. 12.99 *(978-1-4052-7769-3(6))* Egmont Bks., Ltd. GBR. Dist: Independent Pubs. Group.
—Sir Charlie Stinky Socks & the Tale of the Terrible Secret. 2016. (Sir Charlie Stinky Socks Ser.). (ENG., Illus.). 32p. (J). (gr. -1-k). pap. 12.99 *(978-1-4052-7771-6(8))* Egmont Bks., Ltd. GBR. Dist: Independent Pubs. Group.
—Sir Charlie Stinky Socks & the Tale of the Two Treasures. 2016. (Sir Charlie Stinky Socks Ser.). (ENG., Illus.). 32p. (J). (gr. -1-k). pap. 12.99 *(978-1-4052-7772-3(6))* Egmont Bks., Ltd. GBR. Dist: Independent Pubs. Group.
—Sir Charlie Stinky Socks & the Wizard's Whisper. 2016. (Sir Charlie Stinky Socks Ser.). (ENG., Illus.). 32p. (J). (gr. -1-k). pap. 12.99 *(978-1-4052-7773-0(4))* Egmont Bks., Ltd. GBR. Dist: Independent Pubs. Group.
—Sir Charlie Stinkysocks - The Pirate's Curse. 2015. (Sir Charlie Stinky Socks Ser.). (ENG., Illus.). 32p. (J). 17.99 *(978-1-4052-6809-7(3))* Egmont Bks., Ltd. GBR. Dist: Independent Pubs. Group.
Sterling Children's Staff. My Daddy's the Bestest. 2016. (ENG., Illus.). 22p. (J). (— 1). bds. 6.95 *(978-1-4549-1875-2(6))* Sterling Publishing Co., Inc.
—My Mommy's the Bestest. 2016. (ENG., Illus.). 22p. (J). (— 1). bds. 6.95 *(978-1-4549-1876-9(4))* Sterling Publishing Co., Inc.
Sterling Children's, Sterling. Begin Smart(tm) Peek-A-Boo What? Kreloff, Elliot, illus. 2017. (Begin Smart(tm) Ser.). (ENG.). 18p. (J). (— 1). bds. 8.95 *(978-1-4549-2086-1(6))* Sterling Publishing Co., Inc.
—Clothes/la Ropa. 2016. (Say & Play Ser.). (ENG., Illus.). 28p. (J). (— 1). bds. 4.95 *(978-1-4549-1997-1(3))* Sterling Publishing Co., Inc.
—A Day at the Beach: A Book Of 123s. 2016. (ENG., Illus.). 28p. (J). (— 1). bds. 6.95 *(978-1-4114-7588-5(7)*, Spark Publishing Group) Sterling Publishing Co., Inc.
—A Day at the Farm: A Book of ABCs. 2016. (ENG., Illus.). 28p. (J). (— 1). bds. 6.95 *(978-1-4114-7587-8(9)*, Spark Publishing Group) Sterling Publishing Co., Inc.
—Food/Los Alimentos. 2016. (Say & Play Ser.). (ENG., Illus.). 28p. (J). (— 1). bds. 4.95 *(978-1-4549-1998-8(1))* Sterling Publishing Co., Inc.
—Hello, Baby! 2017. (ENG., Illus.). 22p. (J). (— 1). bds. 6.95 *(978-1-4549-2317-6(2))* Sterling Publishing Co., Inc.
—Meow, Moo, Cock-A-Doodle-Doo: A Book of Animals. 2016. (ENG., Illus.). 28p. (J). (— 1). bds. 6.95 *(978-1-4114-7586-1(0)*, Spark Publishing Group) Sterling Publishing Co., Inc.
—Move It! 2017. (ENG., Illus.). 22p. (J). (— 1). bds. 6.95 *(978-1-4549-2311-4(3))* Sterling Publishing Co., Inc.
Sterling, Holly. Hiccups! 2016. (ENG., Illus.). 32p. (J). 17.99 *(978-1-84780-674-1(0)*, Frances Lincoln Children's Bks.) Quarto Publishing Group UK GBR. Dist: Littlehampton Bk Services, Ltd.
Sterling Publishing Co., Inc. Begin Smart(tm) Look at Me! 2016. (Begin Smart(tm) Ser.). (ENG., Illus.). 10p. (J). (— 1). bds. 8.95 *(978-1-4549-1755-7(5))* Sterling Publishing Co., Inc.
—Begin Smart(tm) Meow. 2016. (Begin Smart(tm) Ser.). (ENG., Illus.). 14p. (J). (— 1). bds. 8.95 *(978-1-4549-1877-6(2))* Sterling Publishing Co., Inc.
—Begin Smart(tm) What Does Baby Do? A First Lift-The-Flap Book. 2016. (Begin Smart(tm) Ser.). (ENG., Illus.). 16p. (J). (— 1). bds. 8.95 *(978-1-4549-1879-0(9))* Sterling Publishing Co., Inc.
—Begin Smart(tm) What Does Baby Say? A First Lift-The-Flap Book. 2016. (Begin Smart(tm) Ser.). (ENG., Illus.). 16p. (J). (— 1). bds. 8.95 *(978-1-4549-1880-6(2))* Sterling Publishing Co., Inc.
—Begin Smart(tm) Who Am I? 2016. (Begin Smart(tm) Ser.). (ENG., Illus.). 10p. (J). (— 1). bds. 8.95 *(978-1-4549-1756-4(3))* Sterling Publishing Co., Inc.
—Begin Smart(tm) Woof. 2016. (Begin Smart(tm) Ser.). (ENG., Illus.). 14p. (J). (— 1). bds. 8.95 *(978-1-4549-1878-3(0))* Sterling Publishing Co., Inc.
—Clothes. 2016. (Say & Play Ser.). (ENG., Illus.). 28p. (J). (— 1). bds. 4.95 *(978-1-4549-1971-1(X))* Sterling Publishing Co., Inc.
—Food. 2016. (Say & Play Ser.). (ENG., Illus.). 28p. (J). (— 1). bds. 4.95 *(978-1-4549-1973-5(6))* Sterling Publishing Co., Inc.
—My First Dance: Ballet. 2016. (ENG., Illus.). 22p. (J). (— 1). bds. 6.95 *(978-1-4549-1873-8(X))* Sterling Publishing Co., Inc.
—My First Dance: Tap. 2016. (ENG., Illus.). 22p. (J). (— 1). bds. 6.95 *(978-1-4549-1874-5(8))* Sterling Publishing Co., Inc.
—My First Hockey Book. 2016. (First Sports Ser.). (ENG., Illus.). 22p. (J). (— 1). bds. 6.95 *(978-1-4549-1974-2(4))* Sterling Publishing Co., Inc.
—My First Tennis Book. 2016. (First Sports Ser.). (ENG., Illus.). 22p. (J). (— 1). bds. 6.95 *(978-1-4549-1975-9(2))* Sterling Publishing Co., Inc.
Stern, Beth. Yoda Gets a Buddy. Crane, Devin, illus. 2015. (ENG.). 32p. (J). (gr. -1-3). 17.99 *(978-1-4814-6969-2(X)*, Aladdin) Simon & Schuster Children's Publishing.
Sternberg, Julie. Puppy, Puppy, Puppy. Koehler, Fred, illus. 2017. (ENG.). 32p. (J). (-k). 16.95 *(978-1-62979-466-2(X))* Boyds Mills Pr.
Sterry, Paul. Insects - Pb: A Portrait of the Animal World. 2013. (Portrait of the Animal World Ser.). (Illus.). 72p. pap. 9.95 *(978-1-59764-324-5(6))* New Line Bks.
Steven, Kenneth. Fergus Finds a Friend, 1 vol. Crowe, Louise, illus. 2010. (ENG.). 32p. (J). (gr. -1-1). 11.95 *(978-0-86315-778-3(5))* Floris Bks. GBR. Dist: SteinerBooks, Inc.
Steven, Kenneth C. The Biggest Thing in the World. Mitchell, Melanie, illus. 2013. (ENG.). 32p. (J). (gr. -1-k). 6.99 *(978-0-7459-6402-7(8))* Lion Hudson PLC GBR. Dist: Independent Pubs. Group.
Stevens, Beverly. This Dog Team Lives in the House. 2005. (Illus.). 32p. (J). pap. 9.95 *(978-1-57833-317-2(2))* Todd Communications.
Stevens, Liza. Not Today, Celeste! A Dog's Tale about Her Human's Depression. 2016. (ENG., Illus.). 36p. (J). 17.95 *(978-1-78592-008-0(1)*, 8254) Kingsley, Jessica Pubs. GBR. Dist: Macmillan Distribution Ltd.
Stevenson, Charles. The Adventures of the Glo-Worm Family. 2012. (Illus.). 34p. pap. 9.99 *(978-1-78035-338-8(3)*, Fastprint Publishing) Upfront Publishing Ltd. GBR. Dist: Printondemand-worldwide.com.
Stewart, H. E. The Patched Heart: A Gift of Friendship & Caring, 1 vol. 2010. (ENG., Illus.). 32p. (J). (gr. -1-3). 19.95 *(978-0-9693852-5-7(0))* Tudor Hse. GBR. Dist: Orca Bk. Pubs. USA.
Stewart, Lizzy. There's a Tiger in the Garden. 2016. (ENG., Illus.). 40p. (J). pap. 9.99 *(978-1-84780-807-3(7))*; 18.99 *(978-1-84780-806-6(9))* Quarto Publishing Group UK GBR. (Frances Lincoln Children's Bks.). Dist: Littlehampton Bk Services, Ltd.
Stewart, Melissa & American Museum of Natural History. Caterpillar to Butterfly. 2016. (Science for Toddlers Ser.). (ENG., Illus.). 24p. (J). (gr. -1 — 1). bds. 7.95 *(978-1-4549-1406-8(8))* Sterling Publishing Co., Inc.
Stewart, Pat. Invisible Bugs Magic Picture Book. 2003. (Dover Little Activity Bks.). (ENG., Illus.). 16p. (J). (gr. -1-2). pap. 1.50 *(978-0-486-42635-8(1))* Dover Pubns., Inc.
—Invisible Fairy Tales Magic Picture Book. 2003. (Dover Little Activity Bks.). (ENG., Illus.). 16p. (J). (gr. -1-2). pap. 1.50 *(978-0-486-43022-5(7))* Dover Pubns., Inc.
Stickley, Lisa. Handstand. 2016. (ENG., Illus.). 32p. (J). (gr. -1-1). 14.99 ***(978-1-84365-312-7(5)***, Pavilion) Pavilion Bks. GBR. Dist: Independent Pubs. Group.
—My New Room. 2017. (ENG., Illus.). 32p. (J). pap. 9.99 ***(978-1-84365-327-1(3)***, Pavilion) Pavilion Bks. GBR. Dist: Independent Pubs. Group.
Stiefel, Chana. Daddy Depot. Snair, Andy, illus. 2017. (ENG.). 40p. (J). 17.99 *(978-1-250-05889-8(9)*, 9781250058898) Feiwel & Friends.
Stihler, Chérie B. Wiggle-Waggle Woof 1, 2, 3. Bania, Michael, illus. 2015. (Paws IV Ser.). (ENG.). 20p. (J). (— 1). bds. 8.99 *(978-1-57061-978-6(6)*, Little Bigfoot) Sasquatch Bks.
Stiles, Dan. Today I'm Going to Wear ... 2014. (ENG., Illus.). 16p. (J). (gr. -1-2). bds. 9.95 *(978-1-57687-718-0(3)*, powerHouse Bks.) powerHouse Cultural Entertainment, Inc.
Stil, Teresa B. Tessa Has Two Homes. 2009. 28p. pap. 14.99 *(978-1-4389-8202-1(X))* AuthorHouse.
Stilton, Geronimo. The Race Against Time: The Third Journey Through Time. 2016. (Geronimo Stilton Journey Through Time Ser.: 3). (ENG.). 320p. (J). (gr. 2-5). 14.99 *(978-0-545-87241-6(3)*, Scholastic Paperbacks) Scholastic, Inc.
—Rescue Rebellion. 2015. (Geronimo Stilton Spacemice Ser.: 5). lib. bdg. 17.20 *(978-0-606-37775-1(1))* Turtleback Bks.
—The Underwater Planet. 2016. (Geronimo Stilton Spacemice Ser.: 6). (ENG., Illus.). 128p. (J). (gr. 2-5). pap. 7.99 *(978-0-545-87243-0(X)*, Scholastic Paperbacks) Scholastic, Inc.
Stilton, Geronimo & Pizzelli, Anna. The Underwater Planet. Facciotto, Giuseppe & Verzini, Daniele, illus. 2016. 113p. (J). ***(978-1-5182-0303-9(5))*** Scholastic, Inc.
Stilton, Thea. The Secret of Whale Island, No. 1. Cooper-McGuinness, Nanette, tr. from ITA. 2013. (Thea Stilton Graphic Novels Ser.). (ENG., Illus.). 56p. (J). (gr. 1-5). 9.99 *(978-1-59707-403-2(9)*, 9781597074032) Papercutz.
Stimson, Joan. Brave Lion, Scared Lion. Rubio, Esther, tr. Rutherford, Meg, illus. (J). (gr. k-1). pap. *(978-0-590-90985-3(1)*, SO3690) Scholastic, Inc.
—The Dinosaur Next Door. 2009. (ENG., Illus.). 24p. (J). pap. *(978-0-7787-3904-3(X))*; lib. bdg. *(978-0-7787-3873-2(6))* Crabtree Publishing Co.
Stinson, Kathy. Big or Little? Bell, Jennifer & Goffe, Toni, illus. 2nd ed. 2014. (ENG.). 24p. (J). (gr. -1 — 1). bds. 6.95 *(978-1-55451-610-0(2)*, 9781554516100) Annick Pr., Ltd. CAN. Dist: Publishers Group West (PGW).
—Big or Little? Goffe, Toni & Bell, Jennifer A., illus. 2nd rev. ed. 2009. (ENG.). 32p. (J). (gr. -1-1). pap. 6.95 *(978-1-55451-168-6(2)*, 9781554511686) Annick Pr., Ltd. CAN. Dist: Publishers Group West (PGW).
—Red Is Best. Lewis, Robin Baird, illus. 6th ed. 2011. (ENG.). 26p. (J). (gr. -1 — 1). bds. 7.99 *(978-1-55451-364-2(2)*, 9781554513642) Annick Pr., Ltd. CAN. Dist: Publishers Group West (PGW).
Stockdale, Sean & Strick, Alex. Max the Champion. Asquith, Ros, illus. 2014. 32p. (J). pap. 8.99 *(978-1-84780-519-5(1)*, Frances Lincoln) Quarto Publishing Group UK GBR. Dist: Littlehampton Bk Services, Ltd.
Stockham, Jess, illus. The Boy Who Cried Wolf. 2011. (Flip-Up Fairy Tales Ser.). (ENG.). 24p. (J). audio compact disk *(978-1-84643-407-5(6))* Child's Play International Ltd.
—Little Red Riding Hood. 2011. (Classic Fairy Tales Ser.). (ENG.). 24p. (J). audio compact disk *(978-1-84643-458-7(0))* Child's Play International Ltd.
—Making Friends! 2008. (Just Like Us! Ser.). (ENG.). 12p. (J). (gr. -1). bds. *(978-1-84643-180-7(8))* Child's Play International Ltd.
—Moving House! 2011. (Helping Hands Ser.). (ENG.). 24p. (J). *(978-1-84643-414-3(9))* Child's Play International Ltd.
—Party! 2011. (Helping Hands Ser.). (ENG.). 24p. (J). *(978-1-84643-413-6(0))* Child's Play International Ltd.
—Puss in Boots. 2012. (Classic Fairy Tales Ser.). (ENG.). 24p. (J). *(978-1-84643-441-9(6))* Child's Play International Ltd.
—Recycling! 2011. (Helping Hands Ser.). (ENG.). 24p. (J). *(978-1-84643-415-0(7))* Child's Play International Ltd.
—Shopping! 2011. (Helping Hands Ser.). (ENG.). 24p. (J). *(978-1-84643-412-9(2))* Child's Play International Ltd.
Stockham, Jessica, illus. Doctor. 2011. (First Time Ser.). (ENG.). 24p. (J). (gr. 2-2). pap. *(978-1-84643-334-4(7))* Child's Play International Ltd.
—Visiting the Dentist. 2011. (First Time Ser.). (ENG.). 24p. (J). (gr. 2-2). pap. *(978-1-84643-335-1(5))* Child's Play International Ltd.
—Visiting the Hospital. 2011. (First Time Ser.). (ENG.). 24p. (J). (gr. 2-2). pap. *(978-1-84643-336-8(3))* Child's Play International Ltd.
—Visiting the Vet. 2011. (First Time Ser.). (ENG.). 24p. (J). (gr. 2-2). pap. *(978-1-84643-337-5(1))* Child's Play International Ltd.
Stoddart, Heidi Jardine. Back to the Beach, 1 vol. 2009. (ENG., Illus.). 32p. (J). (gr. -1-3). 10.95 *(978-1-55109-702-2(8))* Nimbus Publishing, Ltd. CAN. Dist: Orca Bk. Pubs. USA.
—East to the Sea, 1 vol. 2007. (ENG., Illus.). 32p. (J). (gr. -1-2). pap. 10.95 *(978-1-55109-577-6(7))* Nimbus Publishing, Ltd. CAN. Dist: Orca Bk. Pubs. USA.
Stoh, Emily. Roger Meets Sam. Stoh, Judy, illus. 2009. 24p. pap. 9.95 *(978-1-935105-41-1(8))* Avid Readers Publishing Group.
Stokes, Brenda. Bella's Blessings. DesRosiers, Trisha, illus. 2012. (ENG.). 50p. (J). (gr. -1-3). 17.95 *(978-1-897476-61-1(2))* Simply Read Bks. CAN. Dist: Ingram Publisher Services.
Stone, Jon. Another Monster at the End of This Book (Sesame Street) Smollin, Michael, illus. 2016. (Little Golden Board Book Ser.). (ENG.). 26p. (J). (-k). bds. 7.99 *(978-1-101-93137-0(X)*, Golden Bks.) Random Hse. Children's Bks.
Stone, Julia. Little Bear's Sparkly Christmas. Muss, Angela, illus. 2014. (ENG.). 6p. (J). (gr. -1-k). 8.99 *(978-0-7459-6262-7(9))* Lion Hudson PLC GBR. Dist: Independent Pubs. Group.
Stoop, Naoko, illus. Love Is Patient, Love Is Kind. 2017. (ENG.). 22p. (J). (— 1). bds. 6.95 *(978-1-4549-1767-0(9))* Sterling Publishing Co., Inc.
Strachan, Linda. Hamish Mchaggis & the Edinburgh Adventure. Collins, Sally J., illus. 2005. (Hamish Mchaggis Ser.). 26p. (J). per. 9.00 *(978-0-9546701-7-7(5))* GW Publishing GBR. Dist: Wilson & Assocs.
—Hamish Mchaggis & the Ghost of Glamis. Collins, Sally J., illus. 2005. (Hamish Mchaggis Ser.). 26p. (J). per. 9.00 *(978-0-9546701-9-1(1))* GW Publishing GBR. Dist: Wilson & Assocs.
—Hamish Mchaggis & the Search for the Loch Ness Monster. Collins, Sally J., illus. 2005. 32p. (J). pap. 9.00 *(978-0-9546701-5-3(9))* GW Publishing GBR. Dist: Wilson & Assocs.
Strambini, Karla. The Extraordinary Mr. Qwerty. Strambini, Karla, illus. 2014. (ENG., Illus.). 32p. (J). (gr. k-3). 16.99 *(978-0-7636-7324-6(2))* Candlewick Pr.
Stranaghan, Crystal. The 13th Floor: Colouring Outside the Lines. Bzymek, Izabela, illus. 2012. 34p. (-18). *(978-1-926691-25-1(3))* Gumboot Bks.
Street Smarts: Picture Book 9x9 with Snipe. 2006. (Illus.). (J). 5.99 *(978-1-933934-17-4(4))* Mighty Kids Media.
Street Smarts: Picture Book (English) 8x8. 2006. (Illus.). (J). 5.99 *(978-1-933934-16-7(6))* Mighty Kids Media.
Sudo, Kumiko. Coco-Chan's Kimono. Sudo, Kumiko, illus. 2010. (ENG., Illus.). 32p. (J). (gr. k-2). 16.95 *(978-1-933308-26-5(5))* Breckling Pr.
Suhay, Lisa. Pardon Me, It's Ham, Not Turkey. Barcita, Pamela, illus. 2007. (J). (gr. -1-3). 17.95 *(978-1-933982-01-4(2))* Bumble Bee Publishing.
Sullivan-Fraser, Deannie. Johnny & the Gypsy Moth, 1 vol. Rose, Hilda, illus. 2009. (ENG.). 32p. (J). (gr. k-5). 10.95 *(978-1-897174-40-1(3)*, Tuckamore Bks) Creative Bk. Publishing CAN. Dist: Orca Bk. Pubs. USA.
Sullivan, Kevin & Morgan, Elizabeth. Anne's New Home. 2010. (Anne of Green Gables Picture Bks.). (ENG.). 32p. (J). (gr. k-2). pap. 4.95 *(978-0-9736803-7-9(7))* Davenport Pr. CAN. Dist: Independent Pubs. Group.
Sunita, Sunita. Gobble You Up! 2013. (ENG & RAJ., Illus.). 40p. (J). (gr. -1). 34.95 *(978-81-923171-4-4(5))* Tara Books Agency IND. Dist: Publishers Group West (PGW).
Surovec, Yasmine. I See Kitty. Surovec, Yasmine, illus. 2015. (ENG., Illus.). 34p. (J). (gr. -1-1). bds. 7.99 *(978-1-62672-093-0(2)*, 9781626720930) Roaring Brook Pr.
Surrey, Ellen, illus. Giving Thanks: 150 Ways to Say Thank You. 2016. (ENG.). 32p. (J). (gr. 1-4). 19.99 *(978-1-84780-879-0(4)*, Frances Lincoln Children's Bks.) Quarto Publishing Group UK GBR. Dist: Hachette Bk. Group.
Sutcliffe, Charlie. Zubert. 2014. (ENG., Illus.). 32p. (J). (gr. -1-3). 18.95 *(978-1-84976-121-5(3))* Tate Publishing, Ltd. GBR. Dist: Abrams, Inc.
Sutherland, Lilli. Jasper at Plumrose Farm. 2016. (ENG., Illus.). 25p. (J). pap. 13.95 *(978-1-78612-614-6(1)*, 3af64d63-73c1-493e-8a08-cb0d3584aae8) Austin, Stan AUS. Dist: Bookmasters Distribution.
Sutton, Benn. Hedgehug's Halloween. Pinto, Dan, illus. 2013. (ENG.). 40p. (J). (gr. -1-3). 9.99 *(978-0-06-196104-5(3))* HarperCollins Pubs.
Swain, Gwenyth. I Wonder as I Wander. Himler, Ronald, illus. 2005. 32p. (J). (gr. k-3). pap. 8.00 *(978-0-8028-5298-4(X)*, Eerdmans Bks For Young Readers) Eerdmans, William B. Publishing Co.
Sweet Dreams Lullabies. (Baby Looney Tunes Song Bks.). (Illus.). 16p. (J). (gr. -1). 7.98 *(978-0-7853-1613-8(2)*, PI13) Publications International, Ltd.
Swensen, Karen, et al. Catherine the Great & Her Teatime Tagalongs, 1 vol. 2005. (ENG., Illus.). 32p. (J). (gr. k-3). 16.99 *(978-1-58980-343-5(4))* Pelican Publishing Co., Inc.
Swift, Gayle H. & Swift, Casey Anne. Abc, Adoption & Me. Griffin, Paul, illus. 2013. 36p. pap. 13.99 *(978-0-9856762-8-5(0))* WRB Pub.
Swinney, Nicola Jane. I Love Horses & Ponies. 2014. (Illus.). 120p. (J). pap. *(978-1-4351-5535-0(1))* Barnes & Noble, Inc.
Swirnow, Linda. What's New at the Zoo? A PhotoPhOnics (c)Reader. 2009. 32p. pap. 12.99 *(978-1-4490-2218-1(9))* AuthorHouse.
Sydor, Colleen & Constantin, Pascale. Camilla Chameleon. Constantin, Pascale, illus. 2007. (ENG., Illus.). 32p. (J). (gr. -1-3). pap. 6.95 *(978-1-55453-164-6(0))* Kids Can Pr., Ltd. CAN. Dist: Hachette Bk. Group.
Sylver, Adrienne. Hot Diggity Dog: The History of the Hot Dog. Smith, Elwood, illus. 2015. (ENG.). 32p. (J). (gr. k-3). 8.99 *(978-0-14-751578-0(5)*, Puffin Books) Penguin Young Readers Group.
Szymanski, Lois. Wild Colt, 1 vol. Kantjas, Linda, illus. 2012. (ENG.). 40p. (J). 16.99 *(978-0-7643-3975-2(3)*, 9780764339752) Schiffer Publishing, Ltd.
Tabby, Abigail. Hokey Pokey Elmo (Sesame Street) Brannon, Tom, illus. 2016. (Little Golden Book Ser.). (ENG.). 24p. (J). (-k). 4.99 *(978-1-101-93725-9(4)*, Golden Bks.) Random Hse. Children's Bks.
Tafuri, Nancy. All Kinds of Kisses. 2014. (ENG., Illus.). 26p. (J). (gr. -1 — 1). bds. 7.99 *(978-0-316-12236-8(X))* Little, Brown Bks. for Young Readers.
—Daddy Hugs. 2014. (ENG., Illus.). 32p. (J). (gr. -1-1). 17.00 *(978-0-316-22923-4(7))* Little, Brown Bks. for Young Readers.
Talbott, Shawn M. Springtime Robins. 2006. (J). lib. bdg. 19.95 *(978-1-933732-05-3(9))* Big Ransom Studio.
Tallarico, Tony. Across America. 2003. (Ultimate Hidden Pictures Ser.). (ENG., Illus.). 48p. (J). (gr. -1-3). 5.99 *(978-0-8431-0265-9(9)*, Price Stern Sloan) Penguin Young Readers Group.
—Under the Sea. 2003. (Ultimate Hidden Pictures Ser.). (ENG., Illus.). 48p. (J). (gr. -1-3). mass mkt. 5.99 *(978-0-8431-0266-6(7)*, Price Stern Sloan) Penguin Young Readers Group.
Tallec, Olivier, illus. Who Done It? 2015. (ENG.). 32p. (J). (gr. -1-k). 15.99 *(978-1-4521-4198-5(3))* Chronicle Bks. LLC.
Tam-McMillan, Gianni. Your Journey Through the Airport. 2012. 28p. pap. 21.99 *(978-1-4797-2112-2(3))* Xlibris Corp.
Tanco, Miguel. You & Me, Me & You. 2017. (ENG., Illus.). 36p. (J). (gr. -1-k). 12.99 *(978-1-4521-4486-3(9))* Chronicle Bks. LLC.
Tang, Greg. Math Fables. Cahoon, Heather, illus. 2004. (ENG.). 40p. (J). (gr. -1-3). 18.99 *(978-0-439-45399-8(2))* Scholastic, Inc.
Tango Books Staff. Armour. Moulder, Bob, illus. 2011. (3-Dimensional Exploration Bks.). (ENG.). 20p. (J). (gr. -1-2). 22.95 *(978-1-85707-664-6(8))* Tango Bks. GBR. Dist: Independent Pubs. Group.
—Car. Abbott, Simon, illus. 2012. (Noisy Pops! Ser.). (ENG.). 10p. (J). (gr. -1-k). 11.99 *(978-1-85707-802-2(0))* Tango Bks. GBR. Dist: Independent Pubs. Group.
—Digger: A Lift-the-Flap & Stand Up. Burton, Terry, illus. 2011. (Mini Trucks Ser.). (ENG.). 12p. (J). (gr. -1-k). 5.99 *(978-1-85707-751-3(2))* Tango Bks. GBR. Dist: Independent Pubs. Group.
Tanner, Martha. And God Said. 2011. 28p. pap. 13.75 *(978-1-4567-3691-0(4))* AuthorHouse.
Taplin, Sam. Noisy Orchestra. 2013. (Noisy Bks). 10p. (J). ring bd. 19.99 *(978-0-7945-3334-2(5)*, Usborne) EDC Publishing.
Tarore, Martha. The Runaway Bubble. 2011. (ENG.). 35p. (J). pap. 16.95 *(978-1-4327-5898-1(5))* Outskirts Pr., Inc.
Tarpley, Natasha Anastasia. I Love My Hair! Lewis, E. B., illus. 2014. 32p. pap. 7.00 *(978-1-61003-348-0(5))* Center for the Collaborative Classroom.
Tarpley, Todd. Beep! Beep! Go to Sleep! Rocco, John, illus. 2015. (ENG.). 40p. (J). (gr. -1-3). 17.00 *(978-0-316-25443-4(6))* Little, Brown Bks. for Young Readers.
Tasmanian Devil. (Looney Tunes Look & Find Bks.). (Illus.). 24p. (J). (gr. -1-5). 7.98 *(978-0-7853-1186-7(6)*, PI1) Publications International, Ltd.
Tavares, Matt. Mudball. Tavares, Matt, illus. 2011. (ENG., Illus.). 32p. (J). (gr. 1-4). pap. 6.99 *(978-0-7636-4136-8(7))* Candlewick Pr.
Taylor, Dereen. Alien Adventure: Peek Inside the Pop-Up Windows! Hutchinson, Tim, illus. 2015. (ENG.). 12p. 16.99 *(978-1-86147-487-2(3)*, Armadillo) Anness Publishing GBR. Dist: National Bk. Network.
—The Dragon's Magic Wish. Hutchinson, Tim, illus. 2012. (ENG.). 12p. (J). (gr. 1-6). 16.99 *(978-1-84322-856-1(4))* Anness Publishing GBR. Dist: National Bk. Network.
—The Fairy Midnight Surprise Party. Stone, Lyn, illus. 2012. (ENG.). 12p. (J). (gr. 1-6). 16.99 *(978-1-84322-763-2(0))* Anness Publishing GBR. Dist: National Bk. Network.
—Journey to the World of the Dinosaurs: Peek Inside the Pop-Up Windows! Kavanagh, Peter, illus. 2014. (ENG.). 12p. (J). (gr. 2-7). 16.99 *(978-1-86147-319-6(2)*, Armadillo) Anness Publishing GBR. Dist: National Bk. Network.
—The Lost Treasure of the Jungle Temple: Peek Inside the 3D Windows! Hutchinson, Tim, illus. 2013. (ENG.). 12p. (J). (gr. 1-8). 16.99 *(978-1-84322-822-6(X)*, Armadillo) Anness Publishing GBR. Dist: National Bk. Network.
—The Mystery of the Vampire Boy: Dare You Peek Through the Pop-Up Windows? Spoor, Mike, illus. 2014. (ENG.). 12p. (J). (gr. k-5). 16.99 *(978-1-86147-410-0(5)*, Armadillo) Anness Publishing GBR. Dist: National Bk. Network.
—Paulo & the Football Thieves: Peek Inside the Pop-Up Windows! Hutchinson, Tim, illus. 2014. (ENG.). 12p. 16.99 *(978-1-86147-409-4(1)*, Armadillo) Anness Publishing GBR. Dist: National Bk. Network.
—Robo-Pup to the Rescue! Hutchinson, Tim, illus. 2013. (ENG.). 12p. (J). (gr. 1-8). 16.99 *(978-1-84322-821-9(1)*, Armadillo) Anness Publishing GBR. Dist: National Bk. Network.
—Rosie Rides to the Rescue: Peek Inside the Pop-Up Windows! Stone, Lyn, illus. 2015. (ENG.). 12p. 16.99 *(978-1-86147-488-9(1)*, Armadillo) Anness Publishing GBR. Dist: National Bk. Network.

—Trapped in the Witch's Lair: Peek Inside the Pop-Up Windows! Catchpole, Diana, illus. 2014. (ENG.). 12p. (J). (gr. 2-7). 16.99 *(978-1-86147-320-2(6)*, Armadillo) Anness Publishing GBR. Dist: National Bk. Network.

Taylor, Kenneth N. The Picture Bible for Little People. 2004. (ENG., Illus.). 256p. (J). 14.99 *(978-0-8423-8734-7(X))* Tyndale Hse. Pubs.

Taylor, Sean. Goal! Vilela, Caio, photos by. 2014. (ENG., Illus.). 40p. (J). (gr. -1-3). 17.99 *(978-1-62779-123-6(X)*, 9781627791236, Holt, Henry & Co. Bks. For Young Readers) Holt, Henry & Co.

—The World-Famous Cheese Shop Break-In. Shaw, Hannah, illus. 2015. (ENG.). 32p. (J). (gr. -1-2). 17.99 *(978-1-84780-430-3(6)*, Frances Lincoln) Quarto Publishing Group UK GBR. Dist: Hachette Bk. Group.

Taylor, Sean & Quarto Generic Staff. Grizzly Bear with the Frizzly Hair. Shaw, Hannah, illus. 2011. (ENG.). 32p. (J). (gr. -1-1). pap. 8.95 *(978-1-84780-144-9(7)*, Frances Lincoln) Quarto Publishing Group UK GBR. Dist: Hachette Bk. Group.

Taylor, Sean & Shaw, Hannah. Who Ate Auntie Iris. 2012. (Illus.). 32p. (J). pap. *(978-1-84780-314-6(8)*, Frances Lincoln) Quarto Publishing Group UK.

Taylor, Thomas. Too Many Tickles! Dann, Penny, illus. 2014. (ENG.). 24p. (J). (gr. -1-k). 17.99 *(978-0-230-75265-8(9))* Pan Macmillan GBR. Dist: Independent Pubs. Group.

Taylor, Trace & Sánchez, Lucía M. Pingülnos de la AntáRtida: Antarctic Penguins. 2010. (2G Animales Marinos Ser.). (ENG & SPA.). 12p. (J). (gr. k-2). pap. 6.99 *(978-1-61541-274-7(3))* American Reading Co.

Taylor Trade Publish. Meet Ranger Rick Jr: Critter Crafts & Recipes. 2016. (Ranger Rick: Animal Fun for Young Children Ser.). (ENG., Illus.). 32p. (J). (gr. -1-1). pap. 5.99 *(978-1-63076-210-0(5))* Taylor Trade Publishing.

Taz TV. (Looney Tunes Song & Sound Bks.). (Illus.). 16p. (J). (gr. -1-k). 7.98 *(978-0-7853-1609-1(4)*, PI9) Publications International, Ltd.

Teckentrup, Britta. Bee: a Peek-Through Picture Book. 2017. (ENG., Illus.). 32p. (J). (gr. -1-2). 14.99 *(978-1-5247-1526-7(3)*, Doubleday Bks. for Young Readers) Random Hse. Children's Bks.

—The Memory Tree. Teckentrup, Britta, illus. 2014. (ENG., Illus.). 32p. (J). (gr. -1-k). pap. 9.99 *(978-1-4083-2634-3(5))* Hodder & Stoughton GBR. Dist: Hachette Bk. Group.

Teckentrup, Britta, illus. Fast & Slow. 2013. (ENG.). 14p. (J). (gr. -1-k). bds. 6.99 *(978-1-84686-952-5(8))* Barefoot Bks., Inc.

Tedder, Elizabeth, illus. Alphabet & Numbers in a New Way. 2011. 32p. pap. 35.95 *(978-1-258-06357-3(3))* Literary Licensing, LLC.

Tekavec, Heather. Stop, Thief! Pratt, Pierre, illus. 2014. (ENG.). 32p. (J). (gr. -1-2). 16.95 *(978-1-77138-012-6(8))* Kids Can Pr., Ltd. CAN. Dist: Hachette Bk. Group.

Tekenteam, illus. My Favorite Safari. 2011. (My Favorite Vehicles Ser.). (ENG.). 12p. (J). (gr. -1-k). bds. 5.99 *(978-0-7641-6412-5(0))* Barron's Educational Series, Inc.

Tekiela, Stan. C Is for Cardinal, 1 vol. 2016. (ENG., Illus.). 64p. (J). (-k). 8.95 *(978-1-59193-533-9(4))* Adventure Pubns.

Terry, Donna. Whose Toes Are Those? 2009. 24p. pap. 11.99 *(978-1-4490-0009-7(6))* AuthorHouse.

Terry, Michael, illus. Who Lives Here? 2012. (ENG.). 12p. (J). (gr. -1-k). 14.99 *(978-1-4088-1943-2(0)*, 9781408819432, Bloomsbury USA Childrens) Bloomsbury Publishing USA.

Tesoro de Libros de Calcomanías V. 2004. (Disney Calcomanias Ser.). (SPA., Illus.). 72p. (J). pap. *(978-970-718-105-2(2)*, Silver Dolphin en Español) Advanced Marketing, S. de R. L. de C. V.

Testa, Maggie. Play with Plex. Zdanowicz, Paul, illus. 2010. (Yo Gabba Gabba! Ser.). (ENG.). 14p. (J). (gr. -1-1). bds. 8.99 *(978-1-4169-9740-5(7)*, Simon Spotlight) Simon Spotlight.

Tewee, Laqaixit. Winterbloom & the Magical Swan: Book 1 Discovery of the Moon Treasure. 2012. 68p. pap. 31.99 *(978-1-4653-9933-5(X))* Xlibris Corp.

Thaler, Mike. The Custodian from the Black Lagoon, 1 vol. 2014. (From the Black Lagoon Ser.). (ENG., Illus.). 32p. (J). (gr. 1-4). lib. bdg. 24.21 *(978-1-61479-196-6(1))* Spotlight.

Thalhamer, Ellen Viola. Let's Play Cashier: I Love to Pretend! 2011. 36p. pap. 15.49 *(978-1-4490-7488-3(X))* AuthorHouse.

The Book Company, ed. Home. (Sparkle Bks.). (ENG.). 10p. (J). bds. 4.99 *(978-1-74047-330-9(2))* Book Co. Publishing Pty, Ltd., The AUS. Dist: Penton Overseas, Inc.

The Ciletti Publishing Group. Story Time Cafe Maisy's Blue Bath Set. The Ciletti Publishing Group, illus. 2010. (Illus.). (J). 24.95 *(978-0-917665-71-4(6))* Ciletti Publishing Group, Inc., The.

The Editors of Sports Illustrated Kids. My First Book of Baseball: A Rookie Book. 2016. (Sports Illustrated Kids Rookie Bks.). (ENG., Illus.). 48p. (J). (gr. -1-1). 11.99 *(978-1-61893-167-2(9))* Time Inc. Bks.

The Okee Dokee Brothers. Thousand Star Hotel. Reese, Brandon, illus. 2017. (ENG.). 40p. (J). (gr. -1). 17.95 *(978-1-4549-1830-1(6))* Sterling Publishing Co., Inc.

The Topps Company & Lucasfilm Ltd Staff. Star Wars Topps Classic Sticker Book. 2017. (ENG., Illus.). 76p. (J). (gr. 1-17). pap. 12.95 ***(978-1-4197-2711-5(7)***, Abrams Bks. for Young Readers) Abrams, Inc.

Thereza, Rowe & Rowe, Thereza. Mister Pip. 2016. (ENG., Illus.). 32p. (J). (gr. -1-k). 16.95 *(978-1-84976-382-0(8))* Tate Publishing, Ltd. GBR. Dist: Abrams, Inc.

Thomas, B. K. Logs. Thomas, B. K., illus. 2013. (Illus.). 36p. 24.95 *(978-1-4512-2170-1(3))* America Star Bks.

Thomas, Glenn. Little Flowers Can't Talk. 2012. 40p. pap. 32.70 *(978-1-4691-6004-7(8))* Xlibris Corp.

Thomas-Logan, Sharon. The Miracles of Jesus Christ. 2009. 24p. pap. 12.99 *(978-1-4389-4615-3(5))* AuthorHouse.

Thomas Nelson Publishing Staff. Daddy Loves You So Much, 1 vol. Parry, Jo, illus. 2015. (ENG.). 20p. (J). bds. 9.99 *(978-0-529-12335-0(5))* Nelson, Thomas Inc.

—Grandma Kisses, 1 vol. 2015. (ENG., Illus.). 20p. (J). bds. 9.99 *(978-0-7180-3659-1(X))* Nelson, Thomas Inc.

—Mommy Loves You So Much, 1 vol. Parry, Jo, illus. 2015. (ENG.). 20p. (J). bds. 9.99 *(978-0-529-12338-1(X))* Nelson, Thomas Inc.

Thomas Nelson, Thomas. I Prayed for You, 1 vol. 2015. (ENG., Illus.). 20p. (J). bds. 8.99 *(978-0-7180-4987-4(X))* Nelson, Thomas Inc.

Thomas, Shelley Moore. No, No, Kitten! Nichols, Lori, illus. 2015. (ENG.). 40p. (J). (gr. -1-2). 16.95 *(978-1-62091-631-5(2))* Boyds Mills Pr.

Thomas, Valerie. Winnie's Big Bad Robot. Paul, Korky, illus. 2015. (ENG.). 32p. ***(978-0-19-273874-5(7))*** Oxford Univ. Pr.

Thompson, Carol. Rain! 2014. (Whatever the Weather Ser.: 4). (ENG., Illus.). 12p. (J). (gr. k-k). bds. *(978-1-84643-683-3(4))* Child's Play International Ltd.

—Snow! 2014. (Whatever the Weather Ser.). (ENG., Illus.). 12p. (J). (gr. k-k). bds. *(978-1-84643-681-9(8))* Child's Play International Ltd.

—Sun! 2014. (Whatever the Weather Ser.). (ENG., Illus.). 12p. (J). (gr. k-k). bds. *(978-1-84643-680-2(X))* Child's Play International Ltd.

—Wind! 2014. (Whatever the Weather Ser.). (ENG., Illus.). 12p. (J). (gr. k-k). bds. *(978-1-84643-682-6(6))* Child's Play International Ltd.

Thompson, Carol, illus. The Emperor's New Clothes. 2016. (Once upon a Timeless Tale Ser.). (ENG.). 32p. (J). (gr. k-2). 9.99 *(978-1-921894-99-2(7))* Little Hare Bks. AUS. Dist: Independent Pubs. Group.

Thompson, Lauren. Cuaquito (Little Quack) Anderson, Derek, illus. 2010. (SPA.). 34p. (J). (gr. -1-1). bds. 7.99 *(978-1-4169-9894-5(2)*, Libros Para Ninos) Libros Para Ninos.

Thompson, Laurie Ann. My Dog Is the Best. Schmid, Paul, illus. 2015. (ENG.). 40p. (J). (gr. -1-1). 17.99 *(978-0-374-30051-7(8)*, 9780374300517, Farrar, Straus & Giroux (BYR)) Farrar, Straus & Giroux.

Thoms, Susan Collins. Jonah & the Big Fish. Stoop, Naoko, illus. 2016. (ENG.). 22p. (J). (— 1). bds. 6.95 *(978-1-4549-1493-8(9)*, 1402423) Sterling Publishing Co., Inc.

Thong, Roseanne Greenfield. Round Is a Mooncake: A Book of Shapes. Lin, Grace, illus. 2014. (ENG.). 40p. (J). (gr. -1-k). 7.99 *(978-1-4521-3644-8(0))* Chronicle Bks. LLC.

—Round Is a Tortilla. Parra, John, illus. 2015. (ENG.). 40p. (J). (gr. -1-k). 7.99 *(978-1-4521-4568-6(7))* Chronicle Bks. LLC.

Thorup, Bryce. Doctor Matthews' Family Christmas. Muller, Ruth, illus. 2005. (J). 18.95 *(978-0-9765964-1-7(5))* Round Tower Pr.

—Two Birthdays. Muller, Daniel, illus. 2005. (J). 18.95 *(978-0-9765964-0-0(7))* Round Tower Pr.

Thuillier, Eléonore, illus. Wolf, Are You There? Learn How to Get Dressed with the Little Wolf. 2012. (ENG.). 14p. (J). (gr. -1). bds. 14.99 *(978-2-7338-1952-4(6))* Auzou, Philippe Editions FRA. Dist: Consortium Bk. Sales & Distribution.

Tibo, Gilles. Au Boulot les Animaux. 2004. (FRE., Illus.). (J). (gr. -1-k). spiral bd. *(978-0-616-11146-8(0))* Canadian National Institute for the Blind/Institut National Canadien pour les Aveugles.

Tiere der Nacht. (GER.). *(978-3-411-09261-1(0))* Bibliographisches Institut & F. A. Brockhaus AG DEU. Dist: i. b. d., Ltd.

Tierney, Tom. Legendary Baseball Stars. 81st ed. 2009. (Dover Paper Dolls Ser.). (ENG.). 32p. (J). (gr. 4-5). 9.99 *(978-0-486-24846-2(1))* Dover Pubns., Inc.

Tiger Tales Staff, ed. Animals Go. Emily, Bolam, illus. 2010. (Touch, Look, & Learn! Ser.). (ENG.). 10p. (J). (gr. -1). bds. 5.95 *(978-1-58925-854-9(1))* Tiger Tales.

Tilley, Sophie. Sparkly Shoes & Picnic Parties. 2015. (ENG., Illus.). 32p. (J). (gr. -1-1). 18.99 *(978-1-4088-3662-0(9)*, 9781408836620, Bloomsbury USA Childrens) Bloomsbury Publishing USA.

Tillworth, Mary. It's Time for Ballet! (Bubble Guppies) MJ Illustrations, illus. 2015. (Glitter Picturebook Ser.). (ENG.). 16p. (J). (gr. -1-2). 5.99 *(978-0-553-52117-7(9)*, Random Hse. Bks. for Young Readers) Random Hse. Children's Bks.

—The Legend of Pinkfoot (Bubble Guppies) MJ Illustrations, illus. 2014. (Pictureback(R) Ser.). (ENG.). 16p. (J). (gr. -1-2). 4.99 *(978-0-385-38411-7(4)*, Random Hse. Bks. for Young Readers) Random Hse. Children's Bks.

—Who's Afraid of Monsters? (Sesame Street) Mathieu, Joe, illus. 2016. (Pictureback(R) Ser.). (ENG.). 24p. (J). (gr. -1-2). 5.99 *(978-1-101-93840-9(4)*, Random Hse. Bks. for Young Readers) Random Hse. Children's Bks.

Timmers, Leo. Franky. Timmers, Leo, illus. 2016. (ENG., Illus.). 40p. (gr. -1-2). 16.99 *(978-1-927271-93-3(2))*; 33.32 *(978-1-77657-053-9(7))*; 33.32 *(978-1-77657-054-6(5))* Gecko Pr. NZL. Dist: Lerner Publishing Group.

—Gus's Garage. Timmers, Leo, illus. 2017. (ENG., Illus.). 32p. (gr. -1-k). 16.99 ***(978-1-77657-092-8(8))***; 9.99 ***(978-1-77657-094-2(4))*** Gecko Pr. NZL. Dist: Lerner Publishing Group.

Timmers, Leo. Oops! Timmers, Leo, illus. 2011. (ENG., Illus.). 32p. (J). (gr. k — 1). 15.95 *(978-1-60537-105-4(X))* Cobblestone Publishing Co.

Timothy, Ering. Frog Belly Rat F & G. 2003. (J). bds. 16.99 *(978-0-7636-2248-0(6))* Candlewick Pr.

Tiny Tots Christmas. 2015. (Tiny Tots Ser.). (ENG., Illus.). 32p. (J). (gr. -1 — 1). 8.99 *(978-0-7459-6455-3(9))* Lion Hudson PLC GBR. Dist: Independent Pubs. Group.

Tischler, Tracey. Heroes in the Sandbox. 2009. 28p. pap. 13.95 *(978-1-4490-5502-8(8))* AuthorHouse.

Tischner, Lukasz. Milosz & the Problem of Evil. Bill, Stanley, tr. from POL. 2015. (ENG.). 272p. (C). pap. 34.95 *(978-0-8101-3177-4(3))* Northwestern Univ. Pr.

Titan Comics Staff. Underworld, Vol. 6. 2015. (Riders of Berk Ser.). (ENG., Illus.). 64p. (J). (gr. 3-7). pap. 6.99 *(978-1-78276-081-8(4))* Titan Bks. Ltd. GBR. Dist: Penguin Random Hse. LLC.

Titan Comics, Titan & Ah-Koon, Didier. Minions, Vol. 1. 2015. (ENG., Illus.). 48p. (J). (gr. 1-4). 14.99 *(978-1-78276-557-8(3))* Titan Bks. Ltd. GBR. Dist: Penguin Random Hse. LLC.

To the Extreme [Really Good Stuff]. 2010. (To the Extreme Ser.). 32p. pap. 79.50 *(978-1-4296-5362-6(0)*, Blazers) Capstone Press of Coughlan Cos.

Todd, Barbara. Edward & the Eureka Lucky Wish Company. Storms, Patricia, illus. 2009. (ENG.). 32p. (J). (gr. -1-2). 16.95 *(978-1-55453-264-3(7))* Kids Can Pr., Ltd. CAN. Dist: Hachette Bk. Group.

Toft, Barbara. Complete Guides Animals. 2012. (ENG.). 144p. (J). *(978-1-4351-4403-3(1))* Barnes & Noble, Inc.

Toft, Kim Michelle. The World That We Want. 2005. (Illus.). 32p. (J). (gr. -1 — 1). pap. 6.95 *(978-1-58089-115-8(2))*; bds. 16.95 *(978-1-58089-114-1(4))* Charlesbridge Publishing, Inc.

Tomlinson, Jill. The Owl Who Was Afraid of the Dark. Howard, Paul, illus. 2017. (ENG.). 28p. (J). (gr. -1-k). bds. 9.99 ***(978-1-4052-8336-6(X))*** Egmont Bks., Ltd. GBR. Dist: Independent Pubs. Group.

Toms, Kate. Twinkle Twinkle Box Set. 2007. (Illus.). 26p. (gr. -1). per. *(978-1-84610-672-9(9))* Make Believe Ideas.

Toole, Anne. Crystal Cadets. Staffaroni, Adam, ed. 2016. (ENG., Illus.). 128p. (J). pap. 12.99 *(978-1-941302-16-3(5)*, 9781941302163) Lion Forge, LLC, The.

Tooth, Lucy. Star the Tooth Fairy Wants to Know If You Need Braces? 2009. 36p. 16.95 *(978-0-557-07542-3(4))* Lulu Pr., Inc.

Toothman, Sherry. I'm Okay, Mommy. Toothman, Lindsey, illus. 2007. 20p. per. 24.95 *(978-1-4241-8733-1(8))* America Star Bks.

Torres, J. Checkers & Dot at the Beach. Lum, J., illus. 2013. (Checkers & Dot Ser.). (ENG.). 16p. (J). (— 1). bds. 7.95 *(978-1-77049-444-2(8)*, Tundra Bks.) Tundra Bks. CAN. Dist: Penguin Random Hse. LLC.

—Checkers & Dot on the Farm. Lum, J., illus. 2013. (Checkers & Dot Ser.). (ENG.). 16p. (J). (— 1). bds. 7.95 *(978-1-77049-443-5(X)*, Tundra Bks.) Tundra Bks. CAN. Dist: Penguin Random Hse. LLC.

Torres, J., et al. Teen Titans Go!: Ready for Action. 2017. (ENG., Illus.). (gr. 2-5). pap. 12.99 *(978-1-4012-6899-2(4))* DC Comics.

Tougas, Chris. Mechanimals, 1 vol. 2012. (ENG.). 32p. (J). (gr. -1-3). 9.95 *(978-1-4598-0273-5(X))* Orca Bk. Pubs. USA.

Tourville, Jacqueline. Albie's First Word: A Tale Inspired by Albert Einstein's Childhood. Evans, Wynne, illus. 2014. (ENG.). 40p. (J). (gr. -1-3). 17.99 *(978-0-307-97893-6(1)*, Schwartz & Wade Bks.) Random Hse. Children's Bks.

Tow, Jack. Up All Night with Howie. Tow, Jack, illus. 2012. (ENG., Illus.). 48p. 16.99 *(978-88-89854-93-8(6))* Officina Libraria srl ITA. Dist: National Bk. Network.

Tow, Jack, illus. Who's Afraid of Howie? 2013. (ENG.). 40p. (gr. -1-3). 16.99 *(978-88-97737-22-3(6))* Officina Libraria srl ITA. Dist: National Bk. Network.

Tracy, Joe. Arnie the Imagination Boy. 2011. 24p. pap. 15.99 *(978-1-4568-9135-0(9))* Xlibris Corp.

Tracy, Kristina, et al. Chris P. Bacon: My Life So Far... 2013. (ENG., Illus.). 32p. 14.95 *(978-1-4019-4439-1(6)*, Hay Hse. Lifestyles) Hay Hse., Inc.

Trasler, Janee. Big Chickie, Little Chickie. Trasler, Janee, illus. 2016. (Illus.). 24p. (J). (gr. -1 — 1). bds. 8.99 *(978-0-06-234231-7(2)*, HarperFestival) HarperCollins Pubs.

Treahy, Iona & Ladybird Books Staff. Jack & the Beanstalk. 2015. (First Favourite Tales Ser.). (ENG., Illus.). 32p. (J). (-k). 7.99 *(978-1-4093-0959-8(2))* Penguin Bks., Ltd. GBR. Dist: Independent Pubs. Group.

Tremblay, Marc. Le Petit Frere du Chaperon Rouge. Fil et al, illus. 2004. (était une Fois Ser.). (FRE.). 24p. (J). (gr. -1). pap. *(978-2-89021-698-3(5))* Diffusion du livre Mirabel (DLM).

Tremblay, Patrick. Poor, Poor Jack. 2010. 40p. pap. 26.00 *(978-0-557-25375-3(6))* Lulu Pr., Inc.

Treml, Renee. Colour for Curlews. Treml, Renee, illus. 2013. (ENG., Illus.). 32p. (J). (gr. -1). 17.99 *(978-1-74275-921-0(1))* Random Hse. Australia AUS. Dist: Independent Pubs. Group.

Trithart, Emma, illus. Crocodile's Burp. 2015. (Pardon Me! Ser.: 4). (ENG.). 14p. (J). *(978-1-84643-750-2(4))* Child's Play International Ltd.

—Leopard's Snore. 2015. (Pardon Me! Ser.: 4). (ENG.). 14p. (J). *(978-1-84643-752-6(0))* Child's Play International Ltd.

Troupe, Thomas Kingsley & Braun, Eric. Origami Science Adventures. Christoph, Jamey, illus. 2013. (Origami Science Adventures Ser.). (ENG.). 24p. (gr. 3-4). pap. 23.80 *(978-1-4048-8074-0(7))*; lib. bdg. 109.28 *(978-1-4048-7973-7(0))* Picture Window Bks.

Trumbauer, Lisa. The Great Reindeer Rebellion. Ho, Jannie, illus. 2014. (ENG.). 32p. (J). (gr. -1). pap. 6.95 *(978-1-4549-1356-6(8))* Sterling Publishing Co., Inc.

Trzpil, Monika Filipina. The Bear Who Loved to Dance. 2016. (ENG., Illus.). 32p. (J). (gr. -1-1). pap. 8.99 *(978-1-78445-245-2(9))* Top That! Publishing PLC GBR. Dist: Independent Pubs. Group.

Tse, Brian. This Is the Greatest Place! A Palace Inspired by the World of Small Animals. Steinhardt, Nancy S., ed. Wang, Ben, tr. from CHI. Mak, Alice, illus. rev. ed. 2014. (ENG.). 44p. (J). (gr. -1-3). 12.95 *(978-0-9893776-2-1(8))* China Institute Gallery, China Institute in America.

Tsurumi, Andrea. Accident! 2017. (ENG., Illus.). 48p. (J). (gr. -1-3). 17.99 ***(978-0-544-94480-0(1)***, HMH Books For Young Readers) Houghton Mifflin Harcourt Publishing Co.

Tucker, Stephen. Jack & the Beanstalk, 2 vols. Sharratt, Nick, illus. 2016. (Lift-The-Flap Fairy Tales Ser.). (ENG.). 24p. (J). (gr. -1-k). bds. 12.99 *(978-1-5098-1714-6(X))* Pan Macmillan GBR. Dist: Independent Pubs. Group.

Tudor, Tasha. A Tale for Easter. Tudor, Tasha, illus. 2004. (ENG., Illus.). 32p. (J). (gr. -1-3). 6.99 *(978-0-689-86694-4(1)*, Aladdin) Simon & Schuster Children's Publishing.

Tugwood, Wendy. I Love You Three. 2016. (ENG., Illus.). 24p. (J). (gr. -1-1). 14.95 *(978-1-77085-784-1(2)*, 9781770857841) Firefly Bks., Ltd.

Tullet, Hervé. The Ball Game. 2014. (ENG., Illus.). 14p. 12.95 *(978-0-7148-6688-8(1))* Phaidon Pr., Inc.

—The Countryside Game. 2013. (ENG., Illus.). 14p. 12.95 *(978-0-7148-6074-9(3))* Phaidon Pr., Inc.

—The Eyes Game. 2014. (ENG., Illus.). 14p. 12.95 *(978-0-7148-6689-5(X))* Phaidon Pr., Inc.

—The Finger Circus Game. Oceano Editorial Staff, ed. 2013. (ENG., Illus.). 14p. 12.95 *(978-0-7148-6531-7(1))* Phaidon Pr., Inc.

—The Game in the Dark. 2012. (Tullet Game Ser.). (ENG., Illus.). 14p. (gr. -1-1). 12.95 *(978-0-7148-6485-3(4))* Phaidon Pr., Inc.

—The Game of Lines. 2015. (ENG., Illus.). 14p. (gr. -1-17). 12.95 *(978-0-7148-6873-8(6))* Phaidon Pr., Inc.

—The Game of Mirrors. 2014. (ENG., Illus.). 14p. (gr. -1-17). 12.95 *(978-0-7148-6687-1(3))* Phaidon Pr., Inc.

—The Game of Red, Yellow & Blue. 2012. (Tullet Game Ser.). (ENG., Illus.). 14p. (gr. -1-1). 9.95 *(978-0-7148-6481-5(1))* Phaidon Pr., Inc.

—The Game of Shadows. 2013. (ENG., Illus.). 14p. 12.95 *(978-0-7148-6532-4(X))* Phaidon Pr., Inc.

—The Game of Tops & Tails. 2015. (ENG., Illus.). 14p. (gr. -1-17). 12.95 *(978-0-7148-6874-5(4))* Phaidon Pr., Inc.

—The Good Morning Game. 2015. (ENG., Illus.). 14p. (gr. -1-17). 12.95 *(978-0-7148-6875-2(2))* Phaidon Pr., Inc.

—Say Zoop! 2017. (ENG., Illus.). 64p. (J). (gr. -1-k). 15.99 ***(978-1-4521-6473-1(8))*** Chronicle Bks. LLC.

Tullet, Hervé. The Trail Game. 2015. (ENG., Illus.). 14p. (gr. -1-17). 12.95 *(978-0-7148-6876-9(0))* Phaidon Pr., Inc.

Turkowski, Einar, illus. Houses Floating Home. 2016. (ENG.). 32p. (J). (gr. -1-3). 16.95 *(978-1-59270-183-4(3))* Enchanted Lion Bks., LLC.

Turnbull, Victoria. Pandora. 2016. (ENG., Illus.). 32p. (J). 18.99 *(978-1-84780-749-6(6)*, Frances Lincoln Children's Bks.) Quarto Publishing Group UK GBR. Dist: Littlehampton Bk Services, Ltd.

Turner-Rahman, Gregory. Ellabug. 2009. 40p. pap. 12.95 *(978-1-935290-09-4(6))* Diversion Pr.

Turner, Sarah Elizabeth. The Littlest Monkey, 1 vol. 2010. (ENG., Illus.). 32p. (J). (gr. -1-3). pap. 9.95 *(978-1-55039-174-9(7))* Sono Nis Pr. CAN. Dist: Orca Bk. Pubs. USA.

Turpin, Nick. Molly Is New. Raga, Silvia, illus. 2010. 32p. pap. *(978-1-84089-650-3(7))* Zero to Ten, Ltd.

Tutu, Desmond & Abrams, Douglas Carlton. God's Dream. Pham, LeUyen, illus. 2008. (ENG.). 40p. (J). (gr. k-12). 17.99 *(978-0-7636-3388-2(7))* Candlewick Pr.

Tuxworth, Nicola. Baby Animals. 2015. (ENG., Illus.). 20p. (J). (gr. -1-12). bds. 6.99 *(978-1-86147-357-8(5)*, Armadillo) Anness Publishing GBR. Dist: National Bk. Network.

—Clothes. 2014. (ENG., Illus.). 20p. (J). (gr. -1 — 1). bds. 6.99 *(978-1-84322-861-5(0)*, Armadillo) Anness Publishing GBR. Dist: National Bk. Network.

—Colours. 2014. (ENG., Illus.). 20p. (J). (gr. -1-12). bds. 6.99 *(978-1-84322-749-6(5)*, Armadillo) Anness Publishing GBR. Dist: National Bk. Network.

—Messy. 2016. (ENG., Illus.). 20p. (J). (gr. -1-k). bds. 6.99 *(978-1-86147-690-6(6)*, Armadillo) Anness Publishing GBR. Dist: National Bk. Network.

—Mix & Match. 2016. (Learn-a-Word Book Ser.). (ENG., Illus.). 20p. (J). (gr. -1-2). bds. 6.99 *(978-1-84322-862-2(9)*, Armadillo) Anness Publishing GBR. Dist: National Bk. Network.

—Nature. 2015. (ENG., Illus.). 20p. bds. 6.99 *(978-1-86147-411-7(3)*, Armadillo) Anness Publishing GBR. Dist: National Bk. Network.

—Numbers. 2015. (Learn-a-Word Book Ser.). (ENG., Illus.). 20p. (J). (gr. -1-2). bds. 6.99 *(978-1-84322-750-2(9)*, Armadillo) Anness Publishing GBR. Dist: National Bk. Network.

—Patterns: Learn-a-Word Book. 2016. (ENG., Illus.). 20p. bds. 6.99 *(978-1-86147-462-9(8)*, Armadillo) Anness Publishing GBR. Dist: National Bk. Network.

—Peekaboo! 2016. (ENG., Illus.). 20p. bds. 6.99 *(978-1-86147-477-3(6)*, Armadillo) Anness Publishing GBR. Dist: National Bk. Network.

—Puppies. (ENG., 2016. Illus.). 20p. bds. 6.99 *(978-1-86147-631-9(0)*, Armadillo) 2013. 12p. (J). (gr. -1-12). bds. 6.99 *(978-0-7548-2210-3(9))* Anness Publishing GBR. Dist: National Bk. Network.

—Shapes. 2015. (ENG., Illus.). 20p. bds. 6.99 *(978-1-86147-648-7(5)*, Armadillo) Anness Publishing GBR. Dist: National Bk. Network.

—Splish Splash. 2013. (ENG.). 12p. (J). (gr. -1 — 1). bds. 6.99 *(978-0-7548-2211-0(7))* Anness Publishing GBR. Dist: National Bk. Network.

Tuxworth, Nicole. Kittens. 2015. (ENG., Illus.). 20p. (J). (gr. -1 — 1). bds. 6.99 *(978-1-86147-384-4(2)*, Armadillo) Anness Publishing GBR. Dist: National Bk. Network.

Twin Sisters(r) Staff, et al. Happy Birthday, Jesus: A Sing-Along Storybook. 2015. (ENG., Illus.). 14p. (J). (-5). 9.99 *(978-1-63409-025-4(X))* Barbour Publishing, Inc.

—Jesus Loves Me More Than... 2015. (Let's Share a Story Ser.). (ENG., Illus.). 10p. (J). (gr. -1-k). bds. 9.99 *(978-1-63058-896-0(2))* Barbour Publishing, Inc.

Twohy, Mike. Oops, Pounce, Quick, Run! An Alphabet Caper. Twohy, Mike, illus. 2016. (Illus.). 32p. (J). (gr. -1-3). 17.99 *(978-0-06-237700-5(0))* HarperCollins Pubs.

Tyler, Brenda. The Tomtes of Hilltop Wood, 1 vol. 2010. (ENG., Illus.). 32p. (J). (gr. -1-3). 17.95 *(978-0-86315-772-1(6))* Floris Bks. GBR. Dist: SteinerBooks, Inc.

Tyler, Michael. The Skin You Live In. Csicsko, David Lee, illus. 2005. (ENG.). 32p. (J). (gr. k-2). 15.95 *(978-0-9759580-0-1(3))* Chicago Children's Museum.

Tyrrell, Melissa. The Gingerbread Man. McMullen, Nigel, illus. 2005. (Fairytale Friends Ser.: Vol. 8). 12p. (J). (gr. -1-k). bds. 5.95 *(978-1-58117-154-9(4)*, Intervisual/Piggy Toes) Bendon, Inc.

Tyson, Leigh Ann. Good Night, Little Dragons. 2012. (Little Golden Book Ser.). (ENG., Illus.). 24p. (J). (gr. k-k). 4.99 *(978-0-307-92957-0(4)*, Golden Bks.) Random Hse. Children's Bks.

U. S. National Geographic Society Staff. Halloween Book of Fun! 2011. (ENG., Illus.). 80p. (J). (gr. 1-4). pap. 6.99 *(978-1-4263-0848-2(5)*, National Geographic Children's Bks.) National Geographic Society.

Uegaki, Chieri. Hana Hashimoto, Sixth Violin. Leng, Qin, illus. 2014. (ENG.). 30p. (J). (gr. -1-3). 16.95 *(978-1-894786-33-1(5))* Kids Can Pr., Ltd. CAN. Dist: Hachette Bk. Group.

Ulkutay Design Group Staff & Random House Children's Books Staff, contrib. by. My Book of Kittens. 2016. (Illus.). (J). *(978-1-4806-9710-2(9)*, Golden Bks.) Random Hse. Children's Bks.

Underwood, Deborah. Here Comes Santa Cat. Rueda, Claudia, illus. 2014. (ENG.). 88p. (J). (gr. -1-k). 16.99 *(978-0-8037-4100-3(6)*, Dial Bks) Penguin Young Readers Group.

—The Loud Book! Padded Board Book. Liwska, Renata, illus. 2015. (ENG.). 32p. (J). (— 1). bds. 8.99 *(978-0-544-43064-8(6)*, HMH Books For Young Readers) Houghton Mifflin Harcourt Publishing Co.

Ungaro, Marley. Darling Dozen of the Deep. 2012. (ENG.). (J). pap. 24.99 *(978-1-4675-4418-4(3))* Independent Pub.

Ungerer, Tomi. Adelaide: The Flying Kangaroo. 2011. (ENG., Illus.). 40p. (gr. -1-3). 16.95 *(978-0-7148-6083-1(2))* Phaidon Pr., Inc.

—Crictor. (J). (gr. -1-3). pap. 12.95 incl. audio Weston Woods Studios, Inc.

—The Mellops Go Spelunking. 2015. (ENG., Illus.). 32p. (gr. -1-k). 14.95 *(978-0-7148-6971-1(6))* Phaidon Pr., Inc.

—Tomi Ungerer: A Treasury of 8 Books. 2016. (ENG.). 320p. (gr. k-3). 49.95 *(978-0-7148-7285-8(7))* Phaidon Pr., Inc.

Universal & King, Trey. Minions: The Road to Villain-Con - Reusable Sticker Book. 2015. (ENG., Illus.). 12p. (J). (gr. -1-1). pap. 6.99 *(978-0-316-29996-1(0))* Little, Brown Bks. for Young Readers.

Upjohn, Rebecca. Lily & the Paper Man, 1 vol. Benoit, Renne & Second Story Press Staff, illus. 2007. (ENG.). 24p. (J). (gr. k-3). 15.95 *(978-1-897187-19-7(X))* Second Story Pr. CAN. Dist: Orca Bk. Pubs. USA.

Urban, Linda. Little Red Henry. Valentine, Madeline, illus. 2015. (ENG.). 40p. (J). (gr. -1-3). 16.99 *(978-0-7636-6176-2(7))* Candlewick Pr.

Urrutia, Cristina. Who Will Save My Planet? 2012. (ENG., Illus.). 32p. (J). (gr. 2-5). 10.95 *(978-1-77049-281-3(X)*, Tundra Bks.) Tundra Bks. CAN. Dist: Penguin Random Hse. LLC.

USCCB Department of Justice, Peace, and Human Development. Green Street Park. 2015. (ENG., Illus.). 32p. (J). (gr. k-3). pap. 7.95 *(978-0-8294-4099-7(2))* Loyola Pr.

Vaid, Stephen. Moo's Walk. 2010. (Illus.). 28p. pap. *(978-0-7552-1236-1(3))* Authors OnLine, Ltd.

Valckx, Catharina & Catharina, Valckx. Bruno: Some of the More Interesting Days in My Life So Far. Hubesch, Nicolas, illus. 2017. (ENG.). 96p. (gr. k-4). 19.99 *(978-1-77657-124-6(X))* Gecko Pr. NZL. Dist: Lerner Publishing Group.

Valentin, Karen. Allie's World: Abuela & Abuelo Move: Abuela & Abuelo Move. 2009. 32p. 6.95 *(978-1-60349-021-4(3)*, Marimba Bks.) Hudson Publishing Group, The.

Van Allsburg, Chris. The Wreck of the Zephyr. 2014. 32p. pap. 9.00 *(978-1-61003-222-3(5))* Center for the Collaborative Classroom.

—The Wreck of the Zephyr. 30th anniv. ed. 2013. (ENG., Illus.). 32p. (J). (gr. -1-3). 18.99 *(978-0-544-05005-1(3))* Houghton Mifflin Harcourt Publishing Co.

Van Camp, Katie. Cookiebot! A Harry & Horsie Adventure. Agnew, Lincoln, illus. 2011. (Harry & Horsie Adventures Ser.: 2). (ENG.). 32p. (J). (gr. -1-1). 16.99 *(978-0-06-197445-8(5))* HarperCollins Pubs.

Van Der Heide, Iris. The Red Chalk. 2006. (ENG., Illus.). 24p. (J). (gr. -1-k). 19.95 *(978-1-932425-79-6(9)*, Lemniscaat) Boyds Mills Pr.

Van Doorn, Sandra. Paper Hearts. 2014. (ENG., Illus.). 32p. (J). (gr. -1-3). 16.95 *(978-1-927018-41-5(2)*, 9781927018415) Simply Read Bks. CAN. Dist: Ingram Publisher Services.

Van Fleet, Matthew. Dog. Stanton, Brian, photos by. 2007. (ENG., Illus.). 20p. (J). (gr. -1-2). 18.99 *(978-1-4169-4137-8(1)*, Simon & Schuster/Paula Wiseman Bks.) Simon & Schuster/Paula Wiseman Bks.

van Genechten, Guido. The Big Woods Orchestra. 2012. (ENG.). 24p. (J). (gr. -1-k). 17.95 *(978-1-60537-113-9(0))* Cobblestone Publishing Co.

van Lieshout, Maria. Flight 1-2-3. 2015. (ENG., Illus.). 32p. (J). (gr. -1 — 1). bds. 7.99 *(978-1-4521-4291-3(2))* Chronicle Bks. LLC.

VanSickle, Vikki. If I Had a Gryphon. Atkinson, Cale, illus. 2016. (ENG.). 32p. (J). (gr. -1-2). 16.99 *(978-1-77049-809-9(5)*, Tundra Bks.) Tundra Bks. CAN. Dist: Penguin Random Hse. LLC.

Various, illus. HarperCollins Treasury of Picture Book Classics: A Child's First Collection. 2015. (ENG.). 464p. (J). (gr. -1-3). 35.00 *(978-0-06-242725-0(3))* HarperCollins Pubs.

Vasiliu, Mircea. A Day at the Beach. 2007. (Illus.). 36p. (J). 7.95 *(978-1-59091-068-9(0))* Eastern National.

Vasquez, Paula. Lili Wool, 1 vol. 2017. (ENG.). 40p. (J). (gr. k-3). 14.99 ***(978-1-4236-4728-7(9))*** Gibbs Smith, Publisher.

Velikanje, Kathryn. Zebras Paint Themselves Rainbow. Hovhannisyan, Nune, illus. 2013. 58p. pap. 12.28 *(978-1-939896-02-5(9))* Levity Pr.

Velthuijs, Max. Where Is Frog? 2017. (ENG., Illus.). 14p. (J). (gr. -1-k). bds. 8.95 ***(978-0-2281-0002-7(X)***, 9780228100027) Firefly Bks., Ltd.

Verrept, Paul. El Pequeno Soldado. Bourgeois, Elodie, tr. Verrept, Paul, illus. 2004. (SPA., Illus.). 26p. (J). (gr. -1-3). 17.99 *(978-84-261-3306-9(1))* Juventud, Editorial ESP. Dist: Lectorum Pubns., Inc.

Verrett, Michael. It Followed Me Home Can I Keep It? (full Color) 2010. 35p. pap. 19.00 *(978-0-557-29796-2(6))* Lulu Pr., Inc.

—The White Alligator (paper Back) 2010. 116p. pap. 17.30 *(978-0-557-28042-1(7))* Lulu Pr., Inc.

Viau, Nancy. Just One Thing!, 1 vol. Young, Timothy, illus. 2016. (ENG.). 144p. (J). 12.99 *(978-0-7643-5162-4(1)*, 9780764351624) Schiffer Publishing, Ltd.

Vickery-Bharadwaj, Janice. Valentino & His Friends: It's Magic! 2012. 28p. pap. 12.99 *(978-1-4691-7709-0(9))* Xlibris Corp.

Vidal, Séverine. Mega Mouse. Barroux, Stephane, illus. 2015. (Mega Hero Bks.). (ENG.). 28p. (J). (gr. k-2). pap. 6.95 *(978-1-77085-655-4(2)*, 9781770856554) Firefly Bks., Ltd.

—Mega Wolf. Barroux, Stephane, illus. 2015. (Mega Hero Bks.). (ENG.). 28p. (J). (gr. k-2). pap. 6.95 *(978-1-77085-653-0(6)*, 9781770856530) Firefly Bks., Ltd.

Vilela, Caio. Goal! Taylor, Sean, tr. from POR. 2015. (ENG., Illus.). 40p. (J). pap. 10.99 *(978-1-84780-597-3(3)*, Frances Lincoln) Quarto Publishing Group UK GBR. Dist: Littlehampton Bk Services, Ltd.

Virján, Emma J. What This Story Needs Is a Hush & a Shush. Virján, Emma J., illus. 2016. (Pig in a Wig Book Ser.). (Illus.). 40p. (J). (gr. -1-3). 9.99 *(978-0-06-241528-8(X))* HarperCollins Pubs.

—What This Story Needs Is a Munch & a Crunch. Virján, Emma J., illus. 2016. (Pig in a Wig Book Ser.). (Illus.). 40p. (J). (gr. -1-3). 9.99 *(978-0-06-241529-5(8))* HarperCollins Pubs.

Viva, Frank. Outstanding in the Rain. 2015. (ENG., Illus.). 32p. (J). (gr. -1-3). 18.00 *(978-0-316-36627-4(7))* Little, Brown Bks. for Young Readers.

Voake, Charlotte. Melissa's Octopus & Other Unsuitable Pets. Voake, Charlotte, illus. 2015. (ENG., Illus.). 32p. (J). (gr. -1-2). 16.99 *(978-0-7636-7481-6(8))* Candlewick Pr.

Voake, Steve. Insect Detective. Voake, Charlotte, illus. 2012. (Read & Wonder Ser.). (ENG.). 32p. (J). (gr. -1-3). pap. 6.99 *(978-0-7636-5816-8(2))* Candlewick Pr.

—Insect Detective. Voake, Charlotte, illus. 2015. 32p. pap. 7.00 *(978-1-61003-407-4(4))* Center for the Collaborative Classroom.

—Insect Detective. 2012. (Read & Wonder Ser.). lib. bdg. 17.20 *(978-0-606-23802-1(6)*, Turtleback) Turtleback Bks.

Volke, Gordon. Big World Activity Sticker Book, Vol. 2. 2004. (Illus.). 16p. 7.25 *(978-1-84161-130-3(1))* Ravette Publishing, Ltd. GBR. Dist: Parkwest Pubns., Inc.

Vrombaut, An. Georgina the Giraffe. 2013. (ENG., Illus.). 32p. (J). (gr. -1-k). pap. 9.99 *(978-1-4449-1298-2(4))* Hodder & Stoughton GBR. Dist: Hachette Bk. Group.

—Henrietta the Hairy Hippo. Vrombaut, An, illus. 2013. (ENG., Illus.). 32p. (J). (gr. -1-k). pap. 8.99 *(978-1-4449-1299-9(2))* Hodder & Stoughton GBR. Dist: Hachette Bk. Group.

—Kevin the Crocodile. 2013. (ENG., Illus.). 32p. (J). (gr. -1-k). pap. 9.99 *(978-1-4449-1301-9(8))* Hodder & Stoughton GBR. Dist: Hachette Bk. Group.

—Zed the Zebra. Vrombaut, An, illus. 2013. (ENG., Illus.). 32p. (J). (gr. -1-k). pap. 8.99 *(978-1-4449-1303-3(4))* Hodder & Stoughton GBR. Dist: Hachette Bk. Group.

Vuillamy, Clara. The Bear with Sticky Paws Won't Go to Bed. Vuillamy, Clara, illus. 2010. (ENG., Illus.). 32p. (J). (gr. -1-2). 15.95 *(978-1-58925-087-1(7))* Tiger Tales.

Vulliamy, Clara. Bear with Sticky Paws Goes to School. Vulliamy, Clara, illus. 2010. (ENG., Illus.). 32p. pap. 7.95 *(978-1-58925-424-4(4))* Tiger Tales.

—Muffin & the Birthday Surprise. Vulliamy, Clara, illus. 2012. (ENG., Illus.). 32p. (J). (gr. -1-k). pap. 9.99 *(978-1-4083-1245-2(X))* Hodder & Stoughton GBR. Dist: Hachette Bk. Group.

Waddell, Martin. Something So Big. Canty, Charlotte, illus. 2004. (ENG.). 24p. (J). lib. bdg. 23.65 *(978-1-59646-706-4(1))* Dingles & Co.

Wadhwa, Vick. A New Take on ABCs - S Is for Smiling Sunrise: An Alphabet Book of Goodness, Beauty, & Wonder [Free Audio-Book Download Included]. Artists, Various, illus. l.t. ed. 2014. 32p. (J). 16.95 *(978-1-940229-12-6(X))* WordsBright.

Wagner, Anke. Help, I Don't Want a Babysitter! Behl, Anne-Kathrin, illus. 2015. (ENG.). 32p. (J). 17.95 *(978-0-7358-4214-4(0))* North-South Bks., Inc.

Wahl, Phoebe. Sonya's Chickens. 2015. (ENG., Illus.). 32p. (J). (gr. -1-3). 17.99 *(978-1-77049-789-4(7)*, Tundra Bks.) Tundra Bks. CAN. Dist: Penguin Random Hse. LLC.

Wakeman, Daniel. Ben's Big Dig, 1 vol. Van Stralen, Dirk, illus. 2005. (ENG.). 32p. (J). (gr. -1-3). 17.95 *(978-1-55143-384-4(2))* Orca Bk. Pubs. USA.

Waldman, David K. How Teddy Bears Find Their Homes. Danner, Maggie, illus. 2nd ed. 2015. (ENG.). 154p. (gr. k-2). pap. 38.40 *(978-0-945522-02-7(9))* Bk.Baby Print.

Waldman, Debby. A Sack Full of Feathers, 1 vol. Revell, Cindy, illus. 2007. (ENG.). 32p. (J). (gr. -1-3). 9.95 *(978-1-55143-863-4(1))* Orca Bk. Pubs. USA.

Walker, Anna. I Love Birthdays. Walker, Anna, illus. 2010. (ENG., Illus.). 32p. (J). (gr. -1-1). 9.99 *(978-1-4169-8320-0(1)*, Simon & Schuster Bks. For Young Readers) Simon & Schuster Bks. For Young Readers.

—I Love My Mom. Walker, Anna, illus. 2010. (ENG., Illus.). 32p. (J). (gr. -1-1). 9.99 *(978-1-4169-8318-7(X)*, Simon & Schuster Bks. For Young Readers) Simon & Schuster Bks. For Young Readers.

Walker, B. Mr Peeze, Say Something Else Please! 2011. 28p. pap. 15.99 *(978-1-4568-2937-7(8))* Xlibris Corp.

Wallace, Chad. The Mouse & the Meadow, 1 vol. Wallace, Chad, illus. 2014. (ENG., Illus.). 32p. (J). (gr. k-4). 16.95 *(978-1-58469-481-6(5))* Dawn Pubns.

Wallace, Ian. The Huron Carol, 1 vol. 2013. (ENG., Illus.). 32p. (J). (gr. -1). 14.95 *(978-1-55498-394-0(0))* Groundwood Bks. CAN. Dist: Publishers Group West (PGW).

Wallace, Mary. The Inuksuk Book. Wallace, Mary & Owlkids Books Inc. Staff, illus. 2004. (Wow Canada! Ser.). (ENG.). 64p. (J). (gr. 3-6). pap. 13.95 *(978-1-897066-13-3(9)*, Owlkids) Owlkids Bks. Inc. CAN. Dist: Publishers Group West (PGW).

Wallner, S. J. Hans & the Golden Stirrup. (Illus.). 48p. (J). (gr. 2-3). lib. bdg. 10.95 *(978-0-87783-016-0(9))*; pap. 3.94 *(978-0-87783-093-1(2))* Oddo Publishing, Inc.

Walsch, Neale Donald. The Little Soul & the Earth: A Children's Parable Adapted from Conversations with God. Riccio, Frank, illus. 2005. (ENG.). 32p. (J). 20.00 *(978-1-57174-451-7(7))* Hampton Roads Publishing Co., Inc.

Walsh, Aly. My Mum Says Blah Blah Blah. Walsh, Marilyn, illus. 2012. 26p. pap. 15.97 *(978-1-61204-854-3(4)*, Strategic Bk. Publishing) Strategic Book Publishing & Rights Agency (SBPRA).

Walsh, Joanna. Did You Ever See? 2016. (ENG., Illus.). 32p. (J). (gr. k-4). 16.95 *(978-1-84976-349-3(6))* Tate Publishing, Ltd. GBR. Dist: Abrams, Inc.

Walter Foster Creative Team. Dinosaurs: Interactive Fun with Reusable Stickers, Fold-Out Play Scene, & Punch-out, Stand-up Figures! Cerato, Mattia, illus. 2015. (Sticker, Punch-Out, & Play! Ser.). (ENG.). 12p. (J). (gr. -1-1). pap. 6.99 *(978-1-63322-000-3(1))* Quarto Publishing Group USA.

—Mighty Machines. 2014. (Look, Read, Learn Ser.). (ENG., Illus.). 90p. (J). (gr. -1-1). 12.95 *(978-0-7603-4712-6(3)*, Walter Foster Jr) Quarto Publishing Group USA.

—Tractors & Farm Trucks. 2014. (Look, Read, Learn Ser.). (ENG., Illus.). 90p. (J). (gr. -1-1). 12.95 *(978-0-7603-4713-3(1)*, Walter Foster Jr) Quarto Publishing Group USA.

Walters, Eric. Hope Springs. Fernandes, Eugenie, illus. 2014. (ENG.). 32p. (J). (gr. 1-4). 17.99 *(978-1-77049-530-2(4)*, Tundra Bks.) Tundra Bks. CAN. Dist: Penguin Random Hse. LLC.

—My Name Is Blessing. Fernandes, Eugenie, illus. 2013. (ENG.). 32p. (J). (gr. 1-4). 17.95 *(978-1-77049-301-8(8)*, Tundra Bks.) Tundra Bks. CAN. Dist: Penguin Random Hse. LLC.

Walton, Ann. Something to Do. Hinrichsen, Natalie, illus. 2010. (ENG.). 24p. (J). (gr. k-2). pap. 6.00 *(978-1-77009-706-3(6))* Jacana Media ZAF. Dist: Independent Pubs. Group.

—The Tale of Sun & Moon. Hinrichsen, Tamsin, illus. 2010. (ENG.). 32p. (J). (gr. k-2). 11.95 *(978-1-77009-705-6(8))* Jacana Media ZAF. Dist: Independent Pubs. Group.

Walton, Rick. Frankenstein's Fright Before Christmas. Hale, Nathan, illus. 2014. (ENG.). 32p. (J). (gr. -1-3). 16.99 *(978-0-312-55367-8(6)*, 9780312553678) Feiwel & Friends.

Wan, Joyce. You Are My Merry Little Christmas. Wan, Joyce, illus. 2016. (ENG., Illus.). 14p. (J). (— 1). 6.99 *(978-0-545-88093-0(9)*, Cartwheel Bks.) Scholastic, Inc.

Wang, Margaret. Eency Weency Spider. Rueda, Claudia, illus. 2006. (ENG.). 22p. (J). (gr. -1-3). bds. 10.95 *(978-1-58117-418-2(7)*, Intervisual/Piggy Toes) Bendon, Inc.

—Postcards from Kitty. Silver-Thompson, Pattie, illus. 2005. 12p. (J). (gr. -1-3). 9.95 *(978-1-58117-427-4(6)*, Intervisual/Piggy Toes) Bendon, Inc.

Wang, Ruowen. To Share One Moon. Xu, Wei & Zheng, Xiaoyan, illus. 2008. 32p. (J). (gr. 2-4). *(978-0-9738799-5-7(5))* Kevin & Robin Bks., Ltd.

Warburg, Sandol Stoddard. The Thinking Book. 2016. (ENG., Illus.). 24p. 14.95 *(978-1-62326-088-0(4))* AMMO Bks., LLC.

Ward, Helen. Moon Dog. 2005. (Illus.). 40p. (J). *(978-1-84011-864-3(4))* Templar Publishing.

—The Town Mouse & the Country Mouse. Ward, Helen, illus. 2012. (ENG., Illus.). 48p. (J). (gr. -1-3). 16.99 *(978-0-7636-6098-7(1)*, Templar) Candlewick Pr.

Ward, Jennifer. What Will Hatch? Ghahremani, Susie, illus. 2016. (ENG.). 30p. (J). bds. 8.99 *(978-1-61963-943-0(2)*, 9781619639430, Bloomsbury USA Childrens) Bloomsbury Publishing USA.

Ward, Nick. The Tadpole Prince. 2003. (Illus.). 32p. (YA). *(978-1-84365-016-4(9)*, Pavilion Children's Books) Pavilion Bks.

Waring, Geoff. Oscar & the Bird: A Book about Electricity. Waring, Geoff, illus. 2011. (Start with Science Ser.). (ENG., Illus.). 32p. (J). (gr. -1-3). pap. 6.99 *(978-0-7636-5302-6(0))* Candlewick Pr.

—Oscar & the Snail: A Book about Things That We Use. Waring, Geoff, illus. 2011. (Start with Science Ser.). (ENG., Illus.). 32p. (J). (gr. -1-3). pap. 6.99 *(978-0-7636-5303-3(9))* Candlewick Pr.

The Water Cycle. (Illus.). (J). (gr. k-5). 112.50 *(978-0-8239-7276-0(3))* Rosen Publishing Group, Inc., The.

Watkins, Kathleen. Pigín of Howth. Suggs, Margaret Anne, illus. 2017. (ENG.). 64p. (J). 28.00 ***(978-0-7171-6972-6(3))*** M.H. Gill & Co. U. C. IRL. Dist: Dufour Editions, Inc.

Watson, Jacqueline. Six Frogs on a Log! 2004. 43p. pap. 24.95 *(978-1-4137-2986-3(X))* PublishAmerica, Inc.

Watson, Jane Werner. Animal Friends. Williams, Garth, illus. 2016. (Little Golden Book Ser.). (ENG.). 24p. (J). (gr. -1-k). 4.99 *(978-0-553-53642-3(7)*, Golden Bks.) Random Hse. Children's Bks.

—The Fuzzy Duckling. Provensen, Martin & Provensen, Alice, illus. 2015. (Little Golden Book Ser.). (ENG.). 24p. (J). (-k). 4.99 *(978-0-553-52213-6(2)*, Golden Bks.) Random Hse. Children's Bks.

Watt, Fiona. Baby's Very First Noisy Book Jungle. 2017. (Picture Bks.). (ENG.). 10p. (J). 15.99 ***(978-0-7945-3986-3(6)***, Usborne) EDC Publishing.

—Este No Es Mi Tren. rev. ed. 2004. (Titles in Spanish Ser.).Tr. of That's Not My Train. 32p. (J). 12.99 *(978-1-58086-585-2(2))* EDC Publishing.

—Polar Bears. Chiara, Francesca De, illus. 2010. (Luxury Touchy-Feely Board Bks). 10p. (J). bds. 15.99 *(978-0-7945-2544-6(X)*, Usborne) EDC Publishing.

—Rainy Day Stroller Book. Baggott, Stella, illus. 2010. 8p. (J). 7.99 *(978-0-7945-2850-8(3)*, Usborne) EDC Publishing.

—Seaside Stroller Book. Baggott, Stella, illus. 2010. 8p. (J). 7.99 *(978-0-7945-2810-2(4)*, Usborne) EDC Publishing.

—That's Not My Dragon... Wells, Rachel, illus. 2006. (Usborne Touchy-Feely Bks.). 10p. (J). (gr. -1-k). bds. 7.99 *(978-0-7945-1285-9(2)*, Usborne) EDC Publishing.

—That's Not My Dragon. rev. ed. 2011. (Touchy-Feely Board Bks). 10p. (J). ring bd. 8.99 *(978-0-7945-3092-1(3)*, Usborne) EDC Publishing.

—That's Not My Prince. Wells, Rachel, illus. 2013. (Usborne Touchy-Feely Board Bks.). (ENG.). 10p. (J). 9.99 *(978-0-7945-2838-6(4)*, Usborne) EDC Publishing.

—That's Not My Santa. rev. ed. 2012. (Touchy-Feely Board Bks). 10p. (J). bds. 8.99 *(978-0-7945-3310-6(8)*, Usborne) EDC Publishing.

Watt, Fiona & Wells, Rachel. Gatitos. 2004. (SPA.). 10p. (J). 11.95 *(978-0-7460-5091-0(7))* EDC Publishing.

Watt, Mélanie. Chester's Back! Watt, Mélanie, illus. (Chester Ser.). (ENG., Illus.). 32p. (J). (gr. -1-3). 2013. 8.95 *(978-1-55453-461-6(5))* 2008. 18.95 *(978-1-55453-287-2(6))* Kids Can Pr., Ltd. CAN. Dist: Hachette Bk. Group.

—Have I Got a Book for You! Watt, Mélanie, illus. 2013. (ENG., Illus.). 32p. (J). (gr. k-4). pap. 7.95 *(978-1-55453-483-8(6))* Kids Can Pr., Ltd. CAN. Dist: Hachette Bk. Group.

—Scaredy Squirrel. 2011. (J). (gr. -1-3). 29.95 *(978-0-545-32740-4(7))*; 18.95 *(978-0-545-32752-7(0))*;Set. 38.75 *(978-0-545-32759-6(8))* Weston Woods Studios, Inc.

—Scaredy Squirrel at Night. Watt, Mélanie, illus. 2009. (ENG., Illus.). 32p. (J). (gr. -1-3). 16.95 *(978-1-55453-288-9(4))* Kids Can Pr., Ltd. CAN. Dist: Hachette Bk. Group.

—Scaredy Squirrel Goes Camping. Watt, Mélanie, illus. 2013. (ENG., Illus.). 32p. (J). (gr. -1-3). pap. 16.95 *(978-1-894786-86-7(6))* Kids Can Pr., Ltd. CAN. Dist: Hachette Bk. Group.

—Scaredy Squirrel Has a Birthday Party. Watt, Mélanie, illus. 2011. (ENG., Illus.). 32p. (J). (gr. -1-3). 16.95 *(978-1-55453-468-5(2))* Kids Can Pr., Ltd. CAN. Dist: Hachette Bk. Group.

—Scaredy Squirrel Prepares for Christmas. Watt, Mélanie, illus. 2012. (ENG., Illus.). 80p. (J). (gr. -1-3). 17.95 *(978-1-55453-469-2(0))* Kids Can Pr., Ltd. CAN. Dist: Hachette Bk. Group.

—Scaredy Squirrel Prepares for Halloween. Watt, Mélanie, illus. 2013. (ENG., Illus.). 64p. (J). (gr. -1-3). 17.95 *(978-1-894786-87-4(4))* Kids Can Pr., Ltd. CAN. Dist: Hachette Bk. Group.

Watts, Bernadette. The Golden Plate. 2014. (ENG., Illus.). 32p. (J). 17.95 *(978-0-7358-4175-8(6))* North-South Bks., Inc.

Watts, Bernadette, et al. Little Red Riding Hood. Watts, Edith M B., illus. 2011. (ENG.). 32p. (J). pap. 7.95 *(978-0-7358-4008-9(3))* North-South Bks., Inc.

Weakly, Chris A. Toby the Little Switch Engine. 2012. 24p. 24.95 *(978-1-4626-4884-9(3))* America Star Bks.

Weale, Andrew. Dinosaur Doo. 2014. (ENG., Illus.). 32p. (J). (gr. -1-k). pap. 10.99 *(978-1-4449-0163-4(X))* Hodder & Stoughton GBR. Dist: Hachette Bk. Group.

Weatherford, Carole Boston. Freedom on the Menu: The Greensboro Sit-Ins. Lagarrigue, Jerome Lagarrigue, illus. 2007. (ENG.). 32p. (J). (gr. -1-3). pap. 5.99 *(978-0-14-240894-0(8)*, Puffin Books) Penguin Young Readers Group.

Weaver, A. J. Big Cats, Little Cats. Budgen, Tim, illus. 2013. 32p. pap. *(978-1-909423-03-9(3))* Bks. to Treasure.

Webb, Sarah & Ranson, Claire. Sally Go Round the Stars: Favourite Rhymes from an Irish Childhood. McCarthy, Steve, illus. 2015. (ENG.). 64p. (J). pap. 17.00 *(978-1-84717-675-2(5))* O'Brien Pr., Ltd., The IRL. Dist: Dufour Editions, Inc.

Webb, Steve. Happy Zappa Cat. Le Huche, Magali, illus. 2014. (ENG.). 32p. 15.99 *(978-0-85707-620-5(5)*, Simon & Schuster Children's) Simon & Schuster, Ltd. GBR. Dist: Simon & Schuster, Inc.

—Rocket Racers. Mantle, Ben, illus. 2014. (ENG.). 24p. (J). (-k). pap. 8.99 *(978-0-552-56673-5(X))* Transworld Publishers Ltd. GBR. Dist: Independent Pubs. Group.

Webber, Helen. Webber Quartet, 4 Vols. deluxe ed. (J). (gr. k-6). 35.00 *(978-0-8392-3070-0(2))* Astor-Honor, Inc.

Webster, Christy. Grumpy Cat Little Golden Book #2 (Grumpy Cat) Golden Books, illus. 2017. (Little Golden Book Ser.). (ENG.). 24p. (J). (gr. -1-1). 4.99 *(978-0-399-55783-5(0)*, Golden Bks.) Random Hse. Children's Bks.

Webster, Jean. Papaito-Piernas-Largas. (SPA.). (YA). (gr. 5-8). pap. *(978-950-08-1515-4(X)*, AA7255) Atlantida ARG. Dist: Lectorum Pubns., Inc.

Wedge, Chris. Bunny: A Picture Book Adapted from the Animated Film. Wedge, Chris, illus. 2004. (Illus.). 30p. (J). (gr. k-4). reprint ed. 19.00 *(978-0-7567-7460-8(8))* DIANE Publishing Co.

Wehr, Julian. Snow White. 2004. (Illus.). 14p. (J). pap. 12.95 *(978-0-9748093-0-4(6))* Wehr Animations.

Weidenbach, Kristin. Meet Banjo Paterson. Hancock, James Gulliver, illus. 2015. (Meet... Ser.: Bk. 7). (ENG.). 32p. (J). (gr. -1-k). 21.99 *(978-0-85798-008-3(4))* Random Hse. Australia AUS. Dist: Independent Pubs. Group.

Weidner, Teri, illus. Sleep, Baby, Sleep. 2009. 20p. (J). (gr. -1-k). 8.95 *(978-1-58925-843-3(6))* Tiger Tales.

Weigand, Jessica. I Have a Monster under My Bed. 2009. 20p. pap. 10.49 *(978-1-4389-7503-0(1))* AuthorHouse.

Weiser, Joey. Mermin Volume 2: the Big Catch: The Big Catch. 2013. (ENG., Illus.). 136p. (J). 19.99 *(978-1-62010-101-8(7)*, 9781620101018) Oni Pr., Inc.

Weiskal, N. J. C Is for the Christ Child. 2009. 32p. pap. 8.00 *(978-1-935125-55-6(9))* Robertson Publishing.

Weiskal, N. j. & Weiskal, N. J. The Skittery Kitten & the Scaredy Cat. Weiskal, N. J., illus. 2009. (Illus.). 36p. pap. 8.00 *(978-1-935125-59-4(1))* Robertson Publishing.

Weiss, Ellen. Simba's Moon. Cuddy, Robin, illus. Date not set. (ENG.). 32p. (J). (gr. -1-2). 12.99 *(978-0-7868-3267-5(3))* Disney Pr.

Wellesley, Rosie. Moonlight Bear. Wellesley, Rosie, illus. 2015. (ENG., Illus.). 32p. (J). (gr. -1-3). pap. 9.99 *(978-1-84365-292-2(7)*, Pavilion) Pavilion Bks. GBR. Dist: Independent Pubs. Group.

—Wide Awake Hedgehog. 2017. (ENG., Illus.). 32p. (J). (gr. -1-1). 9.99 *(978-1-84365-309-7(5)*, Pavilion) Pavilion Bks. GBR. Dist: Independent Pubs. Group.

Wells, E. A. The Butterfly Weed Patch. 2012. 32p. pap. *(978-1-105-50787-8(4))* Lulu.com.

Wells, Mark & Wells, Meagan. Tommy's Lost Tooth. Wells, Mark, illus. 2011. (Illus.). 28p. pap. 11.99 *(978-1-61170-020-6(5))* Robertson Publishing.

Wells, Rosemary. Max & Ruby's Bedtime Book. 2015. (Max & Ruby Ser.). (ENG., Illus.). 42p. (J). (gr. -1-k). 8.99 *(978-0-14-751746-3(X)*, Puffin Books) Penguin Young Readers Group.

—Ruby's Falling Leaves. 2007. (Max & Ruby Ser.). lib. bdg. 13.55 *(978-1-4177-9651-9(0)*, Turtleback) Turtleback Bks.

—Time-Out for Sophie. Wells, Rosemary, illus. 2015. (ENG., Illus.). 26p. (J). (gr. -1). bds. 6.99 *(978-0-451-47766-8(9)*, Viking Books for Young Readers) Penguin Young Readers Group.

Welsh, Karen Leis. Frolicking Friends. 2012. (Illus.). 44p. pap. 21.99 *(978-1-4685-6422-8(6))* AuthorHouse.

Welton, Jude. Tomas Loves... A Rhyming Book about Fun, Friendship - & Autism. Telford, Jane, illus. 2015. (ENG.). 32p. 15.95 *(978-1-84905-544-4(0)*, 7155) Kingsley, Jessica Pubs. GBR. Dist: Macmillan Distribution Ltd.

Weninger, Brigitte. Happy Birthday, Davy! Tharlet, Eve, illus. 2nd rev. ed. 2015. (ENG.). 32p. (J). 15.95 *(978-0-7358-4224-3(8))* North-South Bks., Inc.

—Happy Easter, Davy! Tharlet, Eve, illus. 2014. (ENG.). 32p. (J). (gr. k-3). 15.95 *(978-0-7358-4161-1(6))* North-South Bks., Inc.

—Merry Christmas Davy. Tharlet, Eve, illus. 2014. (ENG.). 32p. (J). 15.95 *(978-0-7358-4186-4(1))* North-South Bks., Inc.

West, Colin. Have You Seen the Crocodile? Read & Share. West, Colin, illus. 2003. (Reading & Math Together Ser.). (ENG., Illus.). 32p. (J). (gr. -1-3). pap. 3.99 *(978-0-7636-0862-0(9))* Candlewick Pr.

West, Tracey & dePaola, Tomie. No Way ... Way! Road Trip. 2015. (Smithsonian Ser.). (ENG., Illus.). 208p. (J). (gr. 3-7). bds. 9.99 *(978-0-448-48211-8(8)*, Grosset & Dunlap) Penguin Young Readers Group.

Wezeman, Phyllis Vos & Liechty, Anna L. Tell Me a Story: 30 Children's Sermons Based on Best-Loved Books. 2005. (New Brown Bag Ser.). (Illus.). 96p. pap. 12.00 *(978-0-8298-1635-8(6))* Pilgrim Pr., The/United Church Pr.

Whale Mail. 2003. (J). spiral bd. 9.95 *(978-0-89610-126-5(6))* Island Heritage Publishing.

Wharton, Eileen. The Shmoogly Boo. Walker, David, illus. 2016. (ENG.). 24p. (J). (gr. -1-1). pap. 9.99 *(978-1-907432-23-1(X))* Hogs Back Bks. GBR. Dist: Independent Pubs. Group.

Wheeler, Lisa. Ugly Pie. Solomon, Heather, illus. 2014. (ENG.). 32p. (J). (gr. -1-3). pap. 7.99 *(978-0-544-23961-6(X)*, HMH Books For Young Readers) Houghton Mifflin Harcourt Publishing Co.

Whelan, Susan & Merritt, Susanne. Don't Think about Purple Elephants. Jones, Gwynneth, illus. 2017. (ENG.). 32p. (J).

(gr. -1-3). pap. 12.99 *(978-1-925335-48-4(8))* Exisle Publishing Pty Ltd. AUS. Dist: Hachette Bk. Group.

When I Go. 2003. (Illus.). (J). bds. 7.98 *(978-0-7525-8657-1(2))* Parragon, Inc.

When I Grow Up - Builder. 2016. (When I Grow Up ... Ser.). (ENG., Illus.). 32p. (J). (gr. -1-2). pap. 8.99 ***(978-0-7232-9471-9(2))*** Penguin Bks., Ltd. GBR. Dist: Independent Pubs. Group.

When I Grow Up - Farmer. 2016. (When I Grow Up ... Ser.). (ENG., Illus.). 32p. (J). (gr. -1-1). pap. 8.99 ***(978-0-7232-9472-6(0))*** Penguin Bks., Ltd. GBR. Dist: Independent Pubs. Group.

White, Howard. The Airplane Ride. Guzek, Greta, illus. unabr. ed. 2006. (ENG.). 32p. (J). bds. 16.95 *(978-0-88971-224-9(7))* Harbour Publishing Co., Ltd. CAN. Dist: Midpoint Trade Bks., Inc.

Whiten, Jan. Chooky-Doodle-Doo. Hanley, Sinéad, illus. 2015. (ENG.). 32p. (J). (-k). 12.99 *(978-0-7636-7327-7(7))* Candlewick Pr.

Whitford Paul, Ann. Fiesta Fiasco. 2012. 29.95 *(978-1-4301-1100-9(3))* Live Oak Media.

Whiting, Sue. Platypus. Jackson, Mark, illus. 2016. (ENG.). 32p. (J). (gr. k-4). 16.99 *(978-0-7636-8098-5(2))* Candlewick Pr.

Whitley, Jeremy. Get over Yourself, Vol. 2. 2013. (ENG., Illus.). 128p. (J). pap. 14.95 *(978-0-9859652-4-2(X)*, 9780985965242) Action Lab Entertainment.

Whitman, Nancy C. Counting Petals: Using Flowers of Hawaii. Chong, Luther, photos by. 2009. (Illus.). 31p. (J). *(978-1-4363-8562-6(8))* Xlibris Corp.

Whybrow, Ian. The Christmas Bear. Scheffler, Axel, illus. 2016. (ENG.). 10p. (J). (gr. -1-2). bds. 8.99 *(978-1-5098-0696-6(2))* Pan Macmillan GBR. Dist: Independent Pubs. Group.

—Say Hello to the Snowy Animals! Eaves, Edward, illus. 2012. (J). *(978-0-7607-9675-7(0))* Barnes & Noble, Inc.

—Tim, Ted & the Pirates. Ayto, Russell, illus. 2014. (ENG.). 32p. (J). 17.99 *(978-0-00-755930-5(5)*, HarperCollins Children's Bks.) HarperCollins Pubs. Ltd. GBR. Dist: HarperCollins Pubs.

—Where's Tim's Ted? It's Time for Bed! Ayto, Russell, illus. 2014. (ENG.). 32p. (J). 17.99 *(978-0-00-755929-9(1)*, HarperCollins Children's Bks.) HarperCollins Pubs. Ltd. GBR. Dist: HarperCollins Pubs.

Whybrow, Ian, et al. Owain A'r Cloc. 2005. (WEL., Illus.). 20p. 6.99 *(978-1-84323-366-4(5))* Gomer Pr. GBR. Dist: Gomer Pr.

Widgen, Susan. A Caring Deed for Becky. Novak, Steven, illus. 2012. 36p. pap. 8.99 *(978-1-60820-579-0(7))* MLR Pr., LLC.

Wiesner, David. Tuesday. 2011. (ENG., Illus.). 32p. (J). (gr. -1-3). pap. 7.99 *(978-0-395-87082-2(8))* Houghton Mifflin Harcourt Publishing Co.

Wigden, Susan. I Want to Learn to Dance. Franzese, Nora Tapp, illus. 2012. 36p. pap. 11.99 *(978-1-60820-725-1(0))* MLR Pr., LLC.

Wilcox, Leah. Waking Beauty. Monks, Lydia, illus. 2011. (ENG.). 32p. (J). (gr. -1-k). pap. 6.99 *(978-0-14-241538-2(3)*, Puffin Books) Penguin Young Readers Group.

Wilde, Irma & dePaola, Tomie. Mr. Wishing Went Fishing. Wilde, George, illus. 2015. (G&d Vintage Ser.). (ENG.). 32p. (J). (gr. -1-k). bds. 7.99 *(978-0-448-48762-5(4)*, Grosset & Dunlap) Penguin Young Readers Group.

Wilder, Laura Ingalls. A Little House Picture Book Treasury: Six Stories of Life on the Prairie: Going to Town, Country Fair, a Little Prairie House, Sugar Snow, Winter Days in the Big Woods, & Christmas in the Big Woods. Graef, Renee, illus. 2017. (Little House Picture Book Ser.). 208p. (J). (gr. -1-3). 24.99 ***(978-0-06-247077-5(9))*** HarperCollins Pubs.

Wilding, Valerie. The Grumpy Queen. Sanfilippo, Simona, illus. 2011. (ENG.). 32p. (J). (gr. -1-k). pap. *(978-1-84089-637-4(X))* Zero to Ten, Ltd.

Wilkes, Ruth. Dancing Fruit Put on a Show! Cross, James, illus. 2013. 48p. 18.99 *(978-1-62314-797-6(2))* Willow Publishing.

Wilkin, Esther. Baby Listens. Wilkin, Eloise, illus. 2012. (Little Golden Book Ser.). (ENG.). 24p. (J). (gr. k-k). 3.99 *(978-0-307-93012-5(2)*, Golden Bks.) Random Hse. Children's Bks.

Wilkins, James Francis. The Queen & Mr Brown: A Day for Dinosaurs. 2015. (ENG., Illus.). 48p. (J). (gr. k-2). pap. 11.99 *(978-0-565-09354-9(1))* Natural History Museum Pubns. GBR. Dist: Independent Pubs. Group.

—The Queen & Mr Brown: a Night in the Natural History Museum. 2016. (ENG., Illus.). 48p. (J). (gr. -1-2). 17.99 *(978-0-565-09376-1(2))* Natural History Museum Pubns. GBR. Dist: Independent Pubs. Group.

Wilkins, Nalini. Doby's First Christmas. Robb, Jonathan, illus. 2012. 28p. pap. 12.50 *(978-1-62212-777-1(3)*, Strategic Bk. Publishing) Strategic Book Publishing & Rights Agency (SBPRA).

Willems, Mo. Don't Let the Pigeon Drive the Bus! Willems, Mo, illus. 2003. (Pigeon Ser.). (ENG., Illus.). 40p. (J). (gr. -1-k). 16.99 *(978-0-7868-1988-1(X))* Hyperion Pr.

—It's a Busload of Pigeon Books! Willems, Mo, illus. 2013. (Pigeon Ser.). (ENG., Illus.). 120p. (J). (gr. -1-k). 24.99 *(978-1-4231-7589-6(1))* Hyperion Pr.

—Knuffle Bunny: A Cautionary Tale. Willems, Mo, illus. 2004. (Knuffle Bunny Ser.). (ENG., Illus.). 40p. (J). (gr. -1-k). 17.99 *(978-0-7868-1870-9(0))* Hyperion Pr.

—The Pigeon Has Feelings, Too! Willems, Mo, illus. 2005. (Pigeon Ser.). (ENG., Illus.). 12p. (J). (gr. -1-k). 6.99 *(978-0-7868-3650-5(4))* Hyperion Pr.

—The Pigeon Loves Things That Go! Willems, Mo, illus. 2005. (Pigeon Ser.). (ENG., Illus.). 12p. (J). (gr. -1-k). 6.99 *(978-0-7868-3651-2(2))* Hyperion Pr.

Willems, Mo, illus. Don't Let the Pigeon Drive the Bus! 2005. 40p. (J). *(978-1-84428-013-1(6))* Walker Bks. Australia Pty, Ltd.

William H. Sadlier Staff. Stop by a Pond. 2005. (Early Library). (gr. k-2). 24.00 net. *(978-0-8215-8942-7(3))* Sadlier, William H. Inc.

Williams, Brenda. Outdoor Opposites. Oldfield, Rachel, illus. 2015. 32p. (J). (gr. -1-2). 9.99 *(978-1-78285-095-3(3))* Barefoot Bks., Inc.

Williams, Chase. The Tale of the Beaver. 2012. 36p. pap. 21.99 *(978-1-4691-7984-1(9))* Xlibris Corp.

Williams, Emma Louise. Harry the Hedgehog Loses His Favorite Sock. 2012. 20p. pap. 7.99 *(978-1-939076-00-7(5))* Wiggies, Piggy.

—What's That Smell Monkey? williams, Emma Louise, illus. 2012. 12p. pap. 7.99 *(978-1-939076-07-6(2))* Wiggies, Piggy.

Williams-Garcia, Rita. Bottle Cap Boys on Royal Street. 2009. (Illus.). 32p. (J). 16.95 *(978-1-60349-030-6(2)*, Marimba Bks.) Hudson Publishing Group, The.

Williams, Garth. Baby Farm Animals. 2016. (Little Golden Board Book Ser.). (ENG., Illus.). 26p. (J). (gr. -1-k). bds. 7.99 *(978-0-553-53632-4(X)*, Golden Bks.) Random Hse. Children's Bks.

Williams, Garth, illus. Garth Williams's Furry Tales. 2016. (Little Golden Book Treasury Ser.). (ENG.). 224p. (J). (-k). 12.99 *(978-1-101-93528-6(6)*, Golden Bks.) Random Hse. Children's Bks.

Williams, Margery. The Velveteen Rabbit: Or How Toys Become Real. Santore, Charles, illus. 2013. (Classic Edition Ser.). (ENG.). 48p. (J). 17.95 *(978-1-60433-277-3(8)*, Applesauce Pr.) Cider Mill Pr. Bk. Pubs., LLC.

Williams, Renee Pierce. Buck the Good Doog. 2012. 28p. pap. 15.99 *(978-1-4691-5325-4(4))* Xlibris Corp.

Williams, Sam. Talk Peace. Moriuchi, Mique, illus. 2005. 32p. (J). 16.95 *(978-0-8234-1936-4(3))* Holiday Hse., Inc.

Williams, Walter. The Bicycle Garden. 2013. 40p. pap. 6.99 *(978-0-9890698-0-9(X))* Fernwood & Hedges Bks.

Williamson, Jennifer. Timmy the Tow Truck, 6 vols. Williamson, Alan, 8th, illus. 2005. 28p. (J). pap. *(978-0-9771678-1-4(X))* Theee Hole Punch Publishing.

Williamson, Karen. Baby Jesus, 1 vol. Conner, Sarah, illus. 2015. (Candle Little Lambs Ser.). (ENG.). 24p. (J). pap. 2.99 *(978-1-78128-188-8(2)*, Candle Bks.) Lion Hudson PLC GBR. Dist: Kregel Pubns.

—Bible Sliders, 1 vol. Selbert, Kathryn, illus. 2015. (ENG.). 10p. (J). bds. 9.99 *(978-1-78128-224-3(2)*, Candle Bks.) Lion Hudson PLC GBR. Dist: Kregel Pubns.

—The First Easter, 1 vol. Conner, Sarah, illus. 2016. (Candle Little Lambs Ser.). (ENG.). 24p. (J). pap. 2.99 *(978-1-78128-243-4(9)*, Candle Bks.) Lion Hudson PLC GBR. Dist: Kregel Pubns.

—The Good Samaritan, 1 vol. Conner, Sarah, illus. 2017. (Candle Little Lambs Ser.). (ENG.). 24p. (J). pap. 2.99 ***(978-1-78128-323-3(0)***, Candle Bks.) Lion Hudson PLC GBR. Dist: Kregel Pubns.

—Lift the Flap Bible, 1 vol. Anglicas, Louise, illus. 2014. (ENG.). 16p. (J). bds. 12.99 *(978-1-78128-130-7(0)*, Candle Bks.) Lion Hudson PLC GBR. Dist: Kregel Pubns.

—Play-Time Noah, 1 vol. Anglicas, Louise, illus. 2014. (ENG.). 8p. (J). bds. 9.99 *(978-1-78128-111-6(4)*, Candle Bks.) Lion Hudson PLC GBR. Dist: Kregel Pubns.

—The Prodigal Son, 1 vol. Conner, Sarah, illus. 2017. (Candle Little Lambs Ser.). (ENG.). 24p. (J). pap. 2.99 ***(978-1-78128-325-7(7)***, Candle Bks.) Lion Hudson PLC GBR. Dist: Kregel Pubns.

—Samuel, 1 vol. Conner, Sarah, illus. 2017. (Candle Little Lambs Ser.). (ENG.). 24p. (J). pap. 2.99 ***(978-1-78128-326-4(5)***, Candle Bks.) Lion Hudson PLC GBR. Dist: Kregel Pubns.

Williamson, Karen. The Wise Men's Story, 1 vol. Barnard, Lucy, illus. 2016. (Bible Mini-Pops Ser.). (ENG.). 10p. (J). 9.99 *(978-1-78128-283-0(8)*, Candle Bks.) Lion Hudson PLC GBR. Dist: Kregel Pubns.

Willis, Jeanne. Caterpillar Dreams. Ross, Tony, illus. 2013. (ENG.). 32p. (J). (gr. -1-k). pap. 8.99 *(978-1-84939-025-5(8))* Andersen Pr. GBR. Dist: Independent Pubs. Group.

—Chicken Clicking. Ross, Tony, illus. 2015. (ENG.). 32p. (J). (gr. -1-k). pap. 9.99 *(978-1-78344-161-7(5))* Andersen Pr. GBR. Dist: Independent Pubs. Group.

—Dr Xargle's Book of Earth Tiggers. Ross, Tony, illus. 2012. (ENG.). 28p. (J). (gr. -1-k). pap. 11.99 *(978-1-84939-297-6(8))* Andersen Pr. GBR. Dist: Independent Pubs. Group.

—Dr Xargle's Book of Earthlets. Ross, Tony, illus. 2012. (ENG.). 28p. (J). (gr. -1-k). pap. 12.99 *(978-1-84939-292-1(7))* Andersen Pr. GBR. Dist: Independent Pubs. Group.

—Mammoth Pie. Ross, Tony, illus. 2008. (ENG.). 32p. (J). (gr. -1-k). 19.99 *(978-1-84270-659-6(4))* Andersen Pr. GBR. Dist: Independent Pubs. Group.

—Prince Charmless. Ross, Tony, illus. 2014. (ENG.). 32p. (J). (gr. -1-k). pap. 9.99 *(978-1-84939-778-0(3))* Andersen Pr. GBR. Dist: Independent Pubs. Group.

—Stomp! Howard, Paul, illus. 2012. (ENG.). 32p. (J). (gr. -1-k). pap. 9.99 *(978-1-84616-795-9(7))* Hodder & Stoughton GBR. Dist: Hachette Bk. Group.

—We're Going to a Party! Ross, Tony, illus. (ENG.). 16p. (J). 2015. (-k). pap. 14.99 *(978-1-84939-456-7(3))* 2013. (gr. -1-k). 12.99 *(978-1-84939-122-1(X))* Andersen Pr. GBR. Dist: Independent Pubs. Group.

—Who's in the Loo? Reynolds, Adrian, illus. 10th ed. 2016. (ENG.). 16p. (J). (— 1). bds. 9.99 *(978-1-78344-420-5(7))* Andersen Pr. GBR. Dist: Independent Pubs. Group.

—The Wind in the Wallows. Ross, Tony, illus. 2013. (ENG.). 32p. (J). (gr. -1-k). pap. 9.99 *(978-1-84939-453-6(9))* Andersen Pr. GBR. Dist: Independent Pubs. Group.

Wilson-Max, Ken. Big Red Fire Engine. 2013. (ENG., Illus.). 12p. (J). (— 1). 11.99 *(978-1-84365-168-0(8)*, Pavilion) Pavilion Bks. GBR. Dist: Independent Pubs. Group.

Wilson-Max, Ken & Quarto Generic Staff. Lenny Goes to Nursery School. Wilson-Max, Ken, illus. 2014. (ENG., Illus.). 32p. (J). (gr. -1-k). 15.99 *(978-1-84780-317-7(2)*, Frances Lincoln) Quarto Publishing Group UK GBR. Dist: Hachette Bk. Group.

Wilson, Troy. Perfect Man, 1 vol. Griffiths, Dean, illus. 2005. (ENG.). 32p. (J). (gr. -1-3). per. 9.95 *(978-1-55143-435-3(0))* Orca Bk. Pubs. USA.

Wilson, Tyrone L. The Spectacle of Lights. 2012. 28p. pap. 15.99 *(978-1-4691-7514-0(2))* Xlibris Corp.

Wing, Natasha. An Eye for Color: The Story of Josef Albers. Breckenreid, Julia, illus. 2009. (ENG.). 40p. (J). (gr. 1-4). 18.99 *(978-0-8050-8072-8(4)*, 9780805080728, Holt, Henry & Co. Bks. For Young Readers) Holt, Henry & Co.

—The Night Before the New Pet. Wummer, Amy, illus. 2016. (Night Before Ser.). (ENG.). 32p. (J). (-k). pap. 4.99 *(978-0-448-48903-2(1)*, Grosset & Dunlap) Penguin Young Readers Group.

Wing, Natasha & dePaola, Tomie. The Night Before Class Picture Day. Wummer, Amy, illus. 2016. (Night Before Ser.). (ENG.). 32p. (J). (-k). bds. 4.99 *(978-0-448-48902-5(3)*, Grosset & Dunlap) Penguin Young Readers Group.

Winstanley, Nicola. The Pirate's Bed. 2015. (ENG., Illus.). 32p. (J). (gr. -1-2). 17.99 *(978-1-77049-616-3(5)*, Tundra Bks.) Tundra Bks. CAN. Dist: Penguin Random Hse. LLC.

Winters, Kari-Lynn. Jeffrey & Sloth, 1 vol. Hodson, Ben, illus. 2008. (ENG.). 32p. (J). (gr. -1-3). per. 9.95 *(978-1-55143-974-7(3))* Orca Bk. Pubs. USA.

—No-Matter-What Friend, 1 vol. Pratt, Pierre, illus. 2014. (ENG.). 32p. (J). (gr. k-2). 16.95 *(978-1-896580-83-8(1))* Tradewind Bks. CAN. Dist: Orca Bk. Pubs. USA.

—On My Bike, 1 vol. Leist, Christina, illus. 2017. (On My ... Ser.). (ENG.). 24p. (J). (gr. -1-k). bds. 12.95 *(978-1-926890-13-5(2))* Tradewind Bks. CAN. Dist: Orca Bk. Pubs. USA.

—On My Skiis, 1 vol. Leist, Christina, illus. 2017. (On My ... Ser.). (ENG.). 24p. (J). (gr. -1-k). bds. 12.95 *(978-1-926890-03-6(5))* Tradewind Bks. CAN. Dist: Orca Bk. Pubs. USA.

Wirth, Beverly. Flowers from Seeds: A Garden Parable. 2012. 40p. pap. 16.99 *(978-1-4624-0101-7(5)*, Inspiring Voices) Author Solutions, Inc.

Witek, Jo. Hello in There! A Big Sister's Book of Waiting. Roussey, Christine, illus. 2013. (Growing Hearts Ser.). (ENG.). 28p. (J). (gr. -1 — 1). 16.95 *(978-1-4197-0371-3(4)*, Abrams Appleseed) Abrams, Inc.

The Wizard of Oz. 2016. (First Favourite Tales Ser.). (ENG., Illus.). 32p. (J). (gr. -1-k). 7.99 *(978-0-7232-9219-7(1))* Penguin Bks., Ltd. GBR. Dist: Independent Pubs. Group.

Wolcott, P. A. The Fox, the Badger, & the Bunny: A Dales Tale. Wolcott, K. Hannah, ed. Schweitzer, Patty, illus. 2009. 20p. pap. 24.95 *(978-1-60749-525-3(2))* America Star Bks.

Wolf, Gita & Anastasio, Andrea. Alone in the Forest. Shyam, Bhajju, illus. 2013. (ENG.). 40p. (J). (gr. -1). 16.95 *(978-81-923171-5-1(3))* Tara Books Agency IND. Dist: Publishers Group West (PGW).

Wolfe, Jane. Cheeky Frog. Benham, Tors, illus. 2016. (ENG.). 8p. (J). (gr. -1-12). bds. 6.99 *(978-1-84322-718-2(5)*, Armadillo) Anness Publishing GBR. Dist: National Bk. Network.

—Crazy Cow. Benham, Tors, illus. 2013. (ENG.). 8p. (J). (gr. -1-k). bds. 6.99 *(978-1-84322-775-5(4)*, Armadillo) Anness Publishing GBR. Dist: National Bk. Network.

—Dizzy Duck. Benham, Tors, illus. 2016. (ENG.). 8p. (J). (gr. -1-12). bds. 6.99 *(978-1-84322-719-9(3)*, Armadillo) Anness Publishing GBR. Dist: National Bk. Network.

—Happy Cat. Benham, Tors, illus. 2016. (ENG.). 8p. bds. 6.99 *(978-1-84322-720-5(7)*, Armadillo) Anness Publishing GBR. Dist: National Bk. Network.

—Hungry Horse. Benham, Tors, illus. 2016. (ENG.). 8p. bds. 6.99 *(978-1-84322-721-2(5)*, Armadillo) Anness Publishing GBR. Dist: National Bk. Network.

—Messy Pig. Benham, Tors, illus. 2013. (ENG.). 8p. (J). (gr. -1-k). bds. 6.99 *(978-1-84322-777-9(0)*, Armadillo) Anness Publishing GBR. Dist: National Bk. Network.

—Noisy Dog. Benham, Tors, illus. 2013. (ENG.). 8p. (J). (gr. -1-k). bds. 6.99 *(978-1-84322-779-3(7)*, Armadillo) Anness Publishing GBR. Dist: National Bk. Network.

—Pull the Lever: Who Does What? Benham, Tors, illus. 2014. (ENG.). 8p. (J). (gr. -1-2). bds. 6.99 *(978-1-86147-392-9(3)*, Armadillo) Anness Publishing GBR. Dist: National Bk. Network.

—Pull the Lever: Who's in Here? Benham, Tors, illus. 2014. (ENG.). 8p. (J). (gr. -1-2). bds. 6.99 *(978-1-86147-394-3(X)*, Armadillo) Anness Publishing GBR. Dist: National Bk. Network.

—Sleepy Sheep. Benham, Tors, illus. 2013. (ENG.). 8p. (J). (gr. -1-k). bds. 6.99 *(978-1-84322-778-6(9)*, Armadillo) Anness Publishing GBR. Dist: National Bk. Network.

Wood, A. J. The Christmas Hat. Kneen, Maggie, illus. 2004. (ENG.). 24p. (J). *(978-1-55168-267-9(2))* Fenn, H. B. & Co., Ltd.

Wood, Audrey. The Napping House Board Book. Wood, Don, illus. 2015. (ENG.). 32p. (J). (— 1). bds. 7.99 *(978-0-544-60225-0(0)*, HMH Books For Young Readers) Houghton Mifflin Harcourt Publishing Co.

Wood, Barbie. The Adventure of Mookin Munchkin. Klick, Gloria, illus. 2013. 32p. pap. 24.95 *(978-1-63004-041-3(X))* America Star Bks.

Wood, Jacqueline & Wood, Jakki. Baby Parade. 2003. (Illus.). 32p. (J). 14.95 *(978-0-7112-2065-2(4))* Fleming, Randall.

Wood, Ramona. Now Caitlin Can: A Donated Organ Helps a Child Get Well. 2004. (Illus.). 32p. (J). 16.00 *(978-0-9758622-0-9(0))* ABC Pr.

Woods-Whitaker, Kim. Elijah's Big Imagination: A Ball of an Adventure. 2010. 20p. 11.49 *(978-1-4490-1518-3(2))* AuthorHouse.

Woodward, Caroline. Singing Away the Dark. Morstad, Julie, illus. 2017. (ENG.). 44p. (J). (gr. -1-3). 16.95 *(978-1-77229-019-6(X))* Simply Read Bks. CAN. Dist: Ingram Publisher Services.

Woolf, Alex. A Photographic View of Crime & Punishment. 2016. (Past in Pictures Ser.). (ENG., Illus.). 32p. (J). (gr. 4-6). pap. 11.99 *(978-0-7502-8348-9(3)*, Wayland) Hachette Children's Group GBR. Dist: Hachette Bk. Group.

—A Photographic View of Hospitals. 2016. (Past in Pictures Ser.). (ENG., Illus.). 32p. (J). (gr. 4-6). pap. 11.99 *(978-0-7502-8354-0(8)*, Wayland) Hachette Children's Group GBR. Dist: Hachette Bk. Group.

Wormell, Chris. Eric!.. the Hero? 2013. (ENG., Illus.). 32p. (J). (gr. -1-k). pap. 15.99 *(978-1-84941-284-1(7)*, Red Fox) Random House Children's Books GBR. Dist: Independent Pubs. Group.

Wormell, Christopher. Scruffy Bear & the Lost Ball. 2014. (ENG., Illus.). 32p. (J). (-k). pap. 12.99 *(978-1-84941-546-0(3)*, Red Fox) Random House Children's Books GBR. Dist: Independent Pubs. Group.

Wotton, Joy. My First Word Book: Pictures & Words to Start Toddlers Reading & to Help Pre-Schoolers Develop Vocabulary Skills. Tulip, Jenny, illus. 2012. (ENG.). 200p. 9.99 *(978-1-84322-617-8(0)*, Armadillo) Anness Publishing GBR. Dist: National Bk. Network.

Wrecks, Billy. Shark Attack! Doescher, Erik, illus. 2017. 24p. (J). ***(978-1-5182-2649-6(3))*** Random Hse., Inc.

Wren, Jenny, illus. In the Jungle. 2017. (First Explorers Ser.). (ENG.). 10p. (J). (— 1). bds. 8.95 ***(978-1-4549-2656-6(2))*** Sterling Publishing Co., Inc.

—Night Animals. 2017. (First Explorers Ser.). (ENG.). 10p. (J). (— 1). bds. 8.95 ***(978-1-4549-2657-3(0))*** Sterling Publishing Co., Inc.

Wyatt, Edwina. Together Always. Masciullo, Lucia, illus. 2017. (ENG.). 48p. (J). (gr. -1-3). 14.95 *(978-1-4549-2326-8(1))* Sterling Publishing Co., Inc.

Wynne, Sarah & Clark, Katie. River Royals: Master the Mississippi. 2014. (ENG., Illus.). 32p. (J). 19.95 *(978-1-939055-71-2(7)*, 011fd19b-d6ae-4840-a0eb-8b2b0a698ba0) Bright Sky Pr.

X-Men. 2003. (J). *(978-1-57657-859-9(3))* Paradise Pr., Inc.

Xinran, Xinran & Mother's Bridge of Love Staff. Motherbridge of Love. Masse, Josée, illus. 2013. (ENG.). 32p. (J). (gr. k-3). 7.99 *(978-1-78285-040-3(6))* Barefoot Bks., Inc.

Yamada, Miho. Miyako from Tokyo. Camcam, Princesse, illus. 2014. (AV2 Fiction Readalong Ser.: Vol. 132). (ENG.). 32p. (J). (gr. -1-3). lib. bdg. 34.28 *(978-1-4896-2268-6(3)*, AV2 by Weigl) Weigl Pubs., Inc.

Yamashita, Masako. Snow Children, 1 vol. 2012. (ENG., Illus.). 32p. (J). (gr. -1-2). 17.95 *(978-1-55498-144-1(1))* Groundwood Bks. CAN. Dist: Publishers Group West (PGW).

Yankey, Lindsey. Bluebird. 2014. (ENG., Illus.). 36p. (J). (gr. -1-3). 17.95 *(978-1-927018-33-0(1))* Simply Read Bks. CAN. Dist: Ingram Publisher Services.

Yarrow, Peter & Lipton, Lenny. Puff, the Magic Dragon. Puybaret, Eric, illus. 2010. (ENG.). 32p. (J). (gr. k-2). cd-rom 9.95 *(978-1-4027-7216-0(5))* Sterling Publishing Co., Inc.

Yates, Irene. The Enormous Turnip. 2015. (First Favourite Tales Ser.). (ENG., Illus.). 32p. (J). (-k). 9.99 *(978-1-4093-0957-4(6))* Penguin Bks., Ltd. GBR. Dist: Independent Pubs. Group.

Yates, Louise. Dog Loves Fairy Tales. 2016. (ENG., Illus.). 32p. (J). pap. 13.99 *(978-1-78295-593-1(3)*, Red Fox) Random House Children's Books GBR. Dist: Independent Pubs. Group.

—Toad & I. 2016. (ENG., Illus.). 32p. (J). (gr. k-2). pap. 12.99 *(978-1-78008-105-2(7))* Transworld Publishers Ltd. GBR. Dist: Independent Pubs. Group.

Yates, Philip. Pirate's Twelve Days of Christmas. Serra, Sebastià, illus. 2016. (ENG.). 24p. (J). (gr. -1 — 1). bds. 7.95 *(978-1-4549-2070-0(X))* Sterling Publishing Co., Inc.

Yayo. Pikiq, 1 vol. 2017. (ENG., Illus.). 32p. (J). (gr. -1-3). 16.95 ***(978-1-926890-05-0(1))*** Tradewind Bks. CAN. Dist: Orca Bk. Pubs. USA.

Yeoman, John. The Bear's Water Picnic. Blake, Quentin, illus. 2011. (ENG.). 40p. (J). (gr. k-k). pap. 12.99 *(978-1-84939-004-0(5))* Andersen Pr. GBR. Dist: Independent Pubs. Group.

—The Heron & the Crane. Blake, Quentin, illus. 2011. (ENG.). 32p. (J). (gr. -1-k). pap. 13.99 *(978-1-84939-200-6(5))* Andersen Pr. GBR. Dist: Independent Pubs. Group.

—Mouse Trouble. Blake, Quentin, illus. 2011. (ENG.). 32p. (J). (gr. -1-k). pap. 12.99 *(978-1-84939-201-3(3))* Andersen Pr. GBR. Dist: Independent Pubs. Group.

—Sixes & Sevens. Blake, Quentin, illus. 2012. (ENG.). 32p. (J). (gr. -1-k). pap. 11.99 *(978-1-84939-308-9(7))* Andersen Pr. GBR. Dist: Independent Pubs. Group.

—Up with Birds! 2013. (ENG., Illus.). 32p. (J). (gr. k-2). pap. 11.99 *(978-1-84939-651-6(5))* Andersen Pr. GBR. Dist: Independent Pubs. Group.

Yeoman, John & Blake, Quentin. The Fabulous Foskett Family Circus. 2014. (ENG., Illus.). 32p. (J). (gr. -1-k). 19.99 *(978-1-84939-564-9(0))* Andersen Pr. GBR. Dist: Independent Pubs. Group.

Yerxa, Leo. Ancient Thunder, 1 vol. 2012. (ENG., Illus.). 40p. (J). (gr. -1-3). 9.95 *(978-1-55498-127-4(1))* Groundwood Bks. CAN. Dist: Publishers Group West (PGW).

Yeva, Laura. Joshua Cleans Up! Likhovidova, Yekaterina, illus. 2017. (ENG.). 36p. (J). pap. 15.95 ***(978-1-78693-648-6(8)***, ca0be078-05cf-48f2-be1a-3ae50fc62a61) Austin, Stan AUS. Dist: Bookmasters Distribution.

Ying, Victoria. Meow! Ying, Victoria, illus. 2017. (Illus.). 32p. (J). (gr. -1-3). 15.99 ***(978-0-06-244096-9(9))*** HarperCollins Pubs.

Yip, Mingmei. Grandma Panda's China Storybook: Legends, Traditions & Fun. 2013. (ENG., Illus.). 32p. (J). (gr. -1-3). 15.95 *(978-0-8048-4149-8(7))* Tuttle Publishing.

Yoon, Salina. Space Walk. 2012. (Lift-The-Flap Adventures Ser.). (ENG., Illus.). 12p. (J). (gr. -1-2). bds. 8.95 *(978-1-4027-8524-5(0))* Sterling Publishing Co., Inc.

Young, Cybèle. Nancy Knows. 2014. (ENG., Illus.). 40p. (J). (gr. -1-2). 17.99 *(978-1-77049-482-4(0)*, Tundra Bks.) Tundra Bks. CAN. Dist: Penguin Random Hse. LLC.

—Ten Birds. Young, Cybèle, illus. 2011. (Ten Birds Ser.). (ENG., Illus.). 32p. (J). (gr. 1-6). 16.95 *(978-1-55453-568-2(9))* Kids Can Pr., Ltd. CAN. Dist: Hachette Bk. Group.

Young, Cybèle, illus. Nancy Knows. 2017. (ENG.). 32p. (J). (— 1). bds. 8.99 *(978-1-101-91892-0(6)*, Tundra Bks.) Tundra Bks. CAN. Dist: Penguin Random Hse. LLC.

Young, Lesley. A Storyteller Book - Red Riding Hood. Williams, Jenny, illus. 2013. (ENG.). 48p. (J). (gr. -1-12). pap. 7.99 *(978-1-84322-909-4(9)*, Armadillo) Anness Publishing GBR. Dist: National Bk. Network.

—A Storyteller Book Sleeping Beauty. Press, Jenny, illus. 2013. (ENG.). 48p. (J). (gr. -1-12). pap. 7.99 *(978-1-84322-910-0(2)*, Armadillo) Anness Publishing GBR. Dist: National Bk. Network.

Young, Timothy, illus. Do Not Open the Box, 1 vol. 2015. (ENG.). 32p. (J). 16.99 *(978-0-7643-5043-6(9)*, 9780764350436) Schiffer Publishing, Ltd.

Younger, Mary. You're Not A Ladybird You've Got No Spots. 2011. (Illus.). 24p. 14.09 *(978-1-4567-7082-2(9))* AuthorHouse.

Yoyo Books, creator. Numbers. 2011. (Baby's First Library). (ENG., Illus.). 40p. (gr. -1-k). bds. *(978-94-6033-702-4(3))* YoYo Bks.

Yu, Jennifer & Jenn, Lady. Texas Animal Ranch: Ricky's Secret Friends Picture Book Series, vols. 6, vol. 2. Yu, Jennifer & Jenn, Lady, illus. 2016. (Ricky's Secret Friends Picturebook Ser.: 6). (ENG & CHI., Illus.). (gr. 1-4). 29.95 *(978-0-9787591-2-4(5))* Direct World Publishing.

Yuly, Toni. Cat Nap. 2017. (ENG., Illus.). 32p. (J). bds. 7.99 *(978-1-250-11261-3(3)*, 9781250112613) Feiwel & Friends.

—The Jelly Bean Tree. Yuly, Toni, illus. 2017. (ENG., Illus.). 40p. (J). 17.99 (978-1-250-09406-3(2), 9781250094063) Feiwel & Friends.

Yun, Yeo-rim. Liang's Treasure: China. Cowley, Joy, ed. Choi, Yang-sook, illus. 2015. (Global Kids Storybooks Ser.). (ENG.). 32p. (gr. 1-4). 26.65 (978-1-925246-05-6(1)); 7.99 (978-1-925246-57-5(4)); 26.65 (978-1-925246-31-5(0)) ChoiceMaker Pty. Ltd., The AUS. (Big and SMALL). Dist: Lerner Publishing Group.

Zeman, Ludmila, illus. & retold by. Sindbad: From the Tales of the Thousand & One Nights. Zeman, Ludmila, retold by. 2011. (ENG.). 32p. (J). (gr. 1-4). pap. 9.95 (978-1-77049-264-6(X), Tundra Bks.) Tundra Bks. CAN. Dist: Penguin Random Hse. LLC.

—Sindbad in the Land of Giants: From the Tales of the Thousand & One Nights. Zeman, Ludmila, retold by. 2011. (ENG.). 32p. (J). (gr. 1-4). pap. 9.95 (978-1-77049-266-0(6), Tundra Bks.) Tundra Bks. CAN. Dist: Penguin Random Hse. LLC.

—Sindbad's Secret: From the Tales of the Thousand & One Nights. Zeman, Ludmila, retold by. 2011. (ENG.). 32p. (J). (gr. 1-4). pap. 9.95 (978-1-77049-265-3(8), Tundra Bks.) Tundra Bks. CAN. Dist: Penguin Random Hse. LLC.

Zeppa, Talaylin. Teddy the Tub. 2011. 32p. pap. 32.70 (978-1-4568-6908-3(6)) Xlibris Corp.

Ziarnik, Natalie. Madeleine's Light: A Story of Camille Claudel. Dunn, Robert, illus. 2012. (ENG.). 32p. (J). (gr. k-2). 17.95 (978-1-59078-855-4(9)) Boyds Mills Pr.

Zimmerman, Andrea & Clemesha, David. Digger Man. Zimmerman, Andrea & Clemesha, David, illus. 2016. (ENG., Illus.). 32p. (J). bds. 7.99 (978-1-62779-444-2(1), 9781627794442, Holt, Henry & Co. Bks. For Young Readers) Holt, Henry & Co.

Zion, Gene. Harry the Dirty Dog. Graham, Margaret Bloy, illus. 50th anniv. ed. 2006. (ENG.). 32p. (J). (gr. -1-3). 17.99 (978-0-06-026865-7(4)) HarperCollins Pubs.

Zoehfeld, Kathleen Weidner. Secrets of the Garden: Food Chains & the Food Web in Our Backyard. Lamont, Priscilla, illus. 2014. (ENG.). 40p. (J). (gr. k-3). 7.99 (978-0-385-75364-7(0), Dragonfly Bks.) Random Hse. Children's Bks.

—What Lives in a Shell? Davie, Helen K., illus. 2015. (Let's-Read-And-Find-Out Science 1 Ser.). (ENG.). 32p. (J). (gr. -1-3). pap. 6.99 (978-0-06-238196-5(2)) HarperCollins Pubs.

Zondervan Staff. All Aboard the Ark, 1 vol. 2016. (ENG., Illus.). 24p. (J). bds. 6.99 (978-0-310-75377-3(5)) Zonderkidz.

Zuckerman, Linda. The Day Is Waiting, 1 vol. Freeman, Don, illus. 2015. (ENG.). 32p. (J). 9.99 (978-0-310-74054-4(1)) Zonderkidz.

Zuill, Andrea. Dance Is for Everyone. 2017. (ENG., Illus.). 32p. (J). (gr. -1). 16.95 (978-1-4549-2114-1(5)) Sterling Publishing Co., Inc.

Zullo, Germano. Jumping Jack. Albertine, illus. 2014. (ENG.). 40p. (J). (gr. k-3). 17.99 (978-1-4521-3152-8(X)) Chronicle Bks. LLC.

Zuppardi, Sam. Things to Do with Dad. Zuppardi, Sam, illus. 2017. (ENG., Illus.). 32p. (J). (gr. -1-3). 16.99 (978-0-7636-8146-3(6)) Candlewick Pr.

Zur Muehlen, Nersel. Monkey in the Mirror. Sanchez, Sara, illus. 2012. 56p. pap. 14.95 (978-0-9829224-2-2(6)) BPM Research LLC.

Zwerger, Lisbeth, illus. Wonderment: The Lisbeth Zwerger Collection. 2014. (ENG.). 164p. (J). 29.95 (978-0-7358-4187-1(X)) North-South Bks., Inc.

PICTURE FRAMES AND FRAMING

Beauvais, Den & creator. Alien Parade Pt. 1: Animated Flip Book. Beauvais, Den, creator. 2004. (Illus.). (YA). per. 4.25 (978-0-9745213-1-2(0)) Dragonfly Entertainment.

PICTURE GALLERIES

see Art Museums

PICTURE POSTERS

see Posters

PICTURE-WRITING

see also Cave Paintings; Hieroglyphics

Award, Anna. Moses in the Bulrushes: See the Picture & Say the Word. 2012. (ENG., Illus.). 24p. (J). pap. 6.50 (978-1-84135-602-0(6)) Award Pubns. Ltd. GBR. Dist: Parkwest Pubns., Inc.

Cortland, D J. A Week of Weather: Learning to Collect & Record Data on a Pictograph. 2004. (Math Big Bookstm Ser.). (ENG., Illus.). 8p. (gr. k-1). 29.95 (978-0-8239-7630-0(0)) Rosen Publishing Group, Inc., The.

Paplow, Paula. Hands upon the Rock. 2013. 48p. 19.99 (978-0-9884268-0-1(3)) Little Cottonwood River Bks.

PICTURES

see also Cartoons and Comics; Portraits

Cocca, Lisa Colozza. Pictographs. 2013. (Explorer Junior Library: Math Explorer Junior Ser.). (ENG.). 24p. (gr. 1-4). 28.50 (978-1-61080-913-9(0), 202631); pap. 12.79 (978-1-61080-938-2(6), 202633) Cherry Lake Publishing.

Dodd, Emma. Forever. Dodd, Emma, illus. 2013. (Emma Dodd's Love You Bks.). (ENG., Illus.). 24p. (J). (-k). 12.99 (978-0-7636-7132-7(0), Templar) Candlewick Pr.

Frederick, Malcolm. Kamal Goes to Trinidad. Das, Prodeepta, illus. 2008. (Children Return to Their Roots Ser.). (ENG.). 40p. (J). (gr. 1-4). 16.95 (978-1-84507-702-0(4), Frances Lincoln Children's Bks.) Quarto Publishing Group UK GBR. Dist: Hachette Bk. Group.

Furgang, Adam. Searching Online for Image, Audio, & Video Files. 2009. (Digital & Information Literacy Ser.). (Illus.). 48p. (YA). (gr. 5-8). lib. bdg. 29.25 (978-1-4358-5318-8(0)) Rosen Publishing Group, Inc., The.

Greene, Joshua M. The Littlest Giant: The Story of Vamana. Moore, Emma V., illus. 2014. (ENG.). 32p. (gr. -1). 16.99 (978-1-60887-303-6(X)) Mandala Publishing.

Group/McGraw-Hill, Wright. Picture This! 6 Each of 1 Anthology, 6 vols. (Wildcats Ser.). 32p. (gr. 2-8). (978-0-322-05627-5(6)) Wright Group/McGraw-Hill.

Harrison, Paul. The Brilliant Book of 3D Thrillers: Get Ready for the Ultimate 3d Adventure! 2012. (ENG., Illus.). 96p. (J). pap. 9.95 (978-1-84837-875-9(0)) Arcturus Publishing GBR. Dist: Bookmasters Distribution.

Harrison, Paul & Arcturus Publishing Staff. The Amazing Book of 3D Thrillers: Fantastic Eye-Popping Experiences. 2012. (ENG., Illus.). 96p. (J). pap. 9.95 (978-1-84837-876-6(9), 9781848378766) Arcturus Publishing GBR. Dist: Bookmasters Distribution.

Paragon Publishing Staff, ed. Words. 2003. (J). per. (978-1-884907-41-8(5)) Paradise Pr., Inc.

Parragon Staff, ed. Words. Date not set. (Illus.). (J). bds. 5.98 (978-0-7525-8559-8(2)) Parragon, Inc.

Rabbat, Suzy. Super Smart Information Strategies: Using Digital Images. 2010. (Explorer Library: Information Explorer Ser.). (ENG.). 32p. (gr. 4-8). lib. bdg. 28.50 (978-1-60279-954-7(7), 200633) Cherry Lake Publishing.

PICTURES, HUMOROUS

see Cartoons and Comics

PIERCE, FRANKLIN, 1804-1869

DiConsoglio, John. Franklin Pierce. 2004. (Encyclopedia of Presidents Ser.). (ENG., Illus.). 110p. (YA). (gr. 5-9). 34.00 (978-0-516-24235-4(0)) Scholastic Library Publishing.

King, David C. Franklin Pierce. 2009. (Presidents & Their Times 3 Ser.). 96p. (gr. 6). 34.21 (978-0-7614-3624-9(3)) Marshall Cavendish Corp.

Lazo, Caroline Evensen. Franklin Pierce. 2007. (Presidential Leaders Ser.). (Illus.). 112p. (J). (gr. 3-7). lib. bdg. 29.27 (978-0-8225-1492-3(3), Twenty-First Century Bks.) Lerner Publishing Group.

Rumsch, BreAnn. Franklin Pierce, 1 vol. (ENG., Illus.). 40p. 2016. (J). (978-1-68078-112-0(X)) 2009. (YA). (gr. 3-6). 27.07 (978-1-60453-469-6(9)) ABDO Publishing Co.

Venezia, Mike. Franklin Pierce: Fourteenth President. Venezia, Mike, illus. 2005. (Getting to Know the U. S. Presidents Ser.). (ENG., Illus.). 32p. (J). (gr. 3-7). lib. bdg. 28.00 (978-0-516-22619-4(3), Children's Pr.) Scholastic Library Publishing.

Zamora, Dulce. How to Draw the Life & Times of Franklin Pierce. (Kid's Guide to Drawing the Presidents of the United States of America Ser.). 2009. 32p. (gr. 4-4). 50.50 (978-1-61511-137-4(9), PowerKids Pr.) 2006. (YA). (gr. 2-5). 26.50 (978-1-4042-2991-4(4)) Rosen Publishing Group, Inc., The.

PIGEONS

Barclay, Marjorie. Flutter: A Very Special Pigeon. 2010. 40p. 24.99 (978-1-4520-6362-1(1)) AuthorHouse.

Dunn, Joeming & Dunn, Ben. Cher Ami: WWI Homing Pigeon, 1 vol. 2011. (Famous Firsts: Animals Making History Ser.). (ENG., Illus.). 32p. (YA). (gr. 3-6). 28.50 (978-1-61641-639-3(4)) Magic Wagon.

Fretland VanVoorst, Jenny. Homing Pigeons. 2013. (We Work! Animals with Jobs Ser.). 24p. (J). (gr. -1-3). lib. bdg. 21.32 (978-1-61772-900-3(0)) Bearport Publishing Co., Inc.

Gagne, Tammy. Care for a Racing Pigeon. 2009. (How to Convince Your Parents You Can ... Ser.). 32p. (J). (gr. 1-4). 25.70 (978-1-58415-801-1(8)) Mitchell Lane Pubs., Inc.

Piehl, Janet. Let's Look at Pigeons. (Lightning Bolt Books (tm) — Animal Close-Ups Ser.). (ENG., Illus.). 32p. 2015. (gr. 2-3). E-Book 39.99 (978-1-5124-1055-6(1), 9781512410556) 2009. (gr. k-2). lib. bdg. 26.60 (978-0-8225-7897-0(2)) Lerner Publishing Group. (Lerner Pubns.).

Roza, Greg. Your Neighbor the Pigeon. 2011. (City Critters Ser.). (ENG., Illus.). 24p. (J). (gr. k-5). pap. 8.25 (978-1-4488-5133-1(5)); lib. bdg. 22.60 (978-1-61533-384-4(3)) Windmill Bks.

Thomas, Isabel. Pigeon: City Safari, 1 vol. 2014. (City Safari Ser.). (ENG., Illus.). 24p. (gr. 1-1). lib. bdg. 23.32 (978-1-4329-8806-7(9), Heinemann Read & Learn) Heinemann-Raintree.

Willis, Danny. Why Pigeons? a Young Boy Discovers Gods Masterpieces. 2009. 40p. pap. 16.95 (978-1-60860-314-5(8), Strategic Bk. Publishing) Strategic Book Publishing & Rights Agency (SBPRA).

PIGEONS—FICTION

Arthur, Anne. The Pigeon with the Sticky Stuck Neck. Liebman, Simean, illus. 2004. (J). per. 7.99 (978-0-9753320-0-9(7)) Riverbank Publishing.

Barnes, Kenneth Edward. A Children's Story Collection. 2011. 216p. (gr. -1). pap. 15.95 (978-1-4634-2863-1(4)); (gr. 1-2). 24.59 (978-1-4634-2864-8(2)) AuthorHouse.

Bauman Wispe, Lisa. Fritter's Spring: A Pocono Rabbit's Tale. 2010. pap. 11.95 (978-0-7414-5796-7(2)) Infinity Publishing.

Bennett, Virginia. The Pigeon Tale. Hardy, E. Stuart, illus. 2007. 48p. per. (978-1-4065-4810-5(3)) Dodo Pr.

Bliss, Harry. Luke on the Loose. Bliss, Harry, illus. 2009. (ENG., Illus.). 32p. (J). (gr. -1-3). 12.95 (978-1-935179-00-9(4)) TOON Books / RAW Junior, LLC.

—Luke on the Loose. 2014. (Toon Books Level 2 Ser.). lib. bdg. 14.75 (978-0-606-32101-3(2), Turtleback) Turtleback Bks.

Brazauski, Vickie. Tweeter the Peachick A True Story, 1 vol. 2010. 26p. 24.95 (978-1-4489-4257-2(8)) PublishAmerica, Inc.

Burnham, Molly B. Teddy Mars: Almost a World Record Breaker. Spencer, Trevor, illus. 2015. (Teddy Mars Ser.: 1). (ENG.). 224p. (J). (gr. 3-7). 16.99 (978-0-06-227810-4(X)) HarperCollins Pubs.

Davies, Nicola. King of the Sky. Carlin, Laura, illus. 2017. (ENG.). 48p. (J). (gr. -1-3). 17.99 (978-0-7636-9568-2(8)) Candlewick Pr.

Dolan, Penny. Plip & Plop. Smith, Lisa, illus. 2004. (Read-It! Readers Ser.). (J). lib. bdg. 18.60 (978-1-4048-0551-4(6)) Picture Window Bks.

Doudna, Kelly. Homing Pigeon, 1 vol. Chawla, Neena, illus. 2007. (Critter Chronicles Ser.). (ENG.). 24p. (J). (gr. k-3). lib. bdg. 24.21 (978-1-59928-440-8(5), SandCastle) ABDO Publishing Co.

Freeman, Don. Fly High, Fly Low. Freeman, Don, illus. (ENG., Illus.). 64p. (J). (gr. -1-k). 2004. reprint ed. 16.99 (978-0-670-03685-1(4), Viking Books for Young Readers) 50th anniv. ed. 2007. 7.99 (978-0-14-240817-9(4), Puffin Books) Penguin Young Readers Group.

—Fly High, Fly Low. Freeman, Don, illus. 2007. (Illus.). 56p. (gr. -1-3). 18.00 (978-0-7569-8001-6(1)) Perfection Learning Corp.

Frossard, Claire, illus. Emma's Journey. Frossard, Etienne, photos by. 2010. (ENG.). 56p. (J). (gr. -1-3). 17.95 (978-1-59270-099-8(3)) Enchanted Lion Bks., LLC.

Gail, Ginnie. The Great Pigeon Race. Griffin, Don, illus. 2008. 28p. per. 24.95 (978-1-4241-9457-5(1)) America Star Bks.

Godden, Rumer. The Mousewife. du Bois, William Pène, illus. 2009. (ENG.). 56p. (J). (gr. -1-2). 16.95 (978-1-59017-310-7(4), NYR Children's Collection) New York Review of Bks., Inc., The.

Greenham, Caz. The Adventures of Eric Seagull. Homfray, Nick, illus. 2013. 40p. pap. (978-1-78132-093-8(4)) SilverWood Bks.

Hamilton, Kersten. The Ire of Iron Claw. Hamilton, James, illus. (Gadgets & Gears Ser.: 2). (ENG.). (J). (gr. 2-5). 2016. 192p. pap. 6.99 (978-0-544-66854-6(5), HMH Books For Young Readers) 2015. 176p. 16.99 (978-0-544-22502-2(3)) Houghton Mifflin Harcourt Publishing Co.

Healey, Richard (Dick). Holly the Christmas Dove. 2005. 36p. (J). 13.28 (978-1-4116-5496-9(X)) Lulu Pr., Inc.

Hub, Ulrich. Be at the Ark by Eight. Mühle, Jörg, illus. 2012. (ENG.). 68p. (J). 12.00 (978-0-8028-5410-0(9), Eerdmans Bks For Young Readers) Eerdmans, William B. Publishing Co.

Hughes, Cheryl. Jackson, the Pigeon Who Was Afraid of Heights. 2008. 44p. pap. 16.99 (978-1-4389-2143-3(8)) AuthorHouse.

Jerry, Spinelli. Wringer. 2014. (ENG.). 256p. (J). (gr. 8-12). 13.24 (978-1-63245-323-5(1)) Lectorum Pubns., Inc.

Kassel, Roger de. Mr P & the Silver Red Bag. 2013. (Illus.). 12p. pap. 7.00 (978-1-78035-536-8(X), Fastprint Publishing) Upfront Publishing Ltd. GBR. Dist: Printondemand-worldwide.com.

—Mr P & the Sticky Gum. 2013. (Illus.). 12p. pap. 7.00 (978-1-78035-537-5(8), Fastprint Publishing) Upfront Publishing Ltd. GBR. Dist: Printondemand-worldwide.com.

Kay, L. M. Frederick's Birthday Surprise. 2009. 36p. pap. 24.95 (978-1-60836-944-7(7)) America Star Bks.

Laurent, Karine. Coo Is in Love, 1 vol. Alastra, Stephanie, illus. 2012. (My Little Picture Book Ser.). (ENG.). 32p. (J). (gr. -1). pap. 6.95 (978-2-7338-1244-0(0)) Auzou, Philippe Editions FRA. Dist: Consortium Bk. Sales & Distribution.

Lloyd, Elizabeth. Piggyon. 2009. (Illus.). 36p. pap. 16.99 (978-1-4490-2654-7(0)) AuthorHouse.

McDavid-Jones, Elizabeth. The Night Flyers. 2009. (Mysteries Through Time Ser.). 144 - 176p. (YA). (gr. 4-8). 31.95 (978-1-60754-197-4(1)); pap. 15.25 (978-1-60754-198-1(X)) Windmill Bks.

McDonald, Jody. Who Is in the Egg? 2010. 28p. pap. 28.03 (978-1-4500-8840-4(6)) Xlibris Corp.

McLaren, Meg. Pigeon P. I. 2017. (ENG., Illus.). 40p. (J). (gr. -1-3). 16.99 **(978-1-328-71561-6(2)**, Clarion Bks.) Houghton Mifflin Harcourt Trade & Reference Pubs.

Mellon, Gray. The Weird Worlds of Willoughby Wren Wren & the Pigeons. 2010. 196p. pap. (978-1-907652-06-6(X)) Grosvenor Hse. Publishing Ltd.

Murray, Diana. City Shapes. Collier, Bryan, illus. 2016. (ENG.). 40p. (J). (gr. -1-3). 17.99 (978-0-316-37092-9(4)) Little Brown & Co.

Naylor, Phyllis Reynolds. Cuckoo Feathers, 0 vols. Ramsey, Marcy, illus. 2009. (Simply Sarah Ser.: 0). (ENG.). 96p. (J). (gr. 2-5). pap. 6.99 (978-0-7614-5541-7(8), 9780761455417, Amazon Children's Publishing) Amazon Publishing.

O'Connor, Barbara. On the Road to Mr. Mineo's, 1 vol. 2012. (ENG.). 192p. (J). (gr. 3-7). 16.99 (978-0-374-38002-1(3), 9780374380021, Farrar, Straus & Giroux (BYR)) Farrar, Straus & Giroux.

—On the Road to Mr. Mineo's. 2014. (ENG., Illus.). 208p. (J). (gr. 3-7). pap. 7.99 (978-1-250-03993-4(2), 9781250039934) Square Fish.

Power, Barry. The First Ice Pigeon of London. 2009. 80p. pap. 10.49 (978-1-4490-3070-4(X)) AuthorHouse.

Redmond, Shirley Raye. Pigeon Hero! Ettlinger, Doris, illus. 2005. (Ready-to-Read Ser.). 31p. (gr. k-2). 14.00 (978-0-7569-5560-1(2)) Perfection Learning Corp.

—Pigeon Hero! Ettlinger, Doris, illus. 2003. (Ready-To-Reads Ser.). (ENG.). 32p. (J). lib. bdg. 11.89 (978-0-689-85487-3(0), Aladdin Library) Simon & Schuster Children's Publishing.

—Pigeon Hero! Ettlinger, Doris, illus. 2003. (Ready-To-Reads Ser.). (ENG.). 32p. (J). (gr. k-2). pap. 3.99 (978-0-689-85486-6(2), Simon Spotlight) Simon Spotlight.

Richmond, Lori. Pax & Blue. Richmond, Lori, illus. 2017. (ENG., Illus.). 32p. (J). (gr. -1-3). 17.99 (978-1-4814-5132-1(4), Simon & Schuster/Paula Wiseman Bks.) Simon & Schuster/Paula Wiseman Bks.

Rudge, Leila. Gary. Rudge, Leila, illus. 2016. (ENG., Illus.). 32p. (J). (gr. -1-2). 16.99 (978-0-7636-8954-4(8)) Candlewick Pr.

Sargent, Dave & Sargent, David M., Jr. Pammie Pigeon: Keep Your Cool, 19 vols., Vol. 12. Lenoir, Jane, illus. 2003. (Feather Tales Ser.: 12). 42p. (J). pap. 10.95 (978-1-56763-742-7(6)); 2nd ed. lib. bdg. 20.95 (978-1-56763-741-0(8)) Ozark Publishing.

—Penny Penguin: Be Kind to Others, 20 vols., Vol. 13. Lenoir, Jane, illus. 2nd ed. 2003. (Feather Tales Ser.: 13). 42p. (J). lib. bdg. 20.95 (978-1-56763-743-4(4)) Ozark Publishing.

Shalev, Michal. How to Be Famous. Shalev, Michal, illus. 2016. (ENG., Illus.). 32p. (gr. -1-1). 16.99 (978-1-77657-029-4(4)); 9.99 (978-1-77657-045-4(6)); 33.32 (978-1-77657-057-7(X)); 33.32 (978-1-77657-047-8(2)) Gecko Pr. NZL. Dist: Lerner Publishing Group.

Stolz, Mary. Pigeon Flight. Tinkelman, Murray, illus. 2012. 62p. 36.95 (978-1-258-25234-2(1)); pap. 21.95 (978-1-258-25387-5(9)) Literary Licensing, LLC.

Sudbury, Dave & Saefkow, Hans. King of Rome. 2008. (ENG., Illus.). 32p. (J). (gr. -1-3). 17.95 (978-1-894965-94-1(9)) Simply Read Bks. CAN. Dist: Ingram Publisher Services.

Thompson, Kimberly. Toulouse Tangled up in Lights. Easey, Chris, illus. 2011. 64p. (J). 19.95 (978-0-9818976-1-5(4)) Little Pigeon Bks.

Van Dixhorn, Brenda. The Pigeon Books: An Instructional Guide for Literature. 2015. (Great Works). (ENG., Illus.). 72p. (gr. k-3). pap. 9.99 (978-1-4807-6992-2(4)) Shell Educational Publishing.

Weathers, Marlon. Henry Baldpate & His Treetop Friends. 2008. 24p. pap. 24.95 (978-1-60672-923-6(3)) America Star Bks.

Webster, Andrea K. Pigeon in the Park. 2012. 28p. pap. 19.99 (978-1-4772-2530-1(7)) AuthorHouse.

Weston Woods Staff, creator. The Pigeon Finds a Hot Dog. 2011. 38.75 (978-0-545-26298-9(4)) Weston Woods Studios, Inc.

Willems, Mo. Don't Let the Pigeon Drive the Bus! Willems, Mo, illus. 2012. (Pigeon Ser.). (ENG., Illus.). 40p. (J). (gr. -1-k). pap. 19.99 (978-1-4231-4514-1(3)) Hyperion Pr.

—Don't Let the Pigeon Finish This Activity Book! Willems, Mo, illus. 2012. (Pigeon Ser.). (ENG., Illus.). 272p. (YA). (gr. 7-12). pap. 19.99 (978-1-4231-3310-0(2)) Hyperion Pr.

—Don't Let the Pigeon Stay Up Late! Willems, Mo, illus. 2006. (Pigeon Ser.). (ENG., Illus.). 40p. (J). (gr. -1-k). 16.99 (978-0-7868-3746-5(2)) Hyperion Pr.

—Don't Let the Pigeon Stay Up Late! 2011. (J). (gr. -1-2). 29.95 (978-0-545-32735-0(0)); pap. 18.95 incl. audio compact disk (978-0-545-32791-6(1));Set. pap. 38.75 incl. audio compact disk (978-0-545-32792-3(X)) Weston Woods Studios, Inc.

—The Duckling Gets a Cookie!? Willems, Mo, illus. 2012. (ENG., Illus.). 40p. (J). (gr. -1-k). 16.99 (978-1-4231-5128-9(3)) Hyperion Pr.

—It's a Busload of Pigeon Books! Willems, Mo, illus. 2013. (Pigeon Ser.). (ENG., Illus.). 120p. (J). (gr. -1-k). 24.99 (978-1-4231-7589-6(1)) Hyperion Pr.

—¡No Dejes Que la Paloma Conduzca el Autobús! Willems, Mo, illus. 2011.Tr. of Don't Let the Pigeon Drive the Bus. (SPA & ENG., Illus.). 40p. (J). (gr. -1-k). pap. 7.99 (978-1-4231-4052-8(4)) Hyperion Pr.

—The Pigeon Finds a Hot Dog! Willems, Mo, illus. 2004. (Pigeon Ser.). (ENG., Illus.). 40p. (J). (gr. -1-k). 16.99 (978-0-7868-1869-3(7)) Hyperion Pr.

—The Pigeon Has Feelings, Too! Willems, Mo, illus. 2005. (Pigeon Ser.). (ENG., Illus.). 12p. (J). (gr. -1-k). 6.99 (978-0-7868-3650-5(4)) Hyperion Pr.

—The Pigeon Loves Things That Go! Willems, Mo, illus. 2005. (Pigeon Ser.). (ENG., Illus.). 12p. (J). (gr. -1-k). 6.99 (978-0-7868-3651-2(2)) Hyperion Pr.

—The Pigeon Needs a Bath! Willems, Mo, illus. 2014. (Pigeon Ser.). (ENG., Illus.). 40p. (J). (gr. -1-k). 16.99 (978-1-4231-9087-5(4)) Hyperion Bks. for Children.

—The Pigeon Wants a Puppy! Willems, Mo, illus. 2008. (Pigeon Ser.). (ENG., Illus.). 40p. (J). (gr. -1-k). 16.99 (978-1-4231-0960-0(0)) Hyperion Pr.

Willems, Mo & Campoy, F. Isabel. ¡La Paloma Encuentra un Perro Caliente! Willems, Mo, illus. 2011. (SPA & ENG., Illus.). 40p. (J). (gr. -1-k). pap. 9.99 (978-1-4231-4051-1(6)) Hyperion Pr.

Willems, Mo & Scieszka, Jon, narrated by. Don't Let the Pigeon Drive the Bus! 2011. (J). (gr. -1-1). 29.95 (978-0-545-13453-8(6)) Weston Woods Studios, Inc.

Willems, Mo & Willems, Trixie, narrated by. The Pigeon Finds a Hot Dog! 2011. (J). (gr. -1-1). 18.95 (978-0-545-26297-2(6)); 29.95 (978-0-545-23795-6(5)) Weston Woods Studios, Inc.

Wyeth, Sharon Dennis. Message in the Sky Bk. 3: Corey's Underground Railroad Diary. 2003. (My America Ser.). (ENG.). 112p. (J). 10.95 (978-0-439-37057-8(4), Scholastic Pr.) Scholastic, Inc.

Yang, Belle. Always Come Home to Me. Yang, Belle, illus. 2007. (ENG., Illus.). 32p. (J). (gr. -1-3). 16.99 (978-0-7636-2899-4(9)) Candlewick Pr.

Yang, Belle & Williams, Marcia. Archie's War: My Scrapbook of the First World War. Williams, Marcia, illus. 2007. (ENG., Illus.). 48p. (J). (gr. 3-7). 18.99 (978-0-7636-3532-9(4)) Candlewick Pr.

Yardley, Liz. The Firefly Legacy - Book Vii. Yardley, Liz, illus. 2013. (Illus.). 314p. pap. (978-0-9872013-2-4(8)) BlueFlower Bks.

PIGGLE-WIGGLE, MRS. (FICTITIOUS CHARACTER)—FICTION

MacDonald, Betty Bard. Happy Birthday, Mrs. Piggle-Wiggle. Boiger, Alexandra, illus. 2007. (Mrs. Piggle-Wiggle Ser.). 193p. (J). (gr. 3-7). lib. bdg. 16.89 (978-0-06-072813-7(2)) HarperCollins Pubs.

—Hello, Mrs. Piggle-Wiggle. Knight, Hilary & Boiger, Alexandra, illus. 2007. (ENG.). 176p. (J). (gr. 3-7). 16.99 (978-0-397-31715-8(8)); pap. 5.99 (978-0-06-440149-4(9)) HarperCollins Pubs.

—Hello, Mrs Piggle Wiggle. unabr. ed. 2004. 125p. (J). (gr. 2-5). pap. 29.00 incl. audio (978-0-8072-1184-7(2), S YA 1018 SP, Listening Library) Random Hse. Audio Publishing Group.

—Mrs. Piggle-Wiggle. Knight, Hilary & Boiger, Alexandra, illus. rev. ed. 2007. (ENG.). 144p. (J). (gr. 3-7). 16.99 (978-0-397-31712-7(3)) HarperCollins Pubs.

—Mrs. Piggle-Wiggle. Boiger, Alexandra, illus. rev. ed. 2007. (Trophy Bk.). (ENG.). 144p. (J). (gr. 3-7). pap. 5.99 (978-0-06-440148-7(0)) HarperCollins Pubs.

—Mrs. Piggle-Wiggle's Magic. Knight, Hilary & Boiger, Alexandra, illus. 2007. (Trophy Bk.). (ENG.). 192p. (J). (gr. 3-7). pap. 5.99 (978-0-06-440151-7(0)) HarperCollins Pubs.

—Mrs. Piggle-Wiggle's Magic. 2004. (Illus.). 144p. (J). (gr. 2-5). pap. 29.00 incl. audio (978-1-4000-9001-3(6), Listening Library) Random Hse. Audio Publishing Group.

MacDonald, Betty Bard & Canham, Anne MacDonald. Happy Birthday, Mrs. Piggle-Wiggle. Boiger, Alexandra, illus. 2008. (ENG.). 208p. (J). (gr. 3-7). pap. 6.99 (978-0-06-072814-4(0)) HarperCollins Pubs.

PIGLET (FICTITIOUS CHARACTER)—FICTION

Champier, Jacqueline. The Little Piggy Goes South. 2012. 28p. pap. 19.99 (978-1-4772-8976-1(3)) AuthorHouse.

Johnson, Carole. Pennie the Piglet. 2007. 60p. per. 16.95 (978-1-4241-7019-7(2)) America Star Bks.

Studio Mouse Staff. Pooh & Piglet. 2008. (ENG., Illus.). 36p. (J). (gr. -1). 7.99 (978-1-59069-419-0(8)) Studio Mouse LLC.

Taylor, W. Y. This Little Piggy Goes Green. 2009. (ENG.). 12p. bds. 3.95 (978-1-58117-925-5(1), Intervisual/Piggy Toes) Bendon, Inc.

Testa, Maggie. OLIVIA & Her Favorite Things. Spaziante, Patrick, illus. 2013. (Olivia TV Tie-In Ser.). (ENG.). 12p. (J). (gr. -1-1). bds. 5.99 (978-1-4424-6587-9(5), Simon Spotlight) Simon Spotlight.

Winnie the Pooh. The Close-up Day. 2010. 16p. 5.99 (978-1-4231-3096-3(0)) Disney Pr.

PIGMENTATION

see Animals—Color; Human Skin Color

PIGS

Adele, Gloria. My Wild Backyard: Wild Hogs. 2012. 32p. pap. 21.99 (978-1-4771-4129-8(4)) Xlibris Corp.

Albright, Rosie. Pig Detectives. 2012. (Animal Detectives Ser.). (ENG.). 24p. (J). (gr. k-3). pap. 8.25 (978-1-4488-6262-7(0));

(Illus.). 22.60 *(978-1-4488-6151-4(9))* Rosen Publishing Group, Inc., The. (PowerKids Pr.).

Alexander, Carol. The Big Squeal: A True Story about a Homeless Pig's Search for Life, Liberty & the Pursuit of Happiness. 2013. (ENG., Illus.). 32p. (J). pap. 16.00 *(978-1-61009-112-1(4),* Acorn) Oak Tree Publishing.

—The Big Squeal: A True Story about a Homeless Pig's Search for Life, Liberty & the Pursuit of Happiness. Kalpart Designs, illus. 2012. (ENG.). 24p. (J). 24.00 *(978-1-61009-036-0(5),* Acorn) Oak Tree Publishing.

Amoroso, Cynthia & Noyed, Bob. Pigs. 2016. (In the Barnyard Ser.). (ENG.). 24p. (J). (gr. k-3). 27.07 *(978-1-5038-0829-4(7),* 210673) Child's World, Inc., The.

Aspen-Baxter, Linda & Kissock, Heather. Cerdos. 2012. (SPA.). (J). *(978-1-61913-190-3(0))* Weigl Pubs., Inc.

Austin, Richard. Pocket Piggies Colors! The Teacup Pigs of Pennywell Farm. Austin, Richard, photos by. 2014. (ENG., Illus.). 22p. (J). bds. 5.95 *(978-0-7611-7980-1(1),* 17980) Workman Publishing Co., Inc.

Barbe-Julien, Colette. Cerditos. 2006. (Nacidos para Ser Salvajes Ser.). (SPA., Illus.). 24p. (gr. k-3). lib. bdg. 23.00 *(978-0-8368-7422-8(6),* Gareth Stevens Learning Library) Stevens, Gareth Publishing LLLP.

—Little Pigs. 2006. (Born to Be Wild Ser.). (Illus.). 24p. (gr. k-3). lib. bdg. 23.00 *(978-0-8368-6698-8(3),* Gareth Stevens Learning Library) Stevens, Gareth Publishing LLLP.

Beck, Angela. Guinea Pigs: Keeping & Caring for Your Pet. 2013. (Keeping & Caring for Your Pet Ser.). 72p. (J). (gr. 6-12). pap. 8.95 *(978-1-4644-0299-9(X))* Enslow Pubs., Inc.

Beck, Isabel L., et al. Trophies Kindergarten: My Pig. 2003. (Trophies Ser.). (gr. k-6). 13.80 *(978-0-15-329535-5(X))* Harcourt Schl. Pubs.

Blake, Jon. House of Fun. Roberts, David, illus. 2005. (ENG.). 128p. (J). (gr. 2-4). pap. 6.95 *(978-0-340-88459-1(2))* Hachette Children's Group GBR. Dist: Hachette Bk. Group.

Blake, Kevin. Feral Pigs: Chomp, Chomp! 2015. (They Don't Belong: Tracking Invasive Species Ser.). (ENG., Illus.). 32p. (J). (gr. 2-7). lib. bdg. 26.60 *(978-1-62724-829-7(3))* Bearport Publishing Co., Inc.

Boothroyd, Jennifer. Meet a Baby Pig. 2016. (Lightning Bolt Books (tm) — Baby Farm Animals Ser.). (ENG., Illus.). 32p. (J). (gr. 1-3). 26.65 *(978-1-5124-0799-0(2))* Lerner Publishing Group.

Borgert-Spaniol, Megan. Warthogs. 2012. (Animal Safari Ser.). (ENG., Illus.). 24p. (J). (gr. k-3). lib. bdg. 25.95 *(978-1-60014-770-8(4),* Blastoff! Readers) Bellwether Media.

Boynton, Sandra. Perfect Piggies! 2010. (ENG., Illus.). 24p. (J). (gr. k — 1). bds. 6.95 *(978-0-7611-5993-3(2),* 15993) Workman Publishing Co., Inc.

Braidich, S. Little Pigs, Big Pigs: Learning the Short I Sound. 2009. (PowerPhonics Ser.). 24p. (gr. 1-1). 39.90 *(978-1-60851-456-4(0),* PowerKids Pr.) Rosen Publishing Group, Inc., The.

Carr, Aaron. Potbellied Pig. 2014. (Illus.). 24p. (J). *(978-1-62127-296-0(6))* Weigl Pubs., Inc.

Carraway, Rose. Pigs on the Farm. 2012. (Farm Animals Ser.). (Illus.). 24p. (gr. k-2). 69.20 *(978-1-4339-8056-5(8));* (J). 22.60 *(978-1-4339-7360-4(X));* (J). pap. 8.15 *(978-1-4339-7361-1(8))* Stevens, Gareth Publishing LLLP.

—Pigs on the Farm: Cerdos de Granja. 2012. (Farm Animals / Animales de granja Ser.). (SPA & ENG., Illus.). 24p. (J). (gr. k-2). lib. bdg. 22.60 *(978-1-4339-7402-1(9))* Stevens, Gareth Publishing LLLP.

Conner, Mac. Ambrose. 2011. 24p. pap. *(978-1-4269-6578-4(8))* Trafford Publishing (UK) Ltd.

Dicker, Katie. Pigs. 2014. (Farm Animals Ser.). (Illus.). 24p. (gr. 2-5). 28.50 *(978-1-62588-023-9(5))* Black Rabbit Bks.

Dieker, Wendy. Pigs. 2012. (Illus.). 24p. (J). lib. bdg. 25.65 *(978-1-62031-005-2(8))* Jump! Inc.

Dolphin, Colleen. Playful Pigs, 1 vol. 2011. (Farm Pets Ser.). (ENG., Illus.). 24p. (J). (gr. k-3). lib. bdg. 24.21 *(978-1-61613-373-3(2))* ABDO Publishing Co.

Doubleday Entertainment USA - Pigs: Down on the Farm. 2006. (J). per. 6.95 *(978-1-59566-228-6(6))* QEB Publishing Inc.

Doyle, Sheri. Pigs, 1 vol. 2012. (Farm Animals Ser.). (ENG., Illus.). 24p. (gr. k-1). lib. bdg. 26.65 *(978-1-4296-8647-1(2),* Pebble Plus) Capstone Press of Coughlan Cos.

Elora, Grace. Piglets. 2011. (Cute & Cuddly: Baby Animals Ser.). (Illus.). 24p. (gr. k-2). 69.20 *(978-1-4339-6152-6(0));* (J). lib. bdg. 22.60 *(978-1-4339-4515-1(0))* Stevens, Gareth Publishing LLLP.

Fretland VanVoorst, Jenny. Pig Detectives. 2013. (We Work! Animals with Jobs Ser.). 24p. (J). (gr. -1-3). lib. bdg. 21.32 *(978-1-61772-899-0(3))* Bearport Publishing Co., Inc.

Gibbs, Maddie. Pigs, 1 vol. 2015. (ENG., Illus.). 24p. (J). lib. bdg. 23.60 *(978-1-4994-0168-4(X),* PowerKids Pr.) Rosen Publishing Group, Inc., The.

Glaser, Rebecca Stromstad. Pigs Oink. 2016. (ENG., Illus.). 14p. (J). (gr. -1 — 1). bds. 7.99 *(978-1-68152-128-2(8))* Amicus.

Gleisner, Jenna Lee. Pig Farmer. 2015. (Gross Jobs Ser.). (ENG.). 24p. (J). (gr. 2-5). 27.07 *(978-1-63143-688-8(0),* 208524) Child's World, Inc., The.

Gorski-Sterner, Gail. The Adventures of Isabelle the Lost Pot Belly Pig: Based on a True Story. 2011. 36p. (gr. -1). pap. 19.99 *(978-1-4520-9040-5(8))* AuthorHouse.

Green, Emily K. Pigs. 2007. (Farm Animals Ser.). (ENG., Illus.). 24p. (J). (gr. k-3). lib. bdg. 25.95 *(978-1-60014-068-6(8))* Bellwether Media.

Harasymiw, R. Mann. Problem Solving with Pigs. 2013. (Animal Math Ser.). (ENG., Illus.). 24p. (J). (gr. 1-3). lib. bdg. 22.60 *(978-1-4339-9323-7(6))* Stevens, Gareth Publishing LLLP.

Harasymiw, Raymond. Problem Solving with Pigs. 2013. (Animal Math Ser.). 24p. (J). (gr. 1-3). pap. 48.90 *(978-1-4339-9325-1(2))* Stevens, Gareth Publishing LLLP.

Harasymiw, Raymond & Harasymiw, R. P. Problem Solving with Pigs. 2013. 24p. (J). (gr. 1-3). pap. 8.15 *(978-1-4339-9324-4(4))* Stevens, Gareth Publishing LLLP.

Hendrix, Emilia. Pigs & Piglets. 2016. (Animal Family Ser.). (ENG., Illus.). 24p. (J). (gr. k-k). pap. 8.15 *(978-1-4824-3783-6(X))* Stevens, Gareth Publishing LLLP.

Howard, Nancy Shroyer. Mischief in Tuscany: Running Wild in a Famous Italian Painting. 2008. (ENG., Illus.). 48p. 17.95 *(978-88-7461-094-5(7))* Mandragora ITA. Dist: National Bk. Network.

Hudak, Heather C. Pigs. 2006. (Farm Animals Ser.). (Illus.). 24p. (J). (gr. 3-7). lib. bdg. 24.45 *(978-1-59036-425-3(2));* per. 8.95 *(978-1-59036-432-1(5))* Weigl Pubs., Inc.

Jeffrey, Gary. Terminator Pig. Poluzz, Alessandro, illus. 2017. (Graphic Prehistoric Animals Ser.). 32p. (gr. 3-7). 31.35 ***(978-1-62588-412-1(5),*** Smart Apple Media) Black Rabbit Bks.

Kalman, Bobbie. Baby Pigs. 2010. (ENG., Illus.). 24p. (J). *(978-0-7787-3962-3(7));* pap. *(978-0-7787-3981-4(3))* Crabtree Publishing Co.

Kalman, Bobbie, contrib. by. Les Bébés Cochons. 2013. (FRE.). 24p. (J). pap. 9.95 *(978-2-89579-482-0(0))* Bayard Canada Livres CAN. Dist: Crabtree Publishing Co.

King-smith, Dick. All Pigs Are Beautiful. Jeram, Anita, illus. 2008. (Read, Listen, & Wonder Ser.). (ENG.). 32p. (J). (gr. -1-3). pap. 8.99 *(978-0-7636-3866-5(8))* Candlewick Pr.

Kishel, Ann-Marie. Pigs & Piglets. 2006. (First Step Nonfiction - Animal Families Ser.). (ENG., Illus.). 8p. (gr. -1-1). pap. 4.95 *(978-0-8225-5651-0(0),* Lerner Pubns.) Lerner Publishing Group.

Kissock, Heather & Aspen-Baxter, Linda. Pigs. 2011. (J). 27.13 *(978-1-61690-928-4(5))* Weigl Pubs., Inc.

Kuskowski, Alex. Portly Potbellied Pigs, 1 vol. Nobens, C. A., illus. 2013. (Unusual Pets Ser.). (ENG.). 24p. (J). (gr. -1-3). 24.21 *(978-1-61783-401-1(7))* ABDO Publishing Co.

Leaf, Christina. Baby Pigs. 2014. (Super Cute! Ser.). (ENG., Illus.). 24p. (J). (gr. k-3). lib. bdg. 25.95 *(978-1-60014-975-7(8),* Blastoff! Readers) Bellwether Media.

Lunis, Natalie. Potbellied Pigs. 2009. (Peculiar Pets Ser.). (Illus.). 24p. (YA). (gr. 2-5). lib. bdg. 22.61 *(978-1-59716-862-5(9))* Bearport Publishing Co., Inc.

Macken, JoAnn Early. Pigs. 2nd rev. ed. 2009. (Animals That Live on the Farm Ser.). (ENG.). 24p. (J). (gr. -1-3). pap. 8.15 *(978-1-4339-2468-2(4));* lib. bdg. 22.60 *(978-1-4339-2399-9(8))* Stevens, Gareth Publishing LLLP. (Weekly Reader Leveled Readers).

—Pigs;Los Cerdos. 2nd rev. ed. 2009. (Animals That Live on the Farm/Animales que viven en la granja Ser.). (ENG & SPA.). 24p. (J). (gr. -1-3). pap. 8.15 *(978-1-4339-2475-0(7));* lib. bdg. 22.60 *(978-1-4339-2431-6(5))* Stevens, Gareth Publishing LLLP. (Weekly Reader Leveled Readers).

MacLean, Kerry Lee. Peaceful Piggy Yoga. MacLean, Kerry Lee, illus. 2014. (ENG., Illus.). 32p. (J). (gr. 1-3). 6.99 *(978-0-8075-6383-0(8))* Whitman, Albert & Co.

McNeil, Niki, et al. HOCPP 1125 Pigs. 2006. spiral bd. 16.00 *(978-1-60308-125-2(9))* In the Hands of a Child.

Meachen Rau, Dana. Adivina Quién Gruñe. 2008. (Adivina Quién Ser.). (SPA.). 32p. (gr. k-2). lib. bdg. 15.95 *(978-0-7614-3455-9(0),* Benchmark Bks.) Marshall Cavendish Corp.

Mercer, Abbie. Pigs on a Farm. 2009. (Barnyard Animals Ser.). 24p. (J). (ENG.). pap. 8.25 *(978-1-4042-8067-0(7));* (Illus.). lib. bdg. 22.60 *(978-1-4042-8053-3(7))* Rosen Publishing Group, Inc., The. (PowerKids Pr.).

Miller, Dave. Dogs, Frogs, & Hogs. 2006. (ENG., Illus.). (J). 3.00 *(978-0-932859-88-4(7))* Apologetics Pr., Inc.

Minden, Cecilia. Farm Animals: Pigs. 2009. (21st Century Junior Library: Farm Animals Ser.). (ENG., Illus.). 24p. (gr. 2-4). lib. bdg. 25.64 *(978-1-60279-542-6(8),* 200275) Cherry Lake Publishing.

Murray, Julie. Pigs, 1 vol. (ENG., 24p. 2015. Illus.). (J). 27.07 *(978-1-62970-942-0(5))* 2003. 25.65 *(978-1-57765-648-7(2),* Buddy Bks.) ABDO Publishing Co.

Nelson, Robin. Pigs. 2009. (First Step Nonfiction - Farm Animals Ser.). (ENG., Illus.). 24p. (gr. k-2). 23.93 *(978-0-7613-4059-1(9),* Lerner Pubns.) Lerner Publishing Group.

Older, Jules. Pig. Severance, Lyn, illus. 2004. (ENG.). 32p. (J). (gr. k-3). 16.95 *(978-0-88106-109-3(3))* Charlesbridge Publishing, Inc.

Olivia's ABC. 2014. (ENG., Illus.). 30p. (J). (gr. -1-k). bds. 7.99 *(978-1-4814-2192-8(1),* Atheneum Bks. for Young Readers) Simon & Schuster Children's Publishing.

Orr, Tamra. Care for a Potbellied Pig. 2008. (How to Convince Your Parents You Can ... Ser.). (Illus.). 32p. (YA). (gr. 1-4). lib. bdg. 25.70 *(978-1-58415-661-1(9))* Mitchell Lane Pubs., Inc.

Otfinoski, Steven. Pigs & Hogs. 2009. (Animals Animals Ser.). 48p. (gr. 3). 29.93 *(978-0-7614-3971-4(4))* Marshall Cavendish Corp.

Owen, Ruth. Warthogs, 1. 2014. (Dr. Bob's Amazing World of Animals Ser.). (ENG.). 32p. (J). (gr. k-5). 27.50 *(978-1-4777-9044-1(6),* Windmill Bks.) Rosen Publishing Group, Inc., The.

Petrie, Kristin. Potbellied Pigs, 1 vol. 2012. (Unique Pets Ser.). (ENG.). 24p. (J). (gr. 3-6). lib. bdg. 25.65 *(978-1-61783-442-4(4),* Checkerboard Library) ABDO Publishing Co.

Pigs. Date not set. (Old MacDonald Stickers Ser.). (Illus.). 16p. (J). 5.98 *(978-0-7525-9968-7(2))* Parragon, Inc.

Randolph, Joanne. My Friend the Potbellied Pig. 2010. (Curious Pet Pals Ser.). (ENG.). 24p. (J). (gr. k-3). lib. bdg. 22.60 *(978-1-60754-975-8(1));* (Illus.). pap. 8.15 *(978-1-60754-982-6(4))* Windmill Bks.

Rau, Dana Meachen. Guess Who Grunts/Adivina Quién Gruñe. 2007. (Guess Who/Adivina Quién Ser.). (SPA & ENG.). 32p. (gr. k-2). 15.95 *(978-0-7614-3481-8(X))* Marshall Cavendish Corp.

Ray, Hannah. Pigs. 2006. (Down on the Farm Ser.). (Illus.). 24p. (J). (gr. 4-7). lib. bdg. 15.95 *(978-1-59566-181-4(6))* QEB Publishing Inc.

Reasoner, Charles. Ooink! 2009. (Lift & Learn Ser.). (Illus.). 10p. (J). (gr. -1-k). 10.99 *(978-1-934650-12-7(9))* Just For Kids Pr., LLC.

Reed, Cristie. Mini Pig. 2015. (ENG.). 32p. (gr. 3-6). 32.79 *(978-1-63430-431-3(4))* Rourke Educational Media.

Rockwood, Leigh. Pigs Are Smart! 2010. (Illus.). 24p. (J). 49.50 *(978-1-4358-9835-6(4),* PowerKids Pr.); pap. 8.25 *(978-1-4358-9834-9(6),* PowerKids Pr.); (gr. 2-5). lib. bdg. 22.60 *(978-1-4358-9373-3(5))* Rosen Publishing Group, Inc., The.

Scieszka, Jon. The True Story of the 3 Little Pigs. Smith, Lane, illus. 2011. (J). (gr. -1-3). 18.95 *(978-0-545-09459-7(3));* 29.95 *(978-0-545-09457-3(7))* Weston Woods Studios, Inc.

Searl, Duncan. Pigs. 2006. (Smart Animals! Ser.). (Illus.). 32p. (J). (gr. 2-5). lib. bdg. 25.27 *(978-1-59716-164-0(0))* Bearport Publishing Co., Inc.

Sexton, Colleen. Piglets. 2008. (Watch Animals Grow Ser.). (ENG., Illus.). 24p. (J). (gr. k-3). lib. bdg. 25.95 *(978-1-60014-169-0(2))* Bellwether Media.

Silverman, Buffy. Mini Pigs. 2017. (J). ***(978-1-5124-8302-4(8))*** Lerner Publishing Group.

Silverstein, Alvin, et al. Potbellied Pigs: Cool Pets! Kelley, Gerald, illus. 2011. (Far-Out & Unusual Pets Ser.). 48p. (J). (gr. 2-5). lib. bdg. 25.27 *(978-0-7660-3687-1(1))* Enslow Pubs., Inc.

Stiefel, Chana. Pigs on the Family Farm. 2013. (Animals on the Family Farm Ser.). 24p. (J). (gr. k-3). pap. 7.95 *(978-1-4644-0359-0(7),* Enslow Elementary); lib. bdg. 22.60 *(978-0-7660-4208-7(1))* Enslow Pubs., Inc.

Stockland, Patricia M. In the Pig Pen, 1 vol. Ouren, Todd, illus. 2007. (Barnyard Buddies Ser.). (ENG.). 24p. (gr. -1-2). 27.07 *(978-1-60270-025-3(7),* Looking Glass Library- Nonfiction) Magic Wagon.

Stone, Tanya Lee. Pigs. 2003. (Wild Wild World Ser.). 24p. (YA). 24.94 *(978-1-56711-819-3(4),* Blackbirch Pr., Inc.) Cengage Gale.

Tait, Leia. Caring for Your Potbellied Pig. 2006. (Caring for Your Pet Ser.). (Illus.). 32p. (J). (gr. 3-7). lib. bdg. 26.00 *(978-1-59036-474-1(0))* Weigl Pubs., Inc.

Thatcher, Henry. Wild Boars & Teacup Pigs, 1 vol., 1. 2014. (Big Animals, Small Animals Ser.). (ENG.). 32p. (J). (gr. k-5). 26.25 *(978-1-4777-6097-0(0),* PowerKids Pr.) Rosen Publishing Group, Inc., The.

Top That Publishing Staff, ed. Wacky Pig. 2004. (Wacky Animals Ser.). (Illus.). 10p. (J). pap. *(978-1-84510-090-2(5))* Top That! Publishing PLC.

Walden, Katherine. Warthogs. 2009. (Safari Animals Ser.). 24p. (gr. 1-1). 42.50 *(978-1-60852-963-6(0));* (J). (gr. -1-2). lib. bdg. 22.60 *(978-1-4358-2688-5(4))* Rosen Publishing Group, Inc., The. (PowerKids Pr.).

Wilsdon, Christina. Pigs. 2009. (Amazing Animals Ser.). (ENG.). 48p. (J). (gr. 2-6). pap. 10.50 *(978-1-4339-2126-1(X),* Gareth Stevens Learning Library); (gr. 3-6). lib. bdg. 28.00 *(978-0-8368-9122-5(8))* Stevens, Gareth Publishing LLLP.

Wood, Alix. Mini Pigs. 2016. (Mini Animals Ser.). 00032p. (J). (gr. 2-3). pap. 10.00 *(978-1-4994-8155-6(1),* Windmill Bks.) Rosen Publishing Group, Inc., The.

PIGS—FICTION

Abadzis, Nick. Pigs Might Fly. Dye, Jerel, illus. 2017. (Pigs Might Fly Ser.). (ENG.). 208p. (J). pap. 15.99 *(978-1-62672-086-2(X),* 9781626720862, First Second Bks.) Roaring Brook Pr.

Acevedo, Ari. Juan Bobo Sends the Pig to Mass. Wrenn, Tom, illus. 2008. (Story Cove Ser.). (SPA & ENG.). 24p. (J). (gr. -1-3). pap. 4.95 *(978-0-87483-883-1(5))* August Hse. Pubs., Inc.

Ackerman, Jill. This Little Piggy. Berg, Michelle, illus. 2007. (Little Scholastic Ser.). (ENG.). 6p. (J). (gr. k — 1). bds. 12.99 *(978-0-545-03038-0(2))* Scholastic, Inc.

Adams, Alison. The Three Little Pigs: Classic Tales Edition. Greenhead, Bill, illus. 2011. (Classic Tales Ser.). (J). *(978-1-936258-71-0(4))* Benchmark Education Co.

Adams, Ben. The Pig with the Curliest Tail. Cameron, Craig, illus. 2013. (Googly Eyes Ser.). (ENG.). 12p. (J). (gr. -1-k). bds. 6.99 *(978-1-84322-618-5(9),* Armadillo) Anness Publishing GBR. Dist: National Bk. Network.

Adams, Jean Ekman. Clarence & the Purple Horse Bounce into Town. Adams, Jean Ekman, illus. 2003. (Illus.). 32p. (J). (gr. -1-3). 15.95 *(978-0-87358-826-3(6),* Rising Moon Bks. for Young Readers) Northland Publishing.

Adventures of the Robber Pig: Level J, 6 vols. (Leveled Books). 128p. (gr. 2-3). 41.95 *(978-0-7699-0987-5(6))* Shortland Pubns. (U. S. A.) Inc.

Aguayo, Sal. The Tiny Telepaths: A Continuing Saga, 1 vol. 2010. 62p. pap. 19.95 *(978-1-4489-5212-0(3))* America Star Bks.

Aina, Olaiya E. Ijapa, the Lion, & the Boar. 2010. 20p. 13.80 *(978-1-4269-3183-3(2))* Trafford Publishing.

Albee, Sarah. Where Is Pig? Velez, Walter, illus. 2006. (Step-By-Step Readers Ser.). (J). pap. *(978-1-59939-056-7(6),* Reader's Digest Young Families, Inc.) Studio Fun International.

Alexander, Lloyd. The Black Cauldron 50th Anniversary Edition. 2015. (Chronicles of Prydain Ser.: 2). (ENG.). 224p. (J). (gr. 3-7). 25.99 *(978-1-62779-323-0(2),* 9781627793230, Holt, Henry & Co. Bks. For Young Readers) Holt, Henry & Co.

—The Book of Three. Wyatt, David, illus. 2006. (Chronicles of Prydain Ser.: 1). (ENG.). 224p. (J). (gr. 3-7). pap. 7.99 *(978-0-8050-8048-3(1),* 9780805080483) Square Fish.

All Pull Together, 6 vols., Pack. (gr. -1-2). 23.00 *(978-0-7635-8789-5(3))* Rigby Education.

Amery & Cartwright. Curly the Pig Kid Kit. 2007. (Kid Kits Ser.). (Illus.). 10p. (J). (gr. -1). bds. 12.99 *(978-1-60130-009-6(3),* Usborne) EDC Publishing.

Amery, H. Where's Curly? Cartwright, Stephen, illus. 2004. (Treasury of Farmyard Tales Ser.). 16p. (J). (gr. 1-18). pap. 7.95 *(978-0-7945-0514-1(7));* lib. bdg. 15.95 *(978-1-58086-563-0(1))* EDC Publishing.

Amery, H. & Cartwright, S. Three Little Pigs. 2004. (First Stories Ser.). 16p. (J). pap. 4.99 *(978-0-7945-0609-4(7))* EDC Publishing.

Amery, Heather. Curly the Pig Board Book. Cartwright, Stephen, illus. 2004. (Young Farmyard Tales Board Books Ser.). 10p. (J). bds. 3.95 *(978-0-7945-0468-7(X),* Usborne) EDC Publishing.

—Three Little Pigs. Tyler, Jenny, ed. 2004. (Usborne First Stories Ser.). 16p. (J). (gr. -1). lib. bdg. 12.95 *(978-1-58086-623-1(9),* Usborne) EDC Publishing.

Anderson, Derek. Ten Hungry Pigs: An Epic Lunch Adventure. Anderson, Derek, illus. 2016. (ENG., Illus.). 40p. (J). (gr. -1-k). 16.99 *(978-0-545-16848-9(1))* Scholastic, Inc.

—Ten Pigs: An Epic Bath Adventure. Anderson, Derek, illus. 2015. (ENG., Illus.). 40p. (J). (gr. -1-k). 16.99 *(978-0-545-16846-5(5))* Scholastic, Inc.

Anderson, Derek. Ten Pigs - An Epic Bath Adventure. 2017. (ENG.). 32p. (J). (— 1). bds. 6.99 ***(978-1-338-13581-7(3),*** Cartwheel Bks.) Scholastic, Inc.

Anderson, Lena & Sandin, Joan. Hedgehog, Pig, & the Sweet Little Friend. Sandin, Joan, tr. from SWE. 2007. (Illus.). 32p. (J). (gr. -1-1). 16.00 *(978-91-29-66742-4(9))* R & S Bks. SWE. Dist: Macmillan.

Andrews, Roxanna. The Adventures of Super Pig. 2006. (Illus.). 68p. (J). 15.95 *(978-1-59879-232-4(6))* Lifevest Publishing, Inc.

Ansley, Frank & Wheeler, Lisa. Who's Afraid of Granny Wolf? Ansley, Frank, tr. 2004. (Fitch & Chip Ser.: 3). (ENG., Illus.). 48p. (J). (gr. 1-3). 16.99 *(978-0-689-84952-7(4),* Simon Spotlight) Simon Spotlight.

Arinola Awokoya. The Adventures of High Jumper. 2009. 112p. pap. 14.99 *(978-1-4269-1792-9(9))* Trafford Publishing.

Artell, Mike. Three Little Cajun Pigs. Harris, Jim, illus. 2006. (ENG.). 32p. (J). (gr. k-3). 17.99 *(978-0-8037-2815-8(8),* Dial Bks) Penguin Young Readers Group.

Asch, Frank. Happy Birthday, Big Bad Wolf. Asch, Frank, illus. 2011. (ENG., Illus.). 32p. (J). (gr. -1-2). 16.95 *(978-1-55337-368-1(5))* Kids Can Pr., Ltd. CAN. Dist: Hachette Bk. Group.

Atlas, Ron. Ten Pigs Fiddling. Flint, Stacie, illus. 2006. (ENG.). 32p. (J). (gr. -1-k). 16.00 *(978-0-9630243-8-1(8),* 1249130) Amberwood Pr.

—Ten Pigs Fiddling. Flint, Stacie, illus. 2nd rev. ed. 2006. (ENG.). 32p. (J). (gr. -1-k). 17.95 *(978-0-9630243-3-6(7))* Amberwood Pr.

Auerbach, Annie & PopCap Games Staff. The Three Little Pigs Fight Back. Grosvenor, Charles & Roberts, Jeremy, illus. 2013. (Plants vs. Zombies Ser.). (ENG.). 24p. (J). (gr. -1-3). pap. 4.99 *(978-0-06-222838-3(2),* HarperFestival) HarperCollins Pubs.

Axelrod, Amy. Pigs in the Corner: Fun with Math & Dance. McGinley-Nally, Sharon, illus. 2005. (ENG.). 40p. (J). (gr. -1-4). 8.99 *(978-1-4169-0335-2(6),* Simon & Schuster/Paula Wiseman Bks.) Simon & Schuster/Paula Wiseman Bks.

Axelrod, Amy & McGinley-Nally, Sharon. Pigs at Odds: Fun with Math & Games. McGinley-Nally, Sharon, illus. 2003. (ENG., Illus.). 40p. (J). (gr. -1-4). 7.99 *(978-0-689-86144-4(3),* Aladdin) Simon & Schuster Children's Publishing.

Ayres, Pam. Piggo & the Fork Lift Truck. (Illus.). 32p. *(978-0-563-36310-1(X))* BBC Worldwide.

Bader, Bonnie. Pig-Piggy-Pigs. 2015. (Penguin Young Readers, Level 2 Ser.). (ENG., Illus.). 32p. (J). (gr. 1-2). 3.99 *(978-0-448-48221-7(5),* Penguin Young Readers) Penguin Young Readers Group.

Bajaj, Subash, illus. The Three Little Pigs. 2010. (J). *(978-1-60617-135-6(6))* Teaching Strategies, LLC.

Baker, E. D. Maggie & the Flying Pigs. 2017. (ENG., Illus.). 128p. (J). 16.99 ***(978-1-68119-489-9(9),*** 9781681194899, Bloomsbury USA Childrens) Bloomsbury Publishing USA.

—Magic Animal Rescue 4: Maggie & the Flying Pigs. 2017. (ENG., Illus.). 128p. (J). pap. 5.99 ***(978-1-68119-485-1(6),*** 9781681194851, Bloomsbury USA Childrens) Bloomsbury Publishing USA.

Barchers, Suzanne I. How Big Is Kip?, 1 vol. 2011. (Targeted Phonics Ser.). (ENG., Illus.). 16p. (J). (gr. k-2). pap. 5.99 *(978-1-4333-2410-9(5))* Teacher Created Materials, Inc.

Barkley, Callie. Ellie & the Good-Luck Pig. Riti, Marsha, illus. 2015. (Critter Club Ser.: 10). (ENG.). 128p. (J). (gr. k-4). pap. 5.99 *(978-1-4814-2402-8(5),* Little Simon) Little Simon.

Barnum, Richard. Squinty the Comical Pig. 2004. reprint ed. pap. 1.99 *(978-1-4192-4865-8(0));* pap. 15.95 *(978-1-4191-4865-1(6))* Kessinger Publishing, LLC.

—Squinty the Comical Pig Illustrated Edit. 2006. (Illus.). pap. *(978-1-4065-0921-2(3))* Dodo Pr.

Barton, Elizabeth & Shaw, Natalie. Olivia Leaps! Osterhold, Jared, illus. 2009. (Olivia TV Tie-In Ser.). (ENG.). 12p. (J). (gr. -1-1). bds. 6.99 *(978-1-4169-8572-3(7),* Simon Spotlight) Simon Spotlight.

Bas, Mercè Escardó I. The Three Little Pigs/Los Tres Cerditos. Joan, Pere, illus. 2006. (Bilingual Fairy Tales Ser.: BILI). (ENG & SPA.). 32p. (J). (gr. -1-7). pap. 6.99 *(978-0-8118-5064-3(1))* Chronicle Bks. LLC.

Bassede, Francine. Dia con los Cerditos. (Buenas Noches Ser.). (SPA.). (J). (gr. 1-3). 8.95 *(978-958-04-5626-1(7))* Norma S.A. COL. Dist: Distribuidora Norma, Inc., Lectorum Pubns., Inc.

Bean, Margo Cronbaugh. Buffaloed Badger. Perry, Aumi Kauffman, illus. 2012. 24p. 19.95 *(978-1-61633-239-6(5));* pap. 11.95 *(978-1-61633-240-2(9))* Guardian Angel Publishing, Inc.

Beaton, Clare & Blackstone, Stella. How Big Is a Pig? Beaton, Clare, illus. 2004. (ENG., Illus.). 24p. (J). (gr. -1-k). pap. 6.99 *(978-1-84148-702-1(3))* Barefoot Bks., Inc.

Bender, Carol. Picky Eater, That Peter. 2011. 25p. (J). 24.95 *(978-1-4327-7055-6(1))* Outskirts Pr., Inc.

Bennicke, Rune Brandt. The Mystery Hat. Jensen, Jakob Hjort, illus. 2014. (ENG.). 32p. (J). (gr. -1-k). 16.95 *(978-1-62914-621-8(8),* Sky Pony Pr.) Skyhorse Publishing Co., Inc.

Benton, Jim. Piggy Paints. 2015. (ENG.). 16p. (J). (— 1). bds. 5.99 *(978-0-545-64785-4(1),* Cartwheel Bks.) Scholastic, Inc.

Bergen, Lara. Tutu Twins. Pastel, Elyse & Pastel, Elyse, illus. 2008. (ENG.). 24p. (J). (gr. k-17). per. 3.99 *(978-1-58476-615-5(8))* Innovative Kids.

Berry, Lynne. Pig & Pug. Correll, Gemma, illus. 2015. (ENG.). 40p. (J). (gr. -1-3). 16.99 *(978-1-4814-2131-7(X),* Simon & Schuster Bks. For Young Readers) Simon & Schuster Bks. For Young Readers.

Between the Lions - Early Literacy Kit - Huff & Puff, 2 bks., 1 cass. 2005. (Between the Lions Ser.). (Illus.). (J). VHS 29.95 *(978-1-59375-283-5(0),* WG38613) WGBH Boston Video.

Biddle, Charles, Jr. The Three Little Pigs. Malak, Annabel, illus. 2011. 16p. (J). pap. 12.95 *(978-2-89558-409-4(5))* Editions Alexandre Stanke CAN. Dist: Bookmasters Distribution.

Bigler, Stephanie, et al. Sir Francis Bacon & the Wolves of Isle Royale: A Little Pig's Big Adventure. 2008. 24p. pap. 13.99 *(978-1-4389-1524-1(1))* AuthorHouse.

Bills, Taylor, illus. Three Little Pigs. 2009. 24p. (J). 12.95 *(978-0-9776845-0-2(4))* 3D Alley, Inc.

Black, Michael Ian. A Pig Parade Is a Terrible Idea. Hawkes, Kevin, illus. 2010. (ENG.). 40p. (J). (gr. -1-3). 17.99 *(978-1-4169-7922-7(0),* Simon & Schuster Bks. For Young Readers) Simon & Schuster Bks. For Young Readers.

Blackford, Andy. The Three Little Pigs & the New Neighbor. 2014. (ENG., Illus.). 32p. (J). *(978-0-7787-0447-8(5));* pap. *(978-0-7787-0482-9(3))* Crabtree Publishing Co.

Blackstone, Stella. Cerdota Grandota. Beaton, Clare, illus. 2003.Tr. of How Big Is a Pig. (SPA.). 24p. (J). (gr. k-2). pap. 6.99 *(978-1-84148-926-1(3))* Barefoot Bks., Inc.
Bloker Cantrell, Jeannette, et al. The Summer of Joanie & Bobo. 2012. 72p. pap. 12.00 *(978-1-4349-1759-1(2))* Dorrance Publishing Co., Inc.
Bloom, Suzanne. No Place for a Pig. Bloom, Suzanne, illus. 2003. (ENG., Illus.). 32p. (J). (gr. k-2). 15.95 *(978-1-59078-047-3(7))* Boyds Mills Pr.
—We Keep a Pig in the Parlor. 2004. (ENG., Illus.). 24p. (J). (gr. k-2). reprint ed. pap. 9.95 *(978-1-59078-084-8(1))* Boyds Mills Pr.
Bloser, Cheryl. Little Mouse & the Muddy Feet. 2012. 28p. pap. 9.99 *(978-0-9836771-1-6(5))* Mindstir Media.
Boldt, Claudia. You're a Rude Pig, Bertie. 2013. (ENG., Illus.). 34p. (J). (gr. -1-3). 17.95 *(978-0-7358-4152-9(7))* North-South Bks., Inc.
Bond, Rebecca. Pig & Goose & the First Day of Spring. Bond, Rebecca, illus. 2017. (ENG., Illus.). 48p. (J). (gr. k-3). lib. bdg. 12.99 *(978-1-58089-594-1(8))* Charlesbridge Publishing, Inc.
Book Company Staff. Who Am I: Pig. 2003. (Board Bks.). (Illus.). (J). bds. 10.95 *(978-1-74047-309-5(4))* Book Co. Publishing Pty, Ltd., The AUS. Dist: Penton Overseas, Inc.
Boonen, Stefan. When Pigs Fly! Loufane, illus. 2004. 32p. (J). 6.95 *(978-1-58925-384-1(1))* Tiger Tales.
Bowater, Alan. A Pig Called Pete. Pascoe, Pete, illus. 2009. (Pig Called Pete Ser.). 32p. (J). (gr. -1-2). 22.60 *(978-1-60754-558-3(6))*; pap. 10.55 *(978-1-60754-559-0(4))* Windmill Bks.
—A Pig Called Pete Meets a Cat Called Kitty. Pascoe, Pete, illus. 2009. (Pig Called Pete Ser.). 32p. (J). (gr. -1-2). 22.60 *(978-1-60754-561-3(6))*; pap. 10.55 *(978-1-60754-562-0(4))* Windmill Bks.
—A Pig Called Pete Meets a Cow Called Carlotta. Pascoe, Pete, illus. 2009. (Pig Called Pete Ser.). 32p. (J). (gr. -1-2). 22.60 *(978-1-60754-567-5(5))*; pap. 10.55 *(978-1-60754-568-2(3))* Windmill Bks.
—A Pig Called Pete Meets a Dog Called Doug. Pascoe, Pete, illus. 2009. (Pig Called Pete Ser.). 32p. (J). (gr. -1-2). 22.60 *(978-1-60754-564-4(0))*; pap. 10.55 *(978-1-60754-565-1(9))* Windmill Bks.
—A Pig Called Pete Meets a Sheep Called Sean. Pascoe, Pete, illus. 2009. (Pig Called Pete Ser.). 32p. (J). (gr. -1-2). 22.60 *(978-1-60754-570-5(5))*; pap. 10.55 *(978-1-60754-571-2(3))* Windmill Bks.
Boynton. Bath Time! 2007. 10p. pap. 7.95 *(978-0-7611-4780-0(2))* Workman Publishing Co., Inc.
Bradman, Tony. The Three Little Pigs Go Camping. 1 vol. Warburton, Sarah, illus. 2014. (After Happily Ever After Ser.). (ENG.). 56p. (gr. 2-3). lib. bdg. 25.32 *(978-1-4342-7952-1(9))*, After Happily Ever After) Stone Arch Bks.
Brave M.A., Kathryn A. & Lavin, Paul J. A Fit ting Fairy Tale. 2006. 60p. pap. 16.95 *(978-1-4241-2992-8(3))* PublishAmerica, Inc.
Breathed, Berkeley. Pete & Pickles. Breathed, Berkeley, illus. 2008. (ENG., Illus.). 48p. (J). (gr. -1-k). 17.99 *(978-0-399-25082-8(4))*, Philomel Bks.) Penguin Young Readers Group.
Briley, Randy W. Big Pigs & Sock Dances. 2013. 36p. pap. 10.99 *(978-0-9896269-2-7(X))* Raven Mad Studios.
Brooke, L. Leslie. The Story of the Three Little Pig & Other Shorts Works. l.t. ed. 2007. 70p. 18.99 *(978-1-4346-1999-0(0))* Creative Media Partners, LLC.
—The Story of the Three Little Pig & Other Shorts Works: The Story of the Three Little Pig & Other Shorts Works. 2007. 70p. 16.99 *(978-1-4346-1975-4(3))* Creative Media Partners, LLC.
Brooks, Nan, illus. This Little Piggy. 2004. (J). 11.99 *(978-1-890647-10-0(1))* TOMY International, Inc.
Brooks, Walter R. The Clockwork Twin: A Freddy the Pig Book on Everything. Wiese, Kurt, illus. 2013. (ENG.). 256p. (gr. 4-13). pap. 10.99 *(978-1-4683-0349-0(X))*, 460349) Overlook Pr., The.
—Freddy & Mr. Camphor. Wiese, Kurt, illus. 2013. (ENG.). 256p. (gr. 4-13). pap. 10.99 *(978-1-4683-0666-8(9))*, 460666) Overlook Pr., The.
—Freddy & Simon the Dictator. Wiese, Kurt, illus. (ENG.). (gr. 4-13). 2014. 256p. pap. 10.99 *(978-1-4683-0976-8(5))*, 460976) 2003. 220p. (J). 23.95 *(978-1-58567-359-9(5))* Overlook Pr., The.
—Freddy & the Baseball Team from Mars. Wiese, Kurt, illus. 2011. (ENG.). 256p. 10.99 *(978-1-59020-696-6(7))*, 902696) Overlook Pr., The.
—Freddy & the Dragon. Wiese, Kurt, tr. 2012. (ENG., Illus.). 240p. (gr. 4-13). pap. 10.99 *(978-1-59020-866-3(8))*, 902866) Overlook Pr., The.
—Freddy & the Flying Saucer Plans. Wiese, Kurt, illus. 2013. (ENG.). 256p. (gr. 4-13). pap. 10.99 *(978-1-4683-0319-3(8))*, 460319) Overlook Pr., The.
—Freddy & the Ignormus, 4 vols. 2003. (Freddy the Pig Ser.). (J). 57.75 *(978-0-7887-2996-6(9))*, 40878) Recorded Bks., Inc.
—Freddy & the Men from Mars. Wiese, Kurt, illus. 2011. (ENG.). 256p. 10.99 *(978-1-59020-695-9(9))*, 902695) Overlook Pr., The.
—Freddy & the North Pole. Wiese, Kurt, illus. 2013. (ENG.). 322p. (gr. 4-13). pap. 10.99 *(978-1-4683-0320-9(1))*, 460320) Overlook Pr., The.
—Freddy & the Perilous Adventure. Wiese, Kurt, illus. 2012. (ENG.). 256p. 10.99 *(978-1-59020-742-0(4))*, 902742) Overlook Pr., The.
—Freddy & the Space Ship. Wiese, Kurt, illus. 2011. (ENG.). 266p. (gr. 2-18). 10.99 *(978-1-59020-469-6(7))* Overlook Pr., The.
—Freddy Goes Camping. Wiese, Kurt, illus. 2014. (ENG.). 272p. (gr. 4-13). pap. 10.99 *(978-1-4683-0831-0(9))*, 460831) Overlook Pr., The.
—Freddy Goes to Florida. Wiese, Kurt, illus. 2012. (ENG.). 224p. (gr. 4-13). 10.99 *(978-1-59020-741-3(6))*, 902741) Overlook Pr., The.
—Freddy Plays Football. Wiese, Kurt, illus. 2013. (ENG.). 288p. (gr. 4-13). pap. 10.99 *(978-1-4683-0667-5(7))*, 460667) Overlook Pr., The.
—Freddy Rides Again. Wiese, Kurt, illus. 2013. (ENG.). 240p. (gr. 4-13). pap. 10.99 *(978-1-4683-0724-5(X))*, 460724) Overlook Pr., The.
—Freddy the Cowboy. Wiese, Kurt, illus. 2014. (ENG.). 240p. (gr. 4-13). pap. 10.99 *(978-1-4683-0830-3(0))*, 460830) Overlook Pr., The.
—Freddy the Detective. Wiese, Kurt, illus. 2010. (ENG.). 272p. (gr. 4-13). 11.99 *(978-1-59020-418-4(2))*, 902418) Overlook Pr., The.
—Freddy the Magician. Wiese, Kurt, illus. 2011. (ENG.). 224p. (gr. 4-13). pap. 10.99 *(978-1-59020-481-8(6))*, 902481) Overlook Pr., The.
—Freddy the Pied Piper. Wiese, Kurt, illus. 2014. (ENG.). 272p. (gr. 4-13). pap. 10.99 *(978-1-4683-0915-7(3))*, 460915) Overlook Pr., The.
—Freddy the Pilot. Wiese, Kurt, tr. 2012. (ENG., Illus.). 256p. (gr. 4-13). pap. 10.99 *(978-1-59020-867-0(6))*, 902867) Overlook Pr., The.
—Freddy's Cousin Weedly. Wiese, Kurt, illus. 2014. (ENG.). 240p. (gr. 4-13). pap. 10.99 *(978-1-4683-0914-0(5))*, 460914) Overlook Pr., The.
Brown, Carron, ed. The Three Little Pigs & Little Red Riding Hood: Two Tales & Their Histories. 2009. (World of Fairy Tales Ser.). (Illus.). 32p. (J). (gr. -1-2). pap. 10.55 *(978-1-60754-641-2(8))*; lib. bdg. 22.60 *(978-1-60754-640-5(X))* Windmill Bks.
Brown, E. Jane. Pinkie. 2005. 76p. pap. 10.00 *(978-1-4116-3115-1(3))* Lulu Pr., Inc.
Brown, Janet. Three Little Pigs (Floor Book) My First Reading Book. Morton, Ken, illus. 2015. (ENG.). 24p. (J). (gr. -1-1). pap. 6.99 *(978-1-86147-396-7(6))*, Armadillo) Anness Publishing GBR. Dist: National Bk. Network.
Bryant, Ann. Tag. 2009. (ENG., Illus.). 24p. (J). pap. *(978-0-7787-3900-5(7))*; lib. bdg. *(978-0-7787-3869-5(8))* Crabtree Publishing Co.
Bryson, Brenda. The Adventures of Roo & Winston. 2007. 78p. pap. 12.95 *(978-1-4357-0145-8(3))* Lulu Pr., Inc.
Burgo, Ann & Shelton, Sherry. A Parable of the Three Little Pigs. 2009. 32p. pap. 14.49 *(978-1-4490-0577-1(2))* AuthorHouse.
Burke, Bob. The Third Pig Detective Agency: The Complete Casebook. 2015. (ENG.). 432p. 8.99 *(978-0-00-747940-5(9))*, Friday Project) HarperCollins Pubs. Ltd. GBR. Dist: HarperCollins Pubs.
Burks, James. Pigs & a Blanket. Burks, James, illus. 2016. (ENG., Illus.). 32p. (J). (gr. -1 — 1). 16.99 *(978-1-4847-2523-8(9))* Hyperion Bks. for Children.
Butler, Ellis Parker. Pigs Is Pigs & Other Favorites. 2004. reprint ed. pap. 20.95 *(978-1-4179-2471-4(3))* Kessinger Publishing, LLC.
Candlewick Press. Peppa Pig & the Backyard Circus. 2017. (Peppa Pig Ser.). (ENG.). 32p. (J). (gr. -1-2). 12.99 *(978-0-7636-9437-1(1))*, Candlewick Entertainment) Candlewick Pr.
—Peppa Pig & the Easter Rainbow. 2017. (Peppa Pig Ser.). (ENG.). 32p. (J). (-k). 12.99 *(978-0-7636-9438-8(X))*, Candlewick Entertainment) Candlewick Pr.
Candlewick Press, Candlewick. Peppa Pig & the Busy Day at School. Candlewick Press, Candlewick & Ladybird Books Staff, illus. 2013. (Peppa Pig Ser.). (ENG.). 32p. (J). (-k). 12.99 *(978-0-7636-6525-8(8))*, Candlewick Entertainment) Candlewick Pr.
—Peppa Pig & the Camping Trip. 2016. (Peppa Pig Ser.). (ENG., Illus.). 32p. (J). (-k). 12.99 *(978-0-7636-8741-0(3))*, Candlewick Entertainment) Candlewick Pr.
—Peppa Pig & the Day at Snowy Mountain. 2014. (Peppa Pig Ser.). (ENG.). 32p. (J). (-k). 12.99 *(978-0-7636-7455-7(9))*, Candlewick Entertainment) Candlewick Pr.
—Peppa Pig & the I Love You Game. 2015. (Peppa Pig Ser.). (ENG.). 32p. (J). (-k). 12.99 *(978-0-7636-8126-5(1))*, Candlewick Entertainment) Candlewick Pr.
—Peppa Pig & the Little Train. 2016. (Peppa Pig Ser.). (ENG., Illus.). 32p. (J). (-k). 12.99 *(978-0-7636-9044-1(9))*, Candlewick Entertainment) Candlewick Pr.
—Peppa Pig & the Lucky Ducks. 2016. (Peppa Pig Ser.). (ENG.). 32p. (J). (-k). 12.99 *(978-0-7636-8740-3(5))*, Candlewick Entertainment) Candlewick Pr.
—Peppa Pig & the Treasure Hunt. 2015. (Peppa Pig Ser.). (ENG.). 32p. (J). (-k). 12.99 *(978-0-7636-7703-9(5))*, Candlewick Entertainment) Candlewick Pr.
—Peppa Pig & the Year of Family Fun. 2016. (Peppa Pig Ser.). (ENG., Illus.). 10p. (J). (gr. -1-2). 17.99 *(978-0-7636-8739-7(1))*, Candlewick Entertainment) Candlewick Pr.
Candlewick Press Editors. Peppa Pig & the Busy Day at School. 2014. (Peppa Pig Ser.). lib. bdg. 16.00 *(978-0-606-35154-6(X))* Turtleback Bks.
—Peppa Pig & the Day at Snowy Mountain. 2015. (Peppa Pig Ser.). lib. bdg. 16.00 *(978-0-606-36867-4(1))* Turtleback Bks.
—Peppa Pig & the Great Vacation. 2015. (Peppa Pig Ser.). lib. bdg. 16.00 *(978-0-606-36857-5(4))* Turtleback Bks.
—Peppa Pig & the I Love You Game. 2016. (Peppa Pig Ser.). (ENG.). 32p. (J). (gr. -1-1). 16.00 *(978-0-606-39091-0(X))* Turtleback Bks.
—Peppa Pig & the Muddy Puddles. 2014. (Peppa Pig Ser.). lib. bdg. 16.00 *(978-0-606-35153-9(1))* Turtleback Bks.
—Peppa Pig & the Treasure Hunt. 2016. (Peppa Pig Ser.). lib. bdg. 16.00 *(978-0-606-37936-6(3))* Turtleback Bks.
—Peppa Pig & the Vegetable Garden. 2015. (Peppa Pig Ser.). lib. bdg. 16.00 *(978-0-606-36856-8(6))* Turtleback Bks.
Candlewick Press Staff. Peppa Pig & the Great Vacation. 2014. (Peppa Pig Ser.). (ENG.). 32p. (J). (-k). 12.99 *(978-0-7636-6986-7(5))*, Candlewick Entertainment) Candlewick Pr.
—Peppa Pig & the Lost Christmas List. Ladybird Books Staff, illus. 2012. (Peppa Pig Ser.). (ENG.). 32p. (J). (gr. k-k). 12.99 *(978-0-7636-6276-9(3))*, Candlewick Entertainment) Candlewick Pr.
—Peppa Pig & the Lost Christmas List. Candlewick Press Staff, illus. 2014. (Peppa Pig Ser.). (ENG., Illus.). 32p. (J). (-k). 5.99 *(978-0-7636-7456-4(7))*, Candlewick Entertainment) Candlewick Pr.
—Peppa Pig & the Lost Christmas List. 2014. (Peppa Pig Ser.). lib. bdg. 16.00 *(978-0-606-35868-2(4))* Turtleback Bks.
—Peppa Pig & the Perfect Day. 2013. (Peppa Pig Ser.). (ENG., Illus.). 8p. (J). (gr. -1-2). 17.99 *(978-0-7636-6825-9(7))*, Candlewick Entertainment) Candlewick Pr.
—Peppa Pig & the Vegetable Garden. 2014. (Peppa Pig Ser.). (ENG.). 32p. (J). (-k). 12.99 *(978-0-7636-6987-4(3))*, Candlewick Entertainment) Candlewick Pr.
Capstone Press Staff. The Three Little Pigs. Blecha, Aaron, illus. 2010. (Graphic Spin Ser.). (ENG.). 40p. (gr. 1-3). pap. 5.95 *(978-1-4342-1395-2(1))*, Graphic Revolve) Stone Arch Bks.
Carlson, Nancy. Get up & Go! 2008. (ENG., Illus.). 32p. (J). (gr. -1-k). pap. 5.99 *(978-0-14-241064-6(0))*, Puffin Books) Penguin Young Readers Group.
—Get up & Go! 2008. (Illus.). (gr. -1-3). 16.00 *(978-0-7569-8922-4(1))* Perfection Learning Corp.
—Louanne Pig in Making the Team. 2005. (Louanne Pig Ser.). (Illus.). 32p. (J). (gr. k-2). lib. bdg. 15.95 *(978-1-57505-914-3(2))*; (ENG., per. 6.95 *(978-1-57505-997-6(5))* Lerner Publishing Group.
—Louanne Pig in the Mysterious Valentine. rev. ed. 2004. (Carolrhoda Picture Books Ser.). (Illus.). 32p. (J). (gr. k-2). 15.95 *(978-1-57505-671-5(2))*; (ENG., per. 6.95 *(978-1-57505-722-4(0))* Lerner Publishing Group.
—Louanne Pig in the Perfect Family. 2nd rev. ed. 2004. (Nancy Carlson's Neighborhood Ser.). (ENG., Illus.). 32p. (J). (gr. k-2). 15.95 *(978-1-57505-611-1(9))*; pap. 6.95 *(978-1-57505-616-6(X))* Lerner Publishing Group.
—Louanne Pig in the Talent Show. 2005. (Louanne Pig Ser.). (Illus.). 32p. (J). (ENG.). (gr. k-2). per. 6.95 *(978-1-57505-996-9(7))*; (gr. -1-3). lib. bdg. 15.95 *(978-1-57505-915-0(0))* Lerner Publishing Group.
—Louanne Pig in Witch Lady. 2006. (Illus.). 32p. (J). (gr. -1-3). lib. bdg. 15.95 *(978-0-8225-6196-5(4))*, Carolrhoda Bks.) Lerner Publishing Group.
—Louanne Pig in Witch Lady. Carlson, Nancy, illus. rev. ed. 2006. (ENG., Illus.). 32p. (J). (gr. k-2). per. 9.95 *(978-0-8225-6197-2(2))*, First Avenue Editions) Lerner Publishing Group.
—Louanne Pig Series, 3 bks. (Illus.). (J). (gr. k-3). pap. 44.95 incl. audio *(978-0-87499-474-2(8))* Live Oak Media.
Cartwright, Stephen, illus. Three Little Pigs. 2006. (First Stories Sticker Bks.). 16p. (J). (gr. -1-3). pap. 6.99 *(978-0-7945-1386-3(7))*, Usborne) EDC Publishing.
Cazet, Denys. Will You Read to Me? Cazet, Denys, illus. 2007. (ENG., Illus.). 32p. (J). (gr. -1-1). 16.99 *(978-1-4169-0935-4(4))*, Atheneum/Richard Jackson Bks.) Simon & Schuster Children's Publishing.
Cerasi, Chris. Angry Birds ICR #2. 2016. (I Can Read Level 2 Ser.). 32p. (J). (gr. -1-3). pap. 3.99 *(978-0-06-245334-1(3))* HarperCollins Pubs.
—Too Many Pigs. 2016. (I Can Read! Level 1 Ser.). (J). lib. bdg. 13.55 *(978-0-606-38186-4(4))* Turtleback Bks.
Chace, Rebecca. June Sparrow & the Million-Dollar Penny. Schwartz, Kacey, illus. 2017. 352p. (J). (gr. 3-7). 16.99 *(978-0-06-246498-9(1))* HarperCollins Pubs.
Chandler, Andrew & Chandler, Amanda. Gertrude & Abigail: The Adventures Thereof. 2006. 35p. (J). 18.90 *(978-1-4116-7572-8(X))* Lulu Pr., Inc.
Charlesworth, Liza. Pig Wants a Peach: An Animal Friends Reader. Smith, Ian, illus. 2015. 16p. (J). pap. ***(978-0-545-85965-3(4))*** Scholastic, Inc.
Chesterfield, Sadie. Let's Make a Snowman! 2007. (Peppa Pig Ser.). 24p. (J). pap. 6.99 *(978-0-06-117367-7(3))*, Harper Entertainment) HarperCollins Pubs.
Chin, Oliver. The Year of the Pig: Tales from the Chinese Zodiac. Alcorn, Miah, illus. 2007. (ENG.). 36p. (J). (gr. -1-3). 15.95 *(978-1-59702-007-7(9))* Immedium.
Chocolate, Debbi. Pigs Can Fly! The Adventures of Harriet Pig & Friends. Tryon, Leslie, illus. 2004. (ENG.). 64p. (J). 15.95 *(978-0-8126-2706-0(7))* Cricket Bks.
Church, Caroline Jayne. Ping Pong Pig. Church, Caroline Jayne, illus. 2008. (ENG., Illus.). 32p. (J). (gr. -1-1). 16.95 *(978-0-8234-2176-3(7))* Holiday Hse., Inc.
Clark, Nicole K. Pigment the Rainbow Pig. Clark, Nicole K., illus. Date not set. (Illus.). (J). (gr. -1-2). *(978-1-892176-18-9(1))* PremaNations Publishing.
Clem, Margaret H. Elbert ein Swine, Genius Pig. Clem, Margaret H., illus. 2003. (ENG., Illus.). 32p. (J). (gr. k-4). pap. 6.95 *(978-1-878044-12-9(5))* Mayhaven Publishing, Inc.
Cloke, Rene, illus. The Three Little Pigs. 2012. (ENG.). 24p. pap. 6.50 *(978-1-84135-544-3(5))* Award Pubns. Ltd. GBR. Dist: Parkwest Pubns., Inc.
Cocca-Leffler, Maryann. A Homemade Together Christmas. Cocca-Leffler, Maryann, illus. 2015. (ENG., Illus.). 32p. (J). (gr. -1-3). 16.99 *(978-0-8075-3366-6(1))* Whitman, Albert & Co.
Cook, Sherry & Johnson, Terri. Pressure Pete, 26 vols. Kuhn, Jesse, illus. l.t. ed. 2006. (Quirkles — Exploring Phonics through Science Ser.: 16). 32p. (J). 7.99 *(978-1-933815-15-2(9))*, Quirkles, The) Creative 3, LLC.
Cook, Teri Ann. The Adventures of Mrs. Patsy's Farm: A Gift! Is a Gift! Is a Gift!, 1 vol. 2009. 24p. pap. 24.95 *(978-1-60749-549-9(X))* America Star Bks.
Cooke, James. Pink Pig in a Boat. 2004. 59p. pap. 16.95 *(978-1-4137-4338-8(2))* America Star Bks.
Cosgrove, Stephen. Jalopy. 2011. (Orig.). (J). *(978-0-86592-797-1(9))* Rourke Enterprises, Inc.
Costello, David Hyde. Little Pig Joins the Band. Costello, David Hyde, illus. 2014. (ENG., Illus.). 32p. (J). (gr. -1-3). pap. 7.95 *(978-1-58089-265-0(5))* Charlesbridge Publishing, Inc.
—Little Pig Joins the Band. Costello, David Hyde, illus. 2012. (Illus.). 29.95 incl. audio compact disk *(978-1-4301-1139-9(9))* Live Oak Media.
—Little Pig Saves the Ship. Costello, David Hyde, illus. 2017. (ENG., Illus.). 32p. (J). (gr. -1-2). 14.99 *(978-1-58089-715-0(0))* Charlesbridge Publishing, Inc.
Coulman, Valerie. When Pigs Fly. l.t. ed. 2012. 63p. (J). pap. *(978-1-4596-3455-8(1))* ReadHowYouWant.com, Ltd.
Cowley, Joy. Mrs. Wishy-Washy's Farm. Fuller, Elizabeth, illus. (ENG.). 32p. (J). (gr. -1-k). 2006. 5.99 *(978-0-14-240299-3(0))*, Puffin Books) 2003. 16.99 *(978-0-399-23872-7(7))*, Philomel Bks.) Penguin Young Readers Group.
Cox, Phil Roxbee. Big Pig on a Dig. Tyler, Jenny, ed. Cartwright, Stephen, illus. rev. ed. 2006. (Phonics Readers Ser.). 16p. (J). (gr. -1-3). pap. 6.99 *(978-0-7945-1501-0(0))*, Usborne) EDC Publishing.
Cox, Rhonda. Pigs Peek. Cox, Rhonda, photos by. 2003. (ENG., Illus.). 12p. (J). pap. 15.00 *(978-1-57274-698-5(X))*, BB2180, Bks. for Young Learners) Owen, Richard C. Pubs., Inc.
Croteau, Marie-Danielle. Fred & the Pig Race. Cummins, Sarah, tr. from FRE. St-Aubin, Bruno, illus. 2007. (Formac First Novels Ser.). (ENG.). 64p. (gr. 2-5). 14.95 *(978-0-88780-733-6(X))*, 9780887807336); (J). 4.95 *(978-0-88780-731-2(3))*, 9780887807312) Formac Publishing Co., Ltd. CAN. Dist: Casemate Pubs. & Bk. Distributors, LLC.
Crump, Fred, Jr. The Three Little Brown Piggies. 2007. (Illus.). 32p. (J). 12.95 *(978-1-934056-21-9(9))* UMI (Urban Ministries, Inc.).
Crump Jr., Fred. The Three Little Brown Piggies. 2007. (Illus.). 32p. (J). pap. 9.95 *(978-1-932715-83-5(5))* UMI (Urban Ministries, Inc.).
Dahl, Michael. Pig Takes a Bath, 1 vol. Vidal, Oriol, illus. 2010. (Hello Genius Ser.). (ENG.). 20p. (gr. 1-2). bds. 7.99 *(978-1-4048-5729-2(X))* Picture Window Bks.
Dakos, Kalli & DesMarteau, Alicia. Our Principal Promised to Kiss a Pig. DiRocco, Carl, illus. (ENG.). 32p. (J). 2017. (gr. -1-3). pap. 7.99 ***(978-0-8075-6635-0(7))*** 2004. (gr. 2-5). 16.99 *(978-0-8075-6629-9(2))* Whitman, Albert & Co.
Davies, Gill & Freeman, Tina. Two Naughty Piglets. 2004. (Tales from Village Barn Farm Ser.). (Illus.). 24p. (J). 3.99 *(978-1-85854-325-3(8))* Brimax Books Ltd. GBR. Dist: Byeway Bks.
Davis, Donald. The Pig Who Went Home on Sunday: An Appalachian Folktale. Mazzucco, Jennifer, illus. 2007. (ENG.). 40p. (J). (gr. -1-3). 8.95 *(978-0-87483-851-0(7))* August Hse. Pubs., Inc.
De Kockere, Geert. Piglet Bo Can Do Anything! Van Hemeldonck, Tineke, illus. 2015. (ENG.). 32p. (J). (gr. -1-k). 16.99 *(978-1-63220-600-8(5))*, Sky Pony Pr.) Skyhorse Publishing Co., Inc.
—Piglet Bo Is Not Scared! Van Hemeldonck, Tineke, illus. 2015. (ENG.). 32p. (J). (gr. -1-k). 16.99 *(978-1-63450-182-8(9))*, Sky Pony Pr.) Skyhorse Publishing Co., Inc.
Dean, James. Pete the Cat's Train Trip. 2015. (Pete the Cat I Can Read Ser.). (J). lib. bdg. 13.55 *(978-0-606-36967-1(8))* Turtleback Bks.
Degman, Lori. Norbert's Big Dream. Bucci, Marco, illus. 2016. (ENG.). 32p. (J). (gr. k-3). 16.99 *(978-1-58536-959-1(4))*, 204108) Sleeping Bear Pr.
Denchfield, Nick. Penelope the Piglet. Parker, Ant, illus. 2008. (ENG.). 16p. (J). (gr. 2-5). bds. 13.95 *(978-0-230-01615-6(4))*, Macmillan) Pan Macmillan GBR. Dist: Trans-Atlantic Pubns., Inc.
deRubertis, Barbara & DeRubertis, Barbara. Hanna Hippo's Horrible Hiccups. Alley, R. W., illus. 2012. (Animal Antics A to Z Ser.). 32p. (J). (gr. 2 — 1). cd-rom 7.95 *(978-1-57565-401-0(6))* Kane Press, Inc.
Desmet, Sara. Scared Silly. Desmet, Sara, illus. 2006. (Illus.). 32p. (J). (gr. -1-3). 15.95 *(978-1-60108-009-7(3))* Red Cygnet Pr.
Dessers, Rik. Rosie & Roger. Schuurmans, Hilde, illus. 2015. (ENG.). 100p. (J). pap. 16.95 *(978-1-931290-09-8(1))* Tallfellow Pr.
DiCamillo, Kate. Mercy Watson: Princess in Disguise. Van Dusen, Chris, illus. 2010. (Mercy Watson Ser.: 4). (ENG.). 80p. (J). (gr. 1-4). pap. 5.99 *(978-0-7636-4951-7(1))* Candlewick Pr.
—Mercy Watson: Something Wonky This Way Comes. Van Dusen, Chris, illus. 2011. (Mercy Watson Ser.: 6). (ENG.). 96p. (J). (gr. 1-4). pap. 5.99 *(978-0-7636-5232-6(6))* Candlewick Pr.
—Mercy Watson: Something Wonky This Way Comes. 2011. 16.00 *(978-1-61383-049-9(1))* Perfection Learning Corp.
—Mercy Watson Boxed Set: Adventures of a Porcine Wonder, 6 vols. Van Dusen, Chris, illus. 2011. (Mercy Watson Ser.). (ENG.). (J). (gr. k-3). pap. 29.99 *(978-0-7636-5709-3(3))* Candlewick Pr.
—Mercy Watson Fights Crime. Van Dusen, Chris, illus. 2010. (Mercy Watson Ser.: 3). (ENG.). 80p. (J). (gr. 1-4). pap. 5.99 *(978-0-7636-4952-4(X))* Candlewick Pr.
—Mercy Watson Fights Crime. DiCamillo, Kate & Van Dusen, Chris, illus. 2006. (Mercy Watson Ser.: 3). (ENG.). 80p. (J). (gr. k-3). 14.99 *(978-0-7636-2590-0(6))* Candlewick Pr.
—Mercy Watson Fights Crime. 2010. (Mercy Watson Ser.: Bk. 3). lib. bdg. 16.00 *(978-0-606-14927-3(9))*, Turtleback) Turtleback Bks.
—Mercy Watson Goes for a Ride. Van Dusen, Chris, illus. 2006. (Mercy Watson Ser.: 2). (ENG.). 80p. (J). (gr. k-4). 14.99 *(978-0-7636-2332-6(6))* Candlewick Pr.
—Mercy Watson Goes for a Ride. 2012. 16.00 *(978-1-61383-702-3(X))* Perfection Learning Corp.
—Mercy Watson Goes for a Ride. Van Dusen, Chris, illus. 2009. (Mercy Watson Ser.: 2). (ENG.). 80p. (J). (gr. 1-4). pap. 5.99 *(978-0-7636-4505-2(2))* Candlewick Pr.
—Mercy Watson Goes for a Ride. 2009. (Mercy Watson Ser.: Bk. 2). lib. bdg. 16.00 *(978-0-606-06699-0(3))*, Turtleback) Turtleback Bks.
—Mercy Watson Thinks Like a Pig. Van Dusen, Chris, illus. (Mercy Watson Ser.: 5). (ENG.). 80p. (J). (gr. 1-4). 2011. pap. 5.99 *(978-0-7636-5231-9(8))* 2008. 12.99 *(978-0-7636-3265-6(1))* Candlewick Pr.
—Mercy Watson to the Rescue. DiCamillo, Kate & Van Dusen, Chris, illus. 2009. (Mercy Watson Ser.: 1). (ENG.). 80p. (J). (gr. 1-4). pap. 5.99 *(978-0-7636-4504-5(4))* Candlewick Pr.
—Mercy Watson to the Rescue. Van Dusen, Chris, illus. 2005. (Mercy Watson Ser.: 1). (ENG.). 80p. (J). (gr. k-4). 14.99 *(978-0-7636-2270-1(2))* Candlewick Pr.
—Mercy Watson to the Rescue. 2009. (Mercy Watson Ser.: Bk. 1). lib. bdg. 16.00 *(978-0-606-06704-1(3))*, Turtleback) Turtleback Bks.
—Something Wonky This Way Comes. Van Dusen, Chris, illus. 2009. (Mercy Watson Ser.: 6). (ENG.). 96p. (J). (gr. 1-4). 14.99 *(978-0-7636-3644-9(4))* Candlewick Pr.
DiCamillo, Kate & Van Dusen, Chris. Mercy Watson: Princess in Disguise. Van Dusen, Chris, illus. 2007. (Mercy Watson Ser.: 4). (ENG., Illus.). 80p. (J). (gr. 1-4). 14.99 *(978-0-7636-3014-0(4))* Candlewick Pr.
Dinner Time. 2005. (Gilbert the Pig Chapter Ser.). (J). 7.67 *(978-1-58453-298-9(X))* Pioneer Valley Bks.
Disney Book Group Staff. Gravity Falls Once upon a Swine. Disney Storybook Artists Staff & No New Art Needed, illus.

2014. (Gravity Falls Chapter Book Ser.: 2). (ENG.). 112p. (J). (gr. 1-3). pap. 4.99 *(978-1-4847-1140-8(8))* Disney Pr.

Disney Press Staff. Once upon a Swine. 2014. (Gravity Falls Ser.: 2). (J). lib. bdg. 14.75 *(978-0-606-35916-0(8))* Turtleback Bks.

Dockery, Marie F. The Three Billy Goats Gruff Find Jesus & the Three Little Souls. 2008. 52p. pap. 12.99 *(978-1-60647-605-5(X))* Salem Author Services.

Dodd, Melissa. Santa Sheds, 1 vol. 2009. 17p. pap. 24.95 *(978-1-60749-208-5(3))* America Star Bks.

Dompierre, Judith. I See Pigs Everywhere, 1 vol. 2010. 28p. pap. 29.95 *(978-1-4489-8838-9(1))* America Star Bks.

Dotlich, Rebecca Kai. Mama Loves. Brown, Kathryn, illus. 2004. 32p. (J). (gr. -1-2). lib. bdg. 15.89 *(978-0-06-029408-3(6))* HarperCollins Pubs.

Dougherty, Jane L. Pig Party. 2008. 36p. pap. 24.95 *(978-1-4241-9045-4(2))* America Star Bks.

Dougherty, John. There's a Pig up My Nose! Hughes, Laura, illus. 2017. (ENG.). 32p. (J). (gr. -1-k). pap. 9.99 ***(978-1-4052-7716-7(5))*** Egmont Bks., Ltd. GBR. Dist: Independent Pubs. Group.

Dowley-Wise, Justine. A Pig Called Harriet. 2008. (ENG.). 112p. pap. 31.99 *(978-1-4389-3388-7(6))* AuthorHouse.

Doyle, Malachy. Big Pig. Bendall-Brunello, John, illus. 2006. (ENG.). 32p. (J). (gr. -1-k). pap. 9.99 *(978-0-689-87485-7(5))* Simon & Schuster, Ltd. GBR. Dist: Simon & Schuster, Inc.

Dubois, Liz Goulet. What Does a Seed Need? 2011. (ENG.). 18p. (J). (gr. -1-k). 7.99 *(978-0-8431-9901-7(6),* Price Stern Sloan) Penguin Young Readers Group.

Edminster, David. Pork Chop. 2010. (Illus.). 36p. (J). pap. 15.95 *(978-1-4327-5345-0(2))* Outskirts Pr., Inc.

Elchgar, Yasmin. Noonoo the Doctor. 2013. 20p. pap. 13.77 *(978-1-4907-1037-2(X))* Trafford Publishing.

Elliot, David. Henry's Map. Elliot, David, illus. 2013. (ENG., Illus.). 40p. (J). (gr. -1-3). 16.99 *(978-0-399-16072-1(8),* Philomel Bks.) Penguin Young Readers Group.

—Henry's Stars. Elliot, David, illus. 2015. (ENG., Illus.). 40p. (J). (gr. k-3). 16.99 *(978-0-399-17116-1(9),* Philomel Bks.) Penguin Young Readers Group.

Elliott, Linda. When Little Pinkie Gets Her Wings. Switzer, Bobbi, illus. 2007. 28p. per. 11.95 *(978-1-59800-871-5(4))* Outskirts Pr., Inc.

Emmett, Jonathan & Dunn, David H. The Princess & the Pig. Bernatene, Poly, illus. 2011. (ENG.). 32p. (J). (gr. k-8). 17.99 *(978-0-8027-2334-5(9),* 9780802723345, Bloomsbury USA Childrens) Bloomsbury Publishing USA.

Eone, illus. Around the World with Peppa. 2017. (Scholastic Reader, Level 1 Ser.). (ENG.). 32p. (J). (gr. -1-k). 3.99 ***(978-1-338-13980-8(0))*** Scholastic, Inc.

—George Catches a Cold (Peppa Pig) 2017. (Peppa Pig Ser.). (ENG.). 24p. (J). (gr. -1-k). pap. 3.99 *(978-1-338-05419-4(8))* Scholastic, Inc.

—Peppa & the Big Train (Peppa Pig) 2017. (Peppa Pig Ser.). (ENG.). 16p. (J). (gr. -1-k). bds. 7.99 *(978-1-338-05420-0(1))* Scholastic, Inc.

—Peppa Goes Swimming. 2015. (Peppa Pig Ser.). (ENG.). 24p. (J). (gr. -1-k). pap. 3.99 *(978-0-545-83491-9(0))* Scholastic, Inc.

—Peppa's Busy Day Magnet Book (Peppa Pig) 2016. (Peppa Pig Ser.). (ENG.). 10p. (J). (gr. -1-k). 12.99 *(978-0-545-92545-7(2))* Scholastic, Inc.

—Peppa's Halloween Party. 2016. (Peppa Pig Ser.). (ENG.). 24p. (J). (gr. -1-k). 4.99 *(978-0-545-92543-3(6))* Scholastic, Inc.

Erickson, John R. The Case of the Missing Bird Dog. Holmes, Gerald L., illus. 2011. (Hank the Cowdog Ser.: No. 40). (ENG.). 126p. (J). (gr. 3-6). pap. 5.99 *(978-1-59188-140-7(4))* Maverick Bks., Inc.

Escardo Bas, Mercè. Los Tres Cerditos. Joan, Pere, illus. 2003. (SPA.). 24p. *(978-84-246-1939-8(0),* GL30510) La Galera, S.A. Editorial ESP. Dist: Lectorum Pubns., Inc.

Evans, Cordelia. Olivia & the Easter Egg Hunt. 2013. (Olivia 8x8 Ser.). lib. bdg. 14.75 *(978-0-606-27062-5(0),* Turtleback) Turtleback Bks.

—OLIVIA & the Fancy Party. Johnson, Shane L., illus. 2014. (Olivia TV Tie-In Ser.). (ENG.). 24p. (J). (gr. -1-2). pap. 3.99 *(978-1-4814-0364-1(8),* Simon Spotlight) Simon Spotlight.

—Olivia & the Fancy Party. 2014. (Olivia 8x8 Ser.). lib. bdg. 13.55 *(978-0-606-35762-3(9))* Turtleback Bks.

Fairley, Melissa. Ding! Dong! Harland, Jackie, illus. 2011. (ENG.). 12p. (J). (gr. -1-k). 15.95 *(978-1-84898-362-5(X),* TickTock Books) Octopus Publishing Group GBR. Dist: Independent Pubs. Group.

Fairy Tales- Three little Pigs. 2005. (J). bds. *(978-1-4194-0044-5(4))* Paradise Pr., Inc.

Falconer, Ian. Olivia. 2004. (Olivia Ser.). (J). (gr. k-3). (FRE., Illus.). spiral bd. *(978-0-616-14599-9(3));* spiral bd. *(978-0-616-07233-2(3));* spiral bd. *(978-0-616-07232-5(5))* Canadian National Institute for the Blind/Institut National Canadien pour les Aveugles.

—Olivia. 2009. (Los Especiales de A la Orilla del Viento Ser.). (SPA.). 32p. (J). 13.99 *(978-968-16-6346-9(2))* Fondo de Cultura Económica.

—Olivia. Mlawer, Teresa, tr. 2004. (Olivia Ser.). (SPA., Illus.). (J). (gr. k-2). 16.00 *(978-1-930332-20-1(3),* LC5675) Lectorum Pubns., Inc.

—Olivia. Falconer, Ian, illus. 2009. (ENG., Illus.). 40p. (J). (gr. -1-3). 12.99 *(978-1-4169-8034-6(2),* Atheneum Bks. for Young Readers) Simon & Schuster Children's Publishing.

—Olivia. High, Amy, tr. from ENG. Falconer, Ian, illus. 2007. (LAT., Illus.). 40p. (J). (gr. 3-7). 17.99 *(978-1-4169-4218-4(1),* Atheneum Bks. for Young Readers) Simon & Schuster Children's Publishing.

—Olivia. Falconer, Ian, illus. unabr. ed. 2004. (Classic Board Bks.). (ENG., Illus.). 34p. (J). (gr. -1-k). bds. 7.99 *(978-0-689-87472-7(3),* Atheneum Bks. for Young Readers) Simon & Schuster Children's Publishing.

—Olivia & the Fairy Princesses. Falconer, Ian, illus. 2012. (ENG., Illus.). 40p. (J). (gr. -1-3). 18.99 *(978-1-4424-5027-1(4),* Atheneum Bks. for Young Readers) Simon & Schuster Children's Publishing.

—Olivia... & the Missing Toy. Falconer, Ian, illus. 2003. (ENG., Illus.). 42p. (J). (gr. -1-3). 18.99 *(978-0-689-85291-6(6),* Atheneum Bks. for Young Readers) Simon & Schuster Children's Publishing.

—Olivia fait son Cirque. (Olivia Ser.). 29.95 *(978-2-02-051642-6(X))* Editions du Seuil FRA. Dist: Distribooks, Inc.

—Olivia Forma una Banda. Mlawer, Teresa, tr. from ENG. Falconer, Ian, illus. 2007. (SPA., Illus.). 39p. (J). (gr. -1-3). 17.99 *(978-1-933032-23-8(5))* Lectorum Pubns., Inc.

—Olivia Forms a Band. Falconer, Ian, illus. (ENG., Illus.). 50p. (J). (gr. -1-3). 2009. 12.99 *(978-1-4169-8037-7(7))* 2006. 18.99 *(978-1-4169-2454-8(X))* Simon & Schuster Children's Publishing. (Atheneum Bks. for Young Readers).

—Olivia Goes to Venice. Falconer, Ian, illus. 2010. (ENG., Illus.). 48p. (J). (gr. -1-2). 17.99 *(978-1-4169-9674-3(5),* Atheneum Bks. for Young Readers) Simon & Schuster Children's Publishing.

—Olivia Helps with Christmas. Falconer, Ian, illus. 2013. (Classic Board Bks.). (ENG., Illus.). 40p. (J). (gr. -1-2). bds. 7.99 *(978-1-4424-9446-6(8),* Atheneum Bks. for Young Readers) Simon & Schuster Children's Publishing.

—Olivia sait Compter. (Olivia Ser.). 18.95 *(978-2-02-056487-8(4))* Editions du Seuil FRA. Dist: Distribooks, Inc.

—Olivia Saves the Circus. 2004. (Olivia Ser.). (J). (gr. k-2). spiral bd. *(978-0-616-11111-6(8));* spiral bd. *(978-0-616-11110-9(X))* Canadian National Institute for the Blind/Institut National Canadien pour les Aveugles.

—Olivia Saves the Circus. Falconer, Ian, illus. 2010. (Classic Board Bks.). (ENG., Illus.). 36p. (J). (gr. -1-2). bds. 7.99 *(978-1-4424-1287-3(9),* Atheneum Bks. for Young Readers) Simon & Schuster Children's Publishing.

—Olivia the Spy. Falconer, Ian, illus. 2017. (ENG., Illus.). 40p. (J). (gr. -1-3). 17.99 *(978-1-4814-5795-8(0),* Atheneum/Caitlyn Dlouhy Books) Simon & Schuster Children's Publishing.

—Olivia y Las Princesas. 2012. (SPA., Illus.). 32p. (J). (gr. -1-1). 17.99 *(978-1-933032-82-5(0))* Lectorum Pubns., Inc.

Falconer, Ian & Simon & Schuster Audio Firm Staff. The Olivia Collection: Olivia; Olivia Saves the Circus; Olivia... & the Missing Toy; Olivia Forms a Band; Olivia Helps with Christmas; Olivia Goes to Venice; Olivia & the Fairy Princesses. Falconer, Ian, illus. 2012. (ENG., Illus.). 322p. (J). (gr. -1-2). 128.99 *(978-1-4424-8299-9(0),* Atheneum Bks. for Young Readers) Simon & Schuster Children's Publishing.

Falconer, Ian & Simon and Schuster/LeapFrog Staff. Olivia. 2008. (Olivia Ser.). (J). 11.99 *(978-1-59319-990-6(2))* LeapFrog Enterprises, Inc.

Falconer, Ian, et al. Olivia & Her Great Adventures. Osterhold, Jared & Johnson, Shane L., illus. 2012. (J). *(978-1-4351-4316-6(7),* Simon Spotlight) Simon Spotlight.

Farhat, Michael. Adventures of the Eastside Pigs: Produced by Funnybook Factory. Chan, Carol, ed. 2012. 40p. pap. 19.99 *(978-1-4669-0289-3(2))* Trafford Publishing.

Farnsworth-Simpson, Patricia Ann. Flick the Karate Pig. 2008. 163p. pap. 16.50 *(978-1-4357-2843-1(2))* Lulu Pr., Inc.

Farrell, Liam. The True Story of the Three Little Pigs & the Big Bad Wolf. 2nd rev. ed. 2012. (ENG.). 192p. (J). pap. 13.95 *(978-1-85635-955-9(7))* Mercier Pr., Ltd., The IRL. Dist: Dufour Editions, Inc.

—True Story of the Three Little Pigs & the Big Bad Wolf. Myler, Terry, illus. 2nd rev. ed. 2012. (ENG.). 192p. (J). pap. 13.95 *(978-1-85635-682-4(5))* Mercier Pr., Ltd., The IRL. Dist: Dufour Editions, Inc.

Fenske, Jonathan. A Pig, a Fox, & Stinky Socks. 2017. (Penguin Young Readers Level 2 Ser.). lib. bdg. 13.55 ***(978-0-606-39771-1(X))*** Turtleback Bks.

Fenske, Jonathan & Bader, Bonnie. A Pig, a Fox, & a Box. Fenske, Jonathan, illus. 2015. (Penguin Young Readers, Level 2 Ser.). (ENG., Illus.). 32p. (J). (gr. 1-2). 3.99 *(978-0-448-48510-2(9),* Penguin Young Readers) Penguin Young Readers Group.

Ferguson, J. M. Bubbles the Little Pig, 1 vol. 2008. (ENG.). 44p. 24.95 *(978-1-60474-229-9(1))* America Star Bks.

Ferrier, Charlotte. The Three Little Pigs. 2016. (Fairytale Cottages Ser.). (ENG., Illus.). 12p. (J). (gr. -1-k). bds. 8.99 *(978-0-7641-6819-2(3))* Barron's Educational Series, Inc.

Field, Matthew S. The Three Pigs, Business School, & Wolf Hash Stew. Hedderich, Tom, illus. 2006. (ENG.). (J). 19.95 *(978-0-9761528-1-1(9))* Matting Leah Publishing Co.

The Fight on the Hill: Individual Title Six-Pack. (Story Steps Ser.). (gr. k-2). 23.00 *(978-0-7635-9837-2(2))* Rigby Education.

Filipek, Nina. The Three Little Pigs. O'Toole, Jeanette, illus. 2009. (Fairy Tale Firsts Ser.). 12p. (J). (gr. -1-k). bds. 11.40 *(978-1-60754-693-1(0))* Windmill Bks.

Fisher, Karin, adapted by. Pig, Pig, & Pig: The Classic Fable of the Three Little Pigs, Retold in One-syllable Words. 2003. (J). pap. 7.95 *(978-0-9744343-0-8(2),* SA-303) Bright Solutions for Dyslexia, LLC.

Fisher, Pam. Pammy the Pig. 2011. 20p. 13.99 *(978-1-4567-1796-4(0))* AuthorHouse.

Fisher, Tina Mollie. Pig's Big Adventure. 2012. 42p. pap. 20.45 *(978-1-4497-5020-6(6),* WestBow Pr.) Author Solutions, Inc.

Flor Ada, Alma. Dear Peter Rabbit. Tryon, Leslie, illus. 2006. (Stories to Go! Ser.). (J). (gr. k-3). 12.65 *(978-0-7569-7322-3(8))* Perfection Learning Corp.

Florian, Douglas. Pig Is Big on Books. Florian, Douglas, illus. 2015. (I Like to Read(r) Ser.). (ENG., Illus.). 24p. (J). (gr. -1-3). 6.99 *(978-0-8234-3424-4(9))* Holiday Hse., Inc.

—Pig Is Big on Books. 2015. (I Like to Read(r) Ser.). (ENG., Illus.). 24p. (J). (gr. -1-3). 14.95 *(978-0-8234-3393-3(5))* Holiday Hse., Inc.

The Flying Pig & the Daredevil Dog: Individual Title Six-Packs. (Action Packs Ser.). 104p. (gr. 3-5). 44.00 *(978-0-7635-2985-7(0))* Rigby Education.

Folgueira, Rodrigo. Ribbit! Bernatene, Poly, illus. (ENG.). (J). 2016. 34p. (-k). bds. 8.99 *(978-0-553-53721-5(0))* 2013. 32p. (gr. -1-k). 15.99 *(978-0-307-98146-2(0))* Random Hse. Children's Bks. (Knopf Bks. for Young Readers).

Forte, Lauren. Olivia Goes to the Library. 2013. (Olivia Ready-To-Read Level 1 Ser.). lib. bdg. 13.55 *(978-0-606-35186-7(8))* Turtleback Bks.

—Olivia Helps Mother Nature. 2014. (Olivia Ready-To-Read Level 1 Ser.). lib. bdg. 13.55 *(978-0-606-35452-3(2))* Turtleback Bks.

—Olivia Makes Memories. 2015. (Olivia 8x8 Ser.). lib. bdg. 13.55 *(978-0-606-37868-0(5))* Turtleback Bks.

French, Lisa S. Eco-Pig, 4 vols., Set. Gott, Barry, illus. Incl. Planet Called Home: Eco-Pig's Animal Protection. 28.50 *(978-1-60270-662-0(X));* Terrible Trash Trail: Eco-Pig Stops Pollution. 28.50 *(978-1-60270-663-7(8));* What Does It Mean to Be Green? Eco-Pig Explains Living Green. 28.50 *(978-1-60270-665-1(4));* Who Turned up the Heat? Eco-Pig Explains Global Warming. 28.50 *(978-1-60270-664-4(6));* (J). (gr. -1-2). (Eco-Pig Ser.). (Illus.). 32p. 2009. 114.00 *(978-1-60270-661-3(1),* Looking Glass Library) ABDO Publishing Co.

—A Planet Called Home: Eco-Pig's Animal Protection, 1 vol. Gott, Barry, illus. 2009. (Eco-Pig Ser.). (ENG.). 32p. (J). (gr. -1-2). 28.50 *(978-1-60270-662-0(X))* ABDO Publishing Co.

—The Terrible Trash Trail: Eco-Pig Stops Pollution, 1 vol. Gott, Barry, illus. 2009. (Eco-Pig Ser.). (ENG.). 32p. (J). (gr. -1-2). 28.50 *(978-1-60270-663-7(8))* ABDO Publishing Co.

—What Does It Mean to Be Green? Eco-Pig Explains Living Green, 1 vol. Gott, Barry, illus. 2009. (Eco-Pig Ser.). (ENG.). 32p. (J). (gr. -1-2). 28.50 *(978-1-60270-665-1(4))* ABDO Publishing Co.

—Who Turned up the Heat? Eco-Pig Explains Global Warming, 1 vol. Gott, Barry, illus. 2009. (Eco-Pig Ser.). (ENG.). 32p. (J). (gr. -1-2). 28.50 *(978-1-60270-664-4(6))* ABDO Publishing Co.

French, Vivian. Pig in Love. Archbold, Tim, illus. 2005. 32p. (J). lib. bdg. 9.00 *(978-1-4242-0889-0(0))* Fitzgerald Bks.

French, Vivian & Melling. Iggy Pig's Skippy Day. (Illus.). 42p. (J). pap. *(978-0-340-71360-0(7))* Hodder & Stoughton.

Fuentes, Marco. Houses for the Three Pigs. 2016. (Spring Forward Ser.). (J). (gr. k). *(978-1-4900-3730-1(6))* Benchmark Education Co.

Galdone, Paul. The Three Little Pigs, 1 vol. Galdone, Paul, illus. 2006. (Paul Galdone Classics Ser.). (ENG., Illus.). 48p. (J). (gr. -1-3). audio compact disk 10.99 *(978-0-618-73277-7(2))* Houghton Mifflin Harcourt Publishing Co.

Galdone, Paul & Galdone, Joanna C. The Three Little Pigs. 2011. (Folk Tale Classics Ser.). (ENG., Illus.). 48p. (J). (gr. -1-3). 8.99 *(978-0-547-37020-0(2))* Houghton Mifflin Harcourt Publishing Co.

Gallion, Sue Lowell. Pug & Pig Trick-or-Treat. Wan, Joyce, illus. 2017. (Pug & Pig Ser.). (ENG.). 40p. (J). (gr. -1-3). 17.99 ***(978-1-4814-4977-9(X),*** Beach Lane Bks.) Beach Lane Bks.

Gallion, Sue Lowell. Pug Meets Pig. Wan, Joyce, illus. 2016. (Pug & Pig Ser.). (ENG.). 40p. (J). (gr. -1-3). 17.99 *(978-1-4814-2066-2(6),* Beach Lane Bks.) Beach Lane Bks.

Gallo, Tina. OLIVIA in the Park. Rose, Drew, illus. 2010. (Olivia TV Tie-In Ser.). (ENG.). 48p. (J). (gr. -1-1). 5.99 *(978-1-4169-9887-7(X),* Simon Scribbles) Simon Scribbles.

—OLIVIA Plays Soccer. Osterhold, Jared, illus. 2013. (Olivia TV Tie-In Ser.). (ENG.). 24p. (J). (gr. -1-1). pap. 3.99 *(978-1-4424-7248-8(0),* Simon Spotlight) Simon Spotlight.

—Olivia Plays Soccer. 2013. (Olivia Ready-To-Read Level 1 Ser.). lib. bdg. 13.55 *(978-0-606-32060-3(1),* Turtleback) Turtleback Bks.

—Olivia Wishes on a Star. 2014. (Olivia 8x8 Ser.). lib. bdg. 13.55 *(978-0-606-36118-7(9))* Turtleback Bks.

—The Three Little Pigs: A Wheel-Y Silly Fairy Tale. Bryne, Kelly, illus. 2011. (Little Simon Sillies Ser.). (ENG.). 14p. (J). (gr. -1-1). 5.99 *(978-1-4424-2107-3(X),* Little Simon) Little Simon.

Galloway, Shannon. The Little Pig That Was Afraid of the Mud. Woodard, Dana, illus. 2007. (J). (gr. -1-3). per. 12.99 *(978-1-59879-244-7(X))* Lifevest Publishing, Inc.

Galvin, Laura. Baby Pig Time to Play. 2008. (Smithsonian Baby Animals Ser.). (ENG., Illus.). 16p. (J). (gr. -1-k). 13.95 *(978-1-59249-788-1(8))* Soundprints.

Galvin, Laura Gates. Baby Pig Time to Play. 2008. (ENG., Illus.). 16p. (J). (gr. -1-k). 6.95 *(978-1-59249-787-4(X))* Soundprints.

Garis, Howard R. Curly & Floppy Twistytail. 2011. 130p. 24.95 *(978-1-4638-9713-0(8));* pap. 10.95 *(978-1-60664-569-7(2))* Rodgers, Alan Bks.

Gaudet, Mary Kate. Peppa Pig: Coloring & Activity Book & Crayons. 2007. (Peppa Pig Ser.). 32p. (J). pap. 4.99 *(978-0-06-117374-5(6),* Harper Entertainment) HarperCollins Pubs.

Gay, Marie-Louise. The Three Little Pigs, 1 vol. 2nd ed. 2004. (ENG., Illus.). 30p. (J). pap. 7.95 *(978-0-88899-639-8(X))* Groundwood Bks. CAN. Dist: Publishers Group West (PGW).

Geisert, Arthur, creator. The Giant Seed. 2012. (Stories Without Words Ser.). (ENG., Illus.). 32p. (J). (gr. -1-3). 14.95 *(978-1-59270-115-5(9))* Enchanted Lion Bks., LLC.

George, Susie. Let's Go on a Treasure Hunt. 2007. (Peppa Pig Ser.). 24p. (J). pap. 3.99 *(978-0-06-117363-9(0),* Harper Entertainment) HarperCollins Pubs.

Gibson, Carol Ann. Loopy. 2003. pap. 16.00 *(978-0-8059-6096-9(1))* Dorrance Publishing Co., Inc.

Gilbert the Pig Chapter Books Set 1. 2005. (J). *(978-1-58453-296-5(3))* Pioneer Valley Bks.

Golden Books Staff & Random House Disney Staff. Three Little Pigs. Walt Disney Company Staff & Random House Disney Staff, illus. 2004. (Little Golden Book Ser.). (ENG.). 24p. (J). (gr. -1-2). 4.99 *(978-0-7364-2312-0(5),* Golden/Disney) Random Hse. Children's Bks.

Gonzalo, Angela. The Pig, Bear, & the Pear: The Pear Meets the Pig & Bear. 2013. 44p. pap. 17.45 *(978-1-4624-0576-3(2),* Inspiring Voices) Author Solutions, Inc.

Grant, Nicola. Don't Be So Nosy, Posy! Warnes, Tim, illus. 2004. 32p. (J). tchr. ed. 15.95 *(978-1-58925-036-9(2))* Tiger Tales.

Grant, Vicki. Pigboy. 2007. (Orca Currents Ser.). 101p. (gr. 5). 19.95 *(978-0-7569-8067-2(4))* Perfection Learning Corp.

Gravett, Emily. Wolf Won't Bite! Gravett, Emily, illus. 2012. (ENG., Illus.). 32p. (J). (gr. -1-1). 16.99 *(978-1-4424-2763-1(9),* Simon & Schuster Bks. For Young Readers) Simon & Schuster Bks. For Young Readers.

Graziani, Mary. Fat Pigs Fly! 2007. 24p. per. 24.95 *(978-1-4241-8344-9(8))* America Star Bks.

Greene, Stephanie. Pig Pickin', 0 vols. Mathieu, Joe, illus. 2013. (Moose & Hildy Ser.). (ENG.). 68p. (J). (gr. -1-3). pap. 9.99 *(978-1-4778-1684-4(4),* 9781477816844, Amazon Children's Publishing) Amazon Publishing.

—The Show-Off, 0 vols. Mathieu, Joe, illus. 2007. (Moose & Hildy Ser.: 0). (ENG.). 64p. (J). (gr. 1-4). lib. bdg. 14.99 *(978-0-7614-5374-1(1),* 9780761453741, Amazon Children's Publishing) Amazon Publishing.

Griffin, Adele & Sheinmel, Courtney. Agnes & Clarabelle. Palacios, Sara, illus. 2017. (Agnes & Clarabelle Ser.). (ENG.). 80p. (J). 9.99 *(978-1-61963-137-3(7),* 9781619631373, Bloomsbury USA Childrens) Bloomsbury Publishing USA.

Griner, Jack. Archibald My Pet Pig. Knudson, Dana, illus. 2011. pap. 8.95 *(978-0-9836081-1-0(3))* Canoed Sun Publishing, LLC.

Griswell, Kim T. Rufus Goes to School. Gorbachev, Valeri, illus. 2013. (ENG.). 32p. (J). (gr. -1-1). 14.95 *(978-1-4549-0416-8(X))* Sterling Publishing Co., Inc.

—Rufus Goes to Sea. Gorbachev, Valeri, illus. 2015. (ENG.). 32p. (J). (gr. -1-1). 14.95 *(978-1-4549-1052-7(6))* Sterling Publishing Co., Inc.

Guarnaccia, Steven. The Three Little Pigs: An Architectural Tale. 2010. (ENG., Illus.). 32p. (J). (gr. -1-2). 19.95 *(978-0-8109-8941-2(7),* Abrams Bks. for Young Readers) Abrams, Inc.

Guess, Catherine Ritch. Rudy & the Magic Sleigh. 2006. (Rudy the Red Pig Ser.). (ENG., Illus.). 32p. 14.95 *(978-1-933341-18-7(1))* CRM.

—Rudy el Puerco Rojo. 2006. (SPA & ENG., Illus.). 32p. 14.95 *(978-1-933341-21-7(1))* CRM.

—Rudy the Red Pig. Haynes, Jason & Oke, Rachel, illus. 2006. (ENG.). 32p. (J). 13.95 *(978-1-933341-13-2(0))* CRM.

Guibert, Emmanuel. A Beautiful Cow. 2014. (Ariol Ser.: 4). (J). lib. bdg. 24.50 *(978-0-606-35103-4(5),* Turtleback) Turtleback Bks.

—Happy as a Pig... 2013. (Ariol Graphic Novels Ser.). (ENG., Illus.). 124p. (J). (gr. 1-5). pap. 12.99 *(978-1-59707-487-2(X),* 9781597074872) Papercutz.

—Happy as a Pig... 2013. (Ariol Ser.: 3). (J). lib. bdg. 24.50 *(978-0-606-32310-9(4),* Turtleback) Turtleback Bks.

Gunderson, Jessica. No Lie, Pigs (and Their Houses) CAN Fly! The Story of the Three Little Pigs As Told by the Wolf. Bernardini, Cristian, illus. 2016. (Other Side of the Story Ser.). (ENG.). 24p. (gr. 2-3). lib. bdg. 27.32 *(978-1-4795-8621-9(8))* Picture Window Bks.

Haley, Carrie. The Three Little Female Pigs. 2010. 32p. pap. 17.49 *(978-1-4269-3028-7(3))* Trafford Publishing.

Hamilton, Elizabeth L. Pansy Pig's Patience Pit. 2004. (Character Critters Ser.: No. 7). (Illus.). 32p. (J). per. 5.95 *(978-0-9754629-3-5(8),* Character-in-Action) Quiet Impact, Inc.

Hanna, Virginie. Rosy Posey Is Not Dirty! Desmoineaux, Christel, illus. 2012. (My Little Picture Book Ser.). (ENG.). 32p. (J). pap. 6.95 *(978-2-7338-1947-0(X))* Auzou, Philippe Editions FRA. Dist: Consortium Bk. Sales & Distribution.

Harrington, Claudia. Book 2: Pickles the Very Hungry Pig. 2016. (Hank the Pet Sitter Ser.). (ENG.). (gr. -1-3). lib. bdg. 27.07 ***(978-1-62402-188-6(3))*** ABDO Publishing Co.

Harris, Brooke. This Little Piggy. Ledger, Bill, illus. 2010. (Rising Readers Ser.). (J). 3.49 *(978-1-60719-696-9(4))* Newmark Learning LLC.

Harrison, Paul. Three Blind Mice Team up with the Three Little Pigs. Epelbaum, Mariano, illus. 2016. (Fairy Tale Mix-Ups Ser.). (ENG.). 24p. (gr. k-2). lib. bdg. 23.32 *(978-1-4109-8301-5(3))* Heinemann-Raintree.

Hartley, Alicia Byrd. I Like Being Me. 2012. 24p. pap. 15.50 *(978-1-4772-9088-0(5))* AuthorHouse.

Harvey, Alex. Olivia & the Kite Party. Spaziante, Patrick, illus. 2012. (Olivia Ready-To-Read Level 1 Ser.). lib. bdg. 13.55 *(978-0-606-26360-3(8),* Turtleback) Turtleback Bks.

Haskamp, Steve, illus. Este Cerdito. 2005.Tr. of This Little Piggy. (SPA & ENG.). 22p. (J). 9.95 *(978-1-58117-328-4(8),* Intervisual/Piggy Toes) Bendon, Inc.

Hawkins, Brett, illus. A Triune Tale of Diminutive Swine. 2012. pap. 15.00 *(978-0-9854699-0-0(0))* Rockshow Comedy, Inc.

Hawkins, Colin & Hawkins, Jacqui. Witch Pigs. 2006. (Illus.). 32p. (J). (gr. 1-2). 19.99 *(978-0-224-06467-5(3),* Jonathan Cape) Random Hse. GBR. Dist: Trafalgar Square Publishing.

Hearne, Betsy. Wishes, Kisses, & Pigs. 2003. (ENG.). 144p. (J). (gr. 3-7). pap. 6.99 *(978-0-689-86347-9(0),* Simon & Schuster/Paula Wiseman Bks.) Simon & Schuster/Paula Wiseman Bks.

Heim, Alastair. Love You Too. Coburn, Alisa, illus. 2016. (ENG.). 32p. (J). (gr. -1-3). 16.99 *(978-1-4998-0174-3(2))* Little Bee Books Inc.

Heiney, Sue P. Zig the Pig Goes to School. Charles, Akins, illus. l.t. ed. 2004. 32p. (J). 7.00 *(978-0-9761700-0-6(0))* Zig the Pig.

Helakoski, Leslie. Big Pigs. Helakoski, Leslie, illus. 2014. (ENG., Illus.). 32p. (J). (gr. -1-2). 16.95 *(978-1-62091-023-8(3))* Boyds Mills Pr.

Herman, Gail. Peppa Pig & Her Best Friend. 2007. (My First I Can Read Bks.). 32p. (J). pap. 3.99 *(978-0-06-117305-9(3),* Harper Trophy) HarperCollins Pubs.

Hickerson, Joel, illus. ImagineLand's Bubble Gum Trouble, Vol. 1. l.t. ed. 2004. 32p. (J). *(978-0-9765038-0-4(8))* Imagineland, Ltd.

Hillert, Margaret. The Three Little Pigs. Dorenkamp, Michelle, illus. 2016. (BeginningtoRead Ser.). (ENG.). 32p. (J). (-2). lib. bdg. 22.60 *(978-1-59953-789-4(3))* Norwood Hse. Pr.

Hillert, Margaret. Los Tres Cerditos. Jack Pullan & Dorenkamp, Michelle, illus. 2017. (BeginningtoRead Ser.).Tr. of Three Little Pigs. (ENG & SPA.). 32p. (J). (-2). 22.60 ***(978-1-59953-852-5(0))*** Norwood Hse. Pr.

Himmelman, John. Pigs to the Rescue. Himmelman, John, illus. 2010. (ENG., Illus.). 32p. (J). (gr. -1-3). 17.99 *(978-0-8050-8683-6(8),* 9780805086836, Holt, Henry & Co. Bks. For Young Readers) Holt, Henry & Co.

Hinkler Studios Staff., ed. Three Little Pigs. 2011. (Fairytale Pop-Ups Ser.). 12p. (J). 12.99 *(978-1-74185-086-4(X))* Hinkler Bks. Pty, Ltd. AUS. Dist: Ideals Pubns.

Hobbie, Holly. I'll Be Home for Christmas. 2008. (Toot & Puddle Ser.: 5). (ENG.). 32p. (gr. -1-3). pap. 6.99 *(978-0-316-03383-1(9))* Little, Brown Bks. for Young Readers.

—Toot & Puddle. 2010. (Toot & Puddle Ser.: 1). (ENG., Illus.). 32p. (J). (gr. -1-3). pap. 7.99 *(978-0-316-08080-4(2))* Little, Brown Bks. for Young Readers.

—Toot & Puddle. Hobbie, Holly, illus. 2007. (Toot & Puddle Ser.: 1). (ENG., Illus.). 32p. (J). (gr. -1-3). 17.99

P Q R

(978-0-316-16702-4(9)) Little, Brown Bks. for Young Readers.
—Toot & Puddle: Let It Snow. 2016. (Toot & Puddle Ser.: 11). (ENG.). 32p. (J). (gr. -1-3). 6.99 (978-0-316-35224-6(1)) Little, Brown Bks. for Young Readers.
—Top of the World. 2008. (Toot & Puddle Ser.: 6). (ENG.). 32p. (gr. -1-3). pap. 7.99 (978-0-316-03384-8(7)) Little, Brown Bks. for Young Readers.
—You Are My Sunshine. 2010. (Toot & Puddle Ser.: 3). (ENG., Illus.). 32p. (J). (gr. -1-3). pap. 7.99 (978-0-316-16703-1(7)) Little, Brown Bks. for Young Readers.
Holden, Pam. Huff & Puff!, 6 pack. Storey, Jim, illus. 2009. (Red Rocket Readers Ser.). (ENG.). 16p. (gr. 2-2). pap. (978-1-877363-58-0(8), Red Rocket Readers) Flying Start Bks.
Hollaway, David. Quigley Mccormick: And the Curse of the Polka Dotted Pig, 3 vols. l.t. ed. 2005. (Illus.). 156p. (J). (gr. -1-3). per. 15.95 (978-1-933211-54-1(7)) Quackenworth Publishing.
Housel, Debra. Charlotte's Web: An Instructional Guide for Literature. rev. ed. 2015. (Great Works). (ENG., Illus.). 72p. (gr. 3-5). pap. 9.99 (978-1-4807-6995-3(9)) Shell Educational Publishing.
Howell, Julie Ann. Mrs Owl's Nest of Rhymes. LaGrange, Tiffany, illus. 2008. 24p. pap. 12.95 (978-0-9818683-8-7(X)) Peppertree Pr., The.
Hulst, W. G. van de & Hulst, Willem G. van de, illus. The Pig under the Pew. 2014. (J). (978-1-928136-10-1(9)) Inheritance Pubns.
Hupf, Zetta & Hupf, Mitchell. Henry Goes to the Park, 1 vol. Hupf, Zetta, illus. 2009. (Illus.). 33p. pap. 24.95 (978-1-61546-279-7(1)) America Star Bks.
Image Books Staff & Chronicle Books Staff. Little Pig. Put, Klaartje van der, illus. 2012. (Little Finger Puppet Board Bks.). (ENG.). 12p. (J). (gr. -1 — 1). bds. 6.99 (978-1-4521-0817-9(X)) Chronicle Bks. LLC.
Imperato, Teresa. This Little Piggy. Haskamp, Steve, illus. 2006. (ENG.). 22p. (J). 9.95 (978-1-58117-281-2(8), Intervisual/Piggy Toes) Bendon, Inc.
Inkpen, Mick. Everyone Hide from Wibbly Pig. 2010. (ENG., Illus.). 20p. (J). (gr. -1-k). pap. 10.99 (978-0-340-99754-3(0)) Hodder & Stoughton GBR. Dist: Hachette Bk. Group.
—Kipper's A to Z: An Alphabet Adventure. 2006. (Kipper Ser.). (Illus.). 54p. (gr. -1-2). 18.00 (978-0-7569-6557-0(8)) Perfection Learning Corp.
—Tickly Christmas. 2016. (Wibbly Pig Ser.). (ENG., Illus.). 32p. (J). (gr. -1-k). pap. 8.99 (978-1-4449-2410-7(9)) Hachette Children's Group GBR. Dist: Hachette Bk. Group.
—Wibbly Pig Has 10 Balloons. 2012. (ENG., Illus.). 32p. (J). (gr. -1-k). pap. 9.99 (978-1-4449-0267-9(9)) Hodder & Stoughton GBR. Dist: Hachette Bk. Group.
Jackson, Brenda. Henrietta & the Pot-Bellied Pig. 2005. (J). 16.95 (978-0-9773146-0-7(X)) Krisaran Publishing Co.
James, Andrea. Adventures at Ja-Mar Farms: Pup-Pup, Padluck & PIG Take a Walk in the Wet Woods, 1 vol. 2010. 48p. 24.95 (978-1-4512-1005-7(1)) PublishAmerica, Inc.
James, Dalton. The Mudhogs. 2009. 30p. (J). pap. 13.95 (978-1-4327-4560-8(3)) Outskirts Pr., Inc.
James, Larry W. Captain Petey: An Adventure at Sea. Ramos, Violet M., ed. James, Larry W. & Freshman, Floris R., illus. 2003. 28p. pap. 6.99 (978-0-9742154-0-2(6)) Cross Pointe Printing.
James, Shilah & James, Michael. Little Land Adventures - Little Pig. Castles, Heather, illus. 2010. 24p. pap. (978-1-926635-35-4(3)) Adibbed, Ltd.
Jamieson, Victoria. Olympig! 2016. lib. bdg. 19.65 (978-0-606-38844-3(3)) Turtleback Bks.
Jeong, SoYun. Lulu the Shy Piglet. Orsolini, Laura, illus. rev. ed. 2014. (MySELF Bookshelf Ser.). (ENG.). 32p. (J). (gr. k-2). pap. 11.94 (978-1-60357-654-3(1)); lib. bdg. 25.27 (978-1-59953-645-3(5)) Norwood Hse. Pr.
Jim Pig Is Mad: Short Vowel i: Level A, 6 vols. (Wright Skills Ser.). 12p. (gr. k-3). 17.95 (978-0-322-03115-9(X)) Wright Group/McGraw-Hill.
Johns, Linda. The Three Shapely Pigs. 2004. (Shared Connections Ser.). (J). pap., instr.'s gde. ed. 27.00 (978-1-4108-1614-6(1)) Benchmark Education Co.
—The Three Shapley Pigs. 2004. (Shared Connections Ser.). (J). pap. (978-1-4108-1638-2(9)) Benchmark Education Co.
Johnson, Angela. Julius. Pilkey, Dav, illus. 2015. 32p. pap. 7.00 (978-1-61003-548-4(8)) Center for the Collaborative Classroom.
Johnson, K. Ii. Pig Farm: Adventures of Sal & Snapper. 2011. 52p. pap. 31.99 (978-1-4653-5058-9(6)) Xlibris Corp.
Johnson, Richard, illus. Three Little Pigs. (Flip-Up Fairy Tales Ser.). (ENG.). 24p. (J). 2007. (gr. -1-2). audio compact disk (978-1-84643-087-9(9)) 2005. pap. (978-1-904550-21-1(5)) Child's Play International Ltd.
Johnson, Shane, illus. OLIVIA Paints a Mural. 2011. (Olivia TV Tie-In Ser.). (ENG.). 12p. (J). (gr. -1-1). bds. 5.99 (978-1-4424-1674-1(2), Simon Spotlight) Simon Spotlight.
Johnson, Shane L., illus. OLIVIA Trains Her Cat. 2009. (Olivia TV Tie-In Ser.). (ENG.). 24p. (J). (gr. -1-1). pap. 3.99 (978-1-4169-8296-8(5), Simon Spotlight) Simon Spotlight.
Jones, Brandy. Petunia: The Plump Princess, 1 vol. 2010. 32p. 24.95 (978-1-4489-4874-1(6)) PublishAmerica, Inc.
Josiah, Iris. Tiny Pig. 2012. (Illus.). 28p. (J). pap. (978-0-9572728-1-1(2)) Tiny Island Pr.
Joyner, Andrew. Boris for the Win. 2013. (Boris Ser.: 3). lib. bdg. 14.75 (978-0-606-31976-8(X), Turtleback) Turtleback Bks.
—Boris Gets a Lizard. 2013. (Boris Ser.: 2). lib. bdg. 14.75 (978-0-606-31975-1(1), Turtleback) Turtleback Bks.
—Boris on the Move. 2013. (Boris Ser.: 1). lib. bdg. 14.75 (978-0-606-31974-4(3), Turtleback) Turtleback Bks.
—Boris Sees the Light. 2013. (Boris Ser.: 4). lib. bdg. 14.75 (978-0-606-32363-5(5), Turtleback) Turtleback Bks.
Jugran, Jan. Ibaby - Rub-a-Dub-Dub. Larranaga, Ana Martin, illus. 2007. (ENG.). 6p. (J). (gr. -1 — 1). 14.99 (978-1-58476-555-4(0), IKIDS) Innovative Kids.
Kasza, Keiko. El Dia de Campo de Don Chancho. (Buenas Noches Ser.). (SPA., Illus.). (J). (gr. 1-3). 8.95 (978-958-04-1426-1(2)) Norma S.A. COL. Dist: Distribuidora Norma, Inc., Lectorum Pubns., Inc.
—My Lucky Birthday. Kasza, Keiko, illus. 2013. (ENG., Illus.). 32p. (J). (gr. -1-k). 16.99 (978-0-399-25763-6(2), G.P. Putnam's Sons Books for Young Readers) Penguin Young Readers Group.
—My Lucky Day. Kasza, Keiko, illus. (ENG., Illus.). 32p. (J). (gr. -1-3). 2005. pap. 5.99 (978-0-14-240456-0(X), Puffin Books) 2003. 16.99 (978-0-399-23874-1(3), G.P. Putnam's Sons Books for Young Readers) Penguin Young Readers Group.
—My Lucky Day. Kasza, Keiko, illus. 2005. (Illus.). (gr. -1-3). lib. bdg. 16.00 (978-0-7569-5492-5(4)) Perfection Learning Corp.
—My Lucky Day. 2006. (J). (gr. k-3). incl. audio (978-0-8045-6937-8(1), SAC6937); 29.95 incl. audio compact disk (978-0-8045-4136-7(1), SACD4136) Spoken Arts, Inc.
Katzler, Eva. Florentine & Pig. Mikhail, Jess, illus. 2012. (ENG.). 32p. (J). 17.89 (978-1-59990-949-3(9), 9781599909493); (gr. -1-6). 16.99 (978-1-59990-847-2(6), 9781599908472) Bloomsbury Publishing USA. (Bloomsbury USA Childrens).
Kaufmann, Nancy. Bye, Bye! Spetter, Jung-Hee, illus. 2004. (ENG.). 32p. (J). (gr. -1-1). 14.95 (978-1-886910-95-9(2), Lemniscaat) Boyds Mills Pr.
Kendall, Jodi. The Unlikely Story of a Pig in the City. Campion, Pascal, illus. 2017. 336p. (J). (gr. 3-7). 16.99 **(978-0-06-248453-6(2))** HarperCollins Pubs.
Kennemore, Tim. Alice's Birthday Pig. Spoor, Mike, illus. 2008. 54p. (J). (gr. 2-5). 12.00 (978-0-8028-5335-6(8)) Eerdmans, William B. Publishing Co.
Kerby, Johanna. Little Pink Pup. Kerby, Johanna, photos by. 2010. (ENG., Illus.). 32p. (J). (gr. -1-k). 16.99 (978-0-399-25435-2(8), G.P. Putnam's Sons Books for Young Readers) Penguin Young Readers Group.
Kim, Cecil. The Three Pig Sisters. Park, Keun, illus. 2014. (MySELF Bookshelf Ser.). (ENG.). 32p. (J). (gr. k-2). pap. 11.94 (978-1-60357-689-5(4)); lib. bdg. 25.27 (978-1-59953-654-5(4)) Norwood Hse. Pr.
King-smith, Dick. Lady Lollipop. Barton, Jill, illus. 2003. (ENG.). 128p. (J). (gr. 2-5). pap. 7.99 (978-0-7636-2181-0(1)) Candlewick Pr.
Kinney, Jessica. The Pig Scramble, 1 vol. Brannen, Sarah S., illus. 2011. (ENG.). 32p. (J). 17.95 (978-1-934031-61-2(5), bd7fa2f2-9ea3-439a-9713-9f7979711a16) Islandport Pr., Inc.
Kirk, Daniel. Ten Things I Love about You. Kirk, Daniel, illus. 2012. (ENG., Illus.). 36p. (J). (gr. k-3). 16.99 (978-0-399-25288-4(6), Nancy Paulsen Books) Penguin Young Readers Group.
Kline, Trish & Donev, Mary. Coming Home: KA Reader 8. 2007. (Illus.). 32p. (J). per. 20.00 (978-1-934307-01-4(7)) Ghost Hunter Productions.
Kneen, Maggie. The Christmas Surprise. Kneen, Maggie, illus. 2006. (Illus.). 18p. (J). (gr. k-4). reprint ed. 16.00 (978-0-7567-9837-6(X)) DIANE Publishing Co.
Kneen, Maggie, illus. Some Pig! A Charlotte's Web Picture Book. 2006. (Charlotte's Web Ser.). 32p. (J). (gr. k-2). 17.89 (978-0-06-078162-0(9)) HarperCollins Pubs.
Knight, Chris. Piggy's Party. 2011. (Illus.). 36p. (gr. 1-2). pap. 17.07 (978-1-4520-9585-1(X)) AuthorHouse.
Koch, Claus. The Three Little Wolves & the Big Bad Boar. 2011. 68p. pap. 9.99 (978-1-4520-5321-9(9)) AuthorHouse.
Koenig, Albert. Wood, Hay, & Pigs. Compton, Donna, illus. 2005. (J). 8.99 (978-1-4183-0078-4(0)) Christ Inspired, Inc.
Kramer, Alan. The Three Little Pigs Wise up & the Princess Prince & the Vegetables. 2011. (Navigators Ser.). (J). pap. (978-1-61672-962-2(7)) Benchmark Education Co.
Krensky, Stephen. The Three Little Pigs' Sledding Adventure. Shortley, Michele, illus. 2011. 28p. (J). pap. (978-0-7680-3486-8(8)) SAE Intl.
Kuczenski, Tyler & Schumacher, Dan. Twelve Little Piggies. 2011. 28p. pap. 12.03 (978-1-4567-5313-9(4)) AuthorHouse.
Kurtz, Chris. The Adventures of a South Pole Pig: A Novel of Snow & Courage. (ENG., Illus.). 288p. (J). (gr. 5-7). 2015. pap. 7.99 (978-0-544-54070-5(0), HMH Books For Young Readers) 2013. 16.99 (978-0-547-63455-5(2)) Houghton Mifflin Harcourt Publishing Co.
La Rue, Coco. A New Pig in Town. May, Kyla, illus. 2013. 127p. (J). pap. (978-0-545-46607-3(5)) Scholastic, Inc.
Ladybird Books Staff. Three Little Pigs. (First Fairy Tales Ser.: No. S852-2). (Illus.). (J). (gr. -1-2). pap. 3.95 (978-0-7214-5059-9(8), Dutton Juvenile) Penguin Publishing Group.
Ladybird Books Staff & Candlewick Press Staff. Peppa Pig & the Muddy Puddles. Ladybird Books Staff, illus. 2013. (Peppa Pig Ser.). (ENG., Illus.). 32p. (J). (-k). 12.99 (978-0-7636-6523-4(1), Candlewick Entertainment) Candlewick Pr.
Laird, Donivee Martin. The Magic Shark Learns to Cook. Johnson, Carol Ann, illus. 2004. 48p. (J). 9.95 (978-1-57306-233-6(2)) Bess Pr., Inc.
Lambert, Nat. Three Little Pigs. Butcher, Rosie, illus. 2016. (Press Out & Build Fairy-Tale Scenes Ser.). (ENG.). 24p. (J). (gr. -1-1). 14.99 (978-1-78244-899-0(3)) Top That! Publishing PLC GBR. Dist: Independent Pubs. Group.
Landolf, Diane Wright. Hog & Dog. Harris, Jennifer Beck, illus. 2005. (Step into Reading Ser.: Vol. 1). (ENG.). 32p. (J). (gr. -1-1). per. 3.99 (978-0-375-83165-2(7), Random Hse. Bks. for Young Readers) Random Hse. Children's Bks.
LaReau, Kara. The Infamous Ratsos. Myers, Matt, illus. 2016. (Infamous Ratsos Ser.). (ENG.). 64p. (J). (gr. k-3). 14.99 (978-0-7636-7636-0(5)) Candlewick Pr.
Larson, D. J. Pigsley Brew. Larson, D. J., illus. 2003. (Illus.). 39p. (J). (gr. k-2). pap. 5.95 (978-0-9728234-0-1(9)) Don't Look Publishing.
LaSala, Paige. Pig Kissing. Gullotti, Pat, illus. 2010. 24p. pap. 12.99 (978-1-4520-2849-1(4)) AuthorHouse.
Latsch, Oliver, tr. from GER. The Pirate Pig. 2015. (ENG., Illus.). 80p. (J). (gr. 2-5). 9.99 (978-0-385-37544-3(1), Random Hse. Bks. for Young Readers) Random Hse. Children's Bks.
Lawson, Barbara. Three Little Pigs Go to School. 2012. 28p. pap. 24.95 (978-1-4626-8185-3(9)) America Star Bks.
Laybourn, Emma. Dungeon Dragon. 2008. (ENG.). 156p. (J). (gr. 3-6). pap. 9.95 (978-1-84270-736-4(1)) Andersen Pr. GBR. Dist: Independent Pubs. Group.
Lee, George Douglas. Twyla the Truffle Pig. Lee, Brenda Donaloio, ed. Lee, George Douglas, illus. 2012. (Illus.). 34p. pap. 10.95 (978-0-9848486-0-7(6)) Electric Theatre Radio Hour.
Lee, Michelle. Play with Me! Lee, Michelle, illus. 2017. (ENG., Illus.). 32p. (J). (-k). 16.99 (978-0-399-54601-3(4), G.P. Putnam's Sons Books for Young Readers) Penguin Young Readers Group.
Leech, Carlyle & Leech, Thirma. Ha-Ha Farm. 2009. (ENG., Illus.). 24p. (J). (gr. -1-1). 14.95 (978-1-59583-396-9(X), 9781595833969, Green Tiger Pr.) Laughing Elephant.
Lehrhaupt, Adam. Chicken in School. Kober, Shahar, illus. 2017. 40p. (J). (gr. -1-3). 17.99 (978-0-06-236413-5(8)) HarperCollins Pubs.
—Chicken in Space. Kober, Shahar, illus. 2016. 40p. (J). (gr. -1-3). 17.99 (978-0-06-236412-8(X)) HarperCollins Pubs.
Leonard, Barry, ed. The Three Little Pigs. 2003. (Illus.). 12p. (J). (gr. k-4). reprint ed. 17.00 (978-0-7567-6860-7(8)) DIANE Publishing Co.
—Three Little Pigs. 2006. (Illus.). 61p. (J). (gr. k-4). reprint ed. 25.00 (978-1-4223-5245-8(5)) DIANE Publishing Co.
Lester, Helen. Me First. Munsinger, Lynn, illus. 2013. (Laugh-Along Lessons Ser.). (ENG.). 32p. (J). (gr. -1-3). 8.99 (978-0-544-00321-7(7)) Houghton Mifflin Harcourt Publishing Co.
—Miss Nelson Is Missing! Munsinger, Lynn, illus. 2015. 32p. pap. 7.00 (978-1-61003-507-1(0)) Center for the Collaborative Classroom.
Lindgren, Barbro. Benny's Had Enough! Dyssegaard, Elisabeth Kallick, tr. from SWE. Landstrom, Olof, illus. 2005. 28p. (J). (gr. -1-1). reprint ed. 6.95 (978-91-29-66338-9(5)) R & S Bks. SWE. Dist: Macmillan.
Lindgren, Barbro & Lindgren, B. L. Oink, Oink Benny. Dyssegaard, Elisabeth Kallick, tr. from SWE. Landstrom, Olof, illus. 2008. 28p. (J). (gr. -1-1). 16.00 (978-91-29-66855-1(7)) R & S Bks. SWE. Dist: Macmillan.
Liu, Eleanor. Lao Li & His Beancurd. 2011. 28p. pap. 21.99 (978-1-4653-3712-2(1)) Xlibris Corp.
Liz, Pichon. Three Horrid Little Pigs. Liz, Pichon, illus. 2010. (ENG., Illus.). 32p. (J). pap. 7.95 (978-1-58925-423-7(6)) Tiger Tales.
Lodge, Jo. Cosy Cuddlers: Pig. 2006. (ENG., Illus.). 8p. (J). (gr. -1-k). bds. 7.99 (978-0-333-98752-0(7)) Macmillan Pubs., Ltd. GBR. Dist: Trafalgar Square Publishing.
Long, Ethan. Pig Has a Plan. 2013. (I Like to Read(r) Ser.). (ENG.). 24p. (J). (gr. -1-3). pap. 6.99 (978-0-8234-2911-0(3)) Holiday Hse., Inc.
—Pig Has a Plan. Long, Ethan, illus. 2012. (I Like to Read(r) Ser.). (ENG., Illus.). 24p. (J). (gr. -1-3). 14.95 (978-0-8234-2428-3(6)) Holiday Hse., Inc.
Lowell, Susan. Los Tres Pequenos Jabalies: The Three Little Javelinas. Harris, Jim, illus. 2004. (SPA, ENG & MUL.). 32p. (J). (gr. -1-3). 15.95 (978-0-87358-661-0(1), NP611) Rowman & Littlefield Publishers, Inc.
Lucero, Len & Tracy, Kristina. Woo-Hoo ... Chris P. Is 2! Weber, Penny, illus. 2015. (ENG.). 32p. 14.99 (978-1-4019-4441-4(8), Hay Hse. Lifestyles) Hay Hse., Inc.
Ludwig, Sabine. The Story of the Little Pig Who Couldn't Say No. Wilharm, Sabine, illus. 2013. (ENG.). 32p. (J). (gr. -1-1). 16.95 (978-1-62087-684-8(1), 620684, Sky Pony Pr.) Skyhorse Publishing Co., Inc.
Lyon, Tammie Speer, illus. This Little Piggy. gif. ed. 2006. 10p. (J). bds. 10.95 (978-1-57791-212-5(8)) Brighter Minds Children's Publishing.
Lyons, Fergus. Muckeen & the UFO. 2004. (Pandas Ser.: 28). (ENG., Illus.). 64p. (J). pap. 9.95 (978-0-86278-832-2(3)) O'Brien Pr., Ltd., The IRL. Dist: Dufour Editions, Inc.
Maccarone, Grace. The Three Little Pigs Count To 100. Pistacchio, illus. 2015. (ENG.). 32p. (J). (gr. -1-3). 16.99 (978-0-8075-7901-5(7)) Whitman, Albert & Co.
MacDonald, Alan. The Pig in a Wig. Hess, Paul, illus. 2003. 32p. (J). (gr. k-3). pap. 6.95 (978-1-56145-299-6(8), Q32523) Peachtree Pubs.
MacDonald, Betty Bard. Happy Birthday, Mrs. Piggle-Wiggle. Boiger, Alexandra, illus. 2007. (Mrs. Piggle-Wiggle Ser.). 193p. (J). (gr. 3-7). lib. bdg. 16.89 (978-0-06-072813-7(2)) HarperCollins Pubs.
—Hello, Mrs. Piggle-Wiggle. Knight, Hilary & Boiger, Alexandra, illus. 2007. (ENG.). 176p. (J). (gr. 3-7). 16.99 (978-0-397-31715-8(8)); pap. 5.99 (978-0-06-440149-4(9)) HarperCollins Pubs.
—Mrs. Piggle-Wiggle. Knight, Hilary & Boiger, Alexandra, illus. rev. ed. 2007. (ENG.). 144p. (J). (gr. 3-7). 16.99 (978-0-397-31712-7(3)) HarperCollins Pubs.
—Mrs. Piggle-Wiggle. Boiger, Alexandra, illus. rev. ed. 2007. (Trophy Bk.). (ENG.). 144p. (J). (gr. 3-7). pap. 5.99 (978-0-06-440148-7(0)) HarperCollins Pubs.
—Mrs. Piggle-Wiggle's Magic. 2004. (Illus.). 144p. (J). (gr. 2-5). pap. 29.00 incl. audio (978-1-4000-9001-3(6), Listening Library) Random Hse. Audio Publishing Group.
MacKoul, Eva. The Pig Who Didn't Want to Be Pink. 2013. 24p. pap. 12.45 (978-1-4908-0071-4(9), WestBow Pr.) Author Solutions, Inc.
MacLean, Kerry Lee. Peaceful Piggy Meditation. MacLean, Kerry Lee, illus. 2016. (ENG., Illus.). 32p. (J). (gr. -1-3). 12.99 (978-0-8075-6389-2(7)) Whitman, Albert & Co.
—Peacefully Piggy Meditation. MacLean, Kerry Lee, illus. 2004. (ENG., Illus.). 32p. (J). (gr. k-3). 6.99 (978-0-8075-6381-6(1)) Whitman, Albert & Co.
MacLean, Kerry Lee, creator. Pigs Ski over Colorado: The Top Ten Reasons Winter Is the Piggies Favorite Season. 2005. (J). per. 15.95 (978-0-9652998-7-9(2)) On the Spot! Bks.
Madou, Carol. When Pigs Can Fly! 2011. 40p. pap. 18.99 (978-1-4567-3534-0(9)) AuthorHouse.
Maggiora, Linda Jean. The Three Little Pigs. 2012. 28p. (-18). pap. 11.00 (978-1-4349-1288-6(4)) Dorrance Publishing Co., Inc.
Magnayon, Megan Coy. PuzzlePal Books: Pretty Pig. Cohen, Melissa, illus. 2013. (PuzzlePal Bks.). (ENG.). 10p. (J). (gr. -1). bds. 14.95 (978-1-60710-698-2(1), Silver Dolphin Bks.) Readerlink Distribution Services, LLC.
Make Believe Ideas. Three Little Pigs. 2014. (ENG.). 12p. (J). bds. 9.99 (978-1-78235-908-1(7)) Make Believe Ideas GBR. Dist: Nelson, Thomas Inc.
Malepart, Celine, illus. When Pigs Fly: A Piggy Pop-up Book! 2008. (ENG.). 12p. 16.95 (978-1-58117-671-1(6), Intervisual/Piggy Toes) Bendon, Inc.
Maloney, Brenna. Philomena's New Glasses. 2017. (ENG., Illus.). 40p. (J). (gr. -1-1). 16.99 **(978-0-425-28814-6(5),** Viking Books for Young Readers) Penguin Young Readers Group.
Marchesani, Laura & Medina, Zenaides A., Jr. Pig & Pug. Jarvis, illus. 2015. (Penguin Young Readers, Level 2 Ser.). (ENG.). 32p. (J). (gr. 1-2). pap. 3.99 (978-0-448-48342-9(4), Penguin Young Readers) Penguin Young Readers Group.
Marko, Cyndi. This Little Piggy: An Owner's Manual. Marko, Cyndi, illus. 2017. (Pix Ser.). (ENG., Illus.). 64p. (J). (gr. 1-4). 14.99 **(978-1-4814-6826-8(X),** Aladdin) Simon & Schuster Children's Publishing.
Marshall, James. Swine Lake. 2004. (Illus.). (J). (gr. k-5). spiral bd. (978-0-616-01712-8(X)) Canadian National Institute for the Blind/Institut National Canadien pour les Aveugles.
—The Three Little Pigs. 2015. 32p. pap. 4.00 (978-1-61003-557-6(7)) Center for the Collaborative Classroom.
Marshall, Natalie. This Little Piggy: A Fingers & Toes Nursery Rhyme Book. Marshall, Natalie, illus. 2015. (ENG., Illus.). 12p. (J). (— 1). bds. 6.99 (978-0-545-76761-3(X), Cartwheel Bks.) Scholastic, Inc.
Martin, David Lozell. Piggy & Dad Play Big Book: Brand New Readers. Remkiewicz, Frank, illus. 2009. (Brand New Readers Ser.). (ENG.). 48p. (J). (gr. -1-3). pap. 24.99 (978-0-7636-4455-0(2)) Candlewick Pr.
McCarroll, Barbara. There's Always Two Sides to Every Story. 2005. 9.00 (978-0-8059-9917-4(5)) Dorrance Publishing Co., Inc.
McCully, Emily Arnold. Pete Likes Bunny. McCully, Emily Arnold, illus. 2016. (I Like to Read(r) Ser.). (ENG., Illus.). 24p. (J). (gr. -1-2). 6.99 (978-0-8234-3687-3(X)) Holiday Hse., Inc.
—Pete Likes Bunny. 2016. (I Like to Read(r) Ser.). (ENG., Illus.). 24p. (J). (gr. -1-2). 14.95 (978-0-8234-3653-8(5)) Holiday Hse., Inc.
—Pete Won't Eat. McCully, Emily Arnold, illus. 2014. (I Like to Read(r) Ser.). (ENG., Illus.). 24p. (J). (gr. -1-3). pap. 6.99 (978-0-8234-3183-0(5)) Holiday Hse., Inc.
—Pete Won't Eat. 2013. (I Like to Read(r) Ser.). (ENG., Illus.). 24p. (J). (gr. -1-3). 14.95 (978-0-8234-2853-3(2)) Holiday Hse., Inc.
McDonald, Lisa. The Adventures of Penelope the Tea Cup Pig. 2012. 36p. pap. 32.70 (978-1-4771-3182-4(5)) Xlibris Corp.
McDonald, Megan. Bad Luck Charm. Reynolds, Peter H., illus. 2013. (Judy Moody Ser.: 11). (ENG.). 176p. (J). (gr. 1-4). pap. 5.99 (978-0-7636-4348-5(3)) Candlewick Pr.
McDoogle, Farrah. OLIVIA & the Sea Lions. Spaziante, Patrick, illus. 2013. (Olivia TV Tie-In Ser.). (ENG.). 16p. (J). (gr. -1-1). pap. 5.99 (978-1-4424-7364-5(9), Simon Spotlight) Simon Spotlight.
—OLIVIA Makes a Charm Bracelet. Osterhold, Jared, illus. 2012. (Olivia TV Tie-In Ser.). (ENG.). 16p. (J). (gr. -1-2). pap. 6.99 (978-1-4424-4163-7(1), Simon Spotlight) Simon Spotlight.
Mcdoogle, Farrah. Olivia Says Good Night. 2016. (Olivia 8x8 Ser.). lib. bdg. 13.55 (978-0-606-39244-0(0)) Turtleback Bks.
McDoogle, Farrah. OLIVIA Talks Turkey. Osterhold, Jared, illus. 2011. (Olivia TV Tie-In Ser.). (ENG.). 16p. (J). (gr. -1-1). pap. 5.99 (978-1-4424-3061-7(3), Simon Spotlight) Simon Spotlight.
—A Sweet Surprise for Mom. Osterhold, Jared, illus. 2015. (Olivia TV Tie-In Ser.). (ENG.). 24p. (J). (gr. -1-2). pap. 3.99 (978-1-4814-2763-0(6), Simon Spotlight) Simon Spotlight.
McDoogle, Farrah & Pulliam, Gabe. OLIVIA Says Good Night. Spaziante, Patrick, illus. 2011. (Olivia TV Tie-In Ser.). (ENG.). 24p. (J). (gr. -1-1). 16.99 (978-1-4424-2947-5(X), Simon Spotlight) Simon Spotlight.
McMullan, Kate. Pig Latin — Not Just for Pigs!, 1 vol. Basso, Bill, illus. 2006. (Dragon Slayers' Academy Ser.: No. 14). (ENG.). 112p. (gr. 1-7). 24.21 (978-1-59961-127-3(9)) Spotlight.
McNaughton, Colin. Gôl! Williams, Dylan, tr. from ENG. McNaughton, Colin, illus. 2005.Tr. of Goal! (WEL., Illus.). 30p. (978-0-948930-79-9(9)) Cymdeithas Lyfrau Ceredigion.
—M. W. S. G. Williams, Dylan, tr. 2005.Tr. of S. W. A. L. K. (WEL., Illus.). 32p. (978-1-902416-62-5(7)) Cymdeithas Lyfrau Ceredigion.
McNaughton, Colin, et al. Wps! 2005.Tr. of Oops! (WEL., Illus.). 28p. (978-1-902416-29-8(5)) Cymdeithas Lyfrau Ceredigion.
McPhail, David. Baby Pig Pig Talks. McPhail, David, illus. 2014. (ENG., Illus.). 14p. (J). (— 1). bds. 6.95 (978-1-58089-597-2(2)) Charlesbridge Publishing, Inc.
—Baby Pig Pig Walks. McPhail, David, illus. 2014. (ENG., Illus.). 14p. (J). (— 1). bds. 6.95 (978-1-58089-596-5(4)) Charlesbridge Publishing, Inc.
—Big Pig & Little Pig. 2003. (Green Light Readers Level 1 Ser.). (ENG., Illus.). 24p. (J). (gr. -1-3). pap. 3.95 (978-0-15-204857-0(X)) Houghton Mifflin Harcourt Publishing Co.
—Big Pig & Little Pig. 2003. (Green Light Readers — Level 1 Ser.). (gr. k-3). lib. bdg. 13.50 (978-0-613-63254-6(0), Turtleback) Turtleback Bks.
—Big Pig & Little Pig(Cerdo y Cerdito) 2009. (SPA & ENG., Illus.). 32p. (J). (gr. -1-1). 12.99 Houghton Mifflin Harcourt Trade & Reference Pubs.
—Cerdo y Cerdito. Flor Ada, Alma & Campoy, F. Isabel, trs. from ENG. 2009. (Green Light Readers Level 1 Ser.).Tr. of Big Pig & Little Pig. (SPA & ENG., Illus.). 32p. (J). (gr. -1-3). pap. 3.99 (978-0-15-206561-4(X)) Houghton Mifflin Harcourt Publishing Co.
—Pig Pig Meets the Lion. McPhail, David, illus. 2012. (Illus.). pap. 15.95 (978-1-60734-080-5(1)); (ENG., 32p. (J). (gr. -1-3). 15.95 (978-1-58089-358-9(9)) Charlesbridge Publishing, Inc.
—Pig Pig Returns. McPhail, David, illus. 2011. (ENG., Illus.). 32p. (J). (gr. -1-3). 15.95 (978-1-58089-356-5(2)) Charlesbridge Publishing, Inc.
Meade, Rita. Edward Gets Messy. 2016. (ENG., Illus.). 32p. (J). (gr. -1-3). 17.99 (978-1-4814-3777-6(1), Simon & Schuster Bks. For Young Readers) Simon & Schuster Bks. For Young Readers.
Meadows, Michelle. Piggies in Pajamas. Hoyt, Ard, illus. 2013. (ENG.). 32p. (J). (gr. -1-2). 15.99 (978-1-4169-4982-4(8), Simon & Schuster Bks. For Young Readers) Simon & Schuster Bks. For Young Readers.
—Piggies in the Kitchen. Hoyt, Ard, illus. 2011. (ENG.). 32p. (J). (gr. -1-2). 14.99 (978-1-4169-3787-6(0), Simon & Schuster Bks. For Young Readers) Simon & Schuster Bks. For Young Readers.

Meredith, Christopher. The King & Queen of Slop. 2013. 50p. 23.95 (978-1-937912-89-5(2)) Cordon Pubns.
Merry, Margaret. The Wise Old Boar. 2009. 72p. pap. 21.50 (978-1-60693-728-0(6), Strategic Bk. Publishing) Strategic Book Publishing & Rights Agency (SBPRA).
Messimer, Wanda Fay. Tiny Teacup & Pot Belly Pig Go to Africa to Meet the 'Great Lion' 2013. 24p. pap. 24.95 (978-1-4626-8736-7(9)) America Star Bks.
The Midnight Pig, 6 vols., Pack. (Action Packs Ser.). 120p. (gr. 3-5). 44.00 (978-0-7635-8399-6(5)) Rigby Education.
Milhander, Laura Aron. Not for All the Hamantaschen in Town. Chernyak, Inna, illus. 2016. (ENG.). 32p. (gr. -1-3). 17.99 (978-1-4677-5928-1(7), Kar-Ben Publishing) Lerner Publishing Group.
Miller, Carol. Maurice the Mole: Can You Guess Series. 2007. (ENG., Illus.). 24p. (J). lib. bdg. 18.95 (978-0-9771641-3-4(6)) Defiance In Print.
Milne, A. A. In Which Piglet Meets a Heffalump. Shepard, Ernest H., illus. unabr. ed. (Winnie-the-Pooh Ser.). (J). incl. audio (978-1-57375-014-1(X), 70124) Audioscope.
Milway, Alex. Pigsticks & Harold & the Incredible Journey. Milway, Alex, illus. (Candlewick Sparks Ser.). (ENG., Illus.). 84p. (J). (gr. k-4). 2015. pap. 3.99 (978-0-7636-8105-0(9)) 2014. 12.99 (978-0-7636-6615-6(7)) Candlewick Pr.
Mlawer, Teresa, tr. from ENG. Olivia Se Prepara para la Navidad. Falconer, Ian, illus. 2008.Tr. of Olivia Helps with Christmas. (SPA.). 58p. (J). (gr. k-1). 16.99 (978-1-933032-42-9(1)) Lectorum Pubns., Inc.
Moerbeck, Kees, illus. & des. Three Little Pigs. Moerbeck, Kees, des. 2006. (Roly Poly Box Bks.). (ENG.). 24p. (J). (978-1-84643-018-3(6)) Child's Play International Ltd.
Moerbeek, Kees. The Three Little Pigs. 2011. (My Secret Scrapbook Diary Ser.). (ENG., Illus.). 10p. (J). (978-1-84643-448-8(3)) Child's Play International Ltd.
Molly's Magic: Evaluation Guide. 2006. (J). (978-1-55942-417-2(6)) Witcher Productions.
Montgomery, Lewis B. The Case of the Poisoned Pig. Montgomery, Lewis B., illus. 2009. (Milo & Jazz Mysteries Ser.). (Illus.). 96p. (J). (gr. 2-5). 22.60 (978-1-57565-289-4(7)) Kane Press, Inc.
—The Case of the Poisoned Pig. Wummer, Amy, illus. 2009. (Milo & Jazz Mysteries Ser.). (ENG.). 96p. (J). (gr. 2-6). pap. 6.95 (978-1-57565-286-3(2)) Kane Press, Inc.
Mortensen, Lori. Dirty Gertie, 1 vol. Perry, Gina Marie, illus. 2009. (Read-It! Readers: Character Education Ser.). (ENG.). 32p. (gr. k-2). 21.32 (978-1-4048-4234-2(9), Easy Readers) Picture Window Bks.
Mr. Pig & Jumbo's Birthday Cake. 2004. (J). per. 15.99 (978-0-9744205-7-8(3)) Golden Eagle Publishing Hse., Inc.
Mrs Molesworth & Molesworth, Mary Louisa S. The Thirteen Little Black Pigs & Other Stories. 2011. 66p. 16.95 (978-1-4638-9845-8(2)) Rodgers, Alan Bks.
Mrs Molesworth, et al. The Thirteen Little Black Pigs & Other Stories. 2011. 66p. pap. 8.95 (978-1-4638-0052-9(5)) Rodgers, Alan Bks.
Munsch, Robert. Pigs. Martchenko, Michael, illus. 2014. (ENG.). 26p. (J). (gr. -1-k). bds. 7.99 (978-1-55451-628-5(5), 9781554516285) Annick Pr., Ltd. CAN. Dist: Publishers Group West (PGW).
Muntean, Michaela. Do Not Open This Book. Lemaître, Pascal, illus. 2006. (ENG.). 40p. (J). (gr. -1-3). 17.99 (978-0-439-69839-9(1), Scholastic Pr.) Scholastic, Inc.
Namm, Diane. The Three Little Pigs. Wakefield, Scott, illus. 2012. (Silver Penny Stories Ser.). (ENG.). 48p. (J). (gr. -1-1). 4.95 (978-1-4027-8434-7(1)) Sterling Publishing Co., Inc.
Nanette. Oinky the Yellow Pig. 2004. (Life on Granny's Farm Ser.). (J). 12.95 (978-0-9741269-4-4(2)) St. Bernard Publishing, LLC.
Needham B.Ed, Louise. Flossie's Escape to Freedom. 2010. (Illus.). 44p. pap. 16.99 (978-1-4490-9385-3(X)) AuthorHouse.
Nelid, Piper. Emilio & the Baby Pig, 01 vols., 1. 2016. (Rosen REAL Readers: STEM & STEAM Collection). (ENG.). 8p. (J). pap. 5.46 (978-1-5081-1404-8(8), Rosen Classroom) Rosen Publishing Group, Inc., The.
Nero, Molly. Smarty Pig & the Test Taking Terror. Turchan, Monique, illus. 2012. 28p. pap. 12.95 (978-1-61244-055-2(X)) Halo Publishing International.
Never Bring a Pigout Home. Date not set. 5.95 (978-0-89868-355-4(6)) ARO Publishing Co.
Newman, Diana Marie. Gramps' Tales: Pig Ride. 2008. 14p. pap. 24.95 (978-1-4241-9396-7(6)) America Star Bks.
—Gramps' Tales: Pig Ride, 1 vol. 2010. 16p. 24.95 (978-1-4512-1479-6(0)) PublishAmerica, Inc.
Newth, Rebecca. Tinkum's Dog. Primm, Thomas, illus. 2005. 32p. (J). 15.00 (978-0-9630310-7-5(4)) Will Hall Bks.
Nicholson, Melissa. Prissy & Pop - Big Day Out. Nicholson, Melissa, illus. 2016. (Illus.). 32p. (J). (gr. -1-3). 17.99 (978-0-06-243995-6(2)) HarperCollins Pubs.
Nicolle, Ethan. Kill the Devil. 2008. (ENG., Illus.). 120p. (YA). pap. 10.95 (978-1-59362-099-8(3), 9781593620998) Slave Labor Bks.
Nilsen, Morten. Snyder: The Pig's Tale. Osenchakov, Yuri, illus. 2007. 116p. 24.95 (978-0-9774906-0-8(2)) Counterbalance Bks.
Nordquist, Donna M. Petey the Pigasaurus. Fortune, Leslie, illus. 2011. 32p. pap. 24.95 (978-1-4560-6051-0(1)) America Star Bks.
Norman, Kim. I Know a Wee Piggy. Cole, Henry, illus. 2012. (ENG.). 32p. (J). (gr. -1-k). 16.99 (978-0-8037-3735-8(1), Dial Bks) Penguin Young Readers Group.
—Puddle Pug. Yamaguchi, Keika, illus. 2014. (ENG.). 40p. (J). (gr. -1). 14.95 (978-1-4549-0436-6(4)) Sterling Publishing Co., Inc.
Norris II, Charles H. Fat Little Ugly Friend. 2008. 12p. per. 24.95 (978-1-4241-9222-9(6)) America Star Bks.
North, Laura. The Big Bad Wolf & the Robot Pig. 2014. (ENG., Illus.). 32p. (J). (978-0-7787-1291-6(5)) Crabtree Publishing Co.
Norton Kreider, Barbara. Mr Squealy Goes to Town. Dimbylow, Jube, illus. 2013. 24p. pap. (978-1-921883-41-5(3), MBS Pr.) Pick-a-Woo Woo Pubs.
—Mr Squealy Makes a Friend. Dimbylow, Jube, illus. 2013. 24p. pap. (978-1-921883-52-1(9)) Pick-a-Woo Woo Pubs.
—Mr Squealy Meets Scarecrow. Dimbylow, Jube, illus. 2013. 24p. pap. (978-1-921883-53-8(7)) Pick-a-Woo Woo Pubs.
Nosy Crow Staff. The Three Little Pigs: A Nosy Crow Fairy Tale. Bryan, Ed, illus. 2016. (ENG.). (J). (gr. -1-2). 9.99 (978-0-7636-8655-0(7), Nosy Crow) Candlewick Pr.
Numeroff, Laura Joffe. Happy Valentine's Day, Mouse! Bond, Felicia, illus. 2009. (If You Give... Ser.). (ENG.). 24p. (J). (gr. -1-3). bds. 6.99 (978-0-06-180432-8(0)) HarperCollins Pubs.
—If You Give a Pig a Pancake. Bond, Felicia, illus. Date not set. (J). 6.99 (978-0-694-01430-9(3)) HarperCollins Pubs.
—If You Give a Pig a Pancake Big Book. braille ed. 2004. (Illus.). (J). (gr. k-3). spiral bd. (978-0-616-07244-8(9)); spiral bd. (978-0-616-07243-1(0)) Canadian National Institute for the Blind/Institut National Canadien pour les Aveugles.
—If You Give a Pig a Party. Bond, Felicia, illus. 2005. (If You Give... Ser.). 32p. (J). (gr. -1-2). (ENG.). 16.99 (978-0-06-028326-1(2)); lib. bdg. 17.89 (978-0-06-028327-8(0)) HarperCollins Pubs.
—If You Give a Pig a Pumpkin: Book & Doll. Bond, Felicia, illus. Date not set. (J). 19.99 (978-0-694-01432-3(X)) HarperCollins Pubs.
—Pig Stroller Songs. Bond, Felicia, illus. Date not set. (J). 10.99 (978-0-694-01428-6(1)) HarperCollins Pubs.
—Si le Haces una Fiesta a una Cerdita, 1 vol. Mlawer, Teresa, tr. from ENG. Bond, Felicia, illus. 2006. (If You Give... Ser.).Tr. of If You Give a Pig a Party. (SPA.). 32p. (J). (gr. -1-2). 16.99 (978-0-06-081532-5(9)) HarperCollins Pubs.
Oddo, Jennifer M. Asim the Awesome Possum: Asim Gets His Awesome. Lamb, T. S., illus. 2012. 36p. 16.95 (978-0-9855906-2-8(9)) Pie Plate Publishing Co.
Ohi, Ruth. Chicken, Pig, Cow & the Purple Problem. Ohi, Ruth, illus. 2010. (Chicken, Pig, Cow Ser.). (ENG., Illus.). 32p. (J). (gr. -1-k). 19.95 (978-1-55451-219-5(0), 9781554512195); 2nd ed. pap. 6.95 (978-1-55451-218-8(2), 9781554512188) Annick Pr., Ltd. CAN. Dist: Publishers Group West (PGW).
—Chicken, Pig, Cow Horse Around. Ohi, Ruth, illus. 2010. (Chicken, Pig, Cow Ser.). (ENG., Illus.). 32p. (J). (gr. -1-k). 19.95 (978-1-55451-245-4(X), 9781554512454) Annick Pr., Ltd. CAN. Dist: Publishers Group West (PGW).
—Chicken, Pig, Cow on the Move. Ohi, Ruth, illus. 3rd ed. 2009. (Chicken, Pig, Cow Ser.). (ENG., Illus.). 32p. (J). (gr. -1-k). 19.95 (978-1-55451-194-5(1), 9781554511945); pap. 6.95 (978-1-55451-193-8(3), 9781554511938) Annick Pr., Ltd. CAN. Dist: Publishers Group West (PGW).
Ohi, Ruth, illus. Chicken, Pig, Cow Horse Around. 3rd ed. 2010. (Chicken, Pig, Cow Ser.). (ENG.). 32p. (J). (gr. -1-k). pap. 6.95 (978-1-55451-244-7(1), 9781554512447) Annick Pr., Ltd. CAN. Dist: Publishers Group West (PGW).
Oldenburg, Richard. The Three Little Green Pigs, Llc: A Recycling Pig Tale. Samantha May Cerney, illus. 2013. 28p. 23.50 (978-1-62516-753-8(9), Strategic Bk. Publishing) Strategic Book Publishing & Rights Agency (SBPRA).
—The Three Little Green Pigs, Llc: A Recycling Pig Tale. Cerney, Samantha May, illus. 2013. 28p. pap. 12.50 (978-1-62516-649-4(4), Strategic Bk. Publishing) Strategic Book Publishing & Rights Agency (SBPRA).
Oliver, Ilanit. Olivia & the Best Teacher Ever. 2012. (Olivia 8x8 Ser.). lib. bdg. 13.55 (978-0-606-26367-2(5), Turtleback) Turtleback Bks.
OLIVIA Helps the Tooth Fairy. 2015. (Olivia TV Tie-In Ser.). (ENG., Illus.). 24p. (J). (gr. -1-2). pap. 3.99 (978-1-4814-1906-2(4), Simon Spotlight) Simon Spotlight.
Once upon a Time Spanish Version-the Three Little Pigs. 2005. (J). (978-1-57022-565-9(6)) ECS Learning Systems, Inc.
Ondrias, Rachel. There's a Pig in My Fridge. Scarborough, Casey, illus. 2006. (ENG.). 28p. (J). 16.95 (978-1-933660-30-1(9), Tadpole Pr. 4 Kids) Smooth Sailing Pr., LLC.
Oshiro, Kimberley. The Saga of Simon the Skinny Pig: Simon Saves the Day. Yee, Jeanne, illus. 2012. 38p. pap. 12.50 (978-1-61170-089-3(2)) Robertson Publishing.
Osterhold, Jared, illus. Cooks up a Surprise. 2011. (Olivia TV Tie-In Ser.). (ENG.). 24p. (J). (gr. -1-2). pap. 3.99 (978-1-4424-1384-9(0), Simon Spotlight) Simon Spotlight.
—OLIVIA & the Pet Project. 2015. (Olivia TV Tie-In Ser.). (ENG.). 24p. (J). (gr. -1-1). pap. 3.99 (978-1-4814-2895-8(0), Simon Spotlight) Simon Spotlight.
—OLIVIA Becomes a Vet. 2011. (Olivia TV Tie-In Ser.). (ENG.). 24p. (J). (gr. -1-1). 16.99 (978-1-4424-2860-7(0)); pap. 3.99 (978-1-4424-2859-1(7)) Simon Spotlight. (Simon Spotlight).
—OLIVIA Goes Camping. 2011. (Olivia TV Tie-In Ser.). (ENG.). 24p. (J). (gr. -1-1). 15.99 (978-1-4424-2253-7(X)); pap. 3.99 (978-1-4424-2135-6(5)) Simon Spotlight. (Simon Spotlight).
—OLIVIA Goes to the Library. 2013. (Olivia TV Tie-In Ser.). (ENG.). 24p. (J). (gr. -1-1). 16.99 (978-1-4424-8479-5(9)); pap. 3.99 (978-1-4424-8478-8(0)) Simon Spotlight. (Simon Spotlight).
—OLIVIA Helps Mother Nature. 2014. (Olivia TV Tie-In Ser.). (ENG.). 24p. (J). (gr. -1-1). pap. 3.99 (978-1-4424-9664-4(9), Simon Spotlight) Simon Spotlight.
—OLIVIA Plants a Garden. 2011. (Olivia TV Tie-In Ser.). (ENG.). 24p. (J). (gr. -1-1). pap. 3.99 (978-1-4424-1675-8(0), Simon Spotlight) Simon Spotlight.
—OLIVIA Plays Soccer. 2013. (Olivia TV Tie-In Ser.). (ENG.). 24p. (J). (gr. -1-1). 16.99 (978-1-4424-7249-5(9), Simon Spotlight) Simon Spotlight.
—OLIVIA Wishes on a Star. 2014. (Olivia TV Tie-In Ser.). (ENG.). 24p. (J). (gr. -1-2). pap. 3.99 (978-1-4814-1769-3(X), Simon Spotlight) Simon Spotlight.
Oulton, Harry. Heather's Piglets. 2017. (Pig Called Heather Ser.: 3). (ENG., Illus.). 240p. (J). (gr. 4-7). pap. 8.99 **(978-1-84812-479-0(1))** Bonnier Publishing GBR. Dist: Independent Pubs. Group.
—A Pig Called Heather. 2015. (ENG.). 192p. (J). (gr. 3-7). 16.95 (978-0-8234-3290-5(4)) Holiday Hse., Inc.
Oulton, Harry. The Return of a Pig Called Heather. 2017. (Pig Called Heather Ser.: 2). (ENG., Illus.). 192p. (J). (gr. 4-7). pap. 8.99 **(978-1-84812-473-8(2))** Bonnier Publishing GBR. Dist: Independent Pubs. Group.
Oxenbury, Helen. Pig Tale. Oxenbury, Helen, illus. 2010. (ENG., Illus.). 32p. (J). (gr. -1-1). 16.99 (978-1-4424-2153-0(3), McElderry, Margaret K. Bks.) McElderry, Margaret K. Bks.
Pace, Anne Marie. Pigloo. Hussey, Lorna, illus. 2016. (ENG.). 32p. (J). 16.99 (978-1-62779-202-8(3), 9781627792028, Holt, Henry & Co. Bks. For Young Readers) Holt, Henry & Co.
Page, Nick. Read with Me Three Little Pigs. 2011. 32p. (J). 3.99 (978-1-78065-013-5(2)) Make Believe Ideas GBR. Dist: Nelson, Thomas Inc.
Paine, Walter. Cousin John: The Story of a Boy & a Small Smart Pig. Dodson, Bert, illus. 2006. (ENG.). 96p. (J). (gr. 3-4). 17.95 (978-1-59373-057-4(8)) Bunker Hill Publishing, Inc.
Palatini, Margie. Hogg, Hogg, & Hog. Palatini, Margie, illus. 2011. (ENG., Illus.). 32p. (J). (gr. -1-3). 15.99 (978-1-4424-0322-2(5), Simon & Schuster Bks. For Young Readers) Simon & Schuster Bks. For Young Readers.
—Oink? Cole, Henry, illus. 2006. (ENG.). 40p. (J). (gr. -1-3). 17.99 (978-0-689-86258-8(X), Simon & Schuster Bks. For Young Readers) Simon & Schuster Bks. For Young Readers.
—Under a Pig Tree: A History of the Noble Fruit. Groenink, Chuck, illus. 2015. (ENG.). 40p. (J). (gr. -1-3). 16.95 (978-1-4197-1488-7(0), Abrams Bks. for Young Readers) Abrams, Inc.
Pan, Hui-Mei. El Cochinito en mi Bolsillo, 1 vol. Vernescu, Maritza, tr. from ENG. Pan, Hui-Mei, illus. 2004.Tr. of Piggy in My Pocket. (SPA., Illus.). 32p. (J). bds. 5.95 (978-1-932065-04-6(0), 1-718-784-9112) Star Bright Bks., Inc.
—Piggy in My Pocket. 2004. (Illus.). 14p. (J). bds. 5.95 (978-1-887734-96-7(1)) Star Bright Bks., Inc.
—Piggy in My Pocket (Spanish/English), 1 vol. del Risco, Eida, tr. Pan, Hui-Mei, illus. 2004. (ENG & SPA., Illus.). 32p. (J). bds. 5.95 (978-1-932065-11-4(3)) Star Bright Bks., Inc.
Parragon Staff, ed. Cerdito. 2010. pap. 4.95 (978-1-4054-4915-1(2)) Parragon, Inc.
Pastis, Stephan. Beginning Pearls. 2013. lib. bdg. 20.85 (978-0-606-31764-1(3), Turtleback) Turtleback Bks.
Paulson, Michael W. The Baker Street Bunch No. 1: A Double Mystery Book. l.t. ed. 2004. (Illus.). 154p. (J). per. (978-0-9754241-0-0(6)) MiMar Publishing.
—The Baker Street Bunch & the Missing Pig Mystery. l.t. ed. 2004. (Illus.). 90p. (J). per. 3.95 (978-0-9754241-1-7(4)) MiMar Publishing.
PC Treasures Staff, prod. The Three Little Pigs. 2007. (J). (978-1-60072-016-1(1)) PC Treasures, Inc.
Penguin Books Staff, ed. The Three Little Pigs. (Fairy Tale Fun Ser.). (J). 3.95 (978-0-7214-5431-3(3), Dutton Juvenile) Penguin Publishing Group.
Pennart, Geoffroy de. SOFIA LA VACA QUE AMABA LA MUSICA. 2005. (SPA.). 40p. (J). (gr. k-2). 22.95 (978-84-8470-027-2(5)) Corimbo, Editorial S.L. ESP. Dist: Iaconi, Mariuccia Bk. Imports.
Peters, Rob. The Wolf & Pig Report. 2009. 60p. pap. 12.00 (978-0-557-08112-7(2)) Lulu Pr., Inc.
Peterson, Mary & Rofé, Jennifer. Piggies in the Pumpkin Patch. Peterson, Mary, illus. 2010. (ENG., Illus.). 28p. (J). (gr. -1-2). 16.95 (978-1-57091-460-7(5)); pap. 7.95 (978-1-57091-461-4(3)) Charlesbridge Publishing, Inc.
Petkovich, David. The Story of Pete the Pig: A Truly Twisted Tail. 2012. 52p. pap. 24.99 (978-1-4817-0043-6(X)) AuthorHouse.
Petty, Colin, illus. The Three Little Pigs: A Tale about Working Hard. 2006. (J). 6.99 (978-1-59939-016-1(7)) Cornerstone Pr.
Phelan, Connie. The Little Pink Pig That Was Different. 2009. 16p. pap. 8.95 (978-1-4389-5180-5(9)) AuthorHouse.
Pichon, Liz. The Three Horrid Little Pigs. Pichon, Liz, illus. 2008. (Illus.). 32p. (J). (gr. -1-2). 15.95 (978-1-58925-077-2(X)) Tiger Tales.
Pig & Small, 1 vol. 2014. (ENG., Illus.). 32p. (J). (gr. -1-3). 15.95 (978-1-56145-797-7(3)) Peachtree Pubs.
Pig in a Blanket. 2004. (J). per. (978-1-57657-517-8(9)) Paradise Pr., Inc.
Pinkowski, Vern V. A Twisted Pig's Tale. 2008. 144p. pap. 11.95 (978-0-595-46595-8(1), iUniverse, Inc.) iUniverse, Inc.
Pinkowski, Vernon V. A Twisted Pig's Tale. 2008. 148p. 21.95 (978-0-595-49022-6(0), iUniverse, Inc.) iUniverse, Inc.
Pittar, Gill. Milly, Molly & Betelgeuse (book W/dolls) 2006. 28p. pap. (978-1-86972-095-7(4)) Milly Molly Bks.
—Milly, Molly & Oink. 28p. 2006. pap. (978-1-86972-093-3(8)) 2004. (Illus.). (978-1-86972-002-5(4)) Milly Molly Bks.
Plitt, Kay. Why Isn't Bobby Like Me, Mom? 2010. 32p. 14.75 (978-1-4269-4038-5(6)) Trafford Publishing.
Polacco, Patricia. Ginger & Petunia. Polacco, Patricia, illus. 2007. (ENG., Illus.). 40p. (J). (gr. -1-3). 17.99 (978-0-399-24539-8(1), Philomel Bks.) Penguin Young Readers Group.
Ponting, Susan. The Revenge of BB Wolf. 2011. 140p. (gr. -1). 28.98 (978-1-4567-7528-5(6)); (Illus.). pap. 17.23 (978-1-4567-7011-2(X)) AuthorHouse.
Portis, Antoinette. Not a Stick. Portis, Antoinette, illus. 2007. (ENG., Illus.). 32p. (J). (gr. -1-1). 14.99 (978-0-06-112325-2(0)) HarperCollins Pubs.
Price, Mathew. Este Cerdito. (SPA.). pap. 3.95 (978-950-07-2058-8(2)) Editorial Sudamericana S.A. ARG. Dist: Distribooks, Inc.
Publications International Ltd. Staff, ed. Record Story Three Little Pigs. 2011. 18p. 17.98 (978-1-4508-1911-4(7)) Phoenix International Publications, Inc.
R. Friend -Panic in the PigPen. 2007. (J). per. (978-0-9743627-7-9(8)) Sunflower Seeds Pr.
Ransom, Jeanie Franz. Don't Squeal Unless It's a Big Deal: A Tale of Tattletales. Urbanovic, Jackie, illus. 2005. (J). 32p. 14.95 (978-1-59147-239-1(3)); 28p. (gr. -1-3). pap. 9.95 (978-1-59147-240-7(7)) American Psychological Assn. (Magination Pr.).
Ray Charles Lockamy, Inez Eason. The Adventures of Tracks & Cookout. 2010. 40p. pap. (978-1-4269-2159-9(4)) Trafford Publishing (UK) Ltd.
Reed, Adolph, ed. Ice. 2011. (Stories Without Words Ser.). (ENG., Illus.). 32p. (J). (gr. -1-2). 14.95 (978-1-59270-098-1(5)) Enchanted Lion Bks., LLC.
Ressy-Nieves, Cynthia Ann. Keek-A-Poo's Adventures. 2010. 48p. pap. 24.99 (978-1-4535-1479-5(1)) Xlibris Corp.
Rhiger, Tenna. The Story about How the Spotted Wobblepig Got Its Spots. 2012. 40p. pap. (978-1-84903-152-3(5)) Schiel & Denver Publishing Ltd.
Rigby Education Staff. Goodness Me, Mr. Magee! (Sails Literacy Ser.). (Illus.). 16p. (gr. 1-2). 27.00 (978-0-7635-9904-1(2), 699042C99) Rigby Education.
—The Three Little Pigs. (Illus.). 16p. (J). pap. 30.00 (978-0-7635-6442-1(7), 764427C99) Rigby Education.
Rigo, L., illus. Little Pig. 2010. (Look at Me Bks.). (ENG.). 10p. (J). (gr. -1-k). bds. 7.99 (978-0-7641-6355-5(8)) Barron's Educational Series, Inc.
Rivers-Moore, Debbie. Pig. Larranaga, Ana Martin, illus. 2012. (Come Out & Play Bks.). (ENG.). 10p. (J). bds. 2.99 (978-0-7641-6519-1(4)) Barron's Educational Series, Inc.
Robe, Adam D. Robbie's Trail Through Adoption. Robe, Kim A., ed. Gavet, Nathalie, illus. 2010. 44p. pap. 23.99 (978-1-935831-03-7(8)) Robe Communications, Inc.
—Robbie's Trail Through Adoption — Activity Book. Robe, Kim A., ed. Gavet, Nathalie, illus. 2010. 36p. pap. 16.99 (978-1-935831-04-4(6)) Robe Communications, Inc.
—Robbie's Trail Through Adoption — Adult Guide. Robe, Kim A., ed. Gavet, Nathalie, illus. 2010. 28p. pap. 16.99 (978-1-935831-05-1(4)) Robe Communications, Inc.
—Robbie's Trail Through Foster Care. Robe, Kim A., ed. Gavet, Nathalie, illus. 2010. 40p. pap. 23.99 (978-1-935831-00-6(3)) Robe Communications, Inc.
—Robbie's Trail Through Foster Care — Activity Book. Robe, Kim A., ed. Gavet, Nathalie, illus. 2010. 36p. pap. 16.99 (978-1-935831-01-3(1)) Robe Communications, Inc.
—Robbie's Trail Through Foster Care — Adult Guide. Robe, Kim A., ed. Gavet, Nathalie, illus. 2010. 28p. pap. 16.99 (978-1-935831-02-0(X)) Robe Communications, Inc.
—Robbie's Trail Through Open Adoption. Robe, Kim A., ed. Gavet, Nathalie, illus. 2010. 44p. pap. 23.99 (978-1-935831-06-8(2)) Robe Communications, Inc.
Roberts, Angela. The Pig Tale. 2006. (ENG.). 232p. (J). pap. 13.95 (978-0-86243-867-8(5)) Y Lolfa GBR. Dist: Dufour Editions, Inc.
Robinson, Hilary. Three Pigs & a Gingerbread Man. Sanfilippo, Simona, illus. 2012. (ENG.). 32p. (J). (978-0-7787-8026-7(0)); pap. (978-0-7787-8037-3(6)) Crabtree Publishing Co.
Robinson, Janie. Preston, the Not-So-Perfect-Pig. Snider, K. C., illus. 2009. 20p. pap. 10.95 (978-1-935137-84-9(0)) Guardian Angel Publishing, Inc.
Romay, Alexis, tr. OLIVIA Vende Galletas (OLIVIA Sells Cookies) Spaziante, Patrick, illus. 2013. (Olivia TV Tie-In Ser.). (SPA.). 24p. (J). (gr. -1-2). pap. 3.99 (978-1-4424-5967-0(0), Libros Para Ninos) Libros Para Ninos.
Roots, Robert. Prepararse para el Lobo: Los secretos del exito a partir de Los Tres Cerditos. 2005. (SPA.). (YA). (978-0-9715336-2-2(8)) Roots, Robert.
Rosen, Michael & Langley, Jonathan. Oww! 2004. (ENG., Illus.). 32p. (J). (gr. k-2). pap. 9.99 (978-0-00-712443-5(0), HarperCollins Children's Bks.) HarperCollins Pubs. Ltd. GBR. Dist: Independent Pubs. Group.
Rosenthal, Amy Krouse. Little Oink. Corace, Jen, illus. (ENG.). (J). 2017. 24p. bds. 7.99 (978-1-4521-5319-3(1)) 2009. 36p. (gr. -1-17). 14.99 (978-0-8118-6655-2(6)) 2009. 14.99 (978-0-8118-8331-3(0)) Chronicle Bks. LLC.
Rosie's House, 6, Pack. (Literatura 2000 Ser.). (gr. 2-3). 33.00 (978-0-7635-0237-9(5)) Rigby Education.
Roth, Carol. Ten Dirty Pigs: An Upside-Down Turn Around. Paparone, Pamela, illus. 2008. (ENG.). 22p. (J). (gr. -1-k). bds. 7.95 (978-0-7358-2213-9(1)) North-South Bks., Inc.
Rottenberg, David Ira & Rottenberg, David Ira. Gwendolyn Goes Hollywood. Anderson, Lesley, illus. 2011. 40p. (J). 16.99 (978-0-910291-11-8(X)) Cedar Crest Bks.
Rueda, Claudia. Huff & Puff: Can You Blow down the Houses of the Three Little Pigs? 2012. (ENG., Illus.). 32p. (J). (gr. -1-k). 15.95 (978-1-4197-0170-2(3), Abrams Appleseed) Abrams, Inc.
Rusackas, Francesca. Daddy All Day Long. Burris, Priscilla, tr. Burris, Priscilla, illus. 2004. 32p. (J). (gr. -1-k). lib. bdg. 13.89 (978-0-06-050285-0(1)) HarperCollins Pubs.
—I Love You All Day Long. Burris, Priscilla, illus. 2004. (ENG.). 32p. (J). (gr. -1-k). reprint ed. pap. 6.99 (978-0-06-050278-2(9)) HarperCollins Pubs.
Rusu, Meredith. Peppa Visits the Aquarium (Peppa Pig) 2017. (Peppa Pig Ser.). (ENG.). 32p. (J). (gr. -1-k). pap. 5.99 (978-1-338-05417-0(1)) Scholastic, Inc.
—Play Time for Peppa & George (Peppa Pig) Eone, illus. 2016. (Peppa Pig Ser.). (ENG.). 32p. (J). (gr. -1-k). 8.99 (978-1-338-03280-2(1)) Scholastic, Inc.
Rylant, Cynthia. Poppleton. Teague, Mark, illus. 2015. 56p. pap. 4.00 (978-1-61003-551-4(8)) Center for the Collaborative Classroom.
—Poppleton in Spring. Teague, Mark, illus. 2009. (Scholastic Reader Level 3 Ser.). (ENG.). 48p. (J). (gr. -1-3). pap. 3.99 (978-0-545-07867-2(9), Cartwheel Bks.) Scholastic, Inc.
—Poppleton in Winter. Teague, Mark, illus. 2008. 48p. (gr. -1-3). 14.00 (978-0-7569-8910-1(8)) Perfection Learning Corp.
—Poppleton in Winter, Level 3. Teague, Mark, illus. 2008. (Scholastic Reader Level 3 Ser.). (ENG.). 56p. (J). (gr. -1-3). pap. 3.99 (978-0-545-06823-9(1), Cartwheel Bks.) Scholastic, Inc.
—Poppleton Se Divierte. Teague, Mark, illus. 2006. (Poppleton Ser.). (SPA.). 48p. pap. 11.73 (978-0-15-356487-1(3)) Harcourt Children's Bks.
Sally Spencer. Juanita's Flowers. Phil Brannan & Sunni Brannan, illus. 2009. 32p. pap. 14.49 (978-1-4389-4841-6(7)) AuthorHouse.
Saltzberg, Barney. Cornelius P. Mud, Are You Ready for School? 2007. (Illus.). (J). (978-1-4287-4764-7(8)) Candlewick Pr.
Sandu, Anca. Churchill's Tale of Tails, 1 vol. Sandu, Anca, illus. (ENG., Illus.). 32p. (J). (gr. -1-3). 2016. pap. 7.95 (978-1-56145-782-3(5)) 2013. 16.95 (978-1-56145-738-0(8)) Peachtree Pubs.
Santillo, LuAnn. The Pig. Santillo, LuAnn, ed. 2003. (Half-Pint Kids Readers Ser.). (Illus.). 7p. (J). (gr. -1-1). pap. 1.00 (978-1-59256-064-6(4)) Half-Pint Kids, Inc.
Sarfatti, Esther, tr. from ENG. Los Tres Cerditos (The Three Little Pigs) Rius, Maria, illus. 2006. (Bilingual Tales Ser.). (SPA.). 24p. (J). (gr. -1-3). pap. 3.99 (978-0-439-77382-9(2), Scholastic en Espanol) Scholastic, Inc.
Sattler, Jennifer. Pig Kahuna. (Pig Kahuna Ser.). (ENG., Illus.). (J). (gr. -1-1). 2014. 30p. bds. 7.99 (978-1-61963-196-0(2),

P
Q
R

9781619631960) 2011. 32p. 16.99 *(978-1-59990-635-5(X),* 9781599906355) Bloomsbury Publishing USA. (Bloomsbury USA Childrens).
—Pig Kahuna Pirates! 2014. (Pig Kahuna Ser.). (ENG., Illus.). 32p. (J). (gr. -1-1). 16.99 *(978-1-61963-200-4(4),* 9781619632004, Bloomsbury USA Childrens) Bloomsbury Publishing USA.
—Who's That Pig? 2015. (Pig Kahuna Ser.). (ENG., Illus.). 32p. (J). (gr. -1-1). 16.99 *(978-1-61963-632-3(8),* 9781619636323, Bloomsbury USA Childrens) Bloomsbury Publishing USA.
Sattler, Jennifer Gordon, illus. Pig Kahuna Pirates! 2014. (J). *(978-1-61963-203-5(9))* Bloomsbury Pr.
Say Ahhh! Finley Pig. 2008. (Picture Books Ser.). 32p. *(978-1-4075-1841-1(0))* Parragon, Inc.
Scarry, Richard. Best Little Board Book Ever. Random House Staff, illus. 2013. (ENG.). 24p. (J). (— 1). bds. 4.99 *(978-0-449-81901-2(9),* Golden Bks.) Random Hse. Children's Bks.
—The Night Before the Night Before Christmas! Scarry, Richard, illus. 2014. (ENG., Illus.). 48p. (J). (gr. -1-2). 14.99 *(978-0-385-38804-7(7),* Golden Bks.) Random Hse. Children's Bks.
—Richard Scarry's Pig Will & Pig Won't. Scarry, Richard, illus. 2014. (Pictureback(R) Ser.). (ENG., Illus.). 24p. (J). (gr. -1-2). 4.99 *(978-0-385-38337-0(1),* Random Hse. Bks. for Young Readers) Random Hse. Children's Bks.
—Richard Scarry's Postman Pig & His Busy Neighbors. 2015. lib. bdg. 14.75 *(978-0-606-36401-0(3))* Turtleback Bks.
Schaefer, Elizabeth. Ballet Lesson. 2014. (Peppa Pig Ser.). (ENG.). 24p. (J). (gr. -1-k). pap. 3.99 *(978-0-545-74775-2(9))* Scholastic, Inc.
—Ballet Lesson. 2014. (Peppa Pig 8X8 Ser.). lib. bdg. 13.55 *(978-0-606-35866-8(8))* Turtleback Bks.
Scheunemann, Pam. El Bolígrafo del Cerdo, 1 vol. Nobens, C. A., illus. 2007. (Cuentos de Animales Ser.). (SPA & ENG.). 24p. (J). (gr. k-3). lib. bdg. 24.21 *(978-1-59928-659-4(9),* SandCastle) ABDO Publishing Co.
—Pig Pens, 1 vol. Nobens, Cheryl A., illus. 2006. (Animal Tales Ser.). (ENG.). 24p. (J). (gr. k-3). lib. bdg. 24.21 *(978-1-59679-959-2(5),* SandCastle) ABDO Publishing Co.
—Pig Pens. Nobens, C. A., illus. 2006. (Fact & Fiction Ser.). 24p. (J). pap. 48.42 *(978-1-59679-960-8(9))* ABDO Publishing Co.
Schindel, John. Busy Piggies. Holt, Steven, illus. Holt, Steven, photos by. 2006. (Busy Book Ser.). (ENG.). 20p. (J). (gr. k — 1). bds. 6.99 *(978-1-58246-169-4(4),* Tricycle Pr.) Random Hse. Children's Bks.
Scholastic. Fun at the Fair: a Sticker Storybook (Peppa Pig) Eone, illus. 2016. (Peppa Pig Ser.). (ENG.). 24p. (J). (gr. -1-k). pap. 7.99 *(978-1-338-03281-9(X))* Scholastic, Inc.
Scholastic. Peppa's First Colors (Peppa Pig) Eone, illus. 2017. (Peppa Pig Ser.). (ENG.). 10p. (J). (gr. -1-k). bds. 7.99 ***(978-1-338-18257-6(9))*** Scholastic, Inc.
Scholastic Editors. Bedtime for Peppa. 2015. (Peppa Pig 8X8 Ser.). (Illus.). (J). lib. bdg. 13.55 *(978-0-606-37768-3(9))* Turtleback Bks.
—George Catches a Cold. 2017. (Peppa Pig 8X8 Ser.). lib. bdg. 13.55 ***(978-0-606-39735-3(3))*** Turtleback Bks.
Scholastic Editors. Peppa's Easter Egg Hunt. 2015. (Peppa Pig 8X8 Ser.). lib. bdg. 13.55 *(978-0-606-38112-3(0))* Turtleback Bks.
Scholastic, Inc. Staff. Dentist Trip. 2015. (Peppa Pig 8X8 Ser.). (ENG.). 24p. (J). (gr. -1-k). lib. bdg. 14.75 *(978-0-606-38113-0(9))* Turtleback Bks.
—Dentist Trip (Peppa Pig) 2015. (Peppa Pig Ser.). (ENG.). 24p. (J). (gr. -1-k). 4.99 *(978-0-545-89146-2(9))* Scholastic, Inc.
—Good Night, Peppa (Peppa Pig) 2015. (Peppa Pig Ser.). (ENG., Illus.). 16p. (J). (gr. -1-k). bds. 7.99 *(978-0-545-88132-6(3))* Scholastic, Inc.
—My Mommy. 2014. (Peppa Pig Ser.). (ENG.). 16p. (J). (gr. -1-k). bds. 7.99 *(978-0-545-46804-6(3))* Scholastic, Inc.
—Peppa's Chalk ABCs. 2015. (Peppa Pig Ser.). (ENG.). 16p. (J). (gr. -1-k). bds. 10.99 *(978-0-545-82111-7(8))* Scholastic, Inc.
—Peppa's Easter Egg Hunt (Peppa Pig) Eone, illus. 2015. (Peppa Pig Ser.). (ENG.). 24p. (J). (gr. -1-k). 3.99 *(978-0-545-88130-2(7))* Scholastic, Inc.
—Peppa's First Pet. 2015. (Peppa Pig Ser.). (ENG.). 16p. (J). (gr. -1-k). bds. 7.99 *(978-0-545-88127-2(7))* Scholastic, Inc.
—Peppa's First Sleepover. Eone, François René, illus. 2014. (Peppa Pig Ser.). (ENG.). 24p. (J). (gr. -1-k). pap. 3.99 *(978-0-545-69093-5(5))* Scholastic, Inc.
—Peppa's Windy Fall Day. Scholastic, Inc. Staff, illus. 2015. (Peppa Pig Ser.). (ENG., Illus.). 24p. (J). (gr. -1-k). 3.99 *(978-0-545-84818-3(0))* Scholastic, Inc.
—Peppa's Windy Fall Day. 2015. (Peppa Pig 8X8 Ser.). (Illus.). (J). lib. bdg. 13.55 *(978-0-606-37088-2(9))* Turtleback Bks.
—The Tooth Fairy. 2014. (Peppa Pig Ser.). (ENG.). 24p. (J). (gr. -1-k). pap. 3.99 *(978-0-545-46806-0(X))* Scholastic, Inc.
—The Tooth Fairy. 2014. (Peppa Pig 8X8 Ser.). lib. bdg. 13.55 *(978-0-606-35415-8(8))* Turtleback Bks.
Scholastic, Inc. Staff, contrib. by. Class Trip. 2013. (Peppa Pig Ser.). (ENG., Illus.). 24p. (J). (gr. -1-k). pap. 3.99 *(978-0-545-52402-5(4))* Scholastic, Inc.
—Fun with Friends. 2013. (Peppa Pig Ser.). (ENG.). 16p. (J). (gr. -1-k). 6.99 *(978-0-545-49861-6(9))* Scholastic, Inc.
—Peppa's Christmas Wish. 2013. (Peppa Pig Ser.). (ENG.). 24p. (J). (gr. -1-k). 4.99 *(978-0-545-56511-0(1))* Scholastic, Inc.
—Peppa's Storytime Box. 2016. (Peppa Pig Ser.). (ENG.). (J). (gr. -1-k). pap. 10.99 *(978-0-545-92544-0(4))* Scholastic, Inc.
—The Story of Peppa Pig. 2013. (Peppa Pig Ser.). (ENG.). 32p. (J). (gr. -1-k). 8.99 *(978-0-545-46805-3(1))* Scholastic, Inc.
Scholastic, Inc. Staff, ed. Class Trip. 2013. (Peppa Pig 8X8 Ser.). lib. bdg. 13.55 *(978-0-606-32021-4(0),* Turtleback) Turtleback Bks.
Scholastic, Inc. Staff & Ladybird Books Staff. Peppa's First Sleepover. 2014. (Peppa Pig 8X8 Ser.). lib. bdg. 13.55 *(978-0-606-36374-7(2))* Turtleback Bks.
Schwartz, Betty Ann & Seresin, Lynn. Run, Run Piglet. Ng, Neiko, illus. 2015. (Follow-Along Book Ser.). (ENG.). 10p. (J). (gr. -1 — 1). bds. 9.99 *(978-1-4521-2467-4(1))* Chronicle Bks. LLC.
Schwartz, Corey Rosen. The Three Ninja Pigs. Santat, Dan, illus. 2012. (ENG.). 40p. (J). (gr. k-3). 16.99 *(978-0-399-25514-4(1),* G.P. Putnam's Sons Books for Young Readers) Penguin Young Readers Group.
Scieszka, Jon. ¡La Verdadera Historia de los Tres Cerditos! 2009. (ENG & SPA.). 64p. (J). (gr. k-3). pap. 8.99 *(978-0-14-241447-7(6),* Puffin Books) Penguin Young Readers Group.
Seal, Julia. Three Little Pigs. 2013. (Classic Fairy Tale Pop-Ups Ser.). (ENG.). 12p. (J). (gr. -1-1). 12.99 *(978-0-7641-6599-3(2))* Barron's Educational Series, Inc.
Sebring, Ruthie. Itty's Guinea Pig. 2009. 24p. pap. 24.95 *(978-1-61582-555-4(X))* America Star Bks.
Seibert, Patricia. The Three Little Pigs, Grades Pk - 3. 2005. (Keepsake Stories Ser.).Tr. of Los Tres Cerditos. (SPA & ENG., Illus.). 32p. (gr. -1-3). pap. 3.99 *(978-0-7696-3818-8(X),* Brighter Child) Carson-Dellosa Publishing, LLC.
Sendak, Maurice. Bumble-Ardy. Sendak, Maurice, illus. 2011. (ENG., Illus.). 40p. (J). 17.95 *(978-0-06-205198-1(9))* HarperCollins Pubs.
Sharratt, Nick & Tucker, Stephen. The Three Little Pigs, 2 vols. Sharratt, Nick, illus. 2016. (Lift-The-Flap Fairy Tales Ser.). (ENG., Illus.). 24p. (J). (gr. -1-k). bds. 11.99 *(978-1-5098-1713-9(1))* Pan Macmillan GBR. Dist: Independent Pubs. Group.
Shaw, Natalie. A Guide to Being a Big Sister. 2014. (Olivia 8x8 Ser.). lib. bdg. 16.00 *(978-0-606-35761-6(0))* Turtleback Bks.
—A Guide to Being a Friend. 2014. (Olivia 8x8 Ser.). lib. bdg. 16.00 *(978-0-606-36117-0(0))* Turtleback Bks.
—A Guide to Life. Spaziante, Patrick, illus. 2015. (Olivia TV Tie-In Ser.). (ENG.). 16p. (J). (gr. -1-2). 5.99 *(978-1-4814-2788-3(1),* Simon Spotlight) Simon Spotlight.
—I Can Do Anything! 2016. (Illus.). (J). *(978-1-5182-0411-1(2))* Simon & Schuster Children's Publishing.
—I Can Do Anything! 2016. (Olivia 8x8 Ser.). lib. bdg. 13.55 *(978-0-606-38242-7(9))* Turtleback Bks.
—Olivia & the Perfect Valentine. 2013. (Olivia 8x8 Ser.). lib. bdg. 14.75 *(978-0-606-35200-0(7))* Turtleback Bks.
—A Special Day with Dad. Johnson, Shane L., illus. 2014. (Olivia TV Tie-In Ser.). (ENG.). 24p. (J). (gr. -1-2). pap. 4.99 *(978-1-4424-9751-1(3),* Simon Spotlight) Simon Spotlight.
Shepherd, Jodie. Olivia & the Haunted Hotel. Spaziante, Patrick, illus. 2010. (Olivia TV Tie-In Ser.). (ENG.). 24p. (J). (gr. -1-2). pap. 4.99 *(978-1-4424-0182-2(6),* Simon Spotlight) Simon Spotlight.
—Olivia & the Haunted Hotel. 2010. (Olivia 8x8 Ser.). lib. bdg. 14.75 *(978-0-606-26573-7(2),* Turtleback) Turtleback Bks.
Simpson, Patrica Ann. Flick the little Runt. 2006. (J). lib. bdg. *(978-0-9779662-6-4(7))* Creative Bk. Pubs.
Sinha, Rhea. Latte's Vacation. Sinha, Rhea, illus. 2011. (Illus.). 20p. pap. 7.50 *(978-1-61170-045-9(0))* Robertson Publishing.
Sisco, Joann Ellen. Priscilla, the Graceful Greased Pig: 11. 2013. 80p. pap. 13.95 *(978-1-4772-7092-9(2))* AuthorHouse.
Sleator, William. Interstellar Pig. (Interstellar Pig Ser.: Bk. 1). 196p. (J). (gr. 4-6). pap. 4.99 *(978-0-8072-1381-0(0),* Listening Library) Random Hse. Audio Publishing Group.
Smart Kidz, creator. This Little Piggy Went to Market. 2013. (Sing N Play Songs Ser.). (ENG., Illus.). (gr. -1). bds. 12.99 *(978-1-891100-09-3(2),* Smart Kids) Penton Overseas, Inc.
Smith, Dee. The Pigs of Pineapple Beach Anthology. 2009. (Illus.). 80p. pap. 15.00 *(978-1-59858-961-0(X))* Dog Ear Publishing, LLC.
Smith, Elwood. I'm Not a Pig in Underpants. Smith, Elwood, illus. 2013. (ENG., Illus.). 40p. (J). (gr. 1-3). 18.99 *(978-1-56846-229-5(8),* Creative Editions) Creative Co., The.
Smith, Jeffrey B. Stubby. 2006. 15p. 8.28 *(978-1-4116-8215-3(7))* Lulu Pr., Inc.
Smith, John C. Popee the Purple Pig-a-Saurus. 2010. 40p. pap. 16.99 *(978-1-4490-9285-6(3))* AuthorHouse.
Smith, Lynda Faye. The Revenge of the Big Bad Wolf. 2012. pap. 9.95 *(978-0-7414-6529-0(9))* Infinity Publishing.
Snyder, Laurel. Baxter, the Pig Who Wanted to Be Kosher. Goldin, David, illus. 2010. (ENG.). 32p. (J). (gr. -1-2). 15.99 *(978-1-58246-315-6(8),* Tricycle Pr.) Random Hse. Children's Bks.
—Baxter, the Pig Who Wanted to Be Kosher. 2010. (J). pap. 2.46 *(978-1-58246-373-5(5),* Tricycle Pr.) Ten Speed Pr.
Sollinger, Emily. OLIVIA Plants a Garden. Osterhold, Jared, illus. 2011. (Olivia TV Tie-In Ser.). (ENG.). 24p. (J). (gr. -1-1). 16.99 *(978-1-4424-2011-3(1),* Simon Spotlight) Simon Spotlight.
Solomon, Philippa. Settle down for Storytime. 2009. (Illus.). 64p. pap. 23.49 *(978-1-4389-6032-6(8))* AuthorHouse.
Sommer, Carl. Three Little Pigs. Budwine, Greg, illus. 2014. (J). pap. *(978-1-57537-968-5(6))* Advance Publishing, Inc.
—Three Little Pigs Read-Along. 2003. (Another Sommer-Time Story Ser.). (Illus.). 48p. (J). lib. bdg. 23.95 incl. audio *(978-1-57537-761-2(6))* Advance Publishing, Inc.
—Three Little Pigs(Los Tres Cerditos) Budwine, Greg & Vignolo, Enrique, illus. 2009. (Another Sommer-Time Story Bilingual Ser.). (SPA & ENG.). 48p. (J). lib. bdg. 16.95 *(978-1-57537-168-9(5))* Advance Publishing, Inc.
Soo, Kean, illus. The Baker's Run. 2015. (March Grand Prix Ser.). (ENG.). 48p. (gr. 1-3). lib. bdg. 33.32 *(978-1-4342-9640-5(7))* Capstone Young Readers of Coughlan Cos.
—The Great Desert Rally. 2015. (March Grand Prix Ser.). (ENG.). 48p. (gr. 1-3). lib. bdg. 33.32 *(978-1-4342-9641-2(5))* Capstone Young Readers of Coughlan Cos.
Spaziante, Patrick, illus. Olivia Acts Out. 2009. (Olivia TV Tie-In Ser.). (ENG.). 24p. (J). (gr. -1-1). 16.99 *(978-1-4169-8571-6(9),* Simon Spotlight) Simon Spotlight.
—OLIVIA & Her Alien Brother. 2014. (Olivia TV Tie-In Ser.). (ENG.). 24p. (J). (gr. -1-2). pap. 3.99 *(978-1-4424-9749-8(1),* Simon Spotlight) Simon Spotlight.
—OLIVIA & the Fashion Show. 2011. (Olivia TV Tie-In Ser.). (ENG.). 16p. (J). (gr. -1-1). pap. 5.99 *(978-1-4424-2026-1(6),* Simon Spotlight) Simon Spotlight.
—OLIVIA Learns to Surf. 2010. (Olivia TV Tie-In Ser.). (ENG.). 12p. (J). (gr. -1-1). bds. 6.99 *(978-1-4424-0330-7(6),* Simon Spotlight) Simon Spotlight.
—OLIVIA Sells Cookies. 2013. (Olivia TV Tie-In Ser.). (ENG.). 24p. (J). (gr. -1-2). pap. 3.99 *(978-1-4424-5965-6(4),* Simon Spotlight) Simon Spotlight.
—OLIVIA the Superhero. 2016. (Olivia TV Tie-In Ser.). (ENG.). 24p. (J). (gr. -1-2). pap. 3.99 *(978-1-4814-6055-2(2),* Simon Spotlight) Simon Spotlight.
Spelman, Cornelia Maude. When I Feel Good about Myself. Parkinson, Kathy, illus. 2003. (Way I Feel Bks.). (ENG.). 24p. (J). (gr. -1-3). pap. 6.99 *(978-0-8075-8901-4(2))* Whitman, Albert & Co.
—When I Miss You. Parkinson, Kathy, illus. 2004. (Way I Feel Bks.). (ENG.). 24p. (J). (gr. -1-3). pap. 6.99 *(978-0-8075-8903-8(9))* Whitman, Albert & Co.
Sperling, Thomas, illus. The Three Little Pigs. 2005. (J). *(978-0-7664-1051-0(X))* Abrams, Inc.
Spratt, R. A. The Adventures of Nanny Piggins. Santat, Dan, illus. 2012. (Nanny Piggins Ser.: 1). (ENG.). 272p. (J). (gr. 3-7). pap. 7.00 *(978-0-316-06818-5(7))* Little, Brown Bks. for Young Readers.
—Nanny Piggins & the Runaway Lion. 2014. (Nanny Piggins Ser.: 3). (ENG., Illus.). 320p. (J). (gr. 3-7). 17.00 *(978-0-316-25453-3(3))* Little, Brown Bks. for Young Readers.
—Nanny Piggins & the Wicked Plan. 2013. (Nanny Piggins Ser.: 2). (ENG.). 320p. (J). (gr. 3-7). pap. 7.99 *(978-0-316-19922-3(2))* Little, Brown Bks. for Young Readers.
Stanek, Linda. The Pig & Miss Prudence, 1 vol. Castillo, Lauren, illus. 2008. (ENG.). 32p. (J). (gr. -1-3). 15.95 *(978-1-59572-125-9(8))* Star Bright Bks., Inc.
Stanton, Elizabeth Rose. Peddles. Stanton, Elizabeth Rose, illus. 2016. (ENG., Illus.). 40p. (J). (gr. -1-3). 17.99 *(978-1-4814-1691-7(X),* Simon & Schuster Bks. For Young Readers) Simon & Schuster Bks. For Young Readers.
Steers, Billy. Tractor Mac Farmers' Market. 2015. (Tractor Mac Ser.). (ENG., Illus.). 32p. (J). (gr. -1-k). 8.99 *(978-0-374-30107-1(7),* 9780374301071, Farrar, Straus & Giroux (BYR)) Farrar, Straus & Giroux.
—Tractor Mac Farmers Market: Farmer's Market. Steers, Billy, illus. 2009. (ENG., Illus.). (J). 7.95 *(978-0-9826870-1-7(X))* Tractor Mac Inc.
—Tractor Mac Worth the Wait. 2017. (Tractor Mac Ser.). (ENG., Illus.). 32p. (J). 8.99 *(978-0-374-30115-6(8),* 9780374301156, Farrar, Straus & Giroux (BYR)) Farrar, Straus & Giroux.
Steig, William. The Amazing Bone. Steig, William, illus. 2011. (ENG., Illus.). 32p. (J). (gr. k-3). pap. 7.99 *(978-0-312-56421-6(X),* 9780312564216) Square Fish.
—Farmer Palmer's Wagon Ride. Steig, William, illus. 2014. (ENG., Illus.). 32p. (J). (gr. -1-3). 6.99 *(978-1-250-05791-4(4),* 9781250057914) Square Fish.
—Roland the Minstrel Pig. 2016. (ENG., Illus.). 32p. (J). (gr. -1-3). 18.99 *(978-0-374-30088-3(7),* 9780374300883, Farrar, Straus & Giroux (BYR)) Farrar, Straus & Giroux.
Stein, Erin K. Peppa Pig: Family Fun Reusable Sticker Book. 2007. (Peppa Pig Ser.). 12p. (J). pap. 6.99 *(978-0-06-117373-8(8),* Harper Entertainment) HarperCollins Pubs.
—Peppa Pig: Paint Book. 2007. (Peppa Pig Ser.). 32p. (J). pap. 4.99 *(978-0-06-117376-9(2),* Harper Entertainment) HarperCollins Pubs.
Steps To Literacy Staff, compiled by. Mercy Watson Collection: Class Pack (4 Titles, 6 Each) 2010. (ENG., Illus.). (J). pap. 136.75 *(978-1-60923-560-4(6))* Steps To Literacy, LLC.
—Mercy Watson Collection: Variety Pack (4 Titles, 1 Each) 2010. (ENG., Illus.). (J). pap. 23.95 *(978-1-60923-559-8(2))* Steps To Literacy, LLC.
Stolz, Mary. Emmett's Birthday Pig. 32p. (J). (gr. -1-2). Date not set. pap. 5.99 *(978-0-06-443633-5(0))* 2003. (Illus.). 16.89 *(978-0-06-028747-4(0))* HarperCollins Pubs.
Storad, Conrad J. Don't Ever Cross That Road! An Armadillo Story. Jensen, Nathaniel P., illus. 2006. (Sonoran Desert Tails Ser.). 32p. (J). (gr. k-4). 15.95 *(978-1-891795-08-4(2))* RGU Group, The.
Surplice, Holly. Guinea Pig Party. Surplice, Holly, illus. 2012. (ENG., Illus.). 32p. (J). (gr. -1-k). 14.99 *(978-0-7636-6269-1(0),* Nosy Crow) Candlewick Pr.
Swartz, Patricia. Pig-A-Poo Moves to the Zoo. 2009. (Illus.). 28p. pap. 14.99 *(978-1-4490-4616-3(9))* AuthorHouse.
Tait, Elena. The Twisted Fairy Tale. 2009. 36p. pap. 16.99 *(978-1-4389-2774-9(6))* AuthorHouse.
Teague, Mark. Pigsty. 2007. (ENG., Illus.). (J). (gr. -1-3). 9.95 *(978-0-545-00361-2(X))* Scholastic, Inc.
—The Three Little Pigs & the Somewhat Bad Wolf. 2013. (ENG., Illus.). 48p. (J). (gr. -1-k). 17.99 *(978-0-439-91501-4(5),* Orchard Bks.) Scholastic, Inc.
Teague, Mark. The Three Little Pigs & the Somewhat Bad Wolf (a StoryPlay Book) 2017. (StoryPlay Ser.). (ENG.). 48p. (J). (gr. -1-k). 5.99 ***(978-1-338-15774-1(4),*** Cartwheel Bks.) Scholastic, Inc.
Ted in a Red Bed Kid Kit. 2004. (Kid Kits Ser.). (Illus.). 10p. (J). bds. 9.95 *(978-1-58086-404-6(X))* EDC Publishing.
Testa, Maggie. Olivia & Her Alien Brother. 2014. (Olivia 8x8 Ser.). lib. bdg. 13.55 *(978-0-606-35199-7(X))* Turtleback Bks.
—Olivia & the Rain Dance. 2012. (Olivia Ready-To-Read Level 1 Ser.). lib. bdg. 13.55 *(978-0-606-23688-1(0),* Turtleback) Turtleback Bks.
—OLIVIA Loves Halloween. Osterhold, Jared, illus. 2014. (Olivia TV Tie-In Ser.). (ENG.). 24p. (J). (gr. -1-1). pap. 3.99 *(978-1-4814-0462-4(8),* Simon Spotlight) Simon Spotlight.
Thomas, Jan. Pumpkin Trouble. Thomas, Jan, illus. 2011. (ENG., Illus.). 40p. (J). (gr. -1-3). 9.99 *(978-0-06-169284-0(0))* HarperCollins Pubs.
Thomas Nelson. Three Little Pigs. 2015. (ENG., Illus.). 12p. (gr. -1). bds. *(978-1-78393-500-0(6))* Make Believe Ideas.
Thompson, Carol. I Like You the Best. Thompson, Carol, illus. 2011. (ENG., Illus.). 32p. (J). (gr. -1-1). 16.95 *(978-0-8234-2341-5(7))* Holiday Hse., Inc.
Thompson, Kate. I'm Just a Little Pig. Reasoner, Charles, illus. 2014. (ENG.). 12p. (gr. -1). *(978-1-78244-590-6(0))* Top That! Publishing PLC.
—I'm Just a Little Pig. Green, Barry, illus. 2017. (Googley-Eye Bks.). (ENG.). 12p. (J). (gr. -1-k). bds. 7.99 *(978-1-78445-871-3(6))* Top That! Publishing PLC GBR. Dist: Independent Pubs. Group.
Three Little Pigs. 2005. (J). bds. 3.99 *(978-1-933200-13-2(8))* Family Bks. at Home.
Three Little Pigs. 2004. (Treasure Tree Ser.). (Illus.). 32p. (J). *(978-0-7166-1602-3(5))* World Bk., Inc.
The Three Little Pigs. (Read-Along Ser.). (J). 7.99 incl. audio *(978-1-55723-015-7(3))* Walt Disney Records.
The Three Little Pigs: Lap Book. (Pebble Soup Explorations Ser.). 16p. (gr. -1-18). 21.00 *(978-0-7578-2111-0(1))* Rigby Education.
The Three Little Pigs: Small Book. (Pebble Soup Explorations Ser.). 16p. (gr. -1-18). 5.00 *(978-0-7578-2112-7(X))* Rigby Education.
Thydell, Johanna & Martens, Helle. There's a Pig in My Class! Ramel, Charlotte, illus. 2014. (ENG.). 32p. (J). (gr. -1-3). 16.95 *(978-0-8234-3168-7(1))* Holiday Hse., Inc.
Tiger Tales, ed. Three Little Pigs. Jatkowska, Ag, illus. 2016. (My First Fairy Tales Ser.). (ENG.). 32p. (J). (gr. -1-2). pap. 7.99 *(978-1-58925-479-4(1))* Tiger Tales.
Timmers, Leo. Oops! Timmers, Leo, illus. 2011. (ENG., Illus.). 32p. (J). (gr. k — 1). 15.95 *(978-1-60537-105-4(X))* Cobblestone Publishing Co.
Toms, Kate. Funny Faces Moo-Riel Cow. 2006. (Funny Faces (Make Believe Ideas) Ser.). (Illus.). 4p. (gr. -1). *(978-1-84610-288-2(X))* Make Believe Ideas.
Torgrimsen, Reidun. Timmy's Christmas, a Very Special Pig from Sugar Valley & His Best Friend. 2012. 30p. 24.95 *(978-1-62709-149-7(1))* America Star Bks.
Townsend, Amber C. Once upon a Time. 2007. (J). 7.95 *(978-0-9796978-6-9(7))* G Publishing LLC.
Los tres Cerditos: Lap Book. (Pebble Soup Exploraciones Ser.). (SPA.). 16p. (gr. -1-18). 21.00 *(978-0-7578-1674-1(6))* Rigby Education.
Trivizas, Eugene. The Three Little Wolves & the Big Bad Pig. Oxenbury, Helen, illus. 2004. (ENG.). 16p. (J). 24.95 *(978-1-4052-0669-3(1))* Egmont Bks., Ltd. GBR. Dist: Trafalgar Square Publishing.
—The Three Little Wolves & the Big Bad Pig: A Pop-up Storybook. Oxenbury, Helen, illus. 2006. 16p. (J). (gr. k-4). reprint ed. 27.00 *(978-0-7567-9913-7(9))* DIANE Publishing Co.
—Los Tres Lobitos y el Cochino Feroz. Oxenbury, Helen, illus. 2003. (SPA.). 32p. (J). (gr. k-3). pap. 12.99 *(978-980-257-246-5(2),* EK1366) Ekare, Ediciones VEN. Dist: Kane Miller, Lectorum Pubns., Inc.
Les Trois Petits Cochons.Tr. of Three Little Pigs. (FRE.). 48p. (J). pap. 12.95 incl. audio compact disk *(978-2-89558-053-9(7))* Coffragants CAN. Dist: Penton Overseas, Inc.
Les Trois Petits Cochons. (Musicontes Ser.).Tr. of Three Little Pigs. (FRE.). (J). 24.95 incl. audio *(978-2-09-230469-3(0))* Nathan, Fernand FRA. Dist: Distribooks, Inc.
Turner, Daniel. Cinnamon the Adventurous Guinea Pig Goes to Devil's Island. Skinner, Gayle, illus. 2013. (ENG.). 48p. (J). pap. 10.95 *(978-1-4787-1753-9(X))* Outskirts Pr., Inc.
Two naughty Piglets. 2006. (J). per. 3.99 *(978-1-934004-17-3(0))* Byeway Bks.
Twohy, Mike. Poindexter Makes a Friend. Twohy, Mike, illus. 2011. (ENG., Illus.). 32p. (J). (gr. -1-3). 15.99 *(978-1-4424-0965-1(7),* Simon & Schuster/Paula Wiseman Bks.) Simon & Schuster/Paula Wiseman Bks.
Tyler, Jenny. Big Pig on a Dig. Cartwright, Stephen, illus. 2004. (Easy Words to Read Ser.). (ENG.). 1p. (J). (gr. 1-18). pap. 6.99 *(978-0-7460-3021-9(5))* EDC Publishing.
U. S. National Geographic Society Staff. The Great Cheese Chase. 2008. (Toot & Puddle Ser.). (ENG., Illus.). 24p. (J). (gr. -1-2). lib. bdg. 11.90 *(978-1-4263-0371-5(8),* National Geographic Children's Bks.) National Geographic Society.
—How Does Your Garden Grow? 2009. (Toot & Puddle Ser.). (ENG., Illus.). 24p. (J). (gr. -1-2). pap. 3.99 *(978-1-4263-0482-8(X),* National Geographic Children's Bks.) National Geographic Society.
—The Mystery of the Disappearing Swing. 2008. (Toot & Puddle Ser.). (ENG., Illus.). 24p. (J). (gr. -1-2). pap. 3.99 *(978-1-4263-0224-4(X));* lib. bdg. 11.90 *(978-1-4263-0372-2(6))* National Geographic Society. (National Geographic Children's Bks.).
Ungerer, Tomi. Christmas Eve at the Mellops' 2011. (ENG., Illus.). 32p. (gr. -1-2). 12.95 *(978-0-7148-6250-7(9))* Phaidon Pr., Inc.
Usera, Abe. The Pigs & Friends. 2012. 52p. pap. 21.99 *(978-1-4685-6152-4(9))* AuthorHouse.
Uwe, Timm. Rennschwein Rudi Rüssel. (GER.). pap. 16.95 *(978-3-423-70285-0(0))* Deutscher Taschenbuch Verlag GmbH & Co KG DEU. Dist: Distribooks, Inc.
Vail, Rachel. Piggy Bunny. Tankard, Jeremy, illus. 2012. (ENG.). 32p. (J). (gr. -1-1). 14.99 *(978-0-312-64988-3(6),* 9780312649883) Feiwel & Friends.
van Genechten, Guido. Alex & the Tart. 2005. (Von Hamm Family Ser.). (Illus.). 32p. (J). (gr. -1-2). 6.95 *(978-1-58925-393-0(3))* Tiger Tales.
Van Leeuwen, Jean. Amanda Pig & Her Big Brother Oliver. Schweninger, Ann, illus. (Oliver Pig Ser.). 56p. (J). (gr. k-2). pap. 3.99 *(978-0-8072-1341-4(1),* Listening Library) Random Hse. Audio Publishing Group.
—Amanda Pig & the Really Hot Day. Schweninger, Ann, illus. 2007. (Oliver & Amanda Ser.). (ENG.). 48p. (J). (gr. 1-3). pap. 3.99 *(978-0-14-240775-2(5),* Penguin Young Readers) Penguin Young Readers Group.
—Amanda Pig & the Really Hot Day. Schweninger, Ann, illus. 2007. (Oliver & Amanda Ser.). 47p. (J). (gr. -1-3). 11.65 *(978-0-7569-8152-5(2))* Perfection Learning Corp.
—Amanda Pig & the Wiggly Tooth. Schweninger, Ann, illus. 2009. (Oliver & Amanda Ser.). (ENG.). 48p. (J). (gr. 1-3). mass mkt. 3.99 *(978-0-14-241290-9(2),* Penguin Young Readers) Penguin Young Readers Group.
—Amanda Pig, First Grader. Schweninger, Ann, illus. 2007. (Oliver & Amanda Ser.). 40p. (J). *(978-1-4287-4781-4(8),* Dial) Penguin Publishing Group.
—Amanda Pig, First Grader. Schweninger, Ann, illus. 2009. (Oliver & Amanda Ser.). (ENG.). 48p. (J). (gr. 1-3). mass mkt. 3.99 *(978-0-14-241276-3(7),* Penguin Young Readers) Penguin Young Readers Group.
—Tales of Oliver Pig. Schweninger, Ann, illus. (Oliver Pig Ser.). 64p. (J). (gr. k-2). pap. 3.99 *(978-0-8072-1334-6(9),* Listening Library) Random Hse. Audio Publishing Group.
Vasquez, Elisa Irene. My Little Piggy: A Bilingual English-Spanish Children's Book. 2010. 28p. 14.95 *(978-1-4490-8716-6(7))* AuthorHouse.
Verville, Claudia. Piggy with the Curly Tail. 2013. 26p. pap. 14.50 *(978-1-4817-1270-5(5))* AuthorHouse.

Vidal, Séverine. Mega Pig. Barroux, Stephane, illus. 2015. (Mega Hero Bks.). (ENG.). 28p. (J). (gr. k-2). 12.95 (978-1-77085-636-3(6), 9781770856363); pap. 6.95 (978-1-77085-652-3(8), 9781770856523) Firefly Bks., Ltd.
Virjan, Emma J. What This Story Needs Is a Bang & a Clang. Virjan, Emma J., illus. 2017. (Pig in a Wig Book Ser.). (Illus.). 40p. (J). (gr. -1-3). 9.99 (978-0-06-241530-1(1)) HarperCollins Pubs.
Virjan, Emma J. What This Story Needs Is a Vroom & a Zoom. Virjan, Emma J., illus. 2017. (Pig in a Wig Book Ser.). (Illus.). 40p. (J). (gr. -1-3). 9.99 **(978-0-06-249431-3(7))** HarperCollins Pubs.
Vosloo, Isak. Kerneelsie Droom Groot. 2012. 32p. pap. 21.35 (978-1-4772-2329-1(0)) AuthorHouse.
Waddell, Martin. Captain Small Pig, 1 vol. Varley, Susan, illus. 2010. (ENG.). 32p. (J). (gr. -1-3). 15.95 (978-1-56145-519-5(9)) Peachtree Pubs.
—Captain Small Pig, 1 vol. Varley, Susan, illus. 2017. (ENG.). 32p. (J). (gr. -1-3). pap. 7.95 (978-1-56145-982-7(8)) Peachtree Pubs.
Walton, Rick. Pig Pigger Piggest. Holder, Jimmy, illus. 2003. (ENG.). 32p. (J). (gr. 1). reprint ed. pap. 6.99 (978-1-58685-318-1(X)) Gibbs Smith, Publisher.
Waterbury, Matthew. The Little Pig. Muro, Jenny, illus. 2013. 16p. pap. 24.95 (978-1-4512-2919-6(4)) America Star Bks.
Watt, Fiona. That's Not My Pig... Its Nose Is Too Fuzzy. Wells, Rachel, illus. 2014. (Usborne Touchy-Feely Board Bks.). (ENG.). 10p. (gr. -1). bds. 9.99 (978-0-7945-2666-5(7), Usborne) EDC Publishing.
Weatherly, Lee. Pigwitchery. Reed, Nathan, illus. 2008. (ENG.). 32p. (J). (978-1-4050-9234-0(3), Macmillan Children's Bks.) Pan Macmillan.
Weeks, Sarah. I'm a Pig. Berry, Holly, illus. 2005. 32p. (J). (gr. -1-2). lib. bdg. 16.89 (978-0-06-074344-4(1), Geringer, Laura Book) HarperCollins Pubs.
Weinberg, Jennifer Liberts. This Little Piggy (Disney Junior: Minnie's Bow-Toons) RH Disney Staff, illus. 2014. (Little Golden Book Ser.). (ENG.). 24p. (J). (-k). 3.99 (978-0-7364-3234-4(5), Golden/Disney) Random Hse. Children's Bks.
Weiss, Ellen & Friedman, Mel. Porky & Bess. Winborn, Marsha, illus. 2011. (Step into Reading Ser.). (ENG.). 48p. (J). (gr. 2-4). pap. 3.99 (978-0-375-86113-0(0), Random Hse. Bks. for Young Readers) Random Hse. Children's Bks.
Welling, Peter J. Michael le Soufflé & the April Fool, 1 vol. Welling, Peter J., illus. 2003. (ENG., Illus.). 32p. (J). (gr. k-3). 16.99 (978-1-58980-105-9(9)) Pelican Publishing Co., Inc.
Wells, Zachariah, et al. Anything but Hank! Orchard, Eric, illus. 2008. (ENG.). 50p. (J). (gr. k-3). 19.95 (978-1-897231-36-4(9)) Biblioasis CAN. Dist: Consortium Bk. Sales & Distribution.
Wesley, Valerie Wilson. Willimena & Mrs. Sweetly's Guinea Pig. 2005. (Illus.). (J). pap. (978-0-7868-1321-6(0)) Hyperion Bks. for Children.
Weston Woods Staff, creator. I Like Me! 2011. 38.75 (978-0-545-23378-1(X)); 18.95 (978-0-545-23376-7(3)); 29.95 (978-0-545-23373-6(9)) Weston Woods Studios, Inc.
—The Three Little Pigs. 2011. 18.95 (978-0-439-72901-7(7)); 38.75 (978-0-439-72902-4(5)) Weston Woods Studios, Inc.
—The True Story of the 3 Little Pigs. 2011. 38.75 (978-0-545-09460-3(7)) Weston Woods Studios, Inc.
Whatley, Bruce & Whatley. Wait! No Paint! Whatley, Bruce, illus. 2005. (ENG., Illus.). 32p. (J). (gr. -1-3). pap. 7.99 (978-0-06-443546-8(6)) HarperCollins Pubs.
Wheeler, Lisa. Invasion of the Pig Sisters. Ansley, Frank, illus. 2006. (Fitch & Chip Ser.: 4). (ENG.). 48p. (J). (gr. 1-3). 16.99 (978-0-689-84953-4(2)); pap. 3.99 (978-0-689-84958-9(3)) Simon Spotlight. (Simon Spotlight).
—New Pig in Town. Ansley, Frank, illus. 2005. 48p. (J). lib. bdg. 15.00 (978-1-59054-997-1(X)) Fitzgerald Bks.
—New Pig in Town. Ansley, Frank, illus. 2003. (Fitch & Chip Ser.: 1). (ENG.). 48p. (J). (gr. 1-3). 16.99 (978-0-689-84950-3(8), Atheneum/Richard Jackson Bks.) Simon & Schuster Children's Publishing.
—New Pig in Town. Ansley, Frank, illus. 2005. (Fitch & Chip Ser.: 1). (ENG.). 48p. (J). (gr. 1-3). pap. 3.99 (978-0-689-84955-8(9), Simon Spotlight) Simon Spotlight.
—When Pigs Fly. Ansley, Frank, illus. 2005. 48p. (J). lib. bdg. 15.00 (978-1-59054-996-4(1)) Fitzgerald Bks.
—When Pigs Fly. Ansley, Frank, illus. 2005. (Fitch & Chip Ser.). 48p. (gr. 1-3). 14.00 (978-0-7569-5472-7(X)) Perfection Learning Corp.
—When Pigs Fly. Ansley, Frank, illus. 2003. (Fitch & Chip Ser.: 2). (ENG.). 48p. (J). (gr. 1-3). 16.99 (978-0-689-84951-0(6), Atheneum/Richard Jackson Bks.) Simon & Schuster Children's Publishing.
—When Pigs Fly. Ansley, Frank, illus. 2005. (Fitch & Chip Ser.: 2). (ENG.). 48p. (J). (gr. 1-3). pap. 3.99 (978-0-689-84956-5(7), Simon Spotlight) Simon Spotlight.
—Who's Afraid of Granny Wolf? Ansley, Frank, illus. 2006. (Fitch & Chip Ser.: 3). (ENG.). 48p. (J). (gr. 1-3). pap. 3.99 (978-0-689-84957-2(5), Simon Spotlight) Simon Spotlight.
Wheiler, Robert. Wink's , Boo, & Who! 2012. 64p. pap. 13.49 (978-1-105-49858-9(1)) Lulu Pr., Inc.
White. Tela di Carlotta. pap. 13.95 (978-88-04-46241-5(8)) Mondadori ITA. Dist: Distribooks, Inc.
White, E. B. Charlotte's Web. Williams, Garth, illus. 2005. (Charming Classics). 192p. (J). pap. 7.99 (978-0-06-084594-0(5), HarperFestival) HarperCollins Pubs.
—Charlotte's Web. movie tie-in ed. 2006. (Charlotte's Web Ser.). (ENG., Illus.). 192p. (J). (gr. 4-7). per. 7.99 (978-0-06-112026-8(X)) HarperCollins Pubs.
—Charlotte's Web. Williams, Garth, illus. movie tie-in ed. 2006. (Charlotte's Web Ser.). (J). 192p. mass mkt. 7.99 (978-0-06-122874-2(5), Harper Trophy);Set. pap. 19.99 (978-0-06-121502-5(3)) HarperCollins Pubs.
—Charlotte's Web. Williams, Garth, illus. 2004. (CHI.). 158p. (YA). pap. (978-957-08-2568-8(5)) Linking Publishing Co., Ltd.
—Charlotte's Web. Williams, Garth, illus. 184p. (J). pap. 5.95 (978-0-8072-8305-9(3), Listening Library) Random Hse. Audio Publishing Group.
—Charlotte's Web. unabr. ed. 2004. 184p. (J). (gr. 3-7). pap. 36.00 incl. audio (978-0-8072-8304-2(5), YYA156SP, Listening Library) Random Hse. Audio Publishing Group.
—Charlotte's Web. 2012. (J). (gr. 3-6). 18.40 (978-0-8085-3772-4(5), Turtleback) Turtleback Bks.
—Wilbur's Adventure: A Charlotte's Web Picture Book. Kneen, Maggie, illus. 2008. (Charlotte's Web Ser.). 32p. (J). (gr. k-2). lib. bdg. 17.89 (978-0-06-078165-1(3)) HarperCollins Pubs.
White, E. B. & DiCamillo, Kate. Charlotte's Web. Williams, Garth, illus. (ENG.). 192p. (J). (gr. 3-7). 2012. 8.99 (978-0-06-112495-2(8)) 2012. 16.99 (978-0-06-026385-0(7)) 2012. pap. 8.99 (978-0-06-440055-8(7)) 2006. 16.99 (978-0-06-088261-7(1)) HarperCollins Pubs.
Whitfield, Willie. Big Pigpen Willie's Inheritance. 2006. (Illus.). 40p. (J). (gr. -1-3). pap. 12.95 (978-1-56167-958-4(5)) American Literary Pr.
Wiesner, David. Los Tres Cerditos. 2003.Tr. of Three Little Pigs. (SPA.). 40p. (J). (gr. k-2). 21.99 (978-84-261-3291-8(X)) Juventud, Editorial ESP. Dist: Lectorum Pubns., Inc.
Wild, Margaret. Old Pig. Brooks, Ron, illus. 2017. (ENG.). 32p. (J). (gr. -1-1). 17.99 **(978-1-76029-389-5(X))** Allen & Unwin AUS. Dist: Independent Pubs. Group.
—Piglet & Granny. King, Stephen Michael, illus. 2009. (ENG.). 32p. (J). (gr. -1-k). 15.95 (978-0-8109-4063-5(9), Abrams Bks. for Young Readers) Abrams, Inc.
—This Little Piggy Went Dancing. Niland, Deborah, illus. 2014. (ENG.). 24p. (J). (-k). 15.99 (978-1-74331-511-8(2)) Allen & Unwin AUS. Dist: Independent Pubs. Group.
Willems, Mo. A Big Guy Took My Ball! Willems, Mo, illus. 2013. (Elephant & Piggie Ser.). (ENG., Illus.). 64p. (J). (gr. 1-3). 9.99 (978-1-4231-7491-2(7)) Hyperion Bks. for Children.
—Can I Play Too? 2012. (Elephant & Piggie Bks.). (CHI & JPN.). (J). (gr. -1-3). pap. **(978-986-189-329-7(6))** Grimm Cultural Ent., Co., Ltd.
—Can I Play Too? Willems, Mo, illus. 2010. (Elephant & Piggie Book Ser.). (ENG., Illus.). 64p. (J). (gr. -1-k). 9.99 (978-1-4231-1991-3(6)) Hyperion Pr.
—An Elephant & Piggie Biggie! Willems, Mo, illus. 2017. (Elephant & Piggie Book Ser.). (ENG., Illus.). 320p. (J). (gr. 1-3). 16.99 **(978-1-4847-9967-3(4))** Hyperion Bks. for Children.
—Elephants Cannot Dance! 2012. (Elephant & Piggie Bks.). (CHI & ENG.). (J). pap. **(978-986-189-325-9(3))** Grimm Cultural Ent., Co., Ltd.
—Elephants Cannot Dance! Willems, Mo, illus. 2009. (Elephant & Piggie Book Ser.). (ENG., Illus.). 64p. (J). (gr. -1-k). 9.99 (978-1-4231-1410-9(8)) Hyperion Pr.
—Elephants Cannot Dance! 2011. (ENG & KOR.). (J). **(978-89-7184-930-9(4))** Pu-Reun-Sup Publishing Co., Ltd.
—¡Esperar No Es Fácil! Willems, Mo, illus. 2017. (Elephant & Piggie Book Ser.). (ENG & SPA., Illus.). 64p. (J). (gr. 1-3). 9.99 (978-1-4847-8698-7(X)) Hyperion Bks. for Children.
—Happy Pig Day! Willems, Mo, illus. 2011. (Elephant & Piggie Book Ser.). (ENG., Illus.). 64p. (J). (gr. -1-k). 9.99 (978-1-4231-4342-0(6)) Hyperion Pr.
—I Am Going! Willems, Mo, illus. 2010. (Elephant & Piggie Book Ser.). (ENG., Illus.). 64p. (J). (gr. -1-k). 9.99 (978-1-4231-1990-6(8)) Hyperion Pr.
—I Am Invited to a Party! Willems, Mo, illus. rev. ed. 2007. (Elephant & Piggie Book Ser.). (ENG., Illus.). 64p. (J). (gr. -1-k). 9.99 (978-1-4231-0687-6(3)) Hyperion Pr.
—I Broke My Trunk! Willems, Mo, illus. 2011. (Elephant & Piggie Book Ser.). (ENG., Illus.). 64p. (J). (gr. -1-k). 9.99 (978-1-4231-3309-4(9)) Hyperion Pr.
—I Love My New Toy! Willems, Mo, illus. 2008. (Elephant & Piggie Book Ser.). (ENG., Illus.). 64p. (J). (gr. -1-k). 9.99 (978-1-4231-0961-7(9)) Hyperion Pr.
—I Really Like Slop! Willems, Mo, illus. 2015. (Elephant & Piggie Book Ser.). (ENG., Illus.). 64p. (J). (gr. 1-3). 9.99 (978-1-4847-2262-6(0)) Hyperion Bks. for Children.
—I Will Surprise My Friend! Willems, Mo, illus. 2008. (Elephant & Piggie Book Ser.). (ENG., Illus.). 64p. (J). (gr. -1-k). 9.99 (978-1-4231-0962-4(7)) Hyperion Pr.
—I Will Take a Nap! Willems, Mo, illus. 2015. (Elephant & Piggie Ser.). (ENG., Illus.). 64p. (J). (gr. 1-3). 9.99 (978-1-4847-1630-4(2)) Hyperion Bks. for Children.
—I'm a Frog! Willems, Mo, illus. 2013. (Elephant & Piggie Ser.). (ENG., Illus.). 64p. (J). (gr. 1-3). 9.99 (978-1-4231-8305-1(3)) Hyperion Pr.
—Let's Go for a Drive! Willems, Mo, illus. 2012. (Elephant & Piggie Book Ser.). (ENG., Illus.). 64p. (J). (gr. -1-k). 9.99 (978-1-4231-6482-1(2)) Hyperion Pr.
—Listen to My Trumpet! Willems, Mo, illus. 2012. (Elephant & Piggie Book Ser.). (ENG., Illus.). 64p. (J). (gr. -1-k). 9.99 (978-1-4231-5404-4(5)) Hyperion Pr.
—My Friend Is Sad. Willems, Mo, illus. 2007. (Elephant & Piggie Book Ser.). (ENG., Illus.). 64p. (J). (gr. -1-k). 9.99 (978-1-4231-0297-7(5)) Hyperion Pr.
—Pigs Make Me Sneeze! Willems, Mo, illus. 2009. (Elephant & Piggie Book Ser.). (ENG., Illus.). 64p. (J). (gr. -1-k). 9.99 (978-1-4231-1411-6(6)) Hyperion Pr.
—Should I Share My Ice Cream? Willems, Mo, illus. 2011. (Elephant & Piggie Book Ser.). (ENG., Illus.). 64p. (J). (gr. -1-k). 9.99 (978-1-4231-4343-7(4)) Hyperion Pr.
—The Thank You Book. Willems, Mo, illus. 2016. (Elephant & Piggie Book Ser.). (ENG., Illus.). 64p. (J). (gr. 1-3). 9.99 (978-1-4231-7828-6(9)) Hyperion Bks. for Children.
—There Is a Bird on Your Head! Willems, Mo, illus. rev. ed. 2007. (Elephant & Piggie Book Ser.). (ENG., Illus.). 64p. (J). (gr. -1-k). 9.99 (978-1-4231-0686-9(5)) Hyperion Pr.
—¡Tienes un Pájaro en la Cabeza! Willems, Mo, illus. 2017. (Elephant & Piggie Book Ser.). (ENG & SPA., Illus.). 64p. (J). (gr. 1-3). 9.99 (978-1-4847-8697-0(1)) Hyperion Bks. for Children.
—Today I Will Fly! Willems, Mo, illus. 2007. (Elephant & Piggie Book Ser.). (ENG., Illus.). 64p. (J). (gr. -1-k). 9.99 (978-1-4231-0295-3(9)) Hyperion Pr.
—Waiting Is Not Easy! Willems, Mo, illus. 2014. (Elephant & Piggie Ser.). (ENG., Illus.). 64p. (J). (gr. 1-3). 9.99 (978-1-4231-9957-1(X)) Hyperion Bks. for Children.
—Watch Me Throw the Ball! Willems, Mo, illus. 2009. (Elephant & Piggie Book Ser.). (ENG., Illus.). 64p. (J). (gr. -1-k). 9.99 (978-1-4231-1348-5(9)) Hyperion Pr.
—We Are in a Book! Willems, Mo, illus. 2010. (Elephant & Piggie Book Ser.). (ENG., Illus.). 64p. (J). (gr. -1-k). 9.99 (978-1-4231-3308-7(0)) Hyperion Pr.
Willems, Mo & Campoy, F. Isabel. ¿Debo Compartir Mi Helado? Willems, Mo, illus. 2015. (Elephant & Piggie Book Ser.). (SPA., Illus.). 64p. (J). (gr. -1-k). 9.99 (978-1-4847-2291-6(4)) Disney Publishing Worldwide.
—¡Estamos en un Libro! Willems, Mo, illus. 2015. (Elephant & Piggie Book Ser.). (SPA., Illus.). 64p. (J). (gr. 1-3). 9.99 (978-1-4847-2288-6(4)) Hyperion Bks. for Children.
—¡Hoy Volaré! Willems, Mo, illus. 2015. (Elephant & Piggie Book Ser.). (SPA., Illus.). 64p. (J). (gr. 1-3). 9.99 (978-1-4847-2287-9(6)) Disney Publishing Worldwide.
—¡Un Tipo Grande Se Llevó Mi Pelota! Willems, Mo, illus. 2015. (Elephant & Piggie Book Ser.). (SPA., Illus.). 64p. (J). (gr. 1-3). 9.99 (978-1-4847-2285-5(X)) Disney Publishing Worldwide.
Williams, Becky. Good Night Little Piggy. Howarth, Daniel, illus. 2007. (Night Light Book Ser.). 10p. (gr. -1-k). bds. (978-1-84666-129-7(3), Tide Mill Pr.) Top That! Publishing PLC.
Williams, Billie A. Fourteen Is Too Many: The Survivors. 2013. 24p. pap. 24.95 (978-1-63004-179-3(3)) America Star Bks.
Williams, Mark. Hooty & Pig: The Missing Christmas Pudding. Garrett, Keith, illus. 2013. 24p. pap. (978-1-78132-133-1(7)) SilverWood Bks.
Williams, Rose. Tres Porculi. L and L Enterprises, ed. Este, James, illus. 2006. (LAT.). spiral bd. 18.00 (978-0-9760046-5-3(8)) L & L Enterprises.
Wilson, Karma. Hogwash! McMullan, Jim, illus. 2011. (ENG.). 40p. (J). (gr. -1-3). 17.99 (978-0-316-98840-7(5)) Little, Brown Bks. for Young Readers.
Winter, Milo, illus. The Three Little Pigs. 2008. (Shape Bks.). (ENG.). 16p. (J). (gr. -1-3). per. 9.95 (978-1-59583-265-8(3), 9781595832658, Green Tiger Pr.) Laughing Elephant.
Winthrop, Elizabeth. Dumpy la Rue. Lewin, Betsy, illus. rev. ed. 2004. (ENG.). 40p. (J). (gr. -1-3). reprint ed. pap. 8.99 (978-0-8050-7535-9(6), 9780805075359, Holt, Henry & Co. Bks. For Young Readers) Holt, Henry & Co.
Witkowski, Teri. Bunny & Piggy at the Beach. Ackley, Peggy Jo, illus. 2005. (J). (978-1-58485-961-1(X)) American Girl Publishing, Inc.
Wojtowycz, David. Let's Play, Dudley! Colors. 2003. (Dudley Ser.). (Illus.). (J). 3.95 (978-1-58925-667-5(0)) Tiger Tales.
Wolek, Guy, illus. OLIVIA Builds a Snowlady. 2011. (Olivia TV Tie-In Ser.). (ENG.). 24p. (J). (gr. -1-2). pap. 4.99 (978-1-4424-3286-4(1), Simon Spotlight) Simon Spotlight.
Wolfe, Jane. Messy Pig. Benham, Tors, illus. 2013. (ENG.). 8p. (J). (gr. -1-k). bds. 6.99 (978-1-84322-777-9(0), Armadillo) Anness Publishing GBR. Dist: National Bk. Network.
Wood, Audrey. Piggy Pie Po. Wood, Don, illus. (ENG.). (J). 2016. 30p. (— 1). bds. 7.99 (978-0-544-79113-6(4), HMH Books For Young Readers) 2010. 32p. (gr. -1-3). 17.99 (978-0-15-202494-9(8)) Houghton Mifflin Harcourt Publishing Co.
Wood, Audrey & Wood, Don. Piggies. 2016. (ENG., Illus.). 30p. (J). (— 1). bds. 7.99 (978-0-544-79114-5(2), HMH Books For Young Readers) Houghton Mifflin Harcourt Publishing Co.
Yamaguchi, Kristi. Dream Big, Little Pig! Bowers, Tim, illus. 2011. (ENG.). 32p. (J). (gr. -1-3). 16.99 (978-1-4022-5275-4(7), Sourcebooks Jabberwocky) Sourcebooks, Inc.
—It's a Big World, Little Pig! Bowers, Tim, illus. 2012. (ENG.). 32p. (J). (gr. k-3). 16.99 (978-1-4022-6644-7(8), Sourcebooks Jabberwocky) Sourcebooks, Inc.
Yonge, Charlotte M. The Stokesley Secret. 2005. 28.95 (978-1-4218-0319-7(4), 1st World Library - Literary Society) 1st World Publishing, Inc.
Young, Cynthia Anne. The Muddy Little Piggy's. 2011. 16p. pap. 24.95 (978-1-4560-8090-7(3)) America Star Bks.
Young, Polly G. Pokey Pig's Picnic. Raymond, Janet Y., illus. 2007. (J). pap. 15.00 (978-0-8059-7298-6(6)) Dorrance Publishing Co., Inc.

PIGS—POETRY

Wohnoutka, Mike, illus. This Little Piggy. 2005. (J). (978-1-58987-106-9(5)) Kindermusik International.

PIKAS

Bill, Tannis. Pika: Life in the Rocks. Jacobson, Jim, photos by. 2010. (ENG., Illus.). 32p. (J). (gr. k-2). 18.95 (978-1-59078-803-5(6)) Boyds Mills Pr.

PIKE, ZEBULON MONTGOMERY, 1779-1813

Magoon, Kekla. The Zebulon Pike Expedition, 1 vol. 2009. (Essential Events Set 3 Ser.). (ENG., Illus.). 112p. (J). (gr. 6-12). lib. bdg. 35.64 (978-1-60453-518-1(0)) ABDO Publishing Co.
Maynard, Charles W. Zebulon Pike: Soldier Explorer of the American Southwest. 2003. (Famous Explorers of the American West Ser.). (Illus.). 24p. (J). lib. bdg. 22.60 (978-0-8239-6286-0(5), PowerKids Pr.) Rosen Publishing Group, Inc., The.
—Zebulon Pike: Soldier-Explorer of the American Southwest. 2009. (Famous Explorers of the American West Ser.). 24p. (gr. 3-4). 42.50 (978-1-61512-506-7(X), PowerKids Pr.) Rosen Publishing Group, Inc., The.
Sanford, William R. & Green, Carl R. Zebulon Pike: Courageous Rocky Mountain Explorer. 2012. (Courageous Heroes of the American West Ser.). (Illus.). 48p. (J). (gr. 5-18). lib. bdg. 22.60 (978-0-7660-4012-0(7)) Enslow Pubs., Inc.
Walsh, Steve. Zebulon Montgomery Pike: Explorer & Military Officer. 2011. (ENG & SPA., Illus.). 54p. (J). pap. 8.95 (978-0-86541-123-4(9)) Filter Pr., LLC.

PILGRIM FATHERS

see Pilgrims (New Plymouth Colony)

PILGRIMS (NEW PLYMOUTH COLONY)

Allen, Nancy Kelly. My Life As an Early Settler. 2012. (ENG.). 24p. (gr. k-2). pap. 8.95 (978-1-61810-273-7(7)) Rourke Educational Media.
Arenstam, Peter, et al. MayFlower 1620: A New Look at a Pilgrim Voyage. 2004. (Illus.). 47p. (J). (gr. k-4). 18.00 (978-0-7567-7967-2(7)) DIANE Publishing Co.
Barber, Nicola. Who Journeyed on the Mayflower?, 1 vol. HL Studios Staff, illus. 2014. (Primary Source Detectives Ser.). (ENG.). 64p. (gr. 7-8). lib. bdg. 35.99 (978-1-4329-9602-4(9)) Heinemann-Raintree.
Bartlett, Robert Merrill. The Story of Thanksgiving. Comport, Sally Wern, illus. rev. ed. 2004. 30p. (J). (gr. k-4). reprint ed. (978-0-7567-7757-9(7)) DIANE Publishing Co.
—The Story of Thanksgiving. Comport, Sally Wern, illus. Date not set. 40p. (J). (gr. 2-5). 5.99 (978-0-06-446238-9(2)) HarperCollins Pubs.
Benge, Janet & Benge, Geoff. William Bradford: Plymouth's Rock. 2016. (ENG., Illus.). 200p. (J). pap. 9.99 (978-1-62486-092-8(3)) Emerald Bks.
Caswell, Max. My Journey Aboard the Mayflower. 2017. (My Place in History Ser.). 24p. (J). (gr. 2-3). pap. 8.15 **(978-1-5382-0217-3(4))** Stevens, Gareth Publishing LLLP.
—My Life in the Plymouth Colony. 2017. (My Place in History Ser.). 24p. (J). (gr. 2-3). pap. 8.15 **(978-1-5382-0305-7(7))**; pap. 48.90 **(978-1-5382-0306-4(5))** Stevens, Gareth Publishing LLLP.
Clark, Mary. Biographical Sketches of the Fathers of New England. 2003. 180p. 89.00 (978-0-7950-4738-1(X)) New Library Press LLC.
Connors, Kathleen. The First Thanksgiving, Vol. 1. 2014. (What You Didn't Know about History Ser.). (Illus.). 24p. (J). (gr. 2-3). (ENG.). 22.60 (978-1-4824-0581-1(4)); pap. 8.15 (978-1-4824-0582-8(2)) Stevens, Gareth Publishing LLLP.
Cook, Peter. You Wouldn't Want to Sail on the Mayflower! A Trip That Took Entirely Too Long. Whelan, Kevin, illus. rev. ed. 2013. (ENG.). 40p. (J). (gr. 3-12). pap. 9.95 (978-0-531-23858-5(X)) Scholastic Library Publishing.
Cook, Peter & Whelan, Kevin. You Wouldn't Want to Sail on the Mayflower! A Trip That Took Entirely Too Long. rev. ed. 2013. (ENG.). 32p. (J). 29.00 (978-0-531-27107-0(2), Watts, Franklin) Scholastic Library Publishing.
Crane, Carol. P Is for Pilgrim: A Thanksgiving Alphabet. Urban, Helle, illus. rev. ed. 2007. (ENG.). 40p. (J). (gr. k-6). 7.95 (978-1-58536-353-7(7)) Sleeping Bear Pr.
Crawford, Laura. The Pilgrims' Thanksgiving from A to Z, 1 vol. Hierstein, Judith, illus. 2005. (ENG.). 32p. (J). (gr. k-3). per. 8.99 (978-1-58980-238-4(1)) Pelican Publishing Co., Inc.
Davis, Daniel K. Miles Standish. 2010. (Leaders of the Colonial Era Ser.). 120p. (gr. 5-8). 35.00 (978-1-60413-739-2(8), Chelsea Hse.) Facts On File, Inc.
Davis, Kenneth C. Don't Know Much About the Pilgrims. Schindler, S. D., illus. 2006. (Don't Know Much About Ser.). (ENG.). 48p. (J). (gr. 1-4). pap. 6.99 (978-0-06-446228-0(5)) HarperCollins Pubs.
Dyan, Penelope. The Place of Tales — - a Kid's Guide to Canterbury, Kent, England. Weigand, John, photos by. 2011. (Illus.). 40p. pap. 12.95 (978-1-935630-66-1(0)) Bellissima Publishing, LLC.
Edwards, Judith. The Plymouth Colony & the Pilgrim Adventure in American History. 2003. (In American History Ser.). (Illus.). 128p. (J). (gr. 5-12). lib. bdg. 26.60 (978-0-7660-1989-8(6)) Enslow Pubs., Inc.
Englar, Mary. The Pilgrims & the First Thanksgiving, 1 vol. McDonnell, Peter, illus. 2006. (Graphic History Ser.). (ENG.). 32p. (gr. 3-4). 8.10 (978-0-7368-9656-6(2)); 30.65 (978-0-7368-5492-4(4)) Capstone Press of Coughlan Cos. (Graphic Library).
Florence, Sarah. Pilgrim Foods & Recipes. 2009. (Reading Room Collection 2 Ser.). 24p. (gr. 3-4). 42.50 (978-1-60851-983-5(X), PowerKids Pr.) Rosen Publishing Group, Inc., The.
Fradin, Dennis Brindell. The Mayflower Compact. 2006. (Turning Points in U. S. History Ser.). (Illus.). 47p. (J). (gr. 3-7). lib. bdg. 31.36 (978-0-7614-2125-2(4), Benchmark Bks.) Marshall Cavendish Corp.
Greenwood, Mark. The Mayflower. Lessac, Frané, illus. 2014. (ENG.). 32p. (J). (gr. -1-3). 16.95 (978-0-8234-2943-1(1)) Holiday Hse., Inc.
Griffis, William Elliot. Young People's History of the Pilgrims. 353p. reprint ed. 98.00 (978-0-7222-6679-3(0)) Library Reprints, Inc.
Gunderson, Jessica. Life on the Mayflower, 1 vol. Dumm, Brian Caleb, illus. 2011. (Thanksgiving Ser.). (ENG.). 24p. (gr. 1-2). pap. 7.95 (978-1-4048-6719-2(8)) Picture Window Bks.
—The Pilgrims' First Thanksgiving, 1 vol. Lucke, Deb, illus. (Thanksgiving Ser.). (ENG.). 24p. (gr. 1-2). 2011. pap. 8.95 (978-1-4048-6720-8(1)) 2010. lib. bdg. 27.32 (978-1-4048-6285-2(4)) Picture Window Bks.
Harness, Cheryl. The Adventurous Life of Myles Standish & the Amazing-but-True Survival Story of Plymouth Colony. Harness, Cheryl, illus. 2006. (Cheryl Harness Histories Ser.). (ENG., Illus.). 144p. (J). (gr. 5-9). 16.95 (978-0-7922-5918-3(1)); lib. bdg. 25.90 (978-0-7922-5919-0(X)) National Geographic Society. (National Geographic Children's Bks.).
—The Adventurous Life of Myles Standish & the Amazing-but-True Survival Story of Plymouth Colony: Barbary Pirates, the Mayflower, the First Thanksgiving, & Much, Much More. 2008. (Cheryl Harness Histories Ser.). (ENG., Illus.). 144p. (J). (gr. 5-9). 9.95 (978-1-4263-0284-8(3), National Geographic Children's Bks.) National Geographic Society.
Harte, May. Thanksgiving. 2009. (My Library of Holidays Ser.). 24p. (gr. 1-1). 37.50 (978-1-61514-697-0(0), PowerKids Pr.) Rosen Publishing Group, Inc., The.
Holub, Joan. What Was the First Thanksgiving? 2013. (What Was? Ser.). (ENG., Illus.). 112p. (J). (gr. 3-7). pap. 5.99 (978-0-448-46463-3(2), Penguin Workshop) Penguin Young Readers Group.
—What Was the First Thanksgiving? 2013. (What Was... ? Ser.). lib. bdg. 16.00 (978-0-606-31687-3(6), Turtleback) Turtleback Bks.
Honders, Christine. Mayflower Compact. 2016. (Documents of American Democracy Ser.). (Illus.). 32p. (J). (gr. 5-5). pap. 10.00 (978-1-4994-2085-2(4), PowerKids Pr.) Rosen Publishing Group, Inc., The.
Isbell, Hannah. Squanto. 2017. (J). pap. **(978-0-7660-9065-1(5))** Enslow Pubs., Inc.
Jones, Emma. Recipes of the Pilgrims. 2017. (Cooking Your Way Through American History Ser.). (J). (gr. 3-3). 24p. pap. 10.60 **(978-1-5345-2096-7(1))**; pap. 63.60 **(978-1-5345-2097-4(X))**; 24p. lib. bdg. 27.25 **(978-1-5345-2098-1(8))** Greenhaven Publishing LLC. (KidHaven Publishing).
Kallio, Jamie. Mayflower Compact, 1 vol. 2013. (Foundations of Our Nation Ser.). (ENG.). 48p. (J). (gr. 3-6). lib. bdg. 32.79 (978-1-61783-711-1(3)); (Illus.). pap. 15.64 (978-1-61783-761-6(X), Core Library) ABDO Publishing Co.
Kauffman, Dorothy. Two Villages: Two Hundred Years Apart. 2005. (Oxford Picture Dictionary for the Content Areas Ser.). (ENG., Illus.). 22p. pap. 7.56 (978-0-19-430952-3(5)) Oxford Univ. Pr., Inc.

Kessel, Joyce K. Squanto & the First Thanksgiving. Donze, Lisa, illus. rev. ed. 2003. (On My Own Holidays Ser.). (ENG.). 48p. (gr. 2-4). pap. 6.95 *(978-1-57505-585-5(6))*; lib. bdg. 25.26 *(978-0-87614-941-6(7))* Lerner Publishing Group.
—Squanto y el Primer Dia de Accion de Gracias. Donze, Lisa, illus. 2007. (Yo Solo - Festividades (on My Own - Holidays) Ser.). 48p. (J). (gr. 4-7). per. 6.95 *(978-0-8225-7795-9(X))* Lerner Publishing Group.
—Squanto y el Primer Día de Acción de Gracias. Translations.com Staff, tr. from ENG. Donze, Lisa, illus. 2007. (Yo Solo - Festividades (on My Own - Holidays) Ser.). (SPA.). 48p. (gr. 2-4). lib. bdg. 25.26 *(978-0-8225-7792-8(5))* Lerner Publishing Group.
—Squanto Y el Primer Dia de Accion de Gracias; Squanto & the First Thanksgiving. 2008. pap. 40.95 *(978-0-8225-9678-3(4))* Lerner Publishing Group.
Koestler-Grack, Rachel A. Pilgrims, 1 vol. 2005. (American Moments Ser.). (ENG., Illus.). 48p. (gr. 4-8). 27.07 *(978-1-59197-937-1(4)*, Abdo & Daughters) ABDO Publishing Co.
Landau, Elaine. Celebrate the First Thanksgiving with Elaine Landau. 2006. (Explore Colonial America with Elaine Landau Ser.). (Illus.). 48p. (J). (gr. 3-7). lib. bdg. 25.27 *(978-0-7660-2556-1(X)*, Enslow Elementary) Enslow Pubs., Inc.
Lassieur, Allison. El Viaje del Mayflower. McDonnell, Peter, illus. 2006. (Historia Gráficas Ser.). (SPA.). 32p. (gr. 3-4). 30.65 *(978-0-7368-6613-2(2))* Capstone Press of Coughlan Cos.
Lynch, P. J. The Boy Who Fell off the Mayflower, or John Howland's Good Fortune. Lynch, P. J., illus. 2015. (ENG., Illus.). 64p. (J). (gr. 2-5). 17.99 *(978-0-7636-6584-5(3))* Candlewick Pr.
Marsh, Carole. I'm Reading about the Pilgrims. 2016. (I'm Reading About Ser.). (ENG., Illus.). (J). lib. bdg. 24.99 ***(978-0-635-12191-2(3))***; pap. 7.99 ***(978-0-635-12192-9(1))*** Gallopade International.
McNeese, Tim. Plymouth. 2007. (Colonial Settlements in America Ser.). (Illus.). 112p. (YA). (gr. 5-9). lib. bdg. 30.00 *(978-0-7910-9339-9(5))* Facts On File, Inc.
Metaxas, Eric. Squanto & the First Thanksgiving: The Legendary American Tale. Donato, Michael A., illus. 2004. 36p. (J). (gr. 3-8). reprint ed. 19.00 *(978-0-7567-7123-2(4))* DIANE Publishing Co.
Newman-D'Amico, Fran. The Story of the Pilgrims. 2005. (Dover History Coloring Book Ser.). (ENG., Illus.). 30p. (J). (gr. -1-3). 3.99 *(978-0-486-44430-7(9))* Dover Pubns., Inc.
Osborne, Mary Pope & Boyce, Natalie Pope. Pilgrims: A Nonfiction Companion to Thanksgiving on Thursday. Murdocca, Sal, illus. 2005. (Magic Tree House - Fact Tracker Ser.: 13). (ENG.). 128p. (J). (gr. 2-5). 6.99 *(978-0-375-83219-2(X)*, Random Hse. Bks. for Young Readers) Random Hse. Children's Bks.
Owens, L. L. Pilgrims in America. 2006. (Events in American History Ser.). (Illus.). 48p. (J). (gr. -1-1). lib. bdg. 31.36 *(978-1-60044-122-6(X))* Rourke Educational Media.
Philbrick, Nathaniel. The Mayflower & the Pilgrims' New World. 2009. (ENG.). 368p. (J). (gr. 5-18). 8.99 *(978-0-14-241458-3(1)*, Puffin Books) Penguin Young Readers Group.
Plimoth Plantation Staff, et al. Mayflower 1620: A New Look at a Pilgrim Voyage. 2013. (ENG.). 48p. (J). (gr. 3-7). lib. bdg. 27.00 *(978-1-4263-1631-9(3)*, National Geographic Children's Bks.) National Geographic Society.
—Mayflower 1620: A New Look at a Pilgrim Voyage. Coulson, Cotton, photos by. 2007. (ENG., Illus.). 48p. (J). (gr. 3-7). per. 6.95 *(978-0-7922-6276-3(X)*, National Geographic Children's Bks.) National Geographic Society.
Poolos, J. The Mayflower. 2004. (Primary Sources in American History Ser.). (Illus.). 64p. (J). (gr. 5-8). lib. bdg. 31.95 *(978-0-8239-4514-6(6)*, Rosen Reference) Rosen Publishing Group, Inc., The.
—The Mayflower: A Primary Source History of the Pilgrims' Journey to the New World. 2009. (Primary Sources in American History Ser.). 64p. (gr. 5-8). 58.50 *(978-1-60851-499-1(4))* Rosen Publishing Group, Inc., The.
Pumphrey, Margaret B. Stories of the Pilgrims. 2005. pap. 27.95 *(978-1-4179-1115-8(8))* Kessinger Publishing, LLC.
—Stories of the Pilgrims (Yesterday's Classics) 2006. (J). per. 10.95 *(978-1-59915-123-6(5))* Yesterday's Classics.
Rajczak, Michael. Life on the Mayflower, Vol. 1. 2014. (What You Didn't Know about History Ser.). (ENG.). 24p. (J). (gr. 2-3). 22.60 *(978-1-4824-0591-0(1))* Stevens, Gareth Publishing LLLP.
Raum, Elizabeth. The Mayflower Compact, 1 vol. 2012. (Documenting U. S. History Ser.). (ENG.). 48p. (gr. 3-6). pap. 9.95 *(978-1-4329-6759-8(2))*; lib. bdg. 32.65 *(978-1-4329-6750-5(9))* Heinemann-Raintree. (NA-h).
Roop, Peter & Roop, Connie. Did Pilgrims Really Wear Black & White? And Other Questions about Colonial Times. 2007. (Illus.). 44p. (J). pap. *(978-0-439-02522-5(2))* Scholastic, Inc.
Santella, Andrew. The First Thanksgiving. 2003. (Cornerstones of Freedom Ser.). (ENG., Illus.). 48p. (YA). (gr. 4-7). 26.00 *(978-0-516-24204-0(0))* Scholastic Library Publishing.
Skarmeas, Nancy J. The Story of Thanksgiving. Venturi-Pickett, Stacy, illus. 2012. 22p. (J). bds. 6.99 *(978-0-8249-1883-5(5)*, Ideal Pubns.) Worthy Publishing.
Smith, Andrea P. The First Thanksgiving. 2012. (Illus.). 24p. (J). 63.60 *(978-1-4488-5213-0(7))*; pap. 10.60 *(978-1-4488-5212-3(9))*; lib. bdg. 25.25 *(978-1-4488-5187-4(4))* Rosen Publishing Group, Inc., The. (PowerKids Pr.).
—The Journey of the Mayflower. 2012. (Illus.). 24p. (J). 63.60 *(978-1-4488-5211-6(0))*; pap. 10.60 *(978-1-4488-5210-9(2))*; lib. bdg. 25.25 *(978-1-4488-5186-7(6))* Rosen Publishing Group, Inc., The. (PowerKids Pr.).
Stilwell, Norma Minturn. A Thought for Thanksgiving. Bingham, Pamela E., illus. 2011. 24p. pap. 14.95 *(978-1-936343-93-5(2))* Peppertree Pr., The.
Sullivan, Laura L. Life As a Passenger on the Mayflower. 2016. (Life As... Ser.). (Illus.). 32p. (J). (gr. 3-3). 28.50 *(978-1-5026-1789-7(7))* Cavendish Square Publishing.
Wagner, Heather Lehr. William Bradford. 2010. (Leaders of the Colonial Era Ser.). 120p. (gr. 5-8). 35.00 *(978-1-60413-743-9(6)*, Chelsea Hse.) Facts On File, Inc.
Waters, Kate. A Day in the Life of a Pilgrim Girl. Kendall, Russell, illus. 2008. (Sarah Morton's Day Ser.). (ENG.). 32p. (J). (gr. -1-3). pap. 7.99 *(978-0-439-81220-7(8)*, Scholastic Paperbacks) Scholastic, Inc.
Waxman, Laura Hamilton. Why Did the Pilgrims Come to the New World? And Other Questions about the Plymouth Colony. 2010. (Six Questions of American History Ser.). (ENG., Illus.). 48p. (gr. 4-6). lib. bdg. 30.60 *(978-1-58013-665-5(6))* Lerner Publishing Group.
—Why Did the Pilgrims Come to the New World? & Other Questions about the Plymouth Colony. 2010. (Six Questions of American History Ser.). 48p. (J). pap. 9.95 *(978-0-7613-6123-7(5))*; pap. 56.72 *(978-0-7613-6951-6(1))* Lerner Publishing Group.
Whitcraft, Melissa. The Mayflower Compact. 2003. (Cornerstones of Freedom Ser.). (ENG., Illus.). 48p. (YA). (gr. 4-7). 26.00 *(978-0-516-24203-3(2))* Scholastic Library Publishing.
Whitehurst, Susan. The Mayflower. 2009. (Library of the Pilgrims Ser.). 24p. (gr. 3-4). 42.50 *(978-1-60853-914-7(8)*, PowerKids Pr.) Rosen Publishing Group, Inc., The.
—The Pilgrims Before the Mayflower. 2009. (Library of the Pilgrims Ser.). 24p. (gr. 3-4). 42.50 *(978-1-60853-915-4(6)*, PowerKids Pr.) Rosen Publishing Group, Inc., The.
—Plymouth Partnership: Pilgrims & Native Americans. 2009. (Library of the Pilgrims Ser.). 24p. (gr. 3-4). 42.50 *(978-1-60853-912-3(1)*, PowerKids Pr.) Rosen Publishing Group, Inc., The.
—William Bradford & Plymouth: A Colony Grows. 2009. (Library of the Pilgrims Ser.). 24p. (gr. 3-4). 42.50 *(978-1-60853-916-1(4)*, PowerKids Pr.) Rosen Publishing Group, Inc., The.
Williams, Gianna & Riehecky, Janet. La Colonia de Plymouth. 2006. (Hitos de la historia de Estados Unidos (Landmark Events in American History) Ser.). (SPA.). 48p. (gr. 5-12). pap. 11.70 *(978-0-8368-7471-6(4)*, Gareth Stevens Learning Library); (Illus.). lib. bdg. 27.00 *(978-0-8368-7464-8(1)*, Gareth Stevens Secondary Library) Stevens, Gareth Publishing LLLP.
Yero, Judith Lloyd & National Geographic Learning Staff. The Mayflower Compact. 2007. (Reading Expeditions Ser.). (ENG., Illus.). 32p. (J). pap. 17.95 *(978-0-7922-4553-7(9))* CENGAGE Learning.

PILGRIMS (NEW PLYMOUTH COLONY)—FICTION

Bruchac, Joseph. Squanto's Journey: The Story of the First Thanksgiving. Shed, Greg, illus. 2007. (ENG.). 32p. (J). (gr. -1-3). pap. 7.99 *(978-0-15-206044-2(8)*, HMH Books For Young Readers) Houghton Mifflin Harcourt Publishing Co.
—Squanto's Journey: The Story of the First Thanksgiving. 2014. 17.00 *(978-1-63419-743-4(7))* Perfection Learning Corp.
Burton, Jeffrey. The Itsy Bitsy Pilgrim. Rescek, Sanja, illus. 2016. (Itsy Bitsy Ser.). (ENG.). 16p. (J). (gr. -1 — 1). bds. 5.99 *(978-1-4814-6852-7(9)*, Little Simon) Little Simon.
Dougherty, Brandi. The Littlest Pilgrim. Richards, Kirsten, illus. 2008. (ENG.). 32p. (J). (gr. -1-k). pap. 3.99 *(978-0-545-05372-3(2)*, Cartwheel Bks.) Scholastic, Inc.
Greene, Rhonda Gowler. The Very First Thanksgiving Day. Gaber, Susan, illus. 2006. (ENG.). 32p. (J). (gr. -1-1). 6.99 *(978-1-4169-1916-2(3)*, Atheneum Bks. for Young Readers) Simon & Schuster Children's Publishing.
Hillert, Margaret. Why We Have Thanksgiving. Marchesi, Stephen, illus. 2016. (BeginningtoRead Ser.). (ENG.). 32p. (J). (gr. 1-2). 22.60 *(978-1-59953-809-9(1))* Norwood Hse. Pr.
Klimo, Kate. Dash. 2014. (Dog Diaries: 5). lib. bdg. 18.40 *(978-0-606-36021-0(2))* Turtleback Bks.
—Dog Diaries #5: Dash. Jessell, Tim, illus. 2014. (Dog Diaries). (ENG.). 160p. (J). (gr. 2-5). pap. 7.99 *(978-0-385-37338-8(4)*, Random Hse. Bks. for Young Readers) Random Hse. Children's Bks.
Krulik, Nancy. Don't Be Such a Turkey! John and Wendy Staff, illus. 2010. (Katie Kazoo, Switcheroo Ser.). (ENG.). 160p. (J). (gr. 2-4). pap. 4.99 *(978-0-448-45448-1(3)*, Grosset & Dunlap) Penguin Young Readers Group.
Lasky, Kathryn. A Journey to the New World: The Diary of Remember Patience Whipple, Mayflower 1620. 2010. (Dear America Ser.). (ENG.). 192p. (J). (gr. 3-7). 12.99 *(978-0-545-23801-4(3)*, Scholastic Pr.) Scholastic, Inc.
Lawton, Wendy G. Almost Home: A Story Based on the Life of the Mayflower's Mary Chilton. 2003. (Daughters of the Faith Ser.). (ENG.). 160p. (YA). (gr. 3). pap. 7.99 *(978-0-8024-3637-5(4))* Moody Pubs.
Limbaugh, Rush H., III. Rush Revere & the Brave Pilgrims: Time-Travel Adventures with Exceptional Americans. 2013. (ENG., Illus.). 224p. 19.99 *(978-1-4767-5586-1(8)*, Threshold Editions) Threshold Editions.
Osborne, Mary Pope, et al. Jueves de Acción de Gracias. Murdocca, Sal, illus. 2014. 27. (SPA.). 88p. (J). (gr. 2-4). pap. 5.99 *(978-1-933032-94-8(4))* Lectorum Pubns., Inc.
Stanley, Diane. Thanksgiving on Plymouth Plantation. Berry, Holly, illus. 2004. (Time-Traveling Twins Ser.). (ENG.). 48p. (J). (gr. k-5). 16.99 *(978-0-06-027069-8(1))* HarperCollins Pubs.

PILOTING (AERONAUTICS)

see Airplanes—Piloting

PILOTS, AIRPLANE

see Air Pilots

PILOTS AND PILOTAGE

see also Navigation

Gordon, Nick. Fighter Pilot. 2013. (Dangerous Jobs Ser.). (ENG., Illus.). 24p. (J). (gr. 3-7). lib. bdg. 25.95 *(978-1-60014-894-1(6)*, Torque Bks.) Bellwether Media.
Hense, Mary, et al. How Fighter Pilots Use Math. 2009. (Math in the Real World Ser.). 32p. (gr. 4-6). 28.00 *(978-1-60413-605-0(7)*, Chelsea Clubhouse) Facts On File, Inc.
Loveless, Antony. Fighter Pilots. 2009. (World's Most Dangerous Jobs Ser.). (ENG., Illus.). 32p. (J). (gr. 3-6). pap. *(978-0-7787-5110-6(4))*; lib. bdg. *(978-0-7787-5096-3(5))* Crabtree Publishing Co.
Loveless, Antony & Oxlade, Chris. Support Helicopter Pilots. 2012. (ENG.). 32p. (J). *(978-0-7787-5102-1(3))* Crabtree Publishing Co.
West, David. Fighter Pilots. 2008. 52p. (gr. 5-8). pap. 29.25 *(978-1-4358-3785-0(1))* Rosen Publishing Group, Inc., The.
Youngblood, Wayne. Mark Twain along the Mississippi. 2006. (In the Footsteps of American Heroes Ser.). (Illus.). 64p. (gr. 5-12). pap. 14.05 *(978-0-8368-6435-9(2))*; lib. bdg. 34.00 *(978-0-8368-6430-4(1))* Stevens, Gareth Publishing LLLP. (Gareth Stevens Secondary Library).

PINCKNEY, ELIZA LUCAS, 1723-1793

Krebs, Laurie. A Day in the Life of a Colonial Indigo Planter. (Library of Living & Working in Colonial Times Ser.). 24p. 2009. (gr. 3-3). 42.50 *(978-1-60853-732-7(3)*, PowerKids Pr.) 2004. (Illus.). (J). lib. bdg. 19.95 *(978-0-8239-6229-7(6))* Rosen Publishing Group, Inc., The.

PINKERTON, ALLAN, 1819-1884

Seiple, Samantha. Lincoln's Spymaster: Allan Pinkerton, America's First Private Eye. 2015. (ENG., Illus.). 224p. (J). (gr. 5-9). 17.99 *(978-0-545-70897-5(4)*, Scholastic Pr.) Scholastic, Inc.

PINOCCHIO (FICTITIOUS CHARACTER)—FICTION

The Adventures of Pinocchio. 2011. 130p. pap. 9.99 *(978-1-61203-094-4(7))* Bottom of the Hill Publishing.
The Adventures of Pinocchio. (Twelve-Point Ser.). 2003. (J). lib. bdg. 25.00 *(978-1-58287-248-3(1))* 2004. 229p. 25.00 *(978-1-58287-732-7(7))* North Bks.
Las Aventuras de Pinocho. (SPA., Illus.). 160p. (YA). 14.95 *(978-84-7281-190-4(5)*, AF1905) Auriga, Ediciones S.A. ESP. Dist: Continental Bk. Co., Inc.
Le Avventure di Pinocchio, Level B. (ITA.). (J). pap. 9.95 *(978-0-88436-050-6(4)*, 55254) EMC/Paradigm Publishing.
Bemis, John Claude. Out of Abaton, Book 1 the Wooden Prince. 2017. (Out of Abaton Ser.). (ENG.). 336p. (J). (gr. 3-7). pap. 7.99 *(978-1-4847-0742-5(7))* Hyperion Bks. for Children.
Brown, Janet. Pinocchio: My First Reading Book. Morton, Ken, illus. 2015. (ENG.). 24p. pap. 6.99 *(978-1-86147-475-9(X)*, Armadillo) Anness Publishing GBR. Dist: National Bk. Network.
Campillo, Carlo Collodi. Ilustrado por Susana. Las Aventuras de Pinocho. (Coleccion Cuentos Universales). (SPA.). (YA). (gr. 4-18). *(978-84-261-3145-4(X)*, JV30301) Juventud, Editorial ESP. Dist: Lectorum Pubns., Inc.
Carsey, Alice, illus. Pinocchio. 2003. (Library of Tale Ser.).Tr. of Avventure di Pinocchio. (SPA.). 12p. (J). (gr. -1-7). pap. *(978-958-30-0986-0(5))* Panamericana Editorial.
—Pinocchio. 2005.Tr. of Avventure di Pinocchio. (ENG.). 136p. (J). (gr. 2-5). 19.95 *(978-1-933327-00-6(6))* Purple Bear Bks., Inc.
—Pinocchio, the Tale of a Puppet. 2011. 140p. pap. 12.99 *(978-1-61203-095-1(5))* Bottom of the Hill Publishing.
Carter, Scott William. Wooden Bones. (ENG., Illus.). 160p. (J). (gr. 3-7). 2013. pap. 6.99 *(978-1-4424-2752-5(3))* 2012. 15.99 *(978-1-4424-2751-8(5))* Simon & Schuster Bks. For Young Readers. (Simon & Schuster Bks. For Young Readers).
Cherubini, E. Pinocchio in Africa. 2007. pap. *(978-1-4065-1442-1(X))* Dodo Pr.
Collodi, C. The Adventures of Pinocchio. 2005. 216p. 27.95 *(978-1-4218-0608-2(8)*, 1st World Library - Literary Society) 1st World Publishing, Inc.
—The Adventures of Pinocchio. Della Chiesa, Carol, tr. 2007. (ENG.). 160p. per. *(978-1-4065-1463-6(2))* Dodo Pr.
—The Adventures of Pinocchio. 2007. 108p. (gr. 4-7). per. 7.99 *(978-1-60459-012-8(2))* Wilder Pubns., Corp.
—Pinocchio: the Tale of a Puppet. Carsey, Alice, illus. 2007. (ENG.). 196p. per. *(978-1-4065-1462-9(4))* Dodo Pr.
Collodi, Carlo. Adventures of Pinocchio. Lucas, Ann Lawson, tr. from ITA. 2009. (Oxford World's Classics Ser.). (ENG., Illus.). 256p. pap. 10.95 *(978-0-19-955398-3(X))* Oxford Univ. Pr., Inc.
—The Adventures of Pinocchio. Staino, Franco & Innocenti, Roberto, illus. rev. ed. 2004. (ENG.). 192p. (J). (gr. 1-3). 35.00 *(978-1-56846-190-8(9))* Creative Co., The.
—The Patua Pinocchio. Chiesa, Carol Della, tr. from ITA. Chitrakar, Swarna, illus. 2015. (ENG.). 188p. (gr. 6). 18.95 *(978-93-83145-12-6(9))* Tara Books Agency IND. Dist: Publishers Group West (PGW).
Fairy Tales - Pinocchio. 2005. (J). bds. *(978-1-4194-0101-5(7))* Paradise Pr., Inc.
Fairy Tales- Pinocchio. 2005. (J). bds. *(978-1-4194-0041-4(X))* Paradise Pr., Inc.
Fairy Tales s/s - Pinocchio. 2005. (J). bds. *(978-1-4194-0067-4(3))* Paradise Pr., Inc.
Kunhardt, Dorothy, ed. Pinocchio. (FRE.). 96p. (J). (gr. k-5). pap. 9.95 *(978-0-7859-8845-8(9))* French & European Pubns., Inc.
Leigh, Tom, illus. Pinocchio: A Tale of Honesty. 2006. (J). 6.99 *(978-1-59939-005-5(1))* Cornerstone Pr.
Leonard, Barry, ed. Pinocchio. 2003. (Illus.). 12p. (J). (gr. k-5). reprint ed. 17.00 *(978-0-7567-6862-1(4))* DIANE Publishing Co.
Linares, Jairo, illus. Pinocho. 2004. (Literatura Juvenil (Panamericana Editorial) Ser.).Tr. of Pinocchio. (SPA.). 283p. (J). (gr. 4-7). pap. *(978-958-30-0803-0(6)*, PV30464) Centro de Informacion y Desarrollo de la Comunicacion y la Literatura MEX. Dist: Lectorum Pubns., Inc.
Murray, M. A., tr. Pinocchio, As First Translated into English by M a Murray & Illustrated by Charles Folkard. Folkard, Charles, illus. 2009. 280p. pap. 11.95 *(978-1-59915-177-9(4))* Yesterday's Classics.
Nickel. Pinocchio. Date not set. (J). 4.99 *(978-0-7214-5404-7(6))* Nickel Pr.
Parragon Staff. Pinocchio: The Magical Story. 2010. (Disney Padded Magical Storybks.). (Illus.). 32p. (J). (gr. -1-1). *(978-1-4075-8451-5(0))* Parragon, Inc.
Pinocchio. (J). 22.95 *(978-0-88411-249-5(7))* Amereon Ltd.
Pinocchio. *(978-1-894998-20-8(0))* Lake, Jack Productions, Inc. CAN. Dist: Hushion Hse. Publishing, Ltd.
Pinocchio. 2005. (WEL., Illus.). 40p. *(978-1-899877-05-8(3))* Y Ddraig Fach.
Pinocchio: A Classic Story about Honesty. 2003. (Illus.). 32p. per. 3.95 *(978-0-9747133-2-8(5)*, Values to Live By Classic Stories) Thomas, Frederic Inc.
Pinocchio: The Human Body, Sea Life, The Bedroom. (FRE & ENG., Illus.). 24p. (J). (gr. -1-5). pap., stu. ed. 5.95 *(978-88-8148-243-6(6))* EMC/Paradigm Publishing.
RH Disney Staff & Winkelman, Barbara Gaines. Pinocchio's Nose Grows. 2013. (Step into Reading Ser.). (ENG., Illus.). 32p. (J). (gr. -1-1). lib. bdg. 12.99 *(978-0-7364-8001-7(3)*, RH/Disney) Random Hse. Children's Bks.
Rossendale, Helen. Tales from Pinocchio. Philpot, Graham, illus. 2011. (10-Minute Bedtime Stories Ser.). (ENG.). 88p. (J). (gr. k-4). 14.99 *(978-1-84365-147-5(5)*, Pavilion) Pavilion Bks. GBR. Dist: Independent Pubs. Group.
Ruiz, Margarita, illus. Pinocho. (SPA & ENG.). (J). (gr. -1-5). pap. 5.95 incl. audio compact disk *(978-88-8148-253-5(3))* EMC/Paradigm Publishing.
Tyrrell, Melissa. Pinocchio. McMullen, Nigel, illus. 2005. (Fairytale Friends Ser.: Vol. 7). 12p. (J). (gr. -1-k). bds. 5.95 *(978-1-58117-151-8(X)*, Intervisual/Piggy Toes) Bendon, Inc.

PIONEER LIFE

see Frontier and Pioneer Life

PIONEERS

see also Frontier and Pioneer Life

Adler, David A. & Adler, Michael S. A Picture Book of Daniel Boone. Collins, Matt, illus. 2013. (ENG.). 32p. (J). (gr. -1-3). 17.95 *(978-0-8234-2748-2(X))* Holiday Hse., Inc.
Allen, Nancy Kelly. Daniel Boone: Trailblazer, 1 vol. Waites, Joan C., illus. 2005. (ENG.). 32p. (J). (gr. k-3). 16.99 *(978-1-58980-212-4(8))* Pelican Publishing Co., Inc.
Alter, Judy & Alter, Judy. Laura Ingalls Wilder: Pioneer & Author. 2003. (Our People Ser.). (ENG., Illus.). 32p. (J). (gr. 3-6). 29.93 *(978-1-59296-007-1(3)*, 200644) Child's World, Inc., The.
Améz, Lynda. My Life As a Pioneer. 2016. (My Place in History Ser.). (ENG., Illus.). 24p. (J). (gr. 2-3). pap. 8.15 *(978-1-4824-3988-5(3))* Stevens, Gareth Publishing LLLP.
Arnez, Lynda. My Wagon Train Adventure. 2016. (My Place in History Ser.). (ENG., Illus.). 24p. (J). (gr. 2-3). pap. 8.15 *(978-1-4824-4002-7(4))* Stevens, Gareth Publishing LLLP.
Beckwith, Cheryl. William Bent: Frontiersman. 2011. (ENG & SPA., Illus.). 60p. (J). pap. 8.95 *(978-0-86541-117-3(4))* Filter Pr., LLC.
Benge, Janet. Richard Wurmbrand: Love Your Enemies. 2017. (J). pap. ***(978-1-57658-987-8(0))*** YWAM Publishing.
Benge, Janet & Benge, Geoff. Davy Crockett: Ever Westward. 2011. (ENG.). 192p. (YA). pap. 9.99 *(978-1-932096-67-5(1))* Emerald Bks.
Bennett, Doraine. Laura Ingalls Wilder: Little World Biographies. 2013. (ENG.). 24p. (gr. k-3). pap. 8.95 *(978-1-61810-293-5(1))* Rourke Educational Media.
Blair, Eric. Daniel Boone, 1 vol. Chambers-Goldberg, Micah, illus. (My First Classic Story Ser.). (ENG.). 32p. (gr. k-3). 2013. pap. 7.10 *(978-1-4795-1859-3(X))* 2011. lib. bdg. 22.65 *(978-1-4048-6578-5(0))* Picture Window Bks. (My First Classic Story).
Bliss, John. Pioneers to the West, 1 vol. 2011. (Children's True Stories: Migration Ser.). (ENG.). 32p. (gr. 3-3). pap. 8.29 *(978-1-4109-4082-7(9)*, Raintree Perspectives) Heinemann-Raintree.
Boothroyd, Jennifer. William Penn. 2009. pap. 6.95 *(978-0-8225-6431-7(9))* Lerner Publishing Group.
Brandt, Keith & Macken, JoAnn Early. Daniel Boone: Frontier Explorer. Lawn, John, illus. 2008. 55p. (J). pap. *(978-0-439-02020-6(4))* Scholastic, Inc.
Buffalo Bill Cody. 2010. (Legends of the Wild West Ser.). (Illus.). 136p. (gr. 6-12). 35.00 *(978-1-60413-528-2(X)*, Chelsea Hse.) Facts On File, Inc.
Byers, Ann. Life As a Homesteader in the American West. 2016. (Life As... Ser.). (Illus.). 32p. (J). (gr. 3-3). 28.50 *(978-1-5026-1787-3(0))* Cavendish Square Publishing.
Calamity Jane. 2010. (Legends of the Wild West Ser.). (Illus.). 128p. (gr. 6-12). 35.00 *(978-1-60413-595-4(6)*, Chelsea Hse.) Facts On File, Inc.
Callery, Sean. The Dark History of America's Old West. 2010. (Dark Histories Ser.). 64p. (gr. 5). 32.79 *(978-1-60870-086-8(0))* Marshall Cavendish Corp.
Capek, Michael. Davy Crockett. 2017. 25.70 *(978-1-61228-974-8(6))* Mitchell Lane Pubs., Inc.
Chemerka, William R. Davy Crockett from a to Z, 1 vol. Dillon, Wade, illus. 2013. (ENG.). 32p. (J). (gr. k-3). 16.99 *(978-1-4556-1835-4(7))* Pelican Publishing Co., Inc.
Coddington, Andrew. Davy Crockett. Lapegue, Matias, illus. 2016. (American Legends & Folktales Ser.). 32p. (J). 28.50 *(978-1-5026-2193-1(2))* Cavendish Square Publishing.
Davy Crockett. 2010. (Legends of the Wild West Ser.). (Illus.). 120p. (gr. 6-12). 35.00 *(978-1-60413-592-3(1)*, Chelsea Hse.) Facts On File, Inc.
Demuth, Patricia Brennan. Who Was Laura Ingalls Wilder? 2013. (Who Was... ? Ser.). lib. bdg. 16.00 *(978-0-606-32134-1(9)*, Turtleback) Turtleback Bks.
Doeden, Matt. Oregon Trail: An Interactive History Adventure. 2013. (You Choose: History Ser.). (ENG.). 112p. (gr. 3-4). pap. 6.95 *(978-1-4765-3607-1(4))*; 31.99 *(978-1-4765-0254-0(4))* Capstone Press of Coughlan Cos. (You Choose Bks.).
Doherty, Kieran. Voyageurs, Lumberjacks & Farmers: Pioneers of the Midwest. 2003. (Shaping America Ser.: Vol. 5). (Illus.). 176p. (gr. 7-18). lib. bdg. 22.95 *(978-1-881508-54-0(4))* Oliver Pr., Inc.
Domnauer, Teresa. Life in the West. 2010. (True Book Ser.). (ENG.). 48p. (J). (gr. 2-5). 29.00 *(978-0-531-20583-9(5))* Scholastic Library Publishing.
Figley, Marty Rhodes. Who Was William Penn? And Other Questions about the Founding of Pennsylvania. 2012. (Six Questions of American History Ser.). (ENG.). 48p. (gr. 4-6). pap. 56.72 *(978-0-7613-9241-5(6))*; pap. 9.95 *(978-0-7613-8571-4(1))*; (Illus.). lib. bdg. 30.60 *(978-0-7613-5328-7(3))* Lerner Publishing Group.
Fleming, Candace. Presenting Buffalo Bill: The Man Who Invented the Wild West. 2016. (ENG., Illus.). 288p. (J). 19.99 *(978-1-59643-763-0(4)*, 9781596437630) Roaring Brook Pr.
Ford, Anne. Davy Crockett. Vosburgh, Leonard, illus. 2011. 48p. 35.95 *(978-1-258-06913-1(X))* Literary Licensing, LLC.
Ford, Carin T. Laura Ingalls Wilder: Real-Life Pioneer of the Little House Books. 2003. (People to Know Ser.). (Illus.). 112p. (J). lib. bdg. 26.60 *(978-0-7660-2105-1(X))* Enslow Pubs., Inc.
Freedman, Jeri. Life As a Pioneer on the Oregon Trail. 2016. (Life As... Ser.). (ENG., Illus.). 32p. (J). (gr. 3-3). pap. 10.58 *(978-1-5026-1075-1(2))* Cavendish Square Publishing.
Friedman, Mel. The Oregon Trail. (Cornerstones of Freedom, Third Ser.). (ENG., (J). 2012. Illus.). 64p. pap. 8.95 *(978-0-531-28163-5(9))* 2012. (Illus.). 64p. lib. bdg. 30.00 *(978-0-531-23063-3(5))* 2010. 48p. pap. 6.95 *(978-0-531-21247-9(5)*, Children's Pr.) Scholastic Library Publishing.

Furstinger, Nancy. Davy Crockett. 2003. (Folk Heroes Ser.). (Illus.). 24p. (J). lib. bdg. 24.45 *(978-1-59036-073-6(7))* Weigl Pubs., Inc.

Gaines, Ann. Jim Bowie: Legendary Hero of the Alamo. 2015. (Legendary American Biographies Ser.). 96p. (J). (gr. 6-12). pap. 10.95 *(978-0-7660-6471-3(9))* Enslow Pubs., Inc.

Gaines, Ann Graham. Jim Bowie: Legendary Hero of the Alamo. 2015. (Legendary American Biographies Ser.). 96p. (J). (gr. 6-12). 27.94 *(978-0-7660-6470-6(0))* Enslow Pubs., Inc.

Giff, Patricia Reilly. Laura Ingalls Wilder. 2014. (Women of Our Time Ser.). (ENG., Illus.). 80p. (J). (gr. 3-7). pap. 7.99 *(978-0-14-751364-9(2)*, Puffin Books) Penguin Young Readers Group.

Gunderson, Jessica. Your Life As a Pioneer on the Oregon Trail. Dougherty, Rachel, illus. 2012. (Way It Was Ser.). (ENG.). 32p. (gr. 2-3). pap. 8.95 *(978-1-4048-7250-9(7))*; lib. bdg. 26.65 *(978-1-4048-7157-1(8))* Picture Window Bks.

Haldy, Emma E. Davy Crockett. Bane, Jeff, illus. 2017. (My Early Library: My Itty-Bitty Bio Ser.). (ENG.). 24p. (J). (gr. k-1). lib. bdg. 28.50 *(978-1-63472-151-6(9)*, 209176) Cherry Lake Publishing.

Hale, Nathan. Donner Dinner Party. 2013. (Nathan Hale's Hazardous Tales Ser.). (ENG., Illus.). 128p. (J). (gr. 3-7). 12.99 *(978-1-4197-0856-5(2)*, Amulet Bks.) Abrams, Inc.

Harkins, Susan Sales & Harkins, William H. The Donner Party. 2008. (What's So Great About... ? Ser.). (Illus.). 32p. (J). (gr. 2-4). lib. bdg. 25.70 *(978-1-58415-669-7(4))* Mitchell Lane Pubs., Inc.

Harness, Cheryl. The Tragic Tale of Narcissa Whitman & a Faithful History of the Oregon Trail. Harness, Cheryl, illus. 2006. (Cheryl Harness Histories Ser.). (ENG., Illus.). 144p. (J). (gr. 5-9). lib. bdg. 25.90 *(978-0-7922-5921-3(1)*, National Geographic Children's Bks.) National Geographic Society.

Hay, John & Harwich, Mary Belle. Dancing Hands: Signs of Learning. Wapahi, Robert, illus. 2013. 78p. pap. 16.95 *(978-0-9888972-0-5(2))* Scotland Gate, Inc.

Hayhurst, Chris. John Sutter: California Pioneer / Pionero de California. 2009. (Famous People in American History/Grandes personajes en la historia de los Estados Unidos Ser.). (ENG & SPA.). 32p. (gr. 2-3). 47.90 *(978-1-61512-549-4(3)*, Editorial Buenas Letras) Rosen Publishing Group, Inc., The.

—John Sutter: Pionero de California (John Sutter: California Pioneer) 2009. (Grandes personajes en la historia de los Estados Unidos (Famous People in American History) Ser.). (SPA.). 32p. (gr. 2-3). 47.90 *(978-1-61512-803-7(4)*, Editorial Buenas Letras) Rosen Publishing Group, Inc., The.

Herman, Gail. Who Was Davy Crockett? Squier, Robert & Harrison, Nancy, illus. 2013. (Who Was? Ser.). (ENG.). 112p. (J). (gr. 3-7). 5.99 *(978-0-448-46704-7(6)*, Grosset & Dunlap) Penguin Young Readers Group.

—Who Was Davy Crockett? 2013. (Who Was... ? Ser.). lib. bdg. 16.00 *(978-0-606-32133-4(0)*, Turtleback) Turtleback Bks.

Hicks, Peter. You Wouldn't Want to Live in a Wild West Town! Dust You'd Rather Not Settle. Antram, David, illus. 2013. (ENG.). (J). 32p. 29.00 *(978-0-531-27106-3(4))*; 40p. pap. 9.95 *(978-0-531-23857-8(1))* Scholastic Library Publishing. (Watts, Franklin).

Isecke, Harriet. Stephen F. Austin: The Father of Texas, 1 vol. 2012. (Primary Source Readers Ser.). (ENG.). 32p. (J). (gr. 3-3). pap. 8.99 *(978-1-4333-5045-0(9))* Teacher Created Materials, Inc.

Jeffrey, Gary. The Oregon Trail. Poluzzi, Allesandro, illus. 2012. (Graphic History of the American West Ser.). (ENG.). 24p. (J). (gr. 3-8). pap. 8.15 *(978-1-4339-6745-0(6)*, Gareth Stevens Learning Library); (gr. 4-7). lib. bdg. 23.95 *(978-1-4339-6743-6(X))* Stevens, Gareth Publishing LLLP.

Johnston, Marianne. Daniel Boone. 2009. (American Legends Ser.). 24p. (gr. 3-3). 42.50 *(978-1-61511-380-4(0)*, PowerKids Pr.) Rosen Publishing Group, Inc., The.

Kennedy, Emily. Daniel Boone. 2014. (Illus.). 31p. (J). lib. bdg. *(978-1-62712-280-1(X))* Cavendish Square Publishing.

Klepeis, Alicia. Calamity Jane: Frontierswoman. Lapegüe, Matias, illus. 2016. (American Legends & Folktales Ser.). 32p. (J). pap. 10.58 *(978-1-5026-2200-6(9))*; lib. bdg. 28.50 *(978-1-5026-2202-0(5))* Cavendish Square Publishing.

Kundiger, Marion S. Izzie of Fergus Falls: A Minnesota Childhood in The 1880s. Kundiger, Marion S., illus. 2008. (ENG., Illus.). 56p. (J). 29.95 *(978-0-9659712-8-7(7))* Ravenstone Pr.

Landau, Elaine. The California Gold Rush: Would You Go for the Gold? 2010. (What Would You Do? Ser.). (Illus.). 48p. (J). pap. 8.95 *(978-1-59845-193-1(6)*, Enslow Elementary) Enslow Pubs., Inc.

—The Gold Rush in California: Would You Catch Gold Fever? 2015. (What Would You Do? Ser.). 48p. (J). (gr. 3-4). 25.27 *(978-0-7660-6300-6(3))*; pap. 8.95 *(978-0-7660-6301-3(1)*, Enslow Elementary) Enslow Pubs., Inc.

Lappi, Megan. The Church: Pioneers of Canada. 2011. 24p. (YA). (gr. 2-4). *(978-1-77071-678-0(5))*; pap. *(978-1-77071-682-7(3))* Weigl Educational Pubs. Ltd.

Leaf, Christina. Laura Ingalls Wilder. 2015. (Children's Storytellers Ser.). (ENG., Illus.). 24p. (J). (gr. 2-5). lib. bdg. 25.95 *(978-1-62617-269-2(2)*, Blastoff! Readers) Bellwether Media.

Levy, Janey. William Penn: Shaping a Nation. 2009. (Real Life Readers Ser.). 32p. (J). (ENG., Illus.). (gr. 5-6). pap. 10.00 *(978-1-4358-0195-0(4)*, 1291824); (gr. 4-6). lib. bdg. 25.25 *(978-1-4358-3016-5(4))*; (Illus.). 60.00 *(978-1-4358-0196-7(2)*, 1291824) Rosen Publishing Group, Inc., The. (PowerKids Pr.).

Lightfoot, D. J. Trail Fever: The Life of a Texas Cowboy. Bobbish, John, illus. exp. ed. 2003. 88p. (J). (gr. 3-18). pap. 12.95 *(978-0-9728768-0-3(4))* Seven Rivers Publishing.

Linde, Barbara M. The Price of a Pioneer Journey: Adding & Subtracting Two-Digit Dollar Amounts. 2009. (Math for the REAL World Ser.). 16p. (gr. 2-3). pap. 7.05 *(978-0-8239-8906-5(2)*, Rosen Classroom) Rosen Publishing Group, Inc., The.

Macy, Sue. Basketball Belles: How Two Teams & One Scrappy Player Put Women's Hoops on the Map. Collins, Matt & Matt, Collins, illus. 2011. (ENG.). 32p. (J). (gr. 1-5). 17.95 *(978-0-8234-2163-3(5))* Holiday Hse., Inc.

Mara, Wil. Laura Ingalls Wilder. 2003. (Rookie Biographies Ser.). (ENG., Illus.). 32p. (J). (gr. 1-2). 20.50 *(978-0-516-22855-6(2)*, Children's Pr.) Scholastic Library Publishing.

Mara, Wil & National Geographic Learning Staff. Laura Ingalls Wilder. 2010. (Rise & Shine Ser.). (ENG.). 32p. (C). (gr. 1-2). pap. 7.95 *(978-0-516-27840-7(1))* National Geographic School Publishing, Inc.

Matzke, Ann H. My Life As a Pioneer. 2012. (ENG.). 24p. (gr. k-2). pap. 8.95 *(978-1-61810-280-5(X))* Rourke Educational Media.

Maynard, Charles W. Jedediah Smith: Mountain Man of the American West. 2003. (Famous Explorers of the American West Ser.). (Illus.). 24p. (J). lib. bdg. 22.60 *(978-0-8239-6287-7(3)*, PowerKids Pr.) Rosen Publishing Group, Inc., The.

—Jim Bridger: Frontiersman & Mountain Guide. (Famous Explorers of the American West Ser.). 24p. 2009. (gr. 3-4). 42.50 *(978-1-61512-502-9(7))* 2003. (Illus.). (J). lib. bdg. 22.60 *(978-0-8239-6288-4(1))* Rosen Publishing Group, Inc., The. (PowerKids Pr.).

McCaslin, Nellie. Johnny Appleseed. 2003. (Players Press Nellie McCaslin Ser.). (Illus.). 16p. (J). (gr. 1-8). pap. 5.00 *(978-0-88734-447-3(X))* Players Pr., Inc.

McDonough, Yona Zeldis. Little Author in the Big Woods: A Biography of Laura Ingalls Wilder. Thermes, Jennifer, illus. 2014. (ENG.). 176p. (J). (gr. 3-7). 16.99 *(978-0-8050-9542-5(X)*, 9780805095425, Holt, Henry & Co. Bks. For Young Readers) Holt, Henry & Co.

Mead, James R., et al. Hunting & Trading in Kansas, 1859-1875. 2015. (J). *(978-1-929731-25-1(6))* Rowfant Pr.

Miller, Brandon Marie. Women of the Frontier: 16 Tales of Trailblazing Homesteaders, Entrepreneurs, & Rabble-Rousers. 2013. (Women of Action Ser.). (ENG., Illus.). 256p. (J). (gr. 7). 19.95 *(978-1-883052-97-3(1))* Chicago Review Pr., Inc.

Morley, Jacqueline. You Wouldn't Want to... Be an American Pioneer! Antram, David, illus. rev. ed. 2012. (ENG.). (J). 40p. pap. 9.95 *(978-0-531-28025-6(X))*; 32p. lib. bdg. 29.00 *(978-0-531-27500-9(0))* Scholastic Library Publishing.

Nichols, Kaitlyn. Davey Crockett. 2009. pap. 13.25 *(978-1-60559-057-8(6))* Hameray Publishing Group, Inc.

Oachs, Emily Rose. Death in the Donner Party: A Cause-And-Effect Investigation. 2016. (Cause-And-Effect Disasters Ser.). (ENG., Illus.). 40p. (J). (gr. 4-6). 46.65 *(978-1-5124-1126-3(4)*, Lerner Pubns.) Lerner Publishing Group.

Peppas, Lynn. Why Charles Goodnight Matters to Texas. 2014. (Illus.). 32p. (J). lib. bdg. 26.25 *(978-1-4777-0907-8(X))* Rosen Publishing Group, Inc., The.

—Why Martin de Léon Matters to Texas. 2014. (Illus.). 32p. (J). lib. bdg. 26.25 *(978-1-4777-0916-0(9))* Rosen Publishing Group, Inc., The.

—Why Stephen F. Austin Matters to Texas. 2014. (Illus.). 32p. (J). lib. bdg. 26.25 *(978-1-4777-0914-6(2))* Rosen Publishing Group, Inc., The.

Pioneer Spirit: The Westward Expansion. 2013. (Pioneer Spirit: the Westward Expansion Ser.). 24p. (J). (gr. 3-6). 135.60 *(978-1-4777-1145-3(7))*; pap. 49.50 *(978-1-4777-1247-4(X))*; pap. 297.00 *(978-1-4777-1248-1(8))* Rosen Publishing Group, Inc., The. (PowerKids Pr.).

Rajczak, Kristen. The Donner Party. 2015. (Doomed! Ser.). (ENG., Illus.). 32p. (J). (gr. 4-5). pap. 10.50 *(978-1-4824-2928-2(4))* Stevens, Gareth Publishing LLLP.

—Laura Ingalls Wilder in Her Own Words. 2016. (Eyewitness to History Ser.). (ENG.). 32p. (J). (gr. 4-5). pap. 10.50 *(978-1-4824-4070-6(9))* Stevens, Gareth Publishing LLLP.

—Life on a Wagon Train. 2013. (What You Didn't Know about History Ser.). (Illus.). 24p. (J). (gr. 2-5). pap. 8.15 *(978-1-4339-8445-7(8))*; lib. bdg. 22.60 *(978-1-4339-8444-0(X))* Stevens, Gareth Publishing LLLP.

—20 Fun Facts about Pioneer Women. 2015. (Fun Fact File: Women in History Ser.). (ENG., Illus.). 32p. (J). (gr. 2-3). 25.25 *(978-1-4824-2806-3(7))* Stevens, Gareth Publishing LLLP.

Rau, Margaret. Belle of the West: The True Story of Belle Starr. 2004. (Women of the Frontier Ser.). (Illus.). 160p. (YA). (gr. 6-12). 23.95 *(978-1-883846-68-8(4)*, First Biographies) Reynolds, Morgan Inc.

Revolutionary Discoveries of Scientific Pioneers. 2013. (Revolutionary Discoveries of Scientific Pioneers Ser.). 80p. (YA). (gr. 7-12). 266.00 *(978-1-4777-1818-6(4))* Rosen Publishing Group, Inc., The.

Reynolds, Toby & Calver, Paul. Fearless Women: Courageous Females Who Refused to Be Denied. 2017. (Real Lives Ser.). (ENG., Illus.). 64p. (J). (gr. 4-10). 8.99 *(978-0-7641-6886-4(X))* Barron's Educational Series, Inc.

Rice, Katelyn. Settling & Unsettling the West (America in The 1800s) 2017. (Primary Source Readers Ser.). (Illus.). 32p. (J). (gr. 4-5). pap. 8.99 ***(978-1-4938-3797-7(4))*** Teacher Created Materials, Inc.

Russell, Greta. Olive Boone: Frontier Woman. Hare, John, illus. 2014. (Notable Missourians Ser.). (ENG.). 48p. (J). lib. bdg. 24.00 *(978-1-61248-118-0(3))* Truman State Univ. Pr.

Sandler, Martin W. Who Were the American Pioneers? And Other Questions about Westward Expansion. Barrett, Robert, illus. 2014. (Good Question! Ser.). (ENG.). 32p. (J). pap. 5.95 *(978-1-4027-9047-8(3))* Sterling Publishing Co., Inc.

Sanford, William R. & Green, Carl R. Buffalo Bill Cody: Courageous Wild West Showman. 2012. (Courageous Heroes of the American West Ser.). (Illus.). 48p. (J). pap. 8.95 *(978-1-4644-0090-2(3))*; (gr. 5-18). 22.60 *(978-0-7660-4007-6(0))* Enslow Pubs., Inc.

—Calamity Jane: Courageous Wild West Woman. 2012. (Courageous Heroes of the American West Ser.). (Illus.). 48p. (J). pap. 8.95 *(978-1-4644-0093-3(8))*; (gr. 5-18). 22.60 *(978-0-7660-4010-6(0))* Enslow Pubs., Inc.

—Daniel Boone: Courageous Frontiersman. 2012. (Courageous Heroes of the American West Ser.). (Illus.). 48p. (J). pap. 8.95 *(978-1-4644-0085-8(7))*; (gr. 5-18). 22.60 *(978-0-7660-4002-1(X))* Enslow Pubs., Inc.

—Davy Crockett: Courageous Hero of the Alamo. 2012. (Courageous Heroes of the American West Ser.). (Illus.). 48p. (J). pap. 8.95 *(978-1-4644-0086-5(5))*; (gr. 5-18). 22.60 *(978-0-7660-4005-2(4))* Enslow Pubs., Inc.

—Kit Carson: Courageous Mountain Man. 2012. (Courageous Heroes of the American West Ser.). 48p. (J). pap. 8.95 *(978-1-4644-0094-0(6))*; (Illus.). (gr. 5-18). 22.60 *(978-0-7660-4011-3(9))* Enslow Pubs., Inc.

Savage, Jeff. Pioneering Women: True Tales of the Wild West. 2012. (True Tales of the Wild West Ser.). (Illus.). 48p. (J). (gr. 5-18). lib. bdg. 22.60 *(978-0-7660-4022-9(4))* Enslow Pubs., Inc.

Schwartz, Heather E. The Foul, Filthy American Frontier: The Disgusting Details about the Journey Out West. 2011. (Disgusting History Ser.). (ENG.). 32p. (gr. 3-4). pap. 47.70 *(978-1-4296-6478-3(9)*, Fact Finders) Capstone Press of Coughlan Cos.

Shoup, Kate. The Gold Rush. 2017. (J). ***(978-1-5026-2640-0(3))*** Cavendish Square Publishing.

Smith, Andrea P. Daniel Boone. 2012. (Illus.). 24p. (J). 63.60 *(978-1-4488-5227-7(7))*; pap. 10.60 *(978-1-4488-5226-0(9))*; lib. bdg. 25.25 *(978-1-4488-5194-2(7))* Rosen Publishing Group, Inc., The. (PowerKids Pr.).

—Davy Crockett. 2012. (Illus.). 24p. (J). 63.60 *(978-1-4488-5223-9(4))*; pap. 10.60 *(978-1-4488-5222-2(6))*; lib. bdg. 25.25 *(978-1-4488-5192-8(0))* Rosen Publishing Group, Inc., The. (PowerKids Pr.).

—Jim Bowie. 2012. (Illus.). 24p. (J). 63.60 *(978-1-4488-5231-4(5))*; pap. 10.60 *(978-1-4488-5230-7(7))*; lib. bdg. 25.25 *(978-1-4488-5196-6(3))* Rosen Publishing Group, Inc., The. (PowerKids Pr.).

Smith-Llera, Danielle. Stranded in the Sierra Nevada: The Story of the Donner Party. 2015. (Adventures on the American Frontier Ser.). (ENG., Illus.). 32p. (gr. 3-4). pap. 7.95 *(978-1-4914-4912-7(8))* Capstone Press of Coughlan Cos.

Spies, Karen Bornemann. Buffalo Bill Cody: Legend of the Wild West. 2015. (Legendary American Biographies Ser.). 96p. (J). (gr. 6-12). 27.94 *(978-0-7660-6450-8(6))*; pap. 10.95 *(978-0-7660-6451-5(4))* Enslow Pubs., Inc.

Stefoff, Rebecca. Surviving the Oregon Trail. 2012. (Stories in American History Ser.). (Illus.). 128p. (J). (gr. 5-18). 33.27 *(978-0-7660-3955-1(2))* Enslow Pubs., Inc.

—Surviving the Oregon Trail: Stories in American History. 2012. (Stories in American History Ser.). (Illus.). 128p. (J). (gr. 5-18). pap. 10.95 *(978-1-4644-0025-4(3))* Enslow Pubs., Inc.

Stuckey, Rachel. Go West with Famous Trailblazers. 2016. (ENG.). 32p. (J). *(978-0-7787-2324-0(0))* Crabtree Publishing Co.

Transgender Pioneers. 2016. (Transgender Pioneers Ser.). 112p. (gr. 6-6). 148.40 *(978-1-4777-8549-2(3)*, Rosen Young Adult) Rosen Publishing Group, Inc., The.

Wade, Mary Dodson. David Crockett: Creating a Legend. Hein, Joy Fisher, illus. 2009. (ENG.). 24p. (J). (gr. k-2). 16.95 *(978-1-933979-12-0(7)*, 9781933979120) Bright Sky Pr.

—Henrietta King: La Patrona. Farnsworth, Bill, illus. 2012. (ENG.). 64p. 16.95 *(978-1-933979-63-2(1)*, 7e8171df-3905-4241-a084-108e6384ddaf) Bright Sky Pr.

Wadsworth, Ginger. Survival in the Snow. Orback, Craig, illus. 2011. 48p. (J). pap. 6.95 *(978-0-7613-3941-0(8)*, First Avenue Editions) Lerner Publishing Group.

Warren, Andrea. The Boy Who Became Buffalo Bill: Growing up Billy Cody in Bleeding Kansas, 0 vols. 2015. (ENG., Illus.). 256p. (J). 19.99 *(978-1-4778-2718-5(8)*, 9781477827185, Two Lions) Amazon Publishing.

PIONEERS—FICTION

Abbott, E. F. Mary Jemison: Native American Captive. 2016. (Based on a True Story Ser.). (ENG., Illus.). 224p. (J). 15.99 *(978-1-250-06838-5(X)*, 9781250068385) Feiwel & Friends.

Drummond, Ree. Stuck in the Mud. 2015. (I Can Read! Level 1 Ser.). (J). lib. bdg. 13.55 *(978-0-606-36469-0(2))* Turtleback Bks.

Johnson, Mary L. Flinthills Frannie, 1 vol. 2009. 43p. pap. 24.95 *(978-1-61546-886-7(2))* America Star Bks.

Monroe, George. The Secret Cave on the Hill. 2012. 50p. pap. 21.99 *(978-1-4772-8840-5(6))* AuthorHouse.

Monson, Marianne. Pioneer Puzzle. 2010. (J). *(978-1-60641-669-3(3))* Deseret Bk. Co.

Parker, Amy Christine. Gated. 2014. (ENG.). 368p. (YA). (gr. 9). pap. 9.99 *(978-0-449-81600-4(1)*, Ember) Random Hse. Children's Bks.

Santrey, Laurence & Macken, JoAnn Early. Davy Crockett: Young Pioneer. Livingston, Francis, illus. 2008. 55p. (J). pap. *(978-0-439-02048-0(4))* Scholastic, Inc.

Scott, Dan. The Secret of Fort Pioneer: A Bret King Mystery. Beeler, Joe, illus. 2011. 190p. 42.95 *(978-1-258-09951-0(9))* Literary Licensing, LLC.

Webster, Raelyn & Rasmussen, Kenneth L. My Grandma Mary. Johnson, Kimberli Anne, illus. 2013. 38p. 22.95 *(978-1-940379-00-5(8))* Telling Family Tales.

Winters, Kay. Voices from the Oregon Trail. Day, Larry, illus. 2014. (ENG.). 48p. (J). (gr. 2-4). 17.99 *(978-0-8037-3775-4(0)*, Dial Bks) Penguin Young Readers Group.

PIPE FITTING—VOCATIONAL GUIDANCE

Payment, Simone. A Career as a Plumber. 2010. (Essential Careers Ser.). (ENG.). 80p. (YA). lib. bdg. 33.25 *(978-1-4358-9473-0(1))* Rosen Publishing Group, Inc., The.

PIRATES

see also Privateering; United States—History—Tripolitan War, 1801-1805; Women Pirates

AZ Books Staff. Secrets of Pirates. Naumovets, Elena, ed. 2012. (Mysteries of History Ser.). (ENG.). 18p. (J). (gr. 1-3). bds. 17.95 *(978-1-61889-089-4(1))* AZ Bks. LLC.

Barefoot Books, et al. Pirates Fun Activities. 2008. (ENG., Illus.). 16p. (J). pap. 4.99 *(978-1-84686-217-5(5))* Barefoot Bks., Inc.

Bearce, Stephanie. Top Secret Files: Pirates & Buried Treasure: Secrets, Strange Tales, & Hidden Facts about Pirates. rev. ed. 2015. (Top Secret Files of History Ser.: 0). (ENG., Illus.). 125p. (J). (gr. 4-7). pap. 8.95 *(978-1-61821-421-8(7))* Prufrock Pr.

Believe It Or Not, Ripley, compiled by. Ripley Twists: Pirates. 2015. (Twist Ser.: 14). (ENG., Illus.). 48p. (J). 12.95 *(978-1-60991-139-3(3))* Ripley Entertainment, Inc.

Bell, Robin. My Adventure with Pirates: Advanced My Adventure. 2009. (ENG.). 44p. (J). 8.99 *(978-1-59092-462-4(2))* Blue Forge Pr.

Biskup, Agnieszka. Captured by Pirates! An Isabel Soto History Adventure. Stewart, Roger, illus. 2012. (Graphic Expeditions Ser.). (ENG.). 32p. (gr. 3-4). pap. 47.70 *(978-1-4296-8471-2(2))*; lib. bdg. 30.65 *(978-1-4296-7545-1(4))* Capstone Press of Coughlan Cos. (Graphic Library).

Bloomsbury USA. My Pirate Activity & Sticker Book: Bloomsbury Activity Books. 2014. (ENG., Illus.). 32p. (J). (gr. -1-1). pap. 4.99 *(978-1-61963-306-3(X)*, 9781619633063, Bloomsbury USA Childrens) Bloomsbury Publishing USA.

Bodden, Valerie. Pirates. 2017. (J). ***(978-1-60818-814-7(0)***, Creative Education) Creative Co., The.

Boshouwers, Suzan. Pirates. Hund, Marjolein & Burr, Dan, illus. 2012. (Want to Know Ser.). (ENG.). 30p. (J). (gr. k-2). 16.95 *(978-1-60537-135-1(1))* Cobblestone Publishing Co.

Bowman, Bianca. National Geographic Kids Funny Fill-In: My Pirate Adventure. Tharp, Jason, illus. 2014. (ENG.). 48p. (J). (gr. 3-7). pap. 4.99 *(978-1-4263-1480-3(9)*, National Geographic Children's Bks.) National Geographic Society.

Brew, Jim. Pirates. 2012. (History's Greatest Warriors Ser.). (ENG., Illus.). 24p. (J). (gr. 3-7). lib. bdg. 25.95 *(978-1-60014-747-0(X)*, Torque Bks.) Bellwether Media.

Brown, Chris. Shiver Me Timbers: A Fun Book of Pirates, Sailors, & Other Sea-Farers. 2006. (ENG., Illus.). 32p. (J). (gr. 4-7). pap. 8.95 *(978-0-7145-3303-2(3))* Consortium Bk. Sales & Distribution.

Buckley, James. Who Was Blackbeard? 2015. (Who Was... ? Ser.). lib. bdg. 16.00 *(978-0-606-37556-6(2))* Turtleback Bks.

Buckley, James & dePaola, Tomie. Who Was Blackbeard? Harrison, Nancy & Qiu, Joseph J. M. , illus. 2015. (Who Was? Ser.). (ENG.). 112p. (J). (gr. 3-7). 5.99 *(978-0-448-48308-5(4)*, Grosset & Dunlap) Penguin Young Readers Group.

Butzer, Anna. A Pirate Alphabet: The ABCs of Piracy! Jevons, Chris, illus. 2016. (Alphabet Connection Ser.). (ENG.). 32p. (gr. k-1). lib. bdg. 27.32 *(978-1-4795-6886-4(4))* Picture Window Bks.

Callery, Sean. Treasure Hunt. 2011. (ENG.). 24p. (J). pap. *(978-0-7787-7874-5(6))*; (gr. 3-6). *(978-0-7787-7852-3(5))* Crabtree Publishing Co.

Caviezel, Giovanni. Pirates! Mesturini, C., illus. 2011. (Mini People Shape Bks.). (ENG.). 10p. (J). bds. 5.99 *(978-0-7641-6441-5(4))* Barron's Educational Series, Inc.

Chrisp, Peter. Navigators: Pirates. 2014. (Navigators Ser.). (ENG., Illus.). 48p. (J). (gr. 4-7). pap. 8.99 *(978-0-7534-7131-9(0)*, 9780753471319, Kingfisher) Roaring Brook Pr.

Claybourne, Anna. Pirate Secrets Revealed. 2010. (Extreme! Ser.). (ENG.). 32p. (gr. 3-4). pap. 47.70 *(978-1-4296-5024-3(9)*, Fact Finders) Capstone Press of Coughlan Cos.

—Treasure Hunter's Handbook. 2011. (ENG.). 24p. (J). pap. *(978-0-7787-7866-0(5))*; (gr. 3-6). *(978-0-7787-7844-8(4))* Crabtree Publishing Co.

Clifford, Barry. Real Pirates: The Untold Story of the Whydah from Slave Ship to Pirate Ship. Manchess, Gregory, illus. Garrett, Kenneth, photos by. 2008. (ENG.). 32p. (J). (gr. 5). 16.95 *(978-1-4263-0279-4(7))*; lib. bdg. 25.90 *(978-1-4263-0280-0(0))* National Geographic Society. (National Geographic Children's Bks.).

Clissold, Caroline. All about Pirates. 2007. (Trackers-Math Ser.). (gr. 2-5). pap. 5.00 *(978-1-59055-918-5(5))* Pacific Learning, Inc.

Cooke, Tim. Blackbeard: A Notorious Pirate in the Caribbean. 2016. (Wanted! Famous Outlaws Ser.). (ENG., Illus.). 48p. (J). (gr. 6-8). pap. 14.05 *(978-1-4824-4247-2(7))* Stevens, Gareth Publishing LLLP.

Davies, Kate & Stowell, Louie. Sticker Dressing Pirates. 2012. (Sticker Dressing Ser.). 24p. (J). pap. 8.99 *(978-0-7945-3165-2(2)*, Usborne) EDC Publishing.

Davis, Sarah K. Pirates. 2016. (Uncommon Women Ser.). (ENG., Illus.). 48p. (gr. 3-8). 27.99 *(978-1-62920-584-7(2))* Scobre Pr. Corp.

DeGagne, Mandie. Pirates. Dennis, Peter, illus. 2012. 31p. (J). *(978-1-58865-594-3(6))* Kidsbooks, LLC.

Design Eye Publishing Staff, et al. Amazing Automata — Pirates! 2013. (Dover Origami Papercraft Ser.). (ENG.). 24p. (J). (gr. 5). 14.99 *(978-0-486-49980-2(4))* Dover Pubns., Inc.

Donaldson, Madeline. Pirates, Scoundrels, & Scallywags. (ShockZone (tm) — Villains Ser.). (ENG., Illus.). 32p. (gr. 5-8). 2015. 21.32 *(978-1-4677-6005-8(6)*, Lerner Digital) 2013. pap. 8.95 *(978-1-4677-0897-5(6))* 2013. lib. bdg. 26.60 *(978-1-4677-0606-3(X)*, Lerner Pubns.) Lerner Publishing Group.

Dorling Kindersley Publishing Staff. DK Findout! Pirates. 2017. (DK Find Out! Ser.). (ENG., Illus.). 64p. (J). (gr. 1-4). pap. 10.99 *(978-1-4654-5752-3(6)*, DK Children) Dorling Kindersley Publishing, Inc.

—Factivity Fun: Pirates. 2017. (ENG.). 96p. (J). (gr. 1-4). pap. 12.99 *(978-1-4654-5681-6(3)*, DK Children) Dorling Kindersley Publishing, Inc.

—Pirate Glow-in-the-Dark. 2004. (Ultimate Sticker Bks.). (ENG.). 16p. (J). (gr. k-3). pap. 6.99 *(978-0-7566-0219-2(X)*, DK Children) Dorling Kindersley Publishing, Inc.

—Ultimate Sticker Book: Pirates. 2017. (Ultimate Sticker Bks.). (ENG.). 32p. (J). (gr. k-2). pap. 6.99 *(978-1-4654-6289-3(9)*, DK Children) Dorling Kindersley Publishing, Inc.

Drechsler, Lawrence. The Pirates. (Illus.). (Orig.). (J). (gr. 6-18). pap. *(978-0-935143-01-0(7))* Treadle Pr.

Elborough, Travis. Highwayman, Outlaws & Bandits of London. 2004. (.... of London Ser.). (ENG., Illus.). 96p. pap. 8.99 *(978-1-904153-13-9(5))* Watling St., Ltd. GBR. Dist: Trafalgar Square Publishing.

Farndon, John. How to Live Like a Caribbean Pirate. Campidelli, Maurizio & Viana, Tatio, illus. 2016. (How to Live Like... Ser.). (ENG.). 32p. (J). (gr. 3-6). 26.65 *(978-1-5124-0631-3(7))* Lerner Publishing Group.

Feder, Joshua B. Pirates. 2003. (Illus.). 66p. (YA). (gr. 5-9). reprint ed. 22.00 *(978-0-7567-6684-9(2))* DIANE Publishing Co.

Forest, Christopher. The Crude, Unpleasant Age of Pirates: The Disgusting Details about the Life of Pirates. (Disgusting History Ser.). (ENG.). 32p. (gr. 3-4). 2011. pap. 47.70 *(978-1-4296-6476-9(2))* 2010. lib. bdg. 27.32 *(978-1-4296-4542-3(3))* Capstone Press of Coughlan Cos. (Fact Finders).

Fox, E. T. Pirates. 2017. (Illus.). 64p. (J). ***(978-1-5182-2427-0(X))*** Dorling Kindersley Publishing, Inc.

Gelletly, LeeAnne. Modern-Day Pirates. 2013. (J). *(978-1-61900-038-4(5))*; 34.95 *(978-1-61900-037-7(7))* Eldorado Ink.

Gilpin, Rebecca. Pirate Things to make & Do. 2005. 32p. (J). pap. 6.95 *(978-0-7945-1061-9(2)*, Usborne) EDC Publishing.

Gunderson, Jessica. Your Life as a Cabin Boy on a Pirate Ship. Burns, Mike, illus. 2012. (Way It Was Ser.). (ENG.). 32p. (gr. 2-3). pap. 8.95 *(978-1-4048-7249-3(3))*; lib. bdg. 26.65 *(978-1-4048-7159-5(4))* Picture Window Bks.

Hamilton, John. A History of Pirates, 1 vol. 2007. (Pirates! Ser.). (ENG., Illus.). 32p. (gr. 4-8). 27.07 *(978-1-59928-761-4(7)*, Abdo & Daughters) ABDO Publishing Co.

—Pirate Ships & Weapons, 1 vol. 2007. (Pirates Ser.). (ENG., Illus.). 32p. (gr. 4-8). 27.07 *(978-1-59928-763-8(3)*, Abdo & Daughters) ABDO Publishing Co.

—A Pirate's Life, 1 vol. 2007. (Pirates! Ser.). (ENG., Illus.). 32p. (gr. 4-8). 27.07 *(978-1-59928-762-1(5)*, Abdo & Daughters) ABDO Publishing Co.

Hamilton, Sue. Bartholomew Roberts, 1 vol. 2007. (Pirates Ser.). (ENG., Illus.). 32p. (gr. 4-8). 27.07 *(978-1-59928-757-7(9)*, Abdo & Daughters) ABDO Publishing Co.

Hamilton, Sue L. Blackbeard, 1 vol. 2007. (Pirates! Ser.). (ENG., Illus.). 32p. (gr. 4-8). 27.07 *(978-1-59928-758-4(7)*, Abdo & Daughters) ABDO Publishing Co.

—Captain Kidd, 1 vol. 2007. (Pirates! Ser.). (ENG., Illus.). 32p. (gr. 4-8). 27.07 *(978-1-59928-759-1(5)*, Abdo & Daughters) ABDO Publishing Co.

—Henry Morgan, 1 vol. 2007. (Pirates! Ser.). (ENG., Illus.). 32p. (gr. 4-8). 27.07 *(978-1-59928-760-7(9)*, Abdo & Daughters) ABDO Publishing Co.

—Pirates!, 8 vols., Set. Incl. Blackbeard. 27.07 *(978-1-59928-758-4(7))*; Captain Kidd. 27.07 *(978-1-59928-759-1(5))*; Henry Morgan. 27.07 *(978-1-59928-760-7(9))*; (Illus.). 32p. (gr. 4-8). (Pirates Ser.). 2007. 216.56 *(978-1-59928-756-0(0)*, Abdo & Daughters) ABDO Publishing Co.

Hanel, Rachel. Pirates. 2007. (Fearsome Fighters Ser.). (Illus.). 48p. (YA). (gr. 3-6). lib. bdg. 31.35 *(978-1-58341-537-5(8))* Creative Co., The.

Hanson, Anders & Hengel, Katherine. Biggest, Baddest Book of Pirates, 1 vol. 2012. (Biggest, Baddest Books for Boys Ser.). (ENG.). 24p. (J). (gr. k-4). 25.65 *(978-1-61783-408-0(4))* ABDO Publishing Co.

Harris, Nicholas. Let's Explore a Pirate Ship. Lee, Brian, illus. 2010. 36p. (J). 13.99 *(978-0-8437-1378-7(X))* Hammond World Atlas Corp.

Harrison, Paul. Pirates. (Up Close Ser.). 24p. (gr. 3-3). 2009. 47.90 *(978-1-60854-699-2(3))* 2008. (Illus.). (J). lib. bdg. 25.25 *(978-1-4042-4226-5(0))* Rosen Publishing Group, Inc., The. (PowerKids Pr.)

Havercroft, Elizabeth. A Year on a Pirate Ship. 2008. (Time Goes By Ser.). (ENG.). (gr. k-3). pap. 39.62 *(978-0-7613-4716-3(X))*; (Illus.). 24p. lib. bdg. 22.60 *(978-1-58013-547-4(1))* Lerner Publishing Group.

Heilbrough, Emma. A Day in the Life of a Pirate. 2009. (Day in the Life Ser.). 32p. (gr. 4-5). 47.90 *(978-1-61511-007-0(0)*, PowerKids Pr.) Rosen Publishing Group, Inc., The.

Hibbert, Clare. Real Pirates. James, John, illus. 2003. (ENG.). 48p. (J). (gr. 3). 15.95 *(978-1-59270-018-9(7))* Enchanted Lion Bks., LLC.

Howard, Barnaby. The Best Book of Pirates. 2006. (Best Book Of Ser.). (ENG., Illus.). 32p. (J). (gr. k-3). pap. 6.99 *(978-0-7534-5936-2(1)*, 9780753459362, Kingfisher) Roaring Brook Pr.

Hunter, Nick. Pirate Treasure, 1 vol. 2013. (Treasure Hunters Ser.). (ENG., Illus.). 48p. (gr. 5-8). pap. 9.25 *(978-1-4109-4960-8(5))*; lib. bdg. 29.99 *(978-1-4109-4953-0(2))* Heinemann-Raintree.

Jackman, Vernon. Bunnies & Butterflies in the Backyard & the Pirates Who Know Where They Live: Stories That Help Children Learn & Remember Their Address & Telephone Number. Theagene, Jeannisse, illus. l.t. ed. 2010. (ENG.). 32p. (J). pap. 6.99 *(978-0-9829371-1-2(3))* New Kid Safety.

Jacobs, Pat. I Wonder Why Pirates Wore Earrings: And Other Questions about Piracy. 2012. (I Wonder Why Ser.). (ENG., Illus.). 32p. (J). (gr. k-3). 6.99 *(978-0-7534-6791-6(7)*, 9780753467916, Kingfisher) Roaring Brook Pr.

Jenson-Elliott, Cindy. Pirate Ships Ahoy!, 1 vol. 2012. (Pirates! Ser.). (ENG.). 32p. (gr. 1-2). lib. bdg. 26.65 *(978-1-4296-8610-5(3))* Capstone Press of Coughlan Cos.

Jenson-Elliott, Cindy & Sautter, Aaron. The Most Famous Pirates. 2013. (Illus.). 32p. (J). *(978-91-620-6520-1(3))* Capstone Press of Coughlan Cos.

Jones, Rob Lloyd & Gower, Teri. 1001 Pirate Things to Spot. 2007. (ENG., Illus.). 32p. *(978-0-7460-7694-1(0)*, Usborne) EDC Publishing.

Kaplan, Arie. Swashbuckling Scoundrels: Pirates in Fact & Fiction. 2015. (ENG., Illus.). 72p. (gr. 5-12). (J). lib. bdg. 33.32 *(978-1-4677-5252-7(5))*; 33.32 *(978-1-4677-5253-4(3))* Lerner Publishing Group. (Twenty-First Century Bks.).

Keppeler, Jill. Pirate Legends. 2017. (Famous Legends Ser.). 32p. (J). (gr. 2-3). pap. 10.50 ***(978-1-5382-0245-6(X))*** Stevens, Gareth Publishing LLLP.

Keyworth, R. L. Do Pirates Like to Play Pattie Cake? A Pirate's Guide to Playing Nice. 2009. 40p. pap. 17.99 *(978-1-4389-4667-2(8))* AuthorHouse.

Krull, Kathleen. Lives of the Pirates: Swashbucklers, Scoundrels (Neighbors Beware!) Hewitt, Kathryn, illus. 2013. (Lives Of ... Ser.). (ENG.). 96p. (J). (gr. 5-7). pap. 8.99 *(978-0-544-10495-2(1))* Houghton Mifflin Harcourt Publishing Co.

LaBaff, Stephanie. Draw Pirates in 4 Easy Steps: Then Write a Story. LaBaff, Tom, illus. 2012. (Drawing in 4 Easy Steps Ser.). 48p. (J). (gr. 3-18). 25.27 *(978-0-7660-3839-4(4))* Enslow Pubs., Inc.

Langley, Andrew. Pirates. 2015. (100 Facts You Should Know Ser.). (ENG., Illus.). 48p. (J). (gr. 4-5). lib. bdg. 31.95 *(978-1-4824-2181-1(X))* Stevens, Gareth Publishing LLLP.

Leapfrog Learners - Pirates. (Awesome Adventures Ser.). 16p. (J). *(978-2-7643-0117-3(0))* Phidal Publishing, Inc./Editions Phidal, Inc.

Leblanc, Catherine. How to Pulverize Pirates. Garrigue, Roland, illus. 2013. (ENG.). 32p. (J). (gr. -1). 14.99 *(978-1-60887-192-6(4))* Insight Editions.

Leigh, Susannah. Puzzle Pirates. Haw, Brenda, illus. 2006. (Usborne Young Puzzles Ser.). 32p. (J). (gr. 1). lib. bdg. 14.99 *(978-1-58086-973-7(4)*, Usborne) EDC Publishing.

Lethbridge, Lucy. True Stories of Pirates. 2005. (True Adventure Stories Ser.). (Illus.). 144p. (J). pap. 4.99 *(978-0-7945-0875-3(8)*, Usborne) EDC Publishing.

Lewis, Jan, illus. Pirate Ship: Lift the Flaps to Follow the Clues & Discover the Fabulous Treasure. 2016. (ENG.). 10p. (J). (gr. -1-12). 7.99 *(978-1-86147-767-5(8)*, Armadillo) Anness Publishing GBR. Dist: National Bk. Network.

Lichtenheld, Tom. Everything I Know about Pirates. Lichtenheld, Tom, illus. 2003. (ENG., Illus.). 40p. (J). (gr. -1-3). pap. 7.99 *(978-0-689-86009-6(9)*, Simon & Schuster Bks. For Young Readers) Simon & Schuster Bks. For Young Readers.

Lincoln, Margarette. The Pirate's Handbook: How to Become a Rogue of the High Seas. (Illus.). (J). pap. 15.99 *(978-0-590-24558-6(9))* Scholastic, Inc.

Little & Large Sticker Activity Pirates. 2008. 24p. pap. *(978-1-84810-061-9(2))* Miles Kelly Publishing, Ltd.

Llimós, Anna. Pirate Ship Adventure Crafts. 2010. (Fun Adventure Crafts Ser.). (Illus.). 32p. (J). pap. 7.95 *(978-0-7660-3729-8(0)*, Enslow Elementary) Enslow Pubs., Inc.

Llimós, Anna & Library Association Staff. Pirate Ship Adventure Crafts. 2010. (Fun Adventure Crafts Ser.). (Illus.). 32p. (J). 23.94 *(978-0-7660-3728-1(2)*, Enslow Elementary) Enslow Pubs., Inc.

Lubber, William. Pirateology: The Pirate Hunter's Companion. Steer, Dugald A., ed. 2006. (Ologies Ser.). (ENG., Illus.). 32p. (J). (gr. 3-7). 21.99 *(978-0-7636-3143-7(4))* Candlewick Pr.

Macdonald, Fiona. Nasty Pirates: You Wouldn't Want to Meet! 2010. (Top 10 Worst Ser.). (Illus.). 32p. (J). (gr. 3-6). (ENG.). pap. 10.50 *(978-1-4339-4086-6(8))*; lib. bdg. 26.60 *(978-1-4339-4085-9(X))* Stevens, Gareth Publishing LLLP. (Gareth Stevens Learning Library).

Macdonald, Fiona & Salariya, Daivid. Top 10 Worst Nasty Pirates: You Wouldn't Want to Meet! Antram, David, illus. 2013. 32p. (J). *(978-1-4351-5037-9(6))* Barnes & Noble, Inc.

Malam, John. Do You Want to Be a Pirate? 2015. (Do You Want to Be... Ser.). (Illus.). 32p. (gr. 3-6). 28.50 *(978-1-909645-36-3(2))* Book Hse. GBR. Dist: Black Rabbit Bks.

—How to Be a Pirate. Antram, Dave, illus. 2005. (How to Be Ser.). (ENG.). 32p. (J). (gr. 3-7). 14.95 *(978-0-7922-7448-3(2))*; 21.90 *(978-0-7922-7497-1(0))* National Geographic Society. (National Geographic Children's Bks.).

—How to Be a Pirate. Bergin, Mark, illus. 2008. (How to Be Ser.). (ENG.). 32p. (J). (gr. 3-7). pap. 5.95 *(978-1-4263-0283-1(5)*, National Geographic Children's Bks.) National Geographic Society.

—You Wouldn't Want to... Be a Pirate's Prisoner! Antram, David, illus. rev. ed. 2012. (ENG.). 32p. (J). lib. bdg. 29.00 *(978-0-531-27502-3(7))* Scholastic Library Publishing.

—You Wouldn't Want to Be a Pirate's Prisoner! Horrible Things You'd Rather Not Know. Antram, David, illus. rev. ed. 2012. (You Wouldn't Want to...: History of the World Ser.). (ENG.). 40p. (J). pap. 9.95 *(978-0-531-28027-0(6))* Scholastic Library Publishing.

Marley, David F. Daily Life of Pirates, 1 vol. 2012. (Daily Life Ser.). (Illus.). 259p. (C). 64.00 *(978-0-313-39563-5(2)*, A3426C, Greenwood) ABC-CLIO, LLC.

Mason, Paul. Pirate Adventures! 2011. (ENG.). 24p. (J). pap. *(978-0-7787-7878-3(9))*; (gr. 3-6). *(978-0-7787-7856-1(8))* Crabtree Publishing Co.

McCarthy, Tom. Pirates & Shipwrecks: True Stories. 2016. (Mystery & Mayhem Ser.). (ENG.). 128p. (gr. 3). 19.95 *(978-1-61930-471-0(6))* Open City Bks.

Mcdonald, Jake. The Pirate Colouring Book. 2015. (ENG.). 32p. (J). (gr. -1-3). pap. 6.99 ***(978-1-78055-310-8(2))*** O'Mara, Michael Bks., Ltd. GBR. Dist: Independent Pubs. Group.

McLeese, Don. Pirates. 2009. 32p. pap. 7.99 *(978-0-8249-1449-3(X)*, Ideal Pubns.) Worthy Publishing.

McNeil, Niki, et al. HOCPP 1139 Pirates. 2006. spiral bd. 19.00 *(978-1-60308-139-9(9))* In the Hands of a Child.

Meinking, Mary & Peschke, Marci. Kylie Jean Pirate Craft Queen, 1 vol. Mourning, Tuesday, illus. 2014. (Kylie Jean Craft Queen Ser.). (ENG.). 32p. (gr. 2-3). lib. bdg. 26.65 *(978-1-4795-2192-0(2))* Picture Window Bks.

Menges, Jeff A. Haunted Pirate Tattoos. 2004. (Dover Tattoos Ser.). (ENG., Illus.). 2p. (J). (gr. 1-4). pap. 1.50 *(978-0-486-43320-2(X))* Dover Pubns., Inc.

Miles, Liz. Meet the Pirates. 2014. (Encounters with the Past Ser.). 32p. (J). (gr. 3-6). 26.60 *(978-1-4824-0893-5(7))* Stevens, Gareth Publishing LLLP.

Morris, Neil. Pirates. 2009. (Amazing History Ser.). (Illus.). 32p. (J). (gr. 4-7). pap. 7.95 *(978-1-59920-205-1(0))* Black Rabbit Bks.

Nemmers, Tom. Pirates Scratch & Sketch: For Adventurous Artists & Explorers of All Ages. Zschock, Martha Day, illus. 2007. 64p. (J). 12.99 *(978-1-59359-871-6(8))* Peter Pauper Pr. Inc.

Nilsen, Anna. Pirates: All Aboard for Hours of Puzzling Fun! 2006. (Illus.). 32p. pap. *(978-1-921049-71-2(5))* Little Hare Bks. AUS. Dist: HarperCollins Pubs. Australia.

—Pirates Galore: The Biggest Treasure Hunt Ever! 2008. (ENG., Illus.). 32p. (J). (gr. 2-7). pap. 8.99 *(978-1-921049-97-2(9))* Little Hare Bks. AUS. Dist: Independent Pubs. Group.

O'Donnell, Liam. Crack the Pirate Code. 2017. (Pirates! Ser.). (ENG.). 32p. (gr. 1-3). lib. bdg. 29.99 ***(978-1-4109-8706-8(X)***, Read Me!) Heinemann-Raintree.

—Get into Pirate Gear. 2017. (Pirates! Ser.). (ENG.). 32p. (gr. 1-3). lib. bdg. 29.99 ***(978-1-4109-8705-1(1)***, Read Me!) Heinemann-Raintree.

—Hop on the Pirate History Boat. 2017. (Pirates! Ser.). (ENG.). 32p. (gr. 1-3). lib. bdg. 29.99 ***(978-1-4109-8703-7(5)***, Read Me!) Heinemann-Raintree.

—Pirates! 2017. (Pirates! Ser.). (ENG.). 32p. (gr. 1-3). 119.96 ***(978-1-4109-8723-5(X)***, Read Me!) Heinemann-Raintree.

—Sink or Swim with Pirate Ships. 2017. (Pirates! Ser.). (ENG.). 32p. (gr. 1-3). lib. bdg. 29.99 ***(978-1-4109-8704-4(3)***, Read Me!) Heinemann-Raintree.

Owen, James A. & Owen, Jeremy. Lost Treasures of the Pirates of the Caribbean. Owen, James A., illus. 2011. (ENG., Illus.). 32p. (J). (gr. 3-7). pap. 16.99 *(978-1-4424-3093-8(1)*, Simon & Schuster Bks. For Young Readers) Simon & Schuster Bks. For Young Readers.

Owen, Ruth. The Life of a Caribbean Pirate. 2015. (It's a Fact Ser.). (ENG.). 32p. (J). (gr. 3-6). lib. bdg. 26.60 *(978-1-909673-92-2(7))* Bearport Publishing Co., Inc.

Platt, Richard. Discovering Pirates, 1 vol. 2004. (ENG., Illus.). 32p. (J). (gr. k-3). 16.99 *(978-1-58980-227-8(6))* Pelican Publishing Co., Inc.

Platt, Richard & Dorling Kindersley Publishing Staff. Pirate. Chambers, Tina, photos by. 2007. (DK Eyewitness Bks.). (ENG., Illus.). 72p. (J). (gr. 3-7). 16.99 *(978-0-7566-3005-8(3)*, DK Children) Dorling Kindersley Publishing, Inc.

Pope, Miller. ABC-Pirate-Coloring Book. 2012. (ENG.). (J). pap. 5.99 *(978-1-4507-8603-4(0))* Independent Pub.

Price, Roger & Stern, Leonard. Pirates Mad Libs. 2007. (Mad Libs Ser.). (ENG.). 48p. (J). (gr. 3-7). 4.99 *(978-0-8431-2313-5(3)*, Mad Libs) Penguin Young Readers Group.

Price, Sean Stewart. Pirates: Truth & Rumors, 1 vol. Doty, Eldon, illus. 2010. (Truth & Rumors Ser.). (ENG.). 32p. (gr. 3-4). lib. bdg. 27.99 *(978-1-4296-4746-5(9)*, Edge Bks.) Capstone Press of Coughlan Cos.

Punter, R. Pirates. 2004. (Young Reading Ser.: Vol. 1). 48p. (J). (gr. 2-18). lib. bdg. 13.99 *(978-1-58086-608-8(5)*, Usborne) EDC Publishing.

Punter, Russell. Pirates Kid Kit. 2004. (Kid Kits Ser.). 48p. (J). 15.99 *(978-1-58086-735-1(9))*; 15.99 *(978-1-58086-732-0(4))* EDC Publishing. (Usborne).

Radtke, Becky. Pirates Ahoy! Activity Book. 2006. (Dover Little Activity Bks.). (ENG., Illus.). 64p. (J). (gr. 3-5). per., act. bk. ed. 1.99 *(978-0-486-45170-1(4))* Dover Pubns., Inc.

Reid, Struan & Stowell, Louie. My First Pirate Book. Allen, Peter, illus. 2012. (My First Book Ser.). 16p. (J). ring bd. 6.99 *(978-0-7945-3228-4(4)*, Usborne) EDC Publishing.

Rice, Dona & Herweck Rice, Dona. Chicas y Chicos Malos de Alta Mar. 2016. (TIME for Kids en Español - Level 5 Ser.). (SPA & ENG.). 64p. (gr. 5-5). lib. bdg. 31.99 *(978-1-5157-2955-6(9))* Time for Kids Inc AUS. Dist: Capstone Pub.

Rice, Dona Herweck. Bad Guys & Gals of the High Seas, 1 vol. 2nd rev. ed. 2013. (Nonfiction Readers Ser.). (ENG., Illus.). 64p. (J). (gr. 5-5). pap. 31.96 *(978-1-4333-7425-8(0))* Teacher Created Materials, Inc.

—Bad Guys & Gals on the High Seas, 1 vol. 2nd rev. ed. 2013. (TIME for KIDS(r) Nonfiction Readers Ser.). (ENG.). 64p. (J). (gr. 5-5). pap. 10.99 *(978-1-4333-4902-7(7))* Teacher Created Materials, Inc.

Riggs, Kate. Pirates. 2011. (Great Warriors Ser.). 24p. (J). (gr. k-2). 16.95 *(978-1-60818-002-8(6)*, Creative Education); (ENG.). (gr. 1-17). pap. 9.99 *(978-0-89812-573-3(1)*, Creative Paperbacks) Creative Co., The.

Robson, Kirsteen. Wipe-Clean Pirate Activities. 2015. (Wipe-Clean Bks.). (ENG.). 22p. (J). (gr. k-5). pap. 7.99 *(978-0-7945-3543-8(7)*, Usborne) EDC Publishing.

Ryland Peters and Small Staff, creator. Now I am a Pirate. 2008. (ENG., Illus.). 48p. *(978-1-84597-743-6(2))* Ryland Peters & Small.

Savery, Annabel. Pirates. 2012. (It's Amazing Ser.). (Illus.). 32p. (gr. 3-6). lib. bdg. 31.35 *(978-1-59920-690-5(0))* Black Rabbit Bks.

Shirley, Rebekah Joy. I Want to Be a Pirate. 2011. (Let's Play Dress up Ser.). (ENG., Illus.). 24p. (J). (gr. k-3). pap. 10.60 *(978-1-61533-393-6(2))*; lib. bdg. 25.25 *(978-1-61533-355-4(X))* Windmill Bks.

Smith, Helen. Pirates, Swashbucklers & Buccaneers of London. 2004. (... of London Ser.). (ENG., Illus.). 96p. pap. 8.99 *(978-1-904153-17-7(8))* Watling St., Ltd. GBR. Dist: Trafalgar Square Publishing.

Smith, Jeremy. Why Why Why... Did Pirates Bury Their Treasure? 2010. (Why Why Why Ser.). (Illus.). 32p. (J). (gr. 1-3). lib. bdg. 18.95 *(978-1-4222-1576-0(8))* Mason Crest.

Spence, David. Pirates. 2004. (Illus.). 32p. (J). (gr. 4-7). pap. 5.95 *(978-1-86007-001-3(9)*, TickTock Books) Octopus Publishing Group GBR. Dist: Independent Pubs. Group.

Spenceley, Angela, compiled by. Pirate Coloring & Sticker Book: Your Complete Guide to Famous Pirates. l.t. ed. 2006. (Illus.). 24p. (J). pap. 8.95 *(978-0-9702168-6-1(6))* Coconut Pr., LLC.

Steele, Philip. The Amazing History of Pirates: See What a Buccaneer's Life Was Really Like, with over 350 Exciting Pictures. 2016. (ENG., Illus.). 64p. 12.99 *(978-1-86147-711-8(2)*, Armadillo) Anness Publishing GBR. Dist: National Bk. Network.

—Wow! Surprising Facts about Pirates. Aspinall, Marc, illus. 2014. (ENG.). 32p. (J). (gr. k-3). 15.99 *(978-0-7534-7188-3(4)*, 9780753471883, Kingfisher) Roaring Brook Pr.

Steele, Philip & Smith, Miranda. The World of Pirates. 2004. (ENG., Illus.). 64p. (J). (gr. 3-7). pap. 8.99 *(978-0-7534-5786-3(5)*, 9780753457863, Kingfisher) Roaring Brook Pr.

Stefoff, Rebecca. Captain Kidd. 2015. (J). lib. bdg. *(978-1-62713-529-0(4))*; (ENG.). 48p. (gr. 3-3). 31.36 *(978-1-5026-0205-3(9))* Cavendish Square Publishing.

—Redbeard. 2015. (J). lib. bdg. *(978-1-62713-533-7(2))*; (ENG.). 48p. (gr. 3-3). 31.36 *(978-1-5026-0199-5(0))* Cavendish Square Publishing.

Stewart, Alex. Pirates. 2013. (Greatest Warriors Ser.). 32p. (gr. 3-7). 28.50 *(978-1-78212-401-6(2))* Arcturus Publishing GBR. Dist: Black Rabbit Bks.

Stockton, Frank Richard. Buccaneers & Pirates. Varian, George & Clinedinst, B. West, illus. 2007. (Dover Maritime Ser.). (ENG.). 368p. per. 12.95 *(978-0-486-45425-2(8))* Dover Pubns., Inc.

—Buccaneers & Pirates of Our Coasts. 2008. 232p. 24.99 *(978-0-559-13822-5(9))* 2008. 232p. pap. 24.75 *(978-0-559-13821-8(0))* 2008. 228p. (gr. 4-7). 24.99 *(978-0-554-35563-4(9))* 2008. 228p. (gr. 4-7). 27.99 *(978-0-554-26260-4(6))* 2007. (ENG.). 206p. pap. 20.99 *(978-1-4346-0736-2(4))* 2007. 224p. pap. 22.99 *(978-1-4346-0796-6(8))* Creative Media Partners, LLC.

—Buccaneers & Pirates of Our Coasts. 2007. (ENG., Illus.). 216p. (J). (gr. 4-7). per. *(978-1-4065-6187-6(8))* Dodo Pr.

—Buccaneers & Pirates of Our Coasts. Varian, George & Clinedinst, B. West, illus. 2008. 364p. (gr. 4-7). 46.95 *(978-1-4369-8234-4(0))*; pap. 31.95 *(978-1-4367-9391-9(2))* Kessinger Publishing, LLC.

—Buccaneers & Pirates of Our Coasts. 2013. (Notable American Authors Ser.). reprint ed. lthr. 79.00 *(978-0-7812-8936-8(X))* Reprint Services Corp.

—Buccaneers & Pirates of Our Coasts. 2005. pap. 30.95 *(978-1-885529-90-9(2))* Stevens Publishing.

—Buccaneers & Pirates of Our Coasts. 2005. 35.00 *(978-1-55742-497-6(7))*; pap. 15.95 *(978-1-55742-486-0(1))* Wildside Pr., LLC.

Storey, Rita. Pirates. 2013. (Have Fun with Arts & Crafts Ser.). 32p. (gr. 4-7). 31.35 *(978-1-59920-900-5(4))* Black Rabbit Bks.

Sullivan, Laura L. Black Bart Roberts. 2015. (J). lib. bdg. *(978-1-62713-527-6(8))*; (ENG.). 48p. (gr. 3-3). lib. bdg. 31.36 *(978-1-5026-0207-7(5))* Cavendish Square Publishing.

—Blackbeard. 2015. (J). lib. bdg. *(978-1-62713-525-2(1))* Cavendish Square Publishing.

—Sir Henry Morgan. 2015. (J). lib. bdg. *(978-1-62713-308-1(9))* Cavendish Square Publishing.

Sutherland, Adam. The Fact or Fiction Behind Pirates. 2016. (Fact or Phony? Ser.). (ENG.). 96p. (J). (gr. 5-6). lib. bdg. 33.25 *(978-1-4824-4271-7(X))* Stevens, Gareth Publishing LLLP.

Taplin, Sam. Pirates First Coloring Book. 2012. (First Sticker Coloring Bks). 16p. (J). pap. 6.99 *(978-0-7945-3260-4(8)*, Usborne) EDC Publishing.

Teach, William. Pirates: The Secrets of Blackbeard's World. 2015. (ENG., Illus.). 80p. (J). (gr. 3). pap. 16.95 *(978-1-78312-116-8(5))* Carlton Kids GBR. Dist: Sterling Publishing Co., Inc.

Teach, William, retold by. Blackbeard's Pirateworld: Cut-Throats of the Caribbean. 2011. (ENG., Illus.). 80p. (J). (gr. 3). 19.95 *(978-1-84732-973-8(X))* Carlton Bks., Ltd. GBR. Dist: Sterling Publishing Co., Inc.

Temple, Bob. The Golden Age of Pirates: An Interactive History Adventure. 2016. (You Choose: History Ser.). (ENG.). 112p. (gr. 3-4). pap. 6.95 *(978-1-5157-4255-5(5)*, You Choose Bks.) Capstone Press of Coughlan Cos.

True-Life Pirates. 2015. (True-Life Pirates Ser.). (ENG.). 48p. (J). (gr. 3-3). 188.16 *(978-1-5026-0305-0(5))* Cavendish Square Publishing.

Tucker, Rosalyn. Famous Pirates. 2015. (Pirates Ahoy! Ser.). (ENG.). 24p. (gr. k-1). lib. bdg. 26.65 *(978-1-4914-2111-6(8)*, Pebble Plus) Capstone Press of Coughlan Cos.

—Pirate Gear. 2015. (Pirates Ahoy! Ser.). (ENG.). 24p. (gr. k-1). lib. bdg. 26.65 *(978-1-4914-2112-3(6)*, Pebble Plus) Capstone Press of Coughlan Cos.

—Pirate Ships. 2015. (Pirates Ahoy! Ser.). (ENG.). 24p. (gr. k-1). lib. bdg. 26.65 *(978-1-4914-2113-0(4)*, Pebble Plus) Capstone Press of Coughlan Cos.

—Pirate Treasure. 2015. (Pirates Ahoy! Ser.). (ENG.). 24p. (gr. k-1). lib. bdg. 26.65 *(978-1-4914-2114-7(2)*, Pebble Plus) Capstone Press of Coughlan Cos.

—Pirates Ahoy! 2015. (Pirates Ahoy! Ser.). (ENG.). 24p. (gr. k-1). lib. bdg. 106.60 *(978-1-4914-2564-0(4)*, Pebble Plus) Capstone Press of Coughlan Cos.

Usborne Books Staff, creator. Pirate Treasure Kid Kit. 2007. (Kid Kits Ser.). 32p. (J). (gr. 4-7). 19.99 *(978-1-60130-004-1(2)*, Usborne) EDC Publishing.

Vonne, Mira. Gross Facts about Pirates. 2017. (Gross History Ser.). (ENG., Illus.). 32p. (gr. 1-2). lib. bdg. 26.65 *(978-1-5157-4157-2(5)*, Blazers) Capstone Press of Coughlan Cos.

Watt, Fiona. Pirate Sticker Book. Nichols, Paul, illus. 2011. (Sticker Activity Books Ser.). 24p. (J). pap. 8.99 *(978-0-7945-2915-4(1)*, Usborne) EDC Publishing.

Weintraub, Aileen. The Barbarossa Brothers: 16th-Century Pirates of the Barbary Coast. 2009. (Library of Pirates Ser.). 24p. (gr. 3-3). 42.50 *(978-1-60853-814-0(1)*, PowerKids Pr.) Rosen Publishing Group, Inc., The.

—Captain Kidd: 17th-Century Pirate of the Indian Ocean & African Coast. 2009. (Library of Pirates Ser.). 24p. (gr. 3-3). 42.50 *(978-1-60853-811-9(7)*, PowerKids Pr.) Rosen Publishing Group, Inc., The.

—Henry Morgan: 17th-Century Buccaneer. 2009. (Library of Pirates Ser.). 24p. (gr. 3-3). 42.50 *(978-1-60853-812-6(5)*, PowerKids Pr.) Rosen Publishing Group, Inc., The.

—Jean Lafitte: Pirate Hero of the War Of 1812. 2009. (Library of Pirates Ser.). 24p. (gr. 3-3). 42.50 *(978-1-60853-813-3(3)*, PowerKids Pr.) Rosen Publishing Group, Inc., The.

—The Library of Pirates, 6 bks. Incl. Barbarossa Brothers: 16th-Century Pirates of the Barbary Coast. (YA). (gr. 2-5). lib. bdg. 22.60 *(978-0-8239-5799-6(3))*; Captain Kidd: 17th-Century Pirate of the Indian Ocean & African Coast. (YA). (gr. 2-5). lib. bdg. 22.60 *(978-0-8239-5797-2(7))*; Henry Morgan: 17th-Century Buccaneer. (J). (gr. 3). lib. bdg. 22.60 *(978-0-8239-5798-9(5)*, PowerKids Pr.); Jean Lafitte: Pirate Hero of the War of 1812. (J). (gr. 3). lib. bdg. 22.60 *(978-0-8239-5796-5(9)*, PowerKids Pr.); 24p. 2002. (Illus.). 112.50 *(978-0-8239-7133-6(3)*, PowerKids Pr.) Rosen Publishing Group, Inc., The.

West, David. Lots of Things You Want to Know about Pirates... & Some You Don't! 2015. (Lots of Things You Want to Know About Ser.). 24p. (J). 28.50 *(978-1-62588-092-5(8))* Black Rabbit Bks.

Wharton, Ellie. Preschool Pirates. Enright, Amanda & Lee, Maxine, illus. 2013. (ENG.). 10p. (J). (gr. -1-k). 9.99 *(978-1-78244-875-4(6))* Top That! Publishing PLC GBR. Dist: Independent Pubs. Group.

White, Graham. A Maze Adventure: Search for Pirate Treasure. 2009. (ENG., Illus.). 32p. (J). (gr. 4-7). pap. 8.95 *(978-1-4263-0459-0(5)*, National Geographic Children's Bks.) National Geographic Society.

Williams, Brian. Pirates. 2009. (History Explorers Ser.). (ENG.). 24p. (J). (gr. k-2). pap. 5.95 *(978-1-84696-211-0(0)*, TickTock Books) Octopus Publishing Group GBR. Dist: Independent Pubs. Group.

Wood, Alix. Pirates on the Map. 2014. (Fun with Map Skills Ser.). 32p. (J). (gr. 3-6). lib. bdg. 26.25 *(978-1-4777-6964-5(1)*, PowerKids Pr.) Rosen Publishing Group, Inc., The.

Wren, Laura Lee. Pirates & Privateers of the High Seas. 2003. (Collective Biographies Ser.). (Illus.). 128p. (J). (gr. 6-12). lib. bdg. 26.60 *(978-0-7660-1542-5(4))* Enslow Pubs., Inc.
Yancey, Diane. Piracy on the High Seas. 2012. (World History Ser.). (ENG., Illus.). 128p. (gr. 7-10). 39.90 *(978-1-4205-0679-2(X))* Cengage Gale.
Yomtov, Nelson. Modern Pirates. 2016. (True Book(tm), a — The New Criminals Ser.). (ENG., Illus.). 48p. (J). lib. bdg. 31.00 *(978-0-531-21466-4(4)*, Children's Pr.) Scholastic Library Publishing.
Zepke, Terrance. Pirates of the Carolinas for Kids. 2009. (Carolinas for Kids Ser.). (ENG.). 71p. (J). (gr. 4-18). pap. 9.95 *(978-1-56164-459-9(5))* Pineapple Pr., Inc.

PIRATES—FICTION

Abbott, Tony. The Race to Doobesh. 2005. (Secrets of Droon Ser.: No. 24). (Illus.). 127p. (J). lib. bdg. 15.38 *(978-1-4242-0311-6(2))* Fitzgerald Bks.
Ackelsberg, Amy. Happy New Year! 2014. (Strawberry Shortcake Ser.). (ENG., Illus.). 24p. (J). (gr. -1-k). 4.99 *(978-0-448-48248-4(7)*, Grosset & Dunlap) Penguin Young Readers Group.
Adamson, Ged, illus. Meet the Mckaws. 2015. (ENG.). 32p. (J). (gr. -1-k). 16.95 *(978-1-62914-618-8(8)*, Sky Pony Pr.) Skyhorse Publishing Co., Inc.
Aguilar, Jose. Jovenes piratas/Youngs Pirates. 2008. 36p. *(978-84-934160-7-2(X))* Atalante.
Aikins, Dave. Haunted Houseboat. 2013. (SpongeBob Squarepants 8X8 Ser.). lib. bdg. 13.55 *(978-0-606-32220-1(5)*, Turtleback) Turtleback Bks.
Allabach, P. R. Dragon & Captain. Tumbloom, Lucas, illus. 2015. (ENG.). 32p. (J). (gr. k-2). 17.95 *(978-1-936261-33-8(2))* Flashlight Pr.
Anderson, Jon A. My T-Rex. 2010. 108p. 23.99 *(978-1-4520-0496-9(X))*; pap. 14.99 *(978-1-4520-0495-2(1))* AuthorHouse.
Anderson, Scoular. Pirate Treasure. Anderson, Scoular, illus. 2009. (Get Set Readers Ser.). (Illus.). 32p. (J). (gr. -1-2). lib. bdg. 22.60 *(978-1-60754-266-7(8))* Windmill Bks.
Andreae, Giles. Captain Flinn & the Pirate Dinosaurs. Ayto, Russell, illus. 2005. (Captain Flinn & the Pirate Dinosaurs Ser.). (ENG.). 32p. (J). (gr. -1-1). 17.99 *(978-1-4169-0713-8(0)*, McElderry, Margaret K. Bks.) McElderry, Margaret K. Bks.
—Missing Treasure! Ayto, Russell, illus. 2008. (Captain Flinn & the Pirate Dinosaurs Ser.). (ENG.). 32p. (J). (gr. -1-3). 17.99 *(978-1-4169-6745-3(1)*, McElderry, Margaret K. Bks.) McElderry, Margaret K. Bks.
Arena, Felice & Kettle, Phil. Pirate Ship: By Felice Arena & Phil Kettle: Illustrated by Susy Boyer. Boyer, Susy, illus. 2004. (J). pap. *(978-1-59336-362-8(1))* Mondo Publishing.
Arrigan, Mary. Milo & the Pirate Sisters. 2015. (ENG., Illus.). 176p. (J). pap. 13.00 *(978-1-84717-562-5(7))* O'Brien Pr., Ltd., The IRL. Dist: Dufour Editions, Inc.
Awdry, W. Pirate Treasure. Durk, Jim, illus. 2015. (Glow-In-the-Dark Sticker Book Ser.). (ENG.). 48p. (J). (gr. -1-2). pap. 4.99 *(978-0-553-52478-9(X)*, Golden Bks.) Random Hse. Children's Bks.
—Sodor's Legend of the Lost Treasure. 2015. (Big Golden Book Ser.). (ENG., Illus.). 32p. (J). (gr. -1-2). 9.99 *(978-0-553-52076-7(8)*, Golden Bks.) Random Hse. Children's Bks.
Bakewell, Lori. Savannah Adventure: Pirate's Treasure. 2007. 173p. (J). pap. 12.95 *(978-0-9799473-9-1(1))* Tailwind Press.
Ballantyne, R. The Coral Island. 2006. pap. 14.95 *(978-1-55742-666-6(X))* Wildside Pr., LLC.
Ballantyne, R. M. Blown to Bits; or, the Lonely Man of Rak. 2006. pap. *(978-1-4065-0515-3(3))* Dodo Pr.
Ballantyne, Robert Michael. The Battery & the Boiler: Adventures in Laying of Submarine Electric Cables. 2007. 254p. pap. 21.99 *(978-1-4346-3754-3(9))*; (ENG.). 282p. pap. 23.99 *(978-1-4346-3768-0(9))* Creative Media Partners, LLC.
Bardhan-Quallen, Sudipta. The Pirate Princess. McElmurry, Jill, illus. 2012. (ENG.). 40p. (J). (gr. -1-3). 17.99 *(978-0-06-114242-0(5))* HarperCollins Pubs.
Bargellini, Demetrio & Stilton, Geronimo. The Coliseum Con. Cooper-McGuinness, Nanette, tr. 2009. (Geronimo Stilton Graphic Novels Ser.). (ENG., Illus.). 56p. (J). (gr. 2-6). 9.99 *(978-1-59707-172-7(2)*, 9781597071727) Papercutz.
Barrie, J. M. Peter Pan. 2013. (Puffin Chalk Ser.). (ENG.). 224p. (J). (gr. 3-7). pap. 7.99 *(978-0-14-750865-2(7)*, Puffin Books) Penguin Young Readers Group.
—Peter Pan. 2013. (ENG., Illus.). 256p. (J). (gr. 4-7). pap. 10.99 *(978-0-09-957304-3(0))* Random Hse. GBR. Dist: Independent Pubs. Group.
—Peter Pan: The Story of Peter & Wendy [Photoplay Edition]. 2007. 244p. (gr. 4-7). 29.95 *(978-1-4344-8379-9(7))*; per. 17.95 *(978-1-4344-8378-2(9))* Wildside Pr., LLC.
—Peter Pan & Wendy: Centenary Edition. Ingpen, Robert R., illus. 2010. (Sterling Illustrated Classics Ser.). (ENG.). 216p. (J). (gr. 5-18). 19.95 *(978-1-4027-2868-6(9))* Sterling Publishing Co., Inc.
Barry, Dave & Pearson, Ridley. Peter & the Starcatchers. Call, Greg, illus. rev. ed. 2006. (Peter & the Starcatchers Ser.). (ENG.). 480p. (J). (gr. 5-9). reprint ed. pap. 9.99 *(978-0-7868-4907-9(X)*, Disney Editions) Disney Pr.
Bass, Guy. The Pirate's Eye, 1 vol. Williamson, Pete, illus. 2013. (Stitch Head Ser.). (ENG.). 208p. (gr. 3-4). 10.95 *(978-1-62370-008-9(6))* Capstone Young Readers of Coughlan Cos.
Bateman, Teresa. Fluffy: Scourge of the Sea. Chesworth, Michael, illus. 2006. (ENG.). 32p. (J). (gr. -1-2). pap. 7.95 *(978-1-58089-152-3(7))* Charlesbridge Publishing, Inc.
Bateson, Maggie. My Pirate Adventure: A Pop-up & Play Book. Eaves, Ed, illus. 2008. (ENG.). 20p. (J). (gr. 4-7). 23.50 *(978-0-230-53036-2(2)*, Macmillan) Pan Macmillan GBR. Dist: Trans-Atlantic Pubns., Inc.
Batson, Wayne Thomas. Isle of Fire, 1 vol. 2009. (ENG.). 352p. pap. 9.99 *(978-1-4003-1512-3(3))* Nelson, Thomas Inc.
—Isle of Swords, 1 vol. 2008. (ENG.). 352p. pap. 9.99 *(978-1-4003-1363-1(5))* Nelson, Thomas Inc.
Bauer, Christina. The Pirate Queen: A Timewalker Journey. 2005. 280p. (YA). 14.99 *(978-1-59092-224-8(7))* Blue Forge Pr.
Baxter, Nicola. The Great Pirate Adventure: Peek Inside the 3D Windows. Goulding, June, illus. 2012. (ENG.). 12p. (J). (gr. -1-12). 16.99 *(978-1-84322-966-7(8))* Anness Publishing GBR. Dist: National Bk. Network.
—The Perils of Pirates & Other Dastardly Deeds: A Compendium of Swashbuckling Pirate Adventure Stories. King, Colin, illus. 2012. (ENG.). 80p. (J). (gr. k-4). pap. 9.99 *(978-1-84322-802-8(5))* Anness Publishing GBR. Dist: National Bk. Network.
Bee, William. Stanley's Numbers, 1 vol. Bee, William, illus. 2017. (Stanley Ser.). (ENG., Illus.). 20p. (J). (gr. -1 — 1). bds. 6.95 ***(978-1-56145-976-6(3))*** Peachtree Pubs.
Beeke, Joel R. & Kleyn, Diana. How God Stopped the Pirates. Anderson, Jeff, illus. 2008. (Building on the Rock Ser.). (ENG.). 176p. (J). pap. 8.99 *(978-1-85792-816-7(4)*, 9781857928167, CF4Kids) Christian Focus Pubns. GBR. Dist: Bookmasters Distribution.
Bell, Hilari. Crown of Earth. Willis, Drew, illus. 2010. (Shield, Sword, & Crown Ser.: 3). (ENG.). 272p. (J). (gr. 3-7). pap. 5.99 *(978-1-4169-0599-8(5)*, Aladdin) Simon & Schuster Children's Publishing.
—Crown of Earth. Willis, Drew, illus. 2009. (Shield, Sword, & Crown Ser.: 3). (ENG.). 272p. (J). (gr. 3-7). 16.99 *(978-1-4169-0598-1(7)*, Simon & Schuster/Paula Wiseman Bks.) Simon & Schuster/Paula Wiseman Bks.
Bell, Rebecca. Capitano Ricco. Bell, Rebecca, illus. 2005. (Illus.). 36p. (J). 9.95 *(978-1-934138-06-9(1))* Bouncing Ball Bks., Inc.
Bell, Ted. Nick of Time. 2009. (Nick Mciver Adventures Through Time Ser.: 1). (ENG., Illus.). 464p. (J). (gr. 5-9). pap. 8.99 *(978-0-312-58143-5(2)*, 9780312581435) Square Fish.
—The Time Pirate. 2011. (Nick Mciver Adventures Through Time Ser.: 2). (ENG., Illus.). 480p. (J). (gr. 5-9). pap. 10.99 *(978-0-312-66549-4(0)*, 9780312665494) Square Fish.
Bellville, Sharyn. The Pirate of Smith Point Beach. 2005. 85p. pap. 16.95 *(978-1-4137-8353-7(8))* PublishAmerica, Inc.
Bently, Peter. Captain Jack & the Pirates. Oxenbury, Helen, illus. 2016. (ENG.). 32p. (J). (-k). 17.99 *(978-0-525-42950-0(6)*, Dial Bks) Penguin Young Readers Group.
Benton, Lynne. Pirate Pete. Chapman, Neil, illus. 2008. (Tadpoles Ser.). (ENG.). 24p. (J). (gr. -1-3). pap. *(978-0-7787-3892-3(2))* Crabtree Publishing Co.
Berenstain, Mike. The Berenstain Bears' Pirate Adventure. Berenstain, Mike, illus. 2016. (Berenstain Bears Ser.). (Illus.). 24p. (J). (gr. -1-3). pap. 3.99 *(978-0-06-235021-3(8)*, HarperFestival) HarperCollins Pubs.
Berger, Samantha. Pirate Potty. Cartwright, Amy, illus. 2010. (ENG.). 24p. (J). (gr. -1 — 1). pap. 5.99 *(978-0-545-17295-0(0)*, Cartwheel Bks.) Scholastic, Inc.
Bergeron, Alain M. & Sampar. Le Tresor des Tresors. 2004. (Boreal Maboul Ser.). (FRE., Illus.). 56p. (J). *(978-2-7646-0337-6(1)*, Spotlight Poets) Editions du Boreal, Les.
Big Idea, Inc. Staff. The Pirates Who Don't Do Anything: VBS Superkit. 2008. (J). 179.99 *(978-1-4003-1144-6(6))* Nelson, Thomas Inc.
Blain, Christophe. Los Hielos, Vol. 2. 2005. (Isaac el Pirata Ser.). (SPA., Illus.). 48p. (YA). (gr. 8-17). 19.95 *(978-1-59497-114-3(5))* Public Square Bks.
Bleu, Kennedy. Cotter Otter in Treasure Water. Goembel, Ponder, illus. 2014. (ENG.). 24p. (J). pap. 24.95 *(978-1-63004-814-3(3))* America Star Bks.
Bliven, Jeremy. Captain Stumpy the Pirate Cat. 2004. (ENG., Illus.). 44p. (J). pap. *(978-0-9713890-8-3(X))* Outer Banks Pr.
Bloomsbury USA. Lift-The-Flap Friends: Pirates. 2017. (ENG.). 14p. (J). bds. 9.99 *(978-1-68119-241-3(1)*, 9781681192413, Bloomsbury Activity Bks.) Bloomsbury Publishing USA.
Blum, Alex A., et al. Treasure Island. 2015. (Classics Illustrated Ser.: 21). (ENG., Illus.). 48p. pap. 9.95 *(978-1-906814-47-2(3))* Classic Comic Store, Ltd. GBR. Dist: Casemate Pubs. & Bk. Distributors, LLC.
Bondor-Stone, Annabeth & White, Connor. The Shivering. Holden, Anthony, illus. 2016. (Shivers! Ser.: 2). 208p. (J). (gr. 3-7). 12.99 *(978-0-06-231389-8(4))* HarperCollins Pubs.
—Shivers! - The Pirate Who's Afraid of Everything. Holden, Anthony, illus. 2015. (Shivers! Ser.: 1). (ENG.). 192p. (J). (gr. 3-7). 12.99 *(978-0-06-231387-4(8))* HarperCollins Pubs.
Bossley, Michele Martin. Bio-Pirate, 1 vol. 2008. (Orca Currents Ser.). (ENG.). (J). (gr. 5-9). 112p. 16.95 *(978-1-55143-895-5(X))*; 128p. pap. 9.95 *(978-1-55143-893-1(3))* Orca Bk. Pubs. USA.
Bowen, Carl & Fuentes, Benny. Sea Demon, 1 vol. Tortosa, Wilson, illus. 2013. (Shadow Squadron Ser.). (ENG.). 112p. (gr. 4-8). lib. bdg. 26.65 *(978-1-4342-4604-2(3))* Stone Arch Bks.
Bradford, Chris. Hostage, Bk. 2. 2017. (Bodyguard Ser.). (ENG.). 224p. (J). (gr. 5). pap. 8.99 *(978-1-5247-3699-6(6)*, Philomel Bks.) Penguin Young Readers Group.
Bradman, Tony. Polly & the Pirates. Davies, James, illus. 2nd ed. 2016. (Reading Ladder Ser.). (ENG.). 48p. (J). (gr. k-2). 7.99 *(978-1-4052-8249-9(5))* Egmont Bks., Ltd. GBR. Dist: Independent Pubs. Group.
Bradman, Tony & Banana, Red. Polly & the Pirates. Davies, James, illus. 2014. (Red Bananas Ser.). (ENG.). 48p. (J). (gr. k-2). pap. 5.99 *(978-1-4052-6412-9(8))* Egmont Bks., Ltd. GBR. Dist: Independent Pubs. Group.
Brady, Carolyn. The Adventures of Pelican Mcfeet: The Big Lumpy Green Monster. Phillips, Deborah, illus. 2008. 32p. pap. 16.95 *(978-1-4389-3539-3(0))* AuthorHouse.
Bramucci, Stephen. The Danger Gang & the Pirates of Borneo! Chung, Arree, illus. 2017. (ENG.). 384p. (J). 16.99 *(978-1-61963-692-7(1)*, 9781619636927, Bloomsbury USA Childrens) Bloomsbury Publishing USA.
Bray, Libba. Beauty Queens. (ENG.). 400p. (J). (gr. 7). 2012. pap. 10.99 *(978-0-439-89598-9(7)*, Scholastic Paperbacks) 2011. 18.99 *(978-0-439-89597-2(9)*, Scholastic Pr.) Scholastic, Inc.
Brian, Kate, pseud. Confessions. 2007. (Private Ser.: No. 4). (ENG.). 240p. (YA). (gr. 9-12). pap. 9.99 *(978-1-4169-1876-9(0)*, Simon & Schuster Bks. For Young Readers) Simon & Schuster Bks. For Young Readers.
Brown, Barbara. The Adventures of Captain Crick, Super Hero. 2011. 28p. pap. 21.99 *(978-1-4568-5005-0(9))* Xlibris Corp.
Brown, Calef. Pirateria: The Wonderful Plunderful Pirate Emporium. Brown, Calef, illus. 2012. (ENG., Illus.). 40p. (J). (gr. -1-3). 16.99 *(978-1-4169-7878-7(X)*, Atheneum Bks. for Young Readers) Simon & Schuster Children's Publishing.
Brown, Cathie. Today I am a Pirate. 2010. 24p. 11.49 *(978-1-4520-0461-7(7))* AuthorHouse.
Brownlow, Mike, illus. Dinosaurs of Doom! 2011. (Time Pirates Ser.). (ENG.). 12p. (J). (gr. k-2). bds. 24.99 *(978-0-230-74179-9(7))* Macmillan Pubs., Ltd. GBR. Dist: Independent Pubs. Group.
Bruton, Georgia. Escape. 2012. 210p. pap. 11.95 *(978-1-938083-10-5(5))* Silver Knight Publishing, LLC.
Bunting, Eve. Pirate Boy. Fortenberry, Julie, illus. (ENG.). 32p. (J). (gr. -1-2). 2012. pap. 7.99 *(978-0-8234-2546-4(0))* 2011. 16.95 *(978-0-8234-2321-7(2))* Holiday Hse., Inc.
—The Pirate Captain's Daughter. (Pirate Captain's Daughter Ser.). (ENG.). (J). 2012. 192p. pap. 8.95 *(978-1-58536-790-0(7))* 2012. 192p. lib. bdg. 15.95 *(978-1-58536-789-4(3))* 2011. 208p. (gr. 6-18). pap. 8.95 *(978-1-58536-525-8(4))* 2011. 208p. (gr. 6-18). lib. bdg. 15.95 *(978-1-58536-526-5(2))* Sleeping Bear Pr.
Burchett, Jan & Vogler, Sara. The Ghost Ship. Hartas, Leo, illus. 2012. (ENG.). 128p. (J). (gr. 2-4). 7.99 *(978-1-4440-0585-1(5)*, Orion Children's Bks.) Hachette Children's Group GBR. Dist: Hachette Bk. Group.
—Kidnapped. Hartas, Leo, illus. 2012. (ENG.). 128p. (J). (gr. 2-4). pap. 7.99 *(978-1-4440-0586-8(3)*, Orion Children's Bks.) Hachette Children's Group GBR. Dist: Hachette Bk. Group.
—Skeleton Island. Hartas, Leo, illus. 2012. (ENG.). 128p. (J). (gr. 2-4). pap. 7.99 *(978-1-4440-0584-4(7)*, Orion Children's Bks.) Hachette Children's Group GBR. Dist: Hachette Bk. Group.
Burghard, Marie. Captain's Best Imbecile: A Young Pirate's Story. 2008. 184p. pap. 12.99 *(978-1-4357-3807-2(1))* Lulu Pr., Inc.
—Captain's Best Imbecile: A Young Pirate's Story: Collector's Edition. 2008. 184p. 29.99 *(978-1-4357-4521-6(3))* Lulu Pr., Inc.
Burlington, Marie. Lighthouse Joey. 2006. (Pandas Ser.: 33). (ENG., Illus.). 64p. (J). pap. 9.95 *(978-0-86278-945-9(1))* O'Brien Pr., Ltd., The IRL. Dist: Dufour Editions, Inc.
Burnett, Melissa. Even Pirates Need Their Sleep. 2010. 32p. (J). pap. 15.00 *(978-1-4490-7092-2(2))* AuthorHouse.
Butterman, Stephen. Rootbeer Beard. 2012. 74p. pap. 8.95 *(978-1-61477-055-8(7))* Bellissima Publishing, LLC.
Cadell, Ava. NeuroLoveology: The Power to Mindful Love & Sex. 2014. (ENG.). 310p. pap. 14.99 *(978-1-4976-6112-7(9))* Open Road Integrated Media, Inc.
Campos, Llanos & Campos Martinez, Llanos. The Treasure of Barracuda. Sardà, Júlia, illus. 2016. (ENG.). 156p. (J). (gr. 3-7). 15.95 *(978-1-939775-14-6(0))* March 4th, Inc.
Cannon, Deborah. The Pirate Vortex: Elizabeth Latimer, Pirate Hunter. 2009. 260p. pap. 20.00 *(978-1-4269-0532-2(7))* Trafford Publishing.
Carlson, Caroline. The Buccaneers' Code. (Very Nearly Honorable League of Pirates Ser.: 3). 320p. (J). (gr. 3-7). 2016. pap. 6.99 *(978-0-06-219440-4(2))* 2015. (ENG.). 16.99 *(978-0-06-219439-8(9))* HarperCollins Pubs.
—Magic Marks the Spot. Phillips, Dave, illus. 2013. (ENG.). 368p. (J). pap. *(978-0-06-231467-3(X))* Harper & Row Ltd.
—Magic Marks the Spot. Phillips, Dave, illus. 2013. (Very Nearly Honorable League of Pirates Ser.: 1). (ENG.). 368p. (J). (gr. 3-7). 16.99 *(978-0-06-219434-3(8))* HarperCollins Pubs.
—The Terror of the Southlands. Phillips, Dave, illus. 2014. (ENG.). 336p. (J). pap. *(978-0-06-236178-3(3))* Harper & Row Ltd.
—The Very Nearly Honorable League of Pirates - The Terror of the Southlands. Phillips, Dave, illus. 2014. (Very Nearly Honorable League of Pirates Ser.: 2). (ENG.). 336p. (J). (gr. 3-7). 16.99 *(978-0-06-219436-7(4))* HarperCollins Pubs.
Carretero, Mónica. Pirate Handbook. 2011. (Handbooks Ser.). (ENG., Illus.). 32p. (J). (gr. k-2). *(978-84-937814-8-4(7))* D P & G Military Pubs.
Carris, Joan D. A Ghost of a Chance. 2003. (Legends of the Carolinas Ser.). 155p. (J). 8.95 *(978-1-928556-40-4(X))* Coastal Carolina Pr.
Castroman, Nicole. Blackhearts. 2016. (ENG., Illus.). 384p. (YA). (gr. 9). 17.99 *(978-1-4814-3269-6(9)*, Simon Pulse) Simon Pulse.
Chantler, Scott. Pirates of the Silver Coast. Chantler, Scott, illus. 2014. (Three Thieves Ser.). (ENG., Illus.). 96p. (J). (gr. 4-7). 17.95 *(978-1-894786-53-9(X))* Kids Can Pr., Ltd. CAN. Dist: Hachette Bk. Group.
Child, Lauren. I Can Do Anything That's Everything All on My Own. 2008. (Charlie & Lola Ser.). (ENG., Illus.). 24p. (J). (gr. -1-k). mass mkt. 3.99 *(978-0-448-44792-6(4)*, Grosset & Dunlap) Penguin Young Readers Group.
—Ruby Redfort Take Your Last Breath. Child, Lauren, illus. 2013. (Ruby Redfort Ser.: 2). (ENG., Illus.). 432p. (J). (gr. 5-9). 16.99 *(978-0-7636-5468-9(X))* Candlewick Pr.
Chin, Oliver. Baltazar & the Flying Pirates. Roth, Justin, illus. 2009. (ENG.). 36p. (J). (gr. -1-3). 15.95 *(978-1-59702-018-3(4))* Immedium.
Chizuru, Mio. The Pirate & the Princess Volume 1: the Timelight Stone: The Timelight Stone. 2007. 110p. (J). pap. 5.99 *(978-1-933164-43-4(3))* Seven Seas Entertainment, LLC.
—The Pirate & the Princess Volume 2: the Red Crystal: The Red Crystal. 2007. 110p. (J). pap. 5.99 *(978-1-933164-44-1(1))* Seven Seas Entertainment, LLC.
Cima, Alessandro V. Pirate Jack. 2007. 180p. pap. 11.95 *(978-0-615-14024-7(6))* Candlelight Stories, Inc.
Citak, Michael J. The Adventures of Leo- & the Treasure Cave. 2009. 51p. pap. 22.95 *(978-0-557-02994-5(5))* Lulu Pr., Inc.
Coats, Lucy. Captain Beastlie's Pirate Party. Mould, Chris, illus. 2014. (ENG.). 32p. (J). (gr. -1-2). 15.99 *(978-0-7636-7399-4(4)*, Nosy Crow) Candlewick Pr.
Cobb, Daryl K. Do Pirates Go to School. 2010. pap. 11.99 *(978-0-578-05535-0(X))* 10 To 2 Children's Bks.
Collard, Liz. The Secret of Pirate Taz. 2011. 28p. 13.54 *(978-1-4269-5268-5(6))* Trafford Publishing.
Collingwood, Harry. Across the Spanish Main. 204p. 2011. 26.95 *(978-1-4638-9643-0(3))* 2009. pap. 14.95 *(978-1-60664-390-7(8))* Rodgers, Alan Bks.
—The Cruise of The 'Esmeralda' 2009. 220p. pap. 15.95 *(978-1-60664-391-4(6))* Rodgers, Alan Bks.
—The Rover's Secret. 2011. 274p. 29.95 *(978-1-4638-9505-1(4))* Rodgers, Alan Bks.
—The Strange Adventures of Eric Blackburn. 2008. 164p. 25.95 *(978-1-60664-711-0(3))*; pap. 13.95 *(978-1-60664-210-8(3))* Rodgers, Alan Bks.
Cosson, M. J. The Pirate, Big Fist, & Me, 1 vol. Garvey, Brann, illus. 2006. (Vortex Bks.). (ENG.). 112p. (gr. 2-3). 26.65 *(978-1-59889-068-6(9)*, Vortex Bks.) Stone Arch Bks.
Coughlin, Shirley. Toby & the Pirates. 2012. 58p. pap. 13.00 *(978-1-61204-745-4(9)*, Strategic Bk. Publishing) Strategic Book Publishing & Rights Agency (SBPRA).
Courtauld, Sarah. On a Pirate Ship. Davies, Benji, illus. 2007. (Picture Bks). 24p. (J). (gr. -1-3). 9.99 *(978-0-7945-1712-0(9)*, Usborne) EDC Publishing.
Cousins, Lucy. Maisy's Pirate Ship: A Pop-Up-and-Play Book. Cousins, Lucy, illus. 2015. (Maisy Ser.). (ENG., Illus.). 10p. (J). (-k). 16.99 *(978-0-7636-7941-5(0))* Candlewick Pr.
Cowell, Cressida. How to Be a Pirate. 2010. (ENG., Illus.). 240p. (J). *(978-0-340-99908-0(X)*, Hodder Children's Books) Hachette Children's Group GBR. Dist: Hachette Bk. Group.
—How to Be a Pirate. (How to Train Your Dragon Ser.: 2). (ENG.). (J). (gr. 3-7). 2010. 240p. pap. 8.99 *(978-0-316-08528-1(6))* 2005. (Illus.). 224p. 13.99 *(978-0-316-15598-4(5))* Little, Brown Bks. for Young Readers.
Craddock, Erik. Pirate Palooza. Craddock, Erik, illus. 2009. (Stone Rabbit Ser.: Bk. 2). (ENG., Illus.). 96p. (J). (gr. 3-7). pap. 6.99 *(978-0-375-85660-0(9)*, Random Hse. Bks. for Young Readers) Random Hse. Children's Bks.
Crimi, Carolyn. Henry & the Buccaneer Bunnies. Manders, John, illus. 2009. (ENG.). 40p. (J). (gr. -1-3). pap. 7.99 *(978-0-7636-4540-3(0))* Candlewick Pr.
—Henry & the Crazed Chicken Pirates. Manders, John, illus. 2010. (ENG.). 40p. (J). (gr. -1-3). pap. 7.99 *(978-0-7636-4999-9(6))* Candlewick Pr.
Croce, Pat & Slutsky, Adam. Plunder. 2015. (Plunder Ser.: 1). (ENG.). 336p. 31.95 *(978-1-68162-373-3(0))*; 338p. (J). pap. 16.95 *(978-1-63026-893-0(3))* Turner Publishing Co.
Crowe, Caroline. Pirates in Pajamas. Knight, Tom, illus. 2017. (ENG.). 28p. (J). (gr. -1-k). bds. 7.99 ***(978-1-68010-516-2(7))*** Tiger Tales.
—Pirates in Pajamas. Knight, Tim, illus. 2015. (ENG.). 32p. (J). (gr. -1-3). 16.99 *(978-1-58925-190-8(3))* Tiger Tales.
Crowe, Ellie & Fry, Juliet. HOKU the Stargazer: The Exciting Pirate Adventure! Petosa-Sigel, Kristi, illus. 2009. (ENG.). 28p. (J). *(978-1-59700-601-9(7))* Island Heritage Publishing.
Cuillain, Adam & Cuillain, Charlotte. The Pirates on Holiday. Van Wyk, Rupert, illus. 2014. (ENG.). 32p. (J). *(978-0-7787-1311-1(3))* Crabtree Publishing Co.
Cullen, Sean. Hamish X Goes to Providence, Rhode Island. 2008. (ENG.). 336p. (J). ***(978-0-670-06854-8(3))*** Penguin Bks., Ltd.
Curtis, Alice. A Little Maid of New Orleans. 2011. (Little Maid Ser.). (ENG.). 236p. pap. 12.95 *(978-1-4290-9746-8(9))* Applewood Bks.
Czajak, Paul. Monster Needs a Party. Grieb, Wendy, illus. 2015. (Monster & Me Ser.). (ENG.). 32p. (J). (-k). 16.95 *(978-1-938063-55-8(4)*, Mighty Media Kids) Mighty Media Pr.
Daffern, Brian. Prince Albert Bk. 3: The Realm Pirates. 2004. 192p. (YA). per. 13.95 *(978-0-9709104-7-9(9))* Hickory Tales Publishing.
Dahl, Michael. Pirate. Ho, Jannie, illus. 2015. (Baby Face Ser.). (ENG.). 10p. (gr. -1 — 1). bds. 9.99 *(978-1-62370-294-6(1))* Capstone Young Readers of Coughlan Cos.
Dale, Jay. Lazy Old Pirates, 1 vol. Diggory, Nick, illus. 2012. (Wonder Words Ser.). (ENG.). 32p. (gr. k-2). pap. 5.99 *(978-1-4296-8930-4(7)*, Engage Literacy) Capstone Press of Coughlan Cos.
—Two Old Pirates, 1 vol. Diggory, Nick, illus. 2012. (Wonder Words Ser.). (ENG.). 32p. (gr. k-2). pap. 5.99 *(978-1-4296-8928-1(5)*, Engage Literacy) Capstone Press of Coughlan Cos.
Dale, Penny. Dinosaur Pirates! Dale, Penny, illus. 2017. (ENG., Illus.). 32p. (J). (-k). 15.99 *(978-0-7636-9330-5(8)*, Nosy Crow) Candlewick Pr.
Dalton, Annie. Making Waves: Mission - Foil the Pirates. 2010. (Mel Beeby, Agent Angel Ser.: 7). (ENG.). 208p. (J). (gr. 4-7). pap. 9.99 *(978-0-00-720477-9(9))* HarperCollins Pubs. Ltd. GBR. Dist: HarperCollins Pubs.
David, B. The Littlest Pirate King. 2010. (ENG., Illus.). 48p. 16.99 *(978-1-60699-403-0(4)*, 699403) Fantagraphics Bks.
Davidson, Susanna. Stories of Mermaids. 2009. (Young Reading 1 Ser.). 48p. (J). (gr. 2). 6.99 *(978-0-7945-2589-7(X)*, Usborne) EDC Publishing.
Davis, Mike. Pirates, Bats, & Dragons. Simpson, William, illus. 2004. 174p. (J). 15.95 *(978-0-9747078-2-2(1))* Perceval Pr.
Day, Jan. Pirate Pink & Treasures of the Reef, 1 vol. Mason, Janeen, illus. 2003. (ENG.). 32p. (J). (gr. k-3). 16.99 *(978-1-58980-086-1(9))* Pelican Publishing Co., Inc.
DeGorsky, Gregory J. The Christmas Pirate. DeGorsky, Jon, ed. 2007. (ENG., Illus.). 80p. (J). pap. 4.95 *(978-0-9678542-3-6(7))* Magnetic Image, Inc.
Delibero, Bob. Petrucchio. 2012. 234p. 24.95 *(978-1-4626-6155-8(6))* America Star Bks.
Demas, Corinne. Pirates Go to School. Manders, John, illus. 2011. (ENG.). 32p. (J). (gr. -1-3). 16.99 *(978-0-545-20629-7(4)*, Orchard Bks.) Scholastic, Inc.
Demas, Corinne & Roehrig, Artemis. Are Pirates Polite? Catrow, David, illus. 2016. (ENG.). 40p. (J). (gr. -1-k). 16.99 *(978-0-545-62874-7(1))* Scholastic, Inc.
Dennis, Peter & Rawson, Christopher. Treasure Island. 2004. (Young Reading Ser.). (Illus.). 64p. (J). (gr. 2-18). pap. 5.95 *(978-0-7945-0411-3(6)*, Usborne) EDC Publishing.
Deutsch, Stacia, adapted by. The Pirate Fairy: The Chapter Book. 2014. 117p. *(978-0-316-33346-7(8))* Little Brown & Co.
DiCamillo, Kate. Louise, the Adventures of a Chicken. Bliss, Harry, illus. 2009. (J). (gr. -1-2). 29.95 incl. audio compact disk *(978-1-4301-0688-3(3))* Live Oak Media.
Dickins, Rosie. Illustrated Pirate Stories IR. 2015. (Illustrated Stories Ser.). (ENG.). 269p. (J). (gr. k-5). 19.99 *(978-0-7945-3213-0(6)*, Usborne) EDC Publishing.
Disney Book Club Staff. Pirates of the Caribbean - On Stranger Tides: Six Sea Chanties - An Original Graphic Novel Anthology. 2011. (ENG.). 128p. (YA). (gr. 8-18). pap. 10.99 *(978-1-4231-3320-9(X))* Disney Pr.
Disney Book Group & Rudnick, Elizabeth. Pirates of the Caribbean: Dead Men Tell No Tales Novelization. Disney

PQR

Storybook Art Team, illus. 2017. (ENG.). 272p. (J). (gr. 5-9). 16.99 *(978-1-4847-8719-9(6))* Disney Pr.

Disney Book Group & Rusu, Meredith. Pirates of the Caribbean: Dead Men Tell No Tales: the Brightest Star in the North. Disney Storybook Art Team, illus. 2017. (ENG.). 240p. (J). (gr. 3-7). 12.99 *(978-1-4847-8720-5(X))* Disney Pr.

Disney Book Group, et al. Pirates of the Caribbean. Disney Storybook Art Team & Wall, Mike, illus. 2017. (Disney Parks Presents Ser.). (ENG.). 32p. (J). (gr. -1-k). 17.99 *(978-1-4847-2786-7(X))* Disney Pr.

Disney Book Group Staff. Captain Jake & the Never Land Pirates the Great Never Sea Conquest. Disney Storybook Art Team, illus. 2015. (ENG.). 24p. (J). (gr. -1-k). pap. 4.99 *(978-1-4847-1150-7(5))* Disney Pr.

—Tinker Bell & the Pirate Fairy. Disney Storybook Art Team, illus. 2014. (Read-Along Storybook & CD Ser.). (ENG.). 32p. (J). (gr. -1-k). pap. 6.99 *(978-1-4231-7407-3(0))* Disney Pr.

Disney Book Group Staff & Kelman, Marcy. All Hands on Hooks. Disney Storybook Art Team, illus. 2014. (Flap 'n Tab Ser.). (ENG.). 10p. (J). (gr. -1-k). bds. 6.99 *(978-1-4231-8494-2(7))* Disney Pr.

Disney Book Group Staff & LaRose, Melinda. Jake & the Never Land Pirates - Winter Never Land. Disney Storybook Art Team, illus. 2014. (ENG.). 12p. (J). (gr. -1-k). bds. 7.99 *(978-1-4231-9424-8(1))* Disney Pr.

Disney Book Group Staff & Lewis, Kevin. Hide & Hug Olaf: A Fun Family Experience! Disney Storybook Art Team & Mosqueda, Olga, illus. 2014. (ENG.). 48p. (J). (gr. -1-k). 26.99 *(978-1-4847-2150-6(0))* Disney Pr.

Disney Book Group Staff & Scollon, William. Jake & the Never Land Pirates Battle for the Book. Disney Storybook Art Team, illus. 2014. (ENG.). 24p. (J). (gr. -1-k). pap. 4.99 *(978-1-4231-8397-6(5))* Disney Pr.

Disney Press Staff, ed. Pirates of the Caribbean 3: Swann. 2007. (ENG.). 24p. (J). (gr. -1-2). pap. 3.99 *(978-1-4231-0375-2(0))* Disney Pr.

Disney Publishing Staff. Playing Pirates, 15 vols. 2003. (It's Fun to Learn Ser.). (Illus.). 32p. (J). (gr. -1-3). 3.99 *(978-1-57973-136-6(8))* Advance Pubs. LLC.

Dogiakis, Helen. Captain Terry the Pirate Cow's Adventure to Greece. 2012. 24p. pap. 17.99 *(978-1-4685-9403-4(6))* AuthorHouse.

—Captain Terry the Pirate Cow's Adventure to Italy. 2011. 32p. pap. 14.99 *(978-1-4567-3131-1(9))* AuthorHouse.

Donaldson, Julia. Charlie Cook's Favorite Book. Scheffler, Axel, illus. 2008. (ENG.). 32p. (J). (gr. -1-k). pap. 7.99 *(978-0-14-241138-4(8),* Puffin Books) Penguin Young Readers Group.

—The Troll, 2. Roberts, David, illus. 3rd ed. 2010. (ENG.). 32p. (J). (gr. -1-k). pap. 11.99 *(978-0-230-01794-8(0))* Pan Macmillan GBR. Dist: Independent Pubs. Group.

Dorison, Xavier. Lady Vivian Hastings. Saincantin, Jerome, tr. from FRE. Lauffray, Mathieu, illus. 2011. (Long John Silver Ser.: 1). (ENG.). 56p. pap. 13.95 *(978-1-84918-062-7(8))* CineBook GBR. Dist: National Bk. Network.

—Neptune Vol. 2: Long John Silver. Lauffray, Mathieu, illus. 2011. (Long John Silver Ser.: 2). (ENG.). 56p. pap. 13.95 *(978-1-84918-072-6(5))* CineBook GBR. Dist: National Bk. Network.

Dorling Kindersley Publishing Staff & Buller, Laura. Pirate Attack! 2014. (DK Readers Ser.). (ENG.). 32p. (J). (gr. k-4). 14.99 *(978-1-4654-1606-3(4));* pap. 3.99 *(978-1-4654-1721-3(4))* Dorling Kindersley Publishing, Inc. (DK Children).

Dorman, Brandon. Pirates of the Sea! Dorman, Brandon, illus. 2011. (ENG., Illus.). 32p. (J). (gr. -1-3). 16.99 *(978-0-06-204068-8(5),* Greenwillow Bks.) HarperCollins Pubs.

Doudna, Kelly. Parrot Crackers, 1 vol. Haberstroh, Anne, illus. 2007. (Critter Chronicles Ser.). (ENG.). 24p. (J). (gr. k-3). lib. bdg. 24.21 *(978-1-59928-458-3(8),* SandCastle) ABDO Publishing Co.

Downey, Lisa & Fox, Kathleen. The Pirates of Plagiarism. Downey, Lisa, illus. 2010. (Illus.). 32p. (J). (gr. 1-4). lib. bdg. 17.95 *(978-1-60213-053-1(1),* Upstart Bks.) Highsmith Inc.

Duddle, Jonny. The Jolley-Rogers & the Ghostly Galleon. Duddle, Jonny, illus. 2016. (ENG., Illus.). 160p. (J). (gr. 1-4). pap. 6.99 *(978-0-7636-8910-0(6),* Templar) Candlewick Pr.

—The Pirate Cruncher. Duddle, Jonny, illus. 2010. (ENG., Illus.). 38p. (J). (gr. -1-2). 15.99 *(978-0-7636-4876-3(0),* Templar) Candlewick Pr.

—The Pirates Next Door. 2012. (ENG., Illus.). 44p. (J). (gr. -1-2). 15.99 *(978-0-7636-5842-7(1),* Templar) Candlewick Pr.

Duey, Kathleen. Rex. Epstein, Eugene, illus. Gould, Robert, photos by. 2006. (Time Soldiers Ser.: Bk. 1). (ENG.). 96p. (gr. -1-7). 24.21 *(978-1-59961-226-3(7))* Spotlight.

—Time Soldiers - Patch. Epstein, Eugene, illus. Gould, Robert, photos by. 2005. (Time Soldiers Ser.: Bk. 3). (ENG.). 96p. (J). (gr. k-2). per. 5.95 *(978-1-929945-55-9(8))* Big Guy Bks., Inc.

Durango, Julia. Sea of the Dead. 2009. (ENG.). 144p. (J). (gr. 3-7). 16.99 *(978-1-4169-5778-2(2),* Simon & Schuster Bks. For Young Readers) Simon & Schuster Bks. For Young Readers.

Durbin, Amanda. Tree Houses & Treasures. 2013. 24p. pap. 24.95 *(978-1-63004-353-7(2))* America Star Bks.

Durrant, Geraldine. Pirate Gran. Forshall, Rose, illus. 2009. 32p. (J). 19.95 *(978-0-948065-96-5(6))* National Maritime Museum GBR. Dist: Independent Pubs. Group.

—Twinbane: an Appalling True History. 2010. 142p. pap. 16.95 *(978-1-4457-7998-0(6))* Lulu Pr., Inc.

Eames, Brian. The Dagger Quick. (Dagger Chronicles Ser.). (ENG., (J). (gr. 3-7). 2013. Illus.). 352p. pap. 6.99 *(978-1-4424-8368-2(7))* 2011. 336p. 15.99 *(978-1-4424-2311-4(0))* Simon & Schuster/Paula Wiseman Bks. (Simon & Schuster/Paula Wiseman Bks.).

—The Dagger X. 2013. (Dagger Chronicles Ser.). (ENG.). 368p. (J). (gr. 3-7). 15.99 *(978-1-4424-6855-9(6),* Simon & Schuster Bks. For Young Readers) Simon & Schuster Bks. For Young Readers.

—The Dagger X. 2013. (Dagger Chronicles Ser.). (ENG., Illus.). 368p. (J). (gr. 3-7). pap. 6.99 *(978-1-4424-6856-6(4),* Simon & Schuster/Paula Wiseman Bks.) Simon & Schuster/Paula Wiseman Bks.

Easton, Tom. Pirates Can Be Honest, 01 vols., 1. 2016. (Pirate Pals Ser.). (ENG.). 32p. (J). pap. 10.00 *(978-1-5081-9141-4(7),* Windmill Bks.) Rosen Publishing Group, Inc., The.

—Pirates Can Be Kind, 01 vols., 1. 2016. (Pirate Pals Ser.). (ENG.). 32p. (J). pap. 10.00 *(978-1-5081-9145-2(X),* Windmill Bks.) Rosen Publishing Group, Inc., The.

—Pirates Can Be Polite, 01 vols., 1. 2016. (Pirate Pals Ser.). (ENG.). 32p. (J). pap. 10.00 *(978-1-5081-9149-0(2),* Windmill Bks.) Rosen Publishing Group, Inc., The.

—Pirates Can Pay Attention, 01 vols., 1. 2016. (Pirate Pals Ser.). (ENG.). 32p. (J). pap. 10.00 *(978-1-5081-9152-0(2),* Windmill Bks.) Rosen Publishing Group, Inc., The.

—Pirates Can Share, 01 vols., 1. 2016. (Pirate Pals Ser.). (ENG.). 32p. (J). pap. 10.00 *(978-1-5081-9155-1(7),* Windmill Bks.) Rosen Publishing Group, Inc., The.

—Pirates Can Work Together, 01 vols., 1. 2016. (Pirate Pals Ser.). (ENG.). 32p. (J). pap. 10.00 *(978-1-5081-9159-9(X),* Windmill Bks.) Rosen Publishing Group, Inc., The.

Edward Stratemeyer. The Rover Boys on Treasure Isle: Or - the Strange Cruise of the Steam Yacht. l.t. ed. 2007. (ENG.). 202p. pap. 22.99 *(978-1-4264-8951-8(X))* Creative Media Partners, LLC.

Eifrig, Kate. I'll Be a Pirate: World of Discovery II. Graves, Dennis, illus. l.t. ed. 2006. (SPA & ENG.). 12p. (gr. k-2). pap. 7.95 *(978-1-57874-053-6(3),* Kaeden Bks.) Kaeden Corp.

Elkington, John. The Pirates of the Gayoso Bayou. 2012. 24p. pap. 15.99 *(978-1-4797-3940-0(5))* Xlibris Corp.

Emmett, Jonathan. The Treasure of Captain Claw. Cox, Steve, illus. 2012. (ENG.). 32p. (J). (gr. -1-k). pap. 9.99 *(978-1-84616-741-6(8))* Hodder & Stoughton GBR. Dist: Hachette Bk. Group.

Enderle, Dotti. Book 13: Yo Ho No!, 1 vol. 2014. (Ghost Detectors Set 3 Ser.). (ENG., Illus.). 80p. (J). (gr. 2-5). lib. bdg. 27.07 *(978-1-62402-001-8(1),* Calico Chapter Bks) Magic Wagon.

Eschler, Linda. The Strawberry Fairies & the Secret of Mystery Island. 2008. 57p. pap. 16.95 *(978-1-60610-960-1(X))* America Star Bks.

Evelyn Gill Hilton. Kidnapped by Pirates: Based on the true story of a fourteen year-old boy, Charles Tilton, who was kidnapped alone from an Amer. 2010. 124p. (gr. 1-2). pap. 11.95 *(978-1-4269-2017-2(2))* Trafford Publishing.

—Kidnapped by Pirates: Based on the true story of a fourteen year-old boy, Charles Tilton, who was kidnapped alone from an Amer. 2010. 124p. *(978-1-4269-2018-9(0))* Trafford Publishing (UK) Ltd.

Fafoutakis, Anne. Enchanted Talisman & Other Stories for Children of All Ages. 2004. 132p. pap. 13.50 *(978-1-84426-296-0(0))* Upfront Publishing Ltd. GBR. Dist: Printondemand-worldwide.com.

Farren, Rick. Grandpa & the Pirate. 2003. (J). per. 9.95 *(978-0-9728716-4-8(0))* Journey Pubns., LLC.

—Grandpa & the Pirate. 2007. 49p. (J). per. 9.95 *(978-0-9794863-6-4(X))* Summerland Publishing.

Feldman, Thea. Backyard Pirates. Conger, Holli, illus. 2007. (Magnix Imagination Activity Bks.). 6p. bds. 5.99 *(978-1-932915-40-2(0))* Sandvik Innovations, LLC.

Ferrone, John M. Gus & the Pirate Treasure. Ferrone, John M., illus. Date not set. (Illus.). 36p. (J). (gr. -1-5). pap. 16.95 *(978-1-928811-01-5(9))* Story Stuff, Inc.

Ferry, Beth. Pirate's Perfect Pet. Myers, Matt, illus. 2016. (ENG.). 32p. (J). (gr. -1-3). 15.99 *(978-0-7636-7288-1(2))* Candlewick Pr.

Fisch, Sholly, et al. Starro & the Pirates, 1 vol. 2014. (DC Super Friends Ser.). (ENG., Illus.). 32p. (J). (gr. 1-2). 22.60 *(978-1-4342-9225-4(8))* Stone Arch Bks.

Flanagan, John. The Ghostfaces. 2016. (Brotherband Chronicles Ser.: 6). (ENG.). 400p. (J). (gr. 5). 18.99 *(978-0-399-16357-9(3),* Philomel Bks.) Penguin Young Readers Group.

—The Hunters. (Brotherband Chronicles Ser.: 3). (ENG.). (J). (gr. 5). 2014. 448p. pap. 8.99 *(978-0-14-242664-7(4),* Puffin Books) 2012. 416p. 18.99 *(978-0-399-25621-9(0),* Philomel Bks.) Penguin Young Readers Group.

—The Hunters. 2014. (Brotherband Chronicles Ser.: 3). lib. bdg. 19.65 *(978-0-606-35708-1(4))* Turtleback Bks.

—The Invaders. (Brotherband Chronicles Ser.: 2). (ENG.). (J). (gr. 5). 2013. 448p. pap. 8.99 *(978-0-14-242663-0(6),* Puffin Books) 2012. 432p. 18.99 *(978-0-399-25620-2(2),* Philomel Bks.) Penguin Young Readers Group.

—The Invaders. 2013. (Brotherband Chronicles Ser.: 2). lib. bdg. 19.65 *(978-0-606-26637-6(2),* Turtleback) Turtleback Bks.

—Slaves of Socorro. 2014. (Brotherband Chronicles Ser.: Bk. 4). (ENG., Illus.). 480p. (J). 18.99 *(978-0-399-16355-5(7),* Philomel Bks.) Penguin Publishing Group.

—Slaves of Socorro. 2015. (Brotherband Chronicles Ser.: 4). (ENG.). 496p. (J). (gr. 5). pap. 8.99 *(978-0-14-242726-2(8),* Puffin Books) Penguin Young Readers Group.

—Slaves of Socorro. 2015. (Brotherband Chronicles Ser.: 4). lib. bdg. 19.65 *(978-0-606-36771-4(3))* Turtleback Bks.

Fleischman, Sid. The Ghost in the Noonday Sun. Sís, Peter, illus. 2007. (ENG.). 256p. (J). (gr. 3-7). per. 5.99 *(978-0-06-134502-9(4),* Greenwillow Bks.) HarperCollins Pubs.

—The Giant Rat of Sumatra. Hendrix, John, illus. 2006. (ENG.). 208p. (J). (gr. 5-9). reprint ed. pap. 6.99 *(978-0-06-074240-9(2),* Greenwillow Bks.) HarperCollins Pubs.

Fletcher, Corina. Playbook Pirates. Teckentrup, Britta, illus. 2013. (ENG.). 12p. (J). (gr. -1-2). 24.00 *(978-0-7636-6606-4(8),* Nosy Crow) Candlewick Pr.

Fliess, Sue. How to Be a Pirate. Dyson, Nikki, illus. 2014. (Little Golden Book Ser.). (ENG.). 24p. (J). (-k). 4.99 *(978-0-449-81309-6(6),* Golden Bks.) Random Hse. Children's Bks.

Foley, Lizzie K. Remarkable. 2013. (ENG.). 336p. (J). (gr. 3-7). pap. 7.99 *(978-0-14-242410-0(2),* Puffin Books) Penguin Young Readers Group.

Foley, Lizzie K. & Foley, Elizabeth. Remarkable. 2012. (ENG.). 336p. (J). (gr. 3-7). 16.99 *(978-0-8037-3706-8(8),* Dial Bks) Penguin Young Readers Group.

Fontes, Ron & Fontes, Justine. Captured by Pirates. Witt, David, illus. 2007. (Twisted Journeys (r) Ser.: 1). (ENG.). 112p. (J). (gr. 4-7). lib. bdg. 27.93 *(978-0-8225-6201-6(4),* Graphic Universe™); per. 7.95 *(978-0-8225-6202-3(2))* Lerner Publishing Group.

Foster, Emily. The Drowning Eyes. 2016. (ENG.). 144p. pap. 12.99 *(978-0-7653-8768-4(9),* 9780765387684, Tor Bks.) Doherty, Tom Assocs., LLC.

Francis, Pauline, retold by. Treasure Island. 2010. (Essential Classics - Adventure Ser.). (Illus.). 48p. pap. *(978-0-237-54085-2(1))* Evans Brothers, Ltd.

Franks, Kevin. Scurvy Dogs. Franks, Kevin, illus. 2017. (ENG., Illus.). 96p. (J). pap. 5.99 *(978-1-61067-459-1(6))* Kane Miller.

Fravel, Gale. Fellsmere the Pirate, Chipley's Adventure. Fravel, Harold, illus. 2011. 28p. pap. 12.95 *(978-1-936343-79-9(7))* Peppertree Pr., The.

Freedman, Claire. Pirates Love Underpants. Cort, Ben, illus. 2013. (Underpants Bks.). (ENG.). 32p. (J). (gr. -1-2). 17.99 *(978-1-4424-8512-9(4),* Simon & Schuster/Paula Wiseman Bks.) Simon & Schuster/Paula Wiseman Bks.

Friesen, Ray. Pirate Penguin vs Ninja Chicken Volume 1: Troublems with Frenemies: Troublems with Frenemies. 2011. (Pirate Penguin vs Ninja Chicken Ser.). (ENG., Illus.). 96p. (J). (gr. 2-5). 9.95 *(978-1-60309-071-1(1),* 9781603090711) Top Shelf Productions.

Frisch, Aaron. Pirates at the Plate. Summers, Mark, illus. 2012. (ENG.). 32p. (J). (gr. 1-3). 17.99 *(978-1-56846-210-3(7),* Creative Editions) Creative Co., The.

Fry, Jason. The Jupiter Pirates: Hunt for the Hydra. 2013. (Jupiter Pirates Ser.: 1). (ENG.). 256p. (J). (gr. 3-7). 16.99 *(978-0-06-223020-1(4))* HarperCollins Pubs.

—The Jupiter Pirates #2: Curse of the Iris. 2016. (Jupiter Pirates Ser.: 2). 368p. (J). (gr. 3-7). pap. 6.99 *(978-0-06-223024-9(7))* HarperCollins Pubs.

—The Jupiter Pirates #3: the Rise of Earth. 2016. (Jupiter Pirates Ser.: 3). (Illus.). 448p. (J). (gr. 3-7). 16.99 *(978-0-06-223026-3(3))* HarperCollins Pubs.

—The Jupiter Pirates: Hunt for the Hydra. 2014. (Jupiter Pirates Ser.: 1). (ENG.). 272p. (J). (gr. 3-7). pap. 6.99 *(978-0-06-223021-8(2))* HarperCollins Pubs.

Fry, Jason. Leia & the Great Island Escape. 2016. (Star Wars: Force Awakens 8X8 Ser.). (J). lib. bdg. 14.75 ***(978-0-606-39934-0(8))*** Turtleback Bks.

Fuerst, Jeffrey B. & Benchmark Education Co., LLC. Robert Louis Stevenson's Treasure Island: My Sea Adventure Israel Hands. Hondru, Ovi, illus. 2014. (Text Connections Ser.). (J). (gr. 3). *(978-1-4509-9652-5(3))* Benchmark Education Co.

Funk, Josh. Pirasaurs! Slack, Michael H., illus. 2016. (ENG.). 40p. (J). (gr. -1-k). 14.99 *(978-0-545-75049-3(0),* Orchard Bks.) Scholastic, Inc.

Gaiman, Neil. The Dangerous Alphabet. Grimly, Gris, illus. (ENG.). 32p. (J). (gr. k). 2010. pap. 6.99 *(978-0-06-078335-8(4))* 2008. 17.99 *(978-0-06-078333-4(8))* HarperCollins Pubs.

Gamble, Adam & Jasper, Mark. Good Night Pirate Ship. Kelly, Cooper, illus. 2015. (Good Night Our World Ser.). (ENG.). 26p. (J). (— 1). bds. 9.95 *(978-1-60219-217-1(0))* Good Night Bks.

Gamble, Paul. The Ministry of S. U. I. T. S. 2016. (Ministry of SUITs Ser.: 1). (ENG.). 384p. (J). 16.99 *(978-1-250-07682-3(X),* 9781250076823) Feiwel & Friends.

Gardner, Lyn. Fright in the Night. Asquith, Ros, illus. 2016. (Ghastly Mcnastys Ser.: 3). (ENG.). 192p. (J). (gr. k-3). pap. 9.99 *(978-1-84812-392-2(2))* Bonnier Publishing GBR. Dist: Independent Pubs. Group.

Gates, Susan. Pirate! Band 15. McClellan, Maddy, illus. 2007. (Collins Big Cat Ser.). (ENG.). 48p. (J). (gr. 3-4). pap. 8.99 *(978-0-00-723095-2(8))* HarperCollins Pubs. Ltd. GBR. Dist: Independent Pubs. Group.

Gelsey, James & Duendes Del Sur Staff. Scooby-Doo & the Sunken Ship, 1 vol. 2011. (Scooby-Doo Mysteries Ser.). (ENG., Illus.). 64p. (J). (gr. 3-6). 24.21 *(978-1-59961-893-7(1))* Spotlight.

Geronimo Stilton Staff. Sea Monster Surprise. 2016. (Geronimo Stilton Cavemice Ser.: 11). (ENG.). 128p. (J). (gr. 2-5). pap. 6.99 *(978-0-545-87248-5(0),* Scholastic Paperbacks) Scholastic, Inc.

The Ghost Ship. 2013. (Illus.). (J). *(978-1-4351-4725-6(1))* Barnes & Noble, Inc.

Gilbert, Heather. Skyler the Pirate, 1 vol. 2009. 25p. pap. 24.95 *(978-1-60813-820-3(8))* America Star Bks.

Gilkerson, William. Pirate's Passage. 2014. (ENG., Illus.). 376p. (J). (gr. 4-7). pap. 16.95 *(978-1-61180-247-4(4),* Trumpeter) Shambhala Pubns., Inc.

Gilligan, Alison. Pirate Treasure of the Onyx Dragon. 2011. 144p. (J). (gr. 2-18). pap. 6.99 *(978-1-933390-99-4(9))* Chooseco LLC.

Golden Books. Bubble Pirates! (Bubble Guppies) Unten, Eren, illus. 2013. (Little Golden Book Ser.). (ENG.). 24p. (J). (-k). 4.99 *(978-0-449-81769-8(5),* Golden Bks.) Random Hse. Children's Bks.

—Night of the Ghost Pirate (Paw Patrol) Lovett, Nate, illus. 2015. (Hologramatic Sticker Book Ser.). (ENG.). 64p. (J). (gr. -1-2). pap. 4.99 *(978-0-553-52390-4(2),* Golden Bks.) Random Hse. Children's Bks.

Golden Books Staff. Pirate Pups! (Paw Patrol) Petrossi, Fabrizio, illus. 2016. (Little Golden Book Ser.). (ENG.). 24p. (J). (gr. -1-k). 4.99 *(978-0-553-53888-5(8),* Golden Bks.) Random Hse. Children's Bks.

Golden, Christopher & Lebbon, Tim. The Sea Wolves Bk. 2, Bk. 2. Ruth, Greg, illus. 2012. (Secret Journeys of Jack London Ser.: 2). (ENG.). 400p. (YA). (gr. 8). 16.99 *(978-0-06-186320-2(3),* HarperTeen) HarperCollins Pubs.

Golding, Julia. The Silver Sea, 0 vols. 2013. (ENG.). 352p. (YA). (gr. 7-11). pap. 9.99 *(978-1-4778-1598-4(8),* 9781477815984, Amazon Children's Publishing) Amazon Publishing.

The Great Pirate Adventure. 2016. (ENG., Illus.). 16p. (J). (gr. -1-k). 7.99 ***(978-0-241-20355-2(4))*** Penguin Bks., Ltd. GBR. Dist: Independent Pubs. Group.

Greene, Rhonda Gowler. No Pirates Allowed! Said Library Lou. Ajhar, Brian, illus. 2013. (ENG.). 40p. (J). (gr. 1-3). 15.95 *(978-1-58536-796-2(6),* 202364) Sleeping Bear Pr.

Griswell, Kim T. Rufus Goes to Sea. Gorbachev, Valeri, illus. 2015. (ENG.). 32p. (J). (gr. -1-1). 14.95 *(978-1-4549-1052-7(6))* Sterling Publishing Co., Inc.

Grossmann-Hensel, Katharina. Papa is a Pirate. Grossmann-Hensel, Katharina, illus. 2009. (ENG., Illus.). 32p. (J). (gr. -1-3). 16.95 *(978-0-7358-2237-5(9))* North-South Bks., Inc.

Guerra, Elisa Puricelli. The City of Lizards. Zeni, Marco, tr. from ITA. Bernstein, Gabriel León, illus. 2015. (Minerva Mint Ser.). (ENG.). 160p. (gr. 2-4). lib. bdg. 25.32 *(978-1-4342-9671-9(7))* Stone Arch Bks.

—The Legend of Black Bart, 1 vol. Pernigotti, Chiara, tr. from ITA. Bernstein, Gabo León, illus. 2014. (Minerva Mint Ser.). (ENG.). 160p. (gr. 2-4). pap. 7.99 *(978-1-4342-6515-9(3))* Capstone Young Readers of Coughlan Cos.

—The Legend of Black Bart, 1 vol. Pernigotti, Chiara, tr. from ITA. Bernstein, Gabo León, illus. 2014. (Minerva Mint Ser.). (ENG.). 160p. (gr. 2-4). 25.32 *(978-1-4342-6512-8(9))* Stone Arch Bks.

Guillain, Adam & Guillain, Charlotte. The Pirate Pie Ship. Van Wyk, Rupert, illus. 2014. (ENG.). 32p. (J). *(978-0-7787-1309-8(1));* pap. *(978-0-7787-1368-5(7))* Crabtree Publishing Co.

Guillain, Adam & Guillain, Charlotte. Pizza for Pirates. Wildish, Lee, illus. 2nd ed. 2016. (George's Amazing Adventures Ser.). (ENG.). 32p. (J). (gr. -1-k). pap. 10.99 *(978-1-4052-7361-9(5))* Egmont Bks., Ltd. GBR. Dist: Independent Pubs. Group.

Haarsma, P. J. The Softwire: Wormhole Pirates on Orbis 3. 2010. (Softwire Ser.: 3). (ENG., Illus.). 400p. (YA). (gr. 7). 8.99 *(978-0-7636-4777-3(2))* Candlewick Pr.

—Wormhole Pirates on Orbis, Vol. 3. 2009. (Softwire Ser.: 3). (ENG., Illus.). 384p. (YA). (gr. 7). 16.99 *(978-0-7636-2711-9(9))* Candlewick Pr.

Hamilton, Libby. The Ultimate Pirate Handbook. Leyssenne, Mathieu & Kraft, Jason, illus. 2015. (ENG.). 20p. (J). (gr. k-3). 19.99 *(978-0-7636-7963-7(1),* Templar) Candlewick Pr.

Hamilton, Tim. But! Hamilton, Tim, illus. 2014. (ENG., Illus.). 32p. (J). (gr. -1-2). 16.95 *(978-0-8234-3046-8(4))* Holiday Hse., Inc.

Hamilton, Tisha. Piratas del Caribe. el viaje al fin del Mundo: Pirates of the Caribbean: at the World's End. 2007. (Illus.). 38p. (J). *(978-970-718-532-6(5),* Silver Dolphin en Español) Advanced Marketing, S. de R. L. de C. V.

Harley, Bill. Dirty Joe the Pirate: A True Story. Davis, Jack E., illus. 2008. (ENG.). 32p. (J). (gr. k-3). 17.99 *(978-0-06-623780-0(7))* HarperCollins Pubs.

Havercroft, Elizabeth. A Year on a Pirate Ship. 2009. (Time Goes By Ser.). (ENG.). 24p. (gr. k-3). pap. 6.95 *(978-1-58013-799-7(7),* First Avenue Editions) Lerner Publishing Group.

Hawes, Charles Boardman. The Dark Frigate. 2005. pap. 27.95 *(978-1-4179-3209-2(0))* Kessinger Publishing, LLC.

Hawkins, Colin. Pirate Ship: A Pop-up Adventure. Hawkins, Colin et al, illus. 2006. 28p. (J). (gr. 4-8). reprint ed. 20.00 *(978-0-7567-9827-7(2))* DIANE Publishing Co.

Hawkins, Mia K. The Broken Guild of Twelve Pirates, 1 vol. 2009. 201p. pap. 24.95 *(978-1-61546-333-6(X))* PublishAmerica, Inc.

Hawley, Mabel C. Four Little Blossoms on Apple Tree Island. 2007. 80p. per. *(978-1-4068-1704-1(X))* Echo Library.

Head, Mat. Warduff & the Pelican Pirates. 2014. (ENG., Illus.). 32p. (J). (-k). pap. 9.99 *(978-1-84939-567-0(5))* Andersen Pr. GBR. Dist: Independent Pubs. Group.

Heilig, Heidi. The Girl from Everywhere. 2016. 464p. (YA). (gr. 8). 17.99 *(978-0-06-238075-3(3),* Greenwillow Bks.) HarperCollins Pubs.

Helmer, Marilyn. Pirate Island Treasure, 1 vol. Parkins, David, illus. 2013. (Orca Echoes Ser.). (ENG.). 64p. (J). (gr. 2-3). pap. 6.95 *(978-1-4598-0165-3(2))* Orca Bk. Pubs. USA.

Helquist, Brett. Roger, the Jolly Pirate. Helquist, Brett, illus. 2004. (Illus.). 40p. (J). (gr. -1-3). lib. bdg. 17.89 *(978-0-06-623806-7(4))* HarperCollins Pubs.

Helquist, Brett & Helquist, Brett. Roger: The Jolly Pirate. Helquist, Brett, illus. 2004. (ENG., Illus.). 40p. (J). (gr. -1-3). 16.99 *(978-0-06-623805-0(6))* HarperCollins Pubs.

—Roger, the Jolly Pirate. Helquist, Brett, illus. 2007. (ENG., Illus.). 40p. (J). (gr. -1-2). pap. 6.99 *(978-0-06-443851-3(1))* HarperCollins Pubs.

Hemyng, Bracebridge. Jack Harkaway & His Son's Escape from the Brigand's of Greece. 2007. (ENG.). 342p. pap. 23.99 *(978-1-4264-2290-4(3));* 386p. pap. 26.99 *(978-1-4264-2325-3(X))* Creative Media Partners, LLC.

—Jack Harkaway & His Son's Escape from the Brigands of Greece. 2004. reprint ed. pap. 1.99 *(978-1-4192-2705-9(X))* Kessinger Publishing, LLC.

Henry, James. The Cabinet of Curiosities. 2010. 240p. pap. 21.50 *(978-0-9559851-0-2(2))* Blue Cat GBR. Dist: Lulu Pr., Inc.

Herwick Rice, Dona & Paris, Stephanie. Sal Fink, 1 vol. 2009. (Building Fluency Through Reader's Theater Ser.). (ENG.). 24p. (J). (gr. 2-4). pap. 6.99 *(978-1-4333-0995-3(5))* Teacher Created Materials, Inc.

Herz, Henry L. Cap'n Rex & His Clever Crew. Schipper, Benjamin, illus. 2017. (ENG.). 32p. (J). (gr. k). 16.95 ***(978-1-4549-2088-5(2))*** Sterling Publishing Co., Inc.

Higgins, Nadia. Avast, Ye Dog Thief!, 1 vol. Holder, Jimmy, illus. 2008. (Barnacle Barb & Her Pirate Crew Ser.). (ENG.). 32p. (gr. -1-3). 28.50 *(978-1-60270-089-5(3),* Looking Glass Library) ABDO Publishing Co.

—Aye, My Eye!, 1 vol. Holder, Jimmy, illus. 2008. (Barnacle Barb & Her Pirate Crew Ser.). (ENG.). 32p. (gr. -1-3). 28.50 *(978-1-60270-090-1(7),* Looking Glass Library) ABDO Publishing Co.

—Blimey, That's Slimy!, 1 vol. Holder, Jimmy, illus. 2008. (Barnacle Barb & Her Pirate Crew Ser.). (ENG.). 32p. (gr. -1-3). 28.50 *(978-1-60270-091-8(5),* Looking Glass Library) ABDO Publishing Co.

—Break a Sea Leg, Shrimp-Breath!, 1 vol. Holder, Jimmy, illus. 2008. (Barnacle Barb & Her Pirate Crew Ser.). (ENG.). 32p. (gr. -1-3). 28.50 *(978-1-60270-092-5(3),* Looking Glass Library) ABDO Publishing Co.

—Pegleg Gets Stumped, 1 vol. Holder, Jimmy, illus. 2008. (Barnacle Barb & Her Pirate Crew Ser.). (ENG.). 32p. (gr. -1-3). 28.50 *(978-1-60270-093-2(1),* Looking Glass Library) ABDO Publishing Co.

—Walk the Plank, Plankton, 1 vol. Holder, Jimmy, illus. 2008. (Barnacle Barb & Her Pirate Crew Ser.). (ENG.). 32p. (gr. -1-3). 28.50 *(978-1-60270-094-9(X),* Looking Glass Library) ABDO Publishing Co.

Higginson, Sheila Sweeny. Cubby's Mixed-Up Map. 2014. (Jake & the Never Land Pirates Ser.). (J). lib. bdg. 14.75 *(978-0-606-35262-8(7))* Turtleback Bks.

Hoena, B. A. & Barrie, J. M. Peter Pan. Cano, Fernando, illus. 2015. (Graphic Revolve: Common Core Editions Ser.). (ENG.). 72p. (gr. 2-3). lib. bdg. 27.99 *(978-1-4965-0372-5(4))* Stone Arch Bks.

Hoena, Blake. Robert Louis Stevenson's Treasure Island, 1 vol. 2013. (Can You Survive? Ser.). (ENG.). 160p. (J). (gr. 4-6). pap. 8.95 *(978-0-9883662-6-8(6))* Lake 7 Creative, LLC.

Holden, Pam. Greedy Gus the Pirate, 6 pack. Whimp, Pauline, illus. 2009. (Red Rocket Readers Ser.). (ENG.). 16p. (gr. 2-2). pap. *(978-1-877363-74-0(X))* Flying Start Bks.

—Two Pirates, 6 pack. Whimp, Pauline, illus. 2009. (Red Rocket Readers Ser.). (ENG.). 16p. (gr. 2-2). pap. *(978-1-877363-71-9(5))* Flying Start Bks.

Holmes, Anna. Tickety Toc: Pirate Time. 2014. (ENG.). 24p. (J). (gr. -1-k). pap. 3.99 *(978-0-545-61475-7(9))* Scholastic, Inc.

Hope, B. T. The Curse of the Bone Pirates: Nui Island Eco-Logical Adventures. 2008. 198p. (J). pap. 9.95 *(978-0-9817388-0-2(X))* Nui Media & Entertainment, LLC.

Hopkins, Douglas. Princess June & the Shadow Pirates, 1 vol. 2007. (ENG., Illus.). 32p. (J). (gr. -1-2). per. 8.95 *(978-1-894294-88-1(2)*, Tuckamore Bks) Creative Bk. Publishing CAN. Dist: Orca Bk. Pubs. USA.

Hoppey, Tim. Pedro, the Pirate. Bonder, Dianna, illus. 2012. (ENG & SPA.). 32p. (J). lib. bdg. 16.95 *(978-1-936299-18-8(6)*, Raven Tree Pr.,Csi) Continental Sales, Inc.

Hord, Colleen. Keep Your Chin Up. Dufalla, Anita, illus. 2012. (ENG.). 24p. (gr. 1-2). pap. 8.95 *(978-1-61810-315-4(6))* Rourke Educational Media.

Horn, Shannon. Pirates of the Mississippian: The Adventures of Jerry & Draco. 2012. 24p. pap. 17.99 *(978-1-4772-6991-6(6))* AuthorHouse.

Horowitz, Dave. Twenty-Six Pirates: An Alphabet Book. Horowitz, Dave, illus. 2013. (ENG., Illus.). 32p. (J). (gr. -1-k). 16.99 *(978-0-399-25777-3(2)*, Nancy Paulsen Books) Penguin Young Readers Group.

Howard, Jenny. Bittersweet Voyage. 2012. 172p. pap. 12.95 *(978-1-4685-7573-6(2))* AuthorHouse.

Hritzay, Tami. The Hole in the Wall: J. B. & the Pirates. 2013. pap. 11.45 *(978-0-7414-8266-2(5))* Infinity Publishing.

Hunt, Elizabeth Singer. The Search for the Sunken Treasure. Williamson, Brian, illus. 2007. (Secret Agent Jack Stalwart Ser.: 2). (ENG.). 128p. (J). (gr. 1-4). per. 5.99 *(978-1-60286-002-5(5)*, Weinstein Bks.) Perseus Bks. Group.

Hunter, Derek. Brainwash Escape Victims, Vol. 2. 2006. (ENG., Illus.). 144p. (YA). pap. 12.95 *(978-1-59362-051-6(9)*, 9781593620516) Slave Labor Bks.

Icanberry, Mark. A Pirate's Feast. 2011. (Illus.). 48p. 14.95 *(978-1-893327-08-5(6))*; pap. 7.95 *(978-1-893327-09-2(4))* Ten Speed Pr. (Tricycle Pr.).

Jacques, Brian. The Angel's Command. Elliot, David & Schoenherr, Ian, illus. 2005. (ENG.). 384p. (J). (gr. 3-7). 7.99 *(978-0-14-240285-6(0)*, Firebird) Penguin Young Readers Group.

—The Angel's Command. 2003. (Castaways of the Flying Dutchman Ser.: No. 2). 1.00 *(978-1-4175-5393-8(6))* Recorded Bks., Inc.

—Mariel of Redwall. 2004. (Redwall Ser.). 1.00 *(978-1-4175-6449-1(0))* Recorded Bks., Inc.

James, Brian. Ahoy, Ghost Ship Ahead! Zivoin, Jennifer, illus. 2007. (Pirate School Ser.: 2). (ENG.). 64p. (J). (gr. 1-3). pap. 3.99 *(978-0-448-44625-7(1)*, Grosset & Dunlap) Penguin Young Readers Group.

—Treasure Trouble. Zivoin, Jennifer, illus. 2008. (Pirate School Ser.: 5). (ENG.). 64p. (J). (gr. 1-3). pap. 3.99 *(978-0-448-44782-7(7)*, Grosset & Dunlap) Penguin Young Readers Group.

—Yo-Ho-Ho! Zivoin, Jennifer, illus. 2008. (Pirate School Ser.: 7). (ENG.). 64p. (J). (gr. 1-3). pap. 3.99 *(978-0-448-44887-9(4)*, Grosset & Dunlap) Penguin Young Readers Group.

James, Larry W. Captain Petey: An Adventure at Sea. Ramos, Violet M., ed. James, Larry W. & Freshman, Floris R., illus. 2003. 28p. pap. 6.99 *(978-0-9742154-0-2(6))* Cross Pointe Printing.

Jardine, Alan. Sloop John B: A Pirate's Tale. Pickering, Jimmy, illus. 2005. (ENG.). 32p. (J). (gr. 4-7). 17.95 *(978-1-59687-181-6(4))* IBks., Inc.

—Sloop John B: A Pirate's Tale. Pickering, Jimmy, illus. 2005. 32p. 17.95 *(978-0-689-03596-8(9)*, Milk & Cookies) ibooks, Inc.

Jardine, Alan. Sloop John B -A Pirate's Tale. Pickering, Jimmy, illus. 2016. (ENG.). (J). (gr. k-4). 32.00 ***(978-1-59687-511-1(9)***, ipicturebooks) ibooks, Inc.

Jarman, Julia. Class Three at Sea. Chapman, Lynne, illus. 2008. (ENG.). 32p. (J). (gr. k-3). 16.95 *(978-0-8225-7617-4(1)*, Carolrhoda Bks.) Lerner Publishing Group.

Jeffrey, Rosemary. Allio, Are you Free. 2010. 176p. pap. 12.00 *(978-0-557-75342-0(2))* Lulu Pr., Inc.

Jenkins, Amanda & Reeves, Tara McClary. The Pirate & the Firefly: A Boy, a Bug, & a Lesson in Wisdom. Fernandez, Daniel, illus. 2017. (Firefly Chronicles Ser.). (ENG.). 32p. (J). (gr. -1-3). pap. 3.99 ***(978-1-4627-4521-0(0)***, B&H Kids) B&H Publishing Group.

Johnson, Myrna. Let's Take a Hike. 2013. (ENG., Illus.). 32p. (gr. -1-1). pap. 13.95 *(978-1-936205-79-0(3))* Austin, Stephen F. State Univ. Pr.

Jones, Gareth P. Are You the Pirate Captain? Parsons, Garry, illus. 2016. (ENG.). 32p. (gr. -1-3). (J). 17.99 *(978-1-5124-0427-2(6))*; 35.99 *(978-1-5124-0446-3(2))* Lerner Publishing Group.

Jones, Rob Lloyd. See Inside Pirate Ships. Muhle, Jorg, illus. 2007. (See Inside Board Bks). 15p. (J). (gr. -1-3). bds. 12.99 *(978-0-7945-1601-7(7)*, Usborne) EDC Publishing.

—The Story of Pirates. Dutrait, Vincent, illus. 2007. (Young Reading Series 3 Gift Bks). 63p. (J). (gr. 4-7). 8.99 *(978-0-7945-1618-5(1)*, Usborne) EDC Publishing.

Jorgensen, Norman. Smuggler's Curse The. 2017. (ENG.). 356p. (J). (gr. 4-7). 8.95 ***(978-1-925164-19-0(5))*** Fremantle Pr. AUS. Dist: Independent Pubs. Group.

Joyce, Melanie. What Pirates Really Do. Paterson, Alex, illus. 2016. (ENG.). 32p. (J). (gr. -1-3). 16.99 *(978-1-4998-0257-3(9))* Little Bee Books Inc.

The Jupiter Pirates - Curse of the Iris. 2014. (Jupiter Pirates Ser.: 2). (ENG.). 352p. (J). (gr. 3-7). 16.99 *(978-0-06-223023-2(9))* HarperCollins Pubs.

Kaserman, James & Kaserman, Sarah Jane. How the Pirates Saved Christmas. 2005. (Illus.). 64p. (J). per. 5.99 *(978-0-9674081-2-5(1)*, (239)939-4845) Pirate Publishing International.

Katar, Al. Captain Scratch: The Island of Sirmarj. 2008. 48p. pap. 21.99 *(978-1-4363-4188-2(4))* Xlibris Corp.

Keats, Israel. The Zephyr Conspiracy. 2017. (Level Up Ser.). (ENG.). (YA). (gr. 6-12). 120p. pap. 7.99 ***(978-1-5124-5361-4(7))***; lib. bdg. 26.65 ***(978-1-5124-3985-4(1))*** Lerner Publishing Group. (Darby Creek).

Keene, Carolyn. Treasure Trouble. Pamintuan, Macky, illus. 2009. (Nancy Drew & the Clue Crew Ser.: 20). (ENG.). 112p. (J). (gr. 1-4). pap. 4.99 *(978-1-4169-7809-1(7)*, Aladdin) Simon & Schuster Children's Publishing.

Kehne, Carroll Harrison, Jr. Buried Treasure, a Pirate's Tale, 1 vol. 2009. (ENG., Illus.). 34p. (J). (gr. 3-7). 12.95 *(978-0-87033-601-0(0)*, 9780870336010, Cornell Maritime Pr./Tidewater Pubs.) Schiffer Publishing, Ltd.

Kelly, John. The Beastly Pirates. 2015. (ENG., Illus.). 32p. (J). (gr. -1-1). 18.99 *(978-1-4088-4983-5(6)*, 9781408849835, Bloomsbury USA Childrens) Bloomsbury Publishing USA.

Kelman, Marcy & Disney Book Group Staff. Ahoy, Izzy! Disney Storybook Art Team, illus. 2013. (ENG.). 24p. (J). (gr. -1-k). pap. 3.99 *(978-1-4231-6393-0(1))* Disney Pr.

—Trick or Treasure? Disney Storybook Artists Staff, illus. 2013. (ENG.). 24p. (J). (gr. -1-k). pap. 5.99 *(978-1-4231-7140-9(3))* Disney Pr.

Kennedy, Kim. Misty Gordon & the Mystery of the Ghost Pirates. 2010. (ENG., Illus.). 240p. (YA). (gr. 3-7). 15.95 *(978-0-8109-9357-0(0)*, Amulet Bks.) Abrams, Inc.

—Pirate Pete. Kennedy, Doug & Kennedy, Roy D., illus. 2010. (ENG.). 40p. (J). (gr. 1-4). pap. 8.95 *(978-0-8109-8923-8(9))* Abrams, Inc.

—Pirate Pete's Talk Like a Pirate. Kennedy, Doug, illus. 2007. (ENG.). 40p. (J). (gr. k-17). 16.95 *(978-0-8109-9348-8(1)*, Abrams Bks. for Young Readers) Abrams, Inc.

Kessler, Liz. Poppy the Pirate Dog & the Missing Treasure. Phillips, Mike, illus. (Candlewick Sparks Ser.). (ENG.). 64p. (J). (gr. k-4). 2016. pap. 3.99 *(978-0-7636-8772-4(3))* 2015. 14.99 *(978-0-7636-7497-7(4))* Candlewick Pr.

—Poppy the Pirate Dog's New Shipmate. Phillips, Mike, illus. (Candlewick Sparks Ser.). (ENG.). 64p. (J). (gr. k-4). 2015. pap. 3.99 *(978-0-7636-8031-2(1))* 2014. 14.99 *(978-0-7636-6751-1(X))* Candlewick Pr.

Kettle, Shey. Girl Pirates. Thomas, Meredith, illus. 2005. (Girlz Rock! Ser.). (J). pap. *(978-1-59336-701-5(5))* Mondo Publishing.

Kidd, Rob. City of Gold, 1 vol. Orpinas, Jean-Paul, illus. 2009. (Pirates of the Caribbean, Jack Sparrow Ser.: Bk. 7). (ENG.). 128p. (gr. 3-6). 24.21 *(978-1-59961-529-5(0))* Spotlight.

—Day of the Shadow. 4th ed. 2009. (Pirates of the Caribbean Ser.: No. 5). 256p. (YA). (gr. 5-18). pap. 6.99 *(978-1-4231-1041-5(2))* Disney Pr.

—Jack Sparrow: The Siren Song. Orpinas, Jean-Paul, illus. 2006. 122p. (J). lib. bdg. 16.00 *(978-1-4242-1571-3(4))* Fitzgerald Bks.

—The Siren Song, 1 vol. Orpinas, Jean-Paul, illus. 2009. (Pirates of the Caribbean, Jack Sparrow Ser.: Bk. 2). (ENG.). 128p. (gr. 3-6). 24.21 *(978-1-59961-524-0(X))* Spotlight.

Kimmelman, Leslie. Trick ARRR Treat: A Pirate Halloween. Monlongo, Jorge, illus. 2017. (ENG.). 32p. (J). (gr. -1-k). pap. 7.99 ***(978-0-8075-8066-0(X))*** Whitman, Albert & Co.

Kimmelman, Leslie. Trick Arrr Treat: A Pirate Halloween. Monlongo, Jorge, illus. 2015. (ENG.). 32p. (J). (gr. -1-3). 16.99 *(978-0-8075-8061-5(9))* Whitman, Albert & Co.

Kladstrup, Kristin. The Gingerbread Pirates. Tavares, Matt, illus. (ENG.). 32p. (J). (gr. -1-3). 2009. 16.99 *(978-0-7636-3223-6(6))* 2012. 9.99 *(978-0-7636-6233-2(X))* Candlewick Pr.

Kloepfer, John. The Zombie Chasers - Zombies of the Caribbean. DeGrand, David, illus. 2014. (Zombie Chasers Ser.: 6). (ENG.). 224p. (J). (gr. 3-7). 16.99 *(978-0-06-229024-3(X))* HarperCollins Pubs.

Knapman, Timothy. A Very Pirate Christmas. Ayto, Russell, illus. 2015. (ENG.). 32p. (J). (gr. -1-k). pap. 11.99 *(978-1-4052-6504-1(3))* Egmont Bks., Ltd. GBR. Dist: Independent Pubs. Group.

Knotoff, Karenann. The Island of Rouge. 2007. 96p. per. 19.95 *(978-1-4241-7575-8(5))* America Star Bks.

Knowlton, Laurie Lazzaro. Pirates Don't Say Please!, 1 vol. Tans, Adrian, illus. 2012. (ENG.). 32p. (J). (gr. k-3). 16.99 *(978-1-58980-982-6(3))* Pelican Publishing Co., Inc.

Kramer, Andrew. Pajama Pirates. Lammle, Leslie, illus. 2010. (ENG.). 40p. (J). (gr. k-3). 16.99 *(978-0-06-125194-8(1))* HarperCollins Pubs.

Kuhl, Debra. Black Bert the Pirate, 1 vol. 2009. 83p. pap. 19.95 *(978-1-60749-968-8(1))* America Star Bks.

La Rose, Melinda. Jake & the Neverland Pirates: X Marks the Croc!, 1 vol. Batson, Alan, illus. 2014. (World of Reading Pre-1 Ser.). (ENG.). 32p. (J). (gr. 3-5). lib. bdg. 24.21 *(978-1-61479-247-5(X))* Spotlight.

La Rose, Melinda & Ward, Kelly. Treasure of the Tides. 2014. (Illus.). (J). *(978-1-4844-3449-9(8))* Disney Publishing Worldwide.

Lake, Nick. Hostage Three. 2014. (ENG.). 400p. (YA). (gr. 7). pap. 9.99 *(978-1-61963-438-1(4)*, 9781619634381, Bloomsbury USA Childrens) 2013. (ENG.). 384p. (YA). (gr. 7). 17.99 *(978-1-61963-123-6(7)*, 9781619631236, Bloomsbury USA Childrens) 2013. 368p. 17.99 *(978-1-61963-149-6(0))* Bloomsbury Publishing USA.

Lamphere-Slaughter, Sharyn. Droopy Drawers & the Peg Leg Pirate. 2009. 24p. pap. 12.99 *(978-1-4490-6055-8(2))* AuthorHouse.

Landers, Melissa. Starflight. 2017. (ENG.). 384p. (YA). (gr. 9-17). pap. 9.99 *(978-1-4847-4786-5(0))* Hyperion Bks. for Children.

—Starflight. 2016. (ENG., Illus.). 364p. (YA). (gr. 7-12). 17.99 *(978-1-4847-2324-1(4))* Hyperion Pr.

LaReau, Kara. Unintentional Adventures of the Bland Sisters. Hill, Jen, illus. 2017. (ENG.). 176p. (J). (gr. 3-7). 14.95 *(978-1-4197-2136-6(4)*, Amulet Bks.) Abrams, Inc.

Larose, Melinda. After a While, Crocodile. 2014. (Jake & the Never Land Pirates Ser.). (J). lib. bdg. 13.55 *(978-0-606-35267-3(8))* Turtleback Bks.

—Treasure of the Tides. 2014. (Jake & the Never Land Pirates Ser.). (J). lib. bdg. 13.55 *(978-0-606-35269-7(4))* Turtleback Bks.

LaRose, Melinda & Disney Book Group Staff. Birthday Bash! Disney Storybook Art Team, illus. 2014. (ENG.). 32p. (J). (gr. -1-k). pap. 4.99 *(978-1-4231-9935-9(9))* Disney Pr.

—Bucky Makes a Splash! Disney Storybook Artists Staff, illus. 2013. (ENG.). 16p. (J). (gr. -1-k). pap. 4.99 *(978-1-4231-6389-3(3))* Disney Pr.

—The Croc Takes the Cake. Disney Storybook Artists Staff, illus. 2012. (World of Reading Ser.). (ENG.). 32p. (J). (gr. -1-k). pap. 3.99 *(978-1-4231-5543-0(2))* Disney Pr.

—Jake & the Never Land Pirates after a While, Crocodile. Disney Storybook Artists Staff, illus. 2014. (ENG.). 32p. (J). (gr. -1-k). pap. 3.99 *(978-1-4231-8387-7(8))* Disney Pr.

—Jake & the Never Land Pirates Treasure of the Tides. Disney Storybook Artists Staff, illus. 2014. (ENG.). 32p. (J). (gr. -1-k). pap. 3.99 *(978-1-4231-9422-4(5))* Disney Pr.

—X Marks the Croc!, Pre-Level 1. Disney Storybook Art Team, illus. 2013. (World of Reading Ser.). (ENG.). 32p. (J). (gr. -1-k). pap. 3.99 *(978-1-4231-6392-3(3))* Disney Pr.

Lasky, Kathryn. Pirate Bob. Clark, David, illus. alt. ed. 2008. (ENG.). 32p. (J). (gr. k-3). per. 8.95 *(978-1-57091-647-2(0))* Charlesbridge Publishing, Inc.

Latsch, Oliver, tr. from GER. The Pirate Pig. 2015. (ENG., Illus.). 80p. (J). (gr. 2-5). 9.99 *(978-0-385-37544-3(1)*, Random Hse. Bks. for Young Readers) Random Hse. Children's Bks.

Laurence, Daniel. Captain & Matey Set Sail. Muñoz, Claudio, illus. 2003. (I Can Read Bks.). 64p. (gr. 1-3). 15.00 *(978-0-7569-1402-8(7))* Perfection Learning Corp.

Lawrence, Caroline. The Pirates of Pompeii. 2004. (Roman Mysteries Ser.). (Illus.). 159p. (J). (gr. 3-7). 13.65 *(978-0-7569-5938-8(1))* Perfection Learning Corp.

Lawrence, Iain. The Buccaneers. 2003. (High Seas Trilogy). (Illus.). 244p. (gr. 5-9). 16.50 *(978-0-7569-1454-7(X))* Perfection Learning Corp.

—The Buccaneers. 2003. (ENG., Illus.). 256p. (J). (gr. 3-7). 7.99 *(978-0-440-41671-5(X)*, Yearling) Random Hse. Children's Bks.

Lawrenson, Judith. Petunia the Pirate of Port Royal Sound. 2007. (Illus.). (J). 14.95 *(978-0-9767278-0-4(3))* Mrs. L's Reading Room.

Layboum, Emma. Dungeon Dragon. 2008. (ENG.). 156p. (J). (gr. 3-6). pap. 9.95 *(978-1-84270-736-4(1))* Andersen Pr. GBR. Dist: Independent Pubs. Group.

Le Gras, Gilbert. Joaquin & Olivier en Haute Mer! On the High Seas. 2009. 24p. pap. 8.20 *(978-1-4251-1980-5(8))* Trafford Publishing.

LeapFrog Staff. Pirates: The Treasure of Turtle Island. 2008. (J). 13.99 *(978-1-59319-927-2(9))* LeapFrog Enterprises, Inc.

Lee, Brian, illus. A Pirate Ship. 2005. (What's Inside? Ser.). *(978-0-7607-6809-9(9))* backpackbook.

Lee, Maxine. Pi-Rat! Lee, Maxine, illus. 2013. (ENG., Illus.). 32p. (J). (gr. -1-k). 14.99 *(978-1-58925-143-4(1))* Tiger Tales.

Lee, Tanith. Piratica: Being a Daring Tale of a Singular Girl's Adventure upon the High Seas. 2006. (ENG.). 304p. (YA). (gr. 7-18). per. 8.99 *(978-0-14-240644-1(9)*, Firebird) Penguin Young Readers Group.

Leigh, S. Uncle Pete's Pirate Adventure. rev. ed. 2004. (Young Puzzle Adventures Ser.). 32p. (J). (gr. 2-18). pap. 4.95 *(978-0-7945-0401-4(9))*; lib. bdg. 12.95 *(978-1-58086-545-6(3))* EDC Publishing.

Leigh, Susannah. Uncle Pete the Pirate. 2004. (Usborne Young Puzzle Adventures Ser.). (Illus.). 32p. (J). (gr. 2-18). pap. 4.95 *(978-0-7945-0400-7(0)*, Usborne) EDC Publishing.

—Uncle Pete's Pirate Adventure. Stowell, Louie, ed. Haw, Brenda & Dawes, Will, illus. rev. ed. 2007. (Young Puzzle Adventures Ser.). 32p. (J). (gr. -1-3). pap. 4.99 *(978-0-7945-1848-6(6)*, Usborne) EDC Publishing.

LernerClassroom Editors, ed. Twisted Journeys, Set 1. 2008. (Twisted Journeys (r) Ser.). (ENG.). (J). (gr. 4-7). pap. 271.89 *(978-1-58013-276-3(6))* Lerner Publishing Group.

Leung, Peyton. The Pirate Girl's Treasure. Leung, Hilary, illus. 2012. (ENG.). 32p. (J). (gr. -1-3). 16.95 *(978-1-55453-660-3(X))* Kids Can Pr., Ltd. CAN. Dist: Hachette Bk. Group.

Levenseller, Tricia. Daughter of the Pirate King. 2017. (Daughter of the Pirate King Ser.). (ENG.). 320p. (YA). 17.99 *(978-1-250-09596-1(4)*, 9781250095961) Feiwel & Friends.

Lewis, Michael G. The Great Pirate Christmas Battle, 1 vol. Jaskiel, Stan, illus. 2014. (ENG.). 32p. (J). (gr. k-3). 16.99 *(978-1-4556-1934-4(5))* Pelican Publishing Co., Inc.

Lindgren, Astrid. Ferien auf Saltkroken. pap. 19.95 *(978-3-423-70773-2(9))* Deutscher Taschenbuch Verlag GmbH & Co KG DEU. Dist: Distribooks, Inc.

Linklater, Eric. The Pirates in the Deep Green Sea. 2013. (ENG.). 314p. (YA). pap. 16.99 *(978-1-4482-0582-0(4)*, 9781448205820, Bloomsbury Reader) Bloomsbury Publishing Plc GBR. Dist: Macmillan.

Lloyd, Hugh. Among the River Pirates. Fogel, Seymour, illus. 2011. 204p. 44.95 *(978-1-258-06703-8(X))* Literary Licensing, LLC.

Lock, Deborah. Pirate Attack! 2017. (DK Readers Ser.). (ENG.). 48p. (J). (gr. k-2). 14.99 ***(978-1-4654-6474-3(3))***; pap. 3.99 ***(978-1-4654-6473-6(5))*** Dorling Kindersley Publishing, Inc. (DK Children).

London, C. Alexander. Honor Bound. 2014. (Tides of War Ser.: 2). (ENG.). 224p. (J). (gr. 5-9). pap. 5.99 *(978-0-545-66301-4(6)*, Scholastic Paperbacks) Scholastic, Inc.

Long, Melinda. How I Became a Pirate. Shannon, David, illus. 2003. (ENG.). 44p. (J). (gr. -1-3). 16.99 *(978-0-15-201848-1(4))* Houghton Mifflin Harcourt Publishing Co.

—Pirates Don't Change Diapers. Shannon, David, illus. 2007. (ENG.). 44p. (J). (gr. -1-3). 17.99 *(978-0-15-205353-6(0))* Houghton Mifflin Harcourt Publishing Co.

Lopez, Patricia A. Corky & Pirate Dan, 1 vol. 2009. 43p. pap. 24.95 *(978-1-61546-096-0(9))* PublishAmerica, Inc.

Lord, Kenniston. The Pirates of Peary Village. 2004. 182p. (J). pap. 9.18 *(978-1-4116-7893-4(1))* Lulu Pr., Inc.

The Lost Treasure of Skull Island. 2012. (Illus.). (J). *(978-1-4351-4328-9(0))* Barnes & Noble, Inc.

Lowery, Mike. The Pursuit of the Pesky Pizza Pirate! 2016. (Doodle Adventures Ser.). (ENG., Illus.). 112p. (J). (gr. 2-5). 12.95 *(978-0-7611-8720-2(0))* Workman Publishing Co., Inc.

Lubber, William & Steer, Dugald A. Pirateology Guidebook & Model Set. 2007. (Ologies Ser.). (ENG., Illus.). 24p. (J). (gr. 3-7). 17.99 *(978-0-7636-3582-4(0))* Candlewick Pr.

LUCAS, David. The Skeleton Pirate. 2013. (ENG., Illus.). 30p. (J). (gr. -1-2). 15.99 *(978-0-7636-6107-6(4))* Candlewick Pr.

Lynes, William. Pirates, Scoundrels, & Kings. 2013. 450p. (gr. 10-12). 33.95 *(978-1-4759-6562-9(1))*; pap. 23.95 *(978-1-4759-6561-2(3))* iUniverse, Inc.

Lytle, Robert A. Pirate Party. Williams, Bill, illus. 2006. (Mackinac Passage Ser.). 258p. (J). (gr. 4-7). pap. 9.95 *(978-0-9749412-5-7(5))* EDCO Publishing, Inc.

Mabbitt, Will. Mabel Jones & the Doomsday Book. 2016. (Mabel Jones Ser.). (ENG., Illus.). 336p. (J). (gr. 3-7). 16.99 *(978-1-101-99962-2(4)*, Viking Books for Young Readers) Penguin Young Readers Group.

—The Unlikely Adventures of Mabel Jones. Collins, Ross, illus. 2015. (Mabel Jones Ser.). (ENG.). 304p. (J). (gr. 3-7). 16.99 *(978-0-451-47196-3(2)*, Viking Books for Young Readers) Penguin Young Readers Group.

—The Unlikely Adventures of Mabel Jones. 2016. lib. bdg. 19.65 *(978-0-606-38422-3(7))* Turtleback Bks.

MacKenzie, Ross. Zac & the Dream Stealers. (J). 2013. 297p. *(978-0-545-40107-4(0))* 2012. (ENG.). 304p. (gr. 3-7). 16.99 *(978-0-545-40106-7(2))* Scholastic, Inc. (Chicken Hse., The).

Mackowiak Elson, Maya. Transformers: Rescue Bots: the Mystery of the Pirate Bell. 2013. (Transformers Rescue Bots Ser.). (ENG., Illus.). 24p. (J). (gr. -1-3). 3.99 *(978-0-316-22833-6(8))* Little, Brown Bks. for Young Readers.

MacNeil, Stephen. Woolies & Worms. Sandford, John, illus. 2007. (ENG.). 192p. (J). (gr. 1-5). 16.95 *(978-0-8126-2751-0(2))* Cricket Bks.

MacPhail, C. & Cosson, M. J. The Pirate, Big Fist, & Me, 1 vol. Garvey, Brann, illus. 2006. (Vortex Bks.). (ENG.). 112p. (gr. 2-3). 7.19 *(978-1-59889-279-6(7)*, Vortex Bks.) Stone Arch Bks.

Malcolm, Jahnna N. Pirate's Revenge. Comport, Sally Wern, illus. 2003. 77p. (J). *(978-1-931020-09-1(4))* HOP, LLC.

Manushkin, Fran. Pirate Pedro. Lyon, Tammie, illus. 2017. (Pedro Ser.). (ENG.). 32p. (J). (gr. k-2). lib. bdg. 21.32 *(978-1-5158-0872-5(6))* Pedro Pubns. GBR. Dist: Capstone Pub.

Marillier, Juliet. Cybele's Secret. 2011. (ENG.). 444p. (YA). (gr. 7). pap. 9.99 *(978-0-553-49486-0(4)*, Knopf Bks. for Young Readers) Random Hse. Children's Bks.

Marks, Graham. Radio Radio. (ENG.). (YA). (gr. 7). 2007. 219p. pap. 11.95 *(978-0-7475-9087-3(7))* 2003. 224p. pap. 12.99 *(978-0-7475-5939-9(2))* Bloomsbury Publishing Plc GBR. Dist: Independent Pubs. Group.

Marsh, Carole. The Mystery of Blackbeard the Pirate. Marsh, Carole, photos by. 2009. (Real Kids, Real Places Ser.). (Illus.). 150p. (J). 18.99 *(978-0-635-06992-4(X)*, Marsh, Carole Mysteries) Gallopade International.

Masefield, John. Jim Davis. l.t. ed. 2007. (ENG.). 142p. pap. 19.99 *(978-1-4264-2384-0(5))* Creative Media Partners, LLC.

Mayer, Kirsten. Disney Fairies: the Pirate Fairy: Adventure at Skull Rock. 2014. (ENG., Illus.). 24p. (J). (gr. -1-3). 3.99 *(978-0-316-28331-1(2))* Little, Brown Bks. for Young Readers.

—Disney Fairies: the Pirate Fairy: Reusable Sticker Book. 2014. (ENG., Illus.). 12p. (J). (gr. -1-3). pap. 6.99 *(978-0-316-28334-2(7))* Little, Brown Bks. for Young Readers.

McClatchy, Lisa. Eloise's Pirate Adventure. Lyon, Tammie Speer & Lyon, Tammie, illus. 2007. (Eloise Ser.). (ENG.). 32p. (J). (gr. -1-1). pap. 3.99 *(978-1-4169-4979-4(8)*, Simon Spotlight) Simon Spotlight.

McDavid-Jones, Elizabeth. Mystery on Skull Island. 2009. (Mysteries Through Time Ser.). 192p. (YA). (gr. 4-8). 31.95 *(978-1-60754-286-5(2))*; pap. 15.25 *(978-1-60754-302-2(8))* Windmill Bks.

McDonald, Megan. Judy Moody & Stink: La Loca, Loca Busqueda del Tesoro. Reynolds, Peter, illus. 2011. (SPA.). 256p. (J). (gr. 2-5). pap. 14.95 *(978-1-61605-137-2(X))* Ediciones Alfaguara ESP. Dist: Two Rivers Distribution.

—Judy Moody & Stink: The Mad, Mad, Mad, Mad Treasure Hunt. Reynolds, Peter H., illus. 2009. (Judy Moody Ser.: No. 2). (ENG.). 128p. (J). (gr. 1-4). 14.99 *(978-0-7636-3962-4(1))* Candlewick Pr.

—The Mad, Mad, Mad, Mad Treasure Hunt. Reynolds, Peter H., illus. 2010. (Judy Moody Ser.: Bk. 2). (ENG.). 128p. (J). (gr. 1-4). pap. 7.99 *(978-0-7636-4351-5(3))* Candlewick Pr.

—The Mad, Mad, Mad, Mad Treasure Hunt. 2010. (Judy Moody & Stink Ser.: 2). lib. bdg. 18.40 *(978-0-606-01311-6(3)*, Turtleback) Turtleback Bks.

McKinley, Ryan. The Lost Crew. 2012. (ENG.). 144p. pap. 14.95 *(978-1-4327-9659-4(3))*; pap. 9.95 *(978-1-4327-9658-7(5))* Outskirts Pr., Inc.

—The Pirate Bride. 2010. 105p. 21.95 *(978-1-4327-5546-1(3))*; (Illus.). pap. 14.95 *(978-1-4327-5545-4(5))* Outskirts Pr., Inc.

McNee, Ian, illus. Treasure Island. 2006. 158p. (J). (gr. 5-9). per. 4.99 *(978-0-7945-1230-9(5)*, Usborne) EDC Publishing.

Meisel, Peter. Stinky Spike & the Royal Rescue. Meisel, Paul, illus. 2017. (ENG.). 80p. (J). 9.99 *(978-1-61963-883-9(5)*, 9781619638839, Bloomsbury USA Childrens) Bloomsbury Publishing USA.

—Stinky Spike the Pirate Dog. Meisel, Paul, illus. 2017. (ENG.). 80p. (J). 9.99 *(978-1-61963-778-8(2)*, 9781619637788, Bloomsbury USA Childrens) Bloomsbury Publishing USA.

Meyer, Kai. Pirate Wars. Crawford, Elizabeth D., tr. 2008. (Wave Walkers Ser.: 3). (ENG.). 384p. (J). (gr. 5-9). pap. 6.99 *(978-1-4169-2477-7(9)*, McElderry, Margaret K. Bks.) McElderry, Margaret K. Bks.

Meyer, L. A. Under the Jolly Roger: Being an Account of the Further Nautical Adventures of Jacky Faber. 2010. (Bloody Jack Adventures Ser.: 3). (ENG., Illus.). 528p. (YA). (gr. 7). pap. 9.99 *(978-0-15-205673-9(7))* Houghton Mifflin Harcourt Publishing Co.

Michaels, Craig. Blackbeard's Treasure. 2008. (J). *(978-0-936389-99-8(0))* Tudor Pubs., Inc.
Miles, Colin. Naughty Nicky & the Good Ship Oggy. Miles, Gail, illus. 2013. 24p. pap. *(978-1-909202-16-0(9))* Little Acorns Publishing.
Miller, Bobbi. Big River's Daughter. 2013. (ENG.). 224p. (J). (gr. 2-7). 16.95 *(978-0-8234-2752-9(8))* Holiday Hse., Inc.
Miller, Jeff. The Nerdy Dozen #3: 20,000 Nerds under the Sea. 2016. (Nerdy Dozen Ser.: 3). 208p. (J). (gr. 3-7). pap. 6.99 *(978-0-06-227269-0(1))* HarperCollins Pubs.
Miller, Suzanne. Pirates! That Is Who We Be! 2010. 28p. pap. 13.50 *(978-1-4490-6362-7(4))* AuthorHouse.
Milway, Alex. The Curse of Mousebeard. 2011. (ENG.). 368p. (J). (gr. 3-7). pap. 6.99 *(978-0-316-07745-3(3))* Little, Brown Bks. for Young Readers.
—Pigsticks & Harold & the Pirate Treasure. Milway, Alex, illus. 2016. (ENG., Illus.). 64p. (J). (gr. k-4). 12.99 *(978-0-7636-8157-9(1))* Candlewick Pr.
Miraucourt, Christophe. Pirate Treasure. 2015. (Race Further with Reading Ser.). (ENG., Illus.). 48p. (J). *(978-0-7787-2031-7(4))* Crabtree Publishing Co.
—The Pirate's Daughter. 2015. (Race Further with Reading Ser.). (ENG., Illus.). 48p. (J). *(978-0-7787-2088-1(8))* Crabtree Publishing Co.
Mone, Gregory. Fish. 2010. (J). *(978-0-545-11631-2(7),* Scholastic Pr.) Scholastic, Inc.
Mongredien, Sue & Taylor, Dan. The Best Pirate: With Pirate Hat, Eyepatch, & Treasure! 2016. (ENG.). 32p. (J). (gr. -1-2). pap. 7.99 *(978-1-4380-0948-3(8))* Barron's Educational Series, Inc.
Morley, P. Kevin. The Stinky Pirate & the Princess. 2009. 36p. pap. 17.99 *(978-1-4490-4062-8(4))* AuthorHouse.
Morse, William A. Kurkle Kids: Pirate Lostman's Great Adventure. 2010. 44p. pap. 16.99 *(978-1-4490-6187-6(7))* AuthorHouse.
Mould, Chris. Pirates 'n' Pistols. 2013. (ENG., Illus.). 96p. (J). (gr. 4-6). pap. 8.99 *(978-0-340-99935-6(7))* Hodder & Stoughton GBR. Dist: Hachette Bk. Group.
Moulder, Holly. Eyes of the Calusa. 2007. 111p. (J). pap. 8.95 *(978-0-9790405-0-4(7))* White Pelican Pr.
Muller, Carrie & Halsey, Jacqueline. The Terrible, Horrible, Smelly Pirate, 1 vol. Orchard, Eric, illus. 2008. (ENG.). 32p. (J). (gr. k-3). pap. 11.95 *(978-1-55109-655-1(2))* Nimbus Publishing, Ltd. CAN. Dist: Orca Bk. Pubs. USA.
Murray, Diana. Ned the Knitting Pirate. Lammle, Leslie, illus. 2016. (ENG.). 40p. (J). 16.99 *(978-1-59643-890-3(8),* 9781596438903) Roaring Brook Pr.
Murray, Pamela. Pirates of Texas. 2012. 28p. (-18). pap. 24.95 *(978-1-4626-9996-4(0))* America Star Bks.
Myklusch, Matt. The Lost Prince. (ENG.). 400p. (J). (gr. 3-6). 2017. (Seaborne Ser.). pap. 9.99 ***(978-1-5124-8175-4(0))*** 2015. 16.99 *(978-1-5124-0185-1(4))* 2015. (Seaborne Ser.: No. 1). 16.99 *(978-1-60684-525-7(X))* Lerner Publishing Group. (Carolrhoda Bks.).
—Strangers in Atlantis. 2017. (Seaborne Ser.: 2). (ENG.). 280p. (gr. 3-6). (J). 18.99 *(978-1-5124-1375-5(5))*; 38.65 ***(978-1-5124-2691-5(1))*** Lerner Publishing Group. (Carolrhoda Bks.).
Nannini, Randi. My Brother's A Pirate, 1 vol. Clark, Wendy, illus. 2010. 14p. pap. 24.95 *(978-1-4489-8576-0(5))* America Star Bks.
Nash, Scott. The High-Skies Adventures of Blue Jay the Pirate. Nash, Scott, illus. 2012. (ENG., Illus.). 368p. (J). (gr. 4-7). 17.99 *(978-0-7636-3264-9(3))* Candlewick Pr.
Nash, Tim. The Club. 2009. 112p. pap. 12.49 *(978-1-4490-2087-3(9))* AuthorHouse.
Newland, Trevor. The Scallywag Solution, 1 vol. 2014. (ENG., Illus.). 64p. (J). (gr. k-7). 15.95 *(978-0-88962-990-5(0),* 9780889629905) Mosaic Pr. CAN. Dist: Independent Pubs. Group.
Newman, Marjorie. Yo Ho Ho! Sheppard, Kate, illus. 2014. (Colour First Reader Ser.). (ENG.). 80p. (J). (gr. k-2). pap. 9.99 *(978-0-552-56897-5(X))* Transworld Publishers Ltd. GBR. Dist: Independent Pubs. Group.
Nicholls, Paul, illus. I Want to Be A... Pirate. 2014. (J). *(978-1-4351-5500-8(9))* Barnes & Noble, Inc.
Nilsson, Frida. The Ice Sea Pirates. 2017. (ENG.). 300p. (J). (gr. 3-8). 17.99 ***(978-1-77657-145-1(2))*** Gecko Pr. NZL. Dist: Lerner Publishing Group.
Nix, Garth. Drowned Wednesday. 2006. (Keys to the Kingdom Ser.: No. 3). 389p. (gr. 4-7). 18.00 *(978-0-7569-6939-4(5))* Perfection Learning Corp.
Nolen, Jerdine. Block Party Surprise. Henninger, Michelle, illus. 2015. 41p. (J). *(978-1-4806-8574-1(7))* Harcourt.
Nosy Crow Staff. Pirate Adventure. Davies, Benji, illus. 2013. (Bizzy Bear Ser.). (ENG.). 8p. (J). (— 1). bds. 6.99 *(978-0-7636-6519-7(3),* Nosy Crow) Candlewick Pr.
Oda, Eiichiro. Recipe for Disaster. 2007. 90p. (J). pap. *(978-0-439-89722-8(X))* Scholastic, Inc.
O'Malley, Kevin & O'Brien, Patrick. Captain Raptor & the Space Pirates. O'Brien, Patrick, illus. 2007. (Captain Raptor Ser.). (ENG., Illus.). 32p. (J). (gr. k-3). 16.95 *(978-0-8027-9571-7(4),* 9780802795717) Walker & Co.
Oppel, Kenneth. Airborn. (Illus.). (YA). (gr. 8-18). 2004. 368p. 18.99 *(978-0-06-053180-5(0))* 2005. 544p. reprint ed. pap. 8.99 *(978-0-06-053182-9(7))* HarperCollins Pubs.
—Skybreaker. (Illus.). 2007. 560p. (YA). (gr. 8). per. 9.99 *(978-0-06-053229-1(7))* 2005. (ENG.). 384p. (J). (gr. 6-10). 16.99 *(978-0-06-053227-7(0))* HarperCollins Pubs.
—Skybreaker. 2007. (Illus.). 544p. (YA). (gr. 8-12). lib. bdg. 20.85 *(978-1-4177-8130-0(0),* Turtleback) Turtleback Bks.
Orsi, Tea. Tinker Bell & the Pirate Fairy. 2015. (Disney Fairies Graphic Novels Ser.: 16). (J). lib. bdg. 18.40 *(978-0-606-37294-7(6))* Turtleback Bks.
Osborne, Mary Pope. Piratas Despues Del Mediodia. 2004. (Casa del Arbol Ser.: 4). (SPA.). (J). pap. 5.99 *(978-1-930332-52-2(1))* Lectorum Pubns., Inc.
Osteen, Victoria. Unexpected Treasures. Palmisciano, Diane, illus. 2009. (ENG.). 32p. (J). (gr. -1-3). 17.99 *(978-1-4169-5550-4(X),* Little Simon Inspirations) Little Simon Inspirations.
Owen, Chris. Hairy Mole the Pirate 1. 2007. (Hairy Mole the Pirate Ser.). (ENG., Illus.). 82p. pap. *(978-1-84167-562-6(8))* Ransom Publishing Ltd.
Owen, Christopher. Hairy Mole's Adventures on the High Seas. Mostyn, David, illus. 2007. (Hairy Mole the Pirate Ser.). (ENG.). 80p. (J). per. *(978-1-84167-563-3(6))* Ransom Publishing Ltd.
Owens, Greg. Rupert the Wrong-Word Pirate. Beaky, Suzanne, illus. 2006. (J). *(978-1-58987-143-4(X))* Kindermusik International.
Parker, Danny. Lola's Toybox: on the Story Sea. 2017. (Lola's Toy Box Ser.: 2). (ENG.). 96p. (J). (gr. k-2). pap. 6.99 *(978-1-76012-437-3(0))* Hardie Grant Egmont Pty, Ltd. AUS. Dist: Independent Pubs. Group.
Parker, Emma. The Lucky Pearl. 2010. (Illus.). 20p. pap. *(978-1-877561-18-4(5))* First Edition Ltd.
—One Leg Ned. 2010. (Illus.). pap. *(978-1-877561-12-2(6))* First Edition Ltd.
Parus, M. V. The Adventures of Mamma Simone, Jodie & Zed: The Mystery of the Pirate's Lost Treasure. 2006. 115p. (YA). per. 12.95 *(978-1-58374-148-1(8))* Chicago Spectrum Pr.
Patterson, Rebecca. The Pirate House. 2013. (Illus.). (J). *(978-1-4351-4762-1(6))* Barnes & Noble, Inc.
Pavanello, Roberto. The Pirate with the Golden Tooth, 1 vol. Zeni, Marco, tr. from ITA. Pisapia, Blasco & Brughera, Pamela, illus. (Echo & the Bat Pack Ser.). (ENG.). 128p. (gr. 2-3). 2013. 9.95 *(978-1-4342-4888-6(7))* 2012. 25.32 *(978-1-4342-3836-8(9),* Echo & the Bat Pack) Stone Arch Bks.
Pearson Education Staff. Pirates of the Caribbean the Curse of the Black Pearl. 2nd ed. 2008. (ENG.). 48p. pap. 11.99 *(978-1-4058-8170-8(4))* Pearson Education.
Pearson, Maggie. The Pop Star Pirates. 2015. (Race Further with Reading Ser.). (ENG., Illus.). 48p. (J). *(978-0-7787-2089-8(6))* Crabtree Publishing Co.
Peck, Dale. Drift House: The First Voyage. 2006. (ENG.). 464p. (YA). (gr. 5). per. 7.95 *(978-1-59990-005-6(X),* 9781599900056, Bloomsbury USA Childrens) Bloomsbury Publishing USA.
Peck, Jan. Pirate Treasure Hunt!, 1 vol. Tans, Adrian, illus. 2008. (ENG.). 32p. (J). (gr. k-3). 16.99 *(978-1-58980-549-1(6))* Pelican Publishing Co., Inc.
Penn, Audrey & Miller, Joshua. Blackbeard & the Gift of Silence. 2009. (ENG.). 350p. (J). (gr. 2-7). pap. 8.95 *(978-1-933718-32-3(3))* Tanglewood Pr.
—Blackbeard & the Sandstone Pillar: When Lightning Strikes. 2009. (ENG.). 350p. (J). (gr. 2-7). pap. 8.95 *(978-1-933718-31-6(5))* Tanglewood Pr.
Perkins, T. J. Wound Too Tight. 2006. (Illus.). 141p. (YA). 10.99 *(978-0-9777538-5-7(9))* GumShoe Press.
Perry, Fred. Gold Digger, Vol. 8. 2006. (ENG., Illus.). 200p. (YA). pap. 9.99 *(978-0-9768043-0-7(1),* 9780976804307) Antarctic Pr., Inc.
Peschke, Marci. Pirate Queen. Mourning, Tuesday, illus. (Kylie Jean Ser.). (ENG.). 112p. (gr. 2-3). 2015. pap. 5.95 *(978-1-4795-8020-0(1))* 2013. 8.95 *(978-1-4048-8103-7(4))* 2013. lib. bdg. 22.65 *(978-1-4048-7581-4(6))* Picture Window Bks. (Kylie Jean).
Phillips, Dee. Pirate, 1 vol., Bk. 11. 2015. (Yesterday's Voices Ser.). (ENG.). 48p. (YA). (gr. 9-12). pap. 8.95 *(978-1-62250-913-3(7))* Saddleback Educational Publishing, Inc.
—Pirate: The Story of a Buccaneer. 2015. (Yesterday's Voices Ser.). (YA). lib. bdg. 19.60 *(978-0-606-36673-1(3))* Turtleback Bks.
Pigott, Louise. Squirrel Me Timbers. 2016. (Fiction Picture Bks.). (ENG., Illus.). 24p. (gr. k-1). lib. bdg. 24.65 *(978-1-4795-9177-0(7),* Fiction Picture Bks.) Picture Window Bks.
Pinnington, Andrea. The Pirate Creativity Book. 2011. (Creativity Bks.). (ENG.). 80p. (J). (gr. 1-4). pap. 12.99 *(978-0-7641-4778-4(1))* Barron's Educational Series, Inc.
Pirates of the Caribbean Dead Mans Chest. 2006. incl. audio compact disk *(978-1-4054-7260-9(X))* Parragon Bk. Service Ltd.
Pirotta, Saviour. The Buccaneering Book of Pirates. 2013. (ENG., Illus.). 24p. (J). (gr. 1-4). 19.95 *(978-1-4549-0414-4(3))* Sterling Publishing Co., Inc.
Platt, Richard. Pirate Diary: The Journal of Jake Carpenter. Riddell, Chris, illus. 2014. (ENG.). 128p. (J). (gr. 4-7). pap. 6.99 *(978-0-7636-7361-1(7))* Candlewick Pr.
Posner-Sanchez, Andrea. Jake & the Never Land Pirates LGB Favorites (Jake & the Never Land Pirates) Random House Disney Staff, illus. 2015. (Little Golden Book Favorites Ser.). (ENG.). 80p. (J). (-k). 7.99 *(978-0-7364-3404-1(6),* Golden/Disney) Random Hse. Children's Bks.
—The Pirate Games. Random House Disney Staff, illus. 2012. (Little Golden Book Ser.). (ENG.). 24p. (J). (-k). 4.99 *(978-0-7364-3028-9(8),* Golden/Disney) Random Hse. Children's Bks.
—Shadow Play! Random House Disney Staff, illus. 2014. (Little Golden Book Ser.). (ENG.). 24p. (J). (-k). 3.99 *(978-0-7364-3086-9(5),* Golden/Disney) Random Hse. Children's Bks.
—A Skipping Day (Disney Junior: Jake & the Neverland Pirates) Random House Disney Staff, illus. 2012. (Little Golden Book Ser.). (ENG.). 24p. (J). (gr. k-k). 4.99 *(978-0-7364-3029-6(6),* Golden/Disney) Random Hse. Children's Bks.
Poth, Karen. Pirates, a Super Hero, & a Mess Detective, 1 vol. 2014. (I Can Read! / Big Idea Books / VeggieTales Ser.). (ENG.). 96p. (J). 9.99 *(978-0-310-74204-3(8))* Zonderkidz.
Poth, Karen, et al. The Pirates Who Don't Do Anything & Me! 2004. (Big Idea Books / VeggieTales Ser.). (ENG., Illus.). 32p. (J). 7.99 *(978-0-310-70725-7(0))* Zonderkidz.
Powell, Huw. The Lost Sword: A Spacejackers Novel. 2016. (Spacejackers Ser.: 2). (ENG.). 320p. (J). 16.99 *(978-1-61963-836-5(3),* 9781619638365, Bloomsbury USA Childrens) Bloomsbury Publishing USA.
—The Pirate King. 2017. (Spacejackers Ser.). (ENG.). 320p. (J). 16.99 *(978-1-68119-074-7(5),* 9781681190747, Bloomsbury USA Childrens) Bloomsbury Publishing USA.
—Spacejackers. 2015. (Spacejackers Ser.). (ENG.). 336p. (YA). (gr. 3-6). 16.99 *(978-1-61963-515-9(1),* 9781619635159, Bloomsbury USA Childrens) Bloomsbury Publishing USA.
Preller, James. A Pirate's Guide to First Grade. Ruth, Greg, illus. 2013. (ENG.). 48p. (J). (gr. -1-1). 7.99 *(978-1-250-02721-4(7),* 9781250027214) Square Fish.
—A Pirate's Guide to First Grade. 2013. (J). lib. bdg. 18.40 *(978-0-606-31896-9(8),* Turtleback) Turtleback Bks.
—A Pirate's Guide to Recess. Ruth, Greg, illus. 2013. (ENG.). 36p. (J). (gr. -1-1). 16.99 *(978-1-250-00515-1(9),* 9781250005151) Feiwel & Friends.
Priddy, Roger. Let's Be... Pirates. 2015. (Tiny Travelers Ser.). (ENG., Illus.). 12p. (J). (gr. -1-2). bds. 12.99 *(978-0-312-51902-5(8),* 9780312519025, Priddy Bks.) St. Martin's Pr.
Pritchett, Georgia. Wilf the Mighty Worrier: Battles a Pirate. 2016. (Wilf the Mighty Worrier Ser.: 2). (ENG., Illus.). 208p. (J). 16.99 *(978-1-68144-320-1(1))* Quercus NA.
Pryor, Bonnie. Captain Hannah Pritchard: The Hunt for Pirate Gold. 2011. (Historical Fiction Adventures (HFA) Ser.). (Illus.). 160p. (J). (gr. 3-18). pap. 10.95 *(978-1-59845-283-9(5))*; (gr. 4-7). lib. bdg. 29.27 *(978-0-7660-3817-2(3))* Enslow Pubs., Inc.
—Hannah Pritchard: Pirate of the Revolution. 2008. (Historical Fiction Adventures (HFA) Ser.). (Illus.). 160p. (J). (gr. 3-7). lib. bdg. 29.27 *(978-0-7660-2851-7(8))* Enslow Pubs., Inc.
—Pirate Hannah Pritchard: Captured! 2009. (Historical Fiction Adventures (HFA) Ser.). (Illus.). 160p. (J). (gr. 3-6). lib. bdg. 29.27 *(978-0-7660-3310-8(4))* Enslow Pubs., Inc.
Publications International Ltd. Staff. Interactive Sound Pirates of the Caribbean 3. 2007. 24p. (J). 16.98 *(978-1-4127-8111-4(6))* Publications International, Ltd.
Publications International Ltd. Staff, ed. Jake & the Neverland Pirates: Playful Pirates: Play-A-Sound Book. 2013. 10p. (J). (gr. k-3). bds. 7.99 *(978-1-4508-6772-6(3),* 922eff8e-f9be-4736-a025-2bb18924e404) Phoenix International Publications, Inc.
—Jake & the Neverland Pirates: What Do You See? Pop up Book & Flashlight Set. 2013. 8p. (J). (gr. k-4). bds. 10.99 *(978-1-4508-6836-5(3),* 2baa77ff-d973-4d57-acdb-676cb1d56b2d) Phoenix International Publications, Inc.
—Look & Find Pirates of the Caribbean 3. 2007. 24p. (J). 7.10 *(978-1-4127-8019-3(5))* Publications International, Ltd.
—Pirate. 2008. (J). bds. 9.98 *(978-1-4127-9357-5(2))* Publications International, Ltd.
Punter, R. Pirate Adventures. 2009. (Kid Kits Ser.). 48p. (J). 16.99 *(978-0-60130-155-0(3))*; 16.99 *(978-1-60130-154-3(5))* EDC Publishing. (Usborne).
—Stories of Pirates. 2004. (Young Reading Ser.: Vol. 1). 48p. (J). (gr. 2-18). pap. 5.99 *(978-0-7945-0583-7(X))* EDC Publishing.
Punter, Russell. Percy & the Pirates. 2007. 48p. (J). 8.99 *(978-0-7945-1545-4(2),* Usborne) EDC Publishing.
—Pirate Adventures. Fox, Christyan, illus. 2007. (Usborne Young Reading: Series One Ser.). 48p. (J). (gr. 2). 13.99 *(978-1-58086-985-0(8))*; (gr. 4-7). pap. 5.99 *(978-0-7945-1447-1(2))* EDC Publishing. (Usborne).
—Pirate Stories for Little Children. 2015. (Stories for Little Children Gift Bks.). (ENG.). 176p. (J). 19.99 *(978-0-7945-2260-5(2),* Usborne) EDC Publishing.
Purtle, Louise. Potato Pie Pirate. Guiza, Victor, illus. 2009. 24p. (J). 15.99 *(978-0-9818145-0-6(6))* Biggaloo Bks.
Pyle, Howard. The Ruby of Kishmoor. 2004. reprint ed. pap. 15.95 *(978-1-4191-8126-9(2))*; pap. 1.99 *(978-1-4192-8126-6(7))* Kessinger Publishing, LLC.
—The Story of Jack Ballister's Fortunes: Being the Narrative of the Adventures of a Young Gentleman of Good Family, Who Was Kidnapped in the Year 1719 & Carried to the Plantations of the Continent of Virginia, Where He Fell in with That Famous Pirate Captain Edward Teach, or Blackbeard: of His Escape from the Pirates & the Rescue of a Young Lady from Out Their Hands. unabr. ed. 2012. (Illus.). 436p. 49.99 *(978-1-4622-8858-8(0))* Repressed Publishing LLC.
Quillen, Carl. Dragon Girl Myra. 2009. 53p. pap. 5.56 *(978-0-557-08268-1(4))* Lulu Pr., Inc.
Raine, Bonnie. Islands. MacMenamin, John, illus. 2003. 48p. (J). per. *(978-1-931456-74-6(7))* Athena Pr.
Ramos, María Cristina. Ruedamares Pirata de la Mar Bravía. (Torre de Papel Ser.). (SPA.). (J). (gr. 4-18). 8.95 *(978-958-04-3814-4(5))* Norma S.A. COL. Dist: Distribuidora Norma, Inc.
Random House. Thomas & the Lost Pirate / the Sunken Treasure, 2 bks. in 1. Stubbs, Tommy, illus. 2015. (Pictureback(R) Ser.). (ENG.). 24p. (J). (gr. -1-2). 4.99 *(978-0-553-52078-1(4),* Random Hse. Bks. for Young Readers) Random Hse. Children's Bks.
Random House Disney Staff. Peter Pan Step into Reading (Disney Peter Pan) Random House Disney Staff, illus. 2013. (Step into Reading Ser.). (ENG., Illus.). 32p. (J). (gr. -1-1). 3.99 *(978-0-7364-3114-9(4),* RH/Disney) Random Hse. Children's Bks.
Random House Editors. Disney Peter Pan. 2013. (Step into Reading Level 1 Ser.). lib. bdg. 13.55 *(978-0-606-26973-5(8),* Turtleback) Turtleback Bks.
Reasoner, Charles. Inside Jolly Rodger's Pirate Ship. 2014. (Illus.). (J). *(978-1-4351-5466-7(5))* Barnes & Noble, Inc.
—Inside Jolly Roger's Pirate Ship. Reasoner, Charles, illus. 2007. (Story Book Ser.). (Illus.). 12p. (J). (gr. k). bds. *(978-1-84666-149-5(8),* Tide Mill Pr.) Top That! Publishing PLC.
Reeder, Marty. How to Become a Pirate Hunter. 2017. (ENG.). (J). pap. 14.99 ***(978-1-4621-1980-6(8)***, Sweetwater Bks.) Cedar Fort, Inc./CFI Distribution.
Rees, Celia. Pirates! 2003. (ENG., Illus.). 368p. *(978-0-7475-5950-4(3))* Bloomsbury Publishing Plc GBR. Dist: Trafalgar Square Publishing.
—Pirates! 2003. (ENG.). 384p. (YA). (gr. 7). 16.95 *(978-1-58234-816-2(2),* 9781582348162, Bloomsbury USA Childrens) Bloomsbury Publishing USA.
Rees, Douglas. Uncle Pirate. Auth, Tony, illus. (ENG.). 112p. (J). (gr. 2-5). 2009. pap. 6.99 *(978-1-4169-4763-9(9))* 2008. 15.99 *(978-1-4169-4762-2(0))* McElderry, Margaret K. Bks. (McElderry, Margaret K. Bks.).
—Uncle Pirate to the Rescue. Auth, Tony, illus. 2010. (ENG.). 112p. (J). (gr. 2-5). pap. 6.99 *(978-1-4169-7505-2(5),* McElderry, Margaret K. Bks.) McElderry, Margaret K. Bks.
Rees, Lesley. How to Be a Pirate in 7 Days or Less. Lewis, Jan, illus. 2006. (How to be A Ser.). 32p. (J). (gr. k-3). 12.95 *(978-0-7534-6041-2(6),* Kingfisher) Roaring Brook Pr.
Regan, Dian. Space Boy & the Space Pirate. Neubecker, Robert, illus. 2016. (Space Boy Ser.). (ENG.). 40p. (J). (gr. k-5). 16.95 *(978-1-59078-956-8(3))* Boyds Mills Pr.
Remphry, Martin. Pirates Are Stealing Our Cows. 2014. (ENG., Illus.). 32p. (J). *(978-0-7787-1330-2(X))* Crabtree Publishing Co.
Renier, Aaron. The Unsinkable Walker Bean. Renier, Aaron, illus. 2010. (Unsinkable Walker Bean Ser.: 1). (ENG., Illus.). 208p. (J). (gr. 4-9). pap. 15.99 *(978-1-59643-453-0(8),* 9781596434530, First Second Bks.) Roaring Brook Pr.
Reynolds, Aaron. Pirates vs. Cowboys. Barneda, David, illus. 2013. (ENG.). 40p. (J). (gr. k-3). 16.99 *(978-0-375-85874-1(1),* Knopf Bks. for Young Readers) Random Hse. Children's Bks.
RH Disney. Beware the Kakamora! RH Disney, illus. 2016. (Pictureback(R) Ser.). (ENG., Illus.). 24p. (J). (gr. -1-2). 4.99 *(978-0-7364-3601-4(4),* RH/Disney) Random Hse. Children's Bks.
Riddell, Andrew G. The Curse of Blackbeard's Ghost. 2010. 122p. (gr. 4-6). pap. 10.95 *(978-1-4502-6952-0(4))* iUniverse, Inc.
Riddell, Chris & Stewart, Paul. The Curse of the Gloamglozer. 2009. (Edge Chronicles Ser.). (ENG.). 384p. (J). (gr. 3-7). 8.99 *(978-0-440-42099-6(7),* Yearling) Random Hse. Children's Bks.
Rider, Cynthia. Pirate Treasure, 1 vol. Aguilar, Sandra, illus. 2013. (Start Reading Ser.). (ENG.). 24p. (gr. k-1). pap. 7.95 *(978-1-4765-4129-7(9))* Capstone Press of Coughlan Cos.
Rits, Susan Katherine. The Pirates of Bair Island. 2013. 234p. pap. 12.99 *(978-0-9894891-1-9(6))* Imprint.li.
Roberts, Scott A. The Rollicking Adventures of Tam O'Hare. Roberts, Scott A., illus. 2007. (ENG., Illus.). 228p. (J). (gr. 4-7). per. 16.95 *(978-1-60037-289-6(9))* Morgan James Publishing.
Robertson, Barry & Smith, Jeff. Pirates of the "I Don't Care" -Ibbean: A Kids' Musical about Storing up Treasures in Heaven. 2007. (ENG.). 104p. pap. 7.99 *(978-0-8341-7595-2(9),* 0834175959) Lillenas Publishing Co.
Robinson, Michelle. Goodnight Pirate: The Perfect Bedtime Book! 2015. (Goodnight Ser.). (ENG., Illus.). 32p. (J). (gr. -1 — 1). pap. 7.99 *(978-1-4380-0662-8(4))* Barron's Educational Series, Inc.
Rockwell, Carey. On the Trail of Space Pirates. Ley, Willy, ed. 2007. 140p. per. 11.95 *(978-1-60312-283-2(4))* Aegypan.
Roddy, Lee. Peril at Pirate's Point. 2006. (Ladd Family Adventure Ser.: Vol. 7). (Illus.). 153p. (J). (gr. 4-7). per. 7.99 *(978-0-88062-256-1(3))* Mott Media.
Roger, Moore & Ron, Kurtz. Arfie Plays Pirates. 2007. 40p. 17.95 *(978-0-9710343-5-8(4))* Photographs Naturally, Inc.
Rolt-Wheeler, Francis. Plotting in Pirate Seas. 2007. (ENG.). 166p. pap. 19.99 *(978-1-4346-4415-2(4))*; 186p. pap. 21.99 *(978-1-4346-4416-9(2))* Creative Media Partners, LLC.
Romeu, Emma. Gregorio y el Pirata. 2003.Tr. of Gregorio & the Pirate. (SPA., Illus.). 152p. (J). pap. 9.95 *(978-968-19-0553-8(9))* Santillana USA Publishing Co., Inc.
Root, Phyllis. Lilly & the Pirates. Shepperson, Rob, illus. (ENG.). (J). 2013. 180p. (gr. 3-7). pap. 8.95 *(978-1-62091-027-6(6))* 2010. 116p. (gr. 4-6). 16.95 *(978-1-59078-583-6(5),* Front Street) Boyds Mills Pr.
Rosen, Lucy. Disney Fairies: the Pirate Fairy: Meet Zarina the Pirate Fairy. 2014. (Passport to Reading Level 1 Ser.). (ENG., Illus.). 32p. (J). (gr. -1-3). 3.99 *(978-0-316-28330-4(4))* Little, Brown Bks. for Young Readers.
Rossell, Judith. Jack Jones & the Pirate Curse. 2006. 166p. *(978-1-921049-29-3(4))* Little Hare Bks. AUS. Dist: HarperCollins Pubs. Australia.
Rotstein, Adira. Little Jane & the Nameless Isle: A Little Jane Silver Adventure (Large Print 16pt) 2013. 324p. pap. *(978-1-4596-6322-0(5))* ReadHowYouWant.com, Ltd.
—Little Jane Silver. 2011. (Little Jane Silver Adventure Ser.: 1). (ENG., Illus.). 288p. (YA). (gr. 7). pap. 12.99 *(978-1-55488-878-8(6),* Dundurn Pr.) Dundurn CAN. Dist: Ingram Publisher Services.
Rowland, Lucy. Pirate Pete & His Smelly Feet. Chambers, Mark, illus. 2017. (ENG.). 32p. (J). (gr. -1-1). 16.99 ***(978-1-5098-1776-4(X))*** Pan Macmillan GBR. Dist: Independent Pubs. Group.
Roy, Oscar. I Was Captured by Pirates. 2013. 110p. pap. 11.00 *(978-1-62212-790-0(0),* Strategic Bk. Publishing) Strategic Book Publishing & Rights Agency (SBPRA).
Roy, Philip. Seas of South Africa. 2013. (ENG.). 250p. pap. 11.95 *(978-1-55380-247-1(0))* Ronsdale Pr. CAN. Dist: SPD-Small Pr. Distribution.
Ryan, Carrie & Davis, John Parke. City of Thirst. (Map to Everywhere Ser.: 2). (ENG., Illus.). (J). (gr. 3-7). 2016. 416p. pap. 7.99 *(978-0-316-24082-6(6))* 2015. 400p. 17.00 *(978-0-316-24084-0(2))* Little, Brown Bks. for Young Readers.
—The Map to Everywhere. 2014. (Map to Everywhere Ser.: Bk. 1). (ENG., Illus.). 448p. (J). (gr. 3-7). 17.00 *(978-0-316-24077-2(X))* Little Brown & Co.
—Shadows of the Lost Sun. 2017. (Map to Everywhere Ser.: 3). (ENG., Illus.). 368p. (J). (gr. 3-7). 17.99 *(978-0-316-24088-8(5))* Little, Brown Bks. for Young Readers.
Ryan, John. Captain Pugwash: A Pirate Story. (Illus.). 32p. (J). pap. 8.95 *(978-0-09-940874-1(0),* Arrow Bks., Ltd.) Random Hse. GBR. Dist: Trafalgar Square Publishing.
—Pugwash Aloft. Ryan, John, illus. 2008. (ENG., Illus.). 32p. (J). (gr. -2-1). 16.95 *(978-1-84507-822-5(5),* Frances Lincoln) Quarto Publishing Group UK GBR. Dist: Hachette Bk. Group.
Sabatini, Rafael. The King's Messenger. 2004. reprint ed. pap. 1.99 *(978-1-4192-6824-3(4))* Kessinger Publishing, LLC.
Sabuda, Robert, illus. Peter Pan: A Pop-Up Adaptation of J. M. Barrie's Original Tale. 2008. (ENG.). 16p. (J). 39.99 *(978-0-689-85364-7(5),* Little Simon) Little Simon.
Sagar, Marie. Pirate Hill. 2008. 17p. pap. 24.95 *(978-1-60610-705-8(4))* America Star Bks.
Sage, Angie. Skeleton Island. 2016. (Araminta Spookie Adventure Ser.: 2). (ENG.). 176p. (J). 16.99 *(978-1-61963-945-4(9),* 9781619639454, Bloomsbury USA Childrens) Bloomsbury Publishing USA.
Sams, Laura & Sams, Robert. A Pirate's Quest: For His Family Heirloom Peg Leg. Hertling, Heiner, illus. 2008. 48p. (J). 19.95 *(978-0-9770108-7-5(2))* Sams, II, Carl R. Photography, Inc.

Samuel, R. Skull & Bones: A Pirate's Odyssey. 2011. 192p. (gr. 1-2). 27.99 *(978-1-4634-0319-5(4))*; (gr. 10-12). pap. 18.49 *(978-1-4634-0320-1(8))* AuthorHouse.

Sander, Sonia. Scooby-Doo in Shiver Me Timbers, 1 vol. 2016. (Scooby-Doo! Set 3 Ser.). (ENG., Illus.). 32p. (J). (gr. k-4). lib. bdg. 24.21 *(978-1-61479-408-0(1)*, 1401184) Spotlight.

Sava, Scott Christian. Gary the Pirate. 2008. (Illus.). 112p. 12.95 *(978-0-9789168-5-5(9))* Blue Dream Studios.

Savitsky, Steve, illus. Dora's Pirate Treasure Hunt. 2010. (Dora the Explorer Ser.). (ENG.). 12p. (J). (gr. -1-1). 6.99 *(978-1-4169-9927-0(2)*, Simon Spotlight/Nickelodeon) Simon Spotlight/Nickelodeon.

Schade, Susan. Riff Raff the Mouse Pirate. Kennedy, Anne, illus. 2014. (I Can Read Level 2 Ser.). (ENG.). 24p. (J). (gr. -1-3). pap. 3.99 *(978-0-06-230507-7(7))* HarperCollins Pubs.

Schaub, Michelle. The Lost Pirate. 2006. (Early Explorers Ser.). (J). pap. *(978-1-4108-6109-2(0))* Benchmark Education Co.

Scholastic, Inc. Staff & Weisman, Greg. Traveler. Didier, Samwise, illus. 2016. (World of Warcraft Ser.). (ENG.). 384p. (J). (gr. 3-7). 14.99 *(978-0-545-90667-8(9))* Scholastic, Inc.

Schrowang, Irene. Sam & Joey's Pirate Ship Adventure. 2013. 16p. pap. 15.99 *(978-1-4817-0333-8(1))* AuthorHouse.

Schulz, Heidi. Hook's Revenge. Hendrix, John, illus. (Hook's Revenge Ser.: Bk. 1). (ENG.). (J). (gr. 3-7). 2015. 310p. pap. 7.99 *(978-1-4847-1188-0(2))* 2015. 344p. 16.99 *(978-1-4847-1717-2(1))* 2014. 304p. 16.99 *(978-1-4231-9867-3(0))* Hyperion Bks. for Children.

—Hook's Revenge, Book 2: the Pirate Code. Hendrix, John, illus. 2016. (Hook's Revenge Ser.: 2). (ENG.). (J). (gr. 3-7). lib. bdg. 18.40 ***(978-0-606-39169-6(X))*** Turtleback Bks.

Schulz, Heidi. The Pirate Code. Hendrix, John, illus. 2016. (Hook's Revenge Ser.: Bk. 2). (ENG.). 352p. (J). (gr. 3-7). pap. 7.99 *(978-1-4847-2369-2(4))* Hyperion Bks. for Children.

Scieszka, Jon. El Pirata Barbanegra. Smith, Lane, illus. (SPA.). (J). (gr. 5-8). 7.95 *(978-958-04-3401-6(8)*, NR8584) Norma S.A. COL. Dist: Distribuidora Norma, Inc., Lectorum Pubns., Inc.

Scollon, Bill. The Pirate Pup. 2013. (Picture Viewer Ser.: 1). (ENG.). 24p. (J). (gr. -1-2). 12.99 *(978-0-7944-2592-0(5))* Reader's Digest Assn., Inc., The.

Scollon, William. Jake & the Never Land Pirates: Pirate Campout. 2014. (World of Reading Ser.). (J). lib. bdg. 13.55 *(978-0-606-35266-6(X))* Turtleback Bks.

Scollon, William & Disney Book Group Staff. The Key to Skull Rock, Level 1. Disney Storybook Art Team, illus. 2013. (World of Reading Ser.). (ENG.). 32p. (J). (gr. -1-k). pap. 3.99 *(978-1-4231-6397-8(4))* Disney Pr.

Sconyers, Jennifer. The Map. 2010. 24p. pap. 12.99 *(978-1-4490-5731-2(4))* AuthorHouse.

Scott, Janine. The Noisy Parrot. Rigby, Deborah, illus. 2009. (Treasure Chest Readers Ser.). 24p. (J). (gr. -1-2). pap. 8.15 *(978-1-60754-680-1(9))*; lib. bdg. 22.60 *(978-1-60754-679-5(5))* Windmill Bks.

Seaworthy, Oscar. Port Side Pirates. 2008. (ENG., Illus.). 32p. (J). 9.99 *(978-1-84686-153-6(5))*; 6.99 *(978-1-84686-205-2(1))* Barefoot Bks., Inc.

—Port Side Pirates Puzzle. Harter, Debbie, illus. 2011. (ENG.). n/ap. (J). 14.99 *(978-1-84686-666-1(9))* Barefoot Bks., Inc.

Seuling, Barbara. Robert & the Happy Endings. Brewer, Paul, illus. 2007. (Robert Bks.). (ENG.). 160p. (J). (gr. 1-4). 16.95 *(978-0-8126-2748-0(2))* Cricket Bks.

Sharp, Michael. Captain Tristan Am I. Van Tine, Laura, illus. 2009. 20p. (J). pap. *(978-1-897455-10-4(0))* Avatar Pubns., Inc.

Shreve, Steve. Pirates: Or the Truth about Life on the High Seas. Shreve, Steve, illus. 2010. (Adventures of Charlie Ser.). (Illus.). 32p. pap. *(978-0-237-54286-3(2))* Evans Brothers, Ltd.

Simon, Nadine. The Treasured Dream. 2009. 52p. pap. 9.95 *(978-1-60693-274-2(8)*, Eloquent Bks.) Strategic Book Publishing & Rights Agency (SBPRA).

Simon Spotlight, creator. Dora & Diego's Adventures! 2007. (Dora the Explorer Ser.). (ENG., Illus.). 80p. (J). (gr. -1-2). 7.99 *(978-1-4169-3532-2(0)*, Simon Spotlight/Nickelodeon) Simon Spotlight/Nickelodeon.

Skrutskie, Emily. The Abyss Surrounds Us. 2016. (ENG., Illus.). 288p. (YA). pap. 11.99 *(978-0-7387-4691-3(6)*, Flux) North Star Editions.

—The Abyss Surrounds Us. 2016. lib. bdg. 23.30 *(978-0-606-38499-5(5))* Turtleback Bks.

Skrutskie, Emily. The Edge of the Abyss. 2017. lib. bdg. 23.30 ***(978-0-606-40232-3(2))*** Turtleback Bks.

Smith, Danna. Pirate Nap: A Book of Colors. Petrone, Valeria, illus. 2011. (ENG.). 40p. (J). lib. bdg. 14.99 *(978-0-547-57531-5(9))* Houghton Mifflin Harcourt Publishing Co.

Snow, Alan. Worse Things Happen at Sea! A Tale of Pirates, Poison, & Monsters. Snow, Alan, illus. 2014. (Ratbridge Chronicles Ser.: 2). (ENG., Illus.). 352p. (J). (gr. 3-9). pap. 9.99 *(978-0-689-87050-7(7)*, Atheneum Bks. for Young Readers) Simon & Schuster Children's Publishing.

Sobel, June. Shiver Me Letters: A Pirate ABC. Cole, Henry, illus. (ENG.). 32p. (J). (gr. -1-3). 2009. pap. 7.99 *(978-0-15-206679-6(9))* 2006. 16.99 *(978-0-15-216732-5(3))* Houghton Mifflin Harcourt Publishing Co.

Soderberg, Erin. Catnapped! 2016. (Puppy Pirates Ser.). (ENG., Illus.). 96p. (J). (gr. 1-4). lib. bdg. 12.99 *(978-0-553-51174-1(2)*, Random Hse. Bks. for Young Readers) Random Hse. Children's Bks.

—Ghost Ship. 2016. (Puppy Pirates Ser.: 1). (ENG., Illus.). 128p. (J). (gr. 1-4). 5.99 *(978-1-101-93773-0(4)*, Random Hse. Bks. for Young Readers) Random Hse. Children's Bks.

—Puppy Pirates #5: Search for the Sea Monster. 2016. (Puppy Pirates Ser.). (ENG., Illus.). 96p. (J). (gr. 1-4). 4.99 *(978-1-101-93776-1(9)*, Random Hse. Bks. for Young Readers) Random Hse. Children's Bks.

—Puppy Pirates Super Special #2: Best in Class. 2017. (Puppy Pirates Ser.: 2). (ENG.). 128p. (J). (gr. 1-4). lib. bdg. 12.99 ***(978-1-5247-1329-4(5))***; (Illus.). 5.99 ***(978-1-5247-1328-7(7))*** Random Hse. Children's Bks. (Random Hse. Bks. for Young Readers).

Soderberg, Erin. Sea Sick. 2016. (Puppy Pirates Ser.). (ENG., Illus.). 96p. (J). (gr. 1-4). 4.99 *(978-0-553-51176-5(9)*, Random Hse. Bks. for Young Readers) Random Hse. Children's Bks.

Soderberg, Erin & Wasserman, Robin. Stowaway! 2015. (Puppy Pirates Ser.: 1). (ENG., Illus.). 96p. (J). (gr. 1-4). pap. 4.99 *(978-0-553-51167-3(X))*; lib. bdg. 12.99 *(978-0-553-51168-0(8))* Random Hse. Children's Bks. (Random Hse. Bks. for Young Readers).

Somper, Justin. Black Heart. 2010. (Vampirates Ser.: 4). (ENG.). 512p. (J). (gr. 3-7). pap. 8.99 *(978-0-316-02088-6(5))* Little, Brown Bks. for Young Readers.

—Blood Captain. 2009. (Vampirates Ser.: 3). (ENG.). 592p. (J). (gr. 3-7). pap. 10.99 *(978-0-316-02086-2(9))* Little Brown & Co.

—Dead Deep. 2009. pap. 1.00 *(978-1-4074-4559-5(6))* Recorded Bks., Inc.

—Demons of the Ocean. 2007. (Vampirates Ser.: 1). (ENG.). 352p. (J). (gr. 3-7). per. 8.99 *(978-0-316-01444-1(3))* Little, Brown Bks. for Young Readers.

—Demons of the Ocean. 2006. 1.00 *(978-1-4294-1974-1(1))* Recorded Bks., Inc.

—Demons of the Ocean. 2007. (Vampirates Ser.: 1). (Illus.). 330p. (J). 19.65 *(978-1-4177-8287-1(0)*, Turtleback) Turtleback Bks.

—Empire of Night. (Vampirates Ser.: 5). (ENG.). (J). (gr. 3-7). 2011. 512p. pap. 10.99 *(978-0-316-03323-7(5))* 2010. 496p. 15.99 *(978-0-316-03322-0(7))* Little, Brown Bks. for Young Readers.

—Immortal War. 2013. (Vampirates Ser.: 6). (ENG.). 512p. (J). (gr. 3-7). pap. 10.99 *(978-0-316-03325-1(1))* Little, Brown Bks. for Young Readers.

—Immortal War. 2013. (Vampirates Ser.: 6). (J). lib. bdg. 22.10 *(978-0-606-26696-3(8)*, Turtleback) Turtleback Bks.

—Tide of Terror. 2008. (Vampirates Ser.: 2). (ENG.). 480p. (J). (gr. 3-7). pap. 10.99 *(978-0-316-01445-8(1))* Little, Brown Bks. for Young Readers.

Southard, Patricia. Captain Andre's Adventure in the Sky. 2008. 27p. pap. 24.95 *(978-1-4241-8613-6(7))* America Star Bks.

Spangler, Brie, illus. We Both Read-the Mystery of Pirate's Point. 2007. (We Both Read Ser.). 40p. (J). (gr. 1-5). 7.99 *(978-1-60115-009-7(1))* Treasure Bay, Inc.

—We Both Read-The Mystery of Pirate's Point: Level 3. 2008. (We Both Read Ser.). 40p. (J). (gr. 1-5). per. 4.99 *(978-1-60115-010-3(5))* Treasure Bay, Inc.

Specter, Baron. Drama at Dungeon Rock: #6, 1 vol. Evans, Dustin, illus. 2010. (Ghostly Graphic Adventures Ser.). (ENG.). 32p. (J). (gr. 3-6). 28.50 *(978-1-60270-775-7(8))* ABDO Publishing Co.

—The Star Island Spirits: #5, 1 vol. Evans, Dustin, illus. 2010. (Ghostly Graphic Adventures Ser.). (ENG.). 32p. (J). (gr. 3-6). 28.50 *(978-1-60270-774-0(X))* ABDO Publishing Co.

Spendlove, Owen. Stanley Brambles & the Pirate's Treasure. 2007. 320p. per. 18.95 *(978-0-595-43792-4(3))* iUniverse, Inc.

Spires, Ashley. Small Saul. Spires, Ashley, illus. 2011. (ENG., Illus.). 32p. (J). (gr. -1-2). 16.95 *(978-1-55453-503-3(4))* Kids Can Pr., Ltd. CAN. Dist: Hachette Bk. Group.

Staley, Samuel. The Pirate of Panther Bay Classroom Guide. 2007. 75p. spiral bd. 15.00 *(978-0-9764684-2-4(5))* IZS, Inc.

Steele, Michael Anthony. Skeleton Crew Showdown. Jeralds, Scott, illus. 2017. (Scooby-Doo! Beginner Mysteries Ser.). (ENG.). 112p. (gr. 2-3). lib. bdg. 22.65 ***(978-1-4965-4769-9(1))*** Capstone Press of Coughlan Cos.

Steele, Michael Anthony & Oda, Eiichiro. Shonen Jump's One Piece. 2007. 88p. (J). *(978-0-439-89720-4(3))* Scholastic, Inc.

Stevens, Cara. Let's Save Pirate Day! (Dora & Friends) Aikins, David, illus. 2014. (Pictureback(R) Ser.). (ENG.). 24p. (J). (gr. -1-2). 4.99 *(978-0-385-37440-8(2)*, Random Hse. Bks. for Young Readers) Random Hse. Children's Bks.

Stevenson, Robert Louis. La Isla del Tesoro. (Coleccion Clasicos de la Juventud).Tr. of Treasure Island. (SPA., Illus.). 188p. (J). 12.95 *(978-84-7189-017-7(8)*, ORT301) Ortells, Alfredo Editorial S.L. ESP. Dist: Continental Bk. Co., Inc.

—La Isla del Tesoro. (Coleccion Estrella).Tr. of Treasure Island. (SPA., Illus.). 64p. (J). 14.95 *(978-950-11-0009-9(X)*, SGM009) Sigmar ARG. Dist: Continental Bk. Co., Inc.

—Secuestrado. 3rd ed. (Coleccion Clasicos en Accion).Tr. of Kidnapped. (SPA., Illus.). 80p. (YA). (gr. 5-8). 15.95 *(978-84-241-5781-4(8)*, EV1487) Everest Editora ESP. Dist: Lectorum Pubns., Inc.

—Treasure Island. Corvino, Lucy, illus. 2005. (Classic Starts(tm) Ser.). (ENG.). 160p. (J). (gr. 2-4). 6.95 *(978-1-4027-1318-7(5))* Sterling Publishing Co., Inc.

—Treasure Island. 2009. (Foundation Classics Ser.). (Illus.). 56p. (J). (gr. 5-9). lib. bdg. 27.95 *(978-1-60754-543-9(8))* Windmill Bks.

—Treasure Island. Lawrence, John, illus. 2009. (Candlewick Illustrated Classics Ser.). (ENG.). 272p. (J). (gr. 4-7). 24.99 *(978-0-7636-4445-1(5))* Candlewick Pr.

—Treasure Island. 2014. (Graphic Classics Ser.). 48p. (gr. 3-6). 37.10 *(978-1-908973-91-7(9))* Book Hse. GBR. Dist: Black Rabbit Bks.

—Treasure Island. 2016. (ENG., Illus.). (J). pap. ***(978-3-7433-2049-9(5))*** Creation Pubs.

—Treasure Island. 2016. (ENG., Illus.). (J). 26.95 ***(978-1-358-35578-3(9))*** Creative Media Partners, LLC.

—Treasure Island. 2005. 116p. per. 5.95 *(978-1-4209-2258-5(0))* Digireads.com Publishing.

—Treasure Island. 2004. reprint ed. pap. 1.99 *(978-1-4192-9097-8(5))* Kessinger Publishing, LLC.

—Treasure Island. (Young Collector's Illustrated Classics Ser.). (Illus.). 192p. (J). (gr. 3-7). 9.95 *(978-1-56156-456-9(7))* Kidsbooks, LLC.

—Treasure Island. Rhead, Louis, illus. 2015. (J). pap. *(978-1-4677-7821-3(4)*, First Avenue Editions) Lerner Publishing Group.

—Treasure Island. 2014. (Word Cloud Classics Ser.). (ENG., Illus.). 208p. pap. 14.99 *(978-1-62686-256-2(7)*, Thunder Bay Pr.) Readerlink Distribution Services, LLC.

—Treasure Island, 1 vol. Gully, Mario & Davidson, Pat, illus. 2009. (Treasure Island Ser.). (ENG.). 24p. (gr. 5-8). 24.21 *(978-1-59961-601-8(7))*;Pt. 2. 24.21 *(978-1-59961-602-5(5))* Spotlight.

—Treasure Island. Corvino, Lucy, illus. abr. ed. 2010. (Classic Starts(tm) Ser.). (ENG.). 160p. (J). (gr. 2-4). cd-rom 9.95 *(978-1-4027-7358-7(7))* Sterling Publishing Co., Inc.

—Treasure Island: The Treasure Map. Comport, Sally Wern, illus. 2008. (Easy Reader Classics Ser.). (ENG.). 32p. (gr. -1-3). lib. bdg. 24.21 *(978-1-59961-342-0(5))* Spotlight.

—Treasure Island: With a Discussion of Courage. 2003. (Values in Action Illustrated Classics Ser.). (J). *(978-1-59203-054-5(8))* Learning Challenge, Inc.

—Treasure Island: With Story of the Treasure of Normon Island. Date not set. (J). (gr. 5-6). reprint ed. lib. bdg. 22.95 *(978-0-89190-236-2(8)*, American Reprint Co.) Amereon Ltd.

Stevenson, Robert Louis & Ballaz, Jesus. Treasure Island. 2007. (Illustrated Classics Ser.). (Illus.). 40p. (gr. 3-6). lib. bdg. 26.00 *(978-0-8368-7665-9(2)*, Gareth Stevens Learning Library) Stevens, Gareth Publishing LLLP.

Stevenson, Robert Louis & Gaston, Charles Robert. Treasure Island. 2016. (ENG., Illus.). (J). 25.95 ***(978-1-358-93415-5(0))*** Creative Media Partners, LLC.

Stevenson, Robert Louis & Vance, Hiram Albert. Treasure Island. 2016. (ENG., Illus.). (J). 25.95 ***(978-1-359-06744-9(2))***; 25.95 ***(978-1-358-73513-4(1))*** Creative Media Partners, LLC.

Stevenson, Robert Louis, et al. Treasure Island. 2016. (ENG., Illus.). (J). 26.95 ***(978-1-357-83050-2(5))*** Creative Media Partners, LLC.

Stewart, Paul & Riddell, Chris. Far-Flung Adventures: Fergus Crane. 2011. (Far-Flung Adventures Ser.). (ENG.). 240p. (J). (gr. 3-7). 7.99 *(978-0-385-75112-4(5)*, Yearling) Random Hse. Children's Bks.

Stilton, Geronimo. Attack of the Bandit Cats. Wolf, Matt, illus. 2004. (Geronimo Stilton Ser.: 8). (ENG.). 128p. (J). (gr. 2-5). pap. 7.99 *(978-0-439-55970-6(7)*, Scholastic Paperbacks) Scholastic, Inc.

—Who Stole the Mona Lisa? Cooper-McGuinness, Nanette, tr. 2010. (Geronimo Stilton Graphic Novels Ser.). (ENG., Illus.). 56p. (J). (gr. 2-6). 9.99 *(978-1-59707-221-2(4)*, 9781597072212) Papercutz.

Stine, R. L. Creep from the Deep. 2008. (Goosebumps HorrorLand Ser.: No. 2). 137p. (gr. 4-7). 17.00 *(978-0-7569-8815-9(2))* Perfection Learning Corp.

Stockton, Frank Richard. Buccaneers & Pirates of Our Coasts. 2006. 168p. (gr. 4-7). per. 13.95 *(978-1-59818-872-1(0))*; 25.95 *(978-1-59818-255-2(2))* Aegypan.

—Kate Bonnet: The Romance of a Pirate's Daughter. reprint ed. pap. 28.00 *(978-1-4047-8937-1(5))* Classic Textbooks.

—Kate Bonnet: The Romance of a Pirate's Daughter. 2007. 364p. (J). (gr. -1-7). 46.95 *(978-0-548-02295-5(X))* Kessinger Publishing, LLC.

—Kate Bonnet: The Romance of a Pirate's Daughter. 2005. 29.95 *(978-1-59818-254-5(4))* Wildside Pr., LLC.

Stowell, Louie. Wind-Up Pirate Ship. Fox, Christyan, illus. 2010. (Wind-up Bks). 13p. (J). bds. 29.99 *(978-0-7945-2835-5(X)*, Usborne) EDC Publishing.

Strangway, Melissa. Finding Hope. 2012. 82p. pap. 11.65 *(978-1-61933-676-6(6))* FastPrncil, Inc.

Stratemeyer, Edward. The Rover Boys on Treasure Isle. 2007. 268p. 27.95 *(978-1-4218-4148-9(7))*; per. 12.95 *(978-1-4218-4246-2(7))* 1st World Publishing, Inc. (1st World Library - Literary Society).

Strong, Jeremy. The Indoor Pirates on Treasure Island. Sharratt, Nick, illus. (ENG.). 96p. (J). 7.95 *(978-0-14-038637-0(8))* Penguin Bks., Ltd. GBR. Dist: Trafalgar Square Publishing.

Suen, Anastasia. The Pirate Map: A Robot & Rico Story. Laughead, Mike, illus. 2010. (Robot & Rico Ser.). (ENG.). 32p. (gr. 1-2). pap. 6.25 *(978-1-4342-2301-2(9))* Stone Arch Bks.

Surget, Alain. The Ghost Ship. 2015. (Jolly Roger Ser.). (Illus.). 96p. (gr. 3-6). 28.50 *(978-1-909645-41-7(9))* Book Hse. GBR. Dist: Black Rabbit Bks.

Surget, Alain & Yeardley, Glynne. Caesar, Who's He? Parme, Fabrice, illus. 2014. 95p. (J). *(978-1-4351-5328-8(6))* Barnes & Noble, Inc.

Sutherland, Jon, et al. The Emerald Pirate. 2005. (F. E. A. R. Adventures S. Ser.). (ENG., Illus.). 110p. (J). 8.00 *(978-1-84046-690-4(1)*, Wizard Books) Icon Bks., Ltd. GBR. Dist: Publishers Group Canada.

Taplin, Sam. Noisy Pirates. Chambers, Mark, illus. 2014. (ENG.). (J). 19.99 *(978-0-7945-2814-0(7)*, Usborne) EDC Publishing.

—The Usborne Official Pirate's Handbook. McNee, Ian, illus. 2007. (Usborne Official Handbooks Ser.). 80p. (J). (gr. -1-3). 12.99 *(978-0-7945-1463-1(4)*, Usborne) EDC Publishing.

Taylor, Richard A. Ships of Children. 2nd rev. ed. 2006. (Illus.). 191p. (YA). lib. bdg. 37.95 *(978-0-9764403-7-6(7))* Klare Taylor Pubs.

Teacher Created Resources Staff & Collins, Susan. A Guide for Using Time Soldiers in the Classroom. 2009. (ENG.). 48p. pap. 9.99 *(978-1-4206-2003-0(7))* Teacher Created Resources, Inc.

Teague, Mark. The Pirate Jamboree. 2016. (ENG., Illus.). 40p. (J). (gr. -1-k). 17.99 *(978-0-545-63221-8(8))* Scholastic, Inc.

Terry, Michael. Captain Wag & the Big Blue Whale. Terry, Michael, illus. 2008. (Captain Wag Ser.). (ENG., Illus.). 32p. (J). (gr. k-k). pap. 13.95 *(978-0-7475-9254-9(3))* Bloomsbury Publishing Plc GBR. Dist: Independent Pubs. Group.

Thomas Nelson Publishing Staff. The Pirates Who Don't Do Anything - Veggietales Movie: Squawk-Along Songs & Games. 2008. (Adventures in Odyssey Activity Pack Ser.). 48p. (J). pap. 12.99 *(978-1-4003-1235-1(3))* Nelson, Thomas Inc.

—The Pirates Who Don't Do Anything: A VeggieTales Movie: Cheesecurl Cave Snacks & Science. 2008. 48p. (J). pap. 12.99 *(978-1-4003-1233-7(7))* Nelson, Thomas Inc.

—The Pirates Who Don't Do Anything: A VeggieTales Movie: Clapping Rocks Crafts. 2008. 48p. (J). pap. 12.99 *(978-1-4003-1230-6(2))* Nelson, Thomas Inc.

—The Pirates Who Don't Do Anything: A VeggieTales Movie: Discovery Bay. 2008. 64p. (J). pap. 12.99 *(978-1-4003-1234-4(5))* Nelson, Thomas Inc.

—The Pirates Who Don't Do Anything: A VeggieTales Movie: Elementary Director's Guide. 2008. 128p. (J). pap. 17.99 *(978-1-4003-1226-9(4))* Nelson, Thomas Inc.

—The Pirates Who Don't Do Anything: A VeggieTales Movie: Preschool Director's Guide. 2008. 64p. (J). pap. 12.99 *(978-1-4003-1231-3(0))* Nelson, Thomas Inc.

—The Pirates Who Don't Do Anything: A VeggieTales Movie: Rock Monster Science Lab. 2008. 48p. (J). pap. 12.99 *(978-1-4003-1228-3(0))* Nelson, Thomas Inc.

—The Pirates Who Don't Do Anything: A VeggieTales Movie: Rowboat Bible Stories. 2008. 64p. (J). pap. 17.99 *(978-1-4003-1232-0(9))* Nelson, Thomas Inc.

—The Pirates Who Don't Do Anything: A VeggieTales Movie: Spyglass Bible Theater Guide. 2008. 64p. (J). pap. 12.99 *(978-1-4003-1227-6(2))* Nelson, Thomas Inc.

—The Pirates Who Don't Do Anything: A VeggieTales Movie: Whipcrack Island Games. 2008. 64p. (J). pap. 12.99 *(978-1-4003-1229-0(9))* Nelson, Thomas Inc.

—The Pirates Who Don't Do Anything: A VeggieTales Movie: Yo-Ho-Ho Opening & Closing Show. 2008. 64p. (J). pap. 5.99 *(978-1-4003-1236-8(1))* Nelson, Thomas Inc.

Thompson, Bill. The Legend of Gunners Cove. 2012. (ENG.). 132p. pap. 14.95 *(978-1-4327-9817-8(0))* Outskirts Pr., Inc.

Thomson, Sarah L. Pirates, Ho!, 0 vols. Gilpin, Stephen, illus. 2012. (ENG.). 32p. (J). (gr. k-3). pap. 7.99 *(978-0-7614-6247-7(3)*, 9780761462477, Amazon Children's Publishing) Amazon Publishing.

Tillworth, Mary. Nickelodeon 5-Minute Stories Collection. Random House, illus. 2016. (5-Minute Story Collection). (ENG.). 160p. (J). (gr. -1-2). 12.99 *(978-0-399-55314-1(2)*, Random Hse. Bks. for Young Readers) Random Hse. Children's Bks.

Timothy E. Dillinger. The Pick Pocket Pirate: An Original Pirate Tale. 2009. 126p. (gr. 2-2). 21.99 *(978-1-4389-4042-7(4))*; pap. 15.99 *(978-1-4389-4043-4(2))* AuthorHouse.

Tolcser, Sarah. Song of the Current. 2017. (ENG.). 384p. (YA). 17.99 *(978-1-68119-297-0(7)*, 9781681192970, Bloomsbury USA Childrens) Bloomsbury Publishing USA.

ToyBox Innovations, creator. The Curse of the Black Pearl. 2006. (Pirates of the Caribbean Ser.). (ENG., Illus.). 24p. (J). (gr. -1-3). pap. *(978-0-7634-2176-2(6))* Walt Disney Records.

—Dead Man's Chest. 2006. (Pirates of the Caribbean Ser.). (ENG., Illus.). 24p. (J). (gr. -1-3). pap. *(978-0-7634-2177-9(4))* Walt Disney Records.

Toybox Innovations, creator. Pirates of the Caribbean: the Complete Collection: The Curse of the Black Pearl/Dead Man's Chest/at World's End. 2007. (Disney's Read along Collection). (ENG., Illus.). (J). (gr. -1-3). pap. *(978-0-7634-2194-6(4))* Walt Disney Records.

Toybox Innovations & Toybox Innovations, creators. At Worlds End. 2007. (Pirates of the Caribbean Ser.). (ENG., Illus.). (J). (gr. -1-3). pap. *(978-0-7634-2186-1(3))* Walt Disney Records.

Trine, Greg. Pinkbeard's Revenge. Dormer, Frank W., illus. (Adventures of Jo Schmo Ser.: 4). (ENG.). 128p. (J). (gr. 1-4). 2015. pap. 5.99 *(978-0-544-45601-3(7)*, HMH Books For Young Readers) 2013. 12.99 *(978-0-547-80797-3(X))* Houghton Mifflin Harcourt Publishing Co.

Tucker, Kathy. Do Pirates Take Baths? 2015. (Illus.). 27p. (J). *(978-1-4896-3861-8(X))* Weigl Pubs., Inc.

Tullson, Diane. Red Sea, 1 vol. 2005. (ENG.). 176p. (YA). (gr. 8-12). per. 13.00 *(978-1-55143-331-8(1))* Orca Bk. Pubs. USA.

Underwood, Deborah. Pirate Mom. Gilpin, Stephen, illus. 2006. (Step into Reading Ser.: Vol. 3). (ENG.). 48p. (J). (gr. k-3). per. 3.99 *(978-0-375-83323-6(4)*, Random Hse. Bks. for Young Readers) Random Hse. Children's Bks.

Valor, De. Pirate Adventures of Sea Worthy: Featuring: the Treasure of Captain Blue Beard & the Return of Captain Blue Beard. 2013. 150p. (gr. 2-2). 20.35 *(978-1-4669-7483-8(4))*; pap. 10.35 *(978-1-4269-9551-4(2))* Trafford Publishing.

VeggieTales, contrib. by. The Pirates Who Don't Do Anything. 2007. (VeggieTales (EMI-CMG Audio) Ser.). (J). (gr. -1-3). 12.99 *(978-5-557-52681-4(1))* Big Idea Productions.

Verne, Jules. The Secret of the Island. Kingston, W. H. G., tr. 2008. 160p. 24.95 *(978-1-60664-753-0(9))* Rodgers, Alan Bks.

Vischer, Lisa. Three Pirates & You! 2004. (Big Idea Books / VeggieTales Ser.). (ENG., Illus.). 32p. (J). 7.99 *(978-0-310-70724-0(2))* Zonderkidz.

Viz Media Staff & Mizobuchi, Makoto. Pokémon: Ranger & the Temple of the Sea. Mizobuchi, Makoto, illus. 2008. (ENG., Illus.). 192p. (J). (gr. 1). pap. 9.99 *(978-1-4215-2288-3(8))* Viz Media.

Vogel-Placides, Joan Katherine. The Safe Place. Placides, Del S., illus. 2013. 58p. 13.99 *(978-0-9888718-3-0(1))* DOMINIONHOUSE Publishing & Design.

Walker, Richard. The Barefoot Book of Pirates. Whelan, Olwyn, illus. (Barefoot Bks.). (ENG.). 64p. (J). 2008. 19.99 *(978-1-84686-237-3(X))* 2004. (gr. 3-6). 16.99 *(978-1-84148-131-9(9))* Barefoot Bks., Inc.

Warner, Penny. Mystery of the Pirate's Treasure. 2013. (Code Busters Club Ser.). (ENG.). 192p. (J). (gr. 4-7). 16.99 *(978-1-60684-457-1(1)*, Darby Creek) Lerner Publishing Group.

Wasserman, Robin & Soderberg, Erin. X Marks the Spot. 2015. (Puppy Pirates Ser.: No. 2). (ENG., Illus.). 96p. (J). (gr. 1-4). 4.99 *(978-0-553-51170-3(X)*, Random Hse. Bks. for Young Readers) Random Hse. Children's Bks.

Waters, Erica-Jane. Petticoat Pirates: The Mermaids of Starfish Reef. 2013. (ENG., Illus.). 96p. (J). (gr. 2-4). 7.99 *(978-1-907411-96-0(8))* Little, Brown Book Group Ltd. GBR. Dist: Hachette Bk. Group.

Watt, Fiona. That's Not My Pirate. Wells, Rachel, illus. 2007. (Touchy-Feely Board Bks). 10p. (J). (gr. -1-k). bds. 8.99 *(978-0-7945-1702-1(1)*, Usborne) EDC Publishing.

Weaver, Jack W. Cat & Dog Breath Meet the Last Pirates: How to Fly a Basset Hound. 2012. 164p. 24.95 *(978-1-4626-6652-2(3))* America Star Bks.

Weinert, Matthias. No Bath, No Cake! Polly's Pirate Party. 2013. (ENG., Illus.). 48p. (J). (gr. -1-3). 17.95 *(978-0-7358-4112-3(8))* North-South Bks., Inc.

West, Tracey. Pirates vs. Ninja. 2013. (Ninjago Readers Ser.: 6). lib. bdg. 13.55 *(978-0-606-32026-9(1)*, Turtleback) Turtleback Bks.

Weston, Greg. Ocean View Terrace & the Blue Pirate Eater. 2008. 232p. pap. 14.95 *(978-1-4092-0278-3(X))* Lulu Pr., Inc.

Whybrow, Ian. Little Wolf, Terror of the Shivery Sea. Ross, Tony, illus. 2004. (Little Wolf Adventures Ser.). (ENG.). 144p. (J). (gr. 3-6). 14.95 *(978-1-57505-629-6(1))* Lerner Publishing Group.

—Tim, Ted & the Pirates. Ayto, Russell, illus. 2014. (ENG.). 32p. (J). 17.99 *(978-0-00-755930-5(5)*, HarperCollins Children's Bks.) HarperCollins Pubs. Ltd. GBR. Dist: HarperCollins Pubs.

Whybrow, Ian & Ayto, Russell. Tim, Ted & the Pirates. 2nd ed. 2008. (ENG., Illus.). 32p. (J). (gr. k-3). pap. 9.95 (978-0-00-713124-2(0)) HarperCollins Pubs. Ltd. GBR. Dist: Independent Pubs. Group.

Wigington, Patti. Pirate's Alphabet. Umscheid, Kit, illus. 2007. (ENG.). 32p. (J). (gr. -1-3). lib. bdg. 15.95 (978-0-9766805-8-1(0)) Keene Publishing.

Wilhelm, Doug. Curse of the Pirate Mist. 2011. (Illus.). 144p. (J). pap. 6.99 (978-1-937133-02-3(8)) Chooseco LLC.

Williams, Rozanne Lanczak. Captain Jack's Journal. Grayson, Rick, illus. 2006. (Learn to Write Ser.). 16p. (J). (gr. k-2). pap. 2.99 (978-1-59198-303-3(7), 6197) Creative Teaching Pr., Inc.

—Captain Jack's Journal. Maio, Barbara, ed. Grayson, Rick, illus. 2006. (J). per. 8.99 (978-1-59198-361-3(4)) Creative Teaching Pr., Inc.

Winbolt-Lewis, Martin. The Soggy Saga of Samuel Sprat. Mason, Abi, illus. 2013. 24p. pap. (978-1-78222-152-4(2)) Paragon Publishing, Rothersthorpe.

Winfield, A. C. The Star Pirate. 2013. (Illus.). 184p. pap. (978-1-909202-11-5(8)) Little Acorns Publishing.

Wininger, Stephen T. The Adventure of Pirate Pete Moss. 2004. (J). pap. (978-1-59196-466-7(0)) Instant Pub.

Winstanley, Nicola. The Pirate's Bed. 2015. (ENG., Illus.). 32p. (J). (gr. -1-2). 17.99 (978-1-77049-616-3(5), Tundra Bks.) Tundra Bks. CAN. Dist: Penguin Random Hse. LLC.

Winters, Kari-Lynn. Good Pirate. Griffiths, Dean, illus. 2016. (ENG.). 32p. (J). (gr. k-3). 17.95 (978-1-927485-80-4(0)) Pajama Pr. CAN. Dist: Ingram Publisher Services.

Wishinsky, Frieda. Beware, Pirates! Griffiths, Dean & Owlkids Books Inc. Staff, illus. 2007. (Canadian Flyer Adventures Ser.: 1). (ENG.). 96p. (J). (gr. 1-4). pap. 7.95 (978-1-897066-80-5(5), Owlkids) Owlkids Bks. Inc. CAN. Dist: Publishers Group West (PGW).

Wolfe, Myra & Monescillo, Maria. Charlotte Jane Battles Bedtime. Monescillo, Maria, illus. 2011. (ENG., Illus.). 32p. (J). (gr. -1-3). 16.99 (978-0-15-206150-0(9)) Houghton Mifflin Harcourt Publishing Co.

Wood, Francis. The SnowPeople. Larsen, Dan, illus. 2003. 96p. (YA). per. 14.95 (978-0-9746372-0-4(3)) Tip-Of-The-Moon Publishing Co.

Wood, James Playsted. The Queen's Most Honorable Pirate. Fisher, Leonard Everett, illus. 2011. 192p. 42.95 (978-1-258-09722-6(2)) Literary Licensing, LLC.

Wood, Jane R. Adventures on Amelia Island: A Pirate, a Princess, & Buried Treasure. Blacker, Elizabeth A., illus. Wood, Jane R., photos by. 2007. (ENG.). 132p. (J). (gr. 3-8). pap. 8.99 (978-0-9792304-0-0(3)) Florida Kids Pr., Inc.

Wronski, Gareth. Holly Farb & the Princess of the Galaxy. 2017. (ENG., Illus.). 320p. (J). (gr. 3-7). 16.99 **(978-1-4814-7177-0(5)**, Aladdin) Simon & Schuster Children's Publishing.

Wygand, Melissa. Where the Pirates Arrgh! (SpongeBob SquarePants) Martinez, Heather, illus. 2013. (Little Golden Book Ser.). (ENG.). 24p. (J). (-k). 3.99 (978-0-307-98174-5(6), Golden Bks.) Random Hse. Children's Bks.

Yolen, Jane. The Ballad of the Pirate Queens. 2004. (J). (gr. k-3). spiral bd. (978-0-616-01821-7(5)) Canadian National Institute for the Blind/Institut National Canadien pour les Aveugles.

Young, Jessica. All Paws on Deck. Burks, James, illus. 2016. (Haggis & Tank Unleashed Ser.: 1). (ENG.). 80p. (J). (gr. k-2). pap. 4.99 (978-0-545-81886-5(9)) Scholastic, Inc.

Zellerhoff, Christi. Princesses Can Be Pirates Too! Davis, Amy, illus. 2012. 38p. 17.99 (978-1-935961-68-0(3)); pap. 8.99 (978-1-935961-95-6(0)) Booktrope. (Booktrope Editions).

Ziegler-Sullivan, Ursula. Pirate Pups! Petrossi, Fabrizio, illus. 2016. (J). (978-1-4806-9717-1(6), Golden Bks.) Random Hse. Children's Bks.

Zullo, Allan. Kid Pirates: Their Battles, Shipwrecks, & Narrow Escapes. 2007. 147p. (J). pap. (978-0-439-91813-8(8)) Scholastic, Inc.

PITTSBURGH PIRATES (BASEBALL TEAM)

Connery-Boyd, Peg. Pittsburgh Pirates. 2016. (Hawk's Nest Activity Bks.: 0). (ENG.). 64p. (J). (gr. k-3). pap., act. bk. ed. 8.99 (978-1-4926-3369-3(0)) Sourcebooks, Inc.

Frager, Ray. Pittsburgh Pirates, 1 vol. (Inside MLB Ser.). (ENG., Illus.). 48p. (gr. 3-6). 2011. (YA). lib. bdg. 32.79 (978-1-61714-055-6(4)) 2014. (J). lib. bdg. 32.79 (978-1-62403-481-7(0), SportsZone) ABDO Publishing Co.

Goodman, Michael E. The Story of the Pittsburgh Pirates. 2007. (Baseball, the Great American Game Ser.). (Illus.). 48p. (YA). (gr. 4-7). lib. bdg. 32.80 (978-1-58341-498-9(3)) Creative Co., The.

LeBoutillier, Nate. The Story of the Pittsburgh Pirates. 2011. (Illus.). 48p. (J). 35.65 (978-1-60818-052-3(2), Creative Education) Creative Co., The.

Marsh, Carole. Roberto Clemente: Baseball Hero & Humanitarian: Baseball Hero & Humanitarian. 2003. 12p. (gr. k-4). 2.95 (978-0-635-02140-3(4)) Gallopade International.

Stewart, Mark. The Pittsburgh Pirates. 2012. (Team Spirit Ser.). 48p. (J). (gr. 3-6). lib. bdg. 29.27 (978-1-59953-493-0(2)) Norwood Hse. Pr.

Winter, Jonah. Roberto Clemente: Pride of the Pittsburgh Pirates. Colón, Raúl, illus. (ENG.). 40p. (J). (gr. -1-3). 2008. 7.99 (978-1-4169-5082-0(6)) 2005. 17.99 (978-0-689-85643-3(1)) Simon & Schuster Children's Publishing. (Atheneum Bks. for Young Readers).

PIUS V, SAINT, POPE, 1566-1572

Daughters of St. Paul Staff. No Place for Defeat. Date not set. (Encounter Ser.). 96p. (J). (gr. 3-9). pap. 2.00 (978-0-8198-5100-0(0)) Pauline Bks. & Media.

PIUS XII, POPE, 1876-1958

Marchione, Margherita. Pope Pius XII: Bilingual Coloring Book. Elliott, John, illus. 2004. (SPA & ENG.). 32p. 1.00 (978-0-8091-6721-0(2), 6721-2) Paulist Pr.

PIZARRO, FRANCISCO, APPROXIMATELY 1475-1541

Baicker, Karen. Conquistador: Francisco Pizarro Ravages the Inca Empire. 2011. (J). pap. (978-0-545-32940-8(X)) Scholastic, Inc.

DiConsiglio, John. Francisco Pizarro: Destroyer of the Inca Empire. 2008. (Wicked History Ser.). (ENG., Illus.). 128p. (J). 31.00 (978-0-531-18551-3(6), Watts, Franklin) Scholastic Library Publishing.

Hoogenboom, Lynn. Francisco Pizarro. 2009. (Primary Source Library of Famous Explorers Ser.). 24p. (gr. 4-4). 42.50 (978-1-60854-121-8(5), PowerKids Pr.) Rosen Publishing Group, Inc., The.

—Francisco Pizarro: A Primary Source Biography. 2006. (Primary Source Library of Famous Explorers Ser.). (Illus.). 24p. (YA). (gr. 2-5). lib. bdg. 22.60 (978-1-4042-3038-5(6)) Rosen Publishing Group, Inc., The.

Kachurek, Sandra J. Francisco Pizarro: Explorer of South America. 2004. (Explorers! Ser.). (Illus.). 48p. (J). lib. bdg. 23.93 (978-0-7660-2178-5(5)) Enslow Pubs., Inc.

Meltzer, Milton. Francisco Pizarro: The Conquest of Peru. 2003. (Great Explorations Ser.). (J). 29.93 (978-0-7614-1607-4(2), Benchmark Bks.) Marshall Cavendish Corp.

Mountjoy, Shane. Francisco Pizarro & the Conquest of the Inca. Goetzmann, William H., ed. 2005. (Explorers of New Lands Ser.). (Illus.). 100p. (gr. 5-8). 30.00 (978-0-7910-8614-8(3), Chelsea Hse.) Facts On File, Inc.

O'Brien, Cynthia. Explore with Francisco Pizarro. 2015. (Travel with the Great Explorers Ser.). (ENG., Illus.). 32p. (J). (gr. 3-6). (978-0-7787-1700-3(3)) Crabtree Publishing Co.

Ramen, Fred. Francisco Pizarro: The Exploration of Peru & the Conquest of the Inca. (Library of Explorers & Exploration Ser.). 112p. (gr. 5-8). 2009. 66.50 (978-1-60853-603-0(3)) 2004. (Illus.). lib. bdg. 34.60 (978-0-8239-3618-2(X)) Rosen Publishing Group, Inc., The. (Rosen Reference).

Somervill, Barbara A. Francisco Pizarro: Conqueror of the Incas, 1 vol. 2005. (Signature Lives: Renaissance Era Ser.). (ENG., Illus.). 112p. (gr. 6-7). 35.32 (978-0-7565-0815-9(0), 1240121, Signature Lives) Compass Point Bks.

Sonneborn, Liz. Pizarro: Conqueror of the Mighty Incas. 2010. (Great Explorers of the World Ser.). (Illus.). 112p. (J). (gr. 7-12). 33.27 (978-1-59845-128-3(6)) Enslow Pubs., Inc.

Zronik, John Paul & Zronik, John. Francisco Pizarro: Journeys Through Peru & South America. 2005. (In the Footsteps of Explorers Ser.). (ENG., Illus.). 32p. (J). (gr. -1-9). pap. (978-0-7787-2447-6(6)) Crabtree Publishing Co.

PLACE NAMES

see Names, Geographical

PLAGUE

see also Black Death

Andrews, Lawrence. The Plague. 2015. (J). lib. bdg. (978-1-62713-377-7(1)); (ENG.). 64p. (gr. 7-7). 34.21 (978-1-5026-0087-5(0)) Cavendish Square Publishing.

Cunningham, Kevin. The Bubonic Plague, 1 vol. 2011. (Essential Events Set 6 Ser.). (ENG., Illus.). 112p. (J). (gr. 6-12). lib. bdg. 35.64 (978-1-61714-762-3(1)) ABDO Publishing Co.

Elliott, Lynne. Medieval Medicine & the Plague. 2005. (Medieval World Ser.). (ENG., Illus.). 32p. (J). (gr. 5-9). pap. (978-0-7787-1390-6(3)) Crabtree Publishing Co.

Emmeluth, Donald. Plague, Second Edition. 2nd rev. ed. 2009. (Deadly Diseases & Epidemics Ser.). (Illus.). 120p. (C). (gr. 9-18). 34.95 (978-1-60413-237-3(X), Chelsea Hse.) Facts On File, Inc.

Hardman, Lizabeth. Plague. 2009. (Diseases & Disorders Ser.). (ENG.). 128p. (gr. 7-12). 39.90 (978-1-4205-0145-2(3)) Cengage Gale.

Jarrow, Gail. Bubonic Panic: When Plague Invaded America. 2016. (ENG., Illus.). 200p. (J). (gr. 4). 18.95 (978-1-62091-738-1(6), 1405837, Calkins Creek) Boyds Mills Pr.

Leone, Bruno. Disease in History. 2016. (ENG.). 104p. (J). (gr. 5-12). 38.60 (978-1-60152-960-2(0)) ReferencePoint Pr., Inc.

Levy, Janey. Plaga: La Peste Negra (Plague: the Black Death) Sarfatti, Esther, tr. from ENG. 2015. (Desastres Ser.). (SPA., Illus.). 32p. (J). (gr. 4-5). lib. bdg. 26.60 (978-1-4824-3248-0(X)) Stevens, Gareth Publishing LLLP.

MacDonald, Fiona. The Plague & Medicine in the Middle Ages. 2005. (World Almanac Library of the Middle Ages). (Illus.). 48p. (gr. 5-12). pap. 14.05 (978-0-8368-5907-2(3), Gareth Stevens Secondary Library) Stevens, Gareth Publishing LLLP.

Narayan, Natasha. Black Death & Other Putrid Plagues of London. 2004. (... . of London Ser.). (Illus.). 96p. 8.99 (978-1-904153-01-6(1)) Watling St., Ltd. GBR. Dist: Independent Pubs. Group.

Ollhoff, Jim. The Black Death, 1 vol. 2009. (History of Germs Ser.). (ENG., Illus.). 32p. (YA). (gr. 5-9). 27.07 (978-1-60453-497-9(4)) ABDO Publishing Co.

Orme, David. Plagues. 2010. (Fact to Fiction Grafx Ser.). (Illus.). 36p. (J). lib. bdg. 16.95 (978-1-60686-472-2(6)) Perfection Learning Corp.

Peppas, Lynn. Plague! 2013. (ENG.). 48p. (J). (978-0-7787-1102-5(1)); pap. (978-0-7787-1122-3(6)) Crabtree Publishing Co.

Person, Stephen. Bubonic Plague: The Black Death! (Nightmare Plagues Ser.). 32p. (gr. 4-9). 2016. (ENG.). (J). pap. 8.95 (978-1-944998-69-1(1)) 2010. (YA). lib. bdg. 25.27 (978-1-936088-03-4(7)) Bearport Publishing Co., Inc.

Throp, Claire. The Horrors of the Bubonic Plague. 2017. (Deadly History Ser.). (ENG.). 48p. (gr. 3-4). lib. bdg. 33.32 **(978-1-4846-4167-5(1)**, Heinemann InfoSearch) Heinemann-Raintree.

Walker, Richard. KFK Epidemics & Plagues. 2007. (Kingfisher Knowledge Ser.). 8.95 (978-0-7534-6181-5(1), Kingfisher) Roaring Brook Pr.

Whiting, Jim. Bubonic Plague. 2006. (Natural Disasters Ser.). (Illus.). 32p. (J). (gr. 1-4). lib. bdg. 25.70 (978-1-58415-494-5(2)) Mitchell Lane Pubs., Inc.

PLAGUE—FICTION

Barker, M. A. R. Lords of Tsamra 2003. (Illus.). 296p. (YA). per. 19.95 (978-0-9725880-1-0(9), 2) Zottola Publishing, Inc.

Brennan, Herbie. The Doomsday Box: A Shadow Project Adventure. 2011. (Shadow Project Ser.: 2). (ENG.). 352p. (J). (gr. 5). pap. 6.99 (978-0-06-175650-4(4)) HarperCollins Pubs.

Choldenko, Gennifer. Chasing Secrets. 2015. (ENG.). 288p. (J). (gr. 4-7). lib. bdg. 19.99 (978-0-375-99063-2(1), Lamb, Wendy Bks.) Random Hse. Children's Bks.

—Chasing Secrets. 2016. lib. bdg. 18.40 (978-0-606-38879-5(6)) Turtleback Bks.

Collins, Suzanne. Gregor & the Curse of the Warmbloods. 2006. (Underland Chronicles: Bk. 3). 358p. (gr. 4-7). 17.00 (978-0-7569-6766-6(X)) Perfection Learning Corp.

—Gregor & the Curse of the Warmbloods, Bk. 3. 2006. (Underland Chronicles Ser.: 3). (ENG.). 368p. (J). (gr. 3-7). pap. 7.99 (978-0-439-65624-5(9), Scholastic Paperbacks) Scholastic, Inc.

Cullen, Lyn. I Am Rembrandt's Daughter. 2011. 8.88 (978-0-7848-3491-6(1), Everbind) Marco Bk. Co.

Dahme, Joanne, et al. The Plague. 2009. (ENG., Illus.). 272p. (YA). (gr. 7-17). 16.95 (978-0-7624-3344-5(2)) Running Pr. Bk. Pubs.

Dixon, Heather. Illusionarium. 2015. (ENG.). 368p. (YA). (gr. 8). 17.99 (978-0-06-200105-4(1), Greenwillow Bks.) HarperCollins Pubs.

Furlong, C. T. Killer Genes. 2012. (Arctic6 Adventure Ser.). 192p. (YA). (gr. 4-6). pap. 45.54 (978-0-7613-9209-5(2)) Lerner Publishing Group.

Furlong, Carol T. Killer Genes. 2012. (Arctic6 Adventure Ser.). 192p. (YA). (gr. 4-6). pap. 7.99 (978-0-9562315-7-4(8)) Lerner Publishing Group.

Goodman, Gabriel. Plague Riders. 2012. (After the Dust Settled Ser.). (ENG.). 112p. (YA). (gr. 6-12). pap. 7.95 (978-0-8225-9033-0(6), Darby Creek); lib. bdg. 27.93 (978-0-7613-8330-7(1)) Lerner Publishing Group.

Grant, Michael. Plague. (Gone Ser.: 4). (ENG.). (YA). (gr. 8). 2014. 528p. pap. 9.99 (978-0-06-144914-7(8)) 2011. 512p. 17.99 (978-0-06-144912-3(1)) HarperCollins Pubs. (Tegen, Katherine Bks).

Griffin, Bethany. Masque of the Red Death. 2013. (Masque of the Red Death Ser.: 1). (ENG.). 336p. (YA). (gr. 9). pap. 9.99 (978-0-06-210780-0(1), Greenwillow Bks.) HarperCollins Pubs.

Kaufman, Amie. Illuminae. 2017. lib. bdg. 24.50 **(978-0-606-39847-3(3))** Turtleback Bks.

Kaufman, Amie & Kristoff, Jay. Illuminae. 2015. (Illuminae Files Ser.). (ENG., Illus.). 608p. (YA). (gr. 9). lib. bdg. 21.99 (978-0-553-49912-4(2)); 18.99 (978-0-553-49911-7(4)) Random Hse. Children's Bks. (Knopf Bks. for Young Readers).

Keeling, Annie E. Andrew Golding A Tale of the Great Plague. 2004. reprint ed. pap. 1.99 (978-1-4192-0694-8(X)); pap. 15.95 (978-1-4191-0694-1(5)) Kessinger Publishing, LLC.

Kristoff, Amie Kaufman/Jay. ILLUMINAE. EXPEDIENTE_01 (ILLUMINAE 1) 2016. (SPA.). 592p. (J). (gr. 6). pap. 17.95 (978-84-204-8355-9(9), Alfaguara Juvenil) Santillana USA Publishing Co., Inc.

Lu, Marie. Champion. 2013. (Legend Trilogy: 3). (ENG.). 384p. (YA). (gr. 7). 18.99 (978-0-399-25677-6(6), G.P. Putnam's Sons Books for Young Readers) Penguin Publishing Group.

—Champion. 2014. (Legend Ser.: 3). (ENG.). 416p. (YA). (gr. 7). pap. 9.99 (978-0-14-751228-4(X), Speak) Penguin Young Readers Group.

—Champion. 2014. (Legend Ser.: 3). lib. bdg. 20.85 (978-0-606-36605-2(9)) Turtleback Bks.

—Legend. aut. ltd. collector's ed. 2013. (Legend Trilogy: Bk. 1). (Illus.). 306p. (YA). mass mkt. 100.00 net. (978-1-934267-38-7(4)) Gauntlet, Inc.

—Legend. 2011. (Legend Trilogy: Bk. 1). (ENG.). (YA). (gr. 8-12). 54.99 (978-1-61657-044-6(X), Penguin AudioBooks) Penguin Publishing Group.

—Legend. Kaaris, illus. 2015. (Legend Ser.). (ENG.). 160p. (YA). (gr. 7). pap. 14.99 (978-0-399-17189-5(4), G.P. Putnam's Sons Books for Young Readers) Penguin Young Readers Group.

—Legend. (Legend Ser.: 1). (ENG.). (YA). (gr. 7). 2013. 352p. pap. 9.99 (978-0-14-242207-6(X), Speak) 2011. 320p. 17.99 (978-0-399-25675-2(X), G.P. Putnam's Sons Books for Young Readers) Penguin Young Readers Group.

—Legend. l.t. ed. 2012. (Legend Trilogy: Bk. 1). (ENG.). 394p. (J). (gr. 7-12). 23.99 (978-1-4104-4606-0(9)) Thorndike Pr.

—Legend. (Legend Graphic Novels Ser.: 1). 2015. lib. bdg. 26.95 (978-0-606-38424-7(3)) 2013. lib. bdg. 20.85 (978-0-606-31701-6(5), Turtleback) Turtleback Bks.

Marriott, Zoë. Darkness Hidden: the Name of the Blade, Book Two. 2015. (ENG.). 352p. (J). (gr. 7). 16.99 (978-0-7636-6958-4(X)) Candlewick Pr.

O'Hearn, Kate. Origins of Olympus. 2015. (Pegasus Ser.: 4). lib. bdg. 19.65 (978-0-606-38366-0(2)) Turtleback Bks.

The Origins of Olympus. 2014. (Pegasus Ser.: 4). (ENG., Illus.). 432p. (J). (gr. 3-7). 18.99 (978-1-4424-9715-3(7), Simon & Schuster/Paula Wiseman Bks.) Simon & Schuster/Paula Wiseman Bks.

Orme, David. Plagues. 2010. (Fact to Fiction Grafx Ser.). (Illus.). 36p. (J). pap. 7.45 (978-0-7891-7997-5(0)) Perfection Learning Corp.

Russell, Christopher. Hunted. 2007. (J). (gr. 5-9). 254p. 15.99 (978-0-06-084119-5(2)); 272p. lib. bdg. 16.89 (978-0-06-084120-1(6), Greenwillow Bks.) HarperCollins Pubs.

Taranta, Mary. Shimmer & Burn. 2017. (YA). pap. **(978-1-4814-7200-5(3)**, McElderry, Margaret K. Bks.) McElderry, Margaret K. Bks.

Turnbull, Ann. Forged in the Fire. 2007. (ENG.). 320p. (YA). (gr. 7-12). 16.99 (978-0-7636-3144-4(2)) Candlewick Pr.

Zarcinas, Scott. The Golden Chalice: A Pilgrim's Chronicle. 2013. 200p. pap. (978-0-9875975-9-5(0)) DoctorZed Publishing.

—The Golden Chalice: A Pilgrim's Chronicle (Large Print 16pt) l.t. ed. 2013. 284p. (YA). pap. (978-1-4596-7063-1(9)) ReadHowYouWant.com, Ltd.

PLANE CRASHES

see Aircraft Accidents

PLANE GEOMETRY

see Geometry

PLANE TRIGONOMETRY

see Trigonometry

PLANETS

see also Life on Other Planets; Solar System; Stars
also names of planets, e.g. Venus (Planet)

Aguilar, David A. Cosmic Catastrophes. 2016. (Smithsonian Ser.). (ENG., Illus.). 80p. (J). (gr. 3-7). 18.99 (978-0-451-47684-5(0), Viking Books for Young Readers) Penguin Young Readers Group.

—Seven Wonders of the Solar System. 2017. (Smithsonian Ser.). (ENG., Illus.). 80p. (J). (gr. 5). 18.99 (978-0-451-47685-2(9), Viking Books for Young Readers) Penguin Young Readers Group.

—13 Planets: The Latest View of the Solar System. 2011. (ENG., Illus.). 64p. (J). (gr. 3-7). 16.95 (978-1-4263-0770-6(5)); lib. bdg. 25.90 (978-1-4263-0771-3(3)) National Geographic Society. (National Geographic Children's Bks.).

Anderson, Michael. The Nature of Planets, Dwarf Planets, & Space Objects. 2011. (Illus.). 96p. (J). lib. bdg. 31.70 (978-1-61530-517-9(3)) Rosen Publishing Group, Inc., The.

Arlon, Penelope & Arlon, Penny. Planets. 2012. (Scholastic Discover More Ser.). (ENG., Illus.). 80p. (J). (gr. 2-5). 12.99 (978-0-545-33028-2(9), Scholastic Reference) Scholastic, Inc.

Arlon, Penelope & Gordon-Harris, Tory. Planets. 2012. (J). lib. bdg. (978-0-531-22957-6(2)) Scholastic, Inc.

Arlon, Penelope & Gordon-Harris, Tory. Planets: A LEGO Adventure in the Real World. 2016. (Illus.). 64p. (J). **(978-1-4844-8522-4(X))** Scholastic, Inc.

Ashby, Ruth. The Outer Planets. 2003. (New Solar System Ser.). (J). lib. bdg. 28.50 (978-1-58340-290-0(X)) Black Rabbit Bks.

Asimov, Isaac & Hantula, Richard. Marte: Nuestro Misteriosos Vecino. Porras, Carlos & D'Andrea, Patricia, trs. from ENG. 2003. (Isaac Asimov's Biblioteca del Universo del Siglo XXI).Tr. of Mars: Our Mysterious Neighbor. (SPA., Illus.). 32p. (gr. 2-6). lib. bdg. 26.00 (978-0-8368-3856-5(4), Gareth Stevens Learning Library) Stevens, Gareth Publishing LLLP.

—Plutón y Caronte. Porras, Carlos & D'Andrea, Patricia, trs. from ENG. 2003. (Isaac Asimov's Biblioteca del Universo del Siglo XXI). (SPA., Illus.). 32p. (gr. 2-6). lib. bdg. 26.00 (978-0-8368-3859-6(9), Gareth Stevens Learning Library) Stevens, Gareth Publishing LLLP.

Askew, Amanda. Complete Guides Space. 2012. (ENG.). 144p. (J). (978-1-4351-4409-5(0)) Barnes & Noble, Inc.

Aspen-Baxter, Linda & Kissock, Heather. Los Planetas, with Code. 2012. (Mirando Al Cielo Ser.). (SPA., Illus.). 24p. (J). (gr. k-2). lib. bdg. 27.13 (978-1-61913-215-3(X), AV2 by Weigl) Weigl Pubs., Inc.

Baines, Becky. Explore My World Planets. 2016. (Explore My World Ser.). (ENG., Illus.). 32p. (J). (gr. -1-2). pap. 4.99 (978-1-4263-2322-5(0), National Geographic Children's Bks.) National Geographic Society.

Bauer, Jeff. The Planets. 2007. (Illus.). 16p. (J). 3.95 (978-0-545-00733-7(X)) Scholastic, Inc.

Bell, Trudy E. The Inner Planets. 2003. (New Solar System Ser.). (J). lib. bdg. 28.50 (978-1-58340-288-7(8)) Black Rabbit Bks.

Berger, Melvin & Berger, Gilda. Planets. 2010. (Scholastic True or False Ser.: 9). (ENG.). 48p. (J). (gr. 2-5). pap. 4.99 (978-0-545-20204-6(3), Scholastic Paperbacks) Scholastic, Inc.

Berkes, Marianne Collins. Going Around the Sun: Some Planetary Fun, 1 vol. Mason, Janeen, illus. 2008. (ENG.). 32p. (J). (gr. -1-4). 16.95 (978-1-58469-099-3(2)); pap. 8.95 (978-1-58469-100-6(X)) Dawn Pubns.

Berne, Emma Carlson. Totally Wacky Facts about Planets & Stars. 2015. (Mind Benders Ser.). (ENG., Illus.). 112p. (gr. 1-3). lib. bdg. 23.32 (978-1-4914-6523-3(9)) Capstone Press of Coughlan Cos.

Berne, Emma Carlson, et al. Planets. 2015. (Planets Ser.). (ENG.). 32p. (gr. 2-4). 255.92 (978-1-4914-6957-6(9)) Capstone Press of Coughlan Cos.

Bing & Bong's Tiny Planets. (Bing & Bong's Tiny Planets Ser.). (Illus.). 12p. (J). pap. (978-1-84222-875-3(7)) Carlton Bks., Ltd.

Birch, Robin. Dwarf Planets. 2nd rev. ed. 2008. (New Solar System Ser.). 32p. (YA). (gr. 3-6). 23.00 (978-1-60413-216-8(7)) Facts On File, Inc.

Blevins, Wiley. Planets, 6 vols., Set. 2004. (Phonics Readers Books 37-72 Ser.). (ENG.). 8p. (gr. k-1). pap. 35.70 (978-0-7368-4066-8(4), Phonics Readers) Capstone Press of Coughlan Cos.

Bloom, J. P. Planets, 1 vol. 2014. (Planets Ser.: 8). (ENG.). 24p. (J). (gr. 2-4). lib. bdg. 228.00 (978-1-62970-714-3(7)) ABDO Publishing Co.

Bowman, Donna H. What Is the Moon Made Of? And Other Questions Kids Have about Space, 1 vol. Lubach, Peter, illus. (Kids' Questions Ser.). (ENG.). 24p. (gr. 1-2). 2011. pap. 7.49 (978-1-4048-6726-0(0)) 2009. lib. bdg. 26.65 (978-1-4048-5529-8(7)) Picture Window Bks.

Branley, Franklyn M. The Planets in Our Solar System. O'Malley, Kevin, illus. 2015. (Let's-Read-And-Find-Out Science 2 Ser.). (ENG.). 32p. (J). (gr. -1-3). pap. 6.99 (978-0-06-238194-1(6)) HarperCollins Pubs.

Brasch, Pamela. J Is for Jupiter: A-Z of People, Places & Things in Jupiter, Florida. Kindt, Kathleen G., illus. 2011. 52p. (J). pap. 19.95 (978-0-9846071-7-4(X)) Middle River Pr.

Carney, Elizabeth. Planets (1 Hardcover/1 CD) 2017. (National Geographic Kids Ser.). (ENG.). (J). 29.95 **(978-1-4301-2677-5(9))** Live Oak Media.

—Planets (1 Paperback/1 CD) 2017. (National Geographic Kids Ser.). (ENG.). (J). pap. 19.95 **(978-1-4301-2676-8(0))** Live Oak Media.

—Planets (4 Paperbacks/1 CD), 4 vols. 2017. (National Geographic Kids Ser.). (ENG.). (J). pap., pap. 31.95 **(978-1-4301-2678-2(7))** Live Oak Media.

Carson, Mary Kay. How Many Planets Circle the Sun? And Other Questions about Our Solar System. Miller, Ron, illus. 2014. (Good Question! Ser.). (ENG.). 40p. (J). (gr. 1). 12.95 (978-1-4549-0668-1(5)) Sterling Publishing Co., Inc.

—Life on Mars. 2016. (Scholastic Reader, Level 2 Ser.). (ENG., Illus.). 32p. (J). (gr. 1-3). pap. 3.99 (978-0-545-93548-7(2), Scholastic Nonfiction) Scholastic, Inc.

Carson, Mary Kay & Carson, Mary K. Extreme Planets Q & A. 2008. (Illus.). 48p. (J). (gr. k-4). 17.99 (978-0-06-089975-2(1)) HarperCollins Pubs.

Channing, Margot. Stars & Planets. 2014. (Closer Look At... Ser.). (Illus.). 32p. (gr. 3-6). 31.35 (978-1-905087-08-2(X), 1374553) Book Hse. GBR. Dist: Black Rabbit Bks.

Chiger, Arielle & Elkin, Matthew. 20 Fun Facts about Gas Giants. 2014. (Fun Fact File: Space! Ser.). 32p. (J). (gr. 2-5). 25.25 (978-1-4824-1001-3(X)); pap. 10.50 (978-1-4824-1002-0(8)) Stevens, Gareth Publishing LLLP.

Clissold, Caroline. Out of This World. 2007. (Trackers-Math Ser.). (gr. 2-5). pap. 5.00 (978-1-59055-917-8(7)) Pacific Learning, Inc.

Cole, Joanna. Lost in the Solar System. Degen, Bruce, illus. 2010. (Magic School Bus Ser.). (ENG.). (J). (gr. -1-3). 18.95 *(978-0-545-22337-9(7))* Scholastic, Inc.

Crabtree Editors & Donaldson, Chelsea. The Planets. 2012. (Journey Through Space Ser.). (ENG.). 24p. (J). (gr. 3-6). lib. bdg. *(978-0-7787-5307-0(7))* Crabtree Publishing Co.

Culp, Jennifer. How We Find Other Earths: Technology & Strategies to Detect Planets Similar to Ours, 01 vols., 1. 2016. (Search for Other Earths Ser.). (ENG., Illus.). 112p. (J). 35.60 *(978-1-4994-6292-0(1)*, Rosen Young Adult) Rosen Publishing Group, Inc., The.

Dalmatian Press Staff. My Race into Space! 2008. (ENG.). 9p. bds. 4.95 *(978-1-58117-717-6(8)*, Intervisual/Piggy Toes) Bendon, Inc.

The Deep Blue Planet, 5 bks., Set. Incl. Along the Coasts. Massa, Renato. Davenport, Neil F., tr. (YA). 1998. lib. bdg. 28.54 *(978-0-8172-4654-9(1))*; Back to the Sea. Massa, Renato. Davenport, Neil F., tr. (YA). 1998. lib. bdg. 28.54 *(978-0-8172-4653-2(3))*; Coral Reef. Massa, Renato. Serio, Linda, tr. (YA). 1997. lib. bdg. 28.54 *(978-0-8172-4652-5(5))*; Ocean Environments. Voglino, Alex & Massa, Renato. Davenport, Neil F., tr. (YA). 1998. lib. bdg. 28.54 *(978-0-8172-4651-8(7))*; Oceans & Seas. Voglino, Alex. (J). 1997. lib. bdg. 28.54 *(978-0-8172-4650-1(9))*; 56p. (gr. 6-12). (Illus.). Set lib. bdg. 142.70 *(978-0-8172-4655-6(X))* Heinemann-Raintree.

DeYoe, Aaron. Planets, 1 vol. 2015. (ENG., Illus.). 24p. (J). *(978-1-62403-744-3(5))* ABDO Publishing Co.

DiSiena, Laura Lyn & Eliot, Hannah. Saturn Could Sail: And Other Fun Facts. Oswald, Pete & Spurgeon, Aaron, illus. 2014. (Did You Know? Ser.). (ENG.). 32p. (J). (gr. -1-3). 17.99 *(978-1-4814-1429-6(1))*; pap. 6.99 *(978-1-4814-1428-9(3))* Little Simon. (Little Simon).

Donaldson, Chelsea. The Planets. 2012. (ENG.). 24p. (J). pap. *(978-0-7787-5312-4(3))* Crabtree Publishing Co.

Dorling Kindersley Publishing Staff. DK Eyewitness Books: Planets. 2017. (DK Eyewitness Bks.). (ENG.). 72p. (J). (gr. 3-7). pap. 9.99 ***(978-1-4654-6250-3(3)***, DK Children) Dorling Kindersley Publishing, Inc.

—My Best Pop-Up Space Book. 2015. (ENG., Illus.). 18p. (J). (-k). bds. 14.99 *(978-1-4654-3914-7(5)*, DK Children) Dorling Kindersley Publishing, Inc.

—Planets. 2017. (DK Eyewitness Bks.). (ENG.). 72p. (J). (gr. 3-7). lib. bdg. 19.99 ***(978-1-4654-6251-0(1)***, DK Children) Dorling Kindersley Publishing, Inc.

—Smithsonian Geography. 2013. (Visual Encyclopedia Ser.). (ENG.). 304p. (J). (gr. 3-7). pap. 19.99 *(978-1-4654-0885-3(1)*, DK Children) Dorling Kindersley Publishing, Inc.

—Stars & Planets: Glow in the Dark. 2014. (ENG.). 24p. (J). (gr. k-4). 19.99 *(978-1-4654-1420-5(7)*, DK Children) Dorling Kindersley Publishing, Inc.

Dorling Kindersley Publishing Staff & Last, Shari. Miles from Tomorrowland. 2016. (Ultimate Sticker Collections). (ENG.). 96p. (J). (gr. -1-1). pap. 12.99 *(978-1-4654-5461-4(6)*, DK Children) Dorling Kindersley Publishing, Inc.

Evert, Laura. Planets, Moons, & Stars. Garrow, Linda, illus. 2003. (Take along Guides). (ENG.). 48p. (J). (gr. 2-5). pap. 7.95 *(978-1-55971-842-4(0))* Cooper Square Publishing Llc.

Extreme Planet, 6 vols. 2010. (Extreme Planet Ser.). (ENG.). 24p. (gr. 1-2). lib. bdg. 126.60 *(978-1-4296-4416-7(8)*, First Facts) Capstone Press of Coughlan Cos.

Extreme Planet [Capstone Sole Source]. 2010. (Extreme Planet Ser.). 24p. lib. bdg. 143.94 *(978-1-4296-5857-7(6)*, First Facts) Capstone Press of Coughlan Cos.

Farndon, John. The Awesome Book of Planets & Their Moons. Paiva, Johannah Gilman, ed. Various & Thompson, Ian, illus. 2014. (ENG.). 32p. (J). (gr. 3-7). 7.99 *(978-1-4867-0342-5(9))* Flowerpot Children's Pr. Inc. CAN. Dist: Cardinal Pubs. Group.

Faust, Daniel R. After Earth: Living on a Different Planet. 2009. (Jr. Graphic Environmental Dangers Ser.). (ENG., Illus.). 24p. (gr. 3-8). pap. 10.60 *(978-1-4042-4596-9(0)*, PowerKids Pr.) Rosen Publishing Group, Inc., The.

—Más Allá de la Tierra: Vivir en Otro Planeta. 2009. (Historietas Juveniles: Peligros Del Medioambiente (Jr. Graphic Environmental Dangers) Ser.). (SPA., Illus.). 24p. (gr. 3-6). (YA). lib. bdg. 25.25 *(978-1-4358-8471-7(X))*; pap. 10.60 *(978-1-4358-8472-4(8))* Rosen Publishing Group, Inc., The.

Finton, Nancy. Explore the Solar System! 2010. (Illus.). 29p. (J). *(978-0-545-28884-2(3))* Scholastic, Inc.

Galvin, Laura Gates. I Love My Planet Earth. 2010. (ENG.). 16p. (J). (gr. -1). 5.95 *(978-1-60727-140-6(0))* Soundprints.

Gendell, Megan & Sweitzer, James. Spinning 'round the Sun: Everything You Wanted to Know about the Solar System & Everything in It. 2008. (Illus.). 32p. (J). pap. *(978-0-545-04459-2(6))* Scholastic, Inc.

Gibbons, Gail. The Planets. rev. ed. 2005. (ENG., Illus.). 32p. (J). 16.95 *(978-0-8234-1957-9(6))*; pap. 6.95 *(978-0-8234-1958-6(4))* Holiday Hse., Inc.

—The Planets. Gibbons, Gail, illus. 3rd rev. ed. 2008. (ENG., Illus.). 32p. (J). (gr. -1-3). 7.99 *(978-0-8234-2157-2(0))* Holiday Hse., Inc.

Gilpin, Daniel & Basher, Simon. Planet Earth: What Planet Are You On? Basher, Simon, illus. 2010. (Basher Science Ser.). (ENG., Illus.). 128p. (J). (gr. 5-9). pap. 8.99 *(978-0-7534-6412-0(8)*, 9780753464120, Kingfisher) Roaring Brook Pr.

Goldsmith, Mike. Stars & Planets. 2011. (Navigators Ser.). (ENG., Illus.). 48p. (J). (gr. 4-7). pap. 8.99 *(978-0-7534-6682-7(1)*, 9780753466827, Kingfisher) Roaring Brook Pr.

Goldstein, Margaret J. The Sun. 2003. (Our Universe Ser.). (ENG., Illus.). 32p. (gr. 2-4). lib. bdg. 22.60 *(978-0-8225-4647-4(7))* Lerner Publishing Group.

Graham, Ian. Earth & the Universe. 2008. (World of Wonder Ser.). (ENG.). 32p. (J). (gr. 1-4). pap. 9.95 *(978-0-531-23821-9(0)*, Children's Pr.) Scholastic Library Publishing.

—Planets Far from Earth. 2015. (Space Ser.). (Illus.). 24p. (gr. 3-6). lib. bdg. 28.50 *(978-1-62588-211-0(4))* Black Rabbit Bks.

—Planets near Earth. 2015. (Space Ser.). (Illus.). 24p. (gr. 3-6). lib. bdg. 28.50 *(978-1-62588-212-7(2))* Black Rabbit Bks.

Grant, Donald. In the Sky. Grant, Donald, illus. 2013. (ENG., Illus.). 36p. (J). (gr. -1-k). 12.99 *(978-1-85103-419-2(6))* Moonlight Publishing, Ltd. GBR. Dist: Independent Pubs. Group.

Group/McGraw-Hill, Wright. Earth & Physical Science: Our Solar System, 6 vols. (Book2WebTM Ser.). (gr. 4-8). 36.50 *(978-0-322-04427-2(8))* Wright Group/McGraw-Hill.

Halpern, Paul. Faraway Worlds: Planets Beyond Our Solar System. Cook, Lynette R., illus. 2004. (ENG.). 32p. (J). (gr. 2-5). pap. 7.95 *(978-1-57091-617-5(9))* Charlesbridge Publishing, Inc.

Hand, Carol. Is There Life Out There? The Likelihood of Alien Life & What It Would Look Like, 01 vols., 1. 2016. (Search for Other Earths Ser.). (ENG., Illus.). 112p. (J). 35.60 *(978-1-4994-6294-4(8)*, Rosen Young Adult) Rosen Publishing Group, Inc., The.

Harman, Alice. Planets, 01 vols., 1. 2016. (Fact Finders: Space Ser.). (ENG., Illus.). 24p. (J). pap. 8.25 *(978-1-5081-9133-9(6)*, 1397743, Windmill Bks.) Rosen Publishing Group, Inc., The.

Hirschmann, Kris. Space & the Planets. Bollinger, Peter, illus. 2003. (Magic School Bus Fact Finder Ser.). (ENG.). 96p. (J). pap. 4.99 *(978-0-439-38175-8(4))* Scholastic, Inc.

Hiton, Lisa. Gravity, Orbiting Objects, & Planetary Motion. 2016. (Space Systems Ser.). 112p. (J). 42.79 *(978-1-5026-2287-7(4))* Cavendish Square Publishing.

Hoffmann, Sara. The Little Book of Space. 2005. (Little Bks.). (ENG., Illus.). 24p. (J). (gr. -1-2). 9.95 *(978-1-58728-485-4(5))* Cooper Square Publishing Llc.

Hollar, Sherman. The Outer Planets: Jupiter, Saturn, Uranus, & Neptune. 2011. (J). lib. bdg. 31.70 *(978-1-61530-518-6(1))* Rosen Publishing Group, Inc., The.

Holt, Rinehart and Winston Staff. Holt Science & Technology Chapter 21: Earth Science: The Family of Planets. 5th ed. 2004. (Illus.). pap. 12.86 *(978-0-03-030346-3(X))* Holt McDougal.

Hopping, Lorraine Jean. Space Rocks: The Story of Planetary Geologist Adriana Ocampo. 2006. (ENG., Illus.). 128p. (gr. 7-9). per. 19.95 *(978-0-309-09555-6(7)*, Joseph Henry Pr.) National Academies Pr.

Howard, Fran. Dwarf Planets, 1 vol. 2008. (Universe Ser.). (ENG.). 32p. (gr. k-4). 27.07 *(978-1-59928-926-7(1)*, Buddy Bks.) ABDO Publishing Co.

James, Brian. Eight Spinning Planets. Benfanti, Russell, illus. 2010. (ENG.). 16p. (J). (gr. k — 1). 12.99 *(978-0-545-23517-4(0)*, Cartwheel Bks.) Scholastic, Inc.

Jemison, Mae & Rau, Dana Meachen. Discovering New Planets. 2013. (True Book™—Dr. Mae Jemison & 100 Year Starship™ Ser.). (ENG., Illus.). 48p. (J). pap. 6.95 *(978-0-531-24063-2(0))*; lib. bdg. 29.00 *(978-0-531-25503-2(4))* Scholastic Library Publishing.

Karam, P. Andrew & Stein, Ben P. Planetary Motion. 2009. (Science Foundations Ser.). (Illus.). 120p. (gr. 6-12). lib. bdg. 35.00 *(978-1-60413-017-1(2)*, Chelsea Hse.) Facts On File, Inc.

Kazunas, Ariel. Saturn. 2011. (21st Century Junior Library: Solar System Ser.). (ENG.). 24p. (gr. 2-5). lib. bdg. 25.64 *(978-1-61080-087-7(7)*, 201084) Cherry Lake Publishing.

Kenney, Karen Latchana. Exoplanets. 2017. (ENG., Illus.). 88p. (YA). (gr. 8-12). 35.99 *(978-1-5124-0086-1(6)*, Twenty-First Century Bks.) Lerner Publishing Group.

Kenney, Karen Latchana. Exoplanets: Worlds Beyond Our Solar System. 2017. (Nonfiction — Young Adult Ser.). (ENG.). 88p. (YA). (gr. 8-12). 19.99 ***(978-1-5124-3908-3(8))***; 53.32 ***(978-1-5124-3909-0(6))***; 53.32 ***(978-1-5124-2849-0(3))*** Lerner Publishing Group. (Twenty-First Century Bks.).

Kerrod, Robin. Jupiter. 2005. (Planet Library). (Illus.). 32p. (gr. 3-8). lib. bdg. 21.27 *(978-0-8225-3907-0(1))* Lerner Publishing Group.

—Mercury & Venus. 2005. (Planet Library). (Illus.). 32p. (gr. 3-8). 21.27 *(978-0-8225-3904-9(7))* Lerner Publishing Group.

—Planet Earth. 2005. (Planet Library). (Illus.). 32p. (gr. 3-8). lib. bdg. 21.27 *(978-0-8225-3902-5(0))* Lerner Publishing Group.

—Saturn. 2005. (Planet Library). (Illus.). 32p. (gr. 3-8). lib. bdg. 21.27 *(978-0-8225-3909-4(8))* Lerner Publishing Group.

—Uranus, Neptune, & Pluto. 2005. (Planet Library). (Illus.). 32p. (J). (gr. 3-8). lib. bdg. 21.27 *(978-0-8225-3908-7(X))* Lerner Publishing Group.

Kissock, Heather. Planets. 2011. (J). *(978-1-61690-604-7(9))*; *(978-1-61690-958-1(7))* Weigl Pubs., Inc.

Kops, Deborah. Exploring Exoplanets. 2011. (Searchlight Books Whats Amazing about Space Ser.). (ENG., Illus.). (gr. 3-5). pap. 51.01 *(978-0-7613-8415-1(4))*; 40p. pap. 8.95 *(978-0-7613-7878-5(2))* Lerner Publishing Group.

Kortenkamp, Steve. The Dwarf Planets, 1 vol. 2011. (Solar System & Beyond Ser.). (ENG., Illus.). 32p. (gr. 3-4). pap. 8.10 *(978-1-4296-6242-0(5)*, Fact Finders) Capstone Press of Coughlan Cos.

—The Planets of Our Solar System, 1 vol. (Solar System & Beyond Ser.). (ENG., 32p. (gr. 3-4). 2011. Illus.). pap. 8.10 *(978-1-4296-6241-3(7))* 2011. pap. 47.70 *(978-1-4296-6410-3(X))* 2010. lib. bdg. 27.32 *(978-1-4296-5396-1(5))* Capstone Press of Coughlan Cos. (Fact Finders).

La Bella, Laura. The Goldilocks Zone: Conditions Necessary for Extraterrestrial Life, 01 vols., 1. 2016. (Search for Other Earths Ser.). (ENG., Illus.). 112p. (J). 35.60 *(978-1-4994-6298-2(0)*, Rosen Young Adult) Rosen Publishing Group, Inc., The.

Lancaster, Juliana. PBIS- Planetary Forecaster. 2005. pap. 8.00 *(978-1-58591-567-5(X))* It's About Time, Herff Jones Education Div.

Lawrence, Ellen. Earth: Our Home in the Solar System. 2013. (Zoom into Space Ser.). 24p. (J). (gr. -1-3). lib. bdg. 23.93 *(978-1-909673-06-9(4))* Ruby Tuesday Books Limited GBR. Dist: Bearport Publishing Co., Inc.

Leigh, Autumn. A Trip Through Our Solar System. (Reading Room Collection 1 Ser.). 16p. 2009. (gr. 2-3). 37.50 *(978-1-60851-940-8(6))* 2006. (Illus.). (J). (gr. 3-7). lib. bdg. 17.25 *(978-1-4042-3345-4(8))* Rosen Publishing Group, Inc., The. (PowerKids Pr.).

Levy, Janey. Viaje Al Centro de la Tierra (a Trip to the Center of the Earth) 2015. (Maravillosos Viajes a Través de la Ciencia (Fantastic Science Journeys) Ser.). (SPA., Illus.). 32p. (J). (gr. 2-3). 25.25 *(978-1-4824-2025-8(2)*, 1384039) Stevens, Gareth Publishing LLLP.

Llimós, Anna. Space Adventure Crafts. 2010. (Fun Adventure Crafts Ser.). (Illus.). 32p. (J). pap. 7.95 *(978-0-7660-3733-5(9)*, Enslow Elementary) Enslow Pubs., Inc.

Llimós, Anna & Library Association Staff. Space Adventure Crafts. 2010. (Fun Adventure Crafts Ser.). (Illus.). 32p. (J). 23.94 *(978-0-7660-3732-8(0)*, Enslow Elementary) Enslow Pubs., Inc.

Loewen, Nancy. Amazing Science - Planets, 9 vols., Set. Yesh, Jeff, illus. Incl. Farthest from the Sun: The Planet Neptune. lib. bdg. 26.65 *(978-1-4048-3955-7(0)*, 1278900); Nearest to the Sun: The Planet Mercury. lib. bdg. 26.65 *(978-1-4048-3954-0(2)*, 1278902); Our Home Planet: Earth. lib. bdg. 26.65 *(978-1-4048-3951-9(8)*, 1278903); Seeing Red: The Planet Mars. lib. bdg. 26.65 *(978-1-4048-3953-3(4)*, 1278905); (gr. k-4). (Amazing Science: Planets Ser.). (ENG., Illus.). 24p. 2008. Set lib. bdg. 106.60 *(978-1-4048-4360-8(4))* Picture Window Bks.

London, Jude. Powering Our Planet. 2013. (Rosen Readers Ser.). (ENG.). 24p. (J). (gr. 2-3). pap. 8.25 *(978-1-4777-2286-2(6))*; pap. 49.50 *(978-1-4777-2287-9(4))* Rosen Publishing Group, Inc., The. (Rosen Classroom).

The Magic School Bus: Lost in the Solar System. 2011. (J). audio compact disk 9.99 *(978-0-545-22880-0(8))* Scholastic, Inc.

Magic Wagon Staff & ABDO Publishing Company Staff. The Planets, 1 vol. 2011. (Planets Ser.). (ENG., Illus.). 32p. 228.00 *(978-1-61641-676-8(9)*, Looking Glass Library) Magic Wagon.

Mapua, Jeff. What Is a Planet? 2014. (Let's Find Out! Ser.). 32p. (J). (gr. 3-6). 23.45 *(978-1-62275-456-4(5))*; pap. 77.40 *(978-1-62275-459-5(X))*; pap. 12.90 *(978-1-62275-458-8(1))* Rosen Publishing Group, Inc., The.

Marsh, Laura & Carney, Elizabeth. National Geographic Readers: Planets. 2012. (Readers Ser.). (ENG., Illus.). 32p. (J). (gr. k-3). lib. bdg. 13.90 *(978-1-4263-1037-9(4)*, National Geographic Children's Bks.) National Geographic Society.

—Planets. 2012. (Readers Ser.). (ENG., Illus.). 32p. (J). (gr. k-3). pap. 3.99 *(978-1-4263-1036-2(6)*, National Geographic Children's Bks.) National Geographic Society.

Martin, Justin McCory. Planets. 2010. (Illus.). 16p. (J). pap. *(978-0-545-13738-6(1))* Scholastic, Inc.

Mason Crest. Giant Planets, Vol. 7. 2016. (Solar System Ser.: Vol. 7). (ENG., Illus.). 48p. (J). (gr. 5-8). 20.95 *(978-1-4222-3551-5(3))* Mason Crest.

—Near Planets, Vol. 7. 2016. (Solar System Ser.: Vol. 7). (ENG.). 48p. (J). (gr. 5-8). 20.95 *(978-1-4222-3552-2(1))* Mason Crest.

Massey, Steve. Space, Stars & Planets. 2009. (Young Reed Ser.). (ENG.). 64p. (J). 14.95 *(978-1-921073-06-9(3))* New Holland Pubs. Pty, Ltd. AUS. Dist: Tuttle Publishing.

Mazurkiewicz, Jessica, et al. Skyscapes. 2012. (Adult Coloring Ser.). (ENG.). 32p. (J). (gr. 3). pap. 5.99 *(978-0-486-48834-9(9))* Dover Pubns., Inc.

McGranaghan, John. Conoce Los Planetas, 1 vol. Klein, Laurie Allen, illus. 2011. (SPA.). 32p. (J). (gr. k-5). pap. 9.95 *(978-1-62855-411-3(8))* Arbordale Publishing.

—Meet the Planets, 1 vol. Klein, Laurie Allen, illus. 2011. (ENG.). 32p. (J). (gr. k-5). 16.95 *(978-1-60718-123-1(1))*; pap. 9.95 *(978-1-60718-869-8(4))* Arbordale Publishing.

Meachen Rau, Dana & Picture Window Books Staff. Giran en el Espacio: Un Libro Sobre Los Planetas. Robledo, Sol, tr. from ENG. Shea, Denise, illus. 2007. (Ciencia Asombrosa: Exploremos el Espacio Ser.). (SPA.). 24p. (gr. k-4). 26.65 *(978-1-4048-3231-2(9))* Picture Window Bks.

Mi Planeta, 6 Packs. (Chiquilibros Ser.). (SPA.). (gr. k-1). 23.00 *(978-0-7635-8620-1(X))* Rigby Education.

Miller, Ron. Seven Wonders Beyond the Solar System. 2011. (Seven Wonders Ser.). (ENG., Illus.). 80p. (gr. 5-8). 33.26 *(978-0-7613-5454-3(9))* Lerner Publishing Group.

—Seven Wonders of the Gas Giants & Their Moons. 2011. (Seven Wonders Ser.). (ENG.). 80p. (gr. 5-8). lib. bdg. 33.26 *(978-0-7613-5449-9(2))* Lerner Publishing Group.

—Seven Wonders of the Rocky Planets & Their Moons. 2011. (Seven Wonders Ser.). (ENG.). 80p. (gr. 5-8). lib. bdg. 33.26 *(978-0-7613-5448-2(4))* Lerner Publishing Group.

—Uranus & Neptune. 2003. (Worlds Beyond Ser.). (Illus.). 80p. (gr. 7-18). lib. bdg. 27.93 *(978-0-7613-2357-0(0)*, Twenty-First Century Bks.) Lerner Publishing Group.

Mitton, Jacqueline. The Planet Gods: Myths & Facts about the Solar System. Balit, Christina, illus. 2008. (ENG.). 32p. (J). (gr. 1-4). 7.95 *(978-1-4263-0448-4(X))*; 25.90 *(978-1-4263-0449-1(8))* National Geographic Society. (National Geographic Children's Bks.).

Moore Niver, Heather. 20 Fun Facts about Rocky Planets. 2014. (Fun Fact File: Space! Ser.). 32p. (J). (gr. 2-5). 25.25 *(978-1-4824-1008-2(7))*; pap. 10.50 *(978-1-4824-1009-9(5))* Stevens, Gareth Publishing LLLP.

Moving & Shaking: Individual Title Six-Packs. (Bookweb Ser.). 32p. (gr. 4-18). 34.00 *(978-0-7635-3743-2(8))* Rigby Education.

Nicolson, Cynthia. Discover the Planets. Slavin, Bill, illus. 2005. 32p. (J). lib. bdg. 15.38 *(978-1-4242-1194-4(8))* Fitzgerald Bks.

Nussbaum, Ben. All about Planets: Stitch Explores the Solar System. 2005. (All about Ser.). (ENG., Illus.). 40p. (J). (gr. -1-3). 12.99 *(978-1-59069-452-7(X)*, 1A703) Studio Mouse LLC.

Olien, Rebecca. Exploring the Planets in Our Solar System. (Objects in the Sky Ser.). 24p. (gr. 3-3). 2009. 42.50 *(978-1-60851-141-9(3))* 2007. (Illus.). (J). lib. bdg. 22.60 *(978-1-4042-3467-3(5))* Rosen Publishing Group, Inc., The. (PowerKids Pr.).

Our Solar System. (Jump Ser.). 36p. (J). (gr. 2-7). pap. *(978-1-882210-23-7(9))* Action Publishing, Inc.

Owen, Ruth. Objects in Space, 1 vol. 2015. (Objects in Space Ser.). (ENG.). 32p. (J). pap. 60.00 *(978-1-4994-0318-3(6)*, PowerKids Pr.) Rosen Publishing Group, Inc., The.

Oxlade, Chris. Space Watch: The Sun. 2010. (Eye on Space Ser.). 24p. (J). pap. 8.25 *(978-1-61532-548-1(4)*, PowerKids Pr.); (ENG.). lib. bdg. 22.60 *(978-1-61532-542-9(5))* Rosen Publishing Group, Inc., The.

Paris, Stephanie. Siglo Xxi: Misterios Del Espacio Sideral. 2016. (TIME for Kids en Español - Level 5 Ser.). (SPA.). 64p. (gr. 5-5). lib. bdg. 31.99 *(978-1-5157-2937-2(0))* Time for Kids Inc AUS. Dist: Capstone Pub.

Parker, Steve. Probes to the Planets. West, David, illus. 2015. (Story of Space Ser.). (ENG.). 32p. (J). (gr. 3-6). 31.35 *(978-1-62588-077-2(4))* Black Rabbit Bks.

Parr, Todd. Todd Parr Create Your Own Planet. 2010. (ENG.). 240p. (J). (gr. -1-4). 14.99 *(978-0-8118-7146-4(0))* Chronicle Bks. LLC.

Peters, Elisa. The Planets. 2012. (PowerKids Readers: the Universe Ser.). (ENG., Illus.). 24p. (J). (gr. k-2). pap. 8.25 *(978-1-4488-7468-2(8))*; lib. bdg. 22.60 *(978-1-4488-7389-0(4))* Rosen Publishing Group, Inc., The. (PowerKids Pr.).

—The Planets: Los Planetas. 2012. (PowerKids Readers: the Universe / el universo Ser.). (SPA & ENG., Illus.). 24p. (J). (gr. k-2). lib. bdg. 22.60 *(978-1-4488-7825-3(X)*, PowerKids Pr.) Rosen Publishing Group, Inc., The.

Petrikowski, Nicki Peter. Critical Perspectives on the Viability of Human Life on Other Planets. 2016. (Analyzing the Issues Ser.). 208p. (J). (gr. 8-8). 47.93 *(978-0-7660-7674-7(1))* Enslow Pubs., Inc.

Planetary Exploration. 2016. (Planetary Exploration Ser.). 00032p. (J). (gr. 2-3). 220.05 *(978-1-5081-0288-5(0)*, Britannica Educational Publishing) Rosen Publishing Group, Inc., The.

Los Planetas, 6 vols., Vol. 2. (Explorers. Exploradores Nonfiction Sets Ser.). (SPA.). 32p. (gr. 3-6). 44.95 *(978-0-7699-0642-3(7))* Shortland Pubns. (U. S. A.) Inc.

Planetas y Satelites. (SPA.). (J). 10.00 *(978-84-342-1468-2(7))* Parramon Ediciones S.A. ESP. Dist: Distribuidora Norma, Inc.

Planets: Level L, 6 vols. (Wonder Worldtm Ser.). 16p. 34.95 *(978-0-7802-2020-1(X))* Wright Group/McGraw-Hill.

The Planets: Level P, 6 vols., Vol. 2. (Explorers Ser.). 32p. (gr. 3-6). 44.95 *(978-0-7699-0606-5(0))* Shortland Pubns. (U. S. A.) Inc.

Portman, Michael. Could We Live on Other Planets? 2013. 32p. (J). (gr. 2-5). 25.25 *(978-1-4339-9213-1(2))*; pap. 10.50 *(978-1-4339-9214-8(0))*; pap. 63.00 *(978-1-4339-9215-5(9))* Stevens, Gareth Publishing LLLP.

—Why Isn't Pluto a Planet? 2013. (Space Mysteries Ser.). (Illus.). 32p. (J). (gr. 2-5). 25.25 *(978-1-4339-8282-8(X))*; pap. 10.50 *(978-1-4339-8283-5(8))* Stevens, Gareth Publishing LLLP. (Gareth Stevens Learning Library).

PRESS, Celebration. The Case of the Missing Planet. 2003. (ENG.). (J). (gr. 2-5). pap., stu. ed. 34.95 *(978-0-673-62845-9(0)*, Celebration Pr.) Pearson Schl.

Price, Jane. Underworld: Exploring the Secret World Beneath Your Feet, 0 vols. Hancock, James Gulliver, illus. 2014. (ENG.). 96p. (J). (gr. 3-7). 18.95 *(978-1-894786-89-8(0))* Kids Can Pr., Ltd. CAN. Dist: Hachette Bk. Group.

Prinja, Raman. In Focus: Space. 2017. (In Focus Ser.). (ENG.). 64p. (J). 17.99 *(978-0-7534-7349-8(6)*, 9780753473498, Kingfisher) Roaring Brook Pr.

Pulliam, Christine & Daniels, Patricia. Space Encyclopedia: A Tour of Our Solar System & Beyond. Aguilar, David A., illus. 2013. 191p. (J). *(978-1-4263-1629-6(1))* National Geographic Society.

Rabe, Tish. Planet Name Game. 2015. (Step into Reading Level 2 Ser.). lib. bdg. 13.55 *(978-0-606-37271-8(7))* Turtleback Bks.

Red Bird Press Staff, creator. Planets. 2005. (Glow in the Dark Ser.). (Illus.). 19p. (J). (gr. -1 — 1). *(978-1-902626-73-4(7))* Red Bird Publishing.

Reilly, Carmel. The Planets. 2011. (Sky Watching Ser.). 32p. (gr. 2-4). 28.50 *(978-1-60870-582-5(X))* Marshall Cavendish Corp.

Reyes, Sonja. How Do Planets Move? What Will Happen? 2017. (Computer Science for the Real World Ser.). 16p. (gr. 7-8). pap. 7.95 ***(978-1-5383-5234-2(6)***, Rosen Classroom) Rosen Publishing Group, Inc., The.

Ridpath, Ian. Facts on File Stars & Planets Atlas: New Edition. 3rd rev. ed. 2005. (Facts on File Atlas Ser.). 96p. (gr. 4-6). 18.95 *(978-0-8160-6294-2(3)*, Checkmark Bks.) Facts On File, Inc.

Riggs, Kate. Across the Universe: Planets. 2015. (Across the Universe Ser.). (ENG.). 24p. (J). (gr. 1-3). pap. 9.99 *(978-1-62832-084-8(2)*, Creative Paperbacks) Creative Co., The.

—Planets. 2015. (J). *(978-1-60818-484-2(6)*, Creative Education) Creative Co., The.

Ring, Susan & Roumanis, Alexis. Dwarf Planets. 2016. (Illus.). 24p. (J). *(978-1-5105-0968-9(2))* SmartBook Media, Inc.

Rosen Publishing Staff. Objects in Space, 1 vol. 2015. (Objects in Space Ser.). (ENG.). 32p. (J). 157.50 *(978-1-4777-5728-4(7)*, PowerKids Pr.) Rosen Publishing Group, Inc., The.

Roumanis, Alexis. Dwarf Planets. 2015. (J). *(978-1-4896-3312-5(X))* Weigl Pubs., Inc.

Royal Observatory Greenwich Staff & Collins Maps Staff. Stars & Planets. 2013. (ENG., Illus.). 32p. (YA). (gr. 4-10). 31.99 *(978-0-00-753226-1(1))* HarperCollins Pubs. Ltd. GBR. Dist: Independent Pubs. Group.

Roza, Greg. Pluto: The Dwarf Planet. 2010. (Our Solar System Ser.). 24p. (J). (gr. k-3). (ENG.). pap. 8.15 *(978-1-4339-3837-5(5))*; (Illus.). lib. bdg. 22.60 *(978-1-4339-3836-8(7))* Stevens, Gareth Publishing LLLP.

Rustad, Martha E. H. Los Planetas. 2012. (En el Espacio/Out in Space Ser.).Tr. of Planets. (MUL.). 24p. (gr. k-1). pap. 35.70 *(978-1-4296-8555-9(7))*; pap. 5.95 *(978-1-4296-8554-2(9))* Capstone Press of Coughlan Cos.

—Planets. 2016. (Space Ser.). (ENG., Illus.). 24p. (gr. k-1). lib. bdg. 21.99 *(978-1-4914-8322-0(9)*, Pebble Bks.) Capstone Press of Coughlan Cos.

—The Planets. rev. ed. 2008. (Out in Space Ser.). (ENG., Illus.). 24p. (gr. k-1). pap. 6.29 *(978-1-4296-2814-3(6)*, 1284182, Pebble Bks.) Capstone Press of Coughlan Cos.

—The Planets [Scholastic]. 2009. (Out in Space Ser.). 24p. (gr. k-1). pap. 2.50 *(978-1-4296-4050-3(2)*, Pebble Bks.) Capstone Press of Coughlan Cos.

Ryback, Carol. The Planets. 2006. (In the Sky Ser.). (Illus.). 24p. (gr. 1-4). pap. 8.15 *(978-0-8368-6349-9(6))*; lib. bdg. 22.00 *(978-0-8368-6344-4(5))* Stevens, Gareth Publishing LLLP. (Weekly Reader Leveled Readers).

Salas, Laura Purdie. Eight Great Planets! A Song about the Planets, 1 vol. De Giorgi, Sergio, illus. 2010. (Science Songs Ser.). (ENG.). 24p. (gr. 1-3). lib. bdg. 26.65 *(978-1-4048-5765-0(6))* Picture Window Bks.

P
Q
R

Scholastic, Inc. Staff. Planets: A LEGO(r) Adventure in the Real World. 2016. (LEGO Nonfiction Ser.). (ENG., Illus.). 64p. (J). (gr. 1-3). pap. 8.99 *(978-0-545-94765-7(0))* Scholastic, Inc.

Sian revision Planets&stars. 2004. (J). *(978-1-59242-057-5(5))* Delta Education, LLC.

Simon, Seymour. Planets. 2006. (Illus.). 24p. (J). *(978-0-439-77702-5(X))* Scholastic, Inc.

Solway, Andrew. Jupiter & the Outer Planets, 1 vol. 2012. (Astronaut Travel Guides). (ENG.). 48p. (gr. 3-6). lib. bdg. 32.65 *(978-1-4109-4569-3(3),* NA-r) Heinemann-Raintree.

Space!, 12 vols., Set. Incl. Asteroids, Meteors, & Comets. Sherman, Josepha. lib. bdg. 32.79 *(978-0-7614-4252-3(9));* Dwarf Planet Pluto. Lew, Kristi. lib. bdg. 32.79 *(978-0-7614-4243-1(X));* Earth & the Moon. Hicks, Terry Allan. lib. bdg. 32.79 *(978-0-7614-4254-7(5));* Jupiter. Capaccio, George. lib. bdg. 32.79 *(978-0-7614-4244-8(8));* Mars. Capaccio, George. lib. bdg. 32.79 *(978-0-7614-4247-9(2));* Mercury. Colligan, L. H. lib. bdg. 32.79 *(978-0-7614-4239-4(1));* Neptune. Sherman, Josepha. lib. bdg. 32.79 *(978-0-7614-4246-2(4));* Saturn. Hicks, Terry Allan. lib. bdg. 32.79 *(978-0-7614-4249-3(9));* Stars. Mack, Gail. lib. bdg. 32.79 *(978-0-7614-4250-9(2));* Sun. Capaccio, George. lib. bdg. 32.79 *(978-0-7614-4242-4(1));* Uranus. Sherman, Josepha. lib. bdg. 32.79 *(978-0-7614-4248-6(0));* Venus. Bjorklund, Ruth. lib. bdg. 32.79 *(978-0-7614-4251-6(0));* 64p. (gr. 5-18). (Space! Ser.). 2009. Set lib. bdg. 393.48 o.p. *(978-0-7614-4237-0(5))* Marshall Cavendish Corp.

Sparrow, Giles. Earth & the Inner Planets. 2011. (Exploring Space: Space Travel Guides). 32p. (gr. 3-6). 31.35 *(978-1-59920-663-9(3))* Black Rabbit Bks.

—The Outer Planets. 2011. (Exploring Space: Space Travel Guides). 32p. (gr. 3-6). lib. bdg. 31.35 *(978-1-59920-664-6(1))* Black Rabbit Bks.

—Planets & Moons. 2006. (Secrets of the Universe Ser.). (Illus.). 48p. (gr. 6-12). pap. 14.05 *(978-0-8368-7285-9(1));* lib. bdg. 31.00 *(978-0-8368-7278-1(9))* Stevens, Gareth Publishing LLLP. (Gareth Stevens Secondary Library).

Storad, Conrad J. Our Sun Brings Life. 2011. (ENG., Illus.). 24p. (gr. k-1). pap. 8.95 *(978-1-61741-925-6(7))* Rourke Educational Media.

Stott, Carole. Mission: Space: Explore the Galaxy. 2016. (Illus.). 128p. (J). *(978-1-4654-5376-1(8))* Dorling Kindersley Publishing, Inc.

Sutter, Debra, et al. Moons of Jupiter. Klofkorn, Lisa, illus. Hoyt, Richard & Bergman Publishing Co. Staff, photos by. 2003. (Great Explorations in Math & Science Ser.). 116p. (J). pap., tchr. ed. 16.00 *(978-0-924886-87-4(0),* GEMS) Univ. of California, Berkeley, Lawrence Hall of Science.

Time for Kids Editors. Time for Kids - Planets! 2005. (Time for Kids Ser.). (ENG., Illus.). 32p. (J). 14.99 *(978-0-06-078203-0(X))* HarperCollins Pubs.

Watt, E. Planeta Tierra: Ciencia y Experimentos. (SPA.). (J). pap. *(978-950-724-135-2(3))* Lumen.

Wells, Robert E. What's So Special about Planet Earth? 2012. (J). *(978-1-61913-154-5(4))* Weigl Pubs., Inc.

Whiting, Sue. Ancient Orbiters: A Guide to the Planets. 2006. (Science Chapters Ser.). (ENG., Illus.). 48p. (J). (gr. 1-4). lib. bdg. 17.90 *(978-0-7922-5945-9(9),* National Geographic Children's Bks.) National Geographic Society.

Wilkins, Mary-Jane. The Inner Planets. 2017. (Fast Track: Our Solar System Ser.). (Illus.). 24p. (gr. k-3). 28.50 ***(978-1-78121-366-7(6))*** Brown Bear Bks.

—The Outer Planets. 2017. (Fast Track: Our Solar System Ser.). (Illus.). 24p. (gr. k-3). 28.50 ***(978-1-78121-367-4(4))*** Brown Bear Bks.

Willett, Edward. Space Q&a. 2014. (Science Discovery Ser.). (ENG., Illus.). 48p. (J). (gr. 4-7). lib. bdg. 28.55 *(978-1-4896-0692-1(0),* AV2 by Weigl) Weigl Pubs., Inc.

World Book, Inc Staff, contrib. by. Alien Planets. 2010. (J). *(978-0-7166-9551-6(0))* World Bk., Inc.

Yakola, Carrie C. Clayton & the Planets. 2009. 32p. pap. 15.99 *(978-1-4343-5275-0(7))* AuthorHouse.

Yoon, Salina. Space Walk. 2012. (Lift-The-Flap Adventures Ser.). (ENG., Illus.). 12p. (J). (gr. -1-2). bds. 8.95 *(978-1-4027-8524-5(0))* Sterling Publishing Co., Inc.

Young-Brown, Fiona. The Universe to Scale: Similarities & Differences in Objects in Our Solar System. 2016. (Space Systems Ser.). 112p. (YA). 42.79 *(978-1-5026-2289-1(0))* Cavendish Square Publishing.

PLANETS, LIFE ON OTHER

see Life on Other Planets

PLANNED PARENTHOOD

see Birth Control

PLANNING, CITY

see City Planning

PLANNING, ECONOMIC

see Economic Policy; Social Policy

see names of countries, states, etc. with the subdivision Economic Policy, e.g. United States—Economic Policy

PLANNING, NATIONAL

see Economic Policy; Social Policy

see names of countries with the subdivision Economic Policy, Social Policy; e.g. United States—Economic Policy; United States—Social policy

PLANS

see Architectural Drawing; Geometrical Drawing; Map Drawing; Maps; Mechanical Drawing

PLANT ANATOMY

Aloian, Molly. Plants Are Alive! 2012. (ENG., Illus.). 24p. (J). *(978-0-7787-4219-7(9));* pap. *(978-0-7787-4224-1(5))* Crabtree Publishing Co.

—What Are Bulbs & Roots? 2012. (ENG., Illus.). 24p. (J). *(978-0-7787-4220-3(2));* pap. *(978-0-7787-4225-8(3))* Crabtree Publishing Co.

—What Are Seeds? 2012. (ENG., Illus.). 24p. (J). *(978-0-7787-4221-0(0));* pap. *(978-0-7787-4226-5(1))* Crabtree Publishing Co.

—What Are Stems? 2012. (ENG., Illus.). 24p. (J). *(978-0-7787-4222-7(9));* pap. *(978-0-7787-4227-2(X))* Crabtree Publishing Co.

Bodach, Vijaya K. Roots [Scholastic]. 2010. (Plant Parts Ser.). 24p. pap. 0.52 *(978-1-4296-5059-5(1),* Pebble Plus) Capstone Press of Coughlan Cos.

Braun, Eric. Plant Parts Smarts: Science Adventures with Charlie the Origami Bee, 1 vol. Christoph, Jamey, illus. 2013. (Origami Science Adventures Ser.). (ENG.). 24p. (gr. 3-4). pap. 6.95 *(978-1-4048-8072-6(0));* lib. bdg. 27.32 *(978-1-4048-7970-6(6))* Picture Window Bks.

Dickmann, Nancy. Plant Structures. 2016. (Earth Figured Out Ser.). (ENG., Illus.). 32p. (J). (gr. 4-4). pap. 10.58 *(978-1-5026-0874-1(X))* Cavendish Square Publishing.

Griffin, Maeve. Plant Parts: Roots, Stems, & Leaves. 2009. (Real Life Readers Ser.). 16p. (gr. 2-3). pap. 7.05 *(978-1-4358-0037-3(0),* Rosen Classroom) Rosen Publishing Group, Inc., The.

Hansen, Grace. Plant Anatomy. 2016. (Plant Anatomy Ser.: 6). (ENG.). 24p. (J). (gr. k-2). lib. bdg. 171.00 *(978-1-68080-134-7(1))* ABDO Publishing Co.

Hill, Christina. Inside a Plant, 1 vol. rev. ed. 2014. (Science Readers: Content & Literacy Ser.). (ENG., Illus.). 24p. (gr. 1-1). pap. 8.99 *(978-1-4807-4560-5(X))* Teacher Created Materials, Inc.

Hollar, Sherman. A Closer Look at Plant Classifications, Parts, & Uses. 2011. (J). lib. bdg. 31.70 *(978-1-61530-529-2(7))* Rosen Publishing Group, Inc., The.

Johnson, Rebecca L. Powerful Plant Cells. 2008. pap. 52.95 *(978-0-8225-9383-6(1))* Lerner Publishing Group.

—Powerful Plant Cells. Desrocher, Jack & Fairman, Jennifer, illus. 2007. (Microquests Ser.). (ENG.). 48p. (gr. 3-5). lib. bdg. 29.27 *(978-0-8225-7141-4(2),* Millbrook Pr.) Lerner Publishing Group.

Konicek-Moran, Richard. From Flower to Fruit. Konicek-Moran, Kathleen, illus. 2017. (ENG.). 30p. (J). (gr. k-2). pap. 11.95 *(978-1-941316-34-4(4))* National Science Teachers Assn.

LernerClassroom Editors. First Step Nonfiction-Parts of Plants. 2009. pap., tchr. ed. 7.95 *(978-0-8225-1798-6(1))* Lerner Publishing Group.

Midthun, Joseph. Plant Structure & Classification. 2014. (Illus.). 32p. (J). *(978-0-7166-2823-1(6))* World Bk., Inc.

Plant Parts [Scholastic]. 2010. (Plant Parts Ser.). pap. 2.08 *(978-1-4296-5061-8(3),* Pebble Plus) Capstone Press of Coughlan Cos.

Rake, Jody Sullivan. Roots, Bulbs, & Bacteria: Growths of the Underground. 2015. (Underground Safari Ser.). (ENG., Illus.). 24p. (gr. 1-2). lib. bdg. 25.32 *(978-1-4914-5062-8(2))* Capstone Press of Coughlan Cos.

Ripley, Mark. Picking Fruit. 2017. (Plants in My World Ser.). 24p. (gr. 4-6). pap. 8.25 ***(978-1-5081-6163-9(1),*** PowerKids Pr.) Rosen Publishing Group, Inc., The.

Rissman, Rebecca. Plants. 2013. (Real Size Science Ser.). (ENG.). 24p. (gr. -1-1). 22.65 *(978-1-4329-7880-8(2));* pap. 6.95 *(978-1-4329-7887-7(X))* Heinemann-Raintree. (Acorn).

Senker, Cath. Plant Reproduction: How Do You Grow a Giant Pumpkin?, 1 vol. 2014. (Show Me Science Ser.). (ENG.). 32p. (gr. 3-5). lib. bdg. 30.65 *(978-1-4329-8749-7(6),* Raintree Perspectives) Heinemann-Raintree.

Spilsbury, Louise. What Is the Structure of a Plant?, 1 vol., 1. 2014. (Let's Find Out! Ser.). (ENG.). 32p. (gr. 3-6). 23.45 *(978-1-62275-251-5(1))* Rosen Publishing Group, Inc., The.

Spilsbury, Louise & Spilsbury, Richard. Why Do Plants Have Flowers? 2016. (World of Plants Ser.). (ENG.). 32p. pap. 8.29 *(978-1-4846-3824-8(7),* Heinemann First Library) Heinemann-Raintree.

Stephens, Nicholas. Plant Cells & Tissues. Hopkins, William G., ed. 2006. (Green World Ser.). (Illus.). 136p. (gr. 6-12). lib. bdg. 37.50 *(978-0-7910-8560-8(0))* Facts On File, Inc.

Sterling, Kristin. Exploring Flowers. 2011. (First Step Nonfiction / Let's Look at Plants Ser.). pap. 33.92 *(978-0-7613-8614-8(9));* (ENG.). 24p. pap. 6.95 *(978-0-7613-7832-7(4));* (ENG.). 24p. lib. bdg. 23.93 *(978-0-7613-5779-7(3))* Lerner Publishing Group.

—Exploring Leaves. 2011. (First Step Nonfiction / Let's Look at Plants Ser.). pap. 33.92 *(978-0-7613-8615-5(7));* lib. bdg. 21.27 *(978-0-7613-5780-3(7));* (ENG.). 24p. pap. 6.95 *(978-0-7613-7833-4(2))* Lerner Publishing Group.

—Exploring Roots. 2011. (First Step Nonfiction / Let's Look at Plants Ser.). pap. 33.92 *(978-0-7613-8616-2(5));* (Illus.). 23p. lib. bdg. 21.27 *(978-0-7613-5781-0(5));* (ENG.). 24p. pap. 6.95 *(978-0-7613-7834-1(0))* Lerner Publishing Group.

—Exploring Seeds. 2011. (First Step Nonfiction / Let's Look at Plants Ser.). pap. 33.92 *(978-0-7613-8617-9(3));* lib. bdg. 21.27 *(978-0-7613-5782-7(3));* (ENG.). 24p. pap. 6.95 *(978-0-7613-7835-8(9))* Lerner Publishing Group.

—Exploring Stems. 2011. (First Step Nonfiction / Let's Look at Plants Ser.). pap. 33.92 *(978-0-7613-8618-6(1));* (ENG.). 24p. pap. 6.95 *(978-0-7613-7836-5(7));* (ENG.). 24p. lib. bdg. 23.93 *(978-0-7613-5783-4(1))* Lerner Publishing Group.

Thrope, Claire. All about Flowers. (All about Plants Ser.). (ENG.). 24p. (gr. -1-1). 2016. pap. 5.99 *(978-1-4846-3846-0(8))* 2014. 22.65 *(978-1-4846-0506-6(3))* Heinemann-Raintree. (Acorn).

—All about Leaves. (All about Plants Ser.). (ENG.). 24p. (gr. -1-1). 2016. pap. 5.99 *(978-1-4846-3847-7(6))* 2014. 22.65 *(978-1-4846-0507-3(1))* Heinemann-Raintree. (Acorn).

—All about Roots. (All about Plants Ser.). (ENG.). 24p. (gr. -1-1). 2016. pap. 5.99 *(978-1-4846-3848-4(4))* 2014. 22.65 *(978-1-4846-0508-0(X))* Heinemann-Raintree. (Acorn).

—All about Seeds. (All about Plants Ser.). (ENG.). 24p. (gr. -1-1). 2016. pap. 5.99 *(978-1-4846-3849-1(2))* 2014. 22.65 *(978-1-4846-0509-7(8))* Heinemann-Raintree. (Acorn).

—All about Stems. (All about Plants Ser.). (ENG.). 24p. (gr. -1-1). 2016. pap. 5.99 *(978-1-4846-3850-7(6))* 2014. 22.65 *(978-1-4846-0510-3(1))* Heinemann-Raintree. (Acorn).

Waldron, Melanie. Plant Parts, 1 vol. 2014. (Plant Parts Ser.). (ENG.). 32p. (gr. 2-4). lib. bdg. 153.25 *(978-1-4109-5425-1(0),* Raintree Perspectives) Heinemann-Raintree.

—Roots, 1 vol. 2014. (Plant Parts Ser.). (ENG., Illus.). 32p. (gr. 2-4). pap. 8.95 *(978-1-4109-6281-2(4));* lib. bdg. 30.65 *(978-1-4109-5422-0(6))* Heinemann-Raintree. (Raintree Perspectives).

—Seeds & Fruits, 1 vol. 2014. (Plant Parts Ser.). (ENG.). 32p. (gr. 2-4). lib. bdg. 30.65 *(978-1-4109-5423-7(4),* Raintree Perspectives) Heinemann-Raintree.

—Stems & Trunks, 1 vol. 2014. (Plant Parts Ser.). (ENG.). 32p. (gr. 2-4). lib. bdg. 30.65 *(978-1-4109-5424-4(2),* Raintree Perspectives) Heinemann-Raintree.

Weiss, Ellen. From Bulb to Daffodil. 2007. (Scholastic News Nonfiction Readers Ser.). (ENG., Illus.). 24p. (J). (gr. 1-2). 22.00 *(978-0-531-18534-6(6));* pap. 6.95 *(978-0-531-18787-6(X))* Scholastic Library Publishing.

PLANT BREEDING

see also Plant Propagation

Boothroyd, Jennifer. Animal Pollinators. 2015. (First Step Nonfiction - Pollination Ser.). (ENG., Illus.). 24p. (gr. k-2). lib. bdg. 23.99 *(978-1-4677-5741-6(1),* Lerner Pubns.) Lerner Publishing Group.

—Insect Pollinators. 2015. (First Step Nonfiction - Pollination Ser.). (ENG., Illus.). 24p. (gr. k-2). lib. bdg. 23.99 *(978-1-4677-5738-6(1),* Lerner Pubns.) Lerner Publishing Group.

Ransom, Candice. Cross-Pollination. 2015. (First Step Nonfiction - Pollination Ser.). (ENG., Illus.). 24p. (gr. k-2). lib. bdg. 23.99 *(978-1-4677-5737-9(3),* Lerner Pubns.) Lerner Publishing Group.

PLANT DISEASES

Halfmann, Janet. Plant Tricksters. 2003. (Watts Library). (Illus.). 64p. (J). 25.50 *(978-0-531-12278-5(6),* Watts, Franklin) Scholastic Library Publishing.

Lay, Richard & Zamnnaal, Laura Nienhaus. A Green Kid's Guide to Preventing Plant Diseases, 1 vol. 2013. (Green Kid's Guide to Gardening! Ser.). (ENG.). 24p. (J). (gr. -1-4). 27.07 *(978-1-61641-946-2(6))* Magic Wagon.

Stewart, Melissa & Young, Allen M. No Monkeys, No Chocolate. Wong, Nicole, illus. 2013. (ENG.). 32p. (J). (gr. k-3). 16.95 *(978-1-58089-287-2(6))* Charlesbridge Publishing, Inc.

Wright, Russell G. Blight! Investigations in Plant Diseases. (Event-Based Science Ser.). 32p. (gr. 5-9). pap., tchr.'s training gde. ed. 25.95 incl. VHS *(978-0-7690-0022-0(3))* Seymour, Dale Pubns.

PLANT DISTRIBUTION

Wade, Mary Dodson. Plants Live Everywhere! 2009. (I Like Plants! Ser.). (Illus.). 24p. (J). (gr. k-3). lib. bdg. 22.60 *(978-0-7660-3155-5(1));* (gr. 1-3). pap. 7.95 *(978-0-7660-3615-4(4),* Enslow Elementary) Enslow Pubs., Inc.

PLANT ECOLOGY

Anderson, Michael. A Closer Look at Plant Reproduction, Growth, & Ecology. 2011. (J). lib. bdg. 31.70 *(978-1-61530-530-8(0))* Rosen Publishing Group, Inc., The.

Belback, Elsie. Masters of Disguise: Animal Mimicry. 2014. (ENG.). 24p. (gr. k-3). 28.50 *(978-1-62717-636-1(5))* Rourke Educational Media.

Bodden, Valerie. Critical Plant Life. 2010. (Earth Issues Ser.). 48p. (YA). (gr. 5-18). 23.95 *(978-1-58341-984-7(5),* Creative Education) Creative Co., The.

Boothroyd, Jennifer. Plants & the Environment. 2008. pap. 34.95 *(978-0-8225-9358-4(0));* (ENG., Illus.). 24p. lib. bdg. 23.93 *(978-0-8225-8603-6(7),* Lerner Pubns.) Lerner Publishing Group.

Cohn, Scotti. Animal Partners, 1 vol. Bersani, Shennen, illus. 2015. (ENG.). 32p. (J). (gr. 2-5). 17.95 *(978-1-62855-448-9(7))* Arbordale Publishing.

Exploring the Native Plant World Grades 3-4: Survival. 2004. 74p. (J). pap. 14.95 *(978-1-57168-835-4(8),* Eakin Pr.) Eakin Pr.

Gibson, J. Phil & Gibson, Terri R. Plant Ecology. 2006. (Green World Ser.). (Illus.). 189p. (gr. 6-12). lib. bdg. 37.50 *(978-0-7910-8566-0(X))* Facts On File, Inc.

Gould, Margee. Prickly Plants. 2012. (Strangest Plants on Earth Ser.). (Illus.). 24p. (J). (gr. 2-5). lib. bdg. 22.60 *(978-1-4488-4991-8(8))* Rosen Publishing Group, Inc., The.

Hwang, Jay. Amazing Animals: Strange Animal Partnerships: Multiplying Fractions (Grade 4) 2017. (Mathematics Readers Ser.). (Illus.). 32p. (J). (gr. 4-4). pap. 8.99 ***(978-1-4258-5555-0(5))*** Teacher Created Materials, Inc.

Jang, Ki-hwa. Good Friends: Symbiotic Relationships. Cowley, Joy, ed. Oh, Seung-min, illus. 2015. (Science Storybooks Ser.). (ENG.). 32p. (J). (gr. k-3). 26.65 *(978-1-925233-58-2(8))* Lerner Publishing Group.

Jang, Ki-hwa & Kim, In-sook. Good Friends: Symbiotic Relationships. Cowley, Joy, ed. Oh, Seung-min, illus. 2015. (Science Storybooks Ser.). (ENG.). 32p. (gr. k-3). 7.99 *(978-1-925246-72-8(8));* 26.65 *(978-1-925246-20-9(5))* ChoiceMaker Pty. Ltd., The AUS. (Big and SMALL). Dist: Lerner Publishing Group.

Jenkins, Steve & Page, Robin. How to Clean a Hippopotamus: A Look at Unusual Animal Partnerships. 2013. lib. bdg. 18.40 *(978-0-606-31663-7(9),* Turtleback) Turtleback Bks.

Kalman, Bobbie. Hogares de los Seres Vivos. 2008.Tr. of Living Things Need Water. (SPA.). 24p. (J). pap. *(978-0-7787-8687-0(0))* Crabtree Publishing Co.

—Symbiosis: How Different Animals Relate. 2016. (ENG., Illus.). 32p. (J). lib. bdg. *(978-0-7787-2785-9(8))* Crabtree Publishing Co.

Lady Bird Johnson Wildflower Center Staff, Lady Bird Johnson, compiled by. Exploring the Native Plant World Grades 1-2: Changes. 2004. 62p. (J). pap. *(978-1-57168-827-9(7),* Eakin Pr.) Eakin Pr.

—Exploring the Native Plant World Pre-K-K: Patterns & Shapes. 2004. 44p. (J). pap. 14.95 *(978-1-57168-680-0(0),* Eakin Pr.) Eakin Pr.

Lawrence, Ellen. Prickly Plants: Stuck! 2012. (Science Slam: Plant-Ology Ser.). 24p. (J). (gr. -1-3). lib. bdg. 23.93 *(978-1-61772-588-3(9))* Bearport Publishing Co., Inc.

Owen, Ruth. How Do Plants Defend Themselves? 2014. (World of Plants Ser.). 32p. (J). (gr. 2-5). lib. bdg. 26.25 *(978-1-4777-7157-0(3),* PowerKids Pr.) Rosen Publishing Group, Inc., The.

Pascoe, Elaine. The Ecosystem of a Milkweed Patch. 2003. (Library of Small Ecosystems Ser.). (Illus.). 24p. (J). lib. bdg. 25.25 *(978-0-8239-6309-6(8))* Rosen Publishing Group, Inc., The.

Pryor, Kimberley Jane. Mimicry & Relationships. 2009. (Animal Attack & Defense Ser.). 32p. (gr. 3). 28.50 *(978-0-7614-4421-3(1))* Marshall Cavendish Corp.

Rhodes, Mary Jo & Hall, David. Partners in the Sea. Hall, David, photos by. 2006. (Undersea Encounters Ser.). (ENG., Illus.). 48p. (J). (gr. 3-7). per. 6.95 *(978-0-516-25492-0(8),* Children's Pr.) Scholastic Library Publishing.

Russell, Margaret. Exploring the Native Plant World: A Life Science Curriculum, 5th-6th Grade: Adaptations in the Native Plant World. Thompson, Maria, illus. 2004. 63p. (J). (gr. 5-6). per. 14.95 *(978-1-57168-851-4(X),* Eakin Pr.) Eakin Pr.

Rustad, Martha E. H. Ants & Aphids Work Together. 2011. (Animals Working Together Ser.). (ENG.). 24p. (gr. k-1). pap. 41.70 *(978-1-4296-6366-3(9),* Pebble Plus) Capstone Press of Coughlan Cos.

—Clown Fish & Sea Anemones Work Together, 1 vol. (Animals Working Together Ser.). (ENG., 24p. (gr. k-1). 2011. Illus.). pap. 7.29 *(978-1-4296-6198-0(4))* 2011. pap. 41.70 *(978-1-4296-6367-0(7))* 2010. lib. bdg. 26.65 *(978-1-4296-5297-1(7))* Capstone Press of Coughlan Cos. (Pebble Plus).

—Moray Eels & Cleaner Shrimp Work Together. (Animals Working Together Ser.). (ENG.). 24p. (gr. k-1). 2011. pap. 41.70 *(978-1-4296-6368-7(5))* 2010. lib. bdg. 26.65 *(978-1-4296-5299-5(3))* Capstone Press of Coughlan Cos. (Pebble Plus).

—Zebras & Oxpeckers Work Together. 2011. (Animals Working Together Ser.). (ENG.). 24p. (gr. k-1). pap. 41.70 *(978-1-4296-6369-4(3),* Pebble Plus) Capstone Press of Coughlan Cos.

Silverstein, Alvin, et al. Symbiosis. rev. ed. 2007. (Science Concepts, Second Ser.). (Illus.). 96p. (YA). (gr. 5-9). lib. bdg. 31.93 *(978-0-8225-6799-8(7))* Lerner Publishing Group.

Walker, Kate. Plants. 2011. (Investigating Earth Ser.). 32p. (gr. 2). 28.50 *(978-1-60870-559-7(5))* Marshall Cavendish Corp.

Zayarny, Jack. Symbiosis. (Illus.). 24p. (J). 2017. ***(978-1-5105-0944-3(5))*** 2016. *(978-1-5105-0942-9(9))* SmartBook Media, Inc.

PLANT INTRODUCTION

Batten, Mary. Aliens from Earth: When Animals & Plants Invade Other Ecosystems, 1 vol. Doyle, Beverly J., illus. 2008. (ENG.). 32p. (J). (gr. 3-7). pap. 8.95 *(978-1-56145-450-1(8))* Peachtree Pubs.

—Aliens from Earth: When Animals & Plants Invade Other Ecosystems, 1 vol. Doyle, Beverly, illus. 2003. (ENG.). 32p. (J). (gr. 3-7). 15.95 *(978-1-56145-236-1(X))* Peachtree Pubs.

PLANT PHYSIOLOGY

see also Growth (Plants)

Amstutz, Lisa J. Which Seed Is This? 2012. (Nature Starts Ser.). (ENG.). 32p. (gr. 1-2). pap. 47.70 *(978-1-4296-8297-8(3),* Aplus Bks.) Capstone Press of Coughlan Cos.

Griffin, Maeve. Plant Parts: Roots, Stems, & Leaves. 2009. (Real Life Readers Ser.). 16p. (gr. 2-3). pap. 7.05 *(978-1-4358-0037-3(0),* Rosen Classroom) Rosen Publishing Group, Inc., The.

Holt, Rinehart and Winston Staff. Holt Science & Technology Chapter 13: Life Science: Plant Processes. 5th ed. 2004. (Illus.). pap. 12.86 *(978-0-03-030217-6(X))* Holt McDougal.

Jordan, Helene J. How a Seed Grows. Krupinski, Loretta, illus. 2015. (Let's-Read-And-Find-Out Science 1 Ser.). (ENG.). 32p. (J). (gr. -1-3). pap. 6.99 *(978-0-06-238188-0(1))* HarperCollins Pubs.

Julivert, Maria Angels. La Vida de Las Plantas. (SPA.). 288p. (J). 10.00 *(978-84-342-1465-1(2))* Parramon Ediciones S.A. ESP. Dist: Distribuidora Norma, Inc.

Kalman, Bobbie & Sjonger, Rebecca. Las Plantas de Distintos Habitats. 2006. (Cambios Que Suceden en la Naturaleza Ser.). (SPA., Illus.). 32p. (J). (gr. 3-7). pap. *(978-0-7787-8391-6(X));* lib. bdg. *(978-0-7787-8377-0(4))* Crabtree Publishing Co.

Lundgren, Julie K. Reproduction in Plants. 2012. (ENG.). 24p. (gr. 3-4). pap. 8.95 *(978-1-61810-223-2(0))* Rourke Educational Media.

Oxlade, Edwin. Plant Physiology: The structure of plants Explained. 2007. Orig. Title: Understanding Plant Physiology. (Illus.). 156p. (C). *(978-1-84285-048-0(2))* GLMP Ltd.

Royston, Angela. Flowers. (Illus.). 32p. (YA). (gr. 2-18). lib. bdg. 27.10 *(978-1-932333-39-8(8))* Chrysalis Education.

Somervill, Barbara A. Plant Cells & Life Processes, 1 vol. 2010. (Investigating Cells Ser.). (ENG.). 48p. (gr. 3-6). 33.32 *(978-1-4329-3878-9(9),* Heinemann InfoSearch) Heinemann-Raintree.

Troupe, Thomas Kingsley. Do Plants Have Heads? Learning about Plant Parts with the Garbage Gang. Toye, Derek, illus. 2015. (Garbage Gang's Super Science Questions Ser.). (ENG.). 24p. (gr. k-2). lib. bdg. 26.65 *(978-1-4795-7059-1(1))* Picture Window Bks.

PLANT PROPAGATION

see also Plant Breeding; Seeds

Colby, Jennifer. Growing New Plants. 2014. (21st Century Junior Library: Plants Ser.). (ENG., Illus.). 24p. (J). (gr. 2-5). 25.64 *(978-1-63188-036-0(5),* 205551) Cherry Lake Publishing.

PLANT STRUCTURE

see Plant Anatomy

PLANTATION LIFE

Bober, Natalie S. Thomas Jefferson: Draftsman of a Nation. 2008. (ENG., Illus.). 376p. per. 16.95 *(978-0-8139-2732-9(3))* University of Virginia Pr.

Dickmann, Nancy. Watch It Grow, 1 vol., Set. Incl. Apple's Life. (Illus.). pap. 6.29 *(978-1-4329-4150-5(X));* Bean's Life. (Illus.). pap. 6.29 *(978-1-4329-4151-2(8));* Bee's Life. (Illus.). pap. 6.29 *(978-1-4329-4146-8(1));* Butterfly's Life. (Illus.). pap. 6.29 *(978-1-4329-4147-5(X));* Chicken's Life. (Illus.). pap. 6.29 *(978-1-4329-4148-2(8));* Dog's Life. pap. 6.29 *(978-1-4329-4232-8(8));* Frog's Life. pap. 6.29 *(978-1-4329-4149-9(6));* Oak Tree's Life. (Illus.). pap. 6.29 *(978-1-4329-4152-9(6));* Penguin's Life. (Illus.). pap. 6.29 *(978-1-4329-4233-5(6));* Sunflower's Life. (Illus.). pap. 6.29 *(978-1-4329-4153-6(4));* Turtle's Life. pap. 6.29 *(978-1-4329-4234-2(4));* (gr. -1-1). (Watch It Grow Ser.). (ENG.). 24p. 2010. Set pap. 69.19 *(978-1-4329-4154-3(2),* Acorn) Heinemann-Raintree.

Draper, Allison Stark. What People Wore on Southern Plantations. 2009. (Clothing, Costumes, & Uniforms Throughout American History Ser.). 24p. (gr. 3-3). 42.50 *(978-1-61511-882-3(9),* PowerKids Pr.) Rosen Publishing Group, Inc., The.

Erickson, Paul. Daily Life on a Southern Plantation. Gabbey, Terry, illus. Slingsby, Miki, photos by. 2006. 48p. (J). (gr. 2-5). reprint ed. pap. 8.00 *(978-1-4223-5727-9(9))* DIANE Publishing Co.

Gullo, Jim. A Travel Guide to the Plantation South. 2005. (Travel Guide To Ser.). (ENG., Illus.). 112p. (J). (gr. 5-8). lib. bdg. 30.85 *(978-1-59018-360-1(6),* Lucent Bks.) Cengage Gale.

Hill, George. The Fall of Irish Chiefs & Clans & the Plantation of Ulster: Including the Names of Irish Catholics, & Protestant Settlers. 2004. Orig. Title: An Historical Account of the Plantation in Ulster at the Commencement of the 17th Century. (Illus.). 276p. lib. bdg. 39.00 *(978-0-940134-42-3(X))* Irish Genealogical Foundation.

Krebs, Laurie. A Day in the Life of a Colonial Indigo Planter. (Library of Living & Working in Colonial Times Ser.). 24p. 2009. (gr. 3-3). 42.50 *(978-1-60853-732-7(3),* PowerKids Pr.) 2004. (Illus.). (J). lib. bdg. 19.95 *(978-0-8239-6229-7(6))* Rosen Publishing Group, Inc., The.

Levy, Debbie. Slaves on a Southern Plantation. 2004. (Daily Life Ser.). (ENG., Illus.). 48p. (J). 27.50 *(978-0-7377-1827-0(7),* Greenhaven Pr., Inc.) Cengage Gale.

Rikson, Paule. Daily Life on a Southern Plantation 1853. 2004. (Illus.). 48p. (J). (gr. 4-8). reprint ed. 17.00 *(978-0-7567-7709-8(7))* DIANE Publishing Co.

Worth, Richard. Slave Life on the Plantation: Prisons Beneath the Sun. 2004. (Slavery in American History Ser.). (Illus.). 128p. (J). lib. bdg. 27.94 *(978-0-7660-2152-5(1))* Enslow Pubs., Inc.

PLANTING

see Agriculture; Gardening; Landscape Gardening; Tree Planting

PLANTS

see also Desert Plants; Endangered Plants; Flower Gardening; Flowers; Forest Plants; Freshwater Plants; Gardening; Marine Plants; Shrubs; Weeds also names of plants (e.g. Mosses, etc.)

Abdo Publishing. A Green Kid's Guide to Gardening!, 1 vol. 2013. (Green Kid's Guide to Gardening! Ser.: 6). (ENG.). 24p. (J). (gr. -1-4). lib. bdg. 162.42 *(978-1-61641-942-4(3),* Looking Glass Library) Magic Wagon.

Aitken, Stephen. Plants & Insects. 2013. 64p. (J). (gr. 5-8). 31.36 *(978-1-60870-462-0(9));* pap. 15.28 *(978-1-62712-042-5(4))* Cavendish Square Publishing.

Akeroyd, John. Plant: An Eyewitness 3-D Book. 2004. (Illus.). 52p. (gr. 4-8). reprint ed. 17.00 *(978-0-7567-7415-8(2))* DIANE Publishing Co.

Aldrich, William, et al. Annuals for Illinois, 1 vol. rev. ed. 2004. (ENG., Illus.). 296p. (gr. 4). pap. 18.95 *(978-1-55105-380-6(2),* 1551053802) Lone Pine Publishing USA.

—Perennials for Illinois, 1 vol. rev. ed. 2003. (ENG., Illus.). 344p. (gr. 4). pap. 19.95 *(978-1-55105-378-3(0),* 1551053780) Lone Pine Publishing USA.

All about Plants, 6 vols., Pack. (gr. k-1). 23.00 *(978-0-7635-8839-7(3))* Rigby Education.

Allaire, Caroline. Let's Look at the Stream. Hugo, Pierre de, illus. 2012. (ENG.). 38p. (J). (gr. 1-4). pap. 11.99 *(978-1-85103-359-1(9))* Moonlight Publishing, Ltd. GBR. Dist: Independent Pubs. Group.

Allyn, Daisy. Seeds & Plants. 2012. (InfoMax Readers Ser.). (ENG., Illus.). 16 pp.p. (J). (gr. k-1). pap. 7.00 *(978-1-4488-8932-7(4),* Rosen Classroom) Rosen Publishing Group, Inc., The.

Aloian, Molly. Plants Are Alive! 2012. (ENG., Illus.). 24p. (J). *(978-0-7787-4219-7(9));* pap. *(978-0-7787-4224-1(5))* Crabtree Publishing Co.

Amstutz, L. J. Investigating Plant Life Cycles. 2015. (ENG., Illus.). 40p. (gr. 3-5). 29.32 *(978-1-4677-8056-8(1))* Lerner Publishing Group.

Andersen, Jill. Plants Need Light. 2016. (Rosen REAL Readers: STEM & STEAM Collection). 8p. (gr. 1-k). pap. 5.46 *(978-1-5081-2386-6(1),* Rosen Classroom) Rosen Publishing Group, Inc., The.

Anderson, Michael. A Closer Look at Plant Reproduction, Growth, & Ecology. 2011. (J). lib. bdg. 31.70 *(978-1-61530-530-8(0))* Rosen Publishing Group, Inc., The.

Apple Tree. 2003. stu. ed. 36.95 *(978-0-8136-9258-6(X))* Modern Curriculum Pr.

Bailey, Diane. Pollination Problems: The Battle to Save Bees & Other Vital Animals. 2017. (J). ***(978-1-4222-3876-9(8))*** Mason Crest.

Baillie, Marilyn, et al. How to Save a Species. 2014. (ENG.). 48p. (J). (gr. 3-7). 17.95 *(978-1-77147-063-6(1),* Owlkids) Owlkids Bks. Inc. CAN. Dist: Publishers Group West (PGW).

Baker, Wendy & Haslam, Andrew. Plants. (Make It Work! (Eureka!) Ser.). (Illus.). (J). (FRE.). pap. 9.99 *(978-0-590-24331-5(4));* pap. 15.95 *(978-0-590-74523-9(9))* Scholastic, Inc.

Ballard, Carol. Living Processes: Plant Variation & Classification. 2017. (Living Processes Ser.). (ENG., Illus.). 48p. (J). (gr. 7-11). pap. 11.99 *(978-0-7502-9655-7(0),* Wayland) Hachette Children's Group GBR. Dist: Hachette Bk. Group.

—Plant Variation & Classification. 2010. (Living Processes Ser.). (Illus.). 48p. (J). pap. 11.75 *(978-1-61532-346-3(5));* (YA). (gr. 5-8). lib. bdg. 29.25 *(978-1-61532-345-6(7))* Rosen Publishing Group, Inc., The. (Rosen Reference).

Bang, Molly & Chisholm, Penny. Ocean Sunlight: How Tiny Plants Feed the Seas. Bang, Molly, illus. 2012. (ENG., Illus.). 48p. (J). (gr. -1-3). 18.99 *(978-0-545-27322-0(6),* Blue Sky Pr., The) Scholastic, Inc.

Barlowe, Dot. Grand Canyon Plants & Animals. 2010. (Dover Nature Coloring Book Ser.). (ENG., Illus.). 32p. (gr. 3-8). pap. 3.99 *(978-0-486-47294-2(9))* Dover Pubns., Inc.

Bartholomew, Linda & Bartholomew, Al. The Rain Forest Book for Kids. Bartholomew, Linda & Bartholomew, Al, photos by. 2005. (Illus.). 32p. (J). 9.00 *(978-0-9764802-0-4(4))* Solutions for Human Services, LLC.

Bateman, Donna M. Deep in the Swamp. Lies, Brian, illus. 2007. (ENG.). 32p. (J). (gr. -1-3). 16.95 *(978-1-57091-596-3(2));* pap. 7.95 *(978-1-57091-597-0(0))* Charlesbridge Publishing, Inc.

Bath, Louella. Plants That Mimic. 2016. (Plant Defenses Ser.). 24p. (J). (gr. 3-3). pap. 8.25 *(978-1-4994-2151-4(6),* PowerKids Pr.) Rosen Publishing Group, Inc., The.

Bayden, Maya. What Is Chemical Energy? 2017. (Let's Find Out! Forms of Energy Ser.). 32p. (gr. 6-8). pap. 12.90 ***(978-1-68048-693-3(4),*** Britannica Educational Publishing) Rosen Publishing Group, Inc., The.

Benbow, Ann & Mably, Colin. Lively Plant Science Projects. Labaff, Tom & LaBaff, Tom, illus. 2009. (Real Life Science Experiments Ser.). 48p. (J). (gr. 2-5). lib. bdg. 25.27 *(978-0-7660-3146-3(2))* Enslow Pubs., Inc.

Benchmark Education Company, compiled by. Amazing Plants & Plantas Asombrosas. 2005. (J). 62.00 net. *(978-1-4108-4495-8(1))* Benchmark Education Co.

Benchmark Education Company, LLC Staff, compiled by. Plants: Theme Set. 2006. (J). spiral bd. 195.00 *(978-1-4108-7107-7(X))* Benchmark Education Co.

—Plants & Animal Life: Theme Set. 2006. (J). 178.00 *(978-1-4108-7083-4(9))* Benchmark Education Co.

—Plants & Animals: Theme Set. 2006. (J). 173.00 *(978-1-4108-7137-4(1));* spiral bd. 174.00 *(978-1-4108-7063-6(4))* Benchmark Education Co.

Bennett, Doraine. Coastal Plain. 2009. (J). *(978-1-935077-51-0(1));* pap. *(978-1-935077-52-7(X))* State Standards Publishing, LLC.

Berger, Melvin & Berger, Gilda. The Wacky World of Living Things! 273 Facts! Miller, Ed, illus. 2017. (Fact Attack Ser.: 1). (ENG.). 96p. (J). (gr. 1-3). pap. 7.99 ***(978-1-338-03839-2(7))*** Scholastic, Inc.

Beullens-Maoui, Nathalie, ed. Plants: Armenian, 01 vols., 1. 2016. (Our Wonderful World Ser.). (ENG & SPA.). 8p. (J). pap. 9.35 *(978-1-5081-1212-9(6),* Rosen Classroom) Rosen Publishing Group, Inc., The.

—Plants: Cantonese, 01 vols., 1. 2016. (Our Wonderful World Ser.). (ENG & SPA.). 8p. (J). pap. 9.35 *(978-1-5081-1224-2(X),* Rosen Classroom) Rosen Publishing Group, Inc., The.

—Plants: Filipino, 01 vols., 1. 2016. (Our Wonderful World Ser.). (ENG & SPA.). 8p. (J). pap. 9.35 *(978-1-5081-1218-1(5),* Rosen Classroom) Rosen Publishing Group, Inc., The.

—Plants: Hmong Green, 01 vols., 1. 2016. (Our Wonderful World Ser.). (ENG & SPA.). 8p. (J). pap. 9.35 *(978-1-5081-1230-3(4),* Rosen Classroom) Rosen Publishing Group, Inc., The.

—Plants: Hmong White, 01 vols., 1. 2016. (Our Wonderful World Ser.). (ENG & SPA.). 8p. (J). pap. 9.35 *(978-1-5081-1236-5(3),* Rosen Classroom) Rosen Publishing Group, Inc., The.

—Plants: Korean, 01 vols., 1. 2016. (Our Wonderful World Ser.). (ENG & SPA.). 8p. (J). pap. 9.35 *(978-1-5081-1242-6(8),* Rosen Classroom) Rosen Publishing Group, Inc., The.

—Plants: Russian, 01 vols., 1. 2016. (Our Wonderful World Ser.). (ENG & SPA.). 8p. (J). pap. 9.35 *(978-1-5081-1248-8(7),* Rosen Classroom) Rosen Publishing Group, Inc., The.

—Plants: Spanish, 01 vols., 1. 2016. (Our Wonderful World Ser.). (ENG & SPA.). 8p. (J). pap. 9.35 *(978-1-5081-1254-9(1),* Rosen Classroom) Rosen Publishing Group, Inc., The.

—Plants: Vietnamese, 01 vols., 1. 2016. (Our Wonderful World Ser.). (ENG & SPA.). 8p. (J). pap. 9.35 *(978-1-5081-1260-0(6),* Rosen Classroom) Rosen Publishing Group, Inc., The.

Bishop, Celeste. ¿Por Qué Las Plantas Tienen Raíces? / Why Do Plants Have Roots?, 01 vols., 1. 2016. (Partes de la Planta / Plant Parts Ser.). (ENG & SPA., Illus.). 24p. (J). 23.60 *(978-1-5081-4742-8(6),* PowerKids Pr.) Rosen Publishing Group, Inc., The.

—¿Por Qué Las Plantas Tienen Semillas? / Why Do Plants Have Seeds?, 01 vols., 1. 2016. (Partes de la Planta / Plant Parts Ser.). (ENG & SPA., Illus.). 24p. (J). 23.60 *(978-1-5081-4732-9(9),* PowerKids Pr.) Rosen Publishing Group, Inc., The.

—¿Por Qué Las Plantas Tienen Tallos? / Why Do Plants Have Stems?, 01 vols., 1. 2016. (Partes de la Planta / Plant Parts Ser.). (ENG & SPA., Illus.). 24p. (J). 23.60 *(978-1-5081-4731-2(0),* PowerKids Pr.) Rosen Publishing Group, Inc., The.

—Why Do Plants Have Roots?, 01 vols., 1. 2016. (Plant Parts Ser.). (ENG., Illus.). 24p. (J). pap. 8.25 *(978-1-5081-4225-6(4),* PowerKids Pr.) Rosen Publishing Group, Inc., The.

—Why Do Plants Have Seeds?, 01 vols., 1. 2016. (Plant Parts Ser.). (ENG., Illus.). 24p. (J). pap. 8.25 *(978-1-5081-4229-4(7),* PowerKids Pr.) Rosen Publishing Group, Inc., The.

—Why Do Plants Have Stems?, 01 vols., 1. 2016. (Plant Parts Ser.). (ENG., Illus.). 24p. (J). 23.60 *(978-1-4994-1851-4(5),* PowerKids Pr.) Rosen Publishing Group, Inc., The.

Blackaby, Susan. Buds & Blossoms: A Book about Flowers, 1 vol. DeLage, Charlene, illus. 2003. (Growing Things Ser.). (ENG.). 24p. (gr. -1-2). per. 8.95 *(978-1-4048-0388-6(2))* Picture Window Bks.

—Green & Growing: A Book about Plants. DeLage, Charlene, illus. 2003. (Growing Things Ser.). (ENG.). 24p. (gr. -1-2). 26.65 *(978-1-4048-0107-3(3))* Picture Window Bks.

—Plant Packages: A Book about Seeds, 1 vol. Delage, Charlene, illus. 2003. (Growing Things Ser.). (ENG.). 24p. (gr. -1-2). per. 8.95 *(978-1-4048-0384-8(X))* Picture Window Bks.

Blashfield, Jean F. Plant Life. 2007. (Gareth Stevens Vital Science Ser.). (Illus.). 48p. (gr. 5-12). lib. bdg. 27.00 *(978-0-8368-8442-5(6),* Gareth Stevens Secondary Library) Stevens, Gareth Publishing LLLP.

Blevins, Wiley. Ninja Plants: Survival & Adaptation in the Plant World. 2017. (ENG.). 96p. (YA). (gr. 8-12). 35.99 *(978-1-5124-1013-6(6));* 19.99 ***(978-1-5124-3914-4(2));*** 53.32 ***(978-1-5124-3915-1(0));*** 53.32 ***(978-1-5124-2853-7(1))*** Lerner Publishing Group. (Twenty-First Century Bks.).

Bocknek, Jonathan. Plants. 2007. (Life Science (Weigl Hardcover) Ser.). (Illus.). 32p. (J). (gr. 4-7). lib. bdg. 26.00 *(978-1-59036-717-9(0));* per. 9.95 *(978-1-59036-718-6(9))* Weigl Pubs., Inc.

Bodach, Vijaya Khisty. Stems. 2016. (Plant Parts Ser.). (ENG.). 24p. (gr. k-1). pap. 7.29 *(978-1-5157-4247-0(4),* Pebble Plus) Capstone Press of Coughlan Cos.

Boothroyd, Jennifer. Self-Pollination. 2015. (First Step Nonfiction - Pollination Ser.). (ENG., Illus.). 24p. (gr. k-2). 39.99 *(978-1-4677-8908-0(9),* Lerner Digital) Lerner Publishing Group.

Bow, James. Wetlands Inside Out. 2014. (ENG.). 32p. (J). *(978-0-7787-0641-0(9))* Crabtree Publishing Co.

Brooks, Marigold. Let's Plant a Tree. 2017. (Plants in My World Ser.). 24p. (gr. 4-6). pap. 8.25 ***(978-1-5383-2120-1(3),*** PowerKids Pr.) Rosen Publishing Group, Inc., The.

Brown, Carron. Secrets of the Rain Forest. Nassner, Alyssa, illus. 2015. (ENG.). 36p. (J). 12.99 *(978-1-61067-325-9(5))* Kane Miller.

Bryan, Lynn. Where Do Plants Grow? 2005. (IOpeners Ser.). (Illus.). 8p. (J). pap. 7.56 *(978-0-7652-5145-9(0))* Celebration Pr.

Brynie, Faith Hickman. What Helps Plants Grow? The Nitrogen Cycle Case. 2003. (J). *(978-1-58417-151-5(0))* Lake Street Pubs.

Buchanan, Shelly. Plant Reproduction. 2015. (Science Readers: Content & Literacy Ser.). (ENG., Illus.). 32p. (J). (gr. 4-4). pap. 8.99 *(978-1-4807-4676-3(2))* Teacher Created Materials, Inc.

Burnie, David. Eyewitness Plant. 2011. (DK Eyewitness Bks.). (ENG.). 72p. (J). (gr. 3-7). 16.99 *(978-0-7566-6035-2(1),* DK Children) Dorling Kindersley Publishing, Inc.

Burton, Margie, et al. Plants & Las Plantas: 6 English, 6 Spanish Adaptations. 2011. (J). spiral bd. 75.00 net. *(978-1-4108-5638-8(0))* Benchmark Education Co.

Butt, Kyle. God Made Plants. 2007. (ENG., Illus.). (J). 3.00 *(978-0-932859-85-3(2))* Apologetics Pr., Inc.

Butterfield, Moira & Jacobs, Pat. Plants. 2016. (Know It All Ser.). (ENG., Illus.). 32p. (J). (gr. 5-5). pap. 10.58 *(978-1-5026-0894-9(4),* 1398905) Cavendish Square Publishing.

Cameron, Ken. La genética de las Plantas. Hanner, Albert & Hortens, Mike, illus. 2011. (SPA.). 32p. (J). pap. 49.00 net. *(978-1-4108-2341-0(5),* A23415) Benchmark Education Co.

Canavan, Thomas. Do Plants Really Eat Insects? Questions & Answers about the Science of Plants. 2013. (Science F. A. Q. Ser.). (Illus.). 32p. (gr. 3-6). 31.35 *(978-1-78212-392-7(X))* Arcturus Publishing GBR. Dist: Black Rabbit Bks.

Capon, Brian. Plant Survival: Adapting to a Hostile World. Capon, Brian, illus. 2009. (ENG., Illus.). 144p. pap. 15.95 *(978-0-88192-287-5(0),* 682287) Timber Pr., Inc.

Carle, Eric. The Tiny Seed. Carle, Eric, illus. 2015. (World of Eric Carle Ser.). (ENG., Illus.). 32p. (J). (gr. k-2). pap. 3.99 *(978-1-4814-3575-8(2),* Simon Spotlight) Simon Spotlight.

Carr, Aaron. Plants. 2013. lib. bdg. 20.00 *(978-1-62127-492-6(6))* Weigl Pubs., Inc.

Carr, Joaquin. Habitats of South America: Text Pairs. 2008. (Bridges/Navigators Ser.). (J). (gr. 3). 81.00 *(978-1-4108-8361-2(2))* Benchmark Education Co.

Carter, David A. Spring: A Pop-up Book. 2016. (Seasons Pop-Up Ser.). (ENG., Illus.). 12p. (J). (gr. -1-k). 14.95 *(978-1-4197-1912-7(2),* Abrams Appleseed) Abrams, Inc.

Cavell-Clarke, Steffi. Plant Parts. 2017. (Closer Look at Living Things Ser.). 24p. (J). (gr. 2-2). pap. 8.25 ***(978-1-5345-2069-1(4));*** lib. bdg. 24.60 ***(978-1-5345-2070-7(8))*** Greenhaven Publishing LLC. (KidHaven Publishing).

Charman, Andrew. I Wonder Why Leaves Change Color: And Other Questions about Plants. 2012. (I Wonder Why Ser.). (ENG., Illus.). (J). (gr. k-3). pap. 6.99 *(978-0-7534-6697-1(X),* 9780753466971, Kingfisher) Roaring Brook Pr.

Cheshire, Gerald. Living World. 2013. (World of Wonder Ser.). (ENG., Illus.). 32p. (J). (gr. 1-3). lib. bdg. 31.35 *(978-1-908973-99-3(4))* Book Hse. GBR. Dist: Black Rabbit Bks.

Clasky, Leonard. My Little Plant: If... Then. 2017. (Computer Science for the Real World Ser.). 8p. (gr. 5-6). pap. 6.20 ***(978-1-5383-5104-8(8),*** Rosen Classroom) Rosen Publishing Group, Inc., The.

Claybourne, Anna. Killer Plants & Other Green Gunk. 2014. (ENG., Illus.). 32p. (J). *(978-0-7787-1400-2(4))* Crabtree Publishing Co.

Colby, Jennifer. Growing New Plants. 2014. (21st Century Junior Library: Plants Ser.). (ENG., Illus.). 24p. (J). (gr. 2-5). 25.64 *(978-1-63188-036-0(5),* 205551) Cherry Lake Publishing.

—Plants Need Sunlight. 2014. (21st Century Junior Library: Plants Ser.). (ENG.). 24p. (J). (gr. 2-5). 25.64 *(978-1-63188-038-4(1),* 205559) Cherry Lake Publishing.

—Poison Ivy Makes Me Itch. 2015. (Tell Me Why Library). (ENG., Illus.). 24p. (J). (gr. 2-5). 27.07 *(978-1-63362-615-7(6),* 206644) Cherry Lake Publishing.

—What Is a Plant? 2014. (21st Century Junior Library: Plants Ser.). (ENG.). 24p. (J). (gr. 2-5). 25.64 *(978-1-63188-042-1(X),* 205575) Cherry Lake Publishing.

Cole, Tayler. Corpse Flowers Smell Nasty! 2016. (World's Weirdest Plants Ser.). 00024p. (J). pap. 8.15 *(978-1-4824-5607-3(9))* Stevens, Gareth Publishing LLLP.

Collier, Elise. What Grows in an Orchard? 2017. (Plants in My World Ser.). 24p. (gr. 4-6). pap. 8.25 ***(978-1-5081-6159-2(3),*** PowerKids Pr.) Rosen Publishing Group, Inc., The.

Colson, Mary. Gmos. 2016. (Cutting-Edge Technology Ser.). (ENG.). 48p. (YA). (gr. 8-6). lib. bdg. 31.95 *(978-1-4824-5157-3(3))* Stevens, Gareth Publishing LLLP.

Colvin, L. Living World Encyclopedia. 2009. pap. 14.99 *(978-0-7945-2784-6(1))* EDC Publishing.

Connolly, Randy, et al. Poison Ivy, Pets & People: Scratching the Poison Ivy, Oak & Sumac Itch. 2005. (10thingstoknow about ... Ser.). (Illus.). 104p. pap. 9.95 *(978-0-9722400-1-7(2))* 2Lakes Publishing.

Cook, Trevor. Experiments with Plants & Other Living Things. 2009. (Science Lab Ser.). (J). (ENG., Illus.). 32p. (J). (gr. 4-6). pap. 10.00 *(978-1-4358-3219-0(1),* 1291701); lib. bdg. 26.50 *(978-1-4358-2806-3(2))* Rosen Publishing Group, Inc., The. (PowerKids Pr.).

De la Bédoyère, Camilla. Plants. 2013. (Illus.). 40p. (J). *(978-1-4351-5095-9(3))* Barnes & Noble, Inc.

Delafosse, Claude & Broutin, Christian. Let's Look at the Jungle. Broutin, Christian, illus. 2012. (ENG., Illus.). 38p. (J). (gr. k-3). pap. 11.99 *(978-1-85103-332-4(7))* Moonlight Publishing, Ltd. GBR. Dist: Independent Pubs. Group.

Los Desiertos. (Coleccion Planeta Vivo).Tr. of Deserts. (SPA.). (J). (gr. 5-8). 12.00 *(978-84-342-1947-2(6))* Parramon Ediciones S.A. ESP. Dist: Distribuidora Norma, Inc.

Dickmann, Nancy. Las Plantas de la Granja, 1 vol. 2011. (Mundo de la Granja Ser.). (Illus.). 24p. (J). (gr. -1-1). (SPA & ENG.). 22.65 *(978-1-4329-5310-2(9));* (ENG & SPA., pap. 6.29 *(978-1-4329-5317-1(6))* Heinemann-Raintree. (Bellota).

—Plants on a Farm, 1 vol. 2010. (World of Farming Ser.). (ENG.). 24p. (gr. -1-1). pap. 6.29 *(978-1-4329-3950-2(5),* Acorn) Heinemann-Raintree.

—World of Farming, 1 vol., Set. Incl. Farm Animals. pap. 6.29 *(978-1-4329-3941-0(6));* Farm Machines. pap. 6.29 *(978-1-4329-3942-7(4));* Food from Farms. pap. 6.29 *(978-1-4329-3943-4(2));* Jobs on a Farm. (Illus.). pap. 6.29 *(978-1-4329-3945-8(9));* Plants on a Farm. pap. 6.29 *(978-1-4329-3950-2(5));* Seasons on a Farm. pap. 6.29 *(978-1-4329-3953-3(X));* (gr. -1-1). (World of Farming Ser.). (ENG.). 24p. 2010. Set pap. 35.94 *(978-1-4329-3935-9(1),* Acorn) Heinemann-Raintree.

Duke, Shirley Smith. Perennial Plants & Annual Plants Explained. 2016. (Distinctions in Nature Ser.). (Illus.). 32p. (J). (gr. 3-3). 28.50 *(978-1-5026-1742-2(0))* Cavendish Square Publishing.

DuneCraft & Soffer, Ruth. DuneCraft Weird & Wacky Plantlife. 2015. (ENG., Illus.). 32p. (J). (gr. 3-5). pap. 3.99 *(978-0-486-79386-3(9))* Dover Pubns., Inc.

Eason, Sarah, ed. Plants & Microorganisms. 2011. (FAYFT: Introducing Biology Ser.). 64p. (gr. 4-10). lib. bdg. 39.95 *(978-1-936333-02-8(3))* Brown Bear Bks.

Edom, Helen. Science with Plants. Abel, Simone, illus. rev. ed. 2007. (Science Activities Ser.). 24p. (J). (gr. 3-7). pap. 5.99 *(978-0-7945-1485-3(5),* Usborne) EDC Publishing.

Edwards, Nicola. Flowers. 2007. (See How Plants Grow Ser.). (Illus.). 24p. (J). (gr. 4-7). lib. bdg. 22.60 *(978-1-4042-3699-8(6))* Rosen Publishing Group, Inc., The.

Encyclopaedia Britannica, Inc. Staff. Britannica Illustrated Science Library Series (18 Title Series), 18 vols. 2010. 599.00 *(978-1-61535-423-8(9))* Encyclopaedia Britannica, Inc.

Encyclopaedia Britannica, Inc. Staff, compiled by. Britannica Illustrated Science Library: Plants, 16 vols. 2008. (Illus.). (J). 29.95 *(978-1-59339-394-6(6))* Encyclopaedia Britannica, Inc.

—My First Britannica: Plants. 2008. (gr. 7-12). *(978-1-59339-410-3(1))* Encyclopaedia Britannica, Inc.

Encyclopedia Britannica Staff, creator. Plants, Algae, & Fungi. 2011. (Britannica Illustrated Science Library Ser.). 104p. (J). 37.44 *(978-1-61535-461-0(1))* Encyclopaedia Britannica, Inc.

Engebretson, Don & Williamson, Don. Annuals for Minnesota & Wisconsin, 1 vol., Vol. 1. rev. ed. 2004. (ENG., Illus.). 296p. (gr. 4). pap. 19.95 *(978-1-55105-381-3(0),* 1551053810) Lone Pine Publishing USA.

Farndon, John. Flowers. 2005. 24p. (J). (gr. 2-4). pap. 22.45 *(978-1-4103-0517-6(1),* Blackbirch Pr., Inc.) Cengage Gale.

Felix, Rebecca. What Happens to Plants in Summer? 2014. (21st Century Basic Skills Library: Let's Look at Summer Ser.). (ENG.). 24p. (J). (gr. k-3). 22.79 *(978-1-63137-603-0(9),* 205195) Cherry Lake Publishing.

—What Happens to Plants in Winter? 2014. (21st Century Basic Skills Library: Let's Look at Winter Ser.). (ENG.). 24p. (J). (gr. k-3). 22.79 *(978-1-63137-608-5(X),* 205215) Cherry Lake Publishing.

Fleisher, Paul. Forest Food Webs in Action. 2013. (Searchlight Books What Is a Food Web Ser.). (ENG., Illus.). 40p. (gr. 3-5). pap. 8.95 *(978-1-4677-1553-9(0))* Lerner Publishing Group.

—Grassland Food Webs in Action. 2013. (Searchlight Books What Is a Food Web Ser.). (ENG., Illus.). 40p. (gr. 3-5). pap. 8.95 *(978-1-4677-1554-6(9));* lib. bdg. 27.93 *(978-1-4677-1293-4(0),* Lerner Pubns.) Lerner Publishing Group.

—Lake & Pond Food Webs in Action. 2013. (Searchlight Books What Is a Food Web Ser.). (ENG., Illus.). 40p. (gr. 3-5). pap. 8.95 *(978-1-4677-1555-3(7));* lib. bdg. 27.93 *(978-1-4677-1256-9(6),* Lerner Pubns.) Lerner Publishing Group.

Fortuna, Lois. Growing Plants. 2016. (We Can Do It! Ser.). (ENG., Illus.). 24p. (J). (gr. k-k). pap. 8.15 *(978-1-4824-3803-1(8))* Stevens, Gareth Publishing LLLP.

La Fresa. (Coleccion Ciclos Vitales). (SPA., Illus.). (J). (gr. 3-5). pap. *(978-84-236-2653-3(9),* ED4700) Edebé ESP. Dist: Lectorum Pubns., Inc.

Fuhr, Ute & Allaire, Caroline. Let's Look at the Rainforest. Sautai, Raoul, illus. 2012. (ENG.). 38p. (J). (gr. 1-4). pap. 11.99 *(978-1-85103-360-7(2))* Moonlight Publishing, Ltd. GBR. Dist: Independent Pubs. Group.

Gagliano, Eugene. V Is for Venus Flytrap: A Plant Alphabet. Traynor, Elizabeth, illus. 2009. (Science Ser.). (ENG.). 40p. (J). (gr. k-8). 17.95 *(978-1-58536-350-6(2))* Sleeping Bear Pr.

Gaines, Alison. Invasive Plants & Birds. 2016. (Invasive Species Ser.). (Illus.). 48p. (J). (gr. 4-4). 31.36 *(978-1-5026-1834-4(6))* Cavendish Square Publishing.

Ganeri, Anita. All Kinds of Plants Blue Band. 2016. (Cambridge Reading Adventures Ser.). (ENG.). 16p. pap. 6.56 *(978-1-316-60579-0(5))* Cambridge Univ. Pr.

—Peculiar Plants, 1 vol. 2012. (Extreme Nature Ser.). (ENG.). 32p. (gr. 1-3). pap. 8.29 *(978-1-4109-4703-1(3));* lib. bdg. 29.99 *(978-1-4109-4698-0(3))* Heinemann-Raintree. (Read Me!).

Garassino, Alessandro. Las Plantas. (SPA.). 40p. (YA). (gr. 5-8). 10.36 *(978-84-207-5190-0(1))* Grupo Anaya, S.A. ESP. Dist: Lectorum Pubns., Inc.

Gardner, Robert. Experimenting with Plants Science Projects. 2013. (Exploring Hands-On Science Projects Ser.). 128p. (J). (gr. 5-12). pap. 10.95 *(978-1-4644-0220-3(5));* 27.94 *(978-0-7660-4144-8(1))* Enslow Pubs., Inc.

Gardner, Robert & Perry, Phyllis Jean. Ace Your Plant Science Project: Great Science Fair Ideas. 2009. (Ace Your Biology Science Project Ser.). (Illus.). 104p. (J). (gr. 5-9). lib. bdg. 33.27 *(978-0-7660-3221-7(3))* Enslow Pubs., Inc.

Gibbons, Gail. From Seed to Plant. Gibbons, Gail, illus. 2012. (Illus.). audio compact disk 18.95 *(978-1-4301-1079-8(1))* Live Oak Media.

Gleisner, Jenna Lee. What Blossoms in Spring? 2014. (21st Century Basic Skills Library: Let's Look at Spring Ser.). (ENG.). 24p. (J). (gr. k-3). 22.79 *(978-1-62431-659-3(X),* 203148); pap. 12.79 *(978-1-62431-686-9(7),* 203149) Cherry Lake Publishing.

Goldstein, Natalie. Photosynthesis & Other Plant Life Processes. 2012. (YA). 35.00 *(978-1-61753-026-5(3),* Chelsea Hse.) Facts On File, Inc.

Goldsworthy, Kaite. Producers. 2016. (J). ***(978-1-4896-5779-4(7))*** 2011. (J). (gr. 4-6). pap. 12.95 *(978-1-61690-716-7(9),* AV2 by Weigl) 2011. (Illus.). 24p.

P
Q
R

(YA). (gr. 2-5). 27.13 *(978-1-61690-710-5(X))* Weigl Pubs., Inc.

Goodman, Emily. Plant Secrets. Tildes, Phyllis Limbacher, illus. 2009. (ENG.). 40p. (J). (gr. -1-3). pap. 7.95 *(978-1-58089-205-6(1))* Charlesbridge Publishing, Inc.

Gray, Leon. Plant Classification. 2013. (Life Science Stories Ser.). (Illus.). 32p. (J). (gr. 3-5). pap. 10.50 *(978-1-4339-8720-5(1))*; lib. bdg. 26.60 *(978-1-4339-8719-9(8))* Stevens, Gareth Publishing LLLP.

Gray, Rita. Flowers Are Calling. Pak, Kenard, illus. 2015. (ENG.). 32p. (J). (gr. -1-3). 16.99 *(978-0-544-34012-1(4))*, HMH Books For Young Readers) Houghton Mifflin Harcourt Publishing Co.

Gray, Susan H. Experiment with Plants. 2010. (Explorer Junior Library: Science Explorer Junior Ser.). (ENG.). 32p. (gr. 3-6). lib. bdg. 28.50 *(978-1-60279-839-7(7)*, 200544) Cherry Lake Publishing.

—Super Cool Science Experiments: Plants. 2009. (Explorer Library: Science Explorer Ser.). (ENG., Illus.). 32p. (gr. 4-8). lib. bdg. 28.50 *(978-1-60279-522-8(3)*, 200286) Cherry Lake Publishing.

Green, Jen. Projects with Plants. 2014. (Make & Learn Ser.). (Illus.). 32p. (J). (gr. 3-6). 27.50 *(978-1-4777-7161-7(1)*, PowerKids Pr.) Rosen Publishing Group, Inc., The.

Gregoire, Maryellen. We All Need Plants, 1 vol. 2011. (Wonder Readers Emergent Level Ser.). (ENG.). (gr. -1-1). 32p. pap. 5.99 *(978-1-4296-7878-0(X))*; 16p. pap. 35.94 *(978-1-4296-8200-8(0))* Capstone Press of Coughlan Cos. (Wonder Readers).

Griffiths, Rachel. Why Do Leaves Change Colour? Level 3 Factbook. 2010. (Cambridge Young Readers Ser.). (ENG., Illus.). 16p. pap. 6.00 *(978-0-521-13715-7(2))* Cambridge Univ. Pr.

Group/McGraw-Hill, Wright. Donde Viven Algunos Animales, 6 vols. (First Explorers. Primeros Exploradores Nonfiction Sets Ser.). (SPA.). (gr. 1-2). 29.95 *(978-0-7699-1472-5(1))* Shortland Pubns. (U. S. A.) Inc.

—El Mundo de Las Plantas, 6 vols. (First Explorers. Primeros Exploradores Nonfiction Sets Ser.). (SPA.). (gr. 1-2). 29.95 *(978-0-7699-1474-9(8))* Shortland Pubns. (U. S. A.) Inc.

Guest, John. Amazing True Facts. 2012. (Illus.). 224p. *(978-1-4351-4353-1(1))* Barnes & Noble, Inc.

Haelle, Tara. Edible Sunlight. 2016. (Let's Explore Science Ser.). (ENG., Illus.). 48p. (gr. 5-8). 35.64 *(978-1-68191-399-5(2))* Rourke Educational Media.

Halpern, Monica. Venus Flytraps, Bladderworts & Other Wild & Amazing Plants. 2006. (Science Chapters Ser.). (ENG., Illus.). 48p. (J). (gr. 1-4). 17.90 *(978-0-7922-5957-2(2)*, National Geographic Children's Bks.) National Geographic Society.

Harkrader, Lisa. Unusual Plants. 2016. (Spring Forward Ser.). (J). (gr. 1). *(978-1-4900-2243-7(0))* Benchmark Education Co.

Head, Honor. Amazing Plants. 2008. (Amazing Life Cycles Ser.). (Illus.). 32p. (J). (gr. 2-6). lib. bdg. 26.00 *(978-0-8368-8897-3(9)*, Gareth Stevens Learning Library) Stevens, Gareth Publishing LLLP.

Heddle, Becca. Plants, Pollen & Pollinators. 2016. (ENG., Illus.). 32p. (J). (gr. 2-3). pap. 8.95 *(978-0-00-816385-3(5))* HarperCollins Pubs. Ltd. GBR. Dist: Independent Pubs. Group.

Hedegaard, Lise. Plants in Disguise: Features of Creatures in Flowers & Foliage. Schmid, Debi, illus. 2017. (J). 15.00 ***(978-0-87842-673-7(6))*** Mountain Pr. Publishing Co., Inc.

Heller, Ruth. The Reason for a Flower. (FRE.). (J). 6.99 *(978-0-590-71999-5(8))* Scholastic, Inc.

Herrington, Lisa M. Seed to Plant. 2014. (Rookie Read-About(tm) Science — Life Cycles Ser.). (ENG.). 32p. (J). lib. bdg. 25.00 *(978-0-531-21056-7(1))* Scholastic Library Publishing.

Hewitt, Sally. Amazing Plants. 2007. (Amazing Science Ser.). (ENG.). 32p. (J). pap. *(978-0-7787-3628-8(8))* Crabtree Publishing Co.

—Plants. (Illus.). 32p. (YA). (gr. 2-18). lib. bdg. 27.10 *(978-1-932333-30-5(4))* Chrysalis Education.

Hibbert, Clare. Seaside Plants & Animals. 2016. (Beside the Seaside Ser.). (ENG., Illus.). 24p. (J). (gr. k-2). 16.99 *(978-1-4451-3766-7(6)*, Franklin Watts) Hachette Children's Group GBR. Dist: Hachette Bk. Group.

Higgins, Nadia. Experiment with a Plant's Living Environment. 2015. (Lightning Bolt Books (tm) — Plant Experiments Ser.). (ENG., Illus.). 32p. (gr. k-2). pap. 8.99 *(978-1-4677-6072-0(2))*; lib. bdg. 26.65 *(978-1-4677-5731-7(4))* Lerner Publishing Group. (Lerner Pubns.).

—Experiment with a Plant's Roots. 2015. (Lightning Bolt Books (tm) — Plant Experiments Ser.). (ENG., Illus.). 32p. (gr. k-2). pap. 8.99 *(978-1-4677-6073-7(0))*; lib. bdg. 26.65 *(978-1-4677-5729-4(2))* Lerner Publishing Group. (Lerner Pubns.).

—Experiment with Parts of a Plant. 2015. (Lightning Bolt Books (tm) — Plant Experiments Ser.). (ENG., Illus.). 32p. (gr. k-2). lib. bdg. 26.65 *(978-1-4677-5733-1(0)*, Lerner Pubns.) Lerner Publishing Group.

—Experiment with Photosynthesis. 2015. (Lightning Bolt Books (tm) — Plant Experiments Ser.). (ENG., Illus.). 32p. (gr. k-2). 26.65 *(978-1-4677-5732-4(2))*; pap. 8.99 *(978-1-4677-6075-1(7))* Lerner Publishing Group. (Lerner Pubns.).

—Experiment with Pollination. 2015. (Lightning Bolt Books (tm) — Plant Experiments Ser.). (ENG., Illus.). 32p. (gr. k-2). lib. bdg. 26.65 *(978-1-4677-5734-8(9)*, Lerner Pubns.) Lerner Publishing Group.

—Experiment with What a Plant Needs to Grow. 2015. (Lightning Bolt Books (tm) — Plant Experiments Ser.). (ENG., Illus.). 32p. (gr. k-2). lib. bdg. 26.65 *(978-1-4677-5730-0(6)*, Lerner Pubns.) Lerner Publishing Group.

Hileman, Jane. The Life of a Dandelion. 2016. (1G Our Natural World Ser.). (ENG., Illus.). 20p. (J). pap. 5.99 *(978-1-63437-411-8(8))* American Reading Co.

Hill, Christina. Inside a Plant, 1 vol. rev. ed. 2014. (Science Readers: Content & Literacy Ser.). (ENG., Illus.). 24p. (gr. 1-1). (J). 22.96 *(978-1-4938-1147-2(9))*; pap. 8.99 *(978-1-4807-4560-5(X))* Teacher Created Materials, Inc.

—What Makes a Plant?, 1 vol. rev. ed. 2014. (Science Readers: Content & Literacy Ser.). (ENG., Illus.). 24p. (gr. 1-1). (J). 22.96 *(978-1-4938-1146-5(0))*; pap. 8.99 *(978-1-4807-4559-9(6))* Teacher Created Materials, Inc.

Hirsch, Rebecca. The Life Cycles of Plants. 2011. (Explorer Library: Language Arts Explorer Ser.). (ENG.). 32p. (gr. 4-8). pap. 14.21 *(978-1-61080-293-2(4)*, 201215) Cherry Lake Publishing.

—Science Lab: The Life Cycles of Plants. 2011. (Explorer Library: Language Arts Explorer Ser.). (ENG.). 32p. (gr. 4-8). lib. bdg. 28.50 *(978-1-61080-204-8(7)*, 201184) Cherry Lake Publishing.

Hirsch, Rebecca E. Plants Can't Sit Still. Posada, Mia, illus. 2016. (ENG.). 32p. (gr. k-4). (J). 19.99 *(978-1-4677-8031-5(6))*; 38.65 *(978-1-5124-1109-6(4))* Lerner Publishing Group. (Millbrook Pr.).

Hirschmann, Kris. Real Life Zombies. 2013. (Illus.). 32p. (J). *(978-0-545-53563-2(8))* Scholastic, Inc.

Hodge, Judith. Plants We Use: Set Of 6. 2010. (Navigators Ser.). (J). 48.00 net. *(978-1-4108-0435-8(6))* Benchmark Education Co.

—Plants We Use & Las plantas que Usamos: 6 English, 6 Spanish Adaptations. 2011. (ENG & SPA.). (J). 97.00 net. *(978-1-4108-5708-8(5))* Benchmark Education Co.

Hoff, Mary. Pollination. 2003. (World of Wonder Ser.). (Illus.). 32p. (J). lib. bdg. *(978-1-58341-270-1(0)*, Creative Education) Creative Co., The.

Hoffman, Mary Ann. Plant Experiments: What Affects Plant Growth? 2009. (Real Life Readers Ser.). 24p. (gr. 3-4). pap. 8.25 *(978-1-4358-0131-8(8)*, Rosen Classroom); (J). lib. bdg. 22.60 *(978-1-4358-2971-8(9)*, PowerKids Pr.) Rosen Publishing Group, Inc., The.

Hoffmann, Sara. Kinds of Flowers. 2012. (First Step Nonfiction - Kinds of Plants Ser.). (ENG., Illus.). 8p. (gr. -1-1). pap. 4.95 *(978-1-4677-0500-4(4)*, Lerner Pubns.) Lerner Publishing Group.

Hollar, Sherman. A Closer Look at Plant Classifications, Parts, & Uses. 2011. (J). lib. bdg. 31.70 *(978-1-61530-529-2(7))* Rosen Publishing Group, Inc., The.

Holmes, Porter. Plants in My Pond. 2017. (Plants in My World Ser.). 24p. (gr. 4-6). pap. 8.25 ***(978-1-5383-2124-9(6)***, PowerKids Pr.) Rosen Publishing Group, Inc., The.

Holt, Rinehart and Winston Staff. Holt Science & Technology Chapter 12: Life Science: Introduction to Plants. 5th ed. 2004. (Illus.). pap. 12.86 *(978-0-03-030216-9(1))* Holt McDougal.

Hopkins, William G. Photosynthesis & Respiration. 2006. (Green World Ser.). (Illus.). 168p. (gr. 6-12). lib. bdg. 37.50 *(978-0-7910-8561-5(9))* Facts On File, Inc.

Hotchkins, Dewayne. The Biggest Tomato. 2016. (Rosen REAL Readers: STEM & STEAM Collection). 12p. (gr. 1-k). pap. 6.33 *(978-1-5081-2673-7(9)*, Rosen Classroom) Rosen Publishing Group, Inc., The.

Huntington, Harriet E. Forest Giants: The Story of the California Redwoods. 2011. 52p. 36.95 *(978-1-258-02773-5(9))* Literary Licensing, LLC.

Iasevoli, Brenda, told to. Plants! 2006. (Time for Kids Science Scoops Ser.). (ENG., Illus.). 32p. (J). (gr. 1-3). 14.99 *(978-0-06-078219-1(6))* HarperCollins Pubs.

Jacobs, Pat. Why Do Plants Have Flowers? And Other Questions about Evolution & Classification. 2016. (Wildlife Wonders Ser.). 00032p. (J). (gr. 3-3). 26.25 *(978-1-4994-3273-2(9)*, PowerKids Pr.) Rosen Publishing Group, Inc., The.

James, Wayan. Food for Plants. 2016. (Rosen REAL Readers: STEM & STEAM Collection). 8p. (gr. 1-k). pap. 5.46 *(978-1-5081-2377-4(2)*, Rosen Classroom) Rosen Publishing Group, Inc., The.

Jennings, Dorothy. Our Flower Garden. 2017. (Plants in My World Ser.). 24p. (gr. 4-6). pap. 8.25 ***(978-1-5383-2117-1(3)***, PowerKids Pr.) Rosen Publishing Group, Inc., The.

Jennings, Rosemary. I Can Grow Plants! 2012. (InfoMax Readers Ser.). (ENG., Illus.). 24p. (J). (gr. 1-2). pap. 8.25 *(978-1-4488-8989-1(8)*, Rosen Classroom) Rosen Publishing Group, Inc., The.

Johnson, Terry. Growing New Plants. 2008. (21st Century Junior Library: Plants Ser.). (ENG., Illus.). 24p. (gr. 2-5). lib. bdg. 25.64 *(978-1-60279-279-1(8)*, 200183) Cherry Lake Publishing.

Kallio, Jamie. 12 Things to Know about Invasive Species. 2015. (ENG., Illus.). 32p. (J). *(978-1-63235-030-5(0))* Pr. Room Editions LLC.

Kalman, Bobbie. The ABCs of Plants. 2007. (ABCs of the Natural World Ser.). (ENG., Illus.). 32p. (J). (gr. 1-4). pap. *(978-0-7787-3433-8(1))* Crabtree Publishing Co.

—Los Animales Crecen y Cambian. 2008.Tr. of Plants are Living Things. (SPA.). 24p. (J). pap. *(978-0-7787-8686-3(2))* Crabtree Publishing Co.

—¿Cómo Se Mueve? 2009. (SPA.). 24p. (J). *(978-0-7787-8704-4(4))*; pap. *(978-0-7787-8743-3(5))* Crabtree Publishing Co.

—How Do Plants Help Us? 2011. (ENG.). 16p. (J). pap. *(978-0-7787-9586-5(1))*; lib. bdg. *(978-0-7787-9561-2(6))* Crabtree Publishing Co.

—How Does It Move? 2008. (Looking at Nature Ser.). (ENG., Illus.). 24p. (J). (gr. -1-2). pap. *(978-0-7787-3342-3(4))*; lib. bdg. *(978-0-7787-3322-5(X))* Crabtree Publishing Co.

—Plants Are Living Things. 2007. (Introducing Living Things Ser.). (ENG., Illus.). 24p. (J). (gr. 1-4). pap. *(978-0-7787-3257-0(6))* Crabtree Publishing Co.

—?Que Son Las Plantas? 2005. (Ciencia de los Seres Vivos Ser.). (SPA., Illus.). 32p. (J). (gr. 3-4). lib. bdg. *(978-0-7787-8759-4(1))* Crabtree Publishing Co.

—¿Qué Son Las Plantas? 2005. (Ciencia de los Seres Vivos Ser.). (SPA., Illus.). 32p. (J). (gr. 7-12). pap. *(978-0-7787-8805-8(9))* Crabtree Publishing Co.

Kalman, Bobbie & Sjonger, Rebecca. Plants in Different Habitats. 2006. (Nature's Changes Ser.). (ENG., Illus.). 32p. (J). (gr. 4-7). pap. *(978-0-7787-2316-5(X))* Crabtree Publishing Co.

Kavanagh, James. My First Arctic Nature. Leung, Raymond, illus. 2011. (Nature Activity Book Ser.). (ENG.). 32p. (J). (gr. 2-4). act. bk. ed. 6.95 *(978-1-58355-586-6(2))* Western National Parks Assn.

Kim, Cecil. One Little Bean: Observation - Life Cycle. Cowley, Joy, ed. Dattola, Chiara, illus. 2015. (Step up - Creative Thinking Ser.). (ENG.). 32p. (J). (gr. -1-2). 26.65 *(978-1-925186-40-6(7))* Lerner Publishing Group.

Kinsner, Kathy. Amazing Plants. 2004. (Shared Connections Ser.). (J). pap. *(978-1-4108-1647-4(8))*; instr.'s gde. ed. 27.00 *(978-1-4108-1623-8(0))* Benchmark Education Co.

Knapke, Debra & Beck, Alison. Annuals for Ohio, 1 vol. rev. ed. 2003. (ENG., Illus.). 296p. (gr. 4). pap. 18.95 *(978-1-55105-388-2(8)*, 1551053888) Lone Pine Publishing USA.

—Perennials for Ohio, 1 vol. rev. ed. 2003. (ENG., Illus.). 352p. (gr. 4). pap. 19.95 *(978-1-55105-386-8(1)*, 1551053861) Lone Pine Publishing USA.

Krezel, Cindy. 101 Kid-Friendly Plants: Fun Plants & Family Garden Projects. 2008. (ENG., Illus.). 160p. (J). (gr. 1-7). pap. 19.95 *(978-1-883052-54-6(8))* Chicago Review Pr., Inc.

Kuskowski, Alex. Super Simple Hanging Gardens: A Kid's Guide to Gardening, 1 vol. 2014. (Super Simple Gardening Ser.). (ENG.). 32p. (gr. k-4). 27.07 *(978-1-62403-523-4(X))* ABDO Publishing Co.

Lawrence, Ellen. Freaky Plant Facts: Extreme Greens. 2012. (Science Slam: Plant-Ology Ser.). 24p. (J). (gr. -1-3). lib. bdg. 23.93 *(978-1-61772-591-3(9))* Bearport Publishing Co., Inc.

—How Plants Clean the Air. 2014. (Science Slam: Plant-Ology Ser.). (ENG.). 24p. (J). (gr. -1-3). lib. bdg. 23.93 *(978-1-62724-305-6(4))* Bearport Publishing Co., Inc.

—Plants. 2016. (FUN-Damental Experiments Ser.). (ENG., Illus.). 24p. (J). (gr. -1-3). 17.95 *(978-1-943553-17-4(3))* Bearport Publishing Co., Inc.

—Why Do Most Plants Need Soil? 2015. (Down & Dirty Ser.). (ENG., Illus.). 24p. (J). (gr. -1-3). lib. bdg. 23.93 *(978-1-62724-837-2(4))* Bearport Publishing Co., Inc.

Lay, Richard & Zarrinnaal, Laura Nienhaus. A Green Kid's Guide to Watering Plants, 1 vol. 2013. (Green Kid's Guide to Gardening! Ser.). (ENG.). 24p. (J). (gr. -1-4). 27.07 *(978-1-61641-948-6(2))* Magic Wagon.

Leedy, Loreen & Schuerger, Andrew. Amazing Plant Powers: How Plants Fly, Fight, Hide, Hunt, & Change the World. 2015. (ENG.). 32p. (J). (gr. -1-2). 17.95 *(978-0-8234-2256-2(9))* Holiday Hse., Inc.

Legalizing Marijuana. 2nd rev. ed. 2010. (Point/Counterpoint Ser.). (Illus.). 128p. (C). (gr. 9). 35.00 *(978-1-60413-690-6(1)*, Chelsea Hse.) Facts On File, Inc.

Legg, Gerald & Weston, Steve. The World of Plant Life. 2012. (ENG., Illus.). 48p. (J). 15.00 *(978-1-899762-75-0(2))* Award Pubns. Ltd. GBR. Dist: Parkwest Pubns., Inc.

LernerClassroom Editors. Plant Life Cycles. 2009. (Illus.). pap. 7.95 *(978-0-8225-4786-0(4))* Lerner Publishing Group.

Levine, Shar. Plants: Flowering Plants, Ferns, Mosses, & Other Plants. 2010. (Class of Their Own Ser.). (ENG., Illus.). 48p. (J). (gr. 5-8). pap. *(978-0-7787-5390-2(5))*; lib. bdg. *(978-0-7787-5376-6(X))* Crabtree Publishing Co.

Levy, Janey. Freaky Stories about Plants. 2016. (Freaky True Science Ser.). 32p. (J). (gr. 5-4). pap. 10.50 *(978-1-4824-4831-3(9))* Stevens, Gareth Publishing LLLP.

—Life in a Rain Forest Ecosystem. 2009. (Real Life Readers Ser.). (J). (ENG., Illus.). 32p. (gr. 5-6). pap. 10.00 *(978-1-4358-0189-9(X))*; lib. bdg. 25.25 *(978-1-4358-2997-8(2))* Rosen Publishing Group, Inc., The. (PowerKids Pr.).

Lilly, Melinda. Make It Grow. Thompson, Scott M., illus. 2003. (Rourke Discovery Library). 24p. (J). 22.79 *(978-1-58952-637-2(6))* Rourke Educational Media.

Linde, Barbara M. Pitcher Plants Eat Meat! 2016. (World's Weirdest Plants Ser.). 00024p. (J). pap. 8.15 ***(978-1-4824-5632-5(X))*** Stevens, Gareth Publishing LLLP.

Lindstrom, Karin. Tiny Life on Plants. (Rookie Read-About Science Ser.). (ENG., Illus.). 32p. (J). (gr. 1-2). 2006. per. 4.95 *(978-0-516-25478-4(2))* 2005. lib. bdg. 20.50 *(978-0-516-25297-1(6))* Scholastic Library Publishing. (Children's Pr.).

Littlefield, Angie & Littlefield, Jennifer. The 10 Deadliest Plants. 2007. (J). 14.99 *(978-1-55448-511-6(8))* Scholastic Library Publishing.

Llewellyn, Claire. How Plants Grow. 2006. (I Know That, Growth & Change Set Ser.). (Illus.). 24p. (J). lib. bdg. 24.25 *(978-1-59771-021-3(0))* Sea-To-Sea Pubns.

—The Life of Plants. 2007. (Understanding Plants/Watts Ser.). (Illus.). 30p. (YA). (gr. 2-5). lib. bdg. 28.50 *(978-1-59920-033-0(3))* Black Rabbit Bks.

—Plants of the World. 2007. (Understanding Plants/Watts Ser.). (Illus.). 30p. (YA). (gr. 2-5). lib. bdg. 28.50 *(978-1-59920-032-3(5))* Black Rabbit Bks.

Lomberg, Michelle. Plant Cells. 2016. (Illus.). 32p. (J). *(978-1-5105-1188-0(1))* SmartBook Media, Inc.

Long, Erin. Plants & Their Environments. 2016. (Spotlight on Ecology & Life Science Ser.). 00024p. (J). (gr. 4-6). pap. 10.00 *(978-1-4994-2587-1(2)*, PowerKids Pr.) Rosen Publishing Group, Inc., The.

Lundgren, Julie K. Plant Adaptations. 2011. (ENG., Illus.). 24p. (gr. 1-2). pap. 8.95 *(978-1-61741-937-9(0))* Rourke Educational Media.

—Plant Life Cycles. 2011. (ENG., Illus.). 24p. (gr. 1-2). pap. 8.95 *(978-1-61741-936-2(2))* Rourke Educational Media.

—Seeds, Bees, & Pollen. 2011. (ENG., Illus.). 24p. (gr. 2-3). pap. 8.95 *(978-1-61741-950-8(8))* Rourke Educational Media.

Lynch, Wayne. The Arctic. Lynch, Wayne, photos by. 2007. (Our Wild World Ser.). (ENG., Illus.). 64p. (J). (gr. 3-7). pap. 8.95 *(978-1-55971-961-2(3))* Cooper Square Publishing Llc.

Lynette, Rachel. Plants, 1 vol. 2012. (Science Behind Ser.). (ENG., Illus.). 32p. (gr. 3-3). pap. 8.29 *(978-1-4109-4495-5(6)*, Raintree Perspectives) Heinemann-Raintree.

MacAulay, Kelley. How Do Plants Survive? 2013. (ENG., Illus.). 24p. (J). *(978-0-7787-1285-5(0))*; pap. *(978-0-7787-0003-6(8))* Crabtree Publishing Co.

Macceca, Michael L. The World of Plants, 1 vol. 2007. (Science Readers Ser.). (SPA & ENG.). 32p. (J). (gr. 4-4). pap. 8.99 *(978-0-7439-0589-3(X))* Shell Educational Publishing.

MacDonald, Margaret. Spring Plants. 2011. (Learn-Abouts Ser.). (Illus.). 16p. (J). pap. 7.95 *(978-1-59920-651-6(X))* Black Rabbit Bks.

Machajewski, Sarah. We Need Plants. 2015. (Creatures We Can't Live Without Ser.). (ENG.). 24p. (J). (gr. 3-4). 23.60 *(978-1-4994-1042-6(5)*, PowerKids Pr.) Rosen Publishing Group, Inc., The.

Mack, Molly. Plants That Move. 2016. (Plant Defenses Ser.). 24p. (J). (gr. 3-3). pap. 8.25 *(978-1-4994-2147-7(8)*, PowerKids Pr.) Rosen Publishing Group, Inc., The.

Madgwick, Wendy. Animals & Plants: 10 Easy-to-Follow Experiments for Learning Fun - Find Out about Nature & How Things Live! 2014. (ENG., Illus.). 270p. (J). (gr. -1-12). 8.99 *(978-1-86147-349-3(4)*, Armadillo) Anness Publishing GBR. Dist: National Bk. Network.

Maloof, Torrey. Photosynthesis, 1 vol. 2015. (Science Readers: Content & Literacy Ser.). (ENG., Illus.). 32p. (gr. 3-3). pap. 8.99 *(978-1-4807-4640-4(1))* Teacher Created Materials, Inc.

Mann, Rachel. Plants Grow from Seeds, 6 vols., Set. 2003. (Phonics Readers 1-36 Ser.). (ENG.). 8p. (gr. k-1). pap. 29.70 *(978-0-7368-3207-6(6)*, Phonics Readers) Capstone Press of Coughlan Cos.

El Manzano. (Coleccion Ciclos Vitales). (SPA., Illus.). (J). (gr. 3-5). pap. 7.96 *(978-84-236-2659-5(8)*, ED4704) Edebé ESP. Dist: Lectorum Pubns., Inc.

La Mariposa y la Oruga. (Coleccion Ciclos Vitales). (SPA., Illus.). (J). (gr. 3-5). pap. 7.96 *(978-84-236-2663-2(6)*, ED4702) Edebé ESP. Dist: Lectorum Pubns., Inc.

La Mariquita. (Coleccion Ciclos Vitales). (SPA., Illus.). (J). (gr. 3-5). pap. 7.96 *(978-84-236-2661-8(X)*, ED4701) Edebé ESP. Dist: Lectorum Pubns., Inc.

Marshall Cavendish Corporation Staff, contrib. by. Wildlife & Plants, 20 Vols., Set. 3rd ed. 2007. (Illus.). 1280p. (J). (gr. 4-8). lib. bdg. 514.21 *(978-0-7614-7693-1(8))* Marshall Cavendish Corp.

Marsico, Katie. Step-by-Step Experiments with Life Cycles. Ostrom, Bob, illus. 2012. (Step-By-Step Experiments Ser.). (ENG.). 32p. (J). (gr. 1-4). lib. bdg. 29.93 *(978-1-60973-587-6(0)*, 201232) Child's World, Inc., The.

Matheson, Christie. Plant the Tiny Seed. Matheson, Christie, illus. 2017. (Illus.). 40p. (J). (gr. -1-3). 15.99 *(978-0-06-239339-5(1)*, Greenwillow Bks.) HarperCollins Pubs.

May, Suellen. Invasive Terrestrial Plants. 2006. (Invasive Species Ser.). (Illus.). 100p. (gr. 6-12). lib. bdg. 30.00 *(978-0-7910-9128-9(7)*, Chelsea Hse.) Facts On File, Inc.

McEvoy, Paul. Plants. (Make it Work Ser.). (J). 42p. (gr. 4-8). pap. *(978-1-882210-41-1(7))*; (Illus.). 32p. (gr. 2-7). pap. 4.95 *(978-1-882210-31-2(X))* Action Publishing, Inc.

McGowan, Timothy. Plants Around the World. 2012. (InfoMax Readers Ser.). (ENG., Illus.). 24p. (J). (gr. 1-2). pap. 8.25 *(978-1-4488-9016-3(0)*, Rosen Classroom) Rosen Publishing Group, Inc., The.

McGraw-Hill, Wright. Amazing Plants, 6 vols. (Comprehension Strand Ser.). (gr. 4-8). 54.00 *(978-0-322-06030-2(3))* Wright Group/McGraw-Hill.

Midthun, Joseph. Plant Structure & Classification. 2014. (Illus.). 32p. (J). *(978-0-7166-2823-1(6))* World Bk., Inc.

Milet Publishing Staff. My First Bilingual Book - Plants. 2014. (My First Bilingual Book Ser.). (Illus.). 20p. (J). (— 1). (ENG & TUR.). bds. 7.99 *(978-1-84059-887-2(5))*; (ENG & ARA., bds. 7.99 *(978-1-84059-874-2(3))*; (POR & ENG., bds. 7.99 *(978-1-84059-883-4(2))*; (ENG & CHI., bds. 7.99 *(978-1-84059-876-6(X))*; (ENG & SOM., bds. 7.99 *(978-1-84059-885-8(9))* Milet Publishing.

—My First Bilingual Book - Plants (English-Farsi) 2014. (My First Bilingual Book Ser.). (ENG & PER., Illus.). 20p. (J). (— 1). bds. 7.99 *(978-1-84059-877-3(8))* Milet Publishing.

—My First Bilingual Book - Plants (English-Korean) 2014. (My First Bilingual Book Ser.). (ENG & KOR., Illus.). 20p. (J). (— 1). bds. 7.99 *(978-1-84059-881-0(6))* Milet Publishing.

—Plants - My First Bilingual Book. 2014. (My First Bilingual Book Ser.). (Illus.). 20p. (J). (— 1). (ENG & ITA.). bds. 7.99 *(978-1-84059-880-3(8))*; (FRE & ENG., bds. 7.99 *(978-1-84059-878-0(6))*; (ENG, POL & POR., bds. 7.99 *(978-1-84059-882-7(4))*; (ENG & BEN., bds. 7.99 *(978-1-84059-875-9(1))*; (ENG & VIE., bds. 7.99 *(978-1-84059-889-6(1))*; (ENG & URD., bds. 7.99 *(978-1-84059-888-9(3))*; (SPA & ENG., bds. 7.99 *(978-1-84059-886-5(7))*; (ENG & RUS., bds. 7.99 *(978-1-84059-884-1(0))* Milet Publishing.

Mills, Nathan & Abbott, Henry. How Plants Live & Grow. 2012. (Rosen Readers Ser.). (ENG., Illus.). 24p. (J). (gr. 1-2). pap. 8.25 *(978-1-4488-8770-5(4)*, Rosen Classroom) Rosen Publishing Group, Inc., The.

Mills, Nathan & Herman, Alley. Plants Live Everywhere. 2012. (Rosen Readers Ser.). (ENG., Illus.). 24p. (J). (gr. 1-2). pap. 8.25 *(978-1-4488-8797-2(6)*, Rosen Classroom) Rosen Publishing Group, Inc., The.

Mills, Nathan & Lewis, Charlotte. Plant Parts. 2012. (Rosen Readers Ser.). (ENG., Illus.). 16p. (J). (gr. k-1). pap. 7.00 *(978-1-4488-8725-5(9)*, Rosen Classroom) Rosen Publishing Group, Inc., The.

Mis, Melody S. Exploring Canyons. 2009. (Geography Zone: Landforms Ser.). (Illus.). 24p. (J). (gr. 2-4). pap. 8.25 *(978-1-4358-3114-8(4))*; 24p. (gr. 2-3). 42.50 *(978-1-61512-692-7(9))*; (J). lib. bdg. 22.60 *(978-1-4358-2716-5(3))* Rosen Publishing Group, Inc., The. (PowerKids Pr.).

Misztal, Yvonne. How Bugs & Plants Live Together. 2013. (InfoMax Readers Ser.). (ENG.). 24p. (J). (gr. 2-3). pap. 49.50 *(978-1-4777-2447-7(8))*; (Illus.). pap. 8.25 *(978-1-4777-2446-0(X))* Rosen Publishing Group, Inc., The. (Rosen Classroom).

Mitchell, Melanie S. Flowers. 2004. (First Step Nonfiction - Parts of Plants Ser.). (ENG., Illus.). 8p. (gr. -1-1). pap. 4.95 *(978-0-8225-3917-9(9)*, Lerner Pubns.) Lerner Publishing Group.

—Roots. 2004. (First Step Nonfiction - Parts of Plants Ser.). (ENG., Illus.). 8p. (gr. -1-1). pap. 4.95 *(978-0-8225-3919-3(5)*, Lerner Pubns.) Lerner Publishing Group.

—Stems. 2004. (First Step Nonfiction - Parts of Plants Ser.). (ENG., Illus.). 8p. (gr. -1-1). pap. 4.95 *(978-0-8225-3921-6(7)*, Lerner Pubns.) Lerner Publishing Group.

Monster Plants. 2004. (I-Quest Ser.). (Illus.). 48p. (J). per. *(978-1-84510-192-3(8))* Top That! Publishing PLC.

Mooney, Carla. Sunscreen for Plants. 2009. (Great Idea Ser.). (Illus.). 48p. (J). (gr. 4-6). lib. bdg. 26.60 *(978-1-59953-344-5(8))* Norwood Hse. Pr.

Morgan, Sally. How We Use Plants for Making Everyday Things. 2009. (How We Use Plants Ser.). 32p. (gr. 2-5). pap.

10.60 *(978-1-4358-2614-4(0),* Rosen Classroom) Rosen Publishing Group, Inc., The.

—How We Use Plants to Make Everyday Things. 2008. (How We Use Plants Ser.). (Illus.). 32p. lib. bdg. 26.50 *(978-1-4042-4424-5(7),* PowerKids Pr.) Rosen Publishing Group, Inc., The.

—The Plant Cycle. 2009. (Nature's Cycles Ser.). (J). (ENG.). 32p. (gr. 4-6). pap. 10.00 *(978-1-4358-2949-7(2));* lib. bdg. 26.50 *(978-1-4358-2867-4(4))* Rosen Publishing Group, Inc., The. (PowerKids Pr.).

—Plant Life Cycles. 2011. (Earth Cycles Ser.). 32p. (YA). (gr. 3-6). lib. bdg. 28.50 *(978-1-59920-524-3(6))* Black Rabbit Bks.

Morley, Margaret W. Little Wanderers. 2009. (Illus.). 116p. pap. 8.95 *(978-1-59915-317-9(3))* Yesterday's Classics.

Mullins, Matt. Think Like a Scientist in the Backyard. 2011. (Explorer Junior Library: Science Explorer Junior Ser.). (ENG.). 32p. (gr. 4-8). lib. bdg. 28.50 *(978-1-61080-167-6(9),* 201104) Cherry Lake Publishing.

—Think Like a Scientist in the Garden. 2011. (Explorer Junior Library: Science Explorer Junior Ser.). (ENG.). 32p. (gr. 4-8). lib. bdg. 28.50 *(978-1-61080-166-9(0),* 201102) Cherry Lake Publishing.

Nelson, Robin. Apple Trees. 2009. (First Step Nonfiction - Plant Life Cycles Ser.). (ENG.). 24p. (gr. k-2). 23.93 *(978-0-7613-4071-3(8),* Lerner Pubns.) Lerner Publishing Group.

El Nido del Pajaro. (Coleccion Ciclos Vitales). (SPA., Illus.). (J). (gr. 3-5). pap. 7.96 *(978-84-236-2651-9(2),* ED4699) Edebé ESP. Dist: Lectorum Pubns., Inc.

Nsrc. Science & Technology for Children Books: Experiments with Plants. 2004. (Illus.). 64p. (J). *(978-1-933008-08-0(3))* Smithsonian Science Education Ctr. (SSEC).

Nunn, Daniel. Food, 1 vol. 2012. (Why Living Things Need Ser.). (ENG.). 24p. (gr. -1-1). pap. 6.29 *(978-1-4329-5920-3(4));* lib. bdg. 22.65 *(978-1-4329-5914-2(X))* Heinemann-Raintree. (Acorn).

Los Oceanos.Tr. of Oceans. (SPA.). (J). (gr. 5-8). 12.00 *(978-84-342-1949-6(2))* Parramon Ediciones S.A. ESP. Dist: Distribuidora Norma, Inc.

O'Gorman, Neil. Plants & Their Environments. 2009. (Real Life Readers Ser.). 16p. (gr. 2-3). pap. 7.05 *(978-1-4358-0067-0(2),* Rosen Classroom) Rosen Publishing Group, Inc., The.

Ohanesian, Diane C. Seeds & Plants: Grades 2 & 3. (Illus.). (J). pap., wbk. ed. 4.99 *(978-0-88743-961-2(6))* School Zone Publishing Co.

Olson, Nathan. Plant Patterns. 2016. (Finding Patterns Ser.). (ENG.). 32p. (gr. 1-2). pap. 8.10 *(978-1-5157-3510-6(9),* Aplus Bks.) Capstone Press of Coughlan Cos.

Orme, Helen. Seeds, Bulbs, Plants & Flowers. 2010. (Science Everywhere! Ser.). 24p. 24.25 *(978-1-84898-291-8(7))* Black Rabbit Bks.

Owen, Ruth. How Do Plants Make Their Own Food? 2014. (World of Plants Ser.). 32p. (J). (gr. 2-5). lib. bdg. 26.25 *(978-1-4777-7149-5(2),* PowerKids Pr.) Rosen Publishing Group, Inc., The.

—Science & Craft Projects with Plants & Seeds. 2013. (Get Crafty Outdoors Ser.). (ENG., Illus.). 32p. (J). (gr. k-3). 26.50 *(978-1-4777-0247-5(4));* pap. 11.75 *(978-1-4777-0257-4(1))* Rosen Publishing Group, Inc., The. (PowerKids Pr.).

—What Do Roots, Stems, Leaves, & Flowers Do? 2014. (World of Plants Ser.). 32p. (J). (gr. 2-5). lib. bdg. 26.25 *(978-1-4777-7137-2(9),* PowerKids Pr.) Rosen Publishing Group, Inc., The.

Paderewski, Elliot. Plants, Animals, & People Live Together. 2016. (Rosen REAL Readers: STEM & STEAM Collection). 8p. (gr. 1-k). pap. 5.46 *(978-1-5081-2398-9(5),* Rosen Classroom) Rosen Publishing Group, Inc., The.

El Paisaje. (Coleccion Planeta Vivo).Tr. of Topography. (SPA.). (YA). (gr. 5-8). 10.36 *(978-84-342-1948-9(4))* Parramon Ediciones S.A. ESP. Dist: Lectorum Pubns., Inc.

Palazeti, Toulla. A Seed Was Planted. 2009. (ENG.). 32p. (J). (gr. -1-3). 16.95 *(978-1-934960-09-7(8),* Raven Tree Pr.,Csi) Continental Sales, Inc.

—A Seed Was Planted/Sembré una Semilla. Barcita, Pamela, illus. 2009. (ENG & SPA.). 32p. (J). (gr. -1-3). 16.95 *(978-1-932748-89-5(X));* pap. 7.95 *(978-1-932748-88-8(1))* Continental Sales, Inc. (Raven Tree Pr.,Csi).

Paris, Stephanie. Garden Invasion. 2015. (Building Fluency Through Reader's Theater Ser.). (ENG., Illus.). 32p. (gr. 5-5). pap. 7.99 *(978-1-4938-1293-6(9))* Teacher Created Materials, Inc.

Parker, Steve. Survival & Change. (Life Processes Ser.). 32p. pap. 7.50 *(978-1-4034-4076-1(X))* Heinemann-Raintree.

Parker, Steve & Collins UK Staff. Mega Plants. 2016. (ENG.). 32p. (J). (gr. 2-3). pap. 8.95 *(978-0-00-816379-2(0))* HarperCollins Pubs. Ltd. GBR. Dist: Independent Pubs. Group.

Parsons, Alexandra & Barnes, Jon. Plants. (Make It Work! Ser.). (Illus.). 48p. (J). pap. 7.95 *(978-0-590-24403-9(5))* Scholastic, Inc.

Pascoe, Elaine. The Ecosystem of a Milkweed Patch. 2009. (Library of Small Ecosystems Ser.). 24p. (gr. 3-4). 47.90 *(978-1-60853-854-6(0),* PowerKids Pr.) Rosen Publishing Group, Inc., The.

—Plant Clones. 2003. (Illus.). 48p. (J). 27.45 *(978-1-56711-444-7(X),* Blackbirch Pr., Inc.) Cengage Gale.

La Patata. (Coleccion Ciclos Vitales). (SPA., Illus.). pap. 7.96 *(978-84-236-2657-1(1),* ED4698) Edebé ESP. Dist: Lectorum Pubns., Inc.

Pearson, Scott. Kudzu. 2017. (Invasive Species Takeover Ser.). (ENG.). 32p. (gr. 3-7). 31.35 ***(978-1-68072-015-0(5),*** Bolt) Black Rabbit Bks.

Penguin Books Staff, ed. Plants. (Learners Ser.). (Illus.). 48p. (J). 3.50 *(978-0-7214-1709-7(4),* Dutton Juvenile) Penguin Publishing Group.

Perish, Patrick. Disgusting Plants. 2014. (Totally Disgusting Ser.). (ENG., Illus.). 24p. (J). (gr. 3-7). 25.95 *(978-1-62617-132-9(7),* Epic Bks.) Bellwether Media.

Petersen, Christine. Plants Need Sunlight. 2008. (21st Century Junior Library: Plants Ser.). (ENG.). 24p. (gr. 2-5). lib. bdg. 27.07 *(978-1-60279-273-9(9),* 200178) Cherry Lake Publishing.

Peterson, Cris. Seed, Soil, Sun: Earth's Recipe for Food. Lundquist, David R., photos by. 2012. (ENG., Illus.). 32p. (J). (gr. k-4). pap. 7.95 *(978-1-59078-947-6(4))* Boyds Mills Pr.

Phillips, Dee. Find It in the Park. 2006. (Can You Find It? Ser.). (Illus.). 24p. (gr. k-3). lib. bdg. 23.00 *(978-0-8368-6301-7(1),* Gareth Stevens Learning Library) Stevens, Gareth Publishing LLLP.

Plant Defenses. 2016. (Plant Defenses Ser.). 24p. (gr. 3-3). 141.60 *(978-1-4994-1917-7(1));* pap. 49.50 *(978-1-4994-2454-6(X))* Rosen Publishing Group, Inc., The. (PowerKids Pr.).

The Plant Kingdom: Level Q, 6 vols., Vol. 2. (Explorers Ser.). 32p. (gr. 3-6). 44.95 *(978-0-7699-0605-8(2))* Shortland Pubns. (U. S. A.) Inc.

Plants. 2010. (Discovering the Earth Ser.). (Illus.). 240p. (C). (gr. 9-18). 39.95 *(978-0-8160-6102-0(5))* Facts On File, Inc.

Plants & Seeds, 6 vols. (Sunshinetm Science Ser.). 24p. (gr. 1-2). 31.50 *(978-0-7802-0291-7(0))* Wright Group/McGraw-Hill.

Plants in My World. 2017. (Plants in My World Ser.). 24p. (gr. 4-6). 141.60 ***(978-1-5081-6185-1(2));*** pap. 49.50 ***(978-1-5081-6187-5(9))*** Rosen Publishing Group, Inc., The. (PowerKids Pr.).

Probst, Jeff. Remarkable Plants. 2017. (Challenge Yourself Ser.: 3). (ENG., Illus.). 176p. (J). (gr. 3-7). pap. 8.99 *(978-0-14-751808-8(3),* Puffin Books) Penguin Young Readers Group.

Puri, Devi. Plants That Hide. 2016. (Plant Defenses Ser.). (Illus.). 24p. (J). (gr. 3-3). pap. 8.25 *(978-1-4994-2143-9(5),* PowerKids Pr.) Rosen Publishing Group, Inc., The.

—Seeds, Bulbs, & Sprouts. 2015. (Garden Squad! Ser.). (ENG., Illus.). 24p. (J). (gr. 3-4). pap. 8.25 *(978-1-4994-0977-2(X),* PowerKids Pr.) Rosen Publishing Group, Inc., The.

Questions about Plants. 2003. 62p. pap. *(978-7-80051-848-5(5))* Dolphin Books, China.

Raintree. Itip 2004 Sprouts Pkg (29 Titl. 2004. pap. *(978-1-4109-1565-8(4))* Harcourt Schl. Pubs.

Rappoport, Bernice. Habitats of Africa: Text Pairs. 2008. (Bridges/Navigators Ser.). (J). (gr. 3). 81.00 *(978-1-4108-8359-9(0))* Benchmark Education Co.

Rattini, Kristin Baird. Seed to Plant. 2014. (Readers Ser.). (ENG., Illus.). 32p. (J). (gr. -1-1). pap. 3.99 *(978-1-4263-1470-4(1),* National Geographic Children's Bks.) National Geographic Society.

Rau, Dana Meachen. Plants. 2009. (Bookworms Ser.). 32p. (gr. 1-2). 15.95 *(978-0-7614-4097-0(6))* Marshall Cavendish Corp.

—Plants/Las Plantas. 2009. (Bookworms Ser.). (SPA & ENG.). 32p. (gr. 1-2). lib. bdg. 15.95 *(978-0-7614-4790-0(3))* Marshall Cavendish Corp.

Reader dsm-3 classroom plants Ea. 2004. (J). *(978-1-59242-521-1(6))* Delta Education, LLC.

Reader dsm-3 plant&animal population Ea. 2004. (J). *(978-1-59242-524-2(0))* Delta Education, LLC.

Readman, Jo & Roberts, Ley Honor. The World Came to My Place Today. 2003. (ENG., Illus.). 32p. 19.99 *(978-1-903919-01-9(0),* Eden Project Children's) Random House Children's Books GBR. Dist: Trafalgar Square Publishing.

Relf, Patricia. Magic School Plants Seeds. 2014. 14.00 *(978-1-63419-672-7(4))* Perfection Learning Corp.

Rice, Dona. Good Work. 2015. (TIME for KIDS(r) Nonfiction Readers Ser.). (ENG., Illus.). 12p. (gr. k-k). 4.99 *(978-1-4938-2139-6(3))* Teacher Created Materials, Inc.

—Pollination, 1 vol. rev. ed. 2014. (Science Readers: Content & Literacy Ser.). (ENG.). 32p. (gr. 2-2). pap. 8.99 *(978-1-4807-4598-8(7))* Teacher Created Materials, Inc.

Rice, Dona Herweck. Buen Trabajo. 2016. (TIME for KIDS(r) Nonfiction Readers Ser.). (SPA.). 12p. (J). (gr. k-k). 4.99 *(978-1-4938-3020-6(1))* Teacher Created Materials, Inc.

—How Plants Grow, 1 vol. 2nd rev. ed. 2013. (Nonfiction Readers Ser.). (ENG., Illus.). 12p. (J). (gr. 1-1). pap. 15.96 *(978-1-4807-1016-0(4))* Shell Educational Publishing.

Richardson, Gillian. 10 Plants That Shook the World. Rosen, Kim, illus. 2013. (World of Tens Ser.). (ENG.). 132p. (J). (gr. 5-7). pap. 14.95 *(978-1-55451-444-1(4),* 9781554514441); 2nd ed. 24.95 *(978-1-55451-445-8(2),* 9781554514458) Annick Pr., Ltd. CAN. Dist: Publishers Group West (PGW).

Richter, Sandy. Grow a Plant Inch by Inch. 2003. (Real Readers Series: Level Blue Ser.). (ENG., Illus.). 12p. (gr. 1-2). pap. 5.90 *(978-0-8239-6352-2(7))* Rosen Publishing Group, Inc., The.

Rigby Education Staff. Bugs on the Menu. (Sails Literacy Ser.). (Illus.). 16p. (gr. 2-3). 27.00 *(978-0-7635-9954-6(9),* 699549C99) Rigby Education.

Riggs, Kate. A Seed Needs Sun. Dogi, Fiammetta, illus. 2014. (ENG.). 14p. (J). (gr. -1-k). 7.99 *(978-1-56846-254-7(9),* Creative Editions) Creative Co., The.

Riggs, Sandy. Habitats of Australia: Text Pairs. 2008. (Bridges/Navigators Ser.). (J). (gr. 3). 94.00 *(978-1-4108-8360-5(4))* Benchmark Education Co.

Riley, Peter. All about Plants. 2016. (Ways into Science Ser.). (ENG., Illus.). 32p. (J). (gr. k-2). pap. 11.99 *(978-1-4451-3470-3(5),* Franklin Watts) Hachette Children's Group GBR. Dist: Hachette Bk. Group.

Rissman, Rebecca. Plants. 2013. (Real Size Science Ser.). (ENG.). 24p. (gr. -1-1). 22.65 *(978-1-4329-7880-8(2));* pap. 6.95 *(978-1-4329-7887-7(X))* Heinemann-Raintree. (Acorn).

Rivera, Sheila. Wetland. 2005. (First Step Nonfiction Ser.). (Illus.). 23p. (J). (gr. 3-7). lib. bdg. 18.60 *(978-0-8225-2598-1(4),* Lerner Pubns.) Lerner Publishing Group.

Robinson, Fay. Plants in Different Habitats. 2016. (Spring Forward Ser.). (J). (gr. 2). *(978-1-4900-9480-9(6))* Benchmark Education Co.

Romero, Libby. Characteristics of Plants. 2006. (J). pap. *(978-1-4108-6480-2(4))* Benchmark Education Co.

—Discover Plants. 2006. (J). pap. *(978-1-4108-6483-3(9))* Benchmark Education Co.

Root, Phyllis. Plant a Pocket of Prairie. Bowen, Betsy, illus. 2014. (ENG.). 40p. 14.95 *(978-0-8166-7980-5(0))* Univ. of Minnesota Pr.

Rosenberg, Pam. What Is a Plant? 2008. (21st Century Junior Library: Plants Ser.). (ENG.). 24p. (gr. 2-5). lib. bdg. 25.64 *(978-1-60279-272-2(0),* 200177) Cherry Lake Publishing.

Rushworth, Gary. What Makes a Plant a Plant? Set Of 6. 2011. (Navigators Ser.). (J). pap. 48.00 net. *(978-1-4108-6229-7(1))* Benchmark Education Co.

—What Makes a Plant a Plant: Text Pairs. 2008. (Bridges/Navigators Ser.). (J). (gr. 4). 89.00 *(978-1-4108-8400-8(7))* Benchmark Education Co.

Rustad, Martha E. H. Do Trees Get Hungry? Noticing Plant & Animal Traits. Moran, Mike, illus. 2015. (ENG.). 24p. (gr. k-2). lib. bdg. 25.32 *(978-1-4677-8559-4(8));* pap. 6.99 *(978-1-4677-8605-8(5))* Lerner Publishing Group. (Millbrook Pr.).

—Plants in Spring, 1 vol. 2012. (All about Spring Ser.). (ENG.). 24p. (gr. k-1). pap. 7.29 *(978-1-4296-9362-2(2));* pap. 41.70 *(978-1-4296-9363-9(0));* lib. bdg. 26.65 *(978-1-4296-8656-3(1))* Capstone Press of Coughlan Cos. (Pebble Plus).

Saavedra, Eusebio. The Tree & Anniy el Árbol y Annly. Rowley, Jillian, illus. 2011. 8p. (J). 7.00 *(978-0-9742432-9-0(9))* Flying Scroll Publishing, LLC.

Saddleback Educational Publishing Staff, creator. Plants. 2008. (Factoscope Ser.). (Illus.). 64p. (YA). per. 10.95 *(978-1-59905-236-6(9))* Saddleback Educational Publishing, Inc.

Samson, Tess. They Grow Plants. 2010. (Sight Word Readers Ser.). (J). 3.49 *(978-1-60719-616-7(6))* Newmark Learning LLC.

Sanchez, Anita. Leaflets Three, Let It Be! The Story of Poison Ivy. Brickman, Robin, illus. 2015. (ENG.). 32p. (J). (gr. -1-3). 16.95 *(978-1-62091-445-8(X))* Boyds Mills Pr.

Schaefer, Lola M. Pick, Pull, Snap! Where Once a Flower Bloomed. George, Lindsay Barrett, illus. 2003. (ENG.). 32p. (J). (gr. k-5). 17.99 *(978-0-688-17834-5(0),* Greenwillow Bks.) HarperCollins Pubs.

Scholastic, Inc. Staff, contrib. by. What Happens Next? Seed to Plant. 2013. (ENG.). 12p. (J). bds. 6.95 *(978-0-531-27255-8(9))* Scholastic Library Publishing.

School Zone Publishing Company Staff. Seeds & Plants. (Illus.). (J). 19.99 incl. audio compact disk *(978-0-88743-922-3(5))* School Zone Publishing Co.

Schuh, Mari. Carrots Grow Underground, 1 vol. 2011. (How Fruits & Vegetables Grow Ser.). (ENG., Illus.). 24p. (gr. k-1). pap. 6.29 *(978-1-4296-6185-0(2),* Pebble Bks.) Capstone Press of Coughlan Cos.

—Lettuce Grows on the Ground, 1 vol. 2011. (How Fruits & Vegetables Grow Ser.). (ENG., 24p. (gr. k-1). Illus.). pap. 6.29 *(978-1-4296-6188-1(7));* pap. 35.70 *(978-1-4296-6356-4(1))* Capstone Press of Coughlan Cos. (Pebble Bks.).

Science & Technology for Children Books, Experiments with Plants Set, 8 vols. 2004. (Illus.). 64p. (J). *(978-1-933008-20-2(2))* Smithsonian Science Education Ctr. (SSEC).

Science Stories Foss Spanish New Plants EA CR05. 2005. (J). *(978-1-59242-583-9(6))* Delta Education, LLC.

Scott, Janine. Growing a Plant. 2011. (Early Connections Ser.). (J). *(978-1-61672-230-2(4))* Benchmark Education Co.

Selwyn, Josephine. What Do Plants Need? 2014. (Little Books of Answers: Level a Ser.). (Illus.). 16p. (gr. k-2). pap. 7.95 *(978-1-927136-08-9(3))* Three Crows Media NZL. Dist: RiverStream Publishing.

Serafini, Frank. The Garden. Serafini, Frank, illus. 2008. (Looking Closely Ser.). (ENG., Illus.). 40p. (J). (gr. -1-2). 16.95 *(978-1-55453-210-0(8))* Kids Can Pr., Ltd. CAN. Dist: Hachette Bk. Group.

Shea, Therese. Watch Peas Grow / ¡Mira cómo crecen los Guisantes! 2011. (Watch Plants Grow! / ¡Mira cómo crecen las plantas! Ser.). (SPA., Illus.). 24p. (J). (gr. -1-2). 22.60 *(978-1-4339-4837-4(0))* Stevens, Gareth Publishing LLLP.

Sian Flowering Plants. 2004. (J). *(978-1-59242-030-8(3))* Delta Education, LLC.

Silvey, Anita. The Plant Hunters: True Stories of Their Daring Adventures to the Far Corners of the Earth, 1 vol. 2012. (ENG., Illus.). 96p. (J). (gr. 3-7). 21.99 *(978-0-374-30908-4(6),* 9780374309084, Farrar, Straus & Giroux (BYR)) Farrar, Straus & Giroux.

Slade, Suzanne. What Do You Know about Plant Life? (20 Questions: Science Ser.). 24p. (gr. 2-3). 2009. 42.50 *(978-1-60854-965-8(8),* PowerKids Pr.) 2008. (Illus.). (J). lib. bdg. 22.60 *(978-1-4042-4200-5(7))* Rosen Publishing Group, Inc., The.

Slingerland, Janet. The Secret Lives of Plants!, 1 vol. Kemarskaya, Oksana, illus. 2012. (Adventures in Science Ser.). (ENG.). 32p. (gr. 3-4). pap. 8.10 *(978-1-4296-7989-3(1));* pap. 47.70 *(978-1-4296-8467-5(4));* lib. bdg. 30.65 *(978-1-4296-7686-1(8))* Capstone Press of Coughlan Cos. (Graphic Library).

Smith, Jodene Lynn & Garbani, Tony. Oats, Peas, Beans, & Barley Grow, 1 vol. 2010. (Early Childhood Themes Ser.). (ENG., Illus.). 16p. (J). (gr. -1-2). pap. 6.99 *(978-1-4333-1489-6(4));* pap. 19.99 *(978-1-4333-1490-2(8))* Shell Educational Publishing.

Smith, Jodene Lynn & Reid, Stephanie. Las Plantas, 1 vol. rev. ed. 2010. (Early Childhood Themes Ser.). (SPA., Illus.). 16p. (J). (gr. -1-2). pap. 19.99 *(978-1-4333-2121-4(1))* Shell Educational Publishing.

—Plantas, 1 vol. rev. ed. 2010. (Early Childhood Themes Ser.).Tr. of Plants. (SPA., Illus.). 16p. (J). (gr. -1-2). pap. 6.99 *(978-1-4333-2120-7(3))* Shell Educational Publishing.

—Plants, 1 vol. 2010. (Early Childhood Themes Ser.). (ENG., Illus.). 16p. (J). (gr. -1-2). pap. 6.99 *(978-1-4333-1485-8(1));* pap. 19.99 *(978-1-4333-1486-5(X))* Shell Educational Publishing.

Smith, Jodene Lynn & Rice, Dona. Si Fuera un Árbol, 1 vol. rev. ed. 2010. (Early Childhood Themes Ser.). (SPA., Illus.). 16p. (J). (gr. -1-2). pap. 6.99 *(978-1-4333-2101-6(7))* Shell Educational Publishing.

Smith, Jodene Lynn & Rice, Dona Herweck. Si Fuera un Arbol, 1 vol. rev. ed. 2010. (Early Childhood Themes Ser.).Tr. of If I Were a Tree. (SPA., Illus.). 16p. (J). (gr. -1-2). pap. 19.99 *(978-1-4333-2102-3(5))* Shell Educational Publishing.

Sohn, Emily & Ash Sullivan, Erin. New Plants: Seeds in the Soil Patch. 2011. (iScience Readers Ser.). 24p. (J). (gr. k-2). lib. bdg. 21.27 *(978-1-59953-408-4(8))* Norwood Hse. Pr.

Souza, Dorothy M. Plant Invaders. 2003. (Watts Library). (Illus.). 64p. (J). 25.50 *(978-0-531-12211-2(5),* Watts, Franklin) Scholastic Library Publishing.

Spilsbury, Louise. Creeping Killers: Extreme Plants. 2015. (Extreme Biology Ser.). (ENG., Illus.). 48p. (J). (gr. 4-4). lib. bdg. 31.95 *(978-1-4824-2234-4(4))* Stevens, Gareth Publishing LLLP.

—Superstar Plants. 2014. (Nature's Got Talent Ser.). 32p. (J). (gr. k-5). lib. bdg. 26.25 *(978-1-4777-7072-6(0),* PowerKids Pr.) Rosen Publishing Group, Inc., The.

Spilsbury, Louise & Spilsbury, Richard. Killer Plants. 2017. (Engineered by Nature Ser.). (ENG., Illus.). 32p. (J). (gr. 3-8). lib. bdg. 25.95 *(978-1-62617-590-7(X),* Pilot Bks.) Bellwether Media.

Stanos, Dimi, et al. Plants in the Park. 2007. (Windows on Literacy Ser.). (ENG., Illus.). 8p. (J). pap. 9.95 *(978-0-7922-8463-5(1))* CENGAGE Learning.

Stefoff, Rebecca. The Flowering Plant Division. 2005. (Family Trees Ser.). (Illus.). 96p. (gr. 6-7). lib. bdg. 34.21 *(978-0-7614-1817-7(2),* Benchmark Bks.) Marshall Cavendish Corp.

Stephens, Catherine. Classification Clues. 2007. (Nonfiction Reading & Writing Workshops Ser.). (ENG., Illus.). 32p. (J). pap. 17.95 *(978-0-7922-4576-6(8))* CENGAGE Learning.

Stewart, Melissa. How Does a Seed Sprout? And Other Questions about Plants. Schwartz, Carol, illus. 2014. (Good Question! Ser.). (ENG.). 32p. (J). (gr. 1). pap. 5.95 *(978-1-4549-0671-1(5))* Sterling Publishing Co., Inc.

Stockland, Patricia M. Look at an Ash Tree. 2012. (First Step Nonfiction - Look at Trees Ser.). (ENG., Illus.). 8p. (gr. -1-1). pap. 4.95 *(978-1-4677-0526-4(8),* Lerner Pubns.) Lerner Publishing Group.

Stone, Lynn. Stems. 2007. (ENG., Illus.). 24p. (gr. 2-3). per. 8.95 *(978-1-60044-696-2(5))* Rourke Educational Media.

Stradling, Jan. Plants all Around: Level H, 6 vols. (First Explorers Ser.). 24p. (gr. 1-2). 29.95 *(978-0-7699-1450-3(0))* Shortland Pubns. (U. S. A.) Inc.

Sullivan, Laura. Flowering & Nonflowering Plants Explained. 2016. (Distinctions in Nature Ser.). 32p. (J). pap. 10.58 *(978-1-5026-2177-1(0));* lib. bdg. 28.50 *(978-1-5026-2179-5(7))* Cavendish Square Publishing.

Sundance/Newbridge LLC Staff. Where Plants Live. 2004. (Reading PowerWorks Ser.). (gr. 1-3). 37.50 *(978-0-7608-7799-9(8));* pap. 6.10 *(978-0-7608-7800-2(5))* Sundance/Newbridge Educational Publishing.

Swain, Cynthia. A Plant Has Parts. 2006. (Early Explorers Ser.). (J). pap. *(978-1-4108-6024-8(8))* Benchmark Education Co.

Taylor, Barbara. Inside Plants. 2010. (Invisible Worlds Ser.). 48p. (gr. 4). 28.50 *(978-0-7614-4189-2(1))* Marshall Cavendish GBR. Dist: Marshall Cavendish Corp.

Taylor-Butler, Christine. Experiments with Plants, 1 vol. 2011. (My Science Investigations Ser.). (ENG.). 32p. (gr. 1-3). pap. 8.29 *(978-1-4329-5368-3(0));* 27.32 *(978-1-4329-5362-1(1))* Heinemann-Raintree. (Heinemann First Library).

—Experiments with Plants. 2011. (True Bk Ser.). (Illus.). 48p. (J). (ENG.). pap. 6.95 *(978-0-531-26647-2(8));* lib. bdg. 29.00 *(978-0-531-26347-1(9))* Scholastic Library Publishing. (Children's Pr.).

Tell Me Why, Tell Me How, 6 vols., Group 3. Incl. How Do Caterpillars Become Butterflies? Bailer, Darice. 29.93 *(978-0-7614-3987-5(0));* How Do Mountains Form? Hicks, Terry Allan. 29.93 *(978-0-7614-3992-9(7));* Why Do Bears Hibernate? Bailer, Darice. 29.93 *(978-0-7614-3990-5(0));* Why Do Volcanoes Erupt? Mara, Wil. 29.93 *(978-0-7614-3989-9(7));* Why Does It Rain? Mara, Wil. 29.93 *(978-0-7614-3991-2(9));* Why Does the Sun Set? Hicks, Terry Allan. 29.93 *(978-0-7614-3993-6(5));* 32p. (gr. 3-18). (Tell Me Why, Tell Me How 3 Ser.). 2009. Set lib. bdg. 179.58 o.p. *(978-0-7614-3986-8(2))* Marshall Cavendish Corp.

Thomas, Isabel. Experiments with Plants. 2015. (Read & Experiment Ser.). (ENG., Illus.). 32p. (gr. 2-4). 30.65 *(978-1-4109-7924-7(5))* Heinemann-Raintree.

Throp, Claire. All about Plants. (All about Plants Ser.). (ENG.). 24p. (gr. -1-1). 2016. pap. 29.95 *(978-1-4846-3861-3(1))* 2014. 113.25 *(978-1-4846-0511-0(X))* Heinemann-Raintree. (Acorn).

Tidey, John & Tidey, Jackie. Plants. 2008. (China Ser.). 32p. (gr. 4-18). lib. bdg. 18.56 *(978-0-7614-3159-6(4),* Benchmark Bks.) Marshall Cavendish Corp.

Time for Kids Editors & Iasevoli, Brenda. Plants! 2006. (Time for Kids Ser.). (ENG., Illus.). 32p. (J). (gr. 1-3). pap. 3.99 *(978-0-06-078218-4(8))* HarperCollins Pubs.

Top That Publishing Staff, ed. Monster Plants. 2004. 48p. (J). pap. *(978-1-84510-193-0(6))* Top That! Publishing PLC.

Tornqvist, Carl-Erik. Plant Genetics. Hopkins, William G., ed. 2006. (Green World Ser.). (Illus.). 124p. (gr. 6-12). lib. bdg. 37.50 *(978-0-7910-8563-9(5),* Chelsea Hse.) Facts On File, Inc.

Twist, Clint. A Little Book of Slime: Everything That Oozes, from Killer Slime to Living Mold. 2012. (ENG., Illus.). 80p. (J). (gr. 4-18). 9.95 *(978-1-77085-006-4(6),* 9781770850064) Firefly Bks., Ltd.

Van Manen, Dave. Plants of the Pueblo Mountain Park. 2005. (Illus.). 120p. per. 19.95 *(978-0-9743791-7-3(4))* Medici Publishing, Inc.

Veitch, Catherine. Learning about Plants, 1 vol. 2013. (Natural World Ser.). (ENG., Illus.). 24p. (gr. -1-1). 22.65 *(978-1-4109-5401-5(3));* pap. 6.95 *(978-1-4109-5406-0(4))* Heinemann-Raintree. (NA-r).

—The Natural World. 2013. (Natural World Ser.). (ENG.). 24p. (gr. -1-1). lib. bdg. 90.60 *(978-1-4109-5405-3(6),* NA-r) Heinemann-Raintree.

Wade, Mary Dodson. Plants Grow! 2009. (I Like Plants! Ser.). (Illus.). 24p. (J). (gr. 1-3). pap. 7.95 *(978-0-7660-3612-3(X),* Enslow Elementary) Enslow Pubs., Inc.

—Seeds Sprout! 2009. (I Like Plants! Ser.). (Illus.). 24p. (J). (gr. 1-3). pap. 7.95 *(978-0-7660-3614-7(6),* Enslow Elementary) Enslow Pubs., Inc.

—Trees, Weeds, & Vegetables- So Many Kinds of Plants! 2009. (I Like Plants! Ser.). (Illus.). 24p. (J). (gr. 1-3). pap. 7.95 *(978-0-7660-3616-1(2),* Enslow Elementary) Enslow Pubs., Inc.

—Trees, Weeds, & Vegetables-So Many Kinds of Plants! 2009. (I Like Plants! Ser.). (Illus.). 24p. (J). (gr. k-3). lib. bdg. 22.60 *(978-0-7660-3156-2(X))* Enslow Pubs., Inc.

Wadsworth, Pamela. Golwg Gyntaf Ar Bethau Byw. Owen, Ken & Owen, Siân, illus. 2005. (WEL.). 24p. pap. *(978-1-85596-250-7(0))* Dref Wen.

—Golwg Gyntaf Ar Wahanol Blanhigion AC Anifeiliaid. 2005. (WEL., Illus.). 24p. pap. *(978-1-85596-254-5(3))* Dref Wen.

—Gwahanol Blanhigion AC Anifeiliaid. Owen, Ken & Owen, Siân, illus. 2005. (WEL.). 24p. pap. *(978-1-85596-223-1(3))* Dref Wen.

—Rhagor Am Bethau Byw Ar Waith. 2005. (WEL., Illus.). 24p. pap. (978-1-85596-234-7(9)) Dref Wen.
—Rhagor Am Wahanol Blanhigion Ac Anifeiliaid. 2005. (WEL., Illus.). 24p. pap. (978-1-85596-224-8(1)) Dref Wen.
Waldron, Melanie. Plants, 1 vol. (Essential Life Science Ser.). (ENG.). 48p. (gr. 4-6). 2014. 33.32 (978-1-4329-7812-9(8)) 2013. pap. 9.95 (978-1-4329-7843-3(8)) Heinemann-Raintree. (Heinemann InfoSearch).
—Variation & Classification, 1 vol. 2014. (Essential Life Science Ser.). (ENG.). 48p. (gr. 4-6). lib. bdg. 33.32 (978-1-4329-7813-6(6), Heinemann InfoSearch) Heinemann-Raintree.
Waldron, Melanie, et al. Essential Life Science, 1 vol. 2014. (Essential Life Science Ser.). (ENG.). 48p. (gr. 4-6). lib. bdg. 133.28 (978-1-4329-7814-3(4), Heinemann InfoSearch) Heinemann-Raintree.
Walker, Colin. Plants Grow Almost Anywhere. Simons, Sally, illus. 2012. (Concept Science: Plants Ser.). (ENG.). 16p. (J). (gr. k-3). pap. 8.50 (978-0-8136-7331-8(3)) Modern Curriculum Pr.
Walker, Colin, et al. Las Differentes Cosas Que Vienende las Plantas. (Coleccion Conceptos de Ciencia en Big Books). (SPA.). (J). (gr. k-3). 12.00 (978-0-8136-6753-9(4)) Modern Curriculum Pr.
Walker, Kate. Plants. 2011. (Investigating Earth Ser.). 32p. (gr. 2). 28.50 (978-1-60870-559-7(5)) Marshall Cavendish Corp.
Wallace, Marianne D. America's Seashores: Guide to Plants & Animals. 2005. (America's Ecosystems Ser.). (ENG., Illus.). 48p. (J). (gr. 3-7). pap. 11.95 (978-1-55591-483-7(7), 1250708) Fulcrum Publishing.
Wanjie, Anne, ed. The Basics of Plant Structures. 2013. (Core Concepts Ser.). (ENG., Illus.). 96p. (YA). (gr. 7-12). lib. bdg. 34.60 (978-1-4777-0553-7(8)) Rosen Publishing Group, Inc., The.
Ward, Jennifer. What Will Grow? Ghahremani, Susie, illus. 2017. (ENG.). 40p. (J). 16.99 (978-1-68119-030-3(3), 9781681190303, Bloomsbury USA Childrens) Bloomsbury Publishing USA.
Warren, Howard. The Life Cycle of Plants: Set Of 6. 2010. (Navigators Ser.). (J). pap. 44.00 net. (978-1-4108-6224-2(0)) Benchmark Education Co.
—The Life Cycle of Plants: Text Pairs. 2008. (Bridges/Navigators Ser.). (J). (gr. 3). 89.00 (978-1-4108-8363-6(9)) Benchmark Education Co.
Watts, Barrie. Bean. 2004. (Watch It Grow Ser.). (J). (gr. k-3). lib. bdg. 27.10 (978-1-58340-503-1(8)) Black Rabbit Bks.
—El Hámster. (Coleccion Ciclos Vitales). (SPA., Illus.). 32p. (J). (gr. 3-5). (978-84-236-2665-6(2), ED4704) Edebé ESP. Dist: Lectorum Pubns., Inc.
Weakland, Mark. Yogi Bear's Guide to Plants. Cornia, Christian, illus. 2015. (Yogi Bear's Guide to the Great Outdoors Ser.). (ENG.). 32p. (gr. 1-2). lib. bdg. 27.99 (978-1-4914-6547-9(6)) Capstone Press of Coughlan Cos.
Weekly Reader Editorial Staff. Things at the Park. 2006. (Things in My World Ser.). (Illus.). 16p. (gr. -1-2). lib. bdg. 19.00 (978-0-8368-6809-8(9), Weekly Reader Leveled Readers) Stevens, Gareth Publishing LLLP.
—Things at the Park (Las Cosas Del Parque) 2006. (Things in My World/ Las cosas de mi mundo Ser.). (ENG & SPA., Illus.). 16p. (gr. -1-2). pap. 5.30 (978-0-8368-7228-6(2), Weekly Reader Leveled Readers) Stevens, Gareth Publishing LLLP.
—Things at the Park/Las Cosas del Parque. 2006. (Things in My World/ Las cosas de mi mundo Ser.). (ENG & SPA., Illus.). 16p. (gr. -1-2). lib. bdg. 19.00 (978-0-8368-7221-7(5), Weekly Reader Leveled Readers) Stevens, Gareth Publishing LLLP.
Weekly Reader Editorial Staff, contrib. by. Things at the Park. 2006. (Things in My World Ser.). (Illus.). 16p. (gr. -1-2). pap. 5.30 (978-0-8368-6816-6(1), Weekly Reader Leveled Readers) Stevens, Gareth Publishing LLLP.
Whited, Zillah. Flower Fables. 2011. 28p. pap. 35.95 (978-1-258-02350-8(4)) Literary Licensing, LLC.
Wiedenhoeft, Alex C. Plant Nutrition. Hopkins, William G., ed. 2006. (Green World Ser.). (Illus.). 144p. (gr. 6-12). lib. bdg. 37.50 (978-0-7910-8564-6(3), Chelsea Hse.) Facts On File, Inc.
Wilkins, John-Paul. What Can Live in the Snow?, 1 vol. 2014. (What Can Live There? Ser.). (ENG., Illus.). 24p. (gr. -1-1). 22.65 (978-1-4846-0577-6(2), Heinemann Read & Learn) Heinemann-Raintree.
—What Can Live There?, 1 vol. 2014. (What Can Live There? Ser.). (ENG.). 24p. (gr. -1-1). 67.95 (978-1-4846-0579-0(9), Heinemann Read & Learn) Heinemann-Raintree.
Williams, Kathryn. Plants. 2017. (Readers Ser.). (ENG., Illus.). 48p. (J). (-k). pap. 4.99 (978-1-4263-2694-3(7), National Geographic Children's Bks.) National Geographic Society.
Wiseman, Blaine. The Midwest. 2014. (Illus.). 32p. (J). (978-1-4896-1226-7(2)) Weigl Pubs., Inc.
—The Northeast. 2014. (Illus.). 32p. (J). (978-1-4896-1230-4(0)) Weigl Pubs., Inc.
—The Southeast. 2014. (Illus.). 32p. (J). (978-1-4896-1234-2(3)) Weigl Pubs., Inc.
—The Southwest. 2014. (Illus.). 32p. (J). (978-1-4896-1238-0(6)) Weigl Pubs., Inc.
—The West. 2014. (Illus.). 32p. (J). (978-1-4896-1242-7(4)) Weigl Pubs., Inc.
World Book, Inc Staff, contrib. by. Encyclopedia of Plants. 2013. (J). (978-0-7166-7522-8(6)) World Bk., Inc.
—Learning about Plants. 2011. (J). (978-0-7166-0230-9(X)) World Bk., Inc.
—Plants Around the World. 2010. (J). (978-0-7166-7742-0(3)) World Bk., Inc.
—Resources & Cumulative Index. 2005. (World Book's Science & Nature Guides Ser.). 80p. (J). (978-0-7166-4216-9(6)) World Bk., Inc.
The World of Plants. 2014. (World of Plants Ser.). 32p. (J). (gr. 2-5). 157.50 (978-1-4777-7093-1(3), PowerKids Pr.) Rosen Publishing Group, Inc., The.
World's Weirdest Plants. 2016. (World's Weirdest Plants Ser.). 00024p. (J). pap. 48.90 **(978-1-4824-5837-4(3))** Stevens, Gareth Publishing LLLP.
York, M. J. Plants in Spring. 2017. (Welcome, Spring! Ser.). (ENG.). 24p. (J). (gr. -1-2). lib. bdg. 27.07 (978-1-5038-1654-1(0), 211507) Child's World, Inc., The.
Zondervan Staff. Weird & Wonderful Creations, 1 vol. 2014. (Made by God Ser.). (ENG., Illus.). 128p. (J). 9.99 (978-0-310-73124-5(0)) Zonderkidz.
Zorzi, Gina & Sánchez, Lucía M. Desiertos: This Is a Desert. 2011. (2G Ecosistemas Ser.). (SPA.). 36p. (J). (gr. k-2). pap. 6.99 (978-1-61541-424-6(X)) American Reading Co.
Zuchora-Walske, Christine. That Bull Is Seeing Red! Science's Biggest Mistakes about Animals & Plants. 2014. (Science Gets It Wrong Ser.). (Illus.). 32p. (gr. 4-6). pap. 7.95 (978-1-4677-4550-5(2)); (ENG.). lib. bdg. 26.60 (978-1-4677-3660-2(0), Lerner Pubns.) Lerner Publishing Group.

PLANTS—ANATOMY
see Plant Anatomy

PLANTS—DISEASES
see Plant Diseases

PLANTS—ECOLOGY
see Plant Ecology

PLANTS, EDIBLE

Amstutz, Lisa J. Edible Gardening: Growing Your Own Vegetables, Fruits, & More. 2016. (Gardening Guides). (ENG., Illus.). 32p. (gr. 3-4). lib. bdg. 27.99 (978-1-4914-8235-3(4), Snap Bks.) Capstone Press of Coughlan Cos.
Colby, Jennifer. Plants We Eat. 2014. (21st Century Junior Library: Plants Ser.). (ENG.). 24p. (J). (gr. 2-5). 25.64 (978-1-63188-039-1(X), 205563) Cherry Lake Publishing.
—Plants We Wear. 2014. (21st Century Junior Library: Plants Ser.). (ENG.). 24p. (J). (gr. 2-5). 25.64 (978-1-63188-040-7(3), 205567) Cherry Lake Publishing.
Domnauer, Teresa & Kenah, Katharine. Incredible Edibles. 2006. (Extreme Readers: Level 3 Ser.). (Illus.). 32p. (gr. 1-2). 13.95 (978-0-7569-6851-9(8)) Perfection Learning Corp.
Encyclopaedia Britannica, Inc. Staff, compiled by. Food Plants. 2003. (Illus.). 64p. 14.95 (978-1-59339-044-0(0)) Encyclopaedia Britannica, Inc.
Encyclopaedia Britannica Publishers, Inc. Staff. Food Plants. 2003. (Illus.). 64p. 14.95 (978-1-59339-013-6(0)) Encyclopaedia Britannica, Inc.
Feldman, Sarah. Incredible, Edible Plants. 2011. (Early Connections Ser.). (J). (978-1-61672-664-5(4)) Benchmark Education Co.
—Incredible, Edible Plants: Set Of 6. 2011. (Early Connections Ser.). (J). pap. 39.00 net. (978-1-4108-1541-5(2)) Benchmark Education Co.
Hollar, Sherman. A Closer Look at Plant Classifications, Parts, & Uses. 2011. (J). lib. bdg. 31.70 (978-1-61530-529-2(7)) Rosen Publishing Group, Inc., The.
Lundgren, Julie K. Plants As Food, Fuel, & Medicine. 2012. (ENG.). 24p. (gr. 4-5). pap. 8.95 (978-1-61810-235-5(4)) Rourke Educational Media.
Morgan, Sally. How We Use Plants: For Food. (How We Use Plants Ser.). 32p. 2009. (gr. 2-5). pap. 10.60 (978-1-4358-2611-3(6), Rosen Classroom) 2008. (Illus.). (J). lib. bdg. 26.50 (978-1-4042-4421-4(2), PowerKids Pr.) Rosen Publishing Group, Inc., The.
Piper, Ross. Survival! Staying Alive in the Wild, 1 vol. 2009. (Extreme! Ser.). (ENG.). 32p. (gr. 3-4). pap. 7.95 (978-1-4296-3130-3(9), Fact Finders) Capstone Press of Coughlan Cos.
Rockwell, Lizzy. Plants Feed Me. Rockwell, Lizzy, illus. 2015. (ENG., Illus.). 32p. (J). (gr. -1-1). 6.99 (978-0-8234-3307-0(2)) Holiday Hse., Inc.
—Plants Feed Me. 2014. (ENG.). 32p. (J). (gr. -1-1). 16.95 (978-0-8234-2526-6(6)) Holiday Hse., Inc.
Sweet, Muriel. Common Edible & Useful Plants of the West. rev. ed. 2003. (Illus.). 64p. (J). pap. 7.95 (978-0-87961-046-3(8)) Naturegraph Pubs., Inc.
Wade, Mary Dodson. People Need Plants! 2009. (I Like Plants! Ser.). (Illus.). 24p. (J). (gr. k-3). lib. bdg. 22.60 (978-0-7660-3153-1(5)); (gr. 1-3). pap. 7.95 (978-0-7660-3613-0(8), Enslow Elementary) Enslow Pubs., Inc.

PLANTS, EXTINCT
see Plants, Fossil

PLANTS—FICTION

Anthony, Joseph. The Dandelion Seed's Big Dream. Arbo, Cris, illus. 2014. 32p. (J). (gr. k-4). 16.95 (978-1-58469-496-0(3)); (ENG.). pap. 8.95 (978-1-58469-497-7(1)) Dawn Pubns.
Archambault, Marc. Teevert the Little Green Leaf. 2010. 31p. 18.98 (978-0-557-17967-1(X)) Lulu Pr., Inc.
Bardsley-Sirois, Lois. Katherine's Winter Garden. 2012. 24p. pap. 12.99 (978-1-4525-6269-8(5)) Balboa Pr.
Barkow, Henriette. The Giant Turnip. Johnson, Richard, illus. 2004. 32p. (J). (ENG & BEN.). pap. (978-1-85269-734-1(2)); (ENG & PAN.). pap. (978-1-85269-742-6(3)); (POL & ENG.). pap. (978-1-85269-743-3(1)); (ENG & POR.). pap. (978-1-85269-744-0(X)); (ENG & URD.). pap. (978-1-85269-750-1(4)) Mantra Lingua.
Barton, Tamra Clum. The Adventures of Lucky the Leaf. 2007. 32p. per. 18.65 (978-1-4257-3026-0(4)) Xlibris Corp.
Beer, Barbara Vagnozzi. Jack & the Beanstalk. Vagnozzi, Barbara, illus. 2005. (Flip-Up Fairy Tales Ser.). (ENG.). 24p. (J). pap. (978-1-904550-20-4(7)) Child's Play International Ltd.
Belew, Elizabeth A. There's Always a Place for Mr. Plant. 2010. 24p. 11.32 (978-1-4520-8656-9(7)) AuthorHouse.
Bennett, Marilyn J. The Poinsettia Adventure. 2010. 60p. pap. 21.99 (978-1-4490-7108-0(2)) AuthorHouse.
Brenner, Barbara & Sweet, Melissa. The Plant That Kept on Growing. 2015. (ENG., Illus.). 34p. (J). pap. 11.95 (978-1-899694-59-4(5), ipicturebooks) ibooks, Inc.
Bryan, Marcia. Dandy Lion: The Adventure Begins. 2006. (Illus.). 40p. (J). (gr. -1-5). 18.95 (978-1-57736-376-7(0)) Providence Hse Pubs.
Burton-Hupp, Lynne. Venus the Very Proper Fly Trap. 2009. 28p. pap. 24.95 (978-1-60563-993-2(1)) America Star Bks.
Canetti, Yanitzia. ABC's of Plants. 2010. (ENG.). 40p. (J). pap. 8.99 (978-1-59835-118-7(4), BrickHouse Education) Cambridge BrickHouse, Inc.
—Abecedario de Plantas. 2010. (SPA.). 40p. (J). pap. 8.99 (978-1-59835-119-4(2), BrickHouse Education) Cambridge BrickHouse, Inc.
Capeci, Anne. Little Lab or Horrors. 2003. (Dexter's Laboratory Science Log Ser.: Vol. 4). (Illus.). 78p. (J). (978-0-439-47242-5(3)) Scholastic, Inc.
Carbone, Courtney. Flower Power! (DC Super Friends) Schoening, Dan, illus. 2014. (Little Golden Book Ser.). (ENG.). 24p. (J). (-k). 4.99 (978-0-385-37396-8(1), Golden Bks.) Random Hse. Children's Bks.
Carle, Eric. The Tiny Seed. Carle, Eric, illus. 2009. (World of Eric Carle Ser.). (ENG., Illus.). 36p. (J). (gr. -1). 7.99 (978-1-4169-7917-3(4), Little Simon) Little Simon.
Ching, Brent & Santos, Jordan. Little Lima Bean. 2009. 16p. pap. 9.95 (978-0-9821698-5-8(X)) Watermark Publishing, LLC.
Clark, Danell. Daisy. Irwin, April, illus. 2008. 28p. pap. 11.95 (978-1-59858-642-8(4)) Dog Ear Publishing, LLC.
Coates, Theresa. Imaginary Time of Life. 2007. 102p. pap. 10.95 (978-0-7414-4067-9(9)) Infinity Publishing.
Cordone Warner, Debra. Buddy & A Walk in the Woods. 2010. 38p. pap. 18.99 (978-0-557-60690-0(X)) Lulu Pr., Inc.
Corwin, Jeff. The Wild, Wild Southwest!, 3 vols. 2010. (Jeff Corwin Ser.: 3). (ENG.). 112p. (J). (gr. 1-3). 4.99 (978-0-14-241440-8(9), Puffin Books) Penguin Young Readers Group.
Dompierre, Judith E. Wow, What's That? 2012. 48p. pap. 24.95 (978-1-4626-9332-0(6)) America Star Bks.
DuTemple, Leslie A. One Little Balsam Fir: A Northwoods Counting Book. Robinson, Susan, illus. 2006. 32p. (J). per. (978-1-892384-37-9(X)) Avery Color Studios, Inc.
Edwards, Tanille & Edwards, Latoya. Jordan & Justine's Weekend Adventures Pt. 1-2: Plants. 2007. (SPA.). 32p. (J). (gr. k-3). 12.95 (978-0-9787302-3-9(2)) Fire Flies Entertainment, LLC.
Ehlert, Lois. Leaf Man. 2005. (ENG., Illus.). 40p. (J). (gr. -1-3). 17.99 (978-0-15-205304-8(2)) Houghton Mifflin Harcourt Publishing Co.
Eisele, Barbara. Miss Thistle & Friends. 2009. 48p. pap. 12.99 (978-1-4490-2007-1(0)) AuthorHouse.
Ering, Timothy Basil. The Story of Frog Belly Rat Bone. Ering, Timothy Basil, illus. 2013. (ENG., Illus.). 48p. (J). (gr. -1-3). 17.99 (978-0-7636-6661-3(0)) Candlewick Pr.
Everett, Clare. Henrietta - a Rabbit's Tale of Summer Time Fun. 2012. 116p. pap. (978-1-84914-296-0(3)) CompletelyNovel.com.
Falwell, Cathryn. Mystery Vine. Falwell, Cathryn, illus. 2009. (Illus.). 32p. (J). lib. bdg. 17.89 (978-0-06-177197-2(X), Greenwillow Bks.) HarperCollins Pubs.
Fleischman, Paul. Weslandia. braille ed. 2004. (Illus.). (J). (gr. k-3). spiral bd. (978-0-616-01641-1(7)) Canadian National Institute for the Blind/Institut National Canadien pour les Aveugles.
—Weslandia. Hawkes, Kevin, illus. 2006. (gr. -1-3). 17.00 (978-0-7569-6566-2(7)) Perfection Learning Corp.
Frommer, Julia. Happiness Is Yours. 2007. 24p. 13.95 (978-1-4303-1176-8(2)) Lulu Pr., Inc.
Gellman, Ellie B. Netta & Her Plant. Ugliano, Natascia, illus. 2014. (Tu B'Shevat Ser.). (ENG.). 32p. (J). (gr. -1-2). 17.95 (978-1-4677-0422-9(9), Kar-Ben Publishing) Lerner Publishing Group.
Gibbs, Lynne. Time to Share: A Story of Sharing. Mitchell, Melanie, illus. 2009. (Let's Grow Together Ser.). 32p. (J). (gr. -1-2). lib. bdg. 22.60 (978-1-60754-757-0(0)) Windmill Bks.
Giff, Patricia Reilly. The Garden Monster. Palmisciano, Diane, illus. (Fiercely & Friends Ser.). (J). (gr. k-2). 2014. (ENG.). 40p. 16.99 (978-0-545-43379-2(7)) 2013. (978-0-545-24460-2(9)) Scholastic, Inc. (Orchard Bks.).
Glennon, Michelle. My Big Green Teacher: Taking the Green Road. Glennon, Michelle, illus. 2008. (Illus.). 32p. (J). 19.95 (978-0-9796625-7-7(5)) GDG Publishing.
Gordon, Michele Lynne. The Springing Singing Sprout: Little Tales of a Little Sprout. 2008. 54p. pap. 19.95 (978-1-4241-8942-7(X)) America Star Bks.
Grandma Carol's Plant: Individual Title Six-Packs. (gr. k-1). 23.00 (978-0-7635-9039-0(8)) Rigby Education.
Hapka, Catherine, pseud. Plants vs. Zombies. 2014. (I Can Read! Level 2 Ser.). (J). lib. bdg. 13.55 (978-0-606-35477-6(8)) Turtleback Bks.
—Plants vs. Zombies: Save Your Brains! 2014. (I Can Read Level 2 Ser.). (ENG.). 32p. (J). (gr. -1-3). pap. 3.99 (978-0-06-229496-8(2)) HarperCollins Pubs.
Harris, Joel Chandler. Nights with Uncle Remus. 2008. 288p. 29.95 (978-1-60664-915-2(9)) Aegypan.
Heidari, Mahdi. Little Red Fire. Taylor, Adam, illus. 2012. 40p. (J). pap. 12.99 (978-0-9838321-8-8(8)) Higher Ground Pr.
Hofmeister, Alan, et al. The Seed. (Reading for All Learners Ser.). (Illus.). (J). pap. (978-1-56861-112-9(9)) Swift Learning Resources.
Hood, Susan. Rooting for You. Cordell, Matthew, illus. 2014. (ENG.). 32p. (J). (gr. -1-k). 16.99 (978-1-4231-5230-9(1)) Disney Pr.
Howard, Ellen. The Big Seed. 2007. (ENG.). 36p. (J). (gr. -1-3). 10.99 (978-1-4169-6155-0(0), Simon & Schuster/Paula Wiseman Bks.) Simon & Schuster/Paula Wiseman Bks.
Hughes, Mónica. The Big Turnip. Williams, Lisa, illus. 2006. (Collins Big Cat Ser.). (ENG.). 32p. (J). (gr. -1-k). pap. 5.99 (978-0-00-718644-0(4)) HarperCollins Pubs. Ltd. GBR. Dist: Independent Pubs. Group.
Hulin, Pamela. Down under in Australia. Mendoza, Carlos, illus. 2007. 20p. per. 24.95 (978-1-4241-8929-8(2)) America Star Bks.
Hunt, Connie. Planting Love: A Tale of Love & Growing. 2012. 48p. 18.10 (978-1-4669-0965-6(X)); pap. 8.10 (978-1-4669-0967-0(6)) Trafford Publishing.
Ingalls, Ann. Biggety Bat: Chow down, Biggety! Zenz, Aaron, illus. 2015. (Scholastic Reader, Level 1 Ser.). (ENG.). 32p. (J). (gr. -1-1). pap. 3.99 (978-0-545-66264-2(8)) Scholastic, Inc.
Ioan, Elwyn. Ici'r Dŵl A'r Corrach Coch. 2005. (WEL., Illus.). 36p. pap. (978-0-86243-428-1(9)) Y Lolfa.
Jarrell, Pamela R. Planting a Seed. Meier, Kerry L., illus. l.t. ed. 2006. 12p. (J). (gr. -1-k). pap. 10.95 (978-1-57332-350-5(0), HighReach Learning, Incorporated) Carson-Dellosa Publishing, LLC.
Jenson-Elliott, Cindy. Weeds Find a Way. Fisher, Carolyn, illus. 2014. (ENG.). 40p. (J). (gr. -1-3). 17.99 (978-1-4424-1260-6(7)) Simon & Schuster Children's Publishing.
Johnson, Richard, illus. The Giant Turnip. 2004. (J). 24p. (978-1-85269-737-2(7)); 24p. (978-1-85269-739-6(3)); 24p. (978-1-85269-740-2(7)); 24p. (978-1-85269-741-9(5)); 24p. (978-1-85269-745-7(8)); 24p. (978-1-85269-746-4(6)); 24p. (978-1-85269-747-1(4)); 24p. (978-1-85269-748-8(2)); 24p. (978-1-85269-749-5(0)); 24p. (978-1-85269-789-1(X)); 24p. (978-1-85269-736-5(9)); 24p. (978-1-85269-735-8(0)); 24p. (978-1-85269-733-4(4)); (ENG & RUS.). 32p. pap. (978-1-85269-788-4(1)) Mantra Lingua.
Juslin, Lee. Nurse Frosty Saves the Day. 2009. 35p. pap. 22.00 (978-0-557-09486-8(0)) Lulu Pr., Inc.
Kaplan, Madeline. Planet Earth Gets Well. 2008. (ENG.). 24p. pap. 9.99 (978-1-4196-8986-4(X)) CreateSpace Independent Publishing Platform.
Kiernan, Tim. Liams Luck & Finnegans Fortune. 2009. (ENG.). 144p. pap. 10.95 (978-1-933916-48-4(6), Ferne Pr.) Nelson Publishing & Marketing.
Kim, Cecil. One Little Bean: Observation - Life Cycle. Cowley, Joy, ed. Dattola, Chiara, illus. 2015. (Step up - Creative Thinking Ser.). (ENG.). 32p. (gr. -1-2). 26.65 (978-1-925246-12-4(4)); 7.99 (978-1-925246-64-3(7)); 26.65 (978-1-925246-38-4(8)) ChoiceMaker Pty. Ltd., The AUS. (Big and SMALL). Dist: Lerner Publishing Group.
Kitami, Yoko. Cactus. 2005. (Los Especiales de A la Orilla del Viento Ser.).Tr. of Cactus. (SPA., Illus.). 36p. (J). (gr. 2-4). (978-968-16-7386-4(7), FC15223) Fondo de Cultura Economica.
Klempner, Rebecca. A Dozen Daises for Raizy: A Shavuos Story. Chava, illus. 2008. 30p. (J). (gr. -1-2). 10.95 (978-1-929628-41-4(2)) Hachai Publishing.
Krauss, Ruth & Krauss. The Carrot Seed. Johnson, Crockett, illus. 60th anniv. ed. 2004. (Rise & Shine Ser.). (ENG.). 32p. (J). (gr. -1-3). pap. 6.99 (978-0-06-443210-8(6)) HarperCollins Pubs.
The Laughing Lavender Field. 2005. (J). 5.00 (978-0-9765731-0-4(5)) DTJ, LLC.
Leszczynski, Diana. Fern Verdant & the Silver Rose. 2009. (Playaway Children Ser.). (J). 59.99 (978-1-4332-7708-5(5)) Findaway World, LLC.
Lettrick, Robert. The Murk. Disney Storybook Art Team, illus. 2015. (ENG.). 320p. (J). (gr. 5-9). 16.99 (978-1-4231-8695-3(8)) Hyperion Bks. for Children.
Loos, Jody C. Alex the Alien: Bubble Magic. 2013. 24p. pap. 14.95 (978-1-4787-0322-8(9)) Outskirts Pr., Inc.
Lotfy, Evelyn. Ms. Plant & Friends. 2011. 24p. (gr. -1). pap. 14.98 (978-1-4567-5448-8(3)) AuthorHouse.
Lucas, Nancy T. Peppy's Coral Kingdom. 2008. (ENG.). 24p. pap. 12.99 (978-1-4196-9046-4(9)) CreateSpace Independent Publishing Platform.
Lucas, Ronne Kay. How the Cactus Got Its Thorns. 2013. 20p. pap. 24.95 (978-1-4626-8915-6(9)) America Star Bks.
Luke, Melinda. The Green Dog. Manning, Jane K., illus. 2006. (Science Solves It Ser.). 32p. (J). pap. 7.99 (978-0-15-356581-6(0)) Houghton Mifflin Harcourt School Pubs.
MacLachlan, Patricia. Prairie Days. Moser, Barry, illus. 2014. (J). (978-1-4424-4191-0(7), McElderry, Margaret K. Bks.) McElderry, Margaret K. Bks.
Magers, Ramona Hirsch. Walter's Discovery. Hirsch, Charmaine, illus. 2008. 26p. pap. 24.95 (978-1-60563-623-8(1)) America Star Bks.
Martin, Dawn L. Freeze Dance: A Story of the Dancing Cactus. 2011. 36p. pap. (978-1-4269-8196-8(1)) Trafford Publishing (UK) Ltd.
May, Eleanor. Let's Go, Snow! Temperature Measurement. Pillo, Cary, illus. 2017. (Math Matters (r) Ser.). (ENG.). 32p. (gr. k-3). 23.99 **(978-1-57565-808-7(9))** Kane Press, Inc.
McArthur, Nancy. The Mystery of the Plant That Ate Dirty Socks. 2004. 162p. pap. 11.95 (978-0-595-33693-7(0), Backinprint.com) iUniverse, Inc.
—The Plant That Ate Dirty Socks. (Plant That Ate Dirty Socks Ser.: Bk. 1). 119p. (J). (gr. k-3). pap. 4.50 (978-0-8072-1494-7(9), Listening Library) Random Hse. Audio Publishing Group.
McQuinn, Anna, et al. A Leo le Gusta Bebelandia. Hearson, Ruth, illus. 2015. (SPA & ENG.). 24p. (J). (— 1). lib. bdg. 9.95 (978-1-58089-704-4(5)) Charlesbridge Publishing, Inc.
Merchant, Richard. The Anise Seed. 2013. 24p. pap. 24.95 (978-1-63004-371-1(0)) America Star Bks.
Metzger, Steve. The Biggest Leaf Pile. Dubin, Jill, illus. 2003. (J). (978-0-439-55657-6(0)) Scholastic, Inc.
—We're Going on a Leaf Hunt. Sakamoto, Miki, illus. (J). 2008. (ENG.). 32p. (gr. -1-3). pap. 6.99 (978-0-439-87377-2(0), Cartwheel Bks.) 2005. pap. (978-0-439-77361-4(X)) Scholastic, Inc.
Minger, Janet. How Do Strawberries & Green Beans Sleep at Night? 2011. 28p. pap. 13.54 (978-1-4567-2239-5(5)) AuthorHouse.
Morgan, Ruth. Jess & the Bean Root. Vagnozzi, Barbara, illus. 2005. (ENG.). 24p. (J). lib. bdg. 23.65 (978-1-59646-732-3(0)) Dingles & Co.
Nolen, Jerdine. Plantzilla Goes to Camp. Catrow, David, illus. 2006. (ENG.). 32p. (J). (gr. k-3). 17.99 (978-0-689-86803-0(0), Simon & Schuster/Paula Wiseman Bks.) Simon & Schuster/Paula Wiseman Bks.
Nolen, Jerdine & Keliher, Brian. Plantzilla. Catrow, David, illus. 2005. (ENG.). 32p. (J). (gr. -1-3). reprint ed. pap. 7.99 (978-0-15-205392-5(1)) Houghton Mifflin Harcourt Publishing Co.
O'Connor, Jane. Poison Ivy Expert. Glasser, Robin Preiss & Enik, Ted, illus. 2008. (Fancy Nancy - I Can Read! Ser.). 32p. (J). lib. bdg. 13.55 (978-1-4364-5050-6(0), Turtleback) Turtleback Bks.
Oliver, Jane. The Birthday Surprise. Raga, Silvia, illus. 2009. (Get Ready (Windmill Books) Ser.). 32p. (J). (gr. k-2). lib. bdg. 22.60 (978-1-60754-257-5(9)) Windmill Bks.
Ozgur, Lynne Emily. Darryl & the Mountain. Abay, Ismail, illus. 2009. (ENG.). 32p. (J). (gr. 2-4). 9.95 (978-1-59784-138-2(2)) Tughra Bks.
Pacheco, Maria & Garcia-Martinez, Julia. The Hamburger Tree. Hergenroeder, Ernie, illus. 2006. 24p. (J). (978-0-9776835-0-5(8)) Run With Me Publishing.
Palazetti, Toulla. Seed Was Planted. Barcita, Pamela, illus. 2010. (ENG.). 32p. (J). (gr. -1-3). pap. 7.95 (978-1-934960-10-3(1), Raven Tree Pr.,Csi) Continental Sales, Inc.

Park, Linda Sue. Forest of Wonders. Madsen, Jim, illus. 2016. (Wing & Claw Ser.: 1). 352p. (J). (gr. 3-7). 16.99 (978-0-06-232738-3(0)) HarperCollins Pubs.

Parker, Emma. Chuck the Chilli. 2010. (Illus.). pap. (978-1-877547-92-8(1)) First Edition Ltd.

Pier, Daniel Wayne. Ferrous the Venus Fly Trap Meets the Cactus. 2008. 36p. pap. 24.95 (978-1-60441-645-9(9)) PublishAmerica, Inc.

Pike, Aprilynne. Hechizos. 2012.Tr. of Spells. (UND & SPA.). 352p. (YA). pap. 18.95 (978-84-96886-27-8(1)) Ediciones Urano S. A. ESP. Dist: Spanish Pubs., LLC.

—Spells. (Wings Ser.: 2). (ENG.). (YA). (gr. 8). 2011. 384p. pap. 9.99 (978-0-06-166808-1(7)) 2010. 368p. 16.99 (978-0-06-166806-7(0)) HarperCollins Pubs. (HarperTeen).

—Spells, 7 vols. 2010. (YA). 78.75 (978-1-4407-8375-3(6)) Recorded Bks., Inc.

—Wings. 2011. (Wings Ser.: 1). (ENG.). 320p. (YA). (gr. 8). pap. 8.99 (978-0-06-166805-0(2), HarperTeen) HarperCollins Pubs.

Pittar, Gill. Milly, Molly & Jimmy's Seeds. 2004. (Illus.). 28p. (978-1-86972-000-1(8)) Milly Molly Bks.

Pizzoli, Greg. The Watermelon Seed. Pizzoli, Greg, illus. 2013. (ENG., Illus.). 40p. (J). (gr. -1-k). 16.99 (978-1-4231-7101-0(2)) Disney Pr.

Polette, Keith. Paco & the Giant Chile Plant/Paco y la Planta de Chile Gigante. Dulemba, Elizabeth, illus. 2008. (ENG & SPA.). 32p. (J). (gr. -1-3). pap. 7.95 (978-0-9794462-3-8(6), Raven Tree Pr.,Csi) Continental Sales, Inc.

Press, Applesauce. Grow Your Own Flesh-Eating Plant! Everything You Need for the Care & Feeding of Your Venus Fly Trap. 2012. (ENG.). 64p. (J). 18.95 (978-1-60433-223-0(9), Applesauce Pr.) Cider Mill Pr. Bk. Pubs., LLC.

Prignano, Barbara. How Bunnies Got Their Cottontails. 2009. (Illus.). 20p. pap. 11.95 (978-1-60860-675-7(9), Eloquent Bks.) Strategic Book Publishing & Rights Agency (SBPRA).

Prose, Francine. Rhino, Rhino, Sweet Potato. Armstrong, Matthew S., illus. 2009. 32p. (J). (gr. -1-1). lib. bdg. 18.89 (978-0-06-008079-2(5)) HarperCollins Pubs.

Pugliano-Martin, Carol. The Great Big Giant Turnip: Set Of 6. 2010. (Early Connections Ser.). (J). pap. 39.00 net. (978-1-4108-1553-8(6)) Benchmark Education Co.

Rere The Storyteller. I Am a Wish. 2013. 36p. 25.99 (978-1-4808-0090-8(2)) Archway Publishing.

Rey, H. A. Curious George Plants a Seed. 2007. (Curious George Ser.). (ENG., Illus.). 24p. (J). (gr. -1-3). 4.99 (978-0-618-77710-5(5)) Houghton Mifflin Harcourt Publishing Co.

—Jorge el Curioso Siembra Una Semilla. Zappy, Erica, ed. Canetti, Yanitzia, tr. 2007. (Curious George Ser.). (ENG & SPA., Illus.). 24p. (J). (gr. -1-3). mass mkt. 3.99 (978-0-618-89688-2(0)) Houghton Mifflin Harcourt Publishing Co.

Rey, H. A. & Rey, Margret. The H. A. Rey Treasury of Stories. 2015. (Dover Children's Classics Ser.). (ENG., Illus.). 112p. (J). (gr. 2-4). pap. 14.99 (978-0-486-78468-7(1)) Dover Pubns., Inc.

Robinson, Bonita. The Little Seed That Could. 2011. 24p. pap. 24.95 (978-1-4626-4234-2(9)) America Star Bks.

Rochelin, Ghyslaine. The Coconut Tree. Bertoni, Oliver, illus. 2010. (HAT.). 32p. (J). pap. 14.95 (978-1-60195-319-3(4)) International Step by Step Assn.

Root, Phyllis. One North Star: A Counting Book. Prange, Beckie & Bowen, Betsy, illus. 2016. (ENG.). 36p. (J). 16.95 (978-0-8166-5063-7(2)) Univ. of Minnesota Pr.

Rovetch, L. Bob. TLC Grow with Me! McLeod, Chum, illus. 2005. (J). (978-1-58987-114-4(6)) Kindermusik International.

Santos, Penelope. A Seed's Story. 2015. (Rosen REAL Readers: STEM & STEAM Collection). (ENG.). 8p. pap. 5.46 (978-1-4994-9569-0(2), Rosen Classroom) Rosen Publishing Group, Inc., The.

Shivers, Juliette. Brenda Doesn't Like Broccoli. 2004.Tr. of Brenda no le Gusta Bróculi. (Illus.). 25p. (J). 6.50 (978-0-9769379-0-6(5)) Ingram's Nutrition Consultations.

Simonson, Louise. Harley Quinn's Crazy Creeper Caper. Vecchio, Luciano, illus. 2017. (Batman & Robin Adventures Ser.). (ENG.). 88p. (gr. 2-3). lib. bdg. 26.65 **(978-1-4965-5347-8(0)**, DC Super Heroes) Stone Arch Bks.

Sommer, Cindy. Salvando Las Flores de Camelia, 1 vol. Klein, Laurie Allen, illus. 2016. (SPA.). 32p. (J). (gr. k-3). pap. 9.95 (978-1-62855-872-2(5)) Arbordale Publishing.

Spalding, Esta. Knock about with the Fitzgerald-Trouts. Smith, Sydney, illus. 2017. (ENG.). 320p. (J). (gr. 3-7). 16.99 (978-0-316-29860-5(3)) Little, Brown Bks. for Young Readers.

Splawn, "E". Planting Fruitful Seeds. 2011. 32p. pap. 12.77 (978-1-4567-3896-9(8)) AuthorHouse.

Stephens, Sarah Hines. Poison Ivy's Rainforest Revenge. Levins, Tim, illus. 2017. (Batman & Robin Adventures Ser.). (ENG.). 88p. (gr. 2-3). lib. bdg. 26.65 **(978-1-4965-5352-2(7)**, DC Super Heroes) Stone Arch Bks.

Swain, Cynthia. Sorting at the Nature Center. 2006. (Early Explorers Ser.). (J). pap. (978-1-4108-6039-2(6)) Benchmark Education Co.

Swanson, Tina M. Silly Sierra & the Mysterious Mushroom. 2011. 28p. pap. 13.99 (978-1-4634-3594-3(0)) AuthorHouse.

Switzer, Vern. Lucy the Cantaloupe. Connally, Perry L., Sr., illus. 2005. 32p. (J). 15.95 (978-0-9753542-1-6(3)) Rural Farm Productions.

—Puffy the Watermelon. Listokin, David & Connally, Perry L., Sr., illus. 2004. 24p. (J). 15.95 (978-0-9753542-0-9(5)) Rural Farm Productions.

Thompson, Holly. The Wakame Gatherers. Wilds, Kazumi, illus. 2007. (Wakame Gatherers Ser.). 32p. (J). (gr. -1-3). 16.95 (978-1-885008-33-6(3), Shen's Bks.) Lee & Low Bks., Inc.

Tolstoy, Aleksei. The Gigantic Turnip. Sharkey, Niamh, illus. 2005. (ENG.). 40p. (J). (gr. -1-2). pap. 8.99 (978-1-905236-58-9(1)) Barefoot Bks., Inc.

Walker, Richard. Jack & the Beanstalk. 2009. (ENG., Illus.). (J). 16.99 (978-1-84686-297-7(3)) Barefoot Bks., Inc.

—Juan y los Frijoles Magicos. 2008. (ENG & SPA., Illus.). 40p. (J). (gr. -1-1). 10.99 (978-1-84686-216-8(7)) Barefoot Bks., Inc.

Weisenfluh, Craig. ABC's in the Trees, a LittleWeeds Adventure: A book for Little Ones. 2007. (Illus.). (J). 11.95 (978-0-9746782-1-4(X)) B'Squeak Productions.

Wheeler, Eliza. Miss Maple's Seeds. Wheeler, Eliza, illus. (ENG., Illus.). 32p. (J). 2017. (-k). pap. 8.99 (978-0-425-28889-4(7), Puffin Books) 2013. (gr. -1-k). 17.99 (978-0-399-25792-6(6), Nancy Paulsen Books) Penguin Young Readers Group.

—Miss Maple's Seeds. 2017. lib. bdg. 19.65 **(978-0-606-40087-9(7))** Turtleback Bks.

Williams, Dawn. Very Little Venus & the Very Friendly Fly. Chou, Joey, illus. 2007. 48p. (J). 15.00 (978-0-9770783-2-5(9)) SunriseHouse Pubs.

Wolchansky, Molly Kay. The Cactus & the Balloon. 2009. 24p. pap. 12.99 (978-1-4490-1037-9(7)) AuthorHouse.

Woodbridge, Nancy Garfield. A Bouquet of Fairy Tales. 2012. 108p. pap. 15.99 (978-1-4771-4492-3(7)) Xlibris Corp.

Wortche, Allison. Rosie Sprout's Time to Shine. Barton, Patrice, illus. 2011. (ENG.). 40p. (J). (gr. -1-2). 17.99 (978-0-375-86721-7(X), Knopf Bks. for Young Readers) Random Hse. Children's Bks.

PLANTS, FOSSIL

Aspen-Baxter, Linda. Plants. 2004. (Prehistoric Life Ser.). (Illus.). 32p. (J). lib. bdg. 26.00 (978-1-59036-114-6(8)) Weigl Pubs., Inc.

Aspen-Baxter, Linda & Lomberg, Michelle. Planets. 2004. (Prehistoric Life Ser.). (Illus.). 24p. (J). (gr. -1-3). pap. 9.95 (978-1-59036-174-0(1)) Weigl Pubs., Inc.

Connors, Kathleen. Petrified Forests. 2012. (Fossilized! Ser.). (Illus.). 24p. (J). (gr. 2-5). pap. 8.15 (978-1-4339-6422-0(8)); lib. bdg. 22.60 (978-1-4339-6420-6(1)) Stevens, Gareth Publishing LLLP.

Hyde, Natalie. Plant Fossils. 2013. (ENG., Illus.). 32p. (J). (978-0-7787-1264-0(8)); pap. (978-0-7787-1268-8(0)) Crabtree Publishing Co.

Sohn, Emily & Kentor Schmauss, Judy. Structures of Life: What Is this Fossil? 2011. (IScience Readers Ser.). 32p. (J). (gr. 3-4). lib. bdg. 22.60 (978-1-59953-420-6(7)) Norwood Hse. Pr.

PLANTS—GROWTH

see Growth (Plants)

PLANTS, MEDICINAL

see Botany, Medical

PLANTS—PROPAGATION

see Plant Propagation

PLANTS—STRUCTURE

see Plant Anatomy

PLANTS, USEFUL

see Botany, Economic; Plants, Edible

PLASTIC MATERIALS

see Plastics

PLASTICS

see also Synthetic Products

Barraclough, Sue & Ridley, Sarah. A Plastic Toy. 2006. (How It's Made Ser.). (Illus.). 32p. (gr. 1-4). lib. bdg. 26.00 (978-0-8368-6704-6(1), Gareth Stevens Learning Library) Stevens, Gareth Publishing LLLP.

Blaxland, Wendy. Helmets. 2009. (How Are They Made? Ser.). (Illus.). 32p. (gr. 4-6). lib. bdg. 18.56 (978-0-7614-4755-9(5)) Marshall Cavendish Corp.

Blevins, Wiley. The Not-So-Right Day. Kreloff, Elliott, illus. 2016. (Basic Concepts Ser.). (ENG.). 24p. (J). (gr. -1-1). lib. bdg. 14.99 (978-1-63440-083-1(6)) Red Chair Pr.

Colich, Abby. Plastic, 1 vol. 2013. (Exploring Materials Ser.). (ENG.). 24p. (gr. -1-1). 22.65 (978-1-4329-8017-7(3)); pap. 6.95 (978-1-4329-8025-2(4)) Heinemann-Raintree. (Acorn).

Ditchfield, Christin. The Story Behind Plastic, 1 vol. 2011. (True Stories Ser.). (ENG.). 32p. (gr. 3-3). 30.65 (978-1-4329-5441-3(5), NA-h) Heinemann-Raintree.

Edison, Erin. Shred It!, 1 vol. 2013. (Destruction Ser.). (ENG., Illus.). 12p. (gr. k-1). bds. 9.99 (978-1-4765-3529-6(9), Pebble Plus) Capstone Press of Coughlan Cos.

Fix, Alexandra. Plastic. 2016. (Reduce, Reuse, Recycle Ser.). (ENG.). 32p. (gr. 1-3). pap. 8.29 (978-1-4846-3590-2(6), Heinemann First Library) Heinemann-Raintree.

Goodstein, Madeline P. Plastics & Polymers Science Fair Projects. LaBaff, Tom & LaBaff, Stephanie, illus. rev. exp. ed. 2010. (Chemistry Science Projects Using the Scientific Method Ser.). 160p. (J). (gr. 5-18). 35.94 (978-0-7660-3412-9(7)) Enslow Pubs., Inc.

—Plastics & Polymers Science Fair Projects Using Hair Gel, Soda Bottles, & Slimy Stuff. 2004. (Chemistry! Best Science Projects Ser.). (Illus.). 128p. (J). lib. bdg. 27.94 (978-0-7660-2123-5(8)) Enslow Pubs., Inc.

Graham, Ian. You Wouldn't Want to Live Without Plastic! Antram, David, illus. 2015. (You Wouldn't Want to Live Without... Ser.). (ENG.). 32p. (J). lib. bdg. 29.00 (978-0-531-21929-4(1), Watts, Franklin) Scholastic Library Publishing.

—You Wouldn't Want to Live Without Plastic! 2015. (You Wouldn't Want to Live Without... Ser.). lib. bdg. 20.80 (978-0-606-37472-9(8)) Turtleback Bks.

Jennings, Terry. Plastic. 2006. (Illus.). 32p. (YA). (gr. 1-18). lib. bdg. 27.10 (978-1-932333-03-9(7)) Chrysalis Education.

Kachur, Matthew. A Miracle Material & un material Milagroso: 6 English, 6 Spanish Adaptations. 2011. (ENG & SPA.). (J). 97.00 net. (978-1-4108-5717-0(4)) Benchmark Education Co.

Knight, Geof. Plastic Pollution, 1 vol. 2012. (Hot Topics Ser.). (ENG.). 64p. (gr. 7-8). pap. 10.95 (978-1-4329-6047-6(4), NA-h) Heinemann-Raintree.

Langley, Andrew. Plastic. 2008. (Everyday Materials Ser.). (ENG., Illus.). 24p. (J). (gr. k-3). pap. (978-0-7787-4136-7(2)) Crabtree Publishing Co.

Lepetit, Angie. Trash Magic: A Book about Recycling a Plastic Bottle. 2013. (Earth Matters Ser.). (ENG.). 32p. (gr. 1-2). pap. 47.70 (978-1-62065-744-7(9)); pap. 8.10 (978-1-62065-743-0(0)); lib. bdg. 27.32 (978-1-62065-049-3(5)) Capstone Press of Coughlan Cos. (Aplus Bks.).

Llewellyn, Claire. Plastic. 2005. (I Know That! Ser.). (Illus.). 24p. (J). (gr. 1-3). lib. bdg. 22.80 (978-1-932889-53-6(1)) Sea-To-Sea Pubns.

Macken, JoAnn Early. Take a Closer Look at Plastic. 2016. (Core Content Science — Take a Closer Look Ser.). (ENG., Illus.). 40p. (J). (gr. 2-4). lib. bdg. 26.65 (978-1-63440-050-3(X)) Red Chair Pr.

Malam, John. Journey of a Toy, 1 vol. 2012. (Journey of A... Ser.). (ENG.). 32p. (gr. 1-3). pap. 8.29 (978-1-4329-6612-6(X), Heinemann First Library) Heinemann-Raintree.

Malue, Jenna. Recycling Plastic: Understand Place Value. 2014. (Math Masters: Number & Operations in Base Ten Ser.). (Illus.). 24p. (J). (gr. 2-3). 23.60 (978-1-4777-6427-5(5)); (ENG., pap. 8.25 (978-1-4777-4651-6(X)) Rosen Publishing Group, Inc., The. (Rosen Classroom).

Mitchell, Melanie S. Plastic. 2003. (First Step Nonfiction - Materials Ser.). (ENG., Illus.). 24p. (gr. k-2). lib. bdg. 23.93 (978-0-8225-4620-7(5)) Lerner Publishing Group.

Morris, Neil. Plastics. 2010. (Materials That Matter Ser.). 32p. (YA). (gr. 4-7). 28.50 (978-1-60753-068-8(6)) Amicus Publishing.

Newman, Patricia. Plastic, Ahoy! Investigating the Great Pacific Garbage Patch. Crawley, Annie, illus. 2014. (ENG.). 48p. (gr. 3-6). lib. bdg. 30.60 (978-1-4677-1283-5(3), Millbrook Pr.) Lerner Publishing Group.

Oxlade, Chris. Global Warming. 2012. (Mapping Global Issues Ser.). 48p. (J). (gr. 7-9). lib. bdg. 34.25 (978-1-59920-508-3(4)) Black Rabbit Bks.

Rae, Alison. Oil, Plastics, & Power. 2010. (Development Without Damage Ser.). (YA). (gr. 5-9). 34.25 (978-1-59920-251-8(4)) Black Rabbit Bks.

Rau, Dana Meachen. Plastic. 2011. (Bookworms Chapter Books: Use It! Reuse It! Ser.). 24p. (gr. 2-3). 22.79 (978-1-60870-518-4(8)) Marshall Cavendish GBR. Dist: Marshall Cavendish Corp.

Royston, Angela. Plastic: Let's Look at the Frisbee. 2005. (J). (978-1-4109-1820-8(3)); (ENG.). 24p. pap. (978-1-4109-1829-1(7)) Steck-Vaughn.

Shores, Lori. Cómo Hacer Slime. 2010. (Divertirse con la Ciencia/Hands-On Science Fun Ser.).Tr. of How to Make Slime. (SPA, MUL & ENG.). 24p. (gr. k-1). lib. bdg. 26.65 (978-1-4296-6106-5(2)) Capstone Press of Coughlan Cos.

—How to Make Slime, 1 vol. 2010. (Hands-On Science Fun Ser.). (ENG., 24p. (gr. k-1). Illus.). pap. 7.29 (978-1-4296-5575-0(5)); 26.65 (978-1-4296-4492-1(3)); pap. 41.70 (978-1-4296-5576-7(3)) Capstone Press of Coughlan Cos. (Pebble Plus).

Sterngass, Jon & Kachur, Matthew. Plastics. 2005. (Great Inventions Ser.). (Illus.). 48p. (gr. 5-12). lib. bdg. 31.00 (978-0-8368-5878-5(6), Gareth Stevens Secondary Library) Stevens, Gareth Publishing LLLP.

Troupe, Thomas Kingsley. Shred It!, 1 vol. 2013. (Destruction Ser.). (ENG.). 24p. (gr. k-1). 26.65 (978-1-4765-2089-6(5), Pebble Plus) Capstone Press of Coughlan Cos.

Walker, Kate. Plastic Bottles & Bags. 2010. (Recycling Ser.). (Illus.). 32p. (J). (gr. 1). 28.50 (978-1-60870-133-9(6)) Marshall Cavendish GBR. Dist: Marshall Cavendish Corp.

Wallace, Holly. Plastic. 2007. (How We Use Materials/Watts Ser.). (Illus.). 30p. (J). (gr. 4-7). lib. bdg. 28.50 (978-1-59920-005-7(8)) Black Rabbit Bks.

PLATYPUS

Antill, Sara. Platypus. 2010. (Unusual Animals Ser.). (Illus.). 24p. (J). (gr. k-3). (ENG.). pap. 8.15 (978-1-60754-997-0(2)); lib. bdg. 22.60 (978-1-60754-991-8(3)) Windmill Bks.

Borgert-Spaniol, Megan. Platypuses. 2015. (Animal Safari Ser.). (ENG., Illus.). 24p. (J). (gr. k-3). lib. bdg. 25.95 (978-1-62617-212-8(9), Blastoff! Readers) Bellwether Media.

Caper, William. Platypus: A Century-Long Mystery. 2008. (Uncommon Animals Ser.). (Illus.). 32p. (YA). (gr. 2-5). lib. bdg. 25.27 (978-1-59716-735-2(5), 1284359) Bearport Publishing Co., Inc.

Clarke, Ginjer L. Platypus! Mirocha, Paul, illus. 2004. (Step into Reading Ser.). (ENG.). 32p. (J). (gr. -1-1). pap. 3.99 (978-0-375-82417-3(0), Random Hse. Bks. for Young Readers) Random Hse. Children's Bks.

Collard, Sneed B., III. A Platypus, Probably. Plant, Andrew, illus. 2005. (ENG.). 32p. (J). (gr. k-3). per. 7.95 (978-1-57091-584-0(9)) Charlesbridge Publishing, Inc.

Ganeri, Anita. Discover the Platypus. 2016. (Fabulous Animals Ser.). (ENG., Illus.). 32p. (gr. 1-3). lib. bdg. 27.32 (978-1-4846-2710-5(5), Heinemann First Library) Heinemann-Raintree.

Hirsch, Rebecca. Platypuses: Web-Footed Billed Mammals. 2015. (Comparing Animal Traits Ser.). (ENG., Illus.). 32p. (J). (gr. 2-4). pap. 8.99 (978-1-4677-6064-5(1)) Lerner Publishing Group.

Hirsch, Rebecca E. Platypuses: Web-Footed Billed Mammals. 2015. (Comparing Animal Traits Ser.). (ENG., Illus.). 32p. (J). (gr. 2-4). lib. bdg. 26.65 (978-1-4677-5581-8(8), Lerner Pubns.) Lerner Publishing Group.

Leaf, Christina. Platypus. 2014. (Extremely Weird Animals Ser.). (ENG., Illus.). 24p. (J). (gr. 3-8). lib. bdg. 25.95 (978-1-62617-076-6(2), Pilot Bks.) Bellwether Media.

Lunis, Natalie. Electric Animals. 2011. (Animals with Super Powers Ser.). 24p. (YA). (gr. 2-5). lib. bdg. 22.61 (978-1-61772-121-2(2)) Bearport Publishing Co., Inc.

Meister, Cari. Do You Really Want to Meet a Platypus? Fabbri, Daniele, illus. 2014. (Do You Really Want to Meet... ? Ser.). (ENG.). 24p. (J). (gr. 1-4). 27.10 (978-1-60753-460-0(6)) Amicus Publishing.

Murray, Julie. Platypuses, 1 vol. 2011. (Australian Animals Ser.). (ENG., Illus.). 32p. (J). (gr. 2-5). 28.50 (978-1-61783-013-6(5)) ABDO Publishing Co.

Rudolph, Jessica. Platypus. 2017. (Weirder & Cuter Ser.). (ENG.). 24p. (J). (gr. -1-3). 17.95 **(978-1-68402-264-9(9))** Bearport Publishing Co., Inc.

Whiting, Sue. Platypus. Jackson, Mark, illus. 2016. (ENG.). 32p. (J). (gr. k-4). 16.99 (978-0-7636-8098-5(2)) Candlewick Pr.

PLAY

see also Amusements; Games; Recreation; Sports

Alizadeh, Kate. Quiet! Alizadeh, Kate, illus. 2017. (Child's Play Library). (ENG., Illus.). 32p. (J). (978-1-84643-887-5(X)) Child's Play International Ltd.

Allan, Delores. Magical Moments with Roy & Toni: Fun at the Fair. 2011. 28p. pap. 13.59 (978-1-4634-1546-4(X)) AuthorHouse.

Atlantic, Leonard. We Play with Pets! 2017. (Ways to Play Ser.). 24p. (gr. k-k). pap. 8.15 **(978-1-4824-6357-6(1))** Stevens, Gareth Publishing LLLP.

Baker, Sue & Stockham, Jessica. Sleep Tight! Stockham, Jess, illus. 2006. (Blanket Babies Ser.). (ENG.). 12p. (J). (gr. -1-k). bds. (978-1-904550-90-7(8)) Child's Play International Ltd.

The Bees & the Bear: Individual Title Six-Packs. (Story Steps Ser.). (gr. k-2). 32.00 (978-0-7635-9806-8(2)) Rigby Education.

Benchmark Education Co., LLC. Play, Play, Play All Day Big Book. 2014. (Shared Reading Foundations Ser.). (J). (gr. -1). (978-1-4509-9434-7(2)) Benchmark Education Co.

Bidder, Jane. Inventions We Use for Play. 2006. (Everyday Inventions Ser.). (Illus.). 32p. (gr. 1-4). lib. bdg. 26.00 (978-0-8368-6900-2(1), Gareth Stevens Learning Library) Stevens, Gareth Publishing LLLP.

Cartwright, Mary. Splish, Splash, Splosh Bath Bk. Wells, Rachel, illus. 2007. 8p. (J). 14.99 (978-0-7945-1619-2(X), Usborne) EDC Publishing.

Carver, Patty, et al. The Amazing Adventures of Peter Rabbit: An Interactive Musical Based on the Story by Beatrix Potter. 2013. 43p. **(978-0-87602-395-2(2))** Family Plays.

Colich, Abby. A Babysitter's Guide to Keeping the Kids Entertained. 2017. (Go-To Guides). (ENG., Illus.). 32p. (gr. 3-4). lib. bdg. 27.99 (978-1-5157-3664-6(4), Snap Bks.) Capstone Press of Coughlan Cos.

Conner, Bobbi. Unplugged Play: No Batteries. No Plugs. Pure Fun. Patacchiola, Amy, illus. 2007. (ENG.). 516p. (J). (gr. -1-5). pap. 16.95 (978-0-7611-4390-1(4), 14390) Workman Publishing Co., Inc.

D'Andrea, Deborah & Borlasca, Hector. Pretend & Play Kitty: With Real Crown You Can Wear! 2004. 10p. (J). (gr. -1-18). bds. (978-1-57151-735-7(9)) Playhouse Publishing.

Desalle, Nicole. Safe at Play. 2011. pap. 39.95 (978-0-7664-3752-4(3)) Abrams & Co. Pubs., Inc.

Dewberry, Melba. Rainy Day Fun. 2016. (We Love Spring! Ser.). 00024p. (J). pap. 8.15 **(978-1-4824-5503-8(X))** Stevens, Gareth Publishing LLLP.

Dixon, Dallas L. Little Boys Run. Little Boys Play. Williams, Nancy E., ed. Cappoen, Jennifer Tipton, illus. 2013. 44p. (J). pap. 12.98 (978-1-938526-40-4(6)) Laurus Bks.

Dorling Kindersley Publishing Staff. Playtime. 2012. (Touch & Feel Ser.). (ENG.). 12p. (J). (gr. -1-k). bds. 6.99 (978-1-4654-0166-3(0), DK Children) Dorling Kindersley Publishing, Inc.

Dorsey, Colleen. Super Sands! Awesome Activities for Sands Alive! And Kinetic Sand. 2014. (ENG., Illus.). 48p. (J). pap. 9.99 (978-1-57421-980-7(4), Design Originals) Fox Chapel Publishing Co., Inc.

Dymock, Melissa. Sliding in the Snow: Winter Activities for Kids, 1 vol. Lee, Frances Cook, illus. 2015. (ENG.). 64p. (J). pap. 9.99 (978-1-4236-3893-3(X)) Gibbs Smith, Publisher.

Finn, Carrie. Comportamiento y Modales en el Patio de Juegos. Lensch, Chris, illus. 2011. (¡Así Debemos Ser!: Buenos Modales, Buen Comportamiento/Way to Be!: Manners Ser.).Tr. of Manners on the Playground. (ENG, SPA & MUL.). 24p. (gr. -1-2). lib. bdg. 26.65 (978-1-4048-6699-7(X)) Picture Window Bks.

Foy, Debbie. Toys, Play, Tidy Away! 2016. (All by Myself Ser.). (ENG., Illus.). 20p. (J). (gr. -1-k). pap. 6.99 (978-0-7502-9616-8(X), Wayland) Hachette Children's Group GBR. Dist: Hachette Bk. Group.

Hall, Pamela. A Bully-Free Playground, 1 vol. Ostrom, Bob, illus. 2012. (Bully-Free World Ser.). (ENG.). 24p. (J). (gr. -1-4). 27.07 (978-1-61641-846-5(X)) Magic Wagon.

Harbison, Lawrence. 5-Minute Plays for Teens. 2017. (ENG.). 272p. pap. 16.99 (978-1-4950-6925-3(7), 1495069257, Applause Theatre & Cinema) Leonard, Hal Corp.

Higgins, Melissa. Let's Play! Awesome Activities Every Babysitter Needs to Know, 1 vol. 2014. (Babysitter's Backpack Ser.). (ENG., Illus.). 32p. (gr. 3-4). lib. bdg. 27.99 (978-1-4914-0763-9(8), Snap Bks.) Capstone Press of Coughlan Cos.

Hirose, George, photos by. I Catch My Moment: Art & Writing by Children on the Life of Play. 2008. (Illus.). 56p. (J). (gr. -1-3). pap. 10.00 (978-1-929299-06-5(0)) Touchstone Ctr. Pubns.

Holden, Pam. Toys That Can Go, 6 pack. 2009. (Red Rocket Readers Ser.). (ENG., Illus.). 16p. (gr. -1-1). pap. (978-1-877435-93-5(7)) Flying Start Bks.

Jordan, Pat. Plays from Around the World: Every Teacher's Friend Classroom Plays. Alliger, Richard, illus. 2010. (ENG.). 128p. (J). spiral bd. 25.00 (978-0-88734-975-1(7)) Players Pr., Inc.

Kingsland, Robin. Porky Pies: Wolves, Squeals & Dodgy Deals: A Play with Songs for School Performances. 2012. (978-0-88734-076-5(8)) Players Pr., Inc.

Kramer, Daniel Elihu. Coyote Tales. 2008. 52p. per. 6.50 (978-0-87440-297-1(2)) Baker's Plays.

Kulsa, Wha. Childs Play: Positive Affirmations for Children to Sing & Dramatize. Gardner, Stephen, illus. Date not set. 30p. (J). (gr. 1-7). pap. (978-1-886942-08-0(0)) White Lion Pr.

Latchana Kenney, Karen. Cool School Drama & Theater: Fun Ideas & Activities to Build School Spirit, 1 vol. 2011. (Cool School Spirit Ser.). (ENG., Illus.). 32p. (gr. 3-6). 28.50 (978-1-61714-668-8(4), Checkerboard Library) ABDO Publishing Co.

Lindeen, Mary. Playing Together. 2015. (BeginningtoRead Ser.). (ENG., Illus.). 32p. (J). (gr. k-2). pap. 11.94 (978-1-60357-762-5(9)) Norwood Hse. Pr.

Lindeen, Mary & Peggy, Nille. Playing Together. 2015. (BeginningtoRead Ser.). (ENG., Illus.). 32p. (J). (gr. k-2). lib. bdg. 22.60 (978-1-59953-702-3(8)) Norwood Hse. Pr.

Lobdell-Bulson, Jodi. The Toddler Room: Free Play. 2013. 16p. pap. 7.95 (978-1-4582-1256-6(4), Abbott Pr.) Author Solutions, Inc.

MacDonald, John. Child's Play in Poetry. 2013. 60p. pap. 11.99 (978-1-62839-169-5(3)) Salem Author Services.

Macdonald, Margaret. What Things Did Your Parents Play With? 2014. (Little Books of Answers: Level e Ser.). (Illus.). 16p. (gr. k-2). pap. 7.95 (978-1-927136-41-6(5)) Three Crows Media NZL. Dist: RiverStream Publishing.

Marsico, Katie. Good Manners on the Playground, 1 vol. Haslam, John, illus. 2009. (Good Manners Matter! Ser.). (ENG.). 32p. (J). (gr. -1-2). 28.50 (978-1-60270-612-5(3)) Magic Wagon.

—Play Fair! 2012. (21st Century Basic Skills Library: Kids Can Make Manners Count Ser.). (ENG.). 24p. (gr. k-3). 22.79 (978-1-61080-438-7(4), 202048); pap. 12.79 (978-1-61080-612-1(3), 202222) Cherry Lake Publishing.

Massie, Elizabeth. Playing Fair. 2016. (Spring Forward Ser.). (J). (gr. 1). (978-1-4900-9378-9(8)) Benchmark Education Co.

McLeod, Len & Martens, Elisabeth. The Faery Flag of Dunvegan. 2012. (Illus.). 38p. 17.00 (978-1-84426-877-1(2), Fastprint Publishing) Upfront Publishing Ltd. GBR. Dist: Printondemand-worldwide.com.

McPhail, David. I Play. 2015. (ENG., Illus.). 12p. (J). (gr. -1 — 1). bds. 5.99 (978-1-62672-148-7(3), 9781626721487) Roaring Brook Pr.

Meiners, Cheri J. Join in & Play. 2003. (Learning to Get Along(r) Ser.). (ENG., Illus.). 40p. (J). (gr. -1-3). pap. 10.95 (978-1-57542-152-0(6)) Free Spirit Publishing, Inc.

Michaels, Chris. Playtime at Home. 2010. (Sight Word Readers Ser.). (J). 3.49 (978-1-60719-624-2(7)) Newmark Learning LLC.

Miller, Amanda. This Is the Way We Play. 2009. (Scholastic News Nonfiction Readers Ser.). (ENG.). 24p. (J). (gr. 1-2). pap. 6.95 (978-0-531-21442-8(7), Children's Pr.); lib. bdg. 22.00 (978-0-531-21342-1(0)) Scholastic Library Publishing.

Moerbeek, Kees, illus. & des. Jungle Explorers. Moerbeek, Kees, des. 2008. (Roly Poly Box Bks.). (ENG.). 24p. (J). (gr. -1-1). (978-1-84643-243-9(X)) Child's Play International Ltd.

—Ocean Explorers. Moerbeek, Kees, des. 2008. (Roly Poly Box Bks.). (ENG.). 24p. (J). (gr. -1-1). (978-1-84643-245-3(6)) Child's Play International Ltd.

—Snow Explorers. Moerbeek, Kees, des. 2008. (Roly Poly Box Bks.). (ENG.). 24p. (J). (gr. -1-1). (978-1-84643-244-6(8)) Child's Play International Ltd.

—Space Explorers. Moerbeek, Kees, des. 2008. (Roly Poly Box Bks.). (ENG.). 24p. (J). (gr. -1-1). (978-1-84643-246-0(4)) Child's Play International Ltd.

Mortensen, Lori. Manners Matter on the Playground. Hunt, Lisa, illus. (First Graphics: Manners Matter Ser.). (ENG.). 24p. (gr. 1-2). 2011. pap. 35.70 (978-1-4296-6395-3(2)) 2010. lib. bdg. 23.99 (978-1-4296-5332-9(9)) Capstone Press of Coughlan Cos.

Nelson, Robin. Playing Safely. 2006. (Pull Ahead Books: Health Ser.). (ENG., Illus.). 32p. (gr. k-3). pap. 7.95 (978-0-8225-2770-1(7)) Lerner Publishing Group.

Onyefulu, Ifeoma. Look at This! - Play. 2013. (ENG., Illus.). 32p. (J). (gr. -1-k). 17.99 (978-1-84780-267-5(2), Frances Lincoln) Quarto Publishing Group UK GBR. Dist: Hachette Bk. Group.

Oppenheim, Joanne F. & Oppenheim, Stephanie. A Leer y Jugar! con Bebés y Niños Pequeños. Auclair, Joan, illus. 2006.Tr. of Read It! Play It! with Babies & Toddlers. (SPA.). 102p. pap. 10.00 (978-0-9721050-5-7(0)) Oppenheim Toy Portfolio, Inc.

—Read It! Play It! with Babies & Toddlers. 2006. (Illus.). pap. 10.00 (978-0-9721050-4-0(2)) Oppenheim Toy Portfolio, Inc.

Petty, Kate. Playtime. 2006. (World Show-And-Tell Ser.). (ENG., Illus.). 32p. (J). (gr. -1-1). 14.95 (978-1-58728-549-3(5)); pap. 8.95 (978-1-58728-546-2(0)) Cooper Square Publishing Llc.

Priddy, Roger. Picture Play: Playtime. 2016. (Picture Play Ser.). (ENG., Illus.). 10p. (J). bds. 5.99 (978-0-312-51960-5(5), 9780312519605, Priddy Bks.) St. Martin's Pr.

Publications International Ltd. Staff, ed. Sesame Play a Sound Stero. 2011. 24p. (J). 9.39 net. (978-1-4508-1704-2(1), 145081704I) Phoenix International Publications, Inc.

Redmond, Diane. The Odyssey. Smith, Barry, illus. 2012. 48p. (978-0-88734-067-3(9)) Players Pr., Inc.

Rice, Dona Herweck. I Can, 1 vol. 2nd rev. ed. 2014. (TIME for KIDS(r) Nonfiction Readers Ser.). (ENG., Illus.). 12p. (J). (gr. 1-1). pap. 15.96 (978-1-4807-1008-5(3)) Shell Educational Publishing.

Rissman, Rebecca. Play, 1 vol. 2013. (Say What You See Ser.). (ENG., Illus.). 24p. (gr. -1-1). 22.65 (978-1-4109-5049-9(2)); pap. 7.10 (978-1-4109-5054-3(9)) Heinemann-Raintree.

—Playing with Friends: Comparing Past & Present, 1 vol. 2014. (Comparing Past & Present Ser.). (ENG., Illus.). 24p. (gr. -1-1). lib. bdg. 22.65 (978-1-4329-8993-4(6), Acorn) Heinemann-Raintree.

The Roach Approach, Don't Miss the Boat! Coloring & Activity Book. 2003. (J). 5.99 (978-0-9742997-3-0(1)) Wacky World Studios LLC.

Rosen, Michael J. & Kaboom! Staff. Let's Build a Playground. Kelson, Ellen & Cecil, Jennifer, illus. 2013. (ENG.). 32p. (J). (gr. 1-4). 15.99 (978-0-7636-5532-7(5)) Candlewick Pr.

Schumacher, Bev. Play Action (Chinese-English) 2008. 20p. (J). lib. bdg. 9.95 (978-1-935292-02-9(1)) Learning Props.

Schumacher, Bev, creator. Play Action. 2005. (Illus.). 20p. (J). lib. bdg. 9.95 (978-0-9768706-1-6(4)) Learning Props.

Senker, Cath. Exercise & Play. 2008. (Healthy Choices Ser.). (Illus.). 24p. (J). (gr. 3-7). lib. bdg. 22.60 (978-1-4042-4305-7(4), PowerKids Pr.) Rosen Publishing Group, Inc., The.

Studio Mouse, creator. Let's Play: Nursery Rhymes for Playing & Learning. 2005. (Read-Aloud Book Ser.). (ENG., Illus.). 36p. (J). 7.95 (978-1-59249-535-1(4), 1D205) Soundprints.

Taylor, Dereen. Toys. 2017. (Popcorn: in the Past Ser.). (ENG., Illus.). 24p. (J). (gr. k-2). pap. 10.99 (**978-0-7502-6423-5(3)**, Wayland) Hachette Children's Group GBR. Dist: Hachette Bk. Group.

Thalhamer, Ellen Viola. I'm a Daddy: I Love to Pretend! 2010. 36p. pap. 16.49 (978-1-4490-7489-0(8)) AuthorHouse.

The Toddler Room: Free Play. 2013. 16p. pap. 7.95 (978-1-4582-1259-7(9), Abbott Pr.) Author Solutions, Inc.

Tuxworth, Nicola. Messy. 2016. (ENG., Illus.). 20p. (J). (gr. -1-k). bds. 6.99 (978-1-86147-690-6(6), Armadillo) Anness Publishing GBR. Dist: National Bk. Network.

Umansky, Kaye. The Emperor's New Clothes. Crossland, Caroline, illus. 2012. (978-0-88734-074-1(1)) Players Pr., Inc.

—Noah's Ark. Richardson-Jones, Tessa, illus. 2012. (978-0-88734-071-0(7)) Players Pr., Inc.

—Sleeping Beauty. Crossland, Caroline, illus. 2012. (978-0-88734-070-3(9)) Players Pr., Inc.

Verdick, Elizabeth & Lisovskis, Marjorie. Play. 2014. (Happy Healthy Baby Ser.). (ENG., Illus.). 22p. (J). bds. 6.99 (978-1-57542-426-2(6)) Free Spirit Publishing, Inc.

Ways to Play. 2017. (Ways to Play Ser.). 24p. (gr. k-k). pap. 48.90 (**978-1-5382-0230-2(1)**); lib. bdg. 135.60 (**978-1-5382-0229-6(8)**) Stevens, Gareth Publishing LLLP.

Weekly Reader Early Learning Library Staff. Las Cosas con las Que Juego. 2006. (Things in My World/ Las cosas de mi mundo Ser.). (ENG & SPA., Illus.). 16p. (gr. -1-2). lib. bdg. 19.00 (978-0-8368-7223-1(1), Weekly Reader Leveled Readers) Stevens, Gareth Publishing LLLP.

—Things I Play With. 2006. (Things in My World Ser.). (Illus.). 16p. (gr. -1-2). lib. bdg. 19.00 (978-0-8368-6811-1(0), Weekly Reader Leveled Readers) Stevens, Gareth Publishing LLLP.

Weekly Reader Editorial Staff. Things I Play With/Las Cosas con las Que Juego. 2006. (Things in My World/ Las cosas de mi mundo Ser.). (ENG & SPA.). 16p. (gr. -1-2). pap. 5.30 (978-0-8368-7230-9(4), Weekly Reader Leveled Readers) Stevens, Gareth Publishing LLLP.

Woehlke, Joshua. Shakespeare's Painless Romeo & Juliet. 2008. 64p. pap. 12.50 (978-0-557-02661-6(X)) Lulu Pr., Inc.

Wood, David. The Christmas Story. 2012. (978-0-88734-069-7(5)) Players Pr., Inc.

Woodruff, Elvira. The Christmas Doll (Full) 2014. 110p. (J). pap. 9.95 (978-1-58342-870-2(4)) Dramatic Publishing Co.

PLAY—FICTION

Abbott, Jacob. Rollo at Play. 2009. 148p. pap. 8.95 (978-1-59915-343-8(2)) Yesterday's Classics.

—Rollo at Work. 2009. 124p. 23.95 (978-1-60664-636-6(2)); pap. 10.95 (978-1-60664-261-0(8)) Rodgers, Alan Bks.

Adams, Colleen. Jugando en la Nieve (Playing in the Snow) 2007. (Lecturas del barrio (Neighborhood Readers) Ser.). (SPA.). 8p. 29.95 (978-1-4042-7064-0(7), Rosen Classroom) Rosen Publishing Group, Inc., The.

—Playing in the Snow. (Neighborhood Readers Ser.). (ENG.). 8p. 2007. 29.95 (978-1-4042-7059-6(0)) 2006. (gr. -1-3). pap. 5.15 (978-1-4042-5657-6(1)) Rosen Publishing Group, Inc., The. (Rosen Classroom).

Adams, Tonya. Sam the Walrus: A Grumpy Day to Play. Johnson, Amber W., illus. 2008. 28p. pap. 24.95 (978-1-60672-861-1(X)) America Star Bks.

Aiken, Zora & Aiken, David. Busy Bodies: Play Like the Animals, 1 vol. 2011. (ENG., Illus.). 32p. (J). 14.99 (978-0-7643-3832-8(3), 9780764338328, Schiffer Publishing Ltd) Schiffer Publishing, Ltd.

Ainsworth, Kimberly. Little Monkey. Berg, Michelle, illus. 2008. (Little Green Bks.). (ENG.). 8p. (J). (gr. -1 — 1). 9.99 (978-1-4169-6175-8(5), Little Simon) Little Simon.

—Little Panda. Berg, Michelle, illus. 2008. (Little Green Bks.). (ENG.). 8p. (J). (gr. -1 — 1). 9.99 (978-1-4169-6173-4(9), Little Simon) Little Simon.

Albee, Sarah. Clever Trevor. Billin-Frye, Paige, illus. 2003. (Science Solves It! Ser.). 32p. (J). pap. 5.95 (978-1-57565-123-1(8)) Kane Press, Inc.

—Fun in the Sun. Williams, Sue, illus. 2006. (Step-By-Step Readers Ser.). (J). pap. (978-1-59939-058-1(2), Reader's Digest Young Families, Inc.) Studio Fun International.

Allen, J. J. Hello Kitty's Fun Friend Day! 2003. (Illus.). 32p. (J). pap. (978-0-439-44917-5(0)) Scholastic, Inc.

Alley, R. W. Annabelle at the South Pole. 2016. (ENG., Illus.). 32p. (J). (gr. -1-3). 14.99 (978-0-547-90704-8(4), Clarion Bks.) Houghton Mifflin Harcourt Trade & Reference Pubs.

Amatangelo, Sergio Lino. Forever Four, Finally Five. 2008. (Illus.). 32p. (J). pap. 8.00 (978-0-8059-7680-9(9)) Dorrance Publishing Co., Inc.

Amato, Gaetano. Upside Right: A Children's Guide to Movement. 2010. (J). 19.95 (978-0-615-38545-7(1)) Amato, G. J.

Anderson, Lynne. Charlie's Championships: Set Of 6. 2010. (Early Connections Ser.). (J). pap. 37.00 net. (978-1-4108-1370-1(3)) Benchmark Education Co.

Anderson, Peggy Perry. Joe on the Go. 2012. (Green Light Readers — Level 1 Ser.). lib. bdg. 13.55 (978-0-606-24018-5(7), Turtleback) Turtleback Bks.

Arena, Felice & Kettle, Phil. Olympics. Cox, David, illus. 2004. (J). pap. (978-1-59336-374-1(5)) Mondo Publishing.

—Pirate Ship: By Felice Arena & Phil Kettle: Illustrated by Susy Boyer. Boyer, Susy, illus. 2004. (J). pap. (978-1-59336-362-8(1)) Mondo Publishing.

—Secret Agent Heroes. Vane, Mitch, illus. 2004. (J). pap. (978-1-59336-355-0(9)) Mondo Publishing.

Asani, Samantha. Everyone Is Special: A Lesson in Teamwork. 2012. 28p. pap. 19.99 (978-1-4685-5320-8(8)) AuthorHouse.

Ashbe, Jeanne. Eso No Se Hace! 2003. (SPA.). 32p. (978-84-95150-35-6(2)) Corimbo, Editorial S.L.

At Play. 2003. (J). per. (978-1-57657-963-3(8)) Paradise Pr., Inc.

Atkinson, Cale. Explorers of the Wild. Atkinson, Cale, illus. 2016. (ENG., Illus.). 40p. (J). (gr. -1-k). 16.99 (978-1-4847-2340-1(6)) Disney Pr.

Bader, Bonnie. Go to Bed, Blue. Robertson, Michael, illus. 2014. (Penguin Young Readers, Level 1 Ser.). (ENG.). 32p. (J). (gr. k-1). pap. 3.99 (978-0-448-48219-4(3), Penguin Young Readers) Penguin Young Readers Group.

—Play with Blue. Robertson, Michael, illus. 2013. (Penguin Young Readers, Level 1 Ser.). (ENG.). 32p. (J). (gr. k-1). mass mkt. 3.99 (978-0-448-46254-7(0), Penguin Young Readers) Penguin Young Readers Group.

Baker, Karle Wilson. The Garden of the Plynck (Illustrated Ed. 2006. (Illus.). pap. (978-1-4065-0482-8(3)) Dodo Pr.

The Ball: KinderReaders Individual Title Six-Packs. (Kinderstarters Ser.). 8p. (gr. -1-1). 21.00 (978-0-7635-8645-4(5)) Rigby Education.

Ballard, Peg & Amoroso, Cynthia. Fun! The Sound of Short U. 2015. (Long & Short Vowels Ser.). (ENG.). 24p. (J). (gr. -1-2). 25.64 (978-1-63407-022-5(4), 208857) Child's World, Inc., The.

Balouch, Kristen. The Little Little Girl with the Big Big Voice. Balouch, Kristen, illus. 2011. (ENG., Illus.). 32p. (J). (gr. -1-k). 12.99 (978-1-4424-0808-1(1), Little Simon) Little Simon.

Banks, Kate. Max's Castle. Kulikov, Boris, illus. 2011. (Max's Words Ser.: 3). (ENG.). 40p. (J). (gr. -1-3). 18.99 (978-0-374-39919-1(0), 9780374399191, Farrar, Straus & Giroux (BYR)) Farrar, Straus & Giroux.

—Max's Dragon. Kulikov, Boris, illus. 2008. (Max's Words Ser.: 2). (ENG.). 32p. (J). (gr. -1-3). 17.99 (978-0-374-39921-4(2), 9780374399214, Farrar, Straus & Giroux (BYR)) Farrar, Straus & Giroux.

Barchers, Suzanne I. Rose & Dad, 1 vol. 2011. (Targeted Phonics Ser.). (ENG.). 16p. (J). (gr. k-2). pap. 5.99 (978-1-4333-2912-8(3)) Teacher Created Materials, Inc.

Bardhan-Quallen, Sudipta. Caveboy Is Bored! Wight, Eric, illus. 2017. (Caveboy Ser.). (ENG.). 80p. (J). 9.99 (978-1-68119-045-7(1), 9781681190457, Bloomsbury USA Childrens) Bloomsbury Publishing USA.

Barnett, Penny. Matilda & Puppy's Beach Adventure. 2012. 24p. pap. 15.99 (978-1-4797-1106-2(3)) Xlibris Corp.

Barton, Chris. Shark vs. Train. Lichtenheld, Tom, illus. (ENG.). (J). (gr. -1 — 1). 2015. 20p. bds. 6.99 (978-0-316-37814-7(3)) 2010. 40p. 18.99 (978-0-316-00762-7(5)) Little, Brown Bks. for Young Readers.

Batchelor, Louise. Whoops! (Illus.). 21p. (978-1-84089-079-2(7), 26143) Zero to Ten, Ltd.

Baumgarten, Josephine & Baumgarten, Michael. My Baby Monsters & I went to the Park. 2005. 32p. pap. 14.99 (978-1-4116-6348-0(9)) Lulu Pr., Inc.

Beard, Alex. Monkey See, Monkey Draw. 2011. (ENG., Illus.). 48p. (J). (gr. k-2). 17.95 (978-0-8109-8970-2(0), Abrams Bks. for Young Readers) Abrams, Inc.

Beckford, Avril. I Love You 65 Bulldozers. 2009. 36p. pap. 15.49 (978-1-4389-4048-9(3)) AuthorHouse.

Bedford, David. Big Bears Can! Hansen, Gaby, illus. 2007. (Storytime Board Bks.). 16p. (J). (gr. -1-k). bds. 6.95 (978-1-58925-826-6(6)) Tiger Tales.

Bella & Rosie Play Hide & Seek. 2003. (Bella & Rosie Set 1 Ser.). (J). 7.67 (978-1-932570-11-3(X)) Pioneer Valley Bks.

Bennett, Bonnie. Meet Cinnamon Bear. 2009. 48p. pap. 16.95 (978-1-60749-496-6(5)) America Star Bks.

Bennett, Kelly. One Day I Went Rambling. Murphy, Terri, illus. 2012. (ENG.). 24p. (J). (gr. k-3). 17.95 (978-1-936474-06-6(9)) Bright Sky Pr.

Bently, Peter. King Jack & the Dragon. Oxenbury, Helen, illus. 2011. (ENG.). 32p. (J). (gr. -1-k). 17.99 (978-0-8037-3698-6(3), Dial Bks) Penguin Young Readers Group.

—King Jack & the Dragon Board Book. Oxenbury, Helen, illus. 2013. (ENG.). 14p. (J). (gr. -1 — 1). bds. 7.99 (978-0-8037-3987-1(7), Dial Bks) Penguin Young Readers Group.

—Look Out, Cub! A Lift-the-Flap Story about Lions. 2013. (ENG.). 20p. (J). (gr. -1-2). bds. 9.99 (978-1-4263-1096-6(X), National Geographic Children's Bks.) National Geographic Society.

Berenstain, Stan, et al. The Berenstain Bears Discover God's Creation, 1 vol. 2010. (Berenstain Bears/Living Lights Ser.). (ENG.). 40p. (J). (gr. -1-2). 6.99 (978-0-310-71936-6(4)) Zonderkidz.

Bertier, Anne, creator. Wednesday. 2014. (ENG., Illus.). 48p. (J). (gr. -1-2). 17.95 (978-1-59270-152-0(3)) Enchanted Lion Bks., LLC.

Bianchi, John. We Can Play. 2016. (1-3Y Bird, Bunny & Bear Ser.). (ENG., Illus.). 16p. (J). pap. 5.99 (978-1-63437-486-6(X)) American Reading Co.

Bittle Jr., Paul. Me too, Little Puppies, Me Too, 1 vol. 2010. 16p. pap. 24.95 (978-1-61582-922-4(9)) PublishAmerica, Inc.

Black, Robyn Hood. Sir Mike. Murphy, David, illus. 2006. (Rookie Reader Skill Set Ser.). (ENG.). 32p. (J). (gr. k-2). per. 4.95 (978-0-516-25020-5(5), Children's Pr.) Scholastic Library Publishing.

Blackaby, Susan. El Lugar de Luis, 1 vol. Ruíz, Carlos, tr. from ENG. Gallagher-Cole, Mernie, illus. 2006. (Read-It! Readers en Español: Story Collection).Tr. of Place for Mike. (SPA.). 24p. (gr. -1-3). 21.32 (978-1-4048-1688-6(7), Easy Readers) Picture Window Bks.

Blackmon, Rodney Allan. A Kitten Named Buddy: Buddy Stays Clean. 2013. 20p. pap. 24.95 (978-1-62709-675-1(2)) America Star Bks.

Blackstone, Stella. A Dragon on the Doorstep. Harter, Debbie, illus. 2012. (ENG.). 32p. (J). (gr. -1-2). 9.99 (978-1-84686-826-9(2)) Barefoot Bks., Inc.

Blake, Michel. Out to Play. Candlewick Press Staff, illus. 2005. (Easy Open Board Book Ser.). (ENG.). 16p. (J). (— 1). bds. 5.99 (978-0-7636-2767-6(4)) Candlewick Pr.

Bledsoe, Josh. Hammer & Nails. Warrick, Jessica, illus. 2016. (ENG.). 32p. (J). (gr. k-2). 17.95 (978-1-936261-36-9(7)) Flashlight Pr.

Blevins-Counts, Charlotte. A Pot Full of Te. 2009. 24p. pap. 12.95 (978-1-59858-962-7(8)) Dog Ear Publishing, LLC.

Bloom, Suzanne. A Mighty Fine Time Machine. Bloom, Suzanne, illus. 2014. (ENG., Illus.). 32p. (J). (gr. k-2). pap. 6.95 (978-1-62091-605-6(3)) Boyds Mills Pr.

—What about Bear? (Goose & Bear Stories Ser.). (ENG., Illus.). 32p. (J). (gr. -1-1). 2012. pap. 7.95 (978-1-59078-913-1(X)) 2010. 16.95 (978-1-59078-528-7(2)) Boyds Mills Pr.

Bloomfield, Kevin. Mr. Biggs in the City. Bloomfield, Kevin, illus. 2011. (ENG & SPA., Illus.). 32p. (gr. -1-3). lib. bdg. 16.95 (978-1-936299-26-3(7), Raven Tree Pr.,Csi) Continental Sales, Inc.

Bogart, Mike. Ice Warriors, 1 vol. 2010. 72p. pap. 19.95 (978-1-4489-3885-8(6)) America Star Bks.

Boland, Janice. Zippers. Pfeiffer, Judith, illus. 2003. (Books for Young Learners). (ENG.). 8p. (J). pap. 15.00 (978-1-57274-700-5(5), BB2220, Bks. for Young Learners) Owen, Richard C. Pubs., Inc.

Bolton, Robin. Sunny Goes Out to Play. 2011. 28p. pap. 12.03 (978-1-4634-2530-2(9)) AuthorHouse.

Boukov, Lubima. The Magic Swing, 1 vol. 2009. 15p. pap. 24.95 (978-1-60749-612-0(7)) America Star Bks.

Boyd, Lizi. Inside Outside. Boyd, Lizi, illus. 2013. (ENG., Illus.). 40p. (J). (gr. -1-1). 15.99 (978-1-4521-0644-1(4)) Chronicle Bks. LLC.

Boyle, Bob. Rosie & Rex: A Nose for Fun! Boyle, Bob, illus. 2014. (ENG., Illus.). 40p. (J). (gr. -1-3). 15.99 (978-0-06-221131-6(5)) HarperCollins Pubs.

Brabham, Barbara. Donkey Tales — Color with Paco! [English/Spanish Versions]. 2006. (J). 2.95 (978-1-882185-86-3(2)) Cornerstone Publishing, Inc.

Brandy. DID & DIDN't Learn When to Study & When to Play: Big Life Lessons for Little Kids. 2017. (ENG., Illus.). 40p. 10.00 (**978-981-4771-31-3(7)**) Marshall Cavendish International (Asia) Private Ltd. SGP. Dist: National Bk. Network.

Brimner, Larry Dane. Summer Fun. Tripp, Christine, illus. 2003. (Rookie Choices Ser.). (ENG.). 32p. (J). (gr. 1-2). 20.50 (978-0-516-22548-7(0), Children's Pr.) Scholastic Library Publishing.

Britton, Faith. If You'D Only Believe. 2009. 24p. pap. 12.99 (978-1-4490-1741-5(X)) AuthorHouse.

Brooks, Yvonne & Grant, Steven. Meet the Goat Kids. Lt. ed. 2006. (Illus.). 32p. (J). 14.95 (978-0-9791021-0-3(3), 978-0-9791021-0-3) Lotus Pond Media.

Brown, Jo. Hoppity Skip Little Chick. 2005. (Illus.). 32p. (J). 15.95 (978-1-58925-045-1(1)) Tiger Tales.

Brown, Susan Taylor. Oliver's Must-Do List. Sullivan, Mary, illus. 2005. (ENG.). 32p. (J). (gr. -1-1). 15.95 (978-1-59078-198-2(8)) Boyds Mills Pr.

Browne, Anthony. Things I Like. 2014. 24p. pap. 7.00 (978-1-61003-372-5(8)) Center for the Collaborative Classroom.

Brunel, Aude. Let's Go to Work. Mancek, Marjan, illus. 2007. 32p. (J). (POL & ENG.). pap. 16.95 (978-1-60195-101-4(9)); (ARA & ENG.). pap. 16.95 (978-1-60195-089-5(6)) International Step by Step Assn.

Bug, Judy. A Day to Play, 1 vol. 2010. 26p. 24.95 (978-1-4489-4007-3(9)) PublishAmerica, Inc.

Butler, John. Ten in the Meadow. Butler, John, illus. 2006. (ENG., Illus.). 32p. (J). (gr. k-1). 15.95 (978-1-56145-372-6(2)) Peachtree Pubs.

Byrne, Marlene. Follow the Leader. Graber, Jesse, illus. 2009. (ENG.). 39p. (J). 14.99 (978-0-9777135-1-6(2)) Celtic Marketing Inc.

Calder, C. J. Busy Truck, 1 vol. Rooney, Ronnie & Peterson, Shauna, illus. 2012. (Truck Buddies Ser.). (ENG.). 16p. (gr. -1-k). bds. 7.95 (978-1-4342-4388-1(5)) Stone Arch Bks.

Campbell, Susan. Little Jimmy: The Itty Bitty Fifty Foot Tall Giraffe. 2011. 24p. pap. 24.95 (978-1-4626-2929-9(6)) America Star Bks.

Candlewick Press, Candlewick. Peppa Pig & the Year of Family Fun. 2016. (Peppa Pig Ser.). (ENG., Illus.). 10p. (J). (gr. -1-2). 17.99 (978-0-7636-8739-7(1), Candlewick Entertainment) Candlewick Pr.

Cano, Felipe. Bonjour Camille. Aguilar, Laia, illus. 2014. (ENG & SPA.). 32p. (J). (gr. 1-4). 12.99 (978-1-4521-2407-0(8)) Chronicle Bks. LLC.

Capucilli, Alyssa Satin. Biscuit & the Little Pup. Schories, Pat, illus. 2007. (My First I Can Read Ser.). (ENG.). 32p. (J). (gr. -1 — 1). 16.99 (978-0-06-074170-9(8)) HarperCollins Pubs.

—Biscuit's Big Field Trip. Schories, Pat, illus. 2008. (Biscuit Ser.). 32p. (J). pap. 3.99 (978-0-06-112844-8(9), HarperFestival) HarperCollins Pubs.

—Biscuit's Pet & Play Christmas. Schories, Pat & Young, Mary O'Keefe, illus. 2006. (Biscuit Ser.). (ENG.). 12p. (J). (gr. -1-1). bds. 7.99 (978-0-06-009470-6(2), HarperFestival) HarperCollins Pubs.

—Katy Duck Makes a Friend. Cole, Henry, illus. 2012. (Katy Duck Ser.). (ENG.). 24p. (J). (gr. -1-1). 16.99 (978-1-4424-1977-3(6)); pap. 3.99 (978-1-4424-1976-6(8)) Simon Spotlight. (Simon Spotlight).

—Ralph & the Rocket Ship. Cole, Henry, illus. 2016. (Ready-To-Reads Ser.). (ENG.). 24p. (J). (gr. -1-1). pap. 3.99 (978-1-4814-5866-5(3), Simon Spotlight) Simon Spotlight.

Carey, Catherine Elaine. The Colorful & Playful Animal Friends, 1 vol. 2009. 73p. pap. 16.95 (978-1-60749-480-5(9)) PublishAmerica, Inc.

Carpenter, Cindy. The Little Inchworm. 2008. 16p. per. 24.95 (978-1-4241-9681-4(7)) America Star Bks.

Carter, Candace. Sid's Surprise. Kim, Joung Un, illus. 2005. (Green Light Readers Level 1 Ser.). (gr. -1-3). 13.95 (978-0-7569-5242-6(5)) Perfection Learning Corp.

Carter, David A. Bugs at the Beach. Carter, David A., illus. 2016. (David Carter's Bugs Ser.). (ENG., Illus.). 24p. (J). (gr. -1-1). pap. 3.99 (978-1-4814-4050-9(0), Simon Spotlight) Simon Spotlight.

—Busy Bug Builds a Fort. Carter, David A., illus. 2016. (David Carter's Bugs Ser.). (ENG., Illus.). 24p. (J). (gr. -1-1). pap. 3.99 (978-1-4814-4047-9(0), Simon Spotlight) Simon Spotlight.

Carver, David. Leafy Leafs Where Is Lester?, 1 vol. Carver, Erin, illus. 2009. 34p. pap. 19.95 (978-1-4489-2203-1(8)) PublishAmerica, Inc.

Chase, Kit. Charlie's Boat. Chase, Kit, illus. 2017. (ENG., Illus.). 32p. (J). (-k). 16.99 (978-0-399-25702-5(0), G.P. Putnam's Sons Books for Young Readers) Penguin Young Readers Group.

Child, Lauren. Slightly Invisible. Child, Lauren, illus. 2011. (Charlie & Lola Ser.). (ENG., Illus.). 40p. (J). (gr. -1-2). 16.99 (978-0-7636-5347-7(0)) Candlewick Pr.

Chorao, Kay. Ed & Kip. Chorao, Kay, illus. (I Like to Read(r) Ser.). (ENG., Illus.). 24p. (J). (gr. -1-3). 2015. 6.99 (978-0-8234-3398-8(6)) 2014. 14.95 (978-0-8234-2903-5(2)) Holiday Hse., Inc.

Christelow, Eileen. Five Little Monkeys Play Hide & Seek. 2010. (Five Little Monkeys Story Ser.). (ENG., Illus.). 40p. (J). (gr. -1-3). pap. 6.99 (978-0-547-33787-6(6)) Houghton Mifflin Harcourt Publishing Co.

Christopher, Kathleen. Janie's First Day of School. 2012. 32p. pap. 24.95 (978-1-62709-914-1(X)) America Star Bks.

Chung, Arree. Ninja! Chung, Arree, illus. (Ninja! Ser.). (ENG., Illus.). 40p. (J). 2016. 16.99 (978-0-8050-9916-4(6), 9780805099164) 2014. (gr. -1-2). 17.99 (978-0-8050-9911-9(5), 9780805099119) Holt, Henry & Co. (Holt, Henry & Co. Bks. For Young Readers).

Ciminera, Siobhan, adapted by. Get the Sillies Out! 2009. (Yo Gabba Gabba! Ser.). (ENG.). 16p. (J). (gr. -1-1). pap. 5.99 (978-1-4169-7099-6(1), Simon Spotlight) Simon Spotlight.

Clish, Marian L. I Wonder What a Fish Would Wish For? Swaim, Mike, illus. 2009. 29p. pap. 24.95 (978-1-60836-289-9(2)) America Star Bks.

Come & Play, Jack. 2008. (Jack Flocked Board Ser.). 8p. bds. (978-1-4075-1815-2(1)) Parragon, Inc.

Come Out to Play. (J). 7.95 (978-0-8126-0082-7(7)) Open Court Publishing Co.

Cook, Gary. The Best Saturday Ever! Sward, Adam, illus. 2013. (Robbie's Big Adventures Ser.). (ENG.). 40p. (J). (gr. k-3). 15.95 (978-1-938063-25-1(2), Mighty Media Kids) Mighty Media Pr.

Cordwell, Mary Hebert. The Dirty-Foot Fairy. 2010. 28p. 13.99 (978-1-4490-9153-8(9)) AuthorHouse.

Cossi, Olga. Playing Your Heart Out. 2013. 138p. pap. 9.95 (978-1-938083-21-1(0)) Silver Knight Publishing, LLC.

Costales, Amy. Lupe Vargas & Her Super Best Friend/Lupe Vargas y Su Super Mejor Amiga. 2006. (ENG, SPA & MUL.,

Illus.). 32p. (J). (gr. -1-3). 15.95 *(978-0-87358-888-1(6))* Cooper Square Publishing Llc.

Coulton, Mia. Danny & Abby Play Tag. Coulton, Mia, photos by. 2004. (ENG., Illus.). pap. 5.35 *(978-0-9746475-3-1(5))* Maryruth Bks., Inc.

Courtin, Thierry. L imagier de T Choupi. 19.95 *(978-2-09-202283-2(0))* Nathan, Fernand FRA. Dist: Distribooks, Inc.

Cousineau-Peiffer, Trisha. Have You Ever Heard of a Rainbow Farm. Everett-Hawkes, Bonnie, illus. 2006. 32p. (J). 12.95 *(978-0-9792084-1-6(6))* Dream Ridge Pr.

—Have You Ever Heard of a Rainbow Farm: The Missing Color Kittens. Everett-Hawkes, Bonnie, illus. 2007. 48p. (J). per. 15.95 *(978-0-9792084-2-3(4))* Dream Ridge Pr.

Cousins, Lucy. Maisy's Fairground: A Maisy Pop-Up-and-Play Book. 2013. (Maisy Ser.). (ENG., Illus.). 16p. (J). (gr. k-k). 17.99 *(978-0-7636-6491-6(X))* Candlewick Pr.

—Where Is Maisy? Cousins, Lucy, illus. 2010. (Maisy Ser.). (ENG., Illus.). 14p. (J). (gr. k-k). bds. 5.99 *(978-0-7636-4673-8(3))* Candlewick Pr.

Cowell, Cressida. That Rabbit Belongs to Emily Brown. Layton, Neal, illus. 2007. (ENG.). 40p. (gr. -1-3). 16.99 *(978-1-4231-0645-6(8))* Hyperion Pr.

Cowley, Joy. Freddy Bear & the Beach. Webb, Philip, illus. 2016. (Freddy Bear Ser.). (ENG.). 20p. (J). (gr. -1-k). bds. 12.99 *(978-1-927262-56-6(9))* Upstart Pr. NZL. Dist: Independent Pubs. Group.

Coyle, Carmela Lavigna. Do Princesses Have Best Friends Forever? Gordon, Mike & Gordon, Carl, illus. 2010. (J). *(978-1-58979-543-3(1))* Taylor Trade Publishing.

—Do Princesses Have Best Friends Forever? Gordon, Carl & Gordon, Mike, illus. 2010. (ENG.). 32p. (J). (gr. -1-3). 15.95 *(978-1-58979-542-6(3))* Taylor Trade Publishing.

—Do Princesses Scrape Their Knees? 2006. (ENG., Illus.). 32p. (J). (gr. -1-2). 15.95 *(978-0-87358-909-3(2))* Cooper Square Publishing Llc.

—Do Princesses Scrape Their Knees? Keepsake Sticker Doodle Book. Gordon, Mike & Gordon, Carl, illus. 2014. (ENG.). 96p. (J). (gr. -1-2). 15.95 *(978-1-58979-948-6(8))* Taylor Trade Publishing.

Crane, Noelle L. The Clever Pug. Crane, Noelle L., illus. 2013. (Illus.). 66p. pap. 9.99 *(978-0-9846119-8-0(3))* Pluriverse Publishing.

Crews, Donald. Cloudy Day Sunny Day. 2010. (Rise & Shine Ser.). (ENG., Illus.). 24p. (C). (gr. -1-3). pap. 6.95 *(978-0-15-204850-1(2))* National Geographic School Publishing, Inc.

—Cloudy Day Sunny Day. 2003. (Green Light Readers — Level 1 Ser.). (gr. -1-2). 13.50 *(978-0-613-62277-6(4),* Turtleback) Turtleback Bks.

Cronick, Mitch. In the Garden. 2005. (Big Cat Ser.). (gr. k-2). pap. 6.50 *(978-1-60457-007-6(5))* Pacific Learning, Inc.

Crow, Melinda Melton. Camiones Amigos/Truck Buddies, 1 vol. Heck, Claudia M., tr. from ENG. Rooney, Ronnie, illus. 2012. (Camiones Amigos/Truck Buddies Ser.). (ENG, SPA & MUL.). 32p. (gr. -1-1). pap. 5.05 *(978-1-4342-3913-6(6))*; lib. bdg. 22.65 *(978-1-4342-3774-3(5))* Stone Arch Bks. (Bilingual Stone Arch Readers).

Curry, Don L. Fall Leaves. Jasinski, Aaron, illus. (Rookie Reader Skill Set Ser.). (J). (gr. k-2). 2005. (ENG.). 24p. pap. 4.95 *(978-0-516-26831-6(7))* 2004. 23p. 19.50 *(978-0-516-25904-8(0))* Scholastic Library Publishing. (Children's Pr.).

Curtis, Jennifer Keats. Baby Owl's Rescue, 1 vol. Jacques, Laura, illus. 2009. (ENG.). 32p. (J). (gr. -1-3). 16.95 *(978-1-934359-95-2(5),* 9781934359952) Arbordale Publishing.

Dadoo Stops Playing. . . 2003. (J). per. 5.50 *(978-0-9742714-0-8(3))* I C Creative, Inc.

Dagostino, Argus. Belcher Bomb. 2008. 53p. pap. 16.95 *(978-1-60441-596-4(7))* America Star Bks.

Dahl, Michael. Little Dinos Don't Push, 1 vol. Record, Adam, illus. 2013. (Little Dinos Ser.). (ENG.). 20p. (gr. -1-k). bds. 7.99 *(978-1-4048-7534-0(4))* Picture Window Bks.

—Me & My Cat. Persico, Zoe, illus. 2016. (Me & My Pet Ser.). (ENG.). 24p. (gr. 1-2). lib. bdg. 22.65 *(978-1-5158-0239-6(6),* Fiction Picture Bks.) Picture Window Bks.

—Me & My Cat. Persico, Zoe, illus. 2016. (Me & My Pet Ser.). (ENG.). 24p. (gr. 1-2). 6.95 *(978-1-62370-794-1(3))* Capstone Young Readers of Coughlan Cos.

—Me & My Dog. Persico, Zoe, illus. 2016. (Me & My Pet Ser.). (ENG.). 24p. (gr. 1-2). 6.95 *(978-1-62370-793-4(5))* Capstone Young Readers of Coughlan Cos.

—Me & My Dog. Persico, Zoe, illus. 2016. (Me & My Pet Ser.). (ENG.). 24p. (gr. 1-2). lib. bdg. 22.65 *(978-1-5158-0238-9(8),* Fiction Picture Bks.) Picture Window Bks.

—Playdate for Panda. Vidal, Oriol, illus. 2016. (Hello Genius Ser.). (ENG.). 20p. (gr. 1-2). bds. 7.99 *(978-1-4795-8741-4(9))* Picture Window Bks.

Darling, Helen. Hide-n-seek Monday. Glickstein, Jennifer, ed. Sona and Jacob, illus. 2007. (J). 10.00 *(978-0-9797674-0-1(7))* My Darling-Tots Pubns.

Davis, Jacky. The Amazing Adventures of Bumblebee Boy. Soman, David, illus. 2011. (Ladybug Girl Ser.). (ENG.). 40p. (J). (gr. -1-k). 16.99 *(978-0-8037-3418-0(2),* Dial Bks) Penguin Young Readers Group.

—I Love You, Bingo. 2015. (Penguin Young Readers Level 2 Ser.). lib. bdg. 13.55 *(978-0-606-37578-8(3))* Turtleback Bks.

—Ladybug Girl. Soman, David, illus. 2015. (Ladybug Girl Ser.). (ENG.). 40p. (J). (-k). 18.99 *(978-1-101-99433-7(9),* Dial Bks) Penguin Young Readers Group.

—Ladybug Girl & the Best Ever Playdate. Soman, David, illus. 2015. (Ladybug Girl Ser.). (ENG.). 40p. (J). (gr. -1-k). 17.99 *(978-0-8037-4030-3(1),* Dial Bks) Penguin Young Readers Group.

Davis, Jacky & Soman, David. Ladybug Girl. Soman, David, illus. 2008. (Ladybug Girl Ser.). (ENG., Illus.). 40p. (J). (gr. -1-k). 17.99 *(978-0-8037-3195-0(7),* Dial Bks) Penguin Young Readers Group.

—Ladybug Girl & Bumblebee Boy. Soman, David, illus. 2009. (Ladybug Girl Ser.). (ENG., Illus.). 40p. (J). (gr. -1-k). 17.99 *(978-0-8037-3339-8(9),* Dial Bks) Penguin Young Readers Group.

—Ladybug Girl & the Bug Squad. Soman, David, illus. 2011. (Ladybug Girl Ser.). (ENG., Illus.). 40p. (J). (gr. -1-k). 16.99 *(978-0-8037-3419-7(0),* Dial Bks) Penguin Young Readers Group.

—Ladybug Girl Loves... Soman, David, illus. 2010. (Ladybug Girl Ser.). (ENG., Illus.). 12p. (J). (gr. -1 — 1). bds. 5.99 *(978-0-448-45374-3(6),* Grosset & Dunlap) Penguin Young Readers Group.

—Ladybug Girl Makes Friends. Soman, David, illus. 2012. (Ladybug Girl Ser.). (ENG., Illus.). 12p. (J). (gr. -1 — 1). bds. 5.99 *(978-0-448-45764-2(4),* Grosset & Dunlap) Penguin Young Readers Group.

—Ladybug Girl Plays. Soman, David, illus. 2013. (Ladybug Girl Ser.). (ENG., Illus.). 14p. (J). (gr. -1 — 1). bds. 5.99 *(978-0-8037-3892-8(7),* Dial Bks) Penguin Young Readers Group.

—Who Can Play? Soman, David, illus. 2013. (Ladybug Girl Ser.). (ENG., Illus.). 32p. (J). (gr. k-1). pap. 3.99 *(978-0-448-46501-2(9),* Penguin Young Readers) Penguin Young Readers Group.

de Brunhoff, Laurent. Babar's Little Girl. rev. ed. 2012. (ENG., Illus.). 40p. (J). (gr. k-2). 16.95 *(978-1-4197-0340-9(4),* Abrams Bks. for Young Readers) Abrams, Inc.

De Sena, Joseph. Little Sammy Sunshine & the Frightful Forest. 2008. 64p. pap. 27.95 *(978-1-4327-3119-9(X))* Outskirts Pr., Inc.

Dean, James. Pete the Cat - Robo-Pete. Dean, James, illus. 2015. (Pete the Cat Ser.). (ENG., Illus.). 24p. (J). (gr. -1-3). pap. 4.99 *(978-0-06-230427-8(5),* HarperFestival) HarperCollins Pubs.

Delval, Marie-Hélène. Lili et Mistigri jouent a Cache. (FRE.). pap. 14.95 *(978-2-227-75602-1(0))* Bayard Editions FRA. Dist: Distribooks, Inc.

Dempsey, Kristy. A Hop Is Up. Richmond, Lori, illus. 2016. (ENG.). 40p. (J). 16.99 *(978-1-61963-390-2(6),* 9781619633902, Bloomsbury USA Childrens) Bloomsbury Publishing USA.

Denos, Julia. Swatch: the Girl Who Loved Color. Denos, Julia, illus. 2016. (Illus.). 40p. (J). (gr. -1-3). 17.99 *(978-0-06-236638-2(6))* HarperCollins Pubs.

Derby, Sally & Burrowes, Adjoa J. My Steps. 2005. (ENG., Illus.). 32p. (J). (gr. 1-4). pap. 9.95 *(978-1-880000-84-7(9))* Lee & Low Bks., Inc.

Derrick, David G., Jr. Play with Your Food. 2014. (ENG., Illus.). 36p. (J). (gr. -1-3). 15.95 *(978-1-59702-102-9(4))* Immedium.

Dewdney, Anna. Llama Llama Zippity-Zoom! 2012. (Llama Llama Ser.). (ENG.). 14p. (J). (gr. -1 — 1). bds. 5.99 *(978-0-670-01328-9(5),* Viking Books for Young Readers) Penguin Young Readers Group.

—Nelly Gnu & Daddy Too. (ENG., Illus.). (J). 2017. 36p. (-k). bds. 9.99 *(978-0-425-28977-8(X))* 2014. 40p. (gr. -1-k). 17.99 *(978-0-670-01227-5(0))* Penguin Young Readers Group. (Viking Books for Young Readers).

Disney Princess Staff, adapted by. Princess Enchanted Palace: Storybook & Play Castle. 2010. (Playbox Ser.). (ENG., Illus.). 32p. (J). (gr. -1-2). bds. 19.99 *(978-0-7944-2035-2(4))* Reader's Digest Assn., Inc., The.

Doerrfeld, Cori. Maggie & Wendel: Imagine Everything! Doerrfeld, Cori, illus. 2016. (ENG., Illus.). 48p. (J). (gr. -1-3). 17.99 *(978-1-4814-3974-9(X),* Simon & Schuster Bks. For Young Readers) Simon & Schuster Bks. For Young Readers.

Dorling Kindersley Publishing Staff. Pop-Up Peekaboo! - Playtime. 2011. (ENG.). 12p. (J). (gr. -1 — 1). bds. 9.99 *(978-0-7566-7171-6(X),* DK Children) Dorling Kindersley Publishing, Inc.

Dorling Kindersley Publishing Staff, creator. Bedtime Peekaboo! 2006. (ENG., Illus.). 12p. (J). (gr. -1-k). bds. 6.99 *(978-0-7566-1622-9(0),* DK Children) Dorling Kindersley Publishing, Inc.

Dwyer, Kevin & Dwyer, Shawnae. The Blue Baboon. Harman, Micah, illus. 2007. 40p. per. 13.95 *(978-1-59800-247-8(3))* Outskirts Pr., Inc.

D'yans, Masha. Razzle-Dazzle Ruby. D'yans, Masha, illus. 2011. (ENG., Illus.). 20p. (J). (— 1). bds. 17.99 *(978-0-545-22500-7(0))* Scholastic, Inc.

Earley, Catherine. Outside Fun, 1. Earley, Catherine, ed. Art&Script, illus. 2005. 12p. (J). 6.95 *(978-0-9769589-1-8(0))* Naynay Bks.

Eaton, Deborah J. My Wild Woolly. Karas, G. Brian, illus. 2005. (Green Light Readers Level 2 Ser.). (ENG.). 24p. (J). (gr. -1-3). pap. 3.95 *(978-0-15-205147-1(3))* Houghton Mifflin Harcourt Publishing Co.

—My Wild Woolly. Karas, G. Brian, illus. 2005. (Green Light Readers Level 2 Ser.). (gr. k-2). 13.95 *(978-0-7569-5445-1(2))* Perfection Learning Corp.

Edwards, Jean Pearce. Little Jean's War. 2008. (Illus.). 208p. pap. 14.49 *(978-1-4343-9133-9(7))* AuthorHouse.

Elk, Ronit. A Surprise at Dancing Fields. 2009. 76p. pap. 10.49 *(978-1-4490-2064-4(X))* AuthorHouse.

Ellery, Amanda. If I Had a Dragon. Ellery, Tom, illus. 2006. (ENG.). 40p. (J). (gr. -1-3). 17.99 *(978-1-4169-0924-8(9),* Simon & Schuster Bks. For Young Readers) Simon & Schuster Bks. For Young Readers.

Escoffier, Michaël. The Day I Lost My Superpowers. Di Giacomo, Kris, illus. 2014. (ENG.). 32p. (J). (gr. -1-3). 16.95 *(978-1-59270-144-5(2))* Enchanted Lion Bks., LLC.

Farley, Brianne. Secret Tree Fort. Farley, Brianne, illus. 2016. (ENG., Illus.). 32p. (J). (gr. -1-3). 16.99 *(978-0-7636-6297-4(6))* Candlewick Pr.

Farrow, Nancy L. Lucas & Leroy, 1 vol. Schoonmaker, Christina, illus. 2009. 32p. pap. 24.95 *(978-1-60836-232-5(9))* America Star Bks.

Feather, Tami Flaming. A Wondrous World of Home. Porter, Tammy, illus. 2012. 24p. pap. 24.95 *(978-1-4626-4544-2(5))* America Star Bks.

Fenwick, Margaret. Stella's Hair. 2009. 36p. pap. 14.75 *(978-1-60693-857-7(6),* Eloquent Bks.) Strategic Book Publishing & Rights Agency (SBPRA).

Fergus, Maureen. Buddy & Earl, 1 vol. Sookocheff, Carey, illus. 2015. (Buddy & Earl Ser.: 1). (ENG.). 32p. (J). (gr. -1-2). 16.95 *(978-1-55498-712-2(1))* Groundwood Bks. CAN. Dist: Publishers Group West (PGW).

Ferreri, Della Ross. Star of the Show. Weinstock, Tony, illus. 2009. (ENG.). 36p. (J). (gr. -1-3). 15.95 *(978-1-934860-03-8(4))* Shenanigan Bks.

Ficocelli, Elizabeth. Kid Tea. Dibley, Glin, illus. 2009. 32p. (J). (gr. -1). bds. 7.99 *(978-0-7614-5533-2(7))* Marshall Cavendish Corp.

Fine, Anne. Jamie & Angus Together. Dale, Penny, illus. 2007. (ENG.). 112p. (J). (gr. -1-1). 15.99 *(978-0-7636-3374-5(7))* Candlewick Pr.

Fleming, David. Charlie Blue Berry Fipple Berry. 2012. 88p. 19.95 *(978-1-4759-1945-5(X))*; pap. 9.95 *(978-1-4759-1944-8(1))* iUniverse, Inc.

Flying Frog Pub, creator. ABC Fun with Elmo & Friends. 2011. (Sesame Street (Publications International) Ser.). (ENG., Illus.). 14p. (J). (gr. -1). bds. 3.99 *(978-1-60745-030-6(5))* Flying Frog Publishing.

—Big & Small Fun with Elmo & Friends. 2011. (ENG., Illus.). 14p. (gr. -1-k). bds. 3.99 *(978-1-60745-033-7(X))* Flying Frog Publishing.

Franco, Betsy. Double Play: Monkeying Around with Addition. Cushman, Doug, illus. 2011. (ENG.). 32p. (J). (gr. -1-2). 15.99 *(978-1-58246-384-1(0),* Tricycle Pr.) Random Hse. Children's Bks.

Franklin, Teii L. Ameelia's Adventures: Ameelia's First Play. 2010. 32p. pap. 16.49 *(978-1-4520-3613-7(6))* AuthorHouse.

Friedman, Becky. Daniel Learns to Share. 2016. (Simon & Schuster Ready-To-Read Level 1 Ser.). lib. bdg. 13.55 ***(978-0-606-39754-4(X))*** Turtleback Bks.

Fruchter, Jason, illus. Daniel Plays at School. 2016. (Daniel Tiger's Neighborhood Ser.). (ENG.). 32p. (J). (gr. -1-k). pap. 3.99 *(978-1-4814-6102-3(8),* Simon Spotlight) Simon Spotlight.

Fucile, Tony. Let's Do Nothing! Fucile, Tony, illus. 2012. (ENG., Illus.). 40p. (J). (gr. -1-3). pap. 6.99 *(978-0-7636-5269-2(5))* Candlewick Pr.

Fudge, Keith. The Rainy Day Discovery. 2006. (J). per. 11.95 *(978-1-889743-37-0(2))* Robbie Dean Pr.

Fujikawa, Gyo. Oh, What a Busy Day. 2010. (ENG., Illus.). 72p. (J). (gr. -1-2). 9.95 *(978-1-4027-6819-4(2))* Sterling Publishing Co., Inc.

Fujikawa, Gyo, illus. Let's Play. 2010. (ENG.). 20p. (J). (gr. k-k). bds. 5.95 *(978-1-4027-6821-7(4))* Sterling Publishing Co., Inc.

Fuller, Bob, illus. The Costume Trunk. 2011. (J). *(978-1-936169-01-6(0))* Paddywhack Lane LLC.

Galvin, Laura Gates. Baby Lamb Finds a Friend. 2008. (Smithsonian Baby Animals Ser.). (ENG., Illus.). 16p. (gr. -1-k). 13.95 *(978-1-59249-790-4(X))* Soundprints.

—Baby Pig Time to Play. 2008. (ENG., Illus.). 16p. (J). (gr. -1-k). 6.95 *(978-1-59249-787-4(X))* Soundprints.

—Baby Polar Bear Learns to Swim. 2008. (ENG., Illus.). 16p. (J). (gr. -1-k). 6.95 *(978-1-59249-785-0(3))* Soundprints.

—Black Bear Cub at Sweet Berry Trail. 2008. (ENG., Illus.). 32p. (J). (gr. k-2). 9.95 *(978-1-59249-779-9(9))* Soundprints.

—Black Bear Cub at Sweet Berry Trail. Nelson, Will, illus. 2008. (ENG.). 32p. (J). (gr. k-2). 6.95 *(978-1-59249-775-1(6))*; pap. 8.95 *(978-1-59249-777-5(2))*; 19.95 *(978-1-59249-776-8(4))*; 16.95 *(978-1-59249-773-7(X))*; pap. 6.95 *(978-1-59249-774-4(8))* Soundprints.

Galvin, Laura Gates & Odierno, Lisa. Puppy Explores. 2008. (ENG.). 16p. (J). (gr. -1-k). 6.95 *(978-1-59249-863-5(9))* Soundprints.

Gammell, Stephen. Mudkin. Gammell, Stephen, illus. 2011. (Carolrhoda Picture Bks.). (ENG., Illus.). 32p. (J). (gr. k-3). 16.95 *(978-0-7613-5790-2(4))* Lerner Publishing Group.

Garland, Sally Anne. Share. Garland, Sally Anne, illus. 2014. (ENG., Illus.). 32p. (J). (gr. -1-3). 17.95 *(978-1-77147-005-6(4),* Owlkids) Owlkids Bks. Inc. CAN. Dist: Publishers Group West (PGW).

Gasior, Julie. Samy the Star. 2008. 46p. 27.95 *(978-0-615-18884-3(2))* Gasior, Julie.

Gates, Josephine Scribner. The live dolls' play Days. Keep, Virginia, illus. 2007. 110p. (J). lib. bdg. 59.00 *(978-1-60304-008-2(0))* Dollworks.

—The Story of Live Dolls: Being an Account of How, on a Certain June Morning. unabr. ed. 2012. (Illus.). 104p. 39.99 *(978-1-4622-8158-9(3))* Repressed Publishing LLC.

Gauch, Patricia Lee. Christina Katerina & the Box. 2012. (ENG.). 32p. (J). (gr. -1-3). 7.95 *(978-1-59078-915-5(6))* Boyds Mills Pr.

Gay, Marie-Louise. Stella, Queen of the Snow. 2004. (J). (gr. -1-1). spiral bd. *(978-0-616-08493-9(5))* Canadian National Institute for the Blind/Institut National Canadien pour les Aveugles.

—Stella, Reine des Neiges. 2004.Tr. of Stella, Queen of the Snow. (FRE., Illus.). (J). (gr. k-3). spiral bd. *(978-0-616-14596-8(9))* Canadian National Institute for the Blind/Institut National Canadien pour les Aveugles.

Gay, Marie-Louise, illus. Stella, Queen of the Snow. braille ed. 2004. (J). (gr. -1-1). spiral bd. *(978-0-616-08492-2(7))* Canadian National Institute for the Blind/Institut National Canadien pour les Aveugles.

Ghigna, Charles. Adeline Porcupine. East, Jacqueline, illus. 2015. (Tiny Tales Ser.). (ENG.). 64p. (gr. -1-2). lib. bdg. 23.99 *(978-1-4795-6530-6(X))* Tiny Tales.

Giggle & grow with Plush. 2007. bds. 15.95 *(978-1-58117-644-5(9),* Intervisual/Piggy Toes) Bendon, Inc.

Gigi, Jessy. The Sky Ride of Jimmy & Friends. 2011. 20p. pap. 24.95 *(978-1-4626-2723-3(4))* America Star Bks.

Gilbert in the Snow. 2005. (Gilbert the Pig Chapter Ser.). (J). 7.67 *(978-1-58453-297-2(1))* Pioneer Valley Bks.

Gillis, Jennifer Blizin. What Do You Say? Losa, Ann, illus. 2006. (Reader's Clubhouse Level 2 Reader Ser.). (ENG.). 24p. (J). (gr. 1-4). pap. 3.99 *(978-0-7641-3298-8(9))* Barron's Educational Series, Inc.

Gordon, David. Extremely Cute Animals Operating Heavy Machinery. Gordon, David, illus. 2016. (ENG., Illus.). 48p. (J). (gr. -1-3). 17.99 *(978-1-4169-2441-8(8),* Simon & Schuster Bks. For Young Readers) Simon & Schuster Bks. For Young Readers.

Graham, Tamara. Little Miss Litterbug. 2008. 24p. pap. 12.99 *(978-1-4389-2519-6(0))* AuthorHouse.

Grandma Sue. Bubba the Bear. 2010. 12p. pap. 8.49 *(978-1-4490-1813-9(0))* AuthorHouse.

Green, Corey. Managing Stan: Buckley School Books #1. 2007. (ENG.). 162p. (J). 16.95 *(978-1-934437-01-8(8))*; pap. 7.99 *(978-1-934437-02-5(6))* Aligio Bks.

Gritton, Steve. ... & Then I... 2007. (Illus.). (J). 17.95 *(978-0-9795361-1-3(1))* Bad Frog Art/SMG Bks.

Groves. Mud Cake, Bk. 3A. Date not set. (Illus.). 16p. (J). pap. 129.15 *(978-0-582-18794-8(X))* Addison-Wesley Longman, Ltd. GBR. Dist: Trans-Atlantic Pubns., Inc.

Gudeon, Adam. Me & Meow. Gudeon, Adam, illus. 2011. (ENG., Illus.). 32p. (J). (gr. -1-k). 12.99 *(978-0-06-199821-8(4))* HarperCollins Pubs.

Guerin, F. A. The Witch at NO46: Verbrola. 2011. (Illus.). 140p. pap. 14.69 *(978-1-4567-7118-8(3))* AuthorHouse.

Gutman, Dan. Miss Small Is off the Wall! Paillot, Jim, illus. 2005. (My Weird School Ser.: 5). (ENG.). 112p. (J). (gr. 1-5). pap. 4.99 *(978-0-06-074518-9(5))* HarperCollins Pubs.

Guy, Ginger Foglesong. Bravo! Moreno, Rene King, illus. 2010. (SPA & ENG.). 32p. (J). (gr. -1-k). 16.99 *(978-0-06-173180-8(3),* Greenwillow Bks.) HarperCollins Pubs.

H & T Imaginations Unlimited, Inc. Sand Castles with Professor Woodpecker. 2009. 12p. pap. 8.49 *(978-1-4389-7262-6(8))* AuthorHouse.

Haesche, Richard, Sr. A Dog Named Wishbone. 2007. 155p. (J). 6.75 *(978-0-9798536-2-3(1))* Kreative X-Pressions Pubns.

Haladay, Max. Max Gets Mad. 2006. (Neighborhood Readers Ser.). (ENG.). 8p. (gr. 1-3). pap. 5.15 *(978-1-4042-6811-1(1),* Rosen Classroom) Rosen Publishing Group, Inc., The.

Hall, Bureda Ann Greathouse. Stories of My Little Blue Monkey. 2007. (Illus.). 32p. (J). pap. 15.00 *(978-0-8059-7397-6(4))* Dorrance Publishing Co., Inc.

Hannigan, Katherine. Dirt + Water = Mud. Hannigan, Katherine, illus. 2016. (Illus.). 40p. (J). (gr. -1-3). 17.99 *(978-0-06-234517-2(6),* Greenwillow Bks.) HarperCollins Pubs.

Hapka, Cathy, pseud. Pretend & Play Kitty: With Real Crown You Can Wear! Borlasca, Hector, illus. 2004. (Role Play Ser.). 10p. (J). (gr. -1-18). bds. 6.99 *(978-1-57151-742-5(1))* Playhouse Publishing.

Harper, Charise Mericle. Mae & June & the Wonder Wheel. Spires, Ashley, illus. 2017. (ENG.). 128p. (J). (gr. 1-4). 15.99 *(978-0-544-63063-5(7),* HMH Books For Young Readers) Houghton Mifflin Harcourt Publishing Co.

Harris, Angela. Night Light. 2008. 28p. pap. 12.95 *(978-1-4389-1971-3(9))* AuthorHouse.

Harris, Donna. Lucie & the Garden Fairies. 2008. (Illus.). 40p. pap. 18.49 *(978-1-4389-1312-4(5))* AuthorHouse.

Hatton, Jenny. Swimming in the Sun. Rankin, Joan, illus. 2012. (Lucy Bks.). (ENG.). 32p. (J). (gr. -1-k). pap. 6.95 *(978-1-4314-0218-2(4))* Jacana Media ZAF. Dist: Independent Pubs. Group.

Havill, Juanita. Jamaica's Find. O'Brien, Anne Sibley, illus. 2009. (ENG.). 32p. (J). (gr. -1-3). audio compact disk 10.99 *(978-0-547-11961-8(5))* Houghton Mifflin Harcourt Publishing Co.

HB Staff. Where Babies Play. 97th ed. 2003. (First-Place Reading Ser.). (gr. 1-18). pap. 16.50 *(978-0-15-308136-1(8))* Harcourt Schl. Pubs.

Heape, David. R. That's What Friends Do. l.t. ed. 2006. (ENG., Illus.). 28p. per. 9.95 *(978-1-4327-0177-2(0))* Outskirts Pr., Inc.

Heiman, Laura. My Favorite Michael. Keen, Sophie, illus. 2009. (J). (gr. -1-2). 32p. 15.95 *(978-1-58925-086-4(9))*; 24p. pap. 7.95 *(978-1-58925-419-0(8))* Tiger Tales.

Helou, Sandra & Chown, Xanna Eve. Grover on the Case: Follow the Reader Level 1. 2008. (Sesame Street Ser.). (ENG.). 24p. (J). 24.99 *(978-1-4169-5852-9(5),* Simon Scribbles) Simon Scribbles.

Higginson, Sheila Sweeny & Disney Book Group Staff. Brontosaurus Breath. Disney Storybook Art Team, illus. 2013. (World of Reading Ser.). (ENG.). 32p. (J). (gr. -1-k). pap. 3.99 *(978-1-4231-6894-2(1))* Disney Pr.

Hilb, Nora, illus. Itsy Bitsy Spider. 2012. (Classic Books with Holes Board Book Ser.). (ENG.). (J). 14p. bds. *(978-1-84643-509-6(9))*; 16p. pap. *(978-1-84643-498-3(X))* Child's Play International Ltd.

Hill, Eric. Spot Goes to the Park. Hill, Eric, illus. 2005. (Spot Ser.). (ENG., Illus.). 24p. (J). (gr. -1 — 1). bds. 7.99 *(978-0-399-24363-9(1),* Warne) Penguin Young Readers Group.

Hill, Ros. Unexpected Tails. 2010. (ENG.). 32p. (J). (gr. -1-3). 15.95 *(978-1-59687-861-7(4),* Milk & Cookies) ibooks, Inc.

Hillert, Margaret. The Birthday Car. Girouard, Patrick, illus. 2016. (BeginningtoRead Ser.). (ENG.). 32p. (J). (gr. -1-2). pap. 11.94 *(978-1-60357-936-0(2))* Norwood Hse. Pr.

—Play Ball. Kemarskaya, Oksana, illus. 2016. (BeginningtoRead Ser.). (ENG.). 32p. (J). (gr. k-2). 22.60 *(978-1-59953-819-8(9))* Norwood Hse. Pr.

—Where Is Dear Dragon? Schimmell, David, illus. 2012. (BeginningtoRead Ser.). 32p. (J). (-2). lib. bdg. 22.60 *(978-1-59953-546-3(7))* Norwood Hse. Pr.

Hoban, Russell. How Tom Beat Captain Najork & His Hired Sportsmen. Blake, Quentin, illus. 2006. (ENG.). 32p. (J). (gr. k-4). pap. 7.95 *(978-1-56792-322-3(4))* Godine, David R. Pub.

Hochman, Marisa. A Walk in Pirate's Cove. Woodland, Bette, illus. 2012. (ENG.). 32p. (J). *(978-0-9865679-0-2(6))* Fitzhenry & Whiteside, Ltd.

Hoffman, Eric. A Dark, Dark Cave. Tabor, Corey R., illus. 2016. (ENG.). 40p. (J). (gr. -1-1). 17.99 *(978-0-670-01636-5(5),* Viking Books for Young Readers) Penguin Young Readers Group.

Hofmeister, Alan, et al. Fun with the Sheet. (Reading for All Learners Ser.). (Illus.). (J). pap. *(978-1-56861-115-0(3))* Swift Learning Resources.

—In the Mud. (Reading for All Learners Ser.). (Illus.). (J). pap. *(978-1-56861-127-3(7))* Swift Learning Resources.

—Will We Win? (Reading for All Learners Ser.). (Illus.). (J). pap. *(978-1-56861-110-5(2))* Swift Learning Resources.

Holden, Pam. Hunting for Treasure, 6 pack. Whimp, Pauline, illus. 2009. (Red Rocket Readers Ser.). (ENG.). 16p. (gr. 2-2). pap. *(978-1-877363-65-8(0),* Red Rocket Readers) Flying Start Bks.

—Pin the Tail on the Donkey, 6 pack. Hawley, Kelvin, illus. 2009. (Red Rocket Readers Ser.). (ENG.). 16p. pap. *(978-1-877363-78-8(2))* Flying Start Bks.

—Too Big & Heavy, 6 pack. Hatam, Samer, illus. 2009. (Red Rocket Readers Ser.). (ENG.). 16p. (gr. 2-2). pap. *(978-1-877363-70-2(7))* Flying Start Bks.

Hollon, Frank Turner, et al. Glitter Girl & the Crazy Cheese. Dulemba, Elizabeth O., illus. 2006. (ENG.). 32p. (J). (gr.

P
Q
R

-1-3). (978-1-59692-137-5(4)) MacAdam/Cage Publishing, Inc.

Holub, Joan. Dig, Scoop, Ka-Boom! Gordon, David, illus. 2013. (Step into Reading Ser.). (ENG.). 24p. (J). (gr. -1-1). pap. 3.99 (978-0-375-86910-5(7), Random Hse. Bks. for Young Readers) Random Hse. Children's Bks.

—Itty Bitty Kitty & the Rainy Play Day. Burks, James, illus. 2016. 32p. (J). (gr. -1-3). 17.99 (978-0-06-232220-3(6)) HarperCollins Pubs.

Hooper, Jaci. Gary: #Exodus 20. 2013. 32p. pap. 16.95 (978-1-4908-1120-8(6), WestBow Pr.) Author Solutions, Inc.

Hope, Laura Lee. Freddie & Flossie & Snap. Pyle, Chuck, illus. 2005. (Bobbsey Twins Ser.). (ENG.). 32p. (J). (gr. -1-k). pap. 13.99 (978-1-4169-0267-6(8), Simon Spotlight) Simon Spotlight.

Howard-Parham, Pam. Playing on the Playground. Crowell, Knox, illus. l.t. ed. 2005. (HRL Little Book Ser.). (J). (gr. k-18). pap. 10.95 (978-1-57332-336-9(5)); pap. 10.95 (978-1-57332-335-2(7)) Carson-Dellosa Publishing, LLC. (HighReach Learning, Incorporated).

—Spending Time Outdoors. Teeple, Jackie, illus. l.t. ed. 2005. (HRL Big Book Ser.). (J). (gr. k-18). pap. 10.95 (978-1-57332-333-8(0)); pap. 10.95 (978-1-57332-334-5(9)) Carson-Dellosa Publishing, LLC. (HighReach Learning, Incorporated).

Huber, Mike. Bree Finds a Friend. Cowman, Joseph, illus. 2014. (ENG.). 32p. (gr. -1). 15.95 (978-1-60554-211-9(3)) Redleaf Pr.

—Rita & the Firefighters. Cowman, Joseph, illus. 2014. (ENG.). 32p. (gr. -1-k). 15.95 (978-1-60554-208-9(3)) Redleaf Pr.

Hudson, Wade. Places I Love to Go. 2008. (Illus.). 24p. (J). (gr. -1-3). 3.99 (978-1-60349-008-5(6), Marimba Bks.) Hudson Publishing Group, The.

Hulst, W. G. van de & Hulst, Willem G. van de, illus. The Rockity Rowboat. 2014. (J). (978-1-928136-18-7(4)) Inheritance Pubns.

Hunter, Sally. Humphrey's Playtime. 2013. (Illus.). (J). (978-1-4351-4766-9(9)) Barnes & Noble, Inc.

Hupf, Zetta & Hupf, Mitchell. Henry Goes to the Park, 1 vol. Hupf, Zetta, illus. 2009. (Illus.). 33p. pap. 24.95 (978-1-61546-279-7(1)) America Star Bks.

Hutton, John. Blocks: Baby Unplugged. Hutton, John, ed. Kang, Andrea, illus. 2013. (Baby Unplugged Ser.). (ENG.). 14p. (J). (— 1). bds. 7.99 (978-1-936669-13-4(7)) Blue Manatee Press.

I DOUBLE Dare You. 2008. (Illus.). 36p. (J). (978-0-9792686-5-6(6)) Lehman Publishing.

I Love to Play. 2003. (J). per. (978-1-57657-962-6(X)) Paradise Pr., Inc.

I Want a Friend. 2017. (ENG., Illus.). 32p. (J). (gr. -1-k). 16.99 (978-0-7459-7707-2(3)) Lion Hudson PLC GBR. Dist: Independent Pubs. Group.

I Want to Go to. . . the All-American Soap Box Derby Race. 2003. (Illus.). 40p. (J). per. 9.99 (978-0-9742667-0-1(1)) Creative Image Pubs.

Image Books Staff. Little Dolphin. Put, Klaartje van der, illus. 2012. (Little Finger Puppet Board Bks.: FING). (ENG.). 12p. (J). (gr. -1 — 1). bds. 6.99 (978-1-4521-0816-2(1)) Chronicle Bks. LLC.

ImageBooks Staff. Little Shark: Finger Puppet Book. Put, Klaartje van der, illus. 2013. (Little Finger Puppet Board Bks.). (ENG.). 12p. (J). (gr. -1 — 1). bds. 6.99 (978-1-4521-1251-0(7)) Chronicle Bks. LLC.

Intrater, Roberta Grobel. Peek-a-Boo, You! Intrater, Roberta Grobel, photos by. 2nd rev. l.t. ed. 2005. (Illus.). 14p. (J). 14.99 (978-0-9764985-0-6(2)) 1212 Pr.

Isaacs, Latricia. Mason & Lilly Visit Grandpa. 2011. 16p. 8.32 (978-1-4567-2788-8(5)) AuthorHouse.

Isabel, Delgado Maria. Chave's Memories / Los Recuerdos de Chave. Yvonne, Symank, illus. 2008. 32p. (J). pap. 7.95 (978-1-55885-244-0(1), Piñata Books) Arte Publico Pr.

Ismail, Yasmeen. Imagine That! 2017. (ENG., Illus.). 32p. (J). 16.99 (978-1-68119-362-5(0), 9781681193625, Bloomsbury USA Childrens) Bloomsbury Publishing USA.

It's a Bit Tricky: Individual Title Six-Packs. (gr. k-1). 23.00 (978-0-7635-9022-2(3)) Rigby Education.

Jackson, Richard. This Beautiful Day. Lee, Suzy, illus. 2017. (ENG.). 40p. (J). (gr. -1-3). 15.99 (978-1-4814-4139-1(6), Atheneum/Caitlyn Dlouhy Books) Simon & Schuster Children's Publishing.

Jakubowski, Michele. Outside Surprise. Waters, Erica-Jane, illus. 2015. (Perfectly Poppy Ser.). (ENG.). 32p. (gr. k-2). 22.65 (978-1-4795-5802-5(8)) Picture Window Bks.

—Snowy Blast. Waters, Erica-Jane, illus. 2014. (Perfectly Poppy Ser.). (ENG.). 32p. (gr. k-2). lib. bdg. 22.65 (978-1-4795-2283-5(X)) Picture Window Bks.

James, Thomas & Thomas, James. What Will I Play While You Are Away? 2010. 28p. pap. 16.09 (978-1-4269-2924-3(2)) Trafford Publishing.

Jarrell, Pamela R. Who Is in the Backyard? Crowell, Knox, illus. l.t. ed. 2004. (HRL Board Book Ser.). 8p. (J). (gr. -1). pap. 10.95 (978-1-57332-281-2(4), HighReach Learning, Incorporated) Carson-Dellosa Publishing, LLC.

Jeffries, Alison. Sam & the Bag. Andreasen, Dan, illus. 2004. (Green Light Readers Level 1 Ser.). (gr. -1-1). 13.95 (978-0-7569-4331-8(0)) Perfection Learning Corp.

Jenson-Elliott, Cindy. Dig In! Peterson, Mary, illus. 2016. (ENG.). 40p. (J). (gr. -1-3). 17.99 (978-1-4424-1261-3(5), Beach Lane Bks.) Beach Lane Bks.

Jobes, Cecily. Playtime. 2016. (It's Time Ser.). 24p. (gr. 1-1). pap. 8.25 (978-1-4994-2284-9(9), PowerKids Pr.) Rosen Publishing Group, Inc., The.

Johnson, Linda Louisa. Needle in a Haystack. 2003. 78p. (YA). pap. 10.95 (978-0-7414-1541-7(0)) Infinity Publishing.

Jolin, Dominique. Toupie Veut Jouer. braille ed. 2004. (FRE.). (J). (gr. 1). spiral bd., bds. (978-0-616-07270-7(8)) Canadian National Institute for the Blind/Institut National Canadien pour les Aveugles.

Judybee. The Zoo Crew Play Ball. LittlePinkPebble, illus. 2011. 40p. pap. (978-1-78092-000-9(8)) MX Publishing, Ltd.

Kalar, Bonnie. Ann Paints & Plays. Spreen, Kathe, illus. Date not set. 12p. (J). (gr. -1-2). pap. (978-1-891619-40-3(3)) Corona Pr.

Kathleen, Jo Ann. Buddy Can't Tie Shoes. l.t. ed. 2006. (ENG., Illus.). 28p. per. 9.95 (978-1-4327-0238-0(6)) Outskirts Pr., Inc.

Katz, Alan. Stalling. Smith, Elwood H., illus. 2010. (ENG.). 40p. (J). (gr. -1-2). 16.99 (978-1-4169-5567-2(4), McElderry, Margaret K. Bks.) McElderry, Margaret K. Bks.

Katz, Danny. Little Lunch Four. Vane, Mitch, illus. 2005. (Little Lunch Ser.). 64p. (J). pap. (978-1-876372-84-2(2), Black Dog Books) Walker Bks. Australia Pty, Ltd.

Katz, Karen. ¡Cu-Cú, Bebé! Katz, Karen, illus. 2009. (SPA., Illus.). 14p. (J). (gr. -1 — 1). bds. 7.99 (978-1-4169-7938-8(7), Libros Para Ninos) Libros Para Ninos.

—Peek-a-Baby. Katz, Karen, illus. 2010. (ENG., Illus.). 14p. (J). (gr. -1 — 1). 11.99 (978-1-4424-0790-9(5), Little Simon) Little Simon.

Kawai, Ritsuko. Hamtaro. Kawai, Ritsuko, illus. 2003. (ENG., Illus.). 16p. (J). pap. 7.95 (978-1-56931-815-7(8)) Viz Media.

—Hamtaro, Vol. 1. Kawai, Ritsuko, illus. 2003. (ENG., Illus.). 16p. (J). pap. 7.95 (978-1-56931-814-0(X)) Viz Media.

Kearney, Rena. Mimi Fairy's Purple Hair. 2009. 32p. pap. 15.99 (978-1-4490-1554-1(9)) AuthorHouse.

Keats, Ezra Jack. Regards to the Man in the Moon. 2009. (ENG.). 40p. (J). (gr. -1-2). 15.99 (978-0-670-01137-7(1), Viking Books for Young Readers) Penguin Young Readers Group.

Kemble, Mai S., illus. I'm So Not Wearing a Dress! 2010. (ENG.). 32p. (J). 11.99 (978-1-935703-05-1(6)) Downtown Bookworks.

Kettle, Shey. Girl Pirates. Thomas, Meredith, illus. 2005. (Girlz Rock! Ser.). (J). pap. (978-1-59336-701-5(5)) Mondo Publishing.

Klein, Adria F. Max Goes to the Playground, 1 vol. Gallagher-Cole, Mernie, illus. 2007. (Read-It! Readers: the Life of Max Ser.). (ENG.). 24p. (gr. -1-2). lib. bdg. 21.32 (978-1-4048-3681-5(0), Easy Readers) Picture Window Bks.

Koehler, Fred. Super Jumbo. Koehler, Fred, illus. 2016. (ENG., Illus.). 32p. (J). (-k). 16.99 (978-0-8037-3923-9(0), Dial Bks) Penguin Young Readers Group.

Koppens, Judith. The Seesaw. van Lindenhuizen, Eline, illus. 2013. (Animal Square Ser.). (ENG.). 32p. (J). (gr. -1-k). 13.95 (978-1-60537-152-8(1)) Cobblestone Publishing Co.

Krauss, Ruth. I Can Fly. Blair, Mary, illus. 2003. (Little Golden Book Ser.). (ENG.). 24p. (J). (gr. -1-2). 4.99 (978-0-307-00146-7(6), 312-12, Golden Bks.) Random Hse. Children's Bks.

Krebs, Patricia, illus. On Your Mark, Get Set, Go! 2009. 32p. (J). 16.95 (978-0-9796380-1-5(1)) Three Wishes Publishing Co.

Krensky, Stephen. What Do You See? A Lift-the-Flap Book about Endangered Animals. Schimler, Amy, illus. 2009. (Little Green Bks.). (ENG.). 16p. (J). (gr. -1-k). 6.99 (978-1-4169-7123-8(8), Little Simon) Little Simon.

Krutop, Lee, creator. Go Out to Play. 2008. (Illus.). 10p. (J). (gr. -1-1). bds. (978-1-74178-572-2(3)) Brimax Books Ltd.

Kuhlman, Evan. Hank's Big Day: The Story of a Bug. Groenink, Chuck, illus. 2016. (ENG.). 40p. (J). (gr. -1-2). 16.99 (978-0-553-51150-5(5), Schwartz & Wade Bks.) Random Hse. Children's Bks.

Kula, Cheryl. Play Day with Daddy. Trolenberg, Karl, illus. 2013. 20p. pap. 6.95 (978-1-4575-2336-6(1)) Dog Ear Publishing, LLC.

Ladd, Debbie. Puddles. Morejon, Tom, illus. 2006. 32p. (J). pap. 8.95 (978-0-9727615-4-3(3)) Deb on Air Bks.

Lamb, Anne. Beat Bugs: Rain. 2017. (Beat Bugs Ser.). 16p. (J). (gr. -1 — 1). bds. 6.99 (978-0-06-264073-4(9), HarperFestival) HarperCollins Pubs.

Landolf, Diane Wright. Hog & Dog. Harris, Jennifer Beck, illus. 2005. (Step into Reading Ser.: Vol. 1). (ENG.). 32p. (J). (gr. -1-1). per. 3.99 (978-0-375-83165-2(7), Random Hse. Bks. for Young Readers) Random Hse. Children's Bks.

Latty, Jasmin. Oh, My Boring Toes! 2005. (J). pap. 12.00 (978-0-8059-6668-8(4)) Dorrance Publishing Co., Inc.

Lawlor, Laurie. The Biggest Pest on Eighth Avenue. Fisher, Cynthia, illus. (Holiday House Reader Ser.). (ENG.). 47p. (J). (gr. k-3). tchr. ed. 14.95 (978-0-8234-1321-8(7)) Holiday Hse., Inc.

Leah. The Alligator Named Ally, 1 vol. 2009. 20p. pap. 24.95 (978-1-60749-726-4(3)) America Star Bks.

Lee, Michelle. Play with Me! Lee, Michelle, illus. 2017. (ENG., Illus.). 32p. (J). (-k). 16.99 (978-0-399-54601-3(4), G.P. Putnam's Sons Books for Young Readers) Penguin Young Readers Group.

Lee, Suzy. Mirror. 2010. (ENG., Illus.). 48p. (J). (gr. -1). 15.95 (978-1-934734-39-1(X)) Seven Footer Pr.

Lehman, Barbara. Rainstorm. 2007. (ENG., Illus.). 32p. (J). (gr. -1-3). 17.99 (978-0-618-75639-1(6)) Houghton Mifflin Harcourt Publishing Co.

Lenart, Claudia, illus. Seasons of Joy: Every Day Is for Outdoor Play. 2017. (J). pap. (978-1-61599-317-8(7)) Loving Healing Pr., Inc.

Lendler, Ian & Bloch, Serge. Saturday. 2016. (ENG., Illus.). 40p. (J). 16.99 (978-1-59643-965-8(3), 9781596439658) Roaring Brook Pr.

Leonard, Marcia. Saltar, Brincar, Correr. Translations.com Staff, tr. from ENG. Handelman, Dorothy, photos by. 2007. (Lecturas para niños de Verdad - Nivel 1 (Real Kids Readers - Level 1) Ser.).Tr. of Hop, Skip, Run. (SPA., Illus.). 32p. (gr. k-2). per. 5.95 (978-0-8225-7799-7(2), Ediciones Lerner) Lerner Publishing Group.

—Saltar, Brincar, Correr; Hop, Skip, Run. 2008. pap. 34.95 (978-0-8225-9497-0(8)) Lerner Publishing Group.

LeTourneau, Marie, illus. Argyle Fox. 2017. (ENG.). 32p. (J). (gr. -1-2). 17.99 (978-1-939100-09-2(7)) Tanglewood Pr.

Let's Play at the Playground. 2013. (Illus.). 38p. 19.95 (978-0-9885741-1-3(X)) Community Voice Media, LLC.

Let's Pretend: Individual Title Six-Packs. (gr. -1-2). 23.00 (978-0-7635-9001-7(0)) Rigby Education.

Levy, Janey. Play Ball! 2006. (Neighborhood Readers Ser.). (ENG.). 8p. (gr. -1-3). pap. 5.15 (978-1-4042-5659-0(8), Rosen Classroom) Rosen Publishing Group, Inc., The.

Lewis, Edwina. Who Plays? Parker, Ant, illus. 2003. (Who... Ser.). 16p. (J). (978-1-85602-469-3(5), Pavilion Children's Books) Pavilion Bks.

Lin, Grace. Ling & Ting: Together in All Weather. 2015. (ENG., Illus.). 48p. (J). (gr. 1-4). 16.00 (978-0-316-33549-2(5)) Little Brown & Co.

—Ling & Ting: Together in All Weather. 2016. (ENG.). 48p. (J). (gr. 1-4). pap. 4.99 (978-0-316-33548-5(7)) Little, Brown Bks. for Young Readers.

—Ling & Ting: Twice As Silly. 2014. (ENG., Illus.). 48p. (J). (gr. 1-4). 16.00 (978-0-316-18402-1(0)) Little, Brown Bks. for Young Readers.

Little Blue Kite & Friends Activity Book. 2005. (YA). per. (978-1-59872-122-5(4)) Instant Pub.

Litwin, Eric. The Nuts: Bedtime at the Nut House. Magoon, Scott, illus. 2014. (ENG.). 32p. (J). (gr. -1-3). 18.00 (978-0-316-32244-7(X)) Little, Brown Bks. for Young Readers.

—The Nuts: Sing & Dance in Your Polka Dot Pants. Magoon, Scott, illus. 2015. (ENG.). 32p. (J). (gr. -1-3). 18.00 (978-0-316-32250-8(4)) Little Brown & Co.

Liwska, Renata. The Red Wagon. Liwska, Renata, illus. 2011. (ENG., Illus.). 32p. (J). (gr. -1-k). 16.99 (978-0-399-25237-2(1), Philomel Bks.) Penguin Young Readers Group.

Llewellyn, Claire. Sand!, 1 vol. Beard, Lauren, illus. 2013. (Start Reading Ser.). (ENG.). 24p. (gr. k-1). pap. 7.95 (978-1-4765-3187-8(0)); pap. 41.94 (978-1-4765-3230-1(3)) Capstone Press of Coughlan Cos.

Long, Ethan. Clara & Clem Take a Ride. 2012. (Penguin Young Readers Level 1 Ser.). lib. bdg. 13.55 (978-0-606-26639-0(9), Turtleback) Turtleback Bks.

—Lion & Tiger & Bear: Tag! You're It! 2016. (Lion & Tiger & Bear Ser.). (ENG., Illus.). 40p. (J). (gr. k-2). 14.95 (978-1-4197-1896-0(7)) Abrams, Inc.

Loti, Pierre. The Story of a Child. 2007. (ENG.). 200p. pap. 19.99 (978-1-4264-4968-0(2)); 210p. pap. 22.99 (978-1-4264-5269-7(1)) Creative Media Partners, LLC.

—The Story of a Child. 2004. reprint ed. pap. 20.95 (978-1-4191-8367-6(2)) Kessinger Publishing, LLC.

—The Story of A Child. 2004. reprint ed. pap. 1.99 (978-1-4192-8367-3(7)) Kessinger Publishing, LLC.

Love, Pamela. Dos Pies Suben, Dos Pies Bajan. Chapman, Lynne, illus. 2005. (Rookie Reader Español Ser.). (SPA & ESP.). 31p. (J). (gr. k-2). per. 4.95 (978-0-516-25532-3(0), Children's Pr.) Scholastic Library Publishing.

Lovell, Patty. Have Fun, Molly Lou Melon. Lovell, Patty & Catrow, David, illus. 2012. (ENG.). 32p. (J). (gr. k-3). 16.99 (978-0-399-25406-2(4), G.P. Putnam's Sons Books for Young Readers) Penguin Young Readers Group.

Lowery, Marie Hayes. Beau & Friends. 2012. 20p. pap. 17.99 (978-1-4817-0106-8(1)) AuthorHouse.

Lundquist, Mary. Cat & Bunny. Lundquist, Mary, illus. 2015. (ENG., Illus.). 32p. (J). (gr. -1-3). 17.99 (978-0-06-228780-9(X)) HarperCollins Pubs.

Lynn, Cheryl. Kayla's Day at the Park. 2008. 16p. pap. 24.95 (978-1-60813-169-3(6)) America Star Bks.

Lynn, Sarah. 1-2-3 Va-Va-Vroom! A Counting Book, 0 vols. Griffo, Daniel, illus. 2012. (ENG.). 32p. (J). (gr. -1-3). 16.99 (978-0-7614-6162-3(0), 9780761461623, Amazon Children's Publishing) Amazon Publishing.

Maccarone, Grace. The Gingerbread Family: A Scratch-and-Sniff Book. Gardner, Louise, illus. 2010. (ENG.). 14p. (J). (gr. -1-k). bds. 7.99 (978-1-4424-0678-0(X), Little Simon) Little Simon.

Maddox, Jake. Striker Assist, 1 vol. Tiffany, Sean, illus. 2012. (Jake Maddox Sports Stories Ser.). (ENG.). 72p. (gr. 2-3). pap. 5.95 (978-1-4342-4208-2(0)) Stone Arch Bks.

Mahoney, Daniel J., illus. I See a Monster. 2008. (ENG.). 12p. (J). bds. 5.95 (978-1-58117-729-9(1), Intervisual/Piggy Toes) Bendon, Inc.

Mahoney, Jean. Swan Lake Ballet Theatre. Seddon, Viola Anne, illus. 2009. (ENG.). 16p. (J). (gr. 1-4). 24.99 (978-0-7636-4396-6(3)) Candlewick Pr.

Maldonado, Luis, illus. Friends Having Fun. Maldonado, Luis, . 2007. 48p. (J). 3.95 (978-0-9790699-1-8(2)) Empty Harbor Productions, LLC.

Mallat, Kathy. Just Ducky. 2004. (Illus.). 24p. (J). (gr. -1-1). 16.85 (978-0-8027-8825-2(4)) Walker & Co.

Manushkin, Fran. Pirate Pedro. Lyon, Tammie, illus. 2017. (Pedro Ser.). (ENG.). 32p. (gr. k-2). lib. bdg. 21.32 (978-1-5158-0872-5(6)) Pedro Pubns. GBR. Dist: Capstone Pub.

Marconi, Martina. Birthday Wishes, 1 vol. 2010. 20p. pap. 24.95 (978-1-4489-6067-5(3)) PublishAmerica, Inc.

Marino Walters, Jennifer. Sweet Summer. Nez, John, illus. 2016. (Seasons Ser.). (ENG.). 24p. (J). (gr. -1-1). lib. bdg. 25.32 (978-1-63440-048-0(8)) Red Chair Pr.

Martin, David. Peep & Ducky. Walker, David, illus. (ENG.). (J). (— 1). 2015. 24p. bds. 6.99 (978-0-7636-7243-0(2)) 2013. 32p. 14.99 (978-0-7636-5039-1(0)) Candlewick Pr.

—Three Little Bears Play All Day. Gutierrez, Akemi, illus. 2010. (Brand New Readers Ser.). (ENG.). 48p. (J). (gr. -1-3). pap. 5.99 (978-0-7636-4230-3(4)) Candlewick Pr.

Matchett, Gillian. The Adventures of Weston Super Cat with Activities. 2009. (Illus.). 92p. pap. 30.49 (978-1-4389-2241-6(8)) AuthorHouse.

Matsutani, Miyoko. Peek-A-Boo. Segawa, Yasuo, illus. 2006. 20p. (J). (gr. -1). 10.95 (978-1-74126-047-2(7)) R.I.C. Pubns. AUS. Dist: SCB Distributors.

May, Sophie. Dotty Dimple at Play. 2004. reprint ed. pap. 1.99 (978-1-4192-1661-9(9)); pap. 15.95 (978-1-4191-1661-2(4)) Kessinger Publishing, LLC.

Mayer, Mercer. The Bravest Knight. Mayer, Mercer, illus. 2007. (ENG., Illus.). 32p. (J). (gr. -1-3). 16.99 (978-0-8037-3206-3(6), Dial Bks) Penguin Young Readers Group.

McBratney, Sam. A Surprise for the Nutbrown Hares. Jeram, Anita, illus. 2009. (J). (978-0-7636-4903-6(1)) Candlewick Pr.

McClure, Brian D. The Bubble. 2006. (Illus.). 64p. (J). 14.95 (978-1-933426-05-1(5)) Universal Flag Publishing.

McClure, Leigh. Donna Plays Double Dutch: Working at the Same Time. 2017. (Computer Science for the Real World Ser.). 12p. (gr. 6-7). pap. 7.05 (978-1-5383-5174-1(9), Rosen Classroom) Rosen Publishing Group, Inc., The.

McClure, Nikki. In. 2015. (ENG., Illus.). 36p. (J). (gr. -1-k). 16.95 (978-1-4197-1486-3(4)) Abrams, Inc.

McCully, Emily Arnold. 3, 2, 1, Go! McCully, Emily Arnold, illus. 2015. (I Like to Read(r) Ser.). (ENG., Illus.). 24p. (J). (gr. -1-3). 6.99 (978-0-8234-3314-8(5)); 14.95 (978-0-8234-3288-2(2)) Holiday Hse., Inc.

McDonald, Kirsten. The Big Rain, 1 vol. Meza, Erika, illus. 2016. (Carlos & Carmen Ser.). (ENG.). 32p. (J). (gr. k-3). 27.07 (978-1-62402-137-4(9)) Magic Wagon.

McDonald, Megan. Judy Moody & the Not Bummer Summer. Reynolds, Peter H., illus. movie tie-in ed. (Judy Moody Ser.: Bk. 10). (ENG.). (J). (gr. 1-4). 2011. 128p. pap. 5.99 (978-0-7636-5351-4(9))Bk. 10. 2012. 208p. 15.99 (978-0-7636-5711-6(5))Bk. 10. 2012. 208p. pap. 5.99 (978-0-7636-5710-9(7)) Candlewick Pr.

—Judy Moody & the Not Bummer Summer. 2012. (Judy Moody Ser.: 10). lib. bdg. 16.00 (978-0-606-23800-7(X), Turtleback) Turtleback Bks.

McGougan, Kathy. Buddy Plays Ball. 2007. (J). pap. 5.00 (978-0-9799980-4-1(2)) Buddy Bks. Publishing.

McKay, Sindy. We Both Read-Jack & the Toddler. Zivoin, Jennifer, illus. 2011. (ENG.). 44p. (J). 9.95 (978-1-60115-249-7(3)); pap. 4.99 (978-1-60115-250-3(7)) Treasure Bay, Inc.

McKenzie, Heath. I Wanna Be a Great Big Dinosaur. 2016. (ENG.). 48p. (J). (-4). 16.99 (978-1-4926-3299-3(6), 9781492632993, Sourcebooks Jabberwocky) Sourcebooks, Inc.

McLerran, Alice & Mclerran, Alice. Roxaboxen. Cooney, Barbara, illus. 2004. (ENG.). 32p. (J). (gr. -1-3). pap. 6.99 (978-0-06-052633-7(5)) HarperCollins Pubs.

McMahon, Kara. Playdates Are Not Scary! McClellan, Maddy, illus. 2015. (Friday the Scaredy Cat Ser.). (ENG.). 24p. (J). (gr. -1-1). pap. 3.99 (978-1-4814-3591-8(4), Simon Spotlight) Simon Spotlight.

McOmber, Rachel B., ed. McOmber Phonics Storybooks: A Nifty Ball of String. rev. ed. (Illus.). (J). (978-0-944991-50-3(5)) Swift Learning Resources.

McPhail, David. Olivia Loves Owl. 2016. (ENG., Illus.). 20p. (J). (gr. -1 — 1). bds. 8.95 (978-1-4197-2127-4(5), Abrams Appleseed) Abrams, Inc.

—Peter Loves Penguin. 2014. (David Mcphail's Love Ser.). (ENG., Illus.). 22p. (J). (gr. -1 — 1). bds. 8.95 (978-1-4197-1337-8(X), Abrams Appleseed) Abrams, Inc.

McQuinn, Anna. Leo Loves Baby Time. Hearson, Ruth, illus. 2014. (ENG.). 24p. (J). (— 1). lib. bdg. 9.95 (978-1-58089-665-8(0)) Charlesbridge Publishing, Inc.

McQuinn, Anna, et al. A Leo le Gusta Bebelandia. Hearson, Ruth, illus. 2015. (SPA & ENG.). 24p. (J). (— 1). lib. bdg. 9.95 (978-1-58089-704-4(5)) Charlesbridge Publishing, Inc.

Meachen Rau, Dana. A Rodar! 2006. (En Movimiento Ser.). (SPA., Illus.). 24p. (gr. k-1). lib. bdg. 15.95 (978-0-7614-2419-2(9), Benchmark Bks.) Marshall Cavendish Corp.

—A Trepar! 2006. (En Movimiento Ser.). (SPA., Illus.). 24p. (gr. k-1). lib. bdg. 15.95 (978-0-7614-2424-6(5), Benchmark Bks.) Marshall Cavendish Corp.

Meddaugh, Susan. Toy Trouble. 2010. (Martha Speaks Ser.). (ENG., Illus.). 24p. (J). (gr. -1-3). pap. 3.99 (978-0-547-21078-0(7)) Houghton Mifflin Harcourt Publishing Co.

Merry, Margaret. The Adventures of Princess the Pony. 2009. 64p. pap. 19.50 (978-1-60860-936-9(7), Eloquent Bks.) Strategic Book Publishing & Rights Agency (SBPRA).

Metz, Teresa L. Friends for Phoebe. 2010. 43p. pap. 24.40 (978-0-557-16884-2(8)) Lulu Pr., Inc.

Metzger, Steve. Five Little Bunnies Hopping on a Hill. 2006. (J). (978-0-439-80382-3(9)) Scholastic, Inc.

—Five Little Penguins Slipping on the Ice. Bryant, Laura, illus. 2008. (ENG.). (J). (gr. -1-3). 18.95 (978-0-545-07408-7(8)) Scholastic, Inc.

Meyer, Ken, Jr., illus. Lucky Lionel. 2009. (J). (978-1-60108-020-2(4)) Red Cygnet Pr.

Meyers, Susan. This Is the Way a Baby Rides. Nakata, Hiroe, illus. 2005. (ENG.). 32p. (J). (gr. -1-1). 15.95 (978-0-8109-5763-3(9), Abrams Bks. for Young Readers) Abrams, Inc.

Milbourne, Anna. The Snowy Day. Temporin, Elena, illus. 2007. (J). (978-0-439-88988-9(X)) Scholastic, Inc.

Miller, Paula K. Amy, Louise & Me. 2008. 24p. pap. 24.95 (978-1-4241-9757-6(0)) America Star Bks.

Mlawer, Teresa. If I Had a Dragon/Si Yo Tuviera un Dragon. Ellery, Tom & Ellery, Amanda, illus. 2006. (ENG & SPA.). (J). (gr. -1-3). per. 3.99 (978-1-933032-17-7(0)); 32p. (gr. 5-6). 12.99 (978-1-933032-16-0(2)) Lectorum Pubns., Inc.

Moncure, Jane Belk. The Bears Upstairs: A Book of Creative Dramatics. Girouard, Patrick, illus. 2013. (Magic Castle Readers Ser.). (ENG.). 32p. (J). (gr. -1-2). 25.64 (978-1-62323-564-2(2), 206302) Child's World, Inc., The.

—Yes, No, Little Hippo: A Book about Safety. DeSantis, Susan, illus. 2013. (Magic Castle Readers Ser.). (ENG.). 32p. (J). (gr. -1-2). 25.64 (978-1-62323-571-0(5), 206306) Child's World, Inc., The.

Moore, Julianne. Best Friends Forever. Pham, LeUyen, illus. 2017. (Step into Reading Ser.). (ENG.). 32p. (J). (gr. -1-1). 15.99 (978-0-375-97369-7(9), Random Hse. Bks. for Young Readers) Random Hse. Children's Bks.

Morgante, Roxanne & Callies, Pat. Justin & Travis: Games They Play, 1 vol. 2010. 62p. pap. 19.95 (978-1-4489-4458-3(9)) PublishAmerica, Inc.

Murguia, Bethanie Deeney. Princess! Fairy! Ballerina! 2016. (ENG., Illus.). 40p. (J). (gr. -1-k). 17.99 (978-0-545-73240-6(9)) Scholastic, Inc.

—Zoe's Jungle. 2014. (ENG.). 40p. (J). (gr. -1-k). 16.99 (978-0-545-55869-3(7), Levine, Arthur A. Bks.) Scholastic, Inc.

Murphy, Jill. All for One. 2004. (Illus.). (J). (gr. -1-2). spiral bd. (978-0-616-14592-0(6)); spiral bd. (978-0-616-14591-3(8)) Canadian National Institute for the Blind/Institut National Canadien pour les Aveugles.

Murphy, Stuart J. Freda Says Please. Jones, Tim, illus. 2013. (I See I Learn Ser.). (ENG.). 32p. (J). (-k). pap. 6.95 (978-1-58089-475-3(5)) Charlesbridge Publishing, Inc.

—Freda Says Please. Jones, Tim, illus. 2013. (I See I Learn Ser.). (ENG.). 32p. (J). (-k). lib. bdg. 14.95 (978-1-58089-474-6(7)) Charlesbridge Publishing, Inc.

—Happy, Healthy Ajay! 2012. (I See I Learn Ser.). (ENG., Illus.). 32p. (J). (-k). 14.95 (978-1-58089-470-8(4)); pap. 6.95 (978-1-58089-471-5(2)) Charlesbridge Publishing, Inc.

—Percy Juega con Cuidado. 2011. (I See I Learn Ser.). (SPA & ENG., Illus.). 32p. (J). (-k). 14.95 (978-1-58089-484-5(4)); pap. 6.95 (978-1-58089-485-2(2)) Charlesbridge Publishing, Inc.

—Percy Plays It Safe. 2010. (I See I Learn Ser.). (ENG., Illus.). 32p. (J). (gr. -1-k). 14.95 (978-1-58089-452-4(6)) Charlesbridge Publishing, Inc.

Nelid, Piper. The Turkey Day Play, 01 vols., 1. 2016. (Rosen REAL Readers: STEM & STEAM Collection). (ENG.). 8p.

(J). pap. 5.46 *(978-1-5081-1492-5(7)*, Rosen Classroom) Rosen Publishing Group, Inc., The.

Neubecker, Robert. What Little Boys Are Made Of. Neubecker, Robert, illus. 2012. (ENG., Illus.). 32p. (J). (gr. -1-3). 14.99 *(978-0-06-202355-1(1))* HarperCollins Pubs.

Nolan, Allia Zobel. God's Winter Wonderland. Mitchell, Melanie, illus. 2006. 10p. (J). bds. 8.99 *(978-0-8254-5526-1(X))* Kregel Pubns.

Nolen, Gale. Johnny, My Favorite Mouse. Cain, Doreyl Ammons, illus. 2007. 32p. (J). per. 18.95 *(978-0-9753023-7-8(X))* Ammons Communications, Ltd.

Nora Juega Todo el Dia: Nora Plays All Day. 2005. (Take-Home Bks.). (SPA.). (YA). (gr. -1-3). 15.75 *(978-0-8215-1204-3(8))* Sadlier, William H. Inc.

Nora Juega Todo el Dia/Nora Plays All Day. 2005. (Libros en Espanol Para Ninos Ser.). (SPA.). (YA). (gr. -1-1). 11.97 *(978-0-8215-0994-4(2))* Sadlier, William H. Inc.

Nora Plays All Day: Take-Home Book. 2005. (Emergent Library: Vol. 2). (YA). (gr. -1-1). 12.60 *(978-0-8215-7259-7(8))* Sadlier, William H. Inc.

Nosy Crow Staff. Bizzy Bear: Let's Go & Play. Davies, Benji, illus. 2011. (Bizzy Bear Ser.). (ENG.). 8p. (J). (gr. k — 1). bds. 6.99 *(978-0-7636-5880-9(4)*, Nosy Crow) Candlewick Pr.

—Pip & Posy: the New Friend. Scheffler, Axel, illus. 2017. (Pip & Posy Ser.). (ENG.). 32p. (J). (-k). 12.99 *(978-0-7636-9339-8(1)*, Nosy Crow) Candlewick Pr.

November, Deborah, et al. Let's Visit Sesame Street. Mathieu, Joe, illus. 2010. (ENG.). 24p. (J). bds. 14.99 *(978-0-7944-2101-4(6))* Reader's Digest Assn., Inc., The.

Nugent, Penn. Come down & Play. 2004. (Illus.). 40p. (J). 7.95 *(978-1-880849-90-3(9))* Chapel Hill Press, Inc.

O'Connor, George. Kapow! O'Connor, George, illus. 2007. (ENG., Illus.). 48p. (J). (gr. -1-3). 12.99 *(978-1-4169-6847-4(4)*, Aladdin) Simon & Schuster Children's Publishing.

O'Connor, Jane. Fancy Nancy - There's No Day Like a Snow Day. 2012. (Fancy Nancy Picture Bks.). (J). lib. bdg. 14.75 *(978-0-606-26857-8(X)*, Turtleback) Turtleback Bks.

Odierno, Lisa. Bunny Hide-and-Seek. 2009. (Smithsonian Baby Animals Ser.). (ENG., Illus.). 16p. (J). (gr. -1-k). 6.95 *(978-1-60727-092-8(7))* Soundprints.

—Kitten & Her Sister. 2009. (ENG.). 16p. (J). 6.95 *(978-1-60727-000-3(5))* Soundprints.

Odierno, Lisa & Soundprints Staff. Bunny Hide-and-Seek. 2009. (Smithsonian Baby Animals Ser.). (ENG., Illus.). 16p. (J). (gr. -1-k). 6.95 *(978-1-60727-105-5(2))* Soundprints.

O'Donnell, Mabel & Monro, Rona. Janet & John: Off to Play. 2007. (Janet & John Bks.). (ENG., Illus.). 40p. (J). (gr. -1-2). 9.99 *(978-1-84024-615-5(4))* Summerdale Pubs. GBR. Dist: Independent Pubs. Group.

O'Keefe, Lauren. Raindrop Flies a Kite. 2012. 16p. pap. 12.68 *(978-1-4669-7000-7(6))* Trafford Publishing.

Olsen, Leigh & S. I. International. What Do You Say? A Book about Manners. 2009. (Playskool Ser.). (ENG.). 16p. (J). (gr. -1). pap. 6.99 *(978-1-4169-8518-1(2)*, Simon Spotlight) Simon Spotlight.

Onyefulu, Ifeoma & Quarto Generic Staff. Omer's Favorite Place. 2011. (First Experiences Ser.). (ENG., Illus.). 32p. (J). (gr. -1-1). 17.95 *(978-1-84780-241-5(9)*, Frances Lincoln) Quarto Publishing Group UK GBR. Dist: Hachette Bk. Group.

Oram, Hiawyn. Ned & the Joybaloo. Kitamura, Satoshi, illus. 2012. (ENG.). 32p. (J). (gr. -1-k). pap. 10.99 *(978-1-84270-605-3(5))* Andersen Pr. GBR. Dist: Independent Pubs. Group.

Ostow, Micol. GoldenGirl. 2009. (Bradford Ser.). (ENG.). 224p. (YA). (gr. 9-18). pap. 9.99 *(978-1-4169-6118-5(6)*, Simon Pulse) Simon Pulse.

Pace, Anne Marie. Pigloo. Hussey, Lorna, illus. 2016. (ENG.). 32p. (J). 16.99 *(978-1-62779-202-8(3)*, 9781627792028, Holt, Henry & Co. Bks. For Young Readers) Holt, Henry & Co.

Pagratis, Maggie & Pagratis, Illustrator Liliane, MaggieGrenier. Go Away Booboo! 2005. 29p. (J). 11.88 *(978-1-4116-3689-7(9))* Lulu Pr., Inc.

Parker, Ant & Denchfield, Nick. Charlie Chick Wants to Play. Parker, Ant, illus. 2017. (Charlie Chick Ser.: 6). (ENG., Illus.). 10p. (J). (-k). bds. 9.99 ***(978-1-5098-2900-2(8))*** Pan Macmillan GBR. Dist: Independent Pubs. Group.

Parker, David. We Can All Play. Lucas, Margeaux, illus. 2007. (J). *(978-0-545-00390-2(3))* Scholastic, Inc.

Parnell, Declan. Playground Fun, 01 vols., 1. 2016. (Rosen REAL Readers: STEM & STEAM Collection). (ENG.). 12p. (J). pap. 6.33 *(978-1-5081-1557-1(5)*, Rosen Classroom) Rosen Publishing Group, Inc., The.

Parragon Staff, ed. Cerdito. 2010. pap. 4.95 *(978-1-4054-4915-1(2))* Parragon, Inc.

—Corderito. 2010. pap. 5.95 *(978-1-4054-4914-4(4))* Parragon, Inc.

Parton, Paula. I Always Wondered. Parton, Paula, illus. 2009. (Illus.). 44p. pap. 11.95 *(978-1-935118-48-0(X))* Bellissima Publishing, LLC.

Patricelli, Leslie. Higher! Higher! Patricelli, Leslie, illus. 2010. (Leslie Patricelli Board Bks.). (ENG., Illus.). 30p. (J). (-k). bds. 6.99 *(978-0-7636-4433-8(1))* Candlewick Pr.

Paulhus, Jonathan. Chester, the Light Golden Retriever. 2013. 36p. pap. 24.95 *(978-1-63004-640-8(X))* America Star Bks.

Paz, Veronica. Play Pretend with Muno. 2009. (Yo Gabba Gabba! Ser.). (ENG.). 12p. (J). (gr. -1-1). bds. 6.99 *(978-1-4169-8508-2(5)*, Simon Spotlight) Simon Spotlight.

Pendergrass, Daphne. Daniel Plays at School. 2016. (Daniel Tiger's Neighborhood Ready-To-Read Ser.). lib. bdg. 13.55 *(978-0-606-38991-4(1))* Turtleback Bks.

Perez, Irene. Rain or Shine. 2008. 16p. pap. 12.50 *(978-1-4389-0873-1(3))* AuthorHouse.

Peters, Lou. The Owl & the Turtle. 2010. 32p. pap. 15.95 *(978-0-557-51727-5(3))* Lulu Pr., Inc.

Peto, Judith E. & Talwar, Robert B. Jenny & Benny: Friends 2005. (Illus.). 28p. (J). (gr. -1-3). 16.95 *(978-0-9767511-0-6(0))* Lasting Bks. Publishing Co.

Petty, Dev. There's Nothing to Do! Boldt, Mike, illus. 2017. (ENG.). 32p. (J). (gr. -1-2). lib. bdg. 19.99 ***(978-0-399-55804-7(7)***, Doubleday Bks. for Young Readers) Random Hse. Children's Bks.

Phillips, Dee. What Can I Be? 2010. (Look at Me! Ser.). (ENG.). 5p. (J). (gr. -1-k). bds. 6.95 *(978-1-84696-199-1(8)*, TickTock Books) Octopus Publishing Group GBR. Dist: Independent Pubs. Group.

—Who Can I Be? 2010. (Look at Me! Ser.). (ENG.). 5p. (J). (gr. -1-k). bds. 6.95 *(978-1-84696-200-4(5)*, TickTock Books) Octopus Publishing Group GBR. Dist: Independent Pubs. Group.

Phillips, Dee & Ticktock Media, Ltd. Staff. What Do Kangaroos Do? 2009. (What Do Animals Do? Ser.). (ENG.). 5p. (J). (gr. k — 1). bds. 4.95 *(978-1-84696-959-1(X)*, TickTock Books) Octopus Publishing Group GBR. Dist: Independent Pubs. Group.

—What Do Monkeys Do? 2009. (What Do Animals Do? Ser.). (ENG.). 5p. (J). (gr. k — 1). bds. 4.95 *(978-1-84696-960-7(3)*, TickTock Books) Octopus Publishing Group GBR. Dist: Independent Pubs. Group.

—What Do Rabbits Do? 2009. (What Do Animals Do? Ser.). (ENG.). 5p. (J). (gr. k — 1). bds. 4.95 *(978-1-84696-961-4(1)*, TickTock Books) Octopus Publishing Group GBR. Dist: Independent Pubs. Group.

Piantedosi, John J. The Cat That Purred. Maglio-Macullar, Andrea, illus. 2014. (ENG.). (J). pap. 11.95 *(978-1-56548-540-2(8))* New City Press of the Focolare.

Piggy Toes Press, creator. Color Party! 2007. (ENG., Illus.). 12p. (gr. -1-k). bds. 7.99 *(978-1-58117-585-1(X)*, Intervisual/Piggy Toes) Bendon, Inc.

—Giggle & Grow Baby's Body! 2007. (ENG., Illus.). 14p. (gr. -1-k). bds. 7.99 *(978-1-58117-586-8(8)*, Intervisual/Piggy Toes) Bendon, Inc.

Piggy Toes Press Staff, creator. Little Feet Like: A Tiny Tootsie Touch & Feel Book. 2008. (ENG., Illus.). 12p. (gr. -1-k). 9.95 *(978-1-58117-692-6(9)*, Intervisual/Piggy Toes) Bendon, Inc.

Pitt, Marilyn & Hileman, Jane. My Babies. 2010. pap. 39.62 *(978-1-61541-066-8(X))* American Reading Co.

—Pretty Cat. 2010. pap. 39.62 *(978-1-61541-068-2(6))* American Reading Co.

The Playful Kitten. 2003. (J). per. *(978-1-57657-888-9(7))* Paradise Pr., Inc.

Ponko, Cindy A. Busy Busy Days. 2006. (Illus.). (J). *(978-0-9768230-1-8(2))* Some Kids I Know.

Ponti, Claude. Chick & Chickie in Play All Day! 2013. (Toon Books Level 1 Ser.). lib. bdg. 14.75 *(978-0-606-31595-1(0)*, Turtleback) Turtleback Bks.

—Chick & Chickie Play All Day!, 1 vol. 2013. (Toon Bks). (ENG.). 36p. (J). (gr. k-1). lib. bdg. 27.07 *(978-1-61479-150-8(3))* Spotlight.

—Chick & Chickie Play All Day! Ponti, Claude, illus. 2012. (ENG., Illus.). 36p. (J). (gr. -1-3). 12.95 *(978-1-935179-14-6(4))* TOON Books / RAW Junior, LLC.

Poole, Catherine Cheyenne. Batboy's Crazy Day. Murphy, Fredrick, illus. 2008. 24p. pap. 8.95 *(978-1-935105-18-3(3))* Avid Readers Publishing Group.

Portis, Antoinette. Not a Stick. Portis, Antoinette, illus. 2007. (ENG., Illus.). 32p. (J). (gr. -1-1). 14.99 *(978-0-06-112325-2(0))* HarperCollins Pubs.

Posner-Sanchez, Andrea. Miles from Tomorrowland (Disney Junior: Miles from Tomorrowland) RH Disney, illus. 2016. (Big Golden Book Ser.). (ENG.). 32p. (J). (-k). 9.99 *(978-0-7364-3494-2(1)*, Golden/Disney) Random Hse. Children's Bks.

Powell-Tuck, Maudie. Pumpkin Party! Guile, Gill, illus. 2015. (ENG.). 22p. (J). (gr. -1-2). bds. 8.99 *(978-1-58925-206-6(3))* Tiger Tales.

Preston, Helen M. Gra Gra's Stories. 2012. 72p. pap. 28.99 *(978-1-4772-9783-4(9))* AuthorHouse.

Raden, Tammy. Priscilla Play. 2010. 28p. 12.49 *(978-1-4520-0808-0(6))* AuthorHouse.

Raghbeer, Anjali. A Royal Deck: Ganjifa Art. Modak, Tejas, illus. 2012. (Art Tales from India Ser.). (ENG.). 23p. 14.95 *(978-81-8328-187-4(7))* Wisdom Tree IND. Dist: SCB Distributors.

Rand, Edward A. The Knights of the White Shield: Up-the-Ladder Club Series Round One Play. 2007. 166p. pap. 19.99 *(978-1-4264-8273-1(6))*; (ENG.). 184p. pap. 21.99 *(978-1-4264-8310-3(4))* Creative Media Partners, LLC.

—The Knights of the White Shield; or, up-the-Ladder Club Series, Round One Play. 2007. 120p. per. *(978-1-4068-3739-1(3))* Echo Library.

Rankin, Laura. My Turn! Rankin, Laura, illus. 2016. (ENG., Illus.). 32p. (J). 16.99 *(978-1-59990-174-9(9)*, 9781599901749, Bloomsbury USA Childrens) Bloomsbury Publishing USA.

Rao, Lisa. Playtime in Trucktown. Shannon, David et al, illus. 2008. (Jon Scieszka's Trucktown Ser.). (ENG.). 24p. (J). (gr. -1-1). 5.99 *(978-1-4169-4197-2(5)*, Simon Scribbles) Simon Scribbles.

Raudenbush, Amy. Lucy More Needs Less. 2006. 48p. (J). pap. 13.99 *(978-1-4116-6120-2(6))* Lulu Pr., Inc.

Rayner, Shoo, concept. Cat & Dog Play Hide & Seek. 2006. (Collins Big Cat Ser.). (ENG., Illus.). 80p. (J). (gr. -1-k). pap. 5.99 *(978-0-00-718660-0(6))* HarperCollins Pubs. Ltd. GBR. Dist: Independent Pubs. Group.

Rea, Ba. Monarch! Come Play with Me. Rea, Ba, illus. 2006. (Illus.). 32p. (J). per. 10.95 *(978-0-9657472-5-7(5))* Bas Relief, LLC.

Reasoner, Charles. No Peeking! 2003. (ENG., Illus.). 14p. bds. 4.99 *(978-0-8431-0227-7(6)*, Price Stern Sloan) Penguin Publishing Group.

Red Fox Picture Books Staff & Transworld Publishing Staff. Better Play Times. 2006. (ENG., Illus.). 24p. (J). (gr. k-k). pap. 7.95 *(978-1-86230-164-1(6)*, Red Fox) Random House Children's Books GBR. Dist: Independent Pubs. Group.

Reed, Jennifer. That's Not Fair! Dufalla, Anita, illus. 2012. (ENG.). 24p. (gr. 1-2). pap. 8.95 *(978-1-61810-309-3(1))* Rourke Educational Media.

Reidy, Jean. Too Princessy! Leloup, Geneviève, illus. (Too! Bks.). (ENG.). (J). (gr. -1 — 1). 2013. 26p. bds. 7.99 *(978-1-59990-955-4(3)*, 9781599909554) 2012. 32p. 12.99 *(978-1-59990-722-2(4)*, 9781599907222) Bloomsbury Publishing USA. (Bloomsbury USA Childrens).

Reilly, Carmel. The Boy at the Park. Reynolds, Pat, illus. 2009. 24p. pap. 10.67 *(978-1-4190-5517-1(8))* Rigby Education.

Rey, H. A. & Rey, Margret. Curious George Hide-and-Seek. 2008. (Curious George Ser.). (ENG., Illus.). 10p. (J). (gr. -1 — 1). bds. 6.99 *(978-0-618-89199-3(4))* Houghton Mifflin Harcourt Publishing Co.

Reynolds, Luke. Bedtime Blast-Off! Yamada, Mike, illus. 2016. (ENG.). 40p. (J). (gr. -1-1). 16.99 *(978-0-545-77855-8(7)*, Orchard Bks.) Scholastic, Inc.

Rice, Dona. What Kind of Weather?, 1 vol. 2009. (Early Childhood Themes Ser.). (ENG., Illus.). 16p. (J). (gr. -1-2). pap. 19.99 *(978-1-4333-1459-9(2))* Shell Educational Publishing.

Riley, Kellee, illus. Tolee's Rhyme Time. 2009. (Ni Hao, Kai-Lan Ser.). (ENG.). 24p. (J). pap. 3.99 *(978-1-4169-9024-6(0)*, Simon Spotlight/Nickelodeon) Simon Spotlight/Nickelodeon.

Rim, Sujean, illus. Birdie's Big-Girl Shoes. 2009. (Birdie Ser.). (ENG.). 40p. (J). (gr. -1-3). 17.99 *(978-0-316-04470-7(9))* Little, Brown Bks. for Young Readers.

Rinne, Teresa & Dillon, Preston. Snail Tails: Let's Play Ball! 2009. 40p. pap. 16.99 *(978-1-4389-7076-9(5))* AuthorHouse.

Rippin, Sally. The Crazy Cousins. Spartels, Stephanie, illus. 2012. 42p. (J). *(978-1-61067-135-4(X))* Kane Miller.

Rivers-Moore, Debbie. Five Little Snowmen. Everitt-Stewart, Andrew, illus. 2015. (ENG.). 10p. (J). (gr. -1 — 1). bds. 8.99 *(978-1-4998-0170-5(X))* Little Bee Books Inc.

Rodriguez, Paul. Let's All Play! Character Education/ Anti-Bullying. Rodriguez, Paul, illus. 2003. (Illus.). 32p. (J). lib. bdg. 15.99 *(978-0-9744770-0-8(1))* Rodro.

Romano, Melissa. Mama, Lions Don't Listen. 2008. 24p. pap. 11.99 *(978-1-4343-9907-6(9))* AuthorHouse.

Rose, C. T. Don't Play with the Craft, 1 vol. 2009. 82p. pap. 19.95 *(978-1-61582-871-5(0))* America Star Bks.

Rosenthal, Amy Krouse. Little Hoot. Corace, Jen, illus. 2016. (ENG.). 28p. (J). (gr. -1-k). bds. 7.99 *(978-1-4521-5207-3(1))* Chronicle Bks. LLC.

Ross, Theodore J. Lucy Wants to Play. 2003. (Illus.). 16p. (J). 3.99 *(978-1-59384-029-7(2))* Parklane Publishing.

Rubiano, Brittany. Frozen Anna Loves Elsa. Lee, Brittney, illus. 2015. (ENG.). 14p. (J). (gr. -1-k). bds. 9.99 *(978-1-4847-2470-5(4))* Disney Pr.

Ruiz, Jackson. It's Cool in the Furnace: The first graphic novel by Jackson Ruiz. 2010. 32p. pap. 16.99 *(978-1-4520-2634-3(3))* AuthorHouse.

Russell, James. The Dragon Hunters. Choi, Link, illus. 2017. (Dragon Brothers Ser.: 1). (ENG.). 32p. (J). (-4). 16.99 *(978-1-4926-4861-1(2)*, 9781492648611, Sourcebooks Jabberwocky) Sourcebooks, Inc.

Rusu, Meredith. Play Time for Peppa & George (Peppa Pig) Eone, illus. 2016. (Peppa Pig Ser.). (ENG.). 32p. (J). (gr. -1-k). 8.99 *(978-1-338-03280-2(1))* Scholastic, Inc.

Rylant, Cynthia. Annie & Snowball & the Magical House. Stevenson, Suçie, illus. (Annie & Snowball Ser.: 7). (ENG.). 40p. (J). (gr. k-2). 2011. pap. 3.99 *(978-1-4169-3949-8(0))* 2010. 16.99 *(978-1-4169-3945-0(8))* Simon Spotlight. (Simon Spotlight).

—Brownie & Pearl Get Dolled Up. Biggs, Brian, illus. 2010. (Brownie & Pearl Ser.). (ENG.). 24p. (J). (gr. -1-3). 14.99 *(978-1-4169-8631-7(6)*, Beach Lane Bks.) Beach Lane Bks.

—Brownie & Pearl Get Dolled Up. Biggs, Brian, illus. 2014. (Brownie & Pearl Ser.). (ENG.). 24p. (J). (gr. -1-k). 16.99 *(978-1-4424-9568-5(5))*; pap. 3.99 *(978-1-4424-9567-8(7))* Simon Spotlight. (Simon Spotlight).

—Mr. Putter & Tabby Drop the Ball. Howard, Arthur, illus. 2013. (Mr. Putter & Tabby Ser.: 22). (ENG.). 44p. (J). (gr. 1-4). 14.99 *(978-0-15-205072-6(8))* Houghton Mifflin Harcourt Publishing Co.

Sakai, Komako. Hannah's Night. 2014.Tr. of Hanna-chan ga Me wo Samashitara. (ENG., Illus.). 32p. (J). (gr. -1-2). 17.95 *(978-1-877579-54-7(8))* Gecko Pr. NZL. Dist: Lerner Publishing Group.

Sandall, Ellie. Everybunny Dance! 2017. (ENG., Illus.). 32p. (J). (gr. -1-3). 17.99 *(978-1-4814-9822-7(3)*, McElderry, Margaret K. Bks.) McElderry, Margaret K. Bks.

Sanders, Rob. Rodzilla. Santat, Dan, illus. 2017. (ENG.). 48p. (J). (gr. -1-3). 17.99 ***(978-1-4814-5779-8(9)***, McElderry, Margaret K. Bks.) McElderry, Margaret K. Bks.

Sansone, V. K. A Daunting Quest for Quincy & Quigley. 2009. 32p. pap. 8.98 *(978-0-557-03594-6(5))* Lulu Pr., Inc.

Santillo, LuAnn. Mike. Santillo, LuAnn, ed. 2003. (Half-Pint Kids Readers Ser.). (Illus.). 7p. (J). (gr. -1-1). pap. 1.00 *(978-1-59256-100-1(4))* Half-Pint Kids, Inc.

Santirso, Liliana. Me Gusta Jugar Con los Libros. Gomez, Patricio & Villagomez, Raul, illus. (SPA.). (J). (gr. k-1). pap. *(978-968-6465-48-8(0))* Casa de Estudios de Literatura y Talleres Artisticos Amaquemecan A.C. MEX. Dist: Lectorum Pubns., Inc.

Santos de las Heras, José María. Cachicos. 2007. 176p. pap. 20.95 *(978-1-84799-885-9(2))* Lulu Pr., Inc.

Sarah, Linda. Big Friends. Davies, Benji, illus. 2016. (ENG.). 32p. (J). 16.99 *(978-1-62779-330-8(5)*, 9781627793308, Holt, Henry & Co. Bks. For Young Readers) Holt, Henry & Co.

Sateren, Shelley Swanson. Max & Zoe at School, 1 vol. Sullivan, Mary, illus. 2013. (Max & Zoe Ser.). (ENG.). 32p. (gr. k-2). pap. 5.19 *(978-1-4048-8059-7(3)*, Max & Zoe) Picture Window Bks.

Sattler, Jennifer. Pig Kahuna Pirates! 2014. (Pig Kahuna Ser.). (ENG., Illus.). 32p. (J). (gr. -1-1). 16.99 *(978-1-61963-200-4(4)*, 9781619632004, Bloomsbury USA Childrens) Bloomsbury Publishing USA.

Sattler, Jennifer Gordon, illus. Pig Kahuna Pirates! 2014. (J). *(978-1-61963-203-5(9))* Bloomsbury Pr.

Sauer, Tammi. Truck, Truck, Goose! Waring, Zoe, illus. 2017. 40p. (J). (gr. -1-3). 14.99 ***(978-0-06-242153-1(0))*** HarperCollins Pubs.

Saunders, Brianna. The Magic Marble. 2013. 32p. pap. 24.95 *(978-1-63004-598-2(5))* America Star Bks.

Saxon, Victoria. Anna & Elsa's Secret Playtime (Disney Frozen) RH Disney, illus. 2016. (Big Golden Book Ser.). (ENG.). 32p. (J). (-k). 9.99 *(978-0-7364-3493-5(3)*, Golden/Disney) Random Hse. Children's Bks.

Scarry, Patricia. Richard Scarry's Just for Fun. Scarry, Richard, illus. 2016. (Little Golden Book Ser.). (ENG.). 24p. (J). (gr. -1-k). 4.99 *(978-0-553-53662-1(1)*, Golden Bks.) Random Hse. Children's Bks.

Schaefer, Lola M. One Busy Day: A Story for Big Brothers & Sisters. Meserve, Jessica, illus. 2014. (ENG.). 40p. (J). (gr. -1-k). 16.99 *(978-1-4231-7112-6(8))* Hyperion Bks. for Children.

Schertle, Alice. The Adventures of Old Bo Bear. Parkins, David, illus. 2005. (J). 16.95 *(978-978-081-183-9(4))* Chronicle Bks. LLC.

Schoenherr, Ian. Cat & Mouse. Schoenherr, Ian, illus. 2008. (Illus.). 40p. (J). (gr. -1). lib. bdg. 17.89 *(978-0-06-136314-6(6)*, Greenwillow Bks.) HarperCollins Pubs.

Scholastic, Inc. Staff & Hudson, Cheryl Willis. What Do You Know? Snow! Walker, Sylvia, illus. 2004. (Just for You Ser.). (ENG.). 32p. pap. 3.99 *(978-0-439-56851-7(X)*, Teaching Resources) Scholastic, Inc.

Schories, Pat. Pants for Chuck. 2014. (I Like to Read(r) Ser.). (ENG., Illus.). 24p. (J). (gr. -1-3). 14.95 *(978-0-8234-3066-6(9))* Holiday Hse., Inc.

Schories, Pat & Capucilli, Alyssa Satin. Biscuit & the Little Pup. Schories, Pat, illus. 2007. (My First I Can Read Ser.). (ENG., Illus.). 32p. (J). (gr. -1 — 1). pap. 3.99 *(978-0-06-074172-3(4))* HarperCollins Pubs.

Schwartz, Joanne. Pinny in Summer, 1 vol. Malenfant, Isabelle, illus. 2016. (ENG.). 32p. (J). (gr. -1-2). 16.95 *(978-1-55498-782-5(2))* Groundwood Bks. CAN. Dist: Publishers Group West (PGW).

Sconyers, Jennifer. The Map. 2010. 24p. pap. 12.99 *(978-1-4490-5731-2(4))* AuthorHouse.

Scott, Lucy. Busy Busy! Scott, Lucy, illus. 2016. (ENG., Illus.). 32p. (J). (gr. -1-k). 15.99 *(978-1-939547-25-5(3))* Creston Bks.

Scotton, Rob. And the Snowy Day Surprise. Scotton, Rob, illus. 2014. (Splat the Cat Ser.). (ENG., Illus.). 16p. (J). (gr. -1-3). pap. 6.99 *(978-0-06-197864-7(7)*, HarperFestival) HarperCollins Pubs.

Shaw, Natalie. Be Careful, Friend! Craig, Karen, illus. 2010. (Yo Gabba Gabba! Ser.). (ENG.). 26p. (J). (gr. -1 — 1). bds. 5.99 *(978-1-4169-9534-0(X)*, Simon Spotlight) Simon Spotlight.

Shea, Bob. Ballet Cat: The Totally Secret Secret. Shea, Bob, illus. 2015. (Ballet Cat Ser.). (ENG., Illus.). 56p. (J). (gr. 1-3). 9.99 *(978-1-4847-1378-5(8))* Disney Pr.

Shepherd, Donna J. OUCH! Sunburn. Collier, Kevin Scott, illus. 2007. 27p. (J). E-Book 9.95 incl. cd-rom *(978-1-933090-60-3(X))* Guardian Angel Publishing, Inc.

Sheridan, Sara. I'm Me! Chamberlain, Margaret, illus. 2011. (ENG.). 32p. (J). (gr. -1-k). 17.99 *(978-0-545-28222-2(5)*, Chicken Hse., The) Scholastic, Inc.

Shields, Gillian. Library Lily. Chessa, Francesca, illus. 2011. (ENG.). 26p. (YA). 16.00 *(978-0-8028-5401-8(X))* Eerdmans, William B. Publishing Co.

Short, Carol. Todd's Nine Lives. 2009. 28p. pap. 12.49 *(978-1-4389-3893-6(4))* AuthorHouse.

Siddals, Mary McKenna. Bringing the Outside In. Barton, Patrice, illus. 2016. (ENG.). 32p. (J). (gr. -1-2). 20.99 *(978-0-375-97165-5(3)*, Random Hse. Bks. for Young Readers) Random Hse. Children's Bks.

Siewart, Pauline, illus. Look What I Can Do! 2009. (Watch This! Ser.). 32p. (J). (gr. -1-k). 22.60 *(978-1-60754-452-4(0))*; pap. 10.55 *(978-1-60754-453-1(9))* Windmill Bks.

—Look What I Can Make! 2009. (Watch This! Ser.). 32p. (J). (gr. -1-k). 22.60 *(978-1-60754-446-3(6))*; pap. 10.55 *(978-1-60754-447-0(4))* Windmill Bks.

—Look What I Can Play! 2009. (Watch This! Ser.). 32p. (J). (gr. -1-k). 22.60 *(978-1-60754-458-6(X))*; pap. 10.55 *(978-1-60754-586-6(1))* Windmill Bks.

—See What I Can Do! 2009. (Watch This! Ser.). 32p. (J). (gr. -1-k). 22.60 *(978-1-60754-455-5(5))*; pap. 10.55 *(978-1-60754-456-2(3))* Windmill Bks.

—See What I Can Make! 2009. (Watch This! Ser.). 32p. (J). (gr. -1-k). 22.60 *(978-1-60754-449-4(0))*; pap. 10.55 *(978-1-60754-450-0(4))* Windmill Bks.

—See What I Can Play! 2009. (Watch This! Ser.). 32p. (J). (gr. -1-k). 22.60 *(978-1-60754-461-6(X))*; pap. 10.55 *(978-1-60754-462-3(8))* Windmill Bks.

Siewart, Pauline. Look What I Can Play! 2009. (YA). pap. 10.55 *(978-1-80754-586-4(5))* Windmill Bks.

Slegers, Liesbet. Playing. 2011. (Clavis Toddler: Daily Life Ser.). (ENG.). 12p. (J). (gr. k — 1). bds. 5.95 *(978-1-60537-091-0(6))* Cobblestone Publishing Co.

Smith, Danna. Pirate Nap: A Book of Colors. Petrone, Valeria, illus. 2011. (ENG.). 40p. (J). lib. bdg. 14.99 *(978-0-547-57531-5(9))* Houghton Mifflin Harcourt Publishing Co.

Smith, Joy V. Why Won't Anyone Play with Me? 2007. 20p. per. 24.95 *(978-1-4241-8634-1(X))* America Star Bks.

Smith, Kathy Jo. Come Play with Me. 2009. 26p. (J). pap. 17.95 *(978-1-4327-3464-0(4))* Outskirts Pr., Inc.

Smith, Michael. My Ducky Buddy. Oliva, Octavio, illus. 2011. 23p. (J). *(978-0-9821675-4-0(7))* East West Discovery Pr.

Smith, Michael & Wang, Emily. My Ducky Buddy. Oliva, Octavio, illus. 2011. (CHI & ENG.). 23p. (J). *(978-0-9821675-7-1(1))* East West Discovery Pr.

Smith, Mildred M. Louie the Blue Frog. 2012. 24p. pap. 24.95 *(978-1-62709-122-0(X))* America Star Bks.

Snyder, Betsy E., illus. I Can Play. 2015. (ENG.). 14p. (J). (gr. -1 — 1). bds. 8.99 *(978-1-4521-2905-1(3))* Chronicle Bks. LLC.

Soman, David & Davis, Jacky. Who Can Play? 2013. (Penguin Young Readers Level 1 Ser.). lib. bdg. 13.55 *(978-0-606-32148-8(9)*, Turtleback) Turtleback Bks.

Spaceboy Plays Hide & Seek. 2003. (Spaceboy Set 1 Ser.). (J). 7.33 *(978-1-932570-05-2(5))* Pioneer Valley Bks.

Spalding, Andrea. Dance Baby Dance, 1 vol. 2009. (ENG.). 24p. (J). (gr. -1 — 1). bds. 9.95 *(978-1-55469-079-4(X))* Orca Bk. Pubs. USA.

Spence, Ann. Elmo's Play Day. 2010. (Illus.). 6p. (J). bds. 12.98 *(978-0-7853-8441-0(3)*, 7186300) Phoenix International Publications, Inc.

Spinelli, Eileen. God's Amazing World! Florian, Mlanie, illus. 2014. 32p. (J). 15.99 *(978-0-8249-5661-5(3)*, Ideal Pubns.) Worthy Publishing.

Spinelli, Jerry. Hokey Pokey. 2013. (J). 282p. pap. *(978-0-375-83201-7(7))*; (ENG.). 304p. (gr. 5). 15.99 *(978-0-375-83198-0(3))*; (ENG.). 304p. (gr. 5). lib. bdg. 18.99 *(978-0-375-93198-7(8))* Random Hse. Children's Bks. (Knopf Bks. for Young Readers).

Stanisha, Terésa (Tracey). Especially for Rachel - Butterflies Abound. 2009. 84p. pap. 16.97 *(978-0-557-04450-4(2))* Lulu Pr., Inc.

Steig, William. Pedro Es una Pizza. (Buenas Noches Ser.). (SPA., Illus.). (J). (gr. -1-5). 7.95 *(978-958-04-6034-3(5))*

Norma S.A. COL. Dist: Distribuidora Norma, Inc., Lectorum Pubns., Inc.

—Pete's a Pizza. 2004. (Illus.). 32p. (J). (gr. -1-2). 28.95 incl. audio compact disk *(978-1-59112-740-6(8))* Live Oak Media.

Steve Cormey. The Brothers Foot: A Hare Raising Story. Ronda Eden, illus. 2009. 56p. pap. 21.99 *(978-1-4389-4269-8(9))* AuthorHouse.

Stevenson-Spurgon, Barbara J. Have You Ever Made Mud Pies on a Hot Summer Day? This Is a Bitty Book. Ruffin, Aurzella, illus. 2006. 36p. (J). (gr. -1-4). per. 19.95 *(978-1-60002-234-0(0)*, 4073) Mountain Valley Publishing, LLC.

Stewart, Joel. Dexter Bexley & the Big Blue Beastie. Stewart, Joel, illus. 2007. (ENG., Illus.). 32p. (J). (gr. -1-3). 16.95 *(978-0-8234-2068-1(X))* Holiday Hse., Inc.

Still, Cynthia W. Gypsy Travels the World. 2012. 48p. pap. 21.99 *(978-1-4685-5839-5(0))* AuthorHouse.

Stinson, Aimee. The Championship Game, 1 vol. 2009. 52p. pap. 16.95 *(978-1-60813-645-2(0))* PublishAmerica, Inc.

Stockham, Jess, illus. Having Fun! 2008. (Just Like Us! Ser.). (ENG.). 12p. (J). (gr. -1). bds. *(978-1-84643-178-4(6))* Child's Play International Ltd.

Stockham, Jessica. Taking It Easy! 2008. (Just Like Us! Ser.). (ENG., Illus.). 12p. (J). (gr. -1). bds. *(978-1-84643-181-4(6))* Child's Play International Ltd.

Strom, Maria Diaz. Joe Arco Iris y Yo. Strom, Maria Diaz, illus. 2008.Tr. of Rainbow Joe & Me. (SPA., Illus.). 32p. (J). (gr. -1-3). pap. 9.95 *(978-1-60060-278-8(9))* Lee & Low Bks., Inc.

Suen, Anastasia. The Pirate Map: A Robot & Rico Story. Laughead, Mike, illus. 2010. (Robot & Rico Ser.). (ENG.). 32p. (gr. 1-2). pap. 6.25 *(978-1-4342-2301-2(9))* Stone Arch Bks.

—We're Going on a Dinosaur Dig. Myer, Ed, illus. 2012. (ENG.). 24p. (gr. k-1). pap. 8.95 *(978-1-61810-299-7(0))* Rourke Educational Media.

Sullivan, Deirdre. Ming Goes to School. Löfdahl, Maja, illus. 2016. (ENG.). 32p. (J). (gr. -1-k). 16.99 *(978-1-5107-0050-5(1)*, Sky Pony Pr.) Skyhorse Publishing Co., Inc.

Teague, Mark. The Pirate Jamboree. 2016. (ENG., Illus.). 40p. (J). (gr. -1-k). 17.99 *(978-0-545-63221-8(8))* Scholastic, Inc.

Thomas, Jan. Here Comes the Big, Mean Dust Bunny! Thomas, Jan, illus. 2009. (ENG., Illus.). 40p. (J). (gr. -1-3). 15.99 *(978-1-4169-9150-2(6)*, Beach Lane Bks.) Beach Lane Bks.

Thomas, Janet. Can I Play? Bartlett, Alison, illus. 2005. 32p. (J). 8.99 *(978-1-4052-0597-9(0))* Egmont Bks., Ltd. GBR. Dist: Trafalgar Square Publishing.

Thomas, Shelley Moore. No, No, Kitten! Nichols, Lori, illus. 2015. (ENG.). 40p. (J). (gr. -1-2). 16.95 *(978-1-62091-631-5(2))* Boyds Mills Pr.

Thompson, Elissa. Tryin' Ryan. 2006. (J). 15.00 *(978-0-9787341-0-7(6))* Aidan's Butterfly Pubns.

Thompson, Lauren. Little Quack's New Friend. Anderson, Derek, illus. 2008. (Classic Board Bks.). (ENG.). 34p. (J). (gr. -1-1). bds. 7.99 *(978-1-4169-4923-7(2)*, Little Simon) Little Simon.

—Little Quack's New Friend. Anderson, Derek, illus. 2006. (ENG.). 32p. (J). (gr. -1-3). 17.99 *(978-0-689-86893-1(6)*, Simon & Schuster Bks. For Young Readers) Simon & Schuster Bks. For Young Readers.

Thompson, Lauren & Anderson, Derek. Little Quack's Hide & Seek. 2007. (Classic Board Bks.). (ENG., Illus.). 34p. (J). (gr. -1-k). bds. 7.99 *(978-1-4169-0325-3(9)*, Little Simon) Little Simon.

Thorpe, Kiki. Dónde Está Boots? - Cuento para Levantar la Tapita. Savitsky, Steven, illus. 2005. (Dora the Explorer Ser.).Tr. of Where Is Boots? - A Lift-the-Flap Story. (SPA.). 16p. (J). pap. 5.99 *(978-1-4169-0621-6(5)*, Libros Para Ninos) Libros Para Ninos.

Thrasher, Grady. Tim & Sally's Beach Adventure. Rabon, Elaine Hearn, illus. 2008. 48p. (J). (gr. -1-3). 18.95 *(978-1-58818-161-9(8))* Hill Street Pr., LLC.

Tidhar, Lavie. Central Station, 1 vol. unabr. ed. 2017. (ENG.). 9.99 ***(978-1-5436-2453-3(7)***, 9781543624533) Brilliance Publishing, Inc.

Toki, Sela Tuita. Pati Loves to Walk Barefoot to School. 2009. 44p. pap. 24.95 *(978-1-60749-433-1(7))* America Star Bks.

Top That. Press Out & Play Magic Castle. 2008. *(978-1-84666-600-1(7))* Top That! Publishing PLC.

Torrey, Richard. Ally-Saurus & the Very Bossy Monster. 2017. (Ally-Saurus Ser.). (ENG., Illus.). 40p. (J). (gr. -1-1). 16.95 ***(978-1-4549-2123-3(4))*** Sterling Publishing Co., Inc.

Torrey, Richard. The Almost Terrible Playdate. Torrey, Rich, illus. 2016. (ENG.). 40p. (J). (gr. -1-2). 19.99 *(978-0-375-97430-4(X)*, Doubleday Bks. for Young Readers) Random Hse. Children's Bks.

Tougas, Chris. Dojo Daycare. 2014. (Dojo Ser.: 1). (ENG., Illus.). 32p. (J). (gr. -1-3). 16.95 *(978-1-77147-057-5(7)*, Owlkids) Owlkids Bks. Inc. CAN. Dist: Publishers Group West (PGW).

Tullet, Hervé. Let's Play! 2016. (ENG., Illus.). 68p. (J). (gr. -1-k). 15.99 *(978-1-4521-5477-0(5))* Chronicle Bks. LLC.

Turner, Dannie E. You Don't Know Beans: the Great Frog Adventure. 2008. 28p. pap. 24.95 *(978-1-60474-711-9(0))* America Star Bks.

Twin Sister Produtions. Sesame Street What Did Elmo Say? 2008. (ENG.). 20p. (J). (gr. -1-3). 9.99 *(978-1-59069-657-6(3))* Studio Mouse LLC.

Twin Sister Produtions & Galvin, Laura Gates. Sesame Street What Did Elmo Say? 2010. (J). (gr. k-2). 14.99 *(978-1-59922-633-0(2))* Twin Sisters IP, LLC.

Twin Sister Produtions Staff & Galvin, Laura Gates. Sesame Street What Did Elmo Say? 2010. (J). (gr. k-2). 14.99 *(978-1-59922-524-1(7))* Twin Sisters IP, LLC.

U. S. National Geographic Society Staff. Anybody Home? 2008. (Mama Mirabelle Ser.). (ENG., Illus.). 24p. (J). (gr. -1-2). pap. 3.99 *(978-1-4263-0303-6(3))*; lib. bdg. 11.90 *(978-1-4263-0304-3(1))* National Geographic Society. (National Geographic Children's Bks.).

—Hide & Seek. 2008. (Mama Mirabelle Ser.). (ENG., Illus.). 24p. (J). (gr. -1-2). pap. 3.99 *(978-1-4263-0305-0(X))*; lib. bdg. 11.90 *(978-1-4263-0306-7(8))* National Geographic Society. (National Geographic Children's Bks.).

Ulbrich, Jasper. The Little Owl. 2009. (Illus.). 32p. pap. 16.50 *(978-1-60860-047-2(5)*, Eloquent Bks.) Strategic Book Publishing & Rights Agency (SBPRA).

Valentino, Carla. When Can We Run, Play & Dance Again? An Enchanting Story about Family, Learning & Imagination. 2011. 32p. (gr. 2-4). pap. 17.95 *(978-1-4567-5495-2(5))* AuthorHouse.

Van Camp, Katie. Harry & Horsie. Agnew, Lincoln, illus. 2009. (Harry & Horsie Adventures Ser.: 1). (ENG.). 32p. (J). (gr. -1-1). 16.99 *(978-0-06-175598-9(2))* HarperCollins Pubs.

Van Der Heide, Iris. The Red Chalk. 2006. (ENG., Illus.). 24p. (J). (gr. -1-k). 19.95 *(978-1-932425-79-6(9)*, Lemniscaat) Boyds Mills Pr.

Veil, Karney. Sun & Moon Play Hide & Seek: A Children's Story. 2012. 24p. (-18). pap. 24.95 *(978-1-4626-9401-3(2))* America Star Bks.

Vilarrubias, Pía. ¿A QUÉ JUEGAN NICO Y MAX? (SPA.). 36p. 11.95 *(978-84-207-1250-5(7))* Grupo Anaya, S.A. ESP. Dist: Distribooks, Inc.

—Juguemos a Volar! (SPA.). 36p. 11.95 *(978-84-207-1255-0(8))* Grupo Anaya, S.A. ESP. Dist: Distribooks, Inc.

—LINA TAMBIÉN JUEGA. (SPA.). 36p. 11.95 *(978-84-207-1251-2(5))* Grupo Anaya, S.A. ESP. Dist: Distribooks, Inc.

Voght, Victor A. Fun with Huff & Puff, 1 vol. 2009. 15p. pap. 24.95 *(978-1-60749-853-7(7))* America Star Bks.

Voigtsberger, Sandra A. Jack's Pockets. 2008. 17p. pap. 24.95 *(978-1-60563-546-0(4))* America Star Bks.

Waddell, Martin. You & Me, Little Bear. 2004. (Illus.). (J). (gr. -1-2). spiral bd. *(978-0-616-01802-6(9))*; spiral bd. *(978-0-616-01803-3(7))* Canadian National Institute for the Blind/Institut National Canadien pour les Aveugles.

Wales, Sid. Freddie & Mee. Bryant, Kerry, illus. 2013. 28p. pap. *(978-1-78222-097-8(6))* Paragon Publishing, Rothersthorpe.

Ward, M. The Evergreens Get Wet: The Evergreens. 2009. (Illus.). 28p. pap. 12.49 *(978-1-4389-8960-0(1))* AuthorHouse.

Watts, Jan. CAKE! A comedy script for young People. 2010. 55p. pap. 21.95 *(978-1-4452-4587-4(6))* Lulu Pr., Inc.

Weatherall, Barry. Jay & the Worm Save the Day. 2005. 40p. 14.28 *(978-1-4116-4717-6(3))* Lulu Pr., Inc.

Weiner, Brian. Toad Catchers' Creek. Weintraub, Claudia & Frederick, Robin, eds. Cannon, Martin, illus. 2005. 40p. (J). lib. bdg. 17.99 *(978-1-932949-58-2(5))* Illusion Factory, The.

Weiss, Ellen. Playtime for Twins. Williams, Sam, illus. 2012. (ENG.). 30p. (J). (gr. -1 — 1). bds. 7.99 *(978-1-4424-3027-3(3)*, Little Simon) Little Simon.

Wells, Rosemary. Max & Ruby Play School. Wells, Rosemary, illus. 2003. (Max & Ruby Ser.). (ENG., Illus.). 32p. (J). (gr. -1-k). pap. 3.99 *(978-0-448-43182-6(3)*, Grosset & Dunlap) Penguin Young Readers Group.

—Max & Ruby Play School. 2003. (All Aboard Reading Ser.). (gr. -1-2). lib. bdg. 13.55 *(978-0-613-64064-0(0)*, Turtleback) Turtleback Bks.

—Max & Ruby's Preschool Pranks. 2016. (Max & Ruby Ser.). (ENG., Illus.). 40p. (J). (-k). 17.99 *(978-0-670-78462-2(1)*, Viking Books for Young Readers) Penguin Young Readers Group.

Wenger, Brahm. Dewey Doo-It at the Jingle Jangle Jamboree: A Musical Storybook Inspired by Arnold Schwarzenegger to Benefit Inner-City Games. 2006. (ENG.). 32p. (J). (gr. -1-3). 18.95 *(978-0-9745143-4-5(9))* RandallFraser Publishing.

Weston Woods Staff, creator. Pete's a Pizza. 2011. 29.95 *(978-0-439-74519-2(5))* Weston Woods Studios, Inc.

—A Weeekend with Wendell. 2004. 29.95 *(978-1-55592-129-3(9))*; (J). 18.95 *(978-1-55592-116-3(7))* Weston Woods Studios, Inc.

—A Weekend with Wendell. 2004. (J). 38.75 *(978-1-55592-647-2(9))* Weston Woods Studios, Inc.

What Shall We Play. 2004. (J). per. *(978-1-57657-459-1(8))* Paradise Pr., Inc.

Wheeler, Lisa. Invasion of the Pig Sisters. Ansley, Frank, illus. 2006. (Fitch & Chip Ser.: 4). (ENG.). 48p. (J). (gr. 1-3). 16.99 *(978-0-689-84953-4(2)*, Simon Spotlight) Simon Spotlight.

White. Naja Plays Hide-Go-Seek, 1 vol. Hyatt, Sean, illus. 2010. 28p. pap. 24.95 *(978-1-4489-8842-6(X))* America Star Bks.

White, Ramy Allison. Sunny Boy & His Playmates. 2006. pap. *(978-1-4068-3390-4(8))* Echo Library.

Wilkenstanley, Ellen. Berryville Bully. 2011. 24p. pap. 11.50 *(978-1-61204-527-6(8)*, Strategic Bk. Publishing) Strategic Book Publishing & Rights Agency (SBPRA).

Willems, Mo. Are You Ready to Play Outside? Willems, Mo, illus. 2008. (Elephant & Piggie Book Ser.). (ENG., Illus.). 64p. (J). (gr. -1-k). 9.99 *(978-1-4231-1347-8(0))* Hyperion Pr.

—A Big Guy Took My Ball! Willems, Mo, illus. 2013. (Elephant & Piggie Ser.). (ENG., Illus.). 64p. (J). (gr. 1-3). 9.99 *(978-1-4231-7491-2(7))* Hyperion Bks. for Children.

—Can I Play Too? 2012. (Elephant & Piggie Bks.). (CHI & JPN.). (J). (gr. -1-3). pap. ***(978-986-189-329-7(6))*** Grimm Cultural Ent., Co., Ltd.

—Can I Play Too? Willems, Mo, illus. 2010. (Elephant & Piggie Book Ser.). (ENG., Illus.). 64p. (J). (gr. -1-k). 9.99 *(978-1-4231-1991-3(6))* Hyperion Pr.

Willems, Mo & Campoy, F. Isabel. ¡Un Tipo Grande Se Llevó Mi Pelota! Willems, Mo, illus. 2015. (Elephant & Piggie Book Ser.). (SPA., Illus.). 64p. (J). (gr. 1-3). 9.99 *(978-1-4847-2285-5(X))* Disney Publishing Worldwide.

William H. Sadlier Staff. Nora Plays All Day. 2005. (Emergent Library: Vol. 2). (gr. -1-1). 24.00 net. *(978-0-8215-8929-8(6))* Sadlier, William H. Inc.

Wilson, Karma. Horseplay! McMullan, Jim, illus. 2012. (ENG.). 40p. (gr. -1-3). 16.99 *(978-0-316-93842-6(4))* Little Brown & Co.

Wineinger, Cherylann. Corgy & His Friends: A Trip to the Unknown. 2011. 24p. pap. 12.79 *(978-1-4520-0349-8(1))* AuthorHouse.

Wishinsky, Frieda. You're Mean, Lily Jean! Denton, Kady MacDonald, illus. 2011. (ENG.). 32p. (J). (gr. -1-3). 16.99 *(978-0-8075-9476-6(8))* Whitman, Albert & Co.

Witek, Jo. In My Room: A Book of Creativity & Imagination. Roussey, Christine, illus. 2017. (Growing Hearts Ser.). (ENG.). 32p. (J). (gr. -1 — 1). 16.95 ***(978-1-4197-2644-6(7)***, Abrams Appleseed) Abrams, Inc.

Wojtowycz, David. Let's Play, Dudley! Colors. 2003. (Dudley Ser.). (Illus.). (J). 3.95 *(978-1-58925-667-5(0))* Tiger Tales.

Won, Brian. Hooray for Today! 2016. (ENG., Illus.). 40p. (J). (gr. -1-3). 16.99 *(978-0-544-74803-3(4)*, HMH Books For Young Readers) Houghton Mifflin Harcourt Publishing Co.

Wood, Douglas. Nothing to Do. Halperin, Wendy Anderson, illus. 2006. (ENG.). 32p. (J). (gr. -1-3). 16.99 *(978-0-525-47656-6(3)*, Dutton Books for Young Readers) Penguin Young Readers Group.

Woodcock, Fiona. Hiding Heidi. 2016. (ENG., Illus.). 32p. (J). (gr. -1-3). 16.99 *(978-1-4998-0350-1(8))* Little Bee Books Inc.

Yacoubou, Jeanne. Wanna Play? Coloring-Story Book. Stebakova, Elena, illus. 2005. 16p. (J). *(978-0-9788737-5-2(0))* Alaafia Kids Co.

Ying, Jonathan. Not Quite Black & White Board Book. Ying, Victoria, illus. 2017. 28p. (J). (gr. -1 — 1). bds. 7.99 ***(978-0-06-238067-8(2)***, HarperFestival) HarperCollins Pubs.

Yolen, Jane. How Do Dinosaurs Play with Their Friends? Teague, Mark, illus. 2006. (How Do Dinosaurs... Ser.). (ENG.). 12p. (J). (gr. -1-k). bds. 6.99 *(978-0-439-85654-6(X)*, Blue Sky Pr., The) Scholastic, Inc.

—What to Do with a Box. Sheban, Chris, illus. 2016. (ENG.). 32p. (J). (gr. 1-3). 18.99 *(978-1-56846-289-9(1)*, Creative Editions) Creative Co., The.

Yoo, Paula. Want to Play? Ng-Benitez, Shirley, illus. 2016. (Confetti Kids Ser.). (ENG.). 32p. (J). (gr. k-2). 14.95 *(978-1-62014-250-9(3))* Lee & Low Bks., Inc.

Yorinks, Arthur. Flappy & Scrappy. Ivanov, Olga & Ivanov, Aleksey, illus. 2010. (I Can Read Level 2 Ser.). (ENG.). 48p. (J). (gr. k-3). 16.99 *(978-0-06-205117-2(2))* HarperCollins Pubs.

—Flappy & Scrappy. Ivanov, Aleksey & Ivanov, Olga, illus. 2010. (I Can Read Level 2 Ser.). (ENG.). 48p. (J). (gr. k-3). pap. 3.99 *(978-0-06-205913-0(0))* HarperCollins Pubs.

Young, Cybèle. A Few Blocks, 1 vol. 2011. (ENG., Illus.). 48p. (J). (gr. -1-2). 18.95 *(978-0-88899-995-5(X))* Groundwood Bks. CAN. Dist: Publishers Group West (PGW).

Young, Jessica. All Paws on Deck. Burks, James, illus. 2016. (Haggis & Tank Unleashed Ser.: 1). (ENG.). 80p. (J). (gr. k-2). pap. 4.99 *(978-0-545-81886-5(9))* Scholastic, Inc.

Young, T. M. Playing Church. Washington, Victoria, ed. Cromwell, Danielle, illus. 2012. 32p. pap. 24.95 *(978-1-4626-7883-9(1))* America Star Bks.

Zepeda, Gwendolyn. Level up / Paso de Nivel. Baeza Ventura, Gabriela, tr. from ENG. Torrecilla, Pablo, illus. 2012. (SPA & ENG.). (J). (gr. 5-9). 16.95 *(978-1-55885-747-6(8)*, Piñata Books) Arte Publico Pr.

123 Sesame Street, ed. When Zoe Grows Up. 2009. (ENG.). 20p. 9.99 *(978-1-59069-820-4(7))* Studio Mouse LLC.

PLAY CENTERS

see Playgrounds

PLAY DIRECTION (THEATER)

see Theater—Production and Direction

PLAY PRODUCTION

see Theater—Production and Direction

PLAY WRITING

see Drama—Technique

PLAYGROUNDS

Bloom, Paul. Rules on the Playground. 2015. (School Rules Ser.). (ENG.). 24p. (gr. k-k). pap. 8.15 *(978-1-4824-2657-1(9))* Stevens, Gareth Publishing LLLP.

Bradman, Tony & Quarto Generic Staff. In a Minute. Browne, Eileen, illus. 2012. (ENG.). 32p. (J). (gr. -1-1). pap. 8.99 *(978-1-84780-180-7(3)*, Frances Lincoln) Quarto Publishing Group UK GBR. Dist: Hachette Bk. Group.

Donahue, Jill Urban. Juega Con Cuidado. Masheris, Bob, illus. 2011. (Cómo Mantenernos Seguros/How to Be Safe Ser.).Tr. of Play It Smart. (ENG, SPA & MUL.). 24p. (gr. k-2). 26.65 *(978-1-4048-6886-1(0))* Picture Window Bks.

Enz, Tammy. Hidden Worlds, 4 vols., Set. Incl. Behind the Racks: Exploring the Secrets of a Shopping Mall. lib. bdg. 26.65 *(978-1-4296-3386-4(7))*; Beyond the Bars: Exploring the Secrets of a Police Station. lib. bdg. 26.65 *(978-1-4296-3377-2(8))*; Under the Lights: Exploring the Secrets of a Sports Stadium. lib. bdg. 26.65 *(978-1-4296-3376-5(X))*; (gr. 1-2). (Hidden Worlds Ser.). (ENG.). 32p. 2010. Set lib. bdg. 79.95 *(978-1-4296-3777-0(3)*, Blazers) Capstone Press of Coughlan Cos.

Finn, Carrie. Comportamiento y Modales en el Patio de Juegos. Lensch, Chris, illus. 2011. (¡Así Debemos Ser!: Buenos Modales, Buen Comportamiento/Way to Be!: Manners Ser.).Tr. of Manners on the Playground. (ENG, SPA & MUL.). 24p. (gr. -1-2). lib. bdg. 26.65 *(978-1-4048-6699-7(X))* Picture Window Bks.

—Manners on the Playground. Lensch, Chris, illus. (Way to Be!: Manners Ser.). 24p. (gr. -1-2). 2009. pap. 0.63 *(978-1-4048-5995-1(0)*, Nonfiction Picture Bks.) 2009. pap. 2.76 *(978-1-4048-6053-7(3)*, Nonfiction Picture Bks.) 2007. (ENG.). per. 7.95 *(978-1-4048-3559-7(8))* Picture Window Bks.

Finn, Carrie & Picture Window Books Staff. Manners on the Playground, 1 vol. Lensch, Chris, illus. 2007. (Way to Be!: Manners Ser.). (ENG.). 24p. (gr. -1-2). 26.65 *(978-1-4048-3154-4(1))* Picture Window Bks.

Gorman, Jacqueline Laks. The Playground. 2005. (I Like to Visit/Me Gusta Visitar Ser.). (ENG & SPA.). 24p. (gr. k-3). pap. 8.15 *(978-0-8368-4461-0(0)*, Weekly Reader Leveled Readers) Stevens, Gareth Publishing LLLP.

—The Playground. Acosta, Tatiana & Gutiérrez, Guillermo, trs. 2005. (I Like to Visit Ser.). (ENG & SPA., Illus.). 24p. (gr. k-3). lib. bdg. 22.00 *(978-0-8368-4454-2(8)*, Weekly Reader Leveled Readers) Stevens, Gareth Publishing LLLP.

—The Playground: El Parque. 2005. (I Like to Visit/ Me gusta visitar Ser.). (ENG & SPA., Illus.). 24p. (gr. k-3). pap. 8.15 *(978-0-8368-4605-8(2)*, Weekly Reader Leveled Readers) Stevens, Gareth Publishing LLLP.

Gorman, Jacqueline Laks & Laks Gorman, Jacqueline. The Playground/El Parque. 2005. (I Like to Visit/Me Gusta Visitar Ser.). (SPA & ENG., Illus.). 24p. (gr. k-3). lib. bdg. 22.00 *(978-0-8368-4598-3(6)*, Weekly Reader Leveled Readers) Stevens, Gareth Publishing LLLP.

Hall, Pamela. A Bully-Free Playground, 1 vol. Ostrom, Bob, illus. 2012. (Bully-Free World Ser.). (ENG.). 24p. (J). (gr. -1-4). 27.07 *(978-1-61641-846-5(X))* Magic Wagon.

Heos, Bridget. Be Safe on the Playground. Baroncelli, Silvia, illus. 2015. (Be Safe! Ser.). 24p. (J). 25.65 *(978-1-60753-446-4(0))* Amicus Publishing.

Hidden Worlds [Capstone Sole Source]. 2010. (Hidden Worlds Ser.). 32p. lib. bdg. 101.28 *(978-1-4296-5865-2(7)*, Blazers) Capstone Press of Coughlan Cos.

Hurley, Michael. The World's Most Amazing Stadiums, 1 vol. 2011. (Landmark Top Tens Ser.). (ENG., Illus.). 32p. (gr. 3-5). pap. 8.29 *(978-1-4109-4256-2(2)*, Raintree Perspectives) Heinemann-Raintree.

James, Dawn. Playground Math. 2015. (Math Around Us Ser.). (ENG.). 24p. (J). (gr. 1-1). pap. 24.21 *(978-1-5026-0152-0(4))* Cavendish Square Publishing.

Knowlton, MaryLee. Safety at the Playground. Andersen, Gregg, photos by. 2008. (Staying Safe Ser.). (ENG., Illus.). 32p. (J). (gr. -1-3). lib. bdg. *(978-0-7787-4318-7(7))* Crabtree Publishing Co.

Knowlton, MaryLee & Dowdy, Penny. Safety at the Playground. Andersen, Gregg, photos by. 2008. (Staying Safe Ser.). (ENG., Illus.). 32p. (J). (gr. -1-3). pap. *(978-0-7787-4323-1(3))* Crabtree Publishing Co.

Mara, Wil. What Should I Do? On the Playground. 2011. (Community Connections: What Should I Do? Ser.). (ENG.). 24p. (gr. 2-5). lib. bdg. 25.64 *(978-1-61080-054-9(0)*, 201050) Cherry Lake Publishing.

Marsico, Katie. Good Manners on the Playground, 1 vol. Haslam, John, illus. 2009. (Good Manners Matter! Ser.). (ENG.). 32p. (J). (gr. -1-2). 28.50 *(978-1-60270-612-5(3))* Magic Wagon.

Mortensen, Lori. Manners Matter on the Playground. Hunt, Lisa, illus. (First Graphics: Manners Matter Ser.). (ENG.). 24p. (gr. 1-2). 2011. pap. 35.70 *(978-1-4296-6395-3(2))* 2010. lib. bdg. 23.99 *(978-1-4296-5332-9(9))* Capstone Press of Coughlan Cos.

Myers, Edward. Let's Build a Playground. 2012. (ENG., Illus.). 48p. (J). (gr. 2-3). pap. 9.50 *(978-0-7652-0882-8(2)*, Modern Curriculum Pr.) Pearson Schl.

The Playground: Individual Title Two-Packs. (Chiquilibros Ser.). (gr. -1-1). 12.00 *(978-0-7635-8528-0(9))* Rigby Education.

Raatma, Lucia. Staying Safe on the Playground, 1 vol. 2011. (Staying Safe Ser.). (ENG.). 24p. (gr. 1-2). pap. 7.29 *(978-1-4296-7197-2(1))*; pap. 41.70 *(978-1-4296-7198-9(X))*; lib. bdg. 25.32 *(978-1-4296-6822-4(9))* Capstone Press of Coughlan Cos. (First Facts).

Randolph, Joanne. The Slide at School. 2015. (Rosen REAL Readers: STEM & STEAM Collection). (ENG.). 8p. pap. 5.46 *(978-1-4994-9733-5(4)*, Rosen Classroom) Rosen Publishing Group, Inc., The.

Rosen, Michael J. & Kaboom! Staff. Let's Build a Playground. Kelson, Ellen & Cecil, Jennifer, illus. 2013. (ENG.). 32p. (J). (gr. 1-4). 15.99 *(978-0-7636-5532-7(5))* Candlewick Pr.

Sandler, Michael. Stupendous Sports Stadiums. 2011. (So Big Compared to What? Ser.). 24p. (YA). (gr. 1-4). lib. bdg. 22.61 *(978-1-61772-302-5(9))* Bearport Publishing Co., Inc.

Thomas, Mark. Maracaná: El estadio de fútbol más grande del mundo (the Maracaná: World's Largest Soccer Stadium) 2009. (Estructuras extraordinarias (Record-Breaking Structures) Ser.). (SPA.). 24p. (gr. 1-2). 42.50 *(978-1-61512-315-5(6)*, Editorial Buenas Letras) Rosen Publishing Group, Inc., The.

Urban Donahue, Jill. Play It Smart: Playground Safety, 1 vol. Masheris, Bob, illus. 2008. (How to Be Safe! Ser.). (ENG.). 24p. (gr. k-2). 26.65 *(978-1-4048-4823-8(1))* Picture Window Bks.

What Happens When You Recycle? Individual Title Six-Packs. (Discovery World Ser.). 16p. (gr. 1-2). 28.00 *(978-0-7635-8464-1(9))* Rigby Education.

PLAYGROUNDS—FICTION

Baltazar, Art & Aureliani, Franco. Tiny Titans vs. the Fearsome Five, 1 vol. Baltazar, Art & Aureliani, Franco, illus. 2012. (Tiny Titans Ser.). (ENG., Illus.). 32p. (gr. 1-2). lib. bdg. 22.60 *(978-1-4342-4538-0(1))* Stone Arch Bks.

Becker, Kate M. My Dream Playground. Henry, Jed, illus. 2013. (ENG.). 32p. (J). (gr. -1-3). 15.99 *(978-0-7636-5531-0(7))* Candlewick Pr.

Benenfeld, Rikki. Let's Go to the Park. 2015. (ENG., Illus.). 36p. (J). 10.95 *(978-1-929628-82-7(X))* Hachai Publishing.

Bond, Roland. Harvey Plumstead & the Dinnertime Dog. 2012. (Illus.). 96p. (gr. 4-18). pap. 13.66 *(978-1-4772-4317-6(8))* AuthorHouse.

Bonnell, Kris. Too Big to Play. 2006. (J). pap. 5.95 *(978-1-933727-35-6(7))* Reading Reading Bks., LLC.

Brown, Cornelia. Constance the Little Angel Wants Curls. 2009. 28p. pap. 15.99 *(978-1-4490-3962-2(6))* AuthorHouse.

Clanchy, Kate. Our Cat Henry Comes to the Swings. Bird, Jemima, illus. 2007. 32p. (J). (gr. -1-1). 16.00 *(978-1-56148-563-5(2)*, Good Bks.) Skyhorse Publishing Co., Inc.

Copeland, Cynthia L. What Are You Waiting For? Gordon, Mike, illus. 2003. (Silly Millies Ser.: 1). 32p. lib. bdg. 17.90 *(978-0-7613-2804-9(1)*, Millbrook Pr.) Lerner Publishing Group.

Copeland, Cynthia L. & Gordon, Mike. What Are You Waiting For? 2003. (Silly Millies Ser.: Vol.1). (Illus.). 32p. (J). (gr. -1-1). pap. 4.99 *(978-0-7613-1828-6(3))* Lerner Publishing Group.

Coppock, Phil & Bower's 2008-2009 4th Grade Class. Rubber Tuesday. 2010. 70p. pap. 12.95 *(978-1-4327-5751-9(2))* Outskirts Pr., Inc.

Dean, James. Construction Destruction. Dean, James, illus. 2015. (Pete the Cat Ser.). (ENG., Illus.). 24p. (J). (gr. -1-3). pap. 4.99 *(978-0-06-219861-7(0)*, HarperFestival) HarperCollins Pubs.

—Construction Destruction. 2015. (Pete the Cat (HarperCollins) Ser.). (J). lib. bdg. 14.75 *(978-0-606-36489-8(7))* Turtleback Bks.

dePaola, Tomie, illus. When Andy Met Sandy. 2016. (Andy & Sandy Book Ser.). (ENG.). 32p. (J). (gr. -1-3). 8.99 *(978-1-4814-4155-1(8)*, Simon & Schuster Bks. For Young Readers) Simon & Schuster Bks. For Young Readers.

Evans, Nate & Brown, Stephanie Gwyn. Bang! Boom! Roar! A Busy Crew of Dinosaurs. Santoro, Christopher, illus. 2012. (ENG.). 40p. (J). (gr. -1-2). 15.99 *(978-0-06-087960-0(2))* HarperCollins Pubs.

—Dinosaur ABC. Santoro, Christopher, illus. 2011. (J). lib. bdg. 16.89 *(978-0-06-087962-4(9))* HarperCollins Pubs.

Feldman, Thea. Fun Around the Town. 2006. 3p. 5.99 *(978-1-932915-34-1(6))* Sandvik Publishing.

Harrar, Frank W. Wee Dragonslayers. Galan-Robles, Francisco, illus. 2008. 45p. pap. 24.95 *(978-1-60610-851-2(4))* America Star Bks.

Harrison, Kenny. Hide & Seek Harry at the Playground. Harrison, Kenny, illus. 2015. (ENG., Illus.). 20p. (J). (-k). bds. 6.99 *(978-0-7636-7347-5(1))* Candlewick Pr.
Hillert, Margaret. Juega, Juega, Juega, Querido Dragón/Play, Play, Play Dear Dragon. del Risco, Eida, tr. Schimmell, David, illus. 2010. (BeginningtoRead Ser.). 32p. (J). (-2). pap. 11.94 *(978-1-60357-551-5(0))* Norwood Hse. Pr.
—Play, Play, Play Dear Dragon. Schimmell, David, illus. 2009. (BeginningtoRead Ser.). 32p. (J). (gr. k-2). lib. bdg. 22.60 *(978-1-59953-294-3(8))* Norwood Hse. Pr.
—Play, Play, Play, Dear Dragon (Juega, Juega, Juega, Querido Dragon) Del Risco, Eida, tr. Schimmell, David, illus. 2010. (BeginningtoRead Ser.). (SPA & ENG.). 32p. (J). (gr. k-2). lib. bdg. 22.60 *(978-1-59953-363-6(4))* Norwood Hse. Pr.
Howard-Parham, Pam. Playing on the Playground. Crowell, Knox, illus. l.t. ed. 2005. (HRL Little Book Ser.). (J). (gr. k-18). pap. 10.95 *(978-1-57332-336-9(5))*; pap. 10.95 *(978-1-57332-335-2(7))* Carson-Dellosa Publishing, LLC. (HighReach Learning, Incorporated).
Kaputa, Christine C. Jungle Gym Me & Him! 2008. 24p. pap. 10.95 *(978-1-59858-781-4(1))* Dog Ear Publishing, LLC.
Kemp, Hill & Kemp, Siena. Lucky Penny. 2007. 88p. pap. 6.95 *(978-1-933090-87-0(1))* Guardian Angel Publishing, Inc.
Klein, Adria F. Max Goes to the Playground, 1 vol. Gallagher-Cole, Mernie, illus. 2007. (Read-It! Readers: the Life of Max Ser.). (ENG.). 24p. (gr. -1-2). lib. bdg. 21.32 *(978-1-4048-3681-5(0)*, Easy Readers) Picture Window Bks.
—Sophie Screwdriver, 1 vol. Rowland, Andrew, illus. 2011. (Tool School Ser.). (ENG.). 32p. (gr. 1-2). pap. 6.25 *(978-1-4342-3386-8(3))*; lib. bdg. 22.65 *(978-1-4342-3044-7(9))* Stone Arch Bks.
Leman, Nora. The Alpha Building Crew. Hartmann, April, illus. 2005. (J). *(978-1-58987-110-6(3))* Kindermusik International.
Lewis, Joan Lane. See with Me. Hough, Hannah Bliss, illus. 2011. 32p. pap. 24.95 *(978-1-4626-2347-1(6))* America Star Bks.
Merz, Jennifer. Playground Day. 2007. 32p. 16.00 *(978-978-061-896-4(1)*, Clarion Bks.) Houghton Mifflin Harcourt Trade & Reference Pubs.
Parnell, Declan. Playground Fun, 01 vols., 1. 2016. (Rosen REAL Readers: STEM & STEAM Collection). (ENG.). 12p. (J). pap. 6.33 *(978-1-5081-1557-1(5)*, Rosen Classroom) Rosen Publishing Group, Inc., The.
Peschke, Marci. Green Queen, 1 vol. Mourning, Tuesday, illus. 2014. (Kylie Jean Ser.). (ENG.). 112p. (gr. 2-3). 22.65 *(978-1-4795-2351-1(8)*, Kylie Jean) Picture Window Bks.
Priddy, Roger & Crimi-Trent, Ellen. My First Day at School. 2013. (Schoolies Ser.). (ENG., Illus.). 28p. (J). (gr. -1-1). 4.99 *(978-0-312-51612-3(6)*, 9780312516123, Priddy Bks.) St. Martin's Pr.
Queen Latifah. Queen of the Scene. Morrison, Frank, illus. 2006. 32p. (J). (gr. -1-3). 17.89 incl. audio compact disk *(978-0-06-077857-6(1)*, Geringer, Laura Book) HarperCollins Pubs.
Reidy, Jean. Busy Builders, Busy Week! Timmers, Leo, illus. 2016. (ENG.). 32p. (J). 16.99 *(978-1-61963-556-2(9)*, 9781619635562, Bloomsbury USA Childrens) Bloomsbury Publishing USA.
Rodgers, Ilona. Musgrove in Kensington Gardens. 2007. (ENG.). 50p. 10.95 *(978-1-905299-49-2(4)*, Stacey International) Stacey Publishing GBR. Dist: Casemate Pubs. & Bk. Distributors, LLC.
Sandra De Mos. Cleo's Playground Adventure. 2009. 40p. pap. 16.99 *(978-1-4389-2049-8(0))* AuthorHouse.
Schorr, Titus. A Playground Adventure, 01 vols., 1. 2016. (Rosen REAL Readers: STEM & STEAM Collection). (ENG.). 8p. (J). pap. 5.46 *(978-1-5081-1469-7(2)*, Rosen Classroom) Rosen Publishing Group, Inc., The.
Shaw, Mary. Brady Brady & the Cleanup Hitters. Temple, Chuck, illus. 2008. 32p. (J). pap. *(978-1-897169-11-7(6))* Brady Brady, Inc.
Shofner, Melissa Raé. Good Manners at the Playground. 2017. (Manners Matter Ser.). 24p. (gr. 4-6). 23.60 ***(978-1-5081-5729-8(4)***, PowerKids Pr.) Rosen Publishing Group, Inc., The.
Stefanescu, Estera. Megan's Great Day. 2009. 20p. pap. 15.99 *(978-1-4389-6318-1(1))* AuthorHouse.
Trasler, Janee. Mimi & Bear Make a Friend. Trasler, Janee, illus. 2017. (Mimi & Bear Ser.). (ENG., Illus.). 32p. (J). 16.99 *(978-0-374-30360-0(6)*, 9780374303600, Farrar, Straus & Giroux (BYR)) Farrar, Straus & Giroux.
Yolen, Jane. Romping Monsters, Stomping Monsters. Murphy, Kelly, illus. 2013. (ENG.). 32p. (J). (gr. -1-2). 14.99 *(978-0-7636-5727-7(1))* Candlewick Pr.

PLAYHOUSES

see Theaters

PLAYING CARDS

see Cards

PLAYS

Adam & Eve Playbook. 2006. (J). *(978-0-9792640-2-3(2))* GSP Players, LLC.
Adam & Eve Workbook. 2006. (J). *(978-0-9792640-1-6(4))* GSP Players, LLC.
Adams, Jennifer. Pride & Prejudice: Counting Primer Book & Playset, 1 vol. Oliver, Alison, illus. 2013. (ENG.). 22p. (J). (gr. k-1). bds. 19.99 *(978-1-4236-3515-4(9))* Gibbs Smith, Publisher.
Adams, Karin. Lights! Curtains! Cows!, 1 vol. 2009. (Lorimer Streetlights Ser.). (ENG.). 132p. (J). (gr. 2-4). 8.95 *(978-1-55277-426-7(0)*, 9781552774267) Lorimer, James & Co., Ltd., Pubs. CAN. Dist: Casemate Pubs. & Bk. Distributors, LLC.
Agbaje, Salihah. Mouth Almighty a Play. Akhtar, Waheed, illus. 2012. 144p. pap. *(978-0-9565861-0-0(4))* Spoken World Productions.
Alcott, Louisa May. Comic Tragedies. 2010. 334p. pap. 31.75 *(978-1-144-55721-6(6))* 2009. 324p. 25.99 *(978-1-103-79747-9(6))* 2009. 324p. pap. 19.99 *(978-1-103-79738-7(7))* Creative Media Partners, LLC.
—Comic Tragedies. 2010. 82p. pap. 19.83 *(978-1-151-98760-0(3))* 2009. 88p. pap. 14.14 *(978-1-151-52805-6(6))* General Bks. LLC.
—Comic Tragedies. 2008. 324p. pap. *(978-1-4097-0064-7(X))* Read Bks.
—Comic Tragedies. 2013. 110p. pap. 3.99 *(978-1-61720-909-3(0))* Wilder Pubns., Corp.
—Comic Tragedies: Written by Jo & Meg & Acted by the Little Women. 2010. 320p. 36.76 *(978-1-163-54988-9(6))* 2010. 320p. pap. 24.76 *(978-1-163-28090-4(9))* 2007. (ENG.). 318p. 45.95 *(978-0-548-24869-0(9))* 2007. (ENG.). 320p. per. 30.95 *(978-1-4326-5113-8(7))* Kessinger Publishing, LLC.
—Comic Tragedies/ Written by Jo & Meg & Acted by the Little Women. 2012. 334p. (-18). pap. *(978-1-4076-6141-4(8))* HardPr.
Alcott, Louisa May & Meg, Meg. Comic Tragedies/ Written by Jo & Meg & Acted by the Little Women. 2010. (ENG.). 328p. pap. 31.75 *(978-1-177-42111-9(9))* Creative Media Partners, LLC.
Alcott, Louisa May & Pratt, Anna Bronson Alcott. Comic Tragedies. 2010. 326p. pap. 30.75 *(978-1-177-67911-4(6))*; 334p. pap. 31.75 *(978-1-177-69933-4(8))* Creative Media Partners, LLC.
Alfreda. Taestella A Black Cinderella Folder Leaf Edition. 2007. (YA). 3.25 *(978-1-56820-442-0(6)*, folder leaf) Story Time Stories That Rhyme.
Allen, Laurie. Middle School Mania: Comedy Duos for Guy / Girl, 8 bklts. 2003. (YA). pap. 19.95 *(978-1-932404-53-1(8)*, 915) Brooklyn Pubs.
—Thirty-Three Short Comedy Plays for Teens: Plays for Small Casts. 2011. (ENG.). 208p. (J). pap. 17.95 *(978-1-56608-181-8(5))* Meriwether Publishing, Ltd.
Andersen, Hans Christian. The Little Mermaid. 2005. (ENG.). 96p. (gr. 3-7). per. 16.95 *(978-1-84002-487-6(9))* Theatre Communications Group, Inc.
Armstrong, James. The New Mrs. Jones: A One-Act Comedy Play. 2003. (YA). pap. 4.50 *(978-1-932404-62-3(7)*, 760) Brooklyn Pubs.
Asher, Sandra Fenichel. Blackbirds & Dragons, Mermaids & Mice. 2003. (Illus.). 150p. (YA). pap. 9.95 *(978-1-58342-174-1(2)*, BB1) Dramatic Publishing Co.
Aston, Nell, contrib. by. Bailed Up. 22p. pap. *(978-1-875739-29-5(7))* Wizard Bks.
Atkinson, Lawrence. Great Ideas. 2003. (YA). 8.00 *(978-0-9679552-3-0(8))* Mushroom Cloud Pr. of Orlando.
Averill, Ric. The Pied Piper of Hamelin (musical) 2014. 58p. (J). pap. 9.95 *(978-1-58342-898-6(4))* Dramatic Publishing Co.
Avi, et al. Acting Out: Six One-Act Plays! Six Newbery Stars! 2010. (ENG.). 192p. (J). (gr. 3-7). pap. 6.99 *(978-1-4169-3849-1(4)*, Atheneum Bks. for Young Readers) Simon & Schuster Children's Publishing.
Baillie, Allan. Archie the Big Good Wolf Vol. 9: Band 15/Emerald. Ogden, Betina, illus. 2007. (Collins Big Cat Ser.). (ENG.). 32p. (J). pap. 8.99 *(978-0-00-723421-9(X))* HarperCollins Pubs. Ltd. GBR. Dist: Independent Pubs. Group.
Baker, Thomas. The Fine Lady's Airs. 2006. pap. *(978-1-4065-0502-3(1))* Dodo Pr.
Balkin, Alfred & Grimm, Jacob. The Musicians of Bremen: A Not-So-Grimm Modern Musical Fairy Tale. 2013. 62p. ***(978-0-87602-428-7(2))*** Family Plays.
Baptist, Leona. Daniel Boone. (Illus.). (YA). (gr. 6-12). 6.00 *(978-0-87602-118-7(6))* Family Plays.
Barchers, Suzanne I. War Stories for Readers Theatre: World War II. 2010. 214p. (ENG.). E-Book *(978-1-59884-676-8(0))*; (C). pap. 40.00 *(978-1-59158-750-7(6)*, TIP8750) ABC-CLIO, LLC. (Libraries Unlimited).
Barchers, Suzanne I. & Ruscoe, Michael. Against All Odds: Readers Theatre for Grades 3-8, 1 vol. 2008. (Readers Theatre Ser.). 264p. (C). pap. 40.00 *(978-1-59158-677-7(1)*, TIP8677, Libraries Unlimited) ABC-CLIO, LLC.
Bartlett, Lynne, et al, adapted by. H. M. S. Pinafore: Or the Lass That Loved a Sailor. 2012. (ENG.). 64p. pap. 8.95 *(978-1-58342-727-9(9))* Dramatic Publishing Co.
Bawden, Nina. Carrie's War. 2007. (ENG.). 96p. per. 20.95 *(978-1-84002-720-4(7))* Oberon Bks., Ltd. GBR. Dist: Consortium Bk. Sales & Distribution.
Beissel, Henry. Inuk & the Sun (Inuk et le Soleil) Barton, Bruce, ed. Franciere, Arlette, tr. 2010. (FRE & ENG., Illus.). 232p. pap. 25.00 *(978-0-88754-593-1(9))* Theatre Communications Group, Inc.
Benchmark Education Company, LLC Staff. Reader's Theater for Fluency & Comprehension Handbook. 2004. (Reader's Theater Ser.). pap., instr.'s hndbk. ed. 10.00 *(978-1-4108-1320-6(7))* Benchmark Education Co.
Bennett, Doraine. Readers Theatre for Global Explorers, 1 vol. 2010. (Readers Theatre Ser.). 190p. (C). pap. 40.00 *(978-1-59884-515-0(2)*, A3007P, Libraries Unlimited) ABC-CLIO, LLC.
Bergman, Steven. Critic's Carnival: A Ten-Minute Dramatic Monologue. 2003. 12p. (YA). pap. 4.50 *(978-1-932404-26-5(0)*, 279) Brooklyn Pubs.
Bernardi, Philip & Havens, Diane. Twice upon a Time. 2003. (Theater for Young Audiences Ser.). (Illus.). 24p. (J). (gr. k-6). pap. 6.00 *(978-0-88734-425-1(9))* Players Pr., Inc.
Beth, Georgia. The Swimming Hole (Science) 2015. (Building Fluency Through Reader's Theater Ser.). (Illus.). 24p. (gr. 2-2). pap. 6.99 *(978-1-4938-1515-9(6))* Teacher Created Materials, Inc.
Bevington, David. Twelfth Night. Laurel Associates Inc. Staff & Saddleback Educational Publishing Staff, eds. 2006. (Graphic Shakespeare Ser.). (ENG., Illus.). 16p. (YA). (gr. 9-12). pupil's gde. ed. 7.95 incl. cd-rom *(978-1-59905-279-3(2))* Saddleback Educational Publishing, Inc.
Bible Drama: 136 Stories to Be Read or Acted as Plays. 2004. pap. 29.95 *(978-1-879415-41-6(0)*, Bearly Cooking) Mountain n' Air Bks.
Bland, Janice. Allie's Class. 2010. (YA). pap. 12.00 *(978-0-88734-984-3(6))* Players Pr., Inc.
Blane, Francisco. The Little Girl with Curl. Kelley, Gerald, illus. 2009. (Reader's Theater Nursery Rhymes & Songs Set B Ser.). 48p. (J). pap. *(978-1-60859-157-2(3))* Benchmark Education Co.
—Little Jack Horner Eats Pie. Price, Nick, illus. 2009. (Reader's Theater Nursery Rhymes & Songs Set B Ser.). 48p. (J). pap. *(978-1-60859-158-9(1))* Benchmark Education Co.
—One Raining, Pouring Morning. 2008. (Reader's Theater Nursery Rhymes & Songs Ser.). (Illus.). 48p. (J). (gr. k-1). pap. *(978-1-60437-977-8(4))* Benchmark Education Co.
—Tim Rows a Boat Gently down the Stream. 2008. (Reader's Theater Nursery Rhymes & Songs Ser.). (Illus.). 48p. (J). (gr. k-1). pap. *(978-1-60437-980-8(4))* Benchmark Education Co.
Blum, Renon. California Wax Museum. 2003. (Ideal for Teens Ser.). 16p. (J). (gr. 4-8). pap. 5.00 *(978-0-88734-518-0(2))* Players Pr., Inc.
Bogard, Jerrod. Jack & the Soy Beanstalk. 2010. (ENG.). 47p. pap. 8.95 *(978-0-87440-659-7(5))* Baker's Plays.
Booth, David. Molly Whuppie & the Giant: Band 13/Topaz. Ross, Christine, illus. 2007. (Collins Big Cat Ser.). (ENG.). 24p. (J). pap. 8.99 *(978-0-00-722874-4(0))* HarperCollins Pubs. Ltd. GBR. Dist: Independent Pubs. Group.
Boylan, Eleanor. The Brementown Musicians Vol. 1: Band 13/Topaz. Jensz, Penny, illus. 2007. (Collins Big Cat Ser.). (ENG.). 24p. (J). pap. 8.99 *(978-0-00-722864-5(3))* HarperCollins Pubs. Ltd. GBR. Dist: Independent Pubs. Group.
Bradley, Jeffery & Miller, Britt Ekland. Positive African American Plays for Children Book 2: Building High Self Esteem & Confidence Through Plays. 2005. 128p. (J). per. 19.95 *(978-1-884163-92-0(0)*, Juba Bks.) NetNia Publishing Co.
Bradman, Tony & Bradman, Tom. The Great Fire of London. 2017. (Putting on a Play Ser.). (ENG., Illus.). 32p. (J). (gr. 2-4). pap. 9.99 *(978-0-7502-9753-0(0)*, Wayland) Hachette Children's Group GBR. Dist: Hachette Bk. Group.
—The Gunpowder Plot. 2017. (Putting on a Play Ser.). (ENG., Illus.). 32p. (J). (gr. 2-4). pap. 9.99 *(978-0-7502-9754-7(9)*, Wayland) Hachette Children's Group GBR. Dist: Hachette Bk. Group.
Breslin, Theresa, et al. Divided City. 2013. (Critical Scripts Ser.). (ENG., Illus.). 144p. (J). pap. 14.95 *(978-1-4081-8157-7(6)*, 9781408181577, Bloomsbury Methuen Drama) Bloomsbury Publishing Plc GBR. Dist: Macmillan.
Brooks, Laurie. Franklin's Apprentice. 2006. 48p. pap. 9.00 *(978-0-8222-2069-5(5))* Dramatists Play Service, Inc.
Brown, Susan Taylor. Enrique Esparza & the Battle of the Alamo. Reeves, Jeni, illus. 2010. (History Speaks: Picture Books Plus Reader's Theater Ser.). (ENG.). 48p. (gr. 2-4). pap. 9.95 *(978-0-7613-3942-7(6))*; lib. bdg. 27.93 *(978-0-8225-8566-4(9)*, Millbrook Pr.) Lerner Publishing Group.
Bruchac, Joseph. Pushing up the Sky. Flavin, Teresa, illus. 2015. 96p. pap. 10.00 *(978-1-61003-552-1(6))* Center for the Collaborative Classroom.
Buchanan, Matt. Ernie's Place: A Play for Young Audiences. 2006. 36p. (YA). pap. 5.95 *(978-1-60003-200-4(1)*, 618) Brooklyn Pubs.
—Prince Ugly: One Act Youth Play. rev. ed. 2005. 40p. (YA). pap. 5.95 *(978-1-60003-169-4(2)*, 613) Brooklyn Pubs.
—Sleeping Walter: One Act Youth Play. rev. ed. 2005. 32p. (YA). pap. 5.95 *(978-1-60003-170-0(6)*, 614) Brooklyn Pubs.
Bushore-Fallis, Martha. Book of Lyrics: Freedom Found, the Musical Drama. 2013. 106p. 44.95 *(978-1-4582-1195-8(9)*, Abbott Pr.) Author Solutions, Inc.
Cain, Candice. The Tortoise & the Hare. 2010. (ENG.). 23p. pap. 4.50 *(978-0-87440-739-6(7))* Baker's Plays.
Carr, Diane. River Dragon Activity Book: Just Add Kids. 2003. (J). 15.00 *(978-1-59094-051-8(2)*, Jawbreakers for Kids) Jawbone Publishing Corp.
Carrière, Jean-Claude. The Little Black Book. 2003. (ENG.). 86p. pap. 18.95 *(978-0-9542330-7-5(7))* Aurora Metro Pubns. Ltd. GBR. Dist: Consortium Bk. Sales & Distribution.
Carsey, Alice & Collodi, Carlo. Pinocchio. 2005.Tr. of Avventure di Pinocchio. (ENG.). 96p. per. 16.95 *(978-1-84002-529-3(8))* Theatre Communications Group, Inc.
Carter, Pip. Double Dare. (Illus.). 128p. (J). (gr. 4-6). *(978-1-875739-48-6(3))* Wizard Bks.
—The Little People. (Illus.). 112p. (J). (gr. 3-5). *(978-1-875739-70-7(X))* Wizard Bks.
Carter, Richard. A Community Shakespeare Company Edition of the TWO GENTLEMEN of VERONA. 2007. 80p. (J). per. 10.95 *(978-0-595-45825-7(4))* iUniverse, Inc.
Carthew, Mark. Hairy Toe. Lindsey, Cath, illus. 2007. (Collins Big Cat Ser.). (ENG.). 24p. (J). pap. 8.99 *(978-0-00-722867-6(8))* HarperCollins Pubs. Ltd. GBR. Dist: Independent Pubs. Group.
Carthew, Mark & Allen, Pamela. Brown Bread & Honey. Allen, Pamela, illus. 2007. (Collins Big Cat Ser.). (ENG., Illus.). 1p. (J). pap. 7.99 *(978-0-00-722877-5(5))* HarperCollins Pubs. Ltd. GBR. Dist: Independent Pubs. Group.
Carthew, Mark & Rosen, Michael. Kaleidoscope. Denton, Terry, illus. 2007. (Collins Big Cat Ser.). (ENG.). 1p. (J). pap. 8.99 *(978-0-00-722870-6(8))* HarperCollins Pubs. Ltd. GBR. Dist: Independent Pubs. Group.
—There Was an Old Lady Who Swallowed a Fly. James, Ann, illus. 2007. (Collins Big Cat Ser.). (ENG.). 16p. (J). pap. 7.99 *(978-0-00-722872-0(4))* HarperCollins Pubs. Ltd. GBR. Dist: Independent Pubs. Group.
Cerio, Johnathan. The Cathedral. 2003. (YA). 7.99 *(978-0-9679552-8-5(9))* Mushroom Cloud Pr. of Orlando.
Chanko, Pamela. 25 Fun Phonics Plays for Beginning Readers: Engaging, Reproducible Plays That Target & Teach Key Phonics Skills - And Get Kids Eager to Read! 2009. (ENG.). 64p. (gr. k-2). pap. 11.99 *(978-0-545-10339-8(8)*, Teaching Resources) Scholastic, Inc.
Charles, Nancy Linehan. Romeo & Juliet or the Old You-Know-I-Really-Love-You-but-My-Father-Really-Hates-Yo u Blues. 2004. 72p. (YA). pap. 4.50 *(978-1-58342-236-6(6)*, R74) Dramatic Publishing Co.
Charles, Nancy Linehan, adapted by. A Midsummer Night's Dream or the Night They Missed the Forest for the Trees. (Illus.). 78p. (YA). 6.25 *(978-1-58342-092-8(4)*, MD1) Dramatic Publishing Co.
Chesterton, G. K. Magic: A Fantastic Comedy in Three Acts. 2007. 64p. per. 11.99 *(978-1-59547-789-7(6))* NuVision Pubns., LLC.
Children's Theatre Company Staff. Igniting Wonder: Plays for Preschoolers. Brosius, Peter & Adams, Elissa, eds. 2013. (ENG., Illus.). 152p. 48.00 *(978-0-8166-8113-6(9))*; pap. 15.95 *(978-0-8166-8114-3(7))* Univ. of Minnesota Pr.
Child's Play. Getting Ready. Cocoretto, illus. 2016. (Tactile Bks.). (ENG.). 12p. (J). *(978-1-84643-886-8(1))* Child's Play International Ltd.
Chorpenning, Charlotte B. The Indian Captive. (Illus.). (YA). (gr. 6-12). 6.00 *(978-0-87602-139-2(9))* Family Plays.
Christiansen, Diane. Scenes for Teens, by Teens: A collection by Diane Christiansen. 2010. 76p. pap. 10.95 *(978-1-4502-1878-8(4))* iUniverse, Inc.
Christopher, Garrett. Good Masters! Sweet Ladies! A Study Guide. Friedland, Joyce & Kessler, Rikki, eds. 2008. (Novel-Ties Ser.). (Illus.). 41p. pap. 16.95 *(978-0-7675-4257-9(6))* Learning Links Inc.
Clark, Ouida Ouijella. He Planned to Be A Leader: First Drama of Children of the 21st Century. 2006. pap. 25.00 *(978-0-9777289-4-7(3))* Clark Productions Ltd. Inc.
Clark, Phil & Wilde, Oscar. Oscar Wilde: Three Plays for Children. 2008. (ENG.). 128p. (J). pap. 23.95 *(978-1-84002-816-4(5))* Oberon Bks., Ltd. GBR. Dist: Consortium Bk. Sales & Distribution.
Coble, Eric. Cinderella Confidential. 2004. 48p. (YA). pap. 6.50 *(978-1-58342-201-4(3)*, CB5) Dramatic Publishing Co.
—Pecos Bill & the Ghost Stampede. 2003. (Illus.). 48p. (YA). pap. 6.50 *(978-1-58342-202-1(1)*, PA3) Dramatic Publishing Co.
Coble, Eric, adapted by. The Giver. 2010. (ENG.). 64p. pap. 7.50 *(978-1-58342-662-3(0))* Dramatic Publishing Co.
Coburn, Ann. Alex & the Warrior. 2005. (ENG., Illus.). 96p. per. 16.95 *(978-1-84002-502-6(6))* Theatre Communications Group, Inc.
—Alex & the Winter Star. 2009. (ENG.). 96p. (J). pap. 18.95 *(978-1-84002-849-2(1))* Oberon Bks., Ltd. GBR. Dist: Consortium Bk. Sales & Distribution.
Cohen, Frumi. The Magic Flute RELOADED: (play Script) 2006. (YA). pap. 7.00 *(978-0-87602-415-7(0))* Family Plays.
—Try a Little Shakespeare. 2003. (J). pap. 10.00 *(978-0-88734-519-7(0))* Players Pr., Inc.
Coleman, Wim & Perrin, Pat. Follow the Drinking Gourd: Come along the Underground Railroad. Martin, Courtney, illus. 2014. (Setting the Stage for Fluency Ser.). 40p. (gr. 3-5). pap. 8.95 *(978-1-939656-10-0(9))* Red Chair Pr.
—La Llorona: Retelling a Mexican Legend. Weber Feeney, Siri, illus. 2014. (Setting the Stage for Fluency Ser.). 40p. (gr. 3-5). pap. 8.95 *(978-1-939656-13-1(3))* Red Chair Pr.
—My Sprig of Lilac: Remembering Abraham Lincoln. Catalano, Dominic, illus. 2014. (Setting the Stage for Fluency Ser.). (ENG.). 40p. (gr. 3-5). lib. bdg. 27.93 *(978-1-939656-54-4(0))* Red Chair Pr.
—Runaway Train: Saved by Belle of the Mines & Mountains. Renaud, Joanne, illus. 2015. (Setting the Stage for Fluency Ser.). (ENG.). 40p. (gr. 3-5). lib. bdg. 27.93 *(978-1-939656-71-1(0))* Red Chair Pr.
—Sequoyah & His Talking Leaves: A Play about the Cherokee Syllabary. Weber Feeney, Siri, illus. 2014. (Setting the Stage for Fluency Ser.). 40p. (gr. 3-5). pap. 8.95 *(978-1-939656-35-3(4))* Red Chair Pr.
—A Slave's Education in Courage: The Life of Frederick Douglass. Ward, Damian, illus. 2014. (Setting the Stage for Fluency Ser.). 40p. (gr. 3-5). pap. 8.95 *(978-1-939656-38-4(9))* Red Chair Pr.
—Steam! Taming the River Monster. Todd, Sue, illus. 2015. (Setting the Stage for Fluency Ser.). (ENG.). 40p. (gr. 3-5). lib. bdg. 27.93 *(978-1-939656-74-2(5))* Red Chair Pr.
Collette, Paul & Wright, Robert. Huddles: Playscript. 2003. (Musicals for Young Audiences Ser.). 28p. (Orig.). (YA). (gr. 3-12). pap. 7.00 *(978-0-88734-512-8(3))* Players Pr., Inc.
Conner, Daniel. The Tempest, 1 vol. Martin, Cynthia, illus. 2008. (Graphic Shakespeare Ser.). (ENG.). 48p. (gr. 5-10). 29.93 *(978-1-60270-194-6(6)*, Graphic Planet- Fiction) ABDO Publishing Co.
Cook, Christopher. Washington Irving's the Legend of Sleepy Hollow. 2008. 158p. 23.00 *(978-1-4259-3427-9(7))* AuthorHouse.
—Washington Irving's The Legend of Sleepy Hollow: A Play in Two Acts. 2008. 158p. pap. 12.00 *(978-1-4259-3428-6(5))* AuthorHouse.
Cooper, John. Putting on Your Pantos. 2012. (Illus.). 96p. 17.00 *(978-1-78035-412-5(6)*, Fastprint Publishing) Upfront Publishing Ltd. GBR. Dist: Printondemand-worldwide.com.
Cosgrove, Stephen & Higgins, Kitty. The el juicio del pastelero & Tasty Tort Trial. 2005. spiral bd. 76.00 *(978-1-4108-5793-4(X))* Benchmark Education Co.
—Semillas de Estrellamelón Star-Melon Seeds. 2005. spiral bd. 76.00 *(978-1-4108-5791-0(3))* Benchmark Education Co.
—Star-Melon Seeds. 2004. (Reader's Theater Ser.). (J). pap. *(978-1-4108-1139-4(5))* Benchmark Education Co.
Craddock, Chris. Naked at School: Three Plays for Teens. 2005. (Prairie Plays Ser.). (ENG., Illus.). 162p. pap. 12.95 *(978-1-896300-46-7(4))* NeWest Pubs., Ltd. CAN. Dist: Strauss Consultants.
Crawley, Brian. Halloween Math. Beckes, Shirley, illus. 2004. (Reader's Theater Ser.). (J). pap. *(978-1-4108-2300-7(8)*, A23008) Benchmark Education Co.
Croft, Steven. Othello. Beal, Duncan & Jurksaitis, Dinah, eds. 2004. (Nelson Thornes Shakespeare Ser.). (ENG., Illus.). 208p. (YA). pap. 14.95 *(978-0-7487-8601-5(5))* Nelson Thornes Ltd. GBR. Dist: Trans-Atlantic Pubns., Inc.
Crouch, Tim. I, Cinna (the Poet) 2013. (ENG., Illus.). 96p. pap. 16.95 *(978-1-84943-403-4(4))* Oberon Bks., Ltd. GBR. Dist: Consortium Bk. Sales & Distribution.
—I, Shakespeare. 2012. (ENG.). 128p. pap. 22.95 *(978-1-84943-126-2(4))* Oberon Bks., Ltd. GBR. Dist: Consortium Bk. Sales & Distribution.
Crozier, Eric. Let's Make an Opera! - an Entertainment for Young People in Three Acts. 2008. 100p. pap. 26.45 *(978-1-4437-0249-2(8))* Audubon Pr. & Christian Bk. Service.
Cruz Gonzalez, Jose. Thaddeus & Tila (A Crane & Frog Tale) 2006. pap. 6.50 *(978-1-58342-352-3(4))* Dramatic Publishing Co.
Cudney, Chriss. The Brothers Are Here! Preschool Years. 2011. 60p. 24.99 *(978-1-4628-5275-8(0))*; pap. 15.99 *(978-1-4628-5274-1(2))* Xlibris Corp.
Dabrowski, Kristen. My First Scene Book: 51 One-Minute Scenes about Etiquette. 2009. (My First Acting Ser.). 288p. (J). (gr. k-4). pap. *(978-1-57525-603-0(7))* Smith & Kraus Pubs., Inc.
Dahl, Roald. The BFG. Walmsley, Jane, illus. 2007. (ENG.). 128p. (J). (gr. 3-7). 5.99 *(978-0-14-240792-9(5)*, Puffin Books) Penguin Young Readers Group.

PQR

—The BFG. Walmsley, Jane, illus. 2008. 119p. 16.00 *(978-0-7569-8346-6(0))* Perfection Learning Corp.

—Charlie & the Chocolate Factory: A Play. 2007. (ENG., Illus.). 96p. (J). (gr. 3-7). 6.99 *(978-0-14-240790-5(9)*, Puffin Books) Penguin Young Readers Group.

—James & the Giant Peach: A Play. 2007. (ENG., Illus.). 96p. (J). (gr. 3-7). 5.99 *(978-0-14-240791-2(7)*, Puffin Books) Penguin Young Readers Group.

Dahl, Roald & Wood, David. The BFG. 2010. (Illus.). 46p. pap. *(978-0-573-05094-7(5))* French, Samuel Ltd.

—The Twits: Stage Adaptation. 2015. 45p. *(978-0-573-05125-8(9))* French, Samuel Ltd.

David, Peter, et al. Cyrano de Bergerac: A Heroic Comedy in Five Acts. (Classics Illustrated Ser.). (Illus.). 52p. (YA). pap. 4.95 *(978-1-57209-019-4(7))* Classics International Entertainment, Inc.

Davis, Buddy, et al. Buddy Davis' Cool Critters of the Ice Age. 2015. (ENG., Illus.). 60p. (J). 13.99 *(978-0-89051-858-8(0))* Master Bks.

DeFerie, Steph. After the Rain King. 2003. 101p. *(978-0-87440-197-4(6))* Baker's Plays.

Deferie, Steph. Ghost Rider: The Final Journey on the Underground Railroad. 2008. 60p. mass mkt. 6.50 *(978-0-87440-181-3(X))* Baker's Plays.

Desmarattes, J. Lyonel. Lakòl Medam Yo. 2004. Orig. Title: L' Ecole des Femmes. (CRP.). 80p. (YA). per. 15.00 *(978-1-58432-170-5(9))* Educa Vision Inc.

Desmon, Jeremy. Cyrano de BurgerShack: A Pop Musical. 2014. 90p. (J). pap. 9.99 *(978-1-62384-479-0(7))* Playscripts, Inc.

Diaz, Enrique Perez. Letters from Alain. 2008. (ENG., Illus.). 130p. pap. 16.95 *(978-0-9551566-4-9(5))* Theatre Communications Group, Inc.

Dirksing, Donna. First Stage: A Collection of Musical Plays for Children's First Performances Arranged with Orff Instruments for Grades 1-3. 2006. 24.95 *(978-0-89328-020-8(8))* Heritage Music Pr.

Donaldson, Julia. Bombs & Blackberries: A World War Two Play. Dupasquier, Philippe, illus. 48p. (YA). *(978-0-7502-4124-3(1)*, Wayland) Hachette Children's Group.

—Play Time: A Selection of Plays by the Best Selling Author of the Gruffalo. unabr. ed. 2013. (ENG., Illus.). 240p. (J). (gr. k-2). pap. 9.99 *(978-1-4472-3159-2(7))* Pan Macmillan GBR. Dist: Independent Pubs. Group.

Donnelly, Rebecca. How to Stage a Catastrophe. 2017. (Middle-Grade Novels Ser.). (ENG.). 256p. (gr. 4-7). lib. bdg. 26.65 *(978-1-4965-4053-9(0))* Stone Arch Bks.

Doolittle, Joyce, ed. Playhouse: Six Fantasy Plays for Children, 1 vol. 2003. (Drama Ser.). (ENG., Illus.). 208p. (J). (gr. 6-12). pap. 9.95 *(978-0-88995-028-3(8))* Red Deer Pr. CAN. Dist: Ingram Publisher Services.

Doyle, Alfreda C. Alfreda's Reader's Theatre: Comedy Club. Date not set. (Illus.). (J). spiral bd. 8.95 *(978-1-56820-362-1(4))* Story Time Stories That Rhyme.

—Alfreda's Reader's Theatre: Dialogues. Date not set. (Illus.). (J). spiral bd. 10.95 *(978-1-56820-361-4(6))* Story Time Stories That Rhyme.

—Alfreda's Reader's Theatre: Public Transportation. Date not set. (Illus.). (J). spiral bd. 8.95 *(978-1-56820-360-7(8))* Story Time Stories That Rhyme.

—The Missing Sugar Beet. Date not set. (Illus.). (J). (gr. 5-8). spiral bd. 8.95 *(978-1-56820-355-3(1))* Story Time Stories That Rhyme.

Duffield, Neil. Plays for Youth Theatres & Large Casts. Duffield, Neil, ed. 2010. (ENG., Illus.). 232p. (J). pap. 28.95 *(978-1-906582-06-7(8))* Aurora Metro Pubns. Ltd. GBR. Dist: Consortium Bk. Sales & Distribution.

Duffield, Neil, et al. The Jungle Book, Bk. 1. 2012. (ENG., Illus.). 88p. (J). (gr. k). pap. 20.95 *(978-1-906582-26-5(2))* Aurora Metro Pubns. Ltd. GBR. Dist: Consortium Bk. Sales & Distribution.

Dugan, Michael. Life's a Riot! 21p. (J). (gr. 4-6). pap. *(978-1-875739-30-1(0))* Wizard Bks.

Dunn, Joeming. Macbeth, 1 vol. Hutchinson, David, illus. 2008. (Graphic Shakespeare Ser.). (ENG.). 48p. (gr. 5-10). 29.93 *(978-1-60270-190-8(3)*, Graphic Planet- Fiction) ABDO Publishing Co.

—Romeo & Juliet, 1 vol. Espinosa, Rod, illus. 2008. (Graphic Shakespeare Ser.). (ENG.). 48p. (gr. 5-10). 29.93 *(978-1-60270-193-9(8)*, Graphic Planet- Fiction) ABDO Publishing Co.

Dunn, Rebecca. Hamlet, 1 vol. Dunn, Ben, illus. 2008. (Graphic Shakespeare Ser.). (ENG.). 48p. (gr. 5-10). 29.93 *(978-1-60270-188-5(1)*, Graphic Planet- Fiction) ABDO Publishing Co.

Dyer, Kevin. Monster under the Bed: A Play for Children. 2010. (ENG., Illus.). 90p. (J). pap. 20.95 *(978-1-906582-07-4(6))* Aurora Metro Pubns. Ltd. GBR. Dist: Consortium Bk. Sales & Distribution.

El-Bushra, Suhayla, et al. National Theatre Connections 2017: Fomo; Extremism; Musical Differences; Status Update; the School Film; the Monstrum; the Snow Dragons; Three; #YOLO; Zero for the Young Dudes! 2017. (ENG.). 680p. pap. 26.95 ***(978-1-350-03359-7(6)***, 9781350033597, Bloomsbury Methuen Drama) Bloomsbury Publishing Plc GBR. Dist: Macmillan.

Elish, Dan, et al. 13: The Complete Book & Lyrics of the Broadway Musical the Applause Libretto Library. 2011. (ENG.). 104p. pap. 16.99 *(978-1-55783-777-6(5)*, 1557837775, Applause Theatre & Cinema) Leonard, Hal Corp.

Elzbieta. Mimi's Scary Theater: A Play in Nine Scenes for Seven Characters & an Egg. Elzbieta & Hawcock, David, illus. 2004. 20p. (J). (gr. -1-3). reprint ed. 15.00 *(978-0-7567-8299-3(6))* DIANE Publishing Co.

Euripides & Burian, Peter. Helen. 2007. (Aris & Phillips Classical Texts). (GEC & ENG.). 292p. (C). 99.00 *(978-0-85668-650-4(6))*; pap. 35.00 *(978-0-85668-651-1(4))* Liverpool Univ. Pr. GBR. Dist: Oxford Univ. Pr., Inc.

Evans, Olive. Secrets of the Forest: Playscript. 2003. (Theater for Young Audiences Ser.). 44p. (J). (gr. 3-12). reprint ed. pap. 6.00 *(978-0-88734-502-9(6))* Players Pr., Inc.

Ewald, Thomas. Christian Reader's Theater. Flint, Russ, illus. 2005. 64p. (J). per. 8.99 *(978-1-59441-077-2(1)*, CD-204004) Carson-Dellosa Publishing, LLC.

Falconer, Ian. Teatro Olivia: Swan Lake; Romeo & Juliet; Turandot. Falconer, Ian, illus. 2004. (Olivia Ser.). (Illus.). 10p. (J). 19.95 *(978-0-689-87816-9(8))* Simon & Schuster, Inc.

Fenichel Asher, Sandra. Too Many Frogs! 2007. pap. 6.95 *(978-1-58342-404-9(0))* Dramatic Publishing Co.

Figley, Marthy Rhodes. Clara Morgan & the Oregon Trail Journey. Orback, Craig, illus. 2011. (History Speaks: Picture Books Plus Reader's Theater Ser.). (ENG.). 48p. (gr. 2-4). 27.93 *(978-0-7613-5878-7(1)*, Millbrook Pr.) Lerner Publishing Group.

Figley, Marty Rhodes. John Greenwood's Journey to Bunker Hill. Orback, Craig, illus. 2010. (History Speaks: Picture Books Plus Reader's Theater Ser.). (ENG.). 48p. (gr. 2-4). pap. 9.95 *(978-0-7613-6134-3(0))*; lib. bdg. 27.93 *(978-1-58013-673-0(7)*, Millbrook Pr.) Lerner Publishing Group.

—President Lincoln, Willie Kettles, & the Telegraph Machine. Riley, David, illus. 2010. (History Speaks: Picture Books Plus Reader's Theater Ser.). (ENG.). 48p. (gr. 2-4). pap. 9.95 *(978-0-7613-6131-2(6))* Lerner Publishing Group.

Flagg, Phyllis. Five Fun Plays for Christian Kids: Including Two Christmas Plays. 2012. 64p. pap. 13.95 *(978-1-4497-3151-9(1)*, WestBow Pr.) Author Solutions, Inc.

Fleischman, Paul. Zap: A Play. (ENG.). 96p. (YA). (gr. 9). 2015. pap. 7.99 *(978-0-7636-8013-8(3))* 2005. 16.99 *(978-0-7636-2774-4(7))* Candlewick Pr.

—Zap: A Play. 2003. 160p. (YA). (gr. 7-11). 16.95 *(978-0-8126-2687-2(7))* Cricket Bks.

Fogg, Scott. Power Skits for Youth & Young Adults: 25 Faith-Awakening, Disciple-Making Drama Presentations. 2006. 175p. pap. *(978-0-8280-1883-8(9))* Review & Herald Publishing Assn.

Foon, Dennis. Kindness. 2010. (ENG.). 64p. pap. 14.95 *(978-0-88754-857-4(1))* Playwrights Canada Pr. CAN. Dist: Consortium Bk. Sales & Distribution.

—Rick: The Rick Hansen Story. 2012. (ENG.). 80p. pap. 16.95 *(978-1-77091-037-9(9))* Playwrights Canada Pr. CAN. Dist: Consortium Bk. Sales & Distribution.

—War. 2008. (ENG.). 96p. pap. 13.95 *(978-0-88754-826-0(1))* Playwrights Canada Pr. CAN. Dist: Consortium Bk. Sales & Distribution.

France, Anatole. The Man Who Married a Dumb Wife. Landes, William-Alan, ed. 2003. 28p. (YA). (gr. 8-12). pap. 7.00 *(978-0-88734-850-1(5))* Players Pr., Inc.

Francis, Claudette. Jesus Is Risen: An Easter Play for Children. 2009. 52p. pap. 11.99 *(978-1-4389-8103-1(1))* AuthorHouse.

Frankie Dolan, Ragtime Orphan. 2nd ed. 2006. (YA). pap. *(978-1-932663-13-6(4))* History Compass, LLC.

Frazier, Bessie. Decisions: A Teenage Play. 2009. 64p. pap. 10.49 *(978-1-4490-4014-7(4))* AuthorHouse.

Fredericks, Anthony D. & Bongaman. African Legends, Myths, & Folktales for Readers Theatre, 1 vol. 2008. (Readers Theatre Ser.). (Illus.). 192p. (C). pap. 40.00 *(978-1-59158-633-3(X)*, TIP8633, Libraries Unlimited) ABC-CLIO, LLC.

Friedman, Rosalind. Hannukah Holiday. Friedman, Rosalind, . 2008. (ENG.). 16p. mass mkt. 5.50 *(978-0-87440-303-9(0))* Baker's Plays.

Fuerst, Jeffrey B. Baa Baa Black Sheep Sells Her Wool. 2008. (Reader's Theater Nursery Rhymes & Songs Ser.). (Illus.). 48p. (J). (gr. k-1). pap. *(978-1-60437-965-5(0))* Benchmark Education Co.

—Bear Goes over the Mountain. 2008. (Reader's Theater Nursery Rhymes & Songs Ser.). (Illus.). 48p. (J). (gr. k-1). pap. *(978-1-60437-972-3(3))* Benchmark Education Co.

—Bingo, Come Home! Greenhead, Bill, illus. 2009. (Reader's Theater Nursery Rhymes & Songs Set B Ser.). 48p. (J). pap. *(978-1-60859-151-0(4))* Benchmark Education Co.

—Chuck, Woodchuck, Chuck! Greenhead, Bill, illus. 2009. (Reader's Theater Nursery Rhymes & Songs Set B Ser.). 48p. (J). pap. *(978-1-60859-152-7(2))* Benchmark Education Co.

—Hickory Dickory Dock; or, Go, Mouse, Go! 2008. (Reader's Theater Nursery Rhymes & Songs Ser.). (Illus.). 48p. (J). (gr. k-1). pap. *(978-1-60437-960-0(X))* Benchmark Education Co.

—Hot Cross Buns for Everyone. Abbott, Jason, illus. 2009. (Reader's Theater Nursery Rhymes & Songs Set B Ser.). 48p. (J). pap. *(978-1-60859-153-4(0))* Benchmark Education Co.

—Hunting We Will Go. 2008. (Reader's Theater Nursery Rhymes & Songs Ser.). (Illus.). 48p. (J). (gr. k-1). pap. *(978-1-60437-974-7(X))* Benchmark Education Co.

—Itsy Bitsy Spider Climbs Again. 2008. (Reader's Theater Nursery Rhymes & Songs Ser.). (Illus.). 48p. (J). (gr. k-1). pap. *(978-1-60437-968-6(5))* Benchmark Education Co.

—Jack B. Nimble Jumps. Colby, Garry, illus. 2009. (Reader's Theater Nursery Rhymes & Songs Set B Ser.). 48p. (J). pap. *(978-1-60859-154-1(9))* Benchmark Education Co.

—Lazy Mary Gets Up. Kelley, Gerald, illus. 2009. (Reader's Theater Nursery Rhymes & Songs Set B Ser.). 48p. (J). pap. *(978-1-60859-156-5(5))* Benchmark Education Co.

—Lunch with Little Miss Muffet. 2008. (Reader's Theater Nursery Rhymes & Songs Ser.). (Illus.). 48p. (J). (gr. k-1). pap. *(978-1-60437-961-7(8))* Benchmark Education Co.

—Miss Mary Mack & the Jumping Elephants. Workman, Terry, illus. 2009. (Reader's Theater Nursery Rhymes & Songs Set B Ser.). 48p. (J). pap. *(978-1-60859-161-9(1))* Benchmark Education Co.

—The Old Gray Mare IS What She Used to Be. Currant, Gary, illus. 2009. (Reader's Theater Nursery Rhymes & Songs Set B Ser.). 48p. (J). pap. *(978-1-60859-162-6(X))* Benchmark Education Co.

—Old MacDonald. Greenhead, Bill, illus. 2010. (Rising Readers Ser.). (J). 3.49 *(978-1-60719-694-5(8))* Newmark Learning LLC.

—Old MacDonald's Noisy Farm. 2008. (Reader's Theater Nursery Rhymes & Songs Ser.). (Illus.). (J). (gr. k-1). pap. *(978-1-60437-967-9(7))* Benchmark Education Co.

—Party Time with Old King Cole. 2008. (Reader's Theater Nursery Rhymes & Songs Ser.). (Illus.). 48p. (J). (gr. k-1). pap. *(978-1-60437-962-4(6))* Benchmark Education Co.

—Peter Pumpkin Eater Loses His Appetite. Greenhead, Bill, illus. 2009. (Reader's Theater Nursery Rhymes & Songs Set B Ser.). 48p. (J). pap. *(978-1-60859-164-0(6))* Benchmark Education Co.

—Pies for Simple Simon. Ledger, Bill, illus. 2009. (Reader's Theater Nursery Rhymes & Songs Set B Ser.). 48p. (J). pap. *(978-1-60859-165-7(4))* Benchmark Education Co.

—Run, Three Blind Mice! Walker, Sholto, illus. 2009. (Reader's Theater Nursery Rhymes & Songs Set B Ser.). 48p. (J). pap. *(978-1-60859-168-8(9))* Benchmark Education Co.

—Sing a Song of Sixpence, the King's Special Pie. 2008. (Reader's Theater Nursery Rhymes & Songs Ser.). (Illus.). 48p. (J). (gr. k-1). pap. *(978-1-60437-979-2(0))* Benchmark Education Co.

—Wishing on a Bright Star. 2008. (Reader's Theater Nursery Rhymes & Songs Ser.). (Illus.). 48p. (J). (gr. k-1). pap. *(978-1-60437-971-6(5))* Benchmark Education Co.

—The Woman Who Lived in a Shoe. Greenhead, Bill, illus. 2009. (Reader's Theater Nursery Rhymes & Songs Set B Ser.). 48p. (J). pap. *(978-1-60859-172-5(7))* Benchmark Education Co.

Gabridge, Pat. Den of Iniquity: A Ten-Minute Comedy Duet. 2003. 16p. (YA). pap. 4.50 *(978-1-932404-19-7(8)*, 155A) Brooklyn Pubs.

—Flying the Friendly Skies: A Ten-Minute Dramatic Duet. 2003. 16p. (YA). pap. 4.50 *(978-1-932404-20-3(1)*, 156A) Brooklyn Pubs.

—The Invisible Husband: A Ten-Minute Dramatic Duet. 2003. 16p. (YA). pap. 4.50 *(978-1-931805-99-5(7)*, 151A) Brooklyn Pubs.

—It's a Girl! A Ten-Minute Comedy Duet. 2003. (YA). pap. 4.50 *(978-1-931805-95-7(4)*, 147A) Brooklyn Pubs.

—Measuring Matthew: A Ten-Minute Comedy Duet. 2003. (YA). pap. 4.50 *(978-1-931805-92-6(X)*, 144A) Brooklyn Pubs.

—Phoenix Funeral Draft 3: A Ten-Minute Comedy Duet. 2003. 16p. (YA). pap. 4.50 *(978-1-931805-98-8(9)*, 150A) Brooklyn Pubs.

Gabridge, Patrick. The Sky Is Falling: A One-Act Comedy Play. 2003. (YA). pap. 4.50 *(978-1-932404-58-6(9)*, 756) Brooklyn Pubs.

Gallina, Jill, et al. Sing Me a Story: Classic Stories Throughout Time Come to Life in Song & Rhyme. 2011. (ENG.). 76p. pap. 49.99 incl. audio compact disk *(978-1-4234-9972-5(7)*, 1423499727) Shawnee Pr., Inc.

Gardiner, Meghan, et al. The Green Thumb Theatre Anthology. Green Thumb Theatre Staff, ed. 2012. (ENG.). 240p. (gr. 4). pap. 29.95 *(978-1-77091-024-9(7))* Playwrights Canada Pr. CAN. Dist: Consortium Bk. Sales & Distribution.

Giannakeff, Dianne D., adapted by. The Young Actor's Bible: Stories from the Bible. 2004. (J). spiral bd. 39.95 *(978-0-9762297-0-4(6))* Lucia Pubs.

Gibson, Rex & Shakespeare, William. As You Like It. Andrews, Richard, ed. 2nd ed. 2009. (Cambridge School Shakespeare Ser.). (ENG., Illus.). 208p. pap. 13.95 *(978-0-521-73437-0(1))* Cambridge Univ. Pr.

Gill, Jim. A Soup Opera. Moose, David, illus. 2009. (ENG.). 32p. (J). lib. bdg. *(978-0-9815721-0-9(3))* Gill, Jim Music.

Gingerich, Neeltje. Mini-Musicals for Christmas. 2011. 32p. (J). pap. 7.00 *(978-0-88734-998-0(6))* Players Pr., Inc.

Glavich, Mary Kathleen. Gospel Theater for the Whole Community: 92 Plays for Education & Worship. 2006. 215p. per. 29.95 *(978-1-58595-563-3(9))* Twenty-Third Pubns./Bayard.

Glennon, William. The Trial of the Arkansas Bear. 2003. 52p. (YA). pap. 6.25 *(978-1-58342-158-1(0)*, TE5) Dramatic Publishing Co.

Goldberg, Moses. Sleeping Beauty (Dornroschen) (Play Script) 2006. (J). pap. 6.00 *(978-0-87602-416-4(9))* Family Plays.

Golden, Joseph. Johnny Moonbeam & the Silver Arrow: An Adventure for Young People in Narration & Mime. 2011. 42p. 35.95 *(978-1-258-09981-7(0))* Literary Licensing, LLC.

Goldenthal, Jolene. The Beautiful Truth: A One-Act Comedy Play. 2003. (YA). pap. 4.50 *(978-1-932404-64-7(3)*, 762) Brooklyn Pubs.

Goode, Jeff. PRINCESS GRAY & the BLACK & WHITE KNIGHT. 2008. 39p. per. *(978-0-87440-281-0(6))* Baker's Plays.

—Rumpelstiltskin. 2009. 48p. mass mkt. 9.95 *(978-0-87440-314-5(6))* Baker's Plays.

Goodwin, Debbie Salter. Quick Start Drama for Kids: No Rehearsal Bible Skits for Classroom or Performance. 2005. (ENG.). 40p. pap. 19.99 *(978-0-8341-7410-8(3)*, MP-858) Lillenas Publishing Co.

Goodwin, Vincent. Othello, 1 vol. Allen, Chris, illus. 2008. (Graphic Shakespeare Ser.). (ENG.). 48p. (gr. 5-10). 29.93 *(978-1-60270-192-2(X)*, Graphic Planet- Fiction) ABDO Publishing Co.

Goodwin, Vincent & Shakespeare, William. Twelfth Night, 1 vol. Martin, Cynthia, illus. 2008. (Graphic Shakespeare Ser.). (ENG.). 48p. (gr. 5-10). 29.93 *(978-1-60270-195-3(4)*, Graphic Planet- Fiction) ABDO Publishing Co.

Gordon, Mick. The Ride of Your Life. 2010. (ENG.). 96p. (gr. k). pap. 18.95 *(978-1-84002-958-1(7))* Oberon Bks., Ltd. GBR. Dist: Consortium Bk. Sales & Distribution.

Gorky, Maxim. The Lower Depths. Landes, William-Alan, ed. Covan, Jennie, tr. from RUS. unabr. ed. 2003. (Players Press Classic Plays Ser.). 64p. (YA). (gr. 4-12). pap. 7.50 *(978-0-88734-815-0(7))* Players Pr., Inc.

Gourlay, Catherine. Family Matters: Plays about Family Changes. 2010. (Get into Character Ser.). (ENG., Illus.). 32p. (J). (gr. 3-6). pap. *(978-0-7787-7375-7(2))*; lib. bdg. *(978-0-7787-7361-0(2))* Crabtree Publishing Co.

—Flashpoints! Plays about Controlling Anger. 2010. (Get into Character Ser.). (ENG., Illus.). 32p. (J). (gr. 3-6). pap. *(978-0-7787-7376-4(0))*; lib. bdg. *(978-0-7787-7362-7(0))* Crabtree Publishing Co.

—Friend or Foe? Plays about Bullying. 2010. (Get into Character Ser.). (ENG., Illus.). 32p. (J). (gr. 3-6). pap. *(978-0-7787-7377-1(9))*; lib. bdg. *(978-0-7787-7363-4(9))* Crabtree Publishing Co.

—The Invisible Me: Plays about Self-Image. 2010. (Get into Character Ser.). (ENG., Illus.). 32p. (J). (gr. 3-6). pap. *(978-0-7787-7379-5(5))*; lib. bdg. *(978-0-7787-7365-8(5))* Crabtree Publishing Co.

—What's the Difference? Plays about Tolerance. 2010. (Get into Character Ser.). (ENG., Illus.). 32p. (J). (gr. 3-6). pap. *(978-0-7787-7378-8(7))*; lib. bdg. *(978-0-7787-7364-1(7))* Crabtree Publishing Co.

—Where Do I Belong? Plays about Fitting In. 2010. (Get into Character Ser.). (ENG., Illus.). 32p. (J). (gr. 3-6). pap. *(978-0-7787-7380-1(9))*; lib. bdg. *(978-0-7787-7366-5(3))* Crabtree Publishing Co.

Graham, Joseph. Who's Gonna Save Me? It's Time to Tell Your Secrets. 2005. 126p. (YA). pap. 14.00 *(978-0-9767778-0-9(0)*, 704-724-1683) Alpha & Omega Publishing.

Gravois, Michael. Aesop's Fable-Ous Barnyard Bash. 2014. 63p. (J). pap. 9.95 *(978-1-58342-975-4(1))* Dramatic Publishing Co.

Greenidge, Kirsten. Familiar. 2004. (YA). pap. 6.50 *(978-1-58342-175-8(0)*, F79) Dramatic Publishing Co.

Gregg, Stephen. S. P. A. R. a play / 2003. 26p. (YA). pap. 4.25 *(978-1-58342-157-4(2)*, SH5) Dramatic Publishing Co.

Greig, Noel, adapted by. The Tin Soldier: And Other Plays for Children. 2011. (ENG., Illus.). 112p. (J). (gr. 1). pap. 22.95 *(978-1-906582-19-7(X))* Aurora Metro Pubns. Ltd. GBR. Dist: Consortium Bk. Sales & Distribution.

Grose, Carl. Hansel & Gretel. 2011. (ENG.). 96p. (J). (gr. 2). pap. 18.95 *(978-1-84943-057-9(8))* Oberon Bks., Ltd. GBR. Dist: Consortium Bk. Sales & Distribution.

Group/McGraw-Hill, Wright. Queen of the Trail Play 8: Decodable Plays, 6 vols. (Fast Track Reading Ser.). 24p. (gr. 4-8). 40.95 *(978-0-322-05999-3(2))* Wright Group/McGraw-Hill.

—Saws Don't Pounce Play 9: Decodable Plays, 6 vols. (Fast Track Reading Ser.). 24p. (gr. 4-8). 40.95 *(978-0-322-06001-2(X))* Wright Group/McGraw-Hill.

Groves. Six Silly Plays. Date not set. (Illus.). 58p. pap. 65.00 *(978-0-582-24379-8(3))* Addison-Wesley Longman, Ltd. GBR. Dist: Trans-Atlantic Pubns., Inc.

Grudzina, Rebecca. A Baby Bumblebee for Mommy. Boyer, Lyn, illus. 2009. (Reader's Theater Nursery Rhymes & Songs Set B Ser.). 48p. (J). pap. *(978-1-60859-149-7(2))* Benchmark Education Co.

—Pease Porridge, Please! Harrington, David, illus. 2009. (Reader's Theater Nursery Rhymes & Songs Set B Ser.). 48p. (J). pap. *(978-1-60859-163-3(8))* Benchmark Education Co.

—Red Roses, Blue Violets, And... ? Ledger, Bill, illus. 2009. (Reader's Theater Nursery Rhymes & Songs Set B Ser.). 48p. (J). pap. *(978-1-60859-167-1(0))* Benchmark Education Co.

Guderjahn, Ernie L. A Children's Trilogy: Ali's Flying Rug, the Shadow Workers, & the Magic Cricket (Playscript) 2003. (Theater for Young Audiences Ser.). 32p. (Orig.). (J). (gr. 3-18). pap. 6.00 *(978-0-88734-504-3(2))* Players Pr., Inc.

Haddon, Mark. The Curious Incident of the Dog in the Night-Time. 2013. (Critical Scripts Ser.). (ENG., Illus.). 144p. (J). pap. 14.95 *(978-1-4081-8521-6(0)*, 9781408185216, A&C Black) Bloomsbury Publishing Plc GBR. Dist: Macmillan.

Haehnel, Alan. The Blender: A One-Act Dark Comedy Play. 2003. (YA). pap. 4.50 *(978-1-932404-57-9(0)*, 755) Brooklyn Pubs.

—The Twisting-Turning Death Machine: Ten-Minute Comedy Duet. 2003. (YA). pap. 9.00 *(978-1-932404-02-9(3)*, 139A) Brooklyn Pubs.

—What the Doctor Ordered: Ten-Minute Comedy Duet. 2003. (YA). pap. 9.00 *(978-1-932404-00-5(7)*, 137A) Brooklyn Pubs.

Halligan, Terry. Funny Skits & Sketches. Behr, Joyce, illus. unabr. ed. 2003. 128p. (YA). (gr. 4-12). pap. 15.00 *(978-0-88734-688-0(X))* Players Pr., Inc.

Harder, Eleanor. What'd Ya Do Today, Billy Joe? 2003. 40p. (YA). pap. 4.50 *(978-1-58342-188-8(2)*, W98) Dramatic Publishing Co.

Harris, Brooke. Baby Gets a Cake. Beckstrand, Jared, illus. 2009. (Reader's Theater Nursery Rhymes & Songs Set B Ser.). 48p. (J). pap. *(978-1-60859-150-3(6))* Benchmark Education Co.

—Brother John, Wake Up! 2008. (Reader's Theater Nursery Rhymes & Songs Ser.). (Illus.). 48p. (J). (gr. k-1). pap. *(978-1-60437-973-0(1))* Benchmark Education Co.

—Jack & Jill Play on the Hill. 2008. (Reader's Theater Nursery Rhymes & Songs Ser.). (Illus.). 48p. (J). (gr. k-1). pap. *(978-1-60437-964-8(2))* Benchmark Education Co.

—Little Boy Blue, Where are You? 2008. (Reader's Theater Nursery Rhymes & Songs Ser.). (Illus.). 48p. (J). (gr. k-1). pap. *(978-1-60437-976-1(6))* Benchmark Education Co.

—London Bridge Has Fallen Down. Boyer, Lyn, illus. 2009. (Reader's Theater Nursery Rhymes & Songs Set B Ser.). 48p. (J). pap. *(978-1-60859-159-6(X))* Benchmark Education Co.

—Mary's Garden: How Does it Grow? Xin, Xiao, illus. 2009. (Reader's Theater Nursery Rhymes & Songs Set B Ser.). 48p. (J). pap. *(978-1-60859-160-2(3))* Benchmark Education Co.

—The Purple Cow. Hohnstadt, Cedric, illus. 2009. (Reader's Theater Nursery Rhymes & Songs Set B Ser.). 48p. (J). pap. *(978-1-60859-166-4(2))* Benchmark Education Co.

—This Little Pig, That Little Pig. 2008. (Reader's Theater Nursery Rhymes & Songs Ser.). (Illus.). 48p. (J). (gr. k-1). pap. *(978-1-60437-969-3(3))* Benchmark Education Co.

—The Twinkling Stars. Harrington, David, illus. 2009. (Reader's Theater Nursery Rhymes & Songs Set B Ser.). 48p. (J). pap. *(978-1-60859-170-1(0))* Benchmark Education Co.

—Where Has My Little Dog Gone? 2008. (Reader's Theater Nursery Rhymes & Songs Ser.). (Illus.). 48p. (J). (gr. k-1). pap. *(978-1-60437-975-4(8))* Benchmark Education Co.

—Working on the Railroad. 2008. (Reader's Theater Nursery Rhymes & Songs Ser.). (Illus.). 48p. (J). (gr. k-1). pap. *(978-1-60437-981-5(2))* Benchmark Education Co.

Harris, Valerie. The Saga of Henry Box Brown: A Play for Black History Month. 2004. (Illus.). 35p. spiral bd. 12.95 *(978-0-9772126-0-6(2))* BPT Media.

Harrison, Jordan & Gray, Richard. Hans Christian Anderson's the Flea & the Professor. 2012. (J). pap. 8.95 *(978-0-573-70095-8(8))* French, Samuel Inc.

Haupt, Wolfgang & Bland, Janice. Tales of the Little Hedgehogs: Fairy Plays. Mouraviova, Yulia, illus. 2009. (J). *(978-0-88734-978-2(1))* Players Pr., Inc.

Hendrickson, Clyde. The Altos: A Clyde Hendrickson Joint. 2003. (YA). 7.99 *(978-0-9679552-7-8(0))* Mushroom Cloud Pr. of Orlando.

—Special Places. 2003. (AFR.). 20p. (YA). 8.50 *(978-0-9679552-5-4(4))* Mushroom Cloud Pr. of Orlando.

—Squirrel. 2003. (YA). 11.00 (978-0-9679552-6-1(2)) Mushroom Cloud Pr. of Orlando.

Henry, Lenworth. Gilbert the Mighty Hurricane: A Jamaican Experience. 2010. 48p. pap. 9.95 (978-0-595-48923-7(0)) iUniverse, Inc.

Herweck, Diana. The Indestructible Pele (Science) 2015. (Building Fluency Through Reader's Theater Ser.). (Illus.). 24p. (gr. 1-2). 6.99 (978-1-4938-1516-6(4)) Teacher Created Materials, Inc.

Heslep, William. Tower of London. 2003. 23p. (J). pap. 6.00 (978-0-88734-418-3(6)) Players Pr., Inc.

Hezlep, William. Bigfoot! 2004. (Travelers Ser.). 24p. (J). (gr. 3-6). pap. 5.00 (978-0-88734-485-5(2)) Players Pr., Inc.

—Bog Bodies. 2004. (Travelers Ser.). 20p. (J). pap. 5.00 (978-0-88734-467-1(4)) Players Pr., Inc.

—Cayman Duppy: Playscript. 2003. 16p. (J). (gr. 5-18). pap. 5.00 (978-0-88734-403-9(8)) Players Pr., Inc.

—Curse of the Tomb Raiders. 2005. (Travelers Ser.). 32p. (J). pap. 6.00 (978-0-88734-565-4(4)) Players Pr., Inc.

—How Come Christmas? 2003. (Theater for Young Audiences Ser.). 18p. (J). pap. 5.00 (978-0-88734-424-4(0)) Players Pr., Inc.

—Kokopelli's Cave. 2003. (Travelers Ser.). 24p. (J). (gr. k-6). pap. 5.00 (978-0-88734-466-4(6)) Players Pr., Inc.

—Merlin's Cave. 2003. (Theater for Young Audiences Ser.). 55p. (Orig.). (YA). (gr. k-12). pap. 6.00 (978-0-88734-420-6(8)) Players Pr., Inc.

—Nessie: Playscript. 2003. 24p. (J). (gr. 3-12). reprint ed. pap. 6.00 (978-0-88734-401-5(1)) Players Pr., Inc.

—Pharaoh's Dagger: Playscript. 2003. 70p. (Orig.). (J). (gr. 3-12). reprint ed. pap. 6.00 (978-0-88734-404-6(6)) Players Pr., Inc.

—Shipwrecked. Landes, William Alan, ed. unabr. ed. 2003. (Ideal for Teens Ser.). 21p. (J). (gr. 3-8). pap. 5.00 (978-0-88734-484-8(4)) Players Pr., Inc.

—Time Travelers, 16 vols. 2006. (Travelers Ser.). 36p. (J). (gr. 3-6). pap. 6.00 (978-0-88734-573-9(5)) Players Pr., Inc.

—Treasure of the Mayans. 2003. 28p. (Orig.). (J). (gr. 3-8). pap. 6.00 (978-0-88734-405-3(4)) Players Pr., Inc.

Higgins, Frank. The Slave Dancer's Choice. 2003. (Illus.). 40p. (YA). pap. 6.50 (978-1-58342-166-6(1), SH6) Dramatic Publishing Co.

Higgins, Kitty. As the Crow Flies. Leon, Karen, illus. 2004. (Reader's Theater Ser.). (J). pap. (978-1-4108-2304-5(0), A23040) Benchmark Education Co.

—The Three Sisters. Corcoran, Mark, illus. 2004. (Reader's Theater Ser.). (J). pap. (978-1-4108-2312-0(1), A23121) Benchmark Education Co.

Hilderbrandt, Sandra June. Wilbur's Great Adventure. Merrell, Vernon R., illus. 2011. 32p. (J). 19.95 (978-1-59649-587-6(1)) Whispering Pine Pr. International, Inc.

Hoban, Russell. The Mouse & His Child. 2013. (ENG.). 96p. pap. 17.95 (978-1-84943-465-2(4)) Oberon Bks., Ltd. GBR. Dist: Consortium Bk. Sales & Distribution.

Hodge, Bill. Cyril: Tales of a Teenage Cyrano. 31p. (YA). (gr. 7-12). pap. 4.00 (978-1-57514-153-4(1), 1160) Encore Performance Publishing.

Hollindale, Peter & Barrie, J. M. Peter Pan & Other Plays: The Admirable Crichton; Peter Pan; When Wendy Grew up; What Every Woman Knows; Mary Rose. 2008. (Oxford World's Classics Ser.). (ENG.). 384p. pap. 14.95 (978-0-19-953783-9(6)) Oxford Univ. Pr., Inc.

Hoover, Nicolas. The Red Merit Badge of Courage. 2010. (ENG.). 23p. pap. 4.50 (978-0-87440-392-3(8)) Baker's Plays.

Howard, Annabelle. Alex in Numberland. DuFalla, Anita, illus. 2004. (Reader's Theater Ser.). (J). pap. (978-1-4108-2303-8(2), A23032) Benchmark Education Co.

—Battle for the Ballot. Leon, Karen, illus. 2004. (Reader's Theater Ser.). (J). pap. (978-1-4108-2305-2(9), A23059) Benchmark Education Co.

Howard, Jane R. Maria's Loom: An Original Fairy Tale with Music (play Script) 2007. (ENG.). 48p. (J). pap. 7.00 (978-0-87602-417-1(7)) Family Plays.

Hutchins, Laurence. I'm the King of the Castle! And Other Plays for Children. Hutchins, Laurence, illus. 2005. (ENG., Illus.). 107p. per. 16.95 (978-1-84002-486-9(0)) Theatre Communications Group, Inc.

Ibsen, Henrik. A Doll's House - Literary Touchstone Edition. 2005. 88p. (YA). per. 3.99 (978-1-58049-598-1(2), PWH5982) Prestwick Hse., Inc.

In the Mind of the Beholder: A Ten-Minute Dramatic Duet. 2003. (YA). pap. 4.50 (978-1-932404-22-7(8), 158A) Brooklyn Pubs.

Janet & Donald Play 7: Decodable Plays, 6 vols. (Fast Track Reading Ser.). 24p. (gr. 4-8). 40.95 (978-0-322-05998-6(4)) Wright Group/McGraw-Hill.

Jasspon, Ethel Reed. Ritual & Dramatized Folkways. 2006. (Illus.). pap. 24.95 (978-1-4286-6016-8(X)) Kessinger Publishing, LLC.

Jeffries, Katherine. Tim's Head, Shoulders, Knees, & Toes. Price, Nick, illus. 2009. (Reader's Theater Nursery Rhymes & Songs Set B Ser.). 48p. (J). pap. (978-1-60859-169-5(7)) Benchmark Education Co.

Jenkins, Diana R. All Year Long! Funny Readers Theatre for Life's Special Times, 1 vol. 2007. (Illus.). 264p. (C). per. 35.00 (978-1-59158-436-0(1), TIP4361, Libraries Unlimited) ABC-CLIO, LLC.

—Just Deal with It! Funny Readers Theatre for Life's Not-So-Funny Moments, 1 vol. 2004. (Readers Theatre Ser.). (Illus.). 256p. (C). pap. 32.00 (978-1-59158-043-0(9), LU0439, Libraries Unlimited) ABC-CLIO, LLC.

—Spotlight on Saints! A Year of Funny Readers Theater for Today's Catholic Kids. Richards, Virginia Helen, illus. 2009. 180p. (J). (gr. 4-7). pap. 18.95 (978-0-8198-7119-0(2)) Pauline Bks. & Media.

—STALKER MOM & OTHER PLAYS. 2009. 60p. mass mkt. 5.50 (978-0-87440-220-9(4)) Baker's Plays.

Jennings, Coleman A. & Berghammer, Gretta, eds. Theatre for Youth II: More Plays with Mature Themes. 2016. (ENG.). 488p. pap. 29.95 (978-1-4773-1004-5(5)) Univ. of Texas Pr.

John, Rob. The Spaceman. 2014. (ENG., Illus.). 104p. pap. 13.00 (978-1-4085-1977-6(1)) Oxford Univ. Pr., Inc.

Johnson, Judith. Scary Play. 2007. (Collins National Theatre Plays Ser.). (ENG.). 320p. (YA). (gr. 7-10). pap. 13.99 (978-0-00-725489-7(X)) HarperCollins Pubs. Ltd. GBR. Dist: Independent Pubs. Group.

Johnson, Ramona. All Steamed Up. 2009. 36p. pap. 15.49 (978-1-4389-8590-9(8)) AuthorHouse.

Jonas, J. J. Conflagration: A Ten-Minute Dramatic Duet. 2003. 20p. pap. 4.50 (978-1-932404-17-3(1), 153A) Brooklyn Pubs.

—Last of the Lotto Laity: A Ten-Minute Comedy Monologue. 2003. 16p. (YA). pap. 4.50 (978-1-932404-29-6(5), 282) Brooklyn Pubs.

—Revenge of the Coach's Daughter: A Ten-Minute Comedy Monologue. 2003. 12p. (YA). pap. 4.50 (978-1-932404-28-9(7), 281) Brooklyn Pubs.

—Running on Empty: A Ten-Minute Dramatic Monologue. 2003. 16p. (YA). pap. 4.50 (978-1-932404-27-2(9), 280) Brooklyn Pubs.

—Twitcher: A Ten-Minute Dramatic Duet. 2003. (YA). pap. 4.50 (978-1-931805-93-3(8), 145A) Brooklyn Pubs.

Jordan, Pat. Adventures of King Arthur: From the Every Teacher's Friend Classroom Plays Series. 2010. 20p. (J). pap. 5.00 (978-0-88734-986-7(2)) Players Pr., Inc.

—Alice in Wonderland: From the Every Teacher's Friend Classroom Plays Series. 2010. 20p. (YA). pap. 5.00 (978-0-88734-987-4(0)) Players Pr., Inc.

—Classic Literature for Teens: Every Teachers Friend Classroom Plays. Alliger, Richard, illus. 2007. 118p. pap. 25.00 (978-0-88734-692-7(8)) Players Pr., Inc.

—Little Women, or the March Girls of New England: From the Every Teacher's Friend Classroom Plays Series. 2010. 20p. (YA). pap. 5.00 (978-0-88734-989-8(7)) Players Pr., Inc.

—Mini-Myths: Eleven Short Plays & Mimes of Favorite Greek & Roman Myths. 2010. 72p. pap. 8.00 (978-0-88734-993-5(5)) Players Pr., Inc.

—Mini-Myths for Pre-Teens & Teens Vol. 2: Every Teacher's Friend Classroom Plays. Alliger, Richard, illus. 2008. (Every Teacher's Friend Classroom Plays Ser.: Vol. 2). 122p. pap. 25.00 (978-0-88734-964-5(1)) Players Pr., Inc.

—Mother Goose Plays: From Every Teacher's Friend Classroom Plays Vol. 4: Mother Goose Plays. 2011. 36p. (J). pap. 5.00 (978-0-88734-065-9(2)) Players Pr., Inc.

—Oliver Twist: From the Every Teacher's Friend Classroom Plays Series. 2010. 20p. (YA). pap. 5.00 (978-0-88734-990-4(0)) Players Pr., Inc.

—The Secret Garden: From the Every Teacher's Friend Classroom Plays Series. 2010. 20p. (YA). pap. 5.00 (978-0-88734-988-1(9)) Players Pr., Inc.

Jordan, Shirley. Benjamin Brown & the Great Steamboat Race. Chayka, Doug & Kemly, Kathleen, illus. 2011. (History Speaks: Picture Books Plus Reader's Theater Ser.). (ENG.). 48p. (gr. 2-4). lib. bdg. 27.93 (978-1-58013-674-7(5), Millbrook Pr.) Lerner Publishing Group.

Juwell, et al. The Ab-Solute Truth. 2006. (Platinum Teen Ser.: Vol. 2). 111p. (J). (gr. 5-11). per. 6.99 (978-0-9729325-4-7(2)) Precioustymes Entertainment, LLC.

Karczewski, Deborah. Cheerleader Meets the Goth: A Ten-Minute Comedy Monologue. 2003. 16p. (YA). pap. 4.50 (978-1-932404-25-8(2), 278) Brooklyn Pubs.

Katz, Leon. Fables: A Collection for Youth. 2006. 68p. (YA). pap. 5.95 (978-1-60003-199-1(4), 617) Brooklyn Pubs.

Kaye, Leon. Cooking on the Street: A Comedy Monologue. 2003. (YA). pap. 4.50 (978-1-932404-33-3(3), 286) Brooklyn Pubs.

—Eat a Can: A Comedy Skit, 3 Booklets. 2003. (YA). pap. 9.00 (978-1-932404-36-4(8), 324) Brooklyn Pubs.

Keene, Daniel. Terminus & Other Plays. 2003. (Modern Drama Ser.). (ENG.). 280p. pap. (978-1-876857-18-9(8)) Salt Publishing.

Kehret, Peg. Tell It Like It Is: Fifty Monologs for Talented Teens, 1 vol. 2007. (ENG.). 118p. per. 15.95 (978-1-56608-144-3(0)) Meriwether Publishing, Ltd.

Kelso, Brendan. Shakespeare's a Midsummer Night's Dream for Kids: 3 Short Melodramatic Plays for 3 Group Sizes. Lopez, Shana, illus. 2008. (ENG.). 54p. pap. 9.99 (978-1-4196-8552-1(X)) CreateSpace Independent Publishing Platform.

Kemp, Robert. The Other Dear Charmer. 2006. 80p. (YA). (gr. 6-12). pap. 6.00 (978-0-88734-566-1(2)) Players Pr., Inc.

Kheroufi, Allel. I Want to Fly: A Play for Children in Four Parts. 2012. (ENG.). 201p. pap. 12.95 (978-1-4327-8007-4(7)) Outskirts Pr., Inc.

Kingsland, Robin. Porky Pies. unabr. ed. 2003. (Plays & Play Collections). (ENG., Illus.). 64p. (J). (gr. 1-6). reprint ed. pap. 15.00 (978-0-7136-5370-0(1), A&C Black) Bloomsbury Publishing Plc GBR. Dist: Players Pr., Inc.

Kirkeby, Jennifer. Dot & Tot of Merryland - 2004. 80p. (J). pap. 7.50 (978-1-58342-237-3(4), D04) Dramatic Publishing Co.

—Harriet & Walt. 2010. 57p. pap. 7.00 (978-0-87440-234-6(4)) Baker's Plays.

Korty, Carol. Plays from African Folktales. Landes, William-Alan, ed. unabr. ed. 2003. (International Black Plays & Folk Tales Ser.). (Illus.). 98p. (J). (gr. 3-12). pap. 17.00 (978-0-88734-659-0(6)) Players Pr., Inc.

—Silly Soup. Landes, William-Alan, ed. Colombo, David, illus. Helms, Tina, photos by. 2003. (Plays & Play Collections). 128p. (Orig.). (J). (gr. k-6). pap. 17.00 (978-0-88734-679-8(0)) Players Pr., Inc.

Kramer, Alan. Bajo el mar con Jacques Cousteau & under the Sea with Jacques Cousteau. 2005. spiral bd. 76.00 (978-1-4108-5789-7(1)) Benchmark Education Co.

—Escape de la extinción & Path from Extinction. 2005. spiral bd. 76.00 (978-1-4108-5794-1(8)) Benchmark Education Co.

Krensky, Stephen. Lizzie Newton & the San Francisco Earthquake. Tugeau, Jeremy, illus. 2010. (History Speaks: Picture Books Plus Reader's Theater Ser.). (ENG.). 48p. (gr. 2-4). pap. 9.95 (978-0-7613-3944-1(2)); lib. bdg. 27.93 (978-0-8225-9031-6(X), Millbrook Pr.) Lerner Publishing Group.

Kroll, Virginia L. The Christmas Cow. 2003. 55p. (Orig.). (J). (gr. 1-6). pap. 5.00 (978-0-88734-481-7(X)) Players Pr., Inc.

Kropp, Paul & Jamison, Lori. HIP Readers' Theater Plays. (978-1-897039-40-3(9)) High Interest Publishing (HIP).

Kruh, David. Top of the World, Ma! A Ten-Minute Comedy Duet. 2003. 12p. (YA). pap. 4.50 (978-1-932404-16-6(3), 152A) Brooklyn Pubs.

Lamedman, Debbie. Twenty 10-Minute Plays For Teens By Teens, Vol. 3. 2007. 176p. 14.95 (978-1-57525-456-2(5)) Smith & Kraus Pubs., Inc.

Landes, William-Alan. Aladdin n' His Magic Lamp. rev. ed. 2003. (Wondrawhopper Ser.). 51p. (J). (gr. 3-12). pap. 6.00 (978-0-88734-102-1(0)) Players Pr., Inc.

—Alice n' Wonderland. 2003. (Wondrawhopper Ser.). 32p. (Orig.). (YA). (gr. 3-18). pap. 6.00 (978-0-88734-112-0(8)) Players Pr., Inc.

—Jack 'n the Beanstalk: Playscript. rev. ed. 2003. (Wondrawhopper Ser.). 40p. (J). (gr. 3-12). pap. 6.00 (978-0-88734-101-4(2)) Players Pr., Inc.

—Peter 'n the Wolf: Acting Edition. rev. ed. 2003. (Wondrawhopper Ser.). 36p. (J). (gr. 3-12). pap. 6.00 (978-0-88734-106-9(3)) Players Pr., Inc.

—Rapunzel 'n the Witch. rev. ed. 2003. (Wondrawhopper Ser.). 48p. (J). (gr. 3-12). pap. 6.00 (978-0-88734-107-6(1)) Players Pr., Inc.

—Rhyme Tyme: Playscript. rev. ed. 2003. (Wondrawhopper Ser.). 40p. (J). (gr. 3-12). pap. 6.00 (978-0-88734-108-3(X)) Players Pr., Inc.

—Rumpelstiltskin. 2011. (Wondrawhopper Ser.). (J). (978-0-88734-117-5(9)) Players Pr., Inc.

—Rumpelstiltskin: Playscript. rev. ed. 2003. (Wondrawhopper Ser.). 52p. (J). (gr. 3-12). pap. 6.00 (978-0-88734-104-5(7)) Players Pr., Inc.

Landes, William-Alan & Lasky, Mark A. Grandpa's Bedtime Story. rev. ed. 2003. (Theater for Young Audiences Ser.). 36p. (YA). (gr. 3-12). pap. 6.00 (978-0-88734-505-0(0)) Players Pr., Inc.

Landes, William-Alan & Standish, Marilyn. The Wizard of Oz. rev. ed. 2003. (Wondrawhopper Ser.). 40p. (J). (gr. 3-12). pap. 6.00 (978-0-88734-105-2(5)) Players Pr., Inc.

Landry, Deb. Sticks Stones & Stumped the Play & Teacher's Guide. 2008. (Illus.). 40p. pap. 29.95 (978-0-9773738-2-6(7)) Bryson Taylor Publishing.

Lawall, Gilbert & Kindel, Gerde. The Phaedra of Seneca. 2nd ed. 2007. (Illus.). 238p. (J). (gr. 9-12). 39.00 (978-0-86516-016-3(3)) Bolchazy-Carducci Pubs.

Leaf, Claudia. Radical Will. unabr. ed. 2003. (Shakespeare Ser.). 28p. (YA). (gr. 6-12). pap. 6.00 (978-0-85343-614-0(2)) Miller, J. Garnet Ltd. GBR. Dist: Empire Publishing Service.

Lee, Nate. The Invitation & 5 Other Dramas for Tweens. 2008. 48p. pap. 6.00 (978-0-687-64713-2(4)) Abingdon Pr.

—Words from the Cross & 5 Other Dramas for Tweens. 2009. pap. 6.00 (978-0-687-65859-6(4)) Abingdon Pr.

Leese, Joan, et al. Three Plays for Women. 2003. (Full-Length Plays Ser.). 44p. (YA). (gr. 8-12). pap. 6.00 (978-0-88734-932-4(3)) Players Pr., Inc.

LeMaster, David. Sir Saddlesore & the Dragon: One-Act Children's Comedy Play. rev. ed. 2005. 12p. (YA). pap. 4.95 (978-1-60003-094-9(7), 783) Brooklyn Pubs.

LeMaster, David J. Homeland Insecurity: A Comedy Skit, 4 Booklets. 2003. (YA). pap. 4.50 (978-1-932404-38-8(4), 322) Brooklyn Pubs.

—Paper, Rock, Scissors, Bomb! A Ten-Minute Comedy Duet. 2003. 16p. (YA). pap. 4.50 (978-1-932404-18-0(X), 154A) Brooklyn Pubs.

—Shakespeare, Horny Toads & Banana Peels: Ten-Minute Comedy Duet. 2003. (YA). pap. 9.00 (978-1-932404-04-3(X), 141A) Brooklyn Pubs.

Levine, Karen. Hana's Suitcase on Stage, 1 vol. 2007. (Holocaust Remembrance Ser.). (ENG., Illus.). 175p. (J). (gr. 3-12). pap. 18.95 (978-1-897187-05-0(X)) Second Story Pr. CAN. Dist: Orca Bk. Pubs. USA.

Liebenow, Todd, et al. Beyond Words 2. 2003. (Illus.). 56p. (YA). 20.00 (978-1-58302-228-3(7)) One Way St., Inc.

Lieberman, Paulette (Peshe Razel) Fein. Jewish Plays for Children: For successful educational fun & fundraising Purposes. 2008. 236p. pap. 18.95 (978-0-595-52944-5(5)) iUniverse, Inc.

Lodato, Victor & Pen, Polly. Arlington. 2015. 49p. **(978-0-8222-3165-3(4))** Dramatists Play Service, Inc.

Mabian, Mercy. The Little Crying Hearts: A Play. 2009. 116p. pap. 13.99 (978-1-4389-5035-8(7)) AuthorHouse.

MacDonald, Margaret. The Skit Book: 101 Skits from Kids. Scull, Marie-Louise, illus. 2006. (ENG.). 160p. (J). (gr. -1-12). per. 17.95 (978-0-87483-785-8(5)) August Hse. Pubs., Inc. (978-0-87483-655-4(7)); pap. 17.95 (978-0-87483-650-9(6)) August Hse. Pubs., Inc.

MacDougal, P. Paullette. Waiting for MacArthur. 2003. (Illus.). 58p. (YA). (gr. 10). pap. 6.50 (978-1-58342-183-3(1), W97) Dramatic Publishing Co.

Mahfouz, Sabrina, et al. National Theatre Connections 2014: Plays for Young People: Same; Horizon; the Wardrobe; Heritage; a Letter to Lacey; a Shop Selling Speech; Angels; Hearts; Pronoun; Tomorrow. Banks, Anthony, ed. 2014. (ENG.). 728p. pap. 29.95 (978-1-4725-7143-4(6), 9781472571434, Bloomsbury Methuen Drama) Bloomsbury Publishing Plc GBR. Dist: Macmillan.

Mamet, Clara & Quaid, Jack. Solvit Kids. 2012. 41p. (J). 8.95 (978-0-573-70087-3(7)) French, Samuel Inc.

Mankowski, Sarah. Fallout: An original Screenplay. 2004. (YA). spiral bd. 10.95 (978-0-9745268-6-7(X)) WordThunder Pubns.

Manning, Mick & Brita, Granström. Mi Primer Libro de Teatro. Granström, Brita, illus.Tr. of Drama School. (SPA.). (J). (gr. 3-5). 15.16 (978-84-241-7922-9(6)) Everest Editora ESP. Dist: Lectorum Pubns., Inc.

Mapleson, Peter & Mapleson, Robyn. Bill the Bunyip. (J). (gr. 3-6). pap. (978-1-875739-82-0(3)) Wizard Bks.

Marlin, Therese. Cindyrella. 2006. 32p. 5.50 (978-0-87440-254-4(9), 1726-B) Baker's Plays.

Martin, Judith. Out of the Bag: The Paper Bag Players Book of Plays. Chwast, Seymour, illus. 2005. 48p. (J). (gr. k-4). reprint ed. pap. 14.00 (978-0-7567-8530-7(8)) DIANE Publishing Co.

Maupassant, Guy de. The Necklace. Kelley, Gary, illus. 2004. (ENG.). 48p. (J). (gr. 4-7). 19.95 (978-1-56846-193-9(3)) Creative Co., The.

Maxwell, Glyn. Merlin & the Woods of Time. 2012. (ENG.). 96p. (J). (gr. k). pap. 20.95 (978-1-84943-224-5(4)) Oberon Bks., Ltd. GBR. Dist: Consortium Bk. Sales & Distribution.

Maxwell-Snyder, Hope. Lullaby for George. 2005. (J). 9.95 (978-0-9753285-4-5(9)) H.B.P., Inc.

May, Bob. Snowmen, elves & Nutcrackers. 2008. (ENG.). 144p. mass mkt. (978-0-87440-306-0(5)) Baker's Plays.

Mayer, Mindy & Mayer, Allie. Sheltered Friends. 2008. mass mkt. 6.50 (978-0-87440-248-3(4)) Baker's Plays.

McBride-Smith, Barbara. Tell It Together: Foolproof Scripts for Story Theatre. 2005. (ENG.). 192p. (gr. 3-6). 24.95 (978-0-87483-655-4(7)); pap. 17.95 (978-0-87483-650-9(6)) August Hse. Pubs., Inc.

McCaslin, Nellie. Angel of the Battlefield. 2003. (Players Press Nellie McCaslin Ser.). (Illus.). 20p. (YA). (gr. 4-12). pap. 5.00 (978-0-88734-430-5(5)) Players Pr., Inc.

—The Bailiff's Wonderful Coat. 2003. (Players Press Nellie McCaslin Ser.). 55p. (J). (gr. 1-6). pap. 5.00 (978-0-88734-453-4(4)) Players Pr., Inc.

—Bluebonnets. 2003. (Players Press Nellie McCaslin Ser.). 18p. (YA). (gr. 4-12). pap. 5.00 (978-0-88734-439-8(9)) Players Pr., Inc.

—Brave New Banner. 2003. (Players Press Nellie McCaslin Ser.). (Illus.). 20p. (YA). (gr. 6-12). pap. 5.00 (978-0-88734-436-7(4)) Players Pr., Inc.

—Broken Rehearsal. 2006. 16p. (gr. 6-12). pap. 6.00 (978-0-88734-580-7(8)) Players Pr., Inc.

—Cold Face - Warm Heart. 2003. 20p. (J). (gr. k-6). pap. 5.00 (978-0-88734-440-4(2)) Players Pr., Inc.

—The Legend of Minna Lamourrie. 2003. (Players Press Nellie McCaslin Ser.). (Illus.). 20p. (J). (gr. k-6). pap. 5.00 (978-0-88734-438-1(0)) Players Pr., Inc.

—Legends in Action: Ten Plays of Ten Lands. 2003. (Plays & Play Collections). (Illus.). xii, 142p. (J). pap. 20.00 (978-0-88734-633-0(2)) Players Pr., Inc.

—Paul Bunyan: Lumberjack. 2003. (Players Press Nellie McCaslin Ser.). 55p. (Orig.). (J). (gr. 1-6). pap. 5.00 (978-0-88734-477-0(1)) Players Pr., Inc.

—A Straight Shooter (Playscript) 2003. (Players Press Nellie McCaslin Ser.). 16p. (YA). (gr. 6-12). pap. 5.00 (978-0-88734-429-9(1)) Players Pr., Inc.

—Three Meals a Day. 2003. 55p. (J). (gr. 1-7). pap. 5.00 (978-0-88734-445-9(3)) Players Pr., Inc.

—Too Many Cooks. 2003. (Players Press Nellie McCaslin Ser.). (Illus.). 20p. (J). pap. 5.00 (978-0-88734-434-3(8)) Players Pr., Inc.

McCullough, L. E. Classroom Plays for Social Studies America in the 1800s, 4 vols. Mason, Mark, illus. 2003. 48p. (J). per. 7.99 (978-1-56472-242-3(2)) Edupress, Inc.

—Classroom Plays for Social Studies American Biographies, 4. Mason, Mark, illus. 2003. 48p. (J). per. 7.99 (978-1-56472-243-0(0)) Edupress, Inc.

—Classroom Plays for Social Studies Ancient Civilizations, 4 vols. Mason, Mark, illus. 2003. 48p. (J). per. 7.99 (978-1-56472-240-9(6)) Edupress, Inc.

—Classroom Plays for Social Studies Early America, 4 vols. Mason, Mark, illus. 2003. 48p. (J). per. 7.99 (978-1-56472-241-6(4)) Edupress, Inc.

McDonald, Trevy. Time Will Tell. 2nd ed. 2017. pap. 15.00 (978-0-9670712-2-0(4)) zReyomi Publishing.

McGregor, Rex. Girls on the Brink: Seven Female-Forward Plays for Young Adults. 2016. (ENG.). 72p. pap. 7.95 (978-1-62088-584-0(0)) YouthPlays.

McKinnon, Robert Scott. The Tooth Fairy Came to Gopher Gulch. 2010. 64p. (J). 3.00 (978-0-9651943-4-1(5)) McKinnon, Robert Scott.

McLaren, Maria. Seven with One Blow. 2003. (Theater for Young Audiences Ser.). 24p. (J). (gr. 1-6). pap. 6.00 (978-0-88734-517-3(4)) Players Pr., Inc.

Mead, Maggie. Exploring the West: Tales of Courage on the Lewis & Clark Expedition. Jacobsen, Laura, illus. 2015. (Setting the Stage for Fluency Ser.). (ENG.). 40p. (gr. 3-5). lib. bdg. 27.93 (978-1-939656-65-0(6)) Red Chair Pr.

—Suffrage Sisters: The Fight for Liberty. Feeney, Siri, illus. 2015. (Setting the Stage for Fluency Ser.). (ENG.). 40p. (gr. 3-5). lib. bdg. 27.93 (978-1-939656-68-1(0)) Red Chair Pr.

Meadows, Kelly. Dumping Ground: A Ten-Minute Comedy Duet. 2003. (YA). pap. 4.50 (978-1-931805-94-0(6), 146A) Brooklyn Pubs.

—A Ghost of a Chance: A One-Act Comedy Play. 2003. (YA). pap. 4.50 (978-1-932404-59-3(7), 757) Brooklyn Pubs.

—Not Ready! A Ten-Minute Comedy Monologue. 2003. 12p. (YA). pap. 4.50 (978-1-932404-31-9(7), 284) Brooklyn Pubs.

—Teen Comedy Playlets: A Collection of Six Skits: Third Time's a Charm, 8 Booklets. 2003. (YA). pap. 19.95 (978-1-932404-49-4(X), 911) Brooklyn Pubs.

—Ten Easy Steps to Humiliation: A Ten-Minute Comedy Duet. 2003. (YA). pap. 4.50 (978-1-931805-96-4(2), 148A) Brooklyn Pubs.

Meighan, Julie. Drama Start Two Drama Activities & Plays for Children. 2012. 92p. pap. (978-0-9568966-1-2(8)) JemBks.

—Stage Start 20 Plays for Children. 2013. 76p. pap. (978-0-9568966-2-9(6)) JemBks.

Mercafi, Cindy. Faces of Freedom. 2003. 48p. (YA). pap. 6.50 (978-1-58342-199-4(8), F81) Dramatic Publishing Co.

Middleton, Alasdair & Dove, Jonathon. The Enchanted Pig. 2007. (ENG.). 96p. per. 18.95 (978-1-84002-717-4(7)) Oberon Bks., Ltd. GBR. Dist: Consortium Bk. Sales & Distribution.

Mihalko, Ross & Swift, Donna. Ant & the Grasshopper (Play) 2013. pap. 8.95 (978-0-573-70111-5(3)) French, Samuel Inc.

—Beanstalk! the Play! 2012. 32p. (J). pap. 8.95 (978-0-573-70113-9(X)) French, Samuel Inc.

Mini Plays & Folktale Plays that Build Reading Skills. 2005. (J). pap. (978-1-60015-036-4(5)) Steps To Literacy, LLC.

Molnar, Ferenc. Liliom. 2003. 68p. (YA). (gr. 4-12). pap. 7.50 (978-0-88734-798-6(3)) Players Pr., Inc.

Montgomery, L. M. Anne of Green Gables. 2006. (ENG.). 96p. (gr. k-3). per. 16.95 (978-1-84002-538-5(7)) Consortium Bk. Sales & Distribution.

Morgan, Robert F. The Partners: A Three Act Play. 2007. 20p. (J). (gr. 6). pap. 25.00 (978-1-885679-05-5(X)) Morgan Foundation Pubs.: International Published Innovations.

Morpurgo, Michael. Private Peaceful. 2013. (ENG.). 96p. pap. 17.95 (978-1-84943-501-7(4)) Oberon Bks., Ltd. GBR. Dist: Consortium Bk. Sales & Distribution.

Morreale, Vin, Jr. The Day the Woods Were One. 2003. (Theater for Young Audiences Ser.). 20p. (Orig.). (J). (gr. 3-18). pap. 6.00 (978-0-88734-507-4(7)) Players Pr., Inc.

—Nicky's Secret. 2003. 48p. (YA). pap. 6.50 (978-1-58342-186-4(6), N53) Dramatic Publishing Co.

Morris, Kathleen. Lost & Found - a Children's Christmas Play. 2013. 32p. pap. (978-1-927828-25-0(2)) Rouge Publishing.

Morss, Ben. Cinderella's Mice. Morss, Ben, . 2009. 48p. (J). mass mkt. 7.00 (978-0-87440-216-2(6)) Baker's Plays.

Morton, Carlos. The Drop-Out. Landes, William-Alan, ed. 2003. (Players Press Carlos Morton Collection). 55p. (Orig.). (YA). (gr. 6-12). pap. 5.00 (978-0-88734-443-5(7)) Players Pr., Inc.

—Drug-O. Landes, William-Alan, ed. 2003. (Carlos Morton Collection). 55p. (Orig.). (YA). (gr. 6-12). pap. 6.00 (978-0-88734-444-2(5)) Players Pr., Inc.

—Los Fatherless. Landes, William-Alan, ed. 2003. (Players Press Carlos Morton Collection). 55p. (YA). (gr. 6-12). pap. 5.00 (978-0-88734-376-6(7)) Players Pr., Inc.

Mowery, Milo. El Zorrito. 2014. (SPA & ENG.). 64p. (J). pap. 9.95 (978-1-58342-992-1(1)) Dramatic Publishing Co.

Muir, Kerry. Three New Plays for Young Actors: From the Young Actor's Studio. 2004. (ENG., Illus.). 216p. (Orig.). pap. 19.99 (978-0-87910-957-8(2), 0879109572, Limelight Editions) Leonard, Hal Corp.

Muschell, David. The Invisible Princess: A Full-Length Comedy-Dramatic Play. 2003. (YA). pap. 5.00 (978-1-932404-67-8(8), 609) Brooklyn Pubs.

Nehls, David & Kelso, Betsy. The Great American Trailer Park Christmas Musical. 2014. 62p. pap. 10.00 (978-0-8222-3104-2(2)) Dramatists Play Service, Inc.

Neipris, Janet. Jeremy & the Thinking Machine: A Musical for Young Audiences. 2004. 26p. (YA). pap. (978-0-573-05139-5(9)) French, Samuel Inc.

Nesbit, E. Beautiful Stories from Shakespeare (Yesterday's Classics) 2006. (J). per. 11.95 (978-1-59915-029-1(8)) Yesterday's Classics.

Nield, Maureen. How Different from Us. 2003. 28p. (YA). (gr. 4-12). pap. 5.00 (978-0-88734-767-2(3)) Players Pr., Inc.

Nimmo, Paul. Will Shakespeare Save Us! Will Shakespeare Save the King! 2003. (Shakespeare Ser.). 58p. (J). (gr. k-8). pap. 12.00 (978-0-88734-658-3(8)) Players Pr., Inc.

Nolan, Ernie. Snow White & the Seven Dwarfs as Performed by Professor TJ Barker's Troupe of Theatricals. 2011. (Illus.). 78p. pap. 7.50 (978-1-58342-713-2(9)) Dramatic Publishing Co.

Norden, Barbara. Meteorite. 2004. (ENG.). 96p. pap. 16.95 (978-1-84002-401-2(1)) Theatre Communications Group, Inc.

Nyberg, Judy. Just Pretend. 2007. pap. 12.95 (978-1-59647-259-4(6)) Good Year Bks.

Nyman, Debbie & Wortzman, Ricki. The 10 Best Plays. 2008. 14.99 (978-1-55448-503-1(7)) Scholastic Library Publishing.

Orr, Wendy. Nim's Island. 2008. lib. bdg. 17.20 (978-1-4178-1829-7(8), Turtleback) Turtleback Bks.

Osment, Philip. Duck! 2008. (ENG.). 96p. (J). pap. 18.95 (978-1-84002-822-5(X)) Oberon Bks., Ltd. GBR. Dist: Consortium Bk. Sales & Distribution.

—Palace of Fear. 2006. (ENG., Illus.). 96p. per. 16.95 (978-1-84002-505-7(0)) Oberon Bks., Ltd. GBR. Dist: Consortium Bk. Sales & Distribution.

—Plays for Young People: Who's Breaking - Listen - Sleeping Dogs - Wise Guys. 2006. (ENG.). 216p. per. 36.95 (978-1-84002-272-8(8)) Oberon Bks., Ltd. GBR. Dist: Consortium Bk. Sales & Distribution.

Osment, Philip, et al. Class Acts. 2010. (ENG.). 96p. (J). pap. 23.95 (978-1-84002-933-8(1)) Oberon Bks., Ltd. GBR. Dist: Consortium Bk. Sales & Distribution.

Owen, Gary. Mrs Reynolds & the Ruffian. 2011. (ENG.). 96p. (gr. 7). pap. 18.95 (978-1-84943-065-4(9)) Oberon Bks., Ltd. GBR. Dist: Consortium Bk. Sales & Distribution.

Pagnol, Marcel. Manon des Sources, Level C. (FRE.). (YA). (gr. 7-12). 9.95 (978-0-8219-1865-4(6), 40341) EMC/Paradigm Publishing.

Palacios, John, illus. Readers' Theater: Scripts for Young Readers: How the Tiger Got Its Stripes. 2009. 16p. (J). pap. 16.95 (978-1-60184-162-9(0)) Primary Concepts, Inc.

Palacious, John, illus. Readers' Theater Paul Bunyan: Scripts for Young Readers. 2009. 16p. (J). pap. (978-1-60184-144-5(2)) Primary Concepts, Inc.

Perkins, David & Dooley, Caroline. The Selfish Giant: A Children's Musical. 2003. (J). pap. (978-0-573-08123-1(9)) French, Samuel Inc.

Peters, Andrew & Peters, Polly. Dragon Chaser. (Illus.). 64p. 19.99 (978-0-7502-3457-3(1)) Hodder & Stoughton GBR. Dist: Trafalgar Square Publishing.

Pettus, Tiffany. The Sweetness of Christmas: The Candy Cane Story. 2009. 54p. pap. 19.95 (978-1-4327-4964-4(1)) Outskirts Pr., Inc.

Phillips, Louis. Late Night in the Rain Forest. Strozier, M. Stefan & Torke, Kyle, eds. 2009. 122p. pap. 17.99 (978-1-935444-99-2(9)) World Audience Pubs.

Polsky, Milton, et al. Houdini - The King of Escapes: Playscript. 2003. (Musicals Ser.). 32p. (Orig.). (J). (gr. 3-12). pap. 8.00 (978-0-88734-510-4(7)) Players Pr., Inc.

Pommerat, Joël, et al. Theatre Cafe - Plays One: Invasion! - This Child - Respect. 2009. (ENG.). 96p. (J). pap. 24.95 (978-1-84002-893-5(9)) Oberon Bks., Ltd. GBR. Dist: Consortium Bk. Sales & Distribution.

Pop-Out Play-Pak: Bats. Orig. Title: Child's Play. (Illus.). 14p. (J). (gr. -1-4). reprint ed. (978-1-881469-81-0(6)) Safari, Ltd.

Pop-Out Play-Pak: Butterfly. Orig. Title: Child's Play. (Illus.). 14p. (J). (gr. -1-4). reprint ed. (978-1-881469-78-0(6)) Safari, Ltd.

Pop-Out Play-Pak: Frogs. Orig. Title: Child's Play. (Illus.). 14p. (J). (gr. -1-4). reprint ed. (978-1-881469-82-7(4)) Safari, Ltd.

Pop-Out Play-Pak: Spider. Orig. Title: Child's Play. (Illus.). 14p. (J). (gr. -1-4). reprint ed. (978-1-881469-79-7(4)) Safari, Ltd.

Pop-Out Play-Pak: Time Tunnel. Orig. Title: Child's Play. (Illus.). 24p. (J). (gr. -1-4). (978-1-881469-76-6(X)) Safari, Ltd.

Porter, Phil. Two Plays for Young People: The Flying Machine; Smashed Eggs. 2009. (ENG.). 96p. (J). pap. 18.95 (978-1-84002-864-5(5)) Oberon Bks., Ltd. GBR. Dist: Consortium Bk. Sales & Distribution.

Porter, Steven. The Prairie Man. 2003. 62p. (YA). pap. 6.00 (978-0-9625372-0-2(9)) Phantom Pubns., Inc.

Porter Zasada, Marc. Alice Through the Looking Glass - a Children's Play. 2011. 62p. pap. 19.95 (978-0-557-74883-9(6)) Lulu Pr., Inc.

Post, Sam. Responsibility: A Comedy Skit, 3 Booklets. 2003. (YA). pap. 9.00 (978-1-932404-40-1(6), 326) Brooklyn Pubs.

Potter, Beatrix. Two Beatrix Potter Plays. 2010. (ENG.). 96p. pap. 16.95 (978-1-84002-519-4(0)) Oberon Bks., Ltd. GBR. Dist: Consortium Bk. Sales & Distribution.

Powell, Jenny. The Chief's Bride: An African Tale. 2016. (Putting on a Play Ser.). (ENG., Illus.). 32p. (J). (gr. 2-4). pap. 9.99 (978-0-7502-9708-0(5), Wayland) Hachette Children's Group GBR. Dist: Hachette Bk. Group.

—Stop Bullying Me! 2016. (Putting on a Play Ser.). (ENG., Illus.). 32p. (J). (gr. 2-4). pap. 9.99 (978-0-7502-9707-3(7), Wayland) Hachette Children's Group GBR. Dist: Hachette Bk. Group.

Pratchett, Terry & Holmes, Matthew. Terry Pratchett's the Amazing Maurice & His Educated Rodents, 1 vol. 2011. (and C Black Musicals Ser.). (ENG.). 76p. (J). (gr. 4). pap. 47.95 incl. audio compact disk (978-1-4081-4563-0(4)) HarperCollins Pubs. Ltd. GBR. Dist: Independent Pubs. Group.

Pratt, Anna Bronson Alcott. Comic Tragedies. 2010. 332p. pap. 31.75 (978-1-144-42717-5(7)) Creative Media Partners, LLC.

Pugliano-Martin, Carol. Famous Americans: Fluency-Building Plays with Activities That Expand Vocabulary & Content Knowledge. 2009. (15 Plays for Beginning Readers Ser.). (ENG.). 48p. pap. 11.99 (978-0-545-11082-2(3), Teaching Resources) Scholastic, Inc.

—Greek Myth Plays: 10 Readers Theater Scripts Based on Favorite Greek Myths That Students Can Read & Reread to Develop Their Fluency. 2008. (ENG.). 72p. pap. 11.99 (978-0-439-64014-5(8), Teaching Resources) Scholastic, Inc.

Pullman, Philip. The Firework-Maker's Daughter. 2011. (ENG.). 96p. (gr. 2). pap. 18.95 (978-1-84943-069-2(1)) Oberon Bks., Ltd. GBR. Dist: Consortium Bk. Sales & Distribution.

—Scarecrow & His Servant. 2009. (ENG.). 96p. (J). pap. 18.95 (978-1-84002-899-7(8)) Oberon Bks., Ltd. GBR. Dist: Consortium Bk. Sales & Distribution.

Pullman, Philip & Adams, Emma. Ugly. 2011. (ENG.). 98p. pap. 18.95 (978-1-84943-021-0(7)) Oberon Bks., Ltd. GBR. Dist: Consortium Bk. Sales & Distribution.

Pyle, Howard. The Wonder Clock. 2009. (Illus.). 440p. pap. 15.95 (978-1-59915-339-1(4)) Yesterday's Classics.

Quinn, Stephanie. Little Stars Creative Drama for Preschoolers. 2008. 100p. per. 19.95 (978-0-9773099-5-5(9)) Quinn Entertainment.

Rabushka, Jerry. The Casket & the Casserole: A Ten-Minute Comedy Duet. 2003. 16p. (YA). pap. 4.50 (978-1-932404-23-4(6), 159A) Brooklyn Pubs.

—The Frying Pan: A Dramatic Skit, 4 Booklets. 2003. (YA). pap. 4.50 (978-1-932404-37-1(6), 323) Brooklyn Pubs.

—On Location: A Ten-Minute Comedy Duet. 2003. 16p. (YA). pap. 4.50 (978-1-931805-97-1(0), 149A) Brooklyn Pubs.

—Saucy Mamasita: A Dramatic Monologue. 2003. (YA). pap. 4.50 (978-1-932404-30-2(9), 283) Brooklyn Pubs.

—White Elephant: Comedy Monologue. 2003. (YA). pap. 4.50 (978-1-932404-08-1(2), 276) Brooklyn Pubs.

Rajagopal, P. & Pullens, Evelien. Aiyappan & the Magic Horse. 2005. (Illus.). 70p. (978-81-8146-153-7(3)) Tulika Pubs.

Ramirez, Frank. The Bee Attitudes: And 5 More Extraordinary Plays for Ordinary Days. 2007. 84p. (J). pap. 12.95 (978-0-7880-2435-1(3)) CSS Publishing Co.

Ransome, Arthur. Swallows & Amazons. 2012. (ENG.). 96p. pap. 20.95 (978-1-84842-237-7(7)) Hern, Nick Bks., Ltd. GBR. Dist: Consortium Bk. Sales & Distribution.

Rapier, Darren. The Little Mermaid. 2008. 68p. pap. 16.95 (978-0-9556798-1-0(8)) Tualen GBR. Dist: Lulu Pr., Inc.

Raspanti, Celeste. The Terezin Promise. 2004. 40p. (YA). pap. 4.50 (978-1-58342-200-7(5), TF7) Dramatic Publishing Co.

Ravenhill, Mark. Plays for Young People: Citizenship; Scenes from Family Life; Totally over You. 2010. (Play Anthologies Ser.). (ENG., Illus.). 160p. pap. 20.95 (978-1-4081-2861-9(6), 9781408128619, Bloomsbury Methuen Drama) Bloomsbury Publishing Plc GBR. Dist: Macmillan.

Rechenspiele. (Duden-Schuelerhilfen Ser.). (GER.). 79p. (J). (gr. 4-5). (978-3-411-02611-1(1)) Bibliographisches Institut & F. A. Brockhaus AG DEU. Dist: International Bk. Import Service, Inc.

Redmond, Diane. The Odyssey, Vol. 4. Smith, Barry, illus. unabr. ed. 2003. (Curtain Up Ser.: Vol. 4). (ENG.). 48p. (J). (gr. 1-4). pap. 15.00 (978-0-7136-4628-3(4), A&C Black) Bloomsbury Publishing Plc GBR. Dist: Players Pr., Inc.

Reese, Kevin M., adapted by. Chicken Little Henny Penny (Non-Musical Version) 2004. (J). (978-1-932240-60-3(8)) KMR Scripts.

—The Pied Piper (Non-Musical Version) 2004. (J). 4.00 net. (978-1-932240-62-7(4)) KMR Scripts.

—The True Story of the Tortoise & the Hare (Non-Musical Version) 2005. (J). 4.00 net. (978-1-932240-64-1(0)) KMR Scripts.

Reese, Kevin M., adapted by. Chicken Little Henny Penny. Reese, Kevin M., . 2004. (J). 4.00 (978-1-932240-59-7(4)) KMR Scripts.

—The Pied Piper. Reese, Kevin M., . 2004. (J). 4.00 net. (978-1-932240-61-0(6)) KMR Scripts.

—The True Story of the Tortoise & the Hare. Reese, Kevin M., . 2005. (J). 4.00 net. (978-1-932240-63-4(2)) KMR Scripts.

Rice, Dona. Alice in the Garden of Flowers (Science) 2015. (Building Fluency Through Reader's Theater Ser.). (Illus.). 24p. (gr. 2-2). pap. 6.99 (978-1-4938-1514-2(8)) Teacher Created Materials, Inc.

Riosley, Lane. The Attack of the Crab Nebula. (Lucky Hightops & the Cosmic Cat Patrol Ser.: No. 2). (Illus.). (J). (gr. 2-8). pap. 4.00 (978-1-57514-268-5(6), 1027) Encore Performance Publishing.

—Captives of the Dog Star. (Lucky Hightops & the Cosmic Cat Patrol Ser.: No. 1). (Illus.). (J). (gr. 2-8). pap. 4.00 (978-1-57514-267-8(8), 1026) Encore Performance Publishing.

—Polaris, the Robot King. (Lucky Hightops & the Cosmic Cat Patrol Ser.: No. 3). (Illus.). (J). (gr. 2-8). pap. 4.00 (978-1-57514-269-2(4), 1028) Encore Performance Publishing.

—Revenge of the Dog Robber. (Lucky Hightops & the Cosmic Cat Patrol Ser.: No. 4). (Illus.). (J). (gr. 2-8). pap. 4.00 (978-1-57514-270-8(8), 1116) Encore Performance Publishing.

Rizzo, Joe. On the Same Frequency: A One-Act Comedy Play. 2003. (YA). pap. 4.50 (978-1-932404-63-0(5), 761) Brooklyn Pubs.

Robinetie, Joseph & Tierney, Thomas. The Fabulous Fable Factory. 2004. 56p. (YA). pap. 6.50 (978-1-58342-216-8(1), F82) Dramatic Publishing Co.

Robinette, Joseph. Dorothy Meets Alice or the Wizard of Wonderland. 2004. 48p. (YA). pap. 6.50 (978-1-58342-221-2(8), D82) Dramatic Publishing Co.

Romer, Marcus & Hinton, S. E. Rumble Fish. 2003. (Illus.). 62p. pap. 6.25 (978-1-58342-154-3(8), R69) Dramatic Publishing Co.

Romer, Ruth. The Pattern Hike, 6 vols. Dufalla, Anita, illus. 2004. (Reader's Theater Ser.). (J). pap. (978-1-4108-2290-1(7), A22907) Benchmark Education Co.

Rooyackers, Paul, et al. 101 Dialogues, Sketches & Skits: Instant Theatre for Teens & Tweens. 2014. (SmartFun Activity Bks.). (ENG., Illus.). 144p. (gr. 1). pap. 14.95 (978-0-89793-677-4(9), Hunter Hse.) Turner Publishing Co.

Rosenberg, Joe, ed. Aplauso! Hispanic Children's Theater. 2nd ed. 2003. (Latin-American Play Anthologies Ser.). (Illus.). 274p. (YA). (gr. 4-10). pap. 10.00 (978-1-55885-127-6(5), Piñata Books) Arte Publico Pr.

Ross, Kathryn & Pruitt, Kimberly. Artic Skits. Utley, David, illus. 2006. 88p. (J). per. 24.95 (978-0-9725803-9-7(5)) Children's Publishing.

Ruditis, Paul. The Devil's in the Diva: The Four Dorothys - Everyone's a Critic. 2010. (Drama! Ser.). (ENG.). 496p. (YA). (gr. 7). pap. 9.99 (978-1-4424-1444-0(8), Simon Pulse) Simon Pulse.

—Everyone's a Critic. 2007. (Drama! Ser.). (ENG.). 256p. (YA). (gr. 7-12). pap. 12.99 (978-1-4169-3392-2(1), Simon Pulse) Simon Pulse.

—The Four Dorothys. 2007. (Drama! Ser.: No. 1). (ENG., Illus.). 256p. (YA). (gr. 7-12). pap. 11.99 (978-1-4169-3391-5(3), Simon Pulse) Simon Pulse.

Rumble, P. Barry. Full Moon. 2003. (One Act Plays Ser.). 14p. (J). pap. 5.00 (978-0-88734-422-0(4)) Players Pr., Inc.

Russell, Willy & Gunton, Mark. Our Day Out: Improving Standards in English Through Drama at Key Stage 3 & GCSE. 2011. (Critical Scripts Ser.). (ENG., Illus.). 144p. pap. 14.95 (978-1-4081-3485-6(3), 9781408134856, Bloomsbury Methuen Drama) Bloomsbury Publishing Plc GBR. Dist: Macmillan.

Ryan, Tammy. The Music Lesson. 2003. 72p. (YA). pap. 6.50 (978-1-58342-207-6(2), MD8) Dramatic Publishing Co.

Sabato, George F. The New Improved Santa. Landes, William-Alan, ed. 2003. (Theater for Young Audiences Ser.). 55p. (Orig.). (J). (gr. k-7). pap. 5.00 (978-0-88734-457-2(7)) Players Pr., Inc.

Sanders, D. J. Metatheatre: A Ten-Minute Comedy Duet. 2003. (YA). pap. 4.50 (978-1-932404-43-2(0), 131A) Brooklyn Pubs.

Schlitz, Laura Amy. A Drowned Maiden's Hair. 2006. (ENG., Illus.). 400p. (J). (gr. 5-9). 16.99 (978-0-7636-2930-4(8)) Candlewick Pr.

—Good Masters! Sweet Ladies! Voices from a Medieval Village. Byrd, Robert, illus. (ENG.). 96p. (J). (gr. 5-9). 2011. pap. 6.99 (978-0-7636-5094-0(3)) 2008. pap. 10.99 (978-0-7636-4332-4(7)) Candlewick Pr.

Schnitzler, Arthur. Anatol. Landes, William-Alan, ed. unabr. ed. 2003. (Players Press Classic Plays Ser.). (Illus.). 68p. (J). (gr. 4-6). pap. 7.50 (978-0-88734-817-4(3)) Players Pr., Inc.

Schnupp, Al. Censored. 2003. (Full-Length Plays Ser.). 76p. (YA). (gr. 8-12). pap. 15.00 (978-0-88734-868-6(8)) Players Pr., Inc.

Schoenfeld, Jeff. Information: A Ten-Minute Comedy Duet. 2003. 16p. (YA). pap. 4.50 (978-1-932404-24-1(4), 160A) Brooklyn Pubs.

Scholastic, Inc. Staff. Goldilocks & the Three Bears Fairy Tale Masks with Easy-to-Read Play! 2006. (ENG.). 11.99 (978-0-439-82428-6(1), Teaching Resources) Scholastic, Inc.

—Three Little Pigs Fairy Tale Masks with Easy-to-Read Play! 2006. (ENG.). 11.99 (978-0-439-82427-9(3), Teaching Resources) Scholastic, Inc.

Scholastic, Inc. Staff, contrib. by. Short Plays for Building Fluency: Famous Americans - 22 Reproducible Plays That Build Fluency, Vocabulary, & Comprehension. 2008. (Short Plays for Building Fluency Ser.). (ENG.). 200p. pap. 19.99 (978-0-545-07216-8(6), Teaching Resources) Scholastic, Inc.

Schreibspiele. (Duden-Schuelerhilfen Ser.). (GER.). 79p. (J). (gr. 3-4). (978-3-411-02612-8(X)) Bibliographisches Institut & F. A. Brockhaus AG DEU. Dist: International Bk. Import Service, Inc.

Schroeder-Arce, Roxanne. Mariachi Girl. 2014. 53p. (J). pap. 9.50 (978-1-58342-932-7(8)) Dramatic Publishing Co.

Shakespeare, William. As You Like It. 2008. (Easy Reading Shakespeare Ser.). (ENG., Illus.). 72p. pap., act. bk. ed. 10.95 (978-1-55576-329-9(4), EDSC301B) EDCON Publishing Group.

—Macbeth. Cheung, Charly, illus. 2013. (William Shakespeare Ser.). (ENG.). 64p. pap. 6.95 (978-1-906230-47-0(1)) Real Reads Ltd. GBR. Dist: Casemate Pubs. & Bk. Distributors, LLC.

—The Merchant of Venice. 2004. (Saddleback Classics Ser.). (Illus.). 48p. (J). per. 17.95 (978-1-56254-634-2(1), SP6341) Saddleback Educational Publishing, Inc.

—A Midsummer Night's Dream. Cheung, Charly, illus. 2013. (William Shakespeare Ser.). (ENG.). 64p. pap. 6.95 (978-1-906230-44-9(7)) Real Reads Ltd. GBR. Dist: Casemate Pubs. & Bk. Distributors, LLC.

—Pyramus & Thisbe: A Dramatization Arranged from Shakespeare's A Midsummer Night's Dream. Landes, William-Alan, ed. rev. ed. 2003. (One Act Plays Ser.). 55p. (Orig.). (J). (gr. 4-12). pap. 5.00 (978-0-88734-103-8(9)) Players Pr., Inc.

—Romeo & Juliet. Cheung, Charly, illus. 2013. (William Shakespeare Ser.). (ENG.). 64p. pap. 6.95 (978-1-906230-45-6(5)) Real Reads Ltd. GBR. Dist: Casemate Pubs. & Bk. Distributors, LLC.

—The Tempest. 2008. (Shakespeare Ser.: Level 2). (Illus.). 72p. pap., act. bk. ed. 10.95 (978-1-55576-327-5(8), EDSC-201B) EDCON Publishing Group.

—The Tempest. Cheung, Charly, illus. 2014. (William Shakespeare Ser.). (ENG.). 64p. pap. 6.95 (978-1-906230-46-3(3)) Real Reads Ltd. GBR. Dist: Casemate Pubs. & Bk. Distributors, LLC.

—Three Great Plays of Shakespeare, Pack. 2007. (ENG., Illus.). 80p. pap. 17.32 incl. cd-rom (978-1-4058-5221-0(6)) Pearson Education.

—Twelfth Night: Classicscript. Landes, William-Alan, ed. abr. ed. 2003. (Shakespeare Ser.: Vol. 3). 68p. (YA). (gr. 4-12). pap. 7.00 (978-0-88734-530-2(1)) Players Pr., Inc.

—The Two Gentlemen of Verona. 2008. (Easy Reading Shakespeare Ser.). (ENG., Illus.). 72p. pap., act. bk. ed. 10.95 (978-1-55576-350-3(2), EDSC-305B) EDCON Publishing Group.

Shakespeare, William & SparkNotes Staff. King Lear. Crowther, John, ed. 2003. (No Fear Shakespeare Ser.). (ENG., Illus.). 320p. pap. 6.95 (978-1-58663-853-5(X), Spark Notes) Sterling Publishing Co., Inc.

—Macbeth. Crowther, John, ed. 2003. (No Fear Shakespeare Ser.). (ENG., Illus.). 240p. pap. 5.95 (978-1-58663-846-7(7), Spark Notes) Sterling Publishing Co., Inc.

—Much Ado about Nothing. 2004. (No Fear Shakespeare Ser.). (ENG., Illus.). 256p. per. 5.95 (978-1-4114-0101-3(8), Spark Notes) Sterling Publishing Co., Inc.

Shakespeare, William, et al. The Tempest. 2003. (No Fear Shakespeare Ser.). (ENG., Illus.). 224p. pap. 5.95 (978-1-58663-849-8(1), Spark Notes) Sterling Publishing Co., Inc.

Shapiro, Gordon & Crafts, Gregory. Super Sidekick: The Musical. 2012. 55p. (J). pap. 8.95 (978-0-573-70096-5(6)) French, Samuel Inc.

Shaw, George Bernard. Annajanska. Landes, William-Alan, ed. 2003. (George Bernard Shaw Collection). 20p. (YA). (gr. 6-12). 8.00 (978-0-88734-863-1(7)) Players Pr., Inc.

—The Dark Lady of the Sonnets. abr. ed. 2005. (Stratford Festival Ser.). (gr. 9-12). (978-0-660-17979-7(2)) Canadian Broadcasting Corp./Societe Radio-Canada.

—The Inca of Perusalem. Landes, William-Alan, ed. 2003. (Players Press G. B. Shaw Collection). 28p. (YA). (gr. 4-12). 8.00 (978-0-88734-864-8(5)) Players Pr., Inc.

—O'Flaherty V. C. Landes, William-Alan, ed. 2003. (George Bernard Shaw Collection). 28p. (YA). (gr. 6-12). pap. 8.00 (978-0-88734-350-6(3)) Players Pr., Inc.

Shepard, Aaron. Folktales on Stage: Children's Plays for Readers Theater, with 16 Reader's Theatre Play Scripts from World Folk & Fairy Tales & Legends, Including Asian, African, Middle Eastern, & Native American. 2004. 180p. pap. 10.00 (978-0-938497-20-2(0)) Shepard Pubns.

Shepherd, C. A., et al. The Sly Fox (Playscript) 2003. (Musicals for Young Audiences Ser.). 32p. (Orig.). (YA). (gr. 3-12). pap. 8.00 (978-0-88734-503-6(4)) Players Pr., Inc.

Shockey, Marilyn. What's a Wolf to Do? (Musical) 42p. (YA). pap. 7.50 (978-1-58342-182-6(3), WD7) Dramatic Publishing Co.

Shucart, Deborah. ABC Scripts. 2010. 120p. 21.49 (978-1-4520-0407-5(2)); pap. 10.99 (978-1-4520-0406-8(4)) AuthorHouse.

Simandan, Voicu Mihnea. The Ironman. A Play. 2009. 32p. pap. 15.10 (978-0-557-06395-6(7)) Lulu Pr., Inc.

SINGH, H. Happy peace Day. 2008. 52p. per. 15.95 (978-1-4357-0773-3(7)) Lulu Pr., Inc.

Smith, Carrie. Humpty Dumpty's Fall. 2008. (Reader's Theater Nursery Rhymes & Songs Ser.). (Illus.). 48p. (J). (gr. k-1). pap. (978-1-60437-958-7(8)) Benchmark Education Co.

—The Jumping Monkeys. Harpster, Steve, illus. 2009. (Reader's Theater Nursery Rhymes & Songs Set B Ser.). 48p. (J). pap. (978-1-60859-155-8(7)) Benchmark Education Co.

—Mary Has a Little Lamb. 2008. (Reader's Theater Nursery Rhymes & Songs Ser.). (Illus.). 48p. (J). (gr. k-1). pap. (978-1-60437-978-5(2)) Benchmark Education Co.

—One Silly Hey Diddle Day. 2008. (Reader's Theater Nursery Rhymes & Songs Ser.). (Illus.). 48p. (J). (gr. k-1). pap. (978-1-60437-963-1(4)) Benchmark Education Co.

—Where Are Bo Peep's Sheep? Abbott, Jason, illus. 2009. (Reader's Theater Nursery Rhymes & Songs Set B Ser.). 48p. (J). pap. (978-1-60859-171-8(9)) Benchmark Education Co.

Smith, Laura Lundgren. Sending down the Sparrows. 2005. (SPA & ENG.). 48p. per. 21.95 (978-1-903392-11-9(X)) Salmon Publishing IRL. Dist: Dufour Editions, Inc.

Snyder, Geraldine Ann. Johnny Appleseed: Musical. 2003. (Illus.). 41p. (YA). pap. 6.95 (978-1-58342-127-7(0), J04) Dramatic Publishing Co.

Soto, Gary. Novio Boy: A Play. 2006. 78p. (gr. 7-12). 17.00 (978-0-7569-6684-3(1)) Perfection Learning Corp.

Sr. Hariette. Princess Frisky. 2008. 28p. pap. 13.99 (978-1-4389-0466-5(5)) AuthorHouse.

Stevenson, Robert Louis. Treasure Island. 2003. (More for Teens Ser.). 64p. (Orig.). (YA). (gr. 6-12). pap. 6.00 (978-0-88734-412-1(7)) Players Pr., Inc.

Stewart, Kelly, ed. Readers' Theater: Scripts for Young Readers. Palacios, John, illus. 2009. 16p. (J). pap. 16.95 (978-1-60184-166-7(3)); pap. 16.95 (978-1-60184-160-5(4)); pap. 16.95 (978-1-60184-154-4(X)); pap. 16.95 (978-1-60184-152-0(3)); pap. 16.95 (978-1-60184-150-6(7)); pap. 16.95 (978-1-60184-148-3(5)); pap. 16.95 (978-1-60184-146-9(9)) Primary Concepts, Inc.

—Readers' Theater: Scripts for Young Readers: the Monkey & the Crocodile. Palacios, John, illus. 2009. 16p. (J). pap. 16.95 (978-1-60184-164-3(7)) Primary Concepts, Inc.

—Readers' Theater: Scripts for Young Readers: the Peach Boy. Palacios, John, illus. 2009. 16p. (J). pap. 16.95 (978-1-60184-156-8(6)) Primary Concepts, Inc.

—Readers' Theater: Scripts for Young Readers: the Spear Throwing Contest. Palacios, John, illus. 2009. 16p. (J). pap. 16.95 (978-1-60184-158-2(2)) Primary Concepts, Inc.

Stewart, Kelly, retold by. Readers' Theater Stone Soup: Scripts for Young Readers. 2008. (Illus.). 16p. (J). 12.95 (978-1-60184-121-6(3)) Primary Concepts, Inc.

—Readers' Theater the Magic Porridge Pot: Scripts for Young Readers: the Magic Porridge Pot. 2008. (Illus.). 16p. (J). 12.95 (978-1-60184-117-9(5)) Primary Concepts, Inc.

—Readers' Theater the Mitten: Scripts for Young Readers: the Mitten. 2008. (Illus.). 16p. (J). 12.95 (978-1-60184-123-0(X)) Primary Concepts, Inc.

—Readers' Theater the Princess & the Pea: Scripts for Young Readers: the Princess & the Pea. 2008. (Illus.). 16p. (J). 12.95 (978-1-60184-115-5(9)) Primary Concepts, Inc.

Stickland, Eugene. Two Plays: Sitting on Paradise & a Guide to Mourning. 2003. (Plays & Play Collections). 168p. (YA). (gr. 6-12). pap. 15.00 (978-0-88734-931-7(5)) Players Pr., Inc.

Stickler, LeeDell. Busy Boogie: And Other Dramas for Preschool. 2004. (Just Add Kids Ser.). 112p. pap. 16.99 *(978-0-687-07645-1(5))* Abingdon Pr.
Strand, John. The Diaries. 2004. 104p. (J). pap. 6.50 *(978-1-58342-232-8(3),* D83) Dramatic Publishing Co.
Sturkie, Joan & Cassady, Marsh. Acting It Out - Junior. 2003. (Plays & Play Collections). 249p. (YA). (gr. 6-8). pap. 22.00 *(978-0-89390-240-7(3))* Resource Pubns., Inc.
Sugarek, Trisha. The Exciting Exploits of an Effervescent Elf. 2009. 58p. mass mkt. 9.95 *(978-0-87440-217-9(4))* Baker's Plays.
Surface, Mary Hall. Spirit Shall Fly: (play Script) 2007. (YA). 7.00 *(978-0-87602-418-8(5))* Family Plays.
Swajeski, Donna M. One Magic Kiss: Snow White & the Seven Dwarfs. 2014. 72p. (J). pap. 9.50 *(978-1-58342-948-8(4))* Dramatic Publishing Co.
—The Revolution Machine: Playscript. rev. ed. 2003. (Musicals Ser.). 55p. (Orig.). (J). (gr. 3-12). pap. 8.00 *(978-0-88734-511-1(5))* Players Pr., Inc.
Taylor, Ali. Cotton Wool. 2009. (ENG.). 64p. (J). pap. 18.95 *(978-1-85459-536-2(9))* Hern, Nick Bks., Ltd. GBR. Dist: Consortium Bk. Sales & Distribution.
Thistle, Louise. Little Red Snares the Wolf. (J). pap. 4.25 *(978-1-58342-036-2(3),* L49) Dramatic Publishing Co.
Thurston, Cheryl M. A Frog King's Daughter Is Nothing to Sneeze At: Playscript. 2003. (Musicals for Young Audiences Ser.). 32p. (Orig.). (YA). (gr. k-12). pap. 10.00 *(978-0-88734-513-5(1))* Players Pr., Inc.
Top Cat: Individual Title Six-Packs. (Story Steps Ser.). (gr. k-2). 32.00 *(978-0-7635-9851-8(8))* Rigby Education.
ToyBox Innovations, creator. Disney's Cinderella Read-along. 2006. (Disney's Read Along Ser.). (Illus.). 24p. (J). pap. *(978-0-7634-2171-7(5))* Walt Disney Records.
Treasure, Kevin A. Decisions Determine Destiny: Stories & Scenarios. 2010. 128p. pap. 13.99 *(978-1-4520-3102-6(9))* AuthorHouse.
Trussell-Cullen, Alan. Maui Tames the Sun Vol. 7: Band 15/Emerald. Grimwood, Tracie, illus. 2007. (Collins Big Cat Ser.). (ENG.). 32p. (J). pap. 8.99 *(978-0-00-722871-3(6))* HarperCollins Pubs. Ltd. GBR. Dist: Independent Pubs. Group.
Twead, Victoria. Morgan & the Martians. 2012. 60p. pap. *(978-1-78176-111-3(6))* FeedARead.com.
Twentieth Century Fox Home Entertainment Staff & Anderson, Wes. The Making of Fantastic Mr. Fox. 2009. (ENG., Illus.). 192p. 35.00 *(978-0-8478-3354-2(2))* Rizzoli International Pubns., Inc.
Umansky, Kaye. Cinderella. Crossland, Caroline, illus. 2012. 48p. *(978-0-88734-072-7(5))* Players Pr., Inc.
—The Emperor's New Clothes. 2003. (Curtain Up Ser.: Vol. 6). (ENG., Illus.). 48p. (J). (gr. 1-4). pap. *(978-0-7136-4624-5(1),* A&C Black) Bloomsbury Publishing Plc.
—Sleeping Beauty. Crossland, Caroline, illus. 2003. (Plays & Play Collections). (ENG.). 48p. (J). pap. 15.00 *(978-0-7136-5371-7(X),* A&C Black) Bloomsbury Publishing Plc GBR. Dist: Players Pr., Inc.
Ure, Jean. Star Crazy Me! 2008. (ENG.). 192p. (J). (gr. 4-7). pap. 9.95 *(978-0-00-722461-6(3),* HarperCollins Children's Bks.) HarperCollins Pubs. Ltd. GBR. Dist: HarperCollins Pubs.
Varod, Gil, et al. Oedipus for Kids. 2009. 88p. pap. 9.95 *(978-0-573-66358-1(0))* French, Samuel Inc.
Verrier, Steven. Don't Needle Me: A Ten-Minute Comedy Duet. 2003. 16p. (YA). pap. 4.50 *(978-1-932404-21-0(X),* 157A) Brooklyn Pubs.
—Golf Doctor: A Ten-Minute Comedy Duet. 2003. 16p. (YA). pap. 4.50 *(978-1-932404-41-8(4),* 108) Brooklyn Pubs.
Walker, Geof. William Shakespeare's 'A Midsummer Night's Dream' - a playscript for younger Students. 2006. 49p. pap. 19.45 *(978-1-4116-4407-6(7))* Lulu Pr., Inc.
Walker, George F. Moss Park & Tough! The Bobby & Tina Plays. 2015. (ENG.). 192p. pap. 19.95 *(978-0-88922-954-9(6))* Talonbooks, Ltd. CAN. Dist: Consortium Bk. Sales & Distribution.
Walker, Lois. Crazy Critters. Boyer, Susy, illus. 2007. (Collins Big Cat Ser.). (ENG.). 24p. (J). pap. 7.99 *(978-0-00-722869-0(4))* HarperCollins Pubs. Ltd. GBR. Dist: Independent Pubs. Group.
—Gigantic Turnip Tug. Guthridge, Bettina, illus. 2007. (Collins Big Cat Ser.). (ENG.). 1p. (J). pap. 7.99 *(978-0-00-722873-7(2))* HarperCollins Pubs. Ltd. GBR. Dist: Independent Pubs. Group.
Wallace, Nancy K. Ghosts & Gummy Worms: A Readers' Theater Script & Guide, 1 vol. Fleming, Lucy, illus. 2016. (ENG.). 32p. (J). *(978-1-62402-113-8(1))* Magic Wagon.
—Groundhogs & Guinea Pigs: A Readers' Theater Script & Guide, 1 vol. Fleming, Lucy, illus. 2016. (ENG.). 32p. (J). *(978-1-62402-114-5(X))* Magic Wagon.
—Medals & Memorials: A Readers' Theater Script & Guide, 1 vol. Mata, Nina, illus. 2016. (ENG.). 32p. (J). *(978-1-62402-115-2(8))* Magic Wagon.
—Pickles & Parks: A Readers' Theater Script & Guide, 1 vol. Fleming, Lucy, illus. 2016. (ENG.). 32p. (J). *(978-1-62402-116-9(6))* Magic Wagon.
—Princedom of Pea: A Readers' Theater Script & Guide. Mata, Nina, illus. 2013. (Readers' Theater: How to Put on a Production Ser.). 32p. (J). (gr. 2-6). lib. bdg. 28.50 *(978-1-61641-988-2(1),* Looking Glass Library- Nonfiction) Magic Wagon.
—Princess & the Frog: A Readers' Theater Script & Guide. Henninger, Michelle, illus. 2013. (Readers' Theater: How to Put on a Production Ser.). 32p. (J). (gr. 2-6). lib. bdg. 28.50 *(978-1-61641-989-9(X),* Looking Glass Library- Nonfiction) Magic Wagon.
—Snow White & the Seven Dorks: A Readers' Theater Script & Guide. Mata, Nina, illus. 2013. (Readers' Theater: How to Put on a Production Ser.). 32p. (J). (gr. 2-6). lib. bdg. 28.50 *(978-1-61641-990-5(3),* Looking Glass Library- Nonfiction) Magic Wagon.
—Turkey & Take-Out: A Readers' Theater Script & Guide, 1 vol. Fleming, Lucy, illus. 2016. (ENG.). 32p. (J). *(978-1-62402-117-6(4))* Magic Wagon.
Walter, Kristin. The Elves & the Shoemaker. 2010. 47p. pap. 8.95 *(978-0-87440-730-3(3))* Baker's Plays.
—Hansel & Gretel. 2010. (ENG.). 59p. pap. 7.00 *(978-0-87440-269-8(7))* Baker's Plays.
—Last of the Dragons: Based on the sotry by Edith Nesbit. 2011. 41p. pap. 8.95 *(978-0-87440-258-2(1))* Baker's Plays.
Washington Sr., Von H. The Journey Begins: Seven Stops to Freedom & Contact in Harmonia. 2009. 108p. 20.95 *(978-0-595-51190-7(2));* pap. 10.95 *(978-0-595-50468-8(X))* iUniverse, Inc.
Watson, James. Gotcha! 2007. (Collins Drama Ser.). (ENG., Illus.). 96p. (J). pap. 13.99 *(978-0-00-725870-3(4))* HarperCollins Pubs. Ltd. GBR. Dist: Independent Pubs. Group.
Watts, Irene N. Munsch at Play: Eight Stage Adaptations for Young Performers. 2nd ed. 2010. (ENG., Illus.). 80p. (J). (gr. 1-4). 24.95 *(978-1-55451-230-0(1),* 9781554512300) Annick Pr., Ltd. CAN. Dist: Publishers Group West (PGW).
Way, Charles. The Classic Fairytales. 2003. (ENG., Illus.). 200p. pap. 25.95 *(978-0-9542330-0-6(X))* Aurora Metro Pubns. Ltd. GBR. Dist: Consortium Bk. Sales & Distribution.
—Classic Fairytales 2: Retold for the Stage. 2008. (ENG., Illus.). 250p. pap. 26.95 *(978-0-9551566-7-0(X))* Aurora Metro Pubns. Ltd. GBR. Dist: Consortium Bk. Sales & Distribution.
—New Plays for Young People. 2014. (ENG.). 224p. pap. 34.95 *(978-1-906582-51-7(3))* Aurora Metro Pubns. Ltd. GBR. Dist: Consortium Bk. Sales & Distribution.
Welch, Fay. The Magic Swap Shop. rev. ed. 2003. 48p. (YA). (gr. 3-12). pap. 6.00 *(978-0-88734-509-8(3))* Players Pr., Inc.
Westley, Joan. Readers' Theater the Emperor's New Clothes: Scripts for Young Readers: 2008. (Illus.). 32p. (J). 12.95 net. *(978-1-60184-125-4(6))* Primary Concepts, Inc.
Westley, Joan, retold by. Readers' Theater the Ugly Duckling: Scripts for Young Readers: the Ugly Duckling. 2008. (Illus.). 16p. (J). 12.95 *(978-1-60184-119-3(1))* Primary Concepts, Inc.
Wheeler, Jacque & Hartsfield, Mariella G. Tall Betsy & the Crackerbarrel Tales. 2003. 32p. (YA). (gr. k-12). pap. 6.00 *(978-0-88734-265-3(5))* Players Pr., Inc.
Wignell, Edel. Bendelomena. Goss, Mini, illus. 2007. (Collins Big Cat Ser.). (ENG.). 1p. (J). pap. 8.99 *(978-0-00-722868-3(6))* HarperCollins Pubs. Ltd. GBR. Dist: Independent Pubs. Group.
Williams, David L. The Bully. 2014. 53p. pap. 9.95 *(978-1-58342-906-8(9))* Dramatic Publishing Co.
Williams, Guy. Billy Budd. 2003. (More for Teens Ser.). 32p. (Orig.). (YA). (gr. 6-12). pap. 5.00 *(978-0-88734-415-2(1))* Players Pr., Inc.
—David & Goliath. 2003. (Players Press Classicscripts Ser.). (Illus.). 20p. (Orig.). (J). (gr. 3-18). pap. 6.00 *(978-0-88734-411-4(9))* Players Pr., Inc.
—Nicholas Nickleby: Playscript. 2003. (Ideal for Teens Ser.). 36p. (YA). (gr. 6-12). pap. 6.00 *(978-0-88734-515-9(8))* Players Pr., Inc.
Williams, Marcia. More Tales from Shakespeare. Williams, Marcia, illus. 2005. (ENG., Illus.). 40p. (J). (gr. 3-7). pap. 8.99 *(978-0-7636-2693-8(7))* Candlewick Pr.
Wilson, Jacqueline. Beauty & the Beast. Kavanagh, Peter, illus. 2012. *(978-0-88734-073-4(3))* Players Pr., Inc.
Wim, Coleman. Classroom Plays by Wim Coleman. 2012. 48p. (J). pap. 12.95 *(978-1-935178-26-2(1),* ChironBooks) Coleman/Perrin.
Winther, Barbara. India, Burma/Thailand, Vietnam. 2004. (Plays from Asian Tales Ser.: No. 1). 52p. (YA). (gr. 3-12). pap. 10.00 *(978-0-88734-486-2(0))* Players Pr., Inc.
—India, Indonesia/Malaysia, China. 2004. (Plays from Asian Tales Ser.: No. 2). 60p. (YA). (gr. 3-12). pap. 10.00 *(978-0-88734-487-9(9))* Players Pr., Inc.
—Japan & Korea. 2004. (Plays from Asian Tales Ser.: No. 3). 56p. (J). pap. 10.00 *(978-0-88734-488-6(7))* Players Pr., Inc.
Wistrand, Carolyn Nur. Beauty in Black Performance: Plays for African American Youth. 2006. (Illus.). (YA). 151p. *(978-1-59221-379-5(0));* (ENG., 158p. pap. *(978-1-59221-380-1(4))* Africa World Pr.
Wolak, Camilla H. Squire Gullible & the Dragon. rev. ed. 2003. (Theater for Young Audiences Ser.). 40p. (YA). (gr. 3-12). pap. 6.00 *(978-0-88734-508-1(5))* Players Pr., Inc.
Wood, David. The Twits. 62p. (YA). (gr. 6). pap. 6.25 *(978-1-58342-172-7(6),* TD6) Dramatic Publishing Co.
Wood, David & Dahl, Roald. Danny the Champion of the World. 2006. 70p. pap. *(978-0-573-15016-6(8))* French, Samuel Inc.
Wood, Nick. Warrior Square. 2004. (ENG.). 64p. pap. 18.95 *(978-0-9546912-0-2(2))* Aurora Metro Pubns. Ltd. GBR. Dist: Consortium Bk. Sales & Distribution.
Wordwindow, illus. Shakespeare for Children Picture Book. 2007. 32p. (J). 14.95 *(978-0-9774484-8-7(7))* Wordwindow LLC.
Woyiwada, Allison. The Little Fir Tree: A Musical for Primary Children Based on a Story by Hans Christian Andersen. 2003. (Musicals for Young Audiences Ser.). 16p. (J). (gr. k-6). pap. 5.00 *(978-0-88734-428-2(3))* Players Pr., Inc.
Wray, Charles. A Spell of Cold Weather. 2004. (ENG.). 96p. pap. 18.95 *(978-0-9542330-8-2(5))* Aurora Metro Pubns. Ltd. GBR. Dist: Consortium Bk. Sales & Distribution.
Wright, Roosevelt, Jr. Deacon Willie's Last Will & Testament. 2004. (YA). *(978-0-943751-36-8(5))* Free Pr. Pubs.
—For Such a Time As This. 2004. (YA). 5.00 *(978-0-943751-31-3(4))* Free Pr. Pubs.
Wright, Roosevelt, Sr. The Prodigals. 2004. (YA). *(978-0-943751-35-1(7))* Free Pr. Pubs.
Wright, Roosevelt, Jr. Shoe Shine. 2004. (YA). 8.00 *(978-0-943751-38-2(1))* Free Pr. Pubs.
Wright, Roosevelt, Jr. & Wright, Roosevelt. Honey Babe's Treasure: A Black Heritage Drama in Two Acts. 2003. 24p. 6.00 *(978-0-943751-22-1(5))* Free Pr. Pubs.
Yee, Lauren D. How to Be the Perfect Parent: A Comedy Monologue. 2003. (YA). pap. 4.50 *(978-1-932404-35-7(X),* 288) Brooklyn Pubs.
—My Mother's Touch: A Dramatic Monologue. 2003. (YA). pap. 4.50 *(978-1-932404-34-0(1),* 287) Brooklyn Pubs.
Zacarias, Karen. Chasing George Washington: A White House Adventure. 2013. 59p. (J). pap. 9.95 *(978-1-58342-828-3(3))* Dramatic Publishing Co.
Zacarias, Karen. Einstein Is a Dummy. 2013. 80p. (J). pap. *(978-1-58342-825-2(9))* Dramatic Publishing Co.
Zacarias, Karen. Einstein Is a Dummy (small-Cast Musical) 2013. 62p. (J). pap. 9.95 *(978-1-58342-826-9(7))* Dramatic Publishing Co.
Zacarias, Karen. Looking for Roberto Clemente. 2013. (Illus.). 72p. (J). pap. *(978-1-58342-827-6(5))* Dramatic Publishing Co.
Zeder, Suzan. Wiley & the Hairy Man (musical) 2014. 69p. pap. 9.95 *(978-1-58342-916-7(6))* Dramatic Publishing Co.
Zephaniah, Benjamin, et al. Theatre Centre - Plays for Young People Vol. 1: Celebrating 50 Years of Theatre Centre. 2003. (ENG., Illus.). 300p. pap. 28.95 *(978-0-9542330-5-1(0))* Aurora Metro Pubns. Ltd. GBR. Dist: Consortium Bk. Sales & Distribution.
Zindel, Paul. The Effect of Gamma Rays on Man-in-the-Moon Marigolds. 2005. (ENG.). 112p. (YA). (gr. 8-18). pap. 8.99 *(978-0-06-075738-0(8),* HarperTeen) HarperCollins Pubs.
Zuber, Diane. The Broken Doll A Musical Play for Christmas. 2006. (J). 29.95 *(978-0-9785551-0-8(4))* Zuber Publishing.

PLAYS—FICTION

Bryant, Annie. Out of Bounds. 2005. (Beacon Street Girls Ser.: No. 4). 255p. (J). 7.99 *(978-0-9746587-9-7(0),* Beacon Street Girls) B*tween Productions, Inc.
Butler, Dori Hillestad. The Ghost Backstage. Damant, Aurore, illus. 2014. (Haunted Library: 3). (ENG.). 128p. (J). (gr. 1-3). 5.99 *(978-0-448-46246-2(X),* Grosset & Dunlap) Penguin Young Readers Group.
Child, Lauren. I Can't Stop Hiccuping! 2010. (Charlie & Lola Ser.). lib. bdg. 13.55 *(978-0-606-10629-0(4),* Turtleback) Turtleback Bks.
Christopher, Lawrence. The Tickle Fingers: Where Is Pinky? Christopher, Lawrence, illus. 2006. (ENG., Illus.). 24p. (J). (gr. -1-18). 9.95 *(978-0-9712278-3-5(7))* MF Unlimited.
Cook, Gina J. Just a Little Lion: A Little Cheetah Learns the Truth about Little Lions As We Learn the Truth about Little Lies. 2012. 38p. pap. 13.95 *(978-1-4497-6352-7(9),* WestBow Pr.) Author Solutions, Inc.
Divine, L. Hustlin' 2009. (ENG., Illus.). 256p. (YA). (gr. 9). pap. 15.00 *(978-0-7582-3105-5(9),* K-Teen/Dafina) Kensington Publishing Corp.
Doti, James. Jimmy Finds His Voice. Mertins, Lisa, illus. 2013. (J). 14.95 *(978-1-935204-47-3(5))* Salem Author Services.
Emily Reed-Guldin, Reed-Guldin & Emily Reed-Guldin. Sarah & Sammi's Playhouse Bedroom. 2009. 32p. pap. 14.49 *(978-1-4389-5881-1(1))* AuthorHouse.
Engelbreit, Mary. Queen of the Class. Engelbreit, Mary, illus. 2007. (Illus.). 24p. (J). 16.00 *(978-1-4223-6705-6(3))* DIANE Publishing Co.
Ficocelli, Elizabeth. Kid Tea, 0 vols. Dibley, Glin, illus. 2013. (ENG.). 36p. (J). (gr. -1-k). pap. 9.99 *(978-1-4778-4738-1(3),* 9781477847381, Amazon Children's Publishing) Amazon Publishing.
Gilman, Phoebe. Jillian Jiggs & the Secret Surprise. 2004. (J). (gr. -1-2). spiral bd. *(978-0-616-01655-8(7))* Canadian National Institute for the Blind/Institut National Canadien pour les Aveugles.
Hairston, Kennard Lee. Rosie Bear Plays Baseball. 2009. 48p. pap. 19.49 *(978-1-4389-7343-2(8))* AuthorHouse.
Harper, Charise Mericle. Just Grace, Star on Stage. 2014. (Just Grace Ser.: 9). (ENG., Illus.). 208p. (J). (gr. 1-4). pap. 5.99 *(978-0-544-22533-6(3),* HMH Books For Young Readers) Houghton Mifflin Harcourt Publishing Co.
Holmes, Sara. Operation Yes. 2009. 234p. (J). pap. *(978-0-545-20418-7(6))* Scholastic, Inc.
Hutchins, Hazel. Robyn's Monster Play, 1 vol. Cathcart, Yvonne, illus. 2008. (Formac First Novels Ser.). (ENG.). 64p. (J). (gr. 2-5). 5.95 *(978-0-88780-748-0(8),* 9780887807480) Formac Publishing Co., Ltd. CAN. Dist: Casemate Pubs. & Bk. Distributors, LLC.
—Robyn's Monster Play. Cathcart, Yvonne, illus. 2008. (Formac First Novels Ser.). (ENG.). 64p. (J). (gr. 2-5). 14.95 *(978-0-88780-750-3(X),* 9780887807503) Formac Publishing Co., Ltd. CAN. Dist: Casemate Pubs. & Bk. Distributors, LLC.
ImageBooks Staff. Little Horse: Finger Puppet Book. Put, Klaartje van der, illus. 2013. (Little Finger Puppet Board Bks.). (ENG.). 12p. (J). (gr. -1 — 1). bds. 6.99 *(978-1-4521-1249-7(5))* Chronicle Bks. LLC.
Jakubowski, Michele. Sidney & Sydney, 1 vol. 2014. (Sidney & Sydney Ser.). (ENG.). 128p. (gr. 1-3). 75.96 *(978-1-4795-5749-3(8))* Picture Window Bks.
Koch, Joann. Annie's World. 2009. 20p. (J). pap. 9.95 *(978-1-4327-4063-4(6))* Outskirts Pr., Inc.
Koontz, Robin. Zelda la Cenicienta. 2012. (SPA & ENG.). 24p. (gr. 2-3). pap. 8.95 *(978-1-61810-544-8(2))* Rourke Educational Media.
Korda, Lerryn. It's Vacation Time. Korda, Lerryn, illus. 2010. (Playtime with Little Nye Ser.). (ENG., Illus.). 26p. (J). (— 1). 8.99 *(978-0-7636-4813-8(2))* Candlewick Pr.
Kristina Takes the Stage. 2008. (Illus.). 56p. (J). mass mkt. 10.95 *(978-0-9792361-3-6(4))* Inspire U., LLC.
Lawlor, Laurie. The Biggest Pest on Eighth Avenue. Fisher, Cynthia, illus. (Holiday House Reader Ser.). (ENG.). 47p. (J). (gr. k-3). tchr. ed. 14.95 *(978-0-8234-1321-8(7))* Holiday Hse., Inc.
Little Engine - Playing Together. 2005. (J). bds. *(978-1-4194-0022-3(3))* Paradise Pr., Inc.
Madonna, pseud. A Rose by Any Other Name. Fulvimari, Jeffrey, illus. 2007. (English Roses Ser.: 4). (ENG.). 144p. (J). (gr. 3-7). 10.99 *(978-0-14-240685-8(9),* Puffin Books) Penguin Young Readers Group.
Mason, Jane B. & Hines-Stephens, Sarah. Let Sleeping Dogs Spy. Phillips, Craig, illus. 2012. 91p. (J). pap. *(978-0-545-37470-5(7))* Scholastic, Inc.
O'Connor, George. Ker-Splash! O'Connor, George, illus. 2010. (ENG., Illus.). 40p. (J). (gr. -1-3). 19.99 *(978-1-4424-2196-7(7),* Simon & Schuster Bks. For Young Readers) Simon & Schuster Bks. For Young Readers.
Reed-Guldin, Emily. Sarah & Sammi's Playhouse: Mermaid Adventure. 2009. 36p. pap. 16.99 *(978-1-4389-9342-3(0))* AuthorHouse.
Renna, G. M. Meticulous Nicholas Goes to Camp. 2009. 64p. pap. 10.49 *(978-1-4490-2784-1(9))* AuthorHouse.
Routley, Becky. Moon Golf. 2009. (Illus.). 28p. pap. 12.49 *(978-1-4490-4713-9(0))* AuthorHouse.
Rud, Jeff. Crossover, 1 vol. 2008. (Orca Sports Ser.). (ENG.). 176p. (YA). (gr. 6-10). pap. 9.95 *(978-1-55143-981-5(6))* Orca Bk. Pubs. USA.
Schmidt, Gary D. The Wednesday Wars. (ENG.). 272p. (J). (gr. 5-7). 2009. pap. 7.99 *(978-0-547-23760-2(X))* 2007. 16.99 *(978-0-618-72483-3(4))* Houghton Mifflin Harcourt Publishing Co.
—The Wednesday Wars. 2008. *(978-0-545-10562-0(5))* Scholastic, Inc.
—The Wednesday Wars. 2009. lib. bdg. 18.40 *(978-0-606-10573-6(5),* Turtleback) Turtleback Bks.
The School Play: Individual Title Six-Packs. (gr. -1-2). 27.00 *(978-0-7635-9473-2(3))* Rigby Education.
Su, Lucy. Play Hide & Seek. Su, Lucy, illus. 2003. (Kitten & Baby Kitten Ser.). (Illus.). 42p. (J). pap. *(978-1-85602-538-6(1),* Pavilion Children's Books) Pavilion Bks.
Ventura, Marne. Jittery Jake Conquers Stage Fright. Trinidad, Leo, illus. 2016. (Worry Warriors Ser.). (ENG.). 96p. (gr. 2-4). lib. bdg. 25.99 *(978-1-4965-3612-9(6))* Stone Arch Bks.
Wallace, Nancy K. Claim to Fame, 1 vol. Chronister, Amanda, illus. 2013. (Abby & the Book Bunch Ser.). (ENG.). 80p. (J). (gr. 2-5). 27.07 *(978-1-61641-912-7(1))* Magic Wagon.
Walters, Celeste. Treading the Boards. 2007. 208p. *(978-1-921049-80-4(4))* Little Hare Bks. AUS. Dist: HarperCollins Pubs. Australia.
Wheeler, Lisa. Invasion of the Pig Sisters. Ansley, Frank, illus. 2006. (Fitch & Chip Ser.: 4). (ENG.). 48p. (J). (gr. 1-3). pap. 3.99 *(978-0-689-84958-9(3),* Simon Spotlight) Simon Spotlight.
Winkler, Henry & Oliver, Lin. Bookmarks Are People Too! Garrett, Scott, illus. 2014. (Here's Hank Ser.: 1). (ENG.). 128p. (J). (gr. 1-3). 14.99 *(978-0-448-48239-2(8));* No. 1. 5.99 *(978-0-448-47997-2(4))* Penguin Young Readers Group. (Grosset & Dunlap).
—Bookmarks Are People Too! 2014. (Here's Hank Ser.: 1). lib. bdg. 16.00 *(978-0-606-34142-4(0),* Turtleback) Turtleback Bks.

PLAYS, CHRISTMAS

see Christmas Plays

PLAYS FOR CHILDREN

see Plays

PLAYWRIGHTS

see Dramatists

PLAYWRITING

see Drama—Technique

PLESKIT (FICTITIOUS CHARACTER)—FICTION

Coville, Bruce. I Lost My Grandfather's Brain. unabr. ed. 2004. (I Was a Sixth Grade Alien Ser.: Vol. 3). 160p. (J). (gr. 3-6). pap. 29.00 incl. audio *(978-0-8072-8385-1(1),* YA180SP, Listening Library) Random Hse. Audio Publishing Group.
—I Was a Sixth Grade Alien. (I Was a Sixth Grade Alien Ser.: Vol. 1). 170p. (J). (gr. 4-6). pap. 3.99 *(978-0-8072-8202-1(2));* 2004. (gr. 3-6). pap. 29.00 incl. audio *(978-0-8072-8201-4(4),* S YA 138 SP) Random Hse. Audio Publishing Group. (Listening Library).

PLOT-YOUR-OWN STORIES

Here are entered works of fiction in which the reader chooses from a number of possible options for developing the story.

Baxendale, Trevor & BBC. Choose the Future - Terror Moon. 2016. (ENG.). 208p. (J). pap. 9.99 *(978-1-4059-2651-5(1),* 9781405926515) Penguin Bks., Ltd. GBR. Dist: Diamond Comic Distributors, Inc.
Becket, Jim. Inca Gold: Choose Your Own Adventure #20. 2007. (Choose Your Own Adventure Ser.: 20). (Illus.). 144p. (J). per. 6.99 *(978-1-933390-20-8(4),* CHCL20) Chooseco LLC.
Blade, Adam. The Dagger of Doom. 2014. (Beast Quest Ser.). (ENG., Illus.). 128p. (J). (gr. 2-4). 5.99 *(978-1-4083-1406-7(1))* Hodder & Stoughton GBR. Dist: Hachette Bk. Group.
—The Dark Cauldron. 2014. (Beast Quest Ser.). (ENG., Illus.). 112p. (J). (gr. 2-4). pap. 5.99 *(978-1-4083-0943-8(2))* Hodder & Stoughton GBR. Dist: Hachette Bk. Group.
—The Pirate's Curse. 2016. (Beast Quest Ser.). (ENG., Illus.). 144p. (J). (gr. 2-4). pap. 5.99 *(978-1-4083-1840-9(7))* Hodder & Stoughton GBR. Dist: Hachette Bk. Group.
Blashfield, Jean F. Realm of the Enchanter. 2007. (Paths of Doom Ser.). (Illus.). 127p. (J). per. 4.99 *(978-1-931567-73-2(5))* Margaret Weis Productions, Ltd.
Borgenicht, David & Khan, Hena. Amazon: You Decide How to Survive! 2015. (WorstCase Scenario Ultimate Adventure Ser.). (ENG., Illus.). 204p. (gr. 3-8). 47.10 *(978-1-59920-980-7(2),* 1389530) Black Rabbit Bks.
Borgenicht, David & Lurie, Alexander. Deadly Seas: You Decide How to Survive! 2015. (WorstCase Scenario Ultimate Adventure Ser.). (ENG., Illus.). 204p. (gr. 3-8). 47.10 *(978-1-59920-981-4(0))* Black Rabbit Bks.
Borgenicht, David, et al. The Worst-Case Scenario: Everest - You Decide How to Survive! Labat, Yancey, illus. 2011. (Worst Case Scenario Ser.). (ENG.). 208p. (J). (gr. 4-5). 12.99 *(978-0-8118-7123-5(1))* Chronicle Bks. LLC.
Bosch, Pseudonymous. Write This Book: A Do-It-Yourself Mystery. (Secret Ser.). (ENG., Illus.). (J). (gr. 3-7). 2014. 304p. pap. 8.99 *(978-0-316-20780-5(2))* 2013. 288p. 16.99 *(978-0-316-20781-2(0))* Little, Brown Bks. for Young Readers.
Braun, Eric. Goldilocks & the Three Bears: An Interactive Fairy Tale Adventure. Lopez, Alex, illus. 2015. (You Choose: Fractured Fairy Tales Ser.). (ENG.). 112p. (gr. 3-4). lib. bdg. 31.99 *(978-1-4914-5855-6(0),* You Choose Bks.) Capstone Press of Coughlan Cos.
—Little Red Riding Hood: An Interactive Fairy Tale Adventure. Epelbaum, Mariano, illus. 2015. (You Choose: Fractured Fairy Tales Ser.). (ENG.). 112p. (gr. 3-4). pap. 6.95 *(978-1-4914-5929-4(8),* You Choose Bks.) Capstone Press of Coughlan Cos.
Braun, Eric & Gunderson, Jessica. Cinderella: An Interactive Fairy Tale Adventure. Lopez, Ayesha, illus. 2015. (You Choose: Fractured Fairy Tales Ser.). (ENG.). 112p. (gr. 3-4). lib. bdg. 31.99 *(978-1-4914-5854-9(2),* You Choose Bks.) Capstone Press of Coughlan Cos.
Brezenoff, Steven. The Missing Bully: An Interactive Mystery Adventure. Calo, Marcos, illus. 2017. (You Choose Stories: Field Trip Mysteries Ser.). (ENG.). 112p. (gr. 3-7). lib. bdg. 32.65 *(978-1-4965-2642-7(2))* Stone Arch Bks.
Bright, J. E. The Case of the Cheese Thief, 1 vol. Neely, Scott, illus. 2014. (You Choose Stories: Scooby-Doo Ser.). (ENG.). 112p. (gr. 2-3). pap. 6.95 *(978-1-4342-7927-9(8),* You Choose Bks.) Capstone Press of Coughlan Cos.

P
Q
R

—Seed Bank Heist. Beavers, Ethen, illus. 2015. (You Choose Stories: Batman Ser.). (ENG.). 112p. (gr. 2-3). pap. 6.95 *(978-1-4342-9709-9(8))* Stone Arch Bks.

Brooks, Minnie. Carl, Colonel of the Carrot Colony. 2012. 40p. pap. 24.99 *(978-1-62230-714-2(3))* Salem Author Services.

Burgan, Michael. World War II Pilots: An Interactive History Adventure. 2013. (You Choose: World War II Ser.). (ENG.). 112p. (gr. 3-4). pap. 41.70 *(978-1-62065-719-5(8),* You Choose Bks.) Capstone Press of Coughlan Cos.

Cannella, Marco & Marron, Jose Luis, illus. Tattoo of Death. 2007. (Choose Your Own Adventure Ser.: No. 22). 113p. (J). (gr. 4-7). pap. 6.99 *(978-1-933390-22-2(0))* Chooseco LLC.

Caravan. 2007. (Choose Your Own Adventure - Dragonlarks Ser.). (Illus.). 64p. (J). (gr. 4-7). pap. 7.99 *(978-1-933390-54-3(9))* Chooseco LLC.

Chooseco, creator. Choose Your Own Adventure 4 Book Boxed Set #1: The Abominable Snowman/Journey under the Sea/Space & Beyond/the Lost Jewels of Nabooti. 2006. (ENG., Illus.). 576p. (J). (gr. 2-9). pap. 22.99 *(978-1-933390-94-9(8))* Chooseco LLC.

—Choose Your Own Adventure 4 Book Boxed Set #2: Mystery of the Maya/House of Danger/Race Forever/Escape. 2006. (ENG., Illus.). 144p. (J). pap. 22.99 *(978-1-933390-95-6(6))* Chooseco LLC.

Clark, Bridie. Maybe Tonight? 2013. (Snap Decision Ser.: 1). (ENG.). 224p. (YA). (gr. 7). pap. 9.99 *(978-1-59643-816-3(9))* Roaring Brook Pr.

—You Only Live Once. 2014. (Snap Decision Ser.: 2). (ENG.). 224p. (YA). (gr. 7). pap. 9.99 *(978-1-59643-817-0(7),* 9781596438170) Roaring Brook Pr.

Croall, Marie P. School of Evil. Carruthers, Sandy, illus. 2010. (Twisted Journeys (r) Ser.: 13). (ENG.). 112p. (J). (gr. 4-7). pap. 7.95 *(978-0-8225-9271-6(1),* Graphic Universe™); lib. bdg. 27.93 *(978-0-8225-9263-1(0))* Lerner Publishing Group.

Croall, Marie P. & Jolley, Dan. Agent Mongoose & the Attack of the Giant Insects. Wendt, Matt, illus. 2010. (Twisted Journeys (r) Ser.: 15). (ENG.). 112p. (J). (gr. 4-7). lib. bdg. 27.93 *(978-0-8225-9251-8(7))* Lerner Publishing Group.

David, Juliet. The Christmas Story, 1 vol. Parry, Jo, illus. 2009. (Candle Read & Play Ser.). 12p. (J). bds. 11.99 *(978-0-8254-7400-2(0),* Candle Bks.) Lion Hudson PLC GBR. Dist: Kregel Pubns.

DeHoratius, Ed. The Journey of Odysseus. Delandro Hardison, Brian, illus. 2009. (Follow Your Fates Ser.). 116p. (J). pap. 12.00 *(978-0-86516-710-0(9))* Bolchazy-Carducci Pubs.

—Wrath of Achilles. 2009. 62p. pap. 12.00 *(978-0-86516-708-7(7))* Bolchazy-Carducci Pubs.

Dever, Joe. Caverns of Kalte. 2007. (ENG., Illus.). 320p. (YA). pap. 14.95 *(978-1-906103-20-0(8))* Mongoose Publishing GBR. Dist: Diamond Bk. Distributors.

Doeden, Matt. At Battle in World War II: An Interactive Battlefield Adventure. 2015. (You Choose: Battlefields Ser.). (ENG., Illus.). 112p. (gr. 3-4). lib. bdg. 31.99 *(978-1-4914-2152-9(5),* You Choose Bks.) Capstone Press of Coughlan Cos.

—The Berlin Wall: An Interactive Modern History Adventure, 1 vol. 2014. (You Choose: Modern History Ser.). (ENG.). 112p. (gr. 3-4). 31.99 *(978-1-4914-0354-9(3),* You Choose Bks.) Capstone Press of Coughlan Cos.

—Can You Survive a Global Blackout? An Interactive Doomsday Adventure. Nathan, James, illus. 2015. (You Choose: Doomsday Ser.). (ENG.). 112p. (gr. 3-4). lib. bdg. 31.99 *(978-1-4914-5850-1(X),* You Choose Bks.) Capstone Press of Coughlan Cos.

—Can You Survive a Virus Outbreak? An Interactive Doomsday Adventure. 2015. (You Choose: Doomsday Ser.). (ENG., Illus.). 112p. (gr. 3-4). lib. bdg. 31.99 *(978-1-4914-5851-8(8),* You Choose Bks.) Capstone Press of Coughlan Cos.

—Can You Survive an Artificial Intelligence Uprising? An Interactive Doomsday Adventure. Fisher-Johnson, Paul, illus. 2016. (You Choose: Doomsday Ser.). (ENG.). 112p. (gr. 3-4). lib. bdg. 31.99 *(978-1-4914-8107-3(2),* You Choose Bks.) Capstone Press of Coughlan Cos.

—Can You Survive an Asteroid Strike? An Interactive Doomsday Adventure. Davidson, Paul, illus. 2016. (You Choose: Doomsday Ser.). (ENG.). 112p. (gr. 3-4). lib. bdg. 31.99 *(978-1-4914-8109-7(9),* You Choose Bks.) Capstone Press of Coughlan Cos.

—The Civil War [Scholastic]: An Interactive History Adventure. 2010. (You Choose: History Ser.). 112p. pap. 0.90 *(978-1-4296-5977-2(7),* You Choose Bks.) Capstone Press of Coughlan Cos.

—The Queen Mary: A Chilling Interactive Adventure. 2016. (You Choose: Haunted Places Ser.). (ENG., Illus.). 112p. (gr. 3-4). lib. bdg. 31.99 *(978-1-5157-2578-7(2),* You Choose Bks.) Capstone Press of Coughlan Cos.

Donploypetch, Jintanan & Montgomery, R. A. Mystery of the Maya. Pornkerd, Vorrarit & Yaweera, Sasiprapa, illus. 2006. (Choose Your Own Adventure Ser.: No. 5). 144p. (J). (gr. 4-8). per. 6.99 *(978-1-933390-05-5(0),* CHCL05) Chooseco LLC.

Doyle, Bill & Borgenicht, David. Everest: You Decide How to Survive! 2015. (WorstCase Scenario Ultimate Adventure Ser.). (ENG., Illus.). 204p. (gr. 3-8). 47.10 *(978-1-59920-978-4(0))* Black Rabbit Bks.

Dragonology: Pocket Adventures, 4 vols. 2007. (Illus.). (J). *(978-0-7636-3698-2(3)); (978-0-7636-3699-9(1)); (978-0-7636-3697-5(5)); (978-0-7636-3696-8(7))* Candlewick Pr.

Enderle, Dotti. Beyond the Grave: An Up2U Mystery Adventure, 1 vol. Uhles, Mary, illus. 2013. (Up2U Adventures Ser.). (ENG.). 80p. (J). (gr. 2-5). 27.07 *(978-1-61641-964-6(4),* Calico Chapter Bks) Magic Wagon.

—Clawed! An Up2U Horror Adventure, 1 vol. To, Vivienne, illus. 2013. (Up2U Adventures Ser.). (ENG.). 80p. (J). (gr. 2-5). lib. bdg. 27.07 *(978-1-61641-965-3(2),* Calico Chapter Bks) Magic Wagon.

Fabregat, Antonio-Manuel. Los Cuentos de Mi Escuela. (SPA.). 128p. (J). (gr. 4-6). *(978-84-216-1185-2(2),* BU3866) Bruño, Editorial ESP. Dist: Lectorum Pubns., Inc.

Fields, Jan. Ghost Light Burning: An Up2U Mystery Adventure, 1 vol. Fabbretti, Valerio, illus. 2015. (ENG.). 80p. (J). *(978-1-62402-092-6(5))* Magic Wagon.

—Really New School: An Up2U Action Adventure, 1 vol. To, Vivienne, illus. 2013. (Up2U Adventures Ser.). (ENG.). 80p. (J). (gr. 2-5). lib. bdg. 27.07 *(978-1-61641-969-1(5),* Calico Chapter Bks) Magic Wagon.

Fison, Julie. The Call of the Wild. 2015. (ENG.). 288p. (J). pap. *(978-1-61067-388-4(3))* Kane Miller.

Fontes, Justine & Fontes, Ron. The Fifth Musketeer. Meconis, Dylan, illus. 2012. (Twisted Journeys Ser.: 19). (ENG.). 112p. (J). (gr. 4-7). lib. bdg. 27.93 *(978-0-7613-4594-7(9),* Graphic Universe™) Lerner Publishing Group.

Gilligan, Alison. Pirate Treasure of the Onyx Dragon. 2011. 144p. (J). (gr. 2-18). pap. 6.99 *(978-1-933390-99-4(9))* Chooseco LLC.

—Search for the Black Rhino. 2011. (Illus.). 144p. (J). pap. 6.99 *(978-1-937133-01-6(X))* Chooseco LLC.

Gilligan, Shannon. The Case of the Silk King. Pornkerd, Vorrarit et al, illus. 2006. (Choose Your Own Adventure Ser.). 144p. (J). (gr. 4-8). per. 6.99 *(978-1-933390-14-7(X),* CHCL14) Chooseco LLC.

—The Case of the Silk King. 2005. 116p. (J). pap. *(978-0-7608-9702-7(6))* Sundance/Newbridge Educational Publishing.

—Choose Your Own Adventure: The Case of the Silk King. 2007. 144p. (J). pap. *(978-1-74169-069-9(2))* Chooseco LLC.

—Cup of Death. Nugent, Suzanne, illus. 2006. (Choose Your Own Adventure Ser.). 144p. (J). (gr. 4-8). per. 6.99 *(978-1-933390-70-3(0))* Chooseco LLC.

—Ghost Island. Newton, Keith, illus. 2008. (Dragonlarks Ser.). 80p. (J). (gr. k-3). pap. 7.99 *(978-1-933390-57-4(3))* Chooseco LLC.

—The Lake Monster Mystery. Newton, Keith, illus. 2009. (Dragonlarks Ser.). 80p. (J). (gr. k-3). pap. 7.99 *(978-1-933390-60-4(3))* Chooseco LLC.

—Princess Island. 2015. (ENG.). (J). pap. 7.99 *(978-1-937133-50-4(8))* Chooseco LLC.

—Struggle down Under. Burphon, S. et al, illus. 2007. (Choose Your Own Adventure Ser.: No. 21). 123p. (J). (gr. 4-7). pap. 6.99 *(978-1-933390-21-5(2))* Chooseco LLC.

Goodhart, Pippa & Sharratt, Nick. You Choose! (ENG., Illus.). 32p. (J). 19.99 *(978-0-385-60176-4(X),* Doubleday Children's) Random House Children's Books GBR. Dist: Trafalgar Square Publishing.

Gunderson, Jessica. Olympians vs. Titans: An Interactive Mythological Adventure. Arcabascio, Carolyn, illus. 2017. (You Choose: Ancient Greek Myths Ser.). (ENG.). 112p. (gr. 3-4). lib. bdg. 31.99 *(978-1-5157-4820-5(0),* You Choose Bks.) Capstone Press of Coughlan Cos.

Gunderson, Jessica, et al. You Choose: Fractured Fairy Tales. 2015. (You Choose: Fractured Fairy Tales Ser.). (ENG.). 112p. (gr. 3-4). 127.96 *(978-1-4914-6969-9(2),* You Choose Bks.) Capstone Press of Coughlan Cos.

The Haunted House. 2007. (Choose Your Own Adventure Ser.). (Illus.). 80p. (J). (gr. 4-7). pap. 7.99 *(978-1-933390-51-2(4))* Chooseco LLC.

Hoena, B. A. Can You Survive an Alien Invasion? An Interactive Doomsday Adventure. Fisher-Johnson, Paul, illus. 2015. (You Choose: Doomsday Ser.). (ENG.). 112p. (gr. 3-4). lib. bdg. 31.99 *(978-1-4914-5853-2(4),* You Choose Bks.) Capstone Press of Coughlan Cos.

—Jack & the Beanstalk: An Interactive Fairy Tale Adventure. Tayal, Amit, illus. 2015. (You Choose: Fractured Fairy Tales Ser.). (ENG.). 112p. (gr. 3-4). pap. 6.95 *(978-1-4914-5930-0(1),* You Choose Bks.) Capstone Press of Coughlan Cos.

Hoena, Blake. Can You Survive a Supervolcano Eruption? An Interactive Doomsday Adventure. Vanzo, Filippo, illus. 2016. (You Choose: Doomsday Ser.). (ENG.). 112p. (gr. 3-4). lib. bdg. 31.99 *(978-1-4914-8108-0(0),* You Choose Bks.) Capstone Press of Coughlan Cos.

—Jason, the Argonauts, & the Golden Fleece: An Interactive Mythological Adventure. Nathan, James, illus. 2016. (You Choose: Ancient Greek Myths Ser.). (ENG.). 112p. (gr. 3-4). lib. bdg. 31.99 *(978-1-4914-8113-4(7),* You Choose Bks.) Capstone Press of Coughlan Cos.

—The Quest of Theseus: An Interactive Mythological Adventure. Arcabascio, Carolyn, illus. 2017. (You Choose: Ancient Greek Myths Ser.). (ENG.). 112p. (gr. 3-4). pap. 6.95 *(978-1-5157-4826-7(X),* You Choose Bks.) Capstone Press of Coughlan Cos.

—The Quest of Theseus: An Interactive Mytholoical Adventure. Arcabascio, Carolyn, illus. 2017. (You Choose: Ancient Greek Myths Ser.). (ENG.). 112p. (gr. 3-4). lib. bdg. 31.99 *(978-1-5157-4821-2(9))* Capstone Press of Coughlan Cos.

—The Riddler's Ransom. Beavers, Ethen, illus. 2015. (You Choose Stories: Batman Ser.). (ENG.). 112p. (gr. 2-3). lib. bdg. 32.65 *(978-1-4342-9706-8(3))* Stone Arch Bks.

—The Trojan War: An Interactive Mythological Adventure. Takvorian, Nadine, illus. 2017. (You Choose: Ancient Greek Myths Ser.). (ENG.). 112p. (gr. 3-4). lib. bdg. 31.99 *(978-1-5157-4822-9(7),* You Choose Bks.) Capstone Press of Coughlan Cos.

Hoena, Blake & Doeden, Matt. You Choose: Doomsday. Nathan, James, illus. 2015. (You Choose: Doomsday Ser.). (ENG.). 112p. (gr. 3-4). 127.96 *(978-1-4914-6968-2(4),* You Choose Bks.) Capstone Press of Coughlan Cos.

Indian Trail. 2007. (Choose Your Own Adventure - Dragonlarks Ser.). (Illus.). 64p. (J). (gr. 4-7). pap. 7.99 *(978-1-933390-53-6(0))* Chooseco LLC.

Iparraguirre, Sylvia, et al. Terminemos el Cuento. 2003. (SPA., Illus.). 128p. (YA). (gr. 9-12). 9.95 *(978-84-204-4965-4(2))* Ediciones Alfaguara ESP. Dist: Santillana USA Publishing Co., Inc.

Jackson, Sharinese. Choices: Upper Elementary. Nyamor, Eric, illus. 2010. 112p. pap. 12.95 *(978-0-9840660-3-2(9))* Second Time Media & Communications.

Jackson, Steve. The Citadel of Chaos. 2003. 208p. pap. *(978-0-7434-7510-5(0))* ibooks, Inc.

Jackson, Steve & Livingstone, Ian. The Worlock of Firetop Mountain. 2003. 192p. pap. 6.99 *(978-0-7434-7511-2(9))* ibooks, Inc.

Johnson, Alaya Dawn. Detective Frankenstein. Ota, Yuko, illus. 2011. (Twisted Journeys (r) Ser.: 17). (ENG.). 112p. (J). (gr. 4-7). pap. 7.95 *(978-0-8225-8943-3(5));* pap. 45.32 *(978-0-7613-7613-2(5))* Lerner Publishing Group. (Graphic Universe™).

Jolley, Dan. Alien Adventure on Planet J. Wendt, Matt, illus. 2008. (Twisted Journeys (r) Ser.: 8). (ENG.). 112p. (J). (gr. 4-7). 27.93 *(978-0-8225-6998-5(1),* Graphic Universe™) Lerner Publishing Group.

—Attack of the Mutant Meteors. Witt, David, illus. 2010. (Twisted Journeys (r) Ser.: 14). (ENG.). 112p. (J). (gr. 4-7). pap. 7.95 *(978-0-8225-9255-6(X),* Graphic Universe™); lib. bdg. 27.93 *(978-0-8225-9249-5(5))* Lerner Publishing Group.

—Shipwrecked on Mad Island, No. 11. Huddleston, Courtney, illus. 2009. (Twisted Journeys (r) Ser.: 11). (ENG.). 112p. (J). (gr. 4-7). 27.93 *(978-0-8225-7911-3(1),* Graphic Universe™) Lerner Publishing Group.

—Vampire Hunt. Titus, Gregory, illus. 2008. (Twisted Journeys (r) Ser.: 7). (ENG.). 112p. (J). (gr. 4-7). pap. 7.95 *(978-0-8225-8879-5(X))* Lerner Publishing Group.

Lassieur, Allison. At Battle in World War I: An Interactive Battlefield Adventure. 2015. (You Choose: Battlefields Ser.). (ENG., Illus.). 112p. (gr. 3-4). lib. bdg. 31.99 *(978-1-4914-2151-2(7),* You Choose Bks.) Capstone Press of Coughlan Cos.

—The Attack on Pearl Harbor [Scholastic]: An Interactive History Adventure. 2009. (You Choose: History Ser.). 112p. (gr. 3-4). pap. 0.86 *(978-1-4296-4046-6(4),* You Choose Bks.) Capstone Press of Coughlan Cos.

Lay, Kathryn. The Substitutes: An Up2U Action Adventure, 1 vol. Calo, Marcos, illus. 2015. (ENG.). 80p. (J). *(978-1-62402-095-7(X))* Magic Wagon.

Leibold, Jay. Secret of the Ninja. Nugent, Suzanne & Marron, Jose, illus. 2007. (Choose Your Own Adventure Ser.: Vol. 16). 124p. (J). (gr. 4-7). per. 6.99 *(978-1-933390-16-1(6))* Chooseco LLC.

Livingstone, Ian. Deathtrap Dungeon. 2003. 224p. pap. 6.99 *(978-0-7434-7967-7(X))* ibooks, Inc.

Manning, Matthew K. The Mystery of the Mayhem Mansion. Neely, Scott, illus. 2016. (You Choose Stories: Scooby-Doo Ser.). (ENG.). 112p. (gr. 2-3). lib. bdg. 32.65 *(978-1-4965-2661-8(9),* You Choose Bks.) Capstone Press of Coughlan Cos.

Matthews, T. J. The Canoeing Safari. Rheburg, Judy, illus. 2004. (J). *(978-0-938978-35-0(7))* Wycliffe Bible Translators.

Mayhall, Robin. The Quest for Dragon Mountain. Martinez, Alitha E., illus. 2010. (Twisted Journeys (r) Ser.: 16). (ENG.). 112p. (J). (gr. 4-7). lib. bdg. 27.93 *(978-0-8225-9261-7(4))* Lerner Publishing Group.

—The Quest for Dragon Mountain. Martinez, Alitha, illus. 16th rev. ed. 2010. (Twisted Journeys (r) Ser.: 16). (ENG.). (J). (gr. 4-7). pap. 45.32 *(978-0-7613-6999-8(6))* Lerner Publishing Group.

McMurtry, Ken. Zombie Penpal. 2010. (Illus.). 144p. (J). pap. 6.99 *(978-1-933390-34-5(4))* Chooseco LLC.

Millet, Jason, et al, illus. Beyond Escape! 2007. (Choose Your Own Adventure Ser.: No. 15). 118p. (J). (gr. 4-7). per. 6.99 *(978-1-933390-15-4(8),* CHCL15) Chooseco LLC.

Mizielinska, Aleksandra & Mizielinski, Daniel. The World of Mamoko in the Year 3000. 2014. (ENG.). 16p. (J). (gr. k-3). 17.99 *(978-0-7636-7125-9(8),* Big Picture Press) Candlewick Pr.

Montgomery, Anson. Dragon Day. 2011. (Illus.). 80p. (J). (gr. k-3). 7.99 *(978-1-933390-61-1(1))* Chooseco LLC.

—Escape from the Haunted Warehouse. 2015. (ENG.). 144p. (J). pap. 6.99 *(978-1-937133-47-4(8))* Chooseco LLC.

—Moon Quest. Semionov, Vladimir, illus. 2008. (Choose Your Own Adventure Ser.: No. 26). 144p. (J). (gr. 2-7). pap. 6.99 *(978-1-933390-26-0(3))* Chooseco LLC.

—Search for the Dragon Queen. 2011. (Illus.). 80p. (J). (gr. k-3). pap. 7.99 *(978-1-933390-56-7(5))* Chooseco LLC.

Montgomery, R. A. The Abominable Snowman Peguy, Laurence, illus. 2006. (Choose Your Own Adventure Ser.). 144p. (J). (gr. 4-8). per. 6.99 *(978-1-933390-01-7(8),* CHCL01) Chooseco LLC.

—Always Picked Last. 2009. 64p. (J). pap. 7.99 *(978-1-933390-38-3(7))* Chooseco LLC.

—Behind the Wheel. 2010. 144p. pap. 6.99 *(978-1-933390-35-2(2))* Chooseco LLC.

—Beyond Escape. 2005. (Choose Your Own Adventure Ser.). (Illus.). 118p. (gr. 4-8). pap. 5.50 *(978-0-7608-9703-4(4))* Sundance/Newbridge Educational Publishing.

—Blood on the Handle. 2010. (Illus.). 144p. (J). pap. 6.99 *(978-1-933390-33-8(6))* Chooseco LLC.

—The Brilliant Dr. Wogan. 2005. (Choose Your Own Adventure Ser.). (Illus.). 112p. (gr. 4-8). pap. 5.50 *(978-0-7608-9705-8(0))* Sundance/Newbridge Educational Publishing.

—Chinese Dragons. Semionov, Vladimir, illus. 2009. (Choose Your Own Adventure Ser.: No. 30). 144p. (J). (gr. 2-7). pap. 6.99 *(978-1-933390-30-7(1))* Chooseco LLC.

—Choose Your Own Adventure 4 Book Boxed Set #3: Lost on the Amazon; Prisoner of the Ant People; Trouble on Planet Earth; War with the Evil Power Master. 2006. (Illus.). 144p. (J). pap. 22.99 *(978-1-933390-96-3(4))* Chooseco LLC.

—Choose Your Own Adventure 6 Book Boxed Set #1: The Abominable Snowman, Journey under the Sea, Space & Beyond, the Lost Jewels of Nabooti, Mystery of the Maya, House of Danger, nos. 2, no. 2. 2005. (ENG., Illus.). 144p. (J). pap. 33.99 *(978-1-933390-91-8(3),* CHCL91) Chooseco LLC.

—Choose Your Own Adventure 6 Book Boxed Set #2: Race Forever; Escape, Lost on the Amazon; Prisoner of the Ant People; Trouble on Planet Earth; War with the Evil Power Master, vols. 2, vol. 2. 2006. (Illus.). 144p. (J). per. 33.99 *(978-1-933390-92-5(1),* CHCL92) Chooseco LLC.

—Escape. Millet, Jason, illus. 2006. (Choose Your Own Adventure Ser.: No. 8). 144p. (J). (gr. 4-8). per. 6.99 *(978-1-933390-08-6(5),* CHCL08) Chooseco LLC.

—Fire! 2015. (ENG.). 80p. (Orig.). (J). pap. 7.99 *(978-1-937133-49-8(4))* Chooseco LLC.

—House of Danger. 2005. (Choose Your Own Adventure Ser.). (Illus.). 108p. (gr. 4-8). pap. 5.50 *(978-0-7608-9694-5(1))* Sundance/Newbridge Educational Publishing.

—House of Danger. Sundaravej, Sittisan, illus. 2006. (Choose Your Own Adventure Ser.: No. 6). 144p. (J). (gr. 4-8). per. 6.99 *(978-1-933390-06-2(9),* CHCL06) Chooseco LLC.

—Island of Time. Louie, Wes & Cannella, Marco, illus. 2008. 144p. (J). (gr. 2-7). pap. 6.99 *(978-1-933390-28-4(X))* Chooseco LLC.

—Journey under the Sea. Sundaravej, Sittisan, illus. 2006. (Choose Your Own Adventure Ser.: No. 2). 144p. (J). (gr. 4-8). per. 6.99 *(978-1-933390-02-4(6),* CHCL02) Chooseco LLC.

—Journey under the Sea. 2006. (Choose Your Own Adventure Ser.: 2). 17.20 *(978-1-4177-6410-5(4),* Turtleback) Turtleback Bks.

—Lost Dog! 2011. (Dragonlarks Ser.). (Illus.). 80p. (J). (gr. k-3). pap. 7.99 *(978-1-933390-00-0(X))* Chooseco LLC.

—The Lost Jewels of Nabooti. Kornmaneeroj, T. et al, illus. 2006. (Choose Your Own Adventure Ser.: No. 4). 144p. (J). (gr. 4-8). per. 6.99 *(978-1-933390-04-8(2),* CHCL04) Chooseco LLC.

—Lost on the Amazon. 2007. 144p. (J). pap. *(978-1-86504-931-1(X))* Chooseco LLC.

—Lost on the Amazon. Millet, Jason, illus. 2006. (Choose Your Own Adventure Ser.: No. 9). 144p. (J). (gr. 4-8). per. 6.99 *(978-1-933390-09-3(3),* CHCL09) Chooseco LLC.

—Lost on the Amazon. 2005. (Choose Your Own Adventure Ser.). (Illus.). 114p. (gr. 4-8). pap. 5.50 *(978-0-7608-9697-6(6))* Sundance/Newbridge Educational Publishing.

—Monsters of the Deep. 2010. 64p. pap. 7.99 *(978-1-933390-37-6(9))* Chooseco LLC.

—The Owl Tree. 2010. (Illus.). 64p. (Orig.). (J). pap. 7.99 *(978-1-933390-80-2(8))* Chooseco LLC.

—Prisoner of the Ant People. 2007. 144p. (J). pap. *(978-1-86504-932-8(8))* Chooseco LLC.

—Prisoner of the Ant People. Millet, Jason, illus. 2006. (Choose Your Own Adventure Ser.: No. 10). 144p. (J). (gr. 4-8). per. 6.99 *(978-1-933390-10-9(7),* CHCL10) Chooseco LLC.

—Prisoner of the Ant People. 2005. (Illus.). 115p. (J). pap. *(978-0-7608-9698-3(4))* Sundance/Newbridge Educational Publishing.

—Project UFO. Semionov, Vladimir & Cannella, Marco, illus. 2008. 144p. (J). (gr. 4-7). pap. 6.99 *(978-1-933390-27-7(1))* Chooseco LLC.

—Punishment: Earth. 2010. 144p. pap. 6.99 *(978-1-933390-36-9(0))* Chooseco LLC.

—Race Forever. 2005. (Illus.). 122p. (J). *(978-0-7608-9695-2(X))* Sundance/Newbridge Educational Publishing.

—Race Forever. Sundaravej, Sittisan, illus. 2006. (Choose Your Own Adventure Ser.: No. 7). 144p. (J). (gr. 4-8). per. 6.99 *(978-1-933390-07-9(7),* CHCL07) Chooseco LLC.

—Return to Atlantis. 2005. (Choose Your Own Adventure Ser.). (Illus.). 119p. (gr. 4-8). pap. 5.50 *(978-0-7608-9706-5(9))* Sundance/Newbridge Educational Publishing.

—Return to Haunted House. 2010. (Illus.). 80p. (J). pap. 7.99 *(978-1-933390-40-6(9))* Chooseco LLC.

—Sand Castle. Newton, Keith, illus. 2008. 80p. (J). (gr. k-3). pap. 7.99 *(978-1-933390-59-8(X))* Chooseco LLC.

—Smoke Jumpers. Peguy, Laurence, illus. 2009. (Choose Your Own Adventure Ser.: No. 29). 144p. (J). (gr. 2-7). pap. 6.99 *(978-1-933390-29-1(8))* Chooseco LLC.

—Space & Beyond. Yaweera, Sasiprapa & Donploypetch, Jintanan, illus. 2006. (Choose Your Own Adventure Ser.: No. 3). 144p. (J). (gr. 4-8). pap. 6.99 *(978-1-933390-03-1(4),* CHCL03) Chooseco LLC.

—Track Star! 2009. (Choose Your Own Adventure Ser.: No. 31). (Illus.). 144p. (J). (gr. 2-7). pap. 6.99 *(978-1-933390-31-4(X))* Chooseco LLC.

—The Trail of Lost Time. 2011. (Illus.). 144p. (J). mass mkt. 6.99 *(978-1-937133-03-0(6))* Chooseco LLC.

—Trouble on Planet Earth. 2007. 144p. (J). pap. *(978-1-86504-933-5(6))* Chooseco LLC.

—Trouble on Planet Earth. Trod, Mariano et al, illus. 2006. (Choose Your Own Adventure Ser.: No. 11). 144p. (J). (gr. 4-8). per. 6.99 *(978-1-933390-11-6(5),* CHCL11) Chooseco LLC.

—Trouble on Planet Earth. 2005. (Illus.). 113p. (J). pap. *(978-0-7608-9699-0(2))* Sundance/Newbridge Educational Publishing.

—War with the Evil Power Master. 2005. (Illus.). 123p. (J). pap. *(978-0-7608-9700-3(X))* Sundance/Newbridge Educational Publishing.

—War with the Evil Power Master. Millet, Jason, illus. 2006. (Choose Your Own Adventure Ser.: No. 12). 144p. (J). (gr. 4-8). per. 6.99 *(978-1-933390-12-3(3),* CHCL12) Chooseco LLC.

—Your Grandparents Are Zombies! 2010. (Illus.). 64p. (J). pap. 7.99 *(978-1-933390-90-1(5))* Chooseco LLC.

—Your Very Own Robot Goes Cuckoo Bananas. 2009. (Illus.). 80p. (J). pap. 7.99 *(978-1-933390-39-0(5))* Chooseco LLC.

Montgomery, Ramsey. U. N. Adventure: Mission to Molowa. 2009. 144p. (J). pap. 6.99 *(978-1-933390-32-1(8))* Chooseco LLC.

Morris, Dave. Crypt of the Vampire. Hartas, Leo, illus. 2013. 122p. pap. *(978-1-909905-05-4(4))* Fabled Lands Publishing.

Mullarkey, John & Mullarkey, Lisa. Johnstown Flood: An Up2U Historical Fiction Adventure, 1 vol. Martin, Dana, illus. 2013. (Up2U Adventures Ser.). (ENG.). 80p. (J). (gr. 2-5). lib. bdg. 27.07 *(978-1-61641-967-7(9),* Calico Chapter Bks) Magic Wagon.

Mystery of the Maya: Choose Your Own Adventure. 2004. per. 5.95 *(978-0-9745356-3-0(X))* Chooseco LLC.

Packard, Edward. Return to the Cave of Time. Willis, Drew, illus. 2012. (U-Ventures Ser.). (ENG.). 160p. (Orig.). (J). (gr. 3-7). pap. 5.99 *(978-1-4424-3427-1(9),* Simon & Schuster Bks. For Young Readers) Simon & Schuster Bks. For Young Readers.

—Through the Black Hole. Willis, Drew, illus. 2012. (U-Ventures Ser.). (ENG.). 160p. (J). (gr. 3-7). pap. 5.99 *(978-1-4424-3426-4(0),* Simon & Schuster Bks. For Young Readers) Simon & Schuster Bks. For Young Readers.

Pomaska, Anna. Scruffy & Muffin in the Land of Enchantment: A Dot-to-Dot Storybook. 2004. (Dover Children's Activity Bks.). (ENG., Illus.). 32p. (J). (gr. -1-2). pap. 3.95 *(978-0-486-43566-4(0))* Dover Pubns., Inc.

Raum, Elizabeth. The Aztec Empire: An Interactive History Adventure. 2012. (You Choose: Historical Eras Ser.). (ENG.). 112p. (gr. 3-4). pap. 41.70 *(978-1-4296-9475-9(0),* You Choose Bks.) Capstone Press of Coughlan Cos.

—Christmas Crossroads. 2015. 133p. (J). *(978-1-62856-046-6(0)*, Bloomsbury Visual Arts) BJU Pr.
—Crossroads in Galilee. 2016. (Illus.). xii, 139p. (J). *(978-1-62856-239-2(0))* BJU Pr.
Ray, Cindy & Kids Write On, creators. The Stapler Caper: You Write the Story. 2008. (ENG., Illus.). 28p. (J). 16.95 *(978-0-615-23574-5(3))* Kids Write On, LLC.
Santopolo, Jill. Summer Love. 2014. (Follow Your Heart Ser.: 1). (ENG.). 224p. (YA). (gr. 7). pap. 9.99 *(978-0-14-751092-1(9)*, Speak) Penguin Young Readers Group.
Sazaklis, John. Clayface Returns. Beavers, Ethen, illus. 2016. (You Choose Stories: Batman Ser.). (ENG.). 112p. (gr. 2-3). lib. bdg. 32.65 *(978-1-4965-3089-9(6)*, DC Super Heroes) Stone Arch Bks.
—The Lazarus Plan. Beavers, Ethen, illus. 2016. (You Choose Stories: Batman Ser.). (ENG.). 112p. (gr. 2-3). lib. bdg. 32.65 *(978-1-4965-3088-2(8)*, DC Super Heroes) Stone Arch Bks.
—The Mystery of the Maze Monster, 1 vol. Neely, Scott, illus. 2014. (You Choose Stories: Scooby-Doo Ser.). (ENG.). 112p. (gr. 2-3). pap. 6.95 *(978-1-4342-7928-6(6)*, You Choose Bks.) Capstone Press of Coughlan Cos.
—Super-Villain Smackdown! Beavers, Ethen, illus. 2015. (You Choose Stories: Batman Ser.). (ENG.). 112p. (gr. 2-3). lib. bdg. 32.65 *(978-1-4965-0528-6(X))* Stone Arch Bks.
Schweizer, Chris. Tricky Coyote Tales. Thomas, Chad, illus. 2011. (Tricky Journeys Ser.: 1). (ENG.). (J). (gr. 2-4). pap. 39.62 *(978-0-7613-8625-4(4))*;No. 1. 64p. pap. 6.95 *(978-0-7613-7859-4(6))*;No. 1. 64p. lib. bdg. 27.93 *(978-0-7613-6601-0(6))* Lerner Publishing Group.
—Tricky Fox Tales. Paroline, Shelli & Paroline, Michelle, illus. 2011. (Tricky Journeys Ser.: 3). (ENG.). (J). (gr. 2-4). pap. 39.62 *(978-0-7613-8627-8(0))* Lerner Publishing Group.
—Tricky Fox Tales. Paroline, Shelli, illus. 2011. (Tricky Journeys Ser.: 3). (ENG.). 64p. (J). (gr. 2-4). pap. 6.95 *(978-0-7613-7861-7(8))* Lerner Publishing Group.
—Tricky Fox Tales, No. 3. Paroline, Shelli & Paroline, Michelle, illus. 2011. (Tricky Journeys Ser.: 3). (ENG.). 64p. (J). (gr. 2-4). lib. bdg. 27.93 *(978-0-7613-6605-8(9))* Lerner Publishing Group.
—Tricky Monkey Tales. Thomas, Chad, illus. 2011. (Tricky Journeys Ser.: 6). (ENG.). (J). (gr. 2-4). pap. 39.62 *(978-0-7613-8630-8(0))*; 64p. pap. 6.95 *(978-0-7613-7860-0(X))*;No. 6. 64p. lib. bdg. 27.93 *(978-0-7613-6611-9(3))* Lerner Publishing Group.
—Tricky Rabbit Tales. Giallongo, Zack, illus. 2011. (Tricky Journeys Ser.: 2). (ENG.). (J). (gr. 2-4). pap. 39.62 *(978-0-7613-8626-1(2))*; 64p. pap. 6.95 *(978-0-7613-7862-4(6))*;No. 2. 64p. lib. bdg. 27.93 *(978-0-7613-6607-2(5))* Lerner Publishing Group.
—Tricky Raven Tales. Witt, David, illus. 2011. (Tricky Journeys Ser.: 4). (ENG.). (J). (gr. 2-4). pap. 39.62 *(978-0-7613-8628-5(9))*;No. 4. 64p. pap. 6.95 *(978-0-7613-7863-1(4))* Lerner Publishing Group.
—Tricky Spider Tales. Huddleston, Courtney, illus. 2011. (Tricky Journeys Ser.: 5). (ENG.). (J). (gr. 2-4). pap. 39.62 *(978-0-7613-8629-2(7))*; 64p. pap. 6.95 *(978-0-7613-7864-8(2))*;No. 5. 64p. lib. bdg. 27.93 *(978-0-7613-6609-6(1))* Lerner Publishing Group.
Semionov, Vladimir, illus. Silver Wings. 2007. (Choose Your Own Adventure Ser.: No. 23). 107p. (J). (gr. 4-7). pap. 6.99 *(978-1-933390-23-9(9))* Chooseco LLC.
Semionov, Vladimir & Louie, Wes, illus. Forecast from Stonehenge. 2007. (Choose Your Own Adventure Ser.: No. 19). 127p. (J). (gr. 4-7). pap. 6.99 *(978-1-933390-19-2(0))* Chooseco LLC.
Shiga, Jason. Meanwhile: Pick Any Path. 3,856 Story Possibilities. 2010. (ENG., Illus.). 80p. (J). (gr. 3-7). 16.95 *(978-0-8109-8423-3(7)*, Amulet Bks.) Abrams, Inc.
Simpson, C. E. & Smith, C. E. Eighth Grade Witch. Utomo, Gabhor, illus. 2014. (ENG.). 144p. (J). mass mkt. 6.99 *(978-1-937133-45-0(1))* Chooseco LLC.
Smith, Anne & Smith, Owen. Safari Survivor. Rayas, Rubén, illus. 2012. (Twisted Journeys (r) Ser.: 21). (ENG.). 112p. (J). (gr. 4-7). pap. 7.95 *(978-1-57505-943-3(6)*, Graphic Universe™) Lerner Publishing Group.
Smith, Owen & Smith, Anne. Safari Survivor. Rubine, illus. 2012. (Twisted Journeys (r) Ser.: 21). (ENG.). 112p. (J). (gr. 4-7). lib. bdg. 27.93 *(978-0-7613-6727-7(6)*, Graphic Universe™) Lerner Publishing Group.
Steele, Michael Anthony. The Case of the Fright Flight. Neely, Scott, illus. 2016. (You Choose Stories: Scooby-Doo Ser.). (ENG.). 112p. (gr. 2-3). lib. bdg. 32.65 *(978-1-4965-2662-5(7)*, You Choose Bks.) Capstone Press of Coughlan Cos.
Stern, Leonard & Price, Roger. Hello Kitty Loves Mad Libs. 2013. (Hello Kitty Ser.). (ENG.). 48p. (J). (gr. 3-7). 3.99 *(978-0-8431-7609-4(1)*, Mad Libs) Penguin Young Readers Group.
Stine, R. L. Please Don't Feed the Vampire! A Give Yourself Goosebumps Book. 2015. (Classic Goosebumps Ser.: 32). (ENG.). 144p. (J). (gr. 3-7). pap. 6.99 *(978-0-545-82887-1(2)*, Scholastic Paperbacks) Scholastic, Inc.
—Slappy's Tales of Horror. 2015. (Goosebumps Graphix Ser.). lib. bdg. 24.50 *(978-0-606-37761-4(1))* Turtleback Bks.
Storrie, Paul D., et al. Twisted Journeys(r): Spring 2012 New Releases. 2012. (Twisted Journeys Ser.). (Illus.). 112p. (J). (gr. 4-7). lib. bdg. 55.86 *(978-0-7613-8910-1(5)*, Graphic Universe™) Lerner Publishing Group.
Suen, Anastasia. A Great Idea? An Up2U Character Education Adventure, 1 vol. Dippold, Jane, illus. 2015. (ENG.). 80p. (J). *(978-1-62402-093-3(3))* Magic Wagon.
—New Girl: An Up2U Character Education Adventure, 1 vol. Dippold, Jane, illus. 2013. (Up2U Adventures Ser.). (ENG.). 80p. (J). (gr. 2-5). lib. bdg. 27.07 *(978-1-61641-968-4(7)*, Calico Chapter Bks) Magic Wagon.
Sundaravej, Sittisan & Thongmoon, Kriangsak, illus. Return to Atlantis. 2007. (Choose Your Own Adventure Ser.: No. 18). 119p. (J). (gr. 4-7). per. 6.99 *(978-1-933390-18-5(2)*, CHCL18) Chooseco LLC.
Sutton, Laurie S. The Fright at Zombie Farm. Neely, Scott, illus. 2015. (You Choose Stories: Scooby-Doo Ser.). (ENG.). 112p. (gr. 2-3). lib. bdg. 32.65 *(978-1-4342-9713-6(6)*, You Choose Bks.) Capstone Press of Coughlan Cos.
—The Ghost of the Bermuda Triangle, 1 vol. Neely, Scott, illus. 2014. (You Choose Stories: Scooby-Doo Ser.). (ENG.). 112p. (gr. 2-3). 32.65 *(978-1-4342-9126-4(X)*, You Choose Bks.) Capstone Press of Coughlan Cos.
—The House on Spooky Street. Neely, Scott, illus. 2015. (You Choose Stories: Scooby-Doo Ser.). (ENG.). 112p. (gr. 2-3). lib. bdg. 32.65 *(978-1-4342-9714-3(4)*, You Choose Bks.) Capstone Press of Coughlan Cos.
—The Joker's Dozen. Beavers, Ethen, illus. 2015. (You Choose Stories: Batman Ser.). (ENG.). 112p. (gr. 2-3). lib. bdg. 32.65 *(978-1-4342-9707-5(1))* Stone Arch Bks.
—The Mystery of the Aztec Tomb, 1 vol. Neely, Scott, illus. 2014. (You Choose Stories: Scooby-Doo Ser.). (ENG.). 112p. (gr. 2-3). 32.65 *(978-1-4342-9127-1(8)*, You Choose Bks.) Capstone Press of Coughlan Cos.
—The Secret of the Flying Saucer. Neely, Scott, illus. 2015. (You Choose Stories: Scooby-Doo Ser.). (ENG.). 112p. (gr. 2-3). lib. bdg. 32.65 *(978-1-4965-0478-4(X))* Stone Arch Bks.
—The Secret of the Sea Creature, 1 vol. Neely, Scott, illus. 2014. (You Choose Stories: Scooby-Doo Ser.). (ENG.). 112p. (gr. 2-3). pap. 6.95 *(978-1-4342-7925-5(1)*, You Choose Bks.) Capstone Press of Coughlan Cos.
—The Terrible Trio. Beavers, Ethen, illus. 2015. (You Choose Stories: Batman Ser.). (ENG.). 112p. (gr. 2-3). lib. bdg. 32.65 *(978-1-4965-0529-3(8))* Stone Arch Bks.
—You Choose: Scooby-Doo. 2013. (You Choose Stories: Scooby Doo Ser.). (ENG.). 112p. pap. 166.80 *(978-1-4342-9604-7(0))* Stone Arch Bks.
Terman, Douglas. By Balloon to the Sahara. 2015. (ENG.). 144p. (J). pap. 6.99 *(978-1-937133-48-1(6))* Chooseco LLC.
Terrell, Brandon. Greek Mythology's Twelve Labors of Hercules, 1 vol. 2013. (Can You Survive? Ser.). (ENG.). 164p. (J). (gr. 4-6). pap. 8.95 *(978-0-9883662-9-9(0))* Leadership Institute for Urban Education.
—Summer Freeze! Beavers, Ethen, illus. 2015. (You Choose Stories: Batman Ser.). (ENG.). 112p. (gr. 2-3). lib. bdg. 32.65 *(978-1-4342-9708-2(X))* Stone Arch Bks.
Trod, Mariano, et al, illus. The Brilliant Dr. Wogan. 2007. (Choose Your Own Adventure Ser.: No. 17). 112p. (J). (gr. 4-7). per. 6.99 *(978-1-933390-17-8(4)*, CHC17) Chooseco LLC.
Tsang, Evonne. Kung Fu Masters, No. 12. Martinez, Alitha E., illus. 2009. (Twisted Journeys (r) Ser.: 12). (ENG.). 112p. (J). (gr. 4-7). 27.93 *(978-0-8225-8878-8(1)*, Graphic Universe™) Lerner Publishing Group.
Tsang, Evonne & Jimenez, Adan. Hero City. BarÓN, Lara & Torres, German, illus. 2012. (Twisted Journeys (r) Ser.: 22). (ENG.). 112p. (J). (gr. 4-7). pap. 7.95 *(978-1-57505-945-7(2)*, Graphic Universe™) Lerner Publishing Group.
—Hero City. Barón, Lara & Torres, German, illus. 2012. (Twisted Journeys (r) Ser.: 22). (ENG.). 112p. (J). (gr. 4-7). lib. bdg. 27.93 *(978-0-7613-4595-4(7)*, Graphic Universe™) Lerner Publishing Group.
Turner, Tracey. Lost in the Crater of Fear. 2016. (ENG., Illus.). 128p. (J). *(978-0-7787-2353-0(4))* Crabtree Publishing Co.
—Lost in the Desert of Dread. 2014. (ENG., Illus.). 128p. (J). *(978-0-7787-0725-7(3))* Crabtree Publishing Co.
—Lost in the Jungle of Doom. 2014. (ENG., Illus.). 128p. (J). *(978-0-7787-0727-1(X))* Crabtree Publishing Co.
—Lost in the Mountains of Death. 2014. (ENG., Illus.). 128p. (J). *(978-0-7787-0729-5(6))* Crabtree Publishing Co.
—Lost in the Sea of Despair. 2014. (ENG., Illus.). 128p. (J). *(978-0-7787-0731-8(8))* Crabtree Publishing Co.
—Lost in the Swamp of Terror. 2016. (ENG., Illus.). 128p. (J). *(978-0-7787-2354-7(2))* Crabtree Publishing Co.
Wacholtz, Anthony. Can You Survive in a Dystopia? An Interactive Doomsday Adventure. Nathan, James, illus. 2016. (You Choose: Doomsday Ser.). (ENG.). 112p. (gr. 3-4). lib. bdg. 31.99 *(978-1-4914-8110-3(2)*, You Choose Bks.) Capstone Press of Coughlan Cos.
Wallace, Jim. Search for the Mountain Gorillas. Nugent, Suzanne & Donploypetch, Jintanan, illus. 2008. (Choose Your Own Adventure Ser.: No. 25). 125p. (J). (gr. 4-7). pap. 6.99 *(978-1-933390-25-3(5))* Chooseco LLC.
—Terror on the Titanic. Sundaravej, Sittisan & Barchus, Nathan, illus. 2007. (Choose Your Own Adventure Ser.: No. 24). (ENG.). 122p. (J). (gr. 4-7). pap. 6.99 *(978-1-933390-24-6(7))* Chooseco LLC.
Wallace, Rich. Double-Crossed at Cactus Flats: An Up2 U Western Adventure, 1 vol. Mitchell, Hazel, illus. 2013. (Up2U Adventures Ser.). (ENG.). 80p. (J). (gr. 2-5). lib. bdg. 27.07 *(978-1-61641-966-0(0)*, Calico Chapter Bks) Magic Wagon.
—The Room of Woe: An Up2U Horror Adventure, 1 vol. Emroca Flores, Jose, illus. 2015. (ENG.). 80p. (J). *(978-1-62402-094-0(1))* Magic Wagon.
Weetman, Nova. A Hot Cold Summer: Choose Your Own Ever After. 2016. (ENG.). 256p. (J). pap. 5.99 *(978-1-61067-354-9(9))* Kane Miller.
Wilder, Chase. Jungle Trek. 2016. (Temple Run Ser.: 1). (ENG., Illus.). 160p. (J). (gr. 2-4). pap. 9.99 *(978-1-4052-7167-7(1))* Egmont Bks., Ltd. GBR. Dist: Independent Pubs. Group.
Wilhelm, Doug. Curse of the Pirate Mist. 2011. (Illus.). 144p. (J). pap. 6.99 *(978-1-937133-02-3(8))* Chooseco LLC.
Windover, Liz. Blood Island. Utomo, Gabhor, illus. 2014. (ENG.). 144p. (J). mass mkt. 6.99 *(978-1-937133-46-7(X))* Chooseco LLC.
Young, J. E. Horror in Space. Huddleston, Courtney, illus. 2011. (Twisted Journeys Ser.: 18). (ENG.). 112p. (J). (gr. 4-7). pap. 45.32 *(978-0-7613-7614-9(3))*; lib. bdg. 27.93 *(978-0-8225-9265-5(7))* Lerner Publishing Group. (Graphic Universe™).
Your Purrr-Fect Birthday. 2007. (Dragonlarks Ser.). (Illus.). 64p. (J). (gr. k-3). per. 7.99 *(978-1-933390-55-0(7))* Chooseco LLC.
Your Very Own Robot. 2007. (Choose Your Own Adventure Ser.). (Illus.). 80p. (J). (gr. 4-7). pap. 7.99 *(978-1-933390-52-9(2))* Chooseco LLC.
Zuckerman, Lilla & Zuckerman, Nora. Beauty Queen Blowout. 2003. (ENG.). 240p. pap. 15.99 *(978-0-7432-3846-5(X)*, Touchstone) Touchstone.

PLUMBING

Freedman, Jeri. Plumber. 2016. (Careers in Construction Ser.). (ENG., Illus.). 112p. (J). (gr. 7-7). lib. bdg. 42.79 *(978-1-5026-0982-3(7))* Cavendish Square Publishing.
Isle, Mick. Everything You Need to Know about Food Poisoning. 2009. (Need to Know Library). 64p. (gr. 5-5). 58.50 *(978-1-60854-069-3(3))* Rosen Publishing Group, Inc., The.
Meister, Cari. Plumbers. 2014. (Illus.). 24p. (J). lib. bdg. 25.65 *(978-1-62031-095-3(3)*, Bullfrog Bks.) Jump! Inc.
Payment, Simone. A Career as a Plumber. 2010. (Essential Careers Ser.). (ENG.). 80p. (YA). lib. bdg. 33.25 *(978-1-4358-9473-0(1))* Rosen Publishing Group, Inc., The.
Plumbing, Heating, Air Conditioning & Refrigeration Student Activity. 2004. (YA). cd-rom *(978-1-57078-954-0(1)*, CEV60033) C E V Multimedia, Ltd.
Rose, Simon. Plumber. 2014. (Illus.). 24p. (J). *(978-1-4896-2994-4(7))* Weigl Pubs., Inc.
Yomtov, Nelson. The Grimy, Gross Unusual History of the Toilet, 1 vol. 2011. (Unusual Histories Ser.). (ENG.). 48p. (gr. 3-4). lib. bdg. 31.99 *(978-1-4296-5489-0(9))* Capstone Press of Coughlan Cos.

PLUMBING—FICTION

Adinolfi, Joanne. Tina's Diner. Adinolfi, Joanne, illus. 2014. (ENG., Illus.). 32p. (J). (gr. -1-3). 13.99 *(978-1-4814-4459-0(X)*, Simon & Schuster Bks. For Young Readers) Simon & Schuster Bks. For Young Readers.
Candlewick Press Staff. FETCH! with Ruff Ruffman: Doggie Duties. WGBH Educational Foundation Staff, illus. 2014. (Fetch! with Ruff Ruffman Ser.). (ENG.). 48p. (J). (gr. 1-4). pap. 4.99 *(978-0-7636-6815-0(X)*, Candlewick Entertainment) Candlewick Pr.
Rey, H. A. Plumber's Helper. Meyer, Emily, ed. 2010. (Curious George Ser.). (ENG., Illus.). 24p. (J). (gr. -1-3). pap. 4.99 *(978-0-547-23589-9(5))* Houghton Mifflin Harcourt Publishing Co.

PLUMBING—VOCATIONAL GUIDANCE

Gregory, Josh. Plumber. 2011. (21st Century Skills Library: Cool Careers Ser.). (ENG.). 32p. (gr. 4-8). lib. bdg. 28.50 *(978-1-60279-984-4(9)*, 200974) Cherry Lake Publishing.
Lüsted, Marcia Amidon. Working As a Plumber in Your Community. 2015. (Careers in Your Community Ser.). (ENG.). 80p. (YA). (gr. 7-8). 34.25 *(978-1-4994-6119-0(4)*, Rosen Young Adult) Rosen Publishing Group, Inc., The.
Worthington, Niles. A Plumber's Job. 2015. (Community Workers Ser.). (ENG., Illus.). 24p. (J). (gr. 1-1). pap. 8.22 *(978-1-5026-0433-0(7))* Cavendish Square Publishing.

PLUTO (DWARF PLANET)

Adamson, Thomas K. Pluto [Scholastic]: A Dwarf Planet. 2010. (Exploring the Galaxy Ser.). (ENG.). 24p. pap. 0.49 *(978-1-4296-5817-1(7)*, Pebble Plus) Capstone Press of Coughlan Cos.
Asimov, Isaac & Hantula, Richard. Plutón y Caronte. Porras, Carlos & D'Andrea, Patricia, trs. from ENG. 2003. (Isaac Asimov's Biblioteca del Universo del Siglo XXI). (SPA., Illus.). 32p. (gr. 2-6). lib. bdg. 26.00 *(978-0-8368-3859-6(9)*, Gareth Stevens Learning Library) Stevens, Gareth Publishing LLLP.
Buckley, James. Curious about Pluto. 2016. (Smithsonian Ser.). (ENG., Illus.). 32p. (J). (gr. 1-3). pap. 3.99 *(978-0-399-54218-3(3)*, Grosset & Dunlap) Penguin Young Readers Group.
Carson, Mary Kay. The Mission to Pluto: The First Visit to an Ice Dwarf & the Kuiper Belt. Uhlman, Tom, photos by. 2017. (Scientists in the Field Ser.). (ENG., Illus.). 80p. (J). (gr. 5-7). 18.99 *(978-0-544-41671-0(6)*, HMH Books For Young Readers) Houghton Mifflin Harcourt Publishing Co.
Elkins-Tanton, Linda T. Uranus, Neptune, Pluto, & the Outer Solar System. 2nd rev. ed. 2010. (Solar System Ser.). (Illus.). 272p. (C). (gr. 9). 39.50 *(978-0-8160-7701-4(0))* Facts On File, Inc.
Glaser, Chaya & Sawyer, J. Clark. Pluto: Not a Planet. 2015. (Out of This World Ser.). (ENG.). 24p. (J). (gr. -1-3). lib. bdg. 23.93 *(978-1-62724-571-5(5))* Bearport Publishing Co., Inc.
Goldstein, Margaret. Pluto. 2009. pap. 6.95 *(978-0-8225-4766-2(X))* Lerner Publishing Group.
Goldstein, Margaret J. Pluto. 2003. (Our Universe Ser.). (ENG., Illus.). 32p. (gr. 2-4). lib. bdg. 22.60 *(978-0-8225-4656-6(6))* Lerner Publishing Group.
Hayhurst, Chris. Pluto. 2009. (Library of Planets Ser.). 48p. (gr. 5-8). 55.90 *(978-1-60853-820-1(6)*, Rosen Reference) Rosen Publishing Group, Inc., The.
—Pluto & Other Dwarf Planets. 2006. (Library of Planets Ser.). (J). 29.25 *(978-1-4042-1965-6(X))* Rosen Publishing Group, Inc., The.
Higgins, Nadia. Dwarf Planets: Pluto & the Lesser Planets. 2014. (ENG.). 24p. (gr. k-3). 28.50 *(978-1-62717-729-0(9))* Rourke Educational Media.
Jefferis, David. Ice Dwarfs: Pluto & Beyond. 2008. (Exploring Our Solar System Ser.). (ENG., Illus.). 32p. (J). (gr. 3-7). pap. *(978-0-7787-3752-0(7))* Crabtree Publishing Co.
Kaspar, Anna. A Look at Pluto & Other Dwarf Planets. 2009. (Astronomy Now! Ser.). 24p. (gr. 2-3). 42.50 *(978-1-61511-472-6(6)*, PowerKids Pr.) Rosen Publishing Group, Inc., The.
Korba, Joanna & Benchmark Education Co., LLC. Pluto, the Planet That Was. 2014. (Text Connections Ser.). (J). (gr. 3). *(978-1-4509-9662-4(0))* Benchmark Education Co.
Kortenkamp, Steve. Demoting Pluto: The Discovery of the Dwarf Planets. 2015. (Exploring Space & Beyond Ser.). (ENG., Illus.). 48p. (gr. 3-4). lib. bdg. 29.32 *(978-1-4914-4162-6(3))* Capstone Press of Coughlan Cos.
Lawrence, Ellen. Pluto & the Dwarf Planets. 2013. (Zoom into Space Ser.). 24p. (J). (gr. -1-3). lib. bdg. 23.93 *(978-1-909673-20-5(X))* Ruby Tuesday Books Limited GBR. Dist: Bearport Publishing Co., Inc.
Lew, Kristi. The Dwarf Planet Pluto. 2009. (Space!). 64p. (gr. 5-18). lib. bdg. 32.79 *(978-0-7614-4243-1(X))* Marshall Cavendish Corp.
Miller, Ron. Mercury & Pluto. 2003. (Worlds Beyond Ser.). (Illus.). 80p. (J). (gr. 7-18). lib. bdg. 27.93 *(978-0-7613-2361-7(9)*, Twenty-First Century Bks.) Lerner Publishing Group.
O'Connell, Kim A. Pluto: A Myreportlinks. com Book. 2005. (Solar System Ser.). (Illus.). 48p. (J). (gr. 4-10). lib. bdg. 26.60 *(978-0-7660-5210-9(9)*, MyReportLinks.com Bks.) Enslow Pubs., Inc.
Orme, Helen & Orme, David. Let's Explore Pluto & Beyond. 2007. (Space Launch! Ser.). (Illus.). 24p. (gr. 1-4). lib. bdg. 23.00 *(978-0-8368-7945-2(7)*, Gareth Stevens Learning Library) Stevens, Gareth Publishing LLLP.
Owen, Ruth. Pluto & Other Dwarf Planets. 2013. (Explore Outer Space Ser.). 32p. (J). (gr. 3-6). 25.25 *(978-1-61533-730-9(X))*; pap. 10.00 *(978-1-61533-777-4(6))*; pap. 60.00 *(978-1-61533-778-1(4))* Windmill Bks.
Owens, L. L. Pluto & Other Dwarf Planets. McGeehan, Dan, illus. 2011. (Space Neighbors Ser.). (ENG.). 32p. (J). (gr. 1-4). lib. bdg. 27.07 *(978-1-60954-386-0(6)*, 200891) Child's World, Inc., The.
Oxlade, Chris. Jupiter, Neptune, & Other Outer Planets. 2007. (Earth & Space Ser.). (Illus.). 48p. (YA). (gr. 5-9). lib. bdg. 29.25 *(978-1-4042-3736-0(4))* Rosen Publishing Group, Inc., The.
Portman, Michael. Why Isn't Pluto a Planet? 2013. (Space Mysteries Ser.). (Illus.). 32p. (J). (gr. 2-5). 25.25 *(978-1-4339-8282-8(X))*; pap. 10.50 *(978-1-4339-8283-5(8))* Stevens, Gareth Publishing LLLP. (Gareth Stevens Learning Library).
Ring, Susan. Pluto. (Exploring Planets Ser.). (J). 2004. pap. 8.95 *(978-1-59036-228-0(4))* 2003. (Illus.). 24p. lib. bdg. 24.45 *(978-1-59036-101-6(6))* Weigl Pubs., Inc.
Roland, James. Pluto: A Space Discovery Guide. 2017. (Space Discovery Guides). (ENG.). 48p. (J). (gr. 4-6). 16.99 ***(978-1-5124-3812-3(X)***, Lerner Pubns.); 47.99 ***(978-1-5124-2796-7(9)***, Lerner Pubns.); 47.99 ***(978-1-5124-3813-0(8)***, Lerner Pubns.); (Illus.). 31.99 *(978-1-5124-2587-1(7))* Lerner Publishing Group.
Rusch, Elizabeth & Francis, Guy. The Planet Hunter: The Story Behind What Happened to Pluto. 2007. (ENG., Illus.). 32p. (J). (gr. -1-3). 15.95 *(978-0-87358-926-0(2))* Cooper Square Publishing Llc.
Sawyer, J. Clark. PlutÓN: No Es un Planeta. 2015. (Fuera de Este Mundo Ser.). (SPA., Illus.). 24p. (J). (gr. -1-3). lib. bdg. 23.93 *(978-1-62724-595-1(2))* Bearport Publishing Co., Inc.
Sparrow, Giles. Destination Uranus, Neptune, & Pluto. 2009. (Destination Solar System Ser.). (Illus.). 32p. (J). 25.25 *(978-1-4358-3446-0(1))*; pap. 10.00 *(978-1-4358-3463-7(1))* Rosen Publishing Group, Inc., The. (PowerKids Pr.).
Stewart, Kellie. Journey to Pluto & Other Dwarf Planets, 1 vol. 2014. (Spotlight on Space Science Ser.). (ENG.). 32p. (J). (gr. 5-5). pap. 11.75 *(978-1-4994-0375-6(5)*, PowerKids Pr.) Rosen Publishing Group, Inc., The.
Taylor-Butler, Christine. Pluto: Dwarf Planet. (Scholastic News Nonfiction Readers Ser.). (ENG., Illus.). 24p. (J). (gr. 1-2). 2008. pap. 6.95 *(978-0-531-14766-5(5))* 2007. 22.00 *(978-0-531-14751-1(7))* Scholastic Library Publishing.
Vogt, Gregory. The Dwarf Planet Pluto. 2009. (Early Bird Astronomy Ser.). (ENG.). 48p. (gr. 2-5). lib. bdg. 26.60 *(978-0-7613-4157-4(9))* Lerner Publishing Group.
—Pluto: A Dwarf Planet. 2009. (Early Bird Astronomy Ser.). (ENG., Illus.). 48p. (gr. 2-5). pap. 8.95 *(978-0-7613-4988-4(X)*, Lerner Pubns.) Lerner Publishing Group.
Weitekamp, Margaret & DeVorkin, David. Pluto's Secret: An Icy World's Tale of Discovery. Kidd, Diane, illus. (ENG.). 40p. (J). (gr. 1-4). 2015. pap. 9.95 *(978-1-4197-1526-6(7))* 2013. 16.95 *(978-1-4197-0423-9(0))* Abrams, Inc. (Abrams Bks. for Young Readers).
Weitekamp, Margaret & Devorkin, David. Pluto's Secret: An Icy World's Tale of Discovery. 2015. (J). lib. bdg. 20.80 *(978-0-606-37376-0(4))* Turtleback Bks.
World Book, contrib. by. Neptune & the Distant Dwarf Planets. 2nd ed. 2006. (World Book's Solar System & Space Exploration Library). (Illus.). 64p. (J). *(978-0-7166-9518-9(9))* World Bk., Inc.
World Book, Inc Staff, contrib. by. Neptune & Pluto. 2006. (World Book's Solar System & Space Exploration Library). (Illus.). 63p. (J). *(978-0-7166-9507-3(3))* World Bk., Inc.

PLUTO (FICTITIOUS CHARACTER)—FICTION

Disney Staff. The Story of Pluto the Pup. 2004. (Illus.). 96p. (J). 35.00 incl. audio compact disk *(978-1-55709-356-1(3))* Applewood Bks.
Disney Storybook Artists Staff, illus. Disney Mickey Mouse Clubhouse Movie Theater: Storybook & Movie Projector. 2012. (Movie Theater Ser.). (ENG.). 32p. (J). (gr. k-3). 19.99 *(978-0-7944-2587-6(9))* Reader's Digest Assn., Inc., The.

PLUTO (PLANET)

see Pluto (Dwarf Planet)

PLYMOUTH (MASS.)—HISTORY

Cipriano, Jeri. Three Historical Communities of North America: Text Pairs. 2008. (Bridges/Navigators Ser.). (J). (gr. 3). 89.00 *(978-1-4108-8375-9(2))* Benchmark Education Co.
Samo, Melissa. If You Were a Kid at the First Thanksgiving Dinner. Farré, Lluís, illus. 2017. (If You Were a Kid Ser.). (ENG.). 32p. (J). pap. 7.95 *(978-0-531-23097-8(X)*, Children's Pr.) Scholastic Library Publishing.
Samo, Melisa. If You Were a Kid at the First Thanksgiving Dinner. 2017. (If You Were a Kid Ser.). (ENG., Illus.). 32p. (J). lib. bdg. 26.00 *(978-0-531-22383-3(3)*, Children's Pr.) Scholastic Library Publishing.
Wagner, Heather Lehr. William Bradford. 2010. (Leaders of the Colonial Era Ser.). 120p. (gr. 5-8). 35.00 *(978-1-60413-743-9(6)*, Chelsea Hse.) Facts On File, Inc.

POCAHONTAS, -1617

Adams, Colleen. Pocahontas. 2009. (Reading Room Collection 1 Ser.). 16p. (gr. 2-3). 37.50 *(978-1-60851-949-1(X)*, PowerKids Pr.) Rosen Publishing Group, Inc., The.
—Pocahontas: The Life of an Indian Princess. 2006. (Rosen Publishing Group's Reading Room Collection). (Illus.). 16p. (J). (gr. 3-7). lib. bdg. 17.25 *(978-1-4042-3348-5(2)*, PowerKids Pr.) Rosen Publishing Group, Inc., The.
—The True Story of Pocahontas. 2009. (What Really Happened? Ser.). 24p. (gr. 2-3). 42.50 *(978-1-60854-765-4(5)*, PowerKids Pr.); (Illus.). (J). (gr. 3-6). lib. bdg. 22.60 *(978-1-4042-4475-7(1))* Rosen Publishing Group, Inc., The.
Alter, Judy & Rosenberg, Pam. Jane Addams: Social Reformer & Nobel Prize Winner. 2003. (Our People Ser.). (ENG., Illus.). 32p. (J). (gr. 3-6). 29.93 *(978-1-59296-010-1(3)*, 200641) Child's World, Inc., The.
Becker, Sandra. Pocahontas. 2003. (Folk Heroes Ser.). (Illus.). 24p. (J). lib. bdg. 24.45 *(978-1-59036-074-3(5))* Weigl Pubs., Inc.
Benjamin, Andrew. Pocahontas. 2014. (Illus.). 32p. (J). lib. bdg. *(978-1-62712-292-4(3))* Cavendish Square Publishing.
Brimner, Larry Dane. Pocahontas: Bridging Two Worlds. 2008. (American Heroes Ser.). 48p. (gr. 3-18). lib. bdg. 29.93 *(978-0-7614-3065-0(2)*, Benchmark Bks.) Marshall Cavendish Corp.

Bruchac, Joseph. Pocahontas. 2005. (ENG., Illus.). 192p. (YA). (gr. 7-12). pap. 6.99 *(978-0-15-205465-6(0))* Houghton Mifflin Harcourt Publishing Co.
—Pocahontas. 2005. (Illus.). 173p. (gr. 7). 15.95 *(978-0-7569-5604-2(8))* Perfection Learning Corp.
Edison, Erin. Pocahontas. 2013. (Great Women in History Ser.). (ENG.). 24p. (gr. k-1). pap. 35.70 *(978-1-62065-862-8(3))*; pap. 6.29 *(978-1-62065-861-1(5))*; lib. bdg. 21.99 *(978-1-62065-074-5(6))* Capstone Press of Coughlan Cos. (Pebble Bks.).
Ford, Carin T. Pocahontas: American Indian Princess. 2006. (Heroes of American History Ser.). (Illus.). 32p. (J). (gr. 4-7). lib. bdg. 23.94 *(978-0-7660-2604-9(3)*, Enslow Elementary) Enslow Pubs., Inc.
Fritz, Jean. The Double Life of Pocahontas. l.t. ed. 2003. (Children's Large Print Ser.). 24.95 *(978-1-58118-109-8(4))* LRS.
Harkins, Susan Sales & Harkins, William H. Pochantas. 2008. (What's So Great About... ? Ser.). (Illus.). 32p. (J). (gr. 2-4). lib. bdg. 25.70 *(978-1-58415-682-6(1))* Mitchell Lane Pubs., Inc.
Jenner, Caryn. Pocahontas, Level 2. 2009. (DK Readers Ser.). (ENG.). 32p. (J). (gr. 1-3). 3.99 *(978-0-7566-5611-9(7)*, DK Children) Dorling Kindersley Publishing, Inc.
Jones, Victoria Garrett. Pocahontas: A Life in Two Worlds. 2010. (Sterling Biographies(r) Ser.). (ENG., Illus.). 128p. (J). (gr. 5-18). pap. 5.95 *(978-1-4027-5158-5(3))* Sterling Publishing Co., Inc.
Kirkman, Marissa. The Life & Times of Pocahontas & the First Colonies. 2016. (Life & Times Ser.). (ENG., Illus.). 24p. (gr. 1-2). lib. bdg. 25.32 *(978-1-5157-2477-3(8)*, First Facts) Capstone Press of Coughlan Cos.
Ledgerwood, Maja. Pocahontas: Princess of Faith & Courage. 2008. (Illus.). 48p. pap. 17.99 *(978-1-4343-4394-9(4))* AuthorHouse.
Mattern, Joanne. Pocahontas. 2015. (Rookie Biographies(tm) Ser.). (ENG., Illus.). 32p. (J). lib. bdg. 25.00 *(978-0-531-20596-9(7))* Scholastic Library Publishing.
Nagle, Jeanne. Pocahontas: Facilitating Exchange Between the Powhatan & the Jamestown Settlers. 2017. (Women Who Changed History Ser.). 48p. (gr. 10-12). pap. 14.05 ***(978-1-68048-653-7(5)***, Britannica Educational Publishing) Rosen Publishing Group, Inc., The.
Nettleton, Pamela Hill. Pocahontas: Peacemaker & Friend to the Colonists. Yesh, Jeff, illus. 2003. (Biographies Ser.). (ENG.). 24p. (gr. k-3). 26.65 *(978-1-4048-0187-5(1))* Picture Window Bks.
Patterson, Marie. Pocahontas, 1 vol. 2004. (Primary Source Readers Ser.). (ENG.). 24p. (J). (gr. 4-4). pap. 8.99 *(978-0-7439-8745-5(4))* Shell Educational Publishing.
Polette, Nancy. Pocahontas. 2003. (Rookie Biographies Ser.). (ENG., Illus.). 32p. (J). (gr. 1-2). 20.50 *(978-0-516-22859-4(5)*, Children's Pr.) Scholastic Library Publishing.
—Rookie Biographies: Pocahontas. 2003. (Rookie Biographies Ser.). (ENG.). 32p. (J). (gr. 1-2). pap. 4.95 *(978-0-516-27782-0(0)*, Children's Pr.) Scholastic Library Publishing.
Schwartz, Heather E. Pocahontas: Her Life & Legend. 2016. (Primary Source Readers Ser.). (Illus.). 32p. (J). (gr. 4-5). pap. 8.99 *(978-1-4938-3072-5(4))* Teacher Created Materials, Inc.
Sita, Lisa. Pocahontas: The Powhatan Culture & the Jamestown Colony. 2009. (Library of American Lives & Times Ser.). 112p. (gr. 5-5). 69.20 *(978-1-60853-500-2(2))* Rosen Publishing Group, Inc., The.
Sjonger, Rebecca & Kalman, Bobbie. Life of the Powhatan. 2004. (Native Nations of North America Ser.). (ENG., Illus.). 32p. (J). (gr. 2-5). pap. *(978-0-7787-0472-0(6))*; (gr. 5). lib. bdg. *(978-0-7787-0380-8(0))* Crabtree Publishing Co.
Weinberger, Kimberly. Let's Read About— Pocahontas. Marchesi, Stephen, illus. 2003. (Scholastic First Biographies Ser.). (J). pap. *(978-0-439-56148-8(5))* Scholastic, Inc.

POCAHONTAS, -1617—FICTION

Kudlinski, Kathleen V. My Lady Pocahontas, 0 vols. unabr. ed. 2013. (ENG.). 288p. (gr. 5-9). pap. 9.99 *(978-1-4778-1711-7(5)*, 9781477817117, Amazon Children's Publishing) Amazon Publishing.
Lawton, Wendy G. The Captive Princess: A Story Based on the Life of Young Pocahontas. 2008. (Daughters of the Faith Ser.). (ENG.). 144p. (gr. 3-7). per. 7.99 *(978-0-8024-7640-1(6))* Moody Pubs.
LeSourd, Nancy. Adventures in Jamestown, 1 vol. 2008. (Liberty Letters Ser.). (ENG.). 240p. (J). pap. 7.99 *(978-0-310-71392-0(7))* Zonderkidz.
Marsh, Carole. Pocahontas. (Read-Along Ser.). (J). 7.99 incl. audio *(978-1-55723-739-2(5))* Walt Disney Records.
Smith, Andrea P. Pocahontas & John Smith. 2012. (Illus.). 24p. (J). 63.60 *(978-1-4488-5219-2(6))*; pap. 10.60 *(978-1-4488-5218-5(8))*; lib. bdg. 25.25 *(978-1-4488-5190-4(4))* Rosen Publishing Group, Inc., The. (PowerKids Pr.).
Walt Disney Company Staff. Pocahontas. 2005. (WEL., Illus.). 24p. *(978-1-899877-04-1(5))* Y Ddraig Fach.

POE, EDGAR ALLAN, 1809-1849

Amper, Susan. Bloom's How to Write about Edgar Allan Poe. 2007. (Bloom's How to Write about Literature Ser.). 232p. (C). (gr. 9-12). 45.00 *(978-0-7910-9488-4(X)*, Chelsea Hse.) Facts On File, Inc.
Binns, Tristan Boyer. Edgar Allan Poe: Master of Suspense. 2005. (Great Life Stories Ser.). (ENG., Illus.). 128p. (J). (gr. 6-8). lib. bdg. 30.50 *(978-0-531-16751-9(8)*, Watts, Franklin) Scholastic Library Publishing.
Burlingame, Jeff. Edgar Allan Poe: Deep into That Darkness Peering. 2008. (Americans—the Spirit of a Nation Ser.). (Illus.). 128p. (J). (gr. k-5). lib. bdg. 33.27 *(978-0-7660-3020-6(2))* Enslow Pubs., Inc.
Frisch, Aaron. Edgar Allan Poe. 2005. (Voices in Poetry Ser.). (Illus.). 48p. (J). (gr. 5-9). lib. bdg. 21.95 *(978-1-58341-344-9(8)*, Creative Education) Creative Co., The.
—Edgar Allan Poe. Kelley, Gary, illus. 2014. (Voices in Poetry Ser.). 47p. (J). lib. bdg. 35.65 *(978-1-60818-324-1(6)*, Creative Education) Creative Co., The.
Frish, Aaron. Voices in Poetry: Edgar Allan Poe. 2015. (Voices in Poetry Ser.). (ENG.). 48p. (J). (gr. 5-8). pap. 12.00 *(978-1-62832-052-7(4)*, Creative Paperbacks) Creative Co., The.
Gigliotti, Jim. Who Was Edgar Allan Poe? Foley, Tim, illus. 2015. 105p. (J). *(978-1-4844-6178-5(9)*, Grosset & Dunlap) Penguin Publishing Group.
Lacey, Saskia. The Prehistoric Masters of Literature: Discover Literary History with a Prehistoric Twist! 2016. (Jurassic Classics Ser.). (ENG., Illus.). 40p. (J). (gr. 2-6). 14.95 *(978-1-63322-098-0(2))* Quarto Publishing Group USA.
Mcarthur, Debra. Reading & Interpreting the Works of Edgar Allan Poe. 2016. (Lit Crit Guides). (ENG., Illus.). 160p. (J). (gr. 8-8). lib. bdg. 39.93 *(978-0-7660-7342-5(4))* Enslow Pubs., Inc.
McArthur, Debra. A Student's Guide to Edgar Allan Poe. 2006. (Understanding Literature Ser.). (Illus.). 160p. (YA). (gr. 8-12). lib. bdg. 27.93 *(978-0-7660-2437-3(7))* Enslow Pubs., Inc.
Meltzer, Milton. Edgar Allan Poe: A Biography. 2003. (Literary Greats Ser.). (ENG., Illus.). 144p. (gr. 7-12). lib. bdg. 33.26 *(978-0-7613-2910-7(2)*, Twenty-First Century Bks.) Lerner Publishing Group.
Peltak, Jennifer. Edgar Allan Poe. 2003. (Who Wrote That? Ser.). (Illus.). 112p. (gr. 6-12). 35.00 *(978-0-7910-7622-4(9)*, Chelsea Hse.) Facts On File, Inc.
Schoell, William. Mystery & Terror: The Story of Edgar Allan Poe. 2004. (Illus.). 128p. (YA). (gr. 6-12). 23.95 *(978-1-931798-39-6(7))* Reynolds, Morgan Inc.
Streissguth, Thomas. Edgar Allan Poe. 2005. (Biography Ser.). (Illus.). 112p. (J). (gr. 6-12). lib. bdg. 27.93 *(978-0-8225-4991-8(3))* Lerner Publishing Group.
Streissguth, Tom. Edgar Allan Poe. 2007. (Just the Facts Biographies Ser.). (ENG., Illus.). 112p. (gr. 5-12). lib. bdg. 27.93 *(978-0-8225-6800-1(4)*, Lerner Pubns.) Lerner Publishing Group.
Whiting, Jim. Edgar Allan Poe. 2005. (Classic Storytellers Ser.). (Illus.). 48p. (J). (gr. 4-8). lib. bdg. 29.95 *(978-1-58415-373-3(3))* Mitchell Lane Pubs., Inc.

POE, EDGAR ALLAN, 1809-1849—FICTION

Bowen, Carl & Poe, Edgar Allen. The Murders in the Rue Morgue, 1 vol. Dimaya, Emerson & Calero, Dennis, illus. 2013. (Edgar Allan Poe Graphic Novels Ser.). (ENG.). 72p. (gr. 2-3). 27.99 *(978-1-4342-3033-1(3))*; pap. 6.10 *(978-1-4342-4259-4(5))* Stone Arch Bks.
Creagh, Kelly. Enshadowed. 2012. (ENG., Illus.). 448p. (YA). (gr. 7). 17.99 *(978-1-4424-0204-1(0)*, Atheneum Bks. for Young Readers) Simon & Schuster Children's Publishing.
—Enshadowed: A Nevermore Book. 2013. (ENG., Illus.). 464p. (YA). (gr. 7). pap. 9.99 *(978-1-4424-0206-5(7))* Simon & Schuster Children's Publishing.
—Nevermore. (ENG., Illus.). (YA). (gr. 9). 2011. 576p. pap. 9.99 *(978-1-4424-0201-0(6))* 2010. 560p. 17.99 *(978-1-4424-0200-3(8))* Simon & Schuster Children's Publishing. (Atheneum Bks. for Young Readers).
—Oblivion. 2015. (ENG.). 448p. (YA). (gr. 7). 18.99 *(978-1-4424-3627-5(1))* Simon & Schuster Children's Publishing.
Dunn, Joeming. Cask of Amontillado, 1 vol. 2014. (Graphic Horror Set 3 Ser.). (ENG.). 32p. (J). (gr. 5-8). lib. bdg. 28.50 *(978-1-62402-015-5(1)*, Graphic Planet) Magic Wagon.
—Raven, 1 vol. 2014. (Graphic Horror Set 3 Ser.). (ENG.). 32p. (J). (gr. 5-8). lib. bdg. 28.50 *(978-1-62402-017-9(8)*, Graphic Planet) Magic Wagon.
Edgar Allan Poe. 2013. (Edgar Allan Poe Graphic Novels Ser.). (ENG.). 72p. (gr. 2-3). 111.96 *(978-1-4342-4129-0(7))* Stone Arch Bks.
Edgar Allan Poe Collection of Stories Student Packet. 2004. (YA). 12.99 *(978-1-58130-510-4(9))* Novel Units, Inc.
Edgar Allan Poe Graphic Novels. 2013. (Edgar Allan Poe Graphic Novels Ser.). (ENG.). 72p. (gr. 2-3). pap. 23.80 *(978-1-4342-4351-5(6))* Stone Arch Bks.
Fields, Jan. A Novel Nightmare: The Purloined Story, 1 vol. Altmann, Scott, illus. 2013. (Adventures in Extreme Reading Ser.). (ENG.). 112p. (J). (gr. 3-6). 27.07 *(978-1-61641-924-0(5))* Magic Wagon.
Gustafson, Scott. Eddie: The Lost Youth of Edgar Allan Poe. Gustafson, Scott, illus. (ENG., Illus.). 208p. (J). (gr. 3-7). 2012. pap. 6.99 *(978-1-4169-9765-8(2))* 2011. 15.99 *(978-1-4169-9764-1(4))* Simon & Schuster Bks. For Young Readers. (Simon & Schuster Bks. For Young Readers).
Harper, Benjamin & Poe, Edgar Allen. The Tell-Tale Heart, 1 vol. Calero, Dennis, illus. 2013. (Edgar Allan Poe Graphic Novels Ser.). (ENG.). 72p. (gr. 2-3). lib. bdg. 27.99 *(978-1-4342-3023-2(6))* Stone Arch Bks.
Kirov, Erica. Magickeepers: The Eternal Hourglass. Fortune, Eric, illus. 2010. (ENG.). 256p. (J). (gr. 4-7). pap. 10.99 *(978-1-4022-3855-0(X)*, Sourcebooks Jabberwocky) Sourcebooks, Inc.
Manning, Matthew K. & Poe, Edgar Allen. The Fall of the House of Usher, 1 vol. Jimenz, Jim & Calero, Dennis, illus. 2013. (Edgar Allan Poe Graphic Novels Ser.). (ENG.). 72p. (gr. 2-3). 27.99 *(978-1-4342-3024-9(4))*; pap. 6.10 *(978-1-4342-4258-7(7))* Stone Arch Bks.
McAlpine, Gordon. Once upon a Midnight Eerie: Book #2. Zuppardi, Sam, illus. 2014. (Misadventures of Edgar & Allan Poe Ser.: 2). (ENG.). 192p. (J). (gr. 3-7). 16.99 *(978-0-670-78493-6(1)*, Viking Books for Young Readers) Penguin Young Readers Group.
—The Tell-Tale Start. Zuppardi, Sam, illus. 2013. (Misadventures of Edgar & Allan Poe Ser.: 1). (ENG.). (J). (gr. 3-7). 208p. pap. 7.99 *(978-0-14-242346-2(7)*, Puffin Books); 192p. 15.99 *(978-0-670-78491-2(5)*, Viking Books for Young Readers) Penguin Young Readers Group.
Poe, Edgar Allen. Edgar Allan Poe's Tales of Death & Dementia. Grimly, Gris, illus. 2009. (ENG.). 144p. (J). (gr. 6-9). 19.99 *(978-1-4169-5025-7(7)*, Atheneum Bks. for Young Readers) Simon & Schuster Children's Publishing.
Poe, Edgar Allen & Harper, Benjamin. The Tell-Tale Heart, 1 vol. Calero, Dennis, illus. 2013. (Edgar Allan Poe Graphic Novels Ser.). (ENG.). 72p. (gr. 2-3). pap. 6.10 *(978-1-4342-4261-7(7))* Stone Arch Bks.
Tulien, Sean & Poe, Edgar Allen. The Pit & the Pendulum, 1 vol. Fabul, J. C. & Calero, Dennis, illus. 2013. (Edgar Allan Poe Graphic Novels Ser.). (ENG.). 72p. (gr. 2-3). pap. 6.10 *(978-1-4342-4260-0(9))*; lib. bdg. 27.99 *(978-1-4342-4024-8(X))* Stone Arch Bks.

POETICS

Here are entered works on the appreciation and technique of poetry. Works on the appreciation and philosophy of poetry are entered under Poetry.
see also Rhythm; Versification

Bodden, Valerie. Picturing Words in a Poem. 2016. (Illus.). 22p. (J). *(978-1-60818-621-1(0)*, Creative Education) Creative Co., The.
Early Macken, JoAnn. Read, Recite, & Write Narrative Poems. 2014. (ENG., Illus.). 32p. (J). *(978-0-7787-0410-2(6))* Crabtree Publishing Co.
Fandel, Jennifer. Metaphors, Similes, & Other Word Pictures. 2005. (Understanding Poetry Ser.). (Illus.). 48p. (YA). (gr. 4-7). lib. bdg. 21.95 *(978-1-58341-340-1(5))* Creative Co., The.
—Puns, Allusions, & Other Word Secrets. 2005. (Understanding Poetry Ser.). (Illus.). 48p. (YA). (gr. 4-7). lib. bdg. 21.95 *(978-1-58341-341-8(3))* Creative Co., The.
—Rhyme, Meter, & Other Word Music. 2005. (Understanding Poetry Ser.). (Illus.). 48p. (YA). (gr. 4-7). lib. bdg. 21.95 *(978-1-58341-342-5(1))* Creative Co., The.
Lázaro León, Georgina & Genovés, Graciela. Jorge Luis Borges. Genovés, Graciela, illus. 2009. (Cuando los Grandes Eran Pequenos Ser.). (SPA., Illus.). 32p. (J). (gr. 4-6). 14.99 *(978-1-933032-40-5(5))* Lectorum Pubns., Inc.
Lesynski, Loris. I Did It Because... How a Poem Happens. Martchenko, Michael, illus. 2006. (ENG.). 64p. (J). (gr. 2-5). 19.95 *(978-1-55451-018-4(X)*, 9781554510184); 3rd ed. pap. 9.95 *(978-1-55451-017-7(1)*, 9781554510177) Annick Pr., Ltd. CAN. Dist: Publishers Group West (PGW).
Lombardo, Mary A. Poetry & Pop-Ups: An Art-Enhanced Approach to Writing Poetry, 1 vol. 2003. (Illus.). 96p. (C). (gr. 4-6). pap. 10.95 *(978-1-58683-082-3(1)*, A2385P, Linworth Publishing, Inc.) ABC-CLIO, LLC.
Lyon, George Ella. Where I'm From. 2004. (Writers & Young Writers Ser.: 2). 98p. pap. 13.95 *(978-1-888842-18-0(0))* Absey & Co.
Prelutsky, Jack. Pizza, Pigs, & Poetry: How to Write a Poem. 2008. (ENG.). 208p. (J). (gr. 2-5). pap. 6.99 *(978-0-06-143448-8(5))*; (Illus.). 16.99 *(978-0-06-143449-5(3))* HarperCollins Pubs. (Greenwillow Bks.).
Roza, Greg. Patterns in Poetry: Recognizing & Analyzing Poetic Form & Meter. (PowerMath Ser.). 32p. 2009. (ENG.). (gr. 5-6). pap. 10.00 *(978-1-4042-5146-5(4))* 2009. (gr. 4-5). 47.90 *(978-1-60851-415-1(3))* 2005. (Illus.). (J). (gr. 3-6). lib. bdg. 25.25 *(978-1-4042-2941-9(8))* Rosen Publishing Group, Inc., The. (PowerKids Pr.).
Walsh, Brendan, et al. Opinions about Three Victorian Era Poets: Christina Rossetti, Robert Louis Stevenson, Emily Dickinson. 2014. (Text Connections Ser.). (J). (gr. 3). *(978-1-4509-9657-0(4))* Benchmark Education Co.

POETRY

see also Ballads; Free Verse; Hymns; Love Poetry; Nature—Poetry
also American Poetry; English Poetry, etc.; and general subjects, names of historical events, places and famous persons with the subdivision Poetry, e.g. Animals—poetry

La Abajita que Habla (the Talking Bumblebee) 2003. (J). *(978-1-56870-477-7(1))* Hewell Publishing.
ABC Memory Verses. 2003. 32p. (J). per. 9.99 *(978-0-88724-137-6(9))* Carson-Dellosa Publishing, LLC.
Abell, Angel Morgan. The Alphabliss of Miss: Poems & Pictures. 2005. (Illus.). 54p. (J). 30.00 *(978-1-885679-20-8(3))* Morgan Foundation Pubs.: International Published Innovations.
Abodehman, Ahmed. El Cinturón. Lovillo, Pilar Ortiz, tr. Sanchez, Andres & Tagle, illus. 2006. (la Orilla del Viento Ser.). (SPA.). 121p. (J). per. 8.50 *(978-968-16-6670-5(4))* Fondo de Cultura Economica USA.
Academy of American Poets Staff. Poem in Your Pocket for Young Poets. 2011. (ENG.). 232p. (J). (gr. 7-17). 18.95 *(978-0-8109-9882-7(3)*, Amulet Bks.) Abrams, Inc.
Acheson, Alison & Gutiérrez, Elisa. Night Sky - Wheel Ride, 1 vol. 2012. (ENG., Illus.). 88p. (J). (gr. 2-4). pap. 8.95 *(978-1-896580-99-9(8))* Tradewind Bks. CAN. Dist: Orca Bk. Pubs. USA.
Adam, Ryan. New Orleans Mother Goose, 1 vol. Gentry, Marita, illus. 2014. (ENG.). 40p. (J). 17.99 *(978-1-4556-1953-5(1))* Pelican Publishing Co., Inc.
Adedjouma, Davida. The Palm of My Heart: Poetry by African American Children. Christie, Gregory R., illus. 2013. (ENG.). 32p. (J). (gr. -1-18). pap. 9.95 *(978-1-880000-76-2(8))* Lee & Low Bks., Inc.
Ageledis, Ida. First Foil Poetry Seasons, 2 vols. Berg, Michelle, illus. 2005. (First Foil Poetry Haikus Ser.). 10p. (J). 6.95 *(978-1-58117-188-4(9)*, Intervisual/Piggy Toes) Bendon, Inc.
Alarcón, Francisco X. Angels Ride Bikes & Other Fall Poems: Los Angeles Andan Bicicletas y Otros Poemas de Otoño. Gonzalez, Maya Christina, illus. 2013. (ENG & SPA.). 32p. (J). (gr. 1-4). per. 9.95 *(978-0-89239-198-1(7))* Lee & Low Bks., Inc.
—Animal Poems of the Iguazú: Animalario del Iguazú. Gonzalez, Maya Christina, illus. 2008. (SPA & ENG.). 32p. (J). (gr. k). 16.95 *(978-0-89239-225-4(8))* Lee & Low Bks., Inc.
—From the Bellybutton of the Moon & Other Summer Poems: Del Ombligo de la Luna y Otros Poemas de Verano. Gonzalez, Maya Christina, illus. 2013. (ENG & SPA.). 32p. (J). (gr. 1-4). per. 9.95 *(978-0-89239-201-8(0))* Lee & Low Bks., Inc.
—Iguanas in the Snow & Other Winter Poems: Iguanas en la Nieve y Otros Poemas de Invierno. Gonzalez, Maya Christina, illus.Tr. of Iguanas in the Snow & Other Winter Poems. (ENG & SPA.). 32p. (J). (gr. 1-4). 2013. per. 9.95 *(978-0-89239-202-5(9))* 2004. 16.95 *(978-0-89239-168-4(5))* Lee & Low Bks., Inc.
—Laughing Tomatoes & Other Spring Poems: Jitomates Risueños y Otros Poemas de Primavera. Gonzalez, Maya Christina, illus. 2013. (ENG & SPA.). 32p. (J). (gr. 1-4). per. 9.95 *(978-0-89239-199-8(5))* Lee & Low Bks., Inc.
—Poems to Dream Together: Poemas para Soñar Juntos. Barragán, Paula, illus. 2005. (ENG & SPA.). 32p. (J). (gr. 2-5). 16.95 *(978-1-58430-233-9(X))* Lee & Low Bks., Inc.
Alarcón, Francisco X., et al. Border Voices: The San Diego Celebration of Poetry & Music: the 10th Annual Anthology of Poetry. 2003. (ENG.). per. 12.95 *(978-0-9719906-1-6(1))* Webb, Jack.
Alberti, Rafael. Rafael Alberti para Ninos. Gaban, Jesus, illus. (SPA.). 164p. (J). (gr. 4-6). 20.76 *(978-84-305-9290-6(3)*, SU0175) Susaeta Ediciones, S.A. ESP. Dist: Lectorum Pubns., Inc.
Alderson, Sue Ann. The Eco-Diary of Kiran Singer, 1 vol. Ballance, Millie, illus. 2007. (ENG.). 64p. (YA). (gr. 7-12). 15.95 *(978-1-896580-47-0(5))* Tradewind Bks. CAN. Dist: Orca Bk. Pubs. USA.
Alexander, Elizabeth & Nelson, Marilyn. Miss Crandall's School for Young Ladies & Little Misses of Color. Cooper, Floyd, illus. 2007. (ENG.). 48p. (J). (gr. 6-9). 17.95 *(978-1-59078-456-3(1)*, Wordsong) Boyds Mills Pr.
Alexander-Heaton, Susanne & Gabriell, Chantal T. The ABC Field Guide to Faeries: Inspiring Reminders of Respect for Ourselves, Each Other & the Environment. 2nd ed. 2009. *(978-0-9813048-0-9(X))* Alexander-Heaton, Susanne.
Alexander, Jessica & Shore, Diane Z. This Is the Dream. Ransome, James E., illus. 2005. (ENG.). 40p. (J). (gr. k-5). 16.99 *(978-0-06-055519-1(X)*, Amistad) HarperCollins Pubs.
Alexander, Kwame, et al. Out of Wonder: Poems Celebrating Poets. Holmes, Ekua, illus. 2017. (ENG.). 56p. (J). (gr. 3-7). 16.99 *(978-0-7636-8094-7(X))* Candlewick Pr.
Alexander, Martha, illus. & selected by. Poems & Prayers for the Very Young. Alexander, Martha, selected by. 32p. (J). Random Hse. Children's Bks.
Allan, Shaun. Zits'n'bits. 2012. 56p. pap. 6.50 *(978-1-4716-1244-2(9))* Lulu Pr., Inc.
Allison, Hugh A. Intrigue of Love. 2012. 108p. (gr. -1). pap. 19.40 *(978-1-4343-9444-6(1))* AuthorHouse.
Alston, Stanley E. Faith, Love & Life. Sharps, Angelique, ed. Alston, Sheila Y., photos by. (Illus.). 48p. (YA). (gr. 4-18). pap. 12.95 *(978-0-9719897-0-2(2))* Magnatic Music.
Altein, Chani. The Aleph Bias Ship on the Aleph Bias Trip. Rosenfeld, D. L. & Leverton, Yossi, eds. Becker, Baruch, illus. 2009. 30p. (J). 10.95 *(978-1-929628-25-4(0))* Hachai Publishing.
—Oif der Aleph Bais Shif. Brod, Chani, tr. from ENG. Becker, Baruch, illus. 2014.Tr. of Aleph Bais Trip on the Aleph Bais Ship. 32p. (J). 10.95 *(978-1-929628-77-3(3))* Hachai Publishing.
Arnholt, Laurence. Collins Big Cat - Royal Rap. Morenton, Alice, illus. 2015. (Collins Big Cat Ser.). (ENG.). 24p. (J). (gr. 2-2). pap. 7.95 *(978-0-00-759113-8(6))* HarperCollins Pubs. Ltd. GBR. Dist: Independent Pubs. Group.
Andersen, Hans Christian & Stevenson, Robert Louis. The Swing. Morriss, Deborah & Morstad, Julie, illus. 2012.Tr. of Nattergalen. (ENG.). 16p. (J). 8.95 *(978-1-897476-48-2(5))* Simply Read Bks. CAN. Dist: Ingram Publisher Services.
Anderson, Lillian. My Sandwich. Uhlig, Elizabeth, illus. 2012. 32p. (J). pap. 12.95 *(978-0-9834030-3-6(1))* Marble Hse. Editions.
Andreacchi, Grace. Little Poems for Children. 2010. (Illus.). 64p. pap. 26.95 *(978-1-4457-6338-5(9))* Lulu Pr., Inc.
Andreae, Giles. Cock-A-Doodle-Doo! Barnyard Hullabaloo. Wojtowycz, David, illus. 2004. (ENG.). 32p. (J). reprint ed. pap. 7.95 *(978-1-58925-387-2(6))* Tiger Tales.
Andrews, Julie & Hamilton, Emma Walton. Julie Andrews' Treasury for All Seasons: Poems & Songs to Celebrate the Year. Priceman, Marjorie, illus. 2012. (ENG.). 192p. (J). (gr. -1-3). 19.99 *(978-0-316-04051-8(7))* Little, Brown Bks. for Young Readers.
Andricain, Sergio. Arco Iris de Poesia: Poemmas de las Americas y Espana. Cuellar, Olga, illus. 2008. (SPA.). 40p. (J). (gr. -1-3). 15.99 *(978-1-930332-59-1(9))* Lectorum Pubns., Inc.
Anon. A Collection of Animal Poems for Children. 2012. 26p. pap. 8.45 *(978-1-4474-5458-8(8))* Palmer Pr., The.
Anonymous. The Child's Book of Poetry a Selection of Poems, Ballads & Hymns. 2011. (Illus.). 238p. pap. 26.75 *(978-1-241-56870-2(7)*, British Library, Historical Print Editions) Creative Media Partners, LLC.
—Required Poems for Reading & Memorizing: Third & Fourth Grades, Prescribed by State Courses of Study. l.t. ed. 2007. (ENG.). 168p. pap. 19.99 *(978-1-4264-3925-4(3))* Creative Media Partners, LLC.
Antunes, Ana Claudia. The Sea Sons. 2009. 53p. pap. 9.99 *(978-1-4357-2479-2(8))* Lulu Pr., Inc.
Antwine, Tajiye Lavonne. Changing the World 1 Poem @ a Time. 2012. 42p. pap. 9.95 *(978-0-9834275-1-3(8))* Blacktastic.net.
Appelt, Kathi. Just People & Paper - Pen - Poem: A Young Writer's Way to Begin. Appelt, Kenneth, photos by. 2004. (Writers & Young Writers Ser.: Vol. 1). (Illus.). 91p. (YA). pap. 11.95 *(978-1-888842-07-4(5)*, 1020) Absey & Co.
Archer, Peggy. From Dawn to Dreams: Poems for Busy Babies. Wakiyama, Hanako, illus. 2007. (ENG.). 32p. (J). (gr. k-k). 15.99 *(978-0-7636-2467-5(5))* Candlewick Pr.
Argueta, Jorge. Arroz con Leche / Rice Pudding: Un Poema para Cocinar / a Cooking Poem, 1 vol. Amado, Elisa, tr. Vilela, Fernando, illus. 2016. (Bilingual Cooking Poems Ser.). (ENG & SPA.). 32p. (J). (gr. -1-2). 8.95 *(978-1-55498-887-7(X))* Groundwood Bks. CAN. Dist: Publishers Group West (PGW).
—Guacamole: A Cooking Poem / Guacamole: un Poema para Cocinar. 2016. (ENG & SPA.). lib. bdg. 19.60 *(978-0-606-38493-3(6))* Turtleback Bks.
—Guacamole: Un Poema para Cocinar (A Cooking Poem), 1 vol. Amado, Elisa, tr. Sada, Margarita, illus. 2016. (Bilingual Cooking Poems Ser.). (ENG & SPA.). 32p. (J). (gr. -1-2). pap. 8.95 *(978-1-55498-888-4(8))* Groundwood Bks. CAN. Dist: Publishers Group West (PGW).
—Una Pelicula en Mi Almohada. Gomez, Elizabeth & Gómez, Elizabeth, illus. 2013.Tr. of Movie in My Pillow. (ENG & SPA.). 32p. (J). (gr. k). pap. 9.95 *(978-0-89239-219-3(3))* Lee & Low Bks., Inc.
—Somos Como las Nubes / We Are Like the Clouds, 1 vol. Amado, Elisa, tr. Ruano, Alfonso, illus. 2016. (ENG & SPA.). 36p. (J). (gr. 1-7). 18.95 *(978-1-55498-849-5(7))* Groundwood Bks. CAN. Dist: Publishers Group West (PGW).
—Sopa de Frijoles / Bean Soup, 1 vol. Yockteng, Rafael, illus. 2017. (ENG & SPA.). 32p. (J). (gr. -1-2). 8.95 *(978-1-77306-002-6(3))* Groundwood Bks. CAN. Dist: Publishers Group West (PGW).

—Tamalitos: Un Poema para Cocinar. Amado, Elisa, tr. from SPA. Domi, illus. 2013. (Bilingual Cooking Poems Ser.).Tr. of A Cooking Poem. (ENG & SPA.). 32p. (J). (gr. -1-2). 18.95 *(978-1-55498-300-1(2))* Groundwood Bks. CAN. Dist: Publishers Group West (PGW).

Armstrong, Charles. Laugh & Pray Today. 2013. 58p. 21.99 *(978-1-62839-199-2(5))*; pap. 12.99 *(978-1-62839-156-5(1))* Salem Author Services.

Arneson, Guy. Kiddy Ditties. 2009. 32p. pap. 14.50 *(978-1-4389-8137-6(6))*; 36p. pap. 16.99 *(978-1-4389-8165-9(1))*; 28p. pap. 14.50 *(978-1-4389-8126-0(0))*; 40p. pap. 18.49 *(978-1-4389-8127-7(9))*; 32p. pap. 14.50 *(978-1-4389-6783-7(7))* AuthorHouse.

Asher, Melissa. Magical, Mystical, Majestic. 2009. 88p. pap. 19.95 *(978-1-4489-8991-1(4))* America Star Bks.

Asher, Sandra Fenichel. Somebody Catch My Homework. 2004. (YA). pap. 4.50 *(978-1-58342-171-0(8)*, SH8) Dramatic Publishing Co.

Ashman, Linda. The Essential Worldwide Monster Guide. Small, David, illus. 2010. (ENG.). 40p. (J). (gr. -1-3). 13.99 *(978-1-4424-1436-5(7)*, Simon & Schuster Bks. For Young Readers) Simon & Schuster Bks. For Young Readers.

Asquith, Ros. Vanishing Trick: Poems by Ros Asquith. Asquith, Ros, illus. 2015. (ENG., Illus.). 112p. (J). (gr. 3-7). pap. 7.99 *(978-1-84780-539-3(6)*, Frances Lincoln) Quarto Publishing Group UK GBR. Dist: Hachette Bk. Group.

Atkins, Jeannine. Borrowed Names: Poems about Laura Ingalls Wilder, Madam C. J. Walker, Marie Curie, & Their Daughters. 2010. (ENG.). 224p. (YA). (gr. 7-12). 29.99 *(978-0-8050-8934-9(9)*, 9780805089349, Holt, Henry & Co. Bks. For Young Readers) Holt, Henry & Co.

Atwood, Megan. Connor & Clara Build a Concrete Poem. Butler, Reginald, illus. 2011. (Poetry Builders Ser.). 32p. (J). (gr. 2-4). lib. bdg. 25.27 *(978-1-59953-434-3(7))* Norwood Hse. Pr.

Audet, Martine. Que Ferais-Je du Jour? Sylvestre, Daniel, tr. 2003. (New Poetry Ser.). (FRE.). 36p. (J). (gr. 7). pap. *(978-2-89021-621-1(7))* Diffusion du livre Mirabel (DLM).

Austin, Norma J. Baby's Bedtime Poems: Sleepy Time Rhymes. 2010. 48p. pap. 8.95 *(978-1-4401-9403-0(3))* iUniverse, Inc.

Avery, Carrie L. A String of Pearls. 2003. 68p. (YA). pap. 9.95 *(978-0-7414-1540-0(2))* Infinity Publishing.

Ayers, Linda. There's Something in My Sandwich. Hunt, Jane, illus. 50p. (J). 2006. 13.95 *(978-0-9760505-7-5(9))* 2005. per. 6.95 *(978-0-9760505-5-1(2))* Blue Thistle Pr.

AZ Books, creator. Being a Princess. 2013. (Jingle-Jangle Ser.). (ENG., Illus.). 10p. (J). (gr. -1-k). bds. 9.95 *(978-1-61889-236-2(3))* AZ Bks. LLC.

—Come & Play. 2013. (Everyday Rhymes Ser.). (ENG., Illus.). 14p. (J). (gr. -1-k). bds. 15.95 *(978-1-61889-225-6(8))* AZ Bks. LLC.

—Do Like Me. 2013. (Jingle-Jangle Ser.). (ENG., Illus.). 10p. (J). (gr. -1-k). bds. 9.95 *(978-1-61889-238-6(X))* AZ Bks. LLC.

—It's Playtime. 2013. (Jingle-Jangle Ser.). (ENG., Illus.). 10p. (J). (-k). bds. 9.95 *(978-1-61889-237-9(1))* AZ Bks. LLC.

—My Favorite Toy. 2013. (Everyday Rhymes Ser.). (ENG., Illus.). 14p. (J). (gr. -1-k). bds. 15.95 *(978-1-61889-227-0(4))* AZ Bks. LLC.

—What I Say. 2013. (Everyday Rhymes Ser.). (ENG., Illus.). 14p. (J). (gr. -1-k). bds. 15.95 *(978-1-61889-228-7(2))* AZ Bks. LLC.

AZ Books Staff. Animal Wonder. 2013. (Everyday Rhymes Ser.). (ENG., Illus.). 14p. (J). (gr. -1-k). bds. 15.95 *(978-1-61889-226-3(6))* AZ Bks. LLC.

—Animals on the Go. 2013. (Jingle-Jangle Ser.). (ENG., Illus.). 10p. (J). (gr. -1-k). bds. 9.95 *(978-1-61889-239-3(8))* AZ Bks. LLC.

B. A. O'Reilly. You've Got a Friend in Me. 2012. 52p. pap. 17.50 *(978-1-61897-713-7(X)*, Strategic Bk. Publishing) Strategic Book Publishing & Rights Agency (SBPRA).

Bagert, Brod. Shout! Little Poems That Roar. Yoshikawa, Sachiko, illus. 2007. (ENG.). 32p. (J). (gr. -1-3). 17.99 *(978-0-8037-2972-8(3)*, Dial Bks) Penguin Young Readers Group.

Bagert, Brod, ed. Edgar Allan Poe. Cobleigh, Carolynn, illus. 2008. (Poetry for Young People Ser.). (ENG.). 48p. (J). (gr. 3-7). pap. 6.95 *(978-1-4027-5472-2(8))* Sterling Publishing Co., Inc.

—Poetry for Young People: Edgar Allan Poe. Cobleigh, Carolynn, illus. 2014. (Poetry for Young People Ser.). (ENG.). 48p. (J). (gr. 3). 14.95 *(978-1-4549-1348-1(7))* Sterling Publishing Co., Inc.

Bain, A. Watson, compiled by. A Poetry Book for Children. 2012. (ENG.). 122p. pap. 35.99 *(978-1-107-66147-9(1))* Cambridge Univ. Pr.

Baker, Jaime. Bedtime Baby, 1 vol. Noble, Roger, illus. 2010. 16p. pap. 24.95 *(978-1-4489-6234-1(X))* PublishAmerica, Inc.

Baker, Kenneth, ed. Children's English History in Verse. Stower, Adam, illus. 2007. 289p. pap. 20.00 *(978-1-4223-9012-2(8))* DIANE Publishing Co.

Bannatyne, Lesley Pratt. Witches' Night Before Halloween, 1 vol. Tans, Adrian, illus. 2007. (ENG.). 32p. (J). (gr. k-3). 16.99 *(978-1-58980-485-2(6))* Pelican Publishing Co., Inc.

Bar-el, Dan. Pussycat, Pussycat, Where Have You Been? Mate, Rae, illus. 2011. (ENG.). 32p. (J). (gr. -1-3). 16.95 *(978-1-897476-46-8(9))* Simply Read Bks. CAN. Dist: Ingram Publisher Services.

Barbe, Walter B. A School Year of Poems: 180 Favorites from Highlights. Hockerman, Dennis, illus. 2005. (ENG.). 116p. (J). (gr. 2-4). pap. 11.95 *(978-1-59078-395-5(6))* Boyds Mills Pr.

Bardsley, Jacqueline. Dandelion Days. 2011. 28p. pap. 15.99 *(978-1-4568-2219-4(5))* Xlibris Corp.

Barker, Cicely Mary. Flower Fairies of the Summer. 2008. (Flower Fairies Ser.). (ENG., Illus.). 48p. (J). (gr. -1-2). 7.99 *(978-0-7232-6282-4(9)*, Warne) Penguin Young Readers Group.

—A Flower Fairies Treasury. 2007. 14.99 *(978-0-7232-5973-2(9))* Penguin Publishing Group.

Barnett, Mac. Guess Again! Rex, Adam, illus. 2009. (ENG.). 32p. (J). (gr. -1-3). 17.99 *(978-1-4169-5566-5(6)*, Simon & Schuster Bks. For Young Readers) Simon & Schuster Bks. For Young Readers.

Bartlett, Irene. The New Testament: Bible Poems for Children. 2007. (Illus.). 96p. per. *(978-1-84748-207-5(4))* Athena Pr.

Barton, Matthew. The Winding Road: A Child's Treasury of Poems, Verses, & Prayers. 2005. (Festivals Ser.). (ENG.). 224p. pap. 23.50 *(978-1-903458-47-1(1))* Hawthorn Pr. GBR. Dist: SteinerBooks, Inc.

Bauer, Marion Dane. The Halloween Forest. Shelley, John, illus. 2012. (ENG.). 32p. (J). 16.95 *(978-0-8234-2324-8(7))* Holiday Hse., Inc.

Baxter, Nicola. Childrens's Book of Classic Poems & Rhymes. 2013. (ENG., Illus.). 240p. (J). (gr. 3-7). pap. 14.99 *(978-1-84322-920-9(X))* Anness Publishing GBR. Dist: National Bk. Network.

—Classic Poetry for Children. Shuttleworth, Cathie, illus. 2013. (ENG.). 80p. (J). (gr. k-4). pap. 9.99 *(978-1-84322-820-2(3))* Anness Publishing GBR. Dist: National Bk. Network.

—The Ultimate Treasury of Stories & Rhymes: A Collection of 215 Tales & Poems. 2013. (ENG., Illus.). 576p. (J). (gr. -1-3). 16.99 *(978-1-84322-886-8(6)*, Armadillo) Anness Publishing GBR. Dist: National Bk. Network.

Baxter, Nicola, ed. Christmas Lullabies for Children. Finn, Rebecca, illus. 2014. (ENG.). 12p. (J). (gr. k-5). bds. 14.99 incl. audio compact disk *(978-1-84322-931-5(5)*, Armadillo) Anness Publishing GBR. Dist: National Bk. Network.

Beal, Jane. Magical poems for Girls. 2009. 76p. pap. 9.99 *(978-0-557-09280-2(9))* Lulu Pr., Inc.

Beaton, Clare & Kletter, Dana. Mrs. Moon: Lullabies for Bedtime. 2007. (ENG., Illus.). 48p. (J). 19.99 *(978-1-84686-067-6(9))* Barefoot Bks., Inc.

The Beginning of Love. 2005. per. 12.00 net. *(978-0-9720046-2-6(9))* Bluestone Bks.

Beglau, Judy. Spark Story Bible Psalm Book: Prayers & Poems for Kids. Krueger, Naomi Joy, ed. Grosshauser, Peter, illus. 2016. (ENG.). 112p. (J). (gr. -1-3). 14.99 *(978-1-5064-1768-4(X))* Augsburg Fortress, Pubs.

Belgrove, Teresa. A Collection of Children's Poems, Verses & Rhymes for All Ages. 2007. (Illus.). 216p. per. 20.78 *(978-1-4251-0945-5(4))* Trafford Publishing.

Bell, Marvin. A Primer about the Flag. Raschka, Chris, illus. 2011. (ENG.). 32p. (J). (gr. -1-3). 15.99 *(978-0-7636-4991-3(0))* Candlewick Pr.

Benjamin, Lisa & Benchmark Education Co. Staff. The Story of Casey at the Bat. 2014. (Text Connections Ser.). (J). (gr. 5). *(978-1-4900-1365-7(2))* Benchmark Education Co.

A Benji's Pup Set, 6 vols. 32p. (gr. 1-3). 37.50 *(978-0-322-00338-5(5))*; 31.50 incl. 5.25 hd *(978-0-7802-8045-8(8))* Wright Group/McGraw-Hill.

Benson, Catherine. It Must Have Been a Sunday, Vol. 2005. 32p. pap. *(978-1-902382-79-1(X))* Smith/Doorstop Books.

Bernier-Grand, Carmen T. Cesar: Si, Se Puede! Yes, We Can!, 0 vols. Diaz, David, illus. 2011. (ENG.). 50p. (J). (gr. 3-7). pap. 7.99 *(978-0-7614-5833-3(6)*, 9780761458333, Amazon Children's Publishing) Amazon Publishing.

Berry, James. Classic Poems to Read Aloud. Mayhew, James, illus. 2003. (Classic Collections). (ENG.). 256p. (J). (gr. 2-5). pap. 8.99 *(978-0-7534-5688-0(5)*, 9780753456880, Kingfisher) Roaring Brook Pr.

—A Nest Full of Stars. Bryan, Ashley, illus. 2004. 104p. (J). (gr. 2-18). 16.89 *(978-0-06-052748-8(X))* HarperCollins Pubs.

Bilkan, Ali Fuat. Tales from Rumi: Mathnawi Selections for Young Readers. 2008. (ENG., Illus.). 160p. (J). (gr. 7-17). 9.95 *(978-1-59784-124-5(2))* Tughra Bks.

Bills, Taylor, illus. Twas the Night before Christmas. 2009. 24p. 12.95 *(978-0-9776845-4-0(7))* 3D Alley, Inc.

Bint Mahmood, Ayesha. Thank You O Allah! 2016. (ENG., Illus.). 24p. (J). (gr. -1-k). 8.95 *(978-0-86037-335-3(5))* Kube Publishing Ltd. GBR. Dist: Consortium Bk. Sales & Distribution.

Birchall, Lorrie L. The Purple Glurple. 2012. 76p. pap. 12.95 *(978-0-9857816-0-6(2))* Birchall Publishing.

Birkelbach, Alan. Smurglets Are Everywhere. Halbower, Susan J., illus. 2010. (ENG.). 48p. (J). (gr. -1-6). 19.95 *(978-0-87565-415-7(0))* Texas Christian Univ. Pr.

Bits & Pieces: The Poems of Melvin E. Giles, 1 vol. 2004. (Illus.). 235p. per. 14.50 *(978-0-9656364-1-4(0))* Oakdale Pr.

Blanco, Alberto. Tambien Los Insectos Son Perfectos. Radaviciute, Diana, illus. 2005.Tr. of Insects Are Perfect, Too: (SPA.). (J). (gr. k-2). pap. 10.95 *(978-968-494-054-3(8))* Centro de Informacion y Desarrollo de la Comunicacion y la Literatura MEX. Dist: Iaconi, Mariuccia Bk. Imports.

Blane, Francisco. Looking for the Muffin Man. 2008. (Reader's Theater Nursery Rhymes & Songs Ser.). (Illus.). 48p. (J). (gr. k-1). pap. *(978-1-60437-966-2(9))* Benchmark Education Co.

Blatz-Harvey, Elizabeth. The Windows of My World. Blatz-Harvey, Elizabeth, illus. 2011. (Illus.). 32p. *(978-0-9868730-3-4(9))* Cheaper Cheeper Copy.

Blazek, Sarah Kirwan. An Irish Night Before Christmas, 1 vol. Rice, James, illus. 2009. (Night Before Christmas Ser.). (ENG.). 32p. (J). (gr. k-3). pap. 3.95 *(978-1-58980-704-4(9))* Pelican Publishing Co., Inc.

Bleck, Linda, illus. A Children's Treasury of Poems. 2015. (ENG.). 32p. (J). (-k). pap. 6.95 *(978-1-4549-1474-7(2))* Sterling Publishing Co., Inc.

Bloom, Valerie. Hot Like Fire. Lush, Debbie, illus. 2009. (ENG.). 192p. (J). (gr. 4-7). pap. 11.95 *(978-0-7475-9973-9(4))* Bloomsbury Publishing Plc GBR. Dist: Independent Pubs. Group.

—Let Me Touch the Sky: Selected Poems for Children. 2003. (Illus.). 90p. (J). 19.99 *(978-0-333-78067-1(1))* Macmillan Pubs., Ltd. GBR. Dist: Trafalgar Square Publishing.

—Mighty Mountains, Swirling Seas. Cimatoribus, Alessandra, illus. 2015. (Collins Big Cat Ser.). (ENG.). 32p. (J). (gr. 2-2). pap. 7.95 *(978-0-00-759126-8(8))* HarperCollins Pubs. Ltd. GBR. Dist: Independent Pubs. Group.

Bloomquist, Stephen, ed. The Sun with Loving Light, 1 vol. Dalton, Pamela, illus. 2014. Orig. Title: Der Sonne Licht. (ENG.). 110p. (J). *(978-1-936367-63-4(7))* Waldorf Publications.

Blue Set. (Dias y Dias de Poesia Ser.). (SPA.). (gr. -1-6). 293.52 *(978-1-56334-270-7(7)*, DI8630) CENGAGE Learning.

Bodden, Valerie. Finding the Rhyme in a Poem. 2016. (Write Me a Poem Ser.). (ENG.). 24p. (J). (gr. 2-4). pap. 9.99 *(978-1-62832-252-1(7)*, Creative Paperbacks) Creative Co., The.

—Picturing Words in a Poem. 2016. (Write Me a Poem Ser.). (J). (ENG.). 24p. (gr. 2-4). pap. 9.99 *(978-1-62832-253-8(5)*, Creative Paperbacks); (Illus.). 22p. *(978-1-60818-621-1(0)*, Creative Education) Creative Co., The.

—Poking Fun in a Poem. 2016. (Write Me a Poem Ser.). (J). (ENG.). 24p. (gr. 2-4). pap. 9.99 *(978-1-62832-254-5(3)*, Creative Paperbacks); (Illus.). 22p. *(978-1-60818-622-8(9)*, Creative Education) Creative Co., The.

—Who Is a Poet? 2016. (Illus.). 22p. (J). *(978-1-60818-623-5(7)*, Creative Education) Creative Co., The.

—Write Me a Poem: Finding the Rhyme in a Poem. 2016. (Illus.). 22p. (J). *(978-1-60818-620-4(2)*, Creative Education) Creative Co., The.

Bogdan, Diane. Twigs Is a Poet. 2010. 108p. pap. 10.95 *(978-1-4502-1971-6(3))* iUniverse, Inc.

Bolden, Tonya. 12 Days of New York. Ford, Gilbert, illus. 2013. (ENG.). 32p. (J). (gr. k-2). 17.95 *(978-1-4197-0542-7(3)*, Abrams Bks. for Young Readers) Abrams, Inc.

Bolding, Clarissa. Life Is A Song Worth Singing. 2005. 88p. per. 12.00 *(978-0-9762924-7-0(5))* InnerCircle Publishing.

Bolin, Frances Schoonmaker, ed. Carl Sandburg. Arcella, Steven, illus. 2008. (Poetry for Young People Ser.). (ENG.). 48p. (J). (gr. 3-7). pap. 6.95 *(978-1-4027-5471-5(X))* Sterling Publishing Co., Inc.

—Emily Dickinson. Chung, Chi, illus. 2008. (Poetry for Young People Ser.). (ENG.). 48p. (J). (gr. 3). pap. 6.95 *(978-1-4027-5473-9(6))* Sterling Publishing Co., Inc.

—Poetry for Young People: Emily Dickinson. Chung, Chi, illus. 2014. (Poetry for Young People Ser.). (ENG.). 48p. (J). (gr. 3). 14.95 *(978-1-4549-1346-7(0))* Sterling Publishing Co., Inc.

Bollen, Christine. Three Munch-y Cherries. 2007. (J). per. 11.99 *(978-1-59879-376-5(4))* Lifevest Publishing, Inc.

Bolocan, D. Stephie learns about Animals. 2010. 54p. pap. 10.50 *(978-1-4457-7447-3(X))* Lulu Pr., Inc.

Bond, Felicia. Tumble Bumble. braille ed. 2004. (Illus.). (J). (gr. 1). spiral bd., bds. *(978-0-616-03081-3(9))* Canadian National Institute for the Blind/Institut National Canadien pour les Aveugles.

Booth, Philip. Crossing. Ibatoulline, Bagram, illus. 2013. (ENG.). 40p. (J). (gr. k-4). pap. 6.99 *(978-0-7636-6664-4(5))* Candlewick Pr.

Borisov, Vadim & Borisova, Alina. Krylataia Mechta. 2012. (RUS., Illus.). 39p. pap. 24.55 *(978-1-4678-8959-9(8))* AuthorHouse.

Boulden, Lowell E. Why Not Me? 2008. 40p. pap. 20.99 *(978-1-4389-1505-0(5))* AuthorHouse.

Bowcut~, ~Jan. Seasons of Poetry: A Guide for Young Writers Grades 3-6. 2012. 40p. pap. 20.99 *(978-1-4772-3708-3(9))* AuthorHouse.

BOWE, Andi. Alphabet book 1: a to z in song & Verse. 2009. 48p. pap. 28.50 *(978-0-557-04239-5(9))* Lulu Pr., Inc.

—Alphabet book 2: a to z in song & Verse. 2009. 44p. pap. 27.95 *(978-0-557-02784-2(5))* Lulu Pr., Inc.

Bower, Gary. The Garden Where I Grow: And Other Poems for Cultivating a Happy Family. Bower, Jan, illus. 2012. (Bright Future Bks.). (ENG.). 32p. (J). 11.99 *(978-0-9845236-2-7(6))* Storybook Meadow Publishing.

Bowyer, Mary. Tony Turtle & Friends. 2004. 56p. (J). pap. 9.95 *(978-0-595-32152-0(6))* iUniverse, Inc.

Boychuk, Carol. The Tiny World: Poems by Carol Boychuk. 2010. 24p. 14.95 *(978-1-4269-3186-4(7))* Trafford Publishing.

Boynton, Sandra. Belly Button Book! 2005. (ENG., Illus.). 24p. (J). (gr. k — 1). bds. 6.95 *(978-0-7611-3799-3(8)*, 13799) Workman Publishing Co., Inc.

—Snuggle Puppy! A Love Song. (ENG., Illus.). 144p. 101.70 *(978-0-7611-4101-3(4)*, 24101); 1p. (J). bds. 83.40 *(978-0-7611-3455-8(7)*, 23455) Workman Publishing Co., Inc.

Bradbury, Ken & Crowe, Robert L. Wait ... Don't Leave Yet. Crowe, Robert L., ed. 2003. (YA). ring bd. 10.00 *(978-0-9707173-7-5(7))* Consortium Publishing Co.

Bradford, Imani. People Can't Save You. 2004. (J). pap. 7.00 *(978-0-9671796-0-5(2))* Segue Pubs.

Bradley, B. D. Wonderful Willie: What He & Tommy Did to Spain. 2013. (ENG., Illus.). 52p. (J). (gr. 4-8). pap. 24.95 *(978-1-4290-9806-9(6))* New-York Historical Society.

Breckon, Brett, illus. Dragon Days. 2004. (ENG.). 82p. 17.95 *(978-1-84323-301-5(0))* Beekman Bks., Inc.

Brenna, Beverley. The Bug House Family Restaurant, 1 vol. Mongeau, Marc, illus. 2014. (ENG.). 64p. (J). (gr. 3-5). pap. 12.95 *(978-1-926890-01-2(9))* Tradewind Bks. CAN. Dist: Orca Bk. Pubs. USA.

Brennan, Michael. The Imageless World. 2004. (ENG., Illus.). 108p. pap. 14.99 *(978-1-84471-005-8(X))* Salt Publishing GBR. Dist: SPD-Small Pr. Distribution.

Brewin, Barbara. Treasure Box of Children's Poetry: A magical world for Children. 2009. (Illus.). 56p. pap. 23.99 *(978-1-4389-5592-6(8))* AuthorHouse.

Bride of the Wolf (UNCUT EDITION), 5 vols., Vol. 2. anniv. ed. 2012. (ENG., Illus.). 162p. (YA). per. 11.99 *(978-0-9769819-4-7(7)*, M.S.C. Bks.) Mustard Seed Comics.

Brilis, Michael Nicholas. Joy & Tears in Life: Perspectives of a Greek Immigrant. 2004. (GRE.). 49p. pap. 24.95 *(978-0-9753454-0-5(0)*, CQ-003) ComQwest, LLC.

Brock, Justin. Have You Seen My Pencil? Poems & Musings. Wright, Christopher, illus. 2007. (J). pap. *(978-0-9796210-0-0(3))* OPUS II Bks.

Brockett, Keith. The Nutcracker's Night Before Christmas. Cowman, Joseph, illus. 2015. (ENG.). 32p. (J). (gr. 1-3). 15.99 *(978-1-58536-889-1(X)*, 203954) Sleeping Bear Pr.

Brockway, Margaret. David, the Son of Jesse. 2011. 20p. (gr. 1-2). pap. 10.03 *(978-1-4567-4915-6(3))* AuthorHouse.

Brookman, Darin. Where Sagebrush Grows. 2004. per. 20.00 *(978-0-9749518-0-5(3))* Pair'a Spurs Pr.

Brooks, Gwendolyn. Bronzeville Boys & Girls. Ringgold, Faith, illus. 2007. 48p. (J). (gr. 2-5). 18.89 *(978-0-06-029506-6(6))* HarperCollins Pubs.

—Bronzeville Boys & Girls. 2015. (J). lib. bdg. 17.20 *(978-0-606-36468-3(4))* Turtleback Bks.

Brothers, Karen. Rhythm & Rhyme Literacy Time, Level K. rev. ed. 2015. (Getting to the Core of Poetry Ser.). (ENG., Illus.). 128p. (gr. k-k). pap. 15.99 *(978-1-4258-1336-9(4))* Shell Educational Publishing.

Brown, Calef. Hypnotize a Tiger: Poems about Just about Everything. Brown, Calef, illus. 2015. (ENG., Illus.). 144p. (J). (gr. 3-7). 17.99 *(978-0-8050-9928-7(X)*, 9780805099287, Holt, Henry & Co. Bks. For Young Readers) Holt, Henry & Co.

—Soup for Breakfast. 2008. (ENG., Illus.). 32p. (J). (gr. -1-3). 16.00 *(978-0-618-91641-2(5))* Houghton Mifflin Harcourt Publishing Co.

Brown, Daniel. Gerard Manley Hopkins. 2004. (ENG., Illus.). 144p. (C). 80.00 *(978-0-7463-1017-5(X))*; pap. 19.95 *(978-0-7463-0975-9(9))* Northcote Hse. Publishers, Ltd. GBR. Dist: Casemate Academic.

Brown, Margaret Wise. The Fathers Are Coming Home. Savage, Stephen, illus. 2010. (ENG.). 32p. (J). (gr. -1-k). 16.99 *(978-0-689-83345-8(8)*, McElderry, Margaret K. Bks.) McElderry, Margaret K. Bks.

—The Friendly Book. Williams, Garth, illus. 2012. (Little Golden Book Ser.). (ENG.). 24p. (J). (gr. k-k). 4.99 *(978-0-307-92962-4(0)*, Golden Bks.) Random Hse. Children's Bks.

—Give Yourself to the Rain: Poems for the Very Young. Weidner, Teri, illus. 2012. (ENG.). 32p. (J). (gr. -1-3). pap. 16.99 *(978-1-4424-6063-8(6)*, McElderry, Margaret K. Bks.) McElderry, Margaret K. Bks.

—Where Have You Been? Dillon, Leo & Dillon, Diane, illus. 2004. 32p. (J). (gr. -1-1). lib. bdg. 16.89 *(978-0-06-028379-7(3))* HarperCollins Pubs.

Brown, Skila. Slickety Quick: Poems about Sharks. Kolar, Bob, illus. 2016. (ENG.). 32p. (J). (gr. 1-4). 16.99 *(978-0-7636-6543-2(6))* Candlewick Pr.

Brown, Suzanne. The Night Before Christmas in Ski Country. Schlingman, Dana, illus. 2013. 32p. (J). 17.95 *(978-1-56579-658-4(6)*, Westcliffe Pubs.) Bower Hse.

Browning, Robert. The Pied Piper of Hamelin, Illustrated by Hope Dunlap. Dunlap, Hope, illus. 2008. 52p. pap. 12.95 *(978-1-59915-265-3(7))* Yesterday's Classics.

Brunette, Steffan. Cough, Achoo, & Roar! 2013. 16p. pap. 7.99 *(978-1-4624-0632-6(7)*, Inspiring Voices) Author Solutions, Inc.

Bruno, Elsa Knight. Punctuation Celebration. Whitehead, Jenny, illus. 2012. (ENG.). 32p. (J). (gr. 1-4). pap. 7.99 *(978-1-250-00335-5(0)*, 9781250003355) Square Fish.

Brush & Paint. 2003. (Gateways to the Sun Ser.). 32p. (J). (gr. 1-2). pap. 11.95 *(978-1-58105-575-7(7))* Santillana USA Publishing Co., Inc.

Bryan, Ashley. Ashley Bryan's Puppets: Making Something from Everything. Bryan, Ashley, illus. 2014. (ENG., Illus.). 80p. (J). (gr. -1). 19.99 *(978-1-4424-8728-4(3)*, Atheneum Bks. for Young Readers) Simon & Schuster Children's Publishing.

Bryce, Clara. Just My Imagination: Children's Poems. 2010. 44p. pap. 16.99 *(978-1-4490-6615-4(1))* AuthorHouse.

Bryer, Tom. Fun Poems for Kids. Bryer, Tom, illus. 2012. (Illus.). 26p. *(978-1-908341-74-7(2))* Paragon Publishing, Rothersthorpe.

Bulion, Leslie. At the Sea Floor Café: Odd Ocean Critter Poems, 1 vol. Evans, Leslie, illus. 2016. (ENG.). 48p. (J). (gr. 3-6). pap. 6.95 *(978-1-56145-920-9(8))* Peachtree Pubs.

Bunnaby Bunny (G) Toddler Reader. 2006. (Illus.). 20p. (J). bds. *(978-0-9712816-3-9(7))* Third Week Bks.

Burroughs, William S. Live Performance, Vol. 1. Hoffman, Kathelin, ed. Phillips, Zelmer, illus. (C). 12.95 incl. audio *(978-0-929856-00-1(7))* Caravan of Dreams Productions.

Buscher, Nancy Tancey. Kaleidoscope of Children's Poems. 2009. 28p. pap. 12.95 *(978-1-936051-53-3(2))* Peppertree Pr., The.

Bush Rage: Collected Verse. 2nd ed. 2005. *(978-0-9765948-0-2(3))* Diomo Square Bks.

Butler, Rosemary. My Merry Menagerie: Lighthearted Verses & Drawings. Butler, Rosemary, illus. 2013. (Illus.). 144p. 19.99 *(978-1-883378-22-6(2))* Sun on Earth Bks.

Byrd, Bill Scott. The Story of Rap & Tap. Ayzenberg, Nina, illus. 2006. 9.95 *(978-0-9776805-0-4(9))* Byrd, Fay T.

Cabreros, Beryl. Melting Pot of Children's Poetry, 1 vol. 2010. 77p. pap. 19.95 *(978-1-4489-5765-1(6))* America Star Bks.

Cain, Vernice. The Little Green Tree. 2012. 24p. (-18). pap. 17.99 *(978-1-4685-9446-1(X))* AuthorHouse.

Calderon, Marcela, illus. Poems by the Sea. 2017. (Poems Just for Me Ser.). 32p. (gr. 7-8). 27.25 ***(978-1-4994-8388-8(0)**, Windmill Bks.)* Rosen Publishing Group, Inc., The.

A Camel Called Bump-Along, 6 vols., Set B. 32p. (gr. 1-3). 31.50 *(978-0-7802-8049-6(0))* Wright Group/McGraw-Hill.

Canetti, Yanitzia. Canciones para Dormir a Las Munecas: Dulce Compania. 2010. (SPA.). 32p. (J). pap. 6.99 *(978-1-59835-256-6(3)*, BrickHouse Education) Cambridge BrickHouse, Inc.

—Canciones para dormir a los Peluches. 2010. (SPA.). 32p. (J). pap. *(978-1-59835-258-0(X)*, BrickHouse Education) Cambridge BrickHouse, Inc.

—I'm Proud to Be Me! 2010. (Illus.). 32p. (J). pap. 9.99 *(978-1-59835-286-3(5)*, BrickHouse Education) Cambridge BrickHouse, Inc.

—Imagina un mundo Mejor. 2010. (SPA., Illus.). 32p. (J). pap. *(978-1-59835-283-2(0)*, BrickHouse Education) Cambridge BrickHouse, Inc.

—Soy Original, ¡genial! 2010. (SPA.). (J). pap. *(978-1-59835-285-6(7))* Cambridge BrickHouse, Inc.

Cannon, Nick. Neon Aliens Ate My Homework & Other Poems. 2015. (Illus.). 142p. (J). *(978-0-545-80178-2(8))* Scholastic, Inc.

Canton, William. Invisible Playmate A Story of the Unseen. 2006. pap. 19.95 *(978-1-4286-3869-3(5))* Kessinger Publishing, LLC.

Capstone Press. The Poet's Toolbox: Set of 4, 4 vols. (Poet's Toolbox Ser.). (ENG., Illus.). 32p. (C). (gr. 3-5). 90.40 *(978-0-7565-0713-8(8))* Compass Point Bks.

Carangelo, Audrey. On the Street: Poems about Paintings. 2006. (Illus.). 8p. (J). *(978-0-439-73410-3(X))* Scholastic, Inc.

Carle, Eric. Dragons Dragons: And Other Creatuers That Never Were. 2004. (ENG., Illus.). 68p. (J). (gr. 1-4). pap. 12.99 *(978-0-14-240103-3(X)*, Puffin Books) Penguin Young Readers Group.

Carlson, Lori Marie. Cool Salsa: Bilingual Poems on Growing up Latino in the United States. 2013. (SPA & ENG.). (J). lib. bdg. 22.10 *(978-0-606-28551-3(2)*, Turtleback) Turtleback Bks.

Carlson, Lori Marie, ed. Cool Salsa: Bilingual Poems on Growing up Latino in the United States. 2013. (ENG & SPA.,

P
Q
R

Illus.). 160p. (J). (gr. 4-7). pap. 10.99 (978-1-250-01678-2(9), 9781250016782) Square Fish.

Carney, Audrey McDonald. It's Me Mommy, I've Been Sent from Heaven Above. 2011. 28p. pap. 24.95 (978-1-4560-3472-6(3)) America Star Bks.

Carney, Larry, adapted by. Three Billy Goats Gruff. 2009. (ENG., Illus.). 24p. (J). 6.95 (978-1-60072-114-4(1)) PC Treasures, Inc.

Carney-Nunes, Charisse. I Dream for You a World: A Covenant for Our Children. Williams, Ann Marie, illus. 2007. (ENG.). 32p. (J). (gr. k-2). 16.95 (978-0-9748142-3-0(7), Brand Nu Words) Nunes Productions, LLC.

Carr, Holly, illus. What Is Pink? 2003. 24p. (J). (gr. -1-1). (978-0-921156-92-5(8)) Rubicon Publishing, Inc.

Carroll, Lewis, pseud. Jabberwocky. Jorisch, Stéphane, illus. 2008. (Visions in Poetry Ser.). (ENG.). 40p. (J). (gr. 2-9). pap. 9.95 (978-1-55453-266-7(3)) Kids Can Pr., Ltd. CAN. Dist: Hachette Bk. Group.

—The Nonsense Verse of Lewis Caroll. Hussey, Lorna, illus. 2004. (ENG.). 32p. (J). (gr. 4). pap. 12.99 (978-0-7475-5019-8(0)) Bloomsbury Publishing Plc GBR. Dist: Independent Pubs. Group.

Carroll, Yvonne & Waters, Fiona, as told by. A Child's Treasury of Irish Stories & Poems. 2004. (ENG., Illus.). 194p. (J). 32.95 (978-0-7171-3795-4(3)) M.H. Gill & Co. U. C. IRL. Dist: Dufour Editions, Inc.

Carter, Cheri. The Misfitz: A Book of Poems. 2011. 108p. (gr. -1). 21.23 (978-1-4567-5890-5(X)); pap. 12.84 (978-1-4567-5891-2(8)) AuthorHouse.

Carter, James. Around the World. 2007. (Collins Big Cat Ser.). (ENG.). 24p. (J). (gr. k-1). pap. 5.99 (978-0-00-718658-7(4)) HarperCollins Pubs. Ltd. GBR. Dist: Independent Pubs. Group.

—Homes Sweet Homes. 2015. (Collins Big Cat Ser.). (ENG.). 24p. (J). (gr. 2-2). pap. 6.95 (978-0-00-759110-7(1)) HarperCollins Pubs. Ltd. GBR. Dist: Independent Pubs. Group.

—Journey to the Centre of My Brain, 1. unabr. ed. 2012. (ENG., Illus.). 96p. (J). (gr. 1). pap. 7.99 (978-0-230-75195-8(4)) Pan Macmillan GBR. Dist: Independent Pubs. Group.

Carter, James & Denton, Graham. Grrr! Dinos, Dragons & Other Beastie Poems. Morgan, Gaby, ed. unabr. ed. 2013. (ENG., Illus.). 96p. (J). (gr. 4). pap. 7.99 (978-1-4472-2034-3(X)) Pan Macmillan GBR. Dist: Independent Pubs. Group.

Carter, James & Moses, Brian. Spooky Poems. 2015. (ENG., Illus.). 96p. (J). (gr. 2-4). pap. 7.99 (978-1-4472-7258-8(7)) Pan Macmillan GBR. Dist: Independent Pubs. Group.

Carter, K. D. Vacation into Nonsense. 2009. 60p. pap. 16.95 (978-1-4489-2590-2(8)) America Star Bks.

Carthew, Mark. Flabbergaster, 1 vol. rev. ed. 2013. (Fiction Readers Ser.). (ENG., Illus.). 28p. (J). (gr. 3-3). pap. 8.99 (978-1-4333-5603-2(1)) Shell Educational Publishing.

—Speak Up!, 1 vol. rev. ed. 2013. (Fiction Readers Ser.). (ENG., Illus.). 20p. (J). (gr. 1-1). 4.99 (978-1-4333-5496-0(9)); pap. 15.96 (978-1-4807-1152-5(7)) Shell Educational Publishing.

—Vroom! Vroom! Poems about Things with Wheels, 1 vol. 2013. (Fiction Readers Ser.). (ENG., Illus.). 24p. (J). (gr. 2-2). pap. 6.99 (978-1-4333-5521-9(3)) Shell Educational Publishing.

Casey, Barbara. Slightest in the House. 2003. 100p. pap. 12.95 (978-1-932162-23-3(2)) Benoy Publishing.

Casey, Dawn. A Lullaby for Little One. Fuge, Charles, illus. 2017. (ENG.). 20p. (J). (-k). bds. 8.99 (978-0-7636-8661-1(1), Nosy Crow) Candlewick Pr.

Cashman, Seamus. Something Beginning with P: New Poems from Irish Poets. Askin, Corrina & Clarke, Alan, illus. 2004. (ENG.). 160p. (978-0-86278-868-1(4)) O'Brien Pr., Ltd., The.

Caswell, Deanna. Guess Who, Haiku. Shea, Bob, illus. 2016. (Guess Who Haiku Ser.). (ENG.). 24p. (J). (gr. -1-k). 14.95 (978-1-4197-1889-2(4), Abrams Appleseed) Abrams, Inc.

Catalano, Tom. Rhymes for Teens: Poems Older Students Can Enjoy. Romango, Jim, illus. 2004. 80p. (YA). per. 9.95 (978-1-882646-48-7(7)) Wordsmith Bks.

Celebrate Freedom: Songs, Symbols, & Sayings of the United States. 2003. (Scott Foresman Social Study Ser.). (Illus.). 32p. (gr. k-2). (978-0-328-03672-1(2)); 48p. (gr. 3-6). (978-0-328-03674-5(9)) Addison-Wesley Educational Pubs., Inc. (Scott Foresman).

Center for Learning Network Staff. Paradise Lost: Curriculum Unit. 2003. (Novel Ser.). 100p. (YA). tchr. ed., spiral bd. 19.95 (978-1-56077-732-8(X)) Center for Learning, The.

Cephas, Shelley A. Animal Tales: Poetry for Children & the Child at Heart. 2013. 70p. pap. 12.47 (978-1-61704-171-6(8)) River Styx Publishing Co.

Chafer, E. I., ed. The Illustrated Book of Children's Verse. 2014. (Foiled Gift Bks.). (ENG., Illus.). 160p. 15.99 (978-1-78361-130-0(8), 8cbffa92-0ac4-483f-bcbd-0203786ae90e) Flame Tree Publishing GBR. Dist: Bookmasters Distribution.

Champagne, Elena. Where Do Raindrops Go? Sarna, Billy, illus. l.t. ed. 2006. 24p. (J). (gr. -1-3). per. 10.99 (978-1-59879-233-1(4)) Lifevest Publishing, Inc.

Champlin, DeeAnn. Eddie E & the Eggs. Champlin, DeeAnn, illus. Date not set. (Little Lyrics Short Vowel Collection: Vol. 2). (Illus.). (J). (gr. k-2). pap. 12.00 (978-1-893429-26-0(1)) Little Lyrics Pubns.

Chandler, Tom. Sad Jazz. 2003. 80p. 18.00 (978-0-9726869-0-7(8)) Table Rock Bks.

Chanko, Pamela. Leveled Poems for Small-Group Reading Lessons: 40 Just-Right Poems for Guided Reading Levels e-N with Mini-Lessons That Teach Key Phonics Skills, Build Fluency, & Meet the Common Core. 2014. (ENG.). 96p. (gr. 1-3). pap. 14.99 (978-0-545-59363-2(8), Teaching Resources) Scholastic, Inc.

Cheng, Ainsley. Being Just Me, Myself, & I! 2006. (J). pap. 16.00 (978-0-8059-7189-7(0)) Dorrance Publishing Co., Inc.

Chiasson, Herménégilde. L' Oiseau Tatoué. Lafrance, David, illus. 2004. (Poetry Ser.). (FRE.). 36p. (J). (gr. 7). pap. (978-2-89021-675-4(6)) Diffusion du livre Mirabel (DLM).

A Chicago Winds Set, 6 vols. 32p. (gr. 1-3). 26.50 (978-0-7802-8047-2(4)) Wright Group/McGraw-Hill.

Child, Lydia Maria. Bitty Bear's Sleigh Ride. Ackley, Peggy Jo, illus. 2006. (J). (978-1-59369-157-8(2)) American Girl Publishing, Inc.

—Over the River & Through the Woods. Edelson, Wendy, illus. 2012. 16p. (J). 12.99 (978-0-8249-1881-1(9), Ideal Pubns.) Worthy Publishing.

Chronicle Books Staff. Nick Jr. Nursery Rhyme Time: A Touch-and-See Activity Book. (J). 15.95 (978-0-8118-4726-1(8)) Chronicle Bks. LLC.

Cinar, Lisa. Paulina P. 2009. (ENG., Illus.). 32p. (J). (gr. -1-3). 16.95 (978-1-897476-09-3(4)) Simply Read Bks. CAN. Dist: Ingram Publisher Services.

Cirillo, Todd, et al. Roxy: The Girl in the Platform Shoes, with the Black Dress On. 2003. (Illus.). 94p. per. 12.95 (978-0-9722958-0-2(1)) Crow, R.L. Pubns.

Claiborn, Trevor M. Li'l Missy & Antman: Colors. 2012. 28p. pap. 19.99 (978-1-4772-0983-7(2)) AuthorHouse.

Clark, Ann Nolan. In My Mother's House. Herrera, Velino, illus. 2004. 56p. (J). (gr. k-3). reprint ed. pap. 14.00 (978-0-7567-7104-1(8)) DIANE Publishing Co.

Class Pack. (Cuentacuentos Ser.). (SPA.). (gr. k-18). 813.22 (978-1-56334-799-3(7)) CENGAGE Learning.

Clay Lamberton Elementary School Students. Who Let the Cougars Out? 2006. (ENG., Illus.). 209p. per. (978-1-59146-095-4(6), Crystal Dreams Publishing) Multi-Media Pubns., Inc.

Clayton, Dallas. Make Magic! Do Good! Clayton, Dallas, illus. 2012. (ENG., Illus.). 112p. (J). (gr. 2-5). 17.99 (978-0-7636-5746-8(8)) Candlewick Pr.

Cleary, Brian P. I Saw an Invisible Lion Today: Quatrains. Watson, Richard, illus. 2016. (Poetry Adventures Ser.). (ENG.). 32p. (J). (gr. 2-5). 39.99 (978-1-4677-9732-0(4), Millbrook Pr.) Lerner Publishing Group.

—Peanut Butter & Jellyfishes: A Very Silly Alphabet Book. Snyder, Betsy E., illus. 2007. (ENG.). 32p. (J). (gr. -1-2). 15.95 (978-0-8225-6188-0(3), Millbrook Pr.) Lerner Publishing Group.

—Underneath My Bed: List Poems. Watson, Richard, illus. 2016. (Poetry Adventures Ser.). (ENG.). 32p. (gr. 2-5). 39.99 (978-1-5124-1112-6(4), Millbrook Pr.) Lerner Publishing Group.

Clemens, Edgar T. Trail Back: Epic Verse & Poems of The 1800s. 2003. (Illus.). 96p. pap. 11.95 (978-0-9718677-1-0(2)) Infusionmedia Publishing.

Coach B. God's Animal Tales. 2008. 36p. pap. 16.99 (978-1-4389-3047-3(X)) AuthorHouse.

Cobb, Soozi Bruun. Skis for Feet. 2012. 36p. pap. 19.99 (978-0-557-26740-8(4)) Lulu Pr., Inc.

Coelho, Joseph. Werewolf Club Rules. 2014. (ENG., Illus.). 96p. (J). (gr. 2-6). pap. 7.99 (978-1-84780-452-5(7), Frances Lincoln) Quarto Publishing Group UK GBR. Dist: Hachette Bk. Group.

Cohn, Jessica. Poems about Choices, 1 vol. 2014. (Experiencing Poetry Ser.). (ENG., Illus.). 64p. (gr. 7-8). lib. bdg. 35.99 (978-1-4329-9560-7(X)) Heinemann-Raintree.

Collins, Katrina. The voice from our Souls. 2009. 41p. pap. 10.02 (978-0-557-20475-5(5)) Lulu Pr., Inc.

Collins-Philippe, Jane. Sail Away with Me. Beingessner, Laura, illus. 2010. (ENG.). 32p. (J). (gr. -1-2). 15.95 (978-0-88776-842-2(3), Tundra Bks.) Tundra Bks. CAN. Dist: Penguin Random Hse. LLC.

Constant, Clare, et al. Experiencing Poetry, 1 vol. 2014. (Experiencing Poetry Ser.). (ENG.). 64p. (gr. 7-8). lib. bdg. 215.94 (978-1-4329-9562-1(6)) Heinemann-Raintree.

Conway, Kathleen E. Journey to the Stars: A Child's Dream. 2008. 72p. pap. 10.49 (978-1-4343-8627-4(9)) AuthorHouse.

Cookson, Paul. Crazy Classrooms. Wells, Steve, illus. 2015. (ENG.). 96p. (J). (gr. 2-6). pap. 7.99 (978-1-84780-505-8(1), Frances Lincoln) Quarto Publishing Group UK GBR. Dist: Hachette Bk. Group.

—How to Embarrass Teachers. unabr. ed. 2013. (ENG., Illus.). 96p. (J). (gr. 2-4). pap. 7.99 (978-1-4472-4126-3(6)) Pan Macmillan GBR. Dist: Independent Pubs. Group.

—I'd Rather Be a Footballer: The Very Best of Paul Cookson, 1. unabr. ed. 2008. (ENG., Illus.). 96p. (J). pap. 7.99 (978-0-330-45713-2(6)) Pan Macmillan GBR. Dist: Independent Pubs. Group.

—Paul Cookson's Joke Shop. unabr. ed. 2014. (ENG., Illus.). 128p. (J). pap. 9.99 (978-1-4472-5465-2(1)) Pan Macmillan GBR. Dist: Independent Pubs. Group.

—Unzip Your Lips. (ENG., Illus.). 144p. (J). pap. 9.99 (978-0-330-37062-2(6)) Pan Macmillan GBR. Dist: Trafalgar Square Publishing.

—The Works. 9. 5th rev. ed. 2010. (ENG., Illus.). 608p. (J). (gr. 1). pap. 12.99 (978-0-330-48104-5(5)) Pan Macmillan GBR. Dist: Independent Pubs. Group.

—The Works: Every Poem You Will Ever Need at School. 2014. (ENG.). 608p. (J). pap. 12.99 (978-1-4472-7349-3(4)) Pan Macmillan GBR. Dist: Independent Pubs. Group.

—100 Brilliant Poems for Children. 2016. (ENG.). 192p. (J). (gr. 2-5). pap. 11.99 (978-1-5098-2416-8(2)) Pan Macmillan GBR. Dist: Independent Pubs. Group.

Cookson, Paul & Harmer, David. It Came from Outer Space! unabr. ed. 2013. (ENG., Illus.). 96p. (J). (gr. 2). pap. 9.95 (978-1-4472-2035-0(8)) Pan Macmillan GBR. Dist: Independent Pubs. Group.

—It's Behind You! unabr. ed. 2013. (ENG.). 96p. (J). (gr. 2). pap. 7.99 (978-1-4472-4210-9(6)) Pan Macmillan GBR. Dist: Independent Pubs. Group.

Coolidge, Susan. Verses. 2007. (ENG.). 124p. per. (978-1-4065-1526-8(4)) Dodo Pr.

Coombs, Kate. Monster School. Gatlin, Lee, illus. 2017. (J). (978-1-4521-2938-9(X)) Chronicle Bks. LLC.

Cope, Steven R. Crow 2. Baumgardner, Julie, illus. 2012. 158p. pap. 16.00 (978-1-936138-49-4(2)) Wind Pubns.

Corr, Christopher, illus. Heaven in a Poem: An Anthology of Poems. 48p. 19.99 (978-0-7459-4259-9(8), Lion Books) Lion Hudson PLC GBR. Dist: Trafalgar Square Publishing.

Craig, Sienna R. A Sacred Geography: Sonnets of the Himalaya & Tibet. Heebner, Mary D., illus. 100th collector's ed. 2005. 24p. bds. 85.00 (978-0-9766811-0-6(2)) Simplemente Maria Pr.

Crawley, Dave. Dog Poems. Petrosino, Tamara, illus. 2007. (ENG.). 32p. (J). (gr. 4-6). 16.95 (978-1-59078-454-9(5), Wordsong) Boyds Mills Pr.

Crebbin, June, et al. We See a Cloud. Warren, Celia, illus. 2015. (Collins Big Cat Ser.). (ENG.). 32p. (J). (gr. 2-2). pap. 7.95 (978-0-00-759125-1(X)) HarperCollins Pubs. Ltd. GBR. Dist: Independent Pubs. Group.

Cribbs, Randy, narrated by. Tales from the Oldest City: Selected Readings Vol 1. 2005. (YA). cd-rom 8.95 (978-0-9725796-3-6(X)) River Pr.

Cricket Books Staff. Ladybug, Ladybug: And Other Favorite Poems. 2007. (ENG., Illus.). 40p. (J). (gr. k-k). 17.95 (978-0-8126-7936-6(9)) Cricket Bks.

Crozier, Lorna. Lots of Kisses, 1 vol. 2014. (ENG.). 24p. (J). (gr. -1-k). bds. 9.95 (978-1-4598-0745-7(6)) Orca Bk. Pubs. USA.

Crystian, Carol Payne. Jas & Poetic Lucy. Crystian, Carol Payne, illus. l.t. ed. 2006. (Illus.). 21p. (J). (gr. -1-3). per. 10.99 (978-1-59879-154-9(0)) Lifevest Publishing, Inc.

Cullinan, Bernice E. & Wooten, Deborah, eds. Another Jar of Tiny Stars: Poems by More NCTE Award-Winning Poets. rev. ed. 2010. (ENG.). 152p. (J). (gr. 4-6). 19.95 (978-1-59078-726-7(9), Wordsong) Boyds Mills Pr.

Culver, Kathy. Things I See When I Open My Eyes. Hauck, Christie, illus. 2007. 32p. per. 13.95 (978-1-59858-306-9(9)) Dog Ear Publishing, LLC.

Cummings, Priscilla. Beddy Bye in the Bay, 1 vol. Ramsey, Marcy Dunn, illus. 2010. (ENG.). 32p. (J). 14.99 (978-0-7643-3450-4(6), 9780764334504) Schiffer Publishing, Ltd.

Cushion, Hazel. Triplet Tales. Platt, Brian, illus. 2006. 32p. pap. (978-0-9547092-1-1(7)) Accent Pr. Ltd.

Cushman, Doug. Pigmares: Porcine Poems of the Silver Screen. 2012. 44p. 12.95 (978-1-60734-457-5(2)); (YA). pap. 12.95 (978-1-58089-402-9(X)) Charlesbridge Publishing, Inc.

—Pigmares: Porcine Poems of the Silver Screen. Cushman, Doug, illus. 2012. (ENG., Illus.). 44p. (J). (gr. 2-5). 12.95 (978-1-58089-401-2(1)) Charlesbridge Publishing, Inc.

Dafydd, Myrddin ap & Gwalch, Gwasg Carreg. Mae Modfedd Yn Llawer Mewn Trwyn. 2005. (Barddoniaeth Poetry Ser.). (WEL., Illus.). 117p. pap. (978-0-86381-857-8(9)) Gwasg Carreg Gwalch.

Dailey, Victoria, afterword by. Let's Play. 2009. (ENG., Illus.). 50p. 75.00 (978-0-9819597-0-2(9)) Bk. Club of California, The.

Dakos, Kalli. A Funeral in the Bathroom: And Other School Poems. Beech, Mark, illus. 2017. (ENG.). 48p. (J). (gr. -1-3). pap. 7.99 (978-0-8075-2676-7(2)) Whitman, Albert & Co.

Dallas SCORES Students. Learning Kicks! a Dallas Scores Anthology. 2006. 148p. per. 15.95 (978-0-9779530-9-7(2)) Pen & Publish Inc.

Dance me a Poem. 2005. (YA). per. 15.00 (978-1-59872-089-1(9)) Instant Pub.

Daniel, Claire & Benchmark Education Co. Staff. The True Story of Paul Revere's Ride. 2014. (Text Connections Ser.). (J). (gr. 6). (978-1-4900-1523-1(X)) Benchmark Education Co.

Daniels, Nicole M. Potpourri in the Wind: Nursery Rhymes from One Kid to Another. 2005. (Illus.). 64p. (J). pap. 19.95 (978-0-9771447-8-5(X)) Twinkle Twinkle Little Bks.

Dannenbring, Cheryl & Hess, Anna. Beaver, Bear, & Snowshoe Hare: Mammal poems. 2009. (Illus.). 32p. (J). (gr. 1-2). pap. 9.95 (978-0-9819307-1-8(9)) Raven Productions, Inc.

—Beaver, Bear, & Snowshoe Hare: Mammal Poems. 2009. (Illus.). 32p. (gr. 1-2). 18.95 (978-0-9819307-0-1(0)) Raven Productions, Inc.

d'Aquino, Alfonso. Fauna Mayor. Riglietti, Serena, illus. 2005. (SPA.). (J). (gr. k-2). pap. 10.95 (978-968-494-100-7(5)) Centro de Informacion y Desarrollo de la Comunicacion y la Literatura MEX. Dist: Iaconi, Mariuccia Bk. Imports.

Darkhor, P. H. Silent Being. 2010. 36p. pap. 15.49 (978-1-4520-2998-6(9)) AuthorHouse.

David C. Cook Publishing Company Staff. Nursery Rhymes. 2003. (My Jesus Pocket Bks.). (Illus.). 32p. (J). pap., pap. 8.90 (978-1-55513-102-9(6), 1555131026) Cook, David C.

David, Carole. Averses et Réglisses Noires. Athanassiadis, Kiki, illus. 2004. (Poetry Ser.). (FRE.). 36p. (J). (gr. 7). pap. (978-2-89021-674-7(8)) Diffusion du livre Mirabel (DLM).

David Cook Publishers, creator. God Is My Song. 2008. (Land of Milk & Honey Ser.). (Illus.). 32p. (J). (gr. -1-k). bds. 9.99 (978-1-4347-9944-9(1)) Cook, David C.

Davidson, Arden. Playing Hopscotch on a Rubber Roof. 2006. 56p. pap. 16.95 (978-1-4241-1170-1(6)) America Star Bks.

Davidson, Margot, creator. Stories with a View. 2004. (J). pap. 21.50 (978-0-9766386-1-2(4)) Hillside Education.

Davis, Crystal. School Rhymes. 2011. 70p. pap. 10.00 (978-1-4568-7578-7(7)) Xlibris Corp.

Davis, David. Southern Mother Goose, 1 vol. Leonhard, Herb, illus. 2013. (ENG.). 40p. (J). (gr. k-4). 17.99 (978-1-4556-1760-9(1)) Pelican Publishing Co., Inc.

—The Twelve Days of Christmas — in Texas, That Is, 1 vol. Camling, Candace, illus. 2011. (ENG.). 32p. (J). (gr. k-3). 16.99 (978-1-58980-924-6(6)) Pelican Publishing Co., Inc.

Davis, Will. Simply for Kids. 2012. 48p. (gr. 2-2). pap. 11.50 (978-1-4634-3048-1(5)) AuthorHouse.

Dawson, Kate & Glucksman, Jodi, compiled by. Over the Moon: The Broadway Lullaby Project. 2012. (ENG., Illus.). 48p. (J). (gr. -1-3). 18.95 (978-1-935212-70-6(2)) Easton Studio Pr., LLC.

A Day for JJ & Me Set B, 6 vols. 32p. (gr. 1-3). 31.50 (978-0-7802-8050-2(4)) Wright Group/McGraw-Hill.

Day, Lucille. Chain Letter. Dworkin, Doug, illus. 2005. 32p. (J). (gr. 3-7). 14.95 (978-1-59714-011-9(2)) Heyday.

de la Mare, Walter. Rhymes & Verses: Collected Poems for Young People. Blaisdell, Elinore, illus. 2005. 351p. (J). (gr. 4-8). reprint ed. 19.00 (978-0-7567-8944-2(3)) DIANE Publishing Co.

De Vos, Philip. Carnival of the Animals. Grobler, Piet, illus. 32p. (J). (978-0-7981-3823-9(8)) Human & Rousseau.

Deltoro, Antonio. La Plaza. Ochoa, Francisco, illus. 2004. Tr. of Plaza. (SPA.). (J). (gr. k-2). pap. 11.99 (978-968-494-045-1(9)) Centro de Informacion y Desarrollo de la Comunicacion y la Literatura MEX. Dist: Lectorum Pubns., Inc.

Demery, Ramona. Hey, Little Bird: Verses for Children. 2012. 48p. (gr. 10-12). pap. 9.95 (978-1-4759-2766-5(5)) iUniverse, Inc.

Derby, Sally. A New School Year: Poem Stories in Six Voices. Song, Mika, illus. 2017. (ENG.). 48p. (J). (gr. k-4). lib. bdg. 16.99 (978-1-58089-730-3(4)) Charlesbridge Publishing, Inc.

Desautels, Denise. La Marathonienne. Chronopoulos, Maria, illus. 2004. (Poetry Ser.). (FRE.). 36p. (J). (gr. 7). pap. (978-2-89021-673-0(X)) Diffusion du livre Mirabel (DLM).

Di Bella, Brenda. I'm up to Big Things. 2010. 14.95 (978-0-615-38253-1(3)) Di Bella, Brenda.

Diane Bogdan. Twigs Is a Poet! 2009. 104p. pap. 9.95 (978-1-4401-6202-2(6)) iUniverse, Inc.

Dias y Dias de Poesia. (Dias y Dias de Poesia Ser.). (SPA.). (gr. -1-6). 388.10 (978-1-56334-279-0(0), CO9637); 632.60 (978-1-56334-280-6(4), CO9638); suppl. ed. 207.23 (978-1-56334-269-1(3), PO9639) CENGAGE Learning.

Dickinson, Emily. Emily Dickinson. Snively, Susan, ed. Davenier, Christine, illus. 2016. (Poetry for Kids Ser.). (ENG.). 48p. (J). (gr. 3-7). 14.95 (978-1-63322-117-6(2), Moondance) Quarto Publishing Group USA.

—My Letter to the World & Other Poems. Arsenault, Isabelle, illus. 2008. (Visions in Poetry Ser.). (ENG.). 48p. (J). (gr. 5-9). 17.95 (978-1-55453-103-5(9)); pap. 9.95 (978-1-55453-339-8(2)) Kids Can Pr., Ltd. CAN. Dist: Hachette Bk. Group.

Dictionary, Oxford, ed. Oxford Children's Rhyming Dictionary. 2014. (ENG., Illus.). 160p. pap. 15.95 (978-0-19-273558-4(6)) Oxford Univ. Pr., Inc.

Diehn, Andi. Explore Poetry! With 25 Great Projects. Stone, Bryan, illus. 2015. (Explore Your World Ser.). (ENG.). 96p. (gr. 1-5). 19.95 (978-1-61930-279-2(9)) Open City Bks.

Dieter, Debra. Lightning & Mikey. 2012. 16p. (-18). pap. 15.99 (978-1-4772-8405-6(2)) AuthorHouse.

Disney Book Group. Tsum Tsum Book of Haiku. Disney Storybook Art Team, illus. 2015. (ENG.). 64p. (J). (gr. 5-9). 9.99 (978-1-4847-2925-0(0)) Disney Pr.

DKSmith. My Inner Child. 2006. 57p. pap. 16.95 (978-1-4241-0689-9(3)) America Star Bks.

Dodds, John Thomas. A Sneaky Twitch of an Itch. 2010. 44p. pap. 19.95 (978-0-557-44341-3(5)) Lulu Pr., Inc.

Donaldson, Julia. Crazy Mayonnaisy Mum. Sharratt, Nick, illus. 2015. (ENG.). 112p. (J). (gr. 2-4). pap. 8.99 (978-1-4472-9322-4(3)) Pan Macmillan GBR. Dist: Independent Pubs. Group.

—Shuffle & Squelch. Sharratt, Nick, illus. 2015. (ENG.). 32p. (J). (-k). pap. 11.99 (978-1-4472-7681-4(7)) Pan Macmillan GBR. Dist: Independent Pubs. Group.

—Wriggle & Roar! Sharratt, Nick, illus. 2015. (ENG.). 32p. (J). (gr. -1-1). pap. 9.99 (978-1-4472-7665-4(5)) Pan Macmillan GBR. Dist: Independent Pubs. Group.

Dotlich, Rebecca Kai. In the Spin of Things: Poetry of Motion. Dugan, Karen, illus. 2010. (ENG.). 32p. (J). pap. 11.95 (978-1-59078-828-8(1), Wordsong) Boyds Mills Pr.

—When Riddles Come Rumbling: Poems to Ponder. Dugan, Karen, illus. 2013. (ENG.). 32p. (J). (gr. 2-4). pap. 6.95 (978-1-62091-031-3(4), Wordsong) Boyds Mills Pr.

Drake, Michael. The Growing Books: My Inside Is Outside. 2009. 68p. pap. 25.49 (978-1-4389-6337-2(8)); (Illus.). 60p. pap. 23.99 (978-1-4389-6336-5(X)) AuthorHouse.

Dranoel, Eittem. Eittem Dranoel: Judgement Day. 2003. 110p. (YA). pap. 11.95 (978-0-595-26320-2(8), Writers Club Pr.) iUniverse, Inc.

Dressler, Craig. Kids' Bible Poems. 2006. (J). per. 4.99 (978-0-9679062-7-0(X)) Dressler, Craig.

Driscoll, Michael & Hamilton, Meredith. A Child's Introduction to Poetry: Listen While You Learn about the Magic Words That Have Moved Mountains, Won Battles, & Made Us Laugh & Cry. Hamilton, Meredith, illus. 2003. (ENG., Illus.). 96p. (J). (gr. -1-17). tchr. ed. 19.99 (978-1-57912-282-9(5), 81282, Black Dog & Leventhal Pubs. Inc.) Hachette Bks.

Dromgoole, Glenn & Clack, Barbra. Good Night Cowgirl. Clack, Barbra, illus. 2006. (ENG., Illus.). 24p. (J). (gr. -1-k). 15.95 (978-1-931721-80-6(7), 2b775fed-84a0-4c63-9402-a94e6e772dbd) Bright Sky Pr.

Duffy, Carol Ann. New & Collected Poems for Children. 2014. (ENG., Illus.). 288p. 24.95 (978-0-571-31819-3(3)) Faber & Faber, Inc.

Duggan, Laurie. Mangroves. 2003. 186p. (J). pap. (978-0-7022-3351-7(X)) Univ. of Queensland Pr.

Dyan, Penelope. A Book for Girls about Being a Girl. 2006. (J). per. 7.95 (978-0-9771916-9-7(9)) Bellissima Publishing, LLC.

—Flying High in the Sky — -for Boys Only. Weigand, John D., photos by. 2009. (Illus.). 42p. pap. 13.95 (978-1-935118-66-4(8)) Bellissima Publishing, LLC.

—For Boys Only! No Girls Allowed! 2005. (Illus.). 80p. (J). per. 7.95 (978-0-9768417-1-5(1)) Bellissima Publishing, LLC.

—For the Matterhorn's Face, Zermatt Is the Place, a Kid's Guide to Zermatt, Switzerland. Weigand, John D., photos by. 2010. (Illus.). 50p. pap. 11.95 (978-1-935630-04-3(0)) Bellissima Publishing, LLC.

—Hair We Are! Dyan, Penelope, illus. 2009. (Illus.). 44p. pap. 11.95 (978-1-935118-61-9(7)) Bellissima Publishing, LLC.

—I Am a Monster! Dyan, Penelope, illus. 2010. (Illus.). 34p. pap. 11.95 (978-1-935630-24-1(5)) Bellissima Publishing, LLC.

—I Am Eight! Dyan, Penelope, illus. 2010. (Illus.). 34p. pap. 11.95 (978-1-935630-17-3(2)) Bellissima Publishing, LLC.

—Just Look Out the Window! Dyan, Penelope, illus. 2010. (Illus.). 34p. pap. 11.95 (978-1-935630-25-8(3)) Bellissima Publishing, LLC.

—Life in the Pits. Dyan, Penelope, illus. 2010. (Illus.). 34p. pap. 11.95 (978-1-935630-18-0(0)) Bellissima Publishing, LLC.

—A Nose by Any Other Name Is Still a Nose! Dyan, Penelope, illus. 2009. (Illus.). 44p. pap. 11.95 (978-1-935118-62-6(5)) Bellissima Publishing, LLC.

—Over the Edge, a Kid's Guide to Niagara Falls, Ontario, Canad. Weigand, John D., photos by. 2010. (Illus.). 48p. pap. 11.95 (978-1-935630-07-4(5)) Bellissima Publishing, LLC.

—Pink Patti Pinkerton. Dyan, Penelope, illus. 2009. (Illus.). 44p. pap. 11.95 (978-1-935118-63-3(3)) Bellissima Publishing, LLC.

—Spend a Day in Old Pompeii, a Kid's Travel Guide to Ancient Pompeii, Italy. Weigand, John D., photos by. 2010. (Illus.). 50p. pap. 11.95 (978-1-935630-01-2(6)) Bellissima Publishing, LLC.

—Sticks — -Because Sticks Are Also People. Dyan, Penelope, illus. 2008. (Illus.). 52p. pap. 11.95 (978-1-935118-07-7(2)) Bellissima Publishing, LLC.

—There Are Bees in My Trees! Dyan, Penelope, illus. 2009. (Illus.). 44p. pap. 11.95 (978-1-935118-59-6(5)) Bellissima Publishing, LLC.

—There's a Chicken in My Kitchen! Dyan, Penelope, illus. 2009. (Illus.). 44p. pap. 11.95 *(978-1-935118-60-2(9))* Bellissima Publishing, LLC.
—There's a Racoon in My House! Dyan, Penelope, illus. 2009. (Illus.). 44p. pap. 11.95 *(978-1-935118-58-9(7))* Bellissima Publishing, LLC.
—There's an Alligator in My Closet! Dyan, Penelope, illus. 2009. (Illus.). 44p. pap. 11.95 *(978-1-935118-64-0(1))* Bellissima Publishing, LLC.
—This Means War! for Boys Only. Dyan, Penelope, illus. 2009. (Illus.). 44p. pap. 11.95 *(978-1-935118-65-7(X))* Bellissima Publishing, LLC.
—When in Rome, a Kid's Guide to Rome. Weigand, John, photos by. 2010. (Illus.). 50p. pap. 11.95 *(978-1-935630-00-5(8))* Bellissima Publishing, LLC.
—Who's the Fairest of Them All? Dyan, Penelope, illus. 2010. (Illus.). 34p. pap. 11.95 *(978-1-935630-20-3(2))* Bellissima Publishing, LLC.
Eastwick, Ivy O. Some Folks Like Cats: And Other Poems. Maass, Mary Kurnick, illus. 2003. (ENG.). 32p. (J). (gr. k-2). 15.95 *(978-1-56397-450-2(9))* Boyds Mills Pr.
Ebia, Iris. When the Wind Blows What Is That Noise? 2010. 28p. pap. 12.88 *(978-1-4490-2939-5(6))* AuthorHouse.
Eckles, Alice. My Life as a Flower Chapters 1&2: Color, Fragrance. 2004. 66p. 6.85 *(978-0-9742516-2-2(3))* Minimal Pr., The.
Edgar, M. G. A Treasury of Poems for Children. Pogány, Willy, illus. 2010. (Dover Children's Classics Ser.). (ENG.). 272p. (J). (gr. -1-3). pap. 9.99 *(978-0-486-47376-5(7))* Dover Pubns., Inc.
Eleven. Spirit Comes to Earth: Renewing Your Heart's Mission. Eleven, illus. 2005. (Illus.). 128p. (YA). per. 13.95 *(978-0-9743540-0-2(7),* By title) Peace Love Karma Publishing.
Elliot, Zetta & Strickland, Shadra. Bird. 2017. (ENG.). (J). pap. 11.95 ***(978-1-62014-348-3(8))*** Lee & Low Bks., Inc.
Elliott, David. In the Wild. Meade, Holly, illus. 2013. (ENG.). 32p. (J). (gr. -1-3). pap. 6.99 *(978-0-7636-6337-7(9))* Candlewick Pr.
Engelbreit, Mary. Mary Engelbreit's Mother Goose: One Hundred Best-Loved Verses. Engelbreit, Mary, illus. 2005. (ENG., Illus.). 128p. (J). (gr. -1-k). 19.99 *(978-0-06-008171-3(6))* HarperCollins Pubs.
Engle, Janice. Rainbows Stories & Poetry for Children. 2004. 277p. (J). pap. 15.08 *(978-1-4116-8612-0(8))* Lulu Pr., Inc.
Engle, Margarita. The Firefly Letters: A Suffragette's Journey to Cuba. 2010. (ENG.). 160p. (YA). (gr. 5-18). 17.99 *(978-0-8050-9082-6(7),* 9780805090826, Holt, Henry & Co. Bks. For Young Readers) Holt, Henry & Co.
—Hurricane Dancers: The First Caribbean Pirate Shipwreck. 2011. (ENG.). 160p. (YA). (gr. 7-12). 29.99 *(978-0-8050-9240-0(4),* 9780805092400, Holt, Henry & Co. Bks. For Young Readers) Holt, Henry & Co.
—The Lightning Dreamer. 2015. lib. bdg. 18.40 *(978-0-606-37463-7(9))* Turtleback Bks.
—The Lightning Dreamer: Cuba's Greatest Abolitionist. 2015. (ENG.). 192p. (YA). (gr. 7). pap. 7.99 *(978-0-544-54112-2(X),* HMH Books For Young Readers) Houghton Mifflin Harcourt Publishing Co.
—Miguel's Brave Knight: Young Cervantes & His Dream of Don Quixote, 1 vol. Colón, Raúl, illus. 2017. (ENG.). 32p. (J). (gr. 3-6). 17.95 ***(978-1-56145-856-1(2))*** Peachtree Pubs.
Engle, Margarita. The Surrender Tree: Poems of Cuba's Struggle for Freedom. 2008. (ENG.). 176p. (YA). (gr. 7-12). 16.95 *(978-0-8050-8674-4(9),* 9780805086744, Holt, Henry & Co. Bks. For Young Readers) Holt, Henry & Co.
—The Surrender Tree: Poems of Cuba's Struggle for Freedom. 2010. (ENG.). 384p. (YA). (gr. 7-12). pap. 10.99 *(978-0-312-60871-2(3),* 9780312608712) Square Fish.
—The Surrender Tree: Poems of Cuba's Struggle for Freedom. 2010. (YA). lib. bdg. 22.10 *(978-0-606-10545-3(X),* Turtleback) Turtleback Bks.
Engler, Jerry. Highly Embellished Truth & Some Poetry Just Folks Three. 2008. 232p. pap. 14.95 *(978-0-9771255-2-4(1))* 6-mile Roots.
Ernst, Carol. Messages to the Heart. 2nd ed. 2003. spiral bd. 9.95 net. *(978-0-9668868-3-2(6))* Leadership Horizons, LLC.
Espinosa Guerra, Julio. Poesia Del Siglo Xx en Chile la; antologia. 2006. (SPA.). 506p. pap. 36.99 *(978-84-7522-788-7(0))* Visor Libros ESP. Dist: AIMS International Bks., Inc.
Estrada, Xinia M. Pluma en Silencio. 2004. (SPA.). 54p. (YA). per. 10.95 *(978-0-9746855-5-7(0))* Refined Savage Editions / Ediciones El Salvaje Refinado, The.
Evans, Olive. The Thrift Store Bears. Woolley, Patricia, illus. 2004. (ENG.). 41p. (J). 18.97 *(978-0-9748954-0-6(7))* Teddy Traveler Co.
Everett, Melissa. The Owl & the Kitty Cat. Kummer, Mark, illus. 2013. (ENG.). 20p. (J). (gr. -1-3). 8.99 *(978-1-77093-535-8(5))* Flowerpot Children's Pr. Inc. CAN. Dist: Cardinal Pubs. Group.
Ewing, Juliana Horatia. Verses for Children & Songs for Music. 2007. (Illus.). 136p. per. *(978-1-4065-2521-2(9))* Dodo Pr.
Ewing, Thor, ed. 50 Classic Poems Every Boy Should Know. 2015. (ENG., Illus.). 144p. (J). pap. *(978-1-910075-03-6(5))* Welkin Bks.
Fajardo, Alexis E. Kid Beowulf: the Blood-Bound Oath. 2016. (Kid Beowulf Ser.: 1). (ENG.). 240p. (J). pap. 12.99 *(978-1-4494-7589-5(2))* Andrews McMeel Publishing.
Fandel, Jennifer. Keats, Shakespeare, & Other Wordsmiths. 2005. (Understanding Poetry Ser.). (Illus.). 48p. (YA). (gr. 4-7). lib. bdg. 21.95 *(978-1-58341-343-2(X))* Creative Co., The.
Fandel, Jennifer & Miller, Connie Colwell. Thorns, Horns, & Crescent Moons: Reading & Writing Nature Poems, 1 vol. Burkes-Larrañaga, Dustin et al, illus. 2014. (Poet in You Ser.). (ENG.). 32p. (gr. 2-4). lib. bdg. 27.32 *(978-1-4795-2197-5(3))* Picture Window Bks.
Fandel, Jennifer, et al. Poet in You, 1 vol. Smith, Simon et al, illus. 2014. (Poet in You Ser.). (ENG.). 32p. (gr. 2-4). lib. bdg. 109.28 *(978-1-4795-3358-9(0))* Picture Window Bks.
—Trust, Truth, & Ridiculous Goofs: Reading & Writing Friendship Poems, 1 vol. Smith, Simon et al, illus. 2014. (Poet in You Ser.). (ENG.). 32p. (gr. 2-4). lib. bdg. 27.32 *(978-1-4795-2199-9(X))* Picture Window Bks.
Farjeon, Eleanor & Harvey, Anne. Blackbird Has Spoken: Selected Poems for Children. 2003. (ENG.). 112p. (J). 16.95 *(978-0-333-74133-7(1))* Macmillan Pubs., Ltd. GBR. Dist: Trafalgar Square Publishing.
Farnsworth, Scott & Hoyt, Peggy R. Like a Library Burning. 2008. 144p. pap. 19.95 *(978-0-9719177-7-4(9))* Legacy Planning Partners, LLC.
Farrell, Eric L. & Holmes, Will, Jr. Seeking Solace: In a Time of Distress. 2003. (Illus.). 128p. 19.95 *(978-1-931855-33-4(1),* 1-800-Bookway) Emaculate Publishing.
Faulks, Rebecca Rachel. The Curtains Ate My Grandma. 2010. (Illus.). 40p. pap. 16.99 *(978-1-4490-7454-8(5))* AuthorHouse.
Fessler, Bob. Hey! You Aren't the Boss of Me! 2007. (ENG., Illus.). 48p. (J). pap. 19.95 *(978-1-59299-262-1(5))* Inkwater Pr.
Field, Eugene. Dibdin's Ghost. 2013. (Notable American Authors Ser.). 425p. reprint ed. lthr. 79.00 *(978-0-7812-2649-3(X))* Reprint Services Corp.
—Love Songs of Childhood. 2006. 124p. per. 16.99 *(978-1-4255-0825-8(1))* Michigan Publishing.
—The Love Songs of Children. 2013. (Notable American Authors Ser.). 425p. reprint ed. lthr. 79.00 *(978-0-7812-2645-5(7))* Reprint Services Corp.
—Lullaby Land: Songs of Childhood. Robinson, Charles, illus. 2006. 236p. per. 20.99 *(978-1-4255-1951-3(2))* Michigan Publishing.
—Lullaby Land: Songs of Childhood. 2013. (Notable American Authors Ser.). 231p. reprint ed. lthr. 79.00 *(978-0-7812-2646-2(5))* Reprint Services Corp.
—Second Book of Verse. 2013. (Notable American Authors Ser.). 260p. reprint ed. lthr. 79.00 *(978-0-7812-2644-8(9))* Reprint Services Corp.
—Songs & Other Verse. 2007. 140p. per. *(978-1-4065-2394-2(1))* Dodo Pr.
—The Sugar-Plum Tree & Other Verses: Includes a Read-and-Listen. Peat, Fern Bisel, illus. 2010. (Dover Read & Listen Ser.). (ENG.). 80p. (J). (gr. 1-5). pap. 14.99 *(978-0-486-47675-9(8))* Dover Pubns., Inc.
—With Trumpet & Drum. 2006. 140p. per. 16.99 *(978-1-4255-1004-6(3))* Michigan Publishing.
Figueroa, Ephraim. The Prince of Belverdere & Other Poems. 2003. 11.95 *(978-0-9745799-0-0(4))* Tabor Pr.
Fitch, Janet. White Olander. 2010. mass mkt. 10.99 *(978-0-316-01757-2(4))* Little Brown & Co.
Fitch, Sheree. Mabel Murple, 1 vol. Smith, Sydney, illus. 2014. (ENG.). 24p. (J). (gr. -1-3). pap. 12.95 *(978-1-55109-859-3(8))* Nimbus Publishing, Ltd. CAN. Dist: Orca Bk. Pubs. USA.
—Night Sky Wheel Ride, 1 vol. Yayo, illus. 2013. (ENG.). 32p. (J). (gr. k-2). 16.95 *(978-1-896580-67-8(X))* Tradewind Bks. CAN. Dist: Orca Bk. Pubs. USA.
—Sleeping Dragons All Around, 1 vol. Nidenoff, Michele, illus. 2014. (ENG.). 32p. (J). (gr. -1-3). pap. 12.95 *(978-1-55109-772-5(9))* Nimbus Publishing, Ltd. CAN. Dist: Orca Bk. Pubs. USA.
—There Were Monkeys in My Kitchen, 1 vol. Smith, Sydney, illus. 2014. (ENG.). 32p. (J). (gr. -1-3). pap. 12.95 *(978-1-55109-994-1(2))* Nimbus Publishing, Ltd. CAN. Dist: Orca Bk. Pubs. USA.
—Toes in My Nose: And Other Poems, 1 vol. Smith, Sydney, illus. 2014. (ENG.). 32p. (J). (gr. -1-3). 19.95 *(978-1-55109-939-2(X))* Nimbus Publishing, Ltd. CAN. Dist: Orca Bk. Pubs. USA.
Fitch, Sheree & Hunt, Anne, eds. Whispers of Mermaids & Wonderful Things, 1 vol. 2017. (ENG., Illus.). 160p. (J). (gr. -1-7). 29.95 ***(978-1-77108-471-0(5))*** Nimbus Publishing, Ltd. CAN. Dist: Orca Bk. Pubs. USA.
Fitzmaurice, Gabriel. G. F. Woz Ere. MacDonald, Stella, illus. 2009. (ENG.). 96p. (J). pap. 12.95 *(978-1-85635-622-0(1))* Mercier Pr., Ltd., The IRL. Dist: Dufour Editions, Inc.
—I'm Proud to Be Me: Poems for Children & Their Parents. Phelan, Nicky, illus. 2005. (ENG.). 96p. (J). pap. 12.95 *(978-1-85635-474-5(1))* Mercier Pr., Ltd., The IRL. Dist: Dufour Editions, Inc.
—Will You Be My Friend? 2016. (ENG., Illus.). 178p. pap. 14.99 *(978-1-910742-45-7(7))* Liberties Pr., Ltd. IRL. Dist: Casemate Pubs. & Bk. Distributors, LLC.
Fitzmaurice, Gabriel & Macdonald, Stella. Splat: And Other Great Poems. Phelan, Nicky, illus. 2012. (ENG.). 96p. (J). pap. 13.95 *(978-1-85635-953-5(0))* Mercier Pr., Ltd., The IRL. Dist: Dufour Editions, Inc.
Fitzpatrick, Deanne & Fitch, Sheree. Singily Skipping Along, 1 vol. 2014. (ENG., Illus.). 32p. (J). (gr. k-3). 19.95 *(978-1-77108-091-0(4))* Nimbus Publishing, Ltd. CAN. Dist: Orca Bk. Pubs. USA.
Flavin, Dick. Red Sox Rhymes: Verses & Curses by Fenway Park's Poet Laureate. 2015. (ENG.). 224p. 19.99 *(978-0-06-239152-0(6),* Morrow, William & Co.) HarperCollins Pubs.
Fleischman, Paul. Joyful Noise: Poems for Two Voices. Beddows, Eric, illus. rev. ed. 2005. (Charlotte Zolotow Bk.). (ENG.). 64p. (J). (gr. 3-7). pap. 5.99 *(978-0-06-446093-4(2))* HarperCollins Pubs.
—Joyful Noise: Poems for Two Voices. 2005. (J). (gr. 3-6). 16.00 *(978-0-8335-8555-4(X),* Turtleback) Turtleback Bks.
Fleming, Maria & Franco, Betsy. Poem of the Month Flip Chart: 12 Joyful Read-Aloud Poems with Skill-Building Lessons & Writing Springboards. 2005. (ENG.). 24p. (gr. k-3). pap. 21.99 *(978-0-439-47123-7(0))* Scholastic, Inc.
Fletcher, Ralph J. A Writing Kind of Day: Poems for Young Poets. 2005. (ENG., Illus.). 32p. (J). (gr. 3-7). pap. 9.95 *(978-1-59078-353-5(0))* Boyds Mills Pr.
Fletter, Sharon Sofia. My Guardian Angel. Fletter, Sharon Sofia, illus. l.t. ed. 2007.Tr. of Mi Angel Guardian, il Mio Angelo, Meu Anjo Da Guarda, Mein Schutzengel, Mon Ange Guardian. (SPA, ITA, POR, GER & FRE., Illus.). 44p. (J). per. 17.95 *(978-0-9793113-0-7(6))* SoulSong Publishing.
FLH Students & Lutz, Suzanne. Many Voices: Where Dreams Take Flight III. 2008. 149p. pap. 14.95 *(978-0-7414-4569-8(7))* Infinity Publishing.
Flint, Norman. Rag & Bone: Visit London. 2010. 28p. pap. 12.49 *(978-1-4520-4093-6(1))* AuthorHouse.
Flor Ada, Alma & Campoy, F. Isabel. Chuchurumbe. (Literature Collection of Puertas Al Sol Ser.). (SPA.). 32p. (J). (gr. k-6). pap. 12.95 *(978-1-59437-709-9(X))* Santillana USA Publishing Co., Inc.
—Dreaming Fish. (Literature Collection of Gateways to the Sun Ser.). 32p. (J). (gr. k-6). pap. 12.95 *(978-1-59437-712-9(X))* Santillana USA Publishing Co., Inc.
—Flying Dragon. (Literature Collection of Gateways to the Sun Ser.). 32p. (J). (gr. k-6). pap. 12.95 *(978-1-59437-721-1(9))* Santillana USA Publishing Co., Inc.
—Laughing Crocodiles. (Literature Collection of Gateways to the Sun Ser.). 32p. (J). (gr. k-6). pap. 12.95 *(978-1-59437-715-0(4))* Santillana USA Publishing Co., Inc.
—Mambru. (Literature Collection of Puertas Al Sol Ser.). (SPA.). 32p. (J). (gr. k-6). pap. 12.95 *(978-1-59437-706-8(5))* Santillana USA Publishing Co., Inc.
—Pimpon. (Literature Collection of Puertas Al Sol Ser.). (SPA.). 32p. (J). (gr. k-6). pap. 12.95 *(978-1-59437-700-6(6))* Santillana USA Publishing Co., Inc.
Florian, Douglas. Comets, Stars, the Moon, & Mars: Space Poems & Paintings. 2007. (ENG., Illus.). 56p. (J). (gr. -1-3). 17.99 *(978-0-15-205372-7(7))* Houghton Mifflin Harcourt Publishing Co.
—Dinothesaurus: Prehistoric Poems & Paintings. Florian, Douglas, illus. 2009. (ENG., Illus.). 56p. (J). (gr. 1-5). 17.99 *(978-1-4169-7978-4(6),* Beach Lane Bks.) Beach Lane Bks.
—Lizards, Frogs, & Polliwogs. 2005. (ENG., Illus.). 48p. (J). (gr. 1-4). reprint ed. pap. 7.99 *(978-0-15-205248-5(8))* Houghton Mifflin Harcourt Publishing Co.
—Poem Depot: Aisles of Smiles. (ENG.). 160p. (J). (gr. 4-7). 2015. Illus.). 8.99 *(978-0-14-750917-8(3),* Puffin Books) 2014. 16.99 *(978-0-8037-4042-6(5),* Dial Bks) Penguin Young Readers Group.
—Shiver Me Timbers! Pirate Poems & Paintings. Neubecker, Robert, illus. 2012. (ENG.). 32p. (J). (gr. 1-5). 16.99 *(978-1-4424-1321-4(2),* Beach Lane Bks.) Beach Lane Bks.
—UnBEElievables: Honeybee Poems & Paintings. Florian, Douglas, illus. 2012. (ENG., Illus.). 32p. (J). (gr. k-3). 17.99 *(978-1-4424-2652-8(7),* Beach Lane Bks.) Beach Lane Bks.
Follett, C. B. & Terris, Susan, eds. Runes, a Review of Poetry: Memory. 2003. (Illus.). 162p. pap. 12.00 *(978-0-9657015-9-4(X))* Arctos Pr.
Fondo de Cultura Económica (Mexico) Staff, creator. Despertar del Jaguar, Vol. 2. 2003. (Vida Y Palabra de Los Indios de America Ser.). (SPA., Illus.). 229p. (J). 20.99 *(978-968-16-6593-7(7))* Fondo de Cultura Economica USA.
Forler, Nan. Winterberries & Apple Blossoms: Reflections & Flavors of a Mennonite Year. Snyder, Peter Etril, illus. 2011. (ENG.). 40p. (J). (gr. k-12). 22.95 *(978-1-77049-254-7(2),* Tundra Bks.) Tundra Bks. CAN. Dist: Penguin Random Hse. LLC.
Forman, Ruth. Young Cornrows Callin Out the Moon. Bayoc, Cbabi, illus. 2007. (ENG.). 24p. (J). (gr. -1-3). lib. bdg. 16.95 *(978-0-89239-218-6(5))* Lee & Low Bks., Inc.
Forrest, George. Echoes with a Western Air. 2007. 192p. (YA). per. 16.95 *(978-0-595-45286-6(8))* iUniverse, Inc.
Fort, Gary W. Mom, I Love Spaghetti. Schultz, Michael, illus. 2011. 86p. pap. 24.00 *(978-1-60911-562-3(7),* Eloquent Bks.) Strategic Book Publishing & Rights Agency (SBPRA).
Foster, John. Dinosaur Poems. Paul, Korky, illus. 2nd rev. ed. 2004. (ENG.). 32p. (YA). 10.95 *(978-0-19-276305-1(9))* Oxford Univ. Pr., Inc.
—I've Got a Poem for You. 2010. (ENG., Illus.). 96p. (YA). pap. 10.95 *(978-0-19-276354-9(7))* Oxford Univ. Pr., Inc.
—The Poetry Chest. 2015. (ENG.). 336p. (J). pap. 13.95 *(978-0-19-276341-9(5))* Oxford Univ. Pr., Inc.
Foster, John, ed. Ridiculous Rhymes. 2011. (ENG., Illus.). 96p. (J). (gr. k-4). pap. 5.99 *(978-0-00-711212-8(2))* HarperCollins Pubs. Ltd. GBR. Dist: HarperCollins Pubs.
Foster, John, selected by. Century of Childrens Poems. 2011. (ENG., Illus.). 160p. (J). pap. 7.99 *(978-0-00-714001-5(0),* HarperCollins Children's Bks.) HarperCollins Pubs. Ltd. GBR. Dist: HarperCollins Pubs.
—Dead Funny. 2011. (ENG., Illus.). 96p. (J). (gr. k-4). pap. 5.99 *(978-0-00-711213-5(0))* HarperCollins Pubs. Ltd. GBR. Dist: HarperCollins Pubs.
—Teasing Tongue Twisters. 2011. (ENG., Illus.). 96p. (J). pap. 5.99 *(978-0-00-711214-2(9))* HarperCollins Pubs. Ltd. GBR. Dist: HarperCollins Pubs.
Foster, John L. Dragon Poems. Paul, Korky, illus. 2nd rev. ed. 2004. (ENG.). 32p. (YA). pap. 10.95 *(978-0-19-276307-5(5))* Oxford Univ. Pr., Inc.
Foston, Rebera E. Beyond a Reasonable Doubt. 2003. 96p. (YA). pap. *(978-1-930362-04-8(8))* Foston Adolescent Workshop, Inc.
—A New Day. 2003. 96p. (YA). pap. *(978-1-930362-03-1(X))* Foston Adolescent Workshop, Inc.
—No Cross, No Crown. 2003. 96p. (YA). per. *(978-1-930362-08-6(0))* Foston Adolescent Workshop, Inc.
—No Forwarding Address. 2003. 96p. (YA). per. *(978-1-930362-09-3(9))* Foston Adolescent Workshop, Inc.
—Pictures of the Wedding. 2003. 96p. (YA). per. *(978-1-930362-11-6(0))* Foston Adolescent Workshop, Inc.
—Sweet Memories. 2003. 96p. (YA). per. *(978-1-930362-12-3(9))* Foston Adolescent Workshop, Inc.
—When You Have Been Alone. 2003. 96p. (YA). per. *(978-1-930362-14-7(5))* Foston Adolescent Workshop, Inc.
—While You Were Gone. 2003. 96p. (YA). per. *(978-1-930362-15-4(3))* Foston Adolescent Workshop, Inc.
Foxworthy, Jeff. Silly Street. Björkman, Steve, illus. (I Can Read Level 2 Ser.). 32p. (J). 2010. (ENG.). (gr. k-3). pap. 3.99 *(978-0-06-176528-5(7))* 2009. (ENG.). (gr. -1-2). 17.99 *(978-0-06-171918-9(8))* 2009. (gr. k-2). lib. bdg. 18.89 *(978-0-06-171919-6(6))* HarperCollins Pubs.
Frampton, David. Mr. Ferlinghetti's Poem. Frampton, David, illus. 2006. (Illus.). 32p. (J). (gr. k-4). 18.00 *(978-0-8028-5290-8(4),* Eerdmans Bks For Young Readers) Eerdmans, William B. Publishing Co.
Franco, Betsy. Bees, Snails, & Peacock Tails: Patterns & Shapes... Naturally. Jenkins, Steve, illus. 2008. (ENG.). 40p. (J). (gr. -1-3). 18.99 *(978-1-4169-0386-4(0),* McElderry, Margaret K. Bks.) McElderry, Margaret K. Bks.
—Messing Around on the Monkey Bars: And Other School Poems for Two Voices. Hartland, Jessie, illus. 2009. (ENG.). 48p. (J). (gr. 3-7). 18.99 *(978-0-7636-3174-1(4))* Candlewick Pr.
—A Spectacular Selection of Sea Critters: Concrete Poems. Wertz, Michael, illus. 2015. (ENG.). 32p. (J). (gr. 2-5). 19.99 *(978-1-4677-8849-6(X),* Millbrook Pr.) Lerner Publishing Group.
Franco, Betsy, ed. Falling Hard: 100 Love Poems by Teenagers. 2010. (ENG., Illus.). 160p. (YA). (gr. 9). pap. 6.99 *(978-0-7636-4839-8(6))* Candlewick Pr.
Frank, John. Lend a Hand: Poems About Giving. Ladd, London, illus. 2014. (ENG.). 32p. (J). 17.95 *(978-1-60060-970-1(8))* Lee & Low Bks., Inc.
Franskevich, Ala, compiled by. Underwater World. 2013. (Everyday Rhymes Ser.). (ENG., Illus.). 14p. (J). (-k). bds. 15.95 *(978-1-61889-229-4(0))* AZ Bks. LLC.
Freeman, Ken. I Hope You Know: A Message from Dad. 2012. 32p. pap. 19.99 *(978-1-4685-7466-1(3))* AuthorHouse.
Freese, Susan M. Guppies to Puppies: Reading, Writing, & Reciting Poems about Pets, 1 vol. Westberg, Jan, illus. 2008. (Poetry Power Ser.). (ENG.). 32p. (J). (gr. 1-4). 27.07 *(978-1-60453-005-6(7))* ABDO Publishing Co.
—Nicknames to Nightmares: Reading, Writing, & Reciting Poems about Me, 1 vol. Westberg, Jan, illus. 2008. (Poetry Power Ser.). (ENG.). 32p. (J). (gr. 1-4). 27.07 *(978-1-60453-006-3(5))* ABDO Publishing Co.
Frodsham, Ken. The Mobile Phone of Jeremy Bone. 2014. (ENG., Illus.). 118p. pap. 14.95 *(978-1-4918-7950-4(5),* ccd1116e-7ccc-4130-862c-c81bb3f3b5d9) AuthorHouse.
Froh, Joanne. Imagine This! Plagens, Frances, illus. 2006. 32p. (J). 19.95 *(978-0-9777640-0-6(1))* Joanne Frances Pr.
Frost, Helen. Among a Thousand Fireflies. Lieder, Rick, illus. 2016. (ENG.). 32p. (J). (gr. -1-2). 15.99 *(978-0-7636-7642-1(X))* Candlewick Pr.
Frost, Robert. The Cow in Apple Time. Yeagle, Dean, illus. 2005. 32p. (J). 15.95 *(978-0-9758970-1-0(2))* Beekman & Hathaway.
Frost, Robert. Poetry for Kids: Robert Frost. Parini, Jay, ed. Paraskevas, Michael, illus. 2017. (Poetry for Kids Ser.). (ENG.). 48p. (J). (gr. 3-8). 14.95 ***(978-1-63322-220-5(9),*** Moondance) Quarto Publishing Group USA.
Fuerst, Jeffrey B. Peter Piper Picks & Pickles Peppers. 2008. (Reader's Theater Nursery Rhymes & Songs Ser.). (Illus.). 48p. (J). (gr. k-1). pap. *(978-1-60437-970-9(7))* Benchmark Education Co.
Fuertes, Gloria. Diccionario Estrafalario. 2003. (SPA.). 168p. *(978-84-305-8462-8(5),* SU3166) Susaeta Ediciones, S.A. ESP. Dist: Lectorum Pubns., Inc.
—4 Poemas de Gloria Fuertes y Una Calabaza Vestida de Luna. Aguilar, Jose, illus. 2007. (SPA.). 36p. (J). *(978-84-934160-9-6(6))* Atalante.
Fugate, Alonzo. Pumpkin Guts. 2008. 96p. pap. 13.93 *(978-0-557-01914-4(1))* Lulu Pr., Inc.
Furlong, Frank. Before We Were. 2011. 24p. pap. 10.95 *(978-1-4575-0269-9(0))* Dog Ear Publishing, LLC.
Furlong, Frank, illus. Not Yet: Poems for Kids Five & Up. 2011. 24p. pap. 14.95 *(978-1-4575-0467-9(7))* Dog Ear Publishing, LLC.
Fuschia. China Doll's Charm. 2012. 28p. pap. 16.95 *(978-1-4525-4674-2(6))* Balboa Pr.
Fusek Peters, Andrew, compiled by. Poems about Earth. 2007. (Elements in Poetry Ser.). (Illus.). 30p. (J). *(978-0-237-52887-4(8))* Evans Brothers, Ltd.
Fusek Peters, Andrew & Peters, Polly. Poems with Attitude. 2003. 96p. pap. *(978-0-7502-4189-2(6),* Wayland) Hachette Children's Group.
Gagliano, Eugene. My Teacher Dances on the Desk. Mai-Wyss, Tatjana, illus. 2009. (ENG.). 48p. (J). (gr. k-6). pap. 6.95 *(978-1-58536-446-6(0))* Sleeping Bear Pr.
Galdone, Paul. Three Little Kittens. 2013. (Paul Galdone Classics Ser.). (ENG., Illus.). 32p. (J). (gr. -1-3). 26.99 *(978-0-547-99480-2(X))* Houghton Mifflin Harcourt Publishing Co.
Galdone, Paul & Lear, Edward. The Owl & the Pussycat. 2015. (Folk Tale Classics Ser.). (ENG., Illus.). 40p. (J). (gr. -1-3). 8.99 *(978-0-544-39295-3(7),* HMH Books For Young Readers) Houghton Mifflin Harcourt Publishing Co.
Gallegos, Michael. Mommy Do You Love Me? 2013. 20p. pap. 24.95 *(978-1-62709-265-4(X))* America Star Bks.
Ganeri, Anita. I Can Write Poems, 1 vol. 2013. (I Can Write Ser.). (ENG., Illus.). 32p. (gr. 1-3). pap. 8.29 *(978-1-4329-6943-1(9));* lib. bdg. 27.32 *(978-1-4329-6936-3(6))* Heinemann-Raintree. (Heinemann First Library).
García Lorca, Federico. Canciones (1921-1924) (SPA.). 96p. (J). 13.25 *(978-84-206-6106-3(6),* AZ6106) Alianza Editorial, S. A. ESP. Dist: Continental Bk. Co., Inc.
—Canciones y Poemas para Ninos. (Coleccion Poemas Juvenil). (SPA., Illus.). 96p. (J). 9.50 *(978-84-335-8401-4(4),* DD4014) Labor, Editorial S. A. ESP. Dist: Continental Bk. Co., Inc.
—Canciones y Poemas para Ninos. (SPA., Illus.). 64p. (J). (gr. 4-6). pap. 6.95 net. *(978-1-887578-59-2(5),* SQ0128) SpanPress, Inc.
—FEDERICO GARCÍA LORCA PARA NIÑOS. (Coleccion Grandes Autores para Ninos). (SPA., Illus.). 154p. (J). (gr. 4-6). 20.76 *(978-84-305-9302-6(0),* SU4866) Susaeta Ediciones, S.A. ESP. Dist: Lectorum Pubns., Inc.
García Lorca, Federico & Aguilar, José. 4 Poemas de Lorca y un Viaje a Nueva York. 2008. (SPA., Illus.). 36p. *(978-84-934160-3-4(7))* Atalante.
García Ordaz, Daniel. You Know What I'm Sayin'? Poetry Drama. 2nd rev. ed. 2006. (ENG & SPA.). 80p. (YA). per. 10.00 *(978-0-9789954-1-6(4))* El Zarape Pr.
Garfield, Carl. After All, I'm Just a Ball: Children's Poetry Guessing Book. 2005. 32p. pap. 18.00 *(978-1-4208-2492-6(9))* AuthorHouse.
Garrison, Tommy. Imagination Celebration. 2009. 50p. pap. 10.00 *(978-0-557-07835-6(0))* Lulu Pr., Inc.
Gasca, Theresa & Juarez, Amanda. Mere Words Can Only Say... 2003. 162p. (YA). pap. 14.95 *(978-0-595-27669-1(5))* iUniverse, Inc.
Gatell, Angelina. Mis Primeras Lecturas Poeticas. (SPA.). 256p. (J). (gr. 5-8). *(978-84-7175-180-5(1),* EN1279) Twenty-Nine Ediciones ESP. Dist: Lectorum Pubns., Inc.
Gauthier, Glenn G. The A to Z Book. Gauthier, Glenn G., illus. 2006. (Illus.). 32p. (J). 16.95 *(978-1-887542-42-5(6))* Book Pubs. Network.
Gbala, Deswin R. Rock University: A Collection of Short Stories & Poems. Gbala, Deswin R., illus. Date not set. (Illus.). 51p. (Orig.). (J). (gr. 3-10). pap. 8.50 *(978-0-9650629-2-3(9))* Coulee Region Pubns., Inc.
Gedichte Analysieren. (Duden Abiturhilfen Ser.). (GER.). 112p. (YA). (gr. 12-13). *(978-3-411-70141-4(2))* Bibliographisches

P Q R

Institut & F. A. Brockhaus AG DEU. Dist: International Bk. Import Service, Inc.

George, Elizabeth. A Little Girl after God's Own Heart: Learning God's Ways in My Early Days. Luenebrink, Judy, illus. 2006. (ENG.). 32p. (J). 14.99 *(978-0-7369-1545-8(1))* Harvest Hse. Pubs.

George, Kristine O'Connell. Emma Dilemma: Big Sister Poems. Carpenter, Nancy, illus. 2011. (ENG.). 48p. (J). (gr. 1-4). 17.99 *(978-0-618-42842-7(9))* Houghton Mifflin Harcourt Publishing Co.

—The Great Frog Race: And Other Poems. Kiesler, Kate, illus. 2005. (ENG.). 48p. (J). (gr. -1-3). reprint ed. 6.99 *(978-0-618-60478-4(2))* Houghton Mifflin Harcourt Publishing Co.

—Old Elm Speaks. Kiesler, Kate, illus. 2007. (ENG.). 48p. (J). (gr. -1-3). 6.99 *(978-0-618-75242-3(0))* Houghton Mifflin Harcourt Publishing Co.

Gerber, Carole. Seeds, Bees, Butterflies, & More! Poems for Two Voices. Yelchin, Eugene, illus. 2013. (ENG.). 32p. (J). (gr. -1-3). 17.99 *(978-0-8050-9211-0(0),* 9780805092110, Holt, Henry & Co. Bks. For Young Readers) Holt, Henry & Co.

Ghigna, Charles. Animal Tracks: Wild Poems to Read Aloud. Speirs, John, tr. Speirs, John, illus. 2004. (ENG.). 36p. (J). (gr. -1-1). 14.95 *(978-0-8109-4841-9(9))* Abrams, Inc.

—Little Seeds [Scholastic]. AG Jatkowska, illus. 2012. (My Little Planet Ser.). (ENG.). 24p. (gr. -1 — 1). pap. 0.50 *(978-1-4795-1671-1(6),* My Little Planet) Picture Window Bks.

—Score! 50 Poems to Motivate & Inspire. Gorton, Julia, illus. 2008. (ENG.). 48p. (J). (gr. 2-7). 16.95 *(978-0-8109-9488-1(7),* Abrams Bks. for Young Readers) Abrams, Inc.

Giles, W. Marie. Open Your Mind, Open Your Heart: A Collection of Words of Wisdom, Heartfelt Thoughts, & Original Poetry. 2003. 112p. per. 19.95 *(978-0-9728944-0-1(3))* Giles, Willie M.

Gillespie, Esther A. & Clark, Thomas Curtis, eds. A Child's Thought of God: Religious Poems for Children. 2006. (ENG.). 136p. per. 20.95 *(978-1-4286-2999-8(8))* Kessinger Publishing, LLC.

Gillooly, Eileen, ed. Poetry for Young People: Rudyard Kipling. Spector, Joel & Sharpe, Jim, illus. 2010. (Poetry for Young People Ser.). (ENG.). 48p. (J). (gr. 3). pap. 6.95 *(978-1-4027-7293-1(9))* Sterling Publishing Co., Inc.

Gilmartin, Erin. Stretched into Shadow with No End: A Collection of Poems, 1 book. 2004. (Illus.). 88p. (YA). pap. 11.95 *(978-0-9702497-0-8(5),* Meister-Home Pr.) Meister-Home, Inc.

Gittens, Sandra L. Hooray! We're Making Memories Today! PA Illustrator, illus. 2011. 48p. pap. 24.95 *(978-1-4560-0914-4(1))* America Star Bks.

Givens, Florence Rosie. A Little More Cream Please Poem Collection by Florence Rosie Givens. 2003. (Illus.). 232p. per. 12.95 *(978-0-9705819-3-8(9))* FloBound Poems Publications.

Glaser, Linda. Our Big Home: An Earth Poem. Kleven, Elisa, illus. 2010. (Rise & Shine Ser.). (ENG.). 32p. (C). (gr. 2-4). pap. 13.95 *(978-0-7613-1776-0(7))* National Geographic School Publishing, Inc.

Godden, Rumer. Cockcrow to Starlight: A Day Full of Poetry. Kneen, Maggie, illus. 2003. (ENG.). 144p. (J). pap. 13.99 *(978-0-330-34302-2(5),* Pan) Pan Macmillan GBR. Dist: Trafalgar Square Publishing.

Godula, Ellen Kjelgaard & Godula, Brian. Queen Mab, Musical Verses Volume 3. 2007. (J). audio compact disk 16.99 *(978-0-9764109-3-5(1))* Pillar Rock Publishing.

Goel, Samir. My Favorite Children's Poems. 2009. 28p. pap. 12.49 *(978-1-4389-7306-7(3))* AuthorHouse.

Goff-Tuttle, Marie Jaume. The Colors of Christmas: A Christmas Poem for Young & Old. Reschofsky, Jean, illus. 2013. (ENG.). 16p. (J). 12.95 *(978-1-939621-09-2(7))* ORO Editions.

Goldstone, Bruce. Great Estimations. Goldstone, Bruce, illus. rev. ed. 2006. (ENG., Illus.). 32p. (J). (gr. 2-5). 18.99 *(978-0-8050-7446-8(5),* 9780805074468, Holt, Henry & Co. Bks. For Young Readers) Holt, Henry & Co.

Gonsalves, Gloria D. Diamonds Forever: Never Let Your Inner Child Stop from Glittering. 2008. (ENG., Illus.). 100p. pap. 31.99 *(978-1-4389-0428-3(2))* AuthorHouse.

Gonzalez, Ray. El Conejito Claudio (G) Para Bebés de 1 a 3 Años. Giannini, Claudia, tr. 2006. (SPA., Illus.). 20p. (J). bds. *(978-0-9712816-4-6(5))* Third Week Bks.

Goodridge, Walt F. J. Lyrics for Living Vol. 2: Just Because I Am. Owens-Waters, Zelda, ed. 2003. 64p. (C). 10.00 *(978-0-9629202-5-7(8),* LL002) Passion Profit Co., The/NicheMarket.

Gooseberry, Philbert. Philbert Gooseberry's Book of Preposterous Poems. 2016. (ENG.). 92p. (J). pap. 10.95 *(978-1-78554-168-1(4),* 3e8965a0-ede4-461a-8d6a-158bf020b668) Austin, Stan AUS. Dist: Bookmasters Distribution.

Gorey, Edward & Lear, Edward, illus. Jumblies. 2010. 48p. 14.95 *(978-0-7649-5426-9(1))* Pomegranate Communications, Inc.

Granados, Antonio. Poemas de Juguete 1. 2003. (SPA., Illus.). 191p. 8.95 *(978-968-19-0627-6(6))* Aguilar, Altea, Taurus, Alfaguara, S.A. de C.V MEX. Dist: Santillana USA Publishing Co., Inc.

—Versos de Dulce y de Sal. (SPA.). 166p. (J). pap. 13.95 *(978-968-7205-28-1(8),* AIM288) Amaquemecan, Editorial MEX. Dist: Continental Bk. Co., Inc.

Grandits, John. Blue Lipstick: Concrete Poems. Grandits, John, illus. 2007. (ENG., Illus.). 48p. (J). (gr. 5-7). 7.99 *(978-0-618-85132-4(1))* Houghton Mifflin Harcourt Publishing Co.

—Technically, It's Not My Fault: Concrete Poems. 2005. (Illus.). 40p. (gr. 4-8). 17.00 *(978-0-7569-5513-7(0))* Perfection Learning Corp.

Grant, Shauntay. Apples & Butterflies: A Poem for Prince Edward Island, 1 vol. Thiebaux-Heikalo, Tamara, illus. 2013. (ENG.). 32p. (J). (gr. k-3). 19.95 *(978-1-55109-935-4(7))* Nimbus Publishing, Ltd. CAN. Dist: Orca Bk. Pubs. USA.

—Up Home, 1 vol. Tooke, Susan, illus. 2012. (ENG.). 32p. (J). (gr. k-5). pap. 12.95 *(978-1-55109-911-8(X))* Nimbus Publishing, Ltd. CAN. Dist: Orca Bk. Pubs. USA.

Graves, Robert. Ann at Highwood Hall. Ardizzone, Edward, illus. 2017. (ENG.). 56p. (J). (gr. k-4). 16.95 *(978-1-60980-743-6(X),* Triangle Square) Seven Stories Pr.

Green, Paula. Flamingo Bendalingo: Poems from the Zoo. Hight, Michael, illus. 2006. (ENG.). 100p. (gr. 4-7). 24.95 *(978-1-86940-353-9(3))* Auckland Univ. Pr. NZL. Dist: Independent Pubs. Group.

Green Set. (Dias y Dias de Poesia Ser.). (SPA.). (gr. -1-6). 207.23 *(978-1-56334-273-8(1),* DI8633); 293.52 *(978-1-56334-274-5(X),* DI8634) CENGAGE Learning.

Greenberg, Jan, ed. Side by Side: New Poems Inspired by Art from Around the World. 2008. (MUL & ENG., Illus.). 88p. (J). (gr. 2-7). 21.95 *(978-0-8109-9471-3(2),* Abrams Bks. for Young Readers) Abrams, Inc.

Greene, Leslie. Papa & Breannah Bear on a Treasure Hunt. 2008. 31p. pap. 24.95 *(978-1-60563-985-7(0))* America Star Bks.

Greenfield Educational Center Staff. Words Through Poetry, Level 2. 2005. (CHI., Illus.). 31p. (J). pap. 7.99 *(978-962-563-029-8(5));* pap., wbk. ed. 4.99 *(978-962-563-030-4(9))* Greenfield Enterprises, Ltd. HKG. Dist: Cheng & Tsui Co.

Greenfield, Eloise. Brothers & Sisters. 2009. (J). 18.89 *(978-0-06-056285-4(4))* HarperCollins Pubs.

—Brothers & Sisters: Family Poems. Gilchrist, Jan Spivey, illus. 2008. (ENG.). 32p. (J). (gr. k-4). 17.99 *(978-0-06-056284-7(6),* Amistad) HarperCollins Pubs.

—The Friendly Four. Gilchrist, Jan Spivey, illus. 2006. (ENG.). 48p. (J). (gr. -1-3). 17.99 *(978-0-06-000759-1(1),* Amistad) HarperCollins Pubs.

Grimes, Nikki. Thanks a Million. Cabrera, Cozbi A., illus. 2006. 32p. (J). (gr. k-3). 17.99 *(978-0-688-17292-3(X));* 17.89 *(978-0-688-17293-0(8),* Greenwillow Bks.) HarperCollins Pubs.

—When Daddy Prays. Ladwig, Tim, illus. 2004. 32p. (J). pap. 8.00 *(978-0-8028-5266-3(1));* 16.00 *(978-0-8028-5152-9(5))* Eerdmans, William B. Publishing Co.

Gs Troop 1358. A Thanksgiving Poem. 2011. 24p. pap. 9.99 *(978-1-4575-0749-6(8))* Dog Ear Publishing, LLC.

Guillain, Charlotte. What Is a Poem? 2015. (Connect with Text Ser.). (ENG.). 32p. (gr. 2-4). 30.65 *(978-1-4109-6829-6(4),* Raintree Perspectives) Heinemann-Raintree.

Guillén, Nicolás. Por el Mar de las Antillas Anda un Barco de Papel. 3rd ed. 2003. (Rosa y Manzana Ser.). (SPA., Illus.). 44p. *(978-84-85334-32-2(9),* LG1397) Lóguez Ediciones ESP. Dist: Lectorum Pubns., Inc.

Guilmette, Patty. Finding Kyle Some Style, 1 vol. Whitman, Diana McManus, illus. 2009. 32p. pap. 24.95 *(978-1-60703-962-4(1))* America Star Bks.

Hablandole A Tu Corazon. 2005. (SPA.). (YA). 11.99 *(978-0-9765663-1-1(1))* Guevara, Alexis S.

Hale, Glorya, ed. Read-Aloud Poems: 50 of the World's Best-Loved Poems for Parent & Child to Share. 2012. (ENG., Illus.). 232p. (J). (gr. -1-17). 14.95 *(978-1-57912-921-7(8),* 1352599, Black Dog & Leventhal Pubs. Inc.) Hachette Bks.

Hall, Jennifer. Winston Rabbit & other Poems. 2010. (ENG., Illus.). 48p. pap. *(978-1-84748-735-3(1))* Athena Pr.

Hallworth, Grace. Down by the River: Afro-Caribbean Rhymes, Games, & Songs for Children. Binch, Caroline, illus. 2011. (ENG.). 32p. (J). (gr. -1-2). pap. 7.95 *(978-1-84780-082-4(3),* Frances Lincoln) Quarto Publishing Group UK GBR. Dist: Hachette Bk. Group.

Hamburger, Maria. The Story of Aum. 2006. (J). *(978-0-9759226-1-3(0))* BrainFriendly Learning.

Hamilton, Carol. I'm Not from Neptune. 2003. 117p. (YA). (gr. 4-5). pap. 9.99 *(978-0-88092-537-2(X))* Royal Fireworks Publishing Co.

Hansen, Doug, illus. Mother Goose in California. 2009. (J). 16.95 *(978-1-59714-101-7(1))* Heyday.

Hansen, Nichole. When I Was a Grown-Up. Hansen, Tevin, illus. 2015. (ENG.). 28p. (YA). pap. 9.49 *(978-1-941429-13-6(0))* Handersen Publishing.

Hanson, Sharon. The 10 Best Love Poems. 2008. 14.99 *(978-1-55448-543-7(6))* Scholastic Library Publishing.

Hardy, Ed & Young, Jim. Pollywogs & Other Friends. Motley, Chris and Jim Young, illus. 2007. 28p. per. 24.95 *(978-1-4137-2834-7(0))* America Star Bks.

Harmer, David. There's a Monster in the Garden: The Best of David Harmer. Archbold, Tim, illus. 2015. (ENG.). 96p. (J). (gr. 2-6). pap. 7.99 *(978-1-84780-538-6(8),* Frances Lincoln) Quarto Publishing Group UK GBR. Dist: Hachette Bk. Group.

Harris, Elle. Lullaby World. 2013. 26p. pap. 13.95 *(978-1-4908-1456-8(6),* WestBow Pr.) Author Solutions, Inc.

Harrison, David L. Connecting Dots: Poems of My Journey. Cousineau, Kelley & Cunningham, Kelley, illus. 2004. (ENG.). 64p. (J). (gr. 5-6). 15.95 *(978-1-59078-260-6(7))* Boyds Mills Pr.

—Cowboys: Voices in the Western Wind. Burr, Dan, illus. 2012. (ENG.). 48p. (J). (gr. 2-4). 17.95 *(978-1-59078-877-6(X),* Wordsong) Boyds Mills Pr.

—Farmer's Garden: Rhymes for Two Voices. Johnson-Petrov, Arden, illus. 2003. (ENG.). 32p. (J). (gr. k-2). pap. 10.95 *(978-1-59078-177-7(5))* Boyds Mills Pr.

—Pirates. Burr, Dan, illus. (ENG.). 48p. (J). (gr. 4-6). 2012. pap. 9.95 *(978-1-59078-912-4(1))* 2008. 17.95 *(978-1-59078-455-6(3))* Boyds Mills Pr. (Wordsong).

Harrison, Michael & Stuart-Clark, Christopher. One Hundred Years of Poetry for Children. rev. ed. 2007. (ENG., Illus.). 192p. (YA). (gr. 3). per. 12.95 *(978-0-19-276350-1(4))* Oxford Univ. Pr., Inc.

Harter, Penny. The Beastie Book: An Alphabestiary. Miller, Alexandra, illus. 2009. (ENG.). 56p. (J). 21.95 *(978-1-934860-05-2(0))* Shenanigan Bks.

Hattrup, Cheryl. The Little Woman Handbook. 2008. 25p. pap. 11.95 *(978-1-4327-1636-3(0))* Outskirts Pr., Inc.

Headstream, John H. Bright Stories & Little Literature for Children. 2007. pap. 10.00 *(978-0-8059-7028-9(2))* Dorrance Publishing Co., Inc.

Heard, Georgia. The Arrow Finds Its Mark: A Book of Found Poems. Guilloppé, Antoine, illus. 2012. (ENG.). 48p. (J). (gr. 3-7). 16.99 *(978-1-59643-665-7(4),* 9781596436657) Roaring Brook Pr.

Heard, Georgia, ed. Falling down the Page. 2011. (ENG.). 48p. (J). (gr. 3-7). pap. 9.99 *(978-1-59643-666-4(2),* 9781596436664) Square Fish.

Hearn, Emily. Batchawana Silly Stuff. Valleau, Gailon, illus. 2011. *(978-1-897475-70-6(5))* Hidden Brook Pr.

Heart of the Moment. 2005. (YA). per. *(978-1-59872-142-3(9))* Instant Pub.

Hedlund, Stephanie. Bedtime with Mother Goose, 1 vol. Tugeau, Jeremy, illus. 2011. (Mother Goose Nursery Rhymes Ser.). (ENG.). 32p. (J). (gr. k-2). 28.50 *(978-1-61641-143-5(0),* Looking Glass Library) ABDO Publishing Co.

Hegley, John. I Am a Poetato: An a-Z of Poems about People, Pets & Other Creatures. 2016. (ENG., Illus.). 80p. (J). (gr. 3-7). pap. 12.99 *(978-1-84780-600-0(7),* Frances Lincoln) Quarto Publishing Group UK GBR. Dist: Littlehampton Bk Services, Ltd.

Heidbreder, Robert. Lickety-Split. Petricic, Dusan, illus. 2007. (ENG.). 32p. (J). (gr. -1-2). 15.95 *(978-1-55337-710-8(9))* Kids Can Pr., Ltd. CAN. Dist: Hachette Bk. Group.

—A Sea-Wishing Day. Denton, Kady MacDonald, illus. 2007. (ENG.). 32p. (J). (gr. -1-3). 15.95 *(978-1-55337-707-8(9))* Kids Can Pr., Ltd. CAN. Dist: Hachette Bk. Group.

—See Saw Saskatchewan. Ritchie, Scot, illus. 2005. (ENG.). 32p. (J). (gr. -1-4). 7.95 *(978-1-55337-968-3(3))* Kids Can Pr., Ltd. CAN. Dist: Hachette Bk. Group.

—Shake Awakes, 1 vol. Mongeau, Marc, illus. 2012. (ENG.). 48p. (J). (gr. -1-3). 18.95 *(978-1-896580-71-5(8))* Tradewind Bks. CAN. Dist: Orca Bk. Pubs. USA.

Heiman, Diane & Suneby, Liz. That's a Mitzvah. Molk, Laurel, illus. 2014. (ENG.). 24p. (J). bds. 8.99 *(978-1-58023-804-5(1),* 9781580238045, Jewish Lights Publishing) LongHill Partners, Inc.

Hemphill, Stephanie. Your Own, Sylvia: A Verse Portrait of Sylvia. 2011. 9.84 *(978-0-7848-3501-2(2),* Everbind) Marco Bk. Co.

—Your Own, Sylvia: A Verse Portrait of Sylvia Plath. 2008. (ENG.). 272p. (YA). (gr. 7). pap. 7.99 *(978-0-440-23968-0(0),* Knopf Bks. for Young Readers) Random Hse. Children's Bks.

Hempstead, Jim. Come, Journey to Bethlehem. 2012. 34p. pap. 14.95 *(978-1-105-90106-5(8))* Lulu Pr., Inc.

Henchey, Agnes Braceland. This 'N' That. 2012. 84p. pap. 41.99 *(978-1-4691-3124-5(2))* Xlibris Corp.

Henderson, Scott. I Want to Be a Pig. 2013. 116p. 24.95 *(978-1-62646-415-5(4))* Booklocker.com, Inc.

Henderson, Stewart. All Things Weird & Wonderful. Baines, Nigel, illus. 2003. (ENG.). 96p. (J). (gr. 2-4). 19.99 *(978-0-7459-4678-8(X),* Lion Books) Lion Hudson PLC GBR. Dist: Independent Pubs. Group.

Henry, Lori. Silent Screams: Into & Out of Bulimia Through Poetry. 3rd ed. 2014. (ENG., Illus.). 150p. (J). pap. *(978-0-9918659-3-2(6))* Dancing Traveller Media.

Heppermann, Christine. Poisoned Apples: Poems for You, My Pretty. 2014. (ENG.). 128p. (YA). (gr. 8). 17.99 *(978-0-06-228957-5(8),* Greenwillow Bks.) HarperCollins Pubs.

Herford, Oliver. The Peter Pan Alphabet. Herford, Oliver, illus. 2015. (ENG., Illus.). 62p. pap. 5.99 *(978-1-61242-874-1(6),* Serenity Pubs.) Arc Manor.

Heymann, Irene Rommel. Fanciful Tales & Poems: For Grandchildren of Any Age. Heyman, Frank J., ed. Bessey, Vance, illus. 2012. 102p. (-18). pap. 14.95 *(978-1-934949-63-4(9))* Just Write Bks.

Higgins, Nadia. Henry & Hala Build a Haiku. Dumm, Brian, illus. 2011. (Poetry Builders Ser.). 32p. (J). (gr. 2-4). lib. bdg. 25.27 *(978-1-59953-435-0(5))* Norwood Hse. Pr.

High School, West Scranton & Mazzino, Christopher. Four Years to Life. 2004. 339p. (YA). 33.95 *(978-0-595-66333-0(8))* iUniverse, Inc.

Hillert, Margaret. Come Play with Me. Chow, Derrick, illus. 2016. (BeginningtoRead Ser.). (ENG.). 32p. (J). (-2). 22.60 *(978-1-59953-814-3(8))* Norwood Hse. Pr.

Hinckley, Betts. Adventure's of Charlie Girl. 2012. 44p. pap. 21.99 *(978-1-4691-4364-4(X))* Xlibris Corp.

Hines, Anna Grossnickle. Peaceful Pieces: Poems & Quilts about Peace. Hines, Anna Grossnickle, illus. 2011. (ENG., Illus.). 32p. (J). (gr. -1-3). 17.99 *(978-0-8050-8996-7(9),* 9780805089967, Holt, Henry & Co. Bks. For Young Readers) Holt, Henry & Co.

—Winter Lights: A Season in Poems & Quilts. Hines, Anna Grossnickle, illus. 2005. (Illus.). 32p. (J). lib. bdg. 17.89 *(978-0-06-000818-5(0))* HarperCollins Pubs.

Hirschfield, Beth. What's Eating You, Girls 'n Boysenberries? Veno, Joe, illus. 2009. 32p. (J). 16.95 *(978-0-9818126-3-2(5))* Ampersand, Inc.

Hoberman, Mary Ann. The Llama Who Had No Pajama: 100 Favorite Poems. Fraser, Betty, illus. 2006. (ENG.). 68p. (J). (gr. 1-4). pap. 8.99 *(978-0-15-205571-4(1))* Houghton Mifflin Harcourt Publishing Co.

—My Song Is Beautiful: Poems & Pictures in Many Voices. 2009. (Illus.). 32p. pap. 6.99 *(978-0-316-06835-2(7))* Little, Brown Bks. for Young Readers.

—You Read to Me, I'll Read to You: Very Short Fairy Tales to Read Together. 2012. (J). lib. bdg. 17.20 *(978-0-606-26685-7(2),* Turtleback) Turtleback Bks.

—You Read to Me, I'll Read to You: Very Short Scary Tales to Read Together. Emberley, Michael, illus. 2007. (ENG.). 32p. (J). (gr. -1-3). 17.99 *(978-0-316-01733-6(7))* Little, Brown Bks. for Young Readers.

Hogg, James. The Magical Mermaids. Atkins, Alison, illus. 2007. (Sparkling Jigsaw Book Ser.). 10p. (J). (gr. k-3). *(978-1-84666-373-4(3),* Tide Mill Pr.) Top That! Publishing PLC.

Hoguet, Susan Ramsay. Maine ABC. 2013. (ENG.). 32p. (J). (gr. -1-k). 14.99 *(978-1-60893-182-8(X))* Down East Bks.

Holbrook, Sara. Zombies! Evacuate the School! Sandstrom, Karen, illus. 2014. (ENG.). 56p. (J). (gr. 3-6). pap. 7.95 *(978-1-62979-110-4(5),* Wordsong) Boyds Mills Pr.

Holbrook, Sara & Wolf, Allan. More Than Friends: Poems from Him & Her. 2008. (ENG.). 64p. (J). (gr. 6-10). 16.95 *(978-1-59078-587-4(8),* Wordsong) Boyds Mills Pr.

Hollins, Paula. Christopher Makes Words! A Personalized World of Words Based on the Letters in the Name Christopher, with Humorous Poems & Colorful Illustrations. 2013. (Illus.). 42p. pap. 9.25 *(978-0-9897278-5-3(8))* PHD Ink.

—Isabella Makes Words! A Personalized World of Words Based on the Letters in the Name Isabella, with Humorous Poems & Colorful Illustrations. 2013. 36p. pap. 9.25 *(978-1-941104-00-2(2))* PHD Ink.

—Isabelle Makes Words! A Personalized World of Words Based on the Letters in the Name Isabelle, with Humorous Poems & Colorful Illustrations. 2013. 36p. pap. 9.25 *(978-1-941104-01-9(0))* PHD Ink.

—Katherine Makes Words! A Personalized World of Words Based on the Letters in the Name Katherine, with Humorous Poems & Colorful Illustrations. 2013. 38p. pap. 9.25 *(978-0-9897278-7-7(4))* PHD Ink.

—Michael Makes Words! A Personalized World of Words Based on the Letters in the Name Michael, with Humorous Poems & Colorful Illustrations. 2013. (Illus.). 38p. pap. 9.25 *(978-0-9897278-6-0(6))* PHD Ink.

—Sophie Makes Words! A Personalized World of Words Based on the Letters in the Name Sophie, with Humorous Poems & Colorful Illustrations. 2013. 30p. pap. 9.25 *(978-0-9897278-4-6(X))* PHD Ink.

Hollowell, Lorraine L. The Oatmeal Bath: And Other Poems That Make Kids Laugh. 2013. 112p. (gr. 2-4). pap. 12.06 *(978-1-4669-7926-0(7))* Trafford Publishing.

—Outside Is Where I'd Rather Be: And Other Poems for Kids Like Me. 2013. 84p. (gr. 2-4). pap. 9.10 *(978-1-4669-9012-8(0))* Trafford Publishing.

Holt, Lindsey Leann. The Green Jellybean: A Book of Children's Poems, 1 vol. 2010. 72p. pap. 19.95 *(978-1-4489-8559-3(5))* America Star Bks.

Homer. The Odyssey. Fagles, Robert, tr. from GRE. 2006. (ENG., Illus.). 560p. (gr. 12-18). 17.00 *(978-0-14-303995-2(4),* Penguin Classics) Penguin Publishing Group.

Homewood, Terry Stewart. From Then until Now. 2011. 116p. (gr. -1). 23.89 *(978-1-4634-2397-1(7));* pap. 12.01 *(978-1-4634-2396-4(9))* AuthorHouse.

Hood, Karen Jean Matsko. Tanka Thoughts: A Collection of Poetry, bk. 11. Whispering Pine Press International, ed. Artistic Design Service Staff, illus. 2014. (Hood Poetry Ser.). 224p. pap. 19.95 *(978-1-930948-52-5(2),* 1-930948-52-2) Whispering Pine Pr. International, Inc.

—Under the Lilacs: A Collection of Children's Poetry, Vol. 1. Whispering Pine Press International, ed. Artistic Design Service Staff, illus. 2014. (Hood Children's Poetry Book Ser.). 160p. (J). 29.95 *(978-1-930948-51-8(4),* 1-930948-51-4) Whispering Pine Pr. International, Inc.

Hopkins, Lee Bennett. All the World's a Stage. Billout, Guy, illus. 2013. (ENG.). 40p. (J). (gr. 4-7). 19.99 *(978-1-56846-218-9(2),* Creative Editions) Creative Co., The.

—Alphathoughts. Baggetta, Marla, illus. 2015. (ENG.). 32p. (J). (gr. k-2). 6.95 *(978-1-62091-792-3(0),* Wordsong) Boyds Mills Pr.

—Amazing Faces. Soentpiet, Chris K., illus. 2011. (ENG.). 40p. (J). (gr. 1-18). 18.95 *(978-1-60060-334-1(3))* Lee & Low Bks., Inc.

—Been to Yesterdays: Poems of a Life. Rendeiro, Charlene, illus. 2007. 64p. (gr. 3-7). 21.45 *(978-0-7569-7966-9(8))* Perfection Learning Corp.

—Give Me Wings. Goembel, Ponder, illus. 2010. (ENG.). 32p. (J). (gr. -1-3). 16.95 *(978-0-8234-2023-0(X))* Holiday Hse., Inc.

—Got Geography! Stanton, Philip, illus. 2006. (ENG.). 32p. (J). (gr. k-5). 16.99 *(978-0-06-055601-3(3),* Greenwillow Bks.) HarperCollins Pubs.

—Hamsters, Shells, & Spelling Bees: School Poems. Yoshikawa, Sachiko, illus. 2008. (I Can Read Bks.). 48p. (J). (gr. -1-3). lib. bdg. 17.89 *(978-0-06-074113-6(9))* HarperCollins Pubs.

—I Am the Book. Yayo, illus. 2011. (ENG.). 32p. (J). (gr. -1-3). 17.95 *(978-0-8234-2119-0(8))* Holiday Hse., Inc.

—Lullaby & Kisses Sweet: Poems to Love with Your Baby. Nassner, Alyssa, illus. 2015. (ENG.). 44p. (J). (gr. -1-1). bds. 15.95 *(978-1-4197-1037-7(0))* Abrams, Inc.

—Worlds of Poetry, 9 bks. 2005. (Poetry Ser.). (gr. k-3). 270.00 *(978-0-8215-0539-7(4))* Sadlier, William H. Inc.

Hopkins, Lee Bennett, ed. Amazing Faces, 1 vol. Soentpiet, Chris K., illus. 2015. (ENG.). 40p. (J). (gr. 2-5). pap. 11.95 *(978-1-62014-223-3(6))* Lee & Low Bks., Inc.

Hopkins, Lee Bennett & Alcorn, Stephen. Little Bill: Extra Thankful Thanksgiving. 2004. (Illus.). (J). pap. 3.99 *(978-0-439-35244-4(4),* Orchard Bks.) Scholastic, Inc.

Hopkins, Lee Bennett & Boyds Mills Press Staff. Alphathoughts: Alphabet Poems. Baggetta, Marla, illus. 2003. (ENG.). 32p. (J). (gr. 1-3). 16.95 *(978-1-56397-979-8(9))* Boyds Mills Pr.

Hopwood, Mererid, et al. Byd Llawn Hud. Glynn, Chris, illus. 2005. (WEL.). 32p. pap. 4.99 *(978-1-84323-342-8(8));* pap. 12.99 *(978-1-84323-343-5(6))* Gomer Pr. GBR. Dist: Gomer Pr.

Horton, Joan. I Brought My Rat for Show-and-Tell. Siegel, Melanie, tr. Siegel, Melanie, illus. 2004. (Penguin Young Readers, Level 3 Ser.). (ENG.). 48p. (J). (gr. 1-3). mass mkt. 3.99 *(978-0-448-43364-6(8),* Penguin Young Readers) Penguin Young Readers Group.

Hosford, Kate. Feeding the Flying Fanellis: And Other Poems from a Circus Chef. Kawa, Cosei, illus. 2015. (ENG.). 32p. (J). (gr. 1-3). 17.99 *(978-1-4677-7511-3(8));* lib. bdg. 17.99 *(978-1-4677-3905-4(7))* Lerner Publishing Group. (Carolrhoda Bks.).

Hotaling, Gwenn. A Child's Book of Seasons. 2003. (Illus.). 64p. 19.95 *(978-0-9728838-0-1(0))* Little Bird Publishing.

Hovey, Kate. Ancient Voices. Kimber, Murray, illus. 2007. (ENG.). 40p. (J). (gr. 3-7). 11.99 *(978-1-4169-6818-4(0),* Simon & Schuster/Paula Wiseman Bks.) Simon & Schuster/Paula Wiseman Bks.

—Arachne Speaks. Drawson, Blair, illus. 2014. (ENG.). 40p. (J). (gr. 5). 13.99 *(978-1-4814-5069-0(7),* McElderry, Margaret K. Bks.) McElderry, Margaret K. Bks.

—Voices of the Trojan War. Gore, Leonid, illus. 2012. (ENG.). 128p. (J). (gr. 3-7). pap. 7.99 *(978-1-4424-8880-9(8),* McElderry, Margaret K. Bks.) McElderry, Margaret K. Bks.

Howard, Cheryl L. It's Turtle Time. Kapart, illus. 2011. 28p. pap. 24.95 *(978-1-4560-6676-5(5))* America Star Bks.

Howitt, Mary. The Spider & the Fly. DiTerlizzi, Tony, illus. 2012. (ENG.). 40p. (J). (gr. 1-4). 17.99 *(978-1-4424-5454-5(7),* Simon & Schuster Bks. For Young Readers) Simon & Schuster Bks. For Young Readers.

Hudson, Cheryl Willis. Many Colors of Mother Goose. 2004. (Illus.). 32p. (J). (gr. -1-3). pap. 7.95 (978-0-940975-91-0(2), Sankofa Bks.) Just Us Bks., Inc.

Hudson, Wade. Poetry from the Masters: The Pioneers. Hudson, Stephen J., illus. 2003. (Poetry from the Masters Ser.). (ENG.). 88p. (J). pap. 9.95 (978-0-940975-96-5(3), Sankofa Bks.) Just Us Bks., Inc.

Hughes, Langston. I, Too, Am America. Collier, Bryan, illus. 2012. (ENG.). 40p. (J). (gr. -1-3). 16.99 (978-1-4424-2008-3(1), Simon & Schuster Bks. For Young Readers) Simon & Schuster Bks. For Young Readers.

Hughes, Shirley. Out & About: A First Book of Poems. Hughes, Shirley, illus. 2015. (ENG., Illus.). 56p. (J). (-k). 16.99 (978-0-7636-7644-5(6)) Candlewick Pr.

Hughes, Ted & Downer, Jim. Timmy the Tug. Hughes, Ted, illus. 2010. (ENG., Illus.). 40p. (J). 19.95 (978-0-500-51496-2(8), 551496) Thames & Hudson.

Hullinger, C. D. & Brighter Child Publishing Staff. Mother Goose Rhymes (Las Rimas de Mama Oca), Grades PK - 3. 2007. (Keepsake Stories Ser.). (ENG & SPA., Illus.). 32p. (gr. -1-3). pap. 3.99 (978-0-7696-5416-4(9), Brighter Child) Carson-Dellosa Publishing, LLC.

Hulme, Joy N. & Guthrie, Donna. How to Write, Recite, & Delight in All Kinds of Poetry. 2003. (Single Titles Ser.: Vol. 8). 96p. (J). (gr. 3-6). pap. 9.95 (978-0-7613-1831-6(3)) Lerner Publishing Group.

Hutchins, Hazel J. A Second Is a Hiccup: A Child's Book of Time. Denton, Kady MacDonald, illus. 2004. (ENG.). 32p. (J). (978-0-439-97400-4(3), North Winds Pr) Scholastic Canada, Ltd.

If You're Happy & You Know It & Other Favorites. 2005. (Meet Mother Goose Ser.). (ENG., Illus.). 36p. (J). 10.95 (978-1-59069-211-0(X), MD1108) Studio Mouse LLC.

Intermediate School, Parkview, compiled by. School Memories. 2006. per. 19.95 (978-0-9768391-3-2(X)) Pen & Publish Inc.

Irish, Janice. The Gift of Words: A Resource for Parents & Educators. 2011. 92p. pap. 9.99 (978-1-4567-1969-2(6)) AuthorHouse.

Isaac, Denise. Agape to You. 2003. (YA). per. 12.99 (978-1-59352-038-0(7)) Christian Services Publishing.

Iyengar, Malathai. Tan to Tamarind: Poems about the Color Brown. Akib, Jamel, illus. 2017. (ENG.). 32p. (J). pap. 9.95 **(978-0-89239-412-8(9)**, Children's Book Press) Lee & Low Bks., Inc.

Iyengar, Malathi Michelle. Tan to Tamarind: Poems about the Color Brown. Akib, Jamel, illus. 2013. (ENG.). 32p. (J). (gr. k). 16.95 (978-0-89239-227-8(4)) Lee & Low Bks., Inc.

Jackson, Anna. Catullus for Children. 2004. (ENG.). 64p. pap. 12.95 (978-1-86940-308-9(8)) Auckland Univ. Pr. NZL. Dist: Independent Pubs. Group.

Jackson, Demond, Sr. The Turnaround Book of Poetry: Complete Series. 2004. (YA). per. 20.00 (978-0-9753028-6-6(8), TA-04) Turnaround Bk. Publishing Corp.

Jager, Phyllis. Introducing Myself. Jager, Korin Elizabeth, illus. 2005. (J). 9.95 (978-1-59571-080-2(9)) Word Association Pubs.

James, Corinne M. A Zoo Party. 2008. 24p. pap. 11.49 (978-1-4389-1828-0(3)) AuthorHouse.

James, Simon, illus. & compiled by. Days Like This: A Collection of Small Poems. James, Simon, compiled by. 2005. (ENG.). 48p. (J). (gr. 1-4). reprint ed. pap. 6.99 (978-0-7636-2314-2(8)) Candlewick Pr.

Janeczko, Paul B. The Death of the Hat: A Brief History of Poetry in 50 Objects. Raschka, Chris, illus. 2015. (ENG.). 80p. (J). (gr. 3-7). 17.99 (978-0-7636-6963-8(6)) Candlewick Pr.

—A Foot in the Mouth: Poems to Speak, Sing, & Shout. Raschka, Chris, illus. 2012. (ENG.). 64p. (J). (gr. 3-7). pap. 8.99 (978-0-7636-6083-3(3)) Candlewick Pr.

—Poetry from A to Z: A Guide for Young Writers. Bobak, Cathy, illus. 2012. (ENG.). 144p. (J). (gr. 4-7). pap. 8.99 (978-1-4424-6061-4(X), Simon & Schuster Bks. For Young Readers) Simon & Schuster Bks. For Young Readers.

—Requiem: Poems of the Terezin Ghetto. 2011. (ENG., Illus.). 102p. (YA). (gr. 9). 16.99 (978-0-7636-4727-8(6)) Candlewick Pr.

—Worlds Afire. 2007. (ENG., Illus.). 112p. (YA). (gr. 7-18). per. 7.99 (978-0-7636-3400-1(X)) Candlewick Pr.

Jeffs, Stephanie. Come into the Ark with Noah. Reynolds, Annette, ed. Saunderson, Chris, illus. 2007. (Action Rhymes Ser.). (ENG.). 16p. (J). (gr. -1-2). pap. 4.99 (978-0-9789056-6-8(0)) New Day Publishing, Inc.

—Follow the Star with the Wise Men. Reynolds, Annette, ed. Saunderson, Chris, illus. 2007. (Action Rhymes Ser.). (ENG.). 16p. (J). (gr. -1-3). per. 4.99 (978-0-9789056-3-7(6)) New Day Publishing, Inc.

—March Round the Walls with Joshua. Reynolds, Annette, ed. Saunderson, Chris, illus. 2007. (Action Rhymes Ser.). (ENG.). 16p. (J). (gr. -1-2). pap. 4.99 (978-0-9789056-7-5(9)) New Day Publishing, Inc.

Jenkins, Mike. Poems for Underage Thinkers. 2004. (ENG., Illus.). 48p. pap. 12.95 (978-1-84323-359-6(2)) Beekman Bks., Inc.

Jenkins-Tate, Nesha L. The 10 Love Poems to Empower Young Souls: A Gift Book to Encourage Young People You Love. 2004. 56p. (YA). per. 21.00 (978-0-9753245-0-9(0), BBR) BBR: Books for Brilliance & Resilience.

Jiang, Emily. Summoning the Phoenix: Poems & Prose about Chinese Musical Instruments, 1 vol. Chu, April, illus. 2014. (ENG.). 32p. (J). 18.95 (978-1-885008-50-3(3)) Lee & Low Bks., Inc.

Jilson, Emily. The Five Little Mice: A Collection of Children's Poems. 2010. 24p. pap. 13.99 (978-1-4490-9739-4(1)) AuthorHouse.

Jiménez, Juan Ramón. Canta Pajaro Lejano. 14th ed. (SPA., Illus.). 128p. (J). (gr. 4-6). 14.95 (978-84-239-8892-1(9), EC2591) Espasa Calpe, S.A. ESP. Dist: Lectorum Pubns., Inc., Distribooks, Inc.

John Blake. Pound a Poem. 2010. (ENG., Illus.). 288p. 16.95 (978-1-84454-833-0(3)) Blake, John Publishing, Ltd. GBR. Dist: Independent Pubs. Group.

John Blake Publishing Staff. Pound a Poem: The Winning Entries from the National Schools Poetry Competition. Sayers, Myrna, illus. 2007. (ENG.). 256p. 19.95 (978-1-84454-436-3(2)) Blake, John Publishing, Ltd. GBR. Dist: Independent Pubs. Group.

John, Rebecca Mary. The Musings of a Young Girl. 2012. 48p. pap. 21.99 (978-1-4772-9280-8(2)) AuthorHouse.

Johnson, Celia, ed. 100 Great Poems for Girls. 2011. (ENG.). 208p. pap., pap. 13.00 (978-0-446-56384-0(6)) Grand Central Publishing.

Johnson-Hall, Wanda. You Can Be: Yes! He Can! 2005. 16p. (YA). 10.00 (978-1-59633-000-9(7)) Goose Creek Pubs., Inc.

Johnson, Julia. Humpy Grumpy Saves the Day! Styles, Emily, illus. 2007. (ENG.). 32p. 16.95 (978-1-905299-43-0(5), Stacey International) Stacey Publishing GBR. Dist: Casemate Pubs. & Bk. Distributors, LLC.

Johnson, William. Every Second Something Happens: Poems for the Mind & Senses. Hall, Melanie W., illus. 2009. (ENG.). 48p. (J). (gr. k-2). 17.95 (978-1-59078-622-2(X), Wordsong) Boyds Mills Pr.

Johnston, Gail. Whispers in the Mist. 2010. 144p. pap. 11.70 (978-1-4520-9673-5(2)) AuthorHouse.

Johnston, Tony. Voice from Afar: Poems of Peace. Guevara, Susan, illus. 2008. (ENG.). 32p. (YA). (gr. 5-18). 16.95 (978-0-8234-2012-4(4)) Holiday Hse., Inc.

Jones, Andy. Poo-Etry - Raps, Rhymes, Riddles & Rocking Poetry. 2017. 272p. 6.99 (978-0-7333-3566-2(7)) ABC Bks. AUS. Dist: HarperCollins Pubs.

Jones, Susan Smith & Warren, Dianne. Vegetable Soup - The Fruit Bowl. Lindman, Amy Sorvaag, illus. rev. ed. 2006. 64p. (J). (gr. -1-3). per. 14.95 (978-0-9652736-0-2(1)) Oasis Pubns.

Jones, V. C. When You're Sick. 2010. 16p. 8.49 (978-1-4490-8265-9(3)) AuthorHouse.

Joyner, A. Bernard. Out of the Mouths of Babes! A Book of Childrenrsquo;s Poetry. 2007. (ENG.). 68p. per. 16.95 (978-1-4241-6643-5(8)) PublishAmerica, Inc.

Judd, Lissa Elaine. A Slightly Larger Book of Kick-Arse Poetry. 2013. 90p. pap. (978-0-473-26612-7(1)) Idea Factory, The.

—A Small Book of Kick-Arse Poetry. 2012. 62p. pap. (978-0-473-22562-9(X)) Idea Factory, The.

Judy Kohl. Little Heavenly Poems. 2009. (Illus.). 44p. pap. 14.99 (978-1-4251-7869-7(3)) Trafford Publishing.

Kahla, Robert. Mr. X from Planet X: And Other Animules. (Animules Ser.). (Illus.). 64p. (J). pap. 8.95 (978-1-882820-00-9(2)) kahla, bob.

Kalantary, Tanya. So Can You! 2010. 34p. pap. 14.50 (978-1-60911-928-7(2), Eloquent Bks.) Strategic Book Publishing & Rights Agency (SBPRA).

Kamerling, Yvonne. TLC for Teenagers & their Parents: Inspirational Quotes, Poetry, Touching Stories. 2004. 122p. (YA). 22.95 (978-0-595-66340-8(0)) iUniverse, Inc.

Kammeraad, Kevin & Kammeraad, Stephanie. A Curious Glimpse of Michigan. Kammeraad, Kevin & Hipp, Ryan, illus. 2004. 32p. (J). (gr. 3-7). 19.95 (978-0-9712692-9-3(7)) EDCO Publishing, Inc.

Kanaan. Literati: A Revolution of Living. 2003. 230p. (YA). pap. 18.95 (978-0-595-30381-6(1)) iUniverse, Inc.

Kasper, Catherine. Field Stone: Poems. 2005. 57p. per. 14.00 (978-0-9764726-0-5(0), 1A) Winnow Pr.

Kass, Ed. D. Playground Time: A Skip-Counting Rhyme. 2010. 32p. pap. 13.49 (978-1-4490-6795-3(6)) AuthorHouse.

Kasten, David Scott & Kastan, Marina, eds. William Shakespeare. Harrington, Glenn, illus. 2008. (Poetry for Young People Ser.). (ENG.). 48p. (J). (gr. 3). pap. 6.95 (978-1-4027-5478-4(7)) Sterling Publishing Co., Inc.

Katz, Alan. Oops! Koren, Edward, illus. 2008. (ENG.). 176p. (J). (gr. 2-5). 19.99 (978-1-4169-0204-1(X), McElderry, Margaret K. Bks.) McElderry, Margaret K. Bks.

Kauenhofen, Jessica. My First A B C Book. Kauenhofen, Jessica, illus. 2007. (Little Jewel Book Ser.). (Illus.). 24p. (J). (gr. 2). pap. 2.70 (978-0-7399-2385-6(4)) Rod & Staff Pubs., Inc.

Kay, Francesca. One Busy Book. Glynn, Chris, illus. 2004. (ENG.). 32p. pap. 12.95 (978-1-84323-344-2(4)) Beekman Bks., Inc.

Keane, Sarah. My Foot Fell Asleep, 1 vol. 2013. (Fiction Readers Ser.). (ENG., Illus.). 28p. (J). (gr. 2-2). pap. 6.99 (978-1-4333-5567-7(1)) Shell Educational Publishing.

Kearney, Meg. The Secret of Me. 2005. (Karen & Michael Braziller Bks.). (ENG.). 128p. (YA). (gr. 7). 17.95 (978-0-89255-322-8(7)) Persea Bks., Inc.

Keaton, Bobby J. The Closet Monster. 2011. 48p. pap. 19.26 (978-1-4567-3087-1(8)) AuthorHouse.

Keats, John. A Song about Myself. Raschka, Chris, illus. 2017. (ENG.). 40p. (J). (gr. 1-4). 17.99 (978-0-7636-5090-2(0)) Candlewick Pr.

Keller-Miller, LeAnn Marie, illus. When I Grow Up: An A-Z Poem Book for Children & Their Dreams. 2005. (978-0-9711480-4-8(X)) ICanPublish.

Kelman, Louise & Kelman, Suzanne. Big Purple Undies. Dowling, Jane, ed. Baker, Penny, illus. 2004. 64p. (J). pap. (978-0-9580869-6-7(6)) Inhoa Publishing.

Kennedy, Caroline. A Family of Poems: My Favorite Poetry for Children. Muth, Jon J., illus. 2005. (ENG.). 144p. (J). (gr. -1-17). 21.99 (978-0-7868-5111-9(2)) Hyperion Pr.

—Poems to Share. Muth, Jon J., illus. 2008. 32p. 17.99 (978-1-4231-1658-5(5)) Hyperion Pr.

Kennedy, X. J. City Kids: Street & Skyscraper Rhymes, 1 vol. Beha, Phillippe, illus. 2010. (ENG.). 86p. (J). (gr. 4-7). 17.95 (978-1-896580-44-9(0)) Tradewind Bks. CAN. Dist: Orca Bk. Pubs. USA.

Kids: Sagebrush Prairie. 2004. (J). 1.00 (978-1-888631-34-0(1)) Project WET Foundation.

Kim, Aerim. A Tiny Bud. Kim, Lindsey, illus. 2008. 80p. (J). 29.95 (978-0-9789624-0-1(0)) Blue Lotus Wave.

Kim, Isabel Joy & Prasad, Siona. Tangled in Beauty: Contemplative Nature Poems. Kim, Isabel Joy, illus. 2013. (Illus.). 74p. pap. 7.99 (978-0-9912472-0-2(5)) Philokalos Pr.

Kimble, George J. Poetry for the Road, 1. annot. ed. 2005. (Illus.). 157p. per. 15.00 (978-0-9767024-0-5(1)) Kimble, George J.

King, Michael Riano, Jr. Let's Learn Together. 2007. (J). 8.00 (978-0-8059-7295-5(1)) Dorrance Publishing Co., Inc.

Klanot, Khaya Dawn. Just Hanging Out, a Collection of Poems for Kids. Pirnot, Karen Hutchins, illus. 2008. 48p. pap. 16.95 (978-0-9814894-5-2(1)) Peppertree Pr., The.

Klein, A. M. Doctor Dwarf & Other Poems for Children. Date not set. (Illus.). 32p. 12.95 (978-0-919627-41-3(2)); pap. 6.95 (978-0-919627-43-7(9)) Quarry Pr. CAN. Dist: LPC/InBook.

Klunder, Barbara. Other Goose: Recycled Rhymes for Our Fragile Times..., 1 vol. 2007. (ENG., Illus.). 48p. (J). (gr. 1-4). 17.95 (978-0-88899-829-3(5)) Groundwood Bks. CAN. Dist: Publishers Group West (PGW).

Knight, Nelson & Knight, Suzanne. The ABCs of Southern Virginia University. 2013. (J). 14.95 (978-1-62086-063-2(5)) Mascot Bks., Inc.

Kochner, Donna Rose Porta. Through the Night. 2012. 20p. pap. 10.95 (978-1-4497-6999-4(3), WestBow Pr.) Author Solutions, Inc.

Koertge, Ronald. The Brimstone Journals. 2004. (ENG., Illus.). 128p. (YA). (gr. 9-18). pap. 7.99 (978-0-7636-1742-4(3)) Candlewick Pr.

Korhel, Erik. My Tooth Fell in My Soup: And Other Poems. Baker, Celia M., illus. 2009. 26p. (J). 14.95 (978-1-935359-02-9(9)) Book Pubs. Network.

Kovner, Vladimir, tr. from ENG. Prilaskaite L'va: Amerikanskiye i Angliiskiye Stikhi Dlya Detei. Braslavskii, Felix, illus. 2010. (RUS.). 110p. (J). pap. (978-1-934881-43-9(0), M-Graphics) M-Graphics Publishing.

Koziara, Colleen. Thirteen Silver Moons. Koziara, Colleen, illus. 2004. (Illus.). (J). per. (978-0-9763205-0-0(9)) Mystical Willow Productions.

Kram, T. Gooey Desserts & Messy Shirts Poetry F. 2007. 125p. pap. 19.95 (978-1-4241-6072-3(3)) America Star Bks.

Krensky, Stephen, et al. Arturo y el Concurso de Poesia. 2004.Tr. of Arthur & the Poetry Contest. (SPA., Illus.). (J). pap. 4.95 (978-1-930332-61-4(0)) Lectorum Pubns., Inc.

Kroelinger, Melanie. Ocean: A Lullaby Book. 2013. 20p. pap. 17.99 (978-1-4817-0817-3(1)) AuthorHouse.

Kubler, Annie, illus. Hop a Little, Jump a Little! 2010. (Baby Board Bks.). (ENG.). 12p. (J). bds. (978-1-84643-341-2(X)) Child's Play International Ltd.

—Humpty Dumpty. 2010. (Baby Board Bks.). (ENG.). 12p. (J). bds. (978-1-84643-339-9(8)) Child's Play International Ltd.

—Pat-A-Cake! 2010. (Baby Board Bks.). (ENG.). 12p. (J). bds. (978-1-84643-338-2(X)) Child's Play International Ltd.

—Pussy Cat, Pussy Cat. 2010. (Baby Board Bks.). (ENG.). 12p. (J). bds. (978-1-84643-340-5(1)) Child's Play International Ltd.

Kumuhana High, Kukulu. The Hala Grove of Wakiu, Vol. II. 2005. (YA). per. 19.95 (978-1-59571-047-5(7)) Word Association Pubs.

Kurkela, Robert W. Lilies on the Moon. Kurkela, Cassidy S., illus. 2005. 32p. (J). 16.95 (978-0-9760220-0-8(1)) Kidzpoetz Publishing.

Laing, Robin. The Whisky Muse: Collected & Introduced by Robin Laing. Dewar, Bob, illus. 2nd ed. 2003. (ENG.). 224p. per. 19.95 (978-1-84282-041-4(9)) Luath Pr. Ltd. GBR. Dist: Midpoint Trade Bks., Inc.

Laisney, Sarah. Ice Flowers & Pomegranates, 1 vol. 2010. 98p. pap. 19.95 (978-1-4489-4900-7(9)) America Star Bks.

Lalli, Judy. I Like Being Me: Poems about Kindness, Friendship, & Making Good. rev. ed. 2016. (ENG., Illus.). 64p. (J). (gr. -1-2). pap. 9.99 (978-1-63198-092-3(0)) Free Spirit Publishing, Inc.

Lambert, Kelly. Sounds of a Coo. 2012. (ENG.). 45p. (J). pap. 23.95 (978-1-4327-8303-7(3)); pap. 32.95 (978-1-4327-8316-7(5)) Outskirts Pr., Inc.

Land, Autumn. The Monarch & the Monarch. 2009. 112p. pap. 11.99 (978-1-60647-428-0(6)) Salem Author Services.

Lane, Diane Luby & Get Lit Players, the. Get Lit Rising: Words Ignite. Claim Your Poem. Claim Your Life. 2016. (ENG., Illus.). 272p. (YA). (gr. 7). 21.99 (978-1-58270-576-7(3)) Simon Pulse/Beyond Words.

Lane, Leena. Climb up the Tree with Zacchaeus. Reynolds, Annette, ed. Saunderson, Chris, illus. 2007. (Action Rhymes Ser.). (ENG.). 16p. (J). (gr. -1-2). pap. 4.99 (978-0-9789056-2-0(8)) New Day Publishing, Inc.

Lang, Tiffany. Mango Leaves Strings in Your Teeth. 2003. (J). per. (978-1-59196-409-4(1)) Instant Pub.

Language Through Poetry (Gr. PreK-5) 2003. (J). (978-1-58232-119-6(1)) ECS Learning Systems, Inc.

Lanksy, Bruce. Rolling in the Aisles: A Collection of Laugh-Out-Loud Poems. Carpenter, Stephen, illus. 2004. 116p. (J). (978-0-88166-473-7(1)) Meadowbrook Pr.

Lansana, Quraysh Ali & Lightfoot, Toni Asante. The Sixth Wave. 2008. 88p. (YA). (gr. 4-18). pap. 9.95 (978-1-933491-14-1(0)) Just Us Bks., Inc.

Lansky, Bruce, ed. Dinner with Dracula. Gordon, Mike & Gordon, Carl, illus. 2006. 32p. (J). (978-0-88166-512-3(6)) Meadowbrook Pr.

Lansky, Bruce & Carpenter, Stephen. My Teacher's in Detention: Kids' Favorite Funny School Poems. 2006. (Giggle Poetry Ser.). (ENG., Illus.). 80p. (J). (gr. k-6). per. 8.95 (978-0-689-05245-3(6)) Meadowbrook Pr.

Larkin, Eric-Shabazz, illus. A Moose Boosh: A Few Choice Words about Food. 2014. (ENG.). 96p. (J). (gr. 4-7). 18.95 (978-0-9836615-5-9(3)) READERS to EATERS.

Larsen, Alison. What Makes You Smile? Larsen, Alison, illus. 2006. (Illus.). 23p. (J). (gr. -1-3). per. 13.95 (978-1-60002-094-0(1)) Mountain Valley Publishing, LLC.

Lassiter, Gianna Bari. Rosy Proses: Whimsical Verses & Sanity Journal for Big People Who Have Little People in Their Lives. gif. ed. 2005. (Illus.). 40p. (YA). spiral bd. 10.00 (978-0-9773324-0-3(3)) MentorSource, LLC.

Latham, Irene. Fresh Delicious. Moriuchi, Mique, illus. 2016. (ENG.). 40p. (J). (gr. -1-3). 16.95 (978-1-62979-103-6(2), Wordsong) Boyds Mills Pr.

Latham, Irene & Waters, Charles. Can I Touch Your Hair? Poems of Race, Mistakes, & Friendship. Alko, Selina & Qualls, Sean, illus. 2017. (ENG.). 40p. **(978-1-5124-0442-5(X)**, Millbrook Pr.) Lerner Publishing Group.

Law, Felicia. Family. Knight, Paula, illus. 2015. (Patchwork Ser.). (ENG.). 24p. (J). (gr. k-3). pap. 11.94 (978-1-60357-801-1(3)) Norwood Hse. Pr.

—Feelings. Knight, Paula, illus. 2015. (Patchwork Ser.). (ENG.). 24p. (J). (gr. k-3). pap. 11.94 (978-1-60357-802-8(1)) Norwood Hse. Pr.

—Numbers. Knight, Paula, illus. 2015. (Patchwork Ser.). (ENG.). 24p. (J). (gr. k-3). pap. 11.94 (978-1-60357-800-4(5)) Norwood Hse. Pr.

Lawson, JonArno. Black Stars in a White Night Sky. Tjia, Sherwin, illus. 2008. (ENG.). 128p. (J). (gr. 6-9). 16.95 (978-1-59078-521-8(5), Wordsong) Boyds Mills Pr.

—Black Stars in a White Night Sky. Tjia, Sherwin, illus. 2006. (ENG.). 80p. (978-1-897141-07-6(6)) Pedlar Pr.

—Down in the Bottom of the Bottom of the Box. 2012. (ENG., Illus.). 80p. (J). pap. 16.95 (978-0-88984-354-7(6)) Porcupine's Quill, Inc. CAN. Dist: Univ. of Toronto Pr.

—The Man in the Moon-Fixer's Mask. Tjia, Sherwin, illus. 2004. (ENG.). 88p. (J). (gr. 3-7). (978-0-9732140-9-3(0)) Pedlar Pr.

—Think Again. Morstad, Julie, illus. 2010. (ENG.). 64p. (J). (gr. 5-9). 16.95 (978-1-55453-423-4(2)) Kids Can Pr., Ltd. CAN. Dist: Hachette Bk. Group.

—A Voweller's Bestiary: From Aardvark to Guineafowl. 2008. (ENG., Illus.). 96p. (J). (gr. 4-7). pap. 14.95 (978-0-88984-300-4(7)) Porcupine's Quill, Inc. CAN. Dist: Univ. of Toronto Pr.

Layne, Steven. The Principal's Night Before Christmas, 1 vol. Rice, James, illus. 2004. (Night Before Christmas Ser.). (ENG.). 32p. (J). (gr. k-3). 16.99 (978-1-58980-252-0(7)) Pelican Publishing Co., Inc.

Layne, Steven L. Teachers' Night Before Halloween, 1 vol. Hoyt, Ard, illus. 2008. (ENG.). 32p. (gr. -1-3). 16.99 (978-1-58980-585-9(2)) Pelican Publishing Co., Inc.

Le, Le Pham. From Where the Wind Blows. Arbuthnot, Nancy, tr. 2003.Tr. of Gio Thoi Phuong Nao. (VIE.). per. 12.00 (978-0-9746300-0-7(4)) Vietnamese International Poetry Society.

Lear, Edward. Nonsense Drolleries: The Owl & the Pussy-Cat, the Duck & the Kangaroo. Foster, William, illus. 2007. 32p. pap. 10.95 (978-1-60355-050-5(X)) Juniper Grove.

—The Table & the Chair. Ebbeler, Jeffrey, illus. 2011. (Poetry for Children Ser.). (ENG.). 24p. (J). (gr. k-3). 27.07 (978-1-60973-156-4(5), 201185) Child's World, Inc., The.

Lear, Edward & Campbell, Lori M. The Complete Nonsense Books of Edward Lear. 2008. (Illus.). xxxiii, 409p. pap. (978-1-4351-0325-2(4)) Barnes & Noble Bks.-Imports.

Lear, Edward & Mortimer. The Owl & the Pussycat. Mortimer, Anne, illus. 2006. (ENG.). 32p. (J). (gr. -1-4). 16.99 (978-0-06-027228-9(7), Tegen, Katherine Bks) HarperCollins Pubs.

Learn along with Lily. 2008. (Illus.). 32p. (J). 15.95 (978-0-9799677-0-2(8)) Raindrop Bks.

Lebachen, Medyhne. Hilhairyass Poems: By a Six Year Old Adult. Payne, Mark, illus. 2012. 76p. (YA). (978-0-9872816-4-7(X)) Heart Space Pubns Pty Ltd (Australia).

Lee, Dennis. Alligator Pie Board Book. 2014. (ENG., Illus.). 13p. (J). bds. 10.50 (978-1-4434-1161-5(2)) HarperCollins Pubs.

—Alligator Pie Classic Edition. Nichols, Sandy & Newfeld, Frank, illus. 2012. (ENG.). 64p. (J). 15.99 **(978-1-4434-1151-6(5))** HarperCollins Pubs.

—Bubblegum Delicious. 2014. 32p. (J). (gr. -1-3). 17.99 (978-0-06-231347-8(9)) HarperCollins Pubs.

—The Cat & the Wizard. 2004. (Illus.). (J). (gr. k-3). spiral bd. (978-0-616-11115-4(0)); spiral bd. (978-0-616-11116-1(9)) Canadian National Institute for the Blind/Institut National Canadien pour les Aveugles.

—The Dreadful Doings of Jelly Belly. Hilb, Nora, illus. rev. ed. 2009. (ENG.). 16p. (J). (gr. k-k). bds. (978-1-55263-767-8(0)) Me to We.

—The Kitty Ran up the Tree. Hilb, Nora, illus. rev. ed. 2009. (ENG.). 16p. (J). (gr. k-k). bds. (978-1-55263-813-2(8)) Me to We.

—Silverly/Good Night, Good Night. Hilb, Nora, illus. rev. ed. 2008. (ENG.). 16p. (J). (gr. k-k). bds. (978-1-55263-769-2(7)) Me to We.

—Skyscraper. Hilb, Nora, illus. rev. ed. 2009. (ENG.). 16p. (J). (gr. k-k). bds. (978-1-55263-811-8(1)) Me to We.

—Willoughby Wallaby Woo. Hilb, Nora, illus. rev. ed. 2008. (ENG.). 16p. (J). (gr. k-k). bds. (978-1-55263-676-3(3)) Me to We.

Lee, Patty. Wild Animals: What Is That I Ask? Lee, Jack, illus. 2013. 30p. pap. 14.00 (978-1-4349-3518-2(3), RoseDog Bks.) Dorrance Publishing Co., Inc.

Lee, Patty & Lee, Jack. Biblical: Who Is That I Ask? a Children's Poetry Book. 2013. 28p. pap. 19.99 (978-1-4817-1096-1(6)) AuthorHouse.

Lehman, David. Great American Prose Poems: From Poe to the Present. 2003. (ENG.). 352p. pap. 18.00 (978-0-7432-4350-6(1), Scribner) Scribner.

Leppanen, Debbie. Trick-or-Treat: A Happy Haunter's Halloween. Carpenter, Tad, illus. 2013. (ENG.). 40p. (J). (gr. k-3). 16.99 (978-1-4424-3398-4(1)) Simon & Schuster Children's Publishing.

Lesynski, Loris. Cabbagehead. Lesynski, Loris, illus. 2003. (ENG., Illus.). 32p. (J). (gr. k-3). 18.95 (978-1-55037-805-4(8), 9781550378054); pap. 6.95 (978-1-55037-804-7(X), 9781550378047) Annick Pr., Ltd. CAN. Dist: Publishers Group West (PGW).

—Crazy about Basketball! Rasmussen, Gerry, illus. 2013. (Crazy about Sports Ser.). (ENG.). 32p. (J). (gr. 3-5). 22.95 (978-1-55451-541-7(6), 9781554515417); pap. 12.95 (978-1-55451-540-0(8), 9781554515400) Annick Pr., Ltd. CAN. Dist: Publishers Group West (PGW).

—Crazy about Hockey! Rasmussen, Gerry, illus. 2015. (Crazy about Sports Ser.). (ENG.). 32p. (J). (gr. 3-5). pap. 9.95 (978-1-55451-711-4(7), 9781554517114) Annick Pr., Ltd. CAN. Dist: Publishers Group West (PGW).

—Crazy about Soccer. Rasmussen, Gerry, illus. 2012. (Crazy about Sports Ser.). (ENG.). 48p. (J). (gr. 2-5). 22.95 (978-1-55451-422-9(3), 9781554514229); pap. 12.95 (978-1-55451-421-2(5), 9781554514212) Annick Pr., Ltd. CAN. Dist: Publishers Group West (PGW).

—Shoe Shakes. Martchenko, Michael, illus. 2007. (ENG.). 32p. (J). (gr. -1-k). 19.95 (978-1-55451-106-8(2), 9781554511068); pap. 9.95 (978-1-55451-105-1(4), 9781554511051) Annick Pr., Ltd. CAN. Dist: Publishers Group West (PGW).

Levin, Jonathan, ed. Walt Whitman. Burke, Jim, illus. 2008. (Poetry for Young People Ser.). (ENG.). 48p. (J). (gr. 3-7). pap. 6.95 (978-1-4027-5477-7(9)) Sterling Publishing Co., Inc.

Levin, Vadim. Silly Horse. Wolfson, Tanya & Zunshine, Tatiana, trs. from RUS. Antonenkov, Evgeny, illus. 2005. (ENG.). 32p. (J). (gr. -1-4). 15.95 (978-0-9646010-1-7(X), 1241074) Pumpkin Hse., Ltd.

Levine, Diana. The Dancing Waves. 2007. 68p. per. 10.00 (978-1-4257-5337-5(X)) Xlibris Corp.

Lewis, Anthony, illus. Humpty Dumpty: Asl. 2013. (Hands-On Songs Ser.). (ENG.). 12p. (J). bds. (978-1-84643-627-7(3)) Child's Play International Ltd.

Lewis, J. Patrick. Black Swan/White Crow. Manson, Christopher, illus. 2007. (ENG.). 32p. (J). (gr. 2-5). 9.99 (978-1-4169-6158-1(5), Simon & Schuster/Paula Wiseman Bks.) Simon & Schuster/Paula Wiseman Bks.

—Blackbeard the Pirate King. 2006. (ENG., Illus.). 32p. (J). (gr. 2-5). 16.95 (978-0-7922-5585-7(2)); lib. bdg. 25.90 (978-0-7922-5586-4(0)) National Geographic Society. (National Geographic Children's Bks.).

—Edgar Allan Poe's Pie: Math Puzzlers in Classic Poems. Slack, Michael, illus. 2012. (ENG.). 40p. (J). (gr. 1-4). 16.99 (978-0-547-51338-6(0)) Houghton Mifflin Harcourt Publishing Co.

—Everything Is a Poem: the Best of J. Patrick Lewis. Pritelli, Maria Cristina, illus. 2014. (ENG.). 88p. (J). (gr. 1-3). 24.99 (978-1-56846-240-0(9), Creative Editions) Creative Co., The.

—Face Bug. Murphy, Kelly, illus. Siskind, Fred, photos by. 2013. (ENG.). 36p. (J). (gr. 1-5). 16.95 (978-1-59078-925-4(3), Wordsong) Boyds Mills Pr.

—Freedom Like Sunlight: Praisesongs for Black Americans. 2014. (ENG.). 40p. (J). (gr. 5-17). pap. 9.99 (978-0-89812-973-1(7), Creative Paperbacks) Creative Co., The.

—God Made the Skunk: And Other Animal Poems. King, Jerry, illus. 2005. 60p. (J). 14.95 (978-0-9722820-1-7(7)) Doggerel Daze.

—The House. Innocenti, Roberto, illus. 2009. (ENG.). 64p. (J). (gr. 4-7). 19.95 (978-1-56846-201-1(8), 1300178, Creative Editions) Creative Co., The.

—Keep a Pocket in Your Poem: Classic Poems & Playful Parodies. Wright, Johanna, illus. 2017. (ENG.). 32p. (J). (gr. k-5). 17.95 (978-1-59078-921-6(0), Wordsong) Boyds Mills Pr.

—Self-Portrait with Seven Fingers: The Life of Marc Chagall in Verse. Chagall, Marc, illus. 2011. (ENG.). 40p. (J). (gr. 4-7). 18.99 (978-1-56846-211-0(5), Creative Editions) Creative Co., The.

—Under the Kissletoe: Christmastime Poems. Shepperson, Rob, illus. 2007. (ENG.). 32p. (J). (gr. 2-4). 16.95 (978-1-59078-438-9(3), Wordsong) Boyds Mills Pr.

—The Underwear Salesman: And Other Jobs for Better or Verse. Bloch, Serge, illus. 2009. (ENG.). 64p. (J). (gr. 2-5). 18.99 (978-0-689-85325-8(4), Atheneum Bks. for Young Readers) Simon & Schuster Children's Publishing.

—World Rat Day: Poems about Real Holidays You've Never Heard Of. Raff, Anna, illus. 2013. (ENG.). 40p. (J). (gr. k-3). 15.99 (978-0-7636-5402-3(7)) Candlewick Pr.

—The World's Greatest. Graves, Keith, illus. 2008. (ENG.). 36p. (J). (gr. k-4). 16.99 (978-0-8118-5130-5(3)) Chronicle Bks. LLC.

Lewis, J. Patrick & Thompson, John. Freedom Like Sunlight. 2005. (Illus.). pap. 7.95 (978-0-89812-382-1(8)) Creative Co., The.

Lewis, Ophelia S. My Dear Liberia: Recollections, Poetic Memoirs from My Heart. 2004. (YA). per. 9.95 (978-0-9753609-0-3(6)) Village Tales Publishing.

Lewis, Richard. Cave: An Evocation of the Beginnings of Art. Crawford, Elizabeth, illus. Hirose, George, photos by. 2003. 56p. pap. 14.00 (978-1-929299-03-4(6)) Touchstone Ctr. Pubns.

—Play, Said the Earth to Air. Neilson, Heidi, illus. 2013. (ENG.). 44p. (J). (gr. -1). pap. 12.00 (978-1-929299-12-6(5)) Touchstone Ctr. Pubns.

—A Tree Lives. Baen, Noah, illus. 2006. 48p. per. 12.00 (978-1-929299-04-1(4)) Touchstone Ctr. Pubns.

Lewis, Siân. Dim Mwnci'n y Dosbarth. Glynn, Chris, illus. 2005. (WEL.). 64p. pap. 4.99 (978-1-84323-427-2(0)) Gomer Pr. GBR. Dist: Gomer Pr.

Liddle-Pirouet, Leasal. I Love You More Than Ice Cream Dipped in Sprinkles. 2010. 28p. pap. 14.95 (978-1-4251-7577-1(5)) Trafford Publishing.

Linda (Mimi') Wise. Come Grow with Me: Inspirational Poems for Children. 2009. 28p. pap. 12.49 (978-1-4389-2754-1(1)) AuthorHouse.

Little, Jean. Hey World, Here I Am! Truesdell, Sue, illus. 2015. 96p. pap. 6.00 (978-1-61003-607-8(7)) Center for the Collaborative Classroom.

Littlewood, Graham. Restless Owl & Other Stories. Preston, Carole, illus. 2010. (ENG.). 56p. pap. (978-1-84748-778-0(5)) Athena Pr.

Llanas, Sheila Griffin. Modern American Poetry: Echoes & Shadows. 2009. (Poetry Rocks! Ser.). (Illus.). 160p. (YA). (gr. 9-12). lib. bdg. 35.94 (978-0-7660-3275-0(2)) Enslow Pubs., Inc.

Lloyd, Sophie. Behind Brown Eyes. 2012. (Illus.). 44p. pap. (978-0-9568247-5-2(7)) Cloister Hse. Pr., The.

Lofficier, Randy. If Your Possum Go Daylight. OKeefe, Raven, illus. 2009. (ENG.). 60p. (J). pap. 12.95 (978-1-934543-78-8(0)) HollywoodComics.com, LLC.

Longfello, Henry Wadsworth. Paul Revere's Ride. Vachula, Monica, illus. 2011. (ENG.). 32p. (J). (gr. 4-6). pap. 11.95 (978-1-59078-869-1(9)) Boyds Mills Pr.

Longfellow, Henry Wadsworth. The Children's Hour. Lang, Glenna, illus. 2008. (ENG.). 32p. (YA). (gr. 8-12). pap. 9.95 (978-1-56792-344-5(5)) Godine, David R. Pub.

—The Children's Own Longfellow & the Golden Legend. 2007. (ENG.). 224p. pap. 20.99 (978-1-4346-0835-2(2)); pap. 23.99 (978-1-4346-0909-0(X)) Creative Media Partners, LLC.

—Paul Revere's Ride: The Landlord's Tale. Encarnacion, Elizabeth, ed. Santore, Charles, illus. 2014. (ENG.). 40p. (J). 17.95 (978-1-60433-493-7(2), Applesauce Pr.) Cider Mill Pr. Bk. Pubs., LLC.

—Paul Revere's Ride: The Landlord's Tale. Santore, Charles, illus. 2005. 28p. (J). (gr. 4-8). reprint ed. 17.00 (978-0-7567-9202-2(9)) DIANE Publishing Co.

—Paul Revere's Ride: The Landlord's Tale. Santore, Charles, illus. 2003. 40p. (J). lib. bdg. 17.89 (978-0-06-623747-3(5)) HarperCollins Pubs.

—Song of Hiawatha. 2003. 252p. pap. 14.95 (978-1-59224-329-7(0)) Wildside Pr., LLC.

Lorenz, Colton. I Am a New York City. 2008. 180p. pap. 16.95 (978-0-595-51062-7(0)) iUniverse, Inc.

Loski, Krystle C. Ode to Me & My Day. 2011. 24p. pap. 24.95 (978-1-4626-0668-9(7)) America Star Bks.

Lottridge, Celia. Mother Goose. Clement, Gary et al, illus. 2009. (ENG.). 32p. (J). (gr. k — 1). bds. 9.95 (978-0-88899-933-7(X)) Groundwood Bks. CAN. Dist: Publishers Group West (PGW).

Low, Elizabeth Cothen. Big Book of Seasons, Holidays, & Weather: Rhymes, Fingerplays, & Songs for Children, 1 vol. 2011. (Illus.). 156p. (C). pap. 40.00 (978-1-59884-623-2(X), A3162P) Pearson Education GBR. Dist: ABC-CLIO, LLC.

Lucas, Scott. Lies Nostalgia & Cow Gas. 2008. 192p. pap. 14.95 (978-0-615-16630-8(X)) Feather River Publishing.

Luján, Jorge. Colors! / ¡Colores! Simon, John Oliver & Parfitt, Rebecca, trs. Grobler, Piet, illus. 2008.Tr. of Colors! (SPA & ENG.). 36p. (J). (gr. k-4). 18.95 (978-0-88899-863-7(5)) Groundwood Bks. CAN. Dist: Publishers Group West (PGW).

—Numeralia, 1 vol. Ouriou, Susan, tr. from SPA. Isol Staff, illus. 2014. (ENG.). 32p. (J). (gr. -1). 18.95 (978-1-55498-444-2(0)) Groundwood Bks. CAN. Dist: Publishers Group West (PGW).

—Rooster / Gallo, 1 vol. Amado, Elisa, tr. from SPA. Monroy, Manuel, illus. 2016. (ENG & SPA.). 24p. (J). 8.95 (978-1-55498-936-2(1)) Groundwood Bks. CAN. Dist: Publishers Group West (PGW).

LuzMarie. Suicidal Beauty, 1 vol. 2010. 88p. pap. 19.95 (978-1-4489-4950-2(5)) America Star Bks.

Lynch, Ryan. Just a Pup: And Other Poems for Children. 2007. 216p. per. 24.95 (978-1-4241-5640-5(8)) America Star Bks.

Lynette, Shannon. A Place with No Name. 2003. 120p. (YA). pap. 14.95 (978-0-7414-1534-9(8)) Infinity Publishing.

Lyons, John. Dancing in the Rain. 2016. (Books for Children Ser.). (ENG., Illus.). 64p. (J). (gr. 4-7). pap. 17.95 (978-1-84523-301-3(8)) Peepal Tree Pr., Ltd. GBR. Dist: Independent Pubs. Group.

Mac, Gi Gi. Poetry Stories for the Rug Rat the Ankle Biter & the Bun in the Oven. 2013. 24p. pap. (978-1-4602-0945-5(1)) FriesenPress.

Mac, Janie. The Moon over Americ. 2013. 20p. pap. 13.77 (978-1-4669-7697-9(7)) Trafford Publishing.

MacCormick SEcure Center, Residents. Another Sad Inning: Incarcerated Youth Reveal Their Trials, Tribulations & Loves. MacCormick Secure Center, Residents, illus. 2003. 90p. (YA). per. 17.00 (978-0-9740184-1-6(4), MAC-2) Durland Alternatives Library.

MacDonald, John. Child's Play in Poetry. 2013. 60p. pap. 11.99 (978-1-62839-169-5(3)) Salem Author Services.

MacGregor, Kim. Button, Buckle, Tie. Snider, Sharon & Reny, Todd, trs. 2004. (Illus.). 24p. (978-0-9731301-4-0(8)); pap. (978-0-9731301-3-3(X)) Beautiful Beginnings Youth, Inc.

—Yummy Yummy Nummy Nummy, Should I Put This in My Tummy? Ioannou, Gregory Phillip, ed. Snider, Sharon & Reny, Todd, illus. 2004. 24p. (978-0-9731301-0-2(5)) Beautiful Beginnings Youth, Inc.

Machado, Antonio. Yo Voy Sonando Caminos. (Coleccion Poemas Juvenil). (SPA., Illus.). 96p. (J). 9.50 (978-84-335-8423-6(5), DD4236) Labor, Editorial S. A. ESP. Dist: Continental Bk. Co., Inc.

Macken, JoAnn Early. Read, Recite, & Write Cinquains. 2015. (ENG., Illus.). 32p. (J). (978-0-7787-1962-5(6)) Crabtree Publishing Co.

—Read, Recite, & Write Concrete Poems. 2015. (ENG., Illus.). 32p. (J). (978-0-7787-1963-2(4)) Crabtree Publishing Co.

—Read, Recite, & Write List Poems. 2015. (ENG., Illus.). 32p. (J). (978-0-7787-1965-6(0)) Crabtree Publishing Co.

MacLachlan, Patricia & Charest, Emily MacLachlan. Cat Talk. Moser, Barry, illus. 2013. 32p. (J). (gr. -1-3). (ENG.). 17.99 (978-0-06-027978-3(8)); lib. bdg. 18.89 (978-0-06-027979-0(6)) HarperCollins Pubs. (Tegen, Katherine Bks).

MacMillan, Lesley. Draw Me a Picture. 2006. (Illus.). 37p. (J). per. 12.90 (978-1-59879-301-7(2)) Lifevest Publishing, Inc.

Mair, J. Samia & Whamsby, Dawud. Colours of Islam. Adams, Shireen, illus. 2013. (ENG.). 40p. (J). (gr. k-2). 22.95 (978-0-86037-591-3(9)) Kube Publishing Ltd. GBR. Dist: Consortium Bk. Sales & Distribution.

Make a Joyful Sound. 2003. (J). 13.95 (978-0-590-28205-5(0)) Scholastic, Inc.

Malenfant, Paul Chanel. Si Tu Allais Quelque Part. 2003. (New Poetry Ser.). (FRE.). 36p. (J). (gr. 7). pap. (978-2-89021-622-8(5)) Diffusion du livre Mirabel (DLM).

Manley, Molly. On a Vineyard Veranda. Marshall, Janet, illus. 2007. (Little Limericks Ser.). (ENG.). 24p. (J). (gr. k-3). 12.95 (978-1-933212-46-3(2), Commonwealth Editions) Applewood Bks.

Mannis, Celeste Davidson. One Leaf Rides the Wind. Hartung, Susan Kathleen, illus. 2005. (gr. -1-3). 17.00 (978-0-7569-5213-6(1)) Perfection Learning Corp.

Marcamo, Thais. Vivencias & Despertar. Vilma Muises, ed. 2004. (SPA., Illus.). 96p. (YA). pap. 15.00 (978-1-931481-34-2(2)) LiArt-Literature & Art.

Margaret Scollan. The Gods of Rome: Dei Romae. 2009. 20p. pap. 15.00 (978-1-4269-1871-1(2)) Trafford Publishing.

Mari?I?, ?Uro. How Children Grow. 2013. (Illus.). 86p. pap. 13.66 (978-1-4817-7605-9(3)) AuthorHouse.

Marjorie, as told by. A Flower Unfolds: Inspirational Teachings in Verse from Kwan Yin, Bodhisattva of Mercy & Compassion. l.t. ed. 2003. (Illus.). 52p. 12.95 (978-0-9745712-0-1(2)) Sun Sprite Publishing.

Mark, Jan. A Jetblack Sunrise: Poems about War & Conflict. 2005. (Illus.). (J). 16.99 (978-0-7502-4293-6(0)) Hodder & Stoughton GBR. Dist: Trafalgar Square Publishing.

Marrero, Rafelito. Amar sin decir Nada. 1000th l.t. ed. 2003. 137p. per. 14.95 net. (978-0-9747569-0-5(3)) Marrero, Rafael.

Marston, J. D., photos by. The Poems for Pequenines (Poemas Para Pequenines) 2004. (Baby Einstein Ser.). (SPA., Illus.). 12p. (J). bds. (978-970-718-159-5(1), Silver Dolphin en Español) Advanced Marketing, S. de R. L. de C. V.

Martin, Bill, Jr., ed. The Bill Martin Jr Big Book of Poetry. 2008. (ENG., Illus.). 176p. (J). (gr. -1-3). 24.99 (978-1-4169-3971-9(7), Simon & Schuster Bks. For Young Readers) Simon & Schuster Bks. For Young Readers.

Martin, Tamara. Little Robin Redbreast: An Illustrated Poem. l.t. ed. 2014. (Illus.). 24p. (J). 14.95 (978-1-935656-07-4(4), Little Red Acorns) Little Red Tree Publishing LLC.

Mataya, Marybeth. Luke & Leo Build a Limerick. Richard, Ilene, illus. 2011. (Poetry Builders Ser.). 32p. (J). (gr. 2-4). lib. bdg. 25.27 (978-1-59953-436-7(3)) Norwood Hse. Pr.

Matthews, Jennifer V. For A Ghetto Child: An Anthology of Poems & Art. 2010. 40p. pap. 16.99 (978-1-4259-1752-4(6)) AuthorHouse.

Maude, Tony. Without Surprise. Monica, Brufton, illus. 2013. 60p. pap. (978-2-917183-29-8(2)) Nigeria Baptist Convention, Pubns. Dept.

Maxey, Ann. Country Style Oklahoma. 2005. (Illus.). 71p. (YA). per. 15.95 (978-0-9771939-1-2(8), 0001) New World Publishing.

Mays, Charli. A Lifetime from Before, 1 vol. 2009. (ENG.). 103p. pap. 19.95 (978-1-61546-102-8(7)) America Star Bks.

McClarrin Vaupel, Lynn. The Queen of Hearts. 2007. 9.00 (978-0-8059-8378-4(3)) Dorrance Publishing Co., Inc.

McClellan, Cheryl. Bunny Flu Flu Gets Well. 2004. (J). per. 7.99 (978-0-9719241-9-2(8)) Chosen Word Publishing.

McConduit, Denise & Harrington, David. The Boy Who Wouldn't Read, 1 vol. Harrington, David, illus. 2013. (ENG., Illus.). 32p. (J). (gr. k-3). 16.99 (978-1-4556-1829-3(2)) Pelican Publishing Co., Inc.

McDermott, Mustafa Yusuf. Muslim Nursery Rhymes. Norridge, Terry, illus. 2nd ed. 2009. (ENG.). 29p. (J). (gr. -1-k). 8.95 (978-0-86037-342-1(8)) Kube Publishing Ltd. GBR. Dist: Consortium Bk. Sales & Distribution.

McDevitt, Brian. Ode to General George Washington. 2003. 20p. (YA). 6.00 (978-1-888032-14-7(6)) Library Sales of N.J.

McDonald, J. Donnelly. I Gazed in Amazement: (Ordinary Creatures Do Extraordinary Things) 2008. 40p. pap. 16.99 (978-1-4343-9211-4(2)) AuthorHouse.

McDougal-Littell Publishing Staff. Literature Connections English: Dogsong. 2004. (McDougal Littell Literature Connections Ser.). (ENG.). 224p. (gr. 6-8). 16.90 (978-0-395-77527-1(2), 2-80096) Great Source Education Group, Inc.

McDougall, Carol & LaRamee-Jones, Shanda. Baby Play, 1 vol. 2012. (Baby Steps Ser.). (ENG., Illus.). 14p. (J). (gr. -1 — 1). bds. 8.95 (978-1-55109-902-6(0)) Nimbus Publishing, Ltd. CAN. Dist: Orca Bk. Pubs. USA.

McDougall, Jill. Anna the Goanna: And Other Poems. Taylor, Jenny, illus. 2009. (ENG.). 48p. (J). (gr. k-6). pap. 17.95 (978-0-85575-616-1(0)) Aboriginal Studies Pr. AUS. Dist: Independent Pubs. Group.

McGougan, Kathy. NO, Buddy! 2007. (J). pap. 5.00 (978-0-9799980-6-5(9)) Buddy Bks. Publishing.

McGough, Roger. Sensational! Poems Inspired by the Five Senses. 3rd unabr. ed. 2005. (ENG., Illus.). 240p. (J). (gr. 3-7). pap. 10.99 (978-0-330-41344-2(9)) Macmillan Pubs., Ltd. GBR. Dist: Independent Pubs. Group.

—Wicked Poems. Layton, Neal, illus. 2004. (ENG.). 208p. (gr. 2-4). pap. 15.00 (978-0-7475-6195-8(8)) Bloomsbury Publishing Plc GBR. Dist: Independent Pubs. Group.

McGough, Roger, et al. You Tell Me! Paul, Korky, illus. 2015. (ENG.). 96p. (J). (gr. 2-6). pap. 7.99 (978-1-84780-444-0(6), Frances Lincoln) Quarto Publishing Group UK GBR. Dist: Hachette Bk. Group.

McGrath, Noelle. The Dupes & How Not to Be Them: A Primer on the Perils of Political Correctness. 2010. 76p. pap. 76.00 (978-1-4520-1221-6(0)) AuthorHouse.

McHenry, Eric. Mommy Daddy Evan Sage. Garland, Nicholas, illus. 2011. (ENG.). 72p. (J). 16.95 (978-1-904130-45-1(3)) Waywiser Pr., The GBR. Dist: Dufour Editions, Inc.

Mckenzie, Natalie. The Children of New York City: Straight from the Heart 2009. 2009. 64p. pap. 14.99 (978-1-4269-1300-6(1)) Trafford Publishing.

McKeown, Theresa. The ABCs of Being Me. 2007. (J). 17.00 (978-0-8059-7235-1(8)) Dorrance Publishing Co., Inc.

McMachan, Susan K. The Forest of the Leprechauns. Skiadas, Melissa & Skiadas, Stephanie, illus. 2008. 36p. pap. 15.95 (978-1-4389-1325-4(7)) AuthorHouse.

McMahon, Jeff & Warrick, Jessica. Running to the Sun: Another Collection of Rhymes Without Reason. 2015. (ENG., Illus.). 192p. (J). 19.98 (978-0-9890270-1-4(5)) Leisure Time Pr.

McMahon, Michael. Space Ace, 1 vol. rev. ed. 2013. (Fiction Readers Ser.). (ENG., Illus.). 32p. (J). (gr. 3-3). pap. 8.99 (978-1-4333-5638-4(4)) Shell Educational Publishing.

McNabb, Vincent. The Children's Hour of Heaven on Earth. Symington, Lindsay, illus. 2007. 48p. per. 21.95 (978-0-9782985-2-4(7)) Catholic Authors Pr.

Me, Myself, & I! Take-Home Book. 2005. (Lee Bennett Hopkins Worlds of Poetry Classroom Library). (YA). (gr. k-3). 13.50 (978-0-8215-0565-6(3)) Sadlier, William H. Inc.

Meinderts, Koos. In Our Street. Fienieg, Annette, illus. 2013. (ENG.). 32p. (J). (gr. -1). 12.95 (978-1-935954-24-8(5), 9781935954248) Lemniscaat USA.

Meinke, Peter & Meinke, Jeanne, illus. The Elf Poem, or, Nine Not Very Golden Rules for Children Who Like to Write Poetry. 2015. 104p. (J). pap. (978-1-59732-129-7(X)) Univ. of Tampa Pr.

Memoirs on Love & Life: A Poetic Expression, 4. 2003. (YA). per. 13.00 (978-0-9742010-0-9(6)) California Is Me.

Mena Ccc-Slp, Gretchen. I Won't Bite. 2009. 16p. pap. 10.49 (978-1-4389-6449-2(8)) AuthorHouse.

Mendelson, Edward, ed. Lewis Carroll. Copeland, Eric, illus. 2008. (Poetry for Young People Ser.). (ENG.). 48p. (J). (gr. 3). pap. 6.95 (978-1-4027-5474-6(4)) Sterling Publishing Co., Inc.

—Poetry for Young People: Edward Lear. Huliska-Beith, Laura, illus. 2010. (Poetry for Young People Ser.). (ENG.). 48p. (J). (gr. 3). pap. 6.95 (978-1-4027-7294-8(7)) Sterling Publishing Co., Inc.

Mercer, Gerald. What's Going on at the Time Tonight?, 1 vol. DeWolf, Holly, illus. 2013. (ENG.). 32p. (J). (gr. -1-3). 19.95 (978-1-77108-004-0(3)) Nimbus Publishing, Ltd. CAN. Dist: Orca Bk. Pubs. USA.

Merrill, Karen Grill. Rhyme Time. 2007. 48p. per. 10.00 (978-1-4257-4947-7(X)) Xlibris Corp.

Michelson, Richard. Animals Anonymous. Fischer, Scott M., illus. 2008. (ENG.). 96p. (YA). (gr. 9-18). 14.99 (978-1-4169-1424-2(2), Simon & Schuster Bks. For Young Readers) Simon & Schuster Bks. For Young Readers.

Middleton, Peter. Aftermath. 2003. (Modern Poets Ser.). (ENG.). 188p. pap. (978-1-876857-63-9(3)) Salt Publishing.

Mike. Lemon Drop Rain: Poems & Drawings by Mr. Mike. Mike, illus. l.t. ed. 2003. (ENG., Illus.). 180p. (J). pap. 14.95 (978-0-9658365-6-2(8)) Beetle Bug Bks.

Miles, Liz. Humorous & Nonsensical Poems, 1 vol. 2014. (Experiencing Poetry Ser.). (ENG.). 64p. (gr. 7-8). lib. bdg. 35.99 (978-1-4329-9559-1(6)) Heinemann-Raintree.

Miller, Ann. Proverbs, Prayers, Poems for Children & Teens. 2005. (J). lib. bdg. 14.95 (978-0-9748165-1-7(5)) Jaylil Publishing Co.

Miller, Connie Colwell, et al. Tickles, Pickles, & Floofing Persnickles: Reading & Writing Nonsense Poems, 1 vol. Smith, Simon et al, illus. 2014. (Poet in You Ser.). (ENG.). 32p. (gr. 2-4). pap. 9.95 (978-1-4795-2949-0(4)); lib. bdg. 27.32 (978-1-4795-2198-2(1)) Picture Window Bks.

Miller, Susan. Cowboy Nativity: A Narrative Poem. 2016. (ENG., Illus.). (J). (gr. 2-5). pap. 9.95 **(978-1-61984-492-6(3))** Price World Publishing.

Millman, Selena. Ever Notice. 2006. (Illus.). (J). 11.18 (978-1-4243-2354-8(1)) Independent Publisher Services.

Mills, Lois. Saddles & Sails. 2005. reprint ed. pap. 15.95 (978-1-4191-0458-9(6)) Kessinger Publishing, LLC.

Milne, A. A. When We Were Very Young. Shepard, Ernest H., illus. deluxe ed. 2009. (Winnie-The-Pooh Ser.). (ENG.). 112p. (J). (gr. 3-7). 19.99 (978-0-525-47930-7(9), Dutton Books for Young Readers) Penguin Young Readers Group.

Milstein, Larry. Spring's Bright Colors. 2007. (Illus.). 24p. (J). 15.99 (978-0-9798421-0-8(7)) Wonderful Publishing.

Minden, Cecilia & Roth, Kate. How to Write a Poem. 2011. (Explorer Junior Library: Language Arts Explorer Junior Ser.). (ENG.). 24p. (gr. 1-4). lib. bdg. 25.64 (978-1-60279-995-0(4), 200990) Cherry Lake Publishing.

Minter, Peter. Blue Grass. 2006. (ENG.). 128p. per. (978-1-84471-246-5(X)) Salt Publishing.

Miracles Can Happen. 2003. 96p. (YA). per. (978-1-930362-07-9(2)) Foston Adolescent Workshop, Inc.

Mistral, Gabriela. Poesia Infantil. (Coleccion Poemas Juvenil). (SPA.). (J). (gr. 2-4). pap. 9.50 (978-956-13-1083-4(X), AB0120) Bello, Andres CHL. Dist: Continental Bk. Co., Inc.

Mitchell, Gail A. Learning English the Cultural Way. Mitchell, Gail A., photos by. 2004. (Illus.). 40p. (J). per. 20.00 (978-0-9653308-9-3(3)) Africana Homestead Legacy Pubs., Inc.

Mitchell, Katherine. Another Day & Lots to Do. 2012. 16p. pap. 15.99 (978-1-4772-0541-9(1)) AuthorHouse.

Mitchell, Stephen. The Wishing Bone, & Other Poems. Pohrt, Tom, illus. 2003. (ENG.). 56p. (J). (gr. k-12). 16.99 (978-0-7636-1118-7(2)) Candlewick Pr.

Mohanraj, Amirthi. The Poet's Journey. 2008. 30p. 16.95 (978-0-615-18889-8(3)) Serendib Pr.

Mondragon, Philip. Going Beyond. 2009. 120p. pap. 12.95 (978-0-595-53051-9(6)) iUniverse, Inc.

Montale, Eugenio. Selected Poems. Young, David et al, trs. from ITA. 2004. (FIELD Translation Ser.: 26). (ENG & ITA.). 164p. pap. 19.95 (978-0-932440-98-3(3)) Oberlin College Pr.

Moolenaar Bernier, Ashley-Ruth. Sand, Sea & Poetry. Fundora, Yolanda V., illus. 2014. (J). pap. (978-1-934370-35-3(5)) Editorial Campana.

Moon, Jo, illus. Twinkle, Twinkle Little Star. 2016. (Carousel Bks.). (ENG.). 10p. (J). (gr. -1 — 1). bds. 8.99 (978-0-7641-6860-4(6)) Barron's Educational Series, Inc.

Moore, Clement C. The Night Before Christmas: Peek Inside the 3D Windows. Alderson, Lisa, illus. 2013. (ENG.). 12p. (J). (gr. -1-3). 16.99 (978-1-84322-923-0(4), Armadillo) Anness Publishing GBR. Dist: National Bk. Network.

—The Night Before Christmas: The Classic Rhyme with Flaps to Lift & Sparkling Surprises! Downer, Maggie, illus. 2015. (ENG.). 10p. (J). (gr. k-3). bds. 7.99 (978-1-86147-293-9(5), Armadillo) Anness Publishing GBR. Dist: National Bk. Network.

—Night Before Christmas Board Book: The Classic Edition. Santore, Charles, illus. 2013. (ENG.). 26p. (J). bds. 8.95 (978-1-60433-438-8(X), Applesauce Pr.) Cider Mill Pr. Bk. Pubs., LLC.

—Twas the Night Before Christmas. Goodell, Jon, illus. 2013. (ENG.). 26p. (J). bds. 9.99 (978-1-4494-3557-8(2)) Andrews McMeel Publishing.

—Twas the Night Before Christmas. 2016. (ENG., Illus.). (J). pap. 9.99 **(978-1-5324-0083-4(7))** Xist Publishing.

Moore, Lilian. Mural on Second Avenue & Other City Poems. Karas, Roma, illus. 2013. (ENG.). 32p. (J). (gr. k-4). pap. 6.99 (978-0-7636-6349-0(2)) Candlewick Pr.

Moore, Mel. Way Cool Book of Poetry. 2006. (Illus.). 21p. (J). per. (978-0-9775919-0-9(5)) Carpe Diem Publishing.

Moore, Natalia, illus. Animal Poems. 2017. (Poems Just for Me Ser.). 32p. (gr. 7-8). pap. 10.00 **(978-1-4994-8389-5(9)**, Windmill Bks.) Rosen Publishing Group, Inc., The.

Moore, Shelbie. Words Scribbled in My Notebook. 2008. 100p. pap. 9.99 (978-0-9814650-4-3(8)) G Publishing LLC.

Mora, Pat. Confeti: Poemas para Ninos, 1 vol. Mora, Pat & Fernandez, Queta, trs. Sanchez, Enrique O., illus. 2006. (SPA.). 32p. (J). (gr. -1-5). pap. 10.95 (978-1-58430-270-4(4)) Lee & Low Bks., Inc.

—The Desert is My Mother/El Desierto Es Mi Madre: CD & Book Set. Lechon, Daniel, illus. 2008. 32p. (J). pap. 18.95 (978-0-9815686-2-1(9)) Lorito Bks., Inc.

—Join Hands! The Ways We Celebrate Life. Ancona, George, photos by. 2008. (ENG., Illus.). 32p. (J). (gr. -1-3). 15.95 (978-1-58089-202-5(7)) Charlesbridge Publishing, Inc.

—Yum! Mmmm! Que Rico! America's Sproutings, 1 vol. López, Rafael, illus. 2007. 32p. (J). (gr. -1-3). lib. bdg. 16.95 (978-1-58430-271-1(2)) Lee & Low Bks., Inc.

—Yum! ¡Mmmm! ¡Qué Rico! Americas' Sproutings. López, Rafael, illus. 2007. (ENG & SPA.). 32p. (J). pap. 10.95 (978-1-60060-892-6(2)) Lee & Low Bks., Inc.

—Yum! ¡MmMm! ¡Qué Rico! Brotes de las Américas. López, Rafael, illus. 2009.Tr. of Yum! ¡MmMm! ¡Qué rico! America's Sproutings. (SPA.). 32p. (J). 17.95 (978-1-60060-430-0(7)) Lee & Low Bks., Inc.

Mora, Pat & López, Rafael. Yum! Mmmm! Que Rico! America's Sproutings. Mora, Pat & López, Rafael, illus. 2008. (SPA & ENG., Illus.). (J). (gr. k-6). 7.95 (978-1-60060-267-2(3)) Lee & Low Bks., Inc.

Mora, Pat & Sanchez, Enrique O. Confetti: Poems for Children. 2006. (ENG., Illus.). 32p. (J). (gr. 2-18). pap. 9.95 (978-1-880000-85-4(7)) Lee & Low Bks., Inc.

Mora, Pat, et al. Yum! Mmmm! Qué Rico! Brotes de las Américas. López, Rafael & Flor Ada, Alma, illus. 2009.Tr. of

Yum! ¡MmMm! ¡Qué rico! America's Sproutings. (SPA & ENG.). 32p. (J). (gr. k-6). pap. 8.95 *(978-1-60060-268-9(1))* Lee & Low Bks., Inc.

More, Francisco J., Sr. Carousel de Fantasias, 1. 2000th l.t. ed. 2003. (SPA., Illus.). 26p. (J). lib. bdg. 4.95 *(978-0-9747851-0-3(5))* More, Francisco J.

Moreillon, Judi. Vamos a Leer. Mercado, Mary M., tr. from ENG. Teis, Kyra, illus.Tr. of Read to Me. (SPA.). 12p. (J). 2005. bds. 6.95 *(978-1-59572-015-3(4))* 2004. 6.95 *(978-1-932065-50-3(4))* Star Bright Bks., Inc.

Morenz, Justin, creator. Cardlings. 2004. (Illus.). 30p. (YA). 10.95 *(978-0-9760108-0-7(1))* Cardlings.

Morgan, Michaela, ed. Alice in Poetry. 2016. (Macmillan Alice Ser.). (ENG., Illus.). 128p. (J). (gr. 4-6). pap. 8.99 *(978-1-5098-1884-6(7))* Pan Macmillan GBR. Dist: Independent Pubs. Group.

Morgenstern, Constance. Waking Day. 2006. (Picture Book Ser.). (ENG., Illus.). 32p. (J). (gr. k-17). 17.95 *(978-1-55971-919-3(2))* Cooper Square Publishing Llc.

Mornard, Germaine & Farish, Catherine. La Fille Orange. 2003. (New Poetry Ser.). (FRE., Illus.). 36p. (J). (gr. 7). pap. *(978-2-89021-623-5(3))* Diffusion du livre Mirabel (DLM).

Morpurgo, Michael & Morpurgo, Clare. Where My Wellies Take Me. Lomenech Gill, Olivia, illus. 2013. (ENG.). 110p. (J). (gr. 1-4). 29.99 *(978-0-7636-6629-3(7),* Templar) Candlewick Pr.

Morris, Jackie. The Barefoot Book of Classic Poems. 2006. (ENG., Illus.). 128p. (J). (gr. 3-6). 19.99 *(978-1-905236-56-5(5))* Barefoot Bks., Inc.

Morrison, Lillian. Guess Again! Riddle Poems. Hale, Christy, illus. 2006. (ENG.). 48p. (J). (gr. 1-4). 16.95 *(978-0-87483-730-8(8))* August Hse. Pubs., Inc.

Morrissey, Tricia. Everyday Life: Through Chinese Peasant Art. Mak, Ding Sang, illus. 2009. (ENG.). 36p. (J). (gr. -1-5). pap. 9.95 *(978-1-934159-18-7(2))* ThingsAsian Pr.

Mortensen, Lyn. My Favorite Flower Is the Daisy... & other Silly Poems. Mortensen, Lyn, illus. 2005. (Illus.). 48p. (J). per. *(978-0-9767570-0-9(1))* Whitegate Bks.

Morton, Jim. Let's Make Memories ... 2004. 100p. per. 9.00 net. *(978-0-9763253-0-7(6),* 004) Windchimes Publishing.

Moses, Brian. Brian Moses' School Report: Very Funny Poems about School! unabr. ed. 2014. (ENG., Illus.). 96p. (J). pap. 7.99 *(978-1-4472-5464-5(3))* Pan Macmillan GBR. Dist: Independent Pubs. Group.

—Lost Magic: The Very Best of Brian Moses. 2016. (ENG.). 208p. (J). (gr. 4-7). 19.99 ***(978-1-5098-3874-5(0))*** Pan Macmillan GBR. Dist: Independent Pubs. Group.

—Lost Magic: the Very Best of Brian Moses. 2017. (ENG., Illus.). 208p. (J). (gr. 4-7). 9.99 ***(978-1-5098-3876-9(7))*** Pan Macmillan GBR. Dist: Independent Pubs. Group.

Moses, Brian, ed. Performance Poems. Pascoe, Jed, illus. 2013. (ENG.). 80p. pap. 16.50 *(978-1-85741-087-7(4))* Southgate Pubs. GBR. Dist: Parkwest Pubns., Inc.

Moses, Brian & Stevens, Roger. Olympic Poems - 100% Unofficial!, 1. unabr. ed. 2012. (ENG., Illus.). 96p. (J). (gr. 1-4). pap. 7.99 *(978-1-4472-0552-4(9))* Pan Macmillan GBR. Dist: Independent Pubs. Group.

—1066 & Before That - History Poems. 2016. (ENG., Illus.). 112p. (J). (gr. 2-4). pap. 10.99 *(978-1-4472-8394-2(5))* Pan Macmillan GBR. Dist: Independent Pubs. Group.

Moses, Will. Will Moses' Mother Goose. Moses, Will, illus. 2003. (ENG., Illus.). 64p. (J). (gr. -1-2). 18.99 *(978-0-399-23744-7(5),* Philomel Bks.) Penguin Young Readers Group.

Mozz. In Search of the Holey Whale: The Top Secret Riddles & Left-Handed Scribbles of Mozz. Mozz, illus. 2008. (Illus.). 176p. (J). (gr. 3-6). lib. bdg. 17.95 *(978-0-9726130-3-3(X))* Goofy Guru Publishing.

Muldrow, Diane. We Planted a Tree. Staake, Bob, illus. 2016. (ENG.). 40p. (J). (gr. -1-2). 7.99 *(978-0-553-53903-5(5),* Dragonfly Bks.) Random Hse. Children's Bks.

Munro, David. Lyrical Poetry for Boys & Girls 1891. 2006. 156p. per. *(978-1-4067-1339-8(2),* Hesperides Pr.) Read Bks.

Murdock Elementary Student Council. Gallop to Glory: Mustangs Write Like the Wind: Volume 2. 2008. pap. 14.95 *(978-0-7414-4779-1(7))* Infinity Publishing.

Murphy, Charles R. The Waking Hour: A Collection of Illustrated Verse. 2010. 32p. 24.95 *(978-0-9845798-0-8(X))* True North Studio.

Murray, Barbara. The Seasons of Life. Corbin, Marissa, illus. 2013. 36p. 19.95 *(978-0-9885370-8-8(7))* RIVERRUN BOOKSTORE INC.

Murray, P. D. Cat & Caboodle. 2008. 82p. pap. 9.50 *(978-0-615-20153-5(9))* Oh My Stars Publishing.

Musmanno, Albert J. Little Poems about Big Ideas in Science. 2012. 198p. pap. 23.95 *(978-1-4759-3988-0(4))* iUniverse, Inc.

Mussari, Mark. Poetry. 2011. (Craft of Writing Ser.). 96p. (gr. 6). 34.21 *(978-1-60870-500-9(5))* Marshall Cavendish Corp.

My Voice Matters. 2004. (J). 5.00 *(978-0-9664455-6-5(2))* Rhode Island State Council, International Reading Assn.

Myers, Walter Dean. Blues Journey. Myers, Christopher A. & Myers, Christopher, illus. 2007. (ENG.). 48p. (J). (gr. -1-3). pap. 8.95 *(978-0-8234-2079-7(5))* Holiday Hse., Inc.

Myers, Walter Dean & Myers, Christopher. Jazz. Myers, Christopher, illus. 2008. (ENG., Illus.). 48p. (J). pap. 12.95 *(978-0-8234-2173-2(2))* Holiday Hse., Inc.

Myrddin ap Dafydd. Briwsion Yn y Clustiau: Cyfrol O Farddoniaeth I Blant. 2005. (WEL., Illus.). 76p. pap. *(978-0-86381-300-9(3))* Gwasg Carreg Gwalch.

—Mul Bach Ar Gefn Ei Geffyl: Cerddi Am Greaduriaid. 2005. (WEL., Illus.). 76p. pap. *(978-0-86381-314-6(3))* Gwasg Carreg Gwalch.

Myrddin ap Dafydd & Morris, Siôn. Armadilo Ar Fy Mhen. 2005. (WEL., Illus.). 64p. pap. *(978-0-86381-625-3(8))* Gwasg Carreg Gwalch.

—Chwarae Plant. 2005. (WEL., Illus.). 68p. pap. *(978-0-86381-431-0(X))* Gwasg Carreg Gwalch.

—Sach Gysgu Yn Llawn O Greision. 2005. (WEL., Illus.). 80p. pap. *(978-0-86381-626-0(6))* Gwasg Carreg Gwalch.

—Tabledi-Gwneud-'Chi-Wenu: Dôs Arbennig O Farddoniaeth Loerig Am Salwch AC Afiechydon. 2005. (WEL., Illus.). 72p. pap. *(978-0-86381-678-9(9))* Gwasg Carreg Gwalch.

Myrddin ap Dafydd, et al. Caneuon y Coridorau: Barddoniaeth Ar Gyfer Pobl Ifanc. 2005. (WEL., Illus.). 84p. pap. *(978-0-86381-970-4(2))* Gwasg Carreg Gwalch.

Nathan, Jeff. Calling All Animals: The First Book of PunOETRY. Ball, Liz, illus. 2003. 96p. per. 9.95 *(978-0-9702730-1-7(0))* Chucklebks. Publishing.

Neal, Kathleen A. The Sun Begins Its Daily Flight. 2013. 32p. pap. 24.95 *(978-1-63004-158-8(0))* America Star Bks.

Nelson, Alexis Andria. Sing Mommie Sing: Lullabies from the Heart. 2010. 36p. 21.99 *(978-1-4490-9405-8(8))* AuthorHouse.

Nelson, Marilyn. The Freedom Business: Including a Narrative of the Life & Adventures of Venture, a Native of Africa. Dancy, Deborah & Muirhead, Deborah, illus. 2008. (ENG.). 72p. (YA). (gr. 6-18). 18.95 *(978-1-932425-57-4(8),* Wordsong) Boyds Mills Pr.

—How I Discovered Poetry. Hooper, Hadley, illus. 2014. (ENG.). 112p. (YA). (gr. 7). 17.99 *(978-0-8037-3304-6(6),* Dial Bks) Penguin Young Readers Group.

Nesbitt, Ken. When the Teacher Isn't Looking: And Other Funny School Poems. Gordon, Mike, illus. 2010. (Giggle Poetry Ser.). (ENG.). 80p. (J). (gr. 1-6). per. 8.95 *(978-0-684-03128-6(0))* Meadowbrook Pr.

Nesbitt, Kenn. Kiss, Kiss Good Night. Elliott, Rebecca, illus. 2013. (ENG.). 12p. (J). (— 1). bds. 8.99 *(978-0-545-47957-8(6),* Cartwheel Bks.) Scholastic, Inc.

—One Minute till Bedtime: 60-Second Poems to Send You off to Sleep. Niemann, Christoph, illus. 2016. (ENG.). 176p. (J). (gr. -1-3). 19.99 *(978-0-316-34121-9(5))* Little, Brown Bks. for Young Readers.

—Revenge of the Lunch Ladies: The Hilarious Book of School Poetry. Gordon, Mike & Gordon, Carl, illus. 2007. 80p. *(978-0-88166-527-7(4))* Meadowbrook Pr.

—When the Teacher Isn't Looking: And Other Funny School Poems. Gordon, Mike, illus. 2005. 80p. (J). *(978-0-88166-489-8(8))* Meadowbrook Pr.

New, William. Dream Helmet. Bevis, Vivian, illus. 2005. (ENG.). 32p. (J). 11.95 *(978-1-55380-021-7(4))* Ronsdale Pr. CAN. Dist: Literary Pr. Group of Canada.

—Llamas in the Laundry. Bevis, Vivian, illus. 2005. (ENG.). 32p. (J). 12.95 *(978-0-921870-97-5(3))* Ronsdale Pr. CAN. Dist: Literary Pr. Group of Canada.

New, William H. The Year I Was Grounded, 1 vol. 2009. (ENG., Illus.). 64p. (J). (gr. 5-8). pap. 12.95 *(978-1-896580-35-7(1))* Tradewind Bks. CAN. Dist: Orca Bk. Pubs. USA.

Newbold, Dale L. Funny Facts & Fun Facts! 2006. 20.00 *(978-0-8059-9019-5(4))* Dorrance Publishing Co., Inc.

Newell, Peter. The Slant Book. 2007. (Illus.). 52p. per. *(978-1-4065-3053-7(0))* Dodo Pr.

Nicholls, Judith. The Sun in Me: Poems about the Planet. Krommes, Beth, illus. 2008. (ENG.). 40p. (J). (gr. -1). 12.99 *(978-1-84686-161-1(6))* Barefoot Bks., Inc.

Nicholls, Judith, ed. The Sun in Me: Poems about the Planet. Krommes, Beth, illus. 2003. 40p. (J). pap. 16.99 *(978-1-84148-058-9(4))* Barefoot Bks., Inc.

Nicolson, Paula. The Love Book Healing Poems for Broken Hearts. (Illus.). 40p. (J). 9.95 *(978-1-880976-18-0(8))* Brookshire Pubns., Inc.

Nield, Sue. Raps & Rhymes about Primary School Times: A Children's Poetry Anthology. 2012. 112p. (gr. 4-6). pap. 14.95 *(978-1-4678-8893-6(1))* AuthorHouse.

—Raps & Rhymes about Tudor Times: A Poetic Interpretation of History. 2012. (Illus.). 56p. pap. 11.95 *(978-1-4678-8001-5(9))* AuthorHouse.

Nino, Jairo Anibal. Los Papeles de Miguela. Rincon, Fernando, illus. 2003. (Literatura Juvenil (Panamericana Editorial) Ser.). (SPA.). 78p. (J). (gr. -1-7). pap. *(978-958-30-0336-3(0),* PV30462) Centro de Informacion y Desarrollo de la Comunicacion y la Literatura MEX. Dist: Lectorum Pubns., Inc.

Niqo, Jairo Anmbal. Preguntario. Gonzalez, Henry, illus. 2007. (Literatura Juvenil (Panamericana Editorial) Ser.). (SPA.). 188p. (gr. 5-7). pap. 18.99 *(978-958-30-0497-1(9),* PV30461) Panamericana Editorial COL. Dist: Lectorum Pubns., Inc.

Nishat-Botero, Hannah. Hannah Banana's Book of Poems. 2012. (Illus.). 48p. pap. 18.31 *(978-1-4567-9693-8(3))* AuthorHouse.

Nnamoko, Johanan U. The Greatest Mom, 1 vol. 2009. 25p. pap. 24.95 *(978-1-61546-678-8(9))* PublishAmerica, Inc.

Noda, Takayo. Dear World. 2005. (ENG., Illus.). 32p. (J). (gr. k-3). reprint ed. pap. 6.99 *(978-0-14-240280-1(X),* Puffin Books) Penguin Young Readers Group.

November, Deena & Rosenberg, Liz, eds. I Just Hope It's Lethal: Poems of Sadness, Madness, & Joy. 2005. (ENG.). 208p. (YA). (gr. 7-12). pap. 13.95 *(978-0-618-56452-1(7))* Houghton Mifflin Harcourt Publishing Co.

Noyes, Alfred. The Highwayman. Kimber, Murray, illus. 2009. (Visions in Poetry Ser.). (ENG.). 48p. (J). (gr. 5-9). 9.95 *(978-1-55453-384-8(8))* Kids Can Pr., Ltd. CAN. Dist: Hachette Bk. Group.

—The Highwayman. Keeping, Charles, illus. 2015. (ENG.). 32p. pap. 12.95 *(978-0-19-279442-0(6))* Oxford Univ. Pr., Inc.

—The Highwayman. Riswold, Gilbert, illus. 2003. (ENG.). 31p. (gr. 6-6). cd-rom 147.47 net. *(978-0-13-036517-0(3),* Prentice Hall) Pearson Schl.

Nuno, Fran & Nuño, Fran. Poebromario. 2013. (SPA.). 54p. (J). pap. 5.99 *(978-84-15207-62-7(X))* Almadraba Infantil y Juvenil ESP. Dist: Lectorum Pubns., Inc.

Nuttall, Neil & Hawkins, Andy, eds. Second Thoughts. Fell, Jenny, illus. 2004. (ENG.). 64p. pap. 14.95 *(978-1-84323-046-5(1))* Beekman Bks., Inc.

Nye, Naomi Shihab. Honeybee: Poems & Short Prose. 2008. (ENG.). 176p. (J). (gr. 5-9). 16.99 *(978-0-06-085390-7(5),* Greenwillow Bks.) HarperCollins Pubs.

—Time You Let Me In: 25 Poets under 25. 2010. 256p. (YA). (gr. 8-18). (ENG.). 17.99 *(978-0-06-189637-8(3));* lib. bdg. 17.89 *(978-0-06-189638-5(1))* HarperCollins Pubs. (Greenwillow Bks.).

—19 Varieties of Gazelle: Poems of the Middle East. 2005. (ENG.). 160p. (YA). (gr. 5). reprint ed. pap. 8.99 *(978-0-06-050404-5(8),* Greenwillow Bks.) HarperCollins Pubs.

Ode, Eric. Sea Star Wishes: Poems from the Coast. Brooks, Erik, illus. 2013. (ENG.). 32p. (J). (gr. -1-3). 16.99 *(978-1-57061-790-4(2),* Little Bigfoot) Sasquatch Bks.

—Tall Tales of the Wild West: A Humorous Collection of Cowboy Poems & Songs. Crane, Ben, illus. 2007. 32p. *(978-0-88166-524-6(X))* Meadowbrook Pr.

—When You're a Pirate Dog & Other Pirate Poems, 1 vol. Harris, Jim, illus. 2012. (ENG.). 40p. (J). (gr. k-3). 17.99 *(978-1-4556-1493-6(9))* Pelican Publishing Co., Inc.

Oelschlager, Vanita. Ivan's Great Fall: Poetry for Summer & Autumn from Great Poets & Writers of the Past. Blackwood, Kristin, illus. 2009. (ENG.). 44p. (J). (gr. -1-3). 15.95 *(978-0-9819714-1-4(5));* pap. 8.95 *(978-0-9819714-2-1(3))* VanitaBooks.

Of Love Expressed. 2005. per. 8.50 *(978-0-9770594-2-3(1))* Grimes, Richard.

Oliver, Lin. Little Poems for Tiny Ears. dePaola, Tomie, illus. 2014. (ENG.). 32p. (J). (gr. -1 — 1). 16.99 *(978-0-399-16605-1(X),* Nancy Paulsen Books) Penguin Young Readers Group.

—Steppin' Out: Jaunty Rhymes for Playful Times. dePaola, Tomie, illus. 2017. (ENG.). 32p. (J). (-k). 17.99 *(978-0-399-17434-6(6),* Nancy Paulsen Books) Penguin Young Readers Group.

Olowoyeye, Ola. Rhythm & Motion. 2010. 28p. pap. 12.49 *(978-1-4520-2584-1(3))* AuthorHouse.

The Open Door. 2004. per. *(978-0-9747704-0-6(X))* Writers in the Schools (WITS).

Opie, Ian, ed. My Very First Mother Goose. Wells, Rosemary, illus. 2004. 107p. (J). reprint ed. 17.00 *(978-0-7567-8384-6(4))* DIANE Publishing Co.

Orgill, Roxane. Jazz Day: The Making of a Famous Photograph. Vallejo, Francis, illus. 2016. (ENG.). 66p. (J). (gr. 3-7). 18.99 *(978-0-7636-6954-6(7))* Candlewick Pr.

Orme, Nicholas. Fleas, Flies, & Friars: Children's Poetry from the Middle Ages. 2012. (ENG., Illus.). 116p. 52.50 *(978-0-8014-5102-7(7),* 80140100993970); pap. 15.95 *(978-0-8014-7775-1(1),* 80140100993970) Cornell Univ. Pr.

Ortberg, John. Your Magnificent Chooser. Dunn, Robert, illus. 2017. (ENG.). 40p. (J). 14.99 *(978-1-4964-1742-8(9),* Tyndale Kids) Tyndale Hse. Pubs.

Ortegon, Sharon A. You. 2013. 40p. pap. 19.57 *(978-1-4669-9981-7(0))* Trafford Publishing.

Ostashevsky, Eugene. The Fire Horse: Children's Poems by Vladimir Mayakovsky, Osip Mandelstam & Daniil Kharms. 2017. (ENG.). 48p. (J). (gr. 1-3). 16.95 *(978-1-68137-092-7(1),* NYR Children's Collection) New York Review of Bks., Inc., The.

Osundare, Niyi. Early Birds: Poems for Junior Secondary Schools. 2004. (Illus.). 100p. pap. *(978-978-029-530-1(5))* Spectrum Bks., Ltd. NGA. Dist: Michigan State Univ. Pr.

Pace, Yolantha. Wing-Plucked Butterfly: A Survivor Speaks One Woman's War on Hate Crimes Against Women & Children. 2004. 146p. per. 15.00 *(978-0-9747017-8-3(5))* Neshee Pubn.

Pacheva, Svetla & Cholakova, Maiia. Kushtichka S Gatanki. 2008. (Illus.). 17p. *(978-954-443-730-5(4))* Balgarski pisatel, Izdatelstvo.

Page, P. K. A Brazilian Alphabet for the Younger Reader. 2005. (ENG., Illus.). 64p. (J). (gr. -1-1). pap. 16.95 *(978-0-88984-265-6(5))* Porcupine's Quill, Inc. CAN. Dist: Univ. of Toronto Pr.

—Jake, the Baker, Makes a Cake. Campbell, Ruth, illus. 2008. (ENG.). 40p. pap. 19.95 *(978-0-88982-245-0(X))* Oolichan Bks. CAN. Dist: Univ. of Toronto Pr.

Pahn, Latosha. Come go on a Read along Ride with Me: Read along Ride. 2008. 68p. pap. 9.95 *(978-1-4184-4896-7(6))* AuthorHouse.

Paolilli, Paul & Brewer, Dan. Silver Seeds. Fancher, Lou & Johnson, Steve, illus. 2003. (ENG.). 32p. (J). (gr. k-4). pap. 6.99 *(978-0-14-250010-1(0),* Puffin Books) Penguin Young Readers Group.

Park, Linda Sue. Tap Dancing on the Roof: Sijo (Poems) Banyai, Istvan, illus. (ENG.). 48p. (J). (gr. -1-3). 2015. 6.99 *(978-0-544-55551-8(1),* HMH Books For Young Readers) 2007. 16.00 *(978-0-618-23483-7(7))* Houghton Mifflin Harcourt Publishing Co.

Parower, Alec. So I Wrote It Down. 2008. 84p. pap. 11.95 *(978-0-595-51259-1(3))* iUniverse, Inc.

Parveen, Tahmina. Realistic Rhymes. 2004. 92p. pap. *(978-1-84401-287-9(5))* Athena Pr.

Paschen, Elise. Poetry Speaks to Children. Collins, Billy et al, eds. Love, Judy et al, illus. 2005. (Poetry Speaks Experience Ser.: 0). (ENG.). 112p. (gr. k-3). 19.95 *(978-1-4022-0329-9(2),* Sourcebooks MediaFusion) Sourcebooks, Inc.

Paschen, Elise & Raccah, Dominique. Poetry Speaks Who I Am: Poems of Discovery, Inspiration, Independence, & Everything Else. 2010. (Poetry Speaks Experience Ser.: 0). (ENG.). 176p. (J). (gr. 7-12). 19.99 *(978-1-4022-1074-7(4),* Sourcebooks Jabberwocky) Sourcebooks, Inc.

Patten, Brian & Assorted Staff. The Puffin Book of Utterly Brilliant Poetry. Patten, Brian, ed. (ENG., Illus.). 144p. (J). pap. 15.00 *(978-0-14-038421-5(9))* Penguin Bks., Ltd. GBR. Dist: Trafalgar Square Publishing.

Paul, Julia Marian. Song of the Teapot: Poems about Little Babies, Little Jerry, Little Susie, & Other Things. 2007. (ENG.). 60p. per. 16.95 *(978-1-4241-4299-6(7))* PublishAmerica, Inc.

Paz Lozano, Octavio. La Rama. Kitora, Tetsuo, illus. 2005.Tr. of Branch. (SPA.). (J). (gr. k-2). pap. 10.95 *(978-968-494-046-8(7))* Centro de Informacion y Desarrollo de la Comunicacion y la Literatura MEX. Dist: Iaconi, Mariuccia Bk. Imports.

Pearl, Beverly. Little Cat Snowshoes. 2010. 56p. pap. 22.30 *(978-0-557-24481-2(1))* Lulu Pr., Inc.

Pearson, Debora. Leo's Tree. Hilb, Nora, illus. 2004. (ENG.). 24p. (J). (gr. -1-1). 2nd ed. 19.95 *(978-1-55037-845-0(7),* 9781550378450) 5th ed. pap. 5.95 *(978-1-55037-844-3(9),* 9781550378443) Annick Pr., Ltd. CAN. Dist: Publishers Group West (PGW).

Pearson, Susan. Grimericks, 0 vols. Grimly, Gris, illus. 2005. (ENG.). 32p. (J). (gr. 1-4). pap. 9.99 *(978-0-7614-5444-1(6),* 9780761454441, Amazon Children's Publishing) Amazon Publishing.

Pearson, Susan & Pearson. Who Swallowed Harold? And Other Poems about Pets, 1 vol. Slonim, David, illus. 2005. (ENG.). 32p. (J). (gr. k-4). 16.95 *(978-0-7614-5193-8(5))* Marshall Cavendish Corp.

Pearson, Yvonne. Concrete Poems. Petelinsek, Kathleen, illus. 2015. (Poetry Party Ser.). (ENG.). 24p. (J). (gr. 2-5). 27.07 *(978-1-63143-694-9(5),* 208529) Child's World, Inc., The.

—Narrative Poems. Petelinsek, Kathleen, illus. 2015. (Poetry Party Ser.). (ENG.). 24p. (J). (gr. 2-5). 27.07 *(978-1-63143-699-4(6),* 208534) Child's World, Inc., The.

—Prose Poems. Petelinsek, Kathleen, illus. 2015. (Poetry Party Ser.). (ENG.). 24p. (J). (gr. 2-5). 27.07 *(978-1-63143-697-0(X),* 208530) Child's World, Inc., The.

Pedigo, Kim Tran. Having Fun with Kandai the Elephant. Pedigo, Kim Tran, illus. 2012. (Illus.). 36p. pap. 12.95 *(978-1-61244-105-4(X))* Halo Publishing International.

Perkins, Jill E. Cherubs Chatter: A Collection of Original Songs & Poems. 2004. (Illus.). 88p. (J). per. 7.95 *(978-0-9749862-2-7(4))* Theragogy.com.

Perkins, Useni Eugene. The Black Arts Movement. 2009. (Poetry from the Masters Ser.). 88p. (YA). (gr. 4-18). pap. 9.95 *(978-1-933491-13-4(2))* Just Us Bks., Inc.

Perry, Andrea. The Snack Smasher: And Other Reasons Why It's Not My Fault. Snow, Alan, illus. 2007. (ENG.). 40p. (J). (gr. -1-3). 17.99 *(978-0-689-85469-9(2),* Atheneum Bks. for Young Readers) Simon & Schuster Children's Publishing.

Perry, Robert. My Vancouver Sketchbook. Guzek, Greta, illus. unabr. ed. 2010. (ENG.). 32p. (J). pap. 9.95 *(978-0-88971-248-5(4))* Nightwood Editions CAN. Dist: Midpoint Trade Bks., Inc.

Peters, Andrew Fusek. Mad, Bad & Dangerously Haddock. 2006. (ENG., Illus.). 96p. (J). (gr. 2-7). pap. 8.99 *(978-0-7459-6021-0(9))* Lion Hudson PLC GBR. Dist: Independent Pubs. Group.

Peters, Lisa Westberg. Volcano Wakes Up! 2016. (J). lib. bdg. 19.65 *(978-0-606-38430-8(8))* Turtleback Bks.

Peters, Lisa Westberg & Peters. Earthshake: Poems from the Ground Up. Felstead, Cathie, illus. 2003. (ENG.). 32p. (J). (gr. k-5). 17.99 *(978-0-06-029265-2(2),* Greenwillow Bks.) HarperCollins Pubs.

Petway, Jessie. A Child's Book of Poetry. 2007. per. 12.00 *(978-0-9791154-5-5(0),* MSP) Main St Publishing, Inc.

Phelps Williams, Janice, illus. Still Her Spirit Sings: One Dog's Love, Lessons, Life & Legacy. 2010. 32p. (J). (gr. k-2). 16.95 *(978-0-9760220-1-5(X))* Kidzpoetz Publishing.

Phethean, Ellen. Wall. 2014. (ENG.). 152p. pap. 18.00 *(978-0-9551061-6-3(8))* Smokestack Bks. GBR. Dist: Dufour Editions, Inc.

Phillips, Dee. Samurai, 1 vol., Bk. 7. 2015. (Yesterday's Voices Ser.). (ENG.). 48p. (YA). (gr. 9-12). pap. 8.95 *(978-1-62250-909-6(9))* Saddleback Educational Publishing, Inc.

Phinn, Gervase. What I Like! Poems for the Very Young. Eccles, Jane, illus. 2004. (Poetry Ser.). (ENG.). 32p. (J). (gr. 2-3). pap. *(978-1-904550-12-9(6))* Child's Play International Ltd.

Pickard, Ben & Pickard, Carolyn. A Fish! Don't You Wish. 2003. 265p. 29.95 *(978-0-595-65747-6(8));* pap. 19.95 *(978-0-595-28229-6(6))* iUniverse, Inc.

Pierre, Manes. Spinning the Globe. 2008. 132p. 23.95 *(978-0-595-49576-4(1));* pap. 13.95 *(978-0-595-49925-0(2))* iUniverse, Inc.

Piper, Sophie. My Guardian Angel. Rescek, Sanja, illus. 2014. (ENG.). 48p. (J). (gr. -1-k). 9.99 *(978-0-7459-6397-6(8))* Lion Hudson PLC GBR. Dist: Independent Pubs. Group.

Pirie, Mark. Gallery: A Selection. 2003. (Modern Poets Ser.). (ENG.). 116p. pap. *(978-1-876857-24-0(2))* Salt Publishing.

Pittman, Rickey. Scottish Alphabet, 1 vol. McLennan, Connie, illus. 2008. (ENG.). 32p. (J). (gr. 1-3). 16.99 *(978-1-58980-596-5(8))* Pelican Publishing Co., Inc.

Plaza, José María & María, Plaza José. Alibaru: La Ronda de las Estaciones. (SPA.). 120p. *(978-84-392-8119-1(6))* Gaviota Ediciones ESP. Dist: Lectorum Pubns., Inc.

—Pajarulí: Poemas para Seguir Andando. Villamuza, Noemi, illus. (SPA.). (J). *(978-84-392-8120-7(X),* EV0782) Gaviota Ediciones ESP. Dist: Lectorum Pubns., Inc.

—Tungaira: Miss Primeras Poesias. Lucini, Carmen, illus. (SPA.). 96p. (J). 8.99 *(978-84-392-8115-3(3),* EV4870) Gaviota Ediciones ESP. Dist: Lectorum Pubns., Inc.

Plourd, Brenden. My New Brother. 2011. 20p. pap. 24.95 *(978-1-4489-6811-4(9))* America Star Bks.

Pockell, Leslie, ed. 100 Great Poems for Boys. 2011. (ENG.). 256p. pap., pap. 14.00 *(978-0-446-56382-6(X))* Grand Central Publishing.

Poe, Edgar Allen. The Raven: Includes Sound! 2011. (ENG.). 48p. pap. 8.95 *(978-0-7624-4282-9(4))* Running Pr. Bk. Pubs.

Poemas y Cantares de America y el Mundo. (SPA.). (YA). (gr. 5-8). pap. *(978-956-13-1606-5(4),* AB2725) Bello, Andres CHL. Dist: Lectorum Pubns., Inc.

Poems & Rhymes (Gr. 1-2) 2003. (J). *(978-1-58232-070-0(5))* ECS Learning Systems, Inc.

Poems Just for Me. 2017. (Poems Just for Me Ser.). 32p. (gr. 7-8). 109.00 ***(978-1-4994-8273-7(6));*** pap. 40.00 ***(978-1-4994-8407-6(0))*** Rosen Publishing Group, Inc., The. (Windmill Bks.).

Poesia Una Al Dia. (SPA.). 32p. (J). (gr. 3-5). 15.95 *(978-84-204-4334-8(4))* Santillana USA Publishing Co., Inc.

Poetry & Rhymes. Date not set. 256p. (J). 5.98 *(978-0-7525-7690-9(9))* Parragon, Inc.

Poetry Power ESL: Complete Set. 2003. (SPA., Illus.). 225.50 *(978-0-8136-0715-3(9))* Modern Curriculum Pr.

Poetry Tapes & Small Books. (Dias y Dias de Poesia Ser.). (SPA.). (gr. -1-6). 182.43 *(978-1-56334-281-3(2))* CENGAGE Learning.

Poetry Works! Complete Set. 2003. (SPA., Illus.). (J). (gr. -1-k). 183.95 *(978-0-8136-0719-1(1))* Modern Curriculum Pr.

Polisar, Barry Louis. Something Fishy. Clark, David, illus. 2013. (Rainbow Morning Music Picture Bks.). (ENG.). 32p. (J). (gr. 2-4). 14.95 *(978-0-938663-53-9(4))* Rainbow Morning Music Alternatives.

Polk, James G. Gift of Love, Vol. 2. Rudkin, Shawn, ed. Rudkin, Tracy, illus. (YA). *(978-0-9727753-1-1(5))* New Wave Bks. & CD.

Pomerantz, Charlotte. Thunderboom! Poems for Everyone. Shepperson, Rob, illus. 2012. (ENG.). 48p. (J). (gr. 2-5). pap. 7.95 *(978-1-59078-909-4(1),* Wordsong) Boyds Mills Pr.

Popper, Garry. Big World. Johnson, Andi, illus. 2004. 36p. (gr. -1-7). 4.00 *(978-1-84161-052-8(6))* Ravette Publishing, Ltd. GBR. Dist: Parkwest Pubns., Inc.

Pottle, Robert. I'm Allergic to School: Funny Poems & Songs about School. Gordon, Mike & Gordon, Carl, illus. 2007. 32p. *(978-0-88166-522-2(3))* Meadowbrook Pr.

—Maine: A Wicked Good Book of Verse: the Way Wildlife Should Be. Hardwick, Holly, illus. 2005. 64p. (J). per. 8.95 *(978-0-9709569-3-4(2))* Blue Lobster Pr.

—Moxie Day the Prankster: Another Laugh & Learn Book of Poetry. Jonathan Siruno, illus. 2004. 64p. (J). per. 8.95 *(978-0-9709569-2-7(4)*, MDTP) Blue Lobster Pr.

—Poems with Moxie: Funny Poems & Funny Songs. 2008. (Illus.). 96p. (J). per. 9.95 *(978-0-9709569-4-1(0))* Blue Lobster Pr.

Potts, William. Under My Pillow. 2010. 38p. pap. 17.50 *(978-0-557-51217-1(4))* Lulu Pr., Inc.

Powell, Amy. Me. 2006. (Illus.). 21p. (J). (gr. -1-3). per. 15.00 *(978-0-9773608-3-3(0))* Shiny Red Ball Publishing.

Powers, Lillian. Girl Child: (The Transition - in Poetic Form) 2004. 64p. (YA). per. 9.95 *(978-0-9761523-2-3(0))* Mama Incense Publishing.

Prelutsky, Jack. Awful Ogre Running Wild. Zelinsky, Paul O., illus. 2008. 40p. (J). (gr. -1-3). lib. bdg. 18.89 *(978-0-06-623867-8(6)*, Greenwillow Bks.) HarperCollins Pubs.

—Behold the Bold Umbrellaphant: And Other Poems. Berger, Carin, illus. 2006. (ENG.). 40p. (J). (gr. -1-4). 16.99 *(978-0-06-054317-4(5)*, Greenwillow Bks.) HarperCollins Pubs.

—It's Raining Pigs & Noodles. Stevenson, James, illus. 2012. (ENG.). 160p. (J). (gr. k-5). reprint ed. pap. 9.99 *(978-0-06-076390-9(6)*, Greenwillow Bks.) HarperCollins Pubs.

—It's Snowing! It's Snowing! Winter Poems. Abolafia, Yossi, illus. 2006. (I Can Read Bks.). 48p. (J). (gr. -1-3). lib. bdg. 16.89 *(978-0-06-053716-6(7))* HarperCollins Pubs.

—It's Thanksgiving! Hafner, Marylin, illus. 2008. (I Can Read Level 3 Ser.). (ENG.). 48p. (J). (gr. k-3). pap. 3.99 *(978-0-06-053711-1(6))* HarperCollins Pubs.

—It's Valentine's Day! Hafner, Marylin, illus. 2013. (I Can Read Level 3 Ser.). (ENG.). 48p. (J). (gr. -1-3). pap. 3.99 *(978-0-06-053714-2(0)*, Greenwillow Bks.) HarperCollins Pubs.

—Me I Am! Davenier, Christine, illus. 2007. (ENG.). 32p. (J). (gr. -1-1). 18.99 *(978-0-374-34902-8(9)*, 9780374349028, Farrar, Straus & Giroux (BYR)) Farrar, Straus & Giroux.

—My Dog May Be a Genius. Stevenson, James, illus. 2008. (ENG.). 160p. (J). (gr. k-5). 18.99 *(978-0-06-623862-3(5)*, Greenwillow Bks.) HarperCollins Pubs.

—My Parents Think I'm Sleeping. Abolafia, Yossi, illus. (I Can Read Level 3 Ser.). 48p. (J). (gr. k-3). 2008. (ENG.). pap. 3.99 *(978-0-06-053722-7(1))* 2007. lib. bdg. 16.89 *(978-0-06-053721-0(3))* HarperCollins Pubs.

—Scranimals. Sís, Peter, illus. 2006. (ENG.). 48p. (J). (gr. -1-3). reprint ed. pap. 6.99 *(978-0-06-075368-9(4)*, Greenwillow Bks.) HarperCollins Pubs.

—Something Big Has Been Here. Stevenson, James, illus. 2010. (ENG.). 160p. (J). (gr. k-5). pap. 9.99 *(978-0-06-185775-1(0)*, Greenwillow Bks.) HarperCollins Pubs.

—Stardines Swim High Across the Sky: And Other Poems. Berger, Carin, illus. 2013. 40p. (J). (gr. -1-3). (ENG.). 17.99 *(978-0-06-201464-1(1))*; lib. bdg. 18.89 *(978-0-06-201465-8(X))* HarperCollins Pubs. (Greenwillow Bks.).

—There's No Place Like School. Manning, Jane, illus. 2010. (ENG.). 32p. (J). (gr. k-5). 16.99 *(978-0-06-082338-2(0)*, Greenwillow Bks.) HarperCollins Pubs.

—There's No Place Like School: Classroom Poems. Manning, Jane, illus. 2010. 32p. (J). (gr. k-5). lib. bdg. 17.89 *(978-0-06-082339-9(9)*, Greenwillow Bks.) HarperCollins Pubs.

—What a Day It Was at School! Cushman, Doug, illus. 2009. (ENG.). 40p. (J). (gr. k-5). pap. 6.99 *(978-0-06-082337-5(2)*, Greenwillow Bks.) HarperCollins Pubs.

Prendergast, R. L. Baby, Please Go to Sleep. Maciborski, Charmaine, illus. 2013. 16p. (J). pap. *(978-0-9784548-4-5(7))* Dekko Publishing.

Prescott, Brian. Chloe Saves Christmas. 2013. 24p. pap. *(978-1-909192-45-4(7))* Beaten Track Publishing.

—Chloe the Campervan Goes on Holiday. 2013. 28p. pap. *(978-1-909192-40-9(6))* Beaten Track Publishing.

Price, Aleksandra. What Do You See? Poems for Young Children. 2008. 16p. pap. 12.95 *(978-1-59858-811-8(7))* Dog Ear Publishing, LLC.

Price, Erika. The Turnaround: Book of Poetry, 2004. (YA). per. 7.00 *(978-0-9753028-0-4(9))* Turnaround Bk. Publishing Corp.

Price, Erika, contrib. by. The Turnaround: Book of Poetry. 2004. (YA). per. 7.00 *(978-0-9753028-1-1(7))*; per. 7.00 *(978-0-9753028-2-8(5))* Turnaround Bk. Publishing Corp.

Price, Margaret Evans, illus. & as told by. Mother Goose: Book of Rhymes. Price, Margaret Evans, as told by. 2007. (Shape Bks.). (ENG.). 16p. (J). (gr. 4-7). pap. 9.95 *(978-1-59583-134-7(7)*, 9781595831347, Green Tiger Pr.) Laughing Elephant.

Priest, Robert. Rosa Rose. Krygsman, Joan, illus. 2013. (ENG.). 56p. pap. 10.00 *(978-1-894987-73-8(X))* Wolsak & Wynn Pubs., Ltd. CAN. Dist: Independent Pubs. Group.

Pritchard, Mary. Mrs P's Poems. Gasking, Terry, ed. 2013. 52p. pap. *(978-1-907953-58-3(2))* TwigBooks.

Professor Bubbledunk. Stories from the Mugglewhuft. 2013. 36p. pap. 15.50 *(978-1-4669-6044-2(2))* Trafford Publishing.

Proudfit, Benjamin. Writing Poems. 2014. (Write Right! Ser.). 24p. (J). (gr. 2-5). 22.60 *(978-1-4824-1124-9(5))* Stevens, Gareth Publishing LLLP.

Pruitt, Christine Lee. I'm Alright Day & Night! 2012. 16p. pap. 12.68 *(978-1-4669-6065-7(5))* Trafford Publishing.

Pujari, M. Nathalie. 20 Umbrellas. Sananmuang, Chatree, illus. 2007. (J). *(978-0-9715865-0-5(0))* Abuzz Bks.

Pyle, Howard. The Wonder Clock Or, Four & Twenty Marvelous Tales. 2012. (Dover Children's Classics Ser.). (ENG., Illus.). 319p. (J). (gr. 3-8). per. 12.95 *(978-0-486-21446-7(X))* Dover Pubns., Inc.

Pynn, Susan. The Colours of My Home: A Portrait of Newfoundland & Labrador, 1 vol. Keating, Nancy, illus. 2007. (ENG.). 32p. (J). (gr. -1-2). pap. 8.95 *(978-1-897174-06-7(3))* Creative Bk. Publishing CAN. Dist: Orca Bk. Pubs. USA.

—A Puppy Story, 1 vol. Keating, Nancy, illus. 2007. (ENG.). 32p. (J). (gr. -1-3). pap. 8.95 *(978-1-897174-18-0(7))* Creative Bk. Publishing CAN. Dist: Orca Bk. Pubs. USA.

Quattlebaum, Mary. Family Reunion. Shine, Andrea, illus. 2004. 32p. (J). 16.00 *(978-0-8028-5237-3(8))* Eerdmans, William B. Publishing Co.

Quiñones, Magaly. Quiero una Noche Azul. 2007. 64p. 14.95 *(978-0-8477-0732-4(6))* Univ. of Puerto Rico Pr.

Quintero, Aramis. Todo el Cielo un Juguete Poemas para Ninos. 2003. (J). *(978-956-240-374-0(2))* Arrayán Editores S.A.

Rabisa, Tabitha. I Dream of Angels... yet I Live with Demons. 2008. 76p. pap. 10.95 *(978-0-595-52719-9(1))* iUniverse, Inc.

Raczka, Bob. Lemonade: And Other Poems Squeezed from a Single Word. Doniger, Nancy, illus. 2011. (ENG.). 48p. (J). (gr. 3-7). 16.99 *(978-1-59643-541-4(0)*, 9781596435414) Roaring Brook Pr.

—Wet Cement: A Mix of Concrete Poems. 2016. (ENG.). 48p. (J). 17.99 *(978-1-62672-236-1(6)*, 9781626722361) Roaring Brook Pr.

Randall, Alex. Rhyming Book. 2010. 32p. pap. 15.00 *(978-0-557-66356-9(3))* Lulu Pr., Inc.

Random House Disney Staff. Mother Goose. Walt Disney Company Staff & Random House Disney Staff, illus. 2004. (Little Golden Book Ser.). (ENG.). 24p. (J). (gr. -1-2). 4.99 *(978-0-7364-2310-6(9)*, Golden/Disney) Random Hse. Children's Bks.

Raschka, Chris, illus. A Kick in the Head: An Everyday Guide to Poetic Forms. (ENG.). 64p. (J). 2009. (gr. 3-7). pap. 9.99 *(978-0-7636-4132-0(4))* 2005. (gr. 2-5). 17.99 *(978-0-7636-0662-6(6))* Candlewick Pr.

Raschka, Chris & Radunsky, Vladimir. Alphabetabum: An Album of Rare Photographs & Medium Verses. 2014. (ENG., Illus.). 80p. (J). (gr. -1-3). 19.95 *(978-1-59017-817-1(3)*, NYR Children's Collection) New York Review of Bks., Inc., The.

Rasmussen, Halfdan Wedel, et al. A Little Bitty Man & Other Poems for the Very Young. Hawkes, Kevin, illus. 2011. (ENG.). 32p. (J). (gr. k-12). 15.99 *(978-0-7636-2379-1(2))* Candlewick Pr.

Ravishankar, Anushka. Catch That Crocodile! Biswas, Pulak, illus. 2008. (ENG.). 40p. (J). (gr. k-1). *(978-81-86211-63-2(2))* Tara Publishing.

—Catch That Crocodile! Biswas, Pulak, illus. collector's ed. 2007. 40p. (J). (gr. -1-2). 25.00 *(978-81-86211-94-6(2))* Tara Publishing IND. Dist: Consortium Bk. Sales & Distribution.

Rebelo, Gabriel Bastos. Let's Go To... Work!: the Let's Go! Children's Book Series. 2004. (Illus.). 54p. pap. *(978-1-84401-197-1(6))* Athena Pr.

Reddin, Brian. What Do Rabbits Think? And Other Fun Poems for Kids. Fox, Woody, illus. 2006. (ENG.). 64p. (J). pap. 17.95 *(978-1-85635-517-9(9))* Mercier Pr., Ltd., The IRL. Dist: Dufour Editions, Inc.

Reflections of a Fool. 2004. (Illus.). 115p. (YA). per. 14.95 *(978-1-931084-33-8(5))* Balloon Magic.

Required Poems for Reading & Memorizing: Third & Fourth Grades, Prescribed by State Courses of Study. l.t. ed. 2006. 200p. pap. 21.99 *(978-1-4264-4013-7(8))* Creative Media Partners, LLC.

Resnicoff, Stan. Tom, the Talking Toilet. 2012. (ENG.). (J). pap. *(978-1-4675-1536-8(1))* Independent Pub.

Rex, Adam. Frankenstein Makes a Sandwich. 2011. (ENG., Illus.). 40p. (J). (gr. 1-4). pap. 7.99 *(978-0-547-57683-1(8))* Houghton Mifflin Harcourt Publishing Co.

—Frankenstein Takes the Cake. 2012. lib. bdg. 18.40 *(978-0-606-26615-4(1)*, Turtleback) Turtleback Bks.

Rexroad, Danese. Naked Baby. 2012. 20p. pap. 12.70 *(978-1-4669-5409-0(4))* Trafford Publishing.

Reynolds, Jason & Griffin, Jason. My Name Is Jason. Mine Too: Our Story. Our Way. 2011. (ENG.). (YA). 13.08 *(978-0-7848-3419-0(9)*, Everbind) Marco Bk. Co.

Reynolds, Lauren F. Deep Sea Poetry: For Children. 2012. (Illus.). 28p. pap. 19.99 *(978-1-4772-8019-5(7))* AuthorHouse.

Rhatigan, Joe. Everyone Toots. O'Kif, Alejandro, illus. 2017. (ENG.). 28p. (J). (gr. -1-1). 14.95 ***(978-1-63322-224-3(1)***, Moondance) Quarto Publishing Group USA.

Rhodes, Sam. Native American Rhymes: The People of the Far North, 9 vols. Howard, Kimberley, ed. Haas, Deborah, illus. 2003. 92p. (J). (gr. 3-5). mass mkt. 7.50 *(978-0-9743214-0-0(0))* Rhodes Educational Pubns.

Richardson, Bill. The Alphabet Thief, 1 vol. Bikadoroff, Roxanna, illus. 2017. (ENG.). 40p. (J). (gr. k-4). 16.95 *(978-1-55498-877-8(2))* Groundwood Bks. CAN. Dist: Publishers Group West (PGW).

Richardson, Sandra Lee. The Backyard Series: Volume One, 1 vol. 2009. 37p. pap. 24.95 *(978-1-60836-945-4(5))* America Star Bks.

Richmond, Marianne. The Gift of an Angel Vol. 1: For Parents Welcoming a New Child. l.t. ed. 2003. (ENG., Illus.). 40p. (YA). 15.95 *(978-0-9741465-2-2(8)*, Marianne Richmond Studios, Inc.) Sourcebooks, Inc.

Riddell, Chris, illus. A Great Big Cuddle: Poems for the Very Young. 2015. (ENG.). 80p. (J). (gr. -1-2). 19.99 *(978-0-7636-8116-6(4))* Candlewick Pr.

Riddle, Peter H. No Room: A Read-Aloud Story of Christmas. Hustins, Shelley, illus. 2009. 40p. (J). pap. *(978-1-926585-43-7(7)*, CCB Publishing) CCB Publishing.

Riehle, Mary Ann McCabe. The Little Kid's Table. Uhles, Mary, illus. 2015. (ENG.). 32p. (J). (gr. k-3). 16.99 *(978-1-58536-913-3(6)*, 203952) Sleeping Bear Pr.

Ritter-Henley, Sharlene. 123 Count Drive Nursery Rhyme, 1 vol. 2010. 20p. pap. 24.95 *(978-1-4489-8141-0(7))* PublishAmerica, Inc.

Roberts, Emrys. Pwdin Semolina: Cerddi Cynganeddol I Blant. 2005. (WEL.). 80p. pap. *(978-0-86381-402-0(6))* Gwasg Carreg Gwalch.

Robinson, Gary. Native American Night Before Christmas. Hummingbird, Jesse T., illus. 2007. 40p. (J). *(978-1-57416-093-2(1))* Clear Light Pubs.

Roche, Patricia Jo. I Am More Than a Name. 2009. 187p. pap. 24.95 *(978-1-60703-520-6(0))* America Star Bks.

Rodda, Geri. Lyme in Rhyme. 2005. (J). 7.50 *(978-0-9793602-1-3(8))* Pumpkin Hill Productions.

Rojas, Emilio. Poemas de Amor de un Adolescente. 2003. (SPA.). 66p. (YA). 9.95 *(978-968-5432-09-2(0))* EDITER'S Publishing Hse. MEX. Dist: EDITER'S Publishing Hse.

Rolando Elementary School. Children's Words of Wonder: A Poetry Anthology. 2008. 133p. pap. 13.95 *(978-0-7414-4828-6(9))* Infinity Publishing.

Rondeno, Lisa. Fly, Boys & Girls Fly! 2012. 24p. pap. 17.99 *(978-1-4772-5259-8(2))* AuthorHouse.

Rooney, Rachel. My Life As a Goldfish. 2014. (ENG., Illus.). 96p. (J). (gr. 3-7). pap. 7.99 *(978-1-84780-482-2(9)*, Frances Lincoln) Quarto Publishing Group UK GBR. Dist: Hachette Bk. Group.

Rose, Dilys. When I Wear My Leopard Hat: Poems for Young Children. Allan, Gill, illus. 40p. pap. 6.95 *(978-1-899827-70-1(6))* Scottish Children's Pr. GBR. Dist: Wilson & Assocs.

Rose, Elizabeth. Daft Doggerels. 2013. 38p. pap. 12.99 *(978-0-9851157-1-5(8))* Quillrunner Publishing LLC.

—Dotty Ditties. 2013. 36p. pap. 12.99 *(978-0-9851157-2-2(6))* Quillrunner Publishing LLC.

Rosen, Michael. Even My Ears Are Smiling. Cole, Babette, illus. 2012. (ENG.). 128p. (J). (gr. 3). 26.99 *(978-1-4088-0297-7(X)*, 9781408802977, Bloomsbury USA Childrens) Bloomsbury Publishing USA.

—Nonsense. Mackie, Clare, illus. 2003. 48p. pap. *(978-0-7500-2671-0(5)*, Wayland) Hachette Children's Group.

—Something's Drastic. Archbold, Tim, illus. 2007. (Collins Big Cat Ser.). (ENG.). 32p. (J). (gr. 2-4). pap. 7.99 *(978-0-00-723077-8(X))* HarperCollins Pubs. Ltd. GBR. Dist: Independent Pubs. Group.

Rosen, Michael. You Wait till I'm Older Than You! 2016. (Puffin Poetry Ser.). (ENG., Illus.). 128p. (J). (gr. 4-6). pap. 11.99 ***(978-0-14-137421-5(7))*** Penguin Bks., Ltd. GBR. Dist: Independent Pubs. Group.

Rosenberg, Pam. Tongue Twisters. Ostrom, Bob, illus. 2014. (Laughing Matters Ser.). (ENG.). 24p. (J). (gr. 1-4). 27.07 *(978-1-62687-000-0(4)*, 206789) Child's World, Inc., The.

Rosenblatt, Danielle. The Ant in the Cellar. Kirk, Jacqueline, illus. 2008. 127p. per. 19.95 *(978-0-9788985-3-3(2))* Better Be Write Pub., A.

Rosenstock, Gabriel. I Met a Man from Artikelly: Verse for the Young & Young at Heart. Staunton, Mathew, illus. 2013. 96p. pap. *(978-1-78201-032-6(7))* Evertype.

Ross, H. K., ed. & intro. Great American Story Poems. Ross, H. K., intro. 160p. (YA). (gr. 5-12). lib. bdg. 13.95 *(978-0-87460-363-7(3))* Lion Bks.

Ross, Mandy. Wake up, Sleepyhead! Early Morning Poems. Kalanovic, Dubravka, illus. 2004. (Poems for the Young Ser.). (ENG.). 32p. (J). (gr. 2-3). pap. *(978-1-904550-33-4(9))* Child's Play International Ltd.

Rowan, Charles A. I Like to Love. 2012. 28p. pap. 24.95 *(978-1-4626-8110-5(7))* America Star Bks.

Roy, Brenda & Lantis, Lora. Night Noise. 2010. 40p. pap. 16.99 *(978-1-4490-5426-7(9))* AuthorHouse.

Roza, Greg. Patterns in Poetry: Recognizing & Analyzing Poetic Form & Meter. (PowerMath Ser.). 32p. 2009. (ENG.). (gr. 5-6). pap. 10.00 *(978-1-4042-5146-5(4))* 2009. (gr. 4-5). 47.90 *(978-1-60851-415-1(3))* 2005. (Illus.). (J). (gr. 3-6). lib. bdg. 25.25 *(978-1-4042-2941-9(8))* Rosen Publishing Group, Inc., The. (PowerKids Pr.).

Rubenz, Sima. Bringing up Parents: A Biography in Verse. 2011. 98p. 38.95 *(978-1-258-08664-0(6))* Literary Licensing, LLC.

Ruddell, Deborah. A Whiff of Pine, a Hint of Skunk: A Forest of Poems. Rankin, Joan E., illus. 2009. (ENG.). 40p. (J). (gr. -1-3). 18.99 *(978-1-4169-4211-5(4)*, McElderry, Margaret K. Bks.) McElderry, Margaret K. Bks.

Rumble, Coral. My Teacher's As Wild As a Bison: Poems Based on the Great Outdoors. 2005. (ENG., Illus.). 96p. (J). (gr. 4-7). pap. 8.99 *(978-0-7459-4954-3(1))* Lion Hudson PLC GBR. Dist: Independent Pubs. Group.

Russo, Joseph Anthony. For My Love Endures Forever: Poetry & Prose. 2013. 64p. (gr. -1). 20.43 *(978-1-4669-9578-9(5))*; pap. 10.43 *(978-1-4669-9579-6(3))* Trafford Publishing.

Ruurs, Margriet. Animal Alphabed. Emery, Jennifer, illus. 2005. (ENG.). 32p. (J). (gr. -1-3). 15.95 *(978-1-59078-200-2(3))* Boyds Mills Pr.

Ryan, Christopher. The Moon & the Mouse. Tillson, Linda L., illus. 2011. 32p. pap. 24.95 *(978-1-4626-1586-5(4))* America Star Bks.

Ryan, Ruth. In the Swamp, Oh Yeah, in the Swamp. Seahorse, Risa, illus. 2012. 54p. pap. *(978-1-55483-922-3(X))* Insomniac Pr.

Rylant, Cynthia. Baby Face: A Book of Love for Baby. Goode, Diane, illus. 2008. (ENG.). 40p. (J). (gr. -1-3). 17.99 *(978-1-4169-4909-1(7)*, Simon & Schuster/Paula Wiseman Bks.) Simon & Schuster/Paula Wiseman Bks.

S., LaTisha & Lee, Mykle. One Giant Leap: Love Poems. Blob, Anjali & Beverly-Patterson, Sylvia Dianne, eds. 2003. 72p. (YA). per. 8.95 *(978-0-9744929-0-2(6))* Leeway Pubs.

Sack, Nancy. Puppies & Poems. Fuchs, Kaitlyn, illus. 2012. (ENG.). 32p. (J). 19.95 *(978-1-4327-8470-6(6))* Outskirts Pr., Inc.

Salas, Laura Purdie. And Then There Were Eight: Poems about Space. 2016. (Poetry Ser.). (ENG.). 32p. pap. 8.10 *(978-1-5157-6153-2(3)*, Aplus Bks.) Capstone Press of Coughlan Cos.

—BookSpeak! Poems About Books. Bisaillon, Josée, illus. 2011. (ENG.). 32p. (J). (gr. -1-3). 17.99 *(978-0-547-22300-1(5))* Houghton Mifflin Harcourt Publishing Co.

—Catch Your Breath: Writing Poignant Poetry. 2015. (Writer's Notebook Ser.). (ENG., Illus.). 64p. (gr. 4-5). lib. bdg. 34.65 *(978-1-4914-5990-4(5))* Capstone Press of Coughlan Cos.

—Picture Yourself Writing Poetry: Using Photos to Inspire Writing, 1 vol. 2011. (See It, Write It Ser.). (ENG.). 32p. (gr. 3-4). lib. bdg. 27.32 *(978-1-4296-6124-9(0)*, Fact Finders) Capstone Press of Coughlan Cos.

Sánchez Beras, César. Sapito Azul. Díaz, Raquel, illus. 2004. (SPA.). 32p. (J). *(978-1-58018-056-6(6))* Cambridge BrickHouse, Inc.

Sandburg, Carl. Carl Sandburg. Benzel, Kathryn N., ed. Crawford, Robert & Steele, Robert, illus. 2017. (ENG.). 48p. (J). (gr. 3-8). 14.95 *(978-1-63322-151-2(2)*, Moondance) Quarto Publishing Group USA.

Santana, Sr. Sabina Stella. Happy Ending Children's Stories, & More: Poems, Tongue-Twisters, Proverbs, & Brain-Teasers. 2008. 64p. pap. 13.50 *(978-1-4303-1344-1(7))* Lulu Pr., Inc.

Sarkisov, Anton G. Curse of the Gemini. 2009. 102p. pap. 15.99 *(978-1-4415-9560-7(0))* Xlibris Corp.

Sarreshtedari, Mehdi, narrated by. Hasht Ketab/ Sohrab Sepehri: Eight Books, 1DVD. 2005. (YA). 42.99 *(978-1-933429-00-7(3))* Ketabe Gooya Publishing LLC.

Sattgast, L. J. & Sattgast, Linda. Rhyme Bible Storybook Bible, 1 vol. Cleyet-Merle, Laurence, illus. 2012. (ENG.). 344p. (J). 17.99 *(978-0-310-72602-9(6))* Zonderkidz.

Saunders, Tom. I Want to Go to the Moon. Nugent, Cynthia, illus. 2012. (ENG.). 32p. (J). (gr. -1-2). 16.95 *(978-1-897476-56-7(6))* Simply Read Bks. CAN. Dist: Ingram Publisher Services.

Savino, Bob. Black Butterfly: Poems for a Muse. 2009. 72p. pap. 11.95 *(978-1-59858-820-0(6))* Dog Ear Publishing, LLC.

Sayre, April Pulley. Go, Go, Grapes! A Fruit Chant. Sayre, April Pulley, photos by. 2012. (ENG., Illus.). 32p. (J). (gr. -1-3). 17.99 *(978-1-4424-3390-8(6)*, Beach Lane Bks.) Beach Lane Bks.

Scanziani, Emanuele, illus. To Market! to Market! 2013. (ENG.). 24p. (J). (gr. -1). 8.95 *(978-81-923171-3-7(7))* Tara Books Agency IND. Dist: Publishers Group West (PGW).

Schaffer, Angel Boi. Blessed Child. 2004. (YA). per. 29.99 *(978-0-9755352-0-2(X))* Angel's Boy Enterprises.

Schaub, Michelle & Huntington, Amy. Fresh-Picked Poetry: A Day at the Farmers' Market. 2017. (ENG., Illus.). 32p. (J). (gr. -1-3). lib. bdg. 16.99 *(978-1-58089-547-7(6))* Charlesbridge Publishing, Inc.

Schertle, Alice. Button Up! Wrinkled Rhymes. Mathers, Petra, illus. 2013. (ENG.). 40p. (J). (gr. -1-3). pap. 7.99 *(978-0-544-02269-0(6))* Houghton Mifflin Harcourt Publishing Co.

—A Lucky Thing: Poems & Paintings. Minor, Wendell, illus. 2006. 28p. (J). (gr. 4-8). reprint ed. 17.00 *(978-1-4223-5417-9(2))* DIANE Publishing Co.

Schiffner, Frederick A. My Back Yard: Poems to Read to Your Children. Guenther, Kim, illus. 2004. 32p. (J). 14.95 *(978-0-9765782-0-8(4))* Schiffner, Frederick A.

Schkade, Jonathan. Icky, Sticky, Hairy Scary Bible Stories: 60 Poems for Kids. Mourning, Tuesday, illus. 2010. 125p. (J). pap. 14.99 *(978-0-7586-2671-4(1))* Concordia Publishing Hse.

Schmidt, Amy. Back to Dog-Gone School. Schmidt, Ron, illus. 2016. (Step into Reading Ser.). (ENG.). 32p. (J). (gr. -1-1). 3.99 *(978-1-101-93511-8(1)*, Random Hse. Bks. for Young Readers) Random Hse. Children's Bks.

—Dog-Gone School. Schmidt, Ron, photos by. 2013. (ENG., Illus.). 40p. (J). (gr. -1-2). 16.99 *(978-0-375-86974-7(3)*, Random Hse. Bks. for Young Readers) Random Hse. Children's Bks.

Schmidt, Gary D., ed. Poetry for Young People: Robert Frost. Sorensen, Henri, illus. 2014. (Poetry for Young People Ser.). (ENG.). 48p. (J). (gr. 3). 14.95 *(978-1-4549-0288-1(4))* Sterling Publishing Co., Inc.

—Robert Frost. Sorensen, Henri, illus. 2008. (Poetry for Young People Ser.). (ENG.). 48p. (J). (gr. 3). pap. 6.95 *(978-1-4027-5475-3(2))* Sterling Publishing Co., Inc.

Schoeder, Alan. In Daddy's Arms I Am Tall: African Americans Celebrating Fathers. Steptoe, Javaka, illus. 2013. (ENG.). 32p. (J). pap. 9.95 *(978-1-58430-016-8(7))* Lee & Low Bks., Inc.

Schoonmaker, Frances, ed. Poetry for Young People: Henry Wadsworth Longfellow. Wallace, Chad, illus. 2010. (Poetry for Young People Ser.). (ENG.). 48p. (J). (gr. 3). pap. 6.95 *(978-1-4027-7292-4(0))* Sterling Publishing Co., Inc.

—Robert Louis Stevenson. Corvino, Lucy, illus. 2008. (Poetry for Young People Ser.). (ENG.). 48p. (J). (gr. 3-7). pap. 6.95 *(978-1-4027-5476-0(0))* Sterling Publishing Co., Inc.

Searles, H. Louise. Sit Down little Sister & Let me Talk to You Vol. 1: The Voices of the Sparkletts. 84p. (Orig.). (J). pap. *(978-0-9706187-0-2(0))* As Sparkle Speaks & Informs/ASSI.

Seaworthy, Oscar & Collins, Mark. Port Side Pirates! Harter, Debbie, illus. 2011. (ENG.). 32p. (J). (gr. -1-2). 9.99 *(978-1-84686-667-8(7))* Barefoot Bks., Inc.

Senchyne, Jonathan & Sikorskyj, Jerod, eds. Living Forge. 2003. (YA). per. 10.00 *(978-1-932583-05-2(X))* digital@batesjackson llc.

Seuss, Dr. Seuss-Isms! A Guide to Life for Those Just Starting Out... & Those Already on Their Way. 2015. (ENG., Illus.). 64p. (J). (gr. k-12). 9.99 *(978-0-553-50841-3(5)*, Random Hse. Bks. for Young Readers) Random Hse. Children's Bks.

Shapiro, Phylis Stacey. Open Your Eyes. 2009. 40p. pap. 21.99 *(978-1-4363-9029-3(X))* Xlibris Corp.

Shapiro, Sheryl. Better Together. Petricic, Dusan, illus. 2011. (ENG.). 32p. (J). (gr. -1-1). 19.95 *(978-1-55451-279-9(4)*, 9781554512799); pap. 8.95 *(978-1-55451-278-2(6)*, 9781554512782) Annick Pr., Ltd. CAN. Dist: Publishers Group West (PGW).

Shapiro, Simon & Shapiro, Sheryl. What Can You Do with Only One Shoe? Reuse, Recycle, Reinvent. Blake, Francis, illus. 2014. (ENG.). 32p. (J). (gr. k-3). pap. 9.95 *(978-1-55451-642-1(0)*, 9781554516421); lib. bdg. 22.95 *(978-1-55451-643-8(9)*, 9781554516438) Annick Pr., Ltd. CAN. Dist: Publishers Group West (PGW).

Shay, Cynthia K. 32 Libritos de Rimas: 32 Spanish Rhyming Flip Books. 2nd ed. 2008. (ENG., Illus.). 48p. (Orig.). (J). (gr. -1-2). pap. 9.95 *(978-1-893447-01-1(4)*, Bilingual Language Materials) MAAT Resources, Inc.

Sheene, Chris. Painted Footsteps: A Creative Collection of Poetry. 2011. 152p. (gr. 4-6). 22.23 *(978-1-4634-2459-6(0))*; pap. 11.70 *(978-1-4634-2460-2(4))* AuthorHouse.

Sherrard, Valerie. There's a Cow under My Bed, 1 vol. Jardine, David, illus. 2008. (ENG.). 32p. (J). (gr. 1-8). 10.95 *(978-1-897174-34-0(9))* Creative Bk. Publishing CAN. Dist: Orca Bk. Pubs. USA.

Shields, Carol Diggory. After the Bell Rings: Poems about After-School Time. Meisel, Paul, illus. 2015. (ENG.). 32p. (J). (gr. 1-4). 16.99 *(978-0-8037-3805-8(6)*, Dial Bks) Penguin Young Readers Group.

Shiner, Jack. Raking Leaves: Poems. 2004. 148p. (YA). per. 14.95 *(978-0-922224-12-8(9))* Tonepoet Publishing.

Shiplett, Danaye. Paint My World with Colors. 2009. 36p. pap. 19.80 *(978-0-557-06342-0(6))* Lulu Pr., Inc.

Showell, Isaiah, Sr. Faith Found New, 1. Nichols, Clayton, illus. 2004. 82p. (YA). per. 15.00 incl. audio compact disk *(978-0-9754489-0-8(0))* Divine Intertwine Publishing.

Shurin, Masha. A Great Time: Children's Poems in Russian & English. Morris, Brian, ed. Barton, Alica, tr. Ginukov, Valentin, illus. 2007. (RUS & ENG.). 32p. (J). 19.95 *(978-0-9792583-2-9(4))* White Stag Pr.

Shuttleworth, Cathie, illus. The Children's Treasury of Classic Poetry. 176p. (J). pap. *(978-1-84322-143-2(8))* Bookmart Ltd.

Shuttleworth, Cathy, illus. Classic Poems for Children: Classic Verse from the Great Poets, Including Lewis Carroll, John Keats & Walt Whitman. 2011. (ENG.). 192p. (J). (gr. -1-12). 9.99 *(978-1-84322-788-5(6))* Anness Publishing GBR. Dist: National Bk. Network.

Sidman, Joyce. Butterfly Eyes & Other Secrets of the Meadow. Krommes, Beth, illus. 2006. (ENG.). 48p. (J). (gr. 2-5). 17.99 *(978-0-618-56313-5(X))* Houghton Mifflin Harcourt Publishing Co.

—Swirl by Swirl: Spirals in Nature. Krommes, Beth, illus. 2011. (ENG.). 40p. (J). (gr. -1-3). 17.99 *(978-0-547-31583-6(X))* Houghton Mifflin Harcourt Publishing Co.

—This Is Just to Say: Poems of Apology & Forgiveness. Zagarenski, Pamela, illus. 2007. (ENG.). 48p. (J). (gr. 5-7). 17.99 *(978-0-618-61680-0(2))* Houghton Mifflin Harcourt Publishing Co.

—What the Heart Knows: Chants, Charms, & Blessings. Zagarenski, Pamela, illus. 2013. (ENG.). 80p. (YA). (gr. 7). 17.99 *(978-0-544-10616-1(4))* Houghton Mifflin Harcourt Publishing Co.

Siebert, Diane. Spring, Summer, Autumn, Winter. Burckhardt, Marc, illus. 2005. (J). *(978-1-59336-299-7(4))*; pap. *(978-1-59336-300-0(1))* Mondo Publishing.

Silvano, Wendi. What Does the Wind Say? Delehanty, Joan M., illus. 2006. (ENG.). 32p. (J). (gr. -1-k). 15.95 *(978-1-55971-954-4(0))* Cooper Square Publishing Llc.

Silverstein, Shel. Cayendo Hacia Arriba. 2011.Tr. of Falling Up. (SPA.). 178p. (J). *(978-1-933032-80-1(4))* Lectorum Pubns., Inc.

—A Light in the Attic. Silverstein, Shel, illus. 2005. (ENG., Illus.). 176p. (J). (gr. -1-3). 19.99 *(978-0-06-025673-9(7))* HarperCollins Pubs.

Simmons, Kenneth. Mr Ken's Rhymes. 2007. 184p. per. 15.95 *(978-0-595-44328-4(1))* iUniverse, Inc.

Simmons, Lynn Sheffield. Sugar Lump's Night Before Christmas, 1 vol. Ward, Sue Marshall, illus. 2007. (Night Before Christmas Ser.). (ENG.). 48p. (J). (gr. k-5). 12.95 *(978-1-58980-439-5(2))* Pelican Publishing Co., Inc.

Simmons, Sukether Williams. Deep in My Soul Poems by Sukether Simmons. 2003. pap. 10.00 *(978-0-9678182-1-4(4))* Shrewsbury Publishing.

Simms, B. D. A Place in My Heart. 2003. 38p. (YA). pap. 10.95 *(978-0-7414-1681-0(6))* Infinity Publishing.

Simons, Lisa M. Bolt. Acrostic Poems. Petelinsek, Kathleen, illus. 2015. (Poetry Party Ser.). (ENG.). 24p. (J). (gr. 2-5). 27.07 *(978-1-63143-692-5(9)*, 208527) Child's World, Inc., The.

—Cinquain Poems. Petelinsek, Kathleen, illus. 2015. (Poetry Party Ser.). (ENG.). 24p. (J). (gr. 2-5). 27.07 *(978-1-63143-693-2(7)*, 208528) Child's World, Inc., The.

—Haikus. Petelinsek, Kathleen, illus. 2015. (Poetry Party Ser.). (ENG.). 24p. (J). (gr. 2-5). 27.07 *(978-1-63143-695-6(3)*, 208531) Child's World, Inc., The.

—Rhyming Poems. Petelinsek, Kathleen, illus. 2015. (Poetry Party Ser.). (ENG.). 24p. (J). (gr. 2-5). 27.07 *(978-1-63143-698-7(8)*, 208533) Child's World, Inc., The.

Simpson, Patricia Ann. The Twinkle Collection. 2006. 19.95 *(978-0-9779662-4-0(0))* Creative Bk. Pubs.

Sin I Si Tou. A Child's Creation: Stories & Poems. 2012. (Illus.). 124p. pap. 41.19 *(978-1-4678-7811-1(1))* AuthorHouse.

Singer, Marilyn. Echo Echo: Reverso Poems About Greek Myths. Masse, Josée, illus. 2016. (ENG.). 32p. (J). (gr. 1-4). 16.99 *(978-0-8037-3992-5(3)*, Dial Bks) Penguin Young Readers Group.

—A Full Moon is Rising. 2013. 31.95 *(978-1-4301-1441-3(X))* Live Oak Media.

—A Stick Is an Excellent Thing: Poems Celebrating Outdoor Play. Pham, LeUyen, illus. 2012. (ENG.). 40p. (J). (gr. -1-3). 17.99 *(978-0-547-12493-3(7))* Houghton Mifflin Harcourt Publishing Co.

—The Superheroes Employment Agency. Jones, Noah Z., illus. 2012. (ENG.). 40p. (J). (gr. 1-4). 16.99 *(978-0-547-43559-6(2))* Houghton Mifflin Harcourt Publishing Co.

Singer, Marilyn & Cairns, Julia. A Full Moon Is Rising. (ENG.). (J). 2014. pap. 10.95 *(978-1-62014-196-0(5))* 2011. (Illus.). 48p. (gr. 1-18). 19.95 *(978-1-60060-364-8(5))* Lee & Low Bks., Inc.

Singh, Belveen. A Kaleidoscopic Life: Poems for the Childrens Heart. 2012. 52p. pap. 37.37 *(978-1-4797-4534-0(0))* Xlibris Corp.

Singing Horse. 2003. (Gateways to the Sun Ser.). 32p. (J). (gr. 2-3). lib. bdg. 9.95 *(978-1-58105-579-5(X))* Santillana USA Publishing Co., Inc.

Skene, Pat. Rhyme Stones, 1 vol. Ross, Graham, illus. 2007. (Orca Echoes Ser.). (ENG.). 64p. (J). (gr. 2-3). per. 6.95 *(978-1-55143-636-4(1))* Orca Bk. Pubs. USA.

Skinner, Ada & Wickes, Frances. A Child's Own Book of Verse, Book One (Yesterday's Classics) Petersham, Maud & Petersham, Miska, illus. 2006. (J). pap. 8.95 *(978-1-59915-051-2(4))* Yesterday's Classics.

—A Child's Own Book of Verse, Book Three (Yesterday's Classics) Petersham, Maud & Petersham, Miska, illus. 2006. (J). pap. 8.95 *(978-1-59915-053-6(0))* Yesterday's Classics.

—A Child's Own Book of Verse, Book Two (Yesterday's Classics) Petersham, Maud & Petersham, Miska, illus. 2006. (J). pap. 8.95 *(978-1-59915-052-9(2))* Yesterday's Classics.

Sklansky, Amy. Out of This World: Poems & Facts about Space. Schuett, Stacey, illus. 2012. (ENG.). 40p. (J). (gr. k-4). 17.99 *(978-0-375-86459-9(8)*, Knopf Bks. for Young Readers) Random Hse. Children's Bks.

Sleith III, Eric. You & Me = We. 2009. 52p. pap. 8.99 *(978-0-557-20616-2(2))* Lulu Pr., Inc.

Smith, Catherine. On My Knees. 2012. 32p. pap. 13.95 *(978-1-4497-6143-1(7)*, WestBow Pr.) Author Solutions, Inc.

Smith, Ernest Lynnwood. Raw Poetry & Prose in Transition. 2005. 50p. 25.00 *(978-0-9729154-2-7(7))* Smith, Ernest.

—The Road to Oneness. 2003. 56p. 25.00 *(978-0-9729154-1-0(9))* Smith, Ernest.

Smith, Hope Anita. Mother Poems. Smith, Hope Anita, illus. 2009. (ENG., Illus.). 80p. (J). (gr. 5-8). 24.99 *(978-0-8050-8231-9(X)*, 9780805082319, Holt, Henry & Co. Bks. For Young Readers) Holt, Henry & Co.

—The Way a Door Closes. Evans, Shane W., illus. 2011. (ENG.). 64p. (J). (gr. 3-7). pap. 9.99 *(978-0-312-66169-4(X)*, 9780312661694) Square Fish.

Smith Meyer, Ruth. Tyson's Sad Bad Day. 2009. 30p. pap. *(978-1-926676-43-2(2))* Word Alive Pr.

Smith, Michael. Relativity. Oliva, Octavio, illus. 2011. 30p. (J). *(978-0-9799339-8-1(6))* East West Discovery Pr.

Smith, Michael & Oliva, Octavio. Relativity: Relatividad. Oliva, Octavio, illus. 2011. (SPA & ENG., Illus.). (J). *(978-0-9832278-3-0(7))* East West Discovery Pr.

Smith, Simon. Reverdy Road. 2003. (Modern Poets Ser.). (ENG.). 252p. pap. *(978-1-84471-027-0(0))* Salt Publishing.

Smith, Vivian. Along the Line. 2006. (ENG.). 132p. per. *(978-1-84471-066-9(1))* Salt Publishing.

Sneed, Nancy Glascock. Grains of Sand: Beach Poems. 2013. 60p. pap. 23.95 *(978-1-4497-9576-4(5)*, WestBow Pr.) Author Solutions, Inc.

Snyder, Betsy E. Haiku Baby. Snyder, Betsy E., illus. 2008. (ENG., Illus.). 14p. (J). (gr. k — 1). bds. 6.99 *(978-0-375-84395-2(7)*, Random Hse. Bks. for Young Readers) Random Hse. Children's Bks.

Snyder, Edward B., et al. Through Tiger's Eyes. 2008. 24p. 24.00 *(978-0-615-18259-9(3))* Cyber Tiger Pr.

Snyder, Max. The King with No Kingdom. Snyder, Max & Snyder, Ili, illus. 2013. 42p. 18.99 *(978-0-9911512-9-5(1))* Mindstir Media.

So, Meilo, illus. Read a Rhyme, Write a Rhyme. 2009. (ENG.). 32p. (J). (gr. 1-4). pap. 7.99 *(978-0-385-73727-2(0)*, Dragonfly Bks.) Random Hse. Children's Bks.

Soentpiet, Chris K. & Hale, Christy, illus. Amazing Places. 2015. (ENG.). 40p. (J). 18.95 *(978-1-60060-653-3(9))* Lee & Low Bks., Inc.

Sones, S. Stop Pretending: What Happened When My Sister Went Crazy. 2004. (YA). 15.65 *(978-0-7569-4250-2(0))* Perfection Learning Corp.

Sorrentino, Dawn. Look at Me. 2012. 20p. pap. 10.49 *(978-1-4678-6813-6(2))* AuthorHouse.

Soto, Gary. Canto Familiar. Nelson, Annika & Diaz, David, illus. 2007. (ENG.). 96p. (J). (gr. 2-5). pap. 7.95 *(978-0-15-205885-2(0))* Houghton Mifflin Harcourt Publishing Co.

—A Fire in My Hands. rev. exp. ed. 2006. (ENG., Illus.). 96p. (YA). (gr. 7-12). 16.00 *(978-0-15-205564-6(9))* Houghton Mifflin Harcourt Publishing Co.

—Neighborhood Odes. Diaz, David, illus. 2005. (ENG.). 80p. (J). (gr. 2-5). pap. 6.99 *(978-0-15-205364-2(6))* Houghton Mifflin Harcourt Publishing Co.

—Partly Cloudy: Poems of Love & Longing. 2012. (ENG., Illus.). 112p. (YA). (gr. 7). pap. 9.99 *(978-0-547-57737-1(0))* Houghton Mifflin Harcourt Publishing Co.

Soundprints Staff. If You're Happy & You Know It & Other Favorites. 2005. (Meet Mother Goose Ser.). (ENG., Illus.). 36p. (J). 14.95 *(978-1-59069-213-4(6)*, MPD1108) Studio Mouse LLC.

—Little Miss Muffet & Other Favorites. 2005. (Meet Mother Goose Ser.). (Illus.). 36p. (J). 10.95 *(978-1-59069-215-8(2))*; bds. 14.95 incl. audio compact disk *(978-1-59069-217-2(9))* Studio Mouse LLC.

Sourcebooks, Inc Staff. Baby's First Mother Goose Treasury. 2013. (ENG., Illus.). 16p. (J). (gr. -1). bds. 8.99 *(978-1-4022-9288-0(0)*, Sourcebooks Jabberwocky) Sourcebooks, Inc.

Southwick Elementary Students. Soaring on the Wings of Eagles. 2008. 200p. per. 14.95 *(978-0-9800429-3-1(3))* Pen & Publish Inc.

Soy de dos lugares: Poesia Juvenil: 6 Small Books. (Saludos Ser.: Vol. 2). (SPA.). (gr. 3-5). 31.00 *(978-0-7635-1767-0(4))* Rigby Education.

Soy de dos lugares: Poesia Juvenil: Big Book. (Saludos Ser.: Vol. 2). (SPA.). (gr. 3-5). 31.00 *(978-0-7635-3162-1(6))* Rigby Education.

Spanish Poetry Packs: Combo Pack. (SPA.). (gr. k-2). 61.62 *(978-1-56334-415-2(7))* CENGAGE Learning.

Spanish Poetry Packs: Jumbo Pack. (SPA.). (gr. k-2). 332.75 *(978-1-56334-414-5(9))* CENGAGE Learning.

Sparkle Little One! 2004. (Illus.). 28p. (J). 6.95 *(978-0-9746779-0-3(6))* Children of Color/The Indra Collection.

Sparshott, Francis. The Naming of the Beasts, 1 vol. 2003. (ENG., Illus.). 80p. pap. *(978-0-88753-055-5(9))* Black Moss Pr. CAN. Dist: LitDistCo.

Spensley, Joe. Home Thoughts from A Broader Perspective. 2005. 96p. (YA). per. 12.00 *(978-1-932496-26-0(2))* Penman Publishing, Inc.

A Spicy-Herby Day, 6 vols.; set. 32p. (gr. 1-3). 26.50 *(978-0-7802-8044-1(X))* Wright Group/McGraw-Hill.

Spinelli, Eileen. Polar Bear, Arctic Hare: Poems of the Frozen North. Fernandes, Eugenie, illus. 2014. (ENG.). 32p. (J). (gr. -1-3). pap. 6.95 *(978-1-62979-112-8(1)*, Wordsong) Boyds Mills Pr.

Spires, Elizabeth. I Heard God Talking to Me: William Edmondson & His Stone Carvings. 2009. (ENG., Illus.). 64p. (YA). (gr. 4-8). 17.95 *(978-0-374-33528-1(1)*, 9780374335281, Farrar, Straus & Giroux (BYR)) Farrar, Straus & Giroux.

St. Pierre, Todd-Michael. A Woolly Mammoth on Amelia Street: Read Aloud Poems4Kids (and Grownups Too!) Douglas, Keith Cartoon Man, illus. 2003. 164p. (J). mass mkt. 15.95 *(978-0-9742602-0-4(7))* Prytania Pr.

Stedman, Edmund Clarence. Rip Van Winkle & His Wonderful Nap. 2011. 18p. pap. 11.99 *(978-1-4181-8988-4(X))* Michigan Publishing.

Steig, Jeanne. Alpha Beta Chowder. Steig, William, illus. 2016. (ENG.). 48p. (J). (gr. -1-3). 17.99 *(978-1-4814-4060-8(8)*, Atheneum/Caitlyn Dlouhy Books) Simon & Schuster Children's Publishing.

Steinberg, D. J. First Grade, Here I Come! Bishop, Tracy, illus. 2016. (ENG.). 32p. (J). (gr. -1-1). pap. 3.99 *(978-0-448-48920-9(1)*, Grosset & Dunlap) Penguin Young Readers Group.

—Grasshopper Pie & Other Poems. Sinnott, Adrian C., tr. Sinnott, Adrian C., illus. 2004. (Penguin Young Readers, Level 3 Ser.). (ENG.). 48p. (J). (gr. 1-3). pap. 3.99 *(978-0-448-43347-9(8)*, Penguin Young Readers) Penguin Young Readers Group.

Stephens, Chris S. Rapping on the Window. Carpenter, Suzanne, illus. 2004. (ENG.). 48p. pap. 12.95 *(978-1-84323-360-2(6))* Beekman Bks., Inc.

Steps To Literacy Staff, compiled by. Bruce Lansky School Poems Collection of 2 Titles: Pro534. 2005. (ENG., Illus.). (J). pap. *(978-1-59564-874-7(7))* Steps To Literacy, LLC.

Stevens, Roger & Quarto Generic Staff. I Wish I Had a Pirate Hat. 2015. (ENG., Illus.). 80p. (J). (gr. -1 — 1). pap. 7.99 *(978-1-84780-618-5(X)*, Frances Lincoln) Quarto Publishing Group UK GBR. Dist: Littlehampton Bk Services, Ltd.

Stevenson, Robert Louis. Bed in Summer. Reisch, Jesse, illus. 2011. (Poetry for Children Ser.). (ENG.). 24p. (J). (gr. k-3). 27.07 *(978-1-60973-151-9(4)*, 201180) Child's World, Inc., The.

—Block City. Kirk, Daniel, illus. 2005. (ENG.). 32p. (J). (gr. -1-3). 19.99 *(978-0-689-86964-8(9)*, Simon & Schuster Bks. For Young Readers) Simon & Schuster Bks. For Young Readers.

—A Child's Garden of Verses: A Collection of Scriptures, Prayers & Poems. Lt. ed. 2005. 64p. pap. *(978-1-84637-255-1(0))* Echo Library.

—A Child's Garden of Verses: A Collection of Scriptures, Prayers & Poems. Robinson, Charles, illus. 2009. (ENG.). 100p. (J). (gr. 4-7). pap. 15.95 *(978-1-59583-350-1(1)*, 9781595833501, Green Tiger Pr.) Laughing Elephant.

—A Child's Garden of Verses: A Collection of Scriptures, Prayers & Poems. Fujikawa, Gyo, illus. 2007. (ENG.). 104p. (J). (gr. -1-2). 9.95 *(978-1-4027-5062-5(5))* Sterling Publishing Co., Inc.

—The Land of Counterpane. Harrison, Nancy, illus. 2011. (Poetry for Children Ser.). (ENG.). 24p. (J). (gr. k-3). 27.07 *(978-1-60973-152-6(2)*, 201183) Child's World, Inc., The.

—The Little Land. Thornburgh, Rebecca McKillip, illus. 2011. (Poetry for Children Ser.). (ENG.). 24p. (J). (gr. k-3). 27.07 *(978-1-60973-153-3(0)*, 201184) Child's World, Inc., The.

—My Shadow. Idle, Molly, illus. 2011. (Poetry for Children Ser.). (ENG.). 24p. (J). (gr. k-3). 27.07 *(978-1-60973-154-0(9)*, 201181) Child's World, Inc., The.

—My Shadow. Sanchez, Sara, illus. 2016. (ENG.). 32p. (J). (gr. -1-k). 16.99 *(978-1-63450-178-1(0)*, Sky Pony Pr.) Skyhorse Publishing Co., Inc.

—Poetry For Young People: Robert Louis Stevenson. 2003. cd-rom 19.00 *(978-0-931968-62-4(3))* Samizdat Express.

Stewart, Es. Who Made the Moon, Mummy? 2013. 24p. pap. 11.95 *(978-1-61897-799-1(7)*, Strategic Bk. Publishing) Strategic Book Publishing & Rights Agency (SBPRA).

Stoneley, Ellie. Milky Moments. D'Alton Goode, Jessica, illus. 2015. (ENG.). 40p. (J). (gr. -1-1). pap. 9.99 *(978-1-78066-256-5(4))* Pinter & Martin Ltd. GBR. Dist: National Bk. Network.

Storad, Conrad J. Don't Ever Cross That Road! An Armadillo Story. Jensen, Nathaniel P., illus. 2006. (Sonoran Desert Tails Ser.). 32p. (J). (gr. k-4). 15.95 *(978-1-891795-08-4(2))* RGU Group, The.

—Lizards for Lunch: A Roadrunner's Tale. 2009. (Sonoran Desert Tails Ser.). (Illus.). 32p. (J). (gr. k-4). 6.95 *(978-1-891795-00-8(7))* RGU Group, The.

Stroud, Bettye. The World's Wide Open. Cummings, Pat, illus. 2016. (J). *(978-0-689-84026-5(8))* Simon & Schuster Bks. For Young Readers.

Students of Fletcher Hills Elementary School. Many Voices: Where Dreams Take Flight II. 2007. 131p. pap. 13.95 *(978-0-7414-3748-8(1))* Infinity Publishing.

Suarez, Nora & Gertz, Mercedes, concepts. When Words Dream, Cuando las Palabras Sueñan: Children's Poetry, Poesía Infantil. 1000th ed. 2006. (ENG & SPA., Illus.). 36p. lib. bdg. 25.95 *(978-0-9789544-0-6(8))* Hundred Ways LLC, A.

Sullivan, E. J. The Tennessee Night Before Christmas. Eldredge, Larry, illus. 2005. (Night Before Christmas Ser.). (J). (gr. -1-3). 12.95 *(978-1-58173-395-2(X))* Sweetwater Pr.

Sullivan, Ellen. The North Carolina Night Before Christmas. Eldredge, Ernie, illus. 2006. (J). *(978-1-60261-163-4(7))* Sweetwater Pr.

Sullivan, Ellen & Moore, Clement C. The Virginia Night Before Christmas. Franks, C. J., illus. 2005. (J). *(978-1-58173-392-1(5))* Sweetwater Pr.

Sullivan, Lisa, compiled by. Happy Days. 2013. (Jingle-Jangle Ser.). (ENG., Illus.). 10p. (J). (-k). bds. 9.95 *(978-1-61889-240-9(1))* AZ Bks. LLC.

Suresh, Shreyas. Joy! a Book of Poems. 2011. (Illus.). 62p. pap. 6.99 *(978-0-557-71631-9(4))* Lulu Pr., Inc.

Swarmer, Kristina, illus. Festival Poems. 2017. (Poems Just for Me Ser.). 32p. (gr. 7-8). 27.25 ***(978-1-4994-8386-4(4)***, Windmill Bks.) Rosen Publishing Group, Inc., The.

Sweeney, Matthew, ed. The New Faber Book of Children's Poems. Fanelli, Sara, tr. Fanelli, Sara, illus. 2003. (ENG.). 304p. (J). pap. 19.95 *(978-0-571-21905-6(5))* Faber & Faber, Inc.

Sycolin Creek Elementary School (Leesburg, Va.) Staff, contrib. by. Greatest Homework Excuse Book Ever. 2009. (Illus.). 25p. *(978-0-545-21329-5(0))* Scholastic, Inc.

Tagore, Rabindranath. Crescent Moon - Child Poems. 2007. 128p. per. 11.45 *(978-1-59462-738-5(X)*, Book Jungle) Standard Pubns., Inc.

The Talking Bumblebee. 2003. (J). *(978-1-56870-476-0(3))* Hewell Publishing.

Tall Tales, 9 vols., Set. 2004. (Tall Tales Ser.). (ENG., Illus.). 32p. (gr. 3-5). 54.64 *(978-0-7565-0712-1(X))* Compass Point Bks.

Tamblyn, Amber. Free Stallion: Poems. 2011. (ENG.). 96p. (YA). (gr. 8). pap. 6.99 *(978-1-4424-3087-7(7)*, Simon & Schuster Bks. For Young Readers) Simon & Schuster Bks. For Young Readers.

Taplin, Sam. Christmas Poems. Luraschi, Anna, illus. 2006. (Christmas Poems Ser.). 95p. (J). 12.99 *(978-0-7945-1471-6(5)*, Usborne) EDC Publishing.

—The Usborne Book of Poems for Little Children. Furukawa, Masumi, illus. 2007. 47p. (J). 11.99 *(978-0-7945-1426-6(X)*, Usborne) EDC Publishing.

Taplin, Sam, compiled by. Poems for Young Children. 2005. (Poems for Young Children Ser.). 96p. (J). 14.95 *(978-0-7945-0924-8(X)*, Usborne) EDC Publishing.

Tavakkoli, Aryan. Abc Animals Are My Friends. 2012. 60p. pap. 31.99 *(978-1-4691-3263-1(X))* Xlibris Corp.

Tavares, Gary Gene. Inspirational & Educational Poems. 2007. 60p. per. 9.95 *(978-0-595-45911-7(0))* iUniverse, Inc.

Taylor, Darlene. Thank You Notes from Grandma. 2013. 24p. pap. *(978-1-4602-0948-6(6))* FriesenPress.

Taylor, Judy. Hidden Pictures 2005. 2004. (ENG., Illus.). 48p. (J). (gr. 6-9). Vol. 2. pap., act. bk. ed. 5.95 *(978-1-59078-295-8(X))* Vol. 3. pap., act. bk. ed. 5.95 *(978-1-59078-296-5(8))* Boyds Mills Pr.

Taylor, K. L. Poetry for Children: Poems Too Make You Smile. 2012. 48p. pap. 8.95 *(978-1-4620-3164-1(1))* iUniverse, Inc.

Taylor, Michelle A. If Bees Rode Shiny Bicycles. 2003. (Illus.). 152p. (J). pap. *(978-0-7022-3382-1(X))* Univ. of Queensland Pr.

Teacher's Selection: Anthology of Eighth Grade Poetry. 2005. 158p. (YA). 16.95 *(978-1-883931-57-5(6))* Anthology of Poetry, Inc.

Teachers Writers Collaborative Staff, ed. A Poem As Big As New York City: Little Kids Write about the Big Apple. D'yans, Masha, illus. 2012. (ENG.). 38p. (J). (gr. k-4). 19.95 *(978-0-7893-2083-4(5))* Universe Publishing.

Tegnér, Esaias. Fritiofs Saga. ANDREW A. STOMBERG, ed. 2007. (ENG.). 258p. pap. 21.99 *(978-1-4264-3043-5(4))*; 304p. pap. 24.99 *(978-1-4264-3108-1(2))* Creative Media Partners, LLC.

Temple, John. Collected Poems. 2003. (Salt Modern Poets). (ENG.). 196p. pap. *(978-1-876857-56-1(0))* Salt Publishing.

Thaxter, Celia. Poems for Children, by Celia Thaxter; with Illustrations by Miss a G Plymptom. 2006. 164p. per. 18.99 *(978-1-4255-1219-4(4))* Michigan Publishing.

Thomas-Bakker, Oslyn. Poetry for Children. 2007. pap. 9.00 *(978-0-8059-8527-6(1))* Dorrance Publishing Co., Inc.

Thomas, Joyce Carol. The Blacker the Berry. Cooper, Floyd, illus. 2008. (ENG.). 32p. (J). (gr. -1-3). 16.99 *(978-0-06-025375-2(4)*, Amistad) HarperCollins Pubs.

Thomas, Mark Lawton. My Lemonade Stand Can't Stand Me. Hoke, Jeenhyun, illus. 114p. 2013. pap. 9.99 *(978-1-935711-23-0(7))* 2012. (ENG.). (J). pap. 9.99 *(978-1-935711-22-3(9))* Peak City Publishing, LLC.

Thomas, Patricia. Nature's Paintbox: A Seasonal Gallery of Art & Verse. Orback, Craig, illus. 2007. (Millbrook Picture Books Ser.). (ENG.). 32p. (J). (gr. 2-4). lib. bdg. 16.95 *(978-0-8225-6807-0(1)*, Millbrook Pr.) Lerner Publishing Group.

Thompson, David. Poems & Illustrations for Preschool Children. 2013. 40p. pap. 19.57 *(978-1-4669-7886-7(4))* Trafford Publishing.

Thornton, Geoffrey. The Illustrated Wynken, Blynken, & Nod. 2007. (Illus.). 28p. per. 19.95 *(978-1-59858-373-1(5))* Dog Ear Publishing, LLC.

Thouw, Jennifer. Under the Rainbow. 2010. 136p. pap. 71.99 *(978-1-4535-0341-6(2))* Xlibris Corp.

Thran, Nick. Halifax Hal. Foreman, Gabe, illus. 2013. (ENG.). 46p. (YA). (gr. 5). pap. 9.95 *(978-1-897411-77-3(4))* Bayeux Arts, Inc. CAN. Dist: Chicago Distribution Ctr.

Thunder from the Earth, 6, Pack. (Greetings Ser.: Vol. 2). (gr. 3-5). 31.00 *(978-0-7635-2062-5(4))* Rigby Education.

Tiger Tales, ed. This Little Light of Mine. Kolvanovic, Dubravka, illus. 2014. (ENG.). 22p. (J). (gr. -1-k). bds. 8.99 *(978-1-58925-569-2(0))* Tiger Tales.

Tize W. Clark. Twin Poems. 2012. (ENG.). per. 24.95 *(978-0-9766770-1-7(6))* BAU Publishing Group.

To Light A Match. 2004. (Illus.). 88p. (YA). spiral bd. 11.95 *(978-1-931084-37-6(8))*; per. 11.95 *(978-1-931084-10-9(6))* Balloon Magic.

To This Day: For the Bullied & Beautiful. 2014. (ENG., Illus.). 72p. (J). (gr. 5-12). 19.95 *(978-1-55451-639-1(0)*, 9781554516391) Annick Pr., Ltd. CAN. Dist: Publishers Group West (PGW).

Toht, Patty & Toht, Patricia. All Aboard the London Bus. Usher, Sam, illus. 2017. (ENG.). 40p. (J). (gr. k-3). 17.99 *(978-1-84780-857-8(3)*, Frances Lincoln Children's Bks.) Quarto Publishing Group UK GBR. Dist: Hachette Bk. Group.

Toland, Mischa P., creator. She Ain't Angry for Nothin' Intervention & Behavior Modification Curriculum. 2008. (ENG.). 160p. (YA). per. 30.00 *(978-0-9754191-1-3(0))* Morals & Values Pr.

Tolkien, Michael G. R. Wish. 2010. (Illus.). 132p. pap. 38.49 *(978-1-4490-9652-6(2))* AuthorHouse.

Torices, Jose Gonzalez, et al. Poemas para la Paz. Noriega, Fernando, illus. 2004.Tr. of Poems for Peace. (SPA.). 68p. (J). (gr. 2-3). 14.99 *(978-84-241-8726-2(1))* Everest Editora ESP. Dist: Lectorum Pubns., Inc.

Tracy, Kathleen. The Life & Times of Homer. 2004. (Biography from Ancient Civilizations Ser.). (Illus.). 48p. (J). (gr. 4-8). lib. bdg. 29.95 *(978-1-58415-260-6(5))* Mitchell Lane Pubs., Inc.

Trainer, Maria T. Kids Are Gifts from Heaven, 1 vol. 2009. 108p. pap. 19.95 *(978-1-4489-8381-0(9))* America Star Bks.

Trueit, Trudi. What Is Poetry? 2014. (Name That Text Type! Ser.). (Illus.). 32p. (gr. 2-4). pap. 7.95 *(978-1-4677-4521-5(9))* Lerner Publishing Group.

Trueit, Trudi Strain. What Is Poetry? 2014. (Name That Text Type! Ser.). (ENG., Illus.). 32p. (gr. 2-4). lib. bdg. 26.60 *(978-1-4677-3667-1(8)*, Lerner Pubns.) Lerner Publishing Group.

Truswell, P. Diane. Star Climber. 2008. 36p. pap. 21.99 *(978-1-4363-2546-2(3))* Xlibris Corp.

Tugeau, Jeremy, illus. Count along with Mother Goose, 1 vol. 2011. (Mother Goose Nursery Rhymes Ser.). (ENG.). 32p. (gr. -1-2). 28.50 *(978-1-61641-144-2(9)*, Looking Glass Library) ABDO Publishing Co.

Tuggle, Le Ann S. Let's Go Fishing. 2006. (Illus.). 32p. (J). (gr. -1). 16.95 *(978-0-9770912-7-0(9)*, Blue Marble Bks.) Sphinx Publishing.

Tully, Sandra M. Cherry Pie Charlie & More Poems for Children. Sadowski, Jeff, illus. 2007. (J). 15.00 *(978-1-933556-86-4(2))* Publishers' Graphics, L.L.C.

Turner, Queen of England Patrenia. Queen Patrenialla - A Canadian Story Poem. Turner, Keeng of England Troyius, ed. 2015. (Illus.). pap. *(978-0-578-18000-7(6))* Royalty Patrenia Turner Publications.

Turner, Steve. Don't Take Your Elephant to School: An Alphabet of Poems. Mostyn, David, illus. 2006. (ENG.). 96p. (J). (gr. 2-4). pap. 8.99 *(978-0-7459-6020-3(0))* Lion Hudson PLC GBR. Dist: Independent Pubs. Group.
Tuttle, Justin J. If My Toes Could Talk. 2009. (Illus.). 20p. pap. 12.99 *(978-1-4389-3953-7(1))* AuthorHouse.
Twain, Mark, pseud, tr. from GER. Slovenly Peter. Kredel, Fritz, illus. 2013. (Calla Editions Ser.). (ENG.). 48p. (gr. 5). 20.00 *(978-1-60660-048-1(6))* Dover Pubns., Inc.
Tyler, Michael. The Skin You Live In. Csicsko, David Lee, illus. 2005. (ENG.). 32p. (J). (gr. k-2). 15.95 *(978-0-9759580-0-1(3))* Chicago Children's Museum.
Tyson, Ian. La Primera: The Story of Wild Mustangs. Halvorson, Adeline, illus. 2009. (ENG.). 32p. (J). (gr. 2-4). 20.95 *(978-0-88776-863-7(6),* Tundra Bks.) Tundra Bks. CAN. Dist: Penguin Random Hse. LLC.
Uhlig, Elizabeth. Children Just Like You. Uhlig, Elizabeth, illus. 2007. (Illus.). (J). pap. 12.95 *(978-0-9786745-6-4(1))* Marble Hse. Editions.
Updike, John. A Child's Calendar, 4 bks. Hyman, Trina Schart, illus. 2004. (J). (gr. k-4). pap. 37.95 incl. audio *(978-1-59112-473-3(5))* Live Oak Media.
The Valentine Poem Book. 10p. (J). bds. *(978-2-89393-865-3(5))* Phidal Publishing, Inc./Editions Phidal, Inc.
Van Camp, Richard. We Sang You Home, 1 vol. Flett, Julie, illus. 2016. (ENG.). 26p. (J). (gr. -1-k). bds. 9.95 *(978-1-4598-1178-2(X))* Orca Bk. Pubs. USA.
Van De Luecht, Susan. Children's Poetry - Dreams & Visons. 2005. 58p. (J). pap. 20.73 *(978-1-4116-6469-2(8))* Lulu Pr., Inc.
Van Os, Erik & Van Lieshout, Elle. How Much Does the Gray in an Elephant Weigh? Hoogstad, Alice, illus. 2013. (ENG.). 32p. (J). (gr. -1). 17.95 *(978-1-935954-27-9(X),* 9781935954279) Lemniscaat USA.
VanAllen, Cindy. Animal ABC's: A little book to make you glad, Hot off the press, from Nana¿s Pad. 2008. 32p. pap. 24.95 *(978-1-60703-255-7(4))* America Star Bks.
Vance, Rodney. De'Monte Love. 2007. (Illus.). (J). per. 17.99 *(978-1-933156-15-6(5),* Visikid Bks.) GSVQ Publishing.
Vanhecke, Susan. Under the Freedom Tree. Ladd, London, illus. 2014. (J). pap. *(978-1-58089-551-4(4));* (ENG.). 32p. (gr. 1-4). lib. bdg. 16.95 *(978-1-58089-550-7(6))* Charlesbridge Publishing, Inc.
VanTine, Karl. Sweet Dreams: A Lullaby. 2012. 16p. pap. 17.99 *(978-1-4685-6477-8(3))* AuthorHouse.
Varikyan, Arpine & Wallace, Dejuanna. From the Inside Out. 2004. (ENG.). 80p. (YA). per. *(978-0-595-33149-9(1))* iUniverse, Inc.
VeJauan, Sherea. Realistically Speaking: Speaking What's Real... Keeping What's Holy. 2003. 85p. (YA). per. 14.99 *(978-0-9727874-0-6(2))* Realistically Speaking Publishing Co.
VERSE! Poetry for Young Children: Lessons for 4 to 6 Year-olds. 2006. spiral bd. *(978-0-9727635-9-2(7))* Univ. of Arizona, Poetry Ctr., Arizona Board of Regents.
Vestergaard, Hope. Digger, Dozer, Dumper. Slonim, David, illus. (ENG.). (J). 2016. 30p. (-k). bds. 7.99 *(978-0-7636-8893-6(2))* 2013. 32p. (gr. -1-3). 15.99 *(978-0-7636-5078-0(1))* Candlewick Pr.
Vigil, Florida. A Child's Imagination: Childhood Poems. 2012. 36p. 24.95 *(978-1-4575-1255-1(6));* pap. 16.95 *(978-1-4575-1430-2(3))* Dog Ear Publishing, LLC.
Voboril, Evan T. Poems about the Natural World, 1 vol. 2014. (Experiencing Poetry Ser.). (ENG.). 64p. (gr. 7-8). lib. bdg. 35.99 *(978-1-4329-9558-4(8))* Heinemann-Raintree.
Vogl, Mark. Confederate Night Before Christmas, 1 vol. Ford, Stephanie, illus. 2015. (ENG.). 32p. (J). (gr. k-3). 16.99 *(978-1-4556-2075-3(0))* Pelican Publishing Co., Inc.
von Rosenberg, Byron. O Christmas Treed. 2006. 30p. (J). 10.95 *(978-0-9759858-5-4(X))* Red Mountain Creations.
Wahid, Kelli. As Children Grow: Poetry for Children. 2011. 86p. pap. 19.95 *(978-1-4560-6692-5(7))* America Star Bks.
Walker, Alice. There Is a Flower at the Tip of My Nose Smelling Me. Vitale, Stefano, illus. 2006. (ENG.). 32p. (J). (gr. -1-3). 17.99 *(978-0-06-057080-4(6))* HarperCollins Pubs.
Walker, Kennesha M. A Word in Due Season. 2003. 47p. (YA). pap. 9.95 *(978-0-7414-1555-4(0))* Infinity Publishing.
Walking: Individual Title Six-Packs. (Literatura 2000 Ser.). (gr. 2-3). 33.00 *(978-0-7635-0215-7(4))* Rigby Education.
Walsh, Russ. Snack Attack & Other Poems for Developing Fluency in Beginning Readers. 2011. pap. 10.95 *(978-0-7414-6431-6(4))* Infinity Publishing.
Wangerin, Walter, Jr. The Bedtime Rhyme. Huang, Benrei, illus. 2008. (ENG.). 32p. (J). (gr. -1-3). 16.95 *(978-1-55725-467-2(2))* Paraclete Pr., Inc.
Ward, Jean Elizabeth. Rabbits Too. 2008. 114p. pap. 18.99 *(978-1-4357-3329-9(0))* Lulu Pr., Inc.
Ward, Jean Elizabeth, Poet Laureate. A BARBARA ANNE BUSHY TALE: Book I. 2008. 101p. pap. 18.99 *(978-1-4357-3223-0(5))* Lulu Pr., Inc.
—A BARBARA ANNE BUSHY TALE Book III. 2008. 148p. pap. 22.50 *(978-1-4357-3216-2(2))* Lulu Pr., Inc.
Warrick, Natalie. A Mighty Warrior Is the Ant. 2013. 52p. pap. 9.99 *(978-0-9886315-7-1(1))* CHB Media.
Washington, Joy Louise. The Gingerbread House. 2009. 12p. pap. 8.99 *(978-1-4389-2805-0(X))* AuthorHouse.
Washington, Peter, ed. Eat, Drink, & Be Merry: Poems about Food & Drink. 2003. (Everyman's Library Pocket Poets Ser.). (ENG.). 256p. 14.95 *(978-1-4000-4023-0(X),* Everyman's Library) Knopf Doubleday Publishing Group.
Waters, Fiona. Fire & Stone, Wind & Tide: Poems About the Elements. Corfield, Robin Bell, illus. 2006. 43p. (gr. 4-8). reprint ed. 24.00 *(978-1-4223-5595-4(0))* DIANE Publishing Co.
Watkins, Bessie. Presidents in Profile: Three Views of One Face. 2003. (Illus.). 60p. (J). per. 11.95 *(978-0-9728674-1-2(4))* Written Expressions Enterprise, Inc.
Watson Bain, E., ed. A Poetry Book for Boys & Girls. 2014. (ENG.). 196p. pap. 13.99 *(978-1-107-44062-3(9))* Cambridge Univ. Pr.
Webster, Keith. Why Can't My Turtle Be a Ninja? 2006. 160p. per. 12.95 *(978-1-59858-193-5(7))* Dog Ear Publishing, LLC.
Weil, Jennifer. Marvin's Lump. 2006. (J). 15.95 *(978-1-889743-47-9(X))* Robbie Dean Pr.
Weinert, Stella, compiled by. Come on Clouds, Fly Away! 2013. 64p. pap. *(978-1-926635-80-4(9))* Adlibbed, Ltd.
Weitl, Joe. My Book of Poems to Enjoy: Volume 1, 1 vol. 2009. 92p. pap. 16.95 *(978-1-61582-540-0(1))* PublishAmerica, Inc.
Wells, Philip. The Alien Guide from Inner Space: And Other Poems. 2013. (ENG.). 80p. pap. *(978-1-84471-816-0(6))* Salt Publishing.
West, Lorraine, illus. I Like You but I Love Me. 2006. 36p. (J). pap. 12.95 *(978-0-9768674-1-8(9))* Hip Hop Schl. Hse.
Wethington, Constance. Mystic Imaginations. 2008. 137p. pap. 24.95 *(978-1-60563-807-2(2))* America Star Bks.
Whamsby, Dawud. Picnic of Poems: In Allah's Green Garden. 2011. (ENG., Illus.). 44p. (J). (gr. k). 22.95 *(978-0-86037-444-2(0))* Kube Publishing Ltd. GBR. Dist: Consortium Bk. Sales & Distribution.
Wheeler, David & Twigg, Natalie. My Pirate Grandad. 2013. (Illus.). 26p. pap. *(978-0-9573384-5-6(7))* Red Axe Bks.
Wheeler, Jordan. Chuck in the City. Auchter, Christopher, illus. rev. ed. 2009. (Chuck Ser.). (ENG.). 32p. (gr. -1-3). pap. 10.95 *(978-1-894778-81-7(2))* Theytus Bks., Ltd. CAN. Dist: Univ. of Toronto Pr.
Wheeler, Tonika Yvonne. Damaged Goods. Attaway, Anelda, ed. Edwards, Cedric, illus. 2013. 100p. pap. 13.99 *(978-0-9892656-0-7(9))* Jazzy Kitty Greetings Marketing & Publishing Co.
White, Eleanor Dantzler. Sincere Sentiments. 2003. 180p. (YA). per. *(978-0-9679516-2-1(3))* Full Effect Gospel Ministries, Inc.
Whitman, Walt. Nothing but Miracles. Roth, Susan L., illus. 2003. (ENG.). 32p. (J). (gr. -1-3). 15.95 *(978-0-7922-6143-8(7),* National Geographic Children's Bks.) National Geographic Society.
Whittingham, Brian. Septimus Pitt & the Grumbleoids. Sinclair, Mandy, illus. 2007. (ENG.). 48p. (J). 17.95 *(978-1-905222-81-0(5),* 9781905222810) Luath Pr. Ltd. GBR. Dist: Midpoint Trade Bks., Inc.
Whittington, Phillip. What a Hullabaloo! 2009. 56p. pap. 10.49 *(978-1-4389-9219-8(X))* AuthorHouse.
Whyman, Jennifer E., text. Heavenly Blessings: Baby's Book of Bible Blessing/Baby's Book of Bible Promises. 2008. (Land of Milk & Honey Ser.). (Illus.). 32p. (J). (gr. -1-k). bds. 9.99 *(978-1-4347-9945-6(X))* Cook, David C.
Wilson, Gabriella S. Anything on Earth Poems: Children's Poetry. l.t. ed. 2005. (Illus.). 34p. (J). per. 9.99 *(978-1-59879-083-2(8))* Lifevest Publishing, Inc.
Willey, Sarah Jo. Lullaby for Birds. 2012. 24p. pap. 17.99 *(978-1-4772-8134-5(7))* AuthorHouse.
Williams, Adele Knight. What's in a Smile. 2010. 28p. pap. 16.95 *(978-1-4490-5638-4(5))* AuthorHouse.
Williams, Caroline. Twinkle, Twinkle Time for Bed. 2009. (Rookie Toddler: Sing along Toddler Ser.). (ENG.). 12p. (J). (gr. -1). bds. 6.95 *(978-0-531-24544-6(6))* Scholastic Library Publishing.
Williams, Julie. Escaping Tornado Season: A Story in Poems. 2004. 272p. (J). 16.89 *(978-0-06-008640-4(8),* HarperTeen) HarperCollins Pubs.
Williams, Laura M. Why Was Jesus Born. 2013. 18p. pap. 9.99 *(978-1-62839-346-0(7))* Salem Author Services.
Williams, Lyndsay. NonSense! It's Banana Cheese! 2007. (ENG.). 84p. per. 19.95 *(978-1-4241-6736-4(1))* America Star Bks.
Williams, Vera B. Amber Was Brave, Essie Was Smart. Williams, Vera B., illus. 2004. (Illus.). 17.00 *(978-0-7569-3181-0(9))* Perfection Learning Corp.
Williamson, Greg. The Hole Story of Kirby the Sneak & Arlo the True. Bowes, Brian, illus. 2016. (ENG.). 119p. pap. 20.00 *(978-1-904130-83-3(6))* Waywiser Pr., The GBR. Dist: Dufour Editions, Inc.
Williamson, Kate T. Hello Kitty Through the Seasons! Butefish, Jennifer & Soares, Maria Fernanda, photos by. 2006. (ENG., Illus.). 96p. (J). (gr. 3-7). 14.95 *(978-0-8109-5993-4(3))* Abrams, Inc.
Willis, Jeanne. Who's in the Loo? Reynolds, Adrian, illus. 2013. (ENG.). 32p. (J). (gr. -1-k). pap. 12.99 *(978-1-84270-698-5(5))* Andersen Pr. GBR. Dist: Independent Pubs. Group.
Wilmot, Rod. The Meal of Magic Cards, 1 vol. 2003. (ENG., Illus.). 41p. pap. *(978-0-88753-010-4(9))* Black Moss Pr. CAN. Dist: LitDistCo.
Wilson, Adele Tolley. Plum Gum & Other Chunk Poems: Teacher Tested Kid Approved Poems for Building Fluency Through Phonics. 2004. 112p. 11.95 *(978-1-4140-5443-8(2))* AuthorHouse.
Wilson, Karma. Bear Hugs: Romantically Ridiculous Animal Rhymes. Watts, Suzanne, illus. 2007. (ENG.). 32p. (J). (gr. -1-3). 7.99 *(978-1-4169-4958-9(5),* McElderry, Margaret K. Bks.) McElderry, Margaret K. Bks.
Wilson, Murray. Goofus & Other Silly Poems, 1 vol. Morrison, Tyler, illus. 2010. 28p. pap. 24.95 *(978-1-4489-6288-4(9))* PublishAmerica, Inc.
Wilson, Vicky, ed. Touch Wood. 2012. (Illus.). 68p. pap. *(978-1-904662-16-7(1))* Categorical Bks.
Winborne, Stephanie. A Peace of Heaven on Earth. 2009. 70p. pap. 15.99 *(978-1-4500-1586-8(7))* Xlibris Corp.
Wing, Natasha. The Night Before Father's Day. Wummer, Amy, illus. 2012. (Night Before Ser.). (ENG.). 32p. (J). (gr. -1-k). pap. 4.99 *(978-0-448-45871-7(3),* Grosset & Dunlap) Penguin Young Readers Group.
—The Night Before Father's Day. 2012. (Night Before Ser.). lib. bdg. 14.75 *(978-0-606-26073-2(0),* Turtleback) Turtleback Bks.
—The Night Before Mother's Day. Wummer, Amy, illus. 2010. (Night Before Ser.). (ENG.). 32p. (J). (gr. -1-k). pap. 4.99 *(978-0-448-45213-5(8),* Grosset & Dunlap) Penguin Young Readers Group.
—The Night Before New Year's. Wummer, Amy, illus. 2009. (Night Before Ser.). (ENG.). 32p. (J). (gr. -1-k). pap. 4.99 *(978-0-448-45212-8(X),* Grosset & Dunlap) Penguin Young Readers Group.
Winners: Poems & Stories, 2003 Spring Writing Contest. 2003. (J). 5.00 *(978-0-9702646-2-6(3));* (YA). 5.00 *(978-0-9702646-3-3(1))* New Sweden Pr.
Winters, Ben H. & Sloan, Price Stern. Literally Disturbed Vol. 2: More Tales to Keep You up at Night. Watkins, Adam F., illus. 2015. (ENG.). 64p. (J). (gr. 3-7). bds. 9.99 *(978-0-8431-7312-3(2),* Price Stern Sloan) Penguin Young Readers Group.
Winters, Kay. Did You See What I Saw? Weston, Martha, illus. 2015. 32p. pap. 7.00 *(978-1-61003-529-3(1))* Center for the Collaborative Classroom.
—Voices of Ancient Egypt. 2009. (ENG., Illus.). 32p. (J). (gr. 3-7). 6.95 *(978-1-4263-0400-2(5),* National Geographic Children's Bks.) National Geographic Society.
Wissinger, Tamera Will. There Was an Old Lady Who Gobbled a Skink. Bermejo, Ana, illus. 2016. (ENG.). 36p. (J). (gr. -1-k). 16.99 *(978-1-63220-428-8(2),* Sky Pony Pr.) Skyhorse Publishing Co., Inc.
Witmer, Edith. Dancing Buttercups: Poems for Little Children. 2003. (Illus.). 83p. (gr. -1-7). 4.95 *(978-0-7399-2303-0(X),* 2183) Rod & Staff Pubs., Inc.
Wodehouse, P. G. William Tell Told Again - Illustrated in Color. Philip Dadd, illus. 2009. 76p. pap. 14.95 *(978-1-60386-208-0(0),* Watchmaker Publishing) Wexford College Pr.
Wolff, Pat. Noah's Faith: A Children's Poem. 2007. (Illus.). (J). bds. 10.99 *(978-0-9788324-2-1(6))* Playing Pig Pr.
Wondrous Tales of Wicked Winston. (Illus.). pap. *(978-0-920236-18-5(9))* Annick Pr., Ltd.
Wong, Janet S. Twist: Yoga Poems. Paschkis, Julie, illus. 2007. (ENG.). 40p. (J). (gr. 2-5). 19.99 *(978-0-689-87394-2(8),* McElderry, Margaret K. Bks.) McElderry, Margaret K. Bks.
Wood, Robert Williams. How to Tell the Birds from the Flowers. 2011. 54p. 16.99 *(978-1-61720-185-1(5));* pap. 6.99 *(978-1-61720-186-8(3))* Wilder Pubns., Corp.
Woodbury, Karl. England Is Truly a Magical Place. 2008. (Illus.). 96p. per. *(978-1-84748-191-7(4))* Athena Pr.
Woodson, Jacqueline. Brown Girl Dreaming. l.t. ed. 2017. (ENG.). 24.99 **(978-1-4328-4315-1(X))** Cengage Gale.
—Brown Girl Dreaming. (ENG.). (J). (gr. 5). 2016. 368p. pap. 10.99 *(978-0-14-751582-7(3),* Puffin Books) 2014. (Illus.). 336p. 17.99 *(978-0-399-25251-8(7),* Nancy Paulsen Books) Penguin Young Readers Group.
—Brown Girl Dreaming. 2016. (ENG.). 368p. (J). (gr. 5). 22.10 *(978-0-606-39310-2(2))* Turtleback Bks.
Wooldridge, Susan. Bathing with Ants. 2004. 30p. pap. 14.00 *(978-0-9719607-4-9(7))* Bear Star Pr.
Woolf-Wade, Sarah J. Nightsong. 2003. (Illus.). 114p. (YA). per. 12.00 *(978-1-930648-45-6(6),* 207-832-6665) Goose River Pr.
Wooten, Terry. When the Bear Came Back: The Whole Story. Lechler, Louan, illus. 2006. (J). per. 9.49 *(978-1-893972-27-8(5))* Wordsmith Pr.
Word, Sharon. The Word Is Alphabet Poems. 2011. 33p. (J). 13.99 *(978-1-935906-29-2(1))* Intermedia Publishing Group.
Worth, Valerie. Animal Poems. Jenkins, Steve, illus. 2007. (ENG.). 48p. (J). (gr. -1-3). 18.99 *(978-0-374-38057-1(0),* 9780374380571, Farrar, Straus & Giroux (BYR)) Farrar, Straus & Giroux.
Wright, Alice & Bridges, LaVon. Alaska Animals We Love You: Chants & Poems for Children. 2005. (J). 16.95 *(978-1-59433-028-5(X),* Publishing Consultants) Publication Consultants.
Wright, Danielle. Japanese Nursery Rhymes: Carp Streamers, Falling Rain & Other Traditional Favorites. Acraman, Helen, illus. 2012. (ENG.). 32p. (J). (gr. -1-3). 16.95 *(978-4-8053-1188-2(6))* Tuttle Publishing.
Wright, Kit. The Magic Box: Poems for Children. Bailey, Peter, illus. unabr. ed. 2010. (ENG.). 240p. (J). (gr. 1-4). pap. 9.99 *(978-0-330-50981-7(0))* Pan Macmillan GBR. Dist: Independent Pubs. Group.
Xinran, Xinran, et al. Motherbridge of Love. Masse, Josée, illus. 2007. (ENG.). 32p. (J). (gr. -1-5). 16.99 *(978-1-84686-047-8(4))* Barefoot Bks., Inc.
Yardman, Barbara M. Crawl, Fly or Run Book. 2009. 60p. pap. 23.99 *(978-1-4389-0872-4(5))* AuthorHouse.
Yolen, Jane. The Alligator's Smile: And Other Poems. Stemple, Jason, photos by. 2016. (ENG., Illus.). 32p. (gr. 3-6). 38.65 *(978-1-5124-1110-2(8),* Millbrook Pr.) Lerner Publishing Group.
—The Alligator's Smile & Other Poems. Stemple, Jason, photos by. 2016. (ENG., Illus.). 32p. (J). (gr. 3-6). 19.99 *(978-1-4677-5575-7(3),* Millbrook Pr.) Lerner Publishing Group.
—An Egret's Day. Stemple, Jason, illus. Stemple, Jason, photos by. 2010. (ENG.). 32p. (J). (gr. 4-6). 17.95 *(978-1-59078-650-5(5),* Wordsong) Boyds Mills Pr.
—Self-Portrait with Seven Fingers. 2014. (ENG.). 40p. (J). (gr. 5-17). pap. 12.00 *(978-0-89812-974-8(5),* Creative Paperbacks) Creative Co., The.
—Snow, Snow: Winter Poems for Children. Stemple, Jason, photos by. 2005. (ENG., Illus.). 32p. (J). (gr. 4-6). pap. 12.95 *(978-1-59078-346-7(8))* Boyds Mills Pr.
—Thunder Underground. Masse, Josée, illus. 2017. (ENG.). 32p. (J). (gr. k-5). 17.95 *(978-1-59078-936-0(9),* Wordsong) Boyds Mills Pr.
—Water Music: Poems for Children. Stemple, Jason, photos by. 2003. (ENG., Illus.). 40p. (J). (gr. 5-7). pap. 11.95 *(978-1-59078-251-4(8))* Boyds Mills Pr.
Yolen, Jane & Dotlich, Rebecca Kai. Grumbles from the Forest: Fairy-Tale Voices with a Twist. Mahurin, Matt, illus. 2013. (ENG.). 40p. (J). (gr. 2). 16.95 *(978-1-59078-867-7(2),* Wordsong) Boyds Mills Pr.
Young, Judy & A12. R Is for Rhyme: A Poetry Alphabet. Juhasz, Victor, illus. 2010. (ENG.). 48p. (J). pap. 7.95 *(978-1-58536-519-7(X))* Sleeping Bear Pr.
Young, Wanda. Joyous Poems for Children. 2007. (YA). per. *(978-1-933594-66-8(7))* FBC Pubns. & Printing.
Yungul, Elizabeth. I'm Looking from My Window — I'm Looking from My Room. 2009. 48p. pap. 17.49 *(978-1-4343-7160-7(3))* AuthorHouse.
Zager, Jack. Where Do the Tigers Go? A Collection of Children's Poetry. 2004. (Illus.). 32p. (J). lib. bdg. 9.95 *(978-1-930580-57-2(6),* Luminary Media Group) Pine Orchard, Inc.
Zavyalov, Diana. The Little Humpy: Derivative Translation from Russian Fairy Tale by Ershov. 2012. 56p. pap. 24.20 *(978-1-4669-6955-1(5))* Trafford Publishing.
Zephaniah, Benjamin. Talking Turkeys. (ENG., Illus.). 96p. (J). 9.95 *(978-0-14-036330-2(0))* Penguin Bks., Ltd. GBR. Dist: Trafalgar Square Publishing.
—When I Grow Up. Das, Prodeepta, photos by. 2012. (ENG., Illus.). 32p. (J). (gr. 2-5). 17.99 *(978-1-84780-059-6(9),* Frances Lincoln) Quarto Publishing Group UK GBR. Dist: Hachette Bk. Group.
Zeringue, Dona. I Am I. Zeringue, Dona, illus. (Illus.). 32p. (Orig.). (YA). (gr. 6-12). pap. 7.50 *(978-1-882913-02-2(7))* Thornton Publishing.
Zimmerman, Mary Joyce. Good Morning Baby! Hartzler, Maria, illus. 2013. 48p. (J). pap. *(978-0-7399-2458-7(3))* Rod & Staff Pubs., Inc.
Zobel-Nolan, Allia. Smelly Feet Sandwich: And Other Silly Poems. Leake, Kate, illus. 2008. 22p. (J). (gr. -1-2). 7.95 *(978-1-58925-836-5(3))* Tiger Tales.
100 Verses about Laura Ingalls Wilder. 2005. (YA). 9.99 *(978-0-9765951-0-6(9))* Little Hse. Site Tours LLC.

POETRY—COLLECTIONS

see also American Poetry—Collections; English Poetry—Collections

Adams, Michelle Medlock. My Funny Valentine. Johnson, Meredith, illus. 2005. (ENG.). 32p. (J). 12.95 *(978-0-8249-5487-1(4),* Ideal Pubns.) Worthy Publishing.
Adedjouma, Davida. The Palm of My Heart: Poetry by African American Children. Christie, Gregory R., illus. 2013. (ENG.). 32p. (J). (gr. -1-18). pap. 9.95 *(978-1-880000-76-2(8))* Lee & Low Bks., Inc.
Akister, Finola, et al, selected by. Sea Poems & Space Poems. 2008. (Illus.). 32p. (J). pap. 10.95 *(978-1-59646-611-1(1))* Dingles & Co.
—Sports Poems & Mouse Poems. 2008. (Illus.). 32p. (J). pap. 10.95 *(978-1-59646-619-7(7))* Dingles & Co.
Akister, Finola, et al. Sea Poems & Space Poems. 2008. (Illus.). 32p. (J). lib. bdg. 23.65 *(978-1-59646-610-4(3))* Dingles & Co.
—Sports Poems & Mouse Poems. 2008. (Illus.). 32p. (J). lib. bdg. 23.65 *(978-1-59646-618-0(9))* Dingles & Co.
Andrew, Moira, et al, selected by. Night Poems & Ghost Poems. 2008. (Illus.). 32p. (J). pap. 10.95 *(978-1-59646-623-4(5))* Dingles & Co.
Andrew, Moira, et al. Night Poems & Ghost Poems. 2008. (Illus.). 32p. (J). lib. bdg. 23.65 *(978-1-59646-622-7(7))* Dingles & Co.
Andrews, David, et al, selected by. Water Poems & Bug Poems. 2008. (Illus.). 32p. (J). pap. 10.95 *(978-1-59646-603-6(0))* Dingles & Co.
Andrews, David, et al. Water Poems & Bug Poems. 2008. (Illus.). 32p. (J). lib. bdg. 23.65 *(978-1-59646-602-9(2))* Dingles & Co.
Barbour, Karen, illus. Wonderful Words: Poems about Reading, Writing, Speaking, & Listening. 2004. (ENG.). 32p. (J). (gr. 1-6). 19.99 *(978-0-689-83588-9(4),* Simon & Schuster Bks. For Young Readers) Simon & Schuster Bks. For Young Readers.
Bennett, Rowena, et al, selected by. Monkey Poems & Seed Poems. 2008. (Illus.). 32p. (J). pap. 10.95 *(978-1-59646-613-5(8))* Dingles & Co.
Bennett, Rowena, et al. Monkey Poems & Seed Poems. 2008. (Illus.). 32p. (J). lib. bdg. 23.65 *(978-1-59646-612-8(X))* Dingles & Co.
Bevan, Clare, et al, selected by. Clothes Poems & Weather Poems. 2008. (Illus.). (J). 32p. pap. 10.95 *(978-1-59646-585-5(9));* 24p. lib. bdg. 23.65 *(978-1-59646-584-8(0))* Dingles & Co.
—Party Poems & Out & about Poems. 2008. (Illus.). 24p. (J). pap. 10.95 *(978-1-59646-583-1(2))* Dingles & Co.
Bevan, Clare, et al. Party Poems & Out & about Poems. 2008. (Illus.). 24p. (J). lib. bdg. 23.65 *(978-1-59646-582-4(4))* Dingles & Co.
Boldes, Gary. Thoughts of a Sailor. 2003. 58p. pap. 7.00 *(978-1-4116-0425-4(3))* Lulu Pr., Inc.
Bradman, Tony, et al, selected by. Castle Poems & Dragon Poems. 2008. (Illus.). 32p. (J). pap. 10.95 *(978-1-59646-615-9(4))* Dingles & Co.
—Machine Poems & Music Poems. 2008. (Illus.). 32p. (J). pap. 10.95 *(978-1-59646-601-2(4))* Dingles & Co.
—Pirate Poems & Monster Poems. 2008. (Illus.). 32p. (J). pap. 10.95 *(978-1-59646-621-0(9))* Dingles & Co.
Bradman, Tony, et al. Castle Poems & Dragon Poems. 2008. (Illus.). 32p. (J). lib. bdg. 23.65 *(978-1-59646-614-2(6))* Dingles & Co.
—Machine Poems & Music Poems. 2008. (Illus.). 32p. (J). lib. bdg. 23.65 *(978-1-59646-600-5(6))* Dingles & Co.
—Pirate Poems & Monster Poems. 2008. (Illus.). 32p. (J). lib. bdg. 23.50 *(978-1-59646-620-3(0))* Dingles & Co.
Brooks, Marie, et al, selected by. Pet Poems & Special Day Poems. 2008. (Illus.). 32p. (J). pap. 10.95 *(978-1-59646-599-2(9))* Dingles & Co.
Clark, Lucinda. View from the Middle of the Road: Where the Greenest Grass Grows, 3 vols., volume I. Brenda, Baratto, ed. Audrey, Crosby, illus. 2004. 55p. per. 9.00 *(978-0-9727703-1-6(3),* 706 855-6173) P.R.A. Publishing.
Colson, Mary. Action Poems, 1 vol. 2014. (Experiencing Poetry Ser.). (ENG., Illus.). 64p. (gr. 7-8). lib. bdg. 35.99 *(978-1-4329-9557-7(X))* Heinemann-Raintree.
Cookson, Paul, et al, selected by. Body Poems & Movement Poems. 2008. (Illus.). 32p. (J). pap. 10.95 *(978-1-59646-589-3(1))* Dingles & Co.
Cooling, Wendy, ed. Come to the Great World: Poems from Around the Globe. Moxley, Sheila, tr. Moxley, Sheila, illus. 2004. (ENG.). 48p. (J). (gr. k-3). tchr. ed. 17.95 *(978-0-8234-1822-0(7))* Holiday Hse., Inc.
Corbett, Pie, et al, selected by. Color Poems & Sounds Poems. 2008. (Illus.). 32p. (J). pap. 10.95 *(978-1-59646-591-6(3))* Dingles & Co.
Corbett, Pie, et al. Color Poems & Sounds Poems. 2008. (Illus.). 32p. (J). lib. bdg. 23.65 *(978-1-59646-590-9(5))* Dingles & Co.
Cordova, Soledad. Poemas de Perros y Gatos. Graullera, Fabiola, illus. 2003. (SPA.). 21p. (J). (gr. 3-5). pap. 7.95 *(978-968-19-0987-1(9))* Santillana USA Publishing Co., Inc.
Corman, Cid. One Man's Moon: Poems by Basho & Other Japanese Poets. exp. ed. 2003. 128p. pap. 15.00 *(978-0-917788-76-5(1))* Gnomon Pr.
Coville, Bruce. The Unicorn Treasury: Stories, Poems, & Unicorn Lore. 2004. (ENG., Illus.). 224p. (J). (gr. 2-5). pap. 7.99 *(978-0-15-205216-4(X))* Houghton Mifflin Harcourt Publishing Co.
Cowling, Sue, et al, selected by. Giant Poems & Wizzard Poems. 2008. (Illus.). 32p. (J). pap. 10.95 *(978-1-59646-607-4(3))* Dingles & Co.

Cruz-Contarini, Rafael & Rafael, Cruz-Contarini. Zaranda. (SPA., Illus.). 84p. (J). 7.50 (978-84-241-3367-2(6)) Everest Editora ESP. Dist: Lectorum Pubns., Inc.

Daly, Catherine. DaDaDa. 2003. (Modern Poets Ser.). (ENG.). 224p. pap. (978-1-876857-95-0(1)) Salt Publishing.

Daniels, John. Love & Pain. 2004. 70p. (YA). mass mkt. 14.95 (978-0-9755489-0-5(5)) New Birth Publishing.

Dawson, Mary, et al, selected by. Snow Poems & Star Poems. 2008. (Illus.). 32p. (J). pap. 10.95 (978-1-59646-617-3(0)) Dingles & Co.

Dawson, Mary, et al. Snow Poems & Star Poems. 2008. (Illus.). 32p. (J). lib. bdg. 23.65 (978-1-59646-616-6(2)) Dingles & Co.

Douthwaite, Gina, et al, selected by. Farm Poems & Seasons Poems. 2008. (Illus.). 32p. (J). pap. 10.95 (978-1-59646-597-8(2)) Dingles & Co.

Douthwaite, Gina, et al. Farm Poems & Seasons Poems. 2008. (Illus.). 32p. (J). lib. bdg. 23.65 (978-1-59646-596-1(4)) Dingles & Co.

Downes, Belinda. Baby Days: A Quilt of Rhymes & Pictures. Downes, Belinda, illus. 2006. (ENG., Illus.). 32p. (J). (— 1). 14.99 (978-0-7636-2786-7(0)) Candlewick Pr.

Eulalie. Buds, Blossoms, & Leaves: Eulalie's Collected Poems. 2003. 200p. lib. bdg. 25.00 (978-0-9708005-3-4(3)) Singing Tree Pr.

Factor. Language Works Jelly Plate. 16p. (J). (978-0-8136-3520-0(9)) Modern Curriculum Pr.

Fairfield Middle School. Poetry 2006 by 6th Grade Students of Fairfield Middle School. 2006. 120p. per. 14.95 (978-1-59540-886-0(X)) 1st World Publishing, Inc.

Favorite Poems. 2015. (Favorite Poems Ser.). (ENG.). 40p. (J). (gr. 2-3). 319.50 (978-1-4824-2169-9(0)) Stevens, Gareth Publishing LLLP.

Field, Eugene. A Little Book of Western Verse. 2013. (Notable American Authors Ser.). 202p. reprint ed. lthr. 79.00 (978-0-7812-2642-4(2)) Reprint Services Corp.

Finney, Eric, et al, selected by. Shopping Poems & Food Poems. 2008. (Illus.). 32p. (J). pap. 10.95 (978-1-59646-595-4(6)) Dingles & Co.

Finney, Eric, et al. Shopping Poems & Food Poems. 2008. (Illus.). 32p. (J). lib. bdg. 23.65 (978-1-59646-594-7(8)) Dingles & Co.

Flowers, Audrey X. Rhymes of the Times II. (Orig.). (J). reprint ed. pap. 10.00 (978-1-56411-146-3(6)) UBUS Communications Systems.

FMS Students. Poetry by 6th Grade Students of FMS. 2005. 21.95 (978-1-59540-968-3(8)); 13.95 (978-1-59540-962-1(9)) 1st World Publishing, Inc. (1st World Publishing).

Foster, John, et al, selected by. Transportation Poems & Senses Poems. 2008. (Illus.). 32p. (J). pap. 10.95 (978-1-59646-605-0(7)) Dingles & Co.

Foster, John & Mellor, Robin. Alphabet Poems & Number Poems. 2008. (Illus.). 32p. (J). lib. bdg. 23.65 (978-1-59646-592-3(1)) Dingles & Co.

Foster, John & Mellor, Robin, selected by. Alphabet Poems & Number Poems. 2008. (Illus.). 32p. (J). pap. 10.95 (978-1-59646-593-0(X)) Dingles & Co.

Foster, John & Williams, Brenda. Animal Poems & Family Poems. 2008. (Illus.). 24p. (J). lib. bdg. 23.65 (978-1-59646-586-2(7)) Dingles & Co.

Foster, John & Williams, Brenda, selected by. Animal Poems & Family Poems. 2008. (Illus.). 32p. (J). pap. 10.95 (978-1-59646-587-9(5)) Dingles & Co.

Foster, John, et al. Body Poems & Movement Poems. 2008. (Illus.). 32p. (J). lib. bdg. 23.65 (978-1-59646-588-6(3)) Dingles & Co.

—Transportation Poems & Senses Poems. 2008. (Illus.). 32p. (J). lib. bdg. 23.65 (978-1-59646-604-3(9)) Dingles & Co.

Fuchs, A. P. The Hand I've Been Dealt: A Collection of Poetry & Song Streams of Thought & Reflection. 2003. 110p. (YA). 22.95 (978-0-595-66096-4(7)); pap. 12.95 (978-0-595-29976-8(8)) iUniverse, Inc.

Fuertes, Gloria. Poesías, Rimas y Disparates: Pienso Mesa y Digo Silla. 2003. (SPA.). 128p. (978-84-305-8535-9(4), SU4859) Susaeta Ediciones, S.A. ESP. Dist: Lectorum Pubns., Inc.

Fujikawa, Gyo, illus. A Child's Book of Poems. 2007. (ENG.). 128p. (J). (gr. -1-2). 9.95 (978-1-4027-5061-8(7)) Sterling Publishing Co., Inc.

Greenfield, Eloise. In the Land of Words: New & Selected Poems. Gilchrist, Jan Spivey, illus. 2016. 48p. (J). (gr. -1-3). pap. 6.99 (978-0-06-443692-2(6), Amistad) HarperCollins Pubs.

Haan, Wanda. The Macaroon Moon: A Book of Poems & Rhymes for Children. Christensen, Donald, illus. 2004. 32p. (J). 17.95 (978-0-913337-51-6(X)) Southfarm Pr.

Hairston, Angelica. Did Noah Have Whales on the Ark? Ferguson, Tamara, illus. l.t. ed. 2004. 44p. (J). (978-0-9716136-1-4(3)) Broadcast Quality Productions, Inc.

Hale, Christy, tr. & illus. It Rained All Day That Night: Autograph Album Verses & Inscriptions. Hale, Christy, illus. 2005. (ENG.). 80p. (J). (gr. 3-7). pap. 9.95 (978-0-87483-726-1(X)) August Hse. Pubs., Inc.

Hopkins, Lee Bennett. Halloween Howls: Holiday Poetry. Schuett, Stacey, illus. 2005. (I Can Read Bks.). 32p. (J). (gr. k-3). 15.99 (978-0-06-008060-0(4)); lib. bdg. 16.89 (978-0-06-008061-7(2)) HarperCollins Pubs.

I Am of Two Places: Children's Poetry, Vol. 2. (Greetings Ser.: Vol. 2). 24p. (gr. 3-5). 31.00 (978-0-7635-3163-8(4)) Rigby Education.

I Am of Two Places: Children's Poetry: 6 Small Books. (Greetings Ser.: Vol. 2). 24p. (gr. 3-5). 31.00 (978-0-7635-1762-5(3)) Rigby Education.

Idaho Writers League Coeur d'Alene Chapter. Kaleidoscope: A Collection of Tantalizing Tales. 2003. (Illus.). (YA). (gr. 6-18). pap. 15.00 (978-0-9740481-0-9(0)) Children's Village Foundation, Inc.

Jauregui, Patricia. Sentimientos. Jauregui, Reginald, ed. Pineda, Jesus, illus. l.t. ed. 2004. (SPA.). 39p. (YA). pap. 19.95 (978-1-931481-41-0(5)) LiArt-Literature & Art.

Johanson, Paula. World Poetry: Evidence of Life. 2010. (Poetry Rocks! Ser.). (Illus.). 160p. (YA). (gr. 9-12). 35.94 (978-0-7660-3280-4(9)) Enslow Pubs., Inc.

—World Poetry- Evidence of Life. 2011. (Poetry Rocks! Ser.). (Illus.). 160p. (YA). (gr. 9-18). pap. 10.95 (978-1-59845-382-9(3)) Enslow Pubs., Inc.

Johnson, Angela. In Daddy's Arms, I Am Tall. 2004. (Illus.). (J). (gr. k-3). spiral bd. (978-0-616-03094-3(0)) Canadian National Institute for the Blind/Institut National Canadien pour les Aveugles.

Johnson, Layne, illus. Grandparent Poems. 2004. (ENG.). 32p. (J). (gr. 1-7). 15.95 (978-1-56397-900-2(4)) Boyds Mills Pr.

Kantor, Stuart. Call Me Collective. 2003. 365p. (YA). pap. 24.95 (978-0-595-27982-1(1)) iUniverse, Inc.

Kassandra, ed. V antologia nuevo Milenio: Narración (Cuentos) y Poesía. Ramírez, Antonio & Morrissey, Kay, photos by. l.t. ed. 2004. (SPA., Illus.). 100p. (YA). pap. 12.00 (978-1-931481-86-1(5)) LiArt-Literature & Art.

Katsuura, Jaden. Glimpses. 2004. 276p. (YA). pap. 20.95 (978-0-595-30896-5(1)) iUniverse, Inc.

Kenward, Jean, et al, selected by. Egg Poems & Fox Poems. 2008. (Illus.). 32p. (J). pap. 10.95 (978-1-59646-609-8(X)) Dingles & Co.

Kenward, Jean, et al. Egg Poems & Fox Poems. 2008. (Illus.). 32p. (J). lib. bdg. 23.65 (978-1-59646-608-1(1)) Dingles & Co.

Lansky, Bruce, ed. Miles of Smiles. Carpenter, Stephen, illus. 2013. (Giggle Poetry Ser.). (ENG.). 126p. (J). (gr. 1-6). pap. 9.95 (978-0-689-03461-9(X)) Meadowbrook Pr.

Larcom. March. Date not set. (Illus.). 32p. (J). (gr. -1-3). 14.99 (978-0-06-024307-4(4)); lib. bdg. 15.89 (978-0-06-024308-1(2)) HarperCollins Pubs.

Lewis, J. Patrick. Monumental Verses. 2005. (ENG., Illus.). 32p. (J). (gr. 3-7). 16.95 (978-0-7922-7135-2(1), National Geographic Children's Bks.) National Geographic Society.

Maddox, Nellie Hazel. Grandmother Nellie's Poems, Vol. I. 2004. (Illus.). 200p. per. 24.95 (978-0-9755255-0-0(6)) Fletcher, C J Publishing LLC.

Mandel, Ruth. How to Tell Your Children about the Holocaust. 2003. (ENG., Illus.). 1p. (J). pap. 22.95 (978-1-894692-06-9(3), Virago Press) McGilligan Bks., Inc. CAN. Dist: Univ. of Toronto Pr.

Mannari, Kaitlyn, et al. Out of Order. 2003. 186p. (YA). pap. 16.95 (978-0-595-30045-7(6)) iUniverse, Inc.

Mao, Xian. Children's Version of 60 Classical Chinese Poems. 2012. 68p. pap. 28.99 (978-1-4685-5904-0(4)) AuthorHouse.

Mboya, Sharif. Heart Fealt Doses of Reality. Mboya, Sharif, illus. 2004. (Illus.). 148p. (YA). per. 14.99 (978-0-9754024-5-0(5)) Doses of Reality, Inc.

McCollough, Aaron. Double Venus. 2003. (Modern Poets Ser.). (ENG.). 108p. pap. (978-1-84471-003-4(3)) Salt Publishing.

McKenzie, Richard. Poems from the Playground & Other Places. Gervasi, Christine, illus. 2004. (J). 12.00 (978-0-9725901-0-5(2)) Lekha Pubs., LLC.

Moore, Ralph. Thoughts of Roses: A Collection of Poems by Ralph S. Moore 2003. (Illus.). 72p. 19.95 (978-0-9741193-1-1(8)) Roland & Eleanor Bergthold.

Morrison, Britta. Zara by the Se. 2011. 24p. pap. 28.03 (978-1-4568-8311-9(9)) Xlibris Corp.

Morrison, Lillian. I Scream, You Scream: A Feast of Food Rhymes. Dunaway, Nancy, illus. 2005. (Story Cove Ser.). (ENG.). 96p. (J). (gr. -1-3). 12.95 (978-0-87483-495-6(3)) August Hse. Pubs., Inc.

Mozz. The Pearls of Wisdumb: The Electric Light Verse & Shocking Scribbles of Mozz. 2003. (ENG., Illus.). 176p. (J). lib. bdg. 17.95 (978-0-9726130-0-2(5)) Goofy Guru Publishing.

Nuestro Mundo en la Poesia: Complete Set. 2003. (SPA., Illus.). (J). 225.50 (978-0-8136-0705-4(1)) Modern Curriculum Pr.

Protopopescu, Orel O. A Thousand Peaks: Poems from China. Liu, Siyu, tr. from CHI. Liu, Siyu, illus. 2003. (CHI & ENG.). 52p. (gr. 7-18). 19.95 (978-1-881896-24-1(2), THPE) Pacific View Pr.

Replogle, Steve & Carlsen, Wendy Vergoz, eds. From a Kid's Life: A Collection of Poetry by Bromwell Students. 2004. 160p. (J). per. 10.00 (978-0-9753345-0-8(6)) Bromwell Bks.

Rette's Last Stand: Poems by Everette Maddox. 2004. (YA). pap. 15.00 (978-0-9746444-0-0(4)) Tensaw Pr., Inc., The.

Robbins, Michelle. Leaving the Scars Behind. 2004. 114p. (YA). pap. 12.95 (978-0-595-31257-3(8)) iUniverse, Inc.

Rodgers, Denise. Great Lakes Rhythmn & Rhyme 2003. (Illus.). 64p. (J). per. 9.95 (978-0-938682-80-6(6)) River Road Pubns., Inc.

Shane, Bill. Hey Batter Batter: A Collection of Baseball Poems for Kids. 2003. (Illus.). 88p. (J). (gr. k-9). pap. 7.95 (978-1-931643-20-7(2)) Seven Locks Pr.

Shapiro, Karen Jo. Because I Could Not Stop My Bike: And Other Poems. Faulkner, Matt, illus. 2005. (ENG.). 32p. (J). (gr. 2-5). pap. 7.95 (978-1-58089-105-9(5)) Charlesbridge Publishing, Inc.

Shea, Pegi Deitz, ed. African American Picture-Poetry Collection for Children. Date not set. (Illus.). (J). 17.95 (978-0-8050-7377-5(9), Holt, Henry & Co. Bks. For Young Readers) Holt, Henry & Co.

Smith, Nikki Siegen. Welcome to the World: A Celebration of Birth & Babies from Many Cultures. 2005. (ENG., Illus.). 48p. (J). 18.99 (978-1-84148-890-5(9)) Barefoot Bks., Inc.

Stepping Stones of Life, 1 vol. 2003. (Illus.). 110p. pap. 19.95 (978-0-9743964-0-8(0)) World of Angels, A.

Stutman, Suzanne. All the Power Rests with You. 2005. 188p. pap. 12.95 (978-0-9648261-7-5(8)) Medical Manor Bks.

Tarazona, Oscar, illus. Volando con Alas Propias. l.t. ed. 2004. (SPA.). 116p. (YA). pap. 12.00 (978-1-931481-88-5(1)) LiArt-Literature & Art.

Thomas, Tamara. ABC Poem Book. Thomas, Tamara, illus. 2004. (Illus.). (YA). (gr. 1-6). pap. (978-1-930200-28-9(5)) Martell Publishing Co.

To Whom It May Concern. 2006. (YA). per. 16.95 (978-0-9661256-8-9(1)) Youth Communication - New York Center.

Washington Elementary School. Principal Dusanek. 2006. 15.95 (978-1-59540-981-2(5), 1st World Publishing) 1st World Publishing, Inc.

Whitman, Walt & Long, Loren. When I Heard the Learn'd Astronomer. Long, Loren, illus. 2004. (ENG., Illus.). 32p. (J). (gr. k-4). 17.99 (978-0-689-86397-4(7), Simon & Schuster Bks. For Young Readers) Simon & Schuster Bks. For Young Readers.

Woods, Gemal. From the Limbs of My Poetree: Selected Poems by Omekongo Dibinga, 1 disc. 2004. (ENG, FRE & SWA., Illus.). 183p. per. 24.95 incl. DVD (978-0-9760056-0-5(3)) Free Your Mind Publishing.

Yolen, Jane. Color Me a Rhyme: Nature Poems for Young People. Stemple, Jason, photos by. 2003. (ENG., Illus.). 32p. (J). (gr. 4-6). pap. 6.95 (978-1-59078-172-2(4)) Boyds Mills Pr.

—Once upon Ice: And Other Frozen Poems. Stemple, Jason, photos by. (ENG., Illus.). 40p. (YA). (gr. 4-6). pap. 9.95 (978-1-59078-174-6(0)) Boyds Mills Pr.

POETRY—FICTION

Amato, Mary. Edgar Allan's Official Crime Investigation Notebook. (ENG.). 176p. (J). 2011. pap. 6.99 (978-0-8234-2386-6(7)) 2010. (gr. 1-5). 16.95 (978-0-8234-2271-5(2)) Holiday Hse., Inc.

Archer, Micha. Daniel Finds a Poem. Archer, Micha, illus. 2016. (ENG., Illus.). 32p. (J). (gr. k-3). 16.99 (978-0-399-16913-7(X), Nancy Paulsen Books) Penguin Young Readers Group.

Arcos, Carrie. Crazy Messy Beautiful. 2017. (ENG.). 320p. (YA). (gr. 7). 17.99 (978-0-399-17553-4(9), Philomel Bks.) Penguin Young Readers Group.

Bennett, Jill. Grandad's Tree: Poems about Families. Cairns, Julia, illus. 2003. 32p. (J). 16.99 (978-1-84148-541-6(1)) Barefoot Bks., Inc.

Bledsoe, Michele & Bledsoe, Richard. The Secret Kingdom. 2013. 36p. 20.95 (978-1-4787-0362-4(8)) Outskirts Pr., Inc.

Bryant, Jen. Call Me Marianne. Johnson, David, illus. 2006. 32p. (J). (gr. 1-4). 16.00 (978-0-8028-5242-7(4), Eerdmans Bks For Young Readers) Eerdmans, William B. Publishing Co.

Burak, Kathryn. Emily's Dress & Other Missing Things. 2012. (ENG.). 240p. (YA). (gr. 8-12). 17.99 (978-1-59643-736-4(7)) Roaring Brook Pr.

Calhoun, Dia. Eva of the Farm. Slater, Kate, illus. 2012. (ENG.). 256p. (J). (gr. 4-7). 16.99 (978-1-4424-1700-7(5), Atheneum Bks. for Young Readers) Simon & Schuster Children's Publishing.

Cartaya, Pablo. The Epic Fail of Arturo Zamora. 2017. (ENG.). 256p. (J). (gr. 5). 16.99 (978-1-101-99723-9(0), Viking Books for Young Readers) Penguin Young Readers Group.

Cassidy, Sara. Skylark, 1 vol. 2014. (Orca Soundings Ser.). (ENG.). 136p. (YA). (gr. 8-12). pap. 9.95 (978-1-4598-0590-3(9)) Orca Bk. Pubs. USA.

Cattell, Bob & Agard, John. Butter-Finger. Smy, Pam, illus. 2006. (ENG.). 128p. (J). (gr. 2-17). per. 7.95 (978-1-84507-376-3(2), Frances Lincoln) Quarto Publishing Group UK GBR. Dist: Hachette Bk. Group.

Cazet, Denys, reader. Minnie & Moo: Will You Be My Valentine? 2004. (Read-Alongs for Beginning Readers Ser.). (Illus.). (J). (gr. -1-3). 25.95 incl. audio (978-1-59112-892-2(7)); pap. 29.95 incl. audio (978-1-59112-893-9(5)); pap. 31.95 incl. audio compact disk (978-1-59112-897-7(8)) Live Oak Media.

Cofer, Judith Ortiz. The Poet Upstairs. Ortiz, Oscar, illus. 2012. (J). (gr. 5-9). 16.95 (978-1-55885-704-9(4), Piñata Books) Arte Publico Pr.

—La Poeta Del Piso de Arriba. Baeza Ventura, Gabriela, tr. from ENG. Ortiz, Oscar, illus. 2014. (SPA.). (J). 17.95 (978-1-55885-788-9(5), Piñata Books) Arte Publico Pr.

Creech, Sharon. Hate That Cat. (ENG.). (J). (gr. 3-7). 2010. 176p. pap. 6.99 (978-0-06-143094-7(3)) 2008. 160p. 16.99 (978-0-06-143092-3(7)) HarperCollins Pubs.

—Love That Dog. 2008. (ENG.). 128p. (J). (gr. 3-7). pap. 6.99 (978-0-06-440959-9(7)) HarperCollins Pubs.

—Love That Dog. 2008. (J). (gr. 3-6). lib. bdg. 17.20 (978-0-613-61715-4(0), Turtleback) Turtleback Bks.

Crossan, Sarah. Apple & Rain. 2015. (ENG.). 352p. (YA). (gr. 7). 17.99 (978-1-61963-690-3(5), 9781619636903, Bloomsbury USA Childrens) Bloomsbury Publishing USA.

Davies, Jacqueline. The Candy Smash. (Lemonade War Ser.). (ENG., Illus.). 240p. (J). (gr. 2-5). 2014. pap. 7.99 (978-0-544-22500-8(7), HMH Books For Young Readers) 2013. 15.99 (978-0-544-02208-9(4)) Houghton Mifflin Harcourt Publishing Co.

Dean, Carolee. Comfort. 2004. (ENG.). 256p. (YA). (gr. 7-18). pap. 14.95 (978-0-618-43912-6(9)) Houghton Mifflin Harcourt Publishing Co.

Dell, Pamela. Shaky Bones: A Story of the Harlem Renaissance. 2003. (Scrapbooks of America Ser.). (ENG., Illus.). 48p. (J). (gr. 3-6). 32.79 (978-1-59187-040-1(2), 200811) Child's World, Inc., The.

Dotlich, Rebecca Kai. Bella & Bean. Leijten, Aileen, illus. 2009. (ENG.). 40p. (J). (gr. -1-3). 17.99 (978-0-689-85616-7(4), Atheneum Bks. for Young Readers) Simon & Schuster Children's Publishing.

Fajardo, Alexis E. Kid Beowulf. 2016. lib. bdg. 22.10 (978-0-606-38999-0(7)) Turtleback Bks.

Finneyfrock, Karen. The Sweet Revenge of Celia Door. 2014. (ENG.). 288p. (YA). (gr. 7). pap. 9.99 (978-0-14-750995-6(5), Speak) Penguin Young Readers Group.

Fitzmaurice, Kathryn. Destiny, Rewritten. 2015. (ENG.). 368p. (J). (gr. 3-7). pap. 6.99 (978-0-06-162503-9(5), Tegen, Katherine Bks) HarperCollins Pubs.

Flores-Scott, Patrick. Jumped In. 2013. (ENG.). 304p. (YA). (gr. 7). 16.99 (978-0-8050-9514-2(4), 9780805095142, Holt, Henry & Co. Bks. For Young Readers) Holt, Henry & Co.

—Jumped In. 2014. (ENG., Illus.). 304p. (YA). (gr. 7). pap. 10.99 (978-1-250-05398-5(6), 9781250053985) Square Fish.

Gilman, Grace. Dixie & the Best Day Ever. Rogers, Jacqueline, illus. 2014. (I Can Read Level 1 Ser.). (ENG.). 32p. (J). (gr. -1-3). pap. 3.99 (978-0-06-208659-4(6)) HarperCollins Pubs.

Grimes, Nikki. Bronx Masquerade. (ENG.). (YA). (gr. 7). 2017. 192p. pap. 8.99 **(978-0-425-28976-1(1))** 2003. 176p. 6.99 (978-0-14-250189-4(1)) Penguin Young Readers Group. (Speak).

—Bronx Masquerade. 2003. (gr. 7-12). lib. bdg. 17.20 (978-0-613-81701-1(X), Turtleback) Turtleback Bks.

—Poems in the Attic. Zunon, Elizabeth, illus. 2015. (ENG.). 48p. (J). 19.95 (978-1-62014-027-7(6)) Lee & Low Bks., Inc.

—Rich. Christie, R. Gregory, illus. 2009. (Dyamonde Daniel Book Ser.: 2). (ENG.). 112p. (J). (gr. 2-4). 12.99 (978-0-399-25176-4(6), G.P. Putnam's Sons Books for Young Readers) Penguin Young Readers Group.

Grover, Lorie Ann. Hit, 1 vol. 2015. (ENG.). 224p. (YA). pap. 8.99 (978-0-310-72938-9(6)) Blink.

Gutman, Dan. Ms. Coco Is Loco! Paillot, Jim, illus. 2007. (My Weird School Ser.: 16). (J). 14.75 (978-1-4177-7428-9(2), Turtleback) Turtleback Bks.

Harris, Teresa E. Gabriela. 2016. (American Girl: Girl of the Year Ser.: 1). (ENG.). 208p. (J). (gr. 3-7). pap. 9.99 (978-1-338-13698-2(4)) Scholastic, Inc.

Herrera, Robin. Hope Is a Ferris Wheel. 2014. (ENG., Illus.). 272p. (YA). (gr. 3-7). 16.95 (978-1-4197-1039-1(7), Amulet Bks.) Abrams, Inc.

Holub, Joan & Williams, Suzanne. Calliope the Muse. 2016. (Goddess Girls Ser.: 20). (ENG., Illus.). 256p. (J). (gr. 3-7). pap. 7.99 (978-1-4814-5004-1(2), Aladdin) Simon & Schuster Children's Publishing.

—Calliope the Muse. 2016. (Goddess Girls Ser.: 20). lib. bdg. 18.40 (978-0-606-38972-3(5)) Turtleback Bks.

Hubbard, Jenny. And We Stay. 2014. (ENG.). 240p. (YA). (gr. 9). lib. bdg. 19.99 (978-0-375-98955-1(2), Delacorte Pr.) Random Hse. Children's Bks.

Johnson, Peter. The Life & Times of Benny Alvarez. 2014. (ENG.). 224p. (J). (gr. 3-7). 16.99 (978-0-06-221596-3(5)) HarperCollins Pubs.

Kephart, Beth. Undercover. 2009. (ENG.). 304p. (YA). (gr. 8). pap. 8.99 (978-0-06-123895-6(3), HarperTeen) HarperCollins Pubs.

Kline, Suzy. Horrible Harry & the Dead Letters. Remkiewicz, Frank et al, illus. 2009. (Horrible Harry Ser.). (ENG.). 80p. (J). (gr. 2-4). 3.99 (978-0-14-241457-6(3), Puffin Books) Penguin Young Readers Group.

Koertge, Ron. Shakespeare Makes the Playoffs. 2012. (ENG., Illus.). 176p. (YA). (gr. 7). pap. 6.99 (978-0-7636-5852-6(9)) Candlewick Pr.

Koertge, Ronald. Shakespeare Bats Cleanup. 2006. 116p. (gr. 7-12). 16.00 (978-0-7569-6571-6(3)) Perfection Learning Corp.

—Shakespeare Makes the Playoffs. 2010. (ENG., Illus.). 176p. (YA). (gr. 7-18). 15.99 (978-0-7636-4435-2(8)) Candlewick Pr.

Kousky, Vern. Otto the Owl Who Loved Poetry. Kousky, Vern, illus. 2015. (ENG., Illus.). 32p. (J). (gr. k-3). 16.99 (978-0-399-16440-8(5), Nancy Paulsen Books) Penguin Young Readers Group.

Lois, Lowry. Gooney Bird Is So Absurd. Thomas, Middy, illus. 2013. (Gooney Bird Greene Ser.). (ENG.). 112p. (J). (gr. 1-4). pap. 5.99 (978-0-547-87559-0(2)) Houghton Mifflin Harcourt Publishing Co.

Mangum, Kay Lynn. When the Bough Breaks. 2007. 352p. (YA). pap. 15.95 (978-1-59038-748-1(1)) Deseret Bk. Co.

Manushkin, Fran. It Doesn't Need to Rhyme, Katie: Writing a Poem with Katie Woo, 1 vol. Lyon, Tammie, illus. 2013. (Katie Woo: Star Writer Ser.). (ENG.). 32p. (gr. k-2). pap. 6.95 (978-1-4795-1923-1(5)); lib. bdg. 20.65 (978-1-4048-8128-0(X)) Picture Window Bks.

McNamara, Margaret. A Poem in Your Pocket. Karas, G. Brian, illus. 2015. (Mr. Tiffin's Classroom Ser.). (ENG.). 40p. (J). (gr. -1-3). 16.99 (978-0-307-97947-6(4), Schwartz & Wade Bks.) Random Hse. Children's Bks.

Murphy, Sally. Pearl Verses the World. Potter, Heather, illus. 2011. (ENG.). 80p. (J). (gr. 3-7). 14.99 (978-0-7636-4821-3(3)) Candlewick Pr.

Nikki, Grimes. Bronx Masquerade. 2014. (ENG.). 176p. (YA). 11.24 (978-1-63245-077-7(1)) Lectorum Pubns., Inc.

O'Connor, Jane. Poet Extraordinaire! Glasser, Robin Preiss, illus. 2010. (Fancy Nancy Ser.). (ENG.). 32p. (J). (gr. -1-2). 12.99 (978-0-06-189643-9(8)) HarperCollins Pubs.

Pearson, Susan. Slugs in Love, 0 vols. O'Malley, Kevin, illus. 2012. (ENG.). 34p. (J). (gr. -1-3). pap. 7.99 (978-0-7614-6248-4(1), 9780761462484, Amazon Children's Publishing) Amazon Publishing.

Roskos, Evan. Dr. Bird's Advice for Sad Poets. 2013. (ENG.). 320p. (YA). (gr. 9). 17.99 (978-0-547-92853-1(X)) Houghton Mifflin Harcourt Publishing Co.

Schroeder, Lisa. Falling for You. 2013. (ENG., Illus.). 384p. (YA). (gr. 9). pap. 9.99 (978-1-4424-4400-3(2), Simon Pulse) Simon Pulse.

Scieszka, Jon. Science Verse. Smith, Lane, illus. 2004. (ENG.). 40p. (J). (gr. 2-5). 17.99 (978-0-670-91057-1(0), Viking Books for Young Readers) Penguin Young Readers Group.

Sharon, Creech. Love That Dog. 2014. (ENG.). 112p. (J). (gr. 7-9). 10.24 (978-1-63245-159-0(X)) Lectorum Pubns., Inc.

Spalding, Andrea & Spalding, David A. E. The Klondike Ring, 1 vol. 2003. (Adventure - Net Ser.). (ENG.). 128p. (J). pap. (978-1-55285-461-7(2)) Whitecap Bks., Ltd.

Spinelli, Eileen. Another Day As Emily. Lew-Vriethoff, Joanne, illus. 2015. (ENG.). 240p. (J). (gr. 3-7). 6.99 (978-0-449-80989-1(7), Yearling) Random Hse. Children's Bks.

Stavans, Ilan. Golemito. Villegas, Teresa, illus. 2013. (ENG.). 32p. (J). 16.95 (978-1-58838-292-4(3), NewSouth Bks.) NewSouth, Inc.

Stone, Tamara Ireland. Every Last Word. 2015. (ENG.). 368p. (YA). (gr. 7-12). 17.99 (978-1-4847-0527-8(0)) Hyperion Bks. for Children.

—Every Last Word. 2017. (ENG.). (YA). (gr. 7-12). lib. bdg. 20.85 **(978-0-606-39885-5(6))** Turtleback Bks.

Weiss, Ellen & Friedman, Mel. Porky & Bess. Winborn, Marsha, illus. 2011. (Step into Reading Ser.). (ENG.). 48p. (J). (gr. 2-4). pap. 3.99 (978-0-375-86113-0(0), Random Hse. Bks. for Young Readers) Random Hse. Children's Bks.

Whybrow, Ian. Little Wolf's Handy Book of Poems. Ross, Tony, illus. 2005. (Little Wolf Adventures Ser.). 80p. (gr. 3-6). pap., lib. bdg. 14.95 (978-0-87614-927-0(1)) Lerner Publishing Group.

Wigden, Susan. Silly Rhymes for Fun Times. Columbin, Corey, illus. 2011. 20p. pap. 11.95 (978-1-60888-107-9(5)) Nimble Bks. LLC.

Yeh, Kat. The Way to Bea. 2017. (ENG.). 352p. (J). (gr. 3-7). 16.99 **(978-0-316-23667-6(5))** Little, Brown Bks. for Young Readers.

POETRY—HISTORY AND CRITICISM

Bodden, Valerie. Concrete Poetry. 2009. (Poetry Basics Ser.). (Illus.). 32p. (J). 19.95 (978-1-58341-775-1(3), 1300261, Creative Education) Creative Co., The.

—Haikus. 2009. (Poetry Basics Ser.). (Illus.). 32p. 19.95 *(978-1-58341-776-8(1)*, 1300262, Creative Education) Creative Co., The.

—Poetry Basics: Concrete Poetry. 2011. (Poetry Basics Ser.). (ENG.). 32p. (J). (gr. 5-17). pap. 8.99 *(978-1-926722-43-6(4)*, Creative Paperbacks) Creative Co., The.

Buckwalter, Stephanie. Death Poetry: Death, Be Not Proud. 2014. (Pure Poetry Ser.). 128p. (J). lib. bdg. 33.27 *(978-0-7660-4257-5(X))* Enslow Pubs., Inc.

Johanson, Paula. Love Poetry: How Do I Love Thee? 2014. (Pure Poetry Ser.). 128p. (J). lib. bdg. 33.27 *(978-0-7660-4284-1(7))* Enslow Pubs., Inc.

—World Poetry: Evidence of Life. 2010. (Poetry Rocks! Ser.). (Illus.). 160p. (YA). (gr. 9-12). 35.94 *(978-0-7660-3280-4(9))* Enslow Pubs., Inc.

—World Poetry- Evidence of Life. 2011. (Poetry Rocks! Ser.). (Illus.). 160p. (YA). (gr. 9-18). pap. 10.95 *(978-1-59845-382-9(3))* Enslow Pubs., Inc.

Llanas, Sheila Griffin. Beauty Poetry: She Walks in Beauty. 2014. (Pure Poetry Ser.). 128p. (J). lib. bdg. 33.27 *(978-0-7660-4243-8(X))* Enslow Pubs., Inc.

—Modern American Poetry- Echoes & Shadows. 2011. (Poetry Rocks! Ser.). (Illus.). 160p. (YA). (gr. 9-18). pap. 10.95 *(978-1-59845-379-9(3))* Enslow Pubs., Inc.

POETRY—PHILOSOPHY

see Poetry

POETRY—SELECTIONS

see Poetry—Collections

POETRY—TECHNIQUE

see Poetics

POETRY FOR CHILDREN

see Nursery Rhymes; Poetry

POETRY OF LOVE

see Love Poetry

POETRY OF NATURE

see Nature—Poetry

POETS

see also Dramatists

Ashby, Ruth. Caedmon's Song. Slavin, Bill, illus. 2006. (ENG.). 32p. (J). (gr. k). 16.00 *(978-0-8028-5241-0(6)*, Eerdmans Bks For Young Readers) Eerdmans, William B. Publishing Co.

Berry, S. L. E. E. Cummings. 2014. (J). *(978-1-60818-325-8(4)*, Creative Education) Creative Co., The.

—Voices in Poetry: E. E. Cummings. 2015. (Voices in Poetry Ser.). (ENG.). 48p. (J). (gr. 5-8). pap. 12.00 *(978-1-62832-053-4(2)*, Creative Paperbacks) Creative Co., The.

Berry, S. L. & Dickinson, Emily. Emily Dickinson. 2014. (Illus.). 47p. (J). *(978-1-60818-326-5(2)*, Creative Education) Creative Co., The.

Bloom, Harold, ed. Bloom's Major Poets. 2005. (Bloom's Major Poets Ser.). 144p. (C). (gr. 9). 670.95 *(978-0-7910-7886-0(8)*, Chelsea Hse.) Facts On File, Inc.

—Contemporary Poets, New Edition. 2nd rev. ed. 2009. (Bloom's Modern Critical Views Ser.). 192p. (C). (gr. 9-18). 45.00 *(978-1-60413-588-6(3)*, Chelsea Hse.) Facts On File, Inc.

Bloom, Harold, et al. Bloom's Major Poets. (Illus.). (J). 780.30 *(978-0-7910-7387-2(4)*, Chelsea Hse.) Facts On File, Inc.

Bodden, Valerie. Who Is a Poet? 2016. (Write Me a Poem Ser.). (ENG.). 24p. (J). (gr. 2-4). pap. 9.99 *(978-1-62832-255-2(1)*, Creative Paperbacks) Creative Co., The.

Bowman, Chris. Nikki Grimes. 2017. (Children's Storytellers Ser.). (ENG., Illus.). 24p. (J). (gr. k-3). lib. bdg. 25.95 ***(978-1-62617-650-8(7)***, Blastoff! Readers) Bellwether Media.

Brown, Monica. Pablo Neruda: Poet of the People. Paschkis, Julie, illus. 2011. (ENG.). 32p. (J). (gr. 1-4). 17.99 *(978-0-8050-9198-4(X)*, 9780805091984, Holt, Henry & Co. Bks. For Young Readers) Holt, Henry & Co.

Bryant, Jennifer. A River of Words: The Story of William Carlos Williams. Sweet, Melissa, illus. 2008. (ENG.). 34p. (J). (gr. 4-7). 17.50 *(978-0-8028-5302-8(1)*, Eerdmans Bks For Young Readers) Eerdmans, William B. Publishing Co.

Buckwalter, Stephanie. Early American Poetry: "Beauty in Words" 2009. (Poetry Rocks! Ser.). (Illus.). 160p. (YA). (gr. 9-12). lib. bdg. 35.94 *(978-0-7660-3277-4(9))* Enslow Pubs., Inc.

—Early American Poetry- Beauty in Words. 2011. (Poetry Rocks! Ser.). (Illus.). 160p. (YA). (gr. 9-18). pap. 10.95 *(978-1-59845-378-2(5))* Enslow Pubs., Inc.

Burgess, Matthew. Enormous Smallness: The Story of e. e. Cummings. Di Giacomo, Kris, illus. 2015. (ENG.). 64p. (J). (gr. -1-3). 17.95 *(978-1-59270-171-1(X))* Enchanted Lion Bks., LLC.

Center for Learning Network Staff. I Know Why the Caged Bird Sings: Curriculum Unit. 2005. (Novel Ser.). 75p. (YA). tchr. ed., spiral bd. 19.95 *(978-1-56077-787-8(7))* Center for Learning, The.

Cheng, Andrea. Etched in Clay: The Life of Dave, Enslaved Potter & Poet. Cheng, Andrea, illus. 2013. (ENG., Illus.). 146p. (J). 17.95 *(978-1-60060-451-5(X))* Lee & Low Bks., Inc.

Cody, Sherwin. Four American Poets. 2009. 198p. pap. 14.14 *(978-0-217-47860-1(3))* General Bks. LLC.

Collard, Sneed B., III. Phillis Wheatley: She Loved Words. 2009. (American Heroes Ser.). 48p. (gr. 3-18). 29.93 *(978-0-7614-4057-4(7))* Marshall Cavendish Corp.

Davis, Rebecca Henry. Fanny Crosby: Queen of Gospel Songs. 2003. (Illus.). 107p. (J). 6.49 *(978-1-57924-970-0(1))* BJU Pr.

Demi. Rumi: Persian Poet, Whirling Dervish, 0 vols. 2009. (ENG.). 40p. (J). (gr. 4-7). 19.99 *(978-0-7614-5527-1(2)*, 9780761455271, Amazon Children's Publishing) Amazon Publishing.

Dennis, John. Heroes of Literature: English Poets, a B. 2006. pap. 34.95 *(978-1-4254-9436-0(6))* Kessinger Publishing, LLC.

Derby, Sally. Jump Back, Paul: The Life & Poems of Paul Laurence Dunbar. Qualls, Sean, illus. 2015. (ENG.). 128p. (J). (gr. 4-7). 16.99 *(978-0-7636-6070-3(1))* Candlewick Pr.

Diggory, Terence. Encyclopedia of the New York School Poets. 2009. (Literary Movements Ser.). (Illus.). 560p. (C). (gr. 9). 75.00 *(978-0-8160-5743-6(5))* Facts On File, Inc.

Doak, Robin S. Phillis Wheatley: The Inspiring Life Story of the American Poet. 2016. (Inspiring Stories Ser.). (ENG., Illus.). 112p. (J). (gr. 5-7). lib. bdg. 35.99 *(978-0-7565-5166-7(8)*, CPB Grades 4-8) Compass Point Bks.

Fine, Anne. An Interview with Anne Fine. (ENG., Illus.). 96p. (YA). pap. 5.50 *(978-1-4052-0053-0(7))* Egmont Bks., Ltd. GBR. Dist: Trafalgar Square Publishing.

Flor Ada, Alma & Campoy, F. Isabel, contrib. by. Paths. (Literature Collection of Gateways to the Sun Ser.). 48p. (J). (gr. k-6). pap. 16.95 *(978-1-59437-722-8(7))* Santillana USA Publishing Co., Inc.

Gallagher, Brigid. Langston Hughes, 1 vol. 2012. (American Biographies Ser.). (ENG.). 48p. (gr. 4-6). pap. 9.95 *(978-1-4329-6466-5(6)*, NA-h) Heinemann-Raintree.

Gigliotti, Jim. Who Was Edgar Allan Poe? Foley, Tim, illus. 2015. 105p. (J). *(978-1-4844-6178-5(9)*, Grosset & Dunlap) Penguin Publishing Group.

Glaser, Linda. Emma's Poem: The Voice of the Statue of Liberty. Nivola, Claire A., illus. 2010. (ENG.). 32p. (J). (gr. -1-3). 17.99 *(978-0-547-17184-5(6))* Houghton Mifflin Harcourt Publishing Co.

Herrera, Juan Felipe. The Upside down Boy. Gómez, Elizabeth, illus. 2011. (Rise & Shine Ser.).Tr. of Nino de Cabeza. (SPA & ENG.). 32p. (C). (gr. k-3). per. 14.95 *(978-0-89239-217-9(7))* National Geographic School Publishing, Inc.

Herstek, Amy Paulson. Emily Dickinson: Solitary & Celebrated Poet. 2003. (Historical American Biographies Ser.). (Illus.). 128p. (J). lib. bdg. 26.60 *(978-0-7660-1977-5(2))* Enslow Pubs., Inc.

Hill, Christine M. Gwendolyn Brooks: Poetry Is Life Distilled. 2005. (African-American Biography Library). (Illus.). 128p. (J). (gr. 6-12). lib. bdg. 33.27 *(978-0-7660-2292-8(7))* Enslow Pubs., Inc.

Hill, Laban Carrick. Dave the Potter: Artist, Poet, Slave. Collier, Bryan, illus. 2010. (ENG.). 40p. (J). (gr. -1-3). 18.99 *(978-0-316-10731-0(X))* Little, Brown Bks. for Young Readers.

Hill, Laban Carrick. Dave the Potter: Artist, Poet, Slave. 2011. (J). *(978-1-4618-1706-2(4))* Recorded Bks., Inc.

Hinds, Maurene. Emily Dickinson, 1 vol. 2013. (Great American Authors Ser.). (ENG.). 48p. (J). (gr. 3-6). lib. bdg. 32.79 *(978-1-61783-716-6(4))* ABDO Publishing Co.

Hoehne, Marcia. Anne Bradstreet: America's Puritan Poet. 2007. 203p. pap. *(978-1-888105-75-9(5))* Avisson Pr., Inc.

Houle, Michelle M. Modern British Poetry- The World Is Never the Same. 2011. (Poetry Rocks! Ser.). (Illus.). 160p. (YA). (gr. 9-18). pap. 10.95 *(978-1-59845-381-2(5))* Enslow Pubs., Inc.

Hubbard-Brown, Janet. Chaucer: Celebrated Poet & Author. 2005. (Makers of the Middle Ages & Renaissance Ser.). (Illus.). 144p. (gr. 5-8). 32.95 *(978-0-7910-8635-3(6)*, Chelsea Hse.) Facts On File, Inc.

Jarnow, Jesse. Phillis Wheatley. 2004. (Primary Sources of Famous People in American History Ser.). (ENG., Illus.). 32p. (gr. 4-8). pap. 10.00 *(978-0-8239-4191-9(4))* Rosen Publishing Group, Inc., The.

—Phillis Wheatley: African American Poet / Poeta Afroamericana. 2009. (Famous People in American History/Grandes personajes en la historia de los Estados Unidos Ser.). (ENG & SPA.). 32p. (gr. 2-3). 47.90 *(978-1-61512-554-8(X)*, Editorial Buenas Letras) Rosen Publishing Group, Inc., The.

—Phillis Wheatley; Poeta afroamericana (Phillis Wheatley: African American Poet) 2009. (Grandes personajes en la historia de los Estados Unidos (Famous People in American History) Ser.). (SPA.). 32p. (gr. 2-3). 47.90 *(978-1-61512-807-5(7)*, Editorial Buenas Letras) Rosen Publishing Group, Inc., The.

Johanson, Paula. Early British Poetry: "Words That Burn" (Poetry Rocks! Ser.). (Illus.). 160p. (YA). (gr. 9-18). 2011. pap. 10.95 *(978-1-59845-383-6(1))* 2009. lib. bdg. 35.94 *(978-0-7660-3276-7(0))* Enslow Pubs., Inc.

—World Poetry- Evidence of Life. 2011. (Poetry Rocks! Ser.). (Illus.). 160p. (YA). (gr. 9-18). pap. 10.95 *(978-1-59845-382-9(3))* Enslow Pubs., Inc.

Jones, Veda Boyd. Jazz Age Poet: A Story about Langston Hughes. Kiwak, Barbara, illus. 2005. (Creative Minds Biographies Ser.). (ENG.). 64p. (gr. 4-8). lib. bdg. 22.60 *(978-1-57505-757-6(3)*, Carolrhoda Bks.) Lerner Publishing Group.

Kanefield, Teri. The Extraordinary Suzy Wright: A Colonial Woman on the Frontier. 2016. (ENG., Illus.). 64p. (J). (gr. 3-7). 19.95 *(978-1-4197-1866-3(5)*, Abrams Bks. for Young Readers) Abrams, Inc.

Kent, Deborah. Phillis Wheatley: First Published African-American Poet. 2003. (Our People Ser.). (ENG., Illus.). 32p. (J). (gr. 3-6). 29.93 *(978-1-59296-009-5(X)*, 200649) Child's World, Inc., The.

Kent, Jacqueline C. Phillis Wheatley. 2003. (Women of the Revolution Ser.). (J). pap. *(978-1-58417-089-1(1))*; lib. bdg. *(978-1-58417-026-6(3))* Lake Street Pubs.

Kerley, Barbara. Walt Whitman: Words for America. Selznick, Brian, illus. 2004. (ENG.). 56p. (J). (gr. 2-5). 17.99 *(978-0-439-35791-3(8)*, Scholastic Pr.) Scholastic, Inc.

Kirkpatrick, Patricia. John Keats. Delessert, Etienne, illus. 2005. (Voices in Poetry Ser.). 43p. (J). (gr. 5-9). 21.95 *(978-1-58341-345-6(6)*, Creative Education) Creative Co., The.

Lasky, Kathryn. A Voice of Her Own: The Story of Phillis Wheatley, Slave Poet. Lee, Paul, illus. 2012. (Candlewick Biographies Ser.). (ENG.). 48p. (J). (gr. 3-7). 14.99 *(978-0-7636-6427-5(8))*; pap. 4.99 *(978-0-7636-6091-8(4))* Candlewick Pr.

Leon, Georgina Lazaro. Conoce a Gabriela Mistral: Get to Know Gabriela Mistral. Palacios, Sara Helena, illus. 2014. (Personajes Del Mundo Hispnico Ser.). (ENG & SPA.). 32p. (J). (gr. -1-3). 15.95 *(978-1-61435-351-5(4)*, Alfaguara) Santillana USA Publishing Co., Inc.

Llanas, Sheila Griffin. Contemporary American Poetry: Not the End, but the Beginning. 2010. (Poetry Rocks! Ser.). (Illus.). 160p. (YA). (gr. 9-12). 35.94 *(978-0-7660-3279-8(5))* Enslow Pubs., Inc.

—Modern American Poetry: Echoes & Shadows. 2009. (Poetry Rocks! Ser.). (Illus.). 160p. (YA). (gr. 9-12). lib. bdg. 35.94 *(978-0-7660-3275-0(2))* Enslow Pubs., Inc.

—Walt Whitman, 1 vol. 2013. (Great American Authors Ser.). (ENG.). 48p. (J). (gr. 3-6). lib. bdg. 32.79 *(978-1-61783-720-3(2))* ABDO Publishing Co.

Loewen, Nancy. Walt Whitman. Day, Rob, illus. 2014. 47p. 35.65 *(978-1-60818-329-6(7)*, Creative Education) Creative Co., The.

Lukes, Bonnie L. Henry Wadsworth Longfellow: America's Beloved Poet. 2nd rev. exp. ed. 2004. (World Writers Ser.). (Illus.). 144p. (YA). (gr. 6-12). 23.95 *(978-1-931798-07-5(9))* Reynolds, Morgan Inc.

Marsh, Carole. Phillis Wheatley. 2003. 12p. (gr. k-4). 2.95 *(978-0-635-02371-1(7))* Gallopade International.

Mattern, Joanne. Geoffrey Chaucer: Medieval Writer, 1 vol. 2012. (Primary Source Readers Ser.). (ENG.). 32p. (J). (gr. 4-4). pap. 8.99 *(978-1-4333-5006-1(8))* Teacher Created Materials, Inc.

McLeese, Don. Phillis Wheatley. 2004. (Heroes of the American Revolution Ser.). (Illus.). 32p. (J). (gr. -1 — 1). pap. 5.95 *(978-1-59515-320-3(9))* Rourke Educational Media.

McLendon, Jacquelyn. Phillis Wheatley: A Revolutionary Poet. 2009. (Library of American Lives & Times Ser.). 112p. (gr. 5-5). 69.20 *(978-1-60853-499-5(5))* Rosen Publishing Group, Inc., The.

McLendon, Jacquelyn Y. Phillis Wheatley: A Revolutionary Poet. 2005. (Library of American Lives & Times). (Illus.). 112p. (YA). (gr. 4-8). lib. bdg. 34.60 *(978-0-8239-5750-7(0))* Rosen Publishing Group, Inc., The.

Meltzer, Milton. Emily Dickinson: A Biography. 2006. (Literary Greats Ser.). (ENG.). 128p. (gr. 7-12). lib. bdg. 33.26 *(978-0-7613-2949-7(8)*, Millbrook Pr.) Lerner Publishing Group.

Moriarty, J. T. Phillis Wheatley: African American Poet. 2009. (Primary Sources of Famous People in American History Ser.). 32p. (gr. 2-3). 47.90 *(978-1-60851-717-6(9))* Rosen Publishing Group, Inc., The.

Nagle, Jeanne & Schull, Jodie A. Pablo Neruda: Nobel Prize-Winning Poet. 2016. (Influential Latinos Ser.). (ENG.). 128p. (J). (gr. 7-8). lib. bdg. 37.27 *(978-0-7660-7314-2(9))* Enslow Pubs., Inc.

Neis, Therese. Extraordinary African-American Poets. 2012. (African-American Collective Biographies Ser.). 112p. (J). (gr. 5-18). 33.27 *(978-1-59845-139-9(1))* Enslow Pubs., Inc.

Poets & Playwrights, 5 vols., Set. Incl. Carl Sandburg. Murcia, Rebecca Thatcher. lib. bdg. 37.10 *(978-1-58415-430-3(6))*; Emily Dickinson. Griskey, Michele. lib. bdg. 37.10 *(978-1-58415-429-7(2))*; Langston Hughes. Gibson, Karen Bush. lib. bdg. 37.10 *(978-1-58415-431-0(4))*; Tennessee Williams. Tracy, Kathleen. lib. bdg. 37.10 *(978-1-58415-427-3(6))*; William Shakespeare. Whiting, Jim. lib. bdg. 37.10 *(978-1-58415-426-6(8))*; (Illus.). 112p. (J). (gr. 3-7). 2007. 2007. Set lib. bdg. 185.50 *(978-1-58415-284-2(2))* Mitchell Lane Pubs., Inc.

Reef, Catherine. The Life of Paul Laurence Dunbar: Portrait of a Poet. 2014. (Legendary African Americans Ser.). (Illus.). 96p. (J). (gr. 6-12). 27.94 *(978-0-7660-6152-1(3))*; pap. 10.95 *(978-0-7660-6153-8(1))* Enslow Pubs., Inc.

—Poetry Came in Search of Me: The Story of Pablo Neruda. 2012. (World Writers Ser.). (gr. 7-12). 28.95 *(978-1-59935-170-4(6))* Reynolds, Morgan Inc.

Rhynes, Martha E. Gwendolyn Brooks: Poet from Chicago. 2004. (World Writers Ser.). (Illus.). 112p. (YA). (gr. 6-12). 23.95 *(978-1-931798-05-1(2))* Reynolds, Morgan Inc.

Rhys, Ann Gruffydd & Bryntirion, Gwasg. Nansi Dolwar. 2005. (WEL., Illus.). 24p. pap. *(978-1-85049-212-2(3))* Bryntirion Pr.

Robertson, David. The Poet: Pauline Johnson. Henderson, Scott B., illus. 2014. (Tales from Big Spirit Ser.: 6). (ENG.). 32p. (J). (gr. 4-6). pap. *(978-1-55379-481-3(8)*, ab04cc8e-58f6-479c-9f04-879c4a722ff3, HighWater Pr.) Portage & Main Pr.

Roby, Cynthia A. & Rohan, Rebecca. Langston Hughes. 2016. (Artists of the Harlem Renaissance Ser.). (ENG.). 128p. (J). (gr. 9-9). lib. bdg. 45.64 *(978-1-5026-1064-5(7))* Cavendish Square Publishing.

Roza, Greg. Guide My Pen: The Poems of Phillis Wheatley. 2009. (Great Moments in American History Ser.). 32p. (gr. 3-3). 47.90 *(978-1-61513-133-4(7))* Rosen Publishing Group, Inc., The.

Santillian, Beatriz & Randall, Bernard. Solon: Athenian Statesman & Poet. 2017. (Leaders of the Ancient World Ser.). 112p. (J). (gr. 12-11). 37.10 ***(978-1-5081-7493-6(8)***, Rosen Young Adult) Rosen Publishing Group, Inc., The.

Simons, Lisa M. B. Nikki Grimes. Byers, Michael, illus. 2017. (Your Favorite Authors Ser.). (ENG.). 24p. (gr. 1-2). lib. bdg. 25.32 *(978-1-5157-3559-5(1))* Capstone Press of Coughlan Cos.

Spivak, Dawnine. Grass Sandals: The Travels of Basho. Demi, illus. 2009. (ENG.). 40p. (J). (gr. 4-6). 13.99 *(978-1-4424-0936-1(3)*, Atheneum Bks. for Young Readers) Simon & Schuster Children's Publishing.

Strong, Amy. Lee Bennett Hopkins: A Children's Poet. 2003. (Great Life Stories: Writers & Poets Ser.). (ENG., Illus.). 112p. (J). 30.50 *(978-0-531-12315-7(4)*, Watts, Franklin) Scholastic Library Publishing.

Taylor, Charlotte. Phillis Wheatley: Colonial African-American Poet. 2016. (Exceptional African Americans Ser.). (ENG.). 24p. (J). (gr. 3-3). pap. 9.35 *(978-0-7660-7324-1(6))* Enslow Pubs., Inc.

Thomas, Dylan. A Child's Christmas in Wales. Raskin, Ellen, illus. 2003. (New Directions Paperbook Ser.: Vol. 972). (ENG.). 32p. reprint ed. pap. 8.00 *(978-0-8112-1560-2(1))* New Directions Publishing Corp.

Tracy, Kathleen. The Life & Times of Homer. 2004. (Biography from Ancient Civilizations Ser.). (Illus.). 48p. (J). (gr. 4-8). lib. bdg. 29.95 *(978-1-58415-260-6(5))* Mitchell Lane Pubs., Inc.

Wallace, Maurice O. Langston Hughes: The Harlem Renaissance. 2007. (Writers & Their Work Ser.). (Illus.). 144p. (J). (gr. 4-7). lib. bdg. 39.93 *(978-0-7614-2591-5(8)*, Benchmark Bks.) Marshall Cavendish Corp.

Watson-Doost, Valeria. Phillis Wheatley. 2008. 35p. pap. 21.50 *(978-0-557-03153-5(2))* Lulu Pr., Inc.

Weidenbach, Kristin. Meet Banjo Paterson. Gulliver Hancock, James, illus. 2016. (ENG.). 32p. (J). (gr. k-2). 14.99 *(978-0-85798-009-0(2))* Random Hse. Australia AUS. Dist: Independent Pubs. Group.

Wheeler, Jill C. Nikki Grimes, 1 vol. 2012. (Children's Authors Set 6 Ser.). (ENG., Illus.). 24p. (J). (gr. 2-5). 25.65 *(978-1-61783-047-1(X))* ABDO Publishing Co.

Wooten, Sara McIntosh. Robert Frost: The Life of America's Poet. 2006. (People to Know Today Ser.). (Illus.). 128p. (J). (gr. 4-7). lib. bdg. 33.27 *(978-0-7660-2627-8(2))* Enslow Pubs., Inc.

POETS—FICTION

Byars, Betsy. Keeper of the Doves. 2004. (ENG., Illus.). 128p. (J). (gr. 3-7). reprint ed. 7.99 *(978-0-14-240063-0(7)*, Puffin Books) Penguin Young Readers Group.

Cooper, Afua. My Name Is Phillis Wheatley: A Story of Slavery & Freedom. 2009. (ENG., Illus.). 152p. (J). (gr. 5-9). 16.95 *(978-1-55337-812-9(1))* Kids Can Pr., Ltd. CAN. Dist: Hachette Bk. Group.

Dana, Barbara. Emily Dickinson: Fictionalized Biography. Date not set. (J). (gr. 3-7). mass mkt. 4.99 *(978-0-06-440843-1(4))* HarperCollins Pubs.

—A Voice of Her Own: Becoming Emily Dickinson. 2009. (ENG.). 368p. (YA). (gr. 8). 17.99 *(978-0-06-028704-7(7)*, HarperTeen) HarperCollins Pubs.

Figley, Marty Rhodes. Emily & Carlo. Stock, Catherine, illus. 2012. (ENG.). 32p. (J). (gr. k-3). 15.95 *(978-1-58089-274-2(4))* Charlesbridge Publishing, Inc.

Furnari, Eva. Fuzz Mcflops. Entrekin, Alison, tr. from POR. 2015. (ENG., Illus.). 56p. (J). (gr. k-3). pap. 12.95 *(978-1-78269-075-7(1)*, Pushkin Press) Steerforth Pr.

Hawes, Louise. The Language of Stars. 2016. (ENG., Illus.). 368p. (J). (gr. 7). 17.99 *(978-1-4814-6241-9(5)*, McElderry, Margaret K. Bks.) McElderry, Margaret K. Bks.

Herrera, Juan Felipe. SkateFate. 2015. 128p. (YA). (gr. 8). pap. 9.99 *(978-0-06-143289-7(X)*, HarperTeen) HarperCollins Pubs.

Leal, Ann Haywood. Also Known As Harper. 2011. (ENG.). 272p. (J). (gr. 5-7). pap. 10.99 *(978-0-312-65934-9(2)*, 9780312659349) Square Fish.

MacColl, Michaela. Nobody's Secret. (ENG.). (gr. 7-17). 2014. 256p. (YA). pap. 9.99 *(978-1-4521-2854-2(5))* 2013. 241p. (J). 16.99 *(978-1-4521-0860-5(9))* Chronicle Bks. LLC.

MacDonald, George. Home Again. 2009. 124p. 22.95 *(978-1-60664-613-7(3))*; pap. 10.95 *(978-1-60664-351-8(7))* Rodgers, Alan Bks.

MacLachlan, Patricia. Fly Away. 2014. (ENG., Illus.). 128p. (J). (gr. 2). 15.99 *(978-1-4424-6008-9(3)*, McElderry, Margaret K. Bks.) McElderry, Margaret K. Bks.

Moody Publishing Staff & Lawton, Wendy G. Freedom's Pen: A Story Based on the Life of Freed Slave & Author Phillis Wheatley 2009. (Daughters of the Faith Ser.). (ENG.). 144p. (gr. 3-7). pap. 7.99 *(978-0-8024-7639-5(2))* Moody Pubs.

Moulton, Mark K. The Visit. Winget, Susan, illus. 2003. 56p. (J). 14.95 *(978-0-8249-5475-8(0)*, Ideal Pubns.) Worthy Publishing.

Moulton, Mark Kimball. The Visit. Winget, Susan, tr. Winget, Susan, illus. 2003. (ENG.). 56p. (J). 14.95 *(978-0-8249-5859-6(4)*, Ideal Pubns.) Worthy Publishing.

—The Visit: The Origin of the Night Before Christmas, 1 vol. Winget, Susan, illus. 2013. (ENG.). 54p. (J). 16.99 *(978-0-7643-4575-3(3)*, 9780764345753) Schiffer Publishing, Ltd.

Muten, Burleigh. Miss Emily. Phelan, Matt, illus. 2014. (ENG.). 144p. (J). (gr. 2-5). 15.99 *(978-0-7636-5734-5(4))* Candlewick Pr.

Myers, Tim J. Basho & the River Stones, 0 vols. Han, Oki, illus. 2013. (ENG.). 34p. (J). (gr. 1-4). pap. 9.99 *(978-1-4778-1682-0(8)*, 9781477816820, Amazon Children's Publishing) Amazon Publishing.

Nilsen, Morten. Snyder: The Pig's Tale. Osenchakov, Yuri, illus. 2007. 116p. 24.95 *(978-0-9774906-0-8(2))* Counterbalance Bks.

Peck, Steven L. The Rifts of Rime (Quickened Chronicles) 2012. pap. 14.99 *(978-1-59955-967-4(6))* Cedar Fort, Inc./CFI Distribution.

The Poet's Basket. 2006. (J). 10.00 *(978-0-9769827-0-8(6))* Wren Song Pr.

Rinaldi, Ann. Hang a Thousand Trees with Ribbons: The Story of Phillis Wheatley. 2005. (Great Episodes Ser.). (ENG.). 352p. (YA). (gr. 7-8). pap. 8.99 *(978-0-15-205393-2(X))* Houghton Mifflin Harcourt Publishing Co.

—Hang a Thousand Trees with Ribbons: The Story of Phillis Wheatley. 2005. (Great Episodes Ser.). 336p. (gr. 5-9). 18.00 *(978-0-7569-5018-7(X))* Perfection Learning Corp.

Ryan, Pam Muñoz. The Dreamer. Sís, Peter, illus. (ENG.). (J). (gr. 4-7). 2012. 400p. pap. 8.99 *(978-0-439-26998-8(9)*, Scholastic Paperbacks) 2010. 384p. 21.99 *(978-0-439-26970-4(9)*, Scholastic Pr.) Scholastic, Inc.

—The Dreamer. 2012. lib. bdg. 19.65 *(978-0-606-23940-0(5)*, Turtleback) Turtleback Bks.

Sharp, Margery. The Rescuers. Williams, Garth, illus. 2016. (ENG.). 160p. (J). (gr. 4-7). pap. 9.99 *(978-1-68137-007-1(7)*, NYRB Kids) New York Review of Bks., Inc., The.

Spinelli, Eileen. Another Day As Emily. Lew-Vriethoff, Joanne, illus. 2014. (ENG.). 240p. (J). (gr. 3-7). 12.99 *(978-0-449-80987-7(0))*; lib. bdg. 15.99 *(978-0-449-80988-4(9))* Random Hse. Children's Bks. (Knopf Bks. for Young Readers).

Tashjian, Janet. Marty Frye, Private Eye Bk. 2: The Case of the Missing Action Figure. Keller, Laurie, illus. 2017. (Marty Frye, Private Eye Ser.). (ENG.). 96p. (J). 15.99 *(978-1-250-11661-1(9)*, 9781250116611, Holt, Henry & Co. Bks. For Young Readers) Holt, Henry & Co.

—Marty Frye, Private Eye Bk. 2: The Case of the Missing Poodle. Keller, Laurie, illus. 2017. (Marty Frye, Private Eye Ser.). (ENG.). 96p. (J). 15.99 *(978-1-62779-460-2(3)*, 9781627794602, Holt, Henry & Co. Bks. For Young Readers) Holt, Henry & Co.

Williams-Garcia, Rita. One Crazy Summer. 2009. (KOR.). 272p. (J). pap. *(978-89-7199-494-8(0))* Dolbegae Publishing Co.

—One Crazy Summer. (J). (gr. 4-7). 2011. (ENG.). 240p. pap. 7.99 *(978-0-06-076090-8(7))* 2010. (ENG.). 224p. 16.99 *(978-0-06-076088-5(5))* 2010. 224p. lib. bdg. 16.89 *(978-0-06-076089-2(3))* HarperCollins Pubs. (Amistad).

—One Crazy Summer. (J). 2011. 1.25 *(978-1-4498-2201-9(0))* 2010. 69.75 *(978-1-4498-2197-5(9))* 2010. 67.75 *(978-1-4498-2199-9(5))* Recorded Bks., Inc.
—One Crazy Summer. 2011. (J). lib. bdg. 17.20 *(978-0-606-23555-6(8)*, Turtleback) Turtleback Bks.

POISONOUS PLANTS

Bradley, Timothy. Terror en Los Trópicos. 2016. (TIME for Kids en Español - Level 5 Ser.). (SPA.). 64p. (gr. 5-5). lib. bdg. 31.99 *(978-1-5157-2939-6(7))* Time for Kids Inc AUS. Dist: Capstone Pub.
Bradley, Timothy J. Terror in the Tropics, 1 vol. 2nd rev. ed. 2013. (Nonfiction Readers Ser.). (ENG., Illus.). 64p. (J). (gr. 5-5). pap. 31.96 *(978-1-4333-7421-0(8))* Teacher Created Materials, Inc.
Claybourne, Anna. 100 Deadliest Things on the Planet. 2012. (100 Most Ser.). lib. bdg. 18.40 *(978-0-606-26744-1(1)*, Turtleback) Turtleback Bks.
Gould, Margee. Poisonous Plants. 2012. (Strangest Plants on Earth Ser.). (Illus.). 24p. (J). (gr. 2-5). lib. bdg. 22.60 *(978-1-4488-4989-5(6))* Rosen Publishing Group, Inc., The.
Hicks, Dwayne. Plants That Poison. 2016. (Plant Defenses Ser.). (Illus.). 24p. (J). (gr. 3-3). pap. 8.25 *(978-1-4994-2155-2(9)*, PowerKids Pr.) Rosen Publishing Group, Inc., The.
Lawler, Janet. Scary Plants! 2017. (Smithsonian Ser.). (ENG., Illus.). 48p. (J). (gr. 1-3). pap. 3.99 *(978-0-451-53371-5(2)*, Penguin Young Readers) Penguin Young Readers Group.
Lawrence, Ellen. Poison Petals: Don't Eat! 2012. (Science Slam: Plant-Ology Ser.). 24p. (J). (gr. -1-3). lib. bdg. 23.93 *(978-1-61772-590-6(0))* Bearport Publishing Co., Inc.
Miller, Connie Colwell. The Deadliest Plants on Earth. 2010. (World's Deadliest Ser.). (ENG.). 32p. (gr. 1-2). lib. bdg. 26.65 *(978-1-4296-3933-0(4)*, Blazers) Capstone Press of Coughlan Cos.
Sanchez, Anita. Itch! Everything You Didn't Want to Know about What Makes You Scratch. Ford, Gilbert, illus. 2017. (ENG.). 80p. (J). *(978-0-544-81101-0(1))* Harcourt.
Spilsbury, Louise. Creeping Killers: Extreme Plants. 2015. (Extreme Biology Ser.). (ENG., Illus.). 48p. (J). (gr. 4-4). lib. bdg. 31.95 *(978-1-4824-2234-4(4))* Stevens, Gareth Publishing LLLP.

POISONS

Albee, Sarah. Poison: Deadly Deeds, Perilous Professions, & Murderous Medicines. 2017. (ENG.). 192p. (J). (gr. 3-7). pap. 17.99 *(978-1-101-93223-0(6)*, Crown Books For Young Readers) Random Hse. Children's Bks.
Bellisario, Gina. Poison Alert! My Tips to Avoid Danger Zones at Home. Conger, Holli, illus. 2014. (Cloverleaf Books — My Healthy Habits Ser.). (ENG.). 24p. (gr. k-2). lib. bdg. 23.93 *(978-1-4677-1353-5(8)*, Millbrook Pr.) Lerner Publishing Group.
Hodge, Susie. Toxic! [Scholastic]: Killer Cures & Other Poisonings. 2011. (Extreme! Ser.). 32p. pap. 1.00 *(978-1-4296-6488-2(6)*, Fact Finders) Capstone Press of Coughlan Cos.
Jackson, Tom. Snake Bite. 2008. (ENG., Illus.). 32p. (J). (gr. 5-9). lib. bdg. *(978-0-7787-3772-8(1))* Crabtree Publishing Co.
Jakubiak, David J. Protecting Our Planet: What Can We Do about Toxins in the Environment? 2012. (Illus.). 24p. (J). 49.50 *(978-1-4488-5122-5(X)*, PowerKids Pr.); (J). pap. 8.25 *(978-1-4488-5121-8(1)*, PowerKids Pr.); (YA). (gr. 2-5). lib. bdg. 22.60 *(978-1-4488-4987-1(X))* Rosen Publishing Group, Inc., The.
Kyi, Tanya Lloyd. 50 Poisonous Questions: A Book with Bite. Kinnaird, Ross, illus. 2011. (50 Questions Ser.). (ENG.). 112p. (J). (gr. 3-18). 21.95 *(978-1-55451-281-2(6)*, 9781554512812); 2nd ed. pap. 12.95 *(978-1-55451-280-5(8)*, 9781554512805) Annick Pr., Ltd. CAN. Dist: Publishers Group West (PGW).
Loh-Hagan, Virginia. Top 10: Venom. 2016. (Illus.). 32p. (J). *(978-1-63470-507-3(6))* Cherry Lake Publishing.
Manley, Claudia B. Crack & Your Circulatory System: The Incredibly Disgusting Story. 2009. (Incredibly Disgusting Drugs Ser.). 48p. (gr. 5-8). 53.00 *(978-1-61513-494-6(8)*, Rosen Reference) Rosen Publishing Group, Inc., The.
Marlowe, Christie. Protecting Your Body: Germs, Super Bugs, Poison & Deadly Diseases. Stephens, Ronald, ed. 2014. (Safety First Ser.: 11). 48p. (J). (gr. 5-18). 20.95 *(978-1-4222-3051-0(1))* Mason Crest.
Meister, Cari. Venomous Animals. Fretland VanVoorst, Jenny, ed. 2016. (Back off! Animal Defenses). 24p. (J). (gr. 2-5). lib. bdg. 25.65 *(978-1-62031-313-8(8)*, Pogo) Jump! Inc.
Prokos, Anna. Killer Wallpaper: True Cases of Deadly Poisonings. 2007. (24/7: Science Behind the Scenes Ser.). (ENG., Illus.). 64p. (YA). (gr. 9-12). 29.00 *(978-0-531-12061-3(9)*, Watts, Franklin) Scholastic Library Publishing.
Riehecky, Janet. Poisons & Venom: Animal Weapons & Defenses, 1 vol. 2012. (Animal Weapons & Defenses Ser.). (ENG.). 32p. (gr. 1-2). pap. 8.10 *(978-1-4296-8008-0(3)*, Blazers) Capstone Press of Coughlan Cos.
Roza, Greg. Sting! The Scorpion & Other Animals That Sting. 2011. (Armed & Dangerous Ser.). (Illus.). 24p. (J). pap. 8.25 *(978-1-4488-2680-3(2)*, PowerKids Pr.); (gr. 1-4). 22.60 *(978-1-4488-2548-6(2))* Rosen Publishing Group, Inc., The.
ShackletonCaroline. POISON: MEDICINE, MURDER, AND MYSTERY HIGH INTERMEDIATE BOOK WITH ONLINE ACCESS. 2014. (ENG., Illus.). 28p. (J). pap. 9.50 *(978-1-107-62260-9(3))* Cambridge Univ. Pr.
Singer, Marilyn. Venom. 2014. (ENG., Illus.). 96p. (gr. 5-12). pap. *(978-1-4677-4909-1(5)*, Millbrook Pr.) Lerner Publishing Group.
Spilsbury, Louise. Harmful Substances. 2012. (Healthy & Happy Ser.). (Illus.). 32p. (J). (gr. 1-4). lib. bdg. 26.50 *(978-1-4488-5276-5(5))* Rosen Publishing Group, Inc., The.

POKEMON (FICTITIOUS CHARACTERS)—FICTION

Barbo, Maria S. The Rescue Mission. 2016. (Pokémon Ser.: 1). (ENG.). 32p. (J). (gr. -1-3). pap. 3.99 *(978-1-338-11290-0(2))* Scholastic, Inc.
—The Rescue Mission. 2016. (Pokemon Reader Ser.: 1). lib. bdg. 13.55 ***(978-0-606-39736-0(1))*** Turtleback Bks.
—Team Rocket to the Rescue. 2016. (Pokemon Reader Ser.: 2). lib. bdg. 13.55 ***(978-0-606-39725-4(6))*** Turtleback Bks.
—Welcome to Alola! 2017. (Pokémon Ser.). (ENG.). 32p. (J). (gr. -1-3). pap. 3.99 ***(978-1-338-14864-0(8))*** Scholastic, Inc.
Foxe, Steve. The Big Book of the Alola Region. Golden Books, illus. 2017. (Big Golden Book Ser.). (ENG.). 48p. (J). (gr. -1-2). 10.99 ***(978-1-5247-7009-9(4)***, Golden Bks.) Random Hse. Children's Bks.
Harukaze, Santa. Pokemon Pocket Comics, Vols. 1 & 2 2016. (Pokemon Ser.: 1). (ENG., Illus.). 576p. (J). pap. 16.99 *(978-1-4215-8964-0(8))* Viz Media.
—Pokémon XY Pocket Comics. 2016. (Pokemon Ser.: 3). (ENG., Illus.). 240p. (J). pap. 10.99 *(978-1-4215-8693-9(2))* Viz Media.
Hijioka, Makoto. Pokemon: Giratina & the Sky Warrior!, Vol. 4. Hijioka, Makoto, illus. 2009. (ENG., Illus.). 192p. (J). pap. 9.99 *(978-1-4215-2701-7(4))* Viz Media.
Ihara, Shigekatsu. Pokémon Vol. 8: Diamond & Pearl Adventure! Ihara, Shigekatsu, illus. 2010. (ENG., Illus.). 192p. (J). pap. 9.99 *(978-1-4215-3671-2(4))* Viz Media.
—Pokémon - Diamond & Pearl Adventure!, Vol. 4. Ihara, Shigekatsu, illus. 2009. (ENG., Illus.). 192p. (J). pap. 9.99 *(978-1-4215-2674-4(3))* Viz Media.
—Pokémon: Diamond & Pearl Adventure!, Vol. 1. Ihara, Shigekatsu, illus. 2008. (ENG., Illus.). 208p. (J). (gr. k). pap. 9.99 *(978-1-4215-2286-9(1))* Viz Media.
—Pokémon: Diamond & Pearl Adventure!, Vol. 2. Ihara, Shigekatsu, illus. 2008. (ENG., Illus.). 192p. (J). (gr. 1). pap. 9.99 *(978-1-4215-2287-6(X))* Viz Media.
—Pokémon: Diamond & Pearl Adventure!, Vol. 3. Ihara, Shigekatsu, illus. 2009. (ENG., Illus.). 200p. (J). pap. 9.99 *(978-1-4215-2574-7(7))* Viz Media.
—Pokémon: Diamond & Pearl Adventure!, Vol. 6. Ihara, Shigekatsu, illus. 2010. (ENG., Illus.). 192p. (J). pap. 9.99 *(978-1-4215-3170-0(4))* Viz Media.
—Pokémon: Diamond & Pearl Adventure!, Vol. 7. Ihara, Shigekatsu, illus. 2010. (ENG., Illus.). 192p. (J). pap. 9.99 *(978-1-4215-3491-6(6))* Viz Media.
Inoue, Momota. Pokémon the Movie: Kyurem vs. The Sword of Justice. 2013. (ENG.). 192p. (J). pap. 9.99 *(978-1-4215-5690-1(1))* Viz Media.
—Pokémon the Movie: White, Vol. 1. movie tie-in ed. 2012. (ENG.). 192p. (J). pap. 9.99 *(978-1-4215-4954-5(9))* Viz Media.
Kamimura, Gin, illus. Pokemon the Movie: Hoopa & the Clash of Ages, Vol. 1. 2016. (ENG.). 192p. (J). pap. 9.99 *(978-1-4215-8782-0(3))* Viz Media.
Kawamoto, Kemon, illus. Pokémon the Movie: Volcanion & the Mechanical Marvel. 2017. (Pokemon Ser.). (ENG.). 200p. (J). pap. 9.99 ***(978-1-4215-9419-4(6))*** Viz Media.
Kitamura, Kenji. Pokémon the Movie: Diancie & the Cocoon of Destruction. 2015. (ENG., Illus.). 200p. (J). pap. 9.99 *(978-1-4215-8051-7(9))* Viz Media.
Kudo, Maki. The Pokémon Cookbook: Easy & Fun Recipes. 2016. (Pokemon Ser.: 1). (ENG., Illus.). 80p. 14.99 *(978-1-4215-8989-3(3))* Viz Media.
Kusaka, Hidenori. Pokemon Adventures. 2015. (Pokemon Adventures Ser.: 29). lib. bdg. 20.85 *(978-0-606-37897-0(9))*; lib. bdg. 20.85 *(978-0-606-37244-2(X))* Turtleback Bks.
—Pokémon Adventures Vol. 1: Black & White. Yamamoto, Satoshi, illus. 2013. (ENG.). 104p. (J). pap. 9.99 *(978-1-4215-5898-1(X))* Viz Media.
—Pokémon Adventures Vol. 1: Diamond & Pearl/Platinum. 2011. (ENG., Illus.). 208p. (J). pap. 9.99 *(978-1-4215-3816-7(4))* Viz Media.
—Pokémon Adventures Vol. 2: Diamond & Pearl/Platinum. 2011. (ENG., Illus.). 208p. (J). pap. 9.99 *(978-1-4215-3817-4(2))* Viz Media.
—Pokémon Adventures Vol. 3: Black & White. Yamamoto, Satoshi, illus. 2014. (ENG.). 208p. (J). pap. 9.99 *(978-1-4215-6178-3(6))* Viz Media.
—Pokémon Adventures Vol. 3: Diamond & Pearl/Platinum. Satoshi, Yamamoto, illus. 2011. (ENG.). 200p. (J). pap. 9.99 *(978-1-4215-3818-1(0))* Viz Media.
—Pokémon Adventures Vol. 5: Diamond & Pearl/Platinum. Yamamoto, Satoshi, illus. 2012. (ENG.). 208p. (J). pap. 9.99 *(978-1-4215-3913-3(6))* Viz Media.
—Pokémon Adventures Vol. 9: Black & White. Yamamoto, Satoshi, illus. 2015. (ENG.). 208p. (J). pap. 9.99 *(978-1-4215-7961-0(8))* Viz Media.
—Pokémon Adventures Vol. 9: Diamond & Pearl/Platinum. Yamamoto, Satoshi, illus. 2013. (Pokemon Ser.: 9). (ENG.). 192p. (J). pap. 9.99 *(978-1-4215-5405-1(4))* Viz Media.
—Pokémon Adventures Vol. 11: Diamond & Pearl/Platinum. Yamamoto, Satoshi, illus. 2014. (ENG.). 192p. (J). pap. 9.99 *(978-1-4215-6179-0(4))* Viz Media.
—Pokémon Adventures - Diamond & Pearl/Platinum. Yamamoto, Satoshi, illus. (ENG.). (J). Vol. 6. 2012. 208p. pap. 9.99 *(978-1-4215-3914-0(4))* Vol. 7. 2013. 192p. pap. 9.99 *(978-1-4215-4247-8(1))* Viz Media.
—Pokémon Adventures: Black 2 & White 2, Vol. 1. Yamamoto, Satoshi, illus. 2017. (Pokemon Ser.: 1). (ENG.). 200p. (J). pap. 9.99 *(978-1-4215-8437-9(9))* Viz Media.
—Pokémon Adventures: Black & White, Vol. 2. Yamamoto, Satoshi, illus. 2013. (ENG.). 192p. (J). pap. 9.99 *(978-1-4215-5899-8(8))* Viz Media.
—Pokémon Adventures: Black & White, Vol. 4. Yamamoto, Satoshi, illus. 2014. (ENG.). 200p. (J). pap. 9.99 *(978-1-4215-6180-6(8))* Viz Media.
—Pokémon Adventures: Black & White, Vol. 6. Yamamoto, Satoshi, illus. 2015. (ENG.). 224p. (J). pap. 9.99 *(978-1-4215-7181-2(1))* Viz Media.
—Pokémon Adventures: Black & White, Vol. 7. Yamamoto, Satoshi, illus. 2015. (ENG.). 208p. (J). pap. 9.99 *(978-1-4215-7836-1(0))* Viz Media.
—Pokémon Adventures: Diamond & Pearl/Platinum, Vol. 10. Yamamoto, Satoshi, illus. 2014. (ENG.). 208p. (J). pap. 9.99 *(978-1-4215-5406-8(2))* Viz Media.
—Pokémon Adventures: Diamond & Pearl/Platinum, Vol. 4. 2012. (ENG., Illus.). 216p. (J). pap. 9.99 *(978-1-4215-3912-6(8))* Viz Media.
—Pokémon Adventures: Diamond & Pearl/Platinum, Vol. 8. Yamamoto, Satoshi, illus. 2013. (ENG.). 192p. (J). pap. 9.99 *(978-1-4215-5404-4(6))* Viz Media.
—Pokémon Adventures Diamond & Pearl / Platinum Box Set, Set, Vols. 1-11. Yamamoto, Satoshi, illus. 2014. (ENG.). 2304p. (J). pap. 89.99 *(978-1-4215-7777-7(1))* Viz Media.
—Pokémon Adventures Fire Red & Leaf Green / Emerald Box Set, Vol. 1. Yamamoto, Satoshi, illus. 2015. (ENG.). 1576p. (J). pap. 54.99 *(978-1-4215-8278-8(3))* Viz Media.
—Pokémon Adventures Gold & Silver Box Set (set includes Vol. 8-14) 2012. (ENG.). 1552p. (J). pap. 54.99 *(978-1-4215-5007-7(5))* Viz Media.
—Pokémon Adventures: Heart Gold Soul Silver, Vol. 1. 2013. (ENG., Illus.). 208p. (J). pap. 9.99 *(978-1-4215-5900-1(5))* Viz Media.
—Pokémon Adventures: Heart Gold Soul Silver, Vol. 2. 2013. (ENG., Illus.). 272p. (J). pap. 9.99 *(978-1-4215-5901-8(3))* Viz Media.
—Pokémon Adventures Red & Blue Box Set (set includes Vol. 1-7) 2012. (ENG., Illus.). 1504p. (J). pap. 54.99 *(978-1-4215-5006-0(7))* Viz Media.
—Pokémon Adventures Ruby & Sapphire Box Set, Set, Vols. 15-22. Yamamoto, Satoshi, illus. 2014. (ENG.). 1576p. (J). pap. 59.99 *(978-1-4215-7776-0(3))* Viz Media.
—Pokémon Adventures, Vol. 1 (2nd Edition) Kusaka, Hidenori, illus. 2nd ed. 2009. (ENG., Illus.). 200p. (J). pap. 9.99 *(978-1-4215-3054-3(6))* Viz Media.
—Pokémon Adventures, Vol. 10. Kusaka, Hidenori, illus. 2010. (ENG., Illus.). 200p. (J). pap. 9.99 *(978-1-4215-3063-5(5))* Viz Media.
—Pokémon Adventures, Vol. 11. Mato, illus. 2011. (ENG.). 208p. (J). pap. 9.99 *(978-1-4215-3545-6(9))* Viz Media.
—Pokémon Adventures, Vol. 12. Mato, illus. 2011. (ENG.). 208p. (J). pap. 9.99 *(978-1-4215-3546-3(7))* Viz Media.
—Pokémon Adventures, Vol. 13. 2011. (ENG., Illus.). 208p. (J). pap. 9.99 *(978-1-4215-3547-0(5))* Viz Media.
—Pokémon Adventures, Vol. 14. 2011. (ENG., Illus.). 208p. (J). pap. 9.99 *(978-1-4215-3548-7(3))* Viz Media.
—Pokémon Adventures, Vol. 15. Mato, illus. 2013. (ENG.). 144p. (J). pap. 9.99 *(978-1-4215-3549-4(1))* Viz Media.
—Pokémon Adventures, Vol. 16. Mato, illus. 2013. (ENG.). 208p. (J). pap. 9.99 *(978-1-4215-3550-0(5))* Viz Media.
—Pokémon Adventures, Vol. 17. Mato, illus. 2013. (ENG.). 208p. (J). pap. 9.99 *(978-1-4215-3551-7(3))* Viz Media.
—Pokémon Adventures, Vol. 18. Mato, illus. 2013. (ENG.). 192p. (J). pap. 9.99 *(978-1-4215-3552-4(1))* Viz Media.
—Pokémon Adventures, Vol. 19. Mato, illus. 2013. (ENG.). 192p. (J). pap. 9.99 *(978-1-4215-3553-1(X))* Viz Media.
—Pokémon Adventures, Vol. 2 (2nd Edition) Kusaka, Hidenori, illus. 2nd ed. 2009. (ENG., Illus.). 200p. (J). pap. 9.99 *(978-1-4215-3055-0(4))* Viz Media.
—Pokémon Adventures, Vol. 20. Mato, illus. 2014. (ENG.). 208p. (J). pap. 9.99 *(978-1-4215-3554-8(8))* Viz Media.
—Pokémon Adventures, Vol. 21. Yamamoto, Satoshi, illus. 2014. (ENG.). 208p. (J). pap. 9.99 *(978-1-4215-3555-5(6))* Viz Media.
—Pokémon Adventures, Vol. 22. Yamamoto, Satoshi, illus. 2014. (ENG.). 184p. (J). pap. 9.99 *(978-1-4215-3556-2(4))* Viz Media.
—Pokémon Adventures, Vol. 26. Mato, illus. 2015. (ENG.). 144p. (J). pap. 9.99 *(978-1-4215-3560-9(2))* Viz Media.
—Pokémon Adventures, Vol. 27. Mato, illus. 2015. (ENG.). 208p. (J). pap. 9.99 *(978-1-4215-3561-6(0))* Viz Media.
—Pokémon Adventures, Vol. 28. Mato, illus. 2015. (ENG.). 208p. (J). pap. 9.99 *(978-1-4215-3562-3(9))* Viz Media.
—Pokémon Adventures, Vol. 29. Yamamoto, Satoshi, illus. 2015. (ENG.). 224p. (J). pap. 9.99 *(978-1-4215-3563-0(7))* Viz Media.
—Pokémon Adventures, Vol. 3 (2nd Edition) Kusaka, Hidenori, illus. 2nd ed. 2009. (ENG., Illus.). 240p. (J). pap. 9.99 *(978-1-4215-3056-7(2))* Viz Media.
—Pokémon Adventures, Vol. 4 (2nd Edition) Kusaka, Hidenori, illus. 2nd ed. 2009. (ENG., Illus.). 216p. (J). pap. 9.99 *(978-1-4215-3057-4(0))* Viz Media.
—Pokémon Adventures, Vol. 5 (2nd Edition) Kusaka, Hidenori, illus. 2nd ed. 2010. (ENG., Illus.). 208p. (J). pap. 9.99 *(978-1-4215-3058-1(9))* Viz Media.
—Pokémon Adventures, Vol. 6 (2nd Edition) Kusaka, Hidenori, illus. 2nd ed. 2010. (ENG., Illus.). 208p. (J). pap. 9.99 *(978-1-4215-3059-8(7))* Viz Media.
—Pokémon Adventures, Vol. 7 (2nd Edition) Kusaka, Hidenori, illus. 2nd ed. 2010. (ENG., Illus.). 200p. (J). pap. 9.99 *(978-1-4215-3060-4(0))* Viz Media.
—Pokémon Adventures, Vol. 8. Kusaka, Hidenori, illus. 2010. (ENG., Illus.). 200p. (J). pap. 9.99 *(978-1-4215-3061-1(9))* Viz Media.
—Pokémon Adventures, Vol. 9. Kusaka, Hidenori, illus. 2010. (ENG., Illus.). 224p. (J). pap. 9.99 *(978-1-4215-3062-8(7))* Viz Media.
—Pokemon Black & White Box Set 2, Vols. 9-14, Set. Yamamoto, Satoshi, illus. 2014. (ENG.). 504p. (J). pap. 25.99 *(978-1-4215-7774-6(7))* Viz Media.
—Pokémon Black & White, Vol. 10. Yamamoto, Satoshi, illus. 2013. (ENG.). 96p. (J). pap. 4.99 *(978-1-4215-5894-3(7))* Viz Media.
—Pokémon Black & White, Vol. 11. Yamamoto, Satoshi, illus. 2013. (ENG.). 96p. (J). pap. 4.99 *(978-1-4215-5895-0(5))* Viz Media.
—Pokémon Black & White, Vol. 12. Yamamoto, Satoshi, illus. 2013. (ENG.). 96p. (J). pap. 4.99 *(978-1-4215-5896-7(3))* Viz Media.
—Pokémon Black & White, Vol. 13. Yamamoto, Satoshi, illus. 2013. (ENG.). 96p. (J). pap. 4.99 *(978-1-4215-5897-4(1))* Viz Media.
—Pokémon Black & White, Vol. 14. Yamamoto, Satoshi, illus. 2014. (ENG.). 88p. (J). pap. 4.99 *(978-1-4215-6766-2(0))* Viz Media.
—Pokémon Black & White, Vol. 15. Yamamoto, Satoshi, illus. 2014. (ENG.). 80p. (J). pap. 4.99 *(978-1-4215-6767-9(9))* Viz Media.
—Pokémon Black & White, Vol. 16. Yamamoto, Satoshi, illus. 2014. (ENG.). 80p. (J). pap. 4.99 *(978-1-4215-6768-6(7))* Viz Media.
—Pokémon Black & White, Vol. 17. Yamamoto, Satoshi, illus. 2014. (ENG.). 88p. (J). pap. 4.99 *(978-1-4215-6769-3(5))* Viz Media.
—Pokémon Black & White, Vol. 18. Yamamoto, Satoshi, illus. 2014. (ENG.). 96p. (J). pap. 4.99 *(978-1-4215-7602-2(3))* Viz Media.
—Pokémon Black & White, Vol. 19. Yamamoto, Satoshi, illus. 2014. (ENG.). 80p. (J). pap. 4.99 *(978-1-4215-7603-9(1))* Viz Media.
—Pokémon Black & White, Vol. 20. Yamamoto, Satoshi, illus. 2015. (ENG.). 80p. (J). pap. 4.99 *(978-1-4215-7604-6(X))* Viz Media.
—Pokémon Black & White, Vol. 4. 2011. (ENG.). 80p. (J). pap. 4.99 *(978-1-4215-4114-3(9))* Viz Media.
—Pokémon Black & White, Vol. 5. Yamamoto, Satoshi, illus. 2012. (ENG.). 96p. (J). pap. 4.99 *(978-1-4215-4280-5(3))* Viz Media.
—Pokémon Black & White, Vol. 7. Yamamoto, Satoshi, illus. 2012. (ENG.). 96p. (J). pap. 4.99 *(978-1-4215-4282-9(X))* Viz Media.
—Pokémon Black & White, Vol. 8. Yamamoto, Satoshi, illus. 2012. (ENG.). 96p. (J). pap. 4.99 *(978-1-4215-4283-6(8))* Viz Media.
—Pokémon Black & White, Vol. 9. Yamamoto, Satoshi, illus. 2013. (ENG.). 96p. (J). pap. 4.99 *(978-1-4215-5893-6(9))* Viz Media.
—Pokémon X Y. Yamamoto, Satoshi, illus. (ENG.). (J). Vol. 1. 2014. 96p. pap. 4.99 *(978-1-4215-7980-1(4))* Vol. 2. 2015. 112p. pap. 4.99 *(978-1-4215-7834-7(4))* Vol. 5. 2015. 96p. pap. 4.99 *(978-1-4215-8250-4(3))* Viz Media.
—Pokémon X Y, Vol. 6. Yamamoto, Satoshi, illus. 2016. (ENG.). 96p. (J). pap. 4.99 *(978-1-4215-8335-8(6))* Viz Media.
—Pokémon X Y, Vol. 7. 2016. (ENG., Illus.). 96p. (J). pap. 4.99 *(978-1-4215-8777-6(7))* Viz Media.
Kusaka, Hidenori. Pokemon Xy, Vol. 11. 2017. (Pokemon X Y Ser.: 11). lib. bdg. 14.75 ***(978-0-606-40299-6(3))*** Turtleback Bks.
Kusaka, Hidenori & Harukaze, Santa. Pokémon Pocket Comics Vol. 1: Black & White. 2013. (ENG., Illus.). 320p. (J). pap. 9.99 *(978-1-4215-5910-0(2))* Viz Media.
MAKOTO, Mizobuchi. Pokémon: Arceus & the Jewel of Life. MAKOTO, Mizobuchi, illus. 2011. (ENG., Illus.). 200p. (J). pap. 9.99 *(978-1-4215-3802-0(4))* Viz Media.
Mayer, Helena. The Lost Riolu: Pokémon Academy. 2009. (Pokémon Ser.). (Illus.). 62p. (J). pap. *(978-0-545-20050-9(4))* Scholastic, Inc.
Miyaki, Tetsuichiro. Pokémon. Yamamoto, Satoshi, illus. 2013. (J). ***(978-1-4844-1630-3(9))*** Viz Media.
Mizobuchi, Makoto. The Complete Pokémon Pocket Guide, Vol. 1. 2017. (Pokemon Ser.: 1). (ENG.). 256p. (J). pap. 10.99 ***(978-1-4215-9543-6(5))*** Viz Media.
—The Complete Pokémon Pocket Guide, Vol. 2. 2017. (Pokemon Ser.: 2). (ENG.). 256p. (J). pap. 10.99 ***(978-1-4215-9544-3(3))*** Viz Media.
Moore, Ken A. Ghost Island & the Mystery of Charmander: An Unofficial Adventure for Pokémon GO Fans. 2016. (ENG.). 236p. (J). (gr. 2-7). pap. 9.99 *(978-1-5107-2296-5(3)*, Sky Pony Pr.) Skyhorse Publishing Co., Inc.
Noll, Katherine & West, Tracey. Sinnoh. 2007. (Pokemon Ser.). (ENG., Illus.). 128p. (J). (gr. 2-5). pap., instr.'s hndbk. ed. 6.99 *(978-0-545-00072-7(6))* Scholastic, Inc.
Pikachu, Press. Pokemon Mini-Sticker Book: White Edition. 2012. (ENG.). 80p. (J). (gr. -1). 4.99 *(978-1-60438-163-4(9))* Pokemon, USA, Inc.
Pikachu Press, . Catch Oshawott! Set: A Pokémon Look & Listen. 2012. (Pokemon Pikachu Press Ser.). (ENG.). 32p. (J). (gr. 3-6). 12.99 *(978-1-60438-158-0(2))* Pokemon, USA, Inc.
—Catch Snivy! A Pokémon Look & Listen Set. 2012. (Pokemon Pikachu Press Ser.). (ENG.). 32p. (J). (gr. 3-6). 12.99 *(978-1-60438-157-3(4))* Pokemon, USA, Inc.
—Catch Tepig! Set: A Pokémon Look & Listen. 2012. (Pokemon Pikachu Press Ser.). (ENG.). 32p. (J). (gr. 3-6). 12.99 *(978-1-60438-159-7(0))* Pokemon, USA, Inc.
—Pokémon Find 'Em All! Welcome to Unova! 2012. (Pokemon Pikachu Press Ser.). (ENG.). 42p. (J). (gr. 3-6). 9.99 *(978-1-60438-161-0(2))* Pokemon, USA, Inc.
Pokemon 1: Advanced Box Set [2 Discs / Subtitles / Box Set]. 2005. 39.98 incl. DVD *(978-1-4215-0214-4(3))* Viz Media.
Pokémon Adventures: Black & White, Vol. 5. 2014. (ENG., Illus.). 208p. (J). pap. 9.99 *(978-1-4215-6181-3(6))* Viz Media.
Pokémon Adventures, Vol. 24. 2014. (ENG., Illus.). 216p. (J). pap. 9.99 *(978-1-4215-3558-6(0))* Viz Media.
Pokémon Adventures, Vol. 25. 2014. (ENG., Illus.). 208p. (J). pap. 9.99 *(978-1-4215-3559-3(9))* Viz Media.
Polan, Alex. Capturing Cresselia: Unofficial Stories for Pokémon Collectors, #2. 2016. (Unofficial Stories for Pokémon Collectors Ser.). (ENG., Illus.). 112p. (J). (gr. 2-7). pap. 7.99 *(978-1-5107-1482-3(0)*, Sky Pony Pr.) Skyhorse Publishing Co., Inc.
—Catching the Jigglypuff Thief. 2016. (Unofficial Adventures for Pokemon GO Players Ser.: 1). lib. bdg. 18.40 ***(978-0-606-39657-8(8))*** Turtleback Bks.
—Chasing Butterfree. 2016. (Unofficial Adventures for Pokemon GO Players Ser.: 3). lib. bdg. 18.40 ***(978-0-606-39655-4(1))*** Turtleback Bks.
—Chasing Butterfree: Unofficial Adventures for Pokémon GO Players, Book Three. 2016. (Unofficial Adventures for Pokémon GO Players Ser.). (ENG.). 112p. (J). (gr. 1-7). pap. 7.99 *(978-1-5107-2204-0(1)*, Sky Pony Pr.) Skyhorse Publishing Co., Inc.
—Cracking the Magikarp Code. 2016. (Unofficial Adventures for Pokemon GO Players Ser.: 4). lib. bdg. 18.40 ***(978-0-606-39656-1(X))*** Turtleback Bks.
—Cracking the Magikarp Code: Unofficial Adventures for Pokémon GO Players, Book Four. 2016. (Unofficial Adventures for Pokémon GO Players Ser.). (ENG.). 112p. (J). (gr. 1-7). pap. 7.99 *(978-1-5107-2205-7(X)*, Sky Pony Pr.) Skyhorse Publishing Co., Inc.
—Following Meowth's Footprints. 2016. (Unofficial Adventures for Pokemon GO Players Ser.: 2). lib. bdg. 18.40 ***(978-0-606-39658-5(6))*** Turtleback Bks.
Polan, Alex. Following Meowth's Footprints: PokéStop Stories, Book Two. 2016. (ENG.). 112p. (J). (gr. 1-7). pap. 7.99 *(978-1-5107-2158-6(4)*, Sky Pony Pr.) Skyhorse Publishing Co., Inc.
Press, Pikachu. Catch Pikachu! DELUXE Look & Listen Set. 2012. (ENG.). 48p. (J). 16.99 *(978-1-60438-171-9(X))* Pokemon, USA, Inc.
—Guide to Pokemon Legends. 2012. (ENG.). 32p. (J). 17.99 *(978-1-60438-175-7(2))* Pokemon, USA, Inc.
—Super Pokemon Pop-Up! Black Kyurem. 2013. (ENG.). 5p. (J). (gr. 3-6). 9.99 *(978-1-60438-179-5(5))* Pokemon, USA, Inc.
—Super Pokemon Pop-Up! - White Kyurem. 2013. (ENG.). 5p. (J). (gr. 3-6). 9.99 *(978-1-60438-180-1(9))* Pokemon, USA, Inc.

Random House. Ash & Pikachu: Alola Region/Team Rocket. Random House, illus. 2017. (Pictureback(R) Ser.). (ENG., Illus.). 32p. (J). (gr. -1-2). pap. 5.99 ***(978-1-5247-7008-2(6)***, Random Hse. Bks. for Young Readers) Random Hse. Children's Bks.

Scholastic. The Pokémon School Challenge. 2017. (Pokémon Ser.: 1). (ENG.). 96p. (J). (gr. 2-5). pap. 4.99 ***(978-1-338-14861-9(3))*** Scholastic, Inc.

Scholastic Editors. Classic Collector's Handbook: An Official Guide to the First 151 Pokemon. 2016. lib. bdg. 19.65 *(978-0-606-39550-2(4))* Turtleback Bks.

Scholastic, Inc. Staff. Kalos Essential Activity Book. 2015. (Pokemon Ser.). (ENG.). 80p. (J). (gr. 2-5). pap. 12.99 *(978-0-545-92749-9(8))* Scholastic, Inc.

—Pokemon: Kalos Region Handbook. 2014. (ENG.). 272p. (J). (gr. 2-5). pap. 8.99 *(978-0-545-64602-4(2))* Scholastic, Inc.

—Super Sinnoh. 2009. (Pokemon Ser.). (ENG.). 48p. (J). (gr. 2-5). pap. 6.99 *(978-0-545-15131-3(7))* Scholastic, Inc.

Scholastic, Inc. Staff, contrib. by. Alola Region Poster Book. 2017. (Pokémon Ser.). (ENG.). 24p. (J). (gr. -1-3). pap. 7.99 *(978-1-338-16122-9(9))* Scholastic, Inc.

—Johto Handbook. 2010. (Pokemon Ser.). (ENG., Illus.). 96p. (J). (gr. 2-5). pap. 7.99 *(978-0-545-15132-0(5)*, Scholastic Paperbacks) Scholastic, Inc.

Scholastic, Inc. Staff & Whitehill, Simcha. Amazing Scenes in 3-D. 2012. (Pokemon Ser.). (ENG.). 16p. (J). (gr. -1-3). pap. 7.99 *(978-0-545-41712-9(0))* Scholastic, Inc.

Sonoda, Hideki. Pokémon: Zoroark: Master of Illusions. 2011. (ENG.). 192p. (J). pap. 7.99 *(978-1-4215-4221-8(8))* Viz Media.

Sweeny, Sheila. Scyther, Heart of a Champion (Pokémon Chapter Book) 2017. (Pokémon Ser.). (ENG.). 96p. (J). (gr. 2-5). pap. 4.99 ***(978-1-338-17579-0(3))*** Scholastic, Inc.

Viz Media Staff & Mizobuchi, Makoto. Pokémon: Ranger & the Temple of the Sea. Mizobuchi, Makoto, illus. 2008. (ENG., Illus.). 192p. (J). (gr. 1). pap. 9.99 *(978-1-4215-2288-3(8))* Viz Media.

Viz Media Staff & Takamisaki, Ryo. Pokémon: The Rise of Darkrai. Takamisaki, Ryo, illus. 2008. (ENG., Illus.). 192p. (J). (gr. 1). pap. 9.99 *(978-1-4215-2289-0(6))* Viz Media.

West, Tracey. The Haunted Gym. 2003. (Pokemon Readers Ser.: No. 3). (ENG.). 32p. (J). pap. 3.99 *(978-0-439-42988-7(9))* Scholastic, Inc.

—Pokémon: Journey to the Orange Islands. 2017. (Pokémon Ser.). (ENG.). 96p. (J). (gr. 2-5). pap. 4.99 ***(978-1-338-17565-3(3))*** Scholastic, Inc.

—Pokémon: Secret of the Pink Pokemon. 2017. (Pokémon Ser.). (ENG.). 96p. (J). (gr. 2-5). pap. 4.99 ***(978-1-338-17567-7(X))*** Scholastic, Inc.

—Race to Danger (Pokémon: Chapter Book) 2017. (Pokémon Ser.). (ENG.). 96p. (J). (gr. 2-5). pap. 4.99 ***(978-1-338-17585-1(8))*** Scholastic, Inc.

—Talent Showdown. 2017. (Pokémon Ser.). (ENG.). 96p. (J). (gr. 2-5). pap. 4.99 ***(978-1-338-17591-2(2))*** Scholastic, Inc.

West, Tracey, adapted by. Bagon Can Fly! 2005. 45p. *(978-0-439-72184-4(9))* Scholastic, Inc.

—Phantom Unmasked. 2006. (Illus.). 62p. (J). pap. *(978-0-439-80000-6(5))* Scholastic, Inc.

—Pokémon: I Feel Skitty. 2005. 45p. *(978-0-439-80940-5(1))* Scholastic, Inc.

West, Tracey & Dewin, Howie. Four-Star Challenge, the (Pokémon Chapter Book) 2017. (Pokémon Ser.). (ENG.). 96p. (J). (gr. 2-5). pap. 4.99 ***(978-1-338-17573-8(4))*** Scholastic, Inc.

Whitehill, Simcha. Official Guide to Legendary & Mythical Pokemon. 2016. lib. bdg. 18.40 *(978-0-606-39551-9(2))* Turtleback Bks.

—World of Sinnoh. 2009. (Pokemon Ser.). (ENG.). 96p. (J). (gr. 2-5). instr.'s gde. ed. 7.99 *(978-0-545-09938-7(2))* Scholastic, Inc.

Yamamoto, Satoshi, illus. Pokemon Omega Ruby Alpha Sapphire. 2016. (Pokemon Ser.: 1). (ENG.). (J). Vol. 1. 96p. pap. 4.99 *(978-1-4215-9070-7(0))* Vol. 2. 112p. pap. 4.99 *(978-1-4215-9016-5(6))* Viz Media.

—Pokémon Omega Ruby Alpha Sapphire, Vol. 3. 2017. (Pokemon Ser.: 3). (ENG.). 96p. (J). pap. 4.99 *(978-1-4215-9156-8(1))* Viz Media.

—Pokemon Omega Ruby & Alpha Sapphire, Vol. 4. 2017. (Pokemon Ser.: 4). (ENG.). 96p. (J). pap. 4.99 ***(978-1-4215-9223-7(1))*** Viz Media.

—Pokémon X*Y, Vol. 8. 2016. (Pokemon Ser.: 8). (ENG.). 96p. (J). pap. 4.99 *(978-1-4215-8779-0(3))* Viz Media.

—Pokémon X*y, Vol. 10. 2017. (Pokemon Ser.: 10). (ENG.). 112p. (J). pap. 4.99 *(978-1-4215-9164-3(2))* Viz Media.

—Pokémon X*y, Vol. 11. 2017. (Pokemon Ser.: 11). (ENG.). 96p. (J). pap. 4.99 ***(978-1-4215-9066-0(2))*** Viz Media.

Yamamoto, Satoshi, illus. Pokémon X*y, Vol. 9. 2017. (Pokemon Ser.: 9). (ENG.). 96p. (J). pap. 4.99 *(978-1-4215-9155-1(3))* Viz Media.

POKEMON (GAME)

Aihara, Kazunori. Let's Find Pokemon! 2017. (Pokemon Ser.). (ENG.). 88p. (J). 16.99 ***(978-1-4215-9579-5(6))*** Viz Media.

Barbo, Maria S. Team Rocket to the Rescue! 2016. (Pokémon Ser.). (ENG.). 32p. (J). (gr. -1-3). pap. 3.99 *(978-1-338-11795-0(5))* Scholastic, Inc.

BradyGames. Pokémon Visual Companion: Second Edition. 2016. (ENG., Illus.). 272p. (J). (gr. 1-4). 16.99 *(978-0-7440-1760-1(2)*, DK) DK Games.

Green, Sara. Pokemon. 2017. (Brands We Know Ser.). (ENG.). 24p. (J). (gr. 3-8). lib. bdg. 25.95 ***(978-1-62617-655-3(8)***, Pilot Bks.) Bellwether Media.

Harukaze, Santa. Pokémon Pocket Comics. 2015. (ENG., Illus.). 256p. (J). pap. 9.99 *(978-1-4215-8128-6(0))* Viz Media.

Noll, Katherine & West, Tracey. Pokémon: Kanto Handbook. 2005. (Illus.). 80p. (J). *(978-0-439-74146-0(7))* Scholastic, Inc.

Pokémon Company International Staff. Pokemon X & Pokemon Y: The Official Kalos Region Guidebook. 2013. (ENG., Illus.). 416p. pap. 19.99 *(978-0-8041-6283-8(2))* Random Hse., Inc.

—Pokémon X & Pokémon y: the Official Kalos Region Guidebook: The Official Pokémon Strategy Guide. 2013. (ENG.). 416p. pap. 16.99 *(978-0-8041-6321-7(9))* Random Hse., Inc.

Prima Games Staff. Pokemon Activity Book. 2009. 80p. pap. 12.99 *(978-0-7615-6164-4(1)*, Prima Games) Random Hse. Information Group.

Scholastic Editors. Pokemon Deluxe Essential Handbook. 2015. lib. bdg. 23.30 *(978-0-606-37083-7(8))* Turtleback Bks.

Scholastic, Inc. Staff & Watson, Silje. Pokémon Classic Collector's Handbook. 2016. (Pokémon Ser.). (ENG., Illus.). 128p. (J). (gr. 2-5). pap. 8.99 *(978-1-338-15823-6(6))* Scholastic, Inc.

Silvestri, Cris. Pokemon. 2015. (Pokémon Ser.). (ENG.). 432p. (J). (gr. 2-5). pap. 11.99 *(978-0-545-79566-1(4))* Scholastic, Inc.

Sterling Children's, Sterling. The Ultimate Pokémon Go Handbook. 2016. (ENG., Illus.). 80p. (J). (gr. 2). pap. 12.95 *(978-1-4549-2481-4(0))* Sterling Publishing Co., Inc.

West, Tracey & Nolls, Katherine. Official Pokémon Pokédex. 2006. (Illus.). 111p. (J). *(978-0-439-85586-0(1))* Scholastic, Inc.

Whitehill, Simcha. Now You See It! Watch Pokémon Evolve — Right Before Your Eyes! 2012. (Illus.). 63p. (J). pap. *(978-0-545-45356-1(9))* Scholastic, Inc.

—Official Guide to Mythical & Legendary Pokémon. 2016. (Pokémon Ser.). (ENG.). 80p. (J). (gr. 2-5). pap. 7.99 *(978-1-338-11291-7(0))* Scholastic, Inc.

—Pokémon: The Official Adventure Guide. 2015. (Pokemon Ser.). (ENG., Illus.). 160p. (J). (gr. 2-5). 12.99 *(978-0-545-84935-7(7))* Scholastic, Inc.

Whitehill, Simcha & Scholastic, Inc. Staff. Kalos Beginner's Handbook. 2014. (ENG.). 64p. (J). (gr. 2-5). pap. 5.99 *(978-0-545-64396-2(1))* Scholastic, Inc.

POLAND

Anderson, Dale. Polish Americans. 2006. (World Almanac Library of American Immigration). (Illus.). 48p. (gr. 5-12). pap. 14.05 *(978-0-8368-7330-6(0))*; lib. bdg. 31.00 *(978-0-8368-7317-7(3))* Stevens, Gareth Publishing LLLP. (Gareth Stevens Secondary Library).

Andronik, Catherine M. Copernicus: Founder of Modern Astronomy. 2009. (Great Minds of Science Ser.). (Illus.). 128p. (J). (gr. 5). lib. bdg. 33.27 *(978-0-7660-3013-8(X))* Enslow Pubs., Inc.

—Copernicus: Genius of Modern Astronomy. 2015. (Genius Scientists & Their Genius Ideas Ser.). 96p. (J). (gr. 5-12). 27.94 *(978-0-7660-6550-5(2))*; pap. 10.95 *(978-0-7660-6551-2(0))* Enslow Pubs., Inc.

Barghoorn, Linda. Cultural Traditions in Poland. 2017. 32p. (J). ***(978-0-7787-8098-4(8))*** Crabtree Publishing Co.

Brandman, Bronia & Bierman, Carol. The Girl Who Survived: A True Story of the Holocaust. 2010. 91p. (J). pap. *(978-0-545-17574-6(7))* Scholastic, Inc.

Brooks, Susie. Let's Visit Poland. 2009. (Around the World Ser.). (Illus.). 32p. (J). (ENG.). pap. 10.00 *(978-1-4358-8614-8(3))*; (gr. 2-5). lib. bdg. 25.25 *(978-1-4358-3030-1(X))* Rosen Publishing Group, Inc., The. (PowerKids Pr.).

Callahan, Kerry P. Mordechai Anielewicz: Hero of the Warsaw Ghetto Uprising. 2005. (Holocaust Biographies Ser.). (Illus.). 112p. (YA). (gr. 7-12). lib. bdg. 34.60 *(978-0-8239-3377-8(6))* Rosen Publishing Group, Inc., The.

Cohen-Janca, Irène. Mister Doctor: Janusz Korczak & the Orphans of the Warsaw Ghetto. Quarello, Maurizio A. C., illus. 2016. (ENG.). 68p. (J). 12.95 *(978-1-55451-861-6(X))* Annick Pr., Ltd. CAN. Dist: Publishers Group West (PGW).

Cregan, Elizabeth R. C. Marie Curie: Pioneering Physicist. 1 vol. 2007. (Science Readers Ser.). (ENG., Illus.). 32p. (J). (gr. 3-3). pap. 8.99 *(978-0-7439-0570-1(9))* Shell Educational Publishing.

Deckker, Zilah. Poland. 2008. (National Geographic Countries of the World Ser.). (ENG., Illus.). 64p. (J). (gr. 5-9). lib. bdg. 27.90 *(978-1-4263-0201-5(0)*, National Geographic Children's Bks.) National Geographic Society.

Docalavich, Heather & Indovino, Shaina C. Poland. Bruton, John, ed. 2012. (Major European Union Nations Ser.). 64p. (J). (gr. 7). 22.95 *(978-1-4222-2254-6(3))* Mason Crest.

Docalavich, Heather & Indovino, Shaina Carmel. Poland. 2012. (J). pap. *(978-1-4222-2285-0(3))* Mason Crest.

Edison, Erin. Marie Curie, 1 vol. 2014. (Great Women in History Ser.). (ENG.). 24p. (gr. k-1). lib. bdg. 21.99 *(978-1-4765-4216-4(3)*, Pebble Bks.) Capstone Press of Coughlan Cos.

Fisher, Teresa. Poland. 2010. (Illus.). 32p. (J). *(978-1-84234-548-1(6))* Cherrytree Bks.

Gifford, Clive. Unpacked - Poland. 2017. (Unpacked Ser.). (ENG., Illus.). 32p. (J). (gr. 4-6). pap. 12.99 ***(978-0-7502-9159-0(1)***, Wayland) Hachette Children's Group GBR. Dist: Hachette Bk. Group.

Goldish, Meish. Poland. 2016. (Countries We Come From Ser.). (ENG.). 32p. (J). (gr. -1-3). lib. bdg. 19.95 *(978-1-944998-30-1(6))* Bearport Publishing Co., Inc.

Guillain, Charlotte. Poland, 1 vol. 2011. (Countries Around the World Ser.). (ENG.). 48p. (gr. 3-6). pap. 9.95 *(978-1-4329-5240-2(4))*; 33.32 *(978-1-4329-5215-0(3))* Heinemann-Raintree. (NA-h).

Hardyman, Robyn. Pierre & Marie Curie. 2014. (Dynamic Duos of Science Ser.). 48p. (YA). (gr. 5-8). pap. 84.30 *(978-1-4824-1287-1(X))* Stevens, Gareth Publishing LLLP.

Henderson, Harry. The Curie Family. 2012. (Trailblazers in Science & Technology Ser.). 136p. (gr. 6-12). 35.00 *(978-1-60413-675-3(8)*, Chelsea Hse.) Facts On File, Inc.

Landau, Abraham, et al. Branded on My Arm & in My Soul: A Holocaust Memoir. 2011. (Illus.). 144p. 50.00 *(978-0-932027-20-7(2))* Spinner Pubns., Inc.

—Branded on My Arm & in My Soul: The Holocaust Memoir of Abraham Landau. 2011. (Illus.). 144p. pap. 25.00 *(978-0-932027-19-1(9))* Spinner Pubns., Inc.

Laub, Frima. Between the Shadows. Laub, Frima & Uhlig, Elizabeth, illus. 2009. 81p. (J). pap. 12.95 *(978-0-9815345-2-7(X))* Marble Hse. Editions.

Leyson, Leon. The Boy on the Wooden Box: How the Impossible Became Possible ... on Schindler's List. (ENG., Illus.). (J). (gr. 4-9). 2015. 256p. pap. 9.99 *(978-1-4424-9782-5(3))* 2013. 240p. 17.99 *(978-1-4424-9781-8(5))* Simon & Schuster Children's Publishing. (Atheneum Bks. for Young Readers).

—The Boy on the Wooden Box: How the Impossible Became Possible ... on Schindler's List. 2015. lib. bdg. 19.65 *(978-0-606-36097-5(2))* Turtleback Bks.

Lin, Yoming S. The Curies & Radioactivity. 2012. (Eureka! Ser.). (Illus.). 24p. (YA). (gr. 3-6). lib. bdg. 22.60 *(978-1-4488-5033-4(9))* Rosen Publishing Group, Inc., The.

Lobel, Anita. No Pretty Pictures: A Child of War. 2008. (J). (gr. 5-8). lib. bdg. 18.40 *(978-0-613-28590-2(5)*, Turtleback) Turtleback Bks.

Malam, John. Hitler Invades Poland. 2007. (Dates with History Ser.). (ENG., Illus.). 48p. (J). pap. 9.99 *(978-1-84234-535-1(4))* Evans Brothers, Ltd. GBR. Dist: Independent Pubs. Group.

Mara, Wil. Poland. 2014. (Enchantment of the World Ser.: 2). (ENG.). 144p. (J). lib. bdg. 40.00 *(978-0-531-22016-0(8))* Scholastic Library Publishing.

McCollum, Sean. Poland. 2009. pap. 52.95 *(978-0-7613-4732-3(1))*; (ENG.). 48p. (gr. 2-4). 29.27 *(978-1-58013-597-9(8))* Lerner Publishing Group.

Mis, Melody S. How to Draw Poland's Sights & Symbols. 2009. (Kid's Guide to Drawing the Countries of the World Ser.). 48p. (gr. 4-4). 53.00 *(978-1-61511-122-0(0)*, PowerKids Pr.) Rosen Publishing Group, Inc., The.

Mrowczynska, Agnieszka. P Is for Poland. Das, Prodeepta, photos by. 2014. (World Alphabets Ser.). (ENG., Illus.). 32p. (J). (gr. -1-2). pap. 8.95 *(978-1-84780-352-8(0)*, Frances Lincoln) Quarto Publishing Group UK GBR. Dist: Hachette Bk. Group.

Opdyke, Irene Gut. In My Hands: Memories of a Holocaust Rescuer. 2016. (ENG., Illus.). 288p. (YA). (gr. 9). pap. 10.99 *(978-0-553-53884-7(5)*, Ember) Random Hse. Children's Bks.

Pavlovic, Zoran. Poland. 2008. (Modern World Nations Ser.). (Illus.). 128p. (gr. 6-12). 35.00 *(978-0-7910-9674-1(2)*, Chelsea Hse.) Facts On File, Inc.

Pohl, Kathleen & Nations, Susan. Descubramos Polonia. 2008. (Descubramos países del mundo (Looking at Countries) Ser.). (SPA., Illus.). 32p. (gr. 1-5). (J). lib. bdg. 26.00 *(978-0-8368-9068-6(X))*; pap. 10.50 *(978-0-8368-9069-3(8))* Stevens, Gareth Publishing LLLP. (Gareth Stevens Learning Library).

—Looking at Poland. 2008. (Looking at Countries Ser.). 32p. (gr. 1-5). (J). lib. bdg. 26.00 *(978-0-8368-9066-2(3))*; pap. 10.50 *(978-0-8368-9067-9(1))* Stevens, Gareth Publishing LLLP. (Gareth Stevens Learning Library).

Poynter, Margaret. Marie Curie: Genius Researcher of Radioactivity. 2015. (Genius Scientists & Their Genius Ideas Ser.). 96p. (J). (gr. 5-12). 27.94 *(978-0-7660-6580-2(4))*; pap. 10.95 *(978-0-7660-6581-9(2))* Enslow Pubs., Inc.

Roberto, Brother. Music for Millions: A Story of Ignace Paderewski. Jagodits, Carolyn Lee, illus. 2011. 94p. 38.95 *(978-1-258-09336-5(7))* Literary Licensing, LLC.

Rubin, Susan Goldman. Irena Sendler & the Children of the Warsaw Ghetto. Farnsworth, Bill, illus. 2016. (ENG.). 40p. (J). (gr. 4-7). pap. 8.99 *(978-0-8234-2595-2(9))* Holiday Hse., Inc.

Sheen, Barbara, ed. Foods of Poland. 2011. (Taste of Culture Ser.). (ENG.). 64p. (gr. 3-6). lib. bdg. 35.20 *(978-0-7377-5951-8(8)*, Kidhaven) Cengage Gale.

Simmons, Walter. Poland. 2012. (Exploring Countries Ser.). (ENG., Illus.). 32p. (J). (gr. 3-7). lib. bdg. 26.95 *(978-1-60014-732-6(1)*, Pilot Bks.) Bellwether Media.

Steele, Philip. Marie Curie: The Woman Who Changed the Course of Science. 2008. (National Geographic World History Biographies Ser.). (ENG., Illus.). 64p. (J). (gr. 3-7). pap. 7.99 *(978-1-4263-0249-7(5)*, National Geographic Children's Bks.) National Geographic Society.

Thomson, Ruth. Poland. 2011. (Countries Ser.). (Illus.). 24p. (J). (gr. k-3). lib. bdg. 22.60 *(978-1-4488-3277-4(2))* Rosen Publishing Group, Inc., The.

Throp, Claire. Marie Curie. 2015. (Against the Odds Biographies Ser.). (ENG., Illus.). 48p. (gr. 3-6). 33.32 *(978-1-4846-2467-8(X))* Heinemann-Raintree.

Vaughan, Marcia & Mazellan, Ron. Irena's Jars of Secrets. 2015. (ENG.). (J). pap. 10.95 *(978-1-62014-252-3(X))* Lee & Low Bks., Inc.

Wallace, Susan Helen. Blessed John Paul II: Be Not Afraid. Craig, Charles, illus. 2011. (Encounter the Saints Ser.). 111p. (J). (gr. 3-7). pap. 7.95 *(978-0-8198-1178-3(5))* Pauline Bks. & Media.

Watts, Franklin & Green, Jen. Living in Poland. 2016. (ENG., Illus.). 24p. (J). (gr. 1-3). 16.99 *(978-1-4451-4856-4(0)*, Franklin Watts) Hachette Children's Group GBR. Dist: Hachette Bk. Group.

Wilson, Rosie. Discover Poland. 2010. (Illus.). 32p. (J). 63.60 *(978-1-61532-295-4(7)*, 1307265); pap. 10.60 *(978-1-61532-294-7(9))* Rosen Publishing Group, Inc., The. (PowerKids Pr.).

Wilson, Rosie & Ward, Chris. Discover Poland. 2010. (Discover Countries Ser.). (Illus.). 32p. (J). (gr. 3-5). 26.50 *(978-1-61532-288-6(4)*, 1307265) Rosen Publishing Group, Inc., The.

Zuchora-Walske, Christine. Poland, 1 vol. 2013. (Countries of the World Set 2 Ser.). (ENG.). 144p. (J). (gr. 6-12). lib. bdg. 37.07 *(978-1-61783-634-3(6)*, Essential Library) ABDO Publishing Co.

Zuehlke, Jeffrey. Poland in Pictures. 2006. (Visual Geography Series, Second Ser.). (ENG., Illus.). 80p. (gr. 5-12). 31.93 *(978-0-8225-2676-6(X))* Lerner Publishing Group.

POLAND—FICTION

Aaron, Chester. Gideon. 2009. (ENG., Illus.). 190p. (YA). pap. 12.99 *(978-1-934841-62-4(5)*, Zumaya Thresholds) Zumaya Pubns. LLC.

Balazy, Elizabeth M. Prince to the Rescue. 2008. 48p. pap. 24.95 *(978-1-60474-812-3(5))* America Star Bks.

Boyne, John. The Boy in the Striped Pajamas. (ENG.). (YA). (gr. 7). 2006. 224p. 17.99 *(978-0-385-75106-3(0))* 2008. 240p. pap. 9.99 *(978-0-385-75189-6(3))* Fickling, David Bks. GBR. Dist: Penguin Random Hse. LLC.

—The Boy in the Striped Pajamas. 2011. 10.54 *(978-0-7848-3514-2(4)*, Everbind) Marco Bk. Co.

—The Boy in the Striped Pajamas. 2008. 215p. (gr. 7-12). 20.00 *(978-0-7569-8943-9(4))* Perfection Learning Corp.

—The Boy in the Striped Pajamas. 2007. (ENG.). 224p. (YA). (gr. 7-18). pap. 9.99 *(978-0-385-75153-7(2)*, Ember) Random Hse. Children's Bks.

—The Boy in the Striped Pajamas. rev. l.t. ed. 2007. (Thorndike Literacy Bridge Ser.). 247p. (YA). (gr. 7-12). 23.95 *(978-0-7862-9425-1(6))* Thorndike Pr.

—The Boy in the Striped Pajamas. 2007. 215p. (YA). (gr. 7-12). 20.85 *(978-1-4178-1823-5(9)*, Turtleback) Turtleback Bks.

Cerrito, Angela. The Safest Lie. 2015. (ENG.). 192p. (J). (gr. 3-7). 16.95 *(978-0-8234-3310-0(2))* Holiday Hse., Inc.

Cohen-Janca, Irène. Mister Doctor: Janusz Korczak & the Orphans of the Warsaw Ghetto. Quarello, Maurizio A. C., illus. 2015. (ENG.). 68p. (J). (gr. 4-7). 24.95 *(978-1-55451-715-2(X)*, 9781554517152) Annick Pr., Ltd. CAN. Dist: Publishers Group West (PGW).

Draus, Naudia Burtwell. My Grandma Wears A Number: How One Girl Survived World War II. 2011. 40p. (gr. 4-6). pap. 19.57 *(978-1-4269-3351-6(7))* Trafford Publishing.

Glaser, Linda. Way Too Many Latkes: A Chelm Hanukkah Story. Zolotic, Aleksander, illus. 2017. (ENG.). 32p. (gr. -1-2). 17.99 ***(978-1-5124-2092-0(1)***, Kar-Ben Publishing) Lerner Publishing Group.

Gleitzman, Morris. Once. 2005. 160p. (J). pap. *(978-0-14-330195-0(0)*, Puffin) Penguin Publishing Group.

—Then. 2013. (Once Ser.: 2). (ENG.). 224p. (YA). (gr. 7). pap. 9.99 *(978-1-250-00341-6(5)*, 9781250003416) Square Fish.

—Then. 2013. (YA). lib. bdg. 20.85 *(978-0-606-31904-1(2)*, Turtleback) Turtleback Bks.

Hemingway, Mike. The Legend of Vysallimore. 2010. 72p. pap. 28.00 *(978-1-4520-5648-7(X))* AuthorHouse.

Jane, Yolen. The Devil's Arithmetic. 2014. (ENG.). 176p. (J). 11.24 *(978-1-63245-218-4(9))* Lectorum Pubns., Inc.

Kacer, Kathy. The Diary of Laura's Twin, 1 vol. 2008. (Holocaust Remembrance Ser.). (ENG., Illus.). 208p. (J). (gr. 4-8). pap. 14.95 *(978-1-897187-39-5(4))* Second Story Pr. CAN. Dist: Orca Bk. Pubs. USA.

Lehman, Theodore H. Defying Odds. 2014. (YA). pap. *(978-1-935604-63-1(5))* Gaon Bks.

Lewis, J. Patrick. The Wren & the Sparrow. Nayberg, Yevgenia, illus. 2014. (J). 6.99 *(978-1-4677-6210-6(5)*, Kar-Ben Publishing) Lerner Publishing Group.

Palmer, Tom. The Real Thing, Bk. 3. 3rd ed. 2009. (Football Academy Ser.). (ENG., Illus.). 176p. (J). (gr. 2-4). pap. 10.99 *(978-0-14-132469-2(4))* Penguin Bks., Ltd. GBR. Dist: Independent Pubs. Group.

Pressler, Mirjam. Malka. Murdoch, Brian, tr. 2005. 280p. (YA). (gr. 7-12). 13.65 *(978-0-7569-5217-4(4))* Perfection Learning Corp.

Pryor, Bonnie. Simon's Escape: A Story of the Holocaust. 2010. (Historical Fiction Adventures (HFA) Ser.). (Illus.). 160p. (J). pap. 10.95 *(978-1-59845-216-7(9))*; (gr. 3-6). 29.27 *(978-0-7660-3388-7(0))* Enslow Pubs., Inc.

Rosner, Mina. I Am a Witness. (Illus.). 112p. (YA). (gr. 3-18). pap. *(978-0-920534-92-2(9))* Hyperion Pr., Ltd.

Roy, Jennifer. Yellow Star, 0 vols. 2014. (ENG.). 256p. (gr. 5-7). pap. 9.99 *(978-0-7614-6310-8(0)*, 9780761463108, Amazon Children's Publishing) Amazon Publishing.

Sasso, Sandy Eisenberg. Butterflies under Our Hats. Rothenberg, Joani Keller, illus. 2014. (ENG.). 32p. (J). (gr. k-5). pap. 15.99 *(978-1-61261-583-7(X))* Paraclete Pr., Inc.

Savit, Gavriel. Anna & the Swallow Man. 2016. (CHI.). 272p. (YA). (gr. 7). pap. ***(978-957-33-3251-0(5))*** Crown Publishing Co., Ltd.

—Anna & the Swallow Man. (ENG.). (YA). (gr. 7). 2017. 256p. pap. 9.99 ***(978-0-553-52208-2(6)***, Ember) 2016. 240p. 17.99 *(978-0-553-51334-9(6)*, Knopf Bks. for Young Readers) Random Hse. Children's Bks.

—Anna & the Swallow Man. 2017. lib. bdg. 20.85 ***(978-0-606-39876-3(7))*** Turtleback Bks.

Sax, Aline. The War Within These Walls. 2013. (ENG., Illus.). 176p. (YA). 17.00 *(978-0-8028-5428-5(1)*, Eerdmans Bks For Young Readers) Eerdmans, William B. Publishing Co.

Stuchner, Joan Betty. Can Hens Give Milk?, 1 vol. Weissmann, Joe, illus. 2013. (ENG.). 32p. (J). (gr. -1-3). 9.95 *(978-1-4598-0427-2(9))* Orca Bk. Pubs. USA.

Surber, Mary Brigid. The Last Stork Summer. 2015. (ENG.). 128p. pap. 13.95 *(978-1-78279-934-4(6)*, Top Hat Bks.) Hunt, John Publishing Ltd. GBR. Dist: National Bk. Network.

Tak, Bibi Dumon & Dumon Tak, Bibi. Soldier Bear. Hopman, Philip, illus. 2011. (ENG.). 158p. (J). 13.00 *(978-0-8028-5375-2(7)*, Eerdmans Bks For Young Readers) Eerdmans, William B. Publishing Co.

Tarshis, Lauren. I Survived the Nazi Invasion 1944. 2014. (I Survived Ser.: 9). (ENG.). 112p. (J). (gr. 2-5). pap. 4.99 *(978-0-545-45938-9(9))* Scholastic, Inc.

—I Survived the Nazi Invasion 1944. 2014. (I Survived . Ser.: No. 9). lib. bdg. 14.75 *(978-0-606-35397-7(6))* Turtleback Bks.

Upjohn, Rebecca. The Secret of the Village Fool, 1 vol. Benoit, Renné, illus. 2012. (ENG.). 32p. (J). (gr. 3-6). lib. bdg. 18.95 *(978-1-926920-75-7(9))* Second Story Pr. CAN. Dist: Orca Bk. Pubs. USA.

Wulf, Linda Press. The Night of the Burning. 2007. (ENG.). 224p. pap. *(978-0-7475-9051-4(6))* Bloomsbury Publishing Plc.

Yolen, Jane. The Devil's Arithmetic. 2004. (Puffin Modern Classics Ser.). (ENG.). 176p. (J). (gr. 5-3). pap. 7.99 *(978-0-14-240109-5(9)*, Puffin Books) Penguin Young Readers Group.

POLAR EXPEDITIONS

see Antarctica; Arctic Regions; North Pole; Polar Regions; South Pole

POLAR REGIONS

see also Antarctica; Arctic Regions; North Pole; South Pole

Algor, Marie. Endangered Animals of Antarctica & the Arctic. 2011. (Save Earth's Animals! Ser.). (Illus.). 24p. (J). pap. 8.25 *(978-1-4488-2652-0(7))*; (gr. 3-4). lib. bdg. 22.60 *(978-1-4488-2534-9(2))* Rosen Publishing Group, Inc., The. (PowerKids Pr.).

—Endangered Tundra Animals. 2012. (Save Earth's Animals! Ser.). (ENG., Illus.). 24p. (J). (gr. k-5). pap. 8.25 *(978-1-4488-7494-1(7))*; lib. bdg. 22.60 *(978-1-4488-7421-7(1))* Rosen Publishing Group, Inc., The. (PowerKids Pr.).

Amstutz, Lisa J. Polar Animal Adaptations. 2011. (Amazing Animal Adaptations Ser.). (ENG.). 32p. (gr. 1-2). pap. 47.70 *(978-1-4296-7039-5(8)*, Aplus Bks.) Capstone Press of Coughlan Cos.

—Show Me Polar Animals: My First Picture Encyclopedia, 1 vol. 2013. (My First Picture Encyclopedias Ser.). (ENG.). 32p. (gr. 1-2). pap. 8.10 *(978-1-4765-3791-7(7))*; (Illus.). 7.95

(978-1-62065-920-5(4)); lib. bdg. 27.32 (978-1-62065-059-2(2)) Capstone Press of Coughlan Cos. (Aplus Bks.).

Apte, Sunita. Polar Regions: Surviving in Antarctica. 2005. (X-treme Places Ser.). (Illus.). 32p. (YA). (gr. 2-5). lib. bdg. 25.27 (978-1-59716-088-9(1)) Bearport Publishing Co., Inc.

Arctic & Antarctic Habitats. 2013. (Discovery Education: Habitats Ser.). 32p. (J). (gr. 3-6). pap. 60.00 (978-1-4777-1482-9(0), PowerKids Pr.) Rosen Publishing Group, Inc., The.

Arlon, Penelope & Hayes, Susan. Polar Animals. 2014. (Scholastic Discover More Ser.). (ENG., Illus.). 80p. (J). (gr. 3-7). 12.99 (978-0-545-66777-7(1), Scholastic Reference) Scholastic, Inc.

AZ Books Staff. Polar Animals. Gorojan, Elena, ed. 2012. (My First Library). (ENG.). 12p. (J). (-k). bds. 8.95 (978-1-61889-122-8(7)) AZ Bks. LLC.

Bailey, Diane. Polar Exploration: Courage & Controversy. 2017. (Exploring the Polar Regions Today Ser.: Vol. 8). (ENG.). (YA). (gr. 7-12). 23.95 **(978-1-4222-3870-7(9))** Mason Crest.

Benduhn, Tea. Living in Polar Regions. 2007. (Life on the Edge Ser.). 24p. (gr. 1-4). pap. 8.15 (978-0-8368-8348-0(9)); (Illus.). lib. bdg. 22.00 (978-0-8368-8343-5(8)) Stevens, Gareth Publishing LLLP. (Weekly Reader Leveled Readers).

—La Vida en las Regiones Polares. 2007. (Vida al Limite (Life on the Edge) Ser.). (SPA., Illus.). 24p. (gr. 1-4). lib. bdg. 22.00 (978-0-8368-8353-4(5), Weekly Reader Leveled Readers) Stevens, Gareth Publishing LLLP.

Berger, Melvin & Berger, Gilda. Polar Animals in Danger. 2006. (Scholastic Reader Ser.). (Illus.). (J). (978-0-439-81535-2(5)) Scholastic, Inc.

Britton, Arthur K. Life at a Polar Research Station. 2013. (Extreme Jobs in Extreme Places Ser.). (Illus.). 32p. (J). (gr. 3-6). pap. 10.50 (978-1-4339-8483-9(0)); lib. bdg. 26.60 (978-1-4339-8482-2(2)) Stevens, Gareth Publishing LLLP.

Burgan, Michael. Climate Change & the Polar Regions. 2017. (Exploring the Polar Regions Today Ser.: Vol. 8). (ENG.). (YA). (gr. 7-12). 23.95 **(978-1-4222-3868-4(7))** Mason Crest.

—Polar Politics: Earth's Next Battlegrounds? 2017. (Exploring the Polar Regions Today Ser.: Vol. 8). (ENG.). (YA). (gr. 7-12). 23.95 **(978-1-4222-3871-4(7))** Mason Crest.

Callery, Sean. Life Cycles: Polar Lands. 2012. (Lifecycles Ser.). (ENG., Illus.). 32p. (J). (gr. 2-5). 6.99 (978-0-7534-6896-8(4), 9780753468968, Kingfisher) Roaring Brook Pr.

Cole, Joanna & O'Brien, Cynthia. Polar Animals. Degen, Bruce & Bracken, Carolyn, illus. 2014. (Magic School Bus Presents Ser.). (ENG.). 32p. (J). (gr. 1-3). pap. 6.99 (978-0-545-68586-3(9), Scholastic Paperbacks) Scholastic, Inc.

Cooper, Wade. Polar Animals. 2009. (Scholastic Reader Level 1 Ser.). (ENG.). 32p. (J). (gr. -1-3). pap. 3.99 (978-0-545-05766-0(3), Cartwheel Bks.) Scholastic, Inc.

Cox, Caroline, et al. Exploring the Polar Regions, Revised Edition. 2nd rev. ed. 2009. (Discovery & Exploration Ser.). (Illus.). 120p. (gr. 5-8). 35.00 (978-1-60413-190-1(X), Chelsea Hse.) Facts On File, Inc.

Cummings, Judy Dodge. Exploring Polar Regions, 1 vol. 2014. (Story of Exploration Ser.). (ENG.). 144p. (J). (gr. 6-12). lib. bdg. 37.07 (978-1-62403-252-3(4), Essential Library) ABDO Publishing Co.

Desonie, Dana. Polar Regions: Human Impacts. 2008. (Our Fragile Planet Ser.). (Illus.). 202p. (YA). (gr. 7-12). lib. bdg. 35.00 (978-0-8160-6218-8(8)) Facts On File, Inc.

Dowswell, Paul. True Polar Adventures. Woodcock, John, illus. 2004. (True Adventure Stories Ser.). 144p. (J). pap. 4.95 (978-0-7945-0404-5(3), Usborne) EDC Publishing.

Editors of Kingfisher. Polar Plunge. 2016. (It's All About... Ser.). (ENG., Illus.). 32p. (J). pap. 5.99 (978-0-7534-7262-0(7), 9780753472620, Kingfisher) Roaring Brook Pr.

Ganeri, Anita. Protecting Polar Regions. 2005. (Protecting Habitats Ser.). 32p. (gr. 4-7). lib. bdg. 26.00 (978-0-8368-4993-6(0), Gareth Stevens Learning Library) Stevens, Gareth Publishing LLLP.

Gifford, Clive. In Focus: Polar Lands. 2017. (In Focus Ser.). (ENG.). 64p. (J). 17.99 (978-0-7534-7351-1(8), 9780753473511); pap. 12.99 (978-0-7534-7352-8(6), 9780753473528) Roaring Brook Pr. (Kingfisher).

Goodman, Susan E. Life on the Ice. Doolittle, Michael J., illus. Doolittle, Michael J., photos by. 2006. 32p. (J). 22.60 (978-0-7613-2775-2(4), Millbrook Pr.) Lerner Publishing Group.

Gordon, Anne. Animals of the Ice & Snow. 2007. (Literacy 2000 Ser.). (Illus.). 24p. (J). (gr. 4-7). pap. (978-0-7327-0888-7(5), Rigby) Pearson Education Australia.

Gray, Leon. Polar Lands. 2015. (Amazing Biomes Ser.). (Illus.). 32p. (gr. 3-6). 31.35 (978-1-78121-245-5(7), 1389655) Brown Bear Bks.

Green, Jen. Deserts & Polar Regions Around the World. 2009. (Geography Now! Ser.). (ENG., Illus.). 32p. (J). (gr. 4-6). pap. 10.00 (978-1-4358-2960-2(3), PowerKids Pr.); (YA). (gr. 3-6). lib. bdg. 26.50 (978-1-4358-2874-2(7)) Rosen Publishing Group, Inc., The.

Guillain, Charlotte. Polar Regions. 2013. (Explorer Travel Guides). (ENG.). 48p. (gr. 3-6). 29.99 (978-1-4109-5431-2(5)); pap. 8.95 (978-1-4109-5438-1(2)) Heinemann-Raintree. (NA-r).

Hall, Katharine. Osos Polares y Pingüinos: Un Libro de Comparación y Contraste. 2014.Tr. of Polar Bears & Penguins: a Compare & Contrast Book. (SPA.). 32p. (J). (gr. -1-3). pap. 9.95 (978-1-62855-227-0(1)) Arbordale Publishing.

Hall, Katherine. Polar Bears & Penguins: A Compare & Contrast Book, 1 vol. 2014. (Compare & Contrast Ser.). (ENG., Illus.). 32p. (J). (gr. -1-3). 17.95 (978-1-62855-209-6(3)) Arbordale Publishing.

Henningfeld, Diane Andrews. North & South Poles. 2009. (Opposing Viewpoints Ser.). (ENG., Illus.). 240p. (J). pap. 42.95 (978-0-7377-4534-4(7)); 224p. (gr. 10-12). pap. 33.80 (978-0-7377-4535-1(5)) Cengage Gale.

Heos, Bridget. Do You Really Want a Hamster? Longhi, Katya, illus. 2013. (Do You Really Want a Pet? Ser.). (ENG.). 24p. (gr. 1-4). 27.10 (978-1-60753-206-4(9)) Amicus Publishing.

Hodge, Deborah. Polar Animals. Stephens, Pat, illus. 2008. (Who Lives Here? Ser.). (ENG.). 24p. (J). (gr. -1-2). 14.95 (978-1-55453-043-4(1)); pap. 5.95 (978-1-55453-044-1(X)) Kids Can Pr., Ltd. CAN. Dist: Hachette Bk. Group.

Holland, Simon. First Animal Encyclopedia Polar Animals. 2015. (First Animal Encyclopedia Ser.). (ENG., Illus.). 64p. (J). (gr. -1-3). 13.99 (978-1-4729-1344-9(2), 9781472913449, Bloomsbury USA Childrens) Bloomsbury Publishing USA.

Hollar, Sherman. Investigating Earth's Polar Biomes. 2011. (J). lib. bdg. 31.70 (978-1-61530-501-8(7)) Rosen Publishing Group, Inc., The.

Hynes, Margaret. Discover Science: Polar Lands. 2017. (Discover Science Ser.). (ENG.). 56p. (J). pap. 7.99 (978-0-7534-7334-4(8), 9780753473344, Kingfisher) Roaring Brook Pr.

—Polar Lands. 2014. 56p. pap. 8.00 (978-1-61003-361-9(2)) Center for the Collaborative Classroom.

Isn't It Cool? Individual Title Six-Packs. (Action Packs Ser.). 128p. (gr. 3-5). 44.00 (978-0-7635-3307-6(6)) Rigby Education.

Jacobs, Pat. I Wonder Why Penguins Can't Fly. 2014. 32p. pap. 7.00 (978-1-61003-350-3(7)) Center for the Collaborative Classroom.

—I Wonder Why Penguins Can't Fly: And Other Questions about Polar Lands. 2011. (I Wonder Why Ser.). (ENG., Illus.). 32p. (J). (gr. k-3). pap. 6.99 (978-0-7534-6530-1(2), 9780753465301, Kingfisher) Roaring Brook Pr.

Johnson, Allen L. Kayaking Around Iceland: Adventures with Grandchildren. 2003. (Illus.). 196p. 15.00 (978-1-880675-07-6(2)) Creative Enterprises.

Kalman, Bobbie & Aloian, Molly. Les Océans Polaires. 2009. (FRE., Illus.). 32p. (J). pap. 9.95 (978-2-89579-248-2(8)) Bayard Canada Livres CAN. Dist: Crabtree Publishing Co.

Katirgis, Jane. Baby Snow Animals. 2010. (All about Baby Animals Ser.). (Illus.). 24p. (J). pap. 7.95 (978-1-59845-160-3(X)); lib. bdg. 22.60 (978-0-7660-3797-7(5)) Enslow Pubs., Inc. (Enslow Elementary).

Kerr, James. Polar Regions. 2016. (Earth's Final Frontiers Ser.). (ENG.). 48p. (gr. 6-6). pap. 8.99 (978-1-4846-3698-5(8), NA-h) Heinemann-Raintree.

Latta, Sara L. Polar Scientists: Studying the Antarctic. 2015. (Extreme Science Careers Ser.). (ENG., Illus.). 128p. (J). (gr. 7-7). 37.27 (978-0-7660-6966-4(4)) Enslow Pubs., Inc.

Love, Ann & Drake, Jane. The Kids Book of the Far North. Bouchard, Jocelyne, illus. 2009. (Kids Book Of Ser.). (ENG.). 48p. (J). (gr. 3-7). 14.95 (978-1-55453-258-2(2)) Kids Can Pr., Ltd. CAN. Dist: Hachette Bk. Group.

Mack, Lorrie & Dorling Kindersley Publishing Staff. Arctic & Antarctic. 2006. (Eye Wonder Ser.). (ENG., Illus.). 48p. (J). (gr. k-3). 10.99 (978-0-7566-1980-0(7), DK Children) Dorling Kindersley Publishing, Inc.

Mason, Paul. Polar Regions. 2004. (Geography Fact Files Ser.). (J). lib. bdg. 28.50 (978-1-58340-428-7(7)) Black Rabbit Bks.

McAllan, Kate. Arctic & Antarctic Habitats. 2013. (Discovery Education: Habitats Ser.). 32p. (J). (gr. 3-6). 25.25 (978-1-4777-1323-5(9)); pap. 10.00 (978-1-4777-1481-2(2)) Rosen Publishing Group, Inc., The. (PowerKids Pr.).

McNeil, Niki, et al. Polar Habitats. 2007. (In the Hands of a Child: Custom Designed Project Pack Ser.). (Illus.). 51p. spiral bd. 22.50 (978-1-60308-119-1(4)) In the Hands of a Child.

Mooney, Carla. Surviving in Cold Places. 2014. (Shockzone: True Survival Stories Ser.). (ENG., Illus.). 32p. (gr. 5-8). lib. bdg. 26.60 (978-1-4677-1434-1(8), Lerner Pubns.) Lerner Publishing Group.

Murphy, Patricia J. Why Are the North & South Poles So Cold? (Library of Why Ser.). 24p. 2009. (gr. 3-4). 42.50 (978-1-60853-962-8(8)) 2004. (Illus.). (J). lib. bdg. 22.60 (978-0-8239-6233-4(4)) Rosen Publishing Group, Inc., The. (PowerKids Pr.).

Nichols, Catherine. Polar Adventures. 2003. (True Tales Ser.). (ENG., Illus.). 48p. (J). 22.50 (978-0-516-22920-1(6), Children's Pr.) Scholastic Library Publishing.

NorthWord Books for Young Readers Editors, contrib. by. Polar Babies. 2003. (Animal Babies Ser.). (ENG., Illus.). 22p. (J). (gr. -1 — 1). bds. 5.95 (978-1-55971-875-2(7)) Cooper Square Publishing Llc.

Polar Regions. 2007. (Geography of Extreme Environments Ser.). (Illus.). 128p. (YA). (gr. 7-12). lib. bdg. 30.00 (978-0-7910-9235-4(6)) Facts On File, Inc.

Pyers, Greg. Biodiversity of Polar Regions. 2010. (Biodiversity Ser.). 32p. (gr. 4-18). 28.50 (978-1-60870-072-1(0)) Marshall Cavendish Corp.

Rissman, Rebecca. Living & Nonliving in the Polar Regions, 1 vol. 2013. (Is It Living or Nonliving? Ser.). (ENG.). 24p. (gr. k-2). 23.32 (978-1-4109-5383-4(1)); pap. 6.95 (978-1-4109-5390-2(4)) Heinemann-Raintree.

Rodriguez, Ana Maria. Polar Bears, Penguins, & Other Mysterious Animals of the Extreme Cold. 2012. (Extreme Animals in Extreme Environments Ser.). (Illus.). 48p. (J). (gr. 5-18). 25.27 (978-0-7660-3695-6(2)) Enslow Pubs., Inc.

Rose, Simon. Polar Ice Caps. 2014. (Illus.). 32p. (J). (978-1-62127-486-5(1)) Weigl Pubs., Inc.

Rose, Simon. Polar Regions. 2017. (J). **(978-1-5105-2173-5(9))** SmartBook Media, Inc.

Senker, Cath. Polar Climates. 2017. (Focus on Climate Zones Ser.). (ENG.). 48p. (gr. 4-6). lib. bdg. 33.32 (978-1-4846-3784-5(4), Heinemann InfoSearch) Heinemann-Raintree.

Sill, Cathryn. About Habitats: Polar Regions, 1 vol. Sill, John, illus. 2015. (About Habitats Ser.). (ENG.). 48p. (J). (gr. -1-2). 16.95 (978-1-56145-832-5(5)) Peachtree Pubs.

Snowden, Maxine. Polar Explorers for Kids: Historic Expeditions to the Arctic & Antarctic with 21 Activities. 2003. (For Kids Ser.). (ENG.). 160p. (J). (gr. 4). pap. 16.95 (978-1-55652-500-1(1)) Chicago Review Pr., Inc.

Soll, Karen. Coldest Places on the Planet. 2016. (Extreme Earth Ser.). (ENG., Illus.). 24p. (gr. k-1). lib. bdg. 26.65 (978-1-4914-8340-4(7), Pebble Plus) Capstone Press of Coughlan Cos.

Spilsbury, Louise. How to Survive in the Arctic & Antarctica. 2012. (Tough Guides). (ENG., Illus.). 32p. (J). (gr. 4-6). pap. 10.00 (978-1-4488-7931-1(0)); lib. bdg. 25.25 (978-1-4488-7866-6(7)) Rosen Publishing Group, Inc., The. (PowerKids Pr.).

—Polar Regions. 2015. (Research on the Edge Ser.). (ENG., Illus.). 32p. (J). (gr. 3-8). 31.35 (978-1-62588-159-5(2)) Black Rabbit Bks.

Spirit of the Polar Regions. 2007. 256p. (978-1-4054-8670-5(8)) Parragon, Inc.

St. John, Sally. Polar Regions. 2010. (Illus.). 16p. (978-0-545-24809-9(4)) Scholastic, Inc.

Taylor, Barbara. Arctic & Antarctic. 2012. (DK Eyewitness Bks.). (ENG.). 72p. (J). (gr. 3-7). 16.99 (978-0-7566-9071-7(4), DK Children) Dorling Kindersley Publishing, Inc.

—Polar Habitats. 2006. (Exploring Habitats Ser.). (Illus.). 36p. (gr. 3-7). lib. bdg. 26.00 (978-0-8368-7256-9(8), Gareth Stevens Learning Library) Stevens, Gareth Publishing LLLP.

Townsend, Emily Rose. Polar Animals, 4 bks. Incl. Seals. (ENG., Illus.). 24p. (gr. k-1). 2004. 21.32 (978-0-7368-2359-3(X), Pebble Bks.); (Polar Animals Ser.). (ENG., Illus.). 24p. 2004. Set lib. bdg. 87.96 o.p. (978-0-7368-2532-0(0), Pebble Bks.) Capstone Press of Coughlan Cos.

Wade, Rosalyn. Polar Worlds. 2011. (Insiders Ser.). (ENG.). 64p. (J). (gr. 3-7). 17.99 (978-1-4424-3275-8(6), Simon & Schuster Bks. For Young Readers) Simon & Schuster Bks. For Young Readers.

Waldron, Melanie. Polar Regions, 1 vol. 2012. (Habitat Survival Ser.). (ENG.). 32p. (gr. 2-4). pap. 8.29 (978-1-4109-4608-9(8)); lib. bdg. 30.65 (978-1-4109-4599-0(5)) Heinemann-Raintree. (Raintree Perspectives).

West, David. Polar Animals. 2016. (Safari Sam's Wild Animals Ser.). 24p. (gr. k-3). 28.50 (978-1-62588-074-1(X), Smart Apple Media) Black Rabbit Bks.

—Ten of the Best Adventures in Frozen Landscapes. 2015. (Ten of the Best: Stories of Exploration & Adventure Ser.). (ENG., Illus.). 24p. (J). (gr. 3-6). (978-0-7787-1834-5(4)) Crabtree Publishing Co.

Woods, Michael & Woods, Mary B. Seven Natural Wonders of the Arctic, Antarctica, & the Oceans. 2009. (Seven Wonders Ser.). (ENG., Illus.). 80p. (gr. 5-8). 33.26 (978-0-8225-9075-0(1)) Lerner Publishing Group.

World Book, Inc Staff, contrib. by. Icy Worlds. 2011. (J). (978-0-7166-1788-4(9)) World Bk., Inc.

—Oceans, Islands, & Polar Regions. 2008. (J). (978-0-7166-1402-9(2)) World Bk., Inc.

POLAR REGIONS—FICTION

Ballantyne, R. M. The World of Ice. 2006. (Illus.). pap. (978-1-4065-0533-7(1)) Dodo Pr.

Bergen, Lara. Polar Bears' Home: A Story about Global Warming. Nguyen, Vincent, illus. 2008. (Little Green Bks.). (ENG.). 24p. (J). (gr. -1-1). pap. 3.99 (978-1-4169-6787-3(7), Little Simon) Little Simon.

Bonnet, Rosalinde. Daddy Honk Honk! Bonnet, Rosalinde, illus. 2017. (ENG., Illus.). 32p. (J). (-k). 16.99 (978-0-399-18676-9(X), Dial Bks) Penguin Young Readers Group.

Brooks, Erik. Polar Opposites, 0 vols. 2010. (ENG., Illus.). 32p. (J). (gr. -1-3). 16.99 (978-0-7614-5685-8(6), 9780761456858, Amazon Children's Publishing) Amazon Publishing.

Freedman, Claire. Where Snowflakes Fall. Macnaughton, Tina, illus. 2012. 24p. (J). (978-1-4351-4321-0(3)) Barnes & Noble, Inc.

Gevry, Claudine, illus. One Little Penguin & His Friends: A Pushing, Turning, Counting Book. 2012. (ENG.). 10p. (J). bds. (978-1-84956-027-6(7)) Top That! Publishing PLC.

Grau, Sheila. Dr. Critchlore's School for Minions: Polar Distress. Sutphin, Joe, illus. 2017. (Dr. Critchlore's School for Minions Ser.). (ENG.). 288p. (J). (gr. 3-7). 14.95 (978-1-4197-2294-3(8), Amulet Bks.) Abrams, Inc.

Heinz, Brian J. Nanuk, Lord of the Ice. Manchess, Gregory, illus. 2005. (J). (978-0-936335-13-1(0)); pap. (978-0-936335-14-8(9)) Ballyhoo BookWorks, Inc.

Lumry, Amanda & Hurwitz, Laura. Polar Bear Puzzle. 2007. (Adventures of Riley Ser.). (Illus.). (J). (gr. -1-3). 33p. 15.95 (978-1-60040-004-9(3)); 36p. 18.95 (978-1-60040-005-6(1)) Eaglemont Pr.

Mackey, Stephen. Miki. Mackey, Stephen, illus. 2010. (ENG., Illus.). 48p. (J). (gr. k-2). pap. 8.99 (978-0-340-95065-4(X)) Hodder & Stoughton GBR. Dist: Hachette Bk. Group.

Rockhill, Dennis. Sueno Polar. 2008. (SPA & ENG.). 32p. (J). (gr. -1-3). pap. 7.95 (978-1-932748-77-2(6), Raven Tree Pr.,Csi) Continental Sales, Inc.

—Sueno Polar. 2008. 32p. 16.95 (978-1-932746-76-1(5)) Sacred Garden Fellowship.

White, Andrea. Surviving Antarctica: Reality TV 2083. 2005. 336p. (J). (gr. 7-18). 16.99 (978-0-06-055454-5(1), HarperCollins) HarperCollins Pubs.

Willis, Jeanne. Poles Apart. Jarvis, illus. 2016. (ENG.). 32p. (J). (gr. -1-2). 15.99 (978-0-7636-8944-5(0), Nosy Crow) Candlewick Pr.

POLARITY

see also Good and Evil

Alda, Arlene. Hello, Good-Bye. 2009. (ENG., Illus.). 32p. (J). (gr. k-k). 16.95 (978-0-88776-900-9(4), Tundra Bks.) Tundra Bks. CAN. Dist: Penguin Random Hse. LLC.

Austin, Richard, photos by. Pocket Piggies Opposites! Featuring the Teacup Pigs of Pennywell Farm. 2016. (ENG., Illus.). 22p. (J). (gr. -1 — 1). bds. 5.95 (978-0-7611-8548-2(8)) Workman Publishing Co., Inc.

Badescu, Ramona. Pomelo's Opposites. Chaud, Benjamin, illus. 2013. (Pomelo the Garden Elephant Ser.). (ENG.). 120p. (J). 15.95 (978-1-59270-132-2(9)) Enchanted Lion Bks., LLC.

Baruzzi, Agnese. Opposites: A Cut-Paper Book. Baruzzi, Agnese, illus. 2013. (ENG., Illus.). 10p. (J). (— 1). 15.99 (978-1-85707-803-9(9)) Tango Bks. GBR. Dist: Independent Pubs. Group.

Blackstone, Stella. You & Me. Manna, Giovanni, illus. 2009. (ENG.). 32p. (J). 14.99 (978-1-84686-336-3(8)) Barefoot Bks., Inc.

Chedru, Delphine. Hello Goodbye: The Magic of Opposites. 2015. (ENG., Illus.). 44p. (J). (-k). 24.95 (978-3-89955-753-4(0)) Die Gestalten Verlag DEU. Dist: Penguin Random Hse. LLC.

Christopher, Jennifer R. What If a Fork Was a Spoon. Christopher, Marie & Christopher, Jennifer, illus. 2006. (ENG.). 29p. (J). (gr. -1-3). per. 19.99 (978-1-4257-0847-4(1)) Xlibris Corp.

Coat, Janik. Hippopposites. 2012. (ENG., Illus.). 38p. (J). (gr. -1 — 1). bds. 15.95 (978-1-4197-0151-1(7), Abrams Appleseed) Abrams, Inc.

Coulton, Mia. Danny & Bee's Book of Opposites. Coulton, Mia, photos by. 2006. (ENG., Illus.). pap. 5.35 (978-1-933624-02-0(7)) Maryruth Bks., Inc.

Davis, Caroline. First Opposites. 2012. (ENG., Illus.). 10p. (J). (gr. -1-1). bds. 7.99 (978-1-84322-844-8(0), Armadillo) Anness Publishing GBR. Dist: National Bk. Network.

Del Moral, S., tr. Contrarios. 2006. (Disney Learning (Silver Dolphin en Espanol) Ser.). (Illus.). 22p. (J). (gr. -1). (978-970-718-428-2(0), Silver Dolphin en Español) Advanced Marketing, S. de R. L. de C. V.

Deneux, Xavier. Opposites. 2013. (ENG., Illus.). 20p. (J). (gr. -1 — 1). bds. 14.99 (978-1-4521-1725-6(X)) Chronicle Bks. LLC.

Dicmas, Courtney. Opposites. Dicmas, Courtney, illus. 2017. (Wild! Concepts Ser.: 4). (ENG., Illus.). 14p. (J). bds. **(978-1-84643-997-1(3))** Child's Play International Ltd.

Dorling Kindersley Publishing Staff. My First Opposites. 2017. (My First Bks.). (ENG.). 36p. (J). (— 1). bds. 5.99 **(978-1-4654-6141-4(8)**, DK Children) Dorling Kindersley Publishing, Inc.

Emberley, Rebecca. My Opposites (Mis Opuestos) braille ed. 2004. (SPA, ENG & FRE.). (J). (gr. 1). spiral bd. bds. (978-0-616-07271-4(6)) Canadian National Institute for the Blind/Institut National Canadien pour les Aveugles.

Erickson, Sharon. The Opposites. Ready, D. M., illus. 2008. 24p. pap. 24.95 (978-1-60672-551-1(3)) America Star Bks.

Evanson, Ashley. London: A Book of Opposites. Evanson, Ashley, illus. 2015. (Hello, World Ser.). (ENG., Illus.). 14p. (J). (— 1). bds. 6.99 (978-0-448-48916-2(3), Grosset & Dunlap) Penguin Young Readers Group.

Fisher, Valorie. Everything I Need to Know Before I'm Five. Fisher, Valorie, illus. 2011. (ENG., Illus.). 40p. (J). (gr. k-k). 17.99 (978-0-375-86865-8(8), Schwartz & Wade Bks.) Random Hse. Children's Bks.

Friedland, Katy & Shoemaker, Maria K. Art Museum Opposites. 2010. (ENG., Illus.). 44p. (J). (gr. -1-3). 16.95 (978-1-4399-0523-4(1)) Temple Univ. Pr.

Friedland, Katy & Shoemaker, Maria K. Art Museum Opposites. 2010. (Illus.). (978-0-87633-222-1(X)) Philadelphia Museum of Art.

Galvin, Laura Gates. Quack's Opposites. 2006. (Peep & the Big Wide World Ser.). (ENG., Illus.). 24p. (J). (gr. -1-2). 15.99 (978-1-59249-520-7(6), 1C302) Soundprints.

George, Patrick & PatrickGeorge. Contrarios. 2012. (SPA.). 26p. (J). (gr. -1-1). pap. 19.99 (978-84-261-3885-9(3)) Juventud, Editorial ESP. Dist: Lectorum Pubns., Inc.

Ghione, Yvette & Gürth, Per-Henrik. Hockey Opposites. Gürth, Per-Henrik, illus. 2010. (ENG., Illus.). 24p. (J). (gr. -1-1). 15.95 (978-1-55453-241-4(8)) Kids Can Pr., Ltd. CAN. Dist: Hachette Bk. Group.

Gordon, Sharon. Arriba Abajo: Exactamente lo Opuesto. 2006. (Bookworms Ser.). (SPA., Illus.). 24p. (gr. k-1). lib. bdg. 15.95 (978-0-7614-2369-0(9)) Marshall Cavendish Corp.

—Duro Blando. 2006. (Bookworms Ser.). (SPA & ENG., Illus.). 24p. (gr. k-1). lib. bdg. 15.95 (978-0-7614-2368-3(0)) Marshall Cavendish Corp.

—Fast/Slow. 2007. (J). pap. 6.99 (978-0-7614-3281-4(7)) Marshall Cavendish Corp.

—Fast/Slow/Rapido/Lento. 2006. (Bookworms Ser.). (ENG & SPA., Illus.). 24p. (gr. k-1). lib. bdg. 15.95 (978-0-7614-2447-5(4)) Marshall Cavendish Corp.

—Grande, Pequeno. 2006. (Bookworms Ser.). (SPA., Illus.). 24p. (gr. k-1). lib. bdg. 15.95 (978-0-7614-2364-5(8), Benchmark Bks.) Marshall Cavendish Corp.

—Hard/Soft. 2007. (J). pap. 6.99 (978-0-7614-3282-1(5)) Marshall Cavendish Corp.

—Hard/Soft/Duro/Blando. 2006. (Bookworms Ser.). (ENG & SPA., Illus.). 24p. (gr. k-1). lib. bdg. 15.95 (978-0-7614-2448-2(2)) Marshall Cavendish Corp.

—Just the Opposite (Exactamente lo Opuesto), 6 bks., Set. Incl. Big/Small/Grande/Pequeno. lib. bdg. 15.95 (978-0-7614-2445-1(8)); Dirty Clean/Sucio Limpio. lib. bdg. 15.95 (978-0-7614-2446-8(6)); Fast/Slow/Rapido/Lento. lib. bdg. 15.95 (978-0-7614-2447-5(4)); Hard/Soft/Duro/Blando. lib. bdg. 15.95 (978-0-7614-2448-2(2)); Up Down (Arriba Abajo) lib. bdg. 15.95 (978-0-7614-2449-9(0)); Wet/Dry/Seco/Mojado. lib. bdg. 15.95 (978-0-7614-2450-5(4)); (Illus.). 24p. (gr. k-1). (Bookworms — Bilingual Editions: Just the Opposite/Exactamente lo Opuesto Ser.). (SPA.). 2006. Set lib. bdg. 95.70 (978-0-7614-2443-7(1)) Marshall Cavendish Corp.

—Mojado Seco. 2006. (Bookworms Ser.). (SPA & ENG., Illus.). 24p. (gr. k-1). lib. bdg. 15.95 (978-0-7614-2370-6(2)) Marshall Cavendish Corp.

—Rapido Lento. 2006. (Bookworms Ser.). (SPA & ENG., Illus.). 24p. (gr. k-1). lib. bdg. 15.95 (978-0-7614-2367-6(2)) Marshall Cavendish Corp.

—Sucio Limpio. 2006. (Bookworms Ser.). (SPA., Illus.). 24p. (gr. k-1). lib. bdg. 15.95 (978-0-7614-2365-2(6), Benchmark Bks.) Marshall Cavendish Corp.

—Wet/Dry. 2007. (J). pap. 6.99 (978-0-7614-3285-2(X)) Marshall Cavendish Corp.

—Wet/Dry/Seco/Mojado. 2006. (Bookworms Ser.). (ENG & SPA., Illus.). 24p. (gr. k-1). lib. bdg. 15.95 (978-0-7614-2450-5(4)) Marshall Cavendish Corp.

Gordon, Sharon & Gordon, Sharon. Exactamente lo Opuesto, 6 bks., Set. Incl. Arriba Abajo: Exactamente lo Opuesto. lib. bdg. 15.95 (978-0-7614-2369-0(9)); Duro Blando. lib. bdg. 15.95 (978-0-7614-2368-3(0)); Grande, Pequeno. lib. bdg. 15.95 (978-0-7614-2364-5(8), Benchmark Bks.); Mojado Seco. lib. bdg. 15.95 (978-0-7614-2370-6(2)); Rapido Lento. lib. bdg. 15.95 (978-0-7614-2367-6(2)); Sucio Limpio. lib. bdg. 15.95 (978-0-7614-2365-2(6), Benchmark Bks.); (Illus.). 24p. (gr. k-1). (Bookworms — Spanish Editions: Exactamente lo Opuesto Ser.). (SPA.). 2006. Set lib. bdg. 95.70 (978-0-7614-2363-8(X), Benchmark Bks.) Marshall Cavendish Corp.

Gunzi, Christiane. Opposites. Murrell, Deborah, ed. 2nd rev. ed. 2015. (ENG., Illus.). 34p. (J). 7.99 (978-1-906572-21-1(6)) Award Pubns. Ltd. GBR. Dist: Parkwest Pubns., Inc.

Heath, Beverly C. Opposites. Floyd, John, Jr., illus. 2006. 8p. (J). (gr. -1). bds. 5.95 (978-0-9752860-3-6(X)) OurRainbow Pr., LLC.

PQR

Hood, Susan. Double Take! A New Look at Opposites. Fleck, Jay, illus. 2017. (ENG.). 32p. (J). (gr. -1-2). 16.99 ***(978-0-7636-7291-1(2))*** Candlewick Pr.
Horácek, Petr. Animal Opposites. Horácek, Petr, illus. 2013. (ENG., Illus.). 20p. (J). (gr. -1-2). 15.99 *(978-0-7636-6776-4(5))* Candlewick Pr.
Hughes, Tom. Tight & Loose. 2016. (All about Opposites Ser.). (Illus.). 24p. (J). pap. 9.35 *(978-0-7660-8116-1(8))* Enslow Pubs., Inc.
Jeffries, Joyce. Big & Small. 2013. (Dinosaur School Ser.). (Illus.). 24p. (J). (gr. -1-1). pap. 8.15 *(978-1-4339-8084-8(3))*; lib. bdg. 22.60 *(978-1-4339-8083-1(5))* Stevens, Gareth Publishing LLLP.
—Heavy & Light. 2013. (Dinosaur School Ser.). (Illus.). 24p. (gr. -1-1). 22.60 *(978-1-4339-8087-9(8))*; pap. 8.15 *(978-1-4339-8088-6(6))* Stevens, Gareth Publishing LLLP.
—Hot & Cold. 2013. (Dinosaur School Ser.). (Illus.). 24p. (gr. -1-1). 22.60 *(978-1-4339-8091-6(6))*; pap. 8.15 *(978-1-4339-8092-3(4))* Stevens, Gareth Publishing LLLP.
—Long & Short. 2013. (Dinosaur School Ser.). (Illus.). 24p. (gr. -1-1). 22.60 *(978-1-4339-8095-4(9))*; pap. 8.15 *(978-1-4339-8096-1(7))* Stevens, Gareth Publishing LLLP.
Kalman, Bobbie. Is It the Same or Different? 2007. (Looking at Nature Ser.). (ENG., Illus.). 24p. (J). (gr. -1-2). pap. *(978-0-7787-3337-9(8))* Crabtree Publishing Co.
—What Are Opposites in Nature? 2010. (Looking at Nature Ser.). (ENG.). 24p. (J). (gr. -1-2). lib. bdg. *(978-0-7787-3326-3(2))* Crabtree Publishing Co.
Katirgis, Jane. Back & Front. 2011. (All about Opposites Ser.). (Illus.). 24p. (J). (gr. -1-18). pap. 7.95 *(978-1-59845-259-4(2)*, Enslow Elementary); (gr. k-3). lib. bdg. 22.60 *(978-0-7660-3916-2(1))* Enslow Pubs., Inc.
—Big & Little. 2011. (All about Opposites Ser.). (Illus.). 24p. (J). (gr. -1-18). pap. 7.95 *(978-1-59845-263-1(0)*, Enslow Elementary); (gr. k-3). lib. bdg. 22.60 *(978-0-7660-3911-7(0))* Enslow Pubs., Inc.
—Day & Night. 2011. (All about Opposites Ser.). (Illus.). 24p. (J). (gr. -1-18). pap. 7.95 *(978-1-59845-262-4(2)*, Enslow Elementary); (gr. k-3). lib. bdg. 22.60 *(978-0-7660-3915-5(3))* Enslow Pubs., Inc.
—Over & Under. 2011. (All about Opposites Ser.). (Illus.). 24p. (J). (gr. -1-18). pap. 7.95 *(978-1-59845-260-0(6)*, Enslow Elementary); (gr. k-3). lib. bdg. 22.60 *(978-0-7660-3914-8(5))* Enslow Pubs., Inc.
—Tall & Short. 2011. (All about Opposites Ser.). (Illus.). 24p. (J). (gr. -1-18). pap. 7.95 *(978-1-59845-261-7(4)*, Enslow Elementary); (gr. k-3). lib. bdg. 22.60 *(978-0-7660-3912-4(9))* Enslow Pubs., Inc.
—Up & Down. 2011. (All about Opposites Ser.). (Illus.). 24p. (J). (gr. -1-18). pap. 7.95 *(978-1-59845-258-7(4)*, Enslow Elementary); (gr. k-3). lib. bdg. 22.60 *(978-0-7660-3913-1(7))* Enslow Pubs., Inc.
Killen, Nicola. Animal Opposites. 2014. (Nicola Killen Animals Ser.). (ENG., Illus.). 10p. (J). (— 1). bds. 9.99 *(978-1-4052-6286-6(9))* Egmont Bks., Ltd. GBR. Dist: Independent Pubs. Group.
Knight, Margy Burns, et al. Who Belongs Here? O'Brien, Anne Sibley, illus. 2nd ed. 2005. 40p. (gr. 3-8). pap., tchr. ed., tchr.'s training gde. ed. 9.95 *(978-0-88448-111-9(5))* Tilbury Hse. Pubs.
Lagonegro, Melissa & Wooster, Devin Ann. Big Dinosaur, Little Dinosaur. Random House Disney Staff, illus. 2016. (Step into Reading Ser.). (ENG.). 24p. (J). (gr. -1-1). 4.99 *(978-0-7364-3247-4(7)*, RH/Disney) Random Hse. Children's Bks.
Larranaga, Ana M. Pull & Play - Opposites. Martín, Ana I., illus. 2013. (Pull & Play Ser.). (ENG.). 10p. (J). (— 1). bds. 7.99 *(978-0-230-75040-1(0))* Pan Macmillan GBR. Dist: Independent Pubs. Group.
Lluch, Alex A. I Like to Learn Opposites: Amazing Bugs. 2011. (ENG.). 32p. (J). (gr. -1-k). bds. 4.95 *(978-1-934386-03-3(0))* WS Publishing.
Marshall Cavendish Benchmark, prod. Heavy/Light. 2nd rev. ed. 2011. (Bookworms 2nd Edition: Opposites Ser.). 16p. (gr. k-1). 21.36 *(978-1-60870-408-8(4))* Marshall Cavendish Corp.
—Hot/Cold. 2nd rev. ed. 2011. (Bookworms 2nd Edition: Opposites Ser.). 16p. (gr. k-1). 21.36 *(978-1-60870-409-5(2))* Marshall Cavendish Corp.
McDonald, Jill. Opposites: A Play-with-Me BK. 2007. (ENG.). 10p. bds. 6.95 *(978-1-58117-605-6(8)*, Intervisual/Piggy Toes) Bendon, Inc.
Mckee, David & McKee, David. Elmer's Opposites. McKee, David, illus. 2012. (Andersen Press Board Bks). (ENG., Illus.). 10p. (J). (gr. -1-2). bds. 7.95 *(978-0-7613-8998-9(9))* Lerner Publishing Group.
National Wildlife Federation Staff. My First Book of Animal Opposites. 2016. (ENG., Illus.). 22p. (J). (— 1). bds. 6.95 *(978-1-62354-062-3(3))* Charlesbridge Publishing, Inc.
National Wildlife Federation Staff & Bové, Jennifer. Ranger Rick Jr. Animal Opposites. 2017. (Ranger Rick: Animal Fun for Young Children Ser.). (ENG., Illus.). 32p. (J). (gr. -1-1). pap. 5.99 *(978-1-63076-292-6(X))* Muddy Boots Pr.
Nunn, Daniel. Eddie & Ellie's Opposites. 2013. (Eddie & Ellie's Opposites Ser.). (ENG.). 24p. (gr. -1-k). pap. 27.80 *(978-1-4109-5349-0(1))*; lib. bdg. 90.60 *(978-1-4109-5344-5(0))* Heinemann-Raintree. (NA-r).
Page, Liza & Innovative Kids Staff. Opposites. Larrañaga, Ana Martín, illus. 2008. (ENG.). 12p. (J). (gr. -1 — 1). bds. 5.99 *(978-1-58476-654-4(9))* Innovative Kids.
Patricelli, Leslie. Grande Pequeño. Rozarena, P., tr. Patricelli, Leslie, illus. 2003. (SPA., Illus.). 25p. (J). (gr. -1-k). bds. 7.95 *(978-970-29-0988-0(0))* Santillana USA Publishing Co., Inc.
—No No Yes Yes. Patricelli, Leslie, illus. 2008. (Leslie Patricelli Board Bks.). (ENG., Illus.). 24p. (J). (— 1). bds. 6.99 *(978-0-7636-3244-1(9))* Candlewick Pr.
Priddy Books Staff. First Concepts: Opposite. 2003. (Illus.). (J). bds. 8.95 *(978-0-312-49231-1(6)*, Priddy Bks.) St. Martin's Pr.
Reich, Kass, illus. Up Hamster, down Hamster, 1 vol. 2015. (ENG.). 24p. (J). (gr. -1-k). bds. 9.95 *(978-1-4598-1013-6(9))* Orca Bk. Pubs. USA.
Saunders, Katie, illus. Let's Learn Opposites. 2013. 10p. (J). ***(978-1-4351-4940-3(8))*** Barnes & Noble, Inc.
Savary, Fabien. Caillou: Que Falta? Tipeo, illus. 2004. (Caillou Ser.).Tr. of What's Missing? (SPA & ENG.). 12p. (J). (gr. -1-17). bds. 4.95 *(978-1-58728-349-9(2))* Cooper Square Publishing Llc.
Savary, Fabien & Vadeboncoeur, Isabelle. Caillou: Los Contrarios. Tipeo, illus. 2004. (Caillou Ser.).Tr. of What's the Difference? (SPA & ENG.). 12p. (J). (gr. -1-17). bds. 4.95 *(978-1-58728-348-2(4))* Cooper Square Publishing Llc.
Saviola, Ava. Dinosaur Opposites. 2012. (Dinosaur School Ser.). (Illus.). 24p. (J). (gr. -1-1). pap. 8.15 *(978-1-4339-7144-0(5))*; lib. bdg. 22.60 *(978-1-4339-7143-3(7))* Stevens, Gareth Publishing LLLP.
Scarry, Richard. My School Backpack: With 4 Books! 2012. (Illus.). (J). *(978-1-4380-8502-9(8))* Barron's Educational Series, Inc.
Shulman, Mark. Big Bagel, Little Bagel. Miline, Bill, photos by. 2006. (Illus.). 10p. (J). (gr. k-4). reprint ed. 6.00 *(978-1-4223-5709-5(0))* DIANE Publishing Co.
Silver Dolphin en Español Editors. Disney Tesoro de libros de Calcomanias: Disney Sticker Book Treasury, Spanish-Language Edition. 2007. (Illus.). 48p. (J). *(978-970-718-447-3(7)*, Silver Dolphin en Español) Advanced Marketing, S. de R. L. de C. V.
Smith, Sian. Hard & Soft, 1 vol. 2014. (Opposites Ser.). (ENG.). 24p. (gr. -1-1). pap. 5.99 *(978-1-4846-0333-8(8)*, Acorn) Heinemann-Raintree.
—Hot & Cold, 1 vol. 2014. (Opposites Ser.). (ENG.). 24p. (gr. -1-1). pap. 5.99 *(978-1-4846-0334-5(6)*, Acorn) Heinemann-Raintree.
—Old & New, 1 vol. 2014. (Opposites Ser.). (ENG.). 24p. (gr. -1-1). pap. 5.99 *(978-1-4846-0335-2(4)*, Acorn) Heinemann-Raintree.
—Opposites, 1 vol. 2014. (Opposites Ser.). (ENG.). 24p. (gr. -1-1). pap. 35.94 *(978-1-4846-0338-3(9)*, Acorn) Heinemann-Raintree.
—Opposites Big Book, 1 vol. 2014. (Opposites Ser.). (ENG., Illus.). 24p. (gr. -1-1). 26.00 *(978-1-4846-0339-0(7)*, Acorn) Heinemann-Raintree.
—Wet & Dry, 1 vol. 2014. (Opposites Ser.). (ENG.). 24p. (gr. -1-1). pap. 5.99 *(978-1-4846-0337-6(0)*, Acorn) Heinemann-Raintree.
Watt, Mélanie. Opposites. Watt, Mélanie, illus. 2005. (Learning with Animals Ser.). (ENG., Illus.). 24p. (J). (gr. -1 — 1). bds. 5.95 *(978-1-55337-832-7(6))* Kids Can Pr., Ltd. CAN. Dist: Hachette Bk. Group.
Wishinsky, Frieda. What's up, Bear? A Book about Opposites. Moore, Sean L., illus. 2012. (ENG.). 32p. (J). (gr. -1-2). 16.95 *(978-1-926973-41-8(0)*, Owlkids) Owlkids Bks. Inc. CAN. Dist: Publishers Group West (PGW).
Yates, Gene. The Dragon Opposites Book. 2005. (Illus.). 14p. (J). *(978-1-58865-283-6(1))* Kidsbooks, LLC.
Yates, Gene, illus. The Dragon Opposites Book. 2006. (J). *(978-1-58865-362-8(5))* Kidsbooks, LLC.

POLARITY—FICTION

Arena, Jen. Marta! Big & Small. Dominguez, Angela, illus. 2016. (ENG & SPA.). 32p. (J). 16.99 *(978-1-62672-243-9(9)*, 9781626722439) Roaring Brook Pr.
Boyd, Lizi. Big Bear Little Chair. 2015. (ENG., Illus.). 36p. (J). (gr. -1-k). 16.99 *(978-1-4521-4447-4(8))* Chronicle Bks. LLC.
Coward, Fiona. Swing High, Swing Low. Manna, Giovanni, illus. 2005. (ENG.). 32p. (J). 16.99 *(978-1-84148-170-8(X))* Barefoot Bks., Inc.
Disney. Big Bear, Little Bear. 2012. (Disney Princess Step into Reading Ser.). lib. bdg. 13.55 *(978-0-606-26391-7(8)*, Turtleback) Turtleback Bks.
Hill, Eric. Spot's Opposites. 2013. (Spot Ser.). (ENG.). 10p. (J). (gr. -1-k). bds. 6.99 *(978-0-7232-7046-1(5)*, Warne) Penguin Young Readers Group.
Idle, Molly. Flora & the Ostrich: An Opposites Book. 2017. (ENG., Illus.). 20p. (J). (gr. -1 — 1). bds. 9.99 *(978-1-4521-4658-4(6))* Chronicle Bks. LLC.
Jordan, Apple. Fast Kart, Slow Kart. 2013. (Step into Reading Level 1 Ser.). lib. bdg. 13.55 *(978-0-606-26980-3(0)*, Turtleback) Turtleback Bks.
Lagonegro, Melissa. Big Friend, Little Friend. 2010. (Disney Princess Step into Reading Ser.). lib. bdg. 13.55 *(978-0-606-07043-0(5)*, Turtleback) Turtleback Bks.
Litton, Jonathan. Tall & Short: A Peek-Through Book of Opposites. Galloway, Fhiona, illus. 2014. (My Little World Ser.). (ENG.). 16p. (J). (gr. -1-k). bds. 7.99 *(978-1-58925-565-4(8))* Tiger Tales.
Makso, Malisa. Inside & Outside. 2010.Tr. of Anndan ak Deyò. (HAT., Illus.). 8p. (J). 4.50 *(978-1-58432-829-2(0))* Educa Vision Inc.
Na, Il Sung, illus. The Opposite Zoo. 2016. (ENG.). 24p. (J). (-k). 16.99 *(978-0-553-51127-7(0)*, Knopf Bks. for Young Readers) Random Hse. Children's Bks.
Preston-Gannon, Frann. What a Hoot! 2015. (ENG., Illus.). 20p. (J). (-k). bds. 12.95 *(978-1-57687-758-6(2)*, powerHouse Bks.) powerHouse Cultural Entertainment, Inc.
Priddy, Roger. On the Go. 2013. (Hello Baby Ser.). (ENG., Illus.). 16p. (J). (gr. -1 — 1). bds. 4.99 *(978-0-312-51599-7(5)*, 9780312515997, Priddy Bks.) St. Martin's Pr.
Prochovnic, Dawn Babb. Opposites Everywhere: Sign Language for Opposites, 1 vol. Bauer, Stephanie, illus. 2012. (ENG.). 32p. 28.50 *(978-1-61641-839-7(7)*, Looking Glass Library) Magic Wagon.
Reidy, Hannah. Crazy Creature Contrasts. Mackie, Clare, illus. 2003. (Crazy Creatures Ser.). 26p. (J). pap. *(978-1-84089-223-9(4))* Zero to Ten, Ltd.
Running Press Staff. Opposites. 2004. (Sticker Math Ser.). (ENG.). 1p. (J). pap., act. bk. ed. 4.95 *(978-0-7945-0042-9(0)*, Usborne) EDC Publishing.
Scholastic, Inc. Staff, contrib. by. Opposites. 2015. (Rookie Toddler(r) Ser.). (ENG.). 12p. (J). bds. 6.95 *(978-0-531-20569-3(X))* Scholastic Library Publishing.
Schwartz, Betty & Seresin, Lynn. Puppies, Puppies, Everywhere! A Back-And-Forth Opposites Book. Powell, Luciana Navarro, illus. 2015. (J). *(978-1-62370-236-6(4))* Capstone Young Readers of Coughlan Cos.
Seuss, Dr. & Seuss. The Foot Book. abr. ed. 2016. (Big Bright & Early Board Book Ser.). (ENG., Illus.). 24p. (J). (gr. -1 — 1). bds. 6.99 *(978-0-553-53630-0(3)*, Random Hse. Bks. for Young Readers) Random Hse. Children's Bks.
Ward, Sarah, illus. Carry & Learn Opposites. 2016. (ENG.). 10p. (J). (— 1). bds. 7.99 *(978-0-545-79789-4(6)*, Cartwheel Bks.) Scholastic, Inc.
Webster, Christy. Big Fish, Little Fish. 2016. (Illus.). 24p. (J). E-Book ***(978-0-7364-3705-9(3))*** Random Hse., Inc.
Williams, Brenda. Outdoor Opposites. Oldfield, Rachel, illus. 2015. 32p. (J). (gr. -1-2). 9.99 *(978-1-78285-095-3(3))* Barefoot Bks., Inc.

POLICE

see also Criminal Investigation; Detectives; Secret Service

ABDO Publishing Company Staff. Emergency Workers. 2012. (Emergency Workers Ser.: 6). (ENG.). 32p. (J). (gr. 5-9). lib. bdg. 162.42 *(978-1-61783-511-7(0)*, Abdo & Daughters) ABDO Publishing Co.
Adamson, Heather. A Day in the Life of a Police Officer, 1 vol. 2003. (Community Helpers at Work Ser.). (ENG., Illus.). 24p. (gr. 1-2). 25.32 *(978-0-7368-2285-5(2)*, First Facts) Capstone Press of Coughlan Cos.
Ames, Michelle. Police Officers in Our Community. 2009. (Illus.). 24p. (J). 49.50 *(978-1-4358-2464-5(4)*, 1300573); (ENG., pap. 8.25 *(978-1-4358-2453-9(9)*, 1300573); (ENG., lib. bdg. 22.60 *(978-1-4042-8057-1(X)*, 1300573) Rosen Publishing Group, Inc., The. (PowerKids Pr.).
Anderson, Sheila. Police Station. 2008. pap. 22.95 *(978-0-8225-9373-7(4))*; (ENG.). 8p. (gr. -1-1). pap. 4.95 *(978-0-8225-8842-9(0))* Lerner Publishing Group.
Apps, Roy. Robbers, Cops, Crime: An Illustrated History of Policing. 2017. (ENG., Illus.). 32p. (J). (gr. 4-6). 16.99 ***(978-1-5263-0081-2(8)***, Wayland) Hachette Children's Group GBR. Dist: Hachette Bk. Group.
Aronin, Miriam. Highway Patrol Officers. 2016. (Police: Search & Rescue! Ser.). (ENG., Illus.). 32p. (J). (gr. 2-7). lib. bdg. 19.95 *(978-1-943553-14-3(9))* Bearport Publishing Co., Inc.
Aronson, Marc. Master of Deceit: J. Edgar Hoover & America in the Age of Lies. 2012. (ENG., Illus.). 230p. (J). (gr. 9). 25.99 *(978-0-7636-5025-4(0))* Candlewick Pr.
Askew, Amanda & Crowson, Andrew. Police Officer. 2012. (Illus.). 24p. (gr. 1-3). pap. 7.95 *(978-1-926853-49-9(0))* Saunders Bk. Co. CAN. Dist: RiverStream Publishing.
Blake, Kevin. City Cops. 2016. (Police: Search & Rescue! Ser.). (ENG., Illus.). 32p. (J). (gr. 2-7). 19.95 *(978-1-943553-11-2(4))* Bearport Publishing Co., Inc.
Bowman, Chris. Police Officer. 2014. (Dangerous Jobs Ser.). (ENG., Illus.). 24p. (J). (gr. 3-7). lib. bdg. 25.95 *(978-1-62617-112-1(2)*, Torque Bks.) Bellwether Media.
Butler, Dori Hillestad. P Is for Police, 1 vol. Waites, Joan, illus. 2009. (ENG.). 32p. (J). (gr. k-3). 16.99 *(978-1-58980-652-8(2))* Pelican Publishing Co., Inc.
Butts, Edward. Behind the Badge: Crimefighters Through History. Williams, Gareth Glyn, illus. 2014. (ENG.). 168p. (J). (gr. 5-8). pap. 14.95 *(978-1-55451-674-2(9)*, 9781554516742) Annick Pr., Ltd. CAN. Dist: Publishers Group West (PGW).
Capici, Gaetano. What Do They Do? Police Officers. 2010. (Community Connections: What Do They Do? Ser.). (ENG.). 24p. (gr. 2-5). lib. bdg. 25.64 *(978-1-60279-803-8(6)*, 200496) Cherry Lake Publishing.
Carr, Aaron. The Police Station. 2013. 24p. pap. 12.95 *(978-1-62127-347-9(4))* Weigl Pubs., Inc.
Caviezel, Giovanni. Policeman's Safety Hints. 2013. (ENG.). 12p. (J). (gr. -1-2). bds. 8.99 *(978-0-7641-6721-8(9))* Barron's Educational Series, Inc.
Chapman, Joan. Visiting the Police Station. 2008. (Rosen Real Readers: Upper Emergent Ser.). (ENG., Illus.). 12p. (gr. 1-2). pap. 5.90 *(978-0-8239-8124-3(X))* Rosen Publishing Group, Inc., The.
Charles, Audrey. I Can Be a Police Officer. 2017. (I Can Be Anything! Ser.). 24p. (gr. k-k). pap. 8.15 ***(978-1-4824-6325-5(3))*** Stevens, Gareth Publishing LLLP.
Christopher, Nick. Que Hacen Los Policias? / What Do Police Officers Do? 2015. (Ayudantes de la Comunidad / Helping the Community Ser.). (ENG & SPA.). 24p. (J). (gr. 1-1). 23.60 *(978-1-4994-0615-3(0)*, PowerKids Pr.) Rosen Publishing Group, Inc., The.
—What Do Police Officers Do? 2015. (Helping the Community Ser.). (ENG., Illus.). 24p. (J). (gr. 1-1). pap. 8.25 *(978-1-4994-0656-6(8)*, PowerKids Pr.) Rosen Publishing Group, Inc., The.
Christy, Lee Louis. I Go to Work as a Police Officer. 2003. (I Go to Work As Ser.). (Illus.). (J). *(978-1-58417-040-2(9))*; pap. *(978-1-58417-103-4(0))* Lake Street Pubs.
Clark, Katie. Police Horses. 2013. (We Work! Animals with Jobs Ser.). (Illus.). 24p. (J). (gr. -1-3). lib. bdg. 21.32 *(978-1-61772-896-9(9))* Bearport Publishing Co., Inc.
Coan, Sharon. Trabajadores Que Me Cuidan (Workers Who Take Care of Me) 2016. (TIME for KIDS(r) Nonfiction Readers Ser.). (SPA.). 12p. (J). (gr. k-k). 4.99 *(978-1-4938-3028-2(7))* Teacher Created Materials, Inc.
Coldwell, Lamar. Shaniqua's Mom Is a Policewoman. 2016. (Rosen REAL Readers: Social Studies Nonfiction / Fiction: Family, Community, & the World Ser.). 12p. (gr. 1-k). pap. 6.33 *(978-1-5081-2314-9(4)*, Rosen Classroom) Rosen Publishing Group, Inc., The.
Crabtree, Marc. Meet My Neighbor, the Police Officer. 2012. (ENG., Illus.). 24p. (J). *(978-0-7787-4561-7(9))*; pap. *(978-0-7787-4566-2(X))* Crabtree Publishing Co.
Crewe, Sabrina. Canadian Mounties. 2015. (Canadian Symbols Ser.). (ENG., Illus.). 24p. (gr. k-1). lib. bdg. 26.65 *(978-1-4914-7094-7(1)*, Pebble Plus) Capstone Press of Coughlan Cos.
Doering Tourville, Amanda. A Visit to the Police Station. Thompson, Jeffrey, illus. 2011. (First Graphics: My Community Ser.). (ENG.). 24p. (gr. 1-2). pap. 35.70 *(978-1-4296-6402-8(9))* Capstone Press of Coughlan Cos.
Dorling Kindersley Publishing Staff & Gersh, Camilla. Emergency Rescuers & Crime Fighters. 2016. (DK Readers Ser.). (ENG., Illus.). 64p. (J). (gr. 2-4). 14.99 *(978-1-4654-4500-1(5)*, DK Children) Dorling Kindersley Publishing, Inc.
Dudley, William. Do Police Abuse Their Powers? 2016. (ENG.). 80p. (J). (gr. 5-12). lib. bdg. *(978-1-68282-072-8(6))* ReferencePoint Pr., Inc.
Entin, Cindy. My First Counting Book: Police. Boldman, Craig, illus. 2014. (ENG.). 10p. (J). bds. 5.99 *(978-1-60433-456-2(8)*, Applesauce Pr.) Cider Mill Pr. Bk. Pubs., LLC.
Enz, Tammy. Beyond the Bars: Exploring the Secrets of a Police Station. 2010. (Hidden Worlds Ser.). (ENG.). 32p. (gr. 1-2). lib. bdg. 26.65 *(978-1-4296-3377-2(8)*, Blazers) Capstone Press of Coughlan Cos.
—Hidden Worlds, 4 vols., Set. Incl. Behind the Racks: Exploring the Secrets of a Shopping Mall. lib. bdg. 26.65 *(978-1-4296-3386-4(7))*; Beyond the Bars: Exploring the Secrets of a Police Station. lib. bdg. 26.65 *(978-1-4296-3377-2(8))*; Under the Lights: Exploring the Secrets of a Sports Stadium. lib. bdg. 26.65 *(978-1-4296-3376-5(X))*; (gr. 1-2). (Hidden Worlds Ser.). (ENG.). 32p. 2010. Set lib. bdg. 79.95 *(978-1-4296-3777-0(3)*, Blazers) Capstone Press of Coughlan Cos.
Espejo, Roman. Community Policing. Greenhaven Press Editors, ed. 2014. (Opposing Viewpoints Ser.). (ENG.). 224p. (gr. 10-12). lib. bdg. 48.80 *(978-0-7377-6951-7(3)*, Greenhaven Pr., Inc.) Cengage Gale.
—Community Policing. Greenhaven Press Editors & Gale Editor, eds. 2014. (Opposing Viewpoints Ser.). (ENG., Illus.). 224p. (gr. 7-12). pap. 33.80 *(978-0-7377-6952-4(1)*, Greenhaven Pr., Inc.) Cengage Gale.
Evans, Colin. New York Police Department. 2011. (Law Enforcement Agencies Ser.). (Illus.). 120p. (gr. 6-12). 35.00 *(978-1-60413-614-2(6)*, Chelsea Hse.) Facts On File, Inc.
Extreme Law Enforcement. 2013. (Extreme Law Enforcement Ser.). 112p. (YA). (gr. 7-12). 207.60 *(978-1-4777-1720-2(X))* Rosen Publishing Group, Inc., The.
Fitzgerald, Lee. Mounted & Canine Police, 01 vols., 1. 2016. (Careers for Heroes Ser.). (ENG., Illus.). 24p. (J). pap. 8.25 *(978-1-5081-4384-0(6)*, PowerKids Pr.) Rosen Publishing Group, Inc., The.
Forest, Anne. SWAT Teams, 01 vols., 1. 2016. (Careers for Heroes Ser.). (ENG., Illus.). 24p. (J). pap. 8.25 *(978-1-5081-4398-7(6)*, PowerKids Pr.) Rosen Publishing Group, Inc., The.
Forrest, Glen C. Police Technology: 21st Century Crime Fighting Tools. 2016. (Law Enforcement & Intelligence Gathering Ser.). 00104p. (YA). (gr. 8-8). lib. bdg. 36.25 *(978-1-5081-0379-0(8))* Rosen Publishing Group, Inc., The.
Freeman, Marcia S. Police Cars [Scholastic]. 2009. (Community Vehicles Ser.). 24p. (gr. k-1). pap. 0.36 *(978-1-4296-4244-6(0)*, Pebble Bks.) Capstone Press of Coughlan Cos.
Gersh, Camilla. Emergency Rescue. 2016. (Illus.). 64p. (J). ***(978-1-4806-9867-3(9))*** Dorling Kindersley Publishing, Inc.
Gilpin, Dan & Brush, Jim. Police Units. 2011. (Action Force Ser.). 32p. (YA). (gr. 4-7). pap. 28.50 *(978-1-59771-293-4(0))* Sea-To-Sea Pubns.
Goldish, Meish. Sheriffs & Deputies. 2016. (Police: Search & Rescue! Ser.). (ENG., Illus.). 32p. (J). (gr. 2-7). 19.95 *(978-1-943553-16-7(5))* Bearport Publishing Co., Inc.
—State Troopers. 2016. (Police: Search & Rescue! Ser.). (ENG., Illus.). 32p. (J). (gr. 2-7). 19.95 *(978-1-943553-15-0(7))* Bearport Publishing Co., Inc.
Gonzalez, Lissette. Police In Action. (Dangerous Jobs Ser.). 24p. 2009. (gr. 2-3). 42.50 *(978-1-61512-134-2(X)*, PowerKids Pr.) 2007. (Illus.). (J). (gr. -1-3). lib. bdg. 22.60 *(978-1-4042-3778-0(X))* Rosen Publishing Group, Inc., The.
Gordon, Sharon. Que Hay Dentro de una Estacion de Policia? 2006. (Bookworms Ser.). (SPA & ENG., Illus.). 32p. (gr. 1-2). lib. bdg. 15.95 *(978-0-7614-2398-0(2))* Marshall Cavendish Corp.
—Que Hay Dentro de una Estacion de Policia? / What's Inside a Police Station? 2006. (Bookworms Ser.). (ENG & SPA., Illus.). 32p. (gr. 1-2). lib. bdg. 15.95 *(978-0-7614-2476-5(8))* Marshall Cavendish Corp.
—What's Inside a Police Station? 2007. (Bookworms: What's Inside Me? Ser.). (Illus.). 31p. (J). (gr. k-2). pap. 6.99 *(978-0-7614-3349-1(X)*, Benchmark Bks.) Marshall Cavendish Corp.
Gorman, Jacqueline Laks. Police Officers. Andersen, Gregg, photos by. 2010. (People in My Community Ser.). (Illus.). 24p. (gr. k-3). pap. 8.15 *(978-1-4339-3351-6(9))* Stevens, Gareth Publishing LLLP.
Gorman, Jacqueline Laks & Laks Gorman, Jacqueline. Police Officers. Andersen, Gregg, photos by. 2010. (People in My Community Ser.). (Illus.). 24p. (gr. k-3). 22.60 *(978-1-4339-3350-9(0))* Stevens, Gareth Publishing LLLP.
Grayson, Robert. SWAT Teams: The Missions, 1 vol. 2013. (American Special Ops Ser.). (ENG.). 48p. (gr. 3-4). 31.99 *(978-1-4765-0112-3(2))* Capstone Press of Coughlan Cos.
Greve, Tom. Police: Protect & Serve. 2014. (ENG.). 32p. (gr. 4-8). 32.79 *(978-1-62717-653-8(5))* Rourke Educational Media.
—Swat: Special Weapons & Tactics. 2014. (ENG.). 32p. (gr. 4-8). 32.79 *(978-1-62717-654-5(3))* Rourke Educational Media.
Herweck, Diana. All in a Day's Work: Police Officer, 1 vol. 2nd rev. ed. 2013. (Nonfiction Readers Ser.). (ENG., Illus.). 64p. (J). (gr. 5-5). pap. 31.96 *(978-1-4333-7428-9(5))* Teacher Created Materials, Inc.
—All in a Day's Work - Police Officer, 1 vol. 2nd rev. ed. 2013. (Nonfiction Readers Ser.). (ENG.). 64p. (J). (gr. 5-5). pap. 10.99 *(978-1-4333-4905-8(1))* Teacher Created Materials, Inc.
Hidden Worlds [Capstone Sole Source]. 2010. (Hidden Worlds Ser.). 32p. lib. bdg. 101.28 *(978-1-4296-5865-2(7)*, Blazers) Capstone Press of Coughlan Cos.
Hutt, Sarah. Missing, 1 vol. unabr. ed. 2012. (Astonishing Headlines Ser.). (ENG.). 92p. (YA). (gr. 9-12). 8.95 *(978-1-61651-923-0(1))* Saddleback Educational Publishing, Inc.
Hynes, Patricia Freeland. Cyber Cop. 2007. (21st Century Skills Library: Cool Science Careers Ser.). (ENG.). 32p. (gr. 4-8). lib. bdg. 28.50 *(978-1-60279-056-8(6)*, 200013) Cherry Lake Publishing.
Jeffries, Joyce. Meet the Policeman. 2012. (People Around Town Ser.). (Illus.). 24p. (gr. k-2). 69.20 *(978-1-4339-8062-6(2))*; (J). 22.60 *(978-1-4339-7336-9(7))*; (J). pap. 8.15 *(978-1-4339-7337-6(5))* Stevens, Gareth Publishing LLLP.
—Meet the Policeman / Te Presento A Los PolicíAs. 2012. (People Around Town / Gente de mi ciudad Ser.). (SPA & ENG., Illus.). 24p. (J). (gr. k-2). 22.60 *(978-1-4339-7390-1(1))* Stevens, Gareth Publishing LLLP.
Kalman, Bobbie. Emergency Workers Are on Their Way! 2004. (My Community & Its Helpers Ser.). (ENG., Illus.). 32p. (J).

pap. *(978-0-7787-2122-2(1))*; lib. bdg. *(978-0-7787-2094-2(2))* Crabtree Publishing Co.

Katz, Samuel M. Global Counterstrike: International Counterterrorism. 2005. (Terrorist Dossiers Ser.). (Illus.). 72p. (J). (gr. 6-12). 26.60 *(978-0-8225-1566-1(0))* Lerner Publishing Group.

—U. S. Counterstrike: American Counterterrorism. 2005. (Terrorist Dossiers Ser.). (Illus.). 72p. (J). (gr. 6-12). 26.60 *(978-0-8225-1569-2(5))* Lerner Publishing Group.

Kenney, Karen L. Police Officers at Work, 1 vol. Dumm, Brian Caleb, illus. 2009. (Meet Your Community Workers Ser.). (ENG.). 32p. (J). (gr. -1-2). 28.50 *(978-1-60270-652-1(2))* Magic Wagon.

Keogh, Josie. A Trip to the Police Station. 2012. (PowerKids Readers: My Community Ser.). (ENG., Illus.). 24p. (J). (gr. k-2). pap. 8.25 *(978-1-4488-7484-2(X))*; lib. bdg. 22.60 *(978-1-4488-7405-7(X))* Rosen Publishing Group, Inc., The. (PowerKids Pr.).

Keogh, Josie & Alamán, Eduardo. A Trip to the Police Station: De Visita en la Estación de Policía. 2012. (PowerKids Readers: My Community / Mi comunidad Ser.). (SPA & ENG., Illus.). 24p. (J). (gr. k-2). lib. bdg. 22.60 *(978-1-4488-7829-1(2)*, PowerKids Pr.) Rosen Publishing Group, Inc., The.

Kerrigan, Michael. Police Crime Prevention. 2004. (Rescue & Prevention Ser.). (Illus.). 96p. (J). (gr. 6-18). lib. bdg. 22.95 *(978-1-59084-406-9(8))* Mason Crest.

Kerrigan, Michael. Stopping Crime: The Police. 2017. (J). ***(978-1-4222-3771-7(0))*** Mason Crest.

Kirby, Lisa. The Life of a Cop. 2017. (Text Connections Guided Close Reading Ser.). (J). (gr. 2). *(978-1-4900-1849-2(2))* Benchmark Education Co.

Knudsen, Shannon. Police Officers. 2005. (Pull Ahead Books: Community Helpers Ser.). (ENG., Illus.). 32p. (gr. k-3). pap. 7.95 *(978-0-8225-2534-9(8))* Lerner Publishing Group.

Labrecque, Ellen. Fighting Crime, 1 vol. 2012. (Heroic Jobs Ser.). (ENG.). 32p. (gr. 1-2). pap. 8.29 *(978-1-4109-4362-0(3))*; lib. bdg. 29.99 *(978-1-4109-4355-2(0))* Heinemann-Raintree. (Read Me!).

Laks Gorman, Jacqueline. Police Officers / Policías. Andersen, Gregg, photos by. 2010. (People in My Community / Mi comunidad Ser.). (SPA., Illus.). 24p. (gr. k-3). pap. 8.15 *(978-1-4339-3769-9(7))* Stevens, Gareth Publishing LLLP.

Larson, Kirsten W. SWAT Teams. 2016. (Protecting Our People Ser.). (ENG., Illus.). 32p. (J). (gr. 1-4). 20.95 *(978-1-60753-985-8(3))* Amicus Publishing.

Liebman, Dan. Policier. Lior, Tsipora, tr. from ENG. 2006. (Je Veux Etre Ser.). (FRE., Illus.). 24p. (J). (gr. -1-2). pap. 5.95 *(978-1-55407-109-8(7)*, 9781554071098) Firefly Bks., Ltd.

Loveless, Antony. Bodyguards. 2009. (World's Most Dangerous Jobs Ser.). (ENG., Illus.). 32p. (J). (gr. 3-6). pap. *(978-0-7787-5108-3(2))*; lib. bdg. *(978-0-7787-5094-9(9))* Crabtree Publishing Co.

Loveless, Antony & Tisdale, Rachel. Police Officers. 2012. (The World's Most Dangerous Jobs Ser.). (ENG.). 32p. (J). pap. *(978-0-7787-5115-1(5))*; lib. bdg. *(978-0-7787-5101-4(5))* Crabtree Publishing Co.

Lowenstein, Felicia. What Does a Police Officer Do? 2005. (What Does a Community Helper Do? Ser.). (Illus.). 24p. (J). lib. bdg. 22.60 *(978-0-7660-2541-7(1)*, Enslow Elementary) Enslow Pubs., Inc.

Mara, Wil. Cyber Cop. 2015. (21st Century Skills Library: Cool STEAM Careers Ser.). (ENG., Illus.). 32p. (J). (gr. 4-7). 29.93 *(978-1-63362-557-0(5)*, 206412) Cherry Lake Publishing.

Márquez, Herón. George W. Bush. 2005. (Just the Facts Biographies Ser.). (ENG., Illus.). 112p. (gr. 5-12). lib. bdg. 27.93 *(978-0-8225-2647-6(6)*, Lerner Pubns.) Lerner Publishing Group.

Mattern, Joanne. Mounted Police. 2009. (Working Together Ser.). 24p. (gr. 1-2). 42.50 *(978-1-60854-831-6(7)*, PowerKids Pr.) Rosen Publishing Group, Inc., The.

—Policia Montada. 2004. (Trabajo en Grupo (Working Together) Ser.). (SPA & ENG., Illus.). 24p. (J). (gr. 3-6). lib. bdg. 22.60 *(978-0-8239-6843-5(X)*, Editorial Buenas Letras) Rosen Publishing Group, Inc., The.

—Policía montada (Mounted Police) 2009. (Trabajo en grupo (Working Together) Ser.). (SPA.). 24p. (gr. 1-2). 42.50 *(978-1-60854-578-0(4)*, Editorial Buenas Letras) Rosen Publishing Group, Inc., The.

Matthews, Kendall J. Mommy I Want to Be a Cop. 2006. 48p. pap. 16.00 *(978-1-4184-6422-6(8))* AuthorHouse.

Mauro, Paul & Melton, H. Keith. Crime Scene & Surveillance Photography. 2004. (Detective Academy Ser.). (Illus.). 48p. (J). *(978-0-439-57182-1(0))* Scholastic, Inc.

Meachen Rau, Dana. Una Oficial de Policia. 2007. (En el Trabajo Ser.). (SPA., Illus.). 24p. (gr. k-1). lib. bdg. 15.95 *(978-0-7614-2786-5(4)*, Benchmark Bks.) Marshall Cavendish Corp.

—Police Officer. 2007. (Jobs in Town Ser.). (SPA., Illus.). 24p. (gr. k-1). lib. bdg. 15.95 *(978-0-7614-2618-9(3)*, Benchmark Bks.) Marshall Cavendish Corp.

Meister, Cari. Police Officers. 2013. (ENG., Illus.). 24p. (J). lib. bdg. 25.65 *(978-1-62031-078-6(3))* Jump! Inc.

Meyer, Jared. Homeland Security Officers. (Extreme Careers Ser.). 64p. 2009. (gr. 5-5). 58.50 *(978-1-61512-398-8(9)*, Rosen Reference) 2007. (Illus.). (J). (gr. 3-7). lib. bdg. 31.95 *(978-1-4042-0945-9(X))* Rosen Publishing Group, Inc., The.

Michele, Tracey. What Do Police Officers Do? 2011. (Learn-Abouts Ser.). (Illus.). 16p. (J). pap. 7.95 *(978-1-59920-624-0(2))* Black Rabbit Bks.

Monnig, Alex. SWAT Team Members in Action. 2017. (Dangerous Jobs in Action Ser.). (ENG.). 32p. (J). (gr. 3-6). lib. bdg. 27.07 *(978-1-5038-1634-3(6)*, 211150) Child's World, Inc., The.

Moskal, Greg. Meet Officer Jerry. 2008. (Real Readers Series: Level Blue Ser.). (ENG., Illus.). 12p. (gr. 1-2). pap. 5.90 *(978-0-8239-8118-2(5))* Rosen Publishing Group, Inc., The.

Murley, Leon. Working the Case: Law Enforcement, Police Work, & Police Organizations. 2016. (Law Enforcement & Intelligence Gathering Ser.). 00104p. (YA). (gr. 8-8). lib. bdg. 36.25 *(978-1-5081-0380-6(1)*, Britannica Educational Publishing) Rosen Publishing Group, Inc., The.

Murray, Aaron R. Police Officers Help Us. 2012. (All about Community Helpers Ser.). (Illus.). 24p. (J). (gr. -1-1). 22.60 *(978-0-7660-4048-9(8)*, Enslow Elementary) Enslow Pubs., Inc.

Murray, Julie. Police Officers, 1 vol. 2015. (ENG., Illus.). 24p. (J). 27.07 *(978-1-62970-916-1(6))* ABDO Publishing Co.

—Policias. 2016. (Trabajos en Mi Comunidad Ser.). (SPA.). 24p. (J). (gr. k-5). pap. 7.95 *(978-1-4966-0725-6(2))* Capstone Classroom.

Newton, Michael. SWAT Teams. 2010. (Law Enforcement Agencies Ser.). (Illus.). 128p. (gr. 6-12). 35.00 *(978-1-60413-625-8(1)*, Chelsea Hse.) Facts On File, Inc.

Niven, Felicia Lowenstein. Lo Que Hacen los Oficiales de Policia. 2007. (What Does a Community Helper Do? Bilingual Ser.).Tr. of What Police Officers Do. (ENG & SPA., Illus.). 24p. (J). (gr. 1-3). lib. bdg. 22.60 *(978-0-7660-2828-9(3)*, Enslow Elementary) Enslow Pubs., Inc.

Noll, Elizabeth. Police Robots. 2017. (World of Robots Ser.). (ENG., Illus.). 32p. (J). (gr. 3-8). lib. bdg. 26.95 ***(978-1-62617-691-1(4)***, Blastoff! Discovery) Bellwether Media.

Oachs, Emily Rose. Police Cars. 2017. (Mighty Machines in Action Ser.). (ENG., Illus.). 24p. (J). (gr. k-3). lib. bdg. 25.95 *(978-1-62617-607-2(8)*, Blastoff! Readers) Bellwether Media.

Ollhoff, Jim. Police. 2012. (Emergency Workers Ser.). 32p. (J). (gr. 5-9). lib. bdg. 27.07 *(978-1-61783-515-5(3)*, Abdo & Daughters) ABDO Publishing Co.

—Swat. 2012. (Emergency Workers Ser.). 32p. (J). (gr. 5-9). lib. bdg. 27.07 *(978-1-61783-517-9(X)*, Abdo & Daughters) ABDO Publishing Co.

Orr, Tamra B. USMC Special Reaction Teams. 2009. (Inside Special Operations Ser.). (Illus.). 64p. (gr. 5-8). pap. 12.95 *(978-1-4358-5130-6(7)*, Rosen Classroom) Rosen Publishing Group, Inc., The.

Owen, Ann. Keeping You Safe: A Book about Police Officers, 1 vol. Thomas, Eric, illus. 2003. (Community Workers Ser.). (ENG.). 24p. (gr. -1-3). per. 8.95 *(978-1-4048-0483-8(8))* Picture Window Bks.

Parkes, Elle. Hooray for Police Officers! 2016. (Bumba Books (tm) — Hooray for Community Helpers! Ser.). (ENG.). 24p. (J). (gr. -1-1). lib. bdg. 25.32 *(978-1-5124-1440-0(9))* Lerner Publishing Group.

Parkes, Elle. ¡Que Vivan Los Oficiales de Policía! (Hooray for Police Officers!) 2017. (Bumba Books (tm) en Español — ¡Que Vivan Los Ayudantes Comunitarios! (Hooray for Community Helpers!) Ser.). (SPA.). 24p. (J). (gr. -1-1). pap. 6.99 ***(978-1-5124-5389-8(7))***; (Illus.). 25.32 ***(978-1-5124-4135-2(X))*** Lerner Publishing Group. (Ediciones Lerner).

Pender, Lionel. To Serve & Protect: The History of Policing. 2016. (Law Enforcement & Intelligence Gathering Ser.). (Illus.). 00104p. (YA). (gr. 8-8). lib. bdg. 36.25 *(978-1-5081-0381-3(X)*, Britannica Educational Publishing) Rosen Publishing Group, Inc., The.

Perish, Patrick. SWAT Team Member. 2015. (Dangerous Jobs Ser.). (ENG., Illus.). 24p. (J). (gr. 3-7). lib. bdg. 25.95 *(978-1-62617-198-5(X)*, Torque Bks.) Bellwether Media.

Perritano, John. SWAT Team, Vol. 12. 2015. (On a Mission Ser.). 48p. (J). (gr. 5). lib. bdg. 20.95 *(978-1-4222-3402-0(9))* Mason Crest.

Petersen, Justin. Bomb Disposal Units: Disarming Deadly Explosives. 2016. (Emergency! Ser.). (ENG., Illus.). 32p. (gr. 3-4). lib. bdg. 27.99 *(978-1-4914-8028-1(9)*, Edge Bks.) Capstone Press of Coughlan Cos.

Pina, Andrew. A Career As a Border Patrol Agent. 2015. (Federal Forces: Careers As Federal Agents Ser.). (ENG., Illus.). 32p. (J). (gr. 4-5). 26.25 *(978-1-4994-1109-6(X)*, PowerKids Pr.) Rosen Publishing Group, Inc., The.

A Police Officer's Job. 2014. (Community Workers Ser.). 24p. (J). (gr. k-2). lib. bdg. 24.21 *(978-1-62712-361-7(X))* Cavendish Square Publishing.

Police Work. 2005. (Book Treks Ser.). (J). (gr. 3-18). stu. ed. 34.95 *(978-0-673-62839-8(6))* Celebration Pr.

Randolph, Joanne. Police Cars. 2008. (To the Rescue! Ser.). (Illus.). 24p. (J). (gr. -1-3). lib. bdg. 22.60 *(978-1-4042-4153-4(1)*, PowerKids Pr.) Rosen Publishing Group, Inc., The.

Ready, Dee. Police Officers Help, 1 vol. 2014. (Our Community Helpers Ser.). (ENG.). 24p. (gr. k-1). lib. bdg. 21.99 *(978-1-4765-3948-5(0)*, Pebble Bks.) Capstone Press of Coughlan Cos.

Reeves, Diane Lindsey. Law & Public Safety. 2017. (Bright Futures Press: World of Work Ser.). (ENG., Illus.). 32p. (J). (gr. 4-7). lib. bdg. 29.93 *(978-1-63472-626-9(X)*, 209538) Cherry Lake Publishing.

Rivera, Sheila. Police Officer. 2005. (First Step Nonfiction - Work People Do Ser.). (ENG.). 8p. (gr. -1-1). pap. 4.95 *(978-0-8225-5359-5(7)*, Lerner Pubns.) Lerner Publishing Group.

Rockwell, Anne F. At the Police Station. 2005. *(978-0-06-056230-4(7))*; *(978-0-06-056231-1(5))* HarperCollins Canada, Ltd.

Rogers, Kate. Police Officers on the Job. 2017. 24p. (J). (gr. 1-1). 24.60 ***(978-1-5345-2155-1(0))***; pap. 49.50 ***(978-1-5345-2154-4(2))***; pap. 8.25 ***(978-1-5345-2153-7(4))*** Greenhaven Publishing LLC. (KidHaven Publishing).

Sanna, Ellyn. Homeland Security Officer. Riggs, Ernestine G. & Gholar, Cheryl, eds. 2013. (Careers with Character Ser.: 18). 96p. (J). (gr. 7-18). 22.95 *(978-1-4222-2757-2(X))* Mason Crest.

Santillo, LuAnn. The Cop. Santillo, LuAnn, ed. 2003. (Half-Pint Kids Readers Ser.). (Illus.). 7p. (J). (gr. -1-1). pap. 1.00 *(978-1-59256-122-3(5))* Half-Pint Kids, Inc.

Settle, Melissa A. Police Then & Now , 1 vol. 2006. (Primary Source Readers Ser.). (ENG., Illus.). 32p. (J). (gr. 2-2). pap. 8.99 *(978-0-7439-9372-2(1))* Shell Educational Publishing.

Shepherd, Jodie. A Day with Police Officers. 2012. (Rookie Read-About Community Ser.). (ENG., Illus.). 32p. (J). pap. 5.95 *(978-0-531-29255-6(X))*; lib. bdg. 23.00 *(978-0-531-28955-6(9))* Scholastic Library Publishing.

Siemens, Jared. Police Officers. 2015. (Illus.). 24p. (J). *(978-1-4896-3653-9(6))* Weigl Pubs., Inc.

Spaight, Anne J. Police Cars on the Go. 2016. (Bumba Books (tm) — Machines That Go Ser.). (ENG., Illus.). 24p. (J). (gr. -1-1). lib. bdg. 25.32 *(978-1-5124-1449-3(2))* Lerner Publishing Group.

Spaight, Anne J. & Granat, Annette. Carros de Policía en Acción. 2017. (Bumba Books (tm) en Español — Máquinas en Acción (Machines That Go) Ser.). (SPA., Illus.). 24p. (J). (gr. -1-1). 25.32 *(978-1-5124-2880-3(9))* Lerner Publishing Group.

Staniford, Linda. Police to the Rescue Around the World. 2016. (To the Rescue! Ser.). (ENG., Illus.). 24p. (gr. k-2). lib. bdg. 23.32 *(978-1-4846-2750-1(4)*, Heinemann Read & Learn) Heinemann-Raintree.

Thomas, William David & Thomas, William David. Working in Law Enforcement. 2005. (My Future Career Ser.). 64p. (gr. 3-7). lib. bdg. 27.00 *(978-0-8368-4775-8(X)*, Gareth Stevens Learning Library) Stevens, Gareth Publishing LLLP.

Torr, James D. Responding to Attack: Firefighters & Police. 2003. (Lucent Library of Homeland Security). (Illus.). 112p. (J). 30.85 *(978-1-59018-375-5(4)*, Lucent Bks.) Cengage Gale.

Tourville, Amanda Doering. Whose Equipment Is This?, 1 vol. 2011. (Community Helper Mysteries Ser.). (ENG.). 24p. (gr. k-1). lib. bdg. 26.65 *(978-1-4296-6080-8(5)*, Pebble Plus) Capstone Press of Coughlan Cos.

Van Meter, Larry A. Miranda V. Arizona: The Rights of the Accused. 2006. (Great Supreme Court Decisions Ser.). (Illus.). 112p. (YA). (gr. 5-9). 32.95 *(978-0-7910-9259-0(3))* Facts On File, Inc.

Weir, William. Border Patrol. 2010. (Law Enforcement Agencies Ser.). (Illus.). 128p. (gr. 6-12). 35.00 *(978-1-60413-635-7(9)*, Chelsea Hse.) Facts On File, Inc.

White, Nancy. Police Officers to the Rescue. 2011. (Work of Heroes: First Responders in Action Ser.). 32p. (YA). (gr. 1-4). lib. bdg. 25.27 *(978-1-61772-283-7(9))* Bearport Publishing Co., Inc.

Wood, Alix. Killer Evidence: Be a Police Detective. 2017. (Crime Solvers Ser.). 48p. (gr. 6-6). pap. 84.30 ***(978-1-5382-0620-1(X))*** Stevens, Gareth Publishing LLLP.

Worth, Richard. Los Angeles Police Department. 2011. (Law Enforcement Agencies Ser.). (Illus.). 128p. (J). (gr. 6-12). 35.00 *(978-1-60413-656-2(1)*, Chelsea Hse.) Facts On File, Inc.

Yomtov, Nel. Peacekeeping. 2016. (Military Missions Ser.). (ENG., Illus.). 24p. (J). (gr. 3-7). 25.95 *(978-1-62617-436-8(9)*, Epic Bks.) Bellwether Media.

Zemlicka, Shannon & Knudsen, Shannon. Police Officers. 2005. (Pull Ahead Bks.). (Illus.). 32p. (J). lib. bdg. 22.60 *(978-0-8225-1693-4(4))* Lerner Publishing Group.

POLICE—FICTION

Balasubramanian, Lalitha. The Twins at the Ancient Villa, 1 vol. 2009. 48p. pap. 16.95 *(978-1-61582-601-8(7))* America Star Bks.

Barnett, Mac. The Case of the Case of Mistaken Identity. Rex, Adam, illus. (Brixton Brothers Ser.: 1). (ENG.). (J). (gr. 3-7). 2010. 208p. pap. 7.99 *(978-1-4169-7816-9(X))* 2009. 192p. 15.99 *(978-1-4169-7815-2(1))* Simon & Schuster Bks. For Young Readers. (Simon & Schuster Bks. For Young Readers).

—Mysterious Case of Cases: The Case of the Case of Mistaken Identity - The Ghostwriter Secret - It Happened on a Train - Danger Goes Berserk. Rex, Adam & Myers, Matthew, illus. 2013. (Brixton Brothers Ser.). (ENG.). 1024p. (J). (gr. 3-7). pap. 29.99 *(978-1-4424-9818-1(8)*, Simon & Schuster Bks. For Young Readers) Simon & Schuster Bks. For Young Readers.

Bayle, B. J. Shadow Riders. 2010. (ENG.). 256p. (YA). (gr. 7). pap. 10.99 *(978-1-55488-724-8(0))* Dundurn CAN. Dist: Ingram Publisher Services.

Beaumier, Randy P. Snapshot Billy: I Remember. 2012. 36p. pap. 24.95 *(978-1-4626-1787-6(5))* America Star Bks.

Becker, Jason Earl. Hero Corps: The Rookie. Moutafis, Greg, illus. 2005. (YA). per. 7.95 *(978-0-9765125-0-9(5))* Baby Shark Productions.

Berrios, Frank. To Protect & Serve. Random House Disney Staff, illus. 2015. (Step into Reading Ser.). (ENG.). 24p. (J). (gr. -1-1). 4.99 *(978-0-7364-3282-5(5)*, RH/Disney) Random Hse. Children's Bks.

Blair, Candice. Rosie's Pink House, 1 vol. Cato, Andrea, illus. 2010. 18p. 24.95 *(978-1-4489-4619-8(0))* America Star Bks.

Bustani, Juma. Adventure in Nairobi. 2005. 72p. pap. *(978-9966-46-842-0(0))* Heinemann Kenya, Limited (East African Educational Publishers Ltd E.A.E.P.) KEN. Dist: Michigan State Univ. Pr.

Caviezel, Giovanni. Police Officer. Mesturini, Cristina, illus. 2009. (Mini People Shape Bks.). (ENG.). 12p. (J). (gr. -1-2). bds. 5.99 *(978-0-7641-6221-3(7))* Barron's Educational Series, Inc.

Clasicos Policiales. (Clasicos Juveniles Coleccion). (SPA.). (YA). (gr. 5-8). pap. *(978-950-11-1284-9(5)*, SG4722) Sigmar ARG. Dist: Lectorum Pubns., Inc.

Cohen, Alana. Heroes! White, David A., illus. 2011. (Lego City Ser.). (ENG.). 10p. (J). (gr. -1-k). bds. 9.99 *(978-0-545-27439-5(7))* Scholastic, Inc.

Cook, Jacqueline. The Little Bear Who Worried Too Much: Suzie Bear Goes to London. 2011. 34p. (gr. 1-4). pap. 13.50 *(978-1-60976-875-1(2)*, Eloquent Bks.) Strategic Book Publishing & Rights Agency (SBPRA).

Davies, Beth & Ripley, Esther. DK Readers L2: LEGO City: Heroes to the Rescue. 2016. (DK Readers Ser.). (ENG., Illus.). 48p. (J). (gr. k-2). pap. 3.99 *(978-1-4654-5189-7(7)*, DK Children) Dorling Kindersley Publishing, Inc.

Deen, Natasha. Burned, 1 vol. 2015. (Retribution Ser.). (ENG.). 168p. (YA). (gr. 8-12). pap. 9.95 *(978-1-4598-0726-6(X))* Orca Bk. Pubs. USA.

Delgado, Linda D. The Visitors. 2006. 169p. (J). per. *(978-0-9767861-1-5(7))* Muslim Writers Publishing.

Dembar Greene, Jacqueline. Speak up, Tommy! Melmon, Deborah, illus. 2012. (Kar-Ben Favorites Ser.). (ENG.). 32p. (J). (gr. -1-3). 7.95 *(978-0-7613-7498-5(1)*, Kar-Ben Publishing) Lerner Publishing Group.

Disney Book Group. Zootopia Picture Book: A Day in the Life of Judy Hopps. 2016. (ENG.). 40p. (J). (gr. -1-k). 16.99 *(978-1-4847-2102-5(0))* Disney Pr.

Echols, Jennifer. Going Too Far. 2009. (ENG.). 256p. pap. 16.99 *(978-1-4165-7173-5(6)*, MTV Bks.) MTV Books.

Ennis, Tom R. The Stranger & the Three Little Children. 2009. 32p. pap. 13.75 *(978-1-60860-509-5(4)*, Strategic Bk. Publishing) Strategic Book Publishing & Rights Agency (SBPRA).

Felsen, Henry Gregor. Rag Top. Felsen, Holly, illus. 2013. 212p. pap. 15.00 *(978-1-62272-001-9(6))* Felsen Ink.

Gianferrari, Maria. Officer Katz & Houndini: A Tale of Two Tails. Chatzikonstantinou, Danny, illus. 2016. (ENG.). 32p. (J). (gr. -1-2). 17.99 *(978-1-4814-2265-9(0)*, Aladdin) Simon & Schuster Children's Publishing.

Giuliani, Alfred. Zootopia. Wu, Vivien, illus. 2016. (J). *(978-1-4806-9720-1(6)*, Golden Bks.) Random Hse. Children's Bks.

Gosling, Sharon. The Diamond Thief. 2014. (Diamond Thief Ser.). (ENG.). 336p. (gr. 9-12). 16.95 *(978-1-63079-002-8(8))* Switch Pr.

—The Ruby Airship. 2015. (Diamond Thief Ser.). (ENG.). 496p. (gr. 9-12). 16.95 *(978-1-63079-004-2(4))* Switch Pr.

Grant, Myrna. Ivan & the Daring Escape. 2006. (Flamingo Fiction 9-13s Ser.). (ENG., Illus.). 144p. (J). (gr. 4-7). per. 6.99 *(978-1-84550-132-7(2)*, 24be2b87-de69-4377-8a1b-bc7b2ad8cd87) Christian Focus Pubns. GBR. Dist: Bookmasters Distribution.

Greene, Jacqueline Dembar. Speak up, Tommy! Melmon, Deborah, illus. 2012. (Kar-Ben Favorites Ser.). (ENG.). 32p. (J). (gr. -1-3). lib. bdg. 17.95 *(978-0-7613-7497-8(3)*, Kar-Ben Publishing) Lerner Publishing Group.

Greene, Janice & Thomas, Terri. Read My Lips, 1 vol. unabr. ed. 2010. (Q Reads Ser.). (ENG.). 32p. (YA). (gr. 9-12). pap. 6.95 *(978-1-61651-216-3(4))* Saddleback Educational Publishing, Inc.

Gundel, Jean. The Mystery Key at Camp Green Meadow. Robertson, R. H., illus. 2011. (J). pap. 14.95 *(978-1-59571-730-6(7))* Word Association Pubs.

Hamilton, Kersten. Police Officers on Patrol. Alley, R. W., illus. 2009. (ENG.). 32p. (J). (gr. -1-k). 15.99 *(978-0-670-06315-4(0)*, Viking Books for Young Readers) Penguin Young Readers Group.

Harber, Chris. Simon the Policeman on Safari - Claude the Camel. Harber, Hulya, illus. 2013. 24p. pap. *(978-0-7552-1552-2(4)*, Bright Pen) Authors OnLine, Ltd.

—Simon the Policeman on the Number Planet. Harber, Hulya, illus. 2013. 28p. pap. *(978-0-7552-1560-7(5)*, Bright Pen) Authors OnLine, Ltd.

Harrison, Michael. Cop's Night Before Christmas, 1 vol. Miles, David, illus. 2010. (Night Before Christmas Ser.). (ENG.). 32p. (J). (gr. k-3). 16.99 *(978-1-58980-800-3(2))* Pelican Publishing Co., Inc.

Helfand, Lewis. Photo Booth. Nagar, Sachin, illus. 2011. (Campfire Graphic Novels Ser.). (ENG.). 80p. (YA). (gr. 3-7). pap. 9.99 *(978-93-80028-65-1(2)*, Campfire) Steerforth Pr.

Hinkes, Enid. Police Cat. 2015. (Illus.). 32p. (J). *(978-1-4896-3873-1(3))* Weigl Pubs., Inc.

Hubbard, L. Ron, contrib. by. Common Core Literature Guide: Dead Men Kill: Literature Guide for Teachers & Librarians Based on Common Core ELA Standards for Classrooms 6-9. 2013. (Stories from the Golden Age Ser.). (ENG.). 35p. (gr. 6-9). pap., tchr. ed. 14.95 *(978-1-61986-218-0(2))* Galaxy Pr., LLC.

Hugo, Victor. Les Misérables. Flores, Catty, illus. adapted ed. 2014. (ENG.). 64p. pap. 6.95 *(978-1-906230-79-1(X))* Real Reads Ltd. GBR. Dist: Casemate Pubs. & Bk. Distributors, LLC.

Hutton, Sam. Countdown. 2011. (Special Agents Ser.: 3). (ENG.). 224p. (J). pap. 9.99 *(978-0-00-714843-1(7)*, HarperCollins Children's Bks.) HarperCollins Pubs. Ltd. GBR. Dist: HarperCollins Pubs.

—Deep End. 2010. (Special Agents Ser.). (ENG.). 240p. (J). (gr. 5-7). pap. 9.99 *(978-0-00-714842-4(9))* HarperCollins Pubs. Ltd. GBR. Dist: HarperCollins Pubs.

—Final Shot. 2010. (Special Agents Ser.: 2). (ENG.). 224p. (J). (gr. 5-7). pap. 9.99 *(978-0-00-714844-8(5))* HarperCollins Pubs. Ltd. GBR. Dist: HarperCollins Pubs.

Jacob, C. W. The Tipperary Bird. 2009. (Illus.). 40p. pap. 18.99 *(978-1-4389-5212-3(0))* AuthorHouse.

Johnson, Gerald J. J. Officer Buck MacDuck. Miltenberger, Dave & Jeri, illus. 2013. 24p. pap. 24.95 *(978-1-62709-429-0(6))* America Star Bks.

Johnson, Virginia. Officer Rick & the Raccoon — a True Story. 2011. 24p. pap. 11.50 *(978-1-60976-114-1(6)*, Eloquent Bks.) Strategic Book Publishing & Rights Agency (SBPRA).

Jones, Patrick & Clark, Marshunna. Duty or Desire. 2016. (Unbarred Ser.). (ENG.). 112p. (YA). (gr. 6-12). lib. bdg. 27.99 *(978-1-5124-0002-1(5)*, Darby Creek) Lerner Publishing Group.

—Duty or Desire. 2016. (Unbarred Ser.). (ENG.). 112p. (YA). (gr. 6-12). pap. 7.99 *(978-1-5124-0089-2(0)*, Darby Creek) Lerner Publishing Group.

—Duty or Desire. 2016. (Unbarred Ser.). (ENG.). 112p. (YA). (gr. 6-12). 42.65 *(978-1-5124-0090-8(4)*, Darby Creek) Lerner Publishing Group.

King, Trey. Detective Chase McCain: Save That Cargo! 2013. (LEGO City 8X8 Ser.). lib. bdg. 13.55 *(978-0-606-32393-2(7)*, Turtleback) Turtleback Bks.

—Detective Chase McCain- Save That Cargo! Primeau, Chuck, illus. 2013. (Lego City Ser.). (ENG.). 24p. (J). (gr. -1-3). 3.99 *(978-0-545-51573-3(4))* Scholastic, Inc.

Krosoczka, Jarrett J. The Frog Who Croaked. Krosoczka, Jarrett J., illus. 2013. (Platypus Police Squad Ser.: 1). (ENG., Illus.). 240p. (J). (gr. 3-7). 12.99 *(978-0-06-207164-4(5)*, Waldon Pond Pr.) HarperCollins Pubs.

Kudina Steinberg, Ganna V. The Princess Conspiracy: an Inspector Poopchyk Mystery. 2009. 143p. 30.00 *(978-0-557-08936-9(0))* Lulu Pr., Inc.

Lenski, Lois. Policeman Small. Lenski, Lois, illus. 2006. (Lois Lenski Bks.). (ENG., Illus.). 32p. (J). (— 1). bds. 6.99 *(978-0-375-83569-8(5)*, Random Hse. Bks. for Young Readers) Random Hse. Children's Bks.

Loughead, Deb. Caught in the Act, 1 vol. 2013. (Orca Currents Ser.). (ENG.). 128p. (J). (gr. 5-9). pap. 9.95 *(978-1-4598-0496-8(1))*; lib. bdg. 16.95 *(978-1-4598-0510-1(0))* Orca Bk. Pubs. USA.

Lyga, Barry. Game. 2014. (ENG.). 544p. (YA). (gr. 10-17). pap. 10.99 *(978-0-316-12585-7(7))* Little, Brown Bks. for Young Readers.

MacAndrew, Richard. The Black Pearls Starter/Beginner. 2008. (Cambridge English Readers Ser.). (ENG.). 32p. pap. 8.50 *(978-0-521-73289-5(1))* Cambridge Univ. Pr.

Maddox, Jake. Free Climb. Tiffany, Sean, illus. 2008. (Jake Maddox Sports Stories Ser.). (ENG.). 72p. (gr. 2-3). 25.32 *(978-1-4342-0784-5(6))*; pap. 5.95 *(978-1-4342-0880-4(X))* Stone Arch Bks.

Magill, Sharon L. Chloe Madison & the Beach Heists. 2009. 60p. pap. 10.49 *(978-1-4389-4191-2(9))* AuthorHouse.

Marano, John. Kody the Kid Cop: And the Case of the Missing Cat. 2012. 20p. pap. 17.99 *(978-1-4685-9555-0(5))* AuthorHouse.

Marsh, Carole. The Adventure Diaries of the Perils of Pauline, the Police Officer!, 2 vols. 2003. 48p. (J). (gr. 1-4). pap. 5.95 *(978-0-635-01144-2(1))* Gallopade International.

McCann, David. Garda Gaby: The Danger of Playing Truant. Brundige, Britt, ed. Bauknecht, Julie, illus. l.t. ed. 2003. 14p. (J). (gr. k-5). spiral bd. 5.99 *(978-1-929063-92-5(X)*, 324) Moons & Stars Publishing For Children.

McCarthy, Rebecca. Save This Christmas! May, Jason J., illus. 2012. (Lego City Ser.). (ENG.). 24p. (J). (gr. -1-3). pap. 3.99 *(978-0-545-45727-9(0))* Scholastic, Inc.

Mccarthy, Rebecca L. Save This Christmas! 2012. (LEGO City 8X8 Ser.). lib. bdg. 13.55 *(978-0-606-26767-0(0)*, Turtleback) Turtleback Bks.

McClintock, Norah. Tell, 1 vol. 2006. (Orca Soundings Ser.). (ENG.). 128p. (YA). (gr. 8-12). per. 9.95 *(978-1-55143-511-4(X))* Orca Bk. Pubs. USA.

McGovan, Michael. The Bobby Dazzlers. 2011. (Illus.). 28p. pap. 14.11 *(978-1-4567-8862-9(0))* AuthorHouse.

Meadows, Michelle. Traffic Pups. Andreasen, Dan, illus. 2011. (ENG.). 32p. (J). (gr. -1-3). 15.99 *(978-1-4169-2485-2(X)*, Simon & Schuster Bks. For Young Readers) Simon & Schuster Bks. For Young Readers.

Meddaugh, Susan. Detective Dog. 2013. (Martha Speaks Ser.). (ENG., Illus.). 96p. (J). (gr. 1-4). pap. 5.99 *(978-0-547-77512-8(1))* Houghton Mifflin Harcourt Publishing Co.

—Martha Speaks: Detective Dog (Chapter Book) 2013. (Martha Speaks Ser.). (ENG., Illus.). 96p. (J). (gr. 1-4). 14.99 *(978-0-547-86021-3(8))* Houghton Mifflin Harcourt Publishing Co.

Mortensen, Denise Dowling. Bug Patrol. Bell, Cece, illus. 2013. (ENG.). 32p. (J). (gr. -1-3). 16.99 *(978-0-618-79024-1(1))* Houghton Mifflin Harcourt Publishing Co.

Myers, Walter Dean & Workman, Ross. Kick. (ENG.). (YA). (gr. 9). 2012. 224p. pap. 9.99 *(978-0-06-200491-8(3))* 2011. 208p. 16.99 *(978-0-06-200489-5(1))* HarperCollins Pubs. (HarperTeen).

Nelson, James Gary. Smileytooth & the Plaque Attack. Bumstead, Debbie, illus. 2008. 20p. pap. 10.95 *(978-1-935137-48-1(4))* Guardian Angel Publishing, Inc.

Newberry, Geoffrey C. The Cape Don Adventure. 2011. 48p. pap. 6.99 *(978-1-61667-262-1(5))* Raider Publishing International.

O'Brien, Jack. Silver Chief's Revenge. Wiese, Kurt, illus. 2011. 222p. 44.95 *(978-1-258-09709-7(5))* Literary Licensing, LLC.

Pass, Emma. Acid. 2014. (ENG.). 384p. (YA). (gr. 9). 17.99 *(978-0-385-74387-7(4)*, Delacorte Pr.) Random Hse. Children's Bks.

Paulsen, Gary. The Glass Cafe or, the Stripper & the State: How My Mother Started a War with the System That Made Us Kind of Rich & a Little Bit Famous. 2004. 99p. (J). 13.65 *(978-0-7569-3105-6(3))* Perfection Learning Corp.

Pierce, Tamora. Bloodhound. 2010. (Beka Cooper Ser.: Bk. 2). (ENG., Illus.). 576p. (YA). (gr. 7-11). pap. 10.99 *(978-0-375-83817-0(1)*, Random Hse. Bks. for Young Readers) Random Hse. Children's Bks.

—Mastiff. 2012. (Beka Cooper Ser.). (ENG.). 608p. (YA). (gr. 7-11). pap. 10.99 *(978-0-375-83818-7(X)*, Ember) Random Hse. Children's Bks.

—Terrier. 2007. (Beka Cooper Ser.: Bk. 1). (ENG.). 608p. (YA). (gr. 7-11). pap. 10.99 *(978-0-375-83816-3(3)*, Ember) Random Hse. Children's Bks.

Pilkey, Dav. Dog Man. Pilkey, Dav, illus. 2016. (Dog Man Ser.: 1). (ENG., Illus.). 240p. (J). (gr. 2). 9.99 *(978-0-545-58160-8(5)*, Graphix) Scholastic, Inc.

—Dog Man Unleashed. 2016. (Dog Man Ser.: 2). (ENG., Illus.). 224p. (J). (gr. 2-7). 9.99 *(978-0-545-93520-3(2)*, Graphix) Scholastic, Inc.

—Dog Man Unleashed. 2016. (Dog Man Ser.: 2). (ENG.). (J). (gr. 2). lib. bdg. 20.85 ***(978-0-606-39709-4(4))***; 240p. 20.85 *(978-0-606-39115-3(0))* Turtleback Bks.

—A Tale of Two Kitties. 2017. (Dog Man Ser.: bk.3). (ENG., Illus.). 256p. (J). (gr. 2-5). 9.99 ***(978-0-545-93521-0(0)***, Graphix) Scholastic, Inc.

—A Tale of Two Kitties. 2017. (Dog Man Ser.: 3). lib. bdg. 20.85 ***(978-0-606-40547-8(X))*** Turtleback Bks.

Poe. Breve Ant de Ctos Policiales. (SPA.). pap. 11.95 *(978-950-07-1006-0(4))* Editorial Sudamericana S.A. ARG. Dist: Distribooks, Inc.

Posner-Sanchez, Andrea & Lagonegro, Melissa. Callie's Cowgirl Twirl (Disney Junior: Sheriff Callie's Wild West) Fruchter, Jason, illus. 2016. (Little Golden Book Ser.). (ENG.). 24p. (J). (-k). 4.99 *(978-0-7364-3442-3(9)*, Golden/Disney) Random Hse. Children's Bks.

Reynolds, Jason & Brendan Kiely. All American Boys. 2017. (ENG.). (YA). lib. bdg. 20.85 *(978-0-606-39493-2(1))* Turtleback Bks.

Reynolds, Jason & Kiely, Brendan. All American Boys. 2015. (ENG., Illus.). 320p. (YA). (gr. 7). 19.99 *(978-1-4814-6333-1(0)*, Atheneum/Caitlyn Dlouhy Books) Simon & Schuster Children's Publishing.

Ripley, Esther. Heroes to the Rescue. 2016. (DK Reader Level 2 Ser.). lib. bdg. 13.55 *(978-0-606-38711-8(0))* Turtleback Bks.

Rossell, Judith. Inspector Stilton & the Missing Jewels. Rossell, Judith, illus. 2005. (Illus.). 32p. pap. *(978-1-921049-09-5(X))* Little Hare Bks. AUS. Dist: HarperCollins Pubs. Australia.

Sander, Sonia. Calling All Cars! 2010. (Lego City Ser.). (ENG.). 32p. (J). (gr. -1-k). pap. 3.99 *(978-0-545-15523-6(1))* Scholastic, Inc.

—Calling All Cars! 2010. (LEGO City Adventures Scholastic Readers Level 1 Ser.: 3). lib. bdg. 13.55 *(978-0-606-07120-8(2)*, Turtleback) Turtleback Bks.

—LEGO City Reader Collection: LEGO City Emergency. 2012. (Illus.). 127p. (J). *(978-1-4351-3985-5(2))* Scholastic, Inc.

Santillo, LuAnn. Jim & the Thug. Santillo, LuAnn, ed. 2003. (Half-Pint Kids Readers Ser.). (Illus.). 7p. (J). (gr. -1-1). pap. 1.00 *(978-1-59256-078-3(4))* Half-Pint Kids, Inc.

Scarry, Huck & Scarry, Richard. A Day at the Police Station. Scarry, Richard, illus. 2004. (Look-Look Ser.). (ENG., Illus.). 24p. (J). (gr. -1-2). pap. 4.99 *(978-0-375-82822-5(2)*, Golden Bks.) Random Hse. Children's Bks.

Scholastic Editors. Stop That Heist! 2013. (LEGO City Scholastic Readers Level 1 Ser.). lib. bdg. 13.55 *(978-0-606-31540-1(3)*, Turtleback) Turtleback Bks.

Sonberg, Caryn. Six Dogs & a Police Officer. Dorenkamp, Michelle, illus. 2006. 31p. pap. 8.40 *(978-1-55501-776-7(2))* Ballard & Tighe Pubs.

Sonnebom, Scott. The North Police. Lozano, Omar, illus. 2015. (North Police Ser.). (ENG.). 32p. (gr. k-2). 85.28 *(978-1-4795-7929-7(7))* Picture Window Bks.

Steele, Michael Anthony. Catch That Crook! Wang, Sean, illus. 2012. 23p. (J). *(978-1-4242-5333-3(0))* Scholastic, Inc.

—Catch That Crook! 2012. (LEGO City 8X8 Ser.). (Illus.). 23p. (J). lib. bdg. 13.55 *(978-0-606-23960-8(X)*, Turtleback) Turtleback Bks.

—LEGO City: Catch That Crook! 2012. (Lego City Ser.). (ENG., Illus.). 24p. (J). (gr. -1-3). pap. 3.99 *(978-0-545-36991-6(6))* Scholastic, Inc.

Steve Van Der Merwe. Policeman Bobby & Stinky. 2009. (Illus.). 24p. pap. 12.99 *(978-1-4389-6935-0(X))* AuthorHouse.

Stewart, Bob. Baily Bumble Bee. 2009. 32p. pap. 14.49 *(978-1-4389-7254-1(7))* AuthorHouse.

Swartout, Jenny. The Little One Behind the Badge. 2017. (ENG., Illus.). (J). (gr. -1-3). pap. 7.99 ***(978-1-935666-95-0(9))*** Nodin Pr.

Taborn, Debbie. When a Feather Fell. 2012. 32p. pap. 16.99 *(978-1-4685-4150-2(1))* AuthorHouse.

Tharp, Tim. Mojo. 2014. (ENG.). 288p. (YA). (gr. 7). pap. 8.99 *(978-0-375-86402-5(4)*, Ember) Random Hse. Children's Bks.

Thompson, Kate. The New Policeman. 2005. (Illus.). 416p. (J). *(978-0-370-32878-2(7)*, Bodley Head Childrens) Random House Children's Books.

Thoughts Staff. Police Stories: the fight Call. 2005. 16p. 8.99 *(978-1-4116-2267-8(7))* Lulu Pr., Inc.

Timothy Nixon. Henry to the Rescue. 2009. (Illus.). 24p. pap. 12.99 *(978-1-4389-4960-4(X))* AuthorHouse.

Turnbull, Ann. Deep Water. 3rd ed. 2013. 102p. pap. *(978-1-78132-160-7(4))* SilverWood Bks.

Van Der Merwe, Steve. Policeman Bobby. 2008. 68p. pap. 11.99 *(978-1-4389-1899-0(2))* AuthorHouse.

A Visit to the Police Station. 2003. (J). per. *(978-1-57657-901-5(8))* Paradise Pr., Inc.

White, Kiersten. Paranormalcy. (Paranormalcy Ser.: 1). (ENG.). (YA). (gr. 8). 2011. 368p. pap. 9.99 *(978-0-06-198585-0(6))* 2010. 352p. 16.99 *(978-0-06-198584-3(8))* HarperCollins Pubs. (HarperTeen).

Wiess, Laura. Leftovers. 2008. (ENG.). 256p. (gr. 8-18). pap. 12.99 *(978-1-4165-4662-7(6)*, MTV Bks.) MTV Books.

POLICE—VOCATIONAL GUIDANCE

Brezina, Corona. Careers in the Homicide Unit. 2013. (Extreme Law Enforcement Ser.). (Illus.). 112p. (J). (gr. 7-12). 34.60 *(978-1-4777-1710-3(2))* Rosen Publishing Group, Inc., The.

Christy, Lee Louis. I Go to Work as a Police Officer. 2003. (I Go to Work As Ser.). (Illus.). (J). *(978-1-58417-040-2(9))*; pap. *(978-1-58417-103-4(0))* Lake Street Pubs.

Harmon, Daniel E. Working As a Law Enforcement Officer in Your Community. 2015. (Careers in Your Community Ser.). (ENG., Illus.). 80p. (J). (gr. 7-8). 34.25 *(978-1-4994-6115-2(1)*, Rosen Young Adult) Rosen Publishing Group, Inc., The.

Safety & Security. 2nd rev. ed. 2007. (What Can I Do Now? Ser.). 200p. (YA). (gr. 7-12). 32.95 *(978-0-8160-6030-6(4))* Facts On File, Inc.

Suen, Anastasia. Careers with Swat Teams. 2013. (Extreme Law Enforcement Ser.). (Illus.). 112p. (J). (gr. 7-12). 34.60 *(978-1-4777-1708-0(0))* Rosen Publishing Group, Inc., The.

Uschan, Michael V. Careers in Law Enforcement. 2017. (ENG.). 80p. (J). (gr. 5-12). ***(978-1-68282-106-0(4))*** ReferencePoint Pr., Inc.

Watson, Stephanie. A Career as a Police Officer. 2010. (Essential Careers Ser.). (ENG.). 80p. (YA). lib. bdg. 33.25 *(978-1-4358-9469-3(3))* Rosen Publishing Group, Inc., The.

Wirths, Claudine G. Choosing a Career in Law Enforcement. rev. ed. 2005. (World of Work Ser.). (Illus.). 64p. (YA). (gr. 7-12). lib. bdg. 31.95 *(978-0-8239-3282-5(6)*, WWLAEN) Rosen Publishing Group, Inc., The.

Woog, Adam. Careers in State, County, & City Police Forces. 2014. (Illus.). 96p. (J). *(978-1-62712-425-6(X))* Cavendish Square Publishing.

POLICE DOGS

Albright, Rosie. Police Dogs. 2012. (Animal Detectives Ser.). (ENG., Illus.). 24p. (J). (gr. k-3). pap. 8.25 *(978-1-4488-6254-2(X))*; lib. bdg. 22.60 *(978-1-4488-6148-4(9))* Rosen Publishing Group, Inc., The. (PowerKids Pr.).

—Police Dogs: Perros Policías. Alamán, Eduardo, tr. from ENG. 2012. (Animal Detectives / Detectives Del Reino Animal Ser.). (SPA & ENG.). 24p. (gr. k-3). lib. bdg. 22.60 *(978-1-4488-6714-1(2)*, PowerKids Pr.) Rosen Publishing Group, Inc., The.

Anderson, Bendix. Security Dogs. 2005. (Dog Heroes Ser.). (Illus.). 32p. (J). lib. bdg. 25.27 *(978-1-59716-015-5(6))* Bearport Publishing Co., Inc.

Bluemel Oldfield, Dawn. Police Dogs. 2014. (Bow Wow! Dog Helpers Ser.). 24p. (J). (gr. -1-3). lib. bdg. 23.93 *(978-1-62724-120-5(5))* Bearport Publishing Co., Inc.

Boothroyd, Jennifer. Hero Law Enforcement Dogs. 2017. (Lightning Bolt Books (tm) — Hero Dogs Ser.). (ENG.). 32p. (J). (gr. 1-3). 7.99 ***(978-1-5124-3645-7(3)***, Lerner Pubns.); 39.99 ***(978-1-5124-2800-1(0)***, Lerner Pubns.); 39.99 ***(978-1-5124-3644-0(5)***, Lerner Pubns.); (Illus.). 26.65 *(978-1-5124-2542-0(7))* Lerner Publishing Group.

Bozzo, Linda & Library Association Staff. Police Dog Heroes. 2010. (Amazing Working Dogs with American Humane Ser.). (Illus.). 48p. (J). (gr. 2-5). 25.27 *(978-0-7660-3197-5(7))* Enslow Pubs., Inc.

Gagne, Tammy. Police Dogs, 1 vol. 2013. (Dogs on the Job Ser.). (ENG.). 32p. (gr. 3-4). 27.99 *(978-1-4765-0129-1(7)*, Edge Bks.) Capstone Press of Coughlan Cos.

Goldish, Meish. Bomb-Sniffing Dogs. 2012. (Dog Heroes Ser.). 32p. (J). (gr. 2-7). lib. bdg. 25.27 *(978-1-61772-455-8(6))* Bearport Publishing Co., Inc.

Green, Sara. Police Dogs. 2013. (Dogs to the Rescue! Ser.). (ENG., Illus.). 24p. (J). (gr. 3-8). lib. bdg. 25.95 *(978-1-60014-957-3(X)*, Pilot Bks.) Bellwether Media.

Hoffman, Mary Ann. Police Dogs. 2011. (Working Dogs Ser.). (Illus.). 24p. (J). (gr. 2-5). lib. bdg. 22.60 *(978-1-4339-4659-2(9))* Stevens, Gareth Publishing LLLP.

Laughlin, Kara L. Bomb-Sniffing Dogs. 2014. (Service Dogs Ser.). (ENG.). 24p. (J). (gr. 1-4). 27.07 *(978-1-62687-308-7(9)*, 207149) Child's World, Inc., The.

—Police Dogs. 2014. (Service Dogs Ser.). (ENG.). 24p. (J). (gr. 1-4). 27.07 *(978-1-62687-310-0(0)*, 207151) Child's World, Inc., The.

Mezzanotte, Jim. Police. 2010. (Working Animals Ser.). 64p. (gr. 5-18). 28.50 *(978-1-60870-166-7(2))* Marshall Cavendish Corp.

Miller, Marie-Therese. Police Dogs. 2007. (Dog Tales: True Stories about Amazing Dogs Ser.). (Illus.). 80p. (gr. 4-6). lib. bdg. 28.00 *(978-0-7910-9036-7(1)*, Chelsea Hse.) Facts On File, Inc.

Moskal, Greg. Meet Officer Jerry. 2008. (Real Readers Series: Level Blue Ser.). (ENG., Illus.). 12p. (gr. 1-2). pap. 5.90 *(978-0-8239-8118-2(5))* Rosen Publishing Group, Inc., The.

Murray, Julie. Crime-Fighting Animals, 1 vol. 2009. (Going to Work:Animal Edition Ser.). (ENG., Illus.). 32p. (J). (gr. 2-5). 27.07 *(978-1-60453-561-7(X))* ABDO Publishing Co.

Raum, Elizabeth. K-9 Police Dogs. 2013. (Animals with Jobs Ser.). (ENG.). 32p. (gr. 1-4). 28.50 *(978-1-60753-377-1(4))* Amicus Publishing.

Ruffin, Frances E. Police Dogs. 2005. (Dog Heroes Ser.). (Illus.). 32p. (J). lib. bdg. 25.27 *(978-1-59716-014-8(8))* Bearport Publishing Co., Inc.

Schuh, Mari C. K-9 Police Dogs, 1 vol. 2010. (Working Dogs Ser.). (ENG.). 24p. (gr. k-1). 26.65 *(978-1-4296-4470-9(2)*, Pebble Plus) Capstone Press of Coughlan Cos.

Terrell, Brandon. Police Dogs on the Job. 2017. (Helping Dogs Ser.). (ENG.). 24p. (J). (gr. 2-5). lib. bdg. 27.07 *(978-1-5038-1614-5(1)*, 211173) Child's World, Inc., The.

Troup, Roxanne. Detection Dogs on the Job. 2017. (Helping Dogs Ser.). (ENG.). 24p. (J). (gr. 2-5). lib. bdg. 27.07 *(978-1-5038-1611-4(7)*, 211170) Child's World, Inc., The.

POLIO

see Poliomyelitis

POLIOMYELITIS

Colson, Mary. Fighting Polio. 2014. (Tiny Battlefields Ser.). 48p. (YA). (gr. 6-8). pap. 84.30 *(978-1-4824-1313-7(2))* Stevens, Gareth Publishing LLLP.

Grayson-Jones, Timothy. Polio. 2015. (J). lib. bdg. *(978-1-62713-379-1(8))*; (ENG.). 64p. (gr. 7-7). 34.21 *(978-1-5026-0088-2(9))* Cavendish Square Publishing.

Hantula, Richard. Jonas Salk. 2004. (Trailblazers of the Modern World Ser.). (Illus.). 48p. (gr. 5-12). lib. bdg. 31.00 *(978-0-8368-5100-7(5)*, Gareth Stevens Secondary Library) Stevens, Gareth Publishing LLLP.

Hecht, Alan. Polio. 2nd rev. ed. 2009. (Deadly Diseases & Epidemics Ser.). (Illus.). 120p. (C). (gr. 9-18). 34.95 *(978-1-60413-238-0(8)*, Chelsea Hse.) Facts On File, Inc.

McLeese, Don. Jonas Salk. 2005. (Rourke Discovery Library). (Illus.). 24p. (J). (gr. 2-5). lib. bdg. *(978-1-59515-436-1(1))* Rourke Educational Media.

Peters, Stephanie. The Battle Against Polio. 2005. (Epidemic! Ser.). (Illus.). 69p. (J). (gr. 4-7). lib. bdg. 32.79 *(978-0-7614-1635-7(8)*, Benchmark Bks.) Marshall Cavendish Corp.

Reis, Ronald A. Jonas Salk: Microbiologist. 2005. (Ferguson Career Biographies Ser.). (Illus.). 120p. (gr. 6-12). 25.00 *(978-0-8160-6186-0(6)*, Ferguson Publishing Co.) Facts On File, Inc.

Rooney, Anne. Jonas Salk & the First Polio Vaccine. 2012. (Miracle Makers Ser.). (ENG.). 48p. (YA). (gr. 5-8). 27.95 *(978-1-4488-6034-0(2)*, Rosen Reference) Rosen Publishing Group, Inc., The.

Sherrow, Victoria. Jonas Salk: Beyond the Microscope. 2nd rev. ed. 2008. (Makers of Modern Science Ser.). (Illus.). 146p. (gr. 6-12). 35.00 *(978-0-8160-6180-8(7)*, Chelsea Hse.) Facts On File, Inc.

Tocci, Salvatore. Jonas Salk: Creator of the Polio Vaccine. 2003. (Great Minds of Science Ser.). (Illus.). 128p. (J). (gr. 4-10). lib. bdg. 27.94 *(978-0-7660-2097-9(5))* Enslow Pubs., Inc.

POLISH AMERICANS

Anderson, Dale. Polish Americans. 2006. (World Almanac Library of American Immigration). (Illus.). 48p. (gr. 5-12). pap. 14.05 *(978-0-8368-7330-6(0))*; lib. bdg. 31.00 *(978-0-8368-7317-7(3))* Stevens, Gareth Publishing LLLP. (Gareth Stevens Secondary Library).

Greene, Meg. Polish Americans. 2003. (Immigrants in America Ser.). (ENG., Illus.). 112p. (J). 30.85 *(978-1-59018-516-2(1)*, Lucent Bks.) Cengage Gale.

Ingram, Scott & Asher, Robert. Polish Immigrants. 2004. (Immigration to the United States Ser.). (Illus.). 96p. (gr. 4-9). 35.00 *(978-0-8160-5686-6(2))* Facts On File, Inc.

Moreno, Barry. The Polish Americans. (Major American Immigration Ser.). (YA). 2010. (Illus.). 64p. (gr. 9-12). 22.95 *(978-1-4222-0616-4(5))* 2007. pap. 9.95 *(978-1-4222-0683-6(1))* Mason Crest.

Nickles, Greg. The Poles: We Came to North America. 2006. (Illus.). 32p. (J). (gr. 4-8). reprint ed. 19.00 *(978-0-7567-9907-6(4))* DIANE Publishing Co.

Wales, Dirk. Twice a Hero: Polish American Heroes of the American Revolution. Peterson, Lynn Ihsen, illus. 2007. 31p. (J). (gr. 4-9). 18.95 incl. audio compact disk *(978-0-9632459-4-6(5))* Great Plains Pr.

POLISH AMERICANS—FICTION

Cushman, Karen. Rodzina. 2016.Tr. of Rodzina. (ENG.). 224p. (J). (gr. 5-7). pap. 6.99 *(978-0-544-54029-3(8)*, HMH Books For Young Readers) Houghton Mifflin Harcourt Publishing Co.

Estes, Eleanor. The Hundred Dresses. Slobodkin, Louis, illus. anniv. ed. 2004. (ENG.). 96p. (J). (gr. 1-4). 16.99 *(978-0-15-205170-9(8))*; pap. 7.99 *(978-0-15-205260-7(7))* Houghton Mifflin Harcourt Publishing Co.

Faigen, Anne G. New World Waiting. 2006. iii, 188p. (J). pap. *(978-0-9744715-5-6(0))* Local History Co., The.

Leighton, Maxinne Rhea. An Ellis Island Christmas. Nolan, Dennis, illus. 2005. (ENG.). 32p. (J). (gr. k-3). pap. 6.99 *(978-0-14-240506-2(X)*, Puffin Books) Penguin Young Readers Group.

Pellowski, Anne. First Farm in the Valley: Anna's Story. Sharpe, Roseanne, illus. 2008. 194p. (J). pap. 12.95 *(978-1-932350-24-1(1))* Bethlehem Bks.

—Stairstep Farm: Anna Rose's Story. Sharpe, Roseanne, illus. 2011. 182p. (J). pap. 12.95 *(978-1-932350-40-1(3))* Bethlehem Bks.

Swigut, Bernadetta. First Star: Vigilja- First Star. 2006. (J). 16.99 *(978-0-9790026-0-1(5))* Steinschneider, Bernadetta.

POLISH LANGUAGE

Kudela, Katy R. My First Book of Polish Words. Translations.com Staff, tr. (Bilingual Picture Dictionaries Ser.). (MUL.). 32p. (gr. 1-2). 2011. pap. 47.70 *(978-1-4296-6168-3(2))* 2010. lib. bdg. 27.32 *(978-1-4296-5964-2(5))* Capstone Press of Coughlan Cos. (Aplus Bks.).

Melling, David, illus. First Polish Words. 2009. (First Words Ser.). (POL & ENG.). 48p. (J). (gr. 3-18). pap. 12.95 *(978-0-19-911715-4(2))* Oxford Univ. Pr., Inc.

Milet Publishing Staff. Animals. 2011. (My First Bilingual Book Ser.). (ENG & POR., Illus.). 24p. (J). (gr. k — 1). bds. 7.99 *(978-1-84059-616-8(3))* Milet Publishing.

—Bilingual Visual Dictionary. 2011. (Milet Multimedia Ser.). (ENG, POL & POR., Illus.). 1p. (J). (gr. k-2). cd-rom 19.95 *(978-1-84059-588-8(4))* Milet Publishing.

—Fruit - My First Bilingual Book. 2011. (My First Bilingual Book Ser.). (ENG & POR., Illus.). 24p. (J). (gr. k — 1). bds. 7.99 *(978-1-84059-632-8(5))* Milet Publishing.

—Home (English-Polish) 2011. (My First Bilingual Book Ser.). (ENG & POR., Illus.). 24p. (J). (gr. k — 1). bds. 7.99 *(978-1-84059-648-9(1))* Milet Publishing.

—Music. 2012. (My First Bilingual Book Ser.). (ENG, POL & POR., Illus.). 24p. (J). (gr. k — 1). bds. 7.99 *(978-1-84059-724-0(0))* Milet Publishing.

—My Bilingual Book-Hearing (English-Polish) 2014. (My Bilingual Book Ser.). (ENG, POL & POR., Illus.). 28p. (J). (gr. -1-k). 9.95 *(978-1-84059-780-6(1))* Milet Publishing.

—My Bilingual Book-Sight (English-Polish) 2014. (My Bilingual Book Ser.). (ENG, POL & POR., Illus.). 28p. (J). (gr. -1-k). 9.95 *(978-1-84059-796-7(8))* Milet Publishing.

—My Bilingual Book-Smell (English-Polish) 2014. (My Bilingual Book Ser.). (ENG, POL & POR., Illus.). 28p. (J). (gr. -1-k). 9.95 *(978-1-84059-812-4(3))* Milet Publishing.

—My Bilingual Book-Taste (English-Polish) 2014. (My Bilingual Book Ser.). (ENG, POL & POR., Illus.). 28p. (J). (gr. -1-k). 9.95 *(978-1-84059-828-5(X))* Milet Publishing.

—My First Bilingual Book - Jobs. 2012. (My First Bilingual Book Ser.). (ENG, POL & POR., Illus.). 24p. (J). (gr. k — 1). bds. 7.99 *(978-1-84059-708-0(9))* Milet Publishing.

—My First Bilingual Book-Opposites (English-Polish) 2012. (My First Bilingual Book Ser.). (ENG, POL & POR., Illus.). 24p. (J). (gr. k — 1). bds. 7.99 *(978-1-84059-741-7(0))* Milet Publishing.

—My First Bilingual Book-Sports (English-Polish) 2012. (My First Bilingual Book Ser.). (ENG, POL & POR., Illus.). 24p. (J). (gr. k — 1). bds. 7.99 *(978-1-84059-756-1(9))* Milet Publishing.

Nunn, Daniel. Colors in Polish: Kolory, 1 vol. 2012. (World Languages - Colors Ser.). (ENG, POL & MUL.). 24p. (gr. 1-3). pap. 6.29 *(978-1-4329-6661-4(8))*; lib. bdg. 22.65 *(978-1-4329-6654-6(5))* Heinemann-Raintree. (Acorn).

—Families in Polish - Rodziny. 2013. (World Languages - Families Ser.). (ENG, MUL & POL., Illus.). 24p. (gr. 1-3). pap. 6.29 *(978-1-4329-7182-3(4))*; lib. bdg. 22.65 *(978-1-4329-7175-5(1))* Heinemann-Raintree. (Acorn).

—Numbers in Polish: Liczby - 1 2 3. 2012. (World Languages - Numbers Ser.). (ENG, POL & MUL.). 24p. (gr. 1-3). pap. 6.29 *(978-1-4329-6682-9(0)*, Acorn) Heinemann-Raintree.

—Numbers in Polish - Liczby: Jeden, Dwa, Trzy... 2012. (World Languages - Numbers Ser.). (ENG, POL & MUL.). 24p. (gr. 1-3). lib. bdg. 22.65 *(978-1-4329-6675-1(8)*, Acorn) Heinemann-Raintree.

The Rosetta Stone Language Library: Polish Level 1. 2005. (J). (gr. 1-18). cd-rom 209.00 *(978-1-58022-035-4(5))* Rosetta Stone Ltd.

POLISH LANGUAGE—DICTIONARIES—ENGLISH

Hippocrene Books Staff, creator. Hippocrene Polish Children's Dictionary: English-Polish/Polish-English. 2006. (ENG & POL., Illus.). 108p. (J). (gr. 3-7). pap. 14.95 *(978-0-7818-1127-9(9))* Hippocrene Bks., Inc.

Milet Publishing Staff. Milet Bilingual Visual Dictionary. 2012. (Milet Bilingual Visual Dictionary Ser.). (ENG, POL & POR., Illus.). 148p. (J). (gr. k-2). 34.95 *(978-1-84059-692-2(9))* Milet Publishing.

—Vegetables. 2011. (My First Bilingual Book Ser.). (ENG & POR., Illus.). 24p. (J). (gr. k — 1). bds. 7.99 *(978-1-84059-664-9(3))* Milet Publishing.

Turhan, Sedat. New Bilingual Visual Dictionary (English-Polish) 2nd ed. 2017. (New Bilingual Visual Dictionary Ser.). (ENG & POL., Illus.). 144p. (J). (gr. k-2). 19.95 *(978-1-78508-889-6(0))* Milet Publishing.

Turhan, Sedat & Hagin, Sally. Milet Picture Dictionary. 2005. (Milet Picture Dictionary Ser.). (ENG & POL., Illus.). 48p. (J). (gr. -1-3). pap. 14.95 *(978-1-84059-466-9(7))* Milet Publishing.

POLITENESS

see Courtesy; Etiquette

POLITICAL CORRUPTION

Brezina, Corona. America's Political Scandals in the Late 1800s: Boss Tweed & Tammany Hall. 2009. (America's Industrial Society in the 19th Century Ser.). 32p. (gr. 4-4). 47.90 *(978-1-61511-336-1(3))* Rosen Publishing Group, Inc., The.

Doeden, Matt. Whistle-Blowers: Exposing Crime & Corruption. 2015. (Illus.). 96p. (J). *(978-1-4677-6312-7(8))* Twenty First Century Bks.

—Whistleblowers. 2015. (ENG., Illus.). 96p. (J). (gr. 8-12). lib. bdg. 33.32 *(978-1-4677-4209-2(0)*, Twenty-First Century Bks.) Lerner Publishing Group.

Espejo, Roman. Voter Fraud. 2010. (At Issue Ser.). (Illus.). 128p. 34.45 *(978-0-7377-4693-8(9))*; pap. 24.45 *(978-0-7377-4694-5(7))* Cengage Gale. (Greenhaven Pr., Inc.).

Gay, Oonagh & Leopold, Patricia, eds. Conduct Unbecoming? The Regulation of Parliamentary Behaviour. Gay, Oonagh & Leopold, Patricia, trs. 2004. vi, 378p. 39.95

(978-1-84275-055-1(0)) Politico's Publishing Ltd. GBR. Dist: Consortium Bk. Sales & Distribution.

Hunt, Jilly. Leaders, 1 vol. 2012. (Ethics of Politics Ser.). (ENG.). 64p. (gr. 6-10). lib. bdg. 35.99 (978-1-4329-6550-1(6)) Heinemann-Raintree.

Lansford, Tom. Corruption & Transparency, Vol. 8. Lansford, Tom, ed. 2016. (Foundations of Democracy Ser.). (Illus.). 64p. (J). (gr. 7). 23.95 (978-1-4222-3627-7(7)) Mason Crest.

Miller, Debra A. Political Corruption. 2007. (Hot Topics Ser.). (ENG., Illus.). 128p. (gr. 7-12). lib. bdg. 39.40 (978-1-59018-982-5(5)) Cengage Gale.

Scherer, Randy. Political Scandals. 2007. (At Issue Ser.). (ENG., Illus.). 128p. (gr. 10-12). pap. 27.80 (978-0-7377-3764-6(6), Greenhaven Pr., Inc.) Cengage Gale.

Young, Mitchell. Political Corruption. 2009. (Issues on Trial Ser.). (ENG., Illus.). 240p. (gr. 10-12). 48.30 (978-0-7377-3981-7(9), Greenhaven Pr., Inc.) Cengage Gale.

POLITICAL CORRUPTION—FICTION

Emerson, Scott. The Case of the Cat with the Missing Ear: From the Notebooks of Edward R. Smithfield, D. V. M. Mullett, Viv, illus. 2011. (Adventures of Samuel Blackthorne Ser.: 1). (ENG.). 240p. (J). (gr. 3-7). pap. 11.99 (978-0-689-87615-8(7), Simon & Schuster Bks. For Young Readers) Simon & Schuster Bks. For Young Readers.

Jones, Frewin. The Seventh Daughter. 2009. (Faerie Path Ser.: 3). (ENG.). 352p. (YA). (gr. 8). pap. 9.99 (978-0-06-087110-9(5), HarperTeen) HarperCollins Pubs.

Mulligan, Andy. Trash. 2011. (ENG., Illus.). 240p. (YA). (gr. 7). pap. 9.99 (978-0-385-75216-9(4), Ember) Random Hse. Children's Bks.

Schraff, Anne. Time of Courage, 1 vol. unabr. ed. 2011. (Urban Underground Ser.). (ENG.). 197p. (YA). (gr. 9-12). pap. 9.95 (978-1-61651-270-5(9)) Saddleback Educational Publishing, Inc.

Skármeta, Antonio. The Composition, 1 vol. Ruano, Alfonso, illus. 2003. (ENG.). 32p. (J). (gr. 3-18). pap. 7.95 (978-0-88899-550-6(4)) Groundwood Bks. CAN. Dist: Publishers Group West (PGW).

Sleator, William. Test. 2010. (ENG.). 320p. (YA). (gr. 7-11). pap. 7.95 (978-0-8109-8989-4(1), Amulet Bks.) Abrams, Inc.

POLITICAL CRIMES AND OFFENSES

see also Anarchism; Assassination; Bombings; Concentration Camps; Terrorism

Archer, Jules. Treason in America: Disloyalty Versus Dissent. 2016. (Jules Archer History for Young Readers Ser.). (ENG.). 208p. (J). (gr. 6). 16.99 (978-1-63450-628-1(6), Sky Pony Pr.) Skyhorse Publishing Co., Inc.

Katz, Samuel M. Raging Within: Ideological Terrorism. 2003. (Terrorist Dossiers Ser.). (Illus.). 72p. (J). (gr. 6-12). 26.60 (978-0-8225-4032-8(0)) Lerner Publishing Group.

Kramer, Ann. Mandela: The Rebel Who Led His Nation to Freedom. 2005. (National Geographic World History Biographies Ser.). (ENG., Illus.). 64p. (J). (gr. 3-7). 17.95 (978-0-7922-3658-0(0), National Geographic Children's Bks.) National Geographic Society.

Shea, Nicole. Poaching & Illegal Trade. 2013. (Animal 911: Environmental Threats Ser.). 48p. (J). (gr. 3-5). pap. 84.30 (978-1-4339-9720-4(7)); (ENG., Illus.). lib. bdg. 31.95 (978-1-4339-9718-1(5)) Stevens, Gareth Publishing LLLP.

Zeinert, Karen. McCarthyism & the Communist Scare in United States History. 2015. (In United States History Ser.). 96p. (J). (gr. 5-12). pap. 10.95 (978-0-7660-6346-4(1)) Enslow Pubs., Inc.

POLITICAL CRIMES AND OFFENSES—FICTION

Dowd, Siobhan. Bog Child. 2010. (ENG.). 336p. (YA). (gr. 7). pap. 9.99 (978-0-375-84135-4(0)) Fickling, David Bks. GBR. Dist: Penguin Random Hse. LLC.

POLITICAL ECONOMY

see Economics

POLITICAL PARTIES

see also Politics, Practical; Right and Left (Political Science)

also names of parties, e.g. Democratic Party

Berlatsky, Noah. Does the U. S. Two-Party System Still Work? 2010. (At Issue Ser.). (Illus.). 128p. (YA). (gr. 8-18). 34.45 (978-0-7377-4644-0(0), Greenhaven Pr., Inc.) Cengage Gale.

Burgan, Michael & Hoena, Blake A. Political Parties, 1 vol. Barnett, Charles et al, illus. 2008. (Cartoon Nation Ser.). (ENG.). 32p. (gr. 3-4). lib. bdg. 30.65 (978-1-4296-1334-7(3), Graphic Library) Capstone Press of Coughlan Cos.

Finne, Stephanie. How Political Parties Work, 1 vol. 2014. (How the US Government Works). (ENG.). 48p. (gr. 3-6). lib. bdg. 32.79 (978-1-62403-634-7(1)) ABDO Publishing Co.

Horn, Geoffrey M. Political Parties, Interest Groups & the Media. 2003. (World Almanac Library of American Government). (Illus.). 48p. (gr. 5-12). pap. 14.05 (978-0-8368-5483-1(7)); lib. bdg. 31.00 (978-0-8368-5478-7(0)) Stevens, Gareth Publishing LLLP. (Gareth Stevens Secondary Library).

Landau, Elaine. Friendly Foes: A Look at Political Parties. 2003. (How Government Works). (ENG., Illus.). 56p. (gr. 4-8). lib. bdg. 25.26 (978-0-8225-1349-0(8)) Lerner Publishing Group.

Leavitt, Amie Jane. A History of the Republican Party. 2012. (J). lib. bdg. 29.95 (978-1-61228-261-9(X)) Mitchell Lane Pubs., Inc.

McCabe, Matthew. 12 Things to Know about Political Parties. 2015. (ENG.). 32p. (J). (978-1-63235-031-2(9)) Pr. Room Editions LLC.

McPherson, Stephanie Sammartino. Political Parties: From Nominations to Victory Celebrations. 2015. (ENG., Illus.). 64p. (J). (gr. 6-8). 26.65 (978-1-4677-7910-4(5), Lerner Pubns.) Lerner Publishing Group.

Payan, Gregory. The Federalists & Anti-Federalists: How & Why Political Parties Were Formed in Young America. 2009. (Life in the New American Nation Ser.). 32p. (gr. 4-4). 47.90 (978-1-61514-283-5(5)) Rosen Publishing Group, Inc., The.

Porterfield, Jason. Problems & Progress in American Politics: The Growth of the Democratic Party in the Late 1800s. 2009. (America's Industrial Society in the 19th Century Ser.). 32p. (gr. 4-4). 47.90 (978-1-61511-339-2(8)) Rosen Publishing Group, Inc., The.

Skahill, Carolyn M. The Socialist Party: Eugene V. Debs & the Radical Politics of the American Working Class. 2009. (Progressive Movement 1900-1920: Efforts to Reform America's New Industrial Society Ser.). 32p. (gr. 3-4). 47.90 (978-1-60854-174-4(6)) Rosen Publishing Group, Inc., The.

Sommers, Michael. Ehud Olmert: Prime Minister of Israel. 2009. (Newsmakers Ser.). 112p. (gr. 9-10). 63.90 (978-1-60851-131-0(6)) Rosen Publishing Group, Inc., The.

Topinka, Joseph Baar. Just Judy: A Citizen & Leader for Illinois. 2017. (ENG.). (J). pap. 16.95 **(978-0-9983282-2-5(7))** Hilton Publishing Co.

Zilber, Jeremy. Why Mommy Is a Democrat. Firsova, Yuliya, illus. 2005. 28p. (J). pap. 8.00 (978-0-9786688-0-8(4)) Zilber, Jeremy.

POLITICAL SCIENCE

see also Anarchism; Aristocracy (Social Class); Church and State; Citizenship; Civil Rights; Civil Service; Communism; Constitutional Law; Democracy; Government, Resistance to; Kings, Queens, Rulers, etc.; Law; Liberty; Local Government; Municipal Government; Political Parties; Power (Social Sciences); Public Administration; Revolutions; Right and Left (Political Science); Socialism; State Governments; Suffrage; World Politics

Aldritt, Jeremy. Thomas Paine & the Power of Common Sense. 2015. (Spotlight on American History Ser.). (ENG., Illus.). 24p. (J). (gr. 4-6). pap. 10.00 (978-1-4994-1765-4(9), PowerKids Pr.) Rosen Publishing Group, Inc., The.

Anderson, Wayne. The ETA: Spain's Basque Terrorists. 2009. (Inside the World's Most Infamous Terrorist Organizations Ser.). 64p. (gr. 5-5). 58.50 (978-1-61513-578-3(2)) Rosen Publishing Group, Inc., The.

Army JROTC: Leadership Education & Training, Cadet Reference. 2nd ed. 2003. (Illus.). vi, 56p. (J). (978-0-536-74189-9(1), Dept. of the Army) United States Government Printing Office.

Baden-Powell, Robert. Scouting for Boys. 2013. pap. 16.99 (978-1-4621-1233-3(1), Horizon Pubs.) Cedar Fort, Inc./CFI Distribution.

Be a Community Leader. 2014. (Be a Community Leader Ser.). 32p. (J). (gr. 4-6). 157.50 (978-1-4777-6654-5(5), PowerKids Pr.) Rosen Publishing Group, Inc., The.

Bedesky, Baron & Bedesky, Baron. What Is a Government? 2008. (Your Guide to Government Ser.). (ENG., Illus.). 32p. (J). (gr. k-5). pap. (978-0-7787-4333-0(0)) Crabtree Publishing Co.

Benchmark Education Company, LLC Staff, compiled by. Power, Authority, & Governance. 2005. spiral bd. 50.00 (978-1-4108-4501-6(X)); spiral bd. 145.00 (978-1-4108-5419-3(1)) Benchmark Education Co.

Block, Marta Segal. Graphing Global Politics, 1 vol. 2010. (Real World Data Ser.). (ENG., Illus.). 32p. (gr. 3-5). lib. bdg. 29.99 (978-1-4329-2624-3(1), NA-h) Heinemann-Raintree.

Brexel, Bernadette. The Populist Party: A Voice for the Farmers in an Industrial Society. 2009. (America's Industrial Society in the 19th Century Ser.). 32p. (gr. 4-4). 47.90 (978-1-61511-344-6(4)) Rosen Publishing Group, Inc., The.

Brezina, Corona. Jean-Jacques Rousseau & the Social Contract. 2016. (J). lib. bdg. (978-1-5081-0227-4(9)) Rosen Publishing Group, Inc., The.

Burgan, Michael. The Branches of U. S. Government. 2011. (Cornerstones of Freedom, Third Ser.). (Illus.). 64p. (J). (ENG.). pap. 8.95 (978-0-531-26553-6(6)); lib. bdg. 30.00 (978-0-531-25028-0(8)) Scholastic Library Publishing. (Children's Pr.).

Byers, Ann. Lebanon's Hezbollah. 2009. (Inside the World's Most Infamous Terrorist Organizations Ser.). 64p. (gr. 5-5). 58.50 (978-1-61513-576-9(6)) Rosen Publishing Group, Inc., The.

Cane, Ella. Our Government, 1 vol. 2014. (Our Government Ser.). (ENG.). 24p. (gr. 1-2). lib. bdg. 101.28 (978-1-4765-7422-6(7), First Facts) Capstone Press of Coughlan Cos.

Careers in Focus - Politics. 2nd rev. ed. 2011. (Careers in Focus Ser.). (Illus.). 194p. (gr. 6-12). 32.95 (978-0-8160-8035-9(6), Ferguson Publishing Co.) Facts On File, Inc.

Cassutto, George. Civics Student Activity Book: Student Activities Book. 2003. (Illus.). stu. ed., ring bd., wbk. ed. (978-1-931680-36-3(1), Expert Systems for Teachers) Teaching Point, Inc.

Cherry Lake Publishing Staff, compiled by. Citizens & their Governments. 2010. 32p. lib. bdg. 199.50 (978-1-60279-108-4(2), 200001) Cherry Lake Publishing.

Cómo Ponerse en Contacto con un Oficial Electo. 2014. (Sé un líder de la Comunidad (Be a Community Leader) Ser.). (SPA., Illus.). 32p. (J). (gr. 4-6). lib. bdg. 26.25 (978-1-4777-6909-6(9), PowerKids Pr.) Rosen Publishing Group, Inc., The.

Connolly, Sean. Monarchy. 2012. (Systems of Government Ser.). (Illus.). 48p. (gr. 6-12). lib. bdg. 37.10 (978-1-59920-805-3(9)) Black Rabbit Bks.

—Political Messages & Propaganda. 2010. (J). 34.25 (978-1-59920-349-2(9)) Black Rabbit Bks.

Csedrik, Alex. Thomas Hobbes & Leviathan. 2016. (J). lib. bdg. (978-1-68048-550-9(4)) Windmill Bks.

De Capua, Sarah. Being a Governor. 2004. (True Bks.). (ENG.). 48p. 25.00 (978-0-516-22797-9(1), Watts, Franklin) Scholastic Library Publishing.

Dorling Kindersley Publishing Staff. Who's in Charge? 2016. (Big Questions Ser.). (ENG., Illus.). 96p. (J). (gr. 3-7). pap. 9.99 (978-1-4654-5139-2(0), DK Children) Dorling Kindersley Publishing, Inc.

Drayton, Bill, frwd. Be a Changemaker: How to Start Something That Matters. 2014. (ENG., Illus.). 240p. (YA). (gr. 7). pap. 14.99 (978-1-58270-464-7(3)) Simon Pulse/Beyond Words.

Ebner, Aviva. Physical Science Experiments. 2011. (Experiments for Future Scientists Ser.). (Illus.). 156p. (gr. 5-8). 35.00 (978-1-60413-855-9(6)) Facts On File, Inc.

Fitzpatrick, Anne & Fandel, Jennifer. Dictatorship. 2017. (Odysseys in Government Ser.). (ENG., Illus.). 80p. (J). (gr. 7-11). pap. 14.99 (978-1-62832-321-4(3), Creative Paperbacks) Creative Co., The.

Fridell, Ron. Dictatorship. 2007. (Political Systems of the World Ser.). (Illus.). 144p. (J). (gr. 4-7). lib. bdg. 42.79 (978-0-7614-2627-1(2), Benchmark Bks.) Marshall Cavendish Corp.

Galè. Junior Worldmark Encyclopedia of the Nations, 10 vols. 6th ed. 2012. (Junior Worldmark Encyclopedia of the Nations Ser.). (ENG., Illus.). 3200p. lib. bdg. 819.00 (978-1-4144-6313-1(8), UXL) Cengage Gale.

Gelletly, LeeAnne. Monarchy. Colton, Timothy J., ed. 2012. (Major Forms of World Government Ser.). (Illus.). 64p. (J). (gr. 5). 22.95 (978-1-4222-2141-9(5)) Mason Crest.

—Oligarchy. Colton, Timothy J., ed. 2012. (Major Forms of World Government Ser.). (Illus.). 64p. (J). (gr. 5). 22.95 (978-1-4222-2142-6(3)) Mason Crest.

Glencoe McGraw-Hill Staff. Civics Today - Citizenship, Economics & You. 4th ed. 2007. (Civics Today: Citzshp Econ You Ser.). (ENG., Illus.). 272p. (gr. 6-10). per., wbk. ed. 11.68 (978-0-07-877672-4(4), 0078776724) McGraw-Hill Education.

Grant, Moyra. Government & Politics. 2005. (ENG., Illus.). 232p. (C). pap. 47.50 (978-0-7487-9032-6(2)) Nelson Thornes Ltd. GBR. Dist: Trans-Atlantic Pubns., Inc.

Hall, Kevin. Montesquieu & the Spirit of Laws. 2016. (J). lib. bdg. (978-1-68048-546-2(6)) Rosen Publishing Group, Inc., The.

Harcourt School Publishers Staff. Our Government, No. 2. 2nd ed. 2003. (Illus.). pap. 139.70 (978-0-15-337566-8(3)) Harcourt Schl. Pubs.

Harkrader, Lisa. Government & You. 2016. (Spring Forward Ser.). (J). (gr. 2). (978-1-4900-9425-0(3)) Benchmark Education Co.

Harris, Nancy. What's Government? 2016. (First Guide to Government Ser.). (ENG.). 32p. (gr. 1-3). pap. 8.29 (978-1-4846-3688-6(0), Heinemann First Library) Heinemann-Raintree.

Harris, Nathaniel. Monarchy. 2005. (Systems of Government Ser.). (Illus.). 48p. (gr. 6-12). pap. 14.05 (978-0-8368-5890-7(5)); lib. bdg. 31.00 (978-0-8368-5885-3(9)) Stevens, Gareth Publishing LLLP. (Gareth Stevens Secondary Library).

Hawker, Louise. Colonialism in Chinua Achebe's Things Fall Apart. 2010. (Social Issues in Literature Ser.). (ENG., Illus.). 224p. pap. 40.95 (978-0-7377-4650-1(5)); pap. 28.45 (978-0-7377-4651-8(3)) Cengage Gale.

Hobbes, Emma. Thomas More & Utopia. 2016. (J). lib. bdg. (978-1-68048-551-6(2)) Rosen Publishing Group, Inc., The.

Holt, Rinehart and Winston Staff. American Civics: Answer Key for Guided Reading Strategies. 5th ed. 2004. pap. 8.00 (978-0-03-038723-4(X)) Holt McDougal.

—American Civics: Chapter Tutorials for Students. 5th ed. 2004. pap. 26.60 (978-0-03-038719-7(1)) Holt McDougal.

—American Civics: Guided Reading Strategies. 5th ed. 2004. pap. 25.80 (978-0-03-038716-6(7)) Holt McDougal.

Hosein, Ann. Political Science: The Study of Nations, Government, & Governing, 01 vols., 1. 2016. (Britannica Guide to the Social Sciences Ser.). (ENG., Illus.). 128p. (J). 35.25 (978-1-62275-546-2(4), Britannica Educational Publishing) Rosen Publishing Group, Inc., The.

How to Contact an Elected Official. 2014. (Be a Community Leader Ser.). 32p. (J). (gr. 4-6). lib. bdg. 26.25 (978-1-4777-6689-7(8), PowerKids Pr.) Rosen Publishing Group, Inc., The.

Keenan, Edward. The Art of the Possible: An Everyday Guide to Politics. McLaughlin, Julie, illus. 2015. (ENG.). 64p. (J). (gr. 5-8). 17.95 (978-1-77147-068-1(2), Owlkids) Owlkids Bks. Inc. CAN. Dist: Publishers Group West (PGW).

Keller, Ellen. Kids Are Citizens. 2007. (Reading Expeditions Ser.). (ENG., Illus.). 32p. (J). pap. 17.95 (978-0-7922-8683-7(9)) CENGAGE Learning.

Kenney, Karen. Civic Responsibilities. 2014. (ENG.). 24p. (gr. 3-5). 28.50 (978-1-62717-685-9(3)) Rourke Educational Media.

Kishel, Ann-Marie. What Is Government? 2007. (First Step Nonfiction - Government Ser.). (ENG., Illus.). 24p. (gr. k-2). lib. bdg. 23.93 (978-0-8225-6393-8(2), Lerner Pubns.) Lerner Publishing Group.

Krieg, Katherine. Supreme Court. 2014. (ENG.). 24p. (gr. 3-5). 28.50 (978-1-62717-680-4(2)) Rourke Educational Media.

LernerClassroom Editors. First Step Nonfiction-Government Teaching Guide. 2009. pap. 7.95 (978-0-8225-6884-1(5)) Lerner Publishing Group.

Let's Find Out! Government. 2015. (Let's Find Out! Government Ser.). (ENG.). 32p. (J). (gr. 2-3). 375.20 (978-1-68048-197-6(5), Britannica Educational Publishing) Rosen Publishing Group, Inc., The.

Lonely Planet Publications Staff. You Rule! Create Your Own Country, 1 vol. 2015. (Lonely Planet Kids Ser.). (ENG., Illus.). 96p. (J). 14.99 (978-1-74360-784-8(9), 4988) Lonely Planet Pubns.

A Look at Your Government. 2017. (Look at Your Government Ser.). 32p. (gr. 2-2). pap. 63.00 **(978-1-4824-6289-0(3))**; lib. bdg. 159.60 **(978-1-4824-6287-6(7))** Stevens, Gareth Publishing LLLP.

Lord, Jonathan. John Locke & the Second Treatise of Civil Government. 2016. (J). lib. bdg. (978-1-68048-548-6(2)) Rosen Publishing Group, Inc., The.

Luthringer, Chelsea. So What Is Citizenship Anyway? 2009. (Student's Guide to American Civics Ser.). 48p. (gr. 5-8). 53.00 (978-1-61511-238-8(3), Rosen Reference) Rosen Publishing Group, Inc., The.

MacDonald, Fiona & Weaver, Clare. Human Rights. 2003. (World Issues Ser.). (Illus.). 57p. (J). (gr. 5-18). lib. bdg. 29.95 (978-1-931983-82-2(8)) Chrysalis Education.

Machajewski, Sarah. What Are State & Local Governments? 2015. (Let's Find Out! Government Ser.). (ENG.). 32p. (J). (gr. 2-3). 46.90 (978-1-62275-988-0(5), Britannica Educational Publishing) Rosen Publishing Group, Inc., The.

Marsh, Carole. Pass the Test! Civics & Economics. (Virginia Experience! Ser.). lab manual ed. 195.00 incl. cd-rom (978-0-635-01593-8(5), 15935); cd-rom 395.00 (978-0-635-01594-5(3), 15943); 2004. cd-rom 24.95 (978-0-635-01592-1(7), 15927) Gallopade International.

—Political Parties & Elections - Common Core Lessons & Activities. 2015. (Common Core Ser.). (ENG.). (J). pap. 4.99 (978-0-635-11987-2(0)) Gallopade International.

—Washington Government Projects: 30 Cool, Activities, Crafts, Experiments & More for Kids to Do to Learn about Your State! 2003. (Washington Experience Ser.). 32p. (gr. k-5). pap. 5.95 (978-0-635-01966-0(3), Marsh, Carole Bks.) Gallopade International.

—West Virginia Government Projects: 30 Cool, Activities, Crafts, Experiments & More for Kids to Do to Learn about Your State! 2003. (West Virginia Experience Ser.). 32p. (gr. k-5). pap. 5.95 (978-0-635-01967-7(1), Marsh, Carole Bks.) Gallopade International.

—Wisconsin Government Projects: 30 Cool, Activities, Crafts, Experiments & More for Kids to Do to Learn about Your State! 2003. (Wisconsin Experience Ser.). 32p. (gr. k-5). pap. 5.95 (978-0-635-01968-4(X), Marsh, Carole Bks.) Gallopade International.

—Wyoming Government Projects: 30 Cool, Activities, Crafts, Experiments & More for Kids to Do to Learn about Your State! 2003. (Wyoming Experience Ser.). 32p. (gr. k-5). pap. 5.95 (978-0-635-01969-1(8), Marsh, Carole Bks.) Gallopade International.

Martin, Bobi. Let's Find Out! Government Set. 2015. (Let's Find Out! Government Ser.). (ENG.). 32p. (J). (gr. 2-3). pap., pap., pap. 103.20 (978-1-68048-149-5(5), Britannica Educational Publishing) Rosen Publishing Group, Inc., The.

Mason, Helen. Be an Active Citizen at Your School. 2016. (Citizenship in Action Ser.). (ENG.). 24p. (J). (gr. 1-4). (978-0-7787-2600-5(2)); pap. (978-0-7787-2606-7(1)) Crabtree Publishing Co.

—Be an Active Citizen in Your Community. 2016. (Citizenship in Action Ser.). (ENG., Illus.). 24p. (J). (gr. 1-4). (978-0-7787-2601-2(0)) Crabtree Publishing Co.

Masters, Nancy Robinson. Airplanes. 2008. (21st Century Skills Library: Global Products Ser.). (ENG.). 32p. (gr. 4-8). lib. bdg. 28.50 (978-1-60279-119-0(8), 200091) Cherry Lake Publishing.

McGraw-Hill Education Editors. Civics Today - Citizenship, Economics & You. 4th ed. 2007. (Civics Today: Citzshp Econ You Ser.). (ENG.). (gr. 6-10). cd-rom 104.00 (978-0-07-879108-6(1), 0078791081) McGraw-Hill Education.

Meredith, Susan Markowitz. Government for All. 2016. (Spring Forward Ser.). (J). (gr. 2). (978-1-4900-9448-9(2)) Benchmark Education Co.

Micronations: Invent Your Own Country & Culture with 25 Projects. 2014. (Build It Yourself Ser.). (ENG., Illus.). 128p. (J). (gr. 3-7). 21.95 (978-1-61930-218-1(7)) Open City Bks.

Miller, Debra A. Politics & Religion. Greenhaven Press Editors, ed. 2013. (Current Controversies Ser.). (ENG., Illus.). 224p. (gr. 10-12). pap. 32.00 (978-0-7377-6885-5(1)); lib. bdg. 46.40 (978-0-7377-6884-8(3)) Cengage Gale. (Greenhaven Pr., Inc.).

Miller, Reagan & Richardson, Hazel. Government in the Ancient World. Crabtree Publishing Co. Staff, ed. 2011. (Life in the Ancient World Ser.: No. 3). (ENG.). 32p. (J). (gr. 5-8). pap. (978-0-7787-1741-6(0)) Crabtree Publishing Co.

Morris, Neil. Modern World Leaders. 2003. (History Makers (Chrysalis) Ser.). (Illus.). 48p. (J). (gr. 5-18). lib. bdg. 29.95 (978-1-932333-79-4(7)) Chrysalis Education.

My Government. 2015. (My Government Ser.). (ENG.). 32p. (J). (gr. 4-4). 171.00 (978-1-5026-0358-6(6)); pap., pap., pap. 63.48 (978-1-5026-0694-5(1)) Cavendish Square Publishing.

Nagelhout, Ryan. Thomas Paine's Common Sense. 2013. 32p. (J). (gr. 4-6). 26.60 (978-1-4339-9013-7(X)); pap. 10.50 (978-1-4339-9014-4(8)) Stevens, Gareth Publishing LLLP.

Ogden, Charlie. Government & Democracy. 2017. (Illus.). 32p. (J). **(978-0-7787-3266-2(5))** Crabtree Publishing Co.

Othello: Activity Pack. 2003. 156p. (YA). pap. (978-1-58049-631-5(8), PA6318) Prestwick Hse., Inc.

Pegis, Jessica. I Can Make a Difference! 2016. (Citizenship in Action Ser.). (ENG., Illus.). 24p. (J). (gr. 1-4). (978-0-7787-2599-2(5)) Crabtree Publishing Co.

Perkins, Anne. Trailblazers in Politics, 1 vol. 2015. (ENG.). 192p. (J). 40.95 (978-1-4777-8144-9(7), Rosen Young Adult) Rosen Publishing Group, Inc., The.

Perl, Lila. Theocracy. 2007. (Political Systems of the World Ser.). (Illus.). 158p. (J). (gr. 4-7). lib. bdg. 42.79 (978-0-7614-2631-8(0), Benchmark Bks.) Marshall Cavendish Corp.

Peters, Marilee. Making It Right: Building Peace, Settling Conflict. 2016. (ENG., Illus.). 136p. (J). (gr. 8). pap. 12.95 (978-1-55451-809-8(1)) Annick Pr., Ltd. CAN. Dist: Publishers Group West (PGW).

Political & Economic Systems. 2014. (Political & Economic Systems Ser.). 312p. (YA). (gr. 9-12). 630.00 (978-1-62275-760-2(2)); 315.00 (978-1-62275-365-9(8)) Rosen Publishing Group, Inc., The.

Porterfield, Jason. Julian Assange & Wikileaks. 2012. (Internet Biographies Ser.). (ENG., Illus.). 128p. (J). (gr. 7-12). lib. bdg. 34.60 (978-1-4488-6915-2(3)) Rosen Publishing Group, Inc., The.

Prentice-Hall Staff. When Legend. 2nd ed. (J). stu. ed. (978-0-13-717281-8(8)) Prentice Hall (Schl. Div.).

Raatma, Lucia. Citizenship. 2009. (21st Century Junior Library: Character Education Ser.). (ENG.). 24p. (J). (gr. 2-5). lib. bdg. 25.64 (978-1-60279-324-8(7), 200220) Cherry Lake Publishing.

Redfern, Nicholas. Top Secret Government Archives: Missing Files & Conspiracy Paper Trails, 1 vol. 2015. (ENG.). 250p. (YA). 38.25 (978-1-4777-8153-1(6), Rosen Young Adult) Rosen Publishing Group, Inc., The.

Rees, Peter. Liberty: Blessing or Burden? 2007. (Shockwave: the Human Experience Ser.). (ENG., Illus.). 36p. (J). (gr. 3-5). 25.00 (978-0-531-17760-0(2), Children's Pr.) Scholastic Library Publishing.

Rodger, Ellen. How Does the Canadian Government Work? 2013. (ENG.). 32p. (J). (978-0-7787-0903-9(5)); pap. (978-0-7787-0908-4(6)) Crabtree Publishing Co.

Saxena, Shalini, ed. Dictatorship, Fascism, & Totalitarianism. 2014. (Political & Economic Systems Ser.). 312p. (YA). (gr. 9-12). 45.00 (978-1-62275-350-5(X)) Rosen Publishing Group, Inc., The.

Schlesinger, Arthur M., Jr., ed. Major World Leaders, 12 vols., Set. (J). 275.40 (978-0-7910-6938-7(9), Chelsea Hse.) Facts On File, Inc.

Stefoff, Rebecca. Monarchy. 2007. (Political Systems of the World Ser.). (Illus.). 143p. (J). (gr. 4-7). lib. bdg. 42.79 (978-0-7614-2630-1(2), Benchmark Bks.) Marshall Cavendish Corp.

Stevenson, Robin. Pride Day: Celebrating Community, 1 vol. 2016. (ENG., Illus.). 120p. (J). (gr. 4-8). pap. 24.95 (978-1-4598-0993-2(9)) Orca Bk. Pubs. USA.

Tears of a Tiger: Activity Pack. 2003. 165p. (YA). pap. (978-1-58049-629-2(6), PA6296) Prestwick Hse., Inc.

Thomas Paine's Common Sense. 2013. (Documents That Shaped America Ser.). 32p. (J). (gr. 4-6). pap. 63.00 (978-1-4339-9015-1(6)) Stevens, Gareth Publishing LLLP.

Turning Points in History, 4 vols., Set. Incl. Britannica Guide to Explorers & Explorations That Changed the Modern World. Pletcher, Kenneth. 352p. lib. bdg. 45.00 (978-1-61530-028-0(7)); Britannica Guide to Inventions That Changed the Modern World. Curley, Robert, ed. 392p. lib. bdg. 45.00 (978-1-61530-020-4(1)); (YA). (gr. 9-12). (Turning Points in History Ser.). (Illus.). 392p. 2009. Set lib. bdg. 180.00 (978-1-61530-034-1(1)) Rosen Publishing Group, Inc., The.

Uschan, Michael V. Careers If You Like Government & Politics. 2016. (ENG.). 80p. (J). (gr. 5-12). lib. bdg. (978-1-68282-000-1(9)) ReferencePoint Pr., Inc.

Wallis, Pete & Wilkins, Joseph. What Are You Staring At? A Comic about Restorative Justice in Schools. 2016. (ENG., Illus.). 36p. (J). 19.95 (978-1-78592-016-5(2), 8283) Kingsley, Jessica Pubs. GBR. Dist: Macmillan Distribution Ltd.

Waxman, Laura Hamilton. An Uncommon Revolutionary: A Story about Thomas Paine. Orback, Craig, illus. 2003. (Creative Minds Biography Ser.). (J). pap. 5.95 (978-1-57505-608-1(9), Carolrhoda Bks.) Lerner Publishing Group.

Weiss, Nancy E. Asking Questions about Political Campaigns. 2015. (21st Century Skills Library: Asking Questions about Media Ser.). (ENG., Illus.). 32p. (J). (gr. 4-8). 29.93 (978-1-63362-490-0(0), 206868) Cherry Lake Publishing.

Williams, Jane A. A Bluestocking Guide - Political Philosophies: Companion Workbook to Richard J. Maybury's Are You Liberal? Conservative? or Confused? Daniels, Kathryn, ed. 2004. (Bluestocking Guide Ser.). (ENG.). 63p. (YA). pap. 12.95 (978-0-942617-47-4(9)) Bluestocking Pr.

Wilson, Christopher. Understanding A/S Level Government Politics. 2003. (Understanding Politics MUP Ser.). (ENG., Illus.). 320p. (C). pap. 25.95 (978-0-7190-6081-6(8), 6921) Manchester Univ. Pr. GBR. Dist: Oxford Univ. Pr., Inc.

Witmer, Scott. Political Systems, 1 vol. 2012. (Ethics of Politics Ser.). (ENG.). 64p. (gr. 6-10). pap. 10.95 (978-1-4329-6556-3(5)); lib. bdg. 35.99 (978-1-4329-6551-8(4)) Heinemann-Raintree.

Zschock, Martha Day. Hello Congress! 2013. (Hello! Ser.). (ENG., Illus.). 16p. (J). (gr. -1-k). bds. 9.95 (978-1-933212-06-7(3), Commonwealth Editions) Applewood Bks.

POLITICIANS

see also Legislators; Presidents; Statesmen

Adler, David A. & Adler, Michael S. A Picture Book of Sam Houston. Collins, Matt, illus. 2012. (ENG.). 32p. (J). (gr. -1-3). 17.95 (978-0-8234-2369-9(7)) Holiday Hse., Inc.

—A Picture Book of Samuel Adams. Himler, Ronald, illus. 2005. (ENG.). 32p. (J). 16.95 (978-0-8234-1846-6(4)) Holiday Hse., Inc.

Alembi, Ezekiel. Jaramogi Oginga Odinga: People's Revolutionary. 2004. (Lion Books). (Illus.). x, 78p. (J). (978-9966-951-24-3(5)) Sasa Sema Publications Ltd.

American Political Biographies, 3 vols., Set. 2010. (Political Biographies Ser.). (C). (gr. 9). 255.00 (978-0-8160-8310-7(X)) Facts On File, Inc.

Aretha, David. Mitt Romney. 2012. (Illus.). 112p. (J). (978-1-59935-344-9(X)) Reynolds, Morgan Inc.

—No Compromise: The Story of Harvey Milk. 2009. (Civil Rights Leaders Ser.). 100p. (YA). (gr. 5-9). lib. bdg. 28.95 (978-1-59935-129-2(3)) Reynolds, Morgan Inc.

Barile, Mary Collins. J. Milton Turner; an American Hero. Guest, Peggy, illus. 2013. 52p. 24.95 (978-0-9889643-0-3(9)) MathisJones Communications, LLC.

Barton, Chris. The Amazing Age of John Roy Lynch. Tate, Don, illus. 2015. (ENG.). 50p. (J). 17.00 (978-0-8028-5379-0(X), Eerdmans Bks For Young Readers) Eerdmans, William B. Publishing Co.

Brezina, Corona. America's Political Scandals in the Late 1800s: Boss Tweed & Tammany Hall. 2009. (America's Industrial Society in the 19th Century Ser.). 32p. (gr. 4-4). 47.90 (978-1-61511-336-1(3)) Rosen Publishing Group, Inc., The.

Doeden, Matt. Muhammad Ali: The Greatest. 2017. (Gateway Biographies Ser.). (ENG.). 48p. (J). (gr. 4-8). 12.99 **(978-1-5124-4433-9(2)**, Lerner Pubns.); 39.99 **(978-1-5124-4434-6(0)**, Lerner Pubns.); (Illus.). 26.65 (978-1-5124-4431-5(6)); 39.99 **(978-1-5124-4432-2(4)**, Lerner Pubns.) Lerner Publishing Group.

Ellis, Carol. African American Activists. 2012. (J). pap. (978-1-4222-2384-0(1)) Mason Crest.

—African American Activists. Hill, Marc Lamont, ed. 2012. (Major Black Contributions from Emancipation to Civil Rights Ser.). 64p. (J). (gr. 5). 22.95 (978-1-4222-2371-0(X)) Mason Crest.

Faulkner, Nicholas, ed. Top 101 Reformers, Revolutionaries, Activists, & Change Agents. 2016. (People You Should Know Ser.). 184p. (J). (gr. 8-8). lib. bdg. 36.25 (978-1-68048-509-7(1)) Rosen Publishing Group, Inc., The.

Favor, Lesli J. Eva Perón. 2010. (Leading Women Ser.). 96p. (gr. 6). 39.93 (978-0-7614-4962-1(0)) Marshall Cavendish Corp.

Field, Jacob & Grant, R. J. Superstars of History. Basher, Simon, illus. 2014. (ENG.). 96p. (J). (gr. 3-7). pap. 7.99 (978-0-545-68024-0(7), Scholastic Paperbacks) Scholastic, Inc.

Frier, Raphaële. Malala: Activist for Girls' Education. Fronty, Aurélia, illus. 2017. 45p. (J). **(978-1-63289-592-9(7))** Charlesbridge Publishing, Inc.

Ganeri, Anita. The Top Ten Leaders That Changed the World. 2009. (J). 60.00 (978-1-4358-9166-1(X), PowerKids Pr.); (ENG., Illus.). 32p. (J). pap. 10.00 (978-1-4358-9165-4(1), PowerKids Pr.); (Illus.). 32p. (YA). (gr. 3-6). 26.50 (978-1-4358-9164-7(3)) Rosen Publishing Group, Inc., The.

Greenhaven Press Staff, ed. Mitt Romney. 2012. (People in the News Ser.). (ENG., Illus.). 128p. (gr. 7-10). lib. bdg. 33.95 (978-1-4205-0877-2(6), Lucent Bks.) Cengage Gale.

Grinapol, Corinne. Harvey Milk: Pioneering Gay Politician, 1 vol. 2015. (ENG., Illus.). 112p. (J). 35.60 (978-1-4777-7899-9(3), Rosen Young Adult) Rosen Publishing Group, Inc., The.

Hart, Joyce. Kim Jong Il: Leader of North Korea. 2009. (Newsmakers Ser.). 112p. (gr. 9-10). 63.90 (978-1-60851-133-4(2)) Rosen Publishing Group, Inc., The.

Hollander, Barbara Gottfried. Harvey Milk: The First Openly Gay Elected Official in the United States. 2017. (J). **(978-1-5383-8093-2(5))**; pap. **(978-1-5383-8092-5(7))** Rosen Publishing Group, Inc., The. (Rosen Young Adult).

Hughes, Chris. The Constitutional Convention. 2005. (People at the Center of Ser.). (Illus.). 48p. (J). (gr. -1-7). lib. bdg. 24.95 (978-1-56711-918-3(2), Blackbirch Pr., Inc.) Cengage Gale.

Johnson, Jen Cullerton. Seeds of Change. Sadler, Sonia Lynn, illus. 2013. (ENG.). 40p. (J). (gr. 1-6). 18.95 (978-1-60060-367-9(X)) Lee & Low Bks., Inc.

Lashnits, Tom. Recep Tayyip Erdogan: Prime Minister ofTurkey. Schlesinger, Arthur M., Jr., ed. 2005. (Major World Leaders Ser.). (Illus.). 144p. (gr. 6-12). 30.00 (978-0-7910-8263-8(6), Chelsea Hse.) Facts On File, Inc.

Macken, Ultan. The Story of Daniel O'Connell. 2009. (Irish Heroes for Children Ser.). (ENG., Illus.). 128p. (J). 17.95 (978-1-85635-596-4(9)) Mercier Pr., Ltd., The IRL. Dist: Dufour Editions, Inc.

Main, Mary & Thomason, Cathy. African-Americans in Law & Politics. 2012. (J). pap. (978-1-4222-2391-8(4)) Mason Crest.

—African-Americans in Law & Politics. Hill, Marc Lamont, ed. 2012. (Major Black Contributions from Emancipation to Civil Rights Ser.). 64p. (J). (gr. 5). 22.95 (978-1-4222-2378-9(7)) Mason Crest.

Malaspina, Ann. Nelson Mandela: Fighting to Dismantle Apartheid. 2017. (Rebels with a Cause Ser.). 128p. (YA). (gr. 8-8). lib. bdg. 37.27 **(978-0-7660-8517-6(1))** Enslow Pubs., Inc.

Mallin, Jay. Al Sharpton: Community Activist. 2007. (Great Life Stories Ser.). (Illus.). 111p. (J). (978-0-531-13672-0(8), Franklin Watts) Hachette Children's Group.

Mapua, Jeff. Hillary Clinton, 1 vol. 2015. (ENG., Illus.). 32p. (J). 23.45 (978-1-62275-689-6(4), Britannica Educational Publishing) Rosen Publishing Group, Inc., The.

Marsh, Carole. John Kerry: Successful Senator & 2004 Presidential Candidate. 2004. (J). 24p. pap. 5.95 (978-0-635-02537-1(X)); 24.95 (978-0-635-02542-5(6)) Gallopade International.

—Samuel Adams. 2003. 12p. (gr. k-4). 2.95 (978-0-635-02367-4(9)) Gallopade International.

McCabe, Matthew. 12 Political Leaders Who Changed the World. 2015. (Change Makers Ser.). (ENG., Illus.). 32p. (J). (gr. 3-5). (978-1-63235-148-7(X), 12-Story Library) Pr. Room Editions LLC.

McCarthy, Pat. Famous Union Generals & Leaders of the North: A MyReportLinks. com Book. 2004. (American Civil War Ser.). (Illus.). 48p. (J). lib. bdg. 26.60 (978-0-7660-5188-1(9), MyReportLinks.com Bks.) Enslow Pubs., Inc.

McCartin, Brian. Thomas Paine: Common Sense, & Revolutionary Pamphleteering. 2009. (Library of American Lives & Times Ser.). 112p. (gr. 5-5). 69.20 (978-1-60853-509-5(6)) Rosen Publishing Group, Inc., The.

McElroy, Lisa Tucker. Alberto Gonzales: Attorney General. 2006. (Gateway Biographies Ser.). (Illus.). 48p. (J). (gr. 4-8). lib. bdg. 23.93 (978-0-8225-3418-1(5)) Lerner Publishing Group.

Miller, Debra A. Women in Politics. 2012. (Current Controversies Ser.). (ENG.). 224p. (gr. 10-12). pap. 32.00 (978-0-7377-6250-1(0)); lib. bdg. 46.40 (978-0-7377-6249-5(7)) Cengage Gale. (Greenhaven Pr., Inc.).

Mis, Melody S. Meet Al Sharpton. (Civil Rights Leaders Ser.). 24p. (gr. 2-3). 2009. 42.50 (978-1-61511-850-2(0), PowerKids Pr.) 2008. (Illus.). (YA). lib. bdg. 22.60 (978-1-4042-4213-5(9)) Rosen Publishing Group, Inc., The.

Ni Dheirg, Iosold. The Story of Michael Collins. 2009. (Irish Heroes for Children Ser.). (ENG.). 123p. (J). 17.95 (978-1-85635-595-7(0)) Mercier Pr., Ltd., The IRL. Dist: Dufour Editions, Inc.

Perkins, Anne. Trailblazers in Politics, 1 vol. 2015. (ENG.). 192p. (J). 40.95 (978-1-4777-8144-9(7), Rosen Young Adult) Rosen Publishing Group, Inc., The.

Rebels with a Cause: Set 1. 2017. (Rebels with a Cause Ser.). 128p. (gr. 8-8). lib. bdg. 298.16 **(978-0-7660-8574-9(0))** Enslow Pubs., Inc.

Sakany, Lois. Progressive Leaders: The Platforms & Policies of America's Reform Politicians. (Progressive Movement 1900-1920: Efforts to Reform America's New Industrial Society Ser.). 32p. 2009. (gr. 3-4). 47.90 (978-1-60854-168-3(1)) 2004. (Illus.). (YA). (gr. 5-9). lib. bdg. 22.50 (978-1-4042-0193-4(9)) Rosen Publishing Group, Inc., The.

Sanna, Ellyn. Politician. Riggs, Ernestine G. & Gholar, Cheryl, eds. 2013. (Careers with Character Ser.: 18). 96p. (J). (gr. 7-18). 22.95 (978-1-4222-2762-6(6)) Mason Crest.

—Politician. 2004. (Careers with Character Ser.). (Illus.). 96p. (YA). (gr. 7-18). lib. bdg. 22.95 (978-1-59084-320-8(7)) Mason Crest.

Southwell, David. Unsolved Political Mysteries. 2009. (Mysteries & Conspiracies Ser.). 80p. (gr. 10-10). 61.20 (978-1-61514-747-2(0)) Rosen Publishing Group, Inc., The.

Southwell, David & Twist, Sean. Unsolved Political Mysteries. 2007. (Mysteries & Conspiracies Ser.). (Illus.). 80p. (YA). (gr. 9-12). lib. bdg. 33.25 (978-1-4042-1083-7(0)) Rosen Publishing Group, Inc., The.

Sutherland, Adam. Political Leaders. 2012. (Black History Makers Ser.). (ENG., Illus.). 24p. (J). (gr. 3-8). pap. 8.25 (978-1-4488-7056-1(9)); lib. bdg. 22.60 (978-1-4488-6639-7(1)) Rosen Publishing Group, Inc., The. (PowerKids Pr.).

Sutoski, Jennifer. Stephen Harper. 2015. (Canadian Biographies Ser.). (ENG.). 24p. (gr. k-1). lib. bdg. 26.65 (978-1-4914-7833-2(0), Pebble Plus) Capstone Press of Coughlan Cos.

Tukan, Jaytoe Anthony, Sr. John Reid Edwards: The People's Senator. 2003. per. 19.95 (978-0-9665909-4-4(5)) Kalawantis Publishing Services, Inc.

Winter, Jeanette. Wangari's Trees of Peace: A True Story from Africa. Winter, Jeanette, illus. 2008. (ENG., Illus.). 32p. (J). (gr. -1-3). 17.99 (978-0-15-206545-4(8)) Houghton Mifflin Harcourt Publishing Co.

Worth, Richard. Pervez Musharraf. 2nd rev. ed. 2007. (Modern World Leaders Ser.). (Illus.). 104p. (YA). (gr. 7-12). lib. bdg. 30.00 (978-0-7910-9264-4(X)) Facts On File, Inc.

Wright, David K. The Life of Paul Robeson: Actor, Singer, Political Activist. 2014. (Legendary African Americans Ser.). 96p. (J). (gr. 6-12). 27.94 (978-0-7660-6157-6(4)) Enslow Pubs., Inc.

Wybomy, Sheila. Kim Jong Il. 2009. (People in the News Ser.). (ENG., Illus.). 128p. (gr. 7-10). lib. bdg. 39.40 (978-1-4205-0091-2(0), LML02109-242095, Lucent Bks.) Cengage Gale.

Yasuda, Anita. Political Leaders. 2010. (Illus.). 48p. (978-1-55388-691-4(7)); pap. (978-1-55388-696-9(8)) Weigl Educational Pubs. Ltd.

POLITICIANS—FICTION

Brockington, Drew. CatStronauts: Mission Moon. 2017. (CatStronauts Ser.: 1). (ENG., Illus.). 160p. (J). (gr. 1-5). 16.99 (978-0-316-30747-5(5)) Little Brown & Co.

Calloway, Cassidy. Secrets of a First Daughter. 2010. (ENG.). 208p. (YA). (gr. 8-18). pap. 8.99 (978-0-06-172442-8(4), HarperTeen) HarperCollins Pubs.

Grainger, A. J. Captive. 2016. (ENG.). 272p. (YA). (gr. 7). pap. 11.99 (978-1-4814-2904-7(3)) Simon & Schuster Children's Publishing.

Jones, Ena. Clayton Stone, Facing Off. 2016. (ENG.). 224p. (J). 16.95 (978-0-8234-3648-4(9)) Holiday Hse., Inc.

Krulik, Nancy. Red, White, & - Achoo! John and Wendy Staff, illus. 2010. (Katie Kazoo, Switcheroo Ser.: 33). (ENG.). 80p. (J). (gr. 2-4). pap. 3.99 (978-0-448-45230-2(8), Grosset & Dunlap) Penguin Young Readers Group.

Lavonne, Victoria. Twas the Night at the Capitol: A Narrative Featuring the First African American Family. 2012. 28p. pap. 24.95 (978-1-4626-9799-1(2)) America Star Bks.

McDonald, Megan. Stink. 2013. (Stink Ser.: 1). lib. bdg. 14.75 (978-0-606-31587-6(X), Turtleback) Turtleback Bks.

Tashjian, Janet. Larry & the Meaning of Life. 2014. (Larry Ser.: 3). (ENG., Illus.). 240p. (YA). (gr. 7-12). pap. 9.99 (978-1-250-05035-9(9), 9781250050359) Square Fish.

Wells, Rosemary, et al. My Havana: Memories of a Cuban Boyhood. Ferguson, Peter, illus. 2010. (ENG.). 72p. (J). (gr. 2-5). 17.99 (978-0-7636-4305-8(X)) Candlewick Pr.

Wilson, Mark A. The Old Man's Secret Friend, 1 vol. 2009. 19p. pap. 19.95 (978-1-61582-315-4(8)) PublishAmerica, Inc.

POLITICS, PRACTICAL

see also Elections; Lobbying; Television in Politics

Beyer, Mark. The Election of 1800: Congress Helps Settle a Three-Way Vote. 2004. (Life in the New American Nation Ser.). (ENG., Illus.). 32p. (gr. 5-8). pap. 10.00 (978-0-8239-4255-8(4)) Rosen Publishing Group, Inc., The.

—The Election Of 1800: Congress Helps Settle a Three-Way Vote. 2009. (Life in the New American Nation Ser.). 32p. (gr. 4-4). 47.90 (978-1-61514-282-8(7)) Rosen Publishing Group, Inc., The.

Christelow, Eileen. Vote! Christelow, Eileen, illus. 2004. (Illus.). 48p. (J). (gr. 1-5). 47.60 (978-0-618-51723-7(5), Clarion Bks.) Houghton Mifflin Harcourt Trade & Reference Pubs.

Donovan, Sandy. Running for Office: A Look at Political Campaigns. 2003. (How Government Works). (ENG., Illus.). 56p. (gr. 4-8). lib. bdg. 25.26 (978-0-8225-4700-6(7)) Lerner Publishing Group.

Ferguson. Careers in Focus: Government. 2nd rev. ed. 2007. (Careers in Focus Ser.). 208p. (gr. 6-12). 32.95 (978-0-8160-6568-4(3), Ferguson Publishing Co.) Facts On File, Inc.

Kowalski, Kathiann M. Campaign Politics: What's Fair, What's Foul? 2005. (Pro/Con Ser.). (Illus.). 144p. (gr. 6-12). lib. bdg. 25.26 (978-0-8225-2630-8(1)) Lerner Publishing Group.

McGowen, Tom. The 1968 Democratic Convention. 2003. (Cornerstones of Freedom Ser.). (ENG., Illus.). 48p. (YA). (gr. 4-7). 26.00 (978-0-516-24220-0(2)) Scholastic Library Publishing.

Shetterly, Robert. Americans Who Tell the Truth. 2008. (Illus.). 46p. (gr. 4-6). 18.00 (978-0-7569-8912-5(4)) Perfection Learning Corp.

Stille, Darlene R. Jackie Robinson: Amazing Athlete & Activist, 1 vol. Sterguiz, Richard, illus. 2013. (Beginner Biographies Set 2 Ser.). (ENG.). 32p. (J). (gr. -1-4). 28.50 (978-1-61641-940-0(7)) Magic Wagon.

World Leaders Set, vols. 8, vol. 8. Incl. Adolf Hitler & Nazi Germany. (Illus.). 176p. (gr. 3-7). 2006. lib. bdg. 28.95 (978-1-931798-78-5(8)); Alexander the Great: Conqueror of the Known World. Nardo, Don. (Illus.). 100p. (J). 2009. 28.95 (978-1-59935-126-1(9)); Che Guevara: In Search of Revolution. Miller, Calvin Craig. (Illus.). 192p. (J). (gr. 6-12). 2006. lib. bdg. 26.95 (978-1-931798-93-8(1)); Cleopatra: Ruler of Egypt. (Illus.). 176p. (gr. 6-12). 2007. lib. bdg. 27.95 (978-1-59935-035-6(1)); Empire in the East: The Story of Genghis Khan. Rice, Earle, Jr. (Illus.). 160p. (gr. 3-7). 2005. 28.95 (978-1-931798-62-4(1)); Fidel Castro & the Cuban Revolution. Naden, Corinne J. & Blue, Rose. (Illus.). 144p. (J). (gr. 3-7). 2006. lib. bdg. 27.95 (978-1-59935-029-5(7)); Fighting Wars, Planning for Peace: The Story of George C. Marshall. Gimpel, Lee. (Illus.). 176p. (J). (gr. 6-12). 2005. lib. bdg. 26.95 (978-1-931798-66-2(4)); Hugo Chavez: Leader of Venezuela. (Illus.). 128p. 2007. lib. bdg. 27.95 (978-1-59935-068-4(8)); Joseph Stalin & the Soviet Union. (Illus.). 208p. (J). (gr. 6-12). 2006. lib. bdg. 26.95 (978-1-931798-94-5(X)); Mao Zedong & the Chinese Revolution. Naden, Corinne J. 144p. (YA). (gr. 6-9). 2008. lib. bdg. 28.95 (978-1-59935-100-1(5)); Velvet Revolution: Vaclav Havel & the Fall of Communism. Duberstein, John. (Illus.). 160p. (gr. 6-12). 2006. lib. bdg. 28.95 (978-1-931798-85-3(0)); Woodrow Wilson & the Progressive Era. Lukes, Bonnie L. (Illus.). 192p. (J). (gr. 6-10). 2006. lib. bdg. 26.95 (978-1-931798-79-2(6)); 2009. Set lib. bdg. 247.60 (978-1-59935-013-4(0)) Reynolds, Morgan Inc.

POLITICS, PRACTICAL—FICTION

Alberto, Daisy. Pete for President! Sims, Blanche, illus. 2004. (Social Studies Connects). 32p. (J). (gr. 1-3). pap. 5.95 (978-1-57565-142-2(4)) Kane Press, Inc.

Angleberger, Tom. Fake Mustache: Or, How Jodie o'Rodeo & Her Wonder Horse (and Some Nerdy Kid) Saved the U. S. Presidential Election from a Mad Genius Criminal Mastermind. 2012. (ENG., Illus.). 208p. (J). (gr. 3-7). 14.95 (978-1-4197-0194-8(0), Amulet Bks.) Abrams, Inc.

Baratz-Logsted, Lauren. Red Girl, Blue Boy: An If Only Novel. 2015. (If Only... Ser.). (ENG.). 304p. (YA). (gr. 7). pap. 9.99 (978-1-61963-685-9(9), 9781619636859, Bloomsbury USA Childrens) Bloomsbury Publishing USA.

Barnes, Peter W. & Barnes, Cheryl. Woodrow for President: A Tail of Voting, Campaigns, & Elections. 2012. (ENG.). 32p. (J). (gr. k-3). 16.95 (978-1-59698-786-9(3)) Regnery Publishing, Inc., An Eagle Publishing Co.

Barshaw, Ruth McNally. The Ellie McDoodle Diaries: Ellie for President. Barshaw, Ruth McNally, illus. 2014. (Ellie Mcdoodle Ser.). (ENG., Illus.). 176p. (J). (gr. 3-6). 12.99 (978-1-61963-061-1(3), 9781619630611, Bloomsbury USA Childrens) Bloomsbury Publishing USA.

Bateman, Anya. The Makeover of James Orville Wickenbee. 2007. 262p. (J). pap. (978-1-59038-707-8(4)) Deseret Bk. Co.

Benton, Jim. The Frandidate. Benton, Jim, illus. 2009. (Franny K. Stein, Mad Scientist Ser.: 7). (ENG., Illus.). 112p. (J). (gr. 2-5). pap. 5.99 (978-1-4169-0234-8(1), Simon & Schuster Bks. For Young Readers) Simon & Schuster Bks. For Young Readers.

—The Frandidate, 1 vol. Benton, Jim, illus. 2011. (Franny K. Stein, Mad Scientist Ser.). (ENG., Illus.). 128p. (gr. 3-6). 24.21 (978-1-59961-823-4(0)) Spotlight.

Bruel, Nick. Bad Kitty for President. 2012. (Bad Kitty Ser.). (ENG., Illus.). 144p. (J). (gr. 2-5). 15.99 (978-1-59643-669-5(7), 9781596436695) Roaring Brook Pr.

—Bad Kitty for President. 2012. (Bad Kitty Ser.). (ENG., Illus.). 160p. (J). (gr. 2-5). pap. 6.99 (978-1-250-01016-2(0), 9781250010162) Square Fish.

—Bad Kitty for President. 2012. (Bad Kitty Chapter Bks.). (J). lib. bdg. 17.20 (978-0-606-26568-3(6), Turtleback) Turtleback Bks.

Calonita, Jen. Belles. 2012. (Belles Ser.: 1). (ENG.). 384p. (YA). (gr. 7-17). pap. 8.99 (978-0-316-09112-1(X), Poppy) Little, Brown Bks. for Young Readers.

Collard, Sneed B., III. The Governor's Dog Is Missing. 2011. (Slate Stephens Mysteries Ser.). 176p. (J). (gr. 4-6). 16.00 (978-0-9844460-1-8(X)) Bucking Horse Bks.

Condie, Ally. Freshman for President. 2008. (ENG.). 304p. (YA). (gr. 8-12). pap. 15.99 (978-1-59038-913-3(1), Shadow Mountain) Shadow Mountain Publishing.

Cronin, Doreen. Duck for President. Lewin, Betsy, illus. 2004. (Click, Clack Book Ser.). (ENG.). 32p. (J). (gr. -1-3). 17.99 (978-0-689-86377-6(2), Atheneum Bks. for Young Readers) Simon & Schuster Children's Publishing.

—Duck for President. Lewin, Betsy, illus. 2006. (Doreen Cronin: Click-Clack & More Ser.). (ENG.). 32p. (gr. -1-3). lib. bdg. 24.21 (978-1-59961-091-7(4)) Spotlight.

—Pato para Presidente. Lewin, Betsy, illus. 2008.Tr. of Duck for President. (SPA.). (J). (gr. k-2). pap. 7.99 (978-1-930332-74-4(2), LC32509) Lectorum Pubns., Inc.

Czajak, Paul. Monster Needs Your Vote. Grieb, Wendy, illus. 2015. (Monster & Me Ser.). (ENG.). 32p. (J). (gr. -1-3). 16.95 (978-1-938063-63-3(5), Mighty Media Kids) Mighty Media Pr.

Doctorow, Cory. Homeland. (ENG.). (YA). (gr. 8). 2014. 448p. pap. 12.99 (978-0-7653-3370-4(8), 9780765333704) 2013. 400p. 17.99 (978-0-7653-3369-8(4), 9780765333698) Doherty, Tom Assocs., LLC. (Tor Teen).

—Homeland. 2014. (YA). lib. bdg. 24.50 (978-0-606-38513-8(4)) Turtleback Bks.

Feiffer, Kate. President Pennybaker. Goode, Diane, illus. 2012. (ENG.). 32p. (J). (gr. -1-3). 7.99 (978-1-4169-1355-9(6), Simon & Schuster/Paula Wiseman Bks.) Simon & Schuster/Paula Wiseman Bks.

—President Pennybaker. Glasser, Robin Preiss & Goode, Diane, illus. 2008. (ENG.). 32p. (J). (gr. -1-3). 16.99 (978-1-4169-1354-2(8), Simon & Schuster/Paula Wiseman Bks.) Simon & Schuster/Paula Wiseman Bks.

FitzGerald, Dawn. Soccer Chick Rules. 2007. (ENG.). 160p. (J). (gr. 5-9). per. 9.99 (978-0-312-37662-8(6), 9780312376628) Square Fish.

Fitzpatrick, Huntley. My Life Next Door. 2012. (ENG.). 400p. (YA). (gr. 7-18). 18.99 (978-0-8037-3699-3(1), Dial Bks) Penguin Young Readers Group.

Freeman, Martha. Fourth-Grade Weirdo. 2004. (Illus.). 147p. (gr. 4-7). 15.50 (978-0-7569-4117-8(2)) Perfection Learning Corp.

Giunta, Brian. The Seven Presidents. Chapin, Patrick O., illus. l.t. ed. 2003. 24p. (J). 8.95 (978-1-58597-172-5(3)) Leathers Publishing.

Gutman, Dan. The Kid Who Ran for President. 2012. (gr. 3-6). 17.20 (978-0-613-03562-0(3), Turtleback) Turtleback Bks.

Hale, Bruce. The Possum Always Rings Twice. Hale, Bruce, illus. 2007. (Chet Gecko Ser.: 11). (ENG., Illus.). 128p. (J). (gr. 2-5). pap. 5.99 (978-0-15-205233-1(X)) Houghton Mifflin Harcourt Publishing Co.

Hall, Kirsten. Vote for Me: All about Civics. Luedecke, Bev, illus. 2003. (Beastieville Ser.). 32p. (J). 19.50 (978-0-516-22897-6(8), Children's Pr.) Scholastic Library Publishing.

Hall, Teri. The Line. 2010. (ENG.). 224p. (J). (gr. 5-18). 16.99 (978-0-8037-3466-1(2), Dial Bks) Penguin Young Readers Group.

Holm, Jennifer L. & Holm, Matthew. Babymouse for President. Holm, Jennifer L. & Holm, Matthew, illus. 2012. (Babymouse Ser.: 16). (ENG., Illus.). 96p. (J). (gr. 2-5). 12.99 (978-0-375-96780-1(X)); pap. 6.99 (978-0-375-86780-4(5)) Random Hse. Children's Bks. (Random Hse. Bks. for Young Readers).

Krulik, Nancy. Vote for Suzanne. John and Wendy Staff, illus. 2008. (Katie Kazoo, Switcheroo Ser.: No. 7). (ENG.). 160p. (J). (gr. 2-4). pap. 4.99 (978-0-448-44678-3(2), Grosset & Dunlap) Penguin Young Readers Group.

Levithan, David. Wide Awake. 2008. (ENG.). 240p. (YA). (gr. 9). pap. 8.99 (978-0-375-83467-7(2), Knopf Bks. for Young Readers) Random Hse. Children's Bks.

Lieb, Josh. I Am a Genius of Unspeakable Evil & I Want to Be Your Class President. 2010. (ENG.). 304p. (J). (gr. 5-7). 8.99 (978-1-59514-354-9(8), Razorbill) Penguin Young Readers Group.

Lupica, Mike. Hero. (ENG.). 304p. (J). (gr. 5-18). 2011. 7.99 (978-0-14-241960-1(5), Puffin Books) 2010. 17.99 (978-0-399-25283-9(5), Philomel Bks.) Penguin Young Readers Group.
—Hero. 2011. lib. bdg. 18.40 (978-0-606-23142-8(0), Turtleback) Turtleback Bks.
Manushkin, Fran. Elect Me!, 1 vol. Demski, James, Jr., illus. 2008. (Read-It! Readers: Social Studies). (ENG.). 32p. (gr. k-2). 21.32 (978-1-4048-4911-2(4), Easy Readers) Picture Window Bks.
Meek, Nora. Sniffing for Democracy. 2004. (J). per. (978-0-9753852-0-3(8)) PM, INK.
Monroe, Ella. Truth or Dare. 2013. (Capital Girls Ser.: 3). (ENG.). 304p. (YA). (gr. 8). pap. 20.99 (978-0-312-62304-3(6), 9780312623043, St. Martin's Griffin) St. Martin's Pr.
Moolenschot, Catherine. A Rough Road. 2008. 142p. pap. 17.96 (978-1-4092-4153-9(X)) Lulu Pr., Inc.
Morgenroth, Kate. Jude. 2006. (ENG., Illus.). 288p. (YA). (gr. 7-12). reprint ed. mass mkt. 7.99 (978-1-4169-1267-5(3), Simon Pulse) Simon Pulse.
Mullarkey, Lisa. The Red, White, & Blue Crew, 1 vol. Harris, Phyllis, illus. 2009. (Katharine the Almost Great Ser.: No. 1). (ENG.). 80p. (J). (gr. 1-4). 27.07 (978-1-60270-583-8(6)) Magic Wagon.
Ogden, Charles. Hot Air. Carton, Rick, illus. 2008. (Edgar & Ellen Nodyssey Ser.: 1). (ENG.). 192p. (J). (gr. 3-7). 9.99 (978-1-4169-5465-1(1), Aladdin) Simon & Schuster Children's Publishing.
Parish, Herman. Amelia Bedelia's First Vote. Avril, Lynne, illus. 2012. (Amelia Bedelia Ser.). 32p. (J). (gr. -1-3). (ENG.). 16.99 (978-0-06-209405-6(X)); lib. bdg. 17.89 (978-0-06-209406-3(8)) HarperCollins Pubs. (Greenwillow Bks.).
Paulsen, Gary. Vote. 2013. (ENG.). 144p. (J). (gr. 4-7). 12.99 (978-0-385-74228-3(2), Lamb, Wendy Bks.) Random Hse. Children's Bks.
—Vote: The Theory, Practice, & Destructive Properties of Politics. 2014. (ENG.). 144p. (J). (gr. 4-7). pap. 6.99 (978-0-385-74229-0(0), Yearling) Random Hse. Children's Bks.
Pollock, Hal. Monster for President. Parisi, Anthony, illus. 2008. 28p. 14.95 (978-0-9816554-1-3(6)) Esquire Publishing, Inc.
Press, J. Double Trouble #2. Kline, Michael, illus. 2013. (Doodles of Sam Dibble Ser.: 2). (ENG.). 128p. (J). (gr. 1-3). pap. 4.99 (978-0-448-46108-3(0), Grosset & Dunlap) Penguin Young Readers Group.
Rhuday-Perkovich, Olugbemisola. 8th Grade Super Zero. 2011. (ENG.). 336p. (J). (gr. 4-7). pap. 7.99 (978-0-545-09725-3(8), Levine, Arthur A. Bks.) Scholastic, Inc.
Rosenberg, Madelyn. Canary in the Coal Mine. 2013. (ENG., Illus.). 192p. (J). (gr. 2-7). 16.95 (978-0-8234-2600-3(9)) Holiday Hse., Inc.
Salvatierra, Dante. The Latchkey Kids & the Escape from California. 2008. 260p. pap. 14.50 (978-1-4357-0876-1(8)) Lulu Pr., Inc.
Sommer, Carl. Mayor for a Day. 2003. (Another Sommer-Time Story Ser.). (Illus.). 48p. (J). (gr. 1-4). 16.95 incl. audio (978-1-57537-562-5(1)) Advance Publishing, Inc.
—Mayor for a Day. Westbrook, Dick, illus. 2003. (Another Sommer-Time Story Ser.). (ENG.). 48p. (J). (gr. k-4). lib. bdg. 23.95 incl. audio compact disk (978-1-57537-713-1(6)); (gr. 1-4). 16.95 incl. audio compact disk (978-1-57537-513-7(3)) Advance Publishing, Inc.
Tashjian, Janet. Vote for Larry. 2008. (Larry Ser.: 2). (ENG.). 256p. (YA). (gr. 7-12). pap. 9.99 (978-0-312-38446-3(7), 9780312384463) Square Fish.
Watson, Stephanie Elaine. Elvis & Olive: Super Detectives. 2010. (ENG.). 288p. (J). (gr. 3-7). 15.99 (978-0-545-15148-1(1), Scholastic Pr.) Scholastic, Inc.
Weissman, Elissa Brent. Standing for Socks. Sonkin, Jessica, illus. (ENG.). 224p. (J). (gr. 3-7). 2010. pap. 6.99 (978-1-4169-9777-1(6)) 2009. 15.99 (978-1-4169-4801-8(5)) Simon & Schuster Children's Publishing. (Atheneum Bks. for Young Readers).
Wells, Rosemary. Otto Runs for President. Wells, Rosemary, illus. 2011. (Illus.). (J). (gr. -1-4). 29.95 (978-0-545-10690-0(7)) Weston Woods Studios, Inc.
Weston Woods Staff, creator. Duck for President. 2004. 29.95 (978-0-7882-0540-8(4)) Weston Woods Studios, Inc.
—Otto Runs for President. 2011. 18.95 (978-0-545-31400-8(3)); 38.75 (978-0-545-31401-5(1)) Weston Woods Studios, Inc.

POLK, JAMES K. (JAMES KNOX), 1795-1849

Bailey, Diane & Nash, Philip. James K. Polk: The 11th President. 2016. (First Look at America's Presidents Ser.). (ENG.). 24p. (J). (gr. -1-3). lib. bdg. 17.95 (978-1-944102-66-1(3)) Bearport Publishing Co., Inc.
Behrman, Carol H. James K. Polk. 2005. (Presidential Leaders Ser.). (ENG., Illus.). 112p. (gr. 6-12). lib. bdg. 29.27 (978-0-8225-1396-4(X)) Lerner Publishing Group.
Gaines, Ann Graham. James K. Polk. 2008. (Presidents of the U. S. A. Ser.). (ENG., Illus.). 48p. (J). (gr. 3-6). 32.79 (978-1-60253-040-9(8), 200675) Child's World, Inc., The.
Mis, Melody S. How to Draw the Life & Times of James K. Polk. (Kid's Guide to Drawing the Presidents of the United States of America Ser.). 2009. 32p. (gr. 4-4). 50.50 (978-1-61511-147-3(6), PowerKids Pr.) 2006. (YA). (gr. 2-5). 26.50 (978-1-4042-2988-4(4)) Rosen Publishing Group, Inc., The.
Rumsch, BreAnn. James K. Polk, 1 vol. 2009. (United States Presidents Ser.). (ENG., Illus.). 40p. (YA). (gr. 3-6). 27.07 (978-1-60453-470-2(2)) ABDO Publishing Co.
Venezia, Mike. James K. Polk: Eleventh President, 1845-1849. Venezia, Mike, illus. 2005. (Getting to Know the U. S. Presidents Ser.). (ENG., Illus.). 32p. (J). (gr. 3-4). 28.00 (978-0-516-22616-3(9), Children's Pr.) Scholastic Library Publishing.

POLLS, ELECTION

see Elections

POLLUTION

Here are entered works on the condition resulting from the action of environmental contaminants.

see also Air—Pollution; Hazardous Wastes; Refuse and Refuse Disposal; Water—Pollution

Addison, D. R. Garbage Trucks at Work. 2009. (Big Trucks Ser.). (Illus.). 24p. (J). (gr. k-2). pap. 8.25 (978-1-4358-3085-1(7), PowerKids Pr.) Rosen Publishing Group, Inc., The.
Bellamy, Rufus. Waste & Pollution. 2010. (Sustaining Our Environment Ser.). 48p. (J). 35.65 (978-1-60753-139-5(9)) Amicus Publishing.
Bily, Cynthia A. Pollution. 2010. (Issues That Concern You Ser.). (Illus.). 144p. 36.95 (978-0-7377-4746-1(3)) Cengage Gale.
Bullard, Lisa. Power up to Fight Pollution. Thomas, Wes, illus. 2011. (Planet Protectors Ser.). pap. 39.62 (978-0-7613-8655-1(6), Millbrook Pr.); (ENG.). 24p. (J). lib. bdg. 23.93 (978-0-7613-6108-4(1)) Lerner Publishing Group.
—Power up to Fight Pollution. Thomas, Wes & Thomas, John, Jr., illus. 2011. (Cloverleaf Books (tm) — Planet Protectors Ser.). (ENG.). 24p. (gr. k-2). pap. 6.95 (978-0-7613-8515-8(0), Millbrook Pr.) Lerner Publishing Group.
Burns, Loree Griffin. Tracking Trash: Flotsam, Jetsam, & the Science of Ocean Motion. 2010. (Scientists in the Field Ser.). (ENG., Illus.). 64p. (J). (gr. 5-7). pap. 9.99 (978-0-547-32860-7(5)) Houghton Mifflin Harcourt Publishing Co.
Burton, Margie, et al. Are We Hurting the Earth? 2011. (Early Connections Ser.). (J). (978-1-61672-480-1(3)) Benchmark Education Co.
Carmichael, L. E. How Can We Reduce Agricultural Pollution? 2016. (Searchlight Books — What Can We Do about Pollution? Ser.). (ENG., Illus.). 40p. (J). (gr. 3-5). lib. bdg. 30.65 (978-1-4677-9514-2(3)) Lerner Publishing Group.
Crelin, Bob. There Once Was a Sky Full of Stars. Ziner, Amie, illus. 2005. 36p. pap. 12.95 (978-1-931559-04-1(X)) Sky Publishing.
Critical Perspectives on Pollution. 2006. (Scientific American Critical Anthologies on Environment & Climate Ser.). (Illus.). 224p. (J). (gr. 3-7). 37.95 (978-1-4042-0690-8(6)) Rosen Publishing Group, Inc., The.
Des Chenes, Elizabeth, ed. Pollution. 2007. (Writing the Critical Essay Ser.). (ENG., Illus.). 130p. (J). (gr. 3-7). lib. bdg. 33.75 (978-0-7377-3198-9(2), Greenhaven Pr., Inc.) Cengage Gale.
Dickmann, Nancy. Burning Out: Energy from Fossil Fuels. 2016. (ENG., Illus.). 32p. (J). (978-0-7787-2372-1(0)) Crabtree Publishing Co.
Dorion, Christiane. Earth's Garbage Crisis. 2007. (What If We Do Nothing? Ser.). (Illus.). 48p. (gr. 5-12). lib. bdg. 31.00 (978-0-8368-7753-3(5), Gareth Stevens Secondary Library) Stevens, Gareth Publishing LLLP.
—Pollution. 2009. (What If We Do Nothing? Ser.). 48p. (YA). (gr. 4-7). lib. bdg. 31.00 (978-1-4339-1984-8(2)) Stevens, Gareth Publishing LLLP.
Eagen, Rachel. Environmental Chemistry. 2011. (Chemtastrophe! Ser.). (ENG.). 32p. (J). (gr. 5-8). pap. (978-0-7787-5302-5(6)); lib. bdg. (978-0-7787-5285-1(2)) Crabtree Publishing Co.
Flynn, Sarah Wassner & National Geographic Kids Staff. This Book Stinks! Gross Garbage, Rotten Rubbish, & the Science of Trash. 2017. (ENG.). 128p. (J). (gr. 3-7). pap. 14.99 (978-1-4263-2730-8(7), National Geographic Children's Bks.) National Geographic Society.
Gold, Susan Dudley. Clean Air & Clean Water Acts. 2011. (Landmark Legislation 2 Ser.). 128p. (J). (gr. 7). 39.93 (978-1-60870-484-2(X)) Marshall Cavendish Corp.
Goldstein, Margaret J. Garbage in Space: A Space Discovery Guide. 2017. (Space Discovery Guides). (ENG.). 48p. (J). (gr. 4-6). 16.99 **(978-1-5124-3806-2(5))**; 47.99 **(978-1-5124-3807-9(3))**; (Illus.). 47.99 **(978-1-5124-2798-1(5))** Lerner Publishing Group. (Lerner Pubns.).
Greeley, August. Poisoned Planet: Pollution in our World. 2009. 24p. (gr. 5-8). pap. 8.25 (978-1-4358-2675-5(2), Rosen Classroom) Rosen Publishing Group, Inc., The.
Green, Jen. Reducing Pollution & Waste, 1 vol. 2011. (Environment Challenge Ser.). (ENG., Illus.). 48p. (gr. 5-6). pap. 9.49 (978-1-4109-4306-4(2), Raintree Freestyle) Heinemann-Raintree.
—Reducing Pollution & Waste, 1 vol. Ward, Geoff, illus. 2011. (Environment Challenge Ser.). (ENG.). 48p. (gr. 3-3). pap. 9.49 (978-1-4109-4327-9(5), Raintree Freestyle Express) Heinemann-Raintree.
—Reducing Pollution & Waste, 1 vol. 2011. (Environment Challenge Ser.). (ENG., Illus.). 48p. (gr. 5-6). 34.65 (978-1-4109-4299-9(6), Raintree Freestyle) Heinemann-Raintree.
—Reducing Pollution & Waste, 1 vol. Ward, Geoff, illus. 2011. (Environment Challenge Ser.). (ENG.). 48p. (gr. 3-3). 34.65 (978-1-4109-4320-0(8), Raintree Freestyle Express) Heinemann-Raintree.
Green, Robert. Pollution. 2008. (21st Century Skills Library: Global Perspectives Ser.). (ENG.). 32p. (gr. 4-8). lib. bdg. 28.50 (978-1-60279-130-5(9), 200105) Cherry Lake Publishing.
Hand, Carol. Dead Zones: Why Earth's Waters Are Losing Oxygen. 2016. (ENG., Illus.). 80p. (YA). (gr. 7-12). 53.32 (978-1-4677-9575-3(5), Twenty-First Century Bks.) Lerner Publishing Group.
Hansen, Amy. Fossil Fuels: Buried in the Earth. 2010. (Powering Our World Ser.). 24p. (J). (ENG.). pap. 8.25 (978-1-4358-9738-0(2)); (Illus.). 49.50 (978-1-4358-9739-7(0), 1307107) Rosen Publishing Group, Inc., The. (PowerKids Pr.).
Hansen, Amy S. Fossil Fuels: Buried in the Earth. 2010. (Powering Our World Ser.). 24p. (J). (gr. 2-5). E-Book 42.50 (978-1-4488-0195-4(8)); (Illus.). lib. bdg. 22.60 (978-1-4358-9325-2(5), PowerKids Pr.) Rosen Publishing Group, Inc., The.
Hay, Jeff. Pollution. 2008. (Issues on Trial Ser.). (ENG., Illus.). 240p. (gr. 10-12). 48.30 (978-0-7377-4181-0(3), Greenhaven Pr., Inc.) Cengage Gale.
Holt, Rinehart and Winston Staff. Decisions for Health Blue, Chptr. 21: Health & Environment. 4th ed. 2004. pap. 11.20 (978-0-03-068057-1(3)) Holt McDougal.
Iyer, Rani. Endangered Energy: Investigating the Scarcity of Fossil Fuels. 2015. (Endangered Earth Ser.). (ENG.). 32p. (gr. 3-4). lib. bdg. 27.32 (978-1-4914-2037-9(5), Fact Finders) Capstone Press of Coughlan Cos.
Jakab, Cheryl. Greenhouse Gases. 2010. (Environment in Focus Ser.). 32p. (gr. 4). 28.50 (978-1-60870-091-2(7)) Marshall Cavendish Corp.
—Pollution. 2010. (Environment in Focus Ser.). 32p. (gr. 4). 28.50 (978-1-60870-089-9(5)) Marshall Cavendish Corp.
Jakubiak, David J. Protecting Our Planet: What Can We Do about Oil Spills & Ocean Pollution? 2012. (Illus.). 24p. (J). 49.50 (978-1-4488-5113-3(0)); pap. 8.25 (978-1-4488-5112-6(2)) Rosen Publishing Group, Inc., The. (PowerKids Pr.).
Jones, Keisha. Halting Pollution. 2016. (Global Guardians Ser.). 00024p. (J). (gr. 3-3). pap. 8.25 (978-1-4994-2756-1(5), PowerKids Pr.) Rosen Publishing Group, Inc., The.
Kortemeier, Todd. Finding an Energy Solution. 2017. (J). (978-1-62143-519-8(9)) Pr. Room Editions LLC.
Kortemeier, Todd & Smibert, Angie. Finding an Energy Solution. 2016. (Science Frontiers Ser.). (ENG., Illus.). 32p. (J). pap. 9.95 (978-1-63235-395-5(4)) Pr. Room Editions LLC.
Lawrence, Ellen. Garbage Galore. 2014. (Science Slam: Green World, Clean World Ser.). 24p. (J). (gr. -1-3). lib. bdg. 23.93 (978-1-62724-102-1(7)) Bearport Publishing Co., Inc.
Leaney, Cindy. Pollution. 2008. (Contemporary Issues Companion Ser.). 240p. (gr. 10-12). 36.20 (978-0-7377-3950-3(9)); pap. 24.95 (978-0-7377-3951-0(7)) Cengage Gale. (Greenhaven Pr., Inc.).
Levete, Sarah. Destroying the Oceans. 2010. (Protecting Our Planet Ser.). (ENG., Illus.). 32p. (J). (gr. 3-6). (978-0-7787-5211-0(9)); pap. (978-0-7787-5228-8(3)) Crabtree Publishing Co.
Linde, Barbara M.. Pollution. 2013. (Habitat Havoc Ser.). 32p. (gr. 3-6). pap. 10.50 (978-1-4339-9857-7(2)) Stevens, Gareth Publishing LLLP.
Linde, Barbara M. Pollution. 2014. (Illus.). 32p. (J). lib. bdg. (978-1-4339-9926-0(9)) Stevens, Gareth Publishing LLLP.
Llewellyn, Claire. Let's Recycle. 2005. (Illus.). 32p. (YA). (gr. 1-18). lib. bdg. 27.10 (978-1-932333-22-0(3)) Chrysalis Education.
—Protect Natural Habitats. 2005. (Illus.). 32p. (YA). (gr. 1-18). lib. bdg. 27.10 (978-1-932333-20-6(7)) Chrysalis Education.
Mara, Wil. The Chernobyl Disaster: Legacy & Impact on the Future of Nuclear Energy. 2010. (Perspectives on 2 Ser.). 112p. (gr. 7). 39.93 (978-0-7614-4984-3(1)) Marshall Cavendish Corp.
McKenzie, Precious. Cleaning up the Earth. 2011. (ENG., Illus.). 24p. (gr. k-2). pap. 8.95 (978-1-61741-970-6(2)) Rourke Educational Media.
Mileham, Rebecca. Global Pollution. 2013. (21st Century Science Ser.). (ENG.). 64p. (J). (gr. 4-7). pap. 7.95 (978-1-84898-193-5(7), TickTock Books) Octopus Publishing Group GBR. Dist: Independent Pubs. Group.
Morrison, Yvonne. Earth Partners: Saving the Planet. 2007. (Shockwave: History & Politics Ser.). (Illus.). 36p. (J). (gr. 4-6). (ENG.). lib. bdg. 25.00 (978-0-531-17753-2(X)); pap. 6.95 (978-0-531-15489-2(0)) Scholastic Library Publishing. (Children's Pr.).
National Geographic Learning Staff. Taking Care of Earth, Level 3. 2011. (World Windows Ser.). (ENG., Illus.). 16p. (J). stu. ed. 9.95 (978-1-133-56615-1(4)) Cengage Heinle.
National Marine Fisheries Service (U.S.), ed. Understanding Marine Debris: Games & Activities for Kids of All Ages. 2009. (ENG., Illus.). 22p. 2.50 (978-0-16-083974-0(2), National Marine Fisheries Service) United States Government Printing Office.
Orme, Helen. Pollution. 2008. (Earth in Danger Ser.). (Illus.). 32p. (YA). (gr. 3-6). lib. bdg. 25.27 (978-1-59716-724-6(X), 1284354) Bearport Publishing Co., Inc.
Parker, Russ. Pollution Crisis. 2009. (Planet in Crisis Ser.). 32p. (gr. 5-8). (ENG.). (J). pap. 10.00 (978-1-4358-0682-5(4)); (YA). lib. bdg. 25.25 (978-1-4358-5252-5(4)) Rosen Publishing Group, Inc., The. (Rosen Reference).
Patent, Dorothy Hinshaw. The Call of the Osprey. Muñoz, William, illus. Muñoz, William, photos by. 2015. (Scientists in the Field Ser.). (ENG.). 80p. (J). (gr. 5-7). 18.99 (978-0-544-23268-6(2), HMH Books For Young Readers) Houghton Mifflin Harcourt Publishing Co.
Paul, Miranda. One Plastic Bag: Isatou Ceesay & the Recycling Women of the Gambia. Zunon, Elizabeth, illus. 2015. (ENG.). 32p. (J). (gr. k-3). lib. bdg. 19.99 (978-1-4677-1608-6(1)) Lerner Publishing Group.
Petersen, Christine. Controlling Earth's Pollutants. 2010. (Environment at Risk Ser.). 112p. (gr. 7-18). 39.93 (978-0-7614-4005-5(4)) Marshall Cavendish Corp.
Pollution: Level H, 6 vols. (Wonder Worldtm Ser.). 16p. 29.95 (978-0-7802-1233-6(9)) Wright Group/McGraw-Hill.
Rake, Jody Sullivan. Endangered Oceans: Investigating Oceans in Crisis. 2015. (Endangered Earth Ser.). (ENG.). 32p. (gr. 3-4). lib. bdg. 27.32 (978-1-4914-2038-6(3), Fact Finders) Capstone Press of Coughlan Cos.
Rice, Dona. Too Much Trash!, 1 vol. (Science Readers: Content & Literacy Ser.). (ENG., Illus.). 24p. (gr. k-k). 2015. (J). 22.96 (978-1-4938-1144-1(4)) 2014. pap. 8.99 (978-1-4807-4534-6(0)) Teacher Created Materials, Inc.
Silverstein, Alvin, et al. Smog, Oil Spills, Sewage, & More: The Yucky Pollution Book. Kelley, Gerald, illus. 2010. (Yucky Science Ser.). 48p. (J). (gr. 5-9). 25.27 (978-0-7660-3313-9(9)) Enslow Pubs., Inc.
Slade, Suzanne. What Can We Do about Pollution? 2009. (Protecting Our Planet Ser.). (Illus.). 24p. (ENG.). (J). pap. 8.25 (978-1-4358-2485-0(7), PowerKids Pr.); (YA). (gr. 2-5). lib. bdg. 22.60 (978-1-4042-8083-0(9)) Rosen Publishing Group, Inc., The.
Solway, Andrew. Secrets of Pollution & Conservation. 2010. (Science Secrets Ser.). 32p. (gr. 4). 28.50 (978-1-60870-140-7(9)) Marshall Cavendish Corp.
—Transportation, 1 vol. 2012. (Impact of Environmentalism Ser.). (ENG.). 64p. (gr. 6-10). lib. bdg. 35.99 (978-1-4329-6520-4(4)) Heinemann-Raintree.
Spilsbury, Louise. Waste & Recycling Challenges. 2009. (Illus.). 48p. (J). 70.50 (978-1-4358-5487-1(X), Rosen Reference); (ENG., pap. 11.75 (978-1-4358-5486-4(1), Rosen Reference); (ENG., (gr. 5-9). lib. bdg. 29.25 (978-1-4358-5355-3(5)) Rosen Publishing Group, Inc., The.
Sturm, Jeanne. Nuestra Huella en la Tierra. 2012. (SPA & ENG.). 48p. (gr. 4-8). pap. 10.95 (978-1-61810-473-1(X)) Rourke Educational Media.
—Our Footprint on Earth. 2009. (ENG., Illus.). 48p. (gr. 4-8). pap. 10.95 (978-1-60694-526-1(2)) Rourke Educational Media.
Watson, Stephanie, ed. Critical Perspectives on Pollution. 2009. (Scientific American Critical Anthologies on Environment & Climate Ser.). 224p. (gr. 9-9). 63.90 (978-1-60853-069-4(8)) Rosen Publishing Group, Inc., The.
West, David & Parker, Steve. Ecological Disasters. 2011. (ENG., Illus.). 32p. (J). pap. (978-0-7787-7578-2(X)); lib. bdg. (978-0-7787-7573-7(9)) Crabtree Publishing Co.
World Book, Inc Staff, contrib. by. Pollution. 2008. (J). (978-0-7166-1406-7(5)) World Bk., Inc.
Young, Karen Romano. Space Junk: The Dangers of Polluting Earth's Orbit. 2016. (Nonfiction - Young Adult Ser.). (ENG.). 64p. (YA). (gr. 7-12). 33.32 (978-1-4677-5600-6(8)); (Illus.). 50.65 (978-1-4677-8806-9(6)) Lerner Publishing Group. (Twenty-First Century Bks.).

POLLUTION—FICTION

Barroux. Starfish, Where Are You? 2016. (ENG., Illus.). 40p. (J). (gr. -1-1). 17.99 (978-1-4998-0258-0(7)) Little Bee Books Inc.
Base, Graeme. Uno's Garden. 2006. (ENG., Illus.). 44p. (J). (gr. -1-3). 19.95 (978-0-8109-5473-1(7)) Abrams, Inc.
Beauregard, Lynda. The Yucky Duck Rescue: A Mystery about Pollution. Torres, German, illus. 2013. (Summer Camp Science Mysteries Ser.: 8). (ENG.). 48p. (gr. 3-6). pap. 6.95 (978-1-4677-0736-7(8)); lib. bdg. 29.27 (978-1-4677-0170-9(X)) Lerner Publishing Group. (Graphic Universe™).
Bottoms, Bud. Davey & the GOM Giant Oil Monster. 2008. (Illus.). 39p. (J). (gr. -1-5). per. 14.95 (978-0-9795444-1-5(6)) Summerland Publishing.
Bradman, Tony. The Ugly Duckling Returns, 1 vol. Warburton, Sarah, illus. 2014. (After Happily Ever After Ser.). (ENG.). 56p. (gr. 2-3). lib. bdg. 25.32 (978-1-4342-7953-8(7), After Happily Ever After) Stone Arch Bks.
Brouwer, Sigmund. Cobra Strike, 1 vol. 2007. (Orca Sports Ser.). (ENG.). 176p. (YA). (gr. 6-10). per. 9.95 (978-1-55143-725-5(2)) Orca Bk. Pubs. USA.
Cornfield, Lynda Ellis. Rocks for Clean Oceans. 2009. 28p. pap. 13.99 (978-1-4389-8417-9(0)) AuthorHouse.
dePaola, Tomie. Michael Bird-Boy. dePaola, Tomie, illus. 2015. (ENG., Illus.). 32p. (J). (gr. -1-3). 16.99 (978-1-4814-4333-3(X), Simon & Schuster Bks. For Young Readers) Simon & Schuster Bks. For Young Readers.
Douglas, Babette. Kiss a Me to the Rescue. Rockwell, Barry, illus. 2006. (Kiss a Me Teacher Creature Stories Ser.). (J). (gr. -1-3). 9.99 (978-1-890343-11-8(0)) Kiss A Me Productions, Inc.
Draper, Rohan. Sunny & Mayo. 2012. 146p. 46.72 (978-1-4771-0446-0(1)); pap. 28.03 (978-1-4771-0445-3(3)) Xlibris Corp.
Foreman, Michael. One World. 2012. (ENG., Illus.). 32p. (J). (gr. -1-k). pap. 12.99 (978-1-84939-304-1(4)) Andersen Pr. GBR. Dist: Independent Pubs. Group.
Fraustino, Lisa Rowe. The Hole in the Wall. 2011. (ENG.). 232p. (J). (gr. 2-8). pap. 8.00 (978-1-57131-698-1(1)) Milkweed Editions.
French, Lisa S. The Terrible Trash Trail: Eco-Pig Stops Pollution, 1 vol. Gott, Barry, illus. 2009. (Eco-Pig Ser.). (ENG.). 32p. (J). (gr. -1-2). 28.50 (978-1-60270-663-7(8)) ABDO Publishing Co.
Galliez, Roxane Marie. The Earth Has Caught Cold. Lhomme, Sandrine, illus. 2009. 24p. (J). (gr. -1-3). 9.99 (978-0-8416-7140-9(0)) Hammond World Atlas Corp.
Geiger, Beth & Fuerst, Jeffrey B. Return to Earth. Wolk-Stanley, Jessica, illus. 2004. (Reader's Theater Ser.). (J). pap. (978-1-4108-2306-9(7), A23067) Benchmark Education Co.
Grabenstein, Chris. Riley Mack Stirs up More Trouble. 2013. (Riley Mack Ser.: 2). (ENG.). 336p. (J). (gr. 3-7). 16.99 (978-0-06-202622-4(4)) HarperCollins Pubs.
Gratz, Alan. Something Rotten. 2009. (ENG.). 224p. (YA). (gr. 7-18). 7.99 (978-0-14-241297-8(X), Puffin Books) Penguin Young Readers Group.
Inches, Alison. I Can Save the Ocean! The Little Green Monster Cleans up the Beach. Garofoli, Viviana, illus. 2010. (Little Green Bks.). (ENG.). 24p. (J). (gr. -1-1). 7.99 (978-1-4169-9514-2(5), Little Simon) Little Simon.
Keene, Carolyn. Green with Envy: Book Two in the Eco Mystery Trilogy. 2010. (Nancy Drew (All New) Girl Detective Ser.: 40). (ENG.). 160p. (J). (gr. 3-7). pap. 6.99 (978-1-4169-7842-8(9), Aladdin) Simon & Schuster Children's Publishing.
—Seeing Green: Book Three in the Eco Mystery Trilogy. 2010. (Nancy Drew (All New) Girl Detective Ser.: 41). (ENG.). 160p. (J). (gr. 3-7). pap. 6.99 (978-1-4169-7845-9(3), Aladdin) Simon & Schuster Children's Publishing.
King, Amy Sarig. Me & Marvin Gardens. 2017. (ENG.). 256p. (J). (gr. 3-7). 16.99 (978-0-545-87074-0(7), Levine, Arthur A. Bks.) Scholastic, Inc.
Liberto, Lorenzo. Save the Planet / Salva el Planeta. Gomez, Rocio, tr. Torres, Irving, illus. 2005. (Matt the Rat Ser. / La Serie de Ratón Mateo). (ENG & SPA.). 32p. (J). lib. bdg. 20.00 (978-0-9743668-5-2(4)) Harvest Sun Pr., LLC.
Manos, John. Samantha Saves the Stream. 2006. (Early Explorers Ser.). (J). pap. (978-1-4108-6125-2(2)) Benchmark Education Co.
Meadows, Daisy. The Earth Fairies #2: Isabella the Air Fairy. 2014. (Earth Fairies Ser.: 2). (ENG.). 80p. (J). (gr. 2-5). pap. 4.99 (978-0-545-60525-0(3), Scholastic Paperbacks) Scholastic, Inc.
Meehan, Patrick & Spratt, Niall. The Shamrogues: Second Challenge. 2013. (ENG.). 228p. (J). pap. 12.95 (978-1-871305-58-6(6)) Orpen Pr. IRL. Dist: Dufour Editions, Inc.
Nelson, Bruce M. The Magician's Hat. 2006. 127p. pap. 19.95 (978-1-4241-2301-8(1)) America Star Bks.
Newton, R. H. Oceannis. 2010. pap. 16.95 (978-0-7414-5911-4(6)) Infinity Publishing.
Oe, Patricia Daly. Where Are My Stripes? Oe, Patricia Daly, illus. 2007. (R. I. C. Story Chest Ser.). (Illus.). 20p. (J). (gr. -1-k). 11.95 incl. audio compact disk (978-1-74126-438-8(3)) R.I.C. Pubs. AUS. Dist: SCB Distributors.
Park, Louise. Odd One Out. May, Kyla & Matthews, Melanie, illus. 2015. (Star Girl Ser.). (ENG.). 80p. (gr. 1-4). lib. bdg. 22.65 (978-1-4795-8276-1(X)) Picture Window Bks.

—Winning Moves. May, Kyla & Matthews, Melanie, illus. 2015. (Star Girl Ser.). (ENG.). 80p. (gr. 1-4). lib. bdg. 22.65 (978-1-4795-8277-8(8)) Picture Window Bks.

Pavanello, Roberto. The Thing in the Sewers, 1 vol. Zeni, Marco, tr. from ITA. Pisapia, Blasco & Brughera, Pamela, illus. 2012. (Echo & the Bat Pack Ser.). (ENG.). 128p. (gr. 2-3). 25.32 (978-1-4342-3824-5(5), Echo & the Bat Pack) Stone Arch Bks.

Pelletier, Maryse. La Chasse au Plomb. Grimard, Gabrielle, illus. 2004. (Roman Jeunesse Ser.). (FRE.). 96p. (J). (gr. 4-7). pap. (978-2-89021-692-1(6)) Diffusion du livre Mirabel (DLM).

Pon, Cindy. Want. 2017. (ENG., Illus.). 336p. (YA). (gr. 9). 18.99 **(978-1-4814-8922-5(4)**, Simon Pulse) Simon Pulse.

Poon, Janice. Claire & the Water Wish. Poon, Janice, illus. 2009. (ENG., Illus.). 120p. (J). (gr. 2-5). 7.95 (978-1-55453-382-4(1)); 15.95 (978-1-55453-381-7(3)) Kids Can Pr., Ltd. CAN. Dist: Hachette Bk. Group.

Reynolds, Paul A. Sydney & Simon: Going Green! Reynolds, Paul A. & Reynolds, Peter H., illus. 2015. (Sydney & Simon Ser.). (ENG.). 48p. (J). (gr. 1-4). lib. bdg. 12.95 (978-1-58089-677-1(4)) Charlesbridge Publishing, Inc.

Santore, Charles, illus. William the Curious: Knight of the Water Lilies. 2012. (J). (978-1-60464-034-2(0)) Appleseed Pr. Bk. Pub. LLC.

Scraper, Katherine. Save the Fairy Penguins. 2005. (J). pap. (978-1-4108-4214-5(2)) Benchmark Education Co.

Spratt, Niall & Meehan, Patrick. The Shamrogues: First Challenge. 2013. (ENG.). 230p. (J). pap. 12.95 (978-1-871305-57-9(8)) Orpen Pr. IRL. Dist: Dufour Editions, Inc.

Stockland, Patricia M. Clean up the Watering Hole!, 1 vol. Haugen, Ryan, illus. 2008. (Safari Friends Ser.). (ENG.). 32p. (gr. -1-3). 28.50 (978-1-60270-084-0(2), Looking Glass Library) ABDO Publishing Co.

Thaler, Mike. Earth Day from the Black Lagoon. Lee, Jared D., illus. 2013. 64p. (J). (978-0-545-47669-0(0)) Scholastic, Inc.

Van Allsburg, Chris. Just a Dream. Van Allsburg, Chris, illus. 2014. (Illus.). 48p. pap. 9.00 (978-1-61003-182-0(2)) Center for the Collaborative Classroom.

—Just a Dream 25th Anniversary Edition. 2015. (ENG., Illus.). 48p. (J). (gr. -1-3). 18.99 (978-0-544-42283-4(X), HMH Books For Young Readers) Houghton Mifflin Harcourt Publishing Co.

Wildsmith, Brian. Professor Noah's Spaceship, 1 vol. Wildsmith, Brian, illus. 2008. (ENG., Illus.). 32p. (J). 16.95 (978-1-59572-124-2(X)) Star Bright Bks., Inc.

Yellowknife, Jessica. Spring Break Adventure. 2011. 84p. pap. 11.11 (978-1-4269-6952-2(X)) Trafford Publishing.

POLLUTION OF AIR

see Air—Pollution

POLLUTION OF WATER

see Water—Pollution

POLO, MARCO, 1254-1323?

Bailey, Gerry & Foster, Karen. Marco Polo's Silk Purse. Radford, Karen & Noyes, Leighton, illus. 2008. (Stories of Great People Ser.). (ENG.). 40p. (J). (gr. 3-8). pap. (978-0-7787-3710-0(1)); lib. bdg. (978-0-7787-3688-2(1)) Crabtree Publishing Co.

Boyd, David. Marco Polo & the Roc. Ng, Drew, illus. 2007. 48p. (J). lib. bdg. 23.08 (978-1-4242-1621-5(4)) Fitzgerald Bks.

Childress, Diana. Marco Polo's Journey to China. 2007. (Pivotal Moments in History Ser.). (ENG.). 160p. (gr. 9-12). lib. bdg. 38.60 (978-0-8225-5903-0(X)) Lerner Publishing Group.

Cooke, Tim. Explore with Marco Polo. 2014. (ENG., Illus.). 32p. (J). (978-0-7787-1428-6(4)) Crabtree Publishing Co.

Crompton, Samuel Willard. Marco Polo: Epic Traveler Throughout Asia. 2017. (Spotlight on Explorers & Colonization Ser.). 48p. (gr. 10-11). 70.50 **(978-1-5081-7504-9(7)**, Rosen Young Adult) Rosen Publishing Group, Inc., The.

Feeney, Kathy. Marco Polo: Explorer of China. 2004. (Explorers! Ser.). (Illus.). 48p. (J). lib. bdg. 23.93 (978-0-7660-2145-7(9)) Enslow Pubs., Inc.

Feinstein, Stephen. Marco Polo: Amazing Adventures in China. 2013. (Great Explorers of the World Ser.). 112p. (gr. 6-12). pap. 10.95 (978-0-7660-5430-1(6)) Enslow Pubs., Inc.

Feinstein, Stephen. Marco Polo: Amazing Adventures in China. 2009. (Great Explorers of the World Ser.). (Illus.). 112p. (J). (gr. 7-12). lib. bdg. 33.27 (978-1-59845-103-0(0)) Enslow Pubs., Inc.

Hain-Jun, Yue & Soldevilla, Juan Manuel. Marco Polo: La Ruta de las Maravillas. 2006.Tr. of Marco Polo & the Route of Wonders. (SPA.). (J). (gr. 6-8). 9.60 (978-84-316-7173-0(4), W32814) Vicens-Vives, Editorial, S.A. ESP. Dist: Lectorum Pubns., Inc.

Holub, Joan. Quién Fue Marco Polo? O'brien, John & Harrison, Nancy, illus. 2012. (Who Was? Ser.). (ENG & SPA.). 112p. (J). (gr. 3-7). pap. 7.99 (978-0-448-46174-8(9), Grosset & Dunlap) Penguin Young Readers Group.

—Who Was Marco Polo? O'brien, John et al, illus. 2007. (Who Was? Ser.). (ENG.). 112p. (J). (gr. 3-7). pap. 5.99 (978-0-448-44540-3(9), Grosset & Dunlap) Penguin Young Readers Group.

—Who Was Marco Polo? O'brien, John, illus. 2007. (Who Was... ? Ser.). 105p. (gr. 4-7). 15.00 (978-0-7569-8165-5(4)) Perfection Learning Corp.

Marsh, Carole. Marco Polo. 2004. 12p. (gr. k-4). 2.95 (978-0-635-02376-6(8)) Gallopade International.

McCarty, Nick. Marco Polo: El Joven Que Viajo Por el Mundo Medieval. 2007. (World History Biographies Ser.). (Illus.). 64p. (J). (gr. 3-7). (978-84-372-2470-1(5)) Altea, Ediciones, S.A. - Grupo Santillana.

—Marco Polo: The Boy Who Traveled the Medieval World. 2006. (National Geographic World History Biographies Ser.). (ENG., Illus.). 64p. (J). (gr. 3-7). 17.95 (978-0-7922-5893-3(2)); lib. bdg. 27.90 (978-0-7922-5894-0(0)) National Geographic Society. (National Geographic Children's Bks.).

—World History Biographies: Marco Polo: The Boy Who Traveled the Medieval World. 2008. (National Geographic World History Biographies Ser.). (ENG., Illus.). 64p. (J). (gr. 3-7). pap. 6.95 (978-1-4263-0296-1(7), National Geographic Children's Bks.) National Geographic Society.

McNeese, Tim. Marco Polo & the Realm of Kublai Khan. Goetzmann, William H., ed. 2005. (Explorers of New Lands Ser.). (Illus.). 100p. (gr. 5-8). lib. bdg. 30.00 (978-0-7910-8612-4(7)) Facts On File, Inc.

Morley, Jacqueline. You Wouldn't Want to Explore with Marco Polo! A Really Long Trip You'd Rather Not Take. Antram, David, illus. 2009. (You Wouldn't Want to Ser.). (ENG.). 32p. (J). (gr. 3-12). 29.00 (978-0-531-21327-8(7)); pap. 9.95 (978-0-531-20518-1(5)) Scholastic Library Publishing.

Ollhoff, Jim. Marco Polo. 2013. (Great Explorers Ser.). 32p. (J). (gr. 5-9). lib. bdg. 27.07 (978-1-61783-968-9(X), Abdo & Daughters) ABDO Publishing Co.

Petrie, Kristin. Marco Polo, 1 vol. 2007. (Explorers Set 2 Ser.). (ENG., Illus.). 32p. (gr. 4-5). 27.07 (978-1-59679-747-5(9), Checkerboard Library) ABDO Publishing Co.

Riddle, John. Marco Polo. 2004. (Great Names Ser.). (Illus.). 32p. (J). (gr. 3-18). lib. bdg. 19.95 (978-1-59084-136-5(0)) Mason Crest.

—Marco Polo: 13th Century Italian Trader. 2013. (People of Importance Ser.: 21). (Illus.). 32p. (J). (gr. 4-18). 19.95 (978-1-4222-2850-0(9)) Mason Crest.

Rosen, Michael J. The Million Stories of Marco Polo. Pritelli, Maria Cristina, illus. 2016. (ENG.). 32p. (J). (gr. 1-3). 18.99 (978-1-56846-290-5(5), Creative Editions) Creative Co., The.

Smalley, Roger. The Adventures of Marco Polo, 1 vol. Carter, Greg & Bascle, Brian, illus. 2005. (Graphic History Ser.). (ENG.). 32p. (gr. 3-4). 30.65 (978-0-7368-3830-6(9), Graphic Library) Capstone Press of Coughlan Cos.

—The Adventures of Marco Polo, 1 vol. Bascle, Brian, illus. 2005. (Graphic History Ser.). (ENG.). 32p. (gr. 3-4). per. 8.10 (978-0-7368-5240-1(9), Graphic Library) Capstone Press of Coughlan Cos.

—Las Aventuras de Marco Polo. Bascle, Brian, illus. 2006. (Historia Gráficas Ser.). (SPA.). 32p. (gr. 3-4). 30.65 (978-0-7368-6054-3(1)) Capstone Press of Coughlan Cos.

Tabilio, Marco & Schwandt, Kerstin. Marco Polo: The Silk Road. Tabilio, Marco, illus. 2017. (ENG., Illus.). 208p. (J). (gr. 9-12). 29.32 (978-1-5124-1182-9(5), Graphic Universe™) Lerner Publishing Group.

Twist, Clint. Marco Polo: History's Great Adventurer. 2011. (Historical Notebooks Ser.). (ENG., Illus.). 30p. (J). (gr. 3-7). 19.99 (978-0-7636-5286-9(5), Templar) Candlewick Pr.

Worth, Richard. The Great Empire of China & Marco Polo in World History. 2003. (In World History Ser.). (Illus.). 112p. (J). lib. bdg. 26.60 (978-0-7660-1939-3(X)) Enslow Pubs., Inc.

Zannos, Susan. The Life & Times of Marco Polo. 2004. (Biography from Ancient Civilizations Ser.). (Illus.). 48p. (J). (gr. 4-8). lib. bdg. 29.95 (978-1-58415-264-4(8)) Mitchell Lane Pubs., Inc.

Zelenyj, Alexander. Marco Polo: Overland to China. 2005. (In the Footsteps of Explorers Ser.). (ENG., Illus.). 32p. (J). (gr. 4-5). pap. (978-0-7787-2453-7(0)) Crabtree Publishing Co.

POLO, MARCO, 1254-1323?—FICTION

Demi. Marco Polo, 0 vols. 2008. (ENG., Illus.). 56p. (J). (gr. 4-7). 19.99 (978-0-7614-5433-5(0), 9780761454335, Amazon Children's Publishing) Amazon Publishing.

Johnson, Vargie. Marco Polo the Adventurer: What Made Them Famous? 2006. 156p. (J). per. 15.00 (978-1-931195-98-0(6)) KiwE Publishing, Ltd.

Jordan, Devin. The Dragon's Pearl. Di Bartolo, Jim, illus. 2010. (ENG.). 352p. (YA). (gr. 5-9). pap. 8.99 (978-1-4169-6411-7(8), Simon & Schuster Bks. For Young Readers) Simon & Schuster Bks. For Young Readers.

Maisner, Heather. Diary of a Princess: A Tale from Marco Polo's Travels. Moxley, Sheila, illus. 2006. 26p. (gr. k-4). reprint ed. pap. 8.00 (978-1-4223-5302-8(8)) DIANE Publishing Co.

Scieszka, Jon. Marco? Polo!, No. 16. McCauley, Adam, illus. 2008. (Time Warp Trio Ser.: 16). (ENG.). 96p. (J). (gr. 2-4). 5.99 (978-0-14-241177-3(9), Puffin Books) Penguin Young Readers Group.

—Marco? Polo! McCauley, Adam, illus. 2008. (Time Warp Trio Ser.: No. 16). 90p. (J). (gr. 4-6). 12.65 (978-0-7569-8923-1(X)) Perfection Learning Corp.

Sylvester, Kevin. Neil Flambé & the Marco Polo Murders. Sylvester, Kevin, illus. 2014. (Neil Flambe Capers Ser.: 1). (ENG., Illus.). 320p. (J). (gr. 3-7). pap. 7.99 (978-1-4424-4605-2(6), Simon & Schuster Bks. For Young Readers) Simon & Schuster Bks. For Young Readers.

POLTERGEISTS

see Ghosts

POLYMERS

see also Plastics

Goodstein, Madeline P. Plastics & Polymers Science Fair Projects. LaBaff, Tom & LaBaff, Stephanie, illus. rev. exp. ed. 2010. (Chemistry Science Projects Using the Scientific Method Ser.). 160p. (J). (gr. 5-18). 35.94 (978-0-7660-3412-9(7)) Enslow Pubs., Inc.

—Plastics & Polymers Science Fair Projects Using Hair Gel, Soda Bottles, & Slimy Stuff. 2004. (Chemistry! Best Science Projects Ser.). (Illus.). 128p. (J). lib. bdg. 27.94 (978-0-7660-2123-5(8)) Enslow Pubs., Inc.

Small, Cathleen. Fab Lab Creating with Vinyl Cutters. 2016. (Getting Creative with Fab Lab Ser.). 00064p. (J). (gr. 6-6). 34.45 (978-1-5081-7350-2(8)) Rosen Publishing Group, Inc., The.

POLYNESIA

Montgomery, Sy. The Octopus Scientists. Ellenbogen, Keith, illus. 2015. (Scientists in the Field Ser.). (ENG.). 80p. (J). (gr. 5-7). 18.99 (978-0-544-23270-9(4), HMH Books For Young Readers) Houghton Mifflin Harcourt Publishing Co.

Webster, Christine. Polynesians. 2003. (Indigenous Peoples Ser.). (J). pap. 9.95 (978-1-59036-158-0(X)); (Illus.). 32p. lib. bdg. 26.00 (978-1-59036-123-8(7)) Weigl Pubs., Inc.

World Book, Inc Staff, contrib. by. The Polynesians. 2009. (J). (978-0-7166-2140-9(1)) World Bk., Inc.

POLYNESIA—FICTION

Disney Storybook Art Team, illus. Moana Read-Along Storybook & CD. 2016. (Read-Along Storybook & CD Ser.). (ENG.). 32p. (J). (gr. 1-3). pap. 6.99 (978-1-4847-4361-4(X)) Disney Pr.

O'Neill, Katrina. The Red Rain of Easter Island. 2007. (Illus.). 52p. (J). pap. (978-1-4207-0723-6(X)) Sundance/Newbridge Educational Publishing.

RH Disney. Quest for the Heart. RH Disney, illus. 2016. (Step into Reading Ser.). (ENG., Illus.). 32p. (J). (gr. -1-1). lib. bdg. 12.99 (978-0-7364-8226-4(1), RH/Disney) Random Hse. Children's Bks.

Sperry, Armstrong. Call It Courage. 2008. (ENG.). 128p. (YA). (gr. 7). mass mkt. 6.99 (978-1-4169-5368-5(X), Simon Pulse) Simon Pulse.

POMPEII (EXTINCT CITY)

Ball, Karen. Pompeii. Cerisier, Emmanuel, illus. 2006. (Usborne Young Reading Ser.). 64p. (J). (gr. 3-7). 8.99 (978-0-7945-1270-5(4), Usborne) EDC Publishing.

Collins, Terry. Escape from Pompeii: An Isabel Soto Archaeology Adventure. 2010. (Graphic Expeditions Ser.). (ENG., Illus.). 32p. (gr. 3-4). pap. 47.70 (978-1-4296-5714-3(6), Graphic Library) Capstone Press of Coughlan Cos.

Conklin, Wendy. You Are There! Pompeii 79. 2017. (TIME for KIDS(r) Nonfiction Readers Ser.). (Illus.). 32p. (J). (gr. 7-7). pap. 8.99 (978-1-4938-3615-4(3)) Teacher Created Materials, Inc.

—You Are There! Pompeii 79. 2017. (Time for Kids Nonfiction Readers Ser.). lib. bdg. 19.65 **(978-0-606-40293-4(4))** Turtleback Bks.

Deem, James M. Bodies from the Ash: Life & Death in Ancient Pompeii. 2005. (ENG., Illus.). 64p. (J). (gr. 5-7). 17.99 (978-0-618-47308-3(4)) Houghton Mifflin Harcourt Publishing Co.

Dunn, Mary. My Adventure at Pompeii. 2006. 44p. (J). 8.99 (978-1-59092-411-2(8)) Blue Forge Pr.

Gimpel, Diane Marczely. Pompeii, 1 vol. 2014. (Digging up the Past Ser.). (ENG.). 112p. (J). (gr. 6-12). lib. bdg. 35.64 (978-1-62403-236-3(2), Essential Library) ABDO Publishing Co.

Ginevra, Dante, contrib. by. Peril in Pompeii! Nickolas Flux & the Eruption of Mount Vesuvius, 1 vol. 2014. (Nickolas Flux History Chronicles Ser.). (ENG., Illus.). 32p. (gr. 3-4). lib. bdg. 30.65 (978-1-4914-0251-1(2), Graphic Library) Capstone Press of Coughlan Cos.

Johnson, Robin. Pompeii. 2012. (ENG.). 48p. (J). (978-0-7787-7927-8(0)); pap. (978-0-7787-7936-0(X)) Crabtree Publishing Co.

Kaplan, Sarah Pitt. Pompeii: City of Ashes. 2005. (High Interest Bks.). (ENG., Illus.). 48p. (J). (gr. 3-7). per. 6.95 (978-0-516-25091-5(4), Children's Pr.) Scholastic Library Publishing.

Levy, Janey. The City of Pompeii. 2015. (Doomed! Ser.). (ENG., Illus.). 32p. (J). (gr. 4-5). pap. 10.50 (978-1-4824-2924-4(1)) Stevens, Gareth Publishing LLLP.

Lindeen, Mary. Ashes to Ashes: Uncovering Pompeii. 2008. (Illus.). 36p. (J). pap. (978-0-531-15544-8(7)) Children's Pr., Ltd.

—Ashes to Ashes: Uncovering Pompeii. 2007. (Shockwave: People & Communities Ser.). (ENG., Illus.). 36p. (J). (gr. 3-5). 25.00 (978-0-531-17745-7(9), Children's Pr.) Scholastic Library Publishing.

Malam, John. Live in Pompeii! A Volcanic Eruption You'd Rather Avoid. Antram, David, illus. 2008. (You Wouldn't Want to Ser.). (ENG.). 32p. (J). (gr. 2-5). 29.00 (978-0-531-18748-7(9)); pap. 9.95 (978-0-531-16900-1(6), Watts, Franklin) Scholastic Library Publishing.

—You Wouldn't Want to Live in Pompeii! (Revised Edition) 2017. (You Wouldn't Want to... Ancient Civilizations Ser.). (ENG., Illus.). 32p. (J). lib. bdg. 29.00 (978-0-531-23836-3(9), Watts, Franklin) Scholastic Library Publishing.

O'Connor, Jim. What Was Pompeii? Harper, Fred & Hinderliter, John, illus. 2014. (What Was? Ser.). (ENG.). 112p. (J). (gr. 3-7). 5.99 (978-0-448-47907-1(9), Penguin Workshop) Penguin Young Readers Group.

—What Was Pompeii? 2014. (What Was... ? Ser.). lib. bdg. 16.00 (978-0-606-34155-4(2), Turtleback) Turtleback Bks.

Osborne, Mary Pope. Pompeii: Lost & Found. Christensen, Bonnie, illus. 2006. (ENG.). 40p. (J). (gr. -1-2). 16.95 (978-0-375-82889-8(3), Knopf Bks. for Young Readers) Random Hse. Children's Bks.

Osborne, Mary Pope & Boyce, Natalie Pope. Ancient Rome & Pompeii: A Nonfiction Companion to Vacation under the Volcano. Murdocca, Sal, illus. 2006. (Magic Tree House (R) Fact Tracker Ser.: 14). (ENG.). 128p. (J). (gr. 2-5). 6.99 (978-0-375-83220-8(3), Random Hse. Bks. for Young Readers) Random Hse. Children's Bks.

O'Shei, Tim. Secrets of Pompeii: Buried City of Ancient Rome, 1 vol. 2014. (Archaeological Mysteries Ser.). (ENG.). 32p. (gr. 3-4). lib. bdg. 27.99 (978-1-4765-9916-8(5)) Capstone Press of Coughlan Cos.

Roberts, Russell. Mt. Vesuvius & the Destruction of Pompei, A. D. 79. 2005. (Natural Disasters Ser.). (Illus.). 32p. (J). (gr. 1-4). lib. bdg. 25.70 (978-1-58415-419-8(5)) Mitchell Lane Pubs., Inc.

Samuel, Charlie. Solving the Mysteries of Pompeii. 2008. (Digging into History Ser.). 32p. (gr. 4-18). lib. bdg. 29.93 (978-0-7614-3105-3(5), Benchmark Bks.) Marshall Cavendish Corp.

Sonnebom, Liz. Pompeii. 2008. (Unearthing Ancient Worlds Ser.). (ENG., Illus.). 80p. (gr. 5-8). lib. bdg. 30.60 (978-0-8225-7505-4(1)) Lerner Publishing Group.

Wagner, Heather Lehr. Pompeii. 2012. (Lost Worlds & Mysterious Civilizations Ser.). (Illus.). 104p. (gr. 6-12). 35.00 (978-1-60413-971-6(4), Chelsea Hse.) Facts On File, Inc.

Waxman, Laura Hamilton. Mysteries of Pompeii. 2017. (Ancient Mysteries Ser.). (ENG.). 32p. (J). (gr. 3-6). 27.99 **(978-1-5124-4017-1(5))** Lerner Publishing Group.

POMPEII (EXTINCT CITY)—FICTION

Collins, Terry & Schulz, Barbara. Escape from Pompeii: An Isabel Soto Archaeology Adventure, 1 vol. 2010. (Graphic Expeditions Ser.). (ENG., Illus.). 32p. (gr. 3-4). pap. 8.10 (978-1-4296-5634-4(4), Graphic Library) Capstone Press of Coughlan Cos.

Collins, Terry, et al. Escape from Pompeii: An Isabel Soto Archaeology Adventure, 1 vol. 2010. (Graphic Expeditions Ser.). (ENG., Illus.). 32p. (gr. 3-4). lib. bdg. 30.65 (978-1-4296-4771-7(X), Graphic Library) Capstone Press of Coughlan Cos.

Collins, Tim. Diary of Dorkius Maximus in Pompeii. Pinder, Andrew, illus. 2015. (Diary of Dorkius Maximus Ser.: 3). (ENG.). 192p. (J). (gr. 4-6). pap. 10.99 (978-1-78055-268-2(8)) O'Mara, Michael Bks., Ltd. GBR. Dist: Independent Pubs. Group.

Osborne, Mary Pope. Vacation under the Volcano. unabr. ed. 2004. (Magic Tree House Ser.: No. 13). 74p. (J). (gr. k-3). pap. 17.00 incl. audio (978-0-8072-0782-6(9), LFTR 241 SP, Listening Library) Random Hse. Audio Publishing Group.

Peacock, L. A. Panic in Pompeii. Hale, Nathan, illus. 2011. 92p. (J). pap. (978-0-545-34062-5(4)) Scholastic, Inc.

Shecter, Vicky Alvear. Curses & Smoke: A Novel of Pompeii. 2014. (ENG.). 336p. (J). (gr. 7). 17.99 (978-0-545-50993-0(9), Levine, Arthur A. Bks.) Scholastic, Inc.

Tarshis, Lauren. I Survived the Destruction of Pompeii, 79 A. D. 2014. (I Survived Ser.: No. 10). (ENG.). 112p. (J). (gr. 2-5). pap. 4.99 (978-0-545-45939-6(7)) Scholastic, Inc.

Tarshis, Lauren. I Survived the Destruction of Pompeii, AD 79. Dawson, Scott, illus. 2014. 95p. (J). **(978-0-545-77568-7(X)**, Scholastic Pr.) Scholastic, Inc.

PONCE DE LEON, JUAN, 1460?-1521

Davenport, John. Juan Ponce de Leon & His Lands of Discovery. Goetzmann, William H., ed. 2005. (Explorers of New Lands Ser.). (Illus.). 110p. (gr. 5-8). lib. bdg. 30.00 (978-0-7910-8607-0(0)) Facts On File, Inc.

Donohue, Moira Rose. Juan Ponce de León. 2013. (Illus.). 24p. (J). (978-1-938813-06-1(5)) State Standards Publishing, LLC.

Eagen, Rachel. Ponce de Leon: Exploring Florida & Puerto Rico. 2005. (In the Footsteps of Explorers Ser.). (ENG., Illus.). 32p. (J). (gr. 4-5). pap. (978-0-7787-2448-3(4)) Crabtree Publishing Co.

Greenberger, Robert. Juan Ponce de Leon: The Exploration of Florida & the Search for the Fountain of Youth. rev. ed. (Library of Explorers & Explorationtm Ser.). (Illus.). 112p. (YA). (gr. 5-8). lib. bdg. 31.95 (978-1-4042-0635-9(3), Rosen Reference) Rosen Publishing Group, Inc., The.

Hoogenboom, Lynn. Juan Ponce de Leon. 2009. (Primary Source Library of Famous Explorers Ser.). 24p. (gr. 4-4). 42.50 (978-1-60854-128-7(2), PowerKids Pr.) Rosen Publishing Group, Inc., The.

—Juan Ponce de Leon: A Primary Source Biography. 2006. (Primary Source Library of Famous Explorers Ser.). (Illus.). 24p. (YA). (gr. 2-5). lib. bdg. 22.60 (978-1-4042-3040-8(8)) Rosen Publishing Group, Inc., The.

Molzahn, Arlene Bourgeois. Ponce de Leon: Explorer of Florida. 2003. (Explorers! Ser.). (Illus.). 48p. (J). lib. bdg. 23.93 (978-0-7660-2071-9(1)) Enslow Pubs., Inc.

O'Brien, Cynthia. Explore with Ponce de León. 2014. (ENG., Illus.). 32p. (J). (978-0-7787-1429-3(2)) Crabtree Publishing Co.

Otfinoski, Steven. Juan Ponce de Leon: Discoverer of Florida. 2004. (Great Explorations Ser.). 80p. (gr. 6). 22.95 (978-0-7614-1610-4(2), Benchmark Bks.) Marshall Cavendish Corp.

Pelleschi, Andrea. Juan Ponce de Leon. 2013. (Jr. Graphic Famous Explorers Ser.). (ENG., Illus.). 24p. (J). (gr. 3-6). pap. 10.60 (978-1-4777-0131-7(1)); lib. bdg. 25.25 (978-1-4777-0073-0(0)) Rosen Publishing Group, Inc., The. (PowerKids Pr.).

Petrie, Kristin. Juan Ponce de Leon, 1 vol. 2007. (Explorers Set 2 Ser.). (ENG., Illus.). 32p. (gr. 4-7). 27.07 (978-1-59679-742-0(8), Checkerboard Library) ABDO Publishing Co.

Sammons, Sandra Wallus. Ponce de Leon & the Discovery of Florida. 2013. (ENG., Illus.). 72p. (J). (gr. 4-6). 12.95 (978-1-56164-592-3(3)); pap. 9.95 (978-1-56164-593-0(1)) Pineapple Pr., Inc.

Shafer, Susan. Ponce de Leon & the Fountain of Youth. 2005. (J). pap. (978-1-4108-4231-2(2)) Benchmark Education Co.

Slavicek, Louise Chipley. Juan Ponce de Leon. 2003. (Great Hispanic Heritage Ser.). (Illus.). 112p. (gr. 6-12). 35.00 (978-0-7910-7255-4(X), Chelsea Hse.) Facts On File, Inc.

Sutcliffe, Jane. Juan Ponce de Leon. 2005. (History Maker Bios Ser.). (Illus.). 48p. (J). (gr. 3-7). lib. bdg. 26.60 (978-0-8225-2944-6(0), Lerner Pubns.) Lerner Publishing Group.

Waxman, Laura Hamilton. A Journey with Juan Ponce de León. 2017. (Primary Source Explorers Ser.). (ENG.). 40p. (J). (gr. 3-5). 30.65 (978-1-5124-0776-1(3)) Lerner Publishing Group.

Worth, Richard. Ponce de Leon & the Age of Spanish Exploration in World History. 2003. (In World History Ser.). (Illus.). 112p. (J). (gr. 5-12). lib. bdg. 26.60 (978-0-7660-1940-9(3)) Enslow Pubs., Inc.

POND ECOLOGY

see Freshwater Biology

PONIES

see also Horses

Andrekson, Judy. Little Squire: The Jumping Pony. Parkins, David, illus. 2007. (True Horse Stories Ser.). (ENG.). 80p. (J). (gr. 4-7). pap. 7.99 (978-0-88776-770-8(2), Tundra Bks.) Tundra Bks. CAN. Dist: Penguin Random Hse. LLC.

Aspen-Baxter, Linda & Kissock, Heather. Ponies. 2012. (SPA.). (J). (978-1-61913-191-0(9)) Weigl Pubs., Inc.

Aspley, Brenda. I Love Ponies. McNicolas, Shelagh, illus. 2013. (ENG.). 20p. (J). (gr. -1-k). 7.99 (978-1-84322-565-2(4), Armadillo) Anness Publishing GBR. Dist: National Bk. Network.

Beylon, Cathy. Let's Color Together — Horses & Ponies. 2014. (ENG., Illus.). 64p. (J). (gr. -1-3). pap. 3.99 (978-0-486-77974-4(2)) Dover Pubns., Inc.

Boone, Mary. Care for a Wild Chincoteague Pony. 2008. (How to Convince Your Parents You Can ... Ser.). (Illus.). 32p. (YA). (gr. 1-4). lib. bdg. 25.70 (978-1-58415-663-5(5)) Mitchell Lane Pubs., Inc.

Brett, Anna. Ponies. 2017. (My First Creativity Bks.). (ENG.). 66p. (J). (gr. -1-2). pap. 9.99 (978-1-4380-0968-1(2)) Barron's Educational Series, Inc.

Crabtree, Marc & Kalman, Bobbie. Les Poneys. 2012. (FRE., Illus.). 32p. (J). pap. 9.95 (978-2-89579-439-4(1)) Bayard Canada CAN. Dist: Crabtree Publishing Co.

Curry, Marion. Horse & Pony Basics. 2006. (Horses & Ponies Ser.). (Illus.). 32p. (gr. 2-6). lib. bdg. 23.00 (978-0-8368-6831-9(5), Gareth Stevens Learning Library) Stevens, Gareth Publishing LLLP.

—Horse & Pony Care. 2006. (Horses & Ponies Ser.). (Illus.). 32p. (gr. 2-6). lib. bdg. 23.00 (978-0-8368-6833-3(1), Gareth Stevens Learning Library) Stevens, Gareth Publishing LLLP.

de la Bédoyere, Camilla. Horses & Ponies. 2015. (100 Facts You Should Know Ser.). (ENG., Illus.). 48p. (J). (gr. 4-5). pap. 14.05 (978-1-4824-3199-5(8)) Stevens, Gareth Publishing LLLP.

Dell, Pamela. Shetland Ponies. 2014. (Majestic Horses Ser.). (ENG.). 24p. (J). (gr. 2-5). 28.50 (978-1-62687-007-9(1), 206796) Child's World, Inc., The.

Dickins, Rosie & Pratt, Leonie. Horse & Pony Treasury. Sims, Lesley, ed. Young, Norman & Ablett, Barry, illus. 2006. (Horse & Pony Treasury Ser.). 93p. (J). 19.99 (978-0-7945-1431-0(6), Usborne) EDC Publishing.

DK. The Amazing Book of My Little Pony. 2017. (ENG.). 48p. (J). (gr. k-3). 14.99 **(978-1-4654-6543-6(X)**, DK Children) Dorling Kindersley Publishing, Inc.

Dorling Kindersley Publishing Staff. Horses & Ponies. 2014. (Eye Wonder Ser.). (ENG.). 56p. (J). (gr. k-4). 10.99 (978-1-4654-1564-6(5), DK Children) Dorling Kindersley Publishing, Inc.

—Ponies. 2013. (Touch & Feel Ser.). (ENG.). 12p. (J). (gr. -1-k). bds. 6.99 (978-1-4654-0919-5(X), DK Children) Dorling Kindersley Publishing, Inc.

—Ponies & Horses. 2009. (DK Readers Ser.). (ENG.). 32p. (J). (gr. -1-1). 3.99 (978-0-7566-4295-2(7), DK Children) Dorling Kindersley Publishing, Inc.

—Ultimate Sticker Book: Horses & Ponies. 2017. (Ultimate Sticker Bks.). (ENG.). 32p. (J). (gr. k-2). pap. 6.99 (978-1-4654-5692-2(9), DK Children) Dorling Kindersley Publishing, Inc.

Draper, Judith & Roberts, Matthew. My First Horse & Pony Book: From Breeds & Bridles to Jophpurs & Jumping. 2005. (My First Horse & Pony Ser.). (ENG., Illus.). 48p. (J). (gr. k-3). 11.99 (978-0-7534-5878-5(0), 9780753458785, Kingfisher) Roaring Brook Pr.

Fodor's Travel Publications, Inc. Staff. Trot, Pony! 2016. (Readers Ser.). (ENG., Illus.). 24p. (J). (-k). pap. 3.99 (978-1-4263-2413-0(8), National Geographic Children's Bks.) National Geographic Society.

Ganeri, Anita. Winnie's Guide to Caring for Your Horse or Pony, 1 vol. Peterson, Rick, illus. 2013. (Pets' Guides). (ENG.). 32p. (gr. 1-3). pap. 8.29 (978-1-4329-7141-0(7)); lib. bdg. 27.32 (978-1-4329-7134-2(4)) Heinemann-Raintree. (Heinemann First Library).

Gates, Josephine Scribner. The land of Delight: Child life on a Pony Farm. 2007. (Illus.). 116p. (J). lib. bdg. 59.00 (978-1-60304-022-8(6)) Dollworks.

Green, Sara. The Shetland Pony. 2011. (Horse Breed Roundup Ser.). (ENG., Illus.). 24p. (J). (gr. 3-8). lib. bdg. 25.95 (978-1-60014-658-9(9), Pilot Bks.) Bellwether Media.

Gunzi, Christiane. Little Ponies: A Feels Real Book to Touch & Share. 2015. (ENG., Illus.). 8p. (J). 9.99 (978-1-909763-10-4(1)) Award Pubns. Ltd. GBR. Dist: Parkwest Pubns., Inc.

Harvey, G. & Dickens, R. Riding & Pony Care. 2004. (Complete Book of Riding & Pony Care Ser.). (Illus.). 144p. (J). (gr. 3-18). lib. bdg. 23.95 (978-1-58086-422-0(8)) EDC Publishing.

Head, Honor. Horses & Ponies. 2007. (QEB Know Your Pet Ser.). (Illus.). 32p. (J). lib. bdg. 19.95 (978-1-59566-219-4(7)) QEB Publishing Inc.

Henry, Lynn. Think Like a Pony: Foundation Book. 2008. (Think Like a Pony Ser.). (ENG., Illus.). 80p. (J). (gr. 3-18). pap. 16.95 (978-1-905693-09-2(5)) Quiller Publishing, Ltd. GBR. Dist: Independent Pubs. Group.

—Think Like a Pony on the Ground, 3 vols. 2008. (Think Like a Pony Ser.). (ENG., Illus.). 112p. (J). (gr. 3-18). pap., wbk. ed. 16.95 (978-1-905693-10-8(9)) Kenilworth Pr., Ltd. GBR. Dist: Independent Pubs. Group.

Horses & Ponies. 2009. (Reference Readers Ser.). 32p. (978-1-4075-1835-0(6)) Parragon, Inc.

Hudak, Heather C. Ponies. 2006. (Farm Animals Ser.). (Illus.). 24p. (J). (gr. 3-7). lib. bdg. 24.45 (978-1-59036-426-0(0)); per. 8.95 (978-1-59036-433-8(3)) Weigl Pubs., Inc.

Kaster, Pam. Molly the Pony: A True Story. 2008. (ENG., Illus.). 36p. (gr. 3-7). 17.95 (978-0-8071-3320-0(5), 9780807133200) Louisiana State Univ. Pr.

—Molly the Pony: A True Story. 2012. (My Readers: Level 3 Ser.). (J). lib. bdg. 13.55 (978-0-606-26125-8(7), Turtleback) Turtleback Bks.

Kelly, Miles. 100 Facts Horses & Ponies. 2017. (ENG.). pap. **(978-1-78617-013-2(2))** Miles Kelly Publishing, Ltd.

Khan, Sarah. Little Book of Horses & Ponies. Lambert, Stephen, illus. 2010. (Miniature Editions Ser.). 64p. (YA). (gr. 3-18). 6.99 (978-0-7945-2791-4(4), Usborne) EDC Publishing.

Kissock, Heather & Aspen-Baxter, Linda. Ponies. 2011. (J). (978-1-61690-575-0(1)); (978-1-61690-929-1(3)) Weigl Pubs., Inc.

Krementz, Jill. A Very Young Rider. Krementz, Jill, photos by. 2006. (Illus.). 124p. (gr. 4-7). 24.95 (978-0-9755516-2-2(0)) DreamHse. Publishing Inc.

Landau, Elaine. Shetland Ponies Are My Favorite! 2012. (My Favorite Horses Ser.). (ENG.). 24p. (gr. 3-5). lib. bdg. 22.60 (978-0-7613-6534-1(6), Lerner Pubns.) Lerner Publishing Group.

Lange, Nikki Bataille. My Little Pony: A Very Minty Christmas. LoRaso, Carlo, illus. gif. ed. 2005. 22p. (J). (gr. -1-1). bds. 13.99 (978-1-57791-191-3(1)) Brighter Minds Children's Publishing.

MacAulay, Kelley & Kalman, Bobbie. Ponies. Crabtree, Marc, illus. Crabtree, Marc, photos by. 2004. (Pet Care Ser.). (ENG.). 32p. (J). pap. (978-0-7787-1790-4(9)) Crabtree Publishing Co.

Make Believe Ideas, creator. Lift Stick & Learn Horse & Pony. 2006. (Lift Stick & Learn Ser.). (Illus.). 12p. (J). (gr. -1-k). pap. (978-1-84610-283-7(9)) Make Believe Ideas.

Marsh, Laura. National Geographic Readers: Ponies. 2011. (Readers Ser.). (ENG., Illus.). 32p. (J). (gr. k-3). lib. bdg. 13.90 (978-1-4263-0850-5(7), National Geographic Children's Bks.) National Geographic Society.

—Ponies. 2011. (Readers Ser.). (ENG., Illus.). 32p. (J). (gr. k-3). pap. 3.99 (978-1-4263-0849-9(3), National Geographic Children's Bks.) National Geographic Society.

—Ponies (1 Hardcover/1 CD) 2016. (National Geographic Readers: Pre-Reader Ser.). (ENG.). (J). (978-1-4301-2105-3(X)) Live Oak Media.

—Ponies (1 Paperback/1 CD) 2016. (National Geographic Readers: Pre-Reader Ser.). (ENG.). (J). pap. (978-1-4301-2104-6(1)) Live Oak Media.

Mason, Theodore. The South Pole Ponies. 2007. 232p. (gr. 7). per. 18.00 (978-1-59048-251-3(4)) Long Riders' Guild Pr., The.

Milbourne, Anna. Horses & Ponies. Gaudenzi, Giacinto & Haggerty, Tim, illus. 2006. (Beginners Nature: Level 1 Ser.). 32p. (J). (gr. k-2). 4.99 (978-0-7945-1397-9(2), Usborne) EDC Publishing.

Monahan, Erin. Ponis Shetland (Shetland Ponies) Strictly Spanish Translation Services Staff, tr. from ENG. 2012. (Cabollos/Horses Ser.). (ENG, SPA & MUL., Illus.). 24p. (gr. k-1). lib. bdg. 21.99 (978-1-4296-9228-1(6)) Capstone Press of Coughlan Cos.

National Geographic Editors. Favorite Animals Collection. 2013. (Readers Ser.). (ENG., Illus.). 128p. (J). (gr. -1-1). pap. 7.99 (978-1-4263-1333-2(0), National Geographic Children's Bks.) National Geographic Society.

National Geographic Kids Staff. Ponies & Horses. 2015. (NG Sticker Activity Bks.). (ENG.). 56p. (J). (gr. -1-3). pap., act. bk. ed. 6.99 (978-1-4263-1902-0(9), National Geographic Children's Bks.) National Geographic Society.

Needham, Kate. Pony Guide. 2006. (Illus.). 31p. (J). (978-0-439-78703-1(3)) Scholastic, Inc.

Needham, Louise. An Adventure with Katy the Pony. 2009. (Illus.). 36p. pap. 15.49 (978-1-4490-3972-1(3)) AuthorHouse.

Patchett, Fiona. Ponies (First Sticker Book) Finn, Rebecca, illus. 2011. (First Sticker Book Ser.). 24p. (J). pap. 6.99 (978-0-7945-2921-5(6), Usborne) EDC Publishing.

Pickeral, Tamsin. The Encyclopedia of Horses & Ponies. 2003. 384p. (YA). pap. 19.95 (978-0-7525-8277-1(1)) Parragon, Inc.

Pollack, Pam & Belviso, Meg. Ponies, Vol. 2. Bonforte, Lisa, illus. 2003. (Penguin Young Readers, Level 2 Ser.: Vol. 2). (ENG.). 48p. (J). (gr. 1-2). mass mkt. 3.99 (978-0-448-42524-5(6), Penguin Young Readers) Penguin Young Readers Group.

Ponies at Play. 12p. (J). (978-2-7643-0191-3(X)) Phidal Publishing, Inc./Editions Phidal, Inc.

Pony Club. 2012. (Illus.). 120p. (J). **(978-1-4351-4412-5(0))** Barnes & Noble, Inc.

Ransford, Sandy. The Kingfisher Illustrated Horse & Pony Encyclopedia. rev. ed. 2010. (ENG., Illus.). 224p. (J). (gr. 5-9). 24.99 (978-0-7534-6485-4(3), 9780753464854, Kingfisher) Roaring Brook Pr.

Reid, Struan. Dictionary of horses & ponies - internet Linked. Khan, Aziz, illus. rev. ed. 2004. 128p. (J). pap. 14.95 (978-0-7945-0843-2(X), Usborne) EDC Publishing.

Silverman, Buffy. Can You Tell a Horse from a Pony? 2012. (Lightning Bolt Books (tm) — Animal Look-Alikes Ser.). 32p. (gr. k-2). (ENG.). pap. 7.95 (978-0-7613-8554-7(1)); pap. 45.32 (978-0-7613-9256-9(4)); (ENG.). lib. bdg. 26.60 (978-0-7613-6740-6(3), Lerner Pubns.) Lerner Publishing Group.

Skeffington, Miranda. My Little Pony: Mini Pony Collector's Guide with Exclusive Figure. 2013. (ENG., Illus.). 240p. (J). (gr. 1-17). 19.00 (978-0-316-24907-2(6)) Little, Brown Bks. for Young Readers.

Smith, L. The Usborne Book of Horses & Ponies. rev. ed. 2004. (Young Nature Ser.). (Illus.). 32p. (Orig.). (J). pap. 6.95 (978-0-7945-0850-0(2), Usborne) EDC Publishing.

Szymanski, Lois. Chincoteague Pony Identification Cards, 1 vol. Kantjas, Linda, photos by. 2013. (ENG., Illus.). 75p. (J). pap. 19.99 (978-0-7643-4453-4(6), 9780764344534) Schiffer Publishing, Ltd.

Turnbull, Stephanie. Ponies. 2015. (My Favorite Horses Ser.). 24p. (gr. 2-5). 28.50 (978-1-62588-181-6(9)) Black Rabbit Bks.

—Ponies. 2015. (ENG., Illus.). 24p. (J). pap. 8.95 (978-1-77092-227-3(X)) RiverStream Publishing.

Van Cleaf, Kristin. Highland Ponies, 1 vol. 2006. (Horses Set 2 Ser.). (ENG., Illus.). 24p. (gr. k-6). 25.65 (978-1-59679-314-9(7), Checkerboard Library) ABDO Publishing Co.

Walker, Kathryn. See How Horses & Ponies Grow. 2009. (See How They Grow Ser.). (J). (gr. k-3). (ENG., Illus.). 24p. pap. 8.25 (978-1-4358-2881-0(X)); lib. bdg. 22.60 (978-1-4358-2832-2(1)) Rosen Publishing Group, Inc., The. (PowerKids Pr.).

Watts, Ana Dearborn & Dearborn, Dorothy. The Pony Princess. Taylor, Carol, illus. 2008. (ENG.). 32p. pap. 6.00 (978-1-896543-32-1(4)) DreamCatcher Publishing CAN. Dist: Univ. of Toronto Pr.

PONIES—FICTION

Abdo Publishing. My Little Pony, 1 vol. 2015. (My Little Pony Ser.: Vol. 6). (ENG.). 24p. (J). 145.26 (978-1-61479-330-4(1), Spotlight) ABDO Publishing Co.

—My Little Pony: Friendship Is Magic. 2015. (My Little Pony: Friendship Is Magic Ser.: Vol. 8). (ENG.). 24p. (J). (gr. 2-5). 193.68 (978-1-61479-375-5(1)) ABDO Publishing Co.

Alexander, Louise. Happy Haunting. 2016. (My Little Pony 8X8 Picture Bks.). (J). lib. bdg. 13.55 (978-0-606-38324-0(7)) Turtleback Bks.

—Legend of Everfree: Save Our Camp! 2016. (ENG.). 24p. (J). (gr. -1-3). pap. 4.99 (978-0-316-39530-4(7)) Little, Brown Bks. for Young Readers.

—My Little Pony: Happy Haunting. 2016. (ENG.). 24p. (J). (gr. -1-3). 8.99 (978-0-316-36150-7(X)) Little, Brown Bks. for Young Readers.

—The Reason for the Season. 2015. (My Little Pony 8X8 Picture Bks.). (J). lib. bdg. 13.55 (978-0-606-37511-5(2)) Turtleback Bks.

—School Spirit! 2015. (My Little Pony 8X8 Picture Bks.). (J). lib. bdg. 13.55 (978-0-606-37225-1(3)) Turtleback Bks.

Alexander, Samantha. Rachel, Vol. 6. 6th ed. (ENG.). 128p. mass mkt. 6.99 (978-0-330-36841-4(9), Pan) Pan Macmillan GBR. Dist: Trafalgar Square Publishing.

Anderson, Ted & Cook, Katie. My Little Pony: Equestria Girls. 2016. lib. bdg. 30.60 (978-0-606-37807-9(3)) Turtleback Bks.

Anderson, Ted, et al. My Little Pony: Pony Tales Volume 2: Pony Tales Volume 2. Mebberson, Amy, illus. 2014. (My Little Pony Ser.). (ENG.). 104p. pap. 17.99 (978-1-61377-873-9(2), 9781613778739) Idea & Design Works, LLC.

Angleberger, Tom. Crankee Doodle. Bell, Cece, illus. 2013. (ENG.). 32p. (J). (gr. -1-3). 16.99 (978-0-547-81854-2(8)) Houghton Mifflin Harcourt Publishing Co.

Ann, Sharrie. Granddaughter & King Green Warts. 2008. 24p. pap. 12.99 (978-1-4343-9470-5(0)) AuthorHouse.

Asquith, Ros. Trixie & the Dream Pony of Doom. 2010. (ENG., Illus.). 208p. (J). (gr. 3-6). pap. 9.99 (978-0-00-722358-9(7)) HarperCollins Pubs. Ltd. GBR. Dist: HarperCollins Pubs.

Baglio, Ben M. Searching for Sunshine. Beckett, Andrew & Aubrey, Meg Kelleher, illus. 2005. 158p. (J). (978-0-439-79249-3(5)) Scholastic, Inc.

Bak, Jenny. Color & Poster Book. Middleton, Gayle & Edwards, Ken, illus. 2006. (My Little Pony Ser.). 32p. (J). (gr. -1-1). 3.99 (978-0-06-079470-5(4), HarperFestival) HarperCollins Pubs.

Barkhouse, Joyce & Barkhouse, Janet. Pit Pony: The Picture Book. Smith, Sydney, illus. 2012. (ENG.). 32p. (J). (gr. -1-2). 14.95 (978-1-4595-0143-0(8), 9781459501430) Formac Publishing Co., Ltd. CAN. Dist: Casemate Pubs. & Bk. Distributors, LLC.

Bates, M. The Perfect Pony. 2004. (Sandy Lane Stables Ser.). (ENG.). 118p. (J). pap. 4.99 (978-0-7945-0505-9(8)) EDC Publishing.

Batts, Laura. Love Your Pony, Love Your Planet: All about Pony Poo & Other Helpful Things We Can Do! 2013. (ENG., Illus.). 16.95 (978-1-62086-303-9(0)) Mascot Bks., Inc.

Baxter, Nicola. My Book of Magical Pony Tales: 12 Beautifully Illustrated Stories. Shuttleworth, Cathie, illus. 2013. (ENG.). 80p. (J). (gr. -1-12). pap. 9.99 (978-1-84322-965-0(X)) Anness Publishing GBR. Dist: National Bk. Network.

Beaton, Kate. The Princess & the Pony. 2015. (ENG., Illus.). 40p. (J). (gr. -1-3). 17.99 (978-0-545-63708-4(2)) Scholastic, Inc.

Belle, Magnolia. My Little Pony: Power Ponies to the Rescue! 2015. (Passport to Reading Level 1 Ser.). (J). lib. bdg. 13.55 (978-0-606-37224-4(5)) Turtleback Bks.

—My Little Pony: Crusaders of the Lost Mark. 2016. (ENG., Illus.). 24p. (J). (gr. -1-3). pap. 4.99 (978-0-316-26545-4(4)) Little, Brown Bks. for Young Readers.

—My Little Pony: Pinkie Pie Keeps a Secret. 2016. (Passport to Reading Level 1 Ser.). (ENG., Illus.). 32p. (J). (gr. -1-3). pap. 4.99 (978-0-316-26734-2(1)) Little, Brown Bks. for Young Readers.

—My Little Pony: Rainbow Dash & the Great Cookie Prank. 2017. (ENG., Illus.). 32p. (J). (gr. -1-3). pap. 4.99 **(978-0-316-43176-7(1))** Little, Brown Bks. for Young Readers.

Belle, Magnolia. Pinkie Pie Keeps a Secret. 2016. (Passport to Reading Level 1 Ser.). (Illus.). 32p. (J). lib. bdg. 14.75 (978-0-606-38323-3(9)) Turtleback Bks.

Beloat, Betty. The Winged Pony. Schwartz, Wendy, illus. 2005. 32p. (J). (gr. k-5). pap. 5.99 (978-0-9701008-8-7(4)) Bicast, Inc.

Benjamin, Ruth. My Little Pony: A Secret Gift. Middleton, Gayle, illus. 2006. 24p. (J). lib. bdg. 15.00 (978-1-4242-1536-2(6)) Fitzgerald Bks.

—A Secret Gift/el Regalo Secreto. Abboud, Adela, tr. from ENG. Middleton, Gayle, illus. 2006. (I Can Read Bks.). (SPA & ENG.). 24p. (J). (gr. k-3). per. 3.99 (978-0-06-112391-7(9), Rayo) HarperCollins Pubs.

Bentley, Sue. Circus Surprise #7. Swan, Angela, illus. 2014. (Magic Ponies Ser.: 7). (ENG.). 128p. (J). (gr. 1-3). 4.99 (978-0-448-46734-4(8), Grosset & Dunlap) Penguin Young Readers Group.

—New Beginning, No. 1. Swan, Angela & Farley, Andrew, illus. 2009. (Magic Puppy Ser.: 1). (ENG.). 128p. (J). (gr. 1-3). pap. 5.99 (978-0-448-45044-5(5), Grosset & Dunlap) Penguin Young Readers Group.

—A New Friend, No. 1. Swan, Angela, illus. 2013. (Magic Ponies Ser.: 1). (ENG.). 128p. (J). (gr. 1-3). pap. 5.99 (978-0-448-46205-9(2), Grosset & Dunlap) Penguin Young Readers Group.

—A New Friend. 2013. (Magic Ponies Ser.: 1). lib. bdg. 16.00 (978-0-606-29584-0(4), Turtleback) Turtleback Bks.

—Pony Camp. 2014. (Magic Ponies Ser.: 8). lib. bdg. 16.00 (978-0-606-34139-4(0), Turtleback) Turtleback Bks.

—Pony Camp #8. Swan, Angela, illus. 2014. (Magic Ponies Ser.: 8). (ENG.). 128p. (J). (gr. 1-3). 5.99 (978-0-448-46787-0(9), Grosset & Dunlap) Penguin Young Readers Group.

—Riding Rescue #6. Swan, Angela, illus. 2013. (Magic Ponies Ser.: 6). (ENG.). 128p. (J). (gr. 1-3). 4.99 (978-0-448-46735-1(6), Grosset & Dunlap) Penguin Young Readers Group.

—Show-Jumping Dreams. 2013. (Magic Ponies Ser.: 4). lib. bdg. 14.75 (978-0-606-31679-8(5), Turtleback) Turtleback Bks.

—Show-Jumping Dreams #4. Swan, Angela, illus. 2013. (Magic Ponies Ser.: 4). (ENG.). 128p. (J). (gr. 1-3). pap. 5.99 (978-0-448-46208-0(7), Grosset & Dunlap) Penguin Young Readers Group.

—A Special Wish, No. 2. Swan, Angela, illus. 2013. (Magic Ponies Ser.: 2). (ENG.). 128p. (J). (gr. 1-3). pap. 4.99 (978-0-448-46206-6(0), Grosset & Dunlap) Penguin Young Readers Group.

—A Special Wish. 2013. (Magic Ponies Ser.: 2). lib. bdg. 14.75 (978-0-606-29758-5(8), Turtleback) Turtleback Bks.

—A Twinkle of Hooves #3. Swan, Angela, illus. 2013. (Magic Ponies Ser.: 3). (ENG.). 128p. (J). (gr. 1-3). pap. 4.99 (978-0-448-46207-3(9), Grosset & Dunlap) Penguin Young Readers Group.

—Winter Wonderland. 2013. (Magic Ponies Ser.: 5). lib. bdg. 16.00 (978-0-606-32118-1(7), Turtleback) Turtleback Bks.

—Winter Wonderland #5. Swan, Angela, illus. 2013. (Magic Ponies Ser.: 5). (ENG.). 128p. (J). (gr. 1-3). 5.99 (978-0-448-46786-3(0), Grosset & Dunlap) Penguin Young Readers Group.

Berenstain, Jan & Berenstain, Mike. The Berenstain Bears & the Shaggy Little Pony. Berenstain, Jan & Berenstain, Mike, illus. 2011. (I Can Read Level 1 Ser.). (ENG., Illus.). 32p. (J). (gr. k-3). 16.99 (978-0-06-168972-7(6)); pap. 3.99 (978-0-06-057419-2(4)) HarperCollins Pubs.

Berrow, G. M. Discord & the Ponyville Players Dramarama. 2015. (My Little Pony Chapter Bks.). (J). lib. bdg. 16.00 (978-0-606-37226-8(1)) Turtleback Bks.

—Fluttershy & the Fine Furry Friends Fair. 2015. (My Little Pony Chapter Bks.). (J). lib. bdg. 16.00 (978-0-606-35942-9(7)) Turtleback Bks.

—Friendship Is Magic. 2016. (ENG., Illus.). 144p. (J). (gr. 3-7). pap. 5.99 (978-0-316-26631-4(0)) Little, Brown Bks. for Young Readers.

—Lyra & Bon Bon & the Mares from S. M. I. L. E. 2016. (My Little Pony Chapter Bks.). (J). lib. bdg. 16.00 (978-0-606-38301-1(8)) Turtleback Bks.

—My Little Pony: Applejack & the Honest-To-Goodness Switcheroo. 2014. (ENG.). 160p. (J). (gr. 3-7). pap. 5.99 (978-0-316-24825-9(8)) Little, Brown Bks. for Young Readers.

—My Little Pony: Daring Do & the Eternal Flower. 2016. (Daring Do Adventure Collection). (ENG.). 208p. (J). (gr. 5-7). 9.99 (978-0-316-38934-1(X)) Little, Brown Bks. for Young Readers.

—My Little Pony: Equestria Girls: Through the Mirror. 2013. (Equestria Girls Ser.: 1). (ENG.). 240p. (J). (gr. 3-7). 9.99 (978-0-316-24762-7(6)) Little, Brown Bks. for Young Readers.

—My Little Pony: Pinkie Pie & the Rockin' Ponypalooza Party! 2013. (ENG.). 160p. (J). (gr. 3-7). pap. 5.99 (978-0-316-22818-3(4)) Little, Brown Bks. for Young Readers.

—My Little Pony: Princess Cadance & the Spring Hearts Garden. 2016. (Princess Collection). (ENG., Illus.). 160p. (J). (gr. 3-7). 9.99 (978-0-316-38930-3(7)) Little, Brown Bks. for Young Readers.

—My Little Pony: Rarity & the Curious Case of Charity. 2014. (ENG.). 176p. (J). (gr. 3-7). pap. 5.99 (978-0-316-24808-2(8)) Little, Brown Bks. for Young Readers.

—My Little Pony: Twilight Sparkle & the Forgotten Books of Autumn. 2016. (Princess Collection). (ENG., Illus.). 160p. (J). (gr. 3-7). 9.99 (978-0-316-38996-9(X)) Little, Brown Bks. for Young Readers.

—Pinkie Pie & the Rockin' Ponypalooza Party! 2013. (My Little Pony Chapter Bks.). (J). lib. bdg. 16.00 (978-0-606-35299-4(6)) Turtleback Bks.

—Rainbow Dash & the Daring Do Double Dare. 2014. (My Little Pony Chapter Bks.). (J). lib. bdg. 16.00 (978-0-606-34089-2(0), Turtleback) Turtleback Bks.

—Rarity & the Curious Case of Charity. 2014. (My Little Pony Chapter Bks.). (J). lib. bdg. 16.00 (978-0-606-35300-7(3)) Turtleback Bks.

—Trixie & the Razzle-Dazzle Ruse. 2017. (ENG.). 144p. (J). (gr. 3-7). pap. 5.99 (978-0-316-30163-3(9)) Little, Brown Bks. for Young Readers.

—The Trouble with Trixie. 2017. (My Little Pony Chapter Bks.). (J). lib. bdg. 16.00 (978-0-606-39477-2(X)) Turtleback Bks.

—Twilight Sparkle & the Crystal Heart Spell. 2013. (My Little Pony Chapter Bks.). (J). lib. bdg. 16.00 (978-0-606-31733-7(3), Turtleback) Turtleback Bks.

Betancourt, Jeanne. Penny & Pepper. Riley, Kellee, illus. 2011. (Scholastic Reader Level 3 Ser.). (ENG.). 48p. (J). (gr. 1-4). pap. 3.99 (978-0-545-11508-7(6), Cartwheel Bks.) Scholastic, Inc.

Bhakta, Sanjini. The Chocolate Pony. 2010. 28p. pap. 12.99 (978-1-4490-9761-5(8)) AuthorHouse.

Blyton, Enid. Pretty Star the Pony: And Other Stories. 2013. (ENG., Illus.). 192p. (J). 9.95 (978-1-84135-459-0(7)) Award Pubns. Ltd. GBR. Dist: Parkwest Pubns., Inc.

Braddock, Pauline. Humbug. 2010. 108p. pap. 8.48 (978-1-4452-9227-4(0)) Lulu Pr., Inc.

Brooks, Heather. Hercules: A Matter of Trust. 2009. (Running Horse Ridge Ser.: 2). (ENG.). 224p. (J). (gr. 5-18). pap. 6.99 (978-0-06-142981-1(3)) HarperCollins Pubs.

Brown, Kathryn. Adventures at Aaron Loch Farm. 2009. 50p. pap. 23.50 (978-1-4092-6961-8(2)) Lulu Pr., Inc.

Burgess, Pauline. Pony Palace Camp. 2014. (Pony Friends Forever Ser.). (ENG., Illus.). 128p. (J). pap. 12.00 (978-0-85640-923-3(5)) Blackstaff Pr., Ltd. GBR. Dist: Dufour Editions, Inc.

—Pony Surprise. 2014. (Pony Friends Forever Ser.). (ENG., Illus.). 93p. (J). pap. 12.00 (978-0-85640-936-3(7)) Blackstaff Pr., Ltd. GBR. Dist: Dufour Editions, Inc.

Campbell, James & Mould, Chris. Boyface & the Uncertain Ponies. 2015. (Boyface Ser.). (ENG., Illus.). 144p. (J). (gr. 2-4). pap. 8.99 (978-1-4449-1805-2(2)) Hodder & Stoughton GBR. Dist: Hachette Bk. Group.

Carithers, Rochelle. The Purple with Pink Polka Dot Ponies. Weber, Caressa, illus. 2010. 102p. pap. 7.95 (978-1-936107-31-5(7)) Salem Author Services.

Carlson, Nolan. Lame Eagle & Wind Chaser. 2005. (YA). per. (978-0-9772745-1-2(9)) Mennonite Pr. Inc.

Causton, Linda. Lester's Rainy Lake Pony. l.t. ed. 2004. (Illus.). 32p. (J). 12.00 (978-1-930374-09-6(7)) DeForest Pr.

Chapman, Linda. Flying High. Hull, Biz & Farley, Andrew, illus. 2004. (My Secret Unicorn Ser.). 118p. (J). (978-0-439-65273-5(1)) Scholastic, Inc.

—Starlight Surprise, Vol. 4. 4th ed. 2003. (ENG., Illus.). 144p. pap. (978-0-14-131344-3(7), Puffin) Penguin Bks., Ltd.

—Starlight Surprise. Hull, Biz, illus. 2003. (My Secret Unicorn Ser.). 130p. (J). (978-0-439-65275-9(8)) Scholastic, Inc.

—Twilight Magic. Kronheimer, Ann, illus. 2008. 149p. (J). pap. (978-0-545-03160-8(5)) Scholastic, Inc.

Chapman, Marian. The Purple Pony. 2004. 56p. pap. 20.99 (978-1-4134-2363-1(9)) Xlibris Corp.

Chase, Diana. Daisy Street. Bradley, Vanessa, illus. 2005. 128p. (Orig.). (J). pap. 13.50 (978-1-920731-11-3(3)) Fremantle Pr. AUS. Dist: Independent Pubs. Group.

Chasing Gold. 2014. (Marguerite Henry's Ponies of Chincoteague Ser.: 3). (ENG., Illus.). 192p. (J). (gr. 3-7). pap. 6.99 (978-1-4814-0342-9(7), Aladdin) Simon & Schuster Children's Publishing.

Chester, Laura. Marvel the Marvelous. Lippincott, Gary A., illus. 2008. (ENG.). 176p. (J). 18.95 (978-1-59543-841-6(6)) Willow Creek Pr., Inc.

Clay, Tim. Pippa the Pony. 2017. (ENG.). 30p. (J). pap. 11.95 **(978-1-78693-515-1(5)**, 780386c6-116d-495a-9918-b7f18386f44a) Austin, Stan AUS. Dist: Bookmasters Distribution.

Clover, Peter. Rescue Riders: Ghost Pony. l.t. ed. 2007. 92p. per. (978-1-905665-28-0(8)) Pollinger In Print.

—Rescue Riders: Race Against Time. l.t. ed. 2007. 88p. per. (978-1-905665-29-7(6)) Pollinger In Print.

—Sheltie & the Stray. 2005. (Illus.). 91p. (J). *(978-0-439-68890-1(6))* Scholastic, Inc.

—Sheltie in Trouble. 2005. 89p. (J). *(978-0-439-68889-5(2))* Scholastic, Inc.

Cochrane, Ian. Shian & the Corryvreckan. 2013. (Illus.). 96p. pap. *(978-1-909465-09-1(7))* Cloister Hse. Pr., The.

Cook, Katie. Friendship Is Magic, Vol. 1. Price, Andy, illus. 2014. (My Little Pony Ser.). (ENG.). 104p. pap. 17.99 *(978-1-61377-605-6(5)*, 9781613776056) Idea & Design Works, LLC.

—My Little Pony: Friendship Is Magic Part 1: Friendship Is Magic Part 1. Price, Andy, illus. 2013. (My Little Pony Ser.). (ENG.). 52p. (J). (gr. 2-5). pap. 6.99 *(978-1-61377-628-5(4)*, 9781613776285) Idea & Design Works, LLC.

—My Little Pony: Friendship Is Magic Part 2: Friendship Is Magic Part 2. Price, Andy, illus. 2014. (My Little Pony Ser.). (ENG.). 52p. (J). (gr. 2-5). pap. 6.99 *(978-1-61377-860-9(0)*, 9781613778609) Idea & Design Works, LLC.

—My Little Pony: Friendship Is Magic Volume 3: Friendship Is Magic Volume 3. Price, Andy, illus. 2014. (My Little Pony Ser.). (ENG.). 104p. pap. 17.99 *(978-1-61377-854-8(6)*, 9781613778548) Idea & Design Works, LLC.

Cotten, Cynthia. Snow Ponies. Cockcroft, Jason, illus. 2013. (ENG.). 32p. (J). (gr. -1-1). 6.99 *(978-1-250-03429-8(9)*, 9781250034298) Square Fish.

Crawford, Hannah. The Fight for Light by Hannah Crawford. 2012. (Illus.). 86p. pap. 8.50 *(978-1-78035-335-7(9)*, Fastprint Publishing) Upfront Publishing Ltd. GBR. Dist: Printondemand-worldwide.com.

—The Fight with Darkness. 2013. (Illus.). 79p. pap. 8.49 *(978-1-78035-586-3(6)*, Fastprint Publishing) Upfront Publishing Ltd. GBR. Dist: Printondemand-worldwide.com.

Dahl, Michael. Pony Brushes His Teeth, 1 vol. Vidal, Oriol, illus. 2010. (Hello Genius Ser.). (ENG.). 20p. (gr. 1-2). bds. 7.99 *(978-1-4048-5727-8(3))* Picture Window Bks.

David, Erica. The Big Pony Race. Fruchter, Jason, illus. 2006. 27p. (J). *(978-0-7172-9869-3(8))* Scholastic, Inc.

Davidson, Susanna. Princess Polly & the Pony. Hill, Dave, illus. 2007. (First Reading Level 4 Ser.). 48p. (J). 8.99 *(978-0-7945-1756-4(0)*, Usborne) EDC Publishing.

—Stories of Magic Ponies. Costa, Jana, illus. 2007. (Young Reading Series 1 Gift Bks). 48p. (J). 8.99 *(978-0-7945-1790-8(0)*, Usborne) EDC Publishing.

Davis, David Denton. Polly's Promise: A Story about Thriving Rather Than Simply Surviving... Turning Apparent Disability into Gifted Ability. 2013. 80p. pap. 21.95 *(978-1-4787-0275-7(3))* Outskirts Pr., Inc.

Dawson, JoAnn S. Lady's Big Surprise. 2004. 288p. pap. 8.95 *(978-0-9746561-6-8(X))*; (Illus.). 15.95 *(978-0-9746561-5-1(1))* FT Richards Publishing.

—Star of Wonder. 2005. (Illus.). 268p. pap. 8.95 *(978-0-9746561-4-4(3))* FT Richards Publishing.

Doty, Jean Slaughter. Can I Get There by Candlelight? 2012. (ENG.). 128p. (YA). (gr. 7). pap. 7.99 *(978-1-4424-8608-9(2)*, Simon & Schuster Bks. For Young Readers) Simon & Schuster Bks. For Young Readers.

—Summer Pony. Sanderson, Ruth, illus. 2008. (Stepping Stone Book Ser.). (ENG.). 144p. (J). (gr. 1-4). pap. 3.99 *(978-0-375-84709-7(X)*, Random Hse. Bks. for Young Readers) Random Hse. Children's Bks.

—The Valley of the Ponies. 2012. (ENG.). 96p. (YA). (gr. 7-7). pap. 6.99 *(978-1-4424-8607-2(4)*, Simon & Schuster Bks. For Young Readers) Simon & Schuster Bks. For Young Readers.

—Winter Pony. Sanderson, Ruth, illus. 2008. (Stepping Stone Book Ser.). (ENG.). 144p. (J). (gr. 1-4). 3.99 *(978-0-375-84710-3(3)*, Random Hse. Bks. for Young Readers) Random Hse. Children's Bks.

Doucet, Patricia. The Adventures of Blackie & Brownie. 2012. 26p. pap. 19.99 *(978-1-62230-887-3(5))* Salem Author Services.

Dowling, Iris Gray. A Pony for My Birthday. Bouthyette, Valerie, illus. 2012. 36p. pap. 10.99 *(978-1-937129-50-7(0))* Faithful Life Pubs.

Dream Pony (revised) 2017. (Sandy Lane Stables Ser.). (ENG.). (J). pap. 5.99 ***(978-0-7945-3624-4(7)***, Usborne) EDC Publishing.

Earhart, Kristin. Finding Luck. Geddess, Serena, illus. 2016. (Marguerite Henry's Misty Inn Ser.: 4). (ENG.). 128p. (J). (gr. 2-5). pap. 5.99 *(978-1-4814-1422-7(4)*, Aladdin) Simon & Schuster Children's Publishing.

—Roscoe & the Pony Parade. Gurney, John Steven, illus. 2008. (Little Apple Ser.). 88p. (J). *(978-0-545-08094-1(0))* Scholastic, Inc.

Edmonds, Lin. Jaden & the Terrible Terrible Toad. 2011. 36p. pap. 15.14 *(978-1-4634-1112-1(X))* AuthorHouse.

—Patric the Pony & the Golden Salamander. 2009. 32p. pap. 13.99 *(978-1-4389-8021-8(3))* AuthorHouse.

Eveleigh, Victoria. Katy's Pony Challenge. 2016. (Katy's Exmoor Ponies Ser.). (ENG., Illus.). 144p. (J). (gr. 2-4). 7.99 *(978-1-4440-1451-8(X)*, Orion Children's Bks.) Hachette Children's Group GBR. Dist: Hachette Bk. Group.

—Katy's Pony Surprise. 2012. (ENG., Illus.). 128p. (J). (gr. 2-4). 7.99 *(978-1-4440-0553-0(7)*, Orion Children's Bks.) Hachette Children's Group GBR. Dist: Hachette Bk. Group.

Feaster, Raven Joye Raye. Merrileggs of Macon County. 2011. 72p. (gr. -1). pap. 10.75 *(978-1-4567-6971-0(5))* AuthorHouse.

Finn, Perdita. Equestria Girls: Friendship Games. 2015. (Equestria Girls Ser.: 5). (ENG., Illus.). 208p. (J). (gr. 3-7). 9.99 *(978-0-316-41080-9(2))* Little, Brown Bks. for Young Readers.

—The Mane Event. 2014. (Equestria Girls Ser.: 3). (ENG.). 240p. (J). (gr. 3-7). 9.99 *(978-0-316-24777-1(4))* Little, Brown Bks. for Young Readers.

—My Little Pony: Equestria Girls: Magic, Magic Everywhere! 2017. (Equestria Girls Ser.: 8). (ENG.). 208p. (J). (gr. 3-7). 9.99 ***(978-0-316-43186-6(9))*** Little, Brown Bks. for Young Readers.

—My Little Pony: Equestria Girls: the Legend of Everfree. 2016. (Equestria Girls Ser.: 7). (ENG.). 240p. (J). (gr. 3-7). 10.99 *(978-0-316-39537-3(4))* Little, Brown Bks. for Young Readers.

—Rainbow Rocks. 2014. (Equestria Girls Ser.: 2). (ENG.). 192p. (J). (gr. 3-7). 9.99 *(978-0-316-28486-8(6))* Little, Brown Bks. for Young Readers.

Fisher, Marilyn Anne. Pony Tales. 2005. (Illus.). 75p. (J). per. 20.00 *(978-1-890306-90-8(8))* Warwick Hse. Publishing.

Flaxenwick, Dim. Dobbin, Our Favourite Pony: Dobbin & the Little Red Squirrel. 2012. 44p. pap. 20.72 *(978-1-4669-2179-5(X))* Trafford Publishing.

Foltz, Joanna "Gwen". The Owl Tree. 2011. 28p. pap. 13.59 *(978-1-4634-1199-2(5))* AuthorHouse.

Fox, Jennifer. My Little Pony: Hearts & Hooves. 2013. (Passport to Reading Level 1 Ser.). (ENG., Illus.). 32p. (J). (gr. -1-3). 4.99 *(978-0-316-24797-9(9))* Little, Brown Bks. for Young Readers.

—We Like Spike! 2015. (Passport to Reading Level 1 Ser.). (J). lib. bdg. 13.55 *(978-0-606-37512-2(0))* Turtleback Bks.

Francis, Anwen. Siani Shetland. 2008. (ENG.). 84p. (J). pap. 9.95 *(978-1-905762-62-0(3))* Parthian Bks. GBR. Dist: Independent Pubs. Group.

Garis, Howard R. The Curlytops & Their Pets. 2009. 120p. 22.95 *(978-1-60664-609-0(5))*; pap. 10.95 *(978-1-60664-341-9(X))* Rodgers, Alan Bks.

—The Curlytops at Uncle Frank's Ranch; or, Little Folks on Ponyback. 2007. 160p. per. *(978-1-4065-2763-6(7))* Dodo Pr.

Gaydos, Nora. Phonics Comics: Pony Tales - Level 1. Hamilton, Pamela, illus. 2007. (ENG.). 24p. (J). (gr. 1-17). per. 3.99 *(978-1-58476-553-0(4))* Innovative Kids.

Gleadhill, Christa J. Here Comes Lucky! 2011. 16p. pap. 9.99 *(978-1-257-03275-4(5))* Lulu Pr., Inc.

Golden Books. Barbie: My Book of Ponies (Barbie) 2016. (Little Golden Book Ser.). (ENG., Illus.). 24p. (J). (-k). 4.99 *(978-0-399-54960-1(9)*, Golden Bks.) Random Hse. Children's Bks.

Gorman, Patrick. Alicia & Policia, 1 vol. Gorman, Kyrsten, illus. 2010. 24p. 24.95 *(978-1-4489-6425-3(3))* PublishAmerica, Inc.

Green, D. L. Sparkling Jewel. Wallis, Emily, illus. 2015. (Silver Pony Ranch Ser.: 1). (ENG.). 96p. (J). (gr. 1-3). pap. 4.99 *(978-0-545-79765-8(9))* Scholastic, Inc.

—Sweet Buttercup. Wallis, Emily, illus. 2016. (Silver Pony Ranch Ser.: 2). (ENG.). 96p. (J). (gr. 1-3). 15.99 *(978-0-545-79770-2(5))* Scholastic, Inc.

Gregg, Stacy. Comet & the Champion's Cup, 5. 2015. (Pony Club Secrets Ser.: 5). (ENG., Illus.). 256p. (J). pap. 6.99 *(978-0-00-727030-9(5)*, HarperCollins Children's Bks.) HarperCollins Pubs. Ltd. GBR. Dist: HarperCollins Pubs.

—Stardust & the Daredevil Ponies, 4. 2015. (Pony Club Secrets Ser.: 4). (ENG., Illus.). 240p. (J). pap. 6.99 *(978-0-00-724516-1(5)*, HarperCollins Children's Bks.) HarperCollins Pubs. Ltd. GBR. Dist: HarperCollins Pubs.

Griffiths, Gary Wayne. Hawaiian Ponies: A Mystery in Paradise, 1 vol. 2010. 48p. pap. 16.95 *(978-1-4489-4793-5(6))* America Star Bks.

Grimes, Terri & Timmons, Jasmine. A Pony Named Penny. 2007. 16p. 11.95 *(978-0-615-15990-4(7))* Dm Productions.

Grovet, Heather. Blondie's Big Ride. 2008. (Illus.). 95p. (J). pap. 5.97 *(978-0-8163-2225-1(2))* Pacific Pr. Publishing Assn.

—A Friend for Zipper. 2008. (J). pap. 5.97 *(978-0-8163-2226-8(0))* Pacific Pr. Publishing Assn.

—Super Star Problems. 2008. (J). pap. 5.97 *(978-0-8163-2255-8(4))* Pacific Pr. Publishing Assn.

Haas, Jessie. Birthday Pony. Apple, Margot, illus. 2004. 80p. (J). (gr. 2-18). 15.99 *(978-0-06-057359-1(7))* HarperCollins Pubs.

Haberler, Julia. Carnival Pony. 2008. 46p. pap. 18.95 *(978-0-557-03179-5(6))* Lulu Pr., Inc.

Hagman, Harvey Dixon. Majesty from Assateague, 1 vol. Aiken, David, illus. 2009. (ENG.). 80p. (J). pap. 8.95 *(978-0-87033-552-5(9)*, 9780870335525, Cornell Maritime Pr./Tidewater Pubs.) Schiffer Publishing, Ltd.

Hapka, Catherine, pseud. ASPCA Pet Rescue Club: the Lonely Pony. 2015. (Pet Rescue Club Ser.: 3). (ENG., Illus.). 128p. (J). (gr. 1-3). lib. bdg. 16.99 *(978-0-7944-3454-0(1))* Reader's Digest Assn., Inc., The.

—At the Show. Kennedy, Anne, illus. 2011. (I Can Read Level 2 Ser.). (ENG.). 32p. (J). (gr. -1-3). pap. 3.99 *(978-0-06-125544-1(0))* HarperCollins Pubs.

—Back in the Saddle. Kennedy, Anne, illus. 2011. (I Can Read Level 2 Ser.). (ENG.). 32p. (J). (gr. k-3). 16.99 *(978-0-06-125539-7(4))*; pap. 3.99 *(978-0-06-125541-0(6))* HarperCollins Pubs.

—Back in the Saddle. 2016. (Marguerite Henry's Ponies of Chincoteague Ser.: 7). (ENG., Illus.). 192p. (J). (gr. 3-7). pap. 6.99 *(978-1-4814-5993-8(7)*, Aladdin) Simon & Schuster Children's Publishing.

—Blue Ribbon Day. Kennedy, Anne, illus. 2013. (I Can Read Level 2 Ser.). (ENG.). 32p. (J). (gr. -1-3). 16.99 *(978-0-06-208677-8(4))* HarperCollins Pubs.

—Blue Ribbon Summer. 2014. (Marguerite Henry's Ponies of Chincoteague Ser.: 2). (ENG., Illus.). 208p. (J). (gr. 3-7). pap. 6.99 *(978-1-4814-0339-9(7)*, Aladdin) Simon & Schuster Children's Publishing.

—The Camping Trip. 2014. (Pony Scouts: I Can Read! Ser.). (J). lib. bdg. 13.55 *(978-0-606-35069-3(1)*, Turtleback) Turtleback Bks.

—Moonlight Mile. 2015. (Marguerite Henry's Ponies of Chincoteague Ser.: 4). (ENG., Illus.). 192p. (J). (gr. 3-7). pap. 6.99 *(978-1-4814-0345-0(1)*, Aladdin) Simon & Schuster Children's Publishing.

—The New Pony. Kennedy, Anne, illus. 2013. (I Can Read Level 2 Ser.). (ENG.). 32p. (J). (gr. -1-3). 16.99 *(978-0-06-208674-7(X))* HarperCollins Pubs.

—Pony Crazy. Kennedy, Anne, illus. 2009. (I Can Read Level 2 Ser.). (ENG.). 32p. (J). (gr. -1-3). 16.99 *(978-0-06-125533-5(5))* HarperCollins Pubs.

—Pony Scouts - Pony Party. Kennedy, Anne, illus. 2013. (I Can Read Level 2 Ser.). (ENG.). 32p. (J). (gr. -1-3). 16.99 *(978-0-06-208680-8(4))*; pap. 3.99 *(978-0-06-208679-2(0))* HarperCollins Pubs.

—Pony Scouts - The Camping Trip. Kennedy, Anne, illus. 2014. (I Can Read Level 2 Ser.). (ENG.). 32p. (J). (gr. -1-3). pap. 3.99 *(978-0-06-208663-1(4))* HarperCollins Pubs.

—Pony Scouts: the Camping Trip. Kennedy, Anne, illus. 2014. (I Can Read Level 2 Ser.). (ENG.). 32p. (J). (gr. -1-3). 16.99 *(978-0-06-208665-5(0))* HarperCollins Pubs.

—Runaway Ponies! Kennedy, Anne, illus. 2012. (I Can Read Level 2 Ser.). (ENG.). 32p. (J). (gr. -1-3). 16.99 *(978-0-06-208669-3(3))*; pap. 3.99 *(978-0-06-208667-9(7))* HarperCollins Pubs.

—The Trail Ride. Kennedy, Anne, illus. 2012. (I Can Read Level 2 Ser.). (ENG.). 32p. (J). (gr. -1-3). 16.99 *(978-0-06-208671-6(5))*; pap. 3.99 *(978-0-06-208670-9(7))* HarperCollins Pubs.

—True Riders. 2015. (Marguerite Henry's Ponies of Chincoteague Ser.: 6). (ENG., Illus.). 192p. (J). (gr. 3-7). 17.99 *(978-1-4814-3972-5(3)*, Aladdin) Simon & Schuster Children's Publishing.

—A Winning Gift. 2015. (Marguerite Henry's Ponies of Chincoteague Ser.: 5). (ENG., Illus.). 192p. (J). (gr. 3-7). pap. 6.99 *(978-1-4814-3968-8(5)*, Aladdin) Simon & Schuster Children's Publishing.

—A Winning Gift. 2015. (Ponies of Chincoteague Ser.: 5). lib. bdg. 17.20 *(978-0-606-37135-3(4))* Turtleback Bks.

Harlow, Joan Hiatt. Secret of the Night Ponies. (ENG.). (J). (gr. 3-7). 2010. 352p. pap. 7.99 *(978-1-4169-0784-8(X))* 2009. 336p. 16.99 *(978-1-4169-0783-1(1))* McElderry, Margaret K. Bks. (McElderry, Margaret K. Bks.).

HarperCollins Publishers Ltd. Staff. A My Little Pony. 2003. 115.84 *(978-0-06-056197-0(1))* HarperCollins Pubs.

Hasbro. Around Equestria! 2016. (ENG.). 160p. (J). (gr. -1-3). 11.99 *(978-0-316-39529-8(3))* Little, Brown Bks. for Young Readers.

—My Little Pony: Chapter Book Bind-Up. 2016. (ENG., Illus.). 416p. (J). (gr. 3-7). pap. 12.99 *(978-0-316-27259-9(0))* Little, Brown Bks. for Young Readers.

—My Little Pony: Make Your Own Pop-Up Book. 2016. (ENG.). 36p. (J). (gr. 1-3). 14.99 *(978-0-7944-3666-7(8)*, Reader's Digest Children's Bks.) Studio Fun International.

—My Little Pony: Ponyville Reading Adventures. 2015. (Passport to Reading Level 2 Ser.). (ENG., Illus.). 192p. (J). (gr. -1-3). 9.99 *(978-0-316-33740-3(4))* Little, Brown Bks. for Young Readers.

Hasbro & Finn, Perdita. My Little Pony: Friendship Is Magic. 2016. (Equestria Girls Ser.: 6). (ENG., Illus.). 208p. (J). (gr. 3-7). 9.99 *(978-0-316-26699-4(X))* Little, Brown Bks. for Young Readers.

Hasbro & Quill, Penumbra. My Little Pony. 2017. (Ponyville Mysteries Ser.: 1). (ENG.). 112p. (J). (gr. 1-5). pap. 5.99 ***(978-0-316-43168-2(0))*** Little, Brown Bks. for Young Readers.

—Tail of the Timberwolf. 2017. (Ponyville Mysteries Ser.: 2). (ENG.). 112p. (J). (gr. 1-5). pap. 5.99 ***(978-0-316-43190-3(7))*** Little, Brown Bks. for Young Readers.

Hasbro Inc. Staff & Begin, Mary Jane. My Little Pony: The Art of Equestria. 2015. (ENG., Illus.). 216p. 29.95 *(978-1-4197-1577-8(1))* Abrams, Inc.

Hasbro Industries Incorporated Staff. My Little Pony Winning Style: Stories, Activites, & Tattoos. 2014. (ENG.). 24p. (J). (gr. -1-1). pap. 7.99 *(978-0-7944-3030-6(9)*, Reader's Digest Children's Bks.) Studio Fun International.

Hasbro Industries Incorporated Staff & Snider, Brandon T. Wonderbolts Academy Handbook. 2016. (ENG.). 192p. (J). (gr. 3-7). 17.99 *(978-0-316-39499-4(8))* Little, Brown Bks. for Young Readers.

Hasbro My Little Pony, Hasbro My. My Little Pony New Episode 2014. 2014. (Panorama Sticker Storybook Ser.: 12). (ENG.). 24p. (J). (gr. -1-2). pap. 7.99 *(978-0-7944-3117-4(8))* Reader's Digest Assn., Inc., The.

—My Little Pony Pony Friends Are Forever/La Amistad de los Ponis Es Para Siempre: An English/Spanish Lift-the-Flap Book. 2014. (Lift-The-Flap Ser.: 30). (ENG.). 10p. (J). (gr. -1-1). bds. 9.99 *(978-0-7944-3144-0(5))* Reader's Digest Assn., Inc., The.

Henry, Marguerite. Misty of Chincoteague. Dennis, Wesley, illus. 2007. 173p. (gr. 3-7). 17.00 *(978-0-7569-8227-0(8))* Perfection Learning Corp.

—Misty of Chincoteague. Dennis, Wesley, illus. 60th ed. 2006. (ENG.). 176p. (J). (gr. 3-7). pap. 7.99 *(978-1-4169-2783-9(2)*, Aladdin) Simon & Schuster Children's Publishing.

—Sea Star: Orphan of Chincoteague. Dennis, Wesley, illus. 2007. (ENG.). 176p. (J). (gr. 3-7). pap. 7.99 *(978-1-4169-2784-6(0)*, Aladdin) Simon & Schuster Children's Publishing.

—Stormy, Misty's Foal. Dennis, Wesley, illus. (ENG.). (J). (gr. 3-7). 2015. 256p. 19.99 *(978-1-4814-2561-2(7))* 2007. 224p. pap. 6.99 *(978-1-4169-2788-4(3))* Simon & Schuster Children's Publishing. (Aladdin).

Herman, R. A. Pal Saves the Day. Ogden, Betina, illus. 2004. (Pal the Pony Ser.). 32p. (J). pap. *(978-0-439-64985-8(4))*; pap. *(978-0-439-57746-5(2))* Scholastic, Inc.

Hesse, Laura. The Great Pumpkin Ride. 2004. ix, 133p. (J). *(978-0-9734013-1-8(1))* Running L. Productions.

Higginson, Hadley. Keeker & the Crazy, Upside-Down Birthday. Perrett, Lisa, illus. 2008. (ENG.). 56p. (J). (gr. k-3). pap. 4.99 *(978-0-8118-6256-1(9))* Chronicle Bks. LLC.

—Keeker & the Springtime Surprise. Perrett, Lisa, illus. 2007. (Keeker & the Sneaky Pony Ser.: KEEK). (ENG.). 58p. (J). (gr. k-3). per. 4.99 *(978-0-8118-5599-0(6))* Chronicle Bks. LLC.

Hilburn, L. M. Little Princesses to the Rescue. 2008. 24p. pap. 24.95 *(978-1-60672-783-6(4))* America Star Bks.

Hope, Lee Laura. Bunny Brown & His Sister Sue & Their Shetland Pony. 2007. 172p. 41.99 *(978-1-4280-7508-5(9))*; per. 35.99 *(978-1-4280-7514-6(3))* IndyPublish.com.

Hughes, Emily C. My Little Pony: Ponies Love Pets! 2014. (Passport to Reading Level 1 Ser.). (ENG., Illus.). 32p. (J). (gr. -1-3). pap. 3.99 *(978-0-316-36885-8(7))* Little, Brown Bks. for Young Readers.

—My Little Pony: the Cutie Mark Crusaders Doodle Book. 2013. (My Little Pony Ser.). (ENG., Illus.). 128p. (J). (gr. 1-17). 12.99 *(978-0-316-24906-5(8))* Little, Brown Bks. for Young Readers.

—Ponies Love Pets! 2014. (Passport to Reading Level 1 Ser.). (J). lib. bdg. 13.55 *(978-0-606-35298-7(8))* Turtleback Bks.

Jaegly, Peggy. Sweetheart's Gift: A Healing Chincoteague Pony Story. 2011. 28p. pap. 14.95 *(978-1-4575-0287-3(9))* Dog Ear Publishing, LLC.

Jakobs, D. Holly, Jolly Harmony. 2013. (Passport to Reading Level 2 Ser.). (J). lib. bdg. 14.75 *(978-0-606-32276-8(0)*, Turtleback) Turtleback Bks.

—My Little Pony: Holly, Jolly Harmony. 2013. (Passport to Reading Level 2 Ser.). (ENG., Illus.). 32p. (J). (gr. -1-3). 4.99 *(978-0-316-22816-9(8))* Little, Brown Bks. for Young Readers.

—My Little Pony: Tricks & Treats. 2014. (ENG., Illus.). 24p. (J). (gr. -1-3). pap. 5.99 *(978-0-316-24795-5(2))* Little, Brown Bks. for Young Readers.

—Tricks & Treats. 2014. (My Little Pony 8X8 Picture Bks.). (J). lib. bdg. 16.00 *(978-0-606-35302-1(X))* Turtleback Bks.

James, Scilla. Ponies at Owls' Wood. 2013. 112p. pap. *(978-0-9568148-2-1(4))* Swift Publishing.

Jeffers, Susan. Jingle Bells. Jeffers, Susan, illus. 2017. (Illus.). 40p. (J). (gr. -1-3). 17.99 ***(978-0-06-236020-5(5))*** HarperCollins Pubs.

Jeffers, Susan. My Pony. Jeffers, Susan, illus. 2008. (ENG., Illus.). 32p. (J). (gr. -1-3). 6.99 *(978-1-4231-1295-2(4))* Hyperion Pr.

Johnson, Gwen & Johnson, Carl. The Treasure of Diamond's Shoal. l.t. ed. 2007. (ENG., Illus.). 24p. (J). 8.95 *(978-0-9795860-0-2(3))* Fish Tales Publishing.

Johnston, Gail. The Shaggy Pony & the Spotted Pup. 2010. 24p. 11.32 *(978-1-4520-9653-7(8))* AuthorHouse.

Jones, Anouska. Patch & Ruby. Jones, Gwynneth, illus. 2016. (ENG.). 32p. (J). (gr. -1-3). 17.99 *(978-1-925335-22-4(4)*, EK Bks.) Exisle Publishing Pty Ltd. AUS. Dist: Hachette Bk. Group.

Jones, Janey Louise. Dancer the Wild Pony. Poh, Jennie, illus. 2016. (Superfairies Ser.). (ENG.). 56p. (gr. k-3). lib. bdg. 23.99 *(978-1-4795-8642-4(0))* Picture Window Bks.

Kaster, Pam. Molly the Pony: A True Story. 2012. (My Readers Ser.). (ENG., Illus.). 48p. (J). (gr. 1-3). pap. 4.99 *(978-0-312-61121-7(8)*, 9780312611217) Square Fish.

Katschke, Judy. Teacher's Pet. Geddes, Serena, illus. 2017. (Marguerite Henry's Misty Inn Ser.: 7). (ENG.). 128p. (J). (gr. 2-5). pap. 5.99 ***(978-1-4814-6991-3(6)***, Aladdin) Simon & Schuster Children's Publishing.

Keene, Carolyn. Pony Problems. Pamintuan, Macky, illus. 3rd ed. 2006. (Nancy Drew & the Clue Crew Ser.: 3). (ENG.). 96p. (J). (gr. 1-4). pap. 5.99 *(978-1-4169-1815-8(9)*, Aladdin) Simon & Schuster Children's Publishing.

—Pony Problems, 1 vol. Pamintuan, Macky, illus. 2007. (Nancy Drew & the Clue Crew Ser.). (ENG.). 80p. (gr. 1-4). 24.21 *(978-1-59961-346-8(8))* Spotlight.

Kelly, Bernadette & Ward, Krista. Naughty Norton, 1 vol. Alger, Liz, illus. (Pony Tales Ser.). (ENG.). 56p. (gr. 2-2). 2013. pap. 5.05 *(978-1-4795-2067-1(5))* 2009. lib. bdg. 21.32 *(978-1-4048-5504-5(1))* Picture Window Bks. (Chapter Readers).

—Norton Saves the Day, 1 vol. Alger, Liz, illus. 2009. (Pony Tales Ser.). (ENG.). 56p. (gr. 2-2). lib. bdg. 21.32 *(978-1-4048-5505-2(X)*, Chapter Readers) Picture Window Bks.

—Norton's First Show, 1 vol. Alger, Liz, illus. (Pony Tales Ser.). (ENG.). 56p. (gr. 2-2). 2013. pap. 5.05 *(978-1-4795-2068-8(3))* 2009. lib. bdg. 21.32 *(978-1-4048-5506-9(8))* Picture Window Bks. (Chapter Readers).

—Pony Tales. Alger, Liz, illus. 2013. (Pony Tales Ser.). (ENG.). 56p. (gr. 2-2). pap. 9.90 *(978-1-4795-3784-6(5)*, Chapter Readers) Picture Window Bks.

—Who Stole Norton?, 1 vol. Alger, Liz, illus. 2009. (Pony Tales Ser.). (ENG.). 56p. (gr. 2-2). lib. bdg. 21.32 *(978-1-4048-5503-8(3)*, Chapter Readers) Picture Window Bks.

Kelly, Lynda. Magazine-Page Pony. 2013. 190p. pap. *(978-1-903053-37-9(4))* Kelly Pubns.

—The Most Horrible Pony! 2013. 202p. pap. *(978-1-903053-36-2(6))* Kelly Pubns.

Kelly, Theresa. Tony the Pony. Sampson, Jody, illus. l.t. ed. 2003. 12p. (J). 5.95 *(978-1-59466-003-0(4))* Port Town Publishing.

—Tony the Pony: Bugs Are Not Bad. Sampson, Jody, illus. 2005. (J). per. 7.95 *(978-1-59466-030-6(1))* Port Town Publishing.

Kimpton, Diana. Pony-Crazed Princess: Princess Ellie's Mystery. Finlay, Lizzie, illus. 3rd rev. ed. 2006. (ENG.). 96p. (gr. 1-4). pap. 3.99 *(978-0-7868-4872-0(3))* Hyperion Pr.

—Pony-Crazed Princess Super Special: Princess Ellie's Summer Vacation. Finlay, Lizzie, illus. 2007. (ENG.). 144p. (gr. 1-4). pap. 4.99 *(978-1-4231-0616-6(4))* Hyperion Pr.

—Princess Ellie Solves a Mystery. Finlay, Lizzie, illus. 8th rev. ed. 2007. (ENG.). 96p. (gr. 1-4). pap. 3.99 *(978-1-4231-0901-3(5))* Hyperion Pr.

—Princess Ellie to the Rescue. Finlay, Lizzie, illus. 2006. (ENG.). 96p. (gr. 1-4). pap. 3.99 *(978-0-7868-4870-6(7))* Hyperion Pr.

—Princess Ellie's Moonlight Mystery. 2015. (Pony-Crazed Princess Ser.). (ENG.). 96p. (J). (gr. k-5). pap. 4.99 *(978-0-7945-3431-8(7)*, Usborne) EDC Publishing.

—Princess Ellie's Royal Jamboree No. 11. Finlay, Lizzie, illus. 11th ed. 2008. (ENG.). 96p. (gr. 1-4). pap. 3.99 *(978-1-4231-1531-1(7))* Hyperion Pr.

—Princess Ellie's Secret No. 2. Finlay, Lizzie, illus. 2nd rev. ed. 2006. (ENG.). 96p. (gr. 1-4). pap. 3.99 *(978-0-7868-4871-3(5))* Hyperion Pr.

—Princess Ellie's Snowy Ride. Finlay, Lizzie, illus. 2007. (Pony-Crazed Princess Ser.). 90p. (J). 11.65 *(978-0-7569-8352-9(5))* Perfection Learning Corp.

—Princess Ellie's Snowy Ride No. 9. Finlay, Lizzie, illus. 9th rev. ed. 2007. (ENG.). 96p. (gr. 1-4). pap. 3.99 *(978-1-4231-0902-0(3))* Hyperion Pr.

—Princess Ellie's Treasure Hunt No. 10. Finlay, Lizzie, illus. 10th ed. 2008. (ENG.). 96p. (gr. -1-3). pap. 3.99 *(978-1-4231-1414-7(0))* Hyperion Pr.

—A Surprise for Princess Ellie. 2015. (Pony-Crazed Princess Ser.). (ENG.). 96p. (J). (gr. k-5). pap. 4.99 *(978-0-7945-3432-5(5)*, Usborne) EDC Publishing.

—A Surprise for Princess Ellie. Finlay, Lizzie, illus. 6th rev. ed. 2006. (ENG.). 96p. (gr. 1-4). pap. 3.99 *(978-0-7868-4875-1(8))* Hyperion Pr.

Klein-Carroll, Theodora. Tippy & the Runaway Cloud. 2013. 28p. pap. 16.95 *(978-1-4525-7390-8(5)*, Balboa Pr.) Author Solutions, Inc.

Knight, Barbara. The Cowboys with penny the mustang Pony. 2006. (Penny the Mustang Pony Ser.). (Illus.). 16p. (J). 14.95 net. *(978-0-9766270-1-2(9))* Mustang BKS.

—The Rescue, with Penny the Mustang Pony. 2005. (Penny the Mustang Pony Ser.). *(978-0-9766270-0-5(0))* Mustang BKS.

Knight, Barbara Maxine. The Storm. 2007. (Penny the Mustang Pony Ser.). (Illus.). 32p. (J). 14.95 *(978-0-9766270-2-9(7))* Mustang BKS.

Kuc, Jessica. Mawby the Christmas Pony. 2011. 36p. pap. 15.14 *(978-1-4634-2521-0(X))* AuthorHouse.

Larson, Mitch & McCarthy, Meghan. When Cutie Calls. 2014. (My Little Pony Ser.). (ENG., Illus.). 128p. (J). (gr. 2-5). pap. 7.99 *(978-1-61377-830-2(9)*, 9781613778302) Idea & Design Works, LLC.

Lawrence, Iain. The Winter Pony. 2012. (ENG., Illus.). 256p. (J). (gr. 4-7). 7.99 *(978-0-440-23972-7(9)*, Yearling) Random Hse. Children's Bks.

Lawson, Dorie McCullough. Tex: A Book for Little Dreamers. 2011. (ENG., Illus.). 44p. (J). (gr. -1-k). 15.95 *(978-1-57076-501-8(4))* Trafalgar Square Bks.

Lee, Barbara R. Pookey the Pony. 2004. 35p. pap. 24.95 *(978-1-4137-3396-9(4))* PublishAmerica, Inc.

Leigh, S. Runaway Pony. 2004. (Sandy Lane Stables Ser.). (J). (ENG.). 118p. pap. 4.95 *(978-0-7945-0507-3(4))*; 100p. lib. bdg. 12.95 *(978-1-58086-575-3(5))* EDC Publishing.

Lester, Alison. Noni the Pony. Lester, Alison, illus. 2012. (ENG., Illus.). 32p. (J). (gr. -1-k). 15.99 *(978-1-4424-5959-5(X)*, Beach Lane Bks.) Beach Lane Bks.

—Noni the Pony Goes to the Beach. Lester, Alison, illus. 2015. (ENG., Illus.). 32p. (J). (gr. -1-3). 17.99 *(978-1-4814-4625-9(8)*, Beach Lane Bks.) Beach Lane Bks.

—The Snow Pony. 2006. (ENG.). 208p. (J). (gr. 5-7). pap. 12.95 *(978-0-618-77125-7(5))* Houghton Mifflin Harcourt Publishing Co.

Lindsay, Elizabeth. Annie Saves the Day. Eastwood, John, illus. 2003. 92p. (J). *(978-0-439-44651-8(1))* Scholastic, Inc.

—Ghost in the House. 2010. (Magic Pony Ser.: 2). (ENG.). 112p. (J). (gr. 2-5). 4.99 *(978-0-545-21321-9(5)*, Scholastic Paperbacks) Scholastic, Inc.

—Unicorn Dreams (Book 1) 2011. (Silverlake Fairy School Ser.). 96p. (J). pap. 4.99 *(978-0-7945-3062-4(1)*, Usborne) EDC Publishing.

London, Olivia. Meet the Ponies of Ponyville. 2013. (Passport to Reading Level 1 Ser.). (J). lib. bdg. 14.75 *(978-0-606-31732-0(5)*, Turtleback) Turtleback Bks.

—My Little Pony: Meet the Ponies of Ponyville. 2013. (Passport to Reading Level 1 Ser.). (ENG., Illus.). 32p. (J). (gr. -1-3). 4.99 *(978-0-316-22815-2(X))* Little, Brown Bks. for Young Readers.

—My Little Pony: Welcome to Equestria! 2013. (ENG., Illus.). 24p. (J). (gr. -1-3). 3.99 *(978-0-316-22814-5(1))* Little, Brown Bks. for Young Readers.

—Welcome to Equestria! 2013. (My Little Pony 8X8 Picture Bks.). (J). lib. bdg. 13.55 *(978-0-606-31731-3(7)*, Turtleback) Turtleback Bks.

—Welcome to Rainbow Falls! 2014. (My Little Pony Ser.). (ENG., Illus.). 24p. (J). (gr. -1-3). 4.99 *(978-0-316-24796-2(0))* Little, Brown Bks. for Young Readers.

—Welcome to Rainbow Falls! 2014. (My Little Pony 8X8 Picture Bks.). (J). lib. bdg. 14.75 *(978-0-606-35297-0(X))* Turtleback Bks.

—Welcome to the Crystal Empire! 2013. (My Little Pony 8X8 Picture Bks.). (J). lib. bdg. 14.75 *(978-0-606-32275-1(2)*, Turtleback) Turtleback Bks.

—Welcome to the Everfree Forest! 2014. (My Little Pony 8X8 Picture Bks.). (J). lib. bdg. 13.55 *(978-0-606-35940-5(0))* Turtleback Bks.

Mackall, Dandi Daley. A Perfect Pony, 1 vol. Wolf, Claudia, illus. 2011. (I Can Read! / a Horse Named Bob Ser.). (ENG.). 32p. (J). pap. 3.99 *(978-0-310-71783-6(3))* Zonderkidz.

Man-Kong, Mary. Pretty Ponies (Barbie) 2015. (Hologramatic Sticker Book Ser.). (ENG.). 64p. (J). (gr. -1-2). pap. 4.99 *(978-0-553-51260-1(9)*, Golden Bks.) Random Hse. Children's Bks.

Mattern, Joanne. My Little Pony: Phonics Box. 2015. (ENG., Illus.). 144p. (J). (gr. -1-1). 12.99 *(978-0-316-25762-6(1))* Little, Brown Bks. for Young Readers.

Mattern, Joanne & Toohey, Cathy. My Little Pony Phonics Fun/[stories by Joanne Mattern]; [phonics Scope & Sequence by Cathy Toohey; Pictures by Carlo Lo Rosa ... [et Al.], 12 vols. Lo Raso, Carlo et al, illus. 2008. (J). *(978-0-06-123184-1(3))*; *(978-0-06-123183-4(5))*; *(978-0-06-123178-0(9))*; *(978-0-06-123180-3(0))*; *(978-0-06-123179-7(7))*; *(978-0-06-123176-6(2))*; *(978-0-06-123175-9(4))*; *(978-0-06-123174-2(6))*; *(978-0-606-123173-5(8))*; *(978-0-06-123171-1(1))*; *(978-0-06-123182-7(7))*; *(978-0-06-123181-0(9))* HarperCollins Pubs. (Harper Trophy).

Matty & the Problem Ponies. 2006. (J). *(978-1-933343-18-1(4))* Stabenfeldt Inc.

McKain, Kelly. Megan & Mischief. 2008. (Pony Camp Diaries: Vol. 1). 96p. (J). (gr. 3-5). 3.99 *(978-1-56148-646-5(9)*, Good Bks.) Skyhorse Publishing Co., Inc.

—Poppy & Prince. 2008. (Pony Camp Diaries: Vol. 2). 96p. (J). (gr. 3-5). 3.99 *(978-1-56148-647-2(7)*, Good Bks.) Skyhorse Publishing Co., Inc.

Meadows, Daisy. Penny the Pony Fairy. 2008. (Rainbow Magic — the Pet Fairies Ser.). lib. bdg. 14.75 *(978-1-4178-3008-4(5)*, Turtleback) Turtleback Bks.

Melchionno, Marion. Patty & the Little Ponies That Could: Hunt for the Collar of Sparkle. 2013. 28p. pap. 24.95 *(978-1-4626-9973-5(1))* America Star Bks.

—Patty & the Little Pony That Could. 2012. 44p. 24.95 *(978-1-4626-9475-4(6))*; pap. 24.95 *(978-1-4626-7552-4(2))* America Star Bks.

Milbourne, Anna. Little Pony. Roberti, Alessandra, illus. 2009. (Picture Bks.). 24p. (J). (gr. -1). 9.99 *(978-0-7945-2198-1(3)*, Usborne) EDC Publishing.

Miller, Debra J. The Pony Tale: The Truth about Timberlin. 2005. 4.00 *(978-0-9776014-1-7(2))* Miller, Debra Juanita.

Miller, Lorna. Jumper the Pony: Thomas Learns a Lesson. 2008. 32p. per. 24.95 *(978-1-4241-9578-7(0))* America Star Bks.

Mills, Enos A. Cricket, A Mountain Pony, 1 vol. l.t. ed. 2006. (Illus.). 67p. 9.95 *(978-1-928878-37-7(7))* Temporal Mechanical Pr.

Ms. T. A Chincoteague Pony Finds a Friend. 2009. 28p. pap. 12.49 *(978-1-4389-7981-6(9))* AuthorHouse.

Mullarkey, Lisa. Pony Girls. 2016. (Pony Girls Ser.: 4). (ENG.). 112p. (J). (gr. 1-4). lib. bdg. 108.28 *(978-1-62402-126-8(3)*, Calico Chapter Bks.) ABDO Publishing Co.

Muschinske, Victoria. Honey Pie Pony's Book: A Fun with Fillies Adventure. 2005. (Illus.). 39p. *(978-0-439-70471-7(5))* Scholastic, Inc.

My Little Pony. 2003. (J). 144.80 *(978-0-06-056336-3(2))*; (Illus.). 115.84 *(978-0-06-056195-6(5))* HarperCollins Pubs.

My Little Pony, My Little. My Little Pony Equestria Girls - Rainbow Rocks! 2015. (Panorama Sticker Storybook Ser.: 3). (ENG.). 24p. (J). (gr. -1-2). pap. 7.99 *(978-0-7944-3323-9(5)*, Reader's Digest Children's Bks.) Studio Fun International.

Myers, Linda. Stoney the Pony's Most Inspiring Year: Teaching Children about Addiction Through Metaphor. 2012. 36p. pap. 16.99 *(978-1-4624-0311-0(5)*, Inspiring Voices) Author Solutions, Inc.

Nanette. Pancake the Purple Pony. 2004. (Life on Granny's Farm Ser.). (J). 12.95 *(978-0-9741269-8-2(5))* St. Bernard Publishing, LLC.

Natsukawa, Maiko. Rachel, Grace, & Pony Club. 2013. 32p. pap. 13.95 *(978-1-4525-7543-8(6)*, Balboa Pr.) Author Solutions, Inc.

Nault, Susan. Mr Scruffpot's Pony. Nault, S. &R, illus. 2013. 30p. pap. *(978-0-9870744-1-6(5))* Kingdom Pr.

Newbery, L. El Poni de Mermelada. (Raton de Biblioteca Coleccion). (SPA.). 80p. (J). (gr. 3). 7.95 *(978-84-88061-68-3(4))* Serres, Ediciones, S. L. ESP. Dist: Lectorum Pubns., Inc.

Nicholas, Soraya. Gymkhana Hijinks. 2017. (Starlight Stables Ser.: 2). (ENG.). 192p. (J). (gr. 2-4). 8.99 ***(978-0-14-330863-8(7))*** Random Hse. Australia AUS. Dist: Independent Pubs. Group.

Numeroff, Laura Joffe & Evans, Nate. Ponyella. Munsinger, Lynn, illus. 2011. (ENG.). 32p. (J). (gr. -1-k). 16.99 *(978-1-4231-0259-5(2))* Hyperion Pr.

O'Donnell, Liam. Daisy on the Farm. 2005. (ENG., Illus.). 32p. (J). (gr. -1-2). 9.95 *(978-1-59249-452-1(8)*, 1B037) Soundprints.

—Daisy on the Farm. Hatala, Dan, illus. 2005. (Pet Tales Ser.). (ENG.). 32p. (J). (gr. -1-2). 2.95 *(978-1-59249-451-4(X)*, 1B036) Soundprints.

—Daisy the Farm Pony. Hatala, Dan, illus. 2005. (Pet Tales Ser.). (ENG.). 32p. (J). (gr. -1 — 1). 4.95 *(978-1-59249-450-7(1)*, 1B035) Soundprints.

Oldfield, Jenny. Dawn Light. Bright, Alasdair, illus. 2006. (ENG.). 144p. (J). (gr. 2-4). pap. 6.95 *(978-0-340-91078-8(X))* Hachette Children's Group GBR. Dist: Hachette Bk. Group.

—Midnight Snow. Bright, Alasdair, illus. 2006. (ENG.). 144p. (J). (gr. 2-4). pap. 6.95 *(978-0-340-91076-4(3))* Hachette Children's Group GBR. Dist: Hachette Bk. Group.

—New Beginnings. 2007. (ENG., Illus.). 144p. (J). (gr. 4-6). pap. 6.95 *(978-0-340-93246-9(5))* Hachette Children's Group GBR. Dist: Hachette Bk. Group.

—Red Skies. 2006. (ENG., Illus.). 144p. (J). (gr. 4-6). pap. 6.95 *(978-0-340-93020-5(9))* Hachette Children's Group GBR. Dist: Hachette Bk. Group.

—Secret Whispers. 2007. (ENG., Illus.). 144p. (J). (gr. 4-6). pap. 6.95 *(978-0-340-93245-2(7))* Hodder & Stoughton GBR. Dist: Hachette Bk. Group.

Oliver, Charles Folkes. Little Willy & the Party Animals. 2011. (Illus.). 20p. (gr. -1). pap. 14.99 *(978-1-4567-5138-8(7))* AuthorHouse.

Olson, John J. Wild Child & Annie. 2010. 44p. pap. 26.49 *(978-0-557-32534-4(X))* Lulu Pr., Inc.

Ongman, Gudrun. Sleep Pony Dreams. l.t. ed. 2006. (Illus.). 32p. (J). pap. 16.95 *(978-0-9677204-2-5(7))* Mindcastle Bks., Inc.

Orr, Wendy. Stolen! - A Pony Called Pebbles. 2012. (Rainbow Street Shelter Ser.: 5). (J). lib. bdg. 16.00 *(978-0-606-26719-9(0)*, Turtleback) Turtleback Bks.

Parker, Vic, ed. The Goblin Pony & Other Stories. 2015. (Scary Fairy Tales Ser.). (ENG.). 40p. (J). (gr. 3-4). pap. 14.05 *(978-1-4824-3077-6(0))* Stevens, Gareth Publishing LLLP.

Pearce, Arline June. Sunrise the Barnegat Pony. 2011. 28p. pap. 15.99 *(978-1-4628-8601-2(9))* Xlibris Corp.

Peck, Jan. Way Out West on My Little Pony, 1 vol. Leonhard, Herb, illus. 2010. (ENG.). 32p. (J). (gr. k-3). 16.99 *(978-1-58980-697-9(2))* Pelican Publishing Co., Inc.

Pegg, Laura Wittman. The Patch Quilt Pony. 2006. 17.00 *(978-0-8059-7346-4(X))* Dorrance Publishing Co., Inc.

Pelizzari, Nora. Crystal Princess: The Runaway Rainbow. 2006. (My Little Pony Ser.). (Illus.). 12p. (J). (gr. -1-1). 6.99 *(978-0-06-111692-6(0)*, HarperFestival) HarperCollins Pubs.

Pennell, Kathleen. The Phantom Stallion. Pennell, Lauren, illus. 2003. (Pony Investigators Ser.: Vol. 4). 118p. (J). (gr. 3-7). pap. 5.95 *(978-1-930353-73-2(1))* Masthof Pr.

—The Secret Passage: Pony Investigators Series #5. 2005. (Pony Investigators Ser.: 5). (Illus.). 108p. (J). pap. 5.95 *(978-1-932864-42-7(3))* Masthof Pr.

Perfect Pony (revised) 2017. (Sandy Lane Stables Ser.). (ENG.). (J). pap. 5.99 ***(978-0-7945-3623-7(9)***, Usborne) EDC Publishing.

Picciolo, Sharon. The Dream Pony. 2016. (ENG.). 37p. (J). (gr. 1-2). 13.95 *(978-1-78554-559-7(0)*, e68b694f-84db-4147-a277-d3a1d7c426e7) Austin, Stan AUS. Dist: Bookmasters Distribution.

Pinnington, Andrea. Horse & Pony Pocket Activity Fun & Games: Games & Puzzles, Fold-Out Scenes, Patterned Paper, Stickers! 2014. (Pocket Activity Fun & Games Ser.). (ENG.). 96p. (J). (gr. 1-5). pap. 7.99 *(978-1-4380-0446-4(X))* Barron's Educational Series, Inc.

Powell, Jillian. Hurry up, Pony!, 1 vol. Colnaghi, Stefania, illus. 2013. (Start Reading Ser.). (ENG.). 24p. (gr. k-1). pap. 7.95 *(978-1-4765-4105-1(1))* Capstone Press of Coughlan Cos.

Prentice-Hall Staff. The Red Pony. 2nd ed. (J). stu. ed. *(978-0-13-717133-0(1))* Prentice Hall (Schl. Div.).

Price, Cheryl A. Follow the Sun. 2010. (Calico Pony Ser.: Bk. 1). 48p. (J). pap. 17.49 *(978-1-4490-7217-9(8))* AuthorHouse.

Randolph, Joanne. The Pony Ride. 2015. (Rosen REAL Readers: STEM & STEAM Collection). (ENG.). 8p. pap. 5.46 *(978-1-4994-9617-8(6)*, Rosen Classroom) Rosen Publishing Group, Inc., The.

Redbank, Tennant. Blondie: Rapunzel's Royal Pony. Random House Disney Staff, illus. 2014. (Stepping Stone Book(TM) Ser.). (ENG.). 64p. (J). (gr. 2-5). 5.99 *(978-0-7364-3267-2(1)*, RH/Disney) Random Hse. Children's Bks.

Reinhart, Matthew. My Little Pony: the Castles of Equestria: An Enchanted My Little Pony Pop-Up Book. 2015. (ENG., Illus.). 10p. (J). (gr. 1-17). 24.99 *(978-0-316-18832-6(8))* Little, Brown Bks. for Young Readers.

Renne. The Ice Horse, 1 vol. 2003. (ENG., Illus.). 32p. (J). 17.95 *(978-0-86315-384-6(4))* Floris Bks. GBR. Dist: SteinerBooks, Inc.

Ricchiazzi, Lisa Gail. The Adventures of Fella & Dawn: Help One Another. 2012. 20p. pap. 13.77 *(978-1-4669-7170-7(3))* Trafford Publishing.

—Fella Finds a Friend: (You Are Never Alone) 2012. 24p. pap. 14.93 *(978-1-4669-2985-2(5))* Trafford Publishing.

Riddle, Peter H. The Painted Ponies of Partequineus & the Summer of the Kittens: Two Novels for Young Readers. 2009. (Illus.). 260p. (J). pap. *(978-1-926585-19-2(4)*, CCB Publishing) CCB Publishing.

Rigo, L. Little Pony. 2011. (Look at Me Bks.). (ENG., Illus.). 10p. (J). bds. 8.99 *(978-0-7641-6448-4(1))* Barron's Educational Series, Inc.

Rigo, L., illus. Little Pony. 2014. (Mini Look at Me Bks.). (ENG.). 10p. (J). (gr. -1 — 1). bds. 4.99 *(978-0-7641-6733-1(2))* Barron's Educational Series, Inc.

Rippin, Sally. The Bumpy Ride: Hey Jack! Spartels, Stephanie, illus. 2014. (ENG.). 48p. (J). pap. 4.99 *(978-1-61067-187-3(2))* Kane Miller.

Rising, Janet. Pony Whisperer. 2010. (ENG.). 208p. (J). (gr. 4-7). pap. 6.99 *(978-1-4022-3952-6(1)*, Sourcebooks Jabberwocky) Sourcebooks, Inc.

—Runaway Rescue. 2010. (Pony Whisperer Ser.: Bk. 3). (ENG.). 256p. (J). pap. *(978-0-340-98843-5(6)*, Hodder Children's Books) Hachette Children's Group GBR. Dist: Hachette Bk. Group.

—Team Challenge. 2010. (Pony Whisperer Ser.: Bk. 2). (ENG.). 256p. (J). pap. *(978-0-340-98842-8(8)*, Hodder Children's Books) Hachette Children's Group GBR. Dist: Hachette Bk. Group.

—The Word on the Yard. 2010. (Pony Whisperer Ser.: Bk. 1). (ENG.). 256p. (J). pap. *(978-0-340-98841-1(X)*, Hodder Children's Books) Hachette Children's Group GBR. Dist: Hachette Bk. Group.

Rivers-Moore, Debbie. Pony. Larranaga, Ana Martin, illus. 2012. (Come Out & Play Bks.). (ENG.). 10p. (J). bds. 2.99 *(978-0-7641-6520-7(8))* Barron's Educational Series, Inc.

Rogers, Amy Keating. The Journal of the Two Sisters: The Official Chronicles of Celestia & Luna. 2014. (ENG., Illus.). 192p. (J). (gr. 3-17). 14.99 *(978-0-316-28224-6(3))* Little, Brown Bks. for Young Readers.

Rosen, Lucy. My Little Pony: Meet Princess Twilight Sparkle. 2014. (Passport to Reading Level 1 Ser.). (J). lib. bdg. 13.55 *(978-0-606-35939-9(7))* Turtleback Bks.

—My Little Pony - Meet the Princess of Friendship. 2014. (Passport to Reading Level 1 Ser.). (ENG., Illus.). 32p. (J). (gr. -1-3). pap. 4.99 *(978-0-316-28230-7(8))* Little, Brown Bks. for Young Readers.

—My Little Pony: Cutie Map Quest: Punch Out & Play. 2016. (ENG., Illus.). 36p. (J). (gr. 1-5). pap. 12.99 *(978-0-316-39293-8(6))* Little, Brown Bks. for Young Readers.

Roy, Ron. July Jitters. Gurney, John Steven, illus. 2012. (Calendar Mysteries Ser.: 7). (ENG.). 80p. (J). (gr. 1-4). 4.99 *(978-0-375-86882-5(8)*, Random Hse. Bks. for Young Readers) Random Hse. Children's Bks.

—July Jitters. 2012. (Calendar Mysteries Ser.: 7). lib. bdg. 14.75 *(978-0-606-26402-0(7)*, Turtleback) Turtleback Bks.

Runaway Pony (revised) 2017. (Sandy Lane Stables Ser.). (ENG.). (J). pap. 5.99 ***(978-0-7945-3622-0(0)***, Usborne) EDC Publishing.

Ryder, Chloe. Best Friends Forever! 2015. (Princess Ponies Ser.). (ENG., Illus.). 128p. (YA). (gr. 2-4). pap. 5.99 *(978-1-61963-405-3(8)*, 9781619634053, Bloomsbury USA Childrens) Bloomsbury Publishing USA.

—A Dream Come True. 2014. (Princess Ponies Ser.). (ENG., Illus.). 128p. (YA). (gr. 1-3). pap. 5.99 *(978-1-61963-167-0(9)*, 9781619631670, Bloomsbury USA Childrens) Bloomsbury Publishing USA.

—A Magical Friend. 2014. (Princess Ponies Ser.). (ENG., Illus.). 128p. (J). (gr. 1-3). pap. 5.99 *(978-1-61963-165-6(2)*, 9781619631656, Bloomsbury USA Childrens) Bloomsbury Publishing USA.

—Princess Ponies: An Amazing Rescue. 2015. (Princess Ponies Ser.). (ENG., Illus.). 128p. (YA). (gr. 2-4). pap. 5.99 *(978-1-61963-403-9(1)*, 9781619634039, Bloomsbury USA Childrens) Bloomsbury Publishing USA.

—Princess Ponies 3: the Special Secret. 2014. (Princess Ponies Ser.). (ENG., Illus.). 128p. (J). (gr. 2-4). pap. 5.99 *(978-1-61963-237-0(3)*, 9781619632370, Bloomsbury USA Childrens) Bloomsbury Publishing USA.

—Princess Ponies 4: a Unicorn Adventure! 2014. (Princess Ponies Ser.). (ENG., Illus.). 128p. (J). (gr. 2-4). pap. 5.99 *(978-1-61963-294-3(2)*, 9781619632943, Bloomsbury USA Childrens) Bloomsbury Publishing USA.

—Princess Ponies 7: a Special Surprise. 2015. (Princess Ponies Ser.). (ENG., Illus.). 128p. (J). (gr. 2-4). pap. 5.99 *(978-1-61963-565-4(8)*, 9781619635654, Bloomsbury USA Childrens) Bloomsbury Publishing USA.

—Princess Ponies 8: a Singing Star. 2015. (Princess Ponies Ser.). (ENG., Illus.). 128p. (J). (gr. 2-4). pap. 5.99 *(978-1-61963-567-8(4)*, 9781619635678, Bloomsbury USA Childrens) Bloomsbury Publishing USA.

Sanderson, Whitney. Darcy. Sanderson, Ruth, illus. 2013. (Horse Diaries). 160p. (J). (gr. 3-7). pap. 7.99 *(978-0-307-97635-2(1)*, Random Hse. Bks. for Young Readers) Random Hse. Children's Bks.

—Darcy. 2013. (Horse Diaries: 10). lib. bdg. 18.40 *(978-0-606-27001-4(9)*, Turtleback) Turtleback Bks.

Sargent, Dave & Sargent, Pat. Sweetpea: (Purple Corn Welsh) Be Happy, 30 vols., Vol. 58. Lenoir, Jane, illus. 2003. (Saddle up Ser.: Vol. 58). 42p. (J). pap. 10.95 *(978-1-56763-816-5(3))*; lib. bdg. 23.60 *(978-1-56763-815-8(5))* Ozark Publishing.

Scott, Lisa Ann. All That Glitters (Enchanted Pony Academy #1) 2017. (Enchanted Pony Academy Ser.: 1). (ENG.). 128p. (J). (gr. 2-5). pap. 4.99 *(978-0-545-90887-0(6)*, Scholastic Paperbacks) Scholastic, Inc.

—Dreams That Sparkle (Enchanted Pony Academy #4) 2017. (Enchanted Pony Academy Ser.: 4). (ENG.). 128p. (J). (gr. 2-5). pap. 4.99 *(978-0-545-90897-9(3)*, Scholastic Paperbacks) Scholastic, Inc.

—Wings That Shine (Enchanted Pony Academy #2) 2017. (Enchanted Pony Academy Ser.: 2). (ENG.). 128p. (J). (gr. 2-5). pap. 4.99 *(978-0-545-90891-7(4)*, Scholastic Paperbacks) Scholastic, Inc.

Seeley, Bonnie L. Chincoteague Daisy Chain. Lidard, Kelly & Seeley, Douglas A., illus. 2003. 32p. (J). bds. 12.95 *(978-0-9728380-0-9(7))* Seelcraft Publishing.

Shankman, Ed. I Went to the Party in Kalamazoo. Frank, Dave, illus. 2013. (ENG.). 40p. pap. 12.95 *(978-1-938700-22-4(8)*, Commonwealth Editions) Applewood Bks.

Shea, Bob. Ballet Cat: The Totally Secret Secret. Shea, Bob, illus. 2015. (Ballet Cat Ser.). (ENG., Illus.). 56p. (J). (gr. 1-3). 9.99 *(978-1-4847-1378-5(8))* Disney Pr.

Shepherd, Jodie. Merry Christmas, Rarity! Fletcher, Lyn, illus. 2006. (My Little Pony Ser.). 32p. (J). (gr. -1-1). pap., act. bk. ed. 3.99 *(978-0-06-079472-9(0)*, HarperFestival) HarperCollins Pubs.

Shire, Poppy. Flame the Desert Pony. Berg, Ron, illus. 2008. (Magic Pony Carousel Ser.: 5). (ENG.). 96p. (J). (gr. 2-5). pap. 3.99 *(978-0-06-083794-5(2))* HarperCollins Pubs.

—Jewel the Midnight Pony. Berg, Ron, illus. 2008. (Magic Pony Carousel Ser.: 4). (ENG.). 96p. (J). (gr. 2-5). pap. 3.99 *(978-0-06-083788-4(8))* HarperCollins Pubs.

—Sparkle the Circus Pony. Berg, Ron, illus. 2007. (Magic Pony Carousel Ser.: 1). (ENG.). 96p. (J). (gr. 2-5). pap. 3.99 *(978-0-06-083779-2(9))* HarperCollins Pubs.

—Star the Western Pony. Berg, Ron, illus. 2007. (Magic Pony Carousel Ser.: 3). (ENG.). 96p. (J). (gr. 2-5). pap. 3.99 *(978-0-06-083785-3(3))* HarperCollins Pubs.

Shirt, Virginia. Angels of Clover Farm. Lane, Rob, ed. 2012. 132p. pap. *(978-1-78176-546-3(4))* FeedARead.com.

Silver Dolphin en Español Editors. Mi Pequeno Pony Dibuja con los Ponys. 2006. (Illus.). 22p. (J). (gr. -1). bds. *(978-970-718-361-2(6)*, Silver Dolphin en Español) Advanced Marketing, S. de R. L. de C. V.

—Mi Pequeno Pony Figuras Magicas: Las Maravillosas Estaciones. 2006. (Illus.). 8p. (J). (gr. -1). bds. *(978-970-718-359-9(4)*, Silver Dolphin en Español) Advanced Marketing, S. de R. L. de C. V.

Simon-Kerr, Julia. Princess Party Paint Book. Edwards, Ken, illus. 2005. (My Little Pony Ser.). 32p. (J). 3.99 *(978-0-06-074699-5(8)*, HarperFestival) HarperCollins Pubs.

Simone, Yve. Little Valentine. 2013. 72p. pap. 28.99 *(978-1-4817-0496-0(6))* AuthorHouse.

Sisler, Celeste. My Little Pony: the Rainbow Power Sticker Book. 2014. (ENG., Illus.). 12p. (J). (gr. -1-3). pap. 6.99 *(978-0-316-37631-0(0))* Little, Brown Bks. for Young Readers.

Skeffington, Miranda. My Little Pony: Friendship Is Magic: Collectible Poster Book. 2014. (ENG., Illus.). 40p. (J). (gr. 1-17). pap. 20.00 *(978-0-316-32331-4(4))* Little, Brown Bks. for Young Readers.

Sky Koster, Amy. Cute, Sweet, & Petite! (Disney Princess: Palace Pets) Random House Disney Staff, illus. 2015. (Big Golden Book Ser.). (ENG.). 64p. (J). (gr. -1-2). 9.99 *(978-0-7364-3412-6(7)*, Golden/Disney) Random Hse. Children's Bks.

—Petite's Winter Wonderland. Random House Disney Staff, illus. 2015. (Glitter Picturebook Ser.). (ENG.). 16p. (J). (gr. -1-2). 5.99 *(978-0-7364-3355-6(4)*, RH/Disney) Random Hse. Children's Bks.

Slinkard, Doreen. Wicky Wacky Farm Stories: Peppi Goes to China. 2012. 44p. pap. 14.97 *(978-1-60976-309-1(2)*, Strategic Bk. Publishing) Strategic Book Publishing & Rights Agency (SBPRA).

Small, Lily. Mia the Mouse, Poppy the Pony, & Hailey the Hedgehog Bindup. Small, Lily, illus. 2016. (Fairy Animals of Misty Wood Ser.). (ENG., Illus.). 416p. (J). pap. 10.99 *(978-1-250-11399-3(7)*, 9781250113993, Holt, Henry & Co. Bks. For Young Readers) Holt, Henry & Co.

—Penelope the Pony. 2017. (Fairy Animals of Misty Wood Ser.). (ENG., Illus.). 144p. (J). pap. 5.99 ***(978-1-250-12700-6(9)***, 9781250127006, Holt, Henry & Co. Bks. For Young Readers) Holt, Henry & Co.

—Poppy the Pony. 2016. (Fairy Animals of Misty Wood Ser.). (ENG., Illus.). 144p. (J). pap. 5.99 *(978-1-62779-734-4(3)*, 9781627797344, Holt, Henry & Co. Bks. For Young Readers) Holt, Henry & Co.

Small, Lily. Poppy the Pony & Hailey the Hedgehog Bindup. 2017. (Fairy Animals of Misty Wood Ser.). (ENG., Illus.). 288p. (J). 8.99 ***(978-1-250-13079-2(4))***, 9781250130792, Holt, Henry & Co. Bks. For Young Readers) Holt, Henry & Co.

Smith, Donna Campbell. An Independent Spirit: The Tale of Betsy Dowdy & Black Bess. 2006. (Illus.). 182p. (J). per. 11.95 *(978-0-9779889-0-7(2))* Faithful Publishing.

Snider, Brandon T. My Little Pony: the Elements of Harmony Vol. II. 2017. (ENG.). 256p. (J). (gr. 3-7). 17.99 ***(978-0-316-43197-2(4))*** Little, Brown Bks. for Young Readers.

Spinner, Stephanie. Paddywack. Howarth, Daniel, illus. 2010. (Step into Reading Ser.). (ENG.). 48p. (J). (gr. k-3). pap. 3.99 *(978-0-375-86186-4(6)*, Random Hse. Bks. for Young Readers) Random Hse. Children's Bks.

Stamm, Linda J. Lilly & Zander: A Children's Story about Equine-Assisted Activities. Whitaker, Suzanne, illus. 2014. (J). pap. *(978-1-938313-03-5(8))* Graphite Pr.

Sulkowski, Jennifer Suzanne. A Pony Named Napoleon. 2013. 74p. 30.95 *(978-1-59299-979-8(4))*; pap. 22.95 *(978-1-59299-978-1(6))* Inkwater Pr.

Szymanski, Lois K. A Pony in Need. 2008. (Charming Ponies Ser.). 80p. (J). (gr. 2-5). 4.99 *(978-0-06-128873-9(X)*, HarperFestival) HarperCollins Pubs.

Thompson, Chad. Yankee Doodle, 1 vol. 2011. (Early Childhood Themes Ser.). (ENG.). 16p. (J). (gr. -1-2). pap. 6.99 *(978-1-4333-2364-5(8))*; pap. 19.99 *(978-1-4333-2365-2(6))* Teacher Created Materials, Inc.

Tirey, Rodney. Coppershoo Saves the Sarge's Saddle! Tirey, Rodney, illus. 2007. (Illus.). 32p. (J). 16.95 *(978-0-9789591-0-4(8))* MirthMarks Publishing.

Tull, Linda Handy. Fofo's Journey. 2012. 40p. pap. 24.95 *(978-1-4626-7275-2(2))* America Star Bks.

Tutu el Caballito Volador. 2004. (SPA.). (J). per. *(978-0-9744408-6-6(8))* Editorial Busqueda.

Vanderlaan, Karen. Special Friends. 2008. 28p. pap. 24.95 *(978-1-60813-353-6(2))* America Star Bks.
Vogel, Michael. Good Night, Baby Flurry Heart. 2016. (ENG., Illus.). 40p. (J). (gr. -1-3). 15.99 *(978-0-316-38962-4(5))* Little, Brown Bks. for Young Readers.
Watt, Fiona. That's Not My Pony... Its Mane Is Too Fluffy. Wells, Rachel, illus. 2007. (Usborne Touchy-Feely Board Bks.). 10p. (J). (gr. -1-k). bds. 7.99 *(978-0-7945-1630-7(0),* Usborne) EDC Publishing.
Webster, Frank V. Jack of the Pony Express. 2005. 26.95 *(978-1-4218-1036-2(0));* 172p. pap. 11.95 *(978-1-4218-1136-9(7))* 1st World Publishing, Inc. (1st World Library - Literary Society).
Wedekind, Annie & Haas, Jessie. Little Prince: The Story of a Shetland Pony. 2009. (Breyer Horse Collection: 2). (ENG.). 128p. (J). (gr. 4-7). pap. 5.99 *(978-0-312-59918-8(8),* 9780312599188) Feiwel & Friends.
Whelan, Susan, et al. The Sugar & Spice Collection. 2016. (ENG., Illus.). 32p. (J). (gr. -1-3). 34.99 *(978-1-925335-20-0(8),* EK Bks.) Exisle Publishing Pty Ltd. AUS. Dist: Hachette Bk. Group.
White, Julie. The Secret Pony, 1 vol. 2004. (ENG.). 160p. (J). (gr. 3-7). per. 9.95 *(978-1-55039-148-0(8))* Sono Nis Pr. CAN. Dist: Orca Bk. Pubs. USA.
Wright, Tish. The Boy & the Blue Painted Pony. 2012. 94p. (gr. -1). pap. 13.95 *(978-1-4685-6606-2(7))* AuthorHouse.
Yearling, A. K. My Little Pony Set: The Daring Do Adventure Collection. 2014. (ENG.). 624p. (J). (gr. 5-7). 75.00 *(978-0-316-40612-3(0))* Little, Brown Bks. for Young Readers.
Zimet, Sara Goodman. Hannah & the Perfect Picture Pony: A Story of the Great Depression. Fuller, Sandy Ferguson, illus. 2005. 24p. (J). lib. bdg. 16.95 *(978-0-9645159-2-5(X))* Discovery Pr. Pubns., Inc.

PONY EXPRESS

Brill, Marlene Targ. Bronco Charlie & the Pony Express. Orback, Craig, illus. 2004. (On My Own History Ser.). (ENG.). 48p. (gr. 2-4). pap. 6.95 *(978-1-57505-618-0(6));* lib. bdg. 25.26 *(978-1-57505-587-9(2))* Lerner Publishing Group.
—Bronco Charlie y el Pony Express. Orback, Craig, illus. 2005. (Yo Solo Historia Ser.). (SPA.). 46p. (J). (gr. 2-5). per. 6.95 *(978-0-8225-3093-0(7))* Lerner Publishing Group.
—Bronco Charlie y el Pony Express. Translations.com Staff, tr. Orback, Craig, illus. 2005. (Yo Solo - Historia (on My Own - History) Ser.). (SPA.). 48p. (gr. 2-4). lib. bdg. 25.26 *(978-0-8225-2991-0(2))* Lerner Publishing Group.
—Bronco Charlie Y el Pony Express; Bronco Charlie & the Pony Express. 2008. pap. 40.95 *(978-0-8225-3866-0(0))* Lerner Publishing Group.
Dunn, Joeming W. The Pony Express, 1 vol. Martin, Cynthia, illus. 2008. (Graphic History Ser.). (ENG.). 32p. 28.50 *(978-1-60270-184-7(9),* Graphic Planet- Nonfiction) ABDO Publishing Co.
Jeffrey, Gary. The Pony Express. Riley, Terry, illus. 2012. (Graphic History of the American West Ser.). (ENG.). 24p. (J). (gr. 3-8). pap. 8.15 *(978-1-4339-6749-8(9),* Gareth Stevens Learning Library); (gr. 4-7). lib. bdg. 23.95 *(978-1-4339-6747-4(2))* Stevens, Gareth Publishing LLLP.
Leigh, Autumn. Making History: A Horse Sock Puppet. 2006. (Tony Stead Nonfiction Independent Reading Collection). (ENG.). 24p. (gr. 3-6). pap. 8.85 *(978-1-4042-5588-3(5))* Rosen Publishing Group, Inc., The.
Mattern, Joanne. The Pony Express. 2017. 25.70 *(978-1-61228-964-9(9))* Mitchell Lane Pubs., Inc.
McNeese, Tim. The Pony Express: Bringing Mail to the American West. 2009. (Milestones in American History Ser.). (Illus.). 128p. (gr. 6-12). 35.00 *(978-1-60413-028-7(8),* Chelsea Hse.) Facts On File, Inc.
Micklos, John, Jr. Bold Riders: The Story of the Pony Express. 2015. (Adventures on the American Frontier Ser.). (ENG., Illus.). 32p. (gr. 3-4). pap. 7.95 *(978-1-4914-4910-3(1))* Capstone Press of Coughlan Cos.
Ongman, Gudrun. Sleep Pony Dreams. l.t. ed. 2006. (Illus.). 32p. (J). pap. 16.95 *(978-0-9677204-2-5(7))* Mindcastle Bks., Inc.
Payment, Simone. The Pony Express. 2005. (Primary Sources in American History Ser.). (Illus.). 64p. (J). (gr. 5-8). lib. bdg. 31.95 *(978-1-4042-0181-1(5))* Rosen Publishing Group, Inc., The.
—The Pony Express: A Primary Source History of the Race to Bring Mail to the American West. 2009. (Primary Sources in American History Ser.). 64p. (gr. 5-8). 58.50 *(978-1-60851-502-8(8))* Rosen Publishing Group, Inc., The.
Pierce, Alan. Pony Express, 1 vol. 2005. (American Moments Ser.). (ENG., Illus.). 48p. (gr. 4-8). 27.07 *(978-1-59197-938-8(2),* Abdo & Daughters) ABDO Publishing Co.
Quiri, Patricia R. The Groundbreaking Pony Express. 2017. (Landmarks in U. S. History Ser.). (ENG.). 32p. (gr. 3-4). lib. bdg. 27.32 ***(978-1-5157-7115-9(6),*** Fact Finders) Capstone Press of Coughlan Cos.
Ratliff, Thomas. You Wouldn't Want to Be a Pony Express Rider! A Dusty, Thankless Job You'd Rather Not Do. Bergin, Mark, illus. 2012. (You Wouldn't Want to... Ser.). (ENG.). 32p. (J). pap. 9.95 *(978-0-531-20947-9(4),* Watts, Franklin); lib. bdg. 29.00 *(978-0-531-20872-4(9))* Scholastic Library Publishing.
Rau, Margaret. The Mail Must Go Through: The Story of the Pony Express. 2005. (America's Moving Frontier Ser.). (Illus.). 176p. (J). (gr. 3-7). lib. bdg. 26.95 *(978-1-931798-63-1(X))* Reynolds, Morgan Inc.
Riddle, John. The Pony Express. 2004. (History of the Old West Ser.). (Illus.). 64p. (YA). (gr. 5-18). lib. bdg. 19.95 *(978-1-59084-061-0(5))* Mason Crest.
Savage, Jeff. Daring Pony Express Riders: True Tales of the Wild West. 2012. (True Tales of the Wild West Ser.). (Illus.). 48p. (J). (gr. 5-18). pap. 8.95 *(978-1-4644-0031-5(8));* lib. bdg. 22.60 *(978-0-7660-4023-6(2))* Enslow Pubs., Inc.
Steele, William O. We Were There with the Pony Express. 2007. 125p. (J). pap. 13.95 *(978-0-9779000-3-9(7))* American Home-School Publishing, LLC.
Thompson, Gare. Riding with the Mail: The Story of the Pony Express. 2007. (History Chapters Ser.). (ENG., Illus.). 48p. (J). (gr. 1-4). 17.90 *(978-1-4263-0192-6(8),* National Geographic Children's Bks.) National Geographic Society.
Young, Jeff C. The Pony Express & Its Death-Defying Mail Carriers. 2006. (Wild History of the American West Ser.). (Illus.). 128p. (J). (gr. 5-9). lib. bdg. 34.60 *(978-1-59845-010-1(7),* 1250478, MyReportLinks.com Bks.) Enslow Pubs., Inc.

PONY EXPRESS—FICTION

Bailer, Darice. The Pony Express. Antonishak, Tom, illus. 3rd ed. 2003. (Soundprints' Read-and-Discover Ser.). (ENG.). 48p. (J). (gr. -1-3). pap. 3.95 *(978-1-59249-019-6(0),* S2008) Soundprints.
Brill, Marlene Targ. The Rough-Riding Adventure of Bronco Charlie, Pony Express Rider. 2010. pap. 51.02 *(978-0-7613-6920-2(1))* Lerner Publishing Group.
—The Rough-Riding Adventure of Bronco Charlie, Pony Express Rider. Trover, Zachary, illus. 2010. (History's Kid Heroes Ser.). (ENG.). 32p. (gr. 3-5). pap. 8.95 *(978-0-7613-6195-4(2),* Graphic Universe™); lib. bdg. 26.60 *(978-0-7613-6176-3(6))* Lerner Publishing Group.
Chellis, Marie. The Hayburner, 1 vol. 2010. 60p. pap. 19.95 *(978-1-4512-9053-0(5))* America Star Bks.
Kay, Verla. Whatever Happened to the Pony Express? Root, Kimberly Bulcken & Root, Barry, illus. 2010. (ENG.). 32p. (J). (gr. k-3). 16.99 *(978-0-399-24483-4(2),* G.P. Putnam's Sons Books for Young Readers) Penguin Young Readers Group.
Schnetzler, Pattie L. Fast 'n Snappy. Manning, Jane K., tr. Manning, Jane K., illus. 2004. (Carolrhoda Picture Books Ser.). 32p. (J). (gr. k-3). 16.95 *(978-1-57505-539-8(2))* Lerner Publishing Group.
Wilson, Diane Lee. Black Storm Comin' 2006. (ENG.). 240p. (J). (gr. 5-9). pap. 7.99 *(978-0-689-87138-2(4),* McElderry, Margaret K. Bks.) McElderry, Margaret K. Bks.
—Black Storm Comin' 2006. (Illus.). 291p. (gr. 5-9). 17.00 *(978-0-7569-6908-0(5))* Perfection Learning Corp.

POODLES

Berry, Breanna. Poodles. 2015. (Awesome Dogs Ser.). (ENG., Illus.). 24p. (J). (gr. k-3). lib. bdg. 25.95 *(978-1-62617-243-2(9),* Blastoff! Readers) Bellwether Media.
Bodden, Valerie. Fetch!: Poodles. 2014. (Fetch! Ser.). (ENG., Illus.). 24p. (J). (gr. 1-3). pap. 7.99 *(978-0-89812-942-7(7),* Creative Paperbacks) Creative Co., The.
—Poodles. 2014. (J). 25.65 *(978-1-60818-363-0(7),* Creative Education) Creative Co., The.
Bozzo, Linda. I Like Poodles! 2012. (Discover Dogs with the American Canine Association Ser.). (Illus.). 24p. (J). (gr. k-3). pap. 7.95 *(978-1-4644-0118-3(7),* Enslow Elementary) Enslow Pubs., Inc.
Fitzpatrick, Anne. Poodles. 2003. (Dog Breeds Ser.). 24p. (J). lib. bdg. 21.35 *(978-1-58340-314-3(0))* Black Rabbit Bks.
Johnson, Jinny. Poodle. 2013. (My Favorite Dogs Ser.). 24p. (gr. k-3). 28.50 *(978-1-59920-845-9(8))* Black Rabbit Bks.
Kalman, Bobbie. Les Caniches. 2011. (FRE., Illus.). 32p. (J). pap. 9.95 *(978-2-89579-392-2(1))* Bayard Canada CAN. Dist: Crabtree Publishing Co.
Landau, Elaine. Poodles Are the Best! 2010. (Best Dogs Ever Ser.). (ENG.). 32p. (gr. 2-4). lib. bdg. 25.26 *(978-1-58013-561-0(7),* Lerner Pubns.) Lerner Publishing Group.
MacAulay, Kelley & Kalman, Bobbie. Los Caniches o Poodles. 2007. (Cuidado de las Mascotas Ser.). (SPA & ENG., Illus.). 32p. (J). (gr. -1-4). lib. bdg. *(978-0-7787-8461-6(4))* Crabtree Publishing Co.
—Los Caniches o Poodles. Crabtree, Marc, photos by. rev. ed. 2007. (Cuidado de las Mascotas Ser.). (SPA & ENG., Illus.). 32p. (J). (gr. -1-4). pap. *(978-0-7787-8483-8(5))* Crabtree Publishing Co.
—Poodles. Crabtree, Marc, photos by. 2006. (Pet Care Ser.). (ENG., Illus.). 32p. (J). (gr. -1-4). lib. bdg. *(978-0-7787-1763-8(1),* 1259506) Crabtree Publishing Co.
Mathea, Heidi. Poodles, 1 vol. 2011. (Dogs Set 1 *2011 Ser.). (ENG.). 24p. 25.65 *(978-1-61613-409-9(7),* Checkerboard Library) ABDO Publishing Co.
Rustad, Martha E. H. Poodles. 2017. (Favorite Dog Breeds Ser.). (ENG.). 24p. (gr. 1-4). 20.95 *(978-1-68151-129-0(0))* Amicus Publishing.
Schuh, Mari. Poodles. 2008. (Dog Breeds Ser.). (ENG., Illus.). 24p. (J). (gr. 2-5). lib. bdg. 25.95 *(978-1-60014-220-8(6))* Bellwether Media.
Shores, Erika L. All about Poodles, 1 vol. 2012. (Dogs, Dogs, Dogs Ser.). (ENG., Illus.). 24p. (gr. k-1). lib. bdg. 26.65 *(978-1-4296-8727-0(4),* Pebble Plus) Capstone Press of Coughlan Cos.

POOH (FICTITIOUS CHARACTER)—FICTION

see Winnie-the-Pooh (Fictitious Character)—Fiction

POPES

Costello, Hugh. Pope John Paul II: Pontiff. 2016. (History Makers Ser.). 144p. (J). 45.64 *(978-1-5026-2451-2(6))* Cavendish Square Publishing.
Daughters of St. Paul Staff. No Place for Defeat. Date not set. (Encounter Ser.). 96p. (J). (gr. 3-9). pap. 2.00 *(978-0-8198-5100-0(0))* Pauline Bks. & Media.
Furgang, Kathy. Pope Francis: Priest of the People. 2017. (J). pap. ***(978-0-7660-9049-1(3))*** Enslow Pubs., Inc.
Garza, Fabiola. The Story of Saint John Paul II: A Boy Who Became Pope. Garza, Fabiola, illus. 2014. (Illus.). (J). 15.95 *(978-0-8198-9013-9(8))* Pauline Bks. & Media.
Green, John. Popes Coloring Book. 2015. (ENG.). 32p. (gr. 3). pap. 3.99 *(978-0-486-79236-1(6))* Dover Pubns., Inc.
Hansen, Grace. Pope Francis: Religious Leader, 1 vol. 2014. (History Maker Biographies Ser.). (ENG.). 24p. (J). (gr. 2-4). lib. bdg. 28.50 *(978-1-62970-705-1(8))* ABDO Publishing Co.
Hoffman, Mary Hramiec. Lolek the Boy Who Became Pope John Paul II. Hoffman, Mary Hramiec, illus. 2008. (Illus.). 56p. (J). 18.95 *(978-0-9746901-1-7(2))* Hramiec Hoffman Publishing.
Kramer, Barbara. National Geographic Readers: Pope Francis. 2015. (Readers Bios Ser.). (ENG.). 32p. (J). (gr. -1-1). pap. 3.99 *(978-1-4263-2253-2(4),* National Geographic Children's Bks.) National Geographic Society.
Lanser, Amanda. Pope Francis: Spiritual Leader & Voice of the Poor, 1 vol. 2013. (Essential Lives Set 8 Ser.). (ENG.). 112p. (J). (gr. 6-12). lib. bdg. 35.64 *(978-1-61783-704-3(0),* Essential Library) ABDO Publishing Co.
Mohan, Claire Jordan. Joseph from Germany: The Life of Pope Benedict XVI for Children. Craig, Charlie, illus. 2007. 38p. (J). 8.95 *(978-0-8198-3988-6(4))* Pauline Bks. & Media.
Monge, Marlyn & Wolfe, Jaymie Stuart. Jorge de Argentina: Historia Del Papa Francisco para Ninos. 2013. (Illus.). 64p. (J). pap. 8.95 *(978-0-8198-4007-3(6))* Pauline Bks. & Media.
—Jorge from Argentina: The Story of Pope Francis for Children. Kizlauskas, Diana, illus. 2013. 64p. (J). pap. 8.95 *(978-0-8198-4006-6(8))* Pauline Bks. & Media.
Morreale, Marie. Pope Francis. 2016. (True Book(tm), A — Biographies Ser.). (ENG., Illus.). 48p. (J). lib. bdg. 31.00 *(978-0-531-21973-7(9),* Children's Pr.) Scholastic Library Publishing.
—Pope Francis: A Life of Love & Giving. 2016. (Rookie Biographies(tm) Ser.). (ENG., Illus.). 32p. (J). lib. bdg. 25.00 *(978-0-531-22066-5(4),* Children's Pr.) Scholastic Library Publishing.
Pagotto, Toni. Pope John Paul II. Toppi, Sergio, illus. 2006. (Comic Book Ser.). 64p. (J). pap. 7.95 *(978-0-8198-5957-0(5))* Pauline Bks. & Media.
Perego, Jeanne, et al. Max & Benedict: A Bird's Eye View of the Pope's Daily Life. 2009. 52p. 17.95 *(978-1-58617-407-1(X))* Ignatius Pr.
Sheen, Barbara. Pope Benedict XVI. 2008. (People in the News Ser.). (ENG., Illus.). 128p. (gr. 7-10). lib. bdg. 39.40 *(978-1-4205-0093-6(7),* LML02109-242097, Lucent Bks.) Cengage Gale.
Spinner, Stephanie. Who Is Pope Francis? Putra, Dede, illus. 2017. (Who Was? Ser.). (ENG.). 112p. (J). (gr. 3-7). 5.99 ***(978-0-451-53336-4(4));*** lib. bdg. 15.99 ***(978-0-451-53338-8(0))*** Penguin Young Readers Group. (Penguin Workshop).
Stanley, George E. Pope John Paul II: Young Man of the Church. 2005. (Childhood of World Figures Ser.). (ENG.). 176p. (J). (gr. 3-7). pap. 9.99 *(978-1-4169-1282-8(7),* Aladdin) Simon & Schuster Children's Publishing.
Wallace, Susan Helen. Blessed John Paul II: Be Not Afraid. Craig, Charles, illus. 2011. (Encounter the Saints Ser.). 111p. (J). (gr. 3-7). pap. 7.95 *(978-0-8198-1178-3(5))* Pauline Bks. & Media.
Watson, Stephanie. Pope Francis: First Pope from the Americas. (Gateway Biographies Ser.). (ENG., Illus.). 48p. (gr. 4-8). 2015. 34.65 *(978-1-4677-5977-9(5),* Lerner Digital) 2013. lib. bdg. 26.60 *(978-1-4677-2176-9(X),* Lerner Pubns.) Lerner Publishing Group.
Wheeler, Jill C. Pope John Paul II. 2003. (Breaking Barriers Ser.). (Illus.). 64p. (gr. 3-8). 27.07 *(978-1-57765-740-8(3),* Abdo & Daughters) ABDO Publishing Co.
Wilson, M. Leonora. Karol from Poland: The Life of Pope John Paul II for Children. Koch, Carla, illus. rev. ed. 2006. 38p. (J). pap. 7.95 *(978-0-8198-4209-1(5))* Pauline Bks. & Media.
Woll, Kris. Pope Francis: Catholic Spiritual Leader, 1 vol. 2014. (Newsmakers Ser.). (ENG.). 48p. (gr. 3-6). lib. bdg. 32.79 *(978-1-62403-644-6(9))* ABDO Publishing Co.
Worth, Richard. Pope Francis: The People's Pope. 2016. (Influential Latinos Ser.). (ENG., Illus.). 128p. (J). (gr. 7-8). 37.27 *(978-0-7660-7328-9(9))* Enslow Pubs., Inc.

POPPINS, MARY (FICTITIOUS CHARACTER)—FICTION

Druvert, Hélène. Mary Poppins: Up, up & Away. 2017. (ENG., Illus.). 36p. (gr. k-4). 24.95 *(978-0-500-65104-9(3),* 565104) Thames & Hudson.
Travers, P. L. Mary Poppins. (Mary Poppins Ser.: No. 1). 202p. (J). (gr. 3-5). pap. 6.00 *(978-0-8072-1536-4(8),* Listening Library) Random Hse. Audio Publishing Group.
—Mary Poppins & Mary Poppins Comes Back. Shepard, Mary, illus. 2007. (Mary Poppins Ser.: No 1 and 2). (ENG.). 368p. (J). (gr. 5-7). 19.99 *(978-0-15-205922-4(9))* Houghton Mifflin Harcourt Publishing Co.
—Mary Poppins in the Kitchen: A Cookery Book with a Story. Shepard, Mary, illus. 2006. (Mary Poppins Ser.: No. 6). (ENG.). 88p. (J). (gr. 5-7). 16.99 *(978-0-15-206080-0(4))* Houghton Mifflin Harcourt Publishing Co.
—Mary Poppins in the Park. Shepard, Mary, illus. 2015. (Mary Poppins Ser.). (ENG.). 272p. (J). (gr. 5-7). pap. 6.99 *(978-0-544-51384-6(3),* HMH Books For Young Readers) Houghton Mifflin Harcourt Publishing Co.
—Mary Poppins Opens the Door. Shepard, Mary & Sims, Agnes, illus. 2015. (Mary Poppins Ser.). (ENG.). 256p. (J). (gr. 5-7). pap. 6.99 *(978-0-544-43958-0(9),* HMH Books For Young Readers) Houghton Mifflin Harcourt Publishing Co.

POPULAR GOVERNMENT

see Democracy

POPULAR MUSIC

Anniss, Matt. The History of Modern Music. 2015. (Music Scene Ser.). (J). lib. bdg. 37.10 *(978-1-59920-910-4(1))* Black Rabbit Bks.
—Start a Band! 2013. (Find Your Talent Ser.). (Illus.). 32p. (J). (gr. 5-8). 28.50 *(978-1-84858-571-3(3))* Arcturus Publishing GBR. Dist: Black Rabbit Bks.
—The Story of Pop Music. 2013. (Pop Histories Ser.). 32p. (gr. 4-7). 31.35 *(978-1-59920-970-8(5))* Black Rabbit Bks.
Anniss, Matthew. Create Your Own Music. 2016. (Media Genius Ser.). (ENG.). 48p. (gr. 5-8). lib. bdg. 33.32 *(978-1-4109-8112-7(6))* Heinemann-Raintree.
—The Music Scene: The History of Modern Music. 2016. (Music Scene Ser.). (ENG., Illus.). 48p. (J). (gr. 5-9). pap. 12.99 *(978-1-4451-3936-4(7),* Franklin Watts) Hachette Children's Group GBR. Dist: Hachette Bk. Group.
Barden, Christine H. & Kowalchyk, Gayle. Music for Little Mozarts — Little Mozarts Go to Hollywood: 10 Favorites from TV, Movies & Radio. 2008. (Music for Little Mozarts Ser.: Bk 3-4). (ENG.). 24p. (J). pap. 7.95 *(978-0-7390-5014-9(1))* Alfred Publishing Co., Inc.
Bednar, Chuck. American Idol Profiles Index: Top Finalists from Each Season (82 Contestants) 2009. (Dream Big: American Idol Superstars Ser.). 64p. (YA). (gr. 5-18). pap. 9.95 *(978-1-4222-1593-7(8))* Mason Crest.
—Insights into American Idol. 2009. (Dream Big: American Idol Superstars Ser.). 64p. (YA). (gr. 5-18). pap. 9.95 *(978-1-4222-1600-2(4));* lib. bdg. 22.95 *(978-1-4222-1514-2(8))* Mason Crest.
Carlin, Richard. Folk. 2007. (American Popular Music Ser.). (Illus.). 304p. (gr. 6-12). per. 21.95 *(978-0-8160-7340-5(6),* Checkmark Bks.) Facts On File, Inc.
Carr, Aaron. Pop. 2015. (J). *(978-1-4896-3585-3(8))* Weigl Pubs., Inc.
Cohn, Jessica. The Electronic Music Scene: The Stars, the Fans, the Music. 2009. (Music Scene Ser.). (Illus.). 48p. (J). (gr. 5-9). lib. bdg. 25.27 *(978-0-7660-3398-6(8))* Enslow Pubs., Inc.
Crossingham, John. Learn to Speak Music: A Guide to Creating, Performing, & Promoting Your Songs. Kulak, Jeff & Owlkids Books Inc. Staff, illus. 2009. (ENG.). 96p. (J). (gr. 3-8). pap. 22.95 *(978-1-897349-65-6(3),* Owlkids) Owlkids Bks. Inc. CAN. Dist: Publishers Group West (PGW).
Diver, Lucas. One Direction: Popular Boy Band, 1 vol. 2014. (Pop Bios Ser.). (ENG., Illus.). 24p. (J). (gr. 2-4). lib. bdg. 28.50 *(978-1-62970-726-6(0))* ABDO Publishing Co.
Donovan, Sandy. Music & Theater Top Tens. 2014. (Entertainment's Top 10 Ser.). (Illus.). 32p. (J). (gr. 5-8). lib. bdg. 26.60 *(978-1-4677-3843-9(3),* Lerner Pubns.) Lerner Publishing Group.
Garofoli Zamora, Wendy. Hip-Hop History [Scholastic]. 2010. (Hip-Hop World Ser.). 48p. pap. 1.00 *(978-1-4296-5979-6(3))* Capstone Press of Coughlan Cos.
Gilpin, Daniel. Start Your Own Band. 2013. (Quick Expert's Guide Ser.). 64p. (J). (gr. 5-8). 31.95 *(978-1-4777-2827-7(9));* pap. 77.70 *(978-1-4777-2830-7(9));* pap. 12.95 *(978-1-4777-2829-1(5))* Rosen Publishing Group, Inc., The. (Rosen Reference).
Hal Leonard Corp. Staff, creator. Disney Movie Hits: Tenor Sax. 2003. (ENG.). 20p. pap. 12.99 *(978-0-634-04383-3(8),* 0634043838) Leonard, Hal Corp.
Hapka, Catherine, pseud. Always Dreamin' 2004. (Star Power Ser.: 2). (ENG., Illus.). 160p. (J). (gr. 4-8). pap. 4.99 *(978-0-689-86788-0(3),* Aladdin) Simon & Schuster Children's Publishing.
—Blast from the Past. 2004. (Star Power Ser.: 5). (ENG.). 160p. (J). (gr. 4-8). pap. 8.99 *(978-0-689-86791-0(3),* Simon & Schuster/Paula Wiseman Bks.) Simon & Schuster/Paula Wiseman Bks.
Hegel, Claudette. African-American Musicians. 2012. (J). pap. *(978-1-4222-2387-1(6))* Mason Crest.
—African-American Musicians. Hill, Marc Lamont, ed. 2012. (Major Black Contributions from Emancipation to Civil Rights Ser.). 64p. (J). (gr. 5). 22.95 *(978-1-4222-2374-1(4))* Mason Crest.
Herweck Rice, Dona. Communicate! Pop Song Lyrics (Level 3) 2017. (Exploring Reading Ser.). (Illus.). 32p. (J). (gr. 3-3). pap. 8.99 ***(978-1-4258-4973-3(3))*** Teacher Created Materials, Inc.
Heyer, Sandra. True Stories Behind the Songs. 2010. (ENG.). 112p. (C). pap. 37.32 *(978-0-13-246804-6(2))* Prentice Hall, ESL Dept.
Hoffmann, Frank. Rhythm & Blues, Rap, & Hip-Hop. 2007. (American Popular Music Ser.). (Illus.). 352p. (gr. 6-12). per. 21.95 *(978-0-8160-7341-2(4),* Checkmark Bks.) Facts On File, Inc.
Hubbard, Ben. History of Pop. 2009. (Crabtree Contact Ser.). (ENG., Illus.). 32p. (J). (gr. 6-8). pap. *(978-0-7787-3843-5(4));* lib. bdg. *(978-0-7787-3822-0(1))* Crabtree Publishing Co.
Jones, Edward Huws, ed. Unbeaten Tracks: 8 Contemporary Pieces for Trumpet & Piano. 2003. (Faber Edition: Unbeaten Tracks Ser.). (ENG.). 32p. (gr. 4-7). pap. 13.80 *(978-0-571-52005-3(7))* Faber & Faber, Ltd. GBR. Dist: Alfred Publishing Co., Inc.
Kallen, Stuart A. K-Pop: Korea's Musical Explosion. 2014. (Illus.). 64p. (gr. 6-12). lib. bdg. 33.26 *(978-1-4677-2042-7(9),* Twenty-First Century Bks.) Lerner Publishing Group.
Kallen, Stuart A., ed. The History of American Pop. 2012. (Music Library). (Illus.). 128p. (J). (gr. 7-10). lib. bdg. 34.45 *(978-1-4205-0672-3(2))* Cengage Gale.
Kaplan, Arie. American Pop: Hit Makers, Superstars, & Dance Revolutionaries. 2012. (American Music Milestones Ser.). (ENG., Illus.). 64p. (gr. 5-12). lib. bdg. 30.60 *(978-0-7613-4504-6(3))* Lerner Publishing Group.
Latham, Donna. Music: Investigate the Evolution of American Sound. Stone, Bryan, illus. 2013. (Inquire & Investigate Ser.). (ENG.). 128p. (YA). (gr. 6-10). 21.95 *(978-1-61930-199-3(7));* pap. 16.95 *(978-1-61930-203-7(9))* Open City Bks.
Lindeen, Mary. Cool Latin Music: Create & Appreciate What Makes Music Great!, 1 vol. 2008. (Cool Music Ser.). (ENG., Illus.). 32p. (YA). (gr. 3-6). 28.50 *(978-1-59928-972-4(5))* ABDO Publishing Co.
Mackay, Jennifer & Mackay, Jennifer. The Art of Songwriting. Greenhaven Press Editors, ed. 2013. (Music Library). (ENG., Illus.). 128p. (gr. 7-10). lib. bdg. 39.40 *(978-1-4205-0943-4(8),* Lucent Bks.) Cengage Gale.
Manuel, Peter & Neely, Daniel. The Reggae Scene: The Stars, the Fans, the Music. 2009. (Music Scene Ser.). (Illus.). 48p. (J). (gr. 5-9). lib. bdg. 25.27 *(978-0-7660-3400-6(3))* Enslow Pubs., Inc.
Manzella, Teresa Ryan. How to Analyze the Music of Bob Dylan, 1 vol. 2011. (Essential Critiques Set 2 Ser.). (ENG., Illus.). 112p. (J). (gr. 6-12). lib. bdg. 35.64 *(978-1-61783-090-7(9))* ABDO Publishing Co.
McAneney, Caitie. Gareth's Guide to Becoming a Pop Star. 2017. (Gareth Guides to an Extraordinary Life Ser.). 32p. (gr. 4-5). pap. 63.00 ***(978-1-5382-0335-4(9))*** Stevens, Gareth Publishing LLLP.
Pop Musician. 2008. (Virtual Apprentice Ser.). (Illus.). 64p. (gr. 4-9). 29.95 *(978-0-8160-6752-7(X),* Ferguson Publishing Co.) Facts On File, Inc.
Raffi. Everything Grows. 2004. (ENG., Illus.). 32p. (J). (gr. -1-2). 15.95 *(978-1-57940-097-2(3))* Rounder Bks.
Rauf, Don & Vescia, Monique. Pop Musician. 2008. (Virtual Apprentice Ser.). (Illus.). 64p. (gr. 4-9). per. 9.95 *(978-0-8160-7552-2(2),* Checkmark Bks.) Facts On File, Inc.
Regan, Lisa. Pop Star. 2012. (Stage School Ser.). (ENG., Illus.). 32p. (gr. 3-6). pap. 10.00 *(978-1-4488-8155-0(2))* Windmill Bks.
Robertson, Robbie, et al. Legends, Icons & Rebels: Music That Changed the World. 2016. (ENG., Illus.). 128p. (J). (gr. 4-7). pap. 18.99 *(978-1-101-91868-5(3),* Tundra Bks.) Tundra Bks. CAN. Dist: Penguin Random Hse. LLC.
Salazar, Sam. One Direction. 2013. (Rising Stars Ser.). 32p. (J). (gr. 3-6). 25.25 *(978-1-4339-8985-8(9));* pap. 63.00 *(978-1-4339-8987-2(5));* pap. 10.50 *(978-1-4339-8986-5(7))* Stevens, Gareth Publishing LLLP.
Schweitzer, Karen. Making the Band. 2010. (Major Competitive Reality Shows Ser.). 48p. (YA). (gr. 7-18). lib. bdg. 19.95 *(978-1-4222-1674-3(8))* Mason Crest.
StarNews Media, compiled by. Stars of K-Pop: Boys Edition. 2014. (Illus.). 188p. (J). pap. 24.95 *(978-1-935690-49-8(3))* Watermark Publishing, LLC.
—Stars of K-Pop: Girls Edition. 2014. (Illus.). 192p. (J). pap. 24.95 *(978-1-935690-48-1(5))* Watermark Publishing, LLC.

Stewart, Mark. Music Legends. 2009. (Ultimate 10: Entertainment Ser.). (ENG.). 48p. (J). (gr. 4-8). pap. 10.50 *(978-1-4339-2213-8(4))*; (YA). (gr. 5-9). lib. bdg. 31.00 *(978-0-8368-9165-2(1))* Stevens, Gareth Publishing LLLP.
Trier, George. Music of Heartohopia. 2003. (Illus.). 240p. (YA). (gr. 2-18). per. 19.95 *(978-0-9725184-0-6(1))* Heartohopia Pr.
Triumph Books Staff. One Direction: What Makes You Beautiful. 2012. (ENG.). 112p. (J). (gr. 5). pap. 12.95 *(978-1-60078-777-5(0))* Triumph Bks.
Tsoukanelis, Erika Alexia. The Latin Music Scene: The Stars, the Fans, the Music. 2009. (Music Scene Ser.). (Illus.). 48p. (J). (gr. 5-9). lib. bdg. 25.27 *(978-0-7660-3399-3(6))* Enslow Pubs., Inc.
Weston Woods Staff, creator. The Star Spangled Banner. 2004. 38.75 *(978-1-55592-644-1(4))* Weston Woods Studios, Inc.
Witmer, Scott. Songwriting, 1 vol. 2009. (Rock Band Ser.). (ENG., Illus.). 32p. (YA). (gr. 4-7). 27.07 *(978-1-60453-696-6(9))* ABDO Publishing Co.
Woog, Adam. The History of Gospel Music. Greenhaven Press Editors, ed. 2014. (Music Library). (ENG., Illus.). 128p. (gr. 7-10). lib. bdg. 39.40 *(978-1-4205-0945-8(4)*, Lucent Bks.) Cengage Gale.

POPULAR MUSIC—BIOGRAPHY

Dougherty, Terri. Justin Timberlake. 2008. (People in the News Ser.). (ENG., Illus.). 128p. (gr. 7-10). lib. bdg. 39.40 *(978-1-4205-0056-1(2)*, LML02109-249044, Lucent Bks.) Cengage Gale.
Kanidiadis, Eleni. Healthy Habits Smoothies 2: Conquering the World. 2017. (ENG., Illus.). 70p. pap. 14.95 ***(978-1-925265-10-1(2))*** Wilkinson Publishing AUS. Dist: Independent Pubs. Group.
Orgill, Roxane. Shout, Sister, Shout! Ten Girl Singers Who Shaped a Century. 2007. (ENG.). 160p. (YA). (gr. 7). pap. 12.95 *(978-1-4169-6391-2(X)*, McElderry, Margaret K. Bks.) McElderry, Margaret K. Bks.

POPULAR MUSIC—FICTION

Bruton, Catherine. Pop! 2013. (ENG.). 496p. (YA). (gr. 7). pap. 10.99 *(978-1-4052-6133-3(1))* Egmont Bks., Ltd. GBR. Dist: Independent Pubs. Group.
Calonita, Jen. Battle of the Bands. 2016. (VIP Ser.: 2). (ENG., Illus.). 320p. (J). (gr. 3-7). 16.99 *(978-0-316-25977-4(2))* Little, Brown Bks. for Young Readers.
—VIP: Battle of the Bands. 2017. (VIP Ser.: 2). (ENG.). 320p. (J). (gr. 3-7). pap. 6.99 *(978-0-316-25978-1(0))* Little, Brown Bks. for Young Readers.
Davis, Lisa Selin. Lost Stars. 2016. (ENG.). 288p. (YA). (gr. 9). 17.99 *(978-0-544-78506-9(1)*, HMH Books For Young Readers) Houghton Mifflin Harcourt Publishing Co.
Dimopoulos, Elaine. Material Girls. 2015. (ENG.). 336p. (YA). (gr. 9-12). 17.99 *(978-0-544-38850-5(X)*, HMH Books For Young Readers) Houghton Mifflin Harcourt Publishing Co.
Gadsby, Maggie. Owl Be Home for Christmas. 2012. (J). 14.95 *(978-1-62086-064-9(3))* Mascot Bks., Inc.
Hapka, Catherine, pseud. Over the Top. 2005. (Star Power Ser.: 7). (ENG.). 144p. (J). (gr. 4-8). pap. 8.99 *(978-0-689-87669-1(6)*, Simon & Schuster/Paula Wiseman Bks.) Simon & Schuster/Paula Wiseman Bks.
Philbin, Joanna. The Daughters Take the Stage. 2011. (Daughters Ser.: 3). (ENG.). 304p. (J). (gr. 7-17). pap. 8.99 *(978-0-316-04908-5(5)*, Poppy) Little, Brown Bks. for Young Readers.
Shaw, Deirdre. Fair Play. 2005. (American Dreams Ser.: 5). (ENG.). 176p. (YA). mass mkt. 5.99 *(978-0-689-87850-3(8))* Pocket Books.
Stout, Katie M. Hello, I Love You. 2015. (ENG.). 304p. (YA). pap. *(978-1-250-08195-7(5)*, St. Martin's Griffin) St. Martin's Pr.
—Hello, I Love You: A Novel. 2015. (ENG.). 304p. (YA). (gr. 7-12). 18.99 *(978-1-250-05259-9(9)*, 9781250052599, St. Martin's Griffin) St. Martin's Pr.
Weil, Cynthia. I'm Glad I Did. 2015. (ENG., Illus.). 272p. (YA). (gr. 9). 18.99 *(978-1-61695-356-0(X)*, Soho Teen) Soho Pr., Inc.

POPULARITY

Espejo, Roman. Celebrity Culture. 2010. (Opposing Viewpoints Ser.). 176p. 42.95 *(978-0-7377-5213-7(0))*; 177p. pap. 29.45 *(978-0-7377-5214-4(9))* Cengage Gale. (Greenhaven Pr., Inc.).
Van Wagenen, Maya. Popular: A Memoir. 2015. lib. bdg. 22.10 *(978-0-606-36796-7(9))* Turtleback Bks.

POPULARITY—FICTION

Allen, Crystal. The Laura Line. (J). (gr. 3-7). 2016. 352p. pap. 6.99 *(978-0-06-249021-6(4))* 2013. (ENG.). 336p. 16.99 *(978-0-06-199274-2(7))* HarperCollins Pubs.
Anderson, Jodi Lynn. Loser/Queen. Lee, Brittney, illus. 2010. (ENG.). 272p. (YA). (gr. 7-18). pap. 9.99 *(978-1-4169-9646-0(X)*, Simon & Schuster Bks. For Young Readers) Simon & Schuster Bks. For Young Readers.
Applegate, Katherine. Never Walk in Shoes That Talk. Biggs, Brian, illus. 2009. (Roscoe Riley Rules Ser.: 6). (ENG.). 96p. (J). (gr. 1-5). 14.99 *(978-0-06-114892-7(X))*; pap. 4.99 *(978-0-06-114891-0(1))* HarperCollins Pubs.
—Never Walk in Shoes That Talk. 2009. (Roscoe Riley Rules Ser.: 06). lib. bdg. 14.75 *(978-0-606-05019-7(1)*, Turtleback) Turtleback Bks.
Atkinson, Elizabeth. From Alice to Zen & Everyone in Between. (gr. 4-7). 2013. (ENG.). 248p. (J). pap. 9.95 *(978-1-4677-0861-6(5)*, Carolrhoda Bks.) 2008. 247p. (YA). 16.95 *(978-0-8225-7271-8(0))* Lerner Publishing Group.
Babich, Elaine. You Never Called Me Princess. 2012. 210p. pap. 14.00 *(978-1-105-70209-9(X))* Lulu.com GBR. Dist: Lulu Pr., Inc.
Backes, M. Molly. The Princesses of Iowa. (ENG.). 464p. (YA). (gr. 9). 2014. pap. 9.99 *(978-0-7636-7161-7(4))* 2012. (Illus.). 16.99 *(978-0-7636-5312-5(8))* Candlewick Pr.
Badger, Meredith. Fairy School Dropout Undercover. 2011. (Fairy School Ser.: 2). (ENG., Illus.). 160p. (J). (gr. 2-4). pap. 14.99 *(978-0-312-61951-0(0)*, 9780312619510) Square Fish.
Bailey, Em. Shift. 2016. (ENG.). 288p. (YA). (gr. 9). pap. 17.99 ***(978-1-76012-698-8(5))*** Hardie Grant Egmont Pty, Ltd. AUS. Dist: Independent Pubs. Group.
Balaban, Bob. Boy or Beast. Rash, Andy, illus. (Creature from the 7th Grade Ser.: 1). (ENG.). (J). (gr. 5). 2013. 272p. pap. 7.99 *(978-0-14-242542-8(7)*, Puffin Books) 2012. 256p. 15.99 *(978-0-670-01271-8(8)*, Viking Books for Young Readers) Penguin Young Readers Group.
Barcellona, Kelley Powell. The Hive. 2009. 92p. 14.95 *(978-0-9824095-1-0(6))* Pegasus Bks. for Children.
Baskin, Nora Raleigh. Runt. (ENG., Illus.). 208p. (J). (gr. 3-7). 2014. pap. 6.99 *(978-1-4424-5808-6(9))* 2013. 15.99 *(978-1-4424-5807-9(0))* Simon & Schuster Bks. For Young Readers. (Simon & Schuster Bks. For Young Readers).
Bateman, Anya. The Makeover of James Orville Wickenbee. 2007. 262p. (J). pap. *(978-1-59038-707-8(4))* Deseret Bk. Co.
Bates, Marni. Invisible. 2013. (Smith High Ser.). (ENG.). 288p. (YA). (gr. 9). pap. 9.95 *(978-0-7582-6938-6(2)*, K-Teen) Kensington Publishing Corp.
Birchall, Katy. The It Girl. 2016. (It Girl Ser.: 1). (ENG., Illus.). 352p. (J). (gr. 4-8). 16.99 *(978-1-4814-6362-1(4)*, Aladdin) Simon & Schuster Children's Publishing.
Blackstone, Matt. Sorry You're Lost. 2014. (ENG.). 320p. (J). (gr. 5-9). 15.99 *(978-0-374-38065-6(1)*, 9780374380656, Farrar, Straus & Giroux (BYR)) Farrar, Straus & Giroux.
Bodi, Sari. The Ghost in Allie's Pool. 2007. 192p. (J). (gr. 5-18). pap. 8.95 *(978-0-9768126-6-1(5))* Brown Barn Bks.
Boyce, Frank Cottrell. Desirable. 2012. (Stoke Books Titles Ser.). 64p. (J). (gr. 5-8). pap. 45.32 *(978-0-7613-9216-3(5))* Stoke Bks.
Breen, Steve. Violet the Pilot. 2008. (ENG., Illus.). 32p. (J). (gr. -1-3). 17.99 *(978-0-8037-3125-7(6)*, Dial Bks) Penguin Young Readers Group.
Brian, Kate, pseud. Ambition. 2008. (Private Ser.: No. 7). (ENG.). 288p. (YA). (gr. 9-18). pap. 12.99 *(978-1-4169-5882-6(7)*, Simon & Schuster Bks. For Young Readers) Simon & Schuster Bks. For Young Readers.
—Invitation Only. 2009. (Private Ser.: No. 2). (ENG.). 272p. (YA). pap. 9.99 *(978-1-4169-9947-8(7)*, Simon & Schuster Bks. For Young Readers) Simon & Schuster Bks. For Young Readers.
Brown, Teri. Read My Lips. 2008. (ENG.). 256p. (YA). (gr. 9-12). pap. 8.99 *(978-1-4169-5868-0(1)*, Simon Pulse) Simon Pulse.
Cabot, Meg. How to Be Popular: When You're a Social Reject Like Me, Steph L. (ENG.). (YA). 2008. 320p. (gr. 8-12). pap. 8.99 *(978-0-06-088014-9(7))* 2006. 304p. (gr. 7-12). 16.99 *(978-0-06-088012-5(0))* HarperCollins Pubs. (HarperTeen).
Calame, Don. Beat the Band. 2010. (ENG., Illus.). 400p. (YA). (gr. 9-18). 16.99 *(978-0-7636-4633-2(4))* Candlewick Pr.
Cheva, Cherry. She's So Money. 2009. (ENG.). 304p. (YA). (gr. 8). pap. 8.99 *(978-0-06-128853-1(5)*, HarperTeen) HarperCollins Pubs.
Choldenko, Gennifer. If a Tree Falls at Lunch Period. 2009. (ENG., Illus.). 224p. (J). (gr. 5-7). pap. 7.99 *(978-0-15-206644-4(6))* Houghton Mifflin Harcourt Publishing Co.
Christopher, Matt. QB Blitz. 2011. (ENG.). 144p. (J). (gr. 3-7). pap. 5.99 *(978-0-316-17682-8(6))* Little, Brown Bks. for Young Readers.
Cook, Julia. Cliques Just Don't Make Cents. DuFalla, Anita, illus. 2012. (ENG.). 32p. (J). pap. 10.95 *(978-1-934490-39-6(3))* Boys Town Pr.
Cooney, Caroline B. The Vampire's Promise. 2011. (ENG.). 496p. (J). (gr. 7-7). pap. 9.99 *(978-0-545-28976-4(9))* Scholastic, Inc.
Cooper, Gael. My Name Is Kermeena Kermudgeon. 2009. 28p. pap. 12.49 *(978-1-4490-2932-6(9))* AuthorHouse.
Cooper, Rose. Gossip from the Girls' Room. 2011. (ENG.). 208p. (J). (gr. 3-7). 12.99 *(978-0-385-73947-4(8)*, Delacorte Bks. for Young Readers) Random Hse. Children's Bks.
Cotterill, Colin. Average Alan. 2013. 150p. pap. *(978-616-7503-18-9(4))* Asia Document Bureau, Ltd.
Cronn-Mills, Kirstin. Beautiful Music for Ugly Children. 2012. (ENG.). 288p. (YA). pap. 11.99 *(978-0-7387-3251-0(6)*, Flux) North Star Editions.
Cusick, John M. Girl Parts. 2010. (ENG., Illus.). 240p. (YA). (gr. 9-18). 16.99 *(978-0-7636-4930-2(9))* Candlewick Pr.
De la Cruz, Melissa. The Ashley Project. 2014. (Ashley Project Ser.: 1). (ENG., Illus.). 288p. (J). (gr. 4-8). pap. 6.99 *(978-1-4424-9033-8(0)*, Aladdin) Simon & Schuster Children's Publishing.
—Jealous? 2008. (Ashleys Ser.: Bk. 2). (ENG.). 256p. (J). (gr. 4-8). pap. 9.99 *(978-1-4169-3407-3(3)*, Simon & Schuster Bks. For Young Readers) Simon & Schuster Bks. For Young Readers.
—Popularity Takeover. 2015. (Ashley Project Ser.: 4). (ENG., Illus.). 272p. (J). (gr. 4-8). 17.99 *(978-1-4814-0974-2(3)*, Aladdin) Simon & Schuster Children's Publishing.
—Social Order. 2014. (Ashley Project Ser.: 2). (ENG., Illus.). 288p. (J). (gr. 4-8). 16.99 *(978-1-4814-0667-3(1)*, Simon & Schuster/Paula Wiseman Bks.) Simon & Schuster/Paula Wiseman Bks.
Dean, Carolee. Forget Me Not. (ENG.). (YA). (gr. 9). 2013. 400p. pap. 11.99 *(978-1-4424-3255-0(1))* 2012. 384p. 16.99 *(978-1-4424-3254-3(3))* Simon Pulse. (Simon Pulse).
Dowell, Frances O'Roark. The Sound of Your Voice, Only Really Far Away. 2013. (Secret Language of Girl Trilogy Ser.). (ENG., Illus.). 240p. (J). (gr. 5-9). 16.99 *(978-1-4424-3289-5(6))* Simon & Schuster Children's Publishing.
Echols, Jennifer. Perfect Couple. 2015. (Superlatives Ser.). (ENG., Illus.). 336p. (YA). (gr. 9). pap. 10.99 *(978-1-4424-7448-2(3)*, Simon Pulse) Simon Pulse.
Faris, Stephanie. 25 Roses. 2015. (Mix Ser.). (ENG., Illus.). 224p. (J). (gr. 4-8). pap. 7.99 *(978-1-4814-2420-2(3)*, Aladdin) Simon & Schuster Children's Publishing.
Ficklin, Sherry D. Losing Logan. 2014. (ENG.). 304p. (J). (gr. 10-12). pap. 9.95 *(978-1-940534-41-1(0))* Clean Teen Publishing.
Flinn, Alex. Mirrored. 2015. (Kendra Chronicles Ser.: 3). (ENG.). 384p. (YA). (gr. 8). 17.99 *(978-0-06-213451-6(5))* HarperCollins Pubs.
Frost, Helen. Diamond Willow. 2011. (ENG.). 144p. (J). (gr. 5-9). pap. 7.99 *(978-0-312-60383-0(5)*, 9780312603830) Square Fish.
Garfinkle, D. L. Stuck in the 70's. 2007. 182p. (YA). *(978-1-4287-4661-9(7))* Penguin Publishing Group.
Gephart, Donna. How to Survive Middle School. 2011. (ENG.). 256p. (J). (gr. 3-7). 6.99 *(978-0-375-85411-8(8)*, Yearling) Random Hse. Children's Bks.
Geragotelis, Brittany. What the Spell. (Life's a Witch Ser.). (ENG., Illus.). (YA). (gr. 9). 2014. 352p. pap. 9.99 *(978-1-4424-6707-1(X))* 2013. 336p. 16.99 *(978-1-4424-6815-3(7))* Simon & Schuster Bks. For Young Readers. (Simon & Schuster Bks. For Young Readers).
Giles, Gail. Shattering Glass. 2004. 215p. (J). (gr. 7-18). pap. 37.00 incl. audio *(978-1-4000-9013-6(X)*, Listening Library) Random Hse. Audio Publishing Group.
Gonzalez, Gabriela & Triana, Gaby. Backstage Pass. 2004. (Illus.). 224p. (J). (gr. 7-18). lib. bdg. 16.89 *(978-0-06-056018-8(5))* HarperCollins Pubs.
Goo, Maurene. Since You Asked... 2013. (YA). pap. *(978-0-545-44822-2(0))*; (ENG.). 272p. (J). (gr. 7). 17.99 *(978-0-545-44821-5(2))* Scholastic, Inc. (Scholastic Pr.).
Gorman, Carol. A Midsummer Night's Dork. 2004. (ENG.). 224p. (J). 15.99 *(978-0-06-050718-3(7))* HarperCollins Pubs.
Gownley, Jimmy. True Things: Adults Don't Want Kids to Know. Gownley, Jimmy, illus. 2010. (Amelia Rules! Ser.). (ENG., Illus.). 176p. (J). (gr. 2-7). 19.99 *(978-1-4169-8611-9(1))*; pap. 11.99 *(978-1-4169-8609-6(X))* Simon & Schuster Children's Publishing. (Atheneum Bks. for Young Readers).
—The Tweenage Guide to Not Being Unpopular. Gownley, Jimmy, illus. 2010. (Amelia Rules! Ser.). (ENG., Illus.). 192p. (J). (gr. 2-7). pap. 12.99 *(978-1-4169-8608-9(1)*, Atheneum Bks. for Young Readers) Simon & Schuster Children's Publishing.
Grab, Daphne. Halftime. 2010. (J). *(978-0-385-73783-8(1))*; *(978-0-385-90693-7(5))* Random House Publishing Group. (Delacorte Pr).
Green, Jessica. Diary of a Would-Be Princess: The Journal of Jillian Jones, 5b. 2007. (Illus.). 236p. (J). (gr. 4-7). 15.95 *(978-1-58089-166-0(7))* Charlesbridge Publishing, Inc.
Greenwald, Lisa. Reel Life Starring Us. (ENG.). (YA). (gr. 3-7). 2013. 320p. pap. 7.95 *(978-1-4197-0426-0(5))* 2011. 304p. 16.95 *(978-1-4197-0026-2(X))* Abrams, Inc. (Amulet Bks.).
Gunn, Robin Jones. Christy Miller Collection, Vol 1, Vol. 1. 2005. (Christy Miller Collection: Bks. 1-3). (ENG., Illus.). 496p. (J). (gr. 7-12). 16.99 *(978-1-59052-584-5(1)*, Multnomah) Doubleday Religious Publishing Group, The.
Halpern, Julie. Into the Wild Nerd Yonder. 2011. (ENG.). 272p. (YA). (gr. 8-13). pap. 16.99 *(978-0-312-65307-1(7)*, 9780312653071) Square Fish.
Hapka, Catherine, pseud. Friends 4 Ever? 2008. (High School Musical Stories from East High Ser.). 124p. (J). (gr. 3-7). 12.65 *(978-0-7569-8820-3(9))* Perfection Learning Corp.
Harris, Ashley Rae. The Prank. 2011. (Night Fall Ser.). (ENG.). 120p. (YA). (gr. 6-12). pap. 7.95 *(978-0-7613-7814-3(6))*; lib. bdg. 27.93 *(978-0-7613-7747-4(6))* Lerner Publishing Group.
Harrison, Emma. Toe the Line: A Rival High Novel. 2008. (YA). *(978-1-4114-0526-4(9)*, Spark Publishing Group) Sterling Publishing Co., Inc.
Harrison, Lisi. P. S. I Loathe You. 2008. (Clique Novels Ser.). 208p. 20.00 *(978-1-60686-338-1(X))* Perfection Learning Corp.
—Sealed with a Diss. 2008. (Clique Novels Ser.). 248p. 20.00 *(978-1-60686-345-9(2))* Perfection Learning Corp.
Harvey, Sarah N. Shattered, 1 vol. 2011. (Orca Soundings Ser.). (ENG.). 128p. (YA). (gr. 8-12). pap. 9.95 *(978-1-55469-845-5(6))*; lib. bdg. 16.95 *(978-1-55469-846-2(4))* Orca Bk. Pubs. USA.
Haston, Meg. How to Rock Best Friends & Frenemies. 2013. (How to Rock Ser.: 2). (ENG.). 352p. (J). (gr. 3-7). pap. 8.00 *(978-0-316-06827-7(6)*, Poppy) Little, Brown Bks. for Young Readers.
—How to Rock Braces & Glasses. 2011. (How to Rock Ser.: 1). (ENG.). 336p. (J). (gr. 3-7). 16.99 *(978-0-316-06825-3(X)*, Poppy) Little, Brown Bks. for Young Readers.
—How to Rock Braces & Glasses. 2012. (How to Rock Ser.: 1). (ENG.). 352p. (J). (gr. 3-7). pap. 8.00 *(978-0-316-06824-6(1)*, Poppy) Little, Brown Bks. for Young Readers.
Haworth-Attard, Barbara. My Life from Air-Bras to Zits. 2009. (ENG.). 288p. (YA). (gr. 7-10). pap. 9.95 *(978-0-7387-1483-7(6)*, Flux) North Star Editions.
Holder, Amy. The Lipstick Laws. 2011. (ENG.). 240p. (YA). (gr. 7-18). pap. 13.99 *(978-0-547-36306-6(0))* Houghton Mifflin Harcourt Publishing Co.
Holm, Jennifer L. & Holm, Matthew. Brave New Pond. Holm, Jennifer L. & Holm, Matthew, illus. 2011. (Squish Ser.: No. 2). (ENG., Illus.). 96p. (J). (gr. 3-7). 12.99 *(978-0-375-93784-2(6))*; pap. 6.99 *(978-0-375-84390-7(6))* Random Hse. Children's Bks. (Random Hse. Bks. for Young Readers).
Horowitz, Lena. Dancing with Molly. 2016. (ENG.). 272p. (YA). (gr. 9). pap. 10.99 *(978-1-4814-1551-4(4)*, Simon Pulse) Simon Pulse.
Huang, Charlotte. Going Geek. 2016. (ENG.). 304p. (YA). (gr. 7). 17.99 *(978-0-553-53943-1(4)*, Delacorte Pr.) Random Hse. Children's Bks.
Humphrey, Anna. Mission (un)Popular. 2013. (ENG.). 416p. (J). (gr. 5-9). pap. 6.99 *(978-1-4231-2321-7(2))* Hyperion Pr.
Hurley, Tonya. Ghostgirl. 2010. (Ghostgirl Ser.: 1). (ENG.). 336p. (YA). (gr. 7-17). pap. 9.99 *(978-0-316-03635-1(8))* Little, Brown Bks. for Young Readers.
—Ghostgirl. Frieyro, Alicia, tr. Impey, Allison & Phillips, Craig, illus. 2009. (SPA.). 1200p. (YA). (gr. 8-12). pap. 19.99 *(978-607-11-0185-3(9)*, Alfaguara Juvenil) Santillana USA Publishing Co., Inc.
Ignatow, Amy. The Awesomely Awful Melodies. 2014. (Popularity Papers). (ENG., Illus.). 208p. (J). (gr. 3-7). pap. 8.95 *(978-1-4197-1308-8(6)*, Amulet Bks.) Abrams, Inc.
—The Long-Distance Dispatch Between Lydia Goldblatt & Julie Graham-Chang. 2011. (Popularity Papers). (ENG., Illus.). 208p. (J). (gr. 3-7). 16.95 *(978-0-8109-9724-0(X)*, Amulet Bks.) Abrams, Inc.
—The Popularity Papers. (Popularity Papers). (ENG., Illus.). 208p. (J). (gr. 3-7). 2012. 16.95 *(978-1-4197-0182-5(7))* 2011. pap. 8.95 *(978-0-8109-9723-3(1))* Abrams, Inc. (Amulet Bks.).
—The Popularity Papers: Research for the Social Improvement & General Betterment of Lydia Goldblatt & Julie Graham-Chang. 2010. (Popularity Papers). (ENG., Illus.). 208p. (J). (gr. 3-7). 16.95 *(978-0-8109-8421-9(0)*, Amulet Bks.) Abrams, Inc.
—The Popularity Papers: The Less-Than-Hidden Secrets & Final Revelations of Lydia Goldblatt & Julie Graham-Chang. 2014. (Popularity Papers). (ENG., Illus.). 208p. (J). (gr. 3-7). 15.95 *(978-1-4197-1270-8(5)*, Amulet Bks.) Abrams, Inc.
—The Awesomely Awful Melodies of Lydia Goldblatt & Julie Graham-Chang. 2013. (Popularity Papers). (ENG., Illus.). 208p. (J). (gr. 3-7). 16.95 *(978-1-4197-0536-6(9)*, Amulet Bks.) Abrams, Inc.
—Words of (Questionable) Wisdom. 2013. (Popularity Papers). (ENG., Illus.). 208p. (J). (gr. 3-7). pap. 8.95 *(978-1-4197-0535-9(0)*, Amulet Bks.) Abrams, Inc.
—Words of (Questionable) Wisdom from Lydia Goldblatt & Julie Graham-Chang, Bk. 3. 2011. (Popularity Papers). (ENG., Illus.). 208p. (J). (gr. 3-7). 16.95 *(978-1-4197-0063-7(4)*, Amulet Bks.) Abrams, Inc.
Ignatow, Amy & Allen, Rinne. The Popularity Papers Bk. 2: The Long-Distance Dispatch Between Lydia Goldblatt & Julie Graham-Chang. 2012. (Popularity Papers). (ENG., Illus.). 208p. (J). (gr. 3-7). pap. 8.95 *(978-1-4197-0183-2(5)*, Amulet Bks.) Abrams, Inc.
Jaden, Denise. Never Enough. 2012. (ENG.). 400p. (YA). (gr. 9). pap. 9.99 *(978-1-4424-2907-9(0)*, Simon Pulse) Simon Pulse.
James, Brian. Zombie Blondes. 2009. (ENG.). 256p. (YA). (gr. 7-12). pap. 8.99 *(978-0-312-57375-1(8)*, 9780312573751) Square Fish.
Jennings, Patrick. Lucky Cap. 2011. (ENG.). 224p. (J). (gr. 4-7). 15.99 *(978-1-60684-054-2(1)*, Carolrhoda Bks.) Lerner Publishing Group.
Jerry, Spinelli. Stargirl. 2014. (ENG.). 208p. (YA). 11.24 *(978-1-63245-152-1(2))* Lectorum Pubns., Inc.
Juby, Susan. Getting the Girl: A Guide to Private Investigation, Surveillance, & Cookery. 2010. (ENG.). 352p. (YA). (gr. 8). pap. 8.99 *(978-0-06-076528-6(3)*, HarperTeen) HarperCollins Pubs.
Kaplan, Isabel. Hancock Park. 2010. (ENG.). 272p. (YA). (gr. 9). pap. 8.99 *(978-0-06-137370-1(2)*, HarperTeen) HarperCollins Pubs.
Karre, Elizabeth. All You Are. 2014. (Gift Ser.). 120p. (YA). (gr. 6-12). (ENG.). pap. 7.95 *(978-1-4677-4477-5(8))*; lib. bdg. 27.93 *(978-1-4677-3510-0(8))* Lerner Publishing Group. (Darby Creek).
Kats, Jewel. Miss Popular Steals the Show: Girls in Wheelchairs Rule! Stenton, Murray, illus. 2014. 37p. (J). pap. 14.95 *(978-1-61599-236-2(7))* Loving Healing Pr., Inc.
Keating, Jess. How to Outrun a Crocodile When Your Shoes Are Untied. 2014. (My Life Is a Zoo Ser.: 1). (ENG.). 288p. (J). (gr. 4-7). pap. 7.99 *(978-1-4022-9755-7(6)*, 9781402297557, Sourcebooks Jabberwocky) Sourcebooks, Inc.
—How to Outswim a Shark Without a Snorkel. 2015. (My Life Is a Zoo Ser.: 2). (ENG.). 304p. (J). (gr. 4-7). pap. 7.99 *(978-1-4022-9758-8(0)*, 9781402297588, Sourcebooks Jabberwocky) Sourcebooks, Inc.
Kerr, M. E., pseud. If I Love You, Am I Trapped Forever?, 0 vols. 2011. (ENG.). 192p. (J). (gr. 7-9). pap. 9.99 *(978-0-7614-5839-5(5)*, 9780761458395, Amazon Children's Publishing) Amazon Publishing.
Kittle, Katrina. Reasons to Be Happy. 2011. (ENG.). 288p. (J). (gr. 6-8). pap. 10.99 *(978-1-4022-6020-9(2)*, Sourcebooks Jabberwocky) Sourcebooks, Inc.
Knudson, Mike. Cool Campers. 2011. (Raymond & Graham Ser.). (ENG.). 160p. (J). (gr. 3-7). 6.99 *(978-0-14-241875-8(7)*, Puffin Books) Penguin Young Readers Group.
Kowitt, H. N. The Loser List. 2011. (ENG.). 224p. (J). (gr. 3-7). 9.99 *(978-0-545-24004-8(2)*, Scholastic Paperbacks) Scholastic, Inc.
—Take Me to Your Loser. 2013. (Loser List Ser.: 4). (ENG.). 240p. (J). (gr. 3-7). 9.99 *(978-0-545-50795-0(2)*, Scholastic Pr.) Scholastic, Inc.
Kowitt, Holly. The Principal's Bra Is Missing. Kowitt, Holly, illus. 2017. (ENG., Illus.). 224p. (J). 16.99 *(978-1-250-09132-1(2)*, 9781250091321) Feiwel & Friends.
Kowitt, Holly, illus. The Loser List. 2011. 213p. (J). pap. *(978-0-545-32900-2(0)*, Scholastic Pr.) Scholastic, Inc.
—Revenge of the Loser. 2012. 233p. (J). *(978-0-545-42611-4(1)*, Scholastic Pr.) Scholastic, Inc.
Kramer, Stacy & Thomas, Valerie. Karma Bites. 2010. (ENG.). 348p. (J). (gr. 5-7). pap. 18.99 *(978-0-547-36301-1(X))* Houghton Mifflin Harcourt Publishing Co.
Krys, Michelle. Hexed. 2014. (ENG.). 384p. (YA). (gr. 7). 17.99 *(978-0-385-74337-2(8)*, Delacorte Pr.) Random Hse. Children's Bks.
Lean, Sarah. Hero. 2015. (ENG.). 208p. (J). (gr. 3-7). 16.99 *(978-0-06-212238-4(X))* HarperCollins Pubs.
Lennon, Maria T. Confessions of a So-Called Middle Child. 2014. (ENG.). 304p. (J). (gr. 3-7). pap. 6.99 *(978-0-06-212691-7(1))* HarperCollins Pubs.
Leveen, Tom. Random. 2014. (ENG., Illus.). 224p. (YA). (gr. 9). 17.99 *(978-1-4424-9956-0(7)*, Simon Pulse) Simon Pulse.
Levine, Gail Carson. The Wish. 2005. (ENG.). 256p. (J). (gr. 3-7). pap. 6.99 *(978-0-06-075911-7(9)*, HarperTeen) HarperCollins Pubs.
—The Wish. 2004. 197p. (gr. 3-7). 16.00 *(978-0-7569-4272-4(1))* Perfection Learning Corp.
Long, Ethan. Chamelia & the New Kid in Class. 2013. (ENG., Illus.). 40p. (J). (gr. -1-3). 16.99 *(978-0-316-21042-3(0))* Little Brown & Co.
Lubar, David. My Rotten Life. 2009. (Nathan Abercrombie, Accidental Zombie Ser.: 1). (ENG., Illus.). 160p. (J). (gr. 3-7). pap. 8.99 *(978-0-7653-1634-9(X)*, 9780765316349, Starscape) Doherty, Tom Assocs., LLC.
Ludwig, Trudy. The Invisible Boy. Barton, Patrice, illus. 2013. (ENG.). 40p. (J). (gr. 1-4). 16.99 *(978-1-58246-450-3(2)*, Knopf Bks. for Young Readers) Random Hse. Children's Bks.
Maciejewski, Mark. I Am Fartacus. 2017. (Max Ser.). (ENG., Illus.). 336p. (J). (gr. 4-8). pap. 7.99 *(978-1-4814-6419-2(1)*, Simon & Schuster/Paula Wiseman Bks.) Simon & Schuster/Paula Wiseman Bks.
Mack, Jeff. Clueless Mcgee Gets Famous. Mack, Jeff, illus. 2014. (Clueless Mcgee Ser.: 3). (ENG., Illus.). 288p. (J). (gr. 3-7). 12.99 *(978-0-399-25751-3(9)*, Philomel Bks.) Penguin Young Readers Group.
Maizel, Rebecca. Between Us & the Moon. 2015. (ENG.). 384p. (YA). (gr. 9). 17.99 *(978-0-06-232761-1(5))* HarperCollins Pubs.

Marcionette, Jake. Just Jake: Dog Eat Dog. Villa, Victor Rivas, illus. 2015. (Just Jake Ser.: No. 2). (ENG.). 196p. (J). (gr. 3-7). 11.99 *(978-0-448-46693-4(7)*, Grosset & Dunlap) Penguin Young Readers Group.

Matthews, Owen. How to Win at High School. 2015. (ENG.). 496p. (YA). (gr. 9). 17.99 *(978-0-06-233686-6(X)*, HarperTeen) HarperCollins Pubs.

May, Kyla. Kiki: My Stylish Life. 2013. (Lotus Lane Ser.: 1). (ENG.). 96p. (J). (gr. 1-3). pap. 4.99 *(978-0-545-44512-2(4))* Scholastic, Inc.

—Kiki Bk. 1: My Stylish Life. 2013. (Lotus Lane Ser.: 1). (ENG.). 96p. (J). (gr. 1-3). lib. bdg. 15.99 *(978-0-545-49613-1(6))* Scholastic, Inc.

Mayer, Kirsten. Attack of the Evil Minions! Miller, Ed, illus. 2013. (ENG.). 32p. (J). (gr. -1-3). 12.99 *(978-0-316-23444-3(3))* Little, Brown Bks. for Young Readers.

McCafferty, Megan. Jessica Darling's It List 2: The (Totally Not) Guaranteed Guide to Friends, Foes & Faux Friends. 2015. (Jessica Darling's It List Ser.: 2). (ENG.). 208p. (J). (gr. 3-7). pap. 8.00 *(978-0-316-24503-6(8)*, Poppy) Little, Brown Bks. for Young Readers.

—The (Totally Not) Guaranteed Guide to Popularity, Prettiness & Perfection. 2014. (Jessica Darling's It List Ser.: 1). (ENG.). 240p. (J). (gr. 3-7). pap. 8.99 *(978-0-316-24498-5(8)*, Poppy) Little, Brown Bks. for Young Readers.

—The (Totally Not) Guaranteed Guide to Stressing, Obsessing & Second-Guessing. 2015. (Jessica Darling's It List Ser.: 3). (ENG.). 224p. (J). (gr. 3-7). 17.00 *(978-0-316-33324-5(7))* Little Brown & Co.

McInnes, Nicole. Brianna on the Brink. 2013. (ENG.). 176p. (YA). (gr. 10). 16.95 *(978-0-8234-2741-3(2))* Holiday Hse., Inc.

McNish, Cliff. Angel. 2008. (Exceptional Reading & Language Arts Titles for Intermediate Grades Ser.). 311p. (YA). (gr. 8-12). 16.95 *(978-0-8225-8900-6(1))* Lerner Publishing Group.

Mechling, Lauren, et al. The Rise & Fall of a 10th Grade Social Climber. 2005. (ENG.). 304p. (YA). (gr. 7). pap. 16.99 *(978-0-618-55519-2(6))* Houghton Mifflin Harcourt Publishing Co.

Mellom, Robin. The Classroom Trick Out My School! Gilpin, Stephen, illus. 2014. (Classroom Novel Ser.). (ENG.). 288p. (J). (gr. 3-7). 12.99 *(978-1-4231-5065-7(1))* Hyperion Bks. for Children.

Meyerhoff, Jenny. Class B. U. R. P. Week, Jason, illus. 2014. (Barftastic Life of Louie Burger Ser.: 2). (ENG.). 288p. (J). (gr. 3-6). 13.99 *(978-0-374-30521-5(8)*, 9780374305215, Farrar, Straus & Giroux (BYR)) Farrar, Straus & Giroux.

Mitchell, Todd. The Secret to Lying. (ENG., Illus.). 336p. (YA). (gr. 9). 2011. pap. 7.99 *(978-0-7636-5620-1(8))* 2010. 17.99 *(978-0-7636-4084-2(0))* Candlewick Pr.

Morgan, Melissa J. Freaky Tuesday, 17 vols. 2007. (Camp Confidential Ser.: 17). (ENG.). 160p. (J). (gr. 3-7). pap. 4.99 *(978-0-448-44651-6(0)*, Grosset & Dunlap) Penguin Young Readers Group.

Myracle, Lauren. Rhymes with Witches. (ENG.). (YA). (gr. 8-17). 2006. 272p. pap. 7.95 *(978-0-8109-9215-3(9))* 2005. 224p. 16.95 *(978-0-8109-5859-3(7)*, Amulet Bks.) Abrams, Inc.

Night, P. J. Don't Drink the Punch! 2012. (Creepover Ser.: 11). lib. bdg. 16.00 *(978-0-606-26901-8(0)*, Turtleback) Turtleback Bks.

Nigro, D. M. The Wolfman, the Shrink & the Eighth-Grade Election. 2006. 116p. (J). pap. 13.50 *(978-1-931201-66-7(8))* Twilight Times Bks.

Noël, Alyson. Forever Summer. 2011. (ENG.). 464p. (YA). (gr. 8-12). pap. 9.99 *(978-0-312-60439-4(4)*, 9780312604394, St. Martin's Griffin) St. Martin's Pr.

Oakes, Colleen. Blood of Wonderland. 2017. (Queen of Hearts Ser.: 2). (YA). (gr. 8). 352p. pap. 9.99 ***(978-0-06-240977-5(8))***; 336p. 17.99 *(978-0-06-240976-8(X))* HarperCollins Pubs. (HarperTeen).

O'Connor, Barbara. Fame & Glory in Freedom, Georgia. 2008. (ENG.). 112p. (J). (gr. 3-7). pap. 8.99 *(978-0-374-40018-7(0)*, 9780374400187) Square Fish.

Oliver, Lauren. Before I Fall. (ENG.). (YA). (gr. 9). 2016. 544p. pap. 10.99 *(978-0-06-172681-1(8))* 2010. 480p. 17.99 *(978-0-06-172680-4(X))* HarperCollins Pubs.

—Before I Fall. 2010. 368p. pap. *(978-0-340-98090-3(7)*, Hodder Paperbacks) Hodder & Stoughton.

—Before I Fall. 2016. (YA). lib. bdg. 22.10 *(978-0-606-23576-1(0)*, Turtleback) Turtleback Bks.

Oliver, Lin. Double-Crossed #3. 2013. (Almost Identical Ser.: 3). (ENG.). 224p. (J). (gr. 3-7). pap. 7.99 *(978-0-448-45193-0(X)*, Grosset & Dunlap) Penguin Young Readers Group.

Palmer, Robin. Geek Charming. 2009. (ENG.). 368p. (YA). (gr. 7-18). 7.99 *(978-0-14-241122-3(1)*, Speak) Penguin Young Readers Group.

—Once upon a Kiss. 2016. (ENG.). 304p. (YA). (gr. 7). pap. 9.99 *(978-0-14-750988-8(2)*, Speak) Penguin Young Readers Group.

Patterson, James & Papademetriou, Lisa. Big Fat Liar. Swaab, Neil, illus. 2014. (Middle School Ser.: Bk. 3). (ENG.). 304p. (J). (gr. 3-7). 13.99 *(978-0-316-32203-4(2)*, Jimmy Patterson) Little Brown & Co.

Pearce, Jackson. As You Wish. (ENG.). 304p. (YA). (gr. 8). 2010. pap. 8.99 *(978-0-06-166154-9(6))* 2009. 16.99 *(978-0-06-166152-5(X))* HarperCollins Pubs. (HarperTeen).

Perez, Marlene. The Comeback. 2009. (ENG.). 208p. (J). (gr. 7). pap. 8.99 *(978-0-545-08807-7(0))* Scholastic, Inc.

Petroff, Shani. Careful What You Wish For. McKenney, J. David, illus. 2010. (Bedeviled Ser.: 3). (ENG.). 240p. (J). (gr. 3-7). pap. 6.99 *(978-0-448-45113-8(1)*, Grosset & Dunlap) Penguin Young Readers Group.

—Daddy's Little Angel, No. 1. McKenney, J. David, illus. 2009. (Bedeviled Ser.: 1). (ENG.). 240p. (J). (gr. 5-7). pap. 7.99 *(978-0-448-45111-4(5)*, Grosset & Dunlap) Penguin Young Readers Group.

—The Good, the Bad, & the Ugly Dress. McKenney, J. David, illus. 2010. (Bedeviled Ser.: 2). (ENG.). 240p. (J). (gr. 5-7). pap. 6.99 *(978-0-448-45112-1(3)*, Grosset & Dunlap) Penguin Young Readers Group.

Plank, Alex & Plank, Lisa. How Bad Could It Be? 2007. (ENG.). 64p. per. 19.95 *(978-1-4241-6217-8(3))* America Star Bks.

Polacco, Patricia. Bully. Polacco, Patricia, illus. 2012. (ENG., Illus.). 48p. (J). (gr. 2-5). 17.99 *(978-0-399-25704-9(7)*, G.P. Putnam's Sons Books for Young Readers) Penguin Young Readers Group.

Pons, Lele & De la Cruz, Melissa. Surviving High School: Do It for the Vine: A Novel. 2017. (ENG.). 272p. (gr. 8). pap. 11.99 *(978-1-5011-2054-1(9)*, Gallery Bks.) Gallery Bks.

Portes, Andrea. Anatomy of a Misfit. 2014. (ENG.). 336p. (YA). (gr. 9). 17.99 *(978-0-06-231364-5(9)*, HarperTeen) HarperCollins Pubs.

Preble, Laura. The Queen Geek Social Club. 2006. (ENG.). 336p. (YA). (gr. 7-18). 15.00 *(978-0-425-21164-9(9)*, Berkley) Penguin Publishing Group.

Preller, James. Along Came Spider. 2008. (ENG.). 144p. (J). (gr. 3-7). 15.99 *(978-0-545-03299-5(7)*, Scholastic Paperbacks) Scholastic, Inc.

Prostko, Andrea. Strike One! 2010. 220p. pap. 13.95 *(978-1-60911-546-3(5)*, Eloquent Bks.) Strategic Book Publishing & Rights Agency (SBPRA).

Raskin, Joyce. My Misadventures As a Teenage Rock Star. Chu, Carol, illus. 2011. (ENG.). 112p. (YA). (gr. 7-18). pap. 8.99 *(978-0-547-39311-7(3))* Houghton Mifflin Harcourt Publishing Co.

Robberecht, Thierry. Superhero School. Goossens, Philippe, illus. 2012. (ENG.). 30p. (J). (gr. -1-k). 16.95 *(978-1-60537-140-5(8))* Cobblestone Publishing Co.

Robbins, Jacqui. Two of a Kind. Phelan, Matt, illus. 2009. (ENG.). 32p. (J). (gr. -1-2). 17.99 *(978-1-4169-2437-1(X)*, Atheneum Bks. for Young Readers) Simon & Schuster Children's Publishing.

Rodkey, Geoff. The Tapper Twins Go Viral. 2017. (Tapper Twins Ser.: 4). (ENG., Illus.). 256p. (J). (gr. 3-7). 13.99 *(978-0-316-29784-4(4))* Little Brown & Co.

Romano, Juliana. First There Was Forever. 2016. (ENG.). 416p. (YA). (gr. 9). pap. 10.99 *(978-0-14-751391-5(X)*, Speak) Penguin Young Readers Group.

Rudetsky, Seth. My Awesome - Awful Popularity Plan. 2013. (ENG.). 224p. (YA). (gr. 7). pap. 8.99 *(978-0-375-89997-3(9)*, Ember) Random Hse. Children's Bks.

Rue, Ginger. Brand-New Emily. 2010. (ENG.). 240p. (YA). (gr. 7). pap. 7.99 *(978-1-58246-323-0(9)*, Tricycle Pr.) Random Hse. Children's Bks.

—Rock 'n' Roll Rebel. 2016. (Tig Ripley Ser.). (ENG.). 349p. (J). (gr. 4-7). 16.99 *(978-1-58536-945-4(4)*, 204106) Sleeping Bear Pr.

Russell, Rachel Renée. Dork Diaries Set, Set. Russell, Rachel Renée, illus. 2011. (Dork Diaries: Nos. 1-3). (ENG., Illus.). 928p. (J). (gr. 4-8). 41.99 *(978-1-4424-2662-7(4)*, Aladdin) Simon & Schuster Children's Publishing.

—Tales from a Not-So-Fabulous Life. Russell, Rachel Renée, illus. 2009. (Dork Diaries: 1). (ENG., Illus.). 304p. (J). (gr. 4-8). 13.99 *(978-1-4169-8006-3(7)*, Aladdin) Simon & Schuster Children's Publishing.

—Tales from a Not-So-Fabulous Life. 2009. (Dork Diaries: 1). lib. bdg. 25.75 *(978-0-606-32419-9(4)*, Turtleback) Turtleback Bks.

—Tales from a Not-So-Friendly Frenemy. Russell, Rachel Renée, illus. 2016. (Dork Diaries: 11). (ENG., Illus.). 288p. (J). (gr. 4-8). 13.99 *(978-1-4814-7920-2(2)*, Aladdin) Simon & Schuster Children's Publishing.

—Tales from a Not-So-Graceful Ice Princess. Russell, Rachel Renée, illus. 2012. (Dork Diaries: 4). (ENG., Illus.). 368p. (J). (gr. 4-8). 13.99 *(978-1-4424-1192-0(9)*, Aladdin) Simon & Schuster Children's Publishing.

—Tales from a Not-So-Popular Party Girl. Russell, Rachel Renée, illus. 2010. (Dork Diaries: 2). (ENG., Illus.). 288p. (J). (gr. 4-8). 13.99 *(978-1-4169-8008-7(3)*, Aladdin) Simon & Schuster Children's Publishing.

—Tales from a Not-So-Popular Party Girl. 2010. (Dork Diaries: 2). lib. bdg. 25.75 *(978-0-606-32420-5(8)*, Turtleback) Turtleback Bks.

—Tales from a Not-So-Smart Miss Know-It-All. Russell, Rachel Renée, illus. 2012. (Dork Diaries: 5). (ENG., Illus.). 368p. (J). (gr. 4-8). 13.99 *(978-1-4424-4961-9(6)*, Aladdin) Simon & Schuster Children's Publishing.

—Tales from a Not-So-Talented Pop Star. Russell, Rachel Renée, illus. 2011. (Dork Diaries: 3). (ENG., Illus.). 336p. (J). (gr. 4-8). 13.99 *(978-1-4424-1190-6(2)*, Aladdin) Simon & Schuster Children's Publishing.

Russell, Rachel Renée, et al. Tales from a Not-So-Popular Party Girl. 2010. (ENG.). pap. *(978-1-4424-4042-5(2)*, Aladdin Paperbacks) Simon & Schuster Children's Publishing.

Sachar, Louis. Marvin Redpost #2: Why Pick on Me? Record, Adam, illus. 2015. (Marvin Redpost Ser.: 2). (ENG.). 96p. (J). (gr. 1-4). lib. bdg. 12.99 *(978-0-553-53541-9(2)*, Random Hse. Bks. for Young Readers) Random Hse. Children's Bks.

Sales, Leila. This Song Will Save Your Life. 2013. (ENG.). 288p. (YA). (gr. 7). 18.99 *(978-0-374-35138-0(4)*, 9780374351380, Farrar, Straus & Giroux (BYR)) Farrar, Straus & Giroux.

Sauer, Tammi. Oh, Nuts! Krall, Dan, illus. 2012. (ENG.). 32p. (J). 17.89 *(978-1-59990-467-2(5)*, 9781599904672); (gr. -1-6). 16.99 *(978-1-59990-466-5(7)*, 9781599904665) Bloomsbury Publishing USA. (Bloomsbury USA Childrens).

Schechter, Lynn R. My Big Fat Secret: How Jenna Takes Control of Her Emotions & Eating. Chin, Jason, illus. 2009. 48p. (J). (gr. 3-7). 14.95 *(978-1-4338-0540-0(5))*; pap. 9.95 *(978-1-4338-0541-7(3))* American Psychological Assn. (Magination Pr.).

Schraff, Anne. To Be Somebody. 2008. (Passages Ser.). 120p. (J). (gr. 4-6). lib. bdg. 13.95 *(978-0-7569-8390-1(8))* Perfection Learning Corp.

Schreiber, Ellen. Magic of the Moonlight. (Full Moon Ser.: 2). (ENG.). (YA). (gr. 8). 2012. 256p. pap. 9.99 *(978-0-06-198656-7(9))* 2011. 240p. 17.99 *(978-0-06-198657-4(7))* HarperCollins Pubs. (Tegen, Katherine Bks).

—Once in a Full Moon. 2011. (Full Moon Ser.: 1). (ENG.). 320p. (YA). (gr. 8). pap. 8.99 *(978-0-06-198652-9(6)*, Tegen, Katherine Bks) HarperCollins Pubs.

Scott, Kieran. I Was a Non-Blonde Cheerleader. 2007. (ENG.). 272p. (YA). (gr. 7-18). 8.99 *(978-0-14-240910-7(3)*, Speak) Penguin Young Readers Group.

Sedita, Francesco. Miss Popularity. 2007. 120p. (J). pap. *(978-0-545-00828-0(X))* Scholastic, Inc.

Segal, Zoe. Confessions of a Tenth-Grade Social Climber. 2005. 290p. (YA). *(978-0-618-44981-1(7))* Houghton Mifflin Harcourt Publishing Co.

Shannon, David. A Bad Case of Stripes. 2015. 32p. pap. 7.00 *(978-1-61003-539-2(9))* Center for the Collaborative Classroom.

—A Bad Case of Stripes. 2004. (Scholastic Bookshelf Ser.). (Illus.). (gr. -1-3). 17.00 *(978-0-7569-3183-4(5))* Perfection Learning Corp.

—A Bad Case of Stripes. Shannon, David, illus. 2007. (ENG., Illus.). (J). (gr. -1-3). 9.99 *(978-0-439-92494-8(4))* Scholastic, Inc.

—A Bad Case of Stripes. 2007. (ENG.). (J). (gr. -1-3). 18.95 *(978-0-439-02328-3(9))* Scholastic, Inc.

Shepard, Sara. Ali's Pretty Little Lies. 2013. (Pretty Little Liars Companion Novel Ser.). (ENG.). (gr. 9). 320p. (YA). pap. 9.99 *(978-0-06-223337-0(8))*; 304p. (J). 17.99 *(978-0-06-223336-3(X))* HarperCollins Pubs. (HarperTeen).

—Ali's Pretty Little Lies. 2013. (Pretty Little Liars Ser.). (YA). lib. bdg. 20.85 *(978-0-606-35048-8(9)*, Turtleback) Turtleback Bks.

Shreve, Susan Richards. Kiss Me Tomorrow. 2006. 220p. (J). *(978-1-4156-5592-4(8)*, Levine, Arthur A. Bks.) Scholastic, Inc.

Simon, Coco. Alexis Cool As a Cupcake. 2013. (Cupcake Diaries: 8). (ENG., Illus.). 160p. (J). (gr. 3-7). 16.99 *(978-1-4424-8569-3(8)*, Simon Spotlight) Simon Spotlight.

—Alexis Cool as a Cupcake. 2012. (Cupcake Diaries: 8). lib. bdg. 16.00 *(978-0-606-26334-4(9)*, Turtleback) Turtleback Bks.

—Katie Starting from Scratch. 2014. (Cupcake Diaries: 21). (ENG., Illus.). 160p. (J). (gr. 3-7). pap. 5.99 *(978-1-4814-0471-6(7)*, Simon Spotlight) Simon Spotlight.

—Mia in the Mix. (Cupcake Diaries: 2). (ENG., 160p. (J). (gr. 3-7). 2013. Illus.). 15.99 *(978-1-4424-7491-8(2))* 2011. pap. 6.99 *(978-1-4424-2277-3(7))* Simon Spotlight. (Simon Spotlight).

Sise, Katie. The Boyfriend App. 2013. (ENG.). 320p. (YA). (gr. 8). 17.99 *(978-0-06-219526-5(3))* HarperCollins Pubs.

—The Pretty App. 2015. (ENG.). 352p. (YA). (gr. 8). 17.99 *(978-0-06-219529-6(8))* HarperCollins Pubs.

Slater, David Michael. Comin' Through, 1 vol. Rooney, Ronnie, illus. 2007. (Missy Swiss & More Ser.). (ENG.). 32p. (gr. -1-4). 28.50 *(978-1-60270-008-6(7)*, Looking Glass Library) ABDO Publishing Co.

Smith, Bryan. Is There an App for That? Wish, Katia, illus. 2015. (ENG.). 32p. (J). pap. 10.95 *(978-1-934490-74-7(1))* Boys Town Pr.

Sones, Sonya. What My Girlfriend Doesn't Know. 2011. 9.68 *(978-0-7848-3389-6(3)*, Everbind) Marco Bk. Co.

—What My Girlfriend Doesn't Know. 2013. (ENG., Illus.). 320p. (YA). (gr. 7). pap. 9.99 *(978-1-4424-9384-1(4)*, Simon & Schuster Bks. For Young Readers) Simon & Schuster Bks. For Young Readers.

The Sound of Your Voice, Only Really Far Away. 2014. (Secret Language of Girl Trilogy Ser.). (ENG., Illus.). 256p. (J). (gr. 5-9). pap. 7.99 *(978-1-4424-3290-1(X)*, Atheneum Bks. for Young Readers) Simon & Schuster Children's Publishing.

Spinelli, Jerry. Stargirl. 2003. (EMC Masterpiece Series Access Editions). xiv, 199p. (YA). 12.99 *(978-0-8219-2504-1(0)*, 35378) EMC/Paradigm Publishing.

—Stargirl. unabr. ed. 2004. 192p. (J). (gr. 7-18). pap. 40.00 incl. audio *(978-0-8072-0855-7(8)*, LYA 323 SP, Listening Library) Random Hse. Audio Publishing Group.

—Stargirl. 2004. (ENG.). 208p. (YA). (gr. 7). mass mkt. 7.99 *(978-0-440-41677-7(9)*, Laurel Leaf) Random Hse. Children's Bks.

St. Claire, Roxanne. They All Fall Down. (ENG.). 352p. (YA). (gr. 7). 2016. pap. 9.99 *(978-0-385-74272-6(X)*, Ember) 2014. 17.99 *(978-0-385-74271-9(1)*, Delacorte Pr.) Random Hse. Children's Bks.

Standish, Burt L. Frank Merriwell's Fame. Rudman, Jack, ed. 2003. (Frank Merriwell Ser.). 29.95 *(978-0-8373-9336-0(1))*; pap. 9.95 *(978-0-8373-9036-9(2))* Merriwell, Frank Inc.

Staniszewski, Anna. The Dirt Diary. 2014. (Dirt Diary Ser.: 1). (ENG.). 256p. (J). (gr. 5-9). pap. 6.99 *(978-1-4022-8636-0(8)*, 9781402286360, Sourcebooks Jabberwocky) Sourcebooks, Inc.

—The Gossip File. 2015. (Dirt Diary Ser.: 3). (ENG.). 224p. (J). (gr. 5-9). pap. 6.99 *(978-1-4926-0463-1(1)*, 9781492604631, Sourcebooks Jabberwocky) Sourcebooks, Inc.

Stone, Phoebe. Deep down Popular. 2010. (ENG.). 288p. (J). (gr. 4-7). 6.99 *(978-0-439-80244-4(X)*, Levine, Arthur A. Bks.) Scholastic, Inc.

Summers, Courtney. What Goes Around: Two Books in One: Cracked up to Be & Some Girls Are. 2013. (ENG.). 480p. (YA). (gr. 9-12). pap. 9.99 *(978-1-250-03844-9(8)*, 9781250038449, St. Martin's Griffin) St. Martin's Pr.

Toliver, Wendy. The Secret Life of a Teenage Siren. 2012. (Romantic Comedies Ser.). (ENG.). 304p. (YA). (gr. 7). pap. 14.99 *(978-1-4424-7494-9(7)*, Simon Pulse) Simon Pulse.

Tracy, Kristen. Project (un)Popular Book #1. (Project (un)Popular Ser.). (ENG.). 336p. (J). (gr. 5). 2017. 7.99 ***(978-0-553-51051-5(7)**, Yearling)* 2016. 16.99 *(978-0-553-51048-5(7)*, Delacorte Bks. for Young Readers) Random Hse. Children's Bks.

—Project (un)Popular Book #2: Totally Crushed. 2017. (Project (un)Popular Ser.: 2). (ENG.). 224p. (J). (gr. 5). 16.99 ***(978-0-553-51052-2(5)**,* Delacorte Bks. for Young Readers) Random Hse. Children's Bks.

—Totally Crushed. 2017. 211p. (J). ***(978-0-553-51053-9(3)**,* Delacorte Pr) Random House Publishing Group.

Trueit, Trudi. The Sister Solution. Valencia, Adrian, illus. 2015. (Mix Ser.). (ENG.). 240p. (J). (gr. 4-8). pap. 7.99 *(978-1-4814-3239-9(7)*, Aladdin) Simon & Schuster Children's Publishing.

—Stealing Popular. 2012. (Mix Ser.). (ENG.). 240p. (J). (gr. 4-8). pap. 6.99 *(978-1-4424-4154-5(2)*, Aladdin) Simon & Schuster Children's Publishing.

Vail, Rachel. Lucky. 2009. (Avery Sisters Trilogy Ser.: 1). (ENG.). 256p. (YA). (gr. 8). pap. 8.99 *(978-0-06-089045-2(2))* HarperCollins Pubs.

—Unfriended. (ENG.). (J). (gr. 5). 2015. 304p. 8.99 *(978-0-14-751154-6(2)*, Puffin Books) 2014. 288p. 16.99 *(978-0-670-01307-4(2)*, Viking Books for Young Readers) Penguin Young Readers Group.

Van Dolzer, Krista. Don't Vote for Me. 2016. (ENG.). 240p. (J). (gr. 5-8). pap. 7.99 *(978-1-4926-3184-2(1)*, 9781492631842, Sourcebooks Jabberwocky) Sourcebooks, Inc.

—Don't Vote for Me. 2015. (ENG.). 240p. (J). (gr. 5-8). 15.99 *(978-1-4926-0941-4(2)*, 9781492609414, Sourcebooks Jabberwocky) Sourcebooks, Inc.

Vrettos, Adrienne Maria. The Exile of Gigi Lane. (ENG.). (YA). (gr. 7). 2011. 368p. pap. 8.99 *(978-1-4424-2121-9(5))* 2010. 352p. 16.99 *(978-1-4169-2433-3(7))* McElderry, Margaret K. Bks. (McElderry, Margaret K. Bks.).

Walde, Christine. The Candy Darlings. 2006. (ENG.). 310p. (YA). (gr. 9-12). per. 18.95 *(978-0-618-58969-2(4))* Houghton Mifflin Harcourt Publishing Co.

Wang, Corrie. The Takedown. 2017. (ENG.). 384p. (YA). (gr. 9-17). 17.99 *(978-1-4847-5742-0(4))* Disney Publishing Worldwide.

Weatherly, L. A. Them. 2013. (ENG.). 80p. (YA). (gr. 6-12). pap. 6.95 *(978-1-78112-185-6(0))*; lib. bdg. 22.60 *(978-1-78112-184-9(2))* Lerner Publishing Group.

Whitaker, Alecia. The Queen of Kentucky. 2013. (ENG.). 384p. (YA). (gr. 7-17). pap. 8.99 *(978-0-316-12494-2(X)*, Poppy) Little, Brown Bks. for Young Readers.

Williams, Erika. Through the Shattered Glass, 1 vol. 2010. 62p. pap. 19.95 *(978-1-4489-5149-9(6))* America Star Bks.

Willner-Pardo, Gina. The Hard Kind of Promise. 2011. (ENG.). 204p. (J). (gr. 5-7). pap. 12.99 *(978-0-547-55017-6(0))* Houghton Mifflin Harcourt Publishing Co.

Wong, Janet S. Me & Rolly Maloo. Buttler, Elizabeth, illus. 2010. (ENG.). 128p. (C). (gr. 2-5). pap. 12.95 *(978-1-58089-159-2(4))* National Geographic School Publishing, Inc.

Wright, Lanikka. The Fab Four 2: Eva's Obsession. 2012. (ENG.). 244p. pap. 13.95 *(978-1-4327-9846-8(4))* Outskirts Pr., Inc.

Yee, Lisa. Warp Speed. (ENG.). 320p. (J). 2013. (gr. 3-7). pap. 6.99 *(978-0-545-15400-0(6))* 2011. (gr. 4-7). 16.99 *(978-0-545-12276-4(7))* Scholastic, Inc. (Levine, Arthur A. Bks.).

Yoo, David. The Detention Club. (ENG.). 304p. (J). (gr. 5). 2012. pap. 6.99 *(978-0-06-178380-7(3))* 2011. 16.99 *(978-0-06-178378-4(1))* HarperCollins Pubs.

Zadoff, Allen. Food, Girls, & Other Things I Can't Have. 2011. (ENG., Illus.). 320p. (gr. 9). pap. 9.99 *(978-1-60684-151-8(3)*, Carolrhoda Lab™) Lerner Publishing Group.

Ziegler, Jennifer. How Not to Be Popular. 2010. (ENG.). 348p. (YA). (gr. 7). mass mkt. 8.99 *(978-0-440-24024-2(7)*, Delacorte Bks. for Young Readers) Random Hse. Children's Bks.

POPULATION

see also Birth Control; Migration, Internal
also names of countries, cities, etc. with the subdivision Population, e.g. United States—Population

Anderson, Joanna. The Many People of America. 2012. (I'm an American Citizen Ser.). (ENG., Illus.). 24p. (J). (gr. 1-3). 22.60 *(978-1-4488-8591-6(4)*, PowerKids Pr.) Rosen Publishing Group, Inc., The.

Andregg, Michael. Seven Billion & Counting: The Crisis in Global Population Growth. 2012. (J). lib. bdg. *(978-0-7613-6715-4(2))* Twenty First Century Bks.

Anniss, Matt. Planet under Pressure: Too Many People on Earth? 2013. (Ask the Experts Ser.). (Illus.). 48p. (gr. 6-8). 31.95 *(978-1-4339-8643-7(4))*; pap. 14.04 *(978-1-4339-8644-4(2))* Stevens, Gareth Publishing LLLP. (Gareth Stevens Secondary Library).

Barber, Nicola. Coping with Population Growth, 1 vol. 2011. (Environment Challenge Ser.). (ENG., Illus.). 48p. (gr. 5-6). pap. 9.49 *(978-1-4109-4303-3(8)*, Raintree Freestyle) Heinemann-Raintree.

Bellamy, Rufus. Population Growth. 2010. (Sustaining Our Environment Ser.). 48p. (J). 35.65 *(978-1-60753-137-1(2))* Amicus Publishing.

Bodden, Valerie. The Threat of Overpopulation. 2010. (Earth Issues Ser.). 48p. (YA). (gr. 5-18). 23.95 *(978-1-58341-983-0(7)*, Creative Education) Creative Co., The.

Einspruch, Andrew. Overpopulation. 2012. (Discovery Education: the Environment Ser.). (ENG., Illus.). 32p. (J). (gr. 3-6). pap. 10.00 *(978-1-4488-7978-6(7))*; lib. bdg. 25.25 *(978-1-4488-7890-1(X))* Rosen Publishing Group, Inc., The. (PowerKids Pr.).

Farrell, Courtney. World Population, 1 vol. 2011. (Essential Issues Set 3 Ser.). (ENG., Illus.). 112p. (J). (gr. 6-12). lib. bdg. 35.64 *(978-1-61783-138-6(7))* ABDO Publishing Co.

Green, Robert. Overpopulation. 2008. (21st Century Skills Library: Global Perspectives Ser.). (ENG.). 32p. (gr. 4-8). lib. bdg. 28.50 *(978-1-60279-127-5(9)*, 200102) Cherry Lake Publishing.

Greenhaven Press Editors, ed. Population. 2011. (Opposing Viewpoints Ser.). (Illus.). 240p. pap. 29.45 *(978-0-7377-5756-9(6)*, Greenhaven Pr., Inc.); (YA). (gr. 9-12). 42.95 *(978-0-7377-5755-2(8))* Cengage Gale.

Hardyman, Robyn. The Race to Control the Population. 2014. (World in Crisis Ser.). 48p. (YA). (gr. 5-8). 30.25 *(978-1-4777-7850-0(0)*, Rosen Reference) Rosen Publishing Group, Inc., The.

Haugen, David M., ed. The Millennial Generation. 2012. (Opposing Viewpoints Ser.). (ENG., Illus.). 240p. (J). (gr. 10-12). pap. 29.45 *(978-0-7377-6327-0(2))*; lib. bdg. 42.95 *(978-0-7377-6326-3(4))* Cengage Gale. (Greenhaven Pr., Inc.).

Hyde, Natalie. Population Patterns: What Factors Determine the Location & Growth of Human Settlements? 2010. (Investigating Human Migration & Settlement Ser.). (ENG., Illus.). 48p. (J). (gr. 5-8). *(978-0-7787-5182-3(1))*; pap. *(978-0-7787-5197-7(X))* Crabtree Publishing Co.

Kalman, Bobbie. What Is a Biome? 2008. (ENG.). 32p. (J). *(978-0-7787-7640-6(9))* Crabtree Publishing Co.

Kent, Deborah. The Changing Face of America: Hispanic Roots, Hispanic Pride. 2004. (Proud Heritage: the Hispanic Library). (ENG., Illus.). 40p. (J). (gr. 3-6). 29.93 *(978-1-59296-143-6(6)*, 200015) Child's World, Inc., The.

Kirk, Ellen. Human Footprint: Everything You Will Eat, Use, Wear, Buy, & Throw Out in Your Lifetime. 2011. (ENG., Illus.). 32p. (J). (gr. 3-7). pap. 6.95 *(978-1-4263-0767-6(5)*, National Geographic Children's Bks.) National Geographic Society.

Mason, Paul. Earthquakes. 2012. (Disaster Watch! Ser.). 32p. (gr. 4-6). lib. bdg. 28.50 (978-1-59920-423-9(1)) Black Rabbit Bks.

Newton, David E. Overpopulation: 7 Billion People & Counting. 2016. (End of Life As We Know It Ser.). (ENG., Illus.). 160p. (J). (gr. 7-8). 37.27 (978-0-7660-7312-8(2)) Enslow Pubs., Inc.

Obadina, Tunde. Population & Overcrowding. Ojakorotu, Victor & Rotberg, Robert I., eds. 2013. (Africa: Progress & Problems Ser.: 13). (Illus.). 112p. (J). (gr. 7-18). 24.95 (978-1-4222-2945-3(9)) Mason Crest.

Oxlade, Chris. Infographics, 1 vol. 2014. (Infographics Ser.). (ENG.). 32p. (gr. 1-3). lib. bdg. 119.96 (978-1-4109-6220-1(2), Read Me!) Heinemann-Raintree.

—Population Infographics, 1 vol. 2014. (Infographics Ser.). (ENG.). 32p. (gr. 1-3). lib. bdg. 29.99 (978-1-4109-6218-8(0), Read Me!) Heinemann-Raintree.

Rau, Dana Meachen & National Geographic Learning Staff. In the City. 2010. (Rise & Shine Ser.). (ENG.). (C). pap. 18.95 (978-0-7614-3306-4(6)) National Geographic School Publishing, Inc.

Smith, David J. If: A Mind-Bending New Way of Looking at Big Ideas & Numbers. Adams, Steve, illus. 2014. (ENG.). 40p. (J). (gr. 3-7). 18.95 (978-1-894786-34-8(3)) Kids Can Pr., Ltd. CAN. Dist: Hachette Bk. Group.

—If the World Were a Village: A Book about the World's People. Armstrong, Shelagh, illus. 2nd ed. 2011. (CitizenKid Ser.). (ENG.). 32p. (J). (gr. 3-7). 18.95 (978-1-55453-595-8(6)) Kids Can Pr., Ltd. CAN. Dist: Hachette Bk. Group.

Sterling, Kristin. Living in Urban Communities. 2008. pap. 34.95 (978-0-8225-9480-2(3)) Lerner Publishing Group.

Stewart, Gail B. Population. 2011. (J). (978-1-60217-033-9(9)) Erickson Pr.

—Ripped from the Headlines: Population. 2008. (J). (978-1-60217-026-1(6)) Erickson Pr.

POPULATION, FOREIGN

see Emigration and Immigration

POPULIST PARTY

Brexel, Bernadette. The Populist Party: A Voice for the Farmers in an Industrial Society. 2009. (America's Industrial Society in the 19th Century Ser.). 32p. (gr. 4-4). 47.90 (978-1-61511-344-6(4)) Rosen Publishing Group, Inc., The.

—The Populist Party: A Voice for the Farmers in the Industrialized Society. 2004. (America's Industrial Society in the 19th Century Ser.). (ENG., Illus.). 32p. (gr. 5-8). pap. 10.00 (978-0-8239-4284-8(8)) Rosen Publishing Group, Inc., The.

PORCELAIN

Eng, Loman & Eng, Petula. Collecting American Belleek, 1 vol. 2003. (ENG., Illus.). 160p. 39.95 (978-0-7643-1860-3(8), 9780764318603) Schiffer Publishing, Ltd.

PORCELAIN ENAMELS

see Enamel and Enameling

PORCUPINES

Abrams, Taharra. Growing up Porcupine! 2013. (Rosen Readers Ser.). (ENG.). 24p. (J). (gr. 3-4). pap. 49.50 (978-1-4777-2456-9(7)); pap. 8.25 (978-1-4777-2455-2(9)) Rosen Publishing Group, Inc., The. (Rosen Classroom).

Avery, Sebastian. Porcupines. 2016. (Creatures of the Forest Habitat Ser.). 00024p. (J). (gr. 3-3). pap. 8.25 (978-1-4994-2757-8(3), PowerKids Pr.) Rosen Publishing Group, Inc., The.

Dunn, Mary R. Porcupines, 1 vol. 2011. (Nocturnal Animals Ser.). (ENG., 24p. (gr. k-1). Illus.). pap. 7.29 (978-1-4296-6193-5(3)); pap. 41.70 (978-1-4296-6362-5(6)) Capstone Press of Coughlan Cos. (Pebble Plus).

Green, Emily. Porcupines. 2011. (Backyard Wildlife Ser.). (ENG., Illus.). 24p. (J). (gr. k-3). lib. bdg. 25.95 (978-1-60014-562-9(0), Blastoff! Readers) Bellwether Media.

—Porcupines. 2011. (Backyard Wildlife Ser.). 24p. (J). (gr. k-1). lib. bdg. 22.00 (978-0-531-20488-7(X), Children's Pr.) Scholastic Library Publishing.

Green, Jen. Porcupines. 2008. (Illus.). 52p. (J). (978-0-7172-6278-6(2)) Grolier, Ltd.

James, Lincoln. A Prickle of Porcupines. 2013. (Animal Groups Ser.). (Illus.). 24p. (gr. 1-3). 22.60 (978-1-4339-8219-4(6)); pap. 8.15 (978-1-4339-8220-0(X)) Stevens, Gareth Publishing LLLP.

—A Prickle of Porcupines / una Manada de Puercoespines. 2013. (Animal Groups / Grupos de Animales Ser.). (ENG & SPA., Illus.). 24p. (gr. 1-3). 22.60 (978-1-4339-8812-7(7)) Stevens, Gareth Publishing LLLP.

Jango-Cohen, Judith. Porcupines. 2005. (Animals Animals Ser.). (Illus.). 48p. (J). (gr. 3-7). lib. bdg. (978-0-7614-1868-9(7), Benchmark Bks.) Marshall Cavendish Corp.

Leaf, Christina. Porcupines. 2015. (North American Animals Ser.). (ENG., Illus.). 24p. (J). (gr. k-3). lib. bdg. 25.95 (978-1-62617-262-3(5), Blastoff! Readers) Bellwether Media.

Macken, JoAnn Early. Porcupines. 2nd rev. ed. 2009. (Animals That Live in the Forest Ser.). 24p. (J). (gr. -1-3). pap. 8.15 (978-1-4339-2483-5(8)); lib. bdg. 22.60 (978-1-4339-2407-1(2)) Stevens, Gareth Publishing LLLP.

—Porcupines;Puercoespines. 2nd rev. ed. 2009. (Animals That Live in the Forest/Animales del bosque Ser.). 24p. (J). (gr. -1-3). (SPA & ENG.). pap. 8.15 (978-1-4339-2490-3(0)); (ENG & SPA.). lib. bdg. 22.60 (978-1-4339-2439-2(0)) Stevens, Gareth Publishing LLLP. (Weekly Reader Leveled Readers).

Markle, Sandra. Los Puercoespines (Porcupines) 2009. (SPA.). pap. 46.95 (978-0-7613-4720-0(8)) Lerner Publishing Group.

—Porcupines. (Animal Prey Ser.). 2008. (Illus.). 39p. (J). (gr. 3-7). per. 7.95 (978-0-8225-6442-3(4), First Avenue Editions) 2008. pap. 46.95 (978-0-8225-9322-5(X)) 2007. (ENG., Illus.). 40p. (J). (gr. 3-6). lib. bdg. 25.26 (978-0-8225-6439-3(4)) Lerner Publishing Group.

—Los Puercoespines (Porcupines) 2008. 40p. (J). pap. 7.95 (978-0-7613-3900-7(0), Ediciones Lerner) Lerner Publishing Group.

Nichols, Catherine. Prickly Porcupines. 2008. (Gross-Out Defenses Ser.). (Illus.). 24p. (J). (gr. k-3). lib. bdg. 21.28 (978-1-59716-721-5(5), 1284311) Bearport Publishing Co., Inc.

Rockwood, Leigh. Tell Me the Difference Between a Porcupine & a Hedgehog. 2013. (How Are They Different? Ser.). (ENG., Illus.). 24p. (J). (gr. k-5). pap. 8.25 (978-1-4488-9732-2(7)); lib. bdg. 22.60 (978-1-4488-9637-0(1)) Rosen Publishing Group, Inc., The. (PowerKids Pr.).

Rouche, Jeffrey. Porcupines in the Wild. 2013. (InfoMax Readers Ser.). (ENG.). 24p. (J). (gr. 3-4). pap. 49.50 (978-1-4777-2470-5(2)); (Illus.). pap. 8.25 (978-1-4777-2469-9(9)) Rosen Publishing Group, Inc., The. (Rosen Classroom).

Schuh, Mari. Porcupines. 2016. (My First Animal Library). 24p. (J). (gr. k-2). lib. bdg. 25.65 (978-1-62031-290-2(5), Bullfrog Bks.) Jump! Inc.

Webster, Christine. Porcupines. 2009. (Backyard Animals Ser.). (Illus.). 24p. (J). (gr. 3-5). pap. 8.95 (978-1-60596-079-1(9)); lib. bdg. 24.45 (978-1-60596-078-4(0)) Weigl Pubs., Inc.

Yoon, Salina. Duck, Duck, Porcupine! 2016. (Duck, Duck, Porcupine Book Ser.). (ENG., Illus.). 64p. (J). 9.99 (978-1-61963-723-8(5), 9781619637238, Bloomsbury USA Childrens) Bloomsbury Publishing USA.

—Duck, Duck, Porcupine! 2017. (J). lib. bdg. 16.00 **(978-0-606-40593-5(3))** Turtleback Bks.

Zemlicka, Shannon. Prickly Porcupines. 2003. (Pull Ahead Bks.). (ENG., Illus.). 32p. (J). (gr. k-2). pap. 6.95 (978-0-8225-0966-0(0)) Lerner Publishing Group.

PORCUPINES—FICTION

Avi. Poppy & Ereth. Floca, Brian, illus. 2011. (Poppy Stories Ser.). (ENG.). 224p. (J). (gr. 3-7). pap. 6.99 (978-0-06-111971-2(7)) HarperCollins Pubs.

—Poppy & Rye. Floca, Brian, illus. 2006. (Poppy Stories Ser.). (ENG.). 240p. (J). (gr. 3-7). pap. 6.99 (978-0-380-79717-2(8)) HarperCollins Pubs.

—Poppy & Rye. Floca, Brian, illus. 2006. (Poppy Stories Ser.: 3). 182p. (J). (gr. 3-7). lib. bdg. 17.20 (978-0-613-17447-3(X), Turtleback) Turtleback Bks.

Bentley, Dawn. The Prickly Porcupine. Stover, Beth, illus. 2003. (Soundprints' Read-and-Discover Ser.). (ENG.). 32p. (J). (gr. -1-3). 12.95 (978-1-59249-014-1(X), PS2065); pap. 3.95 (978-1-59249-013-4(1), S2015) Soundprints.

Brown, Derrick. Valentine the Porcupine Dances Funny. Lewis, Jenn, illus. 2011. (ENG.). 44p. 20.00 (978-1-935904-18-2(3)) Write Bloody Publishing.

Burach, Ross. Pine & Boof: the Lucky Leaf. Burach, Ross, illus. 2017. (Illus.). 40p. (J). (gr. -1-3). 17.99 **(978-0-06-241850-0(5))** HarperCollins Pubs.

Burgess, Thornton W. The Adventures of Prickly Porky. 2007. 140p. (gr. 4-7). per. 11.95 (978-1-60312-048-7(3)); 24.95 (978-1-60312-953-4(7)) Aegypan.

—The Adventures of Prickly Porky. 2011. 138p. 25.95 (978-1-4638-9572-3(0)) Rodgers, Alan Bks.

—The Adventures of Reddy Fox & Prickly Porky. 2007. 118p. pap. 18.99 (978-1-4346-4026-0(4)); (ENG.). 136p. pap. 19.99 (978-1-4346-4073-4(6)) Creative Media Partners, LLC.

Cakal, Kimberly. Today I Hugged a Porcupine. 2007. 20p. per. 24.95 (978-1-4241-8561-0(0)) America Star Bks.

Chaconas, Dori. The Babysitters. McCue, Lisa, illus. 2014. (Cork & Fuzz Ser.: 6). (ENG.). 32p. (J). (gr. 1-3). pap. 3.99 (978-0-448-48050-3(6), Penguin Young Readers) Penguin Young Readers Group.

Crenshaw, Glenda. Friends of the Enchanted Forest: How they Save Christmas. 2011. 28p. pap. 15.47 (978-1-4520-0512-6(5)) AuthorHouse.

Day, Ralph M. Peter Porcupine One Quill. 2010. 40p. 19.95 (978-1-4269-3747-7(4)) Trafford Publishing.

deRubertis, Barbara. Polly Porcupine's Painting Prize. Alley, R. W., illus. 2011. (Animal Antics A to Z Ser.). 32p. (J). pap. 45.32 (978-0-7613-7662-0(3)); lib. bdg. 22.60 (978-1-57565-337-2(0)) Kane Press, Inc.

—Polly Porcupine's Painting Prizes. Alley, R. W., illus. 2011. (Animal Antics A to Z Ser.). (ENG.). 32p. (J). (gr. -1-3). pap. 7.95 (978-1-57565-328-0(1)) Kane Press, Inc.

deRubertis, Barbara & DeRubertis, Barbara. Polly Porcupine's Painting Prizes. Alley, R. W., illus. 2012. (Animal Antics A to Z Ser.). 32p. (J). (gr. 2 — 1). cd-rom 7.95 (978-1-57565-409-6(1)) Kane Press, Inc.

Ghigna, Charles. Adeline Porcupine. East, Jacqueline, illus. 2015. (Tiny Tales Ser.). (ENG.). 64p. (gr. -1-2). lib. bdg. 23.99 (978-1-4795-6530-6(X)) Tiny Tales.

Hetzer, Michael. A Hug for Percy Porcupine. Clayton, Kim, illus. 2005. 32p. (J). (gr. k-2). 2nd collector's ed. 18.95 (978-0-9728222-4-4(0)) 3rd ed. 18.95 (978-0-9728222-3-7(2)) Webster Henrietta Publishing.

Isern, Susanna. The Magic Ball of Wool. 2013. (ENG., Illus.). 32p. (J). (gr. -1-k). 16.95 (978-84-15619-89-5(8)) Eastern National.

Isop, Laurie. How Do You Hug a Porcupine? Millward, Gwen, illus. 2011. (ENG.). 32p. (J). (gr. -1-1). 16.99 (978-1-4424-1291-0(7), Simon & Schuster Bks. For Young Readers) Simon & Schuster Bks. For Young Readers.

Kantner, Seth. Pup & Pokey. Hill, Beth, illus. 2014. 48p. pap. 14.95 (978-1-60223-241-9(5)) Univ. of Alaska Pr.

Koehn, Wendel. Love Problematic: And Other Stories. 2012. 24p. pap. 14.93 (978-1-4669-1851-1(9)) Trafford Publishing.

Krensky, Stephen. Pins & Needles. Litten, Kristyna, illus. 2014. (Penguin Core Concepts Ser.). (ENG.). 32p. (J). (gr. -1-k). 3.99 (978-0-448-46209-7(5), Grosset & Dunlap) Penguin Young Readers Group.

Lasher, Shelby. Spiky the Grumpy Porcupine. 2012. 28p. pap. 24.95 (978-1-4626-7844-0(0)) America Star Bks.

Lester, Helen. A Porcupine Named Fluffy. Munsinger, Lynn, illus. 2013. (Laugh-Along Lessons Ser.). (ENG.). 32p. (J). (gr. -1-3). 8.99 (978-0-544-00319-4(5)) Houghton Mifflin Harcourt Publishing Co.

Michalak, Jamie. Larry & Rita. Newton, Jill, illus. 2007. (Brand New Readers Ser.). (ENG.). 48p. (J). (gr. -1-3). 14.99 (978-0-7636-2963-2(4)) Candlewick Pr.

Michie, Brandon J. Caleb the Porcupine: Animal Lessons. 2011. 16p. pap. 10.75 (978-1-4634-3015-3(9)) AuthorHouse.

Morgan, Mary. Pip Sits. 2017. (I Like to Read(r) Ser.). (ENG.). 24p. (J). (gr. -1-3). 6.99 (978-0-8234-3778-8(7)); (Illus.). 14.95 (978-0-8234-3676-7(4)) Holiday Hse., Inc.

Mortensen, Lori, retold by. How Porcupine Got Quills. 2016. (Spring Forward Ser.). (J). (gr. 2). (978-1-4900-9465-6(2)) Benchmark Education Co.

Myers, Bill. My Life As a Prickly Porcupine from the Planet Pluto, 1 vol. 2004. (Incredible Worlds of Wally Mcdoogle Ser.: 23). (ENG.). 128p. pap. 6.99 (978-0-8499-5994-3(2)) Nelson, Thomas Inc.

Nelson, Scott. Patch the Porcupine & the Bike Shop Job. Nelson, Scott, illus. 2004. (Illus.). 28p. (J). 14.95 (978-0-9745715-3-9(9)) KRBY Creations, LLC.

Oramas, Jennifer. Peter's Purpose. Huseman, Ryan, illus. 2012. 34p. 24.95 (978-1-4626-6585-3(3)) America Star Bks.

Raines, Jennifer. Laughs for Porcupine, 1 vol. 2009. 18p. pap. 24.95 (978-1-60836-784-9(3)) America Star Bks.

Ratzlaff, Aaron J. Quills. 2011. (ENG.). 40p. (J). pap. 13.99 (978-0-8361-9509-5(4)) Herald Pr.

Rosenthal, Betsy R. Porcupine's Picnic: Who Eats What? Capizzi, Giusi, illus. 2017. (ENG.). 32p. (gr. -1-2). 19.99 (978-1-4677-9519-7(4)); 30.65 **(978-1-5124-2840-7(X))** Lerner Publishing Group. (Millbrook Pr.).

Saez Castan, Javier. Los Tres Erizos. 2005. (SPA.). (J). (gr. k-1). pap. 6.95 (978-980-257-297-7(7)) Ekare, Ediciones VEN. Dist: Iaconi, Mariuccia Bk. Imports.

Sargent, Dave & Sargent, Pat. Peggy Porcupine: Don't Wander Off, 15 vols., Vol. 13. Huff, Jeane, illus. 2nd rev. ed. 2003. (Animal Pride Ser.: 13). 42p. (J). (AFA.). pap. 10.95 (978-1-56763-784-7(1)); lib. bdg. 20.95 (978-1-56763-783-0(3)) Ozark Publishing.

Schmid, Paul. Hugs from Pearl. Schmid, Paul, illus. 2011. (ENG., Illus.). 40p. (J). (gr. -1-2). 14.99 (978-0-06-180434-2(7)) HarperCollins Pubs.

—Perfectly Percy. Schmid, Paul, illus. 2013. (ENG., Illus.). 40p. (J). (gr. -1-3). 17.99 (978-0-06-180436-6(3)) HarperCollins Pubs.

Sisco, Joann Ellen. Search for the Porcupine: 2. 2012. 92p. pap. 13.95 (978-1-4772-5893-4(0)) AuthorHouse.

Skilbeck, Carol. Adventures of Melonhead. 2011. 56p. 24.99 (978-1-4568-7464-3(0)); pap. 15.99 (978-1-4568-7463-6(2)) Xlibris Corp.

Smith, Ivy. Stickers VIP. 2011. (Illus.). 30p. (J). 19.95 (978-0-9635757-9-1(1)) Red Tail Publishing.

Soundprints. Prickly Porcupine: Wilderness Adventures. 2012. (ENG.). 48p. (J). pap. 3.95 (978-1-60727-870-2(7)) Soundprints.

Tireman, Loyd. Quills. Douglass, Ralph, illus. 2015. (Mesaland Ser.). (ENG.). 48p. (J). 12.95 (978-0-8263-5609-3(5)) Univ. of New Mexico Pr.

Underwood, Deborah. A Balloon for Isabel. Rankin, Laura, illus. 2010. (ENG.). 32p. (J). (gr. -1-2). 16.99 (978-0-06-177987-9(3), Greenwillow Bks.) HarperCollins Pubs.

Wilkinson, Lisa. Prickle Says I'm Sorry. McCord, Kathi, illus. 2015. (Faith That Sticks Bks.). (ENG.). 26p. (J). pap. 3.99 (978-1-4964-0312-4(6)) Tyndale Hse. Pubs.

Wilson, George H. The Path of the Little Porcupine. 2010. (Illus.). 50p. (J). 15.00 (978-0-9778477-2-3(1)) A Story Plus Children Bks.

Yoon, Salina. Duck, Duck, Porcupine! 2017. (Duck, Duck, Porcupine Book Ser.). (ENG., Illus.). 64p. (J). pap. 5.99 **(978-1-61963-724-5(3)**, 9781619637245, Bloomsbury USA Childrens) Bloomsbury Publishing USA.

—My Kite Is Stuck! & Other Stories. 2017. (Duck, Duck, Porcupine Book Ser.). (ENG.). 64p. (J). 9.99 (978-1-61963-887-7(8), 9781619638877, Bloomsbury USA Childrens) Bloomsbury Publishing USA.

Yoon, Salina. That's My Book! & Other Stories. 2017. (Duck, Duck, Porcupine Book Ser.). (ENG., Illus.). 64p. (J). 9.99 **(978-1-61963-891-4(6)**, 9781619638914, Bloomsbury USA Childrens) Bloomsbury Publishing USA.

PORKY PIG (FICTITIOUS CHARACTER)—FICTION

Granny Vanishes. 2008. (Looney Tunes 8*8 Ser.). 24p. pap. (978-1-4075-2641-6(3)); pap. (978-1-4075-2631-7(6)) Parragon, Inc.

Jewel Robbery. 2008. (Looney Tunes 8*8 Ser.). 24p. pap. (978-1-4075-2632-4(4)); pap. (978-1-4075-2642-3(1)) Parragon, Inc.

PORNOGRAPHY

Hurt, Avery Elizabeth. Everything You Need to Know about Sextortion. 2017. (Need to Know Library). 64p. (J). (gr. 12-11). pap. 12.95 **(978-1-5081-7406-6(7)**, Rosen Young Adult) Rosen Publishing Group, Inc., The.

Nathan, Debbie. Pornography, 1 vol. 2007. (Groundwork Guides). (ENG., Illus.). 144p. (gr. 8-12). 15.95 (978-0-88899-766-1(3)) Groundwood Bks. CAN. Dist: Publishers Group West (PGW).

Wilcox, Christine. How Is Online Pornography Affecting Society? 2015. (ENG., Illus.). 96p. (J). lib. bdg. (978-1-60152-882-7(5)) ReferencePoint Pr., Inc.

PORPOISES

Avery, Sebastian. Porpoises, 01 vols., 1. 2016. (Ocean Friends Ser.). (ENG., Illus.). 24p. (J). pap. 8.25 (978-1-5081-4176-1(2), PowerKids Pr.) Rosen Publishing Group, Inc., The.

Brust, Beth Wagner. Dolphins. rev. ed. 2003. (Illus.). 24p. 10.95 (978-1-888153-94-1(6), Zoo Bks.) Wildlife Education, Ltd.

Morgan, Sally. Dolphins & Porpoises: Animal Lives Series. 2008. 32p. (J). lib. bdg. 18.95 (978-1-59566-537-9(4)) QEB Publishing Inc.

Ryndak, Rob. Dolphin or Porpoise? 2015. (Animal Look-Alikes Ser.). (ENG., Illus.). 24p. (J). (gr. 1-2). pap. 8.15 (978-1-4824-2712-7(5)) Stevens, Gareth Publishing LLLP.

Shaskan, Trisha Speed. What's the Difference Between a Dolphin & a Porpoise?, 1 vol. Bandelin, Debra et al, illus. 2010. (What's the Difference? Ser.). (ENG.). 24p. (gr. k-3). lib. bdg. 26.65 (978-1-4048-5545-8(9)) Picture Window Bks.

Silverman, Buffy. Can You Tell a Dolphin from a Porpoise? 2011. (Lightning Bolt Books (tm) — Animal Look-Alikes Ser.). (ENG.). 32p. (gr. k-2). pap. 7.95 (978-0-7613-7848-8(0)) Lerner Publishing Group.

—Can You Tell A Dolphin from A Porpoise? 2011. (Animal Look-Alikes Ser.). pap. 45.32 (978-0-7613-8385-7(9)) Lerner Publishing Group.

Worth, Bonnie. A Whale of a Tale! All about Porpoises, Dolphins, & Whales. Ruiz, Aristides & Mathieu, Joe, illus. 2006. (Cat in the Hat's Learning Library). (ENG.). 48p. (J). (gr. -1-3). 9.99 (978-0-375-82279-7(8), Random Hse. Bks. for Young Readers) Random Hse. Children's Bks.

PORPOISES—FICTION

Edgemon, Darcie. Seamore, the Very Forgetful Porpoise. Seibold, J. Otto, illus. 2008. 48p. (J). (gr. -1-3). lib. bdg. 17.89 (978-0-06-085076-0(0)) HarperCollins Pubs.

Manzel, Michael, illus. Moby's Tale. 2004. 248p. (YA). pap. 19.95 (978-0-9746345-0-0(6)) River of Life Publishing.

Moore, Debbie. Penelope, the Peculiar Purple Porpoise. 2011. 48p. pap. 24.95 (978-1-4560-6577-5(7)) America Star Bks.

Nikolet, C. T. From Bullies to Friends. Howe, Cindy T., illus. 2008. 25p. pap. 24.95 (978-1-60610-121-6(8)) America Star Bks.

PORTRAIT PAINTING

see also Crayon Drawing; Pastel Drawing

Frisch-Schmoll, Joy. Brushes with Greatness: Portraits. 2013. (Brushes with Greatness Ser.). (ENG.). 48p. (J). (gr. 4-7). pap. 12.00 (978-0-89812-765-2(3), Creative Paperbacks) Creative Co., The.

Gittings, Clare. What Are You Looking At? Band 14. 2007. (Collins Big Cat Ser.). (ENG., Illus.). 48p. (J). (gr. 3-4). pap. 8.99 (978-0-00-723091-4(5)) HarperCollins Pubs. Ltd. GBR. Dist: Independent Pubs. Group.

Medina, Mariana & Wooten, Sara McIntosh. Frida Kahlo: Self-Portrait Artist. 2015. (Influential Latinos Ser.). (ENG., Illus.). 128p. (J). (gr. 7-7). 37.27 (978-0-7660-6997-8(4)) Enslow Pubs., Inc.

PORTRAITS

see also Cartoons and Comics

Brooks, Susie. Selfie: The Changing Face of Self Portraits. 2016. (ENG., Illus.). 48p. (J). (gr. 4-6). 7.99 (978-0-7502-9964-0(9), Wayland) Hachette Children's Group GBR. Dist: Hachette Bk. Group.

Brooks, Susie. Selfie: the Changing Face of Self Portraits. 2017. (ENG., Illus.). 48p. (J). (gr. 4-8). pap. 12.99 **(978-1-5263-0025-6(7)**, Wayland) Hachette Children's Group GBR. Dist: Hachette Bk. Group.

Geis, Patricia. Draw Like an Artist: A Self-Portrait Sketchbook. 2016. (ENG.). 48p. (J). (gr. 5-9). pap. 12.99 (978-1-61689-510-5(1)) Princeton Architectural Pr.

Handler, Daniel. Girls Standing on Lawns. Kalman, Maira, illus. 2014. (ENG.). 64p. (gr. 3-7). 14.95 (978-0-87070-908-1(9)) Museum of Modern Art.

Lach, Will. Master-Pieces. 2016. (ENG.). 28p. (J). (-3). 15.95 (978-0-7892-1274-0(9), Abbeville Kids) Abbeville Pr., Inc.

Lozano Carbayo, Pilar. Retratos. (Coleccion Mundo Maravilloso).Tr. of Portraits. (SPA.). 226p. (J). (gr. 3-5). (978-84-348-4448-3(6)) SM Ediciones.

PORTS

see Harbors

PORTSMOUTH (N.H.)—HISTORY

Holbrook, Flannery B. A Great Day in Portsmouth. 2013. 54p. 18.99 (978-1-939739-13-1(6)) RIVERRUN BOOKSTORE INC.

PORTUGAL

Etingoff, Kim. Portugal. 2007. (European Union Ser.). (Illus.). 88p. (YA). (gr. 3-7). lib. bdg. 21.95 (978-1-4222-0059-9(0)) Mason Crest.

Etingoff, Kim & Indovino, Shaina C. Portugal. Bruton, John, ed. 2012. (Major European Union Nations Ser.). 64p. (J). (gr. 7). 22.95 (978-1-4222-2255-3(1)) Mason Crest.

Fischer, David. Cristiano Ronaldo. 2017. (J). **(978-0-7660-9205-1(4))** Enslow Pubs., Inc.

Heale, Jay & Koh, Angeline. Portugal. 2nd rev. ed. 2005. (Cultures of the World Ser.). (Illus.). 144p. (gr. 6-10). lib. bdg. 42.79 (978-0-7614-2053-8(3), Benchmark Bks.) Marshall Cavendish Corp.

Hoogenboom, Lynn. Amerigo Vespucci. 2009. (Primary Source Library of Famous Explorers Ser.). 24p. (gr. 4-4). 42.50 (978-1-60854-118-8(5), PowerKids Pr.) Rosen Publishing Group, Inc., The.

Hurwicz, Claude. Henry the Navigator. 2009. (Primary Source Library of Famous Explorers Ser.). 24p. (gr. 4-4). 42.50 (978-1-60854-124-9(X), PowerKids Pr.) Rosen Publishing Group, Inc., The.

Jokulsson, Illugi. Ronaldo. Jokulsson, Illugi, ed. 2015. (ENG., Illus.). 64p. (J). (gr. 1). 13.95 (978-0-7892-1226-9(9), Abbeville Kids) Abbeville Pr., Inc.

Landau, Jennifer. Vasco Da Gama. 2016. (Spotlight on Explorers & Colonization Ser.). 48p. (J). (gr. 6-6). pap. 11.75 (978-1-4777-8825-7(5)) Rosen Publishing Group, Inc., The.

Logothetis, Paul. Cristiano Ronaldo: International Soccer Star, 1 vol. 2016. (ENG., Illus.). 32p. (J). (978-1-62403-841-9(7), SportsZone) ABDO Publishing Co.

Mis, Melody S. How to Draw Portugal's Sights & Symbols. 2009. (Kid's Guide to Drawing the Countries of the World Ser.). 48p. (gr. 4-4). 53.00 (978-1-61511-123-7(9), PowerKids Pr.) Rosen Publishing Group, Inc., The.

Phillips, Douglas A. Portugal. 2007. (Modern World Nations Ser.). (Illus.). 118p. (YA). (gr. 7-12). lib. bdg. 35.00 (978-0-7910-9257-6(7)) Facts On File, Inc.

Rose, Elizabeth. A Primary Source Guide to Portugal. (Countries of the World). 24p. 2009. (gr. 2-3). 42.50 (978-1-61512-043-7(2)) 2004. (Illus.). (J). (gr. k). lib. bdg. 22.60 (978-0-8239-6733-9(6)) Rosen Publishing Group, Inc., The. (PowerKids Pr.).

Torres, John. Cristiano Ronaldo: Champion Soccer Star. 2017. (Sports Star Champions Ser.). 48p. (J). (gr. 5-6). lib. bdg. 27.93 **(978-0-7660-8688-3(7))** Enslow Pubs., Inc.

Torres, John Albert. Soccer Star Cristiano Ronaldo. 2014. (Goal! Latin Stars of Soccer Ser.). 48p. 14.95 (978-1-62285-222-2(2)) Enslow Pubs., Inc.

PORTUGAL—FICTION

Beck, Barbara. Bill Every Cloud Has a Silver Lining. 2012. 108p. pap. 19.95 (978-1-4626-9718-2(6)) America Star Bks.

Dixon, Franklin W. The Secret of the Soldier's Gold. 2005. (Hardy Boys II Ser.: No. 182). 147p. (J). lib. bdg. 15.00 (978-1-59054-852-3(3)) Fitzgerald Bks.

Kelahan, Renee. Agua, the Mysterious Portuguese Water Dog. 2009. 108p. 20.95 (978-1-4401-5443-0(0)); pap. 10.95 (978-1-4401-5442-3(2)) iUniverse, Inc.

Lerasle, Magdeleine. Songs from a Journey with a Parrot: Lullabies & Nursery Rhymes from Portugal & Brazil. Fronty, Aurélia, illus. 2013. (POR & ENG.). 52p. (J). (gr. -1-k). 16.95 (978-2-923163-99-4(0)) La Montagne Secrete CAN. Dist: Independent Pubs. Group.

PORTUGAL—HISTORY

Draper, Allison Stark. Vasco da Gama: The Portuguese Quest for a Sea Route from Europe to India. rev. ed. (Library of Explorers & Explorationtm Ser.). (Illus.). 112p. (YA). (gr. 5-8). lib. bdg. 31.95 *(978-1-4042-0637-3(X)*, Rosen Reference) Rosen Publishing Group, Inc., The.

Dyan, Penelope. Color Your Life! a Kid's Guide to Lisbon, Portugal. Weigand, John D., photos by. 2012. (Illus.). 34p. pap. 11.95 *(978-1-61477-030-5(1))* Bellissima Publishing, LLC.

Gould, Jane H. Ferdinand Magellan. 2013. (Jr. Graphic Famous Explorers Ser.). (ENG., Illus.). 24p. (J). (gr. 3-6). pap. 10.60 *(978-1-4777-0123-2(0))*; lib. bdg. 25.25 *(978-1-4777-0069-3(2))* Rosen Publishing Group, Inc., The. (PowerKids Pr.).

Heale, Jay, et al. Portugal. 2016. (Cultures of the World (r) Ser.). (Illus.). 144p. (J). (gr. 5-5). 47.07 *(978-1-5026-1693-7(9))* Cavendish Square Publishing.

Ollhoff, Jim. Ferdinand Magellan. 2013. (Great Explorers Ser.). 32p. (J). (gr. 5-9). lib. bdg. 27.07 *(978-1-61783-967-2(1)*, Abdo & Daughters) ABDO Publishing Co.

Parker, Lewis K. Portuguese Colonies in the Americas. 2003. (European Colonies in the Americas Ser.). (Illus.). 24p. (J). lib. bdg. 22.60 *(978-0-8239-6474-1(4)*, PowerKids Pr.) Rosen Publishing Group, Inc., The.

Ray, Michael, ed. Portugal & Spain. 2013. (Britannica Guide to Countries of the European Union Ser.). 344p. (YA). (gr. 9-12). 53.00 *(978-1-61530-967-2(5))* Rosen Publishing Group, Inc., The.

Schuetz, Kari. Portugal. 2012. (Exploring Countries Ser.). (ENG., Illus.). 32p. (J). (gr. 3-7). lib. bdg. 26.95 *(978-1-60014-733-3(X)*, Blastoff! Readers) Bellwether Media.

Sebastian, Emily. The Colonial & Postcolonial Experience in Latin America & the Caribbean. 2016. (Colonial & Postcolonial Experience Ser.). 00128p. (J). (gr. 10-10). 54.00 *(978-1-5081-0439-1(5))* Rosen Publishing Group, Inc., The.

PORTUGUESE—UNITED STATES—FICTION

Lang, Andrew, ed. & compiled by. The Orange Fairy Book. Lang, Andrew, compiled by. 2011. 234p. 27.95 *(978-1-4638-9520-4(8))* Rodgers, Alan Bks.

PORTUGUESE LANGUAGE

Da Guia, Higina. Pajamas O Pijam. 2008. 32p. pap. 18.95 *(978-1-4327-2055-1(4))* Outskirts Pr., Inc.

Juventud Staff & Martin, A - Weissmann. Diccionario Portugues - Espanol. (SPA.). 524p. (J). 29.95 *(978-84-261-2888-1(2))* Juventud, Editorial ESP. Dist: AIMS International Bks., Inc.

Kudela, Katy R. My First Book of Portuguese Words, 1 vol. Translations.com Staff, tr. (Bilingual Picture Dictionaries Ser.). 32p. (gr. 1-2). 2011. (ENG, POR & MUL., Illus.). pap. 8.10 *(978-1-4296-6169-0(0))* 2011. (MUL.). pap. 47.70 *(978-1-4296-6170-6(4))* 2010. (MUL & ENG.). lib. bdg. 27.32 *(978-1-4296-5965-9(3))* Capstone Press of Coughlan Cos. (Aplus Bks.).

Milet Publishing Staff. Animals. 2011. (My First Bilingual Book Ser.). (ENG., Illus.). 24p. (J). (gr. k — 1). bds. 8.99 *(978-1-84059-617-5(1))* Milet Publishing.

—Bilingual Visual Dictionary. 2011. (Milet Multimedia Ser.). (ENG & POR., Illus.). 1p. (J). (gr. k-2). cd-rom 19.95 *(978-1-84059-589-5(2))* Milet Publishing.

—Home (English-Portuguese) 2011. (My First Bilingual Book Ser.). (ENG., Illus.). 24p. (J). (gr. k — 1). bds. 7.99 *(978-1-84059-649-6(X))* Milet Publishing.

—Jobs Empregos. 2012. (My First Bilingual Book Ser.). (ENG & POR., Illus.). 24p. (J). (gr. k — 1). bds. 7.99 *(978-1-84059-709-7(7))* Milet Publishing.

—Milet Bilingual Visual Dictionary (English-Portuguese) 2012. (Milet Bilingual Visual Dictionary Ser.). (ENG & POR., Illus.). 148p. (J). (gr. k-2). 34.95 *(978-1-84059-693-9(7))* Milet Publishing.

—Music - My First Bilingual Book. 2012. (My First Bilingual Book Ser.). (ENG & POR., Illus.). 24p. (J). (gr. k — 1). bds. 7.99 *(978-1-84059-725-7(9))* Milet Publishing.

—My Bilingual Book-Hearing (English-Portuguese) 2014. (My Bilingual Book Ser.). (ENG & POR., Illus.). 28p. (J). (gr. -1-k). 9.95 *(978-1-84059-781-3(X))* Milet Publishing.

—My Bilingual Book-Sight (English-Portuguese) 2014. (My Bilingual Book Ser.). (ENG & POR., Illus.). 28p. (J). (gr. -1-k). 9.95 *(978-1-84059-797-4(6))* Milet Publishing.

—My Bilingual Book-Taste (English-Portuguese) 2014. (My Bilingual Book Ser.). (ENG & POR., Illus.). 28p. (J). (gr. -1-k). 9.95 *(978-1-84059-829-2(8))* Milet Publishing.

—My Bilingual Book-Touch (English-Portuguese) 2014. (My Bilingual Book Ser.). (ENG & POR., Illus.). 28p. (J). (gr. -1-k). 9.95 *(978-1-84059-845-2(X))* Milet Publishing.

—My First Bilingual Book - Colors. 2011. (My First Bilingual Book Ser.). (ENG.). 24p. (J). (gr. k — 1). bds. 7.99 *(978-1-84059-602-1(3))* Milet Publishing.

—My First Bilingual Book - Fruit. 2011. (My First Bilingual Book Ser.). (ENG & POR., Illus.). 24p. (J). (gr. k — 1). bds. 8.99 *(978-1-84059-633-5(3))* Milet Publishing.

—My First Bilingual Book-Opposites. 2012. (My First Bilingual Book Ser.). (ENG & POR., Illus.). 24p. (J). (gr. k — 1). bds. 7.99 *(978-1-84059-740-0(2))* Milet Publishing.

—Smell O olfato. 2014. (My Bilingual Book Ser.). (ENG & POR., Illus.). 28p. (J). (gr. -1-k). 9.95 *(978-1-84059-813-1(1))* Milet Publishing.

—Sports. 2012. (My First Bilingual Book Ser.). (ENG & POR., Illus.). 24p. (J). (gr. k — 1). bds. 7.99 *(978-1-84059-757-8(7))* Milet Publishing.

—Vegetables - My First Bilingual Book. 2011. (My First Bilingual Book Ser.). (ENG., Illus.). 24p. (J). (gr. k — 1). bds. 7.99 *(978-1-84059-665-6(1))* Milet Publishing.

Monckeberg, Paulina. Pascualina 2006 Portuguese. 2005. (Pascualina Family of Products Ser.). (ENG.). 272p. (J). spiral bd. 16.99 *(978-956-8222-29-1(4))* Pascualina Producciones S.A.

The Rosetta Stone Language Library: Portugese Level 2. 2005. (J). (gr. 1-18). cd-rom 239.00 *(978-1-883972-67-7(1))* Rosetta Stone Ltd.

POSSUM

see Opossums

POST-IMPRESSIONISM (ART)

Sabbeth, Carol. Van Gogh & the Post-Impressionists for Kids: Their Lives & Ideas, 21 Activities. 2011. (For Kids Ser.). (ENG., Illus.). 144p. (J). (gr. 4-18). pap. 17.95 *(978-1-56976-275-2(9))* Chicago Review Pr., Inc.

Spence, David. Gauguin. 2010. (Great Artists & Their World Ser.). (Illus.). 48p. (YA). 32.80 *(978-1-84898-316-8(6))* Black Rabbit Bks.

—Picasso. 2010. (Great Artists & Their World Ser.). 48p. 32.80 *(978-1-84898-315-1(8))* Black Rabbit Bks.

POST OFFICE

see Postal Service

POSTAGE STAMPS

Esten, Sidney R. Bird Stamps of All Countries, with a Natural History of Each Bird. Cox, William Drought, ed. 2011. 62p. 36.95 *(978-1-258-07239-1(4))* Literary Licensing, LLC.

Fandel, Jennifer. The Postage Stamp. 2007. (What in the World? Ser.). (Illus.). 48p. (J). (gr. 4-7). lib. bdg. 32.80 *(978-1-58341-554-2(8)*, Creative Education) Creative Co., The.

Price, Pam. Cool Stamps: Creating Fun & Fascinating Collections!, 1 vol. 2007. (Cool Collections Ser.). (ENG., Illus.). 32p. (YA). (gr. 2-5). 28.50 *(978-1-59679-774-1(6))* ABDO Publishing Co.

Smith, Ben. Why Do We Celebrate? 2014. (Little Books of Answers: Level d Ser.). (Illus.). 16p. (gr. k-2). pap. 7.95 *(978-1-927136-31-7(8))* Three Crows Media NZL. Dist: RiverStream Publishing.

POSTAL SERVICE

see also Pony Express

Armentrout, David & Armentrout, Patricia. The Post Office: Our Community. 2008. (Illus.). 24p. (J). lib. bdg. 22.79 *(978-1-60472-340-3(8))* Rourke Educational Media.

At the Post Office, 6, Packs. (gr. -1-2). 27.00 *(978-0-7635-9437-4(7))* Rigby Education.

Bellamy, Adam. This Is My Post Office. 2016. (All about My World Ser.). (Illus.). 24p. (J). pap. 9.35 *(978-0-7660-8102-4(8))* Enslow Pubs., Inc.

Berger, Melvin. Where Does the Mail Go? (Discovery Readers Ser.). (ENG.). 48p. (J). pap. 3.95 *(978-0-8249-5313-3(4)*, Ideal Pubns.) Worthy Publishing.

Bourgeois, Paulette. Postal Workers. LaFave, Kim, illus. 2005. (Kids Can Read Ser.). (ENG.). 32p. (J). (gr. 1-3). 3.95 *(978-1-55337-747-4(8))* Kids Can Pr., Ltd. CAN. Dist: Hachette Bk. Group.

Brill, Marlene Targ. Bronco Charlie & the Pony Express. Orback, Craig, illus. 2004. (On My Own History Ser.). (ENG.). 48p. (gr. 2-4). pap. 6.95 *(978-1-57505-618-0(6))*; lib. bdg. 25.26 *(978-1-57505-587-9(2))* Lerner Publishing Group.

—Bronco Charlie y el Pony Express. Orback, Craig, illus. 2005. (Yo Solo Historia Ser.). (SPA.). 46p. (J). (gr. 2-5). per. 6.95 *(978-0-8225-3093-0(7))* Lerner Publishing Group.

—Bronco Charlie y el Pony Express. Translations.com Staff, tr. Orback, Craig, illus. 2005. (Yo Solo - Historia (on My Own - History) Ser.). (SPA.). 48p. (gr. 2-4). lib. bdg. 25.26 *(978-0-8225-2991-0(2))* Lerner Publishing Group.

—Bronco Charlie Y el Pony Express; Bronco Charlie & the Pony Express. 2008. pap. 40.95 *(978-0-8225-3866-0(0))* Lerner Publishing Group.

Butz, Christopher. Follow That Letter: From the Post Office to Our Mailbox. 2003. (From Here to There Ser.). (J). *(978-1-58417-198-0(7))*; pap. *(978-1-58417-199-7(5))* Lake Street Pubs.

—I Go to Work as a Letter Carrier. 2003. (I Go to Work As Ser.). (Illus.). (J). pap. *(978-1-58417-104-1(9))*; lib. bdg. *(978-1-58417-041-9(7))* Lake Street Pubs.

Capici, Gaetano. How Did That Get to My House? Mail. 2009. (Community Connections: How Did That Get to My House? Ser.). (ENG.). 24p. (gr. 2-5). lib. bdg. 25.64 *(978-1-60279-478-8(2)*, 200249) Cherry Lake Publishing.

Carson-Dellosa Publishing Staff. Mailboxes & Letters. 2009. (ENG.). 34p. (gr. -1-8). 6.99 *(978-1-60418-612-3(7))* Carson-Dellosa Publishing, LLC.

Chiu, David. Choosing a Career in the Post Office. 2009. (World of Work Ser.). 64p. (gr. 5-5). 58.50 *(978-1-60854-339-7(0))* Rosen Publishing Group, Inc., The.

Christopher, Nick. What Do Mail Carriers Do? 2015. (Helping the Community Ser.). (ENG., Illus.). 24p. (J). (gr. 1-1). pap. 8.25 *(978-1-4994-0650-4(9)*, PowerKids Pr.) Rosen Publishing Group, Inc., The.

Chui, David. Choosing a Career in the Post Office. 2005. (World of Work Ser.). (Illus.). 64p. (J). (gr. 7-12). lib. bdg. 31.95 *(978-0-8239-3242-9(7))* Rosen Publishing Group, Inc., The.

Colby, Jennifer. Post Office. 2016. (21st Century Junior Library: Explore a Workplace Ser.). (ENG., Illus.). 24p. (J). (gr. 2-5). 27.07 *(978-1-63471-076-3(2)*, 208383) Cherry Lake Publishing.

Dunn, Joeming W. The Pony Express, 1 vol. Martin, Cynthia, illus. 2008. (Graphic History Ser.). (ENG.). 32p. 28.50 *(978-1-60270-184-7(9)*, Graphic Planet- Nonfiction) ABDO Publishing Co.

Early Macken, JoAnn. Mail Carriers. Andersen, Gregg, photos by. 2010. (People in My Community Ser.). (Illus.). 24p. (gr. k-3). pap. 8.15 *(978-1-4339-3345-5(4))* Stevens, Gareth Publishing LLLP.

—Mail Carriers / Carteros. Andersen, Gregg, photos by. 2010. (People in My Community / Mi comunidad Ser.). (SPA., Illus.). 24p. (gr. k-3). pap. 8.15 *(978-1-4339-3763-7(8))* Stevens, Gareth Publishing LLLP.

Fandel, Jennifer. The Postage Stamp. 2007. (What in the World? Ser.). (Illus.). 48p. (J). (gr. 4-7). lib. bdg. 32.80 *(978-1-58341-554-2(8)*, Creative Education) Creative Co., The.

Finlayson, Reggie & Rivera, Sheila. Postal Carrier. 2005. (First Step Nonfiction - Work People Do Ser.). (ENG.). 8p. (gr. -1-1). pap. 4.95 *(978-0-8225-5360-1(0)*, Lerner Pubns.) Lerner Publishing Group.

Jeffrey, Gary. The Pony Express. Riley, Terry, illus. 2012. (Graphic History of the American West Ser.). (ENG.). 24p. (J). (gr. 3-8). pap. 8.15 *(978-1-4339-6749-8(9)*, Gareth Stevens Learning Library); (gr. 4-7). lib. bdg. 23.95 *(978-1-4339-6747-4(2))* Stevens, Gareth Publishing LLLP.

Kawa, Katie. My First Trip to the Post Office. Livingston, Jessica, illus. 2012. (My First Adventures Ser.). (ENG.). 24p. (J). (gr. k-2). 22.60 *(978-1-4339-6253-0(5))*; pap. 8.15 *(978-1-4339-6255-4(1))* Stevens, Gareth Publishing LLLP.

—My First Trip to the Post Office: Mi Primera Visita Al Correo. Livingston, Jessica, illus. 2012. (My First Adventures / Mis primeras aventuras Ser.). (ENG & SPA.). 24p. (J). (gr. k-2). lib. bdg. 22.60 *(978-1-4339-6633-0(6))* Stevens, Gareth Publishing LLLP.

Kenan, Tessa. Hooray for Mail Carriers! 2017. (Bumba Books (tm) — Hooray for Community Helpers! Ser.). (ENG.). (J). (gr. -1-1). pap. 6.99 ***(978-1-5124-5554-0(7))***; (Illus.). lib. bdg. 25.32 ***(978-1-5124-3354-8(3))*** Lerner Publishing Group.

Kenney, Karen Latchana. Mail Carriers at Work, 1 vol. Dumm, Brian Caleb, illus. 2009. (Meet Your Community Workers Ser.). (ENG.). 32p. (J). (gr. -1-2). 28.50 *(978-1-60270-650-7(6))* Magic Wagon.

Keogh, Josie. A Trip to the Post Office. 2012. (PowerKids Readers: My Community Ser.). (ENG., Illus.). 24p. (J). (gr. k-2). pap. 8.25 *(978-1-4488-7483-5(1))*; lib. bdg. 22.60 *(978-1-4488-7404-0(1))* Rosen Publishing Group, Inc., The.

Keogh, Josie & Alamán, Eduardo. A Trip to the Post Office: De Visita en el Correo. 2012. (PowerKids Readers: My Community / Mi comunidad Ser.). (SPA & ENG., Illus.). 24p. (J). (gr. k-2). lib. bdg. 22.60 *(978-1-4488-7828-4(4)*, PowerKids Pr.) Rosen Publishing Group, Inc., The.

Knudsen, Shannon. Postal Workers. 2005. (Pull Ahead Books: Community Helpers Ser.). (ENG., Illus.). 32p. (gr. k-3). lib. bdg. 22.60 *(978-0-8225-2846-3(0))* Lerner Publishing Group.

Kreisman, Rachelle. Places We Go: A Kids' Guide to Community Sites. Haggerty, Tim, illus. 2015. (Start Smart: Community Ser.). (ENG.). 32p. (gr. 1-3). 26.65 *(978-1-937529-36-9(3))* Red Chair Pr.

Leigh, Autumn. Making History: A Horse Sock Puppet. 2006. (Tony Stead Nonfiction Independent Reading Collection). (ENG.). 24p. (gr. 3-6). pap. 8.85 *(978-1-4042-5588-3(5))* Rosen Publishing Group, Inc., The.

Linde, Barbara M. Working at the Post Office: Learning to Subtract 2 Three-Digit Numbers Without Renaming. 2009. (Math for the REAL World Ser.). 16p. (gr. 2-3). pap. 7.05 *(978-0-8239-8855-6(4)*, Rosen Classroom) Rosen Publishing Group, Inc., The.

Mackey Davis, Cathy. Postal Workers Then & Now, 1 vol. 2006. (Primary Source Readers Ser.). (ENG.). 32p. (J). (gr. 1-1). pap. 8.99 *(978-0-7439-9381-4(0))* Shell Educational Publishing.

A Mail Carrier's Job. 2014. (Community Workers Ser.). 24p. (J). (gr. k-2). pap. 8.22 *(978-1-62712-351-8(2))* Cavendish Square Publishing.

Marsico, Katie. Working at the Post Office. 2009. (21st Century Junior Library: Careers Ser.). (ENG.). 24p. (gr. 2-5). lib. bdg. 25.64 *(978-1-60279-512-9(6)*, 200280) Cherry Lake Publishing.

McNeese, Tim. The Pony Express: Bringing Mail to the American West. 2009. (Milestones in American History Ser.). (Illus.). 128p. (gr. 6-12). 35.00 *(978-1-60413-028-7(8)*, Chelsea Hse.) Facts On File, Inc.

Meachen Rau, Dana. Un Cartero. 2007. (En el Trabajo Ser.). (SPA., Illus.). 24p. (gr. k-1). lib. bdg. 15.95 *(978-0-7614-2785-8(6)*, Benchmark Bks.) Marshall Cavendish Corp.

—Mail Carrier. 2007. (Jobs in Town Ser.). (SPA., Illus.). 24p. (gr. k-1). lib. bdg. 15.95 *(978-0-7614-2620-2(5)*, Benchmark Bks.) Marshall Cavendish Corp.

Meyer, Koston. Where Does the Mail Go? 2012. (Everyday Mysteries Ser.). (ENG., Illus.). 24p. (J). (gr. 2-4). pap. 8.15 *(978-1-4339-6331-5(0))*; lib. bdg. 22.60 *(978-1-4339-6329-2(9))* Stevens, Gareth Publishing LLLP.

Micklos, John, Jr. Bold Riders: The Story of the Pony Express. 2015. (Adventures on the American Frontier Ser.). (ENG., Illus.). 32p. (gr. 3-4). pap. 7.95 *(978-1-4914-4910-3(1))* Capstone Press of Coughlan Cos.

Murray, Julie. Carteros. 2016. (Trabajos en Mi Comunidad Ser.). (SPA.). 24p. (J). (gr. k-5). pap. 7.95 *(978-1-4966-0723-2(6))* Capstone Classroom.

Owen, Ann & National Geographic Learning Staff. Delivering Your Mail: A Book about Mail Carriers. Thomas, Eric, illus. 2003. (Community Workers Ser.). (ENG.). 24p. (gr. -1-3). per. 8.95 *(978-1-4048-0485-2(4))* Picture Window Bks.

Patrick, Roman. Spanish Words at the Post Office, Vol. 1. 2014. (Learn My Language! Spanish Ser.). (ENG & SPA., Illus.). 24p. (J). (gr. 1-2). 22.60 *(978-1-4824-0350-3(1))* Stevens, Gareth Publishing LLLP.

Payment, Simone. The Pony Express. 2005. (Primary Sources in American History Ser.). (Illus.). 64p. (J). (gr. 5-8). lib. bdg. 31.95 *(978-1-4042-0181-1(5))* Rosen Publishing Group, Inc., The.

—The Pony Express: A Primary Source History of the Race to Bring Mail to the American West. 2009. (Primary Sources in American History Ser.). 64p. (gr. 5-8). 58.50 *(978-1-60851-502-8(8))* Rosen Publishing Group, Inc., The.

Phillips, Hannah. Postman. 2016. (Here to Help Ser.). (ENG., Illus.). 24p. (J). (gr. k-2). 16.99 *(978-1-4451-4002-5(0)*, Franklin Watts) Hachette Children's Group GBR. Dist: Hachette Bk. Group.

Pierce, Alan. Pony Express, 1 vol. 2005. (American Moments Ser.). (ENG., Illus.). 48p. (gr. 4-8). 27.07 *(978-1-59197-938-8(2)*, Abdo & Daughters) ABDO Publishing Co.

Quiri, Patricia R. The Groundbreaking Pony Express. 2017. (Landmarks in U. S. History Ser.). (ENG.). 32p. (gr. 3-4). lib. bdg. 27.32 ***(978-1-5157-7115-9(6)***, Fact Finders) Capstone Press of Coughlan Cos.

Ratliff, Thomas. You Wouldn't Want to Be a Pony Express Rider! A Dusty, Thankless Job You'd Rather Not Do. Bergin, Mark, illus. 2012. (You Wouldn't Want to... Ser.). (ENG.). 32p. (J). pap. 9.95 *(978-0-531-20947-9(4)*, Watts, Franklin); lib. bdg. 29.00 *(978-0-531-20872-4(9))* Scholastic Library Publishing.

Riddle, John. The Pony Express. 2004. (History of the Old West Ser.). (Illus.). 64p. (YA). (gr. 5-18). lib. bdg. 19.95 *(978-1-59084-061-0(5))* Mason Crest.

Santillo, LuAnn. The Mailman. Santillo, LuAnn, ed. 2003. (Half-Pint Kids Readers Ser.). (Illus.). 7p. (J). (gr. -1-1). pap. *(978-1-59256-125-4(X))* Half-Pint Kids, Inc.

Savage, Jeff. Daring Pony Express Riders: True Tales of the Wild West. 2012. (True Tales of the Wild West Ser.). (Illus.). 48p. (J). (gr. 5-18). pap. 8.95 *(978-1-4644-0031-5(8))*; lib. bdg. 22.60 *(978-0-7660-4023-6(2))* Enslow Pubs., Inc.

Schaefer, Lola M. Letter to a Friend. 2011. (Early Connections Ser.). (J). *(978-1-61672-639-3(3))* Benchmark Education Co.

Sévigny, Eric, illus. Caillou Sends a Letter. 2012. (Clubhouse Ser.). (ENG.). 24p. (J). (gr. -1-1). pap. 3.99 *(978-2-89450-866-4(2))* Caillouet, Gerry.

Shea, Kitty. Out & about at the Post Office. Shipe, Becky, illus. 2004. (Field Trips Ser.). (ENG.). 24p. (gr. -1-3). 27.32 *(978-1-4048-0294-0(0))* Picture Window Bks.

Shepherd, Jodie. A Day with Mail Carriers. 2012. (Rookie Read-About Community Ser.). (ENG., Illus.). 32p. (J). pap. 5.95 *(978-0-531-29253-2(3))*; lib. bdg. 23.00 *(978-0-531-28953-2(2))* Scholastic Library Publishing.

Stokes, Betty Southard. Postcards from George, 1763-1781: George Rogers Clark Writes Home to Virginia from the Kentucky Wilderness. Cable, Annette, illus. 2010. (J). *(978-1-935497-12-7(X))* Butler Bk. Publishing.

Thomas, Mary Ann. A Trip to the Post Office. 2008. (Rosen Real Readers: Upper Emergent Ser.). (ENG., Illus.). 12p. (gr. 1-2). pap. 5.90 *(978-0-8239-8126-7(6))* Rosen Publishing Group, Inc., The.

Trumbauer, Lisa. What Does a Mail Carrier Do? 2005. (What Does a Community Helper Do? Ser.). (Illus.). 24p. (J). lib. bdg. 22.60 *(978-0-7660-2544-8(6)*, Enslow Elementary) Enslow Pubs., Inc.

Uphall, Margaret. The U. S. Postal Service: The History of America's Mail System. 2017. (Landmarks of Democracy: American Institutions Ser.). 24p. (J). (gr. 7-8). pap. 8.25 ***(978-1-5081-6105-9(4)***, PowerKids Pr.) Rosen Publishing Group, Inc., The.

Young, Jeff C. The Pony Express & Its Death-Defying Mail Carriers. 2006. (Wild History of the American West Ser.). (Illus.). 128p. (J). (gr. 5-9). lib. bdg. 34.60 *(978-1-59845-010-1(7)*, 1250478, MyReportLinks.com Bks.) Enslow Pubs., Inc.

POSTAL SERVICE—FICTION

Arnau, Marta, illus. El cartero de los Suenos. 2004. (Cuentos con miga Ser.). 69p. pap. 12.95 *(978-84-931888-2-5(4))* Editorial Brief ESP. Dist: Independent Pubs. Group.

Bailer, Darice. The Pony Express. Antonishak, Tom, illus. 3rd ed. 2003. (Soundprints' Read-and-Discover Ser.). (ENG.). 48p. (J). (gr. -1-3). pap. 3.95 *(978-1-59249-019-6(0)*, S2008) Soundprints.

Banks, Steven. Special Delivery. DePorter, Vince, illus. 2005. (Ready-to-Read Ser.). 32p. (J). lib. bdg. 15.00 *(978-1-59054-986-5(4))* Fitzgerald Bks.

Blackstone, Stella. Bear at Work. Harter, Debbie, illus. 2011. (ENG & SPA.). 24p. (J). (gr. -1-k). pap. 6.99 *(978-1-84686-554-1(9))* Barefoot Bks., Inc.

—Bear at Work (Oso en el Trabajo) 2012. (ENG & SPA., Illus.). (J). 6.99 *(978-1-84686-769-9(X))* Barefoot Bks., Inc.

—L'Ours au Travail. 2012.Tr. of Bear at Work. (FRE & ENG.). (J). 6.99 *(978-1-84686-770-5(3))* Barefoot Bks., Inc.

Blackstone, Stella & Harter, Debbie. Bear at Work. Harter, Debbie, illus. 2008. (Bear Ser.). (ENG., Illus.). 24p. (J). (gr. -1-1). pap. 6.99 *(978-1-84686-110-9(1))* Barefoot Bks., Inc.

Bourgeois, Paulette. Postal Workers. LaFave, Kim, illus. 2005. 32p. (J). lib. bdg. 15.38 *(978-1-4242-1192-0(1))* Fitzgerald Bks.

Clanton, Ben. It Came in the Mail. Clanton, Ben, illus. 2016. (ENG., Illus.). 40p. (J). (gr. -1-3). 17.99 *(978-1-4814-0360-3(5)*, Simon & Schuster Bks. For Young Readers) Simon & Schuster Bks. For Young Readers.

Clayton, Lisa. Melvin the Mailman. Clayton, Sean & Spears, Ashley, illus. 2005. 8p. (J). 3.49 *(978-0-9773723-0-0(8))* Trent's Prints.

Cunliffe, John. Paints Ceiling. (Postman Pat Ser.: No. 7). (Illus.). 32p. (J). pap. 8.99 *(978-0-340-70407-3(1))* Hodder & Stoughton GBR. Dist: Trafalgar Square Publishing.

—Postman Pat & Frog Pie Dinner. (Illus.). 20p. (J). *(978-0-340-71435-5(2))* Hodder & Stoughton.

—Postman Pat & the Big Surprise. (Postman Pat Ser.: No. 9). (Illus.). 32p. (J). pap. *(978-0-340-70409-7(8))* Hodder & Stoughton.

—Postman Pat & the Hole in the Road. (Illus.). 32p. (J). pap. *(978-0-340-70384-7(9))* Hodder & Stoughton.

—Postman Pat & the Mystery Tour. (Postman Pat Ser.: Bk. 13). (Illus.). 32p. (J). pap. 8.99 *(978-0-340-71333-4(X))* Hodder & Stoughton GBR. Dist: Trafalgar Square Publishing.

—Postman Pat & the Robot. (Illus.). 32p. (J). *(978-0-340-67814-5(3))* Hodder & Stoughton.

—Postman Pat & the Sheep of Many Colours. (Illus.). (J). mass mkt. 7.99 *(978-0-340-73715-6(8))* Hodder & Stoughton GBR. Dist: Trafalgar Square Publishing.

—Postman Pat Follows a Trail. (Illus.). 32p. (J). pap. 8.99 *(978-0-340-70387-8(3))* Hodder & Stoughton GBR. Dist: Trafalgar Square Publishing.

—Postman Pat Has the Best Village. (Postman Pat Ser.: No. 6). (Illus.). 32p. (J). pap. 8.99 *(978-0-340-70388-5(1))* Hodder & Stoughton GBR. Dist: Trafalgar Square Publishing.

—Postman Pat in a Muddle. (Postman Pat Ser.: No. 3). (Illus.). 32p. (J). pap. 8.99 *(978-0-340-70385-4(7))* Hodder & Stoughton GBR. Dist: Trafalgar Square Publishing.

—Postman Pat Misses the Show. (Postman Pat Ser.: No. 4). (Illus.). 32p. (J). pap. 8.99 *(978-0-340-70386-1(5))* Hodder & Stoughton GBR. Dist: Trafalgar Square Publishing.

—Postman Pat Takes Flight. (Illus.). 32p. (J). *(978-0-340-67815-2(1))* Hodder & Stoughton.

—The Robot. (Postman Pat Ser.: Bk. 10). (Illus.). (J). pap. 8.99 *(978-0-340-70915-3(4))* Hodder & Stoughton GBR. Dist: Trafalgar Square Publishing.

Dubuc, Marianne & Ghione, Yvette. Mr. Postmouse's Rounds. Dubuc, Marianne, illus. 2015. (ENG., Illus.). 24p. (J). (gr. -1-2). 17.95 *(978-1-77138-572-5(3))* Kids Can Pr., Ltd. CAN. Dist: Hachette Bk. Group.

Greene, Rhonda Gowler. Mail Monkeys. Bender, Robert, illus. 2006. (J). pap. *(978-1-58669-217-9(8))* Childcraft Education Corp.

Herron, Edward A. The Return of the Alaskan: Mailboat in the Outpost. Langley, Gene, illus. 2011. 190p. 42.95 *(978-1-258-09093-7(7))* Literary Licensing, LLC.

Horning, Sandra. The Giant Hug. Gorbachev, Valeri, illus. 2008. (ENG.). 40p. (J). (gr. -1-2). pap. 7.99 *(978-0-553-11262-7(7)*, Dragonfly Bks.) Random Hse. Children's Bks.

Kay, Verla. Whatever Happened to the Pony Express? Root, Kimberly Bulcken & Root, Barry, illus. 2010. (ENG.). 32p. (J).

(gr. k-3). 16.99 *(978-0-399-24483-4(2)*, G.P. Putnam's Sons Books for Young Readers) Penguin Young Readers Group.

Kelly, Irene. A Small Dog's Big Life: Around the World with Owney. 2005. (ENG., Illus.). 32p. (J). 16.95 *(978-0-8234-1863-3(4))* Holiday Hse., Inc.

Kerby, Mona. Owney, the Mail-Pouch Pooch. Barasch, Lynne, illus. 2008. (ENG.). 40p. (J). (gr. k-3). 17.99 *(978-0-374-35685-9(8)*, 9780374356859, Farrar, Straus & Giroux (BYR)) Farrar, Straus & Giroux.

Kline, Suzy. Horrible Harry & the Dead Letters. Remkiewicz, Frank et al, illus. 2009. (Horrible Harry Ser.). (ENG.). 80p. (J). (gr. 2-4). 3.99 *(978-0-14-241457-6(3)*, Puffin Books) Penguin Young Readers Group.

Klise, Kate. The Phantom of the Post Office. Klise, M. Sarah, illus. (43 Old Cemetery Road Ser.: 4). (ENG.). 160p. (J). (gr. 2-5). 2013. pap. 6.99 *(978-0-544-02281-2(5))* 2012. 16.99 *(978-0-547-51974-6(5))* Houghton Mifflin Harcourt Publishing Co.

—The Phantom of the Post Office. 2013. (43 Old Cemetery Road Ser.: 4). lib. bdg. 17.20 *(978-0-606-31668-2(X)*, Turtleback) Turtleback Bks.

Leigh, Autumn. Door to Door. 2006. (Neighborhood Readers Ser.). (ENG.). 12p. (gr. -1-3). pap. 5.90 *(978-1-4042-6469-4(8)*, Rosen Classroom) Rosen Publishing Group, Inc., The.

Luthardt, Kevin & Luthardt, Kevin. Larabee, 1 vol. 2004. (ENG., Illus.). 32p. (J). (gr. k-1). 15.95 *(978-1-56145-300-9(5))* Peachtree Pubs.

Manos, John. The Mail Comes to Main Street. 2006. (Early Explorers Ser.). (J). pap. *(978-1-4108-6118-4(X))* Benchmark Education Co.

Mcadams, Kate. Flynn the Post Office Mouse. 2010. 28p. pap. 12.49 *(978-1-4520-0816-5(7))* AuthorHouse.

Murray, Eva & Hogan, Jamie. Island Birthday, 1 vol. 2015. (ENG., Illus.). 32p. (gr. 1-7). 16.95 *(978-0-88448-425-7(4)*, 884425) Tilbury Hse. Pubs.

Pryor, Bonnie. Mr. Munday & the Rustlers. 2013. (ENG.). 32p. (J). (gr. -1-3). 16.99 *(978-1-4424-8876-2(X)*, Atheneum Bks. for Young Readers) Simon & Schuster Children's Publishing.

—Mr. Munday & the Space Creatures. 2013. (ENG., Illus.). 32p. (J). (gr. -1-3). 16.99 *(978-1-4424-8877-9(8)*, Atheneum Bks. for Young Readers) Simon & Schuster Children's Publishing.

Rogers, Jacqueline. Jack Jones off to the Post Office. 2012. 20p. pap. 13.77 *(978-1-4669-0808-6(4))* Trafford Publishing.

Tunnell, Michael O. Mailing May. Rand, Ted, illus. 2015. 32p. pap. 7.00 *(978-1-61003-610-8(7))* Center for the Collaborative Classroom.

A Visit to the Post Office. 2003. (J). per. *(978-1-57657-902-2(6))* Paradise Pr., Inc.

POSTERS

see also Signs and Signboards

American Girl Editors & Anton, Carrie, eds. Poster Pack: 60 Cute, Fun, & Inspiring Posters from American Girl! 2010. (ENG.). 64p. (YA). (gr. 3-18). pap. 9.95 *(978-1-59369-795-2(3))* American Girl Publishing, Inc.

Charlesworth, Liza. Personal Poster Set: My Name: 30 Fill-In Personal Posters for Students to Display with Pride. 2013. (ENG.). (gr. -1-2). 15.99 *(978-0-545-53562-5(X)*, Teaching Resources) Scholastic, Inc.

Donahue, Peter. Farm & Zoo. 2010. (Dover Build a Poster Coloring Book Ser.). (ENG., Illus.). 48p. (J). (gr. 3-5). pap. 4.99 *(978-0-486-47947-7(1))* Dover Pubns., Inc.

Gottesman, Eric. Color Your Own Patriotic Posters. 2003. (Dover Art Coloring Book Ser.). (ENG., Illus.). 32p. (J). (gr. 3-8). 3.99 *(978-0-486-42650-1(5))* Dover Pubns., Inc.

McLaren, Thando. My Day, My Way. Villet, Olivia, illus. 2005. (ENG.). 14p. (J). (gr. -1-k). 16.99 *(978-1-85707-633-2(8))* Tango Bks. GBR. Dist: Independent Pubs. Group.

Noble, Marty. Color Your Own Classic Movie Posters. 2006. (Dover Art Coloring Book Ser.). (ENG., Illus.). 32p. (gr. 6-8). pap. 4.99 *(978-0-486-44812-1(6))* Dover Pubns., Inc.

Roytman, Arkady. Fairy Princess. 2010. (Dover Build a Poster Coloring Book Ser.). (ENG., Illus.). 48p. (J). (gr. 3-5). pap. 4.99 *(978-0-486-47943-9(9))* Dover Pubns., Inc.

—Knights & Dragons. 2010. (Dover Build a Poster Coloring Book Ser.). (ENG., Illus.). 48p. (J). (gr. 3-5). pap. 4.99 *(978-0-486-47942-2(0))* Dover Pubns., Inc.

Sovak, Jan. Build a Giant Poster Coloring Book — Under the Sea. 2013. (Dover Build a Poster Coloring Book Ser.). (ENG., Illus.). 48p. (J). (gr. 2-6). pap. 4.99 *(978-0-486-49139-4(0))* Dover Pubns., Inc.

Zourelias, Diana. Build a Giant Poster Coloring Book — United States Map. 2013. (Dover Build a Poster Coloring Book Ser.). (ENG., Illus.). 48p. (J). (gr. 3-5). pap. 4.99 *(978-0-486-49152-3(8))* Dover Pubns., Inc.

POSTIMPRESSIONISM (ART)

see Post-Impressionism (Art)

POTTER, BEATRIX, 1866-1943

Fabiny, Sarah. Who Was Beatrix Potter? Lacey, Mike, illus. 2015. 105p. (J). *(978-1-4806-8934-3(3)*, Grosset & Dunlap) Penguin Publishing Group.

Fabiny, Sarah & dePaola, Tomie. Who Was Beatrix Potter? Lacey, Mike & Harrison, Nancy, illus. 2015. (Who Was? Ser.). (ENG.). 112p. (J). (gr. 3-7). 5.99 *(978-0-448-48305-4(X)*, Grosset & Dunlap) Penguin Young Readers Group.

Guillain, Charlotte. Beatrix Potter, 1 vol. 2012. (Author Biographies Ser.). (ENG., Illus.). 24p. (gr. 1-2). 23.32 *(978-1-4329-5960-9(3))*; pap. 6.79 *(978-1-4329-5966-1(2))* Heinemann-Raintree. (Heinemann Read & Learn).

Hopkinson, Deborah. Beatrix Potter & the Unfortunate Tale of a Borrowed Guinea Pig. Voake, Charlotte, illus. 2016. (ENG.). 44p. (J). (gr. -1-3). 17.99 *(978-0-385-37325-8(2)*, Schwartz & Wade Bks.) Random Hse. Children's Bks.

Hurtig, Jennifer. The Animal World of Beatrix Potter. 2016. (J). ***(978-1-5105-1951-0(3))*** SmartBook Media, Inc.

Hurtig, Jennifer. Beatrix Potter. 2008. (My Favorite Writer Ser.). (Illus.). 32p. (YA). (gr. 5-18). pap. 9.95 *(978-1-59036-923-4(8))*; lib. bdg. 26.00 *(978-1-59036-922-7(X))* Weigl Pubs., Inc.

McPhail, David. Beatrix Potter & Her Paint Box. McPhail, David, illus. 2015. (ENG., Illus.). 40p. (J). (gr. -1-3). 17.99 *(978-0-8050-9170-0(X)*, 9780805091700, Holt, Henry & Co. Bks. For Young Readers) Holt, Henry & Co.

Penguin Young Readers. The Tale of Beatrix Potter. 2016. (Penguin Young Readers, Level 4 Ser.). (ENG.). 48p. (J). (gr. 1-3). pap. 3.99 *(978-0-241-24937-6(6)*, Penguin Young Readers) Penguin Young Readers Group.

Yuan, Margaret Speaker. Beatrix Potter. 2005. (Who Wrote That? Ser.). (Illus.). 120p. (gr. 6-12). lib. bdg. 35.00 *(978-0-7910-8655-1(0)*, Chelsea Hse.) Facts On File, Inc.

POTTER, HARRY (FICTITIOUS CHARACTER)

Bankston, John. Daniel Radcliffe. I.t. ed. 2003. (Blue Banner Biography Ser.). (Illus.). 32p. (J). (gr. 3-8). lib. bdg. 25.70 *(978-1-58415-250-7(8))* Mitchell Lane Pubs., Inc.

Bucholz, Dinah. The Unofficial Harry Potter Cookbook: From Cauldron Cakes to Knickerbocker Glory — More Than 150 Magical Recipes for Muggles & Wizards. 2010. (Unofficial Cookbook Ser.). (ENG.). 256p. 19.95 *(978-1-4405-0325-2(7))* Adams Media Corp.

Davis, Graeme. The Unauthorized Harry Potter Quiz Book: 165 Questions Ranging from the Sorcerer's Stone to the Deathly Hallows. 2008. 76p. pap. 15.38 *(978-1-934840-44-3(0))* Nimble Bks. LLC.

Gaines, Ann Graham. J. K. Rowling. 2004. (Blue Banner Biography Ser.). (Illus.). 32p. (J). (gr. 3-8). lib. bdg. 25.70 *(978-1-58415-325-2(3))* Mitchell Lane Pubs., Inc.

Hallett, Cynthia J. & Huey, Peggy J., eds. New Casebooks - J. K. Rowling: Harry Potter, 1 vol. 2012. (New Casebooks Ser.). (ENG., Illus.). 224p. (C). 85.00 *(978-0-230-00849-6(6)*, 9780230008496); pap. 29.00 *(978-0-230-00850-2(X)*, 9780230008502) Palgrave Macmillan.

Harmin, Karen Leigh. J. K. Rowling: Author of Harry Potter — An Unauthorized Biography. 2006. (People to Know Today Ser.). (Illus.). 128p. (J). (gr. 7-12). lib. bdg. 33.27 *(978-0-7660-1850-1(4))* Enslow Pubs., Inc.

Harrington, Jamie. The Unofficial Guide to Crafting the World of Harry Potter: 30 Magical Crafts for Muggles, Witches, & Wizards Alike. 2016. (ENG., Illus.). 192p. pap. 17.99 *(978-1-4405-9504-2(6))* Adams Media Corp.

Insight Editions. Harry Potter: Magical Film Projections: Patronus Charm. 2017. (J. K. Rowling's Wizarding World Ser.). (ENG.). 16p. (J). (gr. 2-5). 16.99 ***(978-0-7636-9586-6(6))*** Candlewick Pr.

Magic Eye, Inc. Staff. Harry Potter Magic Eye Book: 3D Magical Creatures, Beasts & Beings. 2010. (ENG., Illus.). 32p. (J). 16.99 *(978-0-7407-9770-5(0))* Andrews McMeel Publishing.

—Harry Potter Magic Eye Book: 3D Magical Moments. 2011. (ENG.). 32p. 16.99 *(978-1-4494-0141-2(4))* Andrews McMeel Publishing.

The Magical Worlds of Harry Potter Spellbinding Map & Book of Secrets. 2004. (Illus.). 32p. (J). 8.99 *(978-0-9708442-2-4(0))* Lumina Pr. LLC.

Moore, P.D. About Harry Potter: What Every Kid Should Know... Moore, Rema Harracksingh- & Delande, J., eds. 2003. (Illus.). 170p. (YA). pap. *(978-0-9543596-3-8(1))* Lux-Verbi Bks.

Peterson-Hilleque, Victoria. How to Analyze the Works of J. K. Rowling, 1 vol. 2011. (Essential Critiques Set 2 Ser.). (ENG., Illus.). 112p. (J). (gr. 6-12). lib. bdg. 35.64 *(978-1-61783-093-8(3))* ABDO Publishing Co.

—J. K. Rowling: Extraordinary Author, 1 vol. 2010. (Essential Lives Set 5 Ser.). (ENG.). 112p. (J). (gr. 6-12). lib. bdg. 35.64 *(978-1-61613-517-1(4))* ABDO Publishing Co.

Pezzi, Bryan. J. K. Rowling. (J). 2012. 28.55 *(978-1-61913-057-9(2))* 2012. pap. 13.95 *(978-1-61913-596-3(5))* 2005. (Illus.). 32p. (gr. 5-7). lib. bdg. 26.00 *(978-1-59036-287-7(X))* Weigl Pubs., Inc.

Price, Joan. J. K. Rowling. 2004. (Trailblazers of the Modern World Ser.). (Illus.). 48p. (gr. 5-12). lib. bdg. 31.00 *(978-0-8368-5499-2(3)*, Gareth Stevens Secondary Library) Stevens, Gareth Publishing LLLP.

—J.K. Rowling. 2004. (Trailblazers of the Modern World Ser.). (Illus.). 48p. (gr. 5-12). pap. 14.05 *(978-0-8368-5268-4(0)*, Gareth Stevens Secondary Library) Stevens, Gareth Publishing LLLP.

Pyne, Erin A. A Fandom of Magical Proportions: S: an Unauthorized History of the Harry Potter Phenomenon. 2007. (Illus.). 84p. (J). per. 8.36 *(978-0-9788138-8-8(X))* Nimble Bks. LLC.

Rowling, J. K. Harry Potter & the Chamber of Secrets. Kay, Jim, illus. 2016. (Harry Potter Ser.: 2). (ENG.). 272p. (J). (gr. 3). 39.99 *(978-0-545-79132-8(4))*; 275.00 *(978-1-338-11986-2(9))* Scholastic, Inc. (Levine, Arthur A. Bks.).

Scholastic. Harry Potter: Boxed Set: Cinematic Guide. 2016. (ENG.). (J). (gr. 2-5). 35.96 *(978-1-338-13250-2(4))* Scholastic, Inc.

Scholastic, Inc. Staff, contrib. by. The World of Harry Potter: Harry Potter Poster Book. 2011. (Illus.). 125p. (J). pap. *(978-0-545-31482-4(8))* Scholastic, Inc.

Senker, Cath. J. K. Rowling: Creator of Harry Potter. 2011. (Famous Lives Ser.). (Illus.). 32p. (YA). (gr. 3-6). lib. bdg. 26.50 *(978-1-4488-3288-0(8))* Rosen Publishing Group, Inc., The.

Sexton, Colleen. J. K. Rowling. 2008. pap. 52.95 *(978-1-57505-984-6(3))* Lerner Publishing Group.

Sexton, Colleen A. J. K. Rowling. 2007. (Biography Ser.). (Illus.). 112p. (J). (gr. -1). lib. bdg. 30.60 *(978-0-8225-7949-6(9))* Lerner Publishing Group.

—J.K. Rowling. 2006. (Just the Facts Biographies Ser.). (Illus.). 112p. (J). 27.93 *(978-0-8225-3423-5(1)*, Lerner Pubns.) Lerner Publishing Group.

Shapiro, Marc. J. K. Rowling: The Wizard Behind Harry Potter. 4th ed. 2007. (ENG., Illus.). 288p. pap. 20.99 *(978-0-312-37697-0(9)*, 9780312376970, St. Martin's Griffin) St. Martin's Pr.

Vos MacDonald, Joan. J. K. Rowling: Banned, Challenged, & Censored. 2008. (Authors of Banned Bks). (Illus.). 160p. (YA). (gr. 3-7). lib. bdg. 35.94 *(978-0-7660-2687-2(6))* Enslow Pubs., Inc.

Waters, Galadriel & Mithrandir, Astre. New Clues to Harry Potter: Hints from the Ultimate Unofficial Guide to the Mysteries of Harry Potter, Vol. 5. Waters, Galadriel, illus. 2015. (ENG., Illus.). 100p. (gr. 3-6). pap. 10.95 *(978-0-9723936-2-1(5)*, 1230146) Wizarding World Pr.

POTTER, HARRY (FICTITIOUS CHARACTER)—FICTION

Davis, Graeme. Re-Read Harry Potter & the Chamber of Secrets Today! an Unauthorized Guide. 2008. 112p. pap. 15.49 *(978-1-934840-72-6(6))* Nimble Bks. LLC.

Frankel, Valerie. Henry Potty & the Pet Rock: An Unauthorized Harry Potter Parody. 2006. 112p. (J). pap. *(978-1-59594-088-9(X)*, Wingspan Pr.) WingSpan Publishing.

Petrucha, Stefan. Harry Potty & the Deathly Boring. 2010. (Papercutz Slices Ser.). (ENG., Illus.). 64p. (J). (gr. 5-12). pap. 7.99 *(978-1-59707-217-5(6)*, 9781597072175) Papercutz.

Rowling, J. K. Harrius Potter et Camera Secretorum. Needham, Peter, tr. from ENG. 2007. (Harry Potter Ser.).Tr. of Harry Potter & the Chamber of Secrets. (LAT & ENG., Illus.). 288p. (YA). (gr. 5). 23.95 *(978-1-59990-067-4(X)*, 9781599900674, Bloomsbury USA Childrens) Bloomsbury Publishing USA.

—Harrius Potter et Philosophi Lapis. Needham, Peter, tr. from ENG. 2003. (Harry Potter Ser.).Tr. of Harry Potter & the Philosopher's Stone. (LAT & ENG., Illus.). 256p. (YA). (gr. 7). 29.99 *(978-1-58234-825-4(1)*, 9781582348254, Bloomsbury USA Childrens) Bloomsbury Publishing USA.

—Harry Potter à l'École des Sorciers. Menard, Jean-François, tr. from ENG. 2007. (Harry Potter Ser.: Year 1).Tr. of Harry Potter & the Sorcerer's Stone. 311p. (J). per. 14.95 *(978-2-07-061236-9(8))* Gallimard, Editions FRA. Dist: Distribooks, Inc.

—Harry Potter & the Chamber of Secrets. 2009. 9.64 *(978-0-7848-1444-4(9)*, Everbind) Marco Bk. Co.

—Harry Potter & the Chamber of Secrets. unabr. ed. 2004. (Harry Potter Ser.: Year 2). 352p. (J). (gr. 3-18). pap. 46.00 incl. audio *(978-0-8072-8207-6(3)*, S YA 137 SP, Listening Library) Random Hse. Audio Publishing Group.

—Harry Potter & the Chamber of Secrets. (Harry Potter Ser.: 2). (J). 2006. 1.25 *(978-1-4193-8079-2(6))* 2003. 78.75 *(978-1-4025-6698-1(0))* Recorded Bks., Inc.

—Harry Potter & the Chamber of Secrets. (Harry Potter Ser.: Year 2). (RUS., Illus.). 28.95 *(978-5-8451-0947-7(7))* Rosmen-Izdat RUS. Dist: Distribooks, Inc.

—Harry Potter & the Chamber of Secrets. I.t. ed. 2003. (Harry Potter Ser.: Year 2). (ENG.). 466p. pap. 13.95 *(978-1-59413-001-4(9))* Thorndike Pr.

—Harry Potter & the Chamber of Secrets. 2013. (Harry Potter (Kazu Kibuishi Illustrations) Ser.: 2). lib. bdg. 24.50 *(978-0-606-32346-8(5)*, Turtleback) Turtleback Bks.

—Harry Potter & the Deathly Hallows. (Illus.). 2008. 832p. pap. *(978-0-7475-9586-1(0))* 2007. (ENG., 608p. *(978-0-7475-9106-1(7))* Bloomsbury Publishing Plc.

—Harry Potter & the Deathly Hallows. braille ed. 2007. (Harry Potter Ser.: Year 7). (J). (gr. 4-7). 34.99 *(978-0-939173-57-0(3))* National Braille Pr.

—Harry Potter & the Deathly Hallows. 2010. 25.00 *(978-1-60686-882-9(9))* Perfection Learning Corp.

—Harry Potter & the Deathly Hallows, 17 vols. 2007. (Harry Potter Ser.: 7). (YA). 129.79 *(978-1-4281-6654-7(8))*; 131.75 *(978-1-4281-6652-3(1))* Recorded Bks., Inc.

—Harry Potter & the Deathly Hallows. GrandPré, Mary, illus. (Harry Potter Ser.: 7). (ENG.). (J). 2009. 784p. (gr. 4-7). pap. 14.99 *(978-0-545-13970-0(8)*, Levine, Arthur A. Bks.) 2007. 784p. (gr. 5-9). 34.99 *(978-0-545-01022-1(5))* 2007. 816p. (gr. 4-7). 65.00 *(978-0-545-02937-7(6)*, Levine, Arthur A. Bks.) Scholastic, Inc.

—Harry Potter & the Deathly Hallows. I.t. ed. 2009. (ENG.). 970p. pap. 14.95 *(978-1-59413-355-8(7)*, Large Print Pr.) 2007. (Harry Potter Ser.: Year 7). (Illus.). 969p. (J). (gr. 4-7). 34.95 *(978-0-7862-9665-1(8))* Thorndike Pr.

—Harry Potter & the Deathly Hallows. (Harry Potter (Kazu Kibuishi Illustrations) Ser.: 7). 2013. lib. bdg. 29.40 *(978-0-606-32351-2(1))* 2009. lib. bdg. 26.95 *(978-0-606-00420-6(3))* Turtleback Bks. (Turtleback).

—Harry Potter & the Deathly Hallows. Bar-hillel, Gili, tr. from ENG. 2007. (Harry Potter Ser.: Year 7). (HEB., Illus.). 568p. (J). (gr. 4-7). pap. *(978-965-482-635-8(6))* Yediot Aharonot Bks., Miscal.

—Harry Potter & the Goblet of Fire. 2009. 10.24 *(978-0-7848-1587-8(9)*, Everbind) Marco Bk. Co.

—Harry Potter & the Goblet of Fire. (Harry Potter Ser.: 4). (J). 2006. 1.25 *(978-1-4193-8531-5(3))* 2003. 101.75 *(978-1-4025-6702-5(2))* Recorded Bks., Inc.

—Harry Potter & the Goblet of Fire. GrandPré, Mary, illus. I.t. ed. 2003. (Harry Potter Ser.: Vol. 4). (ENG.). 936p. pap. 11.66 *(978-1-59413-003-8(5))* Thorndike Pr.

—Harry Potter & the Goblet of Fire. 2013. (Harry Potter (Kazu Kibuishi Illustrations) Ser.: 4). lib. bdg. 26.95 *(978-0-606-32348-2(1)*, Turtleback) Turtleback Bks.

—Harry Potter & the Half-Blood Prince. 2005. (ENG.). cd-rom *(978-0-7475-8258-8(0))* Bloomsbury Publishing Plc.

—Harry Potter & the Half-Blood Prince, 9 vols. braille ed. 2005. (Harry Potter Ser.: Year 6). (J). (gr. 4-8). 29.99 *(978-0-939173-39-6(5)*, HALF) National Braille Pr.

—Harry Potter & the Half-Blood Prince. GrandPré, Mary, illus. 2006. (Harry Potter Ser.: Year 6). 652p. (gr. 4-8). 23.00 *(978-0-7569-6765-9(1))* Perfection Learning Corp.

—Harry Potter & the Half-Blood Prince. (Harry Potter Ser.: 6). (J). 2007. 1.25 *(978-1-4193-5430-4(2))* 2006. 110.75 *(978-1-4193-5436-6(1))* 2006. 193.75 *(978-1-4193-5432-8(9))* 2005. 113.75 *(978-1-4193-5434-2(5))* Recorded Bks., Inc.

—Harry Potter & the Half-Blood Prince. GrandPré, Mary, illus. (Harry Potter Ser.: 6). (ENG.). 672p. (J). (gr. 4-8). 2005. 29.99 *(978-0-439-78454-2(9))* 2006. reprint ed. per. 12.99 *(978-0-439-78596-9(0))* Scholastic, Inc. (Levine, Arthur A. Bks.).

—Harry Potter & the Half-Blood Prince. (Illus.). (J). (gr. 4-7). 2007. (ENG.). 832p. per. 14.95 *(978-1-59413-221-6(6))* 2005. (Harry Potter Ser.: Year 6). 831p. 29.95 *(978-0-7862-7745-2(9))* Thorndike Pr. (Large Print Pr.).

—Harry Potter & the Half-Blood Prince. 2013. (Harry Potter (Kazu Kibuishi Illustrations) Ser.: 6). lib. bdg. 26.95 *(978-0-606-32350-5(3)*, Turtleback) Turtleback Bks.

—Harry Potter & the Half Blood Prince - Chinese Language. 2005. (Harry Potter Ser.: Year 6). (CHI.). 496p. (YA). (gr. 4-8). pap. 28.95 *(978-7-02-005323-0(8)*, HAP06) People's Literature Publishing Hse. CHN. Dist: Chinasprout, Inc.

—Harry Potter & the Order of the Phoenix. (ENG.). 768p. (J). (gr. 6-10). pap. *(978-0-7475-6107-1(9))* Bloomsbury Publishing Plc.

—Harry Potter & the Order of the Phoenix. 2008. *(978-977-14-2697-4(4))* Nahdat Misr Bkshop for Printing and Pubs.

—Harry Potter & the Order of the Phoenix, 13 vols. braille ed. 2003. (Harry Potter Ser.: Year 5). (YA). 29.99 *(978-0-939173-38-9(7))* National Braille Pr.

—Harry Potter & the Order of the Phoenix. 2003. (Harry Potter Ser.: Year 5). (CHI.). 575p. (YA). pap. 26.95 *(978-7-02-004327-9(5)*, HAP05) People's Literature Publishing Hse. CHN. Dist: Chinasprout, Inc.

—Harry Potter & the Order of the Phoenix. 2004. (Harry Potter Ser.). 870p. (gr. 4-6). 16.49 *(978-0-7569-4163-5(6))* Perfection Learning Corp.

—Harry Potter & the Order of the Phoenix. 2003. (ENG.). 768p. *(978-1-55192-570-7(2))* Raincoast Bk. Distribution.

—Harry Potter & the Order of the Phoenix. GrandPré, Mary, illus. (Harry Potter Ser.: 5). (ENG.). (J). (gr. 3-7). 2004. 896p. mass mkt. 12.99 *(978-0-439-35807-1(8)*, Scholastic Paperbacks) 2003. 870p. 29.99 *(978-0-439-35806-4(X))* Scholastic, Inc.

—Harry Potter & the Order of the Phoenix. I.t. ed. 2003. (Harry Potter Ser.: Year 5). 1093p. 29.95 *(978-0-7862-5778-2(4)*, Large Print Pr.) Thorndike Pr.

—Harry Potter & the Order of the Phoenix. GrandPré, Mary, illus. I.t. ed. 2003. (Thorndike Young Adult Ser.). (ENG.). 1232p. (J). (gr. 4-7). per. 14.95 *(978-1-59413-112-7(0)*, Large Print Pr.) Thorndike Pr.

—Harry Potter & the Order of the Phoenix. (Harry Potter (Kazu Kibuishi Illustrations) Ser.: 5). 2013. lib. bdg. 26.95 *(978-0-606-32349-9(X))* 2004. lib. bdg. 24.50 *(978-0-613-99916-8(9))* Turtleback Bks. (Turtleback).

—Harry Potter & the Philosopher's Stone. 2014. (ENG., Illus.). 352p. *(978-1-4088-5589-8(5))* Bloomsbury Publishing Plc.

—Harry Potter & the Prisoner of Azkaban. 2009. 9.64 *(978-0-7848-1542-7(9)*, Everbind) Marco Bk. Co.

—Harry Potter & the Prisoner of Azkaban. 2005. (Harry Potter Ser.: Year 3). (CHI.). 260p. (YA). pap. 16.95 *(978-7-02-003345-4(8)*, HAP03) People's Literature Publishing Hse. CHN. Dist: Chinasprout, Inc.

—Harry Potter & the Prisoner of Azkaban, 10 vols. 2003. (Harry Potter Ser.: 3). (J). 84.75 *(978-1-4025-6700-1(6))* Recorded Bks., Inc.

—Harry Potter & the Prisoner of Azkaban. I.t. ed. 2003. (Harry Potter Ser.: Year 3). (ENG.). 592p. pap. 13.95 *(978-1-59413-002-1(7)*, Large Print Pr.) Thorndike Pr.

—Harry Potter & the Prisoner of Azkaban. 2013. (Harry Potter (Kazu Kibuishi Illustrations) Ser.: 3). lib. bdg. 24.50 *(978-0-606-32347-5(3)*, Turtleback) Turtleback Bks.

—Harry Potter & the Sorcerer's Stone. 2014. (ENG.). lthr. 79.00 *(978-1-62715-772-8(7))* Leatherbound Bestsellers.

—Harry Potter & the Sorcerer's Stone. 2009. 8.44 *(978-0-7848-2438-2(X))*; 10.84 *(978-0-7848-1357-7(4))* Marco Bk. Co. (Everbind).

—Harry Potter & the Sorcerer's Stone. 2003. (Harry Potter Ser.: Year 1). (CHI.). 191p. (YA). pap. 14.95 *(978-7-02-003343-0(1)*, HAP01) People's Literature Publishing Hse. CHN. Dist: Chinasprout, Inc.

—Harry Potter & the Sorcerer's Stone. (Harry Potter Ser.: 1). (J). 2004. 1.25 *(978-1-4025-6757-5(X))* 2003. 80.75 *(978-1-4025-6696-7(4))* Recorded Bks., Inc.

—Harry Potter & the Sorcerer's Stone. Kay, Jim, illus. 2015. (Harry Potter Ser.: 1). (ENG.). 256p. (J). (gr. 3). 39.99 *(978-0-545-79035-2(2)*, Levine, Arthur A. Bks.) Scholastic, Inc.

—Harry Potter & the Sorcerer's Stone. Grand Pre, Mary, illus. 10th anniv. ed. 2008. (Harry Potter Ser.: Year 1). (ENG.). 320p. (J). (gr. 2-5). 30.00 *(978-0-545-06967-0(X)*, Levine, Arthur A. Bks.) Scholastic, Inc.

—Harry Potter & the Sorcerer's Stone, Bk. 1. 2013. (Harry Potter Ser.: 1). (ENG., Illus.). 336p. (J). (gr. 4). pap. 12.99 *(978-0-545-58288-9(1))* Scholastic, Inc.

—Harry Potter & the Sorcerer's Stone. 2013. (Harry Potter (Kazu Kibuishi Illustrations) Ser.: 1). lib. bdg. 24.50 *(978-0-606-32345-1(7)*, Turtleback) Turtleback Bks.

—Harry Potter Coffret: Harry Potter à l'École des Sorciers; Harry Potter et la Chambre des Secrets; Harry Potter et le Prisonnier d'Azkaban. (Harry Potter Ser.: Years 1-3).Tr. of Harry Potter Boxed Set: Harry Potter & the Chamber of Secrets; Harry Potter & the Sorcerer's Stone; Harry Potter & the Prisoner of Azkaban. pap. 69.95 *(978-2-07-054972-6(0))* Gallimard, Editions FRA. Dist: Distribooks, Inc.

—Harry Potter e a Camara Secreta. (Harry Potter Ser.: Year 2).Tr. of Harry Potter & the Chamber of Secrets. (POR.). pap. 28.95 *(978-85-325-1166-9(X))* Rocco, Editora, Ltda BRA. Dist: Distribooks, Inc.

—Harry Potter e a Pedra Filosofal. (Harry Potter Ser.: Year 1).Tr. of Harry Potter & the Philosopher's Stone. (POR.). pap. 28.95 *(978-85-325-1101-0(5))* Rocco, Editora, Ltda BRA. Dist: Distribooks, Inc.

—Harry Potter e a Prisioneiro de Azkaban. (Harry Potter Ser.: Year 3).Tr. of Harry Potter & the Prisoner of Azkaban. (POR.). pap. 29.95 *(978-85-325-1206-2(2))* Rocco, Editora, Ltda BRA. Dist: Distribooks, Inc.

—Harry Potter e il Prigioniero di Azkaban. (Harry Potter Ser.: Year 3).Tr. of Harry Potter & the Prisoner of Azkaban. (ITA.). pap. 32.95 *(978-88-7782-852-1(8))* Salani ITA. Dist: Distribooks, Inc.

—Harry Potter e la camera dei segreti. (Harry Potter Ser.: Year 2). (ITA.). pap. 32.95 *(978-88-7782-703-6(3))* Salani ITA. Dist: Distribooks, Inc.

—Harry Potter e la Pietra Filosofale. (Harry Potter Ser.: Year 1).Tr. of Harry Potter & the Philosopher's Stone. (ITA., Illus.). 293p. pap. 32.95 *(978-88-7782-702-9(5))* Salani ITA. Dist: Distribooks, Inc.

—Harry Potter e o Cálice de Fogo. (Harry Potter Ser.: Year 4).Tr. of Harry Potter & the Goblet of Fire. (POR.). pap. 38.95 *(978-85-325-1252-9(6))* Rocco, Editora, Ltda BRA. Dist: Distribooks, Inc.

—Harry Potter et la Coupe de Feu. (Harry Potter Ser.: Year 4).Tr. of Harry Potter & the Goblet of Fire. (FRE., Illus.). 766p. pap. 19.95 *(978-2-07-054351-9(X))* Gallimard, Editions FRA. Dist: Distribooks, Inc.

—Harry Potter I Czara Ognia. (Harry Potter Ser.: Year 4). pap. 29.95 *(978-83-7278-021-8(8))* Media Rodzina POL. Dist: Distribooks, Inc.

—Harry Potter I Kamie D. (Harry Potter Ser.: Year 1). pap. 18.95 *(978-83-7278-000-3(5))* Media Rodzina POL. Dist: Distribooks, Inc.

—Harry Potter I Komnata Tajem. (Harry Potter Ser.: Year 1). pap. 18.95 *(978-83-7278-007-2(2))* Media Rodzina POL. Dist: Distribooks, Inc.
—Harry Potter I wi Zied Azkab. (Harry Potter Ser.: Year 3). pap. 29.95 *(978-83-7278-014-0(5))* Media Rodzina POL. Dist: Distribooks, Inc.
—Harry Potter y el Caliz de Fuego. 2004. (Harry Potter Ser.: Year 4).Tr. of Harry Potter & the Goblet of Fire. (SPA., Illus.). 240p. (YA). 19.95 *(978-84-7888-645-6(1)*, SAL30169) Emece Editores ESP. Dist: Lectorum Pubns., Inc.
—Harry Potter y el Prisionero de Azkaban. 2004. (Harry Potter Ser.: Year 3).Tr. of Harry Potter & the Prisoner of Azkaban. (SPA., Illus.). 360p. (gr. 3-18). 17.95 *(978-84-7888-519-0(6)*, SAL1889) Emece Editores ESP. Dist: Lectorum Pubns., Inc.
—Harry Potter y la Camara Secreta. 2004. (Harry Potter Ser.: Year 2).Tr. of Harry Potter & the Chamber of Secrets. (SPA., Illus.). 288p. (YA). (gr. 3-18). 15.95 *(978-84-7888-495-7(5)*, SAL4595) Emece Editores ESP. Dist: Lectorum Pubns., Inc.
—Harry Potter Y la Orden del Fenix. 2004. (Harry Potter Ser.: Year 5).Tr. of Harry Potter & the Order of the Phoenix. (SPA.). 893p. (YA). 23.99 *(978-84-7888-901-3(9))* Emece Editores ESP. Dist: Lectorum Pubns., Inc.
—Harry Potter Y la Orden del Fenix. Ortega, Gemma Rovira, tr. from ENG. 2004. (Harry Potter Ser.: Year 5).Tr. of Harry Potter & the Order of the Phoenix. (SPA.). 893p. (YA). pap. 17.99 *(978-84-7888-884-9(5))* Emece Editores ESP. Dist: Lectorum Pubns., Inc.
—Harry Potter Y la Orden del Fenix. 2004. (Harry Potter Ser.: Year 5).Tr. of Harry Potter & the Order of the Phoenix. 1000p. 69.95 *(978-0-320-04850-0(0))* French & European Pubns., Inc.
—Harry Potter y la Piedra Filosofal. 2004. (Harry Potter Ser.: Year 1).Tr. of Harry Potter & the Sorcerer's Stone. (SPA., Illus.). 256p. (YA). (gr. 7-18). 15.95 *(978-84-7888-445-2(9)*, SAL2819) Emece Editores ESP. Dist: Lectorum Pubns., Inc.
Rowling, J. K. & Scholastic, Inc. Staff. Harry Potter. 2007. (Harry Potter Ser.: Years 1-7). (ENG.). (J). (gr. 3-7). 205.93 *(978-0-545-04425-7(1)*, Levine, Arthur A. Bks.) Scholastic, Inc.
Rowling, J. K. & Xocuasvili, Cico. Hari Poteri Da Sikvdilis Sacukrebi. 2008. (GEO.). 636p. (J). *(978-9941-40-314-9(7))* Georgian Biographic Ctr., Ltd.
Running Press Staff, ed. Harry Potter Golden Snitch Sticker Kit. Kit. 2006. (Miniature Editions Ser.). (ENG.). 16p. pap. 9.95 *(978-0-7624-2821-2(X))* Running Pr. Bk. Pubs.
Scholastic Teaching Resources Staff. Harry Potter Coloring Book: Celebratory Edition: The Best of Harry Potter Coloring. 2016. (ENG.). 96p. (J). (gr. 3). pap. 15.99 *(978-1-338-16660-6(3))* Scholastic, Inc.
Warner Bros. Entertainment Staff. Harry Potter Poster Collection: The Quintessential Images. 2012. (Insights Poster Collections). (ENG., Illus.). 40p. (gr. 2). pap. 24.99 *(978-1-60887-142-1(8))* Insight Editions.
Warner Bros. Entertainment Staff & Warner Bros. Consumer Products Inc. Staff. Harry Potter Poster Collection: The Definitive Movie Posters. 2012. (Insights Poster Collections). (ENG., Illus.). 40p. (gr. 2). pap. 24.99 *(978-1-60887-113-1(4))* Insight Editions.
Wizard Academies I: The Heart of Darkness. 2006. 658p. pap. 24.96 *(978-1-4116-7787-6(0))* Lulu Pr., Inc.
Zimmerman, W. Frederick. Unauthorized Harry Potter & the Alchemist's Cell News: Half-Blood Prince Analysis & Speculation. 2006. 160p. per. 14.94 *(978-0-9777424-7-9(4))* Nimble Bks. LLC.
—Unauthorized Harry Potter & the Chariots of Light News: Half-Blood Prince Analysis & Speculation. 2006. 160p. per. 14.94 *(978-0-9777424-8-6(2))* Nimble Bks. LLC.

POTTERS

Hill, Laban Carrick. Dave the Potter: Artist, Poet, Slave. Collier, Bryan, illus. 2010. (ENG.). 40p. (J). (gr. -1-3). 18.99 *(978-0-316-10731-0(X))* Little, Brown Bks. for Young Readers.
Hill, Laban Carrik. Dave the Potter: Artist, Poet, Slave. 2011. (J). *(978-1-4618-1706-2(4))* Recorded Bks., Inc.

POTTERS—FICTION

Holliday, Bobby. A Lump of Clay. Price, Rebecca, illus. 2010. 28p. (J). 18.99 *(978-0-9829082-1-1(0))* Lady Hawk Pr.

POTTERY

see also Porcelain

Andrews-Goebel, Nancy. The Pot That Juan Built. Diaz, David, illus. 2013. (ENG.). 32p. (J). (gr. 1-18). 17.95 *(978-1-58430-038-0(8))* Lee & Low Bks., Inc.
—La Vasija Que Juan Fabrico. Diaz, David, illus. 2004. (SPA.). 32p. (J). (gr. 2-5). pap. 10.95 *(978-1-58430-230-8(5))* Lee & Low Bks., Inc.
Clough, Peter. Clay in the Classroom. 2005. (Illus.). 111p. reprint ed. pap. 22.00 *(978-0-7567-9594-8(X))* DIANE Publishing Co.
Greenberg, Jan & Jordan, Sandra. The Mad Potter: George E. Ohr, Eccentric Genius. 2013. (ENG., Illus.). 56p. (J). (gr. 2-6). 17.99 *(978-1-59643-810-1(X)*, 9781596438101) Roaring Brook Pr.
Johnson, Donald-Brian, et al. Ceramic Arts Studio: The Legacy of Betty Harrington, 1 vol. 2003. (ENG., Illus.). 264p. (gr. 10-13). 59.95 *(978-0-7643-1826-9(8)*, 9780764318269) Schiffer Publishing, Ltd.
Kassinger, Ruth. Ceramics: From Magic Pots to Man-Made Bones. 2003. (Material World Ser.). (Illus.). 80p. (gr. 6-8). lib. bdg. 25.90 *(978-0-7613-2108-8(X)*, Twenty-First Century Bks.) Lerner Publishing Group.
Kenney, Karen Latchana. Super Simple Clay Projects: Fun & Easy-to-Make Crafts for Kids, 1 vol. 2009. (Super Simple Crafts Ser.). (ENG., Illus.). 32p. (gr. k-4). 27.07 *(978-1-60453-623-2(3)*, Super SandCastle) ABDO Publishing Co.
Llimós, Anna. Easy Clay Crafts in 5 Steps. 2008. (Easy Crafts in 5 Steps Ser.). (Illus.). 32p. (J). (gr. 3-4). lib. bdg. 23.94 *(978-0-7660-3085-5(7)*, Enslow Elementary) Enslow Pubs., Inc.
Llimos Plomer, Anna & Parramon's Editorial Team Staff. Clay. 2003. (Let's Create! Ser.). (Illus.). 32p. (gr. 1-4). lib. bdg. 26.00 *(978-0-8368-3746-9(0)*, Gareth Stevens Learning Library) Stevens, Gareth Publishing LLLP.
Quan, Adalucia. The Magic of Clay. 2003. (Illus.). 29p. (J). 18.95 *(978-0-9742956-0-2(4))* Cholita Prints & Pub. Co.
Scheunemann, Pam. Cool Glass & Ceramic Projects: Creative Ways to Upcycle Your Trash into Treasure, 1 vol. 2012. (Cool Trash to Treasure Ser.). (ENG., Illus.). 32p. (J). (gr. 3-6). lib. bdg. 27.07 *(978-1-61783-433-2(5)*, Checkerboard Library) ABDO Publishing Co.
Spilsbury, Louise. Decorated Pottery. 2016. (Stories in Art Ser.). (ENG., Illus.). 32p. (J). (gr. 2-4). pap. 11.99 *(978-0-7502-9445-4(0)*, Wayland) Hachette Children's Group GBR. Dist: Hachette Bk. Group.
Spilsbury, Richard. Decorated Pottery. 2009. (Stories in Art Ser.). (Illus.). 30p. (J). lib. bdg. 26.50 *(978-1-4042-4437-5(9)*, PowerKids Pr.) Rosen Publishing Group, Inc., The.
Stephens, Pam. Dropping in on ... Puffer Learns about Ceramics. 2013. (ENG., Illus.). 32p. (J). 15.95 *(978-1-56290-707-5(7))* Crystal Productions.
Zavada, Mary. Lady Head Vases: A Collector's Guide with Prices, 1 vol. 2nd rev. ed. 2003. (ENG., Illus.). 112p. (gr. 10-13). pap. 16.95 *(978-0-7643-1822-1(5)*, 9780764318221) Schiffer Publishing, Ltd.

POTTERY—FICTION

Alexander, Lloyd. The Black Cauldron. Wyatt, David, illus. 2nd rev. ed. 2006. (Chronicles of Prydain Ser.: 2). (ENG.). 208p. (J). (gr. 3-7). pap. 7.99 *(978-0-8050-8049-0(X)*, 9780805080490) Square Fish.
Brandeis, Madeline. The Little Mexican Donkey Boy. 2011. 226p. 44.95 *(978-1-258-09794-3(X))* Literary Licensing, LLC.
Camila & Clay-Old-Woman, 6 pack. (Greetings Ser.: Vol. 1). (gr. 3-5). 31.00 *(978-0-7635-1745-8(3))* Rigby Education.
Carter, Aubrey Smith. The Enchanted Lizard: La Lagartijita Mágica. Nelson, Esther Whitt, ed. Branton, Molly, illus. 2006. (ENG & SPA.). 96p. (J). 18.95 *(978-1-893271-38-8(2)*, Maverick Bks.) Trinity Univ. Pr.
De La Ramee, Louise & Ouida. Bimbi. 2007. 152p. per. 13.95 *(978-1-60312-344-0(X))*; 24.95 *(978-1-60312-682-3(1))* Aegypan.
DiCicco, Sue. Princess Potty Time. 2011. (ENG., Illus.). 14p. (J). (— 1). bds. 7.99 *(978-0-375-87202-0(7)*, Golden Bks.) Random Hse. Children's Bks.
A First Clay Gathering (Review Multiple Meanings), Level C. 2003. ("Plaid" Phonics & Stories Libraries). 43.50 *(978-0-8136-9234-0(2))* Modern Curriculum Pr.
Flegg, Aubrey. Wings over Delft, Vol. 1. 2nd rev. ed. 2004. (Louise Trilogy Ser.: 01). (ENG.). 208p. (J). pap. 12.95 *(978-0-86278-886-5(2))* O'Brien Pr., Ltd., The IRL. Dist: Dufour Editions, Inc.
Krug, R. Lyding. The Treasure of Ferson Creek. 2006. 133p. (YA). pap. 9.95 *(978-1-4116-3683-5(X))* Lulu Pr., Inc.
Meadows, Daisy. Kayla the Pottery Fairy. 2015. (Magical Crafts Fairies Ser.: 1). (ENG., Illus.). 80p. (J). (gr. 2-5). pap. 4.99 *(978-0-545-70829-6(X)*, Scholastic Paperbacks) Scholastic, Inc.
Park, Linda Sue. A Single Shard. unabr. ed. 2004. (Middle Grade Cassette Librariestm Ser.). (J). (gr. 5-9). pap. 36.00 incl. audio *(978-0-8072-1760-3(3)*, S YA 349 SP, Listening Library) Random Hse. Audio Publishing Group.
—A Single Shard. 2011. (gr. 5-8). lib. bdg. 18.40 *(978-0-613-57327-6(7)*, Turtleback) Turtleback Bks.
Stephens, Dawn. The Little Pot. 2009. (Illus.). (J). (gr. -1-3). 17.95 *(978-1-933982-11-3(X)*, bPlus Bks.) Bumble Bee Publishing.

POTTINGER, ROSE RITA (FICTITIOUS CHARACTER)—FICTION

Bellairs, John. The House with a Clock in Its Walls. Gorey, Edward, illus. 2004. (Lewis Barnavelt Ser.: Bk. 1). (ENG.). 192p. (J). (gr. 3-7). pap. 6.99 *(978-0-14-240257-3(5)*, Puffin Books) Penguin Young Readers Group.
—The House with a Clock in Its Walls. (Lewis Barnavelt Ser.: Bk. 1). 179p. (J). (gr. 4-6). pap. 4.50 *(978-0-8072-1423-7(X)*, Listening Library) Random Hse. Audio Publishing Group.

POULTRY

see also names of domesticated birds, e.g. Ducks; Geese; Turkeys, etc.

Harmon, Daniel E. Poultry: From the Farm to Your Table. 2012. (Truth about the Food Supply Ser.). (ENG., Illus.). 48p. (J). (gr. 5-8). lib. bdg. 27.95 *(978-1-4488-6798-1(3)*, Rosen Reference) Rosen Publishing Group, Inc., The.
Mercer, Abbie. Chickens on a Farm. 2009. (Barnyard Animals Ser.). (Illus.). 24p. (J). lib. bdg. 22.60 *(978-1-4358-3840-6(8)*, PowerKids Pr.) Rosen Publishing Group, Inc., The.
Miller, Debra A. Factory Farming. Greenhaven Press Editors, ed. 2013. (Current Controversies Ser.). (ENG., Illus.). 224p. (gr. 10-12). pap. 32.00 *(978-0-7377-6873-2(8))*; lib. bdg. 46.40 *(978-0-7377-6872-5(X))* Cengage Gale. (Greenhaven Pr., Inc.).
Page, Robin. A Chicken Followed Me Home! Questions & Answers about a Familiar Fowl. Page, Robin, illus. 2015. (ENG., Illus.). 40p. (J). (gr. k-5). 17.99 *(978-1-4814-1028-1(8)*, Beach Lane Bks.) Beach Lane Bks.
Quinton, Sasha. Peck-A-peck: A Phonics Reader. 2009. (Illus.). pap. *(978-1-936199-08-2(4))* Book Shop, Ltd., The.
Stone, Tanya Lee. Chickens. 2003. (Wild Wild World Ser.). 24p. (YA). 24.94 *(978-1-56711-812-4(7)*, Blackbirch Pr., Inc.) Cengage Gale.
Walker, Sylvia & Coloring Books Staff. Easter Egg Hunt Coloring Book. 2012. (Dover Holiday Coloring Book Ser.). (ENG., Illus.). 32p. (J). (gr. -1-3). pap. 3.99 *(978-0-486-48521-8(8))* Dover Pubns., Inc.

POULTRY—FICTION

Aimé, Elizabeth Mary. A Peaceful Home for Red Rock Hen. 2012. 32p. pap. 19.99 *(978-1-4772-1340-7(6))* AuthorHouse.
Allen, Christina. A Micro-Chip on my Shoulder: A True Story of a Little Poult. 2010. 28p. pap. 13.99 *(978-1-4490-6681-9(X))* AuthorHouse.
Davis, Peg. After the Storm: A Napoleon & Marigold Adventure. 2009. 40p. pap. 16.50 *(978-1-60860-222-3(2)*, Eloquent Bks.) Strategic Book Publishing & Rights Agency (SBPRA).
Galdone, Paul. The Little Red Hen. 2011. (Folk Tale Classics Ser.). (ENG., Illus.). 48p. (J). (gr. -1-3). 8.99 *(978-0-547-37018-7(0))* Houghton Mifflin Harcourt Publishing Co.
Hayes, Beverly. Charlie Chicken Hawk, 1 vol. Ashcraft Jr, D. C., illus. 2009. 20p. pap. 24.95 *(978-1-60836-673-6(1))* America Star Bks.
Jones, Christianne C. The Little Red Hen, 1 vol. Magnuson, Natalie, illus. 2011. (My First Classic Story Ser.). (ENG.). 32p. (gr. k-3). pap. 7.10 *(978-1-4048-7356-8(2)*, My First Classic Story) Picture Window Bks.
Josiah, Iris. Tiny Hen. 2012. (Illus.). 28p. (J). pap. *(978-0-9572728-3-5(9))* Tiny Island Pr.
Julian, Russell. Happy Cockerel. 2005. (Farm Board Book Ser.). (ENG., Illus.). 12p. (J). bds. 9.99 *(978-1-4052-1030-0(3))* Egmont Bks., Ltd. GBR. Dist: Trafalgar Square Publishing.
Page, P. K. The Old Woman & the Hen. Westergard, Jim, illus. 2008. (ENG.). 32p. (J). pap. 10.95 *(978-0-88984-309-7(0))* Porcupine's Quill, Inc. CAN. Dist: Univ. of Toronto Pr.
Plitt, Kay. Why Isn't Bobby Like Me, Mom? 2010. 32p. 14.75 *(978-1-4269-4038-5(6))* Trafford Publishing.
Simon, Francesca. Higgledy Piggledy the Hen Who Loved to Dance. Moseng, Elisabeth, illus. 2016. (ENG.). 32p. (J). 17.99 *(978-0-00-813946-9(6)*, HarperCollins Children's Bks.) HarperCollins Pubs. Ltd. GBR. Dist: HarperCollins Pubs.
Stoeke, Janet Morgan. The Loopy Coop Hens. Stoeke, Janet Morgan, illus. 2013. (Loopy Coop Hens Ser.). (ENG., Illus.). 32p. (J). (gr. 1-2). mass mkt. 3.99 *(978-0-448-46272-1(9)*, Penguin Young Readers) Penguin Young Readers Group.
Swanberg, Arvon & Spicer, Carolyn. The Big, Blue, Overstuffed Chair. 2013. 46p. pap. 17.99 *(978-1-4808-0432-6(0))* Archway Publishing.
Ungermann Marshall, Yana. Gilda Gets Wise. Ungermann Marshall, Yana, illus. 2008. (Illus.). 34p. (J). pap. *(978-0-9670982-6-5(2))* Yana's Kitchen.
Wiggin, Kate Douglas. The Diary of a Goose Girl. 2007. 108p. per. 9.95 *(978-1-60312-330-3(X))*; 22.95 *(978-1-60312-748-6(8))* Aegypan.
Wolff, Jan, et al. Chiquita's Children: Teaching Children about Foster Families. Dey, Lorraine, illus. 2016. (ENG.). 48p. (gr. -1-4). 9.95 *(978-0-88282-516-8(X))* New Horizon Pr. Pubs., Inc.

POVERTY

see also Homelessness

see also names of countries with the subdivision Economic Conditions and Social Conditions e.g. United States—Economic Conditions; United States—Social Conditions

Black, Donnette. Madam C. J. Walker's Road to Success. 2010. 36p. pap. 17.50 *(978-1-4520-2443-1(X))* AuthorHouse.
Bojang, Ali Brownlie. Aid & Development. 2009. (J). 32.80 *(978-1-59920-099-6(6))* Black Rabbit Bks.
Buckley, A. M. Homelessness, 1 vol. 2011. (Essential Issues Set 3 Ser.). (ENG., Illus.). 112p. (J). (gr. 6-12). lib. bdg. 35.64 *(978-1-61783-134-8(4))* ABDO Publishing Co.
Green, Robert. Poverty. 2008. (21st Century Skills Library: Global Perspectives Ser.). (ENG.). 32p. (gr. 4-8). lib. bdg. 28.50 *(978-1-60279-126-8(0)*, 200106) Cherry Lake Publishing.
Helfand, Lewis. Mother Teresa: Saint of the Slums. Banerjee, Sankha & Nagar, Sachin, illus. 2013. (Campfire Graphic Novels Ser.). (ENG.). 88p. (YA). (gr. 5). pap. 11.99 *(978-93-80028-70-5(9)*, Campfire) Steerforth Pr.
Hopkinson, Deborah. Shutting Out the Sky: Life in the Tenements of New York, 1880-1924. 2003. (ENG., Illus.). 144p. (J). (gr. 3-7). 19.99 *(978-0-439-37590-0(8)*, Orchard Bks.) Scholastic, Inc.
Information Plus Homeless in America November 2005. 2005. 49.00 *(978-1-4144-0418-9(2))* Cengage Gale.
Kalman, Bobbie. ¿Qué Necesito? 2010. (SPA.). 16p. (J). pap. *(978-0-7787-8587-3(4))*; lib. bdg. *(978-0-7787-8561-3(0))* Crabtree Publishing Co.
—What Do I Need? 2010. (My World Ser.). (ENG., Illus.). 16p. (J). (gr. k-2). *(978-0-7787-9436-3(9))*; pap. *(978-0-7787-9480-6(6))* Crabtree Publishing Co.
Kowalski, Kathiann M. Poverty in America: Causes & Issues. 2003. (Issues in Focus Ser.). (Illus.). 128p. (J). lib. bdg. 26.60 *(978-0-7660-1945-4(4))* Enslow Pubs., Inc.
Lusted, Marcia Amidon. Poverty, 1 vol. 2010. (Essential Issues Set 1 Ser.). (ENG.). 112p. (J). (gr. 6-12). lib. bdg. 35.64 *(978-1-60453-957-8(7)*, Essential Library) ABDO Publishing Co.
Maddocks, Steven. World Hunger. 2004. (21st Century Issues Ser.). (Illus.). 48p. (gr. 5-12). lib. bdg. 31.00 *(978-0-8368-5646-0(5)*, Gareth Stevens Secondary Library) Stevens, Gareth Publishing LLLP.
Marsico, Katie. The Salvation Army. 2014. (Community Connections: How Do They Help? Ser.). (ENG.). 24p. (J). (gr. 2-5). 25.64 *(978-1-63188-029-2(2)*, 205523) Cherry Lake Publishing.
Merino, Noël. Poverty & Homelessness. Greenhaven Press Editors, ed. 2014. (Current Controversies Ser.). (ENG., Illus.). 224p. (gr. 10-12). lib. bdg. 46.40 *(978-0-7377-6886-2(X)*, Greenhaven Pr., Inc.) Cengage Gale.
—Poverty & Homelessness. Greenhaven Press Editors & Gale Editors, eds. 2014. (Current Controversies Ser.). (ENG., Illus.). 224p. (gr. 7-12). pap. 32.00 *(978-0-7377-6887-9(8)*, Greenhaven Pr., Inc.) Cengage Gale.
Moore, Elizabeth. Wants or Needs. 2011. (Wonder Readers Emergent Level Ser.). (ENG.). (gr. -1-1). 16p. pap. 35.94 *(978-1-4296-8197-1(7))*; 32p. pap. 5.99 *(978-1-4296-7876-6(3))* Capstone Press of Coughlan Cos. (Wonder Readers).
Muñoz, Mercedes. Is Poverty a Serious Threat? 2006. (At Issue Ser.). (ENG.). 117p. (YA). (gr. 10-13). 24.45 *(978-0-7377-2726-5(8)*, Greenhaven Pr., Inc.); (Illus.). (gr. 9-12). pap. 34.45 *(978-0-7377-2725-8(X))* Cengage Gale.
Saul, Laya. Ways to Help Disadvantaged Youth: A Guide to Giving Back. 2010. (How to Help Ser.). (Illus.). 48p. (J). (gr. 4-8). lib. bdg. 29.95 *(978-1-58415-918-6(9))* Mitchell Lane Pubs., Inc.
Senker, Cath. Poverty. 2007. (What If We Do Nothing? Ser.). (Illus.). 48p. (gr. 5-12). lib. bdg. 31.00 *(978-0-8368-7757-1(8)*, Gareth Stevens Secondary Library) Stevens, Gareth Publishing LLLP.
Spilsbury, Louise. Poverty & Hunger. Kai, Hanane, illus. 2017. (Children in Our World Ser.). (ENG.). 32p. (J). (gr. 1-4). 9.99 ***(978-1-4380-5019-5(4))*** Barron's Educational Series, Inc.
Steinman, Karen. Critical World Issues: Poverty, Vol. 16. 2016. (Critical World Issues Ser.: Vol. 16). (ENG., Illus.). 112p. (J). (gr. 7-12). 25.95 *(978-1-4222-3658-1(7))* Mason Crest.
Wilson, Mike. Poverty. 2009. (Introducing Issues with Opposing Viewpoints Ser.). (ENG.). 144p. (gr. 7-10). 35.75 *(978-0-7377-4340-1(9)*, Greenhaven Pr., Inc.) Cengage Gale.

POVERTY—FICTION

Alexander, James W. Good - Better - Best: Classic Treatment of a Christian's Duty to the Poor. 2009. 224p. pap. 17.00 *(978-1-59925-143-1(4))* Solid Ground Christian Bks.
Alger Jr. Horatio Staff. Herbert Carter's Legacy. rev. ed. 2006. 264p. 28.95 *(978-1-4218-1756-9(X))*; pap. 13.95 *(978-1-4218-1856-6(6))* 1st World Publishing, Inc. (1st World Library - Literary Society).
Ardizzone, Edward. Sarah & Simon & No Red Paint. Ardizzone, Edward, illus. 2011. (Illus.). 48p. (J). 17.95 *(978-1-56792-410-7(7))* Godine, David R. Pub.
Armstrong, William H. Sounder. l.t. ed. 2005. 111p. (YA). pap. 10.95 *(978-0-7862-7915-9(X))* Thorndike Pr.
Avi. The Traitors' Gate. Raude, Karina, illus. 2007. (ENG.). 368p. (J). (gr. 5-8). 17.99 *(978-0-689-85335-7(1)*, Atheneum/Richard Jackson Bks.) Simon & Schuster Children's Publishing.
Bayard, Louis. Lucky Strikes. 2016. (ENG., Illus.). 320p. (YA). 16.99 *(978-1-62779-390-2(9)*, 9781627793902, Holt, Henry & Co. Bks. For Young Readers) Holt, Henry & Co.
—Lucky Strikes. 2017. (YA). lib. bdg. 20.85 ***(978-0-606-39951-7(8))*** Turtleback Bks.
Bennion, Jay B. From Here to There. 2013. 136p. pap. 9.99 *(978-0-9826175-0-2(X))* Pearl Publishing, LLC.
Bertrand, Diane Gonzales. El Momento de Trino. Sanmiguel, Rosario, tr. from ENG. 2006. (SPA.). 181p. (J). (gr. 3-7). per. 9.95 *(978-1-55885-473-4(8)*, Piñata Books) Arte Publico Pr.
Blackwood, Gary. Curiosity. 2015. (ENG.). 336p. (J). (gr. 4-7). 8.99 *(978-0-14-242448-3(X)*, Puffin Books) Penguin Young Readers Group.
Boelts, Maribeth. Those Shoes. Jones, Noah Z., illus. 2009. (ENG.). 40p. (J). (gr. k-3). pap. 6.99 *(978-0-7636-4284-6(3))* Candlewick Pr.
—Those Shoes. Jones, Noah, illus. 2007. (J). *(978-1-4287-6554-2(9))* Candlewick Pr.
—Those Shoes. 2014. 17.00 *(978-1-63419-735-9(6))* Perfection Learning Corp.
Booth, Coe. Tyrell. 2011. 9.04 *(978-0-7848-3385-8(0)*, Everbind) Marco Bk. Co.
Brenner, Summer. Ivy, Homeless in San Francisco. Bowes, Brian, illus. 2nd ed. 2011. (ENG.). 176p. (J). (gr. 4-7). pap. 15.00 *(978-1-60486-317-8(X))* PM Pr.
Casanova, Mary. Ice-Out. 2016. (ENG., Illus.). 264p. (YA). 16.95 *(978-0-8166-9417-4(6))* Univ. of Minnesota Pr.
Condé, Maryse. Reves Amers. pap. 17.95 *(978-2-7470-0350-6(7))* Bayard Editions FRA. Dist: Distribooks, Inc.
Cory, Kim Delmar. Tending Ben's Garden. 2009. (J). pap. *(978-0-88092-778-9(X))* Royal Fireworks Publishing Co.
Cullen, Lyn. I Am Rembrandt's Daughter. 2011. 8.88 *(978-0-7848-3491-6(1)*, Everbind) Marco Bk. Co.
Cummins, Maria S. The Lamplighter. 2011. 308p. pap. 16.99 *(978-1-61203-228-3(1))* Bottom of the Hill Publishing.
Curtis, Christopher Paul. The Mighty Miss Malone. (ENG.). 320p. (J). (gr. 4-7). 2013. pap. 7.99 *(978-0-440-42214-3(0)*, Yearling) 2012. 15.99 *(978-0-385-73491-2(3)*, Lamb, Wendy Bks.) Random Hse. Children's Bks.
—The Mighty Miss Malone. 2013. lib. bdg. 18.40 *(978-0-606-27007-6(8)*, Turtleback) Turtleback Bks.
Cushman, Karen. Alchemy & Meggy Swann. 2011. (ENG.). 176p. (J). (gr. 5-7). pap. 7.99 *(978-0-547-57712-8(5))* Houghton Mifflin Harcourt Publishing Co.
De Los Santos, Elizabeth G. The Secret House. 2011. 18p. pap. 16.95 *(978-1-4626-4409-4(0))* America Star Bks.
Dembkoski, Kacey. Believe. 2004. 60p. (YA). pap. 8.95 *(978-0-595-30549-0(0))* iUniverse, Inc.
Deuker, Carl & Perry, Thomas. Runner. 2007. (ENG.). 224p. (YA). (gr. 7-12). pap. 8.99 *(978-0-618-73505-1(4))* Houghton Mifflin Harcourt Publishing Co.
Dunagan, Ted M. A Yellow Watermelon. 2014. (ENG.). 240p. (J). pap. 17.95 *(978-1-58838-301-3(6)*, NewSouth Bks.) NewSouth, Inc.
Elliott, Ruth & Elliott, David. The Richest Kid in the Poor House. Elliott, Ruth, illus. 2008. (Illus.). (J). pap. *(978-0-9795017-4-6(1))* Edu Designs.
Ellis, Deborah. No Ordinary Day, 1 vol. (ENG.). (J). (gr. 3-7). 2014. 160p. pap. 9.95 *(978-1-55498-108-3(5))* 2011. 144p. 16.95 *(978-1-55498-134-2(4))* Groundwood Bks. CAN. Dist: Publishers Group West (PGW).
Falk, Karen. Tacianna & the Endless Ball of String. 2006. 83p. pap. 19.95 *(978-1-4241-3287-4(8))* PublishAmerica, Inc.
Fine, Edith Hope & Josephson, Judith Pinkerton. Armando & the Blue Tarp School, 1 vol. Sosa, Hernan, illus. 2007. (ENG.). 32p. (J). (gr. -1-3). lib. bdg. 16.95 *(978-1-58430-278-0(X))* Lee & Low Bks., Inc.
—Armando y la Escuela de Lona Azul. Sosa, Hernan, illus. 2015.Tr. of Armando & the Blue Tarp School. (SPA & ENG.). 32p. (J). (gr. k-4). pap. 10.95 *(978-1-60060-449-2(8))* Lee & Low Bks., Inc.
Flake, Sharon G. Begging for Change. rev. ed. 2007. (ENG.). 256p. (J). (gr. 7-12). pap. 7.99 *(978-1-4231-0384-4(X)*, Jump at the Sun) Hyperion Bks. for Children.
—Money Hungry. Disney Press Staff, illus. rev. ed. 2007. (ENG.). 192p. (J). (gr. 5-9). pap. 8.99 *(978-1-4231-0386-8(6)*, Jump at the Sun) Hyperion Bks. for Children.
Foreman, Michael. El Jardin del Nino: Una Historia de Esperanza. Diego, Rapi & Flores, Martha, illus. 2009. (SPA.). 30p. (J). (gr. 1-3). 14.99 *(978-1-933032-56-6(1))* Lectorum Pubns., Inc.
Godby, Ron. The King of Imperial Hill. 2006. 76p. pap. 16.95 *(978-1-4241-1061-2(0))* PublishAmerica, Inc.
Going, K. L. Saint Iggy. 2008. (ENG., Illus.). 272p. (YA). (gr. 9-18). pap. 9.99 *(978-0-15-206248-4(3))* Houghton Mifflin Harcourt Publishing Co.
Goyer, Deb. The Raggedy Beggar. Johnson, Lauren, illus. 2006. 19p. pap. 24.95 *(978-1-60703-698-2(3))* America Star Bks.

Hall, Mary Lou. Wirewalker. 2016. (ENG.). 304p. (YA). (gr. 7). 17.99 *(978-0-670-01646-4(2),* Viking Books for Young Readers) Penguin Young Readers Group.
Harlow, Joan Hiatt. Firestorm! (ENG.). 336p. (J). (gr. 3-7). 2011. pap. 7.99 *(978-1-4169-8486-3(0))* 2010. (Illus.). 16.99 *(978-1-4169-8485-6(2))* McElderry, Margaret K. Bks. (McElderry, Margaret K. Bks.).
Helget, Nicole. The End of the Wild. 2017. (ENG., Illus.). 272p. (J). (gr. 3-7). 16.99 *(978-0-316-24511-1(9))* Little, Brown Bks. for Young Readers.
Hobbs, Valerie. Maggie & Oliver or a Bone of One's Own. Thermes, Jennifer, illus. 2013. (ENG.). 208p. (J). (gr. 3-7). pap. 6.99 *(978-1-250-01672-0(X),* 9781250016720) Square Fish.
Hoffmeister, Peter Brown. This Is the Part Where You Laugh. 2016. (ENG.). 336p. (YA). (gr. 9). 17.99 *(978-0-553-53810-6(1),* Knopf Bks. for Young Readers) Random Hse. Children's Bks.
Horatio Alger Jr. Cast upon the Breakers. l.t. ed. 2007. 226p. pap. 22.99 *(978-1-4264-8224-3(8))* Creative Media Partners, LLC.
Hubbard, Suzanna. The Lady Who Lived in a Car. 2004. (Illus.). 32p. (J). *(978-1-84458-046-0(6),* Pavilion Children's Books) Pavilion Bks.
Hudson, Bonnie Rose. The Hidden Village. 2017. (J). ***(978-1-62856-311-5(7))*** BJU Pr.
Hulst, W. G. van de & Hulst, Willem G. van de, illus. The Search for Christmas. 2014. (J). *(978-1-928136-12-5(5))* Inheritance Pubns.
Jarman, Benjamin. Tony's Last Touchdown. 2012. (Champion Sports Story Ser.). 104p. (J). (gr. 3-18). pap. 10.95 *(978-1-4644-0004-9(0)),* 27.94 *(978-0-7660-3885-1(8))* Enslow Pubs., Inc.
Jesperson, Per. Wonder & Magic: The David Tales. 2003. 50p. pap. *(978-1-84401-017-2(1))* Athena Pr.
Kehret, Peg. Dangerous Deception. 2015. (ENG.). 208p. (J). (gr. 5). 7.99 *(978-0-14-751175-1(5),* Puffin Books) Penguin Young Readers Group.
Kephart, Beth. The Heart Is Not a Size. 2010. (ENG.). 256p. (YA). (gr. 8-18). 16.99 *(978-0-06-147048-6(1),* HarperTeen) HarperCollins Pubs.
Kimmel, Eric A. Even Higher! A Rosh Hashanah Story by I. L. Peretz. Weber, Jill, illus. 2010. (ENG.). 32p. (J). (gr. -1-3). pap. 6.95 *(978-0-8234-2298-2(4))* Holiday Hse., Inc.
Lachenmeyer, Nathaniel. Broken Beaks. Ingpen, Robert R., illus. 2005. 32p. (J). 15.95 *(978-0-85572-335-4(1))* Warwick Publishing CAN. Dist: Two Rivers Distribution.
Lipp, Frederick. Running Shoes. Gaillard, Jason, illus. 2008. 32p. (J). (gr. 2-5). pap. 7.95 *(978-1-58089-176-9(4))* Charlesbridge Publishing, Inc.
Lupita Manana. 3rd ed. (J). pap., stu. ed. *(978-0-13-772500-7(0))* Prentice Hall (Schl. Div.).
Madden, Kerry. Gentle's Holler. 2007. (Maggie Valley Ser.). 237p. (gr. 4-7). 17.00 *(978-0-7569-8090-0(9))* Perfection Learning Corp.
Mancil, Arlene. The Angel Explains Christmas Blessings. McKinnon, Joy, illus. 2008. 16p. pap. 24.95 *(978-1-60813-297-3(8))* America Star Bks.
Massachusetts Sabbath School Society Staff. Winnie Malone Written for the Mass S S Society, & Approved by the Committee of Publication. 2006. 144p. per. 18.99 *(978-1-4255-1163-0(5))* Michigan Publishing.
Meyer, Carolyn. Marie, Dancing. 2007. (ENG., Illus.). 272p. (YA). (gr. 7-18). pap. 15.95 *(978-0-15-205879-1(6))* Houghton Mifflin Harcourt Publishing Co.
Morgan, Nicola. Fleshmarket. 2003. (ENG.). 272p. (J). (gr. 7-17). pap. 9.99 *(978-0-340-85557-7(6))* Hodder & Stoughton GBR. Dist: Hachette Bk. Group.
Morpurgo, Michael. Private Peaceful. 2006. 18.00 *(978-0-7569-6630-0(2))* Perfection Learning Corp.
—Private Peaceful. 2006. (YA). 1.25 *(978-1-4193-2976-0(6))* Recorded Bks., Inc.
—Private Peaceful. 2006. (After Words Ser.). (ENG., Illus.). 224p. (J). (gr. 7-12). per. 7.99 *(978-0-439-63653-7(1),* Scholastic Paperbacks) Scholastic, Inc.
Mulligan, Andy. Trash. 2011. (ENG., Illus.). 240p. (YA). (gr. 7). pap. 9.99 *(978-0-385-75216-9(4),* Ember) Random Hse. Children's Bks.
Naylor, Phyllis Reynolds. I Like Him, He Likes Her: Alice Alone; Simply Alice; Patiently Alice. 2010. (Alice Ser.). (ENG.). 640p. (YA). (gr. 7). pap. 12.99 *(978-1-4424-0978-1(9),* Atheneum Bks. for Young Readers) Simon & Schuster Children's Publishing.
Nesbit, E. The Story of the Treasure Seekers. 2009. 128p. (gr. 4-7). pap. 5.50 *(978-1-60459-695-3(3))* Wilder Pubns., Corp.
—The Story of the Treasure Seekers: Being the Adventures of the Bastable Children in Search of A Fortune. 2006. 132p. (gr. 4-7). per. 10.95 *(978-1-59818-963-6(8));* 24.95 *(978-1-59818-172-2(6))* Aegypan.
Noble, Trinka Hakes. The Orange Shoes. Ettlinger, Doris, illus. rev. ed. 2007. (ENG.). 40p. (J). (gr. k-6). 16.95 *(978-1-58536-277-6(8))* Sleeping Bear Pr.
Optic, Oliver, pseud. Poor & Proud; or, the Fortunes of Katy Redburn a Story for Young Folks by Oliver Optic [Pseud]. 2006. 280p. (gr. 4-7). per. 23.99 *(978-1-4255-2551-4(2))* Michigan Publishing.
Peterson, Lois. The Paper House, 1 vol. 2012. (Orca Young Readers Ser.). (ENG.). 108p. (J). (gr. 3-6). pap. 7.95 *(978-1-4598-0051-9(6))* Orca Bk. Pubs. USA.
Platt, Randall Beth. Liberty's Christmas. 2012. (ENG.). 224p. (YA). (gr. 7-12). 19.95 *(978-0-89672-766-3(1))* Texas Tech Univ. Pr.
Polette, Keith. Moon over the Mountain. 2009. (ENG.). 32p. (J). (gr. -1-3). 16.95 *(978-1-934960-07-3(1),* Raven Tree Pr.,Csi) Continental Sales, Inc.
—Moon over the Mountain/Luna Sobre la Montana. 2009. (ENG & SPA.). 32p. (J). (gr. -1-3). 16.95 *(978-1-932748-85-7(7));* pap. 7.95 *(978-1-932748-84-0(9))* Continental Sales, Inc. (Raven Tree Pr.,Csi).
Qamar, Amjed. Beneath My Mother's Feet. (ENG.). 208p. (YA). (gr. 7). 2011. pap. 10.99 *(978-1-4424-1451-8(0))* 2008. 16.99 *(978-1-4169-4728-8(0))* Simon & Schuster Children's Publishing. (Atheneum Bks. for Young Readers).
Rothshank, Brooke, illus. Cups Held Out. 2006. 40p. (J). (gr. -1-3). per. 12.99 *(978-0-8361-9316-9(4))* Herald Pr.
Schraff, Anne. The One for Me, 1 vol. 2013. (Urban Underground Ser.). (ENG.). 199p. (YA). (gr. 9-12). pap. 9.95 *(978-1-62250-042-0(3))* Saddleback Educational Publishing, Inc.
—Second Chances, 1 vol. 2013. (Urban Underground Ser.). (ENG.). 192p. (YA). (gr. 9-12). pap. 9.95 *(978-1-62250-044-4(X))* Saddleback Educational Publishing, Inc.
Sidney, Margaret. Five Little Peppers & How They Grew. 2006. (Dover Children's Classics Ser.). (ENG., Illus.). 224p. (J). (gr. 3-5). per. 6.95 *(978-0-486-45267-8(0))* Dover Pubns., Inc.
—Five Little Peppers & How They Grew. Andreasen, Dan, illus. 2009. (Classic Starts(tm) Ser.). (ENG.). 160p. (J). (gr. 2-4). 6.95 *(978-1-4027-5420-3(5))* Sterling Publishing Co., Inc.
Sitomer, Alan Lawrence. Caged Warrior. 2014. (ENG., Illus.). 224p. (YA). (gr. 7-12). 16.99 *(978-1-4231-7124-9(1))* Disney Pr.
Smith, Joye. What Does It Mean to Be Poor? 2005. (Illus.). 30p. (J). 8.99 *(978-1-56309-880-2(6))* Woman's Missionary Union.
Snicket, Lemony, pseud. Una Funesta Finestra. pap. 21.95 *(978-88-7782-953-5(2))* Salani ITA. Dist: Distribooks, Inc.
Stellings, Caroline. The Contest, 1 vol. 2009. (ENG.). 160p. (J). (gr. 4-7). pap. 9.95 *(978-0-9779183-5-5(1),* 7th Generation) Book Publishing Co.
Strasser, Todd. If I Grow Up. (ENG.). 240p. (YA). (gr. 7). 2010. pap. 9.99 *(978-1-4169-9443-5(2))* 2009. 17.99 *(978-1-4169-2523-1(6))* Simon & Schuster Bks. For Young Readers. (Simon & Schuster Bks. For Young Readers).
—No Place. 2014. (ENG., Illus.). 272p. (YA). (gr. 7). 17.99 *(978-1-4424-5721-8(X),* Simon & Schuster Bks. For Young Readers) Simon & Schuster Bks. For Young Readers.
Stretton, Hesba. Cassy. Hymper, W. & Stacey, W. S., illus. 2006. (Golden Inheritance Ser.: Vol. 9). 117p. (J). pap. *(978-0-921100-94-2(9))* Inheritance Pubns.
—Jessica's First Prayer. Doe, Charles J., ed. 2008. (ENG., Illus.). 54p. (YA). pap. 7.95 *(978-0-9817505-2-1(4))* Curiosmith.
—Jessica's First Prayer. 2004. reprint ed. pap. 1.99 *(978-1-4192-2751-6(3));* pap. 15.95 *(978-1-4191-2751-9(9))* Kessinger Publishing, LLC.
—Jessica's First Prayer. 2006. 84p. pap. 9.95 *(978-1-59462-373-8(2),* 409, Book Jungle) Standard Pubns., Inc.
—Lost Gip. 2003. (Golden Inheritance Ser.: Vol. 7). (Illus.). 121p. (J). *(978-0-921100-93-5(0))* Inheritance Pubns.
Turk, Cheri. The Stone Between Kings. Turk, Cheri, illus. 2012. (Illus.). 36p. pap. 12.99 *(978-0-9860024-0-3(2))* Specialty Greetings.
Walters, Eric. Hope Springs. Fernandes, Eugenie, illus. 2014. (ENG.). 32p. (J). (gr. 1-4). 17.99 *(978-1-77049-530-2(4),* Tundra Bks.) Tundra Bks. CAN. Dist: Penguin Random Hse. LLC.
Wenxuan, Cao. Bronze & Sunflower. Wang, Helen, tr. So, Meilo, illus. 2017. (ENG.). 400p. (J). (gr. 4-7). 16.99 *(978-0-7636-8816-5(9))* Candlewick Pr.
Wessel-Estes, Pam. A Quilt & a Home. 2012. 36p. pap. 14.95 *(978-1-4575-1489-0(3));* 24.95 *(978-1-4575-1490-6(7))* Dog Ear Publishing, LLC.
Williams, Emma. The Story of Hurry. Quraishi, Ibrahim, illus. 2014. (ENG.). 38p. (J). (gr. -1-2). 16.95 *(978-1-60980-589-0(5),* Triangle Square) Seven Stories Pr.
Wyatt, Leslie J. Poor Is Just a Starting Place. 2005. (ENG.). 192p. (J). (gr. 6-17). 16.95 *(978-0-8234-1884-8(7))* Holiday Hse., Inc.

POWELL, JOHN WESLEY, 1834-1902

Curtis, Suzanne. John Wesley Powell: American Hero. 2013. (ENG & SPA., Illus.). 78p. (J). pap. 8.95 *(978-0-86541-178-4(6))* Filter Pr., LLC.
Maynard, Charles W. John Wesley Powell: Soldier, Scientist, & Explorer. (Famous Explorers of the American West Ser.). 24p. 2009. (gr. 3-4). 42.50 *(978-1-61512-505-0(1),* PowerKids Pr.) 2003. (Illus.). (YA). (gr. 1-4). lib. bdg. 22.60 *(978-0-8239-6290-7(3))* Rosen Publishing Group, Inc., The.
Ross, Michael Elsohn. Exploring the Earth with John Wesley Powell. Smith, Wendy, illus. 2005. (Naturalist's Apprentice Biographies Ser.). 48p. (gr. 3-6). lib. bdg. 19.93 *(978-1-57505-254-0(7))* Lerner Publishing Group.
Souza, Dorothy M. John Wesley Powell. 2004. (Watts Library). (ENG., Illus.). 64p. (J). (gr. 5-7). pap. 8.95 *(978-0-531-16653-6(8),* Watts, Franklin) Scholastic Library Publishing.
Waldman, Stuart. The Last River: John Wesley Powell & the Colorado River Exploring Expedition. Manchess, Gregory, illus. 2015. (ENG.). 48p. (J). (gr. 4-8). pap. 12.95 *(978-1-931414-58-6(0),* 9781931414586) Mikaya Pr.

POWER (MECHANICS)

see also Electric Power; Force and Energy; Machinery; Water Power

Armentrout, David & Armentrout, Patricia. Levers. 2009. (ENG., Illus.). 24p. (J). (gr. 3-6). pap. 8.95 *(978-1-60694-520-9(3))* Rourke Educational Media.
Bishop, Amanda. Energy Conservation. 2008. (Saving Our World Ser.). 32p. (gr. 4-18). lib. bdg. 28.50 *(978-0-7614-3224-1(8),* Benchmark Bks.) Marshall Cavendish Corp.
Braun, Eric. Lance Dragon Defends His Castle with Simple Machines, 1 vol. Briglia, Anthony, illus. 2012. (In the Science Lab Ser.). (ENG.). 24p. (gr. 2-3). pap. 9.95 *(978-1-4048-7708-5(8));* lib. bdg. 26.65 *(978-1-4048-7372-8(4))* Picture Window Bks.
Carlson Berne, Emma. Speeding! Mechanical Energy. 2013. (Energy Everywhere Ser.). (ENG., Illus.). 24p. (J). (gr. 3-6). 22.60 *(978-1-4488-9651-6(7));* pap. 8.25 *(978-1-4488-9760-5(2))* Rosen Publishing Group, Inc., The. (PowerKids Pr.).
Gardner, Robert. Energy: Green Science Projects about Solar, Wind, & Water Power. 2011. (Team Green Science Projects Ser.). (Illus.). 128p. (J). (gr. 5-9). lib. bdg. 33.27 *(978-0-7660-3643-7(X))* Enslow Pubs., Inc.
Greenberger, Robert. How Do We Know the Nature of Energy. (Great Scientific Questions & the Scientists Who Answered Them Ser.). 112p. (gr. 7-12). 2009. 63.90 *(978-1-61513-201-0(5))* 2005. (Illus.). (J). lib. bdg. 34.60 *(978-1-4042-0076-0(2))* Rosen Publishing Group, Inc., The.
Heitkamp, Kristina Lyn. What Is Mechanical Energy? 2017. (Let's Find Out! Forms of Energy Ser.). 32p. (gr. 6-8). pap. 12.90 ***(978-1-68048-709-1(4),*** Britannica Educational Publishing) Rosen Publishing Group, Inc., The.
Herweck, Don. All about Energy, 1 vol. 2007. (Science Readers Ser.). (SPA & ENG.). 32p. (J). (gr. 4-4). pap. 8.99 *(978-0-7439-0571-8(7))* Shell Educational Publishing.
Hyde, Natalie. Pushing & Pulling. 2014. (ENG., Illus.). 24p. (J). *(978-0-7787-0529-1(3))* Crabtree Publishing Co.
Jennings, Terry. Forces. 2009. (Science Alive Ser.). (Illus.). 32p. (J). pap. *(978-1-897563-54-0(X))* Saunders Bk. Co.
Jennings, Terry J. Forces. 2009. (J). 28.50 *(978-1-59920-269-3(7))* Black Rabbit Bks.
Johanson, Paula. What Is Energy? 2014. (Let's Find Out! Ser.). 32p. (J). (gr. 3-6). 23.45 *(978-1-62275-492-2(1))* Rosen Publishing Group, Inc., The.
Nixon, Jonathan. Energy Engineering & Powering the Future. 2016. (Engineering in Action Ser.). (ENG., Illus.). 32p. (J). (gr. 5-8). *(978-0-7787-7539-3(9))* Crabtree Publishing Co.
Petersen, Kristen. Understanding Kinetic Energy. 2015. (J). lib. bdg. *(978-1-62713-435-4(2))* Cavendish Square Publishing.
Phelan, Glen. Introduction to Energy. 2007. (Nonfiction Reading & Writing Workshops Ser.). (ENG., Illus.). 32p. (J). pap. 17.95 *(978-0-7922-4580-3(6))* CENGAGE Learning.
Plummer, Todd. I've Discovered Energy! 2008. (Eureka! Ser.). 32p. (gr. 4-18). lib. bdg. 28.50 *(978-0-7614-3202-9(7),* Benchmark Bks.) Marshall Cavendish Corp.
Rau, Dana Meachen. Super Cool Science Experiments: Levers & Pulleys. 2009. (Explorer Library: Science Explorer Ser.). (ENG., Illus.). 32p. (gr. 4-8). lib. bdg. 28.50 *(978-1-60279-537-2(1),* 200282) Cherry Lake Publishing.
Spilsbury, Richard & Spilsbury, Louise. What Is Energy? Exploring Science with Hands-on Activities. 2008. (In Touch with Basic Science Ser.). (Illus.). 32p. (J). (gr. 3-4). lib. bdg. 23.94 *(978-0-7660-3099-2(7),* Enslow Elementary) Enslow Pubs., Inc.
Stoyles, Pennie & Pentland, Peter. Everyday Technology. 2011. (Energy in Action Ser.). 32p. (gr. 4). 28.50 *(978-1-60870-567-2(6))* Marshall Cavendish Corp.
Walker, Sally M. & Feldmann, Roseann. Palancas. King, Andy, photos by. 2009. (Libros de Física para Madrugadores Ser.). (SPA., Illus.). 47p. (J). (gr. 3-7). pap. 11.95 *(978-0-8225-2973-6(4))* Lerner Publishing Group.
—Put Levers to the Test. 2011. (Searchlight Books (tm) — How Do Simple Machines Work? Ser.). (ENG., Illus.). 40p. (gr. 3-5). lib. bdg. 27.93 *(978-0-7613-5321-8(6))* Lerner Publishing Group.
—Put Pulleys to the Test. 2011. (Searchlight Books (tm) — How Do Simple Machines Work? Ser.). (ENG., Illus.). 40p. (gr. 3-5). lib. bdg. 27.93 *(978-0-7613-5322-5(4))* Lerner Publishing Group.
West, Herbert. Forms of Energy. 2009. (Real Life Readers Ser.). 24p. (gr. 3-4). pap. 8.25 *(978-1-4358-0123-3(7),* Rosen Classroom); (Illus.). (J). (gr. 2-5). lib. bdg. 22.60 *(978-1-4358-2975-6(1),* PowerKids Pr.) Rosen Publishing Group, Inc., The.

POWER (SOCIAL SCIENCES)

Lankford, Ronnie D. Are America's Wealthy Too Powerful? 2010. (At Issue Ser.). (ENG.). 128p. pap. 24.45 *(978-0-7377-5088-1(X),* Greenhaven Pr., Inc.); (gr. 10-12). 39.40 *(978-0-7377-5087-4(1))* Cengage Gale.

POWER BOATS

see Motorboats

POWER RESOURCES

see also Electric Power; Fuel; Solar Energy; Water Power

Aitken, Stephen, illus. How to Cure Earth's Fever. 2011. (J). *(978-1-61641-674-4(2))* Magic Wagon.
Aloian, Molly. Green Energy. 2013. (ENG., Illus.). 24p. (J). *(978-0-7787-0265-8(0));* pap. *(978-0-7787-0284-9(7))* Crabtree Publishing Co.
Armentrout, David & Armentrout, Patricia. Going Green. 2008. (ENG., Illus.). 48p. (gr. 4-8). pap. 10.95 *(978-1-60694-916-0(0))* Rourke Educational Media.
Bailey, Diane. Hydropower. 2015. (Harnessing Energy Ser.). (ENG.). 48p. (J). (gr. 5-8). pap. 12.00 *(978-0-89812-996-0(6),* Creative Paperbacks) Creative Co., The.
—Natural Gas Power. 2015. (Harnessing Energy Ser.). (ENG.). 48p. (J). (gr. 5-8). pap. 12.00 *(978-0-89812-995-3(8),* Creative Paperbacks) Creative Co., The.
Bailey, Gerry. Out of Energy. 2011. (Planet SOS Ser.). (Illus.). 48p. (J). (gr. 3-6). pap. 14.05 *(978-1-4339-4979-1(2));* lib. bdg. 31.95 *(978-1-4339-4978-4(4))* Stevens, Gareth Publishing LLLP. (Gareth Stevens Learning Library).
Barker, Geoff. How Renewable Energy Works. 2013. (EcoWorks Ser.). 32p. (J). (gr. 3-5). pap. 10.50 *(978-1-4339-9569-9(7));* pap. 63.00 *(978-1-4339-9570-5(0))* Stevens, Gareth Publishing LLLP.
Barker, Geoffrey. How Renewable Energy Works. 2013. (EcoWorks Ser.). (ENG., Illus.). 32p. (J). (gr. 3-5). lib. bdg. 26.60 *(978-1-4339-9568-2(9))* Stevens, Gareth Publishing LLLP.
Barnham, Kay. Save Energy. 2007. (Environment Action Ser.). (ENG.). 32p. (J). (gr. 3-7). pap. *(978-0-7787-3670-7(9))* Crabtree Publishing Co.
Bayden, Maya. What Is Chemical Energy? 2017. (Let's Find Out! Forms of Energy Ser.). 32p. (gr. 6-8). pap. 12.90 ***(978-1-68048-693-3(4),*** Britannica Educational Publishing) Rosen Publishing Group, Inc., The.
Benchmark Education Company, LLC Staff. Energy Resources Around the World Teacher's Guide. 2004. *(978-1-4108-2587-2(6))* Benchmark Education Co.
Benduhn, Tea. Etanol y Otros Combustibles Nuevos. 2008. (Energía para el presente (Energy for Today) Ser.). (SPA.). 24p. (gr. 2-6). (J). lib. bdg. 22.00 *(978-0-8368-9266-6(6));* pap. 8.15 *(978-0-8368-9365-6(4))* Stevens, Gareth Publishing LLLP. (Weekly Reader Leveled Readers).
—Ethanol & Other New Fuels. 2008. (Energy for Today Ser.). 24p. (gr. 2-6). (J). lib. bdg. 22.00 *(978-0-8368-9260-4(7));* pap. 8.15 *(978-0-8368-9359-5(X))* Stevens, Gareth Publishing LLLP. (Weekly Reader Leveled Readers).
—Petróleo, Gas y Carbón. 2008. (Energía para el presente (Energy for Today) Ser.). (SPA.). 24p. (gr. 2-6). (J). lib. bdg. 22.00 *(978-0-8368-9267-3(4));* pap. 8.15 *(978-0-8368-9366-3(2))* Stevens, Gareth Publishing LLLP. (Weekly Reader Leveled Readers).
—Solar Power. 2008. (Energy for Today Ser.). 24p. (gr. 2-6). (J). lib. bdg. 22.00 *(978-0-8368-9263-5(1));* pap. 8.15 *(978-0-8368-9362-5(X))* Stevens, Gareth Publishing LLLP. (Weekly Reader Leveled Readers).
Beres, Samantha. Energy Resources Around the World: Set Of 6. 2011. (Navigators Ser.). (J). pap. 50.00 net. *(978-1-4108-2572-8(8))* Benchmark Education Co.
—Energy Resources Around the World & Recursos energéticos alrededor del Mundo: 6 English, 6 Spanish Adaptations. 2011. (ENG & SPA.). (J). 101.00 net. *(978-1-4108-5738-5(7))* Benchmark Education Co.
Bickerstaff, Linda. Oil Power of the Future: New Ways of Turning Petroleum into Energy. 2009. (Library of Future Energy Ser.). 64p. (gr. 5-5). 58.50 *(978-1-60853-628-3(9))* Rosen Publishing Group, Inc., The.
Bishop, Amanda. Energy Conservation. 2008. (Saving Our World Ser.). 32p. (gr. 4-18). lib. bdg. 28.50 *(978-0-7614-3224-1(8),* Benchmark Bks.) Marshall Cavendish Corp.
Bjorklund, Ruth. The Pros & Cons of Algae Biofuel. 2016. (Economics of Energy Ser.). (ENG.). 80p. (J). (gr. 7-7). 35.64 *(978-1-5026-0954-0(1))* Cavendish Square Publishing.
Bow, James. Energy from Earth's Core: Geothermal Energy. 2015. (Next Generation Energy Ser.). (ENG., Illus.). 32p. (J). *(978-0-7787-1979-3(0))* Crabtree Publishing Co.
—Energy from the Sun: Solar Power. 2015. (Next Generation Energy Ser.). (ENG., Illus.). 32p. (J). *(978-0-7787-1982-3(0))* Crabtree Publishing Co.
Bowden, Rob. Energy Sources: The Impact of Science & Technology. 2009. (Pros & Cons Ser.). (ENG.). 64p. (YA). (gr. 5-9). lib. bdg. 35.00 *(978-1-4339-1987-9(7))* Stevens, Gareth Publishing LLLP.
Brennan, Linda Crotta. Geothermal Power. 2013. (J). *(978-1-61080-969-6(6));* (ENG.). 32p. (gr. 4-8). 28.50 *(978-1-61080-894-1(0),* 202555); (ENG.). 32p. (gr. 4-8). pap. 14.21 *(978-1-61080-919-1(X),* 202557) Cherry Lake Publishing.
Brezina, Corona. Jobs in Sustainable Energy. 2010. (Green Careers Ser.). 80p. (YA). (gr. 7-12). E-Book 61.20 *(978-1-4488-0136-7(2));* (Illus.). lib. bdg. 33.25 *(978-1-4358-3569-6(7))* Rosen Publishing Group, Inc., The.
Burgan, Michael. Energy, Vol. 10. 2016. (Stem in Current Events Ser.). (Illus.). 64p. (J). (gr. 7). 23.95 *(978-1-4222-3589-8(0))* Mason Crest.
Caduto, Michael J. Catch the Wind, Harness the Sun: 22 Super-Charged Projects for Kids. 2011. (ENG., Illus.). 224p. (J). (gr. 3-8). pap. 16.95 *(978-1-60342-794-4(5),* 62794) Storey Publishing, LLC.
Cartlidge, Cherese. Alternative Energy. (J). 2011. *(978-1-60217-029-2(0))* 2008. *(978-1-60217-022-3(3))* Erickson Pr.
Casper, Julie Kerr. Energy: Powering the Past, Present, & Future. 2007. (Natural Resources Ser.). (Illus.). 210p. (YA). (gr. 7-12). lib. bdg. 39.50 *(978-0-8160-6354-3(0))* Facts On File, Inc.
Centore, Michael. Renewable Energy, Vol. 12. 2015. (North American Natural Resources Ser.). (Illus.). 64p. (J). (gr. 7). 23.95 *(978-1-4222-3387-0(1))* Mason Crest.
Challoner, Jack & Green, Dan. Energy. 2016. (DK Eyewitness Bks.). (ENG., Illus.). 72p. (J). (gr. 3-7). lib. bdg. 19.99 *(978-1-4654-5105-7(6),* DK Children) Dorling Kindersley Publishing, Inc.
Chambers, Catherine. Energy in Crisis. 2010. (Protecting Our Planet Ser.). (ENG., Illus.). 32p. (J). (gr. 3-6). *(978-0-7787-5212-7(7));* pap. *(978-0-7787-5229-5(1))* Crabtree Publishing Co.
Cunningham, Anne C. Critical Perspectives on Fossil Fuels vs. Renewable Energy. 2016. (Analyzing the Issues Ser.). 208p. (YA). lib. bdg. 47.93 *(978-0-7660-8131-4(1))* Enslow Pubs., Inc.
Davis, Barbara J., et al. Hydrogen Fuel. 2010. (Energy Today Ser.). 48p. (J). (gr. 3-6). 30.00 *(978-1-60413-783-5(5))* Facts On File, Inc.
De Angelis, Therese. Blackout! Cities in Darkness. 2003. (American Disasters Ser.). (Illus.). 48p. (J). (gr. 4-10). lib. bdg. 23.93 *(978-0-7660-2110-5(6))* Enslow Pubs., Inc.
De La Garza, Amanda. Biomass: Energy from Plants & Animals. 2006. (Fueling the Future Ser.). (ENG., Illus.). 120p. (J). (gr. 10-12). lib. bdg. 39.35 *(978-0-7377-3586-4(4),* Greenhaven Pr., Inc.) Cengage Gale.
Dickmann, Nancy. Energy from Nuclear Fission: Splitting the Atom. 2015. (Next Generation Energy Ser.). (ENG., Illus.). 32p. (J). *(978-0-7787-1981-6(2))* Crabtree Publishing Co.
—Harnessing Geothermal Energy. 2016. (Future of Power Ser.). 00032p. (J). (gr. 4-5). pap. 10.00 *(978-1-4994-3211-4(9),* PowerKids Pr.) Rosen Publishing Group, Inc., The.
—Harnessing Hydroelectric Energy. 2016. (Future of Power Ser.). 00032p. (J). (gr. 4-5). pap. 10.00 *(978-1-4994-3212-1(7),* PowerKids Pr.) Rosen Publishing Group, Inc., The.
Doeden, Matt. Finding Out about Wind Energy. 2014. (Searchlight Books — What Are Energy Sources? Ser.). (Illus.). 40p. (gr. 3-5). pap. 8.95 *(978-1-4677-4558-1(8));* (ENG., lib. bdg. 27.93 *(978-1-4677-3656-5(2),* Lerner Pubns.) Lerner Publishing Group.
Draper, Allison Stark. Hydropower of the Future: New Ways of Turning Water into Energy. 2009. (Library of Future Energy Ser.). 64p. (gr. 5-5). 58.50 *(978-1-60853-626-9(2))* Rosen Publishing Group, Inc., The.
Drummond, Alan. Energy Island: How One Community Harnessed the Wind & Changed Their World. 2015. (J). lib. bdg. 18.40 *(978-0-606-37353-1(5))* Turtleback Bks.
Drummond, Allan. Energy Island: How One Community Harnessed the Wind & Changed Their World. Drummond, Allan, illus. 2011. (ENG., Illus.). 40p. (J). (gr. 1-5). 18.99 *(978-0-374-32184-0(1),* 9780374321840, Farrar, Straus & Giroux (BYR)) Farrar, Straus & Giroux.
Eboch, M. M. The 12 Biggest Breakthroughs in Energy Technology. 2014. (ENG.). 32p. (J). *(978-1-63235-013-8(0))* Pr. Room Editions LLC.
The Economics of Energy. 2014. (Economics of Energy Ser.). 80p. (YA). (gr. 7-10). 213.84 *(978-1-62713-132-2(9))* Cavendish Square Publishing.
Einspruch, Andrew. What Is Energy?, 1 vol., 1. 2014. (Discovery Education: How It Works). (ENG.). 32p. (J). (gr. 3-6).

P Q R

26.25 *(978-1-4777-6321-6(X)*, PowerKids Pr.) Rosen Publishing Group, Inc., The.

Enz, Tammy. Harness It: Invent New Ways to Harness Energy & Nature, 1 vol. 2012. (Invent It Ser.). (ENG.). 32p. (gr. 3-4). pap. 8.10 *(978-1-4296-7982-4(4))*; pap. 47.70 *(978-1-4296-8456-9(9))* Capstone Press of Coughlan Cos. (Fact Finders).

Farrell, Courtney. Methane Energy, 1 vol. 2013. (Innovative Technologies Ser.). (ENG.). 112p. (J). (gr. 6-12). 35.64 *(978-1-61783-465-3(3))* ABDO Publishing Co.

—Save the Planet: Using Alternative Energies. 2010. (Explorer Library: Language Arts Explorer Ser.). (ENG.). 32p. (gr. 4-8). pap. 14.21 *(978-1-60279-672-0(6)*, 200919); lib. bdg. 28.50 *(978-1-60279-663-8(7)*, 200356) Cherry Lake Publishing.

Faust, Daniel R. Energy Crisis: The Future of Fossil Fuels. (Jr. Graphic Environmental Dangers Ser.). (ENG., Illus.). 24p. (gr. 3-8). 2009. pap. 10.60 *(978-1-4042-4598-3(7))* 2008. (J). lib. bdg. 25.25 *(978-1-4042-4231-9(7))* Rosen Publishing Group, Inc., The.

Faust, Daniel R. & Obregón, José María. Crisis Energética: El Futuro de Los Combustibles Fósiles. 2009. (Historietas Juveniles: Peligros Del Medioambiente (Jr. Graphic Environmental Dangers) Ser.). (SPA & ENG., Illus.). 24p. (gr. 3-6). (YA). lib. bdg. 25.25 *(978-1-4358-8465-6(5))*; pap. 10.60 *(978-1-4358-8466-3(3))* Rosen Publishing Group, Inc., The.

Fershee, Joshua P. Energy Law: A Context & Practice Casebook. 2014. (Illus.). 646p. 88.00 *(978-1-59460-799-8(0))* Carolina Academic Pr.

Flath, Camden. Careers in Green Energy: Fueling the World with Renewable Resources. 2010. (New Careers for the 21st Century Ser.). 64p. (YA). (gr. 7-18). lib. bdg. 22.95 *(978-1-4222-1812-9(0))* Mason Crest.

Fridell, Ron. Earth-Friendly Energy. 2008. (Saving Our Living Earth Ser.). 72p. (YA). (gr. 4-7). lib. bdg. 30.60 *(978-0-8225-7563-4(9))* Lerner Publishing Group.

The Future of Power. 2016. (Future of Power Ser.). 00032p. (J). (gr. 4-5). 157.50 *(978-1-4994-3187-2(2)*, PowerKids Pr.) Rosen Publishing Group, Inc., The.

Gaarder-Juntti, Oona. What in the World Is Green Energy?, 1 vol. 2010. (Super SandCastle Ser.). (ENG., Illus.). 24p. 25.65 *(978-1-61613-191-3(8)*, 1315123, Super SandCastle) ABDO Publishing Co.

Gerdes, Louise I. Wave & Tidal Power. Kiesbye, Stefan, ed. 2010. (At Issue Ser.). (ENG.). 128p. 34.45 *(978-0-7377-4900-7(8)*, Greenhaven Pr., Inc.) Cengage Gale.

Gibbons, Gail. Clean Energy. 2014. (J). *(978-0-8234-3068-0(5))* Holiday Hse., Inc.

Gillett, Jack & Gillett, Meg. Energy-Resource Maps. 2012. (Maps of the Environmental World Ser.). (ENG., Illus.). 32p. (J). (gr. 4-6). 26.50 *(978-1-4488-8614-2(7))*; pap. 10.60 *(978-1-4488-8621-0(X))* Rosen Publishing Group, Inc., The. (PowerKids Pr.).

Gish, Melissa. Energy. 2005. (My First Look at Science Ser.). (Illus.). 24p. (J). (gr. k-3). lib. bdg. 15.95 *(978-1-58341-372-2(3)*, Creative Education) Creative Co., The.

Goldman, Laurie. Clean Energy. 2010. (Sally Ride Science Ser.). (ENG., Illus.). 44p. (J). (gr. 3-7). pap. 8.99 *(978-1-59643-578-0(X)*, 9781596435780) Roaring Brook Pr.

Goodman, Polly. Energy Today & Tomorrow. 2011. (Earth Alert! Ser.). 32p. (YA). (gr. 3-6). lib. bdg. 26.60 *(978-1-4339-6002-4(8))* Stevens, Gareth Publishing LLLP.

Gordon, Sherri Mabry & Library. Green & Clean Energy: What You Can Do. 2010. (Green Issues in Focus Ser.). (Illus.). 128p. (J). (gr. 7-12). lib. bdg. 33.27 *(978-0-7660-3348-1(1))* Enslow Pubs., Inc.

Gosman, Gillian. Earth-Friendly Energy. 2011. (How to Be Earth Friendly Ser.). (Illus.). 32p. (J). pap. 10.00 *(978-1-4488-2763-3(9)*, PowerKids Pr.); (YA). (gr. 3-6). lib. bdg. 25.25 *(978-1-4488-2587-5(3))* Rosen Publishing Group, Inc., The.

Green, Jen. Energy for the Future. 2006. (Illus.). 32p. (YA). (gr. 4-18). lib. bdg. 27.10 *(978-1-59389-119-0(9))* Chrysalis Education.

—Using Energy Wisely. 2011. (Sherlock Bones Looks at the Environment Ser.). (ENG., Illus.). 32p. (YA). (gr. 3-6). lib. bdg. 25.25 *(978-1-61533-346-2(0))* Windmill Bks.

—Why Should I Save Energy? Gordon, Mike, illus. 2005. (Why Should I? Bks.). (ENG.). 32p. (J). pap. 6.99 *(978-0-7641-3156-1(7))* Barron's Educational Series, Inc.

Green, Robert. How Renewable Energy Is Changing Society. 2015. (ENG., Illus.). 80p. (J). lib. bdg. *(978-1-60152-904-6(X))* ReferencePoint Pr., Inc.

Green Technology Set, 8-Volumes. 2009. (Green Technology Ser.). (C). (gr. 9). 320.00 *(978-0-8160-8278-0(2))* Facts On File, Inc.

Gregory, Joy. Energy. 2017. ***(978-1-5105-1931-2(9))*** SmartBook Media, Inc.

Gunderson, Jessica. The Energy Dilemma. 2010. (Earth Issues Ser.). 48p. (YA). (gr. 5-18). 23.95 *(978-1-58341-980-9(2)*, Creative Education) Creative Co., The.

Hall, Linley Erin, ed. Critical Perspectives on Energy & Power. 2009. (Scientific American Critical Anthologies on Environment & Climate Ser.). 208p. (gr. 9-9). 63.90 *(978-1-60853-065-6(5))* Rosen Publishing Group, Inc., The.

Hand, Carol. Biomass Energy, 1 vol. 2013. (Innovative Technologies Ser.). (ENG.). 112p. (J). (gr. 6-12). 35.64 *(978-1-61783-462-2(9))* ABDO Publishing Co.

—The Great Hope for an Energy Alternative: Laser-Powered Fusion Energy. 2010. (In the News Ser.). (ENG.). 64p. (YA). pap. 12.95 *(978-1-4488-1682-8(3))*; (gr. 7-12). lib. bdg. 31.95 *(978-1-4358-9450-1(2))* Rosen Publishing Group, Inc., The.

Haugen, David M., ed. Renewable Energy. 2012. (Opposing Viewpoints Ser.). (ENG., Illus.). 240p. (J). (gr. 10-12). pap. 29.45 *(978-0-7377-6140-5(7))*; lib. bdg. 42.95 *(978-0-7377-6139-9(3))* Cengage Gale. (Greenhaven Pr., Inc.).

Haugen, David M., et al. Energy Alternatives. 2010. (Opposing Viewpoints Ser.). (ENG., Illus.). 224p. pap. 29.45 *(978-0-7377-4963-2(6))*; (gr. 10-12). 46.45 *(978-0-7377-4962-5(8))* Cengage Gale. (Greenhaven Pr., Inc.).

Hawbacker, Emily. Energy Lab for Kids: 40 Exciting Experiments to Explore, Create, Harness, & Unleash Energy. 2017. (Lab Ser.). (ENG., Illus.). 144p. (J). (gr. 5-9). pap. 22.99 *(978-1-63159-250-8(5)*, Quarry Bks.) Quarto Publishing Group USA.

Heinrichs, Ann. Sustaining Earth's Energy Resources. 2010. (Environment at Risk Ser.). 112p. (gr. 7-18). 39.93 *(978-0-7614-4007-9(0))* Marshall Cavendish Corp.

Herweck, Don. All about Energy, 1 vol. 2007. (Science Readers Ser.). (SPA & ENG.). 32p. (J). (gr. 4-4). pap. 8.99 *(978-0-7439-0571-8(7))* Shell Educational Publishing.

Hewitt, Sally. Using Energy. 2008. (Green Team Ser.). (ENG., Illus.). 32p. (J). (gr. 3-7). pap. *(978-0-7787-4103-9(6)*, 1286252); lib. bdg. *(978-0-7787-4096-4(X)*, 1286252) Crabtree Publishing Co.

Hicks, Dwayne. Solving the Energy Crisis. 2016. (Global Guardians Ser.). 00024p. (J). (gr. 3-3). pap. 8.25 *(978-1-4994-2752-3(2)*, PowerKids Pr.) Rosen Publishing Group, Inc., The.

Higgins, Melissa. Wind Energy, 1 vol. 2013. (Innovative Technologies Ser.). (ENG.). 112p. (J). (gr. 6-12). 35.64 *(978-1-61783-469-1(6))* ABDO Publishing Co.

Higgins, Nadia. Excited about Energy CD+Book. Martinez Ricci, Andres, illus. 2010. (Science Rocks! Set 2 CD+Book Ser.). 32p. lib. bdg. 54.14 incl. cd-rom *(978-1-60270-992-8(0))* ABDO Publishing Co.

Higgins, Nadia & Ricci, Andres Martinez. Excited about Energy, 1 vol. 2008. (Science Rocks Ser.). (ENG., Illus.). 32p. (gr. -1-4). 28.50 *(978-1-60270-277-6(2)*, 1287325, Looking Glass Library- Nonfiction) Magic Wagon.

Hirsch, Rebecca E. Hydrogen & Fuel Cells, 1 vol. 2013. (Innovative Technologies Ser.). (ENG.). 112p. (J). (gr. 6-12). 35.64 *(978-1-61783-464-6(5))* ABDO Publishing Co.

Holt, Rinehart and Winston Staff. Environmental Science Chptr. 17: Nonrenewable Energy. 4th ed. Date not set. pap. 11.20 *(978-0-03-068078-6(6))* Holt McDougal.

—Holt Science & Technology Chapter 5: Earth Science: Energy Resources. 5th ed. 2004. (Illus.). pap. 12.86 *(978-0-03-030286-2(2))* Holt McDougal.

Hord, Colleen. Clean & Green Energy. 2010. (ENG., Illus.). 24p. (gr. k-2). pap. 8.95 *(978-1-61590-539-3(1))* Rourke Educational Media.

Hunter, Nick. Energy for Everyone? the Business of Energy. 2012. (Big-Buck Business Ser.). (Illus.). 48p. (J). (gr. 6-8). 31.95 *(978-1-4339-7751-0(6))*; pap. 14.05 *(978-1-4339-7752-7(4))* Stevens, Gareth Publishing LLLP. (Gareth Stevens Secondary Library).

—Science vs. the Energy Crisis. 2013. (Science Fights Back Ser.). (Illus.). 48p. (gr. 4-6). 31.95 *(978-1-4339-8695-6(7))*; pap. 14.05 *(978-1-4339-8696-3(5))* Stevens, Gareth Publishing LLLP. (Gareth Stevens Learning Library).

Hunter, Rebecca. Energy Supply. 2012. (Eco Alert! Ser.). (Illus.). 32p. (gr. 4-6). lib. bdg. 28.50 *(978-1-59771-296-5(5))* Sea-To-Sea Pubns.

Ivanovich, Nikolai. Sources of Energy. 2013. (InfoMax Readers Ser.). (ENG.). 24p. (J). (gr. 3-4). pap. 8.25 *(978-1-4777-2643-3(8))*; pap. 49.50 *(978-1-4777-2644-0(6))* Rosen Publishing Group, Inc., The. (Rosen Classroom).

Jackson, Tom. Power & Energy. 2012. (FAYT: Invention & Technology Ser.). 64p. (gr. 4-10). lib. bdg. 39.95 *(978-1-936333-39-4(2))* Brown Bear Bks.

Jefferis, David. Green Power: Eco-Energy Without Pollution. 2006. (Science Frontiers Ser.). (ENG., Illus.). 32p. (J). (gr. 4-7). lib. bdg. *(978-0-7787-2857-3(9)*, 1253435) Crabtree Publishing Co.

Johanson, Paula. What Is Energy? 2014. (Let's Find Out! Ser.). 32p. (J). (gr. 3-6). 23.45 *(978-1-62275-492-2(1))* Rosen Publishing Group, Inc., The.

Jones, Susan. Solar Power of the Future: New Ways of Turning Sunlight into Energy. (Library of Future Energy Ser.). 64p. 2009. (gr. 5-5). 58.50 *(978-1-60853-629-0(7))* 2005. (Illus.). (YA). (gr. 7-12). lib. bdg. 31.95 *(978-0-8239-3663-2(5))* Rosen Publishing Group, Inc., The.

Kallen, Stuart A. Cutting Edge Energy Technology. 2016. (ENG.). 80p. (YA). (gr. 5-12). *(978-1-68282-036-4(6))* ReferencePoint Pr., Inc.

Kenney, Karen Lactchana. Energy. 2010. (Everyday Science Ser.). 24p. (J). (gr. k-3). 25.65 *(978-1-60753-018-3(X))* Amicus Publishing.

Kenney, Karen Latchana. Energy Investigations. 2017. (Key Questions in Physical Science Ser.). (ENG.). 32p. (J). (gr. 3-6). 27.99 ***(978-1-5124-4003-4(5))*** Lerner Publishing Group.

Killian, Maryellen. Energy for Earth. 2013. (InfoMax Readers Ser.). (ENG.). 24p. (J). (gr. 2-3). pap. 49.50 *(978-1-4777-2435-4(4))*; (Illus.). pap. 8.25 *(978-1-4777-2434-7(6))* Rosen Publishing Group, Inc., The. (Rosen Classroom).

Knight M J. Why Should I Switch off the Light? 2009. (One Small Step Ser.). (Illus.). 32p. (J). (gr. -1-3). pap. *(978-1-897563-48-9(5))* Saunders Bk. Co.

Koontz, Robin. Poop Is Power. 2016. (Let's Explore Science Ser.). (ENG., Illus.). 48p. (gr. 5-8). 35.64 *(978-1-68191-389-6(5))* Rourke Educational Media.

Kopp, Megan. Energy from Wind: Wind Farming. 2015. (Next Generation Energy Ser.). (ENG., Illus.). 32p. (J). *(978-0-7787-1983-0(9))* Crabtree Publishing Co.

Kowalski, Kathiann M. Alternative Energy Sources. 2010. (Controversy! 2 Ser.). 112p. (gr. 7). 37.07 *(978-0-7614-4899-0(3))* Marshall Cavendish Corp.

Kravetz, Jonathan. Learning about Energy with Graphic Organizers. (Graphic Organizers in Science Ser.). 24p. (gr. 3-4). 2009. 42.50 *(978-1-61513-030-6(6)*, PowerKids Pr.) 2007. (Illus.). (YA). lib. bdg. 22.60 *(978-1-4042-3409-3(8))* Rosen Publishing Group, Inc., The.

Laidlaw, Jill. Cities. 2010. (Sustaining Our Environment Ser.). 48p. (J). lib. bdg. 35.65 *(978-1-60753-135-7(6))* Amicus Publishing.

—Energy. 2010. (Sustaining Our Environment Ser.). 48p. (J). 35.65 *(978-1-60753-136-4(4))* Amicus Publishing.

Laidlaw, Jill A. Cities. 2010. (What's in My Food Ser.). 32p. (gr. 1-4). lib. bdg. 27.10 *(978-1-59920-421-5(5))* Black Rabbit Bks.

—Energy. 2012. (What's in My Food Ser.). 32p. (gr. 1-4). lib. bdg. 27.10 *(978-1-59920-422-2(3))* Black Rabbit Bks.

Landau, Elaine. The History of Energy. 2005. (Major Inventions Through History Ser.). (ENG., Illus.). 56p. (gr. 5-8). lib. bdg. 26.60 *(978-0-8225-3806-6(7)*, Twenty-First Century Bks.) Lerner Publishing Group.

Langley, Andrew. Bridging the Energy Gap, 1 vol. 2011. (Environment Challenge Ser.). (ENG.). 48p. (gr. 3-3). pap. 9.49 *(978-1-4109-4325-5(9)*, Raintree Freestyle Express); (Illus.). (gr. 5-6). 34.65 *(978-1-4109-4297-5(X)*, Raintree Freestyle) Heinemann-Raintree.

Langwith, Jacqueline. Renewable Energy. 2008. (Opposing Viewpoints Ser.). (ENG., Illus.). 242p. (J). (gr. 10-12). 29.45 *(978-0-7377-4227-5(5)*, LML01709-243145); pap. 42.95 *(978-0-7377-4226-8(7)*, LML01709-243112) Cengage Gale. (Greenhaven Pr., Inc.).

Lawrence, Ellen. Poop Power. 2017. (Scoop on Poop Ser.). (ENG.). (J). (gr. -1-3). lib. bdg. 17.95 ***(978-1-68402-246-5(0))*** Bearport Publishing Co., Inc.

Leardi, Jeanette. Making Cities Green. 2009. (Going Green Ser.). (Illus.). 32p. (YA). (gr. 3-6). lib. bdg. 25.27 *(978-1-59716-961-5(7))* Bearport Publishing Co., Inc.

Leedy, Loreen. Shocking Truth about Energy. Leedy, Loreen, illus. 2011. (ENG., Illus.). 32p. (J). pap. 7.95 *(978-0-8234-2388-0(3))* Holiday Hse., Inc.

Let's Find Out! Forms of Energy. 2017. (Let's Find Out! Forms of Energy Ser.). 32p. (gr. 6-8). 146.70 ***(978-1-5081-0533-6(2))***; pap. 77.40 ***(978-1-5081-0535-0(9))*** Rosen Publishing Group, Inc., The. (Britannica Educational Publishing).

The Library of Future Energy. 2005. (Illus.). (gr. 7-12). lib. bdg. 212.00 *(978-0-8239-3901-5(4))* Rosen Publishing Group, Inc., The.

Llewellyn, Claire. Save Energy. 2005. (Illus.). 32p. (YA). (gr. 1-18). lib. bdg. 27.10 *(978-1-932333-23-7(1))* Chrysalis Education.

Macdonald, Margaret. Who Can Save Power? 2014. (Little Books of Answers: Level B Ser.). (Illus.). 16p. (gr. k-2). pap. 7.95 *(978-1-927136-14-0(8))* Three Crows Media NZL. Dist: RiverStream Publishing.

Macken, JoAnn Early. Take a Closer Look at Oil. 2016. (Core Content Science — Take a Closer Look Ser.). (ENG., Illus.). 40p. (J). (gr. 2-4). lib. bdg. 26.65 *(978-1-63440-051-0(8))* Red Chair Pr.

Manolis, Kay. Energy. 2007. (First Science Ser.). (ENG., Illus.). 24p. (J). (gr. 2-5). lib. bdg. 25.95 *(978-1-60014-096-9(3))* Bellwether Media.

—Energy. (Blastoff! Readers Ser.). 24p. (J). 2011. (Illus.). (gr. 2). pap. 5.95 *(978-0-531-28453-7(0))* 2007. (ENG.). (gr. k-2). 20.00 *(978-0-531-14724-5(X))* Scholastic Library Publishing. (Children's Pr.).

Marcovitz, Hal. Can Renewable Energy Replace Fossil Fuels? 2010. (In Controversy Ser.). (Illus.). 96p. (J). (gr. 7-12). 26.95 *(978-1-60152-113-2(8)*, 1316134) ReferencePoint Pr., Inc.

Mason, Paul. How Big Is Your Energy Footprint? 2009. (Environmental Footprints Ser.). 32p. (gr. 4). 28.50 *(978-0-7614-4411-4(4))* Marshall Cavendish Corp.

Massie, Elizabeth. Nonrenewable & Renewable Energy Resources. 2016. (Spring Forward Ser.). (J). (gr. 2). *(978-1-4900-9468-7(7))* Benchmark Education Co.

McKinney, Barbara Shaw. Pass the Energy, Please! Wallace, Chad, illus. 2004. (Sharing Nature with Children Book Ser.). 32p. (YA). (gr. 1-8). pap. 16.95 *(978-1-58469-001-6(1))* Dawn Pubns.

McLeish, Ewan. Challenges to Our Energy Supply. 2009. (J). 70.50 *(978-1-4358-5491-8(8)*, Rosen Reference); (ENG.). 48p. (YA). pap. 11.75 *(978-1-4358-5490-1(X)*, Rosen Reference); (Illus.). 48p. (J). (gr. 5-9). lib. bdg. 29.25 *(978-1-4358-5357-7(1))* Rosen Publishing Group, Inc., The.

McPherson, Stephanie Sammartino. Arctic Thaw: Climate Change & the Global Race for Energy Resources. 2014. (Illus.). 64p. (J). (gr. 6-12). lib. bdg. 34.60 *(978-1-4677-2043-4(7)*, Twenty-First Century Bks.) Lerner Publishing Group.

Meachen Rau, Dana. Alternative Energy: Beyond Fossil Fuels. 2016. (Green Generation Ser.). (ENG.). 64p. (gr. 6-7). pap. 7.10 *(978-0-7565-5554-2(X)*, CPB Grades 4-8) Compass Point Bks.

Miller, Debra A. Energy Production & Alternative Energy. 2010. (Confronting Global Warming Ser.). 112p. (YA). (gr. 10-12). lib. bdg., lib. bdg. 38.95 *(978-0-7377-5106-2(1)*, Greenhaven Pr., Inc.) Cengage Gale.

—Gasoline. 2012. (Current Controversies Ser.). (ENG.). 224p. (gr. 10-12). lib. bdg. 46.40 *(978-0-7377-6227-3(6)*, Greenhaven Pr., Inc.) Cengage Gale.

—Oil. Gale Editors, ed. 2010. (Current Controversies Ser.). (ENG.). 224p. (gr. 10-12). 46.40 *(978-0-7377-4919-9(9))*; pap. 32.00 *(978-0-7377-4920-5(2))* Cengage Gale. (Greenhaven Pr., Inc.).

mooney, carla. What Is the Future of Hydrogen Power? 2012. (Illus.). 80p. (YA). lib. bdg. *(978-1-60152-274-0(6))* ReferencePoint Pr., Inc.

Morris, Neil. The Energy Mix. 2010. (J). 34.25 *(978-1-59920-338-6(3))* Black Rabbit Bks.

—Geothermal Power. 2007. (Energy Sources Ser.). (Illus.). 32p. (YA). (gr. 4-7). lib. bdg. 28.50 *(978-1-58340-906-0(8))* Black Rabbit Bks.

Mulder, Michelle. Brilliant! Shining a Light on Sustainable Energy, 1 vol. (Orca Footprints Ser.). (ENG., Illus.). 48p. (J). (gr. 3-7). 2016. pap. 12.95 *(978-1-4598-1214-7(X))* 2013. 19.95 *(978-1-4598-0221-6(7))* Orca Bk. Pubs. USA.

Muschal, Frank. Bio-fuels. 2007. (21st Century Skills Library: Power Up! Ser.). (ENG., Illus.). 32p. (gr. 4-8). lib. bdg. 28.50 *(978-1-60279-045-2(0)*, 200051) Cherry Lake Publishing.

Nakaya, Andrea C. Energy Alternatives. 2007. (Compact Research Ser.). (Illus.). 112p. (YA). (gr. 7-12). lib. bdg. 25.95 *(978-1-60152-017-3(4))* ReferencePoint Pr., Inc.

Newell, Ella. Energy. 2013. (Physical Science Ser.). 48p. (J). (gr. 4-6). pap. 14.05 *(978-1-4339-9509-5(3))*; pap. 84.30 *(978-1-4339-9510-1(7))*; (ENG., Illus.). lib. bdg. 31.95 *(978-1-4339-9508-8(5))* Stevens, Gareth Publishing LLLP.

Nixon, Jonathan. Energy Engineering & Powering the Future. 2016. (Engineering in Action Ser.). (ENG., Illus.). 32p. (J). (gr. 5-8). *(978-0-7787-7539-3(9))* Crabtree Publishing Co.

Ollhoff, Jim. Fossil Fuels, 1 vol. 2010. (Future Energy Ser.). (ENG.). 32p. (YA). (gr. 4-7). 27.07 *(978-1-60453-935-6(6))* ABDO Publishing Co.

—Geothermal, Biomass, & Hydrogen, 1 vol. 2010. (Future Energy Ser.). (ENG.). 32p. (YA). (gr. 4-7). 27.07 *(978-1-60453-937-0(2))* ABDO Publishing Co.

—World in Crisis, 1 vol. 2010. (Future Energy Ser.). (ENG., Illus.). 32p. (YA). (gr. 4-7). 27.07 *(978-1-60453-940-0(2))* ABDO Publishing Co.

O'Neal, Claire. How to Use Wind Power to Light & Heat Your Home. 2009. (Tell Your Parents Ser.). (Illus.). 48p. (J). (gr. 4-7). lib. bdg. 29.95 *(978-1-58415-762-5(3))* Mitchell Lane Pubs., Inc.

Orme, Helen. Energy for the Future. 2008. (Earth in Danger Ser.). (Illus.). 32p. (YA). (gr. 3-6). lib. bdg. 25.27 *(978-1-59716-727-7(4)*, 1284324) Bearport Publishing Co., Inc.

Orr, Tamra. Geothermal Energy. 2007. (21st Century Skills Library: Power Up! Ser.). (ENG., Illus.). 32p. (gr. 4-8). lib. bdg. 28.50 *(978-1-60279-044-5(2)*, 200053) Cherry Lake Publishing.

Owen, Ruth. Energy from Inside Our Planet: Geothermal Power. 2013. (Power: Yesterday, Today, Tomorrow Ser.). (ENG., Illus.). 32p. (J). (gr. 3-6). 25.25 *(978-1-4777-0268-0(7))*; pap. 11.75 *(978-1-4777-0275-8(X))* Rosen Publishing Group, Inc., The. (PowerKids Pr.).

—Energy from Plants & Trash: Biofuels & Biomass Power. 2013. (Power: Yesterday, Today, Tomorrow Ser.). (ENG., Illus.). 32p. (J). (gr. 3-6). 25.25 *(978-1-4777-0267-3(9))*; pap. 11.75 *(978-1-4777-0273-4(3))* Rosen Publishing Group, Inc., The. (PowerKids Pr.).

Oxlade, Chris. Energy Technology. 2010. (New Technology Ser.). (ENG., Illus.). 48p. (J). 23.99 *(978-0-237-53430-1(4))* Evans Brothers, Ltd. GBR. Dist: Independent Pubs. Group.

Oxlade, Chris & Jennings, Terry. Energy. 2009. (Science Alive Ser.). (Illus.). 32p. (J). pap. *(978-1-897563-53-3(1))* Saunders Bk. Co.

Oxlade, Chris & Jennings, Terry J. Energy. 2009. (J). 28.50 *(978-1-59920-273-0(5))* Black Rabbit Bks.

Paleja, S. N. Power Up! A Visual Exploration of Energy. Tse, Glenda, illus. 2015. (ENG.). 56p. (J). (gr. 4-7). pap. 12.95 *(978-1-55451-726-8(5)*, 9781554517268) Annick Pr., Ltd. CAN. Dist: Publishers Group West (PGW).

Parker, Russ. Energy Supplies in Crisis. 2009. (Planet in Crisis Ser.). 32p. (gr. 5-8). (ENG., Illus.). (J). pap. 10.00 *(978-1-4358-0681-8(6))*; (YA). lib. bdg. 25.25 *(978-1-4358-5251-8(6))* Rosen Publishing Group, Inc., The. (Rosen Reference).

Parker, Steve. Energy & Power. 2010. (How It Works Ser.). 40p. (J). (gr. 3-18). lib. bdg. 19.95 *(978-1-4222-1794-8(9))* Mason Crest.

Parker, Vic. Let's Think about Sustainable Energy, 1 vol. 2014. (Let's Think About Ser.). (ENG., Illus.). 48p. (gr. 3-6). 33.32 *(978-1-4846-0292-8(7))*; pap. 8.99 *(978-1-4846-0297-3(8))* Heinemann-Raintree. (Heinemann InfoSearch).

Parks, Peggy J. Coal Power. 2010. (Compact Research Ser.). 96p. (YA). (gr. 7-12). 26.95 *(978-1-60152-107-1(3))* ReferencePoint Pr., Inc.

Passero, Barbara. Energy Alternatives. 2006. (Opposing Viewpoints Ser.). (ENG., Illus.). 238p. (J). (gr. 3-7). 27.50 *(978-0-7377-3351-8(9))*; pap. 39.70 *(978-0-7377-3350-1(0))* Cengage Gale. (Greenhaven Pr., Inc.).

Peppas, Lynn. Ocean, Tidal & Wave Energy: Power from the Sea. 2008. (Energy Revolution Ser.). (ENG., Illus.). 32p. (J). (gr. 3-8). pap. *(978-0-7787-2933-4(8))*; lib. bdg. *(978-0-7787-2919-8(2))* Crabtree Publishing Co.

Pipe, Jim. Oil. 2010. (J). 28.50 *(978-1-59604-211-7(7))* Black Rabbit Bks.

Povey, Karen D. Energy Alternatives. 2008. (Hot Topics Ser.). (ENG., Illus.). 112p. (J). (gr. 7-12). lib. bdg. 33.45 *(978-1-59018-980-1(9)*, LML02109-229789) Cengage Gale.

The Race to Find Energy. 2014. (World in Crisis Ser.). (Illus.). 48p. (J). (gr. 5-8). 30.25 *(978-1-4777-7842-5(X))* Rosen Publishing Group, Inc., The.

Raum, Elizabeth. Potato Clocks & Solar Cars: Renewable & Nonrenewable Energy. 2016. (Raintree Fusion: Physical Science Ser.). (ENG.). 32p. pap. 8.29 *(978-1-4109-8510-1(5)*, Raintree Fusion) Heinemann-Raintree.

Redmond, Jim. Oil Makes Gasoline Power. 2003. (From Resource to Energy Source Ser.). (J). *(978-1-58417-292-5(4))*; pap. *(978-1-58417-293-2(2))* Lake Street Pubs.

Riddle, John. Coal Power of the Future: New Ways of Turning Coal into Energy. (Library of Future Energy Ser.). 64p. 2009. (gr. 5-5). 58.50 *(978-1-60853-624-5(6))* 2005. (Illus.). (YA). (gr. 7-12). lib. bdg. 31.95 *(978-0-8239-3660-1(0))* Rosen Publishing Group, Inc., The.

Rigsby, Mike. Doable Renewables: 16 Alternative Energy Projects for Young Scientists. 2010. (ENG., Illus.). 224p. (J). (gr. 4-18). pap. 16.95 *(978-1-56976-343-8(7))* Chicago Review Pr., Inc.

Rodger, Ellen. Is There a Future for Fossil Fuels? 2010. (ENG., Illus.). 32p. (J). pap. *(978-0-7787-2937-2(0))*; lib. bdg. *(978-0-7787-2923-5(0))* Crabtree Publishing Co.

Rowell, Rebecca. Energy & Waves Through Infographics. Sciuto, Alex, illus. 2013. (Super Science Infographics Ser.). (ENG.). 32p. (gr. 3-5). pap. 8.95 *(978-1-4677-1590-4(5))*; lib. bdg. 26.60 *(978-1-4677-1290-3(6)*, Lerner Pubns.) Lerner Publishing Group.

Rusch, Elizabeth. The Next Wave: The Quest to Harness the Power of the Oceans. 2014. (Scientists in the Field Ser.). (ENG., Illus.). 80p. (J). (gr. 5-7). 18.99 *(978-0-544-09999-9(0)*, HMH Books For Young Readers) Houghton Mifflin Harcourt Publishing Co.

Saunders, N. & Saunders, Nigel. Geothermal Energy. 2007. (Energy for the Future & Global Warming Ser.). 32p. (gr. 5-8). pap. 11.70 *(978-0-8368-8409-8(4))* Stevens, Gareth Publishing LLLP.

Saunders, Nigel. Geothermal Energy. 2007. (Energy for the Future & Global Warming Ser.). (Illus.). 32p. (gr. 5-8). lib. bdg. 27.00 *(978-0-8368-8400-5(0))* Stevens, Gareth Publishing LLLP.

Saving the Planet Through Green Energy. 2016. (Saving the Planet Through Green Energy Ser.). 24p. (J). lib. bdg. 135.60 *(978-0-7660-8402-5(7))* Enslow Pubs., Inc.

Science & Voege, Debra. Energy Today, 8 vols., Set. 2010. (Energy Today Ser.). (gr. 4-6). 240.00 *(978-1-60413-964-8(1)*, Chelsea Clubhouse) Facts On File, Inc.

Sechrist, Darren. Powerful Planet: Can Earth's Renewable Energy Save Our Future? 2009. (Current Science Ser.). (ENG.). 48p. (gr. 4-7). (YA). lib. bdg. 31.00 *(978-1-4339-2241-1(X))*; (J). pap. 8.95 *(978-1-4339-2245-9(2)*, Gareth Stevens Learning Library) Stevens, Gareth Publishing LLLP.

Silverman, Buffy. Energy All Around. 2012. (ENG.). 24p. (gr. 3-4). pap. 8.95 (978-1-61810-228-7(1)) Rourke Educational Media.

Silverstein, Alvin, et al. Energy. 2008. (Science Concepts Ser.). (YA). (gr. 5-9). lib. bdg. 31.93 (978-0-8225-8655-5(X)) Twenty First Century Bks.

Slade, Suzanne. What Can We Do about the Energy Crisis? 2009. (Protecting Our Planet Ser.). (Illus.). 24p. (ENG.). (J). pap. 8.25 (978-1-4358-2481-2(4), PowerKids Pr.); (YA). (gr. 2-5). lib. bdg. 22.60 (978-1-4042-8081-6(2)) Rosen Publishing Group, Inc., The.

Smith, A. G. Green Power: Earth-Friendly Energy Through the Ages. 2010. (Dover Nature Coloring Book Ser.). (ENG., Illus.). 32p. (J). (gr. 3-8). pap. 3.99 (978-0-486-47447-2(X)) Dover Pubns., Inc.

Smith, Eileen M. ElectriCity Beyond the Curve of Deregulation: Neighborhood Energy Watch Groups & the Ethos of Commerce. 2003. per. (978-0-9741412-9-9(1)) Ethos Of Commerce Pubs., Ltd.

Sneideman, Joshua & Twamley, Erin. Renewable Energy: Discover the Fuel of the Future. Brinesh, Heather Jane, illus. 2016. (Build It Yourself Ser.). (ENG.). 128p. (J). (gr. 3-7). 22.95 (978-1-61930-356-0(6)) Open City Bks.

Sobey, Ed, ed. Solar Cell & Renewable Energy Experiments. 2011. (Cool Science Projects with Technology Ser.). (Illus.). 128p. (J). (gr. 5-18). lib. bdg. 33.27 (978-0-7660-3305-4(8)) Enslow Pubs., Inc.

Sobha, Geeta. Green Technology: Earth-Friendly Innovations. 2007. (In the News Ser.). (Illus.). 64p. (YA). (gr. 7-12). lib. bdg. 31.95 (978-1-4042-1914-4(5)) Rosen Publishing Group, Inc., The.

—Green Technology: Earth-friendly Innovations. 2009. (In the News Ser.). 64p. (gr. 6-6). 58.50 (978-1-61513-467-0(0)) Rosen Publishing Group, Inc., The.

Solway, Andrew. Exploring Energy. 2007. (Exploring Physical Science Ser.). (Illus.). 48p. (YA). (gr. 5-9). lib. bdg. 29.25 (978-1-4042-3748-3(8)) Rosen Publishing Group, Inc., The.

—From Crashing Waves to Music Download: An Energy Journey Through the World of Sound. 2015. (Energy Journeys Ser.). (ENG.). 48p. (gr. 3-6). 33.32 (978-1-4846-0883-8(6), Heinemann InfoSearch) Heinemann-Raintree.

—From Sunlight to Blockbuster Movies: An Energy Journey Through the World of Light. 2015. (Energy Journeys Ser.). (ENG.). 48p. (gr. 3-6). 33.32 (978-1-4846-0882-1(8), Heinemann InfoSearch) Heinemann-Raintree.

—The Scientists Behind Energy, 1 vol. 2011. (Sci-Hi: Scientists Ser.). (ENG.). 48p. (gr. 4-4). pap. 9.95 (978-1-4109-4052-0(7)); lib. bdg. 33.32 (978-1-4109-4045-2(4)) Heinemann-Raintree. (Sci-Hi).

Solway, Andrew & Graham, Ian. Energy Journeys. 2015. (Energy Journeys Ser.). (ENG.). 48p. (gr. 3-6). lib. bdg. 133.28 (978-1-4846-0886-9(0), Heinemann InfoSearch) Heinemann-Raintree.

—Energy Transfers. 2015. (Energy Transfers Ser.). (ENG.). 48p. (gr. 3-6). pap. 35.96 (978-1-4846-0891-3(7), Heinemann InfoSearch) Heinemann-Raintree.

Spilsbury, Louise & Spilsbury, Richard. Energy, 1 vol. 2013. (Essential Physical Science Ser.). (ENG.). 48p. (gr. 4-6). 33.32 (978-1-4329-8144-0(7), Heinemann InfoSearch) Heinemann-Raintree.

Spilsbury, Richard. The Debate about Energy Resources. 2010. (Ethical Debates Ser.). (ENG.). 48p. (YA). lib. bdg. 29.25 (978-1-4358-9651-2(3), Rosen Reference) Rosen Publishing Group, Inc., The.

Spilsbury, Richard & Spilsbury, Louise. What Is Energy? Exploring Science with Hands-on Activities. 2008. (In Touch with Basic Science Ser.). (Illus.). 32p. (J). (gr. 3-4). lib. bdg. 23.94 (978-0-7660-3099-2(7), Enslow Elementary) Enslow Pubs., Inc.

Steele, Philip. Saving Water & Energy. 2009. (Now We Know About... Ser.). (ENG., Illus.). 24p. (J). (gr. k-3). pap. (978-0-7787-4740-6(9)); lib. bdg. (978-0-7787-4723-9(9)) Crabtree Publishing Co.

Stewart, Audrey. Our Natural Resources. 2013. (InfoMax Readers Ser.). (ENG.). 24p. (J). (gr. 2-3). pap. 49.50 (978-1-4777-2357-9(9)); pap. 8.25 (978-1-4777-2356-2(0)) Rosen Publishing Group, Inc., The. (Rosen Classroom).

Stille, Darlene R. Energy: Heat, Light, & Fuel. Boyd, Sheree, illus. 2004. (Amazing Science Ser.). (ENG.). 24p. (gr. k-4). 26.65 (978-1-4048-0249-0(5)) Picture Window Bks.

Stoyles, Pennie & Pentland, Peter. Power & Fuel. 2011. (Energy in Action Ser.). 32p. (gr. 4). 28.50 (978-1-60870-569-6(2)) Marshall Cavendish Corp.

Stuckey, Rachel. Energy from Living Things: Biomass Energy. 2015. (Next Generation Energy Ser.). (ENG., Illus.). 32p. (J). (978-0-7787-1980-9(4)) Crabtree Publishing Co.

Syrewicz, Connor. Energizing Energy Markets: Clean Coal, Shale, Oil, Wind, & Solar. 2013. (Earning $50,000 - $100,000 with a High School Diploma or Less Ser.: 14). 64p. (J). (gr. 7-18). 22.95 (978-1-4222-2894-4(0)) Mason Crest.

Tabak, John. Solar & Geothermal Energy. 2009. (Energy & the Environment Ser.). (Illus.). 206p. (C). (gr. 9-18). 40.00 (978-0-8160-7086-2(5)) Facts On File, Inc.

Tell Your Parents, 5 vols., Set. Incl. All about Electrice & Hybrid Cars. Bearce, Stephanie. (Illus.). 48p. lib. bdg. 25.70 (978-1-58415-763-2(1)); Green Changes You Can Make Around the House. Smalley, Carol. (Illus.). 48p. lib. bdg. 29.95 (978-1-58415-764-9(X)); How to Harness Solar Power for Your Home. Bearce, Stephanie. (Illus.). 48p. lib. bdg. 29.95 (978-1-58415-761-8(5)); How to Use Wind Power to Light & Heat Your Home. O'Neal, Claire. (Illus.). 48p. lib. bdg. 29.95 (978-1-58415-762-5(3)); How You Can Use Waste Energy to Heat & Light Your Home. Brager, Bruce L. 29.95 (978-1-58415-765-6(8)); (J). (gr. 4-7). 2009. 2009. Set lib. bdg. 149.75 (978-1-58415-766-3(6)) Mitchell Lane Pubs., Inc.

Thaddeus, Eva. Powering the Future: New Energy Technologies. 2010. (World's of Wonder Ser.). (ENG., Illus.). 131p. (J). (gr. 4-18). 34.95 (978-0-8263-4901-9(3)) Univ. of New Mexico Pr.

Thomas, Isabel. The Pros & Cons of Biomass Power. 2007. (Energy Debate Ser.). (Illus.). 48p. (YA). (gr. 5-9). lib. bdg. 29.25 (978-1-4042-3742-1(9)) Rosen Publishing Group, Inc., The.

Tiner, John Hudson. Coal Makes Electric Power. 2003. (From Resource to Energy Source Ser.). (J). (978-1-58417-295-6(9)); (978-1-58417-294-9(0)) Lake Street Pubs.

Top That Publishing Staff, ed. Lets Learn about Energy. 2004. (Fun Kits Ser.). (Illus.). 48p. (J). (978-1-904748-98-4(8)) Top That! Publishing PLC.

VanCleave, Janice. Janice VanCleave's Energy for Every Kid: Easy Activities That Make Learning Science Fun. 2005. (Science for Every Kid Ser.: 15). (ENG., Illus.). 236p. (gr. 3-7). pap. 14.95 (978-0-471-33099-8(X), Wiley) Wiley, John & Sons, Inc.

Wachtel, Alan, et al. Geothermal Energy. 2010. (Energy Today Ser.). 48p. (J). (gr. 3-6). 30.00 (978-1-60413-786-6(X)) Facts On File, Inc.

Way, Steve & Bailey, Gerry. Energy. 2008. (Simply Science Ser.). (Illus.). 32p. (J). (gr. 3-6). lib. bdg. 26.00 (978-0-8368-9227-7(5)) Stevens, Gareth Publishing LLLP.

Weakland, Mark. Onion Juice, Poop, & Other Surprising Sources of Alternative Energy, 1 vol. 2011. (Nasty (but Useful!) Science Ser.). (ENG.). 32p. (gr. 3-4). pap. 8.10 (978-1-4296-6347-2(2)); pap. 47.70 (978-1-4296-6473-8(8)) Capstone Press of Coughlan Cos. (Fact Finders).

Weber, Rebecca. El Poder de la Energía. 2011. (Ciencia Física/Physical Science Ser.).Tr. of Power of Energy. (SPA & MUL.). 24p. (gr. k-1). 26.65 (978-1-4296-6907-8(1)) Capstone Press of Coughlan Cos.

Wheeler, Jill C. Everyday Conservation, 1 vol. 2008. (Eye on Energy Ser.). (ENG., Illus.). 32p. (gr. k-6). 27.07 (978-1-59928-804-8(4), Checkerboard Library) ABDO Publishing Co.

—Nature Power, 1 vol. 2008. (Eye on Energy Ser.). (ENG., Illus.). 32p. (gr. k-6). 27.07 (978-1-59928-806-2(0), Checkerboard Library) ABDO Publishing Co.

—Renewable Fuels, 1 vol. 2008. (Eye on Energy Ser.). (ENG., Illus.). 32p. (gr. k-6). 27.07 (978-1-59928-808-6(7), Checkerboard Library) ABDO Publishing Co.

Whitehouse, Patty. Energia Por Dondequiera / Energy Everywhere. 2006. (Construction Forces Discovery Library). (Illus.). 24p. (J). (gr. k-2). lib. bdg. 22.79 (978-1-60044-274-2(9)) Rourke Educational Media.

—Energy Everywhere. 2006. (Construction Forces Discovery Library). (Illus.). 24p. (J). (gr. k-2). lib. bdg. 22.79 (978-1-60044-189-9(0)) Rourke Educational Media.

Whittaker, Helen. Energy. 2011. (Living Green Ser.). 32p. (gr. 3). 28.50 (978-1-60870-573-3(0)) Marshall Cavendish Corp.

Winnick, Nick. Green Energy. 2016. (J). **(978-1-5105-2219-0(0))** SmartBook Media, Inc.

Winnick, Nick. Green Power. 2010. (Being Green Ser.). (Illus.). 32p. (YA). (gr. 3-6). lib. bdg. 27.13 (978-1-61690-097-7(0)); (J). (gr. 4-6). pap. 12.95 (978-1-61690-098-4(9)) Weigl Pubs., Inc.

Zuchora-Walske, Christine. Energy in the Real World. 2013. (Science in the Real World EBook Ser.). (ENG.). 48p. (J). pap. 15.64 (978-1-61783-789-0(X), Core Library); (gr. 3-6). lib. bdg. 32.79 (978-1-61783-739-5(3)) ABDO Publishing Co.

—Solar Energy, 1 vol. 2013. (Innovative Technologies Ser.). (ENG.). 112p. (J). (gr. 6-12). 35.64 (978-1-61783-467-7(X)) ABDO Publishing Co.

POWER SUPPLY

see Power Resources

POWER TRANSMISSION, ELECTRIC

see Electric Lines

POWERPUFF GIRLS (FICTITIOUS CHARACTERS)—FICTION

Little, Troy. Second Chances. 2014. (Powerpuff Girls Ser.). (ENG., Illus.). 152p. pap. 19.99 (978-1-61377-906-4(2), 9781613779064) Idea & Design Works, LLC.

Mccraken, Craig, et al. Power Party, Vol. 1. Carolan, Sean & Denson, Abby, illus. 2013. (Powerpuff Girls Ser.). (ENG.). 148p. pap. 19.99 (978-1-61377-733-6(7), 9781613777336) Idea & Design Works, LLC.

PRACTICAL POLITICS

see Politics, Practical

PRAIRIE DOGS

Bailer, Darice. Prairie Dogs. 2011. (Animals Animals 12 Ser.). (Illus.). 48p. (J). (gr. 3). 23.95 (978-0-7614-4876-1(4)) Marshall Cavendish Corp.

Borgert-Spaniol, Megan. Prairie Dogs. 2016. (North American Animals Ser.). (ENG., Illus.). 24p. (J). (gr. k-3). 25.95 (978-1-62617-402-3(4), Blastoff! Readers) Bellwether Media.

Doudna, Kelly. It's a Baby Prairie Dog!, 1 vol. 2008. (Baby Mammals Ser.). (ENG., Illus.). 24p. (J). (gr. k-3). lib. bdg. 24.21 (978-1-60453-029-2(4)) ABDO Publishing Co.

George, Lynn. Prairie Dogs: Tunnel Diggers. 2010. (Animal Architects Ser.). (ENG.). 24p. (J). pap. 8.25 (978-1-4488-1351-3(4)); lib. bdg. 22.60 (978-1-4488-0695-9(X)) Rosen Publishing Group, Inc., The. (PowerKids Pr.).

Gish, Melissa. Prairie Dogs. 2017. (J). **(978-1-60818-833-8(7)**, Creative Education) Creative Co., The.

Grucella, A. J. Prairie Dogs in Danger. 2013. (Animals at Risk Ser.). 24p. (J). (gr. 2-5). pap. 48.90 (978-1-4339-9166-0(7)); (ENG., Illus.). lib. bdg. 22.60 (978-1-4339-9164-6(0)) Stevens, Gareth Publishing LLLP.

Jackson, Tom. Prairie Dogs. 2008. (Nature's Children Ser.). (Illus.). 52p. (J). (978-0-7172-6242-7(1)) Grolier, Ltd.

Johnson, Jinny. Prairie Dog. 2014. (North American Mammals Ser.). 24p. (gr. 2-5). 28.50 (978-1-62588-034-5(0)) Black Rabbit Bks.

—Prairie Dog. 2014. (North American Mammals Ser.). (ENG., Illus.). 24p. (J). (gr. -1-4). pap. 8.95 (978-1-77092-170-2(2)) Saunders Bk. Co. CAN. Dist: RiverStream Publishing.

Kalman, Bobbie. An Animal Community. 2010. (My World Ser.). (ENG., Illus.). 24p. (J). (gr. k-2). (978-0-7787-9446-2(6)); pap. (978-0-7787-9490-5(3)) Crabtree Publishing Co.

Kopp, Megan. Prairie Dogs. 2011. (J). (gr. 2-4). pap. 12.95 (978-1-61690-630-6(8), AV2 by Weigl); (Illus.). 24p. 27.13 (978-1-61690-624-5(3)) Weigl Pubs., Inc.

Magby, Meryl. Prairie Dogs. 2012. (American Animals Ser.). (ENG., Illus.). 24p. (J). (gr. k-3). lib. bdg. 22.60 (978-1-4488-6182-8(9)); pap. 8.25 (978-1-4488-6323-5(6), PowerKids Pr.) Rosen Publishing Group, Inc., The.

Markle, Sandra. Los Perritos de Las Praders (Prairie Dogs) 2009. (SPA.). pap. 46.95 (978-0-7613-4718-7(6)) Lerner Publishing Group.

—Los Perritos de Las Praderas. Translations.com Staff, tr. from ENG. 2008. (Animales Presa (Animal Prey) Ser.). (SPA.). 40p. (gr. 3-6). 25.26 (978-0-7613-3896-3(9)) Lerner Publishing Group.

—Los perritos de las praderas (Prairie Dogs) 2008. 40p. (J). pap. 7.95 (978-0-7613-3901-4(9), Ediciones Lerner) Lerner Publishing Group.

—Prairie Dogs. 2008. pap. 46.95 (978-0-8225-9323-2(8)) 2008. (ENG., Illus.). 40p. (gr. 3-6). per. 7.95 (978-0-8225-6441-6(6), First Avenue Editions) 2007. (ENG., Illus.). 40p. (J). (gr. 3-6). lib. bdg. 25.26 (978-0-8225-6438-6(6)) Lerner Publishing Group.

Redmond, Shirley Raye. Lewis & Clark: A Prairie Dog for the President. Manders, John, illus. 2003. (Step into Reading Ser.). 48p. 14.00 (978-0-7569-1697-8(6)) Perfection Learning Corp.

Schuetz, Kristin. Prairie Dogs. 2014. (Backyard Wildlife Ser.). (ENG.). 24p. (J). (gr. k-3). lib. bdg. 25.95 (978-1-60014-971-9(5), Blastoff! Readers) Bellwether Media.

Tourville, Amanda Doering. Prairie Dogs Perching: Counting By 3s, 1 vol. Holm, Sharon Lane, illus. 2008. (Count the Critters Ser.). (ENG.). 24p. (J). (gr. k-3). 27.07 (978-1-60270-266-0(7)) Magic Wagon.

Zuchora-Walske, Christine. Peeking Prairie Dogs. 2003. (Pull Ahead Bks.). (Illus.). 32p. (J). (gr. k-2). pap. 5.95 (978-0-8225-3622-2(6)) Lerner Publishing Group.

PRAIRIE DOGS—FICTION

Baum, L. Frank. The Enchanted Buffalo. Montileaux, Donald F., illus. 2010. 31p. (J). (gr. 2-5). 14.95 (978-0-9822749-3-4(9), South Dakota State Historical Society Pr.) South Dakota State Historical Society Pr.

Brix, Liz. Josephine Prairie Dog. 2009. 28p. pap. 12.70 (978-1-4389-4448-7(9)) AuthorHouse.

Horender, Philip M. Head West, Young Mouse: Transcontinental Railroad Traveler, 1 vol. Wolek, Guy, illus. 2013. (Maximilian P. Mouse, Time Traveler Ser.). (ENG.). 112p. (J). (gr. 3-6). lib. bdg. 27.07 (978-1-61641-959-2(8), Calico Chapter Bks) Magic Wagon.

Marable, Justin. Noco. 2010. (ENG., Illus.). 50p. pap. 12.95 (978-0-9831104-0-8(9)) Marable, Justin.

Meyer, Deanna. Buffalo on the Ridge. 2010. pap. 12.95 (978-0-7414-6103-2(X)) Infinity Publishing.

Murray, Caryn Eve. Philomena's Homecoming: The (mostly) true story of a New York prairie dog's search for a Family. 2010. 48p. pap. 8.95 (978-1-4502-2769-8(4)) iUniverse, Inc.

Rheaume, Sherry D. Lulu the Prairie Dog. 2011. 16p. pap. 24.95 (978-1-4626-3987-8(9)) America Star Bks.

Stevens, Janet & Crummel, Susan Stevens. The Great Fuzz Frenzy. (ENG., Illus.). 56p. (J). (gr. -1-3). 2017. pap. 7.99 (978-0-544-94391-9(0), HMH Books For Young Readers) 2005. 17.99 (978-0-15-204626-2(7)) Houghton Mifflin Harcourt Publishing Co.

—The Great Fuzz Frenzy. unabr. ed. 2006. (J). (gr. k-3). 27.99 incl. audio (978-0-8045-6940-8(1), SAC6941) Spoken Arts, Inc.

—The Great Fuzz Frenzy. 2017. (ENG.). (J). (gr. -1-3). lib. bdg. 18.40 **(978-0-606-39816-9(3))** Turtleback Bks.

PRAIRIES

AZ Books Staff. In the Prairie & Desert. Efimova, Tatiana & Goncharik, Irina, eds. 2012. (Animal Sounds Ser.). (ENG.). 14p. (J). (gr. -1-k). bds. 7.95 (978-1-61889-128-0(6)) AZ Bks. LLC.

Bannatyne-Cugnet, Jo. Heartland: A Prairie Sampler. Moore, Yvette, illus. 2005. (ENG.). 40p. (J). (gr. k-12). pap. 9.95 (978-0-88776-722-7(2), Tundra Bks.) Tundra Bks. CAN. Dist: Penguin Random Hse. LLC.

Dayton, Connor. Prairie Animals. 2009. (American Habitats Ser.). (gr. 2-5). (ENG., Illus.). 24p. (J). pap. 8.25 (978-1-4358-3196-4(9), PowerKids Pr.); 24p. 42.50 (978-1-61511-357-6(6), PowerKids Pr.); (YA). lib. bdg. 22.60 (978-1-4358-2767-7(8)) Rosen Publishing Group, Inc., The.

Endres, Hollie. Prairies. 2007. (Learning about the Earth Ser.). (ENG., Illus.). 24p. (J). (gr. k-3). lib. bdg. 25.95 (978-1-60014-114-0(5)) Bellwether Media.

—Prairies. 2011. (Blastoff! Readers Ser.). 24p. (J). pap. 5.95 (978-0-531-26034-0(8), Children's Pr.) Scholastic Library Publishing.

Fredericks, Anthony D. P Is for Prairie Dog: A Prairie Alphabet. Bowles, Doug, illus. 2011. (Sleeping Bear Alphabets Ser.). (ENG.). 32p. (J). (gr. k-6). 16.95 (978-1-58536-508-1(4)) Sleeping Bear Pr.

Frisch, Aaron. Prairies. 2008. (Our World Ser.). (Illus.). 24p. (J). (gr. -1-3). lib. bdg. 24.25 (978-1-58341-572-6(6), Creative Education) Creative Co., The.

Gaarder-Juntti, Oona. What Lives in the Prairie?, 1 vol. 2008. (Animal Habitats Ser.). (ENG., Illus.). 24p. (J). (gr. k-3). 25.65 (978-1-60453-176-3(2)) ABDO Publishing Co.

Heos, Bridget. Do You Really Want to Visit a Prairie? Fabbri, Daniele, illus. 2014. (Do You Really Want to Visit... ? Ser.). (ENG.). 24p. (J). (gr. 1-4). lib. bdg. 27.10 (978-1-60753-452-5(5)) Amicus Publishing.

Lemke, Donald B. The Schoolchildren's Blizzard. 2007. (Disasters in History Ser.). (ENG., Illus.). 32p. (gr. 3-4). 30.65 (978-1-4296-0157-3(4), Graphic Library) Capstone Press of Coughlan Cos.

Levy, Janey. What Lives on a Prairie? (Reading Room Collection 2 Ser.). 24p. 2009. (gr. 3-4). 42.50 (978-1-60852-001-5(3), PowerKids Pr.) 2003. (Illus.). (J). lib. bdg. 22.60 (978-0-8239-3701-1(1)) Rosen Publishing Group, Inc., The.

Lion, David C. La Vida en la Pradera. 2008. (SPA., Illus.). 24p. (J). 22.00 (978-0-531-20722-2(6), Children's Pr.) Scholastic Library Publishing.

McGehee, Claudia. A Tallgrass Prairie Alphabet. McGehee, Claudia, illus. 2004. (Bur Oak Book Ser.). (Illus.). 32p. (J). 17.95 (978-0-87745-897-5(9)) Univ. of Iowa Pr.

Munson Scullin, Wendy. Young Person's Guide to the Prairie. 2006. (Illus.). 160p. (YA). per. 11.95 (978-0-9770764-0-6(7)) South River Pr.

Pettiford, Rebecca. Prairie Food Chains. 2016. (Who Eats What?). 24p. (J). (gr. 2-5). lib. bdg. 25.65 (978-1-62031-303-9(0), Pogo) Jump! Inc.

Tarbox, A. D. A Pairie Food Chain. 2008. (Nature's Bounty Ser.). (Illus.). 43p. 22.95 (978-1-58341-600-6(5), Creative Education) Creative Co., The.

PRAYER

see also Prayers

B&H Kids Editorial Staff. Prayers for Bedtime (padded Board Book) Conger, Holli, illus. 2016. (Little Words Matter(tm) Ser.). (ENG.). 38p. (J). (gr. -1 — 1). 9.99 (978-1-4336-8645-0(7), B&H Kids) B&H Publishing Group.

Baden, Robert. Psalms for Kids. 2004. 64p. (J). 7.49 (978-0-570-07141-9(0)) Concordia Publishing Hse.

Bagley, Val Chadwick & Beckstrand, Tamara, trs. My Little Book about Prayer. Bagley, Val Chadwick, illus. 2004. (Illus.). (J). bds. 10.95 (978-1-59156-096-8(9)) Covenant Communications, Inc.

Batterson, Mark. The Circle Maker for Kids: One Prayer Can Change Everything, 1 vol. Caparo, Antonio Javier, illus. 2013. (ENG.). 32p. (J). 16.99 (978-0-310-72492-6(9)) Zonderkidz.

Becky, Terri And Melissa. Garden Prayer for Little Farmers: Seeds of Evangelism Series (Book 1) 2013. 36p. pap. 15.49 (978-1-4669-8787-6(1)) Trafford Publishing.

Bible Visuals International Staff, compiled by. Prayer: New Testament Volume 09. 2006. (Illus.). (J). pap. (978-1-932381-39-9(2), 1009) Bible Visuals International, Inc.

Billingsley, Mary. The Life of Jesus: Paintings & Meditations on the Rosary. 2010. (ENG., Illus.). 56p. (J). 20.00 (978-0-8028-5362-2(5), Eerdmans Bks For Young Readers) Eerdmans, William B. Publishing Co.

Burrin, Angela M. Jesus Speaks to Me on My First Holy Communion. Lo Cascio, Maria Cristina, illus. 2009. 39p. (J). (gr. 1-5). 12.95 (978-1-59325-149-9(1)) Word Among Us Pr.

Butcher, Sam, illus. Precious Moments: Storybook Bible & Girl Prayer Pal Set. 2003. 14.60 (978-0-7180-0569-6(4)) Nelson, Thomas Inc.

Carr, Josie. IGod: Prayers & Promises to Connect to You with Him. 2008. 86p. (YA). pap. 4.99 (978-1-57794-885-8(8)) Harrison House Pubs.

Center for Learning Staff. Prayer & Worship. 2007. (Religion Ser.). 138p. (YA). spiral bd. 18.95 (978-1-56077-785-4(0)) Center for Learning, The.

Christensen, Catherine. I Can Pray Every Day. Eggbert, Corey, illus. 2015. (J). 14.99 (978-1-4621-1646-1(9), Horizon Pubs.) Cedar Fort, Inc./CFI Distribution.

Cook, LaVelle. Little Jimmie & the Lord's Prayer. 2005. (J). 14.95 (978-1-882185-45-0(5)) Cornerstone Publishing, Inc.

Cursha Pierce-Lunderman. God's Going Too! His Promises for Kids During Deployments. 2009. 20p. pap. 13.00 (978-1-4389-1612-5(4)) AuthorHouse.

Daily Whispers of Wisdom for Girls Journal. 2014. (ENG.). 384p. (J). pap. 14.99 (978-1-62836-945-8(0), Barbour Bks.) Barbour Publishing, Inc.

Daniel, Mikhal. Children's Picture Prayer Book: Sh'ma, V'ahavta & Shemoneh Esrei. 2009. 56p. pap. 29.80 (978-0-557-05763-4(9)) Lulu Pr., Inc.

—Children's Prayer Book: A Messianic Siddur. 2009. 58p. pap. 15.32 (978-0-557-05875-4(9)) Lulu Pr., Inc.

Darens, Cat. My Morning Angel. Oliver, Julia, illus. 2010. 18p. (J). (gr. -1-k). 7.95 (978-0-8091-6753-1(0), Ambassador Bks.) Paulist Pr.

David C. Cook Publishing Company Staff. Land of Milk & Honey. 2007. (LMH Ser.). 16p. (J). (gr. 1-3). Bk. 3. 6.99 (978-0-7814-4526-9(4))Bk. 4. 6.99 (978-0-7814-4527-6(2)) Cook, David C.

David, Juliet. Candle Prayers for Toddlers & Candle Bible for Toddlers, 2 vols. Prole, Helen, illus. 2009. (Candle Bible for Toddlers Ser.). 528p. (J). 24.99 (978-0-8254-7380-7(2), Candle Bks.) Lion Hudson PLC GBR. Dist: Kregel Pubns.

DeVries, Mike & Murphy, Troy. Exodus: The Sacred Journey. 2003. (No Limits Ser.). (ENG.). 112p. (gr. 3-7). per. 12.99 (978-0-8341-5005-8(0), 083-415-0050) Beacon Hill Pr. of Kansas City.

DeWitt, Becky. Destiny's Closet: Circle of Friends. 2010. 68p. pap. 17.99 (978-1-4520-8364-3(9)) AuthorHouse.

DiCianni, Ron. Praying with the Presidents: One Nation's Legacy of Prayer. 2004. 48p. (J). (gr. k-3). 10.99 (978-1-59185-408-1(3), Charisma Kids) Charisma Media.

Donaghy, Thomas J. Joyful Prayers. 2009. (St. Joseph Board Bks.). (Illus.). 12p. bds. 5.95 (978-0-89942-663-1(8)) Catholic Bk. Publishing Corp.

Dowley, Tim. Would You Like to Know How to Pray?, 1 vol. Reeves, Eira, illus. 2015. (ENG.). 28p. (J). pap. 2.99 (978-1-78128-158-1(0), Candle Bks.) Lion Hudson PLC GBR. Dist: Kregel Pubns.

Eddie Ree Stolinski, Ree Stolinski & Stolinski, Eddie Ree. The Prayer Closet. 2010. 28p. 14.93 (978-1-4269-2995-3(1)) Trafford Publishing.

Edwards, Fran. The Lord's Prayer. 2013. 28p. pap. 11.95 (978-1-61244-120-7(3)) Halo Publishing International.

Elkins, Stephen. First Steps in Prayer. Colton, Ellie, illus. 2006. (First Steps Ser.). 32p. (J). 9.99 (978-0-8054-2663-2(9)) B&H Publishing Group.

—Tell Me about Prayer. 2014. (Train 'Em Up Ser.). (ENG.). 24p. (J). pap. 4.99 (978-1-4143-9680-4(5)) Tyndale Hse. Pubs.

Flamini, Lorella, illus. Thank You Dear God! Prayers for Little Ones. 2006. 40p. (J). (gr. -1-k). bds. 11.95 (978-0-8198-7417-7(5)) Pauline Bks. & Media.

Flowerpot Press Staff. A Child's Book of Prayers: Good Night, Dear God. 2013. (ENG., Illus.). 20p. (J). 8.99 (978-1-77093-636-2(X)) Flowerpot Children's Pr. Inc. CAN. Dist: Cardinal Pubs. Group.

Ghani, Aisha. I Can Pray Anywhere! Zulkifli, Azhari, illus. 2010. (ENG.). 15p. (J). (gr. -1-k). bds. 9.95 (978-0-86037-339-1(8)) Kube Publishing Ltd. GBR. Dist: Consortium Bk. Sales & Distribution.

Gibson, Roxie. Talking with God. Gibson, Jim, illus. 2007. (ENG.). 24p. (J). (gr. -1-3). 7.99 (978-1-933725-75-8(3)) Premium Pr. America.

Gold, August. Does God Hear My Prayer? Waller, Diane Hardy, photos by. 2005. (ENG., Illus.). 32p. (J). pap. 8.99 (978-1-59473-102-0(0), 9781594731020, Skylight Paths Publishing) LongHill Partners, Inc.

Goldsmith, Joel S. Class Lessons with Joel Goldsmith. 2008. 116p. pap. (978-0-9793119-3-2(4)) Editorial Benei Noaj.

Goyer, Tricia. Prayers That Changed History: From Christopher Columbus to Helen Keller, How God Used 25 People to Change the World, 1 vol. 2015. (ENG., Illus.). 240p. (J). pap. 12.99 (978-0-310-74801-4(1)) Zonderkidz.

Grace, Will. Thank You Prayer. Geist, Ken, ed. Watanabe, Kaori, illus. 2006. (My First Taggies Book Ser.). (ENG.). 10p. (J). (gr. k — 1). 12.99 *(978-0-439-87564-6(1),* Cartwheel Bks.) Scholastic, Inc.
Grandma's Prayer. 2006. (J). 8.00 *(978-0-9774822-1-4(9))* Crosam Pr.
Groth, Jeanette L. Prayer: Learning How to Talk to God. rev. ed. 2003. (Illus.). 24p. (J). 6.49 *(978-0-570-07188-4(7))* Concordia Publishing Hse.
Grube, Edward C. Teens Pray: Conversations with God. 2003. 96p. (YA). 10.49 *(978-0-7586-0035-6(6))* Concordia Publishing Hse.
Gruen, K. W. Teaching the Message of the Lord's Prayer. 2013. (Illus.). 36p. pap. 16.99 *(978-1-4497-8146-0(2),* WestBow Pr.) Author Solutions, Inc.
Hahn, Samuel J. Stories Told under the Sycamore Tree: Bible Plant Object Lessons. Patton, Scott, tr. Patton, Scott, illus. 2003. 191p. (J). pap. 19.95 *(978-0-7880-1972-2(4))* CSS Publishing Co.
Hartley, Bob. Childrens Adoration Prayer Book. Clonts, E. M. M., illus. 2012. 114p. pap. 24.95 *(978-0-615-58840-7(9))* Deeper Waters.
Hilton, Jennifer Sue & McCurry, Kristen. Ora a Dios. Garton, Michael, illus. 2016. (SPA.). (J). *(978-1-5064-2093-6(1))* Augsburg Fortress, Pubs.
Hoopes, Scott. Joseph's First Prayer. 2017. (ENG.). (J). bds. 12.99 ***(978-1-4621-2033-8(4))*** Cedar Fort, Inc./CFI Distribution.
Hunt, Johnny. Bedtime Devotions with Jesus: My Daily Devotional for Kids, 1 vol. 2015. (ENG., Illus.). 336p. (J). 16.99 *(978-0-7180-3645-4(X))* Nelson, Thomas Inc.
Hydeck, Michelle A. R. Wings Up: All with a Little Help from Our Angels. 2012. 40p. pap. 12.95 *(978-1-4525-5595-9(8))* Balboa Pr.
I Can Pray! 2006. (Faith Discovery Ser.). (Illus.). 24p. (J). bds. 6.99 *(978-0-7847-1398-3(7),* 04058) Standard Publishing.
Jahsmann, Allan Hart & Simon, Martin P. Little Visits with God. White, DeBorah, illus. 4th ed. 2006. (Little Visits Ser.). 413p. (J). (gr. 5-7). per. 13.49 *(978-0-7586-0847-5(0))* Concordia Publishing Hse.
Jelenek, Frank X. Journey to the Heart: Centering Prayer for Children. Boyajian, Ann, illus. 2007. (ENG.). 32p. (J). (gr. -1-5). pap. 15.99 *(978-1-55725-482-5(6))* Paraclete Pr., Inc.
Johnson, Kevin. Pray: Talk to the King of the Universe, 1 vol. 2007. (Deeper Ser.). (ENG., Illus.). 112p. (gr. 13). pap. 7.99 *(978-0-310-27492-6(3))* Zondervan.
Kendrick, Stephen, et al. PrayerWorks: Prayer Strategy & Training for Kids. Manuzak, Lisa, illus. 2015. (ENG.). 128p. (J). (gr. 3-6). 12.99 *(978-1-4336-8869-0(7),* B&H Kids) B&H Publishing Group.
—This Means War: A Strategic Prayer Journal. 2015. (ENG.). 224p. (J). (gr. 8-12). pap. 12.99 *(978-1-4336-8870-6(0),* B&H Kids) B&H Publishing Group.
The Kids Prayed & God Arrived. 2004. (YA). *(978-1-59581-083-0(8))* Brentwood Communications Group.
Kidwai, A. R. & D'Oyen, F. M., compiled by. What Should We Say? 2016. (ENG & ARA., Illus.). 36p. (J). (gr. 2-7). 9.95 *(978-0-86037-267-7(7))* Kube Publishing Ltd. GBR. Dist: Consortium Bk. Sales & Distribution.
Kirgiss, Crystal & Lyon, Christopher. A Teenager's Daily Prayer Book. Publications International Ltd. Staff, ed. 2005. (Illus.). 384p. 10.98 *(978-0-7853-4909-9(X),* 3337100) Publications International, Ltd.
Lafferty, Jill C. Devociones para Niños Chispita. Grosshauser, Peter, illus. 2016. (SPA.). (J). *(978-1-5064-2101-8(6))* Augsburg Fortress, Pubs.
Landreth, Jane. Bible Prayers for Bedtime. 2008. (Bedtime Bible Stories Ser.). (ENG.). 256p. (J). pap. 5.99 *(978-1-60260-066-9(X),* Barbour Bks.) Barbour Publishing, Inc.
Lee, Stephi. Where Do My Prayers Go? Zareba, Lukasz, illus. 2013. (ENG.). 32p. (J). 14.95 *(978-0-578-11938-0(2))* Stephi /Lee.
Legacy. 7.50 *(978-0-8054-5927-2(8))* B&H Publishing Group.
Legacy Press Staff. Gotta Have God: Devotions for Boys. 2004. (Gotta Have God Ser.). (Illus.). 238p. (J). (gr. 5-7). spiral bd. 12.99 *(978-1-885358-98-1(9),* Legacy Pr.) Rainbow Pubs. & Legacy Pr.
Lemon, Willie Sells. Prayer Changes Things. 2011. 24p. (gr. -1). 17.50 *(978-1-4567-3829-7(1))* AuthorHouse.
Lewis, Jan, illus. First Prayers for Little Ones: Prayers for Every Day, Special Occasions & the Family. 2016. (ENG.). 48p. (J). (gr. -1-12). 9.99 *(978-1-86147-716-3(3),* Armadillo) Anness Publishing GBR. Dist: National Bk. Network.
The Lord's Prayer: Prayer Cards. 2004. *(978-0-8294-1406-6(1))* Loyola Pr.
Lounsbury, Pete. Jesus & the Blind Man. 2007. (J). per. 12.95 *(978-1-59879-408-3(6))* Lifevest Publishing, Inc.
Lovasik, Lawrence G. A Child's Prayer Treasury. 2004. (Illus.). (J). *(978-0-89942-719-5(7))* Catholic Bk. Publishing Corp.
MacArthur, John. My Faith & Prayer Journal. 2004. 64p. (J). pap. 4.99 *(978-1-4003-0441-7(5))* Nelson, Thomas Inc.
MacBeth, Sybil. Praying in Color. 2009. (ENG., Illus.). 40p. (J). (gr. 1-5). pap. 16.99 *(978-1-55725-595-2(4))* Paraclete Pr., Inc.
Mackall, Dandi Daley. I'll Talk to God about That. 2014. (ENG.). 32p. (J). 12.99 *(978-0-7369-5875-2(4))* Harvest Hse. Pubs.
Mackall, Dandi Daley & Bostrom, Kathleen Long. Bedtime Stories & Prayers. Kucharik, Elena, illus. 2013. (Little Blessings Ser.). (ENG.). 128p. (J). 14.99 *(978-1-4143-8111-4(5))* Tyndale Hse. Pubs.
MacKenzie, Catherine. Helen Roseveare: What's in the Parcel? 2012. (Little Lights Ser.). (ENG.). 24p. (J). 7.99 *(978-1-84550-383-3(X),* 30e4822e-2a72-488e-8b19-1af61b42efe4) Christian Focus Pubns. GBR. Dist: Bookmasters Distribution.
Mcclure, Gillian. My First Prayers. Fournier, Laure, illus. 2009. (ENG.). 24p. (J). (gr. k-k). *(978-1-84507-535-4(8))* Rough Guides, Ltd.
McIntosh, Kenneth R. Following Aslan: A Book of Devotions for Children Based on the Chronicles of Narnia by C. S. Lewis. 2006. (ENG.). 124p. (J). pap. 11.95 *(978-1-933630-02-1(7),* Anamchara Bks.) Harding Hse. Publishing Sebice Inc.
Meyer, Naama, illus. Siddurchik: Prayer Book for Young Children. 2006. 32p. 12.95 *(978-965-229-328-2(8))* Gefen Publishing Hse., Ltd ISR. Dist: Gefen Bks.
Miller, Ann. Proverbs, Prayers, Poems for Children & Teens. 2005. (J). lib. bdg. 14.95 *(978-0-9748165-1-7(5))* Jaylil Publishing Co.
Montgomery Gibson, Jane. Maker of Prayer. Montgomery Gibson, Jane, illus. 2005. (Illus.). (YA). bds. 8.99 *(978-1-4183-0047-0(0))* Christ Inspired, Inc.
Mordi, Nicku. Know Before You Grow. 2012. 18p. pap. 9.99 *(978-1-61996-394-8(9))* Salem Author Services.
My Rosary. 2006.Tr. of Il Mio Rosario. (Illus.). 32p. pap. 3.95 *(978-0-8189-1235-1(9),* St. Pauls) St Pauls/Alba Hse. Pubs.
Nalls, Charles. Prayer: A field Guide. 2008. 84p. pap. 10.95 *(978-0-595-49142-1(1))* iUniverse, Inc.
Odendahl, Jodi. Praying Hands. 2013. 20p. pap. 12.45 *(978-1-4497-9596-2(X),* WestBow Pr.) Author Solutions, Inc.
Ogunkoya, Olukayode. Godly Children, Praying Children. 2012. 52p. pap. 23.99 *(978-1-61379-470-8(3))* Salem Author Services.
Omartian, Stormie. I Talk to God about How I Feel: Learning to Pray, Knowing He Cares. Warren, Shari, illus. 2010. (Power of a Praying Kid Ser.). (ENG.). 32p. (J). 14.99 *(978-0-7369-2685-0(2))* Harvest Hse. Pubs.
—Little Prayers for Little Kids. Warren, Shari, illus. 2015. (Power of a Praying Kid Ser.). (ENG.). 32p. (J). 14.99 *(978-0-7369-6345-9(6))* Harvest Hse. Pubs.
—The Power of a Praying Kid. 2015. (Power of a Praying Kid Ser.). (ENG.). 112p. (J). pap. 10.99 *(978-0-7369-6603-0(X))* Harvest Hse. Pubs.
—What Happens When I Talk to God? The Power of Prayer for Boys & Girls. Warren, Shari, illus. 2007. (Power of a Praying Kid Ser.). (ENG.). 32p. (J). (gr. -1-3). 14.99 *(978-0-7369-1676-9(8))* Harvest Hse. Pubs.
Omartian, Stormie. What Happens When I Talk to God?/¿Qué Pasa Cuando Hablo con Dios? English/Spanish. Warren, Shari, illus. 2017. (Power of a Praying Kid Ser.). (ENG & SPA.). 32p. (J). (gr. -1-4). pap. 9.99 ***(978-0-7369-7175-1(0))*** Harvest Hse. Pubs.
Paiva, Johannah Gilman, ed. A Child's Book of Prayers: Please. 2013. (ENG., Illus.). 20p. (J). 8.99 *(978-1-77093-637-9(8))* Flowerpot Children's Pr. Inc. CAN. Dist: Cardinal Pubs. Group.
—A Child's Book of Prayers: Thank You. 2013. (ENG., Illus.). 20p. (J). 8.99 *(978-1-77093-638-6(6))* Flowerpot Children's Pr. Inc. CAN. Dist: Cardinal Pubs. Group.
Parker, Amy. Faith, Hope, Love Devotional (padded) 100 Devotions for Kids & Parents to Share. 2016. (Faith, Hope, Love Ser.). (ENG.). 224p. (J). (gr. -1-2). 14.99 *(978-1-4336-9030-3(6),* B&H Kids) B&H Publishing Group.
Parr, Susan Sherwood. Christopher's Adventures: A Prayer on Angel Wings. Paraschiv, Doina, illus. 2004. (ENG.). 16p. 10.95 *(978-0-9728590-3-5(9),* KID-E Bks.) Word Prodns.
—30 Days Out of Depression. 2004. (ENG., Illus.). 58p. 3.95 *(978-0-9728590-5-9(5))* Word Prodns.
Perkins, Nicole. I Believe God Will: Book of Devotion & Prayer for Children. Perkins, Nicole & Frisk, Maria, illus. 2008. 32p. (J). 7.00 *(978-0-9755566-1-0(4))* Azreal Publishing Co.
Pharr, Nancy Elizabeth. When Should I Pray? Rose, Heidi, illus. 2003. 40p. (J). pap. 8.95 *(978-0-8198-8304-9(2),* 332-412) Pauline Bks. & Media.
Piper, Sophie. Blessings for a Baby Boy. Williams, Caroline, illus. 2010. (ENG.). 44p. (J). (gr. k-k). 8.99 *(978-0-7459-6184-2(3))* Lion Hudson PLC GBR. Dist: Independent Pubs. Group.
—Blessings for a Baby Girl. Williams, Caroline, illus. 11th ed. 2010. (ENG.). 48p. (J). (gr. k-k). 8.99 *(978-0-7459-6185-9(1))* Lion Hudson PLC GBR. Dist: Independent Pubs. Group.
—First Prayers for Baby. Spenceley, Annabel, illus. 2014. (ENG.). 48p. (J). (— 1). 8.99 *(978-0-7459-6407-2(9))* Lion Hudson PLC GBR. Dist: Independent Pubs. Group.
Pohl, Mayumi Ishimoto. Morning Prayer. 2012. (ENG.). 23p. (J). pap. 8.95 *(978-1-4327-7153-9(1))* Outskirts Pr., Inc.
Porsenna, Sandy. My first prayer Book. 2010. 34p. pap. 20.00 *(978-0-557-46986-4(4))* Lulu Pr., Inc.
The Prayer for Peace. 2004. 1.75 *(978-0-8294-1073-0(2))* Loyola Pr.
The Prayer Jesus Gave Us. (Two Great Ways to Share God's Love Ser.). 16p. (gr. -1-k). 15.00 *(978-0-570-00315-1(6))* Concordia Publishing Hse.
Praying with the Church Fathers. 2008. (Illus.). 30p. (J). pap. 15.00 *(978-0-9800065-3-7(8))* Saint Paul Brotherhood.
Redden, Vicki, et al. God's Amazing Creation. 2005. (Review Kids Ser.). 375p. (J). *(978-0-8280-1871-5(5))* Review & Herald Publishing Assn.
Reeves, Eira. Oraciones a la Hora de Dormir (Prayers at Bedtime) (SPA.). (J). 1.89 *(978-0-7899-0478-2(0),* 498665) Editorial Unilit.
Roddy, Lauren S. My Scriptural Rosary. Darrenkamp, Julia Mary, illus. rev. ed. 2006. (J). 4.95 *(978-0-8198-4845-1(X))* Pauline Bks. & Media.
The Rosary: Prayer Cards. 2004. *(978-0-8294-1403-5(7))* Loyola Pr.
Rose-Heim, Donna. Dream Walking for Kids: 21 Prayer Activities for Children & Adults. 2011. 64p. (gr. -1). pap. 12.95 *(978-1-4634-4204-0(1))* AuthorHouse.
Rowland, Wil. Wise & Silly. 2011. (Illus.). (J). *(978-1-56722-857-1(7))* Word Aflame Pr.
Rubin, Scott & Oestreicher, Mark. My Future, 1 vol. 2008. (Middle School Survival Ser.). (ENG.). 208p. (YA). pap. 9.99 *(978-0-310-27884-9(8))* Zondervan.
Rue, Nancy N. Everything You Need to Know about Peer Mediation. 2009. (Need to Know Library). 64p. (gr. 5-5). 58.50 *(978-1-60854-080-8(4))* Rosen Publishing Group, Inc., The.
Sainte Croix, Judith. Everything You Need to Know about Meditation. 2009. (Need to Know Library). 64p. (gr. 5-5). 58.50 *(978-1-60854-076-1(6))* Rosen Publishing Group, Inc., The.
Sawyer, Judith L. This Is How I Pray. Sawyer, Judith L., illus. 2008. (Illus.). 24p. (J). pap. *(978-1-926585-11-6(9),* CCB Publishing) CCB Publishing.
Saxon, Terrill. Now I Lay Me down to Sleep. 2006. (Baby Blessings Ser.). (Illus.). 12p. bds. 11.99 *(978-0-7847-1241-2(7),* 04053) Standard Publishing.
Scarfi, Margaret Rose. I Pray the Rosary! Richards, Virginia Helen & Dick, Regina Frances, illus. 2005. 47p. (J). (gr. -1-3). pap. 4.95 *(978-0-8198-3689-2(3),* 332-141) Pauline Bks. & Media.
Schmitt, Betsy & Veerman, David R. 365 Trivia Twist Devotions: An Almanac of Fun Facts & Spiritual Truth for Every Day of the Year. 2005. (ENG., Illus.). 384p. (J). (gr. 4-8). per. 16.99 *(978-0-7847-1737-0(0),* 23350, B&H Kids) B&H Publishing Group.
Setzer, Lee Ann. Tiny Talks #6: I will Trust in Heavenly Father & His Son, Jesus Christ-Their Promises are Sure, Vol. 6. 2005. (J). pap. 7.99 *(978-1-55517-889-5(8))* Cedar Fort, Inc./CFI Distribution.
Shaw, S. B. Children's Edition of Touching Incidents. 2005. pap. 15.95 *(978-1-59605-735-7(1),* Cosimo Classics) Cosimo, Inc.
Shivers, Holly Hawkins. I Can Learn to Pray, 1 vol. 2016. (ENG., Illus.). 224p. (J). 14.99 *(978-0-7180-8169-0(2))* Nelson, Thomas Inc.
Shultz, Karl A. St. Joseph Guide to Lectio Divina. 2010. 192p. pap. 8.95 *(978-0-89942-677-8(8))* Catholic Bk. Publishing Corp.
Silverman, Morris & Silverman, Hillel. Prayer Book for Summer Camps. (J). (gr. 3-12). 8.95 *(978-0-87677-060-3(X));* pap. 6.95 *(978-0-87677-061-0(8))* Prayer Bk. Pr., Inc.
Simon, Mary Manz. Little Visits for Toddlers. Munger, Nancy, illus. 3rd ed. 2006. (Little Visits Ser.). Orig. Title: Little Visits 1-2-3. 275p. (J). (gr. -1-3). per. 13.49 *(978-0-7586-0845-1(4))* Concordia Publishing Hse.
—Little Visits with Jesus. Warren, Beverly, illus. 4th ed. 2006. (Little Visits Ser.). 266p. (J). (gr. -1-3). per. 13.49 *(978-0-7586-0846-8(2))* Concordia Publishing Hse.
Skevington, Andrea. Prayers & Verses Through the Bible. 2016. (ENG., Illus.). 128p. 14.95 *(978-0-7459-7663-1(8))* Lion Hudson PLC GBR. Dist: Independent Pubs. Group.
Small Offerings. 2005. 48p. 15.99 *(978-1-4003-0563-6(2))* Nelson, Thomas Inc.
Spraggett, Daphne. Window on the World: Prayer Atlas for All. 2006. (ENG., Illus.). 221p. pap. 19.99 *(978-1-932805-91-8(5))* Authentic Media GBR. Dist: Send The Light Distribution LLC.
Stortz, Diane. Say & Pray Devotions, 1 vol. 2016. (ENG.). 40p. (J). bds. 9.99 *(978-0-7180-8691-6(0))* Nelson, Thomas Inc.
Stortz, Diane & Holder, Jennifer. I Can Pray! Nobens, C. A., illus. 2014. (Faith That Sticks Bks.). (ENG.). 24p. (J). pap. 3.99 *(978-1-4964-0085-7(2))* Tyndale Hse. Pubs.
Tataryn, Myroslaw. How to Pray with Icons: An Introduction for Children. 2003. (Illus.). 32p. *(978-2-89088-348-2(5))* Novalis Publishing.
Tetz, RosAnne C., told to. God's Big Idea. 2003. 377p. (J). 13.99 *(978-0-8280-1762-6(X))* Review & Herald Publishing Assn.
Thank You God 2001. 2004. (My First Prayers Ser.). 10p. (J). bds. 3.99 *(978-1-85854-405-2(X))* Brimax Books Ltd. GBR. Dist: Byeway Bks.
Thomas Nelson. My Pretty Pink Prayer Purse. 2014. (ENG.). 20p. (J). 9.99 *(978-0-529-12409-8(2))* Nelson, Thomas Inc.
Thomas Nelson, Thomas. My Little Prayers, 1 vol. Le Feyer, Diane, illus. 2016. (ENG.). 96p. (J). 6.99 *(978-0-7180-4019-2(8))* Nelson, Thomas Inc.
Tortorella, Jackie. Our Father: Living the Lord's Prayer, 1 vol. 2009. (ENG.). 49p. pap. 16.95 *(978-1-61582-040-5(X))* America Star Bks.
Twenty-Third Publications, creator. Celebrating Eucharist: A Mass Book for Children. 2012. (ENG., Illus.). 34p. pap. 5.95 *(978-1-58595-855-9(7))* Twenty-Third Pubns./Bayard.
Twin Sisters(r) Staff, et al. My First Bedtime Prayers for Boys. 2016. (Let's Share a Story Ser.). (Illus.). 14p. (J). bds. 5.99 *(978-1-63409-645-4(2))* Barbour Publishing, Inc.
—My First Bedtime Prayers for Girls. 2016. (Let's Share a Story Ser.). (Illus.). 14p. (J). bds. 5.99 *(978-1-63409-646-1(0))* Barbour Publishing, Inc.
Veritas. Children's Everyday Prayerbook: For four to seven year Olds. 2008. (ENG., Illus.). 32p. (J). pap. 10.95 *(978-1-84730-098-0(7))* Veritas Pubns. IRL. Dist: Dufour Editions, Inc.
Wangerin, Walter, Jr., et al. Little Ones Talk with God: A Book of Prayers. Rama, Sue, illus. 2006. 56p. 7.49 *(978-0-7586-1132-1(3))* Concordia Publishing Hse.
Warren, Rick. The Lord's Prayer: Words of Hope & Happiness, 1 vol. Watson, Richard Jesse, illus. 2016. (ENG.). 32p. (J). 16.99 *(978-0-310-75755-9(X))* Zonderkidz.
Williford, Barbara. A Child's Prayer. 2007. (J). 7.95 *(978-0-9796978-7-6(5))* G Publishing LLC.
York Lumbard, Alexis. Everyone Prays: Celebrating Faith Around the World. Sadeghian, Alireza, illus. 2014. (ENG.). 28p. (J). (gr. -1-3). 17.95 *(978-1-937786-19-9(6),* Wisdom Tales) World Wisdom, Inc.
Zondervan. May the Faith Be with You: 180 Devotions That Are Out of This World, 1 vol. 2015. (ENG.). 192p. (J). 9.99 *(978-0-310-75345-2(7))* Zonderkidz.
Zondervan Bible Publishers (Grand Rapids, Mich.) Staff, contrib. by. The Beginner's Bible Kid-Sized Devotions, 1 vol. rev. ed. 2015. (Beginner's Bible Ser.). (ENG., Illus.). 384p. (J). 9.99 *(978-0-310-75142-7(X))* Zonderkidz.

PRAYERS

see also Prayer

Abraham, Ken. Jesus Loves Me Bible Storybook & Devotional Combo. 2003. (Illus.). 672p. (J). 24.99 *(978-1-4003-0185-0(8))* Nelson, Thomas Inc.
Adams, Carol J. God Listens to Your Care: Prayers for All the Animals of the World. 2006. (God Listens Ser.). (Illus.). 48p. (J). (gr. 3-7). per. 8.00 *(978-0-8298-1666-2(6))* Pilgrim Pr., The/United Church Pr.
—God Listens to Your Love: Prayers for Living with Animal Friends. 2005. (God Listens Ser.). 48p. (J). (gr. -1-3). per. 8.00 *(978-0-8298-1665-5(8))* Pilgrim Pr., The/United Church Pr.
—God Listens When You're Afraid: Prayers for When Animals Scare You. 2006. (God Listens Ser.). 48p. (J). (gr. -1). per. *(978-0-8298-1741-6(7))* Pilgrim Pr., The/United Church Pr.
Aiken, Nick, compiled by. Prayers for Teenagers. 2003. 112p. 10.00 *(978-0-281-05543-2(2))* SPCK Publishing GBR. Dist: Pilgrim Pr., The/United Church Pr.
Alcoholics Anonymous World Services. Twenty-Four Hours a Day for Teens: Daily Meditations. 2004. (ENG.). 416p. pap. 15.95 *(978-1-59285-078-5(2),* Z2095) Hazelden.
Allsopp, Sophie, illus. Thank You, God! A Year of Blessings & Prayers for Little Ones. 2009. (ENG.). 16p. (J). (gr. -1-3). 12.99 *(978-1-4169-4754-7(X),* Little Simon Inspirations) Little Simon Inspirations.
Alphonsine, Sister Mary. My Father & Mother on Earth & in Heaven: Our Holy Faith Series Book One. 2014. (Our Holy Faith Ser.: 1). (ENG., Illus.). 96p. (J). (gr. k-2). 18.95 *(978-0-911845-77-8(1),* Neumann Pr.) TAN Bks.
El Alvidadizo David (Bramble Forgets) (Granja Oso de Miel Ser.). (SPA., Illus.). (J). bds. 4.99 *(978-0-7899-0610-6(4),* 495052) Editorial Unilit.
Arterburn, Stephen & Florea, Jesse. The One Year Every Day Devotions: Devotions to Help You Stand Strong. 2008. (ENG.). 384p. (J). pap. 14.99 *(978-1-4143-1814-1(6),* Tyndale Kids) Tyndale Hse. Pubs.
Arthur, Kay & Arndt, Janna. Lord Teach Me to Pray for Kids. 2006. (Discover-4-Yourself for Kids Ser.). 176p. (J). pap. 9.99 *(978-1-888655-30-8(5))* Precept Ministries.
Award Publications Staff. My First Book of Prayers. 2012. (ENG., Illus.). 32p. (J). 8.50 *(978-1-84135-875-8(4))* Award Pubns. Ltd. GBR. Dist: Parkwest Pubns., Inc.
Award Publications Staff & Award, Anna. A Child's Book of Prayers & Graces. 2012. (ENG., Illus.). 36p. (J). 9.95 *(978-1-84135-599-3(2))* Award Pubns. Ltd. GBR. Dist: Parkwest Pubns., Inc.
Barbour Publishing Staff & Biggers, Emily. Power Prayers for Girls. 2015. (ENG.). 224p. (J). pap. 7.99 *(978-1-63058-859-5(8))* Barbour Publishing, Inc.
Barnhill, Carla. The One Year Devotions for Preschoolers 2. Kucharik, Elena, illus. 2010. (Little Blessings Ser.). (ENG.). 384p. (J). 14.99 *(978-1-4143-3445-5(1),* Tyndale Kids) Tyndale Hse. Pubs.
Bernard, M. My First Mass Book. Date not set. (J). (gr. -1-3). pap. 1.95 *(978-0-88271-165-2(2))* Regina Pr., Malhame & Co.
Bicknell, Joanna & Page, Claire. Magnetics Make Your Own Prayers. 2007. (Magnetics Ser.). (Illus.). 14p. (J). (gr. -1-k). *(978-1-84610-466-4(1))* Make Believe Ideas.
Blum, Joyce. A to Z Promises & Prayers for Little Children. 2005. 36p. per. 19.25 *(978-1-4208-5420-6(8))* AuthorHouse.
Bowman, Crystal. The One Year Devotions for Preschoolers. Kucharik, Elena, illus. 2004. (Little Blessings Ser.). (ENG.). 384p. (J). 14.99 *(978-0-8423-8940-2(7),* Tyndale Kids) Tyndale Hse. Pubs.
Box, Su & Brown, Jo. My Rainbow Book of Bedtime Prayers. Brown, Jo & Brown, Joan, illus. 2009. (ENG.). 14p. (J). (gr. k-k). bds. 9.99 *(978-0-7459-6165-1(7))* Lion Hudson PLC GBR. Dist: Independent Pubs. Group.
—My Rainbow Book of Everyday Prayers. Brown, Jo, illus. 2009. (ENG., Illus.). 16p. (J). (gr. k-k). bds. 9.99 *(978-0-7459-6166-8(5))* Lion Hudson PLC GBR. Dist: Independent Pubs. Group.
Boyd, Annalisa. Special Agents of Christ: A Prayer Book for Young Orthodox Saints. 2012. (ENG., Illus.). 96p. (J). pap. 10.95 *(978-1-936270-55-2(2))* Ancient Faith Publishing.
Brewer, Dottie A. Praying 101 for Kids & Teens. 2004. (Illus.). 68p. (J). per. 4.95 *(978-0-9707945-2-9(5))* Billion $ Baby Pubns.
Brichto, Mira Pollak. The God Around Us Vol. 2: The Valley of Blessings. Alko, Selina, illus. 2004. 32p. (gr. -1-3). 13.95 *(978-0-8074-0738-7(0),* 101074) URJ Pr.
Britt, Stephanie. My Little Prayers, 1 vol. 2005. (ENG.). 96p. 6.99 *(978-1-4003-0648-0(5))* Nelson, Thomas Inc.
Britt, Stephanie McFetridge, illus. My First Book of Prayers. 2007. (ENG.). 32p. 3.99 *(978-0-8249-5570-0(6),* Ideal Pubns.) Worthy Publishing.
Brown, Monica & Musgrave, Hilary. Be Still & know... God Is Here: Be Still. 2011. (J). pap. *(978-0-9750732-8-5(1))* Emmaus Productions.
Brown, Rev. Joe. God's Gift, G G Brown: A True Story. 2012. 36p. pap. 24.95 *(978-1-4626-8165-5(4))* America Star Bks.
Burrin, Angela M. A Family Journey with Jesus through Lent: Prayers & Activities for Each Day. 2004. (J). pap. 13.95 *(978-1-59325-050-8(9))* Word Among Us Pr.
Bus, Sabrina. Hail Mary. Deneux, Xavier, illus. 2nd ed. 2006. (ENG.). 12p. (J). (gr. -1). 8.00 *(978-0-8028-5312-7(9),* Eerdmans Bks For Young Readers) Eerdmans, William B. Publishing Co.
Butcher, Sam, illus. Precious Moments: Angel Kisses & Snuggle Time Prayers with Dolly. 2003. 8.40 *(978-0-7180-0575-7(9))* Nelson, Thomas Inc.
—Precious Moments: Angel Kisses & Snuggle Time Prayers with Teddy Bear. 2003. 8.40 *(978-0-7180-0567-2(8))* Nelson, Thomas Inc.
Campbell, Herman. A Child's Prayer from the Heart. 2011. 24p. pap. 14.93 *(978-1-4269-5589-1(8))* Trafford Publishing.
Cannizzo, Karen, ed. Mass Prayers: For Young Catholics. 2006. (Illus.). 31p. (J). (gr. -1-2). per. 2.25 *(978-1-933178-40-0(X))* Pflaum Publishing Group.
Carr, Jacqueline. Tiny Tot Prayers: Baby's First Prayers. 2010. 24p. pap. 11.49 *(978-1-4520-2186-7(4))* AuthorHouse.
Casse-Dasilva, Christel. Little Prayers for the Children. 2012. (Illus.). 24p. pap. *(978-1-908341-96-9(3))* Paragon Publishing, Rothersthorpe.
Catholic Book Publishing Staff, creator. Thank You Prayers. 2008. (St. Joseph Rattle Board Bks.). (Illus.). 14p. (gr. -1-k). bds. 4.95 *(978-0-89942-722-5(7))* Catholic Bk. Publishing Corp.
Cavanaugh, Karen. My First Prayer Book. Luberoff, William, illus. 2007. (Catholic Classics Ser.). 32p. (J). 3.95 *(978-0-88271-216-1(0))* Regina Pr., Malhame & Co.
Chand, Candy. The Twelve Prayers of Christmas. Bernardin, James, illus. 2009. (HarperBlessings Ser.). (ENG.). 32p. (J). (gr. -1-2). 16.99 *(978-0-06-077636-7(6))* HarperCollins Pubs.
Child Evangelism Fellowship Staff, prod. The One Year Real Life Encounters with God: 365 Q & A Devotions. 2003. (ENG.). 416p. (J). pap. 14.99 *(978-0-8423-7206-0(7))* Tyndale Hse. Pubs.
Children's Bible Hour Staff. Tesoros Para Niños, Tomo 2: 365 Historias Devocionales Para Ninos y jovenes, 1 vol., 2. 2005.Tr. of Keys for Kids. (SPA.). 368p. (J). pap. 12.99 *(978-0-8254-1113-7(0),* Editorial Portavoz) Kregel Pubns.
Collins, Rachel. Soul Sprouts. 2010. 41p. pap. 18.21 *(978-0-557-35421-4(8))* Lulu Pr., Inc.
Concordia Publishing House, creator. Happy Birthday: God's Blessings to You! 2007. (Illus.). 22p. (J). (gr. -1-k). bds. 6.49 *(978-0-7586-1331-8(8))* Concordia Publishing Hse.
Concordia Publishing House Staff, contrib. by. A Child's Garden of Prayer. 2005. (Illus.). 80p. 7.99 *(978-0-7586-0785-0(7))* Concordia Publishing Hse.

Cook, Cheryl. Kids Prayer Time Series: Lord, Teach me how to pray, Lord, Teach me how to walk by faith, Lord, Teach me how to love others, Lord, Teach me how to take care of the Temple. 2006. (J). 10.99 (978-0-9746361-5-3(0)) Heavenly C. Publishing.

Cotner, June. House Blessings: Prayers, Poems, & Toasts Celebrating Home & Family. 2005. (ENG., Illus.). 164p. (gr. 8-17). 15.95 (978-0-9748486-0-0(3)) becker&mayer! books.

Dalmatian Press Staff. God Bless Me. (Timeless Treasures Ser.). (ENG.). 28p. (J). bds. 7.99 (978-1-4037-0856-4(8), Spirit Pr.) Bendon, Inc.

—My First Prayers: Happy Tale Storybook. 2005. (ENG.). 24p. (J). 2.99 (978-1-4037-1271-4(9), Spirit Pr.) Bendon, Inc.

Darcy-Bérubé, Françoise & Berube, John Paul. Growing up a Friend of Jesus: A Guide to Discipleship for Children. 2003. (Illus.). 128p. (978-2-89507-041-2(5)) Novalis Publishing.

Darens, Cat. My Bedtime Angel. Oliver, Julia, illus. 2010. 18p. (J). (gr. -1-k). 7.95 (978-0-8091-6745-6(X), Ambassador Bks.) Paulist Pr.

Dateno, Maria Grace. I Pray the Stations of the Cross. Rchards, Virginia Helen, illus. 2006. (J). 4.50 (978-0-8198-3691-5(5)) Pauline Bks. & Media.

David C. Cook Publishing Company Staff. Twenty-Third Psalm, 10 vols. 2003. (Jesus Pocket Bks.). (Illus.). 32p. (J). pap., pap. 8.90 (978-1-55513-134-0(4), 1555131344) Cook, David C.

David, Juliet. Candle Day by Day Prayers: Children's Prayers for Every Day, 1 vol. Heyes, Jane, illus. 2016. (ENG.). 160p. (J). 12.99 (978-1-78128-265-6(X), Candle Bks.) Lion Hudson PLC GBR. Dist: Kregel Pubns.

—Candle Prayers for Toddlers, 1 vol. Prole, Helen, illus. 2010. (Candle Bible for Toddlers Ser.). (ENG.). 128p. (J). 11.99 (978-1-85985-679-6(9), Candle Bks.) Lion Hudson PLC GBR. Dist: Kregel Pubns.

—Prayers for Little Girls, 1 vol. Clay, Julie, illus. 2014. 64p. (J). 12.99 (978-1-85985-990-2(9), Candle Bks.) Lion Hudson PLC GBR. Dist: Kregel Pubns.

David, Juliet & Ayliffe, Alex. My Very First Bible & Prayers, 1 vol. Prole, Helen, illus. 2014. (Candle Bible for Toddlers Ser.). (ENG.). 64p. (J). 9.99 (978-1-78128-152-9(1), Candle Bks.) Lion Hudson PLC GBR. Dist: Kregel Pubns.

DaySpring Greeting Card Staff & Jensen, Bonnie Rickner. Really Woolly Bedtime Prayers, 1 vol. 2009. (Really Woolly Ser.). (ENG.). 40p. bds. 9.99 (978-1-4003-1539-0(5)) Nelson, Thomas Inc.

Dearborn, Sabrina. The Barefoot Book of Blessings: From Many Faiths & Cultures. Whelan, Olwyn, illus. 2007. (ENG.). 40p. (J). (gr. -1-3). 18.99 (978-1-84686-069-0(5)) Barefoot Bks., Inc.

Deffenbaugh, David & McFarland, Bill. Strength for the Journey: A daily devotional Guide. Waldroop, Wista, ed. 2007. 388p. per. 15.99 (978-0-9766703-5-3(6)) Little Acorn LLC.

Derico, Laura. Prayers for a Child's Day. Allen, Joy, illus. 2003. 32p. (J). 7.99 (978-0-7847-1273-3(5), 04033) Standard Publishing.

Dobell, Steve. A Child's Book of Prayer. 2012. (ENG., Illus.). 64p. (J). (gr. 2-7). 9.99 (978-1-84322-867-7(X)) Anness Publishing GBR. Dist: National Bk. Network.

Doxey, Heidi. Tiny Talks, Vol. 14. 2013. pap. 8.99 (978-1-4621-1357-6(5), Horizon Pubs.) Cedar Fort, Inc./CFI Distribution.

D'Oyen, Fatima. Islamic Manners. Zulkifli, Azhar, illus. 2012. (ENG.). 64p. (J). (gr. -1-2). pap., act. bk. ed. 5.95 (978-0-86037-463-3(7)) Kube Publishing Ltd. GBR. Dist: Consortium Bk. Sales & Distribution.

Egbert, Elaine. Nature in a Nutshell. 2003. (Review Kids Ser.). 384p. (J). 13.99 (978-0-8280-1669-8(0)) Review & Herald Publishing Assn.

Elkins, Stephen. The Bible Prayer Collection: 30 Life Changing Prayers from the Bible for Children. Colton, Ellie, illus. 2003. 64p. (J). (gr. k-3). 9.99 incl. audio compact disk (978-0-8054-2758-5(9)) B&H Publishing Group.

—Special Times Bible Prayers for Toddlers. Reagan, Susan Joy, illus. 2004. (Special Times Ser.). 32p. (J). (gr. -1-18). 9.97 (978-0-8054-2660-1(4)) B&H Publishing Group.

—Special Times Bible Promises for Toddlers. Reagan, Susan Joy, illus. 2005. (Special Times Ser.). 32p. (J). (gr. -1-18). 9.97 (978-0-8054-2678-6(7)) B&H Publishing Group.

—Stories That End with a Prayer. Menck, Kevin, illus. 32p. (J). (gr. k-8). 12.98 (978-1-56919-003-6(8)) Wonder Workshop.

Ellis, Gwen. Our Daily Bread: Prayers, Graces, & Slices of Scripture. 2006. (ENG., Illus.). 10p. (J). (gr. -1-k). bds. 10.99 (978-0-7847-1852-0(0), B&H Kids) B&H Publishing Group.

Esquinaldo, Virginia, illus. My Book of Prayers. 2006. 48p. (J). 3.95 (978-0-8198-4843-7(3)) Pauline Bks. & Media.

Everyday Prayers for Sleepyheads. 2003. (J). (978-0-7648-0995-8(4)) Liguori Pubns.

Ficocelli, Elizabeth. Child's Guide to the Rosary. Blake, Anne Catharine, illus. 2009. (J). 10.95 (978-0-8091-6736-4(0)) Paulist Pr.

Field, Rachel. Oración para los Niños. Romay, Alexis, tr. Jones, Elizabeth Orton, illus. 2011.Tr. of Prayer for a Child. (SPA.). 32p. (J). (gr. -1-2). bds. 6.99 (978-1-4424-1350-4(6), Libros Para Ninos) Libros Para Ninos.

—Prayer for a Child. Jones, Elizabeth Orton, illus. 2005. (ENG.). 32p. (J). (gr. -1-k). bds. 7.99 (978-0-689-87886-2(9), Little Simon) Little Simon.

—Prayer for a Child. Jones, Elizabeth Orton, illus. 100th anniv. ed. 2004. (ENG.). 32p. (J). (gr. -1-2). 12.99 (978-0-689-87356-0(5), Simon & Schuster Bks. For Young Readers) Simon & Schuster Bks. For Young Readers.

—Prayer for a Child: Lap Edition. Jones, Elizabeth Orton, illus. 2013. (ENG.). 32p. (J). (gr. -1-2). bds. 12.99 (978-1-4424-7659-2(1), Little Simon) Little Simon.

Fincher, Kathy, illus. A Catholic's Baby's First Prayer Book. 2006. 16p. (gr. -1-k). bds. 9.95 (978-0-88271-706-7(5)) Regina Pr., Malhame & Co.

First Prayers. 192p. (978-1-4054-1716-7(1)) Parragon, Inc.

Flanagan, Anne. Come to Jesus: A Kids' Book for Eucharistic Adoration. Cleary, Janice, illus. 2006. (J). 4.50 (978-0-8198-1577-4(2)) Pauline Bks. & Media.

Florentine, Sister Mary & Naomi, Sister Mary. Jesus Comes: Our Holy Faith Series Book Two. Karch, Paul & Karch, Patricia, illus. 2014. (Our Holy Faith Ser.: 2). (ENG.). 96p. (J). (gr. k-6). reprint ed. 18.95 (978-0-911845-78-5(X), Neumann Pr.) TAN Bks.

Flowerpot Press Staff. A Child's Book of Prayers: Good Morning, Dear God. Paiva, Johannah Gilman, ed. 2013. (ENG., Illus.). 20p. (J). 8.99 (978-1-77093-635-5(1)) Flowerpot Children's Pr. Inc. CAN. Dist: Cardinal Pubs. Group.

Forte, Bruno & Tarzia, Antonio. My Prayers: To God with Love & Joy. 2003. (Illus.). 65p. (J). pap. 6.95 (978-0-8198-4831-4(X), 332-222) Pauline Bks. & Media.

Freedman, Claire. Candle Prayers for Kids, 1 vol. Parry, Jo, illus. 2014. (ENG.). 128p. (J). 12.99 (978-1-78128-102-4(5), Candle Bks.) Lion Hudson PLC GBR. Dist: Kregel Pubns.

—My First Book of Prayers, 1 vol. Atkins, Alison, illus. 2008. 64p. (J). 7.99 (978-0-8254-7389-0(6), Candle Bks.) Lion Hudson PLC GBR. Dist: Kregel Pubns.

Friedl, Natalie. Help Me Pray Today. 2008. (Illus.). 32p. (J). (978-0-9797429-1-0(9)) Halo Publishing International.

Friedrich, Eliza. Play Pray & Hooray. 2004. 128p. 10.99 (978-0-7586-0117-9(4)) Concordia Publishing Hse.

Frotuna, Stan, told to. U Got 2 Pray. 2004. (Illus.). 255p. (YA). per. 9.95 (978-1-931709-96-5(3)) Our Sunday Visitor, Publishing Div.

Fryar, Jane L. & Varvaris, Cathy. Jesus, Can I Talk with You? A Prayer Journal for Kids. 2003. 32p. (J). pap. 2.99 (978-0-9718985-2-3(9)) C T A, Inc.

Gameau, Jean-Yves. Bedtime Prayers. 2004. (ENG., Illus.). 104p. pap. 6.95 (978-0-8146-2890-4(7)) Liturgical Pr.

Geisler, Ruth. It's a Great, Awful, In-Between Day: Devotions for Young Readers. 2003. (Illus.). 112p. (J). (gr. 1-4). 10.99 (978-0-7586-0124-7(7)) Concordia Publishing Hse.

Goble, Paul. Song of Creation. Goble, Paul, illus. 2004. (ENG., Illus.). 32p. (J). 17.00 (978-0-8028-5271-7(8)) Eerdmans, William B. Publishing Co.

God Made 2001. 2004. (My First Prayers Ser.). 10p. (J). bds. 3.99 (978-1-85854-399-4(1)) Brimax Books Ltd. GBR. Dist: Byeway Bks.

God's Awesome Promises. Date not set. (YA). pap. 7.95 (978-0-937347-71-3(X)) C&D International.

Gomez, Elena, illus. A World of Prayers. 2006. (ENG.). 32p. (J). (gr. k). 16.00 (978-0-8028-5285-4(8), Eerdmans Bks For Young Readers) Eerdmans, William B. Publishing Co.

Grand, Dee Ann. A Child's First Prayers. 2003. (SPA & ENG.). 24p. (J). bds. 12.99 (978-0-8254-5504-9(9)) Kregel Pubns.

Groner, Judyth & Wikler, Madeline. Thank You, God! A Jewish Child's Book of Prayers. Haas, Shelly, illus. 2003. (ENG.). 32p. (J). (gr. -1-2). pap. 7.95 (978-1-58013-101-8(8), Kar-Ben Publishing) Lerner Publishing Group.

Hague, Michael. A Child's Book of Prayers. Hague, Michael, ed. 2010. (ENG., Illus.). 20p. (J). (gr. -1 — 1). bds. 7.99 (978-0-8050-9094-9(0), 9780805090949, Holt, Henry & Co. Bks. For Young Readers) Holt, Henry & Co.

Hague, Michael, ed. & illus. A Child's Book of Prayers, Set. Hague, Michael, illus. unabr. ed. 2010. (ENG.). 32p. (J). (gr. -1-k). 9.99 (978-1-4272-0991-7(X), 9781427209917) Macmillan Audio.

Hail Mary: Prayer Cards. 2004. (978-0-8294-1405-9(3)) Loyola Pr.

Hamdani, Ibrahim. Salah: The Prescribed Daily Prayers. 2003. 32p. (YA). (978-0-9769245-5-5(2)) Islamic Ctr. of Sacramento, The.

Hare, Eric B. Skyscrapers: 365 Stories That Build You up: Daily Devotions for Juniors. 2009. (J). (978-0-8280-2466-2(9)) Review & Herald Publishing Assn.

Hascall, Glenn. Power Prayers for Boys. 2015. (ENG.). 224p. (J). pap. 7.99 (978-1-63058-858-8(X)) Barbour Publishing, Inc.

Henley, Karyn. Day by Day Devotions: A Year of Character Building Devotions for Kids. 2004. (ENG.). 416p. (J). per. 13.99 (978-0-8423-7485-9(X), Tyndale Kids) Tyndale Hse. Pubs.

Henriques, S. M. My Little Book of Prayer. 2004. 160p. (gr. -1-3). pap. 6.95 (978-1-58334-034-9(3), F/S) Worthy Publishing.

Herrera, Erik, et al. Acquire the Fire: 40 Teen Devotionals, Vol. 1. Mauss, Doug, ed. 2006. (Teen Mania Ser.). (Illus.). 100p. (J). (gr. 4-7). per. 5.99 (978-0-7814-4352-4(0), 0781443520) Cook, David C.

Hess, Ingrid. Sleep in Peace. 2007. (ENG., Illus.). 40p. (J). (gr. 3-7). per. 12.99 (978-0-8361-9381-7(4)) Herald Pr.

—Walk in Peace. 2009. (ENG.). 44p. (J). (gr. -1-k). pap. 13.99 (978-0-8361-9469-2(1)) Herald Pr.

Hill, Karen. All God's Creatures. Fancher, Lou & Johnson, Steve, illus. 2005. (ENG.). 14p. (J). (gr. -1 — 1). 9.99 (978-0-689-87819-0(2), Little Simon) Little Simon.

Hoagland, Victor. The Illustrated Rosary for Children. 2006. (Catholic Classics Ser.). (Illus.). 32p. (J). 3.95 (978-0-88271-215-4(2)) Regina Pr., Malhame & Co.

Hodgson, Joan. Our Father. Ripper, Peter, illus. 2003. 24p. (gr. k-7). 5.95 (978-0-85487-040-0(7)) White Eagle Publishing Trust GBR. Dist: DeVorss & Co.

Holl, Kristi. What's a Girl to Do? Finding Faith in Everyday Life, 1 vol. 2007. (Faithgirlz Ser.). (ENG.). 192p. (J). (gr. 3-7). pap. 9.99 (978-0-310-71348-7(X)) Zonderkidz.

The Holy Sacrifice of the Mass. (J). 7.00 (978-1-931555-29-6(X)) Our Lady of Victory Schl.

Hopkins, Lee Bennett & Moore, Gigi. Hear My Prayer, 1 vol. 2011. (ENG.). 32p. (J). (gr. -1-2). 12.99 (978-0-310-71811-6(2)) Zonderkidz.

Horwitz, Brad, ed. & tr. With All Your Heart (A Weekday Prayer Book) Horwitz, Brad, tr. 80p. (J). 14.95 (978-1-58013-144-5(1), Kar-Ben Publishing) Lerner Publishing Group.

Hudson, Cheryl Willis. Come by Here Lord: Everyday Prayers for Children. 2004. (Illus.). 32p. (J). (gr. 2). 10.95 (978-0-940975-92-7(0), Sankofa Bks.) Just Us Bks., Inc.

Hudson, Lauriece. Prayers for the Smallest Hands. 2008. (Illus.). 24p. (J). (gr. -1-3). 6.95 (978-1-60349-003-0(5), Marimba Bks.) Hudson Publishing Group, The.

Ippolito, Eva Marie. Hear, O Lord. Ippolito, Eva Marie, ed. l.t. ed. 2009. (Illus.). 72p. (YA). (gr. 7-12). pap. 13.69 (978-1-4389-2422-9(4)) AuthorHouse.

Jeep, Elizabeth McMahon. Blessings & Prayers through the Year: A Resource for School & Parish. 2004. (J). 49.95 incl. audio compact disk (978-1-56854-369-7(7), CLASS) Liturgy Training Pubns.

—Children's Daily Prayer 2005 - 2006. 2005. (J). pap. 16.00 (978-1-56854-538-7(X), CDP06) Liturgy Training Pubns.

John Paul II, Pope, pseud. My Dear Young Friends: Pope John Paul II Speaks to Youth on Life, Love, & Courage. Vitek, John, ed. 2003. (Illus.). 144p. (YA). pap., pap. 9.95 (978-0-88489-748-4(6)) St. Mary's Pr. of MN.

Johnson, Kevin. Total Devotion: 365 Days to Hang Tight with Jesus. 2004. (ENG.). 374p. (YA). reprint ed. pap. 16.00 (978-0-7642-2884-1(6)) Bethany Hse. Pubs.

Johnson, Lois Walfrid. Burnt Cookies. 2006. 96p. (J). pap. 6.99 (978-0-7847-1510-9(6), 42180) Standard Publishing.

Kennedy, Pamela. Prayers at Eastertime. Britt, Stephanie, illus. 2009. (ENG.). 24p. (J). 8.99 (978-0-8249-5609-7(5), Ideal Pubns.) Worthy Publishing.

Kid, Penelope. Teach Me to Pray. Goffe, Toni, illus. 2004. (Teach Me Ser.). 24p. (gr. -1-2). 6.95 (978-0-8294-1368-7(5)) Loyola Pr.

Knox, Lorna Ann. I Came from Joy: Spiritual Affirmations & Activities for Children. 2nd rev. ed. 2004. (ENG., Illus.). 172p. (gr. k-7). pap. 19.95 (978-1-56589-146-3(5)) Crystal Clarity Pubs.

Kowalski, Gary A. Earth Day: An Alphabet Book. Baviera, Rocco, illus. 2009. (ENG.). 32p. (J). (gr. -1-4). 12.00 (978-1-55896-542-3(4), 1297770, Skinner Hse. Bks.) Unitarian Universalist Assn.

Larkin, Jean, ed. Prayers & Guidelines for Young Catholics. 2003. (Illus.). 28p. pap. 1.95 (978-0-89837-231-1(3), 4658) Pflaum Publishing Group.

Larsen, Carolyn. Prayers for Little Boys. Turk, Caron, illus. 2008. (Prayers For... Ser.). 131p. (J). (gr. -1-3). (978-1-86920-527-0(8)) Christian Art Pubs.

—Prayers for Little Girls. Turk, Caron, illus. 2008. (Prayers For... Ser.). 131p. (J). (gr. -1-3). (978-1-86920-526-3(X)) Christian Art Pubs.

Lee, Helen. Where in the World? Stories from Everywhere: Daily Devotions for Juniors. 2006. 373p. (J). (978-0-8280-1874-6(X)) Review & Herald Publishing Assn.

Legacy Press Staff. Gotta Have God: Devotions for Boys. 2004. (Gotta Have God Ser.). (Illus.). 238p. (J). (gr. -1-k). spiral bd. 12.99 (978-1-885358-96-7(2)); (gr. 1-4). spiral bd. 12.99 (978-1-885358-97-4(0)) Rainbow Pubs. & Legacy Pr. (Legacy Pr.).

Levivier, Juliette. Prayers Around the Crib. Gravier, Anne, illus. 2012. (ENG.). 46p. (J). (gr. -1-3). 9.99 (978-1-58617-773-7(7)) Ignatius Pr.

Lewis, Jan. Baby's First Book of Prayers. 2013. (ENG., Illus.). 24p. (J). (gr. -1-12). bds. 6.99 (978-1-86147-340-0(0), Armadillo) Anness Publishing GBR. Dist: National Bk. Network.

Little Folded Hands: Prayers for Childre. 2005. pap. 8.95 (978-1-59605-640-4(1), Cosimo Classics) Cosimo, Inc.

Little Treasury Sac Heart. 15p. pap. (978-0-8198-4461-3(6), 332-164) Pauline Bks. & Media.

Living Out Christ's Love Prayer Journals, 12 vols. 2005. (YA). 9.95 (978-0-9772313-2-4(1)) The 101 Group, Inc.

Living the Good News Staff. Kids in Common: A Children's Book of Common Prayer. 2004. (Illus.). 32p. (J). 4.95 (978-1-931960-29-8(1), Living the Good News) Church Publishing, Inc.

Lonsdale, Mary, illus. My Prayers for Everyday. 2004. 10p. (J). bds. 7.99 (978-1-85854-438-0(6)) Brimax Books Ltd. GBR. Dist: Byeway Bks.

The Lord's Prayer: Forgive Us. 2003. (Illus.). 50p. (J). pap. 6.00 (978-1-58572-052-1(6)) Ambassador Pubns.

Lords Prayer for Children. 2006. 10p. (YA). bds. 11.99 (978-0-7847-1772-1(9), 04724) Standard Publishing.

Lucado, Max & Lucado, Denalyn. Lucado Treasury of Bedtime Prayers: Prayers for Bedtime & Every Time of Day!, 1 vol. 2015. (ENG., Illus.). 160p. (J). 19.99 (978-0-7180-1631-9(9)) Nelson, Thomas Inc.

Lyttle, Marcy. Catching Fireflies: Family Night Devotional Fun. Irwin, Kendra, illus. 2007. 273p. 12.99 (978-1-932307-77-1(X), Ambassador International) Emerald Hse. Group, Inc.

Make Believe Ideas, Ltd. Build Your Own Prayers: Magnetic Prayer Book. 2007. (Illus.). 14p. (J). (gr. k-3). 12.95 (978-1-59145-554-7(5)) Nelson, Thomas Inc.

Manhardt, Laurie Watson. Friends of God: Catholic Bible Study for Children. Co, Aileen & Dayton, Melissa, illus. 2006. (Come & See Kids Ser.). 124p. (J). (gr. -1-2). per. 9.95 (978-1-931018-41-8(3)) Emmaus Road Publishing.

Martin, Carolyn. Book of Childhood Prayers. (Illus.). 63p. (J). (978-0-340-56763-0(5)) Hodder & Stoughton.

Mass, Wendy. Autumn: Poems, Songs, Prayers. 2004. (Weather Windows Ser.). 4.99 (978-0-570-07168-6(2)) Concordia Publishing Hse.

McEntee, Sean & Breen, Michael, eds. The Columba Lectionary for Masses with Children Year C. 2010. (ENG.). 186p. pap. 44.95 (978-1-85607-676-0(8)) Columba Pr. IRL. Dist: Dufour Editions, Inc.

Medina, Sarah. A Day to Remember. Brecknell, Annie, illus. 48p. pap. 8.99 (978-0-7459-4770-9(0), Lion Books) Lion Hudson PLC GBR. Dist: Trafalgar Square Publishing.

Mercer, Gabrielle. Prayers for Boys. 2012. bds. 6.99 (978-1-78065-845-2(1)) Make Believe Ideas GBR. Dist: Nelson, Thomas Inc.

—Prayers for Girls. 2012. bds. 6.99 (978-1-78065-745-5(5)) Make Believe Ideas GBR. Dist: Nelson, Thomas Inc.

Miller, Woody, illus. Tefilat Haderech: The Traveler's Prayer. 2012. (ENG.). 32p. (J). 17.95 (978-0-939144-69-3(7)) EKS Publishing Co.

—Tefilat Haderech: The Traveler's Pryaer. 2012. (ENG.). 32p. (J). pap. 10.95 (978-0-939144-68-6(9)) EKS Publishing Co.

Mundy, Michaelene. A Book of Prayers for All Your Cares. Alley, R. W., illus. 2004. (J). per. 7.95 (978-0-87029-382-5(6)) Abbey Pr.

My First Prayer Book. (Prayer Book Ser.). 9p. (978-1-4075-0359-2(6)) Parragon, Inc.

My Little Book of Prayers. 2008. (Deluxe Charm Book Ser.). 12p. (978-1-4075-3329-2(0)) Parragon, Inc.

Myers, Walter Dean. The Gifts We Bring. Date not set. 96p. (J). (gr. 3-7). 5. 14.99 (978-0-06-027809-0(9))No. 6. 14.99 (978-0-06-027810-6(2)) HarperCollins Pubs.

Oberthür, Rainer. Our Father. Nascimbeni, Barbara, illus. 2016. (ENG.). 58p. (J). 16.00 (978-0-8028-5468-1(0), Eerdmans Bks For Young Readers) Eerdmans, William B. Publishing Co.

Obunge, Adesola. Conversations with God for 5 to 10 Year Olds: Hidden Treasure for Little Minds(r). 2011. (Illus.). 68p. pap. 35.11 (978-1-4490-5382-6(3)) AuthorHouse.

O'Loughlin, Declan & McKenna, Donna, eds. Fone a Friend: A Prayer Book by Children for Children. 2010. (ENG.). 47p. (J). pap. 12.95 (978-1-84730-197-0(5)) Veritas Pubns. IRL. Dist: Dufour Editions, Inc.

Omartian, Stormie. The Prayer That Makes God Smile. Warren, Shari, illus. 2009. (Power of a Praying Kid Ser.). (ENG.). 32p. (J). 14.99 (978-0-7369-2314-9(4)) Harvest Hse. Pubs.

Page, Josephine. Thank You Prayer. Church, Caroline Jayne, illus. 2005. (ENG.). 24p. (J). (gr. -1-k). 8.99 (978-0-439-68099-8(9), Cartwheel Bks.) Scholastic, Inc.

Paltro, Piera. Learning My Prayers, 8 bks. Daughters of St. Paul Staff, tr. Curti, Anna M., illus. Incl. Angel of God. 16p. (gr. k-3). 1981. pap. 2.95 (978-0-8198-0739-7(7), CH0031P); Eternal Rest: A Prayer for People Who Have Died. 15p. (gr. k-3). 1992. pap. 2.50 (978-0-8198-2332-8(5)); Glory to the Father. 21p. (gr. -1-18). 1987. pap. 2.50 (978-0-8198-3043-2(7), CH0227); Hail, Holy Queen. 15p. (gr. k-3). 1992. pap. 2.50 (978-0-8198-3365-5(7)); Hail Mary. 22p. (gr. k-3). 1992. pap. 2.50 (978-0-8198-3316-7(9)); I Believe: The Profession of Faith or Creed. 29p. (gr. k-3). 1992. pap. 2.50 (978-0-8198-3664-9(8)); My Mass. 32p. (gr. k-3). 1992. pap. 2.50 (978-0-8198-4765-2(8)); Our Father. 23p. (gr. -1-1). 1991. pap. 2.95 (978-0-8198-5416-2(6), CH0416P); (J). (Illus.). Set pap. 18.80 (978-0-8198-4483-5(7)) Pauline Bks. & Media.

Pasquali, Elena. Safe This Night: A Book of Bedtime Prayers. Kolanovic, Dubravka, illus. 2013. (ENG.). 64p. (J). (gr. k-2). 12.99 (978-0-7459-6378-5(1)) Lion Hudson PLC GBR. Dist: Independent Pubs. Group.

Paterson, Katherine. Giving Thanks: Poems, Prayers, & Praise Songs of Thanksgiving. Dalton, Pamela, illus. 2013. (ENG.). 56p. (J). (gr. k-17). 18.99 (978-1-4521-1339-5(4)) Chronicle Bks. LLC.

Peralas, Jorge. Oracional Bilingue Para Ninos: A Children's Prayerbook in Spanish-English. Domeier, Renee & Grisewood, Therese U., eds. 2012. (ENG & SPA., Illus.). 96p. (gr. 3-7). pap. 9.95 (978-0-8146-2459-3(6)) Liturgical Pr.

Perseghetti, Jackie & Perseghetti, Jonie. Faith Factor OT: Thru-the-Bible Devotions. 2007. (ENG., Illus.). 384p. (YA). (gr. 3-7). per. 16.99 (978-0-7814-4458-3(6)) Cook, David C.

Peterson, Mary Joseph. Holy Mass in My Pocket. 2008. (Illus.). 32p. (J). 1.95 (978-0-8198-3392-1(4)) Pauline Bks. & Media.

—Rosary in My Pocket. 2008. (Illus.). 32p. (J). 1.95 (978-0-8198-6485-7(4)) Pauline Bks. & Media.

Peterson, Mary Joseph, illus. Basic Prayers in My Pocket. 2009. 32p. (J). pap. 1.95 (978-0-8198-1173-8(4)) Pauline Bks. & Media.

Piper, Sophie. An Arkful of Animal Prayers. Macnaughton, Tina, illus. 2009. (ENG.). 64p. (J). (gr. -1-2). 9.95 (978-0-7459-6064-7(2)) Lion Hudson PLC GBR. Dist: Independent Pubs. Group.

—Goodnight Prayers. Moriuchi, Mique, illus. 2009. (ENG.). 64p. (J). (gr. -1-k). 9.99 (978-0-7459-6065-4(0)) Lion Hudson PLC GBR. Dist: Independent Pubs. Group.

—The Lion Book of Prayers to Read & Know. Lewis, Anthony, illus. 2010. (ENG.). 96p. (J). (gr. k-2). 12.99 (978-0-7459-6147-7(9)) Lion Hudson PLC GBR. Dist: Independent Pubs. Group.

—My Baptism Book. Kolanovic, Dubravka, illus. 2007. (ENG.). 64p. (J). (gr. -1-1). 14.95 (978-1-55725-535-8(0)) Paraclete Pr., Inc.

—My Guardian Angel. Rescek, Sanja, illus. 2014. (ENG.). 48p. (J). (gr. -1-k). 9.99 (978-0-7459-6397-6(8)) Lion Hudson PLC GBR. Dist: Independent Pubs. Group.

—Prayers for Each & Every Day. Wilson, Anne, illus. 2008. (ENG.). 64p. (J). (gr. -1-2). 14.95 (978-1-55725-622-5(5)) Paraclete Pr., Inc.

Piper, Sophie, et al. God Bless. 2nd ed. 2013. (Prayers for Little Hands Ser.). (ENG., Illus.). 8p. (J). (— 1). 8.99 (978-0-7459-6375-4(7)) Lion Hudson PLC GBR. Dist: Independent Pubs. Group.

Poser, Cynthia M. Hotline to Heaven. 2012. pap. 8.95 (978-0-7414-7624-1(X)) Infinity Publishing.

—Hotline to Heaven - Color. 2012. pap. 11.95 (978-0-7414-7625-8(8)) Infinity Publishing.

Prayers for Sleepyheads, Set. 2003. (J). pap. 10.95 net. (978-0-7648-0994-1(6)) Liguori Pubns.

Prayers of Jesus for Children. (J). (978-0-88271-162-1(8)) Regina Pr., Malhame & Co.

Prayers That Avail Much for Teens. (YA). 14.99 (978-0-89274-902-7(4)) Harrison House Pubs.

Promiseland. 2008. (J). per. 8.00 (978-0-9664736-0-5(4)) Grace Walk Resources, LLC.

Publications International Ltd. Staff, ed. My Little Prayer Book. 2010. 384p. 10.98 (978-1-60553-972-0(4)) Publications International, Ltd.

—My Little Treasury: First Prayers & Blessings. 2014. 160p. (J). bds. (978-1-4508-7299-7(9), 1450872999) Publications International, Ltd.

Randazzo, Dottie. Praying 101 for Kids & Teens. 2007. 101p. pap. 10.95 (978-0-615-14725-3(9)) Creative Dreaming Ltd.

Reeves, Eira. El Padre Nuestro (The Lord's Prayer) (SPA.). (J). 1.89 (978-0-7899-0480-5(2), 498667) Editorial Unilit.

Richmond, Marianne. Bedtime Blessings. 2017. (ENG.). 24p. (J). bds. 8.99 (978-1-4926-4183-4(9), 9781492641834, Sourcebooks Jabberwocky) Sourcebooks, Inc.

Roche, Maite. My First Bedtime Prayers. 2011. (ENG., Illus.). 14p. (gr. -1). bds. 6.99 (978-1-58617-503-0(3)) Ignatius Pr.

Rock, Lois. Al Final del Dia. Rawlings, Louise, illus. (Coleccion Luz de Noche). (SPA.). (J). (gr. k-3). (978-84-236-5039-2(1)) Edebé ESP. Dist: Lectorum Pubns., Inc.

—A Child's First Book of Prayers. Jay, Alison, illus. 2012. (ENG.). 224p. (J). (gr. k-2). 12.99 (978-0-7459-6474-6(4)) Lion Hudson PLC GBR. Dist: Independent Pubs. Group.

—A Gift for Baby's Christening. Rescek, Sanja, illus. 2014. (ENG.). 48p. (J). (— 1). 9.99 (978-0-7459-6490-4(7)) Lion Hudson PLC GBR. Dist: Independent Pubs. Group.

—A Gift for Baby's Dedication. Rescek, Sanja, illus. 2014. (ENG.). 48p. (J). (— 1). 9.99 (978-0-7459-6491-1(5)) Lion Hudson PLC GBR. Dist: Independent Pubs. Group.

—Goodnight. 2nd ed. 2013. (Prayers for Little Hands Ser.). (ENG., Illus.). 8p. (J). (— 1). 8.99 (978-0-7459-6376-1(5)) Lion Hudson PLC GBR. Dist: Independent Pubs. Group.

—Here I Am. Widdowson, Kay, illus. 2nd ed. 2013. (Prayers for Little Hands Ser.). (ENG.). 8p. (J). (— 1). 8.99 (978-0-7459-6374-7(9)) Lion Hudson PLC GBR. Dist: Independent Pubs. Group.

—The Lion Book of Prayers to Keep for Ever. Allsopp, Sophie, illus. 2016. (ENG.). 64p. (J). (gr. 2-4). 9.99 (978-0-7459-7641-9(7)) Lion Hudson PLC GBR. Dist: Independent Pubs. Group.

—The Lord's Prayer: And Other Classic Prayers for Children. Allsopp, Sophie, illus. 2014. (ENG.). 32p. (J). (gr. k-2). 6.99 (978-0-7459-6322-8(6)) Lion Hudson PLC GBR. Dist: Independent Pubs. Group.

—My Very First Bible & Prayers, 2 vols. Ayliffe, Alex, illus. 2013. (My Very First Ser.). (ENG.). 416p. (J). (gr. -1-k). 12.99 (978-0-7459-6186-6(X)) Lion Hudson PLC GBR. Dist: Independent Pubs. Group.

—Our Father: And Other Classic Prayers for Children. Allsopp, Sophie, illus. 2010. (ENG.). 32p. (J). (gr. k-2). 12.99 (978-0-7459-6152-1(5)) Lion Hudson PLC GBR. Dist: Independent Pubs. Group.

—Prayers for Your Confirmation. Firmin, Hannah, illus. 2007. (ENG.). 48p. (J). (gr. 4). 9.95 (978-0-7459-6045-6(6)) Lion Hudson PLC GBR. Dist: Independent Pubs. Group.

—Thank You, God. Widdowson, Kay, illus. 2nd ed. 2013. (Prayers for Little Hands Ser.). (ENG.). 8p. (J). (— 1). 8.99 (978-0-7459-6377-8(3)) Lion Hudson PLC GBR. Dist: Independent Pubs. Group.

—Todos los Dias Contigo. Rawlings, Louise, illus. (Coleccion Luz de Noche). (SPA.). (J). (gr. k-3). (978-84-236-4916-7(4)) Edebé ESP. Dist: Lectorum Pubns., Inc.

Ronald, Sister Mary, et al. God's Truths Help Us Live. 2014. (Our Holy Faith Ser.: 3). (ENG., Illus.). 288p. (J). (gr. k-4). reprint ed. 19.95 (978-0-911845-79-2(8), Neumann Pr.) TAN Bks.

Rylant, Cynthia. Give Me Grace: A Child's Daybook of Prayers. Rylant, Cynthia, illus. 2005. (ENG., Illus.). 32p. (J). (gr. -1-k). bds. 7.99 (978-0-689-87885-5(0), Little Simon) Little Simon.

Sabado, Joe, illus. Mommy Teach Us to Pray. Fujii, Jason, photos by. l.t. ed. 2006. 31p. (J). 15.95 (978-1-59879-122-8(2)) Lifevest Publishing, Inc.

Savary, Louis M. Rosary for Children. Date not set. (J). (gr. -1-3). pap. 1.25 (978-0-88271-158-4(X)) Regina Pr., Malhame & Co.

—Way of the Cross. Date not set. (J). (gr. -1-3). pap. 1.95 (978-0-88271-160-7(1)) Regina Pr., Malhame & Co.

Sheeran, Beth. A Child's Book of Prayer. 2005. (ENG.). 90p. pap. 14.00 (978-0-7343-0615-9(6), Penguin Global) Penguin Publishing Group.

Shenton, Tim. Readings from James: Trials + Faith + Riches + Prayer. 2005. (Daily Readings From Ser.). (Illus.). 68p. (J). pap. 6.50 (978-1-903087-61-9(9)) DayOne Pubns. GBR. Dist: Send The Light Distribution LLC.

Simon, Mary Manz. My First Read & Learn Book of Prayers. Duendes Del Sur Staff, illus. 2007. (Little Shepherd Book Ser.). (ENG.). 40p. (J). (gr. -1-k). bds. 9.99 (978-0-439-90632-6(6)) Scholastic, Inc.

Spafford, Suzy, illus. My Little Book of Prayers. gif. ed. 2005. 32p. 9.99 (978-0-7369-1495-6(1)) Harvest Hse. Pubs.

SPCK. I Can Join in Common Worship: A Children's Communion Book. 2003. (Illus.). 24p. 5.00 (978-0-281-05568-5(8)) SPCK Publishing GBR. Dist: Pilgrim Pr., The/United Church Pr.

St. John, Patricia. Talking & Listening to God. 2004. (ENG., Illus.). 128p. (J). pap. 6.99 (978-1-85792-840-2(7), Christian Focus) Christian Focus Pubns. GBR. Dist: Send The Light Distribution LLC.

Stephanie Longfoot Staff. God Bless 2001. 2004. (My First Prayers Ser.). 10p. (J). bds. 3.99 (978-1-85854-403-8(3)) Brimax Books Ltd. GBR. Dist: Byeway Bks.

Strauss, Ed. Devotions to Make You Smarter, 1 vol. 2007. (2:52 Ser.). (ENG., Illus.). 192p. (J). (gr. 3-7). pap. 9.99 (978-0-310-71312-8(9)) Zonderkidz.

—Devotions to Take You Deeper, 1 vol. 2007. (2:52 Ser.). (ENG.). 192p. (J). (gr. 4-7). pap. 9.99 (978-0-310-71313-5(7)) Zonderkidz.

Strong, Cynda. Where Do Angels Sleep? Denos, Julia, illus. 2007. 24p. (J). (gr. -1-3). 14.99 (978-0-7586-1298-4(2)) Concordia Publishing Hse.

Stuckey, Denise. Jesus, I Feel Close to You. Saroff, Phyllis, illus. 2005. 32p. (J). 10.95 (978-0-8091-6718-0(2), 6718-2) Paulist Pr.

Suzanne, Rentz. Daughters of Heaven Devotional. 2004. pap. 12.99 (978-1-57794-560-4(3)) Harrison House Pubs.

Swamp, Jake. Giving Thanks: A Native American Good Morning Message. braille ed. 2004. (Illus.). (J). (gr. k-3). spiral bd. (978-0-616-03096-7(7)) Canadian National Institute for the Blind/Institut National Canadien pour les Aveugles.

Swarner, Kristina, illus. The Bedtime Sh'ma: A Good Night Book. 2007. (ENG & HEB.). 40p. (J). 17.95 (978-0-939144-55-6(7)); pap. 10.95 (978-0-939144-54-9(9)) EKS Publishing Co.

—The BEDTIME SH'MA, Book & CD Set. 2007. (ENG & HEB.). 40p. (J). 24.95 incl. audio compact disk (978-0-939144-58-7(1)) EKS Publishing Co.

—Modeh Ani: A Good Morning Book. 2010. 32p. (J). (HEB.). 17.95 (978-0-939144-64-8(6)); pap. 10.95 (978-0-939144-63-1(8)) EKS Publishing Co.

Talaro, Theresa. Mommy Teach Us to Pray. l.t. ed. 2006. (Illus.). 31p. (J). (gr. -1-5). per. 12.95 (978-1-59879-121-1(4)) Lifevest Publishing, Inc.

—A Mother's Prayer: A Life Changing Prayer for Children. Castulo Aten, Vicky Talaro & Ikaia Aten, Dayle Marc, illus. French, Peter, photos by. 2007. 44p. (J). 23.99 (978-1-59879-335-2(7), Lifevest) Lifevest Publishing, Inc.

Taylor, Caroline. All Things Bright & Beautiful. Longfoot, Stephanie, illus. 2004. (My First Prayers Ser.). 10p. (J). bds. 3.99 (978-1-85854-238-6(3)) Brimax Books Ltd. GBR. Dist: Byeway Bks.

—All Things Wise & Wonderful. Longfoot, Stephanie, illus. 2004. (My First Prayers Ser.). 10p. (J). bds. 3.99 (978-1-85854-239-3(1)) Brimax Books Ltd. GBR. Dist: Byeway Bks.

The Prayer Children. Whispers in God's Ears. 2003. (Illus.). 82p. (J). per. 12.95 (978-0-87029-377-1(X)) Abbey Pr.

Thomas Nelson Publishing Staff. Precious Moments: God Watches over Me: Prayers & Thoughts from Me to God, 1 vol. 2015. (ENG.). 32p. (J). bds. 9.99 (978-0-7180-1108-6(2)) Nelson, Thomas Inc.

Thomas, Scott. Prayers & Pledges. 2010. 24p. pap. 12.99 (978-0-9824931-9-9(3)) Faithful Life Pubs.

Toulmin, Sarah. Baby's Little Bible & Prayers, 2 vols. Stephenson, Kristina, illus. 2011. (ENG.). 224p. (J). (gr. k — 1). pap. 19.99 (978-0-7459-6039-5(1)) Lion Hudson PLC GBR. Dist: Independent Pubs. Group.

—Baby's Tiny Bible & Prayers, 2 vols., Set. Stephenson, Kristina, illus. 2013. (ENG.). 224p. (J). (— 1). 14.99 (978-0-7459-6205-4(X)) Lion Hudson PLC GBR. Dist: Independent Pubs. Group.

Trumpet Of God Ministries. E I I Children's Prayers from the Heart. 2012. (Illus.). 28p. pap. 13.99 (978-1-4497-5478-5(3), WestBow Pr.) Author Solutions, Inc.

Tucker, Terra. Daughter of the King: Daughter of the King: Book with Audio CD. Marsee, Kimberly, illus. 2007. 48p. (J). 19.95 (978-0-9794578-0-7(7)) Tucker, Terra.

Veritas. Children's Everyday Prayer Book. 2008. (ENG., Illus.). 32p. (J). pap. 9.95 (978-1-84730-060-7(X)) Veritas Pubns. IRL. Dist: Dufour Editions, Inc.

Walsh, Sheila. Goodnight Warrior: Bedtime Bible Stories, Devotions, & Prayers, 1 vol. 2008. (God's Mighty Warrior Ser.). (ENG., Illus.). 336p. 16.99 (978-1-4003-1298-6(1)) Nelson, Thomas Inc.

—Sweet Dreams Princess: God's Little Princess Bedtime Bible Stories, Devotions, & Prayers, 1 vol. 2008. (ENG.). 336p. 17.99 (978-1-4003-1297-9(3)) Nelson, Thomas Inc.

Watson, Carol. 365 Children's Prayers: Prayers Old & New for Today & Every Day. 2016. (ENG.). 160p. (J). 14.99 (978-1-4347-1017-8(3)) Cook, David C.

Watson Manhardt, Laurie. In the Beginning: Catholic Bible Study for Children. Aileen Co & Dayton, Melissa, illus. 2008. (Come & See Kids Ser.). 108p. (J). (gr. -1-2). per. 9.95 (978-1-931018-42-5(1)) Emmaus Road Publishing.

Wells, Aurora. Prayers That Bring Deliverance for Teens. 2013. 92p. pap. 10.99 (978-1-62419-669-0(1)) Salem Author Services.

Weston Woods Staff, creator. Giving Thanks. 2011. 18.95 (978-0-439-72673-3(5)); 29.95 (978-0-439-73469-1(X)); 38.75 (978-0-439-72676-4(X)) Weston Woods Studios, Inc.

Widenhouse, Kathy. The Un-Bunny Book. 2004. (Illus.). 168p. (J). pap. 14.99 (978-1-58411-028-6(7), Legacy Pr.) Rainbow Pubs. & Legacy Pr.

Wigger, J. Bradley. Thank You, God. Jago, illus. 2014. (ENG.). 26p. (J). 16.00 (978-0-8028-5424-7(9), Eerdmans Bks For Young Readers) Eerdmans, William B. Publishing Co.

Wiley, Patricia Ann, creator. Time to Change: A Daily Devotinoal. 2nd ed. 2004. Orig. Title: It's Time to Change. (YA). per. 10.00 (978-0-9760734-0-6(4)) Pouring the Oil: Poetic Praise Pubns.

Wilkinson, Bruce & Suggs, Robb. The Prayer of Jabez for Young Hearts. Martinez, Sergio, illus. 2004. 32p. (J). (gr. -1-3). 15.99 (978-0-8499-7932-3(3)) Nelson, Thomas Inc.

Will, Julianne, ed. Catholic Prayer Book for Children. 2004. (J). pap. 3.95 (978-1-59276-047-3(3)); per. 10.95 (978-1-59276-046-6(5)) Our Sunday Visitor, Publishing Div.

William H. Sadlier, Inc Staff, contrib. by. We Believe & Pray: Prayers & Practices for Young Catholics. 2008. 64p. (J). pap. (978-0-8215-5700-6(9)) Sadlier, William H. Inc.

Winter, David. Espresso Prayers: Perfect Shots for Any Time of Day. 2009. (ENG.). 96p. pap. 6.95 (978-0-7459-5311-3(5)) Lion Hudson PLC GBR. Dist: Independent Pubs. Group.

Wright, Sally Ann. A Child's Book of Prayers. Ayres, Honor, illus. 2009. 96p. (J). (gr. -1). 10.99 (978-0-7586-1662-3(7)) Concordia Publishing Hse.

Yaconelli, Mark. Wonder, Fear, & Longing: A Book of Prayers, 1 vol. 2009. (ENG.). 176p. (YA). pap. 9.99 (978-0-310-28360-7(4)) Zondervan.

Young, Jeanna & Johnson, Jacqueline Kinney. Princess Prayers, 1 vol. Aranda, Omar, illus. 2017. (Princess Parables Ser.). (ENG.). 30p. (J). bds. 9.99 (978-0-310-75869-3(6)) Zonderkidz.

Ytreeide, Arnold. Tabitha's Travels: A Family Story for Advent, 1 vol. 2010. (Illus.). 160p. (J). (gr. 7-18). pap. 15.99 (978-0-8254-4172-1(2)) Kregel Pubns.

PRAYING MANTIS

Borgert-Spaniol, Megan. Praying Mantises. 2016. (Creepy Crawlies Ser.). (ENG., Illus.). 24p. (J). (gr. k-3). lib. bdg. 25.95 (978-1-62617-300-2(1)) Bellwether Media.

Goldish, Meish. Deadly Praying Mantises. 2008. (No Backbone! Ser.). (Illus.). 24p. (J). (gr. k-3). lib. bdg. 21.28 (978-1-59716-582-2(4)) Bearport Publishing Co., Inc.

Hesper, Sam. Praying Mantises, 1 vol. 2015. (ENG.). 24p. (J). lib. bdg. 23.60 (978-1-4777-5771-0(6), PowerKids Pr.) Rosen Publishing Group, Inc., The.

Hipp, Andrew. The Life Cycle of a Praying Mantis. 2009. (Life Cycles Library). 24p. (gr. 3-4). 42.50 (978-1-60853-993-2(8), PowerKids Pr.) Rosen Publishing Group, Inc., The.

Hudak, Heather C. Praying Mantises. 2008. (World of Wonder Ser.). (Illus.). 24p. (J). (gr. k-3). pap. 8.95 (978-1-59036-873-2(8)); lib. bdg. 24.45 (978-1-59036-872-5(X)) Weigl Pubs., Inc.

Klepeis, Alicia Z. Praying Mantis vs. Giant Hornet: Battle of the Powerful Predators. 2016. (Bug Wars Ser.). (ENG., Illus.). 32p. (gr. 3-4). lib. bdg. 27.99 (978-1-4914-8067-0(X), Edge Bks.) Capstone Press of Coughlan Cos.

Macheske, Felicia. Lanky Legs. 2016. (Guess What Ser.). (ENG., Illus.). 24p. (J). (gr. k-2). 28.50 (978-1-63470-720-6(6), 207591) Cherry Lake Publishing.

Markle, Sandra. Praying Mantises. 2008. pap. 52.95 (978-1-58013-285-5(5)) Lerner Publishing Group.

—Praying Mantises: Hungry Insect Heroes. 2008. (Insect World Ser.). (ENG., Illus.). 48p. (gr. 4-8). lib. bdg. 27.93 (978-0-8225-7300-5(8), Lerner Pubns.) Lerner Publishing Group.

Meisel, Paul. My Awesome Summer. 2017. (ENG., Illus.). 40p. (J). (gr. -1-3). 16.95 (978-0-8234-3671-2(3)) Holiday Hse., Inc.

Orr, Tamra. Praying Mantis. 2015. (21st Century Junior Library: Creepy Crawly Critters Ser.). (ENG., Illus.). 24p. (J). (gr. k-3). 27.07 (978-1-63362-593-8(1), 206556) Cherry Lake Publishing.

Roza, Greg. Mysterious Mantises. 2011. (World of Bugs Ser.). (Illus.). 24p. (gr. k-2). 69.20 (978-1-4339-6143-4(1)); (J). (gr. -1-2). lib. bdg. 22.60 (978-1-4339-4603-5(3)); (J). (gr. k-2). pap. 8.15 (978-1-4339-4604-2(1)) Stevens, Gareth Publishing LLLP.

Sexton, Colleen. Praying Mantises. 2007. (World of Insects Ser.). (ENG., Illus.). 24p. (J). (gr. k-3). lib. bdg. 25.95 (978-1-60014-053-2(X)) Bellwether Media.

PREACHERS

see Clergy

PRECIOUS METALS

see also Gold; Silver

McDonnell, Julia. How Precious Metals Form. 2016. (From the Earth: How Resources Are Made Ser.). (Illus.). 32p. (J). (gr. 4-3). pap. 10.50 (978-1-4824-4727-9(4)) Stevens, Gareth Publishing LLLP.

PRECIOUS STONES

Here are entered mineralogical and technological works on potential and actual engraved stones and jewels. Antiquarian or artistic works on engraved stones and jewels are entered under Gems.

see also Gems

also names of precious stones, e.g. Diamonds

Cole, Tayler. Aquamarine. 2015. (Gems: Nature's Jewels Ser.). (ENG., Illus.). 24p. (J). (gr. 2-3). pap. 8.15 (978-1-4824-2860-5(1)) Stevens, Gareth Publishing LLLP.

Cole, Taylor. Aquamarine. 2015. (Gems: Nature's Jewels Ser.). (ENG., Illus.). 24p. (J). (gr. 2-3). 22.60 (978-1-4824-2862-9(8)) Stevens, Gareth Publishing LLLP.

Dayton, Connor. Gemstones. (Rocks & Minerals Ser.). 24p. (gr. 2-3). 2009. 42.50 (978-1-60852-500-3(7), PowerKids Pr.) 2007. (Illus.). (YA). lib. bdg. 22.60 (978-1-4042-3686-8(4)) Rosen Publishing Group, Inc., The.

Edwards, Ron & Dickie, Lisa. Diamonds & Gemstones. 2004. (Rocks, Minerals, & Resources Ser.). (ENG., Illus.). 32p. (J). pap. (978-0-7787-1446-0(2)) Crabtree Publishing Co.

Ethan, Eric. Turquoise. 2011. (Gems: Nature's Jewels Ser.). (Illus.). 24p. (J). (gr. 2-5). pap. 8.15 (978-1-4339-4712-4(9)); lib. bdg. 22.60 (978-1-4339-4711-7(0)) Stevens, Gareth Publishing LLLP. (Gareth Stevens Learning Library).

Hansen, Grace. Gems, 1 vol. 2016. (ENG., Illus.). 24p. (J). (978-1-62970-906-2(9), 1391185) ABDO Publishing Co.

Hayes, Amy. Garnets. 2015. (Gems: Nature's Jewels Ser.). (ENG., Illus.). 24p. (J). (gr. 2-3). pap. 8.15 (978-1-4824-2864-3(4)) Stevens, Gareth Publishing LLLP.

Hoffman, Steven M. Gems, Crystals, & Precious Rocks. 2011. (Rock It! Ser.). (Illus.). 24p. (J). 22.60 (978-1-4488-2561-5(X)); pap. 8.25 (978-1-4488-2708-4(6)) Rosen Publishing Group, Inc., The. (PowerKids Pr.).

Keppeler, Jill. How Gems Are Formed. 2016. (From the Earth: How Resources Are Made Ser.). (Illus.). 32p. (J). (gr. 4-3). pap. 10.50 (978-1-4824-4709-5(6)) Stevens, Gareth Publishing LLLP.

Mahoney, Emily Jankowski. Amethysts. 2015. (Gems: Nature's Jewels Ser.). (ENG., Illus.). 24p. (J). (gr. 2-3). pap. 8.15 (978-1-4824-2856-8(3)) Stevens, Gareth Publishing LLLP.

Mcaneney, Caitie. Topaz. 2015. (Gems: Nature's Jewels Ser.). (ENG., Illus.). 24p. (J). (gr. 2-3). pap. 8.15 (978-1-4824-2872-8(5)) Stevens, Gareth Publishing LLLP.

Pellant, Chris & Pellant, Helen. Crystals & Gemstones. 2008. (Rock Stars Ser.). (Illus.). 24p. (J). (gr. 1-4). lib. bdg. 23.00 (978-0-8368-9222-2(4)) Stevens, Gareth Publishing LLLP.

Petersen, Christine. Groovy Gems, 1 vol. 2010. (Rock on!: a Look at Geology Ser.). (ENG.). 32p. (YA). (gr. 3-6). 27.07 (978-1-60453-743-7(4)) ABDO Publishing Co.

—Jade, 1 vol. 2013. (Earth's Treasures Ser.). (ENG.). 32p. (J). (gr. 3-6). lib. bdg. 27.07 (978-1-61783-872-9(1), Checkerboard Library) ABDO Publishing Co.

—Turquoise, 1 vol. 2013. (Earth's Treasures Ser.). (ENG.). 32p. (J). (gr. 3-6). lib. bdg. 27.07 (978-1-61783-875-0(6), Checkerboard Library) ABDO Publishing Co.

Rajczak, Michael. Amber. 2015. (Gems: Nature's Jewels Ser.). (ENG., Illus.). 24p. (J). (gr. 2-3). 22.60 (978-1-4824-2854-4(7)) Stevens, Gareth Publishing LLLP.

Salzano, Tammi J. Rocks, Minerals, & Gemstones. Jankowski, Daniel, illus. 2009. 24p. (J). pap. (978-0-545-19868-4(2)) Scholastic, Inc.

Squire, Ann O. Gemstones. 2012. (True Book Ser.). (ENG.). 48p. (J). pap. 6.95 (978-0-531-26251-1(0)); lib. bdg. 29.00 (978-0-531-26143-9(3)) Scholastic Library Publishing.

Symes, R. F. & Harding, Robert. Crystal & Gem: Eyewitness Books. Keates, Colin, photos by. 2004. (Illus.). 63p. (J). (gr. 4-8). reprint ed. 19.00 (978-0-7567-7687-9(2)) DIANE Publishing Co.

Trueit, Trudi Strain. Rocks, Gems, & Minerals. 2003. (Watts Library). (ENG.). 64p. (gr. 5-7). pap. 8.95 (978-0-531-16241-5(9), Watts, Franklin) Scholastic Library Publishing.

Ward, Charlotte, ed. Gem Care. Ward, Fred, photos by. 2nd ed. 2003. (Fred Ward Gem Book Ser.). (Illus.). 32p. pap. 9.95 (978-1-887651-07-3(1)) Gem Bk. Pubs.

PREGNANCY

see also Childbirth

Adamo, Courtney & van de Paal, Esther. 9 Months: A Month by Month Guide to Pregnancy for the Family to Share. Mirtalipova, Dinara & Stewart, Lizzy, illus. 2017. (ENG.). 32p. (J). (gr. -1-3). 17.99 (978-1-84780-975-9(8), Frances Lincoln) Quarto Publishing Group UK GBR. Dist: Hachette Bk. Group.

Akin, Jessica. Pregnancy & Parenting: The Ultimate Teen Guide. 2016. (It Happened to Me Ser.: 48). (ENG., Illus.). 226p. 45.00 (978-1-4422-4302-6(3)) Rowman & Littlefield Publishers, Inc.

Amos, Janine. Is Helen Pregnant. 2003. (Body Matters Ser.: 1). (ENG., Illus.). 32p. (YA). 19.99 (978-1-84234-107-0(3)) Evans Brothers, Ltd. GBR. Dist: Independent Pubs. Group.

Batten, Mary. Who Has a Belly Button?, 1 vol. Bond, Higgins, illus. 2004. (ENG.). 32p. (J). (gr. 1-5). 15.95 (978-1-56145-235-4(1)) Peachtree Pubs.

Campbell, Carol P. & Orr, Tamra. Frequently Asked Questions about Teen Pregnancy. 2011. (FAQ: Teen Life Ser.). (J). lib. bdg. 31.95 (978-1-4488-4627-6(7)) Rosen Publishing Group, Inc., The.

Colby, Jennifer. I Have a Belly Button. 2015. (Tell Me Why Library). (ENG.). 24p. (J). (gr. 2-5). 27.07 (978-1-63362-612-6(1), 206632) Cherry Lake Publishing.

Cooper, Robbi, creator. Help! We're Having a Baby: Solicited Advice from Family & Friends. 2004. 70p. ring bd. 35.00 (978-0-9749643-0-0(1)) Cooper, Robbi.

Englandar, Anrenee. Dear Diary, I'm Pregnant: Ten Real Life Stories. 2nd rev. ed. 2010. (ENG., Illus.). 160p. (YA). (gr. 7-18). 21.95 (978-1-55451-237-9(9), 9781554512379); pap. 11.95 (978-1-55451-236-2(0), 9781554512362) Annick Pr., Ltd. CAN. Dist: Publishers Group West (PGW).

Frohnapfel-Krueger, Lisa. Teen Pregnancy & Parenting. Gale Editors, ed. 2010. (Current Controversies Ser.). (ENG.). 176-240p. pap. 28.45 (978-0-7377-4924-3(5)); 176240p. (gr. 10-12). 44.10 (978-0-7377-4923-6(7)) Cengage Gale. (Greenhaven Pr., Inc.).

Gordon, Elaine R. Mommy, Did I Grow in Your Tummy? Where Some Babies Come From. Clo, Kathy, illus. Date not set. 28p. (Orig.). (J). (gr. -1-4). pap. 9.95 (978-0-9634561-0-6(5)) EM Greenberg Pr., Inc.

Hammerslough, Jane. Everything You Need to Know about Teen Motherhood. 2009. (Need to Know Library). 64p. (gr. 5-5). 58.50 (978-1-60854-090-7(1)) Rosen Publishing Group, Inc., The.

Harrison, Anne-Marie. Babies Are Noisy: A Book for Big Brothers & Sisters Including Those on the Autism Spectrum. Byrne, Beth, illus. 2013. (ENG.). 40p. (J). 15.95 (978-1-84905-459-1(2), 4085) Kingsley, Jessica Pubs. GBR. Dist: Macmillan Distribution Ltd.

Having a Healthy Baby - Planning Your Pregnancy. 2004. (YA). pap. 4.00 net. (978-1-930996-55-7(1)) Planned Parenthood Federation of America, Inc.

Jamiolkowski, Raymond M. A Baby Doesn't Make the Man: Alternative Sources of Power & Manhood for Young Men. (Teen Pregnancy Prevention Library). 64p. 2009. (gr. 5-5). 58.50 (978-1-60854-244-4(0)) 2005. (Illus.). (YA). (gr. 7-12). lib. bdg. 31.95 (978-0-8239-3470-6(5)) Rosen Publishing Group, Inc., The.

Juettner, Bonnie. Abortion. 2007. (Ripped from the Headlines Ser.). (YA). (gr. 7-12). 23.95 (978-1-60217-020-9(7)) Erickson Pr.

Kamberg, Mary-Lane. Teen Pregnancy & Motherhood. 2012. (Young Woman's Guide to Contemporary Issues Ser.). (ENG., Illus.). 112p. (YA). (gr. 9-12). lib. bdg. 34.60 (978-1-4488-8397-4(0)) Rosen Publishing Group, Inc., The.

Kenney, Karen Latchana. Teen Pregnancy, 1 vol. 2014. (Essential Issues Set 4 Ser.). (ENG.). 112p. (J). (gr. 6-12). lib. bdg. 35.64 (978-1-62403-422-0(5), Essential Library) ABDO Publishing Co.

Lange, Donna. Contraception & Pregnancy. Forman, Sara & McDonnell, Mary Ann, eds. 2013. (Young Adult's Guide to the Science of Health Ser.). (Illus.). 128p. (J). (gr. 7-18). pap. 14.95 (978-1-4222-3005-3(8)) Mason Crest.

—Contraception & Pregnancy. McDonnell, Mary Ann & Forman, Sara, eds. 2013. (Young Adult's Guide to the Science of Health Ser.: 15). (Illus.). 128p. (J). (gr. 7-18). 24.95 (978-1-4222-2805-0(3)) Mason Crest.

Mahoney, Emily & MacKay, Jenny. Dealing with Teen Pregnancy. 2017. (Hot Topics Ser.). 112p. (YA). (gr. 7-7). lib. bdg. 39.40 **(978-1-5345-6019-2(X)**, Lucent Pr.) Greenhaven Publishing LLC.

McDowell, Josh & Stewart, Ed. My Friend Is Struggling with Unplanned Pregnancy. 2009. (Project 17:17 Ser.). (ENG.). 64p. (J). mass mkt. 4.99 (978-1-84550-440-3(2), 088e0695-904e-407d-a6f0-b7042c01cae6) Christian Focus Pubns. GBR. Dist: Bookmasters Distribution.

McDowell, Pamela. Teen Pregnancy. 2010. (ENG.). 48p. (J). pap. (978-0-7787-2139-0(6)); lib. bdg. (978-0-7787-2132-1(9)) Crabtree Publishing Co.

Meister, Deborah. What Catholics Teens Should Know If Pregnant & Panicked. Larkin, Jean K., ed. 2004. (What Catholic Teens Should Know Ser.). (Illus.). 8p. (YA). 7.95 (978-0-89837-237-3(2), 440710) Pflaum Publishing Group.

Murkoff, Heidi. What to Expect When Mommy's Having a Baby. Rader, Laura, illus. 2004. (What to Expect Kids Ser.). (ENG.). 24p. (J). (gr. -1-3). pap. 3.99 (978-0-06-053802-6(3), HarperFestival) HarperCollins Pubs.

Nykiel, Connie. After the Loss of Your Baby: For Teen Mothers. 2004. (ENG.). 24p. (Orig.). (YA). pap. 3.50 (978-1-56123-156-0(8), ALBC) Centering Corp.

Parker, Gary E. Life Before Birth: A Christian Family Book. 2nd ed. 2003. 85p. (J). (gr. 5-7). 12.95 (978-0-89051-164-0(0), LIBEBI) Master Bks.

parks, peggy j. Teenage Sex & Pregnancy. 2011. (Compact Research Ser.). 96p. (YA). (gr. 7-12). lib. bdg. 27.95 (978-1-60152-168-2(5)) ReferencePoint Pr., Inc.

Piehl, Norah. Teenage Pregnancy. 2008. (Social Issues Firsthand Ser.). (ENG., Illus.). 192p. (YA). (gr. 10-12). lib. bdg. 33.75 (978-0-7377-4254-1(2), LML02109-243167, Greenhaven Pr., Inc.) Cengage Gale.

Rigby Education Staff. Carrying Babies. (Sails Literacy Ser.). (Illus.). 16p. (gr. 1-2). 27.00 (978-0-7635-9886-0(0), 698860C99) Rigby Education.

Rodriguez, Gaby. The Pregnancy Project: A Memoir. 2013. (ENG., Illus.). 240p. (YA). (gr. 9). pap. 10.99 (978-1-4424-4623-6(4), Simon & Schuster Bks. For Young Readers) Simon & Schuster Bks. For Young Readers.

Silverberg, Cory. What Makes a Baby. 2013. (ENG., Illus.). 36p. (J). (gr. -1-2). 16.95 (978-1-60980-485-5(6), Triangle Square) Seven Stories Pr.

Simons, Rae. Teen Parents. 2010. (Changing Face of Modern Families Ser.). (Illus.). 64p. (YA). (gr. 5-18). lib. bdg. 22.95 (978-1-4222-1491-6(5)) Mason Crest.

Stroble, Chris. There IS Hope after a Teen Pregnancy: A Collection of Inspiring Mother-Daughter Success Stories plus the Handbook for Teen Moms Anonymous. 2006. pap. 14.95 (978-1-933559-00-1(4)) Wellness pH.

Surprise in Mommy's Tummy. Date not set. (J). (gr. -1-3). 5.50 (978-0-89259-115-2(3)) American Trust Pubns.

Waters, Sophie. The Female Reproductive System. (Girls' Health Ser.). 48p. 2009. (gr. 5-6). 53.00 (978-1-61512-732-0(1), Rosen Reference) 2007. (Illus.). (YA). (gr. 7-12). lib. bdg. 29.25 (978-1-4042-1950-2(1)) Rosen Publishing Group, Inc., The.

Williams, Heidi. Teen Pregnancy. 2009. (Issues That Concern You Ser.). (ENG., Illus.). 144p. (J). 36.95 (978-0-7377-4498-9(7), 1330228) Cengage Gale.

Winkler, Kathleen. High-Tech Babies: The Debate over Assisted Reproductive Technology. 2006. (Issues in Focus Today Ser.). (Illus.). 104p. (J). (gr. 6). lib. bdg. 33.27 (978-0-7660-2528-8(4)) Enslow Pubs., Inc.

Wright, Sally Ann. Where Do Babies Come From? Ayres, Honor, illus. 2007. 29p. (J). 9.95 *(978-0-8198-8311-7(5))* Pauline Bks. & Media.

PREGNANCY—FICTION

Adams, Lenora. Baby Girl. 2007. (ENG.). 240p. (YA). (gr. 9). pap. 6.99 *(978-1-4169-2512-5(0),* Simon Pulse) Simon Pulse.

Arnold, Sarah. I Told You So! Arnold, Sarah, illus. 2009. (Child's Play Library). (ENG., Illus.). 32p. (J). (gr. -1-3). pap. *(978-1-84643-314-6(2))* Child's Play International Ltd.

Atkins, Jill. Cry, Baby. 2004. (Shades Ser.). 62p. (J). pap. *(978-0-237-52810-2(X))* Evans Brothers, Ltd.

Baer, Marianna. The Inconceivable Life of Quinn. 2017. (ENG.). 384p. (YA). 18.95 *(978-1-4197-2302-5(2),* Amulet Bks.) Abrams, Inc.

Baratz-Logsted, Lauren. Angel's Choice. 2006. (ENG.). 256p. (YA). (gr. 9-12). pap. 6.99 *(978-1-4169-2524-8(4),* Simon Pulse) Simon Pulse.

Barrow, Rebecca. You Don't Know Me but I Know You. 2017. 336p. (YA). (gr. 9). 17.99 ***(978-0-06-249419-1(8),*** HarperTeen) HarperCollins Pubs.

Bennett, James W. & Bennett, James. Faith Wish. 2003. (ENG.). 160p. (J). (gr. 7-18). tchr. ed. 16.95 *(978-0-8234-1778-0(6))* Holiday Hse., Inc.

Benway, Robin. Far from the Tree. 2017. 384p. (YA). (gr. 8). 17.99 ***(978-0-06-233062-8(4),*** HarperTeen) HarperCollins Pubs.

Berk, Sheryl & Berk, Carrie. Baby Cakes. 2014. (Cupcake Club Ser.: 5). (ENG.). 160p. (J). (gr. 3-6). pap. 6.99 *(978-1-4022-8330-7(X),* Sourcebooks Jabberwocky) Sourcebooks, Inc.

Blackall, Sophie. The Baby Tree. Blackall, Sophie, illus. 2014. (ENG., Illus.). 32p. (J). (gr. k-3). 17.99 *(978-0-399-25718-6(7),* Nancy Paulsen Books) Penguin Young Readers Group.

Brassill, Amber M. My Greatest Mistake, 1 vol. 2010. 236p. pap. 24.95 *(978-1-4489-9143-3(9))* America Star Bks.

Buckley, Kate. Choices: A Novel. 2009. 208p. (J). pap. 14.95 *(978-1-935359-12-8(6))* Book Pubs. Network.

Burnett, Frances Hodgson. The Head of the House of Coombe. 2008. 252p. 29.95 *(978-1-60664-769-1(5));* pap. 15.95 *(978-1-60664-142-2(5))* Aegypan.

Butler, Dori Hillestad. Alexandra Hopewell, Labor Coach. 2005. 136p. (J). (gr. 3-6). 15.99 *(978-0-8075-0242-6(1))* Whitman, Albert & Co.

Caletti, Deb. The Six Rules of Maybe. (ENG.). (YA). (gr. 7). 2011. 352p. pap. 9.99 *(978-1-4169-7971-5(9))* 2010. 336p. 16.99 *(978-1-4169-7969-2(7))* Simon Pulse. (Simon Pulse).

Calkin, Author & Calkin, Abigail B. The Carolyne Letters: A Story of Birth, Abortion & Adoption. 2013. (ENG., Illus.). 230p. (YA). pap. 14.95 *(978-1-938301-15-5(3))* Familius LLC.

Carter, Caela. Me, Him, Them, & It. (ENG.). (YA). 2014. 336p. (gr. 9). pap. 9.99 *(978-1-61963-186-1(5),* 9781619631861) 2013. 320p. (gr. 7-12). 16.99 *(978-1-59990-958-5(8),* 9781599909585) Bloomsbury Publishing USA. (Bloomsbury USA Childrens).

Castellarin, Loretta & Roberts, Ken. Spike, 1 vol. 2006. (Degrassi Junior High Ser.). (ENG.). 184p. (YA). (gr. 5-10). 7.95 *(978-1-55028-925-1(X),* 9781550289251) Lorimer, James & Co., Ltd., Pubs. CAN. Dist: Casemate Pubs. & Bk. Distributors, LLC.

Choyce, Lesley. Reacción, 1 vol. 2012. (Spanish Soundings Ser.). (SPA.). 112p. (YA). (gr. 8-12). pap. 9.95 *(978-1-4598-0308-4(6))* Orca Bk. Pubs. USA.

Clarke, Kathryn. The Breakable Vow. 2004. 480p. (YA). (gr. 7-18). 16.89 *(978-0-06-051822-6(7))* HarperCollins Pubs.

Clarke, Kathryn Ann. The Breakable Vow. 2004. (ENG.). 480p. (YA). (gr. 8-18). pap. 7.99 *(978-0-06-051821-9(9),* HarperTeen) HarperCollins Pubs.

Coll, Ivar Da. Carlos. Coll, Ivar Da, illus. 2003. (SPA., Illus.). 52p. (J). (gr. k-3). pap. 9.95 *(978-958-8061-64-1(4))* Santillana USA Publishing Co., Inc.

Cook, Makayla. Voice of the Unborn. 2010. 142p. pap. 16.99 *(978-1-60957-924-1(0))* Salem Author Services.

Cousins, Dave. Waiting for Gonzo. 2015. (ENG.). 288p. (YA). pap. 9.99 *(978-0-7387-4199-4(X),* Flux) North Star Editions.

Creech, Sharon. Heartbeat. 2012. (ENG.). 208p. (J). (gr. 3-7). pap. 6.99 *(978-0-06-054024-1(9))* HarperCollins Pubs.

Cupala, Holly. Tell Me a Secret. 2010. (ENG.). 304p. (YA). (gr. 9-18). 16.99 *(978-0-06-176666-4(6),* HarperTeen) HarperCollins Pubs.

Daniels, Babygirl. Glitter. 2009. (ENG., Illus.). 208p. (YA). (gr. 9). pap. 9.95 *(978-1-60162-198-6(1),* Urban Renaissance) Kensington Publishing Corp.

de Gramont, Nina. Every Little Thing in the World. (ENG., Illus.). 288p. (YA). (gr. 9). 2011. pap. 8.99 *(978-1-4169-8015-5(6))* 2010. 16.99 *(978-1-4169-8013-1(X))* Simon & Schuster Children's Publishing. (Atheneum Bks. for Young Readers).

Deriso, Christine Hurley. Thirty Sunsets. 2014. (ENG.). 240p. (YA). pap. 9.99 *(978-0-7387-3991-5(X),* Flux) North Star Editions.

Dessen, Sarah. Someone Like You. 2011. 10.36 *(978-0-7848-3539-5(X),* Everbind) Marco Bk. Co.

—Someone Like You. 2004. (ENG.). 304p. (YA). (gr. 7-7). 10.99 *(978-0-14-240177-4(3),* Speak) Penguin Young Readers Group.

—Someone Like You. 2004. 281p. (YA). (gr. 7). 16.65 *(978-0-7569-4967-9(X))* Perfection Learning Corp.

—Someone Like You. 2004. 281p. (gr. 7). lib. bdg. 22.10 *(978-1-4176-2674-8(7),* Turtleback) Turtleback Bks.

Detweiler, Katelyn & Wells, Rosemary. Immaculate. 2015. (ENG.). 464p. (YA). (gr. 9). bds. 17.99 *(978-0-451-46962-5(3),* Viking Books for Young Readers) Penguin Young Readers Group.

Draper, Sharon M. November Blues. 2011. 9.00 *(978-0-7848-3495-4(4),* Everbind) Marco Bk. Co.

—November Blues. (Jericho Trilogy Ser.: 2). (ENG., Illus.). (YA). (gr. 7). 2017. 336p. pap. 9.99 ***(978-1-4814-9031-3(1),*** Atheneum/Caitlyn Dlouhy Books) 2007. 320p. 19.99 *(978-1-4169-0698-8(3),* Atheneum Bks. for Young Readers) Simon & Schuster Children's Publishing.

Efaw, Amy. After. (ENG.). 368p. (YA). (gr. 7-18). 2010. 8.99 *(978-0-14-241590-0(1),* Speak) 2009. 17.99 *(978-0-670-01183-4(5),* Viking Books for Young Readers) Penguin Young Readers Group.

Evans, Mari. I'm Late: The Story of Laneese & Moonlight & Alisha Who Didn't Have Anyone of Her Own. 2006. (Illus.). 86p. (J). (gr. 7-18). 14.95 *(978-1-933491-00-4(0))* Just Us Bks., Inc.

Fearnley, Jan. A Special Something. 2004. (Illus.). 32p. 7.95 *(978-0-7497-4639-1(4))* Egmont Bks., Ltd. GBR. Dist: Trafalgar Square Publishing.

Feiffer, Kate. The Wild, Wild Inside: A View from Mommy's Tummy! Huliska-Beith, Laura, illus. 2010. (ENG.). 32p. (J). (gr. -1-3). 15.99 *(978-1-4169-4099-9(5),* Simon & Schuster/Paula Wiseman Bks.) Simon & Schuster/Paula Wiseman Bks.

Furniss, Clare. How Not to Disappear. 2017. (ENG., Illus.). 448p. (YA). (gr. 7). 17.99 *(978-1-4814-2102-7(6),* McElderry, Margaret K. Bks.) McElderry, Margaret K. Bks.

Harper, Meg. My Mum & the Gruesome Twosome. 2nd ed. (ENG.). 160p. pap. 9.99 *(978-0-7459-4829-4(4),* Lion Books) Lion Hudson PLC GBR. Dist: Trafalgar Square Publishing.

Hart, Karen. Butterflies in May. 2006. 201p. (YA). (gr. 8-12). pap. 16.95 *(978-1-890862-44-2(4))* Bancroft Pr.

Harvey, Sarah N. The Lit Report, 1 vol. 2008. (ENG.). 208p. (YA). (gr. 7-12). pap. 12.95 *(978-1-55143-905-1(0))* Orca Bk. Pubs. USA.

Hearn, Julie. The Minister's Daughter. 2006. (ENG.). 272p. (YA). (gr. 7-12). pap. 7.99 *(978-0-689-87691-2(2),* Atheneum Bks. for Young Readers) Simon & Schuster Children's Publishing.

Heppermann, Christine. Ask Me How I Got Here. 2016. 240p. (YA). (gr. 9). 17.99 *(978-0-06-238795-0(2),* Greenwillow Bks.) HarperCollins Pubs.

Hoole, Elissa Janine. The Memory Jar. 2016. (ENG.). 336p. (YA). pap. 11.99 *(978-0-7387-4731-6(9),* Flux) North Star Editions.

Hooper, Mary. Newes from the Dead. 2010. (ENG., Illus.). 272p. (YA). (gr. 9-13). pap. 16.99 *(978-0-312-60864-4(0),* 9780312608644) Square Fish.

Hopkins, Ellen. Crank. (ENG., (YA). (gr. 9). 2013. Illus.). 576p. pap. 12.99 *(978-1-4424-7181-8(6))* 2010. 544p. 21.99 *(978-1-4169-9513-5(7))* McElderry, Margaret K. Bks. (McElderry, Margaret K. Bks.).

—Crank. 2013. lib. bdg. 24.50 *(978-0-606-35118-8(3))* Turtleback Bks.

Hornby, Nick. Slam. (ENG.). 320p. (gr. 12). 2009. 16.00 *(978-1-59448-471-1(6))* 2008. 15.00 *(978-1-59448-345-5(0))* Penguin Publishing Group. (Riverhead Bks. (Hardcover)).

Jarwin. Love in the Springtime. 2012. 224p. 24.95 *(978-1-4626-6818-2(6))* America Star Bks.

Johnson, Angela. The First Part Last. 2003. (ENG., Illus.). 144p. (YA). (gr. 7-18). 16.99 *(978-0-689-84922-0(2),* Simon & Schuster Bks. For Young Readers) Simon & Schuster Bks. For Young Readers.

—The First Part Last. 2005. (ENG.). 144p. (YA). (gr. 7). reprint ed. pap. 7.99 *(978-0-689-84923-7(0),* Simon Pulse) Simon Pulse.

—The First Part Last. l.t. ed. 2005. 241p. pap. 10.95 *(978-0-7862-7379-9(8),* Large Print Pr.) Thorndike Pr.

Kelly, Mij. The Bump. Allan, Nicholas, illus. 2012. (ENG.). 32p. (J). *(978-1-58925-107-6(5))* Tiger Tales.

Kephart, Beth. Small Damages. 2013. (ENG., Illus.). 304p. (YA). (gr. 9). pap. 8.99 *(978-0-14-242641-8(5),* Speak) Penguin Young Readers Group.

Kern, Peggy. The Test. 2011. (Bluford Ser.: 18). (J). (gr. k-12). pap. 4.95 *(978-1-59194-234-4(9))* Townsend Pr.

Knowles, Jo. Jumping off Swings. 2011. (ENG., Illus.). 240p. (YA). (gr. 9). pap. 7.99 *(978-0-7636-5296-8(2))* Candlewick Pr.

Larsen, Elizabeth. Kendra's Decision. 2013. 48p. pap. 16.95 *(978-1-63000-662-4(9))* America Star Bks.

Leavitt, Caroline. Girls in Trouble: A Novel. 2005. (ENG.). 368p. pap. 22.99 *(978-0-312-33973-9(9),* 9780312339739, St. Martin's Griffin) St. Martin's Pr.

Lee, Darren. Grown in Sixty Seconds. 2009. (ENG., Illus.). 288p. (YA). (gr. 9). 9.95 *(978-1-933967-72-1(2),* Urban Renaissance) Kensington Publishing Corp.

Lee, Shelley R. Before I Knew You. Lee, Shelley R., ed. Lehman, Denise, illus. 2006. (J). lib. bdg. 20.00 *(978-0-9786757-0-7(3))* Lee, Shelley.

Leicht, Martin & Neal, Isla. Mothership. (Ever-Expanding Universe Ser.: 1). (ENG., Illus.). (YA). (gr. 9). 2013. 336p. pap. 9.99 *(978-1-4424-2961-1(5))* 2012. 320p. 16.99 *(978-1-4424-2960-4(7))* Simon & Schuster Bks. For Young Readers. (Simon & Schuster Bks. For Young Readers).

Levine, Ellen. In Trouble. 2011. (Carolrhoda YA Ser.). (ENG.). 208p. (YA). (gr. 9-12). 17.95 *(978-0-7613-6558-7(3),* Carolrhoda Lab™) Lerner Publishing Group.

Lewis, Ali. Timber Creek Station. 2016. (ENG.). 240p. (YA). (gr. 6-12). 18.99 *(978-1-4677-8117-6(7));* 35.99 *(978-1-4677-8816-8(3),* Carolrhoda Lab™) Lerner Publishing Group.

Liebert, Emily. Those Secrets We Keep. 2015. (ENG.). 336p. (gr. 12). pap. 16.00 *(978-0-451-47187-1(3),* Berkley) Penguin Publishing Group.

Lloyd, Sam. What's in Your Tummy Mummy? Lloyd, Sam, illus. 2007. (ENG., Illus.). 24p. (J). (gr. -1-k). pap. 13.95 *(978-1-84365-091-1(6),* Pavilion) Pavilion Bks. GBR. Dist: Independent Pubs. Group.

Loeffelholz, Sarah, illus. Can You Just Imagine. 2007. 40p. (J). 14.95 *(978-0-9786850-1-0(6))* Overdue Bks.

Look, Lenore. Alvin Ho: Allergic to Babies, Burglars, & Other Bumps in the Night. Pham, LeUyen, illus. 2013. (Alvin Ho Ser.). (ENG.). 192p. (J). (gr. 1-4). 15.99 *(978-0-375-87033-0(4),* Schwartz & Wade Bks.) Random Hse. Children's Bks.

—Alvin Ho: Allergic to Babies, Burglars, & Other Bumps in the Night. Pham, LeUyen, illus. 2014. (Alvin Ho Ser.). (ENG.). 192p. (J). (gr. 1-4). 6.99 *(978-0-385-38600-5(1),* Yearling) Random Hse. Children's Bks.

Mac, Carrie. The Way Back, 1 vol. 2014. (Orca Soundings Ser.). (ENG.). 168p. (YA). (gr. 8-12). pap. 9.95 *(978-1-4598-0715-0(4))* Orca Bk. Pubs. USA.

Mackall, Dandi Daley. There's a Baby in There!, 0 vols. Whitt, Carlynn, illus. 2012. (ENG.). 32p. (J). (gr. -1-3). 16.99 *(978-0-7614-6191-3(4),* 9780761461913, Amazon Children's Publishing) Amazon Publishing.

Madonia, Kristen-Paige. Fingerprints of You. 2013. (ENG., Illus.). 272p. (YA). (gr. 9). pap. 9.99 *(978-1-4424-2921-5(6),* Simon & Schuster Bks. For Young Readers) Simon & Schuster Bks. For Young Readers.

—Fingerprints of You. Ribera, Terry, illus. 2012. (ENG.). 272p. (YA). (gr. 9). 16.99 *(978-1-4424-2920-8(8),* Simon & Schuster Bks. For Young Readers) Simon & Schuster Bks. For Young Readers.

Martinez, Jessica. The Space Between Us. (ENG., (YA). (gr. 9). 2013. Illus.). 416p. pap. 9.99 *(978-1-4424-2056-4(1))* 2012. 400p. 16.99 *(978-1-4424-2055-7(3))* Simon Pulse. (Simon Pulse).

McCafferty, Megan. Bumped. (Bumped Ser.: 1). (ENG.). (YA). (gr. 9). 2012. 352p. pap. 9.99 *(978-0-06-196275-2(9))* 2011. 336p. 16.99 *(978-0-06-196274-5(0))* HarperCollins Pubs.

—Thumped. 2013. (Bumped Ser.: 2). (ENG.). 304p. (YA). (gr. 8). pap. 8.99 *(978-0-06-196277-6(5))* HarperCollins Pubs.

McCaffrey, Kate. Crashing Down. 2015. 304p. (YA). (gr. 7). 14.95 *(978-1-922089-85-4(0))* Fremantle Pr. AUS. Dist: Independent Pubs. Group.

McDaniel, Lurlene. Briana's Gift. 2008. (ENG.). 176p. (YA). (gr. 7-12). mass mkt. 6.50 *(978-0-440-23869-0(2),* Laurel Leaf) Random Hse. Children's Bks.

Mceldowney, Connie. Josiah's Journey. 2009. 34p. pap. 12.99 *(978-1-4490-0489-7(X))* AuthorHouse.

McInnes, Nicole. Brianna on the Brink. 2013. (ENG.). 176p. (YA). (gr. 10). 16.95 *(978-0-8234-2741-3(2))* Holiday Hse., Inc.

Millward, Carol. Star in the Middle. 2009. 304p. (YA). (gr. 9-12). 16.95 *(978-1-934813-13-3(3))* Westside Bks.

Naylor, Phyllis Reynolds. Cricket Man. 2008. (ENG.). 208p. (YA). (gr. 7-18). 16.99 *(978-1-4169-4981-7(X),* Atheneum Bks. for Young Readers) Simon & Schuster Children's Publishing.

Nolan, Han. Pregnant Pause. 2012. (ENG.). 352p. (YA). (gr. 9). pap. 8.99 *(978-0-547-85414-4(5))* Houghton Mifflin Harcourt Publishing Co.

Olsen, Sylvia. The Girl with a Baby, 1 vol. 2003. (ENG.). 208p. (YA). (gr. 7-12). pap. 9.95 *(978-1-55039-142-8(9))* Sono Nis Pr. CAN. Dist: Orca Bk. Pubs. USA.

Orante, Ann-Jeanette P. Best Sisters for Life... 2007. (ENG., Illus.). 36p. (J). per. 11.95 *(978-1-59800-972-9(9))* Outskirts Pr., Inc.

Panzieri, Lucia & Maccarone, Grace. Little Brother Pumpkin Head. Enria, Samantha, illus. 2016. (ENG.). 32p. (J). 16.95 *(978-0-8234-3537-1(7))* Holiday Hse., Inc.

Paratore, Coleen Murtagh. Willa by Heart. 2008. (Wedding Planner's Daughter Ser.). (ENG.). 240p. (J). (gr. 3-7). 15.99 *(978-1-4169-4076-0(6),* Simon & Schuster Bks. For Young Readers) Simon & Schuster Bks. For Young Readers.

—Willa by Heart. 2009. (Wedding Planner's Daughter Ser.). (ENG.). 240p. (J). (gr. 4-8). pap. 6.99 *(978-1-4169-7470-3(9),* Aladdin) Simon & Schuster Children's Publishing.

Poston, Karen. A Baby for Mabel & Frederick. 2005. 20p. (J). 11.28 *(978-1-4116-6024-3(2))* Lulu Pr., Inc.

Pratt, Non. Trouble. 2014. (ENG., Illus.). 384p. (YA). (gr. 9). 17.99 *(978-1-4424-9772-6(6),* Simon & Schuster Bks. For Young Readers) Simon & Schuster Bks. For Young Readers.

—Trouble. 2015. (ENG., Illus.). 400p. (YA). (gr. 9). pap. 10.99 *(978-1-4424-9773-3(4))* Simon & Schuster, Inc.

Quintero, Isabel. Gabi, a Girl in Pieces. 2014. (ENG.). 208p. (J). pap. 11.95 *(978-1-935955-95-5(0));* (YA). 17.95 *(978-1-935955-94-8(2))* Cinco Puntos Pr.

Ritchie, Kate. I Just Couldn't Wait to Meet You. Somerville, Hannah, illus. 2015. (ENG.). 32p. (J). (-k). 22.99 *(978-0-85798-970-3(7))* Random Hse. Australia AUS. Dist: Independent Pubs. Group.

Roth, Carol. Will You Still Love Me? Howarth, Daniel, illus. 2011. (ENG.). 16p. (J). (gr. -1 — 1). bds. 7.99 *(978-0-8075-9116-1(5))* Whitman, Albert & Co.

Royal, Stephen. The Journey Inside the Womb. 2012. (Illus.). 16p. pap. 18.30 *(978-1-4772-2604-9(4))* AuthorHouse.

Ryan, Darlene. Saving Grace, 1 vol. 2006. (Orca Soundings Ser.). (ENG.). 112p. (YA). (gr. 8-12). per. 9.95 *(978-1-55143-508-4(X))* Orca Bk. Pubs. USA.

Rylant, Cynthia. A Kindness. Date not set. (Sky Bks.). 104p. pap. 54.75 *(978-0-582-08106-2(8))* Addison-Wesley Longman, Ltd. GBR. Dist: Trans-Atlantic Pubns., Inc.

Sauer, Tammi. Dear Jack. 2004. 164p. (YA). mass mkt. 6.99 *(978-0-9753367-0-0(3))* Onstage Publishing, LLC.

Scheerger, Sarah Lynn. The Opposite of Love. 2014. (ENG.). 272p. (YA). (gr. 8-12). 16.99 *(978-0-8075-6132-4(0))* Whitman, Albert & Co.

Simon, Charnan. Plan B. (Surviving Southside Ser.). (ENG.). 104p. (YA). (gr. 6-12). 2015. 34.65 *(978-1-4677-6009-6(9),* Lerner Digital) 2011. pap. 7.95 *(978-0-7613-6163-3(4))* 2011. lib. bdg. 27.93 *(978-0-7613-6149-7(9))* Lerner Publishing Group.

Snelson, Brian & Sellars, Rodney. Shaturanga: The Story of Onus. 2003. 244p. pap. 16.95 *(978-0-595-29569-2(X))* iUniverse, Inc.

Sutton, Michelle. It's Not about Him. 2012. (Second Glances Ser.). (ENG.). 228p. pap. 12.99 *(978-0-9838836-0-9(2))* Sword of the Spirit Publishing.

Sweeney, Joyce. Waiting for June, 0 vols. 2006. (ENG.). 158p. (YA). (gr. 10-12). pap. 7.99 *(978-0-7614-5329-1(6),* 9780761453291, Amazon Children's Publishing) Amazon Publishing.

Thomas-Roots, Pamela. FACTS & MEMOIRS of BABY DIARY: A Diary to Record & Save Valuable Information on Facts & Memoirs of Your Pregnancy & Baby from Birth to Age 18. 2010. 48p. pap. 9.99 *(978-0-557-03410-9(8))* Lulu Pr., Inc.

Velasquez, Gloria. Teen Angel. 2003. (Roosevelt High School Ser.). 160p. (J). pap. 9.95 *(978-1-55885-391-1(X),* Piñata Books) Arte Publico Pr.

Watts, Irene N. When the Bough Breaks. 2007. (ENG.). 152p. (YA). (gr. 4-7). pap. 9.95 *(978-0-88776-821-7(0),* Tundra Bks.) Tundra Bks. CAN. Dist: Penguin Random Hse. LLC.

Welford, Sue. Nowhere to Run. l.t. ed. 2006. 180p. per. *(978-1-905665-15-0(6))* Pollinger In Print.

Wells, Maggie. Nine Months. 2016. (Nine Months Ser.: 6). (ENG.). 200p. (YA). (gr. 6-12). lib. bdg. 162.78 *(978-1-68076-189-4(7),* Epic Pr.) ABDO Publishing Co.

Werlin, Nancy. Impossible. 2011. 11.04 *(978-0-7848-3488-6(1),* Everbind) Marco Bk. Co.

—Impossible. 2009. (ENG.). 384p. (YA). (gr. 7-18). 9.99 *(978-0-14-241491-0(3),* Speak) Penguin Young Readers Group.

Whelan, Gloria. Chu Ju's House. 2005. (ENG.). 240p. (J). (gr. 5). reprint ed. pap. 7.99 *(978-0-06-050726-8(8))* HarperCollins Pubs.

Winkler, Henry & Oliver, Lin. Who Ordered This Baby? Definitely Not Me! 2007. (Hank Zipzer Ser.: No. 13). (Illus.). 152p. (gr. 4-7). 15.00 *(978-0-7569-8163-1(8))* Perfection Learning Corp.

Wolfer, Dianne. Choices. 2nd ed. 2010. (ENG.). 256p. (YA). (gr. 7). pap. 13.00 *(978-1-921361-56-2(5))* Fremantle Pr. AUS. Dist: Independent Pubs. Group.

Woodson, Jacqueline. The Dear One. 2010. (ENG.). 176p. (YA). (gr. 7-18). 7.99 *(978-0-14-241705-8(X),* Puffin Books) Penguin Young Readers Group.

—Pecan Pie Baby. Blackall, Sophie, illus. (ENG.). 32p. (J). (gr. k-3). 2013. 7.99 *(978-0-14-751128-7(3),* Puffin Books) 2010. 16.99 *(978-0-399-23987-8(1),* G.P. Putnam's Sons Books for Young Readers) Penguin Young Readers Group.

Writing Club, Dancing Pencils, compiled by. Budding Words: An Anthology. 2007. 60p. pap. *(978-1-86900-871-0(5))* UmSinsi Pr. ZAF. Dist: Michigan State Univ. Pr.

Zarr, Sara. How to Save a Life. 2012. (ENG.). 368p. (YA). (gr. 7-17). pap. 10.99 *(978-0-316-03605-4(6))* Little, Brown Bks. for Young Readers.

PREHISTORIC ANIMALS

see Fossils

PREHISTORIC HUMANS

see Prehistoric Peoples

PREHISTORIC PEOPLES

Brooks, Philip. The Story of Prehistoric Peoples. 2011. (Journey Through History Ser.). (Illus.). 64p. (J). lib. bdg. 31.95 *(978-1-4488-4790-7(7),* Rosen Reference) Rosen Publishing Group, Inc., The.

Brooks, Susie. Prehistoric People. 2009. (Flashback History Ser.). (Illus.). 48p. (J). pap. 11.75 *(978-1-4358-5505-2(1),* PowerKids Pr.); (YA). (gr. 3-6). 29.25 *(978-1-4358-5504-5(3))* Rosen Publishing Group, Inc., The.

Brown, Robin C. The Crafts of Florida's First People. 2003. (ENG., Illus.). 63p. (J). pap. 9.95 *(978-1-56164-282-3(7))* Pineapple Pr., Inc.

Chandler, Fiona. Prehistoric World. 2004. (World History Ser.). (SPA., Illus.). 96p. (J). (gr. 3-18). lib. bdg. 27.95 *(978-1-58086-270-7(5))* EDC Publishing.

Clodd, Edward. Fetish Worship & Idolatry. 2006. pap. 9.95 *(978-1-4286-7861-3(1))* Kessinger Publishing, LLC.

—Myths about the Earth & Man. 2006. pap. 9.95 *(978-1-4286-7865-1(4))* Kessinger Publishing, LLC.

Cole, Joanna. The Human Body. 2014. (Magic School Bus Presents Ser.). lib. bdg. 17.20 *(978-0-606-35815-6(3))* Turtleback Bks.

Cole, Joanna, et al. The Human Body. Degen, Bruce & Bracken, Carolyn, illus. 2014. (Magic School Bus Presents Ser.). (ENG.). 32p. (J). (gr. 1-3). pap. 6.99 *(978-0-545-68364-7(5))* Scholastic, Inc.

Croy, Anita. Exploring the Past. 2010. (Invisible Worlds Ser.). 48p. (gr. 4). 28.50 *(978-0-7614-4194-6(8))* Marshall Cavendish GBR. Dist: Marshall Cavendish Corp.

Deem, James M. Bodies from the Bog. 2003. (ENG., Illus.). 48p. (J). (gr. 5-7). pap. 9.99 *(978-0-618-35402-3(6))* Houghton Mifflin Harcourt Publishing Co.

Diagram Group Staff, contrib. by. The First Humans. 2004. (Life on Earth Ser.). (Illus.). 112p. (gr. 5-8). 35.00 *(978-0-8160-5050-5(3))* Facts On File, Inc.

Dorling Kindersley Publishing Staff. Early Humans. 2005. (DK Eyewitness Bks.). (ENG., Illus.). 72p. (J). (gr. 3-7). 16.99 *(978-0-7566-1067-8(2),* 1241898, DK Children) Dorling Kindersley Publishing, Inc.

—Early People. 2015. (Eye Wonder Ser.). (ENG., Illus.). 56p. (J). (gr. k-4). 10.99 *(978-1-4654-2854-7(2),* DK Children) Dorling Kindersley Publishing, Inc.

Facchini, Fiorenzo. A Day with Homo Sapiens: Life 15,000 Years Ago. 2003. (Early Humans Ser.). (Illus.). 48p. (gr. 6-18). lib. bdg. 23.90 *(978-0-7613-2768-4(1),* Twenty-First Century Bks.) Lerner Publishing Group.

—A Day with Neanderthal Man: Life 70,000 Years Ago. Baldanzi, Alessandro, illus. 2003. (Early Humans Ser.). 48p. (gr. 6-18). lib. bdg. 23.90 *(978-0-7613-2767-7(3),* Twenty-First Century Bks.) Lerner Publishing Group.

Forbes, Claire. Ancient Peoples. 2004. (Discovery Guides Ser.). (SPA., Illus.). 32p. (J). (gr. 2-5). pap. 6.95 *(978-1-58728-217-1(8),* Two-Can Publishing) T&N Children's Publishing.

Ganeri, Anita. How to Live Like a Stone-Age Hunter. Epelbaum, Mariano, illus. 2015. (How to Live Like... Ser.). (ENG.). 32p. (J). (gr. 3-6). pap. 7.99 *(978-1-4677-7207-5(0));* lib. bdg. 26.65 *(978-1-4677-6352-3(7))* Lerner Publishing Group.

Gray, Susan H. Scholastic News Nonfiction Readers: Prehistoric World, 6 bks., Set. Incl. Dinosaur Armor. 22.00 *(978-0-531-17481-4(6));* Dinosaur Digs! 22.00 *(978-0-531-17482-1(4));* Dinosaur Eggs. 22.00 *(978-0-531-17483-8(2));* Dinosaur Teeth. 22.00 *(978-0-531-17484-5(0));* Dinosaur Tracks. 22.00 *(978-0-531-17485-2(9));* (Illus.). 24p. (J). (gr. 1-2). 2007. 114.00 o.p. *(978-0-531-12605-9(6),* Children's Pr.) Scholastic Library Publishing.

Heitkamp, Kristina Lyn. The Rift Valley & the Archaeological Evidence of the First Humans. 2016. (First Humans & Early Civilizations Ser.). 64p. (J). (gr. 6-6). pap. 12.95 *(978-1-4994-6318-7(9))* Rosen Publishing Group, Inc., The.

Holmes, Thom. The Prehistoric Earth Set, 10-Volumes. 2008. (Prehistoric Earth Ser.). (C). (gr. 9-18). 350.00 *(978-0-8160-7841-7(6),* Chelsea Hse.) Facts On File, Inc.

Howell, Izzi. Stone Age to Iron Age. 2017. (Fact Cat: History: Early Britons Ser.). (ENG., Illus.). 24p. (J). (gr. k-2). pap. 9.99 *(978-0-7502-9938-1(X),* Wayland) Hachette Children's Group GBR. Dist: Hachette Bk. Group.

Hynes, Margaret & White, Mike. The Best Book of Early People. 2003. (Best Book Of Ser.). (ENG., Illus.). 32p. (J). (gr. k-3). tchr. ed. 12.99 *(978-0-7534-5577-7(3),* 9780753455777, Kingfisher) Roaring Brook Pr.

Janulis, Klint. Stone Age. 2017. (Illus.). 64p. (J). ***(978-1-5364-0132-5(3))*** Dorling Kindersley Publishing, Inc.

Joseph, Frank. Archaeological Discoveries of Ancient America, 1 vol., 1. 2014. (Discovering Ancient America Ser.). (ENG.). 296p. (YA). (gr. 7-12). 38.25 *(978-1-4777-2809-3(0))* Rosen Publishing Group, Inc., The.

Lanser, Amanda. Ötzi the Iceman, 1 vol. 2014. (Digging up the Past Ser.). (ENG., Illus.). 112p. (J). (gr. 6-12). lib. bdg. 35.64 *(978-1-62403-235-6(4)*, Essential Library) ABDO Publishing Co.

Morris, Neil. Everyday Life in Prehistory. 2005. (Uncovering History Ser.). (Illus.). 46p. (J). (gr. 6-9). lib. bdg. 29.95 *(978-1-58340-709-7(X))* Black Rabbit Bks.

—Everyday Life in Prehistory. 2008. (Uncovering History Ser.). (ENG., Illus.). 48p. (J). (gr. 2-7). 19.95 *(978-88-89272-59-6(7))* McRae Bks. Srl ITA. Dist: Independent Pubs. Group.

Newland, Sonya. Stone, Bronze & Iron Ages. 2017. (Explore! Ser.). (ENG., Illus.). 32p. (J). (gr. 4-6). pap. 12.99 ***(978-0-7502-9736-3(0)***, Wayland) Hachette Children's Group GBR. Dist: Hachette Bk. Group.

Pacchini, Fiorenzo. A Day with Homo Habilis: Life 2,000,000 Years Ago. 2003. (Early Humans Ser.). (Illus.). 48p. (gr. 6-18). lib. bdg. 23.90 *(978-0-7613-2765-3(7)*, Twenty-First Century Bks.) Lerner Publishing Group.

Passport to the Past, 8 vols., Set. Incl. Ancient Egypt. Steele, Philip. 64p. (J). (gr. 4-7). lib. bdg. 31.95 *(978-1-4358-5173-3(0))*; Ancient Greece. Tames, Richard. 61p. (J). (gr. 4-7). lib. bdg. 31.95 *(978-1-4358-5175-7(7))*; Ancient India. Ali, Daud. 64p. (YA). (gr. 4-7). lib. bdg. 31.95 *(978-1-4358-5169-6(2))*; Aztec & Maya Worlds. MacDonald, Fiona. 64p. (J). (gr. 4-7). lib. bdg. 31.95 *(978-1-4358-5170-2(6))*; Chinese Empire. Steele, Philip. 64p. (YA). (gr. 5-8). lib. bdg. 31.95 *(978-1-4358-5174-0(9))*; Mesopotamia. Oakes, Lorna. 64p. (J). (gr. 4-7). lib. bdg. 31.95 *(978-1-4358-5172-6(2))*; Roman Empire. Steele, Philip. 64p. (J). (gr. 4-7). lib. bdg. 31.95 *(978-1-4358-5176-4(5))*; World of North American Indians. Stotter, Mike. 64p. (YA). (gr. 4-7). lib. bdg. 31.95 *(978-1-4358-5171-9(4))*; (Illus.). 2009. Set lib. bdg. 234.00 *(978-1-4358-5215-0(X))* Rosen Publishing Group, Inc., The.

Rice, Dona Herweck. First Fire. 2015. (Building Fluency Through Reader's Theater Ser.). (ENG., Illus.). 32p. (gr. 4-4). pap. 7.99 *(978-1-4938-1291-2(2))* Teacher Created Materials, Inc.

Riggs, Kate. Easter Island. 2009. (Places of Old Ser.). 24p. (J). (gr. 1-5). lib. bdg. 24.25 *(978-1-58341-710-2(9)*, Creative Education) Creative Co., The.

Rubalcaba, Jill & Robertshaw, Peter. Every Bone Tells a Story: Hominin Discoveries, Deductions, & Debates. 2010. (ENG., Illus.). 192p. (J). (gr. 5-8). 18.95 *(978-1-58089-164-6(0))* Charlesbridge Publishing, Inc.

Schomp, Virginia. Prehistoric World, 5 bks., Group 3. Incl. Ceratosaurus: And Other Horned Meat-Eaters. 31p. (J). (gr. 3-7). lib. bdg. *(978-0-7614-2009-5(6))*; Iguanodon: And Other Spiky-Thumbed Plant-Eaters. 32p. (gr. 4-7). lib. bdg. 20.95 *(978-0-7614-2005-7(3))*; Ornithomimus: And Other Speedy Ostrich Dinosaurs. 31p. (J). (gr. 3-7). lib. bdg. *(978-0-7614-2006-4(1))*; Plateosaurus: And Other Early Long-Necked Plant-Eaters. 32p. (gr. 4-7). lib. bdg. 20.95 *(978-0-7614-2008-8(8))*; Therizinosaurus: And Other Colossal-Clawed Plant-Eaters. 32p. (gr. 4-7). lib. bdg. 20.95 *(978-0-7614-2007-1(X))*; (Illus.). 2005. *(978-0-7614-2004-0(5)*, Benchmark Bks.) Marshall Cavendish Corp.

Wood, Robert Muir. Discovering Prehistory. 2012. (ENG., Illus.). 48p. (J). 15.00 *(978-1-899762-87-3(6))* Award Pubns. Ltd. GBR. Dist: Parkwest Pubns., Inc.

PREHISTORIC PEOPLES—FICTION

Angeletti, Roberta. The Cave Painter of Lascaux. 2004. (Illus.). 32p. (J). 16.95 *(978-1-56290-323-7(3))* Crystal Productions.

Bardhan-Quallen, Sudipta. Caveboy Is Bored! Wight, Eric, illus. 2017. (Caveboy Ser.). (ENG.). 80p. (J). 9.99 *(978-1-68119-045-7(1)*, 9781681190457, Bloomsbury USA Childrens) Bloomsbury Publishing USA.

Beckhorn, Susan Williams. The Wolf's Boy. 2016. (ENG., Illus.). 236p. (J). (gr. 3-7). 16.99 *(978-1-4847-2553-5(0))* Disney Pr.

Brenchley, Chaz & Doyle, Arthur Conan. The Lost World. Bennett, Felix, illus. 2009. (Real Reads Ser.). 64p. (J). (gr. 4-8). pap. 13.55 *(978-1-60754-395-4(8))*; lib. bdg. 29.25 *(978-1-60754-394-7(X))* Windmill Bks.

Brett, Jan. The First Dog. Brett, Jan, illus. 2015. (ENG., Illus.). 32p. (J). (gr. -1-k). 17.99 *(978-0-399-17270-0(X)*, G.P. Putnam's Sons Books for Young Readers) Penguin Young Readers Group.

Brooks, Mel & Reiner, Carl. The 2000 Year Old Man Goes to School. Bennett, James, illus. 2006. 32p. (J). (gr. 4-8). reprint ed. 18.00 *(978-1-4223-5622-7(1))* DIANE Publishing Co.

—The 2000 Year Old Man Goes to School. Bennett, James, illus. 2005. (ENG.). 40p. (J). (gr. -1-3). 17.99 *(978-0-06-076676-4(X))* HarperCollins Pubs.

Burroughs, Edgar Rice. The Land That Time Forgot: Graphic Novel. Jones, K. L., illus. 2011. (Campfire Graphic Novels Ser.). (ENG.). 72p. (YA). (gr. 5-12). pap. 9.99 *(978-93-80028-38-5(5)*, Campfire) Steerforth Pr.

Christopher, John. In the Beginning. 2015. (ENG., Illus.). 288p. (J). (gr. 5-9). pap. 7.99 *(978-1-4814-2003-7(8)*, Aladdin) Simon & Schuster Children's Publishing.

Clark, Patricia Nikolina. In the Shadow of the Mammoth. LeTourneau, Anthony Alex, illus. (J). 2005. 14.99 *(978-0-9674602-8-4(X))* 2003. 190p. pap. 6.99 *(978-0-9674602-4-6(7))* Blue Marlin Pubns.

Craddock, Erik. BC Mambo. Craddock, Erik, illus. 2009. (Stone Rabbit Ser.: Bk. 1). (ENG., Illus.). 96p. (J). (gr. 3-7). pap. 6.99 *(978-0-375-84360-0(4)*, Random Hse. Bks. for Young Readers) Random Hse. Children's Bks.

Dolenz, Micky. Gakky Two-Feet. Clark, David, illus. 2006. (J). *(978-1-4156-8089-6(2)*, Putnam Juvenile) Penguin Publishing Group.

Fidler, Kathleen. The Boy with the Bronze Axe. 3rd rev. ed. (ENG., Illus.). 176p. 11.95 *(978-0-86315-488-1(3))* Floris Bks. GBR. Dist: SteinerBooks, Inc.

Fox Mazer, Norma. Saturday, the Twelfth of October. 2015. (ENG.). 274p. (J). (gr. 3). pap. 13.95 *(978-1-939601-31-5(2))* Ig Publishing, Inc.

Fragoso, Sarah. Paleo Pals: Jimmy & the Carrot Rocket Ship. 2012. (ENG., Illus.). 80p. (J). (gr. -1-2). pap. 19.95 *(978-1-936608-88-1(X))* Victory Belt Publishing.

Fraser, Ian. Life with Mammoth, 0 vols. Fraser, Mary Ann, illus. (Ogg & Bob Ser.). (ENG.). 64p. (J). (gr. k-3). 2013. pap. 9.99 *(978-1-4778-1615-8(1)*, 9781477816158) 2010. 14.99 *(978-0-7614-5722-0(4)*, 9780761457220) Amazon Publishing. (Amazon Children's Publishing).

—Meet Mammoth, 0 vols. Fraser, Mary Ann, illus. 2013. (Ogg & Bob Ser.). (ENG.). 64p. (J). (gr. 1-3). pap. 9.99 *(978-1-4778-1617-2(8)*, 9781477816172, Amazon Children's Publishing) Amazon Publishing.

Freedman, Claire. Dinosaurs Love Underpants. Cort, Ben, illus. 2009. (Underpants Bks.). (ENG.). 32p. (J). (gr. -1-2). 16.99 *(978-1-4169-8938-7(2)*, Aladdin) Simon & Schuster Children's Publishing.

Gear, Kathleen O'Neal & Gear, W. Michael. Children of the Dawnland. 2010. (ENG.). 336p. (J). (gr. 4-7). pap. 5.99 *(978-0-7653-5986-5(3)*, 9780765359865, Starscape) Doherty, Tom Assocs., LLC.

Gerstein, Mordicai. The First Drawing. 2013. (ENG., Illus.). 40p. (J). (gr. -1-3). 18.99 *(978-0-316-20478-1(1))* Little, Brown Bks. for Young Readers.

Grant, John. The Explorer. Collins, Ross, illus. 2014. (ENG.). 336p. (J). pap. 8.99 *(978-1-4711-2135-7(6)*, Simon & Schuster Children's) Simon & Schuster, Ltd. GBR. Dist: Simon & Schuster, Inc.

—Littlenose the Magician. Collins, Ross, illus. 2009. (ENG.). 112p. (J). (gr. k-12). pap. 5.99 *(978-1-84738-201-6(0)*, Simon & Schuster Children's) Simon & Schuster, Ltd. GBR. Dist: Simon & Schuster, Inc.

—The Magician. Collins, Ross, illus. 2014. (ENG.). 352p. (J). pap. 8.99 *(978-1-4711-2137-1(2)*, Simon & Schuster Children's) Simon & Schuster, Ltd. GBR. Dist: Simon & Schuster, Inc.

Graves, Keith. Puppy! 2016. (ENG., Illus.). 32p. (J). 16.99 *(978-1-62672-225-5(0)*, 9781626722255) Roaring Brook Pr.

Gravet & Donaldson, Julia. Cave Baby, 3. Gravett, Emily, illus. 2nd ed. 2011. (ENG.). 32p. (J). (gr. -1-k). 11.99 *(978-0-330-52276-2(0))* Pan Macmillan GBR. Dist: Independent Pubs. Group.

Greenburg, J. C. In the Ice Age. Gerardi, Jan, illus. 2005. (Andrew Lost Ser.: 12). (ENG.). 96p. (J). (gr. 1-4). 3.99 *(978-0-375-82952-9(0)*, Random Hse. Bks. for Young Readers) Random Hse. Children's Bks.

Griffin, Adele. Oona Finds an Egg. Wu, Mike, illus. 2016. (Oodlethunks Ser.: Bk. 1). (ENG.). 160p. (J). (gr. 3-7). 12.99 *(978-0-545-73279-6(4)*, Scholastic Pr.) Scholastic, Inc.

Grimaldi. My Amazing Dinosaur. Burrell, Carol klio, tr. from FRE. Bannister, illus. 2014. (Tib & Tumtum Ser.: 2). (ENG.). 48p. (J). (gr. 2-5). lib. bdg. 26.60 *(978-1-4677-1298-9(1)*, Graphic Universe™) Lerner Publishing Group.

—Welcome to the Tribe! Bannister, illus. 2013. (Tib & Tumtum Ser.: 1). (ENG.). 48p. (J). (gr. 2-5). pap. 6.95 *(978-1-4677-1522-5(0))*; lib. bdg. 26.60 *(978-1-4677-1297-2(3))* Lerner Publishing Group. (Graphic Universe™).

Grimaldi, Flora. My Amazing Dinosaur. Burrell, Carol klio, tr. Bannister, illus. 2014. (Tib & Tumtum Ser.: 2). (ENG.). 48p. (J). (gr. 2-5). pap. 7.95 *(978-1-4677-2181-3(6)*, Graphic Universe™) Lerner Publishing Group.

Klio Burrell, Carol. Welcome to the Tribe!, 1. 2013. 48p. pap. 26.60 *(978-1-4677-1656-7(1))* Lerner Publishing Group.

Marshall, Jill. Kave-Tina Rox. Childs, Sam, illus. 2010. (ENG.). 32p. (J). *(978-0-340-95712-7(3)*, Hodder Children's Books) Hachette Children's Group GBR. Dist: Hachette Bk. Group.

McDonnell, Patrick. Tek, the Modern Cave Boy. 2016. (ENG., Illus.). 40p. (J). (gr. -1-3). 15.99 *(978-0-316-33805-9(2))* Little Brown & Co.

Montgomery, R. A. The Trail of Lost Time. 2011. (Illus.). 144p. (J). mass mkt. 6.99 *(978-1-937133-03-0(6))* Chooseco LLC.

Nolan, Alan. Conor's Caveman: The Amazing Adventures of Ogg. 2016. (ENG., Illus.). 144p. (J). pap. 11.00 *(978-1-84717-732-2(8))* O'Brien Pr., Ltd., The IRL. Dist: Dufour Editions, Inc.

Osborne, Mary Pope. Un Tigre Dientes de Sable en el Ocaso. 2004. (Casa del Arbol Ser.: 7).Tr. of Sunset of the Sabretooth. (SPA., Illus.). (J). pap. 5.99 *(978-1-930332-68-3(8))* Lectorum Pubns., Inc.

Paver, Michelle. The Burning Shadow. 2015. (Gods & Warriors Ser.: 2). (ENG.). 320p. (J). (gr. 5). 7.99 *(978-0-14-242285-4(1)*, Puffin Books) Penguin Young Readers Group.

—Ghost Hunter. Taylor, Geoff, illus. (Chronicles of Ancient Darkness Ser.: 6). 304p. (J). (gr. 5). 2011. pap. 7.99 *(978-0-06-072842-7(6))* 2010. 16.99 *(978-0-06-072840-3(X))* HarperCollins Pubs. (Tegen, Katherine Bks).

—Gods & Warriors. 2013. (Gods & Warriors Ser.: 1). (ENG.). 336p. (J). (gr. 5). pap. 8.99 *(978-0-14-242284-7(3)*, Puffin Books) Penguin Young Readers Group.

—HERMANO LOBO: CRÓNICAS DE LA PREHISTORIA I. 2005. (SPA., Illus.). 222p. 17.25 *(978-84-7888-933-4(7))* Emece Editores ESP. Dist: Ediciones Universal.

—Oath Breaker. Taylor, Geoff, illus. (Chronicles of Ancient Darkness Ser.: 5). (J). (gr. 5). 2010. 320p. pap. 6.99 *(978-0-06-072839-7(6))* 2009. 304p. 16.99 *(978-0-06-072837-3(X))* HarperCollins Pubs. (Tegen, Katherine Bks).

—Outcast. Taylor, Geoff, illus. (J). (gr. 5). 2009. (Chronicles of Ancient Darkness Ser.: 4). 352p. pap. 6.99 *(978-0-06-072836-6(1)*, Tegen, Katherine Bks) 2008. (Chronicles of Ancient Darkness: No. 4). 336p. 16.99 *(978-0-06-072834-2(5))* HarperCollins Pubs.

—Soul Eater. Taylor, Geoff, illus. 2008. (Chronicles of Ancient Darkness Ser.: 3). 352p. (J). (gr. 5). pap. 6.99 *(978-0-06-072833-5(7)*, Tegen, Katherine Bks) HarperCollins Pubs.

—Soul Eater. 2007. (Chronicles of Ancient Darkness: No. 3). (Illus.). 323p. (J). (gr. 5-9). 16.99 *(978-0-06-072831-1(0)*, Tegen, Katherine Bks) HarperCollins Pubs.

—Spirit Walker. Taylor, Geoff, illus. 2007. (Chronicles of Ancient Darkness Ser.: 2). 384p. (J). (gr. 5-9). per. 6.99 *(978-0-06-072830-4(2)*, Tegen, Katherine Bks) HarperCollins Pubs.

—Warrior Bronze. 2017. (Gods & Warriors Ser.). (ENG.). 272p. (J). (gr. 3-7). 16.99 *(978-0-8037-3884-3(6)*, Dial Bks) Penguin Young Readers Group.

—Wolf Brother. Taylor, Geoff, illus. 2006. (Chronicles of Ancient Darkness Ser.: 1). 320p. (J). (gr. 5-9). reprint ed. per. 6.99 *(978-0-06-072827-4(2)*, Tegen, Katherine Bks) HarperCollins Pubs.

—Wolf Brother, 6 vols. 2005. (Chronicles of Ancient Darkness Ser.: 1). (J). 89.75 *(978-1-4193-3811-3(0))*; 76.75 *(978-1-4193-2628-8(7))*; 91.75 *(978-1-4193-3809-0(9))*; 73.75 *(978-1-4193-2630-1(9))* Recorded Bks., Inc.

Pilkey, Dav. The Adventures of Ook & Gluk, Kung-Fu Cavemen from the Future. Pilkey, Dav, illus. (Captain Underpants Ser.). (ENG., Illus.). 176p. (J). (gr. 2-5). 2011. 5.99 *(978-0-545-38577-0(6))* 2010. 9.99 *(978-0-545-17530-2(5))* Scholastic, Inc.

—The Adventures of Ook & Gluk, Kung-Fu Cavemen from the Future. 2011. lib. bdg. 16.00 *(978-0-606-16381-1(6)*, Turtleback) Turtleback Bks.

—Las Aventuras de Uuk y Gluk, Cavernícolas del Futuro y Maestros de Kung Fu. Pilkey, Dav, illus. 2011. (Captain Underpants Ser.). (SPA., Illus.). 176p. (J). (gr. 2-5). pap. 5.99 *(978-0-545-27916-1(X)*, Scholastic en Espanol) Scholastic, Inc.

Pilkey, Dav & Beard, George. The Adventures of Ook & Gluk, Kung-Fu Cavemen from the Future. 2010. lib. bdg. 20.85 *(978-0-606-15003-3(X)*, Turtleback) Turtleback Bks.

Popescu, Petru. Footprints in Time. 2008. 256p. (J). (gr. 5). lib. bdg. 17.89 *(978-0-06-088400-0(2)*, Geringer, Laura Book) HarperCollins Pubs.

Posner, Damean. Helix & the Arrival. Faber, Jules, illus. 2015. (ENG.). 288p. (J). (gr. 4-7). pap. 9.99 *(978-0-85798-653-5(8))* Random Hse. Australia AUS. Dist: Independent Pubs. Group.

Randerath, Jeanette & Winterhager, Randerath -. ¡vuela, Yoa, Vuela! 2012. (SPA.). 32p. (J). (gr. 2-3). pap. 19.99 *(978-84-261-3918-4(3))* Juventud, Editorial ESP. Dist: Lectorum Pubns., Inc.

Regan, Dian. The Dragon Stone, 0 vols. Curtis, Stacy, illus. 2013. (ENG.). 96p. (J). (gr. 2-4). pap. 9.99 *(978-1-4778-1632-5(1)*, 9781477816325, Amazon Children's Publishing) Amazon Publishing.

Reynolds, Aaron & Wells, Rosemary. Caveboy Dave: More Scrawny Than Brawny. McAndrew, Phil, illus. 2016. (Caveboy Dave Ser.: 1). (ENG.). 256p. (J). (gr. 3-7). bds. 12.99 *(978-0-14-751658-9(7)*, Viking Books for Young Readers) Penguin Young Readers Group.

Richardson, Faith. The Peacock's Stone. 2003. 192p. (J). 21.95 *(978-0-9744989-0-4(4))*; (Illus.). pap. 12.95 *(978-0-9744989-1-1(2))* Fox Song Bks.

Rolli. Kabungo, 1 vol. Pavlovic, Milan, illus. 2016. (ENG.). 176p. (J). (gr. 1-5). 14.95 *(978-1-55498-804-4(7))* Groundwood Bks. CAN. Dist: Publishers Group West (PGW).

Scieszka, Jon. Your Mother Was a Neanderthal. Smith, Lane, illus. 2004. (Time Warp Trio Ser.: 4). (ENG.). 80p. (J). (gr. 2-4). pap. 5.99 *(978-0-14-240048-7(3)*, Puffin Books) Penguin Young Readers Group.

—Your Mother Was a Neanderthal. Smith, Lane, illus. 2006. (Time Warp Trio Ser.: No. 4). 78p. (gr. 4-7). 15.00 *(978-0-7569-6782-6(1))* Perfection Learning Corp.

—Your Mother Was a Neanderthal. Smith, Lane, illus. 2004. (Time Warp Trio Ser.: 4). 78p. (J). 16.00 *(978-1-4176-3603-7(3))* Turtleback Bks.

Shickman, Allan Richard. Dael & the Painted People. 2011. (Zan-Gah Ser.). 155p. (YA). pap. 9.95 *(978-0-9790357-6-0(7))* Earthshaker Bks.

—Zan-Gah: A Prehistoric Adventure. 2007. 160p. (J). (gr. 4-7). per. 9.95 *(978-0-9790357-0-8(8))* Earthshaker Bks.

—Zan-Gah & the Beautiful Country. 2009. 151p. pap. 9.95 *(978-0-9790357-1-5(6))* Earthshaker Bks.

Stilton, Geronimo. Get the Scoop, Geronimo! 2015. (Geronimo Stilton Cavemice Ser.: 9). 128p. (J). lib. bdg. 17.20 *(978-0-606-37779-9(4))* Turtleback Bks.

—Help, I'm in Hot Lava! 2013. (Geronimo Stilton Cavemice Ser.: 3). (ENG., Illus.). 128p. (J). (gr. 2-5). pap. 7.99 *(978-0-545-64290-3(6)*, Scholastic Paperbacks) Scholastic, Inc.

—Help, I'm in Hot Lava! 2013. (Geronimo Stilton Cavemice Ser.: 3). lib. bdg. 17.20 *(978-0-606-32407-6(0)*, Turtleback) Turtleback Bks.

—The Stone of Fire. 2013. (Geronimo Stilton Cavemice Ser.: 1). lib. bdg. 18.40 *(978-0-606-31526-5(8)*, Turtleback) Turtleback Bks.

Storm, Zed. Will Solvit & the Cannibal Cavemen. 2010. (Will Solvit Ser.: Bk. 5). (Illus.). 128p. (J). (gr. 1-7). pap. *(978-1-4075-8983-1(0))* Parragon, Inc.

Talbott, Hudson. From Wolf to Woof. Talbott, Hudson, illus. 2016. (ENG., Illus.). 40p. (J). (gr. k-3). 16.99 *(978-0-399-25404-8(8)*, Nancy Paulsen Books) Penguin Young Readers Group.

Tankard, Jeremy. Me Hungry! Tankard, Jeremy, illus. (ENG., Illus.). (J). 2010. 34p. (— 1). bds. 7.99 *(978-0-7636-4780-3(2))* 2008. 40p. (gr. -1-2). 15.99 *(978-0-7636-3360-8(7))* Candlewick Pr.

Turnbull, Ann. Maroo of the Winter Caves. 20th anniv. ed. 2004. (ENG., Illus.). 144p. (J). (gr. 2-5). pap. 6.95 *(978-0-618-44299-7(5))* Houghton Mifflin Harcourt Publishing Co.

Williams, Susan. Wind Rider. 2006. 309p. (J). (gr. 5-9). 16.99 *(978-0-06-087236-6(5))* HarperCollins Pubs.

Zeltser, David. Blast from the North. 2016. (Lug Ser.: 2). (ENG., Illus.). 160p. (gr. 3-6). 15.99 *(978-1-5124-0641-2(4))*; 31.99 *(978-1-5124-0890-4(5))* Lerner Publishing Group. (Carolrhoda Bks.).

—Lug, Dawn of the Ice Age, No. 1. 2014. (ENG., Illus.). 182p. (J). (gr. 3-7). 15.99 *(978-1-60684-513-4(6)*, Carolrhoda Bks.) Lerner Publishing Group.

PREHISTORY

see Archaeology; Prehistoric Peoples; Stone Age

PREJUDICES

see also Antisemitism

Adams, Christine. God Made Us One by One: How to See Prejudice & Celebrate Differences. Alley, R. W., illus. 2008. (J). mass mkt. 7.95 *(978-0-87029-418-1(0))* Abbey Pr.

Aikins, Anne Marie. Racism: Deal with It Before It Gets under Your Skin, 1 vol. Murray, Steven, illus. 2010. (Lorimer Deal with It Ser.). (ENG.). 32p. (J). (gr. 4-6). 24.95 *(978-1-55277-495-3(3)*, 9781552774953) Lorimer, James & Co., Ltd., Pubs. CAN. Dist: Casemate Pubs. & Bk. Distributors, LLC.

Baptiste, Tracey & Banas, Sharon L. Overcoming Prejudice. 2009. (Character Education Ser.). (Illus.). 128p. (gr. 6-12). 35.00 *(978-1-60413-119-2(5)*, Chelsea Hse.) Facts On File, Inc.

Cunningham, Anne C., ed. Environmental Racism & Classism. 2017. (At Issue Ser.). 128p. (J). (gr. 10-12). pap. 27.80 ***(978-1-5345-0040-2(5))***; (ESK.). lib. bdg. 39.40 ***(978-1-5345-0016-7(2))*** Greenhaven Publishing LLC. (Greenhaven Publishing).

Davidson, Tish. Prejudice. (Life Balance Ser.). (ENG.). 80p. 2004. (YA). (gr. 5-8). pap. 6.95 *(978-0-531-15572-1(2))* 2003. (Illus.). (J). 20.50 *(978-0-531-12252-5(2))* Scholastic Library Publishing. (Watts, Franklin).

Gay, Kathlyn. Cultural Diversity: Conflicts & Challenges. 2003. (It Happened to Me Ser.: 6). (ENG., Illus.). 144p. pap. 45.00 *(978-0-8108-4805-4(8))* Scarecrow Pr., Inc.

Hanes, Richard Clay, et al. Prejudice in the Modern World. 2007. (J). *(978-1-4144-0206-2(6))*; *(978-1-4144-0205-5(8))* Cengage Gale.

Harrison, Geoffrey C. & Scott, Thomas F. The Fight for Freedom. Stewart, Mark & Kennedy, Mike, eds. 2014. (Great Debates Ser.). (ENG.). 48p. (J). (gr. 5-8). lib. bdg. 29.27 *(978-1-59953-588-3(2))* Norwood Hse. Pr.

Henneberg, Susan, ed. Race in America. 2017. (Opposing Viewpoints Ser.). 224p. (YA). (gr. 10-12). pap. 33.80 ***(978-1-5345-0028-0(6))***; lib. bdg. 48.80 ***(978-1-5345-0022-8(7))*** Greenhaven Publishing LLC. (Greenhaven Publishing).

Hill, Z. B. Gallup Guides for Youth Facing Persistent Prejudice. 2012. (Gallup Guides for Youth Facing Persistent Prejudice Ser.). 64p. (J). (gr. 7-8). 22.95 *(978-1-4222-2463-2(5))* Mason Crest.

McCage, Crystal D., ed. Prejudice. 2009. (Issues That Concern You Ser.). (ENG., Illus.). 144p. (gr. 10-12). lib. bdg. 42.00 *(978-0-7377-4349-4(2)*, LML02109-245305, Greenhaven Pr., Inc.) Cengage Gale.

McIntosh, Kenneth & Walker, Ida. Youth with Cultural/Language Differences: Interpreting an Alien World. 2009. (Helping Youth with Mental, Physical, & Social Challenges Ser.). (Illus.). 128p. (YA). (gr. 7-18). lib. bdg. 24.95 *(978-1-4222-0141-1(4))* Mason Crest.

Palmer, Bill. Gallup Guides for Youth Facing Persistent Prejudice. 2012. (Gallup Guides for Youth Facing Persistent Prejudice Ser.). 64p. (J). (gr. 7-8). 22.95 *(978-1-4222-2466-3(X))* Mason Crest.

Patrick, Denise Lewis. A Lesson for Martin Luther King, Jr. Pate, Rodney S., illus. 2003. (Ready-To-read COFA Ser.). (ENG.). 32p. (J). (gr. k-2). pap. 3.99 *(978-0-689-85397-5(1)*, Simon Spotlight) Simon Spotlight.

Prejudice Throughout History Reference Library 4 Vol Set, 4.0. rev. ed. 2007. (Prejudice in the Modern World Reference Library). (ENG.). 372.00 *(978-1-4144-0203-1(1)*, UXL) Cengage Gale.

Rodger, Marguerite & Rodger, Jessie. Racism & Prejudice. 2010. (Straight Talk about... Ser.). (ENG.). 48p. (J). (gr. 7-10). lib. bdg. *(978-0-7787-2129-1(9))* Crabtree Publishing Co.

Sanna, Ellyn. Gallup Guides for Youth Facing Persistent Prejudice Muslims. 2012. (Gallup Guides for Youth Facing Persistent Prejudice Ser.). 64p. (J). (gr. 7-8). 22.95 *(978-1-4222-2468-7(6))* Mason Crest.

—People with Mental & Physical Challenges. 2012. (Gallup Guides for Youth Facing Persistent Prejudice Ser.). 64p. (J). (gr. 7-8). 22.95 *(978-1-4222-2470-0(8))* Mason Crest.

Scheunemann, Pam. Learning about Differences, 1 vol. 2004. (Keeping the Peace Ser.). (ENG., Illus.). 24p. (J). (gr. k-3). lib. bdg. 24.21 *(978-1-59197-561-8(1)*, SandCastle) ABDO Publishing Co.

—Tolerance. 2003. (United We Stand Ser.). (ENG., Illus.). 24p. (J). (gr. k-3). lib. bdg. 24.21 *(978-1-57765-881-8(7)*, SandCastle) ABDO Publishing Co.

Seba, Jaime. Gallup Guides for Youth Facing Persistent Prejudice: Blacks. 2012. (Gallup Guides for Youth Facing Persistent Prejudice Ser.). 64p. (J). (gr. 7-8). 22.95 *(978-1-4222-2464-9(3))* Mason Crest.

St. Stephen's Community House Staff. It's Not All Black & White: Multiracial Youth Speak Out. 2012. (ENG., Illus.). 120p. (YA). (gr. 7-12). pap. 12.95 *(978-1-55451-380-2(4)*, 9781554513802) Annick Pr., Ltd. CAN. Dist: Publishers Group West (PGW).

Steele, Philip. Race & Crime. 2016. (Illus.). 48p. (J). *(978-0-7787-2588-6(X))* Crabtree Publishing Co.

Thomson Gale Staff. Prejudice in the Modern World. Hanes, Sharon M., ed. rev. ed. 2007. (Prejudice in the Modern World Reference Library). (ENG.). 256p. (YA). 106.00 *(978-1-4144-0208-6(2)*, UXL) Cengage Gale.

—Prejudice in the Modern World - Almanac, 2.0. Hanes, Richard C. et al, eds. rev. ed. 2007. (Prejudice in the Modern World Reference Library). (ENG.). 462p. (YA). 191.00 *(978-1-4144-0204-8(X)*, UXL) Cengage Gale.

Thomson Gale Staff & Hermsen, Sarah. Prejudice in the Modern World: Biographies. Hanes, Richard C. & Rudd, Kelly, eds. rev. ed. 2007. (Prejudice in the Modern World Reference Library). (ENG.). 288p. (YA). 106.00 *(978-1-4144-0207-9(4)*, UXL) Cengage Gale.

—Prejudice in the Modern World: Cumulative Index. rev. ed. 2007. (Prejudice in the Modern World Reference Library). (ENG.). 34p. (YA). 5.00 *(978-1-4144-0209-3(0)*, UXL) Cengage Gale.

Webber, Diane & Mandel, Laurie. Totally Tolerant: Spotting & Stopping Prejudice. 2008. (ENG.). 112p. (J). (gr. 7-18). pap. 8.95 *(978-0-531-20525-9(8))*; (Illus.). 27.00 *(978-0-531-13867-0(4)*, Children's Pr.) Scholastic Library Publishing.

Wright, John D. Race & Crime. 2004. (Crime & Detection Ser.). (Illus.). 96p. (YA). (gr. 7-18). lib. bdg. 22.95 *(978-1-59084-378-9(9))* Mason Crest.

PREJUDICES—FICTION

Ahern, Cecelia. Perfect. 2017. (Flawed Ser.). (ENG.). 352p. (YA). 18.99 *(978-1-250-07412-6(6)*, 9781250074126) Feiwel & Friends.

Alexander, Jill S. The Sweetheart of Prosper County. 2010. (ENG.). 240p. (YA). (gr. 7-12). pap. 18.99 *(978-0-312-54857-5(5)*, 9780312548575) Square Fish.

Allison, Teresa J. Bobble Stories: The Oddbobble's Visit. Allison, Charles T., illus. 2013. 48p. pap. 12.99 *(978-0-9887612-0-9(3))* Tawnsy Publishing.

Armistead, John & Gregory, Fran. The $66 Summer: A Novel of the Segregated South. 2nd ed. 2006. (Milkweed Prize for Children's Literature Ser.). (ENG., Illus.). 240p. (J). (gr. 3-8). reprint ed. per. 8.00 *(978-1-57131-663-9(9))* Milkweed Editions.

Austin, Cassie Rita. Peppermint. Austin, Cassie Rita, illus. 2011. (Illus.). 53p. 15.95 *(978-0-9846151-1-7(3))* Paintbrush Tales Publishing, LLC.

Banks, Jacqueline Turner. A Day for Vincent Chin & Me. 2005. (ENG.). 128p. (J). (gr. 5-7). pap. 11.95 *(978-0-618-54879-8(3))* Houghton Mifflin Harcourt Publishing Co.

Barker, M. P. A Difficult Boy. 2009. (ENG.). 272p. (YA). (gr. 5-18). pap. 7.95 *(978-0-8234-2244-9(5))* Holiday Hse., Inc.

—Mending Horses. 2014. (ENG.). 320p. (J). (gr. 5). 17.95 *(978-0-8234-2948-6(2))* Holiday Hse., Inc.

Baskin, Nora Raleigh. The Truth about My Bat Mitzvah. 2009. (Mix Ser.). (ENG.). 144p. (J). (gr. 4-8). pap. 7.99 *(978-1-4169-7469-7(5),* Aladdin) Simon & Schuster Children's Publishing.

Bell, Anthea. Frog in Love. Velthuijs, Max, illus. 2015. (J). *(978-1-4351-5750-7(8))* Barnes & Noble, Inc.

Beus, Bryan. Westly: A Spider's Tale. Beus, Bryan, illus. 2015. (Illus.). 171p. (J). 15.99 *(978-1-62972-068-5(2),* Shadow Mountain) Deseret Bk. Co.

Blackford, Cheryl. Lizzie & the Lost Baby. 2016. (ENG.). 192p. (J). (gr. 5-7). 16.99 *(978-0-544-57099-3(5),* HMH Books For Young Readers) Houghton Mifflin Harcourt Publishing Co.

Blackman, Malorie. Black & White. 2007. (ENG.). 512p. (YA). (gr. 9-12). pap. 12.99 *(978-1-4169-0017-7(9),* Simon & Schuster Bks. For Young Readers) Simon & Schuster Bks. For Young Readers.

—Knife Edge. 2007. (ENG., Illus.). 368p. (YA). (gr. 9-12). 16.99 *(978-1-4169-0018-4(7),* Simon & Schuster Bks. For Young Readers) Simon & Schuster Bks. For Young Readers.

Blume, Judy. Iggie's House. 2014. (ENG., Illus.). (J). (gr. 3-7). 160p. 17.99 *(978-1-4814-1410-4(0));* 176p. pap. 7.99 *(978-1-4814-1104-2(7))* Simon & Schuster Children's Publishing. (Atheneum Bks. for Young Readers).

Boedoe, Geefwee. Arrowville. Boedoe, Geefwee, illus. 2004. (Illus.). 40p. (J). (gr. -1-2). 16.89 *(978-0-06-055599-3(8),* Geringer, Laura Book) HarperCollins Pubs.

Bradbury, Bianca. Flight into Spring. 2005. (Sally (Bethlehem Books) Ser.). 184p. (YA). (gr. 7). per. 11.95 *(978-1-932350-01-2(2))* Bethlehem Bks.

Bradley, John Ed. Call Me by My Name. (ENG.). (YA). (gr. 7). 2015. 288p. pap. 11.99 *(978-1-4424-9794-8(7))* 2014. (Illus.). 272p. 17.99 *(978-1-4424-9793-1(9),* Atheneum Bks. for Young Readers) Simon & Schuster Children's Publishing.

Brown, Celease N. & Mubarak, Enoch. The Color Orange. 2004. (Illus.). 32p. *(978-1-55306-742-9(8),* Guardian Bks.) Essence Publishing.

Byars, Betsy. The Blossoms Meet the Vulture Lady. 2008. (Blossom Family Book Ser.: 2). (ENG., Illus.). 134p. (J). (gr. 4-7). 6.95 *(978-0-8234-2144-2(9))* Holiday Hse., Inc.

Calhoun, Dia. Avielle of Rhia, 1 vol. 2006. (ENG.). 400p. (J). (gr. 6). 16.99 *(978-0-7614-5320-8(2))* Marshall Cavendish Corp.

Chen, Justina. Nothing but the Truth (And a Few White Lies) 2007. (Justina Chen Novel Ser.). (ENG.). 256p. (J). (gr. 7-17). per. 9.99 *(978-0-316-01131-0(2))* Little, Brown Bks. for Young Readers.

Chotjewitz, David & Orgel, Doris. Daniel, Half Human: And the Good Nazi. 2004. 298p. (J). *(978-3-551-58045-0(6))* Carlsen Verlag DEU. Dist: Distribooks, Inc.

Clements, Andrew. The Jacket. 2014. (ENG.). 96p. (J). (gr. 3-7). 10.24 *(978-1-63245-301-3(0))* Lectorum Pubns., Inc.

—The Jacket. Henderson, McDavid, illus. 2003. (ENG.). 96p. (J). (gr. 3-7). pap. 6.99 *(978-0-689-86010-2(2),* Atheneum Bks. for Young Readers) Simon & Schuster Children's Publishing.

Clifton Wisler, G. All for Texas. 2004. 140p. (J). lib. bdg. 16.92 *(978-1-4242-0767-1(3))* Fitzgerald Bks.

Coats, J. Anderson. The Wicked & the Just. (ENG.). 352p. (YA). (gr. 7). 2012. 16.99 *(978-0-547-68837-4(7))* 2013. pap. 9.99 *(978-0-544-02221-8(1))* Houghton Mifflin Harcourt Publishing Co.

Cohen, Miriam. Layla's Head Scarf, 1 vol. Himler, Ronald, illus. 2009. (ENG.). 32p. (J). (gr. -1-3). 15.95 *(978-1-59572-177-8(0));* pap. 5.95 *(978-1-59572-178-5(9))* Star Bright Bks., Inc.

Coleman, Evelyn. Circle of Fire. 2009. (Mysteries Through Time Ser.). 160p. (YA). (gr. 4-8). 31.95 *(978-1-60754-191-2(2));* pap. 15.25 *(978-1-60754-192-9(0))* Windmill Bks.

Curtis, Christopher Paul. The Watsons Go to Birmingham — 1963. 2013. (ENG.). 224p. (J). (gr. 3-7). 7.99 *(978-0-385-38294-6(4),* Yearling) Random Hse. Children's Bks.

—The Watsons Go to Birmingham 1963. 210p. (YA). (gr. 5-18). pap. 5.50 *(978-0-8072-8336-3(3));* 2004. (J). (gr. 4-18). pap. 38.00 incl. audio *(978-0-8072-8335-6(5),* YA166SP) Random Hse. Audio Publishing Group. (Listening Library).

Curtis, Christopher Paul & Vega, Eida de la. Los Watson Van a Birmingham - 1963. 2016. (SPA.). 200p. (J). (gr. 5-12). pap. 12.99 ***(978-1-63245-640-3(0))*** Lectorum Pubns., Inc.

Cutler, Jane. Susan Marcus Bends the Rules. 2014. (ENG.). 112p. (J). (gr. 3-7). pap. 16.95 *(978-0-8234-3047-5(2))* Holiday Hse., Inc.

Davis, Tanita S. Peas & Carrots. 2016. (ENG.). 288p. (YA). (gr. 7). 17.99 *(978-0-553-51281-6(1));* lib. bdg. 20.99 *(978-0-553-51282-3(X))* Random Hse. Children's Bks. (Knopf Bks. for Young Readers).

Dell, Pamela. Half-Breed: A Story of Two Boys During the Klondike Gold Rush. 2003. (Scrapbooks of America Ser.). (ENG., Illus.). 48p. (J). (gr. 3-6). 32.79 *(978-1-59187-044-9(5),* 200809) Child's World, Inc., The.

Draper, Sharon M. Stella by Starlight. (ENG., Illus.). (J). (gr. 4-8). 2016. 352p. pap. 8.99 *(978-1-4424-9498-5(0))* 2015. 336p. 17.99 *(978-1-4424-9497-8(2),* Atheneum Bks. for Young Readers) Simon & Schuster Children's Publishing.

—Stella by Starlight. 2016. lib. bdg. 18.40 *(978-0-606-38255-7(0))* Turtleback Bks.

Dunagan, Ted M. A Yellow Watermelon. 2014. (ENG.). 240p. (J). pap. 17.95 *(978-1-58838-301-3(6),* NewSouth Bks.) NewSouth, Inc.

Echeverria-Bis, Olivia. The EGGbees. Echeverria Gyorkos, Charmaine, illus. 2009. (ENG & SPA.). 32p. (J). (gr. -1-3). 16.95 *(978-1-55885-529-8(7),* Piñata Books) Arte Publico Pr.

Ecton, Anne Massey. Passing Through Camelot. 2006. (J). *(978-0-88092-620-1(1))* Royal Fireworks Publishing Co.

Eugenio, Johnny. Lil Jordan's 9 Holes of Fear. 2009. 48p. (J). 11.95 *(978-1-60747-706-8(8))* Phoenix Bks., Inc.

Eversole, Robyn. East Dragon, West Dragon. Campbell, Scott, illus. 2012. (ENG.). 40p. (J). (gr. -1-2). 17.99 *(978-0-689-85828-4(0),* Atheneum Bks. for Young Readers) Simon & Schuster Children's Publishing.

Ferrari, G. m. Lake, Sky, Dragonfly. 2009. 44p. pap. 16.99 *(978-1-4490-2895-4(0))* AuthorHouse.

Fine, Sarah. Of Metal & Wishes. 2015. (ENG., Illus.). 352p. (YA). (gr. 9). pap. 11.99 *(978-1-4424-8359-0(8),* McElderry, Margaret K. Bks.) McElderry, Margaret K. Bks.

Finger, Mary E. Charlotte Bakeman Has Her Say. Batti, Kimberly Rose, illus. 2007. 96p. (J). 16.00 *(978-0-9746911-2-1(7))* Little Pear Pr.

Fletcher, Susan. Walk Across the Sea. Jakesevic, Nenad, illus. 2003. (ENG.). 224p. (J). (gr. 4-8). pap. 11.95 *(978-0-689-85707-2(1),* Atheneum Bks. for Young Readers) Simon & Schuster Children's Publishing.

Flood, C. J. Infinite Sky. (ENG., Illus.). 256p. (YA). (gr. 7). 2015. pap. 10.99 *(978-1-4814-0659-8(0))* 2014. 17.99 *(978-1-4814-0658-1(2),* Atheneum Bks. for Young Readers) Simon & Schuster Children's Publishing.

Frazier, Sundee T. The Other Half of My Heart. 2011. (ENG.). 304p. (J). (gr. 3-7). 7.99 *(978-0-440-24006-8(9),* Yearling) Random Hse. Children's Bks.

Fuqua, Jonathon Scott. Darby. 2006. (ENG.). 256p. (J). (gr. 5-7). per. 7.99 *(978-0-7636-2290-9(7))* Candlewick Pr.

Gantos, Jack. Desire Lines. 2006. (ENG.). 144p. (YA). (gr. 7-12). reprint ed. pap. 15.99 *(978-0-374-41703-1(2),* Farrar, Straus & Giroux (BYR)) Farrar, Straus & Giroux.

Garcia, Maria. Las Aventuras de Connie y Diego. 2004. (ENG & SPA., Illus.). (J). (gr. k-3). spiral bd. *(978-0-616-14605-7(1))* Canadian National Institute for the Blind/Institut National Canadien pour les Aveugles.

Going, K. L. The Liberation of Gabriel King. 2007. (ENG.). 160p. (J). (gr. 3-7). 6.99 *(978-0-14-240766-0(6),* Puffin Books) Penguin Young Readers Group.

—The Liberation of Gabriel King. 2007. 151p. (gr. 3-7). 17.00 *(978-0-7569-7762-7(2))* Perfection Learning Corp.

Golding, Julia. The Glass Swallow, 0 vols. 2011. (ENG.). 320p. (gr. 7-12). 17.99 *(978-0-7614-5979-8(0),* 9780761459798, Amazon Children's Publishing) Amazon Publishing.

Gorman, Carol & Findley, Ron J. The Stumptown Kid, 1 vol. 2005. (ENG.). 224p. (J). (gr. 3-7). 15.95 *(978-1-56145-337-5(4))* Peachtree Pubs.

Green, Poppy. A New Friend. Bell, Jennifer A., illus. 2015. (Adventures of Sophie Mouse Ser.: 1). (ENG.). 128p. (J). (gr. k-4). pap. 5.99 *(978-1-4814-2832-3(2),* Little Simon) Little Simon.

Greene, Bette. The Drowning of Stephan Jones. 2012. 220p. pap. 9.99 *(978-0-9834681-3-4(3))* Greene & Sandell.

—Summer of My German Soldier. 2006. (Puffin Modern Classics Ser.). (ENG.). 240p. (J). (gr. 5-18). 7.99 *(978-0-14-240651-9(1),* Puffin Books) Penguin Young Readers Group.

Hall, Amanda, illus. In Andal's House. 2013. (Tales of the World Ser.). (ENG.). 40p. (J). (gr. 2-5). 17.95 *(978-1-58536-603-3(X),* 202358) Sleeping Bear Pr.

Haptie, Charlotte. Otto & the Flying Twins. 2004. (Illus.). 320p. (J). (gr. 4-6). 17.95 *(978-0-8234-1826-8(X))* Holiday Hse., Inc.

Harrison, Lisi. Back & Deader Than Ever. 2013. (Monster High Ser.: 4). (ENG.). 256p. (YA). (gr. 7-17). pap. 9.99 *(978-0-316-18667-4(8),* Poppy) Little, Brown Bks. for Young Readers.

—The Ghoul Next Door. (Monster High Ser.: 2). (ENG.). 256p. (YA). (gr. 7-17). 2012. pap. 8.99 *(978-0-316-18666-7(X))* 2011. 16.99 *(978-0-316-09911-0(2))* Little, Brown Bks. for Young Readers. (Poppy).

—Monster High. 2010. (SPA.). 448p. (YA). (gr. 8-12). mass mkt. 19.99 *(978-607-11-0641-4(9))* Aguilar, Altea, Taurus, Alfaguara, S.A. de C.V MEX. Dist: Two Rivers Distribution.

—Monster High. (Monster High Ser.: 1). (ENG.). 272p. (YA). (gr. 7-17). 2011. pap. 8.99 *(978-0-316-17621-7(4))* 2010. 16.99 *(978-0-316-09918-9(X))* Little, Brown Bks. for Young Readers. (Poppy).

—Monster High. 2011. (Monster High Ser.: 1). (YA). lib. bdg. 19.65 *(978-0-606-23459-7(4),* Turtleback) Turtleback Bks.

—Monster High: Where There's a Wolf, There's a Way. 2011. (Monster High Ser.: 3). (ENG., Illus.). 256p. (YA). (gr. 7-17). 17.99 *(978-0-316-09919-6(8),* Poppy) Little, Brown Bks. for Young Readers.

—Where There's a Wolf, There's a Way. 2012. (Monster High Ser.: 3). (ENG., Illus.). 272p. (YA). (gr. 7-17). pap. 9.99 *(978-0-316-18668-1(6),* Poppy) Little, Brown Bks. for Young Readers.

Hays, Barrett K. Odelette. 2011. 20p. (gr. 1-2). pap. 10.03 *(978-1-4567-2690-4(0))* AuthorHouse.

Hesse, Karen. Witness. 2004. 168p. (J). (gr. 5-9). pap. 29.00 incl. audio *(978-0-8072-2094-8(9),* Listening Library) Random Hse. Audio Publishing Group.

—Witness. 2003. (ENG., Illus.). 176p. (J). (gr. 3-7). pap. 7.99 *(978-0-439-27200-1(9),* Scholastic Paperbacks) Scholastic, Inc.

Hobbs, Valerie. Minnie McClary Speaks Her Mind. 2013. (ENG.). 240p. (J). (gr. 4-8). pap. 9.99 *(978-1-250-03408-3(6),* 9781250034083) Square Fish.

Hoffman, Alice. Incantation. rev. ed. 2007. (ENG., Illus.). 192p. (YA). (gr. 7-17). per. 10.00 *(978-0-316-15428-4(8))* Little, Brown Bks. for Young Readers.

Hoffman, Emily Allen. A Friend of the Enemy. 2003. 108p. (J). pap. 7.95 *(978-1-57249-312-4(7),* White Mane Kids) White Mane Publishing Co., Inc.

Houston, Julian. New Boy. 2008. (ENG.). 288p. (YA). (gr. 7-12). pap. 7.99 *(978-0-618-88405-6(X))* Houghton Mifflin Harcourt Publishing Co.

—New Boy. 2007. 282p. (gr. 7-12). 18.00 *(978-0-7569-8139-6(5))* Perfection Learning Corp.

Hughes, Dean. Four-Four-Two. 2016. (ENG., Illus.). 272p. (YA). (gr. 7). 17.99 *(978-1-4814-6252-5(0),* Atheneum Bks. for Young Readers) Simon & Schuster Children's Publishing.

—Missing in Action. 2010. (ENG.). 240p. (J). (gr. 5-9). 16.99 *(978-1-4169-1502-7(8),* Atheneum Bks. for Young Readers) Simon & Schuster Children's Publishing.

Hughes, Shirley. The Christmas Eve Ghost. Hughes, Shirley, illus. 2010. (ENG., Illus.). 32p. (J). (gr. -1-3). 15.99 *(978-0-7636-4472-7(2))* Candlewick Pr.

Ikeda, Daisaku. Over the Deep Blue Sea. McCaughrean, Geraldine, tr. from JPN. Wildsmith, Brian, illus. 2013. 6.95 *(978-1-935523-59-8(7))* World Tribune Pr.

Ioannides, Mara W. Cohen. A Shout in the Sunshine. 2007. (ENG.). 120p. (gr. 5). per. 14.95 *(978-0-8276-0838-2(1))* Jewish Pubn. Society.

Ish-Kishor, Sulamith. A Boy of Old Prague. Shahn, Ben, illus. 2008. (Dover Children's Classics Ser.). (ENG.). 96p. (J). (gr. 4-6). pap. 3.99 *(978-0-486-46766-5(X))* Dover Pubns., Inc.

Johnson, JoAnne. Pen Pals. 2011. 52p. pap. 16.95 *(978-1-4560-6853-0(9))* America Star Bks.

Jones, Patrick. Heart or Mind. 2016. (Unbarred Ser.). (ENG., Illus.). 120p. (YA). (gr. 6-12). lib. bdg. 27.99 *(978-1-5124-0003-8(3),* Darby Creek) Lerner Publishing Group.

—Heart or Mind. 2016. (Unbarred Ser.). (ENG.). 120p. (YA). (gr. 6-12). 42.65 *(978-1-5124-0092-2(0),* Darby Creek) Lerner Publishing Group.

Jordan, Sherryl. The Raging Quiet. l.t. ed. 2005. 416p. 22.95 *(978-0-7862-7313-3(5),* Large Print Pr.) Thorndike Pr.

Jungle Crossing. 2011. (ENG.). 228p. (J). (gr. 5-7). pap. 13.99 *(978-0-547-55009-1(X))* Houghton Mifflin Harcourt Publishing Co.

Keene, Carolyn. Identity Theft. 34th ed. 2009. (Nancy Drew (All New) Girl Detective Ser.: 34). (ENG.). 176p. (J). (gr. 3-7). pap. 5.99 *(978-1-4169-6831-3(8),* Aladdin) Simon & Schuster Children's Publishing.

Kerr, M. E., pseud. Someone Like Summer. 2007. (gr. 7-12). 272p. (J). lib. bdg. 17.89 *(978-0-06-114100-3(3));* 208p. (YA). 16.99 *(978-0-06-114099-0(6))* HarperCollins Pubs. (HarperTeen).

King, A. S. Ask the Passengers. 2013. (ENG.). 336p. (YA). (gr. 10-17). pap. 10.99 *(978-0-316-19467-9(0))* Little, Brown Bks. for Young Readers.

King-smith, Dick. Dinosaur Trouble. Bruel, Nick, illus. 2012. (ENG.). 128p. (J). (gr. 2-5). pap. 16.99 *(978-1-59643-935-1(1),* 9781596439351) Roaring Brook Pr.

Konigsburg, E. L. T-Backs, T-Shirts, Coat, & Suit. 2008. (ENG.). 192p. (J). (gr. 4-8). pap. 6.99 *(978-1-4169-5877-2(0),* Atheneum Bks. for Young Readers) Simon & Schuster Children's Publishing.

Krisher, Trudy. Fallout. 2006. (ENG.). 272p. (J). (gr. 3-7). 17.95 *(978-0-8234-2035-3(3))* Holiday Hse., Inc.

Krumwiede, Lana. Archon. 2015. (Psi Chronicles Ser.). (ENG.). 320p. (J). (gr. 5). pap. 7.99 *(978-0-7636-7659-9(4))* Candlewick Pr.

—Freaking. 2014. (Psi Chronicles Ser.). (ENG.). 320p. (J). (gr. 5). pap. 7.99 *(978-0-7636-6938-6(5))* Candlewick Pr.

La Valley, Josanne. Factory Girl. 2017. (ENG.). 280p. (YA). (gr. 9). 17.99 *(978-0-544-69947-2(5))* Houghton Mifflin Harcourt Publishing Co.

Lambert, Noelle. Can I Play Too? 2009. (ENG., Illus.). 24p. (J). pap. 18.95 *(978-1-85390-944-3(0))* Veritas Pubns. IRL. Dist: Dufour Editions, Inc.

Lawlor, Laurie. Wind on the River. 2004. 156p. (J). lib. bdg. 16.92 *(978-1-4242-0771-8(1))* Fitzgerald Bks.

Leblanc, Louise. Leo's Midnight Rescue. Prud'homme, Jules, illus. 2004. 62p. (J). lib. bdg. 12.00 *(978-1-4242-1217-0(0))* Fitzgerald Bks.

—Leo's Midnight Rescue, 1 vol. Cummins, Sarah, tr. from FRE. Prud'homme, Jules & Jules, Prud'homme, illus. 2004. (Formac First Novels Ser.: 53). (ENG.). 64p. (J). (gr. 2-5). 4.95 *(978-0-88780-640-7(6),* 9780887806407); 14.95 *(978-0-88780-641-4(4),* 9780887806414) Formac Publishing Co., Ltd. CAN. Dist: Casemate Pubs. & Bk. Distributors, LLC.

Les Becquets, Diane. The Stones of Mourning Creek, 0 vols. 2005. (ENG.). 320p. (YA). (gr. 7-9). reprint ed. pap. 9.99 *(978-0-7614-5238-6(9),* 9780761452386, Amazon Children's Publishing) Amazon Publishing.

Levine, Kristin. The Best Bad Luck I Ever Had. 2010. (ENG.). 272p. (J). (gr. 5-18). 7.99 *(978-0-14-241648-8(7),* Puffin Books) Penguin Young Readers Group.

Levithan, David. Wide Awake. 2008. (ENG.). 240p. (YA). (gr. 9). pap. 8.99 *(978-0-375-83467-7(2),* Knopf Bks. for Young Readers) Random Hse. Children's Bks.

Loney, Andrea J. Bunnybear. Saldaña, Carmen, illus. 2017. (ENG.). 32p. (J). (gr. -1-3). 16.99 *(978-0-8075-0938-8(8))* Whitman, Albert & Co.

Lucado, Max. Best of All. Martinez, Sergio, illus. 2003. (Max Lucado's Wemmicks Ser.: 4). 32p. (J). 16.99 *(978-1-58134-501-8(1))* Crossway.

Lupica, Mike. Point Guard. 2017. (Home Team Ser.). (ENG., Illus.). 272p. (J). (gr. 3-7). 16.99 *(978-1-4814-1003-8(2),* Simon & Schuster Bks. For Young Readers) Simon & Schuster Bks. For Young Readers.

Maddox, Jake. Soccer Stand-Off. 2016. (Jake Maddox JV Ser.). (ENG.). 96p. (gr. 3-4). lib. bdg. 25.99 *(978-1-4965-3983-0(4))* Stone Arch Bks.

Malley, Gemma. The Returners. 2010. (Declaration Ser.). (ENG.). 256p. (YA). (gr. 7-18). 16.99 *(978-1-59990-443-6(8),* 9781599904436, Bloomsbury USA Childrens) Bloomsbury Publishing USA.

Marsden, Carolyn. The Gold-Threaded Dress. 2006. (ENG.). 80p. (J). (gr. 2-4). reprint ed. per. 6.99 *(978-0-7636-2993-9(6))* Candlewick Pr.

—The Gold-Threaded Dress. 2006. 73p. (gr. 2-4). 17.00 *(978-0-7569-6574-7(8))* Perfection Learning Corp.

Martin, Ann M. Here Today. 2005. 308p. (gr. 5-9). 18.00 *(978-0-7569-5104-7(6))* Perfection Learning Corp.

—Here Today. 2005. (ENG.). 336p. (J). (gr. 3-7). pap. 7.99 *(978-0-439-57945-2(7),* Scholastic Paperbacks) Scholastic, Inc.

Mason, Jo-Anne. Paddy, the Goat That Saved Rainbow Island. 2003. 48p. (gr. -1-3). 13.95 *(978-0-333-97062-1(4))* Macmillan Caribbean GBR. Dist: Interlink Publishing Group, Inc.

McAllister, Margaret. The Octave of Angels. 2004. 128p. (J). pap. 8.00 *(978-0-8028-5240-3(8))* Eerdmans, William B. Publishing Co.

McClintock, Norah. Trial by Fire, 1 vol. 2016. (Riley Donovan Ser.). (ENG.). 240p. (YA). (gr. 8-12). pap. 10.95 *(978-1-4598-0936-9(X))* Orca Bk. Pubs. USA.

Meminger, Neesha. Shine, Coconut Moon. 2010. (ENG.). 256p. (YA). (gr. 9). pap. 10.99 *(978-1-4424-0305-5(5),* McElderry, Margaret K. Bks.) McElderry, Margaret K. Bks.

mendelsohn, martha. Bromley Girls. 2015. (ENG.). 192p. (YA). pap. 14.95 *(978-0-89672-922-3(2))* Texas Tech Univ. Pr.

Miklowitz, Gloria D. Secrets in the House of Delgado. 2004. 192p. (J). (gr. 4-18). pap. 8.00 *(978-0-8028-5210-6(6))* Eerdmans, William B. Publishing Co.

Miller, William. Joe Louis, My Champion. Pate, Rodney S., illus. 2004. (ENG.). 32p. (J). pap. 10.95 *(978-1-60060-426-3(9))* Lee & Low Bks., Inc.

—Joe Louis, My Champion, 1 vol. Pate, Rodney, tr. Pate, Rodney, illus. 2004. (ENG.). 32p. (J). 16.95 *(978-1-58430-161-5(9))* Lee & Low Bks., Inc.

Mobin-Uddin, Asma. My Name Is Bilal. Kiwak, Barbara, illus. 2005. (ENG.). 32p. (J). (gr. 1-7). 16.95 *(978-1-59078-175-3(9))* Boyds Mills Pr.

Mochizuki, Ken. Baseball Saved Us. Lee, Dom, illus. (Picture Book Readalong Ser.). pap. 39.95 incl. audio compact disk *(978-1-59112-917-2(6));* 2004. (J). (gr. -1-2). 25.95 incl. audio *(978-1-59112-456-6(5))* Live Oak Media.

Moore, Stephanie Perry. True Friends. 2005. (Carmen Browne Ser.: 1). (ENG.). 128p. (YA). pap. 6.99 *(978-0-8024-8172-6(8),* Lift Every Voice) Moody Pubs.

Myers, Walter Dean. Down to the Last Out: The Journal of Biddy Owens, the Negro Leagues, Birmingham, Alabama, 1948. 2013. (ENG.). 144p. (J). (gr. 3-7). pap. 6.99 *(978-0-545-53050-7(4),* Scholastic Paperbacks) Scholastic, Inc.

—Juba! 2016. (Illus.). 208p. (YA). (gr. 8). pap. 9.99 *(978-0-06-211273-6(2))* HarperCollins Pubs.

—Slam! 2008. (Point Signature Ser.). 266p. (gr. 7-12). lib. bdg. 19.65 *(978-0-613-12111-8(2),* Turtleback) Turtleback Bks.

Napoli, Donna Jo. Alligator Bayou. 2010. (ENG.). 288p. (YA). (gr. 7). pap. 8.99 *(978-0-553-49417-4(1),* Lamb, Wendy Bks.) Random Hse. Children's Bks.

Naylor, Phyllis Reynolds. Alice on the Outside. 2012. (Alice Ser.: 11). (ENG., Illus.). 208p. (J). (gr. 5-9). pap. 6.99 *(978-1-4424-3495-0(3),* Atheneum Bks. for Young Readers) Simon & Schuster Children's Publishing.

—A Shiloh Christmas. 2015. (Shiloh Quartet Ser.). (ENG., Illus.). 256p. (J). (gr. 3-7). 17.99 *(978-1-4814-4151-3(5))* Simon & Schuster Children's Publishing.

Neale, Cynthia. Hope in New York City: The Continuing Story of the Irish Dresser. 2008. (ENG.). 176p. (J). pap. 7.95 *(978-1-57249-387-2(9),* White Mane Kids) White Mane Publishing Co., Inc.

Olivas, Daniel. Benjamin & the Word: Benjamin y la Palabra. Baeza Ventura, Gabriela, tr. Dyen, Don, illus. 2011. 32p. (J). pap. 7.95 *(978-1-55885-687-5(0),* Piñata Books) Arte Publico Pr.

—Benjamin & Word Benjamin Y la Palabra. (SPA & ENG., Illus.). 32p. 15.95 *(978-1-55885-413-0(4),* Piñata Books) Arte Publico Pr.

Olsen, Sylvia. Middle Row, 1 vol. 2008. (Orca Soundings Ser.). (ENG.). (YA). (gr. 8-12). 112p. 16.95 *(978-1-55143-901-3(8));* 136p. pap. 9.95 *(978-1-55143-899-3(2))* Orca Bk. Pubs. USA.

—White Girl, 1 vol. 2004. (ENG., Illus.). 200p. (YA). (gr. 7-12). pap. 9.95 *(978-1-55039-147-3(X))* Sono Nis Pr. CAN. Dist: Orca Bk. Pubs. USA.

Otey Little, Mimi. Yoshiko & the Foreigner. Otey Little, Mimi, illus. 2004. (Illus.). 31p. (J). (gr. 4-8). reprint ed. 16.00 *(978-0-7567-7510-0(8))* DIANE Publishing Co.

Park, Linda Sue. Project Mulberry. 2017. (ENG.). 272p. (J). (gr. 5-7). pap. 6.99 *(978-0-544-93521-1(7),* HMH Books For Young Readers) Houghton Mifflin Harcourt Publishing Co.

—Project Mulberry. 2007. 225p. (gr. 4-7). 17.00 *(978-0-7569-7921-8(8))* Perfection Learning Corp.

—Project Mulberry. 2007. (ENG.). 240p. (J). (gr. 3-7). 6.99 *(978-0-440-42163-4(2),* Yearling) Random Hse. Children's Bks.

Parker, Robert. Edenville Owls. 2008. 194p. (gr. 4-6). 18.00 *(978-0-7569-8920-0(5))* Perfection Learning Corp.

Paul, Curtis Christopher. The Watsons Go to Birmingham 1963. 2014. (ENG.). 224p. (J). (gr. 12-12). 11.24 *(978-1-63245-108-5(5))* Lectorum Pubns., Inc.

Pearsall, Shelley. Jump into the Sky. (ENG.). 352p. (J). 2013. (gr. 4-7). pap. 7.99 *(978-0-440-42140-5(3),* Yearling) 2012. (gr. 5). 16.99 *(978-0-375-83699-2(3),* Knopf Bks. for Young Readers) Random Hse. Children's Bks.

Perera, Anna. Guantanamo Boy. (ENG.). 352p. (YA). (gr. 8-12). 2012. 9.99 *(978-0-8075-3078-8(6))* 2011. 17.99 *(978-0-8075-3077-1(8))* Whitman, Albert & Co.

Plum-Ucci, Carol. What Happened to Lani Garver. 2004. (ENG.). 336p. (YA). (gr. 9). reprint ed. pap. 9.99 *(978-0-15-205088-7(4))* Houghton Mifflin Harcourt Publishing Co.

Porter, Pamela. The Crazy Man. 2013. 164p. pap. *(978-1-4596-6446-3(9))* ReadHowYouWant.com, Ltd.

Rahaman, Vashanti. Divali Rose. Akib, Jamel, illus. 2008. (ENG.). 32p. (J). (gr. 2-4). 16.95 *(978-1-59078-524-9(X))* Boyds Mills Pr.

Raschke, Erik. The Book of Samuel: A Novel. 2009. (ENG.). 256p. (YA). (gr. 4-7). pap. 18.99 *(978-0-312-37969-8(2),* 9780312379698, St. Martin's Griffin) St. Martin's Pr.

Reece, Colleen L. Last Page in the Diary. 2011. 94p. pap. 8.95 *(978-1-61633-179-5(8))* Guardian Angel Publishing, Inc.

Reed, Vernon. Children of the Hollow. 2006. (ENG.). 188p. per. 24.95 *(978-1-4241-3668-1(7))* PublishAmerica, Inc.

Richardson, Faith. The Peacock's Stone. 2003. 192p. (J). 21.95 *(978-0-9744989-0-4(4));* (Illus.). pap. 12.95 *(978-0-9744989-1-1(2))* Fox Song Bks.

Rinaldi, Ann. The Education of Mary: A Little Miss of Color, 1832. 2005. 176p. (J). pap. *(978-0-7868-1377-3(6))* Hyperion Pr.

Robinson, Sharon. The Hero Two Doors Down: A Story of Friendship Between a Boy & a Baseball Legend. 2017. (ENG.). 208p. (J). (gr. 3-7). pap. 6.99 ***(978-0-545-80452-3(3),*** Scholastic Paperbacks) Scholastic, Inc.

Ross, Susan. Kiki & Jacques. 2015. (ENG.). 128p. (J). (gr. 3-7). 16.95 *(978-0-8234-3427-5(3))* Holiday Hse., Inc.

Roy, Keri Anne & Holt, K. A. Brains for Lunch: A Zombie Novel in Haiku?! Wilson, Gahan, illus. 2010. (ENG.). 96p. (J). (gr. 4-9). 22.99 *(978-1-59643-629-9(8)*, 9781596436299) Roaring Brook Pr.

Russ, Tim & Roskilly, Jedda. Bugsters! 2008. (Illus.). 32p. (J). 16.95 *(978-0-9795131-7-6(0))* Woods N' Water Pr., Inc.

Ruzzier, Sergio. Bear & Bee. Ruzzier, Sergio, illus. 2013. (Bear & Bee Ser.). (ENG., Illus.). 48p. (J). (gr. -1-k). 14.99 *(978-1-4231-5957-5(8))* Hyperion Pr.

Scattergood, Augusta. Making Friends with Billy Wong. 2016. (ENG.). 224p. (J). (gr. 3-7). 16.99 *(978-0-545-92425-2(1)*, Scholastic Pr.) Scholastic, Inc.

Schraff, Anne. Freedom Knows No Color. 2008. (Passages to History Ser.). 118p. (J). lib. bdg. 13.95 *(978-0-7569-8392-5(4))*; (YA). (gr. 7-12). pap. 8.50 *(978-0-7891-7567-0(3))* Perfection Learning Corp.

—The Hyena Laughs at Night. 2008. (Passages 2000 Ser.). 111p. lib. bdg. 13.95 *(978-0-7569-8407-6(6))* Perfection Learning Corp.

—Leap of Faith, 1 vol. unabr. ed. 2011. (Urban Underground Ser.). (ENG.). 201p. (YA). (gr. 9-12). pap. 9.95 *(978-1-61651-588-1(0))* Saddleback Educational Publishing, Inc.

Schronk, Julie. The Grass Grows Green. 2007. 208p. per. 24.95 *(978-1-60441-057-0(4))* America Star Bks.

Scoppettone, Sandra. Happy Endings Are All Alike. 2014. (ENG., Illus.). 200p. (gr. 6). pap. 12.95 *(978-1-939601-04-9(5))* Ig Publishing, Inc.

Shabazz, Ilyasah & Magoon, Kekla. X. 2015. (ENG., Illus.). 384p. (YA). (gr. 9). 16.99 *(978-0-7636-6967-6(9))* Candlewick Pr.

Shevah, Emma. Dara Palmer's Major Drama. 2016. (ENG.). 288p. (J). (gr. 3-7). 16.99 *(978-1-4926-3138-5(8)*, 9781492631385, Sourcebooks Jabberwocky) Sourcebooks, Inc.

Siddoway, Richard M. The Cottage Park Puzzle. 2015. 200p. (YA). pap. 14.99 *(978-1-4621-1562-4(4))* Cedar Fort, Inc./CFI Distribution.

Smith, D. James. It Was September When We Ran Away the First Time. 2012. (ENG.). 240p. (J). (gr. 3-7). pap. 11.99 *(978-1-4169-3810-1(9)*, Atheneum Bks. for Young Readers) Simon & Schuster Children's Publishing.

Soria, Destiny. Iron Cast. 2016. (ENG.). 384p. (YA). (gr. 8-17). 17.95 *(978-1-4197-2192-2(5)*, Amulet Bks.) Abrams, Inc.

Speare, Elizabeth George. The Witch of Blackbird Pond. 2011. (ENG.). 272p. (J). (gr. 5-7). pap. 7.99 *(978-0-547-55029-9(4))* Houghton Mifflin Harcourt Publishing Co.

St. James, James. Freak Show. 2008. (ENG.). 304p. (YA). (gr. 9-18). 8.99 *(978-0-14-241231-2(7)*, Puffin Books) Penguin Young Readers Group.

Stanley, Diane. Saving Sky. 2010. (ENG.). 208p. (J). (gr. 3-7). 15.99 *(978-0-06-123905-2(4))* HarperCollins Pubs.

Stiver, Joan. The Door in the Floor: An Underground Railroad Adventure. 2008. 48p. pap. 4.99 *(978-1-4343-2953-0(4))* AuthorHouse.

Strasser, Todd. Fallout. 2013. (ENG.). 272p. (J). (gr. 5). 16.99 *(978-0-7636-5534-1(1))* Candlewick Pr.

Stratton, Allan. Borderline. 2010. (ENG., Illus.). 304p. (YA). (gr. 8-18). 16.99 *(978-0-06-145111-9(8)*, HarperTeen) HarperCollins Pubs.

Suen, Anastasia. Girls Can, Too! A Tolerence Story, 1 vol. Ebbeler, Jeff, illus. 2008. (Main Street School - Kids with Character Ser.). (ENG.). 32p. (gr. -1-4). 28.50 *(978-1-60270-271-4(3)*, Looking Glass Library) ABDO Publishing Co.

Sullivan, Jacqueline Levering. Annie's War. 2007. (Illus.). 183p. (J). (gr. 3-7). 15.00 *(978-0-8028-5325-7(0)*, Eerdmans Bks For Young Readers) Eerdmans, William B. Publishing Co.

Taylor, Mildred D. The Friendship. 2014. (ENG.). 56p. (J). (gr. 3-7). 11.24 *(978-1-63245-342-6(8))* Lectorum Pubns., Inc.

—Roll of Thunder, Hear My Cry. 2004. 276p. (gr. 4-8). reprint ed. pap. 10.00 *(978-0-7567-7955-9(3))* DIANE Publishing Co.

—Roll of Thunder, Hear My Cry. 40th anniv. ed. 2016. (ENG., Illus.). 304p. (J). (gr. 3-7). 19.99 *(978-1-101-99388-0(X)*, Dial Bks) Penguin Young Readers Group.

Taylor, Theodore. The Cay. 2003. (ENG.). 160p. (J). (gr. 5-7). mass mkt. 6.99 *(978-0-440-22912-4(X)*, Laurel Leaf) Random Hse. Children's Bks.

Taylor, Theodore & Taylor, Theodore. The Cay. 2003. (gr. 5-8). lib. bdg. 17.20 *(978-0-613-72282-7(5)*, Turtleback) Turtleback Bks.

Tuttle, Todd. Spot. Tuttle, Todd, illus. 2007. (Illus.). 20p. (J). 19.95 *(978-1-889829-16-6(1))* Window Bks.

Uchida, Yoshiko. Samurai of Gold Hill. Forberg, Ati, illus. 2005. 119p. (J). (gr. 2). per. 8.95 *(978-1-59714-015-7(5))* Heyday.

Ulick, Michael Ackerman. Romeo the Rhino's Rocky Romance: A Cautionary Tale about Differences. Guy, Will, illus. 32p. (J). 15.95 *(978-0-9679813-0-7(1))* Footprints Pr.

Urbain, Catherine. Manuel & the Lobsterman. 2008. (ENG.). 214p. (J). (gr. 4-7). 16.95 *(978-1-59078-516-4(9)*, Front Street) Boyds Mills Pr.

Valdivia, Paloma. Up above & down Below. 2012. (ENG., Illus.). 32p. (J). (gr. -1-2). 15.95 *(978-1-926973-39-5(9)*, Owlkids) Owlkids Bks. Inc. CAN. Dist: Publishers Group West (PGW).

Van Dolzer, Krista. The Sound of Life & Everything. 2015. (ENG.). 272p. (J). (gr. 5). 16.99 *(978-0-399-16775-1(7)*, G.P. Putnam's Sons Books for Young Readers) Penguin Young Readers Group.

Vaughn, Carrie. Voices of Dragons. (ENG.). (YA). (gr. 8). 2011. 336p. pap. 8.99 *(978-0-06-154790-4(5))* 2010. 320p. 16.99 *(978-0-06-179894-8(0))* HarperCollins Pubs. (HarperTeen).

Velthuijs, Max. Frog & the Stranger. 2014. (ENG., Illus.). 32p. (J). (-k). pap. 12.95 *(978-1-78344-143-3(7))* Andersen Pr. GBR. Dist: Independent Pubs. Group.

Vernick, Shirley Reva. The Blood Lie. 2011. (ENG.). 144p. (J). (gr. 7). 15.95 *(978-1-933693-84-2(3))* Cinco Puntos Pr.

Villareal, Ray. Alamo Wars. 2008. 187p. (J). (gr. 6-18). pap. 10.95 *(978-1-55885-513-7(0)*, Piñata Books) Arte Publico Pr.

Volponi, Paul. Homestretch. 2009. (ENG.). 160p. (YA). (gr. 7-18). 16.99 *(978-1-4169-3987-0(3)*, Atheneum Bks. for Young Readers) Simon & Schuster Children's Publishing.

—Response. 2010. (ENG.). 176p. (YA). (gr. 7-18). 6.99 *(978-0-14-241603-7(7)*, Speak) Penguin Young Readers Group.

Wein, Elizabeth. The Pearl Thief. 2017. (ENG.). 336p. (YA). (gr. 7-12). 18.99 *(978-1-4847-1716-5(3))* Hyperion Bks. for Children.

Wildsmith, Brian. The Little Wood Duck, 1 vol. 2007. (ENG., Illus.). 32p. (J). (gr. -1-3). 16.95 *(978-1-59572-042-9(1))* Star Bright Bks., Inc.

—The Little Wood Duck, 1 vol. Wildsmith, Brian, illus. 2006. (ENG., Illus.). 32p. (J). pap. 6.95 *(978-1-59572-049-8(9))* Star Bright Bks., Inc.

Wilson, Diane Lee. Tracks. (ENG., (J). (gr. 5-9). 2013. Illus.). 304p. pap. 6.99 *(978-1-4424-2014-4(6))* 2012. 288p. 16.99 *(978-1-4424-2013-7(8))* McElderry, Margaret K. Bks. (McElderry, Margaret K. Bks.).

Winters, Cat. The Steep & Thorny Way. 2016. (ENG., Illus.). 352p. (YA). (gr. 8-17). 17.95 *(978-1-4197-1915-8(7)*, Amulet Bks.) Abrams, Inc.

Woodson, Jacqueline. Feathers. 2007. (ENG.). 128p. (J). (gr. 5-7). 16.99 *(978-0-399-23989-2(8)*, G.P. Putnam's Sons Books for Young Readers) Penguin Young Readers Group.

Yep, Laurence. The Traitor. 2004. (Golden Mountain Chronicles). 310p. (J). (gr. 5). 14.65 *(978-0-7569-3457-6(5))* Perfection Learning Corp.

Zimmerman, Diana S. Kandide & the Secret of the Mists, Bk. 1. Gadd, Maxine, illus. 2008. (Calabiyau Chronicles Ser.). 289p. (J). (gr. 4-7). pap. 9.99 *(978-0-9794328-2-8(0))* Noesis Publishing.

PRESCHOOL EDUCATION

see Nursery Schools

PRESENTS

see Gifts

PRESERVATION OF FOOD

see Food—Preservation

PRESERVATION OF FORESTS

see Forests and Forestry

PRESERVATION OF NATURAL RESOURCES

see Conservation of Natural Resources

PRESERVATION OF NATURAL SCENERY

see Natural Monuments

PRESERVATION OF WILDLIFE

see Wildlife Conservation

PRESERVATION OF ZOOLOGICAL SPECIMENS

see Zoological Specimens—Collection and Preservation

PRESERVING

see Canning and Preserving

PRESIDENTS

Abrams, Dennis. Hamid Karzai. 2nd rev. ed. 2007. (Modern World Leaders Ser.). (Illus.). 128p. (YA). (gr. 7-12). lib. bdg. 30.00 *(978-0-7910-9267-5(4))* Facts On File, Inc.

—Thabo Mbeki. 2007. (Modern World Leaders Ser.). (Illus.). 126p. (YA). (gr. 7-12). lib. bdg. 30.00 *(978-0-7910-9443-3(X))* Facts On File, Inc.

—Viktor Yushchenko. 2007. (Modern World Leaders Ser.). (Illus.). 120p. (YA). (gr. 7-12). lib. bdg. 30.00 *(978-0-7910-9266-8(6))* Facts On File, Inc.

Allen, John. Idi Amin. 2003. (History's Villains Ser.). (Illus.). 112p. (J). 28.70 *(978-1-56711-759-2(7)*, Blackbirch Pr., Inc.) Cengage Gale.

Allport, Alan. Jacques Chirac. 2007. (Modern World Leaders Ser.). (Illus.). 111p. (YA). (gr. 7-12). lib. bdg. 30.00 *(978-0-7910-9265-1(8))* Facts On File, Inc.

Anderson, Dale. Saddam Hussein. 2004. (A&E Biography Ser.). (Illus.). 112p. (J). 29.27 *(978-0-8225-5005-1(9)*, Lerner Pubns.) Lerner Publishing Group.

Antonio Lopez de Santa Anna. 2010. (Great Hispanic Heritage Ser.). (Illus.). 104p. (gr. 6-12). 35.00 *(978-1-60413-734-7(7)*, Chelsea Hse.) Facts On File, Inc.

Baptiste, Tracey. Nelson Mandela: Nobel Peace Prize-Winning Champion for Hope & Harmony. 2015. (Britannica Beginner Bios Ser.). (ENG.). 32p. (J). (gr. 2-3). 46.90 *(978-1-62275-943-9(5)*, Britannica Educational Publishing) Rosen Publishing Group, Inc., The.

—Nelson Mandela: Nobel Peace Prize-Winning Warrior for Hope & Harmony. 2015. (Britannica Beginner Bios Ser.). (ENG., Illus.). 32p. (J). 23.45 *(978-1-62275-941-5(9)*, Britannica Educational Publishing) Rosen Publishing Group, Inc., The.

Barber, James. Presidents. 2017. (Illus.). 72p. (J). ***(978-1-5364-0120-2(X))*** Dorling Kindersley Publishing, Inc.

Barnham, Kay. Nelson Mandela: Revolutionary President. 2017. (Inspirational Lives Ser.). (ENG., Illus.). 32p. (J). (gr. 4-6). pap. 12.99 ***(978-0-7502-9311-2(X)***, Wayland) Hachette Children's Group GBR. Dist: Hachette Bk. Group.

Barter, James. Idi Amin. 2004. (Heroes & Villains Ser.). (ENG., Illus.). 112p. (J). (gr. 7-10). 32.10 *(978-1-59018-553-7(6)*, Lucent Bks.) Cengage Gale.

Baxter, Kathleen & McConnell, Robert L., contrib. by. Assassination & Its Aftermath: How a Photograph Reassured a Shocked Nation, 1 vol. 2013. (Captured History Ser.). (ENG.). 64p. (gr. 5-7). 34.65 *(978-0-7565-4692-2(3)*, CPB Grades 4-8) Compass Point Bks.

Belviso, Meg & Pollack, Pam. Who Is Nelson Mandela? 2014. (Who Was... ? Ser.). lib. bdg. 16.00 *(978-0-606-34158-5(7)*, Turtleback) Turtleback Bks.

Boothroyd, Jennifer. Nelson Mandela: A Life of Persistence. (Pull Ahead Books-Biographies Ser.). (ENG., Illus.). 32p. (gr. k-3). 2007. pap. 7.95 *(978-0-8225-6434-8(3))* 2006. lib. bdg. 22.60 *(978-0-8225-6385-3(1))* Lerner Publishing Group. (Lerner Pubns.).

Bouma, Paddy, illus. Nelson Mandela: Long Walk to Freedom. 2009. (ENG.). 64p. (J). (gr. 2-6). 18.99 *(978-1-59643-566-7(6)*, 9781596435667) Roaring Brook Pr.

Brexel, Bernadette. Yasser Arafat. 2009. (Middle East Leaders Ser.). 112p. (gr. 5-8). 66.50 *(978-1-61514-649-9(0)*, Rosen Reference) Rosen Publishing Group, Inc., The.

Brill, Marlene Targ. Barack Obama: President for a New Era. rev. ed. 2009. (Gateway Biographies Ser.). (ENG.). 48p. (gr. 4-8). 26.60 *(978-1-57505-950-1(9))* Lerner Publishing Group.

Burch, Joann J. Jefferson Davis: Soldier & President of the Confederacy. 2015. (Legendary American Biographies Ser.). 96p. (J). (gr. 6-12). pap. 10.95 *(978-0-7660-6466-9(2))* Enslow Pubs., Inc.

Capozzi, Suzy. Nelson Mandela: From Prisoner to President. Tadgell, Nicole, illus. 2016. (Step into Reading Ser.). (ENG.). 48p. (J). (gr. 2-4). 12.99 *(978-0-375-97467-0(9)*, Random Hse. Bks. for Young Readers) Random Hse. Children's Bks.

Cefery, Holly. Yasser Arafat. 2004. (Middle East Leaders Ser.). (Illus.). 112p. (J). (gr. 5-8). lib. bdg. 34.60 *(978-0-8239-4469-9(7)*, Rosen Reference) Rosen Publishing Group, Inc., The.

Chambers, Catherine. Dilma Rousseff, 1 vol. 2014. (Extraordinary Women Ser.). (ENG.). 48p. (gr. 6-6). pap. 9.95 *(978-1-4109-5953-9(8))* Heinemann-Raintree.

Childress, Diana. Omar Al-Bashir's Sudan. 2009. (Dictatorships Ser.). (ENG., Illus.). 160p. (J). (gr. 9-12). 38.60 *(978-0-8225-9096-5(4)*, 1299570) Lerner Publishing Group.

Collin, Grace. Man of Destiny: The Life of Leopold Sedar Senghor. Bostic, Alex, illus. 2006. 32p. (J). lib. bdg. 16.95 *(978-1-886366-15-2(2))* Sights Productions.

Cox, Vicki. Oscar Arias Sanchez: Bringing Peace to Central America. 2007. (Modern Peacemakers Ser.). (Illus.). 118p. (YA). (gr. 9-12). lib. bdg. 30.00 *(978-0-7910-8999-6(1))* Facts On File, Inc.

Dakers, Diane. Nelson Mandela: South Africa's Anti-Apartheid Revolutionary. 2014. (ENG., Illus.). 112p. (J). *(978-0-7787-1241-1(9))* Crabtree Publishing Co.

Darraj, Susan Muaddi. Bashar Al-Assad: President of Syria. Schlesinger, Arthur M., Jr., ed. 2005. (Major World Leaders Ser.). (Illus.). 112p. (gr. 6-12). 30.00 *(978-0-7910-8262-1(8)*, Chelsea Hse.) Facts On File, Inc.

—Felipe Calderón. 2008. (Modern World Leaders Ser.). 112p. (YA). (gr. 7-12). 30.00 *(978-1-60413-148-2(9))* Facts On File, Inc.

—Hosni Mubarak. 2007. (Modern World Leaders Ser.). 104p. (YA). (gr. 7-12). 30.00 *(978-0-7910-9280-4(1))* Facts On File, Inc.

Davis, Kenneth C. In the Shadow of Liberty: The Hidden History of Slavery, Four Presidents, & Five Black Lives. 2016. (ENG., Illus.). 304p. (J). 17.99 *(978-1-62779-311-7(9)*, 9781627793117, Holt, Henry & Co. Bks. For Young Readers) Holt, Henry & Co.

Day, Meredith, ed. Lyndon B. Johnson. 2016. (Pivotal Presidents: Profiles in Leadership Ser.). 80p. (gr. 8-8). lib. bdg. 33.90 *(978-1-68048-527-1(X))* Rosen Publishing Group, Inc., The.

Dorling Kindersley Publishing Staff. Presidents Visual Encyclopedia. 2017. (ENG., Illus.). 208p. (J). (gr. 4-7). 16.99 *(978-1-4654-5853-7(0)*, DK Children) Dorling Kindersley Publishing, Inc.

Dougherty, Steve. Idi Amin. 2010. (Wicked History Ser.). 128p. (J). (gr. 6-12). pap. 5.95 *(978-0-531-22354-3(X)*, Watts, Franklin) Scholastic Library Publishing.

Dougherty, Steven. Idi Amin. 2010. (Wicked History Ser.). (ENG., Illus.). 128p. (J). (gr. 5-8). 31.00 *(978-0-531-20754-3(4))* Scholastic Library Publishing.

Finlayson, Reggie. Nelson Mandela. pap. 9.95 *(978-0-8225-5743-2(6))* Lerner Publishing Group.

Friedman, Lita. Mary Robinson: Fighter for Human Rights. 2004. (Avisson Young Adult Ser.). (Illus.). 142p. (YA). pap. 19.95 *(978-1-888105-65-0(8))* Avisson Pr., Inc.

Gaines, Ann Graham & Gaines, Ann. Vicente Fox: The Road to the Mexican Presidency. 2003. (Proud Heritage: the Hispanic Library). (ENG., Illus.). 40p. (J). (gr. 3-6). 29.93 *(978-1-56766-177-4(7)*, 200018) Child's World, Inc., The.

Giraldo, Paola. Gamal Abdel Nasser -el faraón Rojo. 2005. (SPA.). 112p. (YA). *(978-958-30-1689-9(6))* Panamericana Editorial.

Gormley, Beatrice. Nelson Mandela: South African Revolutionary. 2015. (Real-Life Story Ser.). (ENG., Illus.). 256p. (J). (gr. 3-7). 17.99 *(978-1-4814-2059-4(3)*, Aladdin) Simon & Schuster Children's Publishing.

Greenhaven Press Staff, ed. Muammar El-Qaddafi. 2012. (People in the News Ser.). (ENG., Illus.). 128p. (J). (gr. 7-10). lib. bdg. 33.95 *(978-1-4205-0759-1(1)*, Lucent Bks.) Cengage Gale.

Haldy, Emma E. George Washington. Bane, Jeff, illus. 2017. (My Early Library: My Itty-Bitty Bio Ser.). (ENG.). 24p. (J). (gr. k-1). lib. bdg. 28.50 *(978-1-63472-152-3(7)*, 209180) Cherry Lake Publishing.

—Jimmy Carter. Bane, Jeff, illus. 2016. (My Early Library: My Itty-Bitty Bio Ser.). (ENG.). 24p. (J). (gr. k-1). 28.50 *(978-1-63471-014-5(2)*, 208006) Cherry Lake Publishing.

Harmon, Daniel E. Pervez Musharraf: President of Pakistan. 2007. (Newsmakers Ser.). (Illus.). 112p. (YA). (gr. 7-12). lib. bdg. 34.60 *(978-1-4042-1905-2(6))* Rosen Publishing Group, Inc., The.

HARMON, Daniel E. Pervez Musharraf: President of Pakistan. 2009. (Newsmakers Ser.). 112p. (gr. 9-10). 63.90 *(978-1-60851-135-8(9))* Rosen Publishing Group, Inc., The.

Headlam, George. Yasir Arafat. 2004. (A&E Biography Ser.). (Illus.). 112p. (J). 29.27 *(978-0-8225-5004-4(0)*, Lerner Pubns.) Lerner Publishing Group.

Holland, Gini & O'Hern, Kerri. Nelson Mandela. (Biografías Gráficas (Graphic Biographies) Ser.). (Illus.). 32p. (gr. 5-8). 2007. (ENG & SPA.). pap. 10.50 *(978-0-8368-7888-2(4))* 2007. (ENG & SPA., lib. bdg. 27.00 *(978-0-8368-7881-3(7))* 2006. pap. 10.50 *(978-0-8368-6249-2(X))* Stevens, Gareth Publishing LLLP.

—Nelson Mandela. McHargue, D., illus. 2006. (Graphic Biographies Ser.). 32p. (gr. 5-8). lib. bdg. 27.00 *(978-0-8368-6197-6(3))* Stevens, Gareth Publishing LLLP.

Hollingsworth, Tamara. Nelson Mandela: Leading the Way, 1 vol. 2nd rev. ed. 2013. (Nonfiction Readers Ser.). (ENG., Illus.). 48p. (J). (gr. 4-4). pap. 29.96 *(978-1-4807-1116-7(0))* Shell Educational Publishing.

—Nelson Mandela: Marcando el Camino. 2017. (TIME for Kids en Español - Level 4 Ser.). (SPA., Illus.). 48p. (gr. 4-4). lib. bdg. 31.99 *(978-1-5157-5145-8(7))* Time for Kids Inc AUS. Dist: Capstone Pub.

Johnson, Kristin F. Ho Chi Minh: North Vietnamese President, 1 vol. 2011. (Essential Lives Set 7 Ser.). (ENG., Illus.). 112p. (J). (gr. 6-12). lib. bdg. 35.64 *(978-1-61783-006-8(2))* ABDO Publishing Co.

Josephson, Judith Pinkerton. Nelson Mandela. 2009. (History Maker Biographies Ser.). (ENG.). 48p. (gr. 3-6). 27.93 *(978-1-58013-703-4(2)*, Lerner Pubns.) Lerner Publishing Group.

Kawa, Katie. 20 Fun Facts about George Washington. 2017. (Fun Fact File: Founding Fathers Ser.). 32p. (gr. 2-3). pap. 63.00 ***(978-1-5382-0272-2(7))*** Stevens, Gareth Publishing LLLP.

Keller, Bill. Tree Shaker: The Life of Nelson Mandela. 2013. (New York Times Ser.). (ENG., Illus.). 128p. (J). (gr. 5-9). pap. 9.99 *(978-1-59643-533-9(X)*, 9781596435339) Square Fish.

—Tree Shaker: The Story of Nelson Mandela. 2013. (ENG., Illus.). 128p. (J). (gr. 7-12). 17.99 *(978-0-7534-7184-5(1)*, 9780753471845, Kingfisher) Roaring Brook Pr.

Kramer, Ann. Mandela: The Hero Who Led His Nation to Freedom. 2008. (National Geographic World History Biographies Ser.). (ENG., Illus.). 64p. (J). (gr. 3-7). pap. 7.99 *(978-1-4263-0173-5(1)*, National Geographic Children's Bks.) National Geographic Society.

—Mandela: The Rebel Who Led His Nation to Freedom. 2005. (National Geographic World History Biographies Ser.). (ENG., Illus.). 64p. (J). (gr. 3-7). 17.95 *(978-0-7922-3658-0(0)*, National Geographic Children's Bks.) National Geographic Society.

Krull, Kathleen. Lives of the Presidents: Fame, Shame (And What the Neighbors Thought) Hewitt, Kathryn, illus. 2011. (Lives Of ... Ser.). (ENG.). 104p. (J). (gr. 5-7). 21.00 *(978-0-547-49809-6(8))* Houghton Mifflin Harcourt Publishing Co.

Landau, Elaine. Warren G. Harding. 2005. (Presidential Leaders Ser.). (Illus.). 120p. (J). 29.27 *(978-0-8225-0850-2(8)*, Lerner Pubns.) Lerner Publishing Group.

Lange, Brenda. Muammar Qaddafi: President of Libya. Schlesinger, Arthur M., Jr., ed. 2005. (Major World Leaders Ser.). (Illus.). 112p. (J). (gr. 6-12). 30.00 *(978-0-7910-8258-4(X)*, Chelsea Hse.) Facts On File, Inc.

Lewison, Wendy Cheyette. P Is for President. Fabbretti, Valerio, illus. 2016. (ENG.). 32p. (J). (-k). pap. 3.99 *(978-1-101-99611-9(0)*, Grosset & Dunlap) Penguin Young Readers Group.

Liebman, Dan & Liebman, Daniel. President. 2009. (I Want to Be Ser.). (ENG., Illus.). 24p. (J). (gr. -1-2). 14.95 *(978-1-55407-562-1(9)*, 9781554075621); pap. 3.99 *(978-1-55407-563-8(7)*, 9781554075638) Firefly Bks., Ltd.

—Presidente. 2009. (Quiero Ser.). (SPA., Illus.). 24p. (J). (gr. -1-2). pap. 5.99 *(978-1-55407-565-2(3)*, 9781554075652) Firefly Bks., Ltd.

Magoon, Kekla. Nelson Mandela: A Leader for Freedom, 1 vol. 2008. (Essential Lives Set 2 Ser.). (ENG., Illus.). 112p. (J). (gr. 6-12). lib. bdg. 35.64 *(978-1-60453-038-4(3))* ABDO Publishing Co.

Marabini, Sergio. Juan D. Perón. 2004. (Protagonistas Ser.). (SPA.). (YA). *(978-987-1129-46-1(7))* Grupo Visor E.A.S.A.

Marsh, Carole. Jefferson Davis, Civil War Hero. 2004. 12p. (gr. k-4). 2.95 *(978-0-635-02366-7(0))* Gallopade International.

—Jimmy Carter. 2003. 12p. (gr. k-4). 2.95 *(978-0-635-02126-7(9))* Gallopade International.

McCollum, Sean. Deadly Despot: Idi Amin Rains Terror on Uganda. 2011. (J). pap. *(978-0-545-32936-1(1))* Scholastic, Inc.

McConnell, Robert L., contrib. by. Assassination & Its Aftermath: How a Photograph Reassured a Shocked Nation, 1 vol. 2013. (Captured History Ser.). (ENG.). 64p. (gr. 5-7). pap. 9.10 *(978-0-7565-4698-4(2)*, CPB Grades 4-8) Compass Point Bks.

Meyer, Susan. Nelson Mandela: South African President & Anti-Apartheid Activist. 2017. (J). ***(978-1-5383-8089-5(7))***; pap. ***(978-1-5383-8088-8(9))*** Rosen Publishing Group, Inc., The. (Rosen Young Adult).

Nelson, Kadir. Nelson Mandela. Nelson, Kadir, illus. 2013. (Illus.). 40p. (J). (gr. -1-3). (ENG.). 17.99 *(978-0-06-178374-6(9))*; lib. bdg. 18.89 *(978-0-06-178376-0(5))* HarperCollins Pubs. (Tegen, Katherine Bks).

—Nelson Mandela. 2014. (SPA.). (J). (gr. 2-4). 21.99 *(978-84-261-4069-2(6))* Juventud, Editorial ESP. Dist: Lectorum Pubns., Inc.

Nelson Mandela: World Leader for Human Rights. 2014. (Gateway Biographies Ser.). (ENG.). 48p. (gr. 4-8). lib. bdg. 26.60 *(978-1-4677-5197-1(9)*, Lerner Pubns.) Lerner Publishing Group.

Nichols, Susan. Vladimir Putin. 2017. ***(978-0-7660-9204-4(6))*** Enslow Pubs., Inc.

Piven, Hanoch & Thomson, Sarah L. What Presidents Are Made Of. 2004. (ENG., Illus.). 40p. (J). (gr. 1-5). 19.99 *(978-0-689-86880-1(4)*, Atheneum Bks. for Young Readers) Simon & Schuster Children's Publishing.

Rajczak, Kristen. Nelson Mandela. 2015. (Heroes of Black History Ser.). (ENG., Illus.). 32p. (J). (gr. 3-4). pap. 10.50 *(978-1-4824-2908-4(X))* Stevens, Gareth Publishing LLLP.

Rausch, Monica. Thomas Jefferson. 2007. (Great Americans Ser.). (Illus.). 24p. (gr. 1-4). pap. 8.15 *(978-0-8368-7691-8(1))*; lib. bdg. 22.00 *(978-0-8368-7684-0(9))* Stevens, Gareth Publishing LLLP. (Weekly Reader Leveled Readers).

Rice, Dona. Mountain of Presidents (Foundations) 2015. (TIME for KIDS(r) Nonfiction Readers Ser.). (ENG., Illus.). 12p. (gr. k-k). 4.99 *(978-1-4938-2057-3(5))* Teacher Created Materials, Inc.

Riggs, Kate. The Release of Nelson Mandela. 2009. (Days of Change Ser.). (Illus.). 48p. (YA). (gr. 4-7). 22.95 *(978-1-58341-736-2(2))* Creative Co., The.

Rodriguez, Ann Graham Gaines. Nelson Mandela & the End of Apartheid. 2016. (People & Events That Changed the World Ser.). (ENG., Illus.). 128p. (J). (gr. 7-8). 37.27 *(978-0-7660-7300-5(9))* Enslow Pubs., Inc.

Rose, Simon. Nelson Mandela. 2010. (Remarkable People Ser.). (Illus.). 24p. (J). (gr. 3-5). lib. bdg. 25.70 *(978-1-61690-172-1(1))*; (gr. 4-6). pap. 11.95 *(978-1-61690-173-8(X))* Weigl Pubs., Inc.

Rosenberg, Aaron. Gamal-Abdel Nasser. 2004. (Middle East Leaders Ser.). (Illus.). 112p. (gr. 5-8). lib. bdg. 34.60 *(978-0-8239-4466-8(2)*, Rosen Reference) Rosen Publishing Group, Inc., The.

—Vladimir Putin: President of Russia. (Newsmakers Ser.). 112p. 2009. (gr. 9-10). 63.90 *(978-1-60851-136-5(7))* 2007. (Illus.). (YA). (gr. 7-12). lib. bdg. 34.60 *(978-1-4042-1903-8(X))* Rosen Publishing Group, Inc., The.

Rumsch, BreAnn. Abraham Lincoln, 1 vol. 2016. (ENG., Illus.). 40p. (J). *(978-1-68078-106-9(5))* ABDO Publishing Co.

Schroeder, Alan. Abe Lincoln: His Wit & Wisdom from A-Z. O'brien, John, illus. 2016. (ENG.). 32p. (J). 7.99 *(978-0-8234-3575-3(X))* Holiday Hse., Inc.

Senker, Cath. Nelson Mandela. 2015. (Against the Odds Biographies Ser.). (ENG., Illus.). 48p. (gr. 3-6). 33.32 *(978-1-4846-2465-4(3))* Heinemann-Raintree.

Sheafer, Silvia Anne. Roh Moo-Hyun. 2008. (Modern World Leaders Ser.). (Illus.). 136p. (YA). (gr. 7-12). 30.00 *(978-0-7910-9760-1(9))* Facts On File, Inc.

Shields, Charles J. Vladimir Putin. 2nd rev. ed. 2006. (Modern World Leaders Ser.). (Illus.). 120p. (gr. 6-12). lib. bdg. 30.00 *(978-0-7910-9215-6(1),* Chelsea Hse.) Facts On File, Inc.

Shields, Charles J. & Koestler-Grack, Rachel A. Saddam Hussein. 2nd rev. ed. 2005. (Major World Leaders Ser.). (Illus.). 112p. (gr. 6-12). 30.00 *(978-0-7910-8576-9(7),* Chelsea Hse.) Facts On File, Inc.

Shone, Rob. Nelson Mandela: The Life of an African Statesman. 2009. (Graphic Nonfiction Biographies Ser.). (ENG.). 48p. (YA). (gr. 4-5). 58.50 *(978-1-61513-023-8(3),* Rosen Reference) Rosen Publishing Group, Inc., The.

—Nelson Mandela: The Life of an African Statesman. Reed, Neil, illus. 2007. (Graphic Nonfiction Biographies Ser.). (ENG.). 48p. (J). (gr. 4-7). lib. bdg. 31.95 *(978-1-4042-0860-5(7));* (gr. 5-8). pap. 14.05 *(978-1-4042-0923-7(9))* Rosen Publishing Group, Inc., The.

Stamper, G. C. Nelson Mandela. 2005. (Illus.). 32p. (J). pap. *(978-0-7367-2922-2(4))* Zaner-Bloser, Inc.

Trussell-Cullen, Alan. Nelson Mandela. 2009. pap. 13.25 *(978-1-60559-067-7(3))* Hameray Publishing Group, Inc.

Venezia, Mike. Lyndon B. Johnson: Thirty-Sixth President, 1963-1969. Venezia, Mike, illus. 2007. (Getting to Know the U. S. Presidents Ser.). (Illus.). 32p. (J). (gr. 3-4). 28.00 *(978-0-516-22640-8(1),* Children's Pr.) Scholastic Library Publishing.

—Richard M. Nixon: Thirty-Seventh President, 1969-1974. Venezia, Mike, illus. 2007. (Getting to Know the U. S. Presidents Ser.). (Illus.). 32p. (J). (gr. 3-4). 28.00 *(978-0-516-22641-5(X),* Children's Pr.) Scholastic Library Publishing.

Wade, Mary Dodson. Presidents' Day. 2016. (Story of Our Holidays Ser.). (Illus.). 32p. (J). pap. 10.52 *(978-0-7660-8345-5(4))* Enslow Pubs., Inc.

Wheeler, Jill C. Saddam Hussein. 2004. (War in Iraq Ser.). 48p. (gr. 4-8). 27.07 *(978-1-59197-499-4(2),* Abdo & Daughters) ABDO Publishing Co.

Wingate, Brian. Saddam Hussein. 2009. (Middle East Leaders Ser.). 112p. (gr. 5-8). 66.50 *(978-1-61514-648-2(2),* Rosen Reference) Rosen Publishing Group, Inc., The.

—Saddam Hussein: The Rise & Fall of a Dictator. 2004. (Middle East Leaders Ser.). (Illus.). 112p. (J). (gr. 5-8). lib. bdg. 34.60 *(978-0-8239-4468-2(9),* Rosen Reference) Rosen Publishing Group, Inc., The.

Witte, Sam. Gamal Abdel Nasser. 2009. (Middle East Leaders Ser.). 112p. (gr. 5-8). 66.50 *(978-1-61514-646-8(6),* Rosen Reference) Rosen Publishing Group, Inc., The.

Wolny, Philip. Hamid Karzai: President of Afghanistan. (Newsmakers Ser.). 112p. 2009. (gr. 9-10). 63.90 *(978-1-60851-132-7(4))* 2007. (Illus.). (YA). (gr. 7-12). lib. bdg. 34.60 *(978-1-4042-1902-1(1))* Rosen Publishing Group, Inc., The.

Zahler, Kathy A. The Assads' Syria. 2009. (Dictatorships Ser.). (ENG.). 160p. (gr. 9-12). 38.60 *(978-0-8225-9095-8(6))* Lerner Publishing Group.

PRESIDENTS—UNITED STATES

Abbey, Jed. The Life of George Washington. 2012. (InfoMax Readers Ser.). (ENG., Illus.). 24p. (J). (gr. 1-2). pap. 8.25 *(978-1-4488-8986-0(3),* Rosen Classroom) Rosen Publishing Group, Inc., The.

ABDO Publishing. Presidential Perspectives. 2016. (Presidential Perspectives Ser.: 8). (ENG.). 48p. (J). (gr. 3-6). lib. bdg. 262.32 *(978-1-68078-028-4(X))* ABDO Publishing Co.

ABDO Publishing Company Staff & Hansen, Grace. United States President Biographies. 2014. (United States President Biographies Ser.: 6). (ENG.). 24p. (J). (gr. 4-8). lib. bdg. 171.00 *(978-1-62970-084-7(3))* ABDO Publishing Co.

Abnett, Dan. Abraham Lincoln & the Civil War. (Jr. Graphic Biographies Ser.). (ENG.). 24p. 2009. (J). (gr. 2-3). 47.90 *(978-1-61513-807-4(2),* PowerKids Pr.) 2007. (Illus.). (J). (gr. 2-5). lib. bdg. 25.25 *(978-1-4042-3392-8(X))* 2007. (Illus.). (gr. 3-8). pap. 10.60 *(978-1-4042-2145-1(X),* PowerKids Pr.) Rosen Publishing Group, Inc., The.

—Abraham Lincoln y la Guerra Civil. 2009. (Historietas Juveniles: Biografías (Jr. Graphic Biographies) Ser.). (SPA., Illus.). 24p. (J). (gr. 2-5). 25.25 *(978-1-4358-8561-5(9));* (gr. 3-8). pap. 10.60 *(978-1-4358-3316-6(3))* Rosen Publishing Group, Inc., The.

—George Washington & the American Revolution. (Jr. Graphic Biographies Ser.). (ENG.). 24p. 2009. (J). (gr. 2-3). 47.90 *(978-1-61513-813-5(7),* PowerKids Pr.) 2007. (Illus.). (J). (gr. 2-5). lib. bdg. 25.25 *(978-1-4042-3395-9(4))* 2007. (Illus.). (gr. 3-8). pap. 10.60 *(978-1-4042-2148-2(4),* PowerKids Pr.) Rosen Publishing Group, Inc., The.

—George Washington y la Guerra de Independencia. 2009. (Historietas Juveniles: Biografías (Jr. Graphic Biographies) Ser.). (SPA & ENG., Illus.). 24p. (YA). (gr. 2-5). 25.25 *(978-1-4358-8564-6(3));* (gr. 3-8). pap. 10.60 *(978-1-4358-3322-7(8))* Rosen Publishing Group, Inc., The.

Aboff, Marcie. A Day for Presidents. 2016. (Spring Forward Ser.). (J). (gr. 1). *(978-1-4900-9374-1(5))* Benchmark Education Co.

Abraham, Philip. How to Draw the Life & Times of George Washington. (Kid's Guide to Drawing the Presidents of the United States of America Ser.). 32p. 2009. (gr. 4-4). 50.50 *(978-1-61511-140-4(9),* PowerKids Pr.) 2005. (Illus.). (YA). (gr. 2-5). 26.50 *(978-1-4042-2978-5(7))* Rosen Publishing Group, Inc., The.

Adams, Simon. Presidents of the United States. 2004. (Illus.). 96p. (J). (gr. 3-6). pap. 9.95 *(978-1-58728-092-4(2),* Two-Can Publishing) T&N Children's Publishing.

Adelson, Bruce. Benjamin Harrison. 2006. (Presidential Leaders Ser.). (Illus.). 112p. (J). (gr. 3-7). lib. bdg. 29.27 *(978-0-8225-1497-8(4),* Lerner Pubns.) Lerner Publishing Group.

Adler, David A. Colonel Theodore Roosevelt. 2014. (ENG., Illus.). 144p. (J). (gr. 5). 18.95 *(978-0-8234-2950-9(4))* Holiday Hse., Inc.

—George Washington: An Illustrated Biography. 2004. (ENG., Illus.). 288p. (J). (gr. 4-6). tchr. ed. 24.95 *(978-0-8234-1838-1(3))* Holiday Hse., Inc.

—Honest Abe Lincoln: Easy-to-Read Stories about Abraham Lincoln. Wallner, John C., illus. 2009. (Holiday House Reader Level 2 Ser.). (ENG.). 32p. (J). (gr. k-3). 15.95 *(978-0-8234-2057-5(4))* Holiday Hse., Inc.

—A Picture Book of Dwight David Eisenhower. 2004. (ENG., Illus.). 32p. (J). (gr. -1-3). per. 6.95 *(978-0-8234-1830-5(8))* Holiday Hse., Inc.

—President George Washington. Wallner, John C. & Wallner, John, illus. 2005. (Holiday House Reader, Level 2 Ser.). (ENG.). 32p. (J). 14.95 *(978-0-8234-1604-2(6))* Holiday Hse., Inc.

Adler, David A. & Adler, Michael S. A Picture Book of Dolley & James Madison. Himler, Ronald, illus. 2009. (ENG.). 32p. (J). (gr. -1-3). 17.95 *(978-0-8234-2009-4(4))* Holiday Hse., Inc.

—A Picture Book of John & Abigail Adams. Himler, Ronald, illus. 2010. (ENG.). 32p. (J). (gr. -1-3). 17.95 *(978-0-8234-2007-0(8))* Holiday Hse., Inc.

Allen, Susan. The Remarkable Ronald Reagan: Cowboy & Commander in Chief. Harrington, Leslie, illus. 2013. (ENG.). 36p. (J). (gr. 1). 16.95 *(978-1-62157-038-7(X))* Regnery Publishing, Inc., An Eagle Publishing Co.

Allen, Thomas B. George Washington, Spymaster: How the Americans Outspied the British & Won the Revolutionary War. Harness, Cheryl, illus. 2007. (ENG.). 192p. (J). (gr. 5-7). per. 7.95 *(978-1-4263-0041-7(7),* National Geographic Children's Bks.) National Geographic Society.

Aller, Susan Bivin. Ulysses S. Grant. 2006. (History Maker Bios Ser.). (Illus.). 48p. (J). (gr. 3-7). lib. bdg. 26.60 *(978-0-8225-2438-0(4),* Lerner Pubns.) Lerner Publishing Group.

Alphin, Elaine Marie & Alphin, Arthur B. Dwight D. Eisenhower. 2005. (History Maker Bios Ser.). (Illus.). 48p. (J). (gr. 3-5). lib. bdg. 26.60 *(978-0-8225-1544-9(X))* Lerner Publishing Group.

Alter, Judy. Mirabeau B. Lamar: Second President of Texas. Messersmith, Patrick, illus. 2005. (Stars of Texas Ser.: 2). (ENG.). 72p. (gr. 4-7). 17.95 *(978-1-880510-97-1(9))* State Hse. Pr.

Amédékanya, Ben-Kofi. Pillars of Pride. 2011. 32p. pap. 15.99 *(978-1-4567-3458-9(X))* AuthorHouse.

Amoroso, Cynthia. William Mckinley. 2008. (Presidents of the U. S. A. Ser.). (ENG., Illus.). 48p. (J). (gr. 3-6). 32.79 *(978-1-60253-053-9(X),* 200692) Child's World, Inc., The.

Anderson, Catherine Corley. John F. Kennedy. 2004. (Presidential Leaders Ser.). (ENG., Illus.). 112p. (gr. 6-12). 29.27 *(978-0-8225-0812-0(5),* Lerner Pubns.) Lerner Publishing Group.

Anderson, Michael, contrib. by. Abraham Lincoln. 2012. (Pivotal Presidents: Profiles in Leadership Ser.). (ENG., Illus.). 80p. (gr. 7-12). (J). lib. bdg. 32.90 *(978-1-61530-942-9(X));* (YA). 65.80 *(978-1-61530-953-5(5))* Rosen Publishing Group, Inc., The.

—Ronald Reagan. 2012. (Pivotal Presidents: Profiles in Leadership Ser.). (ENG., Illus.). 80p. (YA). (gr. 7-12). 65.80 *(978-1-61530-958-0(6));* lib. bdg. 32.90 *(978-1-61530-944-3(6))* Rosen Publishing Group, Inc., The.

—Thomas Jefferson. 2012. (Pivotal Presidents: Profiles in Leadership Ser.). (ENG.). 80p. (YA). (gr. 7-12). lib. bdg. 32.90 *(978-1-61530-940-5(3));* (Illus.). 65.80 *(978-1-61530-959-7(4))* Rosen Publishing Group, Inc., The.

Anderson, Sheila. Jimmy Carter. 2008. pap. 40.95 *(978-0-8225-9472-7(2))* Lerner Publishing Group.

—Jimmy Carter: A Life of Friendship. 2008. (Pull Ahead Books-Biographies Ser.). (ENG., Illus.). 32p. (gr. k-3). lib. bdg. 22.60 *(978-0-8225-8585-5(5),* Lerner Pubns.) Lerner Publishing Group.

Andronik, Catherine M. & Kenney, Karen Latchana. Abraham Lincoln's Presidency. 2016. (Presidential Powerhouses Ser.). (ENG., Illus.). 104p. (J). (gr. 6-12). 35.99 *(978-1-4677-7925-8(3),* Lerner Pubns.) Lerner Publishing Group.

Appleby, Alex. I Can Be the President. 2014. (When I Grow Up Ser.). 24p. (J). (gr. k-2). 22.60 *(978-1-4824-1030-3(3))* Stevens, Gareth Publishing LLLP.

—Puedo Ser Presidente / I Can Be the President. 2014. (Cuando Sea Grande / When I Grow Up Ser.). (SPA.). 24p. (J). (gr. k-2). 22.60 *(978-1-4824-0867-6(8))* Stevens, Gareth Publishing LLLP.

Aretha, David A. Jefferson Davis. 2009. (Leaders of the Civil War Era Ser.). (Illus.). 144p. (gr. 6-12). 35.00 *(978-1-60413-297-7(3),* Chelsea Hse.) Facts On File, Inc.

Armentrout, David & Armentrout, Patricia. The Emancipation Proclamation. 2005. (Documents that Shaped the Nation Ser.). (Illus.). 48p. (gr. 4-6). 20.95 *(978-1-59515-233-6(4))* Rourke Educational Media.

Aronin, Miriam. Dwight D. Eisenhower. 2016. (First Look at America's Presidents Ser.). (ENG., Illus.). 24p. (J). (gr. -1-3). 17.95 *(978-1-943553-31-0(9))* Bearport Publishing Co., Inc.

—Woodrow Wilson. 2016. (First Look at America's Presidents Ser.). (ENG., Illus.). 24p. (J). (gr. -1-3). 17.95 *(978-1-943553-30-3(0))* Bearport Publishing Co., Inc.

Aronson, Billy. Abraham Lincoln. 2008. (Presidents & Their Times Ser.). 96p. (gr. 6-18). lib. bdg. 34.21 *(978-0-7614-2839-8(9),* Benchmark Bks.) Marshall Cavendish Corp.

—Richard M. Nixon. 2007. (Presidents & Their Times Ser.). (Illus.). 96p. (J). (gr. 4-7). lib. bdg. 34.21 *(978-0-7614-2428-4(8),* Benchmark Bks.) Marshall Cavendish Corp.

—Ulysses S. Grant. 2007. (Presidents & Their Times Ser.). (Illus.). 96p. (J). (gr. 3-7). lib. bdg. 34.21 *(978-0-7614-2430-7(X),* Benchmark Bks.) Marshall Cavendish Corp.

Ashby, Ruth. John & Abigail Adams. 2005. (Presidents & First Ladies Ser.). (Illus.). 48p. (gr. 5-12). lib. bdg. 31.00 *(978-0-8368-5755-9(0),* World Almanac Library) Stevens, Gareth Publishing LLLP.

—Woodrow & Edith Wilson. 2005. (Presidents & First Ladies Ser.). (Illus.). 48p. (gr. 5-12). lib. bdg. 31.00 *(978-0-8368-5759-7(3),* World Almanac Library) Stevens, Gareth Publishing LLLP.

Autrey, Jacquelyn & Yeager, Alice. U.S. Presidents & Their Animal Friends. Passarella, Jennie, illus. 2004. 32p. (J). *(978-1-59421-005-1(5))* Seacoast Publishing, Inc.

B. Yes I Can for Kids. 2009. 36p. pap. 17.95 *(978-1-4490-1585-5(9))* AuthorHouse.

Bader, Bonnie. My Little Golden Book about Abraham Lincoln. Garofoli, Viviana, illus. 2016. (Little Golden Book Ser.). (ENG.). 24p. (J). (-k). 4.99 *(978-1-101-93971-0(0),* Golden Bks.) Random Hse. Children's Bks.

Bailey, Diane & Nash, Philip. James K. Polk: The 11th President. 2016. (First Look at America's Presidents Ser.). (ENG.). 24p. (J). (gr. -1-3). lib. bdg. 17.95 *(978-1-944102-66-1(3))* Bearport Publishing Co., Inc.

—John Quincy Adams: The 6th President. 2016. (First Look at America's Presidents Ser.). (ENG.). 24p. (J). (gr. -1-3). lib. bdg. 17.95 *(978-1-944102-65-4(5))* Bearport Publishing Co., Inc.

—William McKinley, the 25th President. 2016. (First Look at America's Presidents Ser.). (ENG.). 24p. (J). (gr. -1-3). lib. bdg. 17.95 *(978-1-944102-68-5(X))* Bearport Publishing Co., Inc.

Baldwin, James. Four Great Americans. 2006. pap. *(978-1-4065-0509-2(9))* Dodo Pr.

Barber, James. DK Eyewitness Books: Presidents. 2017. (DK Eyewitness Bks.). (ENG., Illus.). 72p. (J). (gr. 3-7). pap. 9.99 *(978-1-4654-5770-7(4),* DK Children) Dorling Kindersley Publishing, Inc.

Barber, James. Presidents. 2017. (Eyewitness Bks.). lib. bdg. 20.85 ***(978-0-606-39897-8(X))*** Turtleback Bks.

Barfell, Judy. Learn & Sign Funtime: The United States Presidents. 2005. (J). per. 29.90 *(978-0-9753717-4-9(6))* Learn & Sign Funtime Bks.

Barnes, Peter W. President Adams' Alligator: And Other White House Pets. Barnes, Cheryl Shaw, illus. 2003. 32p. (J). 16.95 *(978-1-893622-13-5(4),* VSP Bks.) Vacation Spot Publishing.

Barnes, Peter W. & Barnes, Cheryl S., illus. President Adams' Alligator: And Other White House Pets. 2013. (ENG.). 40p. (J). (gr. k-5). 16.95 *(978-1-62157-035-6(5),* Little Patriot Pr.) Regnery Publishing, Inc., An Eagle Publishing Co.

Barretta, Gene. Lincoln & Kennedy: A Pair to Compare. Barretta, Gene, illus. 2016. (ENG., Illus.). 40p. (J). 17.99 *(978-0-8050-9945-4(X),* 9780805099454, Holt, Henry & Co. Bks. For Young Readers) Holt, Henry & Co.

Bartlett, Mel. Meet President Obama. 2012. (InfoMax Readers Ser.). (ENG., Illus.). 24p. (J). (gr. 1-2). pap. 8.25 *(978-1-4488-9058-3(6),* Rosen Classroom) Rosen Publishing Group, Inc., The.

Barton Billman, Hilary. How to Draw the Life & Times of William Henry Harrison. 2009. (Kid's Guide to Drawing the Presidents of the United States of America Ser.). 32p. (gr. 4-4). 50.50 *(978-1-61511-164-0(6),* PowerKids Pr.) Rosen Publishing Group, Inc., The.

Basher, Simon, et al. Basher History: US Presidents: Revised Edition. 2017. (Basher History Ser.). (ENG.). 112p. 14.99 *(978-0-7534-7318-4(6),* 9780753473184, Kingfisher) Roaring Brook Pr.

—U. S. Presidents: Oval Office All-Stars! 2013. (Basher History Ser.). (ENG., Illus.). 112p. (J). (gr. 5-9). pap. 8.99 *(978-0-7534-6924-8(3),* 9780753469248, Kingfisher) Roaring Brook Pr.

—U. S. Presidents: The Oval Office All-Stars! 2013. (Basher History Ser.). (ENG., Illus.). 112p. (J). (gr. 5-9). 14.99 *(978-0-7534-6964-4(2),* 9780753469644, Kingfisher) Roaring Brook Pr.

Bates, Katharine Lee. America the Beautiful: Together We Stand. Collier, Bryan et al, illus. 2013. (ENG.). 32p. (J). 17.99 *(978-0-545-49207-2(6),* Orchard Bks.) Scholastic, Inc.

Bausum, Ann. Our Country's Presidents. 2013. (ENG.). 224p. (J). (gr. 5). 24.95 *(978-1-4263-1089-8(7));* lib. bdg. 28.90 *(978-1-4263-1090-4(0))* National Geographic Society. (National Geographic Children's Bks.).

—Our Country's Presidents: A Complete Encyclopedia of the U. S. Presidency. 2017. (ENG., Illus.). 224p. (J). (gr. 5). 24.99 *(978-1-4263-2685-1(8),* National Geographic Children's Bks.) National Geographic Society.

Bausum, Ann. Our Country's Presidents: A Complete Encyclopedia of the U.S. Presidency. 2017. (Illus.). 224p. (J). ***(978-1-4263-2944-9(X))*** National Geographic Society.

Behnke, Alison. Millard Fillmore. 2005. (Presidential Leaders Ser.). (Illus.). 112p. (J). (gr. 3-7). lib. bdg. 29.27 *(978-0-8225-1495-4(8),* Lerner Pubns.) Lerner Publishing Group.

Behrman, Carol H. Andrew Jackson. 2004. (History Maker Biographies Ser.). (ENG., Illus.). 48p. (gr. 3-6). 27.93 *(978-0-8225-1543-2(1))* Lerner Publishing Group.

—James K. Polk. 2005. (Presidential Leaders Ser.). (ENG., Illus.). 112p. (gr. 6-12). lib. bdg. 29.27 *(978-0-8225-1396-4(X))* Lerner Publishing Group.

—John Adams. 2004. (Presidential Leaders Ser.). (Illus.). 112p. (J). 29.27 *(978-0-8225-0820-5(6),* Lerner Pubns.) Lerner Publishing Group.

Benge, Janet & Benge, Geoff. Heroes of History - Theodore Roosevelt: An American Original. 2004. (ENG., Illus.). 208p. (YA). pap. 9.99 *(978-1-932096-10-1(8))* Emerald Bks.

—Ronald Reagan: Destiny at His Side. 2010. (ENG.). (YA). pap. 9.99 *(978-1-932096-65-1(5))* Emerald Bks.

Bennett, Doraine. Jimmy Carter: Georgia, My State Biographies. Lt. ed. 2008. (ENG., Illus.). 24p. (J). (gr. k-2). 22.60 *(978-1-935077-00-8(7));* pap. 22.60 *(978-1-935077-07-7(4))* State Standards Publishing, LLC.

—Thomas Jefferson. 2012. (Illus.). 24p. (J). *(978-1-935884-39-2(5));* pap. *(978-1-935884-48-4(4))* State Standards Publishing, LLC.

Benoit, Peter. Abraham Lincoln. 2011. (True Book(tm), a — Civil War Ser.). (J). (ENG., Illus.). 48p. lib. bdg. 31.00 *(978-0-531-26308-2(8));* (ENG.). 64p. pap. 8.95 *(978-0-531-26550-5(1));* 64p. lib. bdg. 30.00 *(978-0-531-25025-9(3));* (Illus.). 48p. pap. 6.95 *(978-0-531-26621-2(4))* Scholastic Library Publishing. (Children's Pr.).

Benson, Michael. William H. Taft. 2004. (Presidential Leaders Ser.). (ENG., Illus.). 112p. (gr. 6-12). 29.27 *(978-0-8225-0849-6(4),* Lerner Pubns.) Lerner Publishing Group.

Berlatsky, Noah. Presidential Powers. 2010. (Opposing Viewpoints Ser.). (ENG.). 240p. 42.95 *(978-0-7377-4982-3(2));* 238p. pap. 29.45 *(978-0-7377-4983-0(0))* Cengage Gale. (Greenhaven Pr., Inc.).

Berne, Emma Carlson. The Presidency of Theodore Roosevelt: Leading from the Bully Pulpit, 1 vol. 2014. (Greatest U. S. Presidents Ser.). (ENG.). 64p. (gr. 5-7). lib. bdg. 33.99 *(978-0-7565-4925-1(6))* Compass Point Bks.

—What's Your Story, Abraham Lincoln? 2015. (ENG., Illus.). 32p. (J). (gr. k-3). 26.65 *(978-1-4677-7969-2(5))* Lerner Publishing Group.

Berne, Emma Carlson, et al. The Greatest U. S. Presidents, 1 vol. 2014. (Greatest U. S. Presidents Ser.). (ENG.). 64p. (gr. 5-7). 135.96 *(978-0-7565-4949-7(3),* CPB Grades 4-8) Compass Point Bks.

Best, B. J. Abraham Lincoln, the Emancipation Proclamation, & the 13th Amendment. 2015. (Primary Sources of the Abolitionist Movement Ser.). (ENG., Illus.). 64p. (J). (gr. 6-6). lib. bdg. 34.21 *(978-1-5026-0530-6(9))* Cavendish Square Publishing.

Billman, Hilary Barton. How to Draw the Life & Times of William Henry Harrison. 2006. (Kid's Guide to Drawing the Presidents of the United States of America Ser.). (Illus.). 32p. (YA). (gr. 2-5). 26.50 *(978-1-4042-2986-0(8))* Rosen Publishing Group, Inc., The.

Biskup, Agnieszka. George Washington: The Rise of America's First President, 1 vol. Mallea, Cristian, illus. 2012. (American Graphic Ser.). (ENG.). 32p. (gr. 3-4). lib. bdg. 30.65 *(978-1-4296-8621-1(9),* Graphic Library) Capstone Press of Coughlan Cos.

Blake, Kevin. Harry S. Truman: The 33rd President. 2016. (First Look at America's Presidents Ser.). (ENG., Illus.). 24p. (J). (gr. -1-3). lib. bdg. 17.95 *(978-1-943553-29-7(7))* Bearport Publishing Co., Inc.

—Lyndon B. Johnson. 2016. (First Look at America's Presidents Ser.). (ENG., Illus.). 24p. (J). (gr. -1-3). lib. bdg. 17.95 *(978-1-943553-32-7(7))* Bearport Publishing Co., Inc.

Bober, Natalie S. Thomas Jefferson: Draftsman of a Nation. 2008. (ENG., Illus.). 376p. per. 16.95 *(978-0-8139-2732-9(3))* University of Virginia Pr.

Bolden, Tonya. The Emancipation Proclamation: Lincoln & the Dawn of Liberty. 2013. (ENG., Illus.). 128p. (J). (gr. 3-7). 24.95 *(978-1-4197-0390-4(0),* Abrams Bks. for Young Readers) Abrams, Inc.

Boshier, Rosa. Ronald Reagan: 40th US President, 1 vol. 2013. (Essential Lives Set 8 Ser.). (ENG.). 112p. (J). (gr. 6-12). lib. bdg. 35.64 *(978-1-61783-895-8(0),* Essential Library) ABDO Publishing Co.

Bow, James. What Is the Executive Branch? 2013. (ENG.). 32p. (J). *(978-0-7787-0902-2(7));* pap. *(978-0-7787-0907-7(8))* Crabtree Publishing Co.

Bozonelis, Helen Koutras. 200 Years with Abraham Lincoln: One Man's Life & Legacy. 2008. (Prime (Middle/Senior) Ser.). (Illus.). 64p. (J). (gr. 3-4). lib. bdg. 31.93 *(978-0-7660-3266-8(3))* Enslow Pubs., Inc.

Brain Quest Editors. Brain Quest Presidents. 3rd rev. ed. 2013. (ENG.). 152p. (J). (gr. 3-6). 11.95 *(978-0-7611-7238-3(6),* 17238) Workman Publishing Co., Inc.

Bramwell, Neil D. James Madison: A MyReportLinks. Com Book. 2003. (Presidents Ser.). (Illus.). 48p. (J). (gr. 4-10). lib. bdg. 25.26 *(978-0-7660-5129-4(3),* MyReportLinks.com Bks.) Enslow Pubs., Inc.

Brandt, Keith & Macken, JoAnn Early. Abraham Lincoln: Road to the White House. Lawn, John, illus. 2007. 53p. (J). *(978-0-439-88005-3(X))* Scholastic, Inc.

Brennan, Linda Crotta. Franklin D. Roosevelt's Presidency. 2016. (Presidential Powerhouses Ser.). (ENG., Illus.). 104p. (J). (gr. 6-12). 35.99 *(978-1-4677-7928-9(8));* 53.32 *(978-1-4677-8549-5(0))* Lerner Publishing Group. (Lerner Pubns.).

Britton, Tamara L. Barack Obama, 1 vol. 2013. (United States Presidents Ser.). (ENG.). 40p. (gr. 3-6). lib. bdg. 27.07 *(978-1-61783-492-9(0),* Checkerboard Library) ABDO Publishing Co.

—Dwight D. Eisenhower, 1 vol. 2009. (United States Presidents Ser.). (ENG., Illus.). 40p. (YA). (gr. 3-6). 27.07 *(978-1-60453-449-8(4))* ABDO Publishing Co.

—George Washington, 1 vol. 2009. (United States Presidents Ser.). (ENG., Illus.). 40p. (YA). (gr. 3-6). 27.07 *(978-1-60453-479-5(6))* ABDO Publishing Co.

—Richard Nixon, 1 vol. 2009. (United States Presidents Ser.). (ENG., Illus.). 40p. (YA). (gr. 3-6). 27.07 *(978-1-60453-468-9(0))* ABDO Publishing Co.

—Ronald Reagan, 1 vol. 2009. (United States Presidents Ser.). (ENG., Illus.). 40p. (YA). (gr. 3-6). 27.07 *(978-1-60453-471-9(0))* ABDO Publishing Co.

—Theodore Roosevelt, 1 vol. 2009. (United States Presidents Ser.). (ENG., Illus.). 40p. (YA). (gr. 3-6). 27.07 *(978-1-60453-473-3(7))* ABDO Publishing Co.

Brown, Jonatha A. John F. Kennedy. 2005. (People We Should Know Ser.). (Illus.). 24p. (gr. 1-4). lib. bdg. 22.00 *(978-0-8368-4747-5(4),* Weekly Reader Leveled Readers) Stevens, Gareth Publishing LLLP.

Brunelli, Carol. Chester A. Arthur. 2008. (Presidents of the U. S. A. Ser.). (ENG., Illus.). 48p. (J). (gr. 3-6). 32.79 *(978-1-60253-050-8(5),* 200689) Child's World, Inc., The.

—James A. Garfield. 2008. (Presidents of the U. S. A. Ser.). (ENG., Illus.). 48p. (J). (gr. 3-6). 32.79 *(978-1-60253-049-2(1),* 200688) Child's World, Inc., The.

Buller, Jon, et al. Smart about the Presidents. Buller, Jon et al, illus. 2004. (Smart about History Ser.). (ENG.). 64p. (J). (gr. k-4). mass mkt. 5.99 *(978-0-448-43372-1(9),* Grosset & Dunlap) Penguin Young Readers Group.

Burgan, Michael. Barack Obama. 2016. (Front-Page Lives Ser.). (ENG.). 112p. (gr. 6-9). pap. 11.99 *(978-1-4846-3813-2(1),* NA-h) Heinemann-Raintree.

—George W. Bush. 2011. (Presidents & Their Times 5 Ser.). (Illus.). 96p. (J). (gr. 6). 34.21 *(978-1-60870-184-1(0))* Marshall Cavendish GBR. Dist: Marshall Cavendish Corp.

—James Buchanan. 2010. (Presidents & Their Times 4 Ser.). 96p. (gr. 6). 34.21 *(978-0-7614-4810-5(1))* Marshall Cavendish Corp.

—John F. Kennedy, 1 vol. HL Studios Staff, illus. 2013. (ENG.). 56p. (gr. 4-8). 33.32 *(978-1-4329-8096-2(3));* pap. 10.95 *(978-1-4329-8097-9(1))* Heinemann-Raintree. (NA-h).

—Ronald Reagan. 2011. 128p. pap. 14.99 *(978-0-7566-7739-8(4))* Dorling Kindersley Publishing, Inc.

—Ronald Reagan: A Photographic Story of a Life. 2010. (DK Biography Ser.). (ENG., Illus.). 128p. (J). (gr. 5-12). 6.99 *(978-0-7566-7074-0(8),* DK Children) Dorling Kindersley Publishing, Inc.

—Who Was Theodore Roosevelt? Harrison, Nancy & Hoare, Jerry, illus. 2014. (Who Was? Ser.). (ENG.). 112p. (J). (gr.

P
Q
R

3-7). 5.99 (978-0-448-47945-3(1), Grosset & Dunlap) Penguin Young Readers Group.

Burke, Melissa Blackwell & Sharp, Katie John. Presidents: Profiles in Courage of the Men Who Have Led Our Nation. 2007. (Illus.). 32p. 10.98 (978-1-4127-1335-1(8)) Publications International, Ltd.

Burnett, Iris & Greager, Clay. So You Think You Can Be President? 200 Questions to Determine If You Are Right (Or Left) Enough to Be the Next Commander-in-Chief. 2008. (ENG.). 240p. pap. 12.95 (978-1-60239-202-1(1)) Skyhorse Publishing Co., Inc.

Burns, Ken. Grover Cleveland, Again! A Treasury of American Presidents. Kelley, Gerald, illus. 2016. (ENG.). 96p. (J). (gr. 5-12). 25.00 (978-0-385-39209-9(5)); lib. bdg. 28.00 (978-0-385-39210-5(9)) Random Hse. Children's Bks. (Knopf Bks. for Young Readers).

Cane, Ella. The U. S. Presidency. 2014. (Our Government Ser.). (ENG.). 24p. (gr. 1-2). pap. 6.95 (978-1-4765-5144-9(8)); lib. bdg. 25.32 (978-1-4765-4200-3(7)) Capstone Press of Coughlan Cos.

Canetti, Yanitzia. Yo También Puedo Ser Presidente. 2009. (SPA.). 32p. (J). (gr. k-3). pap. 7.99 (978-1-59835-100-2(1)) Cambridge BrickHouse, Inc.

Canetti, Yanitzia & Keating, Alison. I Can Be President, Too! 2009. (J). (978-1-59835-101-9(X), CBH Bks.) Cambridge BrickHouse, Inc.

Caplan, Jeremy. Franklin D Roosevelt A Leader in Troubled Times. 2006. 44p. (J). lib. bdg. 15.00 (978-1-4242-0848-7(3)) Fitzgerald Bks.

Carey, Charles W., Jr. The Emancipation Proclamation. 2009. (Journey to Freedom Ser.). (ENG., Illus.). 32p. (J). (gr. 4-7). 29.93 (978-1-60253-137-6(4), 200403) Child's World, Inc., The.

Casciato, Daniel. Expansion & Reform: (Early 1800s-1861) 2007. (Presidents of the United States Ser.). (Illus.). 48p. (J). (gr. 4-7). lib. bdg. 29.05 (978-1-59036-741-4(3)) Weigl Pubs., Inc.

—Expansion & Reform: Early 1800s-1861. 2007. (Presidents of the United States Ser.). (Illus.). 48p. (J). (gr. 4-7). per. 11.95 (978-1-59036-742-1(1)) Weigl Pubs., Inc.

Cella, Clara. Presidents' Day. 2012. (Let's Celebrate Ser.). (ENG.). 24p. (gr. k-1). pap. 41.70 (978-1-4296-9393-6(2)); (Illus.). lib. bdg. 26.65 (978-1-4296-8734-8(7)) Capstone Press of Coughlan Cos. (Pebble Plus).

Chandra, Deborah & Comora, Madeleine. George Washington's Teeth. Cole, Brock, illus. 2007. (ENG.). 40p. (J). (gr. -1-3). pap. 7.99 (978-0-312-37604-8(9), 9780312376048) Square Fish.

Childress, Diana. George H. W. Bush. 2007. (Presidential Leaders Ser.). (Illus.). 112p. (J). (gr. 3-7). lib. bdg. 29.27 (978-0-8225-1510-4(5), Lerner Pubns.) Lerner Publishing Group.

Ching, Jacqueline & Dorling Kindersley Publishing Staff. Thomas Jefferson. 2009. (DK Biography Ser.). (ENG.). 128p. (J). (gr. 5-12). 6.99 (978-0-7566-4506-9(9), DK Children) Dorling Kindersley Publishing, Inc.

Chorlian, Meg & Hale, Sarah Elder, eds. Ulysses S. Grant: Confident Leader & Hero. 2005. (ENG., Illus.). 48p. (J). (gr. 3-9). 17.95 (978-0-8126-7906-9(7)) Cobblestone Publishing Co.

Clark, Willow. The True Story of the Emancipation Proclamation. 2013. (What Really Happened? Ser.). (ENG., Illus.). 24p. (J). (gr. 3-6). 22.60 (978-1-4488-9695-0(9)); pap. 8.25 (978-1-4488-9848-0(X)) Rosen Publishing Group, Inc., The. (PowerKids Pr.).

Cleveland, Will & Alvarez, Mark. Yo, Millard Fillmore! And All Those Other Presidents You Don't Know. Nation, Tate, illus. rev. ed. 2011. (ENG.). 128p. (J). (gr. 2-9). pap. 7.95 (978-1-935212-41-6(9), Prospecta Pr.) Easton Studio Pr., LLC.

Coddington, Andrew. Thomas Jefferson: Architect of the Declaration of Independence. 2016. (Great American Thinkers Ser.). (Illus.). 128p. (J). (gr. 9-9). 45.64 (978-1-5026-1924-2(5)) Cavendish Square Publishing.

Colbert, David. Abraham Lincoln. 2009. (10 Days Ser.). (ENG.). 160p. (J). (gr. 3-9). pap. 8.99 (978-1-4169-6807-8(5), Simon & Schuster/Paula Wiseman Bks.) Simon & Schuster/Paula Wiseman Bks.

Colbert, Nancy A. Great Society: The Story of Lyndon Baines Johnson. 2004. (Notable Americans Ser.). (Illus.). 144p. (YA). (gr. 6-12). 23.95 (978-1-883846-84-8(6), First Biographies) Reynolds, Morgan Inc.

Coleman, Wim & Perrin, Pat. George Washington: Creating a Nation. 2004. (America's Founding Fathers Ser.). (Illus.). 128p. (J). lib. bdg. 26.60 (978-0-7660-2290-4(0)) Enslow Pubs., Inc.

Collard, Sneed B., III. Abraham Lincoln: A Courageous Leader. 2006. (American Heroes Ser.). (Illus.). 48p. (gr. 3-7). lib. bdg. 29.93 (978-0-7614-2162-7(9), Benchmark Bks.) Marshall Cavendish Corp.

—George Washington: Our First President. 2009. (American Heroes Ser.). 48p. (gr. 3-18). 29.93 (978-0-7614-4060-4(7)) Marshall Cavendish Corp.

—John Adams: Our Second President. 2006. (American Heroes Ser.). (Illus.). 48p. (gr. 3-7). 29.93 (978-0-7614-2159-7(9), Benchmark Bks.) Marshall Cavendish Corp.

—Thomas Jefferson: Let Freedom Ring! 2008. (American Heroes Ser.). 48p. (gr. 3-18). lib. bdg. 29.93 (978-0-7614-3067-4(9), Benchmark Bks.) Marshall Cavendish Corp.

Combs, Maggie. How to Analyze the Works of John Adams, 1 vol. 2013. (Essential Critiques Set 4 Ser.). (ENG.). 112p. (J). (gr. 6-12). lib. bdg. 35.64 (978-1-61783-646-6(X), Essential Library) ABDO Publishing Co.

Conklin, Wendy. Civil War Leaders, 1 vol. 2005. (Primary Source Readers Ser.). (ENG.). 24p. (J). (gr. 5-5). pap. 8.99 (978-0-7439-8917-6(1)) Shell Educational Publishing.

Connors, Kathleen. What Does the President Do? 2017. (Look at Your Government Ser.). 32p. (J). (gr. 2-2). pap. 10.50 **(978-1-4824-6051-3(3))** Stevens, Gareth Publishing LLLP.

—What's It Like to Be the President? 2014. (White House Insiders Ser.). 24p. (J). (gr. 2-5). 22.60 (978-1-4824-1095-2(8)) Stevens, Gareth Publishing LLLP.

—What's It Like to Be the President's Pet? 2014. (White House Insiders Ser.). 24p. (J). (gr. 2-5). 22.60 (978-1-4824-1105-8(9)) Stevens, Gareth Publishing LLLP.

—What's It Like to Live in the White House? 2014. (White House Insiders Ser.). 24p. (J). (gr. 2-5). 22.60 (978-1-4824-1110-2(5)) Stevens, Gareth Publishing LLLP.

Corey, Shana. Barack Obama: Out of Many, One. Bernardin, James, illus. 2009. (Step into Reading Ser.). (ENG.). 48p. (J). (gr. k-3). pap. 3.99 (978-0-375-86339-4(7), Random Hse. Bks. for Young Readers) Random Hse. Children's Bks.

—Barack Obama: Out of Many, One. 2014. (Step into Reading Ser.). (ENG., Illus.). 48p. (J). (gr. k-3). lib. bdg. 12.99 (978-0-375-97371-0(0), Random Hse. Bks. for Young Readers) Random Hse. Children's Bks.

—A Time to Act: John F. Kennedy's Big Speech. Christie, R. Gregory, illus. 2017. (ENG.). 56p. (J). (gr. 3). 18.95 (978-0-7358-4275-5(2)) North-South Bks., Inc.

Cosson, Jody. Civil War & Reconstruction: 1850-1877. 2007. (Presidents of the United States Ser.). (Illus.). (J). (gr. 4-7). 47p. lib. bdg. 29.05 (978-1-59036-743-8(X)); 48p. per. 10.95 (978-1-59036-744-5(8)) Weigl Pubs., Inc.

—George Washington: 1st U. S. President, 1 vol. Soud, illus. 2008. (Beginner Biographies Ser.). (ENG.). 32p. (gr. -1-3). 28.50 (978-1-60270-253-0(5), Looking Glass Library-Nonfiction) Magic Wagon.

Crabtree Staff & Aloian, Molly. George Washington: Hero of the American Revolution. 2012. (ENG., Illus.). 48p. (J). pap. (978-0-7787-0810-0(1)) Crabtree Publishing Co.

Creative Media Applications Staff, contrib. by. American Presidents in World History, 5 vols., Vol. 1. 2003. (Middle School Reference Ser.). (Illus.). 144p. (C). (gr. 6-8). 242.00 (978-0-313-32564-9(2), MS2564, Greenwood) ABC-CLIO, LLC.

Criscione, Rachel. How to Draw the Life & Times of Chester A. Arthur. 2006. (Kid's Guide to Drawing the Presidents of the United States of America Ser.). (YA). (gr. 2-5). 26.50 (978-1-4042-2998-3(1)) Rosen Publishing Group, Inc., The.

Criscon, R. D. How to Draw the Life & Times of Chester A. Arthur. 2009. (Kid's Guide to Drawing the Presidents of the United States of America Ser.). 32p. (gr. 4-4). 50.50 (978-1-61511-135-0(2), PowerKids Pr.) Rosen Publishing Group, Inc., The.

Crompton, Samuel Willard. Ulysses S. Grant. 2009. (Leaders of the Civil War Era Ser.). (Illus.). 119p. (J). (gr. 6-12). 35.00 (978-1-60413-301-1(5), Chelsea Hse.) Facts On File, Inc.

Cronkite, Walter, frwd. Great American Presidents. (Illus.). (gr. 4-8). pap. (978-0-7910-8048-1(X), Chelsea Hse.) Facts On File, Inc.

Daly, Ruth. John Adams. 2015. (Padres Fundadores Ser.). (SPA.). (J). (gr. -1-3). lib. bdg. 27.13 (978-1-4896-2799-5(5), AV2 by Weigl) Weigl Pubs., Inc.

Darby, Jean. Dwight D. Eisenhower. 2004. (Presidential Leaders Ser.). (Illus.). 112p. (J). (gr. 6-12). lib. bdg. 29.27 (978-0-8225-0813-7(3)) Lerner Publishing Group.

Dash, Meredith. Dia de Los Presidentes. 2015. (Días Festivos Ser.). (SPA & ENG., Illus.). 24p. (gr. k-1). pap. 7.95 (978-1-4966-0419-4(9)) Capstone Classroom.

—Presidents' Day, 1 vol. 2014. (National Holidays Ser.). (ENG., Illus.). 24p. (J). (gr. 4-8). lib. bdg. 28.50 (978-1-62970-046-5(0)) ABDO Publishing Co.

D'Aulaire, Ingri & D'Aulaire, Edgar Parin. Abraham Lincoln. 2008. (Illus.). (978-1-893103-27-6(7)); pap. (978-1-893103-26-9(9)) Beautiful Feet Bks.

D'Aulaire, Ingri & D'Aulaire, Edgar Parin, illus. Abraham Lincoln. 75th ed. 2015. (J). **(978-1-893103-60-3(9))** Beautiful Feet Bks.

Davis, Jenny. The U. S. Lawyer-Presidents Coloring & Activity Book. 2008. (ENG.). 32p. (J). (gr. -1-3). pap. 5.95 (978-1-59031-976-5(1)) American Bar Assn.

Davis, Kenneth C. The Presidents. Martin, Pedro, illus. 2003. (Don't Know Much About Ser.). (ENG.). 64p. (J). (gr. 1-4). reprint ed. pap. 6.99 (978-0-06-446231-0(5)) HarperCollins Pubs.

—Presidents. Martin, Pedro, illus. rev. ed. 2009. (Don't Know Much About Ser.). (ENG.). 64p. (J). (gr. k-4). pap. 6.99 (978-0-06-171823-6(8), Collins) HarperCollins Pubs.

Dayton, Connor. Presidents' Day. 2012. (American Holidays Ser.). (ENG., Illus.). 24p. (J). (gr. k-3). pap. 8.25 (978-1-4488-6242-9(6)); lib. bdg. 22.60 (978-1-4488-6142-2(X)) Rosen Publishing Group, Inc., The. (PowerKids Pr.).

—Presidents' Day: Día de Los Presidentes. Alamán, Eduardo, tr. from ENG. 2012. (American Holidays / Celebraciones en los Estados Unidos Ser.). (SPA & ENG., Illus.). 24p. (J). (gr. k-3). lib. bdg. 22.60 (978-1-4488-6708-0(8), PowerKids Pr.) Rosen Publishing Group, Inc., The.

Dean, Sheri. Presidents' Day. 2010. (Our Country's Holidays Ser.). (ENG.). 24p. (J). (gr. k-3). pap. 8.15 (978-1-4339-3924-2(X)); lib. bdg. 22.60 (978-1-4339-3923-5(1)) Stevens, Gareth Publishing LLLP.

—Presidents Day/dia de los Presidentes. 2006. (Our Country's Holidays/ Las fiestas de nuestra nacion Ser.). (SPA., Illus.). 24p. (gr. k-3). lib. bdg. 22.00 (978-0-8368-6522-6(7), Weekly Reader Leveled Readers) Stevens, Gareth Publishing LLLP.

Deem, James M. Millard Fillmore: A MyReportLinks.com Book. 2003. (Presidents Ser.). 48p. (J). (gr. 4-10). lib. bdg. 25.26 (978-0-7660-5074-7(2), MyReportLinks.com Bks.) Enslow Pubs., Inc.

Dell, Pamela. Show Me the U. S. Presidency: My First Picture Encyclopedia, 1 vol. 2013. (My First Picture Encyclopedias Ser.). (ENG.). 32p. (gr. 1-2). 7.95 (978-1-4765-3345-2(8)); 27.32 (978-1-4765-0115-4(7)); pap. 8.10 (978-1-4765-3349-0(0)) Capstone Press of Coughlan Cos. (Aplus Bks.).

DeMauro, Lisa & Time for Kids Editors. Theodore Roosevelt: The Adventurous President. 2005. (Time for Kids Ser.). (ENG., Illus.). 48p. (J). (gr. 2-4). 15.99 (978-0-06-057606-6(5)); pap. 3.99 (978-0-06-057604-2(9)) HarperCollins Pubs.

Demi. President Lincoln: From Log Cabin to White House. 2016. (ENG., Illus.). 32p. (J). (gr. k-3). 16.95 (978-1-937786-50-2(1), Wisdom Tales) World Wisdom, Inc.

Denenberg, Barry. Lincoln Shot: A President's Life Remembered. Bing, Christopher, illus. 2011. (ENG.). 96p. (J). (gr. 5-9). pap. 14.99 (978-0-312-60442-4(4), 9780312604424) Square Fish.

DeRubertis, Barbara. Let's Celebrate Presidents' Day: George Washington & Abraham Lincoln. Griffith, Gershom, illus. 2014. (Holidays & Heroes Ser.). 32p. (J). (gr. 1-3). pap. 7.95 (978-1-57565-649-6(3)) Kane Press, Inc.

DiCianni, Ron. Praying with the Presidents: One Nation's Legacy of Prayer. 2004. 48p. (J). (gr. k-3). 10.99 (978-1-59185-408-1(3), Charisma Kids) Charisma Media.

DiConsoglio, John. Franklin Pierce. 2004. (Encyclopedia of Presidents Ser.). (ENG., Illus.). 110p. (YA). (gr. 5-9). 34.00 (978-0-516-24235-4(0)) Scholastic Library Publishing.

Diemer, Lauren & Cuthbert, Megan. Abraham Lincoln. 2014. (Illus.). 24p. (J). (978-1-62127-308-0(3)) Weigl Pubs., Inc.

Doak, Robin S. Barack Obama. 2013. (True Book(tm), A — Biographies Ser.). (ENG., Illus.). 48p. (J). lib. bdg. 31.00 (978-0-531-21904-1(6)); pap. 6.95 (978-0-531-23875-2(X)) Scholastic Library Publishing.

Doeden, Matt. George Washington: Leading a New Nation. Martin, Cynthia, illus. 2005. (Graphic Biographies Ser.). (ENG.). 32p. (gr. 3-4). 30.65 (978-0-7368-4963-0(7), Graphic Library) Capstone Press of Coughlan Cos.

—Thomas Jefferson: Great American, 1 vol. Purcell, Gordon & Beatty, Terry, illus. 2006. (Graphic Biographies Ser.). (ENG.). 32p. (gr. 3-4). 30.65 (978-0-7368-5488-7(6), Graphic Library) Capstone Press of Coughlan Cos.

Dolan, Edward F. George Washington. 2007. (Presidents & Their Times Ser.). (Illus.). 96p. (gr. 6-7). lib. bdg. 34.21 (978-0-7614-2427-7(X), Benchmark Bks.) Marshall Cavendish Corp.

Dommermuth-Costa, Carol. Woodrow Wilson. 2003. (Presidential Leaders Ser.). (Illus.). 112p. (J). 29.27 (978-0-8225-0094-0(9), Lerner Pubns.) Lerner Publishing Group.

Donaldson, Madeline. Richard Nixon. 2009. pap. 52.95 (978-0-7613-4956-3(1)) 2008. (ENG.). 48p. (gr. 3-6). 27.93 (978-0-8225-8896-2(X), Lerner Pubns.) Lerner Publishing Group.

Donovan, Sandra & Donovan, Sandy. Did President Grant Really Get a Ticket for Speeding in a Horse-Drawn Carriage? And Other Questions about U. S. Presidents. 2011. (Is That a Fact? Ser.). (ENG.). 40p. (gr. 4-6). 26.60 (978-0-7613-6101-5(4)) Lerner Publishing Group.

Dooling, Sandra. James Madison. 2012. (Jr. Graphic Founding Fathers Ser.). (ENG., Illus.). 24p. (J). (gr. 3-6). pap. 10.60 (978-1-4488-7992-2(2)); lib. bdg. 25.25 (978-1-4488-7898-7(5)) Rosen Publishing Group, Inc., The. (PowerKids Pr.).

Douglas, Lloyd G. The White House. 2003. (Welcome Bks.). (ENG., Illus.). 24p. (J). (gr. -1-2). pap. 4.95 (978-0-516-27878-0(9), Children's Pr.) Scholastic Library Publishing.

Drevitch, Gary. Presidents FYI. 2008. (Illus.). 80p. (J). (gr. 3-7). 16.99 (978-0-06-089992-9(1)); (ENG., pap. 7.99 (978-0-06-089991-2(3), Collins) HarperCollins Pubs.

Duling, Kaitlyn. George Washington. 2017. (J). **(978-1-5026-2784-1(1))** Cavendish Square Publishing.

Dunn, Joe. Abraham Lincoln, 1 vol. Espinosa, Rod, illus. 2007. (Bio-Graphics Ser.). (ENG.). 32p. (gr. 3-6). 28.50 (978-1-60270-064-2(8), Graphic Planet- Nonfiction) ABDO Publishing Co.

Dunn, Joeming. Barack Obama: 44th U. S. President, 1 vol. Espinosa, Rod, illus. 2011. (Presidents of the United States Bio-Graphics Ser.). (ENG.). 32p. (YA). (gr. 3-6). 28.50 (978-1-61641-648-5(3)) Magic Wagon.

—Thomas Jefferson, 1 vol. Espinosa, Rod, illus. 2008. (Bio-Graphics Ser.). (ENG.). 32p. 28.50 (978-1-60270-174-8(1), Graphic Planet- Nonfiction) ABDO Publishing Co.

Dunn, Joeming & Dunn, Ben. Bill Clinton: 42nd U. S. President, 1 vol. 2011. (Presidents of the United States Bio-Graphics Ser.). (ENG., Illus.). 32p. (YA). (gr. 3-6). 28.50 (978-1-61641-645-4(9)) Magic Wagon.

—Richard Nixon: 37th U. S. President, 1 vol. 2011. (Presidents of the United States Bio-Graphics Ser.). (ENG., Illus.). 32p. (YA). (gr. 3-6). 28.50 (978-1-61641-647-8(5)) Magic Wagon.

—Ronald Reagan: 40th U. S. President, 1 vol. 2011. (Presidents of the United States Bio-Graphics Ser.). (ENG., Illus.). 32p. (YA). (gr. 3-6). 28.50 (978-1-61641-649-2(1)) Magic Wagon.

Dunn, Joeming & Espinosa De Santayana, Rodrigo De. Ulysses S. Grant: 18th U. S. President, 1 vol. 2011. (Presidents of the United States Bio-Graphics Ser.). (ENG., Illus.). 32p. (YA). (gr. 3-6). 28.50 (978-1-61641-646-1(7)) Magic Wagon.

Dunn, Joeming & Espinosa, Rod. John Adams: 2nd U. S. President, 1 vol. 2011. (Presidents of the United States Bio-Graphics Ser.). (ENG., Illus.). 32p. (YA). (gr. 3-6). 28.50 (978-1-61641-644-7(0)) Magic Wagon.

Dyan, Penelope. This Is the House George Built! a Kid's Guide to Mount Vernon. Weigand, John D., photos by. 2009. (Illus.). 44p. pap. 11.95 (978-1-935118-83-1(8)) Bellissima Publishing, LLC.

Earl, Sari. George Washington: Revolutionary Leader & Founding Father, 1 vol. 2010. (Military Heroes Ser.). (ENG.). 112p. (J). (gr. 6-12). lib. bdg. 35.64 (978-1-60453-967-7(4)) ABDO Publishing Co.

Edge, Laura Bufano. William Mckinley. 2007. (Presidential Leaders Ser.). (Illus.). 112p. (J). (gr. 3-7). lib. bdg. 29.27 (978-0-8225-1508-1(3), Twenty-First Century Bks.) Lerner Publishing Group.

Edison, Erin. Abraham Lincoln, 1 vol. 2012. (Presidential Biographies Ser.). (ENG., Illus.). 24p. (gr. k-1). lib. bdg. 26.65 (978-1-4296-8735-5(5), Pebble Plus) Capstone Press of Coughlan Cos.

—Franklin D. Roosevelt, 1 vol. (Presidential Biographies Ser.). (ENG.). 24p. (gr. k-1). 2014. pap. 6.29 (978-1-4765-9630-3(1), Pebble Bks.) 2012. (Illus.). lib. bdg. 26.65 (978-1-4296-8736-2(3), Pebble Plus) Capstone Press of Coughlan Cos.

—George Washington, 1 vol. (Presidential Biographies Ser.). (ENG.). 24p. (gr. k-1). 2014. pap. 6.29 (978-1-4765-9631-0(X), Pebble Bks.) 2012. (Illus.). lib. bdg. 26.65 (978-1-4296-8737-9(1), Pebble Plus) Capstone Press of Coughlan Cos.

—John F. Kennedy, 1 vol. (Presidential Biographies Ser.). (ENG.). 24p. (gr. k-1). 2014. pap. 6.29 (978-1-4765-9632-7(8), Pebble Bks.) 2012. lib. bdg. 26.65 (978-1-4296-8738-6(X), Pebble Plus) Capstone Press of Coughlan Cos.

Edwards, Roberta. Barack Obama: Presidente de Estados Unidos. Call, Ken, illus. 2009.Tr. of Barack Obama: United States President. (SPA.). 64p. (J). (gr. 2-5). pap. 9.99 **(978-1-63113-956-7(8)**, Loqueleo) Santillana USA Publishing Co., Inc.

—Hail to the Chiefs, 5 vols. 2013. (Who Was? Ser.). (ENG.). 560p. (J). (gr. 3-7). pap. 24.95 (978-0-448-48122-7(7), Grosset & Dunlap) Penguin Young Readers Group.

—Who Is Barack Obama? Harrison, Nancy & O'brien, John, illus. 2009. (Who Was? Ser.). (ENG.). 112p. (J). (gr. 3-7). pap. 5.99 (978-0-448-45330-9(4), Grosset & Dunlap) Penguin Young Readers Group.

—Who Was George Washington? Kelley, True & Harrison, Nancy, illus. 2009. (Who Was? Ser.). (ENG.). 112p. (J). (gr. 3-7). pap. 5.99 (978-0-448-44892-3(0), Grosset & Dunlap) Penguin Young Readers Group.

—Who Was George Washington? 2009. (Who Was... ? Ser.). lib. bdg. 16.00 (978-0-606-04042-6(0), Turtleback) Turtleback Bks.

Egan, Tracie. George Washington: Padre de la Patria. 2004. (Grandes personajes en la historia de los Estados Unidos Ser.). (SPA.). 32p. (gr. 3-6). pap. 10.00 (978-0-8239-4229-9(5), Rosen Classroom) Rosen Publishing Group, Inc., The.

—George Washington: Padre de la patria (George Washington: Father of the American Nation) 2009. (Grandes personajes en la historia de los Estados Unidos (Famous People in American History) Ser.). (SPA.). 32p. (gr. 2-3). 47.90 (978-1-61512-800-6(X), Editorial Buenas Letras) Rosen Publishing Group, Inc., The.

—George Washington: The Father of the American Nation. 2009. (Primary Sources of Famous People in American History Ser.). 32p. (gr. 2-3). 47.90 (978-1-60851-683-4(0)) Rosen Publishing Group, Inc., The.

—The President & the Executive Branch. 2009. (Primary Source Library of American Citizenship Ser.). 32p. (gr. 5-5). 47.90 (978-1-61511-229-6(4), Rosen Reference) Rosen Publishing Group, Inc., The.

Eldridge, Alison & Eldridge, Stephen. The White House: An American Symbol. 2012. (All about American Symbols Ser.). 24p. (J). (gr. -1-1). (Illus.). pap. 7.95 (978-1-4644-0050-6(4)); 22.60 (978-0-7660-4062-5(3)) Enslow Pubs., Inc. (Enslow Elementary).

Elish, Dan. Franklin Delano Roosevelt. 2008. (Presidents & Their Times Ser.). 96p. (gr. 6-18). lib. bdg. 34.21 (978-0-7614-2841-1(0), Benchmark Bks.) Marshall Cavendish Corp.

—James Madison. 2007. (Presidents & Their Times Ser.). (Illus.). 96p. (gr. 6-7). lib. bdg. 34.21 (978-0-7614-2432-1(6), Benchmark Bks.) Marshall Cavendish Corp.

—John Quincy Adams. 2011. (Presidents & Their Times 5 Ser.). 96p. (gr. 6). 34.21 (978-1-60870-182-7(4)) Marshall Cavendish Corp.

—Theodore Roosevelt. 2007. (Presidents & Their Times Ser.). (Illus.). 96p. (gr. 6-7). lib. bdg. 34.21 (978-0-7614-2429-1(6), Benchmark Bks.) Marshall Cavendish Corp.

Elston, Heidi. Calvin Coolidge, 1 vol. 2016. (ENG., Illus.). 40p. (J). (978-1-68078-090-1(5)) ABDO Publishing Co.

—Chester Arthur, 1 vol. 2016. (ENG.). 40p. (J). (978-1-68078-083-3(2)) ABDO Publishing Co.

—George H. W. Bush, 1 vol. 2009. (United States Presidents Ser.). (ENG., Illus.). 40p. (YA). (gr. 3-6). 27.07 (978-1-60453-443-6(5)) ABDO Publishing Co.

—Harry S. Truman, 1 vol. 2016. (ENG., Illus.). 40p. (J). (978-1-68078-119-9(7)) ABDO Publishing Co.

Elston, Heidi M. D. Calvin Coolidge, 1 vol. 2009. (United States Presidents Ser.). (ENG., Illus.). 40p. (YA). (gr. 3-6). 27.07 (978-1-60453-448-1(6)) ABDO Publishing Co.

—Chester Arthur, 1 vol. 2009. (United States Presidents Ser.). (ENG., Illus.). 40p. (YA). (gr. 3-6). 27.07 (978-1-60453-441-2(9)) ABDO Publishing Co.

—Harry S. Truman, 1 vol. 2009. (United States Presidents Ser.). (ENG., Illus.). 40p. (YA). (gr. 3-6). 27.07 (978-1-60453-476-4(1)) ABDO Publishing Co.

—Jimmy Carter, 1 vol. 2009. (United States Presidents Ser.). (ENG., Illus.). 40p. (YA). (gr. 3-6). 27.07 (978-1-60453-445-0(1)) ABDO Publishing Co.

—John Adams, 1 vol. 2009. (United States Presidents Ser.). (ENG., Illus.). 40p. (YA). (gr. 3-6). 27.07 (978-1-60453-439-9(7)) ABDO Publishing Co.

—John Quincy Adams, 1 vol. 2009. (United States Presidents Ser.). (ENG., Illus.). 40p. (YA). (gr. 3-6). 27.07 (978-1-60453-440-5(0)) ABDO Publishing Co.

—Millard Fillmore, 1 vol. 2009. (United States Presidents Ser.). (ENG., Illus.). 40p. (YA). (gr. 3-6). 27.07 (978-1-60453-450-4(8)) ABDO Publishing Co.

—Thomas Jefferson, 1 vol. 2009. (United States Presidents Ser.). (ENG., Illus.). 40p. (YA). (gr. 3-6). 27.07 (978-1-60453-460-3(5)) ABDO Publishing Co.

—Warren G. Harding, 1 vol. 2009. (United States Presidents Ser.). (ENG., Illus.). 40p. (YA). (gr. 3-6). 27.07 (978-1-60453-454-2(0)) ABDO Publishing Co.

—William H. Harrison, 1 vol. 2009. (United States Presidents Ser.). (ENG., Illus.). 40p. (YA). (gr. 3-6). 27.07 (978-1-60453-456-6(7)) ABDO Publishing Co.

—Zachary Taylor, 1 vol. 2009. (United States Presidents Ser.). (ENG., Illus.). 40p. (YA). (gr. 3-6). 27.07 (978-1-60453-475-7(3)) ABDO Publishing Co.

The Emancipation Proclamation & the End of Slavery in America. 2014. (Celebration of the Civil Rights Movement Ser.). (Illus.). 80p. (J). (gr. 7-12). 34.25 (978-1-4777-7749-7(0)) Rosen Publishing Group, Inc., The.

Encyclopaedia Britannica, ed. The American Presidency. 2009. (Illus.). 144p. (YA). (gr. 7-12). 29.95 (978-1-59339-843-9(3)) Encyclopaedia Britannica, Inc.

Englar, Mary. An Illustrated Timeline of U. S. Presidents, 1 vol. Epstein, Len, illus. 2012. (Visual Timelines in History Ser.). (ENG.). 32p. (gr. 3-4). pap. 7.49 (978-1-4048-7254-7(X)); lib. bdg. 28.65 (978-1-4048-7161-8(6)) Picture Window Bks.

Epstein, Len. Presidents Facts & Fun Activity Book. 2012. (Dover Children's Activity Bks.). (ENG.). 48p. (J). (gr. 3-5). pap. 4.99 (978-0-486-48277-4(4)) Dover Pubns., Inc.

Espinosa, Rod. George Washington, 1 vol. Espinosa, Rod, illus. 2007. (Bio-Graphics Ser.). (ENG., Illus.). 32p. (gr. 3-7). 28.50 (978-1-60270-067-3(2), Graphic Planet- Nonfiction) ABDO Publishing Co.

Etingoff, Kim. Harry Truman: From Farmer to President. 2012. (J). pap. (978-1-4222-2485-4(6)); 64p. (gr. 7-8). 22.95 (978-1-4222-2482-3(1)) Mason Crest.

Falk, Laine. Meet President Barack Obama. 2009. (Scholastic News Nonfiction Readers Ser.). (ENG.). 24p. (J). (gr. 1-2). 20.00 *(978-0-531-23403-7(7),* Children's Pr.) Scholastic Library Publishing.

—Meet President John McCain. 2009. (J). *(978-0-531-23650-5(1))* Children's Pr., Ltd.

Famous Americans, Vol. 3. 2005. (First Biographies Ser.). (YA). (gr. k-3). 118.80 *(978-0-7368-4197-9(0),* Pebble Bks.) Capstone Press of Coughlan Cos.

Feinstein, Stephen. Lee Sobre Abraham Lincoln/Read about Abraham Lincoln. 2006. (I Like Biographies! Bilingual Ser.). (ENG & SPA., Illus.). 24p. (J). (gr. 1-3). lib. bdg. 22.60 *(978-0-7660-2672-8(8),* Enslow Elementary) Enslow Pubs., Inc.

Feldman, Ruth Tenzer. Chester A. Arthur. 2006. (Presidential Leaders Ser.). (Illus.). 111p. (J). (gr. 3-7). lib. bdg. 29.27 *(978-0-8225-1512-8(1),* Twenty-First Century Bks.) Lerner Publishing Group.

Ferry, Joseph. Thomas Jefferson. 2004. (Childhood of the Presidents Ser.). (Illus.). 48p. (J). (gr. 4-18). lib. bdg. 17.95 *(978-1-59084-271-3(5))* Mason Crest.

Ferry, Steven. Martin Van Buren. 2008. (Presidents of the U. S. A. Ser.). (ENG., Illus.). 48p. (J). (gr. 3-6). 32.79 *(978-1-60253-037-9(8),* 200676) Child's World, Inc., The.

Firestone, Mary. The White House, 1 vol. Skeens, Matthew, illus. 2006. (American Symbols Ser.). (ENG.). 24p. (gr. 1-2). 9.95 *(978-1-4048-2223-8(2));* lib. bdg. 26.65 *(978-1-4048-2217-7(8))* Picture Window Bks.

Fisher, Douglas & McGraw-Hill Staff. The American Journey: Reconstruction to the Present. 2004. (Amer Journey Recon/present Ser.). (ENG., Illus.). 310p. (gr. 6-9). stu. ed. 12.80 *(978-0-07-868547-7(8),* 0078685478) McGraw-Hill Higher Education.

Fitzpatrick, Brad. Theodore Roosevelt. 2011. (Conservation Heroes Ser.). (Illus.). 144p. (YA). (gr. 6-12). 35.00 *(978-1-60413-948-8(X),* Chelsea Hse.) Facts On File, Inc.

Flash Kids Editors, Flash Kids. U. S. Presidents FlashCharts. 2017. (FlashCharts Ser.). (ENG., Illus.). 4p. (J). (gr. 5-7). 4.95 ***(978-1-4114-7905-0(X),*** Spark Publishing Group) Sterling Publishing Co., Inc.

Foley, Tim. American Presidents Sticker Book. 2011. (Dover Sticker Bks.). (ENG., Illus.). 4p. (J). (gr. 1-5). 6.99 *(978-0-486-47879-1(3))* Dover Pubns., Inc.

Ford, Carin T. Abraham Lincoln: The 16th President. 2003. (Heroes of American History Ser.). (Illus.). 32p. (J). (gr. 1-4). lib. bdg. 22.60 *(978-0-7660-2000-9(2))* Enslow Pubs., Inc.

—The Emancipation Proclamation, Lincoln, & Slavery Through Primary Sources. 2013. (Civil War Through Primary Sources Ser.). 48p. (J). (gr. 4-10). pap. 8.95 *(978-1-4644-0187-9(X));* lib. bdg. 25.27 *(978-0-7660-4129-5(8))* Enslow Pubs., Inc.

—Franklin D. Roosevelt: The 32nd President. 2006. (Heroes of American History Ser.). (Illus.). 32p. (J). (gr. 4-7). lib. bdg. 23.94 *(978-0-7660-2603-2(5),* Enslow Elementary) Enslow Pubs., Inc.

—John F. Kennedy: The 35th President. 2006. (Heroes of American History Ser.). (Illus.). 32p. (J). (gr. 4-7). lib. bdg. 23.94 *(978-0-7660-2601-8(9),* Enslow Elementary) Enslow Pubs., Inc.

—Lincoln, Slavery, & the Emancipation Proclamation. 2004. (Civil War Library). (Illus.). 48p. (J). lib. bdg. 25.27 *(978-0-7660-2252-2(8))* Enslow Pubs., Inc.

—Thomas Jefferson: The Third President. 2003. (Heroes of American History Ser.). (Illus.). 32p. (J). (gr. 1-4). lib. bdg. 22.60 *(978-0-7660-1861-7(X))* Enslow Pubs., Inc.

Francis, Sandra. Gerald R. Ford. 2008. (Presidents of the U. S. A. Ser.). (ENG., Illus.). 48p. (J). (gr. 3-6). 32.79 *(978-1-60253-066-9(1),* 200705) Child's World, Inc., The.

—Rutherford B. Hayes. 2008. (Presidents of the U. S. A. Ser.). (ENG., Illus.). 48p. (J). (gr. 3-6). 32.79 *(978-1-60253-048-5(3),* 200687) Child's World, Inc., The.

Freedman, Russell. Abraham Lincoln & Frederick Douglass: The Story Behind an American Friendship. 2012. (ENG., Illus.). 128p. (J). (gr. 5-7). 18.99 *(978-0-547-38562-4(5))* Houghton Mifflin Harcourt Publishing Co.

Frith, Margaret. Who Was Franklin Roosevelt? Harrison, Nancy & O'brien, John, illus. 2010. (Who Was? Ser.). (ENG.). 112p. (J). (gr. 3-7). pap. 5.99 *(978-0-448-45346-0(0),* Grosset & Dunlap) Penguin Young Readers Group.

Frith, Margaret & dePaola, Tomie. Who Was Woodrow Wilson? Thomson, Andrew & Harrison, Nancy, illus. 2015. (Who Was? Ser.). (ENG.). 112p. (J). (gr. 3-7). 5.99 *(978-0-448-48428-0(5),* Grosset & Dunlap) Penguin Young Readers Group.

Fry, Sonali. Let's Read About — George W. Bush. Heyer, Carol, illus. 2003. (Scholastic First Biographies Ser.). (J). pap. *(978-0-439-45953-2(2))* Scholastic, Inc.

Fuqua, Nell & Jankowki, Dan. U. S. Presidents: Feats & Foul-Ups. Saunders, Zina, illus. 2003. 48p. (J). pap. *(978-0-439-54081-0(X))* Lemondrop Pr.

Furgang, Kathy. The Declaration of Independence & Thomas Jefferson of Virginia. 2009. (Framers of the Declaration of Independence Ser.). 24p. (gr. 3-3). 42.50 *(978-1-61512-633-0(3),* PowerKids Pr.) Rosen Publishing Group, Inc., The.

Gaff, Jackie. George Washington: The Life of an American Patriot. 2005. (Graphic Nonfiction Biographies Ser.). (ENG., Illus.). 48p. (YA). (gr. 4-7). lib. bdg. 31.95 *(978-1-4042-0236-8(6))* Rosen Publishing Group, Inc., The.

Gaines, Ann Graham. James K. Polk. 2008. (Presidents of the U. S. A. Ser.). (ENG., Illus.). 48p. (J). (gr. 3-6). 32.79 *(978-1-60253-040-9(8),* 200679) Child's World, Inc., The.

—John Adams. 2008. (Presidents of the U. S. A. Ser.). (ENG., Illus.). 48p. (J). (gr. 3-6). 32.79 *(978-1-60253-031-7(9),* 200670) Child's World, Inc., The.

—Richard M. Nixon. 2008. (Presidents of the U. S. A. Ser.). (ENG., Illus.). 48p. (J). (gr. 3-6). 32.79 *(978-1-60253-065-2(3),* 200704) Child's World, Inc., The.

—Ulysses S. Grant. 2008. (Presidents of the U. S. A. Ser.). (ENG., Illus.). 48p. (J). (gr. 3-6). 32.79 *(978-1-60253-047-8(5),* 200686) Child's World, Inc., The.

—William Henry Harrison. 2008. (Presidents of the U. S. A. Ser.). (ENG., Illus.). 48p. (J). (gr. 3-6). 32.79 *(978-1-60253-038-6(6),* 200677) Child's World, Inc., The.

Gamble, Amy. U. S. Government & Presidents, Grades 3 - 5. Fox, Carrie, ed. 2008. (Skills for Success Ser.). (ENG.). 128p. (gr. 3-5). pap. 16.99 *(978-1-60418-602-4(X))* Carson-Dellosa Publishing, LLC.

Garraty, John. Teddy Roosevelt: American Rough Rider. 2017. (Young Voyageur Ser.). (ENG., Illus.). 176p. (YA). (gr. 4-8). pap. 12.99 ***(978-0-7603-5437-7(5),*** Voyageur Pr.) Quarto Publishing Group USA.

Gedacht, Daniel C. George Washington: Leader of a New Nation. (Library of American Lives & Times Ser.). 112p. 2009. (gr. 5-5). 69.20 *(978-1-60853-484-5(7))* 2005. (Illus.). (J). (gr. 4-8). lib. bdg. 34.60 *(978-0-8239-6622-6(4))* Rosen Publishing Group, Inc., The.

Geller, Kevin. Harry S. Truman. 2017. (Pivotal Presidents: Profiles in Leadership Ser.). 80p. (gr. 12-13). lib. bdg. 33.90 ***(978-1-68048-633-9(0),*** Britannica Educational Publishing) Rosen Publishing Group, Inc., The.

Gherman, Beverly. First Mothers. Downing, Julie, illus. 2016. (ENG.). 64p. (J). (gr. 1-4). 6.99 *(978-0-544-66839-3(1),* HMH Books For Young Readers) Houghton Mifflin Harcourt Publishing Co.

—First Son & President: A Story about John Quincy Adams. Bird, Matthew, illus. (Creative Minds Biographies Ser.). (ENG.). 64p. (gr. 4-8). 2006. pap. 8.95 *(978-0-8225-3091-6(0))* 2005. lib. bdg. 22.60 *(978-1-57505-756-9(5),* Carolrhoda Bks.) Lerner Publishing Group.

Gigliotti, Jim. Ronald Reagan, the 40th President. 2016. (First Look at America's Presidents Ser.). (ENG.). 24p. (J). (gr. -1-3). lib. bdg. 17.95 *(978-1-944102-69-2(8))* Bearport Publishing Co., Inc.

Gilpin, Caroline Crosson. National Geographic Readers: Abraham Lincoln. 2012. (Readers Bios Ser.). (ENG.). 32p. (J). (gr. k-3). pap. 3.99 *(978-1-4263-1085-0(4));* lib. bdg. 13.90 *(978-1-4263-1086-7(2))* National Geographic Society. (National Geographic Children's Bks.).

Gimpel, Diane Marczely. Donald Trump. 2017. (Premier Presidents Ser.). (ENG.). 24p. (J). (gr. 1-4). lib. bdg. 27.07 *(978-1-5038-1649-7(4),* 211492) Child's World, Inc., The.

Giovanni, Nikki. Lincoln & Douglass: An American Friendship. Collier, Bryan, illus. 2008. (ENG.). 40p. (J). (gr. 2-6). 16.95 *(978-0-8050-8264-7(6),* 9780805082647, Holt, Henry & Co. Bks. For Young Readers) Holt, Henry & Co.

—Lincoln & Douglass: An American Friendship. Collier, Bryan, illus. 2013. (ENG.). 40p. (J). (gr. 2-6). 8.99 *(978-1-250-01869-4(2),* 9781250018694) Square Fish.

—Lincoln & Douglass: An American Friendship. Collier, Bryan, illus. 2011. (J). (gr. -1-3). 29.95 *(978-0-545-13457-6(9))* Weston Woods Studios, Inc.

Gitlin, Martin. The Great Depression & World War II: 1929-1945. 2007. (Presidents of the United States Ser.). (Illus.). 48p. (J). (gr. 4-7). lib. bdg. 29.05 *(978-1-59036-749-0(9));* per. 10.95 *(978-1-59036-750-6(2))* Weigl Pubs., Inc.

—Post-War United States: 1945-Early 1970s. 2007. (Presidents of the United States Ser.). (Illus.). 48p. (J). (gr. 4-7). lib. bdg. 29.05 *(978-1-59036-751-3(0));* per. 10.95 *(978-1-59036-752-0(9))* Weigl Pubs., Inc.

Goddu, Krystyna Poray. George Washington's Presidency. 2016. (Presidential Powerhouses Ser.). (ENG., Illus.). 104p. (J). (gr. 6-12). 35.99 *(978-1-4677-7924-1(5));* 53.32 *(978-1-4677-8598-3(9),* Lerner Pubns.) Lerner Publishing Group.

Gold, Susan Dudley. Lyndon B. Johnson. 2008. (Presidents & Their Times Ser.). 96p. (gr. 6-18). lib. bdg. 34.21 *(978-0-7614-2837-4(2),* Benchmark Bks.) Marshall Cavendish Corp.

Goldsmith, Howard. John F. Kennedy & the Stormy Sea. Benoit, Renné, illus. 2006. 32p. (J). lib. bdg. 15.00 *(978-1-4242-0958-3(7))* Fitzgerald Bks.

Gomez, Rebecca. Thomas Jefferson, 1 vol. 2003. (First Biographies Ser.). (ENG., Illus.). 32p. (gr. k-4). 27.07 *(978-1-57765-947-1(3),* Buddy Bks.) ABDO Publishing Co.

Goodman, Susan E. See How They Run: Campaign Dreams, Election Schemes, & the Race to the White House. Smith, Elwood, illus. 2nd rev. ed. 2012. (ENG.). 96p. (J). (gr. 3-12). pap. 9.99 *(978-1-59990-897-7(2),* 9781599908977, Bloomsbury USA Childrens) Bloomsbury Publishing USA.

Gorman, Jacqueline Laks. President. 2009. (Know Your Government Ser.). 24p. (gr. 2-4). (J). lib. bdg. 22.00 *(978-1-4339-0095-2(5));* pap. 8.15 *(978-1-4339-0123-2(4))* Stevens, Gareth Publishing LLLP. (Weekly Reader Leveled Readers).

—Presidente. 2009. (Conoce tu gobierno (Know Your Government) Ser.). (SPA.). 24p. (gr. 2-4). (J). lib. bdg. 22.00 *(978-1-4339-0102-7(1));* pap. 8.15 *(978-1-4339-0130-0(7))* Stevens, Gareth Publishing LLLP. (Weekly Reader Leveled Readers).

Gormley, Beatrice. Barack Obama: Our 44th President. 2015. (Real-Life Story Ser.). (ENG., Illus.). 272p. (J). (gr. 3-7). 17.99 *(978-1-4814-4648-8(7),* Aladdin) Simon & Schuster Children's Publishing.

—George W. Bush: Our 43rd President. 2015. (Real-Life Story Ser.). (ENG., Illus.). 256p. (J). (gr. 3-7). 17.99 *(978-1-4814-4645-7(2),* Aladdin) Simon & Schuster Children's Publishing.

Gosman, Gillian. Abraham Lincoln. 2011. (Life Stories Ser.). (Illus.). 24p. (J). pap. 8.25 *(978-1-4488-2753-4(1),* PowerKids Pr.); (gr. 1-4). lib. bdg. 22.60 *(978-1-4488-2582-0(2),* PowerKids Pr.); (SPA., (gr. 1-4). lib. bdg. 22.60 *(978-1-4488-3216-3(0))* Rosen Publishing Group, Inc., The.

—Franklin D. Roosevelt. 2011. (Life Stories Ser.). (Illus.). 24p. (J). pap. 8.25 *(978-1-4488-3182-1(2),* PowerKids Pr.); (ENG & SPA., (gr. 1-4). lib. bdg. 22.60 *(978-1-4488-3222-4(5));* (gr. 1-4). lib. bdg. 22.60 *(978-1-4488-3179-1(2),* PowerKids Pr.) Rosen Publishing Group, Inc., The.

—George Washington. 2011. (Life Stories Ser.). (Illus.). 24p. (J). pap. 8.25 *(978-1-4488-2751-0(5),* PowerKids Pr.); (gr. 1-4). lib. bdg. 22.60 *(978-1-4488-2581-3(4),* PowerKids Pr.); (SPA & ENG., (gr. 1-4). lib. bdg. 22.60 *(978-1-4488-3215-6(2))* Rosen Publishing Group, Inc., The.

—Thomas Jefferson. 2011. (Life Stories Ser.). (Illus.). 24p. (J). pap. 8.25 *(978-1-4488-3180-7(6),* PowerKids Pr.); (gr. 1-4). lib. bdg. 22.60 *(978-1-4488-3178-4(4),* PowerKids Pr.); (SPA & ENG., (gr. 1-4). lib. bdg. 22.60 *(978-1-4488-3221-7(7))* Rosen Publishing Group, Inc., The.

Gottfried, Ted. Millard Fillmore. 2007. (Presidents & Their Times Ser.). (Illus.). 96p. (gr. 6-7). lib. bdg. 34.21 *(978-0-7614-2431-4(8),* Benchmark Bks.) Marshall Cavendish Corp.

Gragg, Rod. George Washington: An Interactive Biography, 1 vol. 2012. (ENG., Illus.). 48p. 34.95 *(978-1-58980-894-2(0))* Pelican Publishing Co., Inc.

Greene, Meg. William H. Harrison. 2007. (Presidential Leaders Ser.). (Illus.). 112p. (J). (gr. 3-7). lib. bdg. 29.27 *(978-0-8225-1511-1(3),* Twenty-First Century Bks.) Lerner Publishing Group.

Gregory, Josh. Abraham Lincoln: The 16th President. 2015. (First Look at America's Presidents Ser.). (ENG.). 24p. (J). (gr. -1-3). lib. bdg. 23.93 *(978-1-62724-554-8(5))* Bearport Publishing Co., Inc.

—Andrew Jackson: The 7th President. 2015. (First Look at America's Presidents Ser.). (ENG.). 24p. (J). (gr. -1-3). lib. bdg. 23.93 *(978-1-62724-556-2(1))* Bearport Publishing Co., Inc.

—Bill Clinton. 2014. (ENG.). 64p. (J). pap. 8.95 *(978-0-531-25825-5(4));* lib. bdg. 30.00 *(978-0-531-21329-2(3))* Scholastic Library Publishing.

—Franklin D. Roosevelt: The 32nd President. 2015. (First Look at America's Presidents Ser.). (ENG.). 24p. (J). (gr. -1-3). lib. bdg. 23.93 *(978-1-62724-555-5(3))* Bearport Publishing Co., Inc.

—George Washington: The 1st President. 2015. (First Look at America's Presidents Ser.). (ENG.). 24p. (J). (gr. -1-3). lib. bdg. 23.93 *(978-1-62724-552-4(9))* Bearport Publishing Co., Inc.

—Theodore Roosevelt: The 26th President. 2015. (First Look at America's Presidents Ser.). (ENG.). 24p. (J). (gr. -1-3). lib. bdg. 23.93 *(978-1-62724-557-9(X))* Bearport Publishing Co., Inc.

—Thomas Jefferson: The 3rd President. 2015. (First Look at America's Presidents Ser.). (ENG.). 24p. (J). (gr. -1-3). lib. bdg. 23.93 *(978-1-62724-553-1(7))* Bearport Publishing Co., Inc.

Gregory, Josh & Bose, Meenekshi. James Madison: The 4th President. 2015. (First Look at America's Presidents Ser.). (ENG.). 24p. (J). (gr. -1-3). lib. bdg. 23.93 *(978-1-62724-559-3(6))* Bearport Publishing Co., Inc.

—John Adams: The 2nd President. 2015. (First Look at America's Presidents Ser.). (ENG.). 24p. (J). (gr. -1-3). lib. bdg. 23.93 *(978-1-62724-558-6(8))* Bearport Publishing Co., Inc.

Gross, M. J. How to Draw the Life & Times of William Jefferson Clinton. 2009. (Kid's Guide to Drawing the Presidents of the United States of America Ser.). 32p. (gr. 4-4). 50.50 *(978-1-61511-166-4(2),* PowerKids Pr.) Rosen Publishing Group, Inc., The.

Gross, Miriam. How to Draw the Life & Times of James Monroe. (Kid's Guide to Drawing the Presidents of the United States of America Ser.). 2009. 32p. (gr. 4-4). 50.50 *(978-1-61511-149-7(2),* PowerKids Pr.) 2006. (YA). (gr. 2-5). 26.50 *(978-1-4042-2982-2(5))* Rosen Publishing Group, Inc., The.

Gross, Miriam J. How to Draw the Life & Times of William Jefferson Clinton. 2007. (Kid's Guide to Drawing the Presidents of the United States of America Ser.). (Illus.). 32p. (YA). (gr. 2-5). 26.50 *(978-1-4042-3018-7(1))* Rosen Publishing Group, Inc., The.

Guernsey, Joann Bren. Hillary Rodham Clinton: Secretary of State. 2009. (USA TODAY Lifeline Biographies Ser.). (ENG.). 112p. (gr. 6-12). lib. bdg. 34.60 *(978-0-7613-5122-1(1))* Lerner Publishing Group.

Gunderson, Jessica. The Election Of 1860: A Nation Divides on the Eve of War. 2016. (Presidential Politics Ser.). (ENG., Illus.). 48p. (gr. 3-4). lib. bdg. 29.32 *(978-1-4914-8240-7(0),* Connect) Stone Arch Bks.

Gunderson, Megan M. Andrew Jackson, 1 vol. (ENG., Illus.). 40p. 2016. (J). *(978-1-68078-101-4(4))* 2009. (YA). (gr. 3-6). 27.07 *(978-1-60453-459-7(1))* ABDO Publishing Co.

—Andrew Johnson, 1 vol. (ENG., Illus.). 40p. 2016. (J). *(978-1-68078-103-8(0))* 2009. (YA). (gr. 3-6). 27.07 *(978-1-60453-461-0(3))* ABDO Publishing Co.

—Benjamin Harrison, 1 vol. (ENG., Illus.). 40p. 2016. (J). *(978-1-68078-097-0(2))* 2009. (YA). (gr. 3-6). 27.07 *(978-1-60453-455-9(9))* ABDO Publishing Co.

—Franklin D. Roosevelt, 1 vol. 2009. (United States Presidents Ser.). (ENG., Illus.). 40p. (YA). (gr. 3-6). 27.07 *(978-1-60453-472-6(9))* ABDO Publishing Co.

—Gerald Ford, 1 vol. 2009. (United States Presidents Ser.). (ENG., Illus.). 40p. (YA). (gr. 3-6). 27.07 *(978-1-60453-451-1(6))* ABDO Publishing Co.

—James A. Garfield, 1 vol. (ENG., Illus.). 40p. 2016. (J). *(978-1-68078-094-9(8))* 2009. (YA). (gr. 3-6). 27.07 *(978-1-60453-452-8(4))* ABDO Publishing Co.

—James Buchanan, 1 vol. 2009. (United States Presidents Ser.). (ENG., Illus.). 40p. (YA). (gr. 3-6). 27.07 *(978-1-60453-442-9(7))* ABDO Publishing Co.

—James Madison, 1 vol. 2009. (United States Presidents Ser.). (ENG., Illus.). 40p. (YA). (gr. 3-6). 27.07 *(978-1-60453-465-8(6))* ABDO Publishing Co.

—James Monroe, 1 vol. 2009. (United States Presidents Ser.). (ENG., Illus.). 40p. (YA). (gr. 3-6). 27.07 *(978-1-60453-467-2(2))* ABDO Publishing Co.

—John F. Kennedy, 1 vol. 2009. (United States Presidents Ser.). (ENG., Illus.). 40p. (YA). (gr. 3-6). 27.07 *(978-1-60453-463-4(X))* ABDO Publishing Co.

—John Tyler, 1 vol. 2009. (United States Presidents Ser.). (ENG., Illus.). 40p. (YA). (gr. 3-6). 27.07 *(978-1-60453-477-1(X))* ABDO Publishing Co.

—Lyndon B. Johnson, 1 vol. 2009. (United States Presidents Ser.). (ENG., Illus.). 40p. (YA). (gr. 3-6). 27.07 *(978-1-60453-462-7(1))* ABDO Publishing Co.

—William McKinley, 1 vol. 2009. (United States Presidents Ser.). (ENG., Illus.). 40p. (YA). (gr. 3-6). 27.07 *(978-1-60453-466-5(4))* ABDO Publishing Co.

Hajeski, Nancy J. The Big Book of Presidents: From George Washington to Barack Obama. 2015. (ENG., Illus.). 144p. (J). (gr. 3-7). 19.95 *(978-1-62914-644-7(7),* Sky Pony Pr.) Skyhorse Publishing Co., Inc.

Haldy, Emma E. Abraham Lincoln. Bane, Jeff, illus. 2016. (My Early Library: My Itty-Bitty Bio Ser.). (ENG.). 24p. (J). (gr. k-1). 28.50 *(978-1-63470-476-2(2),* 207635) Cherry Lake Publishing.

Hale, Sarah Elder, ed. Jefferson Davis & the Confederacy. 2005. (ENG., Illus.). 48p. (J). (gr. 3-9). 17.95 *(978-0-8126-7908-3(3))* Cobblestone Publishing Co.

Hall, Brianna. Freedom from Slavery: Causes & Effects of the Emancipation Proclamation, 1 vol. 2014. (Cause & Effect Ser.). (ENG.). 32p. (gr. 3-4). lib. bdg. 27.32 *(978-1-4765-3930-0(8),* Fact Finders) Capstone Press of Coughlan Cos.

Hally, Ashleigh. Abraham Lincoln. 2012. (Illus.). 24p. (J). *(978-1-935884-41-5(7));* pap. *(978-1-935884-50-7(6))* State Standards Publishing, LLC.

Hamilton, Lynn. Presidents' Day. 2015. (Illus.). 24p. (J). *(978-1-5105-0116-4(9))* SmartBook Media, Inc.

—Presidents' Day. 2010. (American Celebrations Ser.). (Illus.). 24p. (J). (gr. 3-5). pap. 11.95 *(978-1-60596-931-2(1));* lib. bdg. 18.99 *(978-1-60596-773-8(4))* Weigl Pubs., Inc.

Hammond World Atlas Corporation Staff. Presidents: An Illustrated History of America's Leaders. 2009. 144p. (J). (gr. 4-7). 19.99 *(978-0-8437-1848-5(X))* Hammond World Atlas Corp.

Hansen, Grace. Abraham Lincoln, 1 vol. 2014. (United States President Biographies Ser.). (ENG.). 24p. (J). (gr. 4-8). lib. bdg. 28.50 *(978-1-62970-085-4(1))* ABDO Publishing Co.

—Abraham Lincoln. 2015. (Biografías de Los Presidentes de Los Estados Unidos Ser.). (SPA., Illus.). 24p. (gr. k-1). pap. 7.95 *(978-1-4966-0401-9(6))* Capstone Classroom.

—Barack Obama, 1 vol. 2014. (United States President Biographies Ser.). (ENG.). 24p. (J). (gr. 4-8). lib. bdg. 28.50 *(978-1-62970-086-1(X))* ABDO Publishing Co.

—Barack Obama. 2015. (Biografías de Los Presidentes de Los Estados Unidos Ser.). (SPA., Illus.). 24p. (gr. k-1). pap. 7.95 *(978-1-4966-0403-3(2))* Capstone Classroom.

—Bill Clinton, 1 vol. 2014. (United States President Biographies Ser.). (ENG.). 24p. (J). (gr. 4-8). lib. bdg. 28.50 *(978-1-62970-087-8(8))* ABDO Publishing Co.

—Bill Clinton. 2015. (Biografías de Los Presidentes de Los Estados Unidos Ser.). (SPA., Illus.). 24p. (gr. k-1). pap. 7.95 *(978-1-4966-0405-7(9))* Capstone Classroom.

—Franklin D. Roosevelt. 2015. (Biografías de Los Presidentes de Los Estados Unidos Ser.). (SPA., Illus.). 24p. (gr. k-1). pap. 7.95 *(978-1-4966-0407-1(5))* Capstone Classroom.

—Franklin Delano Roosevelt, 1 vol. 2014. (United States President Biographies Ser.). (ENG.). 24p. (J). (gr. 4-8). lib. bdg. 28.50 *(978-1-62970-088-5(6))* ABDO Publishing Co.

—George Washington, 1 vol. 2014. (United States President Biographies Ser.). (ENG.). 24p. (J). (gr. 4-8). lib. bdg. 28.50 *(978-1-62970-089-2(4))* ABDO Publishing Co.

—George Washington. 2015. (Biografías de Los Presidentes de Los Estados Unidos Ser.). (SPA., Illus.). 24p. (gr. k-1). pap. 7.95 *(978-1-4966-0409-5(1))* Capstone Classroom.

—John F. Kennedy, 1 vol. 2014. (United States President Biographies Ser.). (ENG.). 24p. (J). (gr. 4-8). lib. bdg. 28.50 *(978-1-62970-090-8(8))* ABDO Publishing Co.

—John F. Kennedy. 2015. (Biografías de Los Presidentes de Los Estados Unidos Ser.). (SPA., Illus.). 24p. (gr. k-1). pap. 7.95 *(978-1-4966-0411-8(3))* Capstone Classroom.

Harmon, Daniel E. Andrew Jackson. 2004. (Childhoods of the Presidents Ser.). (Illus.). 48p. (J). (gr. 4-18). lib. bdg. 17.95 *(978-1-59084-274-4(X))* Mason Crest.

—Woodrow Wilson. 2004. (Childhoods of the Presidents Ser.). (Illus.). 48p. (J). (gr. 4-18). lib. bdg. 17.95 *(978-1-59084-277-5(4))* Mason Crest.

Harness, Cheryl. Abe Lincoln Goes to Washington: 1837-1865. 2nd ed. 2008. (ENG., Illus.). 48p. (J). (gr. 3-7). pap. 7.95 *(978-1-4263-0436-1(6),* National Geographic Children's Bks.) National Geographic Society.

—The Remarkable Rough-Riding Life of Theodore Roosevelt & the Rise of Empire America. 2007. (Cheryl Harness Histories Ser.). (ENG., Illus.). 144p. (J). (gr. 3-7). 16.95 *(978-1-4263-0008-0(5));* (gr. 4-7). lib. bdg. 25.90 *(978-1-4263-0009-7(3))* National Geographic Society. (National Geographic Children's Bks.).

—The Revolutionary John Adams. 2003. (ENG., Illus.). 48p. (J). (gr. 3-7). 17.95 *(978-0-7922-6970-0(5),* National Geographic Children's Bks.) National Geographic Society.

—Thomas Jefferson. 2007. (ENG., Illus.). 48p. (J). (gr. 2-5). per. 7.95 *(978-1-4263-0043-1(3),* National Geographic Children's Bks.) National Geographic Society.

—Young Abe Lincoln: The Frontier Days: 1809-1837. 2nd ed. 2008. (ENG., Illus.). 32p. (J). (gr. 3-7). pap. 7.95 *(978-1-4263-0437-8(4),* National Geographic Children's Bks.) National Geographic Society.

Harper, Judith E. Andrew Johnson. 2008. (Presidents of the U. S. A. Ser.). (ENG., Illus.). 48p. (J). (gr. 3-6). 32.79 *(978-1-60253-046-1(7),* 200685) Child's World, Inc., The.

Harris, Laurie Lanzen. How to Analyze the Works of Abraham Lincoln, 1 vol. 2013. (Essential Critiques Set 4 Ser.). (ENG.). 112p. (J). (gr. 6-12). lib. bdg. 35.64 *(978-1-61783-642-8(7),* Essential Library) ABDO Publishing Co.

—Presidents of the Uited States. 3rd ed. 2009. (J). lib. bdg. 55.00 *(978-1-931360-45-6(6))* Favorable Impressions.

Harris, Nancy. Mount Rushmore. 2016. (Patriotic Symbols Ser.). (ENG.). 24p. (gr. -1-1). pap. 6.29 *(978-1-4846-3588-9(4),* Acorn) Heinemann-Raintree.

Harrison, Nancy. Who's on Mount Rushmore?, 4 vols., Set. 2014. (Who Was... ? Ser.). (ENG., Illus.). 448p. (J). (gr. 3-7). 19.96 *(978-0-448-48290-3(8),* Grosset & Dunlap) Penguin Young Readers Group.

Hasselius, Michelle M. Lyndon B. Johnson, 1 vol. 2014. (Presidential Biographies Ser.). (ENG.). 24p. (gr. k-1). lib. bdg. 26.65 *(978-1-4765-9611-2(5),* Pebble Plus) Capstone Press of Coughlan Cos.

—Richard M. Nixon, 1 vol. 2014. (Presidential Biographies Ser.). (ENG.). 24p. (gr. k-1). lib. bdg. 26.65 *(978-1-4765-9612-9(3),* Pebble Plus) Capstone Press of Coughlan Cos.

Hasselius, Michelle M. & Tucker, Rosalyn. Presidential Biographies, 1 vol. 2014. (Presidential Biographies Ser.). (ENG.). 24p. (gr. k-1). lib. bdg. 79.95 *(978-1-4765-9623-5(9),* Pebble Plus) Capstone Press of Coughlan Cos.

Havelin, Kate. Andrew Johnson. 2005. (Presidential Leaders Ser.). (Illus.). 112p. (J). (gr. 6-12). lib. bdg. 29.27 *(978-0-8225-1000-0(6))* Lerner Publishing Group.

—John Tyler. 2005. (Presidential Leaders Ser.). (Illus.). 112p. (J). (gr. 3-7). lib. bdg. 29.27 *(978-0-8225-1395-7(1))* Lerner Publishing Group.

—Ulysses S. Grant. 2004. (Presidential Leaders Ser.). (Illus.). 112p. (J). 29.27 *(978-0-8225-0814-4(1),* Lerner Pubns.) Lerner Publishing Group.

P
Q
R

Heiligman, Deborah. High Hopes: A Photobiography of John F. Kennedy. Feresten, Nancy, ed. 2003. (Photobiographies Ser.). (ENG., Illus.). 64p. (J). (gr. 5). 17.95 *(978-0-7922-6141-4(0),* National Geographic Children's Bks.) National Geographic Society.

Helfand, Lewis. Abraham Lincoln: From the Log Cabin to the White House - Campfire Heroes Line. Jones, K. L. & Manikandan, illus. 2013. (Campfire Graphic Novels Ser.). (ENG.). 108p. (YA). (gr. 5-12). pap. 12.99 *(978-93-80741-21-5(9),* Campfire) Steerforth Pr.

Henry, Mike. Tell Me about the Presidents: Lessons for Today's Kids from America's Leaders. 2015. (ENG., Illus.). 128p. 47.00 *(978-1-4758-1703-4(7))* Rowman & Littlefield Publishers, Inc.

Heppermann, Christine & Friedman, Richard D. Bush v. Gore: The Florida Recounts of the 2000 Presidential Election, 1 vol. 2012. (Landmark Supreme Court Cases Ser.). (ENG., Illus.). 160p. (J). (gr. 6-12). 37.07 *(978-1-61783-471-4(8))* ABDO Publishing Co.

Herweck, Dona. George Washington, 1 vol. 2nd rev. ed. 2013. (Nonfiction Readers Ser.). (ENG., Illus.). 28p. (J). (gr. 2-2). pap. 23.96 *(978-1-4807-1061-0(X))* Shell Educational Publishing.

Hess, Deborah. The White House. 2007. (J). pap. 6.99 *(978-0-7614-3394-1(5))* Marshall Cavendish Corp.

Hicks, Kelli L., ed. Complete History of Our Presidents Encyclopedia, 14 vols., Set. 2014. (ENG., Illus.). 896p. (gr. 3-8). lib. bdg. 570.00 *(978-1-60694-293-2(X))* Rourke Educational Media.

Hicks, Kelli L. & Weber, Michael. Rourke's Complete History of Our Presidents Encyclopedia, 14 vols. 2009. (Illus.). (J). *(978-1-60694-297-0(2)); (978-1-60694-298-7(0)); (978-1-60694-307-6(3)); (978-1-60694-296-3(4)); (978-1-60694-306-9(5)); (978-1-60694-305-2(7)); (978-1-60694-304-5(9)); (978-1-60694-294-9(8)); (978-1-60694-295-6(6)); (978-1-60694-299-4(9)); (978-1-60694-300-7(6)); (978-1-60694-301-4(4)); (978-1-60694-302-1(2)); (978-1-60694-303-8(0))* Rourke Educational Media.

Hinkle, Donald. Ronald Reagan: A MyReportLinks.com Book. 2003. (Presidents Ser.). (Illus.). 48p. (J). (gr. 4-10). lib. bdg. 25.26 *(978-0-7660-5112-6(9),* MyReportLinks.com Bks.) Enslow Pubs., Inc.

Hinman, Bonnie. The Executive Branch. 2011. (My Guide to the Constitution Ser.). 48p. (J). (gr. 3-6). pap. 16.50 *(978-1-61228-185-8(0));* (Illus.). lib. bdg. 29.95 *(978-1-58415-943-8(X))* Mitchell Lane Pubs., Inc.

Hinman, Bonnie & Benchmark Education Co. Staff. Opinions about Presidential Speeches. 2014. (Text Connections Ser.). (J). (gr. 5). *(978-1-4900-1368-8(7))* Benchmark Education Co.

Holden, Henry M. Woodrow Wilson: A MyReportLinks.com Book. 2003. (Presidents Ser.). (Illus.). 48p. (J). (gr. 4-10). lib. bdg. 25.26 *(978-0-7660-5123-2(4),* MyReportLinks.com Bks.) Enslow Pubs., Inc.

Hollar, Sherman, contrib. by. Andrew Jackson. 2012. (Pivotal Presidents: Profiles in Leadership Ser.). (ENG., Illus.). 80p. (gr. 7-12). (J). lib. bdg. 32.90 *(978-1-61530-941-2(1));* (YA). 65.80 *(978-1-61530-954-2(3))* Rosen Publishing Group, Inc., The.

—Barack Obama. 2012. (Pivotal Presidents: Profiles in Leadership Ser.). (ENG.). 80p. (gr. 7-12). (J). lib. bdg. 32.90 *(978-1-61530-945-0(4));* (Illus.). (YA). 65.80 *(978-1-61530-955-9(1))* Rosen Publishing Group, Inc., The.

—George Washington. 2012. (Pivotal Presidents: Profiles in Leadership Ser.). (ENG.). 80p. (YA). (gr. 7-12). lib. bdg. 32.90 *(978-1-61530-939-9(X));* (Illus.). 65.80 *(978-1-61530-956-6(X))* Rosen Publishing Group, Inc., The.

—John F. Kennedy. 2012. (Pivotal Presidents: Profiles in Leadership Ser.). (ENG.). 80p. (YA). (gr. 7-12). lib. bdg. 32.90 *(978-1-61530-943-6(8));* (Illus.). 65.80 *(978-1-61530-957-3(8))* Rosen Publishing Group, Inc., The.

Hollihan, Kerrie Logan. Theodore Roosevelt for Kids: His Life & Times, 21 Activities. 2010. (For Kids Ser.). (ENG., Illus.). 144p. (J). (gr. 4-18). pap. 16.95 *(978-1-55652-955-9(4))* Chicago Review Pr., Inc.

Holub, Joan. This Little President: A Presidential Primer. Roode, Daniel, illus. 2016. (This Little Ser.). (ENG.). 26p. (J). (gr. -1-k). bds. 7.99 *(978-1-4814-5850-4(7),* Little Simon) Little Simon.

Hopkinson, Deborah. John Adams Speaks for Freedom. Orback, Craig, illus. 2005. (Ready-To-read SOFA Ser.). (ENG.). 32p. (J). (gr. 1-3). pap. 3.99 *(978-0-689-86907-5(X),* Simon Spotlight) Simon Spotlight.

Hoppe, Ludwig Augustin. Die Epiklesis Der Griechischen Und Orientalischen Liturgieen Und Der Römische Consekrationskanon (German Edition) 2010. 350p. pap. 32.75 *(978-1-142-96440-5(X))* Creative Media Partners, LLC.

Horn, Geoffrey M. The Presidency. 2003. (World Almanac Library of American Government). (Illus.). 48p. (gr. 5-12). lib. bdg. 31.00 *(978-0-8368-5458-9(6),* Gareth Stevens Secondary Library) Stevens, Gareth Publishing LLLP.

Houran, Lori Haskins. My Little Golden Book about George Washington. Garofoli, Viviana, illus. 2016. (Little Golden Book Ser.). (ENG.). 24p. (J). (-k). 4.99 *(978-1-101-93969-7(9),* Golden Bks.) Random Hse. Children's Bks.

Huddle, Lorena. Woodrow Wilson. 2017. (Pivotal Presidents: Profiles in Leadership Ser.). 80p. (gr. 12-13). lib. bdg. 33.90 ***(978-1-68048-635-3(7),*** Britannica Educational Publishing) Rosen Publishing Group, Inc., The.

Isecke, Harriet. Lyndon B. Johnson: A Texan in the White House, 1 vol. 2012. (Primary Source Readers Ser.). (ENG.). 32p. (J). (gr. 3-3). pap. 8.99 *(978-1-4333-5052-8(1))* Teacher Created Materials, Inc.

—Lyndon B. Johnson: Un Texano en la Casa Blanca / Lyndon B. Johnson - A Texan in the White House. 2013. (Primary Source Readers Ser.). (SPA.). lib. bdg. 19.65 *(978-0-606-31873-0(9),* Turtleback) Turtleback Bks.

Jakubiak, David J. What Does the President Do? 2010. (How Our Government Works Ser.). 24p. (J). (ENG.). pap. 8.25 *(978-1-4358-9810-3(9),* PowerKids Pr.); (gr. 3-6). lib. bdg., E-Book 42.50 *(978-1-4488-0020-9(X));* (Illus.). (gr. 3-6). lib. bdg. 22.60 *(978-1-4358-9357-3(3),* PowerKids Pr.) Rosen Publishing Group, Inc., The.

January, Brendan. Air Force One. (Cornerstones of Freedom Ser.). (ENG.). 48p. 2008. (J). pap. 5.95 *(978-0-531-20826-7(5),* Children's Pr.) 2004. (Illus.). (YA). (gr. 4-7). 26.00 *(978-0-516-24236-1(9))* Scholastic Library Publishing.

January, Brendan & Seidman, David. Jimmy Carter: Peacemaker & President. 2004. (Great Life Stories Ser.). (ENG., Illus.). 127p. (J). 30.50 *(978-0-531-12374-4(X),* Watts, Franklin) Scholastic Library Publishing.

Jeffrey, Gary. Abraham Lincoln: The Life of America's Sixteenth President. 2009. (Graphic Nonfiction Biographies Ser.). (ENG.). 48p. (YA). (gr. 4-5). 58.50 *(978-1-61513-011-5(X),* Rosen Reference) Rosen Publishing Group, Inc., The.

—Thomas Jefferson & the Declaration of Independence. 2011. (Graphic Heroes of the American Revolution Ser.). (Illus.). 24p. (J). (gr. 3-6). 23.95 *(978-1-4339-6025-3(7));* pap. 8.15 *(978-1-4339-6026-0(5),* Gareth Stevens Learning Library) Stevens, Gareth Publishing LLLP.

Jennett, Pamela & Marchant, Sherry. Electing Our President: The Process to Elect the Nation's Leader. Jennett, Pamela, ed. Hillam, Corbin & Grayson, Rick, illus. 2004. 48p. pap. 8.99 *(978-0-88160-379-8(1),* LW-436) Creative Teaching Pr., Inc.

Jennings, Ken. U. S. Presidents. Lowery, Mike, illus. 2014. (Ken Jennings' Junior Genius Guides). (ENG.). 160p. (J). (gr. 3-5). pap. 7.99 *(978-1-4424-7332-4(0),* Little Simon) Little Simon.

Johansen, H. L. How to Draw the Life & Times of Calvin Coolidge. 2009. (Kid's Guide to Drawing the Presidents of the United States of America Ser.). 32p. (gr. 4-4). 50.50 *(978-1-61511-134-3(4),* PowerKids Pr.) Rosen Publishing Group, Inc., The.

Johansen, Heidi Leigh. How to Draw the Life & Times of Calvin Coolidge. 2007. (Kid's Guide to Drawing the Presidents of the United States of America Ser.). (Illus.). 32p. (YA). (gr. 2-5). 26.50 *(978-1-4042-3006-4(8))* Rosen Publishing Group, Inc., The.

Johnson, Robin. Why Mirabeau Lamar Matters to Texas. 2014. (Illus.). 32p. (J). lib. bdg. 26.25 *(978-1-4777-0915-3(0))* Rosen Publishing Group, Inc., The.

Jones, Veda Boyd. John F. Kennedy. 2006. (Rookie Biographies Ser.). (ENG., Illus.). 32p. (J). (gr. 1-2). pap. 4.95 *(978-0-516-29797-2(X),* Children's Pr.) Scholastic Library Publishing.

Judson, Karen. Abraham Lincoln: This Nation Shall Have a New Birth of Freedom. rev. ed. 2008. (Americans—the Spirit of a Nation Ser.). (Illus.). 128p. (J). (gr. 3-7). lib. bdg. 33.27 *(978-0-7660-3170-8(5))* Enslow Pubs., Inc.

Junyk, Myra. The 10 Greatest Presidents. 2007. (J). 14.99 *(978-1-55448-457-7(X))* Scholastic Library Publishing.

Jurmain, Suzanne Tripp. George Did It. Day, Larry, illus. 2007. (ENG.). 40p. (J). (gr. k-4). pap. 6.99 *(978-0-14-240895-7(6),* Puffin Books) Penguin Young Readers Group.

—George Did It. Day, Larry, illus. 2007. (gr. -1-3). 17.00 *(978-0-7569-8161-7(1))* Perfection Learning Corp.

—Nice Work, Franklin! Day, Larry, illus. 2016. (ENG.). 32p. (J). (gr. k-4). 17.99 *(978-0-8037-3800-3(5),* Dial Bks) Penguin Young Readers Group.

Katirgis, Jane. Celebrating President Barack Obama in Pictures. 2009. (Obama Family Photo Album Ser.). (Illus.). 32p. (J). (gr. 2-5). lib. bdg. 23.94 *(978-0-7660-3651-2(0))* Enslow Pubs., Inc.

Katz, Vladimir. A Timeline of the Life of George Washington. 2009. (Timelines of American History Ser.). 32p. (gr. 4-4). 47.90 *(978-1-60854-388-5(9),* Rosen Reference) Rosen Publishing Group, Inc., The.

Kawa, Katie. Barack Obama: First African American President. 2012. (Beginning Biographies Ser.). (ENG., Illus.). 24p. (J). (gr. 1-3). 22.60 *(978-1-4488-8595-4(7),* PowerKids Pr.) Rosen Publishing Group, Inc., The.

Keating, Frank. Abraham. Wimmer, Mike, illus. 2017. (Mount Rushmore Presidential Ser.). (ENG.). 32p. (J). (gr. 1-4). 17.99 *(978-1-4424-9319-3(4),* Simon & Schuster/Paula Wiseman Bks.) Simon & Schuster/Paula Wiseman Bks.

—George: George Washington, Our Founding Father. Wimmer, Mike, illus. 2012. (Mount Rushmore Presidential Ser.). (ENG.). 32p. (J). (gr. 1-4). 17.99 *(978-1-4169-5482-8(1),* Simon & Schuster/Paula Wiseman Bks.) Simon & Schuster/Paula Wiseman Bks.

—Theodore. Wimmer, Mike, illus. 2006. (Mount Rushmore Presidential Ser.). (ENG.). 32p. (J). (gr. 1-4). 17.99 *(978-0-689-86532-9(5),* Simon & Schuster/Paula Wiseman Bks.) Simon & Schuster/Paula Wiseman Bks.

Kelley, K. C. Grover Cleveland: The 22nd & 24th President. 2016. (First Look at America's Presidents Ser.). (ENG., Illus.). 24p. (J). (gr. -1-3). 17.95 *(978-1-944102-67-8(1))* Bearport Publishing Co., Inc.

—James Monroe: The 5th President. 2016. (First Look at America's Presidents Ser.). (ENG., Illus.). 24p. (J). (gr. -1-3). 17.95 *(978-1-944102-64-7(7))* Bearport Publishing Co., Inc.

Kenison, Misti. Where's Your Hat, Abe Lincoln? 2017. (ENG.). 28p. (J). bds. 9.99 ***(978-1-4926-5250-2(4),*** Sourcebooks Jabberwocky) Sourcebooks, Inc.

Kennedy, Marge. Pets at the White House. 2009. (Scholastic News Nonfiction Readers Ser.). (Illus.). 24p. (J). (gr. 1-2). 22.00 *(978-0-531-21096-3(0))* Scholastic Library Publishing.

—Scholastic News Nonfiction Readers: Let's Visit the White House, 6 vols., Set. Incl. Having Fun at the White House. Kennedy, Marge M. (Illus.). 22.00 *(978-0-531-21095-6(2));* Pets at the White House. (Illus.). 22.00 *(978-0-531-21096-3(0));* See Inside the White House. (Illus.). 22.00 *(978-0-531-21097-0(9));* Story of the White House. Kennedy, Marge M. (Illus.). 22.00 *(978-0-531-21094-9(4));* Time to Eat at the White House. 22.00 *(978-0-531-21098-7(7));* Who Works at the White House? (Illus.). 22.00 *(978-0-531-21099-4(5));* 24p. (J). (gr. 1-2). 2009. Set lib. bdg. 132.00 *(978-0-531-27902-1(2),* Children's Pr.) Scholastic Library Publishing.

—The Story of the White House. 2009. (Scholastic News Nonfiction Readers Ser.). (ENG.). 24p. (J). (gr. 1-2). pap. 6.95 *(978-0-531-22431-1(7))* Scholastic Library Publishing.

—Who Works at the White House? 2009. (Scholastic News Nonfiction Readers Ser.). (Illus.). 24p. (J). (gr. 1-2). 22.00 *(978-0-531-21099-4(5))* Scholastic Library Publishing.

Kennedy, Marge M. & Kennedy, Marge. Having Fun at the White House. 2009. (Scholastic News Nonfiction Readers Ser.). (Illus.). 24p. (J). (gr. 1-2). 22.00 *(978-0-531-21095-6(2))* Scholastic Library Publishing.

—The Story of the White House. 2009. (Scholastic News Nonfiction Readers Ser.). (Illus.). 24p. (J). (gr. 1-2). 22.00 *(978-0-531-21094-9(4))* Scholastic Library Publishing.

Kenney, Karen Latchana & Andronik, Catherine M. Abraham Lincoln's Presidency. 2016. (Presidential Powerhouses Ser.). (ENG., Illus.). 104p. (J). (gr. 6-12). 53.32 *(978-1-4677-8547-1(4),* Lerner Pubns.) Lerner Publishing Group.

Kent, Deborah. Franklin Delano Roosevelt: Nothing to Fear! 2006. (Defining Moments Ser.). (Illus.). 32p. (YA). (gr. 2-5). lib. bdg. 25.27 *(978-1-59716-272-2(8))* Bearport Publishing Co., Inc.

—James A. Garfield. 2004. (Encyclopedia of Presidents Ser.). (ENG., Illus.). 110p. (YA). (gr. 5-9). 34.00 *(978-0-516-22886-0(2))* Scholastic Library Publishing.

Keppeler, Jill. 20 Fun Facts about Thomas Jefferson. 2017. (Fun Fact File: Founding Fathers Ser.). 32p. (J). (gr. 2-3). pap. 63.00 ***(978-1-5382-0274-6(3))*** Stevens, Gareth Publishing LLLP.

Kerley, Barbara. What to Do about Alice? 2011. (J). (gr. 2-5). 18.95 *(978-0-545-29821-6(0))* Weston Woods Studios, Inc.

Kesselring, Mari. How to Analyze the Works of Franklin D. Roosevelt, 1 vol. 2013. (Essential Critiques Set 4 Ser.). (ENG.). 112p. (J). (gr. 6-12). lib. bdg. 35.64 *(978-1-61783-643-5(5),* Essential Library) ABDO Publishing Co.

King, David C. Have Fun with the Presidents: Activities, Projects, & Fascinating Facts. 2007. (ENG., Illus.). 132p. (J). (gr. 3-9). pap. 14.95 *(978-0-471-67905-9(4),* Jossey-Bass) Wiley, John & Sons, Inc.

—Herbert Hoover. 2009. (Presidents & Their Times 3 Ser.). 96p. (gr. 6). 34.21 *(978-0-7614-3626-3(X))* Marshall Cavendish Corp.

King, Wilma. Children of the Emancipation. 2005. (Picture the American Past Ser.). (Illus.). 48p. (gr. 2-5). 22.60 *(978-1-57505-396-7(9))* Lerner Publishing Group.

Kirkman, Marissa. The Life & Times of Abraham Lincoln & the US Civil War. 2016. (Life & Times Ser.). (ENG., Illus.). 24p. (gr. 1-2). lib. bdg. 25.32 *(978-1-5157-2474-2(3),* First Facts) Capstone Press of Coughlan Cos.

—The Life & Times of George Washington & the American Revolution. 2016. (Life & Times Ser.). (ENG., Illus.). 24p. (gr. 1-2). lib. bdg. 25.32 *(978-1-5157-2476-6(X),* First Facts) Capstone Press of Coughlan Cos.

Kishel, Ann-Marie. Thomas Jefferson: A Life of Patriotism. 2006. (Pull Ahead Books-Biographies Ser.). (ENG., Illus.). 32p. (gr. k-3). lib. bdg. 22.60 *(978-0-8225-3480-8(0),* Lerner Pubns.) Lerner Publishing Group.

—Thomas Jefferson: Una Vida de Patriotismo. Translations.com Staff, tr. 2006. (Libros para Avanzar-Biografías (Pull Ahead Books-Biographies) Ser.). (ENG & SPA., Illus.). 32p. (gr. k-3). lib. bdg. 22.60 *(978-0-8225-6238-2(3),* Ediciones Lerner) Lerner Publishing Group.

Kit, Oscar. A Timeline of the Life of Thomas Jefferson. 2009. (Timelines of American History Ser.). 32p. (gr. 4-4). 47.90 *(978-1-60854-389-2(7),* Rosen Reference) Rosen Publishing Group, Inc., The.

Klein, Adria F. Barack Obama. 2009. pap. 13.25 *(978-1-60559-055-4(X))* Hameray Publishing Group, Inc.

Knudsen, Shannon. When Were the First Slaves Set Free During the Civil War? And Other Questions about the Emancipation Proclamation. 2010. (Six Questions of American History Ser.). (ENG.). (gr. 4-6). pap. 56.72 *(978-0-7613-6948-6(1))* Lerner Publishing Group.

—When Were the First Slaves Set Free During the Civil War? And Other Questions about the Emancipation Proclamation. 2010. (Six Questions of American History Ser.). (ENG.). 48p. (gr. 4-6). pap. 9.95 *(978-0-7613-6121-3(9))* Lerner Publishing Group.

Koestler-Grack, Rachel A. Abraham Lincoln. 2009. (Leaders of the Civil War Era Ser.). (Illus.). 144p. (gr. 6-12). 35.00 *(978-1-60413-298-4(1),* Chelsea Hse.) Facts On File, Inc.

Kops, Deborah. Zachary Taylor: America's 12th President. 2004. (Encyclopedia of Presidents Ser.). (ENG., Illus.). 110p. (YA). (gr. 5-9). 34.00 *(978-0-516-23442-7(0))* Scholastic Library Publishing.

Kozleski, Lisa. James Madison. 2004. (Childhoods of the Presidents Ser.). (Illus.). 48p. (J). (gr. 4-18). lib. bdg. 17.95 *(978-1-59084-269-0(3))* Mason Crest.

Kramer, Barbara. Jimmy Carter: A Life of Service. 2005. (Awesome Values in Famous Lives Ser.). (Illus.). 48p. (J). (gr. 3-7). lib. bdg. 25.27 *(978-0-7660-2379-6(6),* Enslow Elementary) Enslow Pubs., Inc.

Krensky, Stephen. The Emancipaton Proclamation. 2011. (Documents of Democracy Ser.). 96p. (gr. 8). 34.21 *(978-0-7614-4915-7(9))* Marshall Cavendish Corp.

—George Washington's First Victory. Hearn, Diane Dawson, illus. 2005. (Ready-To-read COFA Ser.). (ENG.). 32p. (J). (gr. k-2). pap. 3.99 *(978-0-689-85942-7(2),* Simon Spotlight) Simon Spotlight.

Krieg, Katherine. President & Cabinet. 2014. (ENG.). 24p. (gr. 3-5). 28.50 *(978-1-62717-678-1(0))* Rourke Educational Media.

Krull, Kathleen. A Boy Named FDR: How Franklin D. Roosevelt Grew up to Change America. Johnson, Steve & Fancher, Lou, illus. (ENG.). 48p. (J). (gr. 1-4). 2016. 7.99 *(978-1-101-93251-3(1),* Dragonfly Bks.) 2010. 17.99 *(978-0-375-85716-4(8),* Knopf Bks. for Young Readers) Random Hse. Children's Bks.

—The Brothers Kennedy: John, Robert, Edward. Bates, Amy June, illus. 2010. (ENG.). 40p. (J). (gr. -1-3). 16.99 *(978-1-4169-9158-8(1),* Simon & Schuster Bks. For Young Readers) Simon & Schuster Bks. For Young Readers.

Krull, Kathleen & Brewer, Paul. Lincoln Tells a Joke: How Laughter Saved the President (and the Country) Innerst, Stacy, illus. 2010. (ENG.). 40p. (J). (gr. 1-4). 17.99 *(978-0-15-206639-0(X))* Houghton Mifflin Harcourt Publishing Co.

Kukla, Amy. Thomas Jefferson: Life, Liberty, & the Pursuit of Happiness. 2009. (Library of American Lives & Times Ser.). 112p. (gr. 5-5). 69.20 *(978-1-60853-508-8(8))* Rosen Publishing Group, Inc., The.

Lacey, Saskia. Jurassic Classics: the Presidential Masters of Prehistory: Discover Our Country's Prehistoric Forefathers. 2016. (Jurassic Classics Ser.). (ENG., Illus.). 40p. (J). (gr. 2-6). 14.95 *(978-1-63322-109-3(1),* Walter Foster Jr) Quarto Publishing Group USA.

Landau, Elaine. The Emancipation Proclamation: Would You Do What Lincoln Did? (What Would You Do? Ser.). (Illus.). 48p. (J). 2010. pap. 8.95 *(978-1-59845-194-8(4))* 2008. (gr. 3-7). lib. bdg. 25.27 *(978-0-7660-2899-9(2))* Enslow Pubs., Inc. (Enslow Elementary).

—Lincoln's Emancipation Proclamation: Would You Sign the Great Document? 2015. (What Would You Do? Ser.). 48p. (J). (gr. 3-4). 25.27 *(978-0-7660-6290-0(2));* pap. 8.95 *(978-0-7660-6291-7(0),* Enslow Elementary) Enslow Pubs., Inc.

—The President, Vice President, & Cabinet: A Look at the Executive Branch. 2012. (Searchlight Books How Does Government Work Ser.). (ENG., Illus.). 40p. (gr. 3-5). pap. 51.01 *(978-0-7613-9234-7(3));* pap. 8.95 *(978-0-7613-8563-9(0));* lib. bdg. 27.93 *(978-0-7613-6517-4(6))* Lerner Publishing Group.

—Warren G. Harding. 2005. (Presidential Leaders Ser.). (Illus.). 120p. (J). 29.27 *(978-0-8225-0850-2(8),* Lerner Pubns.) Lerner Publishing Group.

Lazo, Caroline Evensen. Franklin Pierce. 2007. (Presidential Leaders Ser.). (Illus.). 112p. (J). (gr. 3-7). lib. bdg. 29.27 *(978-0-8225-1492-3(3),* Twenty-First Century Bks.) Lerner Publishing Group.

—Harry S. Truman. 2003. (Presidential Biography Ser.). (Illus.). 112p. (J). (gr. 6-12). lib. bdg. 29.27 *(978-0-8225-0096-4(5))* Lerner Publishing Group.

Lee, Sally. George W. Bush, 1 vol. (Presidential Biographies Ser.). (ENG.). 24p. (gr. k-1). 2014. pap. 6.29 *(978-1-4765-9628-0(X),* Pebble Bks.) 2012. (Illus.). lib. bdg. 26.65 *(978-1-4296-8586-3(7),* Pebble Plus) Capstone Press of Coughlan Cos.

—William Jefferson Clinton, 1 vol. (Presidential Biographies Ser.). (ENG.). 24p. (gr. k-1). 2014. pap. 6.29 *(978-1-4765-9627-3(1),* Pebble Bks.) 2012. (Illus.). lib. bdg. 26.65 *(978-1-4296-8585-6(9),* Pebble Plus) Capstone Press of Coughlan Cos.

Lee, Sally & Edison, Erin. Presidential Biographies. 2012. (Presidential Biographies Ser.). (ENG.). 24p. (gr. k-1). lib. bdg. 159.90 *(978-1-4296-9174-1(3),* Pebble Plus) Capstone Press of Coughlan Cos.

Lee, T. S. The Lincoln Story: The Boy Who Embraced a Nation. 4th ed. 2010. (Great Heroes Ser.). 184p. (J). pap. 14.95 *(978-0-9819542-3-3(5))* DASANBOOKS.

—The Obama Story: The Boy with the Biggest Dream! Shin, Janet Jaywan, tr. from KOR. 2009. 207p. (J). (gr. 6-18). pap. 14.95 *(978-0-9819542-0-2(0))* DASANBOOKS.

Leidtke, Leila. If I Were President. 2012. 32p. pap. 16.50 *(978-1-4685-5093-1(4))* AuthorHouse.

Leighton, Marian. George Washington. Salvador, Martin, illus. 2005. (Heroes of America Ser.). 239p. (gr. 3-8). 27.07 *(978-1-59679-262-3(0),* Abdo & Daughters) ABDO Publishing Co.

Levine, Michelle & Waxman, Laura Hamilton. Franklin D. Roosevelt. 2005. (History Maker Bios Ser.). (Illus.). 48p. (J). (gr. 3-5). 26.60 *(978-0-8225-1545-6(8))* Lerner Publishing Group.

Levy, Debbie. James Monroe. 2005. (Presidential Leaders Ser.). (Illus.). 112p. (J). 29.27 *(978-0-8225-0824-3(9),* Lerner Pubns.) Lerner Publishing Group.

—John Quincy Adams. 2004. (Presidential Leaders Ser.). (Illus.). 112p. (J). (gr. 3-7). lib. bdg. 29.27 *(978-0-8225-0825-0(7))* Lerner Publishing Group.

—Lyndon B. Johnson. 2003. (Presidential Leaders Ser.). (Illus.). 112p. (J). 29.27 *(978-0-8225-0097-1(3),* Lerner Pubns.) Lerner Publishing Group.

—Rutherford B. Hayes. 2006. (Presidential Leaders Ser.). (Illus.). 112p. (J). (gr. 3-7). lib. bdg. 29.27 *(978-0-8225-1493-0(1),* Lerner Pubns.) Lerner Publishing Group.

Levy, Janey. 20 Fun Facts about the Presidency. 2013. 32p. (J). (gr. 3-6). 25.25 *(978-1-4339-9188-2(8));* pap. 63.00 *(978-1-4339-9190-5(X));* pap. 10.50 *(978-1-4339-9189-9(6))* Stevens, Gareth Publishing LLLP.

Lewis K., Parker. How to Draw the Life & Times of Richard M. Nixon. 2007. (Kid's Guide to Drawing the Presidents of the United States of America Ser.). (Illus.). 32p. (YA). (gr. 2-5). 26.50 *(978-1-4042-3013-2(0))* Rosen Publishing Group, Inc., The.

Lillard, David. William Henry Harrison: A MyReportLinks. Com Book. 2003. (Presidents Ser.). (Illus.). 48p. (J). lib. bdg. 25.26 *(978-0-7660-5150-8(1),* MyReportLinks.com Bks.) Enslow Pubs., Inc.

Lukes, Bonnie L. John Adams: Public Servant. 2004. (Notable Americans Ser.). (Illus.). 128p. (J). (gr. 6-12). 23.95 *(978-1-883846-80-0(3),* First Biographies) Reynolds, Morgan Inc.

—Woodrow Wilson & the Progressive Era. 2006. (World Leaders Ser.). (Illus.). 192p. (J). (gr. 6-10). lib. bdg. 26.95 *(978-1-931798-79-2(6))* Reynolds, Morgan Inc.

Lusted, Marcia Amidon. Revolution & the New Nation: 1750-Early 1800s. 2007. (Presidents of the United States Ser.). (Illus.). 48p. (J). (gr. 4-7). lib. bdg. 29.05 *(978-1-59036-739-1(1));* per. 10.95 *(978-1-59036-740-7(5))* Weigl Pubs., Inc.

Lynne, Douglas. Contemporary United States: 1968 to the Present. 2007. (Presidents of the United States Ser.). (Illus.). 48p. (J). (gr. 4-7). lib. bdg. 29.05 *(978-1-59036-753-7(7));* per. 10.95 *(978-1-59036-754-4(5))* Weigl Pubs., Inc.

Machajewski, Sarah. Standing in the President's Shoes. 2015. (My Government Ser.). (ENG., Illus.). 32p. (J). (gr. 4-4). pap. 10.58 *(978-1-5026-0460-6(4))* Cavendish Square Publishing.

Magic Wagon Staff. Presidents of the United States Bio-Graphics, 1 vol. 2011. (Presidents of the United States Bio-Graphics Ser.). (ENG., Illus.). 32p. 171.00 *(978-1-61641-643-0(2),* Graphic Planet) Magic Wagon.

Magoon, Kekla. Abraham Lincoln, 1 vol. 2007. (Essential Lives Set 1 Ser.). (ENG., Illus.). 112p. (J). (gr. 6-12). lib. bdg. 35.64 *(978-1-59928-839-0(7))* ABDO Publishing Co.

Maloof, Torrey. Abraham Lincoln: Addressing a Nation. 2017. (Primary Source Readers Ser.). 32p. (J). (gr. 4-5). pap. 8.99 *(978-1-4938-3805-9(9))* Teacher Created Materials, Inc.

—George Washington & the Men Who Shaped America. 2016. (Primary Source Readers Ser.). (Illus.). 32p. (J). (gr. 4-5). pap. 8.99 *(978-1-4938-3081-7(3))* Teacher Created Materials, Inc.

—James Madison & the Making of the United States. 2017. (Primary Source Readers Ser.). (Illus.). 32p. (J). (gr. 4-5). pap. 8.99 *(978-1-4938-3795-3(8))* Teacher Created Materials, Inc.

—Thomas Jefferson & the Empire of Liberty. 2017. (Primary Source Readers Ser.). (Illus.). 32p. (J). (gr. 4-5). pap. 8.99 *(978-1-4938-3792-2(3))* Teacher Created Materials, Inc.

Mansfield, Cheryl. Barack Obama. 2016. (Premier Presidents Ser.). (ENG.). 24p. (J). (gr. 1-4). 27.07 *(978-1-5038-0846-1(7)*, 210696) Child's World, Inc., The.

Mapua, Jeff. Bill & Hillary Clinton. 2014. (Making a Difference: Leaders Who Are Changing the World Ser.). 48p. (YA). (gr. 5-8). 25.85 *(978-1-62275-425-0(5))*; pap. 14.05 *(978-1-62275-427-4(1))*; pap. 84.30 *(978-1-62275-428-1(X))* Rosen Publishing Group, Inc., The.

Mara, Wil. Abraham Lincoln. 2014. (Rookie Biographies(r) Ser.). (ENG.). 32p. (J). lib. bdg. 23.00 *(978-0-531-21058-1(8))* Scholastic Library Publishing.

—Dwight Eisenhower. 2010. (Presidents & Their Times 4 Ser.). 96p. (gr. 6). 34.21 *(978-0-7614-4812-9(8))* Marshall Cavendish GBR. Dist: Marshall Cavendish Corp.

—Franklin D. Roosevelt. 2004. (Rookie Biographies Ser.). (ENG., Illus.). 31p. (J). 20.50 *(978-0-516-21844-1(1)*, Children's Pr.) Scholastic Library Publishing.

—George W. Bush. 2003. (Rookie Biographies Ser.). (ENG.). 32p. (J). (gr. 1-2). pap. 4.95 *(978-0-516-27838-4(X)*, Children's Pr.) Scholastic Library Publishing.

—George Washington. 2013. (Rookie Biographies(tm) Ser.). (ENG.). 32p. (J). lib. bdg. 25.00 *(978-0-531-24736-5(8))*; pap. 5.95 *(978-0-531-24702-0(3))* Scholastic Library Publishing.

—Gerald Ford. 2009. (Presidents & Their Times 3 Ser.). 96p. (gr. 6). 34.21 *(978-0-7614-3629-4(4))* Marshall Cavendish GBR. Dist: Marshall Cavendish Corp.

—Harry Truman. 2011. (Presidents & Their Times 5 Ser.). (Illus.). 96p. (J). (gr. 6). 34.21 *(978-1-60870-185-8(9))* Marshall Cavendish Corp.

—James Garfield. 2011. (Presidents & Their Times 5 Ser.). 96p. (gr. 6). 34.21 *(978-1-60870-183-4(2))* Marshall Cavendish GBR. Dist: Marshall Cavendish Corp.

—John Adams. 2008. (Presidents & Their Times Ser.). 96p. (gr. 6-18). lib. bdg. 34.21 *(978-0-7614-2840-4(2)*, Benchmark Bks.) Marshall Cavendish Corp.

—John F. Kennedy. 2009. (Presidents & Their Times 3 Ser.). 96p. (gr. 6). 34.21 *(978-0-7614-3628-7(6))* Marshall Cavendish Corp.

—Ronald Reagan. 2010. (Presidents & Their Times 4 Ser.). 96p. (gr. 6). 34.21 *(978-0-7614-4814-3(4))* Marshall Cavendish Corp.

—Theodore Roosevelt. 2007. (Rookie Biographies Ser.). (Illus.). 32p. (J). (gr. 1-2). pap. 4.95 *(978-0-516-27304-4(3)*, Children's Pr.) Scholastic Library Publishing.

Marcovitz, Hal. Barack. 2007. (Obamas Ser.). (Illus.). 64p. (YA). (gr. 3-6). pap. 9.95 *(978-1-4222-1484-8(2))*; (gr. 4-7). lib. bdg. 19.95 *(978-1-4222-1477-0(X))* Mason Crest.

—Bill Clinton. 2004. (Childhoods of the Presidents Ser.). (Illus.). 48p. (J). (gr. 4-18). lib. bdg. 17.95 *(978-1-59084-273-7(1))* Mason Crest.

—James Monroe. 2004. (Childhoods of the Presidents Ser.). (Illus.). 48p. (J). (gr. 4-18). lib. bdg. 17.95 *(978-1-59084-283-6(9))* Mason Crest.

—John Adams. 2004. (Childhoods of the Presidents Ser.). (Illus.). 48p. (J). (gr. 4-18). lib. bdg. 17.95 *(978-1-59084-268-3(5))* Mason Crest.

—John F. Kennedy. 2004. (Childhood of the Presidents Ser.). (Illus.). 48p. (J). (gr. 4-18). lib. bdg. 17.95 *(978-1-59084-272-0(3))* Mason Crest.

—The Obama Family Tree. 2007. (Obamas Ser.). (Illus.). 64p. (YA). (gr. 3-6). pap. 9.95 *(978-1-4222-1488-6(5))*; (gr. 4-7). lib. bdg. 19.95 *(978-1-4222-1481-7(8))* Mason Crest.

—Obama Mania. 2007. (Obamas Ser.). (Illus.). 64p. (YA). (gr. 3-6). pap. 9.95 *(978-1-4222-1489-3(3))*; (gr. 4-7). lib. bdg. 19.95 *(978-1-4222-1482-4(6))* Mason Crest.

—Theodore Roosevelt. 2004. (Childhood of the Presidents Ser.). (Illus.). 48p. (J). (gr. 4-18). lib. bdg. 17.95 *(978-1-59084-278-2(2))* Mason Crest.

—The White House: The Home of the U. S. President. Moreno, Barry, ed. 2014. (Patriotic Symbols of America Ser.: 20). 48p. (J). (gr. 4-18). lib. bdg. 20.95 *(978-1-4222-3134-0(8))* Mason Crest.

Margaret, Amy. Franklin D. Roosevelt Library & Museum. (Presidential Libraries Ser.). 24p. 2009. (gr. 3-3). 42.50 *(978-1-60851-483-0(8))* 2004. (Illus.). (J). lib. bdg. 22.60 *(978-0-8239-6268-6(7))* Rosen Publishing Group, Inc., The. (PowerKids Pr.).

—George Bush Presidential Library. 2009. (Presidential Libraries Ser.). 24p. (gr. 3-3). 42.50 *(978-1-60851-484-7(6)*, PowerKids Pr.) Rosen Publishing Group, Inc., The.

—Gerald R. Ford Library & Museum. 2009. (Presidential Libraries Ser.). 24p. (gr. 3-3). 42.50 *(978-1-60851-485-4(4)*, PowerKids Pr.) Rosen Publishing Group, Inc., The.

—John F. Kennedy Library & Museum. 2004. (Presidential Libraries Ser.). (Illus.). 24p. (J). lib. bdg. 22.60 *(978-0-8239-6269-3(5)*, PowerKids Pr.) Rosen Publishing Group, Inc., The.

—Ronald Reagan Presidential Library. (Presidential Libraries Ser.). 24p. 2009. (gr. 3-3). 42.50 *(978-1-60851-488-5(9))* 2004. (Illus.). (J). lib. bdg. 22.60 *(978-0-8239-6272-3(5))* Rosen Publishing Group, Inc., The. (PowerKids Pr.).

Markel, Rita J. Grover Cleveland. 2006. (Presidential Leaders Ser.). (Illus.). 112p. (J). (gr. 3-7). lib. bdg. 29.27 *(978-0-8225-1494-7(X)*, Lerner Pubns.) Lerner Publishing Group.

Marquez, Heron. George W. Bush. 2005. (Presidential Leaders Ser.). (Illus.). 112p. (J). (gr. 6-12). lib. bdg. 29.27 *(978-0-8225-1507-4(5)*, Lerner Pubns.) Lerner Publishing Group.

—Richard M. Nixon. 2003. (Presidential Leaders Ser.). (Illus.). 112p. (J). 29.27 *(978-0-8225-0098-8(1)*, Lerner Pubns.) Lerner Publishing Group.

Marrin, Albert. FDR & the American Crisis. (ENG.). 336p. (YA). (gr. 7). 2016. pap. 15.99 *(978-0-385-75362-3(4)*, Ember) 2015. (Illus.). 24.99 *(978-0-385-75359-3(4)*, Knopf Bks. for Young Readers) 2015. (Illus.). lib. bdg. 27.99 *(978-0-385-75360-9(8)*, Knopf Bks. for Young Readers) Random Hse. Children's Bks.

Marsh, Carole. Andrew Jackson. 2003. 12p. (gr. k-4). 2.95 *(978-0-635-02360-5(1))* Gallopade International.

—Barack Obama: Biography FunBook. 2009. (J). (gr. 2-9). pap. 3.99 *(978-0-635-07053-1(7))* Gallopade International.

—Barack Obama - America's 44th President. 2009. (Here & Now Ser.). 40p. (J). (gr. 2-9). 29.99 *(978-0-635-06983-2(0))* Gallopade International.

—Barack Obama Presidential Coloring Book! 2008. (Here & Now Ser.). (J). 5.99 *(978-0-635-07050-0(2))* Gallopade International.

—I'm Reading about Donald Trump: America's 45th President. 2017. (I'm Reading About Ser.). (ENG., Illus.). (J). lib. bdg. 24.99 ***(978-0-635-12565-1(X))*** Gallopade International.

—John Adams. 2003. 12p. (gr. k-4). 2.95 *(978-0-635-02357-5(1))* Gallopade International.

—John F. Kennedy. 2003. 12p. (gr. k-4). 2.95 *(978-0-635-02127-4(7))* Gallopade International.

—The Obama Family - Life in the White House: President Barack Obama, First Lady Michelle Obama, First Children Malia & Sasha. 2008. (Here & Now Ser.). 32p. (J). (gr. 2-9). pap. 8.99 *(978-0-635-07051-7(0))* Gallopade International.

—Theodore Roosevelt. 2004. 12p. (gr. k-4). 2.95 *(978-0-635-02362-9(8))* Gallopade International.

Marsico, Katie. Andrew Jackson. 2010. (Presidents & Their Times 4 Ser.). 96p. (gr. 6). 34.21 *(978-0-7614-4813-6(6))* Marshall Cavendish GBR. Dist: Marshall Cavendish Corp.

—Woodrow Wilson. 2010. (Presidents & Their Times 4 Ser.). 96p. (gr. 6). 34.21 *(978-0-7614-4815-0(2))* Marshall Cavendish Corp.

Martin, Justin. Easy Reader Biographies: George Washington: George Washington. 2007. (ENG.). 16p. pap. 2.99 *(978-0-439-92331-6(X)*, Teaching Resources) Scholastic, Inc.

Mattern, Joanne. Air Force One: The President's Plane. 2014. (Rookie Read-About(r) American Symbols Ser.). (ENG.). 32p. (J). pap. 5.95 *(978-0-531-21841-9(4))*; lib. bdg. *(978-0-531-21568-5(7))* Scholastic Library Publishing.

—Barack Obama. 2013. (Rookie Biographies(r) Ser.). (ENG.). 32p. (J). pap. 5.95 *(978-0-531-24701-3(5))*; lib. bdg. 23.00 *(978-0-531-24735-8(X))* Scholastic Library Publishing.

—President Donald Trump. 2017. (Rookie Biographies(tm) Ser.). (ENG., Illus.). 32p. (J). lib. bdg. 25.00 ***(978-0-531-23226-2(3)***, Children's Pr.) Scholastic Library Publishing.

—Rookie Biographies: President Donald Trump. 2017. (Rookie Biographies Ser.). (ENG., Illus.). 32p. (J). pap. 5.95 ***(978-0-531-23860-8(1)***, Children's Pr.) Scholastic Library Publishing.

—A True Book: President Donald Trump. 2017. (True Book(tm), A — Biographies Ser.). (ENG.). 48p. (J). 31.00 ***(978-0-531-22718-3(9))***; pap. 7.95 ***(978-0-531-23014-5(7))*** Scholastic Library Publishing. (Children's Pr.).

McAuliffe, Bill. The Presidential Cabinet. 2017. (By the People Ser.). (ENG., Illus.). 48p. (J). (gr. 7-11). pap. 12.00 *(978-1-62832-269-9(1)*, Creative Paperbacks) Creative Co., The.

—The U. S. Presidency. 2017. (By the People Ser.). (ENG., Illus.). 48p. (J). (gr. 7-11). pap. 12.00 *(978-1-62832-272-9(1)*, Creative Paperbacks) Creative Co., The.

—The U.S. Presidency. 2016. (Illus.). 48p. (J). 39.95 *(978-1-60818-676-1(8)*, Creative Education) Creative Co., The.

McClafferty, Carla Killough. The Many Faces of George Washington: Remaking a Presidential Icon. 2011. (Exceptional Social Studies Titles for Intermediate Grades). (ENG.). 120p. (gr. 3-6). lib. bdg. 20.95 *(978-0-7613-5608-0(8))* Lerner Publishing Group.

McDowell, Pamela. James Madison. 2015. (Padres Fundadores Ser.). (SPA.). (J). lib. bdg. 27.13 *(978-1-4896-2796-4(0)*, AV2 by Weigl) Weigl Pubs., Inc.

McLeese, Don. Thomas Jefferson. 2005. (Heroes of the American Revolution Ser.). (Illus.). 32p. (gr. 2-5). 19.95 *(978-1-59515-217-6(2))* Rourke Educational Media.

McPherson, Stephanie. My Dear Husband: Important Letters of Abigail Adams. 2009. (Great Moments in American History Ser.). 32p. (gr. 3-3). 47.90 *(978-1-61513-134-1(5))* Rosen Publishing Group, Inc., The.

McPherson, Stephanie Sammartino. Bill Clinton. 2009. pap. 52.95 *(978-0-7613-4960-0(X))* 2008. (ENG.). 48p. (gr. 3-6). 27.93 *(978-0-8225-7986-1(3)*, Lerner Pubns.) Lerner Publishing Group.

—Theodore Roosevelt. 2005. (Presidential Leaders Ser.). (Illus.). 112p. (J). 29.27 *(978-0-8225-0999-8(7)*, Lerner Pubns.) Lerner Publishing Group.

Meacham, Jon. Thomas Jefferson: President & Philosopher. (ENG., Illus.). 336p. (J). (gr. 5). 2016. pap. 12.99 *(978-0-385-38752-1(0)*, Yearling) 2014. 19.99 *(978-0-385-38749-1(0)*, Crown Books For Young Readers) 2014. lib. bdg. 22.99 *(978-0-385-38750-7(4)*, Crown Books For Young Readers) Random Hse. Children's Bks.

Mead, Wendy. William H. Taft. 2011. (Presidents & Their Times 5 Ser.). 96p. (gr. 6). 34.21 *(978-1-60870-186-5(7))* Marshall Cavendish Corp.

Meltzer, Brad. I Am Abraham Lincoln. Eliopoulos, Christopher, illus. 2014. (Ordinary People Change World Ser.). (ENG.). 40p. (J). (gr. k-3). 14.99 *(978-0-8037-4083-9(2)*, Dial Bks) Penguin Publishing Group.

—I Am George Washington. Eliopoulos, Christopher, illus. 2016. (Ordinary People Change the World Ser.). (ENG.). 40p. (J). (gr. k-3). 14.99 *(978-0-525-42848-0(8)*, Dial Bks) Penguin Young Readers Group.

Metzger, Steve & Kronheimer, Ann. Lincoln & Grace: Why Abraham Lincoln Grew a Beard. 2013. (ENG.). 40p. (J). (gr. 2-5). pap. 6.99 *(978-0-545-48432-9(4)*, Scholastic Paperbacks) Scholastic, Inc.

Miller, Amanda. What Does the President Do? 2009. (Scholastic News Nonfiction Readers Ser.). 24p. (J). (gr. 1-2). (ENG.). pap. 6.95 *(978-0-531-22425-0(2))*; (Illus.). 22.00 *(978-0-531-21088-8(X))* Scholastic Library Publishing.

—What Is Air Force One? 2009. (Scholastic News Nonfiction Readers Ser.). (ENG.). 24p. (J). (gr. 1-2). pap. 6.95 *(978-0-531-22426-7(0))* Scholastic Library Publishing.

Miller, Amanda & Falk, Laine. What Is Air Force One? 2009. (Scholastic News Nonfiction Readers Ser.). 24p. (J). (gr. 1-2). 22.00 *(978-0-531-21089-5(8))* Scholastic Library Publishing.

Miller, Brandon Marie. George Washington for Kids: His Life & Times - 21 Activities. 2007. (For Kids Ser.). (ENG., Illus.). 144p. (J). (gr. 4-7). pap. 16.95 *(978-1-55652-655-8(5))* Chicago Review Pr., Inc.

—Thomas Jefferson for Kids: His Life & Times with 21 Activities. 2011. (For Kids Ser.). (ENG., Illus.). 144p. (J). (gr. 4). pap. 16.95 *(978-1-56976-348-3(8))* Chicago Review Pr., Inc.

Mills, Nathan & Kawa, Katie. Barack Obama: First African American President. 2012. (Rosen Readers Ser.). (ENG., Illus.). 24p. (J). (gr. 1-2). pap. 8.25 *(978-1-4488-8845-0(X)*, Rosen Classroom) Rosen Publishing Group, Inc., The.

Mis, M. S. How to Draw the Life & Times of Franklin Delano Roosevelt. 2009. (Kid's Guide to Drawing the Presidents of the United States of America Ser.). 32p. (gr. 4-4). 50.50 *(978-1-61511-136-7(0)*, PowerKids Pr.) Rosen Publishing Group, Inc., The.

—How to Draw the Life & Times of Lyndon B. Johnson. 2009. (Kid's Guide to Drawing the Presidents of the United States of America Ser.). 32p. (gr. 4-4). 50.50 *(978-1-61511-154-1(9)*, PowerKids Pr.) Rosen Publishing Group, Inc., The.

—How to Draw the Life & Times of Ronald Reagan. 2009. (Kid's Guide to Drawing the Presidents of the United States of America Ser.). 32p. (gr. 4-4). 50.50 *(978-1-61511-158-9(1)*, PowerKids Pr.) Rosen Publishing Group, Inc., The.

—How to Draw the Life & Times of Woodrow Wilson. 2009. (Kid's Guide to Drawing the Presidents of the United States of America Ser.). 32p. (gr. 4-4). 50.50 *(978-1-61511-168-8(9)*, PowerKids Pr.) Rosen Publishing Group, Inc., The.

Mis, Melody S. How to Draw the Life & Times of Andrew Jackson. (Kid's Guide to Drawing the Presidents of the United States of America Ser.). 2009. 32p. (gr. 4-4). 50.50 *(978-1-61511-131-2(X)*, PowerKids Pr.) 2006. (YA). (gr. 2-5). 26.50 *(978-1-4042-2984-6(1))* Rosen Publishing Group, Inc., The.

—How to Draw the Life & Times of Benjamin Harrison. (Kid's Guide to Drawing the Presidents of the United States of America Ser.). 32p. 2009. (gr. 4-4). 50.50 *(978-1-61511-133-6(6)*, PowerKids Pr.) 2007. (Illus.). (YA). (gr. 2-5). 26.50 *(978-1-4042-3000-2(9))* Rosen Publishing Group, Inc., The.

—How to Draw the Life & Times of Franklin Delano Roosevelt. 2007. (Kid's Guide to Drawing the Presidents of the United States of America Ser.). (Illus.). 32p. (YA). (gr. 2-5). 26.50 *(978-1-4042-3008-8(4))* Rosen Publishing Group, Inc., The.

—How to Draw the Life & Times of James Buchanan. (Kid's Guide to Drawing the Presidents of the United States of America Ser.). 2009. 32p. (gr. 4-4). 50.50 *(978-1-61511-146-6(8)*, PowerKids Pr.) 2006. (YA). (gr. 2-5). 26.50 *(978-1-4042-2992-1(2))* Rosen Publishing Group, Inc., The.

—How to Draw the Life & Times of James K. Polk. (Kid's Guide to Drawing the Presidents of the United States of America Ser.). 2009. 32p. (gr. 4-4). 50.50 *(978-1-61511-147-3(6)*, PowerKids Pr.) 2006. (YA). (gr. 2-5). 26.50 *(978-1-4042-2988-4(4))* Rosen Publishing Group, Inc., The.

—How to Draw the Life & Times of Lyndon B. Johnson. 2007. (Kid's Guide to Drawing the Presidents of the United States of America Ser.). (Illus.). 32p. (YA). (gr. 2-5). 26.50 *(978-1-4042-3012-5(2))* Rosen Publishing Group, Inc., The.

—How to Draw the Life & Times of Ronald Reagan. 2007. (Kid's Guide to Drawing the Presidents of the United States of America Ser.). (Illus.). 32p. (YA). (gr. 2-5). 26.50 *(978-1-4042-3016-3(5))* Rosen Publishing Group, Inc., The.

—How to Draw the Life & Times of Rutherford B. Hayes. (Kid's Guide to Drawing the Presidents of the United States of America Ser.). 2009. 32p. (gr. 4-4). 50.50 *(978-1-61511-159-6(X)*, PowerKids Pr.) 2006. (YA). (gr. 2-5). 26.50 *(978-1-4042-2996-9(5))* Rosen Publishing Group, Inc., The.

—How to Draw the Life & Times of Thomas Jefferson. (Kid's Guide to Drawing the Presidents of the United States of America Ser.). 2009. 32p. (gr. 4-4). 50.50 *(978-1-61511-161-9(1)*, PowerKids Pr.) 2006. (YA). (gr. 2-5). 26.50 *(978-1-4042-2980-8(9))* Rosen Publishing Group, Inc., The.

—How to Draw the Life & Times of Woodrow Wilson. 2007. (Kid's Guide to Drawing the Presidents of the United States of America Ser.). (Illus.). 32p. (YA). (gr. 2-5). 26.50 *(978-1-4042-3004-0(1))* Rosen Publishing Group, Inc., The.

Moberg, Julia. Presidential Pets: The Weird, Wacky, Little, Big, Scary, Strange Animals That Have Lived in the White House. 2012. 96p. pap. 14.95 *(978-1-60734-471-1(8))* Charlesbridge Publishing, Inc.

—Presidential Pets: the Weird, Wacky, Little, Big, Scary, Strange Animals That Have Lived in the White House. Jeff Albrecht Studios, Jeff Albrecht, illus. 2016. (ENG.). 96p. (J). (gr. 3-7). pap. 9.95 *(978-1-62354-086-9(0))* Charlesbridge Publishing, Inc.

Modern America 1964-present. 2010. (Discovering U. S. History Ser.). (Illus.). 144p. (gr. 5-8). 35.00 *(978-1-60413-361-5(9)*, Chelsea Hse.) Facts On File, Inc.

Modifica, Lisa. A Timeline of the White House. 2009. (Timelines of American History Ser.). 32p. (gr. 4-4). 47.90 *(978-1-60854-393-9(5)*, Rosen Reference) Rosen Publishing Group, Inc., The.

Mooney, Carla. George Washington: 25 Great Projects You Can Build Yourself. Carbaugh, Samuel, illus. 2010. (Build It Yourself Ser.). (ENG.). 128p. (J). (gr. 3-7). 21.95 *(978-1-934670-64-4(2))* Open City Bks.

Morris, Deborah & Morris, Larry. American History: Presidents: Grade 4-5. Carlson, Andy, illus. 2005. (Skill Builders (Rainbow Bridge Publishing) Ser.). 80p. per. 3.99 *(978-1-59441-267-7(7)*, RB-904000) Carson-Dellosa Publishing, LLC.

Mortensen, Lori. Thomas Jefferson: A Founding Father of the United States of America, 1 vol. Ebert, Len, illus. 2008. (Biographies Ser.). (ENG.). 24p. (gr. k-3). lib. bdg. 26.65 *(978-1-4048-3729-4(9))* Picture Window Bks.

Mulhall, Jill K. James Madison, 1 vol. 2005. (Primary Source Readers Ser.). (ENG.). 24p. (J). (gr. 4-4). pap. 8.99 *(978-0-7439-8908-4(2))* Shell Educational Publishing.

—Thomas Jefferson, 1 vol. 2004. (Primary Source Readers Ser.). (ENG.). 24p. (J). (gr. 4-4). pap. 8.99 *(978-0-7439-8747-9(0))* Shell Educational Publishing.

Murphy, Frank. George Washington & the General's Dog. Walz, Richard, illus. 2015. 48p. pap. 5.00 *(978-1-61003-605-4(0))* Center for the Collaborative Classroom.

—George Washington & the General's Dog. 2003. (J). 1.25 *(978-1-4025-4103-2(1))* Recorded Bks., Inc.

—Thomas Jefferson's Feast. Walz, Richard, illus. 2004. (Step into Reading Ser.). 48p. 14.00 *(978-0-7569-3235-0(1))* Perfection Learning Corp.

—Thomas Jefferson's Feast. Walz, Richard, illus. 2003. (Step into Reading Ser.). (ENG.). 48p. (J). (gr. 2-4). pap. 3.99 *(978-0-375-82289-6(5)*, Random Hse. Bks. for Young Readers) Random Hse. Children's Bks.

Murphy, John A. The Impeachment Process. 2007. (U. S. Government Ser.). (Illus.). 102p. (YA). (gr. 5-9). lib. bdg. 30.00 *(978-0-7910-9465-5(0))* Facts On File, Inc.

Murray, Julie. President's Day, 1 vol. 2005. (Buddy Book Ser.). (ENG., Illus.). 24p. (gr. k-4). 25.65 *(978-1-59197-590-8(5)*, Buddy Bks.) ABDO Publishing Co.

Naden, Corinne J. & Blue, Rose. James Monroe. 2008. (Presidents & Their Times Ser.). 96p. (gr. 6-18). lib. bdg. 34.21 *(978-0-7614-2838-1(0)*, Benchmark Bks.) Marshall Cavendish Corp.

Nagelhout, Ryan. 20 Fun Facts about the White House. 2013. (Fun Fact File: US History! Ser.). 32p. (J). (gr. 3-6). pap. 10.50 *(978-1-4339-9204-9(3))* Stevens, Gareth Publishing LLLP.

Nagle, Jeanne. How George Washington Fought the Revolutionary War. 2017. (Presidents at War Ser.). 128p. (J). (gr. 8-8). lib. bdg. 37.27 ***(978-0-7660-8523-7(6))*** Enslow Pubs., Inc.

Nardo, Don. The Presidency of Abraham Lincoln: The Triumph of Freedom & Unity, 1 vol. 2014. (Greatest U. S. Presidents Ser.). (ENG.). 64p. (gr. 5-7). lib. bdg. 33.99 *(978-0-7565-4926-8(4))* Compass Point Bks.

—The Presidency of Franklin D. Roosevelt: Confronting the Great Depression & World War II. 2014. (Greatest U. S. Presidents Ser.). (ENG.). 64p. (gr. 5-7). lib. bdg. 33.99 *(978-0-7565-4927-5(2))* Compass Point Bks.

National Geographic Kids & DuMont, Brianna. Weird but True! Know-it-All - U. S. Presidents. 2017. (ENG., Illus.). 192p. (J). (gr. 3-7). pap. 12.99 ***(978-1-4263-2796-4(X)***, National Geographic Children's Bks.) National Geographic Society.

—Weird but True Know-It-All: U. S. Presidents. 2017. (ENG.). 192p. (J). (gr. 3-7). lib. bdg. 22.90 ***(978-1-4263-2797-1(8)***, National Geographic Children's Bks.) National Geographic Society.

National Geographic Kids Staff & Gilpin, Caroline Crosson. National Geographic Readers: Barack Obama. 2014. (Readers Bios Ser.). (ENG.). 32p. (J). (gr. k-3). pap. 3.99 *(978-1-4263-1759-0(X)*, National Geographic Children's Bks.) National Geographic Society.

—National Geographic Readers: George Washington. 2014. (Readers Bios Ser.). (ENG., Illus.). 32p. (J). (gr. k-3). pap. 3.99 *(978-1-4263-1468-1(X)*, National Geographic Children's Bks.) National Geographic Society.

N.C.B.L.A. Our White House: Looking in, Looking Out. 2010. (ENG., Illus.). 256p. (J). (gr. 5). pap. 14.99 *(978-0-7636-4609-7(1))* Candlewick Pr.

Nelson, Maria. The Life of Abraham Lincoln. 2012. (Famous Lives Ser.). (ENG., Illus.). 24p. (J). (gr. k-3). lib. bdg. 22.60 *(978-1-4339-6341-4(8))*; (gr. 1-4). pap. 8.15 *(978-1-4339-6343-8(4))* Stevens, Gareth Publishing LLLP.

—The Life of Abraham Lincoln / la Vida de Abraham Lincoln. 2012. (Famous Lives / Vidas extraordinarias Ser.). (ENG & SPA., Illus.). 24p. (J). (gr. k-3). 22.60 *(978-1-4339-6651-4(4))* Stevens, Gareth Publishing LLLP.

—The Life of George Washington. 2012. (Famous Lives Ser.). (ENG.). 24p. (J). (gr. 1-4). pap. 8.15 *(978-1-4339-6351-3(5))* Stevens, Gareth Publishing LLLP.

—The Life of George Washington / la Vida de George Washington. 2012. (Famous Lives / Vidas extraordinarias Ser.). (ENG & SPA., Illus.). 24p. (J). (gr. k-3). 22.60 *(978-1-4339-6655-2(7))* Stevens, Gareth Publishing LLLP.

Nelson, Robin. George Washington: A Life of Leadership. 2006. (Pull Ahead Bks.). (Illus.). 32p. (J). (gr. 3-7). lib. bdg. 22.60 *(978-0-8225-3474-7(6)*, Lerner Pubns.) Lerner Publishing Group.

—George Washington: Una Vida de Liderazgo. 2006. (Libros para Avanzar Ser.). (ENG & SPA., Illus.). 32p. (J). (gr. 3-7). lib. bdg. 22.60 *(978-0-8225-6235-1(9)*, Ediciones Lerner) Lerner Publishing Group.

—George Washington: Una vida de liderazgo (A Life of Leadership) 2006. (Libros para Avanzar-Biografías (Pull Ahead Books-Biographies Ser.). (Illus.). 32p. (J). (gr. -1-3). per. 6.95 *(978-0-8225-6555-0(2)*, Ediciones Lerner) Lerner Publishing Group.

Nicolay, Helen. The Boys' Life of Abraham Lincoln. 2007. 136p. per. *(978-1-4065-4046-8(3))* Dodo Pr.

—The Boys Life of Abraham Lincoln. 2004. 192p. per. 15.95 *(978-1-59540-991-1(2)*, 1st World Library - Literary Society) 1st World Publishing, Inc.

Norwich, Grace. I Am #5: George Washington. 2012. (I Am Ser.: 5). (ENG.). 128p. (J). (gr. 2-5). pap. 5.99 *(978-0-545-48435-0(9)*, Scholastic Paperbacks) Scholastic, Inc.

Oachs, Emily Rose. Thomas Jefferson's Presidency. 2016. (Presidential Powerhouses Ser.). (ENG., Illus.). 104p. (J). (gr. 6-12). 35.99 *(978-1-4677-7923-4(7)*, Lerner Pubns.) Lerner Publishing Group.

Obama, Barack. Our Enduring Spirit: President Barack Obama's First Words to America. Ruth, Greg, illus. 2009. 48p. lib. bdg. 18.89 *(978-0-06-183456-1(4))* HarperCollins Pubs.

O'Connell, Kim A. Slavery, Emancipation, & the Civil War: A MyReportLinks. com Book. 2004. (American Civil War Ser.). (Illus.). 48p. (J). lib. bdg. 26.60 *(978-0-7660-5190-4(0)*, MyReportLinks.com Bks.) Enslow Pubs., Inc.

—William Howard Taft: A MyReportLinks.com Book. 2003. (Presidents Ser.). (Illus.). 48p. (J). (gr. 4-10). lib. bdg. 25.26

(978-0-7660-5078-5(5), MyReportLinks.com Bks.) Enslow Pubs., Inc.
O'Connor, Jane. If the Walls Could Talk: Family Life at the White House. Hovland, Gary, illus. 2004. (ENG.). 48p. (J). (gr. 1-4). 17.99 (978-0-689-86863-4(4), Simon & Schuster/Paula Wiseman Bks.) Simon & Schuster/Paula Wiseman Bks.
Olesen, Andrew. George Washington: The First President of the United States. 2015. (Spotlight on American History Ser.). (ENG., Illus.). 24p. (J). (gr. 4-6). pap. 10.00 (978-1-4994-1751-7(9), PowerKids Pr.) Rosen Publishing Group, Inc., The.
Olson, Nathan. John F. Kennedy: American Visionary, 1 vol. Bascle, Brian, illus. 2007. (Graphic Biographies Ser.). (ENG.). 32p. (gr. 3-4). per. 8.10 (978-0-7368-7904-0(8), 1264943, Graphic Library) Capstone Press of Coughlan Cos.
Olson, Nathan & Capstone Press Staff. John F. Kennedy: American Visionary, 1 vol. Bascle, Brian, illus. 2007. (Graphic Biographies Ser.). (ENG.). 32p. (gr. 3-4). 30.65 (978-0-7368-6852-5(6), Graphic Library) Capstone Press of Coughlan Cos.
Olson, Nathan, et al. Theodore Roosevelt: Bear of a President, 1 vol. Martin, Cynthia et al, illus. 2007. (Graphic Biographies Ser.). (ENG.). 32p. (gr. 3-4). per. 8.10 (978-0-7368-7901-9(3), 1264944, Graphic Library) Capstone Press of Coughlan Cos.
O'Neal, Claire. What's So Great about Barack Obama. 2009. (What's So Great About... ? Ser.). 32p. (J). (gr. 2-4). lib. bdg. 25.70 (978-1-58415-830-1(1)) Mitchell Lane Pubs., Inc.
Oney, Yannick. Abe Lincoln: President for the People. 2005. (World Discovery History Readers Ser.). (Illus.). 32p. (J). pap. (978-0-439-66556-8(6)) Scholastic, Inc.
Orr, Tamra. Ronald Reagan. 2004. (Childhoods of the Presidents Ser.). (Illus.). 48p. (J). (gr. 4-18). lib. bdg. 17.95 (978-1-59084-280-5(4)) Mason Crest.
Osborne, Mary Pope & Boyce, Natalie Pope. Abraham Lincoln: A Nonfiction Companion to Magic Tree House No. 47 - Abe Lincoln at Last! Murdocca, Sal, illus. 2011. (Magic Tree House - Fact Tracker Ser.: No. 25). (ENG.). 128p. (J). (gr. 2-5). 6.99 (978-0-375-87024-8(5), Random Hse. Bks. for Young Readers) Random Hse. Children's Bks.
O'Shei, Tim. Bill Clinton: A MyReportLinks. Com Book. 2003. (Presidents Ser.). (Illus.). 48p. (J). lib. bdg. 25.26 (978-0-7660-5149-2(8), MyReportLinks.com Bks.) Enslow Pubs., Inc.
—Gerald R. Ford: A MyReportLinks.com Book. 2003. (Presidents Ser.). (Illus.). 48p. (J). (gr. 5-10). lib. bdg. 25.26 (978-0-7660-5050-1(5), MyReportLinks.com Bks.) Enslow Pubs., Inc.
Otfinoski, Steven. Calvin Coolidge. 2008. (Presidents & Their Times Ser.). 96p. (gr. 6-18). lib. bdg. 34.21 (978-0-7614-2836-7(4), Benchmark Bks.) Marshall Cavendish Corp.
—Grover Cleveland. 2010. (Presidents & Their Times 4 Ser.). 96p. (gr. 6). 34.21 (978-0-7614-4811-2(X)) Marshall Cavendish GBR. Dist: Marshall Cavendish Corp.
—Zachary Taylor. 2011. (Presidents & Their Times 5 Ser.). (Illus.). 96p. (J). (gr. 6). 34.21 (978-1-60870-187-2(5)) Marshall Cavendish Corp.
Otfinoski, Steven & Otfinoski, Steve. Rutherford B. Hayes. 2004. (Encyclopedia of Presidents Ser.). (ENG., Illus.). 110p. (YA). (gr. 5-9). 34.00 (978-0-516-22866-2(8)) Scholastic Library Publishing.
Our Presidents & First Ladies of the White House. 119.40 (978-0-8249-6046-9(7), Ideal Pubns.) Worthy Publishing.
Owen, John. #Presidents: Follow the Leaders. 2015. (Illus.). 115p. (J). pap. (978-0-545-85127-5(0)) Scholastic, Inc.
Owen, John Bailey. #Presidents: Follow the Leaders. 2015. (ENG., Illus.). 128p. (J). (gr. 3-7). 9.99 (978-0-545-84938-8(1), Scholastic Paperbacks) Scholastic, Inc.
Pace, Betty. Abraham Lincoln. Walker, Bobbie H., illus. 2008. 32p. pap. 12.99 (978-1-4343-7969-6(8)) AuthorHouse.
Panchyk, Richard. Franklin Delano Roosevelt for Kids: His Life & Times with 21 Activities. 2007. (For Kids Ser.). (ENG., Illus.). 160p. (J). (gr. 4-8). pap. 14.95 (978-1-55652-657-2(1)) Chicago Review Pr., Inc.
Parachini, Jodie. The Complete Guide to U.S. Presidents. 2015. (Illus.). 144p. (J). (978-1-4351-6169-6(6)) Barnes & Noble, Inc.
Parker, Christi E. Abraham Lincoln, 1 vol. 2005. (Primary Source Readers Ser.). (ENG.). 24p. (J). (gr. 4-4). pap. 8.99 (978-0-7439-8916-9(3)) Shell Educational Publishing.
—George Washington, 1 vol. 2004. (Primary Source Readers Ser.). (ENG.). 24p. (J). (gr. 4-4). pap. 8.99 (978-0-7439-8749-3(7)) Shell Educational Publishing.
Parker, Lewis. How to Draw the Life & Times of George H. W. Bush. 2009. (Kid's Guide to Drawing the Presidents of the United States of America Ser.). 32p. (gr. 4-4). 50.50 (978-1-61511-138-1(7), PowerKids Pr.) Rosen Publishing Group, Inc., The.
—How to Draw the Life & Times of Harry S. Truman. 2009. (Kid's Guide to Drawing the Presidents of the United States of America Ser.). 32p. (gr. 4-4). 50.50 (978-1-61511-143-5(3), PowerKids Pr.) Rosen Publishing Group, Inc., The.
—How to Draw the Life & Times of James A. Garfield. 2009. (Kid's Guide to Drawing the Presidents of the United States of America Ser.). 32p. (gr. 4-4). 50.50 (978-1-61511-145-9(X), PowerKids Pr.) Rosen Publishing Group, Inc., The.
—How to Draw the Life & Times of Richard M. Nixon. 2009. (Kid's Guide to Drawing the Presidents of the United States of America Ser.). 32p. (gr. 4-4). 50.50 (978-1-61511-157-2(3), PowerKids Pr.) Rosen Publishing Group, Inc., The.
—How to Draw the Life & Times of Warren G. Harding. 2009. (Kid's Guide to Drawing the Presidents of the United States of America Ser.). 32p. (gr. 4-4). 50.50 (978-1-61511-163-3(8), PowerKids Pr.) Rosen Publishing Group, Inc., The.
—How to Draw the Life & Times of William Mckinley. 2009. (Kid's Guide to Drawing the Presidents of the United States of America Ser.). 32p. (gr. 4-4). 50.50 (978-1-61511-167-1(0), PowerKids Pr.) Rosen Publishing Group, Inc., The.
Parker, Lewis K. How to Draw the Life & Times of George H. W. Bush. 2007. (Kid's Guide to Drawing the Presidents of the United States of America Ser.). (Illus.). 32p. (YA). (gr. 2-5). 26.50 (978-1-4042-3017-0(3)) Rosen Publishing Group, Inc., The.
—How to Draw the Life & Times of Harry S. Truman. 2005. (Kid's Guide to Drawing the Presidents of the United States of America Ser.). (Illus.). 32p. (YA). (gr. 2-5). lib. bdg. 26.50 (978-1-4042-3009-5(2)) Rosen Publishing Group, Inc., The.
—How to Draw the Life & Times of James A. Garfield. 2006. (Kid's Guide to Drawing the Presidents of the United States of America Ser.). (YA). (gr. 2-5). 26.50 (978-1-4042-2997-6(3)) Rosen Publishing Group, Inc., The.
—How to Draw the Life & Times of Warren G. Harding. 2007. (Kid's Guide to Drawing the Presidents of the United States of America Ser.). (Illus.). 32p. (J). (gr. 2-5). 26.50 (978-1-4042-3005-7(X)) Rosen Publishing Group, Inc., The.
—How to Draw the Life & Times of William McKinley. 2007. (Kid's Guide to Drawing the Presidents of the United States of America Ser.). (Illus.). 32p. (YA). (gr. 2-5). 26.50 (978-1-4042-3001-9(7)) Rosen Publishing Group, Inc., The.
Pascal, Janet. Who Was Abraham Lincoln? Harrison, Nancy & O'brien, John, illus. 2008. (Who Was? Ser.). (ENG.). 112p. (J). (gr. 3-7). pap. 5.99 (978-0-448-44886-2(6), Grosset & Dunlap) Penguin Young Readers Group.
Patrick, Bethanne Kelly. Ulysses S. Grant. 2004. (Childhoods of the Presidents Ser.). (Illus.). 48p. (J). (gr. 4-18). lib. bdg. 17.95 (978-1-59084-276-8(6)) Mason Crest.
Peacock, L. A. The Truth (and Myths) about the Presidents. Wigsby, Nick, illus. 2014. 94p. (J). pap. (978-0-545-56848-7(X)) Scholastic, Inc.
Peckham, Howard Henry. William Henry Harrison, Young Tippecanoe: Childhood of Famous Americans Series. Laune, Paul, illus. 2011. 190p. 42.95 (978-1-258-07766-2(3)) Literary Licensing, LLC.
Pelleschi, Andrea. George Washington. 2012. (Jr. Graphic Founding Fathers Ser.). (ENG., Illus.). 24p. (J). (gr. 3-6). pap. 10.60 (978-1-4488-7991-5(4)); lib. bdg. 25.25 (978-1-4488-7897-0(7)) Rosen Publishing Group, Inc., The. (PowerKids Pr.).
—Thomas Jefferson. 2012. (Jr. Graphic Founding Fathers Ser.). (ENG., Illus.). 24p. (J). (gr. 3-6). pap. 10.60 (978-1-4488-7994-6(9)); lib. bdg. 25.25 (978-1-4488-7900-7(0)) Rosen Publishing Group, Inc., The. (PowerKids Pr.).
Peppas, Lynn. Presidents' Day. 2009. (Celebrations in My World Ser.). (ENG., Illus.). 32p. (J). (gr. k-2). pap. (978-0-7787-4774-1(3)); (gr. 1-3). (978-0-7787-4756-7(5)) Crabtree Publishing Co.
—Why Anson Jones Matters to Texas. 2014. (Illus.). 32p. (J). lib. bdg. 26.25 (978-1-4777-0911-5(8)) Rosen Publishing Group, Inc., The.
Petty, Kate. Abraham Lincoln: The Life of America's Sixteenth President. 2005. (Graphic Nonfiction Biographies Ser.). (ENG., Illus.). 48p. (YA). (gr. 4-7). lib. bdg. 31.95 (978-1-4042-0237-5(4)) Rosen Publishing Group, Inc., The.
Pflueger, Lynda. Thomas Jefferson: Creating a Nation. 2004. (America's Founding Fathers Ser.). (Illus.). 128p. (J). lib. bdg. 26.60 (978-0-7660-2212-6(9)) Enslow Pubs., Inc.
Pingry, Patricia A. Meet Abraham Lincoln. Britt, Stephanie McFetridge, illus. 2009. (ENG.). 32p. (J). pap. 7.99 (978-0-8249-5613-4(3), Ideal Pubns.) Worthy Publishing.
—Meet George Washington. Britt, Stephanie McFetridge, illus. 2009. (ENG.). 32p. (J). pap. 7.99 (978-0-8249-5612-7(5), Ideal Pubns.) Worthy Publishing.
—Meet Thomas Jefferson. Johnson, Meredith, ed. Johnson, Meredith, illus. 2003. 32p. (J). 9.95 (978-0-8249-5459-8(9), Ideal Pubns.) Worthy Publishing.
—The Story of Abraham Lincoln. Britt, Stephanie, illus. 2016. (J). (978-0-8249-1972-6(6), Ideal Pubns.) Worthy Publishing.
—The Story of George Washington. Britt, Stephanie, illus. 2016. (J). (978-0-8249-1973-3(4), Ideal Pubns.) Worthy Publishing.
—The Story of Ronald Reagan. Mahan, Ben, illus. 2006. (ENG.). 26p. (J). (gr. -1-k). bds. 7.69 (978-0-8249-6621-8(X), Ideal Pubns.) Worthy Publishing.
Piven, Hanoch. What Presidents are Made Of. 2012. lib. bdg. 18.40 (978-0-606-23670-6(8), Turtleback) Turtleback Bks.
Piven, Hanoch, illus. What Presidents Are Made Of. 2012. (ENG.). 40p. (J). (gr. 1-5). 7.99 (978-1-4424-4433-1(9), Atheneum Bks. for Young Readers) Simon & Schuster Children's Publishing.
Piven, Hanoch & Thomson, Sarah L. What Presidents Are Made Of. 2004. (ENG., Illus.). 40p. (J). (gr. 1-5). 19.99 (978-0-689-86880-1(4), Atheneum Bks. for Young Readers) Simon & Schuster Children's Publishing.
Pivotal Presidents: Profiles in Leadership: Set 2. 2016. (Pivotal Presidents: Profiles in Leadership Ser.). 80p. (gr. 8-8). 135.60 (978-1-5081-0225-0(2), Britannica Educational Publishing) Rosen Publishing Group, Inc., The.
Pivotal Presidents: Profiles in Leadership: Set 3. 2017. (Pivotal Presidents: Profiles in Leadership Ser.). 80p. (gr. 12-13). 135.60 **(978-1-5081-0540-4(5)**, Britannica Educational Publishing) Rosen Publishing Group, Inc., The.
Plaut, Michael. How to Draw the Life & Times of Gerald R. Ford. 2009. (Kid's Guide to Drawing the Presidents of the United States of America Ser.). 32p. (gr. 4-4). 50.50 (978-1-61511-141-1(7), PowerKids Pr.) Rosen Publishing Group, Inc., The.
Plaut, Michael F. How to Draw the Life & Times of Gerald R. Ford. 2005. (Kid's Guide to Drawing the Presidents of the United States of America Ser.). (Illus.). 32p. (YA). (gr. 2-5). lib. bdg. 26.50 (978-1-4042-3014-9(9)) Rosen Publishing Group, Inc., The.
Porterfield, Jason. How Lyndon B. Johnson Fought the Vietnam War. 2017. (Presidents at War Ser.). 128p. (J). (gr. 8-8). lib. bdg. 37.27 **(978-0-7660-8531-2(7))** Enslow Pubs., Inc.
Porterfield, Jason. What Is the Executive Branch? 2015. (Let's Find Out! Government Ser.). (ENG., Illus.). 32p. (J). (gr. 2-3). 23.45 (978-1-62275-922-4(2), Britannica Educational Publishing) Rosen Publishing Group, Inc., The.
Powell, Walter. How to Draw the Life & Times of Andrew Johnson. 2009. (Kid's Guide to Drawing the Presidents of the United States of America Ser.). 32p. (gr. 4-4). 50.50 (978-1-61511-132-9(8), PowerKids Pr.) Rosen Publishing Group, Inc., The.
Prentzas, G. S. The Emancipation Proclamation. 2011. (Cornerstones of Freedom, Third Ser.). (Illus.). 64p. (J). (ENG.). pap. 8.95 (978-0-531-26557-4(9)); lib. bdg. 30.00 (978-0-531-25032-7(6)) Scholastic Library Publishing. (Children's Pr.).
Presidential Libraries. (Illus.). (J). (gr. k-5). 112.50 (978-0-8239-6989-0(4)) Rosen Publishing Group, Inc., The.
Presidents. Date not set. (Mini Question & Answers America Ser.). 32p. (J). 3.98 (978-0-7525-9874-1(0)) Parragon, Inc.
Presidents: U.S. Presidents: Feats & Foul-Ups. 2005. (Illus.). 32p. (J). pap. (978-0-439-78476-4(X)) Scholastic, Inc.
Presidents & Their Times - Group 2, 6 bks., Set. Incl. Abraham Lincoln. Aronson, Billy. lib. bdg. 34.21 (978-0-7614-2839-8(9)); Calvin Coolidge. Otfinoski, Steven. lib. bdg. 34.21 (978-0-7614-2836-7(4)); Franklin Delano Roosevelt. Elish, Dan. lib. bdg. 34.21 (978-0-7614-2841-1(0)); James Monroe. Naden, Corinne J. & Blue, Rose. lib. bdg. 34.21 (978-0-7614-2838-1(0)); John Adams. Mara, Wil. lib. bdg. 34.21 (978-0-7614-2840-4(2)); Lyndon B. Johnson. Gold, Susan Dudley. lib. bdg. 34.21 (978-0-7614-2837-4(2)); (gr. 6-18). (Presidents & Their Times 2 Ser.). 96p. 2008. Set lib. bdg. 205.26 (978-0-7614-2834-3(8), Benchmark Bks.) Marshall Cavendish Corp.
Presidents at War. 2017. (Presidents at War Ser.). 128p. (gr. 8-8). lib. bdg. 260.89 **(978-0-7660-8596-1(1))** Enslow Pubs., Inc.
Price, Sean Stewart. U. S. Presidents: Truth & Rumors. Doty, Eldon, illus. 2010. (Truth & Rumors Ser.). (ENG.). 32p. (gr. 3-4). lib. bdg. 27.99 (978-1-4296-3952-1(0), Edge Bks.) Capstone Press of Coughlan Cos.
Qaiser, Annie. How to Analyze the Works of George Washington, 1 vol. 2013. (Essential Critiques Set 4 Ser.). (ENG.). 112p. (J). (gr. 6-12). lib. bdg. 35.64 (978-1-61783-645-9(1), Essential Library) ABDO Publishing Co.
—How to Analyze the Works of Thomas Jefferson, 1 vol. 2013. (Essential Critiques Set 4 Ser.). (ENG.). 112p. (J). (gr. 6-12). lib. bdg. 35.64 (978-1-61783-648-0(6), Essential Library) ABDO Publishing Co.
Raatma, Lucia. Profiles of the Presidents, 42 bks. Incl. John F. Kennedy. (ENG., Illus.). 64p. (gr. 5-6). 2002. lib. bdg. 29.32 (978-0-7565-0205-8(5), Profiles of the Presidents); (Profiles of the Presidents Ser.). (ENG.). Illus.). 64p. 2003. Set lib. bdg. 1169.61 o.p. (978-0-7565-0408-3(2)) Compass Point Bks.
Rabin, Staton. Mr. Lincoln's Boys. Ibatoulline, Bagram, illus. 2008. (ENG.). 36p. (J). (gr. k-3). 16.99 (978-0-670-06169-3(7), Viking Books for Young Readers) Penguin Young Readers Group.
Rajczak, Michael. Becoming President. 2016. (Who's Your Candidate? Choosing Government Leaders Ser.). (ENG., Illus.). 32p. (J). (gr. 3-4). pap. 10.50 (978-1-4824-4039-3(3)) Stevens, Gareth Publishing LLLP.
—Meet the President. 2012. (Guide to Your Government Ser.). (Illus.). 32p. (J). (gr. 4-6). 26.60 (978-1-4339-7256-0(5)); pap. 10.50 (978-1-4339-7257-7(3)) Stevens, Gareth Publishing LLLP. (Gareth Stevens Learning Library).
Rand, Casey. George Washington, 1 vol. Oxford Bible Staff, illus. 2012. (American Biographies Ser.). (ENG.). 48p. (gr. 4-6). lib. bdg. 32.65 (978-1-4329-6452-8(6), NA-h) Heinemann-Raintree.
Randolph, Ryan P. How to Draw the Life & Times of Andrew Johnson. 2006. (Kid's Guide to Drawing the Presidents of the United States of America Ser.). (YA). (gr. 2-5). 26.50 (978-1-4042-2994-5(9)) Rosen Publishing Group, Inc., The.
—How to Draw the Life & Times of Dwight D. Eisenhower. 2007. (Kid's Guide to Drawing the Presidents of the United States of America Ser.). (Illus.). 32p. (YA). (gr. 2-5). 25.25 (978-1-4042-3010-1(6)) Rosen Publishing Group, Inc., The.
—How to Draw the Life & Times of John Adams. (Kid's Guide to Drawing the Presidents of the United States of America Ser.). 2009. 32p. (gr. 4-4). 50.50 (978-1-61511-150-3(6), PowerKids Pr.) 2006. (YA). (gr. 2-5). 26.50 (978-1-4042-2979-2(5)) Rosen Publishing Group, Inc., The.
—How to Draw the Life & Times of Millard Fillmore. (Kid's Guide to Drawing the Presidents of the United States of America Ser.). 2009. 32p. (gr. 4-4). 50.50 (978-1-61511-156-5(5), PowerKids Pr.) 2006. (YA). (gr. 2-5). 26.50 (978-1-4042-2990-7(6)) Rosen Publishing Group, Inc., The.
—How to Draw the Life & Times of William Howard Taft. 2007. (Kid's Guide to Drawing the Presidents of the United States of America Ser.). (Illus.). 32p. (YA). (gr. 2-5). 26.50 (978-1-4042-3003-3(3)) Rosen Publishing Group, Inc., The.
Rappaport, Doreen. Abe's Honest Words. Nelson, Kadir, illus. 2009. (J). (gr. 2-4). 27.95 incl. audio (978-0-8045-6984-2(3)) Spoken Arts, Inc.
—Abe's Honest Words: The Life of Abraham Lincoln. Nelson, Kadir, illus. 2016. (Big Words Ser.). (ENG.). 48p. (J). (gr. 1-3). pap. 8.99 (978-1-4847-4958-6(8)) Hyperion Bks. for Children.
—Abe's Honest Words: The Life of Abraham Lincoln. Kelley, Gary & Nelson, Kadir, illus. 2008. (Big Words Ser.). (ENG.). 48p. (J). (gr. 3-7). 16.99 (978-1-4231-0408-7(0)) Hyperion Pr.
—Jack's Path of Courage: The Life of John F. Kennedy. Tavares, Matt, illus. 2016. (Big Words Ser.). (ENG.). 48p. (J). (gr. 1-3). pap. 8.99 (978-1-4847-4961-6(8)) Hyperion Bks. for Children.
—Jack's Path of Courage: The Life of John F. Kennedy. Tavares, Matt & Borgens, Matthew Todd, illus. 2010. (Big Words Ser.). (ENG.). 48p. (J). (gr. 1-3). 17.99 (978-1-4231-2272-2(0)) Hyperion Pr.
Rauf, Don. Washington's Farewell Address. 2016. (Let's Find Out! Primary Sources Ser.). 00032p. (J). (gr. 2-3). lib. bdg. 24.45 (978-1-5081-0407-0(7)) Rosen Publishing Group, Inc., The.
Raum, Elizabeth. Abraham Lincoln, 1 vol. 2012. (American Biographies Ser.). (ENG.). 48p. (gr. 4-6). pap. 9.95 (978-1-4329-6464-1(X), NA-h) Heinemann-Raintree.
—Abraham Lincoln, 1 vol. Oxford Bible Staff, illus. 2012. (American Biographies Ser.). (ENG.). 48p. (gr. 4-6). lib. bdg. 32.65 (978-1-4329-6453-5(4), NA-h) Heinemann-Raintree.
Rausch, Monica. Andrew Jackson. 2007. (Grandes personajes (Spanish- Great Americans) Ser.). 24p. (gr. 1-4). (ENG & SPA.). pap. 8.15 (978-0-8368-7989-6(9)); (Illus.). pap. 8.15 (978-0-8368-7690-1(3)); (Illus.). lib. bdg. 22.00 (978-0-8368-7683-3(0)) Stevens, Gareth Publishing LLLP. (Weekly Reader Leveled Readers).
—Thomas Jefferson. 2007. (Grandes personajes (Spanish-Great Americans) Ser.). (ENG & SPA.). 24p. (gr. 1-4). pap. 8.15 (978-0-8368-7990-2(2), Weekly Reader Leveled Readers) Stevens, Gareth Publishing LLLP.
Rausch, Monica L. Andrew Jackson. 2007. (Grandes personajes (Great Americans) Ser.). (ENG & SPA., Illus.). 24p. (gr. 1-4). lib. bdg. 22.00 (978-0-8368-7982-7(1), Weekly Reader Leveled Readers) Stevens, Gareth Publishing LLLP.
—Thomas Jefferson. 2007. (Grandes personajes (Great Americans) Ser.). (ENG & SPA., Illus.). 24p. (gr. 1-4). lib. bdg. 22.00 (978-0-8368-7983-4(X), Weekly Reader Leveled Readers) Stevens, Gareth Publishing LLLP.
Reeves, Diane Lindsey & White, Kelly. Choose Your Own Career Adventure at the White House. 2016. (Bright Futures Press: Choose Your Own Career Adventure Ser.). (ENG., Illus.). 32p. (J). (gr. 4-6). 29.93 (978-1-63471-916-2(6), 208985) Cherry Lake Publishing.
Ribke, Simone T. Thomas Jefferson. 2014. (Rookie Biographies(tm) Ser.). (ENG.). 32p. (J). lib. bdg. 25.00 (978-0-531-20560-0(6)); pap. 5.95 (978-0-531-21203-5(3)) Scholastic Library Publishing.
Rice, Dona. Jimmy Carter: For the People. 2016. (Primary Source Readers Ser.). (Illus.). 32p. (gr. 2-2). 8.99 (978-1-4938-2561-5(5)) Teacher Created Materials, Inc.
Rice, Dona Herweck. Teedie: The Boy Who Would Be President. 2015. (Building Fluency Through Reader's Theater Ser.). (ENG., Illus.). 24p. (gr. 1-2). pap. 6.99 (978-1-4938-1513-5(X)) Teacher Created Materials, Inc.
Rice, Earle, Jr. How Franklin D. Roosevelt Fought World War II. 2017. (Presidents at War Ser.). 128p. (J). (gr. 8-8). lib. bdg. 37.27 **(978-0-7660-8527-5(9))** Enslow Pubs., Inc.
Rice, Earle, Jr. Ulysses S. Grant: Defender of the Union. 2005. (Civil War Leaders Ser.). (Illus.). 176p. (gr. 6-12). 28.95 (978-1-931798-48-8(6)) Reynolds, Morgan Inc.
Rissman, Rebecca. Andrew Jackson. 2017. (Premier Presidents Ser.). (ENG.). 24p. (J). (gr. 1-4). lib. bdg. 27.07 (978-1-5038-1643-5(5), 211486) Child's World, Inc., The.
Rivera, Sheila. Abraham Lincoln: A Life of Respect. 2006. (Pull Ahead Bks.). (Illus.). 32p. (J). (gr. 3-7). lib. bdg. 22.60 (978-0-8225-3473-0(8), Lerner Pubns.) Lerner Publishing Group.
—Abraham Lincoln: Una Vida de Respeto. 2006. (Libros para Avanzar Ser.). (ENG & SPA., Illus.). 32p. (J). (gr. 3-7). lib. bdg. 22.60 (978-0-8225-6236-8(7)) Lerner Publishing Group.
Robb, Don. Hail to the Chief: The American Presidency. Witschonke, Alan, illus. rev. ed. 2010. (ENG.). 32p. (J). (gr. 1-4). 17.95 (978-1-58089-285-8(X)); pap. 7.95 (978-1-58089-286-5(8)) Charlesbridge Publishing, Inc.
Roberts, Jeremy. Franklin D. Roosevelt. 2003. (Presidential Leaders Ser.). (Illus.). 112p. (J). (gr. 6-12). lib. bdg. 29.27 (978-0-8225-0095-7(7)) Lerner Publishing Group.
—James Madison. 2004. (Presidential Leaders Ser.). (Illus.). 112p. (J). (gr. 6-12). lib. bdg. 29.27 (978-0-8225-0823-6(0)) Lerner Publishing Group.
Robinson, Tom. Barack Obama: 44th U. S. President, 1 vol. 2009. (Essential Lives Set 3 Ser.). (J). (ENG., Illus.). 112p. (gr. 6-12). lib. bdg. 35.64 (978-1-60453-527-3(X)); lib. bdg. 32.79 (978-1-60453-528-0(8), Essential Library) ABDO Publishing Co.
—The Development of the Industrial United States: 1870-1900. 2007. (Presidents of the United States Ser.). (Illus.). 48p. (J). (gr. 4-7). lib. bdg. 29.05 (978-1-59036-745-2(6)) Weigl Pubs., Inc.
—Development of the Industrial United States: 1870-1900. 2007. (Presidents of the United States Ser.). (Illus.). 48p. (J). (gr. 4-7). per. 10.95 (978-1-59036-746-9(4)) Weigl Pubs., Inc.
Rockwell, Anne. Big George: How a Shy Boy Became President Washington. Phelan, Matt, illus. 2015. (ENG.). 48p. (J). (gr. 1-4). pap. 8.99 (978-0-544-58246-0(2), HMH Books For Young Readers) Houghton Mifflin Harcourt Publishing Co.
Rockwell, Anne F. Big George: How a Shy Boy Became President Washington. Trueman, Matthew & Phelan, Matt, illus. 2009. (ENG.). 48p. (J). (gr. 1-4). 17.99 (978-0-15-216583-3(5)) Houghton Mifflin Harcourt Publishing Co.
Rodhe, Paul. Kids Meet the Presidents 3rd Edition. 2017. (Kids Meet Ser.: 9). (ENG.). 96p. (J). (gr. 3). spiral bd. 14.95 (978-1-60433-657-3(9), Applesauce Pr.) Cider Mill Pr. Bk. Pubs., LLC.
Rodhe, Paul & Beatrice, Paul. Kids Meet the Presidents 2nd Edition. 2013. (Kids Meet Ser.: 1). (ENG.). 96p. (J). 14.95 (978-1-60433-281-0(6), Applesauce Pr.) Cider Mill Pr. Bk. Pubs., LLC.
Roleff, Tamara, ed. What Limits Should Be Placed on Presidential Powers? 2006. (At Issue Ser.). (ENG., Illus.). 128p. (gr. 10-12). 39.40 (978-0-7377-3629-8(1)); pap. 27.80 (978-0-7377-3630-4(5), Greenhaven Pr., Inc.) Cengage Gale.
Roome, Hugh. Franklin D. Roosevelt. 2017. (Rookie Biographies Ser.). (ENG.). 32p. (J). pap. 5.95 **(978-0-531-23863-9(6)**, Children's Pr.) Scholastic Library Publishing.
—Franklin D. Roosevelt: American Hero. 2017. (Rookie Biographies Ser.). (ENG.). 32p. (J). lib. bdg. 25.00 **(978-0-531-23229-3(8)**, Children's Pr.) Scholastic Library Publishing.
Rose, Simon. The Office of the President. 2014. (J). (978-1-4896-1950-1(X)) Weigl Pubs., Inc.
Rose, Simon. Office of the President. 2016. (J). **(978-1-5105-2247-3(6))** SmartBook Media, Inc.
Rowell, Rebecca. John F. Kennedy's Presidency. 2016. (Presidential Powerhouses Ser.). (ENG.). 104p. (J). (gr. 6-12). 53.32 (978-1-4677-8600-3(4), Lerner Pubns.) Lerner Publishing Group.
Roxburgh, Ellis. Thomas Jefferson vs. John Adams: Founding Fathers & Political Rivals. 2016. (History's Greatest Rivals Ser.). (ENG., Illus.). 48p. (J). (gr. 6-8). pap. 14.05 (978-1-4824-4239-7(6)) Stevens, Gareth Publishing LLLP.
Rubel, David. Scholastic Encyclopedia of the Presidents & Their Times. 2013. (ENG.). 256p. (J). (gr. 5-9). 24.99 (978-0-545-49985-9(2), Scholastic Reference) Scholastic, Inc.
Ruffin, Frances E. How to Draw the Life & Times of Theodore Roosevelt. (Kid's Guide to Drawing the Presidents of the

United States of America Ser.). 32p. 2009. (gr. 4-4). 50.50 *(978-1-61511-160-2(3),* PowerKids Pr.) 2007. (Illus.). (YA). (gr. 2-5). 26.50 *(978-1-4042-3002-6(5))* Rosen Publishing Group, Inc., The.

Rumsch, BreAnn. Abraham Lincoln, 1 vol. 2009. (United States Presidents Ser.). (ENG., Illus.). 40p. (YA). (gr. 3-6). 27.07 *(978-1-60453-464-1(8))* ABDO Publishing Co.

—Bill Clinton, 1 vol. 2009. (United States Presidents Ser.). (ENG., Illus.). 40p. (YA). (gr. 3-6). 27.07 *(978-1-60453-447-4(8))* ABDO Publishing Co.

—Franklin Pierce, 1 vol. 2016. (ENG., Illus.). 40p. (J). *(978-1-68078-112-0(X))* ABDO Publishing Co.

—George W. Bush, 1 vol. 2009. (United States Presidents Ser.). (ENG., Illus.). 40p. (YA). (gr. 3-6). 27.07 *(978-1-60453-444-3(3))* ABDO Publishing Co.

—Grover Cleveland, 1 vol. (ENG., Illus.). 40p. 2016. (J). *(978-1-68078-088-8(3))* 2009. (YA). (gr. 3-6). 27.07 *(978-1-60453-446-7(X))* ABDO Publishing Co.

—Herbert Hoover, 1 vol. 2009. (United States Presidents Ser.). (ENG., Illus.). 40p. (YA). (gr. 3-6). 27.07 *(978-1-60453-458-0(3))* ABDO Publishing Co.

—James K. Polk, 1 vol. 2009. (United States Presidents Ser.). (ENG., Illus.). 40p. (YA). (gr. 3-6). 27.07 *(978-1-60453-470-2(2))* ABDO Publishing Co.

—Martin Van Buren, 1 vol. 2009. (United States Presidents Ser.). (ENG., Illus.). 40p. (YA). (gr. 3-6). 27.07 *(978-1-60453-478-8(8))* ABDO Publishing Co.

—Rutherford B. Hayes, 1 vol. 2009. (United States Presidents Ser.). (ENG., Illus.). 40p. (YA). (gr. 3-6). 27.07 *(978-1-60453-457-3(5))* ABDO Publishing Co.

—Ulysses S. Grant, 1 vol. 2009. (United States Presidents Ser.). (ENG., Illus.). 40p. (YA). (gr. 3-6). 27.07 *(978-1-60453-453-5(2))* ABDO Publishing Co.

—William Taft, 1 vol. 2009. (United States Presidents Ser.). (ENG., Illus.). 40p. (YA). (gr. 3-6). 27.07 *(978-1-60453-474-0(5))* ABDO Publishing Co.

—Woodrow Wilson, 1 vol. 2009. (United States Presidents Ser.). (ENG., Illus.). 40p. (YA). (gr. 3-6). 27.07 *(978-1-60453-480-1(X))* ABDO Publishing Co.

Running Press Staff. New Big Book of U. S. Presidents 2016. 2017. (ENG., Illus.). 56p. (J). (gr. -1-2). 13.95 *(978-0-7624-6060-1(1),* Running Pr. Kids) Running Pr. Bk. Pubs.

Ruth, Amy. Herbert Hoover. 2004. (Presidential Leaders Ser.). (Illus.). 112p. (J). (gr. 6-12). lib. bdg. 29.27 *(978-0-8225-0821-2(4))* Lerner Publishing Group.

Saddleback Educational Publishing Staff, ed. Abraham Lincoln, 1 vol. unabr. ed. 2008. (Graphic Biographies Ser.). (ENG., Illus.). 25p. (YA). (gr. 9-12). per. 7.95 *(978-1-59905-211-3(3))* Saddleback Educational Publishing, Inc.

—Franklin Roosevelt, 1 vol. unabr. ed. 2008. (Graphic Biographies Ser.). (ENG., Illus.). 25p. (YA). (gr. 9-12). pap. 7.95 *(978-1-59905-222-9(9))* Saddleback Educational Publishing, Inc.

—George Washington, 1 vol. unabr. ed. 2008. (Graphic Biographies Ser.). (ENG., Illus.). 25p. (YA). (gr. 9-12). pap. 7.95 *(978-1-59905-223-6(7))* Saddleback Educational Publishing, Inc.

—Thomas Jefferson, 1 vol. unabr. ed. 2008. (Graphic Biographies Ser.). (ENG., Illus.). 25p. (YA). (gr. 9-12). pap. 7.95 *(978-1-59905-229-8(6))* Saddleback Educational Publishing, Inc.

Saffer, Barbara. Harry S. Truman. 2004. (Childhoods of the Presidents Ser.). (Illus.). 48p. (J). (gr. 4-18). lib. bdg. 17.95 *(978-1-59084-282-9(0))* Mason Crest.

Santella, Andrew. Air Force One. 2003. (Illus.). 48p. (gr. 4-18). (J). pap. 8.95 *(978-0-7613-1926-9(3));* (Women at War Ser.: up). lib. bdg. 24.90 *(978-0-7613-2617-5(0))* Lerner Publishing Group. (Millbrook Pr.).

Santow, Dan. Millard Fillmore. 2004. (Encyclopedia of Presidents Ser.). (ENG., Illus.). 110p. (YA). (gr. 5-9). 34.00 *(978-0-516-22888-4(9))* Scholastic Library Publishing.

Scarbrough, Mary Hertz. Presidential Politics by the Numbers. 2016. (Presidential Politics Ser.). (ENG., Illus.). 48p. (gr. 3-4). lib. bdg. 29.32 *(978-1-4914-8238-4(9),* Connect) Stone Arch Bks.

Schanzer, Rosalyn. George vs. George: The American Revolution as Seen from Both Sides. 2007. (ENG., Illus.). 64p. (J). (gr. 4-7). per. 6.95 *(978-1-4263-0042-4(5),* National Geographic Children's Bks.) National Geographic Society.

—George vs. George: The Revolutionary War as Seen by Both Sides. 2004. (ENG., Illus.). 64p. (J). (gr. 4-7). 16.95 *(978-0-7922-7349-3(4),* National Geographic Children's Bks.) National Geographic Society.

Schmidt, Roderic. How to Draw the Life & Times of Abraham Lincoln. (Kid's Guide to Drawing the Presidents of the United States of America Ser.). 2009. 32p. (gr. 4-4). 50.50 *(978-1-61511-130-5(1),* PowerKids Pr.) 2006. (YA). (gr. 2-5). 26.50 *(978-1-4042-2993-8(0))* Rosen Publishing Group, Inc., The.

—How to Draw the Life & Times of George W. Bush. (Kid's Guide to Drawing the Presidents of the United States of America Ser.). 32p. 2009. (gr. 4-4). 50.50 *(978-1-61511-139-8(5),* PowerKids Pr.) 2007. (Illus.). (YA). (gr. 2-5). 26.50 *(978-1-4042-3019-4(X))* Rosen Publishing Group, Inc., The.

—How to Draw the Life & Times of James Madison. (Kid's Guide to Drawing the Presidents of the United States of America Ser.). 2009. 32p. (gr. 4-4). 50.50 *(978-1-61511-148-0(4),* PowerKids Pr.) 2006. (YA). (gr. 2-5). 26.50 *(978-1-4042-2981-5(7))* Rosen Publishing Group, Inc., The.

—How to Draw the Life & Times of Martin Van Buren. (Kid's Guide to Drawing the Presidents of the United States of America Ser.). 2009. 32p. (gr. 4-4). 50.50 *(978-1-61511-155-8(7),* PowerKids Pr.) 2006. (YA). (gr. 2-5). 26.50 *(978-1-4042-2985-3(X))* Rosen Publishing Group, Inc., The.

—How to Draw the Life & Times of Zachary Taylor. (Kid's Guide to Drawing the Presidents of the United States of America Ser.). 2009. 32p. (gr. 4-4). 50.50 *(978-1-61511-169-5(7),* PowerKids Pr.) 2006. (YA). (gr. 2-5). 26.50 *(978-1-4042-2989-1(2))* Rosen Publishing Group, Inc., The.

Scholastic & Tracosas, L. J. White House Winners: What You Don't Know about the Presidents. Lynch, Josh, illus. 2017. (ENG.). 64p. (J). (gr. 1-3). 10.99 *(978-1-338-12997-7(X))* Scholastic, Inc.

Schroeder, Alan. Abe Lincoln: His Wit & Wisdom from A to Z. O'brien, John, illus. 2015. (ENG.). 32p. (J). (gr. 1-5). 17.95 *(978-0-8234-2420-7(0))* Holiday Hse., Inc.

Schubert, Barbara. George Washington. 2009. pap. 13.25 *(978-1-60559-060-8(6))* Hameray Publishing Group, Inc.

Schuh, Mari C. The U. S. Presidency, 1 vol. 2012. (U. S. Government Ser.). (ENG.). 24p. (gr. k-1). lib. bdg. 26.65 *(978-1-4296-7566-6(7),* Pebble Plus) Capstone Press of Coughlan Cos.

Schultz, Randy. Dwight D. Eisenhower: A MyReportLinks. Com Book. 2003. (Presidents Ser.). (Illus.). 48p. (J). (gr. 5-10). lib. bdg. 25.26 *(978-0-7660-5102-7(1),* MyReportLinks.com Bks.) Enslow Pubs., Inc.

—Richard M. Nixon: A MyReportLinks. Com Book. 2003. (Presidents Ser.). (Illus.). 48p. (J). (gr. 4-10). lib. bdg. 25.26 *(978-0-7660-5104-1(8),* MyReportLinks.com Bks.) Enslow Pubs., Inc.

—Warren G. Harding: A MyReportLinks. Com Book. 2003. (Presidents Ser.). (Illus.). 48p. (J). (gr. 4-10). lib. bdg. 25.26 *(978-0-7660-5103-4(X),* MyReportLinks.com Bks.) Enslow Pubs., Inc.

Schuman, Michael A. Bill Clinton. rev. ed. 2003. (United States Presidents Ser.). (Illus.). 128p. (J). (gr. 5-12). lib. bdg. 27.94 *(978-0-7660-2032-0(0))* Enslow Pubs., Inc.

Schwartz, Heather E. Theodore Roosevelt's Presidency. 2016. (Presidential Powerhouses Ser.). (ENG., Illus.). 104p. (J). (gr. 6-12). 35.99 *(978-1-4677-7930-2(X),* Lerner Pubns.) Lerner Publishing Group.

Shea, John M. Thomas Jefferson in His Own Words, Vol. 1. 2014. (Eyewitness to History Ser.). 32p. (J). (gr. 4-5). (ENG.). pap. 10.50 *(978-1-4339-9933-8(1));* 26.60 *(978-1-4339-9873-7(4))* Stevens, Gareth Publishing LLLP.

Shepherd, Jodie. Barack Obama: Groundbreaking President. 2016. (Rookie Biographies(tm) Ser.). (ENG., Illus.). 32p. (J). lib. bdg. 25.00 *(978-0-531-21681-1(0),* Children's Pr.) Scholastic Library Publishing.

—Presidents of the United States of America. 2015. (Illus.). 50p. (J). *(978-1-4351-6156-6(4))* Barnes & Noble, Inc.

Sherman, Jill. Donald Trump: Outspoken Personality & President. 2017. (Gateway Biographies Ser.). (ENG., Illus.). 48p. (J). (gr. 4-8). lib. bdg. 26.65 *(978-1-5124-2596-3(6))* Lerner Publishing Group.

Sherman, Patrice. George W. Bush: Texan Governor & U. S. President, 1 vol. 2012. (Primary Source Readers Ser.). (ENG.). 32p. (J). (gr. 3-3). pap. 8.99 *(978-1-4333-5054-2(8))* Teacher Created Materials, Inc.

—What It's Like to Be President Barack Obama? Vega, Eida de la, tr. 2009. (What It's Like to Be/Que se Siente al Ser Ser.). (SPA & ENG., Illus.). 32p. (J). (gr. -1-2). 25.70 *(978-1-58415-843-1(3))* Mitchell Lane Pubs., Inc.

Silate, Jennifer. The White House. (Primary Sources of American Symbols Ser.). 24p. 2009. (gr. 3-3). 42.50 *(978-1-60851-512-7(5),* PowerKids Pr.) 2006. (Illus.). (J). (gr. 4-7). lib. bdg. 22.60 *(978-1-4042-2695-1(8))* Rosen Publishing Group, Inc., The.

Singer, Allison. What Does the President Do? 2017. (DK Readers Ser.). (ENG., Illus.). 48p. (J). (gr. k-2). pap. 3.99 *(978-1-4654-5748-6(8),* DK Children) Dorling Kindersley Publishing, Inc.

Sirvaitis, Karen. Barack Obama: A Leader in a Time of Change. 2009. (USA TODAY Lifeline Biographies Ser.). (ENG.). 112p. (gr. 6-12). lib. bdg. 34.60 *(978-0-7613-4235-9(4))* Lerner Publishing Group.

Slade, Suzanne. The House That George Built. Bond, Rebecca, illus. 2012. (ENG.). 32p. (J). (gr. 1-4). 16.95 *(978-1-58089-262-9(0))* Charlesbridge Publishing, Inc.

Smith, Adam I. P. Abraham Lincoln. 2016. (History Makers Ser.). 144p. (J). (gr. 9-9). 45.64 *(978-1-5026-1912-9(1))* Cavendish Square Publishing.

Smith, Don. Political Power: Richard Nixon. 2012. (ENG.). 32p. pap. 3.99 *(978-0-9855911-3-7(7))* Bluewater Productions, Inc.

Smith-Llera, Danielle. The Presidency of George Washington: Inspiring a Young Nation, 1 vol. 2014. (Greatest U. S. Presidents Ser.). (ENG.). 64p. (gr. 5-7). lib. bdg. 33.99 *(978-0-7565-4928-2(0))* Compass Point Bks.

Snyder, Gail. George Washington. 2004. (Childhoods of the Presidents Ser.). (Illus.). 48p. (J). (gr. 4-18). lib. bdg. 17.95 *(978-1-59084-270-6(7))* Mason Crest.

Somervill, Barbara A. The Life & Times of James Madison. 2008. (Profiles in American History Ser.). (Illus.). 48p. (J). (gr. 4-7). lib. bdg. 29.95 *(978-1-58415-530-0(2))* Mitchell Lane Pubs., Inc.

Sommer, Shelley. John F. Kennedy: His Life & Legacy. 2005. (Illus.). 160p. (J). 16.99 *(978-0-06-054135-4(0))* HarperCollins Pubs.

Souter, Gerry & Souter, Janet. Herbert Hoover. 2008. (Presidents of the U. S. A. Ser.). (ENG., Illus.). 48p. (J). (gr. 3-6). 32.79 *(978-1-60253-059-1(9),* 200698) Child's World, Inc., The.

—James Buchanan. 2008. (Presidents of the U. S. A. Ser.). (ENG., Illus.). 48p. (J). (gr. 3-6). 32.79 *(978-1-60253-044-7(0),* 200683) Child's World, Inc., The.

—John Quincy Adams. 2008. (Presidents of the U. S. A. Ser.). (ENG., Illus.). 48p. (J). (gr. 3-6). 32.79 *(978-1-60253-035-5(1),* 200674) Child's World, Inc., The.

Spalding, Maddie. How the Executive Branch Works. 2016. (How America Works). (ENG.). 24p. (J). (gr. 3-6). 28.50 *(978-1-5038-0903-1(X),* 210660) Child's World, Inc., The.

St. George, Judith. So You Want to Be President? Small, David, illus. 2004. (J). (gr. 1-6). 29.95 *(978-1-55592-132-3(9))* Weston Woods Studios, Inc.

—So You Want to Be President? Small, David, illus. rev. ed. 2004. (ENG.). 56p. (J). (gr. 2-5). 17.99 *(978-0-399-24317-2(8),* Philomel Bks.) Penguin Young Readers Group.

—Stand Tall, Abe Lincoln. Faulkner, Matt, illus. 2015. (ENG.). 48p. (J). (gr. 2-4). 8.99 *(978-0-14-751447-9(9),* Puffin Books) Penguin Young Readers Group.

Stabler, David. Kid Presidents: True Tales of Childhood from America's Presidents. Horner, Doogie, illus. 2014. (Kid Legends Ser.: 1). (ENG.). 224p. (J). (gr. 4-7). 13.95 *(978-1-59474-731-1(8))* Quirk Bks.

Stanley, George Edward. America in Today's World (1969-2004) 2005. (Primary Source History of the United States Ser.). (Illus.). 48p. (gr. 5-12). pap. 14.05 *(978-0-8368-5840-2(9));* lib. bdg. 31.00 *(978-0-8368-5831-0(X))* Stevens, Gareth Publishing LLLP. (Gareth Stevens Secondary Library).

Stevens, Stewart, Sr. The White House Chandeliers: My Experiences While Working for Seven U. S. Presidents. 2016. (ENG., Illus.). xi, 127p. (gr. 6-17). pap. 25.00 *(978-0-9974925-0-7(3))* Lightning Fast Bk. Publishing.

Stier, Catherine. If I Ran for President. Avril, Lynne, illus. 2012. (J). 34.28 *(978-1-61913-115-6(3))* Weigl Pubs., Inc.

Stille, Darlene R. Barack Obama: 44th U.S. President, 1 vol. Stergulz, Richard, illus. 2013. (Beginner Biographies Set 2 Ser.). (ENG.). 32p. (J). (gr. -1-4). 28.50 *(978-1-61641-939-4(3))* Magic Wagon.

—The Emergence of Modern America: 1890-1930. 2007. (Presidents of the United States Ser.). (Illus.). 48p. (J). (gr. 4-7). lib. bdg. 29.05 *(978-1-59036-747-6(2));* per. 10.95 *(978-1-59036-748-3(0))* Weigl Pubs., Inc.

Stine, Megan. Where Is the White House? 2015. (Where Is... ? Ser.). lib. bdg. 16.00 *(978-0-606-36591-8(5))* Turtleback Bks.

—Who Was Ulysses S. Grant? Harrison, Nancy & Geyer, Mark Edward, illus. 2014. (Who Was? Ser.). (ENG.). 112p. (J). (gr. 3-7). 5.99 *(978-0-448-47894-4(3),* Grosset & Dunlap) Penguin Young Readers Group.

Stine, Megan & dePaola, Tomie. Where Is the White House? Groff, David, illus. 2015. (Where Is? Ser.). (ENG.). 112p. (J). (gr. 3-7). 5.99 *(978-0-448-48355-9(6),* Grosset & Dunlap) Penguin Young Readers Group.

Sullivan, Anne Marie. Franklin D. Roosevelt. 2004. (Childhood of the Presidents Ser.). (Illus.). 48p. (J). (gr. 4-18). lib. bdg. 17.95 *(978-1-59084-279-9(0))* Mason Crest.

Sullivan, George. A Book of U. S. Presidents. rev. ed. 2016. (ENG.). 192p. (J). (gr. 3-7). pap. 6.99 *(978-1-338-03807-1(9),* Scholastic Paperbacks) Scholastic, Inc.

Sutcliffe, Jane. Barack Obama. 2010. (History Maker Biographies Ser.). (ENG.). 48p. (gr. 3-6). lib. bdg. 27.93 *(978-0-7613-5205-1(6),* Lerner Pubns.) Lerner Publishing Group.

—John Adams. 2006. (History Maker Biographies Ser.). (ENG., Illus.). 48p. (gr. 3-6). lib. bdg. 27.93 *(978-0-8225-5940-5(4),* Lerner Pubns.) Lerner Publishing Group.

—John F. Kennedy. (History Maker Bios Ser.). (J). 2005. (Illus.). 48p. 26.60 *(978-0-8225-1546-3(6))* 2004. pap. 8.95 *(978-0-8225-2540-0(2))* Lerner Publishing Group. (Lerner Pubns.).

—Ronald Reagan. 2009. pap. 52.95 *(978-0-7613-4958-7(8))* 2008. (ENG.). 48p. (gr. 3-6). 27.93 *(978-0-8225-8894-8(3),* Lerner Pubns.) Lerner Publishing Group.

Swain, Gwenyth. Theodore Roosevelt. 2004. (History Maker Bios Ser.). (J). pap. 8.95 *(978-0-8225-2542-4(9));* (ENG., Illus.). 48p. (gr. 3-6). 27.93 *(978-0-8225-1548-7(2))* Lerner Publishing Group. (Lerner Pubns.).

Taylor-Butler, Christine. The Presidency. (True Book(tm), a — American History Ser.). (Illus.). 48p. (J). (gr. 3-5). 2007. lib. bdg. 31.00 *(978-0-531-12634-9(X))* 2008. (ENG., pap. 6.95 *(978-0-531-14784-9(3))* Scholastic Library Publishing. (Children's Pr.).

Taylor, Charlotte & Feinstein, Stephen. Barack Obama: First African-American President. 2015. (Exceptional African Americans Ser.). (ENG.). 24p. (J). (gr. 3-4). pap. 9.35 *(978-0-7660-7122-3(7));* (Illus.). 22.60 *(978-0-7660-7124-7(3))* Enslow Pubs., Inc.

Tecco, Betsy Dru. How to Draw the Life & Times of Grover Cleveland. (Kid's Guide to Drawing the Presidents of the United States of America Ser.). 2009. 32p. (gr. 4-4). 50.50 *(978-1-61511-142-8(5),* PowerKids Pr.) 2006. (YA). (gr. 2-5). 26.50 *(978-1-4042-2999-0(X))* Rosen Publishing Group, Inc., The.

—How to Draw the Life & Times of John Quincy Adams. (Kid's Guide to Drawing the Presidents of the United States of America Ser.). 2009. 32p. (gr. 4-4). 50.50 *(978-1-61511-152-7(2),* PowerKids Pr.) 2006. (YA). (gr. 2-5). 26.50 *(978-1-4042-2983-9(3))* Rosen Publishing Group, Inc., The.

—How to Draw the Life & Times of Ulysses S. Grant. (Kid's Guide to Drawing the Presidents of the United States of America Ser.). 2009. 32p. (gr. 4-4). 50.50 *(978-1-61511-162-6(X),* PowerKids Pr.) 2006. (YA). (gr. 2-5). 26.50 *(978-1-4042-2995-2(7))* Rosen Publishing Group, Inc., The.

Thomas, Garen. Yes We Can: A Biography of President Barack Obama. 2nd rev. ed. 2008. (ENG., Illus.). 256p. (J). (gr. 3-7). pap. 12.99 *(978-0-312-58639-3(6),* 9780312586393) Feiwel & Friends.

Thomas, Peggy. Thomas Jefferson Grows a Nation. Innerst, Stacy, illus. 2015. (ENG.). 48p. (J). (gr. 3-7). 16.95 *(978-1-62091-628-5(2),* Calkins Creek) Boyds Mills Pr.

Thompson, William & Thompson, Dorcas. George W. Bush. 2004. (Childhoods of the Presidents Ser.). (Illus.). 48p. (J). (gr. 4-18). lib. bdg. 17.95 *(978-1-59084-281-2(2))* Mason Crest.

Thomson, Sarah L. What Lincoln Said. Ransome, James E., illus. 2009. 32p. (J). (gr. k-3). lib. bdg. 18.89 *(978-0-06-084820-0(0))* HarperCollins Pubs.

Thorburn, Mark. The Executive Branch: Leading the Nation. 2008. (Federal Government Ser.). (Illus.). 128p. (J). (gr. 6-18). lib. bdg. 34.60 *(978-1-59845-060-6(3),* MyReportLinks.com Bks.) Enslow Pubs., Inc.

—The President & the Executive Branch: How Our Nation Is Governed. 2012. (Constitution & the United States Government Ser.). (Illus.). 104p. (J). (gr. 5-18). 33.27 *(978-0-7660-4063-2(1))* Enslow Pubs., Inc.

Tieck, Sarah. Barack Obama, 1 vol. 2010. (First Biographies Set 6 Ser.). (ENG.). 32p. (J). (gr. 1-4). 27.07 *(978-1-60453-985-1(2))* ABDO Publishing Co.

Time for Kids Editors. Presidents of the United States. 2006. (Time for Kids Ser.). (ENG., Illus.). 72p. (J). (gr. 2-6). pap. 7.99 *(978-0-06-081556-1(6),* Collins) HarperCollins Pubs.

—Time for Kids: Ronald Reagan: From Silver Screen to Oval Office. 2005. (Time for Kids Ser.). (ENG., Illus.). 48p. (J). (gr. 2-4). per. 3.99 *(978-0-06-057626-4(X))* HarperCollins Pubs.

Time for Kids Magazine Staff. Franklin D. Roosevelt - A Leader in Troubled Times. 2005. (Time for Kids Ser.). (ENG., Illus.). 48p. (J). (gr. 2-4). per. 3.99 *(978-0-06-057615-8(4))* HarperCollins Pubs.

—Presidents of the United States. 2006. (Time for Kids Ser.). (Illus.). 70p. (J). (gr. 2-6). lib. bdg. 18.89 *(978-0-06-081555-4(8))* HarperCollins Pubs.

Townsend, Michael. Where Do Presidents Come From? And Other Presidential Stuff of Super Great Importance. 2012. (ENG.). 160p. (J). (gr. 3-7). 14.99 *(978-0-8037-3748-8(3),* Dial Bks) Penguin Young Readers Group.

Troupe, Thomas Kingsley. If I Were the President [Scholastic]. Heyworth, Heather, illus. 2010. (Dream Big! Ser.). 24p. pap. 0.62 *(978-1-4048-6196-1(3),* Nonfiction Picture Bks.) Picture Window Bks.

Trueit, Trudi Strain. Thomas Jefferson. 2009. (Presidents & Their Times 3 Ser.). 96p. (gr. 6). 34.21 *(978-0-7614-3622-5(7))* Marshall Cavendish Corp.

Trumbauer, Lisa. Abraham Lincoln & the Civil War. 2016. (Life in the Time Of Ser.). (ENG.). 32p. pap. 8.29 *(978-1-4846-3822-4(0),* Heinemann First Library) Heinemann-Raintree.

—Set in Stone. 2005. (Yellow Umbrella Fluent Level Ser.). (ENG.). 16p. (gr. k-1). pap. 35.70 *(978-0-7368-5308-8(1),* Yellow Umbrella Bks.) Capstone Press of Coughlan Cos.

Tucker, Rosalyn. Ronald Reagan, 1 vol. 2014. (Presidential Biographies Ser.). (ENG.). 24p. (gr. k-1). lib. bdg. 26.65 *(978-1-4765-9613-6(1),* Pebble Plus) Capstone Press of Coughlan Cos.

Turner, Juliette. Our Presidents Rock!, 1 vol. Oesch, Brian, illus. 2014. (ENG.). 320p. (J). pap. 16.99 *(978-0-310-73095-8(3))* Zonderkidz.

Upadhyay, Ritu. John F Kennedy the Making of a Leader. 2005. 44p. (J). lib. bdg. 15.00 *(978-1-4242-0851-7(3))* Fitzgerald Bks.

Upadhyay, Ritu & Time for Kids Editors. The Making of a Leader. 2005. (Time for Kids Ser.). (ENG., Illus.). 48p. (J). (gr. 2-4). pap. 3.99 *(978-0-06-057602-8(2))* HarperCollins Pubs.

Vander Hook, Sue. Franklin D. Roosevelt: 32nd U. S. President, 1 vol. 2008. (Essential Lives Set 2 Ser.). (ENG., Illus.). 112p. (J). (gr. 6-12). lib. bdg. 35.64 *(978-1-60453-041-4(3))* ABDO Publishing Co.

Venezia, Mike. Andrew Jackson. Venezia, Mike, illus. 2005. (Getting to Know the U. S. Presidents Ser.). (ENG., Illus.). 32p. (J). (gr. 3-4). 28.00 *(978-0-516-22612-5(6),* Children's Pr.) Scholastic Library Publishing.

—Andrew Jackson: Seventh President, 1829-1837. Venezia, Mike, illus. 2005. (Getting to Know the U. S. Presidents Ser.). (ENG., Illus.). 32p. (J). (gr. 3-4). per. 7.95 *(978-0-516-27481-2(3),* Children's Pr.) Scholastic Library Publishing.

—Andrew Johnson: Seventeenth President. Venezia, Mike, illus. 2005. (Getting to Know the U. S. Presidents Ser.). (ENG., Illus.). 32p. (J). (gr. 3-7). lib. bdg. 28.00 *(978-0-516-22622-4(3),* Children's Pr.) Scholastic Library Publishing.

—Benjamin Harrison. Venezia, Mike, illus. 2006. (Getting to Know the U. S. Presidents Ser.). (ENG., Illus.). 32p. (J). (gr. 3-7). lib. bdg. 28.00 *(978-0-516-22628-6(2),* Children's Pr.) Scholastic Library Publishing.

—Bill Clinton: Forty-Second President, 1993-2001. Venezia, Mike, illus. 2007. (Getting to Know the U. S. Presidents Ser.). (ENG., Illus.). 32p. (J). (gr. 3-4). 28.00 *(978-0-516-22646-0(0),* Children's Pr.) Scholastic Library Publishing.

—Chester A. Arthur. Venezia, Mike, illus. 2006. (Getting to Know the U. S. Presidents Ser.). (ENG., Illus.). 32p. (J). (gr. 3-7). lib. bdg. 28.00 *(978-0-516-22626-2(6),* Children's Pr.) Scholastic Library Publishing.

—Chester A. Arthur: Twenty-First President, 1881-1885. Venezia, Mike, illus. 2006. (Getting to Know the U. S. Presidents Ser.). (ENG., Illus.). 32p. (J). (gr. 3-7). pap. 7.95 *(978-0-516-25401-2(4),* Children's Pr.) Scholastic Library Publishing.

—Dwight D. Eisenhower: Thirty-Fourth President 1953-1961. Venezia, Mike, illus. 2007. (Getting to Know the U. S. Presidents Ser.). (Illus.). 32p. (J). (gr. 3-4). 28.00 *(978-0-516-22638-5(X),* Children's Pr.) Scholastic Library Publishing.

—Franklin Pierce: Fourteenth President. Venezia, Mike, illus. 2005. (Getting to Know the U. S. Presidents Ser.). (ENG., Illus.). 32p. (J). (gr. 3-7). lib. bdg. 28.00 *(978-0-516-22619-4(3),* Children's Pr.) Scholastic Library Publishing.

—George Bush. Venezia, Mike, illus. 2008. (Getting to Know the U. S. Presidents Ser.). (ENG., Illus.). 32p. (J). (gr. 3-4). pap. 7.95 *(978-0-516-25536-1(3),* Children's Pr.) Scholastic Library Publishing.

—Gerald R. Ford: Thirty-Eighth President, 1974-1977. Venezia, Mike, illus. (Getting to Know the U. S. Presidents Ser.). (ENG., Illus.). 32p. (J). (gr. 3-4). 2008. pap. 7.95 *(978-0-516-25597-2(5))* 2007. 28.00 *(978-0-516-22642-2(8))* Scholastic Library Publishing. (Children's Pr.).

—Getting to Know the U. S. Presidents, 6 bks., Set. Venezia, Mike, illus. Incl. Benjamin Harrison. lib. bdg. 28.00 *(978-0-516-22628-6(2));* Chester A. Arthur. lib. bdg. 28.00 *(978-0-516-22626-2(6));* Grover Cleveland: Twenty-Second & Twenty-Fourth President, 1885-1889, 1893-1897. lib. bdg. 28.00 *(978-0-516-22627-9(4));* James A. Garfield. lib. bdg. 28.00 *(978-0-516-22625-5(8));* Rutherford B. Hayes: Nineteenth President, 1877-1881. lib. bdg. 28.00 *(978-0-516-22624-8(X));* William McKinley. lib. bdg. 28.00 *(978-0-516-22629-3(0));* 32p. (J). (gr. 3-7). 2006. (Illus.). 2006. Set lib. bdg. 162.00 o.p. *(978-0-516-25409-8(X),* Children's Pr.) Scholastic Library Publishing.

—Getting to Know the U. S. Presidents, 6 bks., Set. Venezia, Mike, illus. Incl. Dwight D. Eisenhower: Thirty-Fourth President 1953-1961. 28.00 *(978-0-516-22638-5(X));* Harry S. Truman: Thirty-Third President. 28.00 *(978-0-516-22637-8(1));* Lyndon B. Johnson: Thirty-Sixth President, 1963-1969. 28.00 *(978-0-516-22640-8(1));* Richard M. Nixon: Thirty-Seventh President, 1969-1974. 28.00 *(978-0-516-22641-5(X));* (Illus.). 32p. (J). (gr. 3-4). 2007. 162.00 o.p. *(978-0-531-17733-4(5),* Children's Pr.) Scholastic Library Publishing.

—Grover Cleveland: Twenty-Second & Twenty-Fourth President, 1885-1889, 1893-1897. Venezia, Mike, illus. 2006. (Getting to Know the U. S. Presidents Ser.). (ENG., Illus.). 32p. (J). (gr. 3-7). pap. 7.95 *(978-0-516-25402-9(2));* lib. bdg. 28.00 *(978-0-516-22627-9(4))* Scholastic Library Publishing. (Children's Pr.).

—Harry S. Truman: Thirty-Third President. Venezia, Mike, illus. 2007. (Getting to Know the U. S. Presidents Ser.). (Illus.). 32p. (J). (gr. 3-4). 28.00 *(978-0-516-22637-8(1)*, Children's Pr.) Scholastic Library Publishing.

—James A. Garfield. Venezia, Mike, illus. 2006. (Getting to Know the U. S. Presidents Ser.). (ENG., Illus.). 32p. (J). (gr. 3-7). lib. bdg. 28.00 *(978-0-516-22625-5(8)*, Children's Pr.) Scholastic Library Publishing.

—James Buchanan: Fifteenth President. Venezia, Mike, illus. 2005. (Getting to Know the U. S. Presidents Ser.). (ENG., Illus.). 32p. (J). (gr. 3-7). lib. bdg. 28.00 *(978-0-516-22620-0(7)*, Children's Pr.) Scholastic Library Publishing.

—James K. Polk: Eleventh President, 1845-1849. Venezia, Mike, illus. 2005. (Getting to Know the U. S. Presidents Ser.). (ENG., Illus.). 32p. (J). (gr. 3-4). 28.00 *(978-0-516-22616-3(9)*, Children's Pr.) Scholastic Library Publishing.

—Jimmy Carter: Thirty-Ninth President 1977-1981. Venezia, Mike, illus. 2007. (Getting to Know the U. S. Presidents Ser.). (ENG., Illus.). 32p. (J). (gr. 3-4). 28.00 *(978-0-516-22643-9(6)*, Children's Pr.) Scholastic Library Publishing.

—John Tyler: Tenth President, 1841-1845. Venezia, Mike, illus. 2005. (Getting to Know the U. S. Presidents Ser.). (ENG., Illus.). 32p. (J). (gr. 3-4). per. 7.95 *(978-0-516-27484-3(8))*; 28.00 *(978-0-516-22615-6(0))* Scholastic Library Publishing. (Children's Pr.).

—Martin Van Buren. Venezia, Mike, illus. 2005. (Getting to Know the U. S. Presidents Ser.). (ENG., Illus.). 32p. (J). (gr. 3-4). 28.00 *(978-0-516-22613-2(4)*, Children's Pr.) Scholastic Library Publishing.

—Millard Fillmore: Thirteenth President. Venezia, Mike, illus. 2005. (Getting to Know the U. S. Presidents Ser.). (ENG., Illus.). 32p. (J). (gr. 3-7). lib. bdg. 28.00 *(978-0-516-22618-7(5)*, Children's Pr.) Scholastic Library Publishing.

—Millard Fillmore: Thirteenth President, 1850-1853. Venezia, Mike, illus. 2006. (Getting to Know the U. S. Presidents Ser.). (ENG., Illus.). 32p. (J). (gr. 3-7). per. 7.95 *(978-0-516-25487-6(1)*, Children's Pr.) Scholastic Library Publishing.

—Richard M. Nixon: Thirty-Seventh President, 1969-1974. Venezia, Mike, illus. 2007. (Getting to Know the U. S. Presidents Ser.). (ENG., Illus.). 32p. (J). (gr. 3-4). pap. 7.95 *(978-0-531-17949-9(4)*, Children's Pr.) Scholastic Library Publishing.

—Ronald Reagan: Fortieth President, 1981-1989. Venezia, Mike, illus. 2007. (Getting to Know the U. S. Presidents Ser.). (ENG., Illus.). 32p. (J). (gr. 3-4). 28.00 *(978-0-516-22644-6(4)*, Children's Pr.) Scholastic Library Publishing.

—Rutherford B. Hayes: Nineteenth President, 1877-1881. Venezia, Mike, illus. 2006. (Getting to Know the U. S. Presidents Ser.). (Illus.). 32p. (J). (gr. 3-7). pap. 7.95 *(978-0-516-25404-3(9))*; (ENG., lib. bdg. 28.00 *(978-0-516-22624-8(X))* Scholastic Library Publishing. (Children's Pr.).

—Thomas Jefferson: Third President, 1801-1809. Venezia, Mike, illus. 2004. (Gtk Us Presidents Ser.). (ENG., Illus.). (J). 28.00 *(978-0-516-22608-8(8)*, Children's Pr.) Scholastic Library Publishing.

—Ulysses S. Grant. Venezia, Mike, illus. 2005. (Getting to Know the U. S. Presidents Ser.). (ENG., Illus.). 32p. (J). (gr. 3-7). lib. bdg. 28.00 *(978-0-516-22623-1(1)*, Children's Pr.) Scholastic Library Publishing.

—Warren G. Harding: Twenty-Ninth President, 1921-1923. Venezia, Mike, illus. 2006. (Getting to Know the U. S. Presidents Ser.). (ENG., Illus.). 32p. (J). (gr. 3-7). lib. bdg. 28.00 *(978-0-516-22633-0(9))* Scholastic Library Publishing.

—William Henry Harrison. Venezia, Mike, illus. 2005. (Getting to Know the U. S. Presidents Ser.). (ENG., Illus.). 32p. (J). (gr. 3-4). 28.00 *(978-0-516-22614-9(2)*, Children's Pr.) Scholastic Library Publishing.

—William Henry Harrison: Ninth President 1841. Venezia, Mike, illus. 2005. (Getting to Know the U. S. Presidents Ser.). (ENG., Illus.). 32p. (J). (gr. 3-4). per. 7.95 *(978-0-516-27483-6(X)*, Children's Pr.) Scholastic Library Publishing.

—William Howard Taft: Twenty-Seventh President. Venezia, Mike, illus. 2007. (Getting to Know the U. S. Presidents Ser.). (Illus.). 32p. (J). (gr. 3-7). pap. 7.95 *(978-0-516-25239-1(9)*, Children's Pr.) Scholastic Library Publishing.

—William McKinley. Venezia, Mike, illus. 2006. (Getting to Know the U. S. Presidents Ser.). (ENG., Illus.). 32p. (J). (gr. 3-7). lib. bdg. 28.00 *(978-0-516-22629-3(0)*, Children's Pr.) Scholastic Library Publishing.

—Woodrow Wilson: Twenty-Eighth President. Venezia, Mike, illus. 2007. (Getting to Know the U. S. Presidents Ser.). (Illus.). 32p. (J). (gr. 3-7). pap. 7.95 *(978-0-516-25462-3(6)*, Children's Pr.) Scholastic Library Publishing.

—Zachary Taylor: Twelfth President, 1849-1850. Venezia, Mike, illus. 2005. (Getting to Know the U. S. Presidents Ser.). (ENG., Illus.). 32p. (J). (gr. 3-4). 28.00 *(978-0-516-22617-0(7)*, Children's Pr.) Scholastic Library Publishing.

Vescia, Monique. The Emancipation Proclamation. 2016. (Let's Find Out! Primary Sources Ser.). 00032p. (J). (gr. 2-3). lib. bdg. 24.45 *(978-1-5081-0405-6(0))* Rosen Publishing Group, Inc., The.

Vierow, Wendy. The 1864 Presidential Election: A War-Weary Nation Reelects President Abraham Lincoln. 2004. (Headlines from History Ser.). (Illus.). 24p. (J). lib. bdg. 22.60 *(978-0-8239-6224-2(5))* Rosen Publishing Group, Inc., The.

Wade, Mary Dodson. Amazing President Theodore Roosevelt. (Amazing Americans Ser.). (Illus.). 24p. (J). 2013. (gr. k-3). pap. 7.95 *(978-0-7660-5979-5(0)*, Enslow Elementary) 2009. (gr. 1-3). lib. bdg. 22.60 *(978-0-7660-3284-2(1))* Enslow Pubs., Inc.

Wagner, Heather Lehr. The Presidency. 2nd rev. ed. 2007. (U. S. Government Ser.). (Illus.). 112p. (YA). (gr. 5-9). lib. bdg. 30.00 *(978-0-7910-9284-2(4))* Facts On File, Inc.

Waldman, Neil. Voyages: Reminiscences of Young Abe Lincoln. 2009. (ENG., Illus.). 32p. (J). (gr. 5-9). 16.95 *(978-1-59078-471-6(5)*, Calkins Creek) Boyds Mills Pr.

Waryncia, Lou. Abraham Lincoln: Defender of the Union. Hale, Sarah Elder, ed. 2005. (ENG., Illus.). 48p. (J). (gr. 3-9). 17.95 *(978-0-8126-7902-1(4))* Cobblestone Publishing Co.

Waxman, Laura Hamilton. Franklin D. Roosevelt. 2004. (History Maker Bios Ser.). (J). pap. 6.95 *(978-0-8225-2539-4(9)*, Lerner Pubns.) Lerner Publishing Group.

—Gerald R. Ford. 2009. pap. 52.95 *(978-0-7613-4954-9(5))* 2008. (ENG.). 48p. (gr. 3-6). 27.93 *(978-0-8225-7985-4(5)*, Lerner Pubns.) Lerner Publishing Group.

—Jimmy Carter. 2006. (History Maker Biographies Ser.). (ENG., Illus.). 48p. (gr. 3-6). lib. bdg. 27.93 *(978-0-8225-5939-9(0)*, Lerner Pubns.) Lerner Publishing Group.

—Woodrow Wilson. 2006. (History Maker Biographies Ser.). (ENG., Illus.). 48p. (gr. 3-6). lib. bdg. 27.93 *(978-0-8225-6053-1(4)*, Lerner Pubns.) Lerner Publishing Group.

Wearing, Judy. Abraham Lincoln. 2010. (My Life Ser.). 24p. (J). (gr. 2-4). lib. bdg. 25.70 *(978-1-61690-056-4(3))* Weigl Pubs., Inc.

—Abraham Lincoln: My Life. 2010. pap. 9.95 *(978-1-61690-057-1(1))* Weigl Pubs., Inc.

Weintraub, Aileen. Lee Sobre George Washington/Read about George Washington. 2006. (I Like Biographies! Bilingual Ser.). (ENG & SPA., Illus.). 24p. (J). (gr. 1-3). lib. bdg. 21.26 *(978-0-7660-2673-5(6)*, Enslow Elementary) Enslow Pubs., Inc.

—Read about George Washington. 2004. (I Like Biographies! Ser.). (Illus.). 24p. (J). lib. bdg. 22.60 *(978-0-7660-2301-7(X))* Enslow Pubs., Inc.

Weiss, Ellen & Gormley, Beatrice. President George W. Bush: Our Forty-Third President. 2005. (ENG., Illus.). 208p. (J). (gr. 4-9). pap. 10.99 *(978-0-689-87834-3(6)*, Simon & Schuster/Paula Wiseman Bks.) Simon & Schuster/Paula Wiseman Bks.

Welch, Catherine A. George H. W. Bush. 2009. pap. 52.95 *(978-0-7613-4952-5(9))* 2008. (ENG.). 48p. (gr. 3-6). 27.93 *(978-0-8225-8895-5(1)*, Lerner Pubns.) Lerner Publishing Group.

West, David. George Washington: The Life of an American Patriot. 2009. (Graphic Nonfiction Biographies Ser.). (Illus.). 48p. (YA). (gr. 4-5). 58.50 *(978-1-61513-017-7(9)*, Rosen Reference) Rosen Publishing Group, Inc., The.

Weston Woods Staff, creator. What to Do about Alice? 2011. 38.75 *(978-0-545-29822-3(9))* Weston Woods Studios, Inc.

Wheeler, Jill C. Donald Trump. 2016. (United States Presidents Ser.). (ENG.). (J). (gr. 3-6). lib. bdg. 27.07 ***(978-1-68078-363-6(7))*** ABDO Publishing Co.

Whitelaw, Nancy. Andrew Jackson: Frontier President. 2004. (Notable Americans Ser.). (Illus.). 128p. (J). (gr. 6-12). 23.95 *(978-1-883846-67-1(6)*, First Biographies) Reynolds, Morgan Inc.

Wilhelm, Jeffrey. Ulysses S. Grant: From Failure to Hero. 2017. (ENG.). 32p. pap. 5.99 ***(978-1-63437-839-0(3))*** American Reading Co.

Wilson, Jon. The White House. 2014. (United States Landmarks Ser.). (ENG.). 24p. (J). (gr. 1-4). 27.07 *(978-1-62323-960-2(5)*, 206735) Child's World, Inc., The.

Wilson, Natashya. How to Draw the Life & Times of Herbert Hoover. (Kid's Guide to Drawing the Presidents of the United States of America Ser.). 32p. 2009. (gr. 4-4). 50.50 *(978-1-61511-144-2(1)*, PowerKids Pr.) 2007. (Illus.). (YA). (gr. 2-5). 26.50 *(978-1-4042-3007-1(6))* Rosen Publishing Group, Inc., The.

—How to Draw the Life & Times of William Howard Taft. 2009. (Kid's Guide to Drawing the Presidents of the United States of America Ser.). 32p. (gr. 4-4). 50.50 *(978-1-61511-165-7(4)*, PowerKids Pr.) Rosen Publishing Group, Inc., The.

Wilson, Natashya & Natashya, Wilson. How to Draw the Life & Times of James Earl Carter Jr. 2007. (Kid's Guide to Drawing the Presidents of the United States of America Ser.). (Illus.). 32p. (YA). (gr. 2-5). 26.50 *(978-1-4042-3015-6(7))* Rosen Publishing Group, Inc., The.

Winget, Mary Mueller. Gerald R. Ford. 2007. (Presidential Leaders Ser.). (Illus.). 112p. (J). (gr. 3-7). lib. bdg. 29.27 *(978-0-8225-1509-8(1)*, Twenty-First Century Bks.) Lerner Publishing Group.

Winter, Jonah. JFK. Ford, A. G., illus. 2013. (ENG.). 32p. (J). (gr. -1-3). 17.99 *(978-0-06-176807-1(3))* HarperCollins Pubs.

Winters, Kay. Abe Lincoln: The Boy Who Loved Books. Carpenter, Nancy, illus. 2004. 38p. (J). (gr. -1-3). reprint ed. 17.00 *(978-0-7567-7969-6(3))* DIANE Publishing Co.

—Abe Lincoln: The Boy Who Loved Books. Carpenter, Nancy, illus. 2006. (ENG.). 40p. (J). (gr. k-3). reprint ed. 7.99 *(978-1-4169-1268-2(1)*, Aladdin) Simon & Schuster Children's Publishing.

Winters, Kay & Carpenter, Nancy. Abe Lincoln: The Boy Who Loved Books. 2003. (ENG., Illus.). 40p. (J). (gr. k-3). 17.99 *(978-0-689-82554-5(4)*, Simon & Schuster Bks. For Young Readers) Simon & Schuster Bks. For Young Readers.

Wittekind, Erika. James Madison's Presidency. 2016. (Presidential Powerhouses Ser.). (ENG., Illus.). 104p. (J). (gr. 6-12). 35.99 *(978-1-4677-7929-6(6))*; 53.32 *(978-1-4677-8599-0(7)*, Lerner Pubns.) Lerner Publishing Group.

Wong, Angi Ma. Barack Obama: Historymaker. 2009. (Illus.). 104p. (J). *(978-1-928753-86-5(8))* Pacific Heritage Bks.

Wong, Angi Ma, illus. Meet President Obama: America's 44th President. 2009. 32p. (J). *(978-1-928753-28-5(0))* Pacific Heritage Bks.

Wood, Ethel, compiled by. The Presidency. 2004. (Historical Reader Ser.). (Illus.). 240p. (gr. 6-12). 13.32 *(978-0-618-04821-2(9)*, 2-00153) Holt McDougal.

World Book, Inc. Staff, contrib. by. The World Book of America's Presidents, 2 vols. 2005. (Illus.). (gr. 5-12). 99.00 *(978-0-7166-3698-4(0))* World Bk., Inc.

Wukovits, John F. George W Bush: People in the News. 2004. (Illus.). 111p. (J). (gr. 4-8). reprint ed. 22.00 *(978-0-7567-7902-3(2))* DIANE Publishing Co.

Yacka, Douglas. Who Was Andrew Jackson? Murray, Jake, illus. 2017. (Who Was? Ser.). (ENG.). 112p. (J). (gr. 3-7). 5.99 ***(978-0-399-53990-9(5))***; lib. bdg. 15.99 ***(978-0-399-53992-3(1))*** Penguin Young Readers Group. (Penguin Workshop).

Yomtov, Nel. Andrew Jackson: Heroic Leader or Cold-Hearted Ruler?, 1 vol. 2013. (Perspectives on History Ser.). (ENG.). 32p. (gr. 3-4). 27.32 *(978-1-4765-0245-8(5))*; pap. 7.95 *(978-1-4765-3409-1(8))* Capstone Press of Coughlan Cos. (Fact Finders).

Young, Bev. Presidential Cookies. 2nd ed. 2005. Orig. Title: Presidential Cookies the Lure & the Lore. (ENG., Illus.). 168p. (YA). 23.95 *(978-0-9729095-3-2(2)*, SAN 255-1077) Presidential Publishing.

Young, Jeff C. Dwight D. Eisenhower: Soldier & President. 2004. (Notable Americans Ser.). (Illus.). 128p. (YA). (gr. 6-12). 23.95 *(978-1-883846-76-3(5)*, First Biographies) Reynolds, Morgan Inc.

—James A. Garfield: A MyReportLinks.com Book. 2003. (Presidents Ser.). (Illus.). 48p. (J). (gr. 5-10). lib. bdg. 25.26 *(978-0-7660-5100-3(5)*, MyReportLinks.com Bks.) Enslow Pubs., Inc.

—James Buchanan: A MyReportLinks.com Book. 2003. (Presidents Ser.). (Illus.). 48p. (J). (gr. 4-10). lib. bdg. 25.26 *(978-0-7660-5101-0(3)*, MyReportLinks.com Bks.) Enslow Pubs., Inc.

Zahensky, Kenneth, ed. George W. Bush. 2017. (Pivotal Presidents: Profiles in Leadership Ser.). 80p. (J). (gr. 12-13). 33.90 ***(978-1-68048-629-2(2)***, Britannica Educational Publishing) Rosen Publishing Group, Inc., The.

Zamora, Dulce. How to Draw the Life & Times of Franklin Pierce. (Kid's Guide to Drawing the Presidents of the United States of America Ser.). 2009. 32p. (gr. 4-4). 50.50 *(978-1-61511-137-4(9)*, PowerKids Pr.) 2006. (YA). (gr. 2-5). 26.50 *(978-1-4042-2991-4(4))* Rosen Publishing Group, Inc., The.

—How to Draw the Life & Times of John F. Kennedy. 2005. (Kid's Guide to Drawing the Presidents of the United States of America Ser.). (Illus.). 32p. (YA). (gr. 2-5). lib. bdg. 25.25 *(978-1-4042-3011-8(4))* Rosen Publishing Group, Inc., The.

—How to Draw the Life & Times of John Fitzgerald Kennedy. 2009. (Kid's Guide to Drawing the Presidents of the United States of America Ser.). 32p. (gr. 4-4). 50.50 *(978-1-61511-151-0(4)*, PowerKids Pr.) Rosen Publishing Group, Inc., The.

—How to Draw the Life & Times of John Tyler. (Kid's Guide to Drawing the Presidents of the United States of America Ser.). 2009. 32p. (gr. 4-4). 50.50 *(978-1-61511-153-4(0)*, PowerKids Pr.) 2006. (YA). (gr. 2-5). 26.50 *(978-1-4042-2987-7(6))* Rosen Publishing Group, Inc., The.

Zeiger, Jennifer. Barack Obama. 2012. (Cornerstones of Freedom, Third Ser.). (ENG.). 64p. (J). (gr. 4-6). pap. 8.95 *(978-0-531-28150-5(7))*; lib. bdg. 30.00 *(978-0-531-23050-3(3))* Scholastic Library Publishing. (Children's Pr.).

Zuchora-Walske, Christine. Andrew Jackson's Presidency. 2016. (Presidential Powerhouses Ser.). (ENG., Illus.). 104p. (J). (gr. 6-12). 35.99 *(978-1-4677-7926-5(1)*, Lerner Pubns.) Lerner Publishing Group.

Zumbusch, Amelie von. Barack Obama: Man of Destiny. 2010. (Making History: the Obamas Ser.). (Illus.). 24p. (J). pap. 8.25 *(978-1-4358-9866-0(4))*; (gr. 2-3). lib. bdg. 22.60 *(978-1-4358-9387-0(5))* Rosen Publishing Group, Inc., The. (PowerKids Pr.).

—Making History: The Obamas, 4 vols., Set. Incl. Barack Obama: Man of Destiny. lib. bdg. 22.60 *(978-1-4358-9387-0(5))*; Barack Obama's Family Tree: Roots of Achievement. lib. bdg. 22.60 *(978-1-4358-9390-0(5))*; First Family: The Obamas in the White House. lib. bdg. 22.60 *(978-1-4358-9389-4(1))*; Michelle Obama: Our First Lady. lib. bdg. 22.60 *(978-1-4358-9388-7(3))*; (J). (gr. 2-3). (Illus.). 24p. 2010. 85.00 *(978-1-4358-9407-5(3)*, PowerKids Pr.) Rosen Publishing Group, Inc., The.

20 Fun Facts about the White House. 2013. (Fun Fact File: US History! Ser.). 32p. (J). (gr. 3-6). pap. 63.00 *(978-1-4339-9205-6(1))* Stevens, Gareth Publishing LLLP.

PRESIDENTS—UNITED STATES—ASSASSINATION

Denenberg, Barry. Lincoln Shot: A President's Life Remembered. Bing, Christopher, illus. 2008. (ENG.). 40p. (J). (gr. 5-9). 24.95 *(978-0-312-37013-8(X)*, 9780312370138) Feiwel & Friends.

Holzer, Harold. The President Is Shot! The Assassination of Abraham Lincoln. 2004. (ENG., Illus.). 184p. (J). (gr. 3-12). 17.95 *(978-1-56397-985-9(3))* Boyds Mills Pr.

Powell Smith, Brendan. Assassination! The Brick Chronicle Presents Attempts on the Lives of Twelve US Presidents. 2016. (ENG., Illus.). 272p. pap. 19.99 *(978-1-5107-0544-9(9))* Skyhorse Publishing Co., Inc.

Salandria, Vincent J. False Mystery: Essays on the Assassination of JFK. Kelin, John, ed. 2004. 25.00 *(978-0-9754941-0-3(4))* Square Deal Pr.

Smith, Brendan Powell. Assassination! The Brick Chronicle of Attempts on the Lives of Twelve US Presidents. 2013. (ENG., Illus.). 272p. 19.95 *(978-1-62087-998-6(0)*, 620998) Skyhorse Publishing Co., Inc.

Wilson, Antoine. The Assassination of William McKinley. (Library of Political Assassinations Ser.). 64p. 2009. (gr. 5-5). 58.50 *(978-1-60853-830-0(3))* 2003. (Illus.). (YA). (gr. 7-12). lib. bdg. 31.95 *(978-0-8239-3546-8(9))* Rosen Publishing Group, Inc., The.

PRESIDENTS—UNITED STATES—CHILDREN

see Children of Presidents

PRESIDENTS—UNITED STATES—ELECTION

Anderson, Holly Lynn. The Presidential Election Process. 2016. (Illus.). 64p. (J). *(978-1-61900-094-0(6))* Eldorado Ink.

Beyer, Mark. The Election of 1800: Congress Helps Settle a Three-Way Vote. 2004. (Life in the New American Nation Ser.). (ENG., Illus.). 32p. (gr. 5-8). pap. 10.00 *(978-0-8239-4255-8(4))* Rosen Publishing Group, Inc., The.

—The Election Of 1800: Congress Helps Settle a Three-Way Vote. 2009. (Life in the New American Nation Ser.). 32p. (gr. 4-4). 47.90 *(978-1-61514-282-8(7))* Rosen Publishing Group, Inc., The.

Biskup, Agnieszka. Obama: The Historic Election of America's 44th President, 1 vol. Hayden, Seitu, illus. 2011. (American Graphic Ser.). (ENG.). 32p. (gr. 3-4). pap. 8.10 *(978-1-4296-7339-6(7))*; pap. 47.70 *(978-1-4296-7340-2(0))*; lib. bdg. 30.65 *(978-1-4296-6016-7(3))* Capstone Press of Coughlan Cos. (Graphic Library).

Blashfield, Jean F. Hillary Clinton. 2010. (Leading Women Ser.). 96p. (YA). (gr. 7-12). 39.93 *(978-0-7614-4954-6(X))* Marshall Cavendish Corp.

Carole Marsh. Presidential Elections. 2004. (Presidents on Parade Ser.). lib. bdg. 29.95 *(978-0-635-02221-9(4))*; 48p. (gr. 3-8). pap. 7.95 *(978-0-635-02220-2(6))* Gallopade International.

Connell, Kate, et al. The Spirit of a New Nation. 2007. (Avenues Ser.). (ENG., Illus.). 40p. (J). pap. 19.95 *(978-0-7922-8684-4(7))* CENGAGE Learning.

Edwards, Roberta. Barack Obama: United States President. Call, Ken, illus. rev. exp. ed. 2009. (ENG.). 64p. (J). (gr. 1-3). mass mkt. 5.99 *(978-0-448-45234-0(0)*, Grosset & Dunlap) Penguin Young Readers Group.

Election 2004: Choosing America's President. 2004. (Illus.). 22p. (J). *(978-0-439-68921-2(X))* Scholastic, Inc.

Emmett, Dan & Maynard, Charles. I Am a Secret Service Agent: My Life Spent Protecting the President. 2017. (ENG., Illus.). 224p. (YA). 18.99 *(978-1-250-13030-3(1)*, 9781250130303, St. Martin's Griffin) St. Martin's Pr.

Gibson, Karen Bush. The Historic Fight for the 2008 Democratic Presidential Nomination: The Obama View. 2009. (Monumental Milestones Ser.). (Illus.). 48p. (YA). (gr. 4-7). lib. bdg. 29.95 *(978-1-58415-732-8(1))* Mitchell Lane Pubs., Inc.

Goldman, David J. Presidential Losers. 2004. (Middle Grade Nonfiction Ser.). (ENG., Illus.). 72p. (gr. 5-12). 25.26 *(978-0-8225-0100-8(7)*, Carolrhoda Bks.) Lerner Publishing Group.

Greenhaven Press Staff, ed. Mitt Romney. 2012. (People in the News Ser.). (ENG., Illus.). 128p. (gr. 7-10). lib. bdg. 33.95 *(978-1-4205-0877-2(6)*, Lucent Bks.) Cengage Gale.

Gunderson, Cory Gideon. 2000 Presidential Election, 1 vol. 2004. (American Moments Ser.). (ENG.). 48p. (gr. 4-8). 27.07 *(978-1-59197-284-6(1)*, Abdo & Daughters) ABDO Publishing Co.

Gunderson, Jessica. Election of 1860: A Nation Divides on the Eve of War. 2016. (J). pap. *(978-1-4914-8737-2(2))* Capstone Press of Coughlan Cos.

Gutman, Dan. Election! A Kid's Guide to Picking Our President 2012. 2012. (ENG.). 162p. (J). (gr. 2-6). pap. 11.99 *(978-1-4532-7066-0(3))* Open Road Integrated Media, Inc.

Havelin, Kate. Victoria Woodhull: Fearless Feminist. 2006. (Trailblazer Biographies Ser.). (ENG., Illus.). 112p. (gr. 5-9). lib. bdg. 31.93 *(978-0-8225-5986-3(2)*, Lerner Pubns.) Lerner Publishing Group.

Hunt, Santana. What Is the Electoral College? 2017. (Look at Your Government Ser.). 32p. (J). (gr. 2-2). pap. 10.50 ***(978-1-4824-6063-6(7))*** Stevens, Gareth Publishing LLLP.

Klein, Adria F. Barack Obama. 2009. pap. 13.25 *(978-1-60559-055-4(X))* Hameray Publishing Group, Inc.

Krasner, Barbara. A Timeline of Presidential Elections. 2016. (Presidential Politics Ser.). (ENG., Illus.). 48p. (gr. 3-4). lib. bdg. 29.32 *(978-1-4914-8239-1(7)*, Connect) Stone Arch Bks.

Krasner, Barbara, et al. Presidential Politics. 2016. (Presidential Politics Ser.). (ENG.). 48p. (gr. 3-4). 114.61 *(978-1-4914-8738-9(0)*, Connect) Stone Arch Bks.

Krull, Kathleen. A Woman for President: The Story of Victoria Woodhull. Dyer, Jane, illus. 2006. (J). (gr. 2-7). 14.60 *(978-0-7569-8179-2(4))* Perfection Learning Corp.

Mattern, Joanne. President Donald Trump. 2017. (Rookie Biographies(tm) Ser.). (ENG., Illus.). 32p. (J). lib. bdg. 25.00 ***(978-0-531-23226-2(3)***, Children's Pr.) Scholastic Library Publishing.

Morris-Lipsman, Arlene. Presidential Races: Campaigning for the White House. rev. ed. 2011. (People's History Ser.). (ENG., Illus.). 112p. (gr. 5-12). lib. bdg. 33.26 *(978-0-7613-7395-7(0)*, Twenty-First Century Bks.) Lerner Publishing Group.

—Presidential Races: The Battle for Power in the United States. 2007. (People's History Ser.). (ENG., Illus.). 112p. (gr. 5-12). lib. bdg. 33.26 *(978-0-8225-6783-7(0))* Lerner Publishing Group.

Obama, Barack & Nelson, Kadir. Change Has Come: An Artist Celebrates Our American Spirit. Nelson, Kadir, illus. 2009. (ENG., Illus.). 64p. (J). (gr. 1). 12.99 *(978-1-4169-8955-4(2)*, Simon & Schuster Bks. For Young Readers) Simon & Schuster Bks. For Young Readers.

Schlesinger, Arthur M., Jr., et al. History of American Presidential Elections, 1789-2008, 3 vols. 4th rev. ed. 2011. (Illus.). 1742p. (C). (gr. 9). 225.00 *(978-0-8160-8220-9(0))* Facts On File, Inc.

See, Betty. Electing the President: The Electoral Process in Action. 2005. 48p. pap. 14.95 *(978-1-59363-067-6(0))* Prufrock Pr.

St. George, Judith. So You Want to Be President? Small, David, illus. 2004. (J). (gr. 1-6). 29.95 *(978-1-55592-132-3(9))* Weston Woods Studios, Inc.

Stier, Catherine. If I Ran for President. Avril, Lynne, illus. 2012. (J). 34.28 *(978-1-61913-115-6(3))* Weigl Pubs., Inc.

Tolliver, Julia. The Distinguishable Gentleman & the Presidential Race Of '08. 2011. 202p. (gr. 1-1). 29.99 *(978-1-4535-8791-1(8))*; pap. 19.99 *(978-1-4535-8790-4(X))* Xlibris Corp.

Tracy, Kathleen. The Historic Fight for the 2008 Democratic Presidential Nomination: The Clinton View. 2009. (Monumental Milestones Ser.). (Illus.). 48p. (YA). (gr. 4-7). lib. bdg. 29.95 *(978-1-58415-731-1(3))* Mitchell Lane Pubs., Inc.

Vierow, Wendy. The 1864 Presidential Election: A War-Weary Nation Reelects President Abraham Lincoln. 2009. (Headlines from History Ser.). 24p. (gr. 3-3). 42.50 *(978-1-61513-239-3(2)*, PowerKids Pr.) Rosen Publishing Group, Inc., The.

Wagner, Heather Lehr. How the President Is Elected. 2007. (U. S. Government Ser.). (Illus.). 95p. (YA). (gr. 5-9). lib. bdg. 30.00 *(978-0-7910-9418-1(9))* Facts On File, Inc.

Yomtov, Nel. Sarah Palin: Political Rebel, 1 vol. D'Ottavi, Francesca, illus. 2011. (American Graphic Ser.). (ENG.). 32p. (gr. 3-4). pap. 8.10 *(978-1-4296-7341-9(9))*; pap. 47.70 *(978-1-4296-7342-6(7))* Capstone Press of Coughlan Cos. (Graphic Library).

Yomtov, Nelson. Sarah Palin: Political Rebel, 1 vol. D'Ottavi, Francesca, illus. 2011. (American Graphic Ser.). (ENG.). 32p. (gr. 3-4). lib. bdg. 30.65 *(978-1-4296-6018-1(X)*, Graphic Library) Capstone Press of Coughlan Cos.

Zacharias, Jared. Amendment XII: Presidential Election Process. 2008. (Constitutional Amendments Ser.). (ENG., Illus.). 160p. (gr. 9-12). lib. bdg. 43.20 *(978-0-7377-4123-0(6)*, LML02109-243012) Cengage Gale.

PRESIDENTS—UNITED STATES—FAMILY

Davis, Gibbs. First Kids. Comport, Sally Wern, illus. 2009. (Step into Reading Ser.). (ENG.). 48p. (J). (gr. 2-4). pap. 3.99 *(978-0-375-82218-6(6)*, Random Hse. Bks. for Young Readers) Random Hse. Children's Bks.

Holzer, Harold. Father Abraham: Lincoln & His Sons. 2011. (ENG., Illus.). 232p. (J). (gr. 5-18). 17.95 *(978-1-59078-303-0(4)*, Calkins Creek) Boyds Mills Pr.

Hopkinson, Deborah. First Family. Ford, A. G., illus. 2009. (ENG.). 32p. (J). (gr. -1-2). 17.99 *(978-0-06-189680-4(2)*, Tegen, Katherine Bks) HarperCollins Pubs.

Katirgis, Jane. Celebrating the Obama Family in Pictures. 2009. (Obama Family Photo Album Ser.). (Illus.). 32p. (J). (gr. 2-5). lib. bdg. 23.94 *(978-0-7660-3653-6(7))* Enslow Pubs., Inc.

Kerley, Barbara. What to Do about Alice? How Alice Roosevelt Broke the Rules, Charmed the World, & Drove Her Father Teddy Crazy! Fotheringham, Edwin, illus. 2008. (ENG.). 48p. (J). (gr. 2-5). 16.99 *(978-0-439-92231-9(3)*, Scholastic Pr.) Scholastic, Inc.

Marsh, Carole. Barack Obama - America's 44th President. 2008. (Here & Now Ser.). (Illus.). 40p. (J). (gr. 2-9). pap. 9.99 *(978-0-635-06848-4(6))* Gallopade International.

O'Connor, Jane. If the Walls Could Talk: Family Life at the White House. Hovland, Gary, illus. 2004. (ENG.). 48p. (J). (gr. 1-4). 17.99 *(978-0-689-86863-4(4)*, Simon & Schuster/Paula Wiseman Bks.) Simon & Schuster/Paula Wiseman Bks.

Snyder, Gail. Sasha. 2007. (Obamas Ser.). (Illus.). 64p. (YA). (gr. 3-6). pap. 9.95 *(978-1-4222-1487-9(7))*; (gr. 4-7). lib. bdg. 19.95 *(978-1-4222-1480-0(X))* Mason Crest.

Weston Woods Staff, creator. George Washington's Mother. 2011. 38.75 *(978-0-439-72669-6(7))*; 18.95 *(978-0-439-72667-2(0))* Weston Woods Studios, Inc.

Wheeler, Jill C. Harriet Lane, 1 vol. 2010. (First Ladies Set 2 Ser.). (ENG., Illus.). 32p. (YA). (gr. 1-4). 27.07 *(978-1-60453-631-7(4))* ABDO Publishing Co.

White House Insiders. 2014. (White House Insiders Ser.). 24p. (J). (gr. 2-5). pap. 41.70 *(978-1-4824-1595-7(X))* Stevens, Gareth Publishing LLLP.

Zumbusch, Amelie von. Barack Obama's Family Tree: Roots of Achievement. 2010. (Making History: the Obamas Ser.). (Illus.). 24p. (J). pap. 8.25 *(978-1-4358-9872-1(9))*; (gr. 2-3). lib. bdg. 22.60 *(978-1-4358-9390-0(5))* Rosen Publishing Group, Inc., The. (PowerKids Pr.).

—First Family: The Obamas in the White House. 2010. (Making History: the Obamas Ser.). (Illus.). 24p. (J). pap. 8.25 *(978-1-4358-9870-7(2))*; (gr. 2-3). lib. bdg. 22.60 *(978-1-4358-9389-4(1))* Rosen Publishing Group, Inc., The. (PowerKids Pr.).

PRESIDENTS—UNITED STATES—FICTION

Alger, Horatio. From Canal Boy to President: Or the Boyhood & Manhood of James A. Garfield. 2007. (ENG.). 196p. pap. 19.99 *(978-1-4346-2511-3(7))*; 208p. pap. 22.99 *(978-1-4346-2553-3(2))* Creative Media Partners, LLC.

Angleberger, Tom. Fake Mustache: Or, How Jodie o'Rodeo & Her Wonder Horse (and Some Nerdy Kid) Saved the U. S. Presidential Election from a Mad Genius Criminal Mastermind. 2013. (ENG.). 208p. (J). (gr. 3-7). pap. 7.95 *(978-1-4197-1163-3(6)*, Amulet Bks.) Abrams, Inc.

Bailey, Michael. Cartoon Nation, 6 bks., Set. Incl. Citizenship. Skog, Jason. Brown, Kelly, illus. 30.65 *(978-1-4296-1331-6(9))*; Political Elections. Miller, Davis Worth & Brevard, Katherine M. Barnett, Charles, III, illus. 30.65 *(978-1-4296-1333-0(5))*; Political Parties. Burgan, Michael & Hoena, Blake A. Barnett, Charles et al, illus. lib. bdg. 30.65 *(978-1-4296-1334-7(3))*; 32p. (gr. 3-4). (Cartoon Nation Ser.). (ENG.). 2008. 91.95 *(978-1-4296-1675-1(X)*, Graphic Library) Capstone Press of Coughlan Cos.

Barnett, Mac. President Taft Is Stuck in the Bath. Van Dusen, Chris, illus. 2016. (ENG.). 32p. (J). (gr. -1-3). 7.99 *(978-0-7636-6556-2(8))* Candlewick Pr.

Behrens, Rebecca. When Audrey Met Alice. 2014. (ENG.). 304p. (J). (gr. 4-7). 16.99 *(978-1-4022-8642-1(2)*, 9781402286421, Sourcebooks Jabberwocky) Sourcebooks, Inc.

Blundell, Gerald Lee. Bunkalunken Goes to Washington & Other Stories, 1 vol. 2010. 138p. pap. 24.95 *(978-1-4489-5234-2(4))* America Star Bks.

Cabot, Meg. All-American Girl. 2008. (All-American Girl Ser.: Vol. 1). 398p. (YA). (gr. 7-12). 19.65 *(978-1-4178-2386-4(0)*, Turtleback) Turtleback Bks.

—Ready or Not. (All-American Girl Ser.: 2). (ENG.). 2008. 336p. (YA). (gr. 8). pap. 8.99 *(978-0-06-147996-0(9)*, HarperTeen) 2005. 256p. (J). (gr. 7-18). 16.99 *(978-0-06-072450-4(1))* HarperCollins Pubs.

Calabrese, Diane Marie. My Dad's off to War. Swope, Brenda, illus. 2011. 28p. pap. 24.95 *(978-1-4560-0942-7(7))* America Star Bks.

Calloway, Cassidy. Confessions of a First Daughter. 2009. (ENG.). 224p. (YA). (gr. 8-18). pap. 9.99 *(978-0-06-172439-8(4)*, HarperTeen) HarperCollins Pubs.

Cavanah, Frances. Abe Lincoln Gets His Chance. 2007. 72p. per. *(978-1-4068-4447-4(0))* Echo Library.

Cobot, Meg. All-American Girl. 2004. 416p. (J). (gr. 7-18). pap. 44.00 incl. audio *(978-0-8072-2281-2(X)*, Listening Library) Random Hse. Audio Publishing Group.

DeVillers, Julia. Cleared for Takeoff. Pooler, Paige, illus. 2012. (Liberty Porter, First Daughter Ser.: 3). (ENG.). 224p. (J). (gr. 3-7). pap. 7.99 *(978-1-4169-9131-1(X)*, Simon & Schuster/Paula Wiseman Bks.) Simon & Schuster/Paula Wiseman Bks.

—Liberty Porter, First Daughter. Pooler, Paige, illus. (Liberty Porter, First Daughter Ser.: 1). (ENG.). (J). (gr. 3-7). 2010. 192p. pap. 6.99 *(978-1-4169-9127-4(1))* 2009. 176p. 15.99 *(978-1-4169-9126-7(3))* Simon & Schuster/Paula Wiseman Bks. (Simon & Schuster/Paula Wiseman Bks.).

—New Girl in Town. Pooler, Paige, illus. 2010. (Liberty Porter, First Daughter Ser.: 2). (ENG.). 208p. (J). (gr. 3-7). 15.99 *(978-1-4169-9128-1(X)*, Simon & Schuster/Paula Wiseman Bks.) Simon & Schuster/Paula Wiseman Bks.

Dipucchio, Kelly. Grace for President. Pham, LeUyen, illus. 2012. (ENG.). 40p. (J). (gr. 1-3). 16.99 *(978-1-4231-3999-7(2))* Hyperion Pr.

Edwards, Myrtice J. Dirty Sally. 2007. 44p. per. 18.95 *(978-1-4327-0774-3(4))* Outskirts Pr., Inc.

Fosberry, Jennifer. Isabella for President. Litwin, Mike, illus. 2016. (ENG.). 32p. (J). (-4). 16.99 *(978-1-4926-4173-5(1)*, 9781492641735, Sourcebooks Jabberwocky) Sourcebooks, Inc.

Freeman, Martha. The Case of the Bug on the Run. 2014. (First Kids Mystery Ser.: 6). (ENG.). 144p. (J). (gr. 2-7). pap. 6.99 *(978-0-8234-3188-5(6))* Holiday Hse., Inc.

—The Case of the Bug on the Run: First Kids Mystery #6. 2013. (First Kids Mystery Ser.: 6). (ENG.). 144p. (J). (gr. 2-7). 16.95 *(978-0-8234-2872-4(9))* Holiday Hse., Inc.

—The Case of the Diamond Dog Collar. 2nd ed. (First Kids Mystery Ser.: 2). (ENG.). 144p. (J). 2012. Illus.). (gr. 3-5). pap. 6.99 *(978-0-8234-2642-3(4))* 2011. 16.95 *(978-0-8234-2337-8(9))* Holiday Hse., Inc.

—The Case of the Missing Dinosaur Egg. Dibley, Glin, illus. 2014. (First Kids Mystery Ser.: 5). (ENG.). 115p. (J). (gr. 3-7). pap. 6.99 *(978-0-8234-3061-1(8))* Holiday Hse., Inc.

—The Case of the Missing Dinosaur Egg. 2013. (First Kids Mystery Ser.: 5). (ENG.). 144p. (J). (gr. 3-7). 16.95 *(978-0-8234-2523-5(1))* Holiday Hse., Inc.

—The Case of the Piggy Bank Thief: First Kids Mystery #4. 2013. (First Kids Mystery Ser.: 4). (ENG.). 144p. (J). (gr. 1-5). pap. 6.99 *(978-0-8234-2916-5(4))* Holiday Hse., Inc.

—The Case of the Rock 'N' Roll Dog. 2010. (First Kids Mystery Ser.: 1). (ENG., Illus.). 128p. (J). (gr. 1-5). 16.95 *(978-0-8234-2267-8(4))* Holiday Hse., Inc.

—The Case of the Rock 'n' Roll Dog. 2012. (First Kids Mystery Ser.: 1). (ENG.). 128p. (J). (gr. 3-5). pap. 6.99 *(978-0-8234-2549-5(5))* Holiday Hse., Inc.

—The Case of the Ruby Slippers. (First Kids Mystery Ser.: 3). (ENG.). 128p. (J). 2013. pap. 6.99 *(978-0-8234-2764-2(1))* 2012. 16.95 *(978-0-8234-2409-2(X))* Holiday Hse., Inc.

Gilchrist, Jan Spivey. Obama: The Day the World Danced. 2009. (Illus.). 32p. (J). (gr. k-3). 18.99 *(978-0-9824095-0-3(8))* Pegasus Bks. for Children.

Gingrich, Callista. Hail to the Chief. Arciero, Susan, illus. 2016. (Ellis the Elephant Ser.). (ENG.). 40p. (J). (gr. -1-4). 16.99 *(978-1-62157-479-8(2)*, Regnery Kids) Regnery Publishing, Inc., An Eagle Publishing Co.

Gould, Jane H. John Adams. 2012. (Jr. Graphic Founding Fathers Ser.). (ENG., Illus.). 24p. (J). (gr. 3-6). pap. 10.60 *(978-1-4488-7993-9(0))*; lib. bdg. 25.25 *(978-1-4488-7899-4(3))* Rosen Publishing Group, Inc., The. (PowerKids Pr.).

Gutman, Dan. The Kid Who Became President. 2012. (ENG.). 240p. (J). (gr. 3-7). pap. 6.99 *(978-0-545-44214-5(1)*, Scholastic Paperbacks) Scholastic, Inc.

Hill, Genita S. President Obama's Ghost. 2012. 28p. pap. 24.95 *(978-1-4626-4404-9(X))* America Star Bks.

Hutton, John. Flowers for Mr. President. 2012. (Illus.). (J). *(978-0-9789608-3-4(1))* Salem Academy & College.

James, Tina. Sarabeth Palmer: 1963-1964. 2010. 91p. (J). *(978-0-615-37484-0(0))* Afrolez Productions, LLC.

Kelaita, Lynda. Some Houses Are White. 2009. 32p. pap. 10.95 *(978-1-935125-44-0(3))* Robertson Publishing.

Kennedy Center Staff. Chasing George Washington. Hoyt, Ard, illus. 2011. (ENG.). 80p. (J). (gr. 2-5). pap. 5.99 *(978-1-4169-4861-2(9)*, Simon & Schuster Bks. For Young Readers) Simon & Schuster Bks. For Young Readers.

—Teddy Roosevelt & the Treasure of Ursa Major. Hoyt, Ard, illus. 2011. (ENG.). 128p. (J). (gr. 2-5). pap. 5.99 *(978-1-4169-4860-5(0)*, Simon & Schuster Bks. For Young Readers) Simon & Schuster Bks. For Young Readers.

Kidd, Ronald, et al. Chasing George Washington. Hoyt, Ard, illus. 2009. (ENG.). 80p. (J). (gr. 2-5). 12.99 *(978-1-4169-4858-2(9)*, Simon & Schuster Bks. For Young Readers) Simon & Schuster Bks. For Young Readers.

Krause, Robert. The President's Counting Book: The Future Generations of America. 2011. 36p. pap. 18.41 *(978-1-4269-6049-9(2))* Trafford Publishing.

Limbaugh, Rush H., III & Limbaugh, Kathryn Adams. Rush Revere & the Presidency. 2016. (Rush Revere Ser.: 5). (ENG., Illus.). 272p. (gr. 4-7). 19.99 *(978-1-5011-5689-2(6)*, Threshold Editions) Threshold Editions.

Marciano, John Bemelmans. Madeline at the White House. (Madeline Ser.). (ENG., (J). (gr. -1-2). 2016. Illus.). 48p. 8.99 *(978-1-101-99780-2(X)*, Puffin Books) 2011. 45p. 17.99 *(978-0-670-01228-2(9)*, Viking Books for Young Readers) Penguin Young Readers Group.

—Madeline at the White House. 2016. (Madeline Ser.). lib. bdg. 19.65 *(978-0-606-38845-0(1))* Turtleback Bks.

Marie, Cherry. The President Eats Vegetables & So Do I! 2012. 44p. pap. 12.00 *(978-0-9853259-0-9(9))* Professional Publishing Hse. LLC.

McDonald, Megan. Stink: The Incredible Shrinking Kid. Reynolds, Peter H., illus. 2010. (Stink Ser.: No. 1). 112p. (J). (gr. k-4). 24.21 *(978-1-59961-686-5(6))* Spotlight.

—Stink, el Increíble Niño Menguante. 2008. (SPA.). 272p. (J). (gr. 3-5). pap. 7.95 *(978-1-60396-193-6(3))* Ediciones Alfaguara ESP. Dist: Two Rivers Distribution.

McNamara, Margaret. Presidents' Day. Gordon, Mike, illus. 2010. (Robin Hill School Ser.). (ENG.). 32p. (J). (gr. -1-1). pap. 3.99 *(978-1-4169-9170-0(0)*, Simon Spotlight) Simon Spotlight.

Meddaugh, Susan. White House Dog. 2011. (Martha Speaks Ser.). (ENG., Illus.). 96p. (J). (gr. 1-4). 14.99 *(978-0-547-39359-9(8))*; pap. 5.99 *(978-0-547-21076-6(0))* Houghton Mifflin Harcourt Publishing Co.

Nave, Jeff. Obama's Pajamas. 2008. 44p. pap. 18.99 *(978-1-4389-3150-0(6))* AuthorHouse.

Osborne, Mary Pope. Abe Lincoln at Last! Murdocca, Sal, illus. 2013. (Magic Tree House Merlin Mission Ser.: 19). (ENG.). 144p. (J). (gr. 2-5). 5.99 *(978-0-375-86797-2(X)*, Random Hse. Bks. for Young Readers) Random Hse. Children's Bks.

—Abe Lincoln at Last! 2013. (Magic Tree House Merlin Missions Ser.: 19). lib. bdg. 16.00 *(978-0-606-35563-6(4))* Turtleback Bks.

Pollock, Hal. Monster for President. Parisi, Anthony, illus. 2008. 28p. 14.95 *(978-0-9816554-1-3(6))* Esquire Publishing, Inc.

Rolle Williams, Joyce. Chris's Story: A Family Voting Secret Revealed. 2008. 24p. pap. 12.99 *(978-1-4389-4258-2(3))* AuthorHouse.

Roy, Ron. The Election-Day Disaster. Bush, Timothy, illus. 2008. (Capital Mysteries Ser.: No. 10). 87p. (gr. 1-4). 15.00 *(978-0-7569-8802-9(0))* Perfection Learning Corp.

—The Secret at Jefferson's Mansion. Bush, Timothy, illus. 2009. (Capital Mysteries Ser.: 11). (ENG.). 96p. (J). (gr. 1-4). 4.99 *(978-0-375-84533-8(X)*, Random Hse. Bks. for Young Readers) Random Hse. Children's Bks.

Roy, Ronald. Turkey Trouble on the National Mall. Bush, Timothy, illus. 2012. (Capital Mysteries Ser.: 14). (ENG.). 96p. (J). (gr. 1-4). 4.99 *(978-0-307-93220-4(6)*, Random Hse. Bks. for Young Readers) Random Hse. Children's Bks.

Ruiz, Rachel. When Penny Met POTUS. Manwill, Melissa A., illus. 2016. (Fiction Picture Bks.). (ENG.). 32p. (gr. 2-3). lib. bdg. 27.99 *(978-1-5158-0218-1(3)*, Fiction Picture Bks.) Picture Window Bks.

Salamoff, Paul J. Bo Obama: The White House Tails. 2010. (ENG.). 40p. pap. 6.99 *(978-1-61623-925-1(5))* Bluewater Productions, Inc.

Schmidt, Gary D. First Boy. 2007. (ENG.). 224p. (YA). (gr. 5-9). per. 10.99 *(978-0-312-37149-4(7)*, 9780312371494) Square Fish.

Smith, Lane. Madam President. Smith, Lane, illus. 2008. (ENG., Illus.). 40p. (J). (gr. -1-k). 16.99 *(978-1-4231-0846-7(9))* Hyperion Pr.

—Madam President. 2011. (J). (gr. 1-4). 29.95 *(978-0-545-10688-7(5))* Weston Woods Studios, Inc.

St. George, Judith. The Ghost, the White House & Me. 2007. (ENG.). 128p. (J). (gr. 4-7). 16.95 *(978-0-8234-2045-2(0))* Holiday Hse., Inc.

Stier, Catherine. If I Ran for President. Avril, Lynne, illus. 2007. (ENG.). 32p. (J). (gr. 1-3). pap. 6.99 *(978-0-8075-3544-8(3))* Whitman, Albert & Co.

Sun Edit and Book Design, ed. Abraham Lincoln & the Forest of Little Pigeon Creek. 2007. (Illus.). 56p. (J). 19.95 *(978-0-9798739-0-4(8))* AmeriTales Entertainment, LLC.

Tubridy, Ryan. Patrick & the President. Lynch, P. J., illus. 2017. (ENG.). 40p. (J). (gr. 1-4). 16.99 *(978-0-7636-8949-0(1))* Candlewick Pr.

Walter, Aaron T. Mr Lincoln's Hat. 2008. 75p. pap. 16.95 *(978-1-60672-852-9(0))* PublishAmerica, Inc.

Walton, Rick. Mr. President Goes to School, 1 vol. Sneed, Brad, illus. 2010. (ENG.). 32p. (J). (gr. -1-3). 15.95 *(978-1-56145-538-6(5))* Peachtree Pubs.

Wells, Rosemary. Lincoln & His Boys. Lynch, P. J., illus. 2008. (ENG.). 96p. (J). (gr. 3-7). 16.99 *(978-0-7636-3723-1(8))* Candlewick Pr.

Widdemer, Mabel Cleland. James Monroe, Good Neighbor Boy: Childhood of Famous Americans Series. Rawson, Maurice, illus. 2011. 200p. 44.95 *(978-1-258-07964-2(X))* Literary Licensing, LLC.

Worley, Michelle. Buster Goes to the White House, 1 vol. 2009. 48p. pap. 16.95 *(978-1-61546-352-7(6))* PublishAmerica, Inc.

Ziefert, Harriet & National Geographic Learning Staff. I'm Going to Washington to Visit the President. Roitman, Tanya, illus. 2010. (Rise & Shine Ser.). (ENG.). 24p. (C). (gr. -1-k). pap. 6.95 *(978-1-4027-3408-3(5))* National Geographic School Publishing, Inc.

PRESIDENTS—UNITED STATES—POETRY

Katz, Susan. The President's Stuck in the Bathtub: Poems about the Presidents. Neubecker, Robert, illus. 2012. (ENG.). 64p. (J). (gr. 1-4). 18.99 *(978-0-547-18221-6(X))* Houghton Mifflin Harcourt Publishing Co.

Raczka, Bob. Presidential Misadventures: Poems That Poke Fun at the Man in Charge. Burr, Dan E., illus. 2015. (ENG.). 48p. (J). (gr. 3-7). 17.99 *(978-1-59643-980-1(7)*, 9781596439801) Roaring Brook Pr.

Singer, Marilyn. Rutherford B., Who Was He? Poems about Our Presidents. Hendrix, John, illus. 2013. (ENG.). 56p. (YA). (gr. 1-3). 17.99 *(978-1-4231-7100-3(4))* Hyperion Pr.

PRESIDENTS—UNITED STATES—POWER

see Executive Power

PRESIDENTS—UNITED STATES—SPOUSES

see Presidents' Spouses

PRESIDENTS' SPOUSES

Abrams, Dennis. Hillary Rodham Clinton: Politician. 2009. (Women of Achievement Ser.). (Illus.). 144p. (gr. 6-12). 35.00 *(978-1-60413-077-5(6)*, Chelsea Hse.) Facts On File, Inc.

Adler, David A. & Adler, Michael S. A Picture Book of Dolley & James Madison. Himler, Ronald, illus. 2009. (ENG.). 32p. (J). (gr. -1-3). 17.95 *(978-0-8234-2009-4(4))* Holiday Hse., Inc.

—A Picture Book of John & Abigail Adams. Himler, Ronald, illus. 2010. (ENG.). 32p. (J). (gr. -1-3). 17.95 *(978-0-8234-2007-0(8))* Holiday Hse., Inc.

Agins, Donna Brown. Jacqueline Kennedy Onassis: Legendary First Lady. 2004. (People to Know Ser.). (Illus.). 128p. (J). lib. bdg. 26.60 *(978-0-7660-2186-0(6))* Enslow Pubs., Inc.

Alexander, Heather & dePaola, Tomie. Who Is Hillary Clinton? Harrison, Nancy & Putra, Dede, illus. 2016. (Who Was? Ser.). (ENG.). 112p. (J). (gr. 3-7). lib. bdg. 15.99 *(978-0-399-54234-3(5)*, Grosset & Dunlap) Penguin Young Readers Group.

Anthony, Carl Sferrazza. America's Most Influential First Ladies. 2003. (Illus.). 160p. (gr. 5-18). lib. bdg. 19.95 *(978-1-881508-69-4(2))* Oliver Pr., Inc.

Appelt, Kathi. Miss Lady Bird's Wildflowers: How a First Lady Changed America. Hein, Joy Fisher, illus. 2005. 40p. (J). lib. bdg. 17.89 *(978-0-06-001108-6(4))* HarperCollins Pubs.

Ashby, Ruth. John & Abigail Adams. 2005. (Presidents & First Ladies Ser.). (Illus.). 48p. (gr. 5-12). lib. bdg. 31.00 *(978-0-8368-5755-9(0)*, World Almanac Library) Stevens, Gareth Publishing LLLP.

—Woodrow & Edith Wilson. 2005. (Presidents & First Ladies Ser.). (Illus.). 48p. (gr. 5-12). lib. bdg. 31.00 *(978-0-8368-5759-7(3)*, World Almanac Library) Stevens, Gareth Publishing LLLP.

Bader, Bonnie. Who Was Jackie Kennedy? Qiu, Joseph J. M., illus. 2016. (Who Was? Ser.). (ENG.). 112p. (J). (gr. 3-7). lib. bdg. 15.99 *(978-0-399-54242-8(6)*, Grosset & Dunlap) Penguin Young Readers Group.

—Who Was Jacqueline Kennedy? Qiu, Joseph J. M., illus. 2016. (Who Was... ? Ser.). (ENG.). 112p. (J). (gr. 3-7). 16.00 *(978-0-606-39327-0(7))* Turtleback Bks.

Bausum, Ann. Our Country's First Ladies. 2007. (ENG., Illus.). 128p. (J). (gr. 5-9). 19.95 *(978-1-4263-0006-6(9))*; lib. bdg. 28.90 *(978-1-4263-0007-3(7))* National Geographic Society. (National Geographic Children's Bks.).

Belton, Blair. Abigail Adams in Her Own Words, Vol. 1. 2014. (Eyewitness to History Ser.). 32p. (J). (gr. 4-5). (ENG.). pap. 10.50 *(978-1-4339-9871-3(8))*; 26.60 *(978-1-4339-9870-6(X))* Stevens, Gareth Publishing LLLP.

Blashfield, Jean F. Hillary Clinton. 2010. (Leading Women Ser.). 96p. (YA). (gr. 7-12). 39.93 *(978-0-7614-4954-6(X))* Marshall Cavendish Corp.

Blohm, Craig E. Hillary Clinton. 2016. (ENG.). 80p. (J). 38.60 *(978-1-60152-950-3(3))* ReferencePoint Pr., Inc.

Blumenthal, Karen. Hillary Rodham Clinton: A Woman Living History. 2016. (ENG., Illus.). 448p. (J). 18.99 *(978-1-250-06014-3(1)*, 9781250060143) Feiwel & Friends.

Bodden, Valerie. Hillary Clinton: Historic Leader, 1 vol. 2009. (Essential Lives Set 4 Ser.). (ENG., Illus.). 112p. (J). (gr. 6-12). lib. bdg. 35.64 *(978-1-60453-699-7(3))* ABDO Publishing Co.

—Michelle Obama: First Lady & Role Model, 1 vol. 2009. (Essential Lives Set 4 Ser.). (ENG., Illus.). 112p. (J). (gr. 6-12). lib. bdg. 35.64 *(978-1-60453-703-1(5))* ABDO Publishing Co.

Brill, Marlene Targ. Michelle Obama. 2009. (Illus.). 48p. (J). pap. 8.95 *(978-0-7613-5053-8(5))* Lerner Publishing Group.

—Michelle Obama: From Chicago's South Side to the White House. 2009. (Gateway Biographies Ser.). (ENG., Illus.). 48p. (gr. 4-8). 26.60 *(978-0-7613-5033-0(0))* Lerner Publishing Group.

Brophy, David B. Michelle Obama: Meet the First Lady. 2008. 128p. (J). pap. 6.99 *(978-0-06-177990-9(3))* HarperCollins Pubs.

Brophy, David Bergen. Michelle Obama: Meet the First Lady. 2009. (ENG.). 128p. (J). (gr. 3-7). 16.99 *(978-0-06-177991-6(1)*, Collins) HarperCollins Pubs.

Brown, Don. Dolley Madison Saves George Washington. Brown, Don, illus. 2007. (ENG., Illus.). 32p. (J). (gr. -1-3). 16.00 *(978-0-618-41199-3(2))* Houghton Mifflin Harcourt Publishing Co.

Brown, Jonatha A. Eleanor Roosevelt. 2005. (Gente que hay que conocer (People We Should Know- Spanish) Ser.). 24p. (gr. 1-4). (ENG & SPA.). pap. 8.15 *(978-0-8368-4591-4(9))*; (ENG & SPA.). lib. bdg. 22.00 *(978-0-8368-4584-6(6))*; (Illus.). pap. 8.15 *(978-0-8368-4475-7(0))*; (Illus.). lib. bdg. 22.00 *(978-0-8368-4468-9(8))* Stevens, Gareth Publishing LLLP. (Weekly Reader Leveled Readers).

Buller, Jon & Warner, Sally. Smart about the First Ladies: Smart about History. Buller, Jon et al, illus. 2004. (Smart about History Ser.). (ENG.). 48p. (J). (gr. k-4). mass mkt. 5.99 *(978-0-448-43724-8(4)*, Grosset & Dunlap) Penguin Young Readers Group.

Burgan, Michael. Hillary Clinton, 1 vol. 2014. (Extraordinary Women Ser.). (ENG.). 48p. (gr. 6-6). lib. bdg. 32.65 *(978-1-4109-5941-6(4))* Heinemann-Raintree.

Burlingame, Jeff. Hillary Clinton: A Life in Politics. 2008. (People to Know Today Ser.). (Illus.). 112p. (J). (gr. 3-7). lib. bdg. 33.27 *(978-0-7660-2892-0(5))* Enslow Pubs., Inc.

Ching, Jacqueline. Abigail Adams: A Revolutionary Woman. 2009. (Library of American Lives & Times Ser.). 112p. (gr. 5-5). 69.20 *(978-1-60853-469-2(3))* Rosen Publishing Group, Inc., The.

Cohen, Della. Eleanor Roosevelt: Proud & Tall. 2005. (Illus.). 16p. (J). pap. *(978-0-7367-2879-9(1))* Zaner-Bloser, Inc.

Colbert, David. Michelle Obama: An American Story. 2008. (ENG., Illus.). 160p. (J). (gr. 2-5). pap. 6.99 *(978-0-547-24770-0(2))* Houghton Mifflin Harcourt Publishing Co.

Collard, Sneed B., III. Eleanor Roosevelt: Making the World a Better Place. 2008. (American Heroes Ser.). 48p. (gr. 3-18). lib. bdg. 29.93 *(978-0-7614-3069-8(5)*, Benchmark Bks.) Marshall Cavendish Corp.

—Lady Bird Johnson: Keeping America Green. 2009. (American Heroes Ser.). 48p. (gr. 3-18). 29.93 *(978-0-7614-4056-7(9))* Marshall Cavendish Corp.

Connors, Kathleen. What's It Like to Be the First Lady? 2014. (White House Insiders Ser.). 24p. (J). (gr. 2-5). 22.60 *(978-1-4824-1090-7(7))* Stevens, Gareth Publishing LLLP.

Doak, Robin S. Eleanor Roosevelt, 1 vol. 2012. (American Biographies Ser.). (ENG.). 48p. (gr. 4-6). pap. 9.95 *(978-1-4329-6461-0(5)*, NA-h) Heinemann-Raintree.

—Hillary Clinton. 2013. (True Book™—Biographies Ser.). (ENG., Illus.). 48p. (J). pap. 6.95 *(978-0-531-23877-6(6))*; lib. bdg. 29.00 *(978-0-531-21906-5(2))* Scholastic Library Publishing.

—Michelle Obama, 1 vol. 2014. (Extraordinary Women Ser.). (ENG., Illus.). 48p. (gr. 6-6). lib. bdg. 32.65 *(978-1-4109-5940-9(6))* Heinemann-Raintree.

Donnelly, Shannon. Eleanor Roosevelt. Wolek, Guy, illus. 2005. (Heroes of America Ser.). 236p. (gr. 3-8). 27.07 *(978-1-59679-260-9(4)*, Abdo & Daughters) ABDO Publishing Co.

Dorling Kindersley Publishing Staff. DK Eyewitness Books: First Ladies. 2017. (DK Eyewitness Bks.). (ENG., Illus.). 72p. (J). (gr. 3-7). pap. 9.99 *(978-1-4654-5851-3(4)*, DK Children) Dorling Kindersley Publishing, Inc.

Dorling Kindersley Publishing Staff. First Ladies. 2017. (Eyewitness Bks.). lib. bdg. 20.85 ***(978-0-606-39894-7(5))*** Turtleback Bks.

Edge, Laura Bufano. Laura Bush: Portrait of a First Lady. 2006. (People to Know Today Ser.). (Illus.). 128p. (J). (gr. 6). lib. bdg. 31.93 *(978-0-7660-2629-2(9))* Enslow Pubs., Inc.

Edwards, Roberta. Michelle Obama: Primera Dama y Primera Mama. Call, Ken, illus. 2010. (SPA.). 48p. (gr. 3-5). pap. 9.99 *(978-1-60396-946-8(2))* Santillana USA Publishing Co., Inc.

Egan, Jill. Hillary Rodham Clinton. 2009. (People We Should Know Ser.). (ENG., Illus.). 48p. (J). (gr. 3-5). lib. bdg. 31.00 *(978-1-4339-2188-9(X)*, Gareth Stevens Learning Library) Stevens, Gareth Publishing LLLP.

Endsley, Kezia. Michelle Obama: 44th First Lady & Health & Education Advocate. 2014. (Leading Women Ser.). 112p. (YA). (gr. 7-11). lib. bdg. 39.93 *(978-1-62712-975-6(8))* Cavendish Square Publishing.

Epstein, Dwayne. Hillary Clinton. 2010. (People in the News Ser.). (Illus.). 128p. (J). 33.95 *(978-1-4205-0268-8(9)*, Lucent Bks.) Cengage Gale.

PQR

Eva Peron. 2010. (Great Hispanic Heritage Ser.). (Illus.). 104p. (gr. 6-12). 35.00 *(978-1-60413-729-3(0)*, Chelsea Hse.) Facts On File, Inc.

Favor, Lesli J. Eva Perón. 2010. (Leading Women Ser.). 96p. (gr. 6). 39.93 *(978-0-7614-4962-1(0))* Marshall Cavendish Corp.

Feinberg, Barbara Silberdick. Eleanor Roosevelt: Everything She Could Be. 2003. (Gateway Biography Ser.: 4). (Illus.). 48p. lib. bdg. 23.90 *(978-0-7613-2623-6(5)*, Millbrook Pr.) Lerner Publishing Group.

First Ladies. 2010. (First Ladies Ser.). (ENG.). 24p. (gr. k-1). lib. bdg. 133.25 *(978-1-4296-5329-9(9)*, Pebble Plus) Capstone Press of Coughlan Cos.

Fitzgerald, Stephanie. Hillary Clinton. rev. ed. 2017. (Rookie Biographies(tm) Ser.). (ENG., Illus.). 32p. (J). lib. bdg. 25.00 ***(978-0-531-22931-6(9))*** Scholastic Library Publishing.

Fleming, Candace. Our Eleanor: A Scrapbook Look at Eleanor Roosevelt's Remarkable Life. 2005. (ENG., Illus.). 192p. (J). (gr. 4-8). 24.99 *(978-0-689-86544-2(9)*, Atheneum Bks. for Young Readers) Simon & Schuster Children's Publishing.

Freedman, Jeri. Hillary Rodham Clinton: Profile of a Leading Democrat. (Career Profiles Ser.). 112p. 2009. (gr. 9-10). 63.90 *(978-1-61511-794-9(6))* 2007. (YA). (gr. 7-12). lib. bdg. 34.60 *(978-1-4042-1910-6(2))* Rosen Publishing Group, Inc., The.

Glass, Maya. Abigail Adams: Destacada Primera Dama. 2004. (Grandes personajes en la historia de los Estados Unidos Ser.). (SPA.). 32p. (gr. 5-8). pap. 10.00 *(978-0-8239-4218-3(X)*, Rosen Classroom) Rosen Publishing Group, Inc., The.

—Abigail Adams: Destacada Primera Dama (Abigail Adams: Famous First Lady) 2009. (Grandes personajes en la historia de los Estados Unidos (Famous People in American History) Ser.). (SPA.). 32p. (gr. 2-3). 47.90 *(978-1-61512-787-0(9)*, Editorial Buenas Letras) Rosen Publishing Group, Inc., The.

—Abigail Adams: Famous First Lady. (Primary Sources of Famous People in American History Ser.). 32p. 2009. (gr. 2-3). 47.90 *(978-1-60851-643-8(1))* 2004. (ENG., Illus.). (gr. 4-8). pap. 10.00 *(978-0-8239-4172-8(8))* Rosen Publishing Group, Inc., The.

—Abigail Adams: Famous First Lady / Destacada Primera Dama. 2009. (Famous People in American History/Grandes personajes en la historia de los Estados Unidos Ser.). (ENG & SPA.). 32p. (gr. 2-3). 47.90 *(978-1-61512-535-7(3)*, Editorial Buenas Letras) Rosen Publishing Group, Inc., The.

Gormley, Beatrice. Laura Bush: America's First Lady. 2005. 122p. (J). lib. bdg. 15.00 *(978-1-59054-921-6(X))* Fitzgerald Bks.

—Laura Bush: America's First Lady. 2003. (ENG., Illus.). 128p. (J). (gr. 3-7). pap. 4.99 *(978-0-689-85366-1(1)*, Simon & Schuster/Paula Wiseman Bks.) Simon & Schuster/Paula Wiseman Bks.

Guernsey, JoAnn B. Hillary Rodham Clinton. 2005. (Biography Ser.). (Illus.). 112p. (J). (gr. 6-18). pap. 7.95 *(978-0-8225-9613-4(X))* Lerner Publishing Group.

Guernsey, Joann Bren. Hillary Rodham Clinton. 2005. (Biography Ser.). (Illus.). 112p. (J). (gr. 3-7). lib. bdg. 29.27 *(978-0-8225-2372-7(8)*, Lerner Pubns.) Lerner Publishing Group.

—Hillary Rodham Clinton: Secretary of State. 2009. (USA TODAY Lifeline Biographies Ser.). (ENG.). 112p. (gr. 6-12). lib. bdg. 34.60 *(978-0-7613-5122-1(1))* Lerner Publishing Group.

Haldy, Emma E. Eleanor Roosevelt. Bane, Jeff, illus. 2016. (My Early Library: My Itty-Bitty Bio Ser.). (ENG.). 24p. (J). (gr. k-1). 28.50 *(978-1-63470-483-0(5)*, 207663) Cherry Lake Publishing.

Hally, Ashleigh. Rosalynn Carter. 2012. (Illus.). 24p. (J). *(978-1-935884-74-3(3))*; pap. *(978-1-935884-80-4(8))* State Standards Publishing, LLC.

Harness, Cheryl. Hillary Clinton: American Woman of the World. 2016. (Real-Life Story Ser.). (ENG., Illus.). 192p. (J). (gr. 3-7). 17.99 *(978-1-4814-6057-6(9)*, Aladdin) Simon & Schuster Children's Publishing.

Hopkinson, Deborah. Michelle. Ford, A. G., illus. 2009. 32p. (J). (gr. -1-2). 17.99 *(978-0-06-182739-6(8))* HarperCollins Pubs.

Hubbard-Brown, Janet. Abigail Adams: First Lady. 2009. (Women of Achievement Ser.). (Illus.). 128p. (gr. 6-12). 35.00 *(978-1-60413-491-9(7)*, Chelsea Hse.) Facts On File, Inc.

—Eleanor Roosevelt: First Lady. 2009. (Women of Achievement Ser.). 128p. (gr. 6-12). 35.00 *(978-1-60413-076-8(8)*, Chelsea Hse.) Facts On File, Inc.

Hudson, Amanda. Michelle Obama. 2009. (People We Should Know Ser.). (ENG.). 48p. (J). (gr. 3-5). pap. 10.50 *(978-1-4339-2192-6(8))*; lib. bdg. 31.00 *(978-1-4339-2187-2(1))* Stevens, Gareth Publishing LLLP. (Gareth Stevens Learning Library).

Hull, Mary. Mary Todd Lincoln: Civil War's First Lady. 2015. (Legendary American Biographies Ser.). 96p. (J). (gr. 6-12). pap. 10.95 *(978-0-7660-6481-2(6))* Enslow Pubs., Inc.

Hull, Mary E. Mary Todd Lincoln: Civil War's First Lady. 2015. (Legendary American Biographies Ser.). 96p. (J). (gr. 6-12). 27.94 *(978-0-7660-6480-5(8))* Enslow Pubs., Inc.

Jones, Lynda. Mrs. Lincoln's Dressmaker: The Unlikely Friendship of Elizabeth Keckley & Mary Todd Lincoln. 2009. (ENG., Illus.). 80p. (J). (gr. 5). lib. bdg. 27.90 *(978-1-4263-0378-4(5))*; 18.95 *(978-1-4263-0377-7(7))* National Geographic Society. (National Geographic Children's Bks.).

Katirgis, Jane. Celebrating First Lady Michelle Obama in Pictures. 2009. (Obama Family Photo Album Ser.). (Illus.). 32p. (J). (gr. 2-5). lib. bdg. 23.94 *(978-0-7660-3652-9(9))* Enslow Pubs., Inc.

Kawa, Katie. Hillary Clinton. 2016. (Superwomen Role Models Ser.). 32p. (J). (gr. 4-3). 26.25 *(978-1-5081-4806-7(6)*, PowerKids Pr.) Rosen Publishing Group, Inc., The.

Kelley, True. Who Was Abigail Adams? O'brien, John, illus. 2014. (Who Was? Ser.). (ENG.). 112p. (J). (gr. 3-7). 5.99 *(978-0-448-47890-6(0)*, Grosset & Dunlap) Penguin Young Readers Group.

—Who Was Abigail Adams? 2014. (Who Was... ? Ser.). lib. bdg. 16.00 *(978-0-606-34166-0(8)*, Turtleback) Turtleback Bks.

Kent, Zachary. Dolley Madison: The Enemy Cannot Frighten a Free People. 2010. (Americans—the Spirit of a Nation Ser.). (Illus.). 128p. (J). (gr. 7-12). lib. bdg. 33.27 *(978-0-7660-3356-6(2))* Enslow Pubs., Inc.

Kerley, Barbara. What to Do about Alice? 2011. (J). (gr. 2-5). 29.95 *(978-0-545-29679-3(X))* Weston Woods Studios, Inc.

Kimmelman, Leslie & Juhasz, Victor. Hot Dog! Eleanor Roosevelt Throws a Picnic. 2014. (ENG., Illus.). 40p. (J). (gr. 3-6). 16.99 *(978-1-58536-830-3(X)*, 203013) Sleeping Bear Pr.

Klein, Dvora. Eleanor Roosevelt. 2009. pap. 13.25 *(978-1-60559-059-2(2))* Hameray Publishing Group, Inc.

Krull, Kathleen. Dolley Madison: Parties Can Be Patroitic! Fancher, Lou & Johnson, Steve, illus. 2015. (Women Who Broke the Rules Ser.). (ENG.). 48p. (J). (gr. 1-4). 16.99 *(978-0-8027-3793-9(5)*, 9780802737939, Bloomsbury USA Childrens) Bloomsbury Publishing USA.

—Hillary Rodham Clinton: Dreams Taking Flight. Bates, Amy June, illus. 2015. (ENG.). 48p. (J). (gr. k-5). 17.99 *(978-1-4814-5113-0(8)*, Simon & Schuster Bks. For Young Readers) Simon & Schuster Bks. For Young Readers.

—Mary Todd Lincoln: I'm Usually the Smartest Person in the Room. Baddeley, Elizabeth, illus. 2015. (Women Who Broke the Rules Ser.). (ENG.). 48p. (J). (gr. 1-4). pap. 6.99 *(978-0-8027-3825-7(7)*, 9780802738257, Bloomsbury USA Childrens) Bloomsbury Publishing USA.

Lakin, Patricia. Abigail Adams: First Lady of the American Revolution. Bandelin, Debra & Dacey, Bob, illus. 2006. 48p. (J). lib. bdg. 15.00 *(978-1-4242-1560-7(9))* Fitzgerald Bks.

—Abigail Adams: First Lady of the American Revolution. Dacey, Bob & Bandelin, Debra, illus. 2006. (Ready-To-read SOFA Ser.). (ENG.). 48p. (J). (gr. 1-3). pap. 3.99 *(978-0-689-87032-3(9)*, Simon Spotlight) Simon Spotlight.

Larkin, Tanya. What Was Cooking in Dolley Madison's White House? 2009. (Cooking Throughout American History Ser.). 24p. (gr. 3-3). 42.50 *(978-1-61511-950-9(7)*, PowerKids Pr.) Rosen Publishing Group, Inc., The.

—What Was Cooking in Edith Roosevelt's White House? 2009. (Cooking Throughout American History Ser.). 24p. (gr. 3-3). 42.50 *(978-1-61511-951-6(5)*, PowerKids Pr.) Rosen Publishing Group, Inc., The.

—What Was Cooking in Julia Grant's White House? 2009. (Cooking Throughout American History Ser.). 24p. (gr. 3-3). 42.50 *(978-1-61511-952-3(3)*, PowerKids Pr.) Rosen Publishing Group, Inc., The.

—What Was Cooking in Martha Washington's Presidential Mansion? 2009. (Cooking Throughout American History Ser.). 24p. (gr. 3-3). 42.50 *(978-1-61511-953-0(1)*, PowerKids Pr.) Rosen Publishing Group, Inc., The.

Lassieur, Allison. Eleanor Roosevelt: Activist for Social Change. 2006. (Great Life Stories Ser.). (ENG., Illus.). 112p. (J). (gr. 6-8). lib. bdg. 30.50 *(978-0-531-13871-7(2)*, Watts, Franklin) Scholastic Library Publishing.

Lee, Sally. Eleanor Roosevelt, 1 vol. 2010. (First Ladies Ser.). (ENG.). 24p. (gr. k-1). pap. 7.29 *(978-1-4296-5603-0(4))*; pap. 41.70 *(978-1-4296-5604-7(2))*; lib. bdg. 26.65 *(978-1-4296-5010-6(9))* Capstone Press of Coughlan Cos. (Pebble Plus).

—Hillary Clinton, 1 vol. 2010. (First Ladies Ser.). (ENG.). 24p. (gr. k-1). lib. bdg. 26.65 *(978-1-4296-5327-5(2)*, Pebble Plus) Capstone Press of Coughlan Cos.

—Martha Washington, 1 vol. 2010. (First Ladies Ser.). (ENG.). 24p. (gr. k-1). pap. 7.29 *(978-1-4296-5605-4(0))*; pap. 41.70 *(978-1-4296-5606-1(9))*; lib. bdg. 26.65 *(978-1-4296-5011-3(7))* Capstone Press of Coughlan Cos. (Pebble Plus).

Machajewski, Sarah. Michelle Obama. 2016. (Superwomen Role Models Ser.). (Illus.). 32p. (J). (gr. 4-3). 26.25 *(978-1-5081-4812-8(0)*, PowerKids Pr.) Rosen Publishing Group, Inc., The.

MacLeod, Elizabeth. Eleanor Roosevelt: An Inspiring Life. 2006. (Snapshots: Images of People & Places in History Ser.). (ENG., Illus.). 32p. (J). (gr. 3-7). 6.95 *(978-1-55337-811-2(3))* Kids Can Pr., Ltd. CAN. Dist: Hachette Bk. Group.

Maloof, Torrey. Abigail Adams & the Women Who Shaped America. 2016. (Primary Source Readers Ser.). (Illus.). 32p. (J). (gr. 4-5). 8.99 *(978-1-4938-3080-0(5))* Teacher Created Materials, Inc.

Mapua, Jeff. Bill & Hillary Clinton. 2014. (Making a Difference: Leaders Who Are Changing the World Ser.). 48p. (YA). (gr. 5-8). 25.85 *(978-1-62275-425-0(5))*; pap. 84.30 *(978-1-62275-428-1(X))*; pap. 14.05 *(978-1-62275-427-4(1))* Rosen Publishing Group, Inc., The.

—Hillary Clinton, 1 vol. 2015. (ENG., Illus.). 32p. (J). 23.45 *(978-1-62275-689-6(4)*, Britannica Educational Publishing) Rosen Publishing Group, Inc., The.

Mara, Wil. Laura Bush. 2003. (Rookie Biographies Ser.). (ENG., Illus.). 32p. (J). (gr. 1-2). 20.50 *(978-0-516-22854-9(4)*, Children's Pr.) Scholastic Library Publishing.

Marcovitz, Hal. Michelle. 2007. (Obamas Ser.). 64p. (YA). (gr. 3-6). pap. 9.95 *(978-1-4222-1485-5(0))*; (gr. 4-7). lib. bdg. 19.95 *(978-1-4222-1478-7(8))* Mason Crest.

Markel, Michelle. Hillary Rodham Clinton: Some Girls Are Born to Lead. Pham, LeUyen, illus. 2016. 40p. (J). (gr. -1-3). 17.99 *(978-0-06-238122-4(9))* HarperCollins Pubs.

Marsh, Carole. Abigail Adams. 2004. 12p. (gr. k-4). 2.95 *(978-0-635-02372-8(5))* Gallopade International.

—Michelle Obama: Biography FunBook. 2009. (J). (gr. 2-9). pap. 3.99 *(978-0-635-07054-8(5))* Gallopade International.

—The Obama Family - Life in the White House: President Barack Obama, First Lady Michelle Obama, First Children Malia & Sasha. 2008. (Here & Now Ser.). 32p. (J). (gr. 2-9). pap. 8.99 *(978-0-635-07051-7(0))* Gallopade International.

Marsico, Katie. Eleanor Roosevelt: First Lady & Human Rights Advocate, 1 vol. 2008. (Essential Lives Set 2 Ser.). (ENG., Illus.). 112p. (J). (gr. 6-12). lib. bdg. 35.64 *(978-1-60453-040-7(5))* ABDO Publishing Co.

Mattern, Joanne. Barbara Bush, 1 vol. 2008. (First Ladies Set 1 Ser.). (ENG., Illus.). 32p. (J). (gr. 1-4). 27.07 *(978-1-59928-790-4(0))* ABDO Publishing Co.

—Betty Ford, 1 vol. 2008. (First Ladies Set 1 Ser.). (ENG., Illus.). 32p. (YA). (gr. 1-4). 27.07 *(978-1-59928-794-2(3))* ABDO Publishing Co.

—Dolley Madison, 1 vol. 2008. (First Ladies Set 1 Ser.). (ENG., Illus.). 32p. (YA). (gr. 1-4). 27.07 *(978-1-59928-798-0(6))* ABDO Publishing Co.

—Eleanor Roosevelt, 1 vol. 2008. (First Ladies Set 1 Ser.). (ENG., Illus.). 32p. (YA). (gr. 1-4). 27.07 *(978-1-59928-800-0(1))* ABDO Publishing Co.

—Eleanor Roosevelt: More Than a First Lady. (Women Who Shaped History Ser.). 24p. 2009. (gr. 2-3). 42.50 *(978-1-60854-817-0(1))* 2003. (Illus.). (J). lib. bdg. 22.60 *(978-0-8239-6501-4(5))* Rosen Publishing Group, Inc., The. (PowerKids Pr.).

—Grace Coolidge, 1 vol. 2008. (First Ladies Set 1 Ser.). (ENG., Illus.). 32p. (YA). (gr. 1-4). 27.07 *(978-1-59928-793-5(5))* ABDO Publishing Co.

—Hillary Rodham Clinton, 1 vol. 2008. (First Ladies Set 1 Ser.). (ENG., Illus.). 32p. (YA). (gr. 1-4). 27.07 *(978-1-59928-792-8(7))* ABDO Publishing Co.

—Jacqueline Kennedy, 1 vol. 2008. (First Ladies Set 1 Ser.). (ENG., Illus.). 32p. (YA). (gr. 1-4). 27.07 *(978-1-59928-796-6(X))* ABDO Publishing Co.

—Lady Bird Johnson, 1 vol. 2008. (First Ladies Set 1 Ser.). (ENG., Illus.). 32p. (YA). (gr. 1-4). 27.07 *(978-1-59928-795-9(1))* ABDO Publishing Co.

—Laura Bush, 1 vol. 2008. (First Ladies Set 1 Ser.). (ENG., Illus.). 32p. (YA). (gr. 1-4). 27.07 *(978-1-59928-791-1(9))* ABDO Publishing Co.

—Martha Washington, 1 vol. 2008. (First Ladies Set 1 Ser.). (ENG., Illus.). 32p. (J). (gr. 1-4). 27.07 *(978-1-59928-801-7(X))* ABDO Publishing Co.

—Mary Todd Lincoln, 1 vol. 2008. (First Ladies Set 1 Ser.). (ENG., Illus.). 32p. (YA). (gr. 1-4). 27.07 *(978-1-59928-797-3(8))* ABDO Publishing Co.

—Nancy Reagan, 1 vol. 2008. (First Ladies Set 1 Ser.). (ENG., Illus.). 32p. (J). (gr. 1-4). 27.07 *(978-1-59928-799-7(4))* ABDO Publishing Co.

—What's So Great about Michelle Obama. 2009. (What's So Great About...? Ser.). 32p. (J). (gr. 2-4). lib. bdg. 25.70 *(978-1-58415-833-2(6))* Mitchell Lane Pubs., Inc.

McCaffrey, Paul. Michelle Obama. 2010. (Women of Achievement Ser.). 144p. (gr. 6-12). 35.00 *(978-1-60413-911-2(0)*, Chelsea Hse.) Facts On File, Inc.

McPherson, Stephanie. My Dear Husband: Important Letters of Abigail Adams. 2009. (Great Moments in American History Ser.). 32p. (gr. 3-3). 47.90 *(978-1-61513-134-1(5))* Rosen Publishing Group, Inc., The.

McPherson, Stephanie Sammartino. Martha Washington: Legendary First Lady of the United States. 2015. (Legendary American Biographies Ser.). 96p. (J). (gr. 6-12). 27.94 *(978-0-7660-6475-1(1))* Enslow Pubs., Inc.

Merchant, Peter. Eleanor Roosevelt & the Scary Basement. DiVito, Anna, illus. 2006. (Ready-To-read COFA Ser.). (ENG.). 32p. (J). (gr. k-2). pap. 3.99 *(978-0-689-87205-1(4)*, Simon & Schuster/Paula Wiseman Bks.) Simon & Schuster/Paula Wiseman Bks.

Mulhall, Jill K. Abigail Adams, 1 vol. 2004. (Primary Source Readers Ser.). (ENG.). 24p. (J). (gr. 4-4). pap. 8.99 *(978-0-7439-8786-8(1))* Shell Educational Publishing.

Nault, Jennifer. Michelle Obama. 2009. (Remarkable People Ser.). (Illus.). 24p. (J). (gr. 4-6). pap. 8.95 *(978-1-60596-666-3(5))*; lib. bdg. 24.45 *(978-1-60596-665-6(7))* Weigl Pubs., Inc.

Nelson, Maria. The Life of Abigail Adams. 2012. (Famous Lives Ser.). (ENG., Illus.). 24p. (J). (gr. k-3). lib. bdg. 22.60 *(978-1-4339-6337-7(X))*; (gr. 1-4). pap. 8.15 *(978-1-4339-6339-1(6))* Stevens, Gareth Publishing LLLP.

—The Life of Abigail Adams / la Vida de Abigail Adams. 2012. (Famous Lives / Vidas extraordinarias Ser.). (ENG & SPA., Illus.). 24p. (J). (gr. k-3). 22.60 *(978-1-4339-6649-1(2))* Stevens, Gareth Publishing LLLP.

Our Presidents & First Ladies of the White House. 119.40 *(978-0-8249-6046-9(7)*, Ideal Pubns.) Worthy Publishing.

Raatma, Lucia. Jacqueline Kennedy, 1 vol. 2010. (First Ladies Ser.). (ENG.). 24p. (gr. k-1). pap. 7.29 *(978-1-4296-5601-6(8))*; pap. 41.70 *(978-1-4296-5602-3(6))*; lib. bdg. 26.65 *(978-1-4296-5009-0(5))* Capstone Press of Coughlan Cos. (Pebble Plus).

—Michelle Obama, 1 vol. 2010. (First Ladies Ser.). (ENG.). 24p. (gr. k-1). pap. 7.29 *(978-1-4296-5599-6(2))*; pap. 41.70 *(978-1-4296-5600-9(X))*; lib. bdg. 26.65 *(978-1-4296-5008-3(7))* Capstone Press of Coughlan Cos. (Pebble Plus).

Ransom, Candice. Martha Washington. Ritz, Karen, illus. 2003. (On My Own Biographies Ser.). 48p. (J). 25.26 *(978-0-87614-918-8(2))*; (ENG.). (gr. 2-4). per. 6.95 *(978-0-87614-107-6(6))* Lerner Publishing Group. (Carolrhoda Bks.).

Rappaport, Doreen. Eleanor, Quiet No More. Kelley, Gary, illus. 2009. (ENG.). 48p. (J). (gr. 1-3). 16.99 *(978-0-7868-5141-6(4))* Hyperion Pr.

Riddolls, Tom & Wearing, Judy. Hillary Clinton. 2009. (Remarkable People Ser.). (Illus.). 24p. (J). (gr. 4-6). pap. 8.95 *(978-1-60596-621-2(5))*; lib. bdg. 24.45 *(978-1-60596-620-5(7))* Weigl Pubs., Inc.

Rinaldo, Denise. Eleanor Roosevelt: With a Discussion of Respect. 2003. (Values in Action Ser.). (J). *(978-1-59203-063-7(7))* Learning Challenge, Inc.

Rosenberg, Pam. Eleanor Roosevelt: First Lady, Humanitarian, & World Citizen. 2003. (Our People Ser.). (ENG., Illus.). 32p. (J). (gr. 3-6). 29.93 *(978-1-59296-001-9(4)*, 200634) Child's World, Inc., The.

Ruiz, Rachel. When Hillary Rodham Clinton Played Ice Hockey. Doneva, Steliyana, illus. 2017. (Leaders Doing Headstands Ser.). (ENG.). 32p. (gr. 2-3). lib. bdg. 27.99 ***(978-1-5158-1573-0(0))*** Picture Window Bks.

Ryan, Bernard. Hillary Rodham Clinton: First Lady & Senator. 2004. (Ferguson Career Biographies Ser.). (Illus.). 160p. (gr. 6-12). 25.00 *(978-0-8160-5544-9(0)*, Ferguson Publishing Co.) Facts On File, Inc.

Sabin, Francene & Macken, JoAnn Early. Abigail Adams: Young Patriot. Miyake, Yoshi, illus. 2007. 55p. (J). pap. *(978-0-439-88003-9(3))* Scholastic, Inc.

Sawyer, Kem Knapp. Eleanor Roosevelt. 2006. (DK Biography Ser.). (ENG., Illus.). 128p. (J). (gr. 5-12). pap. 6.99 *(978-0-7566-1496-6(1)*, DK Children) Dorling Kindersley Publishing, Inc.

Shamir, Ruby. What's the Big Deal about First Ladies. Faulkner, Matt, illus. 2017. (What's the Big Deal About Ser.). (ENG.). 32p. (J). (gr. -1-3). 17.99 *(978-0-399-54724-9(X)*, Philomel Bks.) Penguin Young Readers Group.

Shea, John M. Eleanor Roosevelt in Her Own Words. 2016. (Eyewitness to History Ser.). (ENG., Illus.). 32p. (J). (gr. 4-5). pap. 10.50 *(978-1-4824-4062-1(8))* Stevens, Gareth Publishing LLLP.

Shepherd, Jodie. Hillary Clinton. 2015. (Rookie Biographies(r) Ser.). (ENG., Illus.). 32p. (J). lib. bdg. 23.00 *(978-0-531-20592-1(4))* Scholastic Library Publishing.

Shulman, Holly. Dolley Madison: Her Life, Letters, & Legacy. 2009. (Library of American Lives & Times Ser.). 112p. (gr. 5-5). 69.20 *(978-1-60853-477-7(4))* Rosen Publishing Group, Inc., The.

Stille, Darlene R. Eleanor Roosevelt: First Lady & Civil Rights Activist, 1 vol. Sprunger, Reed, illus. 2013. (Beginner Biographies Set 2 Ser.). (ENG.). 32p. (J). (gr. -1-4). 28.50 *(978-1-61641-941-7(5))* Magic Wagon.

Stine, Megan. Who Is Michelle Obama? O'brien, John & Harrison, Nancy, illus. 2013. (Who Was? Ser.). (ENG.). 112p. (J). (gr. 3-7). 5.99 *(978-0-448-47863-0(3)*, Grosset & Dunlap) Penguin Young Readers Group.

—Who Is Michelle Obama? 2013. (Who Is... ? Ser.). lib. bdg. 14.75 *(978-0-606-32131-0(4)*, Turtleback) Turtleback Bks.

Summers, Portia. Hillary Clinton: Politician & Activist. 2017. (Junior Biographies Ser.). 24p. (J). (gr. 3-4). lib. bdg. 22.60 ***(978-0-7660-8670-8(4))*** Enslow Pubs., Inc.

Sutcliffe, Jane. Abigail Adams. 2006. (History Maker Biographies Ser.). (ENG., Illus.). 48p. (gr. 3-6). lib. bdg. 27.93 *(978-0-8225-5942-9(0)*, Lerner Pubns.) Lerner Publishing Group.

Taylor-Butler, Christine. Michelle Obama. 2015. (ENG.). 48p. (J). pap. 6.95 *(978-0-531-21206-6(8)*, Orchard Bks.) Scholastic Library Publishing.

Thompson, Gare. Who Was Eleanor Roosevelt? Wolf, Elizabeth, tr. Wolf, Elizabeth & Harrison, Nancy, illus. 2004. (Who Was? Ser.). (ENG.). 112p. (J). (gr. 3-7). pap. 5.99 *(978-0-448-43509-1(8)*, Grosset & Dunlap) Penguin Young Readers Group.

—Who Was Eleanor Roosevelt? Wolf, Elizabeth, illus. 2004. (Who Was... ? Ser.). 106p. (gr. 3-7). 15.00 *(978-0-7569-2829-2(X))* Perfection Learning Corp.

—Who Was Eleanor Roosevelt? 2004. (Who Was... ? Ser.). (gr. 3-6). lib. bdg. 16.00 *(978-0-613-72563-7(8)*, Turtleback) Turtleback Bks.

Tieck, Sarah. Eleanor Roosevelt, 1 vol. 2010. (First Biographies Set 6 Ser.). (ENG., Illus.). 32p. (J). (gr. 1-4). 27.07 *(978-1-60453-986-8(0))* ABDO Publishing Co.

—Hillary Rodham Clinton, 1 vol. 2010. (First Biographies Set 6 Ser.). (ENG.). 32p. (J). (gr. 1-4). 27.07 *(978-1-60453-983-7(6))* ABDO Publishing Co.

Time for Kids Editors. Abigail Adams: Eyewitness to America's Birth. 2009. (Time for Kids Ser.). (ENG.). 48p. (J). (gr. 2-4). 15.99 *(978-0-06-057629-5(4))*; pap. 3.99 *(978-0-06-057628-8(6)*, Collins) HarperCollins Pubs.

Time for Kids Magazine Staff. Time for Kids: Eleanor Roosevelt: First Lady of the World. 2005. (Time for Kids Ser.). (ENG., Illus.). 48p. (J). (gr. 2-4). per. 3.99 *(978-0-06-057613-4(8))* HarperCollins Pubs.

Tracy, Kathleen. The Historic Fight for the 2008 Democratic Presidential Nomination: The Clinton View. 2009. (Monumental Milestones Ser.). (Illus.). 48p. (YA). (gr. 4-7). lib. bdg. 29.95 *(978-1-58415-731-1(3))* Mitchell Lane Pubs., Inc.

Uschan, Michael V. Michelle Obama. 2010. (People in the News Ser.). (Illus.). 128p. (YA). (gr. 8-10). 33.95 *(978-1-4205-0209-1(3)*, Lucent Bks.) Cengage Gale.

Vaughan, Carolyn. First Ladies. Fandex Family Field Guides Staff, ed. 2003. (ENG., Illus.). 50p. (J). (gr. 4-12). 12.95 *(978-0-7611-2944-8(8)*, 12944) Workman Publishing Co., Inc.

Wallner, Alexandra. Abigail Adams. 2005. (ENG., Illus.). 32p. (J). pap. 6.95 *(978-0-8234-1942-5(8))* Holiday Hse., Inc.

Wells, Catherine. Hillary Clinton. 2007. (Political Profiles Ser.). (Illus.). 112p. (YA). (gr. 5-9). lib. bdg. 27.95 *(978-1-59935-047-9(5))* Reynolds, Morgan Inc.

Weston Woods Staff, creator. What to Do about Alice? 2011. 38.75 *(978-0-545-29822-3(9))* Weston Woods Studios, Inc.

Wheeler, Jill C. Edith Wilson, 1 vol. 2010. (First Ladies Set 2 Ser.). (ENG., Illus.). 32p. (YA). (gr. 1-4). 27.07 *(978-1-60453-634-8(9))* ABDO Publishing Co.

—Hillary Rodham Clinton. 2003. (Breaking Barriers Ser.). 64p. (gr. 3-8). 27.07 *(978-1-57765-741-5(1)*, Abdo & Daughters) ABDO Publishing Co.

—Mamie Eisenhower, 1 vol. 2010. (First Ladies Set 2 Ser.). (ENG., Illus.). 32p. (YA). (gr. 1-4). 27.07 *(978-1-60453-630-0(6))* ABDO Publishing Co.

—Patricia Nixon, 1 vol. 2010. (First Ladies Set 2 Ser.). (ENG., Illus.). 32p. (YA). (gr. 1-4). 27.07 *(978-1-60453-632-4(2))* ABDO Publishing Co.

Whiting, Jim. The Life & Times of Abigail Adams. 2007. (Profiles in American History Ser.). (Illus.). 48p. (J). (gr. 4-7). lib. bdg. 29.95 *(978-1-58415-527-0(2))* Mitchell Lane Pubs., Inc.

Winget, Mary. Eleanor Roosevelt. (Biography Ser.). (Illus.). 2005. 112p. (gr. 6-12). lib. bdg. 27.93 *(978-0-8225-4985-7(9))* 2003. 48p. (J). pap. 8.95 *(978-0-8225-4801-0(1)*, Lerner Pubns.) 2003. 48p. (J). (gr. 3-5). lib. bdg. 26.60 *(978-0-8225-4675-7(2))* Lerner Publishing Group.

Winter, Jonah. Hillary. Colón, Raúl, illus. 2016. (ENG.). 40p. (J). (gr. -1-3). lib. bdg. 20.99 *(978-0-553-53389-7(4)*, Schwartz & Wade Bks.) Random Hse. Children's Bks.

Winter, Jonah & Colón, Raúl. Hillary. 2016. (ENG., Illus.). 40p. (J). (gr. -1-3). 17.99 *(978-0-553-53388-0(6)*, Schwartz & Wade Bks.) Random Hse. Children's Bks.

Yasuda, Anita. Lady Bird Johnson. 2010. (My Life Ser.). 24p. (J). (gr. 2-4). lib. bdg. 25.70 *(978-1-61690-062-5(8))* Weigl Pubs., Inc.

—Lady Bird Johnson: My Life. 2010. pap. 9.95 *(978-1-61690-063-2(6))* Weigl Pubs., Inc.

Zourelias, Diana. First Ladies Fascinating Facts. 2012. (Dover History Coloring Book Ser.). (ENG.). 48p. (J). (gr. 3-5). pap. 4.99 *(978-0-486-49832-4(8))* Dover Pubns., Inc.

Zumbusch, Amelie von. Michelle Obama: Our First Lady. 2010. (Making History: the Obamas Ser.). (Illus.). 24p. (J). pap. 8.25 *(978-1-4358-9868-4(0))*; (gr. 2-3). lib. bdg. 22.60 *(978-1-4358-9388-7(3))* Rosen Publishing Group, Inc., The. (PowerKids Pr.).

P
Q
R

PRESLEY, ELVIS, 1935-1977

Alagna, Magdalena. Elvis Presley. (Rock & Roll Hall of Famers Ser.). 112p. (gr. 5-8). 2009. 63.90 *(978-1-60852-474-7(4)*, Rosen Reference) 2006. (Illus.). (YA). lib. bdg. 34.60 *(978-0-8239-3524-6(8))* Rosen Publishing Group, Inc., The.

Brown, Adele Q. Elvis Presley. 2003. (Trailblazers of the Modern World Ser.). (Illus.). 48p. (gr. 5-12). pap. 14.05 *(978-0-8368-5245-5(1)*, Gareth Stevens Secondary Library) Stevens, Gareth Publishing LLLP.

Christensen, Bonnie. Elvis: The Story of the Rock & Roll King. Christensen, Bonnie, illus. 2015. (ENG., Illus.). 32p. (J). (gr. 1-4). 17.99 *(978-0-8050-9447-3(4)*, 9780805094473, Holt, Henry & Co. Bks. For Young Readers) Holt, Henry & Co.

Clayton, Marie. Elvis Presley: Unseen Archives. (Unseen Archives Ser.). (Illus.). 384p. *(978-0-7525-8335-8(2))* Parragon, Inc.

Collins, Terry. Elvis: A Graphic Novel, 1 vol. Melcher, Michele, illus. (American Graphic Ser.). (ENG.). 32p. (gr. 3-4). 2011. pap. 8.10 *(978-1-4296-6266-6(2))* 2011. pap. 47.70 *(978-1-4296-6434-9(7))* 2010. lib. bdg. 30.65 *(978-1-4296-5476-0(7))* Capstone Press of Coughlan Cos. (Graphic Library).

Doll, Susan. Elvis Presley: With Profiles of Muddy Waters & Mick Jagger. 2006. (Biographical Connections Ser.). (Illus.). 112p. (J). *(978-0-7166-1823-2(0))* World Bk., Inc.

Eanes, Jim. Elvis in Virginia. 2003. (Illus.). 78p. (YA). per. 15.95 *(978-0-9717295-2-0(2))* E & H Publishing Co., Inc.

Edgers, Geoff. Who Was Elvis Presley? O'brien, John & Harrison, Nancy, illus. 2007. (Who Was? Ser.). (ENG.). 112p. (J). (gr. 3-7). pap. 5.99 *(978-0-448-44642-4(1)*, Grosset & Dunlap) Penguin Young Readers Group.

—Who Was Elvis Presley? O'brien, John, illus. 2007. (Who Was... ? Ser.). 105p. (gr. 2-5). 15.00 *(978-0-7569-8164-8(6))* Perfection Learning Corp.

Hampton, Wilborn. Elvis Presley: A Twentieth Century Life. 2007. (ENG., Illus.). 192p. (YA). (gr. 7). 26.16 *(978-1-4287-4879-8(2))* Follett School Solutions.

Harper, Betty. Color My World Vol. 1: Early Elvis (Coloring Book) Harper, Betty, illus. 2004. (Illus.). 32p. (J). 4.95 *(978-0-932117-42-7(2))* Osborne Enterprises Publishing.

Micklos, John. Elvis Presley: "I Want to Entertain People" 2010. (American Rebels Ser.). 160p. (YA). (gr. 7-12). 35.94 *(978-0-7660-3382-5(1))* Enslow Pubs., Inc.

Plantz, Connie. Elvis Presley: Music Legend, Movie Star, the King. 2004. (People to Know Ser.). (Illus.). 128p. (J). lib. bdg. 26.60 *(978-0-7660-2103-7(3))* Enslow Pubs., Inc.

Saddleback Educational Publishing Staff, ed. Elvis Presley, 1 vol. unabr. ed. 2008. (Graphic Biographies Ser.). (ENG., Illus.). 25p. (YA). (gr. 9-12). pap. 7.95 *(978-1-59905-221-2(0))* Saddleback Educational Publishing, Inc.

Snyder, R. Bradley, et al. What Every Child Needs to Know about Elvis Presley. 2014. (ENG.). 22p. (J). (-k). bds. 8.95 *(978-1-940705-00-2(2))* Need To Know Publishing.

Watson, Stephanie. Elvis Presley: Rock & Roll's King, 1 vol. 2012. (Lives Cut Short Set 2 Ser.). (ENG.). 112p. (J). (gr. 6-12). 35.64 *(978-1-61783-482-0(3))* ABDO Publishing Co.

PRESS

see Journalism; Newspapers; Periodicals

PRESS LAW

McGlone, Catherine. New York Times V. Sullivan & the Freedom of the Press Debate. 2005. (Debating Supreme Court Decisions Ser.). (Illus.). 112p. (J). (gr. 6-12). lib. bdg. 27.94 *(978-0-7660-2357-4(5))* Enslow Pubs., Inc.

PRESSURE GROUPS

see Lobbying

PRESSURE SUITS

see Astronauts—Clothing

PREVENTION OF ACCIDENTS

see Accidents—Prevention

PREVENTION OF CRUELTY TO ANIMALS

see Animals—Treatment

PREVENTION OF FIRE

see Fire Prevention

PREVENTIVE MEDICINE

see Bacteriology; Health; Immunity; Public Health

PRICE, HOMER (FICTITIOUS CHARACTER)—FICTION

McCloskey, Robert. Homer Price. l.t. ed. 2004. (Beeler Mystery Ser.). 158p. 29.95 *(978-1-58118-123-4(X))* LRS.

—Homer Price. l.t. ed. (J). (gr. 4-6). reprint ed. 10.00 *(978-0-89064-072-2(6))* National Assn. for Visually Handicapped.

PRIESTLEY, JOSEPH, 1733-1804

Bowden, Mary Ellen & Rosner, Linda. Joseph Priestley, Radical Thinker. 2005. (ENG.). 72p. pap. 19.95 *(978-0-941901-38-3(6))* Chemical Heritage Foundation.

Conley, Kate A. Joseph Priestly & the Discovery of Oxygen. 2005. (Uncharted, Unexplored, & Unexplained Ser.). (Illus.). 48p. (J). (gr. 4-8). lib. bdg. 29.95 *(978-1-58415-367-2(9))* Mitchell Lane Pubs., Inc.

PRIMARY EDUCATION

see Education, Elementary

PRIMATES

see also Apes; Human Beings; Lemurs; Monkeys

Aronin, Miriam. Aye-Aye: An Evil Omen. 2008. (Uncommon Animals Ser.). (Illus.). 32p. (YA). (gr. 2-5). lib. bdg. 25.27 *(978-1-59716-731-4(2*, 1284368) Bearport Publishing Co., Inc.

Chimps & Monkeys Are Not Pets! 2013. (When Pets Attack! Ser.). 32p. (J). (gr. 3-6). pap. 63.00 *(978-1-4339-9290-2(6))* Stevens, Gareth Publishing LLLP.

Clark, Willow. Bush Babies. 2012. (Up a Tree Ser.). (ENG., Illus.). 24p. (J). (gr. k-3). lib. bdg. 22.60 *(978-1-4488-6188-0(8))*; pap. 8.25 *(978-1-4488-6335-8(X)*, PowerKids Pr.) Rosen Publishing Group, Inc., The.

Cooper, Sharon Katz. L Is for Lemur: ABCs of Endangered Primates. 2016. (E for Endangered Ser.). (ENG., Illus.). 32p. (gr. 1-2). lib. bdg. 27.32 *(978-1-4914-8034-2(3)*, Aplus Bks.) Capstone Press of Coughlan Cos.

Corwin, Jeffrey, contrib. by. The World of Primates. 2014. (Jeff Corwin's Explorer Ser.). (ENG., Illus.). 12p. 7.95 *(978-1-58355-865-2(9))* Western National Parks Assn.

Curtis, Jennifer Keats. Primate School, 1 vol. 2015. (ENG & SPA., Illus.). 32p. (J). (gr. 2-5). 17.95 *(978-1-62855-555-4(6))* Arbordale Publishing.

De la Bédoyère, Camilla. Monkeys & Apes. 2014. (Animal Q & A Ser.). (Illus.). 24p. (J). (gr. k-3). lib. bdg. 23.60 *(978-1-4777-9190-5(6))* Windmill Bks.

Eck, Thomas Van. Tarsiers in the Dark. 2012. (Creatures of the Night Ser.). (Illus.). 24p. (J). (gr. 1-3). pap. 8.15 *(978-1-4339-6382-7(5))*; lib. bdg. 22.60 *(978-1-4339-6380-3(9))* Stevens, Gareth Publishing LLLP.

Kalman, Bobbie. Baby Primates. 2013. (ENG., Illus.). 24p. (J). *(978-0-7787-1007-3(6))*; pap. *(978-0-7787-1011-0(4))* Crabtree Publishing Co.

—Les Singes et Autres Primates. Sjonger, Rebecca, illus. 2012. (FRE.). 32p. (J). pap. 9.95 *(978-2-89579-440-0(5))* Bayard Canada CAN. Dist: Crabtree Publishing Co.

Kalman, Bobbie & Levigne, Heather. Les Primates. 2005. (Petit Monde Vivant Ser.). (FRE., Illus.). 32p. (J). pap. 9.95 *(978-2-89579-051-8(5))* Bayard Canada Livres CAN. Dist: Crabtree Publishing Co.

McCarthy, Cecilia Pinto. Capuchin Monkeys, 1 vol. 2013. (Monkeys Ser.). (ENG.). 24p. (gr. k-1). lib. bdg. 26.65 *(978-1-62065-108-7(4)*, Pebble Plus) Capstone Press of Coughlan Cos.

Miniature Primates, 1 vol. 2014. (Mini Animal Marvels Ser.). (ENG., Illus.). 24p. (J). (gr. -1-3). 24.21 *(978-1-62403-068-0(8))* ABDO Publishing Co.

Moore Niver, Heather. Chimps & Monkeys Are Not Pets! 2013. (When Pets Attack! Ser.). 32p. (J). (gr. 3-6). 26.60 *(978-1-4339-9288-9(4))*; pap. 10.50 *(978-1-4339-9289-6(2))* Stevens, Gareth Publishing LLLP.

Morgan, Sally. Small Primates. 2004. (J). lib. bdg. *(978-1-59389-178-7(4))* Cherrytree Bks.

Oldfield, Dawn Bluemel. Tarsier. 2016. (Weird but Cute Ser.). (ENG., Illus.). 24p. (J). (gr. -1-3). 17.95 *(978-1-943553-28-0(9))* Bearport Publishing Co., Inc.

Ottaviani, Jim. Primates: The Fearless Science of Jane Goodall, Dian Fossey, & Biruté Galdikas. Wicks, Maris, illus. 2013. (ENG.). 144p. (YA). (gr. 7). 21.99 *(978-1-59643-865-1(7)*, 9781596438651, First Second Bks.) Roaring Brook Pr.

—Primates: The Fearless Science of Jane Goodall, Dian Fossey, & Biruté Galdikas. Wicks, Maris, illus. 2015. (ENG.). 144p. (YA). (gr. 7). pap. 12.99 *(978-1-250-06293-2(4)*, 9781250062932) Square Fish.

Owings, Lisa & Leaf, Christina. Tarsier. 2014. (Extremely Weird Animals Ser.). (ENG., Illus.). 24p. (J). (gr. 3-8). lib. bdg. 25.95 *(978-1-62617-079-7(7)*, Pilot Bks.) Bellwether Media.

Paterson, Samantha. Primates. 2007. (Life Science (Weigl Hardcover) Ser.). (Illus.). 32p. (J). (gr. 4-7). lib. bdg. 26.00 *(978-1-59036-709-4(X))*; per. 9.95 *(978-1-59036-710-0(3))* Weigl Pubs., Inc.

—The Science of Primates. 2003. (Living Science Ser.). (Illus.). 32p. (J). (gr. 1-3). pap. 9.95 *(978-1-930954-36-6(0))* Weigl Pubs., Inc.

Petrie, Kristin. Tarsiers, 1 vol. 2010. (Nocturnal Animals Ser.). (ENG.). 24p. (YA). (gr. 3-6). 25.65 *(978-1-60453-739-0(6))* ABDO Publishing Co.

Rabe, Tish. Can You See a Chimpanzee? All about Primates. Ruiz, Aristides & Mathieu, Joe, illus. 2014. (Cat in the Hat's Learning Library). (ENG.). 48p. (J). (gr. k-3). lib. bdg. 13.99 *(978-0-375-97074-0(6)*, Random Hse. Bks. for Young Readers) Random Hse. Children's Bks.

Rafferty, John P. Primates. 2011. (Britannica Guide to Predators & Prey Ser.). (Illus.). 296p. (YA). (gr. 9-12). lib. bdg. 51.70 *(978-1-61530-339-7(1))* Rosen Publishing Group, Inc., The.

Rafferty, John P., ed. Primates. 2011. (Britannica Guide to Predators & Prey Ser.). (Illus.). 296p. (YA). 103.40 *(978-1-61530-455-4(X))* Rosen Publishing Group, Inc., The.

Redmond, Ian. Gorilas. Anderson, Peter & Brightling, Geoff, illus. 2003. (SPA.). 64p. 14.95 *(978-84-372-2323-0(7))* Altea, Ediciones, S.A. - Grupo Santillana ESP. Dist: Santillana USA Publishing Co., Inc.

Rich, Mari. Rescuing Primates: Gorillas, Chimps, & Monkeys. 2017. (J). ***(978-1-4222-3877-6(6))*** Mason Crest.

Sjonger, Rebecca & Kalman, Bobbie. Monkeys & Other Primates. 2005. (What Kind of Animal Is It? Ser.). (ENG., Illus.). 32p. (J). (gr. 1-2). pap. *(978-0-7787-2223-6(6))*; lib. bdg. *(978-0-7787-2165-9(5))* Crabtree Publishing Co.

Spilsbury, Richard. A Troop of Chimpanzees: And Other Primate Groups, 1 vol. 2012. (Animals in Groups Ser.). (ENG.). 48p. (gr. 4-6). pap. 9.95 *(978-1-4329-6492-4(5))*; lib. bdg. 33.32 *(978-1-4329-6485-6(2))* Heinemann-Raintree. (Heinemann InfoSearch).

Stefoff, Rebecca. The Primate Order. 2005. (Family Trees Ser.). (Illus.). 96p. (gr. 6-7). lib. bdg. 34.21 *(978-0-7614-1816-0(4)*, Benchmark Bks.) Marshall Cavendish Corp.

Willis, John. Baboon. 2016. (J). ***(978-1-4896-5369-7(4))*** Weigl Pubs., Inc.

PRIMATES—FICTION

Browne, Anthony. One Gorilla. Browne, Anthony, illus. 2013. (ENG., Illus.). 32p. (J). (gr. -1-2). 17.99 *(978-0-7636-6352-0(2))* Candlewick Pr.

—One Gorilla: a Counting Book. Browne, Anthony, illus. 2015. (ENG., Illus.). 26p. (J). (— 1). bds. 7.99 *(978-0-7636-7915-6(1))* Candlewick Pr.

Cotter, Amelia. Breakfast with Bigfoot. Swinford, Charles, illus. 2013. 30p. pap. 11.95 *(978-1-61876-017-3(3))* Black Oak Media, Inc.

Doman, Glenn. Nose Is Not Toes. 2010. (Gentle Revolution Ser.). (ENG., Illus.). 144p. (J). 15.95 *(978-0-7570-0208-3(0))* Square One Pubs.

Fontes, Justine & Fontes, Ron. Casebook: Bigfoot. 2009. (Top Secret Graphica Mysteries Ser.). (Illus.). 48p. (YA). (gr. 2-6). 29.25 *(978-1-60754-594-1(2))*; pap. 11.75 *(978-1-60754-595-8(0))* Windmill Bks.

MacHale, D. J. The Lost City of Faar. 2003. (Pendragon Ser.: 2). (ENG.). 400p. (J). (gr. 5-9). pap. 9.99 *(978-0-7434-3732-5(2)*, Aladdin) Simon & Schuster Children's Publishing.

Newton-Perry, Linda. The Little Red Car & Bigfoot. 2009. 70p. pap. 15.95 *(978-0-557-08449-4(0))* Lulu Pr., Inc.

Pankhurst, Kate. Mariella Mystery Investigates the Spaghetti Yeti. 2015. (Mariella Mysteries Ser.). (ENG., Illus.). 176p. (J). (gr. 2-6). pap. 5.99 *(978-1-4380-0705-2(1))* Barron's Educational Series, Inc.

Star, Nancy. Mystery of the Snow Day Bigfoot. Bernardin, James, illus. 2005. (Calendar Club Mysteries Ser.: Vol. 3). 77p. (J). pap. 3.95 *(978-0-439-67262-7(7))* Scholastic, Inc.

Sundance/Newbridge LLC Staff. The Abominable Snowman. 2005. (Choose Your Own Adventure Ser.). (gr. 4-8). pap. 5.50 *(978-0-7608-9693-8(3))* Sundance/Newbridge Educational Publishing.

Torres, J. Into the Woods. Hicks, Faith Erin, illus. 2012. (Bigfoot Boy Ser.: 1). (ENG.). 100p. (J). (gr. 2-5). 17.95 *(978-1-55453-711-2(8))*; pap. 9.95 *(978-1-55453-712-9(6))* Kids Can Pr., Ltd. CAN. Dist: Hachette Bk. Group.

PRIME MINISTERS

Aboff, Marcie. Golda Meir Iron Lady of Israel. 2016. (Spring Forward Ser.). (J). (gr. 2). *(978-1-4900-9454-0(7))* Benchmark Education Co.

Adler, David A. Golda Meir: A Strong Determined Leader. 2015. (Women of Our Time Ser.). (ENG., Illus.). 80p. (J). (gr. 3-7). 7.99 *(978-0-14-751660-2(9)*, Puffin Books) Penguin Young Readers Group.

Darraj, Susan Muaddi. Silvio Berlusconi: Prime Minister of Italy. Schlesinger, Arthur M., Jr., ed. 2005. (Major World Leaders Ser.). (Illus.). 112p. (gr. 6-12). 30.00 *(978-0-7910-8260-7(1)*, Chelsea Hse.) Facts On File, Inc.

Naden, Corinne J. Benazir Bhutto. 2010. (Leading Women Ser.). 96p. (YA). (gr. 7-12). 39.93 *(978-0-7614-4952-2(3))* Marshall Cavendish Corp.

Sylvan, Lu. Vladimir Putin: Russian Leader, 1 vol. 2014. (Newsmakers Ser.). (ENG., Illus.). 48p. (J). (gr. 3-6). lib. bdg. 32.79 *(978-1-62403-645-3(7))* ABDO Publishing Co.

PRIME MINISTERS—CANADA

Hancock, Pat. The Kids Book of Canadian Prime Ministers. Mantha, John, illus. 2005. (Kids Book Of Ser.). (ENG.). 56p. (J). (gr. 3-7). 19.95 *(978-1-55337-740-5(0))* Kids Can Pr., Ltd. CAN. Dist: Hachette Bk. Group.

PRIME MINISTERS—GREAT BRITAIN

Allport, Alan. Gordon Brown. 2009. (Modern World Leaders Ser.). (Illus.). 144p. (YA). (gr. 7-12). 30.00 *(978-1-60413-080-5(6))* Facts On File, Inc.

Collins, Thomas M. Tony Blair. 2005. (Biography Ser.). (Illus.). 112p. (J). (gr. 6-18). pap. 7.95 *(978-0-8225-9622-6(9))*; 29.27 *(978-0-8225-2373-4(6)*, Lerner Pubns.) Lerner Publishing Group.

Daynes, Katie. Winston Churchill. Tomlins, Karen, illus. 2006. (Usborne Famous Lives Gift Bks.). 64p. (J). (gr. 2-5). 8.99 *(978-0-7945-1258-3(5)*, Usborne) EDC Publishing.

Hamilton, Janice. Winston Churchill. 2006. (and E Biography Ser.). (Illus.). 112p. (J). (gr. 3-7). lib. bdg. 27.93 *(978-0-8225-3419-8(3)*, Twenty-First Century Bks.) Lerner Publishing Group.

Hinman, Bonnie. Tony Blair. 2nd rev. ed. 2006. (Modern World Leaders Ser.). (Illus.). 120p. (YA). (gr. 7-12). lib. bdg. 30.00 *(978-0-7910-9216-3(X))* Facts On File, Inc.

Kesselring, Mari. How to Analyze the Works of Winston Churchill, 1 vol. 2013. (Essential Critiques Set 4 Ser.). (ENG.). 112p. (J). (gr. 6-12). lib. bdg. 35.64 *(978-1-61783-649-7(4)*, Essential Library) ABDO Publishing Co.

Labrecque, Ellen & dePaola, Tomie. Who Was Winston Churchill? Hoare, Jerry & Harrison, Nancy, illus. 2015. (Who Was? Ser.). (ENG.). 112p. (J). (gr. 3-7). 5.99 *(978-0-448-48300-9(9)*, Grosset & Dunlap) Penguin Young Readers Group.

Lee, Stephen J. Gladstone & Disraeli. 2005. (Questions & Analysis in History Ser.). (ENG., Illus.). 208p. (C). 110.00 *(978-0-415-32356-7(8)*, RU27027); per. 30.95 *(978-0-415-32357-4(6))* Routledge.

Ridley, Sarah. Winston Churchill: ...And World War II. 2013. (History Makers Ser.). (Illus.). 24p. (J). (gr. 2-4). lib. bdg. 25.65 *(978-1-59771-393-1(7))* Sea-To-Sea Pubns.

Trussell-Cullen, Alan. Winston Churchill. 2009. pap. 13.25 *(978-1-60559-072-1(X))* Hameray Publishing Group, Inc.

Vander Hook, Sue. Winston Churchill: British Prime Minister & Statesman, 1 vol. 2009. (Essential Lives Set 3 Ser.). (ENG., Illus.). 112p. (J). (gr. 6-12). lib. bdg. 35.64 *(978-1-60453-523-5(7))* ABDO Publishing Co.

PRIME MINISTERS—INDIA

Prasad, H.Y. Sharada. Indira Gandhi. 2013. 56p. 10.00 *(978-0-14-333288-6(0))* Penguin Group India IND. Dist: Penguin Publishing Group.

Schupack, Sara. Indira Gandhi. 2013. (Leading Women 2 Ser.). 96p. (gr. 7-12). (YA). pap. 19.99 *(978-1-62712-113-2(7))*; (Illus.). (J). 39.93 *(978-0-7614-4955-3(8))* Cavendish Square Publishing.

PRIME MINISTERS—ISRAEL

Abrams, Dennis. Ehud Olmert. 2008. (Modern World Leaders Ser.). (Illus.). 136p. (YA). (gr. 7-12). 30.00 *(978-0-7910-9761-8(7))* Facts On File, Inc.

Blashfield, Jean F. Golda Meir. 2010. (Leading Women Ser.). 96p. (YA). (gr. 7-12). 39.93 *(978-0-7614-4960-7(4))* Marshall Cavendish GBR. Dist: Marshall Cavendish Corp.

Crompton, Samuel Willard. Ariel Sharon. 2nd rev. ed. 2007. (Modern World Leaders Ser.). (Illus.). 111p. (J). (gr. 7-12). lib. bdg. 30.00 *(978-0-7910-9263-7(1))* Facts On File, Inc.

Finkelstein, Norman H. Ariel Sharon. 128p. (J). (gr. 6-18). 20.95 *(978-1-58013-205-3(7)*, Kar-Ben Publishing); 2005. (Illus.). 112p. (YA). (gr. 7-12). lib. bdg. 29.27 *(978-0-8225-2370-3(1)*, Lerner Pubns.) Lerner Publishing Group.

Krasner, Barbara. Goldie Takes a Stand! Golda Meir's First Crusade. Garrity-Riley, Kelsey, illus. 2014. (ENG.). 32p. (J). (gr. k-4). 17.95 *(978-1-4677-1200-2(0))* Lerner Publishing Group.

—Goldie Takes a Stand: Golda Meir's First Crusade. Garrity-Riley, Kelsey, illus. 2014. (ENG.). 32p. (J). (gr. k-4). 7.95 *(978-1-4677-1201-9(9)*, Kar-Ben Publishing) Lerner Publishing Group.

Sommers, Michael. Ehud Olmert: Prime Minister of Israel. 2009. (Newsmakers Ser.). 112p. (gr. 9-10). 63.90 *(978-1-60851-131-0(6))* Rosen Publishing Group, Inc., The.

Sommers, Michael A. Ehud Olmert: Prime Minister of Israel. 2007. (Newsmakers Ser.). (Illus.). 112p. (YA). (gr. 7-12). lib. bdg. 34.60 *(978-1-4042-1904-5(8))* Rosen Publishing Group, Inc., The.

PRIMERS

see also Alphabet Books

Baby's First Words. 2003. (Illus.). (J). bds. 7.98 *(978-0-7525-8651-9(3))* Parragon, Inc.

Beck, Isabel L., et al. Trophies Kindergarten: A Big, Big Van. 2003. (Trophies Ser.). (gr. k-6). 13.80 *(978-0-15-329546-1(5))* Harcourt Schl. Pubs.

—Trophies Kindergarten: A Bug Can Tug. 2003. (Trophies Ser.). (gr. k-6). 13.80 *(978-0-15-329609-3(7))* Harcourt Schl. Pubs.

—Trophies Kindergarten: A Hat I Like. 2003. (Trophies Ser.). (gr. k-6). 13.80 *(978-0-15-329551-5(1))* Harcourt Schl. Pubs.

—Trophies Kindergarten: But I Can. 2003. (Trophies Ser.). (gr. k-6). 13.80 *(978-0-15-329605-5(4))* Harcourt Schl. Pubs.

—Trophies Kindergarten: Come In. 2003. (Trophies Ser.). (gr. k-6). 13.80 *(978-0-15-329547-8(3))* Harcourt Schl. Pubs.

—Trophies Kindergarten: First Day at School. 2003. (Trophies Ser.). (gr. k-6). 13.80 *(978-0-15-329516-4(3))* Harcourt Schl. Pubs.

—Trophies Kindergarten: Hop In! 2003. (Trophies Ser.). (gr. k-6). 13.80 *(978-0-15-329548-5(1))* Harcourt Schl. Pubs.

—Trophies Kindergarten: Hop on Top. 2003. (Trophies Ser.). (gr. k-6). 13.80 *(978-0-15-329545-4(7))* Harcourt Schl. Pubs.

—Trophies Kindergarten: I Am. 2003. (Trophies Ser.). (gr. k-6). 13.80 *(978-0-15-329525-6(2))* Harcourt Schl. Pubs.

—Trophies Kindergarten: I Can See It! 2003. (Trophies Ser.). (gr. k-6). 13.80 *(978-0-15-329543-0(0))* Harcourt Schl. Pubs.

—Trophies Kindergarten: I Have, You Have. 2003. (Trophies Ser.). (gr. k-6). 13.80 *(978-0-15-329536-2(8))* Harcourt Schl. Pubs.

—Trophies Kindergarten: I Nap. 2003. (Trophies Ser.). (gr. k-6). 13.80 *(978-0-15-329528-7(7))* Harcourt Schl. Pubs.

—Trophies Kindergarten: In a Sub. 2003. (Trophies Ser.). (gr. k-6). 13.80 *(978-0-15-329611-6(9))* Harcourt Schl. Pubs.

—Trophies Kindergarten: Is It a Fish? 2003. (Trophies Ser.). (gr. k-6). 13.80 *(978-0-15-329607-9(0))* Harcourt Schl. Pubs.

—Trophies Kindergarten: Is It for Me? 2003. (Trophies Ser.). (gr. k-6). 13.80 *(978-0-15-329549-2(X))* Harcourt Schl. Pubs.

—Trophies Kindergarten: It Is Fun. 2003. (Trophies Ser.). (gr. k-6). 13.80 *(978-0-15-329608-6(9))* Harcourt Schl. Pubs.

—Trophies Kindergarten: Kip the Ant. 2003. (Trophies Ser.). (gr. k-6). 13.80 *(978-0-15-329539-3(2))* Harcourt Schl. Pubs.

—Trophies Kindergarten: Little Cat, Big Cat. 2003. (Trophies Ser.). (gr. k-6). 13.80 *(978-0-15-329552-2(X))* Harcourt Schl. Pubs.

—Trophies Kindergarten: My Bus. 2003. (Trophies Ser.). (gr. k-6). 13.80 *(978-0-15-329522-5(8))* Harcourt Schl. Pubs.

—Trophies Kindergarten: My Pig. 2003. (Trophies Ser.). (gr. k-6). 13.80 *(978-0-15-329535-5(X))* Harcourt Schl. Pubs.

—Trophies Kindergarten: Pet Day. 2003. (Trophies Ser.). (gr. k-6). 13.80 *(978-0-15-329519-5(8))* Harcourt Schl. Pubs.

—Trophies Kindergarten: Sid Hid. 2003. (Trophies Ser.). (gr. k-6). 13.80 *(978-0-15-329610-9(0))* Harcourt Schl. Pubs.

—Trophies Kindergarten: Sit on My Chair. 2003. (Trophies Ser.). (gr. k-6). 13.80 *(978-0-15-329534-8(1))* Harcourt Schl. Pubs.

—Trophies Kindergarten: Soup. 2003. (Trophies Ser.). (gr. k-6). 13.80 *(978-0-15-329537-9(6))* Harcourt Schl. Pubs.

—Trophies Kindergarten: Tap, Tap, Tap. 2003. (Trophies Ser.). (gr. k-6). 13.80 *(978-0-15-329532-4(5))* Harcourt Schl. Pubs.

—Trophies Kindergarten: The Big Ram. 2003. (Trophies Ser.). (gr. k-6). 13.80 *(978-0-15-329540-9(6))* Harcourt Schl. Pubs.

—Trophies Kindergarten: The Dig. 2003. (Trophies Ser.). (gr. k-6). 13.80 *(978-0-15-329538-6(4))* Harcourt Schl. Pubs.

—Trophies Kindergarten: The Mat. 2003. (Trophies Ser.). (gr. k-6). 13.80 *(978-0-15-329526-3(0))* Harcourt Schl. Pubs.

—Trophies Kindergarten: The Park. 2003. (Trophies Ser.). (gr. k-6). 13.80 *(978-0-15-329533-1(3))* Harcourt Schl. Pubs.

—Trophies Kindergarten: The Party. 2003. (Trophies Ser.). (gr. k-6). 13.80 *(978-0-15-329523-2(6))* Harcourt Schl. Pubs.

—Trophies Kindergarten: The Salad. 2003. (Trophies Ser.). (gr. k-6). 13.80 *(978-0-15-329524-9(4))* Harcourt Schl. Pubs.

—Trophies Kindergarten: Up, up, Up. 2003. (Trophies Ser.). (gr. k-6). 13.80 *(978-0-15-329606-2(2))* Harcourt Schl. Pubs.

—Trophies Kindergarten: We Can Fix. 2003. (Trophies Ser.). (gr. k-6). 13.80 *(978-0-15-329550-8(3))* Harcourt Schl. Pubs.

—Trophies Kindergarten: We Go. 2003. (Trophies Ser.). (gr. k-6). 13.80 *(978-0-15-329527-0(9))* Harcourt Schl. Pubs.

—Trophies Kindergarten: What Can Hop? 2003. (Trophies Ser.). (gr. k-6). 13.80 *(978-0-15-329541-6(4))* Harcourt Schl. Pubs.

—Trophies Kindergarten: What Is in the Box? 2003. (Trophies Ser.). (gr. k-6). 13.80 *(978-0-15-329544-7(9))* Harcourt Schl. Pubs.

—Trophies Kindergarten: Where's My Teddy? 2003. (Trophies Ser.). (gr. k-6). 13.80 *(978-0-15-329517-1(1))* Harcourt Schl. Pubs.

Beech, Linda, et al. Animals. Scholastic, Inc. Staff, ed. 2003. (Sight Word Library). (ENG., Illus.). 8p. pap. 1.25 *(978-0-439-51164-3(X))* Scholastic, Inc.

—City Colors. Scholastic, Inc. Staff, ed. 2003. (Sight Word Library). (ENG., Illus.). 8p. pap. 1.25 *(978-0-439-51158-2(5))* Scholastic, Inc.

—Farm Friends. Scholastic, Inc. Staff, ed. 2003. (Sight Word Library). (ENG.). 8p. pap. 1.25 *(978-0-439-51171-1(2))* Scholastic, Inc.

—Find It! Scholastic, Inc. Staff, ed. 2003. (Sight Word Library). (ENG., Illus.). 8p. pap. 1.25 *(978-0-439-51179-7(8))* Scholastic, Inc.

—Fly Away. Scholastic, Inc. Staff, ed. 2003. (Sight Word Library). (ENG., Illus.). 8p. pap. 1.25 *(978-0-439-51181-0(X))* Scholastic, Inc.

—Go, Go. Scholastic, Inc. Staff, ed. 2003. (Sight Word Library). (ENG., Illus.). 8p. pap. 1.25 *(978-0-439-51169-8(0))* Scholastic, Inc.

—Guessing Game. Scholastic, Inc. Staff, ed. 2003. (Sight Word Library). (ENG., Illus.). 8p. pap. 1.25 *(978-0-439-51161-2(5))* Scholastic, Inc.

—Helpers. Scholastic, Inc. Staff, ed. 2003. (Sight Word Library). (ENG., Illus.). 8p. pap. 1.25 *(978-0-439-51174-2(7))* Scholastic, Inc.

—I Did It! Scholastic, Inc. Staff, ed. 2003. (Sight Word Library). (ENG., Illus.). 8p. pap. 1.25 *(978-0-439-51165-0(8))* Scholastic, Inc.

—Little & Big. Scholastic, Inc. Staff, ed. 2003. (Sight Word Library). (ENG., Illus.). 8p. pap. 1.25 *(978-0-439-51177-3(1))* Scholastic, Inc.

—Me Too! Scholastic, Inc. Staff, ed. 2003. (Sight Word Library). (ENG., Illus.). 8p. pap. 1.25 *(978-0-439-51163-6(1))* Scholastic, Inc.

—The Party. Scholastic, Inc. Staff, ed. 2003. (Sight Word Library). (ENG., Illus.). 8p. pap. 1.25 *(978-0-439-51160-5(7))* Scholastic, Inc.

—Play Time. Scholastic, Inc. Staff, ed. 2003. (Sight Word Library). (ENG., Illus.). 8p. pap. 1.25 *(978-0-439-51167-4(4))* Scholastic, Inc.

—Ride On! Scholastic, Inc. Staff, ed. 2003. (Sight Word Library). (ENG., Illus.). 8p. pap. 1.25 *(978-0-439-51162-9(3))* Scholastic, Inc.

—Run! Scholastic, Inc. Staff, ed. 2003. (Sight Word Library). (ENG., Illus.). 8p. pap. 1.25 *(978-0-439-51168-1(2))* Scholastic, Inc.

—That Hat. Scholastic, Inc. Staff, ed. 2003. (Sight Word Library). (ENG., Illus.). 8p. pap. 1.25 *(978-0-439-51159-9(3))* Scholastic, Inc.

—That Is Funny! Scholastic, Inc. Staff, ed. 2003. (Sight Word Library). (ENG., Illus.). 8p. pap. 1.25 *(978-0-439-51173-5(9))* Scholastic, Inc.

—This Is a Peach. Scholastic, Inc. Staff, ed. 2003. (Sight Word Library). (ENG., Illus.). 8p. pap. 1.25 *(978-0-439-51166-7(6))* Scholastic, Inc.

—Up & Down. Scholastic, Inc. Staff, ed. 2003. (Sight Word Library). (ENG., Illus.). 8p. pap. 1.25 *(978-0-439-51178-0(X))* Scholastic, Inc.

Beech, Linda Ward, et al. Dinner. Scholastic, Inc. Staff, ed. 2003. (Sight Word Library). (ENG., Illus.). 8p. pap. 1.25 *(978-0-439-51176-6(3))* Scholastic, Inc.

—Farm Friends. Scholastic, Inc. Staff, ed. 2003. (Sight Word Library). (ENG., Illus.). 8p. pap. 1.25 *(978-0-439-51157-5(7))* Scholastic, Inc.

—My Bear. Scholastic, Inc. Staff, ed. 2003. (Sight Word Library). (ENG., Illus.). 8p. pap. 1.25 *(978-0-439-51172-8(0))* Scholastic, Inc.

—My Dog. Scholastic, Inc. Staff, ed. 2003. (Sight Word Library). (ENG., Illus.). 8p. pap. 1.25 *(978-0-439-51180-3(1))* Scholastic, Inc.

—New Socks. Scholastic, Inc. Staff, ed. 2003. (Sight Word Library). (ENG., Illus.). 8p. pap. 1.25 *(978-0-439-51170-4(4))* Scholastic, Inc.

—Sharing. Scholastic, Inc. Staff, ed. 2003. (Sight Word Library). (ENG., Illus.). 8p. pap. 1.25 *(978-0-439-51175-9(5))* Scholastic, Inc.

Biddle, Steve & Biddle, Megumi. The Crane's Gift. 2003. (ENG.). 32p. pap. 7.33 *(978-0-582-46143-7(X))* Pearson ESL.

Brown, Jane. Who Has Four Feet? l.t. ed. 2005. (Sadlier Phonics Reading Program: Vol. 1). (Illus.). 8p. (gr. -1-1). 23.00 net. *(978-0-8215-7340-2(3))* Sadlier, William H. Inc.

Crawford, Sheryl Ann Saunders & Sanderson, Ian. Easy-to-Read Mini-Book Plays, 15 bks., Set. 2003. (ENG.). 64p. pap. 10.95 *(978-0-439-20155-1(1))* Scholastic, Inc.

Epstein, Brad M. Columbia University 101: My First Text-Board-Book. l.t. ed. 2005. (101 — My First Text-Board Books). (Illus.). 20p. (J). bds. *(978-0-9727702-1-7(6))* Michaelson Entertainment.

Evans, Mary. Cats! Cats! Cats!, 2. Kovalcik, Terry, illus. l.t. ed. 2005. (Sadlier Phonics Reading Program). 8p. (gr. -1-1). 23.00 net. *(978-0-8215-7348-8(9))* Sadlier, William H. Inc.

—Good Pets, Vol. 3. l.t. ed. 2005. (Sadlier Phonics Reading Program). (Illus.). 8p. (gr. -1-1). 23.00 net. *(978-0-8215-7350-1(0))* Sadlier, William H. Inc.

Goldish, Meish. How Many Are Here? Meyerhoff, Jill, illus. l.t. ed. 2005. (Sadlier Phonics Reading Program). 8p. (gr. -1-1). 23.00 net. *(978-0-8215-7344-0(6))* Sadlier, William H. Inc.

—Nice Vine, Quite Fine, Vol. 2. Sargent, Claudia Karabaic, illus. l.t. ed. 2005. (Little Books & Big Bks.: Vol. 7). 8p. (gr. k-2). 23.00 net. *(978-0-8215-7516-1(3))* Sadlier, William H. Inc.

—Zack Can Fix It!, Vol. 4. Scruton, Clive, illus. l.t. ed. 2005. (Sadlier Phonics Reading Program). 8p. (gr. -1-1). 23.00 net. *(978-0-8215-7359-4(4))* Sadlier, William H. Inc.

Grosset and Dunlap Staff & Penguin Young Readers Group Staff. Away We Go. 2004. (Dick & Jane Ser.: Vol. 7). (ENG., Illus.). 32p. (J). (gr. k-1). mass mkt. 3.99 *(978-0-448-43406-3(7)*, Penguin Young Readers) Penguin Young Readers Group.

—We Play. 2004. (Dick & Jane Ser.: Vol. 11). (ENG., Illus.). 32p. (J). (gr. k-1). mass mkt. 3.99 *(978-0-448-43410-0(5)*, Penguin Young Readers) Penguin Young Readers Group.

—We See. 2004. (Dick & Jane Ser.: Vol. 9). (ENG., Illus.). 32p. (J). (gr. 1-2). mass mkt. 3.99 *(978-0-448-43408-7(3)*, Penguin Young Readers) Penguin Young Readers Group.

—We Work. 2004. (Dick & Jane Ser.: Vol. 10). (ENG., Illus.). 32p. (J). (gr. 1-2). mass mkt. 3.99 *(978-0-448-43409-4(1)*, Penguin Young Readers) Penguin Young Readers Group.

—Who Can Help? 2004. (Dick & Jane Ser.: Vol. 8). (ENG., Illus.). 32p. (J). (gr. 1-2). mass mkt. 3.99 *(978-0-448-43407-0(5)*, Penguin Young Readers) Penguin Young Readers Group.

Harcourt School Publishers Staff. Horizons, Grade 1: Time for Kids Readers. 3rd ed. 2003. (Harcourt Horizons Ser.). pap., tchr. ed. 51.20 *(978-0-15-334646-0(9))* Harcourt Schl. Pubs.

—Horizons, Grade K: Time for Kids Readers. 3rd ed. 2003. (Harcourt Horizons Ser.). pap., tchr. ed. 54.10 *(978-0-15-334645-3(0))* Harcourt Schl. Pubs.

—Trophies Collection. 3rd ed. 2003. (Trophies Ser.). Grade 1. (gr. 1-18). tchr. ed. 596.00 *(978-0-15-327375-9(5))*Grade 2. (gr. 2-18). tchr. ed. 392.80 *(978-0-15-327376-6(3))*Grade 3. (gr. 3-18). tchr. ed. 392.80 *(978-0-15-327377-3(1))*Grade 4. (gr. 4-18). tchr. ed. 419.20 *(978-0-15-327378-0(X))*Grade 5. (gr. 5-18). tchr. ed. 419.20 *(978-0-15-327379-7(8))*Theme 6. (gr. 6-18). tchr. ed. 436.00 *(978-0-15-329239-2(3))* Harcourt Schl. Pubs.

HarperCollins Publishers Ltd. Staff, et al. An I Can Read Halloween Treat, Set. Zimmer, Dirk, illus. 2004. (I Can Read Bks.). (J). (gr. k-3). pap. 11.99 *(978-0-06-054237-5(3)*, Harper Trophy) HarperCollins Pubs.

Herndon, Lynne. Peter & the Wolf. 2003. (ENG.). 32p. pap. 10.00 *(978-0-582-51233-7(6))* Pearson ESL.

Hiebert, Elfrieda H. Ready Read. (J). (gr. -1-3). pap. 179.95 *(978-0-8136-1861-6(4))* Modern Curriculum Pr.

—Ready Read, Stage 1 Take Home Books. (J). (gr. -1-3). pap. 43.50 *(978-0-8136-3277-3(3))* Modern Curriculum Pr.

—Ready Read, Stage 2 Take Home Books, 50 bks. , Set. 2003. (J). (gr. -1-3). pap. 48.50 *(978-0-8136-3278-0(1))* Modern Curriculum Pr.

Hofmeister, Alan, et al. Dash Has Fun. (Reading for All Learners Ser.). (Illus.). (J). pap. *(978-1-56861-145-7(5))* Swift Learning Resources.

Jensen, Patricia. The Mess. Lewis, Anthony, illus. 2003. (My First Reader Ser.). (ENG.). 32p. (J). 18.50 *(978-0-516-22932-4(X)*, Children's Pr.) Scholastic Library Publishing.

Martin, Tyler. I Have a Question, Vol. 4. Williams, Toby, illus. l.t. ed. 2005. (Sadlier Phonics Reading Program). 8p. (gr. -1-1). 23.00 net. *(978-0-8215-7356-3(X))* Sadlier, William H. Inc.

Martinucci, Suzanne. At Space Camp, Vol. 2. l.t. ed. 2005. (Little Books & Big Bks.: Vol. 6). (Illus.). 8p. (gr. k-2). 23.00 net. *(978-0-8215-7515-4(5))* Sadlier, William H. Inc.

Marzollo, Jean. I Spy a Dinosaur's Eye. Wick, Walter, illus. 2003. (Scholastic Reader Level 1 Ser.). (ENG.). 32p. (J). (gr. -1-3). pap. 3.99 *(978-0-439-52471-1(7)*, Cartwheel Bks.) Scholastic, Inc.

MCP Staff. Ready Reader S1. 2003. (J). (gr. -1-3). pap. 227.95 *(978-0-8136-1432-8(5))* Modern Curriculum Pr.

—Stage Two - Early. 2003. (J). (gr. -1-3). pap. 227.95 *(978-0-8136-1433-5(3))* Modern Curriculum Pr.

Michaels, David. Bye-Bye, Katy, Vol. 3. Platt, Pierre, illus. l.t. ed. 2005. (Sadlier Phonics Reading Program). 8p. (gr. -1-1). 23.00 net. *(978-0-8215-7354-9(3))* Sadlier, William H. Inc.

Miranda, Anne. The Best Place. l.t. ed. 2005. (Little Books & Big Bks.: Vol. 5). (Illus.). 8p. (gr. k-2). 23.00 net. *(978-0-8215-7514-7(7))* Sadlier, William H. Inc.

—Looking at Lizards, Vol. 2. l.t. ed. 2005. (Sadlier Phonics Reading Program). (Illus.). 8p. (gr. -1-1). 23.00 net. *(978-0-8215-7346-4(2))* Sadlier, William H. Inc.

—Peach Tree Street, Vol. 2. Lodge, Katherine, illus. l.t. ed. 2005. (Little Books & Big Bks.: Vol. 10). 8p. (gr. k-2). 23.00 net. *(978-0-8215-7519-2(8))* Sadlier, William H. Inc.

—Weather Wise, Vol. 3. l.t. ed. 2005. (Sadlier Phonics Reading Program). (Illus.). 8p. (gr. -1-1). 23.00 net. *(978-0-8215-7351-8(9))* Sadlier, William H. Inc.

Montardre, Hélène. The Cat & the Dog. 2003. (Illus.). 8p. (J). bds. 7.95 *(978-1-58728-483-0(9)*, Two-Can Publishing) T&N Children's Publishing.

—Night & Day. 2003. (Illus.). 8p. (J). bds. 7.95 *(978-1-58728-481-6(2)*, Two-Can Publishing) T&N Children's Publishing.

Nicholas, Melissa. Pumpkin Days, Vol. 3. l.t. ed. 2005. (Sadlier Phonics Reading Program). (Illus.). 8p. (gr. -1-1). 23.00 net. *(978-0-8215-7352-5(7))* Sadlier, William H. Inc.

—Stop by a Pond. Gram, Patrick, illus. l.t. ed. 2005. (Little Books & Big Bks.: Vol. 3). 8p. (gr. k-2). 23.00 net. *(978-0-8215-7512-3(0))* Sadlier, William H. Inc.

—Who Is My Mom? Cassels, Jean, illus. l.t. ed. 2005. (Sadlier Phonics Reading Program). 8p. (gr. -1-1). 23.00 net. *(978-0-8215-7341-9(1))* Sadlier, William H. Inc.

O'Keefe, Ruth A. Starter One Hundred One, Bk. 8. AEVAC, Inc. Staff, ed. (Structured Beginning Reading Program Ser.). 96p. (J). stu. ed. 3.50 *(978-0-913356-14-2(X))* AEVAC, Inc.

Olivia, Cynthia. In January & June, Vol. 4. l.t. ed. 2005. (Sadlier Phonics Reading Program: Vol. 16). (Illus.). 8p. (gr. -1-1). 23.00 net. *(978-0-8215-7355-6(1))* Sadlier, William H. Inc.

Packard, Mary. Surprise! Huang, Benrei, illus. 2003. (My First Reader Ser.). (ENG.). 32p. (J). 18.50 *(978-0-516-22937-9(0)*, Children's Pr.) Scholastic Library Publishing.

Paul, Kate. The Best Ride, Vol. 2. l.t. ed. 2005. (Sadlier Phonics Reading Program). (Illus.). 8p. (gr. -1-1). 23.00 net. *(978-0-8215-7345-7(4))* Sadlier, William H. Inc.

Penguin Young Readers Group Staff. Fun with Dick & Jane. 2004. (Dick & Jane Ser.: Vol. 12). (ENG., Illus.). 32p. (J). (gr. 1-2). mass mkt. 3.99 *(978-0-448-43411-7(3)*, Penguin Young Readers) Penguin Young Readers Group.

Practice Power School Bus Book: Preschool. 2003. 24p. (J). (gr. -1). spiral bd. *(978-1-930355-41-5(6))* Bright of America.

Reading Friends Staff. Peanut Single. (J). *(978-0-8136-3813-3(5))* Modern Curriculum Pr.

—Run Single. (J). *(978-0-8136-3787-7(2))* Modern Curriculum Pr.

Ready Reader Staff. The Ant, Level 6, Bk. 1. 2003. (J). (gr. -1-3). pap. 24.50 *(978-0-8136-1983-5(1))* Modern Curriculum Pr.

—Mr. Wink, 6 bks., Set, Level 8, Bk. 48. (J). pap. 24.50 *(978-0-8136-0781-8(7))* Modern Curriculum Pr.

Rothman, Cynthia Anne. Funny Bugs. Lester, Mike, illus. l.t. ed. 2005. (Little Books & Big Bks.: Vol. 4). 8p. (gr. k-2). 23.00 net. *(978-0-8215-7513-0(9))* Sadlier, William H. Inc.

—I Love to Read, 3. l.t. ed. 2005. (Sadlier Phonics Reading Program). (Illus.). 8p. (gr. -1-1). 23.00 net. *(978-0-8215-7353-2(5))* Sadlier, William H. Inc.

—Violets & Vegetables, Vol. 4. l.t. ed. 2005. (Sadlier Phonics Reading Program). (Illus.). 8p. (gr. -1-1). 23.00 net. *(978-0-8215-7357-0(8))* Sadlier, William H. Inc.

—What Does Sam Sell? Alley, R. W., illus. l.t. ed. 2005. (Sadlier Phonics Reading Program). 8p. (gr. -1-1). 23.00 net. *(978-0-8215-7342-6(X))* Sadlier, William H. Inc.

—Yes, You Can, Vol. 4. l.t. ed. 2005. (Sadlier Phonics Reading Program). (Illus.). 8p. (gr. -1-1). 23.00 net. *(978-0-8215-7358-7(6))* Sadlier, William H. Inc.

Schecter, Deborah & Charlesworth, Liza. My First Little Readers: 25 Reproducible Mini-Books That Give Kids a Great Start in Reading. 2004. (My First Little Readers Ser.). (ENG.). 64p. pap. 11.99 *(978-0-439-57407-5(2)*, Teaching Resources) Scholastic, Inc.

School Zone Publishing. Beginning Reading. 2003. (ENG.). (J). cd-rom 19.99 *(978-1-58947-921-0(1))*; (gr. k-1). cd-rom 19.99 *(978-1-58947-923-4(8))*; (gr. 1-2). cd-rom 19.99 *(978-1-58947-922-7(X))*; (gr. 1-2). cd-rom 19.99 *(978-1-58947-924-1(6))* School Zone Publishing Co.

Schumacher, Stef. Amazing Blue Animals, Vol. 2. l.t. ed. 2005. (Little Books & Big Bks.: Vol. 9). (Illus.). 8p. (gr. k-2). 23.00 net. *(978-0-8215-7518-5(X))* Sadlier, William H. Inc.

Smith, Dodie. 101 Dalmatians. 2003. (ENG., Illus.). 32p. (C). pap. 28.73 *(978-0-582-52979-3(4))* Pearson ESL.

Steck-Vaughn Staff. At-Home Workbooks: Reading. 2004. (Illus.). (gr. 3). pap., wbk. ed. 5.99 *(978-0-7398-8526-0(X))* Steck-Vaughn.

Stuart, Matt. Who Can Run Fast? l.t. ed. 2005. (Little Books & Big Bks.: Vol. 1). (Illus.). 8p. (gr. k-2). 23.00 net. *(978-0-8215-7510-9(4))* Sadlier, William H. Inc.

Taylor, Beth. Tina's Toys. l.t. ed. 2005. (Sadlier Phonics Reading Program). (Illus.). 8p. (gr. -1-1). 23.00 net. *(978-0-8215-7343-3(8))* Sadlier, William H. Inc.

Thryce, Marc & Robinson, Tim. Look at the Pictures. l.t. ed. 2005. (Little Books & Big Bks.: Vol. 2). (Illus.). 8p. (gr. k-2). 23.00 net. *(978-0-8215-7511-6(2))* Sadlier, William H. Inc.

Titzer, Robert C. A Book Your Baby Can Read! Dozier, Brendan et al, photos by. 2003. (Early Language Development Ser.: Vol. 2). (Illus.). 14p. (J). pap. 7.95 *(978-0-9657510-5-6(8)*, 0-9657510-5-8) Infant Learning Co., The.

—A Book Your Baby Can Read! Early Language Development Series. Dozier, Lisa et al, photos by. 2003. (Early Language Development Ser.: Vol. 3). (Illus.). 14p. (J). pap. 7.95 *(978-0-9657510-9-4(0)*, 0-9657510-9-0) Infant Learning Co., The.

—A Book Your Baby Can Read! 5 Book Set: Early Language Development Series, 5 vols., Vol. 1. 2003. (Illus.). 80p. (J). pap. 29.95 *(978-1-931026-05-5(X)*, 1-931026-05-X) Infant Learning Co., The.

—A Book Your Baby Can Read! Review: Early Language Development Series. Dozier, Brendan et al, photos by. 2003. (Early Language Development Ser.). (Illus.). 14p. (J). pap. 7.95 *(978-1-931026-04-8(1)*, 1-931026-04-1) Infant Learning Co., The.

—A Book Your Baby Can Read! Starter: Early Language Development Series, 1, Starter Book. Dozier, Lisa et al, photos by. 2003. (Book Your Baby Can Read!: Starter Book). (Illus.). 14p. (J). pap. 7.95 *(978-1-931026-03-1(3)*, 1-931026-03-3) Infant Learning Co., The.

Unknown, Unknown & Grosset and Dunlap Staff. Dick & Jane Fun Wherever We Are. 2004. (Dick & Jane Ser.). (ENG., Illus.). 144p. (J). (gr. -1-1). 8.99 *(978-0-448-43614-2(0)*, Grosset & Dunlap) Penguin Young Readers Group.

Winter, Max. Did You Know?, Vol. 2. Rechin, Kevin, illus. l.t. ed. 2005. (Little Books & Big Bks.: Vol. 8). 8p. (gr. k-2). 23.00 net. *(978-0-8215-7517-8(1))* Sadlier, William H. Inc.

PRIMITIVE ART

see Art, Primitive

PRINCE EDWARD ISLAND

MacDonald, Hugh. I Is for Island: A Prince Edward Island Alphabet. Jones, Brenda, illus. 2012. (ENG.). 40p. (J). (gr. 1-5). 16.95 *(978-1-58536-367-4(7))* Sleeping Bear Pr.

PRINCE EDWARD ISLAND—FICTION

Boudreau, Hélène. Keep Out!, 1 vol. Lucas, Diane, illus. 2010. (ENG.). 80p. (J). (gr. 1-4). pap. 8.95 *(978-1-55109-753-4(2))* Nimbus Publishing, Ltd. CAN. Dist: Orca Bk. Pubs. USA.

Chronicles of Avonlea. 2004. 142p. (YA). pap. 7.95 *(978-1-57646-893-7(3))* Quiet Vision Publishing.

Helldorfer, M. C. Anne of Green Gables. Beier, Ellen, illus. 2003. (ENG.). 40p. (J). (gr. -1-2). pap. 7.99 *(978-0-440-41614-2(0)*, Dragonfly Bks.) Random Hse. Children's Bks.

Kessler, Deirdre & Montgomery, L. M. Anne of Green Gables, 1 vol. Smith, David Preston, illus. 2008. (ENG.). 46p. (J). (gr. k-5). pap. 10.95 *(978-1-55109-662-9(5))* Nimbus Publishing, Ltd. CAN. Dist: Orca Bk. Pubs. USA.

Knutson, Lori. The Ghost of Northumberland Strait. 2008. (ENG.). 152p. (J). (gr. 5-9). pap. 9.95 *(978-1-894917-43-8(X)*, Napoleon & Co.) Dundurn CAN. Dist: Ingram Publisher Services.

MacDonald, George. Princess & the Goblin. 2006. 128p. per. 10.95 *(978-1-59818-653-6(1))* Aegypan.

—The Princess & the Goblin. 2010. 222p. pap. 13.95 *(978-0-557-47296-3(2))* Lulu Pr., Inc.

Manuel, Lynn. The Summer of the Marco Polo, 1 vol. Charko, Kasia, illus. 2007. (ENG.). 32p. (J). (gr. -1-3). 17.95 *(978-1-55143-330-1(3))* Orca Bk. Pubs. USA.

Montgomery, L. M. Along the Shore: Tales by the Sea. (YA). 22.95 *(978-0-8488-2655-0(8))* Amereon Ltd.

—Ana la de Isla. 4th ed. (Ana la de Tejas Verdes Ser.: 3).Tr. of Anne of the Island. (SPA., Illus.). 240p. (YA). (gr. 5-8). *(978-84-7888-635-7(4)*, SAL5036) Emece Editores ESP. Dist: Lectorum Pubns., Inc.

—Anne of Avonlea. 2005. pap. *(978-1-905432-15-8(1))* Dodo Pr.

—Anne of Avonlea. 2011. (Oxford Children's Classics Ser.). (ENG.). 336p. (YA). (gr. 3-18). 9.95 *(978-0-19-276359-4(8))* Oxford Univ. Pr., Inc.

—Anne of Avonlea. 2005. (Aladdin Classics Ser.). (ENG., Illus.). 416p. (J). (gr. 4-7). pap. 5.99 *(978-1-4169-0328-4(3)*, Aladdin) Simon & Schuster Children's Publishing.

—Anne of Avonlea. Andreasen, Dan, illus. 2009. (Classic Starts(tm) Ser.). (ENG.). 160p. (J). (gr. 2-4). 6.95 *(978-1-4027-5424-1(8))* Sterling Publishing Co., Inc.

—Anne of Avonlea. McKowen, Scott, illus. 2008. (Sterling Unabridged Classics Ser.). (ENG.). 256p. (J). 9.95 *(978-1-4027-5428-9(0))* Sterling Publishing Co., Inc.

—Anne of Avonlea. 2012. (World Classics Ser.). (ENG.). 228p. pap. 19.99 *(978-1-909438-94-1(4)*, Sovereign) Bollinger, Max GBR. Dist: Lightning Source UK, Ltd., Gardners Bks. Ltd.

—Anne of Avonlea. l.t. ed. 2006. (ENG.). pap. *(978-1-4068-3173-3(5))* Echo Library.

—Anne of Green Gables. 400p. 2005. 33.95 *(978-1-4218-0660-0(6)*, 1st World Library - Literary Society) 2004. per. 16.95 *(978-1-59540-110-6(5))* 1st World Publishing, Inc.

—Anne of Green Gables. 2009. 292p. 27.99 *(978-1-60512-375-2(7))*; pap. 14.99 *(978-1-60512-475-9(3))* Akasha Publishing, LLC. (Akasha Classics).

—Anne of Green Gables. 2008. 316p. 28.99 *(978-0-554-32848-5(8))* 2008. 316p. 29.99 *(978-0-554-23545-5(5))* 2007. (ENG.). 312p. pap. 24.99 *(978-1-4264-4662-7(4))* Creative Media Partners, LLC.

—Anne of Green Gables. 2008. (Anne of Green Gables Ser.). (ENG.). 366p. (J). (gr. 4-7). pap. 9.95 *(978-0-9782552-6-8(7))* Davenport Pr. CAN. Dist: Independent Pubs. Group.

—Anne of Green Gables. 2007. per. 6.99 *(978-1-4209-2922-5(4))* Digireads.com Publishing.

—Anne of Green Gables. 2007. 284p. per. *(978-1-4065-6399-3(4))* Dodo Pr.

—Anne of Green Gables. 2007. 572p. *(978-1-84702-773-3(3))* 2006. pap. *(978-1-4068-2170-3(5))* Echo Library.

—Anne of Green Gables. 2008. 316p. pap. 16.95 *(978-1-60096-101-4(0))*; pap. 16.95 *(978-1-60096-565-4(2))* Editorium, The.

—Anne of Green Gables. 2009. 242p. pap. 8.58 *(978-0-217-43952-7(7))* General Bks. LLC.

—Anne of Green Gables. 2005. (My First Classics Ser.). 112p. (J). (gr. k-3). pap., pap. 4.99 *(978-0-06-079147-6(0)*, HarperFestival) HarperCollins Pubs.

—Anne of Green Gables. 2005. 21.99 *(978-1-4142-5125-7(4))* IndyPublish.com.

—Anne of Green Gables. 2008. (ENG.). 376p. (gr. k-12). pap. 14.95 *(978-0-7710-9368-5(3)*, New Can Library) McClelland & Stewart CAN. Dist: Penguin Random Hse. LLC.

—Anne of Green Gables, 1 vol. 2016. (ENG.). 352p. (J). (gr. 2-5). pap. 10.95 *(978-1-55109-249-2(2))* Nimbus Publishing, Ltd. CAN. Dist: National Bk. Network.

—Anne of Green Gables. Rubio, Mary Henley & Waterston, Elizabeth, eds. 2007. (Norton Critical Editions Ser.: 0). (ENG., Illus.). 464p. (C). (gr. 9-12). per. 15.02 *(978-0-393-92695-8(8)*, 92695) Norton, W. W. & Co., Inc.

—Anne of Green Gables. 2003. (ENG.). 320p. (gr. 5-7). 5.95 *(978-0-451-52882-7(4)*, Signet) Penguin Publishing Group.

—Anne of Green Gables. 2008. (Puffin Classics Ser.). (ENG., Illus.). 464p. (J). (gr. 3-7). 5.99 *(978-0-14-132159-2(8)*, Puffin Books) Penguin Young Readers Group.

—Anne of Green Gables. 2003. 320p. (J). (gr. 4-7). 12.60 *(978-0-7569-1848-4(0))* Perfection Learning Corp.

—Anne of Green Gables. 2013. (Word Cloud Classics Ser.). (ENG.). 264p. pap. 14.99 *(978-1-60710-728-6(7)*, Thunder Bay Pr.) Readerlink Distribution Services, LLC.

—Anne of Green Gables. 2009. 224p. pap. 15.45 *(978-1-4385-1847-3(1)*, Book Jungle) Standard Pubns., Inc.

—Anne of Green Gables. McKowen, Scott, illus. 2004. (Sterling Unabridged Classics Ser.). (ENG.). 312p. (J). (gr. 5). 9.95 *(978-1-4027-1451-1(3))* Sterling Publishing Co., Inc.

—Anne of Green Gables. Corvino, Lucy, illus. 2005. (Classic Starts(tm) Ser.). (ENG.). 160p. (J). (gr. 2-4). 6.95 *(978-1-4027-1130-5(1))* Sterling Publishing Co., Inc.

—Anne of Green Gables. 2008. (Modern Library Classics Ser.). (ENG.). 320p. pap. 9.00 *(978-0-8129-7903-9(6)*, Modern Library) Random House Publishing Group.

—Anne of Green Gables. 2012. (World Classics Ser.). (ENG.). 260p. pap. 19.99 *(978-1-909438-96-5(0)*, Sovereign) Bollinger, Max GBR. Dist: Lightning Source UK, Ltd.

—Anne of Green Gables. rev. ed. 2007. 280p. pap. 21.99 *(978-1-4264-4611-5(X))* Creative Media Partners, LLC.

—Anne of Green Gables. l.t. ed. 2006. pap. *(978-1-4068-3174-0(3))* Echo Library.

—Anne of Green Gables. 2004. reprint ed. pap. 27.95 *(978-1-4191-0717-7(8))*; pap. 1.99 *(978-1-4192-0717-4(2))* Kessinger Publishing, LLC.

—Anne of Green Gables. l.t. ed. 2009. (World Classics Ser.). 288p. pap. 21.95 *(978-1-59688-123-5(2))* Large Print Bk. Co., The.

—The Anne of Green Gables Collection: Six Complete & Unabridged Novels in One Volume. 2013. 1140p. *(978-1-78139-344-4(3))* Benediction Classics.

—Anne of the Green Gables. 2014. (Anne of Green Gables Ser.: 1). (ENG.). 352p. (YA). (gr. 5-12). pap. 9.99 *(978-1-4022-8894-4(8))* Sourcebooks, Inc.

—Anne of the Island. 2012. (World Classics Ser.). (ENG.). 212p. pap. 19.99 *(978-1-909438-92-7(8)*, Sovereign) Bollinger, Max GBR. Dist: Lightning Source UK, Ltd.

—Anne of the Island. 2008. (Anne of Green Gables Ser.). (ENG.). 272p. (J). (gr. 4-7). pap. 9.95 *(978-0-9782552-8-2(3))* Davenport Pr. CAN. Dist: Independent Pubs. Group.

—Anne of the Island. 2006. (ENG.). pap. *(978-1-4068-2171-0(3))*; pap. *(978-1-4068-3175-7(1))* Echo Library.

—Anne of the Island. 2004. reprint ed. pap. 1.99 *(978-1-4192-0718-1(0))*; pap. 30.95 *(978-1-4179-0885-1(8))* Kessinger Publishing, LLC.

—Anne of the Island. l.t. ed. 2004. 396p. 26.00 *(978-1-58287-640-5(1))* North Bks.

—Anne of the Island. 2010. (Puffin Classics Ser.). (ENG.). 368p. (J). (gr. 5-7). pap. 5.99 *(978-0-14-132736-5(7)*, Puffin Books) Penguin Young Readers Group.

—Emily Climbs: Emily of New Moon Series. 2014. (Emily Ser.: 2). (ENG.). 368p. (YA). (gr. 5-12). pap. 8.99 *(978-1-4022-8915-6(4))* Sourcebooks, Inc.

—Emily's Quest. 2014. (Emily Ser.: 3). (ENG.). 256p. (YA). (gr. 5-12). pap. 8.99 *(978-1-4022-8918-7(9))* Sourcebooks, Inc.

—The Golden Road. l.t. ed. 2007. (ENG.). 254p. pap. 23.99 *(978-1-4264-7144-5(0))* Creative Media Partners, LLC.

—Jane of Lantern Hill. 2014. (ENG.). 272p. (YA). (gr. 5-12). pap. 11.99 *(978-1-4022-8930-9(8))* Sourcebooks, Inc.

—Kilmeny of the Orchard. 2010. 146p. pap. 16.95 *(978-1-60444-108-6(9))* IndoEuropeanPublishing.com.

—Kilmeny of the Orchard. 2004. 100p. (YA). pap. 7.95 *(978-1-57646-894-4(1))* Quiet Vision Publishing.

—Magic for Marigold. 2014. (ENG.). 336p. (YA). (gr. 5-12). pap. 8.99 *(978-1-4022-8921-7(9))* Sourcebooks, Inc.

—Pat of Silver Bush. 2014. (ENG.). 368p. (YA). (gr. 5-12). pap. 13.99 *(978-1-4022-8924-8(3))* Sourcebooks, Inc.

—Rainbow Valley. 2004. reprint ed. 210p. pap. 24.95 *(978-1-4191-4385-4(9))*; pap. 1.99 *(978-1-4192-4385-1(3))* Kessinger Publishing, LLC.

—Rainbow Valley. 2005. (Twelve-Point Ser.). lib. bdg. 25.00 *(978-1-58287-333-6(X))*; lib. bdg. 26.00 *(978-1-58287-825-6(0))* North Bks.

—Rainbow Valley. 2004. 184p. (YA). pap. 8.95 *(978-1-57646-890-6(9))* Quiet Vision Publishing.

—Rilla of Ingleside. 2007. (ENG.). 284p. pap. 21.99 *(978-1-4346-5285-0(8))*; 314p. pap. 24.99 *(978-1-4346-5286-7(6))* Creative Media Partners, LLC.

—Rilla of Ingleside. 2004. 224p. (YA). pap. 10.95 *(978-1-57646-891-3(7))* Quiet Vision Publishing.

—Rilla of Ingleside. 2006. 384p. pap. 25.45 *(978-1-59462-427-8(5)*, Book Jungle) Standard Pubns., Inc.

—The Story Girl. Date not set. 22.95 *(978-0-8488-2372-6(9))* Amereon Ltd.

—The Story Girl. 2007. (ENG.). 254p. pap. 21.99 *(978-1-4346-5287-4(4))*; 280p. pap. 23.99 *(978-1-4346-5288-1(2))* Creative Media Partners, LLC.

—The Story Girl. 2004. reprint ed. pap. 1.99 *(978-1-4192-8361-1(8))* Kessinger Publishing, LLC.

—The Story Girl. 2005. (Twelve-Point Ser.). lib. bdg. 24.00 *(978-1-58287-336-7(4))*; lib. bdg. 25.00 *(978-1-58287-828-7(5))* North Bks.

—A Tangled Web. 2009. (Voyageur Classics Ser.). (ENG.). 296p. pap. 24.99 *(978-1-55488-403-2(9))* Dundurn CAN. Dist: Ingram Publisher Services.

Montgomery, L. M & Castelao, Patricia. Anne of Green Gables, 1 vol. 2012. (Calico Illustrated Classics Ser.: No. 4). (ENG., Illus.). 112p. (J). (gr. 3-6). 27.07 *(978-1-61641-612-6(2))* Magic Wagon.

Rath, Tom H. Donkey Oatie's Impossible Dream. MacAdam, Reegory, illus. 2012. 24p. pap. *(978-0-9866065-5-7(3))* Wood Islands Prints.

Shecter, Vicky Alvear. Cleopatra's Moon. 2011. (ENG.). 368p. (J). (gr. 9-7). 18.99 *(978-0-545-22130-6(7)*, Levine, Arthur A. Bks.) Scholastic, Inc.

Stretch, Ian. Marty the Mailbox. McNevin, Dale, illus. 2009. 24p. pap. 10.95 *(978-1-4251-8435-3(9))* Trafford Publishing.

PRINCES

Ariganello, Lisa. Henry the Navigator: Prince of Portuguese Exploration. 2006. (In the Footsteps of Explorers Ser.). (ENG., Illus.). 32p. (J). (gr. 4-7). pap. *(978-0-7787-2469-8(7))*; lib. bdg. *(978-0-7787-2433-9(6))* Crabtree Publishing Co.

Braun, Eric. Prince: The Man, the Symbol, the Music. 2017. (Gateway Biographies Ser.). (ENG.). 48p. (J). (gr. 4-8). 12.99 ***(978-1-5124-3861-1(8)***, Lerner Pubns.); 39.99 ***(978-1-5124-3860-4(X)***, Lerner Pubns.); (Illus.). 26.65 *(978-1-5124-3456-9(6))*; 39.99 ***(978-1-5124-3457-6(4)***, Lerner Pubns.) Lerner Publishing Group.

Bryan, Dale-Marie. William & Kate. 2012. (Stars of Today Ser.). (ENG.). 32p. (J). (gr. 2-5). 28.50 *(978-1-61473-287-7(6)*, 205049) Child's World, Inc., The.

Diemer, Lauren & Kissock, Heather. Prince William & Kate Middleton. 2013. (J). *(978-1-62127-392-9(X))* Weigl Pubs., Inc.

Dyan, Penelope. A Royal Residence — A Kid's Guide to Windsor Castle. Weigand, John D., photos by. 2011. (Illus.). 40p. pap. 12.95 *(978-1-935630-65-4(2))* Bellissima Publishing, LLC.

Greenhaven Press Staff, ed. Prince Harry. 2012. (People in the News Ser.). (ENG., Illus.). 128p. (J). (gr. 7-10). lib. bdg. 33.95 *(978-1-4205-0760-7(5)*, Lucent Bks.) Cengage Gale.

Hurwicz, Claude. Henry the Navigator. 2009. (Primary Source Library of Famous Explorers Ser.). 24p. (gr. 4-4). 42.50 *(978-1-60854-124-9(X)*, PowerKids Pr.) Rosen Publishing Group, Inc., The.

Lee, Sally. Princes & Princesses, 1 vol. 2013. (Royalty Ser.). (ENG.). 24p. (gr. k-1). lib. bdg. 26.65 *(978-1-62065-124-7(6)*, Pebble Plus) Capstone Press of Coughlan Cos.

Ribke, Simone T. William & Kate: The Prince & Princess. 2016. (Rookie Biographies(tm) Ser.). (ENG., Illus.). 32p. (J). lib. bdg. 25.00 *(978-0-531-22548-6(8)*, Children's Pr.) Scholastic Library Publishing.

Tieck, Sarah. Prince William: Real-Life Prince, 1 vol. 2011. (Big Buddy Biographies Set 7 Ser.). (ENG., Illus.). 32p. (J). (gr. 2-5). 28.50 *(978-1-61783-022-8(4))* ABDO Publishing Co.

Tracy, Kathleen. Prince William of Wales. 2011. (Blue Banner Biography Ser.). (YA). (gr. 4-7). 25.70 *(978-1-61228-191-9(5))* Mitchell Lane Pubs., Inc.

PRINCES—FICTION

Adrien, Gilles & Broders, Alain. The Planet of the Giant. Élyum Studio, illus. 2013. (Little Prince Ser.: 9). (ENG.). 56p. (J). (gr. 4-8). lib. bdg. 26.60 *(978-0-7613-8759-6(5)*, Graphic Universe™) Lerner Publishing Group.

Adventures in Flatfrost. 2014. (Kingdom of Wrenly Ser.: 5). (ENG., Illus.). 128p. (J). (gr. k-4). pap. 5.99 *(978-1-4814-1388-6(0)*, Little Simon) Little Simon.

Albright, Emily. The Heir & the Spare. 2016. (ENG.). 287p. (YA). 17.99 *(978-1-4405-9010-8(9)*, Simon Pulse) F&W Media, Inc.

Almhjell, Tone. The Twistrose Key. Schoenherr, Ian, illus. 2014. (ENG.). 384p. (J). (gr. 5). pap. 8.99 *(978-0-14-242345-5(9)*, Puffin Books) Penguin Young Readers Group.

Andersen, Hans Christian. The Little Mermaid Retold. Charlotte, J. M., illus. 2013. 48p. 18.00 *(978-0-9895422-0-3(3))* MHC Ministries.

Ant, Exupery. Giorno con il Piccolo Principe. pap. 13.95 *(978-88-451-2269-9(7))* Fabbri Editori - RCS Libri ITA. Dist: Distribooks, Inc.

—Journee avec le Petit Prince. pap. 10.95 *(978-2-07-054268-0(8))* Gallimard, Editions FRA. Dist: Distribooks, Inc.

—L apprends a compter avec Le. pap. 10.95 *(978-2-07-054270-3(X))* Gallimard, Editions FRA. Dist: Distribooks, Inc.

—Piccolo Principe el Suio. pap. 13.95 *(978-88-451-2266-8(2))* Fabbri Editori - RCS Libri ITA. Dist: Distribooks, Inc.

anthony, chance. The Princess of Du'val. 2010. 36p. pap. 7.14 *(978-0-557-03816-9(2))* Lulu Pr., Inc.

Arthur, Felix & Capon, Jenny. Golden Prince. 2012. (IPP Single Titles Ser.). (Illus.). 32p. (J). (gr. -1-1). pap. 7.99 *(978-0-9567122-3-3(1))* Lerner Publishing Group.

At Your Service. 2014. (Mix Ser.). (ENG., Illus.). 272p. (J). (gr. 4-8). pap. 7.99 *(978-1-4814-0283-5(8)*, Aladdin) Simon & Schuster Children's Publishing.

Bacon, Lee. The Battle for Urth. 2016. (Legendtopia Ser.). (ENG., Illus.). 288p. (J). (gr. 4-7). 16.99 *(978-0-553-53402-3(5)*, Delacorte Bks. for Young Readers) Random Hse. Children's Bks.

Bacon, Lee. Legendtopia Book #2: the Shadow Queen. 2017. (Legendtopia Ser.: 2). (ENG.). 272p. (J). (gr. 4-7). 16.99 ***(978-0-553-53406-1(8)***, Delacorte Bks. for Young Readers) Random Hse. Children's Bks.

Baker, E. D. Dragon's Breath: Read-Along/Homework Pack, 6 vols. unabr. ed. 2005. (Frog Princess Ser.: 2). (SPA.). (J). (gr. 5-8). 78.75 *(978-1-4193-3563-1(4)*, 42041) Recorded Bks., Inc.

Baker, Sara, illus. Ready to Read Sleeping Beauty. 2007. (Ready to Read Ser.). 31p. (J). (gr. k-2). *(978-1-84610-441-1(6))* Make Believe Ideas.

Beck, Patricia. Prince Hasmir's High Seas Adventure. 2011. 24p. pap. 15.99 *(978-1-4628-6151-4(2))* Xlibris Corp.

—Princess Feldings & the Academy of Queens. 2010. 28p. 13.99 *(978-1-4490-1376-9(7))* AuthorHouse.

Bell, Hilari. The Prophecy. 2006. (ENG., Illus.). 208p. (J). (gr. 5-9). 15.99 *(978-0-06-059943-0(X))* HarperCollins Pubs.

Beneath the Stone Forest. 2014. (Kingdom of Wrenly Ser.: 6). (ENG., Illus.). 128p. (J). (gr. k-4). pap. 5.99 *(978-1-4814-1391-6(0)*, Little Simon) Little Simon.

Bentley, Douglas W. What Will It Take for a Toad to Kiss a Monkey: The Adventures of Princess Gracie & Prince Wallaby. Bentley, Julia Faye, illus. 2008. 52p. per. 24.95 *(978-1-4137-8849-5(1))* America Star Bks.

Bently, Peter. The Prince & the Porker. Roberts, David, illus. 2017. (ENG.). 32p. (J). (gr. k-2). 16.95 *(978-1-4197-2312-4(X)*, Abrams Bks. for Young Readers) Abrams, Inc.

Berry, Julie. The Amaranth Enchantment. (ENG.). (YA). (gr. 5-8). 2010. 336p. pap. 7.99 *(978-1-59990-449-8(7)*, 9781599904498) 2009. 320p. 16.99 *(978-1-59990-334-7(2)*, 9781599903347) Bloomsbury Publishing USA. (Bloomsbury USA Childrens).

Bidaud, Agnès. The Planet of Libris. Élyum Studio, illus. 2013. (Little Prince Ser.: 11). (ENG.). 48p. (J). (gr. 4-8). lib. bdg. 26.60 *(978-0-7613-8761-9(7)*, Graphic Universe™) Lerner Publishing Group.

Bishop, Anne. Anne Bishop's Christmas Dram: The Gift of Three. 2013. 28p. pap. 24.95 *(978-1-4626-8276-8(6))* America Star Bks.

Blevins, Wiley. Cinderella & the Vampire Prince. Cox, Steve, illus. 2016. (Scary Tales Retold Ser.). (ENG.). 24p. (gr. k-3). lib. bdg. 23.99 *(978-1-63440-090-9(9))* Red Chair Pr.

Bolger, Kevin. Sir Fartsalot Hunts the Booger. Gilpin, Stephen, illus. 2009. (ENG.). 224p. (J). (gr. 3-7). 7.99 *(978-1-59514-284-9(3)*, Razorbill) Penguin Young Readers Group.

Boulton, M. T. Megan Button & the Brim-Tree. 2012. 106p. pap. *(978-1-909039-06-3(3))* Legend Pr.

Bower, Tamara. How the Amazon Queen Fought the Prince of Egypt. Bower, Tamara, illus. 2014. (ENG., Illus.). 36p. (J). (gr. 2-6). 16.99 *(978-1-4814-2526-1(9)*, Atheneum Bks. for Young Readers) Simon & Schuster Children's Publishing.

Brandon, Wendy. The Frog Prince: Board Book & Puppet Theater. Beckes, Shirley V., illus. 2004. (J). *(978-1-883043-46-9(8))* Straight Edge Pr., The.

Bredin, Henrietta & McEwen, Priscilla. The Prince & the Goosegirl: A Story with Activities Based on the Opera by Humperdinck. 2006. (Illus.). 30p. (J). (gr. k-4). reprint ed. pap. 17.00 *(978-1-4223-5538-1(1))* DIANE Publishing Co.

Brubacher, Melody. The Adventures of Princess Penelope. 2012. 68p. pap. 31.99 *(978-1-4691-9274-1(8))* Xlibris Corp.

Bruchac, Joseph. Dragon Castle. 2011. (ENG.). 352p. (J). (gr. 5-18). 16.99 *(978-0-8037-3376-3(3)*, Dial Bks) Penguin Young Readers Group.

Buck, Alicia. Out of the Ashes. 2015. 281p. (YA). pap. 17.99 *(978-1-4621-1727-7(9))* Cedar Fort, Inc./CFI Distribution.

Bunting, Eve. Frog & Friends: Party at the Pond. 2011. (I am A Reader! Ser.). (ENG., Illus.). 40p. (gr. k-3). lib. bdg. 9.95 *(978-1-58536-549-4(1))* Sleeping Bear Pr.

Burden, Meg. The King Commands. 2010. (Tales of the Borderlands Ser.: Bk. 2). 312p. (YA). (gr. 7-18). pap. 8.95 *(978-0-9798824-1-8(9))* Brown Barn Bks.

Burkart, Jeffrey. The Hidden Prince. 2011. (YA). 16.95 *(978-0-9825713-3-0(X))* Clifton Carriage House Pr.

Burkart, Jeffrey E., retold by. The Hidden Prince. 2003. (Illus.). 32p. (J). 9.99 incl. audio compact disk *(978-0-570-07174-7(7))* Concordia Publishing Hse.

Burks, David W. Full Circle: The Story of Outlaw-Prince Edwin, High King of England. 2007. 124p. 20.95 *(978-0-595-70485-9(9))*; per. 10.95 *(978-0-595-46753-2(9))* iUniverse, Inc.

Burnett, Frances Hodgson. The Lost Prince. 2007. 228p. per. 14.95 *(978-1-60312-338-9(5))*; 26.95 *(978-1-60312-676-2(7))* Aegypan.

—The Lost Prince. (J). 25.95 *(978-0-8488-0691-0(3))* Amereon Ltd.

Burnham, Niki. Royally Crushed: Royally Jacked; Spin Control; Do-Over. 2011. (ENG.). 624p. (YA). (gr. 7). pap. 11.99 *(978-1-4424-0648-3(8)*, Simon Pulse) Simon Pulse.

Burns, Jennifer N. Magic in Time: Fairy Tale Stories. 2012. 198p. 24.95 *(978-1-4759-3965-1(5))*; pap. 14.95 *(978-1-4759-3964-4(7))* iUniverse, Inc.

Busch, Jean. Aiden & the Frog Prince, 1 vol. 2009. 48p. pap. 16.95 *(978-1-60836-892-1(0))* America Star Bks.

Carney, Karin. Prince Braden's Animal Kingdom. 2011. 40p. pap. 18.95 *(978-1-4357-9406-1(0))* Lulu Pr., Inc.

Cass, Kiera. The Elite. (Selection Ser.: 2). (ENG.). (YA). (gr. 8). 2014. 352p. pap. 9.99 *(978-0-06-205997-0(1))* 2013. 336p. 17.99 *(978-0-06-205996-3(3))* HarperCollins Pubs. (HarperTeen).

—LA ÉLITE. 2013. (SPA.). 224p. pap. 20.95 *(978-84-9918-613-9(0))* Roca Editorial ESP. Dist: Spanish Pubs., LLC.

—La Elite. 2017. (SPA.). 224p. (YA). (gr. 7-12). pap. 12.95 ***(978-84-16240-61-6(2))*** Roca Bolsillo ESP. Dist: Spanish Pubs., LLC.

—The Elite. 2014. (Selection Ser.: 2). (YA). lib. bdg. 20.85 *(978-0-606-35489-9(1))* Turtleback Bks.

—Happily Ever After. 2015. (Selection Novella Ser.). (ENG., Illus.). 416p. (YA). (gr. 8). 18.99 *(978-0-06-241408-3(9)*, HarperTeen) HarperCollins Pubs.

—Happily Ever After: Companion to the Selection Series. 2016. (Selection Ser.). (YA). lib. bdg. 20.85 *(978-0-606-38919-8(9))* Turtleback Bks.

—The One. 2014. (Selection Ser.). (ENG.). 352p. (J). (gr. 8). 17.99 *(978-0-06-205999-4(8)*, HarperTeen) HarperCollins Pubs.

—The Selection. (Selection Ser.: 1). (ENG.). (YA). (gr. 8). 2013. 352p. pap. 9.99 *(978-0-06-205994-9(7))* 2012. 336p. 17.99 *(978-0-06-205993-2(9))* HarperCollins Pubs. (HarperTeen).

—The Selection, 1. (ENG.). 272p. pap. *(978-0-00-746669-6(2)*, HarperCollins Children's Bks.) HarperCollins Pubs. Ltd.

—The Selection. 2013. (Selection Ser.: 1). (YA). lib. bdg. 20.85 *(978-0-606-35488-2(3))* Turtleback Bks.

—The Selection Stories: The Prince & the Guard. 2014. (Selection Ser.). (ENG.). 240p. (J). (gr. 8). pap. 9.99 *(978-0-06-231832-9(2))* HarperCollins Pubs.

Cerami, Matteo, et al. The Planet of the Grand Buffoon. Smith, Anne & Smith, Owen, trs. from FRE. Élyum Studio, illus. 2014. (Little Prince Ser.: 14). (ENG.). 48p. (J). (gr. 4-8). lib. bdg. 26.60 *(978-0-7613-8764-0(1)*, Graphic Universe™) Lerner Publishing Group.

Chokshi, Roshani. A Crown of Wishes. 2017. (Star-Touched Ser.). (ENG.). 384p. (YA). 18.99 *(978-1-250-08549-8(7)*, 9781250085498, St. Martin's Griffin) St. Martin's Pr.

Christopher, John. Beyond the Burning Lands. 2015. (Sword of the Spirits Ser.: 2). (ENG., Illus.). 272p. (J). (gr. 5-9). pap. 7.99 *(978-1-4814-1994-9(3)*, Aladdin) Simon & Schuster Children's Publishing.

Clarke, Jane. Prince Albert's Birthday. Chatterton, Martin, illus. 2005. 24p. (J). lib. bdg. 23.65 *(978-1-59646-748-4(7))* Dingles & Co.

Clausen, Andrew. Prince Caspian. 2003. stu. ed., ring bd. 14.99 *(978-1-58609-195-8(6))* Progeny Pr.

Coe, Mary. The Prince of Betherland. 2007. 100p. pap. 9.95 *(978-1-4303-2521-5(6))* Lulu Pr., Inc.

Coe, Mary E. The Prince of Betherland. 2008. 117p. 24.95 *(978-0-557-03112-2(5))* Lulu Pr., Inc.

—The Prince of Betherland A Wonderful World of Fantasy. 2009. 66p. pap. 9.95 *(978-0-557-08499-9(7))* Lulu Pr., Inc.

—The Prince of Betherland a Wonderful World of Fantasy. 2009. 112p. pap. 9.95 *(978-0-557-09297-0(3))* Lulu Pr., Inc.

Coia, Kristina. Lymeria. 2007. 120p. (YA). per. 10.95 *(978-0-595-45268-2(X))* iUniverse, Inc.

Coleman, Alice Scovell. Engraved in Stone. Armand, Anjale Renee, illus. 2003. 152p. (J). 14.95 *(978-0-9729846-0-7(7))* Tiara Bks. LLC.

Constantine, Clélia. The Planet of Music. Smith, Owen & Collins Smith, Anne, trs. ÉLyum Studio, illus. 2012. (Little Prince Ser.: 3). (ENG.). 56p. (J). (gr. 4-8). pap. 7.95 *(978-0-8225-9424-6(2)*, Graphic Universe™) Lerner Publishing Group.

Corp, Carey & Langdon, Lorie. Doon, 1 vol. 2014. (Doon Novel Ser.). (ENG.). 416p. (YA). pap. 12.99 *(978-0-310-74239-5(0))* Blink.

Costi, Vincent. The Planet of the Gargand. Smith, Anne & Smith, Owen, trs. from FRE. Élyum Studio, illus. 2014. (Little Prince Ser.: 15). (ENG.). 48p. (J). (gr. 4-8). lib. bdg. 26.60 *(978-0-7613-8765-7(X)*, Graphic Universe™) Lerner Publishing Group.

Cowey, James. William Snottengrout - Gangor's Reign. 2006. 104p. per. *(978-1-84667-006-0(3))* Derwent Pr., The.

Craik, Maria Dinah. The Little Lame Prince. 2008. 120p. 21.99 *(978-0-554-31012-1(0))* Creative Media Partners, LLC.

Cummins, Molly. The Jewel of Fez. 2006. 141p. pap. 24.95 *(978-1-4241-1044-5(0))* PublishAmerica, Inc.

Curtis, Jillian M. The Little Prince & His Magic Wand. 2005. (Illus.). 28p. (J). 24.95 *(978-1-59858-015-0(9))*; pap. 16.95 *(978-1-59858-010-5(8))* Dog Ear Publishing, LLC.

Daffern, Brian. Prince Albert Bk. 2: The Beast School. 2005. 160p. (YA). per. 10.95 *(978-0-9709104-6-2(0))* Hickory Tales Publishing.

—Prince Albert Bk. 3: The Realm Pirates. 2004. 192p. (YA). per. 13.95 *(978-0-9709104-7-9(9))* Hickory Tales Publishing.

—Prince Albert in a Can, Bk. 1. 2004. 256p. (YA). per. 13.95 *(978-0-9709104-5-5(2))* Hickory Tales Publishing.

Dahl, Michael. Dungeon of Seven Dooms, 1 vol. 2011. (Good vs Evil Ser.). (ENG.). 48p. (gr. 1-2). lib. bdg. 23.99 *(978-1-4342-2091-2(5)*, Good vs Evil) Stone Arch Bks.

D'Amico, Carol. Vince, Boy Prince: And the Secrets of How Anyone Can Become a True Prince (or Princess), 1 vol. Cerniga, Kira, illus. 2010. 18p. pap. 24.95 *(978-1-4489-7373-6(2))* PublishAmerica, Inc.

Davison, Gail. Prince Alexander. PellerinUndo, Joel Ray, illus. 2016. (ENG.). 28p. (J). pap. 28.22 ***(978-1-5245-1787-8(9))*** Xlibris Corp.

De Los Santos, Elizabeth G. The Secret House. 2011. 18p. pap. 16.95 *(978-1-4626-4409-4(0))* America Star Bks.

De Saint-Exupéry, Antoine. A Day with the Little Prince. 2015. (Little Prince Ser.). (ENG., Illus.). 10p. (J). (— 1). bds. 7.99 *(978-0-544-69958-8(0)*, HMH Books For Young Readers) Houghton Mifflin Harcourt Publishing Co.

—The Little Prince. 2015.Tr. of Petit Prince. (HEB.). (J). ***(978-965-13-1323-3(4))*** Am Oved Pubs., Ltd.

—The Little Prince.Tr. of Petit Prince. 17.95 *(978-0-89190-331-4(3))* Amereon Ltd.

—The Little Prince. 2003.Tr. of Petit Prince. (Illus.). (J). *(978-0-15-204730-6(1))* Harcourt Trade Pubs.

—The Little Prince. deluxe ed. 2015. (Little Prince Ser.).Tr. of Petit Prince. (ENG., Illus.). 72p. (J). (gr. 5-7). 35.00 *(978-0-544-65649-9(0)*, HMH Books For Young Readers) Houghton Mifflin Harcourt Publishing Co.

—The Little Prince. Kahler, Evan & Woods, Katherine, trs. 2016.Tr. of Petit Prince. (ENG., Illus.). (J). (gr. 3-7). ***(978-1-77323-014-6(X))*** Rehak, David.

—The Little Prince. l.t. ed. 2005.Tr. of Petit Prince. (ENG.). 168p. pap. 10.95 *(978-0-7862-7539-7(1))* Thorndike Pr.

—The Little Prince. Hill, Rowland, tr. Gormand, Caroline, illus. 2016.Tr. of Petit Prince. (ENG.). (J). (gr. 3-6). pap. ***(978-2-89687-592-4(1))*** chouetteditions.com.

—The Little Prince Family Storybook: Unabridged Original Text. 2015. (Little Prince Ser.). (ENG., Illus.). 64p. (YA). (gr. 7). 17.99 *(978-0-544-79256-2(4)*, HMH Books For Young Readers) Houghton Mifflin Harcourt Publishing Co.

—The Little Prince Graphic Novel. Sfar, Joann, illus. 2013. (Little Prince Ser.). (ENG.). 112p. (J). (gr. 5-7). 12.99 *(978-0-547-33800-2(7))* Houghton Mifflin Harcourt Publishing Co.

—The Little Prince Read-Aloud Storybook: Abridged Original Text. Tamm, Vali, tr. 2015. (Little Prince Ser.). (ENG., Illus.). 40p. (J). (gr. 1-4). 9.99 *(978-0-544-79255-5(6)*, HMH Books For Young Readers) Houghton Mifflin Harcourt Publishing Co.

—Meet the Little Prince (padded Board Book) 2015. (Little Prince Ser.). (ENG., Illus.). 10p. (J). (— 1). bds. 7.99 *(978-0-544-70902-7(0)*, HMH Books For Young Readers) Houghton Mifflin Harcourt Publishing Co.

—Le Petit Prince. 2016. (FRE., Illus.). (J). pap. ***(978-5-521-00151-4(4))*** Books on Demand.

—Le Petit Prince. 2010. (CHI., Illus.). 128p. (J). (gr. 3-7). *(978-986-7897-01-5(3))* Ecus Publishing Hse.

—Le Petit Prince. 2010. (CHI.). 132p. (J). (gr. 5-8). pap. *(978-986-189-225-2(7))* Grimm Cultural Ent., Co., Ltd.

—Le Petit Prince. Gormand, Caroline, illus. 2016. (FRE.). (J). (gr. 3-6). pap. ***(978-2-89687-593-1(X))*** chouetteditions.com.

—Il Piccolo Principe.Tr. of Little Prince. (ITA.). 2014. 106p. pap. 6.50 *(978-1-4992-7698-5(2))* 2013. 106p. pap. 6.50 *(978-1-4948-4773-9(6))* 2013. 96p. pap. 12.00 *(978-1-4948-5566-6(6))* CreateSpace Independent Publishing Platform.

—Il Piccolo Principe.Tr. of Little Prince. (ITA.). pap. 17.95 *(978-88-452-4741-5(4))* Fabbri Editori - RCS Libri ITA. Dist: Distribooks, Inc.

—El Principito. (SPA., Illus.). 120p. (J). 10.95 *(978-84-206-3628-3(2)*, AZ6282); 10.95 *(978-84-206-3628-3(2)*, AZ6282) Alianza Editorial, S. A. ESP. Dist: Continental Bk. Co., Inc.

—El Principito. (Coleccion Centro Literario). (SPA.). (J). pap., stu. ed. 7.95 *(978-958-02-0475-6(6)*, CAR005) Editorial Voluntad S.A. COL. Dist: Continental Bk. Co., Inc.

—El Principito. 2003. (SPA., Illus.). 96p. (YA). (gr. 5-8). *(978-84-7888-438-4(6)*, SAL7382) Emece Editores ESP. Dist: Lectorum Pubns., Inc.

—El Principito. (SPA.). (J). pap. 10.95 *(978-950-04-0048-0(0))* Emecé Editores S.A. ARG. Dist: Planeta Publishing Corp.

—El Principito. 2016. (SPA.). 96p. (YA). (gr. 6-9). pap. 11.95 *(978-84-7888-719-4(9))* Publicaciones y Ediciones Salamandra, S.A. ESP. Dist: Spanish Pubs., LLC.

—EL PRINCIPITO. 2016. (SPA., Illus.). 96p. (YA). (gr. 6-9). 20.95 *(978-84-7888-640-1(0))* Publicaciones y Ediciones Salamandra, S.A. ESP. Dist: Spanish Pubs., LLC.

—Travels with the Little Prince. 2015. (Little Prince Ser.). (ENG., Illus.). 10p. (J). (— 1). bds. 7.99 *(978-0-544-70901-0(2)*, HMH Books For Young Readers) Houghton Mifflin Harcourt Publishing Co.

De Saint-Exupéry, Antoine & Hemerman, Ilana. The Little Prince. 2013.Tr. of Petit Prince. (HEB.). (J). ***(978-965-13-0883-3(4))***; 90p. *(978-965-13-2376-8(0))* Am Oved Pubs., Ltd.

Deshpande, Sanjay. In Defense of the Realm: Graphic Novel. Sharma, Lalit Kumar, illus. 2011. (Campfire Graphic Novels Ser.). (ENG.). 104p. (YA). (gr. 3-7). pap. 12.99 *(978-93-80028-64-4(4)*, Campfire) Steerforth Pr.

Despain, Bree. The Eternity Key. 2015. (ENG.). 368p. (YA). (gr. 7). 18.99 *(978-1-60684-467-0(9))*; (Into the Dark Ser.: 2). 18.99 *(978-1-5124-0179-0(X))* Lerner Publishing Group. (Carolrhoda Lab™).

DeSpain, Bree. The Immortal Throne. 2016. (Into the Dark Ser.: 3). (ENG.). 344p. (YA). (gr. 7-12). 18.99 *(978-1-5124-0583-5(3)*, Carolrhoda Bks.) Lerner Publishing Group.

Despain, Bree. The Immortal Throne. 2016. (Into the Dark Ser.: 3). (ENG.). 344p. (YA). (gr. 7-12). 38.65 *(978-1-5124-0897-3(2)*, Carolrhoda Lab™) Lerner Publishing Group.

—The Shadow Prince. (ENG.). 496p. (gr. 7). 2015. (Into the Dark Ser.: Bk. 1). pap. 9.99 *(978-1-60684-567-7(5))* 2014. (J). 18.99 *(978-1-60684-247-8(1))* Lerner Publishing Group. (Carolrhoda Lab™).

Dharma Publishing Staff. The Power of a Promise: A Story about the Power of Keeping Promises. 2010. (ENG.). 36p. (gr. -1-7). pap. 8.95 *(978-0-89800-603-2(1))* Dharma Publishing.

Disney Book Group & Rudnick, Elizabeth. A Frozen Heart. Disney Storybook Art Team, illus. 2015. (ENG.). 304p. (J). (gr. 5-9). 14.99 *(978-1-4847-3051-5(8))* Disney Pr.

Disney Book Group Staff. Cinderella. Disney Storybook Artists Staff, illus. 2nd ed. 2012. (Read-Along Storybook & CD Ser.). (ENG.). 32p. (J). (gr. -1 — 1). pap. 6.99 *(978-1-4231-6321-3(4))* Disney Pr.

—The Little Mermaid Read-Along Storybook & CD. Disney Storybook Artists Staff, illus. 2013. (Read-Along Storybook & CD Ser.). (ENG.). 32p. (J). (gr. -1-k). pap. 6.99 *(978-1-4231-6889-8(5))* Disney Pr.

Disney Press Staff. Valley of Vipers. 2010. 144p. pap. 4.99 *(978-1-4231-1007-1(2))* Disney Pr.

Disney Princess Staff & Disney Book Group Staff. Ariel: The Birthday Surprise. Cagol, Andrea & Studio Iboix Staff, illus. 2010. (Disney Princess Chapter Book: Series #1 Ser.). (ENG.). 96p. (J). (gr. 1-3). pap. 4.99 *(978-1-4231-2971-4(7))* Disney Pr.

Dixon, Ken. Cobweb Jack & the Sacred Khunjar. 2009. 210p. pap. 28.50 *(978-1-4092-8919-7(2))* Lulu Pr., Inc.

Dolamore, Jaclyn. Magic under Glass. (Magic under Glass Ser.). (ENG.). (YA). (gr. 7). 2011. 256p. pap. 8.99 *(978-1-59990-587-7(6)*, 9781599905877) 2010. 240p. 16.99 *(978-1-59990-430-6(6)*, 9781599904306) Bloomsbury Publishing USA. (Bloomsbury USA Childrens).

—Magic under Stone. 2012. (Magic under Glass Ser.). (ENG.). 304p. (YA). 16.99 *(978-1-59990-643-0(0)*, 9781599906430, Bloomsbury USA Childrens) Bloomsbury Publishing USA.

Dower, Laura. Sunny & the Secret Passage. 2013. (Palace Puppies Ser.: 4). (J). lib. bdg. 14.75 *(978-0-606-35108-9(6)*, Turtleback) Turtleback Bks.

Downey, Glen. Rebel Prince. Okum, David, illus. 2007. 48p. (J). lib. bdg. 23.08 *(978-1-4242-1642-0(7))* Fitzgerald Bks.

Drischel, Candy L. Restless with the Dark Moon Rising. 2008. 105p. pap. 19.95 *(978-1-60610-421-7(7))* America Star Bks.

Drobeck, Ronald D. My Name Is Prince Albert. 2012. 152p. (gr. 4-6). 30.95 *(978-1-4582-0205-5(4))*; pap. 12.99 *(978-1-4582-0203-1(8))* Author Solutions, Inc. (Abbott Pr.).

Dubos, Delphine. The Planet of Tear-Eaters. Smith, Anne & Smith, Owen, trs. from FRE. Élyum Studio, illus. 2014. (Little Prince Ser.: 13). (ENG.). 48p. (J). (gr. 4-8). lib. bdg. 26.60 *(978-0-7613-8763-3(3)*, Graphic Universe™) Lerner Publishing Group.

Dugan, David J. The Missing Prince of Distria. 2008. 36p. pap. 24.95 *(978-1-60563-587-3(1))* America Star Bks.

Dumas, Alexandre. Barbie & the Three Musketeers: A Junior Novelization. Choi, Allan, illus. 2009. 93p. (J). *(978-0-545-09413-9(5))* Scholastic, Inc.

Eltoukhy, G.N. Sheherazade Chronicles of the Fairy Tales. 2012. 32p. pap. 17.25 *(978-1-4669-3708-6(4))* Trafford Publishing.

Emmett, Jonathan. Prince Ribbit, 1 vol. Bernatene, Poly, illus. 2017. (ENG.). 32p. (J). (gr. -1-2). 16.95 *(978-1-56145-761-8(2))* Peachtree Pubs.

Engelbreit, Mary. Mary Engelbreit's Nutcracker. Engelbreit, Mary, illus. 2014. (ENG., Illus.). 40p. (J). (gr. -1-3). 9.99 *(978-0-06-222417-0(4))* HarperCollins Pubs.

Essama, Molly Jane. The Prince & the Three Ugly Hags. 2010. 28p. pap. 16.95 *(978-1-4490-5587-5(7))* AuthorHouse.

Everett, Felicity & Rawson, Christopher. Stories of Princes & Princesses. 2004. (Young Reading Ser.). (Illus.). 48p. (J). (gr.

2-18). pap. 5.95 *(978-0-7945-0449-6(3),* Usborne) EDC Publishing.

Faye Morningstar. Little Dream Athe: The Sand Prince. 2012. 20p. pap. 17.99 *(978-1-4772-9540-3(2))* AuthorHouse.

Foster, Jackie. Land of Anear, 1 vol. 2010. 27p. pap. 24.95 *(978-1-61546-634-4(7))* America Star Bks.

French, Vivian. The Heart of Glass: The Third Tale from the Five Kingdoms. Collins, Ross, illus. 2010. (Tales from the Five Kingdoms Ser.: 3). (ENG.). 256p. (J). (gr. 3-7). 14.99 *(978-0-7636-4814-5(0))* Candlewick Pr.

Gaichies, Sarah. Angela & the Prince. 2011. (FRE & ENG., Illus.). 96p. pap. 32.26 *(978-1-4567-8999-2(6))* AuthorHouse.

Gaudin, Thierry. The Planet of Gehom. Smith, Anne & Smith, Owen, trs. from FRE. Elyum Studio, illus. 2014. (Little Prince Ser.: 16). (ENG.). 48p. (J). (gr. 4-8). lib. bdg. 26.60 *(978-0-7613-8766-4(8),* Graphic Universe™) Lerner Publishing Group.

Gaydos, Nora. Now I'm Growing! Prince of the Potty - Little Steps for Big Kids! Gutierrez, Akemi, illus. 2011. (ENG.). 30p. (J). (gr. -1-17). 8.99 *(978-1-60169-077-7(0))* Innovative Kids.

George, Jessica Day. Princess of Glass. (Twelve Dancing Princesses Ser.). (ENG.). 272p. (YA). (gr. 7). 2011. pap. 9.99 *(978-1-59990-659-1(7),* 9781599906591) 2010. 16.99 *(978-1-59990-478-8(0),* 9781599904788) Bloomsbury Publishing USA. (Bloomsbury USA Childrens).

Gordon, Mike, illus. The Frog Prince. rev. ed. 2007. (Young Reading CD Packs Ser.). 48p. (J). (gr. -1-3). 9.99 incl. audio compact disk *(978-0-7945-1868-4(0),* Usborne) EDC Publishing.

Gow, Kailin. Diary of a Discount Donna: A Fashion Fables Book: A Novel. 2005. 274p. (YA). per. 10.95 *(978-1-59748-858-7(5))* Sparklesoup LLC.

Graudin, Ryan. All That Glows. 2014. (ENG.). 480p. (YA). (gr. 8). pap. 9.99 *(978-0-06-218741-3(4),* HarperTeen) HarperCollins Pubs.

Gribble, Julie. Bubblegum Princess. Hanson, Lori, illus. 2013. 32p. (J). 16.99 *(978-0-9890914-0-4(6))* NY Media Works, LLC.

Grimm, J. & W. & Grimm, J. The Frog Prince: Or Iron Henry. Hager, Christian & Schroeder, Binette, illus. 2013. (ENG.). 32p. (J). (gr. -1-3). 17.95 *(978-0-7358-4140-6(3))* North-South Bks., Inc.

Grimm, Jacob & Grimm, Wilhelm K. The Frog Prince/ El Principe Sapo. 2004. (Illus.). (J). *(978-1-933530-21-5(9))* Bingo Bks., Inc.

Guerrera, Jeannette D. The Pot of Gold. 2012. 20p. pap. 17.99 *(978-1-4685-5883-8(8))* AuthorHouse.

Guillain, Charlotte. Ratpunzel, 1 vol. Beacon, Dawn, illus. 2014. (Animal Fairy Tales Ser.). (ENG.). 24p. (gr. 1-2). lib. bdg. 23.99 *(978-1-4109-6112-9(5),* NA-r) Heinemann-Raintree.

Haan, Linda de & Nijland, Stern. King & King. Haan, Linda de & Nijland, Stern, illus. 2003. (ENG., Illus.). 32p. (J). (gr. k-3). 15.99 *(978-1-58246-061-1(2),* Tricycle Pr.) Random Hse. Children's Bks.

Hall, Frank. The Prince Who Did Not Want to be King. 2011. 132p. 28.95 *(978-1-4497-1440-6(4));* (J). pap. 11.95 *(978-1-4497-1438-3(2))* Author Solutions, Inc. (WestBow Pr.).

Hardy, S. F. The Empress' New Hair. 2012. 40p. pap. 10.00 *(978-0-9849360-9-0(2))* G Publishing LLC.

Harkrader, Lisa. The Tadpole Prince. 2016. (Spring Forward Ser.). (J). (gr. 2). *(978-1-4900-9473-1(3))* Benchmark Education Co.

Harrell, Rob. The Trouble with Weasels. 2014. (Life of Zarf Ser.: 1). (ENG.). 288p. (J). (gr. 3-7). 14.99 *(978-0-8037-4103-4(0),* Dial Bks) Penguin Young Readers Group.

Harris, Brenda. Ride Like the Wind. 2011. (Illus.). 40p. (J). pap. 12.95 *(978-1-936076-93-2(4))* Innovo Publishing, LLC.

Harrison, Mette Ivie. The Princess & the Hound. 2007. 410p. (YA). (gr. 7-18). lib. bdg. 18.89 *(978-0-06-113188-2(1),* Eos) HarperCollins Pubs.

Haugaard, Erik. Prince Boghole. 2013. (ENG., Illus.). 32p. (J). (gr. -1-3). 16.99 *(978-1-4814-2167-6(0),* Simon & Schuster Bks. For Young Readers) Simon & Schuster Bks. For Young Readers.

Hawkins, Loreatha V. The Prince & the Musical Castle. 2009. 32p. pap. 14.49 *(978-1-4389-7678-5(X))* AuthorHouse.

Healy, Christopher. The Hero's Guide to Being an Outlaw. Harris, Todd, illus. 2014. (Hero's Guide Ser.: 3). (ENG.). 528p. (J). (gr. 3-7). 16.99 *(978-0-06-211848-6(X),* Waldon Pond Pr.) HarperCollins Pubs.

—The Hero's Guide to Saving Your Kingdom. Harris, Todd, illus. (Hero's Guide Ser.: 1). (ENG.). (J). (gr. 3-7). 2013. 480p. pap. 7.99 *(978-0-06-211745-8(9))* 2012. 448p. 16.99 *(978-0-06-211743-4(2))* HarperCollins Pubs. (Waldon Pond Pr.).

—The Hero's Guide to Storming the Castle. Harris, Todd, illus. 2013. (Hero's Guide Ser.: 2). (ENG.). 496p. (J). (gr. 3-7). 16.99 *(978-0-06-211845-5(5),* Waldon Pond Pr.) HarperCollins Pubs.

Hensley, Judith Victoria. Sir Thomas the Eggslayer. 2008. 156p. pap. 14.95 *(978-0-9795103-8-0(4))* Ascended Ideas.

Herbauts, Anne. Prince Silencio. Bedrick, Claudia Z., tr. from FRE. 2006. (ENG., Illus.). 32p. (J). (gr. -1-3). 14.95 *(978-1-59270-055-4(1))* Enchanted Lion Bks., LLC.

Hewitt, Megan. Eagle Rises. 2013. 118p. (J). pap. 12.99 *(978-1-300-55242-0(5))* Lulu Pr., Inc.

Hill, Leah. The Adventures of Prince Phillip & the Fairytale Creatures: The Giant Problem. 2013. (ENG.). 26p. (J). pap. 10.95 *(978-1-4787-0696-0(1))* Outskirts Pr., Inc.

Hodder, Bridget. The Rat Prince. 2016. (ENG.). 272p. (J). 16.99 *(978-0-374-30213-9(8),* 9780374302139, Farrar, Straus & Giroux (BYR)) Farrar, Straus & Giroux.

Hodgson, Mona. The Princess Twins & the Birthday Party, 1 vol. Olson, Julie, illus. 2016. (I Can Read! / Princess Twins Ser.). (ENG.). 32p. (J). pap. 3.99 *(978-0-310-75067-3(9))* Zonderkidz.

Hofmeyr, Dianne. Eye of the Moon. 2011. (ENG.). 336p. (J). (gr. 3-7). pap. 9.99 *(978-1-4424-1188-3(0),* Aladdin) Simon & Schuster Children's Publishing.

Homberg, Ruth. The Little Mermaid. 2013. (Disney Princess Step into Reading Ser.). lib. bdg. 13.55 *(978-0-606-32202-7(7),* Turtleback) Turtleback Bks.

Howell, Laura. Princess & the Pea. 2009. (Young Reading 1 Ser.). 48p. (J). 6.99 *(978-0-7945-2587-3(3),* Usborne) EDC Publishing.

Hoyt, Holly. The Purple Widow. 2009. 314p. 28.25 *(978-1-60860-688-7(0),* Eloquent Bks.) Strategic Book Publishing & Rights Agency (SBPRA).

Hurley, Jeanette Clinger. The Crystal Prince: Love Is the Only Way. 2010. (Illus.). 77p. pap. 32.95 *(978-0-578-03963-3(X))* Outskirts Pr., Inc.

Ibbotson, Eva. The Dragonfly Pool. 2009. (ENG.). 384p. (J). (gr. 3-7). 7.99 *(978-0-14-241486-6(7),* Puffin Books) Penguin Young Readers Group.

—The Dragonfly Pool, 9 vols. 2008. (Tides of Truth Ser.). (YA). 90.75 *(978-1-4361-5207-5(0));* 92.75 *(978-1-4361-5205-1(4));* 256.75 *(978-1-4361-5206-8(2));* 120.75 *(978-1-4361-5211-2(9));* 1.25 *(978-1-4361-5202-0(X));* 122.75 *(978-1-4361-5209-9(7))* Recorded Bks., Inc.

Ifans, Rhiannon. Owain Glyndwr: Prince of Wales. Jones, Margaret, illus. 2003. (WEL & ENG.). 96p. (J). pap. 13.95 *(978-0-86243-544-8(7))* Y Lolfa GBR. Dist: Dufour Editions, Inc.

Illustrated Stories of Princes & Princesses. 2015. (Illustrated Stories Ser.). (ENG.). (J). 19.99 *(978-0-7945-3416-5(3),* Usborne) EDC Publishing.

Jacques, Brian. The Angel's Command. Elliot, David & Schoenherr, Ian, illus. 2005. (ENG.). 384p. (J). (gr. 3-7). 7.99 *(978-0-14-240285-6(0),* Firebird) Penguin Young Readers Group.

—The Angel's Command. 2003. (Castaways of the Flying Dutchman Ser.: No. 2). 1.00 *(978-1-4175-5393-8(6))* Recorded Bks., Inc.

Jardine, Kathy & Jardine, Ashley. The Durples: Go to School. 2010. 28p. pap. 17.99 *(978-1-4490-3405-4(5))* AuthorHouse.

Jay, Stacey. Princess of Thorns. 2016. (ENG.). 400p. (YA). (gr. 9). pap. 9.99 *(978-0-385-74323-5(8),* Ember) Random Hse. Children's Bks.

Jeffers, Susan. The Nutcracker. Jeffers, Susan, illus. 2007. (Illus.). 40p. (J). (gr. -1-3). 17.89 *(978-0-06-074387-1(5));* (ENG., 17.99 *(978-0-06-074386-4(7))* HarperCollins Pubs.

Jesus, Opal De. The Golden Apple Kingdom, 1 vol. 2009. 48p. pap. 16.95 *(978-1-60749-414-0(0))* America Star Bks.

Jones, Christianne C. Beauty & the Beast, 1 vol. Muehlenhardt, Amy Bailey, illus. 2013. (My First Classic Story Ser.). (ENG.). 32p. (gr. k-3). pap. 7.10 *(978-1-4795-1851-7(4),* My First Classic Story) Picture Window Bks.

Jordan, Annie Laurie. Bogwaddle Pond. La Grange, Myrtle, illus. 2004. 25p. pap. 24.95 *(978-1-4137-2013-6(7))* PublishAmerica, Inc.

Joyce, Sandie May. Little Miss Alice & the Bookworm. 2007. 65p. pap. 24.95 *(978-1-4357-0328-5(6))* Lulu Pr., Inc.

Jungman, Ann. The Footballing Frog. Burnett, Seb, illus. 2007. (Collins Big Cat Ser.). (ENG.). 80p. (J). (gr. 3-4). pap. 8.99 *(978-0-00-723087-7(7))* HarperCollins Pubs. Ltd. GBR. Dist: Independent Pubs. Group.

Justis, Jon. Pumpkin & the Great Dragon Caper. 2012. 32p. pap. 24.95 *(978-1-4626-9733-5(X))* America Star Bks.

Kagawa, Julie. The Iron King. 2010. (Iron Fey Ser.: 1). lib. bdg. 20.85 *(978-0-606-14909-9(0),* Turtleback) Turtleback Bks.

—The Iron Legends. 2012. (Iron Fey Ser.: 5). lib. bdg. 20.85 *(978-0-606-26516-4(3),* Turtleback) Turtleback Bks.

—The Lost Prince. 2012. (Iron Fey Ser.: 5). lib. bdg. 20.85 *(978-0-606-26946-9(0),* Turtleback) Turtleback Bks.

Kale, Ann Stephanian. Marco & Princess Gina. Kale, Ann Stephanian, illus. 2003. (Illus.). 24p. (J). (gr. k-3). pap. 10.00 *(978-0-9704131-5-4(7))* Abril BookStore & Publishing.

Kats, Jewel. Cinderella's Magical Wheelchair: An Empowering Fairy Tale. Kinra, Richa, illus. 2012. (J). 24p. 29.95 *(978-1-61599-113-6(1));* 20p. pap. 16.95 *(978-1-61599-112-9(3))* Loving Healing Pr., Inc.

Kats, Jewel. Prince Preemie: A Tale of a Tiny Puppy Who Arrives Early. Lenart, Claudia, illus. 2016. (J). pap. ***(978-1-61599-306-2(1))*** Loving Healing Pr., Inc.

Kemp, Anna. The Worst Princess. Ogilvie, Sara, illus. 2014. (ENG.). 32p. (J). (gr. -1-2). 16.99 *(978-0-385-37125-4(X),* Random Hse. Bks. for Young Readers) Random Hse. Children's Bks.

Kimmel, Eric A. The Three Princes. Fisher, Leonard Everett, illus. 2005. (Ala Notable Book Ser.). (ENG.). 32p. (J). (gr. k-3). pap. 6.95 *(978-0-8234-1553-3(8))* Holiday Hse., Inc.

Klingele, Lindsey. The Broken World. 2017. 432p. (YA). (gr. 8). 17.99 ***(978-0-06-238036-4(2),*** HarperTeen) HarperCollins Pubs.

Kneblik, Debi. The Shipwreck of Knottingburg. 2009. (J). pap. 12.00 *(978-1-61623-985-5(9))* Independent Pub.

Koch, Claus. The Three Little Wolves & the Big Bad Boar. 2011. 68p. pap. 9.99 *(978-1-4520-5321-9(9))* AuthorHouse.

Kuhl, Debra. Black Bert the Pirate, 1 vol. 2009. 83p. pap. 19.95 *(978-1-60749-968-8(1))* America Star Bks.

L. Prince Cloud & Princess Evergreen, 1 vol. 2010. 26p. pap. 24.95 *(978-1-4512-9016-5(0))* America Star Bks.

Lance, John & Narvarro, Priscilla Holmes & the Case of the Glass Slipper. 2011. 24p. pap. 14.99 *(978-0-9826594-9-6(0))* 4RV Publishing, LLC.

Larson, Sara B. Defy. 2014. (Defy Trilogy: Bk. 1). (ENG.). 336p. (J). (gr. 7). 17.99 *(978-0-545-59758-6(7),* Scholastic Pr.) Scholastic, Inc.

Lehman, Marcus. 5 Novelettes by Marcus Lehman Slipcased: Adopted Princess, Bustenai, Out of the Depths, Rabenu Gershom & Unpaid Ransom. Mindel, Nissan, tr. from GER. Kleiman, Zalman, illus. 2012. (ENG.). (YA). 64.95 *(978-0-8266-0033-2(6))* Kehot Pubn. Society.

Lerangis, Peter. The Promise. 2016. (Seven Wonders Journals: 4). (J). lib. bdg. 12.35 *(978-0-606-38133-8(3))* Turtleback Bks.

Lewison, Wendy Cheyette. The Prince & the Potty. Motoyama, Keiko, illus. 2006. (ENG.). 40p. (J). (gr. -1-3). 16.99 *(978-0-689-87808-4(7),* Simon & Schuster Bks. For Young Readers) Simon & Schuster Bks. For Young Readers.

Liessner, Richard. The Foot Prince. Liessner, Richard, illus. 2006. (Illus.). 24p. (J). 9.95 *(978-0-9766129-5-7(X))* Raindrop Bks.

Limke, Jeff. Jason: Quest for the Golden Fleece, a Greek Myth. Seeley, Tim & Schulz, Barbara, illus. 2008. (Graphic Myths & Legends Ser.). (ENG.). 48p. (gr. 4-8). per. 8.95 *(978-0-8225-6571-0(4))* Lerner Publishing Group.

Lisle, Rebecca. Toad Prince. 2005. (ENG., Illus.). 64p. (J). (gr. k-2). pap. 7.99 *(978-1-84270-315-1(3))* Andersen Pr. GBR. Dist: Independent Pubs. Group.

Liv&Daggerın, Paco. WHAT A SNOUT! 2007. (ENG., Illus.). 48p. (J). 18.95 *(978-84-96788-87-9(3))* OQO, Editora ESP. Dist: Baker & Taylor Bks.

Lobel, Arnold. The Arnold Lobel Treasury. 2014. (ENG., Illus.). 160p. (J). (gr. 1-4). pap. 14.99 *(978-0-486-78078-8(3))* Dover Pubns., Inc.

Loisillier, Maud & Morel, Diane. The Planet of Jade. Smith, Owen & Collins Smith, Anne, trs. ÉLyum Studio, illus. 2012. (Little Prince Ser.: 4). (ENG.). 56p. (J). (gr. 4-8). pap. 7.95 *(978-1-4677-0263-8(3),* Graphic Universe™) Lerner Publishing Group.

Louise, Martha. Why Kings & Queens Don't Wear Crowns. Sevig-Fajardo, Mari Elise, tr. from NOR. Nyhus, Svein, illus. 2005. Orig. Title: Hvorfor de kongelige ikke har krone på Hodet. 32p. (J). 17.95 *(978-1-57534-037-1(2),* CSC 100) Skandisk, Inc.

Love, D. Anne. The Secret Prince. 2012. (ENG.). 240p. (J). (gr. 3-7). pap. 11.99 *(978-1-4424-5931-1(X),* McElderry, Margaret K. Bks.) McElderry, Margaret K. Bks.

Low, Vicki. First Emperor. Mayhew, Sara E., illus. 2007. 48p. (J). lib. bdg. 23.08 *(978-1-4242-1626-0(5))* Fitzgerald Bks.

Maas, Sarah J. Throne of Glass. (Throne of Glass Ser.: 1). (ENG., Illus.). (YA). (gr. 9). 2013. 432p. pap. 10.99 *(978-1-61963-034-5(6),* 9781619630345) 2012. 416p. 18.99 *(978-1-59990-695-9(3),* 9781599906959) Bloomsbury Publishing USA. (Bloomsbury USA Childrens).

—Throne of Glass. 2013. (Throne of Glass Ser.: 1). (YA). lib. bdg. 22.10 *(978-0-606-31888-4(7),* Turtleback) Turtleback Bks.

MacDonald, George. The Light Princess. 2004. reprint ed. pap. 1.99 *(978-1-4192-7001-7(X))* Kessinger Publishing, LLC.

—Light Princess & Other Fairy Stories. 2006. 132p. per. 10.95 *(978-1-59818-618-5(3));* 24.95 *(978-1-59818-236-1(6))* Aegypan.

—Princess & the Goblin. Hughes, Arthur, illus. 2nd ed. 2011. (Puffin Classics Ser.). (ENG.). 256p. (J). (gr. 5-7). 5.99 *(978-0-14-133248-2(4),* Puffin Books) Penguin Young Readers Group.

Magnet, Julien. The Planet of the Firebird. Klio Burrell, Carol, tr. ÉLyum Studio, illus. 2012. (Little Prince Ser.: 2). (ENG.). 56p. (J). (gr. 4-8). pap. 7.95 *(978-0-8225-9423-9(4),* Graphic Universe™) Lerner Publishing Group.

Maguire, Gregory. Egg & Spoon. 2014. (ENG., Illus.). 496p. (YA). (gr. 7). 17.99 *(978-0-7636-7220-1(3))* Candlewick Pr.

Man-Kong, Mary. Barbie as the Island Princess. 2007. (Pictureback(R) Ser.). (ENG., Illus.). 24p. (J). (gr. -1-2). pap. 3.99 *(978-0-375-84218-4(7),* Random Hse. Bks. for Young Readers) Random Hse. Children's Bks.

Manjula Padmanabhan, illus. Unprincess! 2005. 98p. (J). *(978-0-14-333495-8(6),* Puffin) Penguin Publishing Group.

Marsden, John. Hamlet. 2009. (ENG., Illus.). 240p. (YA). (gr. 9-18). 16.99 *(978-0-7636-4451-2(X))* Candlewick Pr.

Martin, Rafe. Birdwing. 2007. (ENG.). 384p. (J). (gr. 7-12). pap. 7.99 *(978-0-439-21168-0(9),* Levine, Arthur A. Bks.) Scholastic, Inc.

Mason & Marisa & Avery & Stella. The Tale of Princess Fluffy & Prince Rupert. 2012. 28p. pap. 19.99 *(978-1-4685-3594-5(3))* AuthorHouse.

Mass, Wendy. Beauty & the Beast: The Only One Who Didn't Run Away. 2012. (Twice upon a Time Ser.: 3). (ENG.). 288p. (J). (gr. 3-7). 16.99 *(978-0-545-31018-5(0),* Scholastic Pr.) Scholastic, Inc.

—Rapunzel: The One with All the Hair. (J). 2012. (Twice upon a Time Ser.: 1). (ENG.). 208p. (gr. 3-7). pap. 6.99 *(978-0-439-79659-0(8),* Scholastic Pr.) 2005. (Illus.). 205p. *(978-0-439-80014-3(5))* Scholastic, Inc.

—Sleeping Beauty: The One Who Took the Really Long Nap. 2012. (Twice upon a Time Ser.: 2). lib. bdg. 17.20 *(978-0-606-26530-0(9),* Turtleback) Turtleback Bks.

McDaniels, Preston, illus. The Prince of Ireland & the Three Magic Stallions. 2003. (ENG.). 32p. (J). (gr. k-3). tchr. ed. 16.95 *(978-0-8234-1573-1(2))* Holiday Hse., Inc.

McEnroe, Jim. The Rabbit King: Kingdom Leporidae. 2011. 32p. pap. 15.95 *(978-1-4520-9199-0(4))* AuthorHouse.

McKay, Laurie. Quest Maker. 2016. (Last Dragon Charmer Ser.: 2). (Illus.). 352p. (J). (gr. 3-7). 16.99 *(978-0-06-230846-7(7))* HarperCollins Pubs.

—The Villain Keeper. 2015. (Last Dragon Charmer Ser.: 1). (ENG.). 352p. (J). (gr. 3-7). 16.99 *(978-0-06-230843-6(2))* HarperCollins Pubs.

McKee, David. El Principe Pedro y el oso de Peluche. (SPA.). (J). 7.95 *(978-958-04-6258-3(5))* Norma S.A. COL. Dist: Distribuidora Norma, Inc.

McKnight, Gillian. To Catch a Prince. 2010. (ENG.). 240p. (YA). (gr. 7). pap. 11.99 *(978-1-4424-2718-1(3),* Simon Pulse) Simon Pulse.

—To Catch a Prince: To Catch a Prince; the Frog Prince. 2011. (ENG., Illus.). 432p. (YA). (gr. 7). pap. 9.99 *(978-1-4424-3139-3(3),* Simon & Schuster Bks. For Young Readers) Simon & Schuster Bks. For Young Readers.

McMakin, Jordan. Prince Ezrick & the Morpheas Curse, 4 vols. 2005. (Illus.). 304p. (J). per. 11.95 *(978-0-9764184-0-5(1))* Canterwine Pr.

McMurtrie, Kevin. The Prince That Always Wore His Top Hat. 2013. 40p. pap. 16.26 *(978-1-4669-9602-1(1))* Trafford Publishing.

McRoberts, Eddison. Sneaking Treats: A Halloween Hunt. Gadra, Jessica, illus. 2012. 48p. 19.95 *(978-1-62137-136-6(0))* Virtualbookworm.com Publishing, Inc.

Meyer, Dana. A Gift for Prince Eli. 2012. 24p. pap. 24.95 *(978-1-4626-5575-5(0))* America Star Bks.

Meyer, Julia & Tabler, Marie. One Pea. Tabler, Marie, illus. 2013. (Illus.). 36p. 14.95 *(978-1-62314-139-4(7))* ePub Bud.

Mihai, Adriana. The Inner of the Diamond Shoes. 2011. 28p. pap. 24.95 *(978-1-4560-0979-3(6))* America Star Bks.

Miller, Michael & Strickland, AdriAnne. Shadow Run. 2017. (ENG.). 400p. (YA). (gr. 7). 17.99 *(978-0-399-55253-3(7),* Delacorte Pr.) Random Hse. Children's Bks.

Miller, Penelope. Farbedrook. 2008. 96p. pap. *(978-1-84748-104-7(3))* Athena Pr.

Millman, Selena. More Than a Hero. 2006. 92p. (YA). per. 11.37 *(978-1-4243-2351-7(7))* Independent Publisher Services.

—The Prince & Me. 2006. 146p. (YA). per. 11.20 *(978-1-4243-2353-1(3))* Independent Publisher Services.

Mirabelli, Eugene. The Queen of the Rain Was in Love with the Prince of the Sky. 2008. pap. 5.00 *(978-0-935891-08-9(0))* Spring Harbor Pr.

Moeling, Nell. The Secret Adventures of Prince Justin & the Dragon. 2010. 40p. 17.99 *(978-1-4520-4996-0(3))* AuthorHouse.

Molina, Angeles. El Principe Que No Queria Ser Principe. 2007. (SPA.). 64p. 14.95 *(978-0-8477-0455-2(6))* Univ. of Puerto Rico Pr.

Monnar, Ana. Heart of Stone. Michaud, Nancy, illus. 2007. 24p. (J). per. 11.99 *(978-0-9768035-5-3(0))* Readers Are Leaders U.S.A., Inc.

Muloch, Miss. The Little Lame Prince & Other Tales. 2007. 304p. 24.95 *(978-1-4344-9379-8(2))* Wildside Pr., LLC.

Mulock, Dinah Maria. The Little Lame Prince & His Traveling Cloak. 2005. reprint ed. pap. 20.95 *(978-1-4179-1940-6(X))* Kessinger Publishing, LLC.

—The Little Lame Prince & the Adventures of a Brownie. Date not set. lib. bdg. 25.95 *(978-0-8488-2095-4(9))* Amereon Ltd.

Mulrain, Sabrina. A Prince's Happy Ever After. 2011. 40p. pap. 24.95 *(978-1-4560-3251-7(8))* America Star Bks.

Munsch, Robert. The Paper Bag Princess. Martchenko, Michael, illus. 10th ed. 2009. (ENG.). 28p. (J). (gr. -1-2). bds. 7.99 *(978-1-55451-211-9(5),* 9781554512119) Annick Pr., Ltd. CAN. Dist: Publishers Group West (PGW).

Myers, Tim J. The Christmas Stick: A Children's Story. Yilmaz, Necdet, illus. 2014. (ENG.). 32p. (J). pap. 13.99 *(978-1-61261-571-4(6))* Paraclete Pr., Inc.

Myklusch, Matt. The Lost Prince. 2015. (Seaborne Ser.: No. 1). (ENG.). 400p. (J). (gr. 3-7). 16.99 *(978-1-60684-525-7(X),* Carolrhoda Bks.) Lerner Publishing Group.

Nevis, Lance. The Pollywog Prince. Laible MBA, Steve William, ed. Piper, Tom, illus. 2012. 46p. pap. 10.99 *(978-0-9850142-8-5(8))* Kodel Group, LLC, The.

Nguy, Hoa X. The Bamboo Girl. 2007. 84p. (J). pap. 20.00 *(978-0-8059-7562-8(4))* Dorrance Publishing Co., Inc.

Nielsen, Amy. Victor & the Sun Orb. 2008. 144p. 21.95 *(978-0-595-50307-0(1));* pap. 11.95 *(978-0-595-51212-6(7))* iUniverse, Inc.

Nielsen, Jennifer A. The False Prince. 2012. (Ascendance Trilogy: Bk. 1). (ENG.). (J). (gr. 5-8). 64.99 *(978-1-61707-596-4(5))* Findaway World, LLC.

—The False Prince. 2013. (False Prince Ser.: Bk. 1). (ENG.). 352p. (J). (gr. 5-9). pap. 7.99 *(978-0-545-28414-1(7),* Scholastic Paperbacks) 2012. (Ascendance Trilogy Ser.: 1). (ENG., Illus.). 352p. (J). (gr. 4-7). 17.99 *(978-0-545-28413-4(9),* Scholastic Pr.) 2012. (Ascendance Trilogy: Bk. 1). 352p. pap. 17.99 *(978-0-545-39249-5(7))* 2012. (Ascendance Trilogy: Bk. 1). (Illus.). 342p. (J). pap. *(978-0-545-43347-1(9),* Scholastic Pr.) Scholastic, Inc.

—The False Prince. 2013. (Ascendance Trilogy Ser.: 1). lib. bdg. 18.40 *(978-0-606-31491-6(1),* Turtleback) Turtleback Bks.

Nix, Garth. A Confusion of Princes. 2012. 352p. (YA). (gr. 8). (ENG.). 17.99 *(978-0-06-009694-6(2));* lib. bdg. 18.89 *(978-0-06-009695-3(0))* HarperCollins Pubs.

Norris, Johanna. The Day Prince Snot Nose Made Friends. 2011. 36p. (gr. -1). pap. 11.32 *(978-1-4567-3283-7(8))* AuthorHouse.

North, Laura. Cinderella's Big Foot. 2014. (ENG., Illus.). 32p. (J). *(978-0-7787-0440-9(8));* pap. *(978-0-7787-0448-5(3))* Crabtree Publishing Co.

—Sleeping Beauty — 100 Years Later. 2014. (ENG., Illus.). 32p. (J). *(978-0-7787-0444-7(0));* pap. *(978-0-7787-0479-9(3))* Crabtree Publishing Co.

O'connell, Tyne. A Royal Match. 2011. (Calypso Chronicles Ser.). (ENG.). 512p. (YA). pap. 9.99 *(978-1-59990-751-2(8),* 9781599907512, Bloomsbury USA Childrens) Bloomsbury Publishing USA.

O'Connell, Tyne. A Royal Mess. 2011. (Calypso Chronicles Ser.). (ENG.). 512p. (YA). pap. 9.99 *(978-1-59990-888-5(3),* 9781599908885, Bloomsbury USA Childrens) Bloomsbury Publishing USA.

Oppenheim, Joanne F. The Prince's Bedtime. Latimer, Miriam, illus. (ENG.). 32p. (J). (gr. -1-3). 2007. pap. 7.99 *(978-1-84686-106-2(3))* 2006. 16.99 *(978-1-84148-597-3(7))* Barefoot Bks., Inc.

Oppenheim, Joanne F. & Barefoot Books Staff. The Prince's Breakfast. Latimer, Miriam, illus. 2014. 32p. (J). (gr. -1-2). 9.99 *(978-1-78285-075-5(9));* 16.99 *(978-1-78285-074-8(0))* Barefoot Bks., Inc.

—El Principe No Duerme. Latimer, Miriam, illus. 2014. (SPA.). 32p. (J). (gr. -1-1). pap. 7.99 *(978-1-78285-077-9(5))* Barefoot Bks., Inc.

Oppenheim, Joanne F. & Latimer, Muriam. The Prince's Bedtime. Latimer, Muriam, illus. 2007. (ENG., Illus.). 32p. (J). (gr. -1-2). 9.99 *(978-1-84686-096-6(2))* Barefoot Bks., Inc.

Pacat, C. S. Kings Rising. 2016. (Captive Prince Trilogy Ser.: 3). (ENG., Illus.). 368p. pap. 16.00 *(978-0-425-27399-9(7),* Berkley) Penguin Publishing Group.

Pace, Terri L. The Christmas Dream, 1 vol. 2009. 116p. pap. 19.95 *(978-1-60813-632-5(2))* America Star Bks.

Parker, Danny. Lola's Toybox: the Plastic Palace. Shield, Guy, illus. 2017. (Lola's Toy Box Ser.: 4). (ENG.). 96p. (J). (gr. k-2). pap. 6.99 ***(978-1-76012-439-7(7))*** Hardie Grant Egmont Pty, Ltd. AUS. Dist: Independent Pubs. Group.

Parker, Vic, ed. The Prince & the Dragon & Other Stories. 2015. (Scary Fairy Tales Ser.). (ENG.). 40p. (J). (gr. 3-4). pap. 14.05 *(978-1-4824-3097-4(5))* Stevens, Gareth Publishing LLLP.

Patten, Linda D. Princess Alese & the Kingdom of Serenity. 2013. 20p. pap. 13.77 *(978-1-4669-8724-1(3))* Trafford Publishing.

Pearson, Kimberly Ann. Mystling Glen Book I: The Tale of A Prince. 2009. 207p. pap. 14.95 *(978-1-4327-4169-3(1))* Outskirts Pr., Inc.

Peattie, Cindy. A Cinderella Atlas. Mountford, Karl, illus. 2017. (Text Connections Guided Close Reading Ser.). (J). (gr. 1). *(978-1-4900-1819-5(0))* Benchmark Education Co.

Pef. Belle lisse poire du prince De. pap. 16.95 *(978-2-07-054806-4(6))* Gallimard, Editions FRA. Dist: Distribooks, Inc.

Perrotti, P. J. Jason & the Enchanted Forest. 2004. 48p. pap. 16.95 *(978-1-4137-4593-1(8))* America Star Bks.

Peterson, Alyson. Ian Quicksilver: The Warrior's Return. 2015. vii, 309p. (YA). pap. 17.99 *(978-1-4621-1629-4(9))* Cedar Fort, Inc./CFI Distribution.

Picoult, Jodi & van Leer, Samantha. Between the Lines. (ENG., Illus.). 368p. (YA). (gr. 7). 2013. pap. 12.99 *(978-1-4516-3581-2(8))* 2012. 19.99 *(978-1-4516-3575-1(3))* Atria/Emily Bestler Bks. (Atria/Emily Bestler Bks.).

—Off the Page. Gilbert, Yvonne, illus. 2015. (YA). lib. bdg. *(978-0-553-53557-0(9)*, Delacorte Pr) Random House Publishing Group.

—Off the Page. Gilbert, Yvonne, illus. (ENG.). (YA). (gr. 7). 2016. 368p. pap. 9.99 *(978-0-553-53559-4(5)*, Ember) 2015. 384p. 19.99 *(978-0-553-53556-3(0)*, Delacorte Pr.) Random Hse. Children's Bks.

Pierce, Tamora. In the Hand of the Goddess. 2014. (Song of the Lioness Ser.: 2). (ENG., Illus.). 272p. (YA). (gr. 7). 19.99 *(978-1-4814-3960-2(X)*, Atheneum Bks. for Young Readers) Simon & Schuster Children's Publishing.

Podd, Gloria. A Royal Runt. 2013. 20p. pap. 24.95 *(978-1-63004-012-3(6))* America Star Bks.

Prince Apple Head Humpledink. 2006. 38p. (J). 13.68 *(978-1-4116-7232-1(1))* Lulu Pr., Inc.

Proulx, Roxanna Darling. The Princes of Pleasant Valley: A Day in the Life of Zyler & Xavier, 1 vol. Sandon, Gina, illus. 2010. 46p. 24.95 *(978-1-4489-7641-6(3))* PublishAmerica, Inc.

Prue, Sally. Big Bad Troll. Knight, Tom, illus. 2017. (Reading Ladder Ser.). (ENG.). 48p. (J). (gr. k-2). pap. 7.99 ***(978-1-4052-7825-6(0))*** Egmont Bks., Ltd. GBR. Dist: Independent Pubs. Group.

Publications International Ltd. Staff. Disney Adventure Look & Find. 2013. (gr. 1-3). 7.98 *(978-1-4127-7146-7(3)*, 1412771463) Phoenix International Publications, Inc.

Publications International Ltd. Staff, creator. Barbie as the Island Princess. 2007. (Play-A-Sound Bks.). (Illus.). 9.98 *(978-1-4127-7413-0(6))* Publications International, Ltd.

Publications International Ltd. Staff, ed. Disney Princess: Cinderella. 2008. (J). 12.98 *(978-1-4127-8475-7(1))* Publications International, Ltd.

Puchner, Willy. The ABC of Fantastic Princes. 2015. (ENG., Illus.). 64p. (J). 19.95 *(978-0-7358-4198-7(5))* North-South Bks., Inc.

Quinn, Jordan. The Bard & the Beast. McPhillips, Robert, illus. 2015. (Kingdom of Wrenly Ser.: 9). (ENG.). 128p. (J). (gr. k-4). pap. 5.99 *(978-1-4814-4396-8(8)*, Little Simon) Little Simon.

—The False Fairy. McPhillips, Robert, illus. 2016. (Kingdom of Wrenly Ser.: 11). (ENG.). 128p. (J). (gr. k-4). pap. 5.99 *(978-1-4814-8586-9(5)*, Little Simon) Little Simon.

—Let the Games Begin! McPhillips, Robert, illus. 2015. (Kingdom of Wrenly Ser.: 7). (ENG.). 128p. (J). (gr. k-4). pap. 5.99 *(978-1-4814-2379-3(7)*, Little Simon) Little Simon.

—The Lost Stone. McPhillips, Robert, illus. 2014. (Kingdom of Wrenly Ser.: 1). (ENG.). 128p. (J). (gr. k-4). pap. 5.99 *(978-1-4424-9690-3(8)*, Little Simon) Little Simon.

—The Lost Stone. 2014. (Kingdom of Wrenly Ser.: 1). lib. bdg. 16.00 *(978-0-606-35443-1(3))* Turtleback Bks.

—The Pegasus Quest. McPhillips, Robert, illus. 2016. (Kingdom of Wrenly Ser.: 10). (ENG.). 128p. (J). (gr. k-4). pap. 5.99 *(978-1-4814-5870-2(1)*, Little Simon) Little Simon.

—The Scarlet Dragon. McPhillips, Robert, illus. 2014. (Kingdom of Wrenly Ser.: 2). (ENG.). 128p. (J). (gr. k-4). pap. 5.99 *(978-1-4424-9693-4(2)*, Little Simon) Little Simon.

—The Scarlet Dragon. 2014. (Kingdom of Wrenly Ser.: 2). lib. bdg. 16.00 *(978-0-606-35444-8(1))* Turtleback Bks.

—Sea Monster! McPhillips, Robert, illus. 2014. (Kingdom of Wrenly Ser.: 3). (ENG.). 128p. (J). (gr. k-4). pap. 5.99 *(978-1-4814-0072-5(X)*, Little Simon) Little Simon.

—The Secret World of Mermaids. McPhillips, Robert, illus. 2015. (Kingdom of Wrenly Ser.: 8). (ENG.). 128p. (J). (gr. k-4). pap. 5.99 *(978-1-4814-3122-4(6)*, Little Simon) Little Simon.

—The Sorcerer's Shadow. McPhillips, Robert, illus. 2017. (Kingdom of Wrenly Ser.: 12). (ENG.). 128p. (J). (gr. k-4). 16.99 ***(978-1-5344-0000-9(1))***; pap. 5.99 ***(978-1-4814-9999-6(8))*** Little Simon. (Little Simon).

Quinn, Jordan. The Witch's Curse. McPhillips, Robert, illus. 2014. (Kingdom of Wrenly Ser.: 4). (ENG.). 128p. (J). (gr. k-4). pap. 5.99 *(978-1-4814-0075-6(4)*, Little Simon) Little Simon.

Rattle, Alison. The Beloved. 2016. (ENG.). 304p. (YA). (gr. 11). pap. 12.99 *(978-1-4714-0379-8(3))* Bonnier Publishing GBR. Dist: Independent Pubs. Group.

Raum, Elizabeth. Cedric & the Dragon. Crittenden, Nina Victor, illus. 2010. (J). *(978-1-934617-05-2(9)*, Alma Little) Elva Resa Publishing, LLC.

Ray, Michelle. Falling for Hamlet. 2012. (ENG.). 368p. (YA). (gr. 10-17). pap. 17.99 *(978-0-316-10161-5(3)*, Poppy) Little, Brown Bks. for Young Readers.

Reeder, Marilou. The Daring Prince Dashing. West, Karl, illus. 2015. (ENG.). 32p. (J). (gr. -1-k). 16.99 *(978-1-63450-161-3(6)*, Sky Pony Pr.) Skyhorse Publishing Co., Inc.

RH Disney Staff. The Princess & the Frog. RH Disney Staff, illus. 2009. (Little Golden Book Ser.). (ENG., Illus.). 24p. (J). (gr. -1-2). 4.99 *(978-0-7364-2628-2(0)*, Golden/Disney) Random Hse. Children's Bks.

Rhodes, Morgan. Gathering Darkness. 2014. (Falling Kingdoms Ser.: 3). (ENG.). 430p. (YA). (gr. 7). 18.99 *(978-1-59514-705-9(5)*, Razorbill) Penguin Young Readers Group.

Riggs, Kate. Princes & Princesses. 2013. (Illus.). 24p. (J). 25.65 *(978-1-60818-243-5(6)*, Creative Education) Creative Co., The.

Riley, Analynn. Legend of the Mountains & the Valleys: The Nine Gifts of Theodosia, the Final Question, Kenelm's Quest, Yedda Sings. 2013. 152p. (J). (gr. 4-6). 30.95 *(978-1-4497-8372-3(4))*; pap. 13.95 *(978-1-4497-8371-6(6))* Author Solutions, Inc. (WestBow Pr.).

Riley, Kana. The Princess & the Wise Woman. Williams, Jenny, illus. 2012. (Ready Readers: Stage 5 Ser.). (ENG.). 24p. (J). (gr. k-2). pap. 6.97 *(978-0-8136-2371-9(5))* Modern Curriculum Pr.

Rios, Yuri M. The Kingdom of Ice. Rios, Margarita, tr. 2012. 26p. pap. 9.99 *(978-1-61897-223-1(5)*, Strategic Bk. Publishing) Strategic Book Publishing & Rights Agency (SBPRA).

Robin, Ink & Rivard, Joanna. A Real Prince Is Hard to Find: A Modern Fairy Tale. 2013. (ENG., Illus.). 32p. (J). (gr. -1-3). 17.89 *(978-1-61963-216-5(0)*, 9781619632165); 16.99 *(978-1-61963-215-8(2)*, 9781619632158) Bloomsbury Publishing USA. (Bloomsbury USA Childrens).

Robinson, Hilary. Beauty & the Pea. Sanfilippo, Simona, illus. 2013. (ENG.). 32p. (J). *(978-0-7787-1155-1(2))* Crabtree Publishing Co.

Roscoe, Charlie. The Red Prince. Cole, Tom Clohosy, illus. 2016. (ENG.). 32p. (J). (-k). 16.99 *(978-0-7636-8912-4(2)*, Templar) Candlewick Pr.

Rudnick, Paul. Gorgeous. (ENG.). 336p. (J). (gr. 9). 2014. pap. 9.99 *(978-0-545-46427-7(1))* 2013. 18.99 *(978-0-545-46426-0(9))* Scholastic, Inc. (Scholastic Pr.).

Rutkoski, Marie. The Cabinet of Wonders. 2013. (Kronos Chronicles Ser.: 1). (ENG.). 288p. (J). (gr. 5-9). pap. 10.99 *(978-1-250-01804-5(8)*, 9781250018045) Square Fish.

—The Celestial Globe. 2013. (Kronos Chronicles Ser.: 2). (ENG.). 320p. (J). (gr. 5-9). pap. 7.99 *(978-1-250-02732-0(2)*, 9781250027320) Square Fish.

Ryan, Rob. The Invisible Kingdom. 2016. (ENG., Illus.). 64p. (J). 19.95 *(978-1-56656-077-1(2)*, Crocodile Bks.) Interlink Publishing Group, Inc.

Sachar, Louis. Marvin Redpost #1: Kidnapped at Birth? Record, Adam, illus. 2015. (Marvin Redpost Ser.: 1). (ENG.). 96p. (J). (gr. 1-4). lib. bdg. 12.99 *(978-0-553-53540-2(4)*, Random Hse. Bks. for Young Readers) Random Hse. Children's Bks.

Sagar, Marie. Princess Samantha? 2009. 20p. pap. 12.49 *(978-1-4389-5297-0(X))* AuthorHouse.

Salisbury, Melinda. The Sin Eater's Daughter. 2015. (ENG.). 320p. (J). (gr. 9). 17.99 *(978-0-545-81062-3(0)*, Scholastic Pr.) Scholastic, Inc.

Schlitt, Jayme & Schlitt, Ron. Rags, Riches & the Robe. 2010. 32p. 17.25 *(978-1-4269-4666-0(X))* Trafford Publishing.

Schnee, Silke. Prince Noah & the School Pirates. Sistig, Heike, illus. 2016. (Prince Noah Book Ser.). (ENG.). 32p. (J). 16.00 *(978-0-87486-765-7(7))* Plough Publishing Hse.

—The Prince Who Was Just Himself. Sistig, Heike, illus. 2015. (Prince Noah Book Ser.). (ENG.). 32p. (J). (gr. -1-4). 16.00 *(978-0-87486-682-7(0))* Plough Publishing Hse.

Scieszka, Jon. The Frog Prince. Johnson, Steve, illus. 2014. 32p. pap. 7.00 *(978-1-61003-314-5(0))* Center for the Collaborative Classroom.

—The Frog Prince, Continued. 2003. (Live Oak Readalong Ser.). (Illus.). (J). 28.95 incl. audio compact disk *(978-1-59112-515-0(4))*; 25.95 incl. audio *(978-1-59112-229-6(5))* Live Oak Media.

—The Frog Prince, Continued. Johnson, Steve, illus. 2003. pap. 39.95 incl. audio compact disk *(978-1-59112-522-8(7))* Live Oak Media.

—The Frog Prince, Continued, 4 bks. 2003. (Live Oak Readalong Ser.). (J). pap. 37.95 incl. audio *(978-1-59112-230-2(9))* Live Oak Media.

Scott, Jeff. Becoming the King: Where's my Father? 2006. 222p. (J). per. 17.95 *(978-0-9787624-0-7(1))* TDO Enterprises.

Seredy, Kate. The Chestry Oak. 2015. (Illus.). 253p. (J). pap. 12.95 *(978-1-930900-81-3(3))* Purple Hse. Pr.

Sharp, Laura. The Key Prince. 2012. 24p. pap. 24.95 *(978-1-4626-8959-0(0))* America Star Bks.

Sharpe, Leah Marinsky. The Goat-Faced Girl: A Classic Italian Folktale. Marinsky, Jane, illus. 2009. 32p. (J). (gr. 1-4). 16.95 *(978-1-56792-393-3(3))* Godine, David R. Pub.

Shirer, Priscilla. The Prince Warriors & the Unseen Invasion. 2016. (Prince Warriors Ser.). (ENG., Illus.). 288p. (J). (gr. 3-7). 12.99 *(978-1-4336-9020-4(9)*, B&H Kids) B&H Publishing Group.

Shirer, Priscilla & Detwiler, Gina. The Prince Warriors. 2016. (Prince Warriors Ser.). (ENG.). 288p. (J). (gr. 3-7). 12.99 *(978-1-4336-9019-8(5)*, B&H Kids) B&H Publishing Group.

Sierra, JulieAnn. Legacy & the Dark Prince, 1 vol. 2009. 209p. pap. 24.95 *(978-1-61582-693-3(9))* America Star Bks.

Silver Dolphin & Andersen, Hans Christian. Little Mermaid: a Coloring Book. Dulac, Edmund, illus. 2017. (Classic Coloring Book Ser.). (ENG.). 96p. (J). (gr. k). pap. 15.99 *(978-1-62686-886-1(7)*, Silver Dolphin Bks.) Readerlink Distribution Services, LLC.

Skye, Evelyn. The Crown's Game. (Crown's Game Ser.: 1). (ENG.). (YA). (gr. 8). 2017. 432p. pap. 9.99 *(978-0-06-242259-0(6))* 2016. 416p. 17.99 *(978-0-06-242258-3(8))* HarperCollins Pubs.

—The Crown's Game. 2017. (Crown's Game Ser.: bk.1). (ENG.). (J). lib. bdg. 20.85 ***(978-0-606-39645-5(4))*** Turtleback Bks.

Smith, Earl. Mainu & the Prince of Bakara: And Other Stories from Africa. 2012. (Illus.). 120p. (YA). (gr. 3-7). pap. 14.95 *(978-1-893731-04-2(9)*, Mandolin Hse.) Kush Univ. Pr.

Smith, Nerissia. Prince de'Mario's Adventure, 1 vol. Dartes, Staci, illus. 2009. 29p. pap. 24.95 *(978-1-61582-972-9(5))* America Star Bks.

Smith, Sindy. Indy the Unicorn Prince. Smith, Sindy, illus. 2012. (Illus.). 46p. 29.95 *(978-1-4626-9864-6(6))* America Star Bks.

—Indy the Unicorn Prince. 2012. 48p. pap. 24.95 *(978-1-4626-7519-7(0))* America Star Bks.

Somper, Justin. A Conspiracy of Princes. 2015. (Allies & Assassins Ser.: 2). (ENG., Illus.). 496p. (J). (gr. 7-17). 18.00 *(978-0-316-25397-0(9))* Little, Brown Bks. for Young Readers.

Sonneveld, Stephen. The Prince of Destiny. 2007. 56p. pap. 30.50 *(978-0-615-16784-8(5))* Splendid Torch.

Stanley, Diane. Bella at Midnight. Ibatoulline, Bagram, illus. 2007. (ENG.). 304p. (J). (gr. 3-7). pap. 7.99 *(978-0-06-077575-9(0))* HarperCollins Pubs.

—The Chosen Prince. 2015. (ENG.). 368p. (J). (gr. 3-7). 16.99 *(978-0-06-224897-8(9))* HarperCollins Pubs.

Stanton, Angie. Royally Lost. 2014. (ENG.). 336p. (YA). (gr. 8). pap. 9.99 *(978-0-06-227258-4(6)*, HarperTeen) HarperCollins Pubs.

Stewig, John Warren. Nobody Asked the Pea. Van Wright, Cornelius, illus. 2013. (ENG.). 32p. (J). (gr. 1-5). 16.95 *(978-0-8234-2224-1(0))* Holiday Hse., Inc.

Stockham, Jess, illus. The Princess & the Pea. 2010. (Flip-Up Fairy Tales Ser.). (ENG.). 24p. (J). (gr. -1-2). audio compact disk *(978-1-84643-332-0(0))* Child's Play International Ltd.

Styles, Walker. Something Smells Fishy. Whitehouse, Ben, illus. 2016. (Rider Woofson Ser.: 2). (ENG.). 128p. (J). (gr. k-4). 16.99 *(978-1-4814-5742-2(X)*, Little Simon) Little Simon.

—Something Smells Fishy. 2016. (Rider Woofson Ser.: 2). lib. bdg. 16.00 *(978-0-606-38263-2(1))* Turtleback Bks.

Surette, Janet H. The Prince & the Gift: A Tale of True Beauty. 2010. 44p. pap. 14.95 *(978-1-4497-0662-3(2)*, WestBow Pr.) Author Solutions, Inc.

Teis, Kyra, adapted by. The Magic Flute: An Opera by Mozart, 1 vol. 2008. (ENG., Illus.). 32p. (J). (gr. k-9). 17.95 *(978-1-59572-058-0(8))* Star Bright Bks., Inc.

Testa, Maggie. Daniel Plays Ball. 2014. (Daniel Tiger's Neighborhood Ready-To-Read Ser.). lib. bdg. 13.55 *(978-0-606-36114-9(6))* Turtleback Bks.

Thomas, Rhiannon. A Wicked Thing. (YA). (gr. 9). 2016. 368p. pap. 9.99 *(978-0-06-230354-7(6))* 2015. (ENG.). 352p. 17.99 *(978-0-06-230353-0(8))* HarperCollins Pubs. (HarperTeen).

Ting, Renee. The Prince's Diary. Dulemba, Elizabeth O., illus. 2005. (Prince's Diary Ser.). 32p. (J). (gr. -1-3). 16.95 *(978-1-885008-27-5(9)*, Shen's Bks.) Lee & Low Bks., Inc.

Tish, Aunty. Kiddiwink Kingdom. 2006. (Illus.). 58p. (J). per. 19.95 *(978-1-59800-587-5(1))* Outskirts Pr., Inc.

Toybox Innovations, creator. Disney's Enchanted. 2007. (Disney's Read along Collection). (Illus.). 24p. (J). (gr. -1-3). pap. *(978-0-7634-2197-7(9))* Walt Disney Records.

Turner, Megan Whalen. A Conspiracy of Kings. (Queen's Thief Ser.: 4). (ENG.). (YA). (gr. 8). 2017. 368p. pap. 9.99 *(978-0-06-264299-8(5))* 2011. 352p. pap. 7.99 *(978-0-06-187095-8(1))* 2010. 336p. 16.99 *(978-0-06-187093-4(5))* HarperCollins Pubs. (Greenwillow Bks.).

—A Conspiracy of Kings, 6 vols. 2010. (Queen's Thief Ser.: BK.4). (YA). 88.75 *(978-1-4498-4573-5(8))*; (ENG.). 230.75 *(978-1-4498-4569-8(X))*; (ENG.). 73.75 *(978-1-4498-4570-4(3))*; 1.25 *(978-1-4498-4574-2(6))*;No. 4. (ENG.). 90.75 *(978-1-4498-4571-1(1))* Recorded Bks., Inc.

Twain, Mark, pseud. The Prince & the Pauper. (J). 19.95 *(978-0-8488-0849-5(5))* Amereon Ltd.

—The Prince & the Pauper. (J). 9.95 *(978-1-56156-311-1(0))* Kidsbooks, LLC.

—The Prince & the Pauper. 2006. (Aladdin Classics Ser.). (ENG.). 352p. (J). pap. 7.99 *(978-1-4169-2805-8(7)*, Aladdin) Simon & Schuster Children's Publishing.

Twain, Mark, pseud & Clemens, Samuel L. The Prince & the Pauper. 2013. (Works of Mark Twain). 425p. reprint ed. lthr. 79.00 *(978-0-7812-1120-8(4))* Reprint Services Corp.

Valentino, Serena & Disney Book Group Staff. The Beast Within: A Tale of Beauty's Prince. Disney Storybook Artists Staff & Disney Storybook Art Team, illus. 2014. (Villains Ser.). (ENG.). 224p. (J). (gr. 5-9). 16.99 *(978-1-4231-5912-4(8))* Disney Pr.

Vaugelade, Anais. The War. Rouffiac, Marie-Christine & Streissguth, Thomas, trs. from FRE. Vaugelade, Anais, illus. 2005. (Picture Bks.). (Illus.). 32p. (J). (gr. k-2). 15.25 *(978-1-57505-562-6(7))* Lerner Publishing Group.

Vaugelade, Anaïs. The War. Vaugelade, Anaïs, illus. 2007. (Carolrhoda Picture Bks.). (ENG., Illus.). 32p. (J). (gr. k-4). per. 6.95 *(978-1-57505-918-1(5)*, First Avenue Editions) Lerner Publishing Group.

Verano, Vladimir, illus. The Prince, the Demon King, & the Monkey Warrior. 2011. (ENG.). 96p. (J). (gr. 3-6). pap. 9.95 *(978-1-934159-30-9(1))* ThingsAsian Pr.

Viguié, Debbie. Violet Eyes. 2010. (Once upon a Time Ser.). (ENG.). 224p. (YA). (gr. 7-18). mass mkt. 7.99 *(978-1-4169-8676-8(6)*, Simon Pulse) Simon Pulse.

Wakeman, Lars. Prince Harry the Hairy Prince: A hairy fairy Tale. 2011. 24p. (gr. -1). pap. 12.56 *(978-1-4269-6304-9(1))* Trafford Publishing.

Walker Styles Staff. Something Smells Fishy. Whitehouse, Ben, illus. 2016. (Rider Woofson Ser.: 2). (ENG.). 128p. (J). (gr. k-4). pap. 5.99 *(978-1-4814-5741-5(1)*, Little Simon) Little Simon.

Wallace II, James C. & Wallace, Amanda D. The Emerald Slippers of Oz. 2013. 156p. pap. 14.99 *(978-0-578-12511-4(0))* Scientia Est Vox Pr.

Ward, Nick. The Tadpole Prince. 2003. (Illus.). 32p. (YA). *(978-1-84365-016-4(9)*, Pavilion Children's Books) Pavilion Bks.

Watt, Fiona. That's Not My Prince. Wells, Rachel, illus. 2013. (Usborne Touchy-Feely Board Bks.). (ENG.). 10p. (J). 9.99 *(978-0-7945-2838-6(4)*, Usborne) EDC Publishing.

Westerfeld, Scott. Behemoth. Thompson, Keith, illus. (Leviathan Trilogy Ser.). (ENG.). (YA). (gr. 7). 2011. 512p. pap. 12.99 *(978-1-4169-7176-4(9))* 2010. 496p. 18.99 *(978-1-4169-7175-7(0))* Simon Pulse. (Simon Pulse).

—Behemoth. Thompson, Keith, illus. l.t. ed. 2010. (Leviathan Trilogy: Bk. 2). (ENG.). 540p. 23.99 *(978-1-4104-3066-3(9))* Thorndike Pr.

—Behemoth. 2011. (Leviathan Ser.: 2). lib. bdg. 24.50 *(978-0-606-22407-9(6)*, Turtleback) Turtleback Bks.

—Goliath, 8 vols. 2011. (YA). 122.75 *(978-1-4618-0617-2(8))*; 124.75 *(978-1-4618-0613-4(5))*; 305.75 *(978-1-4618-0618-9(6))*; 122.75 *(978-1-4618-0614-1(3))*; 1.25 *(978-1-4640-3062-8(6))* Recorded Bks., Inc.

—Goliath. Thompson, Keith, illus. (Leviathan Trilogy Ser.). (ENG.). (YA). (gr. 7). 2012. 576p. pap. 14.99 *(978-1-4169-7178-8(5))* 2011. 560p. 19.99 *(978-1-4169-7177-1(7))* Simon Pulse. (Simon Pulse).

—Goliath. 2012. (Leviathan Ser.: 3). lib. bdg. 24.50 *(978-0-606-26355-9(1)*, Turtleback) Turtleback Bks.

—Leviathan. Thompson, Keith, illus. (Leviathan Trilogy Ser.). (ENG.). (YA). (gr. 7-18). 2010. 464p. pap. 12.99 *(978-1-4169-7174-0(2))* 2009. 448p. 19.99 *(978-1-4169-7173-3(4))* Simon Pulse. (Simon Pulse).

—Leviathan. l.t. ed. 2010. (Leviathan Trilogy: Bk. 1). (ENG.). 526p. 23.95 *(978-1-4104-2572-0(X))* Thorndike Pr.

—Leviathan. 2010. (Leviathan Ser.: 1). lib. bdg. 23.30 *(978-0-606-22393-5(2)*, Turtleback) Turtleback Bks.

—Leviathan: Leviathan; Behemoth; Goliath. Thompson, Keith, illus. 2012. (Leviathan Trilogy Ser.). (ENG.). 1552p. (YA). (gr. 7). pap. 37.99 *(978-1-4424-8377-4(6)*, Simon Pulse) Simon Pulse.

Weston Woods Staff, creator. Harold's Fairy Tale. 2011. 18.95 *(978-0-439-72704-4(9))*; 38.75 *(978-0-439-72706-8(5))* Weston Woods Studios, Inc.

—James Marshall's Cinderella. 2011. 38.75 *(978-0-439-84886-2(5))* Weston Woods Studios, Inc.

White, Lia. Alkis. 2010. (ENG., Illus.). 106p. pap. *(978-1-84748-715-5(7))* Athena Pr.

Whitmore, Gary. Prince Luna & the Space Dreamers. 2011. (ENG.). 204p. pap. 8.50 *(978-1-4565-8438-2(3))* CreateSpace Independent Publishing Platform.

Wilde, Oscar. The Happy Prince & Other Tales. Charles Robinson, illus. 2012. 84p. pap. 3.47 *(978-1-60386-460-2(1)*, Watchmaker Publishing) Wexford College Pr.

—Le Prince Hereux. (FRE.). (J). pap. 15.95 *(978-2-07-051629-2(6))* Gallimard, Editions FRA. Dist: Distribooks, Inc.

Williams, Allix Elise. The Adventures of Prince Thaddeus: The Glamorous Guest. 2010. 56p. pap. 11.49 *(978-1-4520-5437-7(1))* AuthorHouse.

Willis, Jeanne. Prince Charmless. Ross, Tony, illus. 2014. (ENG.). 32p. (J). (gr. -1-k). pap. 9.99 *(978-1-84939-778-0(3))* Andersen Pr. GBR. Dist: Independent Pubs. Group.

Wilson, Diane Lee. To Ride the Gods' Own Stallion. 2010. (ENG.). 256p. (J). (gr. 4-10). pap. 11.99 *(978-1-4022-4028-7(7)*, Sourcebooks Jabberwocky) Sourcebooks, Inc.

Wilson, Tony. The Princess & the Packet of Frozen Peas, 1 vol. deGennaro, Sue, illus. 2012. (ENG.). 32p. (J). 16.95 *(978-1-56145-635-2(7))* Peachtree Pubs.

Wisher, Mark. Don't kiss the Prince. 2010. 33p. pap. 21.50 *(978-1-4457-7238-7(8))* Lulu Pr., Inc.

Wonlah, Ivis. King Ola's Pepper Jar. 2012. 28p. pap. 16.09 *(978-1-4669-1600-5(1))* Trafford Publishing.

Woodward, Kay. Sleeping Handsome & the Princess Engineer. de Ruiter, Jo, illus. 2015. (Fairy Tales Today Ser.). (ENG.). 24p. (gr. 1-2). 23.99 *(978-1-4795-8615-8(3))* Picture Window Bks.

Wu, Nicholas. The Princess & the Pea, 1 vol. rev. ed. 2013. (Fiction Readers Ser.). (ENG., Illus.). 20p. (J). (gr. 1-1). pap. 4.99 *(978-1-4333-5489-2(6))* Shell Educational Publishing.

—The Princess & the Pea: A Retelling of Hans Christian Andersen's Story, 1 vol. rev. ed. 2013. (Fiction Readers Ser.). (ENG., Illus.). 20p. (J). (gr. 1-1). pap. 15.96 *(978-1-4807-1145-7(4))* Shell Educational Publishing.

Wyss, Tyan. The Solitaire Prince. 2006. 168p. (YA). per. 12.95 *(978-1-58939-906-8(4))* Virtualbookworm.com Publishing, Inc.

Yolen, Jane & Stemple, Adam. The Last Changeling. 2014. (Seelie Wars Ser.). (ENG.). 304p. (J). (gr. 3-7). 16.99 *(978-0-670-01435-4(4)*, Viking Books for Young Readers) Penguin Young Readers Group.

—The Seelie King's War. 2016. (Seelie Wars Ser.: 3). (ENG., Illus.). 336p. (J). (gr. 3-7). 17.99 *(978-0-670-01436-1(2)*, Viking Books for Young Readers) Penguin Young Readers Group.

PRINCES AND PRINCESSES

see Princes; Princesses

PRINCESSES

Allen, Nancy Kelly. The Truth about Princesses, 1 vol. Kim, Youngsun, illus. 2010. (Fairy-Tale Superstars Ser.). (ENG.). 32p. (gr. 1-3). lib. bdg. 27.32 *(978-1-4048-5747-6(8))* Picture Window Bks.

Au, May Parker. Princess Huilua & Kamapuaa. 2007.Tr. of Ke Kamalii Wahine o Huilua a me Kamapuaa. (ENG & HAW.). (J). lib. bdg. *(978-0-9773495-4-8(3))* Na Kamalei Koolauloa Early Education Program.

Beauregarde, Constance & Antal, Lara. Princess Diana: Royal Activist & Fashion Icon. 2016. (Leading Women Ser.). (Illus.). 128p. (J). (gr. 7-7). 39.93 *(978-1-5026-1987-7(3))* Cavendish Square Publishing.

Bridges, Shirin Yim & Yim Bridges, Shirin. Qutlugh Terkan Khatun of Kirman. Nguyen, Albert, illus. 2010. (Thinking Girl's Treasury of Real Princesses Ser.). (ENG.). 24p. (J). (gr. 3-8). 18.95 *(978-0-9845098-3-6(6))* Goosebottom Bks. LLC.

Bryan, Dale-Marie. William & Kate. 2012. (Stars of Today Ser.). (ENG.). 32p. (J). (gr. 2-5). 28.50 *(978-1-61473-287-7(6)*, 205049) Child's World, Inc., The.

Cabot, Meg. Princess Lessons. McLaren, Chesley, illus. 2003. (Princess Diaries Guidebook Ser.). (ENG.). 144p. (YA). (gr. 8-18). 15.99 *(978-0-06-052677-1(7)*, HarperTeen) HarperCollins Pubs.

Carbone, Courtney. How to Be a Princess (Disney Princess) RH Disney Staff, illus. 2015. (Ultimate Handbook Ser.). (ENG.). 64p. (J). (gr. 1-4). 9.99 *(978-0-7364-3415-7(1)*, RH/Disney) Random Hse. Children's Bks.

Chapman, Kelly. Princess with a Purpose. Lyon, Tammie, illus. ldr.'s ed. 2009. pap. 12.99 *(978-0-7369-2743-7(3))* Harvest Hse. Pubs.

Davidson, Susanna & Daynes, Katie. Little Princess Treasury. McNicholas, Shelagh & Cascio, Maria Cristina Lo, illus. 2006. (English Heritage Ser.). 96p. (J). 7.99 *(978-0-7945-1442-6(1)*, Usborne) EDC Publishing.

Diemer, Lauren & Kissock, Heather. Prince William & Kate Middleton. 2013. (J). *(978-1-62127-392-9(X))* Weigl Pubs., Inc.

Disney Princess Enchanted Character Guide. 2014. (ENG., Illus.). 144p. (J). (gr. 2-5). 16.99 *(978-1-4654-1569-1(6)*, DK Children) Dorling Kindersley Publishing, Inc.

Disney Storybook Artists Staff. Enchanted Princesses: Learn to Draw Ariel, Cinderella, Belle, Rapunzel, & All of Your Favorite Disney Princesses! 2012. (Licensed Learn to Draw Ser.). (ENG., Illus.). 64p. (J). (gr. 1-17). pap. 9.95 *(978-1-60058-305-6(9)*, 1600583059) Quarto Publishing Group USA.

Doak, Robin S. Kate Middleton. 2015. (True Book(tm), A — Biographies Ser.). (ENG., Illus.). 48p. (J). lib. bdg. 31.00 *(978-0-531-21596-8(2)*, Children's Pr.) Scholastic Library Publishing.

—Kate Middleton: Dutchess of Cambridge. 2015. (True Book(tm) — Biographies Ser.). (ENG., Illus.). 48p. (J). pap. 6.95 *(978-0-531-21758-0(2)*, Children's Pr.) Scholastic Library Publishing.

Eckel, Jessie, illus. How to Be a Princess in 7 Days or Less. 2005. (How to be A Ser.). 32p. (J). (gr. 3-5). 12.95 *(978-0-7534-5921-8(3)*, Kingfisher) Roaring Brook Pr.

English Heritage Staff. My Life as a Princess. 2005. (Illus.). 32p. pap. 19.95 *(978-1-85074-984-4(1))* Historic England Publishing GBR. Dist: Casemate Academic.

Flowerpot Press, creator. Princesses Coloring Book. 2013. (Sockheadz Ser.). (ENG., Illus.). 72p. (J). (gr. -1-3). 4.99 *(978-1-77093-543-3(6))* Flowerpot Pr.

Gamble, Adam & Jasper, Mark. Good Night Princesses. Gardner, Louise, illus. 2016. (Good Night Our World Ser.). (ENG.). 20p. (J). (— 1). bds. 9.95 *(978-1-60219-225-6(1))* Good Night Bks.

Greenwall, Jessica. First Sticker Book Princesses. Finn, Rebecca, illus. 2013. (First Sticker Bks). 16p. (J). pap. 6.99 *(978-0-7945-3357-1(4),* Usborne) EDC Publishing.

Grimm, Jacob & Grimm, Wilhelm. The Twelve Dancing Princesses. McClintock, Barbara, illus. 2017. (J). *(978-0-439-89402-9(6),* Scholastic Pr.) Scholastic, Inc.

Heos, Bridget. Who Wants to Be a Princess? What It Was Really Like to Be a Medieval Princess. Migy, illus. 2017. (ENG.). 32p. (J). 16.99 *(978-0-8050-9769-6(4),* 9780805097696, Holt, Henry & Co. Bks. For Young Readers) Holt, Henry & Co.

Hunter, Nick. Catherine, Duchess of Cambridge, 1 vol. 2014. (Extraordinary Women Ser.). (ENG.). 48p. (gr. 6-6). lib. bdg. 32.65 *(978-1-4109-5942-3(2))* Heinemann-Raintree.

I'm Going to be the Best Princess Ever! 2008. (I'm Going to be Storybooks... Ser.). 32p. *(978-1-4075-1584-7(5))* Parragon, Inc.

Ipcizade, Catherine. T Is for Tiara: A Princess Alphabet, 1 vol. 2010. (Alphabet Fun Ser.). (ENG.). 32p. (gr. 1-2). lib. bdg. 27.32 *(978-1-4296-4462-4(1),* Aplus Bks.) Capstone Press of Coughlan Cos.

Jaycox, Jaclyn. A Princess Alphabet: The ABCs of Royalty! Eriza, Gustavo, illus. 2016. (Alphabet Connection Ser.). (ENG.). 32p. (gr. k-1). lib. bdg. 27.32 *(978-1-4795-6885-7(6))* Picture Window Bks.

Kats, Jewel. The Princess & the Ruby: An Autism Fairy Tale. Kinra, Richa, illus. 2013. 42p. 26.95 *(978-1-61599-193-8(X));* (J). (gr. 3-7). pap. 16.95 *(978-1-61599-175-4(1))* Loving Healing Pr., Inc.

Labrecque, Ellen & Harrison, Nancy. Who Was Princess Diana? Hoare, Jerry, illus. 2017. (Who Was? Ser.). (ENG.). 112p. (J). (gr. 3-7). 5.99 *(978-0-448-48855-4(8),* Grosset & Dunlap) Penguin Young Readers Group.

Lajiness, Katie. Kate Middleton, 1 vol. 2016. (Big Buddy Pop Biographies Ser.). (ENG., Illus.). 32p. (J). (gr. 2-5). 28.50 *(978-1-68078-055-0(7))* ABDO Publishing Co.

Lee, Sally. Princes & Princesses, 1 vol. 2013. (Royalty Ser.). (ENG.). 24p. (gr. k-1). lib. bdg. 26.65 *(978-1-62065-124-7(6),* Pebble Plus) Capstone Press of Coughlan Cos.

Maloof, Torrey. Mary Musgrove: Bringing People Together. 2016. (Primary Source Readers Ser.). (Illus.). 32p. (gr. 2-2). 8.99 *(978-1-4938-2557-8(7))* Teacher Created Materials, Inc.

Matthews, Caitlin. How to Be a Princess. Willey, Bee, illus. 2009. (ENG.). 32p. (J). (gr. 2-3). 21.95 *(978-1-84732-164-0(X))* Carlton Bks., Ltd. GBR. Dist: Sterling Publishing Co., Inc.

—How to Be the Perfect Princess. Willey, Bee, illus. 2011. (ENG.). 32p. (J). (gr. 2). pap. 9.95 *(978-1-84732-326-2(X))* Carlton Bks., Ltd. GBR. Dist: Sterling Publishing Co., Inc.

McDonnell, Peter. The Last Princess. 2005. (Illus.). 16p. *(978-0-7367-2910-9(0))* Zaner-Bloser, Inc.

Miller, Eileen Rudisill. Princess Coloring Book. 2012. (Dover Coloring Bks.). (ENG.). 32p. (J). (gr. -1-3). pap. 3.99 *(978-0-486-49917-8(0))* Dover Pubns., Inc.

Morley, Jacqueline. How to Be an Egyptian Princess. Hewetson, Nicholas J., illus. (How to Be Ser.). (ENG.). 32p. (J). (gr. 4-7). 2008. pap. 5.95 *(978-1-4263-0246-6(0))* 2006. 14.95 *(978-0-7922-7494-0(6))* 2006. lib. bdg. 21.90 *(978-0-7922-7548-0(9))* National Geographic Society. (National Geographic Children's Bks.).

Munro, Fiona. Princesses: With 200 Stickers, Puzzles & Games, Fold-Out Pages, & Creative Play. 2013. (My First Creativity Bks.). (ENG.). 66p. (J). (gr. -1-2). pap. 9.99 *(978-1-4380-0323-8(4))* Barron's Educational Series, Inc.

Norwich, Grace. The Real Princess Diaries. 2015. (ENG.). 96p. (J). (gr. 3-7). pap. 6.99 *(978-0-545-84937-1(3),* Scholastic Paperbacks) Scholastic, Inc.

Owings, Lisa. Diana: The People's Princess, 1 vol. 2012. (Lives Cut Short Set 2 Ser.). (ENG.). 112p. (J). (gr. 6-12). lib. bdg. 35.64 *(978-1-61783-545-2(5),* Essential Library) ABDO Publishing Co.

Pinnington, Andrea. Princess Pocket Activity Fun & Games: Includes Games, Cutouts, Foldout Scenes, Textures, Stickers, & Stencils. 2013. (Pocket Activity Fun & Games Ser.). (ENG.). 96p. (J). (gr. 1-4). pap. 7.99 *(978-1-4380-0313-9(7))* Barron's Educational Series, Inc.

Pohl, Amelia E. Mary Musgrove: Georgia, My State Biographies. l.t. ed. 2008. (ENG., Illus.). 24p. (J). (gr. k-2). 22.60 *(978-1-935077-02-2(3),* Everett Pr.) State Standards Publishing, LLC.

Priddy, Roger. My Pretty Princess. 2013. (Princess World Ser.). (ENG.). 134p. (J). (gr. k-2). pap., act. bk. ed. 12.99 *(978-0-312-51640-6(1),* 9780312516406, Priddy Bks.) St. Martin's Pr.

Princesses. 2007. (Velvet Art Activity Book Ser.). 8p. pap. *(978-1-4075-0362-2(6))* Parragon, Inc.

Publications International Ltd. Staff, ed. Disney Princess: My Own Carriage. 2014. 12p. (J). bds. 12.98 *(978-1-4508-7381-9(2),* 66a3c624-31ec-4290-ae22-6fd5a90376b3) Phoenix International Publications, Inc.

Ribke, Simone T. William & Kate: The Prince & Princess. 2016. (Rookie Biographies(tm) Ser.). (ENG., Illus.). 32p. (J). lib. bdg. 25.00 *(978-0-531-22548-6(8),* Children's Pr.) Scholastic Library Publishing.

Ryland Peters and Small Staff, creator. Now I Am a Princess. 2008. (ENG., Illus.). 48p. *(978-1-84597-741-2(6))* Ryland Peters & Small.

Scholastic Editors. Princess Leia. 2016. (Backstories Ser.: Vol. 7). (ENG., Illus.). 128p. (J). (gr. 3-7). 16.00 *(978-0-606-39146-7(0))* Turtleback Bks.

Shirley, Rebekah Joy. I Want to Be a Princess. 2011. (Let's Play Dress up Ser.). (ENG., Illus.). 24p. (J). (gr. k-3). pap. 10.60 *(978-1-61533-394-3(0));* lib. bdg. 25.25 *(978-1-61533-356-1(8))* Windmill Bks.

Summers, Portia. Kate Middleton: Duchess of Cambridge. 2017. (Junior Biographies Ser.). 24p. (J). (gr. 3-4). pap. 9.35 ***(978-0-7660-8781-1(6));*** lib. bdg. 22.60 ***(978-0-7660-8672-2(0))*** Enslow Pubs., Inc.

Tieck, Sarah. Kate Middleton: Real-Life Princess, 1 vol. 2011. (Big Buddy Biographies Set 7 Ser.). (ENG., Illus.). 32p. (J). (gr. 2-5). 28.50 *(978-1-61783-020-4(8))* ABDO Publishing Co.

Trussell-Cullen, Alan. Princess Diana. 2009. pap. 13.25 *(978-1-60559-068-4(1))* Hameray Publishing Group, Inc.

Webster-Smith, Angela. In the Presence of a King. 2012. 68p. pap. 28.99 *(978-1-4685-5442-7(5))* AuthorHouse.

Woodworth, Viki. Princess Mazes. 2012. (Dover Children's Activity Bks.). (ENG.). 48p. (J). (gr. 1-4). pap. 4.99 *(978-0-486-49058-8(0))* Dover Pubns., Inc.

PRINCESSES—FICTION

Abbott, Tony. The Hidden Stairs & the Magic Carpet. Jessell, Tim, illus. 2004. (Secrets of Droon Ser.: No. 1). 80p. (gr. 2-5). 15.00 *(978-0-7569-3939-7(9))* Perfection Learning Corp.

Abela, Donna. The Princess & the Pea Vol. 9: Band 15/Emerald. Stewart, Chantal, illus. 2007. (Collins Big Cat Ser.). (ENG.). 32p. (J). pap. 8.99 *(978-0-00-722866-9(X))* HarperCollins Pubs. Ltd. GBR. Dist: Independent Pubs. Group.

Ackland, Rachel. Princess Penny & Her Dancing Sister! 2017. (ENG.). 22p. (J). (gr. -1-2). pap. 5.99 *(978-1-4380-0984-1(4))* Barron's Educational Series, Inc.

Adeniyi, Bab. The Servant, the King, & the Princess. 2012. 28p. pap. 15.99 *(978-1-4691-4989-9(3))* Xlibris Corp.

Adkinson, Gina Mary. Growing up with Princess Lizzy: Little Life Lessons. 2012. (ENG.). 50p. pap. 16.95 *(978-1-4787-1993-9(1))* Outskirts Pr., Inc.

The Adventures of Marc John Jefferies: The Missing Princess. l.t. ed. 2004. (Illus.). 110p. (YA). per. *(978-0-9747218-3-5(2),* 100, Young Women Programming) Harper Kids Hse.

Aikins, Dave, illus. Dora Saves the Snow Princess. 2008. (Dora the Explorer Ser.: 27). (ENG.). 24p. (J). (gr. -1-2). pap. 3.99 *(978-1-4169-5866-6(5),* Simon Spotlight/Nickelodeon) Simon Spotlight/Nickelodeon.

Al-Zeheri, Ali. The Princess & the Gold. 2009. 32p. pap. 12.99 *(978-1-4490-2091-0(7))* AuthorHouse.

Alberto, Daisy. A Horse & a Hero. Random House Disney Staff, illus. 2011. (Step into Reading Ser.). (ENG.). 32p. (J). (gr. k-3). pap. 3.99 *(978-0-7364-2746-3(5),* RH/Disney) Random Hse. Children's Bks.

Alexander. Phonic Comics: Princess School - Level 1. 2011. (ENG., Illus.). 24p. (J). (gr. 1-17). pap. 3.99 *(978-1-60169-110-1(6))* Innovative Kids.

Alford, Wade. The Princess & the Golden Ring. 2011. 16p. 8.99 *(978-1-4520-9132-7(3))* AuthorHouse.

Allchin, Rosalind. The Frog Princess. 2004. (Illus.). (J). (gr. k-3). spiral bd. *(978-0-616-14557-9(8))* Canadian National Institute for the Blind/Institut National Canadien pour les Aveugles.

—The Frog Princess. Allchin, Rosalind, illus. 2003. (ENG., Illus.). 32p. (J). (gr. k-3). pap. 5.95 *(978-1-55337-526-5(2))* Kids Can Pr., Ltd. CAN. Dist: Hachette Bk. Group.

Allem, Jolyia. The Maiden & the Prince: A Tale of Devotion. 2009. 16p. pap. 8.75 *(978-1-4490-2350-8(9))* AuthorHouse.

Allen, Joy. Princess Party. Allen, Joy, illus. 2009. (ENG., Illus.). 32p. (J). (gr. -1-k). 16.99 *(978-0-399-25259-4(2),* G.P. Putnam's Sons Books for Young Readers) Penguin Young Readers Group.

Alloway, Kit. Dreamfever: A Novel. 2016. (Dream Walker Trilogy Ser.: 2). (ENG.). 320p. (J). 19.99 *(978-1-250-07811-7(3),* 9781250078117, St. Martin's Griffin) St. Martin's Pr.

Amin, Ahmed. The Mountains of Kohqaf. 2013. 88p. (gr. 4-6). pap. 11.25 *(978-1-4907-0959-8(2))* Trafford Publishing.

Amirkhan, Michele. Princess Elian's Quest. 2008. 112p. 20.95 *(978-0-595-50870-9(7));* pap. 10.95 *(978-0-595-51400-7(6))* iUniverse, Inc.

Amore, Sandra. The Princess Who Lived on the 174th Floor. 2011. 58p. pap. 18.68 *(978-1-4653-5854-7(4))* Xlibris Corp.

Amy, Brooks. Princess Polly Stories. 2007. (ENG.). 196p. pap. 19.99 *(978-1-4346-1976-1(1))* Creative Media Partners, LLC.

Andersen, Hans Christian. The Little Mermaid & the Princess & the Pea: Two Tales & Their Histories. Brown, Carron, ed. 2009. (World of Fairy Tales Ser.). (Illus.). 32p. (J). (gr. -1-2). pap. 10.55 *(978-1-60754-638-2(8));* lib. bdg. 22.60 *(978-1-60754-637-5(X))* Windmill Bks.

Andrews, Julie & Hamilton, Emma Walton. A Fairy Merry Christmas. Davenier, Christine, illus. 2012. (Passport to Reading Level 1 Ser.). (ENG.). 32p. (J). (gr. -1-3). pap. 4.99 *(978-0-316-21962-4(2))* Little, Brown Bks. for Young Readers.

—A Fairy Merry Christmas. 2012. (Passport to Reading Level 1 Ser.). (J). lib. bdg. 14.75 *(978-0-606-26692-5(5),* Turtleback) Turtleback Bks.

—A Spooky, Sparkly Halloween. 2016. (Very Fairy Princess Ser.). (J). lib. bdg. 16.00 *(978-0-606-38317-2(4))* Turtleback Bks.

—Valentines from the Heart. 2015. (Very Fairy Princess Ser.). (J). lib. bdg. 16.00 *(978-0-606-37466-8(3))* Turtleback Bks.

—The Very Fairy Princess. Davenier, Christine, illus. 2010. (Very Fairy Princess Ser.). (ENG.). 32p. (J). (gr. -1-3). 18.00 *(978-0-316-04050-1(9))* Little, Brown Bks. for Young Readers.

—The Very Fairy Princess: A Winter Wonderland Surprise. 2015. (Very Fairy Princess Ser.). (J). lib. bdg. 16.00 *(978-0-606-37465-1(5))* Turtleback Bks.

—The Very Fairy Princess: Here Comes the Flower Girl! Davenier, Christine, illus. 2012. (Very Fairy Princess Ser.). (ENG.). 32p. (J). (gr. -1-3). 16.99 *(978-0-316-18561-5(2))* Little Brown & Co.

—The Very Fairy Princess: Teacher's Pet. Davenier, Christine, illus. 2013. (Passport to Reading Level 1 Ser.). (ENG.). 32p. (J). (gr. -1-3). 4.99 *(978-0-316-21959-4(2))* Little Brown & Co.

—The Very Fairy Princess: Teacher's Pet. 2013. (Passport to Reading Level 1 Ser.). (J). lib. bdg. 14.75 *(978-0-606-31741-2(4),* Turtleback) Turtleback Bks.

—The Very Fairy Princess Follows Her Heart. Davenier, Christine, illus. 2013. (Very Fairy Princess Ser.). (ENG.). 32p. (J). (gr. -1-3). 16.99 *(978-0-316-18559-2(0))* Little Brown & Co.

—The Very Fairy Princess Sparkles in the Snow. Davenier, Christine, illus. 2013. (Very Fairy Princess Ser.). (ENG.). 32p. (J). (gr. -1-1). 18.00 *(978-0-316-21963-1(0))* Little Brown & Co.

—The Very Fairy Princess Takes the Stage. 2011. (Very Fairy Princess Ser.). (ENG., Illus.). 32p. (J). (gr. -1-3). 16.99 *(978-0-316-04052-5(5))* Little Brown & Co.

Andrews, Julie & Walton Hamilton, Emma. The Very Fairy Princess: A Spooky, Sparkly Halloween. 2016. (ENG., Illus.). 32p. (J). (gr. -1-3). pap. 5.99 *(978-0-316-28326-7(6))* Little, Brown Bks. for Young Readers.

—The Very Fairy Princess: Attitude of Gratitude. Davenier, Christine, illus. 2016. (ENG.). 32p. (J). (gr. -1-3). 17.99 *(978-0-316-26588-1(8))* Little, Brown Bks. for Young Readers.

—The Very Fairy Princess: a Spooky, Sparkly Halloween. Davenier, Christine, illus. 2015. (ENG.). 32p. (J). (gr. -1-3). 18.00 *(978-0-316-28304-5(5))* Little, Brown Bks. for Young Readers.

Andrews, Julie, et al. The Very Fairy Princess - Graduation Girl! Davenier, Christine, illus. 2014. (Very Fairy Princess Ser.). (ENG.). 32p. (J). (gr. -1-3). 18.99 *(978-0-316-21960-0(6))* Little, Brown Bks. for Young Readers.

Angelo, Linda. The Three Secrets of Happiness. 2012. (ENG.). 31p. (J). pap. 14.95 *(978-1-4327-9349-4(7))* Outskirts Pr., Inc.

anthony, chance. The Princess of Du'val. 2010. 36p. pap. 7.14 *(978-0-557-03816-9(2))* Lulu Pr., Inc.

Argenta, Joan. The Wicked Princess Torment. 2009. (Illus.). 40p. pap. 16.99 *(978-1-4389-4345-9(8))* AuthorHouse.

Arias, Carlos Ballesteros. The Magic Forest. 2006. (J). pap. 8.00 *(978-0-8059-7022-7(3))* Dorrance Publishing Co., Inc.

Armstrong, Ashley Sage-Taylor. The Adventures of Starlight & Sunny: Book Four in the Adventures of Starlight & Sunny Series, ?Princesses Don't Need a Job !? How to Be an Indepen. 2013. 52p. pap. *(978-1-927863-02-2(3))* Armstrong, Ashley.

Armstrong Nhp, Ashley Sage-Taylor. The Adventures of Starlight & Sunny: Book One in the Adventures of Starlight & Sunny Series, ?the Princess Path?, How to Be True with Good Deeds; 2013. 46p. pap. *(978-0-9919517-7-2(8))* Armstrong, Ashley.

Arps, Melissa & Lagonegro, Melissa. Gwen's Great Gizmos (Disney Junior: Sofia the First) Random House Disney Staff, illus. 2016. (Little Golden Book Ser.). (ENG.). 24p. (J). (gr. -1-k). 4.99 *(978-0-7364-3448-5(8),* Golden/Disney) Random Hse. Children's Bks.

—Polite as a Princess. Harding, Niall & Harchy, Atelier Philippe, illus. 2006. (Pictureback(R) Ser.). (ENG.). 24p. (J). (gr. -1-2). pap. 3.99 *(978-0-7364-2367-0(2),* RH/Disney) Random Hse. Children's Bks.

Aryal, Kusum. The Magic Mermaid Girl. 2011. 36p. pap. *(978-1-4269-8836-3(2))* Trafford Publishing (UK) Ltd.

At Your Service. 2014. (Mix Ser.). (ENG., Illus.). 272p. (J). (gr. 4-8). pap. 7.99 *(978-1-4814-0283-5(8),* Aladdin) Simon & Schuster Children's Publishing.

Attaway-Young, Andrea & Lane Durbin, Deborah. The Secret Treasure - A Fairy Tale. 2010. (ENG.). 40p. 9.95 *(978-1-934363-70-6(7))* Zoe Life Publishing.

Auch, Mary Jane. The Princess & the Pizza. Auch, Herm, illus. 2003. (ENG.). 32p. (J). (gr. k-3). 7.99 *(978-0-8234-1798-8(0))* Holiday Hse., Inc.

Auerbach, Annie. Cindy Big Hair: A Twisted (and Teased & Braided) Cinderella Story. Maxey, David, illus. 2005. 16p. (J). 12.95 *(978-1-58117-387-1(3),* Intervisual/Piggy Toes) Bendon, Inc.

Aveyard, Victoria. Cruel Crown. 2016. (Red Queen Novella Ser.). 208p. (YA). (gr. 8-12). pap. 9.99 *(978-0-06-243534-7(5),* HarperTeen) HarperCollins Pubs.

—Glass Sword. l.t. ed. 2016. (Red Queen Ser.: 2). (ENG.). 656p. 24.99 *(978-1-4104-8668-4(0))* Cengage Gale.

—Glass Sword. (Red Queen Ser.: 2). 464p. (YA). (gr. 8). 2018. pap. 12.99 ***(978-0-06-231067-5(4))*** 2016. (ENG.). 19.99 *(978-0-06-231066-8(6))* HarperCollins Pubs. (HarperTeen).

—King's Cage. 2017. (Red Queen Ser.: 3). (Illus.). 528p. (YA). (gr. 8). 19.99 *(978-0-06-231069-9(0),* HarperTeen) HarperCollins Pubs.

—Red Queen. l.t. ed. 2016. (Red Queen Ser.: 1). (ENG.). 562p. (YA). 24.99 *(978-1-4104-8669-1(9))* Cengage Gale.

—Red Queen. (YA). (gr. 8). 2016. (Red Queen Ser.). 864p. 37.98 *(978-0-06-256866-3(3))* 2016. (Red Queen Ser.: 1). (ENG.). 416p. pap. 12.99 *(978-0-06-231064-4(X))* 2015. (ENG.). 400p. 17.99 *(978-0-06-231063-7(1))* 2015. (Red Queen Ser.: 1). 400p. pap. 12.00 *(978-0-06-236271-1(2))* HarperCollins Pubs. (HarperTeen).

—Red Queen. 2016. (Red Queen Ser.: 1). 416p. lib. bdg. 22.10 *(978-0-606-38918-1(0))* Turtleback Bks.

Ayaz, Huda. Freeze-Land: A New Beginning. 2013. 110p. pap. 11.99 *(978-1-4808-0267-4(0))* Archway Publishing.

AZ Books Staff. Cinderella. Zyl, Olga, ed. 2012. (Classic Fairy Tales Ser.). (ENG.). 10p. (J). (gr. -1-k). bds. 9.95 *(978-1-61889-007-8(7))* AZ Bks. LLC.

Baer, Jill. Just One of the Princes. 2014. (Sofia the First World of Reading Ser.). (J). lib. bdg. 13.55 *(978-0-606-35263-5(5))* Turtleback Bks.

Baer, Jill & Disney Book Group Staff. World of Reading: Sofia the First Just One of the Princes: Level 1. Disney Storybook Artists Staff, illus. 2014. (World of Reading Ser.). (ENG.). 32p. (J). (gr. -1-k). pap. 3.99 *(978-1-4231-9432-3(2))* Disney Pr.

Baker, E. D. The Bravest Princess. (Wide-Awake Princess Ser.: 3). (ENG.). (YA). 2015. 288p. (gr. 3-6). pap. 8.99 *(978-1-61963-570-8(4),* 9781619635708) 2014. (Illus.). 272p. (gr. 5-8). 16.99 *(978-1-61963-136-6(9),* 9781619631366) Bloomsbury Publishing USA. (Bloomsbury USA Childrens).

—The Dragon Princess. (Tales of the Frog Princess Ser.). (ENG.). (YA). 2010. 240p. (gr. 5-8). pap. 7.99 *(978-1-59990-448-1(9),* 9781599904481) 2008. (Illus.). 224p. (gr. 4-8). 16.99 *(978-1-59990-194-7(3),* 9781599901947) Bloomsbury Publishing USA. (Bloomsbury USA Childrens).

—Dragon's Breath: Read-Along/Homework Pack, 6 vols. unabr. ed. 2005. (Frog Princess Ser.: 2). (SPA.). (J). (gr. 5-8). 78.75 *(978-1-4193-3563-1(4),* 42041) Recorded Bks., Inc.

—The Frog Princess Returns. 2017. (Tales of the Frog Princess Ser.). (ENG.). 208p. (J). 16.99 *(978-1-68119-137-9(7),* 9781681191379, Bloomsbury USA Childrens) Bloomsbury Publishing USA.

—A Prince among Frogs. 2nd ed. 2010. (Tales of the Frog Princess Ser.). (ENG.). 224p. (YA). (gr. 5-8). 16.99 *(978-1-59990-349-1(0),* 9781599903491, Bloomsbury USA Childrens) Bloomsbury Publishing USA.

—The Princess & the Pearl. 2017. (Wide-Awake Princess Ser.). (ENG.). 240p. (J). 16.99 *(978-1-68119-135-5(0),* 9781681191355, Bloomsbury USA Childrens) Bloomsbury Publishing USA.

—Princess Between Worlds: A Tale of the Wide-Awake Princess. (Wide-Awake Princess Ser.). (ENG.). (J). 2017. 240p. pap. 8.99 *(978-1-68119-279-6(9),* 9781681192796) 2016. (Illus.). 224p. 16.99 *(978-1-61963-847-1(9),* 9781619638471) Bloomsbury Publishing USA. (Bloomsbury USA Childrens).

—Princess in Disguise. 2015. (Wide-Awake Princess Ser.: 4). (ENG.). 224p. (YA). (gr. 3-6). 16.99 *(978-1-61963-573-9(9),* 9781619635739, Bloomsbury USA Childrens) Bloomsbury Publishing USA.

—Princess in Disguise: A Tale of the Wide-Awake Princess. 2016. (Wide-Awake Princess Ser.: 4). (ENG., Illus.). 240p. (J). pap. 8.99 *(978-1-61963-934-8(3),* 9781619639348, Bloomsbury USA Childrens) Bloomsbury Publishing USA.

—Unlocking the Spell: A Tale of the Wide-Awake Princess. (Wide-Awake Princess Ser.: 2). (ENG.). (YA). 2014. 288p. (gr. 5-6). pap. 8.99 *(978-1-61963-194-6(6),* 9781619631946) 2012. 272p. (gr. 3-12). 16.99 *(978-1-59990-841-0(7),* 9781599908410) Bloomsbury Publishing USA. (Bloomsbury USA Childrens).

—The Wide-Awake Princess. (Wide-Awake Princess Ser.: 1). (ENG.). (YA). (gr. 5-14). 2012. 288p. pap. 8.99 *(978-1-59990-658-4(9),* 9781599906584) 2010. 272p. 16.99 *(978-1-59990-487-0(X),* 9781599904870) Bloomsbury Publishing USA. (Bloomsbury USA Childrens).

Baker, Sara, illus. Ready to Read Sleeping Beauty. 2007. (Ready to Read Ser.). 31p. (J). (gr. k-2). *(978-1-84610-441-1(6))* Make Believe Ideas.

Barbera, Katia. Iron Horse, 1 vol. 2010. 16p. 24.95 *(978-1-4489-4634-1(4))* PublishAmerica, Inc.

Barbie. Barbie in Rock 'N Royals. 2015. (Book & Jewelry Ser.: 1). (ENG.). 10p. (J). (gr. -1-1). bds. 9.99 *(978-0-7944-3556-1(4),* Reader's Digest Children's Bks.) Studio Fun International.

Barbieri, Sandra Birriel. Cristal & the Secret of the Enchanted Forest: Cristal y el Secreto Del Bosque Encantado. 2013. 64p. pap. 23.99 *(978-1-4525-6512-5(0))* Balboa Pr.

Barchers, Suzanne I. One Last Wish: A Tale from India. Todd, Sue, illus. 2013. (Tales of Honor Ser.). (ENG.). 32p. (gr. 1-3). pap. 8.95 *(978-1-937529-60-4(6))* Red Chair Pr.

—The Princess & the Giant: A Tale from Scotland. Lafrance, Marie, illus. 2013. (Tales of Honor Ser.). (ENG.). 32p. (gr. 1-3). pap. 8.95 *(978-1-937529-61-1(4))* Red Chair Pr.

Bardham-Quallen, Sudipta. The Fire Falls. Random House Disney Staff & Gurihiru Staff, illus. 2016. (Stepping Stone Book(TM) Ser.). (ENG.). 128p. (J). (gr. 1-4). 9.99 *(978-0-7364-3291-7(4),* RH/Disney) Random Hse. Children's Bks.

Bardhan-Quallen, Sudipta. Chasing Magic. Random House Disney Staff & Gurihiru Staff, illus. 2016. (Stepping Stone Book Ser.). (ENG.). 128p. (J). (gr. 1-4). 9.99 *(978-0-7364-3290-0(6),* RH/Disney) Random Hse. Children's Bks.

—The Fire Falls. Random House Disney Staff & Gurihiru, illus. 2016. (Stepping Stone Book(TM) Ser.). (ENG.). 128p. (J). (gr. 1-4). lib. bdg. 12.99 *(978-0-7364-8249-3(0),* RH/Disney) Random Hse. Children's Bks.

—The Pirate Princess. McElmurry, Jill, illus. 2012. (ENG.). 40p. (J). (gr. -1-3). 17.99 *(978-0-06-114242-0(5))* HarperCollins Pubs.

—Secret Spell. RH Disney, illus. 2017. (Stepping Stone Book(TM) Ser.). (ENG.). 128p. (J). (gr. 1-4). 9.99 *(978-0-7364-3616-8(2),* RH/Disney) Random Hse. Children's Bks.

—Snoring Beauty. Manning, Jane, illus. 2014. (J). *(978-0-06-087405-6(8))* Harper & Row Ltd.

—Snoring Beauty. Manning, Jane, illus. 2014. (ENG.). 32p. (J). (gr. -1-3). 17.99 *(978-0-06-087403-2(1))* HarperCollins Pubs.

Barnes, Susan. Kelly Karate: Discovers the Ice Princess. 2004. 138p. (J). (gr. 4-8). pap. 5.95 *(978-0-9705777-3-3(7))* McBook Pubs., LLC.

Barnhill, Kelly. Iron Hearted Violet. Bruno, Iacopo, illus. 2014. (ENG.). 448p. (J). (gr. 3-7). pap. 7.00 *(978-0-316-05675-5(8))* Little, Brown Bks. for Young Readers.

Barrett, Tracy. The Missing Heir. 2012. (Sherlock Files Ser.: 4). (ENG., Illus.). 192p. (J). (gr. 3-7). pap. 8.99 *(978-1-250-00480-2(2),* 9781250004802) Square Fish.

—The Missing Heir. 2012. (Sherlock Files Ser.: 4). (J). lib. bdg. 19.65 *(978-0-606-26131-9(1),* Turtleback) Turtleback Bks.

Bartles, Veronica. The Princess & the Frogs. Palacios, Sara, illus. 2016. 40p. (J). (gr. -1-3). 17.99 *(978-0-06-236591-0(6))* HarperCollins Pubs.

Batt, Tanya Robyn. The Princess & White Bear. Ceccoli, Nicoletta, illus. 2008. (ENG.). 40p. (J). (gr. -1-3). 17.99 *(978-1-84686-228-1(0))* Barefoot Bks., Inc.

Baxter, Nicola. My Book of Princess Stories. Lyon, Belinda, illus. 2012. (ENG.). 80p. (J). (gr. k-4). pap. 9.99 *(978-1-84322-801-1(7))* Anness Publishing GBR. Dist: National Bk. Network.

—Princess Stories. Smith, Helen, illus. 2013. (ENG.). 80p. (J). (gr. k-4). pap. 9.99 *(978-1-84322-954-4(4))* Anness Publishing GBR. Dist: National Bk. Network.

Baxter, Nicola & Manson, Beverly. Storybook of Fairy Princesses: Six Tales from an Enchanted Secret World. 2013. (ENG., Illus.). 80p. (J). (gr. 2-8). pap. 9.99 *(978-1-84322-898-1(X))* Anness Publishing GBR. Dist: National Bk. Network.

Bazaldua, Barbara & Bergen, Lara. Rapunzel & the Golden Rule/Jasmine & the Two Tigers (Disney Princess) Studio IBOIX & Disney Storybook Artists Staff, illus. 2011. (Pictureback(R) Ser.). (ENG.). 32p. (J). (gr. -1-2). pap. 4.99 *(978-0-7364-2829-3(1),* RH/Disney) Random Hse. Children's Bks.

Bealer-Wynton, Cheryl. Blinky's Island. 2008. 60p. pap. 6.50 *(978-1-4303-1146-1(0))* Lulu Pr., Inc.

Beaton, Kate. The Princess & the Pony. 2015. (ENG., Illus.). 40p. (J). (gr. -1-3). 17.99 *(978-0-545-63708-4(2))* Scholastic, Inc.

Beck, Patricia. Princess Feldings & the Academy of Queens. 2010. 28p. 13.99 *(978-1-4490-1376-9(7))* AuthorHouse.

Bell, Juliet Clare & Chapman, Laura Kate. The Kite Princess. 2012. (ENG., Illus.). (J). 16.99 *(978-1-84686-803-0(3))* Barefoot Bks., Inc.

Bell, Rebecca. Princess Sara. Bell, Rebecca, illus. 2005. (Illus.). 34p. (J). 9.95 *(978-1-934138-07-6(X))* Bouncing Ball Bks., Inc.

Benjamin, A. H. Wanted: Prince Charming. Fiorin, Fabiano, illus. 2014. (ENG.). 32p. (J). *(978-0-7787-1313-5(X))* Crabtree Publishing Co.

Bentley, Douglas W. What Will It Take for a Toad to Kiss a Monkey: The Adventures of Princess Gracie & Prince Wallaby. Bentley, Julia Faye, illus. 2008. 52p. per. 24.95 *(978-1-4137-8849-5(1))* America Star Bks.

Benton, Lynne. The Sad Princess. Catling, Andy, illus. 2009. (Tadpoles Ser.). (ENG.). 24p. (J). (gr. k-2). pap. *(978-0-7787-3903-6(1))* Crabtree Publishing Co.

Bergen, Lara & Disney Book Group Staff. Enchanted Fashions: A Magnetic Book & Playset. Disney Storybook Artists Staff, illus. rev. ed. 2007. (Book & Magnetic Play Set Ser.). (ENG.). 16p. (J). (gr. -1 — 1). 14.99 *(978-1-4231-0752-1(7))* Disney Pr.

Berger, Glenn. Princess Chantik & the Outside World. 2012. 92p. pap. 39.99 *(978-0-615-61495-3(7))* Marcabru Publishing.

Bergman, Mara. The Twelve Dancing Princesses. 2017. (Collins Big Cat Tales Ser.). (ENG., Illus.). 48p. (J). (gr. 2-3). pap. 8.99 *(978-0-00-817938-0(7))* HarperCollins Pubs. Ltd. GBR. Dist: Independent Pubs. Group.

Bernhardt, William. Princess Alice & the Dreadful Dragon. McGhee, Kerry, illus. 2007. 27p. (J). 19.99 *(978-1-930709-65-2(X))* HAWK Publishing Group.

Bernreuter, Bob J. The Gift. 2006. (Illus.). 25p. (J). *(978-1-4120-7546-6(7))* Trafford Publishing.

Berrios, Frank. A Day in the Sun. 2014. lib. bdg. 13.55 *(978-0-606-35546-9(4))* Turtleback Bks.

Berrow, G. M. My Little Pony: Equestria Girls: Through the Mirror. 2013. (Equestria Girls Ser.: 1). (ENG.). 240p. (J). (gr. 3-7). 9.99 *(978-0-316-24762-7(6))* Little, Brown Bks. for Young Readers.

—My Little Pony: Princess Cadance & the Spring Hearts Garden. 2016. (Princess Collection). (ENG., Illus.). 160p. (J). (gr. 3-7). 9.99 *(978-0-316-38930-3(7))* Little, Brown Bks. for Young Readers.

—My Little Pony: Twilight Sparkle & the Forgotten Books of Autumn. 2016. (Princess Collection). (ENG., Illus.). 160p. (J). (gr. 3-7). 9.99 *(978-0-316-38996-9(X))* Little, Brown Bks. for Young Readers.

—Twilight Sparkle & the Crystal Heart Spell. 2013. (My Little Pony Chapter Bks.). (J). lib. bdg. 16.00 *(978-0-606-31733-7(3)*, Turtleback) Turtleback Bks.

Berry, Erick. The Winged Girl of Knossos. 2017. (ENG., Illus.). 220p. (J). (gr. 3-7). pap. 11.95 *(978-1-58988-120-4(6))* Dry, Paul Bks., Inc.

Bianchi, John & Edwards, Frank B. Princess Frownsalot, 1 vol. rev. ed. 2004. (ENG., Illus.). 127p. (J). pap. 4.95 *(978-1-894323-25-3(4))* Pokeweed Pr. CAN. Dist: Ingram Publisher Services.

Biggs, K. E. The Dawn of Hope. 2010. 112p. pap. 10.99 *(978-1-4490-8931-3(3))* AuthorHouse.

Bilgrey, Marc. And Don't Forget to Rescue the Other Princess. 2009. 252p. 25.95 *(978-1-59414-744-9(2)*, Five Star) Cengage Gale.

Binder, Mark. Kings, Wolves, Princesses & Lions: 28 Illustrated Stories for Young Readers. 2012. (ENG., Illus.). 122p. (J). pap. 14.99 *(978-0-9824707-8-7(9))* Light Pubns.

Birney, Betty G. The Princess & the Peabodys. 2007. (ENG.). 256p. (J). (gr. 5-9). 15.99 *(978-0-06-084720-3(4))* HarperCollins Pubs.

Bishop, Jennie. The Three Gifts of Christmas. McDaniels, Preston, illus. 2009. 32p. (J). (gr. 3-18). 15.99 incl. audio compact disk *(978-1-59317-378-4(4))* Warner Pr., Inc.

Blackaby, Susan. La Princesa Del Guisante: Versión Del Cuento de Hans Christian Anderson. Abello, Patricia, tr. from ENG. Delage, Charlene, illus. 2006. (Read-It! Readers en Español: Cuentos de Hadas Ser.).Tr. of Princess & the Pea - A Retelling of the Grimm's Fairy Tale. (SPA.). 32p. (gr. k-3). 21.32 *(978-1-4048-1634-3(8)*, Easy Readers) Picture Window Bks.

Blair, Eric. The Frog Prince: A Retelling of the Grimm's Fairy Tale, 1 vol. Ouren, Todd, illus. 2013. (My First Classic Story Ser.). (ENG.). 32p. (gr. k-3). pap. 7.10 *(978-1-4795-1853-1(0)*, My First Classic Story) Picture Window Bks.

Blevins, Wiley. Snow White & the Seven Trolls. Cox, Steve, illus. 2016. (Scary Tales Retold Ser.). (ENG.). 24p. (gr. k-3). lib. bdg. 23.99 *(978-1-63440-105-0(0))* Red Chair Pr.

Bliss, Emily. Flash's Dash. Hanson, Sydney, illus. 2017. (Unicorn Princesses Ser.). (ENG.). 128p. (J). 15.99 *(978-1-68119-329-8(9)*, 9781681193298, Bloomsbury USA Childrens) Bloomsbury Publishing USA.

—Sunbeam's Shine. Hanson, Sydney, illus. 2017. (Unicorn Princesses Ser.). (ENG.). 128p. (J). 15.99 *(978-1-68119-325-0(6)*, 9781681193250, Bloomsbury USA Childrens) Bloomsbury Publishing USA.

Block, Betty Mitchell. The Magic Pork Chop Bone. 2013. (ENG.). 76p. (YA). pap. 8.95 *(978-1-4787-1482-8(4))* Outskirts Pr., Inc.

Bloomsbury USA. Lift-The-Flap Friends: Princess. 2017. (ENG.). 14p. (J). bds. 9.99 *(978-1-68119-240-6(3)*, 9781681192406, Bloomsbury Activity Bks.) Bloomsbury Publishing USA.

Blythe, Gary, illus. A Treasury of Princess Stories. 2009. (ENG.). 80p. (J). (gr. 2-5). 19.99 *(978-0-7636-4478-9(1))* Candlewick Pr.

Blyton, Enid. Princess & the Pea. 2012. (ENG., Illus.). 24p. (J). pap. 9.95 *(978-1-84135-608-2(5))* Award Pubns. Ltd. GBR. Dist: Parkwest Pubns., Inc.

—Twelve Dancing Princesses. 2012. (ENG., Illus.). 24p. (J). pap. 9.95 *(978-1-84135-610-5(7))* Award Pubns. Ltd. GBR. Dist: Parkwest Pubns., Inc.

Bohn, Kendall. Fantasy Adventure. 2008. (Kaleidoscopia Coloring Book Ser.). (Illus.). 56p. (J). (gr. -1-7). 8.95 *(978-0-929636-83-2(X))* Syren Bk. Co.

Boie, Kirsten. The Princess Plot. 2010. (ENG.). 400p. (J). (gr. 3-7). 7.99 *(978-0-545-03221-6(0)*, Chicken Hse., The) Scholastic, Inc.

—The Princess Plot. Wilson, David Henry, tr. from GER. 2009. (ENG.). 400p. (J). (gr. 3-7). 17.99 *(978-0-545-03220-9(2)*, Chicken Hse., The) Scholastic, Inc.

—The Princess Trap. (ENG.). 416p. (J). (gr. 5-9). 2012. pap. 7.99 *(978-0-545-22262-4(1))* 2010. 17.99 *(978-0-545-22261-7(3))* Scholastic, Inc. (Chicken Hse., The).

Bondoux, Anne-Laure. The Princetta. Bell, Anthea, tr. 2008. (ENG.). 448p. (YA). (gr. 6-12). pap. 10.99 *(978-1-59990-098-8(X)*, 9781599900988, Bloomsbury USA Childrens) Bloomsbury Publishing USA.

Bosco, Don. Sherlock Hong: The Peranakan Princess. 2016. (Sherlock Hong Adventures Ser.: Volume 2). (ENG.). 80p. pap. 6.99 *(978-981-4721-20-2(4))* Marshall Cavendish International (Asia) Private Ltd. SGP. Dist: National Bk. Network.

Boujie. A Princess from the Heart. 2009. 66p. pap. 15.99 *(978-1-4415-4413-1(5))* Xlibris Corp.

Boulton, M. T. Megan Button & the Brim-Tree. 2012. 106p. pap. *(978-1-909039-06-3(3))* Legend Pr.

Bow, Erin. The Swan Riders. 2016. (Prisoners of Peace Ser.). (ENG., Illus.). 384p. (YA). (gr. 9). 17.99 *(978-1-4814-4274-9(0)*, McElderry, Margaret K. Bks.) McElderry, Margaret K. Bks.

Bracken, Beth & Fraser, Kay. Fate of the Willow Queen. Sawyer, Odessa, illus. 2013. (Faerieground Ser.). (ENG.). 96p. (gr. 1-3). 23.99 *(978-1-4342-4492-5(X)*, Faerieground) Stone Arch Bks.

Bradfield, Roger, illus. The Pickle-Chiffon Pie Olympics. 2011. 64p. (J). (gr. -1-3). 18.95 *(978-1-930900-52-3(X))* Purple Hse. Pr.

Bradman, Tony. Happy Ever After, 1 vol. Warburton, Sarah, illus. 2009. (After Happily Ever After Ser.). (ENG.). 56p. (gr. 2-3). lib. bdg. 25.32 *(978-1-4342-1301-3(3)*, After Happily Ever After) Stone Arch Bks.

—Snow White & the Magic Mirror, 1 vol. Warburton, Sarah, illus. 2014. (After Happily Ever After Ser.). (ENG.). 56p. (gr. 2-3). lib. bdg. 25.32 *(978-1-4342-7950-7(2)*, After Happily Ever After) Stone Arch Bks.

Brandon, Demi. Princess Shakina's Locks. 2007. 48p. per. 16.95 *(978-1-4241-7195-8(4))* America Star Bks.

Braswell, Liz. Once upon a Dream. 2017. (Twisted Tale Ser.). (YA). lib. bdg. 20.85 ***(978-0-606-39935-7(6))*** Turtleback Bks.

—Once upon a Dream: A Twisted Tale. 2016. (Twisted Tale Ser.). (ENG.). 448p. (J). (gr. 7-17). 17.99 *(978-1-4847-0725-8(7))* Disney Pr.

—A Whole New World. 2016. (Twisted Tale Ser.). (YA). lib. bdg. 20.85 *(978-0-606-38511-4(8))* Turtleback Bks.

—A Whole New World: A Twisted Tale. (Twisted Tale Ser.). (ENG.). (YA). (gr. 7-12). 2016. 400p. pap. 9.99 *(978-1-4847-0732-6(X))* 2015. 384p. 17.99 *(978-1-4847-0729-6(X))* Disney Pr.

Brauner, Susan. The Adventures of Sohi: Mystery of Moon Island. 2011. 207p. 28.95 *(978-1-4327-6752-5(6))*; pap. 15.95 *(978-1-4327-6536-1(1))* Outskirts Pr., Inc.

Brazier, Yuvonne. Princess Jordan Saves Golden Tree. 2008. 20p. pap. 12.49 *(978-1-4389-3591-1(9))* AuthorHouse.

Breslin, Jayne. The Princess Jelly Tutu Adventures. 2011. (Illus.). 28p. (gr. -1). pap. 14.09 *(978-1-4567-7611-4(8))* AuthorHouse.

Brian, Kate, pseud. The Princess & the Pauper. 2004. 266p. (J). (gr. 5-9). 14.65 *(978-0-7569-3531-3(8))* Perfection Learning Corp.

—The Princess & the Pauper. 2004. (ENG., Illus.). 272p. (YA). reprint ed. mass mkt. 6.99 *(978-0-689-87042-2(6)*, Simon Pulse) Simon Pulse.

Brice, Ginny. Princess Maddy & Her Blankie. Gary Ripper, illus. 2011. 20p. pap. 24.95 *(978-1-4560-7745-7(7))* America Star Bks.

Brinson, Julie L. Princess Olivia & the Leap Frog, 1 vol. Brinson, Connor J., illus. 2009. 22p. pap. 24.95 *(978-1-60813-802-9(X))* America Star Bks.

Brocklehurst, Ruth. Princess Things to Make & Do. 2005. (Illus.). 32p. (J). pap. 6.95 *(978-0-7945-0908-8(8)*, Usborne) EDC Publishing.

Broderick, Kathy. Disney Princess: Belle (Giant First Play -a-Sound) 2010. 10p. (J). bds. 17.98 *(978-1-60553-543-2(5))* Publications International, Ltd.

Brodsky, Irene. The Adventures of Silly Kitty, Princess Jasmine & First Puppy. 2010. (Illus.). 44p. (J). pap. 23.95 *(978-1-4327-5552-2(8))* Outskirts Pr., Inc.

Brooke, Jasmine. The Princess & the Pea: Pass the Pea Pressure Test! 2017. (Fairy Tale Fixers: Fixing Fairy Tale Problems with STEM Ser.). 32p. (gr. 3-4). pap. 63.00 ***(978-1-5382-0667-6(6))*** Stevens, Gareth Publishing LLLP.

Brooks, Amy. Princess Polly Stories. l.t. ed. 2007. 218p. pap. 22.99 *(978-1-4346-2000-2(X))* Creative Media Partners, LLC.

—Princess Polly's Gay Winter. 2004. reprint ed. pap. 1.99 *(978-1-4192-4299-1(7))*; pap. 15.95 *(978-1-4191-4299-4(2))* Kessinger Publishing, LLC.

—Princess Polly's Playmates. 2004. reprint ed. pap. 19.95 *(978-1-4191-4300-7(X))*; pap. 1.99 *(978-1-4192-4300-4(4))* Kessinger Publishing, LLC.

Brooks, Donna. The Golden Spindle. 2010. 112p. pap. 30.00 *(978-1-60860-852-2(2)*, Eloquent Bks.) Strategic Book Publishing & Rights Agency (SBPRA).

—The Magic Amphor. 2009. 100p. pap. 30.00 *(978-1-60693-027-4(3)*, Eloquent Bks.) Strategic Book Publishing & Rights Agency (SBPRA).

Brothers Grimm. The Twelve Dancing Princesses. Duntze, Dorothee, illus. 2013. (ENG.). 32p. (J). (gr. -1-2). 17.95 *(978-0-7358-4121-5(7))* North-South Bks., Inc.

Brower, Sandra Shane. Princess Zoe & the Mer-Bird. Steele, Andrea M., illus. 2013. 46p. pap. 10.95 *(978-1-936688-77-7(8)*, Compass Flower Pr.) AKA:yoLa.

Brown, Carron, ed. Sleeping Beauty & Snow White & the Seven Dwarfs: Two Tales & Their Histories. 2009. (World of Fairy Tales Ser.). (Illus.). 32p. (J). (gr. -1-2). pap. 10.55 *(978-1-60754-635-1(3))*; lib. bdg. 22.60 *(978-1-60754-634-4(5))* Windmill Bks.

Brown, E.A. Gossamer. 2012. 24p. pap. 24.95 *(978-1-4626-5043-9(0))* America Star Bks.

Brubacher, Melody. The Adventures of Princess Penelope. 2012. 68p. pap. 31.99 *(978-1-4691-9274-1(8))* Xlibris Corp.

Brundage, Frances, illus. Cinderella: A Fairy Story. 2004. reprint ed. pap. 15.95 *(978-1-4179-8713-9(8))* Kessinger Publishing, LLC.

Brundage, Jerome. The Princess & the Bear: Book I: the Battle for Aradam. 2007. 148p. per. 24.95 *(978-1-4241-6346-5(3))* America Star Bks.

Bryant, Ann. Dancing Princess. Benton, Tim, illus. 2006. (Ballerina Dreams Ser.). 102p. (J). per. 4.99 *(978-0-7945-1297-2(6)*, Usborne) EDC Publishing.

—Princess at Silver Spires. 2014. (School Friends Ser.). (ENG.). 145p. (J). (gr. 4-7). pap. 5.99 *(978-0-7945-3152-2(0)*, Usborne) EDC Publishing.

Bryant, Megan & Disney Book Group Staff. Merida: Legend of the Emeralds. Disney Storybook Art Team, illus. 2014. (ENG.). 96p. (J). (gr. 1-3). pap. 4.99 *(978-1-4231-6890-4(9))* Disney Pr.

Buckmaster, Heath L. Box of Hair: A Fairy Tale, 3 bks., Bk. 1. (Illus.). (YA). 2007. 102p. pap. 12.99 *(978-0-9771802-5-7(5))* 2008. 108p. lib. bdg. 25.00 *(978-0-9771802-4-0(7))* Transaltar Publishing.

—Box of Hair: A Fairy Tale. 2008. 104p. pap. 12.50 *(978-1-4357-2690-1(1))* Lulu Pr., Inc.

—The Dragons of Tarnack. 2008. 142p. pap. 13.99 *(978-1-4357-4624-4(4))* Lulu Pr., Inc.

—The Venus Diary. 2008. 136p. pap. 13.50 *(978-0-615-20678-3(6))*;Bk. 2. 132p. (YA). lib. bdg. 19.95 *(978-0-9771802-6-4(3))* Transaltar Publishing.

Burfoot, Ella, illus. Don't Kiss the Frog! Princess Stories with Attitude. 2013. (ENG.). 80p. (YA). (gr. 1-5). pap. 8.99 *(978-0-7534-6946-0(4)*, 9780753469460, Kingfisher) Roaring Brook Pr.

Burgos-Diaz, Mercedes. Meenah, the Mystical Princess of Zantel. 2011. 56p. pap. 8.95 *(978-1-4620-5928-7(7))* iUniverse, Inc.

Burkhart, Jessica. Bella's Birthday Unicorn. Ying, Victoria, illus. 2014. (Unicorn Magic Ser.: 1). (ENG.). 144p. (J). (gr. 1-4). 15.99 *(978-1-4814-1105-9(5))*; pap. 5.99 *(978-1-4424-9822-8(6))* Simon & Schuster Children's Publishing. (Aladdin).

—The Hidden Treasure. Ying, Victoria, illus. 2015. (Unicorn Magic Ser.: 4). (ENG.). 112p. (J). (gr. 1-4). pap. 5.99 *(978-1-4424-9829-7(3)*, Aladdin) Simon & Schuster Children's Publishing.

—Where's Glimmer? Ying, Victoria, illus. 2014. (Unicorn Magic Ser.: 2). (ENG.). 144p. (J). (gr. 1-4). pap. 5.99 *(978-1-4424-9824-2(2)*, Aladdin) Simon & Schuster Children's Publishing.

Burnett, Frances Hodgson. Little Princes. 2015. (ENG.). 267p. (J). 15.99 *(978-1-78270-105-7(2))* Award Pubns. Ltd. GBR. Dist: Parkwest Pubns., Inc.

—A Little Princess. 2017. (First Avenue Classics Ser.). (ENG.). 222p. (gr. 3-8). 19.99 ***(978-1-5124-2605-2(9)***, First Avenue Editions) Lerner Publishing Group.

—La Petit Princesse.Tr. of Little Princess. (J). pap. 12.95 *(978-2-07-056710-2(9))* Gallimard, Editions FRA. Dist: Distribooks, Inc.

—Petite Princess. pap. 19.95 *(978-2-07-051994-1(5))* Gallimard, Editions FRA. Dist: Distribooks, Inc.

—Titus kommt nicht alle Tage.Tr. of Little Princess. pap. 21.95 *(978-3-423-70196-9(X))* Deutscher Taschenbuch Verlag GmbH & Co KG DEU. Dist: Distribooks, Inc.

Burns, Jennifer N. Magic in Time: Fairy Tale Stories. 2012. 198p. 24.95 *(978-1-4759-3965-1(5))*; pap. 14.95 *(978-1-4759-3964-4(7))* iUniverse, Inc.

Burns, Mary Gore. The Magic Room: Mandy & the Lily Pond. 2011. 48p. pap. 17.30 *(978-1-4634-2642-2(9))* AuthorHouse.

Burt, Bethany. I Am Not a Princess!, 1 vol. McCallum, Brenda, illus. 2016. (ENG.). 40p. (J). 16.99 *(978-0-7643-5212-6(1)*, 9780764352126) Schiffer Publishing, Ltd.

Bush, Vicki-Ann. The Queen of IT. Beachamp, Afiyah, illus. 2011. 60p. (J). pap. 9.98 *(978-0-9816949-7-9(7))* Salt of the Earth Pr.

Cabell, Robert W. The Mermaid Adventures of Princess Miranda: Volume One. Cabell, Robert W., illus. 2013. (Illus.). 128p. pap. 7.95 *(978-0-9890974-3-7(9)*, Oceanus Bks.) Warrington Pubns.

Cabot, Meg. Forever Princess, Vol. X. 2009. (Princess Diaries: 10). (ENG.). 416p. (YA). (gr. 8). pap. 9.99 *(978-0-06-123294-7(7)*, HarperTeen) HarperCollins Pubs.

—From the Notebooks of a Middle-School Princess. 2016. (From the Notebooks of a Middle School Princess Ser.: 1). (J). lib. bdg. 18.40 *(978-0-606-38554-1(1))* Turtleback Bks.

—In Waiting. 2008. (Princess Diaries: 4). (ENG.). 256p. (YA). (gr. 8). pap. 9.99 *(978-0-06-154364-7(0)*, HarperTeen) HarperCollins Pubs.

—Journal d'une Princesse.Tr. of Princess Diaries. pap. 13.95 *(978-2-01-321853-5(2))* Hachette Groupe Livre FRA. Dist: Distribooks, Inc.

—Party Princess. (ENG., (YA). 2006. (Princess Diaries: Vol. 7). Illus.). 304p. (gr. 7-12). 16.99 *(978-0-06-072453-5(6))* Vol. VII. 2008. (Princess Diaries: 7). 320p. (gr. 8). pap. 9.99 *(978-0-06-154374-6(8)*, HarperTeen) HarperCollins Pubs.

—The Princess Diaries. 2008. (Princess Diaries: 1). (ENG.). 256p. (YA). (gr. 8). pap. 9.99 *(978-0-06-147993-9(4))*Vols. 1-3, Set. 2006. (Princess Diaries: Vol. I). (J). pap., pap. 19.99 *(978-0-06-115389-1(3))* HarperCollins Pubs. (HarperTeen).

—The Princess Diaries. 2008. 20.00 *(978-0-7569-8793-0(8))* Perfection Learning Corp.

—The Princess Diaries. unabr. ed. 2004. (Princess Diaries: Vol. I). 240p. (J). (gr. 7-18). pap. 38.00 incl. audio *(978-0-8072-0669-0(5)*, Listening Library) Random Hse. Audio Publishing Group.

—The Princess Diaries. 2008. (Princess Diaries: 1). (YA). lib. bdg. 20.85 *(978-1-4178-2328-4(3)*, Turtleback) Turtleback Bks.

—The Princess Diaries Box Set: The Princess Diaries; Princess in the Spotlight; Princess in Love. 2003. (Princess Diaries). 304p. (gr. 7-18). pap. 19.99 *(978-0-06-058745-1(8))* HarperCollins Pubs.

—Princess in Love, Vol. 3. 2008. (Princess Diaries: 3). (ENG.). 256p. (YA). (gr. 8-12). pap. 9.99 *(978-0-06-147995-3(0)*, HarperTeen) HarperCollins Pubs.

—Princess in Love. 2004. (Princess Diaries: Vol. 3). 288p. (J). (gr. 7-18). pap. 38.00 incl. audio *(978-0-8072-2284-3(4)*, Listening Library) Random Hse. Audio Publishing Group.

—Princess in Pink. 2008. (Princess Diaries: 5). (ENG.). 288p. (YA). (gr. 8). pap. 9.99 *(978-0-06-154363-0(2)*, HarperTeen) HarperCollins Pubs.

—Princess in Pink. 2008. (Princess Diaries: 5). 256p. (YA). (gr. 7-12). 20.85 *(978-1-4178-2563-9(4)*, Turtleback) Turtleback Bks.

—Princess in the Spotlight. 2008. (Princess Diaries). 222p. (gr. 7-12). 19.00 *(978-0-7569-8794-7(6))* Perfection Learning Corp.

—Princess in the Spotlight. unabr. ed. 2004. (Princess Diaries: Vol. 2). 272p. (J). (gr. 7-18). pap. 38.00 incl. audio *(978-0-8072-1197-7(4)*, S YA 332 SP, Listening Library) Random Hse. Audio Publishing Group.

—Princess in the Spotlight Vol. 2. 2008. (Princess Diaries: 2). (ENG.). 256p. (YA). (gr. 8-12). pap. 9.99 *(978-0-06-147994-6(2)*, HarperTeen) HarperCollins Pubs.

—Princess in Training. (ENG., 2005. (Princess Diaries: Vol. 6). Illus.). 288p. (J). (gr. 7-18). 16.99 *(978-0-06-009613-7(6))* Vol. VI. 2008. (Princess Diaries: 6). 304p. (YA). (gr. 8). pap. 9.99 *(978-0-06-154365-4(9)*, HarperTeen) HarperCollins Pubs.

—Princess in Waiting, Vol. IV. 2003. (Princess Diaries: 4). (ENG., Illus.). 240p. (YA). (gr. 8-18). 17.99 *(978-0-06-009607-6(1)*, HarperTeen) HarperCollins Pubs.

—Princess Mia. (ENG.). 2008. (Princess Diaries: Vol. 9). 256p. (J). (gr. 7-18). 16.99 *(978-0-06-072461-0(7))* Vol. 9. 2009. (Princess Diaries: 9). 304p. (YA). (gr. 8). pap. 9.99 *(978-0-06-072463-4(3)*, HarperTeen) HarperCollins Pubs.

—Princess Mia. 2009. (Princess Diaries: 9). (YA). lib. bdg. 20.85 *(978-0-606-02178-4(7)*, Turtleback) Turtleback Bks.

—Princess on the Brink. 2007. (ENG.). (Princess Diaries: 8). 272p. (YA). (gr. 8). pap. 9.99 *(978-0-06-072460-3(9)*, HarperTeen); (Princess Diaries: Vol. 8). 256p. (J). 16.99 *(978-0-06-072456-6(0))* HarperCollins Pubs.

—The Princess Present. 2004. (Princess Diaries: 6.5). (ENG.). 96p. (YA). (gr. 8-18). 12.99 *(978-0-06-075433-4(8)*, HarperTeen) HarperCollins Pubs.

—Project Princess. 2003. (Princess Diaries: 4.5). (ENG.). 64p. (YA). (gr. 8-18). pap. 6.99 *(978-0-06-057131-3(4)*, HarperTeen) HarperCollins Pubs.

—Royal Wedding Disaster: From the Notebooks of a Middle School Princess. 2016. (From the Notebooks of a Middle School Princess Ser.). (ENG., Illus.). 288p. (J). 16.99 *(978-1-250-06604-6(2)*, 9781250066046) Feiwel & Friends.

—Valentine Princess. 2006. (Princess Diaries: 7.75). (ENG.). 96p. (YA). (gr. 8-12). 12.99 *(978-0-06-084718-0(2)*, HarperTeen) HarperCollins Pubs.

Cabot, Meg & Cabot, Frank. From the Notebooks of a Middle School Princess. 2015. (From the Notebooks of a Middle School Princess Ser.). (ENG., Illus.). 192p. (J). (gr. 3-7). 16.99 *(978-1-250-06602-2(6)*, 9781250066022) Feiwel & Friends.

Cafaro, Phyllis. Captain Mcfinn & Friends Meet Coral Rose. 2012. (ENG.). 24p. (J). 19.99 *(978-0-9799283-5-2(4)*, 9780979928352) Cold River Pubns.

Calhoun, Dia. Avielle of Rhia, 1 vol. 2006. (ENG.). 400p. (J). (gr. 6). 16.99 *(978-0-7614-5320-8(2))* Marshall Cavendish Corp.

Carbone, Courtney. I Am a Princess (Star Wars) Martinez, Heather, illus. 2016. (Little Golden Book Ser.). (ENG.). 24p. (J). (-k). 4.99 *(978-0-7364-3605-2(7)*, Golden Bks.) Random Hse. Children's Bks.

—Palace Pets: Snuggle Buddies. 2014. (Step into Reading Level 2 Ser.). lib. bdg. 13.55 *(978-0-606-35193-5(0))* Turtleback Bks.

—Snuggle Buddies. Random House Disney Staff, illus. 2014. (Step into Reading Ser.). (ENG.). 32p. (J). (gr. -1-1). 3.99 *(978-0-7364-3155-2(1))*; lib. bdg. 12.99 *(978-0-7364-8158-8(3))* Random Hse. Children's Bks. (RH/Disney).

Cardona, Jose. Mulan (Disney Princess) Golden Books, illus. 2013. (Little Golden Book Ser.). (ENG.). 24p. (J). (-k). 4.99 *(978-0-7364-3053-1(9)*, Golden/Disney) Random Hse. Children's Bks.

Carey, Anna. Rise. 2013. (Eve Ser.: 3). (ENG.). (YA). (gr. 8). 336p. pap. 9.99 *(978-0-06-204858-5(9))*; 320p. 17.99 *(978-0-06-204857-8(0))* HarperCollins Pubs.

—Rise: An Eve Novel. 2013. (Illus.). 320p. (YA). pap. 9.99 *(978-0-06-226273-8(4))* HarperCollins Pubs.

Carey, Janet Lee. Dragon's Keep. 2007. 302p. (J). *(978-1-4287-3929-1(7))* Harcourt Trade Pubs.

—Dragon's Keep. 2008. (ENG., Illus.). 320p. (YA). (gr. 7-18). pap. 7.95 *(978-0-15-206401-3(X))* Houghton Mifflin Harcourt Publishing Co.

Carney, Karin. Princess Bailey & Her Animal Friends. 2011. (Illus.). 46p. pap. 18.95 *(978-0-557-95745-3(1))* Lulu Pr., Inc.

Carroll, Jacquie Lund. The Queen's Jewels. Gillen, Rosemarie, illus. 2013. 26p. pap. 9.99 *(978-1-61286-147-0(4))* Avid Readers Publishing Group.

Carter, David A. Princess Bugs: A Touch-And-Feel Fairy Tale. Carter, David A., illus. 2013. (David Carter's Bugs Ser.). (ENG., Illus.). 16p. (J). (gr. -1-2). 12.99 *(978-1-4424-5055-4(X)*, Little Simon) Little Simon.

Cartwright, Ran. The Adventures of Billy Space Boy, 1 vol. 2010. 208p. pap. 24.95 *(978-1-4489-3901-5(1))* America Star Bks.

Casaluci, Stacy Manning. Miracles Love a Believer. 2011. 32p. pap. 13.00 *(978-1-61204-094-3(2)*, Eloquent Bks.) Strategic Book Publishing & Rights Agency (SBPRA).

Casey, Mark. An African Princess: Deasha's Wild Adventure. 2010. (Illus.). 54p. pap. 11.95 *(978-1-4327-3864-8(X))* Outskirts Pr., Inc.

Cashman, Mary & Whipple, Cynthia. Merrilee Mannerly & Her Magnificent Manners. Johnson, Meredith, illus. 2010. (J). 16.99 *(978-0-615-36448-3(9))* Pink&Brown Publishing, LLP.

Cass, Kiera. The Crown. 2016. (Selection Ser.: 5). (ENG.). 288p. (YA). (gr. 8). 19.99 *(978-0-06-239217-6(4)*, HarperTeen) HarperCollins Pubs.

—Happily Ever After. 2015. (Selection Novella Ser.). (ENG., Illus.). (YA). 416p. (gr. 8). 18.99 *(978-0-06-241408-3(9)*, HarperTeen); 320p. *(978-0-00-814366-4(8))* HarperCollins Pubs.

—Happily Ever After: Companion to the Selection Series. 2016. (Selection Ser.). (YA). lib. bdg. 20.85 *(978-0-606-38919-8(9))* Turtleback Bks.

—The Heir. 2015. (ENG.). 368p. (YA). (Selection Ser.: 4). (gr. 8). 18.99 *(978-0-06-234985-9(6)*, HarperTeen); pap. *(978-0-06-239130-8(5))* HarperCollins Pubs.

—The One. 2015. (Selection Ser.: 3). (ENG.). 368p. (YA). (gr. 8). pap. 9.99 *(978-0-06-206000-6(7)*, HarperTeen) HarperCollins Pubs.

Castner, K. D. Daughters of Ruin. 2017. (ENG.). 320p. (YA). (gr. 9). pap. 11.99 *(978-1-4814-3666-3(X)*, McElderry, Margaret K. Bks.) McElderry, Margaret K. Bks.

Caviezel, Giovanni. Princess. Mesturini, Cristina, illus. 2009. (Mini People Shape Bks.). (ENG.). 12p. (J). (gr. -1-2). bds. 5.99 *(978-0-7641-6219-0(5))* Barron's Educational Series, Inc.

—Princess. Mesturini, C., illus. 2008. (Little People Shape Bks.). (ENG.). 10p. (J). (gr. k-2). bds. 10.99 *(978-0-7641-6103-2(2))* Barron's Educational Series, Inc.

Cech, John. The Princess & the Pea. Oberdieck, Bernhard, illus. 2015. (Classic Fairy Tale Collection). (ENG.). 32p. (J). (gr. -1-2). pap. 6.95 *(978-1-4549-1678-9(8))* Sterling Publishing Co., Inc.

Chambers, Dori. Princesses' Pink Pillows. 2009. 20p. pap. 10.50 *(978-1-60693-431-9(7)*, Eloquent Bks.) Strategic Book Publishing & Rights Agency (SBPRA).

Charvet, Lilian. Princess Dilly & the Kingdom of Pily: Book 1. 2010. 40p. pap. 20.99 *(978-1-4490-8330-4(7))* AuthorHouse.

Cheetham, Natasha. The Princess of the Sky. 2011. (Illus.). 24p. pap. 14.09 *(978-1-4567-7482-0(4))* AuthorHouse.

Childs, Tera Lynn. Forgive My Fins. (Forgive My Fins Ser.: 1). (ENG.). (YA). (gr. 8). 2011. 336p. pap. 8.99 *(978-0-06-191467-6(3))* 2010. 304p. 16.99 *(978-0-06-191465-2(7))* HarperCollins Pubs. (Tegen, Katherine Bks).

—Just for Fins. (Forgive My Fins Ser.: 3). (ENG.). 256p. (YA). (gr. 8). 2013. pap. 9.99 *(978-0-06-219208-0(6))* 2012. 17.99 *(978-0-06-219215-8(9))* HarperCollins Pubs. (Tegen, Katherine Bks).

Chima, Cinda Williams. The Demon King. 2010. (ENG.). 528p. (J). (gr. 5-6). pap. 9.99 *(978-1-4231-2136-7(8))* Hyperion Pr.

—The Exiled Queen. 2011. (Seven Realms Novel Ser.). (ENG.). 608p. (J). (gr. 5-17). pap. 9.99 *(978-1-4231-2137-4(6))* Hyperion Pr.

—The Gray Wolf Throne. 2012. (ENG.). 544p. (YA). (gr. 7-17). pap. 9.99 *(978-1-4231-2138-1(4))* Hyperion Pr.

—The Seven Realms Box Set. 2013. (Seven Realms Novel Ser.). (ENG.). 2272p. (YA). (gr. 7-12). pap. 37.99 *(978-1-4231-9961-8(8))* Hyperion Bks. for Children.

Chinchinian, Harry. The Princess & the Beggar II: Continuing Adventures. Chinchinian, Harry, illus. 2005. (Illus.). 176p. (J). lib. bdg. 18.95 *(978-1-892476-11-1(8))* Plum Tree Pr.

Chiu, Harry. Enve Lopt Unfolded. 2007. 268p. per. 17.95 *(978-0-595-44707-7(4))* iUniverse, Inc.

Chizuru, Mio. The Pirate & the Princess Volume 1: the Timelight Stone: The Timelight Stone. 2007. 110p. (J). pap. 5.99 *(978-1-933164-43-4(3))* Seven Seas Entertainment, LLC.

—The Pirate & the Princess Volume 2: the Red Crystal: The Red Crystal. 2007. 110p. (J). pap. 5.99 *(978-1-933164-44-1(1))* Seven Seas Entertainment, LLC.

Chokshi, Roshani. A Crown of Wishes. 2017. (Star-Touched Ser.). (ENG.). 384p. (YA). 18.99 *(978-1-250-08549-8(7)*, 9781250085498, St. Martin's Griffin) St. Martin's Pr.

Ciccone, Tizania & Linardi, Franca. The Pancake Princess. Bucci, Gino, illus. 2012. 36p. pap. 13.95 *(978-1-61897-720-5(2)*, Strategic Bk. Publishing) Strategic Book Publishing & Rights Agency (SBPRA).

Cinema, Bobby. Princess School. 2012. 68p. 18.66 *(978-1-4669-3968-4(0))*; 18p. pap. 8.66 *(978-1-4669-3967-7(2))* Trafford Publishing.

Claflin, Willy. Rapunzel & the Seven Dwarfs: A Maynard Moose Tale. Stimson, James, illus. 2011. (ENG.). 33p. (J). (gr. -1-3). 18.95 *(978-0-87483-914-2(9))* August Hse. Pubs., Inc.

Claire Hamelin Bruyere. Princess Bonnie & the Dragon. Mary Connors, illus. 2009. 16p. pap. 8.49 *(978-1-4389-8731-6(5))* AuthorHouse.

Clark, Andy S. Heavenly Magic: The Unforgettable Journey of Cassidy, the Valiant. 2013. 64p. pap. 23.95 *(978-1-4497-9874-1(8)*, WestBow Pr.) Author Solutions, Inc.

Clark, Marc. The Princess Fables. Hosford, Eric, illus. 2013. 114p. pap. 5.99 *(978-0-9910345-0-5(3))* Seven C's Productions, Inc.

Clark, Steven & Clark, Justin. The Golden Knight #1: The Boy Is Summoned. Gibson, Taylor, illus. 2011. (ENG.). 80p. (J). pap. 5.99 *(978-0-9647933-9-2(3))* New Horizons Pr.

Clarkson, Stephanie. Sleeping Cinderella & Other Princess Mix-Ups. Barrager, Brigette, illus. 2015. (ENG.). 40p. (J). (gr. -1-3). 17.99 *(978-0-545-56564-6(2)*, Orchard Bks.) Scholastic, Inc.

Clawson, Kimberly. Fun O' Licious. Bellomy, Gail, illus. 2007. (ENG.). 56p. per. 16.95 *(978-1-4241-5556-9(8))* America Star Bks.

Claybourne, Anna. Don't Kiss the Frog! Princess Stories with Attitude. Burfoot, Ella et al, illus. 2008. (ENG.). 80p. (YA). (gr. 1-5). 14.99 *(978-0-7534-5953-9(1)*, 9780753459539, Kingfisher) Roaring Brook Pr.

Cocca-Leffler, Maryann. Princess for a Day. 2012. (Penguin Young Readers, L2 Ser.). (ENG.). 32p. (J). (gr. -1-2). 3.99 *(978-0-448-49485-2(X)*, Grosset & Dunlap) Penguin Publishing Group.

Coe, Mary E. The Prince of Betherland. 2008. 117p. 24.95 *(978-0-557-03112-2(5))* Lulu Pr., Inc.

—The Prince of Betherland A Wonderful World of Fantasy. 2009. 66p. pap. 9.95 *(978-0-557-08499-9(7))* Lulu Pr., Inc.

—The Prince of Betherland a Wonderful World of Fantasy. 2009. 112p. pap. 9.95 *(978-0-557-09297-0(3))* Lulu Pr., Inc.

Coh, Smiljana. Princesses on the Run. 2013. (ENG., Illus.). 40p. (J). (gr. -1-17). 15.95 *(978-0-7624-4612-4(9)*, Running Pr. Kids) Running Pr. Bk. Pubs.

—The Seven Princesses. 2016. (ENG., Illus.). 40p. (J). (gr. -1-17). 16.95 *(978-0-7624-5587-4(X)*, Running Pr. Kids) Running Pr. Bk. Pubs.

Cohen, Warren Lee. Dragon Baked Bread. Ssebulime, John, illus. 2005. 32p. (J). *(978-1-902636-70-2(8))* Clairview Bks.

Coia, Kristina. Lymeria. 2007. 120p. (YA). per. 10.95 *(978-0-595-45268-2(X))* iUniverse, Inc.

Cokal, Susann. The Kingdom of Little Wounds. (ENG.). 576p. (YA). (gr. 11). 2016. pap. 12.99 *(978-0-7636-8757-1(X))* 2013. (Illus.). 22.99 *(978-0-7636-6694-1(7))* Candlewick Pr.

Cole, Babette. Princess Smartypants Breaks the Rules! 2010. (KOR., Illus.). 32p. (J). *(978-89-522-1360-0(2))* Salrim Pubn.

Cole, Nikki. Princess Hope. 2012. 40p. pap. 14.95 *(978-1-886528-39-0(X))* ASA Publishing Corp.

Coleman, Alice Scovell. Engraved in Stone. Armand, Anjale Renee, illus. 2003. 152p. (J). 14.95 *(978-0-9729846-0-7(7))* Tiara Bks. LLC.

Connors, Colleen. A Real Princess. 2009. 32p. pap. 12.99 *(978-1-4389-6884-1(1))* AuthorHouse.

Constable, Cathryn. The Wolf Princess. (ENG.). 320p. (J). (gr. 5-9). 2014. pap. 6.99 *(978-0-545-52841-2(0))* 2013. 16.99 *(978-0-545-52839-9(9))* Scholastic, Inc. (Chicken Hse., The).

Cook, Jacqueline. The Little Bear Who Worried Too Much: Suzie Bear Goes to London. 2011. 34p. (gr. 1-4). pap. 13.50 *(978-1-60976-875-1(2)*, Eloquent Bks.) Strategic Book Publishing & Rights Agency (SBPRA).

Coombs, Kate. The Runaway Princess. l.t. ed. 2007. (Literacy Bridge Middle Reader Ser.). 325p. (J). (gr. 3-7). 22.95 *(978-0-7862-9633-0(X))* Thorndike Pr.

Coonan, Candace N. The Break of Dawn: Tales from Fadreama: Book 3. 2012. 364p. (gr. 4-6). pap. 20.33 *(978-1-4669-3567-9(7))* Trafford Publishing.

Cooper, Michelle. A Brief History of Montmaray. 2011. (Montmaray Journals). (ENG.). 324p. (YA). (gr. 7). pap. 8.99 *(978-0-375-85154-4(2)*, Knopf Bks. for Young Readers) Random Hse. Children's Bks.

Corsetto, Danielle. Adventure Time: Pixel Princesses. 2013. lib. bdg. 23.30 *(978-0-606-35464-6(6))* Turtleback Bks.

—Adventure Time - Seeing Red. 2014. lib. bdg. 23.30 *(978-0-606-35465-3(4))* Turtleback Bks.

—Pixel Princesses, Vol. 2. Sterling, Zack, illus. 2013. (Adventure Time Ser.: 2). (ENG.). 160p. (J). (gr. 3). pap. 11.99 *(978-1-60886-329-7(8))* Boom! Studios.

Coughlin, Jennie Rose. The Purple Scarf. Howes, Bryan Arthur, illus. 2008. 20p. per. 24.95 *(978-1-60441-733-3(1))* America Star Bks.

Coville, Bruce. The Dragonslayers. unabr. ed. 2004. (Words Take Wingtm Ser.), 119p. (J). (gr. 3-6). pap. 29.00 incl. audio *(978-0-8072-7988-5(9)*, S YA 958 SP, Listening Library) Random Hse. Audio Publishing Group.

Cox, Greg. Riese: Kingdom Falling. 2012. (ENG.). 288p. (YA). (gr. 7). 16.99 *(978-1-4424-2969-7(0)*, Simon & Schuster Bks. For Young Readers) Simon & Schuster Bks. For Young Readers.

—Riese: Kingdom Falling. 2013. (ENG., Illus.). 288p. (YA). (gr. 7). pap. 9.99 *(978-1-4424-2970-3(4)*, Simon & Schuster Bks. For Young Readers) Simon & Schuster Bks. For Young Readers.

Coyle, Carmela Lavigna. Do Princesses & Super Heroes Hit the Trails? A National Park Adventure, Vol. 2016. (ENG., Illus.). 32p. (J). (gr. -1-12). 15.95 *(978-1-63076-244-5(X))* Muddy Boots Pr.

—Do Princesses Boogie? Gordon, Mike, illus. 2016. (ENG.). 26p. (J). (gr. -1-2). bds. 7.95 *(978-1-63076-159-2(1))* Taylor Trade Publishing.

—Do Princesses Have Best Friends Forever? Gordon, Mike & Gordon, Carl, illus. 2010. (J). *(978-1-58979-543-3(1))* Taylor Trade Publishing.

—Do Princesses Have Best Friends Forever? Gordon, Carl & Gordon, Mike, illus. 2010. (ENG.). 32p. (J). (gr. -1-3). 15.95 *(978-1-58979-542-6(3))* Taylor Trade Publishing.

—Do Princesses Make Happy Campers? Gordon, Mike, illus. 2015. (ENG.). 32p. (J). (gr. -1-2). 15.95 *(978-1-63076-054-0(4))* Taylor Trade Publishing.

—Do Princesses Really Kiss Frogs? Gordon, Mike & Gordon, Carl, illus. 2014. (ENG.). 96p. (J). (gr. -1-2). 15.95 *(978-1-58979-946-2(1))* Taylor Trade Publishing.

—Do Princesses Scrape Their Knees? 2006. (ENG., Illus.). 32p. (J). (gr. -1-2). 15.95 *(978-0-87358-909-3(2))* Cooper Square Publishing Llc.

—Do Princesses Scrape Their Knees? Keepsake Sticker Doodle Book. Gordon, Mike & Gordon, Carl, illus. 2014. (ENG.). 96p. (J). (gr. -1-2). 15.95 *(978-1-58979-948-6(8))* Taylor Trade Publishing.

—Do Princesses Wear Hiking Boots? Gordon, Mike & Gordon, Carl, illus. 2003. (ENG.). 32p. (J). (gr. -1-2). 15.95 *(978-0-87358-828-7(2))* Cooper Square Publishing Llc.

—Do Princesses Wear Hiking Boots? Gordon, Mike & Gordon, Carl, illus. 2014. (ENG.). 96p. (J). (gr. -1-2). 15.95 *(978-1-58979-945-5(3))* Taylor Trade Publishing.

Cronshaw, Joseph. Podge & Dodge. 2009. 32p. pap. 13.50 *(978-1-60693-868-3(1)*, Strategic Bk. Publishing) Strategic Book Publishing & Rights Agency (SBPRA).

Crossman, David. The Legend of Burial Island: A Bean & Ab Mystery. 2009. (ENG.). 201p. (J). (gr. 3-7). pap. 11.95 *(978-0-89272-797-1(7))* Down East Bks.

Croyle, Paula. Today I'll Be a Princess. Brown, Heather, illus. 2015. (ENG.). 12p. (J). bds. 5.99 *(978-1-4494-6057-0(7))* Andrews McMeel Publishing.

Crump, Fred, Jr. Marigold & the Dragon. 2010. 32p. (J). 12.95 *(978-1-934056-73-8(1))* UMI (Urban Ministries, Inc.).

Cummins, Molly. The Jewel of Fez. 2006. 141p. pap. 24.95 *(978-1-4241-1044-5(0))* PublishAmerica, Inc.

Cuyler, Margery. Princess Bess Gets Dressed. Maione, Heather Harms & Maione, Heather, illus. 2009. (ENG.). 32p. (J). (gr. -1-3). 15.99 *(978-1-4169-3833-0(8)*, Simon & Schuster Bks. For Young Readers) Simon & Schuster Bks. For Young Readers.

Cynthia, A. Sears. A World Divided: The Fairy Princess Chronicles - Book 1. 2012. 656p. *(978-1-4602-0516-7(2))*; pap. *(978-1-4602-0514-3(6))* FriesenPress.

Dadey, Debbie. The Lost Princess. Avakyan, Tatevik, illus. 2013. (Mermaid Tales Ser.: 5). (ENG.). 128p. (J). (gr. 1-4). 15.99 *(978-1-4424-8258-6(3))*; pap. 5.99 *(978-1-4424-8257-9(5))* Simon & Schuster Children's Publishing. (Aladdin).

Dadey, Debby & Dadey, Debbie. Lost Princess, 1 vol., Bk. 5. 2015. (Mermaid Tales Ser.). (ENG.). 120p. (J). (gr. 2-4). 24.21 *(978-1-61479-326-7(3)*, Spotlight) ABDO Publishing Co.

Dahl, Michael. Princess. Ho, Jannie, illus. 2015. (Baby Face Ser.). (ENG.). 10p. (gr. -1 — 1). bds. 7.99 *(978-1-62370-295-3(X))* Capstone Young Readers of Coughlan Cos.

Dahle, Stefanie. Lily, the Little Elf Princess. 2015. (ENG., Illus.). 32p. (J). 17.95 *(978-0-7358-4177-2(2))* North-South Bks., Inc.

D'Angelo, Elaina R. The Magic Book of E, 1 vol. 2010. 48p. pap. 16.95 *(978-1-4489-3949-7(6))* America Star Bks.

Daniels, Sharon. Fifi the Fabulous. 2011. 24p. pap. 15.99 *(978-1-4628-9262-4(0))* Xlibris Corp.

Danson, Lesley, illus. Snow White. 2006. (Flip-Up Fairy Tales Ser.). (ENG.). 24p. (J). (gr. 1-2). *(978-1-84643-023-7(2))* Child's Play International Ltd.

Darlison, Aleesah. Krystal's Charge Cancelled. Brailsford, Jill, illus. 2017. (Unicorn Riders Ser.). (ENG.). 112p. (gr. 3-5). pap. 5.95 *(978-1-4795-6558-0(X))* Picture Window Bks.

David, Erica. Anna & Elsa: Princess in Charge. RH Disney et al, illus. 2017. (Stepping Stone Book(TM) Ser.: 9). (ENG.). 128p. (J). (gr. 1-4). lib. bdg. 12.99 *(978-0-7364-8236-3(9)*, RH/Disney) Random Hse. Children's Bks.

—Anna & Elsa #6: the Arendelle Cup (Disney Frozen) RH Disney Staff et al, illus. 2015. (Stepping Stone Book(TM) Ser.: 6). (ENG.). 128p. (J). (gr. 1-4). 9.99 *(978-0-7364-3437-9(2)*, RH/Disney) Random Hse. Children's Bks.

David, Erica & Foreman, Matthew Sinclair. Disney Frozen - A Year with Elsa & Anna, & Olaf Too! 2016. (Replica Journal Ser.). (ENG.). 96p. (J). (gr. k-3). 9.99 *(978-0-7944-3701-5(X)*, Reader's Digest Children's Bks.) Studio Fun International.

Davidson, S. & Daynes, K. Princess Jewelry Kid Kit (Bag) 2008. (Kid Kits Ser.). 96p. (J). 15.99 *(978-1-60130-104-8(9)*, Usborne) EDC Publishing.

—Princess Jewelry Kid Kit (Box) 2008. (Kid Kits Ser.). 96p. (J). 15.99 *(978-1-60130-115-4(4)*, Usborne) EDC Publishing.

Davidson, Susanna. The Frog Prince. 2005. 48p. (J). (gr. 2-18). 8.95 *(978-0-7945-0969-9(X)*, Usborne) EDC Publishing.

—Princess Handbook. Gordon, Mike, illus. 2006. 80p. (J). (gr. 3-7). 12.99 *(978-0-7945-1329-0(8)*, Usborne) EDC Publishing.

—Princess Polly & the Pony. Hill, Dave, illus. 2007. (First Reading Level 4 Ser.). 48p. (J). 8.99 *(978-0-7945-1756-4(0)*, Usborne) EDC Publishing.

Davies, Kate, illus. Princess Tales. 2012. (ENG.). 96p. 15.00 *(978-1-84135-523-8(2))* Award Pubns. Ltd. GBR. Dist: Parkwest Pubns., Inc.

Davis, Marlo. The Morning Princess. 2013. 26p. pap. 16.95 *(978-1-4497-8792-9(4)*, WestBow Pr.) Author Solutions, Inc.

De Audrade, Norma. The Frog, the Princess, the Purpurine, & the Silk Threads. 2005. (J). pap. 8.00 *(978-0-8059-6524-7(6))* Dorrance Publishing Co., Inc.

De la Cruz, Melissa. Ring & the Crown. 2017. (Ring & the Crown Ser.). (ENG.). 480p. (YA). (gr. 9-17). pap. 9.99 *(978-1-4847-9925-3(9))* Hyperion Bks. for Children.

De Lafayette, Madame. The Princess de Montpensier. 2004. reprint ed. pap. 1.99 *(978-1-4192-7870-9(3))* Kessinger Publishing, LLC.

De Saint-Exupéry, Antoine. Le Petit Prince: Avec les dessins de l'auteur. (FRE., Illus.). 64p. (J). (gr. 1-7). audio, audio compact disk 12.95 *(978-2-921997-41-6(X))* Coffragants CAN. Dist: Penton Overseas, Inc.

—El Principito. (SPA.). 10.98 *(978-968-13-2180-2(4))* Editorial Diana, S.A. MEX. Dist: Continental Bk. Co., Inc.

Dean Wafstet, Cindi. Wings of Light. 2005. 31p. 15.00 *(978-1-4116-5567-6(2))* Lulu Pr., Inc.

Deisher, Kathleen E. Beyond the Gloesmur: In the Gloesmur Scrolls. Deisher, Kathleen E., illus. 2003. (Gloesmur Scrolls Ser.: Bk. 1). (Illus.). 270p. (J). pap. 13.95 *(978-1-892135-00-1(0))* Lamp Post Publishing, Inc.

Depken, Kristen L. A Royal Spring (Disney Princess) Laguna, Fabio & Colletti, Marco, illus. 2016. (Step into Reading Ser.). (ENG.). 24p. (J). (gr. -1-1). 4.99 *(978-0-7364-3452-2(6)*, RH/Disney) Random Hse. Children's Bks.

—Sing Your Song! (Nella the Princess Knight) Myers, Nneka, illus. 2017. (Step into Reading Ser.). (ENG.). 24p. (J). (gr. -1-1). pap. 4.99 ***(978-1-5247-6505-7(8))***; lib. bdg. 12.99 ***(978-1-5247-6506-4(6))*** Random Hse. Children's Bks. (Random Hse. Bks. for Young Readers).

Depken, Kristen L. Sweets & Treats (Disney Princess) RH Disney Staff et al, illus. 2016. (Pictureback(R) Ser.). (ENG.). 16p. (J). (-k). 4.99 *(978-0-7364-3353-2(8)*, RH/Disney) Random Hse. Children's Bks.

Dharma Publishing Staff. The Proud Peacock: A Story about Humility. 3rd ed. 2013. (ENG.). 36p. (gr. -1-7). pap. 8.95 *(978-0-89800-494-6(2))* Dharma Publishing.

DiCicco, Sue. Princess Potty Time. 2011. (ENG., Illus.). 14p. (J). (— 1). bds. 7.99 *(978-0-375-87202-0(7)*, Golden Bks.) Random Hse. Children's Bks.

Disney. Big Bear, Little Bear. 2012. (Disney Princess Step into Reading Ser.). lib. bdg. 13.55 *(978-0-606-26391-7(8)*, Turtleback) Turtleback Bks.

—Disney Frozen: Time for Bed, Olaf! 2016. (ENG.). 12p. (J). (gr. -1-k). bds. 12.99 *(978-0-7944-3754-1(0))* Studio Fun International.

—Disney Princess: Adventure under the Sea. 2008. (J). 13.99 *(978-1-59319-979-1(1))* LeapFrog Enterprises, Inc.

—Disney Princess Movie Theater Storybook & Movie Projector. 2016. (ENG.). 32p. (J). (gr. -1-2). 19.99 *(978-0-7944-3727-5(3))* Reader's Digest Assn., Inc., The.

—Disney Sofia the First: A Gift of Friendship. 2014. (ENG.). 16p. (J). (gr. -1-1). bds. 8.99 *(978-0-7944-3200-3(X))* Reader's Digest Assn., Inc., The.

—Frozen Cinestory, Volume 1. 2014. lib. bdg. 26.95 *(978-0-606-36645-8(8))* Turtleback Bks.

—A Mother's Love. 2012. (Disney Princess Step into Reading Ser.). lib. bdg. 13.55 *(978-0-606-26392-4(6)*, Turtleback) Turtleback Bks.

Disney Book Club Staff. Disney Sofia the First Becoming a Princess: Storybook & Amulet Necklace. 2013. (Storybook with Jewelry Ser.: 1). (ENG.). 24p. (J). (gr. -1-1). 11.99 *(978-0-7944-2873-0(8)*, Reader's Digest Children's Bks.) Studio Fun International.

Disney Book Group. Beauty & the Beast: The Story of Belle. Disney Storybook Art Team, illus. 2016. (ENG.). 112p. (J). (gr. -1-k). 12.99 *(978-1-4847-6720-7(9))* Disney Pr.

—Disney Princess. Disney Storybook Art Team, illus. (Storybook Treasury Ser.). (ENG.). (J). 2016. 256p. (gr. 1-3). 30.00 *(978-1-4847-8959-9(8))* 2015. 304p. (gr. -1-k). 16.99 *(978-1-4847-1283-2(8))* Disney Pr.

—Disney Princess Read-Along Storybook & CD Boxed Set. Disney Storybook Art Team, illus. 2017. (Read-Along Storybook & CD Ser.). (ENG.). 128p. (J). (gr. 1-3). pap. 12.99 *(978-1-368-00262-2(5))* Disney Pr.

—Disney Princess Storybook Collection: Tales to Finish. Disney Storybook Art Team, illus. 2017. (Storybook Collection: Tales to Finish Ser.). (ENG.). 128p. (J). (gr. 1-3). 10.99 *(978-1-4847-8957-5(1))* Disney Pr.

—Elena of Avalor a Palace Fit for a Princess. Disney Storybook Art Team, illus. 2016. (ENG.). 16p. (J). (gr. 1-3). 12.99 *(978-1-4847-5872-4(2))* Disney Pr.

—Frozen: The Story of Anna & Elsa. Disney Storybook Art Team, illus. 2016. (ENG.). 112p. (J). (gr. -1-k). 12.99 *(978-1-4847-6770-2(5))* Disney Pr.

—Frozen 5-Minute Frozen Stories. Disney Storybook Art Team, illus. 2015. (5-Minute Stories Ser.). (ENG.). 192p. (J). (gr. 1-3). 12.99 *(978-1-4847-2330-2(9))* Disney Pr.

—Frozen, Level 1. 2016. (World of Reading Ser.). (ENG.). 96p. (J). (gr. -1-k). pap. 7.99 *(978-1-4847-9032-8(4))* Disney Pr.

—The Princess & the Frog: The Story of Tiana. Disney Storybook Art Team, illus. 2016. (ENG.). 112p. (J). (gr. -1-k). 12.99 *(978-1-4847-6729-0(2))* Disney Pr.

—Sofia the First Let the Good Times Troll: Book with DVD. Disney Storybook Art Team, illus. 2015. (ENG.). 32p. (J). (gr. -1-k). 9.99 *(978-1-4847-0696-1(X))* Disney Pr.

—Sofia the First Sofia's First Christmas. Disney Storybook Art Team, illus. 2015. (ENG.). 40p. (J). (gr. -1-k). 8.99 *(978-1-4847-1556-7(X))* Disney Pr.

—Tangled: The Story of Rapunzel. Disney Storybook Art Team, illus. 2016. (ENG.). 112p. (J). (gr. -1-k). 12.99 *(978-1-4847-6727-6(6))* Disney Pr.

—Tangled & Tangled Ever after Read-Along Storybook & CD Bindup. Disney Storybook Art Team, illus. 2017. (Read-Along Storybook & CD Ser.). (ENG.). 64p. (J). (gr. 1-3). pap. 8.99 ***(978-1-4847-8780-9(3))*** Disney Pr.

Disney Book Group. World of Reading: Sofia the First Adventure Stories: Five Favorites. Disney Storybook Art Team, illus. 2016. (Wonderful World of Reading Ser.). (ENG.). 160p. (J). (gr. -1-k). pap. 7.99 *(978-1-4847-7502-8(3))* Disney Pr.

Disney Book Group & Rudnick, Elizabeth. A Frozen Heart. Disney Storybook Art Team, illus. 2015. (ENG.). 304p. (J). (gr. 5-9). 14.99 *(978-1-4847-3051-5(8))* Disney Pr.

Disney Book Group, et al. Clover Time. 2016. (Sofia the First World of Reading Ser.). (Illus.). 32p. (J). lib. bdg. 13.55 *(978-0-606-37534-4(1))* Turtleback Bks.

Disney Book Group Staff. Brave. 2012. (Read-Along Storybook & CD Ser.). (ENG.). 32p. (J). (gr. -1-k). pap. 6.99 *(978-1-4231-3770-2(1))* Disney Pr.

—Disney Princess, Set. 2012. (ENG.). 272p. pap. 12.99 *(978-1-4231-5533-1(5))* Disney Pr.

—Enchanting Tale. 2010. (ENG.). 128p. (J). (gr. -1-2). 14.99 *(978-1-4231-1938-8(X))* Disney Pr.

—Frozen Read-Along Storybook & CD. Disney Storybook Artists Staff, illus. 2013. (Read-Along Storybook & CD Ser.). (ENG.). 32p. (J). (gr. -1-k). pap. 6.99 *(978-1-4231-7064-8(4))* Disney Pr.

—Princess Adventure Stories. Disney Storybook Artists Staff, illus. 2013. (Storybook Collection). (ENG.). 304p. (J). (gr. -1 — 1). 15.99 *(978-1-4231-4691-9(3))* Disney Pr.

—Royal Kittens: A Palace Pets Book & Magnetic Play Set. 2015. (ENG.). 32p. (J). (gr. -1-k). 14.99 *(978-1-4847-0512-4(2))* Disney Pr.

—Sofia the First Royal Prep Academy. Disney Storybook Artists Staff & Disney Storybook Art Team, illus. 2014. (ENG.). 14p. (J). (gr. -1-k). bds. 8.99 *(978-1-4847-0760-9(5))* Disney Pr.

—Sofia the First S Is for Sofia. Disney Storybook Art Team, illus. 2015. (ENG.). 26p. (J). (gr. -1-k). bds. 12.99 *(978-1-4847-1804-9(6))* Disney Pr.

—Sofia the First Sofia's Princess Adventures: Board Book Boxed Set. Disney Storybook Art Team, illus. 2015. (ENG.). 40p. (J). (gr. -1-k). 10.99 *(978-1-4847-0042-6(2))* Disney Pr.

Disney Book Group Staff & Hapka, Catherine. Sofia the First. Lee, Grace, illus. 2012. (ENG.). 40p. (J). (gr. -1-k). 15.99 *(978-1-4231-6986-4(7))* Disney Pr.

—Sofia the First the Enchanted Science Fair. Disney Storybook Artists Staff, illus. 2014. (ENG.). 24p. (J). (gr. -1-k). pap. 4.99 *(978-1-4847-1309-9(5))* Disney Pr.

Disney Book Group Staff & Hapka, Cathy. Sofia the First the Royal Games. Disney Storybook Artists Staff, illus. 2014. (ENG.). 24p. (J). (gr. -1-k). pap. 3.99 *(978-1-4231-6409-8(1))* Disney Pr.

Disney Book Group Staff & Marsoli, Lisa Ann. World of Reading: Sofia the First the Missing Necklace: Level Pre-1. Disney Storybook Art Team, illus. 2014. (World of Reading Ser.). (ENG.). 32p. (J). (gr. -1-k). pap. 3.99 *(978-1-4231-7164-5(0))* Disney Pr.

Disney Book Group Staff & Richards, Kitty. The Lost Tiara. Disney Storybook Art Team & Studio Iboix Staff, illus. 2012. (Jewel Story Ser.). (ENG.). 96p. (J). (gr. 1-3). pap. 4.99 *(978-1-4231-5197-5(6))* Disney Pr.

Disney Book Group Staff & Rusu, Meredith L. Disney Princess Sleeping Beauty Read-Along Storybook & CD. 2014. (Read-Along Storybook & CD Ser.). (ENG.). 32p. (J). (gr. -1-k). pap. 6.99 *(978-1-4231-9894-9(8))* Disney Pr.

Disney Book Group Staff & Scollon, Bill. Sofia the First: a Royal Mouse in the House. Lee, Grace, illus. 2015. (ENG.). 40p. (J). (gr. -1-k). 8.99 *(978-1-4847-0643-5(9))* Disney Pr.

Disney Book Group Staff, et al. The Curse of Maleficent: The Tale of a Sleeping Beauty. Disney Storybook Artists Staff & Kole, Nicholas, illus. 2014. (ENG.). 240p. (J). (gr. 3-7). 9.99 *(978-1-4231-9751-5(8))* Disney Pr.

Disney Editors. Frozen. 2013. lib. bdg. 14.75 *(978-0-606-32207-2(8)*, Turtleback) Turtleback Bks.

—Frozen - Anna's Icy Adventure. 2013. lib. bdg. 14.75 *(978-0-606-32206-5(X)*, Turtleback) Turtleback Bks.

Disney Editors. Mulan Is Loyal / Merida Is Brave. 2017. (Disney Princess Step into Reading Ser.). lib. bdg. 16.00 ***(978-0-606-40246-0(2))*** Turtleback Bks.

Disney Press Editors. Sofia Takes the Lead. 2014. (Sofia the First World of Reading Ser.). (J). lib. bdg. 13.55 *(978-0-606-34102-8(1)*, Turtleback) Turtleback Bks.

Disney Press Staff & Disney Book Group Staff. 5-Minute Princess Stories. Disney Storybook Artists Staff, illus. 2011. (5-Minute Stories Ser.). (ENG.). 192p. (J). (gr. -1 — 1). 12.99 *(978-1-4231-4657-5(3))* Disney Pr.

Disney Princess, Disney. Disney Princess - Bibbity-Bobbity-Boo! 2015. (ENG.). 12p. (J). (gr. -1-k). bds. 10.99 (978-0-7944-3375-8(8), Reader's Digest Children's Bks.) Studio Fun International.
—Disney Princess Once upon a Castle: Hidden Stories. 2014. (Hidden Stories Ser.: 4). (ENG.). 10p. (J). (gr. -1-1). 15.99 (978-0-7944-3107-5(0)) Reader's Digest Assn., Inc., The.
Disney Princess Dress Up: A Forever Sticker Storybook. 2014. (ENG.). 12p. (J). (gr. -1-1). 14.99 (978-0-7944-3191-4(7), Reader's Digest Children's Bks.) Studio Fun International.
Disney Princess Holiday: Cinderella So This Is Christmas/Beauty & the Beast One Magical Christmas/Ariel's Christmas under the Sea. unabr. ed. 2005. (Disney's Read along Collection Ser.). (J). pap. (978-0-7634-1146-6(9)) Walt Disney Records.
Disney Princess Staff. Movie Theater: Storybook & Movie Projector(r). 2013. (Movie Theater Ser.: 1). (ENG.). 32p. (J). (gr. -1-1). 19.99 (978-0-7944-2842-6(8), Reader's Digest Children's Bks.) Studio Fun International.
Disney Princess Staff, adapted by. Princess Enchanted Palace: Storybook & Play Castle. 2010. (Playbox Ser.). (ENG., Illus.). 32p. (J). (gr. -1-2). bds. 19.99 (978-0-7944-2035-2(4)) Reader's Digest Assn., Inc., The.
Disney Princess Staff & Disney Book Group Staff. Ariel: The Birthday Surprise. Cagol, Andrea & Studio Iboix Staff, illus. 2010. (Disney Princess Chapter Book: Series #1 Ser.). (ENG.). 96p. (J). (gr. 1-3). pap. 4.99 (978-1-4231-2971-4(7)) Disney Pr.
Disney Princess Super Activity Fun Storybook Collection. 2005. (J). (978-1-59487-168-9(X)) Artist Studios, Ltd.
Disney, Sofia the First. Disney Guess Who, Sofia! 2014. (Guess Who Ser.: 1). (ENG.). 10p. (J). (gr. -1-k). 10.99 (978-0-7944-3074-0(0), Reader's Digest Children's Bks.) Studio Fun International.
Disney Sofia the First, Disney Sofia. Disney Sofia the First Movie Theater Storybook & Movie Projector. 2014. (Movie Theater Ser.: 15). (ENG.). 32p. (J). (gr. -1-1). 19.99 (978-0-7944-3138-9(0), Reader's Digest Children's Bks.) Studio Fun International.
—Disney Sofia the First: Please & Thank You: Your Guide to Becoming the Perfect Princess! 2015. (ENG.). 32p. (J). (gr. -1-1). 10.99 (978-0-7944-3279-9(4), Reader's Digest Children's Bks.) Studio Fun International.
—Disney Sofia the First: Where Is My Tiara? 2014. (Open Door Book Ser.: 2). (ENG.). 16p. (J). (gr. -1 — 1). bds. 10.99 (978-0-7944-3109-9(7), Reader's Digest Children's Bks.) Studio Fun International.
Disney Storybook Art Team, illus. Cinderella: The Great Mouse Mistake. 2010. (Disney Princess Chapter Book Ser.). (ENG.). 80p. (J). (gr. 1-3). pap. 4.99 (978-1-4231-2978-3(4)) Disney Pr.
—Royal Lessons. 2014. (ENG.). 10p. (J). (gr. -1-k). bds. 8.99 (978-1-4231-8444-7(0)) Disney Pr.
Disney Storybook Artists Staff, contrib. by. Princess Adventure Stories. 2013. (Illus.). 300p. (J). (978-1-4231-2661-4(0)) Disney Pr.
Disney Storybook Artists Staff & Reader's Digest Staff. Disney Princess Music Player Storybook. 2013. (Music Player Storybook Ser.). (ENG.). 40p. (J). (gr. -1-3). 19.99 (978-0-7944-2804-4(5)) Reader's Digest Assn., Inc., The.
Disney's Read to Me Treasury - Princess. 2011. 400p. (978-1-4231-2393-4(X)) Disney Pr.
Dixon, Heather. Entwined. (ENG.). 480p. (YA). (gr. 8). 2012. pap. 9.99 (978-0-06-200104-7(3)) 2011. 17.99 (978-0-06-200103-0(5)) HarperCollins Pubs. (Greenwillow Bks.).
Donaldson, Julia. Christmas with Princess Mirror-Belle. Monks, Lydia, illus. 2016. (Princess Mirror-Belle Ser.). (ENG.). 112p. (J). (gr. k-6). 14.99 (978-1-5098-1426-8(4)) Pan Macmillan GBR. Dist: Independent Pubs. Group.
—A Gold Star for Zog. Scheffler, Axel, illus. 2012. (ENG.). 32p. (J). (gr. -1-3). 17.99 (978-0-545-41724-2(4), Levine, Arthur A. Bks.) Scholastic, Inc.
—Princess Mirror-Bell & the Sea Monster's Cave. Monks, Lydia, illus. 2016. (Princess Mirror-Belle Ser.). (ENG.). 96p. (J). (gr. 2-4). pap. 8.99 (978-1-4472-8566-3(2)) Pan Macmillan GBR. Dist: Independent Pubs. Group.
—Princess Mirror-Belle. Monks, Lydia, illus. (Princess Mirror-Belle Ser.). (ENG.). (J). 2017. 192p. (gr. k-2). pap. 8.99 **(978-1-5098-3872-1(4))** 2015. 128p. (gr. 2-4). pap. 9.99 (978-1-4472-8562-5(X)) Pan Macmillan GBR. Dist: Independent Pubs. Group.
—Princess Mirror-Belle & Prince Precious Paws. Monks, Lydia, illus. 2016. (Princess Mirror-Belle Ser.). (ENG.). 128p. (J). (gr. 2-4). pap. 8.99 (978-1-4472-8564-9(6)) Pan Macmillan GBR. Dist: Independent Pubs. Group.
—Princess Mirror-Belle & the Flying Horse. Monks, Lydia, illus. 2016. (Princess Mirror-Belle Ser.: 3). (ENG.). 96p. (J). (gr. 2-4). pap. 8.99 (978-1-4472-8565-6(4)) Pan Macmillan GBR. Dist: Independent Pubs. Group.
—Princess Mirror-Belle & the Magic Shoes. Monks, Lydia, illus. (Princess Mirror-Belle Ser.: 2). (ENG.). (J). 2016. 128p. (gr. 2-4). pap. 8.99 (978-1-4472-8563-2(8))1. 2013. 144p. (gr. k-2). pap. 8.99 (978-1-4472-2404-4(3)) Pan Macmillan GBR. Dist: Independent Pubs. Group.
—Princess Mirror-Belle & the Party Hoppers. Monks, Lydia, illus. 2015. (Princess Mirror-Belle Ser.). (ENG.). 128p. (J). (gr. 2-4). pap. 8.99 (978-1-4472-8489-5(5)) Pan Macmillan GBR. Dist: Independent Pubs. Group.
Dorantes, Kathleen. Princess So-Wise. 2005. pap. 11.50 (978-1-59330-330-3(0)) Aventine Pr.
Dorling Kindersley Publishing Staff. Disney Frozen: the Enchanted Guide. 2015. (ENG., Illus.). 96p. (J). (gr. 1-4). 14.99 (978-1-4654-4081-5(X), DK Children) Dorling Kindersley Publishing, Inc.
Dorling Kindersley Publishing Staff, ed. Princess: The Essential Guide. 2012. (ENG.). 96p. (J). (gr. 2-5). 12.99 (978-0-7566-9798-3(0), DK Children) Dorling Kindersley Publishing, Inc.
Dorling Kindersley Publishing Staff & Rose, Eleanor. The Amazing Book of Disney Princess. 2017. (ENG.). 48p. (J). (gr. k-2). 14.99 (978-1-4654-5866-7(2), DK Children) Dorling Kindersley Publishing, Inc.
Doty, Mariel. A Different Kind of Princess: Pictures of You. 2010. 260p. 26.50 (978-1-60911-318-6(7), Eloquent Bks.) Strategic Book Publishing & Rights Agency (SBPRA).
Dower, Laura. Sunny & the Secret Passage. 2013. (Palace Puppies Ser.: 4). (J). lib. bdg. 14.75 (978-0-606-35108-9(6), Turtleback) Turtleback Bks.
Downing, Erin. SPACEPOP: Not Your Average Princesses. 2016. (Spacepop Ser.: 1). (ENG., Illus.). 216p. (J). 14.99 (978-1-250-10227-0(8), 9781250102270) Imprint IND. Dist: Macmillan.
Doyle, Malachy. Tales from Old Ireland. Sharkey, Niamh, illus. 2008. (ENG.). 96p. (J). 21.99 (978-1-84686-241-0(8)) Barefoot Bks., Inc.
Dreissigacker Martin, Susan. Princess Stephanie Stories: The Road Trip & the New School. 2009. 32p. pap. 18.79 (978-1-4389-1836-5(4)) AuthorHouse.
Drobeck, Ronald D. My Name Is Prince Albert. 2012. 152p. (gr. 4-6). 30.95 (978-1-4582-0205-5(4)); pap. 12.99 (978-1-4582-0203-1(8)) Author Solutions, Inc. (Abbott Pr.).
Dube, Pierrette. How to Become a Perfect Princess in Five Days. Melanson, Luc, illus. 2009. (Rainy Day Readers Ser.). 32p. (J). (gr. -1-3). 22.60 (978-1-60754-376-3(1)) Windmill Bks.
Duffy, Carol Ann. The Princess's Blankets. Hyde, Catherine Ryan, illus. 2009. (ENG.). 40p. (J). (gr. k-3). 18.99 (978-0-7636-4547-2(8), Templar) Candlewick Pr.
Dunlap, Susanne. Anastasia's Secret. 2011. (ENG.). 368p. (YA). (gr. 7). pap. 8.99 (978-1-59990-588-4(4), 9781599905884, Bloomsbury USA Childrens) Bloomsbury Publishing USA.
Durkin, Mary Jane. The Shabby Little Princess. 2009. 24p. pap. 14.99 (978-1-4389-5115-7(9)) AuthorHouse.
Durst, Sarah Beth. Journey Across the Hidden Islands. 2017. (ENG., Illus.). 352p. (J). (gr. 5-7). 16.99 (978-0-544-70679-8(X), Clarion Bks.) Houghton Mifflin Harcourt Trade & Reference Pubs.
Duty, William. Boomtown: Darkpit Mountain & the Princess Three, 1 vol. 2010. 76p. pap. 19.95 (978-1-4489-5971-6(3)) America Star Bks.
Dyan, Penelope. Introducing Fabulous Marie, a Girl with a Good Head on Her Shoulders. Dyan, Penelope, illus. 2009. (Illus.). 44p. pap. 11.95 (978-1-935118-55-8(2)) Bellissima Publishing, LLC.
Dyer, Sarah. Princess for a Day: A Clementine & Mungo Story. Dyer, Sarah, illus. (ENG., Illus.). 32p. (J). (gr. -1-k). 2009. pap. 12.95 (978-0-7475-8891-7(0)) 2007. 22.95 (978-0-7475-8753-8(1)) Bloomsbury Publishing Plc GBR. Dist: Independent Pubs. Group.
Dzidrums, Christine. Princess Dessabelle: Tennis Star. Muths, Tohn Fayette, illus. 2013. 50p. pap. 10.99 (978-1-938438-34-9(5)) Creative Media Publishing.
—Princess Dessabelle Makes a Friend. Muths, Tohn, illus. 2011. 32p. (J). pap. 9.99 (978-0-9826435-6-3(X)); 17.99 (978-0-9826435-7-0(8)) Creative Media Publishing.
East, Jacqueline, illus. Princess Palace: A Three-Demensional Playset. 2006. 8p. (J). (gr. -1-3). 22.95 (978-1-58117-492-2(6), Intervisual/Piggy Toes) Bendon, Inc.
Ebbitt, Carolyn Q. The Extra-Ordinary Princess. 2010. (ENG.). 336p. (YA). (gr. 3-6). pap. 7.99 (978-1-59990-484-9(5), 9781599904849, Bloomsbury USA Childrens) Bloomsbury Publishing USA.
Eberly, Chelsea. Magic Friends. 2014. (Step into Reading Ser.). (ENG., Illus.). 32p. (J). (gr. -1-1). 3.99 (978-0-385-38296-0(0), Random Hse. Bks. for Young Readers) Random Hse. Children's Bks.
—Magic Friends. 2014. (Barbie Step into Reading Level 2 Ser.). lib. bdg. 13.55 (978-0-606-35991-7(5)) Turtleback Bks.
Edwards, M. J. Dontayan. 2008. 62p. pap. 19.95 (978-1-60610-026-4(2)) America Star Bks.
Edwards, Marnie. Magical Mix-Ups: Birthdays & Bridesmaids. Hodgkinson, Leigh, illus. 2012. (Magical Mix-Ups Ser.). (ENG.). 96p. (J). (gr. 2-5). pap. 6.99 (978-0-7636-6272-1(0), Nosy Crow) Candlewick Pr.
—Pets & Parties. Hodgkinson, Leigh, illus. 2013. (Magical Mix-Ups Ser.). (ENG.). 96p. (J). (gr. 2-5). pap. 6.99 (978-0-7636-6371-1(9), Nosy Crow) Candlewick Pr.
Edwards, Meinir Wyn. Cantre'r Gwaelod. Wade, Gini, illus. 2007. (ENG.). 24p. (J). pap. 4.95 (978-1-84771-021-5(2)) Y Lolfa GBR. Dist: Dufour Editions, Inc.
Egbert, Charles. The Story of Princess Olivia: Wherein an Optimistic Slip of a Girl Brings Sunshine into the Lives of Her Royal Parents, the Whiny King & the ... & His Magical Minion, the Mischi. 2013. (ENG.). 144p. (gr. 2-7). 14.95 (978-1-59373-147-2(7)) Bunker Hill Publishing, Inc.
Elliot, Rachel. Who Is New York's Prettiest Princess? Spenceley, Annabel, illus. 2012. (ENG.). 32p. (J). (-3). 9.99 (978-1-4022-8221-8(4), Sourcebooks Jabberwocky) Sourcebooks, Inc.
Elliott, Ruth. The Night Princess, 1 disc. Elliott, Ruth, illus. 2007. (SPA., Illus.). (J). per. 12.99 incl. DVD (978-0-9795017-1-5(7)) Edu Designs.
Eltoukhy, G.N. Princess & the Enchanted Pegasus. 2012. 28p. pap. 16.09 (978-1-4669-1831-3(4)) Trafford Publishing.
Elwick, Elissa. The Princess & the Sleep Stealer. Elwick, Elissa, illus. 2012. (ENG., Illus.). 32p. (J). (gr. -1-k). pap. 9.99 (978-0-230-75068-5(0)) Macmillan Pubs., Ltd. GBR. Dist: Independent Pubs. Group.
Emmett, Jonathan & Dunn, David H. The Princess & the Pig. Bernatene, Poly, illus. 2011. (ENG.). 32p. (J). (gr. k-8). 17.99 (978-0-8027-2334-5(9), 9780802723345, Bloomsbury USA Childrens) Bloomsbury Publishing USA.
Espinosa, Rod. Courageous Princess Vol. 1: Beyond the Hundred Kingdoms. Espinosa, Rod, illus. 3rd ed. 2015. (ENG., Illus.). 250p. (J). (gr. 3-7). 19.99 (978-1-61655-722-5(2)) Dark Horse Comics.
—The Courageous Princess Pocket Manga. 2012. (Illus.). 232p. pap. 14.99 (978-0-9841107-9-7(8)) Antarctic Pr., Inc.
—The Dragon Queen. Espinosa, Rod, illus. 2015. (Courageous Princess Ser.). (ENG., Illus.). 180p. (J). (gr. 3-7). 19.99 (978-1-61655-724-9(9)) Dark Horse Comics.
—The Unremembered Lands. Espinosa, Rod, illus. 2015. (ENG., Illus.). 166p. (J). (gr. 3-7). 19.99 (978-1-61655-723-2(0)) Dark Horse Comics.
EsterSonia. Sissi My Story - My life with my loving Owners. 2010. 78p. pap. 33.50 (978-1-4452-1215-9(3)) Lulu Pr., Inc.
Eubank, Patricia Reeder. The Princess & the Snarls. Eubank, Patricia Reeder, illus. 2006. (ENG., Illus.). 32p. (J). (gr. k-3). 16.95 (978-0-8249-5536-6(6), Ideal Pubns.) Worthy Publishing.
Evans, Carolyn, et al. Maggie Malone Gets the Royal Treatment. 2014. (Maggie Malone Ser.: 2). (ENG.). 208p. (J). (gr. 3-6). pap. 6.99 (978-1-4022-9309-2(7), Sourcebooks Jabberwocky) Sourcebooks, Inc.
Evans, Rosemary R. The Little Princesses Magial Party. Taylor, Erin, illus. 2012. 40p. (J). 16.95 (978-1-60743-759-8(7)) Wink Publishing.
Everett, Felicity & Rawson, Christopher. Stories of Princes & Princesses. 2004. (Young Reading Ser.). (Illus.). 48p. (J). (gr. 2-18). pap. 5.95 (978-0-7945-0449-6(3), Usborne) EDC Publishing.
Fackrell, David. Princess, the Collection, Vol. 1. 2005. 78p. pap. 19.99 (978-1-4116-5820-2(5)) Lulu Pr., Inc.
Fairbanks, Letitia. Princess April Morning-Glory: What Kind of a World Would You Create, If You Had to Do Three Dood Deeds to Make li Home Again? Fairbanks, Letitia, illus. 2013. (ENG., Illus.). 66p. pap. 24.00 (978-0-9887848-0-2(7)) Sandramantos Publishing.
Fairy Tale- Cinderella. 2005. (J). bds. (978-1-4194-0039-1(8)) Paradise Pr., Inc.
Fairy tales - Cinderella. 2005. (J). bds. (978-1-4194-0100-8(9)) Paradise Pr., Inc.
Fairy Tales- Sleeping Beauty. 2005. (J). bds. (978-1-4194-0042-1(8)) Paradise Pr., Inc.
Falconer, Ian. Olivia & the Fairy Princesses. Falconer, Ian, illus. 2012. (ENG., Illus.). 40p. (J). (gr. -1-3). 18.99 (978-1-4424-5027-1(4), Atheneum Bks. for Young Readers) Simon & Schuster Children's Publishing.
—Olivia y Las Princesas. 2012. (SPA., Illus.). 32p. (J). (gr. -1-1). 17.99 (978-1-933032-82-5(0)) Lectorum Pubns., Inc.
Farkas, Steven E. Annie Pooh, Princess Pup: How Annie Pooh was lost, was found, & became Princess Pup. 2011. 24p. (gr. 2-4). pap. 15.99 (978-1-4670-3321-3(9)) AuthorHouse.
—Annie Pooh, Princess Pup, Monkey Shines. 2012. 40p. pap. 20.99 (978-1-4772-9484-0(8)) AuthorHouse.
Farley, Christina. The Princess & the Page. 2017. (ENG.). 240p. (J). (gr. 3-7). 17.99 (978-0-545-92409-2(X), Scholastic Pr.) Scholastic, Inc.
Farrey, Brian. The Secret of Dreadwillow Carse. 2016. (ENG.). 256p. (J). (gr. 3-7). 16.95 (978-1-61620-505-8(9)) Algonquin Bks. of Chapel Hill.
Feldman, Thea. Disney Palace Pets: Adventure Tales. 2015. (Hidden Stories Ser.). (ENG.). 10p. (J). (gr. -1-1). 15.99 (978-0-7944-3504-2(1), Reader's Digest Children's Bks.) Studio Fun International.
Ferris, Jean. Once upon a Marigold. 2004. 275p. (gr. 5). 17.00 (978-0-7569-3613-6(6)) Perfection Learning Corp.
—Thrice upon a Marigold: A Royal Kidnapping Caper. 2014. (ENG.). 256p. (J). (gr. 2-5). pap. 6.99 (978-0-544-30262-4(1), HMH Books For Young Readers) Houghton Mifflin Harcourt Publishing Co.
Fimbres, Lorraine. The Gingerbread Princess. 2012. 28p. pap. 16.09 (978-1-4669-1404-9(1)) Trafford Publishing.
Finn, Perdita. The Mane Event. 2014. (Equestria Girls Ser.: 3). (ENG.). 240p. (J). (gr. 3-7). 9.99 (978-0-316-24777-1(4)) Little, Brown Bks. for Young Readers.
—Rainbow Rocks. 2014. (Equestria Girls Ser.: 2). (ENG.). 192p. (J). (gr. 3-7). 9.99 (978-0-316-28486-8(6)) Little, Brown Bks. for Young Readers.
Finney, Shad. Princess Nap. 2008. 28p. pap. 15.99 (978-1-4363-2119-8(0)) Xlibris Corp.
Fitzgerald, D. M. The True Story of the Big Red Onion. Cudd, Savannah, illus. 2013. 36p. 18.99 (978-0-9890288-7-5(9)); pap. 10.99 (978-0-9890288-5-1(2)) Mindstir Media.
Flaker, Tracey. Around the Corner: Gwenever's Quest. 2006. 55p. pap. 16.95 (978-1-4241-1886-1(7)) PublishAmerica, Inc.
Flannigan, Liz. Starlight Grey. Docampo, Valeria, illus. 2013. (Magic Stories Ser.). (ENG.). 48p. (J). (gr. 1-4). pap. 8.99 (978-1-84686-778-1(9)) Barefoot Bks., Inc.
Fleming, Ligia Morales. The Very Special Princess. 2012. (ENG.). 25p. (J). pap. 14.95 (978-1-4327-9665-5(8)) Outskirts Pr., Inc.
Fletcher, Susan. Alphabet of Dreams. 2008. (ENG., Illus.). 432p. (YA). (gr. 7-12). mass mkt. 7.99 (978-0-689-85152-0(9), Simon Pulse) Simon Pulse.
Flinn, Alex. Cloaked. 2011. (YA). 341p. lib. bdg. 17.89 (978-0-06-087423-0(6)); (ENG.). 352p. (gr. 8-18). 16.99 (978-0-06-087422-3(8)) HarperCollins Pubs. (HarperTeen).
—A Kiss in Time. (ENG.). (YA). (gr. 8-18). 2010. 400p. pap. 9.99 (978-0-06-087421-6(X)) 2009. 384p. 17.99 (978-0-06-087419-3(8)) HarperCollins Pubs. (HarperTeen).
Floca, Brian, illus. The Hinky-Pink: An Old Tale. 2008. (ENG.). 48p. (J). (gr. -1-3). 16.99 (978-0-689-87588-5(6), Atheneum/Richard Jackson Bks.) Simon & Schuster Children's Publishing.
Ford, Bernette G. Princess Puppy. Williams, Sam, illus. 2013. (J). (978-0-545-53967-8(6), Cartwheel Bks.) Scholastic, Inc.
Forte, Lauren. When You Wish upon a Well (Disney Junior: Sofia the First) RH Disney, illus. 2016. (Little Golden Book Ser.). (ENG.). 24p. (J). (-k). 4.99 (978-0-7364-3508-6(5), Golden/Disney) Random Hse. Children's Bks.
Foster, Jackie. Land of Anear, 1 vol. 2010. 27p. pap. 24.95 (978-1-61546-634-4(7)) America Star Bks.
Frances, Suzanne & Marsham, Liz. Disney Princess Heart Strong #1 (Disney Princess) Disney Storybook Art Team Staff & Thomas, Jeffrey, illus. 2017. (Step into Reading Ser.). (ENG.). 48p. (J). (gr. -1-1). pap. 5.99 **(978-0-7364-3802-5(5)**, RH/Disney) Random Hse. Children's Bks.
Franz, Kevin. Into the Hidden Lands: A Castle Rose Adventure. Stigler, Marilyn, illus. 2004. 112p. (J). per. 7.99 (978-0-9747774-0-5(4)) Starbell Bks.
Freeman, Mylo. Princess Arabella's Birthday. 2009. (Illus.). 32p. (J). (gr. -1-3). 14.95 (978-0-9815761-7-6(6)) Mackenzie Smiles, LLC.
French, Vivian. The Heart of Glass: The Third Tale from the Five Kingdoms. Collins, Ross, illus. 2010. (Tales from the Five Kingdoms Ser.: 3). (ENG.). 256p. (J). (gr. 3-7). 14.99 (978-0-7636-4814-5(0)) Candlewick Pr.
—The Most Wonderful Thing in the World. Barrett, Angela, illus. 2015. (ENG.). 32p. (J). (gr. -1-3). 18.99 (978-0-7636-7501-1(6)) Candlewick Pr.
—Princess Charlotte & the Enchanted Rose. Gibb, Sarah, illus. 2007. (Tiara Club Ser.: No. 7). 80p. (J). (gr. 1-4). pap. 3.99 (978-0-06-112441-9(3), Tegen, Katherine Bks) HarperCollins Pubs.
—Princess Katie & the Silver Pony. Gibb, Sarah, illus. 2007. (Tiara Club Ser.: No.2). 80p. (J). (gr. 1-4). 15.99 (978-0-06-112432-7(X), Tegen, Katherine Bks) HarperCollins Pubs.
—The Tiara Club at Ruby Mansions No. 5: Princess Lauren & the Diamond Necklace. 2008. (Tiara Club Ser.). (ENG., Illus.). 80p. (J). (gr. 1-4). pap. 3.99 (978-0-06-143488-4(4), Tegen, Katherine Bks) HarperCollins Pubs.
Friesner, Esther M. Deception's Pawn. 2015. (ENG.). 336p. (YA). (gr. 7). 17.99 (978-0-449-81867-1(5), Random Hse. Bks. for Young Readers) Random Hse. Children's Bks.
Froeb, Lori. Disney Frozen: Christmas Magic. 2015. (ENG.). 10p. (J). (gr. -1-1). bds. 8.99 (978-0-7944-3501-1(7)) Reader's Digest Assn., Inc., The.
—Disney Princess: to Be a Princess. 2016. (ENG.). 12p. (J). (gr. -1-k). 15.99 (978-0-7944-3507-3(6), Reader's Digest Children's Bks.) Studio Fun International.
Froeb, Lori C. & Disney Storybook Artists Staff. Cinderella's Shining Moment. 2012. (Fold-Out Figure Ser.). (ENG., Illus.). 32p. (J). (gr. -1-2). 14.99 (978-0-7944-2547-0(X), Reader's Digest Children's Bks.) Studio Fun International.
Funderburg, April. Soul Snatcher. 2009. 84p. pap. 19.95 (978-1-60749-765-3(4)) America Star Bks.
Gabriel, Elizabeth P. & Gabriel, Pamela P. Ziccah Blows Her Horn. 2008. 24p. pap. 12.99 (978-1-4389-2447-2(X)) AuthorHouse.
Gaiman, NEil. The Sleeper & the Spindle. Riddell, Chris, illus. 2015. (ENG.). 64p. (YA). (gr. 8). 19.99 (978-0-06-239824-6(5)) HarperCollins Pubs.
Gallo, Tina. Cinderella: A Wheel-Y Silly Fairy Tale. Scott, Kimberley, illus. 2011. (Little Simon Sillies Ser.). (ENG.). 14p. (J). (gr. -1-1). lib. bdg. 5.99 (978-1-4424-2106-6(1), Little Simon) Little Simon.
Galvin, Laura Gates. Princess Counting Fun. Parisi, Anthony, ed. 2011. (Learning Library). (ENG., Illus.). 24p. (gr. -1). 8.99 (978-1-60727-265-6(2)) Studio Mouse LLC.
Galvin, Laura Gates & Studio Mouse Editorial. Cinderella: Dreams Do Come True. 2008. (Illus.). 36p. (J). (gr. -1). 7.99 (978-1-59069-436-7(8)) Studio Mouse LLC.
—Cinderella & Belle: Kindness Counts. Williams, Tracee, ed. 2008. (ENG., Illus.). 24p. (J). (gr. -1). 4.99 (978-1-59069-652-1(2)) Studio Mouse LLC.
Gardener, Amanda & Sealey, Nanlie. Butterfly Pavilion. 2013. 24p. pap. 10.99 (978-1-60820-898-2(2)) MLR Pr., LLC.
Gardner, Carol. Princess Zelda & the Frog. Young, Shane, photos by. 2011. (ENG., Illus.). 40p. (J). (gr. -1-3). 16.99 (978-0-312-60325-0(8), 9780312603250) Feiwel & Friends.
Gardner, Sally. Book of Princesses. (Illus.). 96p. (J). 19.95 (978-1-85881-350-9(6), Orion) Orion Publishing Group, Ltd. GBR. Dist: Trafalgar Square Publishing.
—The Princess & the Pea. 2011. (ENG., Illus.). 64p. (J). (gr. -1-k). 7.99 (978-1-4440-0245-4(7), Orion Children's Bks.) Hachette Children's Group GBR. Dist: Hachette Bk. Group.
—Snow White. 2011. (ENG., Illus.). 80p. (J). (gr. -1-k). 7.99 (978-1-4440-0243-0(0), Orion Children's Bks.) Hachette Children's Group GBR. Dist: Hachette Bk. Group.
Garey, Barbara J. The Adventures of Princess Naomia, 1 vol. 2009. 32p. pap. 24.95 (978-1-61546-090-8(X)) America Star Bks.
Gavin, Jamila. Three Indian Princesses: The Stories of Savitri, Damayanti & Sita. 2004. (Illus.). 112p. (Orig.). (J). pap. 7.50 (978-0-7497-4613-1(0)) Egmont Bks., Ltd. GBR. Dist: Trafalgar Square Publishing.
Gaydos, Nora. Princess of the Potty - Little Steps for Big Kids! Gutierrez, Akemi, illus. 2011. (ENG.). 30p. (J). (gr. -1-17). 8.99 (978-1-60169-076-0(2)) Innovative Kids.
George, Jessica Day. Fridays with the Wizards. (Tuesdays at the Castle Ser.). (ENG.). 2017. 256p. (J). pap. 7.99 (978-1-68119-204-8(7), 9781681192048) 2016. 240p. (YA). 16.99 (978-1-61963-429-9(5), 9781619634299) Bloomsbury Publishing USA. (Bloomsbury USA Childrens).
—Princess of Glass. (Twelve Dancing Princesses Ser.). (ENG.). 272p. (YA). (gr. 7). 2011. pap. 9.99 (978-1-59990-659-1(7), 9781599906591) 2010. 16.99 (978-1-59990-478-8(0), 9781599904788) Bloomsbury Publishing USA. (Bloomsbury USA Childrens).
—Princess of the Midnight Ball. 2010. (Twelve Dancing Princesses Ser.). (ENG.). 304p. (YA). (gr. 7-9). pap. 9.99 (978-1-59990-455-9(1), 9781599904559, Bloomsbury USA Childrens) Bloomsbury Publishing USA.
—Princess of the Silver Woods. (Twelve Dancing Princesses Ser.). (ENG.). (YA). (gr. 7). 2013. 352p. pap. 9.99 (978-1-61963-126-7(1), 9781619631267) 2012. 336p. 16.99 (978-1-59990-646-1(5), 9781599906461) Bloomsbury Publishing USA. (Bloomsbury USA Childrens).
—Saturdays at Sea. 2017. (Tuesdays at the Castle Ser.). (ENG.). 272p. (J). 16.99 (978-1-61963-957-7(2), 9781619639577, Bloomsbury USA Childrens) Bloomsbury Publishing USA.
—Thursdays with the Crown. (Tuesdays at the Castle Ser.). (ENG.). 2017. 240p. (J). pap. 7.99 (978-1-68119-221-5(7), 9781681192215) 2016. 240p. (J). pap. 7.99 (978-1-61963-796-2(0), 9781619637962) 2014. 224p. (YA). (gr. 3-6). 16.99 (978-1-61963-299-8(3), 9781619632998) Bloomsbury Publishing USA. (Bloomsbury USA Childrens).
—Tuesdays at the Castle. 2011. (Tuesdays at the Castle Ser.: 1). (ENG.). 240p. (YA). (gr. 3-12). 16.99 (978-1-59990-644-7(9), 9781599906447, Bloomsbury USA Childrens) Bloomsbury Publishing USA.
—Wednesdays in the Tower. 2017. (Tuesdays at the Castle Ser.). (ENG.). 256p. (J). pap. 7.99 (978-1-68119-219-2(5), 9781681192192, Bloomsbury USA Childrens) 2014. (Tuesdays at the Castle Ser.: 2). (ENG.). 256p. (YA). (gr. 3-6). pap. 7.99 (978-1-61963-265-3(9), 9781619632653, Bloomsbury USA Childrens) 2013. 240p. E-Book 16.99 (978-1-61963-051-2(6)) 2013. (Tuesdays at the Castle Ser.: 2). (ENG.). 240p. (YA). (gr. 3-6). 16.99 (978-1-59990-645-4(7), 9781599906454, Bloomsbury USA Childrens) Bloomsbury Publishing USA.
George, Joshua. Colors in the Princess Palace. 2016. (ENG.). 10p. (J). (gr. -1-k). 9.99 (978-1-78445-645-0(4)) Top That! Publishing PLC GBR. Dist: Independent Pubs. Group.
Gil, Carmen. It's a Pain to Be a Princess! 2012. (ENG., Illus.). 28p. (J). (gr. k-2). (978-84-15241-78-2(X)) D P & G Military Pubs.
—Que Fastidio Ser Princesa! 2012. (SPA & ENG., Illus.). 28p. (J). (gr. k-2). 14.95 (978-84-15241-14-0(3)) Eastern National.

Giles, Katharine. The Princess of Skye, an Archer Adventure. 2013. (ENG.). 280p. (YA). pap. 12.99 (978-1-939927-79-8(X)) Telemachus Pr., LLC.

Gili, Phillida. Cinderella: A Pop-up Book. Gili, Phillida, illus. 2007. (Illus.). 12p. (J). 25.00 (978-1-4223-9031-3(4)) DIANE Publishing Co.

Gillespie, Tonnika. The Queen's 3 Jewels. Anderson, Susan, illus. 2009. 20p. pap. 13.99 (978-1-4389-3925-4(6)) AuthorHouse.

Gillian, Chelsea, et al. Princess ABCs And 123s. rev. ed. 2007. (Illus.). 24p. (J). (gr. -1-1). 4.99 (978-1-59069-560-9(7)) Studio Mouse LLC.

Gilligan, Shannon. Princess Island. 2015. (ENG.). (J). pap. 7.99 (978-1-937133-50-4(8)) Chooseco LLC.

Gilman, Phoebe. The Balloon Tree. 2004. (J). (gr. k-3). spiral bd. (978-0-616-01650-3(6)) Canadian National Institute for the Blind/Institut National Canadien pour les Aveugles.

—The Balloon Tree. 2011. (ENG., Illus.). 32p. (J). (gr. -1-k). 16.95 (978-1-61608-454-7(5), 608454, Sky Pony Pr.) Skyhorse Publishing Co., Inc.

Glazov, Sheila N. Princess Shayna's Invisible Visible Gift. 2011. (ENG., Illus.). 136p. pap. 18.95 (978-1-61711-035-1(3)) SLACK, Inc.

Gleason, Colleen. The Chess Queen Enigma: A Stoker & Holmes Novel. (ENG.). 360p. (YA). (gr. 7-12). 2016. pap. 9.99 (978-1-4521-5649-1(2)) 2015. (Stoker & Holmes Ser.: 3). 17.99 (978-1-4521-4317-0(X)) Chronicle Bks. LLC.

—The Spiritglass Charade. 2015. (Stoker & Holmes Ser.: 2). (YA). lib. bdg. 20.85 (978-0-606-37441-5(8)) Turtleback Bks.

Gold, Gina. Disney Palace Pets Guess Who Castle Cuties. 2014. (Guess Who Ser.). (ENG.). 10p. (J). (gr. -1-k). 10.99 (978-0-7944-3192-1(5), Reader's Digest Children's Bks.) Studio Fun International.

Golden Books. Purpleberry Surprise! (Nella the Princess Knight) Cespedes-Alicea, Marcela, illus. 2017. (Deluxe Paint Box Book Ser.). (ENG.). 128p. (J). (gr. -1-2). pap. 7.99 **(978-1-5247-1673-8(1)**, Golden Bks.) Random Hse. Children's Bks.

Golden Books, illus. Barbie 9 Favorite Fairy Tales (Barbie) 2013. (Little Golden Book Treasury Ser.). (ENG.). 224p. (J). (-k). 10.99 (978-0-449-81861-9(6), Golden Bks.) Random Hse. Children's Bks.

Gologan, Trena. Alexandru's Gift. 2008. 35p. pap. 17.00 (978-1-4357-3486-9(6)) Lulu Pr., Inc.

Gonnard, Christel, et al. The Planet of Okidians. 2015. (Little Prince Ser.: 21). (ENG., Illus.). 48p. (J). (gr. 4-8). pap. 7.95 (978-1-4677-6024-9(2), Graphic Universe™) Lerner Publishing Group.

Gonyea, Maria. Princess Maria. 2013. 28p. pap. 13.95 (978-1-4525-8189-7(4), Balboa Pr.) Author Solutions, Inc.

Goodhart, Pippa. Cake Test. McCafferty, Jan, illus. 2007. (Blue Bananas Ser.). (ENG.). 48p. (J). (gr. k-2). pap. 5.99 (978-1-4052-2955-5(1)) Egmont Bks., Ltd. GBR. Dist: Independent Pubs. Group.

Gordon, Jennifer. Terrible Tales 2: The Bloodcurdling Truth about the Frog Prince, Jack & the Beanstalk, A Very Fowl Duckling, the Ghoulishly Ghoulish Snow White, A Really Crabby Princess, & A Very Squashed Pea. 2011. 110p. (gr. -1-12). 20.95 (978-1-4620-0941-1(7)); pap. 10.95 (978-1-4620-0940-4(9)) iUniverse, Inc.

Gordon, Mike, illus. The Princess & the Pea. rev. ed. 2007. (Young Reading CD Packs Ser.). 48p. (J). (gr. -1-3). 9.99 incl. audio compact disk (978-0-7945-1875-2(3), Usborne) EDC Publishing.

—Stories of Princesses. 2006. 144p. (J). (gr. 4-7). 14.99 (978-0-7945-1385-6(9), Usborne) EDC Publishing.

Gouveia, Keith. The Goblin Pricess. 2008. 208p. (978-1-897370-49-0(0)) Lachesis Publishing.

Goyer, Katell. Princesses of World. Misstigri, illus. 2009. 3p. (J). (gr. -1-3). 17.99 (978-0-8437-1445-6(X)) Hammond World Atlas Corp.

Grandoit, Jean. In the Quest for Inshalla: Simbies of the Caribbean at the World Under. 2010. 68p. pap. 25.49 (978-1-4520-3900-8(3)) AuthorHouse.

Grant, Cj. The Princess & the Swan. 2012. 48p. pap. 21.88 (978-1-4669-1594-7(3)) Trafford Publishing.

Grant, Holly. The Dastardly Deed. Portillo, Josie, illus. 2016. (League of Beastly Dreadfuls Ser.: Bk. 2). (ENG.). 368p. (J). (gr. 3-7). 16.99 (978-0-385-37025-7(3), Random Hse. Bks. for Young Readers) Random Hse. Children's Bks.

Green, Rich. Pearlsus. 2007. 140p. 20.95 (978-0-595-91189-9(7)) iUniverse, Inc.

Green with Envy. 2014. (Unicorn Magic Ser.: 3). (ENG., Illus.). 144p. (J). (gr. 1-4). pap. 5.99 (978-1-4424-9826-6(9), Aladdin) Simon & Schuster Children's Publishing.

Greenawalt, Kelly. I Am Truly. Rauscher, Amariah, illus. 2017. (ENG.). 40p. (J). (gr. -1-k). 16.99 (978-1-338-16720-7(0), Orchard Bks.) Scholastic, Inc.

Greene, Stephanie. A Pocketful of Princess Posey: First Grade Parade-Perfect Present-Next-Door Dog. Sisson, Stéphanie Roth, illus. 2014. (Princess Posey, First Grader Ser.). (ENG.). 288p. (J). (gr. k-3). 8.99 (978-0-14-751472-1(X), Puffin Books) Penguin Young Readers Group.

—Princess Posey & the Christmas Magic. 2013. (Princess Posey, First Grader Ser.: 7). (ENG.). 96p. (J). (gr. k-3). pap. 4.99 (978-0-14-242734-7(9), Puffin Books) Penguin Young Readers Group.

—Princess Posey & the Christmas Magic. Sisson, Stéphanie Roth, illus. 2013. (Princess Posey, First Grader Ser.: 7). (ENG.). 96p. (J). (gr. k-3). 13.99 (978-0-399-16363-0(8), G.P. Putnam's Sons Books for Young Readers) Penguin Young Readers Group.

—Princess Posey & the First-Grade Boys. Sisson, Stéphanie Roth, illus. 2014. (Princess Posey, First Grader Ser.: 8). (ENG.). 96p. (J). (gr. k-3). pap. 5.99 (978-0-14-242735-4(7), Puffin Books) Penguin Young Readers Group.

Greenway, Beth. A True Princess of Hawai'i. Yee, Tammy, illus. 2017. (ENG & SPA.). 32p. (J). (gr. k-3). 17.95 (978-1-62855-948-4(9)) Arbordale Publishing.

—Una Verdadera Princesa de Hawái. Yee, Tammy, illus. 2017. (SPA.). 32p. (J). (gr. k-3). pap. 9.95 (978-1-62855-950-7(0)) Arbordale Publishing.

Gregg, Stacy. The Princess & the Foal. 2015. (ENG.). 272p. (J). (gr. 5). pap. 7.99 (978-0-14-751242-0(5), Puffin Books) Penguin Young Readers Group.

Grey, Chelsea Gillian. Princess Colors. 2004. (Early Learning Ser.). (Illus.). 36p. (J). (gr. -1-3). 12.99 incl. audio compact disk (978-1-59069-370-4(1), 1A102) Studio Mouse LLC.

Grey, Mini. The Very Smart Pea & the Princess-To-Be. 2011. (ENG.). 32p. (J). (gr. k-3). pap. 7.99 (978-0-375-87370-6(8), Dragonfly Bks.) Random Hse. Children's Bks.

Gribble, Julie. Bubblegum Princess. Hanson, Lori, illus. 2013. 32p. (J). 16.99 (978-0-9890914-0-4(6)) NY Media Works, LLC.

Griffin, Casey. Secrets of a Reluctant Princess. 2017. (ENG.). 354p. (YA). pap. 9.99 (978-1-63375-593-2(2), 9781633755932) Entangled Publishing, LLC.

Grimm, J. & W. & Grimm, J. The Frog Prince: Or Iron Henry. Hager, Christian & Schroeder, Binette, illus. 2013. (ENG.). 32p. (J). (gr. -1-3). 17.95 (978-0-7358-4140-6(3)) North-South Bks., Inc.

Grimm, Jacob & Grimm, Wilhelm. Snow White. Greban, Quentin, illus. 2013. (ENG.). 32p. (J). (gr. -1-3). pap. 7.95 (978-0-7358-4116-1(0)) North-South Bks., Inc.

Grimm, Jacob & Grimm, Wilhelm K. Sleeping Beauty / La Bella Durmiente. 2004. (Illus.). (J). (978-1-933530-18-5(9)) Bingo Bks., Inc.

Grimm, Jacob, et al. Princess Tales, 4 bks., Set. Deru, Myriam et al, illus. 2007. (Abbeville Classic Fairy Tales Ser.). (ENG.). 112p. (J). (gr. -1-3). 19.95 (978-0-7892-0950-4(0)) Abbeville Pr., Inc.

Grizzard, Sue H. Princess Caylee: An Incredible Birthday Wish Come True. 2009. 44p. pap. 19.95 (978-1-4490-4001-7(2)) AuthorHouse.

Guerrera, Jeannette D. The Pot of Gold. 2012. 20p. pap. 17.99 (978-1-4685-5883-8(8)) AuthorHouse.

Guillain, Charlotte. The Frog Prince Saves Sleeping Beauty. Widdowson, Dan, illus. 2016. (Fairy Tale Mix-Ups Ser.). (ENG.). 24p. (gr. k-2). lib. bdg. 23.32 (978-1-4109-8302-2(1)) Heinemann-Raintree.

Guo, Amy. Vhonk. 2012. 588p. pap. 34.95 (978-1-4626-9981-0(2)) America Star Bks.

Hack, Brittany. The Glitter Princess. 2012. 24p. 24.95 (978-1-4626-6638-6(8)) America Star Bks.

Haddix, Margaret Peterson. Just Ella. 2015. (Palace Chronicles Ser.: 1). (ENG., Illus.). 208p. (YA). (gr. 7). pap. 10.99 (978-1-4814-2021-1(6), Simon & Schuster Bks. For Young Readers) Simon & Schuster Bks. For Young Readers.

—Palace of Lies. 2015. (Palace Chronicles Ser.: 3). (ENG., Illus.). 368p. (YA). (gr. 7). 17.99 (978-1-4424-4281-8(6)) Simon & Schuster Children's Publishing.

—Palace of Mirrors. 2010. (Palace Chronicles Ser.: 2). (ENG.). 320p. (J). (gr. 5-9). pap. 7.99 (978-1-4424-0667-4(4), Simon & Schuster Bks. For Young Readers) Simon & Schuster Bks. For Young Readers.

Hahn, Rebecca. A Creature of Moonlight. 2014. (ENG.). 224p. (YA). (gr. 7-12). 17.99 (978-0-544-10935-3(X), HMH Books For Young Readers) Houghton Mifflin Harcourt Publishing Co.

Haile, Carol J. The Princess Tree: A Tale of Fairies, Elves & Magic. l.t. ed. 2005. (ESK., Illus.). 32p. (J). 19.95 (978-0-9711236-1-8(6)) Firenze Pr.

Hale, Shannon. The Forgotten Sisters. 2015. (Princess Academy Ser.: 3). (ENG.). 336p. (YA). (gr. 5-8). 17.99 (978-1-61963-485-5(6), 9781619634855, Bloomsbury USA Childrens) Bloomsbury Publishing USA.

—The Forgotten Sisters. 2016. (Princess Academy Ser.: 3). (J). lib. bdg. 18.40 (978-0-606-38441-4(3)) Turtleback Bks.

—The Goose Girl. (Books of Bayern Ser.: No. 2). (ENG., (YA). 2003. Illus.). 400p. (gr. 5-18). 18.99 (978-1-58234-843-8(X), 9781582348438) 2005. 432p. (gr. 7-17). reprint ed. pap. 9.99 (978-1-58234-990-9(8), 9781582349909) Bloomsbury Publishing USA. (Bloomsbury USA Childrens).

—Princess Academy. (Princess Academy Ser.: 1). (ENG.). (YA). (gr. 5-8). 2005. 320p. 17.99 (978-1-58234-993-0(2), 9781582349930) 2nd. ed. 2015. 336p. pap. 7.99 (978-1-61963-613-2(1), 9781619636132) Bloomsbury Publishing USA. (Bloomsbury USA Childrens).

—Princess Academy. 2009. (Princess Academy Ser.: No. 1). 8.86 (978-0-7848-2867-0(9), Everbind) Marco Bk. Co.

—Princess Academy. 2007. (Princess Academy Ser.: No. 1). 314p. (gr. 5-9). 18.00 (978-0-7569-8180-8(8)) Perfection Learning Corp.

—Princess Academy. (Princess Academy Ser.: No. 1). (978-0-439-88811-0(5), Scholastic) Scholastic, Inc.

—Princess Academy. l.t. ed. 2006. (Princess Academy Ser.: No. 1). 339p. (J). (gr. 5-9). 23.95 (978-0-7862-8733-8(0)) Thorndike Pr.

—Princess Academy. 2015. (Princess Academy Ser.: 1). (YA). lib. bdg. 18.40 (978-0-606-36438-6(2)) Turtleback Bks.

—Princess Academy - The Forgotten Sisters. 2016. (Princess Academy Ser.: 3). (ENG.). 352p. (J). pap. 7.99 (978-1-61963-933-1(5), 9781619639331, Bloomsbury USA Childrens) Bloomsbury Publishing USA.

Hale, Shannon & Hale, Dean. The Princess in Black. Pham, LeUyen, illus. (Princess in Black Ser.). (ENG.). 96p. (J). (gr. k-3). 2015. pap. 6.99 (978-0-7636-7888-3(0)) 2014. 14.99 (978-0-7636-6510-4(X)) Candlewick Pr.

—The Princess in Black. 2015. (Princess in Black Ser.: 1). lib. bdg. 17.20 (978-0-606-36863-6(9)) Turtleback Bks.

—The Princess in Black & the Hungry Bunny Horde. Pham, LeUyen, illus. 2016. (Princess in Black Ser.: 3). (ENG.). (J). (gr. k-3). 96p. pap. 6.99 (978-0-7636-9089-2(9)); 85p. 14.99 (978-0-7636-6513-5(4)) Candlewick Pr.

—The Princess in Black & the Hungry Bunny Horde. Pham, LeUyen, illus. 2016. (Princess in Black Ser.: 3). (ENG.). 85p. (J). (gr. k-3). 17.20 (978-0-606-39109-2(6)) Turtleback Bks.

—The Princess in Black & the Mysterious Playdate. Pham, LeUyen, illus. 2017. (Princess in Black Ser.: 5). (ENG.). 96p. (J). (gr. k-3). 14.99 **(978-0-7636-8826-4(6))** Candlewick Pr.

—The Princess in Black & the Perfect Princess Party. Pham, LeUyen, illus. (Princess in Black Ser.). (ENG.). 96p. (J). (gr. k-3). 2016. pap. 6.99 (978-0-7636-8758-8(8)) 2015. 14.99 (978-0-7636-6511-1(8)) Candlewick Pr.

—The Princess in Black & the Perfect Princess Party. 2016. (Princess in Black Ser.: 2). lib. bdg. 17.20 (978-0-606-37945-8(2)) Turtleback Bks.

—The Princess in Black Takes a Vacation. Pham, LeUyen, illus. 2016. (Princess in Black Ser.). (ENG.). 96p. (J). (gr. k-3). 14.99 (978-0-7636-6512-8(6)) Candlewick Pr.

—The Princess in Black Takes a Vacation. 2017. (Princess in Black Ser.: 4). (ENG.). (J). (gr. k-3). lib. bdg. 17.20 **(978-0-606-39839-8(2))** Turtleback Bks.

Haley, Patty. Princess Pearl's Party (6 Pack) Woodford-Robinson, Rieko, illus. 2010. (ENG.). 12p. (gr. k-2). pap. (978-1-61181-050-9(7), Kaeden Bks.) Kaeden Corp.

Hall, Kirsten. I'm a Princess. DeRosa, Dee, illus. 2004. (My First Reader Ser.). (ENG.). 32p. (J). (gr. k-1). pap. 3.95 (978-0-516-24630-7(5), Children's Pr.) Scholastic Library Publishing.

Halsted, John D., ed. & compiled by. Peachy Princesses & Impetuous Princes - for Girls Only! Halsted, John D., compiled by. 2013. 386p. pap. (978-1-909302-40-2(6)) Abela Publishing.

Hanak, Elizabeth. The Princess of Cliffwood. 2012. 34p. pap. (978-1-105-30501-6(5)) Lulu.com.

Handa, Nimret. Good Night Stories. 2004. (Illus.). 20p. (J). (978-81-291-0373-4(7)) Rupa & Co.

Hanna, Virginie. The Secret Life of Princesses. Delanssay, Cathy, illus. 2009. 26p. (J). (gr. -1-3). 17.99 (978-0-8437-1476-0(X)) Hammond World Atlas Corp.

Hapka, Catherine, pseud. Disney Sofia the First - Sweet Dreams, Sofia! Cardona, Jose, illus. 2015. (ENG.). 12p. (J). (gr. -1-k). 12.99 (978-0-7944-3383-3(9)) Studio Fun International.

—The Enchanted Science Fair. 2014. (Sofia the First Ser.). (J). lib. bdg. 14.75 (978-0-606-35911-5(7)) Turtleback Bks.

—Holiday in Enchancia. 2013. (Sofia the First Ser.). (J). lib. bdg. 24.50 (978-0-606-32289-8(2), Turtleback) Turtleback Bks.

Hapka, Catherine, pseud & Disney Book Group Staff. The Amulet & the Anthem. Disney Storybook Art Team, illus. 2013. (ENG.). 24p. (J). (gr. -1-k). pap. 4.99 (978-1-4231-8023-4(2)) Disney Pr.

—Holiday in Enchancia. Disney Storybook Art Team, illus. 2013. (ENG.). 40p. (J). (gr. -1-k). 12.99 (978-1-4231-8396-9(7)) Disney Pr.

—Sofia the First Princesses to the Rescue! Purchase Includes a Digital Song! Disney Storybook Artists Staff & Lee, Grace, illus. 2014. (ENG.). 40p. (J). (gr. -1-k). 12.99 (978-1-4231-9431-6(4)) Disney Pr.

Hapka, Cathy, pseud. Disney Sofia the First - Sofia's Magical World: The First Hidden Stories. 2015. (Hidden Stories Ser.: 2). (ENG.). 10p. (J). (gr. -1-1). 15.99 (978-0-7944-3201-0(8), Reader's Digest Children's Bks.) Studio Fun International.

—Pretend & Play Kitty: With Real Crown You Can Wear! Borlasca, Hector, illus. 2004. (Role Play Ser.). 10p. (J). (gr. -1-18). bds. 6.99 (978-1-57151-742-5(1)) Playhouse Publishing.

—The Royal Games. 2014. (Sofia the First Ser.). (J). lib. bdg. 13.55 (978-0-606-34098-4(X), Turtleback) Turtleback Bks.

Hapka, Cathy, pseud & Disney Book Group Staff. Sofia Makes a Friend. Disney Storybook Artists Staff, illus. 2013. (World of Reading Ser.). (ENG.). 32p. (J). (gr. -1-k). pap. 3.99 (978-1-4231-6408-1(3)) Disney Pr.

Hapka, Cathy, pseud, et al. The Royal Slumber Party. Disney Storybook Art Team, illus. 2013. (ENG.). 24p. (J). (gr. -1-k). pap. 3.99 (978-1-4231-6410-4(5)) Disney Pr.

Hargreaves, Adam. Little Miss Princess. 2011. (Mr. Men & Little Miss Ser.). (ENG.). 32p. (J). (gr. -1-2). mass mkt. 4.99 (978-0-8431-9834-8(6), Price Stern Sloan) Penguin Young Readers Group.

Hargreaves, Roger. Little Miss Princess & the Very Special Wedding. 2011. (Mr. Men & Little Miss Ser.). (ENG., Illus.). 24p. (J). (gr. -1-3). (978-1-4052-5996-5(5)) Egmont Bks., Ltd.

—Little Miss Splendid & the Princess. Hargreaves, Adam, illus. 2007. (Mr. Men & Little Miss Ser.). (ENG.). 32p. (J). (gr. -1-2). mass mkt. 4.99 (978-0-8431-2489-7(X), Price Stern Sloan) Penguin Young Readers Group.

Harper, Charise Mericle & Mericle Harper, Charise. Princess Patty Finds Her Prince. 2014. (ENG., Illus.). 48p. (J). (gr. -1-k). 16.99 (978-1-4231-0804-7(3)) Hyperion Bks. for Children.

Harris, Kandi. Princess, the Future Queen: A Mother's Guidance. Rippon, Jor-El, illus. l.t. ed. 2006. 32p. (J). bds. 12.99 (978-0-9770331-1-9(2)) Harris, K Publishing, Inc.

Harrison, Christy Gremore. Once upon A Monday. 2010. 40p. pap. 16.99 (978-1-4490-5854-8(X)) AuthorHouse.

Harrison, Mette Ivie. The Princess & the Bear. 2010. (ENG.). 352p. (YA). (gr. 8). pap. 8.99 (978-0-06-155316-5(6), HarperTeen) HarperCollins Pubs.

—The Princess & the Hound. 2008. (ENG.). 432p. (YA). (gr. 8). pap. 8.99 (978-0-06-113189-9(X), HarperTeen) HarperCollins Pubs.

Harrison, Paul. The Perfect Prince. Mason, Sue, illus. 2009. (ENG.). 32p. (J). (gr. -1-k). pap. (978-1-84089-534-6(9)) Zero to Ten, Ltd.

Harrison, Paula. The Golden Shell. 2014. (Rescue Princesses Ser.: 12). lib. bdg. 14.75 (978-0-606-35838-5(2)) Turtleback Bks.

—The Ice Diamond. 2014. (Rescue Princesses Ser.: 1). (ENG.). 128p. (J). (gr. 2-5). pap. 4.99 (978-0-545-66164-5(1), Scholastic Paperbacks) Scholastic, Inc.

—The Ice Diamond. 2014. (Rescue Princesses Ser.: 10). lib. bdg. 14.75 (978-0-606-35422-6(0)) Turtleback Bks.

—The Lost Gold. 2013. (Rescue Princesses Ser.: 7). (ENG.). 128p. (J). (gr. 2-5). pap. 4.99 (978-0-545-50920-6(3), Scholastic Paperbacks) Scholastic, Inc.

—The Lost Gold. 2013. (Rescue Princesses Ser.: 7). lib. bdg. 14.75 (978-0-606-32374-1(0), Turtleback) Turtleback Bks.

—The Magic Rings. 2013. (Rescue Princesses Ser.: 6). (ENG., Illus.). 128p. (J). (gr. 2-5). pap. 4.99 (978-0-545-50918-3(1), Scholastic Paperbacks) Scholastic, Inc.

—The Magic Rings. 2013. (Rescue Princesses Ser.: 6). lib. bdg. 14.75 (978-0-606-32373-4(2), Turtleback) Turtleback Bks.

—The Moonlight Mystery. 2013. (Rescue Princesses Ser.: 3). (ENG., Illus.). 128p. (J). (gr. 2-5). pap. 4.99 (978-0-545-50915-2(7), Scholastic Paperbacks) Scholastic, Inc.

—The Moonlight Mystery. 2013. (Rescue Princesses Ser.: 3). lib. bdg. 14.75 (978-0-606-31988-1(3), Turtleback) Turtleback Bks.

—The Rainbow Opal. 2014. (Rescue Princesses Ser.: 11). lib. bdg. 14.75 (978-0-606-35837-8(4)) Turtleback Bks.

—Secret Promise. 2013. (Rescue Princesses Ser.: 1). (ENG., Illus.). 128p. (J). (gr. 2-5). pap. 4.99 (978-0-545-50913-8(0), Scholastic Paperbacks) Scholastic, Inc.

—Secret Promise. 2013. (Rescue Princesses Ser.: 1). lib. bdg. 14.75 (978-0-606-31986-7(7), Turtleback) Turtleback Bks.

—The Shimmering Stone. 2013. (Rescue Princesses Ser.: 8). (ENG.). 128p. (J). (gr. 2-5). pap. 4.99 (978-0-545-50922-0(X), Scholastic Paperbacks) Scholastic, Inc.

—The Shimmering Stone. 2013. (Rescue Princesses Ser.: 8). lib. bdg. 14.75 (978-0-606-32375-8(9), Turtleback) Turtleback Bks.

—The Silver Locket. 2014. (Rescue Princesses Ser.: 9). (ENG.). 128p. (J). (gr. 2-5). pap. 4.99 (978-0-545-66162-1(5), Scholastic Paperbacks) Scholastic, Inc.

—The Snow Jewel. 2013. (Rescue Princesses Ser.: 5). (ENG.). 128p. (J). (gr. 2-5). pap. 4.99 (978-0-545-50917-6(3), Scholastic Paperbacks) Scholastic, Inc.

—The Snow Jewel. 2013. (Rescue Princesses Ser.: 5). lib. bdg. 14.75 (978-0-606-32372-7(4), Turtleback) Turtleback Bks.

—The Stolen Crystals. 2013. (Rescue Princesses Ser.: 4). (ENG.). 128p. (J). (gr. 2-5). pap. 4.99 (978-0-545-50916-9(5), Scholastic Paperbacks) Scholastic, Inc.

—The Stolen Crystals. 2013. (Rescue Princesses Ser.: 4). lib. bdg. 14.75 (978-0-606-31989-8(1), Turtleback) Turtleback Bks.

—Wishing Pearl. 2013. (Rescue Princesses Ser.: 2). (ENG., Illus.). 128p. (J). (gr. 2-5). pap. 4.99 (978-0-545-50914-5(9), Scholastic Paperbacks) Scholastic, Inc.

—Wishing Pearl. 2013. (Rescue Princesses Ser.: 2). lib. bdg. 14.75 (978-0-606-31987-4(5), Turtleback) Turtleback Bks.

Hart, Caryl. The Princess & the Giant. Warburton, Sarah, illus. 2015. (ENG.). 32p. (J). (gr. -1-2). 16.99 (978-0-7636-8007-7(9), Nosy Crow) Candlewick Pr.

—The Princess & the Peas. Warburton, Sarah, illus. 2013. (ENG.). 32p. (J). (gr. -1-2). 16.99 (978-0-7636-6532-6(0), Nosy Crow) Candlewick Pr.

—The Princess & the Presents. Warburton, Sarah, illus. 2014. (ENG.). 32p. (J). (gr. -1-2). 16.99 (978-0-7636-7398-7(6), Nosy Crow) Candlewick Pr.

Hasbro. My Little Pony: Chapter Book Bind-Up. 2016. (ENG., Illus.). 416p. (J). (gr. 3-7). pap. 12.99 (978-0-316-27259-9(0)) Little, Brown Bks. for Young Readers.

Haskell, Merrie. Handbook for Dragon Slayers. 2013. (ENG.). 336p. (J). (gr. 3-7). 16.99 (978-0-06-200816-9(1)) HarperCollins Pubs.

—The Princess Curse. (ENG.). (J). (gr. 3-7). 2013. 352p. pap. 6.99 (978-0-06-200815-2(3)) 2011. 336p. 16.99 (978-0-06-200813-8(7)) HarperCollins Pubs.

Hatley, Shannon. The Young Princess & the Brave Knight. 2012. 28p. pap. 24.95 (978-1-4626-6779-6(1)) America Star Bks.

Haugaard, Erik. Prince Boghole. 2013. (ENG., Illus.). 32p. (J). (gr. -1-3). 16.99 (978-1-4814-2167-6(0), Simon & Schuster Bks. For Young Readers) Simon & Schuster Bks. For Young Readers.

Hawkins, A. D. The Time Princess. 2013. 208p. pap. (978-1-78299-661-3(3)) FeedARead.com.

Hawkins, Delta Michelle. Cassandra's Journey. 2012. 28p. pap. 24.95 (978-1-4626-9566-9(3)) America Star Bks.

Hawkins, Mia K. The Broken Guild of Twelve Pirates, 1 vol. 2009. 201p. pap. 24.95 (978-1-61546-333-6(X)) PublishAmerica, Inc.

Hayes, Kimberly Wasserman. Princesses & Dinosaurs. 2011. (Illus.). 28p. pap. 14.09 (978-1-4567-8823-0(X)) AuthorHouse.

Heapy, Teresa. Very Little Sleeping Beauty. Heap, Sue, illus. 2016. (Very Little Ser.). (ENG.). 32p. (J). (gr. -1-3). 16.99 (978-0-544-28279-7(5), HMH Books For Young Readers) Houghton Mifflin Harcourt Publishing Co.

Hegarty, Pat. If I Were a... Princess. Pope, Liz & Pope, Kate, illus. 2008. 12p. (J). (gr. -1). bds. 6.95 (978-1-58925-838-9(X)) Tiger Tales.

Hegerhorst, Bethany. The Baseball Princess: Samantha's Summer & the Unicorn Flu. Abbott, Kristin, illus. 2012. 32p. (J). (978-0-9871281-5-7(9)) Murray Bks.

Heide, Florence Parry. Princess Hyacinth. Smith, Lane, illus. 2009. (ENG.). 48p. (J). (gr. -1-3). 17.99 (978-0-375-84501-7(1), Schwartz & Wade Bks.) Random Hse. Children's Bks.

—Princess Hyacinth (the Surprising Tale of a Girl Who Floated) Smith, Lane, illus. 2016. (ENG.). 48p. (J). (gr. -1-3). 7.99 (978-0-553-53804-5(7), Dragonfly Bks.) Random Hse. Children's Bks.

Hendesi, Roya. The Ancient Queendom. 2011. 52p. pap. 29.05 (978-1-4568-2783-0(9)) Xlibris Corp.

Herman, Gail & Studio Iboix Staff. Ariel: The Birthday Surprise, 1 vol. 2012. (Disney Princess Ser.). (ENG., Illus.). 96p. (J). (gr. 2-5). 24.21 (978-1-59961-877-7(X)) Spotlight.

Hewitt, Megan. Eagle Rises. 2013. 118p. (J). pap. 12.99 (978-1-300-55242-0(5)) Lulu Pr., Inc.

Hicks, John. Divided World. 2003. 192p. (YA). per. 6.50 (978-0-9742829-1-6(X)) Quiet Man Publishing.

Hidden. 2014. (ENG., Illus.). 384p. (YA). (gr. 7). 17.99 (978-1-4424-8300-2(8), Simon & Schuster/Paula Wiseman Bks.) Simon & Schuster/Paula Wiseman Bks.

Hiebert, Elfrieda H. & Juel, Connie. The Princess Who Couldn't Cry. (Little Book Practice Reader Ser.). (J). (978-0-8136-0887-7(2)) Modern Curriculum Pr.

Higgins, M. G. Rodeo Princess. 2015. (Gravel Road Ser.). (YA). lib. bdg. 20.80 (978-0-606-37231-2(8)) Turtleback Bks.

Higgins, Wendy. The Great Hunt. (YA). (gr. 8). 2017. 448p. pap. 9.99 (978-0-06-238134-7(2)) 2016. 432p. 17.99 (978-0-06-238133-0(4)) HarperCollins Pubs. (HarperTeen).

—The Great Pursuit. 2017. 512p. (YA). (gr. 8). 17.99 (978-0-06-238136-1(9), HarperTeen) HarperCollins Pubs.

Hilburn, L. M. Little Princesses to the Rescue. 2008. 24p. pap. 24.95 (978-1-60672-783-6(4)) America Star Bks.

Himekawa, Akira. The Legend of Zelda, Vol. 10. Himekawa, Akira, illus. 2010. (ENG., Illus.). 200p. (J). (gr. 2-5). pap. 9.99 (978-1-4215-3724-5(9)) Viz Media.

Hinchliffe, Stuart Jarod. Princess Tiffany Arabella & the Time of Dreams. 2009. 196p. 24.50 *(978-1-60860-627-6(9),* Strategic Bk. Publishing) Strategic Book Publishing & Rights Agency (SBPRA).
Hinkler Books, ed. The Little Princess Tea Party. 2012. 40p. (J). 19.99 *(978-1-74308-402-1(1))* Hinkler Bks. Pty. Ltd. AUS. Dist: Ideals Pubns.
—My Treasury of Princess Tales. 2012. 192p. (J). 12.99 *(978-1-74308-000-9(X))* Hinkler Bks. Pty. Ltd. AUS. Dist: Ideals Pubns.
Hinkler Books Staff. CD Storybook: Beauty & the Beast; The Little Mermaid; Cinderella; Snow White. rev. ed. 2004. (Illus.). 128p. (J). (gr. 4-12). 14.95 incl. cd-rom *(978-1-86515-754-2(6))* Hinkler Bks. Pty. Ltd. AUS. Dist: Penton Overseas, Inc.
Hocking, Amanda. Ascend. 2012. (Trylle Novel Ser.: 3). (ENG.). 336p. (YA). (gr. 7). pap. 8.99 *(978-1-250-00633-2(3),* 9781250006332, St. Martin's Griffin) St. Martin's Pr.
—Ascend. l.t. ed. 2012. (Trylle Trilogy: Bk. 3). (ENG.). 412p. (J). (gr. 8-12). 23.99 *(978-1-4104-5014-2(7))* Thorndike Pr.
—Switched. 2012. (Trylle Novel Ser.: 1). (ENG.). 336p. (YA). (gr. 7). pap. 8.99 *(978-1-250-00631-8(7),* 9781250006318, St. Martin's Griffin) St. Martin's Pr.
—Torn. 2012. (Trylle Novel Ser.: 2). (ENG.). 336p. (YA). (gr. 7-12). pap. 8.99 *(978-1-250-00632-5(5),* 9781250006325, St. Martin's Griffin) St. Martin's Pr.
—Torn. l.t. ed. 2012. (Trylle Trilogy: Bk. 2). (ENG.). 450p. (J). (gr. 7-12). 23.99 *(978-1-4104-5013-5(9))* Thorndike Pr.
Hodge, A. D. The Saucy Bossy Princess. 2012. 32p. *(978-1-4602-1304-9(1));* pap. *(978-1-4602-1305-6(X))* FriesenPress.
Hodgson, Mona. The Princess Twins & the Puppy, 1 vol. Olson, Julie, illus. 2015. (I Can Read! / Princess Twins Ser.). (ENG.). 32p. (J). pap. 3.99 *(978-0-310-75064-2(4))* Zonderkidz.
—The Princess Twins Collection, 1 vol. Olson, Julie, illus. 2017. (I Can Read! / Princess Twins Ser.). (ENG.). 128p. (J). 12.99 *(978-0-310-75319-3(8))* Zonderkidz.
—The Princess Twins Play in the Garden, 1 vol. Olson, Julie, illus. 2015. (I Can Read! / Princess Twins Ser.). (ENG.). 32p. (J). pap. 3.99 *(978-0-310-75050-5(4))* Zonderkidz.
Hodgson, Mona Gansberg. The Princess Twins & the Puppy, 1 vol. Hansen, Red, illus. 2011. (I Can Read! / Princess Twins Ser.). (ENG.). 32p. (J). pap. 3.99 *(978-0-310-72709-5(X))* Zonderkidz.
Hoffman, Mary. Princess Grace. Van Wright, Cornelius & Hu, Ying-Hwa, illus. 2008. (ENG.). 32p. (J). (gr. -1-3). 18.99 *(978-0-8037-3260-5(0),* Dial Bks) Penguin Young Readers Group.
—The Twelve Dancing Princesses. Clara, Miss, illus. 2013. (ENG.). 40p. (J). (gr. 1-5). 17.99 *(978-1-84686-966-2(8))* Barefoot Bks., Inc.
Holland, Dwayne K. Princess Laura & the Magic Waterfall. 2010. 42p. pap. 15.50 *(978-1-60860-744-0(5),* Strategic Bk. Publishing) Strategic Book Publishing & Rights Agency (SBPRA).
Holub, Joan. Isabel Saves the Prince: Based on a True Story of Isabel I of Spain. Aleshina, Nonna, illus. 2007. (Young Princesses Around the World Ser.). (ENG.). 48p. (J). (gr. 1-3). pap. 13.99 *(978-0-689-87197-9(X),* Simon Spotlight) Simon Spotlight.
Holub, Joan & Williams, Suzanne. Artemis the Loyal. 2011. (Goddess Girls Ser.: 7). (ENG.). 288p. (J). (gr. 3-7). pap. 7.99 *(978-1-4424-3377-9(9),* Aladdin) Simon & Schuster Children's Publishing.
Holub, Joan, et al. Aphrodite the Diva. 2011. (Goddess Girls Ser.: 6). (ENG.). 288p. (J). (gr. 3-7). pap. 7.99 *(978-1-4424-2100-4(2),* Aladdin) Simon & Schuster Children's Publishing.
Homberg, Ruth. Across the Sea (Disney Frozen) Random House Disney Staff, illus. 2016. (Step into Reading Ser.). (ENG.). 24p. (J). (gr. -1-1). 4.99 *(978-0-7364-3398-3(8),* RH/Disney) Random Hse. Children's Bks.
—Jewels for a Princess. 2012. (Disney Princess Step into Reading Ser.). lib. bdg. 13.55 *(978-0-606-26395-5(0),* Turtleback) Turtleback Bks.
—Jewels for a Princess (Disney Princess) Random House Disney Staff, illus. 2012. (Step into Reading Ser.). (ENG.). 32p. (J). (gr. -1-1). pap. 3.99 *(978-0-7364-2908-5(5),* RH/Disney) Random Hse. Children's Bks.
—The Little Mermaid. 2013. (Disney Princess Step into Reading Ser.). lib. bdg. 13.55 *(978-0-606-32202-7(7),* Turtleback) Turtleback Bks.
—The Little Mermaid Step into Reading (Disney Princess) RH Disney Staff, illus. 2013. (Step into Reading Ser.). (ENG.). 32p. (J). (gr. -1-1). 3.99 *(978-0-7364-8128-1(1),* RH/Disney) Random Hse. Children's Bks.
Hood, Ann. Anastasia Romanov: The Last Grand Duchess. Zilber, Denis, illus. 2014. (Treasure Chest Ser.: 10). (ENG.). 240p. (J). (gr. 3-7). 15.99 *(978-0-448-46770-2(4));*No. 10. 6.99 *(978-0-448-46771-9(2))* Penguin Young Readers Group. (Grosset & Dunlap).
Hopkins, Douglas. Princess June & the Shadow Pirates, 1 vol. 2007. (ENG., Illus.). 32p. (J). (gr. -1-2). per. 8.95 *(978-1-894294-88-1(2),* Tuckamore Bks) Creative Bk. Publishing CAN. Dist: Orca Bk. Pubs. USA.
Hopper, Celia Brashear. Blade & the Story of the Pearl Princess. 2004. (J). 15.95 *(978-0-9763093-1-4(9))* Creative Bk. Pubs.
Horowitz, Dave. Twenty-Six Princesses. Horowitz, Dave, illus. 2008. (ENG., Illus.). 32p. (J). (gr. -1-k). 15.99 *(978-0-399-24607-4(X),* G.P. Putnam's Sons Books for Young Readers) Penguin Young Readers Group.
—Twenty-Six Princesses: An Alphabet Story. Horowitz, Dave, illus. 2011. (ENG., Illus.). 32p. (J). (gr. -1-k). pap. 6.99 *(978-0-14-241536-8(7),* Puffin Books) Penguin Young Readers Group.
Howard, Cheryl L. Mikhael the Mighty: Be True to Who You Are & You Can Never Go Wrong. 2009. 52p. pap. 18.50 *(978-1-60860-760-0(7),* Strategic Bk. Publishing) Strategic Book Publishing & Rights Agency (SBPRA).
Howard, Peggy Ann. Zorees: Land of Dreams. 2007. (YA). per. 16.95 *(978-0-9795519-0-1(0))* Dream Scape Publishing, LLC.
Howell, Laura. Princess & the Pea. 2009. (Young Reading 1 Ser.). 48p. (J). 6.99 *(978-0-7945-2587-3(3),* Usborne) EDC Publishing.
Howland, Naomi. The Princess Says Goodnight. Small, David, illus. 2010. 32p. (J). (gr. -1-2). (ENG.). 16.99 *(978-0-06-145525-4(3));* lib. bdg. 17.89 *(978-0-06-145526-1(1))* HarperCollins Pubs.
Hughes, Carol. The Princess & the Unicorn. 2010. (ENG.). 288p. (J). (gr. 3-7). 7.99 *(978-0-375-85563-4(7),* Bluefire) Random Hse. Children's Bks.
Hulst, W. G. van de & Hulst, Willem G. van de, illus. The Search for Christmas. 2014. (J). *(978-1-928136-12-5(5))* Inheritance Pubns.
Humphreys, Audrey. The Dragon Princess. 2012. 24p. pap. 24.99 *(978-1-4691-6554-7(6))* Xlibris Corp.
Humphries, Jennifer & DiCampli, Nicki. Rebekah Grace the Practically Perfect Princess. 2012. (Illus.). 34p. (YA). pap. 9.95 *(978-1-60131-138-2(9),* Castlebridge Bks.) Big Tent Bks.
Hurt, John Washington, reader. Rabbit Ears World Tales. 2007. (J). 34.99 *(978-0-7393-7549-5(0))* Findaway World, LLC.
Hush: An Irish Princess' Tale. 2014. (ENG., Illus.). 336p. (YA). (gr. 7). pap. 11.99 *(978-1-4424-9496-1(4),* Simon & Schuster/Paula Wiseman Bks.) Simon & Schuster/Paula Wiseman Bks.
I-Haun. Real - Fake Princess. 2006. (Real/Fake Princess Ser.). (ENG., Illus.). 200p. (YA). pap. 9.95 *(978-1-59796-080-9(2))* DrMaster Pubns. Inc.
—Real/Fake Princess, Vol. 4. Zhao, Yun, tr. 2007. (Real/Fake Princess Ser.). (ENG., Illus.). 200p. pap. 9.95 *(978-1-59796-082-3(9))* DrMaster Pubns. Inc.
I-Huan. Real - Fake Princess, Set, Vols. 1-5. 2007. (ENG., Illus.). 200p. (YA). pap. 34.95 *(978-1-59796-074-8(8))* DrMaster Pubns. Inc.
I-Huan & I-Haun. Real Fake Princess, Vol. 3. 2006. (Real/Fake Princess Ser.). (ENG., Illus.). 200p. (YA). pap. 9.95 *(978-1-59796-081-6(0))* DrMaster Pubns. Inc.
Ibbotson, Eva. The Ogre of Oglefort. 2012. (ENG.). 272p. (J). (gr. 3-7). pap. 6.99 *(978-0-14-242135-2(9),* Puffin Books) Penguin Young Readers Group.
Illustrated Stories of Princes & Princesses. 2015. (Illustrated Stories Ser.). (ENG.). (J). 19.99 *(978-0-7945-3416-5(3),* Usborne) EDC Publishing.
Inkpen, Mick. Lullabyhullaballoo! Inkpen, Mick, illus. 2007. (ENG., Illus.). 32p. (J). (gr. 13-17). pap. 10.99 *(978-0-340-93108-0(6))* Hodder & Stoughton GBR. Dist: Hachette Bk. Group.
An Inner Child Speaks. 2006. (J). 17.99 *(978-0-9779130-0-8(7))* Zy Iman Pubng.
Innis, Amy. The Adventures of Princess Lilyan: The Shimmering Beauty Ball. 2009. 48p. pap. 16.95 *(978-1-60749-318-1(7))* America Star Bks.
Irvine, Patricia McCune. Beyond the Greenest Hill: A Fairy Tale. 2003. 136p. (YA). pap. 11.95 *(978-0-595-26941-9(9))* iUniverse, Inc.
Isadora, Rachel. The Princess & the Pea. 2009. (ENG., Illus.). 32p. (J). (gr. -1-3). pap. 6.99 *(978-0-14-241393-7(3),* Puffin Books) Penguin Young Readers Group.
—The Twelve Dancing Princesses. Isadora, Rachel, illus. 2009. (ENG., Illus.). 32p. (J). (gr. k-3). pap. 6.99 *(978-0-14-241450-7(6),* Puffin Books) Penguin Young Readers Group.
Jackson, Bridgett. The Princess & the Pink Palace: Book Two of Tales from the Creek. 2008. 36p. pap. 16.99 *(978-1-4389-2038-2(5))* AuthorHouse.
Jacobsen, Annie. The Terrible Troll Cat. Hanson, Susan Jo, illus. 2012. 32p. (J). 9.98 *(978-0-9778276-4-0(X))* Pickled Herring Pr.
Jalonen, Nicole. Magical Animal Army Adventures. 2012. 28p. pap. 15.99 *(978-1-4691-7544-7(4))* Xlibris Corp.
James, Kari, adapted by. Barbie & the Magic of Pegasus: A Junior Novelization. 2005. (Illus.). 72p. pap. *(978-0-439-78542-6(1))* Scholastic, Inc.
Jardine, Kathy & Jardine, Ashley. The Durples: Go to School. 2010. 28p. pap. 17.99 *(978-1-4490-3405-4(5))* AuthorHouse.
Jay, Stacey. Of Beast & Beauty. 2014. (ENG.). 400p. (YA). (gr. 9). pap. 9.99 *(978-0-385-74321-1(1),* Ember) Random Hse. Children's Bks.
—Princess of Thorns. 2016. (ENG.). 400p. (YA). (gr. 9). pap. 9.99 *(978-0-385-74323-5(8),* Ember) Random Hse. Children's Bks.
Jeffers, Susan & Ehrlich, Amy. Cinderella. Battcock, Gregory, ed. Jeffers, Susan, illus. 2004. (ENG., Illus.). 32p. (J). (gr. -1-3). 18.99 *(978-0-525-47345-9(9),* Dutton Books for Young Readers) Penguin Young Readers Group.
Jenkins, Emily. Princessland. Tanaka, Yoko, illus. 2017. (ENG.). 32p. (J). 16.99 *(978-0-374-36115-0(0),* 9780374361150, Farrar, Straus & Giroux (BYR)) Farrar, Straus & Giroux.
Jensen, Michael & King, David Powers. Woven. 2015. (ENG., Illus.). 352p. (J). (gr. 7). 18.99 *(978-0-545-68572-6(9),* Scholastic Pr.) Scholastic, Inc.
Jensen, Michael R. & King, David Powers. Woven. 2015. (Illus.). 344p. (J). *(978-0-545-83117-8(2),* Scholastic Pr.) Scholastic, Inc.
Johnson, Amy. The Princess & the Frog. 2010. 24p. 14.93 *(978-1-4269-3712-5(1))* Trafford Publishing.
Johnson, Esther A. The Princess & the Garden. Taylor, Carolyn, illus. 2012. 34p. pap. 19.99 *(978-1-62419-614-0(4))* Salem Author Services.
Johnson, Jacqueline & Young, Jeanna Stolle. Princess Charity's Courageous Heart, 1 vol. Aranda, Omar, illus. 2012. (Princess Parables Ser.). (ENG.). 32p. (J). 14.99 *(978-0-310-72701-9(4))* Zonderkidz.
—Princess Faith's Mysterious Garden, 1 vol. Aranda, Omar, illus. 2012. (Princess Parables Ser.). (ENG.). 32p. (J). 14.99 *(978-0-310-72703-3(0))* Zonderkidz.
Johnson, Jacqueline Kinney & Young, Jeanna. Princess Grace & Poppy, 1 vol. 2012. (I Can Read! / Princess Parables Ser.). (ENG.). 32p. (J). pap. 3.99 *(978-0-310-72677-7(8))* Zonderkidz.
Johnson, Rachel N. No Ordinary Princess. Hill, Jessie, illus. 2012. 32p. pap. 16.97 *(978-1-61204-993-9(1),* Strategic Bk. Publishing) Strategic Book Publishing & Rights Agency (SBPRA).
Johnson, Shane L., illus. OLIVIA la Princesa. 2011. (Olivia TV Tie-In Ser.). (ENG & SPA.). 24p. (J). (gr. -1-2). pap. 3.99 *(978-1-4424-4640-3(4),* Libros Para Ninos) Libros Para Ninos.
—Olivia the Princess. 2011. (Olivia TV Tie-In Ser.). (ENG.). 24p. (J). (gr. -1-2). pap. 3.99 *(978-1-4424-3033-4(8),* Simon Spotlight) Simon Spotlight.
—Princess for a Day: A Pop-Up Storybook. 2011. (Olivia TV Tie-In Ser.). (ENG.). 12p. (J). (gr. -1-1). 17.99 *(978-1-4424-3141-6(5),* Simon Spotlight) Simon Spotlight.
Johnson, Stephen T. My Little Pink Princess Purse. Johnson, Stephen T., illus. 2010. (ENG., Illus.). 16p. (J). (gr. -1-3). 19.99 *(978-1-4169-7979-1(4),* Simon & Schuster/Paula Wiseman Bks.) Simon & Schuster/Paula Wiseman Bks.
Johnson, Vargie. Catherine the Great the Victorious: What Made Them Famous? 2006. 156p. (J). per. 15.00 *(978-1-931195-96-6(X))* KiwE Publishing, Ltd.
Johnson, Young, et al. Princess Hope & the Hidden Treasure, 1 vol. Aranda, Omar, illus. 2012. (I Can Read! / Princess Parables Ser.). (ENG.). 32p. (J). pap. 3.99 *(978-0-310-73250-1(6))* Zonderkidz.
Johnston, E. K. Spindle. 2016. (ENG.). 368p. (YA). (gr. 9-17). 18.99 *(978-1-4847-2228-2(0))* Hyperion Bks. for Children.
Jokisch, Kimberly. I Have Two Homes. 2009. 24p. pap. 11.99 *(978-1-4389-2823-4(8))* AuthorHouse.
Jones, Allan. The Six Crowns: Sargasso Skies. Chalk, Gary, illus. 2013. (Six Crowns Ser.: 5). 176p. (J). (gr. 3-7). 16.99 *(978-0-06-200636-3(3),* Greenwillow Bks.) HarperCollins Pubs.
Jones, Cheri. The Adventures of a Mermaid Princess. 2013. 76p. (gr. -1). pap. 10.84 *(978-1-4907-0598-9(8))* Trafford Publishing.
Jones, Frewin. The Charmed Return. 2011. (Faerie Path Ser.: 6). (ENG.). 368p. (YA). (gr. 8-18). 17.99 *(978-0-06-087161-1(X),* HarperTeen) HarperCollins Pubs.
—Destiny's Path. 2009. (Warrior Princess Ser.: 2). (ENG.). 352p. (YA). (gr. 8-18). 16.99 *(978-0-06-087146-8(6),* HarperTeen) HarperCollins Pubs.
—The Emerald Flame. 2010. (Warrior Princess Ser.: 3). (ENG.). 352p. (YA). (gr. 8-18). 16.99 *(978-0-06-087149-9(0),* HarperTeen) HarperCollins Pubs.
—The Enchanted Quest. 2010. (Faerie Path Ser.: 5). (ENG.). 368p. (YA). (gr. 8-18). 16.99 *(978-0-06-087158-1(X),* HarperTeen) HarperCollins Pubs.
—The Faerie Path Bk. 4: The Immortal Realm. 2010. (Faerie Path Ser.: 4). (ENG.). 368p. (YA). (gr. 8). pap. 9.99 *(978-0-06-087157-4(1),* HarperTeen) HarperCollins Pubs.
—The Lost Queen. (Faerie Path Ser.: 2). (YA). 2008. (ENG.). 352p. (gr. 8). pap. 8.99 *(978-0-06-087107-9(5),* HarperTeen) 2007. 335p. (gr. 7). lib. bdg. 17.89 *(978-0-06-087106-2(7),* Eos) 2007. (ENG.). 352p. (gr. 7-12). 16.99 *(978-0-06-087105-5(9),* Eos) HarperCollins Pubs.
—Warrior Princess. 2009. (YA). 346p. lib. bdg. 17.89 *(978-0-06-087144-4(X));* (ENG.). 352p. (gr. 7-18). 16.99 *(978-0-06-087143-7(1))* HarperCollins Pubs. (Eos).
—Warrior Princess #2: Destiny's Path. 2010. (Warrior Princess Ser.: 2). (ENG.). 352p. (YA). (gr. 8). pap. 8.99 *(978-0-06-087148-2(2),* HarperTeen) HarperCollins Pubs.
Jones, Janey Louise. The Sleepover. 2016. (Princess Poppy Picture Bks.). (ENG., Illus.). 32p. (J). (gr. -1-k). pap. 11.99 ***(978-0-552-57069-5(9))*** Transworld Publishers Ltd. GBR. Dist: Independent Pubs. Group.
Jones, Ursula. The Princess Who Had No Kingdom. 2015. (Illus.). 32p. (J). *(978-1-4896-3882-3(2))* Weigl Pubs., Inc.
—The Princess Who Had No Kingdom. Gibb, Sarah, illus. 2014. (ENG.). 32p. (J). (gr. -1-3). 16.99 *(978-0-8075-6630-5(6))* Whitman, Albert & Co.
Joosse, Barbara M. Lovabye Dragon. Cecil, Randy, illus. 2012. (ENG.). 32p. (J). (gr. -1-2). 15.99 *(978-0-7636-5408-5(6))* Candlewick Pr.
Jordan, Apple. A Fairy-Tale Fall. Legramandi, Francesco, illus. 2010. (Step into Reading Ser.). (ENG.). 32p. (J). (gr. k-3). pap. 3.99 *(978-0-7364-2674-9(4),* RH/Disney) Random Hse. Children's Bks.
—A Fairy-Tale Fall. 2010. (Disney Princess Step into Reading Ser.). lib. bdg. 13.55 *(978-0-606-14879-5(5),* Turtleback) Turtleback Bks.
—Oh, Brother! 2012. (Disney Princess Step into Reading Ser.). lib. bdg. 13.55 *(978-0-606-26560-7(0),* Turtleback) Turtleback Bks.
—A Princess Can! 2015. (Disney Princess Step into Reading Ser.). lib. bdg. 14.75 *(978-0-606-36390-7(4))* Turtleback Bks.
—A Princess Can! (Disney Princess) RH Disney Staff et al, illus. 2015. (Step into Reading Ser.). (ENG.). 24p. (J). (gr. -1-1). 4.99 *(978-0-7364-3341-9(4),* RH/Disney) Random Hse. Children's Bks.
—The Right Track. 2017. (Disney Princess Step into Reading Ser.). lib. bdg. 14.75 ***(978-0-606-39859-6(7))*** Turtleback Bks.
Jordan, Apple. The Sweetest Spring. Matta, Gabriella & Legramandi, Francesco, illus. 2008. (Step into Reading Ser.). (ENG.). 32p. (J). (gr. k-3). pap. 3.99 *(978-0-375-84810-0(X),* RH/Disney) Random Hse. Children's Bks.
Jordan, Apple J. Winter Wishes. Marrucchi, Elisa, illus. 2006. (Step into Reading Ser.). (ENG.). 32p. (J). (gr. k-3). per. 3.99 *(978-0-7364-2409-7(1),* RH/Disney) Random Hse. Children's Bks.
Jordan, Sophie. Reign of Shadows. 2016. (Reign of Shadows Ser.: 1). 304p. (YA). (gr. 8). 17.99 *(978-0-06-237764-7(7),* HarperTeen) HarperCollins Pubs.
Joy, Christine. The Dream Quest. 2013. 162p. pap. *(978-1-78148-790-7(1))* Grosvenor Hse. Publishing Ltd.
Joyce, Melaine. Cinderella. 2009. (Fairydust Fairytales Ser.). (ENG.). 5p. (J). (gr. -1-k). bds. 6.95 *(978-1-84696-964-5(6),* TickTock Books) Octopus Publishing Group GBR. Dist: Independent Pubs. Group.
—Snow White. 2009. (Fairydust Fairytales Ser.). (ENG.). 5p. (J). (gr. -1-k). bds. 6.95 *(978-1-84696-965-2(4),* TickTock Books) Octopus Publishing Group GBR. Dist: Independent Pubs. Group.
Joyce, Rita. Wandawillie. 2005. (J). lib. bdg. 17.95 *(978-1-59094-095-2(4))* Jawbone Publishing Corp.
Joyce, Sandie May. The Crying Princess. 2008. 69p. pap. 25.50 *(978-1-4357-6077-6(8))* Lulu Pr., Inc.
Jules, Jacqueline. The Princess & the Ziz. Kahn, Katherine Janus, illus. 2008. 32p. (J). (gr. -1-3). lib. bdg. 17.95 *(978-0-8225-7377-7(6));* (ENG.). pap. 7.95 *(978-0-8225-7382-1(2))* Lerner Publishing Group. (Kar-Ben Publishing).
Julius, Jessica. A New Reindeer Friend (Disney Frozen) RH Disney Staff, illus. 2015. (Little Golden Book Ser.). (ENG.). 24p. (J). (-k). 4.99 *(978-0-7364-3351-8(1),* Golden/Disney) Random Hse. Children's Bks.
K. B. Kendricks. Travis Taylor & the Dragon Quest. 2010. 344p. 29.95 *(978-1-4502-0261-9(6))* iUniverse, Inc.
Kaesshaefer, Charles. The Lost Princess. 2004. (J). mass mkt. 10.00 *(978-0-9744407-0-5(1))* Shelbykay Publishing Co.
Kagawa, Julie. The Iron King. 2010. (Iron Fey Ser.: 1). lib. bdg. 20.85 *(978-0-606-14909-9(0),* Turtleback) Turtleback Bks.
—The Iron Knight. 2011. (Iron Fey Ser.: 4). lib. bdg. 20.85 *(978-0-606-23259-3(1),* Turtleback) Turtleback Bks.
Kagna, Barbara. Magic of Masara. Gonzalez, Ashley, illus. 2010. 24p. pap. 12.50 *(978-1-4490-5651-3(2))* AuthorHouse.
Kale, Ann Stephanian. Marco & Princess Gina. Kale, Ann Stephanian, illus. 2003. (Illus.). 24p. (J). (gr. k-3). pap. 10.00 *(978-0-9704131-5-4(7))* Abril BookStore & Publishing.
Kang, Hildi. Chengli & the Silk Road Caravan. 2012. (ENG.). 176p. (J). (gr. 2-7). pap. 8.95 *(978-1-933718-78-1(1))* Tanglewood Pr.
Kann, Victoria. The Princess of Pink Slumber Party. Kann, Victoria, illus. 2012. (I Can Read Level 1 Ser.). (ENG., Illus.). 32p. (J). (gr. -1-3). 16.99 *(978-0-06-198963-6(0))* HarperCollins Pubs.
—The Princess of Pink Slumber Party. 2012. (Pinkalicious I Can Read Ser.). (J). lib. bdg. 13.55 *(978-0-606-23581-5(7),* Turtleback) Turtleback Bks.
—The Princess of Pink Treasury. Kann, Victoria, illus. 2011. (Pinkalicious Ser.). (ENG., Illus.). 208p. (J). (gr. -1-3). 19.99 *(978-0-06-210236-2(2))* HarperCollins Pubs.
—Story Time. 2016. (Pinkalicious I Can Read Ser.). (J). lib. bdg. 13.55 *(978-0-606-38758-3(7))* Turtleback Bks.
Karevold, Alison. KenKarta: Battle of the Onoxmon. Malone, Susan Mary, ed. Polinko, Les, illus. 2011. 300p. (J). 25.98 *(978-0-9843166-3-2(9))* Artists' Orchard, LLC, The.
Kats, Jewel. Teddy Bear Princess: A Story about Sharing & Caring. Arts, Richa Kinra, illus. 2012. 24p. (-18). pap. 13.95 *(978-1-61599-163-1(8),* Marvelous Spirit Pr.) Loving Healing Pr., Inc.
Katz, Bebe Weinberg. A Best Friend for Claudia. 2008. 77p. pap. 19.95 *(978-1-60563-485-2(9))* America Star Bks.
—Princess Claudia & the Freckles. 2007. 48p. per. 16.95 *(978-1-4241-6446-2(X))* America Star Bks.
Kearney, G. M. The Apple Trees of Tschlin. 2008. (J). 15.99 *(978-1-59955-098-5(9))* Cedar Fort, Inc./CFI Distribution.
Keithly, Bryan. Princess Tarang. 2009. 24p. pap. 11.49 *(978-1-4343-7601-5(X))* AuthorHouse.
Kemp, Anna. The Worst Princess. Ogilvie, Sara, illus. 2014. (ENG.). 32p. (J). (gr. -1-2). 16.99 *(978-0-385-37125-4(X),* Random Hse. Bks. for Young Readers) Random Hse. Children's Bks.
Khoury, Jessica. The Forbidden Wish. (ENG.). 352p. (YA). (gr. 7). 2017. pap. 9.99 *(978-1-59514-768-4(3))* 2016. 17.99 *(978-1-59514-767-7(5))* Penguin Young Readers Group. (Razorbill).
—The Forbidden Wish. 2017. lib. bdg. 20.85 ***(978-0-606-40000-8(1))*** Turtleback Bks.
Killion, Bette. Princess Rosie's Rainbows. Jacobs, Kim, illus. 2015. (ENG.). 36p. (J). (gr. k-3). 16.95 *(978-1-937786-44-1(7),* Wisdom Tales) World Wisdom, Inc.
Kimpton, Diana. Pony-Crazed Princess: Princess Ellie's Mystery. Finlay, Lizzie, illus. 3rd rev. ed. 2006. (ENG.). 96p. (gr. 1-4). pap. 3.99 *(978-0-7868-4872-0(3))* Hyperion Pr.
—Pony-Crazed Princess Super Special: Princess Ellie's Summer Vacation. Finlay, Lizzie, illus. 2007. (ENG.). 144p. (gr. 1-4). pap. 4.99 *(978-1-4231-0616-6(4))* Hyperion Pr.
—Princess Ellie Solves a Mystery. Finlay, Lizzie, illus. 8th rev. ed. 2007. (ENG.). 96p. (gr. 1-4). pap. 3.99 *(978-1-4231-0901-3(5))* Hyperion Pr.
—Princess Ellie to the Rescue. Finlay, Lizzie, illus. 2006. (ENG.). 96p. (gr. 1-4). pap. 3.99 *(978-0-7868-4870-6(7))* Hyperion Pr.
—Princess Ellie's Moonlight Mystery. 2015. (Pony-Crazed Princess Ser.). (ENG.). 96p. (J). (gr. k-5). pap. 4.99 *(978-0-7945-3431-8(7),* Usborne) EDC Publishing.
—Princess Ellie's Royal Jamboree No. 11. Finlay, Lizzie, illus. 11th ed. 2008. (ENG.). 96p. (gr. 1-4). pap. 3.99 *(978-1-4231-1531-1(7))* Hyperion Pr.
—Princess Ellie's Secret No. 2. Finlay, Lizzie, illus. 2nd rev. ed. 2006. (ENG.). 96p. (gr. 1-4). pap. 3.99 *(978-0-7868-4871-3(5))* Hyperion Pr.
—Princess Ellie's Snowy Ride. Finlay, Lizzie, illus. 2007. (Pony-Crazed Princess Ser.). 90p. (J). 11.65 *(978-0-7569-8352-9(5))* Perfection Learning Corp.
—Princess Ellie's Snowy Ride No. 9. Finlay, Lizzie, illus. 9th rev. ed. 2007. (ENG.). 96p. (gr. 1-4). pap. 3.99 *(978-1-4231-0902-0(3))* Hyperion Pr.
—Princess Ellie's Treasure Hunt No. 10. Finlay, Lizzie, illus. 10th ed. 2008. (ENG.). 96p. (gr. -1-3). pap. 3.99 *(978-1-4231-1414-7(0))* Hyperion Pr.
—A Surprise for Princess Ellie. 2015. (Pony-Crazed Princess Ser.). (ENG.). 96p. (J). (gr. k-5). pap. 4.99 *(978-0-7945-3432-5(5),* Usborne) EDC Publishing.
—A Surprise for Princess Ellie. Finlay, Lizzie, illus. 6th rev. ed. 2006. (ENG.). 96p. (gr. 1-4). pap. 3.99 *(978-0-7868-4875-1(8))* Hyperion Pr.
Kin, Pamphil. The Gorilla Princess. 2012. (ENG.). pap. *(978-1-4675-2345-5(3))* Independent Pub.
The Kind Princess. 2005. (J). 6.50 *(978-0-9773267-1-6(3))* G Publishing LLC.
Kindler, Jennifer. Rita's Fairytale. 2011. 68p. pap. 10.95 *(978-1-4575-0277-4(1))* Dog Ear Publishing, LLC.
King-smith, Dick. Lady Lollipop. Barton, Jill, illus. 2003. (ENG.). 128p. (J). (gr. 2-5). pap. 7.99 *(978-0-7636-2181-0(1))* Candlewick Pr.
Kingsbury, Karen. The Princess & the Three Knights, 1 vol. Grimard, Gabrielle, illus. 2009. (ENG.). 40p. (J). (gr. -1-2). 15.99 *(978-0-310-71641-9(1))* Zonderkidz.
Kiss a Frog, Princess. (Full House Ser.). 96p. (J). (gr. 4-6). pap. 3.25 *(978-0-938753-63-6(0),* PP2) Parachute Publishing, LLC.
Kladstrup, Kristin. Garden Princess. (ENG.). 272p. (J). (gr. 5). 2015. pap. 7.99 *(978-0-7636-7668-1(3))* 2013. (Illus.). 15.99 *(978-0-7636-5685-0(2))* Candlewick Pr.
Kliever, S. I. A Slave's Quest. 2011. 284p. pap. *(978-1-77069-178-0(2))* Word Alive Pr.
Kmiec, Irka. Princess Ella Bell. 2012. 26p. pap. 14.99 *(978-1-4772-4554-5(5))* AuthorHouse.

Knudsen, Michelle. The Dragon of Trelian. (Trelian Ser.: 1). (ENG.). 416p. (J). (gr. 5). 2017. pap. 9.99 *(978-0-7636-9454-8(1))* 2011. (Illus.). pap. 8.99 *(978-0-7636-4993-7(7))* 2009. (Illus.). 16.99 *(978-0-7636-3455-1(7))* Candlewick Pr.

—Mage of Trelian. 2016. (Trelian Ser.). (ENG.). 432p. (J). (gr. 5). 17.99 *(978-0-7636-7436-6(2))* Candlewick Pr.

—The Princess of Trelian. (Trelian Ser.: 2). (ENG.). 448p. (J). (gr. 5). 2017. pap. 9.99 *(978-0-7636-9455-5(X))* 2014. pap. 8.99 *(978-0-7636-6935-5(0))* 2012. (Illus.). 16.99 *(978-0-7636-5062-9(5))* Candlewick Pr.

Kopp, Megan. Scary Folktales, 1 vol. 2010. (Scary Stories Ser.). (ENG.). 32p. (gr. 3-4). lib. bdg. 27.99 *(978-1-4296-4571-3(7)*, Edge Bks.) Capstone Press of Coughlan Cos.

Korba, Joanna. Yeh-shen: A Cinderella Tale from China. 2006. (J). pap. *(978-1-4108-6162-7(7))* Benchmark Education Co.

Koster, Amy Sky. Cuddly Princess Pals. 2014. lib. bdg. 13.55 *(978-0-606-35552-0(9))* Turtleback Bks.

Kraegel, Kenneth. The Song of Delphine. Kraegel, Kenneth, illus. 2015. (ENG., Illus.). 40p. (J). (gr. k-3). 15.99 *(978-0-7636-7001-6(4))* Candlewick Pr.

Krakower, Harold. Sugarland: Princess Sarafina. 2011. 32p. (gr. 1-2). pap. 12.77 *(978-1-4634-0123-8(X))* AuthorHouse.

Kramer, Alan. The Three Little Pigs Wise up & the Princess Prince & the Vegetables. 2011. (Navigators Ser.). (J). pap. *(978-1-61672-962-2(7))* Benchmark Education Co.

Krise, Gale. It's a Colorful Candy Birthday. 2012. 24p. pap. 24.95 *(978-1-4626-7604-0(9))* America Star Bks.

Kronheimer, Ann, illus. Pretty Princesses: Beautiful Princesses to Color! 2014. (ENG.). 96p. (J). (gr. -1-2). 7.99 *(978-1-4424-8385-9(7)*, Little Simon) Little Simon.

Kuenzler, Lou. The Dragon Dance. 2017. (Princess DisGrace Ser.). (ENG., Illus.). 272p. (J). (gr. 3-7). 15.99 *(978-0-553-53781-9(4)*, Random Hse. Bks. for Young Readers) Random Hse. Children's Bks.

—Princess DisGrace: a Royal Disaster. 2016. (Princess DisGrace Ser.). (ENG., Illus.). 240p. (J). (gr. 3-7). 12.99 *(978-0-553-53775-8(X)*, Random Hse. Bks. for Young Readers) Random Hse. Children's Bks.

Kurtz, John, illus. Disney Princess: Look & Find. 2004. (Disney Princess Ser.). 24p. (J). 7.98 *(978-0-7853-7918-8(5)*, 7179200) Phoenix International Publications, Inc.

L. Prince Cloud & Princess Evergreen, 1 vol. 2010. 26p. pap. 24.95 *(978-1-4512-9016-5(0))* America Star Bks.

Lacek, Carolyn. Destiny Awakened. 2009. 52p. pap. 18.25 *(978-1-60860-736-5(4)*, Eloquent Bks.) Strategic Book Publishing & Rights Agency (SBPRA).

Lafrance, Marie, illus. The Princess & the Giant: A Tale from Scotland. 2013. (Tales of Honor (Red Chair Press) Ser.). (ENG.). 32p. (J). (gr. 1-4). lib. bdg. 26.60 *(978-1-937529-77-2(0))* Red Chair Pr.

Lagonegro, Melissa. Barbie in Princess Power - Saving the Day! 2015. (Step into Reading Ser.). (ENG., Illus.). 24p. (J). (gr. -1-1). 4.99 *(978-0-553-50890-1(3)*, Random Hse. Bks. for Young Readers) Random Hse. Children's Bks.

—Beautiful Brides. Marrucchi, Elisa, illus. 2011. (Step into Reading Ser.). (ENG.). 32p. (J). (gr. k-3). pap. 3.99 *(978-0-7364-2685-5(X)*, RH/Disney) Random Hse. Children's Bks.

—Friends for a Princess. 2004. (Disney Princess Step into Reading Ser.). (gr. -1-2). lib. bdg. 13.55 *(978-0-613-73713-5(X)*, Turtleback) Turtleback Bks.

—Friends for a Princess (Disney Princess) Harchy, Atelier Philippe, illus. 2016. (Step into Reading Ser.). (ENG.). 24p. (J). (gr. -1-1). pap. 4.99 *(978-0-7364-3670-0(7)*, RH/Disney) Random Hse. Children's Bks.

—Frozen - A Tale of Two Sisters. 2013. (Disney Princess Step into Reading Ser.). lib. bdg. 13.55 *(978-0-606-32205-8(1)*, Turtleback) Turtleback Bks.

—The Little Mermaid Junior Novelization (Disney Princess) Random House Disney Staff, illus. 2013. (Junior Novel Ser.). (ENG.). 128p. (J). (gr. 3-7). 4.99 *(978-0-7364-2983-2(2)*, RH/Disney) Random Hse. Children's Bks.

—Travel Like a Princess. 2014. (Disney Princess Step into Reading Ser.). lib. bdg. 13.55 *(978-0-606-35554-4(5))* Turtleback Bks.

—Travel Like a Princess (Disney Princess) RH Disney Staff et al, illus. 2014. (Step into Reading Ser.). (ENG.). 24p. (J). (gr. -1-1). 3.99 *(978-0-7364-3089-0(X)*, RH/Disney) Random Hse. Children's Bks.

Lagonegro, Melissa & RH Disney Staff. Ballerina Princess. Harding, Niall, illus. 2007. (Step into Reading Ser.). (ENG.). 32p. (J). (gr. k-3). pap. 3.99 *(978-0-7364-2428-8(8)*, RH/Disney) Random Hse. Children's Bks.

—A Horse to Love: An Enchanted Stables Story. Disney Storybook Artists Staff, illus. 2007. (Pictureback(R) Ser.). (ENG.). 16p. (J). (gr. -1-2). pap. 3.99 *(978-0-7364-2504-9(7)*, RH/Disney) Random Hse. Children's Bks.

Lairamore, Dawn. Ivy & the Meanstalk. 2011. (ENG.). 192p. (J). 16.95 *(978-0-8234-2392-7(1))* Holiday Hse., Inc.

—Ivy's Ever After. (ENG.). 192p. (J). 2013. (gr. 2-7). pap. 7.99 *(978-0-8234-2937-0(7))* 2010. (gr. 3-7). 16.95 *(978-0-8234-2261-6(5))* Holiday Hse., Inc.

Lake, Susan. Ebony & the Five Dwarfs. 2007. 56p. per. 10.00 *(978-1-4257-7841-5(0))* Xlibris Corp.

Lambert, Nat. Magnetic Dressing up Princesses. 2014. (ENG.). 10p. (J). (gr. -1-k). 9.99 *(978-1-78244-799-3(7))* Top That! Publishing PLC GBR. Dist: Independent Pubs. Group.

Lammle, Leslie. Princess Wannabe. Lammle, Leslie, illus. 2014. (ENG., Illus.). 40p. (J). (gr. -1-3). 17.99 *(978-0-06-125197-9(6))* HarperCollins Pubs.

Landers, Melissa. Starfall. 2017. (Starflight Ser.). (ENG.). 368p. (YA). (gr. 9-17). 17.99 *(978-1-4847-5025-4(X))* Hyperion Bks. for Children.

Larousse Mexico Staff, ed. Historias de Princesas y Hadas. 2008.Tr. of Princess & Fairy Stories. (SPA & ENG., Illus.). 35p. 9.95 *(978-970-22-1449-6(1))* Larousse, Ediciones, S. A. de C. V. MEX. Dist: Houghton Mifflin Harcourt Publishing Co.

Larsen, Sharon G. The Parable of the Chocolate Chips. 2008. (J). *(978-1-59038-912-6(3))* Deseret Bk. Co.

Larson, M. A. Pennyroyal Academy. 2014. (Pennyroyal Academy Ser.: 1). (ENG.). 320p. (J). (gr. 5). 16.99 *(978-0-399-16324-1(7)*, G.P. Putnam's Sons Books for Young Readers) Penguin Young Readers Group.

Larson, M. A. The Shadow Cadets of Pennyroyal Academy. 2017. (Pennyroyal Ser.: 2). lib. bdg. 19.65 ***(978-0-606-39792-6(2))*** Turtleback Bks.

Larson, Sara B. Dark Breaks the Dawn. 2017. (ENG.). 320p. (J). (gr. 7). 17.99 ***(978-1-338-06869-6(5)***, Scholastic Pr.) Scholastic, Inc.

L.A.S., Alex. Magnificent Sir Johnny & Santa Claus. 2011. 36p. pap. 24.95 *(978-1-4626-3401-9(X))* America Star Bks.

Lascurain, Anna. Apollo in the Moon House. 2006. Orig. Title: The Moonboy. (J). per. 7.99 *(978-0-9769612-3-9(7))* Darker Intentions Pr.

LaShea, Riley. Bleeding Through Kingdoms: Cinderella's Rebellion. 2005. 256p. (YA). per. 14.95 *(978-0-9766130-1-5(8))* Tattered Essence Publishing LLC.

LeapFrog Staff. Disney Princess Stories - France. 2003. (Illus.). spiral bd. 14.99 *(978-1-59319-005-7(0))* LeapFrog Enterprises, Inc.

—Disney Princess Stories - Latin America. 2003. (Illus.). (J). spiral bd. 14.99 *(978-1-59319-001-9(8))* LeapFrog Enterprises, Inc.

Leavitt, Lindsey. Princess for Hire. 2011. (Princess for Hire Book Ser.). (ENG.). 256p. (J). (gr. 5-9). pap. 7.99 *(978-1-4231-2299-9(2))* Hyperion Pr.

Lechermeier, Philippe & Dautremer, Rebecca. Princesas/Princesses: Mini Album. 2008. (SPA.). 108p. 15.95 *(978-84-263-6701-3(1))* Vives, Luis Editorial (Edelvives) ESP. Dist: Lectorum Pubns., Inc.

Ledeaux, Lola. If A Dog Could Blog. 2010. 28p. 12.49 *(978-1-4520-7575-4(1))* AuthorHouse.

Lee, Y. J. The Little Moon Princess. Lee, Y. J., illus. 2010. (ENG., Illus.). 32p. (J). (gr. -1-3). 16.99 *(978-0-06-154736-2(0))* HarperCollins Pubs.

Lendler, Ian. An Undone Fairy Tale. Martin, Whitney, illus. 2005. (ENG.). 32p. (J). (gr. 1-5). 18.99 *(978-0-689-86677-7(1)*, Simon & Schuster Bks. For Young Readers) Simon & Schuster Bks. For Young Readers.

Lenz, Adrienne. The Glitter Ball: Princess Jewels. 2011. 20p. pap. 24.95 *(978-1-4560-4147-2(9))* PublishAmerica, Inc.

Leprechaun, Seamus T. The o'Shea Chronicles. 2013. 312p. pap. *(978-1-78407-190-5(0))* FeedARead.com.

Leth, Kate. Adventure Time Vol. 4. 2014. lib. bdg. 24.50 *(978-0-606-36119-4(7))* Turtleback Bks.

Levenseller, Tricia. Daughter of the Pirate King. 2017. (Daughter of the Pirate King Ser.). (ENG.). 320p. (YA). 17.99 *(978-1-250-09596-1(4)*, 9781250095961) Feiwel & Friends.

Levert, Mireille. The Princess Who Had Almost Everything. Masse, Josée, illus. 2008. (ENG.). 32p. (J). (gr. -1-3). 19.95 *(978-0-88776-887-3(3)*, Tundra Bks.) Tundra Bks. CAN. Dist: Penguin Random Hse. LLC.

Levine, Gail Carson. The Princess Tales, No. 2. Elliott, Mark, illus. 2004. (Princess Tales Ser.). (ENG.). 256p. (J). (gr. 2-7). pap. 7.99 *(978-0-06-056043-0(6))* HarperCollins Pubs.

—The Two Princesses of Bamarre. (J). 2012. (ENG.). 272p. (gr. 3-7). pap. 6.99 *(978-0-06-440966-7(X))* 2004. (Illus.). 304p. (gr. 7-18). reprint ed. pap. 6.99 *(978-0-06-057580-9(8))* HarperCollins Pubs.

Levine, Gail Carson & Levine, Gail C. The Fairy's Return & Other Princess Tales. 2009. (ENG.). 400p. (J). (gr. 3-7). pap. 7.99 *(978-0-06-176898-9(7))* HarperCollins Pubs.

Lewis, Ellen Parry. An Unremarkable Girl. 2011. 434p. (YA). pap. 19.99 *(978-0-9843437-8-2(4))* Metal Lunchbox Publishing.

Leysen, An. The Princess Who Could Not Sleep. 2012. (ENG.). 30p. (J). (gr. -1-k). 15.95 *(978-1-60537-132-0(7))* Cobblestone Publishing Co.

Liberts, Jennifer. Happy Birthday, Princess! (Disney Princess) Marrucchi, Elisa, illus. 2016. (Step into Reading Ser.). (ENG.). 24p. (J). (gr. -1-1). pap. 4.99 *(978-0-7364-3664-9(2)*, RH/Disney) Random Hse. Children's Bks.

—Princesses & Puppies (Disney Princess) Legramandi, Francesco & Matta, Gabriella, illus. 2016. (Step into Reading Ser.). (ENG.). 24p. (J). (gr. -1-1). pap. 4.99 *(978-0-7364-3660-1(X)*, RH/Disney) Random Hse. Children's Bks.

—What Is a Princess? (Disney Princess) Harchy, Atelier Philippe, illus. 2016. (Step into Reading Ser.). (ENG.). 24p. (J). (gr. -1-1). pap. 4.99 *(978-0-7364-3666-3(9)*, RH/Disney) Random Hse. Children's Bks.

Liguori, Tara. Silly Milly Is a Princess. 2008. 28p. pap. 24.95 *(978-1-60703-349-3(6))* America Star Bks.

Liles, R. D. The Princess & the Troll. 2012. 44p. pap. 21.99 *(978-1-4772-8256-4(4))* AuthorHouse.

Lilibeth, Ethel. Princesses Take Baths Too! 2009. 44p. pap. 18.60 *(978-1-4389-6626-7(1))* AuthorHouse.

Limke, Jeff. Tristan & Isolde: The Warrior & the Princess [A British Legend]. Randall, Ron, illus. 2009. (Graphic Myths & Legends Ser.). (ENG.). 48p. (gr. 4-8). pap. 8.95 *(978-1-58013-889-5(6))* Lerner Publishing Group.

Lincoln, Jerri Kay. Dancing with Unicorns. 2013. 254p. pap. 14.99 *(978-1-938322-21-1(5))* Ralston Store Publishing.

Linker, Julie. Disenchanted Princess. 2007. (ENG.). 240p. (YA). (gr. 9-18). pap. 11.99 *(978-1-4169-3472-1(3)*, Simon Pulse) Simon Pulse.

Linn, Susie. Princesses. Ellis, Lauren, illus. 2017. (Search & Find Ser.). (ENG.). 48p. (J). (gr. k-2). pap. 6.99 *(978-1-78700-034-6(6))* Top That! Publishing PLC GBR. Dist: Independent Pubs. Group.

—Princesses: Sticker Book Fun for Little Ones! Ellis, Lauren, illus. 2017. (My First Sticker Book Ser.). (ENG.). 36p. (J). (gr. -1-k). pap. 8.99 *(978-1-78700-059-9(1))* Top That! Publishing PLC GBR. Dist: Independent Pubs. Group.

Lisa Maria. Princess of the King. 2012. 28p. pap. 17.99 *(978-1-4685-5652-0(5))* AuthorHouse.

Lisle, Rebecca. Toad Prince. 2005. (ENG., Illus.). 64p. (J). (gr. k-2). pap. 7.99 *(978-1-84270-315-1(3))* Andersen Pr. GBR. Dist: Independent Pubs. Group.

Little Princess. 2004. (J). *(978-0-9767179-6-6(4))* ABC Development, Inc.

Little Sticker Dolly Dressing Princesses. 2017. (Little Sticker Dolly Dressing Ser.). (ENG.). (J). pap. 8.99 ***(978-0-7945-3919-1(X)***, Usborne) EDC Publishing.

Littman, Sarah Darer. Charmed, I'm Sure. 2016. (ENG., Illus.). 208p. (J). (gr. 3-7). 17.99 *(978-1-4814-5127-7(8)*, Aladdin) Simon & Schuster Children's Publishing.

Livingston, Lesley. The Valiant. 2017. (ENG.). 384p. (YA). (gr. 7). 17.99 *(978-0-448-49378-7(0)*, Razorbill) Penguin Young Readers Group.

Lodico, Cheryl Madeleine. The Ice Princess Trilogy. 2007. pap. 20.00 *(978-0-8059-8967-0(6))* Dorrance Publishing Co., Inc.

Loewen, Nancy. Believe Me, I Never Felt a Pea! The Story of the Princess & the Pea As Told by the Princess. Bernardini, Cristian, illus. 2016. (Other Side of the Story Ser.). (ENG.). 24p. (gr. 2-3). lib. bdg. 27.32 *(978-1-4795-8622-6(6))* Picture Window Bks.

Loggia, Wendy. Aurora: The Perfect Party, 1 vol. Studio IBOIX, illus. 2012. (Disney Princesses Set 2 Ser.). (ENG.). 96p. (J). (gr. 2-6). lib. bdg. 24.21 *(978-1-59961-181-5(3))* Spotlight.

Lois, Lowry. The Birthday Ball. Feiffer, Jules, illus. 2011. (ENG.). 192p. (J). (gr. 5-7). pap. 7.99 *(978-0-547-57710-4(9))* Houghton Mifflin Harcourt Publishing Co.

Lough, Amber. The Blind Wish. 2015. (Jinni Wars Ser.: 2). (ENG.). 320p. (YA). (gr. 7). 17.99 *(978-0-385-36980-0(8)*, Random Hse. Bks. for Young Readers) Random Hse. Children's Bks.

Louis, Robb. Monster in the Moat. 2011. (Illus.). 44p. (gr. -1). pap. 18.46 *(978-1-4567-4053-5(9))* AuthorHouse.

Lowery, Mark. Attack of the Woolly Jumper. 2017. (Roman Garstang Disaster Ser.). (ENG., Illus.). 224p. (J). (gr. 4-7). pap. 8.99 ***(978-1-84812-582-7(8))*** Bonnier Publishing GBR. Dist: Independent Pubs. Group.

Lowes, Sarah. The Snow Queen. Clara, Miss, illus. 2013. (ENG.). 64p. (J). 17.99 *(978-1-84686-964-8(1))* Barefoot Bks., Inc.

LucasFilm Press Staff, et al. Star Wars Moving Target: A Princess Leia Adventure. Noto, Phil, illus. 2015. (ENG.). 240p. (J). (gr. 5-9). 12.99 *(978-1-4847-2497-2(6)*, Disney Lucasfilm Press) Disney Publishing Worldwide.

Luiz, Fernando, illus. How to Be a Princess: A Girly Girl Book. 2009. 12p. (J). bds. 6.95 *(978-1-58117-850-0(6)*, Intervisual/Piggy Toes) Bendon, Inc.

Lum, Kate. Princesses Are Not Just Pretty. Hellard, Sue, illus. 2014. (ENG.). 32p. (J). (gr. -1-1). 16.99 *(978-1-59990-778-9(X)*, 9781599907789, Bloomsbury USA Childrens) Bloomsbury Publishing USA.

Lundquist, Jenny. The Opal Crown. 2014. (ENG.). 368p. (YA). (gr. 2-17). pap. 9.95 *(978-0-7624-5422-8(9)*, Running Pr. Kids) Running Pr. Bk. Pubs.

—The Princess in the Opal Mask. 2013. (ENG.). 352p. (YA). (gr. 2-17). pap. 9.95 *(978-0-7624-5109-8(2)*, Running Pr. Kids) Running Pr. Bk. Pubs.

Lynn, Kelly. The Princess Transformation, 1 vol. 2010. 132p. pap. 24.95 *(978-1-4512-1417-8(0))* America Star Bks.

MacDonald, George. The Light Princess. 2008. 48p. pap. 5.99 *(978-1-4209-3096-2(6))* Digireads.com Publishing.

—The Light Princess. 2004. reprint ed. pap. 15.95 *(978-1-4191-7001-0(5))* Kessinger Publishing, LLC.

—Light Princess & Other Fairy Stories. 2006. 132p. per. 10.95 *(978-1-59818-618-5(3))*; 24.95 *(978-1-59818-236-1(6))* Aegypan.

—The Light Princess & Other Fairy Stories. 2007. 102p. pap. 18.99 *(978-1-4346-1408-7(5))* Creative Media Partners, LLC.

—The Princess & Curdie. Stratton, Helen, illus. 2003. 162p. pap. 12.99 *(978-1-57646-634-6(5))* Quiet Vision Publishing.

—Princess & Curdie. 2006. 136p. per. 10.95 *(978-1-59818-617-8(5))*; 24.95 *(978-1-59818-235-4(8))* Aegypan.

—The Princess & Curdie. l.t. ed. 2005. 320p. pap. *(978-1-84637-020-5(5))* Echo Library.

—Princess & the Goblin. 2006. 128p. 23.95 *(978-1-59818-234-7(X))* Aegypan.

—The Princess & the Goblin. 2003. (Illus.). 160p. (J). 19.95 *(978-1-81514-970-2(1))* Antique Collectors' Club.

—The Princess & the Goblin. abr. ed. 2007. 191p. (J). (gr. 4-7). per. 8.99 *(978-1-59166-799-5(2))* BJU Pr.

—The Princess & the Goblin. 2008. 176p. 22.99 *(978-0-554-37350-8(5))* 2008. 176p. 25.99 *(978-0-554-28047-9(7))* 2007. 162p. pap. 19.99 *(978-1-4346-4583-8(5))* 2007. 174p. pap. 21.99 *(978-1-4346-4584-5(3))* Creative Media Partners, LLC.

—The Princess & the Goblin. 2005. 108p. per. 5.99 *(978-1-4209-2557-9(1))* Digireads.com Publishing.

—The Princess & the Goblin. 2007. 152p. per. *(978-1-4065-3015-5(8))* Dodo Pr.

—The Princess & the Goblin. l.t. ed. 2005. 292p. pap. *(978-1-84637-021-2(3))* Echo Library.

—The Princess & the Goblin. 2008. 188p. pap. 12.95 *(978-1-60096-531-9(8))*; pap. 12.95 *(978-1-60096-825-9(2))* Editorium, The.

—The Princess & the Goblin. 2007. pap. 5.99 *(978-1-59986-657-4(9)*, FQ Classics) Filiquarian Publishing, LLC.

—The Princess & the Goblin. 2004. reprint ed. pap. 1.99 *(978-1-4192-7868-6(1))* Kessinger Publishing, LLC.

—The Princess & the Goblin. 2011. 174p. pap. 4.95 *(978-1-61427-173-4(9))* Martino Fine Bks.

—The Princess & the Goblin. Hughes, Arthur, illus. 2003. 136p. pap. 12.99 *(978-1-57646-633-9(7))* Quiet Vision Publishing.

—The Princess & the Goblin. 2008. 132p. pap. 4.99 *(978-1-60459-454-6(3))* Wilder Pubns., Corp.

—The Princess & the Goblin. Kirk, Maria L. & Hughes, Arthur, illus. 2011. 260p. pap. 10.95 *(978-1-59915-250-9(9))* Yesterday's Classics.

—The Princess Treasury. 2008. 372p. pap. 12.99 *(978-1-60459-458-4(6))* Wilder Pubns., Corp.

MacDonald, George, ed. The Princess & Curdie. Kirk, Maria L. & Hughes, Arthur, illus. 2011. 260p. pap. 10.95 *(978-1-59915-251-6(7))* Yesterday's Classics.

—The Princess & the Goblin. 2004. reprint ed. pap. 20.95 *(978-1-4191-7868-9(7))* Kessinger Publishing, LLC.

MacGregor, Rose. Princess Bendy. 2012. (Illus.). 12p. pap. 15.99 *(978-1-4678-9038-0(3))* AuthorHouse.

MacHale, D. J. The Monster Princess. Boiger, Alexandra, illus. 2010. (ENG.). 40p. (J). (gr. -1-1). 17.99 *(978-1-4169-4809-4(0)*, Aladdin) Simon & Schuster Children's Publishing.

Macinnis, Katherine. Kelsar. 2006. pap. 12.95 *(978-1-58939-876-4(9))* Virtualbookworm.com Publishing, Inc.

Magic Wand Disney Princess. 2005. (Illus.). 10p. (J). bds. 16.98 *(978-1-4127-3537-7(8)*, 7263500) Publications International, Ltd.

Maisner, Heather. Diary of a Princess: A Tale from Marco Polo's Travels. Moxley, Sheila, illus. 2006. 26p. (gr. k-4). reprint ed. pap. 8.00 *(978-1-4223-5302-8(8))* DIANE Publishing Co.

Malea. Princess Melia. 2007. 145p. (J). pap. 15.95 *(978-1-58909-367-6(4))* Bookstand Publishing.

Malia, Tara Campasano. The Special Princess. 2012. (ENG.). 41p. (J). pap. 15.95 *(978-1-4327-3831-0(3))*; pap. 24.95 *(978-1-4327-7627-5(4))* Outskirts Pr., Inc.

Man-Kong, Mary. Barbie as the Island Princess. 2007. (Pictureback(R) Ser.). (ENG., Illus.). 24p. (J). (gr. -1-2). pap. 3.99 *(978-0-375-84218-4(7)*, Random Hse. Bks. for Young Readers) Random Hse. Children's Bks.

—Dazzling Duet. 2015. (Deluxe Paint Box Book Ser.). (ENG.). 128p. (J). (gr. -1-2). pap. 7.99 *(978-0-553-52164-1(0)*, Golden Bks.) Random Hse. Children's Bks.

—Fairy Dreams. Random House Staff, illus. 2013. (Step into Reading Ser.). (ENG.). 32p. (J). (gr. -1-1). 3.99 *(978-0-449-81628-8(1)*, Random Hse. Bks. for Young Readers) Random Hse. Children's Bks.

—A Fin-Tastic Journey! Golden Books Staff, illus. 2012. (Color Plus Chunky Crayons Ser.). (ENG.). 48p. (J). (gr. k-k). pap. 3.99 *(978-0-307-92978-5(7)*, Golden Bks.) Random Hse. Children's Bks.

—Listen to Your Heart! 2015. (Pictureback(R) Ser.). (ENG., Illus.). 16p. (J). (gr. -1-2). 4.99 *(978-0-553-52341-6(4)*, Random Hse. Bks. for Young Readers) Random Hse. Children's Bks.

—Princess to the Rescue! 2015. (Pictureback(R) Ser.). (ENG., Illus.). 16p. (J). (gr. -1-2). 4.99 *(978-0-553-50737-9(0)*, Random Hse. Bks. for Young Readers) Random Hse. Children's Bks.

—Sleeping Beauty. 2014. (Disney Princess Step into Reading Ser.). lib. bdg. 13.55 *(978-0-606-36001-2(8))* Turtleback Bks.

—Sleeping Beauty Step into Reading (Disney Princess) RH Disney Staff, illus. 2014. (Step into Reading Ser.). (ENG.). 32p. (J). (gr. -1-1). 3.99 *(978-0-7364-3226-9(4)*, RH/Disney) Random Hse. Children's Bks.

—Star Power. Random House Staff, illus. 2012. (Step into Reading Ser.). (ENG.). 32p. (J). (gr. -1-1). pap. 3.99 *(978-0-307-93196-2(X)*, Random Hse. Bks. for Young Readers) Random Hse. Children's Bks.

—Star Power. 2012. (Barbie Step into Reading Level 2 Ser.). lib. bdg. 13.55 *(978-0-606-26550-8(3)*, Turtleback) Turtleback Bks.

—Teachers' Pets (Disney Princess) Marrucchi, Elisa, illus. 2011. (Step into Reading Ser.). (ENG.). 32p. (J). (gr. k-3). pap. 3.99 *(978-0-7364-2778-4(3)*, RH/Disney) Random Hse. Children's Bks.

Man-Kong, Mary & Tillworth, Mary. Princess Charm School (Barbie) Golden Books Staff, illus. 2011. (Little Golden Book Ser.). (ENG.). 24p. (J). (gr. -1-2). 3.99 *(978-0-375-87361-4(9)*, Golden Bks.) Random Hse. Children's Bks.

Manjula Padmanabhan, illus. Unprincess! 2005. 98p. (J). *(978-0-14-333495-8(6)*, Puffin) Penguin Publishing Group.

Marrs, Christie, creator. The Promise Keeper: I B Hoofinit's Horse Tales. l.t. ed. 2003. (Illus.). 53p. (J). mass mkt. 5.99 *(978-1-928890-16-4(4))* I. B. Hoofinit Co.

Marsoli, Lisa Ann. The Missing Necklace. 2014. (Sofia the First World of Reading Ser.). (J). lib. bdg. 13.55 *(978-0-606-35912-2(5))* Turtleback Bks.

Marsoli, Lisa Ann & Disney Book Group Staff. Sofia Takes the Lead, Level 1. Disney Storybook Artists Staff, illus. 2014. (World of Reading Ser.). (ENG.). 32p. (J). (gr. -1-k). pap. 3.99 *(978-1-4231-8345-7(2))* Disney Pr.

—Welcome to Royal Prep, Level 1. Disney Storybook Art Team, illus. 2013. (World of Reading Ser.). (ENG.). 32p. (J). (gr. -1-k). pap. 3.99 *(978-1-4231-6407-4(5))* Disney Pr.

Martin, Alison. Princess of Tabaria. 2004. (Illus.). 104p. pap. *(978-1-84401-151-3(8))* Athena Pr.

Martin, Chandra. Sintacs. 2012. 100p. 19.95 *(978-1-4626-7833-4(5))* America Star Bks.

Martin, Molly. Princess Addison Gets Angry, 1 vol. Florian, Mélanie, illus. 2013. (Princess Heart Ser.). (ENG.). 24p. (gr. -1-1). 6.95 *(978-1-4048-8107-5(7))*; lib. bdg. 22.65 *(978-1-4048-7851-8(3))* Picture Window Bks.

—Princess Harper Gets Happy, 1 vol. Florian, Mélanie, illus. 2013. (Princess Heart Ser.). (ENG.). 24p. (gr. -1-1). 6.95 *(978-1-4048-8108-2(5))*; lib. bdg. 22.65 *(978-1-4048-7852-5(1))* Picture Window Bks.

—Princess Heart. Florian, Mélanie, illus. 2013. (Princess Heart Ser.). (ENG.). 24p. (gr. -1-1). 90.60 *(978-1-4048-8056-6(9))* Picture Window Bks.

—Princess Sophia Gets Scared, 1 vol. Florian, Mélanie, illus. 2013. (Princess Heart Ser.). (ENG.). 24p. (gr. -1-1). 6.95 *(978-1-4048-8110-5(7))*; lib. bdg. 22.65 *(978-1-4048-7854-9(8))* Picture Window Bks.

—Princess Stella Gets Sad, 1 vol. Florian, Mélanie, illus. 2013. (Princess Heart Ser.). (ENG.). 24p. (gr. -1-1). 6.95 *(978-1-4048-8109-9(3))*; lib. bdg. 22.65 *(978-1-4048-7853-2(X))* Picture Window Bks.

Marvin, Susan. Birthday Dreamz. 2011. 36p. (gr. -1). pap. 15.99 *(978-1-4567-4173-0(X))* AuthorHouse.

Mason & Marisa & Avery & Stella. The Tale of Princess Fluffy & Prince Rupert. 2012. 28p. pap. 19.99 *(978-1-4685-3594-5(3))* AuthorHouse.

Mass, Wendy. Beauty & the Beast: The Only One Who Didn't Run Away. 2013. (Twice upon a Time Ser.: 3). (ENG.). 288p. (J). (gr. 3-7). pap. 6.99 *(978-0-545-31019-2(9)*, Scholastic Paperbacks) Scholastic, Inc.

—Rapunzel: The One with All the Hair. (J). 2012. (Twice upon a Time Ser.: 1). (ENG.). 208p. (gr. 3-7). pap. 6.99 *(978-0-439-79659-0(8)*, Scholastic Pr.) 2005. (Illus.). 205p. *(978-0-439-80014-3(5))* Scholastic, Inc.

Matsumoto, Reiko Odate. The Princess with the Magic Bowl: As retold from the Japanese folk tale By. 2008. 48p. pap. 22.49 *(978-1-4389-1225-7(0))* AuthorHouse.

Mattel & Deutsch, Stacia. Ever after High: Dragon Games: The Junior Novel. 2016. (ENG.). 144p. (J). (gr. 3-7). pap. 5.99 *(978-0-316-30184-8(1))* Little, Brown Bks. for Young Readers.

—Ever after High Entertainment Tie-In: the Deluxe Junior Novel. 2016. (ENG.). 144p. (J). (gr. 3-7). 9.99 *(978-0-316-27045-8(8))* Little, Brown Bks. for Young Readers.

Mattel & Green, Margaret. Ever after High. 2016. (ENG., Illus.). 24p. (J). (gr. -1-3). pap. 3.99 *(978-0-316-30179-4(5))* Little, Brown Bks. for Young Readers.
—Ever after High Entertainment Tie-In: Reader. 2016. (Passport to Reading Level 3 Ser.). (ENG., Illus.). 32p. (J). (gr. -1-3). pap. 3.99 *(978-0-316-30180-0(9))* Little, Brown Bks. for Young Readers.
Matter, Sandy. The Great Sea Chase. 2011. 20p. pap. 24.95 *(978-1-4626-2488-1(X))* America Star Bks.
Matthews, Caitlín, et al. The Barefoot Book of Princesses. Whelan, Olwyn, illus. 2008. (Barefoot Bks.). (ENG.). 64p. (J). 19.99 *(978-1-84686-239-7(6))* Barefoot Bks., Inc.
Mawhinney, Art, illus. Look & Find Disney Princess Worlds of Wonder. 2006. (Look & Find Books). (J). pap. 24.98 *(978-1-4127-6490-2(4))* Publications International, Ltd.
Mayhew, James. Katie & the Spanish Princess. Mayhew, James, illus. 2007. (ENG., Illus.). 32p. (J). (gr. -1-k). pap. 10.99 *(978-1-84616-248-0(3))* Hodder & Stoughton GBR. Dist: Hachette Bk. Group.
McClintock. Little Princess Picture Book. Date not set. (Illus.). 40p. (J). (gr. -1-3). pap. 4.99 *(978-0-06-443539-0(3))* HarperCollins Pubs.
McCullough, Kathy. Opposites Attract. 2017. (Stepping Stone Book(TM) Ser.: 2). (ENG., Illus.). 128p. (J). (gr. 1-4). 5.99 ***(978-0-7364-3828-5(9))***; lib. bdg. 12.99 ***(978-0-7364-3829-2(7))*** Random Hse. Children's Bks. (RH/Disney).
—Secrets Unlocked. 2017. (Stepping Stone Book(TM) Ser.: 1). (ENG., Illus.). 128p. (J). (gr. 1-4). 5.99 ***(978-0-7364-3826-1(2))***; lib. bdg. 12.99 ***(978-0-7364-3827-8(0))*** Random Hse. Children's Bks. (RH/Disney).
McCusker, Tammy. Move over! Princess Coming Through!, 1 vol. Greve, Hannah K., illus. 2009. 34p. pap. 24.95 *(978-1-60749-803-2(0))* America Star Bks.
McDoogle, Farrah & Pulliam, Gabe. OLIVIA Says Good Night. Spaziante, Patrick, illus. 2011. (Olivia TV Tie-In Ser.). (ENG.). 24p. (J). (gr. -1-1). 16.99 *(978-1-4424-2947-5(X)*, Simon Spotlight) Simon Spotlight.
McGhee, Heather. The Wild Adventures of a Curious Princess. Myers, Shari, illus. 2008. (J). per. 9.99 *(978-0-9788985-9-5(1))* Better Be Write Pub., A.
McGowan, Maureen. Cinderella: Ninja Warrior. 2010. 320p. pap. 8.95 *(978-1-60747-778-5(5)*, Pickwick Pr.) Phoenix Bks., Inc.
—Sleeping Beauty: Vampire Slayer. 2010. 320p. pap. 8.95 *(978-1-60747-779-2(3)*, Pickwick Pr.) Phoenix Bks., Inc.
McGriff, Shawna A. Princess Pink: Princess Pink Helps Zion, Melinda, & Jasmine Learn to Communicate about Their Parents' Divorces. 2010. 56p. pap. 24.00 *(978-1-4520-3941-1(0))* AuthorHouse.
—Princess Pink: Princess Pink Saves the Girls of Lahappyville. 2010. 44p. pap. 18.49 *(978-1-4520-3936-7(4))* AuthorHouse.
—Princess Pink: Sam Loses Her Mother, but She Gains Her Mother's Heart. 2010. 32p. pap. 15.50 *(978-1-4520-3937-4(2))* AuthorHouse.
McGuire Woods, Molly. Barbie Fall 2014 DVD Junior Novelization (Barbie) 2014. (Junior Novel Ser.). (ENG., Illus.). 128p. (J). (gr. 3-7). 5.99 *(978-0-385-38627-2(3)*, Random Hse. Bks. for Young Readers) Random Hse. Children's Bks.
—Barbie in Rock 'n Royals. 2015. (Barbie Chapters Ser.). (ENG.). 64p. (J). (gr. 1-4). 5.99 *(978-0-553-52435-2(6)*, Random Hse. Bks. for Young Readers) Random Hse. Children's Bks.
—The Pearl Princess. 2014. (Junior Novel Ser.). (ENG.). 128p. (J). (gr. 3-7). 5.99 *(978-0-385-37517-7(4)*, Random Hse. Bks. for Young Readers) Random Hse. Children's Bks.
McKay, Sindy. The Frog Prince/el Príncipe Rana: Spanish/English (We Both Read - Level 1-2) Ulrich, George, illus. 2016. (We Both Read - Level 1-2 Ser.). (ENG & SPA.). (J). pap. 4.99 *(978-1-60115-076-9(8))* Treasure Bay, Inc.
McKenzie, Heath. My Rules for Being a Pretty Princess. 2015. (ENG., Illus.). 32p. (J). (-3). 16.99 *(978-1-4926-1520-0(X))* Sourcebooks, Inc.
McKinley, Robin. Pegasus. 2010. (ENG.). 416p. (YA). (gr. 7-18). 18.99 *(978-0-399-24677-7(0)*, G.P. Putnam's Sons Books for Young Readers) Penguin Young Readers Group.
McRoberts, Eddison. Sneaking Treats: A Halloween Hunt. Gadra, Jessica, illus. 2012. 48p. 19.95 *(978-1-62137-136-6(0))* Virtualbookworm.com Publishing, Inc.
Mead, Richelle. Bloodlines. 2012. (Bloodlines Ser.: 1). (ENG.). 448p. (YA). (gr. 7-18). pap. 10.99 *(978-1-59514-473-7(0)*, Razorbill) Penguin Young Readers Group.
Meadows, Daisy. Aisha the Princess & the Pea Fairy. 2016. (Illus.). (J). (Fairy Tale Fairies Ser.: 6). (ENG.). 80p. (gr. 2-5). pap. 4.99 *(978-0-545-85199-2(8)*, Scholastic Paperbacks); 62p. ***(978-0-545-88741-0(0))*** Scholastic, Inc.
—Eleanor the Snow White Fairy. 2016. (Illus.). (J). (Fairy Tale Fairies Ser.: 2). (ENG.). 80p. (gr. 2-5). pap. 4.99 *(978-0-545-85190-9(4)*, Scholastic Paperbacks); 65p. ***(978-0-545-88738-0(0))*** Scholastic, Inc.
—Faith the Cinderella Fairy. 2016. (Illus.). (J). (Fairy Tale Fairies Ser.: 3). (ENG.). 80p. (gr. 2-5). pap. 4.99 *(978-0-545-85195-4(5)*, Scholastic Paperbacks); 65p. ***(978-0-545-88744-1(5))*** Scholastic, Inc.
—Gwen the Beauty & the Beast Fairy. 2016. (Illus.). (J). (Fairy Tale Fairies Ser.: 5). (ENG.). 80p. (gr. 2-5). pap. 4.99 *(978-0-545-85198-5(X)*, Scholastic Paperbacks); 67p. ***(978-1-5182-1018-1(X))*** Scholastic, Inc.
—Julia the Sleeping Beauty Fairy. 2016. (Illus.). 65p. (J). ***(978-0-545-88737-3(2))*** Scholastic, Inc.
—Lacey the Little Mermaid Fairy. 2016. (Illus.). (J). (Fairy Tale Fairies Ser.: 7). (ENG.). 80p. (gr. 2-5). pap. 4.99 *(978-0-545-85196-1(3)*, Scholastic Paperbacks); 65p. ***(978-0-545-88742-7(9))*** Scholastic, Inc.
Meadows, Daisy. Rita the Frog Princess Fairy. 2016. (Illus.). (J). (Fairy Tale Fairies Ser.: 4). (ENG.). 80p. (gr. 2-5). pap. 4.99 *(978-0-545-85197-8(1)*, Scholastic Paperbacks); 58p. ***(978-0-545-88739-7(9))*** Scholastic, Inc.
Mebberson, Amy, et al. Disney Princess Comics Collection. 2016. (ENG.). 96p. (J). (gr. 4-7). 20.85 *(978-0-606-39073-6(1))* Turtleback Bks.
Mehta, Lila. Anklet for a Princess: A Cinderella Story from India. Tang, Youshan, illus. 2014. (ENG.). 32p. (J). pap. 9.95 *(978-1-885008-46-6(5)*, Shen's Bks.) Lee & Low Bks., Inc.
Meskill, Elizia. The Heart Pendant: A Princess' Search for True Love Resplendent. 2012. (ENG.). 22p. (J). 21.95 *(978-1-4327-8003-6(4))*; pap. 13.95 *(978-1-4327-7774-6(2))* Outskirts Pr., Inc.
Metaxas, Eric. Princess Scargo & the Birthday Pumpkin, 1 vol. Barbour, Karen, illus. 2004. (Rabbit Ears-A Classic Tale Ser.). (ENG.). 40p. (gr. k-5). 25.65 *(978-1-59197-769-8(X))* Spotlight.
Metzger, Steve. Princess Kitty. Okstad, Ella, illus. 2017. 32p. (J). (gr. -1-3). 17.99 *(978-0-06-230662-3(6))* HarperCollins Pubs.
Meyer, Carolyn. Anastasia & Her Sisters. 2015. (ENG., Illus.). 320p. (YA). (gr. 7). 17.99 *(978-1-4814-0326-9(5)*, Simon & Schuster Bks. For Young Readers) Simon & Schuster Bks. For Young Readers.
—Cleopatra Confesses. (ENG.). 304p. (YA). (gr. 7). 2012. pap. 11.99 *(978-1-4169-8728-4(2))* 2011. 16.99 *(978-1-4169-8727-7(4))* Simon & Schuster/Paula Wiseman Bks. (Simon & Schuster/Paula Wiseman Bks.).
Meyer, Julia & Tabler, Marie. One Pea. Tabler, Marie, illus. 2013. (Illus.). 36p. 14.95 *(978-1-62314-139-4(7))* ePub Bud.
Mi-Leing. Chrystal's Castle. 2007. 40p. 18.50 *(978-1-4303-2242-9(X))* Lulu Pr., Inc.
Michaelis, Antonia. Tiger Moon. 2009. (ENG.). 480p. (YA). (gr. 7-11). pap. 9.95 *(978-0-8109-4499-2(5)*, Amulet Bks.) Abrams, Inc.
Miller, Eileen Rudisill. Fairy Tale Princesses Paper Dolls. 2012. (Dover Paper Dolls Ser.). (ENG.). 32p. (J). (gr. k-3). pap. 7.99 *(978-0-486-48990-2(6))* Dover Pubns., Inc.
—Princess Super. 2011. (Dover Sticker Bks.). (ENG., Illus.). 8p. (J). (gr. k-5). 7.99 *(978-0-486-48382-5(7))* Dover Pubns., Inc.
Miller, Holly & Schwartzkopf, Jere. A Horse Named Princess: Hola Princess Adios Thistle. 2009. 48p. pap. 17.49 *(978-1-4343-6976-5(5))* AuthorHouse.
Miller, Samantha A. The Princess & Her Servant. 2012. 24p. pap. 15.99 *(978-1-4691-5580-7(X))* Xlibris Corp.
Miura, Taro. The Big Princess. Miura, Taro, illus. 2015. (ENG., Illus.). 40p. (J). (-k). 14.99 *(978-0-7636-7459-5(1))* Candlewick Pr.
Mlynowski, Sarah. Once upon a Frog. 2015. (Whatever After Ser.: 8). (ENG., Illus.). 176p. (J). (gr. 3-7). 14.99 *(978-0-545-74660-1(4)*, Scholastic Pr.) Scholastic, Inc.
Moerbeck, Kees, illus. & des. Cinderella. Moerbeck, Kees, des. 2006. (Roly Poly Box Bks.). (ENG.). 24p. (J). *(978-1-84643-019-0(4))* Child's Play International Ltd.
Montanari, Eva. Princess Matilda. 2007. (Illus.). 24p. (J). (gr. -1-1). *(978-1-84539-259-8(0))* Meadowside Children's Bks.
Montanari, Eva, illus. Princess Matilda. 2007. 24p. (J). (gr. -1-1). *(978-1-84539-276-5(0))* Meadowside Children's Bks.
Montejo, Victor. Blanca Flor: Una Princessa Maya, 1 vol. Yockteng, Rafael, illus. 2005. (SPA.). 36p. (J). (gr. 1). 16.95 *(978-0-88899-600-8(4))* Groundwood Bks. CAN. Dist: Publishers Group West (PGW).
Montes, Graciela. Había una Vez una Princesa. Torres, Elena, illus. 2006. (Alfaguara Infantil Ser.). 26p. (J). 8.95 *(978-1-59820-215-1(4)*, Alfaguara) Santillana USA Publishing Co., Inc.
Moore, Beth. My Child, My Princess: A Parable about the King. Warren, Beverly, illus. 2014. (ENG.). 32p. (J). (gr. -1-3). 9.99 *(978-1-4336-8468-5(3)*, B&H Kids) B&H Publishing Group.
Moore, Nathan. The Little Princess & the Backyard Mystery: A Children's Story. 2008. 27p. pap. 24.95 *(978-1-60610-805-5(0))* America Star Bks.
Moriarty, Jaclyn. A Corner of White. 2013. (Colors of Madeleine Ser.: 1). (ENG.). 384p. (J). (gr. 7). 18.99 *(978-0-545-39736-0(7)*, Levine, Arthur A. Bks.) Scholastic, Inc.
Morley, P. Kevin. The Stinky Pirate & the Princess. 2009. 36p. pap. 17.99 *(978-1-4490-4062-8(4))* AuthorHouse.
Morningforest, Chris & Raymond, Rebecca. Princess Underdrawers & the Dragon. 2006. 37p. (J). pap. 15.58 *(978-1-4116-8837-7(6))* Lulu Pr., Inc.
Morris, J. & J. Little Black Pearl. 2010. 80p. pap. *(978-1-905553-51-8(X))* BookPublishingWorld.
Morrissey, Lynda I. Princesses Don't Hit. Money, Greg, illus. 2012. 24p. pap. *(978-1-77097-976-5(X))* FriesenPress.
Moss, Yvonne. The Butterfly Princess. 2011. 16p. (gr. -1). pap. 9.49 *(978-1-4567-4044-3(X))* AuthorHouse.
Mowery, Peg K. Once upon A Princess. 2006. 16.50 *(978-0-8059-9027-0(5))* Dorrance Publishing Co., Inc.
Moxilada, J. L. Jonty Jones Takes Guard. 2005. 242p. pap. 16.88 *(978-1-4116-4126-6(4))* Lulu Pr., Inc.
Mulholland, Jane. Ribeye, the Vegetarian Dragon. 2013. 24p. pap. 24.95 *(978-1-4626-9935-3(9))* America Star Bks.
Muloch, Miss. The Little Lame Prince & Other Tales. 2007. 304p. per. 16.95 *(978-1-4344-9378-1(4))* Wildside Pr., LLC.
Mulrain, Sabrina. A Prince's Happy Ever After. 2011. 40p. pap. 24.95 *(978-1-4560-3251-7(8))* America Star Bks.
Munsch, Robert. The Paper Bag Princess. Martchenko, Michael, illus. 10th ed. 2009. (ENG.). 28p. (J). (gr. -1-2). bds. 7.99 *(978-1-55451-211-9(5)*, 9781554512119) Annick Pr., Ltd. CAN. Dist: Publishers Group West (PGW).
—The Paper Bag Princess: The Story Behind the Story. Martchenko, Michael, illus. 3rd anniv. ed. 2005. (ENG.). 64p. (J). (gr. -1-12). 19.95 *(978-1-55037-915-0(1)*, 9781550379150) Annick Pr., Ltd. CAN. Dist: Publishers Group West (PGW).
Murdock, Catherine Gilbert. Princess Ben. 2009. (ENG.). 352p. (YA). (gr. 7). pap. 9.99 *(978-0-547-22325-4(0))* Houghton Mifflin Harcourt Publishing Co.
—Wisdom's Kiss. 2013. (ENG.). 320p. (YA). (gr. 7). pap. 8.99 *(978-0-547-85540-0(0))* Houghton Mifflin Harcourt Publishing Co.
—Wisdom's Kiss: A Thrilling & Romantic Adventure, Incorporating Magic, Villany, & a Cat. 2011. (ENG.). 304p. (YA). (gr. 7). 16.99 *(978-0-547-56687-0(5))* Houghton Mifflin Harcourt Publishing Co.
Murphy, Emily. The Princess of Booray. Smith, Richard G., illus. 2005. (J). *(978-0-9742891-2-0(4))* Marriwell Publishing.
Nasir, Safia. Princess Neelam & Other Stories. 2005. 52p. *(978-969-542-109-3(1))*; *(978-91-21-51821-2(1))* Children Pubns.
Nathan, Sarah. Blue-Ribbon Bunny. 2014. (Sofia the First World of Reading Ser.). (J). lib. bdg. 13.55 *(978-0-606-35264-2(3))* Turtleback Bks.
—Jasmine: The Missing Coin, 1 vol. Studio IBOIX, illus. 2012. (Disney Princesses Set 2 Ser.). (ENG.). 96p. (J). (gr. 2-6). lib. bdg. 24.21 *(978-1-59961-182-2(1))* Spotlight.
—Sofia's Magic Lesson. 2014. (Illus.). 32p. (J). *(978-1-4844-2887-0(0))* Disney Pr.
—Sofia's Magic Lesson. 2014. (Sofia the First Ser.). (J). lib. bdg. 13.55 *(978-0-606-35258-1(9))* Turtleback Bks.
Nathan, Sarah & Disney Book Group Staff. Blue Ribbon Bunny, Level 1. Disney Storybook Art Team, illus. 2014. (World of Reading Ser.). (ENG.). 32p. (J). (gr. -1-k). pap. 3.99 *(978-1-4231-7158-4(6))* Disney Pr.
—Sofia the First Sofia's Magic Lesson. 2014. (ENG.). 32p. (J). (gr. -1-k). pap. 3.99 *(978-1-4231-9854-3(9))* Disney Pr.
Negrin, Fabian. The Princess & the Rainbow Coat. Waters, Fiona, illus. 2005. 32p. (J). *(978-1-84458-411-6(9)*, Pavilion Children's Books) Pavilion Bks.
Nelson, D. J. The One-Eyed Spotogon. 2012. (Illus.). 24p. pap. 19.82 *(978-1-4772-1965-2(X))* AuthorHouse.
Neubert, Oliver. Chantel's Quest for the Silver Leaf. 2012. (Chantel's Quest Ser.). (ENG., Illus.). 200p. (J). (gr. 4-7). pap. 9.95 *(978-1-897476-43-7(4))* Simply Read Bks. CAN. Dist: Ingram Publisher Services.
Newton, Chelle. The Butterfly Princess. Padovano, Chris, illus. 2012. 44p. pap. 11.99 *(978-1-61286-129-6(6))* Avid Readers Publishing Group.
Nguy, Hoa X. The Bamboo Girl. 2007. 84p. (J). pap. 20.00 *(978-0-8059-7562-8(4))* Dorrance Publishing Co., Inc.
Nichills, Dee. Visit the Rainforest. 2013. 42p. pap. 9.99 *(978-1-60820-857-9(5))* MLR Pr., LLC.
Nielsen, Jennifer A. The Runaway King. (Ascendance Trilogy Ser.: 2). (ENG.). 352p. (J). (gr. 4-7). 2014. pap. 7.99 *(978-0-545-28416-5(3)*, Scholastic Paperbacks) 2013. (Illus.). 17.99 *(978-0-545-28415-8(5)*, Scholastic Pr.) Scholastic, Inc.
—The Runaway King. 2014. (Ascendance Trilogy Ser.: 2). lib. bdg. 18.40 *(978-0-606-35663-3(0))* Turtleback Bks.
Nielson, Kelli S. Stone Mage Wars, Book 1: Journey to the Fringe. 2011. (YA). 17.99 *(978-1-60908-833-0(6))* Deseret Bk. Co.
Nix, Garth. Frogkisser! 2017. (ENG.). 384p. (J). (gr. 7). 18.99 *(978-1-338-05208-4(X)*, Scholastic Pr.) Scholastic, Inc.
Nobacon, Danbert. 3 Dead Princes: An Anarchist Fairy Tale. Cox, Alex, illus. 2010. (ENG.). 208p. (gr. 8-18). pap. 13.00 *(978-1-935259-06-0(7))* Exterminating Angel Pr.
Norsgaard, E. Jaediker. How Krokken & Poppen Made Peace. 2008. 31p. pap. 24.95 *(978-1-60672-426-2(6))* America Star Bks.
North, Laura. Cinderella: The Terrible Truth. Dreidemy, Joëlle, illus. 2014. (ENG.). 32p. (J). *(978-0-7787-1326-5(1))* Crabtree Publishing Co.
—The Princess & the Frozen Peas. 2014. (ENG., Illus.). 32p. (J). *(978-0-7787-0446-1(7))*; pap. *(978-0-7787-0481-2(5))* Crabtree Publishing Co.
—Sleeping Beauty — 100 Years Later. 2014. (ENG., Illus.). 32p. (J). *(978-0-7787-0444-7(0))*; pap. *(978-0-7787-0479-9(3))* Crabtree Publishing Co.
North, Ryan. Adventure Time, Vol. 3. 2013. (Adventure Time Graphic Novels Ser.: 3). lib. bdg. 26.95 *(978-0-606-35462-2(X))* Turtleback Bks.
—Adventure Time Volume 2. 2013. (Adventure Time Graphic Novels Ser.: 2). lib. bdg. 26.95 *(978-0-606-35461-5(1))* Turtleback Bks.
North, Ryan & Paroline, Shelli. Adventure Time Vol.4 - Mathematical Edition. 2014. (Illus.). 144p. *(978-1-78276-171-6(3)*, Titan Bks.) Titan Bks. Ltd.
Nosy Crow Staff. Princess Penelope & the Runaway Kitten. Murray, Alison, illus. 2013. (ENG.). 32p. (J). (gr. -1-2). 15.99 *(978-0-7636-6952-2(0)*, Nosy Crow) Candlewick Pr.
Nwokolo, Nwanneka. Zara: The Girl Traveller. 2004. (ENG.). 80p. *(978-1-904744-58-0(3))* Troubador Publishing Ltd.
Oakes, Colleen. Queen of Hearts. 2016. (Queen of Hearts Ser.: 1). 320p. (YA). (gr. 8). 17.99 *(978-0-06-240972-0(7)*, HarperTeen) HarperCollins Pubs.
Ofori-Mankata. Dede Akai. 2012. 48p. pap. 21.88 *(978-1-4669-1569-5(2))* Trafford Publishing.
Ohlin, Nancy. Beauty. 2013. (ENG., Illus.). 208p. (YA). (gr. 7). pap. 9.99 *(978-1-4424-7265-5(0)*, Simon Pulse) Simon Pulse.
Olivas, Silvia. Disney Elena of Avalor: a Sister's Promise: Storybook & Necklace. 2016. (ENG.). 32p. (J). (gr. -1 — 1). 14.99 *(978-0-7944-3842-5(3)*, Reader's Digest Children's Bks.) Studio Fun International.
O'Malley, Kevin. Once upon a Cool Motorcycle Dude. O'Malley, Kevin et al, illus. 2005. (ENG.). 32p. (J). (gr. 1-5). 16.99 *(978-0-8027-8947-1(1)*, 9780802789471, Bloomsbury USA Childrens) Bloomsbury Publishing USA.
O'Neal, Eilis. The False Princess. 2012. (ENG.). 336p. (J). (gr. 7). pap. 8.99 *(978-0-60684-392-5(3)*, Carolrhoda Lab™) Lerner Publishing Group.
Ordal, Stina Langlo. Princess Aasta Event Kit. (J). *(978-1-58234-806-3(5))* Bloomsbury Publishing USA.
Orr, Wendy. The Princess & Her Panther. Stringer, Lauren, illus. 2010. (ENG.). 40p. (J). (gr. -1-3). 16.99 *(978-1-4169-9780-1(6)*, Beach Lane Bks.) Beach Lane Bks.
O'Ryan, Ellie. Jasmine: The Jewel Orchard. 2013. (Disney Princess Early Chapter Bks.). (J). lib. bdg. 14.75 *(978-0-606-27068-7(X)*, Turtleback) Turtleback Bks.
O'Ryan, Ellie & Studio IBOIX. Cinderella: The Great Mouse Mistake, 1 vol. 2012. (Disney Princess Ser.). (ENG., Illus.). 96p. (J). (gr. 2-5). 24.21 *(978-1-59961-879-1(6))* Spotlight.
Osterlund, Anne. Aurelia. 2008. (ENG.). 256p. (YA). (gr. 7-18). 8.99 *(978-0-14-240579-6(5)*, Speak) Penguin Young Readers Group.
Ottolenghi, Carol. The Princess & the Pea. 2009. (Keepsake Stories Ser.). (ENG.). 32p. (gr. -1-3). pap. 3.99 *(978-0-7696-5869-8(5)*, Brighter Child) Carson-Dellosa Publishing, LLC.
—The Princess & the Pea (La Princesa y el Guisante) 2009. (Keepsake Stories Ser.). (ENG & SPA.). 32p. (gr. -1-2). pap. 3.99 *(978-0-7696-5865-0(2)*, Brighter Child) Carson-Dellosa Publishing, LLC.
Owen, Sarah. Sarah the Fairy Princess's Birthday Party. 2009. 32p. pap. 41.50 *(978-1-4452-5921-5(4))* Lulu Pr., Inc.
Page, Nick & Claire. The Autumn Princess. 2006. (Read with Me (Make Believe Ideas) Ser.). (Illus.). 32p. (J). (gr. k-2). *(978-1-84610-171-7(9))* Make Believe Ideas.
Pagnoni, Roberta & Rigo, Laura, illus. My Princess Bag. 2016. (ENG.). 8p. (J). (gr. -1-k). bds. 6.99 *(978-0-7641-6841-3(X))* Barron's Educational Series, Inc.
Pantages, Joanna. Fairytale Fitness: The Goobyland Race. 2009. 20p. pap. 11.95 *(978-1-4389-5480-6(8))* AuthorHouse.
Paquette, Ammi-Joan. Princess Juniper of the Anju. 2016. (Princess Juniper Ser.). (ENG., Illus.). 272p. (J). (gr. 3-7). 16.99 *(978-0-399-17152-9(5)*, Philomel Bks.) Penguin Young Readers Group.
Paquette, Ammi-Joan. Princess Juniper of Torr. 2017. (Princess Juniper Ser.). (ENG.). 256p. (J). (gr. 3-7). 16.99 ***(978-0-399-17153-6(3)***, Philomel Bks.) Penguin Young Readers Group.
Paquette, Ammi-Joan & Mack, Jeff. Princess Juniper of the Hourglass. 2015. (Princess Juniper Ser.). (ENG., Illus.). 288p. (J). (gr. 3-7). bds. 16.99 *(978-0-399-17151-2(7)*, Philomel Bks.) Penguin Young Readers Group.
Parker, Lisa L. Gray. Princesses Do Not Wear Tattoos. Logan, Desiree, illus. 2011. 48p. pap. 24.95 *(978-1-4560-3281-4(X))* America Star Bks.
Parnell, Fran & Fatus, Sophie. Grim, Grunt & Grizzle-Tail: A Story from Chile. Fatus, Sophie, illus. 2013. (Monster Stories Ser.: 6). (ENG., Illus.). 48p. (J). (gr. 1-4). pap. 8.99 *(978-1-84686-910-5(2))* Barefoot Bks., Inc.
Parragon Staff. Disney Princess Sparkling Dreams. 2010. (Disney Twinkly Lights Board Bks.). 6p. (J). (gr. -1-k). bds. *(978-1-4075-9340-1(4))* Parragon, Inc.
Patten, Linda D. Princess Alese & the Kingdom of Serenity. 2013. 20p. pap. 13.77 *(978-1-4669-8724-1(3))* Trafford Publishing.
Patterson, Shannon. The Princess & the Cheese. 2010. 43p. pap. 19.95 *(978-0-557-51615-5(3))* Lulu Pr., Inc.
Patton, Chris. A Totally True Princess Story. Wellman, Mike, ed. St. Aubin, Claude, illus. 2009. 72p. 12.99 *(978-0-615-27602-1(4))* Atomic Basement.
Pau Pau. The Princess' Adventure. 2007. 52p. pap. 16.95 *(978-1-60441-069-3(8))* America Star Bks.
Paulson, Elizabeth. Dead upon a Time. 2015. (ENG.). 224p. (J). (gr. 7). 17.99 *(978-0-545-64046-6(6)*, Scholastic Pr.) Scholastic, Inc.
The Pearl Princess. 2004. (Illus.). 32p. 3.99 *(978-1-894998-00-0(6))* Lake, Jack Productions, Inc. CAN. Dist: Hushion Hse. Publishing, Ltd.
Pearson, Mary E. The Beauty of Darkness. 2016. (Remnant Chronicles Ser.: 3). (ENG., Illus.). 688p. (YA). (gr. 9-12). 18.99 *(978-0-8050-9925-6(5)*, 9780805099256, Holt, Henry & Co. Bks. For Young Readers) Holt, Henry & Co.
—The Beauty of Darkness. 2017. (Remnant Chronicles Ser.: Bk. 3). (ENG.). 688p. (YA). pap. 10.99 *(978-1-250-11531-7(0)*, 9781250115317) Square Fish.
—The Heart of Betrayal. 2015. (Remnant Chronicles: Bk. 2). (ENG.). 480p. (YA). (gr. 9). 18.99 *(978-0-8050-9924-9(7)*, 9780805099249, Holt, Henry & Co. Bks. For Young Readers) Holt, Henry & Co.
—The Heart of Betrayal. 2016. (Remnant Chronicles Ser.: 2). (ENG.). 496p. (YA). pap. 10.99 *(978-1-250-08002-8(9)*, 9781250080028) Square Fish.
—The Kiss of Deception. 2014. (Remnant Chronicles Ser.: 1). (ENG.). 496p. (YA). (gr. 9-12). 18.99 *(978-0-8050-9923-2(9)*, 9780805099232); E-Book *(978-1-62779-218-9(X)*, 9781627792189) Holt, Henry & Co. (Holt, Henry & Co. Bks. For Young Readers).
—The Kiss of Deception. 2015. (Remnant Chronicles Ser.: 1). (ENG.). 512p. (YA). (gr. 9-12). pap. 10.99 *(978-1-250-06315-1(9)*, 9781250063151) Square Fish.
Pef. Belle lisse poire du prince De. pap. 16.95 *(978-2-07-054806-4(6))* Gallimard, Editions FRA. Dist: Distribooks, Inc.
Perelman, Helen. A Candy Fairies Sweet Collection: Chocolate Dreams; Rainbow Swirl; Caramel Moon; Cool Mint. Waters, Erica-Jane, illus. 2013. (Candy Fairies Ser.). (ENG.). 512p. (J). (gr. 2-5). pap. 23.99 *(978-1-4424-9390-2(9)*, Aladdin) Simon & Schuster Children's Publishing.
—Rapunzel: A Day to Remember, 1 vol. Studio IBOIX, illus. 2012. (Disney Princesses Set 2 Ser.). (ENG.). 96p. (J). (gr. 2-6). lib. bdg. 24.21 *(978-1-59961-183-9(X))* Spotlight.
Perelman, Helen & Studio IBOIX. Tiana: The Grand Opening, 1 vol. 2012. (Disney Princess Ser.). (ENG., Illus.). 96p. (J). (gr. 2-5). 24.21 *(978-1-59961-880-7(X))* Spotlight.
Perez, Marlene. Princess Rock & the Royal Inches. 2004. (Shared Connections Ser.). (J). pap. 27.00 *(978-1-4108-1633-7(8))*; instr.'s gde. ed. 27.00 *(978-1-4108-1609-2(5))* Benchmark Education Co.
Perez, Vivian. Stolen Stories for My Nieces. 2007. (ENG.). 68p. per. 19.95 *(978-1-4241-6679-4(9))* America Star Bks.
Perrett, Lisa, illus. Sparkling Princess ABC. 2013. (Sparkling Stories Ser.). (ENG.). 14p. (J). bds. 5.95 *(978-1-4027-8886-4(X))* Sterling Publishing Co., Inc.
Peters, Stephanie True. A Princess Primer: A Fairy Godmother's Guide to Being a Princess. Oberdieck, Bernhard & Gordeev, Denis, illus. 2006. (ENG.). 32p. (J). (gr. k-3). 19.99 *(978-0-525-47765-5(9)*, Dutton Books for Young Readers) Penguin Young Readers Group.
—Sleeping Beauty, Magic Master: A Graphic Novel. Lopez, Alex, illus. 2016. (Far Out Fairy Tales Ser.). (ENG.). 40p. (gr. 3-4). lib. bdg. 25.32 *(978-1-4965-3784-3(X)*, Far Out Fairy Tales) Stone Arch Bks.
Peterson, Alyson. The Cursed Dagger. 2016. (YA). pap. *(978-1-4621-1865-6(8))* Cedar Fort, Inc./CFI Distribution.
—The Exiled Prince. 2017. (ENG.). (YA). (gr. 8-12). pap. 17.99 ***(978-1-4621-2035-2(0)***, Sweetwater Bks.) Cedar Fort, Inc./CFI Distribution.
Peterson, Alyson. Ian Quicksilver: The Warrior's Return. 2015. vii, 309p. (YA). pap. 17.99 *(978-1-4621-1629-4(9))* Cedar Fort, Inc./CFI Distribution.
Petit, Cheryl. Fairy Princess Melina, 1 vol. 2010. 26p. pap. 24.95 *(978-1-4489-7915-8(3))* PublishAmerica, Inc.
Phillips, Deborah. The Parable of the Princesses. 2008. 48p. (J). 19.99 *(978-1-59038-873-0(9))* Deseret Bk. Co.
Phillips, Elizabeth. The Blueberry Princess. Phillips, Elizabeth & Phillips, Andrea, illus. 2008. 25p. pap. 24.95 *(978-1-60672-097-4(X))* America Star Bks.
Phillipson, Fiona. Fairy Princesses: Over 1000 Reusable Stickers! 2014. (Little Hands Creative Sticker Play Ser.).

(ENG.). 64p. (J). (gr. -1-2). pap. 9.99 *(978-1-4380-0396-2(X))* Barron's Educational Series, Inc.

Phoenix International Staff, illus. Princess Sofia. 2012. 10p. (J). bds. 14.98 *(978-1-4508-6822-8(3)*, e41cac27-3be3-41b8-8dc5-7fb934c0ea6b) Phoenix International Publications, Inc.

Piggy Toes Press, creator. Disney Princess Bath Book. 2011. (ENG.). (gr. -1-k). 5.95 *(978-1-61524-416-4(6)*, Intervisual/Piggy Toes) Bendon, Inc.

Pinnington, Andrea. The Princess Creativity Book: Includes Stickers, Fold-Out Scene, Stencils, & Pretty Paper. 2011. (Creativity Bks.). 96p. (J). (gr. 1-4). pap. 12.99 *(978-0-7641-4675-6(0))* Barron's Educational Series, Inc.

Pollett, Allan. For My Little Princess. 2010. 24p. pap. 15.99 *(978-1-4500-7583-1(5))* Xlibris Corp.

Posner-Sanchez, Andrea. Always a Princess (Disney Princess) Disney Storybook Artists Staff, illus. 2011. (Friendship Box Ser.). (ENG.). 48p. (J). (gr. k — 1). bds. 10.99 *(978-0-7364-2848-4(8)*, RH/Disney) Random Hse. Children's Bks.

—Ariel's Dolphin Adventure - Snow White's New Friend, 2 bks. in 1. Random House Disney Staff, illus. 2010. (Pictureback(R) Ser.). (ENG.). 32p. (J). (gr. -1-2). pap. 4.99 *(978-0-7364-2654-1(X)*, RH/Disney) Random Hse. Children's Bks.

—Bunny Magic! (Disney Junior: Sofia the First) RH Disney Staff, illus. 2014. (Little Golden Book Ser.). (ENG.). 24p. (J). (-k). 4.99 *(978-0-7364-3085-2(7)*, Golden/Disney) Random Hse. Children's Bks.

—Cuddly Princess Pals. Random House Disney Staff, illus. 2014. (Pictureback(R) Ser.). (ENG.). 24p. (J). (gr. -1-2). 3.99 *(978-0-7364-3135-4(7)*, RH/Disney) Random Hse. Children's Bks.

—A Frozen Christmas (Disney Frozen) Random House Disney Staff, illus. 2015. (Glitter Board Book Ser.). (ENG.). 12p. (J). (gr. -1 — 1). bds. 8.99 *(978-0-7364-3479-9(8)*, RH/Disney) Random Hse. Children's Bks.

—Good Night, Princess! (Disney Princess) Legramandi, Francesco & Matta, Gabriella, illus. 2012. (Pictureback(R) Ser.). (ENG.). 16p. (J). (gr. -1-2). pap. 4.99 *(978-0-7364-2851-4(8)*, RH/Disney) Random Hse. Children's Bks.

—I Am a Princess. Matta, Gabriella & Legramandi, Francesco, illus. 2012. (Little Golden Book Ser.). (ENG.). 24p. (J). (gr. k-k). 4.99 *(978-0-7364-2906-1(9)*, Golden/Disney) Random Hse. Children's Bks.

—Meet the Princesses (Disney Princess) Random House Disney Staff, illus. 2013. (ENG.). 16p. (J). (-k). bds. 7.99 *(978-0-7364-3146-0(2)*, RH/Disney) Random Hse. Children's Bks.

—Palace Pets Ultimate Handbook (Disney Princess: Palace Pets) Random House Disney Staff, illus. 2015. (Ultimate Handbook Ser.). (ENG.). 64p. (J). (gr. -1-2). 9.99 *(978-0-7364-3421-8(6)*, RH/Disney) Random Hse. Children's Bks.

—The Perfect Tea Party (Disney Junior: Sofia the First) Random House Disney Staff, illus. 2013. (Little Golden Book Ser.). (ENG.). 24p. (J). (-k). 4.99 *(978-0-7364-3109-5(8)*, Golden/Disney) Random Hse. Children's Bks.

—Quiet Time with Belle (Disney Princess) DiCicco, Sue, illus. 2016. (ENG.). 24p. (J). (gr. -1 — 1). bds. 6.99 *(978-0-7364-3441-6(0)*, RH/Disney) Random Hse. Children's Bks.

—A Royal Easter. 2014. (Disney Princess 8x8 Ser.). lib. bdg. 14.75 *(978-0-606-35553-7(7))* Turtleback Bks.

—A Royal Easter (Disney Princess) RH Disney Staff et al, illus. 2014. (Pictureback(R) Ser.). (ENG.). 16p. (J). (gr. -1-2). 4.99 *(978-0-7364-3084-5(9)*, RH/Disney) Random Hse. Children's Bks.

—A Royal Pet Problem. RH Disney Staff, illus. 2015. (Little Golden Book Ser.). (ENG.). 24p. (J). (-k). 4.99 *(978-0-7364-3308-2(2)*, Golden/Disney) Random Hse. Children's Bks.

—A Royal Wedding Album (Disney Princess) RH Disney Staff, illus. 2016. (Picture Book Ser.). (ENG.). 48p. (J). (gr. -1-2). 9.99 *(978-0-7364-3477-5(1)*, RH/Disney) Random Hse. Children's Bks.

—Sleepy Time with Aurora (Disney Princess) RH Disney Staff & DiCicco, Sue, illus. 2015. (Board Book Ser.). (ENG.). 24p. (J). (— 1). bds. 6.99 *(978-0-7364-3311-2(2)*, RH/Disney) Random Hse. Children's Bks.

—Sofia the Second (Disney Junior: Sofia the First) RH Disney Staff, illus. 2014. (Little Golden Book Ser.). (ENG.). 24p. (J). (-k). 4.99 *(978-0-7364-3238-2(8)*, Golden/Disney) Random Hse. Children's Bks.

—Sofia's Royal World (Disney Junior: Sofia the First) Lee, Grace & Disney Storybook Artists Staff, illus. 2014. (Big Golden Book Ser.). (ENG.). 64p. (J). (gr. -1-2). 9.99 *(978-0-7364-3262-7(0)*, Golden/Disney) Random Hse. Children's Bks.

—Teacup to the Rescue! (Disney Princess: Palace Pets) RH Disney Staff & DiCicco, Sue, illus. 2015. (Little Golden Book Ser.). (ENG.). 24p. (J). (-k). 4.99 *(978-0-7364-3364-8(3)*, Golden/Disney) Random Hse. Children's Bks.

—Three Royal Birthdays! (Disney Princess) Legramandi, Francesco & Matta, Gabriella, illus. 2015. (Pictureback(R) Ser.). (ENG.). 24p. (J). (gr. -1-2). 5.99 *(978-0-7364-3403-4(8)*, RH/Disney) Random Hse. Children's Bks.

—Two Princesses & a Baby (Disney Junior: Sofia the First) RH Disney Staff & Studio IBOIX Staff, illus. 2015. (Little Golden Book Ser.). (ENG.). 24p. (J). (-k). 4.99 *(978-0-7364-3358-7(9)*, Golden/Disney) Random Hse. Children's Bks.

—Wish upon a Star (Disney Princess) Random House Disney Staff, illus. 2013. (Pictureback(R) Ser.). (ENG.). 16p. (J). (gr. -1-2). pap. 4.99 *(978-0-7364-3046-3(6)*, RH/Disney) Random Hse. Children's Bks.

Posner-Sanchez, Andrea & Julius, Jessica. Olaf's Perfect Day (Disney Frozen) RH Disney Staff & Disney Storybook Art Team Staff, illus. 2015. (Little Golden Book Ser.). (ENG.). 24p. (J). (-k). 4.99 *(978-0-7364-3356-3(2)*, Golden/Disney) Random Hse. Children's Bks.

Pretty Princess- Royal Party. 2005. (J). bds. *(978-1-4194-0061-2(4))* Paradise Pr., Inc.

Pretty Princess s/s - Beautiful Princess. 2005. (J). bds. *(978-1-4194-0062-9(2))* Paradise Pr., Inc.

Pretty Princess s/s - Fit for a Princess. 2005. (J). bds. *(978-1-4194-0063-6(0))* Paradise Pr., Inc.

Pretty Princess s/s - Wedding Day. 2005. (J). bds. *(978-1-4194-0064-3(9))* Paradise Pr., Inc.

Priddy, Roger. Princess Stories. 2009. (Sing-Along Ser.). (ENG.). 32p. (J). (gr. -1 — 1). bds. 12.95 *(978-0-312-50649-0(X)*, 9780312506490, Priddy Bks.) St. Martin's Pr.

Princesa Stephanie. 2005. (SPA.). (YA). per. 9.95 *(978-0-9764982-8-5(6))* Legacy Publishing Services, Inc.

Princess & Frog. (Ladybird Bks.). (Illus.). 52p. (J). 12.95 incl. audio *(978-0-86685-634-8(X))* International Bk. Ctr., Inc.

The Princess & the Magic Locket. (My Tooth Is Loose!). (Illus.). 32p. (J). *(978-1-4054-1022-9(1))* Parragon, Inc.

Princess Aurora: A Special Day in Her Life. l.t. ed. 2005. (Illus.). 32p. (J). 5.95 *(978-0-9766640-0-0(3)*, 212-279-3492) Attitudes in Dressing, Inc.

Princess Madeline & the Dragon. 2013. (Illus.). 118p. (YA). pap. 5.99 *(978-1-62375-070-1(9)*, Caliburn Bks.) MQuills Publishing.

Princess Protection Program Staff. The Palace of Mystery, No. 4. 2010. (Princess Protection Program Ser.). 144p. pap. 4.99 *(978-1-4231-2727-7(7))* Disney Pr.

Princess Rosa's Winter: Level M, 6 vols. 128p. (gr. 2-3). 49.95 *(978-0-7699-0986-8(8))* Shortland Pubns. (U. S. A.) Inc.

Princesses. 2009. (FACT ATLAS Ser.). 72p. (J). 15.99 *(978-0-8416-1101-6(7))* Hammond World Atlas Corp.

The Priness Who Lost Her Smile. 2006. (J). 19.95 *(978-0-9790682-0-1(7))* Clear Braces L.L.C.

Publications International Ltd. Staff. Disney Adventure Look & Find. 2013. (gr. 1-3). 7.98 *(978-1-4127-7146-7(3)*, 1412771463) Phoenix International Publications, Inc.

—Disney Princess PNO BK. 2010. 10p. (J). 16.98 *(978-1-4127-8997-4(4))* Phoenix International Publications, Inc.

—Disney Princess Songs. 2013. 12p. (J). (gr. k-4). bds. 21.99 *(978-1-4127-8016-2(0)*, fdc578c6-8169-40c1-acde-e3e9449607c7) Phoenix International Publications, Inc.

—Giant Look & Find Disney Princess. 2008. 24p. (J). 15.98 *(978-1-4127-8976-9(1)*, PIL Kids) Publications International, Ltd.

—My 1St Libraries Disney Princess. 2011. 12p. 12.98 *(978-1-4508-1303-7(8))* Publications International, Ltd.

Publications International Ltd. Staff, creator. Barbie as the Island Princess. 2007. (Play-A-Sound Bks.). (Illus.). 9.98 *(978-1-4127-7413-0(6))* Publications International, Ltd.

—Disney Princess Board Books & Bookend Set. 2007. (Illus.). (gr. -1-k). bds. 12.98 *(978-1-4127-8844-1(7))* Publications International, Ltd.

—Disney Princess: Musical Pop-up Treasury. 2007. (Disney Princess Ser.). (Illus.). (J). (gr. -1-3). 15.98 *(978-1-4127-7431-4(4))* Publications International, Ltd.

Publications International Ltd. Staff, ed. Disney Little First Look & Find Pack. 2010. 18p. (J). 14.98 *(978-1-4508-0334-2(2))* Phoenix International Publications, Inc.

—Disney Princess. 2008. (J). 3.98 *(978-1-4127-9248-6(7))* Phoenix International Publications, Inc.

—Disney Princess. (J). 2011. 64p. 9.98 *(978-1-60553-318-6(1)*, PIL Kids) 2007. (SPA.). 10.98 *(978-1-4127-8026-1(8))* Publications International, Ltd.

—Disney Princess: 26 Stories of Virtue. 2010. 12p. (J). 25.98 *(978-1-60553-692-7(X))* Phoenix International Publications, Inc.

—Disney Princess: Cinderella. 2008. (J). 12.98 *(978-1-4127-8475-7(1))* Publications International, Ltd.

—Disney Princess: Dreams Come True (Talking Look & Find) 2010. 16p. (J). bds. 12.98 *(978-1-60553-538-8(9))* Publications International, Ltd.

—Disney Princess: Enchanted Dreams. 2010. 40p. (J). bds. 14.98 *(978-1-60553-685-9(7))* Publications International, Ltd.

—Disney Princess: Follow Your Dreams. 2010. 24p. (J). 19.98 *(978-1-4127-5357-9(0)*, PIL Kids) Publications International, Ltd.

—Disney Princess: Just Like a Princess. 2010. 48p. (J). 2.98 *(978-1-4508-0731-9(3))* Phoenix International Publications, Inc.

—Disney Princess: Please & Thank You. 2011. 12p. (J). bds. *(978-1-4508-0399-1(7))* Phoenix International Publications, Inc.

—Disney Princess: Princess Jewels (Little First Look & Find) 2010. 18p. (J). bds. *(978-1-4508-0279-6(6)*, 1450802796) Phoenix International Publications, Inc.

—Disney Princess: Stories of Virtue. 2010. 10p. (J). bds. 12.98 *(978-1-4508-0164-5(1))* Phoenix International Publications, Inc.

—Disney Princess Ariel. 2011. 14p. (J). bds. 16.98 *(978-1-4127-9206-6(1))* Publications International, Ltd.

—Disney Princess Aurora. 2011. 14p. (J). bds. 16.98 *(978-1-4127-9205-9(3))* Publications International, Ltd.

—Disney Princess (book Block) 2010. (J). 10.98 *(978-1-4508-0672-5(4))* Phoenix International Publications, Inc.

—Disney(r) Princess First Look & Find(r)Palace Pets. 2015. 16p. (J). bds. *(978-1-4508-8634-5(5)*, 1450886345) Publications International, Ltd.

—Disney(r) Princess Little Look & Find(tm) 2014. 24p. (J). *(978-1-4508-9478-4(X)*, 145089478X) Publications International, Ltd.

—Disney Princess (Musical Treasury) 2011. 40p. (J). bds. 15.98 *(978-1-4508-1082-1(9))* Publications International, Ltd.

—Disney(r) Princess Palace Pets: Little Pop-Up Songbook. 2014. 10p. (J). bds. *(978-1-4508-8635-2(3)*, 1450886353) Publications International, Ltd.

—Disney Princess Picture Puzzles. 2010. 128p. (J). pap. 13.98 *(978-1-60553-131-1(6))* Phoenix International Publications, Inc.

—Disney Princess under the Starry Sky. 2013. 8p. (J). bds. *(978-1-4508-7130-3(5)*, 1450871305) Phoenix International Publications, Inc.

—Disney Princesses. 2009. 16p. (J). bds. 9.98 *(978-1-4127-7696-7(1)*, PIL Kids) Publications International, Ltd.

—Disney Tales of Virtue 5 Book Set. 2008. (J). pap. 4.98 *(978-1-4127-9392-6(0))* Phoenix International Publications, Inc.

—Little Sound the Princess & the Frog. 2009. 24p. (J). bds. 10.98 *(978-1-4127-6446-9(7))* Publications International, Ltd.

—Look & Find: Disney Princess: Magical Moments. 2010. 24p. (J). 7.98 *(978-1-60553-064-2(6))* Phoenix International Publications, Inc.

—Musical Disney Princesas. 2004. (ESP & SPA., Illus.). 38p. (J). bds. 12.98 *(978-0-7853-8630-8(0)*, 7176101) Publications International, Ltd.

—Musical Pop up Disney Princess. 2008. (SPA.). (J). 15.98 *(978-1-4127-8980-6(X))* Publications International, Ltd.

—My First Book Block Set Disey Princess. 2011. 5p. (J). bds. 14.98 *(978-1-4508-1630-4(4))* Phoenix International Publications, Inc.

—Once upon a Time. 2009. 24p. (J). bds. 17.98 *(978-1-4127-5369-2(4)*, PIL Kids) Publications International, Ltd.

—Please & Thank You. 2010. 20p. (J). bds. 10.98 *(978-1-60553-439-8(0)*, PIL Kids) Publications International, Ltd.

—PNO BK Spa Disney Princess. 2009. 12p. 15.98 *(978-1-4127-9243-1(6))* Phoenix International Publications, Inc.

—The Princess & the Frog. 2009. 24p. (J). 16.98 *(978-1-4127-6421-6(1))* Publications International, Ltd.

—Princess Magic. 2010. (My First Look & Find Ser.). (Illus.). 12p. (gr. -1). bds. 7.98 *(978-1-4127-3074-7(0)*, 7227000) Phoenix International Publications, Inc.

—Sofia the First - Sofia's Royal Day: Includes 6 Punch-Out Play Pieces. Phoenix Books Staff, illus. 2015. 14p. (J). bds. *(978-1-4508-8884-4(4)*, 1450888844) Publications International, Ltd.

—A Surprise for Belle. 2010. 12p. (J). bds. 9.98 *(978-1-4127-4454-6(7))* Phoenix International Publications, Inc.

Puchner, Willy. The ABC of Fabulous Princesses. 2014. (ENG., Illus.). 64p. (J). (gr. k-3). 19.95 *(978-0-7358-4113-0(6))* North-South Bks., Inc.

Quiller-Couch, Arthur Thomas. The Twelve Dancing Princesses & Other Fairy Tales. Nielsen, Kay, illus. 2012. (Calla Editions Ser.). (ENG.). 208p. (gr. 4). 40.00 *(978-1-60660-025-2(7))* Dover Pubns., Inc.

Rabe, Tish. Frozen. 2013. (Disney Princess Step into Reading Ser.). lib. bdg. 13.55 *(978-0-606-32203-4(5)*, Turtleback) Turtleback Bks.

Rai, Lori. Princess Sheron & the Frog. l.t. ed. 2004. (Illus.). 20p. (J). 10.00 *(978-0-9717419-5-9(6))* Law Offices of Harry Glick.

Rajan, Vithal. Jungu, the Baiga Princess. Kalyan, Srivi, illus. 2015. 112p. pap. 12.00 *(978-93-83074-05-1(1))* 'Zubaan Bks. IND. Dist: Chicago Distribution Ctr.

Rakos, Lynnda, et al. Princesses, Mermaids & Fairies Coloring Book. 2012. (Dover Coloring Bks.). (ENG.). 32p. (J). (gr. -1-2). pap. 3.99 *(978-0-486-48664-2(8))* Dover Pubns., Inc.

Ramius, Edward. Yawnywawnys. 2009. 28p. pap. 14.95 *(978-1-4389-3066-4(6))* AuthorHouse.

Randall, Alice. The Diary of B. B. Bright, Possible Princess. 2012. (J). *(978-1-61858-016-0(7))* Turner Publishing Co.

Randall, Alice & Williams, Caroline Randall. The Diary of B. B. Bright, Possible Princess. Strickland, Shadra, illus. 2012. (ENG.). 192p. (J). (gr. 2-6). 19.95 *(978-1-61858-015-3(9))* Turner Publishing Co.

Random House Disney Staff. Dancing Cinderella/Belle of the Ball. Random House Disney Staff, illus. 2009. (Pictureback(R) Ser.). (ENG., Illus.). 32p. (J). (gr. -1-2). pap. 4.99 *(978-0-7364-2560-5(8)*, RH/Disney) Random Hse. Children's Bks.

—Dream Big, Princess! (Disney Princess) Random House Disney Staff, illus. 2016. (Official Guide Ser.). (ENG., Illus.). 80p. (J). (gr. -1-2). 9.99 *(978-0-7364-3709-7(6)*, RH/Disney) Random Hse. Children's Bks.

—Frozen Story Collection (Disney Frozen) Random House Disney Staff, illus. 2015. (Step into Reading Ser.). (ENG., Illus.). 160p. (J). (gr. -1-2). pap. 7.99 *(978-0-7364-3435-5(6)*, RH/Disney) Random Hse. Children's Bks.

—Jasmine & the Star of Persia (Disney Princess) Random House Disney Staff, illus. 2015. (Pictureback Ser.). (ENG., Illus.). 16p. (J). (gr. -1-2). pap. 4.99 *(978-0-7364-3048-7(2)*, RH/Disney) Random Hse. Children's Bks.

—The Little Mermaid Big Golden Book (Disney Princess) Random House Disney Staff, illus. 2013. (Big Golden Book Ser.). (ENG., Illus.). 64p. (J). (gr. -1-2). 9.99 *(978-0-7364-2988-7(3)*, Golden/Disney) Random Hse. Children's Bks.

—A New Reindeer Friend. Random House Disney Staff, illus. 2014. (Big Golden Book Ser.). (ENG., Illus.). 32p. (J). (gr. -1-2). 9.99 *(978-0-7364-3295-5(7)*, Golden/Disney) Random Hse. Children's Bks.

—A Princess Easter (Disney Princess) 2013. (Glitter Board Book Ser.). (ENG., Illus.). 12p. (J). (gr. -1-2). bds. 6.99 *(978-0-7364-3014-2(8)*, RH/Disney) Random Hse. Children's Bks.

—Princess Story Collection. 2007. (Step into Reading Ser.). (ENG., Illus.). 160p. (J). (gr. k-3). pap. 7.99 *(978-0-7364-2486-8(5)*, RH/Disney) Random Hse. Children's Bks.

—Rapunzel's Royal Wedding/Belle's Royal Wedding (Disney Princess) Random House Disney Staff, illus. 2013. (Pictureback(R) Ser.). (ENG., Illus.). 32p. (J). (gr. -1-2). 4.99 *(978-0-7364-2993-1(X)*, RH/Disney) Random Hse. Children's Bks.

—Sweet & Spooky Halloween. Marrucchi, Elisa, illus. 2007. (Pictureback(R) Ser.). (ENG.). 24p. (J). (gr. -1-2). pap. 3.99 *(978-0-7364-2453-0(9)*, RH/Disney) Random Hse. Children's Bks.

Random House Disney Staff, illus. Anna & Elsa, 6 vols., Bks. 1-6. 2015. (ENG.). 768p. (J). (gr. 1-4). 59.94 *(978-0-7364-3463-8(1)*, RH/Disney) Random Hse. Children's Bks.

Random House Disney Staff & Redbank, Tennant. Teacup: Belle's Star Pup (Disney Princess: Palace Pets) Legramandi, Francesco & Matta, Gabriella, illus. 2015. (Stepping Stone Book(TM) Ser.). (ENG.). 64p. (J). (gr. 1-4). 5.99 *(978-0-7364-3345-7(7)*, RH/Disney) Random Hse. Children's Bks.

Random House Editors & Posner-Sanchez, Andrea. I Am Cinderella. Random House Editors & Disney Storybook Artists Staff, illus. 2011. (Shaped Board Book Ser.). (ENG.). 12p. (J). (— 1). bds. 4.99 *(978-0-7364-2769-2(4)*, Golden/Disney) Random Hse. Children's Bks.

Random House Editors & RH Disney Staff. Aurora & the Helpful Dragon/Tiana & Her Furry Friend. Disney Storybook Artists Staff & Studio Iboix Staff, illus. 2011. (Pictureback(R) Ser.). (ENG.). 32p. (J). (gr. -1-2). pap. 4.99 *(978-0-7364-2757-9(0)*, RH/Disney) Random Hse. Children's Bks.

Random House Staff, illus. Barbie Fairytale Collection. 2011. (Step into Reading Ser.). (ENG.). 160p. (J). (gr. -1-1). pap. 7.99 *(978-0-375-87255-6(8)*, Random Hse. Bks. for Young Readers) Random Hse. Children's Bks.

Ratcliff, Charline. The Princess, the Toad & the Whale. 2012. (ENG.). 36p. (J). (-18). pap. 12.95 *(978-1-4787-1672-3(X))* Outskirts Pr., Inc.

The Real Princess: 6 Small Books. (gr. k-2). 23.00 *(978-0-7635-8505-1(X))* Rigby Education.

Redbank, Tennant. Beauty: Aurora's Sleepy Kitten. Random House Disney Staff, illus. 2014. (Stepping Stone Book Ser.). (ENG.). 64p. (J). (gr. 2-5). 5.99 *(978-0-7364-3266-5(3)*, RH/Disney) Random Hse. Children's Bks.

—Beauty the Sleepiest Kitty. Random House Disney Staff, illus. 2014. (Stepping Stone Book(TM) Ser.). (ENG.). 64p. (J). (gr. 1-4). lib. bdg. 12.99 *(978-0-7364-8163-2(X)*, RH/Disney) Random Hse. Children's Bks.

—Blondie: Rapunzel's Royal Pony. Random House Disney Staff, illus. 2014. (Stepping Stone Book(TM) Ser.). (ENG.). 64p. (J). (gr. 2-5). 5.99 *(978-0-7364-3267-2(1)*, RH/Disney) Random Hse. Children's Bks.

—Pumpkin: Cinderella's Dancing Pup (Disney Princess: Palace Pets) RH Disney Staff et al, illus. 2015. (Disney Chapters Ser.). (ENG.). 64p. (J). (gr. 1-4). 5.99 *(978-0-7364-3423-2(2)*, RH/Disney) Random Hse. Children's Bks.

—Treasure: Ariel's Curious Kitten. 2015. (Disney Princess Palace Pets Ser.). lib. bdg. 16.00 *(978-0-606-36392-1(0))* Turtleback Bks.

—Treasure: Ariel's Curious Kitten (Disney Princess: Palace Pets) RH Disney Staff et al, illus. 2015. (Stepping Stone Book(TM) Ser.). (ENG.). 64p. (J). (gr. 1-4). 5.99 *(978-0-7364-3346-4(5)*, RH/Disney) Random Hse. Children's Bks.

Redbank, Tennant, et al. Disney Princess Little Golden Book Favorites: Volume 3 (Disney Princess) Tyminski, Lori & Ying, Victoria, illus. 2014. (Little Golden Book Favorites Ser.). (ENG.). 80p. (J). (-k). 6.99 *(978-0-7364-3098-2(9)*, Golden/Disney) Random Hse. Children's Bks.

Redwine, C. J. The Shadow Queen. 2016. (YA). (gr. 8). (Ravenspire Ser.: 1). 416p. pap. 9.99 *(978-0-06-236025-0(6))*; (ENG., Illus.). 400p. 17.99 *(978-0-06-236024-3(8))* HarperCollins Pubs.

—The Shadow Queen. 2016. (Ravenspire Ser.: 1). (YA). lib. bdg. 20.85 *(978-0-606-39615-8(2))* Turtleback Bks.

Regan, Dian. Cam's Quest: The Continuing Story of Princess Nevermore & the Wizard's Apprentice. 2007. (Junior Library Guild Selection Ser.). 334p. (J). (gr. 4-8). 17.95 *(978-1-58196-056-3(5)*, Darby Creek) Lerner Publishing Group.

—Princess Nevermore. rev. ed. 2007. (Junior Library Guild Selection Ser.). (ENG.). 256p. (J). (gr. 4-8). 17.95 *(978-1-58196-055-6(7)*, Darby Creek) Lerner Publishing Group.

REID, D. H. Fantasies & Dreams. 2008. 208p. pap. 18.95 *(978-0-557-01592-4(8))* Lulu Pr., Inc.

Reisner, Molly. Dora's Princess Party. Aikins, Dave, illus. 2009. (Dora the Explorer Ser.). (ENG.). 12p. (J). (gr. -1-1). 6.99 *(978-1-4169-9045-1(3)*, Simon Spotlight/Nickelodeon) Simon Spotlight/Nickelodeon.

Rene, Rochelle. Bella & the Bad Mood Busters: The Bad Mood Blues. 2012. (ENG.). 22p. (J). 24.95 *(978-1-4327-7279-6(1))* Outskirts Pr., Inc.

Renner, Ellen. Castle of Shadows. 2013. (ENG., Illus.). 400p. (J). (gr. 5-7). pap. 7.99 *(978-0-544-02270-6(X))* Houghton Mifflin Harcourt Publishing Co.

Rennert, Laura Joy. Emma, the Extra Ordinary Princess. Florian, Melanie, illus. 2009. (J). *(978-0-525-42152-8(1)*, Dutton Juvenile) Penguin Publishing Group.

RH Disney. Belle - Discovery. RH Disney, illus. 2017. (Stepping Stone Book(TM) Ser.). (ENG., Illus.). 128p. (J). (gr. 1-4). 6.99 *(978-0-7364-3579-6(4)*, RH/Disney) Random Hse. Children's Bks.

—Disney Princess Beginnings: Ariel Makes Waves (Disney Princess) RH Disney, illus. 2017. (Stepping Stone Book(TM) Ser.). (ENG., Illus.). 128p. (J). (gr. 1-4). 6.99 ***(978-0-7364-3733-2(9))***; lib. bdg. 12.99 ***(978-0-7364-8196-0(6))*** Random Hse. Children's Bks. (RH/Disney).

—Disney Princess Heart Strong #2 (Disney Princess) RH Disney, illus. 2017. (Step into Reading Ser.). (ENG., Illus.). 48p. (J). (gr. -1-1). pap. 5.99 ***(978-0-7364-3803-2(3)***, RH/Disney) Random Hse. Children's Bks.

—Flounder Loves Ariel (Disney Princess) RH Disney, illus. 2016. (Padded Board Book Ser.). (ENG., Illus.). 26p. (J). (gr. -1-1). bds. 9.99 *(978-0-7364-3707-3(X)*, RH/Disney) Random Hse. Children's Bks.

—Gus Loves Cinderella (Disney Princess) RH Disney, illus. 2016. (Padded Board Book Ser.). (ENG., Illus.). 26p. (J). (gr. -1-1). bds. 9.99 *(978-0-7364-3706-6(1)*, RH/Disney) Random Hse. Children's Bks.

—Journey to the Lights. RH Disney, illus. deluxe ed. 2016. (Stepping Stone Book Ser.). (ENG., Illus.). 224p. (J). (gr. 3-7). 14.99 *(978-0-7364-3659-5(6)*, RH/Disney) Random Hse. Children's Bks.

—Mulan Is Loyal/Merida Is Brave (Disney Princess) RH Disney, illus. 2017. (Step into Reading Ser.). (ENG., Illus.). 48p. (J). (gr. -1-1). lib. bdg. 12.99 ***(978-0-7364-9017-7(5)***, RH/Disney) Random Hse. Children's Bks.

—Nine Disney Princess Tales (Disney Princess) RH Disney, illus. 2016. (Little Golden Book Favorites Ser.). (ENG., Illus.). 224p. (J). (-k). 12.99 *(978-0-7364-3617-5(0)*, Golden/Disney) Random Hse. Children's Bks.

—Princess Spring-Themed Board Book (Disney Princess) RH Disney, illus. 2017. (ENG., Illus.). 22p. (J). (-k). bds. 6.99 *(978-0-7364-3736-3(3)*, RH/Disney) Random Hse. Children's Bks.

RH Disney, illus. Five Enchanting Tales (Disney Princess) 2016. (Step into Reading Ser.). (ENG.). 160p. (J). (gr. -1-2).

pap. 7.99 *(978-0-7364-3518-5(2),* Random Hse. Bks. for Young Readers) Random Hse. Children's Bks.

RH Disney & Olivas, Silvia. Elena of Avalor. RH Disney, illus. 2017. (Big Golden Book Ser.). (ENG., Illus.). 32p. (J). (gr. -1-2). 9.99 *(978-0-7364-3552-9(2),* Golden/Disney) Random Hse. Children's Bks.

RH Disney Staff. Amazing Ariel! (Disney Princess) RH Disney Staff, illus. 2013. (Pictureback(R) Ser.). (ENG., Illus.). 16p. (J). (gr. -1-2). 4.99 *(978-0-7364-2994-8(8),* RH/Disney) Random Hse. Children's Bks.

—Ariel's Royal Wedding/Aurora's Royal Wedding (Disney Princess) RH Disney Staff, illus. 2014. (Pictureback(R) Ser.). (ENG., Illus.). 32p. (J). (gr. -1-2). 4.99 *(978-0-7364-3167-5(5),* RH/Disney) Random Hse. Children's Bks.

—Furry, Fluffy & Fabulous! (Disney Princess: Palace Pets) Disney Storybook Artists Staff, illus. 2014. (Big Golden Book Ser.). (ENG.). 64p. (J). (gr. -1-2). 9.99 *(978-0-7364-3263-4(9),* Golden/Disney) Random Hse. Children's Bks.

—Sparkle Magic! (Disney Frozen) RH Disney Staff, illus. 2015. (Pictureback(R) Ser.). (ENG., Illus.). 16p. (J). (gr. -1-2). 5.99 *(978-0-7364-3366-2(X),* RH/Disney) Random Hse. Children's Bks.

—Welcome to Whisker Haven (Disney Palace Pets: Whisker Haven Tales) RH Disney Staff, illus. 2016. (Big Golden Book Ser.). (ENG., Illus.). 32p. (J). (gr. -1-2). 9.99 *(978-0-7364-3474-4(7),* Golden/Disney) Random Hse. Children's Bks.

RH Disney Staff & Julius, Jessica. Anna's Birthday Surprise. RH Disney Staff, illus. 2015. (Pictureback(R) Ser.). (ENG., Illus.). 24p. (J). (gr. -1-2). 4.99 *(978-0-7364-3439-3(9),* RH/Disney) Random Hse. Children's Bks.

RH Disney Staff & Posner-Sanchez, Andrea. Cinderella Is My Babysitter (Disney Princess) RH Disney Staff et al, illus. 2015. (Little Golden Book Ser.). (ENG.). 24p. (J). (-k). 3.99 *(978-0-7364-3324-2(4),* Golden/Disney) Random Hse. Children's Bks.

Rhodes, Morgan. Falling Kingdoms. (Falling Kingdoms Ser.: 1). (ENG.). (YA). (gr. 7). 2014. 448p. pap. 10.99 *(978-1-59514-585-7(0))* 2012. (Illus.). 432p. 18.99 *(978-1-59514-584-0(2))* Penguin Young Readers Group. (Razorbill).

—Rebel Spring. 2014. (Falling Kingdoms Ser.: 2). (ENG.). 432p. (YA). (gr. 7). pap. 10.99 *(978-1-59514-592-5(3),* Razorbill) Penguin Young Readers Group.

Richards, Kitty. Cinderella: The Lost Tiara. 2012. (Disney Princess Early Chapter Bks.). (J). lib. bdg. 14.75 *(978-0-606-26572-0(4),* Turtleback) Turtleback Bks.

Richemont, Enid. Princess Frog. 2014. (ENG., Illus.). 32p. (J). *(978-0-7787-0443-0(2));* pap. *(978-0-7787-0452-2(1))* Crabtree Publishing Co.

Rigby Education Staff. Real Prince: Jumbled Tumble. (gr. k-2). 21.00 *(978-0-7635-2423-4(9))* Rigby Education.

Riggs, Kate. Princes & Princesses. 2013. (Illus.). 24p. (J). 25.65 *(978-1-60818-243-5(6),* Creative Education) Creative Co., The.

Riggs, Ransom. Tales of the Peculiar. Davidson, Andrew, illus. 2016. (ENG.). 192p. (YA). (gr. 7). 24.99 *(978-0-399-53853-7(4),* Dutton Books for Young Readers) Penguin Young Readers Group.

Rinaldi, Ann. The Redheaded Princess. 2008. (ENG.). 224p. (J). (gr. 3-7). 15.99 *(978-0-06-073374-2(8))* HarperCollins Pubs.

Rizzo, Cynthia Marie. Angela & the Princess. 2006. 89p. pap. 19.95 *(978-1-4241-2599-9(5))* America Star Bks.

Robbins, Trina. The Bark in Space. Page, Tyler, illus. 2013. (Chicagoland Detective Agency Ser.: 5). (ENG.). 64p. (gr. 4-8). (J). lib. bdg. 29.27 *(978-0-7613-8166-2(X));* pap. 6.95 *(978-1-4677-0725-1(2))* Lerner Publishing Group. (Graphic Universe™).

Robinson, Hilary. Beauty & the Pea. Sanfilippo, Simona, illus. 2013. (ENG.). 32p. (J). *(978-0-7787-1155-1(2))* Crabtree Publishing Co.

Robinson, Michelle. Goodnight Princess: The Perfect Bedtime Book! 2015. (Goodnight Ser.). (ENG., Illus.). 32p. (J). (gr. -1 — 1). pap. 7.99 *(978-1-4380-0663-5(2))* Barron's Educational Series, Inc.

Robinson, Rob. The Princess & the Juggler. 2004. 154p. pap. 12.95 *(978-0-595-30831-6(7))* iUniverse, Inc.

Rodriguez, Lourdes. Mandy, Princess of la la Land: The Green Monster. 2013. 52p. pap. 24.99 *(978-1-4817-0077-1(4))* AuthorHouse.

Rodriguez, Marisol. The Princess & the Chocolate Castle. 2012. 24p. pap. 17.99 *(978-1-4685-4911-9(1))* AuthorHouse.

Rogers, Jewels. The Princess & the Dolphin. 2011. 28p. 12.50 *(978-1-4567-3278-3(1))* AuthorHouse.

—The Princess & the Dolphin. 2010. 28p. pap. 16.99 *(978-1-4269-3966-2(3))* Trafford Publishing.

—The Princess & the Parakeet. 2011. 28p. pap. 12.50 *(978-1-4567-5170-8(0))* AuthorHouse.

—The Princess & the Puppy. 2011. 28p. pap. 12.50 *(978-1-4567-3236-3(6))* AuthorHouse.

—The Princess & the Puppy. 2010. 28p. pap. 16.99 *(978-1-4269-4177-1(3))* Trafford Publishing.

—The Princess & the Rabbit. 2011. 28p. pap. 12.50 *(978-1-4567-5171-5(9))* AuthorHouse.

Romansky, Sally Rosenberg. Invincible. Ott, Margot Janet, illus. 2006. (J). pap. 8.95 *(978-0-9723729-4-7(6))* Imagination Stage, Inc.

Rosado, Jessica E. The Princess. 2012. 26p. 24.95 *(978-1-4512-9466-8(2))* America Star Bks.

Rose, Jasmine. The Last Caterpillar Princess. 2011. 16p. pap. 8.64 *(978-1-4634-1953-0(8))* AuthorHouse.

Rose, Marie. Princess Silver Tears & One Feather. l.t. ed. 2006. (Illus.). 32p. (J). lib. bdg. *(978-1-934190-07-4(1))* Ocean Front Bk. Publishing, Inc.

Rosen, Lucy. My Little Pony: Meet Princess Twilight Sparkle. 2014. (Passport to Reading Level 1 Ser.). (J). lib. bdg. 13.55 *(978-0-606-35939-9(7))* Turtleback Bks.

Ross, Tony. Hora de Dormir. 2006. (Little Princess Ser.).Tr. of Bedtime. (SPA.). (J). (gr. -1-k). bds. 7.95 *(978-968-19-1488-2(0),* AT33282) Lectorum Pubns., Inc.

—I Didn't Do It! Ross, Tony, illus. 2016. (ENG., Illus.). 32p. (J). (gr. -1-3). 17.99 *(978-1-5124-0598-9(1))* Lerner Publishing Group.

—I Feel Sick! Ross, Tony, illus. 2015. (ENG., Illus.). 32p. (J). (gr. -1-3). 16.99 *(978-1-4677-5797-3(7))* Andersen Pr. GBR. Dist: Lerner Publishing Group.

—I Want a Bedtime Story! Ross, Tony, illus. 2016. (ENG., Illus.). 32p. (J). (gr. -1-3). 17.99 *(978-1-5124-1629-9(0))* Andersen Pr. GBR. Dist: Lerner Publishing Group.

—I Want a Party! Ross, Tony, illus. 2011. (Andersen Press Picture Books Ser.). (Illus.). (J). 16.95 *(978-0-7613-8069-4(2))* Andersen Pr. GBR. Dist: Lerner Publishing Group.

—I Want My Light On! Ross, Tony, illus. 2010. (Andersen Press Picture Bks). (ENG., Illus.). 32p. (J). (gr. -1-3). 16.95 *(978-0-7613-6443-6(9))* Lerner Publishing Group.

—I Want My Mom! Ross, Tony, illus. 2012. (Andersen Press Picture Bks). (ENG., Illus.). 32p. (J). (gr. -1-3). 16.95 *(978-1-4677-0318-5(4))* Lerner Publishing Group.

—I Want to Do It Myself! Ross, Tony, illus. 2011. (Andersen Press Picture Bks). (ENG., Illus.). 32p. (J). (gr. -1-3). 16.95 *(978-0-7613-7412-1(4))* Lerner Publishing Group.

—I Want to Go Home! Ross, Tony, illus. 2014. (Illus.). 32p. (J). (gr. -1-3). 16.95 *(978-1-4677-5095-0(6))* Lerner Publishing Group.

—I Want to Win! Ross, Tony, illus. 2012. (Andersen Press Picture Bks). (ENG., Illus.). 32p. (J). (gr. -1-3). 16.95 *(978-0-7613-8993-4(8))* Lerner Publishing Group.

—I Want Two Birthdays! Ross, Tony, illus. 2010. (ENG., Illus.). 32p. (J). (gr. -1-3). 16.95 *(978-0-7613-5495-6(6))* Lerner Publishing Group.

—El Tiempo. 2006. (Little Princess Ser.).Tr. of Weather. (SPA.). (J). (gr. -1-k). bds. 7.95 *(978-968-19-1487-5(2),* AT33281) Lectorum Pubns., Inc.

Ross, Tony, illus. I Don't Want to Go to Hospital. 2013. (ENG.). 32p. (J). (gr. -1-3). 16.95 *(978-1-4677-1155-5(1))* Lerner Publishing Group.

—I Feel Sick! 2015. (J). *(978-1-4677-5798-0(5))* Andersen Pr.

Ross, Tony & Ross, Tony. I Want a Sister! 2013. (Illus.). 32p. (J). (gr. -1-3). 16.95 *(978-1-4677-2047-2(X))* Andersen Pr. GBR. Dist: Lerner Publishing Group.

Rothfuss, Patrick. The Adventures of the Princess & Mr. Whiffle: The Thing Beneath the Bed. Taylor, Nate, illus. 2010. 68p. 25.00 *(978-1-59606-313-6(0))* Subterranean Pr.

Rotman, Risa. Azoi Vi Ess Past Fahr a Princessen (Fit for a Princess) Flohr, Perel, tr. Leff, Tova, illus. 2012.Tr. of Fit for a Princess. 32p. (J). 10.95 *(978-1-929628-66-7(6))* Hachai Publishing.

A Royal Tea. 2014. (Mermaid Tales Ser.: 9). (ENG., Illus.). 112p. (J). (gr. 1-4). pap. 5.99 *(978-1-4814-0254-5(4),* Aladdin) Simon & Schuster Children's Publishing.

Ruble, Kam. Princess Annado Tandy's Versery Rhymes. McMullen, T. C., illus. l.t. ed. 2007. 88p. (J). per. *(978-0-9779680-4-6(9))* Global Authors Pubns.

Ryan, Brittney. The Legend of Holly Claus. Long, Laurel, illus. 2004. (Julie Andrews Collection). 544p. (J). (gr. 4-18). 16.99 *(978-0-06-058511-2(0),* Julie Andrews Collection) HarperCollins Pubs.

Ryder, Chloe. Best Friends Forever! 2015. (Princess Ponies Ser.). (ENG., Illus.). 128p. (YA). (gr. 2-4). pap. 5.99 *(978-1-61963-405-3(8),* 9781619634053, Bloomsbury USA Childrens) Bloomsbury Publishing USA.

—A Dream Come True. 2014. (Princess Ponies Ser.). (ENG., Illus.). 128p. (YA). (gr. 1-3). pap. 5.99 *(978-1-61963-167-0(9),* 9781619631670, Bloomsbury USA Childrens) Bloomsbury Publishing USA.

—A Magical Friend. 2014. (Princess Ponies Ser.). (ENG., Illus.). 128p. (J). (gr. 1-3). pap. 5.99 *(978-1-61963-165-6(2),* 9781619631656, Bloomsbury USA Childrens) Bloomsbury Publishing USA.

—Princess Ponies: An Amazing Rescue. 2015. (Princess Ponies Ser.). (ENG., Illus.). 128p. (YA). (gr. 2-4). pap. 5.99 *(978-1-61963-403-9(1),* 9781619634039, Bloomsbury USA Childrens) Bloomsbury Publishing USA.

—Princess Ponies 3: the Special Secret. 2014. (Princess Ponies Ser.). (ENG., Illus.). 128p. (J). (gr. 2-4). pap. 5.99 *(978-1-61963-237-0(3),* 9781619632370, Bloomsbury USA Childrens) Bloomsbury Publishing USA.

—Princess Ponies 4: a Unicorn Adventure! 2014. (Princess Ponies Ser.). (ENG., Illus.). 128p. (J). (gr. 2-4). pap. 5.99 *(978-1-61963-294-3(2),* 9781619632943, Bloomsbury USA Childrens) Bloomsbury Publishing USA.

Sagar, Marie. Princess Samantha? 2009. 20p. pap. 12.49 *(978-1-4389-5297-0(X))* AuthorHouse.

Sage, Angie. Flyte. Zug, Mark, illus. (Septimus Heap Ser.: 2). (ENG.). 544p. (J). (gr. 4-7). 2007. pap. 7.99 *(978-0-06-057736-0(3))* 2006. 17.99 *(978-0-06-057734-6(7))* HarperCollins Pubs. (Tegen, Katherine Bks).

—Flyte. (Septimus Heap Ser.: 2). (J). 2009. 84.49 *(978-1-4361-5831-2(1))* 2008. 1.25 *(978-1-4193-9383-9(9))* 2006. 114.75 *(978-1-4193-9386-0(3))* 2006. 133.75 *(978-1-4193-9390-7(1))* 2006. 282.75 *(978-1-4193-9387-7(1))* 2006. 111.75 *(978-1-4193-9388-4(X))* 2006. 131.75 *(978-1-4193-9392-1(8))* Recorded Bks., Inc.

—Magyk. Zug, Mark, illus. (Septimus Heap Ser.: 1). (J). (gr. 4-18). 2005. (ENG.). 576p. 17.99 *(978-0-06-057731-5(2))* 2005. 576p. lib. bdg. 18.89 *(978-0-06-057732-2(0))* 2006. (ENG.). 608p. reprint ed. pap. 7.99 *(978-0-06-057733-9(9))* HarperCollins Pubs. (Tegen, Katherine Bks).

—Magyk. Zug, Mark, illus. 2007. (Septimus Heap Ser.: Bk. 1). 564p. (gr. 4-7). 18.00 *(978-0-7569-7760-3(6))* Perfection Learning Corp.

—Magyk. (Septimus Heap Ser.: 1). (J). 2008. 79.75 *(978-1-4361-0584-2(6))* 2007. 1.25 *(978-1-4193-2619-6(8))* 2006. 123.75 *(978-1-4193-3807-6(2))* 2005. 106.75 *(978-1-4193-2622-6(8))* 2005. 126.75 *(978-1-4193-3805-2(6))* 2005. 103.75 *(978-1-4193-2624-0(4))* Recorded Bks., Inc.

—Magyk. 2006. (Septimus Heap Ser.: 1). (J). lib. bdg. 18.40 *(978-1-4177-3321-7(7),* Turtleback) Turtleback Bks.

—Septimus Heap, Set. Zug, Mark, illus. 2007. (Septimus Heap Ser.: Bks. 1-2). (J). (gr. 4). pap. 15.99 *(978-0-06-136195-1(X),* Tegen, Katherine Bks) HarperCollins Pubs.

Saito, Taeko. Kiss the Frog. 2010. (Princess & the Frog Ser.). (JPN., Illus.). (J). bds. *(978-4-06-262548-7(2))* Kodansha America, Inc.

Saltzberg, Barney. Would You Rather Be a Princess or a Dragon? 2016. (ENG., Illus.). 32p. (J). 16.99 *(978-1-62672-358-0(3),* 9781626723580) Roaring Brook Pr.

Sauer, Tammi. Princess in Training. Berger, Joe, illus. 2015. (ENG.). 40p. (J). (gr. -1-3). 6.99 *(978-0-544-45609-9(2),* HMH Books For Young Readers) Houghton Mifflin Harcourt Publishing Co.

Saxon, Victoria. Anna & Elsa's Secret Playtime (Disney Frozen) RH Disney, illus. 2016. (Big Golden Book Ser.). (ENG.). 32p. (J). (-k). 9.99 *(978-0-7364-3493-5(3),* Golden/Disney) Random Hse. Children's Bks.

—Frozen (Disney Frozen) Lee, Grace & Cagol, Andrea, illus. 2015. (Little Golden Book Ser.). (ENG.). 24p. (J). (-k). 4.99 *(978-0-7364-3471-3(2),* Golden/Disney) Random Hse. Children's Bks.

Saxon, Victoria & Posner-Sanchez, Andrea. Belle Is My Babysitter (Disney Princess) Laguna, Fabio & Andreu, Meritxell, illus. 2016. (Little Golden Book Ser.). (ENG.). 24p. (J). (-k). 4.99 *(978-0-7364-3502-4(6),* Golden/Disney) Random Hse. Children's Bks.

Saxon, Victoria & RH Disney Staff. Frozen Fever. RH Disney Staff, illus. deluxe ed. 2015. (Junior Novel Ser.). (ENG., Illus.). 96p. (J). (gr. 3-7). 9.99 *(978-0-7364-3440-9(2),* RH/Disney) Random Hse. Children's Bks.

Schlitz, Laura Amy. Princess Cora & the Crocodile. Floca, Brian, illus. 2017. (ENG.). 80p. (J). (gr. -1-3). 16.99 *(978-0-7636-4822-0(1))* Candlewick Pr.

Schneider, Josh. Princess Sparkle-Heart Gets a Makeover. 2017. (ENG., Illus.). 32p. (J). (gr. -1-3). pap. 7.99 *(978-0-544-93033-9(9),* HMH Books For Young Readers) Houghton Mifflin Harcourt Publishing Co.

Schow, Betsy. Spelled. 2015. (Storymakers Ser.: 0). (ENG.). 352p. (YA). (gr. 6-12). pap. 9.99 *(978-1-4926-0871-4(8),* 9781492608714) Sourcebooks, Inc.

Schuette, Eva. The Kingdom of the Wild Gootsies: Meet the Wild Gootsies. 2010. 12p. 8.49 *(978-1-4490-8798-2(1))* AuthorHouse.

Scretching, Dorothy/Janis. Story Time with Princess Dorothy. Walters, Steve, ed. Brunot, Katerina, illus. 2012. 32p. (J). 20.00 *(978-0-9719767-4-0(0),* Crowned Warrior Publishing) Walters, Steve Ministries.

Scribner, Don. Bennie & Thomas & the Rescue at Razor's Edge: Volume I. Scribner, Peter, illus. 2012. 44p. pap. 24.95 *(978-1-4626-8957-6(4))* America Star Bks.

—Bennie & Thomas & the Rescue at Razor's Edge: Volume II. Scribner, Peter, illus. 2012. 48p. pap. 24.95 *(978-1-4626-9472-3(1))* America Star Bks.

Scribner, Meagen & Jensen, Angelina. Princess & the Peasant. 2013. 40p. pap. *(978-1-4602-3308-5(5))* FriesenPress.

Sears, Cynthia A. The Dragon Lord: The Fairy Princess Chronicles - Book 2. 2013. 376p. *(978-1-4602-3081-7(7))* FriesenPress.

Secuban, Andy S. The Papagayo: Magical Bird of Paradise. 2008. 24p. pap. 12.99 *(978-1-4389-0660-7(9))* AuthorHouse.

Seever, Berni. A Supernatural Tale. 2007. 62p. pap. 20.00 *(978-1-4196-7788-5(8))* CreateSpace Independent Publishing Platform.

Seiss, Ellie. Dora's Princess Pals. 2011. (Dora the Explorer Ser.). (ENG.). 12p. (J). (gr. -1-k). 5.99 *(978-1-4424-1203-3(8),* Simon Spotlight/Nickelodeon) Simon Spotlight/Nickelodeon.

Selfors, Suzanne. Ever after High: Hero Training: A Destiny Do-Over Diary. 2015. (ENG., Illus.). 160p. (J). (gr. 3-7). 9.99 *(978-0-316-40139-5(0))* Little, Brown Bks. for Young Readers.

—Next Top Villain. 2015. (School Story Ser.). (ENG., Illus.). 224p. (J). (gr. 3-7). 13.99 *(978-0-316-40128-9(5))* Little Brown & Co.

—A Semi-Charming Kind of Life. 2015. (Ever after High Ser.: Bk. 3). 213p. (J). *(978-0-316-40135-7(8))* Little Brown & Co.

—A Semi-Charming Kind of Life. 2015. (Ever after High Ser.: Bk. 3). (ENG., Illus.). 224p. (J). (gr. 3-7). 13.99 *(978-0-316-40136-4(6))* Little, Brown Bks. for Young Readers.

Senior, Patricia. Pip & the Magic Flute. 2008. (Illus.). 40p. pap. 18.49 *(978-1-4389-0023-0(6))* AuthorHouse.

Sharma, Radhika. The Princess & the Unicorn Prince. 2007. 48p. pap. 19.96 *(978-1-4357-0072-7(4))* Lulu Pr., Inc.

Shecter, Vicky Alvear. Cleopatra's Moon. 2013. (ENG.). 368p. (J). (gr. 9). pap. 9.99 *(978-0-545-22131-3(5),* Levine, Arthur A. Bks.) Scholastic, Inc.

Sholl, Anna. The Faery Tales of Weir. 2006. 116p. per. 9.95 *(978-1-59818-475-4(X))* Aegypan.

Short, Carol. Robert & the Princess. 2008. 16p. pap. 9.94 *(978-1-4389-2203-4(5))* AuthorHouse.

Shughart-Knecht, Kimberly. Princess Kiali & the Purple Box. 2010. 32p. pap. 12.99 *(978-1-4490-0913-7(1))* AuthorHouse.

Shulda, Daron M. Dragon Boots. 2009. 40p. pap. 18.49 *(978-1-4389-7022-6(6))* AuthorHouse.

Shvarts, Andrew. Royal Bastards. 2017. (Royal Bastards Ser.). (ENG.). 352p. (YA). (gr. 9-17). 18.99 ***(978-1-4847-6765-8(9))*** Hyperion Bks. for Children.

Siegel, Terri. Goodnight Princess Scharazad. 2005. (J). lib. bdg. 19.95 *(978-0-9754728-5-9(2))* Big Ransom Studio.

Sierra, JulieAnn. Legacy & the Dark Prince, 1 vol. 2009. 209p. pap. 24.95 *(978-1-61582-693-3(9))* America Star Bks.

Silver Dolphin en Español Editors. Tesoros para llevar Disney: Disney Princess CarryAlong Treasury, Spanish-Language Edition. 2004. (SPA., Illus.). 24p. (J). bds. *(978-970-718-239-4(3),* Silver Dolphin en Español) Advanced Marketing, S. de R. L. de C. V.

Silver Dolphin en Español Editors, creator. Felices para Siempre/Happily Ever After. 2007. (Illus.). 5p. (J). (gr. k). *(978-970-718-448-0(5),* Silver Dolphin en Español) Advanced Marketing, S. de R. L. de C. V.

Silver Dolphin en Español Staff, creator. Caritas Felices. 2007. (Disney Princesa (Silver Dolphin) Ser.). (Illus.). 10p. (J). (gr. -1). bds. *(978-970-718-390-2(X),* Silver Dolphin en Español) Advanced Marketing, S. de R. L. de C. V.

Simon, Charnan. Tressa the Musical Princess. Allen, Joy, illus. 2005. 25p. (J). *(978-1-58987-112-0(X))* Kindermusik International.

Simone, Ni-Ni & Abrams, Amir. Put Your Diamonds Up! 2014. (Hollywood High Ser.: 3). lib. bdg. 20.80 *(978-0-606-35736-4(X))* Turtleback Bks.

Sims, Anthony. Princess Zoe. 2012. (Illus.). 44p. pap. 24.40 *(978-1-4772-2365-9(7))* AuthorHouse.

Sims, C. Bailey. Candlewax. 2012. (ENG., Illus.). 384p. (YA). 18.99 *(978-0-9839877-1-0(8));* pap. 13.99 *(978-0-9839877-0-3(X))* Terabyte Pr. LLC.

Simson, Dana. Princess Ruby's Rainbow Day. 2003. (Sparkle Bks.). (J). bds. 10.95 *(978-1-74047-206-7(3))* Book Co. Publishing Pty, Ltd., The AUS. Dist: Penton Overseas, Inc.

Skidmore, Lauren. The Fairest Poison. 2016. (YA). pap. 16.99 *(978-1-4621-1792-5(9))* Cedar Fort, Inc./CFI Distribution.

Skilbeck, Carol. Adventures of Melonhead. 2011. 56p. 24.99 *(978-1-4568-7464-3(0));* pap. 15.99 *(978-1-4568-7463-6(2))* Xlibris Corp.

Sklyar, Igor. King & the Star. 2005. (Illus.). 50p. pap. *(978-1-84401-048-6(1))* Athena Pr.

Sky Koster, Amy. Cute, Sweet, & Petite! (Disney Princess: Palace Pets) Random House Disney Staff, illus. 2015. (Big Golden Book Ser.). (ENG.). 64p. (J). (gr. -1-2). 9.99 *(978-0-7364-3412-6(7),* Golden/Disney) Random Hse. Children's Bks.

—Petite's Winter Wonderland. Random House Disney Staff, illus. 2015. (Glitter Picturebook Ser.). (ENG.). 16p. (J). (gr. -1-2). 5.99 *(978-0-7364-3355-6(4),* RH/Disney) Random Hse. Children's Bks.

Slater, Dashka. Dangerously Ever After. Docampo, Valeria, illus. 2012. (ENG.). 40p. (J). (gr. k-3). 16.99 *(978-0-8037-3374-9(7),* Dial Bks) Penguin Young Readers Group.

Smith, Carrie. Cinderella: Classic Tales Edition. Greenhead, Bill, illus. 2011. (Classic Tales Ser.). (J). *(978-1-936258-77-2(3))* Benchmark Education Co.

—The Princess & the Pea: Classic Tales Edition. Harpster, Steve, illus. 2011. (Classic Tales Ser.). (J). *(978-1-936258-76-5(5))* Benchmark Education Co.

Smith, Nerissia. Prince de'Mario's Adventure, 1 vol. Dartes, Staci, illus. 2009. 29p. pap. 24.95 *(978-1-61582-972-9(5))* America Star Bks.

Smith, Sherri L. The Toymaker's Apprentice. 2015. (ENG., Illus.). 400p. (J). (gr. 5). 16.99 *(978-0-399-25295-2(9),* G.P. Putnam's Sons Books for Young Readers) Penguin Young Readers Group.

—The Toymaker's Apprentice. 2016. (ENG.). 400p. (J). (gr. 5). 19.65 *(978-0-606-39322-5(6))* Turtleback Bks.

Smyth, Jimmy. The Fairy Princess. 2013. 34p. pap. *(978-0-9569314-5-0(6))* Smith, Jimmy.

Snodgrass, Lady Cecily. The Really Rotten Princess. Lester, Mike, illus. 2012. (Really Rotten Princess Ser.). (ENG.). 32p. (J). (gr. k-2). 15.99 *(978-1-4424-3326-7(4));* pap. 3.99 *(978-1-4424-3325-0(6))* Simon Spotlight. (Simon Spotlight).

—The Really Rotten Princess & the Cupcake Catastrophe. Lester, Mike, illus. 2013. (Really Rotten Princess Ser.). (ENG.). 32p. (J). (gr. k-2). 16.99 *(978-1-4424-8974-5(X));* pap. 3.99 *(978-1-4424-8973-8(1))* Simon Spotlight. (Simon Spotlight).

Snyder, Laurel. Up & down the Scratchy Mountains. Dorman, Brandon & Call, Greg, illus. 2010. (ENG.). 272p. (J). (gr. 3-7). 7.99 *(978-0-375-84720-2(0),* Yearling) Random Hse. Children's Bks.

Solange, Helene. Lala the Little Princess. 2009. (Illus.). 32p. pap. 14.49 *(978-1-4490-1005-8(9))* AuthorHouse.

Solomon, Barbara. The Girl Who Wanted to Become a Princess. 2013. 50p. pap. 12.99 *(978-1-62839-354-5(8))* Salem Author Services.

Sommer, Carl. The Great Royal Race. Westbrook, Dick, illus. 2014. (J). pap. *(978-1-57537-952-4(X))* Advance Publishing, Inc.

—The Great Royal Race. 2003. (Another Sommer-Time Story Ser.). (Illus.). 48p. (J). (gr. k-4). lib. bdg. 23.95 incl. audio *(978-1-57537-758-2(6))* Advance Publishing, Inc.

—The Great Royal Race. Westbrook, Dick, illus. 2003. (Another Sommer-Time Story Ser.). 48p. (J). (gr. k-4). lib. bdg. 23.95 incl. audio compact disk *(978-1-57537-708-7(X))* Advance Publishing, Inc.

—The Great Royal Race. 2003. (Another Sommer-Time Story Ser.). (Illus.). 48p. (J). (gr. 1-4). 16.95 incl. audio *(978-1-57537-557-1(5))* Advance Publishing, Inc.

—The Great Royal Race. Westbrook, Dick, illus. 2003. (Another Sommer-Time Story Ser.). 48p. (J). (gr. 1-4). 16.95 incl. audio compact disk *(978-1-57537-508-3(7))* Advance Publishing, Inc.

—The Great Royal Race(La Gran Carrera Real) Westbrook, Dick, illus. 2009. (Another Sommer-Time Story Bilingual Ser.). (SPA & ENG.). 48p. (J). lib. bdg. 16.95 *(978-1-57537-152-8(9))* Advance Publishing, Inc.

—The Race. Budwine, Greg, illus. 2009. (Quest for Success Ser.). (ENG.). 56p. (YA). lib. bdg. 12.95 *(978-1-57537-256-3(8))* Advance Publishing, Inc.

—The Race(La Carrera) Budwine, Greg, illus. 2009. (Quest for Success Bilingual Ser.). (SPA & ENG.). 104p. (YA). lib. bdg. 14.95 *(978-1-57537-230-3(4))* Advance Publishing, Inc.

—The Racing Fools. Budwine, Greg, illus. 2009. (Quest for Success Ser.). (ENG.). 56p. (YA). pap. 4.95 *(978-1-57537-281-5(9))* Advance Publishing, Inc.

—The Ugly Princess. Martinez, Jorge, illus. 2016. 32p. (J). *(978-1-57537-948-7(1))* Advance Publishing, Inc.

Somper, Justin. Allies & Assassins. 2014. (Allies & Assassins Ser.). (ENG.). 496p. (YA). (gr. 7-17). 18.00 *(978-0-316-25393-2(6))* Little, Brown Bks. for Young Readers.

Sorenson, Margo. Ambrose & the Princess. Szegedi, Katalin, illus. 2005. (ENG.). 32p. (J). (gr. -1-3). 16.95 *(978-0-8146-3043-3(X))* Liturgical Pr.

Soundprints Staff. My Princess Treasury. (Kindness Counts Ser.). (ENG., Illus.). 24p. (J). 14.99 *(978-1-59069-373-5(6),* 1A200); 14.99 *(978-1-59069-381-0(7),* 1A201) Studio Mouse LLC.

St. James, Leah. Lights of Imani. Morse, Nessa Neilson, illus. 2013. 28p. pap. 9.99 *(978-0-9853123-6-7(X))* Allen, Edward Publishing, LLC.

Stanek, Robert, pseud. The Kingdoms & the Elves of the Reaches Ii (Reader's Choice Edition, Keeper Martin's Tales Book 2) 2008. (Illus.). 244p. pap. 15.95 *(978-1-57545-197-8(2))* RP Media.

P
Q
R

Stanfield, Michael. Bucky & Becky - the Magic of Wigglepoo Mountain. 2009. 144p. pap. 14.96 (978-0-557-02614-2(8)) Lulu Pr., Inc.

Stanley, Diane. The Princess of Cortova. (J). 2015. (Silver Bowl Ser.: 3). (ENG.). 336p. (gr. 3-7). pap. 6.99 (978-0-06-204732-8(9)) 2013. (Silver Bowl Ser.: 3). (ENG.). 320p. (gr. 3-7). 16.99 (978-0-06-204730-4(2)) 2013. 311p. lib. bdg. (978-0-06-204731-1(0)) HarperCollins Pubs.

Staunton, Ted. Morgan on Ice, 1 vol. Slavin, Bill, illus. 2013. (Formac First Novels Ser.). (ENG.). 56p. (J). (gr. 2-3). 14.95 (978-1-4595-0289-5(2), 9781459502895); pap. 5.95 (978-1-4595-0290-1(6), 9781459502901) Formac Publishing Co., Ltd. CAN. Dist: Casemate Pubs. & Bk. Distributors, LLC.

Stef. Be Careful What You Wish For. 2008. 380p. 29.99 (978-1-4363-5233-8(9)); pap. 19.99 (978-1-4363-5232-1(0)) Xlibris Corp.

Stein, Mathilde. Dear Daisy Dunnington. Groeninik, Chuck, illus. 2012. (ENG.). 32p. (J). (gr. 1). 17.95 (978-1-935954-18-7(0), 9781935954187) Lemniscaat USA.

Stewart, Joel. Dexter Bexley & the Big Blue Beastie on the Road. 2010. (ENG., Illus.). 32p. (J). (gr. -1-3). pap. 16.95 (978-0-8234-2292-0(5)) Holiday Hse., Inc.

Stewig, John Warren. Nobody Asked the Pea. Van Wright, Cornelius, illus. 2013. (ENG.). 32p. (J). (gr. 1-5). 16.95 (978-0-8234-2224-1(0)) Holiday Hse., Inc.

Stockham, Jess. Cinderella. 2006. (Flip-Up Fairy Tales Ser.). (ENG., Illus.). 24p. (J). (gr. 2-2). (978-1-904550-74-7(6)) Child's Play International Ltd.

Stockham, Jess, illus. Cinderella. 2007. (Flip-Up Fairy Tales Ser.). (ENG.). 24p. (J). (gr. -1-2). audio compact disk (978-1-84643-091-6(7)) Child's Play International Ltd.

Stockham, Jess, et al, illus. The Frog Prince. 2007. (Flip-Up Fairy Tales Ser.). (ENG.). 24p. (J). (gr. 2-2). pap. (978-1-84643-077-0(1)) Child's Play International Ltd.

Stockham, Jess, illus. The Frog Prince. 2007. (Flip-Up Fairy Tales Ser.). (ENG.). 24p. (J). audio compact disk (978-1-84643-143-2(3)) Child's Play International Ltd.

—The Princess & the Pea. 2010. (Flip-Up Fairy Tales Ser.). (ENG.). 24p. (J). (gr. -1-2). audio compact disk (978-1-84643-332-0(0)) Child's Play International Ltd.

Storm, Falcon. The Persnickety Princess (Tales from upon A. Time - Book 1) l.t. ed. 2013. (ENG.). 94p. pap. 9.95 (978-1-62253-047-2(0)) Evolved Publishing.

Studio Mouse, creator. Kindness Counts. rev. ed. 2008. (Learn-Aloud Bks.). (ENG., Illus.). (J). 12.99 (978-1-59069-627-9(1)) Studio Mouse LLC.

Studio Mouse, ed. Disney Preincess Best Friends: Flat Learn & Carry 4 Board Books & CD. rev. ed. 2008. 80p. (J). 12.99 (978-1-59069-553-1(4)) Studio Mouse LLC.

Studio Mouse Staff. Kindness Counts. rev. ed. 2004. (Kindness Counts Ser.). (Illus.). 36p. (J). (gr. -1-3). 12.99 (978-1-59069-364-3(7), 1A500) Studio Mouse LLC.

—Wedding Countdown. 2008. 36p. (J). (gr. -1). 12.99 (978-1-59069-740-5(5)) Studio Mouse LLC.

Sullivan, Chris Mann. Oh No, Not the Shot! 2011. 24p. pap. 11.98 (978-1-4490-8392-2(7)) AuthorHouse.

Sundberg, Norma J. An Odd Fable. Leiper, Esther M., illus. 2007. 32p. (J). pap. 13.95 (978-0-9776958-5-0(9)) CyPress Pubns.

Susaeta, Equipo. La Bella Durmiente -Sleeping Beauty. Susaeta Publishing, Inc., Staff, ed. 2011. (Cuentos Bilingües Ser.). (SPA & ENG.). 34p. (J). (gr. k-2). 6.95 (978-84-305-2453-2(3)) Susaeta Ediciones, S.A. ESP. Dist: Independent Pubs. Group.

Sussman, Elissa. Stray. 2014. (Stray Ser.: 1). (ENG., Illus.). 384p. (YA). (gr. 8). 17.99 (978-0-06-227455-7(4), Greenwillow Bks.) HarperCollins Pubs.

Suttles, Teresa. The Little Gray Box. 2013. 22p. pap. 12.95 (978-1-62646-450-6(2)) Booklocker.com, Inc.

Sutton, S. A. A Hero for Quale. 2009. 72p. pap. 9.99 (978-1-60860-189-9(7), Strategic Bk. Publishing) Strategic Book Publishing & Rights Agency (SBPRA).

Sweet, Susan D. & Miles, Brenda. Jacqueline & the Beanstalk: A Tale of Facing Giant Fears. Docampo, Valeria, illus. 2017. 32p. (J). 15.95 **(978-1-4338-2682-5(8)**, Magination Pr.) American Psychological Assn.

Sweet, Susan D. & Miles, Brenda. Princess Penelopea Hates Peas: A Tale of Picky Eating & Avoiding Catastropeas. 2016. (Illus.). 32p. (J). (978-1-4338-2046-5(3), Magination Pr.) American Psychological Assn.

Swiderska, Barbara. The Fisherman's Bride. Swiderska, Barbara, illus. (Illus.). 32p. (J). (gr. -1-3). 12.95 (978-0-87592-018-4(7)) Scroll Pr., Inc.

Sykes, Julie. Bella at the Ball. Morgan, Richard, illus. 2014. 119p. (J). pap. (978-0-545-69221-2(0)) Scholastic, Inc.

Tanaka, Rika. Kilala Princess, Vol. 2. 2016. (ENG.). 208p. (J). pap. 10.99 (978-1-4278-5663-0(X), 9781427856630) TOKYOPOP, Inc.

Tarnowska, Wafa'. The Seven Wise Princesses: A Medieval Persian Epic. Nilesh, Misty, illus. 2008. (ENG.). 96p. (J). (gr. 5-9). 19.99 (978-1-84686-250-2(7)) Barefoot Bks., Inc.

Tarver, Monroe S. Tales from the Mapmaker: Imagia & the Magic Pearls. 2015. (ENG.). 100p. (J). (gr. k-4). pap. 6.99 (978-0-9723936-5-2(X)) Wizarding World Pr.

Tavares, Victor, illus. Beauty & the Beast. 2007. (Usborne Young Reading: Series Two Ser.). 63p. (J). 8.99 (978-0-7945-1456-3(1), Usborne) EDC Publishing.

Taylor, Kay Lovelace. Princess Aisha & the Cave of Judgment. Rhine, Karen C., illus. 2007. 32p. (J). 19.95 (978-0-9799119-0-3(7)) KLT & Assocs.

Taylor, Roy. Matilda's Magic Wand: Dreamland Adventure. 2008. 36p. (J). pap. 9.00 (978-0-8059-7716-5(3)) Dorrance Publishing Co., Inc.

TBD. DreamWorks Trolls: Storybook with Poppy Collectible. 2016. (ENG.). 24p. (J). (gr. -1-2). 14.99 (978-0-7944-3845-6(8), Reader's Digest Children's Bks.) Studio Fun International.

Teitelbaum, Michael. Disney Princess Little Golden Book Favorites, Vol. 2. Williams, Don et al, illus. 2010. (Little Golden Book Favorites Ser.). (ENG.). 80p. (J). (gr. -1-2). 6.99 (978-0-7364-2656-5(6), Golden/Disney) Random Hse. Children's Bks.

Teitelbaum, Michael, et al. Disney Princess. Random House Disney Staff, illus. 2009. (Little Golden Book Favorites Ser.). (ENG.). 80p. (J). (gr. -1-2). 7.99 (978-0-7364-2567-4(5), Golden/Disney) Random Hse. Children's Bks.

Thanos, Jerald. A Princess Christmas. 2009. 32p. pap. 14.49 (978-1-4389-6752-3(7)) AuthorHouse.

Thomas, Rhiannon. A Wicked Thing. (YA). (gr. 9). 2016. 368p. pap. 9.99 (978-0-06-230354-7(6)) 2015. (ENG.). 352p. 17.99 (978-0-06-230353-0(8)) HarperCollins Pubs. (HarperTeen).

Thompson, Cynthia. Princess Esmeralda of the Land of Ur: The Sharing of Gifts Book Two. 2012. 24p. pap. 12.55 (978-1-4525-0666-1(3)) Balboa Pr.

Tillworth, Mary. Barbie in Princess Power. 2015. (Little Golden Book Ser.). (ENG., Illus.). 24p. (J). (-k). 4.99 (978-0-553-50741-6(9), Golden Bks.) Random Hse. Children's Bks.

—Mariposa & the Fairy Princess (Barbie) Golden Books, illus. 2013. (Little Golden Book Ser.). (ENG.). 24p. (J). (-k). 3.99 (978-0-449-81633-2(8), Golden Bks.) Random Hse. Children's Bks.

Tintera, Amy. Avenged. (Ruined Ser.: 2). (YA). (gr. 8). 2018. (ENG.). 432p. pap. 9.99 **(978-0-06-239664-8(1))** 2017. 416p. 17.99 (978-0-06-239663-1(3)) HarperCollins Pubs. (HarperTeen).

Tintera, Amy. Ruined. (Ruined Ser.: 1). (YA). (gr. 8). 2017. 384p. pap. 9.99 (978-0-06-239661-7(7)) 2016. 368p. 17.99 (978-0-06-239660-0(9)) HarperCollins Pubs. (HarperTeen).

Todd, Sue, illus. One Last Wish: A Tale from India. 2013. (Tales of Honor (Red Chair Press) Ser.). (ENG.). 32p. (J). (gr. 1-4). lib. bdg. 26.60 (978-1-937529-76-5(2)) Red Chair Pr.

Tomlinson, Heather. Aurelie: A Faerie Tale. 2010. (ENG.). 208p. (YA). (gr. 7-12). pap. 18.99 (978-0-312-60275-8(8), 9780312602758) Square Fish.

Top Secret Tiaras. 2009. (Princess Protection Program Ser.: No. 3). (ENG.). 144p. (gr. 3-7). pap. 4.99 (978-1-4231-2392-7(1)) Disney Pr.

Top That. Press Out & Play Princess Castle. 2008. (978-1-84666-611-7(2)) Top That! Publishing PLC.

Torseter, Øyvind. The Heartless Troll. Torseter, Øyvind, illus. 2016. (ENG., Illus.). 120p. (J). (gr. 1-9). 19.95 (978-1-59270-193-3(0)) Enchanted Lion Bks., LLC.

Townley, Roderick. The Great Good Thing. 2003. (Richard Jackson Books (Econo-Clad) Ser.). 216p. (gr. 5). 16.00 (978-0-7569-1435-6(3)) Perfection Learning Corp.

Townsend, S. P. The Star of Persia. 2008. 120p. pap. 12.50 (978-1-84799-532-2(2)) Lulu Pr., Inc.

ToyBox Innovations, creator. Disney Princess: Cinderella/Snow White/Sleeping Beauty. unabr. abr. ed. 2005. (Disney Princess Ser.). (J). pap. (978-0-7634-1150-3(7)) Walt Disney Records.

Toybox Innovations, creator. Disney's Enchanted. 2007. (Disney's Read along Collection). (Illus.). 24p. (J). (gr. -1-3). pap. (978-0-7634-2197-7(9)) Walt Disney Records.

Tran, Hensley. Agatha's Stolen Curve. 2013. 80p. (gr. 4-6). 18.95 (978-1-4759-7312-9(8)); pap. 8.95 (978-1-4759-7310-5(1)) iUniverse, Inc.

Trimble, Irene. Snow Princesses (Disney Princess) RH Disney Staff, illus. 2012. (Glitter Board Book Ser.). (ENG.). 12p. (J). (gr. -1 — 1). bds. 6.99 (978-0-7364-3004-3(0), RH/Disney) Random Hse. Children's Bks.

—Winter Fun for Everyone! (Disney Princess) RH Disney Staff, illus. 2015. (Pictureback(R) Ser.). (ENG.). 16p. (J). (gr. -1-2). 5.99 (978-0-7364-3416-4(X), RH/Disney) Random Hse. Children's Bks.

Triplett, Ginger. The Stringed Princess. 2012. 56p. pap. 31.99 (978-1-4771-2102-3(1)) Xlibris Corp.

Tripp, Ben. The Accidental Highwayman: Being the Tale of Kit Bristol, His Horse Midnight, a Mysterious Princess, & Sundry Magical Persons Besides. 2014. (ENG., Illus.). 304p. (YA). (gr. 6). 17.99 (978-0-7653-3549-4(2), Tor Teen) Doherty, Tom Assocs., LLC.

Tucker, Patricia Wright. The Princess Who Couldn't Laugh. 2012. 24p. pap. 24.95 (978-1-4626-8133-4(6)) America Star Bks.

Tulien, Sean & Hoena, Blake. The Not-So-Helpless Princess. Cunyat, Pol, illus. 2016. (Thud & Blunder Ser.). (ENG.). 56p. (gr. 2-4). pap. 4.95 (978-1-4965-3222-0(8)); lib. bdg. 23.99 (978-1-4965-3218-3(X)) Stone Arch Bks.

Tyrrell, Kevin. Froggy Kisses. Tyrrell, Kayla, illus. 2008. 22p. pap. 24.95 (978-1-60672-066-0(X)) America Star Bks.

Underwood, Deborah. Part-Time Princess. Evans, Cambria, illus. 2013. (ENG.). 40p. (J). (gr. -1-k). 16.99 (978-1-4231-2485-6(5)) Hyperion Pr.

Urbanovic, Jackie. Prince of a Frog. 2015. (ENG., Illus.). 32p. (J). (gr. -1-k). 17.99 (978-0-545-63652-0(3), Orchard Bks.) Scholastic, Inc.

Valle, Anita. Best Princess Coloring Book. 2012. 50p. pap. 10.50 (978-1-105-54804-8(X)) Lulu Pr., Inc.

Van Fleet, Mara. Little Color Fairies. Van Fleet, Mara, illus. 2012. (ENG., Illus.). 16p. (J). (gr. -1-1). 14.99 (978-1-4424-3434-9(1), Simon & Schuster/Paula Wiseman Bks.) Simon & Schuster/Paula Wiseman Bks.

—Night-Night, Princess. Van Fleet, Mara, illus. 2014. (ENG., Illus.). 16p. (J). (gr. -1-1). 14.99 (978-1-4424-8646-1(5), Simon & Schuster/Paula Wiseman Bks.) Simon & Schuster/Paula Wiseman Bks.

Van Fleet, Mara & Wade, Sarah. The Very Mixed-Up Princess. 2009. (Mix & Match Ser.). (ENG., Illus.). 14p. (J). (gr. -1-3). bds. 8.99 (978-0-7944-1775-8(2)) Reader's Digest Assn., Inc., The.

Vande Velde, Vivian. Frogged. 2013. (ENG., Illus.). 208p. (J). (gr. 5-7). 16.99 (978-0-547-94215-5(X)) Houghton Mifflin Harcourt Publishing Co.

—Wizard at Work. 2004. (ENG., Illus.). 144p. (J). (gr. 5-7). pap. 10.95 (978-0-15-205309-3(3)) Houghton Mifflin Harcourt Publishing Co.

Various, illus. Disney Princess Little Golden Book Library (Disney Princess), 6 vols. 2016. (ENG.). 144p. (J). (-k). lib. bdg. 29.94 (978-0-7364-3560-4(3), Golden/Disney) Random Hse. Children's Bks.

Ventura, Marne. The Worry Warriors, 4 vols. Trinidad, Leo, illus. 2016. (Worry Warriors Ser.). (ENG.). 96p. (gr. 2-4). 103.96 (978-1-4965-3665-5(7)) Stone Arch Bks.

Vernon, Ursula. Harriet the Invincible. 2015. (Hamster Princess Ser.: 1). (ENG., Illus.). 208p. (J). (gr. 3-7). 12.99 (978-0-8037-3983-3(4), Dial Bks) Penguin Young Readers Group.

—Of Mice & Magic. 2016. (Hamster Princess Ser.: 2). (ENG., Illus.). 240p. (J). (gr. 3-7). 12.99 (978-0-8037-3984-0(2), Dial Bks) Penguin Young Readers Group.

—Ratpunzel. 2016. (Hamster Princess Ser.: 3). (ENG., Illus.). 240p. (J). (gr. 3-7). 12.99 (978-0-8037-3985-7(0), Dial Bks) Penguin Young Readers Group.

Viguié, Debbie. Violet Eyes. 2010. (Once upon a Time Ser.). (ENG.). 224p. (YA). (gr. 7-18). mass mkt. 7.99 (978-1-4169-8676-8(6), Simon Pulse) Simon Pulse.

Virtue, Queen Petals De. Princess & the Rain. 2012. 28p. pap. 21.99 (978-1-4691-2744-6(X)) Xlibris Corp.

Vize, Dania. My Princess Dress up Storybook. 2005. (Illus.). 12p. (J). (gr. -1-3). bds. (978-1-905051-84-7(0)) Make Believe Ideas.

Voigt, Cynthia. The Tale of Elske. 2015. (Tales of the Kingdom Ser.: 4). (ENG., Illus.). 368p. (YA). (gr. 7). 19.99 (978-1-4814-2189-8(1), Atheneum Bks. for Young Readers) Simon & Schuster Children's Publishing.

Von Buhler, Cynthia. But Who Will Bell the Cats? Von Buhler, Cynthia, illus. 2009. (ENG., Illus.). 32p. (J). (gr. -1-3). 17.00 (978-0-618-99718-3(0)) Houghton Mifflin Harcourt Publishing Co.

Wadsworth, Peter. The Wicked Witch of the Woods. 2012. (Illus.). 28p. pap. 8.49 (978-1-78035-481-1(9), Fastprint Publishing) Upfront Publishing Ltd. GBR. Dist: Printondemand-worldwide.com.

Wallace, Becky. The Storyspinner. 2015. (Keepers' Chronicles Ser.). (ENG., Illus.). 432p. (YA). (gr. 9). 17.99 (978-1-4814-0565-2(9), McElderry, Margaret K. Bks.) McElderry, Margaret K. Bks.

Wallace, Karen. Dragon Hunt, 1 vol. Baines, Nigel, illus. 2013. (Start Reading Ser.). (ENG.). 24p. (gr. k-1). pap. 7.95 (978-1-4765-4095-5(0)) Capstone Press of Coughlan Cos.

—Mirror, Mirror, 1 vol. Brett, Cathy, illus. 2013. (Start Reading Ser.). (ENG.). 24p. (gr. k-1). pap. 7.95 (978-1-4765-4117-4(5)) Capstone Press of Coughlan Cos.

—Stinky Giant. Brett, Cathy, illus. 2013. (Start Reading Ser.). (ENG.). 24p. (gr. k-1). pap. 7.95 (978-1-4765-4139-6(6)) Capstone Press of Coughlan Cos.

Walsh, Sheila. God's Little Princess Treasury, 1 vol. Johnson, Meredith, illus. 2009. (ENG.). 128p. (gr. -1-2). 19.99 (978-1-4003-1472-0(0)) Nelson, Thomas Inc.

Ward, Nick. The Tadpole Prince. 2003. (Illus.). 32p. (YA). (978-1-84365-016-4(9), Pavilion Children's Books) Pavilion Bks.

Waters, Rachel. Wanamea: A Choctaw Princess. 2007. 88p. per. 10.00 (978-1-4257-5976-6(9)) Xlibris Corp.

Watson, Andi. Princess Decomposia & Count Spatula. 2015. (ENG., Illus.). 176p. (YA). (gr. 8). 19.99 (978-1-62672-275-0(7), 9781626722750, First Second Bks.) Roaring Brook Pr.

Watt, Fiona. That's Not My Princess. Wells, Rachel, illus. 2006. (Usborne Touchy-Feely Board Bks.). 10p. (J). (gr. -1). bds. 9.99 (978-0-7945-1325-2(5), Usborne) EDC Publishing.

Watt, J. S. The Hall of Sorrows. 2006. 67p. pap. 16.95 (978-1-4241-2984-3(2)) PublishAmerica, Inc.

Wax, Wendy. Phonics Comics: Clara the Klutz - Level 2. Sullivan, Mary, illus. 2007. (ENG.). 24p. (J). (gr. 1-17). per. 3.99 (978-1-58476-565-3(8)) Innovative Kids.

Wax, Wendy A. Musica en Casa: Libro de Cuentos. de Alba, Arlette, tr. 2005. (Disney Princess Ser.). (SPA., Illus.). 38p. (J). (gr. -1-7). incl. audio compact disk (978-970-718-289-9(X), Silver Dolphin en Español) Advanced Marketing, S. de R. L. de C. V.

Webb, Holly. Rose & the Lost Princess. 2011. (ENG.). 272p. (J). (gr. 4-6). pap. 8.99 (978-1-4083-0448-8(1)) Hodder & Stoughton GBR. Dist: Hachette Bk. Group.

—Rose & the Lost Princess. 2014. (Rose Ser.: 2). (ENG.). 256p. (J). (gr. 3-6). pap. 6.99 (978-1-4022-8584-4(1), Sourcebooks Jabberwocky) Sourcebooks, Inc.

—Rose & the Magician's Mask. 2014. (Rose Ser.: 3). (ENG.). 224p. (J). (gr. 3-6). pap. 6.99 (978-1-4926-0430-3(5), 9781492604303, Sourcebooks Jabberwocky) Sourcebooks, Inc.

Webster, Christy. Anna's Best Friends. 2014. (Disney Princess Step into Reading Ser.). lib. bdg. 13.55 (978-0-606-35547-6(2)) Turtleback Bks.

Weinberg, Jennifer Liberts. Happy Birthday, Princess! 2012. (Disney Princess Step into Reading Ser.). lib. bdg. 13.55 (978-0-606-23725-3(9), Turtleback) Turtleback Bks.

—Pretty Pearl Mermaid. 2014. (Step into Reading Ser.). (ENG., Illus.). 32p. (J). (gr. -1-1). 3.99 (978-0-385-37307-4(4), Random Hse. Bks. for Young Readers) Random Hse. Children's Bks.

—Princess Hearts. 2012. (Disney Princess Step into Reading Ser.). lib. bdg. 13.55 (978-0-606-26975-9(4), Turtleback) Turtleback Bks.

—Princess Hearts (Disney Princess) RH Disney Staff & Legramandi, Francesco, illus. 2012. (Step into Reading Ser.). (ENG.). 32p. (J). (gr. -1-1). pap. 3.99 (978-0-7364-3013-5(X), RH/Disney) Random Hse. Children's Bks.

—Princesses & Puppies. 2013. (Disney Princess Step into Reading Ser.). lib. bdg. 13.55 (978-0-606-32201-0(9), Turtleback) Turtleback Bks.

Weyn, Suzanne. Faces of the Dead. 2014. (ENG.). 208p. (J). (gr. 7). 17.99 (978-0-545-42531-5(X), Scholastic Pr.) Scholastic, Inc.

What's the Time Fairy Princess? 2014. (Illus.). (J). (978-1-4351-5497-1(5)) Barnes & Noble, Inc.

White, J. A. The Thickety: a Path Begins. Offermann, Andrea, illus. 2017. (Thickety Ser.: 4). 512p. (J). (gr. 5). 16.99 (978-0-06-238139-2(3), Tegen, Katherine Bks) HarperCollins Pubs.

White, Kiersten. And I Darken. (ENG.). (YA). (gr. 7). 2017. (And I Darken Ser.: 1). 512p. pap. 10.99 **(978-0-553-52234-1(5)**, Ember) 2016. (Illus.). 496p. 18.99 (978-0-553-52231-0(0), Delacorte Pr.) 2016. (Illus.). 496p. lib. bdg. 21.99 (978-0-553-52232-7(9), Delacorte Pr.) Random Hse. Children's Bks.

—Now I Rise. 2017. (And I Darken Ser.: 2). (ENG.). 480p. (YA). (gr. 7). 18.99 **(978-0-553-52235-8(3))**; lib. bdg. 21.99 **(978-0-553-52236-5(1))** Random Hse. Children's Bks. (Delacorte Pr.).

White, Vernon. Birdhouse. 2010. (ENG., Illus.). 136p. (YA). pap. 10.95 (978-1-59362-185-8(X), 9781593621858) Slave Labor Bks.

Whitehouse, Howard. The Faceless Fiend: Being the Tale of a Criminal Mastermind, His Masked Minions & a Princess with a Butter Knife, Involving Explosives & a Certain Amount of Pushing & Shoving. Slavin, Bill, illus. 2007. (Mad Misadventures of Emmaline & Rubberbones Ser.). (ENG.). 272p. (J). (gr. 4-7). 7.95 (978-1-55453-180-6(2)) Kids Can Pr., Ltd. CAN. Dist: Hachette Bk. Group.

Wildsmith, Sarah. Princess Charming. Paramonova, Lea, illus. 2013. 32p. pap. 14.99 (978-1-62380-970-6(3), Harmony Ink Pr.) Dreamspinner Pr.

Williams, Allix Elise. The Adventures of Prince Thaddeus: The Glamorous Guest. 2010. 56p. pap. 11.49 (978-1-4520-5437-7(1)) AuthorHouse.

Williams, Brenda. The Real Princess. Fatus, Sophie, illus. 2008. (ENG.). 40p. (J). (gr. -1-3). 16.99 (978-1-905236-88-6(3)) Barefoot Bks., Inc.

Williams, Brenda & Barefoot Books Staff. Una Princesa Real: Un Cuento Matemagico. Fatus, Sophie, illus. 2014. (SPA.). 40p. (J). (gr. k-4). pap. 8.99 (978-1-78285-078-6(3)) Barefoot Bks., Inc.

Williams, Sophy. Princess Stories from Around the World. Tym, Kate, illus. 2004. 64p. (J). (978-1-84458-142-9(X), Pavilion Children's Books) Pavilion Bks.

Williams, Suzanne. The Gigantic, Genuine Genie. Gonzales, Chuck, illus. 2007. (Princess Power Ser.: No. 6). 128p. (J). 15.99 (978-0-06-078309-9(5)) HarperCollins Pubs.

—The Mysterious, Mournful Maiden. Gonzales, Chuck, illus. 2007. 112p. (J). 15.99 (978-0-06-078305-1(2)) HarperCollins Pubs.

Williamson, Judithe Anne. Princess Kara in Her Village, 1 vol. 2009. 107p. pap. 19.95 (978-1-60813-817-3(8)) America Star Bks.

Wilson, George H. The Arrival of Grand Princess Leandria. 2010. (Illus.). 50p. (J). 15.00 (978-0-9778477-5-4(6)) A Story Plus Children Bks.

Wilson, Karma. Princess Me. Unzner, Christa, illus. 2007. (ENG.). 32p. (J). (gr. -1-3). 16.99 (978-1-4169-4098-2(7), McElderry, Margaret K. Bks.) McElderry, Margaret K. Bks.

Wilson, Tony. The Princess & the Packet of Frozen Peas, 1 vol. deGennaro, Sue, illus. 2012. (ENG.). 32p. (J). 16.95 (978-1-56145-635-2(7)) Peachtree Pubs.

Wind, Chuck T. The Test of Love. 2011. 24p. pap. 24.95 (978-1-4626-2398-3(0)) America Star Bks.

Winter, Barbara. The Golden Scarab. 2007. (Illus.). 48p. (J). lib. bdg. 15.00 (978-1-4242-1617-8(6)) Dingles & Co.

Wisher, Mark. Don't kiss the Prince. 2010. 33p. pap. 21.50 (978-1-4457-7238-7(8)) Lulu Pr., Inc.

Wonlah, Ivis. King Ola's Pepper Jar. 2012. 28p. pap. 16.09 (978-1-4669-1600-5(1)) Trafford Publishing.

Wood, Audrey. The Princess & the Dragon. 2010. (Child's Play Library). (ENG., Illus.). 32p. (J). audio compact disk (978-1-84643-362-7(2)) Child's Play International Ltd.

—The Princess & the Dragon. 2003. (Child's Play Library). (ENG., Illus.). 10p. (J). (978-0-85953-717-9(X)) Child's Play International Ltd.

—Princess, the Dragon & Scaredy Cats. (J). audio (978-0-85953-375-1(1)) Child's Play International Ltd.

Wood, Jane R. Adventures on Amelia Island: A Pirate, a Princess, & Buried Treasure. Blacker, Elizabeth A., illus. Wood, Jane R., photos by. 2007. (ENG.). 132p. (J). (gr. 3-8). pap. 8.99 (978-0-9792304-0-0(3)) Florida Kids Pr., Inc.

Woods, Valerie. Princess Portia's Enchanted Journey, 1 vol. 2010. 36p. pap. 24.95 (978-1-4489-9673-5(2)) America Star Bks.

Woodward, Kay. Sleeping Handsome & the Princess Engineer. de Ruiter, Jo, illus. (Fairy Tales Today Ser.). (ENG.). 24p. (gr. 1-2). 2016. 9.95 (978-1-4795-8749-0(4)) 2015. 23.99 (978-1-4795-8615-8(3)) Picture Window Bks.

Wooster, Devin Ann. Sing It Out. 2015. (Step into Reading Ser.). (ENG., Illus.). 24p. (J). (gr. -1-1). 4.99 (978-0-553-52438-3(0), Random Hse. Bks. for Young Readers) Random Hse. Children's Bks.

Worrall, Linda, illus. Snow White & the Seven Dwarfs: A Story about Vanity. 2006. (J). 6.99 (978-1-59939-025-3(6)) Cornerstone Pr.

Wright, Peter M. The Stone Prince, 1 vol. 2009. 48p. pap. 16.95 (978-1-4489-2591-9(6)) America Star Bks.

Wright, Sabrina L. & Griffin, Dexter. Kalilah: the Whispered Promise. 2005. 159p. (J). (gr. 4-7). per. 12.95 (978-0-9770363-0-1(8)) First-Sight Publishing.

Written By Tori Velle; Illustrated By Al. Tia Tot Rules! Aguila, Alicia del, illus. 2011. 44p. pap. 24.95 (978-1-4241-7833-9(9)) America Star Bks.

Wronski, Gareth. Holly Farb & the Princess of the Galaxy. 2017. (ENG., Illus.). 320p. (J). (gr. 3-7). 16.99 **(978-1-4814-7177-0(5)**, Aladdin) Simon & Schuster Children's Publishing.

Wu, Nicholas. The Princess & the Pea, 1 vol. rev. ed. 2013. (Fiction Readers Ser.). (ENG., Illus.). 20p. (J). (gr. 1-1). pap. 4.99 (978-1-4333-5489-2(6)) Shell Educational Publishing.

—The Princess & the Pea: A Retelling of Hans Christian Andersen's Story, 1 vol. rev. ed. 2013. (Fiction Readers Ser.). (ENG., Illus.). 20p. (J). (gr. 1-1). pap. 15.96 (978-1-4807-1145-7(4)) Shell Educational Publishing.

Wyss, Tyan. The Solitaire Prince. 2006. 168p. (YA). per. 12.95 (978-1-58939-906-8(4)) Virtualbookworm.com Publishing, Inc.

Yolen, Jane & Harris, Robert J. Girl in a Cage. 2004. 234p. (gr. 5-9). 17.00 (978-0-7569-2946-6(6)) Perfection Learning Corp.

Yolen, Jane & Stemple, Heidi E. Y. Not All Princesses Dress in Pink. Lanquetin, Anne-Sophie, illus. 2010. (ENG.). 32p. (J). (gr. -1-3). 17.99 (978-1-4169-8018-6(0), Simon & Schuster Bks. For Young Readers) Simon & Schuster Bks. For Young Readers.

Young, Jeanna Stolle & Johnson, Jacqueline. Princess Hope & the Hidden Treasure, 1 vol. Aranda, Omar, illus. 2012. (Princess Parables Ser.). (ENG.). 32p. (J). 14.99 (978-0-310-72699-9(9)) Zonderkidz.

Young, Jeanna Stolle & Johnson, Jacqueline Kinney. Princess Grace & the Little Lost Kitten, 1 vol. Aranda, Omar, illus. 2011. (Princess Parables Ser.). (ENG.). 32p. (J). (gr. -1-2). 14.99 (978-0-310-71640-2(3)) Zonderkidz.

—Princess Joy's Birthday Blessing, 1 vol. Aranda, Omar, illus. 2011. (Princess Parables Ser.). (ENG.). 32p. (J). (gr. -1-2). 14.99 (978-0-310-71639-6(X)) Zonderkidz.

Yoyo Books Staff. Princess Charlotte Becomes a Magician. 2005. 32p. (978-90-5843-459-3(1)) YoYo Bks.

Zahler, Diane. Baker's Magic. Price, Mina, illus. 2016. (Middle-Grade Novels Ser.). (ENG.). 336p. (gr. 4-7). lib. bdg. 26.65 *(978-1-4965-2724-0(0))* Stone Arch Bks.
—Princess of the Wild Swans. Gilbert, Yvonne, illus. 2013. (ENG.). 240p. (J). (gr. 3-7). pap. 6.99 *(978-0-06-200495-6(6))* HarperCollins Pubs.
—Sleeping Beauty's Daughters. 2013. 216p. (J). lib. bdg. *(978-0-06-200497-0(2))* Harper & Row Ltd.
—The Thirteenth Princess. 2011. (ENG.). 272p. (J). (gr. 3-7). pap. 6.99 *(978-0-06-182500-2(X))* HarperCollins Pubs.
—A True Princess. (ENG.). (J). (gr. 3-7). 2012. 208p. pap. 6.99 *(978-0-06-182503-3(4))* 2011. 192p. 15.99 *(978-0-06-182501-9(8))* HarperCollins Pubs.
Zanzonico, Gaetana. A Magical Dream. 2011. 52p. pap. 31.99 *(978-1-4568-1562-2(8))* Xlibris Corp.
Zellerhoff, Christi. Princesses Can Be Pirates Too! Davis, Amy, illus. 2012. 38p. 17.99 *(978-1-935961-68-0(3))*; pap. 8.99 *(978-1-935961-95-6(0))* Booktrope. (Booktrope Editions).
Zhao, Yun & I-Haun. Real Fake Princess, Vol. 1. 2006. (Real/Fake Princess Ser.). (ENG., Illus.). 200p. (YA). pap. 9.95 *(978-1-59796-079-3(9))* DrMaster Pubns. Inc.
Ziegler, Argentina Palacios, tr. Dora y la Princesa de la Nieve (Dora Saves the Snow Princess) Aikins, Dave, illus. 2008. (Dora la Exploradora Ser.). (SPA.). 24p. (J). (gr. -1-2). pap. 3.99 *(978-1-4169-5870-3(3),* Libros Para Ninos) Libros Para Ninos.
Zimmerman, Diana S. Kandide & the Secret of the Mists, Bk. 1. Gadd, Maxine, illus. 2008. (Calabiyau Chronicles Ser.). 289p. (J). (gr. 4-7). pap. 9.99 *(978-0-9794328-2-8(0))* Noesis Publishing.
Zinn, Bridget. Poison. 2014. (ENG.). 288p. (YA). (gr. 7-12). pap. 9.99 *(978-1-4231-5330-6(8))* Hyperion Bks. for Children.

PRINTING

see also Books

Abell, Tracy. All about 3D Printing. 2017. (Cutting-Edge Technology (hardcover) Ser.). (ENG.). 32p. (J). (gr. 4-7). lib. bdg. 28.50 ***(978-1-63517-009-2(5),*** Focus Readers) North Star Editions.
Agard, John. Book. Packer, Neil, illus. 2015. (ENG.). 144p. (J). (gr. 5). 15.99 *(978-0-7636-7236-2(X))* Candlewick Pr.
Beckham, Robert. Who in the World Was the Secretive Printer? The Story of Johannes Gutenberg (Audio CD) unabr. ed. 2008. (ENG.). 1p. audio compact disk 12.95 *(978-1-933339-27-6(6),* 333927) Well-Trained Mind Pr.
Carter, Jason. Gutenberg's Bible. 2016. (Let's Find Out! Primary Sources Ser.). 00032p. (J). (gr. 2-3). lib. bdg. 24.45 *(978-1-5081-0403-2(4))* Rosen Publishing Group, Inc., The.
Childress, Diana. Johannes Gutenberg & the Printing Press. 2008. (Pivotal Moments in History Ser.). (ENG., Illus.). 160p. (gr. 9-12). lib. bdg. 38.60 *(978-0-8225-7520-7(5))* Lerner Publishing Group.
Diana, Carla. LEO the Maker Prince: Journeys in 3D Printing. 2013. (ENG., Illus.). 64p. pap. 14.99 *(978-1-4571-8314-0(5),* 9781457183140) O'Reilly Media, Inc.
Feinstein, Stephen. Johannes Gutenberg: The Printer Who Gave Words to the World. 2008. (Inventors Who Changed the World Ser.). (Illus.). 128p. (J). (gr. 3-7). lib. bdg. 34.60 *(978-1-59845-077-4(8),* MyReportLinks.com Bks.) Enslow Pubs., Inc.
Flash Kids Editors, Flash Kids, ed. Write-On Wipe-off Print Writing. 2016. (Write-On Wipe-off Handwriting Cards Ser.). (ENG., Illus.). 80p. (J). (gr. -1-1). 10.95 *(978-1-4114-7891-6(6),* Spark Publishing Group) Sterling Publishing Co., Inc.
Garry-McCord, Kathleen & Sonsky, Kim. Stamp It! Brush-Free Art Prints & Paint Projects. Sonsky, Kim, illus. 2006. (Illus.). 48p. (J). *(978-0-439-81340-2(9))* Scholastic, Inc.
GoBo. Santa Baby: Boxed Set. Boxed Set. 2006. 10p. 9.95 *(978-1-932915-37-2(0))* Sandvik Publishing.
Hamilton, John. Books, 1 vol. 2005. (Straight to the Source Ser.). (ENG.). 32p. (gr. k-6). 27.07 *(978-1-59197-543-4(3),* Checkerboard Library) ABDO Publishing Co.
Hayward, Linda. I Am a Book. Nicklaus, Carol, illus. (Silly Millies Ser.). 32p. (J). (gr. k-2). 2005. pap. 4.99 *(978-0-7613-1826-2(7),* First Avenue Editions) 2004. lib. bdg. 17.90 *(978-0-7613-2905-3(6),* Millbrook Pr.) Lerner Publishing Group.
Hiller, Sandra J. The Life of a Colonial Printer. 2013. (Jr. Graphic Colonial America Ser.). 24p. (J). (gr. 3-6). pap. 63.60 *(978-1-4777-1430-0(8))*; (ENG., Illus.). pap. 10.60 *(978-1-4777-1429-4(4))*; (ENG., Illus.). lib. bdg. 25.25 *(978-1-4777-1306-8(9))* Rosen Publishing Group, Inc., The. (PowerKids Pr.).
Kaergel, Julia. Fingerprints: Let's Make Art with Everyday Things. 2013. (ENG., Illus.). 96p. (J). (gr. 3-7). pap. 12.95 *(978-3-7913-7142-9(8))* Prestel Verlag GmbH & Co KG. DEU. Dist: Penguin Random Hse. LLC.
Malam, John. Journey of a Book, 1 vol. 2012. (Journey of A... Ser.). (ENG.). 32p. (gr. 1-3). pap. 8.29 *(978-1-4329-6607-2(3))*; lib. bdg. 27.32 *(978-1-4329-6600-3(6))* Heinemann-Raintree. (Heinemann First Library).
Medina, Sarah. Having Fun with Printing. 2007. (Fun Art Projects Ser.). (Illus.). 24p. (J). (gr. -1-3). lib. bdg. 25.25 *(978-1-4042-3719-3(4),* PowerKids Pr.) Rosen Publishing Group, Inc., The.
Mismas, L. J., Jr. Write on! Printing: Tutor Kit (English) 2005. (JPN & ENG., Illus.). 20p. (J). bds. incl. DVD *(978-0-9755836-0-9(3),* 0101) Incredible Kid, LLC.
Nicholson, Sue. Printing, 6 vols. 2005. (QEB Learn Art Ser.). (Illus.). (J). per. 8.95 *(978-1-59566-123-4(9))* QEB Publishing Inc.
Owens, L. L. Benjamin Franklin, 1 vol. 2007. (Essential Lives Set 1 Ser.). (ENG., Illus.). 112p. (J). (gr. 6-12). lib. bdg. 35.64 *(978-1-59928-840-6(0))* ABDO Publishing Co.
Petersen, Christine. The Printer. 2010. (Colonial People Ser.). 48p. (gr. 3-18). 29.93 *(978-0-7614-4802-0(0))* Marshall Cavendish Corp.
QEB Let's Start! Art National Book Stores Edition: Printing. 2006. (J). per. *(978-1-59566-299-6(5))* QEB Publishing Inc.
Riley, Gail Blasser. Benjamin Franklin & Electricity. 2004. (Cornerstones of Freedom Ser.). (ENG., Illus.). 48p. (YA). (gr. 4-7). 26.00 *(978-0-516-24240-8(7))* Scholastic Library Publishing.
Rossi, Renzo. The Age of the Book. Baldanzi, Alessandro, illus. 2008. (Reading & Writing Ser.). 32p. (gr. 4-7). 28.50 *(978-0-7614-4321-6(5))* Marshall Cavendish Corp.
Time for Kids Editors. Benjamin Franklin - A Man of Many Talents. 2005. (Time for Kids Ser.). (ENG., Illus.). 48p. (J). (gr. 2-4). pap. 3.99 *(978-0-06-057609-7(X))* HarperCollins Pubs.
Walton, Ruth. Let's Read a Book: Find Out about Books & How They Are Made. 2013. (Let's Find Out Ser.). (Illus.). 32p. (J). (gr. k-5). 28.50 *(978-1-59771-387-0(2))* Sea-To-Sea Pubns.

PRINTING—HISTORY

Crompton, Samuel Willard. The Printing Press. 2003. (Transforming Power of Technology Ser.). (Illus.). 112p. (J). (gr. 9-13). 30.00 *(978-0-7910-7451-0(X),* Chelsea Hse.) Facts On File, Inc.
Guillain, Charlotte. Spreading the Word. 2015. (Collins Big Cat Ser.). (ENG.). 32p. (J). (gr. 2-2). pap. 7.95 *(978-0-00-759127-5(6))* HarperCollins Pubs. Ltd. GBR. Dist: Independent Pubs. Group.
Heinrichs, Ann. The Printing Press. 2005. (Inventions That Shaped the World Ser.). (Illus.). 80p. (J). (gr. 4-7). 17.60 *(978-0-7569-6860-1(7))* Perfection Learning Corp.
Krensky, Stephen. Breaking into Print: Before & after the Invention of the Printing Press. Christensen, Bonnie, illus. 2003. 30p. (J). (gr. 3-8). reprint ed. 18.00 *(978-0-7567-6843-0(8))* DIANE Publishing Co.
Mattern, Joanne. The Printing Press: An Information Revolution. (Technology That Changed the World Ser.). 24p. 2009. (gr. 2-3). 42.50 *(978-1-60853-276-6(3))* 2003. (Illus.). (J). lib. bdg. 22.60 *(978-0-8239-6488-8(4))* Rosen Publishing Group, Inc., The. (PowerKids Pr.).
Mullins, Lisa. Inventing the Printing Press. 2007. (Breakthrough Inventions Ser.). (ENG., Illus.). 32p. (J). (gr. 3-7). lib. bdg. *(978-0-7787-2819-1(6))*; pap. *(978-0-7787-2841-2(2))* Crabtree Publishing Co.
Olson, Kay Melchisedech. Johann Gutenberg & the Printing Press, 1 vol. Smith, Tod G., illus. 2006. (Inventions & Discovery Ser.). (ENG.). 32p. (gr. 3-4). pap. 8.10 *(978-0-7368-9644-3(9),* Graphic Library) Capstone Press of Coughlan Cos.
Rumford, James. From the Good Mountain: How Gutenberg Changed the World. Rumford, James, illus. 2012. (ENG., Illus.). 36p. (J). (gr. -1-3). 17.99 *(978-1-59643-542-1(9),* 9781596435421) Roaring Brook Pr.
Silva, Patricia. Modern Times. Baldanzi, Alessandro, illus. 2008. (Reading & Writing Ser.). 32p. (gr. 4-7). 28.50 *(978-0-7614-4322-3(3),* Benchmark Bks.) Marshall Cavendish Corp.
Spilsbury, Louise. Johannes Gutenberg & the Printing Press, 01 vols., 1. 2016. (Inventions That Changed the World Ser.). (ENG.). 32p. (J). pap. 10.00 *(978-1-5081-4631-5(4),* PowerKids Pr.) Rosen Publishing Group, Inc., The.
Spilsbury, Richard & Spilsbury, Louise. The Printing Press, 1 vol. 2011. (Tales of Invention Ser.). (ENG.). 32p. (gr. 3-5). pap. 8.95 *(978-1-4329-4885-6(7),* NA-h) Heinemann-Raintree.
Vander Hook, Sue. Johannes Gutenberg: Printing Press Innovator, 1 vol. 2009. (Publishing Pioneers Ser.). (ENG., Illus.). 112p. (J). (gr. 6-12). lib. bdg. 35.64 *(978-1-60453-762-8(0),* Essential Library) ABDO Publishing Co.
World Book, Inc. Staff, contrib. by. Hieroglyphics to Hypertext: A Timeline of the Written Word. 2016. (J). *(978-0-7166-3546-8(1))* World Bk.-Childcraft International.

PRINTING INDUSTRY

Otfinoski, Steven. 3D Printing: Science, Technology, & Engineering. 2016. (Calling All Innovators: a Career for You Ser.). (ENG., Illus.). 64p. (J). lib. bdg. 32.00 *(978-0-531-21865-5(1))*; pap. 8.95 *(978-0-531-21988-1(7))* Scholastic Library Publishing. (Children's Pr.).

PRINTS

see also Engraving

AZ Books. Prints. 2013. (Guess What? Ser.). (ENG.). 10p. (J). (— 1). bds. 5.95 *(978-1-61889-315-4(7))* AZ Bks. LLC.
Galat, Joan Marie. Maker Projects for Kids Who Love Printmaking. 2017. (Be a Maker! Ser.). (ENG., Illus.). 32p. (J). (gr. 4-7). ***(978-0-7787-2889-4(7))*** Crabtree Publishing Co.

PRINTS—TECHNIQUE

Hanson, Anders. Cool Print Making: The Art of Creativity for Kids, 1 vol. 2009. (Cool Art Ser.). (ENG.). 32p. (gr. 3-6). 28.50 *(978-1-60453-147-3(9),* Checkerboard Library) ABDO Publishing Co.
Luxbacher, Irene. 123 I Can Make Prints! Luxbacher, Irene, illus. 2008. (Starting Art Ser.). (ENG., Illus.). 24p. (J). (gr. -1-2). 14.95 *(978-1-55453-040-3(7))*; pap. 5.95 *(978-1-55453-153-0(5))* Kids Can Pr., Ltd. CAN. Dist: Hachette Bk. Group.
Rau, Dana Meachen. Learning to Make Prints. 2015. (How-To Library). (ENG., Illus.). 32p. (J). (gr. 3-6). lib. bdg. 29.93 *(978-1-63362-373-6(4),* 206912) Cherry Lake Publishing.
Scrace, Carolyn. Printing & Other Amazing Techniques. 2015. (How to Art Doodle Ser.). (Illus.). 24p. (gr. 3-6). 28.50 *(978-1-909645-51-6(6))* Book Hse. GBR. Dist: Black Rabbit Bks.
—Printing & Other Amazing Techniques. 2015. (ENG., Illus.). 24p. (J). pap. 8.95 *(978-1-910184-38-7(1))* RiverStream Publishing.
Thomas, Isabel. Prints, 1 vol. 2011. (Start with Art Ser.). (ENG.). 24p. (gr. k-2). 23.32 *(978-1-4329-5019-4(3),* Heinemann Read & Learn) Heinemann-Raintree.

PRISON ESCAPES

see Escapes

PRISONS

see also Criminal Law; Escapes

Bakker, T. C. Alcatraz Believe It or Not. House, Charles, illus. 2016. 110p. ***(978-1-932519-36-5(X))*** Golden Gate National Parks Conservancy.
Berlatsky, Noah. America's Prisons. 2010. (Opposing Viewpoints Ser.). (Illus.). 176-240p. (J). 42.95 *(978-0-7377-4956-4(3))*; pap. 29.45 *(978-0-7377-4957-1(1))* Cengage Gale. (Greenhaven Pr., Inc.).
—Imprisonment. 2010. (Global Viewpoints Ser.). (Illus.). 224p. (J). 40.45 *(978-0-7377-4717-1(X))*; pap. 27.95 *(978-0-7377-4718-8(8))* Cengage Gale. (Greenhaven Pr., Inc.).
Bodden, Valerie. Old Jails. 2017. (J). *(978-1-60818-809-3(4),* Creative Education) Creative Co., The.
Burlingame, Jeff. Prisons: Rehabilitate or Severely Punish? 2011. (Controversy! 3 Ser.). 112p. (gr. 7). 37.07 *(978-1-60870-493-4(9))* Marshall Cavendish Corp.
Chandler, Matt. Alcatraz: A Chilling Interactive Adventure. 2016. (You Choose: Haunted Places Ser.). (ENG., Illus.). 112p. (gr. 3-4). lib. bdg. 31.99 *(978-1-5157-2580-0(4),* You Choose Bks.) Capstone Press of Coughlan Cos.
Costain, Meredith. You Wouldn't Want to Be an 18th-Century British Convict! A Trip to Australia You'd Rather Not Take. Antram, David, illus. 2006. (You Wouldn't Want to Ser.). (ENG.). 32p. (J). (gr. 2-5). pap. 9.95 *(978-0-531-16998-8(7),* Watts, Franklin) Scholastic Library Publishing.
Dunn, Dinah. Haunted Prisons. 2014. (Scary Places Ser.). 32p. (J). (gr. 4-8). lib. bdg. 25.27 *(978-1-62724-089-5(6))* Bearport Publishing Co., Inc.
Enz, Tammy. Beyond the Bars: Exploring the Secrets of a Police Station. 2010. (Hidden Worlds Ser.). (ENG.). 32p. (gr. 1-2). lib. bdg. 26.65 *(978-1-4296-3377-2(8),* Blazers) Capstone Press of Coughlan Cos.
Esherick, Joan. Prisoner Rehabilitation: Success Stories & Failures. 2006. (Incarceration Issues Ser.). (Illus.). 111p. (YA). (gr. 7-18). lib. bdg. 22.95 *(978-1-59084-994-1(9))* Mason Crest.
Esherick, Joan. Women Incarcerated. 2017. (J). ***(978-1-4222-3790-8(7))*** Mason Crest.
Faryon, Cynthia J. Real Justice: Guilty of Being Weird: The Story of Guy Paul Morin, 1 vol. 2012. (Lorimer Real Justice Ser.). (ENG., Illus.). 144p. (YA). (gr. 8-12). 18.95 *(978-1-4594-0093-1(3),* 9781459400931); pap. 12.95 *(978-1-4594-0092-4(5),* 9781459400924) Lorimer, James & Co., Ltd., Pubs. CAN. Dist: Casemate Pubs. & Bk. Distributors, LLC.
—Sentenced to Life at Seventeen: The Story of David Milgaard, 1 vol. 2012. (Lorimer Real Justice Ser.). (ENG., Illus.). 120p. (J). (gr. 8-12). 18.95 *(978-1-4594-0169-3(7),* 9781459401693) Lorimer, James & Co., Ltd., Pubs. CAN. Dist: Casemate Pubs. & Bk. Distributors, LLC.
Friedman, Lauri S. Prisons. Des Chenes, Elizabeth, ed. 2007. (Introducing Issues with Opposing Viewpoints Ser.). (ENG., Illus.). 144p. (gr. 10-12). lib. bdg. 42.00 *(978-0-7377-3578-9(3))* Cengage Gale.
Gordon, Nick. Alcatraz. 2013. (Scariest Places on Earth Ser.). (ENG., Illus.). 24p. (J). (gr. 3-7). lib. bdg. 25.95 *(978-1-60014-945-0(6),* Torque Bks.) Bellwether Media.
Gordon, Sharon. What's Inside a Police Station? 2007. (Bookworms: What's Inside Me? Ser.). (Illus.). 31p. (J). (gr. k-2). pap. 6.99 *(978-0-7614-3349-1(X),* Benchmark Bks.) Marshall Cavendish Corp.
Gourley, Catherine. The Horrors of Andersonville: Life & Death Inside a Civil War Prison. 2010. (ENG.). 192p. (gr. 9-12). lib. bdg. 38.60 *(978-0-7613-4212-0(5))* Lerner Publishing Group.
Hamilton, John. Castles & Dungeons, 1 vol. 2006. (Fantasy & Folklore Ser.). (ENG., Illus.). 32p. (gr. 5-8). 27.07 *(978-1-59679-335-4(X),* Abdo & Daughters) ABDO Publishing Co.
Hoena, Blake. The Tower of London: A Chilling Interactive Adventure. 2016. (You Choose: Haunted Places Ser.). (ENG., Illus.). 112p. (gr. 3-4). lib. bdg. 31.99 *(978-1-5157-2579-4(0),* You Choose Bks.) Capstone Press of Coughlan Cos.
Hyde, Natalie. Alcatraz. 2013. (ENG.). 48p. (J). *(978-0-7787-1098-1(X))*; pap. *(978-0-7787-1104-9(8))* Crabtree Publishing Co.
Incarceration Issues: Punishment, Reform, & Rehabilitation, 11 vols., Set. Incl. Alternatives to Prison: Rehabilitation & Other Programs. Russell, Craig. 111p. 2008. lib. bdg. 22.95 *(978-1-59084-991-0(4))*; Incarceration Around the World. Russell, Craig. 112p. 2008. lib. bdg. 22.95 *(978-1-59084-988-0(4))*; Political Prisoners. Smith, Roger. 111p. 2008. lib. bdg. 22.95 *(978-1-59084-987-3(6))*; Prison Conditions: Overcrowding, Disease, Violence, & Abuse. Smith, Roger. 111p. 2008. lib. bdg. 22.95 *(978-1-59084-986-6(8))*; Prisoner Rehabilitation: Success Stories & Failures. Esherick, Joan. 111p. 2006. lib. bdg. 22.95 *(978-1-59084-994-1(9))*; Prisoners on Death Row. Smith, Roger. 111p. 2006. lib. bdg. 22.95 *(978-1-59084-989-7(2))*; Social, Monetary, & Moral Costs of Prisons. Libal, Autumn. 111p. 2008. lib. bdg. 22.95 *(978-1-59084-992-7(2))*; Youth in Prison. Smith, Roger & McIntosh, Marsha & Smith. 111p. 2008. lib. bdg. 22.95 *(978-1-59084-990-3(6))*; (YA). (gr. 7-18). (Incarceration Issues Ser.). (Illus.). 111p. 2007. 252.45 *(978-1-59084-984-2(1))* Mason Crest.
Libal, Autumn. The Social, Monetary, & Moral Costs of Prisons. 2008. (Incarceration Issues Ser.). (Illus.). 111p. (YA). (gr. 7-18). lib. bdg. 22.95 *(978-1-59084-992-7(2))* Mason Crest.
Lock, Joan. Infamous Prisons, Vol. 20. Gomez, Manny, ed. 2016. (Crime & Detection Ser.). (Illus.). 96p. (J). (gr. 7). 24.95 *(978-1-4222-3475-4(4))* Mason Crest.
Macdonald, Fiona. You Wouldn't Want to Be in a Medieval Dungeon! Prisoners You'd Rather Not Meet. Antram, David, illus. 2013. (You Wouldn't Want to... Ser.). (ENG.). (J). 40p. pap. 9.95 *(978-0-531-24504-0(7))*; 32p. 29.00 *(978-0-531-25948-1(X))* Scholastic Library Publishing. (Watts, Franklin).
—You Wouldn't Want to Be in a Medieval Dungeon! Prisoners You'd Rather Not Meet. 2013. (You Wouldn't Want To... Ser.). lib. bdg. 20.80 *(978-0-606-31629-3(9),* Turtleback) Turtleback Bks.
MacDonald, Fiona & Macdonald, Fiona. You Wouldn't Want to Be in a Medieval Dungeon! Prisoners You'd Rather Not Meet. Antram, David, illus. 2003. (You Wouldn't Want to Ser.). (ENG.). 32p. (J). 29.00 *(978-0-531-12312-6(X),* Watts, Franklin) Scholastic Library Publishing.
Markovics, Joyce L. Deserted Prisons. 2017. (Tiptoe into Scary Places Ser.). (ENG., Illus.). 24p. (J). (gr. k-3). 18.95 ***(978-1-68402-052-2(2))*** Bearport Publishing Co., Inc.
Medina, Nico. Where Is Alcatraz? Groff, David, illus. 2016. (Where Is? Ser.). (ENG.). 112p. (J). (gr. 3-7). lib. bdg. 15.99 *(978-0-399-54232-9(9),* Grosset & Dunlap) Penguin Young Readers Group.
Merino, Noël. Prison. 2009. (Issues on Trial Ser.). (ENG., Illus.). 240p. (gr. 10-12). 48.30 *(978-0-7377-4344-9(1),* Greenhaven Pr., Inc.) Cengage Gale.
Oliver, Marilyn Tower. The Infamous Alcatraz Prison in United States History. 2015. (In United States History Ser.). 96p. (J). (gr. 5-12). 27.94 *(978-0-7660-6320-4(8))*; pap. 10.95 *(978-0-7660-6321-1(6))* Enslow Pubs., Inc.
Owings, Lisa. Ghosts in Prisons. 2016. (Ghost Stories Ser.). (ENG., Illus.). 24p. (J). (gr. 3-7). 25.95 *(978-1-62617-431-3(8),* Epic Bks.) Bellwether Media.
Person, Stephen. Ghostly Alcatraz Island. 2010. (HorrorScapes Ser.). 32p. (YA). (gr. 4-7). lib. bdg. 25.27 *(978-1-936087-97-6(9))* Bearport Publishing Co., Inc.
Poole, H. W. Incarceration & Families, Vol. 12. 2016. (Families Today Ser.). (Illus.). 48p. (J). (gr. 5). 20.95 *(978-1-4222-3618-5(8))* Mason Crest.
Rabiger, Joanna. Daily Prison Life, Vol. 20. 2016. (Crime & Detection Ser.: Vol. 20). (ENG., Illus.). 96p. (J). (gr. 7-12). 24.95 *(978-1-4222-3472-3(X))* Mason Crest.
Russell, Craig. Incarceration Around the World. 2008. (Incarceration Issues Ser.). (Illus.). 112p. (YA). (gr. 7-18). lib. bdg. 22.95 *(978-1-59084-988-0(4))* Mason Crest.
Russell, Craig. Prison Conditions Around the World. 2017. (J). ***(978-1-4222-3786-1(9))*** Mason Crest.
Schwartz, Heather E. Locked up for Freedom: Civil Rights Protesters at the Leesburg Stockade. 2017. (ENG., Illus.). 64p. (J). (gr. 5-8). lib. bdg. 33.32 ***(978-1-4677-8597-6(0),*** Millbrook Pr.) Lerner Publishing Group.
Smith, Roger. The History of Punishment & Imprisonment. 2017. (J). ***(978-1-4222-3782-3(6))*** Mason Crest.
—Political Prisoners. 2017. (J). ***(978-1-4222-3784-7(2))*** Mason Crest.
—Prison Conditions: Overcrowding, Disease, Violence, & Abuse. 2008. (Incarceration Issues Ser.). (Illus.). 111p. (YA). (gr. 7-18). lib. bdg. 22.95 *(978-1-59084-986-6(8))* Mason Crest.
Smith, Roger. The Treatment of Prisoners & Prison Conditions. 2017. (Prison System Ser.: Vol. 9). (ENG.). (YA). (gr. 7-12). 24.95 ***(978-1-4222-3787-8(7))*** Mason Crest.
Spalding, Maddie. Guarding Supermax Prisons. 2016. (Highly Guarded Places Ser.). (ENG.). 24p. (J). (gr. 2-5). 28.50 *(978-1-5038-0807-2(6),* 210648) Child's World, Inc., The.
Stewart, David. You Wouldn't Want to Be in a Medieval Dungeon! Antram, David, illus. rev. ed. 2013. (You Wouldn't Want to... Ser.). (ENG.). 32p. (J). 29.00 *(978-0-531-25949-8(8),* Watts, Franklin) Scholastic Library Publishing.
Watson, Stephanie. Incarcerated Youth. 2016. (ENG.). 80p. (J). (gr. 5-12). lib. bdg. *(978-1-60152-982-4(1))* ReferencePoint Pr., Inc.
Williams, Dinah. Haunted Prisons. 2017. (Scary Places Ser.). (ENG.). 32p. (J). (gr. 4-8). 8.95 ***(978-1-68402-603-6(2))*** Bearport Publishing Co., Inc.
Wood, Alix. Ghostly Prisons. 2016. (World's Scariest Places Ser.). 00032p. (J). pap. 10.50 ***(978-1-4824-5904-3(3))*** Stevens, Gareth Publishing LLLP.
Woolf, Alex. A Photographic View of Crime & Punishment. 2016. (Past in Pictures Ser.). (ENG., Illus.). 32p. (J). (gr. 4-6). pap. 11.99 *(978-0-7502-8348-9(3),* Wayland) Hachette Children's Group GBR. Dist: Hachette Bk. Group.
Yomtov, Nel. Tunnelling to Freedom: The Great Escape from Stalag Luft III. Valdrighi, Alessandro, illus. 2017. (Great Escapes of World War II Ser.). (ENG.). 32p. (gr. 3-4). pap. 7.95 *(978-1-5157-3536-6(2),* Graphic Library) Capstone Press of Coughlan Cos.

PRISONS—FICTION

Authords, D. K. Being Alone. 2013. 120p. pap. 19.95 *(978-1-63000-114-8(7))* America Star Bks.
Basye, Dale E. Blimpo Vol. 3: The Third Circle of Heck. Dob, Bob, illus. 2011. (Heck Ser.). (ENG.). 464p. (J). (gr. 3-7). pap. 7.99 *(978-0-375-85677-8(3),* Yearling) Random Hse. Children's Bks.
—Precocia: the Sixth Circle of Heck. Dob, Bob, illus. 2013. (Heck Ser.). (ENG.). 432p. (J). (gr. 3-7). 6.99 *(978-0-375-86807-8(0),* Yearling) Random Hse. Children's Bks.
Breslin, Theresa. Prisoner in Alcatraz. 2012. (Stoke Books Titles Ser.). (ENG.). 80p. (YA). (gr. 8-12). pap. 6.95 *(978-1-78112-124-5(9))*; lib. bdg. 22.60 *(978-1-78112-125-2(7))* Lerner Publishing Group.
Burch, Robert. Queenie Peavey. l.t. ed. 2003. (LRS Large Print Cornerstone Ser.). 166p. (J). lib. bdg. 29.95 *(978-1-58118-115-9(9))* LRS.
Carr, Kathy. Granny, Where Did My Mommy Go? 2008. 24p. pap. 24.95 *(978-1-60610-324-1(5))* America Star Bks.
Crowder, Melanie. An Uninterrupted View of the Sky. 2017. (ENG.). 304p. (YA). (gr. 7). 17.99 *(978-0-399-16900-7(8),* Philomel Bks.) Penguin Young Readers Group.
Darke, J. A. The Grin in the Dark. Evergreen, Nelson, illus. 2015. (Spine Shivers Ser.). (ENG.). 128p. (gr. 3-4). lib. bdg. 26.65 *(978-1-4965-0217-9(5))* Stone Arch Bks.
Dean, Myers Walter. Monster. 2014. (ENG.). 304p. (J). (gr. 12-12). 14.24 *(978-1-63245-060-9(7))* Lectorum Pubns., Inc.
Delaney, Joseph. Ghost Prison. (ENG.). 112p. (YA). (gr. 6-12). 2014. pap. 5.99 *(978-1-4926-0174-6(8))* 2013. 12.99 *(978-1-4022-9318-4(6),* 9781402293184) Sourcebooks, Inc.
Ducie, Joe. The Rig. 2017. (ENG.). 320p. (J). (gr. 5-7). pap. 7.99 *(978-0-544-93674-4(4),* HMH Books For Young Readers) Houghton Mifflin Harcourt Publishing Co.
Finotti, M. C. Paintbrushes & Arrows. 2016. 113p. (J). ***(978-1-56164-968-6(6))*** Pineapple Pr., Inc.
Finotti, M. C. Paintbrushes & Arrows: A Story of St. Augustine. 2016. (ENG.). 112p. (J). pap. 9.95 *(978-1-56164-963-1(5))* Pineapple Pr., Inc.
Fisher, Catherine. Incarceron. 2010. (Playaway Children Ser.). (J). 64.99 *(978-1-61637-331-3(8))* Findaway World, LLC.
—Incarceron. 2010. (Incarceron Ser.). (FRE.). 498p. (YA). (gr. 7-12). pap. *(978-2-266-17793-1(1))* Le Robert.
—Incarceron. November, S., ed. Yuen, Sammy, illus. 2011. (ENG.). 464p. (YA). (gr. 7-18). pap. 10.99 *(978-0-14-241852-9(8),* Firebird) Penguin Young Readers Group.
—Incarceron. 2011. (Incarceron Ser.). (ENG.). 442p. (gr. 7-12). 20.00 *(978-1-61383-117-5(X))* Perfection Learning Corp.
—INCARCERON. 2010. (SPA.). 512p. (J). (gr. 8-12). pap. 19.99 *(978-84-272-0047-0(1))* RBA Libros, S.A. ESP. Dist: Lectorum Pubns., Inc.

PQR

—Incarceron. l.t. ed. 2010. (Incarceron Ser.). (ENG.). 526p. 23.99 *(978-1-4104-2991-9(1))* Thorndike Pr.

—Incarceron. 2011. lib. bdg. 22.10 *(978-0-606-22590-8(0),* Turtleback) Turtleback Bks.

—Sapphique. (ENG.). (YA). (gr. 7-18). 2011. 480p. 10.99 *(978-0-14-241979-3(6),* Firebird) 2010. 464p. 17.99 *(978-0-8037-3397-8(6),* Dial Bks) Penguin Young Readers Group.

Gaffney, Linda. My Daddy Does GOOD Things, Too! Dabney, Undra & Goetting, Nickalas, illus. 2006. 55p. per. 10.99 *(978-0-9787501-0-7(1))* Gaffney, Linda.

Griffin, M. A. Lifers. 2017. (ENG.). 288p. (J). (gr. 7). 17.99 *(978-1-338-06553-4(X),* Chicken Hse., The) Scholastic, Inc.

Hueller, Andy. Skipping Stones at the Center of the Earth: A Middle Grade Novel. 2011. (J). pap. 8.99 *(978-1-59955-488-4(7),* Bonneville Bks.) Cedar Fort, Inc./CFI Distribution.

Ireland, Justina. Promise of Shadows. 2014. (ENG., Illus.). 384p. (YA). (gr. 9). 17.99 *(978-1-4424-4464-5(9),* Simon & Schuster Bks. For Young Readers) Simon & Schuster Bks. For Young Readers.

Kir-on, Callanitte. The 3-D Files: Prisoner on the Loose. 2003. (Illus.). (J). 10.95 *(978-1-931681-47-6(3))* Israel Bookshop Pubns.

Laybourn, Emma. Dungeon Dragon. 2008. (ENG.). 156p. (J). (gr. 3-6). pap. 9.95 *(978-1-84270-736-4(1))* Andersen Pr. GBR. Dist: Independent Pubs. Group.

McClintock, Norah. El Regreso, 1 vol. 2011. (Spanish Soundings Ser.).Tr. of Back. (SPA.). 112p. (YA). (gr. 8-12). pap. 9.95 *(978-1-55469-973-5(8))* Orca Bk. Pubs. USA.

McVoy, Terra Elan. Criminal. 2013. (ENG.). 288p. (YA). (gr. 9). 16.99 *(978-1-4424-2162-2(2),* Simon Pulse) Simon Pulse.

Morgenroth, Kate. Jude. 2006. (ENG., Illus.). 288p. (YA). (gr. 7-12). reprint ed. mass mkt. 7.99 *(978-1-4169-1267-5(3),* Simon Pulse) Simon Pulse.

Muchamore, Robert. Maximum Security. 2011. (Cherub Ser.: 3). (ENG.). 320p. (YA). (gr. 7). lib. bdg. 17.99 *(978-1-4169-9942-3(6),* Simon Pulse) Simon Pulse.

Murphy, Shirley Rousseau & Murphy, Pat J. J. The Cat, the Devil, the Last Escape: A Novel. 2015. (ENG., Illus.). 320p. 24.99 *(978-0-06-226910-2(0),* Morrow, William & Co.) HarperCollins Pubs.

Myers, Walter Dean. Monster. Myers, Christopher, illus. 2004. (Monster Ser.). (ENG.). 304p. (YA). (gr. 8). reprint ed. pap. 9.99 *(978-0-06-440731-1(4),* Amistad) HarperCollins Pubs.

—Monster. unabr. ed. 2004. 281p. (J). (gr. 7-18). pap. 29.00 incl. audio *(978-0-8072-8363-9(0),* YA188CX, Listening Library) Random Hse. Audio Publishing Group.

—Monster. Myers, Christopher A., illus. 2004. (National Book Award Finalist Ser.). 281p. (YA). (gr. 7-12). lib. bdg. 20.85 *(978-0-613-35985-6(2),* Turtleback) Turtleback Bks.

Myers, Walter Dean & Sims, Guy A. Monster. Anyabwile, Dawud, illus. 2015. (YA). lib. bdg. 20.85 *(978-0-606-37629-7(1))* Turtleback Bks.

Parkkola, Seita. The School of Possibilities. Silver, Annira & Gass, Marja, trs. from FIN. Ikonen, Jani, illus. 2010. (ENG.). 368p. (J). (gr. 4-7). 12.99 *(978-1-4022-1835-4(4),* Sourcebooks Jabberwocky) Sourcebooks, Inc.

Phillips, Dee. Doomed on Death Row. 2016. (Cold Whispers II Ser.). (ENG.). 32p. (J). (gr. 2-6). 19.95 *(978-1-944102-35-7(3))* Bearport Publishing Co., Inc.

Pileggi, Leah. Prisoner 88. 2013. (J). 16.95 *(978-1-60734-611-1(7));* (ENG., Illus.). 144p. (gr. 5). 16.95 *(978-1-58089-560-6(3))* Charlesbridge Publishing, Inc.

Schraff, Anne E. Unbroken. 2012. (Urban Underground — Cesar Chavez High School Ser.: 28). (YA). lib. bdg. 20.80 *(978-0-606-26598-0(8),* Turtleback) Turtleback Bks.

Shan, Darren, pseud. Zom-B Family. 2014. (Zom-B Ser.: 9). (ENG.). 208p. (YA). (gr. 7-17). 15.00 *(978-0-316-21434-6(5))* Little Brown & Co.

Sims, Guy A. & Myers, Walter Dean. Monster. Anyabwile, Dawud, illus. 2015. (Monster Ser.). (ENG.). 160p. (YA). (gr. 8). pap. 9.99 *(978-0-06-227499-1(6))* HarperCollins Pubs.

Sitomer, Alan Lawrence. Noble Warrior. 2015. (Caged Warrior Ser.). (ENG., Illus.). 400p. (YA). (gr. 7-12). 17.99 *(978-1-4847-0528-5(9))* Hyperion Bks. for Children.

Smith, Alexander Gordon. Death Sentence. 2011. (Escape from Furnace Ser.: 3). (ENG.). 272p. (YA). (gr. 7-11). 17.99 *(978-0-374-32494-0(8),* 9780374324940, Farrar, Straus & Giroux (BYR)) Farrar, Straus & Giroux.

—Death Sentence. 2012. (Escape from Furnace Ser.: 3). (ENG.). 288p. (YA). (gr. 7-11). pap. 10.99 *(978-0-312-67441-0(4),* 9780312674410) Square Fish.

—Execution. 2012. (Escape from Furnace Ser.: 5). (ENG.). 320p. (YA). (gr. 7-11). 16.99 *(978-0-374-36224-9(6),* 9780374362249, Farrar, Straus & Giroux (BYR)) Farrar, Straus & Giroux.

—Execution. 2013. (Escape from Furnace Ser.: 5). (ENG.). 336p. (YA). (gr. 7-11). pap. 10.99 *(978-1-250-02942-3(2),* 9781250029423) Square Fish.

—Fugitives. 2012. (Escape from Furnace Ser.: 4). (ENG.). 288p. (YA). (gr. 7-11). 17.99 *(978-0-374-32484-1(0),* 9780374324841, Farrar, Straus & Giroux (BYR)) Farrar, Straus & Giroux.

—Fugitives. 2012. (Escape from Furnace Ser.: 4). (ENG.). 304p. (YA). (gr. 7-11). pap. 10.99 *(978-1-250-00339-3(3),* 9781250003393) Square Fish.

—Lockdown. 2009. (Escape from Furnace Ser.: 1). (ENG.). 288p. (YA). (gr. 7-11). 17.99 *(978-0-374-32491-9(3),* 9780374324919, Farrar, Straus & Giroux (BYR)) Farrar, Straus & Giroux.

—Lockdown. 2010. (Escape from Furnace Ser.: 1). (ENG.). 304p. (YA). (gr. 7-11). pap. 10.99 *(978-0-312-61193-4(5),* 9780312611934) Square Fish.

—Solitary. 2010. (Escape from Furnace Ser.: 2). (ENG.). 240p. (YA). (gr. 7-11). 17.99 *(978-0-374-32492-6(1),* 9780374324926, Farrar, Straus & Giroux (BYR)) Farrar, Straus & Giroux.

—Solitary. 2011. (Escape from Furnace Ser.: 2). (ENG.). 256p. (YA). (gr. 7-11). pap. 10.99 *(978-0-312-67476-2(7),* 9780312674762) Square Fish.

Sonneborn, Scott. Prisoner of the Penguin!, 1 vol. Vecchio, Luciano, illus. 2014. (Batman: Comic Chapter Bks.). (ENG.). 88p. (gr. 3-7). 21.32 *(978-1-4342-9131-8(6))* Stone Arch Bks.

Spinelli, Jerry. The Warden's Daughter. 2017. (ENG.). 352p. (J). (gr. 4-7). 16.99 *(978-0-375-83199-7(1));* lib. bdg. 19.99 *(978-0-375-93199-4(6))* Random Hse. Children's Bks. (Knopf Bks. for Young Readers).

Stanglin, Jackie A. Mami, Que Es una Carcel? McGuckie, Cierra Jade, illus. 2007. (J). (gr. -1-3). 36p. 19.99 *(978-1-59879-429-8(9));* 40p. 13.99 *(978-1-59879-428-1(0))* Lifevest Publishing, Inc.

—What Is Jail, Mommy? McGuckie, Cierra Jade, illus. l.t. ed. 2006. 40p. (J). 21.99 *(978-1-59879-252-2(0));* (gr. -1-3). 13.99 *(978-1-59879-248-5(2))* Lifevest Publishing, Inc.

Stasse, Lisa M. The Forsaken. (ENG., (YA). (gr. 7). 2013. Illus.). 400p. pap. 9.99 *(978-1-4424-3266-6(7))* 2012. 384p. 16.99 *(978-1-4424-3265-9(9))* Simon & Schuster Bks. For Young Readers. (Simon & Schuster Bks. For Young Readers).

—The Uprising: The Forsaken Trilogy. (ENG., (YA). (gr. 7). 2014. Illus.). 400p. pap. 9.99 *(978-1-4424-3269-7(1))* 2013. 384p. 16.99 *(978-1-4424-3268-0(3))* Simon & Schuster Bks. For Young Readers. (Simon & Schuster Bks. For Young Readers).

Steven, Ruth Lauren & Lauren, Ruth. Prisoner of Ice & Snow. 2017. (ENG.). 288p. (J). 16.99 *(978-1-68119-131-7(8),* 9781681191317, Bloomsbury USA Childrens) Bloomsbury Publishing USA.

Van Lieshout, Elle & Van Os, Erik. Lovey & Dovey. Van Hout, Mies, illus. 2009. (ENG.). 32p. (J). (gr. k-2). 16.95 *(978-1-59078-660-4(2),* Lemniscaat) Boyds Mills Pr.

Venable, Alan. The Man in the Iron Mask. 2007. (Classic Adventures Ser.). pap. 9.95 *(978-1-4105-0860-7(9))* Johnston, Don Inc.

Volponi, Paul. Rikers High. (ENG.). (YA). (gr. 7-18). 2011. 272p. 7.99 *(978-0-14-241778-2(5),* Speak) 2010. 256p. 16.99 *(978-0-670-01107-0(X),* Viking Books for Young Readers) Penguin Young Readers Group.

PRIVACY, RIGHT OF

Abramovitz, Melissa. Online Predators. 2016. (ENG.). 80p. (J). (gr. 5-12). lib. bdg. *(978-1-68282-092-6(0))* ReferencePoint Pr., Inc.

Berry, Joy. Help Me Be Good about Snooping. 2009. (Help Me Be Good Ser.). 32p. pap. 7.95 *(978-1-60577-122-9(8))* Berry, Joy Enterprises.

Carson, Brian & Ramen, Catherine. Understanding Your Right to Freedom from Searches. 2011. (Personal Freedom & Civic Duty Ser.). (Illus.). 160p. (YA). (gr. 7-12). lib. bdg. 35.95 *(978-1-4488-4670-2(6))* Rosen Publishing Group, Inc., The.

Coddington, Andrew. Mass Government Surveillance: Spying on Citizens. 2017. (J). ***(978-1-5026-2672-1(1))*** Cavendish Square Publishing.

Cunningham, Anne C., ed. Privacy & Security in the Digital Age. 2017. (Current Controversies Ser.). 224p. (J). (gr. 10-12). pap. 32.00 ***(978-1-5345-0032-7(4))***; lib. bdg. 46.40 ***(978-1-5345-0021-1(9))*** Greenhaven Publishing LLC. (Greenhaven Publishing).

Espejo, Roman. Civil Liberties. 2009. (Opposing Viewpoints Ser.). (ENG., Illus.). 240p. (YA). (gr. 10-12). pap. 29.45 *(978-0-7377-4355-5(7),* LML02109-245310);No. 9. pap. 42.95 *(978-0-7377-4356-2(5),* LML02109-245369) Cengage Gale. (Greenhaven Pr., Inc.).

—Privacy. 2010. (Opposing Viewpoints Ser.). (ENG.). 240p. 42.95 *(978-0-7377-4984-7(9));* pap. 29.45 *(978-0-7377-4985-4(7))* Cengage Gale. (Greenhaven Pr., Inc.).

Freedman, Jeri. America Debates Privacy Versus Security. 2007. (America Debates Ser.). (Illus.). 64p. (YA). (gr. 5-9). lib. bdg. 31.95 *(978-1-4042-1929-8(3))* Rosen Publishing Group, Inc., The.

Fridell, Ron. Privacy vs. Security: Your Rights in Conflict. 2004. (Issues in Focus Ser.). (Illus.). 128p. (J). lib. bdg. 26.60 *(978-0-7660-2161-7(0))* Enslow Pubs., Inc.

Furgang, Kathy & Gatta, Frank. Understanding Your Right to Privacy. 2011. (Personal Freedom & Civic Duty Ser.). (YA). (gr. 7-12). lib. bdg. 35.95 *(978-1-4488-4669-6(2))* Rosen Publishing Group, Inc., The.

Garrett, Brandon. The Right to Privacy. 2009. (Individual Rights & Civic Responsibility Ser.). 128p. (gr. 7-12). 63.90 *(978-1-61513-515-8(4))* Rosen Publishing Group, Inc., The.

Glenn, Richard A. The Right to Privacy: Rights & Liberties under the Law, 1 vol. Stephenson, Donald Grier, ed. 2003. (America's Freedoms Ser.). 399p. (C). 75.00 *(978-1-57607-716-0(0),* PRIVRTC) ABC-CLIO, LLC.

Grayson, Robert. Managing Your Digital Footprint. 2011. (Digital & Information Literacy Ser.). (Illus.). 48p. (YA). pap. 11.75 *(978-1-4488-2290-4(4));* lib. bdg. 29.25 *(978-1-4488-1319-3(0))* Rosen Publishing Group, Inc., The. (Rosen Reference).

Henderson, Harry. Online Privacy & Government. 2014. (Privacy in the Online World). (ENG., Illus.). 80p. (J). lib. bdg. *(978-1-60152-726-4(8))* ReferencePoint Pr., Inc.

Jakubiak, David J. A Smart Kid's Guide to Internet Privacy. (J). 2010. pap. 8.25 *(978-1-4358-3356-2(2))* 2009. (Illus.). 24p. (gr. 2-6). lib. bdg. 22.60 *(978-1-4042-8118-9(5))* Rosen Publishing Group, Inc., The. (PowerKids Pr.).

January, Brendan. Information Insecurity: Privacy under Siege. 2015. (ENG.). 96p. (gr. 7-12). lib. bdg. 34.65 *(978-1-4677-2517-0(X));* (Illus.). 34.65 *(978-1-4677-8803-8(1))* Lerner Publishing Group. (Twenty-First Century Bks.).

Kemper, Bitsy. The Right to Privacy: Interpreting the Constitution. 2014. (Understanding the United States Constitution Ser.). (Illus.). 112p. (J). (gr. 7-12). 35.60 *(978-1-4777-7506-6(4))* Rosen Publishing Group, Inc., The.

Kuhn, Betsy. Prying Eyes: Privacy in the Twenty-First Century. 2008. (Exceptional Social Studies Titles for Upper Grades). (ENG., Illus.). 160p. (J). (gr. 7-12). lib. bdg. 38.60 *(978-0-8225-7179-7(X))* Lerner Publishing Group.

Lynette, Rachel. How to Deal with Secrets. 2009. (Let's Work It Out Ser.). (Illus.). 24p. (J). (gr. 2-5). lib. bdg. 22.60 *(978-1-4042-4519-8(7))* Rosen Publishing Group, Inc., The.

Marcovitz, Harold. Privacy Rights & the Patriot Act, 1 vol. 2008. (Essential Viewpoints Set 2 Ser.). (ENG., Illus.). 112p. (J). (gr. 6-12). lib. bdg. 35.64 *(978-1-60453-059-9(6))* ABDO Publishing Co.

McHugh, Jeff. Maintaining a Positive Digital Footprint. 2014. (Explorer Junior Library: Information Explorer Junior Ser.). (ENG.). 24p. (J). (gr. 1-4). 28.50 *(978-1-63137-789-1(2),* 205399); pap. 12.79 *(978-1-63137-809-6(0),* 205400) Cherry Lake Publishing.

Merino, Noel. Civil Liberties. 2013. (Opposing Viewpoints Ser.). (ENG., Illus.). 224p. (gr. 10-12). pap. 33.80 *(978-0-7377-6305-8(1),* Greenhaven Pr., Inc.) Cengage Gale.

Merino, Noël. Civil Liberties. 2013. (Opposing Viewpoints Ser.). (ENG., Illus.). 224p. (gr. 10-12). lib. bdg. 48.80 *(978-0-7377-6304-1(3),* Greenhaven Pr., Inc.) Cengage Gale.

Merino, Noel. Privacy. Greenhaven Press Staff, ed. 2015. (Opposing Viewpoints Ser.). (ENG., Illus.). 224p. (J). (gr. 10-12). pap. 33.80 *(978-0-7377-7283-8(2),* Greenhaven Pr., Inc.) Cengage Gale.

Merino, Noël. Teens & Privacy. Gale Editor, ed. 2011. (Current Controversies Ser.). (ENG.). 224p. (gr. 12-12). pap. 32.00 *(978-0-7377-5134-5(7),* Greenhaven Pr., Inc.) Cengage Gale.

—Teens & Privacy. 2011. (Current Controversies Ser.). 240p. lib. bdg. 40.95 *(978-0-7377-5133-8(9),* Greenhaven Pr., Inc.) Cengage Gale.

Mooney, Carla. Online Privacy & Business. 2014. (Privacy in the Online World). (ENG., Illus.). 80p. (J). lib. bdg. *(978-1-60152-724-0(1))* ReferencePoint Pr., Inc.

—Online Privacy & Social Media. 2014. (Privacy in the Online World). (ENG., Illus.). 80p. (J). lib. bdg. *(978-1-60152-730-1(6))* ReferencePoint Pr., Inc.

Morretta, Alison. How to Maintain Your Privacy Online. 2015. (J). lib. bdg. *(978-1-62713-545-0(6));* (ENG.). 48p. (gr. 5-5). lib. bdg. 31.36 *(978-1-5026-0187-2(7))* Cavendish Square Publishing.

Parks, Peggy J. Online Privacy. 2016. (ENG.). 80p. (J). (gr. 5-12). lib. bdg. *(978-1-60152-988-6(0))* ReferencePoint Pr., Inc.

Porterfield, Jason. The Third Amendment: The Right to Privacy in the Home. 2011. (Amendments to the United States Constitution: the Bill of Rights Ser.). (Illus.). 64p. (YA). (gr. 5-9). lib. bdg. 31.95 *(978-1-4488-1256-1(9))* Rosen Publishing Group, Inc., The.

—Third Amendment: Upholding the Right to Privacy. 2011. (Amendments to the United States Constitution: the Bill of Rights Ser.). (ENG.). 64p. (YA). pap. 12.95 *(978-1-4488-2304-8(8),* Rosen Reference) Rosen Publishing Group, Inc., The.

Rustad, Martha E. H. Learning about Privacy. 2015. (Media Literacy for Kids Ser.). (ENG.). 24p. (gr. k-1). lib. bdg. 26.65 *(978-1-4914-1832-1(X),* Pebble Plus) Capstone Press of Coughlan Cos.

Scherer, Lauri S. Privacy. Gale Editors, ed. 2014. (Introducing Issues with Opposing Viewpoints Ser.). (ENG., Illus.). 144p. (gr. 10-12). lib. bdg. 42.00 *(978-0-7377-6927-2(0),* Greenhaven Pr., Inc.) Cengage Gale.

Senker, Cath. Privacy & Surveillance. 2017. (Ethical Debates Ser.). (ENG., Illus.). 48p. (J). (gr. 6-11). pap. 12.99 ***(978-0-7502-9747-9(6)***, Wayland) Hachette Children's Group GBR. Dist: Hachette Bk. Group.

Smith, Rich. Fourth Amendment: The Right to Privacy, 1 vol. 2007. (Bill of Rights Ser.). (ENG.). 32p. (gr. 4-8). 27.07 *(978-1-59928-916-8(4),* Abdo & Daughters) ABDO Publishing Co.

Stefoff, Rebecca. Security V. Privacy. 2007. (Open for Debate Ser.). (Illus.). 128p. (gr. 7-7). lib. bdg. 42.79 *(978-0-7614-2578-6(0),* Benchmark Bks.) Marshall Cavendish Corp.

Wilcox, Christine. Thinking Critically: Online Privacy. 2014. (Thinking Critically). (ENG., Illus.). 80p. (J). lib. bdg. *(978-1-60152-734-9(9))* ReferencePoint Pr., Inc.

Wilkinson, Colin. Everything You Need to Know about Digital Privacy. 2017. (Need to Know Library). 64p. (J). (gr. 12-11). 34.45 ***(978-1-5081-7400-4(8))***; pap. 12.95 ***(978-1-5081-7398-4(2))*** Rosen Publishing Group, Inc., The. (Rosen Young Adult).

21st Century Safety & Privacy. 2013. (21st Century Safety & Privacy Ser.). 64p. (J). (gr. 5-8). 159.75 *(978-1-4488-9579-3(0));* pap. 388.50 *(978-1-4777-1678-6(5));* pap. 64.75 *(978-1-4777-1677-9(7))* Rosen Publishing Group, Inc., The.

PRIVATE SCHOOLS—FICTION

Brian, Kate, pseud. Ambition. 2008. (Private Ser.: No. 7). (ENG.). 288p. (YA). (gr. 9-18). pap. 12.99 *(978-1-4169-5882-6(7),* Simon & Schuster Bks. For Young Readers) Simon & Schuster Bks. For Young Readers.

—Ominous. 2011. (Private Ser.). (ENG.). 224p. (YA). (gr. 9-18). pap. 9.99 *(978-1-4169-8472-6(0),* Simon & Schuster Bks. For Young Readers) Simon & Schuster Bks. For Young Readers.

—Suspicion. 2009. (Private Ser.: No. 10). (ENG.). 224p. (YA). (gr. 9-18). pap. 9.99 *(978-1-4169-5885-7(1),* Simon & Schuster Bks. For Young Readers) Simon & Schuster Bks. For Young Readers.

Burkhart, Jessica. Home Sweet Drama. 2010. (Canterwood Crest Ser.: 8). (ENG.). 240p. (J). (gr. 4-8). pap. 7.99 *(978-1-4169-9040-6(2),* Aladdin) Simon & Schuster Children's Publishing.

—Jealousy. 2013. (Canterwood Crest Ser.: 17). lib. bdg. 17.20 *(978-0-606-27032-8(9),* Turtleback) Turtleback Bks.

—Popular. 2012. (Canterwood Crest Ser.: 14). (ENG.). 272p. (J). (gr. 4-8). pap. 7.99 *(978-1-4424-1950-6(4),* Aladdin) Simon & Schuster Children's Publishing.

—Rival Revenge. 2010. (Canterwood Crest Ser.: 7). (ENG.). 240p. (J). (gr. 4-8). pap. 7.99 *(978-1-4169-9039-0(9),* Aladdin) Simon & Schuster Children's Publishing.

Carter, Ally. Cross My Heart & Hope to Spy. 2016. (Gallagher Girls Ser.: 2). (J). lib. bdg. 20.85 *(978-0-606-38296-0(8))* Turtleback Bks.

de Campi, Alex. Kat & Mouse. 2017. (ENG., Illus.). 96p. pap. 5.99 *(978-1-59816-549-4(6),* 9781598165494) TOKYOPOP, Inc.

Fisher, Catherine. Darkwater. 2012. (ENG.). 240p. (YA). (gr. 7). 16.99 *(978-0-8037-3818-8(8),* Dial Bks) Penguin Young Readers Group.

Frost, Mark. The Paladin Prophecy, Bk. 1. 2014. (Paladin Prophecy Ser.). (ENG.). 528p. (YA). (gr. 7). pap. 10.99 *(978-0-375-87106-1(3),* Ember) Random Hse. Children's Bks.

Inches, Alison. School Gyrls POW Scrapbook. 2010. (School Gyrls Ser.). (ENG.). 64p. (J). pap. 7.99 *(978-1-4424-0865-4(0),* Simon Spotlight) Simon Spotlight.

Kingsley, Kate. Kiss & Break Up. 2011. (Young, Loaded, & Fabulous Ser.: 3). (ENG.). 320p. (YA). (gr. 9-18). pap. 9.99 *(978-1-4169-9401-5(7),* Simon Pulse) Simon Pulse.

—Pretty on the Outside. 2010. (Young, Loaded, & Fabulous Ser.: 1). (ENG.). 320p. (YA). (gr. 9-18). pap. 9.99 *(978-1-4169-9399-5(1),* Simon Pulse) Simon Pulse.

Kuehn, Stephanie. Complicit. 2014. (ENG.). 256p. (YA). (gr. 8-12). 19.99 *(978-1-250-04459-4(6),* 9781250044594, St. Martin's Griffin) St. Martin's Pr.

Lehman, Barbara. The Secret Box. 2011. (ENG., Illus.). 48p. (J). (gr. -1-3). 16.99 *(978-0-547-23868-5(1))* Houghton Mifflin Harcourt Publishing Co.

Mead, Richelle. Bloodlines. 2012. (Bloodlines Ser.: 1). (ENG.). 448p. (YA). (gr. 7-18). pap. 10.99 *(978-1-59514-473-7(0),* Razorbill) Penguin Young Readers Group.

Middleton, Casey Olsson. Flying the Imaginarium: Book One, Coconut. 2007. 136p. per. 11.50 *(978-1-59330-507-9(9))* Aventine Pr.

Money, Mo. Little Sister. 2011. (School Gyrls Ser.). (ENG.). 112p. (J). pap. 5.99 *(978-1-4424-0879-1(0),* Simon & Schuster/Paula Wiseman Bks.) Simon & Schuster/Paula Wiseman Bks.

Rain, Mandy. Rock 'n' Roll. 2011. (School Gyrls Ser.). (ENG.). 128p. (J). pap. 5.99 *(978-1-4424-0878-4(2),* Simon & Schuster/Paula Wiseman Bks.) Simon & Schuster/Paula Wiseman Bks.

Reid, Kimberly. Sweet 16 to Life. 2013. (ENG., Illus.). 256p. (YA). (gr. 9). pap. 9.95 *(978-0-7582-6742-9(8),* K-Teen/Dafina) Kensington Publishing Corp.

—Sweet 16 to Life. 2013. 233p. (J). lib. bdg. 20.80 *(978-0-606-27166-0(X),* Turtleback) Turtleback Bks.

Ropal, Monica. When You Leave. 2015. (ENG.). 336p. (YA). (gr. 7). pap. 9.95 *(978-0-7624-5455-6(5),* Running Pr. Kids) Running Pr. Bk. Pubs.

Rose, Imogen. Initiation: Japanese Language Edition. Galeano, Tomomi, tr. 2013. 482p. pap. 16.99 *(978-1-940015-04-0(9))* Imogen Rose.

Shields, Gillian. Eternal. 2012. (Immortal Ser.: 3). (ENG.). 384p. (YA). (gr. 8). pap. 9.99 *(978-0-06-200040-8(3),* Tegen, Katherine Bks) HarperCollins Pubs.

Simone, Ni-Ni & Abrams, Amir. Get Ready for War. 2013. (Hollywood High Ser.: 2). (ENG., Illus.). 288p. (YA). (gr. 9). pap. 9.95 *(978-0-7582-7355-0(X),* K-Teen/Dafina) Kensington Publishing Corp.

—Get Ready for War. 2013. (Hollywood High Ser.: 2). 423p. (YA). lib. bdg. 20.80 *(978-0-606-27305-3(0),* Turtleback) Turtleback Bks.

Stanwood Pier, Arthu. The Jester of St. Timothy's. 2006. pap. 14.95 *(978-1-55742-546-1(9))* Wildside Pr., LLC.

Ziegesar, Cecily von. It Had to Be You. 2009. (Gossip Girl Ser.). (ENG.). 432p. (YA). (gr. 10-17). pap. 10.99 *(978-0-316-01769-5(8),* Poppy) Little, Brown Bks. for Young Readers.

PRIVATEERING

Hamilton, Sue L. Henry Morgan, 1 vol. 2007. (Pirates! Ser.). (ENG., Illus.). 32p. (gr. 4-8). 27.07 *(978-1-59928-760-7(9),* Abdo & Daughters) ABDO Publishing Co.

Nick, Charles. Sir Francis Drake: Slave Trader & Pirate. 2010. (ENG., Illus.). 128p. (C). (gr. 6-12). pap. 9.95 *(978-0-531-20740-6(4))* National Geographic School Publishing, Inc.

—Sir Francis Drake: Slave Trader & Pirate. 2009. (Wicked History Ser.). (ENG., Illus.). 128p. (J). (gr. 6-12). 31.00 *(978-0-531-21800-6(7),* Watts, Franklin) Scholastic Library Publishing.

PRIZE FIGHTING

see Boxing

PROBABILITIES

Aboff, Marcie. Pigs, Cows, & Probability. (Data Mania Ser.). (ENG.). 24p. (gr. 1-2). 2011. pap. 41.70 *(978-1-4296-6468-4(1))* 2010. lib. bdg. 25.32 *(978-1-4296-4529-4(6))* Capstone Press of Coughlan Cos. (First Facts).

Adamson, Thomas K. & Adamson, Heather. Give Probability a Chance!, 1 vol. 2012. (Fun with Numbers Ser.). (ENG.). 32p. (gr. 1-2). lib. bdg. 27.32 *(978-1-4296-7558-1(6),* Aplus Bks.) Capstone Press of Coughlan Cos.

Adamson, Thomas K. and Heather. Give Probability a Chance! 2012. (Fun with Numbers Ser.). (ENG.). 32p. (gr. 1-2). pap. 47.70 *(978-1-4296-8305-0(8),* Aplus Bks.) Capstone Press of Coughlan Cos.

Benchmark Education Company, LLC Staff, compiled by. Data Analysis & Probability. 2005. spiral bd. 295.00 *(978-1-4108-5452-0(3));* spiral bd. 215.00 *(978-1-4108-5453-7(1));* spiral bd. 165.00 *(978-1-4108-5863-4(4));* spiral bd. 185.00 *(978-1-4108-5864-1(2));* spiral bd. 205.00 *(978-1-4108-4512-2(5));* spiral bd. 80.00 *(978-1-4108-3915-2(X));* spiral bd. 210.00 *(978-1-4108-3897-1(8));* spiral bd. 60.00 *(978-1-4108-3898-8(6));* spiral bd. 75.00 *(978-1-4108-3908-4(7))* Benchmark Education Co.

—Data & Probability. 2005. spiral bd. 185.00 *(978-1-4108-3901-5(X))* Benchmark Education Co.

Burrill, Gail F., et al. Probability Models. (Data-Driven Mathematics Ser.). 96p. (YA). (gr. 7-12). pap., stu. ed. 18.95 *(978-1-57232-240-0(3))* Seymour, Dale Pubns.

Burton, Margie, et al. We All Scream for Ice Cream. 2011. (Early Connections Ser.). (J). *(978-1-61672-544-0(3))* Benchmark Education Co.

Bussell, Linda. Probabilidad con Juegos y Diversión. 2008. (Matemáticas en Nuestro Mundo - Nivel 3 (Math in Our World - Level 3) Ser.). (SPA.). 24p. (gr. 2-5). (J). lib. bdg. 22.00 *(978-0-8368-9298-7(4));* pap. 8.15 *(978-0-8368-9397-7(2))* Stevens, Gareth Publishing LLLP. (Weekly Reader Leveled Readers).

—Probability with Fun & Games. 2008. (Math in Our World - Level 3 Ser.). 24p. (gr. 2-5). (J). lib. bdg. 22.00 *(978-0-8368-9290-1(9));* pap. 8.15 *(978-0-8368-9389-2(1))* Stevens, Gareth Publishing LLLP. (Weekly Reader Leveled Readers).

Chamberlin, Scott A. Probability for Kids: Using Model-Eliciting Activities to Investigate Probability Concepts. 2016. (ENG.). 160p. (gr. 4-6). pap. 29.95 *(978-1-61821-527-7(2))* Prufrock Pr.

Cohen, Marina. Probability. 2010. (ENG., Illus.). 24p. (J). (978-0-7787-5249-3(6)); pap. (978-0-7787-5296-7(8)) Crabtree Publishing Co.
Colson, Rob. What Are the Chances? Probability, Statistics, Ratios, & Proportions. 2017. (Math Everywhere Ser.). (ENG.). 32p. (J). pap. 8.95 **(978-0-531-23321-4(9))**; lib. bdg. 27.00 **(978-0-531-22885-2(1))** Scholastic Library Publishing. (Children's Pr.).
Cushman, Jean. Do You Wanna Bet? Your Chance to Find Out about Probability. Weston, Martha, illus. 2007. (ENG.). 112p. (J). (gr. 5-7). pap. 6.95 (978-0-618-82999-6(7)) Houghton Mifflin Harcourt Publishing Co.
Data Mania. 2011. (Data Mania Ser.). (ENG.). 24p. (gr. 1-2). pap. 166.80 (978-1-4296-6469-1(X), First Facts) Capstone Press of Coughlan Cos.
Faulkner, Nicholas & Gregersen, Erik. Statistics & Probability. 2017. (J). lib. bdg. **(978-1-68048-779-4(5)**, Britannica Educational Publishing) Rosen Publishing Group, Inc., The.
Fischer, James. Game Math. 2013. (Math 24/7 Ser.: 10). 48p. (J). (gr. 5-18). 19.95 (978-1-4222-2907-1(6)) Mason Crest.
Fried, Ellen. What's the Chance? 2007. (Reading Expeditions Ser.). (ENG., Illus.). 24p. (J). pap. 14.95 (978-0-7922-4590-2(3)) CENGAGE Learning.
Goldstone, Bruce. That's a Possibility! A Book about What Might Happen. 2013. (ENG., Illus.). 32p. (J). (gr. 2-5). 17.99 (978-0-8050-8998-1(5), 9780805089981, Holt, Henry & Co. Bks. For Young Readers) Holt, Henry & Co.
Gott, Robert. How to Be in the Wrong Place at the Wrong Time. 2007. 96p. (J). (978-1-4207-0731-1(0)) Sundance/Newbridge Educational Publishing.
Hammelef, Danielle S. This Book Beats the Odds: A Collection of Amazing & Startling Odds, 1 vol. 2012. (Super Trivia Collection). (ENG.). 32p. (gr. 3-4). lib. bdg. 27.99 (978-1-4296-8420-0(8), Edge Bks.) Capstone Press of Coughlan Cos.
Leech, Bonnie. Gregor Mendel's Genetic Theory: Understanding & Applying Concepts of Probability. (PowerMath: Advanced Proficiency Plus Ser.). 2009. 32p. (gr. 5-5). 47.90 (978-1-60851-356-7(4)) 2007. 36p. pap. 23.95 (978-1-4358-3820-8(3)) Rosen Publishing Group, Inc., The. (PowerKids Pr.).
Leech, Bonnie Coulter. Gregor Mendel's Genetic Theory: Understanding & Applying Concepts of Probability. (Math for the Real World Ser.). (Illus.). 32p. 2009. (ENG.). (gr. 6-7). pap. 10.00 (978-1-4042-6063-4(3)) 2006. (YA). (gr. 5-9). lib. bdg. 25.25 (978-1-4042-3355-3(5)) Rosen Publishing Group, Inc., The.
MacGillivray, Helen & Petocz, Peter. Statistics & Probability in the Australian Curriculum Years 9 And 10. 2013. (ENG.). pap. (978-1-107-65599-7(4)) Cambridge Univ. Pr.
Peters, Elisa. Statistics & Probability, 1 vol. 2015. (ENG.). 64p. (YA). 31.70 (978-1-62275-533-2(2), Britannica Educational Publishing) Rosen Publishing Group, Inc., The.
Roza, Greg. Heads or Tails: Exploring Probability Through Games. 2004. (Math Big Bookstm Ser.). (ENG.). 24p. (gr. 3-4). 43.95 (978-0-8239-7644-7(0)) Rosen Publishing Group, Inc., The.
Sullivan, Erin. Probability. 2011. (Early Connections Ser.). (J). (978-1-61672-648-5(2)) Benchmark Education Co.
Visto, Joy. What Are the Chances? 2015. (Illus.). 48p. (J). (978-1-60818-573-3(7), Creative Education) Creative Co., The.
—What Are the Chances? Making Math Work. 2016. (Making Math Work Ser.). (ENG.). 48p. (J). (gr. 5-9). pap. 12.00 (978-1-62832-174-6(1), Creative Paperbacks) Creative Co., The.

PROBES, SPACE

see Space Probes

PROBLEM CHILDREN

see also Juvenile Delinquency

Chuta, Edith N. Straight Talk to Troubled Kids: Finding Wisdom Underneath Our Pains. 2007. 76p. per. 10.95 (978-0-595-43778-8(8)) iUniverse, Inc.
Hames, Annette & McCaffrey, Monica, eds. Special Brothers & Sisters: Stories & Tips for Siblings of Children with a Disability or Serious Illness. McCaffrey, Brendan, illus. 2005. (ENG.). 96p. (gr. 4-7). per. 17.95 (978-1-84310-383-7(4), 2844) Kingsley, Jessica Pubs. GBR. Dist: Macmillan Distribution Ltd.
Hutchinson, Tim. Battle Scars. 2003. 320p. (J). per. 16.95 (978-1-932133-85-1(2)) Writers' Collective, The.
Lavis, Rose Brenda. Here Comes Trouble & Double Trouble. 2010. 28p. pap. 13.99 (978-1-4490-3607-2(4)) AuthorHouse.
Libal, Autumn. Emotional Disturbance. Albers, Lisa et al, eds. 2014. (Living with a Special Need Ser.: 16). 128p. (J). (gr. 7-18). 25.95 (978-1-4222-3034-3(1)) Mason Crest.
—Runaway Train: Youth with Emotional Disturbance. 2004. (Youth with Special Needs Ser.). (Illus.). 128p. (YA). 24.95 (978-1-59084-732-9(6)) Mason Crest.
—Runaway Train: Youth with Emotional Disturbance. 2003. (Youth with Special Needs Ser.). (Illus.). 127p. (YA). (gr. 7). pap. 14.95 (978-1-4222-0429-0(4)) Mason Crest.
McIntosh, Kenneth & Livingston, Phyllis. Youth with Conduct Disorder: In Trouble with the World. 2007. (Helping Youth with Mental, Physical, & Social Disabilities Ser.). (Illus.). 128p. (YA). pap. 14.95 (978-1-4222-0440-5(5)) Mason Crest.
McIntyre, Thomas. The Survival Guide for Kids with Behavior Challenges: How to Make Good Choices & Stay Out of Trouble. rev. ed. 2013. (ENG., Illus.). 176p. (J). (gr. 4-9). pap. 14.99 (978-1-57542-449-1(5)) Free Spirit Publishing, Inc.
Musselman, Barbara. My Mad Book: I Get Mad & Granny Says It's Ok. 2009. 40p. pap. 19.99 (978-1-4389-9438-3(9)) AuthorHouse.
Nelson, Julie. Families Change: A Book for Children Experiencing Termination of Parental Rights. Gallagher, Mary, illus. 2006. (Kids Are Important Ser.). (ENG.). 32p. (J). (gr. -1-5). pap. 9.99 (978-1-57542-209-1(3)) Free Spirit Publishing, Inc.
Robinson, Tony. Bad Kids Vol. 1: The Naughtiest Children in History, 1. 2012. (ENG., Illus.). 96p. (J). (gr. 4-7). pap. 12.99 (978-0-330-51080-6(0)) Pan Macmillan GBR. Dist: Independent Pubs. Group.
—Bad Kids Vol. 1: The Worst Behaved Children in History, 1. Phillips, Mike, illus. unabr. ed. 2009. (ENG.). 144p. 28.50 (978-0-230-73787-7(0), Macmillan) Pan Macmillan GBR. Dist: Trans-Atlantic Pubns., Inc.

PROBLEM CHILDREN—FICTION

Byrne, Mary. Only Children Hear Me: Jake Is a Friend You Can Talk To. 2007. 96p. (J). per. 10.95 (978-0-595-44359-8(1)) iUniverse, Inc.
Cook, Julia. It's Hard to Be a Verb! Hartman, Carrie, illus. 2008. (ENG.). 32p. (J). (gr. 4-7). pap. 9.95 (978-1-931636-84-1(2)) National Ctr. For Youth Issues.
Diggins, Matthew. Andrew & the Secret Gallery. Diggins, Matthew, illus. 2008. (Illus.). 32p. (J). pap. 6.95 (978-1-60108-026-4(3)) Red Cygnet Pr.
Goerzen, Christy. Explore, 1 vol. 2009. (Orca Currents Ser.). (ENG.). (J). (gr. 5-9). 112p. 16.95 (978-1-55469-120-3(6)); 128p. pap. 9.95 (978-1-55469-119-7(2)) Orca Bk. Pubs. USA.
Jones, Debbie Knatt. Maurice ... As Read to the Students in Room D183 & D184. 2013. 150p. pap. 13.95 (978-1-62516-536-7(6), Strategic Bk. Publishing) Strategic Book Publishing & Rights Agency (SBPRA).
Korobov, Kristine. Allison Marisa Burbank Gets into Trouble. Mahanov, Tanya, ed. Rossi, Andrea, illus. 2008. 172p. 26.90 (978-1-4251-8976-1(8)) Trafford Publishing.
Kropp, Paul & Doherty, Catherine. Juvie. (Illus.). 87p. (978-1-897039-16-8(6)) High Interest Publishing (HIP).
Mac, Carrie. Charmed, 1 vol. 2006. (Orca Soundings Ser.). (ENG.). 112p. (YA). (gr. 8-12). 14.95 (978-1-55143-578-7(0)) Orca Bk. Pubs. USA.
McGinty, Sean. The End of Fun. 2017. (ENG.). 416p. (YA). (gr. 9-17). pap. 9.99 (978-1-4847-2214-5(0)) Hyperion Bks. for Children.
Parkkola, Seita. The School of Possibilities. Silver, Annira & Gass, Marja, trs. from FIN. Ikonen, Jani, illus. 2010. (ENG.). 368p. (J). (gr. 4-7). 12.99 (978-1-4022-1835-4(4), Sourcebooks Jabberwocky) Sourcebooks, Inc.
Polak, Monique. 121 Express, 1 vol. 2008. (Orca Currents Ser.). (ENG.). (J). (gr. 5-9). 144p. pap. 9.95 (978-1-55143-976-1(X)); 112p. lib. bdg. 16.95 (978-1-55143-978-5(6)) Orca Bk. Pubs. USA.
Stevenson, Robin. Inferno, 1 vol. 2009. (ENG.). 240p. (YA). (gr. 7-12). pap. 12.95 (978-1-55469-077-0(3)) Orca Bk. Pubs. USA.
Taylor, Sean & Quarto Generic Staff. A Waste of Good Paper. 2013. (ENG., Illus.). 290p. (J). (gr. 6-9). pap. 8.99 (978-1-84780-268-2(0), Frances Lincoln) Quarto Publishing Group UK GBR. Dist: Hachette Bk. Group.
Walters, Gregory. Fouling Out, 1 vol. 2008. (ENG.). 176p. (J). (gr. 5-10). pap. 8.95 (978-1-55143-714-9(7)) Orca Bk. Pubs. USA.

PROBLEM SOLVING

Abramson, Marcie F. Painless Math Word Problems. 2nd rev. ed. 2010. (Painless Ser.). (ENG.). 288p. pap. 11.99 (978-0-7641-4335-9(2)) Barron's Educational Series, Inc.
Adler, David A. You Can, Toucan, Math: Word Problem-Solving Fun. Miller, Edward, illus. (You Can, Toucan, Math Ser.). (ENG.). 32p. (J). (gr. -1-3). 2007. 6.95 (978-0-8234-2117-6(1)) 2006. 17.95 (978-0-8234-1919-7(3)) Holiday Hse., Inc.
Allanson, Patricia. Parallella's Problem. Allanson, Patricia, illus. 2007. (Illus.). (J). (gr. -1-3). per. 13.99 (978-1-59879-278-2(4)) Lifevest Publishing, Inc.
Amos, Janine. Don't Do That! How Not to Act. 2009. (Best Behavior Ser.). (Illus.). 32p. (J). (gr. -1-2). pap. 10.55 (978-1-60754-052-6(5)) Windmill Bks.
Amos, Janine & Spenceley, Annabel. Don't Do That! How Not to Act. 2009. (Best Behavior Ser.). (Illus.). 32p. (J). (gr. -1-2). lib. bdg. 22.60 (978-1-60754-030-4(4)) Windmill Bks.
—Go Away! What Not to Say. 2009. (Best Behavior Ser.). (Illus.). 32p. (J). (gr. -1-2). pap. 10.55 (978-1-60754-044-1(4)); lib. bdg. 22.60 (978-1-60754-026-7(6)) Windmill Bks.
—It Won't Work! Let's Try Again. 2009. (Best Behavior Ser.). (Illus.). 32p. (J). (gr. -1-2). pap. 10.55 (978-1-60754-046-5(0)); lib. bdg. 22.60 (978-1-60754-027-4(4)) Windmill Bks.
—It's Mine! Let's Try to Share. 2009. (Best Behavior Ser.). (Illus.). 32p. (J). (gr. -1-2). pap. 10.55 (978-1-60754-048-9(7)); lib. bdg. 22.60 (978-1-60754-028-1(2)) Windmill Bks.
—Move Over! Learning to Share Our Space. 2009. (Best Behavior Ser.). (Illus.). 32p. (J). (gr. -1-2). pap. 10.55 (978-1-60754-050-2(9)); lib. bdg. 22.60 (978-1-60754-029-8(0)) Windmill Bks.
Becker, Suzy. The Kids Make It Better: A Write-In, Draw-In Journal. 2010. (ENG., Illus.). 128p. (J). (gr. 1-5). pap. 8.95 (978-0-7611-5845-5(6), 15845) Workman Publishing Co., Inc.
Blackwood, Melissa, et al. Maths - Problem Solving & Reasoning Age 7-9. 2015. (Letts Wild about Learning Ser.). (ENG.). 48p. (J). (gr. 2-4). pap. 8.95 (978-1-84419-788-0(3)) HarperCollins Pubs. Ltd. GBR. Dist: Independent Pubs. Group.
Blaine, Dalton. Where Is My Umbrella? Fixing a Problem. 2017. (Computer Science for the Real World Ser.). 8p. (gr. 5-6). pap. 6.20 **(978-1-5383-5052-2(1)**, Rosen Classroom) Rosen Publishing Group, Inc., The.
Boardworks Learning Centers: Figure It Out. 2006. (J). bds. (978-0-9755252-4-1(7)) Evergreen Pr. of Brainerd, LLC.
Booker, Dwayne. My Science Project: Fixing a Problem. 2017. (Computer Science for the Real World Ser.). 16p. (gr. 7-8). pap. 7.95 **(978-1-5383-5208-3(7)**, Rosen Classroom) Rosen Publishing Group, Inc., The.
—Ty's American Flag: Breaking down the Problem. 2017. (Computer Science for the Real World Ser.). 8p. (gr. 5-6). pap. 6.20 **(978-1-5383-5032-4(7)**, Rosen Classroom) Rosen Publishing Group, Inc., The.
Burstein, John. What Should I Do? Making Good Decisions. 2009. (Slim Goodbody's Life Skills 101 Ser.). (ENG., Illus.). 32p. (J). (gr. 3-6). pap. (978-0-7787-4807-6(3), 1302929); lib. bdg. (978-0-7787-4791-8(3), 1302929) Crabtree Publishing Co.
Canavan, Thomas. Problem Solving: 50 Math Super Puzzles. 2011. (Math Standards Workout Ser.). (ENG., Illus.). 48p. (YA). (gr. 5-8). pap. 11.75 (978-1-4488-6682-3(0), Rosen Reference); lib. bdg. 29.25 (978-1-4488-6675-5(8)) Rosen Publishing Group, Inc., The.
Charles, R., et al. Problem-Solving Experience in Mathematics. 2003. 30.95 (978-0-201-20689-0(7)) Seymour, Dale Pubns.
Colson, Rob. Super Sums: Addition, Subtraction, Multiplication, & Division. 2017. (Math Everywhere Ser.). (ENG.). 32p. (J). pap. 8.95 **(978-0-531-23320-7(0))**; lib. bdg. 27.00 **(978-0-531-22884-5(3))** Scholastic Library Publishing. (Children's Pr.).
Cook-Cottone, Catherine. The brain owner's manual for Kids: Helping the feeling & thinking parts work Together. 2006. (Illus.). (J). pap. 5.00 (978-0-9795773-0-7(6)) Growing & Learning Pr.
Dixon, Dale. Which Materials Float? What's the Problem? 2017. (Computer Science for the Real World Ser.). 16p. (gr. 7-8). pap. 7.95 **(978-1-5383-5202-1(8)**, Rosen Classroom) Rosen Publishing Group, Inc., The.
Dorling Kindersley Publishing Staff. DK Workbooks: Problem Solving, First Grade. 2016. (ENG.). 60p. (J). (gr. k-2). pap. 6.99 (978-1-4654-4479-0(3), DK Children) Dorling Kindersley Publishing, Inc.
—DK Workbooks: Problem Solving, Kindergarten. 2016. (ENG.). 60p. (J). (gr. -1-1). pap. 6.99 (978-1-4654-4458-5(0), DK Children) Dorling Kindersley Publishing, Inc.
—DK Workbooks: Problem Solving, Second Grade. 2016. (ENG.). 60p. (J). (gr. 1-3). pap. 6.99 (978-1-4654-4452-3(1), DK Children) Dorling Kindersley Publishing, Inc.
—DK Workbooks: Problem Solving, Third Grade. 2016. (ENG.). 60p. (J). (gr. 3-4). pap. 6.99 (978-1-4654-4453-0(X), DK Children) Dorling Kindersley Publishing, Inc.
—10 Minutes a Day: Problem Solving, Fourth Grade: Problem Solving, Fourth Grade. 2015. (ENG.). 80p. (J). (gr. 4-7). pap. 9.99 (978-1-4654-3441-8(0), DK Children) Dorling Kindersley Publishing, Inc.
—10 Minutes a Day: Problem Solving, Third Grade: Problem Solving, Third Grade. 2015. (ENG.). 80p. (J). (gr. 2-4). pap. 9.99 (978-1-4654-3440-1(2), DK Children) Dorling Kindersley Publishing, Inc.
Dunham, Bandhu Scott. We Like to Invent! Stark, Ryan, illus. 2010. (J). pap. (978-1-935387-13-8(8)) Hohm Pr.
Ellis, Roman. We Study Wind: Breaking down the Problem. 2017. (Computer Science for the Real World Ser.). 16p. (gr. 7-8). pap. 7.95 **(978-1-5383-5228-1(1)**, Rosen Classroom) Rosen Publishing Group, Inc., The.
—What's Wrong with the Magnet? Fixing a Problem. 2017. (Computer Science for the Real World Ser.). 12p. (gr. 6-7). pap. 7.05 **(978-1-5383-5148-2(X)**, Rosen Classroom) Rosen Publishing Group, Inc., The.
Flash Kids Editors, ed. Problem Solving: Grade 2 (Flash Skills). 2010. (Flash Skills Ser.). (ENG.). 64p. (J). pap. 3.95 (978-1-4114-3463-9(3), Spark Publishing Group) Sterling Publishing Co., Inc.
—Problem Solving: Grade 3 (Flash Skills) 2010. (Flash Skills Ser.). (ENG.). 64p. (J). pap. 3.95 (978-1-4114-3469-1(2), Spark Publishing Group) Sterling Publishing Co., Inc.
—Problem Solving: Grade 4 (Flash Skills) 2010. (Flash Skills Ser.). (ENG.). 64p. (J). pap. 3.95 (978-1-4114-3473-8(0), Spark Publishing Group) Sterling Publishing Co., Inc.
—Problem Solving: Grade 5 (Flash Skills) 2010. (Flash Skills Ser.). (ENG.). 64p. (J). pap. 3.95 (978-1-4114-3474-5(9), Spark Publishing Group) Sterling Publishing Co., Inc.
Gallagher, Jim. A Hassled Guy's Guide: How to Deal. 2014. (ENG.). 64p. (J). (gr. 5-12). 15.95 (978-1-62293-005-0(3)) Enslow Pubs., Inc.
Gerber, Larry. Step-By-Step Guide to Problem Solving at School & Work. 2014. (Winning at Work Readiness Ser.). 64p. (J). (gr. 9-12). 32.95 (978-1-4777-7782-4(2)) Rosen Publishing Group, Inc., The.
Giroux, Lindsay Nina. Goldilocks & the Three Bears: A Problem-Solving Story. Trithart, Emma, illus. 2016. (J). (978-0-87659-707-1(X)) Gryphon Hse., Inc.
—We Are Problem Solvers. Archer, Micha, illus. 2016. (J). (978-0-87659-715-6(0)) Gryphon Hse., Inc.
Golden, Pam. Lulu Learns about Reporting: Ending the Tattle Battle. Outohak, Diana, illus. 2007. 28p. (J). pap. 18.95 (978-0-9659650-8-8(2)) Roedway Pr.
Harasymiw, R. Mann. Problem Solving with Pigs. 2013. (Animal Math Ser.). (ENG., Illus.). 24p. (J). (gr. 1-3). lib. bdg. 22.60 (978-1-4339-9323-7(6)) Stevens, Gareth Publishing LLLP.
Harasymiw, Raymond. Problem Solving with Pigs. 2013. (Animal Math Ser.). 24p. (J). (gr. 1-3). pap. 48.90 (978-1-4339-9325-1(2)) Stevens, Gareth Publishing LLLP.
Harasymiw, Raymond & Harasymiw, R. P. Problem Solving with Pigs. 2013. 24p. (J). (gr. 1-3). pap. 8.15 (978-1-4339-9324-4(4)) Stevens, Gareth Publishing LLLP.
Hoffman, Mary Ann. The History of the Maya: Using Computational Skills in Problem Solving. (Powermath Ser.). 32p. 2009. (ENG., Illus.). (gr. 5-6). pap. 10.00 (978-1-4042-5148-9(0)) 2009. (gr. 4-5). 47.90 (978-1-60851-421-2(8)) 2005. (Illus.). (J). (gr. 3-6). lib. bdg. 25.25 (978-1-4042-2942-6(6)) Rosen Publishing Group, Inc., The. (PowerKids Pr.).
Huffman, Mindy. What's Wrong with the Experiment? Fixing a Problem. 2017. (Computer Science for the Real World Ser.). 16p. (gr. 7-8). pap. 7.95 **(978-1-5383-5232-8(X)**, Rosen Classroom) Rosen Publishing Group, Inc., The.
Kavanaugh, Dorothy. Hassled Girl? Girls Dealing with Feelings. 2014. (ENG.). 64p. (J). (gr. 5-12). 15.95 (978-1-62293-035-7(5)) Enslow Pubs., Inc.
Kelsey, Elin. Wild Ideas. Kim, Soyeon, illus. 2015. (ENG.). 32p. (J). (gr. k-5). 18.95 (978-1-77147-062-9(3)) Owlkids Bks. Inc. CAN. Dist: Publishers Group West (PGW).
Kerstein, Lauren H. A Week of Switching, Shifting, & Stretching: How to Make My Thinking More Flexible. 2013. (ENG., Illus.). 57p. (J). (gr. -1-5). pap. 18.00 (978-1-937473-89-1(9)) Autism Asperger Publishing Co.
Kopp, Megan. Above & Beyond with Critical Thinking & Problem Solving. 2016. (Fueling Your Future! Going above & Beyond in the 21st Cent Ser.). (ENG.). 48p. (J). (gr. 5-8). (978-0-7787-2842-9(0)) Crabtree Publishing Co.
Lawson, Lela. Paco's Winter Plan: What's the Problem? 2017. (Computer Science for the Real World Ser.). 8p. (gr. 5-6). pap. 6.20 **(978-1-5383-5024-9(6)**, Rosen Classroom) Rosen Publishing Group, Inc., The.
Lechner, Judith. Our New Fish Tank: Learning to Estimate & Round Numbers to the Nearest Ones, Tens, & Hundreds Places. 2004. (Math Big Bookstm Ser.). (ENG.). 16p. (gr. 2-3). 37.95 (978-0-8239-7640-9(8)) Rosen Publishing Group, Inc., The.
Leech, Bonnie. Mesopotamia: Creating & Solving World Problems. 2009. (PowerMath: Advanced Proficiency Plus Ser.). 32p. (gr. 5-5). 47.90 (978-1-60851-362-8(9), PowerKids Pr.) Rosen Publishing Group, Inc., The.
Linde, Barbara. Math in Our Solar System: Applying Problem-Solving Strategies. 2009. (PowerMath: Proficiency Plus Ser.). 32p. (gr. 4-5). 47.90 (978-1-60851-413-7(7), PowerKids Pr.) Rosen Publishing Group, Inc., The.
Linde, Barbara M. Math in Our Solar System: Applying Problem-Solving Strategies. (PowerMath Ser.). 32p. 2009. (ENG.). (gr. 5-6). pap. 10.00 (978-1-4042-5135-9(9)) 2005. (Illus.). (J). (gr. 3-6). lib. bdg. 25.25 (978-1-4042-2936-5(1), PowerKids Pr.) Rosen Publishing Group, Inc., The.
Marsico, Katie. Shopping Trip Math. 2014. (Math Everywhere! Ser.). (Illus.). 32p. (gr. 3-4). (J). lib. bdg. 26.60 (978-1-4677-1884-4(X), Lerner Pubns.); pap. 7.95 (978-1-4677-4515-4(4)) Lerner Publishing Group.
McKee, Rosie. My Pet Dinosaur: Breaking down the Problem. 2017. (Computer Science for the Real World Ser.). 12p. (gr. 6-7). pap. 7.05 **(978-1-5383-5138-3(2)**, Rosen Classroom) Rosen Publishing Group, Inc., The.
Middlewood, G. & Debenham, A. 43 Team-Building Activities. 2007. 64p. per. (978-1-903853-57-3(5)) Brilliant Pubns.
Miller, Reagan. Engineers Solve Problems. 2013. (ENG.). 24p. (J). (978-0-7787-0094-4(1)); (Illus.). pap. (978-0-7787-0101-9(8)) Crabtree Publishing Co.
Pezzimenti, Grace. The Pizza Party: Learning Basic Problem-Solving Skills. (Math for the REAL World Ser.). 12p. (gr. 1-2). 2009. pap. 5.90 (978-0-8239-8914-0(3), Rosen Classroom) 2004. (ENG.). 33.50 (978-0-8239-7636-2(X)) Rosen Publishing Group, Inc., The.
Reed, Cristie. Problem Solving. 2012. (ENG., Illus.). 24p. (gr. k-2). pap. 8.95 (978-1-61810-266-9(4)) Rourke Educational Media.
Risby, Bonnie Lou. The Great Honey Robbery: Using Critical Thinking to Solve Problems. 2004. (J). pap. 14.95 (978-1-931334-40-2(4)) Pieces of Learning.
Roza, Greg. The Hoover Dam: Applying Problem-Solving Strategies. (Math for the Real World Ser.). 32p. 2009. (ENG., Illus.). (gr. 6-7). pap. 10.00 (978-1-4042-6065-8(X)) 2009. (gr. 5-5). 47.90 (978-1-60851-369-7(6), PowerKids Pr.) 2006. (Illus.). (YA). (gr. 5-9). lib. bdg. 25.25 (978-1-4042-3356-0(3)) Rosen Publishing Group, Inc., The.
Ruffin, Frances E. Let's Have a Bake Sale: Calculating Profit & Unit Cost. (PowerMath Ser.). (gr. 3-4). 2009. (ENG., Illus.). 224p. pap. 8.25 (978-0-8239-8893-8(7), PowerKids Pr.) 2004. 24p. 43.95 (978-0-8239-7645-4(9)) Rosen Publishing Group, Inc., The.
Sargent, Brian. Guess the Order. 2006. (Rookie Read-About Math Ser.). (ENG., Illus.). 32p. (J). (gr. 1-2). lib. bdg. 20.50 (978-0-516-24963-6(0), Children's Pr.) Scholastic Library Publishing.
—Slumber Party Problem Solving. 2006. (Rookie Read-About Math Ser.). (ENG., Illus.). 32p. (J). (gr. 1-2). lib. bdg. 20.50 (978-0-516-24962-9(2), Children's Pr.) Scholastic Library Publishing.
Saviola, Joseph A. The Tour de France: Solving Addition Problems Involving Renaming. 2009. (PowerMath Ser.). (ENG., Illus.). 24p. (gr. 3-4). pap. 8.25 (978-0-8239-8851-8(1), PowerKids Pr.) Rosen Publishing Group, Inc., The.
—The Tour de France: Solving Addition Problems Using Regrouping. (PowerMath: Intermediate Ser.). 24p. 2009. (gr. 3-4). 45.00 (978-1-60851-386-4(6)) 2004. (Illus.). (J). lib. bdg. 22.50 (978-0-8239-8963-8(1)) Rosen Publishing Group, Inc., The. (PowerKids Pr.).
Shea, Therese. Biosphere 2: Solving Word Problems. (PowerMath Ser.). 32p. 2009. (ENG., Illus.). (gr. 5-6). pap. 10.00 (978-1-4042-5150-2(2), PowerKids Pr.) 2009. (gr. 4-5). 47.90 (978-1-60851-406-9(4), PowerKids Pr.) 2005. (Illus.). (YA). (gr. 5-9). lib. bdg. 25.25 (978-1-4042-2943-3(4)) Rosen Publishing Group, Inc., The.
—The Great Barrier Reef: Using Graphs & Charts to Solve Word Problems. (Math for the Real World Ser.). 32p. 2009. (ENG., Illus.). (gr. 6-7). pap. 10.00 (978-1-4042-6071-9(4)) 2009. (gr. 5-5). 47.90 (978-1-60851-367-3(X), PowerKids Pr.) 2007. (Illus.). (YA). (gr. 5-9). lib. bdg. 25.25 (978-1-4042-3359-1(8)) Rosen Publishing Group, Inc., The.
—The Transcontinental Railroad: Using Proportions to Solve Problems. (Math for the Real World Ser.). 32p. 2009. (ENG., Illus.). (gr. 6-7). pap. 10.00 (978-1-4042-6075-7(7)) 2009. (gr. 5-5). 47.90 (978-1-60851-370-3(X), PowerKids Pr.) 2006. (Illus.). (YA). (gr. 5-9). lib. bdg. 25.25 (978-1-4042-3361-4(X)) Rosen Publishing Group, Inc., The.
Taylor-Butler, Christine. Understanding Diagrams. 2012. (True Book(tm), a — Information Literacy Ser.). (ENG.). 48p. (J). lib. bdg. 31.00 (978-0-531-26008-1(9)); pap. 6.95 (978-0-531-26239-9(1)) Scholastic Library Publishing.
The Violence Prevention Library, 6 bks. Incl. Learning How to Be Kind to Others. Kent, Susan. lib. bdg. 22.60 (978-0-8239-5613-5(X)); Learning How to Feel Good about Yourself. Kent, Susan, contrib. by. lib. bdg. 22.60 (978-0-8239-5615-9(6)); Learning How to Say You Are Sorry. Kent, Susan. lib. bdg. 22.60 (978-0-8239-5614-2(8)); Learning How to Stay Safe at School. Kent, Susan. lib. bdg. 22.60 (978-0-8239-5616-6(4)); 24p. (J). (gr. 3). 2001. (Illus.). Set lib. bdg. 103.50 (978-0-8239-7080-3(9), PowerKids Pr.) Rosen Publishing Group, Inc., The.
Welbourn, Shannon. Step Forward with Problem Solving. 2016. (Step Forward! Ser.). (ENG., Illus.). 24p. (J). (gr. 2-5). (978-0-7787-2768-2(8)) Crabtree Publishing Co.
Williams, Zella & Wingard-Nelson, Rebecca. Word Problems Using Addition & Subtraction. 2016. (Mastering Math Word Problems Ser.). (Illus.). 48p. (J). pap. 11.70 (978-0-7660-8252-6(0)) Enslow Pubs., Inc.
Wingard-Nelson, Rebecca. Big Truck & Car Word Problems Starring Multiplication & Division. 2009. (Math Word Problems Solved Ser.). (Illus.). 48p. (J). (gr. 2-5). lib. bdg. 25.27 (978-0-7660-2918-7(2)) Enslow Pubs., Inc.
—Fun Food Word Problems Starring Fractions: Math Word Problems Solved. 2009. (Math Word Problems Solved Ser.). (Illus.). 48p. (J). (gr. 2-5). lib. bdg. 25.27 (978-0-7660-2919-4(0)) Enslow Pubs., Inc.
—I Can Do Money Word Problems. 2009. (I Like Money Math! Ser.). (Illus.). 24p. (J). pap. 7.95 (978-0-7660-3659-8(6),

Enslow Elementary); (gr. 1-3). lib. bdg. 22.60 *(978-0-7660-3145-6(4))* Enslow Pubs., Inc.
—Problem Solving & Word Problem Smarts! 2011. (Math Smarts! Ser.). (Illus.). 64p. (J). (gr. 5-18). pap. 8.95 *(978-1-59845-325-6(4))*; lib. bdg. 29.27 *(978-0-7660-3943-8(9))* Enslow Pubs., Inc.
—Ready for Word Problems & Problem Solving. LaBaff, Tom, illus. 2014. (Ready for Math Ser.). 48p. (J). pap. 8.95 *(978-1-4644-0443-6(7),* Enslow Elementary) Enslow Pubs., Inc.
—Sports Word Problems Starring Decimals & Percents. 2009. (Math Word Problems Solved Ser.). (Illus.). 48p. (J). (gr. 2-5). lib. bdg. 25.27 *(978-0-7660-2920-0(4))* Enslow Pubs., Inc.
Wingard-Nelson, Rebecca & Library. Graphing & Probability Word Problems: No Problem! 2010. (Math Busters Word Problems Ser.). (Illus.). 64p. (J). lib. bdg. 29.27 *(978-0-7660-3372-6(4))* Enslow Pubs., Inc.
Wingard-Nelson, Rebecca & Williams, Zella. Word Problems Using Ratios & Proportions. 2016. (Mastering Math Word Problems Ser.). 48p. (J). pap. 11.70 *(978-0-7660-8272-4(5))* Enslow Pubs., Inc.
WRITE IT! Problem Solving with Numbers & Words, Grades 5-6. 2004. (J). per. 10.95 *(978-1-58123-365-0(5))* Larson Learning, Inc.
WRITE IT! Problem Solving with Numbers & Words, Grades 7-8. 2004. (J). per. 10.95 *(978-1-58123-367-4(1))* Larson Learning, Inc.
Zuravicky, Orli. Amazing Animals: Multiplying Multidigit Numbers by a One-Digit Number with Regrouping. 2009. (PowerMath Ser.). (Illus.). 24p. (gr. 3-4). pap. 8.25 *(978-0-8239-8861-7(9),* PowerKids Pr.) Rosen Publishing Group, Inc., The.

PROCESSIONS
see Parades

PRODUCTION
see Economics; Industries

PRODUCTS, COMMERCIAL
see Commercial Products

PRODUCTS, DAIRY
see Dairy Products

PRODUCTS, WASTE
see Waste Products

PROFESSION, CHOICE OF
see Vocational Guidance

PROFESSIONS
see also Occupations; Vocational Guidance
also names of professions (e.g. Law; Medicine); also Law—Vocational Guidance; music—Vocational guidance

Antill, Sara. 10 Ways I Can Help My Community. 2012. (I Can Make a Difference Ser.). (ENG., Illus.). 24p. (J). (gr. 2-5). pap. 8.25 *(978-1-4488-6363-1(5))*; lib. bdg. 22.60 *(978-1-4488-6202-3(7))* Rosen Publishing Group, Inc., The. (PowerKids Pr.).
Barberi, Gladys. Pink Fire Trucks. Safar, Lina, illus. 2013.Tr. of Los Camiones de Bomberos de Color Rosado. 30p. (J). 16.95 *(978-1-60131-145-0(1))* Big Tent Bks.
Berendes, Mary. Careers/Las Carreras. Petelinsek, Kathleen, illus. 2008. (WordBooks/Libros de Palabras Ser.). (SPA & ENG.). 24p. (J). (gr. k-3). 25.64 *(978-1-59296-988-3(7),* 201088) Child's World, Inc., The.
Bozzo, Linda & Library. Community Helpers of the Past, Present, & Future. 2010. (Imagining the Future Ser.). (Illus.). 24p. (J). lib. bdg. 22.60 *(978-0-7660-3435-8(6),* Enslow Elementary) Enslow Pubs., Inc.
Calling All Innovators: A Career for You? (Set Of 4) 2013. (J). 120.00 *(978-0-531-27925-0(1))* Scholastic Library Publishing.
Coan, Sharon. Trabajadores de Mi Ciudad (Workers in My City) 2016. (TIME for KIDS(r) Nonfiction Readers Ser.). (SPA.). 12p. (J). (gr. k-k). 4.99 *(978-1-4938-3027-5(9))* Teacher Created Materials, Inc.
Downey, Glen R. The 10 Most Extreme Jobs. 2008. 14.99 *(978-1-55448-536-9(3))* Scholastic Library Publishing.
Durrie, Karen. Diversión. 2012. (SPA.). (J). 27.13 *(978-1-61913-209-2(5))* Weigl Pubs., Inc.
—Fun: Arabic-English Bilingual Edition. 2016. (Community Helpers Ser.). (ENG.). (J). (gr. 3-7). 29.99 *(978-1-61913-902-2(2))* Weigl Pubs., Inc.
—Safety. 2011. (ENG.). (J). lib. bdg. 27.13 *(978-1-61690-951-2(X))* Weigl Pubs., Inc.
—Seguridad. 2012. (SPA & ENG.). (J). *(978-1-61913-211-5(7))* Weigl Pubs., Inc.
Edwards, Clint. Show Me Community Helpers: My First Picture Encyclopedia, 1 vol. 2013. (My First Picture Encyclopedias Ser.). (ENG.). 32p. (gr. 1-2). pap. 8.10 *(978-1-4765-3788-7(7),* Aplus Bks.); 7.95 *(978-1-62065-918-2(2))*; lib. bdg. 27.32 *(978-1-62065-056-1(8))* Capstone Press of Coughlan Cos.
Fiscus, Jim. Careers in the Fashion Industry. rev. ed. 2005. (Career Resource Library). (Illus.). 192p. (YA). (gr. 7-12). lib. bdg. 34.60 *(978-0-8239-4082-0(9))* Rosen Publishing Group, Inc., The.
Guillain, Charlotte. History, 1 vol. 2012. (Jobs If You Like... Ser.). (ENG.). 32p. (gr. 1-3). pap. 8.29 *(978-1-4329-6818-2(1))*; lib. bdg. 27.32 *(978-1-4329-6807-6(6))* Heinemann-Raintree. (Heinemann First Library).
Harcourt School Publishers Staff. Jobs People Do, No. 6. 2nd ed. 2003. (Illus.). pap. 139.70 *(978-0-15-337561-3(2))* Harcourt Schl. Pubs.
—People & Work Big Book No. 6. 2nd ed. 2003. (Illus.). pap. 139.70 *(978-0-15-337571-2(X))* Harcourt Schl. Pubs.
Heling, Kathryn. Clothesline Clues to Jobs People Do. 2014. 17.95 *(978-1-63419-654-3(6))* Perfection Learning Corp.
Heling, Kathryn & Hembrook, Deborah. Clothesline Clues to Jobs People Do. Davies, Andy Robert, illus. 2012. (ENG.). 40p. (J). (gr. -1-2). 14.95 *(978-1-58089-251-3(5))* Charlesbridge Publishing, Inc.
In the Dark Interactive Packages: Nighttime Jobs. (Pebble Soup Explorations Ser.). (SPA.). (gr. -1-18). 52.00 *(978-0-7578-5250-3(5))* Rigby Education.
Jarrell, Jane & Saathoff, Deborah. Off to Work We Go. 2004. 50p. (gr. -1-18). pap., act. bk. ed. 6.99 *(978-0-8054-0823-2(1))* B&H Publishing Group.
Job Connection: Tools to Land the Job. 2nd ed. 2004. (YA). per. 11.95 *(978-1-891818-33-2(3),* 01-WB03) Linx Educational Publishing, Inc.
Kalman, Bobbie. Helpers in My Community. 2010. (My World Ser.). (ENG., Illus.). 24p. (J). (gr. k-2). *(978-0-7787-9444-8(X))*; pap. *(978-0-7787-9488-2(1))* Crabtree Publishing Co.
Malam, John. Be a Skyscraper Builder! A Hazardous Job You'd Rather Not Take. 2009. (You Wouldn't Want to Ser.). (ENG., Illus.). 32p. (J). (gr. 3-18). 29.00 *(978-0-531-20824-3(9),* Watts, Franklin) Scholastic Library Publishing.
—You Wouldn't Want to Be a Skyscraper Builder! A Hazardous Job You'd Rather Not Take. 2009. (You Wouldn't Want to... Ser.). (ENG., Illus.). 32p. (J). (gr. 3-18). pap. 9.95 *(978-0-531-21048-2(0),* Children's Pr.) Scholastic Library Publishing.
Mangrum, Allison. Jobs from A to Z. Capaldi, Gina, illus. 2006. 28p. pap. 9.50 *(978-1-55501-675-3(8))* Ballard & Tighe Pubs.
Owen, Ruth. Asteroid Hunters. 2015. (Get to Work with Science & Technology Ser.). (ENG.). 32p. (J). (gr. 2-7). lib. bdg. 26.60 *(978-1-910549-36-0(3))* Bearport Publishing Co., Inc.
Reece, Richard. Medicine, 1 vol. 2011. (Inside the Industry Ser.). (ENG., Illus.). 112p. (J). (gr. 6-12). lib. bdg. 35.64 *(978-1-61714-802-6(4),* Essential Library) ABDO Publishing Co.
Reeves, Diane Lindsey. Career Ideas for Kids Who Like Talking. Bond, Nancy, illus. 2nd rev. ed. 2007. (Career Ideas for Kids Ser.). 208p. (gr. 4-9). 32.95 *(978-0-8160-6553-0(5),* Checkmark Bks.) Facts On File, Inc.
—Glamorous Jobs. 2009. (Way Out Work Ser.). (Illus.). 48p. (gr. 3-5). 29.95 *(978-1-60413-129-1(2),* Ferguson Publishing Co.) Facts On File, Inc.
Thomas, William David. Mountain Rescuer. 2008. (Cool Careers Ser.). 32p. (gr. 5-8). pap. 10.50 *(978-0-8368-9328-1(X))*; lib. bdg. 26.00 *(978-0-8368-9195-9(3))* Stevens, Gareth Publishing LLLP.
Wolfe, Jane. Pull the Lever: Who Does What? Benham, Tors, illus. 2014. (ENG.). 8p. (J). (gr. -1-2). bds. 6.99 *(978-1-86147-392-9(3),* Armadillo) Anness Publishing GBR. Dist: National Bk. Network.

PROFESSORS
see Teachers

PROGRAMMING (ELECTRONIC COMPUTERS)
see Computer Programming

PROHIBITION

Bearce, Stephanie. Top Secret Files: Gangsters & Bootleggers: Secrets, Strange Tales, & Hidden Facts about the Roaring 20s. rev. ed. 2015. (Top Secret Files Ser.: 0). (ENG., Illus.). 125p. (J). (gr. 4-7). 8.95 *(978-1-61821-461-4(6))* Prufrock Pr.
Beyer, Mark. Temperance & Prohibition: The Movement to Pass Anti-Liquor Laws in America. 2006. (Progressive Movement, 1900-1920 — Efforts to Reform America's New Industrial Society Ser.). (Illus.). 32p. (ENG.). (gr. 4-8). pap. 10.00 *(978-1-4042-0861-2(5))*; (YA). (gr. 5-9). lib. bdg. 22.50 *(978-1-4042-0195-8(5))* Rosen Publishing Group, Inc., The.
—Temperance & Prohibition: The Movement to Pass Anti-liquor Laws in America. 2009. (Progressive Movement 1900-1920: Efforts to Reform America's New Industrial Society Ser.). 32p. (gr. 3-4). 47.90 *(978-1-60854-171-3(1))* Rosen Publishing Group, Inc., The.
Blumenthal, Karen. Bootleg: Murder, Moonshine, & the Lawless Years of Prohibition. 2013. (ENG., Illus.). 176p. (YA). (gr. 7-12). pap. 13.99 *(978-1-250-03427-4(2),* 9781250034274) Square Fish.
Dunn, John M. Prohibition. 2010. (American History Ser.). (Illus.). 128p. (J). 34.80 *(978-1-4205-0134-6(8),* Lucent Bks.) Cengage Gale.
Engdahl, Sylvia. Prohibition. 2012. (Perspectives on Modern World History Ser.). (ENG., Illus.). 224p. (gr. 10-12). lib. bdg. 47.80 *(978-0-7377-6370-6(1),* Greenhaven Pr., Inc.) Cengage Gale.
Graham, Amy. A Look at the Eighteenth & Twenty-First Amendments: The Prohibition & Sale of Intoxicating Liquors. 2007. (Constitution of the United States Ser.). (Illus.). 128p. (J). (gr. 5). lib. bdg. 34.60 *(978-1-59845-063-7(8),* MyReportLinks.com Bks.) Enslow Pubs., Inc.
Lieurance, Suzanne. The Prohibition Era in American History. 2003. (In American History Ser.). (Illus.). 112p. (J). (gr. 5-12). lib. bdg. 27.94 *(978-0-7660-1840-2(7))* Enslow Pubs., Inc.
Worth, Richard. Teetotalers & Saloon Smashers: The Temperance Movement & Prohibition. 2009. (America's Living History Ser.). (Illus.). 128p. (J). (gr. 5-9). lib. bdg. 33.27 *(978-0-7660-2908-8(5))* Enslow Pubs., Inc.

PROHIBITION—FICTION

George, McKelle. Speak Easy, Speak Love. 2017. 432p. (YA). (gr. 8). 17.99 ***(978-0-06-256092-6(1),*** Greenwillow Bks.) HarperCollins Pubs.
Larkin, Jillian. Diva. 2013. (Flappers Ser.). (ENG.). 320p. (YA). (gr. 7). pap. 9.99 *(978-0-385-74042-5(5),* Ember) Random Hse. Children's Bks.
—Ingenue. 2012. (Flappers Ser.). (ENG.). 368p. (YA). (gr. 7). pap. 9.99 *(978-0-385-74037-1(9),* Ember) Random Hse. Children's Bks.
—Vixen. 2011. (Flappers Ser.). (ENG.). 448p. (YA). (gr. 7). pap. 9.99 *(978-0-385-74035-7(2),* Ember) Random Hse. Children's Bks.
Lisle, Janet Taylor. Black Duck. 2007. (ENG.). 256p. (J). (gr. 5-18). 7.99 *(978-0-14-240902-2(2),* Puffin Books) Penguin Young Readers Group.

PROJECT APOLLO (U.S.)

Adamson, Thomas K. Apollo 11 Moon Landing: An Interactive Space Exploration Adventure. 2016. (You Choose: Space Ser.). (ENG., Illus.). 112p. (gr. 3-4). lib. bdg. 31.99 *(978-1-4914-8103-5(X),* You Choose Bks.) Capstone Press of Coughlan Cos.
—The First Moon Landing, 1 vol. Purcell, Gordon & Beatty, Terry, illus. 2006. (Graphic History Ser.). (ENG.). 32p. (gr. 3-4). per. 8.10 *(978-0-7368-9654-2(6),* Graphic Library) Capstone Press of Coughlan Cos.
Aldrin, Buzz. Reaching for the Moon. Minor, Wendell, illus. (ENG.). 40p. (J). (gr. 1-4). 2008. 6.99 *(978-0-06-055447-7(9),* Collins) 2005. 17.99 *(978-0-06-055445-3(2))* HarperCollins Pubs.
—Reaching for the Moon. Minor, Wendell, illus. unabr. ed. 2005. (Picture Book Readalong Ser.). (gr. k-4). 28.95 incl. audio compact disk *(978-1-59519-582-1(3))* Live Oak Media.
Anderson, Dale. The First Moon Landing. 2003. (Landmark Events in American History Ser.). (Illus.). 48p. (gr. 5-12). pap. 14.05 *(978-0-8368-5406-0(3),* Gareth Stevens Secondary Library) Stevens, Gareth Publishing LLLP.
Anderson, Dale & Goff, Elizabeth Hudson. The First Moon Landing. Floor, Guus & Spay, Anthony, illus. 2006. (Graphic Histories Ser.). 32p. (gr. 5-8). lib. bdg. 27.00 *(978-0-8368-6203-4(1))* Stevens, Gareth Publishing LLLP.
Apollo: Stepping Stones to the Moon. (Color & Learn Ser.). 36p. (J). (gr. 1-5). pap. *(978-1-882210-14-5(X))* Action Publishing, Inc.
Bailey, Gerry & Foster, Karen. Armstrong's Moon Rock. Radford, Karen & Noyes, Leighton, illus. 2008. (Stories of Great People Ser.). (ENG.). 40p. (J). (gr. 3-8). lib. bdg. *(978-0-7787-3684-4(9))*; (gr. 5-8). pap. *(978-0-7787-3706-3(3))* Crabtree Publishing Co.
Bodden, Valerie. Man Walks on the Moon. 2009. (Days of Change Ser.). 48p. (YA). (gr. 4-7). 22.95 *(978-1-58341-735-5(4))* Creative Co., The.
—Man Walks on the Moon: Days of Change. 2015. (Illus.). 80p. (J). *(978-1-60818-528-3(1),* Creative Education) Creative Co., The.
—Man Walks on the Moon: Odysseys in History. 2016. (Odysseys in History Ser.). (ENG.). 80p. (J). (gr. 7-10). pap. 14.99 *(978-1-62832-129-6(6),* Creative Paperbacks) Creative Co., The.
—To the Moon. (Great Expeditions Ser.). (Illus.). 48p. (J). 2012. (ENG.). (gr. 4-7). pap. 12.00 *(978-0-89812-666-2(5))* 2011. 35.65 *(978-1-60818-068-4(9))* Creative Co., The. (Creative Education).
Burleigh, Robert. One Giant Leap. Wimmer, Mike, illus. (ENG.). 40p. (J). (gr. 1-3). 2014. 8.99 *(978-0-14-751165-2(8),* Puffin Books) 2009. 16.99 *(978-0-399-23883-3(2),* Philomel Bks.) Penguin Young Readers Group.
Chambers, Catherine. Neil Armstrong, 1 vol. 2014. (Science Biographies Ser.). (ENG.). 32p. (gr. 2-4). lib. bdg. 30.65 *(978-1-4109-6237-9(7),* Raintree Perspectives) Heinemann-Raintree.
Close, Edward. Moon Missions, 1 vol., 1. 2014. (Discovery Education: Earth & Space Science Ser.). (ENG.). 32p. (gr. 3-6). 26.25 *(978-1-4777-6178-6(0),* PowerKids Pr.) Rosen Publishing Group, Inc., The.
Dell, Pamela. Man on the Moon: How a Photograph Made Anything Seem Possible, 1 vol. 2011. (Captured History Ser.). (ENG.). 64p. (gr. 5-7). pap. 9.10 *(978-0-7565-4447-8(5),* CPB Grades 4-8) Compass Point Bks.
Di Piazza, Domenica. NASA Computer Scientist Margaret Hamilton. 2017. (STEM Trailblazer Bios Ser.). (ENG.). 32p. (J). (gr. 2-5). 26.65 ***(978-1-5124-3450-7(7))*** Lerner Publishing Group.
Dunn, Joe. Moon Landing, 1 vol. Espinosa, Rod et al, illus. 2007. (Graphic History Ser.). (ENG.). 32p. (gr. 3-6). 28.50 *(978-1-60270-078-9(8),* Graphic Planet- Nonfiction) ABDO Publishing Co.
Dyer, Alan. Mission to the Moon. 2009. (ENG., Illus.). 80p. (J). (gr. 3-7). 19.99 *(978-1-4169-7935-7(2),* Simon & Schuster Bks. For Young Readers) Simon & Schuster Bks. For Young Readers.
Engdahl, Sylvia, ed. The Apollo 11 Moon Landing. 2011. (Perspectives on Modern World History Ser.). (Illus.). 224p. (J). (gr. 9-12). 42.45 *(978-0-7377-5785-9(X),* 1330286) Cengage Gale.
Feinstein, Stephen. Read about Neil Armstrong. 2005. (I Like Biographies! Ser.). (Illus.). 24p. (J). lib. bdg. 22.60 *(978-0-7660-2593-6(4),* Enslow Elementary) Enslow Pubs., Inc.
Floca, Brian. Moonshot: The Flight of Apollo 11. Floca, Brian, illus. 2009. (ENG., Illus.). 48p. (J). (gr. -1-5). 19.99 *(978-1-4169-5046-2(X),* Atheneum/Richard Jackson Bks.) Simon & Schuster Children's Publishing.
Fradin, Dennis Brindell. The First Lunar Landing. 2009. (Turning Points in U. S. History Ser.). 48p. (gr. 3-18). 31.36 *(978-0-7614-4256-1(1))* Marshall Cavendish Corp.
Friend, Robyn C. The Women of Apollo. Katz, David Arthur, illus. l.t. ed. 2006. 80p. (J). 17.95 *(978-1-880599-80-8(5))*; pap. 12.95 *(978-1-880599-79-2(1))* Cascade Pass, Inc.
Goff, Elizabeth Hudson & Anderson, Dale. The First Moon Landing. 2006. (Graphic Histories Ser.). (Illus.). 32p. (gr. 5-8). pap. 10.50 *(978-0-8368-6255-3(4))* Stevens, Gareth Publishing LLLP.
Goff, Elizabeth Hudson, et al. El Primer Alunizaje. 2007. (Historias Graficas (Graphic Histories) Ser.). (SPA., Illus.). 32p. (gr. 5-8). pap. 10.50 *(978-0-8368-7904-9(X))*; lib. bdg. 27.00 *(978-0-8368-7897-4(3))* Stevens, Gareth Publishing LLLP.
Goldberg, Jan. James Lovell: The Rescue of Apollo 13. 2004. (Library of Astronaut Biographies Ser.). (Illus.). 112p. (gr. 5-8). lib. bdg. 34.60 *(978-0-8239-4459-0(X),* Rosen Reference) Rosen Publishing Group, Inc., The.
Green, Carl R. Apollo 11 Rockets to First Moon Landing: A MyReportLinks. com Book. 2004. (Space Flight Adventures & Disasters Ser.). (Illus.). 48p. (J). lib. bdg. 25.26 *(978-0-7660-5164-5(1),* MyReportLinks.com Bks.) Enslow Pubs., Inc.
—Walking on the Moon: The Amazing Apollo 11 Mission. 2012. (American Space Missions — Astronauts, Exploration, & Discovery Ser.). (Illus.). 48p. (J). (gr. 5-18). 25.27 *(978-0-7660-4076-2(3))* Enslow Pubs., Inc.
Green, Jen. The Story of the Race to the Moon. Mark Bergin, illus. 2017. (Explorers Ser.). 32p. (gr. 3-6). 31.35 ***(978-1-910706-92-3(2))*** Book Hse. GBR. Dist: Black Rabbit Bks.
Hasday, Judy L. The Apollo 13 Mission: Overcoming Adversity. 2006. (Illus.). 120p. (J). (gr. 4-8). reprint ed. 25.00 *(978-1-4223-5546-6(2))* DIANE Publishing Co.
Higgins, Nadia. Moon Landing, 1 vol. 2007. (Essential Events Set 1 Ser.). (ENG., Illus.). 112p. (J). (gr. 6-12). lib. bdg. 35.64 *(978-1-59928-854-3(0))* ABDO Publishing Co.
Holden, Henry M. Danger in Space: Surviving the Apollo 13 Disaster. 2012. (American Space Missions — Astronauts, Exploration, & Discovery Ser.). (Illus.). 48p. (J). (gr. 5-18). 25.27 *(978-0-7660-4072-4(0))* Enslow Pubs., Inc.
—Triumph over Disaster Aboard Apollo 13: A MyReportLinks. com Book. 2004. (Space Flight Adventures & Disasters Ser.). (Illus.). 48p. (J). lib. bdg. 26.60 *(978-0-7660-5167-6(6),* MyReportLinks.com Bks.) Enslow Pubs., Inc.
Hubbard, Ben. Neil Armstrong & Getting to the Moon. 2015. (Adventures in Space Ser.). (ENG., Illus.). 48p. (gr. 4-6). 33.32 *(978-1-4846-2515-6(3))* Heinemann-Raintree.
Irvine, Alex. Far Side of the Moon, 1 vol. Bishop, Ben, illus. 2017. (ENG.). 64p. (gr. 3-7). 16.95 *(978-0-88448-452-3(1),* 884452) Tilbury Hse. Pubs.
Irwin, James. Destination Moon. 15th anniv. ed. 2004. 52p. 16.00 *(978-1-929241-98-9(4))* Send The Light Distribution LLC.
Koestler-Grack, Rachel A. Moon Landing, 1 vol. 2005. (American Moments Ser.). (ENG., Illus.). 48p. (gr. 4-8). 27.07 *(978-1-59197-932-6(3),* Abdo & Daughters) ABDO Publishing Co.
—Neil Armstrong. 2009. (People We Should Know Ser.). 48p. (J). (gr. 3-5). pap. 10.50 *(978-1-4339-2147-6(2))*; lib. bdg. 31.00 *(978-1-4339-1948-0(6))* Stevens, Gareth Publishing LLLP. (Gareth Stevens Learning Library).
Kramer, Barbara. Neil Armstrong: Meet the Famous Astronaut. 2003. (Meeting Famous People Ser.). (Illus.). 32p. (J). lib. bdg. 22.60 *(978-0-7660-2007-8(X))* Enslow Pubs., Inc.
Lassieur, Allison. The Race to the Moon: An Interactive History Adventure, 1 vol. 2014. (You Choose: History Ser.). (ENG.). 112p. (gr. 3-4). 31.99 *(978-1-4765-4185-3(X),* You Choose Bks.) Capstone Press of Coughlan Cos.
Malam, John. Man Walks on the Moon. 2003. (Dates with History Ser.). 45p. (J). lib. bdg. 28.50 *(978-1-58340-407-2(4))* Black Rabbit Bks.
McPherson, Stephanie Sammartino. The First Men on the Moon. 2009. (History Maker Biographies Ser.). (ENG.). 48p. (gr. 3-6). 27.93 *(978-0-7613-4949-5(9),* Lerner Pubns.) Lerner Publishing Group.
Mitchell, Edgar & Mahoney, Ellen. Earthrise: My Adventures As an Apollo 14 Astronaut. 2014. (ENG., Illus.). 192p. (YA). (gr. 7). 19.95 *(978-1-61374-901-2(5))* Chicago Review Pr., Inc.
Morris, Neil. Who Traveled to the Moon?, 1 vol. 2014. (Primary Source Detectives Ser.). (ENG.). 64p. (gr. 7-8). lib. bdg. 35.99 *(978-1-4329-9605-5(3))* Heinemann-Raintree.
Nagelhout, Ryan. The First Moon Walk. 2015. (Incredible True Adventures Ser.). (ENG.). 32p. (J). (gr. 3-4). pap. 10.50 *(978-1-4824-2038-8(4))* Stevens, Gareth Publishing LLLP.
—Neil Armstrong in His Own Words. 2016. (Eyewitness to History Ser.). (ENG., Illus.). 32p. (J). (gr. 4-5). pap. 10.50 *(978-1-4824-4078-2(4))* Stevens, Gareth Publishing LLLP.
Ollhoff, Jim. Neil Armstrong. 2013. (Great Explorers Ser.). 32p. (J). (gr. 5-9). lib. bdg. 27.07 *(978-1-61783-963-4(9),* Abdo & Daughters) ABDO Publishing Co.
Olson, Tod. Lost in Outer Space: The Incredible Journey of Apollo 13. 2017. (Lost Ser.: 2). (ENG.). 224p. (J). (gr. 3-7). 12.99 *(978-0-545-92815-1(X),* Scholastic Nonfiction) Scholastic, Inc.
Ottaviani, Jim. T-Minus: The Race to the Moon. Cannon, Zander & Cannon, Kevin, illus. 2009. (ENG.). 128p. (J). (gr. 3-7). pap. 15.99 *(978-1-4169-4960-2(7),* Aladdin) Simon & Schuster Children's Publishing.
Oxlade, Chris & West, David. The Apollo Missions & Other Adventures in Space. 2011. (Incredible True Adventures Ser.). (ENG., Illus.). 48p. (YA). (gr. 5-8). pap. 11.75 *(978-1-4488-6664-9(2))*; lib. bdg. 29.25 *(978-1-4488-6660-1(X))* Rosen Publishing Group, Inc., The. (Rosen Reference).
Radomski, Kassandra. The Apollo 13 Mission: Core Events of a Crisis in Space, 1 vol. 2014. (What Went Wrong? Ser.). (ENG.). 32p. (gr. 3-4). pap. 7.95 *(978-1-4765-5130-2(8))*; lib. bdg. 27.32 *(978-1-4765-4181-5(7))* Capstone Press of Coughlan Cos.
Riley, Christopher & Dolling, Phil. Inside Apollo 11. 2017. (Geek's Guide to Space Ser.). 192p. (J). (gr. 12-14). 44.60 ***(978-1-4994-6696-6(X),*** Rosen Young Adult) Rosen Publishing Group, Inc., The.
Riley, Christopher & Woods, David. Inside the Lunar Rover. 2017. (Geek's Guide to Space Ser.). 192p. (J). (gr. 12-14). 44.60 ***(978-1-4994-6699-7(4),*** Rosen Young Adult) Rosen Publishing Group, Inc., The.
Robbins, Dean. Margaret & the Moon: How Margaret Hamilton Saved the First Lunar Landing. Knisley, Lucy, illus. 2017. (ENG.). 40p. (J). (gr. -1-3). 17.99 *(978-0-399-55185-7(9),* Knopf Bks. for Young Readers) Random Hse. Children's Bks.
Stone, Adam. The Apollo 13 Mission. 2014. (Disaster Stories Ser.). (ENG., Illus.). 24p. (J). (gr. 3-8). 29.95 *(978-1-62617-149-7(1),* Black Sheep) Bellwether Media.
Tan, Sheri. Handshake in Space: The Apollo-Soyuz Test Project. Bond, Higgins, illus. 2009. 32p. (J). (gr. 1-5). pap. 9.95 incl. audio *(978-1-60727-104-8(4))*; (ENG.). 9.95 *(978-1-60727-115-4(X))*; (ENG.). 17.95 *(978-1-60727-114-7(1))*; pap. 9.95 incl. reel tape *(978-1-59249-203-9(7))* Soundprints.
Thimmesh, Catherine. Team Moon: How 400,000 People Landed Apollo 11 on the Moon. 2006. (ENG., Illus.). 80p. (J). (gr. 5-7). 19.95 *(978-0-618-50757-3(4))* Houghton Mifflin Harcourt Publishing Co.
Watts, Franklin & Howell, Izzi. Neil Armstrong & the Moon Landings. 2016. (ENG., Illus.). 32p. (J). (gr. 1-3). 17.99 *(978-1-4451-4841-0(2),* Franklin Watts) Hachette Children's Group GBR. Dist: Hachette Bk. Group.
Weakland, Mark. When Neil Armstrong Built a Wind Tunnel. Lozano, Luciano, illus. 2017. (Leaders Doing Headstands Ser.). (ENG.). 32p. (gr. 2-3). lib. bdg. 27.99 ***(978-1-5158-1575-4(7))*** Picture Window Bks.
Wilkinson, Philip. Spacebusters. 2012. (DK Reader Level 3 Ser.). lib. bdg. 13.55 *(978-0-606-26544-7(9),* Turtleback) Turtleback Bks.
—Spacebusters: Race to the Moon. 2012. (DK Readers Ser.). (ENG.). 48p. (J). (gr. 2-4). 3.99 *(978-0-7566-9084-7(6),* DK Children) Dorling Kindersley Publishing, Inc.
Yomtov, Nel. The Apollo 11 Moon Landing: July 20 1969, 1 vol. 2014. (24-Hour History Ser.). (ENG.). 48p. (gr. 3-5). pap. 8.95 *(978-1-4329-9298-9(8))*; (Illus.). lib. bdg. 33.32 *(978-1-4329-9292-7(9))* Heinemann-Raintree. (NA-h).
Zelon, Helen. The Apollo 13 Mission: Surviving an Explosion in Space. 2009. (Space Missions Ser.). 24p. (gr. 3-4). 42.50

(978-1-60853-116-5(3), PowerKids Pr.) Rosen Publishing Group, Inc., The.

Zemlicka, Shannon. Neil Armstrong. 2003. (History Maker Bios Ser.). (Illus.). 48p. (J). (gr. 2-4). 26.60 *(978-0-8225-0395-8(6),* Lerner Pubns.) Lerner Publishing Group.

Zoehfeld, Kathleen Weidner. Apollo 13. Lowe, Wesley, illus. 2015. (Totally True Adventures Ser.). (ENG.). 112p. (J). (gr. 2-5). pap. 4.99 *(978-0-385-39125-2(0),* Random Hse. Bks. for Young Readers) Random Hse. Children's Bks.

PROJECT APOLLO (U.S.)—FICTION

Baratz-Logsted, Lauren. I Love You, Michael Collins. 2017. (ENG.). 240p. (J). 16.99 *(978-0-374-30385-3(1),* 9780374303853, Farrar, Straus & Giroux (BYR)) Farrar, Straus & Giroux.

Marazano, Richard. The Sons of Ares, 2 vols. Ponzio, Jean-Michel, illus. 2009. (Chimpanzee Complex Ser.: 1). (ENG.). 56p. pap. 13.95 *(978-1-84918-002-3(4))* CineBook GBR. Dist: National Bk. Network.

PROJECT GEMINI (U.S.)

Green, Carl R. The Gemini 4 Spacewalk Mission: A MyReportLinks. com Book. 2004. (Space Flight Adventures & Disasters Ser.). (Illus.). 48p. (J). lib. bdg. 26.60 *(978-0-7660-5163-8(3),* MyReportLinks.com Bks.) Enslow Pubs., Inc.

—Spacewalk: The Astounding Gemini 4 Mission. 2012. (American Space Missions — Astronauts, Exploration, & Discovery Ser.). (Illus.). 48p. (J). (gr. 5-18). 25.27 *(978-0-7660-4075-5(5))* Enslow Pubs., Inc.

Zelon, Helen. The Gemini IV Mission: The First American Space Walk. 2009. (Space Missions Ser.). 24p. (gr. 3-4). 42.50 *(978-1-60853-119-6(8),* PowerKids Pr.) Rosen Publishing Group, Inc., The.

PROJECT MERCURY (U.S.)

Ashby, Ruth. Rocket Man: The Mercury Adventure of John Glenn, 1 vol. Hunt, Robert, illus. 2004. (ENG.). 144p. (J). (gr. 2-5). 12.95 *(978-1-56145-323-8(4))* Peachtree Pubs.

Myrus, Donald. Keeping up with the Astronauts: The Story of Man's Greatest Adventures in Outer Space Including the John Glenn & Scott Carpenter Flights. 2011. 92p. 38.95 *(978-1-258-10348-4(6))* Literary Licensing, LLC.

Pierce, Philip N. & Schuon, Karl. John H Glenn, Astronaut. 2011. 234p. 46.95 *(978-1-258-00503-0(4))* Literary Licensing, LLC.

Stone, Tanya Lee. Almost Astronauts: 13 Women Who Dared to Dream. 2009. (ENG., Illus.). 144p. (J). (gr. 5). 24.99 *(978-0-7636-3611-1(8))* Candlewick Pr.

Zelon, Helen. The Mercury 6 Mission: The First American Astronaut to Orbit Earth. 2009. (Space Missions Ser.). 24p. (gr. 3-4). 42.50 *(978-1-60853-120-2(1),* PowerKids Pr.) Rosen Publishing Group, Inc., The.

PROJECT METHOD IN TEACHING

Kahn, William A. The Student's Guide to Successful Project Teams. 2008. (ENG., Illus.). 256p. (C). 65.00 *(978-1-84169-893-9(8),* RT8938X) Routledge.

PRONGHORN ANTELOPE

Jackson, Tom. Pronghorns. 2008. (Illus.). 52p. (J). *(978-0-7172-6279-3(0))* Grolier, Ltd.

Lunis, Natalie. Pronghorn: Long-Distance Runner! 2010. (Blink of an Eye: Superfast Animals Ser.). 24p. (J). (gr. k-3). lib. bdg. 22.61 *(978-1-936087-94-5(4))* Bearport Publishing Co., Inc.

PROPAGANDA

see also Advertising

Connolly, Sean. Political Messages & Propaganda. 2010. (J). 34.25 *(978-1-59920-349-2(9))* Black Rabbit Bks.

Roscoe, Kelly & Roberts, Jeremy. Joseph Goebbels, 01 vols., 1. 2016. (Holocaust Ser.). (ENG., Illus.). 112p. (J). 35.60 *(978-1-5081-7049-5(5),* Rosen Young Adult) Rosen Publishing Group, Inc., The.

Shoup, Kate. Nazi Propaganda: Jews in Hitler's Germany. 2016. (Public Persecutions Ser.). 128p. (J). 45.64 *(978-1-5026-2321-8(8))* Cavendish Square Publishing.

PROPAGATION OF PLANTS

see Plant Propagation

PROPHETS

Adil, Hajjah Amina & Sperling, Karima. My Little Lore of Light: A Child's Version of Lore of Light. 2005. (Illus.). x, 193p. (J). 22.00 *(978-1-930409-35-4(4))* Islamic Supreme Council of America.

Bible Visuals International Staff, comment. Prophets to God's People Vol. 24: Old Testament. 2006. (Illus.). (J). pap. *(978-1-932381-84-9(8),* 2024) Bible Visuals International, Inc.

Bible Visuals International Staff, compiled by. Prophets of the Messiah Vol. 32: Old Testament. 2006. (Illus.). (J). pap. *(978-1-932381-91-7(0),* 2032) Bible Visuals International, Inc.

Burrill, Richard L. My Sweet Lord: The Life-Stories of Muhammad & the Five God-Men of History. 2005. (YA). (gr. 9-12). pap. 19.95 *(978-1-878464-53-8(1))* Anthro Co., The.

Demi, Barbara. Muhammad. Demi, Barbara, illus. 2003. (ENG., Illus.). 48p. (J). (gr. 2-5). 19.95 *(978-0-689-85264-0(9),* McElderry, Margaret K. Bks.) McElderry, Margaret K. Bks.

Krull, Kathleen. They Saw the Future: Oracles, Psychics, Scientists, Great Thinkers, & Pretty Good Guessers. Brooker, Kyrsten, illus. 2014. (ENG.). 112p. (J). (gr. -1-3). pap. 45.99 *(978-1-4814-3623-6(6),* Atheneum Bks. for Young Readers) Simon & Schuster Children's Publishing.

Stefoff, Rebecca. Prophets & Prophecy. 2007. (Secrets of the Supernatural Ser.). (Illus.). 79p. (J). (gr. 4-7). lib. bdg. 32.79 *(978-0-7614-2638-7(8),* Benchmark Bks.) Marshall Cavendish Corp.

Van Der Veen, Andrew. Bible Lessons for Juniors, Book 2: Kings & Prophets. 2007. 88p. (J). 6.00 *(978-1-60178-013-3(3))* Reformation Heritage Bks.

Wallis, Mary Alice & Lindstrom, C. G. Prophets & Apostles. 2008. (LDS Puzzle Pals Ser.). 122p. pap. 14.99 *(978-1-59955-126-5(8),* Cedar Fort, Inc.) Cedar Fort, Inc./CFI Distribution.

PROSODY

see Versification

PROSPECTING—FICTION

Kay, Ross. The Go Ahead Boys & Simon's Mine. 2007. 148p. pap. 18.99 *(978-1-4264-8426-1(7));* 168p. pap. 21.99 *(978-1-4264-8484-1(4))* Creative Media Partners, LLC.

PROTECTION OF ANIMALS

see Animals—Treatment

PROTECTION OF BIRDS

see Birds—Protection

PROTECTION OF CHILDREN

see Child Welfare

PROTECTION OF ENVIRONMENT

see Environmental Protection

PROTECTION OF GAME

see Game Protection

PROTECTION OF NATURAL SCENERY

see Natural Monuments

PROTECTION OF WILDLIFE

see Wildlife Conservation

PROTESTANT REFORMATION

see Reformation

PROTESTANTISM

see also Evangelicalism; Reformation

White, Bender Richardson, et al. Protestantism. 3rd rev. ed. 2009. (World Religions Ser.). (Illus.). 144p. (gr. 6-12). 40.00 *(978-1-60413-112-3(8),* Chelsea Hse.) Facts On File, Inc.

PROTOZOA

Graham, Ian. Microscopic Scary Creatures. 2009. (Scary Creatures Ser.). (ENG.). 32p. (J). (gr. 3-5). pap. 8.95 *(978-0-531-21044-4(8),* Watts, Franklin); (Illus.). 27.00 *(978-0-531-21673-6(X),* Children's Pr.) Scholastic Library Publishing.

Hollar, Sherman. A Closer Look at Bacteria, Algae, & Protozoa. 2011. (Illus.). 88p. (J). lib. bdg. 31.70 *(978-1-61530-534-6(3))* Rosen Publishing Group, Inc., The.

PROVERBS

Alvarez O'Neill, Juan, illus. Grano a grano... Refranes Populares. 2005. (SPA.). (J). 8.95 *(978-0-8477-1554-1(X))* Univ. of Puerto Rico Pr.

Brennan-Nelson, Denise. My Daddy Likes to Say. Donovan, Jane Monroe, illus. 2009. (ENG.). 32p. (J). (gr. k-6). 15.95 *(978-1-58536-432-9(0))* Sleeping Bear Pr.

—My Grandma Likes to Say. Donovan, Jane Monroe, illus. rev. ed. 2007. (ENG.). 32p. (J). (gr. k-6). 16.95 *(978-1-58536-284-4(0))* Sleeping Bear Pr.

The Christian Student Compass: KJV Monthly Version with Book of Proverbs. 2003. (YA). spiral bd. *(978-0-9725804-2-7(5))* Salt Pubs.

Davis, Mary J. My Wisdom Journal: A Discovering of Proverbs for Kids. 2004. (Journals Just for Kids Ser.). (Illus.). 160p. (J). (gr. 4-7). pap. 9.99 *(978-1-885358-73-8(3),* Legacy Pr.) Rainbow Pubs. & Legacy Pr.

Dent, Sabrina. Proverbs Kids Fun Activity Book. 2006. (Illus.). 40p. (J). 5.99 *(978-0-9796148-0-4(5))* Joint Heir Multimedia.

Fyne, Olga M. You Can't Teach an Old Dog New Tricks Because. 2010. (Illus.). 26p. pap. 9.99 *(978-1-935105-66-4(3))* Avid Readers Publishing Group.

Gonzalez, Ralfka & Ruiz, Ana, illus. Mi Primer Libro de Dichos. 2014.Tr. of My First Book of Proverbs. (SPA & ENG.). 32p. (J). (gr. -1-3). pap. 9.95 *(978-0-89239-200-1(2))* Lee & Low Bks., Inc.

Herrera, J. Ignacio. 125 Refranes Infantiles. Torcida, María Luisa, illus. (SPA.). (J). (gr. 3-5). 12.76 *(978-84-305-9180-0(X),* SU6580) Susaeta Ediciones, S.A. ESP. Dist: Lectorum Pubns., Inc.

Johnson, Robin. Understanding Sayings. 2015. (Figuratively Speaking Ser.). (ENG., Illus.). 32p. (J). *(978-0-7787-1778-2(X))* Crabtree Publishing Co.

Levin, Mark R., pref. Proverbs for Young People. 2015. (ENG., Illus.). 72p. (J). (gr. -1-3). 17.99 *(978-1-4814-5945-7(7),* Aladdin) Simon & Schuster Children's Publishing.

Libal, Autumn. Folk Proverbs & Riddles. 2004. (North American Folklore Ser.). (Illus.). 112p. (YA). (gr. 7-18). lib. bdg. 22.95 *(978-1-59084-343-7(6))* Mason Crest.

MacKenzie, Carine. Wise Words to Follow: Words of wisdom from the book of Proverbs. 2009. (ENG., Illus.). 24p. (J). 7.99 *(978-1-84550-430-4(5),* df4c3c1d-0da3-460b-89a2-d274e5f6e2d0) Christian Focus Pubns. GBR. Dist: Bookmasters Distribution.

—Wise Words to Obey: Words of wisdom from the book of Proverbs. 2009. (ENG., Illus.). 24p. (J). 7.99 *(978-1-84550-431-1(3),* f9c1af98-7597-4d79-9bcc-9589b7d1ddd8) Christian Focus Pubns. GBR. Dist: Bookmasters Distribution.

—Wise Words to Trust: Words of wisdom from the book of Proverbs. 2009. (ENG., Illus.). 24p. (J). 7.99 *(978-1-84550-432-8(1),* 208c0c67-foed-4e86-9b47-ac39af3768a5) Christian Focus Pubns. GBR. Dist: Bookmasters Distribution.

Miller, Ann. Proverbs, Prayers, Poems for Children & Teens. 2005. (J). lib. bdg. 14.95 *(978-0-9748165-1-7(5))* Jaylil Publishing Co.

Santana, Sr. Sabina Stella. Happy Ending Children's Stories, & More: Poems, Tongue-Twisters, Proverbs, & Brain-Teasers. 2008. 64p. pap. 13.50 *(978-1-4303-1344-1(7))* Lulu Pr., Inc.

Snedeker, Gus. An Apple a Day: Folk Proverbs & Riddles. 2013. (Illus.). 48p. (J). pap. *(978-1-4222-2504-2(6))* Mason Crest.

—An Apple a Day: Folk Proverbs & Riddles. Jabbour, Alan, ed. 2012. (North American Folklore for Youth Ser.). (Illus.). 48p. (J). (gr. 4). 19.95 *(978-1-4222-2493-9(7))* Mason Crest.

Snook, Randy, photos by. Many Ideas Open the Way: A Collection of Hmong Proverbs. 2003. (Illus.). 32p. (J). 16.95 *(978-1-885008-23-7(6),* Shen's Bks.) Lee & Low Bks., Inc.

365 Days of Wonder: Mr. Browne's Book of Precepts. 2014. (ENG.). 432p. (J). (gr. 3-7). 14.99 *(978-0-553-49904-9(1));* lib. bdg. 17.99 *(978-0-553-49905-6(X))* Random Hse. Children's Bks. (Knopf Bks. for Young Readers).

PRUSSIA (GERMANY)

Heuston, Kimberley. Otto von Bismarck: Iron Chancellor of Germany. (Wicked History Ser.). (ENG., Illus.). 128p. (YA). 2010. (gr. 6-12). pap. 5.95 *(978-0-531-22824-1(X),* Watts, Franklin) 2009. (gr. 5-9). 31.00 *(978-0-531-21278-3(5))* Scholastic Library Publishing.

PRYDAIN (IMAGINARY PLACE)—FICTION

Alexander, Lloyd. The Black Cauldron. 2006. (Chronicles of Prydain: Bk. 2). (Illus.). 182p. (gr. 3-7). 17.00 *(978-0-7569-6813-7(5))* Perfection Learning Corp.

—The Black Cauldron. 2004. (Chronicles of Prydain: Bk. 2). 240p. (J). (gr. 4-7). pap. 38.00 incl. audio *(978-1-4000-8636-8(1),* Listening Library) Random Hse. Audio Publishing Group.

—The Castle of Llyr. 2004. (Chronicles of Prydain: Bk. 3). 208p. (J). (gr. 4-7). pap. 36.00 incl. audio *(978-1-4000-9019-8(9),* Listening Library) Random Hse. Audio Publishing Group.

—The High King. 2006. (Chronicles of Prydain: Bk. 5). (Illus.). 253p. (gr. 3-7). 17.00 *(978-0-7569-6816-8(X))* Perfection Learning Corp.

PSALMODY

see Church Music; Hymns

PSYCHIATRISTS

Worth, Richard. Elisabeth Kubler-Ross: Encountering Death & Dying. 2004. (Women in Medicine Ser.). (Illus.). 112p. (gr. 6-12). 30.00 *(978-0-7910-8027-6(7),* Chelsea Hse.) Facts On File, Inc.

PSYCHIATRISTS—FICTION

Gold, Rachel. Being Emily. 2012. (ENG.). 264p. (gr. 9). pap. 15.95 *(978-1-59493-283-0(2))* Bella Bks., Inc.

Henry, April. Shock Point. 2008. (ENG.). 192p. (YA). (gr. 7-18). 7.99 *(978-0-14-241240-4(6),* Speak) Penguin Young Readers Group.

London, Jonathan. Here Comes Doctor Hippo: A Little Hippo Story. Eduar, Gilles, illus. 2013. (Little Hippo Ser.). (ENG.). 32p. (J). (gr. -1-k). pap. 6.95 *(978-1-62091-595-0(2))* Boyds Mills Pr.

Miller, Mary Beth. Aimee. 2004. (ENG., Illus.). 288p. (YA). (gr. 7-18). 8.99 *(978-0-14-240025-8(4),* Speak) Penguin Young Readers Group.

Wells, Helen. Cherry Ames at Hilton Hospital: Book 13. 2007. (Cherry Ames Nurse Stories Ser.). 224p. (J). (gr. 3-7). 14.95 *(978-0-8261-0421-2(5))* Springer Publishing Co., Inc.

PSYCHIATRY

see also Psychotherapy

Brinkerhoff, Shirley. Drug Therapy & Obsessive-Compulsive Disorders. 2004. (Encyclopedia of Psychiatric Drugs & Their Disorders Ser.). (Illus.). 128p. (YA). lib. bdg. 24.95 *(978-1-59084-569-1(2))* Mason Crest.

—Drug Therapy & Schizophrenia. 2004. (Encyclopedia of Psychiatric Drugs & Their Disorders Ser.). (Illus.). 128p. (YA). lib. bdg. 24.95 *(978-1-59084-574-5(9))* Mason Crest.

Docalavich, Heather. The Future of Antidepressants: The New Wave of Research. 2008. (Antidepressants Ser.). (Illus.). 104p. (YA). (gr. 7-18). lib. bdg. 24.95 *(978-1-4222-0103-9(1))* Mason Crest.

Esherick, Joan. The FDA & Psychiatric Drugs: How a Drug Is Approved. 2004. (Encyclopedia of Psychiatric Drugs & Their Disorders Ser.). (Illus.). 128p. (YA). lib. bdg. 24.95 *(978-1-59084-578-3(1))* Mason Crest.

Libal, Autumn. Drug Therapy & Dissociative Disorders. 2004. (Encyclopedia of Psychiatric Drugs & Their Disorders Ser.). (Illus.). 128p. (YA). lib. bdg. 24.95 *(978-1-59084-564-6(1))* Mason Crest.

—Drug Therapy & Impulse Control Disorders. 2004. (Encyclopedia of Psychiatric Drugs & Their Disorders Ser.). (Illus.). 128p. (YA). lib. bdg. 24.95 *(978-1-59084-566-0(8))* Mason Crest.

Libal, Joyce. Drug Therapy & Mental Disorders Due to a Medical Condition. 2003. (Psychiatric Disorders: Drugs & Psychology for the Mind & Bod Ser.). (Illus.). 126p. (YA). (gr. 8-12). pap. 14.95 *(978-1-4222-0391-0(3))* Mason Crest.

—Drug Therapy for Mental Disorders Caused by a Medical Condition. 2004. (Encyclopedia of Psychiatric Drugs & Their Disorders Ser.). (Illus.). 128p. (YA). lib. bdg. 24.95 *(978-1-59084-567-7(6))* Mason Crest.

PSYCHICAL RESEARCH

see Parapsychology

PSYCHOANALYSIS

see also Dreams; Hypnotism; Mind and Body; Psychology; Psychology, Pathological

Docalavich, Heather. Antidepressants & Psychology: Talk Therapy vs. Medication. (Antidepressants Ser.). (Illus.). 104p. (YA). (gr. 7-18). 2008. lib. bdg. 24.95 *(978-1-4222-0096-4(5))* 2007. pap. 14.95 *(978-1-4222-0405-4(7))* Mason Crest.

Gillam, Scott. Sigmund Freud: Famous Neurologist, 1 vol. 2011. (Essential Lives Set 7 Ser.). (ENG., Illus.). 112p. (J). (gr. 6-12). lib. bdg. 35.64 *(978-1-61783-004-4(6))* ABDO Publishing Co.

Hitchcock, Susan Tyler. Karen Horney: Pioneer of Feminine Psychology. 2004. (Women in Medicine Ser.). (Illus.). 112p. (gr. 6-12). 30.00 *(978-0-7910-8025-2(0),* Chelsea Hse.) Facts On File, Inc.

Krull, Kathleen. Sigmund Freud. 2009. (Giants of Science Ser.). (ENG.). 144p. (J). (gr. 3-7). pap. 7.99 *(978-0-14-241266-4(X),* Puffin Books) Penguin Young Readers Group.

PSYCHOLOGICAL WARFARE

Linebarger, Paul M. A. Psychological Warfare. 2010. (ENG.). 336p. pap. 29.95 *(978-0-89556-120-6(4))* Gateways Bks. & Tapes.

PSYCHOLOGY

see also Animal Psychology; Attitude (Psychology); Child Psychology; Educational Psychology; Emotions; Imagination; Individuality; Intellect; Parapsychology; Perception; Personality; Psychoanalysis; Reasoning; Self-acceptance; Senses and Sensation; Social Psychology; Thought and Thinking

Adson, Patricia R. A Princess & Her Garden: A Fable of Awakening & Arrival. 2nd ed. 2011. (J). *(978-0-935652-93-2(0))* Center for Applications of Psychological Type, Inc.

Allyn, Pam. Pam Allyn's Best Books for Boys: How to Engage Boys in Reading in Ways That Will Change Their Lives. 2011. (ENG.). 176p. (gr. k-8). pap. 21.99 *(978-0-545-20455-2(0),* Teaching Resources) Scholastic, Inc.

Anderson, Shannon. Penelope Perfect: A Tale of Perfectionism Gone Wild. Kath, Katie, illus. 2015. (ENG.). 48p. (J). (gr. k-3). 15.99 *(978-1-63198-019-0(X))* Free Spirit Publishing, Inc.

Andrus, Aubre & Bluth, Karen. Project You: More Than 50 Ways to Calm down, de-Stress, & Feel Great. Collignon, Veronica, illus. 2017. (ENG.). 160p. (gr. 4-5). pap. 14.95 ***(978-1-63079-091-2(5))*** Switch Pr.

Antill, Sara. Zest. 2013. (Character Strength Ser.). 24p. (J). (gr. 3-6). pap. 8.25 *(978-1-4488-9812-1(9));* pap. 49.50 *(978-1-4488-9813-8(7));* lib. bdg. 22.60 *(978-1-4488-9677-6(0))* Rosen Publishing Group, Inc., The. (PowerKids Pr.).

Aspden, K. L. Help! - I've Got an Alarm Bell Going off in My Head! How Panic, Anxiety & Stress Affect Your Body. Ra, Zita, illus. 2015. (ENG.). 48p. pap. 12.95 *(978-1-84905-704-2(4),* 8199) Kingsley, Jessica Pubs. GBR. Dist: Macmillan Distribution Ltd.

Ayer, Eleanor H. Everything You Need to Know about Stress. 2009. (Need to Know Library). 64p. (gr. 5-5). 58.50 *(978-1-60854-089-1(8))* Rosen Publishing Group, Inc., The.

Becnel, Barbara, ed. Gangs & the Abuse of Power: Stanley Tookie Williams Street Peace Series, 8 bks., Vol. 1, Bk. 7. 2008. 24p. (J). 6.95 *(978-0-9753584-7-4(2))* Damamli Publishing Co.

Belanger, Jeff. Paranormal Encounters: A Look at the Evidence. 2011. (Haunted: Ghosts & the Paranormal Ser.). (Illus.). 224p. (J). lib. bdg. 37.95 *(978-1-4488-4839-3(3))* Rosen Publishing Group, Inc., The.

Bellamy, Adam. What's Intuition? 2017. (All about My Senses Ser.). 24p. (J). (gr. k-1). pap. 9.35 ***(978-0-7660-8801-6(4))*** Enslow Pubs., Inc.

Berry, Joy. Help Me Be Good about Fighting. 2009. (ENG.). 40p. (J). (gr. k-2). pap. 7.95 *(978-1-60577-128-1(7))* Berry, Joy Enterprises.

—You Can Go for It! 2009. (ENG.). 304p. (J). (gr. 5-7). pap. 12.95 *(978-1-60577-601-9(7))* Berry, Joy Enterprises.

Berry, Joy Wilt. A Book about Fighting. 2005. (Illus.). (J). *(978-0-7172-8584-6(7))* Scholastic, Inc.

Bradshaw, Cheryl M. How to Like Yourself: A Teen's Guide to Quieting Your Inner Critic & Building Lasting Self-Esteem. 2016. (Instant Help Solutions Ser.). (ENG.). 216p. (YA). (gr. 6-12). pap. 16.95 *(978-1-62625-348-3(X))* New Harbinger Pubns.

Brain, Christine. Psychology. 2009. (Illus.). 384p. pap. 62.50 *(978-0-340-96684-6(X))* Hodder Education Group GBR. Dist: Trans-Atlantic Pubns., Inc.

Brenner, Rebecca. Human Life: An Open Heart. Kemmerer, Brooke, illus. 2016. (Kid's User Guide Ser.: 2). (ENG.). 46p. (J). pap. 8.95 *(978-1-63047-866-7(0))* Morgan James Publishing.

Brinkerhoff, Shirley. Psychologist. Riggs, Ernestine G. & Gholar, Cheryl, eds. 2013. (Careers with Character Ser.: 18). 96p. (J). (gr. 7-18). 22.95 *(978-1-4222-2764-0(2))* Mason Crest.

Burloux, Gabriel. Body & Its Pain. Woods, Margaret, tr. from FRE. 2005. 295p. pap. 34.50 *(978-1-85343-794-6(8))* Free Assn. Bks. Ltd. GBR. Dist: ISBS Publisher Services.

Burstein, John. Past Tense: Healthy Ways to Manage Stress. 2010. (ENG., Illus.). 32p. (J). pap. *(978-0-7787-4812-0(X));* lib. bdg. *(978-0-7787-4796-3(4))* Crabtree Publishing Co.

Canetti, Yanitzia. Almost the Same. 2010. 24p. (J). pap. 5.99 *(978-1-59835-146-0(X),* BrickHouse Education) Cambridge BrickHouse, Inc.

—Casi Iguales. 2010. (SPA.). 24p. (J). pap. *(978-1-59835-144-6(3),* BrickHouse Education) Cambridge BrickHouse, Inc.

Cardwell, Mike & Flanagan, Cara. Psychology A2: The Complete Companion. 2003. (ENG., Illus.). 344p. pap. *(978-0-7487-7344-2(4))* Nelson Thornes Ltd.

Carlson, Dale. The Teen Brain Book: Who & What Are You? Teasdale, Nancy, ed. Nicklaus, Carol, illus. 2004. (ENG.). 230p. (gr. 7-12). pap. 14.95 *(978-1-884158-29-2(3))* Team Kreskin Productions, LLC.

Carlson, Hannah. Addiction: The Brain Disease. 2010. (ENG., Illus.). 224p. (gr. 7-18). pap. 14.95 *(978-1-884158-35-3(8),* 03db31a0-ebf1-4ef8-b49f-db048b863aec) Team Kreskin Productions, LLC.

Chan, Paul D. Why Is Mommy Sad? A Child's Guide to Parental Depression. Faust, Laurie A., illus. 2006. 12p. (J). pap. 6.99 *(978-1-929622-71-9(6))* Current Clinical Strategies Publishing.

Cleveland, Don. How Do We Know How the Brain Works. 2005. (Great Scientific Questions & the Scientists Who Answered Them Ser.). (Illus.). 112p. (J). (gr. 7-12). lib. bdg. 34.60 *(978-1-4042-0078-4(9))* Rosen Publishing Group, Inc., The.

Cleveland, Donald. How Do We Know How the Brain Works. 2009. (Great Scientific Questions & the Scientists Who Answered Them Ser.). 112p. (gr. 7-12). 63.90 *(978-1-61513-195-2(7))* Rosen Publishing Group, Inc., The.

Cope, Andy, et al. The Art of Being a Brilliant Teenager. 2014. (ENG., Illus.). 160p. pap. 18.00 *(978-0-85708-578-8(6),* Capstone) Wiley, John & Sons, Inc.

Coping: Set 1. 2017. (Coping Ser.). 112p. (gr. 12-12). 222.60 ***(978-1-4994-6631-7(5),*** Rosen Young Adult) Rosen Publishing Group, Inc., The.

Cox, Erika. Psychology. 2010. 204p. pap. 13.95 *(978-1-4441-1541-3(3))* Hodder Education Group GBR. Dist: Trans-Atlantic Pubns., Inc.

Dobosz, Ann Marie. The Perfectionism Workbook for Teens: Activities to Help You Reduce Anxiety & Get Things Done. 2016. (ENG.). 200p. (YA). (gr. 6-12). pap. 16.95 *(978-1-62625-454-1(0))* New Harbinger Pubns.

Donovan, Sandy. Keep Your Cool! What You Should Know about Stress. 2009. pap. 52.95 *(978-0-7613-4685-2(6))* Lerner Publishing Group.

Dorling Kindersley Publishing Staff. How to Be a Genius. 2013. (ENG.). 192p. (J). (gr. 5-12). pap. 12.99 *(978-1-4654-1424-3(X),* DK Children) Dorling Kindersley Publishing, Inc.

Doudna, Kelly. We Have the Nerve, Now Let's Observe!, 1 vol. 2007. (Science Made Simple Ser.). (ENG., Illus.). 24p. (J). (gr. k-3). lib. bdg. 24.21 *(978-1-59928-624-2(6),* SandCastle) ABDO Publishing Co.

Dwyer, Helen, ed. History of Psychology. 2011. (CC: Psychology Ser.). (Illus.). 112p. (gr. 6-12). lib. bdg. 42.80 *(978-1-936333-15-8(5))* Brown Bear Bks.

P
Q
R

Dyer, Wayne. I Am: Why Two Little Words Mean So Much. 2012. (ENG., Illus.). 32p. 15.99 *(978-1-4019-3975-5(9))* Hay Hse., Inc.

Eason, Sarah. Don't Play Dirty, Gertie: Be Fair. 2013. (You Choose Ser.). 32p. (J). lib. bdg. 23.94 *(978-0-7660-4307-7(X)*, Enslow Elementary) Enslow Pubs., Inc.

Eisenpreis, Bettijane. Coping: A Young Woman's Guide to Breast Cancer Prevention. rev. ed. 2005. (Coping Ser.). (Illus.). 192p. (YA). (gr. 7-12). lib. bdg. 34.60 *(978-0-8239-2967-2(1)*, COBRCA) Rosen Publishing Group, Inc., The.

Engdahl, Sylvia, ed. Dissociative Disorders. 2012. (Perspectives on Diseases & Disorders Ser.). (ENG., Illus.). 144p. (gr. 10-12). lib. bdg. 38.95 *(978-0-7377-6353-9(1)*, Greenhaven Pr., Inc.) Cengage Gale.

Esherick, Joan. Balancing Act: A Teen's Guide to Managing Stress. 2006. (Science of Health Ser.). (Illus.). 128p. (YA). 24.95 *(978-1-59084-853-1(5))* Mason Crest.

—Criminal Psychology & Personality Profiling. Noziglia, Carla Miller & Siegel, Jay A., eds. 2013. (Solving Crimes with Science: Forensics Ser.: 12). (Illus.). 112p. (J). (gr. 7-18). 22.95 *(978-1-4222-2863-0(0))* Mason Crest.

Espeland, Pamela. Knowing Me, Knowing You: The I-Sight Way to Understand Yourself & Others. 2004. (Illus.). 128p. (YA). (gr. 8-12). pap. 13.95 *(978-1-57542-090-5(2))* Free Spirit Publishing, Inc.

Gainer, Cindy. I'm Like You, You're Like Me: A Book about Understanding & Appreciating Each Other. Sakamoto, Miki, illus. 2011. (ENG.). 48p. (J). (gr. -1-3). 14.99 *(978-1-57542-383-8(9))* Free Spirit Publishing, Inc.

Gates, Mariam. Meditate with Me: A Step-By-Step Mindfulness Journey. Sumaite, Margarita, illus. 2017. (ENG.). 40p. (J). (gr. -1-3). 17.99 ***(978-0-399-18661-5(1)***, Dial Bks) Penguin Young Readers Group.

Glimm, Adele. Gene Hunter: The Story of Neuropsychologist Nancy Wexler. 2005. (Women's Adventures in Science Ser.). (ENG., Illus.). 128p. (YA). (gr. 5-9). lib. bdg. 31.50 *(978-0-531-16778-6(X))* Scholastic Library Publishing.

Globe-Fearon Staff. Changes. (YA). pap. 12.95 *(978-0-8359-0922-8(0))* Globe Fearon Educational Publishing.

Grant, Jim & Grant, Caleb. What Gritty Kids Do When No One Is Looking. Regan, Dana, illus. 2016. (ENG.). pap. 10.95 *(978-1-63133-078-0(0))* Staff Development for Educators.

Graves, Sue. But What If? Guicciardini, Desideria, illus. 2013. (Our Emotions & Behavior Ser.). (ENG.). 32p. (J). (gr. -1-3). 12.99 *(978-1-57542-444-6(4))* Free Spirit Publishing, Inc.

Gray, T. L. Keezy's 10 Awesome Rules for Teenaged Dating! 2011. (ENG., Illus.). 95p. pap. 12.00 *(978-0-9834332-4-8(0))* Vabella Publishing.

Grossman, Laurie, et al. Master of Mindfulness: How to Be Your Own Superhero in Times of Stress. 2016. (ENG., Illus.). 72p. (J). (gr. k-5). pap. 14.95 *(978-1-62625-464-0(8))* New Harbinger Pubns.

Hawn Foundation Staff, contrib. by. Brain-Focused Strategies for Learning-And Living. 2011. (MindUP Curriculum Ser.). (ENG., Illus.). 160p. (gr. 3-5). pap. 24.99 *(978-0-545-26713-7(7)*, Teaching Resources) Scholastic, Inc.

—The Mindup Curriculum - Grades Prek-2: Brain-Focused Strategies for Learning-And Living. 2011. (MindUP Curriculum Ser.). (ENG., Illus.). 160p. (gr. -1-2). pap. 24.99 *(978-0-545-26712-0(9)*, Teaching Resources) Scholastic, Inc.

—The Mindup Curriculum, Grades 6-8: Brain-Focused Strategies for Learning-And Living. 2011. (MindUP Curriculum Ser.). (ENG., Illus.). 160p. (gr. 6-8). pap. 24.99 *(978-0-545-26714-4(5)*, Teaching Resources) Scholastic, Inc.

Heinrichs, Ann. Forensic Psychologist. 2009. (21st Century Skills Library: Cool Science Careers Ser.). (ENG.). 32p. (gr. 4-8). lib. bdg. 28.50 *(978-1-60279-309-5(3)*, 200205) Cherry Lake Publishing.

Higgins, Melissa. Celebrating Differences. 2012. (Celebrating Differences Ser.). (ENG.). 24p. (gr. k-1). pap. 166.80 *(978-1-4296-8325-8(2)*, Pebble Plus) Capstone Press of Coughlan Cos.

—Teen Self-Injury, 1 vol. 2014. (Essential Issues Set 4 Ser.). (ENG.). 112p. (J). (gr. 6-12). lib. bdg. 35.64 *(978-1-62403-423-7(3)*, Essential Library) ABDO Publishing Co.

—We All Look Different. 2012. (Celebrating Differences Ser.). (ENG.). 24p. (gr. k-1). pap. 41.70 *(978-1-4296-8323-4(6)*, Pebble Plus) Capstone Press of Coughlan Cos.

Hipp, Earl. Fighting Invisible Tigers: Stress Management for Teens. 3rd rev. ed. 2008. (ENG., Illus.). 160p. (YA). (gr. 6-13). pap. 14.99 *(978-1-57542-282-4(4))* Free Spirit Publishing, Inc.

Hirschmann, Kris. Understanding Motivation. 2017. (ENG.). 80p. (YA). (gr. 5-12). ***(978-1-68282-275-3(3))*** ReferencePoint Pr., Inc.

Hollander, Barbara. What Are Wants & Needs? 2016. (Let's Find Out! Ser.). (ENG.). 32p. (J). (gr. 3-2). lib. bdg. 24.45 *(978-1-68048-407-6(9))* Rosen Publishing Group, Inc., The.

Hoog, Mark. Leadership Journal. 2011. (ENG.). 62p. (J). pap. 9.99 *(978-0-9770391-5-9(3)*, Growing Field) Growing Field Bks.

Hord, Colleen. Need It or Want It? 2011. (ENG., Illus.). 24p. (gr. k-2). pap. 8.95 *(978-1-61741-995-9(8))* Rourke Educational Media.

Huebner, Dawn. What to Do When You Grumble Too Much: A Kid's Guide to Overcoming Negativity. Matthews, Bonnie, illus. 2006. ("What to Do" Guides for Kids Ser.). 88p. (J). (gr. 4-7). per. 15.95 *(978-1-59147-450-0(7)*, Magination Pr.) American Psychological Assn.

Hugel, Bob. I Did It Without Thinking: True Stories about Impulsive Decisions That Changed Lives. 2008. (Scholastic Choices Ser.). (ENG.). 112p. (J). pap. 8.95 *(978-0-531-20526-6(6)*, Watts, Franklin); (Illus.). (gr. 3-7). 27.00 *(978-0-531-13868-7(2)*, Children's Pr.) Scholastic Library Publishing.

Hyde, Natalie. LGBTQ Rights. 2017. 48p. (J). ***(978-0-7787-3942-5(2))*** Crabtree Publishing Co.

Hyman, Bruce M. & Pedrick, Cherry. Obsessive-Compulsive Disorder. 2003. (Twenty-First Century Medical Library). 96p. (gr. 7-18). lib. bdg. 26.90 *(978-0-7613-2758-5(4)*, Twenty-First Century Bks.) Lerner Publishing Group.

Jarvis, Matt Russell, et al. Angles on Psychology. 2nd rev. ed. 2004. (ENG., Illus.). 300p. (YA). pap. 35.75 *(978-0-7487-8032-7(7))* Nelson Thornes Ltd. GBR. Dist: Oxford Univ. Pr., Inc.

Johnson, Spencer. Quién Se Ha Llevado Mi Queso? Para Niños: Una Forma Sorprendente de Cambiar y Ganar ! 2004. (SPA., Illus.). 62p. (J). 19.95 *(978-84-7953-553-7(9))* Ediciones Urano S. A. ESP. Dist: Spanish Pubs., LLC.

Jones, Grace. My Choices. 2017. 24p. (J). ***(978-0-7787-3701-8(2))*** Crabtree Publishing Co.

Kahn, Ada P. & Doctor, Ronald M. Phobias. 2004. (Life Balance Ser.). (ENG., Illus.). 80p. (YA). (gr. 5-8). pap. 6.95 *(978-0-531-15575-2(7)*, Watts, Franklin) Scholastic Library Publishing.

Kaiser, Carducci, et al. Shyness: The Ultimate Teen Guide. 2015. (It Happened to Me Ser.: 44). (ENG., Illus.). 298p. (J). 45.00 *(978-1-4422-3046-0(0))* Rowman & Littlefield Publishers, Inc.

Kalman, Bobbie. ¿Dónde Está? 2008. (SPA.). 24p. (J). pap. *(978-0-7787-8738-9(9))* Crabtree Publishing Co.

—¿Donde Esta? 2008.Tr. of Where Is It? (SPA.). 24p. (J). lib. bdg. *(978-0-7787-8729-7(X))* Crabtree Publishing Co.

—I Can Do It! 2010. (ENG., Illus.). 16p. (J). (gr. k-2). *(978-0-7787-9423-3(7))*; pap. *(978-0-7787-9467-7(9))* Crabtree Publishing Co.

—Today Is a Great Day! 2010. (My World Ser.). (ENG.). 16p. (J). (gr. k-3). *(978-0-7787-9506-3(3))*; pap. *(978-0-7787-9531-5(4))* Crabtree Publishing Co.

—Where Is It? 2007. (Looking at Nature Ser.). (ENG., Illus.). 24p. (J). (gr. -1-2). pap. *(978-0-7787-3341-6(6))* Crabtree Publishing Co.

Kasschau, Richard A., et al. Understanding Psychology. 2006. (Understanding Psychology Ser.). (ENG., Illus.). 704p. (gr. 9-12). stu. ed. 119.28 *(978-0-07-874517-1(9)*, 0078745179) McGraw-Hill Higher Education.

Krasner, Barbara. Returning Soldiers & PTSD. 2017. (J). pap. ***(978-1-5345-0087-7(1))*** Greenhaven Publishing LLC.

La Bella, Laura. Curiosity. 2013. (7 Character Strengths of Highly Successful Students Ser.). 64p. (J). (gr. 5-8). pap. 77.70 *(978-1-4488-9556-4(1))*; (Illus.). 31.95 *(978-1-4488-9542-7(1))*; (Illus.). pap. 12.95 *(978-1-4488-9555-7(3))* Rosen Publishing Group, Inc., The.

Lambillion, Paul. Staying Cool. 2004. (Illus.). 196p. pap. 13.95 *(978-0-7171-3598-1(5))* M.H. Gill & Co. U. C. IRL. Dist: Hushion Hse. Publishing, Ltd.

Langwith, Jacqueline. Mood Disorders. 2009. (Perspectives on Diseases & Disorders Ser.). (ENG., Illus.). 144p. (gr. 10-12). lib. bdg. 44.30 *(978-0-7377-4380-7(8)*, LML02109-245385, Greenhaven Pr., Inc.) Cengage Gale.

Lewis, Anthony, illus. Carrots or Peas? 2008. (Pick & Choose Ser.). (ENG.). 12p. (J). (gr. -1). bds. *(978-1-84643-242-2(1))* Child's Play International Ltd.

—Teddy or Train? 2008. (Pick & Choose Ser.). (ENG.). 12p. (J). (gr. -1). bds. *(978-1-84643-241-5(3))* Child's Play International Ltd.

—Wind or Rain? 2008. (Pick & Choose Ser.). (ENG.). 12p. (J). (gr. -1). bds. *(978-1-84643-240-8(5))* Child's Play International Ltd.

Lynch, Jason. Everyone Has Hope. Hale, Cole, illus. 2011. (J). *(978-0-938467-09-0(3))* Headline Bks., Inc.

Mabry-Gordon, Sherri. Are You at Risk for Public Shaming? 2016. (Got Issues? Ser.). (ENG., Illus.). 112p. (J). (gr. 7-8). lib. bdg. 37.27 *(978-0-7660-7136-0(7))* Enslow Pubs., Inc.

MacAllister, Carol L. The Wisdom Tree & the Red Swing: Thinking Outside the Box for Preteens. 2009. (Wisdom Tree & the Red Swing Ser.). (ENG.). 116p. (J). pap. 3.99 *(978-0-9815818-4-2(6)*, 9780981581842) Take Charge Bks.

Marsico, Katie. Depression & Stress. 2013. 80p. (YA). (gr. 7-12). 34.21 *(978-1-60870-851-2(9))* Cavendish Square Publishing.

McCraty, Rollin, et al. Transforming Stress for Teens: Skills to Help Teens Stay Cool under Pressure. 2016. (Instant Help Solutions Ser.). (ENG., Illus.). 216p. (YA). (gr. 6-12). pap. 16.95 *(978-1-62625-194-6(0))* New Harbinger Pubns.

McGraw-Hill Education Staff. Understanding Psychology Reading Essentials & Study Guide Student Workbook. 2nd ed. 2003. (Understanding Psychology Ser.). (ENG., Illus.). 227p. (gr. 9-12). stu. ed., per. 18.28 *(978-0-07-860607-6(1)*, 0078606071) McGraw-Hill Higher Education.

Meiners, Cheri J. Be Positive! Allen, Elizabeth, illus. 2013. (Being the Best Me Ser.). (ENG.). 40p. (J). (gr. -1-3). 14.99 *(978-1-57542-452-1(5))*; pap. 11.99 *(978-1-57542-441-5(X))* Free Spirit Publishing, Inc.

—Bounce Back! Allen, Elizabeth, illus. 2014. (Being the Best Me Ser.). (ENG.). 40p. (J). (gr. -1-3). 14.99 *(978-1-57542-457-6(6))* Free Spirit Publishing, Inc.

Mental X 2003. (Illus.). 32p. (YA). pap. 5.50 *(978-0-9745066-8-5(0))* Sports In Mind.

Meredith, Susan & Merideth, Susan. Left or Right ? 2010. (ENG., Illus.). 24p. (gr. k-2). pap. 8.95 *(978-1-61590-529-4(4))* Rourke Educational Media.

Mihaly, Mary E. Getting Your Own Way: A Guide to Growing up Assertively. 2014. (ENG.). 176p. pap. 12.95 *(978-1-59077-306-2(3))* Evans, M. & Co., Inc.

Miles, Lisa & Chown, Xanna Eve. How to Survive Being Dumped. 2013. (Girl Talk Ser.). (Illus.). 48p. (J). (ENG.). (gr. 5-8). pap. 11.75 *(978-1-4777-0716-6(6)*, Rosen Classroom); (gr. 5-8). pap. 70.50 *(978-1-4777-0717-3(4)*, Rosen Reference); (ENG., (gr. 8-12). lib. bdg. 29.25 *(978-1-4777-0704-3(2)*, Rosen Reference) Rosen Publishing Group, Inc., The.

Moe, Barbara. Coping with Rejection. 2009. (Coping Ser.). 192p. (gr. 7-12). 63.90 *(978-1-61512-010-9(6))* Rosen Publishing Group, Inc., The.

—Understanding Negative Body Image. 2009. (Teen Eating Disorder Prevention Book Ser.). 192p. (gr. 7-12). 63.90 *(978-1-61511-242-5(1))* Rosen Publishing Group, Inc., The.

Morgan, Nicola. Blame My Brain. 2007. (Illus.). 192p. (YA). pap. *(978-1-4063-1116-7(2))* Walker Bks., Ltd.

Moss, Wendy. School Made Easier: A Kid's Guide to Study Strategies & Anxiety-Busting Tools. 2014. (Illus.). vii, 128p. pap. *(978-1-4338-1336-8(X)*, Magination Pr.) American Psychological Assn.

Moss, Wendy L. & DeLuca-Acconi, Robin. School Made Easier: A Kid's Guide to Study Strategies & Anxiety-Busting Tools. 2013. (Illus.). 128p. 14.95 *(978-1-4338-1335-1(1)*, Magination Pr.) American Psychological Assn.

Mr. Blue. From Underdog to Wonderdog: Top Ten Tricks to Lead Your Pack. 2012. (ENG., Illus.). 52p. (J). (gr. 1-5). pap. 14.95 *(978-1-936354-26-9(8)*, Tremendous Leadership) Tremendous Life Bks.

Mulhall, Jill. Young Adult Literature: The Worlds Inside Us (Grade 6) 2016. (TIME for KIDS(r) Nonfiction Readers Ser.). (Illus.). 48p. (J). (gr. 6-6). pap. 9.99 *(978-1-4938-3598-0(X))* Teacher Created Materials, Inc.

Naik, Anita. Coping with Loss: The Life Changes Handbook. 2009. (Really Useful Handbooks Ser.). (ENG.). 48p. (J). (gr. 5-11). pap. *(978-0-7787-4404-7(3))* Crabtree Publishing Co.

Naik, Anita & Cronin, Ali. Coping with Loss: The Life Changes Handbook. 2009. (Really Useful Handbooks Ser.). (ENG.). 48p. (J). (gr. 5-11). lib. bdg. *(978-0-7787-4391-0(8))* Crabtree Publishing Co.

—Read the Signals: The Body Language Handbook. 2009. (Really Useful Handbooks Ser.). (ENG., Illus.). 48p. (J). (gr. 5-11). pap. *(978-0-7787-4401-6(9))* Crabtree Publishing Co.

Nance, Andrew Jordan. Puppy Mind. Durk, Jim, illus. 2016. (ENG.). (J). (gr. -1-2). 16.95 *(978-1-941529-44-7(5)*, Plum Blossom Bks.) Parallax Pr.

Navarre, Sam. Masculinity, Bullying, & Aggression: A Guy's Guide. 2011. (Young Man's Guide to Contemporary Issues Ser.). (ENG.). 104p. (J). (gr. 9-12). lib. bdg. 34.60 *(978-1-4488-5525-4(X))* Rosen Publishing Group, Inc., The.

Nicolson, Cynthia Pratt. Totally Human: Why We Look & Act the Way We Do. Eastman, Dianne, illus. 2011. (ENG.). 40p. (J). (gr. 4-8). 16.95 *(978-1-55453-569-9(7))* Kids Can Pr., Ltd. CAN. Dist: Hachette Bk. Group.

O'Connor, Frances. Frequently Asked Questions about Academic Anxiety. 2007. (FAQ: Teen Life Ser.). (Illus.). 64p. (YA). (gr. 7-12). lib. bdg. 31.95 *(978-1-4042-1937-3(4))* Rosen Publishing Group, Inc., The.

Ogden, Charlie. Identity & Gender. 2017. (Illus.). 32p. (J). ***(978-0-7787-3268-6(1))*** Crabtree Publishing Co.

Orr, Tamra B. Surprise. 2016. (21st Century Basic Skills Library: Feelings Ser.). (ENG., Illus.). 24p. (J). (gr. k-3). pap. 12.79 *(978-1-63471-246-0(3)*, 208273, Blackbirch Pr., Inc.) Cherry Lake Publishing.

Parker, Vic. Inspiring Others, 1 vol. 2012. (Kids Making a Difference Ser.). (ENG.). 48p. (gr. 3-5). lib. bdg. 32.65 *(978-1-4329-6502-0(6)*, NA-h) Heinemann-Raintree.

—Making Choices. 2016. (Exploring Citizenship Ser.). (ENG.). 32p. pap. 8.29 *(978-1-4846-4000-5(4)*, Heinemann First Library) Heinemann-Raintree.

—Tomar Decisiones, 1 vol. 2010. (Explorar el Civismo Ser.). (SPA & ENG.). 32p. (gr. 1-3). 27.32 *(978-1-4329-4464-3(9))*; pap. 8.29 *(978-1-4329-4472-8(X))* Heinemann-Raintree.

Parks, Peggy J. Anxiety Disorders. 2011. 96p. (YA). lib. bdg. *(978-1-60152-137-8(5))* ReferencePoint Pr., Inc.

Parks, Peggy J. Teens & PTSD. 2017. (ENG.). 80p. (J). (gr. 5-12). ***(978-1-68282-130-5(7))*** ReferencePoint Pr., Inc.

Pessin-Whedbee, Brook. Who Are You? The Kid's Guide to Gender & Identity. Bardoff, Naomi, illus. 2016. (ENG.). 40p. (J). 18.95 *(978-1-78592-728-7(0)*, 8673) Kingsley, Jessica Pubs. GBR. Dist: Macmillan Distribution Ltd.

Peters, Elisa & Killcoyne, Hope Lourie, eds. Psychology, 01 vols., 1. 2016. (Britannica Guide to the Social Sciences Ser.). (ENG.). 128p. (J). 35.25 *(978-1-62275-552-3(9)*, Britannica Educational Publishing) Rosen Publishing Group, Inc., The.

Poole, H. W. Post-Traumatic Stress Disorder, Vol. 13. Walters, Anne S., ed. 2015. (Mental Illnesses & Disorders: Awareness & Understanding Ser.). (Illus.). 48p. (J). (gr. 5). 20.95 *(978-1-4222-3374-0(X))* Mason Crest.

Popkin, Michael H. & Hendrickson, Peggy. Teens in Action: A Teen's Guide for Surviving & Thriving in the 21st Century. 2013. (ENG., Illus.). 216p. (J). (gr. 7-12). pap. 14.95 *(978-1-59723-273-9(4))* Active Parenting Pubs.

Primrose, Alison. Non-Verbal Reasoning, Age 9-11. 2016. 64p. pap., wbk. ed. 14.95 *(978-1-4718-4935-0(X))* Hodder Education Group GBR. Dist: Trans-Atlantic Pubns., Inc.

Psychologie. (Duden-Schuelerduden Ser.). (GER.). 466p. (YA). *(978-3-411-05252-3(X))* Bibliographisches Institut & F. A. Brockhaus AG DEU. Dist: International Bk. Import Service, Inc.

Raatma, Lucia. Making Smart Choices. 2013. (True Book(tm), a — Guides to Life Ser.). (ENG., Illus.). 48p. (J). lib. bdg. 31.00 *(978-0-531-25524-7(7))*; pap. 6.95 *(978-0-531-23924-7(1))* Scholastic Library Publishing.

Rauf, Don, et al. Are You Depressed? 2015. (Got Issues? Ser.). (ENG., Illus.). 128p. (J). (gr. 7-7). lib. bdg. 37.27 *(978-0-7660-6981-7(8))* Enslow Pubs., Inc.

Reade, Clara. Intuition: The Sixth Sense, 1 vol., 1. 2014. (Your Five Senses & Your Sixth Sense Ser.). (ENG.). 24p. (J). (gr. k-2). 23.60 *(978-1-4777-2858-1(9)*, PowerKids Pr.) Rosen Publishing Group, Inc., The.

Reber, Deborah. Doable: The Girls' Guide to Accomplishing Just about Anything. 2015. (ENG., Illus.). 208p. (YA). (gr. 7). pap. 12.99 *(978-1-58270-466-1(X)*, Simon Pulse) Simon Pulse.

Rebman, Renée C. Addictions & Risky Behaviors: Cutting, Bingeing, Snorting, & Other Dangers. 2006. (Issues in Focus Today Ser.). (Illus.). 104p. (J). (gr. 6-12). lib. bdg. 33.27 *(978-0-7660-2165-5(3))* Enslow Pubs., Inc.

Rebman, Renee C. Are You Doing Risky Things? Cutting, Bingeing, Snorting, & Other Dangers. 2014. (Got Issues? Ser.). (Illus.). 112p. (YA). (gr. 6-12). lib. bdg. 33.27 *(978-0-7660-5996-2(0))* Enslow Pubs., Inc.

Reynolds, Shirley & Parkinson, Monika. Am I Depressed & What Can I Do about It? A CBT Self-Help Guide for Teenagers Experiencing Low Mood & Depression. 2015. (ENG., Illus.). 384p. (gr. 16-17). pap. 15.99 ***(978-1-4721-1453-2(1)***, Constable) Little, Brown Book Group Ltd. GBR. Dist: Hachette Bk. Group.

Rissman, Rebecca. Role Models, 1 vol. 2011. (Families Ser.). (ENG., Illus.). 24p. (gr. -1-1). 22.65 *(978-1-4329-4660-9(9))*; pap. 6.29 *(978-1-4329-4668-5(4))* Heinemann-Raintree. (Acorn).

Robinson, Matthew. Making Smart Choices about Relationships. 2009. (Making Smart Choices Ser.). 48p. (gr. 5-5). 53.00 *(978-1-61514-340-5(8)*, Rosen Reference) Rosen Publishing Group, Inc., The.

Rodi, Robert & Ross, Laura. Being Transgender, Vol. 10. Jennings, Kevin, ed. 2016. (Living Proud! Growing up LGBTQ Ser.). (Illus.). 64p. (J). (gr. 7). 23.95 *(978-1-4222-3502-7(5))* Mason Crest.

Roegiers, Maud. Take the Time: Mindfulness for Kids. 2010. (Illus.). 32p. (J). (gr. -1-3). 14.95 *(978-1-4338-0794-7(7))*; pap. 9.95 *(978-1-4338-0796-1(3))* American Psychological Assn. (Magination Pr.).

Roland, James. Careers in Mental Health. 2017. (ENG.). 80p. (J). (gr. 5-12). ***(978-1-68282-108-4(0))*** ReferencePoint Pr., Inc.

Rooney, Anne. The History of Psychology. 2016. (History of the Humanities & Social Sciences Ser.). (ENG.). 208p. (J). (gr. 7-7). lib. bdg. 46.10 *(978-1-4994-6404-7(5))* Rosen Publishing Group, Inc., The.

Rosen, Marvin. Demystifying Dreams. 2004. 64p. (YA). pap. 9.95 *(978-0-595-30290-1(4))* iUniverse, Inc.

Russell, Julia, et al. Cambridge International AS & a Level Psychology Coursebook. 2016. (ENG.). 368p. pap. 60.94 *(978-1-316-60569-1(8))* Cambridge Univ. Pr.

Saltzman, Amy. A Still Quiet Place for Teens: Simple Mindfulness Practices to Ease Stress & Difficult Emotions. 2016. (ENG.). 168p. (YA). (gr. 6-12). pap. 16.95 *(978-1-62625-376-6(5))* New Harbinger Pubns.

Sargent, Brian. Losing It: The Meaning of Loss. 2014. (ENG., Illus.). 28p. (J). pap. 9.50 *(978-1-107-68191-0(X))* Cambridge Univ. Pr.

Schab, Lisa M. The Self-Esteem Workbook for Teens: Activities to Help You Build Confidence & Achieve Your Goals. 2013. (ENG.). 200p. (YA). (gr. 6-12). pap. 15.95 *(978-1-60882-582-0(5)*, Instant Help Books) New Harbinger Pubns.

Sedley, Ben. Stuff That Sucks: A Teen's Guide to Accepting What You Can't Change & Committing to What You Can. 2017. (Instant Help Solutions Ser.). (ENG., Illus.). 96p. (YA). (gr. 6-12). pap. 12.95 *(978-1-62625-865-5(1))* New Harbinger Pubns.

Shoesmith, Geoffrey. Psychology: A Complete GCSE Course. 2003. (ENG., Illus.). 198p. (C). pap. 42.50 *(978-0-7188-3002-1(4))* Lutherworth Pr., The GBR. Dist: Casemate Academic.

Shone, Rob & Spender, Nick. Solving Crimes Through Criminal Profiling. 2008. (Graphic Forensic Science Ser.). (ENG., Illus.). 48p. (YA). 58.50 *(978-1-4488-1666-8(1)*, Rosen Reference) Rosen Publishing Group, Inc., The.

Silverman, Robin Landew. Reaching Your Goals. 2004. (Life Balance Ser.). (ENG.). 80p. (J). 20.50 *(978-0-531-12342-3(1)*, Watts, Franklin) Scholastic Library Publishing.

Slavens, Elaine. Fighting: Without Coming to Blows, 1 vol. Murray, Steven, illus. 2nd ed. 2010. (Lorimer Deal with It Ser.). (ENG.). 32p. (J). (gr. 4-6). 24.95 *(978-1-55277-501-1(1)*, 9781552775011) Lorimer, James & Co., Ltd., Pubs. CAN. Dist: Casemate Pubs. & Bk. Distributors, LLC.

Sokol, Leslie & Fox, Marci G. The Think Confident, Be Confident Workbook for Teens: Activities to Create Unshakable Self-Confidence & Reach Your Goals. 2016. (ENG.). 224p. (YA). (gr. 6-12). pap. 16.95 *(978-1-62625-483-1(4))* New Harbinger Pubns.

Spalding, Maddie. 12 Tips for Managing Stress & Anxiety. 2017. 32p. (J). *(978-1-62143-508-2(3))* Pr. Room Editions LLC.

Spilsbury, Louise. Family & Friends. 2012. (Healthy & Happy Ser.). (Illus.). 32p. (J). (gr. 1-4). lib. bdg. 26.50 *(978-1-4488-5275-8(7))* Rosen Publishing Group, Inc., The.

Staley, Erin. Defeating Stress & Anxiety, 01 vols., 1. 2016. (Effective Survival Strategies Ser.). (ENG., Illus.). 64p. (J). 32.95 *(978-1-4994-6195-4(X)*, Rosen Young Adult) Rosen Publishing Group, Inc., The.

Staniford, Linda. Possessions. 2015. (Wants vs Needs Ser.). (ENG.). 24p. (gr. k-2). 23.32 *(978-1-4846-0945-3(X)*, Heinemann Read & Learn) Heinemann-Raintree.

Statt, David A. A Student's Dictionary of Psychology. 2004. (ENG., Illus.). 176p. (C). per. 23.95 *(978-1-84169-342-2(1)*, RU37524, Psychology Press) Taylor & Francis Group GBR. Dist: Taylor & Francis Group.

Streissguth, Thomas. The Truth about Stress Management. 2011. (Truth about Ser.). (Illus.). 176p. (J). (gr. 9). 35.00 *(978-0-8160-7647-5(2))* Facts On File, Inc.

Stuckey, Rachel. Sexual Orientation & Gender Identity. 2015. (ENG., Illus.). 48p. (J). *(978-0-7787-2203-8(1))* Crabtree Publishing Co.

Subbiah, Seetha. Did You Hear That?: Help for Children Who Hear Voices. 2016. (ENG., Illus.). 120p. *(978-981-3144-14-9(9))* World Scientific Publishing Co. Pte Ltd.

Testa, Rylan Jay, et al. The Gender Quest Workbook for Teens. 2015. (ENG.). 168p. (YA). (gr. 5-12). pap. 17.95 *(978-1-62625-297-4(1))* New Harbinger Pubns.

Treays, Rebecca. Understanding Your Brain - Internet Linked. Fox, Christyan, illus. rev. ed. 2004. (Science for Beginners Ser.). 32p. (J). pap. 7.95 *(978-0-7945-0853-1(7)*, Usborne) EDC Publishing.

—Understanding Your Senses - Internet Linked. Fox, Christyan, illus. rev. ed. 2004. (Science for Beginners Ser.). 32p. (J). pap. 7.95 *(978-0-7945-0852-4(9)*, Usborne) EDC Publishing.

UFlipp. You & Your Military Hero: Building Positive Thinking Skills During Your Hero's Deployment. 2009. 72p. (J). pap. 19.95 *(978-1-59298-268-4(9))* Beaver's Pond Pr., Inc.

Uhl, Xina M. Strengthening Collaborative Project Skills. 2017. (Skills for Success Ser.). 64p. (gr. 12-12). 34.45 ***(978-1-5081-7566-7(7)***, Rosen Young Adult) Rosen Publishing Group, Inc., The.

Verdick, Elizabeth. Bye-Bye Time. Heinlen, Marieka, illus. 2008. (Toddler Tools Ser.). (ENG.). 24p. (J). (gr. k — 1). bds. 7.95 *(978-1-57542-299-2(9))* Free Spirit Publishing, Inc.

Verdick, Elizabeth. Bye-Bye Time/Momento de la Despedida. Heinlen, Marieka, illus. 2017. (Toddler Tools Ser.). (ENG, SPA & MUL.). 24p. (J). bds. 7.95 ***(978-1-63198-151-7(X))*** Free Spirit Publishing, Inc.

Vincent, Denis & Francis, Peter. Non-Verbal Reasoning, Age 8-10. 2016. 56p. pap., wbk. ed. 14.95 *(978-1-4718-4934-3(1))* Hodder Education Group GBR. Dist: Trans-Atlantic Pubns., Inc.

Way, Jennifer & Van Duyne, Sara. What You Can Do about Stress & Anxiety. 2015. (Contemporary Diseases &

Disorders Ser.). (ENG., Illus.). 128p. (J). (gr. 7-7). 37.27 (978-0-7660-7042-4(5)) Enslow Pubs., Inc.

Weeks, Marcus & Dorling Kindersley Publishing Staff. Heads up Psychology. 2014. (Heads Up Ser.). (ENG.). 160p. (YA). (gr. 8-12). 15.99 (978-1-4654-1993-4(4), DK Children) Dorling Kindersley Publishing, Inc.

Weiss, S. I. Coping with the Beauty Myth: A Guide for Real Girls. 2009. (Coping Ser.). 192p. (gr. 7-12). 63.90 (978-1-61512-014-7(9)) Rosen Publishing Group, Inc., The.

Welbourn, Shannon. Step Forward with Empathy. 2016. (Step Forward! Ser.). (ENG., Illus.). 24p. (J). (gr. 2-5). (978-0-7787-2786-6(6)) Crabtree Publishing Co.

—Step Forward with Grit. 2016. (Step Forward! Ser.). (ENG., Illus.). 24p. (J). (gr. 2-5). (978-0-7787-2767-5(X)) Crabtree Publishing Co.

Wilson, Nolan. The Teen's Guide to Getting Ahead: How to Succeed in High School & Beyond. 2008. 192p. (YA). (gr. 8-11). pap. 15.95 (978-1-897073-92-6(5)) Lobster Pr. CAN. Dist: Orca Bk. Pubs. USA.

Wooster, Patricia. Ignite Your Spark: Discovering Who You Are from the Inside Out. 2017. (ENG., Illus.). 224p. (J). (gr. 7). pap. 12.99 (978-1-58270-564-4(X)) Simon Pulse/Beyond Words.

Wroble, Lisa A. Dealing with Stress. 2011. (Life—a How-To Guide Ser.). (Illus.). 128p. (J). lib. bdg. 33.27 (978-0-7660-3439-6(9)) Enslow Pubs., Inc.

Zelinger, Laurie & Zelinger, Jordan. Please Explain Anxiety to Me! Simple Biology & Solutions for Children & Parents. Sabella, Elisa, illus. 2010. 38p. 32.95 (978-1-61599-051-1(8)); 40p. pap. 21.95 (978-1-61599-029-0(1)) Loving Healing Pr., Inc.

Zelinger, Laurie E. & Zelinger, Jordan. Please Explain "Anxiety" to Me! Simple Biology & Solutions for Children & Parents. Sabella, Elisa, illus. 2014. (J). pap. 15.95 (978-1-61599-216-4(2)) Loving Healing Pr., Inc.

PSYCHOLOGY, ABNORMAL

see Psychology, Pathological

PSYCHOLOGY, APPLIED

see also Counseling; Interpersonal Relations; Security (Psychology)

Hanson-Harding, Alexandra. Step-By-Step Guide to Win-Win Negotiating Every Day. 2014. (Winning at Work Readiness Ser.). 64p. (YA). (gr. 9-12). 32.95 (978-1-4777-7790-9(3)) Rosen Publishing Group, Inc., The.

McIntyre, Thomas. The Survival Guide for Kids with Behavior Challenges: How to Make Good Choices & Stay Out of Trouble. rev. ed. 2013. (ENG., Illus.). 176p. (J). (gr. 4-9). pap. 14.99 (978-1-57542-449-1(5)) Free Spirit Publishing, Inc.

PSYCHOLOGY, CHILD

see Child Psychology

PSYCHOLOGY, COMPARATIVE

see also Animal Intelligence; Animal Psychology; Animals—Habits and Behavior

Canetti, Yanitzia. Agarrarse: Ellos lo hacen bien nosotros Tambien. 2010. (SPA.). 24p. (J). 5.99 (978-1-59835-232-0(6), BrickHouse Education) Cambridge BrickHouse, Inc.

—What They Can Do, We Can Too! Grab. 2010. pap. 5.99 (978-1-59835-231-3(8), BrickHouse Education) Cambridge BrickHouse, Inc.

PSYCHOLOGY—DICTIONARIES

Statt, David A. A Student's Dictionary of Psychology. 2004. (ENG., Illus.). 176p. (C). per. 23.95 (978-1-84169-342-2(1), RU37524, Psychology Press) Taylor & Francis Group GBR. Dist: Taylor & Francis Group.

PSYCHOLOGY, EDUCATIONAL

see Educational Psychology

PSYCHOLOGY, INDUSTRIAL

see Psychology, Applied

PSYCHOLOGY, MEDICAL

see Psychology, Pathological

PSYCHOLOGY, PATHOLOGICAL

see also Eating Disorders; Mental Illness; Psychiatry; Psychoanalysis

Bell, Samantha. I Talk in My Sleep. 2014. (Tell Me Why Library). (ENG., Illus.). 24p. (J). (gr. 2-5). 25.64 (978-1-63188-005-6(5), 205427) Cherry Lake Publishing.

Berry, Joy. Good Answers to Tough Questions Trauma. Bartholomew, illus. 2010. (Good Answers to Tough Questions Ser.). (ENG.). 48p. (J). (gr. k-7). pap. 7.99 (978-1-60577-507-4(X)) Berry, Joy Enterprises.

Birmingham, Maria. Tastes Like Music: 17 Quirks of the Brain & Body. Melnychuk, Monika, illus. 2014. (ENG.). 40p. (J). (gr. 3-7). 17.95 (978-1-77147-010-0(0), Owlkids) Owlkids Bks. Inc. CAN. Dist: Publishers Group West (PGW).

Bjornlund, Lydia. Personality Disorders. 2011. 96p. (YA). (gr. 6-10). lib. bdg. (978-1-60152-139-2(1)) ReferencePoint Pr., Inc.

Bonnice, Sherry. Adjustment Disorders. McDonnell, Mary Ann & Esherick, Donald, eds. 2013. (State of Mental Illness & Its Therapy Ser.: 19). 128p. (J). (gr. 7-18). 24.95 (978-1-4222-2820-3(7)) Mason Crest.

Bonnice, Sherry & Hoard, Carolyn. Cognitive Disorders. McDonnell, Mary Ann & Esherick, Donald, eds. 2013. (State of Mental Illness & Its Therapy Ser.: 19). 128p. (J). (gr. 7-18). 24.95 (978-1-4222-2823-4(1)) Mason Crest.

Brinkerhoff, Shirley. Anxiety Disorders. McDonnell, Mary Ann & Esherick, Donald, eds. 2013. (State of Mental Illness & Its Therapy Ser.: 19). 128p. (J). (gr. 7-18). 24.95 (978-1-4222-2821-0(5)) Mason Crest.

—Drug Therapy & Childhood & Adolescent Disorders. (Encyclopedia of Psychiatric Drugs & Their Disorders Ser.). (Illus.). (YA). 2004. 128p. lib. bdg. 24.95 (978-1-59084-563-9(3)) 2003. 125p. (gr. 4-7). pap. 14.95 (978-1-4222-0386-6(7)) Mason Crest.

—Obsessive-Compulsive Disorder. 2014. (Illus.). 128p. (J). (978-1-4222-2819-7(3)) Mason Crest.

—Obsessive-Compulsive Disorder. McDonnell, Mary Ann & Esherick, Donald, eds. 2013. (State of Mental Illness & Its Therapy Ser.: 19). 128p. (J). (gr. 7-18). 24.95 (978-1-4222-2830-2(4)) Mason Crest.

—Personality Disorders. McDonnell, Mary Ann & Esherick, Donald, eds. 2013. (State of Mental Illness & Its Therapy Ser.: 19). 128p. (J). (gr. 7-18). 24.95 (978-1-4222-2831-9(2)) Mason Crest.

Carlson, Dale, et al. Out of Order: Young Adult Manual of Mental Illness & Recovery. 2014. (ENG., Illus.). 256p. (YA). pap. 14.95 (978-1-884158-37-7(4)) Team Kreskin Productions, LLC.

Chou, Joey. Crazy by the Letters. Chou, Joey, illus. 2006. (Illus.). 15.99 (978-0-9788670-0-3(9)) Choo Choo Clan.

Esherick, Joan. Mood Disorders. McDonnell, Mary Ann & Esherick, Donald, eds. 2013. (State of Mental Illness & Its Therapy Ser.: 19). 128p. (J). (gr. 7-18). 24.95 (978-1-4222-2829-6(0)) Mason Crest.

—Sleep Deprivation & Its Consequences. Bridgemohan, Carolyn & Forman, Sara, eds. 2013. (Young Adult's Guide to the Science of Health Ser.: 15). 128p. (J). (gr. 7-18). 24.95 (978-1-4222-2815-9(0)) Mason Crest.

—Sleep Disorders. McDonnell, Mary Ann & Esherick, Donald, eds. 2013. (State of Mental Illness & Its Therapy Ser.: 19). 128p. (J). (gr. 7-18). 24.95 (978-1-4222-2837-1(1)) Mason Crest.

—Smoking-Related Health Issues. 2014. (Illus.). 128p. (J). (978-1-4222-2803-6(7)) Mason Crest.

—Suicide & Self-Destructive Behaviors. McDonnell, Mary Ann & Forman, Sara, eds. 2013. (Young Adult's Guide to the Science of Health Ser.: 15). 128p. (J). (gr. 7-18). 24.95 (978-1-4222-2817-3(7)) Mason Crest.

Giddens, Sandra. Obsessive-Compulsive Disorder. 2009. (Teen Mental Health Ser.). 48p. (gr. 5-6). 53.00 (978-1-60853-297-1(6)) Rosen Publishing Group, Inc., The.

Hyman, Bruce M. & Pedrick, Cherry. Anxiety Disorders. 2012. (USA TODAY Health Reports: Diseases & Disorders Ser.). (ENG.). 112p. (gr. 6-12). lib. bdg. 34.60 (978-0-7613-6084-1(0)) Lerner Publishing Group.

Iorizzo, Carrie. Anxiety & Phobias. 2013. (ENG., Illus.). 48p. (J). (978-0-7787-0082-1(8)); pap. (978-0-7787-0088-3(7)) Crabtree Publishing Co.

Johnson, Maggie & Wintgens, Alison. Can I Tell You about Selective Mutism? A Guide for Friends, Family & Professionals. Gallow, Robyn, illus. 2012. (Can I Tell You About...? Ser.). (ENG.). 56p. pap. 13.95 (978-1-84905-289-4(1), 5165) Kingsley, Jessica Pubs. GBR. Dist: Macmillan Distribution Ltd.

Libal, Autumn. Dissociative Disorders. McDonnell, Mary Ann & Esherick, Donald, eds. 2013. (State of Mental Illness & Its Therapy Ser.: 19). 128p. (J). (gr. 7-18). 24.95 (978-1-4222-2824-1(X)) Mason Crest.

—Impulse-Control Disorders. McDonnell, Mary Ann & Esherick, Donald, eds. 2013. (State of Mental Illness & Its Therapy Ser.: 19). 128p. (J). (gr. 7-18). 24.95 (978-1-4222-2827-2(4)) Mason Crest.

—Postpartum Disorders. McDonnell, Mary Ann & Esherick, Donald, eds. 2013. (State of Mental Illness & Its Therapy Ser.: 19). 128p. (J). (gr. 7-18). 24.95 (978-1-4222-2832-6(0)) Mason Crest.

—Psychosomatic Disorders. McDonnell, Mary Ann & Esherick, Donald, eds. 2013. (State of Mental Illness & Its Therapy Ser.: 19). 128p. (J). (gr. 7-18). 24.95 (978-1-4222-2834-0(7)) Mason Crest.

Marcovitz, Hal & Sheen, Barbara. Personality Disorders. 2009. (Diseases & Disorders Ser.). (ENG., Illus.). 128p. (gr. 7-10). lib. bdg. 39.90 (978-1-4205-0115-5(1), LML02109-245426, Lucent Bks.) Cengage Gale.

McIntosh, Kenneth & Livingston, Phyllis. Youth with Impulse-Control Disorders: On the Spur of the Moment. 2007. (Helping Youth with Mental, Physical, & Social Challenges Ser.). (Illus.). 128p. (YA). pap. 14.95 (978-1-4222-0447-4(2)) Mason Crest.

—Youth with Juvenile Schizophrenia: the Search for Reality. 2007. (Helping Youth with Mental, Physical, & Social Challenges Ser.). (Illus.). 128p. (YA). (gr. 8-12). pap. 14.95 (978-1-4222-0448-1(0)) Mason Crest.

Metcalf, Tom. Phobias. Metcalf, Gena, ed. 2008. (Perspectives on Diseases & Disorders Ser.). (ENG., Illus.). 144p. (gr. 10-12). lib. bdg. 44.30 (978-0-7377-4027-1(2), LML02109-239986, Greenhaven Pr., Inc.) Cengage Gale.

Mooney, Carla. What Is Anxiety Disorder? 2015. (ENG., Illus.). 80p. (J). lib. bdg. (978-1-60152-920-6(1)) ReferencePoint Pr., Inc.

—What Is Panic Disorder? 2015. (ENG., Illus.). 80p. (J). lthr. (978-1-60152-924-4(4)) ReferencePoint Pr., Inc.

Osborne, Jill. Sam Feels Better Now! An Interactive Story for Children. Collier, Kevin Scott, illus. 2008. 44p. (J). pap. 15.95 (978-1-932690-60-6(3)) Loving Healing Pr., Inc.

Owens, Peter. Teens, Health & Obesity. Developed in Association with the Gallup Organization Staff, ed. 2013. (Gallup Youth Survey: Major Issues & Trends Ser.: 14). 112p. (J). (gr. 7-18). 24.95 (978-1-4222-2961-3(0)) Mason Crest.

Patterson, James & Friedman, Hal. Med Head: My Knock-Down, Drag-Out, Drugged-Up Battle with My Brain. 2010. (YA). lib. bdg. 23.30 (978-0-606-14538-1(9), Turtleback) Turtleback Bks.

Pedrick, Cherry, et al. Obsessive-Compulsive Disorder. 2011. (USA TODAY Health Reports: Diseases & Disorders Ser.). (ENG.). 112p. (gr. 6-12). lib. bdg. 34.60 (978-0-7613-5884-8(6)) Lerner Publishing Group.

Poole, H. W. Anxiety Disorders, Vol. 13. Walters, Anne S., ed. 2015. (Mental Illnesses & Disorders: Awareness & Understanding Ser.). (Illus.). 48p. (J). (gr. 5). 20.95 (978-1-4222-3377-1(4)) Mason Crest.

—Obsessive-Compulsive Disorder, Vol. 13. Walters, Anne S., ed. 2015. (Mental Illnesses & Disorders: Awareness & Understanding Ser.). (Illus.). 48p. (J). (gr. 5). 20.95 (978-1-4222-3373-3(1)) Mason Crest.

—Schizophrenia, Vol. 13. Walters, Anne S., ed. 2015. (Mental Illnesses & Disorders: Awareness & Understanding Ser.). (Illus.). 48p. (J). (gr. 5). 20.95 (978-1-4222-3375-7(8)) Mason Crest.

—Sleep Disorders, Vol. 13. Walters, Anne S., ed. 2015. (Mental Illnesses & Disorders: Awareness & Understanding Ser.). (Illus.). 48p. (J). (gr. 5). 20.95 (978-1-4222-3376-4(6)) Mason Crest.

Shea, John M. Self-Injury & Cutting: Stopping the Pain. 2013. (Helpline: Teen Issues & Answers Ser.). (ENG., Illus.). 80p. (YA). (gr. 7-12). lib. bdg. 33.25 (978-1-4488-9448-2(4), Rosen Classroom) Rosen Publishing Group, Inc., The.

Straus, Susan Farber. Healing Days: A Guide for Kids Who Have Experienced Trauma. Bogade, Maria, illus. 2013. 32p. (J). (978-1-4338-1292-7(4)); pap. (978-1-4338-1293-4(2)) American Psychological Assn.

Tourneville, Harry. Attention-Deficit Hyperactivity Disorder. 2013. (ENG., Illus.). 48p. (J). pap. (978-0-7787-0086-9(0)) Crabtree Publishing Co.

Van Duyne, Sara. Stress & Anxiety-Related Disorders. 2003. (Diseases & People Ser.). (Illus.). 112p. (J). lib. bdg. 26.60 (978-0-7660-1900-3(4)) Enslow Pubs., Inc.

Wells, Polly. Freaking Out: Real-Life Stories about Anxiety. Mitchell, Peter, illus. 2013. (ENG.). 136p. (YA). (gr. 7-12). 22.95 (978-1-55451-545-5(9), 9781554515455) Annick Pr., Ltd. CAN. Dist: Publishers Group West (PGW).

Willett, Edward. Frequently Asked Questions about Exercise Addiction. 2009. (FAQ: Teen Life Ser.). 64p. (gr. 5-6). 58.50 (978-1-61512-577-7(9)) Rosen Publishing Group, Inc., The.

Williams, Mary E. Self-Injury. 2013. (Introducing Issues with Opposing Viewpoints Ser.). (ENG., Illus.). 144p. (gr. 7-10). lib. bdg. 42.00 (978-0-7377-6280-8(2), Greenhaven Pr., Inc.) Cengage Gale.

PSYCHOLOGY, PRACTICAL

see Psychology, Applied

PSYCHOLOGY, RELIGIOUS

Rosenberg, concept. Reach Your Goal. 2011. (YID.). 198p. (YA). 21.00 (978-0-9832102-1-4(7)) Roth Pubs.

PSYCHOLOGY, SOCIAL

see Social Psychology

PSYCHOLOGY—VOCATIONAL GUIDANCE

Shaw, Jessica. Dream Jobs in Sports Psychology. 2017. (J). **(978-1-5383-8144-1(3))** Rosen Publishing Group, Inc., The.

PSYCHOPATHOLOGISTS

see Psychiatrists

PSYCHOPATHOLOGY

see Psychology, Pathological

PSYCHOPATHY

see Psychology, Pathological

PSYCHOSES

see Mental Illness

PSYCHOTHERAPY

Borenstein, Gerri C. Therapy. 2004. (Life Balance Ser.). (ENG.). 80p. (YA). (gr. 5-8). pap. 6.95 (978-0-531-15585-1(4), Watts, Franklin) Scholastic Library Publishing.

Collins-Donnelly, Kate. Starving the Anxiety Gremlin: A Cognitive Behavioural Therapy Workbook on Anxiety Management for Young People. 2013. (Gremlin & Thief CBT Workbooks Ser.). (ENG., Illus.). 168p. (C). pap. 19.95 (978-1-84905-341-9(3), 1990) Kingsley, Jessica Pubs. GBR. Dist: Macmillan Distribution Ltd.

Conte, Paola, et al. Someone to Talk To: Getting Good at Feeling Better. 2017. (Illus.). 64p. (J). pap. **(978-1-4338-2672-6(0)**, Magination Pr.) American Psychological Assn.

Esherick, Joan. The Journey Toward Recovery: Youth with Brain Injury. 2004. (Youth with Special Needs Ser.). (Illus.). 128p. (YA). 24.95 (978-1-59084-734-3(2)) Mason Crest.

Fogerty, Ramona. Prince, Labino, & Chrecas from State Parkway. 2005. (YA). per. 24.95 (978-0-9759889-5-4(6)) Potenial Psychotherapy Counseling & Remedial Service.

Libal, Autumn. Runaway Train: Youth with Emotional Disturbance. 2003. (Youth with Special Needs Ser.). (Illus.). 127p. (YA). (gr. 7). pap. 14.95 (978-1-4222-0429-0(4)) Mason Crest.

Rashkin, Rachel. Feeling Better: A Kid's Book about Therapy. Adamson, Bonnie, illus. 2005. 48p. (J). (gr. -1-7). pap. 9.95 (978-1-59147-238-4(5), Magination Pr.) American Psychological Assn.

—Feeling Better: A Kid's Books about Therapy. Adamson, Bonnie, illus. 2005. 48p. (J). 14.95 (978-1-59147-237-7(7), Magination Pr.) American Psychological Assn.

PTOMAINE POISONING

see Food Poisoning

PUBERTY

see also Adolescence

Attwood, Sarah. Making Sense of Sex: A Forthright Guide to Puberty, Sex & Relationships for People with Asperger's Syndrome. Powell, Jonathan, illus. 2008. (ENG.). 320p. (J). (gr. 4-12). pap. 21.95 (978-1-84310-374-5(5), 1254) Kingsley, Jessica Pubs. GBR. Dist: Macmillan Distribution Ltd.

Bailey, Jacqui. Sex, Puberty & All That Stuff: A Guide to Growing Up. 2nd rev. ed. 2016. (ENG., Illus.). 124p. (J). (gr. 5-10). pap. 13.99 (978-1-4380-0857-8(0)) Barron's Educational Series, Inc.

Bob Gresh. It's Great to Be a Guy! 2016. (ENG., Illus.). 128p. (J). pap. 11.99 (978-0-7369-6278-0(6)) Harvest Hse. Pubs.

Bourgeois, Paulette & Martyn, Kim. Changes in You & Me: A Book about Puberty Mostly for Girls. Phillips, Louise, illus. rev. ed. 2005. (ENG.). 64p. (J). pap. 16.95 (978-1-55263-670-1(4)) Kollath-Stensaas Pubs.

Byers, Ann. Frequently Asked Questions about Puberty. (FAQ: Teen Life Ser.). 64p. 2009. (gr. 5-6). 58.50 (978-1-61512-586-9(8)) 2006. (Illus.). (YA). (gr. 7-12). 31.95 (978-1-4042-0966-4(2)) Rosen Publishing Group, Inc., The.

Couwenhoven, Terri. The Boys' Guide to Growing Up: Choices & Changes During Puberty. 2012. (ENG., Illus.). 64p. (J). pap. 16.95 (978-1-60613-089-6(7)) Woodbine Hse.

—Girls' Guide to Growing Up: Choices & Changes in the Tween Years. 2011. (ENG., Illus.). 62p. pap. 16.95 (978-1-60613-026-1(9)) Woodbine Hse.

Daldry, Jeremy. Teenage Guy's Survival Guide. 2011. 11.04 (978-0-7848-3378-0(8), Everbind) Marco Bk. Co.

De la Bédoyère, Camilla. Personal Hygiene & Sexual Health. 2010. (Healthy Lifestyles Ser.). 48p. (J). 35.65 (978-1-60753-087-9(2)) Amicus Publishing.

Deak, JoAnn & Deak, Terrence. The Owner's Manual for Driving Your Adolescent Brain. Harrison, Freya, illus. 2013. (ENG.). 72p. (J). (gr. 3-9). pap. 15.95 (978-1-939775-02-3(7), 9781939775023) March 4th, Inc.

Dunham, Kelli. The Girls Body Book: Everything You Need to Know for Growing up YOU. Tallardy, Laura, illus. 2013. (ENG.). 116p. (J). pap. 11.95 (978-1-60433-353-4(7), Applesauce Pr.) Cider Mill Pr. Bk. Pubs., LLC.

—The Girl's Body Book: Everything You Need to Know for Growing up You! Tallardy, Laura, illus. 3rd rev. ed. 2015. (ENG.). 132p. (J). pap. 12.95 (978-1-60433-575-0(0), Applesauce Pr.) Cider Mill Pr. Bk. Pubs., LLC.

Favor, Lesli J. Everything You Need to Know about Growth Spurts & Delayed Growth. 2005. (Need to Know Library). (Illus.). 64p. (YA). (gr. 4-6). lib. bdg. 31.95 (978-0-8239-3549-9(3)) Rosen Publishing Group, Inc., The.

Favor, Leslie. Everything You Need to Know about Growth Spurts & Delayed Growth. 2009. (Need to Know Library). 64p. (gr. 5-5). 58.50 (978-1-60854-071-6(5)) Rosen Publishing Group, Inc., The.

Firth, Alex. What's Happening to Me? Meredith, Susan, ed. Larkum, Adam, illus. 2007. 48p. (J). (gr. 4-7). pap. 6.99 (978-0-7945-1514-0(2), Usborne) EDC Publishing.

Fiscus, James. Coping with Growth Spurts & Delayed Growth. 2005. (Coping Ser.). (Illus.). 192p. (YA). (gr. 7-12). lib. bdg. 34.60 (978-0-8239-3508-6(6)) Rosen Publishing Group, Inc., The.

Fiscus, Jim. Coping with Growth Spurts & Delayed Growth. 2009. (Coping Ser.). 192p. (gr. 7-12). 63.90 (978-1-61512-000-0(9)) Rosen Publishing Group, Inc., The.

Gray, Leon. Puberty. 2010. (Being Healthy, Feeling Great Ser.). (ENG.). 32p. (J). pap. 10.60 (978-1-61532-378-4(3), PowerKids Pr.); (YA). (gr. 3-6). lib. bdg. 26.50 (978-1-61532-370-8(8)) Rosen Publishing Group, Inc., The.

Gresh, Dannah. It's Great to Be a Girl! A Guide to Your Changing Body. 2015. (Secret Keeper Girl(r) Ser.). (ENG., Illus.). 128p. (J). pap. 11.99 (978-0-7369-6007-6(4)) Harvest Hse. Pubs.

Growing Up, 9 vols., Set. Incl. Going to the Hospital. Parker, Steve & Parker, Vic. 23.32 (978-1-4329-4797-2(4)); Having a Hearing Test. Parker, Steve & Parker, Vic. 23.32 (978-1-4329-4799-6(0)); Having an Eye Test. Parker, Steve & Parker, Vic. 23.32 (978-1-4329-4798-9(2)); Moving. Parker, Steve & Parker, Vic. 23.32 (978-1-4329-4800-9(8)); My First Day at a New School. Guillain, Charlotte. 23.32 (978-1-4329-4796-5(6)); My First Sleepover. Guillain, Charlotte. 23.32 (978-1-4329-4802-3(4)); My First Trip on an Airplane. Parker, Steve & Parker, Vic. 23.32 (978-1-4329-4801-6(6)); New Brother or Sister. Guillain, Charlotte. 23.32 (978-1-4329-4803-0(2)); Visiting the Dentist. Guillain, Charlotte. 23.32 (978-1-4329-4804-7(0)); (gr. k-2). (Growing Up Ser.). (ENG., Illus.). 24p. 2011. Set lib. bdg. 209.88 (978-1-4329-4805-4(9), Heinemann Read & Learn) Heinemann-Raintree.

Hartman, Davida. The Growing up Guide for Girls: What Girls on the Autism Spectrum Need to Know! Suggs, Margaret Anne, illus. 2015. (Growing Up Ser.). (ENG.). 72p. (J). 16.95 (978-1-84905-574-1(2), 2878) Kingsley, Jessica Pubs. GBR. Dist: Macmillan Distribution Ltd.

Hickman, Ruth. Going Through Puberty: A Boy's Manual for Body, Mind, & Health. 2013. (What Now? Ser.). (ENG.). 128p. (gr. 2-10). pap. 15.99 (978-0-9884499-1-6(9)) Lesson Ladder.

—Going Through Puberty: A Girl's Manual for Body, Mind, & Health. 2013. (What Now? Ser.). (ENG.). 128p. (gr. 3-10). pap. 15.99 (978-0-9884499-0-9(0)) Lesson Ladder.

Holmes, Melisa & Hutchison, Patricia. Girlology's There's Something New about You: A Girl's Guide to Growing Up. 2010. (ENG., Illus.). 128p. (J). (gr. 7-11). pap. 12.95 (978-0-7573-1526-8(7), HCI Teens) Health Communications, Inc.

Kahaner, Ellen. Everything You Need to Know about Growing up Female. 2009. (Need to Know Library). 64p. (gr. 5-5). 58.50 (978-1-60854-070-9(7)) Rosen Publishing Group, Inc., The.

Katz, Anne. Girl in the Know: Your Inside-and-Out Guide to Growing Up. Melnychuk, Monika, illus. 2010. (ENG.). 112p. (J). (gr. 5-9). 18.95 (978-1-55453-303-9(1)) Kids Can Pr., Ltd. CAN. Dist: Hachette Bk. Group.

Kelly, Bill. You Ought to Know: A Guy's Guide to Sex. 2005. (Guys' Guides). (Illus.). 48p. (J). (gr. 5-8). lib. bdg. 29.25 (978-0-8239-3084-5(X), GUYOSH) Rosen Publishing Group, Inc., The.

Kershner, Tad. Body Double: Understanding Physical Changes, 1 vol. 2010. (Essential Health: a Guy's Guide Ser.). (ENG.). 112p. (J). (gr. 6-12). lib. bdg. 35.64 (978-1-61613-538-6(7)) ABDO Publishing Co.

Lluch, Isabel B. The Ultimate Girls' Guide Journal to Feel Confident, Pretty & Happy. 2009. (ENG.). 100p. (J). (gr. 6-7). spiral bd. 9.95 (978-1-934386-59-0(6)) WS Publishing.

Loewen, Nancy & Skelley, Paula. Tangles, Growth Spurts, & Being You: Questions & Answers about Growing Up. Mora, Julissa, illus. 2015. (Girl Talk Ser.). (ENG.). 32p. (gr. 3-4). lib. bdg. 27.99 (978-1-4914-1860-4(5), Snap Bks.) Capstone Press of Coughlan Cos.

Madaras, Lynda & Madaras, Area. My Body, My Self for Boys. 2nd rev. ed. 2007. (What's Happening to My Body? Ser.). (ENG., Illus.). 128p. (gr. 4-6). pap. 12.99 (978-1-55704-767-0(7), William Morrow Paperbacks) HarperCollins Pubs.

—My Body, My Self for Girls. 3rd rev. ed. 2007. (What's Happening to My Body? Ser.). (ENG., Illus.). 160p. (gr. 4-6). pap. 12.99 (978-1-55704-766-3(9), William Morrow Paperbacks) HarperCollins Pubs.

—¿Que Pasa en Mi Cuerpo? El Libro para Muchachos: La Guía de Mayor Venta Sobre el Desarrollo, Escrita para Adolescentes y Preadolescentes. 2012. (What's Happening to My Body? Ser.). (SPA., Illus.). 256p. (gr. 4-18). pap. 12.99 (978-1-55704-940-7(8), William Morrow Paperbacks) HarperCollins Pubs.

—¿Que Pasa en Mi Cuerpo? Libro para Muchachas: La Guía de Mayor Venta Sobre el Desarrollo Escrita para Adolescentes y Preadolescentes. 2011. (What's Happening to My Body? Ser.). (SPA & ENG., Illus.). 288p. (gr. 4-18). pap. 12.95 (978-1-55704-939-1(4), William Morrow Paperbacks) HarperCollins Pubs.

Madaras, Lynda, et al. "What's Happening to My Body?" Book for Boys. 3rd rev. ed. 2007. (What's Happening to My Body? Ser.). (ENG., Illus.). 256p. (gr. 5-7). pap. 15.99 (978-1-55704-765-6(0), William Morrow Paperbacks) HarperCollins Pubs.

—"What's Happening to My Body?" Book for Girls. 3rd rev. ed. 2007. (What's Happening to My Body? Ser.). (ENG., Illus.). 288p. (gr. 7-9). pap. 14.99 (978-1-55704-764-9(2), William Morrow Paperbacks) HarperCollins Pubs.

—The "What's Happening to My Body?" Book for Boys. 3rd rev. ed. 2007. (What's Happening to My Body? Ser.). (ENG.,

Illus.). 256p. (gr. 7-9). 24.99 *(978-1-55704-769-4(3),* Morrow, William & Co.) HarperCollins Pubs.
Mason, Paul. Your Growing Body & Remarkable Reproductive System. 2015. (Your Brilliant Body! Ser.). (ENG., Illus.). 32p. (J). (gr. 3-7). lib. bdg. *(978-0-7787-2196-3(5))* Crabtree Publishing Co.
Mejia Soto, Guillermina. Higiene de la Pubertad. 2003. (SPA.). 80p. pap. 12.48 *(978-970-661-099-7(5))* Edamex, Editores Asociados Mexicanos, S. A. de C. V. MEX. Dist: Giron Bks.
Meredith, Susan. What's Happening to Me? (Girls Edition) Leschnikoff, Nancy, illus. 2006. 48p. (J). pap. 6.99 *(978-0-7945-1267-5(4),* Usborne) EDC Publishing.
Miles, Lisa & Chown, Xanna Eve. How to Survive Zits & Bad Hair Days. 2013. (Girl Talk Ser.). 48p. (J). (gr. 5-8). pap. 70.50 *(978-1-4777-0725-8(5),* Rosen Reference); (ENG., Illus.). pap. 11.75 *(978-1-4777-0724-1(7),* Rosen Reference); (ENG., Illus.). lib. bdg. 29.25 *(978-1-4777-0709-8(3),* Rosen Classroom) Rosen Publishing Group, Inc., The.
Moe, Barbara. Coping with Rejection. 2009. (Coping Ser.). 192p. (gr. 7-12). 63.90 *(978-1-61512-010-9(6))* Rosen Publishing Group, Inc., The.
Parker, Steve & Parker, Vic. Growing Up, 9 vols., Set. Incl. My First Trip on an Airplane. (ENG.). 24p. (gr. k-2). 2011. pap. 6.79 *(978-1-4329-4811-5(3),* Heinemann Read & Learn); (Growing Up Ser.). (ENG.). 24p. 2011. Set pap. 13.58 o.p. *(978-1-4329-4815-3(6),* Heinemann Read & Learn) Heinemann-Raintree.
Parker, Vic. The Little Book of Growing Up. 2007. (ENG., Illus.). 128p. (J). (gr. 7-17). pap. 6.99 *(978-0-340-93099-1(3))* Headline Publishing Group GBR. Dist: Hachette Bk. Group.
Picone, Linda. My Changing Body. 2010. (ENG.). 150p. (J). (gr. 4-7). pap. 9.95 *(978-1-57749-181-1(5));* (Illus.). pap. 9.95 *(978-1-57749-187-3(4))* Taylor Trade Publishing.
Plaisted, Caroline. Boy Talk. 2011. (ENG., Illus.). 48p. (J). pap. 11.95 *(978-1-926853-90-1(3))* Saunders Bk. Co. CAN. Dist: RiverStream Publishing.
—Girl Talk: Girl Talk: A Survival Guide to Growing Up. 2011. (ENG., Illus.). 48p. (J). pap. 11.95 *(978-1-926853-91-8(1))* Saunders Bk. Co. CAN. Dist: RiverStream Publishing.
Saltz, Gail. Changing You! A Guide to Body Changes & Sexuality. Cravath, Lynne Avril, illus. 2009. (ENG.). 32p. (J). (gr. 1-3). pap. 6.99 *(978-0-14-241479-8(4),* Puffin Books) Penguin Young Readers Group.
Silverthorne, Sandy. Surviving Zits: How to Cope with Your Changing Self. Silverthorne, Sandy, illus. 2006. (Illus.). 96p. (YA). (gr. 3-6). pap. 5.99 *(978-0-7847-1435-5(5),* 42177) Standard Publishing.
Smith, Liz. A Girl's Guide to Growing up - Booklet, 10 per packet. Perry, Gala, illus. 2005. (J). 63.95 *(978-1-55942-207-9(6))* Witcher Productions.
Stubbs, Lori. Fearfully & Wonderfully Made: A Christian Health & Puberty Guide for Preteen Boys & Girls. Stubbs, Robert Earl, illus. 2nd ed. 2005. 40p. (J). (gr. -1 — 1). pap. 10.00 *(978-1-58597-174-9(X))* Leathers Publishing.
Vermond, Kira. Growing Up. Chin, Carl & Owlkids Books Inc. Staff, illus. 2013. (ENG.). 104p. (J). (gr. 7-7). pap. 11.95 *(978-1-77147-004-9(6),* Owlkids) Owlkids Bks. Inc. CAN. Dist: Publishers Group West (PGW).
—Growing Up, Inside & Out. 2013. 104p. *(978-1-77147-036-0(4))* Owlkids Bks. Inc.
von Holleben, Jan & Helms, Antje. Does This Happen to Everyone? A Budding Adult's Guide to Puberty. 2014. (ENG.). 160p. (J). (gr. 5-12). 24.95 *(978-3-89955-521-9(X))* Die Gestalten Verlag DEU. Dist: Penguin Random Hse. LLC.
Whittaker, Helen. How Toys Roll. 2012. (Toys & Forces Ser.). 32p. (gr. 1-4). lib. bdg. 27.10 *(978-1-59920-468-0(1))* Black Rabbit Bks.

PUBLIC ADMINISTRATION

Bow, James. What Is the Executive Branch? 2013. (ENG.). 32p. (J). *(978-0-7787-0902-2(7));* pap. *(978-0-7787-0907-7(8))* Crabtree Publishing Co.
Donovan, Sandra. Military/Dictators. 2013. (ShockZone (tm) — Villains Ser.). (ENG., Illus.). 32p. (gr. 5-8). lib. bdg. 26.60 *(978-1-4677-0609-4(4),* Lerner Pubns.) Lerner Publishing Group.
Egan, Tracie. The President & the Executive Branch. 2009. (Primary Source Library of American Citizenship Ser.). 32p. (gr. 5-5). 47.90 *(978-1-61511-229-6(4),* Rosen Reference) Rosen Publishing Group, Inc., The.
Hirsch, Rebecca E. How the Executive Branch Works, 1 vol. 2014. (How the US Government Works). (ENG.). 48p. (gr. 3-6). lib. bdg. 32.79 *(978-1-62403-635-4(X))* ABDO Publishing Co.
Kishel, Ann-Marie. Government Services. 2007. (First Step Nonfiction - Government Ser.). (ENG., Illus.). 24p. (gr. k-2). lib. bdg. 23.93 *(978-0-8225-6397-6(5),* Lerner Pubns.) Lerner Publishing Group.
Magoon, Kekla. The Welfare Debate, 1 vol. 2008. (Essential Viewpoints Set 3 Ser.). (ENG.). 112p. (J). (gr. 6-12). lib. bdg. 35.64 *(978-1-60453-114-5(2))* ABDO Publishing Co.
Merino, No'l, ed. Government Spending. 2012. (Opposing Viewpoints Ser.). (ENG., Illus.). 240p. (gr. 10-12). pap. 29.45 *(978-0-7377-6323-2(X));* lib. bdg. 42.95 *(978-0-7377-6322-5(1))* Cengage Gale. (Greenhaven Pr., Inc.).

PUBLIC ADMINISTRATION—VOCATIONAL GUIDANCE

Stemgass, Jon. Great Careers with a High School Diploma: Public Safety, Law, & Security. 2008. (Great Careers with a High School Diploma Ser.). 114p. (C). (gr. 9). 32.95 *(978-0-8160-7049-7(0),* Ferguson Publishing Co.) Facts On File, Inc.

PUBLIC FINANCE

see Finance, Public

PUBLIC HEALTH

see also Cemeteries; Communicable Diseases; Hospitals; Noise; Refuse and Refuse Disposal; Sanitation; Sewage Disposal; Vaccination; Water—Pollution; Water-Supply

Asher, Dana. Epidemiologists: Life Tracking Deadly Diseases. 2009. (Extreme Careers Ser.). 64p. (gr. 5-5). 58.50 *(978-1-61512-392-6(X),* Rosen Reference) Rosen Publishing Group, Inc., The.
Connolly, Sean. The World Health Organization. 2009. (Global Organizations Ser.). (Illus.). 46p. (J). (gr. 4-7). pap. *(978-1-897563-39-7(6))* Saunders Bk. Co.
Davis, Catherine G. USA TODAY(r) Lifeline Biographies: Spring 2012 New Releases. 2012. (USA TODAY Health Reports: Diseases & Disorders Ser.). 112p. (gr. 6-12). lib. bdg. 138.40 *(978-0-7613-8911-8(3),* Twenty-First Century Bks.) Lerner Publishing Group.
Espejo, Roman. Should Vaccinations Be Mandatory? Gale, G., ed. 2014. (At Issue Ser.). (ENG.). 128p. (gr. 10-12). lib. bdg. 39.40 *(978-0-7377-6862-6(2),* Greenhaven Pr., Inc.) Cengage Gale.
Gagne, Tammy & Mangor, Jodie. Battling Against Drug-Resistant Bacteria. 2016. (Science Frontiers Ser.). (ENG., Illus.). 32p. (J). pap. 9.95 *(978-1-63235-390-0(3))* Pr. Room Editions LLC.
Gordon, Sharon. Que Hay Dentro de una Ambulancia? 2006. (Bookworms Ser.). (SPA & ENG., Illus.). 32p. (gr. 1-2). lib. bdg. 15.95 *(978-0-7614-2390-4(7))* Marshall Cavendish Corp.
—What's Inside an Ambulance? 2007. (J). pap. 6.99 *(978-0-7614-3343-9(0))* Marshall Cavendish Corp.
—What's Inside an Ambulance?/Que Hay Dentro de una Ambulancia? 2006. (Bookworms Ser.). (ENG & SPA., Illus.). 32p. (gr. 1-2). lib. bdg. 15.95 *(978-0-7614-2471-0(7))* Marshall Cavendish Corp.
Health Alert Group 3, 6 bks., Set. Incl. Cerebral Palsy. Bjorklund, Ruth. (gr. 4-7). lib. bdg. 32.79 *(978-0-7614-2209-9(9),* Benchmark Bks.); Down Syndrome. Brill, Marlene Targ. (YA). (gr. 4-7). lib. bdg. 32.79 *(978-0-7614-2207-5(2));* Epilepsy. Bjorklund, Ruth. (YA). (gr. 4-7). lib. bdg. 32.79 *(978-0-7614-2206-8(4));* Flu. Hoffmann, Gretchen. (YA). (gr. 4-7). lib. bdg. 32.79 *(978-0-7614-2208-2(0));* Headaches. Petreycik, Rick. (J). (gr. 3-7). lib. bdg. 31.36 *(978-0-7614-2210-5(2),* Benchmark Bks.); Meningitis. Klosterman, Lorrie. (YA). (gr. 4-7). lib. bdg. 32.79 *(978-0-7614-2211-2(0));* (Illus.). 64p. 2006. (Health Alert Ser.). 2007. Set lib. bdg. 188.14 *(978-0-7614-2205-1(6))* Marshall Cavendish Corp.
Hepplewhite, Peter. Thomas Crapper, Corsets, & Cruel Britannia: A Grim History of the Vexing Victorians! 2015. (Awfully Ancient Ser.). (ENG., Illus.). 32p. (J). (gr. 5-5). pap. 10.50 *(978-1-4824-3133-9(5))* Stevens, Gareth Publishing LLLP.
Hundley, Kris. The Disease Detectives: Unraveling How Viruses Go Viral. 2015. (ENG.). 20p. pap. 5.95 *(978-1-942852-05-6(3),* Gatorbytes) Univ. Pr. of Florida.
Hunnicutt, Susan C. Universal Health Care. 2010. (Opposing Viewpoints Ser.). (Illus.). 240p. 42.95 *(978-0-7377-4648-8(3));* pap. 29.45 *(978-0-7377-4649-5(1))* Cengage Gale. (Greenhaven Pr., Inc.).
Jordan, Anna Louise. What Does an EMT Do? 2005. (What Does a Community Helper Do? Ser.). (Illus.). 24p. (J). lib. bdg. 22.60 *(978-0-7660-2540-0(3),* Enslow Elementary) Enslow Pubs., Inc.
Kidder, Tracy. Mountains Beyond Mountains (Adapted for Young People) The Quest of Dr. Paul Farmer, a Man Who Would Cure the World. 2014. (ENG.). (YA). (gr. 7). lib. bdg. 19.60 ***(978-1-68065-029-7(7))*** Perfection Learning Corp.
Kidder, Tracy & French, Michael. Mountains Beyond Mountains (Adapted for Young People) The Quest of Dr. Paul Farmer, a Man Who Would Cure the World. 2014. (ENG.). 288p. (YA). (gr. 7). pap. 9.99 *(978-0-385-74319-8(X),* Ember) Random Hse. Children's Bks.
Lerner Publishing Group Staff. USA Today Health Reports Set: Diseases & Disorders, 5 vols., Set. 2011. (YA). (gr. 6-12). lib. bdg. 173.00 *(978-0-7613-7473-2(6))* Lerner Publishing Group.
Markovics, Joyce L. Blitzed by a Blizzard! 2010. (Disaster Survivors Ser.). (Illus.). 32p. (YA). (gr. 4-7). lib. bdg. 25.27 *(978-1-936087-54-9(5))* Bearport Publishing Co., Inc.
Marsico, Katie. Stinky Sanitation Inventions. 2013. (Awesome Inventions You Use Every Day Ser.). (ENG., Illus.). 32p. (gr. 3-6). lib. bdg. 26.60 *(978-1-4677-1090-9(3),* Lerner Pubns.) Lerner Publishing Group.
—The World Health Organization. 2014. (Community Connections: How Do They Help? Ser.). (ENG., Illus.). 24p. (J). (gr. 2-5). 25.64 *(978-1-63188-030-8(6),* 205527) Cherry Lake Publishing.
Mendenhall, Emily & Koon, Adam, eds. Environmental Health Narratives: A Reader for Youth. Burque, Hannah Adams, illus. 2012. (ENG.). 400p. pap. 34.95 *(978-0-8263-5166-1(2))* Univ. of New Mexico Pr.
Merino, Noel. Health Care. Greenhaven Press Staff, ed. 2014. (Teen Rights & Freedoms Ser.). (ENG., Illus.). 176p. (gr. 10-12). lib. bdg. 42.00 *(978-0-7377-7000-1(7),* Greenhaven Pr., Inc.) Cengage Gale.
Merino, Noël. Medical Testing. Greenhaven Press Editors, ed. 2014. (Opposing Viewpoints Ser.). (ENG.). 224p. (gr. 10-12). lib. bdg. 48.80 *(978-0-7377-6959-3(9),* Greenhaven Pr., Inc.) Cengage Gale.
—Medical Testing. Greenhaven Press Editors & Gale Editors, eds. 2014. (Opposing Viewpoints Ser.). (ENG., Illus.). 224p. (gr. 7-12). pap. 33.80 *(978-0-7377-6960-9(2),* Greenhaven Pr., Inc.) Cengage Gale.
Mitchell, Kirstin. Madame Anopheles. 2008.Tr. of Seòora Anopheles. (Illus.). 26p. (J). pap. 20.00 *(978-0-9816301-0-6(3))* Alexander, Raine.
Murray, Julie. Home, 1 vol. 2009. (That's Gross! A Look at Science Ser.). (ENG., Illus.). 32p. (J). (gr. 2-5). 28.50 *(978-1-60453-555-6(5))* ABDO Publishing Co.
—Hospital, 1 vol. 2009. (That's Gross! A Look at Science Ser.). (ENG., Illus.). 32p. (J). (gr. 2-5). 28.50 *(978-1-60453-556-3(3))* ABDO Publishing Co.
Naden, Corinne J. Patients' Rights. 2007. (Open for Debate Ser.). (Illus.). 128p. (gr. 7-7). lib. bdg. 42.79 *(978-0-7614-2576-2(4),* Benchmark Bks.) Marshall Cavendish Corp.
Perritano, John. Health & Medicine, Vol. 9. van Dijk, Ruud, ed. 2016. (Making of the Modern World: 1945 to the Present Ser.). (Illus.). 64p. (J). (gr. 7). 23.95 *(978-1-4222-3639-0(0))* Mason Crest.
Picklesimer, Olivia. Health Care. 2011. (Issues That Concern You Ser.). (ENG., Illus.). 144p. (gr. 7-10). lib. bdg. 42.00 *(978-0-7377-5207-6(6))* Cengage Gale.
Piddock, Charles. Outbreaks: Science Seeks Safeguards for Global Health. 2008. (National Geographic Investigates Science Ser.). (ENG., Illus.). 64p. (J). (gr. 5). 17.95 *(978-1-4263-0357-9(2));* lib. bdg. 27.90 *(978-1-4263-0263-3(0))* National Geographic Society. (National Geographic Children's Bks.).
Randolph, Joanne. Snowplows. 2009. (Road Machines Ser.). 24p. (gr. k-1). 37.50 *(978-1-60852-466-2(3),* PowerKids Pr.) Rosen Publishing Group, Inc., The.
Ready, Dee. Doctors Help, 1 vol. 2013. (Our Community Helpers Ser.). (ENG.). 24p. (gr. k-1). lib. bdg. 21.99 *(978-1-62065-078-3(9),* Pebble Bks.) Capstone Press of Coughlan Cos.
Riggs, Kate. Ambulances: Seedlings. 2016. (Seedlings Ser.). (ENG.). 24p. (J). (gr. k-2). pap. 7.99 *(978-1-62832-183-8(0),* Creative Paperbacks) Creative Co., The.
Roza, Greg. How Do Sewers Work? 2016. (STEM Waterworks Ser.). 32p. (J). (gr. 5-5). pap. 11.75 *(978-1-4994-2003-6(X),* PowerKids Pr.) Rosen Publishing Group, Inc., The.
Rudolph, Jessica. Erased by a Tornado! 2010. (Disaster Survivors Ser.). (Illus.). 32p. (YA). (gr. 4-7). lib. bdg. 25.27 *(978-1-936087-52-5(9))* Bearport Publishing Co., Inc.
Senker, Cath. Improving Healthcare, 1 vol. 2012. (Charities in Action Ser.). (ENG.). 64p. (gr. 6-10). pap. 10.95 *(978-1-4329-6393-4(7));* lib. bdg. 35.99 *(978-1-4329-6386-6(4))* Heinemann-Raintree.
Yomtov, Nel. Epidemiologist. 2013. (21st Century Skills Library: Cool STEM Careers Ser.). (ENG.). 32p. (gr. 4-8). 28.50 *(978-1-62431-007-2(9),* 202479); pap. 14.21 *(978-1-62431-031-7(1),* 202481) Cherry Lake Publishing.

PUBLIC HEALTH—VOCATIONAL GUIDANCE

Porterfield, Deborah. Great Careers with a High School Diploma: Health Care, Medicine, & Science. 2008. (Great Careers with a High School Diploma Ser.). 115p. (C). (gr. 9). 32.95 *(978-0-8160-7047-3(4),* Ferguson Publishing Co.) Facts On File, Inc.

PUBLIC OPINION

see also Attitude (Psychology); Propaganda
also names of countries with the subdivision Foreign Opinion, e.g., United States—Foreign Opinion

Chant, Christopher. Stalemate: U. S. Public Opinion of the War in Vietnam. 2017. (Vietnam War Ser.: Vol. 5). (ENG.). (YA). (gr. 7-12). 24.95 ***(978-1-4222-3891-2(1))*** Mason Crest.
Gallup Youth Survey: Major Issues & Trends, 6 vols., Set. 2004. (YA). 137.70 *(978-1-59084-720-6(2))* Mason Crest.
Mabry-Gordon, Sherri. Are You at Risk for Public Shaming? 2016. (Got Issues? Ser.). (ENG., Illus.). 112p. (J). (gr. 7-8). lib. bdg. 37.27 *(978-0-7660-7136-0(7))* Enslow Pubs., Inc.
Public Persecutions. 2016. (Public Persecutions Ser.). 128p. (YA). lib. bdg. 273.84 *(978-1-5026-2357-7(9))* Cavendish Square Publishing.

PUBLIC PLAYGROUNDS

see Playgrounds

PUBLIC RELATIONS

Ferguson Publishing Staff, creator. Public Relations. 2007. (Careers in Focus Ser.). (Illus.). 224p. (gr. 6-12). 32.95 *(978-0-8160-6574-5(8),* Ferguson Publishing Co.) Facts On File, Inc.
Harmon, Daniel E. Careers As a Marketing & Public Relations Specialist. 2013. (Essential Careers Ser.). 80p. (YA). (gr. 7-12). 33.25 *(978-1-4777-1793-6(5))* Rosen Publishing Group, Inc., The.
Vaughan, Jenny. Causes & Campaigns. 2010. (Media Power Ser.). 48p. (YA). (gr. 5-9). 35.65 *(978-1-60753-111-1(9))* Amicus Publishing.

PUBLIC SCHOOLS

Marzilli, Alan. Religion in Public Schools. 2003. (Point/Counterpoint Ser.). (Illus.). 112p. (C). (gr. 9-13). 35.00 *(978-0-7910-7484-8(6),* Chelsea Hse.) Facts On File, Inc.

PUBLIC SERVICE CORPORATIONS

see Public Utilities

PUBLIC SPEAKING

see also Acting; Debates and Debating

Athans, Sandra K. & Parente, Robin W. Tips & Tricks for Evaluating an Argument & Its Claims. 2014. (Common Core Readiness Guide to Reading Ser.). 80p. (YA). (gr. 5-8). 32.95 *(978-1-4777-7559-2(5))* Rosen Publishing Group, Inc., The.
Benjamin, Susan J. Speak with Success: A Student's Step-by-Step Guide to Fearless Public Speaking. 2nd ed. 2007. (Illus.). 186p. (J). (gr. 6-11). per. 14.95 *(978-1-59647-127-6(1))* Good Year Bks.
Blumstein, Rachel. Everything You Need to Know about Public Speaking. rev. ed. 2005. (Need to Know Library). (Illus.). 64p. (YA). (gr. 7-12). lib. bdg. 31.95 *(978-0-8239-3087-6(4),* NTPUSP) Rosen Publishing Group, Inc., The.
Bodden, Valerie. Effective Speeches. (Nonfiction Writing Ser.). 48p. 2011. (ENG.). (J). (gr. 4-7). pap. 9.99 *(978-0-89812-545-0(6))* 2010. (YA). (gr. 5-18). 23.95 *(978-1-58341-935-9(7))* Creative Co., The. (Creative Education).
—Giving a Presentation. Williams, Nate, illus. 2015. (Classroom How-To Ser.). (ENG.). 48p. (J). (gr. 5-8). pap. 12.00 *(978-0-89812-986-1(9),* Creative Paperbacks) Creative Co., The.
—Giving a Presentation. 2014. (J). *(978-1-60818-280-0(0),* Creative Education) Creative Co., The.
Boshier, Rosa. How to Analyze the Works of Martin Luther King Jr, 1 vol. 2013. (Essential Critiques Set 4 Ser.). (ENG., Illus.). 112p. (J). (gr. 6-12). lib. bdg. 35.64 *(978-1-61783-647-3(8),* Essential Library) ABDO Publishing Co.
Bullard, Lisa. Ace Your Oral or Multimedia Presentation. 2009. (Ace It! Information Literacy Ser.). (Illus.). 48p. (J). (gr. 2-5). lib. bdg. 25.27 *(978-0-7660-3391-7(0))* Enslow Pubs., Inc.
Burgett, Cindy. Policy Debate. 2007. (National Forensic League Library of Public Speaking & Debate Ser.). (Illus.). 48p. (J). (gr. 5-8). lib. bdg. 29.25 *(978-1-4042-1024-0(5))* Rosen Publishing Group, Inc., The.
Checkmark Books, creator. Communication Skills. 2nd rev. ed. 2007. (Mastering Career Skills Ser.). (Illus.). 144p. per. 12.95 *(978-0-8160-7115-9(2),* Checkmark Bks.) Facts On File, Inc.
Coleman, Miriam. Present It: Understanding Contexts & Audiences. 2012. (Core Skills Ser.). (ENG., Illus.). 32p. (J). (gr. 3-6). 25.25 *(978-1-4488-7455-2(6));* pap. 10.00 *(978-1-4488-7527-6(7))* Rosen Publishing Group, Inc., The. (PowerKids Pr.).
Combs, Maggie. How to Analyze the Works of John Adams, 1 vol. 2013. (Essential Critiques Set 4 Ser.). (ENG.). 112p. (J). (gr. 6-12). lib. bdg. 35.64 *(978-1-61783-646-6(X),* Essential Library) ABDO Publishing Co.
Duffy, Claire. The Australian Schoolkids' Guide to Debating & Public Speaking. 2015. (ENG., Illus.). 192p. pap. 26.99 *(978-1-74223-423-6(2),* UNSW Press) NewSouth Publishing AUS. Dist: Independent Pubs. Group.
Engleberg, Isa N. & Daly, John A. Presentations in Everyday Life: Strategies for Effective Speaking. 2nd ed. 2004. 544p. (YA). pap. 74.36 *(978-0-618-26016-4(1),* 313251) CENGAGE Learning.
Farris, Christine King. March On! The Day My Brother Martin Changed the World. Ladd, London, illus. 2011. (J). (gr. 2-7). 29.95 *(978-0-545-10689-4(3))* Weston Woods Studios, Inc.
Green, Lyric & Bullard, Lisa. Future Ready Oral & Multimedia Presentations. 2017. (Future Ready Project Skills Ser.). 48p. (J). (gr. 3-4). pap. 11.70 ***(978-0-7660-8771-2(9));*** lib. bdg. 27.93 ***(978-0-7660-8659-3(3))*** Enslow Pubs., Inc.
Harper, Leslie. Cómo Dar un Discurso. 2014. (Sé un líder de la Comunidad (Be a Community Leader) Ser.). (SPA.). 32p. (J). (gr. 4-6). lib. bdg. 26.25 *(978-1-4777-6917-1(X),* PowerKids Pr.) Rosen Publishing Group, Inc., The.
—How to Give a Speech. 2014. (Be a Community Leader Ser.). 32p. (J). (gr. 4-6). lib. bdg. 26.25 *(978-1-4777-6697-2(9),* PowerKids Pr.) Rosen Publishing Group, Inc., The.
Harris, Laurie Lanzen. How to Analyze the Works of Abraham Lincoln, 1 vol. 2013. (Essential Critiques Set 4 Ser.). (ENG.). 112p. (J). (gr. 6-12). lib. bdg. 35.64 *(978-1-61783-642-8(7),* Essential Library) ABDO Publishing Co.
Ingalls, Ann. Seth & Savannah Build a Speech. Lee, Karen, illus. 2012. (Writing Builders Ser.). 32p. (J). (gr. 2-4). pap. 11.94 *(978-1-60357-391-7(7));* lib. bdg. 25.27 *(978-1-59953-511-1(4))* Norwood Hse. Pr.
Kesselring, Mari. How to Analyze the Works of Franklin D. Roosevelt, 1 vol. 2013. (Essential Critiques Set 4 Ser.). (ENG.). 112p. (J). (gr. 6-12). lib. bdg. 35.64 *(978-1-61783-643-5(5),* Essential Library) ABDO Publishing Co.
Leverett S. Lyon. Elements of Debating. lt. ed. 2007. 266p. pap. 21.99 *(978-1-4264-7631-0(0))* Creative Media Partners, LLC.
Marx, Jeff. How to Win a High School Election: Advice & Ideas Collected from over 1,000 High School Seniors. 2003. 180p. (gr. 7-12). pap. 14.95 *(978-0-9667824-0-0(2))* Marx, Jeff.
McHugh, Jeff. Speak up! Giving an Oral Presentation. Petelinsek, Kathleen, illus. 2015. (Explorer Junior Library: Information Explorer Junior Ser.). (ENG.). 24p. (J). (gr. 1-4). 29.93 *(978-1-63188-864-9(1),* 206036) Cherry Lake Publishing.
Meany, John & Shuster, Kate. Speak Out: A Guide to Middle School Debate. 2004. (Illus.). 188p. pap. 24.95 *(978-1-932716-02-3(5))* International Debate Education Assn.
Meyer, Susan. Performing & Creating Speeches, Demonstrations, & Collaborative Learning Experiences with Cool New Digital Tools. 2013. (Way Beyond PowerPoint: Making 21st Century Presentations Ser.). 48p. (J). (gr. 5-8). 29.95 *(978-1-4777-1837-7(0));* pap. 11.75 *(978-1-4777-1851-3(6))* Rosen Publishing Group, Inc., The. (Rosen Reference).
Minden, Cecilia & Roth, Kate. How to Write & Give a Speech. 2011. (Explorer Junior Library: Language Arts Explorer Junior Ser.). (ENG.). 24p. (gr. 1-4). lib. bdg. 25.64 *(978-1-61080-108-9(3),* 201118) Cherry Lake Publishing.
The National Forensic League Library of Public Speaking & Debate, 6 bks., Set. Incl. Lincoln-Douglas Debate. Woodhouse, Cynthia. (YA). lib. bdg. 29.25 *(978-1-4042-1025-7(3));* Parliamentary Debate. West, Keith. (YA). lib. bdg. 29.25 *(978-1-4042-1029-5(6));* Persuasive Speaking. Waldo, Dixie. (YA). lib. bdg. 29.25 *(978-1-4042-1028-8(8));* Policy Debate. Burgett, Cindy. (J). lib. bdg. 29.25 *(978-1-4042-1024-0(5));* Public Forum Debate. Kline, Jason. (J). lib. bdg. 29.25 *(978-1-4042-1027-1(X));* Student Congress Debate. Jacobi, Adam J. (J). lib. bdg. 29.25 *(978-1-4042-1026-4(1));* (Illus.). 48p. (gr. 5-8). 2007. 2007. Set lib. bdg. 159.00 *(978-1-4042-0937-4(9))* Rosen Publishing Group, Inc., The.
Performing & Creating Speeches, Demonstrations, & Collaborative Learning Experiences with Cool New Digital Tools. 2013. (Way Beyond PowerPoint: Making 21st Century Presentations Ser.). 48p. (J). (gr. 5-8). pap. 70.50 *(978-1-4777-1852-0(4),* Rosen Reference) Rosen Publishing Group, Inc., The.
Rauf, Don. Strengthening Public Speaking Skills. 2017. (Skills for Success Ser.). 64p. (gr. 12-12). 34.45 ***(978-1-5081-7570-4(5),*** Rosen Young Adult) Rosen Publishing Group, Inc., The.
Roy, Jennifer Rozines & Haney, Johannah. Sharpen Your Debate & Speech Writing Skills. 2011. (Sharpen Your Writing Skills Ser.). (Illus.). 64p. (J). (gr. 6-18). pap. 8.95 *(978-1-59845-341-6(6));* lib. bdg. 29.27 *(978-0-7660-3904-9(8))* Enslow Pubs., Inc.
Shipp, Catherine Elisabeth. 12 Great Tips on Writing a Speech. 2017. (Great Tips on Writing Ser.). (ENG., Illus.). 32p. (J). (gr. 3-6). 21.95 *(978-1-63235-277-4(X))* Pr. Room Editions LLC.
Spilsbury, Louise. Tips for Better Public Speaking. 2016. (Student's Toolbox Ser.). (ENG., Illus.). 32p. (J). (gr. 4-6). 17.99 *(978-0-7502-9106-4(0),* Wayland) Hachette Children's Group GBR. Dist: Hachette Bk. Group.
Taylor, Lacy. Public Speaking Student Activity Book. Matthews, Douglas L., ed. 2003. (Illus.). stu. ed., per., wbk. ed. *(978-1-931680-55-4(8),* Expert Systems for Teachers) Teaching Point, Inc.
Truesdell, Ann. Make Your Point: Creating Powerful Presentations. 2013. (Explorer Library: Information Explorer Ser.). (ENG.). 32p. (gr. 4-8). 28.50 *(978-1-62431-019-5(2),* 202527); pap. 14.21 *(978-1-62431-043-0(5),* 202529) Cherry Lake Publishing.
Ventura, Marne. The 12 Most Influential Speeches of All Time. 2018. (ENG.). 32p. (gr. 3-6). 31.35 ***(978-1-63235-414-3(4),*** 12-Story Library) Pr. Room Editions LLC.

PUBLIC UTILITIES

see also Railroads; Telegraph; Telephone; Water-Supply

Kallan, Stuart A. The Gas Crisis. 2007. (Ripped from the Headlines Ser.). 64p. (YA). (gr. 7-12). 23.95 *(978-1-60217-001-8(0))* Erickson Pr.

Peters, Craig. Larry Ellison: Database Genius of Oracle. 2003. (Internet Biographies Ser.). (Illus.). 48p. (J). (gr. 4-10). lib. bdg. 23.93 *(978-0-7660-1974-4(8))* Enslow Pubs., Inc.

Peterson, Megan Cooley. How Electricity Gets from Power Plants to Homes. 2016. (Here to There Ser.). (ENG., Illus.). 24p. (gr. k-1). lib. bdg. 26.65 *(978-1-4914-8434-0(9)*, Pebble Plus) Capstone Press of Coughlan Cos.

PUBLIC WORKS

see also Municipal Engineering

Beyer, Mark. Homeland Security & Weapons of Mass Destruction: How Prepared Are We? 2009. (Library of Weapons of Mass Destruction Ser.). 64p. (gr. 5-5). 58.50 *(978-1-60853-952-9(0))* Rosen Publishing Group, Inc., The.

Silivanch, Annalise. Rebuilding America's Infrastructure. 2010. (In the News Ser.). (ENG.). 64p. (YA). pap. 12.95 *(978-1-4488-1676-7(9))*; (gr. 7-12). lib. bdg. 31.95 *(978-1-4358-9444-0(8))* Rosen Publishing Group, Inc., The.

PUBLISHERS AND PUBLISHING

see also Book Industries and Trade; Books; Printing

Anderson, Kirsten. Who Was Robert Ripley? 2015. (Who Was... ? Ser.). lib. bdg. 16.00 *(978-0-606-36596-3(6))* Turtleback Bks.

Anderson, Kirsten & dePaola, Tomie. Who Was Robert Ripley? Foley, Tim & Harrison, Nancy, illus. 2015. (Who Was? Ser.). (ENG.). 112p. (J). (gr. 3-7). 5.99 *(978-0-448-48298-9(3)*, Grosset & Dunlap) Penguin Young Readers Group.

Barnett, Mac. How This Book Was Made: Based on a True Story. Rex, Adam, illus. 2016. (ENG.). 48p. (J). (gr. -1-k). 17.99 *(978-1-4231-5220-0(4))* Disney Pr.

Bradshaw, Anne, et al, contrib. by. Publishing Secrets: A Comprehensive Guide to Getting Your Book Published in the LDS Market. 2004. (Illus.). 194p. pap. 14.95 *(978-0-9749241-0-6(5))* Golden Wings Enterprises.

Burden, Peter. News of the World? Fake Sheikhs & Royal Trappings. Dillon, Julia & Hiscocks, Dan, eds. 2009. (ENG., Illus.). 320p. pap. 13.95 *(978-1-903070-72-7(4))* Eye Bks. GBR. Dist: Independent Pubs. Group.

Donovan, Sandy. Pingpong Perry Experiences How a Book Is Made, 1 vol. Christoph, James, illus. 2010. (In the Library). (ENG.). 24p. (gr. k-4). lib. bdg. 26.65 *(978-1-4048-5759-9(1))* Picture Window Bks.

Fox, Kathleen. A Book Is Just Like You! All about the Parts of a Book. Wallace, John, illus. 2012. 32p. (J). 17.95 *(978-1-60213-060-9(4)*, Upstart Bks.) Highsmith Inc.

Gitlin, Martin. Joseph Pulitzer: Historic Newspaper Publisher, 1 vol. 2009. (Publishing Pioneers Ser.). (ENG., Illus.). 112p. (J). (gr. 6-12). lib. bdg. 35.64 *(978-1-60453-765-9(5)*, Essential Library) ABDO Publishing Co.

Goldsmith, Bonnie. William Randolph Hearst: Newspaper Magnate, 1 vol. 2009. (Publishing Pioneers Ser.). (ENG., Illus.). 112p. (J). (gr. 6-12). lib. bdg. 35.64 *(978-1-60453-763-5(9)*, Essential Library) ABDO Publishing Co.

Granahan, Shirley. John Newbery: Father of Children's Literature, 1 vol. 2009. (Publishing Pioneers Ser.). (ENG., Illus.). 112p. (J). (gr. 6-12). lib. bdg. 35.64 *(978-1-60453-764-2(7)*, Essential Library) ABDO Publishing Co.

Greenhaven Press Editors. Are Books Becoming Extinct? 2012. (At Issue Ser.). (ENG.). 128p. (YA). (gr. 9-12). lib. bdg. 34.45 *(978-0-7377-5546-6(6))* Cengage Gale.

Greenhaven Press Editors & Haugen, David. Are Books Becoming Extinct? 2012. (At Issue Ser.). (ENG.). 128p. (gr. 10-12). pap. 27.80 *(978-0-7377-5547-3(4)*, Greenhaven Pr., Inc.) Cengage Gale.

Harmon, Daniel E. Publishing Your E-Book. 2013. (Digital & Information Literacy Ser.). (Illus.). 48p. (J). (gr. 5-8). 29.25 *(978-1-4488-9513-7(8))* Rosen Publishing Group, Inc., The.

Higgins, Melissa. Julian Assange: WikiLeaks Founder, 1 vol. 2011. (Essential Lives Set 7 Ser.). (ENG., Illus.). 112p. (J). (gr. 6-12). lib. bdg. 35.64 *(978-1-61783-001-3(1))* ABDO Publishing Co.

Jeff Bezos & Amazon. 2011. (Graphic Nonfiction Biographies Ser.). (ENG.). 48p. (YA). (gr. 5-8). *(978-1-4488-5549-0(7))*; pap. *(978-1-4488-5648-0(5))* Rosen Publishing Group, Inc., The. (Rosen Reference).

J.G. Ferguson Publishing Company Staff, contrib. by. Publishing. 3rd rev. ed. 2007. (Careers in Focus Ser.). (Illus.). 192p. (gr. 6-12). 32.95 *(978-0-8160-6572-1(1)*, Ferguson Publishing Co.) Facts On File, Inc.

Klein, Rebecca T. Career Building Through Using Digital Publishing Tools. 2013. (Digital Career Building Ser.). (Illus.). 64p. (J). (gr. 7-12). pap. 12.95 *(978-1-4777-1741-7(2))*; pap. 77.70 *(978-1-4777-1742-4(0))*; lib. bdg. 31.95 *(978-1-4777-1724-0(2))* Rosen Publishing Group, Inc., The.

Lange, Brenda. Edward Stratemeyer. 2003. (Who Wrote That? Ser.). (Illus.). 112p. (gr. 6-12). 35.00 *(978-0-7910-7621-7(0)*, Chelsea Hse.) Facts On File, Inc.

Markel, Michelle. Balderdash! John Newbery & the Boisterous Birth of Children's Books. Carpenter, Nancy, illus. 2017. (ENG.). 44p. (J). 17.99 *(978-0-8118-7922-4(4))* Chronicle Bks. LLC.

Morgan, Kayla. Barnes & Noble: Groundbreaking Entrepreneurs, 1 vol. 2009. (Publishing Pioneers Ser.). (ENG., Illus.). 112p. (J). (gr. 6-12). lib. bdg. 35.64 *(978-1-60453-758-1(2)*, Essential Library) ABDO Publishing Co.

PRESS, Celebration. How a Book Gets Published. 2003. (ENG.). (J). (gr. 2-5). pap., stu. ed. 34.95 *(978-0-673-62836-7(1)*, Celebration Pr.) Pearson Schl.

Priddy, Roger. Early Learning Workbook - ABC 1-20: Over 50 Pages of Wipe-Clean Letters & Numbers to Practice. 2013. (ENG.). (J). spiral bd., wbk. ed. 12.95 *(978-0-312-51341-2(0)*, 9780312513412, Priddy Bks.) St. Martin's Pr.

—Santa Express. 2013. (Shaped Board Bks.). (ENG., Illus.). 8p. (J). (gr. -1-k). bds. 9.99 *(978-0-312-51704-5(1)*, 9780312517045, Priddy Bks.) St. Martin's Pr.

Read, Write & Publish. (J). (gr. 5). 125.25 *(978-0-669-17767-1(9))* Houghton Mifflin Harcourt School Pubs.

Roberts, Russell. John Newbery & the Story of the Newbery Medal. 2003. (Great Achiever Awards Ser.). (Illus.). 48p. (J). (gr. 4-8). lib. bdg. 29.95 *(978-1-58415-201-9(X))* Mitchell Lane Pubs., Inc.

Rocha, Toni L. Careers in Magazine Publishing. 2005. (Career Resource Library). (Illus.). 192p. (YA). (gr. 7-12). lib. bdg. 34.60 *(978-0-8239-3188-0(9))* Rosen Publishing Group, Inc., The.

Ross, Allison J. Choosing a Career in Desktop Publishing. 2005. (World of Work Ser.). (Illus.). 64p. (YA). (gr. 7-12). lib. bdg. 31.95 *(978-0-8239-3295-5(8)*, WWDEPU) Rosen Publishing Group, Inc., The.

Ryan, Peter K. Careers in Electronic Publishing. 2013. 80p. (YA). (gr. 9-12). 33.25 *(978-1-4488-9590-8(1))* Rosen Publishing Group, Inc., The.

Sauerwein, Stan. Ma Murray: The Story of Canada's Crusty Queen of Publishing. 2003. (ENG., Illus.). 144p. per. *(978-1-55153-979-9(9))* Heritage Hse.

Townsend, Beth. Publishing, 1 vol. 2011. (Inside the Industry Ser.). (ENG., Illus.). 112p. (J). (gr. 6-12). lib. bdg. 35.64 *(978-1-61714-803-3(2)*, Essential Library) ABDO Publishing Co.

Walton, Ruth. Let's Read a Book: Find Out about Books & How They Are Made. 2013. (Let's Find Out Ser.). (Illus.). 32p. (J). (gr. k-5). 28.50 *(978-1-59771-387-0(2))* Sea-To-Sea Pubns.

Watson, Esther Pearl. Whatcha Mean, What's a Zine? The Art of Making Zines & Mini-Comics. Todd, Mark, illus. 2006. (ENG.). 112p. (YA). (gr. 7). pap. 13.99 *(978-0-618-56315-9(6))* Houghton Mifflin Harcourt Publishing Co.

Whitelaw, Nancy. Let's Go! Let's Publish! Katharine Graham & the Washington Post. 2004. (Makers of the Media Ser.). (Illus.). 112p. (YA). (gr. 6-12). 21.95 *(978-1-883846-37-4(4)*, First Biographies) Reynolds, Morgan Inc.

—William Randolph Hearst & the American Century. rev. exp. ed. 2004. (Makers of the Media Ser.). (Illus.). 128p. (gr. 6-12). 28.95 *(978-1-931798-35-8(4))* Reynolds, Morgan Inc.

PUBLISHERS AND PUBLISHING—FICTION

Chambliss Bertman, Jennifer. Book Scavenger. 2015. (Book Scavenger Ser.). (ENG., Illus.). 368p. (J). (gr. 4-9). 16.99 *(978-1-62779-115-1(9)*, 9781627791151, Holt, Henry & Co. Bks. For Young Readers) Holt, Henry & Co.

—Book Scavenger. 2016. (Book Scavenger Ser.). (ENG.). 368p. (J). pap. 7.99 *(978-1-250-07980-0(2)*, 9781250079800) Square Fish.

Clements, Andrew. The School Story. unabr. ed. 2004. (Middle Grade Cassette Librariestm Ser.). 224p. (J). (gr. 3-7). pap. 29.00 incl. audio *(978-0-8072-1000-0(5)*, S YA 352 SP, Listening Library) Random Hse. Audio Publishing Group.

Edge, Christopher. Twelve Minutes to Midnight. 2014. (Penelope Tredwell Mysteries Ser.: Book 1). (ENG.). 256p. (J). (gr. 3-7). 16.99 *(978-0-8075-8133-9(X))* Whitman, Albert & Co.

Ernst, Kathleen. Whistler in the Dark. 2009. (Mysteries Through Time Ser.). 144 - 176p. (YA). (gr. 4-8). 31.95 *(978-1-60754-429-6(6))*; pap. 15.25 *(978-1-60754-432-6(6))* Windmill Bks.

Hautman, Pete. What Boys Really Want. 2012. (ENG.). 304p. (J). (gr. 7). 17.99 *(978-0-545-11315-1(6)*, Scholastic Pr.) Scholastic, Inc.

McGowan, Patricia. House of Friends. 2012. 242p. 46.95 *(978-1-258-23494-2(7))*; pap. 31.95 *(978-1-258-24543-6(4))* Literary Licensing, LLC.

Messina, Lynn. Savvy Girl. 2008. (ENG., Illus.). 272p. (YA). (gr. 7-18). pap. 15.99 *(978-0-15-206161-6(4))* Houghton Mifflin Harcourt Publishing Co.

Patterson, James & Grabenstein, Chris. Laugh Out Loud. Ebbeler, Jeff, illus. 2017. (ENG.). 304p. (J). (gr. 3-7). 13.99 ***(978-0-316-43146-0(X)***, Jimmy Patterson) Little Brown & Co.

Spizman, Robyn Freedman & Johnston, Mark. Secret Agent. 2006. (ENG.). 240p. (J). (gr. 4-7). pap. 11.99 *(978-1-4169-1862-2(0)*, Atheneum Bks. for Young Readers) Simon & Schuster Children's Publishing.

Trooboff, Rhoda. A Book for Elie. Radjou, Anna Nazaretz, illus. 2008. (ENG.). 31p. pap. 15.00 *(978-0-9773536-1-3(3))* Univ. of Toledo Pr.

Webb Quest, By Sara. Aydil Vice, Author of Kiski the Cat. 2008. 70p. pap. 6.96 *(978-1-4357-5152-1(3))* Lulu Pr., Inc.

PUBLISHING

see Publishers and Publishing

PUERTO RICANS

Conley, Kate A. The Puerto Rican Americans. 2003. (Immigrants in America Ser.). (ENG., Illus.). 112p. (J). (gr. 4-7). lib. bdg. 30.85 *(978-1-59018-432-5(7)*, Lucent Bks.) Cengage Gale.

Hernández, Roger E. 1898 to World War II. 2009. (Hispanic America 2 Ser.). 80p. (gr. 5). 34.21 *(978-0-7614-4176-2(X))* Marshall Cavendish Corp.

PUERTO RICANS—BIOGRAPHY

Andersen, Richard. Abraham Rodriguez. 2013. (Today's Writers & Their Works Ser.). 144p. (YA). (gr. 7-12). pap. 22.34 *(978-1-62712-147-7(1))* Cavendish Square Publishing.

Fischer, David. Roberto Clemente. 2004. (Trailblazers of the Modern World Ser.). (Illus.). 48p. (gr. 5-12). pap. 14.05 *(978-0-8368-5264-6(8))*; lib. bdg. 31.00 *(978-0-8368-5495-4(0))* Stevens, Gareth Publishing LLLP. (Gareth Stevens Secondary Library).

Guzmán, Lila & Guzmán, Rick. Roberto Clemente: Heroe del Beisbol. 2007. (Latinos Famosos Ser.). (SPA., Illus.). 32p. (J). (gr. 3-7). lib. bdg. 23.94 *(978-0-7660-2675-9(2)*, Enslow Elementary) Enslow Pubs., Inc.

Marcovitz, Hal. Puerto Ricans. 2009. (Successful Americans Ser.). 64p. (YA). (gr. 9-12). 22.95 *(978-1-4222-0516-7(9))* Mason Crest.

Marquez, Heron. Roberto Clemente: Baseball's Humanitarian Hero. 2005. (Trailblazer Biography Ser.). (Illus.). 112p. (J). (gr. 3-7). lib. bdg. 30.60 *(978-1-57505-767-5(0))* Lerner Publishing Group.

Mills, Clifford W. Bernie Williams. 2007. (Baseball Superstars Ser.). (Illus.). 122p. (YA). (gr. 7-12). 30.00 *(978-0-7910-9468-6(5))* Facts On File, Inc.

Winter, Jonah. Roberto Clemente: Pride of the Pittsburgh Pirates. Colón, Raúl, illus. (ENG.). 40p. (J). (gr. -1-3). 2008. 7.99 *(978-1-4169-5082-0(6))* 2005. 17.99 *(978-0-689-85643-3(1))* Simon & Schuster Children's Publishing. (Atheneum Bks. for Young Readers).

PUERTO RICANS—FICTION

Delacre, Lulu. Alicia Afterimage. 2008. (ENG.). 144p. (YA). (gr. 7-18). 19.95 *(978-1-60060-242-9(8))* Lee & Low Bks., Inc.

Felicie-Soto, Ada. Arturo & the Hidden Treasure. Ortiz, Abimael, illus. 2015. (ENG.). 32p. (J). (gr. 1-5). lib. bdg. 27.59 *(978-1-4994-1863-7(9)*, PowerKids Pr.) Rosen Publishing Group, Inc., The.

González, Lucía. The Storyteller's Candle: La Velita de Los Cuentos. Delacre, Lulu, illus. 2013. (ENG & SPA.). 32p. (J). pap. 9.95 *(978-0-89239-237-7(1)*, Children's Book Press) Lee & Low Bks., Inc.

Gonzalez, Lucia M. & Delacre, Lulu. The Storyteller's Candle. 2008.Tr. of La Velita de los Cuentos. (SPA & ENG., Illus.). 32p. (J). (gr. k-4). 16.95 *(978-0-89239-222-3(3))* Lee & Low Bks., Inc.

Herrera, Juan Felipe. Cinnamon Girl: Letters Found Inside a Cereal Box. 2016. 176p. (YA). (gr. 8). pap. 9.99 *(978-0-06-244759-3(9)*, HarperTeen) HarperCollins Pubs.

Manzano, Sonia. The Revolution of Evelyn Serrano. 2014. (ENG.). 224p. (J). (gr. 9). pap. 9.99 *(978-0-545-32506-6(4))* Scholastic, Inc.

Manzano, Sonia & Muth, Jon J. No Dogs Allowed! Muth, Jon J., illus. 2004. (ENG., Illus.). 32p. (J). (gr. -1-2). 17.99 *(978-0-689-83088-4(2)*, Atheneum Bks. for Young Readers) Simon & Schuster Children's Publishing.

Nicholasa, Mohr. El Bronx Remembered. 2014. (Trophy Keypoint Bks). (ENG.). 272p. (J). (gr. 8-12). 13.24 *(978-1-63245-280-1(4))* Lectorum Pubns., Inc.

Older, Daniel José. Shadowhouse Fall. 2017. (Shadowshaper Cypher Ser.). (ENG.). 368p. (J). (gr. 7-7). 18.99 ***(978-0-545-95282-8(4)***, Levine, Arthur A. Bks.) Scholastic, Inc.

Ostow, Micol. Emily Goldberg Learns to Salsa. 2007. (ENG.). 208p. (YA). (gr. 7-18). 8.99 *(978-1-59514-144-6(8)*, Razorbill) Penguin Young Readers Group.

Rivera, Rafael, et al. Baseball on Mars/Béisbol en Marte. Rivera, Rafael et al, illus. 2009.Tr. of Béisbol en Marte. (SPA & ENG.). 32p. (J). (gr. -1-3). 16.95 *(978-1-55885-521-2(1))* Arte Publico Pr.

Urbain, Catherine. Manuel & the Lobsterman. 2008. (ENG.). 214p. (J). (gr. 4-7). 16.95 *(978-1-59078-516-4(9)*, Front Street) Boyds Mills Pr.

Valentin, Karen. Allie's World: Abuela & Abuelo Move: Abuela & Abuelo Move. 2009. 32p. 6.95 *(978-1-60349-021-4(3)*, Marimba Bks.) Hudson Publishing Group, The.

Velasquez, Eric. Grandma's Gift. Velasquez, Eric, illus. 2013. (ENG., Illus.). 32p. (J). (gr. k-1). pap. 9.99 *(978-0-8027-3536-2(3)*, 9780802735362, Bloomsbury USA Childrens) Bloomsbury Publishing USA.

Vigilante, Danette. The Trouble with Half a Moon. 2015. (ENG.). 208p. (J). (gr. 5). 7.99 *(978-0-14-751550-6(5)*, Puffin Books) Penguin Young Readers Group.

PUERTO RICANS—NEW YORK (STATE)—NEW YORK—FICTION

Caraballo, Samuel & Torrecilla, Pablo. Estrellita in the Big City/Estrellita en la Ciudad Grande. Caraballo, Samuel & Torrecilla, Pablo, illus. 2008. (SPA & ENG., Illus.). 32p. (J). (gr. -1-4). 16.95 *(978-1-55885-498-7(3)*, Piñata Books) Arte Publico Pr.

Cofer, Judith Ortiz. Call Me Maria. 2011. 8.44 *(978-0-7848-3341-4(9)*, Everbind) Marco Bk. Co.

—Call Me Maria. 2006. (First Person Fiction Ser.). (ENG.). 176p. (J). (gr. 3-7). per. 6.99 *(978-0-439-38578-7(4)*, Scholastic Paperbacks) Scholastic, Inc.

Manzano, Sonia. The Revolution of Evelyn Serrano. 2012. (ENG.). 224p. (J). (gr. 7-9). 17.99 *(978-0-545-32505-9(6)*, Scholastic Pr.) Scholastic, Inc.

Pfeffer, Susan Beth. The Dead & the Gone. 2010. (Last Survivors Ser.: 2). 321p. lib. bdg. 19.65 *(978-0-606-14464-3(1)*, Turtleback) Turtleback Bks.

Velasquez, Eric. Grandma's Records. 2014. 32p. pap. 9.00 *(978-1-61003-346-6(9))* Center for the Collaborative Classroom.

—Grandma's Records. 2004. (Illus.). 32p. (J). (gr. k-3). 17.85 *(978-0-8027-8761-3(4))*; 16.95 *(978-0-8027-8760-6(6))* Walker & Co.

Velasquez, Eric & National Geographic Learning Staff. Grandma's Records. Velasquez, Eric, illus. 2004. (ENG., Illus.). 32p. (J). (gr. k-3). pap. 9.99 *(978-0-8027-7660-0(4)*, 9780802776600, Bloomsbury USA Childrens) Bloomsbury Publishing USA.

PUERTO RICANS—UNITED STATES

Arkham, Thomas. Both Puerto Rican & American. 2012. (J). pap. *(978-1-4222-2333-8(7))* Mason Crest.

—Both Puerto Rican & American. Limón, José E., ed. 2012. (Hispanic Americans: Major Minority Ser.). 64p. (J). (gr. 4). 22.95 *(978-1-4222-2316-1(7))* Mason Crest.

Asselin, Kristine Carlson. Jennifer Lopez: Actress & Pop Superstar, 1 vol. 2013. (Contemporary Lives Set 2 Ser.). (ENG.). 112p. (J). (gr. 6-12). lib. bdg. 35.64 *(978-1-61783-621-3(4)*, Essential Library) ABDO Publishing Co.

Bryan, Nichol. Puerto Rican Americans, 1 vol. 2004. (One Nation Set 2 Ser.). (ENG.). 32p. (gr. k-6). 27.07 *(978-1-59197-532-8(8)*, Checkerboard Library) ABDO Publishing Co.

Marcovitz, Hal. Puerto Ricans. 2009. (Successful Americans Ser.). 64p. (YA). (gr. 9-12). 22.95 *(978-1-4222-0516-7(9))* Mason Crest.

Taus-Bolstad, Stacy. Puerto Ricans in America. 2005. (In America Ser.). (Illus.). 80p. (J). (gr. 5-8). lib. bdg. 27.93 *(978-0-8225-3953-7(5))* Lerner Publishing Group.

PUERTO RICANS—UNITED STATES—FICTION

Cofer, Judith Ortiz. An Island Like You: Stories of the Barrio. 2011. 9.15 *(978-0-7848-3583-8(7)*, Everbind) Marco Bk. Co.

Flor, Ada Alma. My Name Is Maria Isabel. 2014. (ENG.). 64p. (J). (gr. 12-12). 9.24 *(978-1-63245-189-7(1))* Lectorum Pubns., Inc.

Garcia, Richard. Los Espiritus de Mi Tia Otilia. 2004. (ENG & SPA., Illus.). (J). (gr. k-3). spiral bd. *(978-0-616-14606-4(X))* Canadian National Institute for the Blind/Institut National Canadien pour les Aveugles.

Manzano, Sonia. Miracle on 133rd Street. Priceman, Marjorie, illus. 2015. (ENG.). 48p. (J). (gr. -1-3). 17.99 *(978-0-689-87887-9(7))* Simon & Schuster Children's Publishing.

PUERTO RICO

Alvarez O'Neill, Juan, illus. ¡Vamos a Jugar! 2005. (SPA.). 28p. (J). 8.95 *(978-0-8477-1553-4(1))* Univ. of Puerto Rico Pr.

Bjorklund, Ruth. Puerto Rico. 2013. (It's My State 2nd Ed 4 Ser.). 80p. (J). (gr. 4-8). pap. 17.64 *(978-1-62712-096-8(3))* Cavendish Square Publishing.

—Puerto Rico. 2007. (It's My State! Ser.). (Illus.). 80p. (J). (gr. 3-7). lib. bdg. 21.95 *(978-0-7614-2218-1(8))* Marshall Cavendish GBR. Dist: Marshall Cavendish Corp.

Brown, Jonatha A. Puerto Rico & Other Outlying Areas. 2006. (Portraits of the States Ser.). (Illus.). 32p. (gr. 2-6). pap. 10.50 *(978-0-8368-4693-5(1))*; lib. bdg. 26.00 *(978-0-8368-4674-4(5))* Stevens, Gareth Publishing LLLP. (Gareth Stevens Learning Library).

Burgan, Michael. Puerto Rico. 2003. (From Sea to Shining Sea Ser.: 2). (ENG., Illus.). 80p. (J). 30.50 *(978-0-516-22398-8(4)*, Children's Pr.) Scholastic Library Publishing.

—Puerto Rico & Other Outlying Areas. 2003. (World Almanac Library of the States). (Illus.). 48p. (gr. 4-9). pap. 14.05 *(978-0-8368-5329-2(6)*, Gareth Stevens Learning Library) Stevens, Gareth Publishing LLLP.

—Puerto Rico y Otras Areas Perifericas. 2004. (World Almanac Ser.).Tr. of Puerto Rico & Other Outlying Areas. (SPA.). 48p. (gr. 4-9). lib. bdg. 31.00 *(978-0-8368-5726-9(7)*, GHS32693, Gareth Stevens Learning Library) Stevens, Gareth Publishing LLLP.

Fein, E. How to Draw Puerto Rico's Sights & Symbols. 2009. (Kid's Guide to Drawing America Ser.). 32p. (gr. k-k). 50.50 *(978-1-61511-092-6(5)*, PowerKids Pr.) Rosen Publishing Group, Inc., The.

George, Marian M. A Little Journey to Puerto Rico. 2004. reprint ed. pap. 1.99 *(978-1-4192-0211-7(1))* Kessinger Publishing, LLC.

Gutner, Howard. Puerto Rico. 2009. (True Book(tm), A — Countries Ser.). (ENG., Illus.). 48p. (J). (gr. 2-5). 31.00 *(978-0-531-16893-6(X))* Scholastic Library Publishing.

Hernandez, Romel. Puerto Rico. 2010. (Caribbean Today Ser.). (Illus.). 64p. (YA). (gr. 9-12). 21.95 *(978-1-4222-0628-7(9))* Mason Crest.

Johnston, Joyce. Puerto Rico. (J). 2012. lib. bdg. 25.26 *(978-0-7613-4554-1(X)*, Lerner Pubns.) 2nd exp. rev. ed. 2003. (Illus.). 84p. (gr. 3-6). pap. 6.95 *(978-0-8225-4150-9(5))* Lerner Publishing Group.

Levy, Patricia & Bahrawi, Nazry. Puerto Rico. 2nd rev. ed. 2005. (Cultures of the World Ser.). (Illus.). 144p. (gr. 6-10). lib. bdg. 42.79 *(978-0-7614-1970-9(5)*, Benchmark Bks.) Marshall Cavendish Corp.

Maine, Tyler. Puerto Rico. 2016. (States Ser.). (ENG., Illus.). 32p. (gr. 3-4). lib. bdg. 27.32 *(978-1-5157-0426-3(2))* Next Page Pr., The.

Marcus, Amy. Exploring Puerto Rico with the Five Themes of Geography. (Library of the Western Hemisphere Ser.). 24p. 2009. (gr. 4-4). 42.50 *(978-1-60853-930-7(X)*, PowerKids Pr.) 2005. (Illus.). (J). (gr. 5-7). lib. bdg. 22.60 *(978-1-4042-2673-9(7)*, PowerKids Pr.) 2005. (ENG., Illus.). (gr. 3-8). pap. 8.25 *(978-0-8239-4633-4(9))* Rosen Publishing Group, Inc., The.

Milivojevic, JoAnn. Puerto Rico. 2009. pap. 52.95 *(978-0-7613-4733-0(X))* 2005. (Illus.). 48p. (gr. 2-4). 22.60 *(978-1-57505-144-4(3))* Lerner Publishing Group.

Obregon, Jose Maria. Puerto Rico. Brusca, Maria Cristina, tr. from ENG. 2006. (Bilingual Library of the United States of America Ser.: Set 2). (ENG & SPA., Illus.). 32p. (J). (gr. 3-6). lib. bdg. 25.25 *(978-1-4042-3104-7(8))* Rosen Publishing Group, Inc., The.

Obregón, José María. Puerto Rico. 2009. (Bilingual Library of the United States of America Ser.). (ENG & SPA.). 32p. (gr. 2-2). 47.90 *(978-1-60853-383-1(2)*, Editorial Buenas Letras) Rosen Publishing Group, Inc., The.

Reynolds, Jeff E. Puerto Rico. 2005. (A to Z Ser.). (ENG., Illus.). 40p. (J). (gr. 2-4). pap. 6.95 *(978-0-516-25073-1(6)*, Children's Pr.) Scholastic Library Publishing.

Rodríguez Gonzalez, Tania. Roberto Clemente. 2012. (Superstars of Baseball ENGLISH Ser.). 32p. (J). (gr. 4). 19.95 *(978-1-4222-2697-1(2))*; (SPA., Illus.). 19.95 *(978-1-4222-2644-5(1))* Mason Crest.

Roth, Susan L. & Trumbore, Cindy. Parrots over Puerto Rico, 1 vol. Roth, Susan L., illus. 2013. (ENG., Illus.). 48p. (J). 19.95 *(978-1-62014-004-8(7))* Lee & Low Bks., Inc.

Schwabacher, Martin & Otfinoski, Steven. Puerto Rico. 2nd rev. ed. 2009. (Celebrate the States 11 Ser.). 144p. (gr. 6). 42.79 *(978-0-7614-4734-4(2))* Marshall Cavendish GBR. Dist: Marshall Cavendish Corp.

Silva Lee, Alfonso. Mi Isla y Yo: La Naturaleza de Puerto Rico. Hayskar, Bonnie J., ed. Lago, Alexis, illus. 2007. (SPA.). 32p. (J). pap. 8.95 *(978-1-929165-19-3(6))* PANGAEA.

—Mi isla y yo/My Island & I: La naturaleza de Puerto Rico/The Nature of Puerto Rico. Hayskar, Bonnie J., ed. Lago, Alexis, illus. 2003. (SPA & ENG.). 32p. (J). pap. 9.95 *(978-1-929165-12-4(9))* PANGAEA.

Tagliaferro, Linda. Puerto Rico in Pictures. 2nd ed. 2003. (Visual Geography Series, Second Ser.). (ENG., Illus.). 80p. (gr. 5-12). 31.93 *(978-0-8225-0936-3(9))* Lerner Publishing Group.

Zapata, Elizabeth. Puerto Rico. 2006. (Rookie Read-About Geography Ser.). (ENG., Illus.). 32p. (J). (gr. 1-2). lib. bdg. 20.50 *(978-0-516-25387-9(5))* Scholastic Library Publishing.

PUERTO RICO—BIOGRAPHY

Boehme, Gerry. Roberto Clemente: The Pride of Puerto Rico. 2016. (Game-Changing Athletes Ser.). (ENG., Illus.). 112p. (J). (gr. 9-9). lib. bdg. 42.79 *(978-1-5026-1058-4(2))* Cavendish Square Publishing.

Cotts, Nat. Daddy Yankee. 2009. (Hip-Hop Ser.). (Illus.). 64p. (YA). (gr. 4-7). pap. 7.95 *(978-1-4222-0342-2(5))* Mason Crest.

—Don Omar. 2009. (Hip Hop (Mason Crest Paperback) Ser.). (Illus.). 64p. (YA). (gr. 4-7). pap. 7.95 *(978-1-4222-0346-0(8))* Mason Crest.

Etingoff, Kim. Ivy Queen. 2009. (Hip-Hop 2 Ser.). (Illus.). 64p. (YA). (gr. 7-12). lib. bdg. 22.95 *(978-1-4222-0295-1(X))* Mason Crest.

Perdomo, Willie. Clemente! Collier, Bryan, illus. 2010. (ENG.). 32p. (J). (gr. 1-5). 17.99 *(978-0-8050-8224-1(7)*, 9780805082241, Holt, Henry & Co. Bks. For Young Readers) Holt, Henry & Co.

PUERTO RICO—FICTION

A Caribbean Experience Con Amor. There's a Coqui in My Shoe! 2007. (Illus.). 66p. (J). 21.99 *(978-0-9797641-0-3(6))* Chi Chi Rodriguez Bks.

Acevedo, Ari. Juan Bobo Sends the Pig to Mass. Wrenn, Tom, illus. 2008. (Story Cove Ser.). (SPA & ENG.). 24p. (J). (gr. -1-3). pap. 4.95 *(978-0-87483-883-1(5))* August Hse. Pubs., Inc.

Alvarez, Mrinali & Alvarez, Oneill J. Verde Navidad. 2006. (SPA.). 28p. 8.95 *(978-0-8477-1564-0(7))* Univ. of Puerto Rico Pr.

Cofer, Judith Ortiz. Animal Jamboree / La Fiesta de los Animales: Latino Folktales / Leyendas Latinas. Rosales-Yeomans, Natalia, tr. 2012. (SPA & ENG.). (J). pap. 9.95 *(978-1-55885-743-8(5)*, Piñata Books) Arte Publico Pr.

Delacre, Lulu. Rafi & Rosi. 2004. (Illus.). 64p. (J). lib. bdg. 13.85 *(978-1-4242-0596-7(4))* Fitzgerald Bks.

—Rafi & Rosi. Delacre, Lulu, illus. 2005. (I Can Read Bks.). (Illus.). 64p. (J). (gr. k-3). pap. 3.99 *(978-0-06-009897-1(X)*, Rayo) HarperCollins Pubs.

—Rafi & Rosi. Delacre, Lulu, illus. 2016. (Rafi & Rosi Ser.). (ENG., Illus.). 63p. (J). (gr. k-3). pap. 8.95 *(978-0-89239-377-0(7))* Lee & Low Bks., Inc.

—Rafi & Rosi Carnival!, 1 vol. 2016. (Rafi & Rosi Ser.). (ENG., Illus.). 64p. (J). (gr. k-3). pap. 8.95 *(978-0-89239-379-4(3))* Lee & Low Bks., Inc.

—Rafi y Rosi. Delacre, Lulu, illus. 2016. (Rafi & Rosi Ser.).Tr. of Rafi & Rosi. (SPA., Illus.). (J). pap. 8.95 *(978-0-89239-378-7(5))* Lee & Low Bks., Inc.

—Rafi y Rosi ¡Carnaval!, 1 vol. 2016. (Rafi & Rosi Ser.).Tr. of Rafi & Rosi Carnival. (SPA & ENG., Illus.). 64p. (J). pap. 8.95 *(978-0-89239-380-0(7))* Lee & Low Bks., Inc.

Enriquez, Jose. Saving the Mango Farm. 2006. 23p. (J). 10.98 *(978-1-4116-5917-9(1))* Lulu Pr., Inc.

Fontanez, Edwin. En esta hermosa Isla. Fontanez, Edwin, illus. 2nd rev. ed. 2005. (SPA., Illus.). 32p. (J). 16.95 *(978-0-9640868-7-6(5))* Exit Studio.

Garza, Carmen Lomas. Vejigante-Masquerader. (J). (gr. 2-4). *(978-0-590-45777-4(2)*, SO7640) Scholastic, Inc.

Guevara, Melva Vizcarrondo. My Grandma, My Hero. 2007. 58p. pap. 10.00 *(978-0-8059-7296-2(X))* Dorrance Publishing Co., Inc.

Heer, Dusty Rhoades. The Forest That Rains Frogs. 2012. (ENG.). 58p. pap. 19.95 *(978-1-4327-9303-6(9))* Outskirts Pr., Inc.

Hooper, Nancy. Everywhere Coquis. Quinones, Jacqueline, tr. Betancourt, Raymond, illus. 2003.Tr. of En Dondequiera Coquies. (ENG.). 48p. (J). 13.95 *(978-0-942929-14-0(4)*, Omni Arts Publishing) Read Street Publishing, Inc.

Jaffe, Nina. La Flor de Oro: Un Mito Taino de Puerto Rico. Ventura, Gabriela Baeza, tr. from ENG. Sanchez, Enrique O., illus. 2006. (SPA.). 32p. (J). (gr. -1-3). 16.95 *(978-1-55885-463-5(0)*, Piñata Books) Arte Publico Pr.

—Sing, Little Sack! ¡Canta, Saquito!: a Folktale from Puerto Rico. Cruz, Ray, illus. 2006. 48p. (J). (gr. 2-3). reprint ed. 19.00 *(978-1-4223-5573-2(X))* DIANE Publishing Co.

Landrón, Rafael & Landrón, José Rafael. Beba y la Isla Nena: Beba & the Little Island. Ordóñez, María Antonia, illus. 2010. (SPA & ENG.). 32p. (J). *(978-1-934370-05-6(3)*, Campanita Bks.) Editorial Campana.

Mabry, Samantha. A Fierce & Subtle Poison. 2016. (ENG.). 288p. (YA). (gr. 8-12). 17.95 *(978-1-61620-521-8(0))* Algonquin Bks. of Chapel Hill.

Martinez, Lisa Bolivar & Martinez, Matthew. Good Night Puerto Rico. Veno, Joe, illus. 2017. (Good Night Our World Ser.). (ENG.). 20p. (J). (— 1). bds. 9.95 *(978-1-60219-508-0(0))* Good Night Bks.

Montes, Marisa. Get Ready for Gabi No. 5: All in the Familia. Cepeda, Joe, illus. 2004. (ENG.). 112p. (J). (gr. 2-5). pap. *(978-0-439-66156-0(0)*, Scholastic Paperbacks) Scholastic, Inc.

Ortiz, Raquel M. & Ventura, Gabriela Baeza. Sofi & the Magic, Musical Mural. Dominguez, Maria, illus. 2015. (SPA & ENG.). (J). 17.95 *(978-1-55885-803-9(2)*, Piñata Books) Arte Publico Pr.

Peakler, Nicole Danette. Tayno Ti & the Legend of the Coqui. 2012. 28p. 24.95 *(978-1-4626-5940-1(3))* America Star Bks.

Posada, Jorge. Sí, Puedes. Colón, Raúl, illus. 2010.Tr. of Play Ball! (SPA.). 32p. (J). (gr. 1-5). 6.99 *(978-1-4169-9826-6(8)*, Simon & Schuster/Paula Wiseman Bks.) Simon & Schuster/Paula Wiseman Bks.

Reisenauer, Cynthia Mauro. Emerita. Reisenauer, Cynthia Mauro, illus. 2007. (Illus.). 48p. (J). 18.95 *(978-0-9726487-5-2(5))* Puddle Jump Pr., Ltd.

Rodriguez, Ed. Kiki Kokí: La Leyenda Encantada del Coquí. 2015.Tr. of Kiki Kokí - The Enchanted Legend of the Coquí Frog. (SPA & ENG., Illus.). 40p. (J). (gr. -1-3). 17.99 *(978-1-62672-104-3(1)*, 9781626721043) Roaring Brook Pr.

—Kiki Kokí: La Leyenda Encantada Del Coquí (Kiki Kokí: the Enchanted Legend of the Coquí Frog) 2015. (SPA., Illus.). 40p. (J). (gr. -1-3). 8.99 *(978-1-62672-132-6(7)*, 9781626721326) Roaring Brook Pr.

Romeu, Emma. Gregorio y el Pirata. 2003.Tr. of Gregorio & the Pirate. (SPA., Illus.). 152p. (J). pap. 9.95 *(978-968-19-0553-8(9))* Santillana USA Publishing Co., Inc.

Vicente, Alidis. The Case of the Three Kings / el Caso de Los Reyes Magos: The Flaca Files / Los Expedientes de Flaca. 2016. (Flaca Files / Los Expedientes de Flaca Ser.). (MUL, ENG & SPA., Illus.). 96p. (J). (gr. 3-6). pap. 9.95 *(978-1-55885-822-0(9)*, Piñata Books) Arte Publico Pr.

Wallner, Alexandra. Sergio & the Hurricane. 2006. (Illus.). (J). (gr. 1-3). 14.60 *(978-0-7569-6800-7(3))* Perfection Learning Corp.

PUERTO RICO—HISTORY

Alvarez O'Neill, Juan, illus. Grano a grano... Refranes Populares. 2005. (SPA.). (J). 8.95 *(978-0-8477-1554-1(X))* Univ. of Puerto Rico Pr.

Bjorklund, Ruth & Hantula, Richard. Puerto Rico. 2015. (It's My State! (r) Ser.). (ENG., Illus.). 80p. (J). (gr. 4-4). 34.21 *(978-1-62713-216-9(3))* Cavendish Square Publishing.

Clinton, Greg. Puerto Rico & the Spanish-American War. 2016. (Expanding America Ser.). (ENG., Illus.). 96p. (J). (gr. 8-8). 42.79 *(978-1-5026-0972-4(X))* Cavendish Square Publishing.

DaSilva-Gordon, Maria. Puerto Rico: Past & Present. 2010. (United States: Past & Present Ser.). (ENG.). 48p. (YA). pap. 11.75 *(978-1-4358-9529-4(0))*; lib. bdg. 29.25 *(978-1-4358-9502-7(9))* Rosen Publishing Group, Inc., The. (Rosen Reference).

Eagen, Rachel. Ponce de Leon: Exploring Florida & Puerto Rico. 2005. (In the Footsteps of Explorers Ser.). (ENG., Illus.). 32p. (J). (gr. 4-5). pap. *(978-0-7787-2448-3(4))* Crabtree Publishing Co.

Ebon Research Systems Staff. Dare to Be Vol. 4: Luis Munoz Marion. l.t. ed. 2003.Tr. of Atrevete Ser... Un Heroe Luis Munoz Marin. (ENG & SPA., Illus.). 14p. (J). 3.99 *(978-0-9648313-7-7(6))* Ebon Research Systems Publishing, LLC.

Friesen, Helen Lepp. Puerto Rico: Isle of Enchantment. 2012. (J). *(978-1-61913-397-6(0))*; pap. *(978-1-61913-398-3(9))* Weigl Pubs., Inc.

Goldsworthy, Steve. Puerto Rico. 2011. (Guide to American States Ser.). (Illus.). 48p. (YA). (gr. 3-6). 29.99 *(978-1-61690-811-9(4))*; (J). *(978-1-61690-487-6(9))* Weigl Pubs., Inc.

—Puerto Rico: Isle of Enchantment. 2016. (J). *(978-1-4896-4932-4(8))* Weigl Pubs., Inc.

Gutner, Howard. Puerto Rico. 2009. (True Book Ser.). (ENG., Illus.). 48p. (J). (gr. 3-5). pap. 6.95 *(978-0-531-21360-5(9)*, Children's Pr.) Scholastic Library Publishing.

Hantula, Richard & Bjorklund, Ruth. Puerto Rico. 2nd ed. 2013. 80p. (J). (gr. 4-8). 31.36 *(978-1-60870-883-3(7))* Cavendish Square Publishing.

Hernandez, Romel. Puerto Rico, Vol. 11. Henderson, James D., ed. 2015. (Discovering the Caribbean: History, Politics, & Culture Ser.). (Illus.). 64p. (J). (gr. 7). lib. bdg. 22.95 *(978-1-4222-3315-3(4))* Mason Crest.

Lopez, Jose Javier. Puerto Rico. Gritzner, Charles F., ed. 2006. (Modern World Nations Ser.). (Illus.). 108p. (gr. 6-12). lib. bdg. 35.00 *(978-0-7910-8798-5(0))* Facts On File, Inc.

Lusted, Marcia Amidon. Puerto Rico: The Isle of Enchantment. 2010. (Our Amazing States Ser.). (ENG.). 24p. (J). pap. 8.25 *(978-1-4488-0775-8(1))*; lib. bdg. 22.60 *(978-1-4488-0668-3(2))* Rosen Publishing Group, Inc., The. (PowerKids Pr.).

Milivojevic, JoAnn. Puerto Rico. (Country Explorers Ser.). 48p. (gr. 2-4). 2009. (ENG.). 29.27 *(978-1-58013-598-6(6))* 2005. (Illus.). 22.60 *(978-1-57505-144-4(3))* Lerner Publishing Group.

Ollhoff, Jim. Puerto Rico, 1 vol. 2009. (United States Ser.). (ENG., Illus.). 48p. (YA). (gr. 2-5). 27.07 *(978-1-60453-674-4(8))* ABDO Publishing Co.

Riddering, Karenlie Anne. Puerto Rico: Encanto Oculto. 2nd ed. 2005. (ENG & SPA.). 60p. (YA). *(978-0-9765977-2-8(1))* Riddering, Marggie.

Stille, Darlene R. Puerto Rico. rev. ed. 2014. (ENG., Illus.). 144p. (J). lib. bdg. 40.00 *(978-0-531-28290-8(2))* Scholastic Library Publishing.

Tieck, Sarah. Puerto Rico, 1 vol. 2012. (Explore the United States Ser.). (ENG., Illus.). 32p. (J). (gr. 2-5). lib. bdg. 28.50 *(978-1-61783-377-9(0)*, Big Buddy Bks.) ABDO Publishing Co.

Torres, John. We Visit Puerto Rico. 2010. (Your Land & My Land Ser.). (Illus.). 64p. (J). (gr. 3-6). lib. bdg. 33.95 *(978-1-58415-892-9(1))* Mitchell Lane Pubs., Inc.

Worth, Richard. Puerto Rico: From Colony to Commonwealth. 2015. (Our Shared History Ser.). (ENG., Illus.). 128p. (J). (gr. 7-7). lib. bdg. 37.27 *(978-0-7660-7004-2(2))* Enslow Pubs., Inc.

—Puerto Rico in American History. 2008. (From Many Cultures, One History Ser.). (Illus.). 128p. (J). (gr. 5-18). lib. bdg. 33.27 *(978-0-7660-2836-4(4))* Enslow Pubs., Inc.

Yasuda, Anita. What's Great about Puerto Rico? 2015. (Our Great States Ser.). (ENG.). 32p. (J). (gr. 2-5). pap. 7.95 *(978-1-4677-6096-6(X))*; (Illus.). lib. bdg. 26.60 *(978-1-4677-3872-9(7))* Lerner Publishing Group. (Lerner Pubns.).

PUFFINS

Austen, Amy. Puffins, 01 vols., 1. 2016. (Ocean Friends Ser.). (ENG., Illus.). 24p. (J). pap. 8.25 *(978-1-5081-4180-8(0)*, PowerKids Pr.) Rosen Publishing Group, Inc., The.

Beer, Amy-Jane. Puffins. 2008. (Nature's Children Ser.). (Illus.). 52p. (J). *(978-0-7172-6260-1(X))* Grolier, Ltd.

Markovics, Joyce. MIS Patas Son Palmeadas y Anaranjadas (Puffin) 2016. (Pistas de Animales 2 Ser.). (SPA.). 24p. (J). (gr. -1-3). 17.95 *(978-1-944102-80-7(9))* Bearport Publishing Co., Inc.

Markovics, Joyce L. My Feet Are Webbed & Orange. 2016. (Zoo Clues 2 Ser.). (ENG.). 24p. (J). (gr. -1-3). lib. bdg. 17.95 *(978-1-944102-62-3(0))* Bearport Publishing Co., Inc.

Murray, Julie. Puffins, 1 vol. 2013. (Arctic Animals Ser.). (ENG.). 32p. (J). (gr. 2-5). lib. bdg. 28.50 *(978-1-61783-800-2(4)*, Big Buddy Bks.) ABDO Publishing Co.

Owen, Ruth. Puffins. 2013. (Polar Animals: Life in the Freezer Ser.). (ENG., Illus.). 32p. (gr. k-5). 25.25 *(978-1-4777-0224-6(5))*; pap. 10.00 *(978-1-4777-0235-2(0))* Windmill Bks.

Quinlan, Susan E. Puffins. rev. ed. 2009. (Nature Watch Ser.). (ENG.). 48p. (gr. 4-8). 27.93 *(978-1-58013-944-1(2))* Lerner Publishing Group.

Sexton, Colleen. Puffins. 2009. (Oceans Alive Ser.). (ENG., Illus.). 24p. (J). (gr. k-3). lib. bdg. 25.95 *(978-1-60014-251-2(6))* Bellwether Media.

—Puffins. 2009. (Blastoff! Readers Ser.). (ENG., Illus.). 24p. (J). (gr. k-3). 20.00 *(978-0-531-21714-6(0)*, Children's Pr.) Scholastic Library Publishing.

PUGET SOUND (WASH.)

Marsico, Katie. Puget Sound. 2013. (Explorer Library: Social Studies Explorer Ser.). (ENG.). 32p. (J). (gr. 4-8). pap. 14.21 *(978-1-62431-039-3(7)*, 202513) Cherry Lake Publishing.

—The Puget Sound. 2013. (Explorer Library: Social Studies Explorer Ser.). (ENG.). 32p. (J). (gr. 4-8). lib. bdg. 28.50 *(978-1-62431-015-7(X)*, 202511) Cherry Lake Publishing.

PUGET SOUND (WASH.)—FICTION

Arden, Lynne. Guess What Happened to Me, Auntie Kate! Marino, Natalie, illus. 2008. 52p. pap. 18.95 *(978-1-59858-733-3(1))* Dog Ear Publishing, LLC.

Deuker, Carl & Perry, Thomas. Runner. 2007. (ENG.). 224p. (YA). (gr. 7-12). pap. 8.99 *(978-0-618-73505-1(4))* Houghton Mifflin Harcourt Publishing Co.

PUGILISM

see Boxing

PULASKI, KAZIMIERZ, 1748-1779

Flavius, Brother. Father of the American Cavalry: A Story of Brigadier General Casimir Pulaski. Jagodits, Carolyn Lee, illus. 2011. 96p. 38.95 *(978-1-258-07161-5(4))* Literary Licensing, LLC.

Kajencki, AnnMarie Francis. Count Casimir Pulaski: From Poland to America, a Hero's Fight for Liberty. (Library of American Lives & Times Ser.). 112p. 2009. (gr. 5-5). 69.20 *(978-1-60853-475-3(8))* 2005. (Illus.). (YA). (gr. 4-7). lib. bdg. 34.60 *(978-1-4042-2646-3(X))* Rosen Publishing Group, Inc., The.

PULITZER, JOSEPH, 1847-1911

Gitlin, Martin. Joseph Pulitzer: Historic Newspaper Publisher, 1 vol. 2009. (Publishing Pioneers Ser.). (ENG., Illus.). 112p. (J). (gr. 6-12). lib. bdg. 35.64 *(978-1-60453-765-9(5)*, Essential Library) ABDO Publishing Co.

Whitelaw, Nancy. Joseph Pulitzer & the New York World. rev. exp. ed. 2004. (Makers of the Media Ser.). (Illus.). 128p. (J). lib. bdg. 21.95 *(978-1-931798-36-5(2))* Reynolds, Morgan Inc.

PUMA

Archer, Claire. Pumas, 1 vol. 2014. (Big Cats Ser.). (ENG.). 24p. (J). (gr. 4-8). lib. bdg. 28.50 *(978-1-62970-005-2(3))* ABDO Publishing Co.

Archer, Claire, et al. Pumas. 2015. (Grandes Felinos Ser.). (SPA., Illus.). 24p. (gr. k-1). pap. 7.95 *(978-1-4966-0465-1(2))* Capstone Classroom.

Bradley, James V. The Mountain Lion. 2006. (Nature Walk Ser.). (Illus.). 64p. (gr. 4-6). lib. bdg. 28.00 *(978-0-7910-9119-7(8)*, Chelsea Hse.) Facts On File, Inc.

Carr, Aaron. Cougars. 2014. (Illus.). 24p. (J). *(978-1-62127-210-6(9))* Weigl Pubs., Inc.

Cline, Gina. Cougars. Rupp, Kristina, illus. 2012. (1G Predator Animals Ser.). (ENG.). 24p. (J). pap. 5.99 *(978-1-61406-244-8(7))* American Reading Co.

Fox-Parrish, et al. Ghost Cats of the Tetons, Bk. 1. 2010. 40p. pap. 18.99 *(978-1-4490-1939-6(0))* AuthorHouse.

—Ghost Cats of the Tetons: Book 2. 2010. 60p. pap. 23.99 *(978-1-4490-2946-3(9))* AuthorHouse.

—Ghost Cats of the Tetons: Book 3: New Horizons. 2010. 48p. pap. 19.49 *(978-1-4490-2947-0(7))* AuthorHouse.

George, Jean Craighead. Summer Moon. 2003. (J). (gr. 3-7). 20.75 *(978-0-8446-7243-4(2))* Smith, Peter Pub., Inc.

Gish, Melissa. Cougars. 2012. (Living Wild Ser.). (Illus.). 48p. (J). (gr. 5-12). 23.95 *(978-1-60818-167-4(7)*, Creative Education) Creative Co., The.

—Living Wild: Cougars. 2013. (Living Wild Ser.). (ENG., Illus.). 48p. (J). (gr. 4-7). pap. 12.00 *(978-0-89812-774-4(2)*, Creative Paperbacks) Creative Co., The.

Guillain, Charlotte. Pumas, 1 vol. 2014. (Living in the Wild: Big Cats Ser.). (ENG., Illus.). 48p. (gr. 3-6). lib. bdg. 33.32 *(978-1-4329-8109-9(9)*, Heinemann InfoSearch) Heinemann-Raintree.

Guillain, Charlotte, et al. Living in the Wild: Big Cats, 1 vol. 2014. (Living in the Wild: Big Cats Ser.). (ENG.). 48p. (gr. 3-6). lib. bdg. 199.92 *(978-1-4329-8111-2(0)*, Heinemann InfoSearch) Heinemann-Raintree.

Hamilton, Sue. Ambushed by a Cougar, 1 vol. 2010. (Close Encounters of the Wild Kind Ser.). (ENG.). 32p. (YA). (gr. 4-7). 27.07 *(978-1-60453-928-8(3))* ABDO Publishing Co.

Hogan, Christa C. Mountain Lions. 2017. (Animals of North America (paperback) Ser.). (ENG., Illus.). 32p. (J). (gr. 3-5). pap. 9.95 ***(978-1-63517-092-4(3)***, Focus Readers) North Star Editions.

Jackson, Tom. Cougars. 2008. (Nature's Children Ser.). (Illus.). 52p. (J). *(978-0-7172-6220-5(0))* Grolier, Ltd.

Johnson, Jinny. Mountain Lion. 2014. (North American Mammals Ser.). 24p. (gr. 2-5). 28.50 *(978-1-62588-035-2(9))* Black Rabbit Bks.

—Mountain Lion. 2014. (North American Mammals Ser.). (ENG., Illus.). 24p. (J). (gr. -1-4). pap. 8.95 *(978-1-77092-169-6(9))* Saunders Bk. Co. CAN. Dist: RiverStream Publishing.

Karlin, Wade. Pumas. 2012. (Killer Cats Ser.). (Illus.). 24p. (J). (gr. 2-5). pap. 8.15 *(978-1-4339-7012-2(0))*; lib. bdg. 22.60 *(978-1-4339-7011-5(2))* Stevens, Gareth Publishing LLLP.

Macken, JoAnn Early. Cougars. 2nd rev. ed. 2009. (Animals That Live in the Mountains Ser.). 24p. (J). (gr. -1-3). pap. 8.15 *(978-1-4339-2494-1(3))*; lib. bdg. 22.60 *(978-1-4339-2411-8(0))* Stevens, Gareth Publishing LLLP. (Weekly Reader Leveled Readers).

—Cougars;Puma. 2nd rev. ed. 2009. (Animals That Live in the Mountains/Animales de las montañas Ser.). (ENG & SPA.). 24p. (J). (gr. -1-3). pap. 8.15 *(978-1-4339-2501-6(X))*; lib. bdg. 22.60 *(978-1-4339-2443-9(9))* Stevens, Gareth Publishing LLLP. (Weekly Reader Leveled Readers).

Magby, Meryl. Mountain Lions. 2013. 24p. (J). (gr. k-5). 22.60 *(978-1-4777-0788-3(3))*; pap. 49.50 *(978-1-4777-0949-8(5))*; pap. 8.25 *(978-1-4777-0948-1(7))* Rosen Publishing Group, Inc., The. (PowerKids Pr.).

Markle, Sandra. Mountain Lions. 2009. (Animal Predators Ser.). (ENG.). 40p. (gr. 3-6). 26.60 *(978-1-58013-538-2(2))* Lerner Publishing Group.

Owen, Ruth. Pumas, 1. 2014. (Dr. Bob's Amazing World of Animals Ser.). (ENG.). 32p. (J). (gr. k-5). 27.50 *(978-1-4777-9032-8(2)*, Windmill Bks.) Rosen Publishing Group, Inc., The.

Owings, Lisa. Mountain Lion Attack. 2012. (Animal Attacks Ser.). (ENG., Illus.). 24p. (J). (gr. 3-7). lib. bdg. 25.95 *(978-1-60014-769-0(5)*, Torque Bks.) Bellwether Media.

Person, Stephen. Cougar: A Cat with Many Names. 2012. (America's Hidden Animal Treasures Ser.). 32p. (J). (gr. 2-7). lib. bdg. 26.60 *(978-1-61772-569-2(2))* Bearport Publishing Co., Inc.

Raatma, Lucia. How Do We Live Together? Mountain Lions. 2010. (Community Connections: How Do We Live Together? Ser.). (ENG.). 24p. (gr. 2-5). lib. bdg. 25.64 *(978-1-60279-625-6(4)*, 200328) Cherry Lake Publishing.

Rake, Jody Sullivan. Pumas: On the Hunt. 2010. (Killer Animals Ser.). (ENG.). 32p. (gr. 1-2). lib. bdg. 26.65 *(978-1-4296-3928-6(8)*, Blazers) Capstone Press of Coughlan Cos.

Randall, Henry. Cougars. 2011. (Cats of the Wild Ser.). (ENG.). 24p. (J). pap. 8.25 *(978-1-4488-2617-9(9))*; lib. bdg. 22.60 *(978-1-4488-2516-5(4))* Rosen Publishing Group, Inc., The. (PowerKids Pr.).

—Cougars / Pumas. 2011. (Cats of the Wild / Felinos Salvajes Ser.). (SPA.). 24p. 22.60 *(978-1-4488-3128-9(8)*, Editorial Buenas Letras) Rosen Publishing Group, Inc., The.

Rathburn, Betsy. Mountain Lions. 2017. (North American Animals Ser.). (ENG., Illus.). 24p. (J). (gr. k-3). lib. bdg. 25.95 ***(978-1-62617-639-3(6)***, Blastoff! Readers) Bellwether Media.

Read, Tracy C. Exploring the World of Cougars. 2011. (Exploring the World Of Ser.). (ENG., Illus.). 24p. (J). (gr. 3-7). 16.95 *(978-1-55407-785-4(0)*, 9781554077854); pap. 6.95 *(978-1-55407-956-8(X)*, 9781554079568) Firefly Bks., Ltd.

Riggs, Kate. Cougars. 2014. (J). 25.65 *(978-1-60818-347-0(5)*, Creative Education) Creative Co., The.

Ringstad, Arnold. Cougars. 2015. (Wild Cats Ser.). (Illus.). 24p. (J). 27.10 *(978-1-60753-600-0(5))* Amicus Publishing.

Rodriguez, Cindy. Cougars. 2009. (ENG., Illus.). 24p. (gr. 3-6). pap. 8.95 *(978-1-60694-843-9(1))* Rourke Educational Media.

Schuetz, Kristin. Mountain Lions. 2014. (Backyard Wildlife Ser.). (ENG.). 24p. (J). (gr. k-3). lib. bdg. 25.95 *(978-1-60014-970-2(7)*, Blastoff! Readers) Bellwether Media.

Shores, Erika L. Mountain Lions, 1 vol. 2010. (Wildcats Ser.). (ENG & ABK.). 24p. (gr. k-1). lib. bdg. 26.65 *(978-1-4296-4485-3(0)*, Pebble Plus) Capstone Press of Coughlan Cos.

Taylor, Trace & Sánchez, Lucía M. Pumas. 2009. (1G Animales Depredador Ser.). (SPA., Illus.). 32p. (J). (gr. k-2). pap. 6.99 *(978-1-61541-057-6(0))* American Reading Co.

Tomljanovic, Tatiana. Cougars. (J). 2014. *(978-1-4896-0914-4(8))* 2010. (Illus.). 24p. (gr. 2-4). pap. 11.95 *(978-1-60596-950-3(8))* 2010. (Illus.). 24p. (gr. 2-5). lib. bdg. 25.70 *(978-1-60596-949-7(4))* Weigl Pubs., Inc.

Vogel, Elizabeth. Pumas. 2009. (Big Cats (Powerkids Readers) Ser.). 24p. (gr. 1-1). 37.50 *(978-1-61511-571-6(4)*, PowerKids Pr.) Rosen Publishing Group, Inc., The.

von Zumbusch, Amelie. Pumas: Lone Hunters. 2009. (Dangerous Cats Ser.). 24p. (gr. 2-3). 42.50 *(978-1-61512-130-4(7)*, PowerKids Pr.) Rosen Publishing Group, Inc., The.

Zuchora-Walske, Christine. Mountain Lions, 1 vol. 2012. (Big Cats Ser.). (ENG.). 32p. (gr. 3-4). lib. bdg. 27.99 *(978-1-4296-7644-1(2)*, Edge Bks.) Capstone Press of Coughlan Cos.

PUMA—FICTION

Ballantyne, Robert Michael. The Rover of the Andes: A Tale of Adventure in South America. 2007. (ENG.). 266p. pap. 21.99 *(978-1-4346-3753-6(0))*; 296p. pap. 23.99 *(978-1-4346-3767-3(0))* Creative Media Partners, LLC.

Carr, Roger Vaughan. The Climb. 2007. 96p. (J). pap. *(978-1-4207-0730-4(2))* Sundance/Newbridge Educational Publishing.

Cox, Renee K. Sammie Jane Saves Charlie: Cougar's Rescue. 2009. (Illus.). 56p. pap. 11.95 *(978-1-4327-3129-8(7))* Outskirts Pr., Inc.

Haig-Brown, Roderick. Panther. 2007. (ENG., Illus.). 256p. (YA). pap. 14.95 *(978-1-55017-341-3(3))* Harbour Publishing Co., Ltd. CAN. Dist: Midpoint Trade Bks., Inc.

Jordan, Rosa. The Last Wild Place, 1 vol. 2008. (ENG.). 256p. (J). (gr. 3-7). 15.95 *(978-1-56145-458-7(3)*, Peachtree Junior) Peachtree Pubs.

Love, Nicole M. Cool Cougar! Cool Cougar! Cool Cougar! & the Puma Dance. 2012. 24p. pap. 17.99 *(978-1-4685-7541-5(4))* AuthorHouse.

Mitchell, Todd. Species. 2017. (ENG.). 256p. (J). (gr. 3-7). 16.99 *(978-0-399-55558-9(7)*, Delacorte Bks. for Young Readers) Random Hse. Children's Bks.

Mora, Pat. Doña Flor: A Tall Tale about a Giant Woman with a Great Big Heart. Colón, Raúl, illus. 2010. (ENG & SPA.). 32p. (J). (gr. -1-2). pap. 7.99 *(978-0-375-86144-4(0)*, Dragonfly Bks.) Random Hse. Children's Bks.

Nesbit, Troy. Mystery at Rustlers Fort. 2014. (Wilderness Mystery Ser.). (ENG., Illus.). 282p. (J). (gr. 3-7). pap. 12.95 *(978-1-58979-867-0(8))* Taylor Trade Publishing.

Parrish, Amanda. Greyhound Travels: Puma Travels to Italy. 2010. 28p. pap. 12.49 *(978-1-4490-9453-9(8))* AuthorHouse.

Snyder, Adeline. Hunting with Mountain Lions, Vol. 1. 2014. (Animal Attack! Ser.). (ENG.). 32p. (J). (gr. 2-3). 22.60 *(978-1-4824-0516-3(4))* Stevens, Gareth Publishing LLLP.

PUMPKIN

Collier, Polly, reader. The Pumpkin Book. 2004. (Illus.). (J). (gr. -1-2). audio compact disk 28.95 *(978-1-59112-940-0(0))* Live Oak Media.

Farmer, Jacqueline. Calabazas. DelRisco, Eida, tr. from ENG. Tildes, Phyllis Limbacher, illus. 2006. (SPA & ENG.). 32p. (J). (gr. k-3). per. 7.95 *(978-1-57091-696-0(9))* Charlesbridge Publishing, Inc.

—Pumpkins. Tildes, Phyllis Limbacher, illus. 2004. (ENG.). 32p. (J). (gr. k-3). pap. 7.95 *(978-1-57091-558-1(X))* Charlesbridge Publishing, Inc.

Felix, Rebecca. We Harvest Pumpkins in the Fall. 2013. 24p. (J). *(978-1-61080-981-8(5))*; (ENG.). 22.79 *(978-1-61080-906-1(8)*, 202603); (ENG.). pap. 12.79 *(978-1-61080-931-3(9)*, 202605) Cherry Lake Publishing.

Friesen, Helen Lepp. Growing a Pumpkin. 2008. (Discovering & Exploring Science Ser.). (Illus.). 16p. (J). (gr. -1-3). lib. bdg. 12.95 *(978-0-7569-8426-7(2))* Perfection Learning Corp.

Griswold, Cliff. The Pumpkin Patch. 2015. (Fun in Fall Ser.). (ENG.). 24p. (J). (gr. k-k). lib. bdg. 22.60 *(978-1-4824-1788-3(X))* Stevens, Gareth Publishing LLLP.

Hayes, Amy. A Seed Becomes a Pumpkin. 2016. (Transformations in Nature Ser.). (ENG., Illus.). 24p. (J). (gr. 1-1). pap. 8.22 *(978-1-5026-0814-7(6))* Cavendish Square Publishing.

Koontz, Robin Michal. Pick a Perfect Pumpkin: Learning about Pumpkin Harvests, 1 vol. Takvorian, Nadine, illus. 2010. (Autumn Ser.). (ENG.). 24p. (gr. 1-2). lib. bdg. 26.65 *(978-1-4048-6011-7(8))* Picture Window Bks.

Lee, Jackie. Pumpkin. 2015. (See It Grow Ser.). (ENG.). 24p. (J). (gr. -1-3). lib. bdg. 23.93 *(978-1-62724-840-2(4))* Bearport Publishing Co., Inc.

Lindeen, Mary. I Pick Fall Pumpkins. 2016. (First Step Nonfiction — Observing Fall Ser.). (ENG., Illus.). 24p. (J). (gr. k-2). 23.99 *(978-1-5124-0796-9(8))* Lerner Publishing Group.

Malam, John. Grow Your Own Soup, 1 vol. 2011. (Grow It Yourself! Ser.). (ENG.). 32p. (gr. k-2). 27.32

(978-1-4329-5106-1(8), Heinemann First Library) Heinemann-Raintree.

McNeil, Niki, et al. HOCPP 1110 Five Little Pumpkins. 2006. spiral bd. 14.00 (978-1-60308-110-8(0)) In the Hands of a Child.

Michele, Tracey. Pumpkin Time. 2011. (Learn-Abouts Ser.). (Illus.). 16p. (J). pap. 7.95 (978-1-59920-589-2(0)) Black Rabbit Bks.

Nelson, Robin. Pumpkins. 2009. pap. 34.95 (978-0-7613-4118-5(8)); (ENG., Illus.). 24p. 23.93 (978-0-7613-4073-7(4), Lerner Pubns.) Lerner Publishing Group.

Owings, Lisa. From Pumpkin to Pie. 2015. (Start to Finish, Second Ser.). (ENG.). 24p. (gr. k-3). pap. 6.95 (978-1-4677-6112-3(5)); lib. bdg. 23.93 (978-1-4677-6018-8(8)) Lerner Publishing Group. (Lerner Pubns.).

Pfeffer, Wendy. From Seed to Pumpkin. Hale, James Graham, illus. (Let's-Read-And-Find-Out Science 1 Ser.). (ENG.). 40p. (J). (gr. -1-3). 2015. pap. 6.99 (978-0-06-238185-9(7)) 2004. 15.99 (978-0-06-028038-3(7)) HarperCollins Pubs.

Rhatigan, Joe. Grow Your Own Giant Pumpkin. 2013. (ENG.). 64p. (J). 18.95 (978-1-60433-301-5(4), Applesauce Pr.) Cider Mill Pr. Bk. Pubs., LLC.

Rustad, Martha E. H. Fall Pumpkins: Orange & Plump. Enright, Amanda, illus. 2011. (Fall's Here! Ser.). pap. 39.62 (978-0-7613-8647-6(5), Millbrook Pr.); (ENG.). 24p. pap. 6.95 (978-0-7613-8509-7(6), Millbrook Pr.); (ENG.). 24p. lib. bdg. 23.93 (978-0-7613-5065-1(9)) Lerner Publishing Group.

Schuh, Mari. Pumpkins in Fall. 2013. (ENG., Illus.). 24p. (J). lib. bdg. 25.65 (978-1-62031-060-1(0)) Jump! Inc.

Shores, Erika L. Pumpkins. 2015. (Celebrate Fall Ser.). (ENG., Illus.). 24p. (gr. k-1). lib. bdg. 21.99 (978-1-4914-6004-7(0), Pebble Bks.) Capstone Press of Coughlan Cos.

Sundance/Newbridge LLC Staff. Growing Pumpkins. 2007. (Early Science Ser.). (gr. k-3). 18.95 (978-1-4007-6179-1(4)); pap. 6.10 (978-1-4007-6175-3(1)) Sundance/Newbridge Educational Publishing.

PUMPKIN—FICTION

Accord Publishing Staff & Stone, Kate. One Spooky Night: A Halloween Adventure. 2011. (ENG.). 36p. (J). pap. 11.99 (978-1-4494-0330-0(1)) Andrews McMeel Publishing.

The Adventures of the Original Pumpkin Patch Pals. l.t. ed. 2005. (Illus.). 32p. (J). 15.00 (978-0-9770960-1-5(7)) 3 Pals Media, LLC.

Arthur, Sherry. Magical Hallows Eve. 2009. 44p. pap. 24.00 (978-0-557-07264-4(6)) Lulu Pr., Inc.

Atamer, Billie. The Little Purple Pumpkin. 2013. 28p. (gr. -1-3). pap. 11.95 (978-1-61244-235-8(8)) Halo Publishing International.

Bauer, Joan. Squashed. 2005. (ENG.). 208p. (YA). (gr. 7-7). pap. 7.99 (978-0-14-240426-3(8), Speak) Penguin Young Readers Group.

—Squashed. 2005. 194p. (gr. 7-12). 18.00 (978-0-7569-5781-0(8)) Perfection Learning Corp.

Bonnell, Kris. Picking a Pumpkin. 2007. (J). pap. 5.95 (978-1-933727-51-6(9)) Reading Reading Bks., LLC.

Bourgeois, Paulette & Clark, Brenda. Franklin's Pumpkin. Southern, Shelley, illus. 2004. (Kids Can Read Ser.). (ENG.). 32p. (J). (gr. 1-2). 3.95 (978-1-55337-496-1(7)); 14.95 (978-1-55337-495-4(9)) Kids Can Pr., Ltd. CAN. Dist: Hachette Bk. Group.

Bowman, Crystal. My Happy Pumpkin: God's Love Shining Through Me, 1 vol. 2014. (ENG.). 14p. (J). bds. 6.99 (978-0-310-73828-2(8)) Zonderkidz.

Boyd, William T. The Pumpkin Fairy. Roberts, Mary Jo, illus. 2003. 32p. (J). (gr. k-1). 14.95 (978-0-9718161-0-7(7)) Wyatt Pr.

Brown, Desirae. A Pumpkin's Dream, 1 vol. 2009. 29p. pap. 24.95 (978-1-60836-364-3(3)) America Star Bks.

Brown, Margaret Wise. The Fierce Yellow Pumpkin. Egielski, Richard, illus. 2006. (ENG.). 32p. (J). (gr. -1-1). reprint ed. pap. 6.99 (978-0-06-443534-5(2)) HarperCollins Pubs.

Brown, Margaret Wise & Brown. The Fierce Yellow Pumpkin. Egielski, Richard, illus. 2003. (ENG.). 32p. (J). (gr. -1-1). 16.99 (978-0-06-024479-8(8)) HarperCollins Pubs.

Capucilli, Alyssa Satin. Biscuit Visits the Pumpkin Patch. Schories, Pat, illus. 2004. (Biscuit Ser.). (ENG.). 16p. (J). (gr. -1-3). bds. 4.99 (978-0-06-009466-9(4), HarperFestival) HarperCollins Pubs.

Cavanaugh, Wendy. Pumpkin in the Sky: Let's bake a pie together, you & I, with Auntie Wendy. Cavanaugh, Wendy & LeVesque, Sherry, photos by. 2011. (Illus.). 32p. (J). spiral bd. 20.00 (978-0-9743121-1-8(8)) Eastlight Pr.

Chernesky, Felicia Sanzari. The Boy Who Said Nonsense. Anderson, Nicola, illus. 2016. (ENG.). 32p. (J). (gr. -1-3). 16.99 (978-0-8075-5742-6(0)) Whitman, Albert & Co.

Clay Iii, J. Percy. Sampson's Pumpkin Playhouse. 2012. 30p. 24.95 (978-1-4626-7226-4(4)) America Star Bks.

Cody, Christina. The Perfectly Imperfect Pumpkin. 2010. 24p. 12.99 (978-1-4490-7537-8(1)) AuthorHouse.

Condenzio, Mary. Oliver. 2013. 20p. pap. 24.95 (978-1-62709-305-7(2)) America Star Bks.

Cooper, Helen S. Delicious! Cooper, Helen S., illus. 2007. (ENG., Illus.). 32p. (J). (gr. -1-3). 16.99 (978-0-374-31756-0(9), 9780374317560, Farrar, Straus & Giroux (BYR)) Farrar, Straus & Giroux.

—Pumpkin Soup, Set. unabr. ed. 2013. (ENG.). (J). 12.99 (978-1-4272-3920-4(7), 9781427239204) Macmillan Audio.

Cordone Warner, Debra. Pumpkee & the Day of Harvest. 2010. 38p. pap. 19.99 (978-0-557-70397-5(2)) Lulu Pr., Inc.

Crespeno, John. Toby: The Mouse Who Lived in a Pumpkin. 2011. 84p. pap. 28.68 (978-1-4634-1632-4(6)) AuthorHouse.

Denega, Danielle & Bridwell, Norman. Pumpkin Patch Puppy. 2006. (Illus.). 26p. (J). pap. (978-0-439-87764-0(4)) Scholastic, Inc.

Dillon, Jana. Jeb Scarecrow's Pumpkin Patch, 1 vol. 2016. (ENG., Illus.). 32p. (J). (gr. k-3). pap. 8.99 (978-1-4556-2181-1(1)) Pelican Publishing Co., Inc.

Dohr, Robert. The Pumpkin Se. Dewyea, Glenn, illus. 2012. 32p. pap. 13.50 (978-1-61204-337-1(2), Strategic Bk. Publishing) Strategic Book Publishing & Rights Agency (SBPRA).

Donde Esta Belo? (Where's Pipkin?) (Granja Oso de Miel Ser.). (SPA.). (J). bds. 4.99 (978-0-7899-0611-3(2), 495053) Editorial Unilit.

Duke, Kate. Ready for Pumpkins. (ENG., Illus.). 40p. (J). (gr. k-3). 2015. 7.99 (978-0-553-52442-0(9), Dragonfly Bks.) 2012. 16.99 (978-0-375-87068-2(7), Knopf Bks. for Young Readers) Random Hse. Children's Bks.

Evangelista, Gloria. In Search of the Perfect Pumpkin. Shea, Shawn, illus. 2008. (ENG.). 32p. (J). (gr. k). pap. 7.95 (978-1-55591-697-8(X)) Fulcrum Publishing.

Evans, Alwyn & Davis, Anne. Pumpkin in Hollow Countdown. Capelle, Joanna, illus. 16p. (J). pap. 7.49 (978-1-86368-045-5(4)) Fremantle Pr. AUS. Dist: Independent Pubs. Group.

Everett, George W. G. W. Frog & the Pumpkin Patch Bandit. 2010. 40p. 16.95 (978-1-4497-0759-0(9), WestBow Pr.) Author Solutions, Inc.

Fisk, Cindy. Hooga Booga Presents the Little Pumpkin. Fisk, David, illus. 2013. 28p. pap. 11.95 (978-1-938743-02-3(4)) Reimann Bks.

Fry, Sonali. The Itsy Bitsy Pumpkin. Rescek, Sanja, illus. 2014. (Itsy Bitsy Ser.). (ENG.). 16p. (J). (gr. -1 — 1). bds. 5.99 (978-1-4814-0505-8(5), Little Simon) Little Simon.

Fuerst, Jeffrey B. Peter Pumpkin Eater. Greenhead, Bill, illus. 2010. (Rising Readers Ser.). (J). 3.49 (978-1-60719-705-8(7)) Newmark Learning LLC.

Geisler, Ruth. Shine, Smiling Pumpkin. 2004. (J). 0.99 (978-0-9747923-0-9(6)) C T A, Inc.

George, Kallie. Duck, Duck, Dinosaur: Perfect Pumpkin. Vidal, Oriol, illus. 2017. (My First I Can Read Ser.). 32p. (J). (gr. -1-3). 16.99 **(978-0-06-235315-3(2))**; pap. 3.99 **(978-0-06-235314-6(4))** HarperCollins Pubs.

Ghigna, Charles. Oh My, Pumpkin Pie! Spengler, Kenneth, illus. 2005. (Step into Reading Ser.). (ENG.). 32p. (J). (gr. -1-1). pap. 3.99 (978-0-375-82945-1(8), Random Hse. Bks. for Young Readers) Random Hse. Children's Bks.

Gilbert, Jeff. Trick or Shriek. 2006. 72p. pap. 5.97 (978-0-9646781-1-8(X)) Hairball Pr.

Granata, Nancy. The Perfect Porch for Witch Watching. 2008. 52p. pap. 22.49 (978-1-4389-0107-7(0)) AuthorHouse.

Grogan, John. Marley Storybook Treasury. Cowdrey, Richard, illus. 2012. (I Can Read Level 2 Ser.). (ENG.). 192p. (J). (gr. k-3). 11.99 (978-0-06-212331-2(9)) HarperCollins Pubs.

Gruber, Michael. The Legend of the Brog. Gruber, Michael & Graves, Linda, illus. 2005. (J). per. 9.95 (978-0-9770413-0-5(1)) Gruber Enterprises.

Hapka, Cathy, pseud, et al. Pooh's Halloween Pumpkin. Disney Storybook Artists Staff, illus. 2013. (ENG.). 10p. (J). (gr. -1-k). bds. 5.99 (978-1-4231-6767-9(8)) Disney Pr.

Harkrader, Lisa. A Pumpkin Tale. 2016. (Spring Forward Ser.). (J). (gr. 2). (978-1-4900-2247-5(3)) Benchmark Education Co.

Harrod-Eagles, Cynthia. The Biggest Pumpkin Ever! Woodruff, Liza, illus. 2007. (J). pap. (978-0-545-00232-5(X)) Scholastic, Inc.

Harvey, Sharon M. Legend of the Pumpkin Carver. 2010. 100p. pap. 22.95 (978-1-4327-1214-3(4)) Outskirts Pr., Inc.

Hill, Eric. Spot's Thanksgiving. Hill, Eric, illus. 2016. (Spot Ser.). (ENG., Illus.). 10p. (J). (gr. -1-k). bds. 6.99 (978-0-399-24186-4(8), Warne) Penguin Young Readers Group.

Hillert, Margaret. Pumpkin, Pumpkin: For the Earliest Reader. Starfall Education, photos by. 2006. (ENG., Illus.). 32p. (J). (978-1-59577-035-6(6)); pap. (978-1-59577-036-3(4)) Starfall Education.

Hills, Tad. Find a Pumpkin. Hills, Tad, illus. (Duck & Goose Ser.). (ENG., Illus.). 22p. (J). (gr. k-k). 2012. bds. 10.99 (978-0-307-98155-4(X)) 2009. bds. 7.99 (978-0-375-85813-0(X)) Random Hse. Children's Bks. (Schwartz & Wade Bks.).

Holloway, Jamie. Let's Go Pumpkin Picking. 2015. (Rosen REAL Readers: STEM & STEAM Collection). (ENG.). 8p. pap. 5.46 (978-1-4994-9542-3(0), Rosen Classroom) Rosen Publishing Group, Inc., The.

Horning, Sandra. The Biggest Pumpkin, 1 vol. Stone-Barker, Holly, illus. 2014. 32p. (J). 16.99 (978-1-4556-1925-2(6)) Pelican Publishing Co., Inc.

Horowitz, Dave. The Ugly Pumpkin. Horowitz, Dave, illus. 2008. (ENG., Illus.). 40p. (J). (gr. -1-k). pap. 6.99 (978-0-14-241145-2(0), Puffin Books) Penguin Young Readers Group.

Howard, Marie. Punkin & the Peanut. 2012. 30p. 24.95 (978-1-4626-7332-2(5)) America Star Bks.

Inman, George, Jr., et al. The Bumpy Pumpkin. Lyle, Avis, illus. 2004. (ENG.). 18p. (J). 12.95 (978-0-9754696-0-6(6)) Bumpy Pumpkin.

Jacobson, Jennifer Richard. Andy Shane & the Pumpkin Trick. Carter, Abby, illus. 2007. (Andy Shane Ser.: 2). (ENG.). 64p. (J). (gr. k-3). per. 4.99 (978-0-7636-3306-6(2)) Candlewick Pr.

—Andy Shane & the Pumpkin Trick. Carter, Abby, illus. 2008. (Andy Shane Ser.). (J). (gr. -1-3). 25.95 incl. audio (978-1-4301-0313-4(2)); pap. 16.95 incl. audio (978-1-4301-0312-7(4)) Live Oak Media.

Jaeger, Elizabeth. It's Halloween, Little Pumpkin! Boyer, Robin, illus. 2014. 16p. (J). bds. 12.99 (978-0-8249-1942-9(4), Ideal Pubns.) Worthy Publishing.

Jenkins, Emily. Dangerous Pumpkins. Bliss, Harry, illus. 2012. (Invisible Inkling Ser.: 2). (ENG.). 160p. (J). (gr. 1-5). 14.99 (978-0-06-180223-2(9)) HarperCollins Pubs.

Johnson, Jay, illus. Ten Little Pumpkins. 2012. (J). (978-0-545-46862-6(0)) Scholastic, Inc.

Jones, Francesca & Jones, Frankie. Where's the Pumpkin? Galloway, Fhiona, illus. 2015. (ENG.). 16p. (J). (gr. -1 — 1). bds. 5.99 (978-1-4998-0097-5(5)) Little Bee Books Inc.

Kann, Victoria. Pinkalicious & the Pink Pumpkin. Kann, Victoria, illus. 2011. (Pinkalicious Ser.). (ENG., Illus.). 16p. (J). (gr. -1-2). pap. 6.99 (978-0-06-198961-2(4), HarperFestival) HarperCollins Pubs.

Karr, Lily. My Pumpkin. Marts, Doreen Mulryan, illus. 2014. (ENG.). 12p. (J). (gr. -1 — 1). bds. 4.99 (978-0-545-49332-1(3), Cartwheel Bks.) Scholastic, Inc.

Katz, Karen. Where Is Baby's Pumpkin? Katz, Karen, illus. 2006. (ENG., Illus.). 14p. (J). (gr. -1 — 1). bds. 7.99 (978-1-4169-0970-5(2), Little Simon) Little Simon.

Kirby, Ruth M. Claudius Saves the Pumpkin Patch. Larson, Lisa K., illus. 2008. 20p. pap. 24.95 (978-1-60703-827-6(7)) America Star Bks.

Klay, Sharon Joy. Denny Grows a Giant Pumpkin. 2010. 28p. pap. 12.99 (978-1-4520-2871-2(0)) AuthorHouse.

Klein, Abby. The Pumpkin Elf Mystery. McKinley, John, illus. 2007. (Ready, Freddy! Ser.: Bk. 11). 95p. (J). (gr. -1-3). 11.65 (978-0-7569-8301-7(0)) Perfection Learning Corp.

Kleinberg, Naomi. Elmo's Monster Mash. Moroney, Christopher, illus. 2010. (ENG.). 12p. (J). (gr. k — 1). 4.99 (978-0-375-85804-8(0), Random Hse. Bks. for Young Readers) Random Hse. Children's Bks.

Knoll, Linda L. Patient for Pumpkins. 2014. (ENG., Illus.). 32p. (J). (gr. -1-3). 15.95 (978-1-58394-708-1(6)) North Atlantic Bks.

Kramer, K. Out on the Farm with Farmer Jack. 2012. 24p. pap. 15.99 (978-1-4797-0823-9(2)) Xlibris Corp.

Kroll, Steven. The Biggest Pumpkin Ever. Bassett, Jeni, illus. 2007. (ENG.). 32p. (J). (gr. -1-k). pap. 4.99 (978-0-439-92946-2(6)) Scholastic, Inc.

—The Biggest Pumpkin Surprise Ever. Bassett, Jeni, illus. 2012. (ENG.). 10p. (J). (gr. -1-k). bds. 6.99 (978-0-545-40285-9(9), Cartwheel Bks.) Scholastic, Inc.

Kroner, David & Du Houx, Ramona. Seasons. Du Houx, E. M. Cornell, illus. 2007. 70p. (J). per. 6.95 (978-1-882190-54-6(8)) Polar Bear & Co.

Larsen, Kirsten. Dora's Perfect Pumpkin. Miller, Victoria, illus. 2007. (Dora the Explorer Ser.). (ENG.). 24p. (J). (gr. -1-3). pap. 3.99 (978-1-4169-3438-7(3), Simon Spotlight/Nickelodeon) Simon Spotlight/Nickelodeon.

Lay, Kathryn. Josh's Halloween Pumpkin, 1 vol. Bratun, Katy, illus. 2008. (ENG.). 32p. (J). (gr. k-3). 16.99 (978-1-58980-595-8(X)) Pelican Publishing Co., Inc.

Lemire, Roger. Pumpkin & Lumpkin. 2005. 17.00 (978-0-8059-9777-4(6)) Dorrance Publishing Co., Inc.

Lesley, Sharon. The Red Scarf & Other Stories. 2010. 165p. pap. 14.95 (978-1-4457-6720-8(1)) Lulu Pr., Inc.

Lewis, Anne Margaret. The Runaway Pumpkin. Zenz, Aaron, illus. 2015. (ENG.). 40p. (J). (gr. -1-k). 15.99 (978-1-63450-214-6(0), Sky Pony Pr.) Skyhorse Publishing Co., Inc.

Lightburn, Sandra. Pumpkin People, 1 vol. Lightburn, Ron, illus. 2009. (ENG.). 32p. (J). (gr. -1-5). 17.95 (978-1-55109-681-0(1)) Nimbus Publishing, Ltd. CAN. Dist: Orca Bk. Pubs. USA.

Magsamen, Sandra. I Love You, Little Pumpkin. 2017. (ENG.). 10p. (J). (gr. -1 — 1). 7.99 **(978-1-338-11085-2(3)**, Cartwheel Bks.) Scholastic, Inc.

Mama Doo. Zachary & the Magic Pumpkin Seeds, 1 vol. 2007. (ENG.). 35p. 24.95 (978-1-4241-8579-5(3)) America Star Bks.

Marshall, Natalie. Five Little Pumpkins. 2017. (Fingers & Toes Nursery Rhymes Ser.). (ENG.). 12p. (J). (gr. -1 — 1). bds. 6.99 **(978-1-338-09117-5(4)**, Cartwheel Bks.) Scholastic, Inc.

McKy, Katie. Pumpkin Town! or, Nothing Is Better & Worse Than Pumpkins. Bernasconi, Pablo, illus. 2008. (ENG.). 32p. (J). (gr. -1-3). pap. 7.99 (978-0-547-18193-6(0)) Houghton Mifflin Harcourt Publishing Co.

McNamara, Margaret. How Many Seeds in a Pumpkin? Karas, G. Brian, illus. 2007. (Mr. Tiffin's Classroom Ser.). (ENG.). 40p. (J). (gr. -1-2). 17.99 (978-0-375-84014-2(1), Schwartz & Wade Bks.) Random Hse. Children's Bks.

—The Pumpkin Patch. Gordon, Mike, illus. 2005. (Ready-to-Read Ser.). 32p. (J). lib. bdg. 15.00 (978-1-59054-932-2(5)) Fitzgerald Bks.

—The Pumpkin Patch. Gordon, Mike, illus. 2008. (Robin Hill School Ser.). (J). (gr. -1-1). pap. 16.95 (978-1-4301-0622-7(0)) Live Oak Media.

McNamara, Margaret & Gordon, Mike. The Pumpkin Patch. 2003. (Robin Hill School Ser.). (ENG., Illus.). 32p. (J). (gr. -1-1). pap. 3.99 (978-0-689-85874-1(4), Simon Spotlight) Simon Spotlight.

McRoberts, Eddison. Sneaking Treats. Gadra, Jessica, illus. 2013. 48p. pap. 9.95 (978-1-62137-298-1(7)) Virtualbookworm.com Publishing, Inc.

—Sneaking Treats: A Halloween Hunt. Gadra, Jessica, illus. 2012. 48p. 19.95 (978-1-62137-136-6(0)) Virtualbookworm.com Publishing, Inc.

Mcwherter, Barbara. Little Pumpkin & Sally: It's O. K. to Be Different. 2008. 26p. pap. 24.95 (978-1-60563-199-8(X)) America Star Bks.

Meyerhoff, Jenny. Pumpkin Spice. Chatelain, Éva, illus. 2015. (Friendship Garden Ser.: 2). (ENG.). 144p. (J). (gr. 2-5). pap. 5.99 (978-1-4814-3909-1(X), Aladdin) Simon & Schuster Children's Publishing.

—Pumpkin Spice. 2015. (Friendship Garden Ser.: 2). lib. bdg. 16.00 (978-0-606-37833-8(2)) Turtleback Bks.

Minor, Wendell. How Big Could Your Pumpkin Grow? Minor, Wendell, illus. 2013. (ENG., Illus.). 32p. (J). (gr. -1-k). 16.99 (978-0-399-24684-5(3), Nancy Paulsen Books) Penguin Young Readers Group.

Mitchell, Carolyn. The Tale of the Pumpkin Seed Squad. 2006. (ENG.). 40p. per. 16.99 (978-1-4259-7004-8(4)) AuthorHouse.

Mortimer, Anne. Pumpkin Cat. Mortimer, Anne, illus. 2011. (ENG., Illus.). 24p. (J). (gr. -1-2). 14.99 (978-0-06-187485-7(X), Tegen, Katherine Bks) HarperCollins Pubs.

Moulton, Mark. Miss Fiona's Stupendous Pumpkin Pies. Good, Karen Hillard, illus. 2011. 32p. (J). pap. 7.99 (978-0-8249-5635-6(4), Ideal Pubns.) Worthy Publishing.

Moulton, Mark Kimball. Miss Fiona's Stupendous Pumpkin Pies. Crouch, Karen Hillard, illus. 2008. (ENG.). 28p. (J). 14.95 (978-0-8249-5489-5(0), Ideal Pubns.) Worthy Publishing.

—The Very Best Pumpkin. Good, Karen Hillard, illus. 2010. (ENG.). 32p. (J). (gr. -1-3). 12.99 (978-1-4169-8288-3(4), Simon & Schuster/Paula Wiseman Bks.) Simon & Schuster/Paula Wiseman Bks.

Noonan, Julia. My Pumpkin. Lawson, Peter, illus. 2005. (My First Reader Ser.). (ENG.). 32p. (J). (gr. k-1). lib. bdg. 18.50 (978-0-516-24876-9(6), Children's Pr.) Scholastic Library Publishing.

Numeroff, Laura Joffe. It's Pumpkin Day, Mouse! Bond, Felicia, illus. 2012. (If You Give... Ser.). (ENG.). 24p. (J). (gr. -1 — 1). bds. 6.99 (978-0-694-01429-3(X)) HarperCollins Pubs.

Palus, Benji Alexander. The Magic Pumpkin. 2013. 314p. (gr. 10-12). 28.95 (978-1-4759-7046-3(3)); pap. 18.95 (978-1-4759-7048-7(X)) iUniverse, Inc.

Papp, Robert, illus. The Pumpkin Head Mystery, No. 124. 2010. (Boxcar Children Mysteries Ser.: 124). (ENG.). 128p. (J). (gr. 1-5). pap. 5.99 (978-0-8075-6669-5(1)) Whitman, Albert & Co.

Papp, Robert & Papp, Kathy, illus. The Pumpkin Head Mystery. 2010. (Boxcar Children Mysteries Ser.: 124). (ENG.). 128p. (J). (gr. 1-5). 14.99 (978-0-8075-6668-8(3)) Whitman, Albert & Co.

Pasillo, Susan. The Perfect Pumpkin. 2006. (J). lib. bdg. 20.95 (978-1-933732-14-5(8)) Big Ransom Studio.

Patricelli, Leslie. Boo! / ¡Bu! Patricelli, Leslie, illus. 2017. (Leslie Patricelli Board Bks.). (ENG & SPA., Illus.). 26p. (J). (— 1). bds. 6.99 (978-0-7636-9314-5(6)) Candlewick Pr.

Perkins, C. Gale. A Pumpkin for God. 2009. 28p. pap. 14.95 (978-1-4389-4336-7(9)) AuthorHouse.

Peter the Pumpkin-Eater: Individual Title Six-Packs. (Action Packs Ser.). 104p. (gr. 3-5). 44.00 (978-0-7635-8401-6(0)) Rigby Education.

Pilkey, Dav. Dragon's Halloween. Pilkey, Dav, illus. 2003. (Dragon's Tales Ser.: Bk. 5). (ENG., Illus.). 48p. (J). (gr. -1-3). pap. 5.99 (978-0-439-54847-2(0), Orchard Bks.) Scholastic, Inc.

Potter, Beatrix. Peter Rabbit & the Pumpkin Patch. Palmer, Ruth, illus. 2013. (Peter Rabbit Ser.). (ENG.). 32p. (J). (gr. -1-2). pap. 3.99 (978-0-7232-7124-6(0), Warne) Penguin Young Readers Group.

Powell-Tuck, Maudie. Pumpkin Party! Guile, Gill, illus. 2015. (ENG.). 22p. (J). (gr. -1-2). bds. 8.99 (978-1-58925-206-6(3)) Tiger Tales.

Public Domain Staff. Five Little Pumpkins. Yaccarino, Dan, illus. 2003. (ENG.). 16p. (J). (gr. -1-k). pap. 6.99 (978-0-694-01177-3(0), HarperFestival) HarperCollins Pubs.

The Pumpkin House, 6 Packs. (Literatura 2000 Ser.). (gr. 2-3). 33.00 (978-0-7635-0182-2(4)) Rigby Education.

Ransom, Candice. Pumpkin Day! Meza, Erika, illus. 2015. (Step into Reading Ser.). (ENG.). 32p. (J). (gr. -1-1). 12.99 (978-0-375-97466-3(0), Random Hse. Bks. for Young Readers) Random Hse. Children's Bks.

Ray, Christie Jones & Ray, Christie Jones. Pick-A-Pick-a-Pumpkin. 2012. (Illus.). 36p. pap. 12.00 (978-0-9853223-4-2(9)) Rose Water Cottage Pr.

Reasoner, Charles. Pumpkin Shapes. 2015. (Charles Reasoner Halloween Bks.). (ENG., Illus.). 12p. (gr. -1 — 1). bds. 5.99 (978-1-4795-8499-4(1)) Picture Window Bks.

Robinson, Sharon. The Littlest Pumpkin. 2012. 24p. 24.95 (978-1-4626-5963-0(2)) America Star Bks.

Rockwell, Anne F. Apples & Pumpkins. Rockwell, Lizzy, illus. (ENG.). 24p. (J). (gr. -1-3). 2012. 5.99 (978-1-4424-7656-1(7)) 2011. 14.99 (978-1-4424-0350-5(0)) Simon & Schuster Children's Publishing. (Aladdin).

Savage, Stephen. Seven Orange Pumpkins Board Book. 2015. (ENG., Illus.). 28p. (J). (gr. -1 — 1). bds. 6.99 (978-0-8037-4138-6(3), Dial Bks) Penguin Young Readers Group.

—Ten Orange Pumpkins: A Counting Book. 2013. (ENG., Illus.). 48p. (J). (gr. -1-k). 16.99 (978-0-8037-3938-3(9), Dial Bks) Penguin Young Readers Group.

Schulz, Charles. It's the Great Pumpkin, Charlie Brown, 1 vol. 2013. (Peanuts Picture Bks.). (ENG.). 48p. (J). (gr. -1-4). lib. bdg. 24.21 (978-1-61479-032-7(9)) ABDO Publishing Co.

Schulz, Charles M. Waiting for the Great Pumpkin. 2014. (Peanuts Seasonal Ser.: 0). (ENG., Illus.). 64p. 9.99 (978-1-60699-772-7(6), 699772) Fantagraphics Bks.

Scotton, Rob. Splat the Cat & the Pumpkin-Picking Plan. Scotton, Rob, illus. 2014. (Splat the Cat Ser.). (ENG., Illus.). 24p. (J). (gr. -1-3). pap. 4.99 (978-0-06-211586-7(3)) HarperCollins Pubs.

Seal, Kerry. Five Silly Pumpkins: A Pop-up Halloween Book. Smith, Jane, illus. 2009. 10p. (J). 5.95 (978-1-58117-908-8(1), Intervisual/Piggy Toes) Bendon, Inc.

Serfozo, Mary. Plumply, Dumply Pumpkin. Petrone, Valeria, illus. 2006. (Classic Board Bks.). (ENG.). 28p. (J). (gr. -1-1). bds. 6.99 (978-0-689-86277-9(6), Little Simon) Little Simon.

Shepherd, Anita. Scareboo's Halloween Trick. 2013. 50p. pap. 7.95 (978-0-9882368-4-4(2)) New Eden Publishing.

Silva, Amanda. The Day That Jack Became a Jack O'Lantern. 2013. 20p. pap. 24.95 (978-1-62709-387-3(7)) PublishAmerica, Inc.

Simon, Chaman. Pumpkin Fever. Bryan-Hunt, Jan, illus. 2011. (Rookie Ready to Learn Ser.). 40p. (J). (ENG.). pap. 5.95 (978-0-531-26803-2(9)); (gr. -1-k). lib. bdg. 23.00 (978-0-531-25643-5(X)) Scholastic Library Publishing. (Children's Pr.).

Simon, Jenne. Spooky Pumpkin Moon Night. 2016. (ENG.). 24p. (J). (gr. -1-k). 3.99 (978-0-545-93225-7(4)) Scholastic, Inc.

Simon, Mary Manz. The Pumpkin Gospel (die-Cut) A Story of a New Start with God. Scudamore, Angelika, illus. 2016. (ENG.). 14p. (J). (gr. -1 — 1). bds. 12.99 (978-1-4336-9163-8(9), B&H Kids) B&H Publishing Group.

Sisler, Celeste. Disney Fairies: the Perfect Pumpkin. 2015. (ENG., Illus.). 10p. (J). (gr. -1 — 1). bds. 6.99 (978-0-316-37854-3(2)) Little, Brown Bks. for Young Readers.

Sklansky, Amy E. You Are My Little Pumpkin Pie. 2013. (ENG., Illus.). 16p. (J). (gr. -1 — 1). bds. 6.99 (978-0-316-20714-0(4)) Little, Brown Bks. for Young Readers.

Sobel, Gerrie. Jacob & His Magical Flying Bears, a Halloween Story. Torres, Dottie, illus. 2009. 32p. pap. 12.95 (978-1-936051-42-7(7)) Peppertree Pr., The.

Sorenson, Verona. The Pumpkin Patch. 2008. 20p. per. 24.95 (978-1-60441-565-0(7)) America Star Bks.

Souhami, Jessica, illus. No Dinner! The Story of the Old Woman & the Pumpkin. 2012. (ENG.). 32p. (J). (gr. -1-2). pap. 8.99 (978-1-84507-818-8(7), Frances Lincoln) Quarto Publishing Group UK GBR. Dist: Hachette Bk. Group.

Steinberg, Laya. The Best Sukkot Pumpkin Ever. Madden, Colleen M., illus. 2017. (ENG.). 32p. (gr. -1-3). 17.99 **(978-1-5124-0863-8(8)**, Kar-Ben Publishing) Lerner Publishing Group.

Stilton, Geronimo. The Peculiar Pumpkin Thief. 2010. (Geronimo Stilton Ser.: 42). (ENG.). 128p. (J). (gr. 2-5). 7.99 (978-0-545-10372-5(X), Scholastic Paperbacks) Scholastic, Inc.

Swindle, Stephanie. Pumpkin Pants. 2009. 32p. pap. 13.95 (978-1-60860-461-6(6), Strategic Bk. Publishing) Strategic Book Publishing & Rights Agency (SBPRA).

Tegen, Katherine Brown. The Story of the Jack O'Lantern. Dorman, Brandon, illus. 2010. (ENG.). 32p. (J). (gr. -1-3). 12.99 *(978-0-06-143088-6(9))* HarperCollins Pubs.
Thomas, Jan. Pumpkin Trouble. Thomas, Jan, illus. 2011. (ENG., Illus.). 40p. (J). (gr. -1-3). 9.99 *(978-0-06-169284-0(0))* HarperCollins Pubs.
Thomas Nelson. Story Book Five Little Pumpkins. 2016. (ENG.). 14p. (gr. -1). bds. *(978-1-78598-400-6(4))* Make Believe Ideas.
Tiger Tales Staff & Mantle, Ben. Five Little Pumpkins. Tiger Tales Staff, ed. 2010. (ENG., Illus.). 24p. (J). (gr. -1-k). bds. 8.95 *(978-1-58925-856-3(8))* Tiger Tales.
Tim's Pumpkin: Individual Title Six-Packs. (gr. k-1). 23.00 *(978-0-7635-9040-6(1))* Rigby Education.
Titherington, Jeanne. Pumpkin Pumpkin. 2015. 24p. pap. 7.00 *(978-1-61003-615-3(8))* Center for the Collaborative Classroom.
Town, Vicky. The Runaway Pumpkin Pie Man, 1 vol. Baird, Roberta, illus. 2015. (ENG.). 32p. (J). (gr. k-3). 16.99 *(978-1-4556-2025-8(4))* Pelican Publishing Co., Inc.
Townsend, Tamela Ann. Finding Pumpkin, 1 vol. 2010. 48p. pap. 16.95 *(978-1-4489-5983-9(7))* America Star Bks.
Tremblay, Patrick. Poor, Poor Jack. 2010. 40p. pap. 26.00 *(978-0-557-25375-3(6))* Lulu Pr., Inc.
Trooboff, Rhoda. Punkinhead's Veggie Adventure: And the Strange Contraption in the Kitchen. Easton, Susan, illus. Rosenbaum, Elizabeth, photos by. 2013. (ENG.). 56p. (J). (gr. -1). pap. 15.00 *(978-0-9773536-7-5(2))* Transigar Co. LLC.
Tucker, Daniel Deon. The Littlest Pumpkin, 1 vol. 2009. 48p. pap. 16.95 *(978-1-61546-872-0(2))* PublishAmerica, Inc.
Tucker, Peter. Pumpkin Bunch. 2009. 32p. 16.30 *(978-0-615-21675-1(7))* PT Publishing.
Tucker, Peter E. Pumpkin Bunch. 2009. 36p. pap. 16.99 *(978-1-4389-7883-3(9))* AuthorHouse.
Wallace, Nancy Elizabeth. Pumpkin Day, 0 vols. Wallace, Nancy Elizabeth, illus. unabr. ed. 2006. (ENG., Illus.). 32p. (J). (gr. -1-2). per. 9.99 *(978-0-7614-5327-7(X)*, 9780761453277, Amazon Children's Publishing) Amazon Publishing.
Wan, Joyce. You Are My Pumpkin. Wan, Joyce, illus. 2016. (ENG., Illus.). 14p. (J). (— 1). bds. 6.99 *(978-0-545-88092-3(0)*, Cartwheel Bks.) Scholastic, Inc.
Warne, Frederick. The Giant Pumpkin. 2015. (Peter Rabbit Animation Ser.). (ENG.). 32p. (J). (gr. -1-k). 3.99 *(978-0-7232-9599-0(9)*, Warne) Penguin Young Readers Group.
Washburn, Kim. Pumpkin Patch Blessings, 1 vol. East, Jacqueline, illus. 2016. (ENG.). 18p. (J). bds. 8.99 *(978-0-310-75819-8(X))* Zonderkidz.
Waters, George T. The Perfect Little Pumpkin. Duquet, Guy J., illus. l.t. ed. 2006. 30p. (J). per. 14.95 *(978-1-59879-286-7(5))* Lifevest Publishing, Inc.
Wayne, Richard, ed. Poppin's Pumpkin Patch Parade. Carlson, Patrick, illus. 2016. (ENG.). 32p. (J). pap. 12.98 *(978-0-9801692-1-8(6))* Gemstone Literary.
Weathers, R. F. Jill's Joyful Surprise. 2005. 32p. pap. 18.00 *(978-1-4208-5263-9(9))* AuthorHouse.
Webb, M. St. John. Knock Three Times! 2003. (Children's Classics). (ENG.). 160p. (J). (gr. 3-6). pap. *(978-1-85326-132-9(7))* Wordsworth Editions, Ltd.
West, Paul & Denslow, W. W. The Pearl & the Pumpkin: A Classic Halloween Tale. Denslow, W. W., illus. 2009. (Dover Children's Classics Ser.). (ENG., Illus.). 264p. (J). (gr. 2-5). pap. 12.99 *(978-0-486-47031-3(8))* Dover Pubns., Inc.
Whitlock, Matt. Punk 'n Patch. Whitlock, Matt, illus. 2005. (Illus.). 32p. (J). (gr. -1-3). 16.95 *(978-0-9769057-0-7(1))* Little Hero.
Wiles, Faith R. The Pumpkin who couldn't say BOO!, 1 vol. 2010. 20p. 24.95 *(978-1-4489-4242-8(X))* PublishAmerica, Inc.
William H. Sadlier Staff. Pumpkin Days, Vol. 3. 2005. (Emergent Library: Vol. 1). (gr. -1-1). 24.00 net. *(978-0-8215-8912-0(1))* Sadlier, William H. Inc.
Williamson, Hilary & Adams, Lynne. The Magic Pumpkin. 2008. 16p. 9.99 *(978-1-4357-0321-6(9))* Lulu Pr., Inc.
Winters, Kay. Whooo's That? Winston, Jeannie, illus. 2009. (ENG.). 14p. (J). (gr. -1 — 1). 9.99 *(978-0-15-206480-8(X))* Houghton Mifflin Harcourt Publishing Co.
Wunderli, Stephen. Little Boo. Zeltner, Tim, illus. 2014. (ENG.). 32p. (J). (gr. -1-2). 16.99 *(978-0-8050-9708-5(2)*, 9780805097085, Holt, Henry & Co. Bks. For Young Readers) Holt, Henry & Co.
Yolen, Jane. Pumpkin Baby. Mitchell, Susan, illus. 2009. (ENG.). 32p. (J). (gr. -1). *(978-1-55470-141-4(4))* Me to We.
Yoon, Salina. Penguin & Pumpkin. 2014. (Penguin Ser.). (ENG., Illus.). 40p. (J). (gr. -1-1). 14.99 *(978-0-8027-3732-8(3)*, 9780802737328, Bloomsbury USA Childrens) Bloomsbury Publishing USA.
—Penguin & Pumpkin. 2014. (Illus.). (J). *(978-0-8027-3770-0(6))* Walker & Co.

PUNCH AND JUDY

see Puppets

PUNCHED CARD SYSTEMS

see Information Storage and Retrieval Systems

PUNCTUATION

Basher, Simon & Budzik, Mary. Punctuation: The Write Stuff! Basher, Simon, illus. 2010. (Basher Basics Ser.). (ENG., Illus.). 64p. (J). (gr. 3-7). pap. 7.99 *(978-0-7534-6420-5(9)*, 9780753464205, Kingfisher) Roaring Brook Pr.
Blaisdell, Molly. If You Were a Comma, 1 vol. Gray, Sara, illus. 2009. (Word Fun Ser.). (ENG.). 24p. (gr. 2-4). pap. 7.95 *(978-1-4048-5321-8(9))*; 27.99 *(978-1-4048-5320-1(0))* Picture Window Bks.
—If You Were a Comma [LTD Commodities]. Gray, Sara, illus. 2010. (Word Fun Ser.). 24p. pap. 3.50 *(978-1-4048-6251-7(X)*, Nonfiction Picture Bks.) Picture Window Bks.
—If You Were Quotation Marks, 1 vol. Gray, Sara, illus. 2009. (Word Fun Ser.). (ENG.). 24p. (gr. 2-4). pap. 7.95 *(978-1-4048-5330-0(8))*; lib. bdg. 27.99 *(978-1-4048-5329-4(4))* Picture Window Bks.
—If You Were Quotation Marks [LTD Commodities]. Gray, Sara, illus. 2010. (Word Fun Ser.). 24p. pap. 3.50 *(978-1-4048-6255-5(2)*, Nonfiction Picture Bks.) Picture Window Bks.
—If You Were Quotation Marks [Readers World]. Gray, Sara, illus. 2010. (Word Fun Ser.). 24p. pap. 2.72 *(978-1-4048-6706-2(6)*, Nonfiction Picture Bks.) Picture Window Bks.
Blaisdell, Molly & Lyons, Shelly. If You Were an Apostrophe, 1 vol. Gray, Sara, illus. 2009. (Word Fun Ser.). (ENG.). 24p. (gr. 2-4). lib. bdg. 27.99 *(978-1-4048-5317-1(0))* Picture Window Bks.
Bodden, Valerie & Riggs, Kate. Colons & Semicolons. 2017. (Punctuate It! Ser.). (ENG.). 32p. (J). (gr. 3-7). pap. 10.99 *(978-1-62832-327-6(2)*, Creative Paperbacks) Creative Co., The.
Capitalization & Punctuation. 2013. (Core Language Skills Ser.). 24p. (J). (gr. 2-2). pap. 49.50 *(978-1-4777-0981-8(9)*, PowerKids Pr.) Rosen Publishing Group, Inc., The.
Capitalization & Punctuation (Gr. 1-3) 2003. (J). *(978-1-58232-050-2(0))* ECS Learning Systems, Inc.
Carter, Andrew. Punctuation & Sentences. Jones, Bryony, ed. 2009. (Grammar Ray: A Graphic Guide to Grammar Ser.). 24p. (J). (gr. 2-5). pap. 8.15 *(978-1-60754-751-8(1))* Windmill Bks.
Cleary, Brian P. The Punctuation Station. Lew-Vriethoff, Joanne, illus. 2010. (ENG.). 32p. (J). (gr. k-3). lib. bdg. 16.95 *(978-0-8225-7852-9(2)*, 1306583) Lerner Publishing Group.
Collins, Terry. Whatever Says Mark: Knowing & Using Punctuation, 1 vol. Cox, Russ, illus. 2013. (Language on the Loose Ser.). (ENG.). 24p. (gr. 2-4). 27.99 *(978-1-4048-8318-5(5))*; pap. 7.95 *(978-1-4795-1917-0(0))* Picture Window Bks.
Commas & Colons with Your Class. 2013. (Write Right! Ser.). 24p. (J). (gr. 2-5). pap. 48.90 *(978-1-4339-9067-0(9))* Stevens, Gareth Publishing LLLP.
Connors, Kathleen. Punctuation at the Game. 2012. (Word Play Ser.). (Illus.). 24p. (J). (gr. 1-3). pap. 8.15 *(978-1-4339-7196-9(8))*; lib. bdg. 22.60 *(978-1-4339-7195-2(X))* Stevens, Gareth Publishing LLLP.
Dorling Kindersley Publishing Staff. Visual Guide to Grammar & Punctuation. 2017. (ENG.). 128p. (J). (gr. k-3). 16.99 ***(978-1-4654-6258-9(9)**, DK Children)* Dorling Kindersley Publishing, Inc.
Ganeri, Anita. Punctuation: Commas, Periods, & Question Marks, 1 vol. 2012. (Getting to Grips with Grammar Ser.). (ENG.). 32p. (gr. 1-3). lib. bdg. 27.32 *(978-1-4329-5808-4(9)*, Heinemann First Library) Heinemann-Raintree.
Hall, Pamela. Punk-Tuation Celebration, 1 vol. Currant, Gary, illus. 2009. (Grammar's Slammin' Ser.). (ENG.). 32p. (J). (gr. -1-3). 28.50 *(978-1-60270-617-0(4))* Magic Wagon.
HarperCollins UK Staff & Collins Easy Learning Staff. Grammar & Punctuation Practice. 2012. (Collins Easy Learning Age 7-11 Ser.). (ENG.). 96p. (J). pap. 6.99 *(978-0-00-746735-8(4))* HarperCollins Pubs. Ltd. GBR. Dist: Independent Pubs. Group.
Healy, Nicholas M. If You Were a Period, 1 vol. Gray, Sara, illus. 2009. (Word Fun Ser.). (ENG.). 24p. (gr. 2-4). pap. 7.95 *(978-1-4048-5333-1(2))* Picture Window Bks.
—If You Were a Period [LTD Commodities]. Gray, Sara, illus. 2010. (Word Fun Ser.). 24p. pap. 3.50 *(978-1-4048-6252-4(8)*, Nonfiction Picture Bks.) Picture Window Bks.
Healy, Nick & Healy, Nicholas M. If You Were a Period, 1 vol. Gray, Sara, illus. 2009. (Word Fun Ser.). (ENG.). 24p. (gr. 2-4). lib. bdg. 27.99 *(978-1-4048-5332-4(4))* Picture Window Bks.
Herman, Gail & Voege, Debra. Pedaling to Perfect Punctuation. 2009. (Grammar All-Stars: Writing Tools Ser.). 32p. (J). (gr. 2-5). (ENG.). pap. 10.50 *(978-1-4339-2134-6(0))*; lib. bdg. 26.00 *(978-1-4339-1941-1(9))* Stevens, Gareth Publishing LLLP. (Gareth Stevens Learning Library).
Higgins, Nadia. Super Apostrophe Saves the Day! Gallagher-Cole, Memie, illus. 2012. (PunctuationBooks Ser.). (ENG.). 24p. (J). (gr. k-3). 27.07 *(978-1-61473-265-5(5)*, 204962) Child's World, Inc., The.
—Super Comma Saves the Day! Gallagher-Cole, Memie, illus. 2012. (PunctuationBooks Ser.). (ENG.). 24p. (J). (gr. k-3). 27.07 *(978-1-61473-267-9(1)*, 204964) Child's World, Inc., The.
—Super Exclamation Point Saves the Day! Gallagher-Cole, Memie, illus. 2012. (PunctuationBooks Ser.). (ENG.). 24p. (J). (gr. k-3). 27.07 *(978-1-61473-268-6(X)*, 204965) Child's World, Inc., The.
—Super Period Saves the Day! Gallagher-Cole, Memie, illus. 2012. (PunctuationBooks Ser.). (ENG.). 24p. (J). (gr. k-3). 27.07 *(978-1-61473-270-9(1)*, 204967) Child's World, Inc., The.
—Super Question Mark Saves the Day! Gallagher-Cole, Memie, illus. 2012. (PunctuationBooks Ser.). (ENG.). 24p. (J). (gr. k-3). 27.07 *(978-1-61473-271-6(X)*, 204968) Child's World, Inc., The.
—Super Quotation Marks Saves the Day! Gallagher-Cole, Memie, illus. 2012. (PunctuationBooks Ser.). (ENG.). 24p. (J). (gr. k-3). 27.07 *(978-1-61473-272-3(8)*, 204969) Child's World, Inc., The.
Irving, Nicole. Improve Your Punctuation. 2004. (Better English Ser.). 32p. (YA). (gr. 5-18). lib. bdg. 14.95 *(978-1-58086-326-1(4))* EDC Publishing.
Kenan, Tessa. "What Did He Say?" A Book about Quotation Marks. 2015. (Illus.). 16p. (J). *(978-1-60753-727-4(3))* Amicus Publishing.
Law, Karina. Let's Eat Grandma! A Life-Saving Guide to Grammar & Punctuation. Phillips, Mike, illus. 2017. (ENG.). 48p. (J). (gr. 4-7). pap. 12.99 ***(978-1-4451-4201-2(5)**,* Franklin Watts) Hachette Children's Group GBR. Dist: Hachette Bk. Group.
LD COACH. TEH Learns to Read: Beginning Words & Written Characters, Volume One. 2004. (Illus.). 40p. (J). 34.95 *(978-0-9745938-1-4(8))* LD Coach, LLC.
Lynette, Rachel. Super Colon Saves the Day! Gallagher-Cole, Memie, illus. 2012. (PunctuationBooks Ser.). (ENG.). 24p. (J). (gr. k-3). 27.07 *(978-1-61473-266-2(3)*, 204963) Child's World, Inc., The.
—Super Parentheses Saves the Day! Gallagher-Cole, Memie, illus. 2012. (PunctuationBooks Ser.). (ENG.). 24p. (J). (gr. k-3). 27.07 *(978-1-61473-269-3(8)*, 204966) Child's World, Inc., The.
Lyons, Shelly. If You Were a Question Mark, 1 vol. Gray, Sara, illus. 2009. (Word Fun Ser.). (ENG.). 24p. (gr. 2-4). pap. 7.95 *(978-1-4048-5324-9(3))*; lib. bdg. 27.99 *(978-1-4048-5323-2(5))* Picture Window Bks.
—If You Were a Question Mark [LTD Commodities]. Gray, Sara, illus. 2010. (Word Fun Ser.). 24p. pap. 3.50 *(978-1-4048-6253-1(6)*, Nonfiction Picture Bks.) Picture Window Bks.
—If You Were a Question Mark [Readers World]. Gray, Sara, illus. 2010. (Word Fun Ser.). 24p. pap. 2.72 *(978-1-4048-6705-5(8)*, Nonfiction Picture Bks.) Picture Window Bks.
—If You Were an Apostrophe [Readers World]. Gray, Sara, illus. 2010. (Word Fun Ser.). 24p. pap. 2.72 *(978-1-4048-6708-6(2)*, Nonfiction Picture Bks.) Picture Window Bks.
—If You Were an Exclamation Point, 1 vol. Gray, Sara, illus. 2009. (Word Fun Ser.). (ENG.). 24p. (gr. 2-4). pap. 7.95 *(978-1-4048-5327-0(8))*; lib. bdg. 27.99 *(978-1-4048-5326-3(X))* Picture Window Bks.
—If You Were an Exclamation Point [LTD Commodities]. Gray, Sara, illus. 2010. (Word Fun Ser.). 24p. pap. 3.50 *(978-1-4048-6254-8(4)*, Nonfiction Picture Bks.) Picture Window Bks.
—If You Were an Exclamation Point [Readers World]. Gray, Sara, illus. 2010. (Word Fun Ser.). 24p. pap. 2.72 *(978-1-4048-6707-9(4)*, Nonfiction Picture Bks.) Picture Window Bks.
Lyons, Shelly & Blaisdell, Molly. If You Were an Apostrophe, 1 vol. Gray, Sara, illus. 2009. (Word Fun Ser.). (ENG.). 24p. (gr. 2-4). pap. 7.95 *(978-1-4048-5318-8(9))* Picture Window Bks.
Murray, Kara. Capitalization & Punctuation. 2013. 24p. (J). (gr. 2-2). 22.60 *(978-1-4777-0803-3(0))*; (ENG., Illus.). pap. 8.25 *(978-1-4777-0980-1(0))* Rosen Publishing Group, Inc., The. (PowerKids Pr.).
Powell, Marie. Stop Right There: A Book about Periods. 2015. (Punctuation Station Ser.). (ENG., Illus.). 16p. (J). (gr. k-2). 17.95 *(978-1-60753-730-4(3)*, Amicus Readers) Amicus Publishing.
—Take a Pause, Paul: A Book about Commas. Lewis, Anthony, illus. 2015. (Punctuation Station Ser.). (ENG.). 16p. (J). (gr. k-2). 17.95 *(978-1-60753-731-1(1))* Amicus Publishing.
—This Is Exciting! A Book about Exclamation Points. 2015. (Punctuation Station Ser.). (ENG., Illus.). 16p. (J). (gr. k-2). 17.95 *(978-1-60753-728-1(1)*, Amicus Readers) Amicus Publishing.
—We're Going to the Smiths' House: A Book about Apostrophes. 2015. (Punctuation Station Ser.). (ENG., Illus.). 16p. (J). (gr. k-2). 17.95 *(978-1-60753-729-8(X)*, Amicus Readers) Amicus Publishing.
—What Is That? A Book about Question Marks. Lewis, Anthony, illus. 2015. (Punctuation Station Ser.). (ENG.). 16p. (J). (gr. k-2). 17.95 *(978-1-60753-732-8(X))* Amicus Publishing.
Rajczak, Kristen. Commas & Colons with Your Class. 2013. (Write Right! Ser.). (Illus.). 24p. (J). (gr. 2-5). pap. 8.15 *(978-1-4339-9066-3(0))*; (ENG., lib. bdg. 22.60 *(978-1-4339-9065-6(2))* Stevens, Gareth Publishing LLLP.
Riggs, Kate. Quotation Marks & Apostrophes. 2017. (Punctuate It! Ser.). (ENG.). 32p. (J). (gr. 3-7). pap. 10.99 *(978-1-62832-332-0(9)*, Creative Paperbacks) Creative Co., The.
Roy, Jennifer Rozines. Sharpen Your Good Grammar Skills. 2011. (Sharpen Your Writing Skills Ser.). (Illus.). 64p. (J). (gr. 6-18). lib. bdg. 29.27 *(978-0-7660-3902-5(1))* Enslow Pubs., Inc.
Soper, Sandra. Punctuation Practice: Capital. (ENG., Illus.). 32p. (J). pap. 4.95 *(978-0-330-32083-2(1)*, Pan) Pan Macmillan GBR. Dist: Trafalgar Square Publishing.
Stride, Lottie. Write Every Time. 2017. (Buster Reference Ser.). (ENG., Illus.). 128p. (J). (gr. 3-7). pap. 8.99 ***(978-1-78055-469-3(9))*** O'Mara, Michael Bks., Ltd. GBR. Dist: Independent Pubs. Group.
Studio Mouse, creator. Tracing Punctuation! 2005. (Disney's Chicken Little (Studio Mouse) Ser.). (ENG., Illus.). 28p. (J). (gr. -1-3). 14.99 *(978-1-59069-448-0(1)*, 1A603) Studio Mouse LLC.
Truss, Lynne. Eats, Shoots & Leaves: Why, Commas Really Do Make a Difference! Timmons, Bonnie, illus. 2006. (ENG.). 32p. (J). (gr. 1-4). 16.99 *(978-0-399-24491-9(3)*, G.P. Putnam's Sons Books for Young Readers) Penguin Young Readers Group.
—The Girl's Like Spaghetti: Why, You Can't Manage Without Apostrophes! Timmons, Bonnie, illus. 2007. (ENG.). 32p. (J). (gr. 1-4). 16.99 *(978-0-399-24706-4(8)*, G.P. Putnam's Sons Books for Young Readers) Penguin Young Readers Group.
—Twenty-Odd Ducks: Why, Every Punctuation Mark Counts! Timmons, Bonnie, illus. 2008. (ENG.). 32p. (J). (gr. 1-3). 16.99 *(978-0-399-25058-3(1)*, G.P. Putnam's Sons Books for Young Readers) Penguin Young Readers Group.
Using Punctuation (Gr. 3+) 2003. (J). *(978-1-58232-129-5(9))* ECS Learning Systems, Inc.

PUNCTUATION—FICTION

Pulver, Robin. Punctuation Takes a Vacation. Reed, Lynn Rowe, illus. 2004. (ENG.). 32p. (J). (gr. k-3). reprint ed. pap. 7.99 *(978-0-8234-1820-6(0))* Holiday Hse., Inc.
—Punctuation Takes a Vacation. Reed, Lynn Rowe, illus. 2009. (J). (gr. 1-3). 29.95 incl. audio compact disk *(978-1-4301-0708-8(1))* Live Oak Media.
Rosenthal, Amy Krouse. Exclamation Mark. Lichtenheld, Tom, illus. 2013. (ENG.). 56p. (J). 17.99 *(978-0-545-43679-3(6)*, Scholastic Pr.) Scholastic, Inc.
Rosenthal, Amy Krouse & Lichtenheld, Tom. Exclamation Mark. 2013. 56p. (J). (gr. k-3). pap. 6.95 *(978-0-545-63130-3(0)*, Scholastic) Scholastic, Inc.

PUPPET MAKING

D'Cruz, Anna-Marie. Make Your Own Puppets. 2009. (Do It Yourself Projects! Ser.). 24p. (J). (gr. 3-5). (ENG.). pap. 9.40 *(978-1-4358-2919-0(0))*; lib. bdg. 25.25 *(978-1-4358-2851-3(8))* Rosen Publishing Group, Inc., The. (PowerKids Pr.).
Doney, Meryl. Puppets. 2004. (Crafts from Many Cultures Ser.). (Illus.). 32p. (gr. 2-5). lib. bdg. 26.00 *(978-0-8368-4047-6(X)*, Gareth Stevens Learning Library) Stevens, Gareth Publishing LLLP.
Henry, Sally & Cook, Trevor. Making Puppets. 2010. (Make Your Own Art Ser.). (Illus.). 32p. (J). pap. 11.75 *(978-1-4488-1615-6(7))*; (gr. 3-6). 26.50 *(978-1-4488-1584-5(3))* Rosen Publishing Group, Inc., The. (PowerKids Pr.).
Hodge, Susie. Puppets. 2006. (Design & Make Ser.). (Illus.). 32p. (J). (gr. 4-7). lib. bdg. 28.50 *(978-1-58340-954-1(8))* Black Rabbit Bks.
Kennedy, John. Puppet Mania! The World's Most Incredible Puppet Making Book Ever! 2004. (ENG., Illus.). 80p. (J). pap. 14.99 *(978-1-58180-372-3(9)*, North Light Bks.) F&W Media, Inc.
Leigh, Autumn. Making History: A Horse Sock Puppet. 2006. (Tony Stead Nonfiction Independent Reading Collection). (ENG.). 24p. (gr. 3-6). pap. 8.85 *(978-1-4042-5588-3(5))* Rosen Publishing Group, Inc., The.
Petelinsek, Kathleen. Making Sock Puppets. Petelinsek, Kathleen, illus. 2014. (How-To Library). (ENG., Illus.). 32p. (J). (gr. 3-6). 28.50 *(978-1-63137-782-2(5)*, 205371) Cherry Lake Publishing.
Puppets for a Play: Individual Title Six-Packs. (gr. -1-2). 23.00 *(978-0-7635-9000-0(2))* Rigby Education.
Raffaella, Dowling. Make Your Own Finger Puppets! Tips & Techniques for Fabulous Fun. 2009. (Illus.). (J). ***(978-1-60311-206-2(5))*** Mud Puddle, Inc.
Regan, Lisa. Fun Kits Make Your Own Finger Puppets. 2005. (Fun Kits Ser.). (Illus.). 48p. (J). (gr. k-2). *(978-1-84510-312-5(2))* Top That! Publishing PLC.
Smith, Thomasina. Fantastic Finger Puppets to Make Yourself: 25 Fun Ideas for Your Fingers, Thumbs & Even Feet! 2014. (ENG., Illus.). 64p. (J). (gr. -1-12). pap. 9.99 *(978-1-86147-269-4(2)*, Armadillo) Anness Publishing GBR. Dist: National Bk. Network.
Toler, Violet M. Churchmouse Tales: Puppet Book, 10 vols. Koefler, Leatha, illus. rev. ed. 2004. Orig. Title: Charlie Church Mouse. (J). (gr. -1-6). pap. 10.95 *(978-0-9749749-0-3(0))* Wayside Pubns.
—Churchmouse Tales: Puppet Plays, 10 vols., Vol. 2. Koefler, Leatha, illus. 2nd rev. ed. 2004. Orig. Title: "Puppet Plays, Adventures of Charlie & His Friends". (J). (gr. -1-6). pap. 10.95 *(978-0-9749749-1-0(9))* Wayside Pubns.

PUPPET PLAYS

Asphyxia. The Grimstones Collection. Asphyxia, illus. 2015. (Grimstones Ser.). (ENG., Illus.). 488p. (J). (gr. 3-7). pap. 17.99 *(978-1-76011-391-9(3))* Allen & Unwin AUS. Dist: Independent Pubs. Group.
Goldsack, Gaby. Little Lion & Daniel: A Finger Puppet Play & Read Story. 2003. (Snuffleheads Ser.). (Illus.). 14p. (J). 7.99 *(978-0-8254-7268-8(7))* Kregel Pubns.
Katz, Leon. The Greek Myths: Puppet Plays for Children from Ovid's Metamorphoses. 2004. (ENG.). 160p. pap. 12.95 *(978-1-55783-502-4(0)*, 1557835020, Applause Theatre & Cinema) Leonard, Hal Corp.
Landes, William-Alan, ed. Punch & Judy. Cruikshank, George, illus. 2003. (Classic Plays Ser.). 24p. (YA). (gr. 4-12). pap. 7.50 *(978-0-88734-290-5(6))* Players Pr., Inc.
The Laughing Place: Individual Title Six-Packs. (Story Steps Ser.). (gr. k-2). 32.00 *(978-0-7635-9836-5(4))* Rigby Education.
Liebenow, Todd. Sensational Shadows. Washburn, Sue, ed. 2003. 110p. (YA). lib. bdg. 22.00 *(978-1-58302-251-1(1))* One Way St., Inc.
Liebenow, Todd, et al. Plug into the Power. Guibord, Charity, illus. 2003. 28p. (YA). spiral bd. 18.00 *(978-1-58302-231-3(7))* One Way St., Inc.
Stanley, Diane. Mozart: The Wonder Child - A Puppet Play in Three Acts. Stanley, Diane, illus. 2009. (ENG., Illus.). 48p. (J). (gr. 3-7). 17.99 *(978-0-06-072674-4(1)*, Collins) HarperCollins Pubs.

PUPPET SHOWS

see Puppet Theater

PUPPET THEATER

see also Puppet Plays; Puppets

Carreiro, Carolyn. Make Your Own Puppets & Puppet Theaters. Jourdenais-Martin, Norma Jean, illus. 2005. (ENG.). 64p. (YA). 10.95 *(978-0-8249-6776-5(3)*, 1249275); per. 10.95 *(978-0-8249-6770-3(4)*, 1249275) Worthy Publishing. (Ideal Pubns.).
Lawson, Jennifer. Our New Solar System: A Puppet Show. 2010. 27p. 19.95 *(978-0-557-21389-4(4))* Lulu Pr., Inc.
Schultz, Terry L. & Sorenson, Linda M. The Organic Puppet Theatre. 6th ed. 2004. (Illus.). 92p. (J). 18.95 *(978-0-9749936-0-7(3))* Homelight Pr.
Smith, Thomasina. Fantastic Finger Puppets to Make Yourself: 25 Fun Ideas for Your Fingers, Thumbs & Even Feet! 2014. (ENG., Illus.). 64p. (J). (gr. -1-12). pap. 9.99 *(978-1-86147-269-4(2)*, Armadillo) Anness Publishing GBR. Dist: National Bk. Network.

PUPPETRY

see Puppet Making; Puppet Theater

PUPPETS

see also Marionettes

Atkinson, Ruth & Atkinson, Brett. Stick Puppet Templates. Atkinson, Ruth & Atkinson, Brett, illus. (Illus.). (J). (gr. k-2). pap. *(978-1-875739-72-1(6))* Wizard Bks.
Banis, Bud. Me & My Shadows -Shadow Puppet Fun ForKids of All Ages: Enhanced with Practical Paper Pastimes. Banis, Bud, illus. 2012. (Illus.). 122p. (J). pap. 14.95 *(978-1-59630-076-7(0)*, BeachHouse Bks.) Science & Humanities Pr.
Carreiro, Carolyn. Make Your Own Puppets & Puppet Theaters. Jourdenais-Martin, Norma Jean, illus. 2005. (ENG.). 64p. (YA). per. 10.95 *(978-0-8249-6770-3(4)*, 1249275, Ideal Pubns.) Worthy Publishing.
Cummings, Richard. 101 Hand Puppets: A Guide for Puppeteers of All Ages. 2011. 160p. 41.95 *(978-1-258-06260-6(7))* Literary Licensing, LLC.
Doney, Meryl. Puppets. 2004. (Crafts from Many Cultures Ser.). (Illus.). 32p. (gr. 2-5). lib. bdg. 26.00 *(978-0-8368-4047-6(X)*, Gareth Stevens Learning Library) Stevens, Gareth Publishing LLLP.
French, Cathy. Make a Safety Puppet. 2011. (Early Connections Ser.). (J). *(978-1-61672-237-1(1))* Benchmark Education Co.
Group/McGraw-Hill, Wright. Puppets: 6 Each of 1 Anthology, 6 vols. (Wildcats Ser.). 32p. (gr. 2-8). *(978-0-322-05632-9(2))* Wright Group/McGraw-Hill.

Lim, Annalees. Fun with Fabric. 2013. (Clever Crafts Ser.). (ENG., Illus.). 24p. (gr. k-3). 25.25 *(978-1-4777-0180-5(X))*; pap. 10.60 *(978-1-4777-0188-1(5))* Windmill Bks.

Meltzer, Brad. I Am Jim Henson. Eliopoulos, Christopher, illus. 2017. (Ordinary People Change the World Ser.). (ENG.). 40p. (J). (gr. k-3). 14.99 *(978-0-525-42850-3(X)*, Dial Bks) Penguin Young Readers Group.

Nuttall, Gina. Puppets Around the World. 2004. (QEB Start Writing Ser.). (Illus.). 24p. (J). lib. bdg. 15.95 *(978-1-59566-017-6(8))* QEB Publishing Inc.

Petelinsek, Kathleen. Making Sock Puppets. Petelinsek, Kathleen, illus. 2014. (How-To Library). (ENG., Illus.). 32p. (J). (gr. 3-6). 28.50 *(978-1-63137-782-2(5)*, 205371) Cherry Lake Publishing.

Puppets, 6 Packs. (Action Packs Ser.). 104p. (gr. 3-5). 44.00 *(978-0-7635-8410-8(X))* Rigby Education.

Random House. Elmo's ABC Song (Sesame Street) 2015. (Pictureback(R) Ser.). (ENG., Illus.). 24p. (J). (gr. -1-2). pap. 4.99 *(978-0-553-53672-0(9)*, Random Hse. Bks. for Young Readers) Random Hse. Children's Bks.

Smith, Thomasina. Fantastic Finger Puppets to Make Yourself: 25 Fun Ideas for Your Fingers, Thumbs & Even Feet! 2014. (ENG., Illus.). 64p. (J). (gr. -1-12). pap. 9.99 *(978-1-86147-269-4(2)*, Armadillo) Anness Publishing GBR. Dist: National Bk. Network.

Thompson, Kate. Sneaky Snappy Mr Croc. Green, Barry, illus. 2014. (Hand Puppet Bks.). (ENG.). 10p. (J). (gr. -1). 9.99 *(978-1-78244-618-7(4))* Top That! Publishing PLC GBR. Dist: Independent Pubs. Group.

—Sneezy Wheezy Mr Shark. Green, Barry, illus. 2014. (Hand Puppet Bks.). (ENG.). 10p. (J). (gr. -1). 9.99 *(978-1-78244-619-4(2))* Top That! Publishing PLC GBR. Dist: Independent Pubs. Group.

PUPPETS—FICTION

The Adventures of Pinocchio. 2011. 130p. pap. 9.99 *(978-1-61203-094-4(7))* Bottom of the Hill Publishing.

The Adventures of Pinocchio. (Twelve-Point Ser.). 2003. (J). lib. bdg. 25.00 *(978-1-58287-248-3(1))* 2004. 229p. 25.00 *(978-1-58287-732-7(7))* North Bks.

Ajhar, Brian, illus. Pinocchio. 2005. (Rabbit Ears Ser.). 36p. (J). (gr. k-5). 25.65 *(978-1-59679-228-9(0))* Spotlight.

Albee, Sarah. Elmo Says... Leigh, Tom, illus. 2009. (Big Bird's Favorites Board Bks.). (ENG.). 24p. (J). (gr. k — 1). bds. 4.99 *(978-0-375-84540-6(2)*, Random Hse. Bks. for Young Readers) Random Hse. Children's Bks.

Allen, Constance. My Name Is Elmo (Sesame Street) Swanson, Maggie, illus. 2013. (Little Golden Book Ser.). (ENG.). 24p. (J). (-k). 4.99 *(978-0-449-81066-8(6)*, Golden Bks.) Random Hse. Children's Bks.

—Shake a Leg! Swanson, Maggie, illus. 2010. (Big Bird's Favorites Board Bks.). (ENG.). 24p. (J). (gr. k — 1). bds. 4.99 *(978-0-375-85424-8(X)*, Random Hse. Bks. for Young Readers) Random Hse. Children's Bks.

Angleberger, Tom. Darth Paper Strikes Back. 2011. (Origami Yoda Ser.). (ENG., Illus.). 176p. (J). (gr. 3-7). 13.95 *(978-1-4197-0027-9(8)*, Amulet Bks.); pap. *(978-1-4197-0254-9(8))* Abrams, Inc.

—Darth Paper Strikes Back, 3 vols. 2011. (Origami Yoda Ser.: 2). (J). *(978-1-4618-4266-8(2))*; 1.25 *(978-1-4640-2485-6(5))* Recorded Bks., Inc.

—Darth Paper Strikes Back. (Origami Yoda Files Ser.: 2). (J). 2015. lib. bdg. 18.40 *(978-0-606-39395-9(1))* 2011. lib. bdg. 25.70 *(978-0-606-33075-6(5)*, Turtleback) Turtleback Bks.

—Emperor Pickletine Rides the Bus. 2014. (Origami Yoda Ser.). (ENG., Illus.). 224p. (J). (gr. 3-7). 13.95 *(978-1-4197-0933-3(X)*, Amulet Bks.) Abrams, Inc.

—Emperor Pickletine Rides the Bus. 2014. (Origami Yoda Files Ser.: 6). (J). lib. bdg. 25.70 *(978-0-606-36168-2(5))* Turtleback Bks.

—Princess Labelmaker to the Rescue! 2014. (Origami Yoda Ser.). (ENG., Illus.). 208p. (YA). (gr. 3-7). 13.95 *(978-1-4197-1052-0(4)*, Amulet Bks.) Abrams, Inc.

—The Secret of the Fortune Wookiee. Bell, Cece, illus. 2012. (Origami Yoda Ser.: No. 3). (ENG.). 208p. (J). (gr. 3-7). 13.95 *(978-1-4197-0392-8(7)*, Amulet Bks.) Abrams, Inc.

—The Strange Case of Origami Yoda. 2011. (Illus.). 160p. pap. *(978-0-8109-9877-3(7)*, Amulet Bks.) 2010. (ENG., Illus.). 160p. (J). (gr. 3-7). 13.95 *(978-0-8109-8425-7(3)*, Amulet Bks.) 2010. pap. *(978-0-8109-9650-2(2))* Abrams, Inc.

—The Strange Case of Origami Yoda, 2 vols. 2010. (Origami Yoda Ser.: 1). (J). 48.75 *(978-1-4498-4583-4(5))* Recorded Bks., Inc.

—The Surprise Attack of Jabba the Puppett. 2016. (Origami Yoda Ser.). (ENG.). 240p. (YA). (gr. 3-7). pap. 7.95 *(978-1-4197-2030-7(9)*, Amulet Bks.) Abrams, Inc.

—The Surprise Attack of Jabba the Puppett: An Origami Yoda Book. 2013. (Origami Yoda Ser.: No. 4). (ENG., Illus.). 224p. (YA). (gr. 3-7). 13.95 *(978-1-4197-0858-9(9)*, Amulet Bks.) Abrams, Inc.

—The Surprise Attack of Jabba the Puppett: An Origami Yoda Book. 2013. (Origami Yoda Ser.: 4). (J). 50.75 *(978-1-4703-9686-2(6))*; 48.75 *(978-1-4703-9677-0(7))*; 1.25 *(978-1-4703-9695-4(5))*; 48.75 *(978-1-4703-9650-3(5))*; 168.75 *(978-1-4703-9641-1(6))* Recorded Bks., Inc.

—The Surprise Attack of Jabba the Puppett: An Origami Yoda Book. (Origami Yoda Files Ser.: 4). (J). 2016. lib. bdg. 18.40 *(978-0-606-38208-3(9))* 2013. lib. bdg. 25.70 *(978-0-606-33308-5(8)*, Turtleback) Turtleback Bks.

Arps, Melissa & Lagonegro, Melissa. Friends Forever. Random House Disney Staff, illus. 2009. (Step into Reading Ser.). (ENG.). 32p. (J). (gr. k-3). pap. 3.99 *(978-0-7364-2597-1(7)*, RH/Disney) Random Hse. Children's Bks.

Las Aventuras de Pinocho. (SPA., Illus.). 160p. (YA). 14.95 *(978-84-7281-190-4(5)*, AF1905) Auriga, Ediciones S.A. ESP. Dist: Continental Bk. Co., Inc.

Le Aventure di Pinocchio, Level B. (ITA.). (J). pap. 9.95 *(978-0-88436-050-6(4)*, 55254) EMC/Paradigm Publishing.

Baroff, Raina. The Chanukah Puppet Show. 2008. 20p. per. 24.95 *(978-1-4241-8612-9(9))* America Star Bks.

Bedard, Michael. Painted Devil. 2007. (ENG.). 240p. (YA). (gr. 7). pap. 13.95 *(978-1-4169-6139-0(9)*, Atheneum Bks. for Young Readers) Simon & Schuster Children's Publishing.

Boyne, John. Noah Barleywater Runs Away. Jeffers, Oliver, illus. 2011. (ENG.). 240p. (J). (gr. 3-7). 16.99 *(978-0-385-75246-6(6))* Fickling, David Bks. GBR. Dist: Penguin Random Hse. LLC.

—Noah Barleywater Runs Away. Jeffers, Oliver, illus. 2012. (ENG.). 240p. (J). (gr. 3-7). 7.99 *(978-0-385-75264-0(4)*, Yearling) Random Hse. Children's Bks.

Brandon, Wendy. Cinderbear: Board Book & Puppet Theater. Winter, Janet, illus. 2004. (J). *(978-1-883043-47-6(6))* Straight Edge Pr., The.

C. Collodi. The Adventures of Pinocchio. 2007. 104p. per. *(978-1-4068-6037-5(9))* Echo Library.

Campillo, Carlo Collodi. Ilustrado por Susana. Las Aventuras de Pinocho. (Coleccion Cuentos Universales). (SPA.). (YA). (gr. 4-18). *(978-84-261-3145-4(X)*, JV30301) Juventud, Editorial ESP. Dist: Lectorum Pubns., Inc.

Carsey, Alice, illus. Pinocchio. 2005.Tr. of Avventure di Pinocchio. (ENG.). 136p. (J). (gr. 2-5). 19.95 *(978-1-933327-00-6(6))* Purple Bear Bks., Inc.

—Pinocchio, the Tale of a Puppet. 2011. 140p. pap. 12.99 *(978-1-61203-095-1(5))* Bottom of the Hill Publishing.

Carter, Brynn. The Puppet Explained. 2012. 140p. (gr. -1). pap. 14.95 *(978-1-4685-5617-9(7))* AuthorHouse.

Carter, Scott William. Wooden Bones. (ENG., Illus.). 160p. (J). (gr. 3-7). 2013. pap. 6.99 *(978-1-4424-2752-5(3))* 2012. 15.99 *(978-1-4424-2751-8(5))* Simon & Schuster Bks. For Young Readers. (Simon & Schuster Bks. For Young Readers).

Collodi, C. The Adventures of Pinocchio. 2005. 216p. 27.95 *(978-1-4218-0608-2(8)*, 1st World Library - Literary Society) 1st World Publishing, Inc.

—The Adventures of Pinocchio. Della Chiesa, Carol, tr. 2007. (ENG.). 160p. per. *(978-1-4065-1463-6(2))* Dodo Pr.

—The Adventures of Pinocchio. 2007. 108p. (gr. 4-7). per. 7.99 *(978-1-60459-012-8(2))* Wilder Pubns., Corp.

—Pinocchio: the Tale of a Puppet. Carsey, Alice, illus. 2007. (ENG.). 196p. per. *(978-1-4065-1462-9(4))* Dodo Pr.

Collodi, Carlo. Adventures of Pinocchio. Lucas, Ann Lawson, tr. from ITA. 2009. (Oxford World's Classics Ser.). (ENG., Illus.). 256p. pap. 10.95 *(978-0-19-955398-3(X))* Oxford Univ. Pr., Inc.

—The Adventures of Pinocchio. Staino, Franco & Innocenti, Roberto, illus. rev. ed. 2004. (ENG.). 192p. (J). (gr. 1-3). 35.00 *(978-1-56846-190-8(9))* Creative Co., The.

—Pinocchio. 2017. (ENG., Illus.). (J). pap. 9.99 ***(978-1-366-49758-1(9))*** Blurb, Inc.

—Pinocchio. Cowley, Joy, ed. Han, Joon-ho, illus. 2015. (World Classics Ser.). (ENG.). 32p. (gr. k-4). 26.65 *(978-1-925246-43-8(4))*; 7.99 *(978-1-925246-69-8(8))*; 26.65 *(978-1-925246-17-9(5))* ChoiceMaker Pty. Ltd., The AUS. (Big and SMALL). Dist: Lerner Publishing Group.

—Pinocchio. 2017. (ENG., Illus.). 288p. 12.99 ***(978-1-5098-4290-2(X)***, 9781509842902, Collector's Library, The) Pan Macmillan GBR. Dist: Macmillan.

—Pinocchio. McKowen, Scott, illus. 2014. (Sterling Unabridged Classics Ser.). (ENG.). 184p. (J). (gr. 5). 9.95 *(978-1-4549-1220-0(0))* Sterling Publishing Co., Inc.

—Pinocchio. Brock, Geoffrey, tr. from ITA. Testa, Fulvio, illus. 2012.Tr. of Avventure di Pinocchio. (ENG.). 184p. (J). (gr. k-4). 24.95 *(978-1-59017-588-0(3)*, NYR Children's Collection) New York Review of Bks., Inc., The.

—Pinocchio: Candlewick Illustrated Classic. Rose, Emma, tr. from ITA. Fanelli, Sara, illus. 2010. (Candlewick Illustrated Classics Ser.). (ENG.). 192p. (J). (gr. 2-5). pap. 12.99 *(978-0-7636-4731-5(4))* Candlewick Pr.

Cooper, Susan. The Magician's Boy. Riglietti, Serena, illus. 2006. (ENG.). 112p. (J). (gr. 3-7). pap. 9.99 *(978-1-4169-1555-3(9)*, McElderry, Margaret K. Bks.) McElderry, Margaret K. Bks.

Las Cosas Del Jardin. (SPA.). 24p. 7.95 *(978-84-488-1109-9(7))* Beascoa, Ediciones S.A. ESP. Dist: Distribooks, Inc.

Las Cosas Del Salon. (SPA.). 24p. 7.95 *(978-84-488-1108-2(9))* Beascoa, Ediciones S.A. ESP. Dist: Distribooks, Inc.

Cowing, Sue. Call Me Drog. 2014. (ENG.). 320p. (J). 13.99 *(978-0-00-757804-7(0))* HarperCollins Pubs. Ltd. GBR. Dist: Independent Pubs. Group.

—You Will Call Me Drog. 2011. (Exceptional Reading & Language Arts Titles for Intermediate Grades Ser.). (ENG.). 288p. (J). (gr. 4-7). 16.95 *(978-0-7613-6076-6(X)*, Carolrhoda Bks.) Lerner Publishing Group.

Cox, Jason. Puppet. 2005. (Illus.). 51p. (YA). per. *(978-1-59971-005-1(6))* Aardvark Global Publishing.

Cuno, Sabine. Abre, Cierra y Aprende! Caballero, D., tr. Senner, Katja, illus. 2007. 14p. (J). (gr. -1). *(978-970-718-489-3(2)*, Silver Dolphin en Español) Advanced Marketing, S. de R. L. de C. V.

Descoteaux, Chad. Once upon A Crime Syndicate: A mafia fairy Tale. 2006. 151p. pap. 24.95 *(978-1-4241-0893-0(4))* PublishAmerica, Inc.

Disney Editors. Cinderella Takes the Stage. 2017. (Disney Princess Beginnings Ser.). lib. bdg. 17.20 ***(978-0-606-39857-2(0))*** Turtleback Bks.

D'souza, Nadine. Revenge of the Puppets. Rajvanshi, Ayush, illus. 2013. (ENG.). 32p. (J). (gr. -1). pap. 9.95 *(978-81-8190-197-2(5))* Karadi Tales Co. Pvt, Ltd. IND. Dist: Consortium Bk. Sales & Distribution.

Ernie Gets Lost. (J). 5.58 incl. audio NewSound, LLC.

Friedman, Kinky. Curse of the Missing Puppet Head. 2003. lib. bdg. 29.95 *(978-0-9702383-6-8(3)*, CMPH01) Vandam Pr., Inc.

Fuchs, Menucha. Menucha V'Simcha Series #11: All Aboard! Hass, Estie, illus. 2008. (Menucha V'Simcha Ser.). 20p. (J). 8.95 *(978-1-932443-82-0(7)*, PSHH) Judaica Pr., Inc., The.

Gerth, Melanie. Five Little Ladybugs with Hand Puppet. Beith, Laura Huliska, illus. 2009. (ENG.). 12p. 12.95 *(978-1-58117-889-0(1)*, Intervisual/Piggy Toes) Bendon, Inc.

Goldhawk, Emma. Little Lamb. Lambert, Jonathan, illus. 2014. (Snuggle Puppet Ser.). (ENG.). 10p. (J). (gr. -1). bds. 14.95 *(978-1-62686-014-8(9)*, Silver Dolphin Bks.) Readerlink Distribution Services, LLC.

Gonzalez, Jorge & Collodi, Carlo. Pinocchio, 1 vol. Ruiz, Alfonso, illus. 2009. (Classic Fiction Ser.).Tr. of Avventure di Pinocchio. (ENG.). 72p. (gr. 2-3). lib. bdg. 27.99 *(978-1-4342-1583-3(0)*, Graphic Revolve) Stone Arch Bks.

Green, D. L. Zeke Meeks vs the Putrid Puppet Pals, 1 vol. Alves, Josh, illus. 2012. (Zeke Meeks Ser.). (ENG.). 128p. (gr. 2-2). pap. 5.95 *(978-1-4048-7223-3(X))*; lib. bdg. 22.65 *(978-1-4048-6803-8(8))* Picture Window Bks. (Zeke Meeks).

Hillert, Margaret. Let's Have a Play. Flanigan, Ruth, illus. 2016. (BeginningtoRead Ser.). (ENG.). 32p. (J). (gr. -1-2). pap. 11.94 *(978-1-60357-960-3(X))*; (gr. k-2). 22.60 *(978-1-59953-818-1(0))* Norwood Hse. Pr.

—Pinocchio. Schwartz, Carol & Regan, Dana, illus. 2016. (BeginningtoRead Ser.). (ENG.). 32p. (J). (gr. -1-2). pap. 11.94 *(978-1-60357-912-4(5))* Norwood Hse. Pr.

ImageBooks Staff & Chronicle Books Editors. Little Bat Finger Puppet Book. 2010. (Little Finger Puppet Board Bks.). (ENG., Illus.). 12p. (J). (gr. -1 — 1). bds. 6.99 *(978-0-8118-7514-1(8))* Chronicle Bks. LLC.

—Little Turkey. 2010. (Little Finger Puppet Board Bks.). (ENG., Illus.). 12p. (J). (gr. -1 — 1). bds. 6.99 *(978-0-8118-7513-4(X))* Chronicle Bks. LLC.

Keats, Ezra Jack. Louie. Keats, Ezra Jack, illus. 2004. (ENG., Illus.). 40p. (J). (gr. -1-2). pap. 6.99 *(978-0-14-240080-7(7)*, Puffin Books) Penguin Young Readers Group.

—Louie. 2004. (Illus.). 31p. 17.20 *(978-0-613-97780-7(7)*, Turtleback) Turtleback Bks.

Langridge, Roger. The Muppet Show Comic Book: The Treasure of Peg-Leg Wilson. Langridge, Roger, illus. 2010. (Muppet Show Ser.). (ENG., Illus.). 112p. (J). 24.99 *(978-1-60886-530-7(4))*; (gr. 4-7). pap. 9.99 *(978-1-60886-504-8(5))* Boom! Studios.

—The Muppet Show Comic Book - Muppet Mash. Langridge, Roger, illus. 2011. (Muppet Show Ser.). (Illus.). 128p. pap. 9.99 *(978-1-60886-611-3(4))* Boom! Studios.

—On the Road. Langridge, Roger, illus. 2010. (Muppet Show Ser.). (ENG., Illus.). 112p. (J). pap. 9.99 *(978-1-60886-516-1(9))* Boom! Studios.

Lawson, Jennifer. Our New Solar System: A Puppet Show. 2010. 27p. 19.95 *(978-0-557-21389-4(4))* Lulu Pr., Inc.

LeLeu, Lisa. Frenchy the Frog Story Starter: Puppet Show Book Story Starter. 2004. (Puppet Show Bks.). (Illus.). 14p. 1.50 *(978-0-9710537-9-4(4))* LeLeu, Lisa Studios! Inc.

—Miss Moo-Moo the Cow Story Starter: Puppet Book Story Starter. 2004. (Puppet Show Bks.). (Illus.). 14p. 1.50 *(978-0-9710537-1-7(5))* LeLeu, Lisa Studios! Inc.

—Scooter the Cat Gift Set: Puppet Book Gift Set with 2 Books. 2004. (Puppet Show Bks.). (Illus.). 30p. 19.95 *(978-0-9710537-0-0(7))* LeLeu, Lisa Studios! Inc.

—Scooter the Cat Story Teller: Puppet Book Story Starter. 2004. (Puppet Show Bks.). (Illus.). 14p. 1.50 *(978-0-9710537-6-2(6))* LeLeu, Lisa Studios! Inc.

Lemaître, Pascal, illus. Pinocchio. 2014. (Cartoon Classics Ser.). (ENG.). 144p. (J). (gr. 2-5). 12.99 *(978-0-8050-9699-6(X)*, 9780805096996, Holt, Henry & Co. Bks. For Young Readers) Holt, Henry & Co.

Lilly, Evangeline. The Squickerwonkers. Fraser-Allen, Johnny, illus. 2014. (ENG.). 42p. (gr. k-3). 16.99 *(978-1-78329-545-6(7)*, Titan Bks.) Titan Bks. Ltd. GBR. Dist: Penguin Random Hse. LLC.

Love, D. Anne. The Puppeteer's Apprentice. 2004. (ENG., Illus.). 192p. (J). (gr. 3-7). reprint ed. pap. 9.99 *(978-0-689-84425-6(5)*, McElderry, Margaret K. Bks.) McElderry, Margaret K. Bks.

—The Puppeteer's Apprentice. 2004. (Aladdin Historical Fiction Ser.). 185p. (gr. 3-7). 17.00 *(978-0-7569-4323-3(X))* Perfection Learning Corp.

Madore, Michele. Rudee Goes Bananas for Manners. Gravitt, Bill, illus. 2006. (ENG.). 38p. (J). pap. 6.95 *(978-0-615-17967-4(3))* Manners Toy Co., LLC.

Magsamen, Sandra. Love Bug. rev. ed. 2007. (Board Books with Plush Toys Ser.). (ENG., Illus.). 20p. (J). (gr. -1 — 1). 8.99 *(978-0-316-06596-2(X))* Little, Brown Bks. for Young Readers.

Make Believe Ideas, creator. BJ's Finger Puppet Book Assortment. 2007. (Illus.). (J). (gr. -1-3). *(978-1-84610-675-0(3))* Make Believe Ideas.

Mathieu, Joe, et al. Big Bird's Big Book: Counting Colors Country City Opposites Playing. Mathieu, Joe, illus. 2009. (Sesame Street Ser.). (ENG., Illus.). 14p. (J). (gr. k — 1). bds. 45.00 *(978-0-394-89128-6(7)*, Random Hse. Bks. for Young Readers) Random Hse. Children's Bks.

McDonald, Megan. When the Library Lights Go Out. Tillotson, Katherine, illus. 2009. (ENG.). 40p. (J). (gr. -1-1). 8.99 *(978-1-4169-8028-5(8)*, Atheneum Bks. for Young Readers) Simon & Schuster Children's Publishing.

—When the Library Lights Go Out. Tillotson, Katherine, tr. Tillotson, Katherine, illus. 2005. (ENG.). 40p. (J). (gr. -1-3). 19.99 *(978-0-689-86170-3(2)*, Atheneum/Richard Jackson Bks.) Simon & Schuster Children's Publishing.

Melean, Mary & Lascaris, Alexia. The Adventures of Don Quixote of la Mancha. 2011. 44p. pap. 18.46 *(978-1-4567-6131-8(5))* AuthorHouse.

Michael, Melanie. Nerfnerd. Alderton, John, illus. 2011. (J). *(978-0-938467-07-6(7))* Headline Bks., Inc.

Miller, Toby. The Magic Word. 2011. (Illus.). 24p. pap. 14.09 *(978-1-4567-7793-7(9))* AuthorHouse.

Mitchell, Robin. Snowy & Chinook. Steedman, Judith, illus. 2005. (ENG.). 22p. (J). (gr. -1-3). 15.95 *(978-0-9688768-9-3(7))* Simply Read Bks. CAN. Dist: Ingram Publisher Services.

Monster at the End of This Book. 2009. (ENG.). 24p. 14.99 *(978-1-74181-222-0(4)*, Ideal Pubns.) Worthy Publishing.

Murray, M. A., tr. Pinocchio, As First Translated into English by M a Murray & Illustrated by Charles Folkard. Folkard, Charles, illus. 2009. 280p. pap. 11.95 *(978-1-59915-177-9(4))* Yesterday's Classics.

Muss, Angela, illus. Panda & Me. 2012. (Puppet Pals Ser.). (ENG.). 10p. (J). bds. *(978-1-84643-473-0(4))* Child's Play International Ltd.

Nickel. Pinocchio. Date not set. (J). 4.99 *(978-0-7214-5404-7(6))* Nickel Pr.

Page, Nick & Page, Claire. Finger Puppet Books Christmas Story. 2008. (Illus.). 12p. (gr. -1-k). bds. *(978-1-84610-821-1(7))* Make Believe Ideas.

—Finger Puppet Books Christmas Story. 2009. (Finger Puppet Bks.). (Illus.). 12p. (gr. -1-k). bds. 12.99 *(978-1-84610-573-9(0))* Make Believe Ideas GBR. Dist: Nelson, Thomas Inc.

Parragon Staff. Pinocchio: The Magical Story. 2010. (Disney Padded Magical Storybks.). (Illus.). 32p. (J). (gr. -1-1). *(978-1-4075-8451-5(0))* Parragon, Inc.

Paterson, Katherine. El Maestro de las Marionetas.Tr. of Master Puppeteer. (SPA., Illus.). (YA). (gr. 5-8). 9.95 *(978-958-04-4382-7(3)*, NR8770) Norma S.A. COL. Dist: Distribuidora Norma, Inc.

—The Master Puppeteer. 3rd ed. (J). pap. 3.95 *(978-0-13-800095-0(6))* Prentice Hall (Schl. Div.).

Pilegard, Virginia Walton. The Warlord's Puppeteers, 1 vol. Debon, Nicolas, illus. 2003. (Warlord's Ser.: 4). (ENG.). 32p. (J). (gr. k-3). 16.99 *(978-1-58980-077-9(X))* Pelican Publishing Co., Inc.

Pinocchio: The Human Body, Sea Life, The Bedroom. (FRE & ENG., Illus.). 24p. (J). (gr. -1-5). pap., stu. ed. 5.95 *(978-88-8148-243-6(6))* EMC/Paradigm Publishing.

Publications International Ltd. Staff, ed. Elmo Goes to the Doctor. 2010. 14p. (J). bds. 16.98 *(978-1-4127-4609-0(4))* Phoenix International Publications, Inc.

The Puppet Show. (Early Intervention Levels Ser.). 21.30 *(978-0-7362-0362-3(1))* CENGAGE Learning.

Rainey, L. E. Sad Sam, Glad Sam. 2006. (Illus.). 32p. (J). 16.95 *(978-0-9785521-0-7(5))* Shoetree Publishers, Inc.

Rao, Lisa. Don't Bite Your Friends! 2009. (Yo Gabba Gabba! Ser.). (ENG.). 10p. (J). (gr. -1-2). 8.99 *(978-1-4169-9014-7(3)*, Simon Spotlight) Simon Spotlight.

Ross, Katharine. Twinkle, Twinkle, Little Bug. Cooke, Tom & Brannon, Tom, illus. 2014. (Step into Reading Ser.). (ENG.). 32p. (J). (gr. -1-1). pap. 3.99 *(978-0-679-87666-3(9)*, Random Hse. Bks. for Young Readers) Random Hse. Children's Bks.

Ruiz, Margarita, illus. Pinocho. (SPA & ENG.). (J). (gr. -1-5). pap. 5.95 incl. audio compact disk *(978-88-8148-253-5(3))* EMC/Paradigm Publishing.

Schlitz, Laura Amy. Splendors & Glooms. (ENG.). 400p. (J). 2014. (gr. 5-9). pap. 8.99 *(978-0-7636-6926-3(1))* 2012. (Illus.). (gr. 4-7). 17.99 *(978-0-7636-5380-4(2))* Candlewick Pr.

—Splendors & Glooms. 2014. (ENG.). (J). (gr. 4-7). lib. bdg. 18.60 ***(978-1-62765-443-2(7))*** Perfection Learning Corp.

—Splendors & Glooms. 2014. lib. bdg. 18.40 *(978-0-606-35170-6(1))* Turtleback Bks.

Schreiber, Elisheva. The Miniature Puppet Theater Book. Pollack, Gadi & Markovitch, Evgeny, illus. (J). 14.95 *(978-1-58330-617-8(X))* Feldheim Pubs.

Snider, Jesse Blaze. Muppet Snow White. Paroline, Shelli, illus. 2010. (Muppet Show Ser.). 112p. (J). (gr. 3-6). pap. 9.99 *(978-1-60886-574-1(6))* Boom! Studios.

Staino, Franco, illus. The Adventures of Pinocchio. 2012. 312p. *(978-88-492-2206-7(8))* Gangemi.

Stiberth, Elizabeth. Halloween Mystery. 2008. 32p. pap. 14.49 *(978-1-4389-1112-0(2))* AuthorHouse.

Stine, R. L. Dr. Maniac vs. Robby Schwartz. 2008. (Goosebumps Horrorland Ser.: 5). (ENG.). 160p. (J). (gr. 3-7). pap. 6.99 *(978-0-439-91873-2(1)*, Scholastic Paperbacks) Scholastic, Inc.

—Night of the Puppet People. 2015. (Goosebumps Most Wanted Ser.: 8). lib. bdg. 17.20 *(978-0-606-37792-8(1))* Turtleback Bks.

—Revenge of the Living Dummy. 2008. (Goosebumps HorrorLand Ser.: No. 1). 128p. (J). (gr. 4-7). 13.65 *(978-0-7569-8816-6(0))* Perfection Learning Corp.

—Revenge of the Living Dummy. 2008. (Goosebumps HorrorLand Ser.: 1). 128p. (gr. 4-7). lib. bdg. 17.20 *(978-1-4178-1891-4(3)*, Turtleback) Turtleback Bks.

—Son of Slappy. 2013. (Goosebumps Most Wanted Ser.: 2). (ENG.). 160p. (J). (gr. 3-7). pap. 6.99 *(978-0-545-41799-0(6)*, Scholastic Paperbacks) Scholastic, Inc.

—Son of Slappy. 2013. (Goosebumps Most Wanted Ser.: 2). lib. bdg. 17.20 *(978-0-606-31533-3(0)*, Turtleback) Turtleback Bks.

Stone, Jon. The Monster at the End of This Book. Smollin, Michael, illus. 2015. (Little Golden Board Book Ser.). (ENG.). 26p. (J). (— 1). bds. 7.99 *(978-0-553-50873-4(3)*, Golden Bks.) Random Hse. Children's Bks.

Tattum, Stephan. Fun Pup. 2005. (J). 4.95 *(978-1-59792-005-6(3))* F.A.S.T. Learning LLC.

Teitelbaum, Michael. The Cave of No Return. 2015. (Cold Whispers Ser.). (ENG., Illus.). 32p. (J). (gr. 2-6). lib. bdg. 26.60 *(978-1-62724-812-9(9))* Bearport Publishing Co., Inc.

Trimble, Marcia. Peppy's Shadow. Pellegrini, Will, illus. 2003. 32p. (J). (gr. -1-3). 15.95 *(978-1-891577-70-3(0))*; pap. 7.95 *(978-1-891577-71-0(9))* Images Pr.

Tyre, Greg R. Fun with Sockie. 2009. 28p. pap. 14.99 *(978-1-4490-0105-6(X))* AuthorHouse.

Wang, Holman & Wang, Jack. Star Wars Epic Yarns: A New Hope. 2015. (ENG., Illus.). 24p. (J). (gr. -1 — 1). 9.95 *(978-1-4521-3393-5(X))* Chronicle Bks. LLC.

—Star Wars Epic Yarns: Return of the Jedi. 2015. (ENG., Illus.). 24p. (J). (gr. -1 — 1). 9.95 *(978-1-4521-3500-7(2))* Chronicle Bks. LLC.

—Star Wars Epic Yarns: The Empire Strikes Back. 2015. (ENG., Illus.). 24p. (J). (gr. -1 — 1). 9.95 *(978-1-4521-3499-4(5))* Chronicle Bks. LLC.

Wejmeijer, Annelien. Dan & Max. van de Liejgraaf, Deborah, illus. 2013. (My Best Friend & Me Ser.). (ENG.). 10p. (J). (gr. -1 — 1). bds. 6.99 *(978-0-7641-6634-1(4))* Barron's Educational Series, Inc.

PUPPETS AND PUPPET-PLAYS

see Puppet Plays; Puppet Theater; Puppets

PURCHASING

see Shopping

PURIM

Bredeson, Carmen. Purim. 2003. (Rookie Read-About Holidays Ser.). (ENG., Illus.). 32p. (J). (gr. 1-2). pap. 5.95 *(978-0-516-27928-2(9)*, Children's Pr.) Scholastic Library Publishing.

Gottlieb, Wendy Ruth. Purr-Im Cat. 2008. (Illus.). 32p. (J). 16.95 *(978-1-932687-91-0(2)*, Devora Publishing) Simcha Media Group.

Kress, Camille. Purim! Kress, Camille, illus. 2004. (Illus.). 10p. (gr. -1-k). bds. 5.95 *(978-0-8074-0654-0(6)*, 102555) URJ Pr.

Kropf, Latifa Berry. It's Purim Time! Cohen, Tod, photos by. (Purim Ser.). (Illus.). 24p. (J). 2012. (ENG.). (gr. -1-1). pap. 8.95 *(978-0-7613-8493-9(6))* 2005. (gr. 2-6). lib. bdg. 12.95 *(978-1-58013-153-7(0))* Lerner Publishing Group. (Kar-Ben Publishing).

Pollack, Gadi, illus. & contrib. by. Purimshpiel. Pollack, Gadi, contrib. by. (ENG & HEB.). *(978-1-58330-611-6(0))*; (ENG &

FRE.). 21.95 *(978-1-58330-601-7(3))*; 19.99 *(978-1-58330-596-6(3))* Feldheim Pubs.
Schram, Peninnah. The Purim Costume. Keiser, Tammy L., illus. 2004. 13.95 *(978-0-8074-0874-2(3)*, 101312) URJ Pr.
Simon, Norma. Happy Purim Night. Gordon, Ayala, illus. (Festival Series of Picture Storybooks). (J). (gr. -1). vinyl bd. 4.50 *(978-0-8381-0706-5(0)*, 10-706) United Synagogue of America Bk. Service.

PURIM—FICTION

Adelson, Leone. The Mystery Bear: A Purim Story. Howland, Naomi, tr. Howland, Naomi, illus. 2004. 32p. (J). (gr. -1-2). 15.00 *(978-0-618-33727-9(X)*, Clarion Bks.) Houghton Mifflin Harcourt Trade & Reference Pubs.
Barash, Chris. Is It Purim Yet? Psacharopulo, Alessandra, illus. 2017. (ENG.). 32p. (J). (gr. -1-3). 16.99 *(978-0-8075-3391-8(2))* Whitman, Albert & Co.
Cuyler, Margery. Purim Chicken. Pinillos, Puy, illus. 2017. (ENG.). 32p. (J). (gr. -1-3). 16.99 *(978-0-8075-3381-9(5))* Whitman, Albert & Co.
Goldin, Barbara Diamond. Cakes & Miracles: A Purim Tale, 0 vols. Zollars, Jaime, illus. 2010. (ENG.). 32p. (J). (gr. k-3). 17.99 *(978-0-7614-5701-5(1)*, 9780761457015, Amazon Children's Publishing) Amazon Publishing.
Howland, Naomi. The Better-Than-Best Purim, 0 vols. 2012. (ENG.). 32p. (J). (gr. -1-2). 16.99 *(978-0-7614-6203-3(1)*, 9780761462033, Amazon Children's Publishing) Amazon Publishing.
Kushner, Elisabeth. The Purim Superhero. Byrne, Mike, illus. 2013. (Purim Ser.). (ENG.). 32p. (J). (gr. -1-3). 7.95 *(978-0-7613-9062-6(6))*; lib. bdg. 17.95 *(978-0-7613-9061-9(8))* Lerner Publishing Group. (Kar-Ben Publishing).
Marshall, Linda Elovitz. Talia & the Haman-Tushies. Assirelli, Francesca, illus. 2017. (ENG.). 24p. (J). (gr. -1-2). 17.99 *(978-1-5124-0825-6(5)*, Kar-Ben Publishing) Lerner Publishing Group.
Milhander, Laura Aron. Not for All the Hamantaschen in Town. Chernyak, Inna, illus. 2016. (ENG.). 32p. (gr. -1-3). 17.99 *(978-1-4677-5928-1(7)*, Kar-Ben Publishing) Lerner Publishing Group.
Newman, Tracy. Purim Is Coming! Garófoli, Viviana, illus. 2017. (ENG.). 12p. (gr. -1 — 1). 5.99 *(978-1-5124-0827-0(1)*, Kar-Ben Publishing) Lerner Publishing Group.
Rouss, Sylvia A. & Lanton, Sandy. Lots of Latkes: A Hanukkah Story. Kahn, Katherine Janus & Redenbaugh, Vicki Jo, illus. 2003. (ENG.). 32p. (J). (gr. -1-3). pap. 6.95 *(978-1-58013-061-5(5)*, Kar-Ben Publishing) Lerner Publishing Group.
Schotter, Roni. Purim Play, 0 vols. Hafner, Marylin, illus. 2010. (ENG.). 34p. (J). (gr. -1-2). pap. 6.99 *(978-0-7614-5800-5(X)*, 9780761458005, Amazon Children's Publishing) Amazon Publishing.
Simpson, Lesley. The Purim Surprise. Church, Peter, illus. 2004. (Purim Ser.). 32p. (J). (gr. -1-3). pap. 6.95 *(978-1-58013-090-5(9)*, Kar-Ben Publishing) Lerner Publishing Group.
Terwilliger, Kelly. Barnyard Purim. Newman, Barbara Johansen, illus. 2012. (Purim Ser.). (ENG.). 32p. (J). (gr. k-3). pap. 7.95 *(978-0-7613-4514-5(0))*; lib. bdg. 17.95 *(978-0-7613-4513-8(2))* Lerner Publishing Group. (Kar-Ben Publishing).
Watts, Irene N. A Telling Time, 1 vol. Shoemaker, Kathryn E., illus. 2004. (ENG.). 32p. (J). (gr. 2-5). 17.95 *(978-1-896580-39-5(4))* Tradewind Bks. CAN. Dist: Orca Bk. Pubs. USA.
Zolkower, Edie Stoltz. When It's Purim. Bjornson, Barb, illus. 2009. (Very First Board Bks.). (ENG.). 12p. (J). (gr. -1 — 1). 5.95 *(978-0-8225-8947-1(8)*, Kar-Ben Publishing) Lerner Publishing Group.

PURITANS

Abrams, Dennis. Cotton Mather. 2010. (Leaders of the Colonial Era Ser.). 128p. (gr. 5-8). 35.00 *(978-1-60413-736-1(3)*, Chelsea Hse.) Facts On File, Inc.
Marsh, Carole. Anne Hutchinson. 2004. 12p. (gr. k-4). 2.95 *(978-0-635-02370-4(9))* Gallopade International.
Miller, Barbara Kiely. Anne Hutchinson. 2007. (Great Americans Ser.). 24p. (gr. 1-4). pap. 8.15 *(978-0-8368-8324-4(1))*; (SPA.). pap. 8.15 *(978-0-8368-8337-4(3))*; (SPA., Illus.). lib. bdg. 22.00 *(978-0-8368-8330-5(6))*; (Illus.). lib. bdg. 22.00 *(978-0-8368-8317-6(9))* Stevens, Gareth Publishing LLLP. (Weekly Reader Leveled Readers).
Nichols, Joan K. A Matter of Conscience: The Trial of Anne Hutchinson. Krovatin, Dan, illus. 2009. (Steck-Vaughn Stories of America Ser.). (ENG.). 112p. (gr. 3-8). pap. 14.20 *(978-0-8114-8073-4(9))* Houghton Mifflin Harcourt Publishing Co.
Owens, L. L. Pilgrims in America. 2006. (Events in American History Ser.). (Illus.). 48p. (J). (gr. -1-1). lib. bdg. 31.36 *(978-1-60044-122-6(X))* Rourke Educational Media.
The Puritans, Algonkians & Roger Williams (NCHS) (J). (gr. 5-8). spiral bd., tchr.'s planning gde. ed. 13.50 *(978-0-382-44447-0(7))* Cobblestone Publishing Co.
The Puritans, Algonkians & Roger Williams (NCHS) Grades 5-8. (J). tchr. ed. 18.00 *(978-0-382-44537-8(6))* Cobblestone Publishing Co.
Slavicek, Louise Chipley. Anne Hutchinson. 2010. (Leaders of the Colonial Era Ser.). 120p. (gr. 5-8). 35.00 *(978-1-60413-741-5(X)*, Chelsea Hse.) Facts On File, Inc.
Tierney, Tom. Cavalier & Puritan Fashions. 2005. (Dover Fashion Coloring Book Ser.). (ENG., Illus.). 48p. (J). (gr. 6-8). pap. 3.95 *(978-0-486-43655-5(1))* Dover Pubns., Inc.
Williams, Gianna & Riehecky, Janet. La Colonia de Plymouth. 2006. (Hitos de la historia de Estados Unidos (Landmark Events in American History) Ser.). (SPA.). 48p. (gr. 5-12). pap. 11.70 *(978-0-8368-7471-6(4)*, Gareth Stevens Learning Library); (Illus.). lib. bdg. 27.00 *(978-0-8368-7464-8(1)*, Gareth Stevens Secondary Library) Stevens, Gareth Publishing LLLP.
Wolfe, James & Moe, Barbara A. Understanding the Charter of the Massachusetts Bay Colony. 2015. (Primary Sources of American Political Documents Ser.). (ENG., Illus.). 112p. (J). (gr. 7-7). 37.27 *(978-0-7660-6870-4(6))* Enslow Pubs., Inc.

PURITANS—FICTION

Literature Connections English: The Witch of Blackbird Pond. 2004. (gr. 6-12). *(978-0-395-78592-8(8)*, 2-70293) Holt McDougal.
Noyes, Deborah. Angel & Apostle. 2007. (ENG.). 304p. per. 14.95 *(978-1-932961-29-4(1))* Unbridled Bks.
Rees, Celia. Witch Child. unabr. ed. 2004. (Young Adult Cassette Librariestm Ser.). 304p. (J). (gr. 5-9). pap. 40.00 incl. audio *(978-0-8072-1198-4(2)*, S YA 343 SP, Listening Library) Random Hse. Audio Publishing Group.
Smith, Mary P. Wells. The Young Puritans in King Philip's War. Bridgman, L. J., illus. 2011. 396p. 54.95 *(978-1-258-05550-9(3))* Literary Licensing, LLC.
Speare, Elizabeth George. The Witch of Blackbird Pond. 2011. (ENG.). 272p. (J). (gr. 5-7). pap. 7.99 *(978-0-547-55029-9(4))* Houghton Mifflin Harcourt Publishing Co.
—The Witch of Blackbird Pond. 2004. 223p. (J). (gr. 4-7). pap., tchr.'s planning gde. ed. 38.00 incl. audio *(978-0-8072-0862-5(0)*, Listening Library) Random Hse. Audio Publishing Group.
Thompson, Paul B. The Devil's Door: A Salem Witchcraft Story. 2010. (Historical Fiction Adventures (HFA) Ser.). (Illus.). 160p. (J). pap. 10.95 *(978-1-59845-214-3(2))*; (gr. 3-6). 29.27 *(978-0-7660-3387-0(2))* Enslow Pubs., Inc.

PUZZLES

see also Bible Games and Puzzles; Kakuro; Sudoku

Accord Publishing Staff. Flip & Click Christmas Hangman. 2011. (ENG.). 72p. (J). pap. 4.99 *(978-1-4494-0836-7(2))* Andrews McMeel Publishing.
—Go Fun! Big Book of Puzzles. 2014. (ENG.). 216p. (J). pap. 12.99 *(978-1-4494-4386-3(9))* Andrews McMeel Publishing.
Accord Publishing Staff, et al. Stick to It - Pets: A Magnetic Puzzle Book. 2010. (ENG.). 14p. (J). (gr. -1). bds. 16.99 *(978-0-7407-9726-2(3))* Andrews McMeel Publishing.
Adams, Colleen. Tangram Puzzles: Describing & Comparing Attributes of Plane Geometric Shapes. (PowerMath Ser.). 24p. 2009. (ENG., Illus.). (gr. 3-4). pap. 8.25 *(978-0-8239-8921-8(6))* 2009. (gr. 3-4). 45.00 *(978-1-60851-383-3(1))* 2004. (Illus.). (J). lib. bdg. 22.50 *(978-0-8239-8976-8(3))* Rosen Publishing Group, Inc., The. (PowerKids Pr.).
African American Heritage Pictures, Puzzles, & Word Games. 2004. (YA). per. 16.00 *(978-0-9758586-0-8(2))* Jenkins-Simmons, Glenda.
Agee, Jon. Palindromania! Agee, Jon, illus. 2009. (ENG., Illus.). 112p. (J). (gr. 3-8). pap. 9.89 *(978-0-374-40025-5(3)*, 9780374400255) Square Fish.
Aihara, Kazunori. Let's Find Pokemon! 2017. (Pokemon Ser.). (ENG.). 88p. (J). 16.99 ***(978-1-4215-9579-5(6))*** Viz Media.
Akaishi, Shinobu & Sarris, Eno, eds. Animals - My Book of Mazes, Ages 5-6-7. 2006. (Kumon Workbooks Ser.). (ENG., Illus.). 82p. (J). (gr. -1-k). per. 7.95 *(978-1-933241-25-8(X))* Kumon Publishing North America, Inc.
—My Book of Mazes: Things That Go! 2006. (Kumon Workbooks Ser.). (ENG., Illus.). 82p. (J). (gr. -1). per. 7.95 *(978-1-933241-31-9(4))* Kumon Publishing North America, Inc.
All Through the Year (Gr. 1-2) 2003. (J). *(978-1-58232-055-7(1))* ECS Learning Systems, Inc.
All Through the Year (Gr. 1-3) 2003. (J). *(978-1-58232-065-6(9))* ECS Learning Systems, Inc.
All Through the Year (Gr. 2-4) 2003. (J). *(978-1-58232-056-4(X))* ECS Learning Systems, Inc.
Allen, Heather. Earth Day Is Every Day! 2011. (Dover Children's Activity Bks.). (ENG.). 48p. (J). (gr. 1-5). pap. 4.99 *(978-0-486-47765-7(7))* Dover Pubns., Inc.
Allen, Peter, illus. Ancient Egypt Jigsaw Book. 2006. (Jigsaw Bks.). 14p. (J). (gr. k-3). bds. 14.99 *(978-0-7945-1236-1(4)*, Usborne) EDC Publishing.
Allen, Robert. Mensa Mighty Mindbusters for Kids. 2003. 256p. (J). (gr. 4-7). per. *(978-1-84222-897-5(8))* Carlton Bks., Ltd.
—Mensa Presents Secret Codes for Kids. 2003. (Illus.). 128p. (J). pap. *(978-1-84222-767-1(X))* Carlton Bks., Ltd.
Allen, Robert, et al. Mind-Melting Conundrums. 2015. (Train Your Brain Puzzle Bks.). (ENG.). 96p. (J). (gr. 2-6). pap. 7.99 *(978-1-4380-0767-0(1))* Barron's Educational Series, Inc.
—Train Your Brain: Brain-Bending Challenges - Intermediate. 2014. (Train Your Brain Puzzle Bks.). (ENG.). 96p. (J). (gr. 2-6). pap. 7.99 *(978-1-4380-0538-6(5))* Barron's Educational Series, Inc.
—Train Your Brain: Mind-Twisting Puzzles - Beginner. 2014. (Train Your Brain Puzzle Bks.). (ENG.). 96p. (J). (gr. 2-6). pap. 7.99 *(978-1-4380-0537-9(7))* Barron's Educational Series, Inc.
—Train Your Brain: Super Tricky Teasers - Expert. 2014. (Train Your Brain Puzzle Bks.). (ENG.). 96p. (J). (gr. 2-6). pap. 7.99 *(978-1-4380-0539-3(3))* Barron's Educational Series, Inc.
—Train Your Brain Cranium Crunchers. 2016. (Train Your Brain Ser.). (ENG.). 96p. (J). (gr. 2-6). pap. 7.99 *(978-1-4380-0845-5(7))* Barron's Educational Series, Inc.
—Train Your Brain Perplexing Puzzles. 2016. (Train Your Brain Ser.). (ENG.). 96p. (J). (gr. 2-6). pap. 7.99 *(978-1-4380-0846-2(5))* Barron's Educational Series, Inc.
Alphabet Puzzle Pairs. 2004. (J). pap. *(978-1-59461-051-6(7))* eeBoo Corp.
Amery, H. Bible Stories Jigsaw Book. 2004. 20p. (J). 14.95 *(978-0-7945-0558-5(9))* EDC Publishing.
—Navidad en la Granja Libro Con Paginas Puzzle. 2004. Orig. Title: Christmas Jigsaw Book. (SPA.). 6p. (J). 8.95 *(978-0-7460-5092-7(5))* EDC Publishing.
—The Steam Train Jigsaw Book. 2004. 14p. (J). 8.95 *(978-0-7945-0296-6(2))* EDC Publishing.
Amery, H. & Cartwright, S. ABC Jigsaw Book. rev. ed. 2004. 18p. (J). 14.95 *(978-0-7945-0619-3(4))* EDC Publishing.
—Christmas Jigsaw Book. 2004. (Farmyard Tales Ser.). (ENG.). 1p. (J). bds. 8.95 *(978-0-7945-0219-5(9)*, Usborne) EDC Publishing.
—Farm Animal Jigsaw Book. 2004. (Jigsaw Bks.). (ENG., Illus.). 1p. (J). bds. 8.95 *(978-0-7945-0162-4(1)*, Usborne) EDC Publishing.
Amery, Heather. Christmas Story Jigsaw Book. 2004. (Jigsaw Bks.). (Illus.). 14p. (J). 8.95 *(978-0-7945-0223-2(7)*, Usborne) EDC Publishing.
—Usborne Greek Myths Jigsaw Book. Edwards, Linda, illus. 2006. (Usborne Jigsaw Bks.). 14p. (J). bds. 14.99 *(978-0-7945-1183-8(X)*, Usborne) EDC Publishing.

Analogy Challenges Level A. 2004. (J). pap. 12.95 *(978-1-892069-77-1(6))* MindWare Holdings, Inc.
Analogy Challenges Level B. 2004. (J). pap. 12.95 *(978-1-892069-78-8(4))* MindWare Holdings, Inc.
Andrew, Carol B. Little Farm Puppy. 2006. (Illus.). (J). *(978-1-933577-05-0(3))* Learning Wood, LLC.
Andrews McMeel Publishing, LLC Staff & Cole, Jeff. Flip & Click Big Book of Games: 100 Games. 2009. (ENG.). 208p. (J). (gr. -1). pap. 11.99 *(978-0-7407-8154-4(5))* Andrews McMeel Publishing.
Andrews McMeel Publishing Staff. Go Fun! Big Book of Brain Games. 2014. (Go Fun! Ser.: 1). (ENG.). 144p. (J). pap. 8.99 *(978-1-4494-6488-2(2))* Andrews McMeel Publishing.
—Go Fun! Big Book of Brain Games 2. 2016. (Go Fun! Ser.: 12). (ENG.). 128p. (J). pap. 8.99 *(978-1-4494-7883-4(2))* Andrews McMeel Publishing.
—Go Fun! Big Book of Crosswords. 2014. (Go Fun! Ser.: 2). (ENG.). 144p. (J). pap. 8.99 *(978-1-4494-6486-8(6))* Andrews McMeel Publishing.
Anholt, Catherine & Anholt, Laurence. Can You Guess? A Lift-the-Flap Birthday Party Book. 2003. (Illus.). 16p. pap. 7.95 *(978-0-7112-2214-4(2))* Fleming, Randall.
Animal: Puzzles & Games. 2009. (BOREDOM BUSTERS Ser.). 56p. (J). (gr. 2-7). pap. 4.99 *(978-0-8416-1091-0(6))* American Map Corp.
Animal Clues: 6 Small Books. (gr. k-1). 35.00 *(978-0-7635-6226-7(2))* Rigby Education.
Archer, Mandy. Pets: Creative Play, Fold-Out Pages, Puzzles & Games, over 200 Stickers! 2014. (My First Creativity Bks.). (ENG.). 66p. (J). (gr. -1-2). pap. 9.99 *(978-1-4380-0443-3(5))* Barron's Educational Series, Inc.
Arensen, Shel. The First Christmas: Nativity Puzzle Book with 6 Play Pieces. 2003. (Illus.). 16p. (J). 10.99 *(978-0-8254-5509-4(X))* Kregel Pubns.
Armadillo Press Staff. My Book of Baby Animals: A Fun-Packed Picture & Puzzle Book for Little Ones. 2016. (ENG., Illus.). 48p. bds. 9.99 *(978-1-86147-662-3(0)*, Armadillo) Anness Publishing GBR. Dist: National Bk. Network.
Artell, Mike. Backyard Bloodsuckers: Questions, Facts & Tongue Twisters about Creepy Crawlers. 2004. (Illus.). 80p. pap. 14.95 *(978-0-673-59248-4(0))* Good Year Bks.
—Hidden Pictures. 2012. (Dover Children's Activity Bks.). (ENG., Illus.). 64p. (gr. 5). pap. 2.50 *(978-0-486-28153-7(1))* Dover Pubns., Inc.
Bailey, Todd, ed. The Clue Searcher's Discovery Guide To: A Clue Search Puzzles Book: the 50 States, 1. 2004. (Illus.). 60p. spiral bd. 14.99 *(978-0-9753879-0-0(1))* ClueSearchPuzzles.com.
Balkan, Gabrielle. The 50 States: Celebrate the People, Places & Food of the U. S. A! Linero, Sol, illus. 2016. (50 States Ser.). (ENG.). 12p. (J). (gr. 3-6). 19.99 *(978-1-84780-869-1(7)*, Wide Eyed Editions) Quarto Publishing Group UK GBR. Dist: Hachette Bk. Group.
Ball, Liz. Frog Fun Hidden Treasures: Hidden Picture Puzzles, Vol. 8. Ball, Liz, illus. 2008. (Hidden Treasures Ser.: Vol. 8). (Illus.). 56p. (YA). pap. 6.95 *(978-0-9678159-8-5(3))* Hidden Pictures.
Ball, Liz, illus. Bible Stories: Find-the-Picture Puzzles. 2004. (Find-the-Picture Puzzle Ser.: 1). 24p. (J). pap. 2.95 *(978-0-8198-1163-9(7)*, 332-026) Pauline Bks. & Media.
—Miracles & Parables of Jesus: Find-the-Picture Puzzles. 2004. (Find-the-Picture Puzzle Ser.: 2). 24p. (J). pap. 2.95 *(978-0-8198-4830-7(1)*, 332-221) Pauline Bks. & Media.
Balloon Books. Dot to Dot Count to 10. 2003. (ENG.). 64p. (J). pap. 4.95 *(978-1-4027-0630-1(8)*, Balloon Bks.) Sterling Publishing Co., Inc.
Bama. What Am I? 2012. (ENG.). 43p. 14.95 *(978-1-4620-6150-1(8)*, b63c1afb-7535-4777-a6d0-5bdfc94c2226) iUniverse, Inc.
Barbaresi, Nina. Animal Search-a-Word Puzzles. 2003. (Dover Little Activity Bks.). (ENG., Illus.). 64p. (J). (gr. k-3). pap. 1.50 *(978-0-486-42767-6(6))* Dover Pubns., Inc.
—Animal Word Puzzles Coloring Book. 81st ed. 2013. (Dover Coloring Bks.). (ENG., Illus.). 48p. (J). (gr. 1-4). pap. 3.99 *(978-0-486-26848-4(9))* Dover Pubns., Inc.
—Horses. 2005. (Dover Little Activity Bks.). (ENG., Illus.). 64p. (J). (gr. 3-5). pap., act. bk. ed. 1.99 *(978-0-486-44195-5(4))* Dover Pubns., Inc.
—Little Search-a-Word. 2012. (Dover Little Activity Bks.). (ENG., Illus.). 64p. (J). (gr. k-3). pap. 1.99 *(978-0-486-26455-4(6))* Dover Pubns., Inc.
Barberi, Marco, et al, trs. Sabelotodo: 1000 Desafíos para Tu Inteligencia. Bertran, Nuria, illus. 2003. (SPA.). 384p. 35.00 *(978-84-494-2372-7(4)*, GML07104-192209) Oceano Grupo Editoria, S.A. ESP. Dist: Cengage Gale.
Baron, Celia. Brain Sizzlers. 2004. (Illus.). 48p. (J). (gr. 4-7). pap. 5.95 *(978-0-673-59962-9(0))* Good Year Bks.
—Brain Sizzlers: Puzzles for Critical Thinkers. 2nd ed. 2007. (Illus.). 88p. (J). pap. 7.95 *(978-1-59647-232-7(4))* Good Year Bks.
Baron, Puzzle. Puzzle Baron Kid's Puzzles. 2017. (ENG.). 272p. (J). (gr. 5-12). pap. 12.95 ***(978-1-4654-6484-2(0)***, Alpha) Dorling Kindersley Publishing, Inc.
Barth, Linda J. Hidden New Jersey. Mitchell, Hazel, illus. 2012. (Search & Seek Bks.). (ENG.). 32p. (J). (gr. 1-4). 17.95 *(978-1-934133-23-1(X))*; pap. 8.95 *(978-1-934133-40-8(X))* Charlesbridge Publishing, Inc. (Mackinac Island Press, Inc.).
Batterson, Jason. Beast Academy Guide 3C. Owen, Erich, illus. 2012. 112p. pap. 15.00 *(978-1-934124-44-4(3))* AoPS Inc.
Batterson, Jason & Rogers, Shannon. Beast Academy Practice 3A. 2012. (Illus.). 128p. pap. 12.00 *(978-1-934124-41-3(9))* AoPS Inc.
Baumann, Leigh. Jekyll Island Fun Book. 2008. 64p. (J). pap. 9.95 *(978-0-9769510-1-8(0))* Seascape Pr.
—St. Simons Island Fun Book. 2008. 64p. (J). pap. 9.95 *(978-0-9769510-2-5(9))* Seascape Pr.
Baxter, Nicola & Birkinshaw, Marie. A Treasury for Little Ones: Hours of Fun for Babies & Toddlers - Stories & Rhymes, Puzzles to Solve, & Things to Make & Do. Endersby, Frank, illus. 2014. (ENG.). 80p. (J). (gr. -1-6). 14.99 *(978-1-86147-368-4(0)*, Armadillo) Anness Publishing GBR. Dist: National Bk. Network.
Beecroft, Simon & Harvey, Guy. The Tintin & Snowy Big Activity Book. 2011. (ENG., Illus.). 96p. pap. 19.95 *(978-0-86719-761-7(7))* Last Gasp of San Francisco.

Berghof, Michael. The Story of Christmas: Carry-Me Puzzle Book. 2011. 8p. (J). 12.99 *(978-0-7586-2798-8(X))* Concordia Publishing Hse.
Berne, Emma Carlson & Meister, Cari. Mind Benders. 2015. (Mind Benders Ser.). (ENG.). 112p. (gr. 1-3). 93.28 *(978-1-4914-6966-8(8))* Capstone Press of Coughlan Cos.
Berthel, Alice H. Power Puzzles: John. 2007. (J). per. 12.95 *(978-1-59352-193-6(6))* Christian Services Publishing.
—Power Puzzles: Luke. 2007. (J). per. 12.95 *(978-1-59352-192-9(8))* Christian Services Publishing.
—Power Puzzles: Matthew. 2006. (J). per. 12.95 *(978-1-59352-174-5(X))* Christian Services Publishing.
Best Travel Activity Book Ever! (Backseat Bks.). (Illus.). 256p. (J). pap. 3.95 *(978-0-528-96542-5(5))* Rand McNally.
Beylon, Cathy. Easy Beauty & the Beast Sticker Picture Puzzle. 2006. (Dover Little Activity Bks.). (ENG., Illus.). 4p. (J). (gr. -1-2). 1.50 *(978-0-486-44473-4(2))* Dover Pubns., Inc.
—Easy Firehouse Sticker Picture Puzzle. 2005. (Dover Little Activity Bks.). (ENG., Illus.). 4p. (J). (gr. -1-2). pap. 1.50 *(978-0-486-43850-4(3))* Dover Pubns., Inc.
—Easy Nativity Scene Sticker Picture Puzzle. 2012. (Dover Little Activity Bks.). (ENG., Illus.). 4p. (J). (gr. k-3). pap. 1.99 *(978-0-486-44824-4(X))* Dover Pubns., Inc.
—Easy Noah's Ark Sticker Picture Puzzle. 2004. (Dover Little Activity Bks.). (ENG., Illus.). 4p. (J). (gr. k-2). 1.50 *(978-0-486-43864-1(3))* Dover Pubns., Inc.
Big Blue Bubble Inc., Big Blue. My Singing Monsters Search & Find. 2015. (My Singing Monsters Ser.). (ENG., Illus.). 24p. (J). (gr. 1). pap. 11.99 *(978-1-4052-7686-3(X))* Egmont Bks., Ltd. GBR. Dist: Independent Pubs. Group.
Billout, Guy. Somethings Not Quite Right. (ENG.). 32p. pap. 14.95 *(978-1-56792-266-0(X))* Godine, David R. Pub.
Blincoe, Neale. How to Dazzle at Maths Crosswords. 2004. 48p. (J). pap. 30.00 *(978-1-903853-38-2(9))* Brilliant Pubns. GBR. Dist: Parkwest Pubns., Inc.
Block, Cheryl. Think Analogies B1: Learning to Connect Words & Relationships. 2013. (Think Analogies Books ThinkAnalogy Puzzles Software Ser.). 64p. (gr. 6-12). pap. 11.99 *(978-0-89455-792-7(0))* Critical Thinking Co., The.
Bloom, Jonathan. The Must Have Sudoku Holiday Gift 480 Puzzles. 2012. 278p. pap. *(978-0-9814261-5-0(8))* Sudokids.Com.
Blue Ox Technologies Ltd., Blue Ox & York, Christopher. 7 Little Words for Kids: 100 Puzzles. 2014. (ENG.). 112p. (J). pap. 5.99 *(978-1-4494-4200-2(5))* Andrews McMeel Publishing.
Blundell, Kim & Tyler, Jenny. Big Book of Mazes. rev. ed. 2005. 72p. (J). pap. 10.95 *(978-0-7945-0697-1(6)*, Usborne) EDC Publishing.
Blythe, Philip. Nature Hunt! Bewildering Puzzles of the Animal Kingdom. Blythe, Philip, illus. 2005. (Illus.). 32p. pap., act. bk. ed. *(978-1-877003-82-0(4))* Little Hare Bks. AUS. Dist: HarperCollins Pubs. Australia.
Boardworks Learning Centers: Figure It Out. 2006. (J). bds. *(978-0-9755252-4-1(7))* Evergreen Pr. of Brainerd, LLC.
Bodach, Vijaya Khisty. What Is Missing? 2008. (Discovering & Exploring Science Ser.). (Illus.). 16p. (J). (gr. -1-3). lib. bdg. 12.95 *(978-0-7569-8253-9(7))* Perfection Learning Corp.
Book Company Staff. Busy Bugs. 2003. (Puzzles Ser.). (Illus.). (J). bds. 10.95 *(978-1-74047-335-4(3))* Book Co. Publishing Pty, Ltd., The AUS. Dist: Penton Overseas, Inc.
—Ocean Friends. Lassen, Christian R., illus. 2003. (Puzzles Ser.). (J). bds. 14.95 *(978-1-74047-381-1(7))* Book Co. Publishing Pty, Ltd., The AUS. Dist: Penton Overseas, Inc.
Bookworks, Downtown. Eye Q Picture Puzzler. 2010. (ENG.). 24p. (J). bds. 11.99 *(978-1-935703-04-4(8))* Downtown Bookworks.
Boos, Andre, illus. Amazing Animal Puzzle Stickers: #1. 2005. (Amazing Animal Puzzle Stickers Ser.). 10p. (J). pap. 5.99 *(978-1-59496-063-5(1))* Teora USA LLC.
—Amazing Animal Puzzle Stickers: #2, Vol. 2. 2005. (Amazing Animal Puzzle Stickers Ser.). 10p. (J). pap. 5.99 *(978-1-59496-064-2(X))* Teora USA LLC.
—Amazing Animal Puzzle Stickers: #3, Vol. 3. 2005. (Amazing Animal Puzzle Stickers Ser.). 10p. (J). pap. 5.99 *(978-1-59496-065-9(8))* Teora USA LLC.
Booth, Karon. Aslan Is on the Move: Romp in Narnia with Study Helps, Art & Play. 2003. (Illus.). 196p. (J). per. *(978-0-941367-13-4(4))* Peach Blossom Pubns.
Boutavant, Marc, illus. All Aboard Train Puzzle. 2013. (ENG.). 12p. (J). (gr. -1-17). 14.99 *(978-0-8118-7850-0(3))* Chronicle Bks. LLC.
Boyds Mills Press Staff. The Super Colossal Book of Hidden Pictures, Vol. 3. 2003. (ENG., Illus.). 192p. (J). (gr. 6-9). pap. 9.95 *(978-1-56397-952-1(7))* Boyds Mills Pr.
Brallier, Max. Quest for Gem Magic. 2015. (Steven Universe Ser.). (ENG.). 80p. (J). (gr. 3-7). 7.99 *(978-0-8431-8317-7(9)*, Cartoon Network Books) Penguin Young Readers Group.
Brandreth, Gyles. Madcap Book of Brain Teasers. Axworthy, Anni & Miller, Mike, illus. 288p. (J). pap. 6.95 *(978-0-233-99568-7(4))* Andre Deutsch GBR. Dist: Trafalgar Square Publishing.
Brett, Anna. Maze Hop: Around the World. Woolley, Tom, illus. 2016. (ENG.). 64p. (J). (gr. 2). pap. 14.95 *(978-1-78312-134-2(3))* Carlton Kids GBR. Dist: Sterling Publishing Co., Inc.
Brian, Sarah Jane. Brainiac's Mindbenders: Fun Activities for Geniuses of All Ages. 2005. (Activity Journal Ser.). (Illus.). 128p. (J). act. bk. ed. 12.99 *(978-0-88088-591-1(2))* Peter Pauper Pr. Inc.
—Brainiac's Secret Agent: Fun Activities for Spies of All Ages. 2005. (Activity Journal Ser.). 128p. act. bk. ed. 12.99 *(978-0-88088-446-4(0))* Peter Pauper Pr. Inc.
Bridgewater, Glyn. Dot-To-Dot Ancient World: Join the Dots to Discover the Wonders of Antiquity, with up to 1098 Dots. 2017. (ENG.). 96p. (J). (gr. -1-12). pap. 12.99 ***(978-1-78019-511-7(7)***, Southwater) Anness Publishing GBR. Dist: National Bk. Network.
—Dot-To-Dot Natural World: Join the Dots to Discover Fascinating Scenes from Nature, with up to 1324 Dots. 2017. (ENG.). 96p. (J). (gr. -1-12). pap. 12.99 ***(978-1-78019-512-4(5)***, Southwater) Anness Publishing GBR. Dist: National Bk. Network.
Brooke, Jasmine. Goldilocks & the Three Bears: Take the Temperature Test & Solve the Porridge Puzzle! 2017. (Fairy Tale Fixers: Fixing Fairy Tale Problems with STEM Ser.).

32p. (gr. 3-4). pap. 63.00 **(978-1-5382-0665-2(X))** Stevens, Gareth Publishing LLLP.
Brooks, Felicity. Big Red Tractor. Cartwright, Stephen, illus. 2006. (Usborne Farmyard Tales Jigsaw Bks.). 10p. (J). (gr. -1-k). bds. 7.99 *(978-0-7945-1130-2(9)*, Usborne) EDC Publishing.
—Juega con Gabi. 2006. 10p. (J). bds. 8.99 *(978-0-7460-7387-2(9)*, Usborne) EDC Publishing.
—Naughty Woolly. Cartwright, Stephen, illus. 2006. (Usborne Farmyard Tales Jigsaw Bks.). 10p. (J). bds. 7.99 *(978-0-7945-1128-9(7)*, Usborne) EDC Publishing.
—Rusty's Friends. Cartwright, Stephen, illus. 2006. (Usborne Farmyard Tales Jigsaw Bks.). 10p. (J). bds. 7.99 *(978-0-7945-1127-2(9)*, Usborne) EDC Publishing.
—Tractors Chunky Jigsaw Book. 2005. (Chunky Jigsaw Books Ser.). 14p. (J). 7.95 *(978-0-7945-0861-6(8)*, Usborne) EDC Publishing.
—Trains Chunky Jigsaw Book. 2005. (Chunky Jigsaw Books Ser.). 14p. (J). 7.95 *(978-0-7945-0859-3(6)*, Usborne) EDC Publishing.
—Usborne Shapes Jigsaw Book. 2008. (Usborne Jigsaw Bks.). (Illus.). 12p. (J). (gr. -1-3). bds. 9.99 *(978-0-7945-2046-5(4)*, Usborne) EDC Publishing.
Brooks, Felicity & Tyler, Jenny. The Usborne 1,2,3 Jigsaw Book. Cartwright, Stephen, illus. 2006. (Usborne Jigsaw Bks.). 12p. (J). (gr. -1-k). bds. 15.95 *(978-0-7945-1168-5(6)*, Usborne) EDC Publishing.
Brooks, Felicity, et al. The Counting Train. Cartwright, Stephen, illus. 2006. (J). *(978-0-439-89922-2(2))* Scholastic, Inc.
Brown, Jeff. Amazing Washington! A Collection of Puzzlers, Mazes, & Fun! 2005. (Amazing State-by-State Puzzles Ser.). (Illus.). 48p. (J). (gr. 3-7). per. 6.00 *(978-0-87842-508-2(X)*, 345) Mountain Pr. Publishing Co., Inc.
Bruning, Matt. Baby Animal Picture Puzzles, 1 vol. 2009. (Look, Look Again Ser.). (ENG.). 32p. (gr. 1-2). lib. bdg. 27.32 *(978-1-4296-3288-1(7)*, Aplus Bks.) Capstone Press of Coughlan Cos.
—Mighty Machines Picture Puzzles, 1 vol. 2009. (Look, Look Again Ser.). (ENG.). 32p. (gr. 1-2). lib. bdg. 27.32 *(978-1-4296-3289-8(5)*, Aplus Bks.) Capstone Press of Coughlan Cos.
Bryant-Mole, Karen. Dot-to-Dot Animals. rev. ed. 2004. (Dot to Dot Ser.). (Illus.). 24p. (J). pap. 3.99 *(978-0-7945-0497-7(3))* EDC Publishing.
—Dot-to-Dot in Space. 2004. (Dot to Dot Ser.). (Illus.). 24p. (J). pap. 3.95 *(978-0-7945-0495-3(7))* EDC Publishing.
—Dot-to-Dot Machines. Tyler, Jenny, ed. Round, Graham, illus. rev. ed. 2006. (Dot to Dot Ser.). 22p. (J). (gr. -1-2). pap. 3.99 *(978-0-7945-1495-2(2)*, Usborne) EDC Publishing.
—Dot-to-Dot Nature. 2004. (Dot to Dot Ser.). (Illus.). 24p. (J). 3.99 *(978-0-7945-0493-9(0))* EDC Publishing.
Buckley, MacKenzie. PAW Patrol: Jungle Search & Rescue: Storybook with Telescope Viewer. 2016. (ENG.). 24p. (J). (gr. -1-3). 14.99 *(978-0-7944-3586-8(6)*, Reader's Digest Children's Bks.) Studio Fun International.
Bui, Tak. Spot the Difference. 2012. (ENG., Illus.). 44p. (J). (gr. 2-5). pap. 9.95 *(978-1-77049-279-0(8)*, Tundra Bks.) Tundra Bks. CAN. Dist: Penguin Random Hse. LLC.
The Bunty Annual 2004. annuals 2004. 128p. (J). 9.95 *(978-0-85116-882-1(5))* Thomson, D.C. & Co., Ltd. GBR. Dist: APG Sales & Distribution Services.
Burchett, Author Walter; BA. Christian children's circle the Word. 2008. 34p. pap. 6.95 *(978-0-557-02505-3(2))* Lulu Pr., Inc.
Burgess, Mark. Mutiny at Crossbones Bay. Cox, Phil Roxbee, ed. Burgess, Mark, illus. 2006. (Usborne Puzzle Adventures Ser.). (Illus.). 48p. (J). (gr. 3-7). pap. 4.99 *(978-0-7945-1407-5(3)*, Usborne) EDC Publishing.
Busiere, Agnes. What's Hiding Here? 2016. (ENG., Illus.). 96p. 14.95 *(978-1-77085-823-7(7)*, 9781770858237) Firefly Bks., Ltd.
Butterfield, Moira & Golding, Elizabeth. A Moonlight Book: Halloween Hide-And-Seek. Gray, Dean, illus. 2015. (ENG.). 12p. (J). (gr. -1-17). 10.95 *(978-0-7624-5846-2(1)*, Running Pr. Kids) Running Pr. Bk. Pubs.
Capstone Press. Spot It. 2010. (Spot It Ser.). (ENG.). 32p. lib. bdg. 155.94 *(978-1-4296-5911-6(4)*, Aplus Bks.) Capstone Press of Coughlan Cos.
Carlson, George. Fun Time Library Boxed Set. 2008. (ENG., Illus.). 48p. per. 16.95 *(978-1-59583-263-4(7)*, 9781595832634, Green Tiger Pr.) Laughing Elephant.
Carlson, George Leonard & Martin, John. Peter Puzzlemaker: A John Martin Puzzle-Book. 2014. (ENG., Illus.). 112p. (J). (gr. 1-5). pap. 7.99 *(978-0-486-78167-9(4))* Dover Pubns., Inc.
Carlton Books, ed. Eye Twisters: Boggle, Baffle & Blow Your Mind! 2014. (ENG., Illus.). 96p. (J). (gr. 2). pap. 7.95 *(978-1-78312-033-8(9))* Carlton Bks., Ltd. GBR. Dist: Sterling Publishing Co., Inc.
Carlton Books Staff & Allen, Robert. Mensa Mighty Mystery Puzzles for Kids. 2003. (Illus.). 256p. pap. *(978-1-84222-925-5(7))* Carlton Bks., Ltd.
Carlton Publishing Group. Creative Coloring & Dot-To-Dots. 2016. (Cool & Calm Coloring for Kids Ser.). (ENG.). 48p. (J). (gr. 2-6). pap. 6.99 *(978-1-4380-0883-7(X))* Barron's Educational Series, Inc.
Carlton Publishing Group, Carlton Publishing. The Amazing Emoji Puzzle Book: Packed with Totally Tricky Emoji Puzzles & 200 Emoji Stickers. 2017. (ENG.). 96p. (gr. 2-7). pap. 8.99 **(978-1-4380-1075-5(3))** Barron's Educational Series, Inc.
Carpenter, Elizabeth. Mummy Mazes: A Monumental Book. 2010. (ENG., Illus.). 36p. (J). (gr. 3-7). pap. 10.95 *(978-0-7611-6074-8(4)*, 16074) Workman Publishing Co., Inc.
Carson-Dellosa Publishing Staff. Puzzles & Games: Word Play. 2010. (Home Workbooks Ser.). (ENG.). 64p. (gr. k-1). pap. 4.49 *(978-1-60418-782-3(4))* Carson-Dellosa Publishing, LLC.
—Puzzles & Games for Math, Grade 1. 2010. (Home Workbooks Ser.). (ENG.). 64p. (gr. 1-1). pap. 4.49 *(978-1-60418-791-5(3))* Carson-Dellosa Publishing, LLC.
—Puzzles & Games for Math, Grade 3. 2010. (Home Workbooks Ser.). (ENG.). 64p. (gr. 3-3). pap. 4.49 *(978-1-60418-803-5(0))* Carson-Dellosa Publishing, LLC.
—Puzzles & Games, Grade 1. 2010. (Home Workbooks Ser.). (ENG.). 64p. (gr. 1-1). pap. 4.49 *(978-1-60418-793-9(X))* Carson-Dellosa Publishing, LLC.
Carson-Dellosa Publishing Staff, compiled by. Puzzles & Games for Beginners, Grade K. 2010. (Home Workbooks Ser.). (ENG.). 64p. (gr. k-k). pap. 4.49 *(978-1-60418-778-6(6))* Carson-Dellosa Publishing, LLC.
—Puzzles & Games for Math, Grade 2. 2010. (Home Workbooks Ser.). (ENG.). 64p. (gr. 2-2). pap. 4.49 *(978-1-60418-798-4(0))* Carson-Dellosa Publishing, LLC.
—Puzzles & Games, Grade 2. 2010. (Home Workbooks Ser.). (ENG.). 64p. (gr. 2-2). pap. 4.49 *(978-1-60418-799-1(9))* Carson-Dellosa Publishing, LLC.
—Puzzles & Games, Grade 2: Word Play. 2010. (Home Workbooks Ser.). (ENG.). 64p. (gr. 2-2). pap. 4.49 *(978-1-60418-796-0(4))* Carson-Dellosa Publishing, LLC.
Carson, Karen. Horseplay: 50 Puzzles & Games for Horse Lovers. 2004. 68p. (J). pap. 9.95 *(978-1-57779-068-6(5))* Alpine Pubns., Inc.
Cartwright, S. Fairy Jigsaw Puzzle. gif. ed. 2004. (Fairy Jigsaw in A Box Ser.). (Illus.). (J). 11.95 *(978-0-7945-0592-9(9))* EDC Publishing.
Cartwright, Stephen. Abc Floor. Cartwright, Stephen, illus. 2006. (Illus.). 16p. (J). bds. 15.99 *(978-0-7945-1367-2(0)*, Usborne) EDC Publishing.
Catlow, Nikalas, illus. Mind Your Own Business: A File of Super Secret Stuff. 2007. (ENG.). 224p. (J). 8.00 *(978-1-84046-763-5(0)*, Wizard Books) Icon Bks., Ltd. GBR. Dist: Publishers Group Canada.
Cats & Dogs Picture Puzzle Book. 2017. (Picture Puzzle Bks.). (ENG.). (J). bds. 14.99 **(978-0-7945-3925-2(4)**, Usborne) EDC Publishing.
Chamberlain, Kim. The Five-Minute Brain Workout for Kids: 365 Amazing, Fabulous, & Fun Word Puzzles. Chamberlain, Jon, illus. 2015. (ENG.). 416p. (J). (gr. 1). pap. 14.99 *(978-1-63450-159-0(4)*, Sky Pony Pr.) Skyhorse Publishing Co., Inc.
Chaud, Benjamin. The Bear's Song Puzzle. 2015. (ENG., Illus.). 24p. (J). (gr. -1-k). 17.99 *(978-1-4521-4182-4(7))* Chronicle Bks. LLC.
Chedru, Delphine. Spot It Again! Find More Hidden Creatures. 2011. (ENG., Illus.). 40p. (J). (gr. 1-4). 15.95 *(978-0-8109-9736-3(3)*, Abrams Bks. for Young Readers) Abrams, Inc.
Child, Jeni. Dot-To-Dot: Mystery & Magic: Join the Dots to Discover a World of Enchantment. 2017. (ENG.). 96p. (J). (gr. -1-12). pap. 12.99 **(978-1-78019-513-1(3)**, Southwater) Anness Publishing GBR. Dist: National Bk. Network.
—Dot-To-Dot: under the Sea: Join the Dots to Discover the World below the Waves & on the High Seas. 2017. (ENG.). 96p. (J). (gr. -1-12). pap. 12.99 **(978-1-78019-514-8(1)**, Southwater) Anness Publishing GBR. Dist: National Bk. Network.
Children of the World (Gr. 2-4) 2003. (J). *(978-1-58232-057-1(8))* ECS Learning Systems, Inc.
Children's Puzzle Book. 2003. (J). per. *(978-1-884907-26-5(1))*; per. *(978-1-884907-27-2(X))* Paradise Pr., Inc.
Chouette Publishing Staff & Paradis, Anne. Caillou: My Little Bed. Sévigny, Eric, illus. 2012. (ENG.). 10p. (J). (gr. -1-k). 9.99 *(978-2-89450-951-7(0))* Caillouet, Gerry.
Christmas Dot to Dot: Santa's Big Dot to Dot. 2004. (J). per. 6.95 *(978-1-885920-89-8(X))* Pyramid Publishing, Inc.
Chronicle Books Staff. Space Matching Game. 2015. (ENG., Illus.). 56p. (J). (gr. -1-1). bds. 14.99 *(978-1-4521-3390-4(5))* Chronicle Bks. LLC.
Cider Mill Press Staff, ed. What's Missing: Look & Look & Look-Can You Find What's Missing? 2011. (ENG., Illus.). 32p. (J). (gr. 3). 14.95 *(978-1-60433-149-3(6)*, Applesauce Pr.) Cider Mill Pr. Bk. Pubs., LLC.
Cimmet, Brian. Delicious Word Searches. 2013. (ENG.). 160p. spiral bd. 7.95 *(978-1-4549-0052-8(0)*, Puzzlewright) Sterling Publishing Co., Inc.
Clark, Diane C., et al. A Kid's Guide to Washington, D. C. Brown, Richard, illus. rev. ed. 2008. (ENG.). 160p. (J). (gr. 1-4). pap. 15.99 *(978-0-15-206125-8(8))* Houghton Mifflin Harcourt Publishing Co.
Clarke, Catriona. Pirates. McKenna, Terry, illus. 2006. (Beginners Social Studies: Level 2 Ser.). 32p. (J). (gr. 1-3). 4.99 *(978-0-7945-1332-0(8)*, Usborne) EDC Publishing.
Claybourne, Anna. Where's Will? Find Shakespeare Hidden in His Plays. Tilly, illus. 2015. (J). *(978-1-61067-407-2(3))* Kane Miller.
—1001Things to Spot in the Town. 2009. (1001 Things to Spot Ser.). 32p. (J). 9.99 *(978-0-7945-2514-9(8)*, Usborne) EDC Publishing.
Cleary, Brian P. Madam & Nun & 1001: What Is a Palindrome? Gable, Brian, illus. 2012. (Words Are CATegorical (r) Ser.). (ENG.). 32p. (gr. 2-5). lib. bdg. 16.95 *(978-0-7613-4919-8(7)*, Millbrook Pr.) Lerner Publishing Group.
Clifton, Gillian. Puzzle Pieces: Sticking to It. 2017. (Computer Science for the Real World Ser.). 12p. (gr. 6-7). pap. 7.05 **(978-1-5383-5184-0(6)**, Rosen Classroom) Rosen Publishing Group, Inc., The.
Cloutier, Toni Lynn. Word Search USA. 2010. (ENG., Illus.). 128p. (J). (gr. 3-6). spiral bd. 6.95 *(978-1-4027-6905-4(9))* Sterling Publishing Co., Inc.
Cole, Jeff & Stone, Kate. Stick to It - Toys: A Magnetic Puzzle Book. 2011. (ENG., Illus.). 14p. (J). bds. 16.99 *(978-1-4494-0499-4(5))* Andrews McMeel Publishing.
Conceptis Puzzles. Dots! Super Connect-the-Dots Puzzles. 2008. (ENG., Illus.). 96p. (J). (gr. 2). spiral bd. 12.95 *(978-1-4027-5521-7(X)*, Puzzlewright) Sterling Publishing Co., Inc.
Conley, Erin, ed. Dinomite. 2006. (Spinner Bks.). (ENG., Illus.). 160p. (J). (gr. -1-3). pap. 7.95 *(978-1-57528-948-9(2))* Univ. Games.
—Madcap Mazes. 2005. (Made You Laugh for Kids). (ENG., Illus.). 96p. pap. 5.95 *(978-1-57528-931-1(8))* Univ. Games.
Contraire, Bastien. Animals Hide & Sneak. 2017. (ENG., Illus.). 26p. (gr. -1 — 1). bds. 9.95 **(978-0-7148-7422-7(1))** Phaidon Pr., Inc.
Contraire, Bastien. Undercover: One of These Things Is Almost Like the Others. 2016. (ENG., Illus.). 64p. (gr. -1-1). 18.95 *(978-0-7148-7250-6(4))* Phaidon Pr., Inc.
Corr, Christopher. Map of the World Play Scene. 2005. (J). 9.99 *(978-0-7353-0898-5(5))* Galison.
—Whole World: Fun Eco Activities. 2008. (ENG., Illus.). 24p. (J). pap. 4.99 *(978-1-84686-220-5(5))* Barefoot Bks., Inc.
Counting Puzzles. Date not set. (Illus.). 96p. (J). 2.98 *(978-0-7525-7519-3(8))* Parragon, Inc.
Creek, Lorie. Who Is This Jesus? A Hidden Picture Book. Creek, Chris, illus. 2012. (J). 18.99 *(978-1-60908-909-2(X))* Deseret Bk. Co.
Critical Thinking-What's Wrong with This Picture? (Gr. 1-3) 2003. (J). *(978-1-58232-066-3(7))* ECS Learning Systems, Inc.
Crompton, Richmal. Just William's Puzzles. 2003. (ENG.). 64p. (J). pap. 3.95 *(978-0-333-62680-1(X))* Macmillan Pubs., Ltd. GBR. Dist: Trafalgar Square Publishing.
Cronin, B. B. The Lost House. 2016. (ENG., Illus.). 40p. (J). (gr. -1-2). 18.99 *(978-1-101-99921-9(7)*, Viking Books for Young Readers) Penguin Young Readers Group.
Crook, Lydia. Two-Player Big Fun Book: Puzzles & Games for Two to Do! 2015. (ENG.). 112p. (J). (gr. 1-5). pap. 9.99 *(978-1-4380-0605-5(5))* Barron's Educational Series, Inc.
Curry, Don, ed. Jungle Fun: Puzzles & Games. 2008. 10p. (J). bds. 9.99 *(978-0-696-23491-0(2))* Meredith Bks.
Curtis, Dolores. Rhyming Pretzels. 2003. pap. 21.00 *(978-0-8059-5907-9(6))* Dorrance Publishing Co., Inc.
D C Thomson Staff, ed. Animals & You Annual 2004. 2003. (Illus.). 128p. (J). 9.95 *(978-0-85116-840-1(X))* Thomson, D.C. & Co., Ltd. GBR. Dist: APG Sales & Distribution Services.
—Bunty Annual for Girls 2004. 2003. (Illus.). 128p. (J). (gr. -1-4). *(978-0-85116-825-8(6))* Thomson, D.C. & Co., Ltd. GBR. Dist: APG Sales & Distribution Services.
Dahl, Michael. If You Were a Palindrome, 1 vol. Gray, Sara, illus. 2007. (Word Fun Ser.). (ENG.). 24p. (gr. 2-4). lib. bdg. 27.99 *(978-1-4048-3162-9(2))* Picture Window Bks.
Danielle, Sara & James, Danielle. Where's Father Christmas? Find Father Christmas & His Festive Helpers in 15 Fun-Filled Puzzles. Bloom, Harry, illus. 2013. (ENG.). 42p. (J). (gr. 2-5). 16.99 *(978-1-78219-476-7(2))* Blake, John Publishing, Ltd. GBR. Dist: Independent Pubs. Group.
Danna, Mark. Amazing Word Search Puzzles for Kids. 2013. (ENG.). 96p. (J). (gr. 6). pap. 6.95 *(978-1-4549-0950-7(1)*, Puzzlewright) Sterling Publishing Co., Inc.
—Clever Word Search Puzzles for Kids. 2013. (ENG.). 96p. (J). (gr. 6). pap. 6.95 *(978-1-4549-0969-9(2)*, Puzzlewright) Sterling Publishing Co., Inc.
—Word Search Puzzles for Clever Kids. 2017. (ENG.). 96p. (J). (gr. 2-6). pap. 6.95 **(978-1-4549-2280-3(X)**, Puzzlewright) Sterling Publishing Co., Inc.
—Word Search Puzzles for Smart Kids. 2017. (ENG.). 96p. (J). (gr. 2-6). pap. 6.95 **(978-1-4549-2281-0(8)**, Puzzlewright) Sterling Publishing Co., Inc.
Daste, Larry. Easy Gingerbread House Sticker Picture Puzzle. 2004. (Dover Little Activity Bks.). (ENG., Illus.). 4p. (J). (gr. k-3). pap. 1.50 *(978-0-486-43895-5(3))* Dover Pubns., Inc.
Daste, Larry, et al. Hidden Picture Mania. Boddy, Joe, illus. 2006. (Dover Children's Activity Bks.). (ENG.). 96p. (J). (gr. 3-6). per. 7.95 *(978-0-486-45911-0(X))* Dover Pubns., Inc.
Daumain, Thibaut. Minecraft Dot-To-Dot: Awesome Scenes & Incredible Challenges to Complete & Color. 2017. (ENG.). 64p. (J). (gr. 3-7). pap. 9.99 **(978-1-4380-1076-2(1))** Barron's Educational Series, Inc.
David, Juliet. Dot to Dot Coloring & Stickers Bk. 1, 1 vol., 1. Smith, Jan, illus. 2008. (Candle Activity Fun Ser.). 24p. (J). (gr. 4-7). pap. 6.99 *(978-0-8254-7360-9(8)*, Candle Bks.) Lion Hudson PLC GBR. Dist: Kregel Pubns.
David, R. Noahs Ark. 2010. 12p. *(978-965-91286-1-7(4))* Sifrei Bet Shearim Ltd.
David, R., illus. Joseph & His Brothers. 2010. 12p. *(978-965-91286-0-0(6))* Sifrei Bet Shearim Ltd.
Davidson, Susanna & Stowell, Louie. My First Fairyland Book. Raffaella, Ligi, illus. 2012. (My First Book Ser.). 16p. (J). ring bd. 6.99 *(978-0-7945-3227-7(6)*, Usborne) EDC Publishing.
Daynes, Katie. 1001 Things to Spot in the Sea. Gower, Teri, illus. 2009. (1001 Things to Spot Ser.). 32p. (J). (gr. 1). 9.99 *(978-0-7945-2615-3(2)*, Usborne) EDC Publishing.
—1001 Things to Spot in the Sea Sticker Book. 2015. (1001 Things to Spot Sticker Bks.). (ENG.). 32pp + 6p. (J). (gr. k-5). pap. 7.99 *(978-0-7945-3495-0(3)*, Usborne) EDC Publishing.
De La Bédoyère, Camilla. Mega Spot the Difference: Rainforest. 2016. (ENG., Illus.). 80p. (J). (gr. 3). pap. 9.95 *(978-1-78312-165-6(3))* Carlton Kids GBR. Dist: Sterling Publishing Co., Inc.
Del Moral, Susana. El Juego de las Formas. Zaidi, Nadeem, illus. 2005. (Baby Einstein: Libros de Carton Ser.). (SPA.). 6p. (J). (gr. -1). bds. *(978-970-718-303-2(9)*, Silver Dolphin en Español) Advanced Marketing, S. de R. L. de C. V.
Diesen, Deborah. Pout-Pout Fish Wipe Clean Dot to Dot. Hanna, Dan, illus. 2017. (Pout-Pout Fish Novelty Ser.). (ENG.). 56p. (J). spiral bd. 12.99 *(978-0-374-30445-4(9)*, 9780374304454, Farrar, Straus & Giroux (BYR)) Farrar, Straus & Giroux.
Disney Book Group. Disney Princess Dot-To-Dot. 2017. (ENG.). 128p. (YA). (gr. 7-12). pap. 14.99 **(978-1-368-01319-2(8)**, Disney Editions) Disney Pr.
Dixon, Andy. Star Quest. Brooks, Felicity, ed. Harris, Nick, illus. rev. ed. 2006. (Usborne Fantasy Puzzle Bks.). 32p. (YA). (gr. 7). pap. 7.99 *(978-0-7945-1099-2(X)*, Usborne) EDC Publishing.
Doherty, Gillian. Fairyland Jigsaw Bk. Gower, Teri, illus. 2007. 14p. (J). bds. 14.99 *(978-0-7945-1430-3(8)*, Usborne) EDC Publishing.
—1001 Cosas Que Buscar en el Psia de las Hadas. Gower, Teri, illus. 2007. (Titles in Spanish Ser.). 32p. (J). 9.99 *(978-0-7460-8346-8(7)*, Usborne) EDC Publishing.
—1001 Things to Spot in Fairyland. Gower, Teri, illus. 2006. (Usborne 1001 Things to Spot Ser.). 32p. (J). (gr. 1-4). 9.99 *(978-0-7945-1220-0(8)*, Usborne) EDC Publishing.
—1001 Things to Spot Long Ago. 2010. (1001 Things to Spot Ser.). 32p. (J). 9.99 *(978-0-7945-2731-0(0)*, Usborne) EDC Publishing.
—1001 Things to Spot Long Ago. Brooks, Felicity, ed. Gower, Teri, illus. 2006. (Usborne 1001 Things to Spot Ser.). 32p. (J). (gr. 1). lib. bdg. 14.99 *(978-1-58086-963-8(7))* EDC Publishing.
—1001 Things to Spot on the Farm. 2009. (1001 Things to Spot Ser.). 32p. (J). 9.99 *(978-0-7945-2611-5(X)*, Usborne) EDC Publishing.
—1001 Wizard Things to Spot. Gower, Teri, illus. 2008. (Usborne 1001 Things to Spot Ser.). 31p. (J). (gr. 4-7). 9.99 *(978-0-7945-1860-8(5)*, Usborne) EDC Publishing.
Dolby, Karen & Fischel, Emma. Chocolate Island. 2004. (Young Puzzle Adventures Ser.). (Illus.). 32p. (J). (gr. 2-18). pap. 4.95 *(978-0-7945-0231-7(8)*, Usborne); lib. bdg. 12.95 *(978-1-58086-458-9(9))* EDC Publishing.
—Molly's Magic Carpet. 2004. (Young Puzzle Adventures Ser.). (Illus.). 32p. (J). (gr. 2-18). pap. 4.99 *(978-0-7945-0233-1(4)*, Usborne); lib. bdg. 12.99 *(978-1-58086-459-6(7))* EDC Publishing.
—Spooks' Surprise. 2004. (Young Puzzle Adventures Ser.). (Illus.). 32p. (J). (gr. 2-18). pap. 4.95 *(978-0-7945-0234-8(2)*, Usborne) EDC Publishing.
Donahue, Peter. Spot the Differences Picture Puzzles for Kids. 2014. (ENG., Illus.). 64p. (J). (gr. k-5). pap. 9.99 *(978-0-486-78248-5(4))* Dover Pubns., Inc.
Doolittle, John H. Dr. Funster's Creative Thinking Puzzlers A1: Creative Problem-Solving Fun. 2011. (Dr. Funster's Ser.). 45p. (gr. 3-5). pap. 7.99 *(978-0-89455-826-9(9))* Critical Thinking Co., The.
—Dr. Funster's Creative Thinking Puzzlers C1: Creative Problem-Solving Fun. 2003. (Dr. Funster's Ser.). 46p. (gr. 9-12). pap. 7.99 *(978-0-89455-828-3(5))* Critical Thinking Co., The.
Dorling Kindersley Publishing Staff. Leaf it to Cubs. 2008. 16p. (J). (gr. k-5). 2.49 *(978-0-7566-3324-0(9))* Dorling Kindersley Publishing, Inc.
—Little Hide & Seek Words. 2012. (ENG.). 16p. (J). (gr. -1 — 1). bds. 7.99 *(978-0-7566-9274-2(1)*, DK Children) Dorling Kindersley Publishing, Inc.
—Things That Go. 2017. (ENG., Illus.). 16p. (J). (— 1). bds. 6.99 *(978-1-4654-5620-5(1)*, DK Children) Dorling Kindersley Publishing, Inc.
Dorling Kindersley Publishing Staff, ed. Bulldozer. 2004. (Ultimate Sticker Bks.). (ENG.). 16p. (J). (gr. k-3). pap. 6.99 *(978-0-7566-0563-6(6)*, DK Children) Dorling Kindersley Publishing, Inc.
Dover. Animals Activities Dover Chunky Book. 2009. (Dover Little Activity Bks.). (ENG., Illus.). 320p. (J). (gr. -1-5). pap. 6.99 *(978-0-486-47424-3(0))* Dover Pubns., Inc.
Dr. Funster's Think-a-Minutes A1: Fast, Fun Brainwork for Higher Grades & Top Test Scores. 2013. (Dr. Funster's Ser.). 48p. (gr. 2-3). pap. 7.99 *(978-0-89455-806-1(4))* Critical Thinking Co., The.
Dr. Funster's Think-a-Minutes A2: Fast, Fun Brainwork for Higher Grades & Top Test Scores. 2006. (Dr. Funster's Ser.). 48p. (gr. 2-3). pap. 7.99 *(978-0-89455-807-8(2))* Critical Thinking Co., The.
Dr. Funster's Think-a-Minutes B1: Fast, Fun Brainwork for Higher Grades & Top Test Scores. 2008. (Dr. Funster's Ser.). 46p. (gr. 4-5). pap. 7.99 *(978-0-89455-808-5(0))* Critical Thinking Co., The.
Dr. Funster's Think-a-Minutes B2: Fast, Fun Brainwork for Higher Grades & Top Test Scores. 2005. (Dr. Funster's Ser.). 48p. (gr. 4-5). pap. 7.99 *(978-0-89455-809-2(9))* Critical Thinking Co., The.
Dr. Funster's Think-a-Minutes C1: Fast, Fun Brainwork for Higher Grades & Top Test Scores. 2006. (Dr. Funster's Ser.). 45p. (gr. 6-8). pap. 7.99 *(978-0-89455-810-8(2))* Critical Thinking Co., The.
Dr. Funster's Think-a-Minutes C2: Fast, Fun Brainwork for Higher Grades & Top Test Scores. 2005. (Dr. Funster's Ser.). 48p. (gr. 6-8). pap. 7.99 *(978-0-89455-811-5(0))* Critical Thinking Co., The.
Drimmer, Stephanie Warren. Brain Bogglers: Over 100 Games & Puzzles to Reveal the Mysteries of Your Mind. 2017. (ENG., Illus.). 176p. (J). (gr. 3-7). pap. 12.99 *(978-1-4263-2423-9(5)*, National Geographic Children's Bks.) National Geographic Society.
Drimmer, Stephanie Warren & Cohen, Julie K. Mastermind: Over 100 Games, Tests, & Puzzles to Unleash Your Inner Genius. 2016. (ENG., Illus.). 176p. (J). (gr. 3-7). pap. 12.99 *(978-1-4263-2110-8(4)*, National Geographic Children's Bks.) National Geographic Society.
Eck, Kristin. Hide-and-Seek Animals. 2004. (Hide-And-Seek Books). (Illus.). (J). lib. bdg. 21.25 *(978-1-4042-2702-6(4)*, PowerKids Pr.) Rosen Publishing Group, Inc., The.
—Hide & Seek Animals. 2009. (Tough Toddler Bks). 16p. (gr. k-k). 42.50 *(978-1-60854-568-1(7)*, PowerKids Pr.) Rosen Publishing Group, Inc., The.
—Hide-and-Seek Clothes. 2004. (Hide-And-Seek Books). (Illus.). (J). lib. bdg. 21.25 *(978-1-4042-2705-7(9)*, PowerKids Pr.) Rosen Publishing Group, Inc., The.
—Hide & Seek Clothes. 2009. (Tough Toddler Bks). 16p. (gr. k-k). 42.50 *(978-1-60854-569-8(5)*, PowerKids Pr.) Rosen Publishing Group, Inc., The.
—Hide-and-Seek Food. 2004. (Hide-And-Seek Books). (Illus.). 16p. (J). lib. bdg. 21.25 *(978-1-4042-2703-3(2)*, PowerKids Pr.) Rosen Publishing Group, Inc., The.
—Hide & Seek Food. 2009. (Tough Toddler Bks). 16p. (gr. k-k). 42.50 *(978-1-60854-570-4(9)*, PowerKids Pr.) Rosen Publishing Group, Inc., The.
—Hide-and-Seek Toys. 2004. (Hide-And-Seek Books). (Illus.). (J). lib. bdg. 21.25 *(978-1-4042-2704-0(0)*, PowerKids Pr.) Rosen Publishing Group, Inc., The.
—Hide & Seek Toys. 2009. (Tough Toddler Bks). 16p. (gr. k-k). 42.50 *(978-1-60854-573-5(3)*, PowerKids Pr.) Rosen Publishing Group, Inc., The.
Edley, Joe, et al. Bananagrams! For Kids. 2010. (ENG., Illus.). 156p. (J). (gr. 2-12). pap. 10.95 *(978-0-7611-5844-8(8)*, 15844) Workman Publishing Co., Inc.
—Bananagrams! The Official Book. 2009. (ENG., Illus.). 282p. pap. 9.95 *(978-0-7611-5635-2(6)*, 15635) Workman Publishing Co., Inc.
Edwards, Amelia. Name That Dinosaur. Jirankova-Limbrick, Martina, illus. 2009. (ENG.). 40p. (J). (gr. -1-3). 17.99 *(978-0-7636-3473-5(5))* Candlewick Pr.
Edwards, Josh. Bible Stories Gone Crazy!, 1 vol. Migliardo, Emiliano, illus. 2015. (ENG.). 24p. (J). 10.99 *(978-1-78128-190-1(4)*, Candle Bks.) Lion Hudson PLC GBR. Dist: Kregel Pubns.
Elder, Jeremy. Race Against the Clock! Secret Agent. 2011. (Dover Children's Activity Bks.). (ENG.). 48p. (gr. -1-8). pap., act. bk. ed. 4.99 *(978-0-486-47992-7(7))* Dover Pubns., Inc.
—Space Agent. 2010. (Dover Children's Activity Bks.). (ENG., Illus.). 48p. (J). (gr. 2-5). pap. 4.99 *(978-0-486-47828-9(9))* Dover Pubns., Inc.
Elite Find-a-Word Puzzles. 2003. per. *(978-1-884907-16-6(4))* Paradise Pr., Inc.

PQR

Elschner, Gèraldine. Where Is the Frog? A Children's Book Inspired by Claude Monet. Girel, Stephane, illus. 2013. (ENG.). 32p. (J). (gr. -1-3). 14.95 *(978-3-7913-7139-9(8))* Prestel Verlag GmbH & Co KG. DEU. Dist: Penguin Random Hse. LLC.

Engelbreit, Mary. Fun & Games with Ann Estelle. 2007. (ENG., Illus.). 104p. pap. 6.99 *(978-0-7407-7058-6(6))* Andrews McMeel Publishing.

Esparza, Thomas, Jr., prod. Esther's Playhouse, Disk D. 2004. (Illus.). (J). cd-rom *(978-1-879817-45-6(4)*, Children) Star Light Pr.

Farnworth, Lauren. Little Zombie. 2014. (ENG.). 64p. (J). (gr. 3-9). pap., act. bk. ed. 6.99 *(978-1-4380-0449-5(4))* Barron's Educational Series, Inc.

Fatus, Sophie. Journey Home from Grandpa's. Fatus, Sophie, illus. 2012. (ENG., Illus.). (J). (gr. -1-1). 14.99 *(978-1-84686-745-3(2))* Barefoot Bks., Inc.

Felix the Cat/el Gato Felix: A Fun Surprise. 2005. 32p. (J). pap. *(978-0-9762071-1-5(7))* Big City Publishing.

Fink, Jeri & Paltrowitz, Donna. Gizmo's Tail Twisters. 2004. (Illus.). 36p. (J). per. 8.95 *(978-0-9716567-4-1(6))* Book Web Publishing, Limited.

Fitzpatrick, Joe. The Raggedy Snowman. Flowerpot Press, ed. 2012. (Illus.). 18p. (J). *(978-1-77093-112-1(0))* Flowerpot Children's Pr. Inc.

Flash Kids Editors. My First Book of Tracing. 2004. (Illus.). 80p. (J). 7.95 *(978-4-7743-0707-7(6))* Kumon Publishing North America, Inc.

Flash Kids Editors, ed. Number Puzzles & Games: Grade Pre-K-K (Flash Skills) 2010. (Flash Skills Ser.). (ENG.). 64p. (J). pap. 3.95 *(978-1-4114-3464-6(1)*, Spark Publishing Group) Sterling Publishing Co., Inc.

Fleisher, Paul. Brain Food: 100+ Games That Make Kids Think. 2008. (ENG.). 208p. (gr. 4-12). pap. 24.95 *(978-1-59363-331-8(9))* Prufrock Pr.

Flintham, Thomas. Thomas Flintham's Book of Mazes & Puzzles. Flintham, Thomas, illus. 2015. (ENG., Illus.). 192p. (J). (gr. 1-3). pap. 12.99 *(978-0-545-81981-7(4)*, Cartwheel Bks.) Scholastic, Inc.

Ford, Barbara E. Tangrams: The Magnificent Seven Piece Puzzle. 2003. (Illus.). 64p. bds. 19.95 *(978-0-9627337-7-2(6))* Tandora's Box Pr.

Francia, Giada. Alex & Penny's Italy Jigsaw Book. Colombo, Angelo, illus. 2007. (ENG.). 14p. (gr. 1-3). pap. 14.95 *(978-88-544-0242-3(7)*, White Star) Rizzoli International Pubns., Inc.

—Alex & Penny's Wild West Jigsaw Book. Colombo, Angelo, illus. 2007. (ENG.). 14p. (gr. 1-3). pap. 14.95 *(978-88-544-0285-0(0)*, White Star) Rizzoli International Pubns., Inc.

Fremont, Victoria & Flores, Brenda. All Around the World Search-a-Word Puzzles. 2011. (Dover Children's Activity Bks.). (ENG., Illus.). 64p. (gr. 3). pap. 4.00 *(978-0-486-40842-2(6))* Dover Pubns., Inc.

Frey, Daniel J., illus. Jacy's Coloring & Activity Book. 2006. 32p. (J). 3.00 *(978-0-9755314-2-6(5))* Majestic Publishing, LLC.

Frisch-Schmoll, Joy. Before & After, 1 vol. 2013. (Exploring Opposites Ser.). (ENG.). 24p. (gr. k-1). pap. 7.29 *(978-1-62065-895-6(X))*; pap. 41.70 *(978-1-62065-896-3(8))*; lib. bdg. 26.65 *(978-1-62065-118-6(1))* Capstone Press of Coughlan Cos. (Pebble Plus).

Frith, Alex. Travel Pocket Puzzle Book. 2015. (Pocket Activity Bks.). (ENG.). 128p. (J). (gr. k-5). pap. 6.99 *(978-0-7945-2743-3(4)*, Usborne) EDC Publishing.

Gardner, Martin. Mind-Boggling Word Puzzles. Myers, V. G., illus. 2010. (Dover Children's Activity Bks.). (ENG.). 96p. (J). (gr. 3-5). pap. 4.99 *(978-0-486-47496-0(8))* Dover Pubns., Inc.

Gikow, Louise. What Do You See? Ulrich, George, illus. 2005. (My First Reader Ser.). (ENG.). 32p. (J). (gr. k-1). 18.50 *(978-0-516-25177-6(5)*, Children's Pr.) Scholastic Library Publishing.

Giles, Geoff. Match the Views: Cut & Fold Puzzles to Imagine & Solve. 2004. (Illus.). 32p. 10.00 *(978-1-899618-55-2(4))* Tarquin Pubns. GBR. Dist: Parkwest Pubns., Inc.

Gilpen, Rebecca. Boy's Activity Book. 2013. (Doodle Bks). 96p. (J). pap. 12.99 *(978-0-7945-3171-3(7)*, Usborne) EDC Publishing.

Godwin, Edward. Logic Puzzles, 1 vol. 2015. (Brain Games Ser.). (ENG.). 32p. (J). 27.50 *(978-1-4777-5439-9(3)*, Windmill Bks.) Rosen Publishing Group, Inc., The.

Goes, Peter. Timeline: Activity Book Create Your Own Journey Through Time. Goes, Peter, illus. 2017. (ENG., Illus.). 72p. (gr. 5-12). 12.99 ***(978-1-77657-128-4(2))*** Gecko Pr. NZL. Dist: Lerner Publishing Group.

Golding, Elizabeth. My First Dot-To-Dot: Over 50 Fantastic Puzzles. 2017. (My First Activity Bks.). (ENG.). 64p. (J). (gr. -1-2). pap. 5.99 *(978-1-4380-1002-1(8))* Barron's Educational Series, Inc.

—My First Mazes: Over 50 Fantastic Puzzles. 2017. (My First Activity Bks.). (ENG.). 64p. (J). (gr. -1-2). pap. 5.99 *(978-1-4380-1003-8(6))* Barron's Educational Series, Inc.

Gomi, Taro. Taro Gomi's Playful Puzzles for Little Hands: 60+ Guessing Games, Twisty Mazes, Logic Puzzles, & More! 2013. (ENG.). 128p. (J). (gr. -1-3). pap. 14.99 *(978-1-4521-0839-1(0))* Chronicle Bks. LLC.

Goscinny, René. Where's Dogmatix? Uderzo, Albert, illus. 2013. (ENG.). 32p. (J). (gr. 4-6). pap. 9.99 *(978-1-4440-0843-2(9)*, Orion) Orion Publishing Group, Ltd. GBR. Dist: Hachette Bk. Group.

Goscinny, René & Uderzo, Albert. Where's Asterix? 2011. (ENG., Illus.). 32p. (J). (gr. 4-6). 14.99 *(978-1-4440-0444-1(1)*, Orion) Orion Publishing Group, Ltd. GBR. Dist: Hachette Bk. Group.

Gospel Light Publications Staff & Kennelly, Colleen. Big Book of Bible Puzzles. Mejia, Roger, illus. 2015. (Big Bks.). (ENG.). 216p. (J). (gr. 3-6). pap. 19.99 *(978-0-8307-2542-7(3))* Gospel Light Pubns.

Graham, Oakley. Things That Go: Sticker Book Fun for Little Ones! Crisp, Dan, illus. 2017. (My First Sticker Book Ser.). (ENG.). 36p. (J). (gr. -1-k). pap. 8.99 ***(978-1-78700-069-8(9))*** Top That! Publishing PLC GBR. Dist: Independent Pubs. Group.

Greenwald, Todd J., contrib. by. Wizards of Waverly Place Ultimate Puzzle Book. 2009. (Wizards of Waverly Place Ser.). (Illus.). 192p. (J). pap. 4.99 *(978-0-7666-3305-6(5))* Modern Publishing.

Greenwell, Jessica. First Colors Sticker Book. 2015. (Get Ready for School Sticker Bks.). (ENG.). 24+8p. (J). pap. 7.99 *(978-0-7945-3600-8(X)*, Usborne) EDC Publishing.

Griffiths, Andy & Griffiths, Jill. The Treehouse Fun Book. Denton, Terry, illus. 2016. (Treehouse Bks.). (ENG.). 192p. (J). 12.99 *(978-1-250-11775-5(5)*, 9781250117755) Feiwel & Friends.

Group/McGraw-Hill, Wright. And the Winner Is: Level N, 6 vols. 128p. (gr. 3-6). 36.95 *(978-0-322-05885-9(6))* Wright Group/McGraw-Hill.

—Bats about Bats! Level M, 6 vols. (Summer Skies Ser.). 128p. (gr. 3-6). 36.95 *(978-0-322-06724-0(3))* Wright Group/McGraw-Hill.

—Groovy Gran & the Karaoko Kid: Level S, 6 vols. (Whispering Pines Ser.). 128p. (gr. 5-18). 36.95 *(978-0-322-05906-1(2))* Wright Group/McGraw-Hill.

—How not to Catch the Moon: Level L, 6 vols. (Summer Skies Ser.). 128p. (gr. 3-6). 36.95 *(978-0-322-05886-6(4))* Wright Group/McGraw-Hill.

—Samantha's Sea: Level Q, 6 vols. (Whispering Pines Ser.). 128p. (gr. 5-18). 36.95 *(978-0-322-05907-8(0))* Wright Group/McGraw-Hill.

—Survival in Cyberspace: Level T, 6 vols. (Whispering Pines Ser.). 128p. (gr. 5-18). 36.95 *(978-0-322-05904-7(6))* Wright Group/McGraw-Hill.

—Wolf Master: Level R, 6 vols. (Whispering Pines Ser.). 128p. (J). (gr. 5-18). 36.95 *(978-0-322-05900-9(3))* Wright Group/McGraw-Hill.

Guignard, Theo. Labyrinth: Find Your Way Through 15 Magical Mazes. 2017. (ENG., Illus.). 32p. (J). (gr. 2-5). 19.99 *(978-1-84780-998-8(7)*, Wide Eyed Editions) Quarto Publishing Group UK GBR. Dist: Hachette Bk. Group.

Handford, Martin. The Incredible Paper Chase. Handford, Martin, illus. 2009. (Where's Waldo? Ser.). (ENG., Illus.). 24p. (J). (gr. k-4). 14.99 *(978-0-7636-4689-9(X))* Candlewick Pr.

—Where's Waldo? the Sticker Book! Handford, Martin, illus. 2015. (Where's Waldo? Ser.). (ENG., Illus.). 96p. (J). (gr. k-4). pap. 12.99 *(978-0-7636-8128-9(8))* Candlewick Pr.

Harper, Charles. Alphabet Children Puzzle Book. 2013. 40p. pap. 19.57 *(978-1-4907-0660-3(7))* Trafford Publishing.

Harrald-Pilz, Marilee. Hide-and-Seek Puzzles: Animal Friends. 2010. (ENG.). 64p. (J). (gr. k-2). pap. 4.95 *(978-1-4027-5908-6(8))* Sterling Publishing Co., Inc.

Harrison, Erica, illus. Box of Fairies. 2005. 6p. (J). 11.95 *(978-0-7945-1125-8(2)*, Usborne) EDC Publishing.

Harte, May. Hide-and-Seek Kids. 2004. (Hide-And-Seek Books). (Illus.). (J). lib. bdg. 21.25 *(978-1-4042-2816-0(0)*, PowerKids Pr.) Rosen Publishing Group, Inc., The.

—Hide & Seek Kids. 2009. (Tough Toddler Bks). 16p. (gr. k-k). 42.50 *(978-1-60854-571-1(7)*, PowerKids Pr.) Rosen Publishing Group, Inc., The.

—Hide-and-Seek Pets. 2004. (Hide-And-Seek Books). (J). lib. bdg. 21.25 *(978-1-4042-2815-3(2)*, PowerKids Pr.) Rosen Publishing Group, Inc., The.

—Hide & Seek Pets. 2009. (Tough Toddler Bks). 16p. (gr. k-k). 42.50 *(978-1-60854-572-8(5)*, PowerKids Pr.) Rosen Publishing Group, Inc., The.

Haughom, Lisa, illus. Things That Go! 2010. 16p. (J). *(978-1-58865-542-4(3))* Kidsbooks, LLC.

Hayward, Linda, et al. I Spy: A Game to Read & Play. Cooke, Tom, illus. 2014. (Step into Reading Ser.). (ENG.). 32p. (J). (gr. -1-1). pap. 3.99 *(978-0-679-84979-7(3)*, Random Hse. Bks. for Young Readers) Random Hse. Children's Bks.

Heinrich, Erik. Survival Debate: A Rip-Roaring Game of Either-Or Questions. 2012. (This or That? Ser.). (ENG., Illus.). 32p. (gr. 3-4). lib. bdg. 27.99 *(978-1-4296-8594-8(8))* Capstone Press of Coughlan Cos.

—This or That Survival Debate: A Rip-Roaring Game of Either - Or Questions. 2012. (This or That? Ser.). (ENG., Illus.). 32p. (gr. 3-4). pap. 8.29 *(978-1-4296-9278-6(2))* Capstone Press of Coughlan Cos.

—This or That Survival Debate: A Rip-Roaring Game of Either/or Questions. 2012. (This or That? Ser.). (ENG.). 32p. (gr. 3-4). pap. 47.70 *(978-1-4296-9279-3(0)*, Edge Bks.) Capstone Press of Coughlan Cos.

Helbrough, Emma. Great Planet Earth Search. Milbourne, Anna, ed. Jackson, Ian, illus. 2005. (Great Searches Ser.). 32p. (J). (gr. 3). lib. bdg. 15.95 *(978-1-58086-827-3(4))* EDC Publishing.

Herzog, Brad. I Spy with My Little Eye: Baseball. Milne, David, illus. 2011. (I Spy Ser.). (ENG.). 32p. (J). (gr. 3-6). 13.95 *(978-1-58536-496-1(7))* Sleeping Bear Pr.

Heywood, Rosie. Great Balloon Race. 2004. (Picture Puzzles Ser.). (ENG., Illus.). 1p. (J). (gr. k-3). pap. 6.95 *(978-0-7460-3388-3(5))* EDC Publishing.

—Puzzle Car Race. Haw, Brenda, illus. 2004. (Young Puzzles Ser.). 32p. (J). pap. 6.95 *(978-0-7945-0689-6(5)*, Usborne) EDC Publishing.

Heywood, Rosie, ed. Travel Puzzles Sticker Book. Haw, Brenda, illus. rev. ed. 2005. (Travel Puzzles Sticker Book Ser.). 24p. (J). (gr. 1). pap. 6.95 *(978-0-7945-0729-9(8)*, Usborne) EDC Publishing.

Hidden Pictures 1-20 (Gr. K-2) 2003. (J). *(978-1-58232-063-2(2))* ECS Learning Systems, Inc.

Highlights, creator. Old MacDonald Had a Farm. 2016. (Highlights(tm) Song & Puzzle Bks.). (ENG.). 48p. (J). (gr. -1-k). pap. 4.99 *(978-1-62979-609-3(3)*, Highlights) Boyds Mills Pr.

Highlights for Children, compiled by. Fun at School. 2009. (Hidden Pictures Playground Ser.). (ENG., Illus.). 32p. (J). (gr. -1-1). pap. 5.49 *(978-0-87534-319-8(8))* Highlights for Children.

—Playful Pets. 2009. (Hidden Pictures Playground Ser.). (ENG., Illus.). 32p. (J). (gr. -1-1). pap. 5.49 *(978-0-87534-318-1(X))* Highlights for Children.

Highlights for Children Editorial Staff. Amazing Mazes - Follow Your Nose! 2015. (Highlights(tm) Amazing Mazes Ser.). (ENG., Illus.). 72p. (J). (gr. k). 6.95 *(978-1-62979-200-2(4)*, Highlights) Boyds Mills Pr.

—Barnyard Puzzles. 2017. (Highlights(tm) Sticker Hidden Pictures(r) Ser.). (ENG.). 96p. (J). (gr. -1-k). pap. 9.95 *(978-1-62979-778-6(2)*, Highlights) Boyds Mills Pr.

—Dinosaur Puzzles. 2017. (Highlights(tm) Hidden Pictures(r) Ser.). (ENG.). 144p. (J). (gr. k-4). pap. 9.95 *(978-1-62979-780-9(4)*, Highlights) Boyds Mills Pr.

—Farm Puzzles. 2015. (Highlights(tm) Puzzlemania(r) Activity Bks.). (ENG., Illus.). 144p. (J). (gr. k). 9.95 *(978-1-62979-202-6(0)*, Highlights) Boyds Mills Pr.

—Farm Tales. 2017. (Highlights(tm) Hidden Pictures(r) Silly Sticker Stories Ser.). (ENG.). 48p. (J). (gr. k-4). pap. 5.99 *(978-1-62979-766-3(9)*, Highlights) Boyds Mills Pr.

—Hit the Trail. 2015. (Highlights(tm) Amazing Mazes Ser.). (ENG., Illus.). 72p. (J). (gr. k). 6.95 *(978-1-62979-197-5(0)*, Highlights) Boyds Mills Pr.

—Picture Puzzles. 2015. (Highlights(tm) Puzzlemania(r) Puzzle Pads Ser.). (ENG.). 64p. (J). (gr. k). pap. 4.99 *(978-1-62979-424-2(4)*, Highlights) Boyds Mills Pr.

—Puzzlemania(r) Halloween Puzzles. 2014. (Highlights(tm) Puzzlemania(r) Activity Bks.). (ENG., Illus.). 144p. (J). (gr. 1). pap. 9.95 *(978-1-62979-265-1(9))* Boyds Mills Pr.

—Puzzlemania School Puzzles. 2014. (Highlights(tm) Puzzlemania(r) Activity Bks.). (ENG., Illus.). 144p. (J). (gr. 1). pap. 9.95 *(978-1-62979-264-4(0))* Boyds Mills Pr.

—Puzzlemania(r) Winter Puzzles. 2014. (Highlights(tm) Puzzlemania(r) Activity Bks.). (ENG., Illus.). 144p. (J). (gr. 1). pap. 9.95 *(978-1-62979-266-8(7))* Boyds Mills Pr.

—Ticklish Tales. 2015. (Highlights(tm) Hidden Pictures(r) Silly Sticker Stories Ser.). (ENG., Illus.). 128p. (J). (gr. k). pap. 12.95 *(978-1-62979-329-0(9)*, Highlights) Boyds Mills Pr.

—Travel Puzzles. 2015. (Highlights(tm) Puzzlemania(r) Activity Bks.). (ENG., Illus.). 144p. (J). (gr. k). 9.95 *(978-1-62979-203-3(9)*, Highlights) Boyds Mills Pr.

Highlights for Children Editorial Staff, compiled by. Puzzlemania(r) Summer Puzzles. 2016. (Highlights(tm) Puzzlemania(r) Activity Bks.). (ENG.). 144p. (J). (gr. k). pap. 9.95 *(978-1-62979-552-2(6)*, Highlights) Boyds Mills Pr.

Highlights for Children Editorial Staff, creator. Brain Teasers. 2015. (Highlights(tm) Puzzlemania(r) Puzzle Pads Ser.). (ENG.). 64p. (J). (gr. k). pap. 4.99 *(978-1-62979-422-8(8)*, Highlights) Boyds Mills Pr.

—Crazy Codes. 2015. (Puzzlemania#174; Puzzle Pads Ser.). (ENG.). 64p. (J). (gr. k). pap. 4.99 *(978-1-62979-425-9(2)*, Highlights) Boyds Mills Pr.

—Farm Friends. 2015. (Highlights(tm) Write-On Wipe-off Hidden Pictures(r) Ser.). (ENG.). 28p. (J). (gr. -1). pap. 8.99 *(978-1-62979-417-4(1)*, Highlights) Boyds Mills Pr.

—Maze Craze. 2016. (Highlights(tm) Puzzlemania(r) Puzzle Pads Ser.). (ENG.). 64p. (J). (gr. k-4). pap. 4.99 *(978-1-62979-698-7(0)*, Highlights) Boyds Mills Pr.

—More Ticklish Tales. 2015. (Highlights(tm) Hidden Pictures(r) Silly Sticker Stories Ser.). (ENG.). 128p. (J). (gr. k). pap. 12.95 *(978-1-62979-419-8(8)*, Highlights) Boyds Mills Pr.

—Spot the Differences! 2016. (Highlights(tm) Write-On Wipe-off Activity Bks.). (ENG.). 28p. (J). (gr. -1-k). pap. 8.99 *(978-1-62979-545-4(3)*, Highlights) Boyds Mills Pr.

—What's the Word? 2015. (Highlights(tm) Puzzlemania(r) Activity Bks.). (ENG.). 144p. (J). pap. 9.95 *(978-1-62979-421-1(X)*, Highlights) Boyds Mills Pr.

Highlights for Children Staff. Say It Again! 501 Wacky Word Puzzles from Highlights. Dammer, Mike, illus. 2013. (Highlights(tm) Laugh Attack! Joke Bks.). (ENG.). 256p. (J). (gr. k). pap. 5.95 *(978-1-62091-072-6(1))* Boyds Mills Pr.

Highlights Staff, compiled by. Fox's Birthday Surprise. 2016. (Highlights(tm) Story Puzzle Fun Ser.). (ENG.). 24p. (J). (gr. -1-k). pap. 4.99 *(978-1-62979-548-5(8)*, Highlights) Boyds Mills Pr.

Highlights USA for Children Staff. Puzzlemania. (Illus.). 48p. (J). pap. 5.95 *(978-0-87534-710-3(X))*; pap. 5.95 *(978-0-87534-711-0(8))*; pap. 5.95 *(978-0-87534-712-7(6))*; pap. 5.95 *(978-0-87534-709-7(6))* Highlights for Children.

Hinkler Books, ed. Mighty Movers. 2012. (Busy Blocks Ser.). 12p. (J). 5.99 *(978-1-74308-887-6(6))* Hinkler Bks. Pty, Ltd. AUS. Dist: Ideals Pubns.

Hinkler Studios Staff., ed. Sponge Bob Story Vision. 2012. (Story Vision Ser.). 96p. (J). 12.99 *(978-1-74181-226-8(7))* Hinkler Bks. Pty, Ltd. AUS. Dist: Ideals Pubns.

Hinton, Stephanie, illus. Busy Book for Boys: 550 Things to Find. 2014. (J). *(978-1-4351-5358-5(8))* Barnes & Noble, Inc.

—Busy Book for Girls: 550 Things to Find. 2014. (J). *(978-1-4351-5359-2(6))* Barnes & Noble, Inc.

Hockett, Margaret. Punctuation Puzzler - Run-Ons C1. 2005. (Punctuation Puzzler Ser.). 48p. (gr. 7-8). pap. 8.99 *(978-0-89455-819-1(6))* Critical Thinking Co., The.

Holt, Rinehart and Winston Staff. Science Puzzlers, Twisters & Teasers. 5th ed. 2004. (Illus.). pap. 26.46 *(978-0-03-035192-1(8))* Holt McDougal.

Hood, Karen Jean Matsko. Gaited Horse Activity & Coloring Book. Whispering Pine Press International, ed. Artistic Design Service Staff, illus. 2014. (Hood Activity & Coloring Book Ser.). 160p. (J). bk. 4. spiral bd. 21.95 *(978-1-59649-628-6(2))* Vol. 4. (ENG.). per. 19.95 *(978-1-59210-591-5(2))* Whispering Pine Pr. International, Inc.

—Gaited Horse Activity & Coloring Book-English/German/Spanish Edition. Whispering Pine Press International, Inc. Staff, ed. Artistic Book and Web Design, illus. 2010. (ENG, GER & SPA.). 160p. (J). per. 19.95 *(978-1-59649-522-7(7))* Whispering Pine Pr. International, Inc.

HOP, LLC. Hooked on Learning Puzzles & Mazes. 2006. 64p. 3.79 *(978-1-933863-90-0(0))* HOP, LLC.

Hovanec, Helene. Ultimate Puzzle Challenge: Mind Mashers. Luxich, Matt, illus. 2010. (ENG.). 96p. (J). (gr. 2-5). pap. 5.95 *(978-1-4027-6204-8(6))* Sterling Publishing Co., Inc.

Hovanec, Helene & Merrell, Patrick. Chicken Games & Puzzles: 100 Word Games, Picture Puzzles, Fun Mazes, Silly Jokes, Codes, & Activities for Kids. 2012. (Storey's Games & Puzzles Ser.). (ENG.). 144p. (J). (gr. k-5). pap. 9.95 *(978-1-61212-087-4(3)*, 622087) Storey Publishing, LLC.

—The Great Outdoors Games & Puzzles: Bring the Outdoors Inside with 100 Mazes, Word Games, Picture Puzzles, Jokes & Riddles, Brainteasers, & Fun-Packed Activities. 2007. (Storey's Games & Puzzles Ser.). (ENG., Illus.). 144p. (J). (gr. 3-8). pap. 9.95 *(978-1-58017-679-8(8)*, 67679) Storey Publishing, LLC.

Hughes, Emily C. Plants vs. Zombies - Brain Busters. 2013. (Plants vs. Zombies Ser.). (ENG.). 224p. (J). (gr. 1-5). 10.99 *(978-0-06-222844-4(7)*, HarperFestival) HarperCollins Pubs.

Hvass, Nan Na & Hannibal, Sofie, illus. Technicolour Treasure Hunt: Learn to Count with Nature. 2016. (ENG.). 14p. (J). bds. 12.99 *(978-1-84780-744-1(5)*, Wide Eyed Editions) Quarto Publishing Group UK GBR. Dist: Littlehampton Bk Services, Ltd.

I Spy Funhouse. 2003. (J). 129.50 *(978-0-590-66383-0(6))* Scholastic, Inc.

IC4DESIGN Staff & Kamigaki, Hiro. Pierre the Maze Detective - The Sticker Book. 2017. (ENG., Illus.). 44p. (J). (gr. 2-6). pap. 9.99 *(978-1-78067-966-2(1))* King, Laurence Publishing GBR. Dist: Hachette Bk. Group.

IC4DESIGN Staff, et al. Pierre the Maze Detective: The Search for the Stolen Maze Stone. Sakamiya, Emma, tr. 2015. (ENG., Illus.). 36p. (J). (gr. 2-6). 19.95 *(978-1-78067-563-3(1))* King, Laurence Publishing GBR. Dist: Hachette Bk. Group.

IKids, creator. Soft Shapes Chunky Puzzle Playset:outer space (Foam Puzzle & Playset) 2012. (ENG.). 1p. (J). (gr. -1-17). 9.99 *(978-1-60169-271-9(4))* Innovative Kids.

Ikids Staff. Soft Shapes: Dinosaurs (Baby's First Book + Puzzle) Ski, Jenn, illus. 2010. (ENG.). 8p. (J). (gr. -1 — 1). 10.99 *(978-1-60169-043-2(6))* Innovative Kids.

—Soft Shapes: Trucks (Baby's First Book + Puzzle) Ski, Jenn, illus. 2010. (ENG.). 8p. (J). (gr. -1 — 1). 10.99 *(978-1-60169-044-9(4))* Innovative Kids.

—Softs Shapes Ocean. 2011. (ENG., Illus.). 8p. (J). (gr. -1 — 1). 10.99 *(978-1-60169-113-2(0))* Innovative Kids.

Ink, Johnny. Inklings: Kids. 2008. 13p. pap. 12.95 *(978-1-929774-60-9(5))* Greenleaf Book Group.

iSeek Ltd. Odd One Out: 70 Timed Puzzles to Test Your Skills. 2017. (Challenging... Bks.). (ENG.). 96p. (J). (gr. 3-7). pap. 7.99 ***(978-1-4380-1084-7(2))*** Barron's Educational Series, Inc.

Jackson, Sara. Spot the Differences Picture Puzzles for Kids 2. 2017. (Dover Children's Activity Bks.). (ENG., Illus.). 64p. (J). (gr. 1-4). pap. 9.99 *(978-0-486-78249-2(2))* Dover Pubns., Inc.

James, Danielle & Green, Dan. Where's Rudolf? Find Rudolph & His Festive Helpers in 15 Fun-Filled Puzzles. 2015. (ENG., Illus.). 46p. (J). (gr. 2-5). 14.99 *(978-1-78418-016-4(5))* Blake, John Publishing, Ltd. GBR. Dist: Independent Pubs. Group.

James, Diane. Baa, Baa, Black Sheep. 2004. (Jigsaw Nursery Rhymes Ser.). (Illus.). 12p. (J). (gr. -1-k). 9.95 *(978-1-58728-625-4(4)*, Two-Can Publishing) T&N Children's Publishing.

—Here We Go. 2004. (Jigsaw Rhymes Ser.). (Illus.). 12p. (J). (gr. -1-k). 9.95 *(978-1-58728-024-5(8)*, Two-Can Publishing) T&N Children's Publishing.

—Pat-a-Cake. 2004. (Jigsaw Nursery Rhymes Ser.). (Illus.). 12p. (J). (gr. -1-k). 9.95 *(978-1-58728-623-0(8)*, Two-Can Publishing) T&N Children's Publishing.

—Three Blind Mice. 2004. (Jigsaw Nursery Rhymes Ser.). (Illus.). 12p. (J). (gr. -1-k). 9.95 *(978-1-58728-626-1(2)*, Two-Can Publishing) T&N Children's Publishing.

Janeczko, Paul B., ed. Top Secret: A Handbook of Codes, Ciphers & Secret Writing. LaReau, Jenna, illus. 2006. (ENG.). 144p. (J). (gr. 4-7). per. 8.99 *(978-0-7636-2972-4(3))* Candlewick Pr.

Jay, Aye. Punk Rock Fun Time Activity Book. 2009. (ENG., Illus.). 48p. pap. *(978-1-55022-872-4(2))* Filmer Ltd.

Jenkins, Gerald & Bear, Magdalen. Tarquin Number Challenges: A Collection of 50 Puzzles to Test Your Mathematical Skills. 2004. (Illus.). 56p. 10.00 *(978-1-899618-49-1(X))* Tarquin Pubns. GBR. Dist: Parkwest Pubns., Inc.

Jones, Bruce Patrick. Celebrity Scenes: Fun & Games with Hollywood Stars. 2015. (ENG.). 48p. (gr. 6). pap. 4.99 *(978-0-486-79349-8(4))* Dover Pubns., Inc.

Jones, Frankie. Counting. Max & Sid, Max &, illus. 2016. (What Can You Spot? Ser.). (ENG.). 18p. (J). (gr. -1 — 1). bds. 7.99 *(978-1-4998-0269-6(2))* Little Bee Books Inc.

—Muddle & Match Jobs. Hinton, Stephanie, illus. 2016. 16p. (J). bds. 8.99 *(978-1-61067-491-1(X))* Kane Miller.

Jones, Rob Lloyd. 1001 Pirate Things to Spot. Gower, Teri, illus. 2007. (1001 Things to Spot Ser.). 32p. (J). 9.99 *(978-0-7945-1513-3(4)*, Usborne) EDC Publishing.

Jumbo Puzzle Book. 2004. (J). per. *(978-1-57657-006-7(1))* Paradise Pr., Inc.

Junior Puzzles. 2004. 112p. (J). 4.99 *(978-1-85997-389-9(2))* Byeway Bks.

Kalvitis, David. The Greatest Dot-to-Dot Book in the World, Vol. 4. 2003. 48p. (YA). 6.95 *(978-0-9700437-3-3(2))* Monkeying Around.

—The Greatest Dot-to-Dot Super Challenge Book 5, Vol. 5. 2007. (Greatest Dot to Dot! Super Challenge! Ser.). (Illus.). 48p. (J). (gr. 3-16). 7.95 *(978-0-9700437-4-0(0)*, 740) Monkeying Around.

—The Greatest Dot-to-Dot Super Challenge Book 6. 2008. (Greatest Dot to Dot! Super Challenge! Ser.). 48p. (J). (gr. 3-16). pap. 7.95 *(978-0-9700437-5-7(9))* Monkeying Around.

—The Greatest Newspaper Dot-to-Dot! Puzzles, Vol. 7. 2011. (Greatest Newspaper Dot-to-Dot Puzzles Ser.). 40p. (YA). 5.95 *(978-0-9799753-8-7(7))* Monkeying Around.

—The Greatest Newspaper Dot-to-Dot! Puzzles: Volume 5. 2007. (Greatest Newspaper Dot-to-Dot Puzzles Ser.). 40p. (J). (gr. 3-16). pap. 5.95 *(978-0-9799753-6-3(0))* Monkeying Around.

—The Greatest Newspaper Dot-to-Dot! Puzzles: Volume 6. 2007. (Greatest Newspaper Dot-to-Dot Puzzles Ser.). 40p. (J). (gr. 3-16). pap. 5.95 *(978-0-9799753-7-0(9))* Monkeying Around.

Kalz, Jill. Christmas Chaos: Hidden Picture Puzzles, 1 vol. Yamasaki, James, illus. 2012. (Seek It Out Ser.). (ENG.). 32p. (gr. 1-2). 9.95 *(978-1-4048-7724-5(X))*; lib. bdg. 26.65 *(978-1-4048-7494-7(1))* Picture Window Bks.

—Halloween Hide & Seek: Hidden Picture Puzzles, 1 vol. Borlasca, Hector, illus. 2012. (Seek It Out Ser.). (ENG.). 32p. (gr. 1-2). 9.95 *(978-1-4048-7728-3(2))*; lib. bdg. 26.65 *(978-1-4048-7495-4(X))* Picture Window Bks.

—Out-Of-This-World Aliens: Hidden Picture Puzzles, 1 vol. Smith, Simon, illus. 2013. (Seek It Out Ser.). (ENG.). 32p. (gr. 1-2). 26.65 *(978-1-4048-7942-3(0))* Picture Window Bks.

—Pretty Princess Party: Hidden Picture Puzzles, 1 vol. Epstein, Len & Pullan, Jack, illus. 2013. (Seek It Out Ser.). (ENG.). 32p. (gr. 1-2). 9.95 *(978-1-4048-8078-8(X))*; 26.65 *(978-1-4048-7943-0(9))* Picture Window Bks.

—School Shake-Up: Hidden Picture Puzzles, 1 vol. Holgate, Douglas, illus. 2012. (Seek It Out Ser.). (ENG.). 32p. (gr. 1-2). 9.95 (978-1-4048-7726-9(6)); lib. bdg. 26.65 (978-1-4048-7496-1(8)) Picture Window Bks.

—Seek It Out. Smith, Simon & Epstein, Len, illus. 2013. (Seek It Out Ser.). (ENG.). 32p. (gr. 1-2). 19.90 (978-1-4048-8080-1(1)); 59.70 (978-1-4048-8081-8(X)); lib. bdg. 53.30 (978-1-4048-7944-7(7)) Picture Window Bks.

—Seek It Out. Epstein, Len & Smith, Simon, illus. 2013. (Seek It Out Ser.). (ENG.). 32p. (gr. 1-2). lib. bdg. 159.90 (978-1-4048-7945-4(5)) Picture Window Bks.

—Zoo Hideout: Hidden Picture Puzzles, 1 vol. Smith, Simon & Chiacchiera, Moreno, illus. 2012. (Seek It Out Ser.). (ENG.). 32p. (gr. 1-2). 9.95 (978-1-4048-7730-6(4)); lib. bdg. 26.65 (978-1-4048-7497-8(6)) Picture Window Bks.

Keating, Laurel. Find Scruncheon & Touton 2: All Around Newfoundland, 1 vol. Keating, Nancy, illus. 2012. (ENG.). 32p. (J). (gr. k-3). pap. 10.95 (978-1-897174-89-0(6), Tuckamore Bks) Creative Bk. Publishing CAN. Dist: Orca Bk. Pubs. USA.

—Search for Scruncheon & Touton, 1 vol. Keating, Nancy, illus. 2012. (ENG.). 32p. (J). (gr. -1-3). 10.95 (978-1-897174-69-2(1), Tuckamore Bks) Creative Bk. Publishing CAN. Dist: Orca Bk. Pubs. USA.

Ketch, Jack. Hangman Puzzles for Clever Kids. 2017. (ENG.). 96p. (J). (gr. 3-7). pap. 6.95 **(978-1-4549-2276-6(1)**, Puzzlewright) Sterling Publishing Co., Inc.

—Hangman Puzzles for Smart Kids. 2017. (ENG.). 96p. (J). (gr. 3-7). pap. 6.95 **(978-1-4549-2277-3(X)**, Puzzlewright) Sterling Publishing Co., Inc.

Khan, Sarah. Word Puzzles. 2012. (Wipe-Clean Activity Cards Ser.). 53p. (J). pap. 9.99 (978-0-7945-3220-8(9), Usborne) EDC Publishing.

Khanduri, Kamini. The Great World Search. Hancock, David, illus. 2007. (Great Searches (EDC Hardcover) Ser.). 48p. (J). (gr. 3). lib. bdg. 16.99 (978-1-58086-966-9(1), Usborne) EDC Publishing.

Khanduri, Kamini, et al. The Usborne Big Book of Picture Puzzles. Groebner, Dominic, illus. 2006. 173p. (J). (gr. 3-7). per. 18.99 (978-0-7945-1165-4(1), Usborne) EDC Publishing.

KidsLabel Staff. Christmas. 2006. (Spot 7 Ser.: SPOT). (ENG., Illus.). 40p. (J). (gr. -1-17). 12.95 (978-0-8118-5323-1(3)) Chronicle Bks. LLC.

Kleven, Dean, illus. Little Einsteins. 2007. (Look & Find Ser.). (J). (gr. -1-3). 7.98 (978-1-4127-7424-6(1)) Publications International, Ltd.

Kohart, Georgia. A Heritage of the Heart Teaching Companion. 2003. (Illus.). ring bd. 24.95 (978-0-9706348-1-8(1)) Heritage Heart Farm.

Kraft, Ellen Christiansen. Alphabet Hide & Seek. 2014. (ENG.). 32p. (J). (gr. -1-2). pap. 3.99 (978-0-486-49471-5(3)) Dover Pubns., Inc.

Kreloff, Elliot, illus. Matching Puzzle Cards - Numbers. 2012. (ENG.). 36p. (J). (gr. k-12). 9.99 (978-1-60905-221-8(8)) Blue Apple Bks.

Krings, Antoon. Droles de Petites Betes. (FRE.). pap. 18.95 (978-2-07-058437-6(2)) Gallimard, Editions FRA. Dist: Distribooks, Inc.

Kumon Publishing, ed. My First Book of Mazes. 2004. (Illus.). 80p. (J). per. 7.95 (978-4-7743-0709-1(2)) Kumon Publishing North America, Inc.

Kumon Publishing North America, creator. My Book of Easy Mazes, Ages 2-3-4. 2006. (Kumon Workbooks Ser.). (ENG., Illus.). 82p. (J). (gr. -1). per. 7.95 (978-1-933241-24-1(1)) Kumon Publishing North America, Inc.

—My Book of Pasting: Jigsaw Puzzles. 2006. (Kumon Workbooks Ser.). (Illus.). 80p. (J). (gr. k-2). per. 7.95 (978-1-933241-29-6(2)) Kumon Publishing North America, Inc.

Kumon Staff. My Book of Mazes Around the World. Karakida, Toshihiko & Murakami, Yoshiko, illus. 2007. 80p. (J). (gr. -1-3). pap. 7.95 (978-1-933241-40-1(3)) Kumon Publishing North America, Inc.

Kurtz, John. SPARK Amazing Animals! Word Search. 2017. (Dover Children's Activity Bks.). (ENG.). 64p. (J). (gr. 1-4). pap. 5.99 **(978-0-486-81770-5(9))** Dover Pubns., Inc.

—Spot-The-Differences Grumpy Cat Coloring Book. 2017. (Dover Little Activity Bks.). (ENG.). 64p. (gr. k-3). pap. 1.99 **(978-0-486-81959-4(0))** Dover Pubns., Inc.

Kurtz, John & Activity Books Staff. Claus Kids Activity Book. 2011. (Dover Little Activity Bks.). (ENG.). 64p. (J). (gr. -1-5). pap. 2.00 (978-0-486-48293-4(6)) Dover Pubns., Inc.

Kutschbach, Doris. Art Detective: Spot the Difference! 2013. (ENG., Illus.). 48p. (J). (gr. 3-7). 14.95 (978-3-7913-7104-7(5)) Prestel Verlag GmbH & Co KG. DEU. Dist: Penguin Random Hse. LLC.

—The Great Art Treasure Hunt: I Spy Red, Yellow, & Blue. 2013. (ENG., Illus.). 48p. (J). (gr. -1-3). 14.95 (978-3-7913-7106-1(1)) Prestel Verlag GmbH & Co KG. DEU. Dist: Penguin Random Hse. LLC.

LaFosse, Michael G. Making Origami Puzzles Step by Step. 2009. (Kid's Guide to Origami Ser.). 24p. (gr. 3-4). 47.90 (978-1-61511-194-7(8), PowerKids Pr.) Rosen Publishing Group, Inc., The.

Lamb, Stacy, illus. First Puzzles. 2014. (Usborne Wipe-Clean Ser.). (ENG.). 22p. (J). pap. 7.99 (978-0-7945-2524-8(5), Usborne) EDC Publishing.

Lambert, Nat. Puzzle Games. Green, Barry, illus. 2016. (Brain Candy Ser.). (ENG.). 224p. (J). (gr. 4). pap. 12.99 (978-1-78445-547-7(4)) Top That! Publishing PLC GBR. Dist: Independent Pubs. Group.

—Puzzle Quest. Assorted & Green, Barry, illus. 2016. (Brain Candy Ser.). (ENG.). 224p. (J). (gr. 4). pap. 12.99 (978-1-78445-548-4(2)) Top That! Publishing PLC GBR. Dist: Independent Pubs. Group.

—Things That Go. Hinton, Steph, illus. 2017. (Wipe Clean Dot-To-dot Ser.). (ENG.). 24p. (J). (gr. -1-k). bds. 9.99 **(978-1-78700-003-2(6))** Top That! Publishing PLC GBR. Dist: Independent Pubs. Group.

—Under the Sea. Hinton, Steph, illus. 2017. (Wipe Clean Dot-To-dot Ser.). (ENG.). 24p. (J). (gr. -1-k). bds. 9.99 **(978-1-78700-004-9(4))** Top That! Publishing PLC GBR. Dist: Independent Pubs. Group.

Lankford, Mary D. Mazes Around the World. Dugan, Karen, illus. 2008. 26p. (J). **(978-0-688-16519-2(2)**, Collins) HarperCollins Pubs. Ltd.

Larranaga, Ana, illus. Matching Puzzle Cards - Animals. 2012. (ENG.). 36p. (J). (gr. k-12). 9.99 (978-1-60905-225-6(0)) Blue Apple Bks.

Laval, Thierry. Look & Find at School. 2017. (Mini Look & Find Ser.). (ENG.). 14p. (J). 9.95 **(978-0-531-23081-7(3)**, Children's Pr.) Scholastic Library Publishing.

Learn to Juggle. 2004. (How 2 Kits Ser.). (Illus.). 48p. (J). (978-1-84229-929-6(8)) Top That! Publishing PLC.

LeCompte, David & Padrick, Kendell. Eugene Stillwell Wants to Know!, Pt. 2. 2009. (Eugene Stillwell Wants to Know! Ser.). (ENG.). 96p. (J). (gr. 4-6). pap. 4.95 (978-1-929945-74-0(4)) Big Guy Bks., Inc.

—Eugene Stillwell Wants to Know! Part III. 2009. (Eugene Stillwell Wants to Know! Ser.). (ENG.). 96p. (J). (gr. 4-6). pap. 4.95 (978-1-929945-91-7(4)) Big Guy Bks., Inc.

Leichter, Albert. Staunton Treasures Past & Present Connect the Dots. 2005. (J). act. bk. ed. 3.95 (978-0-9704280-6-6(5)) ClockTower Pubns.

Leigh, S. Puzzle Dungeon. 2004. (Young Puzzles Ser.). (Illus.). 32p. (J). pap. 6.95 (978-0-7945-0511-0(2), Usborne) EDC Publishing.

—Puzzle Farm. rev. ed. 2004. (Young Puzzles Ser.). (Illus.). 32p. (J). pap. 6.95 (978-0-7945-0625-4(9)) EDC Publishing.

—Puzzle Jungle. 2004. (Young Puzzles Ser.). (Illus.). 32p. (J). pap. 6.95 (978-0-7945-0435-9(3)); lib. bdg. 14.95 (978-1-58086-534-0(8)) EDC Publishing.

—Puzzle Ocean. 2004. (Young Puzzles Ser.). (Illus.). 32p. (J). pap. 6.95 (978-0-7945-0436-6(1)) EDC Publishing.

—Puzzle Planet. rev. ed. 2004. (Young Puzzles Ser.). (Illus.). 32p. (J). pap. 6.95 (978-0-7945-0437-3(X), Usborne) EDC Publishing.

—Puzzle School. 2004. (Young Puzzles Ser.). (Illus.). 32p. (J). pap. 6.95 (978-0-7945-0512-7(0)) EDC Publishing.

—Puzzle Town. 2004. (Young Puzzles Ser.). (Illus.). 32p. (J). pap. 6.95 (978-0-7945-0438-0(8)) EDC Publishing.

Leigh, Susannah. Ciudad Enigma: Lumen Puzzles Infantiles. (SPA., Illus.). (J). pap. (978-950-724-182-6(5)) Lumen.

—L' Ile Fantastique: Fantastic Island. Gemmell, Kathy & Irving, Nicole, eds. Haw, Brenda, illus. (FRE.). 25p. (J). (gr. 2-3). reprint ed. 17.00 (978-0-7881-9300-2(7)) DIANE Publishing Co.

—Isla Enigma: Lumen Puzzles Infantiles. (SPA., Illus.). (J). pap. (978-950-724-183-3(3)) Lumen.

—Puzzle Castle. Waters, Gaby, ed. Haw, Brenda, illus. 2004. (Usborne Young Puzzles Ser.). 32p. (J). (gr. 1). lib. bdg. 14.95 (978-1-58086-674-3(3)); pap. 6.95 (978-0-7945-0433-5(7)) EDC Publishing. (Usborne).

—Puzzle Dinosaurs. Tyler, Jenny, ed. Haw, Brenda, illus. 2007. (Young Puzzles Ser.). 32p. (J). pap. 6.99 (978-0-7945-1778-6(1), Usborne) EDC Publishing.

—Puzzle Dungeon. Haw, Brenda, illus. 2004. (Young Puzzles Ser.). 32p. (J). (gr. 1). lib. bdg. 14.95 (978-1-58086-599-9(2)) EDC Publishing.

—Puzzle Farm. Waters, Gaby, ed. Haw, Brenda, illus. 2004. (Young Puzzles Ser.). 32p. (J). (gr. 1). lib. bdg. 14.95 (978-1-58086-627-9(1), Usborne) EDC Publishing.

—Puzzle Ocean. Haw, Brenda, illus. 2006. (Young Puzzles Ser.). 32p. (J). (gr. 1). lib. bdg. 14.95 (978-1-58086-535-7(6)) EDC Publishing.

—Puzzle Palace. Tyler, Jenny, ed. Haw, Brenda, illus. 2005. (Usborne Young Puzzles Ser.). 32p. (J). (gr. -1-3). per. 6.95 (978-0-7945-1120-3(1), Usborne) EDC Publishing.

—Puzzle Pirates. Tyler, Jenny, ed. Haw, Brenda, illus. 2006. (Usborne Young Puzzles Ser.). 32p. (J). (gr. 1-4). pap. 6.99 (978-0-7945-1359-7(X), Usborne) EDC Publishing.

—Puzzle Pirates. Haw, Brenda, illus. 2006. (Usborne Young Puzzles Ser.). 32p. (J). (gr. 1). lib. bdg. 14.99 (978-1-58086-973-7(4), Usborne) EDC Publishing.

—Puzzle Planet. Waters, Gaby, ed. Haw, Brenda, illus. 2006. (Young Puzzles Ser.). 32p. (J). (gr. 1). lib. bdg. 14.95 (978-1-58086-536-4(4)) EDC Publishing.

—Puzzle Pyramid. Haw, Brenda, illus. 2004. 32p. (J). pap. 6.95 (978-0-7945-0791-6(3), Usborne) EDC Publishing.

—Puzzle School. Haw, Brenda, illus. 2004. (Young Puzzles Ser.). 32p. (Orig.). (J). (gr. 1). lib. bdg. 14.95 (978-1-58086-600-2(X)) EDC Publishing.

—Puzzle Town. Waters, Gaby, ed. Haw, Brenda, illus. 2006. (Young Puzzles Ser.). 32p. (J). (gr. 1). lib. bdg. 14.95 (978-1-58086-537-1(2), Usborne) EDC Publishing.

—Puzzle Train. Haw, Brenda, illus. 2004. (Young Puzzles Ser.). 32p. (J). (gr. 1). lib. bdg. 14.95 (978-1-58086-633-0(6), Usborne) EDC Publishing.

—Puzzle Train. Waters, Gaby, ed. Haw, Brenda, illus. 2003. (Young Puzzles Ser.). 32p. (J). pap. 6.95 (978-0-7945-0683-4(6), Usborne) EDC Publishing.

—Puzzle World: Combined Volume. Waters, Gaby, ed. Haw, Brenda, illus. 2004. (Young Puzzles Ser.). 96p. (J). pap. 13.95 (978-0-7945-0688-9(7), Usborne) EDC Publishing.

Leighton, Robert, et al. The Brainiest Insaniest Ultimate Puzzle Book! 250 Wacky Word Games, Mystifying Mazes, Picture Puzzles, & More to Boggle Your Brain. 2006. (ENG., Illus.). 194p. (J). (gr. 2-8). pap. 12.95 (978-0-7611-4386-4(6), 14386) Workman Publishing Co., Inc.

Levin, David H. Bridge Puzzles for Children Vol. 1: Simple Card Play Problems to Introduce Them to This Wonderful Game. 2004. (Illus.). 128p. (J). pap. 14.95 (978-0-9638001-2-1(4)) Syllogism Pr.

Levin, Freddie. Outer Space Activity Book. 2009. (Dover Little Activity Bks.). (ENG.). 64p. (J). (gr. k-3). pap. 1.99 (978-0-486-47389-5(9)) Dover Pubns., Inc.

Levy, Barbara Soloff. Dot-To-Dot Fun. 2014. (ENG.). 64p. (J). (gr. -1-3). pap. 4.99 (978-0-486-77962-1(9)) Dover Pubns., Inc.

—The Incredible Dot-To-Dot Book. 2014. (ENG.). 48p. (gr. 3-6). pap. 4.99 (978-0-486-49307-7(5)) Dover Pubns., Inc.

—Little Farm Follow-the-Dots. 2005. (Dover Little Activity Bks.). (ENG., Illus.). 64p. (J). (gr. 3-5). pap. 1.50 (978-0-486-44050-7(8)) Dover Pubns., Inc.

—Little Zoo Animal Mazes. 2006. (Dover Little Activity Bks.). (ENG., Illus.). 64p. (J). (gr. k-3). per. 1.99 (978-0-486-44440-6(6)) Dover Pubns., Inc.

—Pets Follow-the-Dots. 2006. (Dover Little Activity Bks.). (ENG., Illus.). 64p. (J). (gr. k-3). per. 1.99 (978-0-486-44890-9(8)) Dover Pubns., Inc.

—Who's Who in the Zoo? Dot-to-Dot Fun. 2007. (Dover Children's Activity Bks.). (ENG., Illus.). 32p. (J). (gr. 1-3). per. 3.99 (978-0-486-46181-6(5)) Dover Pubns., Inc.

Life Magazine Editors. Picture Puzzle: Can You Spot the Differences? Adams, Mark, ed. 2007. (ENG., Illus.). 176p. (YA). (gr. 8-17). pap. 10.99 (978-1-933821-96-2(5), LIFE Bks.) Time Inc. Bks.

Linn, Susie. Princesses. 2016. (My First Sticker Book Ser.). (ENG.). (J). pap. **(978-1-78445-768-6(X))** Top That! Publishing PLC.

—Princesses. Ellis, Lauren, illus. 2017. (Magnetic Play Ser.). (ENG.). 12p. (J). (gr. -1-1). 12.99 **(978-1-78700-247-0(0))** Top That! Publishing PLC GBR. Dist: Independent Pubs. Group.

Lionni, Leo. What? 2014. (ENG., Illus.). 16p. (J). (— 1). bds. 5.99 (978-0-385-75406-4(X), Knopf Bks. for Young Readers) Random Hse. Children's Bks.

—Where? 2014. (ENG., Illus.). 16p. (J). (— 1). bds. 5.99 (978-0-385-75407-1(8), Knopf Bks. for Young Readers) Random Hse. Children's Bks.

—Who? 2014. (ENG., Illus.). 16p. (J). (— 1). bds. 5.99 (978-0-385-75405-7(1), Knopf Bks. for Young Readers) Random Hse. Children's Bks.

Litchfield, Jo, illus. Box of Trucks. 2004. (Boxed Jigsaws Ser.). 10p. (J). 11.99 (978-0-7945-0916-3(9), Usborne) EDC Publishing.

Little & Large Sticker Activity Bk - Monster Machines. 2008. 24p. pap. (978-1-84810-059-6(0)) Miles Kelly Publishing, Ltd.

Little & Large Sticker Activity Bugs. 2008. 24p. pap. (978-1-84810-057-2(4)) Miles Kelly Publishing, Ltd.

Little & Large Sticker Activity Dinosaurs. 2008. 24p. pap. (978-1-84810-058-9(2)) Miles Kelly Publishing, Ltd.

Little & Large Sticker Activity on the Farm. 2008. 24p. pap. (978-1-84810-060-2(4)) Miles Kelly Publishing, Ltd.

Little & Large Sticker Activity Pirates. 2008. 24p. pap. (978-1-84810-061-9(2)) Miles Kelly Publishing, Ltd.

Little & Large Sticker Activity Sharks. 2008. 24p. pap. (978-1-84810-062-6(0)) Miles Kelly Publishing, Ltd.

Little & Large Sticker Activity Space. 2008. 24p. pap. (978-1-84810-063-3(9)) Miles Kelly Publishing, Ltd.

Little & Large Sticker Activity Whales & Dolphins. 2008. 24p. pap. (978-1-84810-064-0(7)) Miles Kelly Publishing, Ltd.

Littlefield, Cindy A. Sea Life Games & Puzzles: 100 Brainteasers, Word Games, Jokes & Riddles, Picture Puzzles, Matches & Logic Tests. Kline, Michael et al, illus. 2006. (Storey's Games & Puzzles Ser.). (ENG.). 144p. (J). (gr. 3-8). pap. 9.95 (978-1-58017-624-8(0), 67624) Storey Publishing, LLC.

Littlefield, Cindy A. & Littlefield. Horse Games & Puzzles for Kids: 102 Brainteasers, Word Games, Jokes & Riddles, Picture Puzzlers, Matches & Logic Tests for Horse-Loving Kids. 2004. (Storey's Games & Puzzles Ser.). (ENG., Illus.). 144p. (J). (gr. 3-8). pap. 9.95 (978-1-58017-538-8(4), 67538) Storey Publishing, LLC.

Ljungkvist, Laura. Search & Spot: Animals! 2015. (Search & Spot Book Ser.). (ENG., Illus.). 40p. (J). (gr. -1-3). 16.99 (978-0-544-54005-7(0), HMH Books For Young Readers) Houghton Mifflin Harcourt Publishing Co.

Lodge, Katherine. Let's Find Mimi: Around the World. 2014. (ENG., Illus.). 32p. (J). (gr. -1-k). 10.99 (978-1-4449-1292-0(5)) Hodder & Stoughton GBR. Dist: Hachette Bk. Group.

Lombardo, Giulia, illus. Challenging Picture Puzzles: Over 75 Timed Puzzles to Test Your Skills. 2017. (Challenging... Bks.). (ENG.). 96p. (J). (gr. 3-7). pap. 7.99 (978-1-4380-0979-7(8)) Barron's Educational Series, Inc.

—Challenging Spot the Difference: Over 60 Timed Puzzles to Test Your Skills. 2017. (Challenging... Bks.). (ENG.). 96p. (J). (gr. 3-7). pap. 7.99 (978-1-4380-0980-3(1)) Barron's Educational Series, Inc.

Lonely Planet Publications Staff. Adventures in Noisy Places: Packed Full of Activities & over 250 Stickers, 1 vol. 2015. (Lonely Planet Kids Ser.). (ENG., Illus.). 48p. (J). pap. 9.99 (978-1-74360-780-0(6), 4982) Lonely Planet Pubns.

Look & Find Ser., 19 bks. (Illus.). (J). lib. bdg. 284.05 (978-1-56674-907-7(7)) Forest Hse. Publishing Co., Inc.

Look, Look Again: A Picture Puzzle Challenge. 2009. (Look, Look Again Ser.). (ENG., Illus.). 128p. (gr. 1-2). pap. 12.95 (978-1-4296-4253-8(X), Aplus Bks.) Capstone Press of Coughlan Cos.

Lucas Film Book Group. Star Wars Dot-To-Dot. 2017. (ENG.). 128p. (YA). (gr. 7-12). pap. 14.99 **(978-1-368-00567-8(5)**, Disney Lucasfilm Press) Disney Publishing Worldwide.

Lucas, Vivien. A Puzzle a Day: A Collection of Mathematical Problems for Every Day of the Year. 2004. (Illus.). 96p. 14.00 (978-1-899618-52-1(X)) Tarquin Pubns. GBR. Dist: Parkwest Pubns., Inc.

Lucey, Marcia T. Puzzles & Activities for Children Ages 5-7: Year B. 2008. (Catholic Corner Ser.). (Illus.). 67p. (J). (gr. k-2). pap. 14.95 incl. cd-rom (978-1-58459-373-7(3)) World Library Pubns.

—Puzzles & Activities for Children Ages 7-10: Year B. 2008. (Catholic Corner Ser.). (Illus.). 67p. (J). (gr. 2-5). pap. 14.95 incl. audio compact disk (978-1-58459-374-4(1)) World Library Pubns.

Lupton, Hugh. Riddle Me This! Riddles & Stories to Challenge Your Mind. Fatus, Sophie, illus. 2003. 64p. (J). 19.99 (978-1-84148-169-2(6)) Barefoot Bks., Inc.

—Riddles, the Barefoot Book Of. 2016. (ENG.). 64p. (J). (gr. 1-5). pap. 14.99 (978-1-78285-280-3(8)) Barefoot Bks., Inc.

Lyons, Jack. Pyruko: The New Logic Puzzle That's Not for Squares. 2010. (ENG.). 208p. pap. 7.95 (978-1-934734-50-6(0)) Seven Footer Pr.

Mac a'Bháird, Natasha & Nolan, Alan. My Ireland. 2016. (ENG., Illus.). 24p. (J). pap., act. bk. ed. 12.00 (978-1-84717-834-3(0)) O'Brien Pr., Ltd., The IRL. Dist: Dufour Editions, Inc.

MacHale, Des. Puzzleology: Tough Puzzles for Kids. 2006. (ENG., Illus.). 93p. (J). pap. 16.95 (978-1-85635-508-7(X)) Mercier Pr., Ltd., The IRL. Dist: Dufour Editions, Inc.

MacKenzie, Catherine. The Greatest Gift: A Puzzle Book about the Birth of Jesus. 2010. (Puzzle Ser.). (ENG., Illus.). 24p. (J). pap. 4.99 (978-1-84550-593-6(X), 0e3f1c04-517a-4e78-a6a4-7b5d47255af3) Christian Focus Pubns. GBR. Dist: Bookmasters Distribution.

Magma & Bailey, Ella. Ghost Story Box: Create Your Own Spooky Tales. 2017. (Magma for Laurence King Ser.: 2). (ENG., Illus.). (J). (gr. -1-k). 14.99 **(978-1-78627-012-2(9))** King, Laurence Publishing GBR. Dist: Hachette Bk. Group.

Magma & Laval, Anne. Story Box: Create Your Own Fairy Tales. 2016. (Magma for Laurence King Ser.). (ENG., Illus.). (gr. -1-k). 14.99 (978-1-85669-980-8(3)) King, Laurence Publishing GBR. Dist: Hachette Bk. Group.

Magruder, Trula. What a Girl Loves Puzzle Book. Magruder, Trula, ed. Wood, Tracey, illus. 2004. (ENG.). 128p. spiral bd. 7.95 (978-1-58485-909-3(1)) American Girl Publishing, Inc.

Magruder, Trula, ed. The Poster Puzzle Book: Puzzles to Solve & Posters to Share. 2009. (ENG.). 64p. (YA). (gr. 3-18). spiral bd. 9.95 (978-1-59369-591-0(8)) American Girl Publishing, Inc.

Make Believe Ideas. Epic & Awesome. 2015. (ENG.). 62p. (J). spiral bd. 7.99 (978-1-78393-485-0(9)) Make Believe Ideas GBR. Dist: Nelson, Thomas Inc.

—I Love to Learn Math Puzzles. 2013. (ENG.). 40p. (J). pap. 4.99 (978-1-78235-209-9(0)) Make Believe Ideas GBR. Dist: Nelson, Thomas Inc.

Mallet, Lisa & Parchow, Marc, illus. Challenging Mazes: 80 Timed Mazes to Test Your Skill! 2016. (Challenging... Bks.). (ENG.). 96p. (J). (gr. 3-7). pap. 7.99 (978-1-4380-0788-5(4)) Barron's Educational Series, Inc.

Manchester, Richard, ed. Colossal Grab a Pencil Pocket Fill-Ins. 2017. (ENG.). 320p. pap. 7.95 **(978-0-88486-644-2(0))** Bristol Park Bks.

Mansfield, Andy. Find the Dots. Mansfield, Andy, illus. 2017. (ENG., Illus.). 14p. (J). (gr. -1-2). 15.00 (978-0-7636-9558-3(0)) Candlewick Pr.

Maring, Therese, ed. Top-Secret Code Book: Tricky, Fun Codes for You & Your Friends. Lukatz, Casey, illus. 2005. (American Girl Today Ser.). (ENG.). 32p. (J). (gr. 4-7). per. 5.95 (978-1-59369-018-2(5), American Girl) American Girl Publishing, Inc.

Marks, Jennifer L. School Times, 1 vol. 2010. (Spot It Ser.). (ENG.). 32p. lib. bdg. 8.99 (978-1-4296-5761-7(8), Pebble Bks.) Capstone Press of Coughlan Cos.

Martin, Norma. Don Martin Brain Games for Kids. 2007. 68p. pap. 3.95 (978-1-4343-2848-9(1)) AuthorHouse.

Martin, Peter. Bible People Factfile. Buckingham, Matt, illus. 2014. (ENG.). 48p. (J). (gr. 2-4). 14.99 (978-0-7459-6388-4(9)) Lion Hudson PLC GBR. Dist: Independent Pubs. Group.

—Jesus Detective: A Puzzle Search Book. Kent, Peter, illus. 2014. (ENG.). 48p. (J). (gr. 2-4). 14.99 (978-0-7459-6444-7(3)) Lion Hudson PLC GBR. Dist: Independent Pubs. Group.

Marzollo, Jean. A to Z: A Book of Picture Riddles. Wick, Walter, illus. 2009. (I Spy Ser.). (ENG.). 56p. (J). (gr. -1-3). 13.99 (978-0-545-10782-2(2), Cartwheel Bks.) Scholastic, Inc.

—C'est Moi l'Espion: Défis Suprêmes! Duchesne, Lucie, tr. Wick, Walter, photos by. (I Spy Bks.).Tr. of I Spy Fantasy. (FRE., Illus.). 37p. (J). (gr. -1-3). pap. 16.99 (978-0-590-24340-7(3)) Scholastic, Inc.

—C'est Moi l'Espion: Du Monde du Mystère. Wick, Walter, photos by. (I Spy Bks.).Tr. of I Spy Mystery: A Book of Picture Riddles. (FRE., Illus.). 37p. (J). (gr. -1-3). pap. 16.99 (978-0-590-24317-9(9)) Scholastic, Inc.

—A Christmas Tree. Wick, Walter, illus. 2010. (I Spy Ser.). (ENG.). 24p. (J). (gr. -1-3). 9.99 (978-0-545-22092-7(0), Cartwheel Bks.) Scholastic, Inc.

—I Spy: A Scary Monster. Wick, Walter, illus. Wick, Walter, photos by. 2005. (Scholastic Reader Level 1 Ser.). (ENG.). 32p. (J). (gr. -1-3). pap. 3.99 (978-0-439-68054-7(9), Cartwheel Bks.) Scholastic, Inc.

—I Spy a Balloon. Wick, Walter, illus. 2006. (Scholastic Reader Level 1 Ser.). (ENG.). 32p. (J). (gr. -1-3). mass mkt. 3.99 (978-0-439-73864-4(4), Cartwheel Bks.) Scholastic, Inc.

—I Spy a Butterfly. Wick, Walter, illus. 2007. (Scholastic Reader Level 1 Ser.). (ENG.). 32p. (J). (gr. -1-3). pap. 3.99 (978-0-439-73865-1(2), Cartwheel Bks.) Scholastic, Inc.

—I Spy a Candy Can. Wick, Walter, illus. Wick, Walter, photos by. 2004. (Scholastic Reader Level 1 Ser.). (ENG.). 32p. (J). (gr. -1-3). pap. 3.99 (978-0-439-52474-2(1), Cartwheel Bks.) Scholastic, Inc.

—I Spy a Penguin. Wick, Walter, illus. 2005. (Scholastic Reader Level 1 Ser.). (ENG.). 32p. (J). (gr. -1-3). pap. 3.99 (978-0-439-73862-0(8), Cartwheel Bks.) Scholastic, Inc.

—I Spy Adventure: 4 Picture Riddle Books. Wick, Walter, illus. Wick, Walter, photos by. 2012. (J). (978-1-4351-3984-8(4)) Scholastic, Inc.

—I Spy an Apple. Wick, Walter, illus. 2011. (Scholastic Reader Level 1 Ser.). (ENG.). 32p. (J). (gr. -1-2). pap. 3.99 (978-0-545-22095-8(5), Cartwheel Bks.) Scholastic, Inc.

—I Spy an Egg in a Nest. Wick, Walter, illus. Wick, Walter, photos by. 2011. (Scholastic Reader Level 1 Ser.). (ENG.). 32p. (J). (gr. -1-2). pap. 3.99 (978-0-545-22093-4(9), Cartwheel Bks.) Scholastic, Inc.

—I Spy Animals. Wick, Walter, illus. 2012. (I Spy Ser.). (ENG.). 32p. (J). (gr. -1-k). pap. 3.99 (978-0-545-41583-5(7)) Scholastic, Inc.

—I Spy Merry Christmas. Wick, Walter, illus. 2007. (Scholastic Reader Level 1 Ser.). (ENG.). 64p. (J). (gr. -1-3). pap. 5.99 (978-0-545-03945-1(2), Cartwheel Bks.) Scholastic, Inc.

—I Spy Nature: A Book of Picture Riddles. Wick, Walter, photos by. 2006. (Illus.). (J). (978-0-439-80732-6(8)) Scholastic, Inc.

—I Spy Numbers. Wick, Walter, illus. 2012. (I Spy Ser.). (ENG.). 32p. (J). (gr. -1-k). pap. 3.99 (978-0-545-41585-9(3)) Scholastic, Inc.

—I Spy Santa Claus. Wick, Walter, illus. 2006. (Scholastic Reader Level 1 Ser.). (ENG.). 32p. (J). (gr. -1-3). per. 3.99 (978-0-439-78414-6(X)) Scholastic, Inc.

—I Spy School. 2012. (I Spy — Scholastic Readers Level 1 Ser.). lib. bdg. 13.55 (978-0-606-26231-6(8), Turtleback) Turtleback Bks.

—I Spy Spectacular: A Book of Picture Riddles. Wick, Walter, illus. 2011. (I Spy Ser.). (ENG.). 40p. (J). 13.99 (978-0-545-22278-5(8), Cartwheel Bks.) Scholastic, Inc.

—I Spy Thanksgiving. Wick, Walter, illus. 2011. (Scholastic Reader Level 1 Ser.). (ENG.). 32p. (J). (gr. -1-2). pap. 3.99 (978-0-545-22094-1(7), Cartwheel Bks.) Scholastic, Inc.

—Little Bunnies. Wick, Walter, illus. 2006. (I Spy Ser.). (ENG.). 24p. (J). (gr. k — 1). bds. 6.99 (978-0-439-78535-8(9), Cartwheel Bks.) Scholastic, Inc.

—Scholastic Reader Level 1: I Spy School. Wick, Walter, illus. 2012. (Scholastic Reader Level 1 Ser.). (ENG.). 32p. (J). (gr. -1-3). pap. 3.99 (978-0-545-40281-1(6), Cartwheel Bks.) Scholastic, Inc.

—School Bus. Wick, Walter, illus. 2003. (Scholastic Reader Level 1 Ser.). (ENG.). 32p. (J). (gr. -1-3). pap. 3.99 *(978-0-439-52473-5(3)*, Cartwheel Bks.) Scholastic, Inc.
—Sticker Book & Picture Riddles. Wick, Walter, illus. 2012. (I Spy Ser.). (ENG.). 40p. (J). (gr. -1-3). pap. 10.99 *(978-0-545-39074-3(5)*, Cartwheel Bks.) Scholastic, Inc.
—Ultimate Challenger! A Book of Picture Riddles. Wick, Walter, illus. 2003. (I Spy Ser.). (ENG.). 40p. (J). (gr. -1-3). pap. 13.99 *(978-0-439-45401-8(8)*, Cartwheel Bks.) Scholastic, Inc.
Maskel, Hazel. 1001 Things to Spot on Vacation. 2011. (1001 Things to Spot Ser.). 32p. (J). rng bd. 9.99 *(978-0-7945-3087-7(7)*, Usborne) EDC Publishing.
Matthies, Don-Oliver & Arena Verlag Staff. Explorer Mazes. 2004. (ENG., Illus.). 40p. (J). pap. 3.95 *(978-1-4027-1757-4(1))* Sterling Publishing Co., Inc.
Mawhinney, Art & Disney Storybook Artists Staff, illus. Fairies. 2007. (Look & Find Ser.). 7.98 *(978-1-4127-7423-9(3))* Publications International, Ltd.
Mazurkiewicz, Jessica. Dragons Activity Book. 2011. (Dover Little Activity Bks.). (ENG.). 64p. (J). (gr. k-3). pap. 1.99 *(978-0-486-47521-9(2))* Dover Pubns., Inc.
—Winter Fun Activity Book. 2010. (Dover Little Activity Bks.). (ENG., Illus.). 64p. (J). (gr. k-3). 1.99 *(978-0-486-47528-8(X))* Dover Pubns., Inc.
McCurry, Kristen. Alike or Not Alike? A Photo Sorting Game, 1 vol. 2012. (Eye-Look Picture Games Ser.). (ENG.). 32p. (gr. 1-2). lib. bdg. 27.32 *(978-1-4296-7549-9(7)*, Aplus Bks.) Capstone Press of Coughlan Cos.
—Eye-Look Picture Games. 2012. (Eye-Look Picture Games Ser.). (ENG.). 32p. (gr. 1-2). lib. bdg. 81.96 *(978-1-4296-8103-2(9)*, Aplus Bks.) Capstone Press of Coughlan Cos.
—Look & Remember: A Photo Memory Game, 1 vol. 2012. (Eye-Look Picture Games Ser.). (ENG.). 32p. (gr. 1-2). lib. bdg. 27.32 *(978-1-4296-7548-2(9)*, Aplus Bks.) Capstone Press of Coughlan Cos.
—Up-Close Mysteries: Zoomed-In Photo Puzzles, 1 vol. 2012. (Eye-Look Picture Games Ser.). (ENG.). 32p. (gr. 1-2). lib. bdg. 27.32 *(978-1-4296-7550-5(0)*, Aplus Bks.) Capstone Press of Coughlan Cos.
Mcdonald, Jill & Fatus, Sophie. Over in the Meadow Puzzle. Mcdonald, Jill, illus. 2012. (ENG., Illus.). (J). (gr. -1-1). 14.99 *(978-1-84686-746-0(0))* Barefoot Bks., Inc.
McEwan, Elaine K., et al. Word Analysis,Grades 4-8. 2008. (Reading Puzzle Ser.). (ENG., Illus.). 96p. (gr. 4-7). pap. 16.95 *(978-1-4129-5825-7(3)*, B58257P) Corwin Pr.
McKay, Chelsea. A Tangram ABC: Shaping the Alphabet from an Ancient Chinese Puzzle. Firos, Daphne, illus. 2013. 60p. (J). pap. 13.95 *(978-1-939431-04-2(2))* MathWord Pr., LLC.
Mcmahon, Kelly. Mazes, Grade K-1. 2006. (ENG.). 64p. (gr. k-1). pap. 6.99 *(978-1-4206-5990-0(1)*, TCR5990) Teacher Created Resources, Inc.
—More Mazes, Grade K-1. 2006. (ENG.). 64p. (gr. k-1). pap. 6.99 *(978-1-4206-5991-7(X)*, TCR5991) Teacher Created Resources, Inc.
Mega Puzzle Fun. Date not set. 576p. (J). 6.98 *(978-0-7525-9824-6(4))* Parragon, Inc.
Mega Travel Fun. Date not set. 576p. (J). 6.98 *(978-0-7525-9825-3(2))* Parragon, Inc.
Meister, Cari. Mind Benders, 2 vols. 2016. (Mind Benders Ser.). (ENG.). 112p. (gr. 1-3). 139.92 *(978-1-4914-8381-7(4))* Capstone Press of Coughlan Cos.
Menotti, Andrea. How to Tackle Puzzles, Unravel Riddles, Crack Codes, & Other Ways to Bend Your Brain. 2004. (Illus.). 80p. (J). *(978-0-439-57905-6(8))* Scholastic, Inc.
Merrell, Patrick & Bathroom Readers' Institute Staff. Flapjacks from Space - 36 Tear-Off Placemats: Puzzles, Mazes, Brainteasers, Weird Facts, Jokes, & More! 2014. (ENG., Illus.). 72p. (gr. k-4). pap. 10.95 *(978-1-62686-069-8(6)*, Portable Pr.) Readerlink Distribution Services, LLC.
Merrell, Patrick & Hovanec, Helene. Pony Play Games & Puzzles. 2008. (Storey's Games & Puzzles Ser.). (ENG., Illus.). 144p. (J). (gr. k-5). pap. 9.95 *(978-1-60342-063-1(0)*, 62063) Storey Publishing, LLC.
Metsola, Aino-Maija. Animal Parade: Puzzle Book. 2016. (Learning Garden Ser.). (ENG., Illus.). 14p. (J). bds. 14.99 *(978-1-84780-747-2(X)*, Wide Eyed Editions) Quarto Publishing Group UK GBR. Dist: Littlehampton Bk Services, Ltd.
—Animal Parade: Puzzle Book - with a 6 Piece Floor Puzzle! 2016. (Learning Garden Ser.). (ENG.). 14p. (J). (gr. -1-k). bds. 12.99 *(978-1-84780-779-3(1)*, Wide Eyed Editions) Quarto Publishing Group UK GBR. Dist: Hachette Bk. Group.
—Traffic Jam: Puzzle Book - with a 6 Piece Floor Puzzle! 2016. (Learning Garden Ser.). (ENG.). 14p. (J). (gr. -1-k). bds. 12.99 *(978-1-84780-776-2(X)*, Wide Eyed Editions) Quarto Publishing Group UK GBR. Dist: Hachette Bk. Group.
Midda, Sara. How to Build an A. 2008. (ENG., Illus.). 56p. (J). (gr. -1-3). 19.95 *(978-1-57965-378-1(2)*, 85378) Artisan.
Migliardo, Emiliano, illus. Seek & Find Christmas. 2017. (ENG.). 24p. (J). pap. 4.99 ***(978-1-68119-542-1(9)***, 9781681195421, Bloomsbury Activity Bks.) Bloomsbury Publishing USA.
Milbourne, A. Baby Animals Jigsaw Book. 2004. (SPA.). 14p. (J). 8.95 *(978-0-7945-0448-9(5))* EDC Publishing.
Milbourne, Anna. Familias de Animales Libro Con Paginas Puzzle. Butler, John, illus. 2004. (Titles in Spanish Ser.). (SPA.). 8p. (J). 8.95 *(978-0-7460-6108-4(0)*, Usborne) EDC Publishing.
Miles, Lisa. The Book of Girls' Activity Fun: Join Milly & Her Friends for Hours of Puzzle Fun! 2012. (ENG.). 144p. (J). pap. 8.95 *(978-1-84858-391-7(5))* Arcturus Publishing GBR. Dist: Bookmasters Distribution.
Miller, Jonathan, illus. When I Grow Up. 2011. 16p. (J). *(978-1-58865-637-7(3))* Kidsbooks, LLC.
Monkey Business: Level K, 6 vols. 128p. (gr. 2-3). 40.50 *(978-0-7699-0994-3(9))* Shortland Pubns. (U. S. A.) Inc.
Moog, Bob. Do I Bug You? A Who Am I? Book. San Francisco School, illus. 2006. (Spinner Books for Kids Ser.). (ENG.). 32p. (J). (gr. -1-12). 9.95 *(978-1-57528-898-7(2))* Univ. Games.
—I-Ballers: Little Books for Big Minds. 2005. (I-Ballers Ser.). (ENG.). pap. 4.95 *(978-1-57528-937-3(7))* Univ. Games.
—Spinner Books: the Grateful Dead. 2006. 240p. pap. *(978-1-57528-897-0(4))* Univ. Games.
Moon, Jo. Super-Fun Dot-To-Dots. 2016. (ENG.). 96p. (J). pap. 9.95 *(978-1-78599-137-0(X)*, 9781785991370) Arcturus Publishing GBR. Dist: Bookmasters Distribution.
Moore, Gareth. Brain Games for Clever Kids. Dickason, Chris, illus. 2014. (ENG.). 192p. (J). (gr. 3-7). pap. 7.99 *(978-1-78055-249-1(1))* O'Mara, Michael Bks., Ltd. GBR. Dist: Independent Pubs. Group.
—Jungle Puzzles. 2016. (Brain Game Treasure Hunts Ser.). (ENG., Illus.). 32p. (J). (gr. 3-6). 26.65 *(978-1-5124-0621-4(X))* Lerner Publishing Group.
—The Kids' Book of Mazes. Moore, Gareth, illus. 2014. (ENG., Illus.). 192p. (J). (gr. 1-3). pap. 6.99 *(978-1-78055-248-4(3))* O'Mara, Michael Bks., Ltd. GBR. Dist: Independent Pubs. Group.
—Ocean Puzzles. 2016. (Brain Game Treasure Hunts Ser.). (ENG., Illus.). 32p. (J). (gr. 3-6). 26.65 *(978-1-5124-0623-8(6))* Lerner Publishing Group.
—Pyramid Puzzles. 2016. (Brain Game Treasure Hunts Ser.). (ENG., Illus.). 32p. (J). (gr. 3-6). 26.65 *(978-1-5124-0622-1(8))* Lerner Publishing Group.
—Space Puzzles. 2016. (Brain Game Treasure Hunts Ser.). (ENG., Illus.). 32p. (J). (gr. 3-6). 26.65 *(978-1-5124-0624-5(4))* Lerner Publishing Group.
—Think Outside the Box. 2015. (Brain Benders Ser.). (ENG., Illus.). 32p. (J). (gr. 3-6). pap. 7.99 *(978-1-4677-7205-1(4)*, Lerner Pubns.) Lerner Publishing Group.
Moran, Paul. Where's the Meerkat? Journey Through Time. 2014. (ENG., Illus.). 48p. (J). (gr. 2-6). 14.99 *(978-1-84317-804-0(4))* O'Mara, Michael Bks., Ltd. GBR. Dist: Independent Pubs. Group.
—Where's the Meerkat? - Journey Through Time. 2014. (ENG., Illus.). 48p. (J). (gr. 2-6). pap. 7.99 *(978-1-84317-948-1(2))* O'Mara, Michael Bks., Ltd. GBR. Dist: Independent Pubs. Group.
More Time for Bible Puzzles & Games. (Illus.). 32p. (YA). (gr. 5-18). pap. 2.25 *(978-0-87162-664-6(0)*, E9706) Warner Pr., Inc.
More Word Winks: Over 300 Visual Verbal Puzzles. 2004. (J). pap. 12.95 *(978-1-892069-76-4(8))* MindWare Holdings, Inc.
Morgan, Gaby. My Christmas. rev. ed. 2007. 24p. pap., act. bk. ed. 7.99 *(978-0-230-01546-3(8)*, Macmillan Children's Bks.) Pan Macmillan GBR. Dist: Trans-Atlantic Pubns., Inc.
Morris, Michael, illus. Puzzle Cards Letters. gif. ed. 2005. 16p. (J). 9.99 *(978-1-57791-188-3(1))* Brighter Minds Children's Publishing.
—Puzzle Cards Numbers. gif. ed. 2005. 16p. (J). 9.99 *(978-1-57791-187-6(3))* Brighter Minds Children's Publishing.
Mudpuppy Press Staff. Alligator Alphabet Floor Puzzle. 2005. (J). 17.99 *(978-0-7353-1224-1(9))* Galison.
—Dinosaur Block Puzzle. 2005. (J). 12.99 *(978-0-7353-0903-6(5))* Galison.
—Magic Horses 100-piece Puzzle. 2005. (J). 12.99 *(978-0-7353-0512-0(9))* Galison.
Munro, Fiona. Vacation: Creative Play, Fold-Out Pages, Puzzles & Games, over 200 Stickers! 2014. (My First Creativity Bks.). (ENG.). 66p. (J). (gr. -1-2). pap. 9.99 *(978-1-4380-0444-0(3))* Barron's Educational Series, Inc.
Munro, Roxie. Wild West Trail Ride Maze. 2006. (ENG., Illus.). 50p. (J). (gr. k-2). 16.95 *(978-1-931721-67-7(X)*, c7606323-9d58-4d30-ad89-d1aee1920627) Bright Sky Pr.
My First Hidden Pictures (Gr. K-1) 2003. (J). *(978-1-58232-061-8(6))* ECS Learning Systems, Inc.
My Little Pony Surprize Ink! Clipboard I. 2004. 24p. (J). 9.99 *(978-1-932125-92-4(2))* Giddy Up, LLC.
N. E. Thing Enterprises Staff. Garfield's Magic Eye. (FRE., Illus.). 32p. (J). pap. 9.99 *(978-0-590-16004-9(4))* Scholastic, Inc.
—Magic Eye III.Tr. of Oeil Magique III. (FRE., Illus.). (J). pap. 7.99 *(978-0-590-24610-1(0))* Scholastic, Inc.
Napier, Matt. I Spy with My Little Eye - Hockey. Milne, David, photos by. 2008. (ENG., Illus.). 32p. (J). (gr. k-6). 13.95 *(978-1-58536-365-0(0))* Sleeping Bear Pr.
National Geographic Kids Staff. Boredom-Busting Fun Stuff. 2015. (ENG., Illus.). 352p. (J). (gr. 3-7). pap. 14.99 *(978-1-4263-2106-1(6)*, National Geographic Children's Bks.) National Geographic Society.
—What in the World? 2014. (ENG., Illus.). 48p. (J). (gr. 3-7). 16.99 *(978-1-4263-1517-6(1)*, National Geographic Children's Bks.) National Geographic Society.
—What in the World? - A Closer Look: Fun-Tastic Photo Puzzles for Curious Minds. 2016. (ENG., Illus.). 48p. (J). (gr. 3-7). 16.99 *(978-1-4263-2538-0(X)*, National Geographic Children's Bks.) National Geographic Society.
Needham, Kate. Usborne the Great Undersea Search. Brooks, Felicity, ed. Jackson, Ian, illus. rev. ed. 2006. (Great Searches Ser.). 32p. (J). (gr. -1-3). per. 7.99 *(978-0-7945-1228-6(3)*, Usborne) EDC Publishing.
Newman-D'Amico, Fran. Animal Friends Mazes. 2014. (ENG.). 64p. (J). (gr. k-3). pap. 4.99 *(978-0-486-77965-2(3))* Dover Pubns., Inc.
—Animal Spot-the-Differences. 2007. (Dover Little Activity Bks.). (ENG., Illus.). 64p. (J). (gr. k-3). per. 1.99 *(978-0-486-45649-2(8))* Dover Pubns., Inc.
—Bugs Activity & Coloring Book. 2007. (Dover Children's Activity Bks.). (ENG., Illus.). 32p. (J). (gr. 1-3). pap. 3.99 *(978-0-486-46199-1(8))* Dover Pubns., Inc.
—Busy Backyard Coloring & Activity Book. 2014. (ENG.). 64p. (J). (gr. -1-3). pap. 3.99 *(978-0-486-77957-7(2))* Dover Pubns., Inc.
—Fun Farm Animal Mazes. 2006. (Dover Children's Activity Bks.). (ENG., Illus.). 32p. (J). (gr. -1-3). pap. 2.95 *(978-0-486-45184-8(4))* Dover Pubns., Inc.
—Girlfriends Activity Book. 2010. (Dover Little Activity Bks.). (ENG., Illus.). 64p. (J). (gr. k-3). pap. 1.50 *(978-0-486-47525-7(5))* Dover Pubns., Inc.
—Halloween Fun. 2005. (Dover Holiday Coloring Book Ser.). (ENG., Illus.). 32p. (J). (gr. k-3). 3.99 *(978-0-486-44699-8(9))* Dover Pubns., Inc.
—Little Animal Friends Mazes. 2016. (Dover Little Activity Bks.). (ENG.). 64p. (J). (gr. k-3). pap. 1.99 *(978-0-486-81035-6(6))* Dover Pubns., Inc.
—Little Gardener's. 2005. (Dover Coloring Bks.). (ENG., Illus.). 32p. (J). (gr. -1-2). pap., act. bk. ed. 3.99 *(978-0-486-43990-7(9))* Dover Pubns., Inc.
—My First Book of Puzzle Fun. 2005. (Dover Children's Activity Bks.). (ENG., Illus.). 64p. (J). (gr. -1-2). per. 4.95 *(978-0-486-44075-0(3))* Dover Pubns., Inc.
—My Vacation Activity Book. 2014. (ENG.). 64p. (J). (gr. -1-3). pap. 3.99 *(978-0-486-77958-4(0))* Dover Pubns., Inc.
—Spot the Differences Picture Puzzles. 2014. (Dover Little Activity Bks.). (ENG.). 64p. (J). (gr. k-3). pap. 1.99 *(978-0-486-78182-2(8))* Dover Pubns., Inc.
—Spot the Differences Puzzle Fun. 2004. (Dover Little Activity Bks.). (ENG., Illus.). 64p. (J). (gr. k-3). pap. 1.99 *(978-0-486-43841-2(4))* Dover Pubns., Inc.
Nextoy Staff, et al. I Can Kenken! Vol. 1: 75 Puzzles for Having Fun with Math. 2008. (ENG.). 112p. (J). pap. 7.99 *(978-0-312-54641-0(6)*, 9780312546410, St. Martin's Griffin) St. Martin's Pr.
—I Can Kenken! Vol. 2: 75 Puzzles for Having Fun with Math. 2008. (ENG.). 112p. (J). pap. 17.99 *(978-0-312-54642-7(4)*, 9780312546427, St. Martin's Griffin) St. Martin's Pr.
—I Can Kenken! Vol. 3: 75 Puzzles for Having Fun with Math. 2008. (ENG.). 112p. (J). pap. 17.99 *(978-0-312-54643-4(2)*, 9780312546434, St. Martin's Griffin) St. Martin's Pr.
Nicholas, Mother Andrea, compiled by. My Little Orthodox Christian Feast Days Activity Book. 2005. (J). spiral bd. 6.95 *(978-0-9773579-0-1(2))* St. Nicholas Monastery.
Nichols, Roy & Corley, Monte. Bible Puzzles: Match-It. 2004. (Illus.). 64p. (J). pap. 9.95 *(978-0-937282-54-0(5)*, RB36154) Rainbow Pubs. & Legacy Pr.
—Bible Puzzles: Pencil Games. 2004. (Illus.). 64p. (J). pap. 9.95 *(978-0-937282-53-3(7)*, B36153) Rainbow Pubs. & Legacy Pr.
—Bible Puzzles: Word Search. 2004. (Illus.). 64p. (J). pap. 9.95 *(978-0-937282-52-6(9)*, RB36152) Rainbow Pubs. & Legacy Pr.
Niederman, Derrick. Mind-Stretching Math Puzzles. 2005. (Illus.). 112p. (J). *(978-1-4156-0492-2(4))* Sterling Publishing Co., Inc.
Nilsen, Anna. Pirates: All Aboard for Hours of Puzzling Fun! 2006. (Illus.). 32p. pap. *(978-1-921049-71-2(5))* Little Hare Bks. AUS. Dist: HarperCollins Pubs. Australia.
—Pirates Galore: The Biggest Treasure Hunt Ever! 2008. (ENG., Illus.). 32p. (J). (gr. 2-7). pap. 8.99 *(978-1-921049-97-2(9))* Little Hare Bks. AUS. Dist: Independent Pubs. Group.
Noble, Marty. Mandala Mazes. 2010. (Dover Children's Activity Bks.). (ENG.). 48p. (gr. 5). pap. 4.99 *(978-0-486-47653-7(7))* Dover Pubns., Inc.
Noodlers: Elusive Illusions. 2004. (J). pap. 12.95 *(978-1-892069-80-1(6))* MindWare Holdings, Inc.
Noodlers: Eye-Bending Icon. 2004. (J). pap. 12.95 *(978-1-892069-79-5(2))* MindWare Holdings, Inc.
Norman, D. Dinosaurs Sticker & Puzzle Kid Kit (Bag) 2007. (Kid Kits Ser.). 24p. (J). pap. 14.99 *(978-1-60130-054-6(9))* EDC Publishing.
Novelli, Joan & Grundon, Holly. Instant Content Area Vocabulary Packets: 25 Independent Practice Packets That Help Boost Reading Comprehension in Science, Social Studies, & Math - Grades 2-3. 2011. (ENG.). 144p. (gr. 2-3). pap. 18.99 *(978-0-545-23694-2(0)*, Teaching Resources) Scholastic, Inc.
Novick, Mary & Hale, Jenny. Farm Animals Jigsaw Book. 2007. bds. *(978-1-921049-99-6(5))* Little Hare Bks. AUS. Dist: HarperCollins Pubs. Australia.
—Zoo Animals Jigsaw Book. 2007. bds. *(978-1-921272-00-4(7))* Little Hare Bks. AUS. Dist: HarperCollins Pubs. Australia.
Oburkova, Eva. Toby's Travels Through Time: Puzzle Adventures in Dinosaur Days. Oburkova, Eva, illus. 2007. (Toby's Travels Through Time: Puzzle Adventures in Dinosaur Days Ser.). (Illus.). 32p. (gr. k-3). lib. bdg. 28.00 *(978-0-8368-7497-6(8)*, Gareth Stevens Learning Library) Stevens, Gareth Publishing LLLP.
O'Hare, J. The Highlights Big Book of Fun: An Amazing Collection of Jokes, Riddles, Puzzles, & More! 2003. (ENG., Illus.). 96p. (YA). (gr. k-7). pap., act. bk. ed. 9.95 *(978-1-59078-006-0(X))* Boyds Mills Pr.
O'Hare, J., ed. The Big Book of Mazes. 2003. (ENG., Illus.). 72p. (YA). (gr. k-7). pap. 8.95 *(978-1-56397-990-3(X))* Boyds Mills Pr.
Okido Staff. Color Me In! An Activity Book. 2013. (ENG., Illus.). 128p. (J). (gr. k-3). pap. 14.95 *(978-0-500-65017-2(9)*, 565017) Thames & Hudson.
Osborne, Mary Pope & Boyce, Natalie Pope. Animal Games & Puzzles. Murdocca, Sal, illus. 2015. (Magic Tree House Ser.). (ENG.). 256p. (J). (gr. 2-5). 6.99 *(978-0-553-50840-6(7)*, Random Hse. Bks. for Young Readers) Random Hse. Children's Bks.
—Games & Puzzles from the Tree House. Murdocca, Sal, illus. 2010. (Magic Tree House Ser.). (ENG.). 256p. (J). (gr. 1-4). act. bk. ed. 6.99 *(978-0-375-86216-8(1)*, Random Hse. Bks. for Young Readers) Random Hse. Children's Bks.
Otway, Helen. The Christmas Drawing & Activity Book. 2012. (ENG.). 208p. (J). pap. 9.95 *(978-1-84837-589-5(1))* Arcturus Publishing GBR. Dist: Bookmasters Distribution.
Over 100 Things to Do on a Car Trip. 2017. (Activity Puzzle Bks.). (ENG.). (J). pap. 5.99 ***(978-0-7945-3965-8(3)***, Usborne) EDC Publishing.
Owen, James A. & Owen, Jeremy. Lost Treasures of the Pirates of the Caribbean. Owen, James A., illus. 2011. (ENG., Illus.). 32p. (J). (gr. 3-7). pap. 16.99 *(978-1-4424-3093-8(1)*, Simon & Schuster Bks. For Young Readers) Simon & Schuster Bks. For Young Readers.
Pace, Lorenzo. Marching with Martin, 1 vol. 2015. (African American Quartet Ser.). (ENG., Illus.). 48p. (J). 30.25 *(978-1-4777-9285-8(6)*, Windmill Bks.) Rosen Publishing Group, Inc., The.
Padmanabhan, Manjula. I Am Different. 2011. (ENG., Illus.). 40p. (J). (gr. 1-4). 16.95 *(978-1-57091-639-7(X))* Charlesbridge Publishing, Inc.
Pantone. Pantone: Color Puzzles: 6 Color-Matching Puzzles. Carpenter, Tad, illus. 2013. (Pantone Ser.). (ENG.). 12p. (J). (gr. -1-k). 16.95 *(978-1-4197-0939-5(9)*, Abrams Appleseed) Abrams, Inc.
Parchow, Marc, et al, illus. Incredible Dot to Dot: Over 75 Timed Puzzles to Test Your Skills. 2017. (Challenging... Bks.). (ENG.). 96p. (J). (gr. 3-7). pap. 7.99 ***(978-1-4380-1085-4(0))*** Barron's Educational Series, Inc.
Park, Barbara. Junie B.'s These Puzzles Hurt My Brain! Brunkus, Denise, illus. 2011. (Junie B. Jones Ser.). (ENG.). 240p. (J). (gr. 1-4). 5.99 *(978-0-375-87123-8(3)*, Random Hse. Bks. for Young Readers) Random Hse. Children's Bks.
Parkes, Lois. Paper Sport: Activities, Games & Puzzles for Sporty Kids. 2012. 44p. pap. 21.99 *(978-1-4771-2582-3(5))* Xlibris Corp.
Parks, Sandra & Black, Howard. Dr. Funster's Visual B1: Creative Problem-Solving Fun. 2003. (Dr. Funster's Ser.). 30p. (gr. 7-9). pap. 4.99 *(978-0-89455-824-5(2))* Critical Thinking Co., The.
—Dr. Funster's Visual C1: Creative Problem-Solving Fun. 2003. (Dr. Funster's Ser.). 30p. (gr. 10-12). pap. 4.99 *(978-0-89455-825-2(0))* Critical Thinking Co., The.
Parri, Celia. Cyfoeth Cudd y Capten: Llyfr Stori a Phosau. 2005. (WEL., Illus.). 28p. pap. *(978-0-86381-397-9(6))* Gwasg Carreg Gwalch.
Pearcey, Alice. The Usborne Castle Jigsaw Book. Milbourne, Anna, ed. Groebner, Dominic, illus. 2006. (Jigsaw Bks.). 14p. (J). (gr. k-3). bds. 14.95 *(978-0-7945-1137-1(6)*, Usborne) EDC Publishing.
Peirce, Lincoln. Big Nate Boredom Buster. Peirce, Lincoln, illus. 2014. (Big Nate Activity Book Ser.: 1). (ENG., Illus.). 224p. (J). (gr. 3-7). pap. 6.99 *(978-0-06-233800-6(5))* HarperCollins Pubs.
—Big Nate Boredom Buster: Super Scribbles, Cool Comix, & Lots of Laughs. Peirce, Lincoln, illus. 2011. (Big Nate Activity Book Ser.: 1). (ENG., Illus.). 224p. (J). (gr. 3-7). 10.99 *(978-0-06-206094-5(5))* HarperCollins Pubs.
—Big Nate Laugh-O-Rama. Peirce, Lincoln, illus. 2014. (Big Nate Activity Book Ser.: 4). (ENG., Illus.). 224p. (J). (gr. 3-7). pap. 6.99 *(978-0-06-211116-6(7))* HarperCollins Pubs.
Penton, ed. A Happy Bugs. 2003. (J). 12.95 *(978-1-74047-216-6(0))* Penton Overseas, Inc.
Penton Overseas, Inc. Staff. U. S. Presidents. 2006. (ENG., Illus.). (J). pap. 7.95 *(978-1-59125-165-1(6))* Penton Overseas, Inc.
Percy, J.P. At Home. 2013. (Can You Guess What I Am? Ser.). (Illus.). 24p. (gr. k-3). lib. bdg. 28.50 *(978-1-59920-893-0(8))* Black Rabbit Bks.
—In the Street. 2013. (Can You Guess What I Am? Ser.). 24p. (gr. k-3). lib. bdg. 28.50 *(978-1-59920-894-7(6))* Black Rabbit Bks.
Perrin, James W., Jr. Back to School Puzzlers: An Awesome Array of Puzzles & Fun! 2004. (Illus.). 58p. (gr. 4-7). pap. 8.95 *(978-0-673-59963-6(9))* Good Year Bks.
—Holiday Puzzlers: An Awesome Array of Puzzles & Fun for November & December. 2005. (Illus.). 58p. (J). (gr. 4-6). per. 8.95 *(978-1-59647-063-7(1))* Good Year Bks.
Perrin, James W. Winter Puzzlers: An Awesome Array of Puzzles & Fun. 2007. pap. 9.95 *(978-1-59647-258-7(8))* Good Year Bks.
Petruccio, Steven James. Construction Site Sticker Picture Puzzle. 2005. (Dover Little Activity Bks.). (ENG., Illus.). 4p. (J). (gr. -1-2). pap. 1.50 *(978-0-486-44156-6(3))* Dover Pubns., Inc.
Pfister, Marcus. Rainbow Fish Puzzle. 2017. (Rainbow Fish Ser.: 1). (ENG., Illus.). 1p. (J). 14.95 ***(978-0-7358-4291-5(4))*** North-South Bks., Inc.
Phillips, Dave. Americana Mazes. 2011. (Dover Children's Activity Bks.). (ENG.). 48p. (J). (gr. 3-7). pap. 4.99 *(978-0-486-48108-1(5))* Dover Pubns., Inc.
—Ancient Treasure Mazes. 2009. (Dover Children's Activity Bks.). (ENG., Illus.). 48p. (J). (gr. 3-7). pap. 4.99 *(978-0-486-46773-3(2))* Dover Pubns., Inc.
—Haunted Pirates Mazes. 2008. (Dover Children's Activity Bks.). (ENG., Illus.). 48p. (J). (gr. 4). per. 4.95 *(978-0-486-46216-5(1))* Dover Pubns., Inc.
Phoenix International Staff, illus. Write-and-Erase Look & Find(r) Disney: Packed with 'Find 'Ems & Picture Puzzles! Look, Circle, Wipe Clean, & Play Again! 2014. 20p. (J). bds. *(978-1-4508-8033-6(9)*, 1450880339) Phoenix International Publications, Inc.
Poitier, Anton. Challenging Dot-To-Dot: 68 Timed Puzzles to Test Your Skill. Parchow, Marc et al, illus. 2016. (Challenging... Bks.). (ENG.). 96p. (J). (gr. 3-7). pap. 7.99 *(978-1-4380-0932-2(1))* Barron's Educational Series, Inc.
Pomaska, Anna. Anna Pomaska's Big Book of Puzzle Fun. 2013. (Dover Children's Activity Bks.). (ENG., Illus.). 144p. (J). (gr. 1-4). pap. 8.95 *(978-0-486-42790-4(0))* Dover Pubns., Inc.
—Dot-to-Dot. 2005. (Dover Children's Activity Bks.). (ENG., Illus.). 32p. (J). (gr. -1-2). pap. 3.99 *(978-0-486-44700-1(6))* Dover Pubns., Inc.
Prenting, Ruth. I Spy ABC: Totally Crazy Letters. Ancutici, Manuela, photos by. 2017. (ENG., Illus.). 32p. (J). (gr. -1-2). 14.95 ***(978-1-77085-961-6(6)***, 9781770859616) Firefly Bks., Ltd.
Pretty Fabulous: Fashion Activity Book: Super Stylish Puzzles for Hours of Fun! 2012. (ENG.). 96p. (J). pap. 9.95 *(978-1-84858-541-6(1))* Arcturus Publishing GBR. Dist: Bookmasters Distribution.
Priddy, Roger. Around the Town. 2015. (Treasure Hunt Ser.). (ENG., Illus.). 10p. (J). (gr. -1 — 1). bds. 8.99 *(978-0-312-51797-7(1)*, 9780312517977, Priddy Bks.) St. Martin's Pr.
—Baby's Treasure Hunt. 2013. (Baby Basics Ser.). (ENG., Illus.). 16p. (J). (— 1). bds. 9.99 *(978-0-312-51502-7(2)*, 9780312515027, Priddy Bks.) St. Martin's Pr.
—Christmas Color. 2011. (ENG., Illus.). 36p. (J). (gr. -1-1). pap., act. bk. ed. 3.99 *(978-0-312-51097-8(7)*, 9780312510978, Priddy Bks.) St. Martin's Pr.
—Dot-to-Dot for Tiny Tots. 2014. (Dot to Dot Ser.). (ENG.). 64p. (J). (gr. -1 — 1). pap. 6.99 *(978-0-312-51716-8(5)*, 9780312517168, Priddy Bks.) St. Martin's Pr.
—Dot to Dot for Tiny Tots. 2014. (Dot to Dot Ser.). (ENG.). 64p. (J). (gr. -1 — 1). spiral bd. 12.99 *(978-0-312-51772-4(6)*, 9780312517724, Priddy Bks.) St. Martin's Pr.
—Dot-to-Dot Puzzles & Mazes. 2014. (Dot to Dot Ser.). (ENG.). 64p. (J). (gr. -1 — 1). pap. 6.99 *(978-0-312-51717-5(3)*, 9780312517175, Priddy Bks.) St. Martin's Pr.
—Hello Kitty: Wipe Clean Dot to Dot. 2015. (Hello Kitty Ser.). (ENG.). 56p. (J). (gr. -1-1). spiral bd. 12.99 *(978-0-312-51837-0(4)*, 9780312518370, Priddy Bks.) St. Martin's Pr.

—Play & Learn with Wallace: Giant Workbook. 2014. (Play & Learn with Wallace Ser.). (ENG.). 300p. (J). (gr. -1-1). pap. 12.99 *(978-0-312-51727-4(0)*, 9780312517274, Priddy Bks.) St. Martin's Pr.

—Priddy Learning: Number Puzzles. 2017. (ENG., Illus.). 32p. (J). pap. 4.99 *(978-0-312-52212-4(6)*, 9780312522124, Priddy Bks.) St. Martin's Pr.

—Treasure Hunt: Around the House. 2015. (Treasure Hunt Ser.). (ENG.). 10p. (J). (gr. -1 — 1). bds. 8.99 *(978-0-312-51795-3(5)*, 9780312517953, Priddy Bks.) St. Martin's Pr.

—Treasure Hunt: at the Zoo. 2015. (Treasure Hunt Ser.). (ENG., Illus.). 10p. (J). (gr. -1 — 1). bds. 8.99 *(978-0-312-51798-4(X)*, 9780312517984, Priddy Bks.) St. Martin's Pr.

—Treasure Hunt: on the Farm. 2015. (Treasure Hunt Ser.). (ENG., Illus.). 10p. (J). (gr. -1 — 1). bds. 8.99 *(978-0-312-51796-0(3)*, 9780312517960, Priddy Bks.) St. Martin's Pr.

—Wipe Clean: Picture Puzzles. 2015. (Wipe Clean Ser.). (ENG.). 26p. (J). (gr. -1-1). bds. 8.99 *(978-0-312-51789-2(0)*, 9780312517892, Priddy Bks.) St. Martin's Pr.

Publications International Ltd. Staff. Brain Games Picture Puzzle 1. 2008. 192p. spiral bd. 13.98 *(978-1-4127-1607-9(1)*, PIL Kids) Publications International, Ltd.

—Brain Games Picture Puzzle 2. 2008. 192p. spiral bd. 13.98 *(978-1-4127-1608-6(X)*, PIL Kids) Publications International, Ltd.

—Brain Games Picture Puzzle 3. 2008. 192p. spiral bd. 12.98 *(978-1-4127-9965-2(1)*, PIL Kids) Publications International, Ltd.

—Brain Games Picture Puzzle 4. 2008. 192p. spiral bd. 12.98 *(978-1-4127-9966-9(X)*, PIL Kids) Publications International, Ltd.

—Sound Pooh Clues. 2007. 14p. (J). 16.98 *(978-1-4127-6201-4(4))* Publications International, Ltd.

Publications International Ltd. Staff, creator. Disney Enchanted. 2007. (Interactive Play-A-Sound Ser.). (Illus.). (J). (gr. -1). 15.98 *(978-1-4127-8812-0(9))* Publications International, Ltd.

Publications International Ltd. Staff, ed. Brain Games: Logic Puzzles. 2011. 192p. (J). spiral bd. 8.98 *(978-1-4508-1574-1(X))* Publications International, Ltd.

—Brain Games Kids: Amazing Brain Builder Puzzles. 2010. 192p. (J). 13.98 *(978-1-60553-776-4(4))* Phoenix International Publications, Inc.

—Brain Games Kids: Awesome Brain Builder Puzzles. 2010. 192p. (J). 13.98 *(978-1-60553-777-1(2))* Phoenix International Publications, Inc.

—Brain Games Kids: First Grade. 2010. 192p. (J). spiral bd. 13.98 *(978-1-4508-0054-9(8))* Phoenix International Publications, Inc.

—Brain Games Kids: Kindergarten. 2010. 192p. (J). (gr. k-k). spiral bd. 9.99 *(978-1-4508-0053-2(X)*, 145080053X) Phoenix International Publications, Inc.

—Brain Games Kids: Picture Puzzles. 2011. 192p. (J). spiral bd. 13.98 *(978-1-4508-1711-0(4))* Phoenix International Publications, Inc.

—Brain Games Kids: Preschool. 2010. 192p. (J). spiral bd. 13.98 *(978-1-4508-0052-5(1))* Phoenix International Publications, Inc.

—Brain Games Kids: Super Brain Builder Puzzles. 2010. 192p. (J). 13.98 *(978-1-60553-775-7(6))* Phoenix International Publications, Inc.

—Brain Games Kids: Word Search. 2011. 192p. (J). spiral bd. 13.98 *(978-1-4508-1573-4(1))* Phoenix International Publications, Inc.

—Counting Memory Game Puzzle. 2010. (J). 13.98 *(978-1-60553-350-6(5))* Publications International, Ltd.

—Disney Pixar Cars: First Look & Find & Shaped Puzzle Box Set. 2010. (J). 22.98 *(978-1-4508-0136-2(6))* Publications International, Ltd.

—Disney Pixar Picture Puzzle. 2010. 128p. (J). spiral bd. 12.98 *(978-1-60553-132-8(4))* Phoenix International Publications, Inc.

—Disney Princess First Look & Find & Giant Puzzle. 2010. (J). 22.98 *(978-1-4508-0135-5(8))* Publications International, Ltd.

—Disney Princesses. 2009. 16p. (J). bds. 9.98 *(978-1-4127-7696-7(1)*, PIL Kids) Publications International, Ltd.

—Kindergarten Boot Camp. 2010. (J). 20.98 *(978-1-4508-0069-3(6))* Publications International, Ltd.

—My First U.S. Map Puzzle. 2010. (J). 13.98 *(978-1-60553-306-3(8))* Publications International, Ltd.

—Play-a-Puzzle trade; Book: Alphabet. 2010. 12p. (J). bds. 10.98 *(978-1-60553-799-3(3))* Publications International, Ltd.

—Sesame Street Picture Puzzle. 2010. 128p. (J). spiral bd. 12.98 *(978-1-60553-130-4(8)*, PIL Kids) Publications International, Ltd.

—Solar System Puzzle. 2010. (J). 13.98 *(978-1-60553-351-3(3))* Publications International, Ltd.

The Puzzle: Individual Title-Six Packs. (Chiquilibros Ser.). (gr. k-1). 23.00 *(978-0-7635-0440-3(8))* Rigby Education.

Puzzle Society Staff. Girl Hangman 2: 100 Puzzles. 2011. (ENG.). 112p. pap. 7.99 *(978-1-4494-0733-9(1))* Andrews McMeel Publishing.

—Pocket Posh Girl Hangman: 100 Puzzles. 2010. (ENG.). 112p. pap. 7.99 *(978-0-7407-9861-0(8))* Andrews McMeel Publishing.

—Pocket Posh Girl Sudoku: 100 Puzzles. 2010. (ENG.). 128p. pap. 7.99 *(978-0-7407-9858-0(8))* Andrews McMeel Publishing.

—Pocket Posh Girl Sudoku 2 Vol. 2: 100 Puzzles. 2011. (ENG.). 128p. pap. 7.99 *(978-1-4494-0738-4(2))* Andrews McMeel Publishing.

—Pocket Posh Girl Word Search: 100 Puzzles. 2010. (ENG.). 128p. pap. 7.99 *(978-0-7407-9859-7(6))* Andrews McMeel Publishing.

—Pocket Posh Girl Word Search 2 Vol. 2: 100 Puzzles. 2011. (ENG.). 128p. pap. 7.99 *(978-1-4494-0740-7(4))* Andrews McMeel Publishing.

Radtke, Becky. Little Animals Hidden Pictures. 2006. (Dover Little Activity Bks.). (ENG., Illus.). 64p. (J). (gr. 3-5). per. 1.99 *(978-0-486-44899-2(1))* Dover Pubns., Inc.

—Trains Activity Book. 2007. (Dover Little Activity Bks.). (ENG., Illus.). 64p. (J). (gr. k-3). per. 1.99 *(978-0-486-45683-6(8))* Dover Pubns., Inc.

Radtke, Becky J. SPARK Theme Park Maze Craze. 2017. (Dover Children's Activity Bks.). (ENG.). 64p. (J). (gr. 1-4). pap. 5.99 *(978-0-486-81587-9(0))* Dover Pubns., Inc.

—Super Rides & Water Slides Mazes. 2012. (Dover Children's Activity Bks.). (ENG.). 48p. (J). (gr. k-3). pap. 4.99 *(978-0-486-48173-9(5))* Dover Pubns., Inc.

Raffin, Deborah. Mitzi's World: Seek & Discover More Than 150 Details in 15 Works of Folk Art. Scott, Jane Wooster, illus. 2009. (ENG.). 32p. (J). (gr. k-2). 18.95 *(978-0-8109-8004-4(5)*, Abrams Bks. for Young Readers) Abrams, Inc.

Rainbow Publishers Staff. More Bible Puzzles: Life of Jesus. 2004. (Reproducible Activity Books Ser.). (Illus.). 64p. (J). (gr. 4-18). pap. 9.95 *(978-0-937282-57-1(X)*, RB36158) Rainbow Pubs. & Legacy Pr.

—More Bible Puzzles: Memory Verse. 2004. (Reproducible Activity Books Ser.). (Illus.). 64p. (J). (gr. 4-18). pap. 9.95 *(978-0-937282-58-8(8)*, RB36159) Rainbow Pubs. & Legacy Pr.

—More Bible Puzzles: New Testament. 2004. (Reproducible Activity Books Ser.). (Illus.). 64p. (J). (gr. 4-18). pap. 9.95 *(978-0-937282-56-4(1)*, RB36157) Rainbow Pubs. & Legacy Pr.

Rand McNally. Are We There Yet? Awty. 2015. (ENG.). (J). (gr. 4-7). pap. 6.99 *(978-0-528-01340-9(8))* Rand McNally.

Rand McNally, creator. Coast-To-Coast Games. 2015. (ENG.). (J). (gr. 4-7). pap. 6.99 *(978-0-528-01342-3(4))* Rand McNally.

Rao, Lisa. Surf's Up. Merkel, Joe F. & Sazaklis, John, illus. 2007. (Surf's Up Ser.). 32p. (J). (gr. -1-2). 4.99 *(978-0-06-115335-8(4)*, Harper Entertainment) HarperCollins Pubs.

Rath, Robert. Go Wild for Puzzles Glacier National Park. Rath, Robert, illus. 2008. (Illus.). 32p. (J). (gr. k-3). pap. 5.95 *(978-1-56037-428-2(4))* Farcountry Pr.

—Go Wild Puzzles: Great Smoky Mountains National Park. 2007. (Illus.). 32p. (J). pap. 5.95 *(978-1-56037-406-0(3))* Farcountry Pr.

Read, Howard & Chantler, Chris. Little Howard's Big Book. 2011. (ENG., Illus.). 128p. (J). pap. 15.99 *(978-0-00-739125-7(0))* HarperCollins Pubs. Ltd. GBR. Dist: Independent Pubs. Group.

Really Horrible Facts. 2013. (Really Horrible Facts Ser.). 32p. (J). (gr. k-3). 101.00 *(978-1-61533-868-9(3))*; pap. 40.00 *(978-1-61533-876-4(4))*; pap. 240.00 *(978-1-61533-877-1(2))* Windmill Bks.

Red, White & Blue: The Search for Liberty. 2004. (J). cd-rom 19.95 *(978-1-931203-11-1(3))* Inspired Idea.

Regan, Dana, illus. Hidden Pictures Alphabet. 2004. (ENG.). 32p. (J). pap. 2.99 *(978-1-58947-395-9(7)*, 02197) School Zone Publishing Co.

Regan, Lisa. Dinosaur Puzzles. 2012. (ENG.). 144p. (J). pap. 7.95 *(978-1-84858-539-3(X))* Arcturus Publishing GBR. Dist: Bookmasters Distribution.

—Monster Puzzles. 2012. (ENG.). 144p. (J). pap. 7.95 *(978-1-84858-536-2(5))* Arcturus Publishing GBR. Dist: Bookmasters Distribution.

—Pirate Puzzles. 2012. (ENG.). 144p. (J). pap. 7.95 *(978-1-84858-538-6(1))* Arcturus Publishing GBR. Dist: Bookmasters Distribution.

—Princess Puzzles. 2012. (ENG.). 144p. (J). pap. 7.95 *(978-1-84858-537-9(3))* Arcturus Publishing GBR. Dist: Bookmasters Distribution.

—The Totally Brilliant Puzzle & Drawing Book: Can You Be the First to Spot the Yellow Pencil? 2012. (ENG.). 208p. (J). pap. 9.95 *(978-1-84858-472-3(5))* Arcturus Publishing GBR. Dist: Bookmasters Distribution.

—The Totally Brilliant Super Puzzle Book. 2013. (ENG.). 208p. (J). pap. 9.95 *(978-1-84858-941-4(7))* Arcturus Publishing GBR. Dist: Bookmasters Distribution.

Reid, Struan. Pirate Jigsaw Book. Allen, Peter, illus. 2007. (Luxury Jigsaw Bks.). 14p. (J). bds. 14.99 *(978-0-7945-1432-7(4)*, Usborne) EDC Publishing.

Reid, Struan & Stowell, Louie. My First Pirate Book. Allen, Peter, illus. 2012. (My First Book Ser.). 16p. (J). ring bd. 6.99 *(978-0-7945-3228-4(4)*, Usborne) EDC Publishing.

Rey, H. A. Curious Baby Everyday Shapes Puzzle Book: A Puzzle Play Book. 2012. (Curious Baby Curious George Ser.). (ENG., Illus.). 12p. (J). (gr. -1 — 1). bds. 8.99 *(978-0-547-63232-2(0))* Houghton Mifflin Harcourt Publishing Co.

—Where Is Curious George? Around the Town: A Look-And-Find Book. 2015. (Curious George Ser.). (ENG., Illus.). 32p. (J). (gr. -1-3). 9.99 *(978-0-544-38072-1(X)*, HMH Books For Young Readers) Houghton Mifflin Harcourt Publishing Co.

RH Disney Staff. Inside My Mind: A Book about Me! RH Disney Staff, illus. 2015. (Disney Chapters Ser.). (ENG., Illus.). 128p. (J). (gr. 1-4). 6.99 *(978-0-7364-3286-3(8)*, RH/Disney) Random Hse. Children's Bks.

Rhatigan, Joe. The Ultimate Activity Book for Mad Scientists. Owsley, Anthony, illus. 2017. (Just a Pencil Gets You Many Days of Fun Ser.). (ENG.). 144p. (J). (gr. 3-9). pap., act. bk. ed. 7.95 *(978-1-63322-163-5(6)*, Moondance) Quarto Publishing Group USA.

—The Ultimate Brain Bender Activity Book. Owsley, Anthony, illus. 2017. (Just a Pencil Gets You Many Days of Fun Ser.). (ENG.). 144p. (J). (gr. 3-9). pap., act. bk. ed. 7.95 *(978-1-63322-162-8(8)*, Moondance) Quarto Publishing Group USA.

Rhodes, Immacula A. & Scholastic Teaching Resources Staff. Phonics Picture Puzzles for Little Learners: Dozens of Age-Perfect Practice Pages That Help Children Build Key Phonics Skills, Grades K-2. 2011. (ENG.). 48p. (gr. k-2). pap. 10.99 *(978-0-545-31881-5(5)*, Teaching Resources) Scholastic, Inc.

Rinaldo, Luana, illus. Matching Puzzle Cards - Colors. 2012. (ENG.). 36p. (J). (gr. k-12). 9.99 *(978-1-60905-220-1(X))* Blue Apple Bks.

Ritchey, Adam. Out-of-Sight Photo Puzzles: Spot the Differences & More! 2010. (ENG., Illus.). 144p. (gr. 5). pap. 9.95 *(978-1-4027-7080-7(4)*, Puzzlewright) Sterling Publishing Co., Inc.

Ritchie, Scot. Up, up & Away! Ritchie, Scot, illus. 2005. (Illus.). 32p. pap. *(978-1-921049-01-9(4))* Little Hare Bks. AUS. Dist: HarperCollins Pubs. Australia.

Ritchie, Scott. Ghouliest Ever Puzzle Book: Ghosts & Ghouls. 2008. 32p. (J). pap. *(978-1-921272-62-2(7))* Little Hare Bks. AUS. Dist: HarperCollins Pubs. Australia.

Rivera, Nicole. A Glimpse into Max's World (Max's Mini Puzzle Book) 2011. (ENG.). 40p. pap. 7.99 *(978-1-4610-7663-6(3))* CreateSpace Independent Publishing Platform.

Robertson, Barny & Robertson, Carter, told to. The Christmas Puzzle: An Easy-to-Sing, Easy-to-Stage Kids' Christmas Musical about How We're All Part of God's Picture. 2010. (ENG.). 48p. pap. 5.99 *(978-0-8341-7784-0(6)*, 9780834177840) Lillenas Publishing Co.

Robson, Kirsteen. My First Maze Book. 2015. (Maze Bks.). (ENG.). 32p. (J). pap. 5.99 *(978-0-7945-3468-4(6)*, Usborne) EDC Publishing.

—Third Big Maze Book. 2015. (Maze Bks.). (ENG.). 64p. (J). (gr. k-5). pap. 9.99 *(978-0-7945-3491-2(0)*, Usborne) EDC Publishing.

Rogers, Kirsteen. Under the Sea Jigsaw Book. Scott, Peter, illus. 2007. (Luxury Jigsaw Bks.). 14p. (J). bds. 14.99 *(978-0-7945-1330-6(1)*, Usborne) EDC Publishing.

Rosen Publishing Staff. Brain Games, 1 vol. 2015. (Brain Games Ser.). (ENG.). 32p. (J). 110.00 *(978-1-4777-5457-3(1)*, Windmill Bks.) Rosen Publishing Group, Inc., The.

Ross, Jesse Paul & Puzzling Sports Institute Staff. Slapshot Hockey Quizbook: 50 Fun Games Brought to You by the Puzzling Sports Institute. unabr. ed. 2009. (ENG.). 80p. pap. 8.95 *(978-0-88971-234-8(4))* Nightwood Editions CAN. Dist: Midpoint Trade Bks., Inc.

Ross, Suzanne. Nature Mazes. 2012. (Dover Little Activity Bks.). (ENG., Illus.). 64p. (J). (gr. k-3). pap. 1.50 *(978-0-486-28221-3(X))* Dover Pubns., Inc.

Rowe, Jeanette. First 1, 2, 3. 2016. (I Spy with My Little Eye... Bks.). (ENG.). 16p. (J). (gr. -1-k). bds. 9.99 *(978-0-7641-6815-4(0))* Barron's Educational Series, Inc.

—First Words. 2016. (I Spy with My Little Eye... Bks.). (ENG.). 16p. (J). (gr. -1-k). bds. 9.99 *(978-0-7641-6816-1(9))* Barron's Educational Series, Inc.

Roxbee-Cox, Phil. Find the Kitten. Cartwright, Stephen, illus. rev. ed. 2004. (Treasury of Farmyard Tales Ser.). (ENG.). 1p. (J). bds. 3.99 *(978-0-7460-3822-2(4))* EDC Publishing.

Roxbee-Cox, Phil, et al. El Reino de los Juguetes. 2004.Tr. of Magic Toyshop. (SPA., Illus.). 32p. (J). (gr. -1-3). lib. bdg. 14.95 *(978-1-58086-215-8(2)*, EU1202) EDC Publishing.

The Royals: PRINCE WILLIAM & KATE MIDDLETON - Puzzle: PRINCE WILLIAM & KATE MIDDLETON - Puzzle. 2011. 34.95 *(978-1-4507-6248-9(4))* Bluewater Productions, Inc.

Russell, Ken & Carter, Philip. Bumper Quiz Book for Kids. (Illus.). 160p. (J). 17.95 *(978-1-85479-300-3(4))* O'Mara, Michael Bks., Ltd. GBR. Dist: Trans-Atlantic Pubns., Inc.

Russo, David Anson. Around the World: The Great Treasure Hunt. Russo, David Anson, illus. 2011. (ENG., Illus.). 28p. (J). (gr. 4-6). pap. 14.99 *(978-1-4424-4343-3(X)*, Simon & Schuster Bks. For Young Readers) Simon & Schuster Bks. For Young Readers.

Russo, M. Great Book of Dot to Dot: Omnibus Edition. Date not set. (J). 19.95 *(978-0-8069-6140-8(6))* Sterling Publishing Co., Inc.

Russo, Monica. Mythical Animals Dot-to-Dot. 2003. (Illus.). 64p. (J). (gr. 5-7). pap. 5.95 *(978-0-8069-9716-2(8))* Sterling Publishing Co., Inc.

Rutherford, Peter, illus. Giant Fun-to-Find Puzzles Busy Animals: Search for Pictures in Eight Exciting Scenes. 2015. (ENG.). 24p. pap. 6.99 *(978-1-86147-460-5(1)*, Armadillo) Anness Publishing GBR. Dist: National Bk. Network.

Sandau, Carol E. 10 Puzzling Pieces. 2010. 80p. pap. 8.95 *(978-1-4502-6244-6(9))* iUniverse, Inc.

Santana, Sr. Sabina Stella. Happy Ending Children's Stories, & More: Poems, Tongue-Twisters, Proverbs, & Brain-Teasers. 2008. 64p. pap. 13.50 *(978-1-4303-1344-1(7))* Lulu Pr., Inc.

Santa's House Activity Fun. Date not set. (Christmas Activity Bks.). (Illus.). 128p. (J). 3.98 *(978-0-7525-6498-2(6))* Parragon, Inc.

Santillan, Jorge. When's the Doctor? 2012. (ENG., Illus.). 40p. (YA). 14.99 *(978-1-4059-0849-8(1)*, 9781405908498) Penguin Bks., Ltd. GBR. Dist: Diamond Comic Distributors, Inc.

—When's the Doctor? 2nd ed. 2014. (ENG., Illus.). 48p. (YA). pap. 7.99 *(978-1-4059-1720-9(2)*, 9781405917209) Penguin Bks., Ltd. GBR. Dist: Diamond Comic Distributors, Inc.

Sauerhofer, Ulrike. I Spy 123: Totally Crazy Numbers. Ancutici, Manuela, photos by. 2017. (ENG., Illus.). 32p. (J). (gr. -1-2). 14.95 ***(978-1-77085-999-9(3)***, 9781770859999) Firefly Bks., Ltd.

Scarry, Richard. Best Busytown. 2013. (ENG., Illus.). 118p. (J). (gr. -1-2). pap., act. bk. ed. 14.95 *(978-1-4027-7315-0(3))* Sterling Publishing Co., Inc.

Schimmell, David. Wizard of Oz. 2011. (Dover Children's Activity Bks.). (ENG., Illus.). 48p. (J). (gr. 2-5). pap., act. bk. ed. 4.99 *(978-0-486-48095-4(X))* Dover Pubns., Inc.

Schlegl, William. Parable Puzzlers: Word Puzzles from Jesus' Parables. 2008. 64p. pap. 10.99 *(978-0-7586-1336-3(9))* Concordia Publishing Hse.

Scholastic, Inc. Staff. I Spy Treasure Hunt. 2008. 29.99 *(978-0-439-82069-1(3))* Scholastic, Inc.

Scholastic, Inc. Staff, contrib. by. Math Picture Puzzles for Little Learners: Dozens of Age-Perfect Practice Pages That Help Children Build Key Early Math Skills, Grades PreK-K. 2011. (ENG.). 48p. pap. 10.99 *(978-0-545-30068-1(1)*, Teaching Resources) Scholastic, Inc.

School Zone Publishing Company Staff. Vocabulary Puzzles 2. (Illus.). (J). 19.99 incl. audio compact disk *(978-0-88743-968-1(3))* School Zone Publishing Co.

School Zone Staff. Big Mazes & More. 2009. 320p. (J). pap. 12.99 *(978-1-60159-257-6(4))* School Zone Publishing Co.

—Dot-To-Dot Numbers. 2004. (ENG.). 32p. (J). pap. 2.99 *(978-1-58947-385-0(X)*, 02190) School Zone Publishing Co.

—My First Dot-To-Dots. 2009. (J). pap. 1.50 net. *(978-1-60159-246-0(9))* School Zone Publishing Co.

—My First Hidden Pictures. 2009. (J). pap. 2.99 *(978-1-60159-251-4(5))* School Zone Publishing Co.

—My First Mazes. 2009. (J). pap. 2.99 *(978-1-60159-247-7(7))* School Zone Publishing Co.

School Zone Staff, ed. Dot-To-Dot Alphabet. 2006. (ENG.). 32p. (J). pap. 2.99 *(978-1-58947-393-5(0)*, 02195) School Zone Publishing Co.

—Hidden Pictures Around the World. 2006. (ENG.). 32p. (J). pap. 2.99 *(978-1-58947-387-4(6)*, 02192) School Zone Publishing Co.

Schuette, Sarah L. Animals Everywhere: A Spot-It Challenge, 1 vol. 2010. (Spot It Ser.). (ENG.). 32p. (gr. 1-2). lib. bdg. 27.32 *(978-1-4296-4461-7(3)*, Aplus Bks.) Capstone Press of Coughlan Cos.

—Colors & Patterns! A Spot-It, Learn-It Challenge, 1 vol. 2014. (Spot It, Learn It! Ser.). (ENG.). 32p. (gr. 1-2). lib. bdg. 27.32 *(978-1-4765-4011-5(X)*, Aplus Bks.) Capstone Press of Coughlan Cos.

—Football Frenzy: A Spot-It Challenge, 1 vol. 2013. (Spot It Ser.). (ENG.). 32p. (gr. 1-2). lib. bdg. 27.32 *(978-1-62065-062-2(2)*, Aplus Bks.) Capstone Press of Coughlan Cos.

—Happy Birthday! A Spot-It Challenge, 1 vol. 2012. (Spot It Ser.). (ENG., Illus.). 32p. (gr. 1-2). lib. bdg. 27.32 *(978-1-4296-7560-4(8)*, Aplus Bks.) Capstone Press of Coughlan Cos.

—Hockey Scramble: A Spot-It Challenge, 1 vol. 2013. (Spot It Ser.). (ENG.). 32p. (gr. 1-2). lib. bdg. 27.32 *(978-1-62065-063-9(0)*, Aplus Bks.) Capstone Press of Coughlan Cos.

—Pets All Around: A Spot-It Challenge, 1 vol. 2012. (Spot It Ser.). (ENG.). 32p. (gr. 1-2). lib. bdg. 27.32 *(978-1-4296-8713-3(4))* Capstone Press of Coughlan Cos.

—Princesses & Fairy Tales: A Spot-It Challenge, 1 vol. 2011. (Spot It Ser.). (ENG.). 32p. (gr. 1-2). lib. bdg. 27.32 *(978-1-4296-5987-1(4)*, Aplus Bks.) Capstone Press of Coughlan Cos.

—Season Search: A Spot-It Challenge, 1 vol. 2010. (Spot It Ser.). (ENG.). 32p. (gr. 1-2). lib. bdg. 27.32 *(978-1-4296-5261-2(6)*, Aplus Bks.) Capstone Press of Coughlan Cos.

—Sports Zone: A Spot-It Challenge, 1 vol. 2012. (Spot It Ser.). (ENG.). 32p. (gr. 1-2). lib. bdg. 27.32 *(978-1-4296-8712-6(6))* Capstone Press of Coughlan Cos.

—Spot It. (Spot It Ser.). (ENG.). 32p. (gr. 1-2). 2012. lib. bdg. 54.64 *(978-1-4296-9114-7(X))* 2011. lib. bdg. 54.64 *(978-1-4296-6033-4(3))* Capstone Press of Coughlan Cos. (Aplus Bks.).

—100th Day: A Spot-It Challenge, 1 vol. 2012. (Spot It Ser.). (ENG., Illus.). 32p. (gr. 1-2). lib. bdg. 27.32 *(978-1-4296-7559-8(4)*, Aplus Bks.) Capstone Press of Coughlan Cos.

Schuette, Sarah L. & Marks, Jennifer L. Spot It. 2013. (Spot It Ser.). (ENG.). 32p. (gr. 1-2). lib. bdg. 54.64 *(978-1-62065-064-6(9)*, Aplus Bks.) Capstone Press of Coughlan Cos.

Schuh, Mari C. Basketball. 2017. (Spot Sports Ser.). (ENG.). 16p. (gr. k-3). 17.95 ***(978-1-68151-084-2(7))*** Amicus Publishing.

—Football. 2017. (Spot Sports Ser.). (ENG.). 16p. (gr. k-3). 17.95 ***(978-1-68151-086-6(3))*** Amicus Publishing.

—Gymnastics. 2017. (Spot Sports Ser.). (ENG.). 16p. (gr. k-3). 17.95 ***(978-1-68151-087-3(1))*** Amicus Publishing.

—Hockey. 2017. (Spot Sports Ser.). (ENG.). 16p. (gr. k-3). 17.95 ***(978-1-68151-088-0(X))*** Amicus Publishing.

—Soccer. 2017. (Spot Sports Ser.). (ENG.). 16p. (gr. k-3). 17.95 ***(978-1-68151-089-7(8))*** Amicus Publishing.

Schwartz, Linda. Language Critical Thinking, Grades 2-4: Creative Puzzles to Challenge the Brain. Armstrong, Bev & Grayson, Rick, illus. 2005. 64p. (J). pap. 11.99 *(978-0-88160-384-2(8)*, LW423, Learning Works, The) Creative Teaching Pr., Inc.

Scott, Matthew. Search & Find Puzzle Island: Picture Puzzles, Number Games, Amazing Mazes, Treasure Hunt. 2012. (ENG.). 64p. (J). pap. 10.95 *(978-1-84858-358-0(3))* Arcturus Publishing GBR. Dist: Bookmasters Distribution.

Scott, Peter & Justine, Torode, illus. Box of Bugs. 2005. 6p. (J). 11.95 *(978-0-7945-1023-7(X)*, Usborne) EDC Publishing.

Sector, Emma & Smith, Allie. There Are No Wrong Answers: A Book of Quizzes. 2016. (ENG., Illus.). 192p. (J). (gr. 3-7). pap. 7.99 *(978-1-4814-5932-7(5)*, Aladdin) Simon & Schuster Children's Publishing.

Seuss, Dr. Oh, the Places I'll Go! by ME, Myself. Gerardi, Jan, illus. 2016. (ENG.). 64p. (J). (gr. -1-3). 15.00 *(978-0-553-52058-3(X)*, Random Hse. Bks. for Young Readers) Random Hse. Children's Bks.

Sevaly, Karen, ed. Beginning Sound Puzzles. 2006. (Scholastic Hands-on Learning Ser.). (ENG.). 12.99 *(978-0-439-82387-6(0)*, Teaching Resources) Scholastic, Inc.

—Classifying Puzzles. 2006. (Scholastic Hands-on Learning Ser.). (ENG.). 12.99 *(978-0-439-82392-0(7)*, Teaching Resources) Scholastic, Inc.

—Rhyming Puzzles. 2006. (Scholastic Hands-on Learning Ser.). (ENG.). 12.99 *(978-0-439-82390-6(0)*, Teaching Resources) Scholastic, Inc.

Sevaly, Karen & Scholastic, Inc. Staff. Counting Money Puzzles. 2007. (ENG.). (J). (gr. k-2). pap. 12.99 *(978-0-439-91217-4(2))* Scholastic, Inc.

Shadow, Jak. Crime Lord. 2006. (F. E. A. R. Adventures S. Ser.). (ENG., Illus.). 128p. (J). 8.00 *(978-1-84046-693-5(6)*, Wizard Books) Icon Bks., Ltd. GBR. Dist: Publishers Group Canada.

Shaw-Russell, Susan. Seek, Sketch & Color — Alphabet. 2013. (Dover Children's Activity Bks.). (ENG.). 64p. (J). (gr. 1-3). pap. 5.99 *(978-0-486-49772-3(0))* Dover Pubns., Inc.

—Snow White Activity Book. 2012. (Dover Little Activity Bks.). (ENG.). 64p. (J). (gr. k-3). pap. 1.50 *(978-0-486-47226-3(4))* Dover Pubns., Inc.

Shaw-Russell, Susan & Activity Books Staff. Tortoise & the Hare. 2012. (Dover Little Activity Bks.). (ENG., Illus.). 64p. (J). (gr. k-3). pap., act. bk. ed. 1.50 *(978-0-486-47518-9(2))* Dover Pubns., Inc.

Shears, William. My Little Pony. Utopia, illus. 2005. (Look & Find Ser.). 18p. (J). (gr. -1-3). pap. 24.98 *(978-1-4127-3316-8(2)*, 7241700) Publications International, Ltd.

Simon, Francesca. Gold Medal Games. Ross, Tony, illus. 2017. (Horrid Henry Ser.). (ENG.). 24p. (J). (gr. 1-3). pap. 8.99 ***(978-1-5101-0127-2(6)***, Orion Children's Bks.) Hachette Children's Group GBR. Dist: Hachette Bk. Group.

Simpson, Dana. Rainy Day Unicorn Fun: Phoebe & Her Unicorn. 2017. (ENG.). 144p. (J). pap., act. bk. ed. 8.99 **(978-1-4494-8725-6(4))** Andrews McMeel Publishing.

Sims, L. Puzzle Journey Around the World. 2004. (Puzzle Journey Ser.). 32p. (J). pap. 6.95 (978-0-7945-0510-3(4)) EDC Publishing.

—Puzzle Journey into Space. 2004. (Puzzle Journey Ser.). 32p. (J). pap. 6.95 (978-0-7945-0439-7(6)) EDC Publishing.

—Puzzle Journey under the Sea. 2004. (Puzzle Journey Ser.). 32p. (J). pap. 6.95 (978-0-7945-0481-6(7)) EDC Publishing.

Smart, Jamie. Where's the Doctor? 2017. (ENG., Illus.). 40p. (YA). pap. 9.99 (978-1-4059-0904-4(8), 9781405909044) Penguin Bks., Ltd. GBR. Dist: Diamond Comic Distributors, Inc.

SMARTLAB Creative Team. Mega 3D Puzzle Play Dinosaurs. 2010. 3p. mass mkt. 19.99 (978-1-60380-092-1(1)) becker&mayer! books.

—Mega 3D Puzzle Play Sharks. 2010. 3p. mass mkt. 19.99 (978-1-60380-094-5(8)) becker&mayer! books.

Smith, Penny & Dorling Kindersley Publishing Staff. Animal Hide & Seek. 2006. (DK Readers Ser.). (ENG., Illus.). 32p. (J). (gr. k-2). pap. 3.99 (978-0-7566-1961-9(0), DK Children) Dorling Kindersley Publishing, Inc.

Smolik, Jane Petrlik. The Great Massachusetts Puzzle Book: Over 75 Puzzles about Life in the Bay State. rev. ed. 2005. (Illus.). 96p. (J). (gr. 2-7). per. 11.95 (978-0-9664095-5-0(8)) MidRun Pr.

—The Great State of Maine Activity Book: Over 75 Puzzles about Life in Maine. rev. ed. 2006. (Illus.). 96p. (J). (gr. 2-7). per. 11.95 (978-0-9664095-6-7(6)) MidRun Pr.

Snape, Charles & Snape, Juliet. Brain Busters: Games, Puzzles & More! 2012. (Dover Children's Activity Bks.). (ENG., Illus.). 64p. (J). (gr. 3-5). pap. 9.99 (978-0-486-48779-3(2)) Dover Pubns., Inc.

—Mind Twisters: Games, Puzzles & More! 2012. (Dover Children's Activity Bks.). (ENG., Illus.). 64p. (J). (gr. 3-5). pap. 9.99 (978-0-486-48780-9(6)) Dover Pubns., Inc.

Snider, Brandon T. Brain Food. 2013. (Plants vs. Zombies Ser.). (ENG.). 224p. (J). (gr. 1-5). 10.99 (978-0-06-229492-0(X), HarperFestival) HarperCollins Pubs.

Sohn, Emily & Brennan, Joseph. Balance & Motion: Toying with Gravity. 2011. (iScience Readers Ser.). 24p. (J). (gr. k-2). lib. bdg. 21.27 (978-1-59953-405-3(3)) Norwood Hse. Pr.

—Magnetism & Electricity: The Broken Toy Car. 2011. (iScience Readers Ser.). 32p. (J). (gr. 3-4). lib. bdg. 22.60 (978-1-59953-415-2(0)) Norwood Hse. Pr.

Sohn, Emily & Townsend, Laura. Patterns & Textures: Who Took the Pets? 2011. (iScience Readers Ser.). 32p. (J). (gr. 3-4). lib. bdg. 22.60 (978-1-59953-414-5(2)) Norwood Hse. Pr.

Sohn, Emily & Tsang, Nina. Matter & Energy: Finding the Power. 2011. (iScience Readers Ser.). 32p. (J). (gr. 3-4). lib. bdg. 22.60 (978-1-59953-416-9(9)) Norwood Hse. Pr.

Somper, Justin. Pyramid Plot. Wingham, Peter, illus. 2004. (Puzzle Adventures Ser.). 48p. (J). pap. 4.95 (978-0-7945-0139-6(7), Usborne) EDC Publishing.

Space: Puzzles & Games. 2009. (BOREDOM BUSTERS Ser.). 56p. (J). (gr. 2-7). pap. 4.99 (978-0-8416-1092-7(4)) American Map Corp.

Spelling Is Fun. 2004. (Play & Learn Pads Ser.). 48p. (J). 3.99 (978-1-85997-721-7(9)) Byeway Bks.

Sports. 2009. (BOREDOM BUSTERS Ser.). 56p. (J). (gr. 2-7). pap. 4.99 (978-0-8416-1090-3(8)) American Map Corp.

Spot It. 2010. (Spot It Ser.). (ENG.). 32p. (gr. 1-2). lib. bdg. 54.64 (978-1-4296-4724-3(8), Aplus Bks.) Capstone Press of Coughlan Cos.

Stadther, Michael. 101 New Puzzles Clues, Maps, Tantalizing Tales: And Stories of Real Treasure. Stadther, Michael, illus. 2006. (Treasure's Trove Ser.). (ENG., Illus.). 112p. (J). pap. 12.99 (978-1-4169-2655-9(0)) Treasure Trove, Inc.

Standard Publishing Staff. Bible Puzzles for Kids, Ages 6-8. 2016. (ENG., Illus.). 144p. (J). (gr. -1-3). per. 16.99 (978-0-7847-1787-5(7), 02260) Standard Publishing.

Stanley, Stephen. City of Lost Mazes. 2013. (ENG., Illus.). 32p. (J). (gr. 3-8). pap. 5.99 (978-0-486-49133-2(1)) Dover Pubns., Inc.

—The Haunted Maze. 2013. (ENG., Illus.). 32p. (J). (gr. 3-8). pap. 5.99 (978-0-486-49134-9(X)) Dover Pubns., Inc.

Stead, Emily. Things That Go! With 200 Stickers, Puzzles & Games, Fold-Out Pages, & Creative Play. 2013. (My First Creativity Bks.). (ENG.). 66p. (J). (gr. -1-2). pap. 9.99 (978-1-4380-0324-5(2)) Barron's Educational Series, Inc.

Steinbacher, Philip A. Quotation Quizzlers: Puzzling Your Way Through Famous Quotations. 2003. (J). per. 11.95 (978-1-883055-60-8(1), 151) Dandy Lion Pubns.

Steiner, Joan. Look-Alikes: The More You Look, the More You See! Steiner, Joan, illus. Lindley, Thomas, photos by. rev. ed. 2003. (ENG., Illus.). 32p. (J). (gr. -1-3). 17.99 (978-0-316-71348-1(1)) Little, Brown Bks. for Young Readers.

—Look-Alikes Jr. The More You Look, the More You See! Steiner, Joan, illus. rev. ed. 2003. (ENG., Illus.). 32p. (J). (gr. -1-3). 17.99 (978-0-316-71347-4(3)) Little, Brown Bks. for Young Readers.

—Look-Alikes Seek-and-Search Puzzles. 2011. (ENG., Illus.). 56p. (J). (gr. -1-3). pap. 7.99 (978-0-316-07407-0(1)) Little, Brown Bks. for Young Readers.

Sterling Publishing Company Staff, creator. Dot to Dot Count To 25. 2007. (ENG., Illus.). 64p. (J). (gr. -1). per. 4.95 (978-1-4027-4626-0(1)) Sterling Publishing Co., Inc.

Stewart, Trenton Lee. Mr. Benedict's Book of Perplexing Puzzles, Elusive Enigmas, & Curious Conundrums. Sudyka, Diana, illus. 2011. (Mysterious Benedict Society Ser.). (ENG.). 176p. (J). (gr. 3-7). 15.99 (978-0-316-18193-8(5)) Little, Brown Bks. for Young Readers.

—The Mysterious Benedict Society: Mr. Benedict's Book of Perplexing Puzzles, Elusive Enigmas, & Curious Conundrums. Sudyka, Diana, illus. 2016. (Mysterious Benedict Society Ser.). (ENG.). 176p. (J). (gr. 3-7). pap. 9.99 (978-0-316-39475-8(0)) Little, Brown Bks. for Young Readers.

Stride, Lottie. Meerkat Mischief. Stride, Lottie, illus. 2012. (ENG., Illus.). 64p. (J). (gr. 1-4). pap., act. bk. ed. 7.99 (978-1-78055-009-1(X)) O'Mara, Michael Bks., Ltd. GBR. Dist: Independent Pubs. Group.

Studio Mouse Staff. Spelling Fun. 2011. (Cars Ser.). (Illus.). 28p. (J). 15.99 (978-1-59069-938-6(6)) Studio Mouse LLC.

Super Activity Pad. Date not set. 384p. (J). 7.98 (978-0-7525-9573-3(3)) Parragon, Inc.

Super Puzzle Pad. Date not set. (Illus.). 384p. (J). 7.98 (978-0-7525-9575-7(X)) Parragon, Inc.

Super Puzzles. 2004. 112p. (J). 4.99 (978-1-85997-388-2(4)) Byeway Bks.

Super Travel Pad. Date not set. 384p. (J). 7.98 (978-0-7525-9576-4(8)) Parragon, Inc.

Tallarico, Tony, Sr. Everyday Fun for Kids. 2016. (Dover Little Activity Bks.). (ENG.). 64p. (J). (gr. k-3). pap. 1.99 (978-0-486-80760-7(6)) Dover Pubns., Inc.

Tallarico, Tony. Hunt for Hector. 2011. (J). (978-1-56288-047-7(0)) Checkerboard Pr., Inc.

—Sports Spot-The-Differences Activity Book. 2011. (Dover Little Activity Bks.). (ENG., Illus.). 64p. (J). (gr. k-3). pap., act. bk. ed. 1.99 (978-0-486-47527-1(1)) Dover Pubns., Inc.

Tallarico, Tony & Tallarigo, Tony. License Plates Across the States: Travel Puzzles & Games. Tallarico, Tony & Eagle, Cameron, illus. 2005. (ENG.). 24p. (J). (gr. -1-2). mass mkt. 4.99 (978-0-8431-7737-4(3), Price Stern Sloan) Penguin Young Readers Group.

Tallarico, Tony J., Jr. English - Spanish Word Search: Sopa de Letras, Vol. 2. 2011. (Dover Children's Language Activity Bks.). (ENG.). 48p. (J). (gr. 2-5). pap. 4.99 (978-0-486-48098-5(4)) Dover Pubns., Inc.

—English-Spanish Word Search. 2011. (Dover Children's Language Activity Bks.). (ENG., Illus.). 48p. (J). (gr. 2-5). pap. 4.99 (978-0-486-48097-8(6)) Dover Pubns., Inc.

—Presidents Activity Book. 2009. (Dover Little Activity Bks.). (ENG., Illus.). 64p. (J). (gr. k-3). pap. 1.99 (978-0-486-47388-8(0)) Dover Pubns., Inc.

—Spot-the-Differences Around the World. 2009. (Dover Children's Activity Bks.). (ENG., Illus.). 48p. (J). (gr. 3-8). pap. 4.99 (978-0-486-47304-8(X)) Dover Pubns., Inc.

—U. S. A. Constitution Activity Book. 2016. (Dover Children's Activity Bks.). (ENG.). 48p. (J). (gr. 3-6). pap. 4.99 (978-0-486-80934-2(X)) Dover Pubns., Inc.

—U. S. A. Secret Code Puzzles for Kids. 2014. (Dover Children's Activity Bks.). (ENG.). 48p. (J). (gr. 3-6). pap. 4.99 (978-0-486-49459-3(4)) Dover Pubns., Inc.

—Worldwide Secret Code Puzzles for Kids. 2016. (Dover Children's Activity Bks.). (ENG.). 48p. (J). (gr. 3-5). pap. 4.99 (978-0-486-79871-4(2)) Dover Pubns., Inc.

Tallarico, Tony J., Jr. & Tallarico, Tony, Sr. SPARK Nature Fun Facts Mazes. 2017. (Dover Children's Activity Bks.). (ENG.). 64p. (J). (gr. 1-4). pap. 5.99 (978-0-486-81582-4(X)) Dover Pubns., Inc.

Tatchell, Judy & Rogers, Kirsteen. Dragons Jigsaw Book. Scott, Peter, illus. 2005. (Usborne Jigsaw Bks.). 12p. (J). (gr. -1-3). bds. 14.95 (978-0-7945-1117-3(1), Usborne) EDC Publishing.

Tausig, Ben. Mad Tausig vs the Interplanetary Puzzling Peace Patrol. Goopymart, illus. 2007. (ENG.). 94p. (J). (gr. 4-6). per. 7.95 (978-0-9741319-4-8(6)) 4N Publishing LLC.

Taylor, Jody. Hidden Pictures 2008. 2007. (Hidden Pictures Ser.). (ENG., Illus.). 48p. (J). Vol. 2. pap. 5.95 (978-1-59078-542-3(8)) Vol. 4. pap. 5.95 (978-1-59078-544-7(4)) Vol.1. (gr. -1-3). pap. 5.95 (978-1-59078-541-6(X)) Boyds Mills Pr.

Teacher's Friend Publications Staff, creator. Color & Shape Puzzles. 2006. (Scholastic Hands-on Learning Ser.). (ENG., Illus.). 12.99 (978-0-439-82388-3(9), Teaching Resources) Scholastic, Inc.

Teaching Resources Corporation Staff, creator. Number Puzzles. 2006. (Scholastic Hands-on Learning Ser.). (ENG.). 12.99 (978-0-439-82391-3(9), Teaching Resources) Scholastic, Inc.

Teckentrup, Britta. The Odd One Out. Teckentrup, Britta, illus. 2014. (ENG., Illus.). 32p. (J). (-k). 14.99 (978-0-7636-7127-3(4), Big Picture Press) Candlewick Pr.

—One Is Not a Pair. Teckentrup, Britta, illus. 2017. (ENG., Illus.). 32p. (J). (-k). 14.99 (978-0-7636-9319-0(7), Big Picture Press) Candlewick Pr.

Teenage Mutant Ninja Turtles Activity Books. 2004. (J). act. bk. ed. 1.49 (978-0-7666-1295-2(3), 99180) Modern Publishing.

Teitelbaum, Michael. Jigsaw Journey: the 50 States. Allen, Jessica, illus. 2014. (Jigsaw Journey Ser.). (ENG.). 48p. (J). (gr. 1). 15.95 (978-1-60710-950-1(6), Silver Dolphin Bks.) Readerlink Distribution Services, LLC.

Tenah, Ann. Brainiac's Bug Book: Creepy Crawly Activities. McGuinness, Tracy, illus. 2005. (Activity Journals Ser.). 128p. 12.99 (978-0-88088-362-7(6)) Peter Pauper Pr. Inc.

Thomas Nelson. Jigsaw Puzzle & Book Hide & Seek ABC Set. 2017. (ENG.). (J). (gr. -1-7). **(978-1-78692-092-8(1))** Make Believe Ideas.

—Jigsaw Puzzle & Book Itsy Bitsy Spider Set. 2017. (ENG.). (J). (gr. -1-7). **(978-1-78692-093-5(X))** Make Believe Ideas.

—Jigsaw Puzzle & Book My First Bible Stories Set. 2017. (ENG.). (J). (gr. -1-7). **(978-1-78692-094-2(8))** Make Believe Ideas.

Thornburgh, Rebecca. Cars, Trucks & Things That Go. 2010. (ENG.). 64p. (J). (gr. k-2). pap. 4.95 (978-1-4027-5909-3(6)) Sterling Publishing Co., Inc.

Time for Bible Puzzles & Games. (Illus.). 32p. (YA). (gr. 5-18). pap. 2.25 (978-0-87162-662-2(4), E9705) Warner Pr., Inc.

Times Mind Games Staff. Number & Logic Puzzles. 2017. (ENG.). 384p. 9.95 **(978-0-00-819030-9(5))** HarperCollins Pubs. Ltd. GBR. Dist: Independent Pubs. Group.

Tonka Sticker Activity Books. 2004. (J). act. bk. ed. 2.99 (978-0-7666-1142-9(6), 69685); act. bk. ed. 2.99 (978-0-7666-1143-6(4), 69685) Modern Publishing.

Top That Publishing Staff, ed. Brain Workout. 2004. (Illus.). 96p. pap. (978-1-84510-211-1(8)); Vol. 2. pap. (978-1-84510-210-4(X)); Vol. 3. pap. (978-1-84510-209-8(6)); Vol. 4. pap. (978-1-84510-208-1(8)); Vol. 5. pap. (978-1-84510-309-5(2)); Vol. 6. pap. (978-1-84510-310-1(6)) Top That! Publishing PLC.

—101 Brainbender Puzzles. 2005. (Illus.). 48p. pap. (978-1-84510-202-9(9)) Top That! Publishing PLC.

—101 Picture Puzzles. 2005. (Illus.). 48p. pap. (978-1-84510-201-2(0)) Top That! Publishing PLC.

Toufexis, George. Discovering Washington D. C. Activity Book: Awesome Activities about Our Nation's Capital. 2016. (ENG.). 48p. (J). (gr. 3-6). pap. 4.99 (978-0-486-80719-5(3)) Dover Pubns., Inc.

—The Outrageous Human Body Activity Book. 2013. (Dover Children's Science Bks.). (ENG.). 48p. (J). (gr. 3-8). pap. 4.99 (978-0-486-49116-5(1)) Dover Pubns., Inc.

—World Atlas Activity & Coloring Book. 2014. (ENG.). 64p. (J). (gr. 3-5). pap. 5.99 (978-0-486-78121-1(6)) Dover Pubns., Inc.

Trapani, Iza. Rufus & Friends: Rhyme Time. Trapani, Iza, illus. 2008. (ENG., Illus.). 40p. (J). (gr. -1-3). pap. 7.95 (978-1-58089-207-0(8)) Charlesbridge Publishing, Inc.

Tullet, Hervé. The Game of Patterns. 2011. (ENG., Illus.). 14p. (gr. -1 — 1). 8.95 (978-0-7148-6187-6(1)) Phaidon Pr., Inc.

Turnbull, S. Dinosaur Jigsaw Book. 2004. (SPA.). 14p. (J). 8.99 (978-0-7945-0525-7(2)) EDC Publishing.

Turnbull, Stephanie. Los Dinosaurios Con Cuatro Puzzles Sencillos. Scott, Peter, illus. 2004. (Titles in Spanish Ser.). (SPA.). 6p. (J). 8.95 (978-0-7460-6109-1(9), Usborne) EDC Publishing.

Twomey, Emily Golden. Buster's Brilliant Dot to Dot. Twomey, Emily Golden, illus. 2014. (ENG., Illus.). 64p. (J). (gr. k-4). pap. 7.99 (978-1-78055-201-9(7)) O'Mara, Michael Bks., Ltd. GBR. Dist: Independent Pubs. Group.

—The Dot to Dot. Twomey, Emily Golden, illus. 2014. (ENG., Illus.). 64p. (J). (gr. k-4). pap. 4.99 (978-1-78055-115-9(0)) O'Mara, Michael Bks., Ltd. GBR. Dist: Independent Pubs. Group.

Tyler, Jenny. Dot-to-Dot on the Farm. rev. ed. 2004. (Dot to Dot Ser.). (Illus.). 24p. (J). pap. 3.99 (978-0-7945-0492-2(2)) EDC Publishing.

Tyler, Jenny & Blundell, Kim. Animal Mazes. rev. ed. 2004. (Maze Fun Ser.). 24p. (J). pap. 5.95 (978-0-7945-0538-7(4)) EDC Publishing.

—Monster Mazes. rev. ed. 2004. (Maze Fun Ser.). 24p. (J). pap. 5.95 (978-0-7945-0536-3(8)) EDC Publishing.

Tyo, Courtney. Holiday Puzzles. 2004. 47p. (J). (978-0-439-68016-5(6)) Scholastic, Inc.

U. S. Kids Editorial Staff. The Best Adventure of the Puzzle Squad. (Illus.). 48p. (J). (gr. k-6). stu. ed. 6.95 (978-1-885453-75-4(2)) Children's Better Health Institute.

U. S. National Geographic Society Staff. NG Kids Big Book of Fun. 2010. (ENG., Illus.). 80p. (J). (gr. 1-4). pap. 6.99 (978-1-4263-0661-7(X), National Geographic Children's Bks.) National Geographic Society.

Ungerer, Tomi. One, Two, Where's My Shoe? 2014. (ENG., Illus.). 32p. (gr. -1-k). 14.95 (978-0-7148-6798-4(5)) Phaidon Pr., Inc.

Universal. Minions: the Movie Poster Book. 2015. (ENG., Illus.). 24p. (J). (gr. 1-17). pap. 7.99 (978-0-316-30204-3(X)) Little, Brown Bks. for Young Readers.

University Games Staff, compiled by. I-Ballers: Little Books for Big Minds. 2005. (I-Ballers Ser.). (ENG.). pap. 4.95 (978-1-57528-936-6(9)) Univ. Games.

—Made You Laugh for Kids! Books So Fun You'll Pee Your Pants! 2005. (ENG., Illus.). 224p. (J). (gr. -1-3). pap. 14.95 (978-1-57528-995-3(4)) Univ. Games.

Vaicikonis, Kris. Puzzle Me-Brain Twisters. 2012. (Illus.). 32p. (J). pap. 4.99 (978-1-62267-006-2(X)) Bright Connections Media.

Ventura, Marne. Gross Brain Teasers, 1 vol. 2013. (Gross Guides). (ENG.). 32p. (gr. 3-4). 27.99 (978-1-4296-9923-5(X)) Capstone Press of Coughlan Cos.

Ventura, Marne, et al. Gross Guides. 2013. (Gross Guides). (ENG.). 32p. (gr. 3-4). lib. bdg. 111.96 (978-1-4296-9926-6(4), Edge Bks.) Capstone Press of Coughlan Cos.

Vidal, Oriol, illus. Build a Picture Monsters Sticker Book. 2013. (Build a Picture Sticker Bks.). (ENG.). (J). 6.99 (978-0-7945-2947-5(X), Usborne) EDC Publishing.

Vidro, Kenn G. Square Pears. 2003. (Illus.). 112p. (J). spiral bd. 7.95 (978-0-9745308-0-2(8)) Gilbert Square Bks.

Volke, Gordon. Big World Activity Sticker Book, Vol. 2. 2004. (Illus.). 16p. 7.25 (978-1-84161-130-3(1)) Ravette Publishing, Ltd. GBR. Dist: Parkwest Pubns., Inc.

Volke, Gordon, et al, illus. Panda Patrol Big Activity Book. 2004. 24p. 6.00 (978-1-84161-111-2(5)) Ravette Publishing, Ltd. GBR. Dist: Parkwest Pubns., Inc.

Wallace, MaryAlice & Lindstrom, Charlotte. Scripture Puzzlers: Crosswords, Word Searches, & Other Brain Teasers. 2015. (J). pap. 12.99 (978-1-4621-1548-8(9), Horizon Pubs.) Cedar Fort, Inc./CFI Distribution.

Wallis, Mary Alice & Lindstrom, C. G. Prophets & Apostles. 2008. (LDS Puzzle Pals Ser.). 122p. pap. 14.99 (978-1-59955-126-5(8), Cedar Fort, Inc.) Cedar Fort, Inc./CFI Distribution.

Watt, F. & Wells, R. Farm Animals. 2004. 14p. (J). 9.95 (978-0-7945-0561-5(9)) EDC Publishing.

—Pets. 2004. 14p. (J). 9.95 (978-0-7945-0621-6(6)) EDC Publishing.

—Things That Go. 2004. 14p. (J). 9.95 (978-0-7945-0622-3(4)) EDC Publishing.

Watt, Fiona. Animales de la Granja. Wells, Rachel, illus. 2004. (SPA.). 14p. (J). 9.95 (978-0-7460-6113-8(7), Usborne) EDC Publishing.

—Animals. Wells, Rachel, illus. 2006. 10p. (J). (gr. -1-k). bds. 9.99 (978-0-7945-1227-9(5), Usborne) EDC Publishing.

—Baby's Very First Slide & See Animals. 2015. (Baby's Very First Slide & See Board Bks.). (ENG.). 10p. (J). 14.99 (978-0-7945-3479-0(1), Usborne) EDC Publishing.

—Christmas Baby. 2005. 10p. (J). 8.95 (978-0-7945-1185-2(6), Usborne) EDC Publishing.

—Fairies Jigsaw Book. Cartwright, Stephen & Bird, Glen, illus. 2005. (Osborne Sparkly Jigsaws Ser.). 10p. (J). bds. 14.99 (978-0-7945-1131-9(7), Usborne) EDC Publishing.

—Mascotas. Wells, Rachel, illus. 2004. (Titles in Spanish Ser.). (SPA.). 14p. (J). 9.95 (978-0-7460-6112-1(9), Usborne) EDC Publishing.

—Mermaids Jigsaw Book. Cartwright, Stephen & Bird, Glen, illus. 2006. (Osborne Sparkly Jigsaws Ser.). 10p. (J). bds. 14.99 (978-0-7945-1189-0(9), Usborne) EDC Publishing.

Watt, Fiona & Wells, Rachel. Anifeiliaid y Fferm. 2005. (WEL., Illus.). 10p. (978-1-84512-000-9(0)) Cymdeithas Lyfrau Ceredigion.

Wax, Wendy. Easter Bunny on the Loose! Garbot, Dave, illus. 2013. (ENG.). 32p. (J). (gr. -1-3). 7.99 (978-0-06-223709-5(8)) HarperCollins Pubs.

Weber, Bob. Go Fun! Slylock Fox Mystery Puzzles. 2015. (Go Fun! Ser.: 6). (ENG.). 128p. (J). pap. 8.99 (978-1-4494-6900-9(0)) Andrews McMeel Publishing.

—Go Fun! Spot Six Differences. 2015. (Go Fun! Ser.: 7). (ENG.). 128p. (J). pap. 8.99 (978-1-4494-6901-6(9)) Andrews McMeel Publishing.

Weber, Ken. Five-Minute Mysteries, Pack. 2005. (ENG., Illus.). 200p. (gr. 7-12). per. 9.95 (978-0-7624-2437-5(0)) Running Pr. Bk. Pubs.

Weller, Alan & Dover Publications Inc. Staff. Spot the Differences, Bk. 1. 2010. (Dover Children's Activity Bks.: Bk. 1). (ENG., Illus.). 64p. (J). (gr. 3-5). pap. 9.99 (978-0-486-47299-7(X)) Dover Pubns., Inc.

—Spot the Differences Bk. 2, Bk. 2. 2010. (Dover Children's Activity Bks.: Bk. 2). (ENG., Illus.). 64p. (J). (gr. 3-5). pap. 9.99 (978-0-486-47300-0(7)) Dover Pubns., Inc.

West, Tracey & Nolls, Katherine. Challenge. 2008. (Pokemon Ser.). (ENG., Illus.). 64p. (J). (gr. 2-5). pap. 4.99 (978-0-439-53052-1(0)) Scholastic, Inc.

Whelon, Chuck. Alien Invasion! Mazes. 2010. (Dover Children's Activity Bks.). (ENG., Illus.). 48p. (J). (gr. k-3). pap. 4.99 (978-0-486-47233-1(7)) Dover Pubns., Inc.

—Treasure Hunter Activity Book. 2011. (Dover Children's Activity Bks.). (ENG., Illus.). 48p. (J). (gr. 2-5). pap. 4.99 (978-0-486-47878-4(5)) Dover Pubns., Inc.

—Where's the Princess? And Other Fairy Tale Searches. Whelon, Chuck, illus. 2016. (ENG., Illus.). 32p. (J). (gr. k-3). 12.99 (978-1-4814-4633-4(9), Aladdin) Simon & Schuster Children's Publishing.

Wick, Walter. Can You See What I See? Animals. Wick, Walter, illus. 2007. (Scholastic Reader Level 1 Ser.). (ENG., Illus.). 32p. (J). (gr. -1-3). pap. 3.99 (978-0-439-86227-1(2)) Scholastic, Inc.

—Can You See What I See? Dream Machine. Wick, Walter, illus. 2003. (Can You See What I See? Ser.). (ENG., Illus.). 40p. (J). (gr. -1-3). 13.99 (978-0-439-39950-0(5), Cartwheel Bks.) Scholastic, Inc.

—Can You See What I See? Night Before Christmas. Wick, Walter, photos by. 2005. (Can You See What I See? Ser.). (ENG., Illus.). 40p. (J). (gr. -1-3). 13.99 (978-0-439-76927-3(2), Cartwheel Bks.) Scholastic, Inc.

—Can You See What I See? - Christmas Read-and-Seek. Wick, Walter, illus. 2008. (Scholastic Reader Level 1 Ser.). (ENG., Illus.). 32p. (J). (gr. -1-3). pap. 3.99 (978-0-545-07887-0(3)) Scholastic, Inc.

—Can You See What I See? Big Book of Search-and-Find Fun. Wick, Walter, illus. 2016. (Can You See What I See? Ser.). (ENG., Illus.). 160p. (J). (gr. k-2). 12.99 (978-0-545-83863-4(0), Cartwheel Bks.) Scholastic, Inc.

—Hey, Seymour! 2015. (ENG., Illus.). 32p. (J). (gr. -1-k). 18.99 (978-0-545-50216-0(0), Scholastic Pr.) Scholastic, Inc.

—On a Scary Scary Night: Picture Puzzles to Search & Solve. Wick, Walter, illus. 2008. (Can You See What I See? Ser.). (ENG., Illus.). 40p. (J). (gr. -1-3). 13.99 (978-0-439-70870-8(2)) Scholastic, Inc.

—Out of This World: Picture Puzzles to Search & Solve. Wick, Walter, photos by. 2013. (Can You See What I See? Ser.). (ENG., Illus.). 40p. (J). (gr. -1-3). 13.99 (978-0-545-24468-8(4), Cartwheel Bks.) Scholastic, Inc.

—Picture Puzzles to Search & Solve. Wick, Walter, illus. 2004. (Can You See What I See? Ser.). (ENG., Illus.). 40p. (J). (gr. -1-18). 13.99 (978-0-439-61772-7(3), Cartwheel Bks.) Scholastic, Inc.

—Seymour & the Juice Box Boat. Wick, Walter, illus. 2004. (Can You See What I See? Ser.). (ENG., Illus.). 32p. (J). (gr. -1-k). 8.99 (978-0-439-61778-9(2), Cartwheel Bks.) Scholastic, Inc.

—Toyland Express: Picture Puzzles to Search & Solve. Wick, Walter, photos by. 2011. (Can You See What I See? Ser.). (ENG., Illus.). 40p. (J). 13.99 (978-0-545-24483-1(8)) Scholastic, Inc.

—Treasure Ship: Picture Puzzles to Search & Solve. Wick, Walter, illus. 2010. (Can You See What I See? Ser.). (ENG., Illus.). 40p. (J). 13.99 (978-0-439-02643-7(1), Cartwheel Bks.) Scholastic, Inc.

Wick, Walter, photos by. I Spy: Interactive Sound Book of Picture Riddles. 2003. (Illus.). 30p. (J). 15.98 (978-0-7853-8424-3(3)) Publications International, Ltd.

The Wiggles Coloring & Activity Books. 2004. (J). act. bk. ed. 0.99 (978-0-7666-1049-1(7), 99530); act. bk. ed. 0.99 (978-0-7666-1048-4(9), 99530); act. bk. ed. 0.99 (978-0-7666-1047-7(0), 99530) Modern Publishing.

The Wiggles Giant Coloring & Activity Books. 2004. (J). act. bk. ed. 1.99 (978-0-7666-1051-4(9), 49220); act. bk. ed. 1.99 (978-0-7666-1050-7(0), 49220) Modern Publishing.

Williams, Carla. Big Puzzles for Little Hands: Children of the Bible. 2004. (Illus.). 96p. (J). (gr. -1-2). pap. 11.95 (978-1-885358-49-3(0)) Rainbow Pubs. & Legacy Pr.

—Big Puzzles for Little Hands: Jesus' Life & Lessons. 2004. (Illus.). 96p. (J). (gr. -1-2). pap. 11.95 (978-1-885358-79-0(2)) Rainbow Pubs. & Legacy Pr.

—Big Puzzles for Little Hands: The Bible Tells Me So. 2004. (Illus.). 96p. (J). (gr. -1-2). pap. 11.95 (978-1-885358-80-6(6)) Rainbow Pubs. & Legacy Pr.

Woods, Christopher & McClintic, Ben, illus. Where's Hanuman? 2009. (ENG.). 32p. (gr. 3-18). 9.95 (978-0-9779785-8-8(3)) Torchlight Publishing.

Woolley, Steph & Macmillan Audio Staff. Where's Octeelia? A Search-and-Find Adventure. unabr. ed. 2013. (ENG., Illus.). 24p. (J). (gr. 2). pap. 7.99 (978-1-4472-2573-7(2)) Pan Macmillan GBR. Dist: Independent Pubs. Group.

Word Winks: Over 300 Visual Verbal Puzzles. 2004. (J). pap. 12.95 (978-1-892069-75-7(X)) MindWare Holdings, Inc.

World Book-Childcraft International Staff, contrib. by. Brain Games: A Supplement to Childcraft — The How & Why Library. 2010. (J). (978-0-7166-0624-6(0)) World Bk., Inc.

Wos, Joe. A-MAZE-ING Animals: 50 Mazes for Kids. 2017. (ENG., Illus.). 64p. (J). (gr. 3-10). pap. 6.99 (978-1-4380-0994-0(1)) Barron's Educational Series, Inc.

Wos, Joe. Myths & Monsters: 50 Mazes for Kids. 2017. (ENG.). 64p. (J). (gr. 4-8). pap. 6.99 **(978-1-4380-0995-7(X))** Barron's Educational Series, Inc.

Wynne, Patricia J. Easy Dinosaur Mazes. 2006. (Dover Children's Activity Bks.). (ENG., Illus.). 48p. (J). (gr. -1-3). per. 4.99 (978-0-486-45363-7(4)) Dover Pubns., Inc.

Yo-Kai Watch. Seek & Find. 2016. (ENG., Illus.). 24p. (J). (gr. 1-4). 8.99 *(978-0-316-39621-9(4))* Little, Brown Bks. for Young Readers.
Young, Caroline. Big Bug Search. Jackson, Ian, illus. rev. ed. 2005. 32p. (J). pap. 7.99 *(978-0-7945-1045-9(0)*, Usborne) EDC Publishing.
Young, Caroline & Needham, Kate. Great Wildlife Search: Big Bug Search, Great Animal Search & Great Undersea Search. Jackson, Ian, illus. 2004. (Great Searches Ser.). 112p. (J). pap. 15.99 *(978-0-7945-0892-0(8)*, Usborne) EDC Publishing.
Young, Jay, creator. Secret Ziga Zaga. 2003. (Ziga Zaga Ser.). 192p. (YA). *(978-1-84347-034-2(9)*, Pavilion Children's Books) Pavilion Bks.
Yoyo Books Staff. Animals Around Me: Animal Jigsaw Fun. 2004. 12p. bds. *(978-90-5843-550-7(4))* YoYo Bks.
—Baby Animals: Animal Jigsaw Fun. 2004. 12p. bds. *(978-90-5843-551-4(2))* YoYo Bks.
—An Exciting Day Trip: Princess Charlotte's Picture Puzzles. 2005. 32p. *(978-90-5843-456-2(7))* YoYo Bks.
—Farm Animals: Animal Jigsaw Fun. 2004. 12p. bds. *(978-90-5843-549-1(0))* YoYo Bks.
—A Magic Gift: Princess Charlotte's Picture Puzzles. 2005. 32p. *(978-90-5843-457-9(5))* YoYo Bks.
—Wild Animals: Animal Jigsaw Fun. 2004. 12p. bds. *(978-90-5843-552-1(0))* YoYo Bks.
Zourelias, Diana. Fairyland Hidden Pictures. 2006. (Dover Children's Activity Bks.). (ENG., Illus.). 32p. (J). (gr. 3). pap. 3.99 *(978-0-486-45187-9(9))* Dover Pubns., Inc.
—SPARK Adorable Animals Find It! Color It! 2016. (Dover Children's Activity Bks.). (ENG.). 64p. (J). (gr. 1-4). pap. 5.99 *(978-0-486-81067-6(4))* Dover Pubns., Inc.
—SPARK Garden Daze Find It! Color It! 2017. (Dover Coloring Bks.). (ENG.). 64p. (gr. 1-4). pap. 5.99 *(978-0-486-81384-4(3))* Dover Pubns., Inc.
—SPARK Things That Go Find It! Color It! 2017. (Dover Coloring Bks.). (ENG.). 64p. (J). (gr. 1-4). pap. 5.99 *(978-0-486-81383-7(5))* Dover Pubns., Inc.
Zourelias, Diana. SPARK U. S. A. Fun Find It! Color It! 2017. (Dover Coloring Bks.). (ENG.). 64p. (J). (gr. 1-4). pap. 5.99 ***(978-0-486-81893-1(4))*** Dover Pubns., Inc.
3D Circus Puzzle Book. 12p. (J). *(978-2-89393-867-7(1))* Phidal Publishing, Inc./Editions Phidal, Inc.

PYLE, ERNIE, 1900-1945

Boomhower, Ray E. The Soldier's Friend: A Life of Ernie Pyle. 2006. (Illus.). 134p. 17.95 *(978-0-87195-200-4(9))* Indiana Historical Society.
Shone, Rob. War Correspondents. Forsey, Chris, illus. 2008. (Graphic Careers Ser.). (ENG.). 48p. (J). (gr. 5-8). lib. bdg. 31.95 *(978-1-4042-1449-1(6))*; per. 14.05 *(978-1-4042-1450-7(X))* Rosen Publishing Group, Inc., The.

PYRAMIDS

Biskup, Agnieszka. Egypt's Mysterious Pyramids: An Isabel Soto Archaeology Adventure. Stewart, Roger, illus. 2012. (Graphic Expeditions Ser.). (ENG.). 32p. (gr. 3-4). pap. 47.70 *(978-1-4296-8472-9(0)*, Graphic Library) Capstone Press of Coughlan Cos.
Bodden, Valerie. Pyramids. 2008. (Built to Last Ser.). (Illus.). 24p. (J). (gr. 3-7). lib. bdg. 24.25 *(978-1-58341-563-4(7)*, Creative Education) Creative Co., The.
Bolton, Anne. Pyramids & Mummies. 2008. (ENG., Illus.). 32p. (J). (gr. 3-8). 21.99 *(978-1-4169-5873-4(8)*, Simon & Schuster Bks. For Young Readers) Simon & Schuster Bks. For Young Readers.
Chisholm, Jane & Reid, Straun. Who Built the Pyramids? Stitt, Sue, illus. 2004. (Starting Point History Ser.). 32p. (J). (gr. 1). lib. bdg. 12.95 *(978-1-58086-629-3(8)*, Usborne) EDC Publishing.
Duke, Shirley. Pyramids of Egypt. 2015. (ENG.). 48p. (gr. 3-6). 35.64 *(978-1-63430-415-3(2))* Rourke Educational Media.
Forest, Christopher & Wegner, Jennifer Houser. Pyramids of Ancient Egypt, 1 vol. 2012. (Ancient Egyptian Civilization Ser.). (ENG.). 32p. (gr. 3-4). lib. bdg. 27.32 *(978-1-4296-7632-8(9)*, Fact Finders) Capstone Press of Coughlan Cos.
George, Enzo. The Pyramids of Giza. 2017. (Crypts, Tombs, & Secret Rooms Ser.). 48p. (gr. 4-5). pap. 84.30 ***(978-1-5382-0642-3(0))*** Stevens, Gareth Publishing LLLP.
Great Pyramids & the Sphinx. (Butterfly Bks.). (ARA., Illus.). 46p. (YA). (gr. 5-8). 9.95 *(978-0-86685-400-9(2))* International Bk. Ctr., Inc.
Harris, Nicholas. Pyramid. Dennis, Peter, illus. 2006. 31p. (J). *(978-0-7607-7526-4(5))* backpackbooks.
Harris, Nicolas. Pyramids Through Time. 2009. (Fast Forward Ser.). 32p. (YA). (gr. 2-5). lib. bdg. 25.25 *(978-1-4358-2801-8(1))* Rosen Publishing Group, Inc., The.
Henzel, Cynthia Kennedy. Pyramids of Egypt, 1 vol. 2011. (Troubled Treasures: World Heritage Sites Ser.). (ENG., Illus.). 32p. (YA). (gr. 3-6). 27.07 *(978-1-61613-566-9(2))* ABDO Publishing Co.
Herbst, Judith. Lands of Mystery. 2004. (Unexplained Ser.). (Illus.). 48p. (J). pap. 7.95 *(978-0-8225-2407-6(4))*; (ENG., (gr. 5-12). lib. bdg. 26.60 *(978-0-8225-1630-9(6))* Lerner Publishing Group.
Hoobler, Dorothy & Hoobler, Thomas. Where Are the Great Pyramids? 2015. (Where Is...? Ser.). lib. bdg. 16.00 *(978-0-606-37547-4(3))* Turtleback Bks.
Hoobler, Dorothy, et al. Where Are the Great Pyramids? Hoare, Jerry, illus. 2015. (Where Is? Ser.). (ENG.). 112p. (J). (gr. 3-7). 5.99 *(978-0-448-48409-9(9)*, Grosset & Dunlap) Penguin Young Readers Group.
Hooper, Meredith. Who Built the Pyramid? Heighway-Bury, Robin, illus. 2014. (ENG.). 40p. (J). (gr. 2-5). pap. 7.99 *(978-0-7636-7380-2(3))* Candlewick Pr.
Hyman, Teresa L. The Pyramids of Giza. 2004. (Great Structures in History Ser.). (ENG., Illus.). 48p. (J). (gr. 3-7). lib. bdg. 27.50 *(978-0-7377-1560-6(X)*, Greenhaven Pr., Inc.) Cengage Gale.
Kenney, Karen Latchana. Mysteries of the Egyptian Pyramids. 2017. (Ancient Mysteries Ser.). (ENG.). 32p. (J). (gr. 3-6). 27.99 ***(978-1-5124-4014-0(0))*** Lerner Publishing Group.
Keyes, Anna. Pharaohs, Pyramids Mummies & Faraones, pirámides y Momias: 6 English, 6 Spanish Adaptations. 2011. (ENG & SPA.). (J). 101.00 net. *(978-1-4108-5732-3(8))* Benchmark Education Co.
Kissock, Heather. Pyramids. 2011. (J). *(978-1-61690-435-7(6))* Weigl Pubs., Inc.
Kissock, Heather, ed. Pyramids. 2011. (J). (gr. 4-6). pap. 12.95 *(978-1-61690-771-6(1)*, AV2 by Weigl); (Illus.). 24p. (gr. 2-5). 27.13 *(978-1-61690-767-9(3))* Weigl Pubs., Inc.
Leardi, Jeanette. The Great Pyramid: Egypt's Tomb for All Time. 2006. (Castles, Palaces, & Tombs Ser.). (Illus.). 32p. (YA). (gr. 2-5). lib. bdg. 25.27 *(978-1-59716-266-1(3))* Bearport Publishing Co., Inc.
Levy, Janey. The Great Pyramid of Giza: Measuring Length, Area, Volume, & Angles. 2009. (PowerMath: Advanced Proficiency Plus Ser.). 32p. (gr. 5-5). 47.90 *(978-1-60851-368-0(8)*, PowerKids Pr.) Rosen Publishing Group, Inc., The.
MacDonald, Fiona. Solving the Mysteries of the Pyramids. 2008. (Digging into History Ser.). 32p. (gr. 4-18). lib. bdg. 29.93 *(978-0-7614-3106-0(3)*, Benchmark Bks.) Marshall Cavendish Corp.
Malam, John. Pyramids. 2010. (100 Things You Should Know About Ser.). (Illus.). 32p. (YA). (gr. 4-6). lib. bdg. 19.95 *(978-1-4222-1525-8(3))* Mason Crest.
—Pyramids. 2015. (100 Facts You Should Know Ser.). (ENG., Illus.). 48p. (J). (gr. 4-5). lib. bdg. 31.95 *(978-1-4824-2185-9(2))* Stevens, Gareth Publishing LLLP.
Malam, John & Macdonald, Fiona. Pyramids. 2013. (Illus.). 48p. (J). *(978-1-4351-5096-6(1))* Barnes & Noble, Inc.
Mann, Elizabeth. The Great Pyramid: The Story of the Farmers, the God-King & the Most Astonding Structure Ever Built. Turco, Laura Lo, illus. 2006. (Wonders of the World Book Ser.). (ENG.). 48p. (J). (gr. 4-8). pap. 12.95 *(978-1-931414-11-1(4)*, 9781931414111) Mikaya Pr.
Marsh, Laura. Pyramids. 2017. (Readers Ser.). (ENG., Illus.). 32p. (J). (gr. -1-1). pap. 3.99 *(978-1-4263-2690-5(4)*, National Geographic Children's Bks.) National Geographic Society.
Matthews, Sheelagh. Pyramids of Giza. 2007. (Structural Wonders Ser.). (Illus.). 32p. (J). (gr. 4-6). lib. bdg. 26.00 *(978-1-59036-725-4(1))*; per. 9.95 *(978-1-59036-726-1(X))* Weigl Pubs., Inc.
McCall, Henrietta. Pyramid. 2015. (Time Shift History Ser.). (Illus.). 32p. (J). (gr. 3-6). 31.35 *(978-1-905638-63-5(9))* Book Hse. GBR. Dist: Black Rabbit Bks.
McNeil, Niki, et al. Pyramids of Egypt. 2007. (In the Hands of a Child: Project Pack Continent Study Ser.). (Illus.). 47p. spiral bd. 12.00 *(978-1-60308-071-2(6))* In the Hands of a Child.
Meachen Rau, Dana. Bookworms: The Inside Story, 6 bks., Set. Incl. Castle. 32p. (gr. k-2). lib. bdg. 15.95 *(978-0-7614-2272-3(2))*; Igloo. 32p. (gr. k-2). lib. bdg. 15.95 *(978-0-7614-2273-0(0))*; Log Cabin. 31p. (J). (gr. -1-3). lib. bdg. 22.79 *(978-0-7614-2274-7(9))*; Pyramid. 32p. (gr. k-2). lib. bdg. 15.95 *(978-0-7614-2275-4(7))*; Skyscraper. 32p. (gr. k-2). lib. bdg. 15.95 *(978-0-7614-2276-1(5))*; Tepee. 31p. (J). (gr. -1-3). lib. bdg. 22.79 *(978-0-7614-2277-8(3))*; (Illus.). 2006. 2006. Set lib. bdg. 136.71 *(978-0-7614-2271-6(4)*, Benchmark Bks.) Marshall Cavendish Corp.
—Pyramid. 2006. (Bookworms Ser.). (Illus.). 32p. (gr. k-2). lib. bdg. 15.95 *(978-0-7614-2275-4(7)*, Benchmark Bks.) Marshall Cavendish Corp.
Mellett, Peter. Find Out about Pyramids. 2013. (ENG., Illus.). 64p. pap. 9.99 *(978-1-84322-979-7(X)*, Armadillo) Anness Publishing GBR. Dist: National Bk. Network.
Millard, Anne. Misterios de las Piramides. (Coleccion Misterios De). (SPA., Illus.). 48p. (YA). (gr. 5-8). 19.95 *(978-84-348-5690-5(5)*, SM6076) SM Ediciones ESP. Dist: AIMS International Bks., Inc., Lectorum Pubns., Inc.
Moore, Gareth. Pyramid Puzzles. 2016. (Brain Game Treasure Hunts Ser.). (ENG., Illus.). 32p. (J). (gr. 3-6). 26.65 *(978-1-5124-0622-1(8))* Lerner Publishing Group.
Morley, Jacqueline. You Wouldn't Want to Be a Pyramid Builder! A Hazardous Job You'd Rather Not Have. Antram, David, illus. rev. ed. 2013. (ENG.). (J). 32p. 29.00 *(978-0-531-27101-8(3))*; 40p. pap. 9.95 *(978-0-531-23852-3(0))* Scholastic Library Publishing. (Watts, Franklin).
Naden, Corinne J. & Blue, Rose. Ancient Egyptians & the Pyramids. 2003. (J). *(978-1-58417-310-6(6))*; pap. *(978-1-58417-311-3(4))* Lake Street Pubs.
Neuschwander, Cindy. Mummy Math: An Adventure in Geometry. Langdo, Bryan, illus. 2009. (ENG.). 32p. (J). (gr. 2-5). pap. 7.99 *(978-0-312-56117-8(2)*, 9780312561178) Square Fish.
O'Donnell, Kerri. The Pyramids of Egypt. (Reading Room Collection 2 Ser.). 24p. (gr. 3-4). 2009. 42.50 *(978-1-60851-996-5(1)*, PowerKids Pr.) 2003. (ENG.). 43.95 *(978-0-8239-8730-6(2))* Rosen Publishing Group, Inc., The.
Orr, Joel N. Structure Is Destiny: The Dandelion Paradox. 2004. (ALB.). (YA). per. 19.95 *(978-0-9634168-9-6(8))* ZEM Pr.
Peterson, Sheryl. Egyptian Pyramids. 2005. (Ancient Wonders of the World Ser.). (Illus.). 32p. (J). (gr. 4-7). lib. bdg. 18.95 *(978-1-58341-359-3(6)*, Creative Education) Creative Co., The.
Putnam, James. Pyramid. 2011. (DK Eyewitness Bks.). (ENG.). 72p. (J). (gr. 3-7). 16.99 *(978-0-7566-5832-8(2)*, DK Children) Dorling Kindersley Publishing, Inc.
The Pyramids of Giza. 2014. (Great Idea Ser.). (ENG.). 48p. (J). (gr. 4-6). lib. bdg. 26.60 *(978-1-59953-593-7(9))* Norwood Hse. Pr.
Rau, Dana Meachen. Pyramid. 2007. (J). pap. 6.99 *(978-0-7614-3302-6(3))* Marshall Cavendish Corp.
Raum, Elizabeth. Egyptian Pyramids. 2014. (Ancient Wonders Ser.). (Illus.). 32p. (J). 28.50 *(978-1-60753-466-2(5))* Amicus Publishing.
Riggs, Kate. Egyptian Pyramids. 2009. (Places of Old Ser.). 24p. (J). (gr. 1-5). lib. bdg. 24.25 *(978-1-58341-707-2(9)*, Creative Education) Creative Co., The.
Schimel, Lawrence. If You Were a Kid Building a Pyramid. 2017. (If You Were a Kid Ser.). (ENG.). 32p. (J). lib. bdg. 26.00 ***(978-0-531-23748-9(6)***, Children's Pr.) Scholastic Library Publishing.
—If You Were a Kid Building a Pyramid. Ely, Jennifer W., illus. 2017. (If You Were a Kid Ser.). (ENG.). 32p. (J). pap. 7.95 ***(978-0-531-23949-0(7)***, Children's Pr.) Scholastic Library Publishing.
Steele, Philip & Philip, Steele. Las Piramides Fueron Construidas. 2006. (Enciclopedia Me Pregunto Por Que). (SPA., Illus.). 32p. (J). (gr. 3-5). 12.99 *(978-84-241-2171-6(6)*, EV2033) Everest Editora ESP. Dist: Lectorum Pubns., Inc.
Strom, Laura Layton. The Egyptian Science Gazette. 2008. (Illus.). 36p. (J). pap. *(978-0-531-18813-2(2))* Children's Pr., Ltd.
Sullivan, Erin Ash. Pyramids. 2011. (Early Connections Ser.). (J). *(978-1-61672-594-5(X))* Benchmark Education Co.
—Pyramids: Set Of 6. 2011. (Early Connections Ser.). (J). pap. 37.00 net. *(978-1-4108-1067-0(4))* Benchmark Education Co.
Taplin, Sam. Mummies & Pyramids. 2004. (Discovery Program Ser.). (Illus.). 48p. (J). pap. 8.95 *(978-0-7945-0317-8(9)*, Usborne); lib. bdg. 16.95 *(978-1-58086-479-4(1))* EDC Publishing.
Weil, Ann. The World's Most Amazing Pyramids, 1 vol. 2011. (Landmark Top Tens Ser.). (ENG., Illus.). 32p. (gr. 3-5). pap. 8.29 *(978-1-4109-4251-7(1))*; 30.65 *(978-1-4109-4240-1(6))* Heinemann-Raintree. (Raintree Perspectives).
World Book, Inc Staff, contrib. by. The Mysteries of Egypt's Pyramids: The Secrets of the Pharaoh. 2015. (Illus.). 48p. (J). *(978-0-7166-2677-0(2))* World Bk., Inc.

PYTHAGOREAN THEOREM

Ellis, Julie. Pythagoras & the Ratios: A Math Adventure. Peacock, Phyllis Hornung, illus. 2010. (ENG.). 32p. (J). (gr. 2-5). 16.95 *(978-1-57091-775-2(2))*; pap. 7.95 *(978-1-57091-776-9(0))* Charlesbridge Publishing, Inc.
—What's Your Angle, Pythagoras? A Math Adventure. Hornung, Phyllis, illus. 2004. (Math Adventures Ser.). (ENG.). 32p. (J). (gr. 2-5). pap. 7.95 *(978-1-57091-150-7(9))* Charlesbridge Publishing, Inc.

Q

QUACKS AND QUACKERY

Farndon, John. Quacks & con Artists: The Dubious History of Doctors. Dean, Venitia, illus. 2017. (Sickening History of Medicine Ser.). (ENG.). 32p. (J). (gr. 3-6). 26.65 *(978-1-5124-1560-5(X))*; 19.99 ***(978-1-5124-3636-5(4))***; 30.65 ***(978-1-5124-2712-7(8))***; 30.65 ***(978-1-5124-3635-8(6))*** Lerner Publishing Group.

QUACKS AND QUACKERY—FICTION

Hiebert, Elfrieda H. & Juel, Connie. The Quack. (Little Book Practice Reader Ser.). (J). *(978-0-8136-0778-8(7))* Modern Curriculum Pr.
Thompson, Lauren. Little Quack Counts. Anderson, Derek, illus. 2009. (Super Chubbies Ser.). (ENG.). 26p. (J). (gr. -1 — 1). bds. 5.99 *(978-1-4169-6093-5(7)*, Little Simon) Little Simon.
—Little Quack Loves Colors. Anderson, Derek, illus. 2009. (Super Chubbies Ser.). (ENG.). 26p. (J). (gr. -1 — 1). bds. 5.99 *(978-1-4169-6094-2(5)*, Little Simon) Little Simon.

QUAILS

World Book, Inc. Staff, contrib. by. Quail & Other Galliforms. 2005. (World Book's Animals of the World Ser.). (Illus.). 64p. (J). *(978-0-7166-1266-7(6))* World Bk., Inc.

QUAILS—FICTION

Dharma Publishing. The Hunter & the Quail: The Story about the Power of Cooperation. 2010. (ENG.). 36p. (gr. -1-7). pap. 8.95 *(978-0-89800-602-5(3))* Dharma Publishing.
Hays, Summer. Mrs. Gambel the Quirky Quail. 2013. (ENG.). 32p. (J). (gr. k-2). 16.95 *(978-1-57197-517-1(9)*, Ivy House Publishing Group) Pentland Pr., Inc.
Oldenburg, Richard. How the Quail Earned His Topknot. 2010. 30p. pap. 12.50 *(978-1-60911-668-2(2)*, Eloquent Bks.) Strategic Book Publishing & Rights Agency (SBPRA).
Root, Laura L. Quail in My Garden: Book One of Adventures in My Garden. 2012. 64p. pap. 26.99 *(978-1-4490-6963-6(0))* AuthorHouse.
Sparks, Favre. Agnes, the Eggless Quail. 2009. 28p. pap. 16.50 *(978-1-60693-491-3(0)*, Strategic Bk. Publishing) Strategic Book Publishing & Rights Agency (SBPRA).

QUAKERS

see also Society of Friends

Boothroyd, Jennifer. William Penn. 2009. pap. 6.95 *(978-0-8225-6431-7(9))* Lerner Publishing Group.
—William Penn: A Life of Tolerance. 2006. (Pull Ahead Bks.). (Illus.). 32p. (J). (gr. 3-7). lib. bdg. 22.60 *(978-0-8225-6387-7(8)*, Lerner Pubns.) Lerner Publishing Group.
Burton, Margie, et al. Friends. 2011. (Early Connections Ser.). (J). *(978-1-61672-489-4(7))* Benchmark Education Co.
Figley, Marty Rhodes. Who Was William Penn? And Other Questions about the Founding of Pennsylvania. 2012. (Six Questions of American History Ser.). (ENG., Illus.). 48p. (gr. 4-6). lib. bdg. 30.60 *(978-0-7613-5328-7(3))* Lerner Publishing Group.
Friends General Conference (U.S.), Religious Education Committee Staff, contrib. by. Lives That Speak: Stories of Twentieth-Century Quakers. 2004. (Illus.). viii, 168p. (J). *(978-1-888305-32-6(0))* QuakerPress.
Jacobson, Ryan. William Penn: Founder of Pennsylvania. Stiles, Tim, illus. 2006. (Graphic Biographies Ser.). (ENG.). 32p. (gr. 3-4). 30.65 *(978-0-7368-6501-2(2)*, Graphic Library) Capstone Press of Coughlan Cos.
Levy, Janey. William Penn: Shaping a Nation. 2009. (Real Life Readers Ser.). 32p. (ENG., Illus.). (J). (gr. 5-6). pap. 10.00 *(978-1-4358-0195-0(4)*, 1291824); (gr. 5-5). 47.90 *(978-1-61511-376-7(2))*; (J). (gr. 4-6). lib. bdg. 25.25 *(978-1-4358-3016-5(4))*; (Illus.). (J). 60.00 *(978-1-4358-0196-7(2)*, 1291824) Rosen Publishing Group, Inc., The. (PowerKids Pr.).
Marsh, Carole. William Penn. 2003. 12p. (gr. k-4). 2.95 *(978-0-635-02358-2(X))* Gallopade International.
Marsico, Katie. Lucretia Mott: Abolitionist & Women's Rights Leader, 1 vol. 2008. (Essential Lives Set 2 Ser.). (ENG., Illus.). 112p. (J). (gr. 6-12). lib. bdg. 35.64 *(978-1-60453-039-1(1))* ABDO Publishing Co.
Mierka, Gregg A. Nathanael Greene: The General Who Saved the Revolution. 2006. (J). pap. *(978-1-59556-017-9(3))*; (Illus.). 88p. (gr. 5-11). lib. bdg. 23.95 *(978-1-59556-012-4(2))* OTTN Publishing.
Rand, Carol. Lydia Darragh: Quaker Patriot. Marshall, Dan, illus. (J). 15.95 *(978-0-945912-33-0(1))* Pippin Pr.
Swain, Gwenyth. Freedom Seeker: A Story about William Penn. Harvey, Lisa, illus. 2003. (Creative Minds Biographies Ser.). (ENG.). 64p. (gr. 4-8). pap. 8.95 *(978-0-87614-931-7(X)*, Carolrhoda Bks.) Lerner Publishing Group.
Yolen, Jane. Friend: The Story of George Fox & the Quakers. 2nd ed. 2005. (Illus.). xii, 179p. (J). *(978-1-888305-41-8(X))* QuakerPress.

QUALITATIVE ANALYSIS

see Chemistry, Analytic

QUANTITATIVE ANALYSIS

see Chemistry, Analytic

QUANTUM THEORY

see also Chemistry; Force and Energy; Radiation; Relativity (Physics); Thermodynamics

Ferrie, Chris. Quantum Entanglement for Babies. 2017. (J). ***(978-1-4926-5608-1(9))***; (Baby University Ser.: 0). (ENG., Illus.). 24p. bds. 9.99 ***(978-1-4926-5623-4(2)***, Sourcebooks Jabberwocky) Sourcebooks, Inc.
—Quantum Physics for Babies. 2017. (Baby University Ser.: 0). (ENG., Illus.). 24p. (J). bds. 9.99 ***(978-1-4926-5622-7(4)***, Sourcebooks Jabberwocky) Sourcebooks, Inc.
Hagler, Gina. Discovering Quantum Mechanics, 1 vol. 2015. (ENG.). 112p. (YA). 35.60 *(978-1-4777-8002-2(5)*, Rosen Young Adult) Rosen Publishing Group, Inc., The.
McPartland, Randall. Understanding Quantum Physics. 2015. (J). lib. bdg. *(978-1-62713-433-0(6))*; (ENG.). 48p. (gr. 7-7). 31.36 *(978-1-5026-0145-2(1))* Cavendish Square Publishing.
Scientific American Staff. Beyond Extreme Physics. 2009. (Scientific American Cutting-Edge Science Ser.). 160p. (gr. 9-9). 63.90 *(978-1-60853-073-1(6))* Rosen Publishing Group, Inc., The.
—Extreme Physics. 2009. (Scientific American Cutting-Edge Science Ser.). 176p. (gr. 9-9). 63.90 *(978-1-60853-076-2(0))* Rosen Publishing Group, Inc., The.
Spiro, Ruth & Chan, Irene. Baby Loves Quantum Physics! 2017. (ENG., Illus.). 20p. (J). (— 1). bds. 8.99 ***(978-1-58089-769-3(X))*** Charlesbridge Publishing, Inc.
Topp, Patricia. This Strange Quantum World & You. 2006. (Illus.). 68p. (J). (gr. 4-7). per. 10.95 *(978-1-60002-195-4(6)*, 2844) Mountain Valley Publishing, LLC.
Willett, Edward. The Basics of Quantum Physics: Understanding the Photoelectric Effect & Line Spectra. 2004. (Library of Physics Ser.). (Illus.). 48p. (YA). lib. bdg. 29.25 *(978-1-4042-0334-1(6))* Rosen Publishing Group, Inc., The.

QUARANTINE

see Communicable Diseases

QUARTER HORSE

Criscione, Rachel Damon. The Quarter Horse. 2009. (Library of Horses Ser.). 24p. (gr. 3-3). 42.50 *(978-1-60853-724-2(2)*, PowerKids Pr.) Rosen Publishing Group, Inc., The.
Frazel, Ellen. The American Quarter Horse. 2011. (Horse Breed Roundup Ser.). (ENG., Illus.). 24p. (YA). (gr. 3-8). lib. bdg. 25.95 *(978-1-60014-653-4(8)*, Pilot Bks.) Bellwether Media.
Landau, Elaine. American Quarter Horses Are My Favorite! 2012. (My Favorite Horses Ser.). (ENG.). 24p. (gr. 3-5). lib. bdg. 22.60 *(978-0-7613-6532-7(X)*, Lerner Pubns.) Lerner Publishing Group.
Linde, Barbara M. Quarter Horses. 2012. (Horsing Around Ser.). (ENG.). 24p. (J). (gr. 2-5). pap. 8.15 *(978-1-4339-6470-1(8))*; lib. bdg. 22.60 *(978-1-4339-6468-8(6))* Stevens, Gareth Publishing LLLP. (Gareth Stevens Learning Library).
O'Brien, Kim. Caballos Cuarto de Milla. Strictly Spanish LLC. Staff, tr. from ENG. 2012. (Caballos/Horses Ser.).Tr. of American Quarter Horses. (SPA, MUL & ENG.). 24p. (gr. k-1). lib. bdg. 21.99 *(978-1-4296-9224-3(3))* Capstone Press of Coughlan Cos.
Scheff, Matt. Andrew Luck, 1 vol. 2016. (ENG., Illus.). 32p. (J). *(978-1-62403-825-9(5))* ABDO Publishing Co.
Stone, Lynn M. American Quarter Horses. 2007. (Eye to Eye with Horses (High Interest) Ser.). (Illus.). 24p. (J). (gr. 3-6). lib. bdg. 27.07 *(978-1-60044-579-8(9))* Rourke Educational Media.

QUASARS

Owen, Ruth. Quasars. 2012. (Explore Outer Space Ser.). (ENG., Illus.). 32p. (J). (gr. 3-6). 25.25 *(978-1-4488-8076-8(9))*; pap. 10.00 *(978-1-61533-605-0(2))* Windmill Bks.
World Book, Inc Staff, contrib. by. Quasars & Black Holes. 2010. (J). *(978-0-7166-9552-3(9))* World Bk., Inc.

QUASI-STELLAR RADIO SOURCES

see Quasars

QUASIMODO (FICTITIOUS CHARACTER)—FICTION

The Hunchback of Notre Dame. (Read-Along Ser.). (J). 7.99 incl. audio *(978-1-55723-992-1(4))* Walt Disney Records.

QUEBEC (PROVINCE)

Arsenault, Elaine. F Is for French: Un Livre d'Alphabet Sur le Quebec - A Quebec Alphabet. Benoit, Renne, illus. 2013. (Discover Canada Province by Province Ser.). (FRE, ENG & MUL.). 40p. (J). (gr. 1-4). 17.95 *(978-1-58536-435-0(5)*, 202351) Sleeping Bear Pr.
Malarek, Victor. Hey Malarek! The True Story of a Street Kid Who Made It. 2nd ed. 2012. (ENG.). 244p. pap. 22.95 *(978-1-4594-0047-4(X)*, 9781459400474) Lorimer, James & Co., Ltd., Pubs. CAN. Dist: Casemate Pubs. & Bk. Distributors, LLC.

QUEBEC (PROVINCE)—FICTION

Autio, Karen. Second Watch, 1 vol. 2005. (ENG., Illus.). 208p. (J). (gr. 3-7). per. 8.95 *(978-1-55039-151-0(8))* Sono Nis Pr. CAN. Dist: Orca Bk. Pubs. USA.
Brouwer, Sigmund & Gingras, Gaston. La Revanche des Loups Gris, 1 vol. Griffiths, Dean, illus. 2011. (Loups Gris Ser.). (FRE.). 72p. (J). (gr. 2-3). pap. 6.95 *(978-1-4598-0011-3(7))* Orca Bk. Pubs. USA.
Bruchac, Joseph. The Winter People. 2004. (ENG., Illus.). 176p. (J). (gr. 3-7). 7.99 *(978-0-14-240229-0(X)*, Puffin Books) Penguin Young Readers Group.

Burgess, Barbara. The Magic Manuscript: The Nine Companions. 2013. 234p. pap. 12.99 *(978-0-9918574-3-2(7))* Sulby Hall Publishing.
Fitch, Sheree. One More Step, 1 vol. 2006. (Orca Soundings Ser.). (ENG.). 112p. (YA). (gr. 8-12). 14.95 *(978-1-55143-554-1(3))* Orca Bk. Pubs. USA.
Grant, Robert. Jack in the Bush or A Summer on a Salmon River. 2005. pap. 33.95 *(978-1-4179-5573-2(2))* Kessinger Publishing, LLC.
Gunderson, Jessica. Passage to Fortune: Searching for Saguenay. Kurtz, Rory, illus. 2016. (Discovering the New World Ser.). (ENG.). 96p. (gr. 3-4). lib. bdg. 26.65 *(978-1-4965-3481-1(6)*, Connect) Stone Arch Bks.
Henty, George Alfred. With Wolfe in Canad: The Winning of a Continent. 2011. 378p. pap. 19.95 *(978-1-61179-149-5(9))* Fireship Pr.
Littell, William Adams. Guillaume. 2008. 74p. pap. 10.00 *(978-0-8059-7757-8(0))* Dorrance Publishing Co., Inc.
Noel, Michel. Good for Nothing, 1 vol. Tanaka, Shelley, tr. from FRE. 2006. (ENG.). 256p. (J). (gr. 6-10). pap. 14.95 *(978-0-88899-616-9(0)*, Libros Tigrillo) Groundwood Bks. CAN. Dist: Publishers Group West (PGW).
Parker, Gilbert. Wild Youth. 2009. 108p. pap. 9.95 *(978-1-60664-359-4(2))* Rodgers, Alan Bks.
Perkyns, Dorothy. Bridget's Black '47. 2009. (ENG.). 160p. (J). (gr. 5-18). pap. 12.99 *(978-1-55488-400-1(4))* Dundum CAN. Dist: Ingram Publisher Services.
Polak, Monique. The Middle of Everywhere, 1 vol. 2009. (ENG., Illus.). 208p. (YA). (gr. 7-12). pap. 12.95 *(978-1-55469-090-9(0))* Orca Bk. Pubs. USA.
Pont, Beattie. Grandma, Tell Me More: Fishing with Grandpa. 2013. 80p. (gr. 2-4). pap. 19.95 *(978-1-4817-2073-1(2))* AuthorHouse.
Roberts, Dw. Pep Squad Mysteries Book: Trouble on Avalance Mountain. 2010. (Illus.). 86p. pap. 8.99 *(978-0-557-16575-9(X))* Lulu Pr., Inc.
Stoddart, Heidi Jardine. Return to the Sea, 1 vol. 2007. (ENG., Illus.). 32p. (J). (gr. -1-2). pap. 10.95 *(978-1-55109-606-3(4))* Nimbus Publishing, Ltd. CAN. Dist: Orca Bk. Pubs. USA.
Wallace, Karen. Raspberries on the Yangtze. 2013. (ENG.). 160p. (J). pap. 8.99 *(978-1-4711-2122-7(4)*, Simon & Schuster Children's) Simon & Schuster, Ltd. GBR. Dist: Simon & Schuster, Inc.
White, Tara. Where I Belong, 1 vol. 2015. (ENG., Illus.). 148p. (YA). (gr. 7-10). pap. 12.95 *(978-1-896580-77-7(7))* Tradewind Bks. CAN. Dist: Orca Bk. Pubs. USA.

QUEBEC (QUEBEC)—FICTION

Gingras, Marie Claude. Let's Spend Summer with Fred. 2012. 198p. 24.95 *(978-1-4626-4413-1(9))* America Star Bks.
Henty, George Alfred. With Wolfe in Canada: The Winning of a Continent. 2006. per. 8.95 *(978-1-57646-980-4(8))* Quiet Vision Publishing.
Hotte, Sylvain. Power Forward. Roberts, Casey, tr. 2012. (Break Away Ser.). (ENG., Illus.). 180p. (YA). (gr. 8). pap. 16.95 *(978-1-926824-42-0(3))* Baraka Bks. CAN. Dist: Independent Pubs. Group.
Kovacs, Deborah. Catie Copley's Great Escape. Williams, Jared T., illus. 2009. (J). 17.95 *(978-1-56792-382-7(8))*; (ENG.). 32p. (gr. -1-3). 17.95 *(978-1-56792-379-7(8))* Godine, David R. Pub.

QUEBEC CAMPAIGN, 1759, 1759—FICTION

Altsheler, Joseph A. The French & Indian War Novels: The Lords of the Wild & The Sun of Quebec, Vol. 3. 2008. (J). reprint ed. 428p. *(978-1-84677-590-1(6))*; 424p. pap. *(978-1-84677-589-5(2))* Leonaur Ltd.
—The Sun of Quebec: A Story of a Great Crisis. 2006. (French & Indian War Ser.: Vol. 6). 324p. (J). reprint ed. 29.95 *(978-1-4218-2337-9(3))*; pap. 14.95 *(978-1-4218-2437-6(X))* 1st World Publishing, Inc. (1st World Library - Literary Society).
—The Sun of Quebec: A Story of a Great Crisis. (French & Indian War Ser.: Vol. 6). (J). reprint ed. 25.95 *(978-0-8488-0907-2(6))* Amereon Ltd.
—The Sun of Quebec: A Story of a Great Crisis. l.t. ed. (French & Indian War Ser.: Vol. 6). (J). reprint ed. 2007. 296p. pap. 23.99 *(978-1-4264-9822-0(5))* 2008. 300p. 28.99 *(978-0-554-25710-5(6))* 2008. 300p. 25.99 *(978-0-554-35013-4(0))* 2007. (ENG.). 264p. pap. 21.99 *(978-1-4264-9441-3(6))* Creative Media Partners, LLC.
—The Sun of Quebec: A Story of a Great Crisis. 2007. (French & Indian War Ser.: Vol. 6). 280p. (J). reprint ed. per. *(978-1-4065-6552-2(0))* Dodo Pr.
—The Sun of Quebec: A Story of a Great Crisis. 2007. (French & Indian War Ser.: Vol. 6). 196p. (J). reprint ed. per. *(978-1-4068-1689-1(2))* Echo Library.
—The Sun of Quebec: A Story of a Great Crisis. 2010. (French & Indian War Ser.: Vol. 6). (Illus.). 176p. (J). (gr. 4-7). reprint ed. pap. 19.99 *(978-1-153-72258-2(5))* General Bks. LLC.
—The Sun of Quebec: A Story of a Great Crisis. 2011. (French & Indian War Ser.: Vol. 6). (J). (gr. 4-7). reprint ed. *(978-1-164-50609-6(9))* Kessinger Publishing, LLC.
—The Sun of Quebec: A Story of a Great Crisis. Wrenn, Charles L., illus. (French & Indian War Ser.: Vol. 6). 356p. (J). reprint ed. 2010. (gr. 4-7). pap. 25.56 *(978-1-163-19471-3(9))* 2008. 46.95 *(978-1-4366-7287-0(2))* 2007. per. 31.95 *(978-1-4325-9779-5(5))* Kessinger Publishing, LLC.
—The Sun of Quebec: A Story of a Great Crisis. 2012. (French & Indian War Ser.: Vol. 6). 276p. (J). (gr. 4-7). reprint ed. pap. *(978-3-8472-3211-7(8))* Tredition GmbH.

QUEENS

see Kings, Queens, Rulers, etc.

QUERIES

see Questions and Answers

QUESTIONS AND ANSWERS

Abitz, Diana, et al. Know-the-Facts Review Game: 100 Must-Know Facts in a Q & A Game Format to Help Kids Really Remember Standards-Based Social Studies Information. 2005. (Ancient Civilizations Ser.). (ENG.). 144p. pap. 14.99 *(978-0-439-37432-3(4)*, Teaching Resources) Scholastic, Inc.
Adler, David A. A Little at a Time. Tong, Paul, illus. 2010. (ENG.). 32p. (J). (gr. -1-3). 16.95 *(978-0-8234-1739-1(5))* Holiday Hse., Inc.
Amazing Questions & Answers. 2003. 512p. 9.98 *(978-1-4054-0738-0(7))* Parragon, Inc.
American Girl Editorial Staff. Coconut Quiz Book: Tear & Share Quizzes for You & a Friend. 2004. (ENG., Illus.). 80p. (J). pap. 7.95 *(978-1-58485-912-3(1))* American Girl Publishing, Inc.
Anthony, Erin. I-Ballers: Little Books for Big Minds. 2005. (I-Ballers Ser.). (ENG.). pap. 4.95 *(978-1-57528-938-0(5))* Univ. Games.
Avista Products. Blackbook Directory & Yearbook 2010-11: Black Business Year in Review, vol. 1. annuals Media Write, ed. Red Baklava, photos by. aut. collector's ed. 2011. (ENG., Illus.). 160p. 65.00 *(978-0-9798741-0-9(6))* Avista Products.
AZ Books Staff. Countries & People. Borovik, Alija et al, eds. 2013. (Little Genius Ser.). (ENG.). 150p. (J). (gr. 1-3). bds. 19.95 *(978-1-61889-139-6(1))* AZ Bks. LLC.
—History & Discoveries. Shumovich, Nadegda et al, eds. 2013. (Little Genius Ser.). (ENG.). 150p. (J). (gr. 1-3). bds. 19.95 *(978-1-61889-138-9(3))* AZ Bks. LLC.
—Wild Nature. Kokash, Elena et al, eds. 2013. (Little Genius Ser.). (ENG.). 150p. (J). (gr. 1-3). bds. 19.95 *(978-1-61889-140-2(5))* AZ Bks. LLC.
Beaumont, Holly. Why Do Monkeys & Other Mammals Have Fur? 2015. (Animal Body Coverings Ser.). (ENG., Illus.). 24p. (gr. 1-3). pap. 6.99 *(978-1-4846-2539-2(0)*, Heinemann Read & Learn) Heinemann-Raintree.
—Why Do Owls & Other Birds Have Feathers? 2015. (Animal Body Coverings Ser.). (ENG., Illus.). 24p. (gr. 1-3). pap. 6.99 *(978-1-4846-2538-5(2)*, Heinemann Read & Learn) Heinemann-Raintree.
Beilenson, Suzanne. Quiz Book: Who R U? 2008. (Activity Book Ser.). 160p. (J). (gr. k-5). spiral bd. 12.99 *(978-1-59359-807-5(6))* Peter Pauper Pr. Inc.
Berger, Gilda & Berger, Melvin. Dangerous Animals. 2009. (Scholastic True or False Ser.: 5). (ENG.). 48p. (J). (gr. 2-5). pap. 4.99 *(978-0-545-00395-7(4)*, Scholastic Reference) Scholastic, Inc.
Berger, Melvin & Berger, Gilda. Are Mountains Getting Taller? Questions & Answers about the Changing Earth. Carter, Robin, illus. 2003. (Question & Answer Ser.). (ENG.). 48p. (J). pap. 5.95 *(978-0-439-26673-4(4)*, Scholastic Reference) Scholastic, Inc.
—Hurricanes Have Eyes but Can't See: And Other Amazing Facts about Wild Weather. 2003. (Illus.). 48p. (J). *(978-0-439-54980-6(9))* Scholastic, Inc.
—Reptiles. 2008. (Scholastic True or False Ser.: 3). (ENG.). 48p. (J). (gr. 2-5). pap. 4.99 *(978-0-545-00393-3(8)*, Scholastic Reference) Scholastic, Inc.
Biggest Ever Book of Questions & Answers. 2003. 256p. (J). 12.98 *(978-1-4054-1710-5(2))* Parragon, Inc.
Bodden, Valerie. Preparing for an Exam. 2014. (J). *(978-1-60818-282-4(7)*, Creative Education) Creative Co., The.
Bokram, Karen & Faithgirlz! and Girls' Life Magazine Editors. Big Book of Quizzes: Fun, Quirky Questions for You & Your Friends, 1 vol. 2014. (Faithgirlz Ser.). (ENG.). 128p. (J). pap. 12.99 *(978-0-310-74604-1(3))* Zonderkidz.
Boyer, Crispin. This or That? The Wacky Book of Choices to Reveal the Hidden You. 2014. (ENG., Illus.). 176p. (J). (gr. 3-7). pap. 12.99 *(978-1-4263-1557-2(0)*, National Geographic Children's Bks.) National Geographic Society.
Boyer, Crispin. What Would Happen? Serious Answers to Silly Questions. 2017. (ENG.). 176p. (J). (gr. 3-7). lib. bdg. 24.90 ***(978-1-4263-2771-1(4))***; (Illus.). pap. 14.99 ***(978-1-4263-2770-4(6))*** National Geographic Society. (National Geographic Children's Bks.).
Brain Quest Editors. Brain Quest America: 850 Questions 850 Answers Celebrating Our Nation's History People & Culture. rev. ed. 2013. (ENG.). 152p. (J). (gr. 3-6). 11.95 *(978-0-7611-7239-0(4)*, 17239) Workman Publishing Co., Inc.
—Brain Quest for the Car: 1100 Questions, 1100 Answers, All about America. rev. ed. 2013. (ENG.). 152p. (J). (gr. 2-6). 11.95 *(978-0-7611-7401-1(X)*, 17401) Workman Publishing Co., Inc.
—Brain Quest Presidents. 3rd rev. ed. 2013. (ENG.). 152p. (J). (gr. 3-6). 11.95 *(978-0-7611-7238-3(6)*, 17238) Workman Publishing Co., Inc.
Brennan, Linda Crotta. We Have Earthquakes. 2014. (Tell Me Why Library). (ENG., Illus.). 24p. (J). (gr. 2-5). 25.64 *(978-1-63188-011-7(X)*, 205451) Cherry Lake Publishing.
—We Have Tornadoes. 2014. (Tell Me Why Library). (ENG., Illus.). 24p. (J). (gr. 2-5). 25.64 *(978-1-63188-012-4(8)*, 205455) Cherry Lake Publishing.
Brooks, Riley & Hodgin, Molly. One Direction: Quiz Book. 2012. (ENG.). 48p. (J). (gr. 3-7). pap. 3.99 *(978-0-545-50545-1(3))* Scholastic, Inc.
Bryant, Ray, illus. The Book of Space. 2013. (Questions Ser.). (ENG.). 64p. (J). (gr. k-3). 7.99 *(978-0-7534-7099-2(3)*, 9780753470992, Kingfisher) Roaring Brook Pr.
Brynie, Faith Hickman. 101 Questions..., 6 vols. Holm, Sharon Lane, illus. Incl. 101 Questions about Blood & Circulation with Answers Straight from the Heart. 2001. lib. bdg. 27.90 *(978-0-7613-1455-4(5))*; 101 Questions about Food & Digestion: That Have Been Eating at You until Now. 2002. lib. bdg. 30.60 *(978-0-7613-2309-9(0))*; 101 Questions about Your Immune System You Felt Defenseless to Answer until Now. 2000. lib. bdg. 30.60 *(978-0-7613-1569-8(1))*; 101 Questions about Your Skin That Got under Your Skin... until Now. 2000. lib. bdg. 30.60 *(978-0-7613-1259-8(5))*; 176p. (gr. 7-12). (Illus.). 2004. 139.50 o.p. *(978-0-7613-3139-1(5)*, Twenty-First Century Bks.) Lerner Publishing Group.
—101 Questions about Sex & Sexuality: With Answers for the Curious, Cautious, & Confused. Holm, Sharon, illus. 2003. (101 Questions... Ser.). (ENG.). 176p. (gr. 7-12). lib. bdg. 30.60 *(978-0-7613-2310-5(4)*, Twenty-First Century Bks.) Lerner Publishing Group.
Bugbird, Tim. Me Myself & I. 2008. (Illus.). 93p. (J). (gr. 4-7). pap. *(978-1-84610-864-8(0))* Make Believe Ideas.
Burchett, Author Walter, BA. Christian children's questions & answers abraham & keturah to israel & rachel Volume 2. 2009. 32p. pap. 14.28 *(978-0-557-08256-8(0))* Lulu Pr., Inc.
—Christian children's questions & answers adam & eve to abraham & sarah Volume 1. 2009. 36p. pap. 14.44 *(978-0-557-08219-3(6))* Lulu Pr., Inc.
—Christian children's questions & answers birth of christ Volume 5. 2009. 33p. pap. 14.32 *(978-0-557-08275-9(7))* Lulu Pr., Inc.
—Christian children's questions & answers joseph (coat of many colors) Volume 3. 2009. 32p. pap. 14.28 *(978-0-557-08276-6(5))* Lulu Pr., Inc.
—Christian children's questions & answers moses Volume 4. 2009. 32p. pap. 14.28 *(978-0-557-08123-3(8))* Lulu Pr., Inc.
—Christian children's questions & answers resurrection of christ Volume 7. 2009. 32p. pap. 14.28 *(978-0-557-08245-2(5))* Lulu Pr., Inc.
Calhoun, Kelly. Colas Reviradas. 2016. (Adivina (Guess What) Ser.). (SPA., Illus.). 24p. (J). (gr. k-2). 28.50 *(978-1-63471-453-2(9)*, 208875) Cherry Lake Publishing.
—Crines Majestuosas (Majestic Manes) Caballo (Horse) 2016. (Adivina (Guess What) Ser.). (SPA., Illus.). 24p. (J). (gr. k-2). 28.50 *(978-1-63471-450-1(4)*, 208863) Cherry Lake Publishing.
—Fast & Flightless: Ostrich. 2015. (Guess What Ser.). (ENG., Illus.). 24p. (J). (gr. k-2). 28.50 *(978-1-63362-627-0(X)*, 206664) Cherry Lake Publishing.
—Ferocidad Felina (Fiercely Feline) León (Lion) 2016. (Adivina (Guess What) Ser.). (SPA., Illus.). 24p. (J). (gr. k-2). 28.50 *(978-1-63471-448-8(2)*, 208855) Cherry Lake Publishing.
—Fiercely Feline: Lion. 2015. (Guess What Ser.). (ENG.). 24p. (J). (gr. k-2). pap. 12.79 *(978-1-63362-713-0(6)*, 206673) Cherry Lake Publishing.
—Majestic Manes: Horse. 2015. (Guess What Ser.). (ENG., Illus.). 24p. (J). (gr. k-2). pap. 12.79 *(978-1-63362-711-6(X)*, 206685) Cherry Lake Publishing.
—Nadadores Escamosos (Scaly Swimmers) Cocodrilo (Crocodile) 2016. (Adivina (Guess What) Ser.). (SPA.). 24p. (J). (gr. k-2). 28.50 *(978-1-63471-451-8(2)*, 208867) Cherry Lake Publishing.
—Poised & Pink: Flamingo. 2015. (Guess What Ser.). (ENG., Illus.). 24p. (J). (gr. k-2). pap. 12.79 *(978-1-63362-715-4(2)*, 206689) Cherry Lake Publishing.
—Saltarines de Alta Velocidad (High-Speed Hoppers) Canguro (Kangaroo) 2016. (Adivina (Guess What) Ser.). (SPA., Illus.). 24p. (J). (gr. k-2). 28.50 *(978-1-63471-449-5(0)*, 208859) Cherry Lake Publishing.
—Scaly Swimmers: Crocodile. 2015. (Guess What Ser.). (ENG., Illus.). 24p. (J). (gr. k-2). 28.50 *(978-1-63362-629-4(6)*, 206692) Cherry Lake Publishing.
—Slinky Sliders: Rattlesnake. 2015. (Guess What Ser.). (ENG., Illus.). 24p. (J). (gr. k-2). pap. 12.79 *(978-1-63362-721-5(7)*, 206697) Cherry Lake Publishing.
—Twisty Tails: Chameleon. 2015. (Guess What Ser.). (ENG., Illus.). 24p. (J). (gr. k-2). 28.50 *(978-1-63362-628-7(8)*, 206708) Cherry Lake Publishing.
—Velocidad Sin Vuelo (Fast & Flightless) Avestruz (Ostrich) 2016. (Adivina (Guess What) Ser.). (SPA.). 24p. (J). (gr. k-2). 28.50 *(978-1-63471-446-4(6)*, 208847) Cherry Lake Publishing.
Callella, Trisha. I Have, Who Has? Language Arts Grades 1-2. Taylor, Jennifer, ed. Peterson, Barbara, illus. 2007. (J). per. 19.99 *(978-1-59198-429-0(7))* Creative Teaching Pr., Inc.
Callery, Sean. I Wonder Why There's a Hole in the Sky. 2012. (I Wonder Why Ser.). (ENG., Illus.). 32p. (J). (gr. k-3). 6.99 *(978-0-7534-6799-2(2)*, 9780753467992, Kingfisher) Roaring Brook Pr.
Calmenson, Stephanie. Ollie's School Day. Carter, Abby, illus. 2012. (ENG.). 24p. (J). 15.95 *(978-0-8234-2377-4(8))* Holiday Hse., Inc.
Campbell's Comstant Quiz Companion: The Middle/High School Book of Lists, Terms, & Questions. 2004. (YA). per. 24.95 *(978-0-944322-39-0(5))* Patrick's Pr.
Canavan, Thomas. Do Plants Really Eat Insects? Questions & Answers about the Science of Plants. 2013. (Science F. A. Q. Ser.). (Illus.). 32p. (gr. 3-6). 31.35 *(978-1-78212-392-7(X))* Arcturus Publishing GBR. Dist: Black Rabbit Bks.
—Does It Really Rain Frogs? Questions & Answers about Planet Earth. 2013. (Science F. A. Q. Ser.). (Illus.). 32p. (gr. 3-6). 31.35 *(978-1-78212-393-4(8))* Arcturus Publishing GBR. Dist: Black Rabbit Bks.
—What Makes You Hiccup? Questions & Answers about the Human Body. 2013. (Science F. A. Q. Ser.). (Illus.). 32p. (gr. 3-6). 31.35 *(978-1-78212-394-1(6))* Arcturus Publishing GBR. Dist: Black Rabbit Bks.
—Why Do Ice Cubes Float? Questions & Answers about the Science of Everyday Materials. 2013. (Science F. A. Q. Ser.). (Illus.). 32p. (gr. 3-6). 31.35 *(978-1-78212-396-5(2))* Arcturus Publishing GBR. Dist: Black Rabbit Bks.
—Why Do Zebras Have Stripes? Questions & Answers about Animals. 2013. (Science F. A. Q. Ser.). 32p. (gr. 3-6). 31.35 *(978-1-78212-397-2(0))* Arcturus Publishing GBR. Dist: Black Rabbit Bks.
Capstone Press Staff & Time for Kids Magazine Staff. Little Kids Book of Why, 1 vol. 2014. (Little Kids Books of Why Ser.). (ENG.). 48p. (gr. 5-6). 106.60 *(978-1-4914-1930-4(X))* Capstone Press of Coughlan Cos.
Card, Michael. Tell Me Why: Eternal Answers to Children's Timeless Questions. 2004. (Tell Me Ser.). (Illus.). 48p. (gr. -1-3). 17.99 *(978-1-58134-031-0(1))* Crossway.
Carle, Eric. De la Cabeza a los Pies, 1 vol. Carle, Eric, illus. 2007.Tr. of From Head to Toe. (SPA., Illus.). 32p. (J). (gr. -1-3). pap. 6.99 *(978-0-06-051313-9(6))* HarperCollins Pubs.
—From Head to Toe. Carle, Eric, illus. 2007. (ENG., Illus.). 32p. (J). (gr. -1-k). pap. 24.99 *(978-0-06-111972-9(5)*, HarperFestival) HarperCollins Pubs.
Carson, Mary Kay. How Strong Is an Ant? And Other Questions about Bugs & Insects. Schwartz, Carol, illus. 2014. (Good Question! Ser.). (ENG.). 40p. (J). (gr. 1). 12.95 *(978-1-4549-0684-1(7))* Sterling Publishing Co., Inc.
—Who Was Susan B. Anthony Vote? And Other Questions about Women's Suffrage. 2015. (Good Question! Ser.). (ENG., Illus.). 32p. (J). (gr. 2). pap. 5.95 *(978-1-4549-1242-2(1))* Sterling Publishing Co., Inc.
—Why Couldn't Susan B. Anthony Vote? And Other Questions about Women's Suffrage. 2015. (Good Question! Ser.). (ENG., Illus.). 40p. (J). (gr. 2). 12.95 *(978-1-4549-1241-5(3))* Sterling Publishing Co., Inc.
Cave, Holly. Really, Really Big Questions about Science. Aspinall, Marc, illus. 2014. (Really Really Big Questions Ser.). (ENG.). 64p. (J). (gr. 4-7). 16.99 *(978-0-7534-7181-4(7)*, 9780753471814, Kingfisher) Roaring Brook Pr.
Cerasi, Christopher. Star Wars: Fandex Deluxe Edition. deluxe ed. 2008. (ENG., Illus.). 75p. (J). (gr. 4-12). 13.95 *(978-0-7611-5230-9(X)*, 15230) Workman Publishing Co., Inc.
Chadow, Alysa. US States. 2003. pap. 14.00 *(978-0-8059-6054-9(6))* Dorrance Publishing Co., Inc.
Charman, Andrew. I Wonder Why Leaves Change Color: And Other Questions about Plants. 2012. (I Wonder Why Ser.). (ENG., Illus.). (J). (gr. k-3). pap. 6.99 *(978-0-7534-6697-1(X)*, 9780753466971, Kingfisher) Roaring Brook Pr.
—I Wonder Why the Dinosaurs Died Out: And Other Questions about Extinct & Endangered Animals. 2013. (I Wonder Why Ser.). (ENG., Illus.). 32p. (J). (gr. k-3). 6.99 *(978-0-7534-6953-8(7)*, 9780753469538, Kingfisher) Roaring Brook Pr.
Children's Big Book of Questions & Answers. 2011. (Illus.). 224p. (J). *(978-1-4351-3677-9(2))* Barnes & Noble, Inc.
A Child's First Library of Learning, 30 bks. Incl. Animal Friends. Time-Life Staff. (Illus.). 88p. (gr. -1-4). 1999. 14.95 *(978-0-8094-4849-4(1))*; Animals in Action. (Illus.). 88p. (gr. -1-2). 1999. 14.95 *(978-0-8094-4869-2(6))*; Dangerous Animals. Time-Life Books Editors. Kinney, Karin, ed. (Illus.). 88p. (gr. -1-3). 1996. 16.00 *(978-0-8094-9480-4(9))*; Everyday Life. Cfl. (Illus.). 88p. (gr. -1-4). 1999. 14.95 *(978-0-8094-4865-4(3))*; Explorers & Adventurers. Time-Life Books Editors. Fallow, Allan, ed. (Illus.). 88p. (gr. -1-3). 1996. lib. bdg. *(978-0-8094-9482-8(5))*; Famous Places. Gakken Co. Ltd. Editors. Time-Life Books Editors, tr. (Illus.). 88p. (gr. 1-4). 1999. 14.95 *(978-0-8094-4893-7(9))*; Feelings & Manners. Time-Life Books Editors. Fallow, Allan, ed. (Illus.). 88p. (gr. -1-3). 1997. 14.95 *(978-0-8094-9483-5(3))*; Flowers & Trees. Time-Life Staff. (Illus.). 88p. (gr. 1-4). 1999. 14.95 *(978-0-8094-4857-9(2))*; Health & Safety. Time-Life Books Editors. 1996. *(978-0-8094-9479-8(5))*; How Things Work in Your Home. Time-Life Books Editors. (Illus.). 88p. (gr. 1-4). 1999. 14.95 *(978-0-8094-4873-9(4))*; Insect World. Time-Life Books Editors. (Illus.). 88p. (gr. -1-3). 1999. 14.95 *(978-0-8094-4841-8(6))*; Science Starter. Time-Life Books Editors. (Illus.). 88p. (gr. 1-4). 1999. 14.95 *(978-0-8094-4881-4(5))*; Sky & Earth. Time-Life Books Editors. (Illus.). 88p. (gr. 1-4). 1999. 14.95 *(978-0-8094-4837-1(8))*; Things Around Us. Time-Life Staff. (Illus.). 88p. (gr. -1-2). 1999. 14.95 *(978-0-8094-4845-6(9))*; Things to Do. Gakken Co. Ltd. Editors & Time-Life Books Editors. (Illus.). 88p. (gr. 1-4). 1999. 14.95 *(978-0-8094-4897-5(1))*; Wheels & Wings. Gakken Co. Ltd. Editors. Time-Life Books Editors, tr. (Illus.). 88p. (gr. 1-4). 1999. 14.95 *(978-0-8094-4861-6(0))*; Where Things Come From. Time-Life Books Editors. Fallow, Allan, ed. (Illus.). 88p. (gr. -1-3). 1997. *(978-0-8094-9484-2(1))*; Wind & Weather. Gakken Co. Ltd. Editors. Time-Life Books Editors, tr. (Illus.). 88p. (gr. 1-4). 1999. 14.95 *(978-0-8094-4829-6(7))*; World We Live In. Gakken Co. Ltd. Editors. Time-Life Books Editors, tr. (Illus.). 88p. (gr. 1-4). 1999. 14.95 *(978-0-8094-4885-2(8))*; (J). 403.88 *(978-0-8094-9499-6(X))* Time-Life, Inc.
Chorba, April & Phillips, Karen. It's All about Us (... Especially Me!) A Journal of Totally Personal Questions for You & Your Friends. 2013. (ENG.). 126p. (J). (gr. 3). 16.99 *(978-0-545-49280-5(7))* Klutz.
Christensen, Evelyn B. Kentucky Puzzles: Bluegrass Brainteasers for Ages 6 To 106. 2014. Orig. Title: Kentucky Puzzles: Bluegrass Brainteasers for Ages 6 To 106. (ENG., Illus.). 48p. pap. 9.99 *(978-1-62619-328-4(2)*, History Pr., The) Arcadia Publishing.
Ciencias. (Enciclopedias Everest Internacional Ser.). (SPA., Illus.). (YA). (gr. 5-8). 41.95 *(978-84-241-9405-5(5)*, EV7495) Everest Editora ESP. Dist: Lectorum Pubns., Inc.
Cobb, Vicki. What's the BIG Idea? Amazing Science Questions for the Curious Kid. 2013. (ENG., Illus.). 208p. (J). (gr. 2-5). pap. 12.95 *(978-1-62087-685-5(X)*, 620685, Sky Pony Pr.) Skyhorse Publishing Co., Inc.
Continents & Countries. 2008. (Question & Answers Ser.). 320p. *(978-1-4075-2528-0(X))* Parragon, Inc.
Cosgrove, Stephen & Higgins, Kitty. Trivia Pursuit. 2004. (Reader's Theater Ser.). (J). pap. *(978-1-4108-1140-0(9))* Benchmark Education Co.
Craats, Rennay. Construction Q & A. 2013. (J). *(978-1-62127-412-4(8))*; pap. *(978-1-62127-418-6(7))* Weigl Pubs., Inc.
Crompton, Samuel Willard. 100 Relationships That Shaped World History. 2015. (ENG.). 100p. pap. 7.95 *(978-0-912517-40-7(9))* Bluewood Bks.
D C Thomson Staff, ed. Bunty Annual for Girls 2004. 2003. (Illus.). 128p. (J). (gr. -1-4). *(978-0-85116-825-8(6))* Thomson, D.C. & Co., Ltd. GBR. Dist: APG Sales & Distribution Services.
Daniels, Kathryn. A Bluestocking Guide - Justice: Companion Workbook to Richard J. Maybury's Book Whatever Happened to Justice? Williams, Jane A., ed. 2004. (Bluestocking Guide Ser.). (ENG.). (YA). pap. 15.95 *(978-0-942617-45-0(2))* Bluestocking Pr.
—A Bluestocking Guide - the Money Mystery: Based on Richard J. Maybury's book the Money Mystery. Williams, Jane A., ed. 2004. (Bluestocking Guide Ser.). (ENG.). 31p. (YA). pap. 8.95 *(978-0-942617-49-8(5))* Bluestocking Pr.
Davis, Graeme. The Unauthorized Harry Potter Quiz Book: 165 Questions Ranging from the Sorcerer's Stone to the Deathly Hallows. 2008. 76p. pap. 15.38 *(978-1-934840-44-3(0))* Nimble Bks. LLC.
Davis, Kenneth C. Don't Know Much about Abraham Lincoln, Vol. 4. Shepperson, Rob, illus. 2003. (Don't Know Much About Ser.). 144p. (J). (gr. 3-7). pap. 4.99 *(978-0-06-442127-0(9))* HarperCollins Pubs.
—Don't Know Much about Abraham Lincoln Abraham Lincoln, Vol. 4. Shepperson, Rob, illus. 2004. (Don't Know Much About Ser.). 144p. (J). (gr. 2-5). 15.89 *(978-0-06-028820-4(5))* HarperCollins Pubs.
—Don't Know Much about American History. Faulkner, Matt, illus. 2003. (Don't Know Much About Ser.). (ENG.). 224p. (J). (gr. 3-7). pap. 6.99 *(978-0-06-440836-3(1))* HarperCollins Pubs.
—Don't Know Much About American History. 2004. (Don't Know Much about Ser.). 224p. (J). (gr. 4-7). pap. 40.00 incl. audio *(978-0-8072-2092-4(2)*, Listening Library) Random Hse. Audio Publishing Group.
—Don't Know Much about Planet Earth. unabr. ed. 2004. (Don't Know Much about Ser.). 144p. (J). (gr. 4-7). pap.

29.00 incl. audio (978-0-8072-0660-7(1), Listening Library) Random Hse. Audio Publishing Group.

—Don't Know Much about Sitting Bull Sitting Bull, Vol. 2. 2003. (Don't Know Much About Ser.). (Illus.). 144p. (J). (gr. 3-7). 16.89 (978-0-06-028818-1(3)) HarperCollins Pubs.

—Don't Know Much about Space. unabr. ed. 2004. (Don't Know Much about Ser.). 144p. (J). (gr. 4-7). pap. 29.00 incl. audio (978-0-8072-0661-4(X), Listening Library) Random Hse. Audio Publishing Group.

—Don't Know Much about the 50 States. Andriani, Renee, illus. 2004. (Don't Know Much About Ser.). (ENG.). 64p. (J). (gr. 1-4). pap. 7.99 (978-0-06-446227-3(7)) HarperCollins Pubs.

—Presidents. Martin, Pedro, illus. rev. ed. 2009. (Don't Know Much About Ser.). (ENG.). 64p. (J). (gr. k-4). pap. 6.99 (978-0-06-171823-6(8), Collins) HarperCollins Pubs.

Daynes, Katie. Questions & Answers. 2013. (Usborne Lift the Flap Bks.). (ENG., Illus.). 14p. (J). 14.99 (978-0-7945-3207-9(1), Usborne) EDC Publishing.

De La Bedoyere C. Why Why Why Cant Penguins Fly. 2008. 32p. pap. (978-1-84810-000-8(0)) Miles Kelly Publishing, Ltd.

De la Bédoyère, Camilla. Why Why Why Are Orang-Utans So Hairy? 2008. (Why Why Why Ser.). (Illus.). 32p. (J). (gr. 4-7). pap. (978-1-84810-003-9(5)) Miles Kelly Publishing, Ltd.

—Why Why Why Did Dinosaurs Lay Eggs? 2008. (Why Why Why Ser.). (Illus.). 32p. (J). (gr. -1-3). pap. (978-1-84810-001-5(9)) Miles Kelly Publishing, Ltd.

DeRubertis, Barbara. Let's Celebrate Thanksgiving Day. Sperling, Thomas, illus. 2013. (Holidays & Heroes Ser.). 32p. (gr. 1-3). pap. 7.95 (978-1-57565-636-6(1)) Kane Press, Inc.

Dewin, Howard, told to. The Dog: Why Do Dogs Love to Sniff?: The Do's & Don'ts of the Dogs. 2007. (Illus.). 29p. (J). pap. (978-0-439-02255-2(X)) Scholastic, Inc.

Dickason, Chris, et al. Quiz Book for Clever Kids. Dickason, Chris, illus. 2015. (ENG., Illus.). 192p. (J). (gr. 1-5). 7.99 (978-1-78055-314-6(5)) O'Mara, Michael Bks., Ltd. GBR. Dist: Independent Pubs. Group.

DiSiena, Laura Lyn & Eliot, Hannah. Chickens Don't Fly: And Other Fun Facts. Oswald, Pete, illus. 2014. (Did You Know? Ser.). (ENG.). 32p. (J). (gr. -1-3). 17.99 (978-1-4424-9353-7(4)); pap. 6.99 (978-1-4424-9326-1(7)) Little Simon. (Little Simon).

Disiena, Laura Lyn & Eliot, Hannah. Hippos Can't Swim. 2014. (Did You Know? Ser.). lib. bdg. 16.00 (978-0-606-35424-0(7)) Turtleback Bks.

DiSiena, Laura Lyn & Eliot, Hannah. Hippos Can't Swim: And Other Fun Facts. Oswald, Pete, illus. 2014. (Did You Know? Ser.). (ENG.). 32p. (J). (gr. -1-3). 17.99 (978-1-4424-9352-0(6)); pap. 5.99 (978-1-4424-9324-7(0)) Little Simon. (Little Simon).

—Rainbows Never End: And Other Fun Facts. Oswald, Pete, illus. 2014. (Did You Know? Ser.). (ENG.). 32p. (J). (gr. -1-3). 17.99 (978-1-4814-0277-4(3)); pap. 5.99 (978-1-4814-0275-0(7)) Little Simon. (Little Simon).

—Saturn Could Sail: And Other Fun Facts. Oswald, Pete & Spurgeon, Aaron, illus. 2014. (Did You Know? Ser.). (ENG.). 32p. (J). (gr. -1-3). 17.99 (978-1-4814-1429-6(1)); pap. 6.99 (978-1-4814-1428-9(3)) Little Simon. (Little Simon).

Dockrey, Donna. Tell Me about A Place Called Heaven. 2010. 32p. pap. 14.50 (978-0-557-23820-0(X)) Lulu Pr., Inc.

Dorling Kindersley Publishing Staff. Did You Know? Amazing Answers to the Questions You Ask. 2014. (ENG., Illus.). 160p. (J). (gr. 1-3). 21.99 (978-1-4654-2045-9(2), DK Children) Dorling Kindersley Publishing, Inc.

—True or False? 2014. (ENG.). 192p. (J). (gr. 2-5). 19.99 (978-1-4654-2467-9(9), DK Children) Dorling Kindersley Publishing, Inc.

Duden, Jane. Why Do Bears Sleep All Winter? [Chicago]: A Book about Hibernation. 2010. (Why in the World? Ser.). (ENG.). 24p. pap. 6.95 (978-1-4296-5183-7(0), First Facts) Capstone Press of Coughlan Cos.

Editors of TIME For Kids Magazine. Amazing Sports & Science. 2014. (TIME for Kids Big Books of WHY Ser.). (ENG., Illus.). 48p. (J). (gr. 3-17). mass mkt. 4.99 (978-1-60320-986-1(7)) Time Inc. Bks.

—Kids Ask - We Answer. 2013. (TIME for Kids X-WHY-Z Ser.). (ENG., Illus.). 96p. (J). (gr. -1-1). 14.95 (978-1-61893-093-4(1)) Time Inc. Bks.

—Space. 2014. (TIME for Kids X-WHY-Z Ser.). (ENG., Illus.). 96p. (J). (gr. -1-1). 14.95 (978-1-61893-126-9(1)) Time Inc. Bks.

—Time for Kids Big Book of Answers: 1,001 Facts Kids Want to Know. 2015. (TIME for Kids Big Bks.). (ENG., Illus.). 192p. (J). (gr. 3-17). 19.95 (978-1-61893-150-4(4)) Time Inc. Bks.

—Time for Kids Big Book of What? 2012. (TIME for Kids Big Bks.). (ENG., Illus.). 192p. (J). (gr. 3-7). 19.95 (978-1-60320-241-1(2)) Time Inc. Bks.

—Time for Kids Big Book of Where. 2013. (TIME for Kids Big Bks.). (ENG., Illus.). 192p. (J). (gr. 3-17). 19.95 (978-1-61893-042-2(7)) Time Inc. Bks.

Equipo Staff. 1000 Preguntas y Respuestas. (SPA., Illus.). 96p. (J). (gr. 3-5). (978-84-305-8671-4(7), SU2565) Susaeta Ediciones, S.A. ESP. Dist: Lectorum Pubns., Inc.

Esbaum, Jill & National Geographic Kids Staff. Little Kids First Big Book of How. 2016. (National Geographic Little Kids First Big Bks.). (ENG., Illus.). 128p. (J). (gr. -1-3). 14.99 (978-1-4263-2329-4(8), National Geographic Children's Bks.) National Geographic Society.

Falligant, Erin & American Girl Editors, eds. Stand up for Yourself Journal: Quizzes & Questions to Help You Stand Strong Against Bullying. Martini, Angela, illus. 2011. (ENG.). 64p. (J). spiral bd. 9.95 (978-1-59369-910-9(7)) American Girl Publishing, Inc.

FAQ: Teen Life, 6 vols., Set 6. Incl. Frequently Asked Questions about Drinking & Driving. Cefrey, Holly. lib. bdg. 31.95 (978-1-4042-1809-3(2)); Frequently Asked Questions about Exercise Addiction. Willett, Edward. lib. bdg. 31.95 (978-1-4042-1806-2(8)); Frequently Asked Questions about Human Papillomavirus. Gonzalez, Lissette. lib. bdg. 31.95 (978-1-4042-1813-0(0)); Frequently Asked Questions about Migraines & Headaches. Cobb, Allan B. lib. bdg. 31.95 (978-1-4042-1814-7(9)); Frequently Asked Questions about Peer Pressure. Juzwiak, Richard. lib. bdg. 31.95 (978-1-4042-1805-5(X)); Frequently Asked Questions about Suicide. Giddens, Sandra. lib. bdg. 31.95 (978-1-4042-1811-6(4)); (Illus.). 64p. (YA). (gr. 7-12). 2008. 2008. Set lib. bdg. 175.50 (978-1-4042-1887-1(4)) Rosen Publishing Group, Inc., The.

Far from the Madding Crowd: Teaching Unit. 2003. 92p. (YA). ring bd. (978-1-58049-471-7(4), TU4714) Prestwick Hse., Inc.

Feyh, Janelle. Does God Have a Remote Control? Feyh, Alexa & Deghand, Tim, illus. l.t. ed. 2003. 66p. (J). per. 11.95 (978-1-932344-26-4(8)) Thornton Publishing, Inc.

Fougere, Isabelle. Tell Me Why? 2015. (Tell Me Bks.). (ENG., Illus.). 122p. (J). (gr. 2-6). spiral bd. 14.99 (978-0-7641-6794-2(4)) Barron's Educational Series, Inc.

Free Spirit Publishing & Stein, Deborah Jiang. Guy Talk. 2009. (In a Jar(r) Ser.). (ENG.). (J). 9.99 (978-1-57542-906-9(3)) Free Spirit Publishing, Inc.

Freedman, Deborah K. Tacoma's Twenty-One Tales: Every Student Should Be Able to Tell, Teachers, Too! 2010. (Illus.). 48p. (J). (978-0-09-846234-8(2)) Tacoma Historical Society.

Frost, Adam. The Awesome Book of Awesomeness. Bramall, Dan, illus. 2015. (ENG.). 112p. (J). (gr. 2-4). pap. 9.99 (978-1-61963-793-1(6), 9781619637931, Bloomsbury USA Childrens) Bloomsbury Publishing USA.

Gaarder, Jostein. Questions Asked. Bartlett, Don, tr. from NOR. Duezakin, Akin, illus. 2017. (ENG.). 72p. (J). (gr. -1-2). 14.00 (978-0-914671-66-4(9), Elsewhere Editiions) Steerforth Pr.

Gaff, Jackie. I Wonder Why Horses Wear Shoes. 2011. (I Wonder Why Ser.). (ENG., Illus.). 32p. (J). (gr. k-3). pap. 6.99 (978-0-7534-6526-4(4), 9780753465264, Kingfisher) Roaring Brook Pr.

—I Wonder Why the Sahara Is Cold at Night. 2014. 32p. pap. 7.00 (978-1-61003-351-0(5)) Center for the Collaborative Classroom.

—I Wonder Why the Sahara Is Cold at Night. 2nd ed. 2012. (I Wonder Why Ser.). (ENG., Illus.). 32p. (J). (gr. k-3). 6.99 (978-0-7534-6797-8(6), 9780753467978, Kingfisher) Roaring Brook Pr.

Ganeri, Anita. I Wonder Why Camels Have Humps: And Other Questions about Animals. 2012. (I Wonder Why Ser.). (ENG., Illus.). (J). (gr. k-3). pap. 6.99 (978-0-7534-6701-5(1), 9780753467015, Kingfisher) Roaring Brook Pr.

—I Wonder Why the Sea Is Salty. 2014. 32p. pap. 7.00 (978-1-61003-352-7(3)) Center for the Collaborative Classroom.

—I Wonder Why the Sea Is Salty: And Other Questions about the Oceans. 2011. (I Wonder Why Ser.). (ENG., Illus.). 32p. (J). (gr. k-3). pap. 6.99 (978-0-7534-6521-9(3), 9780753465219, Kingfisher) Roaring Brook Pr.

—I Wonder Why the Wind Blows. 2011. (I Wonder Why Ser.). (ENG., Illus.). 32p. (J). (gr. k-3). pap. 6.99 (978-0-7534-6522-6(1), 9780753465226, Kingfisher) Roaring Brook Pr.

Gardeski, Christina Mia. Cats: Questions & Answers. 2016. (Pet Questions & Answers Ser.). (ENG., Illus.). 24p. (gr. k-1). lib. bdg. 26.65 (978-1-5157-0356-3(8), Pebble Plus) Capstone Press of Coughlan Cos.

—Dogs: Questions & Answers. 2016. (Pet Questions & Answers Ser.). (ENG., Illus.). 24p. (gr. k-1). lib. bdg. 26.65 (978-1-5157-0355-6(X), Pebble Plus) Capstone Press of Coughlan Cos.

—Hamsters: Questions & Answers. 2016. (Pet Questions & Answers Ser.). (ENG., Illus.). 24p. (gr. k-1). pap. 6.95 (978-1-5157-0359-4(2)); lib. bdg. 26.65 (978-1-5157-0352-5(5)) Capstone Press of Coughlan Cos. (Pebble Plus).

—Pet Birds: Questions & Answers. 2016. (Pet Questions & Answers Ser.). (ENG., Illus.). 24p. (gr. k-1). lib. bdg. 26.65 (978-1-5157-0354-9(1), Pebble Plus) Capstone Press of Coughlan Cos.

—Pet Fish: Questions & Answers. 2016. (Pet Questions & Answers Ser.). (ENG., Illus.). 24p. (gr. k-1). lib. bdg. 26.65 (978-1-5157-0353-2(3), Pebble Plus) Capstone Press of Coughlan Cos.

George, Lynn. What Do You Know about Colonial America? (20 Questions: History Ser.). 24p. 2009. (gr. 2-3). 42.50 (978-1-60854-955-9(0), PowerKids Pr.) 2008. (Illus.). (J). (gr. 3-7). lib. bdg. 21.25 (978-1-4042-4185-5(X)) Rosen Publishing Group, Inc., The.

—What Do You Know about the American Revolution? (20 Questions: History Ser.). 24p. (gr. 2-3). 2009. 42.50 (978-1-60854-957-3(7), PowerKids Pr.) 2008. (Illus.). (J). lib. bdg. 22.60 (978-1-4042-4186-2(8)) Rosen Publishing Group, Inc., The.

—What Do You Know about the Civil War? (20 Questions: History Ser.). 24p. (gr. 2-3). 2009. 42.50 (978-1-60854-958-0(5), PowerKids Pr.) 2008. (Illus.). (J). lib. bdg. 22.60 (978-1-4042-4187-9(6)) Rosen Publishing Group, Inc., The.

—What Do You Know about the Gold Rush? (20 Questions: History Ser.). 24p. (gr. 2-3). 2009. 42.50 (978-1-60854-959-7(3), PowerKids Pr.) 2008. (J). lib. bdg. 22.60 (978-1-4042-4188-6(4)) Rosen Publishing Group, Inc., The.

—20 Questions: History, 6 vols., Set. 2008. (J). (gr. 2-4). lib. bdg. 127.50 (978-1-4042-4242-5(2)) Rosen Publishing Group, Inc., The.

Gifford, Clive. Around the World in Numbers. Hurley, Josh, illus. 2017. (ENG.). 32p. (J). (gr. k). 14.95 **(978-1-4549-2518-7(3))** Sterling Publishing Co., Inc.

Gifford, Clive. In Focus: Polar Lands. 2017. (In Focus Ser.). (ENG.). 64p. (J). pap. 12.99 (978-0-7534-7352-8(6), 9780753473528, Kingfisher) Roaring Brook Pr.

Graham, Buck. My First Big Book of Questions & Answers: Things That Go. 2005. (Illus.). 10p. bds. 9.98 (978-0-7853-7227-1(X), 7171500) Publications International, Ltd.

Graham, Monty Dr. My First Big Book of Questions & Answers: Under the Sea. 2005. (Illus.). 10p. bds. 9.98 (978-0-7853-7228-8(8), 7171400) Publications International, Ltd.

Gray, Susan H. Bears Hibernate. 2015. (Tell Me Why Library). (ENG., Illus.). 24p. (J). (gr. 2-5). pap. 12.79 (978-1-63362-029-2(8), 205873) Cherry Lake Publishing.

—Camels Have Humps. 2014. (Tell Me Why Library). (ENG.). 24p. (J). (gr. 2-5). 25.64 (978-1-63188-001-8(2), 205411) Cherry Lake Publishing.

—Dolphins Breathe Air. 2015. (Tell Me Why Library). (ENG., Illus.). 24p. (J). (gr. 2-5). pap. 12.79 (978-1-63362-030-8(1), 205877) Cherry Lake Publishing.

Gray, Susan Heinrichs. Bats Sleep Upside Down. 2015. (Tell Me Why Library). (ENG., Illus.). 24p. (J). (gr. 2-5). 27.07 (978-1-63362-608-9(3), 206616) Cherry Lake Publishing.

—Snakes Shed Their Skin. 2015. (Tell Me Why Library). (ENG., Illus.). 24p. (J). (gr. 2-5). 27.07 (978-1-63362-616-4(4), 206648) Cherry Lake Publishing.

Great Americans. Date not set. (Mini Question & Answers America Ser.). 32p. (J). 3.98 (978-0-7525-9872-7(4)) Parragon, Inc.

Great Historic Debates & Speeches, 6 Bks, Set. 2004. (J). 175.50 (978-1-4042-0350-1(8)) Rosen Publishing Group, Inc., The.

Great Scientific Questions & the Scientists Who Answered Them. 2005. (Illus.). 112p. (gr. 7-12). lib. bdg. 319.20 (978-1-4042-0356-3(7)) Rosen Publishing Group, Inc., The.

Greenwood, Rosie. I Wonder Why Volcanoes Blow Their Tops: And Other Questions about Natural Disasters. 2013. (I Wonder Why Ser.). (ENG., Illus.). 32p. (J). (gr. k-3). 6.99 (978-0-7534-6935-4(9), 9780753469354, Kingfisher) Roaring Brook Pr.

Guy, Only A. Hard Questions about Christianity. 2013. 150p. pap. 7.99 (978-1-939670-03-8(9)) VIP Ink Publishing, L.L.C.

—Hard Questions about the End Times. 2013. 80p. pap. 7.99 (978-1-939670-00-7(4)) VIP Ink Publishing, L.L.C.

Halls, Kelly Milner. Dinosaurs. Cosgrove, Lee, illus. 2015. (Lie Detector Ser.). (ENG.). 32p. (gr. k-3). pap. 5.95 (978-1-4795-8514-4(9)) Picture Window Bks.

Hamel, Raymond & Britannica Encyclopaedia, Inc. Staff. Encyclopedia Britannica General KnowledgeTrivia. 2010. (Scratch & Solve(r) Ser.). (ENG.). 160p. pap. 8.95 (978-1-4027-6635-0(1), Puzzlewright) Sterling Publishing Co., Inc.

Hamilton, Gina L. Light Q & A. 2013. (J). (978-1-62127-415-5(2)); pap. (978-1-62127-421-6(7)) Weigl Pubs., Inc.

Harte, May. Hide & Seek Kids. 2009. (Tough Toddler Bks). 16p. (gr. k-k). 42.50 (978-1-60854-571-1(7), PowerKids Pr.) Rosen Publishing Group, Inc., The.

Hazan, Maurice, creator. Dime quien Es: Spanish Dialogues Level 1. (SPA.). (J). 134.95 (978-1-932770-43-8(7), SG4) Symtalk, Inc.

—Dime quien Es: Spanish Dialogues Level 2. (SPA.). (J). 134.95 (978-1-932770-45-2(3), SG6) Symtalk, Inc.

—Dime quien Es: Spanish Dialogues Level 3. (SPA.). (YA). 199.95 (978-1-932770-55-1(0), SG16) Symtalk, Inc.

Heimberg, Justin & Gomberg, David. Radically Repulsive: Over 400 Crazy Questions! 2010. (Would You Rather... ? Ser.). (ENG., Illus.). 216p. (J). (gr. 2-18). pap. 9.95 (978-1-934734-42-1(X)) Seven Footer Pr.

Herrington, Lisa M. Amazing Mammals. 2016. (Rookie Read-About Science(tm): Strange Animals Ser.). (ENG.). 32p. (J). lib. bdg. 25.00 (978-0-531-22600-1(X), Children's Pr.) Scholastic Library Publishing.

—Cheetahs & Leopards. 2015. (Rookie Read-About(tm) Science: What's the Difference? Ser.). (ENG., Illus.). 32p. (J). lib. bdg. 25.00 (978-0-531-21481-7(8), Children's Pr.) Scholastic Library Publishing.

—Crocodiles & Alligators. 2015. (Rookie Read-About(tm) Science: What's the Difference? Ser.). (ENG., Illus.). 32p. (J). lib. bdg. 25.00 (978-0-531-21483-1(4), Children's Pr.) Scholastic Library Publishing.

—Freaky Fish. 2016. (Rookie Read-About Science(tm): Strange Animals Ser.). (ENG., Illus.). 32p. (J). lib. bdg. 25.00 (978-0-531-22601-8(8), Children's Pr.) Scholastic Library Publishing.

—Frogs & Toads. 2015. (Rookie Read-About(tm) Science: What's the Difference? Ser.). (ENG., Illus.). 32p. (J). lib. bdg. 25.00 (978-0-531-21484-8(2), Children's Pr.) Scholastic Library Publishing.

—Incredible Insects. 2016. (Rookie Read-About Science(tm): Strange Animals Ser.). (ENG., Illus.). 32p. (J). lib. bdg. 25.00 (978-0-531-22602-5(6), Children's Pr.) Scholastic Library Publishing.

—Monkeys & Apes. 2015. (Rookie Read-About(tm) Science: What's the Difference? Ser.). (ENG., Illus.). 32p. (J). lib. bdg. 25.00 (978-0-531-21486-2(9), Children's Pr.) Scholastic Library Publishing.

—Turtles & Tortoises. 2015. (Rookie Read-About(tm) Science: What's the Difference? Ser.). (ENG., Illus.). 32p. (J). lib. bdg. 25.00 (978-0-531-21482-4(6), Children's Pr.) Scholastic Library Publishing.

Hirschmann, Kris & Herndon, Ryan. Test Your Smarts! 2009. (Illus.). 80p. (J). (978-0-545-12042-5(X)) Scholastic, Inc.

Holland, Simon. Human Body. Cosgrove, Lee, illus. 2015. (Lie Detector Ser.). (ENG.). 32p. (gr. k-3). pap. 5.95 (978-1-4795-8515-1(7)) Picture Window Bks.

Holub, Joan. Why Do Birds Sing? DiVito, Anna, illus. 2004. (Penguin Young Readers, Level 3 Ser.). (ENG.). 48p. (J). (gr. 1-3). mass mkt. 3.99 (978-0-14-240106-4(4), Penguin Young Readers) Penguin Young Readers Group.

—Why Do Birds Sing? DiVito, Anna, illus. 2004. (Easy-to-Read Ser.). 47p. 14.00 (978-0-7569-3114-8(2)) Perfection Learning Corp.

—Why Do Snakes Hiss? And Other Questions about Snakes, Lizards, & Turtles. DiVito, Anna, illus. 2004. (Penguin Young Readers, Level 3 Ser.). (ENG.). 48p. (J). (gr. 1-3). mass mkt. 3.99 (978-0-14-240105-7(6), Penguin Young Readers) Penguin Young Readers Group.

Horn, Randy & Workman Publishing Company Staff. You Gotta Be Kidding! The Crazy Book of Would You Rather... ? Questions. 2006. (ENG., Illus.). 416p. (J). (gr. 4-12). pap. 8.95 (978-0-7611-4365-9(3), 14365) Workman Publishing Co., Inc.

Hughes-Odgers, Kyle. Can a Skeleton Have an X-Ray? Hughes-Odgers, Kyle, illus. 2016. (ENG., Illus.). 32p. (J). (gr. -1-k). 16.99 (978-1-925162-69-1(9)) Fremantle Pr. AUS. Dist: Independent Pubs. Group.

Humberstone, E. C. The Usborne First Book of Knowledge. 2004. (Explainers Ser.). (ENG.). 1p. (J). 16.95 (978-0-7460-1963-4(7), Usborne) EDC Publishing.

Hunt, Santana. Name That Mammal! 2016. (Guess That Animal! Ser.). 24p. (J). (gr. 2-1). lib. bdg. 22.60 (978-1-4824-4746-0(0)) Stevens, Gareth Publishing LLLP.

Irving, Harry. Picture-Word Quizzes Assessment Sheets & Solution Book: For the Children's Picture-Word & Simple Sentence Book. Graphics Factory, illus. 2009. 196p. pap. 17.14 (978-1-4269-0667-1(6)) Trafford Publishing.

Jacobs, Pat. I Wonder Why Penguins Can't Fly: And Other Questions about Polar Lands. 2011. (I Wonder Why Ser.). (ENG., Illus.). 32p. (J). (gr. k-3). pap. 6.99 (978-0-7534-6530-1(2), 9780753465301, Kingfisher) Roaring Brook Pr.

—I Wonder Why Pirates Wore Earrings: And Other Questions about Piracy. 2012. (I Wonder Why Ser.). (ENG., Illus.). 32p. (J). (gr. k-3). 6.99 (978-0-7534-6791-6(7), 9780753467916, Kingfisher) Roaring Brook Pr.

Jacobs, Pat & MacDonald, Fiona. I Wonder Why Romans Wore Togas. 2012. (I Wonder Why Ser.). (ENG., Illus.). 32p. (J). (gr. k-3). 6.99 (978-0-7534-6795-4(X), 9780753467954, Kingfisher) Roaring Brook Pr.

Jacobs, Pat & Steele, Philip. I Wonder Why Countries Fly Flags. 2012. (I Wonder Why Ser.). (ENG., Illus.). 32p. (J). (gr. k-3). 6.99 (978-0-7534-6793-0(3), 9780753467930, Kingfisher) Roaring Brook Pr.

James, Emily. Do Goldfish Fly? A Question & Answer Book about Animal Movements. 2016. (Animals, Animals! Ser.). (ENG., Illus.). 32p. (gr. 1-2). lib. bdg. 27.32 (978-1-5157-2666-1(5), Aplus Bks.) Capstone Press of Coughlan Cos.

—Do Whales Have Whiskers? A Question & Answer Book about Animal Body Parts. 2016. (Animals, Animals! Ser.). (ENG., Illus.). 32p. (gr. 1-2). lib. bdg. 27.32 (978-1-5157-2664-7(9), Aplus Bks.) Capstone Press of Coughlan Cos.

Jones, Jen & Wittrock, Jeni. Friendship Quizzes. 2011. (Friendship Quizzes Ser.). (ENG.). 32p. (gr. 3-4). lib. bdg. 111.96 (978-1-4296-6543-8(2), Snap Bks.) Capstone Press of Coughlan Cos.

Jones, Tom. Ask the Astronaut: A Galaxy of Astonishing Answers to Your Questions on Spaceflight. 2016. (ENG., Illus.). 224p. (YA). (gr. 5-12). pap. 12.95 (978-1-58834-537-0(8), Smithsonian Bks.) Smithsonian Institution Scholarly Pr.

Jordan, Apple. The Cat: Why Do Cats Purr? & Other True Facts. 2007. (Illus.). 30p. (J). pap. (978-0-545-00088-8(2)) Scholastic, Inc.

Kain, Kathleen. All about Holidays: With Inspector McQ. Mahan, Ben, illus. 2004. (Early Literacy Library). 32p. (J). (gr. 2-5). 219.00 (978-0-7166-1647-4(5)) World Bk., Inc.

—All about Pets. Miyake, Yoshi, illus. 2004. (Treasure Tree Ser.). 32p. (J). (978-0-7166-1626-9(2)) World Bk., Inc.

Katz, Karen A., et al. What Does Being Jewish Mean? Read-Aloud Responses to Questions Jewish Children Ask about History, Culture, & Religion. 2003. (ENG.). 160p. pap. 12.95 (978-0-7432-5413-7(9), Touchstone) Touchstone.

Kaye, Megan. Do You Know Who You Are? Singer, Allison, ed. 2014. (ENG., Illus.). 192p. (YA). (gr. 8-12). pap. 15.99 (978-1-4654-1649-0(8), DK Children) Dorling Kindersley Publishing, Inc.

Ketchum, Ron, illus. Rochestrivia: 2,000 Amazing questions & answers all about Rochester NY, it's people & surrounding Towns. l.t. ed. 2005. 250p. per. 19.95 (978-0-930249-01-4(1)) Big Kids Productions (Publishing).

Kids' Questions Classroom Collection. 2010. (Kids' Questions Ser.). 24p. pap. 125.10 (978-1-4048-6625-6(6), Nonfiction Picture Bks.) Picture Window Bks.

Kiefer, Jeanne. Jobs for Kids: A Smart Kid's Q & A Guide. Green, Anne Canevari, illus. 2003. (Single Titles Ser.). 112p. (gr. 5-8). lib. bdg. 25.90 (978-0-7613-2611-3(1), Millbrook Pr.) Lerner Publishing Group.

Laffon, Martine & De Chabaneix, Hortense. The Book of How. Azam, Jacques, illus. 2007. (ENG.). 90p. (J). (gr. 4-6). 17.95 (978-0-8109-0716-4(X), Abrams Bks. for Young Readers) Abrams, Inc.

Laffon, Martine, et al. Poem in Your Pocket for Young Poets. 2011. (ENG., Illus.). 232p. (J). (gr. 3-7). 13.95 (978-0-8109-9142-2(X), Amulet Bks.) Abrams, Inc.

Lawrence, Paul R. Question Quest HSPA Math Geometry Companion. 2003. (Illus.). (YA). pap. 8.95 (978-1-931104-16-6(6)) L L Teach.

Le Compte, David & Rolland, Carol. Eugene Stillwell Wants to Know! Padrick, Kendell, ed. 2007. (Eugene Stillwell Wants to Know! Ser.). (ENG., Illus.). 96p. (J). (gr. 4-6). per. 4.95 (978-1-929945-71-9(X)) Big Guy Bks., Inc.

LeCompte, David & Padrick, Kendell. Eugene Stillwell Wants to Know!, Pt. 2. 2009. (Eugene Stillwell Wants to Know! Ser.). (ENG.). 96p. (J). (gr. 4-6). pap. 4.95 (978-1-929945-74-0(4)) Big Guy Bks., Inc.

Leipe, Ulla. Lo Que los Ninos Quieren Saber. Limmer, Hannes, illus. (SPA.). 180p. (YA). 11.95 (978-84-241-5501-8(7), EV867) Everest Editora ESP. Dist: Continental Bk. Co., Inc.

Little Kids Book of Why, 1 vol. 2014. (Little Kids Books of Why Ser.). (ENG.). 48p. (gr. 5-6). pap. 17.90 (978-1-4914-1935-9(0)) Capstone Press of Coughlan Cos.

Lluch, Alex A. Let's Leap Ahead 1st Grade Trivia. 2013. (ENG.). 216p. (J). (gr. k). pap. 9.95 (978-1-61351-045-2(4)) WS Publishing.

—Let's Leap Ahead 2nd Grade Trivia. 2013. (ENG.). 216p. (J). (gr. 1). pap. 9.95 (978-1-61351-046-9(2)) WS Publishing.

—Let's Leap Ahead 2nd Grade Trivia Notepad: The Game of 300 Questions for You & Your Friends! 2013. (ENG.). 70p. (J). (gr. 1). pap. 3.95 (978-1-61351-060-5(8)) WS Publishing.

—Let's Leap Ahead 3rd Grade Trivia. 2013. (ENG.). 216p. (J). (gr. 2). pap. 9.95 (978-1-61351-047-6(0)) WS Publishing.

—Let's Leap Ahead 3rd Grade Trivia Notepad: The Game of 300 Questions for You & Your Friends! 2013. (ENG.). 70p. (J). (gr. 2). pap. 3.95 (978-1-61351-061-2(6)) WS Publishing.

—Let's Leap Ahead 4th Grade Trivia. 2013. (ENG.). 216p. (J). (gr. 3). pap. 9.95 (978-1-61351-048-3(9)) WS Publishing.

Lluch, Isabel B. & Lluch, Emily. B. F. F. - Best Friends Forever: Fun Questions & Quizzes for You & Your Best Friends. 2012. (ENG.). 80p. (J). (gr. 6). pap. 6.95 (978-1-936061-55-6(4)) WS Publishing.

—B. F. F. Quizzes. 2013. (ENG.). 128p. (J). (gr. 6). pap. 7.95 (978-1-61351-030-8(6)) WS Publishing.

—iGirl - B. F. F. Quizzes for You & Your Friends. 2012. (ENG.). 130p. (J). (gr. 6). pap. 4.95 (978-1-936061-95-2(3)) WS Publishing.

—iGirl - My B. F. F. S. 2013. (ENG.). 80p. (J). (gr. 6). pap. 7.95 (978-1-61351-016-2(0)) WS Publishing.

—iGirl - My Keepsake. 2013. (ENG.). 80p. (J). (gr. 6). pap. 7.95 *(978-1-61351-015-5(2))* WS Publishing.

Llull, Maria. I-Ballers: Little Books for Big Minds. 2005. (ENG., Illus.). 60p. (J). (gr. 4-7). pap. 4.95 *(978-1-57528-939-7(3))* Univ. Games.

Lonely Planet Publications Staff. Lonely Planet the Round the World Quiz Book, 1 vol. 2017. (Lonely Planet Kids Ser.). (ENG., Illus.). 160p. (J). pap. 11.99 ***(978-1-78657-432-9(2),*** 5370) Lonely Planet Pubns.

Loy, Jessica. Weird & Wild Animal Facts. Loy, Jessica, illus. 2015. (ENG., Illus.). 40p. (J). (gr. -1-3). 17.99 *(978-0-8050-7945-6(9),* 9780805079456, Holt, Henry & Co. Bks. For Young Readers) Holt, Henry & Co.

MacDonald, Fiona. I Wonder Why Greeks Built Temples: And Other Questions about Ancient Greece. 2012. (I Wonder Why Ser.). (ENG., Illus.). 32p. (J). (gr. k-3). pap. 6.99 *(978-0-7534-6705-3(4),* 9780753467053, Kingfisher) Roaring Brook Pr.

MacDonald, Margaret. Job Quiz. 2011. (Learn-Abouts: Level 10 Ser.). (Illus.). 16p. (J). pap. 7.95 *(978-1-59920-599-1(8))* Black Rabbit Bks.

Macheske, Felicia. Blue & Bumpy: Blue Crab. 2016. (Guess What Ser.). (ENG., Illus.). 24p. (J). (gr. k-2). 28.50 *(978-1-63470-717-6(6),* 207579) Cherry Lake Publishing.

—Hefty Hulks: Rhinoceros. 2017. (Guess What Ser.). (ENG., Illus.). 24p. (J). (gr. k-2). lib. bdg. 28.50 *(978-1-63472-169-1(1),* 209248) Cherry Lake Publishing.

—Lanky Legs. 2016. (Guess What Ser.). (ENG., Illus.). 24p. (J). (gr. k-2). 28.50 *(978-1-63470-720-6(6),* 207591) Cherry Lake Publishing.

Maclaine, James. Lift-The-Flap General Knowledge IR. 2015. (Lift-The-Flap Board Bks.). (ENG.). 16p. (J). (gr. k-5). 14.99 *(978-0-7945-3418-9(X),* Usborne) EDC Publishing.

Malloy, Devin. SpookyTalk: Conversation Cards for the Entire Family. 2008. (Tabletalk Conversation Cards Ser.). (Illus.). (J). (gr. 4-7). 6.00 *(978-1-57281-635-0(X))* U.S. Games Systems, Inc.

—WeatherTalk: Conversation Cards for the Entire Family. 2008. (Tabletalk Conversation Cards Ser.). (Illus.). (J). (gr. 4-7). 6.00 *(978-1-57281-632-9(5))* U.S. Games Systems, Inc.

Manning, Mick. Que Hay Debajo de la Cama? Cortes, Eunice, tr. Granström, Brita, illus. 2003. (Descubriendo Mi Mundo Ser.). (SPA.). 32p. (J). *(978-970-690-588-8(X))* Planeta Mexicana Editorial S. A. de C. V.

Marek, Hillary. The smart ass guide to ridiculous Questions. 2010. 139p. pap. 11.06 *(978-0-557-30904-7(2))* Lulu Pr., Inc.

Marrou, Elisabeth. Tell Me What Is That? 2015. (Tell Me Bks.). (ENG., Illus.). 122p. (J). (gr. 2-6). spiral bd. 14.99 *(978-0-7641-6795-9(2))* Barron's Educational Series, Inc.

Marsico, Katie. Chameleons Change Color. 2015. (Tell Me Why Library). (ENG., Illus.). 24p. (J). (gr. 2-5). pap. 12.79 *(978-1-63362-699-7(7),* 206621) Cherry Lake Publishing.

—Elephants Have Trunks. 2014. (Tell Me Why Library). (ENG.). 24p. (J). (gr. 2-5). 25.64 *(978-1-63188-002-5(0),* 205415) Cherry Lake Publishing.

—Giraffes Have Long Necks. 2014. (Tell Me Why Library). (ENG., Illus.). 24p. (J). (gr. 2-5). 25.64 *(978-1-63188-003-2(9),* 205419) Cherry Lake Publishing.

—I Cry. 2014. (Tell Me Why Library). (ENG., Illus.). 24p. (J). (gr. 2-5). 25.64 *(978-1-63188-004-9(7),* 205423) Cherry Lake Publishing.

—I Throw Up. 2014. (Tell Me Why Library). (ENG., Illus.). 24p. (J). (gr. 2-5). 25.64 *(978-1-63188-006-3(3),* 205431) Cherry Lake Publishing.

Martin, Isabel. Animal Kingdom Questions & Answers, 1 vol. 2014. (Animal Kingdom Questions & Answers Ser.). (ENG.). 24p. (gr. k-1). 159.90 *(978-1-4914-0659-5(3),* Pebble Plus) Capstone Press of Coughlan Cos.

—Birds: A Question & Answer Book, 1 vol. 2014. (Animal Kingdom Questions & Answers Ser.). (ENG.). 24p. (gr. k-1). 26.65 *(978-1-4914-0561-1(9));* (Illus.). pap. 6.95 *(978-1-4914-0629-8(1))* Capstone Press of Coughlan Cos. (Pebble Plus).

—Fish: A Question & Answer Book, 1 vol. 2014. (Animal Kingdom Questions & Answers Ser.). (ENG., Illus.). 24p. (gr. k-1). pap. 6.95 *(978-1-4914-0631-1(3),* Pebble Plus) Capstone Press of Coughlan Cos.

Martin, Mary-Jane. Let Me Put It This Way. 2004. (Illus.). 32p. 11.95 *(978-0-9730583-1-4(5))* Lion & Mouse Tales, Inc. CAN. Dist: Hushion Hse. Publishing, Ltd.

Mason, Paul & Barnham, Kay. Questions You Never Thought You'd Ask. 2013. (Questions You Never Thought You'd Ask Ser.). (ENG.). 32p. (gr. 1-3). pap. 39.95 *(978-1-4109-5208-0(8));* lib. bdg. 149.95 *(978-1-4109-5202-8(9))* Heinemann-Raintree. (Read Me!).

Matheson, Murdoch H. Building Wealth for Teens: Answers to Questions Teens Care About. 2007. 116p. 24.65 *(978-1-4251-2358-1(9))* Trafford Publishing.

Maurice, creator. The Spanish Question Game. (SPA.). (YA). 134.95 *(978-1-932770-48-3(8),* SG9) Symtalk, Inc.

Maynard, Christopher. I Wonder Why Planes Have Wings: And Other Questions about Transportation. 2012. (I Wonder Why Ser.). (ENG., Illus.). 32p. (J). (gr. k-3). pap. 6.99 *(978-0-7534-6703-9(8),* 9780753467039, Kingfisher) Roaring Brook Pr.

McGillian, Jamie Kyle. Quiz Me! 2017. (ENG., Illus.). 96p. (J). (gr. 3-7). pap. 6.95 ***(978-1-4549-2336-7(9))*** Sterling Publishing Co., Inc.

Meister, Cari. Totally Wacky Facts about Animals. 2015. (Mind Benders Ser.). (ENG., Illus.). 240p. (gr. 1-3). pap. 7.95 *(978-1-4914-6525-7(5))* Capstone Press of Coughlan Cos.

—Totally Wacky Facts about Land Animals. 2015. (Mind Benders Ser.). (ENG., Illus.). 112p. (gr. 1-3). lib. bdg. 23.32 *(978-1-4914-6522-6(0))* Capstone Press of Coughlan Cos.

—Totally Wacky Facts about Sea Animals. 2015. (Mind Benders Ser.). (ENG., Illus.). 112p. (gr. 1-3). lib. bdg. 23.32 *(978-1-4914-6521-9(2))* Capstone Press of Coughlan Cos.

Miles Kelly Staff. Animals. 2003. (Info Bank Ser.). (Illus.). 96p. (J). 7.95 *(978-1-84236-153-5(8))* Miles Kelly Publishing, Ltd. GBR. Dist: Independent Pubs. Group.

—Geography. 2003. (Info Bank Ser.). (Illus.). 96p. (J). 7.95 *(978-1-84236-055-2(8))* Miles Kelly Publishing, Ltd. GBR. Dist: Independent Pubs. Group.

—History. 2003. (Info Bank Ser.). (Illus.). 96p. (J). 7.95 *(978-1-84236-056-9(6))* Miles Kelly Publishing, Ltd. GBR. Dist: Independent Pubs. Group.

—How Things Work. 2003. (Ask Me a Question Ser.). (Illus.). 20p. spiral bd. 7.95 *(978-1-84236-127-6(9))* Miles Kelly Publishing, Ltd. GBR. Dist: Independent Pubs. Group.

—Nature. 2003. (Ask Me a Question Ser.). (Illus.). 20p. spiral bd. 7.95 *(978-1-84236-125-2(2))* Miles Kelly Publishing, Ltd. GBR. Dist: Independent Pubs. Group.

—Our Planet. 2003. (Ask Me a Question Ser.). (Illus.). 20p. (J). spiral bd. 7.95 *(978-1-84236-128-3(7))* Miles Kelly Publishing, Ltd. GBR. Dist: Independent Pubs. Group.

—People & Places. 2003. (Ask Me a Question Ser.). (Illus.). 20p. spiral bd. 7.95 *(978-1-84236-126-9(0))* Miles Kelly Publishing, Ltd. GBR. Dist: Independent Pubs. Group.

—Science. 2003. (Info Bank Ser.). (Illus.). 96p. (J). 7.95 *(978-1-84236-152-8(X))* Miles Kelly Publishing, Ltd. GBR. Dist: Independent Pubs. Group.

Millman, Christian. Absolutely Crazy Knowledge: The World's Funniest Collection of Amazing Facts. 2015. (ENG., Illus.). 160p. (J). (gr. 3-6). pap. 10.99 *(978-0-7944-3341-3(3))* Reader's Digest Assn., Inc., The.

Moran, Paul, illus. World's Greatest Who What Where When Quiz Book for Kids. 2003. 112p. (J). pap. 3.99 *(978-0-603-56100-9(4))* Egmont Bks., Ltd. GBR. Dist: Trafalgar Square Publishing.

Morse, Jenifer Corr. Scholastic Book of World Records 2015. 2014. (ENG.). 320p. (J). (gr. 3-7). pap. 10.99 *(978-0-545-67950-3(8),* Scholastic Paperbacks) Scholastic, Inc.

Mortimer, J. R. This or That? 2: More Wacky Choices to Reveal the Hidden You. 2014. (ENG., Illus.). 176p. (J). (gr. 3-7). pap. 12.99 *(978-1-4263-1719-4(0),* National Geographic Children's Bks.) National Geographic Society.

Most, Bernard. Dinosaur Questions. 2008. (Illus.). (J). pap. *(978-0-15-206475-4(3),* Red Wagon Bks.) Harcourt Children's Bks.

The Moves Make the Man: Teaching Unit. 2003. 73p. (YA). ring bd. *(978-1-58049-433-5(1),* TU4331) Prestwick Hse., Inc.

Munrriz, Mercedes & Munárriz Guezala, Mercedes. Por Qué? Martinez, Rocio, illus. 2003. (SPA.). 16p. (J). *(978-84-667-2627-6(6))* Grupo Anaya, S.A. ESP. Dist: Lectorum Pubns., Inc.

—Qué Es? Martinez, Rocio, illus. 2003. (SPA.). 16p. (J). *(978-84-667-2626-9(8))* Grupo Anaya, S.A. ESP. Dist: Lectorum Pubns., Inc.

Murphy, Glenn. Why Is Snot Green? And Other Extremely Important Questions (And Answers) Phillips, Mike, illus. 2009. (ENG.). 240p. (J). (gr. 3-7). pap. 13.99 *(978-1-59643-500-1(3),* 9781596435001) Square Fish.

My Big Book of Questions & Answers. 2003. 512p. (J). 9.98 *(978-1-4054-0758-8(1))* Parragon, Inc.

National Geographic. National Geographic Kids Quiz Whiz 2: 1,000 Super Fun Mind-Bending Totally Awesome Trivia Questions. 2013. (ENG.). 176p. (J). (gr. 3-7). lib. bdg. 18.90 *(978-1-4263-1357-8(8),* National Geographic Children's Bks.) National Geographic Society.

National Geographic Kids Staff. Boredom-Busting Fun Stuff. 2015. (ENG., Illus.). 352p. (J). (gr. 3-7). pap. 14.99 *(978-1-4263-2106-1(6),* National Geographic Children's Bks.) National Geographic Society.

—National Geographic Kids Quiz Whiz: 1,000 Super Fun, Mind-Bending, Totally Awesome Trivia Questions. 2012. (ENG., Illus.). 176p. (J). (gr. 3-7). lib. bdg. 18.90 *(978-1-4263-1019-5(6),* National Geographic Children's Bks.) National Geographic Society.

—Weird but True!, 3 vols., Set. 2012. (Weird but True Ser.). (ENG., Illus.). 624p. (J). (gr. 1-4). pap. 23.95 *(978-1-4263-1194-9(X),* National Geographic Children's Bks.) National Geographic Society.

—1,000 Super Fun Mind-Bending Totally Awesome Trivia Questions. 2014. (Quiz Whiz Ser.). (ENG., Illus.). 176p. (J). (gr. 3-7). Illus.). pap. 9.99 *(978-1-4263-1709-5(3));* pap. 9.99 *(978-1-4263-1484-1(1))* National Geographic Society. (National Geographic Children's Bks.).

—1,000 Super Fun, Mind-Bending, Totally Awesome Trivia Questions. 2012. (ENG., Illus.). 176p. (J). (gr. 3-7). pap. 9.99 *(978-1-4263-1018-8(8),* National Geographic Children's Bks.) National Geographic Society.

National Geographic Staff. National Geographic Kids Quiz Whiz 2: 1,000 Super Fun Mind-Bending Totally Awesome Trivia Questions. 2013. (ENG., Illus.). 176p. (J). (gr. 3-7). pap. 9.99 *(978-1-4263-1356-1(X),* National Geographic Children's Bks.) National Geographic Society.

National Parents Council. The Whiz Quiz Book - 3rd Edition: For Children & Grown-Up Children. 3rd rev. ed. 2017. (ENG.). 128p. (J). pap. 10.00 ***(978-1-84889-297-2(7))*** Collins Pr., The IRL. Dist: Dufour Editions, Inc.

National Parents Council - Primary Staff. The Whiz Quiz Book: For Children & Grown-Up Children. 2006. (ENG.). 117p. (J). per. 10.95 *(978-1-903464-98-4(6))* Collins Pr., The IRL. Dist: Dufour Editions, Inc.

National Parents Council - Primary Staff, ed. More Whiz Quiz: For Children & Grown-up Children. 2008. (ENG.). 126p. (J). per. 11.95 *(978-1-905172-50-4(8))* Collins Pr., The IRL. Dist: Dufour Editions, Inc.

Nicholaus, Bret & Lowrie, Paul. KidChat: 222 Creative Questions to Spark Conversations. 2nd rev. ed. 2004. (Illus.). 128p. (J). pap. 9.95 *(978-0-9755801-0-3(8),* KCR) Questmarc Publishing.

—KidChat Too! All-New Questions to Fuel Young Minds & Mouths. 2004. (Illus.). 128p. (J). pap. 9.95 *(978-0-9755801-1-0(6),* KCT) Questmarc Publishing.

Nunn, Daniel. True or False? 2013. (True or False? Ser.). (ENG.). 24p. (gr. -1-1). pap. 29.95 *(978-1-4109-5077-2(8));* lib. bdg. 90.60 *(978-1-4109-5071-0(9))* Heinemann-Raintree. (NA-r).

O'Neill, Amanda. I Wonder Why Snakes Shed Their Skin. 2011. (I Wonder Why Ser.). (ENG., Illus.). 32p. (J). (gr. k-3). pap. 6.99 *(978-0-7534-6531-8(0),* 9780753465318, Kingfisher) Roaring Brook Pr.

—I Wonder Why Spiders Spin Webs: And Other Questions about Creepy Crawlies. 2011. (I Wonder Why Ser.). (ENG., Illus.). 32p. (J). (gr. k-3). pap. 6.99 *(978-0-7534-6524-0(8),* 9780753465240, Kingfisher) Roaring Brook Pr.

Orr, Tamra B. I See Falling Stars. 2015. (Tell Me Why Library). (ENG., Illus.). 24p. (J). (gr. 2-5). pap. 12.79 *(978-1-63362-035-3(2),* 205897) Cherry Lake Publishing.

Osborne, Mary Pope & Boyce, Natalie Pope. Magic Tree House Incredible Fact Book. Murdocca, Sal, illus. 2016. (Magic Tree House Ser.). (ENG.). 144p. (J). (gr. 2-5). 16.99 *(978-0-399-55117-8(4),* Random Hse. Bks. for Young Readers) Random Hse. Children's Bks.

Overdeck, Laura. The Truth Comes Out. Paillot, Jim, illus. 2015. (Bedtime Math Ser.). (ENG.). 96p. (J). (gr. -1-2). 15.99 *(978-1-250-04775-5(7),* 9781250047755) Feiwel & Friends.

Owsley, Anthony, et al. Biggest Trivia Book Ever: And That's a Fact! Burke, Theresa, illus. 2012. (ENG.). 528p. (J). (gr. 3). pap. 16.95 *(978-1-60433-271-1(9),* Applesauce Pr.) Cider Mill Pr. Bk. Pubs., LLC.

Oxlade, Chris. Why Why Why Do Tornadoes Spin. 2008. 32p. pap. *(978-1-84810-004-6(3))* Miles Kelly Publishing, Ltd.

—Why Why Why Does My Heart Begin to Race? 2008. 32p. pap. *(978-1-84810-002-2(7))* Miles Kelly Publishing, Ltd.

Page, Robin & Jenkins, Steve. What Do You Do with a Tail Like This? (ENG., Illus.). 32p. (J). (gr. -1-3). 2008. pap. 7.95 *(978-0-618-99713-8(X))* 2003. 17.99 *(978-0-618-25628-0(8))* Houghton Mifflin Harcourt Publishing Co.

Paquette, Ammi-Joan & Thompson, Laurie Ann. Two Truths & a Lie: It's Alive! Weber, Lisa K., illus. 2017. 176p. (J). (gr. 3-7). 17.99 ***(978-0-06-241879-1(3),*** Walden Pond Pr.) HarperCollins Pubs.

Parker, Janice. Machines Q & A. 2013. (J). *(978-1-62127-416-2(0));* pap. *(978-1-62127-422-3(5))* Weigl Pubs., Inc.

—Weather Q & A. 2013. (J). *(978-1-62127-417-9(9));* pap. *(978-1-62127-423-0(3))* Weigl Pubs., Inc.

Payne, Jan, et al. It Can Rain Frogs & Fish: And Other Facts about Planet Earth. 2016. (True or False? Ser.). 48p. (J). (gr. 3-3). pap. 11.70 *(978-0-7660-7732-4(2))* Enslow Pubs., Inc.

Peters, Celeste A. Health Q & A. 2013. (J). *(978-1-62127-414-8(4));* pap. *(978-1-62127-420-9(9))* Weigl Pubs., Inc.

Pfister, Marcus. Questions, Questions. 2014. (ENG & GER., Illus.). 32p. (J). (gr. -1 — 1). bds. 8.95 *(978-0-7358-4170-3(5),* 9780735841703) North-South Bks., Inc.

Phillips, Karen, ed. What about You? 2009. (ENG., Illus.). 50p. (J). (gr. 3). 16.95 *(978-1-59174-612-6(4))* Klutz.

Potts, Kimberly. Boost Your Guy-Q: Quizzes to Test Your Guy Smarts. 2007. (ENG., Illus.). 160p. (gr. 8-12). per. 12.50 *(978-1-59869-230-3(5))* Adams Media Corp.

Powell, Michael. Do My Ears Ever Stop Growing? And 70 Other Questions That Keep You Awake at Night. 2009. (Illus.). 158p. (J). *(978-1-4351-1200-1(8))* Metro Bks.

Priddy, Roger. Slide & Find Christmas. 2010. (Slide & Find Ser.). (ENG., Illus.). 10p. (J). (gr. -1 — 1). bds. 7.95 *(978-0-312-50969-9(3),* 9780312509699, Priddy Bks.) St. Martin's Pr.

Q & A: Life's Mysteries Solved! 2016. (Q & a: Life's Mysteries Solved! Ser.). 32p. (gr. 4-3). pap. 63.00 *(978-1-4824-5298-3(7));* lib. bdg. 159.60 *(978-1-4824-4606-7(5))* Stevens, Gareth Publishing LLLP.

Questions & Answers of the Natural World. 2003. (Illus.). 256p. (J). 12.98 *(978-1-4054-1682-5(3))* Parragon, Inc.

Questmarc Publishing, creator. Chat Pack for Kids: Creative Questions to Ignite the Imagination. 2009. (J). 9.95 *(978-0-9755801-5-8(9))* Questmarc Publishing.

Raum, Elizabeth. Blue-Ringed Octopuses. 2015. (Poisonous Animals Ser.). (ENG., Illus.). 32p. (J). (gr. 2-4). 19.95 *(978-1-60753-785-4(0))* Amicus Publishing.

—Box Jellyfish. 2015. (Poisonous Animals Ser.). (ENG., Illus.). 32p. (J). (gr. 2-4). 19.95 *(978-1-60753-786-1(9))* Amicus Publishing.

—Poison Dart Frogs. 2015. (Poisonous Animals Ser.). (ENG., Illus.). 32p. (J). (gr. 2-4). 19.95 *(978-1-60753-787-8(7))* Amicus Publishing.

Rey, H. A. & Rey, Margret. Curious George's Big Book of Curiosity. Paprocki, Greg, illus. 2005. (Curious George Ser.). (ENG.). 48p. (J). (gr. -1-3). 11.99 *(978-0-618-58338-6(6))* Houghton Mifflin Harcourt Publishing Co.

Rhatigan, Joe, et al. Head Scratchers Trivia: 708 Numb-Your-Noggin Questions That'll Stump Ya! 2013. (ENG.). 160p. (J). pap. 7.95 *(978-1-60433-340-4(5),* Applesauce Pr.) Cider Mill Pr. Bk. Pubs., LLC.

—Mind Melting Trivia: 715 Head Thumpers That'll Sump Ya! 2013. (ENG.). 160p. (J). pap. 7.95 *(978-1-60433-341-1(3),* Applesauce Pr.) Cider Mill Pr. Bk. Pubs., LLC.

Richards, Jon & Simkins, Ed. Record-Breaking Earth & Space Facts. 2015. (Infographic Top 10s Ser.). (ENG., Illus.). 32p. (J). (gr. 4-6). 26.65 *(978-1-4677-8595-2(4),* Lerner Pubns.) Lerner Publishing Group.

Richmond, Benjamin. Why Is the Sea Salty? And Other Questions about the Ocean. Azhderian, Cecelia, illus. 2014. (Good Question! Ser.). (ENG.). 32p. (J). (gr. 1). pap. 5.95 *(978-1-4549-0677-3(4))* Sterling Publishing Co., Inc.

—Why Is the Sea Salty? And Other Questions about the Oceans. Azhderian, Cecelia, illus. 2014. (Good Question! Ser.). (ENG.). 40p. (J). (gr. 1). 12.95 *(978-1-4549-0676-6(6))* Sterling Publishing Co., Inc.

Ristuccia, Christine & Ristuccia, James. The Entire World of WH? Questions. 2004. (J). 39.99 *(978-0-9723457-9-8(5))* Say It Right.

—The Entire World of WH? Questions Flip Book. 2004. (Illus.). 9p. (J). spiral bd. 14.99 *(978-0-9723457-8-1(7))* Say It Right.

Rooney, Anne. 501 1/2 Horrible Facts. 2013. (ENG., Illus.). 128p. (J). pap. 9.95 *(978-1-84858-760-1(0))* Arcturus Publishing GBR. Dist: Bookmasters Distribution.

Rooney, Anne & Arcturus Publishing Staff. 1001 Horrible Facts: A Yukkopedia of Gross Truths about Everything. 2012. (ENG., Illus.). 207p. (J). pap. 9.95 *(978-1-84193-469-3(0),* 9781841934693) Arcturus Publishing GBR. Dist: Bookmasters Distribution.

Russell, Ken & Carter, Philip. Bumper Quiz Book for Kids. (Illus.). 160p. (J). 17.95 *(978-1-85479-300-3(4))* O'Mara, Michael Bks., Ltd. GBR. Dist: Trans-Atlantic Pubns., Inc.

Scholastic Teaching Resources Staff. The Essential Questions Handbook, Grades 4-8: Hundreds of Guiding Questions That Help You Plan & Teach Successful Lessons in the Content Areas. 2011. (ENG.). 96p. (gr. 4-8). pap. 14.99 *(978-0-545-30585-3(3),* Teaching Resources) Scholastic, Inc.

Seip, Shannon Payette. The Pop Quiz Book: Tons of Trivia! Sheuer, Lauren, illus. 2008. (American Girl Library). (ENG.). 80p. (gr. 3-7). spiral bd. 7.95 *(978-1-58485-844-7(3),* American Girl) American Girl Publishing, Inc.

Shand, Jennifer. Why Do Feet Get So Stinky? 2015. (Why Do... ? Ser.). lib. bdg. 19.65 *(978-1-4867-0623-5(1))* Turtleback Bks.

Shea, Therese. Do Cows Have Two Stomachs? And Other FAQs about Animals. 2016. (Q & a: Life's Mysteries Solved! Ser.). 32p. (J). (gr. 4-3). lib. bdg. 26.60 *(978-1-4824-4778-1(9))* Stevens, Gareth Publishing LLLP.

Shulman, Mark. Are You Normal ? 2: More Than 100 Questions That Will Test Your Weirdness. 2013. (ENG., Illus.). 176p. (J). (gr. 3-7). pap. 12.95 *(978-1-4263-1370-7(5));* lib. bdg. 21.95 *(978-1-4263-1680-7(1))* National Geographic Society. (National Geographic Children's Bks.).

Shulman, Mark & National Geographic Kids Staff. Are You "Normal"? More Than 100 Questions That Will Test Your Weirdness. 2011. (ENG., Illus.). 176p. (J). (gr. 3-7). pap. 12.95 *(978-1-4263-0837-6(X),* National Geographic Children's Bks.) National Geographic Society.

Slade, Suzanne. Who Invented Basketball? And Other Questions Kids Have about Sports, 1 vol. Pillo, Cary, illus. 2011. (Kids' Questions Ser.). (ENG.). 24p. (gr. 1-2). pap. 7.49 *(978-1-4048-6730-7(9))* Picture Window Bks.

Smith, Jeremy. Why Why Why... Did Pirates Bury Their Treasure? 2010. (Why Why Why Ser.). (Illus.). 32p. (J). (gr. 1-3). lib. bdg. 18.95 *(978-1-4222-1576-0(8))* Mason Crest.

Smurd, John & Smidlap, Harley. The 707 Book: (707 Questions-707 Answers) 2008. 140p. pap. 11.95 *(978-0-595-50820-4(0))* iUniverse, Inc.

Snider, Brandon T. LOL: a Keepsake Journal of Hilarious Q&As. 2016. (ENG., Illus.). 368p. (J). (gr. 3-6). pap. 16.95 *(978-1-4549-1833-2(0))* Sterling Publishing Co., Inc.

Solomon, Iris L. & Solomon, Ron. Friendz Pakz: Friends. 2003. (YA). (gr. 3-18). 4.99 *(978-1-930680-04-3(X),* SSP-08FR) Swingset Pr., LLC.

—Friendz Pakz: Future. 2003. (YA). (gr. 3-18). 4.99 *(978-1-930680-05-0(8),* SSP-08FT) Swingset Pr., LLC.

—Friendz Pakz: Love. 2003. (YA). (gr. 3-18). 4.99 *(978-1-930680-07-4(4),* SSP-08LV) Swingset Pr., LLC.

Stewart, Melissa. Why Does T. Rex Have Such Short Arms? And Other Questions about... Dinosaurs. Csotonyi, Julius, illus. 2014. (Good Question! Ser.). (ENG.). (J). (gr. 1). 40p. 12.95 *(978-1-4549-0678-0(2));* 32p. pap. 5.95 *(978-1-4549-0679-7(0))* Sterling Publishing Co., Inc.

Stiekel, Bettina, ed. The Nobel Book of Answers: A the Dalai Lama, Mikhail Gorbachev, Shimon Peres. 2010. (ENG.). 272p. (J). (gr. 5-9). pap. 12.99 *(978-1-4424-2193-6(2),* Atheneum Bks. for Young Readers) Simon & Schuster Children's Publishing.

Stock, Gregory. Kids Book of Questions Review. 2nd rev. expurg. ed. (ENG.). (J). pap. 79.50 *(978-0-7611-3625-5(8),* 23625) Workman Publishing Co., Inc.

Stott, Carole. I Wonder Why Stars Twinkle. 2011. (I Wonder Why Ser.). (ENG., Illus.). 32p. (J). (gr. k-3). pap. 6.99 *(978-0-7534-6520-2(5),* 9780753465202, Kingfisher) Roaring Brook Pr.

Taylor, Barbara. I Wonder Why Zippers Have Teeth. 2012. (I Wonder Why Ser.). (ENG., Illus.). 32p. (J). (gr. k-3). 6.99 *(978-0-7534-6801-2(8),* 9780753468012, Kingfisher) Roaring Brook Pr.

Tears of a Tiger: Teaching Unit. 2003. 88p. (YA). ring bd. *(978-1-58049-429-8(3),* TU4293) Prestwick Hse., Inc.

Theodorou, Rod. I Wonder Why - Triceratops Had Horns: And Other Questions about Dinosaurs. 2011. (I Wonder Why Ser.). (ENG., Illus.). 32p. (J). (gr. k-3). pap. 6.99 *(978-0-7534-6523-3(X),* 9780753465233, Kingfisher) Roaring Brook Pr.

Thomas Nelson Publishing Staff. Solomon Says Bible Trivia: Anything Goes: Test Your Bible Knowledge in this Wacky Game Show! 2008. cd-rom 24.95 *(978-0-9754280-9-2(8))* Nelson, Thomas Inc.

—Solomon Says Bible Trivia for Kids: Amazing Animals: Learn about Animals of the Bible. 2008. cd-rom 24.95 *(978-1-4003-1336-5(8))* Nelson, Thomas Inc.

Thornborough, Kathy. Questions & Answers. Petelinsek, Kathleen, illus. 2014. (Talking Hands Ser.). (ENG.). 24p. (J). (gr. k-3). 25.64 *(978-1-62687-321-6(6),* 207161) Child's World, Inc., The.

Tiede, Karen. Carve Smart. 2004. 189p. (YA). pap. 19.95 *(978-0-7414-2093-0(7))* Infinity Publishing.

Time for Kids Editors. Time for Kids Big Book of How. 2011. 192p. (J). pap. 11.99 *(978-1-60320-907-6(7))* Time Inc. Bks.

Time for Kids Magazine Staff. TIME for Kids Big Book of What. 2012. (ENG.). 192p. (J). (gr. 3-17). pap. 11.99 *(978-1-60320-943-4(3))* Time Inc. Bks.

The Time-Life Library of First Questions & Answers, 18 bks. Incl. Are There Diamonds in My Backyard? First Questions & Answers about the Earth. Time-Life for Children Staff. Mark, Sara, ed. 1995. 14.95 *(978-0-7835-0902-0(2));* Did Triceratops Have Polka Dots? First Questions & Answers about Dinosaurs. Time-Life Books Editors. Fallow, Allan, ed. 1995. 14.95 *(978-0-7835-0903-7(0));* Do Bears Give Bear Hugs? First Questions & Answers about Animals. Time-Life Books Editors. Fallow, Allan, ed. 1994. 14.95 *(978-0-7835-0870-2(0));* Do Buildings Have Bones? First Questions & Answers about Buildings. Time-Life Books Editors. Mark, Sara, ed. 1995. 14.95 *(978-0-7835-0900-6(6));* Do Fish Drink? First Questions & Answers about Water. Time-Life Books Editors. Kagan, Neil, ed. 1993. 14.95 *(978-0-7835-0850-4(6));* Do Mommies Have Mommies? First Questions & Answers about Families. Time-Life Books Editors. Fallow, Allan, ed. 1994. 14.95 *(978-0-7835-0874-0(3));* Do Skyscrapers Touch the Sky? First Questions & Answers about Cities. Time-Life Books Editors. Fallow, Allan, ed. 1994. 14.95 *(978-0-7835-0886-3(7));* How Big Is the Ocean? First Questions & Answers about the Beach. Time-Life Books Editors. Fallow, Allan, ed. 1994. 14.95 *(978-0-7835-0897-9(2));* How Far Can a Butterfly Fly? First Questions & Answers about Bugs. Time-Life Books Editors. Lesk, Sara M., ed. 1994. 14.95 *(978-0-7835-0882-5(4));* What Makes Popcorn Pop? First Questions & Answers about Food. Ward, Elizabeth, ed. 1994. 14.95 *(978-0-7835-0862-7(X));* Where Does the Sun Sleep? First Questions & Answers about Bedtime. Time-Life Books Editors. Kagan, Neil, ed. 1993. 14.95

(978-0-7835-0866-5(2)); Who Named My Street Magnolia? First Questions & Answers about Neighborhoods. Time-Life Books Editors. Mark, Sara, ed. 1995. 14.95 *(978-0-7835-0898-6(0))*; Why Are Wagons Red? First Questions & Answers about Transportation. Time-Life Books Editors. Lesk, Sara M., ed. 1994. 14.95 *(978-0-7835-0878-8(6))*; Why Do Balls Bounce? First Questions & Answers about How Things Work. Time-Life Books Editors. Fallow, Allan, ed. 1995. 14.95 *(978-0-7835-0901-3(4))*; Why Do Roosters Crow? First Questions & Answers about Farms. Time-Life Books Editors. Fallow, Allan, ed. Kavanagh, Peter & Kavanagh, Jim, illus. 1995. 14.95 *(978-0-7835-0899-3(9))*; Why Is the Grass Green? First Questions & Answers about Nature. Time-Life Books Editors. Kagan, Neil, ed. 1993. 14.95 *(978-0-7835-0858-0(1))*; (Illus.). 48p. (J). (gr. k-2). *(978-0-7835-0894-8(8))* Time-Life, Inc.

Todo Sobre Nuestro Mundo. (Coleccion Todo Sobre...). (SPA.). (J). (gr. k-1). *(978-84-243-2966-2(X)*, FH5249) Publicaciones Fher, S.A.

Townsend, John. Gone Missing. 2010. (Amazing Mysteries Ser.). (YA). (gr. 3-6). 28.50 *(978-1-59920-364-5(2))* Black Rabbit Bks.

Traynor, Tracy & Pérez, María. Spanish with Abby & Zak. Hambleton, Laura, illus. 2008. (Abby & Zak Ser.). (SPA & ENG.). 48p. (J). (gr. k-2). pap. 16.95 *(978-1-84059-515-4(9))* Milet Publishing.

Trotter, Pamela D., III. Lantern on a Hitching Post: African-American Heritage Quiz Book 2003. 114p. (YA). per. 12.00 *(978-0-9754540-0-8(5))* Arrinton Pubns.

U. S. National Geographic Society Staff & Harness, Cheryl. Ye Olde Weird but True: 300 Outrageous Facts from History. 2013. (Weird but True Ser.). (ENG.). 208p. (J). (gr. 3-7). lib. bdg. 16.90 *(978-1-4263-1383-7(7)*, National Geographic Children's Bks.) National Geographic Society.

U. S. National Geographic Society Staff, et al. Ye Olde Weird but True: 300 Outrageous Facts from History. 2013. (Weird but True Ser.). (ENG., Illus.). 208p. (J). (gr. 3-7). pap. 7.95 *(978-1-4263-1382-0(9)*, National Geographic Children's Bks.) National Geographic Society.

University Games Staff. More 30 Second Mysteries for Kids. 2007. (Spinner Books for Kids Ser.). (ENG.). 160p. (J). (gr. 4-7). pap. 7.95 *(978-1-57528-839-0(7))* Univ. Games.

Very First Questions & Answers: What Is Poop? 2017. (Lift-The-Flap Very First Questions & Answers* Ser.). (ENG.). (J). bds. 12.99 ***(978-0-7945-3971-9(8)***, Usborne) EDC Publishing.

Walpole, Brenda. I Wonder Why the Sun Rises: And Other Questions about Time & Seasons. 2011. (I Wonder Why Ser.). (ENG., Illus.). 32p. (J). (gr. k-3). pap. 6.99 *(978-0-7534-6529-5(9)*, 9780753465295, Kingfisher) Roaring Brook Pr.

—I Wonder Why the Sun Rises & Other Questions about Time & Seasons. 2008. (I Wonder Why Ser.). (Illus.). 32p. (gr. k-3). 17.00 *(978-0-7569-9054-1(8))* Perfection Learning Corp.

Warner. Ask Quinney. Date not set. 160p. (J). (gr. 3-7). pap. 4.99 *(978-0-06-440762-5(4))* HarperCollins Pubs.

Waxman, Laura Hamilton. Why Did the Pilgrims Come to the New World? & Other Questions about the Plymouth Colony. 2010. (Six Questions of American History Ser.). 48p. (J). pap. 9.95 *(978-0-7613-6123-7(5))* Lerner Publishing Group.

Weber, Belinda. I Wonder Why Caterpillars Eat So Much: And Other Questions about Life Cycles. 2012. (I Wonder Why Ser.). (ENG., Illus.). 32p. (J). (gr. k-3). pap. 6.99 *(978-0-7534-6707-7(0)*, 9780753467077, Kingfisher) Roaring Brook Pr.

Weber, Belinda & Butterfield, Moira. I Wonder Why Cars Go Fast. 2014. (I Wonder Why Ser.). (ENG., Illus.). 24p. (J). (gr. k-3). act. bk. ed. 6.99 *(978-0-7534-7141-8(8)*, 9780753471418, Kingfisher) Roaring Brook Pr.

Williams, Brian. What about HIST. 2008. 40p. pap. *(978-1-84810-068-8(X))* Miles Kelly Publishing, Ltd.

—What about People & Places. 2008. 40p. pap. *(978-1-84810-072-5(8))* Miles Kelly Publishing, Ltd.

—What about Planet Earth. 2008. 40p. pap. *(978-1-84810-073-2(6))* Miles Kelly Publishing, Ltd.

—What about the Natural World. 2008. 40p. pap. *(978-1-84810-071-8(X))* Miles Kelly Publishing, Ltd.

—What about the Universe. 2008. 40p. pap. *(978-1-84810-075-6(2))* Miles Kelly Publishing, Ltd.

—What about World Wonders. 2008. 40p. pap. *(978-1-84810-076-3(0))* Miles Kelly Publishing, Ltd.

Williams, Jane A. A Bluestocking Guide - Building a Personal Model for Success: Companion Workbook to Richard J. Maybury's Uncle Eric Talks about Personal, Career, & Financial Security. Daniels, Kathryn, ed. 2004. (Bluestocking Guide Ser.). (ENG.). 47p. (YA). pap. 10.95 *(978-0-942617-39-9(8))* Bluestocking Pr.

—A Bluestocking Guide - Political Philosophies: Companion Workbook to Richard J. Maybury's Are You Liberal? Conservative? or Confused? Daniels, Kathryn, ed. 2004. (Bluestocking Guide Ser.). (ENG.). 63p. (YA). pap. 12.95 *(978-0-942617-47-4(9))* Bluestocking Pr.

Williams, Jane A. & Daniels, Kathryn, eds. Economics - A Free Market Reader. 2004. (ENG.). 127p. (YA). pap. 12.95 *(978-0-942617-44-3(4))* Bluestocking Pr.

Windeatt, Mary Fabyan & Ignatz, Marie. Vocabulary Quiz Workbook: Based on 6 Great Saints' Lives by Mary Fabyan Windeatt. Lester, Mary Frances, ed. 2004. (ENG.). 200p. (gr. 5-9). pap., wbk. ed. 21.95 *(978-0-89555-743-8(6)*, 1841) TAN Bks.

Witherspoon Press Staff, contrib. by. Belonging to God: A First Catechism. 2003. (J). *(978-1-57153-036-3(3)*, Witherspoon Pr.) Curriculum Publishing, Presbyterian Church (U. S. A.).

Young, Jay. Magic World of Learning. Tucker, Sian, illus. 2003. 32p. *(978-1-903174-42-5(2)*, Pavilion Children's Books) Pavilion Bks.

Young, Jay, creator. Ziga Zaga. 2003. (Illus.). 144p. *(978-1-903174-64-7(3)*, Pavilion Children's Books) Pavilion Bks.

Zakarin, Debra Mostow. Who's Your Superstar BFF? 2010. 112p. pap. 4.95 *(978-1-60747-775-4(0)*, Pickwick Pr.) Phoenix Bks., Inc.

—Who's Your Superstar Soul Mate? 2010. 112p. pap. 4.95 *(978-1-60747-776-1(9)*, Pickwick Pr.) Phoenix Bks., Inc.

Zoehfeld, Kathleen Weidner. How Deep Is the Ocean? Puybaret, Eric, illus. 2016. (Let's-Read-And-Find-Out Science 2 Ser.). 40p. (J). (gr. -1-3). pap. 6.99 *(978-0-06-232819-9(0))* HarperCollins Pubs.

The 5 W's (Gr. 1-3) 2003. (J). *(978-1-58232-075-5(6))* ECS Learning Systems, Inc.

QUILTS

Alyce, Kathie. Flip Flop Block Quilts, 1 vol. 2010. (ENG., Illus.). 64p. 22.95 *(978-1-57432-675-8(9)*, 1574326759, American Quilter's Society) Collector Bks.

Avion, Nicole. The Happy Quilt. 2006. (Neighborhood Readers Ser.). (ENG.). 16p. (gr. 1-3). pap. 6.50 *(978-1-4042-7176-0(7)*, Rosen Classroom) Rosen Publishing Group, Inc., The.

Cardon, Jenny Wilding. The Little Box of Baby Quilts. 2007. (Little Box Of... Ser.). (ENG.). 20p. 22.95 *(978-1-56477-699-0(9)*, That Patchwork Place) Martingale & Co.

CICO Kidz Staff. My First Quilting Book. 2012. (ENG., Illus.). 128p. (J). (gr. 7-11). pap. 14.95 *(978-1-908170-84-2(0)*, CICO Books) Ryland Peters & Small GBR. Dist: WIPRO.

Herkert, Barbara. Sewing Stories: Harriet Powers' Journey from Slave to Artist. Brantley-Newton, Vanessa, illus. 2015. (ENG.). 40p. (J). (gr. -1-3). 17.99 *(978-0-385-75462-0(0)*, Knopf Bks. for Young Readers) Random Hse. Children's Bks.

Hicks, Kyra E. Martha Ann's Quilt for Queen Victoria. Födi, Lee Edward, illus. 2012. 32p. (J). pap. 12.95 *(978-0-9824796-8-1(9))* Black Threads Pr.

—Martha Ann's Quilt for Queen Victoria. Fodi, Lee Edward, illus. 2006. 28p. (J). (gr. -1-3). 16.95 *(978-1-933285-59-7(1))* Brown Books Publishing Group.

Hime, Stanley E. Stanley's Quilt Book / Sue Stays Busy. 2011. 60p. pap. 20.00 *(978-1-935271-88-8(1))* Published by Westview, Inc.

Howard, Judy. Heavenly Patchwork: Quilt Stories Stitched with Love. 2006. (Illus.). 150p. 9.95 *(978-0-9762375-0-1(4))* Dorcas Publishing.

Leisure Arts, creator. Cool Stuff Teach Me to Quilt. 2005. (ENG.). 52p. pap. 10.95 *(978-1-57486-635-3(4))* Leisure Arts, Inc.

Pecorella, Jane. How a Quilt Is Built: Learning to Measure an Object Using Inches. 2009. (Math for the REAL World Ser.). 16p. (gr. 2-3). pap. 7.05 *(978-0-8239-8924-9(0)*, Rosen Classroom) Rosen Publishing Group, Inc., The.

Polydoros, Lori & Benchmark Education Co., LLC. Storytelling on Fabrics: Quilts, Tapestries, Story Cloths, & More. 2014. (Text Connections Ser.). (J). (gr. 3). *(978-1-4509-9646-4(9))* Benchmark Education Co.

Rubin, Susan Goldman. The Quilts of Gee's Bend. 2017. (ENG., Illus.). 56p. (J). (gr. 3-7). 21.95 *(978-1-4197-2131-1(3)*, Abrams Bks. for Young Readers) Abrams, Inc.

Sayre, Hilda L. Kids, Quilts & Reading. 2008. 48p. pap. 24.95 *(978-1-4241-9645-6(0))* America Star Bks.

Schmidt, Carol. Creative Haven Patchwork Quilt Designs Coloring Book. 2014. (Adult Coloring Ser.). (ENG., Illus.). 64p. (gr. 3). pap. 5.99 *(978-0-486-78031-3(7))* Dover Pubns., Inc.

Sturgill, Ruthy. Christmas Tree Advent Calendar: A Country Quilted & Appliquéd Project. 2006. 96p. pap. 24.95 *(978-1-59800-539-4(1))* Outskirts Pr., Inc.

Waldvogel, Merikay. Childhood Treasures: Doll Quilts by & for Children. 2008. (ENG.). 140p. pap. 24.95 *(978-1-56148-599-4(3)*, Good Bks.) Skyhorse Publishing Co., Inc.

QUILTS—FICTION

Avion, Nicole. Un tapiz de felicidad feliz (the Happy Quilt) 2006. (Lecturas del barrio (Neighborhood Readers) Ser.). (SPA.). 16p. (gr. 1-3). pap. 6.50 *(978-1-4042-7178-4(3)*, Rosen Classroom) Rosen Publishing Group, Inc., The.

Barnett, Mac. The Case of the Case of Mistaken Identity. Rex, Adam, illus. (Brixton Brothers Ser.: 1). (ENG.). (J). (gr. 3-7). 2010. 208p. pap. 7.99 *(978-1-4169-7816-9(X))* 2009. 192p. 15.99 *(978-1-4169-7815-2(1))* Simon & Schuster Bks. For Young Readers. (Simon & Schuster Bks. For Young Readers).

Beckman, David. Mika & the Queen's Quilt. 2012. 62p. pap. 17.95 *(978-1-62709-809-0(7))* America Star Bks.

Blomgren, Jennifer. The Tale of Alice's Quilt. 2008. (That Patchwork Place Ser.). (ENG., Illus.). 95p. (YA). (gr. 8-12). per. 14.95 *(978-1-56477-833-8(9)*, That Patchwork Place) Martingale & Co.

Bourgeois, Paulette. Oma's Quilt. 2004. (Illus.). (J). (gr. k-3). spiral bd. *(978-0-616-11099-7(5))*; spiral bd. *(978-0-616-11100-0(2))* Canadian National Institute for the Blind/Institut National Canadien pour les Aveugles.

Bowman, Andy. The Quilt. Travis, Stephanie, illus. 25p. (J). (gr. 1-6). pap. 6.95 *(978-1-931650-04-5(7))*; lib. bdg. 14.95 *(978-1-931650-05-2(5))* Coastal Publishing Carolina, Inc.

Brodine, Linda. Gramma Please Tell Us a Story. 2012. (ENG.). (J). pap. 12.99 *(978-1-4675-1215-2(X))* Independent Pub.

Burnett, Jenifer. My Jungle Quilt. Burnett, Jenifer, illus. 2006. (Illus.). 32p. (J). 19.99 *(978-0-9777570-0-8(5))* Summerside Lane.

Chema. Patch's Country Quilt. Chema, illus. 2013. (Illus.). 54p. 25.95 *(978-1-60571-188-1(8))*; 50p. pap. 17.95 *(978-1-60571-187-4(X))* Northshire Pr.

Coerr, Eleanor. The Josefina Story Quilt. Degen, Bruce, illus. 2003. (I Can Read! Level 3 Ser.). 64p. (J). (gr. 2-4). lib. bdg. 13.55 *(978-0-8335-2723-3(1)*, Turtleback) Turtleback Bks.

Courtney, Kateri. Welby & the Knobby King. 2003. pap. 14.95 *(978-0-9743588-0-2(0))* Castlegate Pr.

Crane, Carol. Handkerchief Quilt. Palmer, Gary, illus. 2010. (ENG.). 32p. (J). (gr. k-3). 15.95 *(978-1-58536-344-5(8))* Sleeping Bear Pr.

Dallas, Sandra. The Quilt Walk. 2012. (ENG.). 216p. (J). 18.95 *(978-1-58536-800-6(8))* Sleeping Bear Pr.

Fitzgerald, Gyleen Xavier. The Dream: A Magical Journey in Colourful Stitches. 2005. (ENG., Illus.). 90p. (J). (gr. 4-7). 29.95 *(978-0-9768215-1-9(6))* FPI Publishing.

Garsee, Linmarie. Annabelle's Vacation with Grandma Hayley: A Mountain Quiltfest Adventure. 2012. 50p. pap. 21.99 *(978-1-4772-7737-9(4))* AuthorHouse.

Geras, Adèle. Apricots at Midnight: And Other Stories from a Patchwork Quilt. 2005. (Illus.). 189p. (J). (gr. -1-17). pap. 5.95 *(978-1-903015-29-2(4))* Barn Owl Bks, London GBR. Dist: Independent Pubs. Group.

Gerdner, Linda & Langford, Sarah. Grandfather's Story Cloth. Loughridge, Stuart, illus. 2008. (Grandfather's Story Cloth Ser.). 32p. (J). (gr. 2-4). 16.95 *(978-1-885008-34-3(1)*, Shen's Bks.) Lee & Low Bks., Inc.

Good, Merle. Reuben & the Quilt. Moss, P. Buckley, illus. rev. ed. 2016. (ENG.). 32p. (J). (gr. -1-3). 16.99 *(978-1-68099-151-2(5)*, Good Bks.) Skyhorse Publishing Co., Inc.

Griffith, Michelle & Conder, Jen. Rosie's Quilt. 2006. (Illus.). (J). 4.99 *(978-0-9789969-4-9(1))* Michelle's Designs.

Hansen, Susan. The Flying Quilt. 2011. pap. 9.95 *(978-0-7414-6469-9(1))* Infinity Publishing.

Kennedy, Pamela. Granny's Cozy Quilt of Memories: Remembering Grandmother's Love Through Her Lasting Gift. Wummer, Amy, illus. 2006. (ENG.). 32p. (J). (gr. k-3). 8.95 *(978-0-8249-5538-0(2)*, Ideal Pubns.) Worthy Publishing.

Keys, Dalen. Just a Quilt? Sponaugle, Kim, illus. 2nd ed. 2012. (ENG.). 32p. (J). 16.00 *(978-1-886068-56-8(9))* Fruitbearer Publishing, LLC.

Kim, Cecil. Friendship Quilt. Jeong, HaJin, illus. rev. ed. 2014. (MySELF Bookshelf Ser.). (ENG.). 32p. (J). (gr. k-2). lib. bdg. 25.27 *(978-1-59953-650-7(1))* Norwood Hse. Pr.

Latham, Irene. Leaving Gee's Bend. 2017. (ENG.). 192p. (gr. 5). pap. 11.95 ***(978-1-58838-332-7(6)***, NewSouth Bks.) NewSouth, Inc.

Marsh, Carole. The Mystery on the Underground Railroad. 2009. (Real Kids, Real Places Ser.). (Illus.). 146p. (J). lib. bdg. 18.99 *(978-0-635-06991-7(1)*, Marsh, Carole Mysteries) Gallopade International.

—The Mystery on the Underground Railroad (Hardcover) 2003. 160p. (gr. 2-8). 14.95 *(978-0-635-02110-6(2))* Gallopade International.

McKissack, Patricia C. Stitchin' & Pullin' A Gee's Bend Quilt. Cabrera, Cozbi A., illus. 2016. (ENG.). 48p. (J). (gr. k-4). 19.65 *(978-0-606-39338-6(2))* Turtleback Bks.

O'Connor, Crystal Ball. Katherine's Quilt. 2007. (J). 18.95 *(978-0-9774038-4-4(X))* Monarch Pubs.

Paschkis, Julie. Mooshka, a Quilt Story, 1 vol. Paschkis, Julie, illus. 2012. (ENG., Illus.). 32p. (J). 16.95 *(978-1-56145-620-8(9))* Peachtree Pubs.

Polacco, Patricia. The Keeping Quilt. 2007. 18.00 *(978-0-7569-1720-3(4))* Perfection Learning Corp.

—The Keeping Quilt: 25th Anniversary Edition. Polacco, Patricia, illus. 25th ed. 2013. (ENG., Illus.). 64p. (J). (gr. -1-3). 17.99 *(978-1-4424-8237-1(0)*, Simon & Schuster/Paula Wiseman Bks.) Simon & Schuster/Paula Wiseman Bks.

Stroud, Bettye. The Patchwork Path: A Quilt Map to Freedom. Bennett, Erin Susanne, illus. 2007. (ENG.). 32p. (J). (gr. k-3). pap. 7.99 *(978-0-7636-3519-0(7))* Candlewick Pr.

Turner, Ann Warren. Sewing Quilts. Allen, Thomas B., illus. 2012. (ENG.). 32p. (J). (gr. k-3). pap. 16.99 *(978-1-4424-6042-3(3)*, Simon & Schuster Bks. For Young Readers) Simon & Schuster Bks. For Young Readers.

von Olfers, Sibylle. Mother Earth & Her Children: A Quilted Fairy Tale. Zipes, Jack, tr. from GER. Schoen-Smith, Sieglinde, illus. 2007. (ENG.). 32p. (J). (gr. -1-2). 17.95 *(978-1-933308-18-0(4))* Breckling Pr.

Wang, Sarah. My Quilt. 2009. (Illus.). 24p. pap. 11.49 *(978-1-4490-3422-1(5))* AuthorHouse.

Werner, Teresa Orem. A Quilt of Wishes. Tremlin, Nathan, illus. l.t. ed. 2005. 26p. (J). 16.95 *(978-1-59879-147-1(8))* Lifevest Publishing, Inc.

Wessel-Estes, Pam. A Quilt & a Home. 2012. 36p. pap. 14.95 *(978-1-4575-1489-0(3))*; 24.95 *(978-1-4575-1490-6(7))* Dog Ear Publishing, LLC.

Woodson, Jacqueline. Show Way. Talbott, Hudson, illus. 2005. (ENG.). 48p. (J). (gr. -1-3). 17.99 *(978-0-399-23749-2(6)*, G.P. Putnam's Sons Books for Young Readers) Penguin Young Readers Group.

QUIMBY, RAMONA (FICTITIOUS CHARACTER)—FICTION

Cleary, Beverly. Beezus & Ramona. Darling, Louis & Rogers, Jacqueline, illus. 2013. (Ramona Ser.: 1). (ENG.). 208p. (J). (gr. 3-7). pap. 6.99 *(978-0-380-70918-2(X))* HarperCollins Pubs.

—Beezus & Ramona. Darling, Louis et al, illus. 2013. (Ramona Ser.: 1). (ENG.). 208p. (J). (gr. 3-7). 16.99 *(978-0-688-21076-2(7))* HarperCollins Pubs.

—Beezus & Ramona. Dockray, Tracy & Rogers, Jacqueline, illus. movie tie-in ed. 2010. (Ramona Ser.: 1). (ENG.). 208p. (J). (gr. 3-7). pap. 5.99 *(978-0-06-191461-4(4)*, HarperFestival) HarperCollins Pubs.

—Beezus & Ramona. 2011. 9.01 *(978-0-7848-3570-8(5)*, Everbind) Marco Bk. Co.

—Beezus & Ramona. (Ramona Quimby Ser.). 142p. (J). (gr. 3-5). pap. 4.99 *(978-0-8072-1441-1(8)*, Listening Library) Random Hse. Audio Publishing Group.

—Beezus & Ramona. Darling, Louis, illus. (gr. 3-5). pap. *(978-0-545-24980-5(5))* Scholastic, Inc.

—Beezus & Ramona. (Ramona Quimby Ser.: 1). (J). 2013. lib. bdg. 17.20 *(978-0-88103-289-5(1))* 2010. lib. bdg. 16.00 *(978-0-606-15072-9(2))* Turtleback Bks. (Turtleback).

—Ramona & Her Family. (J). Random House Publishing Group.

—Ramona & Her Father. Tiegreen, Alan & Rogers, Jacqueline, illus. 2013. (Ramona Ser.: 4). (ENG.). 192p. (J). (gr. 3-7). pap. 6.99 *(978-0-380-70916-8(3))* HarperCollins Pubs.

—Ramona & Her Father. Tiegreen, Alan et al, illus. 2013. (Ramona Ser.: 4). (ENG.). 192p. (J). (gr. 3-7). 16.99 *(978-0-688-22114-0(9))* HarperCollins Pubs.

—Ramona & Her Father. 2009. 8.32 *(978-0-88483-705-3(X)*, Everbind) Marco Bk. Co.

—Ramona & Her Father. (Ramona Quimby Ser.). 186p. (J). (gr. 3-5). pap. 4.99 *(978-0-8072-1439-8(6)*, Listening Library) Random Hse. Audio Publishing Group.

—Ramona & Her Mother. Tiegreen, Alan et al, illus. 2013. (Ramona Ser.: 5). (ENG.). 224p. (J). (gr. 3-7). 16.99 *(978-0-688-22195-9(5))* HarperCollins Pubs.

—Ramona & Her Mother. Tiegreen, Alan & Rogers, Jacqueline, illus. 2013. (Ramona Ser.: 5). (ENG.). 224p. (J). (gr. 3-7). reprint ed. pap. 7.99 *(978-0-380-70952-6(X))* HarperCollins Pubs.

—Ramona & Her Mother. (Ramona Quimby Ser.). 208p. (J). (gr. 3-5). pap. 4.99 *(978-0-8072-1435-0(3)*, Listening Library) Random Hse. Audio Publishing Group.

—The Ramona Collection Vol. 1: Beezus & Ramona, Ramona & Her Father, Ramona the Brave, Ramona the Pest, Vol. 1. Dockray, Tracy & Rogers, Jacqueline, illus. 2013. (Ramona Ser.). (ENG.). (J). (gr. 3-7). pap. 22.99 *(978-0-06-124647-0(6))* HarperCollins Pubs.

—Ramona Empieza el Curso, 1 vol. Bustelo, Gabriela, tr. Giegreen, Alan et al, illus. 2006. (Ramona Ser.: 6).Tr. of Ramona Quimby, Age 8. (SPA.). 224p. (J). (gr. 3-7). pap. *(978-0-688-15487-5(5)*, MR7554) HarperCollins Pubs.

—Ramona Forever. Tiegreen, Alan et al, illus. 2013. (Ramona Ser.: 7). (ENG.). 208p. (J). (gr. 3-7). 16.99 *(978-0-688-03785-7(2))* HarperCollins Pubs.

—Ramona Forever. Tiegreen, Alan & Rogers, Jacqueline, illus. 2013. (Ramona Ser.: 7). (ENG.). 208p. (J). (gr. 3-7). reprint ed. pap. 7.99 *(978-0-380-70960-1(0))* HarperCollins Pubs.

—Ramona Forever. (Ramona Quimby Ser.). 182p. (J). (gr. 3-5). pap. 4.99 *(978-0-8072-1437-4(X)*, Listening Library) Random Hse. Audio Publishing Group.

—Ramona Forever. 2013. (Ramona Quimby Ser.: 7). (J). (gr. 3-6). lib. bdg. 17.20 *(978-0-8085-5273-4(2)*, Turtleback) Turtleback Bks.

—Ramona la Chinche, 1 vol. Darling, Louis et al, illus. 2006. (Ramona Ser.: 2).Tr. of Ramona the Pest. (SPA.). 192p. (J). (gr. 3-7). pap. 5.99 *(978-0-688-14888-1(3)*, MR2295) HarperCollins Pubs.

—Ramona la Chinche. Palacios, Argentina, tr. Darling, Louis, illus. 2006. (Ramona Quimby Spanish Ser.: 2).Tr. of Ramona the Pest. (SPA.). 181p. (J). (gr. 4-7). lib. bdg. 16.00 *(978-0-613-00464-0(7)*, Turtleback) Turtleback Bks.

—Ramona la Valiente. 2003.Tr. of Ramona the Brave. (SPA., Illus.). 124p. (J). pap. 15.95 *(978-84-239-7099-5(X)*, AV2133) Espasa Calpe, S.A. ESP. Dist: Distribooks, Inc.

—Ramona Quimby, Age 8. Tiegreen, Alan & Rogers, Jacqueline, illus. 2016. (Ramona Ser.: 6). (ENG.). 208p. (J). (gr. 3-7). pap. 6.99 *(978-0-380-70956-4(2))* HarperCollins Pubs.

—Ramona Quimby, Age 8. Tiegreen, Alan et al, illus. 2014. (Ramona Ser.: 6). (ENG.). 208p. (J). (gr. 3-7). 16.99 *(978-0-688-00477-4(6))* HarperCollins Pubs.

—Ramona Quimby, Age 8. (Ramona Quimby Ser.). (J). (gr. 3-5). Random House Publishing Group.

—Ramona Quimby, Age 8. (Ramona Quimby Ser.). 190p. (J). (gr. 3-5). pap. 4.99 *(978-0-8072-1436-7(1)*, Listening Library) Random Hse. Audio Publishing Group.

—Ramona the Brave. Tiegreen, Alan et al, illus. 2013. (Ramona Ser.: 3). (ENG.). 208p. (J). (gr. 3-7). 16.99 *(978-0-688-22015-0(0))*; pap. 6.99 *(978-0-380-70959-5(7))* HarperCollins Pubs.

—Ramona the Brave. (Ramona Quimby Ser.). 190p. (J). (gr. 3-5). pap. 4.99 *(978-0-8072-1440-4(X)*, Listening Library) Random Hse. Audio Publishing Group.

—Ramona the Pest. Darling, Louis & Rogers, Jacqueline, illus. 2013. (Ramona Ser.: 2). (SPA & ENG.). 240p. (J). (gr. 3-7). pap. 6.99 *(978-0-380-70954-0(6))* HarperCollins Pubs.

—Ramona the Pest. Darling, Louis et al, illus. 2013. (Ramona Ser.: 2). (ENG.). 240p. (J). (gr. 3-7). 16.99 *(978-0-688-21721-1(4))* HarperCollins Pubs.

—Ramona the Pest. (Ramona Quimby Ser.). (J). (gr. 3-5). Random House Publishing Group.

—Ramona the Pest. (Ramona Quimby Ser.). 192p. (J). (gr. 3-5). pap. 4.99 *(978-0-8072-1438-1(8)*, Listening Library) Random Hse. Audio Publishing Group.

—Ramona y Su Padre. 10th ed. 2003.Tr. of Ramona & Her Father. (SPA., Illus.). 136p. (J). (gr. 3-5). 15.95 *(978-84-239-9020-7(6)*, EC1443) Espasa Calpe, S.A. ESP. Dist: Lectorum Pubns., Inc., Distribooks, Inc.

—Ramona's World. Tiegreen, Alan et al, illus. 2014. (Ramona Ser.: 8). (ENG.). 240p. (J). (gr. 3-7). 16.99 *(978-0-688-16816-2(7))* HarperCollins Pubs.

—Ramona's World. Tiegreen, Alan & Rogers, Jacqueline, illus. 2013. (Ramona Ser.: 8). (ENG.). 240p. (J). (gr. 3-7). pap. 7.99 *(978-0-380-73272-2(6))* HarperCollins Pubs.

—Ramona's World. unabr. ed. 2004. (Ramona Quimby Ser.). 194p. (J). (gr. 3-7). pap. 29.00 incl. audio *(978-0-8072-8169-7(7)*, Listening Library) Random Hse. Audio Publishing Group.

—Ramona's World. 2013. (Ramona Quimby Ser.: 8). (J). (gr. 3-6). lib. bdg. 17.20 *(978-0-613-35794-4(9)*, Turtleback) Turtleback Bks.

QUIZ BOOKS

see Questions and Answers

QUOTATIONS

see also Proverbs

Bates, Katharine Lee. America the Beautiful: Together We Stand. Collier, Bryan et al, illus. 2013. (ENG.). 32p. (J). 17.99 *(978-0-545-49207-2(6)*, Orchard Bks.) Scholastic, Inc.

Beilenson, Evelyn. A Warm & Fuzzy Christmas. Giordano, illus. 2013. (ENG.). 80p. 5.95 *(978-1-4413-1358-4(3))* Peter Pauper Pr. Inc.

Bodden, Michelle. Well My Teacher Said. Williams, Brittney, illus. 2007. 32p. (J). 14.95 *(978-0-9753089-2-9(0))* Water Daughter Publishing.

Brady, Tom, et al. Tom Brady. 2015. (Quotes from the Greatest Athletes Ser.). (ENG., Illus.). 24p. (J). lib. bdg. 12.95 *(978-1-4896-3381-1(2)*, AV2 by Weigl) Weigl Pubs., Inc.

Carlson, Dale. Who Said What? Philosophy Quotes for Teens. Nicklaus, Carol, illus. 2003. (ENG.). 224p. (gr. 7-12). pap. 14.95 *(978-1-884158-28-5(5))* Team Kreskin Productions, LLC.

Celebrate Freedom: Songs, Symbols, & Sayings of the United States. 2003. (Scott Foresman Social Study Ser.). (Illus.). 32p. (gr. k-2). *(978-0-328-03672-1(2))*; 48p. (gr. 3-6). *(978-0-328-03674-5(9))* Addison-Wesley Educational Pubs., Inc. (Scott Foresman).

Countryman, Jack & Parker, Amy. God's Promises for Girls, 1 vol. 2010. (ENG.). 128p. (gr. 1-5). 12.99 *(978-1-4003-1591-8(3))* Nelson, Thomas Inc.

Crosby, Sidney, et al. Sidney Crosby. 2015. (Quotes from the Greatest Athletes Ser.). (ENG., Illus.). 24p. (J). lib. bdg. 12.95 *(978-1-4896-3377-4(4)*, AV2 by Weigl) Weigl Pubs., Inc.

Dean, James & Dean, Kimberly. Pete the Cat's Groovy Guide to Life. Dean, James, illus. 2015. (Pete the Cat Ser.). (ENG., Illus.). 48p. (J). (gr. -1-3). 12.99 *(978-0-06-235135-7(4))* HarperCollins Pubs.

P
Q
R

Engelbreit, Mary. The Blessings of Friendship Treasury, 1 vol. 2014. (ENG., Illus.). 40p. (J). 15.99 *(978-0-310-74509-9(8))* Zonderkidz.

Farina von Buchwald, Martin & Prado Farina, Gabriela. The Joy of Giving. Avendano, Dolores, illus. Testino, Mario et al, photos by. 2005. 89p. (J). 18.00 *(978-0-9777266-0-8(6))* von Buchwald, Martin Farina.

Foldvary-Anderson, Carol. Words of Love Stained Glass Coloring Book. 2011. (Dover Design Stained Glass Coloring Book Ser.). (ENG., Illus.). 32p. (gr. 3-8). pap. 6.99 *(978-0-486-47707-7(X))* Dover Pubns., Inc.

Free Spirit Publishing. Questions & Quotes for Girls. 2nd rev. ed. 2015. (In a Jar(r) Ser.). (ENG.). (J). (gr. 5). 9.99 *(978-1-57542-488-0(6))* Free Spirit Publishing, Inc.

Free Spirit Publishing & Stein, Deborah Jiang. Quotes & Quotables. 2009. (In a Jar(r) Ser.). (ENG.). (YA). 9.99 *(978-1-57542-900-7(4))* Free Spirit Publishing, Inc.

Hamm, Mia, et al. Mia Hamm. 2015. (Quotes from the Greatest Athletes Ser.). (ENG., Illus.). 24p. (J). lib. bdg. 12.95 *(978-1-4896-3365-1(0),* AV2 by Weigl) Weigl Pubs., Inc.

Hudson, Katura J. Afro-Bets Quotes for Kids: Words for Kids to Live By. Simpson, Howard, illus. 2004. (Afro-Bets Ser.). 64p. (J). (gr. k-4). pap. 5.95 *(978-0-940975-89-7(0),* Sankofa Bks.) Just Us Bks., Inc.

I Love Babies. 2004. per. 9.95 *(978-0-9754779-1-5(9))* Chosen Word Publishing.

Jordan, Michael. Michael Jordan. 2015. (Quotes from the Greatest Athletes Ser.). (ENG., Illus.). 24p. (J). lib. bdg. 12.95 *(978-1-4896-3369-9(3),* 1393457, AV2 by Weigl) Weigl Pubs., Inc.

Kamerling, Yvonne. TLC for Teenagers & their Parents: Inspirational Quotes, Poetry, Touching Stories. 2004. 122p. (YA). 22.95 *(978-0-595-66340-8(0))* iUniverse, Inc.

Kerrigan, Michael. Greeks. 2010. (Ancients in Their Own Words Ser.). 64p. (gr. 5). 32.79 *(978-1-60870-065-3(8))* Marshall Cavendish GBR. Dist: Marshall Cavendish Corp.

—Mesopotamians. 2010. (Ancients in Their Own Words Ser.). 64p. (gr. 5). 32.79 *(978-1-60870-066-0(6))* Marshall Cavendish GBR. Dist: Marshall Cavendish Corp.

—Romans. 2010. (Ancients in Their Own Words Ser.). 64p. (gr. 5). 32.79 *(978-1-60870-067-7(4))* Marshall Cavendish Corp.

Kuchler, Bonnie Louise, compiled by. Just Kids: Pictures, Poems & Other Silly Animal Stuff Just for Kids! 2003. (ENG., Illus.). 32p. tchr. ed. 12.95 *(978-1-57223-598-4(5),* 5985) Willow Creek Pr., Inc.

Manning, Peyton, et al. Peyton Manning. 2015. (Quotes from the Greatest Athletes Ser.). (ENG., Illus.). 24p. (J). lib. bdg. 12.95 *(978-1-4896-3373-6(1),* AV2 by Weigl) Weigl Pubs., Inc.

Ogburn, Jacqueline. Little Treasures: Endearments from Around the World. Raschka, Chris, illus. 2012. (ENG.). 32p. (J). (gr. -1-3). 16.99 *(978-0-547-42862-8(6))* Houghton Mifflin Harcourt Publishing Co.

Petrie, H. D., photos by. All God's Creatures; Jesus Loves Me. 2005. (Illus.). 32p. (J). spiral bd. *(978-0-9774115-0-4(8))* AGC Outreach Ministry.

Seabrook, Lochlainn. The Quotable Nathan Bedford Forrest: Selections from the Writings & Speeches of the Confederacy's Most Brilliant Cavalryman. 2012. (Illus.). 130p. pap. 12.95 *(978-0-9838185-5-7(X))* Sea Raven Pr.

Seduction by Shakespeare: Advice, Observations & Quotes on Love, Lust, Beauty & Desire. 2004. 128p. (YA). (gr. 11-18). per. 11.95 *(978-0-9674898-6-5(5))* TCB-Cafe Publishing.

Venus & Serena Williams. 2015. (Quotes from the Greatest Athletes Ser.). (ENG.). (J). lib. bdg. 12.95 *(978-1-4896-3385-9(5),* AV2 by Weigl) Weigl Pubs., Inc.

Weiner, Miriam. Shakespeare's Seasons. Whitt, Shannon, illus. 2012. (ENG.). 32p. (J). (gr. -1). 16.99 *(978-1-935703-57-0(9))* Downtown Bookworks.

365 Days of Wonder: Mr. Browne's Book of Precepts. 2014. (ENG.). 432p. (J). (gr. 3-7). 14.99 *(978-0-553-49904-9(1));* lib. bdg. 17.99 *(978-0-553-49905-6(X))* Random Hse. Children's Bks. (Knopf Bks. for Young Readers).

R

RABBIS

Finkelman, Shimon. The Story of Reb Moshe: A Biography for Young Readers. 2015. (Illus.). 308p. (J). ***(978-1-4226-1665-9(7),*** ArtScroll Series) Mesorah Pubns., Ltd.

Lumer, Marc, illus. When Miracles Happened- Wondrous Stories of Tzaddikim. 2009. 22p. (J). *(978-1-56871-484-4(X))* Targum Pr., Inc.

Mindel, Nissan. Maharal to the Rescue. Ayache, Avraham, illus. 2010. 67p. (YA). 10.95 *(978-0-8266-0032-5(8))* Kehot Pubn. Society.

Rose, Or N. Abraham Joshua Heschel: Man of Spirit, Man of Action. 2003. (ENG., Illus.). 80p. pap. 9.95 *(978-0-8276-0758-3(X))* Jewish Pubn. Society.

Simon, Solomon & Bial, Morrison D. The Rabbi's Bible Vol. 1: Torah. (J). (gr. 5-6). pap., stu. ed. 3.95 *(978-0-87441-319-9(2));*Wkbk. 2. pap., stu. ed. 3.95 *(978-0-87441-320-5(6))* Behrman Hse., Inc.

RABBITS

Alderton, David. How to Look after Your Pet Rabbit: A Practical Guide to Caring for Your Pet, in Step-By-Step Photographs. 2014. (ENG., Illus.). 20p. (J). (gr. -1-3). 8.99 *(978-1-84322-834-9(3),* Armadillo) Anness Publishing GBR. Dist: National Bk. Network.

Antol, Jenna. "Do" The Once Forgotten Little Bunny Who Grew to Become a World Record Holder. 2012. (ENG.). 36p. (J). pap. 14.95 *(978-1-4787-1593-1(6))* Outskirts Pr., Inc.

Baker, Alan. Black & White Rabbit's ABC. 2017. (Little Rabbit Bks.). (ENG.). 24p. 12.99 *(978-0-7534-7322-1(4),* 9780753473221, Kingfisher) Roaring Brook Pr.

—Brown Rabbit's Shapes. 2017. (Little Rabbit Bks.). (ENG.). (J). 12p. bds. 7.99 ***(978-0-7534-7365-8(8),*** 9780753473658); 24p. 12.99 *(978-0-7534-7326-9(7),* 9780753473269) Roaring Brook Pr. (Kingfisher).

—White Rabbit's Colors. 2017. (Little Rabbit Bks.). (ENG.). (J). 12p. bds. 7.99 ***(978-0-7534-7362-7(3),*** 9780753473627); 24p. 12.99 *(978-0-7534-7320-7(8),* 9780753473207) Roaring Brook Pr. (Kingfisher).

Barbe-Julien, Colette. Conejitos. 2006. (Nacidos para Ser Salvajes Ser.). (SPA., Illus.). 24p. (J). (gr. k-3). lib. bdg. 23.00 *(978-0-8368-7423-5(4),* Gareth Stevens Learning Library) Stevens, Gareth Publishing LLLP.

—Little Rabbits. 2006. (Born to Be Wild Ser.). (Illus.). 24p. (gr. k-3). lib. bdg. 23.00 *(978-0-8368-6699-5(1),* Gareth Stevens Learning Library) Stevens, Gareth Publishing LLLP.

Barnes, Julia. Pet Rabbits. 2006. (Pet Pals Ser.). (Illus.). 32p. (gr. 2-6). lib. bdg. 26.00 *(978-0-8368-6781-7(5),* Gareth Stevens Learning Library) Stevens, Gareth Publishing LLLP.

Beck, Angela. Rabbits: Keeping & Caring for Your Pet. 2013. (Keeping & Caring for Your Pet Ser.). 72p. (J). lib. bdg. 29.27 *(978-0-7660-4183-7(2));* (gr. 6-12). pap. 8.95 *(978-1-4644-0297-5(3))* Enslow Pubs., Inc.

Beer, Amy-Jane. Pet Rabbits. 2009. (Illus.). 52p. (J). *(978-0-7172-8050-6(0))* Grolier, Ltd.

Bekkering, Annalise. Rabbits. (J). 2012. 12.95 *(978-1-61913-265-8(6))* 2012. 27.13 *(978-1-61913-068-5(8))* 2007. (Illus.). 24p. (gr. -1-3). lib. bdg. 24.45 *(978-1-59036-679-0(4))* Weigl Pubs., Inc.

—Rabbits. Hudak, Heather C., ed. 2007. (Backyard Animals Ser.). (Illus.). 24p. (J). (gr. -1-3). pap. 8.95 *(978-1-59036-680-6(8))* Weigl Pubs., Inc.

Biniok, Janice. Rabbits. (J). 2009. (Illus.). 112p. 14.95 *(978-1-932904-40-6(9))* 2008. *(978-1-932904-32-1(8))* Eldorado Ink.

Bissell, Robert, illus. Robert Bissell's Rabbits & Bears. 2013. (ENG.). (J). 7.95 *(978-0-7649-6476-3(3))* Pomegranate Communications, Inc.

Bjorklund, Ruth. Rabbits. 2007. (Great Pets Ser.). (Illus.). 48p. (gr. 3-7). lib. bdg. 29.93 *(978-0-7614-2708-7(2),* Benchmark Bks.) Marshall Cavendish Corp.

Bodden, Valerie. Rabbits. (My First Look At Ser.). 24p. (J). 2011. (ENG.). (gr. 1-17). pap. 7.99 *(978-1-926722-42-9(6),* Creative Paperbacks) 2006. (Illus.). (gr. -1-3). lib. bdg. 15.95 *(978-1-58341-460-6(6),* Creative Education) Creative Co., The.

Boothroyd, Jennifer. Meet a Baby Rabbit. 2016. (Lightning Bolt Books (tm) — Baby Farm Animals Ser.). (ENG., Illus.). 32p. (J). (gr. 1-3). 26.65 *(978-1-5124-0802-7(6))* Lerner Publishing Group.

Bunnies. 2003. (Three Minute Tales Ser.). 32p. (J). 5.98 *(978-0-7525-8914-5(8));* 7.95 *(978-0-7525-4758-9(5))* Parragon, Inc.

Butterfield, Moira. Rabbit. (Illus.). 32p. lib. bdg. 24.25 *(978-1-930643-93-2(4))* Chrysalis Education.

Carr, Aaron. El Conejo. 2012. (SPA.). (J). *(978-1-61913-185-9(4))* Weigl Pubs., Inc.

—Rabbit. 2011. (J). *(978-1-61690-570-5(0));* *(978-1-61690-924-6(2))* Weigl Pubs., Inc.

Chung, Liz. Inside Rabbit Burrows. 2015. (Inside Animal Homes Ser.). (ENG., Illus.). 24p. (J). (gr. 2-3). pap. 8.25 *(978-1-4994-0876-8(5),* PowerKids Pr.) Rosen Publishing Group, Inc., The.

—Madrigueras de Conejos (Inside Rabbit Burrows) 2015. (Las Casas de Los Animales (Inside Animal Homes) Ser.). (ENG & SPA.). 24p. (J). (gr. 2-3). 23.60 *(978-1-4994-0565-1(0),* PowerKids Pr.) Rosen Publishing Group, Inc., The.

Colson, Mary. The Truth about Rabbits: What Rabbits Do When You're Not Looking. 2017. (Pets Undercover! Ser.). (ENG., Illus.). 32p. (gr. 2-4). lib. bdg. 29.99 *(978-1-4109-8608-5(X),* Read Me!) Heinemann-Raintree.

Coppendale, Jean. Rabbit. 2004. (QEB You & Your Pet Ser.). (Illus.). 32p. (J). lib. bdg. 18.95 *(978-1-59566-053-4(4))* QEB Publishing Inc.

Dorling Kindersley Publishing Staff. Bunny. 2011. (Baby Touch & Feel Ser.). (ENG.). 14p. (J). (gr. -1 — 1). bds. 5.99 *(978-0-7566-8987-2(2),* DK Children) Dorling Kindersley Publishing, Inc.

Doudna, Kelly. Rascally Rabbits, 1 vol. 2007. (Perfect Pets Ser.). (ENG., Illus.). 24p. (J). (gr. k-3). lib. bdg. 24.21 *(978-1-59928-753-9(6),* SandCastle) ABDO Publishing Co.

Dummies Press Staff, et al. Rabbits for Dummies(r). 2nd ed. 2009. (ENG., Illus.). 312p. pap. 16.99 *(978-0-470-43064-4(8),* For Dummies) Wiley, John & Sons, Inc.

Elora, Grace. Bunnies. 2011. (Cute & Cuddly: Baby Animals Ser.). (Illus.). 24p. (gr. k-2). 69.20 *(978-1-4339-6149-6(0));* pap. 8.15 *(978-1-4339-4504-5(5));* (J). 22.60 *(978-1-4339-4503-8(7))* Stevens, Gareth Publishing LLLP.

Endres, Hollie. Rabbits. 2007. (Farm Animals Ser.). (ENG., Illus.). 24p. (J). (gr. k-3). lib. bdg. 25.95 *(978-1-60014-085-3(8))* Bellwether Media.

Fletcher, Ann L. Angora Rabbits, the Complete Owner's Guide. Includes English, French, Giant, Satin & German Breeds. Care, Breeding, Wool, Farming, Lifespan, Colors. 2013. 158p. (J). pap. *(978-1-909820-07-4(5))* EKL Publishing.

Foran, Jill. Caring for Your Rabbit. 2005. (Caring for Your Pet Ser.). (Illus.). 32p. (J). (gr. 4-7). lib. bdg. 26.00 *(978-1-59036-034-7(6))* Weigl Pubs., Inc.

—Caring for Your Rabbit. Marshall, Diana & Nault, Jennifer, eds. 2003. (Caring for Your Pet Ser.). (Illus.). 32p. (J). pap. 9.95 *(978-1-59036-064-4(8))* Weigl Pubs., Inc.

—Rabbit. 2008. (My Pet Ser.). (Illus.). 32p. (J). (gr. 3-5). pap. 9.95 *(978-1-59036-909-8(2));* lib. bdg. 26.00 *(978-1-59036-908-1(4))* Weigl Pubs., Inc.

Ganeri, Anita. Bunny's Guide to Caring for Your Rabbit, 1 vol. Peterson, Rick, illus. 2013. (Pets' Guides). (ENG.). 32p. (gr. 1-3). pap. 8.29 *(978-1-4329-7142-7(5));* lib. bdg. 27.32 *(978-1-4329-7135-9(2))* Heinemann-Raintree. (Heinemann First Library).

Gardeski, Christina Mia. Pet Rabbits: Questions & Answers. 2016. (Pet Questions & Answers Ser.). (ENG., Illus.). 24p. (gr. k-1). lib. bdg. 26.65 *(978-1-5157-0342-6(8),* Pebble Plus) Capstone Press of Coughlan Cos.

Gillespie, Katie. Rabbits. 2017. (Illus.). 24p. (J). ***(978-1-4896-4503-6(9),*** AV2 by Weigl) Weigl Pubs., Inc.

Glaser, Rebecca. Bunnies Hop. 2017. (Amicus Ink Board Bks.). (ENG., Illus.). 14p. (J). (gr. -1 — 1). bds. 7.99 ***(978-1-68152-199-2(7))*** Amicus.

Glover, David & Glover, Penny. Owning a Pet Rabbit. 2008. (Owning a Pet Ser.). (Illus.). 32p. (J). (gr. 2-5). lib. bdg. 24.25 *(978-1-59771-055-8(5))* Sea-To-Sea Pubns.

Goodbody, Slim & Burstein, John. Rabbits. McGinnis, Ben, illus. 2008. (Slim Goodbody's Inside Guide to Pets Ser.). 32p. (gr. 2-6). lib. bdg. 26.00 *(978-0-8368-8958-1(4),* Gareth Stevens Learning Library) Stevens, Gareth Publishing LLLP.

Graubart, Norman D. How to Track a Rabbit, 1 vol. 2015. (ENG., Illus.). 24p. (J). lib. bdg. 23.60 *(978-1-4777-5434-4(2),* Windmill Bks.) Rosen Publishing Group, Inc., The.

Gray, Leon. Flemish Giant Rabbit: The World's Biggest Bunny. 2013. (Even More SuperSized! Ser.). 24p. (J). (gr. k-3). lib. bdg. 23.93 *(978-1-61772-729-0(6))* Bearport Publishing Co., Inc.

Green, Jen. Rabbits. 2008. (Illus.). 52p. (J). *(978-0-7172-6280-9(4))* Grolier, Ltd.

Gregory, Josh. Rabbits. 2016. (Nature's Children Ser.). (ENG., Illus.). 48p. (J). pap. 6.95 *(978-0-531-21934-8(8),* Children's Pr.) Scholastic Library Publishing.

Guillain, Charlotte. Rabbits. Elsom, Clare, illus. 2013. (Animal Family Albums Ser.). (ENG.). 32p. (gr. 2-4). 30.65 *(978-1-4109-4938-7(9),* Raintree Perspectives) Heinemann-Raintree.

—Rabbits - Animal Family Albums. Elsom, Clare, illus. 2013. (Animal Family Albums Ser.). (ENG.). 32p. (gr. 2-4). pap. 8.29 *(978-1-4109-4943-1(5),* Raintree Perspectives) Heinemann-Raintree.

Haakonsen, Jens. Lynx Chase, Hares Dash. 2017. (Hunter & Hunted: Animal Survival Ser.). 24p. (J). (gr. 7-8). 23.60 ***(978-1-5081-5664-2(6),*** PowerKids Pr.) Rosen Publishing Group, Inc., The.

Hall, Kirsten. Bunny, Bunny. Wilburn, Kathy, illus. 2003. (My First Reader Ser.). (ENG.). 32p. (J). 18.50 *(978-0-516-22923-2(0),* Children's Pr.) Scholastic Library Publishing.

Harkins, Susan Sales & Harkins, William H. Care for a Pet Bunny. 2008. (How to Convince Your Parents You Can ... Ser.). (Illus.). 32p. (J). (gr. 1-4). lib. bdg. 25.70 *(978-1-58415-659-8(7))* Mitchell Lane Pubs., Inc.

Heneghan, Judith. Love Your Rabbit. 2013. (Your Perfect Pet Ser.). (ENG., Illus.). 32p. (gr. k-5). 25.25 *(978-1-4777-0187-4(7));* pap. 10.00 *(978-1-4777-0202-4(4))* Windmill Bks.

Hurley, Jorey. Hop. Hurley, Jorey, illus. 2016. (ENG., Illus.). 40p. (J). (gr. -1-2). 17.99 *(978-1-4814-3272-6(9),* Simon & Schuster/Paula Wiseman Bks.) Simon & Schuster/Paula Wiseman Bks.

Jackman, Vernon. Bunnies & Butterflies in the Backyard & the Pirates Who Know Where They Live: Stories That Help Children Learn & Remember Their Address & Telephone Number. Theagene, Jeannisse, illus. l.t. ed. 2010. (ENG.). 32p. (J). pap. 6.99 *(978-0-9829371-1-2(3))* New Kid Safety.

Jacobs, Pat. Rabbit Pals. 2017. 32p. (J). ***(978-0-7787-3561-8(3))*** Crabtree Publishing Co.

Johnson, Jinny. Rabbit. 2014. (My New Pet Ser.). 24p. (gr. k-3). lib. bdg. 28.50 *(978-1-62588-028-4(6))* Black Rabbit Bks.

—Rabbit. 2014. (My New Pet Ser.). (ENG., Illus.). 24p. (J). (gr. -1-3). pap. 8.95 *(978-1-77092-210-5(5))* Saunders Bk. Co. CAN. Dist: RiverStream Publishing.

—Rabbits. 2009. (Get to Know Your Pet Ser.). (J). 28.50 *(978-1-59920-090-3(2))* Black Rabbit Bks.

—Rabbits. 2009. (Get to Know Your Pet Ser.). (Illus.). 32p. (J). (gr. 4-7). pap. *(978-1-897563-32-8(9))* Saunders Bk. Co.

Jordan, Apple. Guess Who Hops. 2nd rev. ed. 2011. (Bookworms 2nd Edition: Guess Who Ser.). (Illus.). 24p. (J). (gr. k-2). 21.36 *(978-1-60870-427-9(0))* Marshall Cavendish Corp.

Kalman, Bobbie. Baby Bunnies. 2010. (ENG., Illus.). 24p. (J). *(978-0-7787-3958-6(9));* pap. *(978-0-7787-3977-7(5))* Crabtree Publishing Co.

Kalman, Bobbie, photos by. Les Bébés Lapins. 2012. (FRE., Illus.). 24p. (J). pap. 9.95 *(978-2-89579-441-7(3))* Bayard Canada CAN. Dist: Crabtree Publishing Co.

Kawa, Katie. Cuddly Rabbits. 2011. (Pet Corner Ser.). (Illus.). 24p. (gr. k-2). (J). 22.60 *(978-1-4339-5615-7(2));* (J). pap. 8.15 *(978-1-4339-5617-1(9));* 69.20 *(978-1-4339-6885-3(1))* Stevens, Gareth Publishing LLLP.

—Cuddly Rabbits: Conejos Encantadores. 2011. (Pet Corner / RincóN de Las Mascotas Ser.). (SPA & ENG., Illus.). 24p. (J). (gr. k-3). lib. bdg. 22.60 *(978-1-4339-5619-5(5))* Stevens, Gareth Publishing LLLP.

Kennard, Philippa. Bunny Island. Fukuda, Yukihiro, photos by. 2015. (ENG., Illus.). 32p. (J). (gr. -1-1). pap. 4.99 *(978-1-77085-657-8(9),* 9781770856578) Firefly Bks., Ltd.

Knott, Marie, ed. Why Waabooz Has Long Ears. 2007. (Illus.). 27p. (J). pap. 8.95 net. *(978-0-9779895-2-2(6))* Knott, Joan.

Lake, G. G. Rabbits. 2016. (Woodland Wildlife Ser.). (ENG., Illus.). 24p. (gr. k-1). lib. bdg. 26.65 *(978-1-5157-0816-2(0),* Pebble Plus) Capstone Press of Coughlan Cos.

Lambert, Hines. Hunting Rabbits. 2013. (Let's Go Hunting Ser.). (ENG., Illus.). 32p. (J). (gr. 4-6). 25.25 *(978-1-4488-9662-2(2));* pap. 10.00 *(978-1-4488-9782-7(3))* Rosen Publishing Group, Inc., The. (PowerKids Pr.).

Leach, Michael. Hare. 2009. (Animal Neighbors Ser.). 32p. (gr. k-5). pap. 10.60 *(978-1-4042-4574-7(X),* Rosen Classroom); (Illus.). (J). lib. bdg. 25.25 *(978-1-4358-4997-6(3),* PowerKids Pr.) Rosen Publishing Group, Inc., The.

Leaf, Christina. Jackrabbits. 2015. (North American Animals Ser.). (ENG., Illus.). 24p. (J). (gr. k-3). lib. bdg. 25.95 *(978-1-62617-191-6(2),* Blastoff! Readers) Bellwether Media.

Leighton, Christina. Cottontail Rabbits. 2017. (North American Animals Ser.). (ENG., Illus.). 24p. (J). (gr. k-3). lib. bdg. 25.95 *(978-1-62617-566-2(7),* Blastoff! Readers) Bellwether Media.

Los Conejos: Individual Title Six-Packs. (Literatura 2000 Ser.). (SPA.). (gr. 2-3). 33.00 *(978-0-7635-1259-0(1))* Rigby Education.

MacAulay, Kelley & Kalman, Bobbie. Rabbits. Crabtree, Marc, illus. Crabtree, Marc, photos by. 2004. (Pet Care Ser.). (ENG.). 32p. (J). pap. *(978-0-7787-1788-1(7))* Crabtree Publishing Co.

MacAulay, Kelley, et al. Les Lapins. 2011. (Petit Monde Vivant (Small Living World) Ser.: No. 78). (FRE., Illus.). 32p. (J). pap. 9.95 *(978-2-89579-372-4(7))* Bayard Canada Livres CAN. Dist: Crabtree Publishing Co.

MacDonald, Margaret. I Want to Buy a Rabbit. 2011. (Learn-Abouts Ser.). (Illus.). 16p. (J). pap. 7.95 *(978-1-59920-631-8(5))* Black Rabbit Bks.

Macken, JoAnn Early. Jackrabbits. 2nd rev. ed. 2009. (Animals That Live in the Desert Ser.). (ENG.). 24p. (J). (gr. -1-3). pap. 8.15 *(978-1-4339-2450-7(1));* lib. bdg. 22.60 *(978-1-4339-2194-0(4))* Stevens, Gareth Publishing LLLP. (Weekly Reader Leveled Readers).

—Jackrabbits;Liebres Americanas. 2nd rev. ed. 2009. (Animals That Live in the Desert/Animales del desierto Ser.). (SPA & ENG.). 24p. (J). (gr. -1-3). pap. 8.15 *(978-1-4339-2458-3(7));* lib. bdg. 22.60 *(978-1-4339-2131-5(6))* Stevens, Gareth Publishing LLLP. (Weekly Reader Leveled Readers).

—Rabbits. 2003. (Weekly Reader Early Learning Library). (Illus.). 24p. (gr. k-3). pap. 8.15 *(978-0-8368-3849-7(1),* Weekly Reader Leveled Readers) Stevens, Gareth Publishing LLLP.

Mara, Wil. Rabbits. 2014. 31p. 28.50 *(978-1-62712-310-5(5))* Cavendish Square Publishing.

Markovics, Joyce L. Angora Rabbit. 2016. (Weird but Cute Ser.: 8). (ENG., Illus.). 24p. (J). (gr. -1-3). lib. bdg. 17.95 *(978-1-62724-847-1(1))* Bearport Publishing Co., Inc.

Marsico, Katie. How Do We Live Together? Rabbits. 2010. (Community Connections: How Do We Live Together? Ser.). (ENG.). 24p. (gr. 2-5). lib. bdg. 25.64 *(978-1-60279-622-5(X),* 200329) Cherry Lake Publishing.

McBratney, Sam. Colors Everywhere. Jeram, Anita, illus. 2007. (Guess How Much I Love You Ser.). (ENG.). 24p. (J). (-k). bds. 7.99 *(978-0-7636-3545-9(6))* Candlewick Pr.

McBride, Anne. Rabbits, Vol. 12. 2016. (Understanding & Caring for Your Pet Ser.: Vol. 12). (ENG., Illus.). 128p. (J). (gr. 5-8). 25.95 *(978-1-4222-3703-8(6))* Mason Crest.

McDowell, Pamela. Liebres. 2013. (Animales en Mi Patio Ser.). (SPA., Illus.). 24p. (J). (gr. -1-3). lib. bdg. 27.13 *(978-1-62127-597-8(3),* AV2 by Weigl) Weigl Pubs., Inc.

—Rabbits. 2012. (J). 27.13 *(978-1-61913-269-6(9));* pap. *(978-1-61913-273-3(7))* Weigl Pubs., Inc.

McGrath, Barbara Barbieri. The Little Gray Bunny. Kim, Violet, illus. 2013. (ENG.). 32p. (J). (gr. -1-2). 16.95 *(978-1-58089-394-7(5));* pap. 7.95 *(978-1-58089-395-4(3))* Charlesbridge Publishing, Inc.

Meachen Rau, Dana. El Conejo en el Huerto. 2006. (Naturaleza Ser.). (SPA., Illus.). 24p. (gr. k-1). lib. bdg. 15.95 *(978-0-7614-2413-0(X),* Benchmark Bks.) Marshall Cavendish Corp.

—The Rabbit in the Garden. 2006. (Nature Ser.). (SPA., Illus.). 24p. (gr. k-1). lib. bdg. 15.95 *(978-0-7614-2308-9(7),* Benchmark Bks.) Marshall Cavendish Corp.

Meade, Jean McCurdy. The Tale of Rebekah Rabbit. Clark, Barbara Hoserman, illus. 2009. 28p. pap. 12.95 *(978-1-59858-970-2(9))* Dog Ear Publishing, LLC.

Meister, Cari. Rabbits. 2014. (Illus.). 24p. (J). lib. bdg. 25.65 *(978-1-62031-125-7(9),* Bullfrog Bks.) Jump! Inc.

Miller, Amanda & Mayer, Sandra. I Love Bunnies. 2017. (Rookie Toddler(tm) Ser.). (ENG.). 12p. (J). bds. 6.95 *(978-0-531-22975-0(0),* Children's Pr.) Scholastic Library Publishing.

Minden, Cecilia. Kits Grow up to Be Rabbits. 2010. (21st Century Basic Skills Library: Animals Grow Up Ser.). (ENG.). 24p. (gr. k-3). lib. bdg. 22.79 *(978-1-60279-854-0(0),* 200574) Cherry Lake Publishing.

Mitchell, Melanie S. Rabbits. (First Step Nonfiction Ser.). (Illus.). (gr. k-2). 2005. 24p. lib. bdg. 17.27 *(978-0-8225-4604-7(3))* 2003. 23p. (J). pap. 5.95 *(978-0-8225-4605-4(1),* Lerner Pubns.) Lerner Publishing Group.

Morgan, Sally. Rabbits. 2012. (Pets Plus Ser.). (Illus.). 32p. (gr. 3-6). lib. bdg. 31.35 *(978-1-59920-700-1(1))* Black Rabbit Bks.

Neuman, Susan B. Hop, Bunny! (1 Hardcover/1 CD) 2017. (National Geographic Kids Ser.). (ENG.). (J). 29.95 ***(978-1-4301-2645-4(0))*** Live Oak Media.

—Hop, Bunny! (1 Paperback/1 CD) 2017. (National Geographic Kids Ser.). (ENG.). (J). pap. 19.95 ***(978-1-4301-2644-7(2))*** Live Oak Media.

—Hop, Bunny! (4 Paperbacks/1 CD), 4 vols. 2017. (National Geographic Kids Ser.). (ENG.). (J). pap., pap. 31.95 ***(978-1-4301-2646-1(9))*** Live Oak Media.

Newman, Aline Alexander. Rascally Rabbits! And More True Stories of Animals Behaving Badly! 2016. (NGK Chapters Ser.). (ENG., Illus.). 112p. (J). (gr. 2-5). pap. 5.99 *(978-1-4263-2308-9(5),* National Geographic Children's Bks.) National Geographic Society.

Niven, Felicia Lowenstein. Learning to Care for Small Mammals. 2010. (Beginning Pet Care with American Humane Ser.). 48p. (J). 25.27 *(978-0-7660-3195-1(0),* Enslow Elementary) Enslow Pubs., Inc.

Olson, Bethany. Baby Rabbits. 2013. (Super Cute! Ser.). (ENG., Illus.). 24p. (J). (gr. k-3). lib. bdg. 25.95 *(978-1-60014-932-0(4),* Blastoff! Readers) Bellwether Media.

Petrie, Kristin. Cottontail Rabbits, 1 vol. 2014. (Backyard Animals Ser.). (ENG.). 32p. (gr. 3-6). 27.07 *(978-1-62403-659-0(7))* ABDO Publishing Co.

Phillips, Clifton C. Rabbits Rule at Night School. 2008. 28p. pap. 8.99 *(978-1-935105-02-2(7))* Avid Readers Publishing Group.

Phillips, Dee. Snowshoe Hare. 2015. (Arctic Animals: Life Outside the Igloo Ser.). (ENG.). 24p. (J). (gr. -1-3). lib. bdg. 23.93 *(978-1-62724-527-2(8))* Bearport Publishing Co., Inc.

Rabbit's Nap. (Acorn Wood Lift-the-Flap Bks.). (YA). bds. 3.50 net. *(978-1-56021-380-2(9))* W.J. Fantasy, Inc.

Randolph, Joanne. Rabbits. (Classroom Pets Ser.). 24p. 2009. (gr. 2-3). 42.50 *(978-1-61511-858-8(6))* 2007. (Illus.). (J). (gr. 3-7). lib. bdg. 22.60 *(978-1-4042-3680-6(5))* Rosen Publishing Group, Inc., The. (PowerKids Pr.).

Raum, Elizabeth. Los Orangutanes y Sus Nidos (Orangutans Build Tree Nests) Romina Martí, illus. 2017. (Animal Builders Ser.). (ENG & SPA.). 24p. (J). (gr. 1-4). 20.95 ***(978-1-68151-283-9(1),*** Amicus Illustrated) Amicus Publishing.

—Rabbits Dig Burrows. Romina Martí, illus. 2017. (Animal Builders Ser.). (ENG.). 24p. (J). (gr. 1-4). 20.95 ***(978-1-68151-173-3(8),*** Amicus Illustrated) Amicus Publishing.

Rayner, Matthew & BVetMed MRCVS Staff. Rabbit. Burton, Jane & Greenaway, Frank, photos by. 2004. (I Am Your Pet Ser.). (Illus.). 32p. (gr. k-4). lib. bdg. 26.00

(978-0-8368-4105-3(0), Gareth Stevens Learning Library) Stevens, Gareth Publishing LLLP.
Robbins, Lynette. Rabbits & Hares. 2012. (J). 49.50 (978-1-4488-5170-6(X), PowerKids Pr.); pap. 8.25 (978-1-4488-5169-0(6), PowerKids Pr.); lib. bdg. 22.60 (978-1-4488-5018-1(5)) Rosen Publishing Group, Inc., The.
Rockwood, Leigh. Tell Me the Difference Between a Rabbit & a Hare. 2013. (How Are They Different? Ser.). (ENG., Illus.). 24p. (J). (gr. k-5). pap. 8.25 (978-1-4488-9734-6(3)); lib. bdg. 22.60 (978-1-4488-9638-7(X)) Rosen Publishing Group, Inc., The. (PowerKids Pr.).
Royston, Angela. Rabbit. 2004. (J). lib. bdg. 27.10 (978-1-59389-160-2(1)) Chrysalis Education.
Schuh, Mari C. Rabbits. 2015. (Backyard Animals Ser.). (ENG.). 24p. (gr. k-1). lib. bdg. 26.65 (978-1-4914-2086-7(3), Pebble Plus) Capstone Press of Coughlan Cos.
Sexton, Colleen. Bunnies. 2008. (Watch Animals Grow Ser.). (ENG., Illus.). 24p. (J). (gr. k-3). lib. bdg. 25.95 (978-1-60014-166-9(8)) Bellwether Media.
—Caring for Your Rabbit. 2010. (Pet Care Library). (ENG., Illus.). 24p. (J). (gr. 2-5). lib. bdg. 25.95 (978-1-60014-471-4(3), Blastoff! Readers) Bellwether Media.
Shea, Therese. Arctic Hares. 2010. (Animals That Live in the Tundra Ser.). (ENG.). 24p. (J). (gr. -1-3). pap. 8.15 (978-1-4339-3891-7(X)); lib. bdg. 22.60 (978-1-4339-3890-0(1)) Stevens, Gareth Publishing LLLP.
Steinkraus, Kyla. Rabbits on the Farm. 2010. (Farm Animals Ser.). (Illus.). 24p. (J). (gr. k-3). 22.79 (978-1-61590-268-2(6)) Rourke Educational Media.
Stewart, Melissa. Rabbits. 2007. (Animals Animals Ser.). (Illus.). 48p. (gr. 3-7). lib. bdg. 29.93 (978-0-7614-2528-1(4)) Marshall Cavendish Corp.
Stockland, Patricia M. In the Rabbit Hutch, 1 vol. Ouren, Todd, illus. 2009. (Barnyard Buddies Set 2 Ser.). (ENG.). 24p. (gr. -1-2). 27.07 (978-1-60270-645-3(X), Looking Glass Library-Nonfiction) Magic Wagon.
Stoltman, Joan. My First Bunny. 2017. (Let's Get a Pet! Ser.). 24p. (gr. 1-2). pap. 8.15 **(978-1-4824-6441-2(1))** Stevens, Gareth Publishing LLLP.
Tagliaferro, Linda. Rabbits & Their Burrows [Scholastic]. 2010. (Animal Homes Ser.). 24p. pap. 0.49 (978-1-4296-5796-9(0), Pebble Plus) Capstone Press of Coughlan Cos.
Treselt, Alvin & Ewing, Carolyn. The Rabbit Story.Tr. of Histoire de Lapins. (FRE.). (J). pap. 6.99 (978-0-590-74143-9(8)) Scholastic, Inc.
Vogel, Julia. Are You My Rabbit?, 1 vol. Williams, Matthew, illus. 2008. (Are You My Pet? Ser.). (ENG.). 32p. (J). (gr. 1-4). 28.50 (978-1-60270-245-5(4)) Magic Wagon.
Walker, Kathryn. See How Rabbits Grow. 2009. (See How They Grow Ser.). (J). (gr. k-3). (ENG., Illus.). 24p. pap. 8.25 (978-1-4358-2879-7(8)); lib. bdg. 22.60 (978-1-4358-2831-5(3)) Rosen Publishing Group, Inc., The. (PowerKids Pr.).
Why Rabbits Have Long Ears: Individual Title Six-Packs. (Literatura 2000 Ser.). (gr. 2-3). 33.00 (978-0-7635-0270-6(7)) Rigby Education.
Why the Rabbit Has Such Long Ears: Lap Book. (Pebble Soup Explorations Ser.). (SPA.). 16p. (gr. -1-18). 21.00 (978-0-7578-1667-3(3)) Rigby Education.
Why the Rabbit Has Such Long Ears: Small Book. (Pebble Soup Explorations Ser.). (SPA.). 16p. (gr. -1-18). 5.00 (978-0-7578-1707-6(6)) Rigby Education.
Wittrock, Jeni. A Baby Rabbit Story. 2011. (Baby Animals Ser.). (ENG.). 24p. (gr. k-1). pap. 41.70 (978-1-4296-7100-2(9), Pebble Plus) Capstone Press of Coughlan Cos.
—Pet Rabbits up Close. (Pets up Close Ser.). (ENG.). 24p. (gr. k-1). 2015. pap. 6.95 (978-1-4914-7766-3(0)) 2014. 26.65 (978-1-4914-0584-0(8)) Capstone Press of Coughlan Cos. (Pebble Plus).
World Book, Inc Staff, contrib. by. Holland Lops & Other Rabbits. 2007. (World Book's Animals of the World Ser.). (Illus.). 64p. (J). (978-0-7166-1330-5(1)) World Bk., Inc.
Worthington, Niles. A Rabbit's Burrow. 2016. (Animal Builders Ser.). 24p. (J). pap. 8.22 (978-1-5026-2086-6(3)) Cavendish Square Publishing.
Zobel, Derek. Rabbits. 2010. (Backyard Wildlife Ser.). (ENG., Illus.). 24p. (J). (gr. k-3). lib. bdg. 25.95 (978-1-60014-443-1(8), Blastoff! Readers) Bellwether Media.

RABBITS—FICTION

ABDO Publishing Company Staff. Rabbit Ears: A Classic Tale. 2004. (Rabbit Ears-A Classic Tale Ser.). (ENG.). (J). (gr. k-5). 230.85 (978-1-59197-745-2(2)) Spotlight.
Abramson, Laurin. Coco. Abramson, Stephen, photos by. 2010. (Illus.). 28p. pap. 8.75 (978-1-935125-95-2(8)) Robertson Publishing.
Acreman, Hayley. Found You Rabbit! Acreman, Hayley, illus. 2011. (ENG., Illus.). 34p. (J). (gr. k-2). pap. 9.95 (978-1-905762-87-3(9)) Parthian Bks. GBR. Dist: Independent Pubs. Group.
Adams, Adrienne. Christmas Party. 2017. (ENG.). 32p. (J). (gr. -1-3). 13.99 **(978-1-5344-1244-6(1)**, Aladdin) Simon & Schuster Children's Publishing.
—The Easter Egg Artists. 2017. (ENG.). 32p. (J). (gr. -1-3). 13.99 **(978-1-5344-1245-3(X)**, Aladdin) Simon & Schuster Children's Publishing.
Adams, Alison. Brer Rabbit Hears a Noise: Classic Tales Series. Greenhead, Bill, illus. 2011. (Classic Tales Ser.). (J). (978-1-936258-64-2(1)) Benchmark Education Co.
Adams, Richard. Watership Down. 2005. (ENG., Illus.). 496p. pap. 18.99 (978-0-7432-7770-9(8), Scribner) Scribner.
Afetian, "Uncle Ted". The Adventures of Midas & the Little Red Airplane. 2005. (Illus.). 32p. (J). 16.95i (978-0-9752749-0-3(2)) Snyder-Winston Pr.
Agaoglu, Basak. The Almost Impossible Thing. Green, Michael, ed. 2017. (ENG., Illus.). 32p. (J). (gr. -1-2). 16.99 (978-0-399-54827-7(0), Philomel Bks.) Penguin Young Readers Group.
Aggs, Patrice. Strawberry Squirt. 2004. (Pandas Ser.: 27). (ENG., Illus.). 64p. (J). pap. 9.95 (978-0-86278-805-6(6)) O'Brien Pr., Ltd., The IRL. Dist: Dufour Editions, Inc.
Albee, Sarah. The Bunny Hop. Swanson, Maggie, illus. 2004. (Big Bird's Favorites Board Bks.). (ENG.). 24p. (J). (gr. k — 1). bds. 4.99 (978-0-375-82693-1(9), Random Hse. Bks. for Young Readers) Random Hse. Children's Bks.
Alexander, Brad. Antiniak: A Different Kind of Village. 2011. 76p. pap. 15.50 (978-1-257-10163-4(3)) Lulu Pr., Inc.
Anderson, Dee, retold by. Otter Gets Tricked! A Cherokee Trickster Story. l.t. ed. 2004. (Illus.). 32p. (J). pap. 6.00 (978-0-9755934-1-7(2)) Colonel Davenport Historical Foundation.
Anderson, Derek. How the Easter Bunny Saved Christmas. Anderson, Derek, illus. 2006. (ENG., Illus.). 40p. (J). (gr. -1-3). 17.99 (978-0-689-87634-9(3), Simon & Schuster Bks. For Young Readers) Simon & Schuster Bks. For Young Readers.
Anderson, Laurie Halse. New Beginnings #13, 13 vols. 2012. (Vet Volunteers Ser.: 13). (ENG.). 192p. (J). (gr. 3-7). 6.99 (978-0-14-241675-4(4), Puffin Books) Penguin Young Readers Group.
Anderson, R. P., et al. Happy Easter, Curious George. Young, Mary O'Keefe, illus. 2010. (Curious George Ser.). (ENG.). 24p. (J). (gr. -1-3). 9.99 (978-0-547-04825-3(4)) Houghton Mifflin Harcourt Publishing Co.
Andrews McMeel Publishing Staff & Wang, Dorthea Deprisco. Five Minutes until Bed. Vaux, Patricia, illus. 2009. (ENG.). 14p. (J). (gr. 4-7). 14.99 (978-0-7407-8428-6(5)) Andrews McMeel Publishing.
Andros, Camille. Charlotte the Scientist Is Squished. Farley, Brianne, illus. 2017. (ENG.). 40p. (J). (gr. -1-3). 16.99 (978-0-544-78583-0(5)) Houghton Mifflin Harcourt Publishing Co.
Animal Friends Squeaky- Bunny. 2005. (J). bds. (978-1-4194-0091-9(6)) Paradise Pr., Inc.
Antonia, Miller, illus. Baby's Very First Little Book of Bunnies. 2011. (Baby's Very First Board Bks). 10p. (J). ring bd. 6.99 (978-0-7945-2955-0(0), Usborne) EDC Publishing.
Armantrout, Denise. Pink & Green Story Time: Book One. 2013. 32p. pap. 13.99 (978-1-4525-7581-0(9), Balboa Pr.) Author Solutions, Inc.
Arnold, Robyn. Branli Says Bye-Bye to Binky. 2007. 32p. 16.50 (978-0-615-15292-9(9)) Robyn Z Moon Publishing.
Arnosky, Jim. Rabbits & Raindrops. 2014. 16.00 (978-1-63419-679-6(1)) Perfection Learning Corp.
Arrington, R. Region. Tommy Hop the Bunny, 1 vol. 2009. 16p. pap. 24.95 (978-1-4489-2134-8(1)) America Star Bks.
Arzave, Jose. Rabbit the Shepherd. 2013. 24p. pap. 10.99 (978-1-62509-572-5(4)) Salem Author Services.
Ashby, Gaylene. STORY TIME A Collection of Three Children's Stories. 2008. 28p. 14.95 (978-1-4357-1929-3(8)) Lulu Pr., Inc.
Asher, Sandy. Too Many Frogs! Graves, Keith, illus. 2005. (ENG.). 32p. (J). (gr. -1-k). 16.99 (978-0-399-23978-6(2), Philomel Bks.) Penguin Young Readers Group.
—Why Rabbit's Nose Twitches. 2003. (Illus.). 14.95 (978-1-59319-019-4(0)) LeapFrog Enterprises, Inc.
Austin, Jeanne J. Unlikely Friends. 2009. 24p. pap. 14.99 (978-1-4343-2348-4(X)) AuthorHouse.
Auty, Rob. A Hare's Tale 2 - the Golden Hare. Wood, Chaz, illus. 2013. 102p. pap. (978-1-908098-90-0(2)) 2QT, Ltd. (Publishing).
Auty, Robert C. A Hare's Tale. 2011. (ENG., Illus.). 80p. pap. 9.99 (978-1-908098-40-5(6)) 2QT, Ltd. (Publishing) GBR. Dist: Printondemand-worldwide.com.
Award, Anna, et al. The Sick Lion & Hare & the Tortoise. 2014. (ENG.). 24p. (J). pap. 6.95 (978-1-84135-954-0(8)) Award Pubns. Ltd. GBR. Dist: Parkwest Pubns., Inc.
AZ Books Staff. Who Is the Hare Looking For? Zajceva, Ira, ed. 2012. (Who Is There Ser.). (ENG.). 10p. (J). (-k). bds. 11.95 (978-1-61889-040-5(9)) AZ Bks. LLC.
Bachelet, Gilles. Mrs. White Rabbit. 2017. (ENG., Illus.). 32p. (J). 17.00 **(978-0-8028-5483-4(4)**, Eerdmans Bks For Young Readers) Eerdmans, William B. Publishing Co.
Baglio, Ben M. Bunny in a Basket. Baum, Ann, illus. 2005. 142p. (J). (978-0-439-68761-4(6)) Scholastic, Inc.
—Runaway Rascal. 2006. (Illus.). 157p. (J). (978-0-439-79250-9(9)) Scholastic, Inc.
Baguley, Elizabeth. A Long Way from Home. Chapman, Jane, illus. 2008. 32p. (J). (gr. 4-7). 15.95 (978-1-58925-074-1(5)) Tiger Tales.
Bailey, Arthur Scott. The Tale of Peter Mink. 2005. pap. 20.95 (978-0-7661-9699-5(2)) Kessinger Publishing, LLC.
Bailey, Rosemary. Benjamin Bunny A Childrens Story. 2004. 12p. (J). pap. 10.33 (978-1-4116-1043-9(1)) Lulu Pr., Inc.
Baker, Alan. Brown Rabbit's Busy Day. 2017. (Little Rabbit Bks.). (ENG.). 24p. (J). 12.99 (978-0-7534-7337-5(2), 9780753473375, Kingfisher) Roaring Brook Pr.
—Gray Rabbit's 1,2,3. 2017. (Little Rabbit Bks.). (ENG.). 24p. (J). 12.99 (978-0-7534-7324-5(0), 9780753473245, Kingfisher) Roaring Brook Pr.
—Gray Rabbit's 123. 2017. (Little Rabbit Bks.). (ENG.). 12p. (J). bds. 7.99 **(978-0-7534-7364-1(X)**, 9780753473641, Kingfisher) Roaring Brook Pr.
—Gray Rabbit's 123. 2017. (Little Rabbit Bks.). (J). lib. bdg. 18.40 **(978-0-606-39601-1(2))** Turtleback Bks.
Baker, Alan. Gray Rabbit's Favorite Things. 2017. (Little Rabbit Bks.). (ENG.). 24p. (J). 12.99 (978-0-7534-7338-2(0), 9780753473382, Kingfisher) Roaring Brook Pr.
Balian, Lorna. Humbug Rabbit. 2004. (Illus.). 32p. (J). 15.95 (978-1-932065-40-4(7)) Star Bright Bks., Inc.
Banks, Steven. Show Me the Bunny! Greenblatt, C. H. & Reiss, William, illus. 2004. (Spongebob Squarepants Ser.). 32p. (J). 11.65 (978-0-7569-5643-1(9)) Perfection Learning Corp.
Barbo, Maria S. The Velveteen Rabbit Christmas. Hague, Michael, illus. 2013. (My Readers Ser.). (ENG.). 32p. (J). (gr. -1-1). 15.99 (978-1-250-01768-0(8), 9781250017680) Square Fish.
Barlone, M. J. A Mouse & Rabbits Tale. 2010. (Illus.). 40p. pap. 16.99 (978-1-4490-7771-6(4)) AuthorHouse.
Barton, Chris. That's Not Bunny! Jack, Colin, illus. 2016. (ENG.). 32p. (J). (gr. -1-k). 16.99 (978-1-4231-9086-8(6)) Disney Pr.
Base, Graeme, et al. Dinosaurs in Your Backyard: The Coolest, Scariest Creatures Ever Found in the USA! 2009. (ENG., Illus.). 32p. (J). (gr. 1-4). 16.95 (978-0-8109-7099-1(6), Abrams Bks. for Young Readers) Abrams, Inc.
Bauman Wispe, Lisa. Fritter's Spring: A Pocono Rabbit's Tale. 2010. pap. 11.95 (978-0-7414-5796-7(2)) Infinity Publishing.
Baumbach, Rudolph. Summer Legends. 2004. reprint ed. pap. 1.99 (978-1-4192-4993-8(2)); pap. 21.95 (978-1-4191-4993-1(8)) Kessinger Publishing, LLC.
Baxter, Nicola. The Bunny Tales Collection: Twelve Lively Stories of Rascally Rabbits. Shuttleworth, Cathie, illus. 2014. (ENG.). 80p. (J). (gr. -1-3). pap. 9.99 (978-1-84322-934-6(X), Armadillo) Anness Publishing GBR. Dist: National Bk. Network.
Beachy, Elaine. Biff & Becka's Stupendous Vacation. 2013. 156p. (J). 30.95 (978-1-4497-9069-1(0)); pap. 13.95 (978-1-4497-9070-7(4)) Author Solutions, Inc. (WestBow Pr.).
Beckstedt, Cynthia. Hopsy. 2008. 24p. pap. 24.95 (978-1-4241-9122-2(X)) America Star Bks.
Bedford, David. Love Is a Magical Feeling. Butler, John, illus. 2016. (Snuggle Time Stories Ser.). (ENG.). 32p. (J). (gr. -1-k). 9.95 (978-1-4549-1684-0(2)) Sterling Publishing Co., Inc.
Bell, Cece. Rabbit & Robot. 2014. (Candlewick Sparks Ser.). lib. bdg. 13.55 (978-0-606-35169-0(8)) Turtleback Bks.
—Rabbit & Robot: The Sleepover. Bell, Cece, illus. 2012. (ENG., Illus.). 56p. (J). (gr. k-4). 14.99 (978-0-7636-5475-7(2)) Candlewick Pr.
—Rabbit & Robot - The Sleepover. Bell, Cece, illus. 2014. (Candlewick Sparks Ser.). (ENG., Illus.). 56p. (J). (gr. k-4). pap. 3.99 (978-0-7636-6875-4(3)) Candlewick Pr.
—Rabbit & Robot & Ribbit. Bell, Cece, illus. 2016. (ENG., Illus.). 48p. (J). (gr. k-4). 14.99 (978-0-7636-7935-4(6)) Candlewick Pr.
Benoist, Cathy & Gilmore, Cathy. El Conejito de Pascua: El Cuento de un Dia Extraordinario. Sundy, Jonathan, illus. 2014. (SPA.). 40p. (J). (gr. 4-7). 16.99 (978-0-7648-2456-2(2), Libros Liguori) Liguori Pubns.
Bentley, Catherine & Bentley, Dawn. Hoppy Goes to School. Huerta, Catherine, illus. 2006. (Pet Tales Ser.). (ENG.). 32p. (J). 2.95 (978-1-59249-558-0(3)) Soundprints.
Bentley, Dawn. Hoppy Goes to School. Huerta, Catherine, illus. 2006. (ENG.). 32p. (J). pap. 9.95 (978-1-59249-559-7(1)); (gr. -1-3). 4.95 (978-1-59249-556-6(7)) Soundprints.
Bentley, Sue. Chocolate Wishes. 2013. (Magic Bunny Ser.: 1). lib. bdg. 14.75 (978-0-606-31675-0(2), Turtleback) Turtleback Bks.
—Chocolate Wishes #1. Swan, Angela, illus. 2013. (Magic Bunny Ser.: 1). (ENG.). 128p. (J). (gr. 1-3). pap. 5.99 (978-0-448-46727-6(5), Grosset & Dunlap) Penguin Young Readers Group.
—Classroom Capers. 2014. (Magic Bunny Ser.: 4). lib. bdg. 14.75 (978-0-606-34134-9(X), Turtleback) Turtleback Bks.
—Classroom Capers #4. Swan, Angela & Farley, Andrew, illus. 2014. (Magic Bunny Ser.: 4). (ENG.). 128p. (J). (gr. 1-3). 4.99 (978-0-448-46792-4(5), Grosset & Dunlap) Penguin Young Readers Group.
—Dancing Days. 2014. (Magic Bunny Ser.: 5). lib. bdg. 14.75 (978-0-606-34135-6(8), Turtleback) Turtleback Bks.
—Dancing Days #5. Swan, Angela & Farley, Andrew, illus. 2014. (Magic Bunny Ser.: 5). (ENG.). 128p. (J). (gr. 1-3). 4.99 (978-0-448-46793-1(3), Grosset & Dunlap) Penguin Young Readers Group.
—A Splash of Magic. 2013. (Magic Bunny Ser.: 3). lib. bdg. 14.75 (978-0-606-31677-4(9), Turtleback) Turtleback Bks.
—A Splash of Magic #3. Swan, Angela, illus. 2013. (Magic Bunny Ser.: 3). (ENG.). 128p. (J). (gr. 1-3). pap. 5.99 (978-0-448-46729-0(1), Grosset & Dunlap) Penguin Young Readers Group.
—Vacation Dreams. 2013. (Magic Bunny Ser.: 2). lib. bdg. 16.00 (978-0-606-31676-7(0), Turtleback) Turtleback Bks.
—Vacation Dreams #2. Swan, Angela, illus. 2013. (Magic Bunny Ser.: 2). (ENG.). 128p. (J). (gr. 1-3). pap. 5.99 (978-0-448-46728-3(3), Grosset & Dunlap) Penguin Young Readers Group.
Berenstain, Jan & Berenstain, Mike. The Berenstain Bears' Baby Easter Bunny. Berenstain, Jan & Berenstain, Mike, illus. 2008. (Berenstain Bears Ser.). (ENG., Illus.). 16p. (J). (gr. -1-1). pap. 6.99 (978-0-06-057420-8(8), HarperFestival) HarperCollins Pubs.
Berger, Carin. Forever Friends. Berger, Carin, illus. 2010. (ENG., Illus.). 40p. (J). (gr. -1-1). 16.99 (978-0-06-191528-4(9), Greenwillow Bks.) HarperCollins Pubs.
Berglund, Andrea Lloyd. A Good Little Horse: Thunder's Morning Stroll. 2009. 36p. (J). pap. 19.95 (978-1-4327-3822-8(4)) Outskirts Pr., Inc.
Berkes, Marianne. The Tortoise & Hare's Amazing Race, 1 vol. Morrison, Cathy, illus. 2015. (ENG & SPA.). 32p. (J). (gr. k-3). 17.95 (978-1-62855-635-3(8)) Arbordale Publishing.
Berner, R. Thomas. The Cottontails & the Jackrabbits. Berner, Paulette L., illus. 2008. 22p. (J). per. 19.95 (978-0-922993-06-2(8)) Marquette Bks., LLC.
Berner, Rotraut Susanne. Hound & Hare, 1 vol. Tanaka, Shelley, tr. from GER. 2011. (ENG., Illus.). 80p. (J). (gr. k-4). 18.95 (978-0-88899-987-0(9)) Groundwood Bks. CAN. Dist: Publishers Group West (PGW).
Bernstein, Dan. The Tortoise & the Hare Race Again. Glass, Andrew, illus. 2006. (ENG.). (J). 36p. (gr. -1-3). 6.95 (978-0-8234-2070-4(1)); 32p. (gr. 4-8). 16.95 (978-0-8234-1867-1(7)) Holiday Hse., Inc.
Berry, Eileen M. Buttercup Hill. Harrald-Pilz, Marilee, illus. 2006. 39p. (J). (gr. -1-3). pap. (978-1-59166-667-7(8)) BJU Pr.
Bianchi, John, illus. Where Is Here? 2013. (1G Bird, Bunny, & Bear Ser.). (ENG.). 12p. (J). pap. 5.99 (978-1-61406-592-0(6)) American Reading Co.
Bianco, Margery Williams. The Velveteen Rabbit, or, How Toys Become Real. Nicholson, William, illus. 2015. iii, 27p. (J). pap. (978-1-4677-9307-0(8), First Avenue Editions) Lerner Publishing Group.
Billings, David Joseph. Road Trip with Rabbit & Squash. Billings, David Joseph, illus. 2006. (Illus.). 48p. (J). per. (978-0-9789036-0-2(9)) Billings, David J.
Billingsley, Victoria. Happy Hoppy's Orchestra & Other Stories. 2010. 44p. 16.99 (978-1-4520-6753-7(8)) AuthorHouse.
Binkow, Howard. Howard B. Wigglebottom Learns to Listen. Cornelison, Susan F., illus. 2006. (ENG.). 32p. (J). (gr. -1-k). 15.00 (978-0-9715390-1-3(4)) We Do Listen Foundation.
—Howard B. Wigglebottom Listens to His Heart. Cornelison, Susan F., illus. 2nd ed. 2008. (ENG.). 32p. (J). 15.00 (978-0-9715390-2-0(2)) We Do Listen Foundation.
Birchall, Mark. Rabbit's Birthday Surprise. Birchall, Mark, illus. 2003. (Illus.). 32p. (J). (gr. -1-3). 15.95 (978-0-87614-910-2(7), Carolrhoda Bks.) Lerner Publishing Group.
—Rabbit's Wooly Sweater. Birchall, Mark, illus. 2003. (Picture Bks.). (Illus.). 32p. (J). (gr. -1-3). 15.95 (978-1-57505-465-0(5), Carolrhoda Bks.) Lerner Publishing Group.
Bishop, Poppy. Bear's House of Books. Edgson, Alison, illus. 2017. (ENG.). 32p. (J). (gr. -1-2). 16.99 **(978-1-68010-038-9(6))** Tiger Tales.
Blake, Linda. My Pet Rabbit. 2012. 24p. 24.95 (978-1-4626-6187-9(4)) America Star Bks.
Blake, Stephanie. New Baby! 2016. (ENG., Illus.). 40p. (J). 15.95 (978-0-7358-4255-7(8)) North-South Bks., Inc.
—No Quiero Ir a la Escuela. 2007. (SPA., Illus.). 40p. (gr. k-2). 17.99 (978-84-8470-268-9(5)) Corimbo, Editorial S.L. ESP. Dist: Lectorum Pubns., Inc.
—Poop-Di-Doop! 2015. (ENG., Illus.). 40p. (J). 15.95 (978-0-7358-4204-5(3)) North-South Bks., Inc.
—Super Bunny. Blake, Stephanie, illus. 2015. (ENG., Illus.). 38p. (J). 15.95 (978-0-7358-4223-6(X)) North-South Bks., Inc.
Blumberg, Margie. Sunny Bunnies. Goulding, June, illus. 2008. (ENG.). 32p. (gr. -1-k). 15.95 (978-0-9624166-4-4(9)) MB Publishing, LLC.
Blunt, Fred, illus. The Rabbit's Tale. 2013. (Usborne First Reading: Level 1 Ser.). (ENG.). 32p. (J). (gr. -1-3). 6.99 (978-0-7945-3346-5(9), Usborne) EDC Publishing.
Book Buddy: Rabbit with Story Book. Orig. Title: Child's Play. (Illus.). 10p. (J). (gr. -1-3). reprint ed. (978-1-881469-47-6(6)) Safari, Ltd.
Book Company Staff. Who Am I: Rabbit. 2003. (Board Bks.). (Illus.). (J). bds. 10.95 (978-1-74047-308-8(6)) Book Co. Publishing Pty, Ltd., The AUS. Dist: Penton Overseas, Inc.
Bowman, Crystal. The Best Thing about My Birthday. 2014. (Happy Day Ser.). (ENG.). 16p. (J). pap. 2.49 (978-1-4143-9485-5(3)) Tyndale Hse. Pubs.
Boynton, Sandra. The Bunny Rabbit Show! Boynton, Sandra, illus. 2014. (ENG., Illus.). 24p. (J). (gr. -1). bds. 6.95 (978-0-7611-8060-9(5), 18060) Workman Publishing Co., Inc.
Brackett, Michael. The Adventures of Bunny & Hare. 2010. 138p. pap. 11.00 (978-1-60911-296-7(2), Eloquent Bks.) Strategic Book Publishing & Rights Agency (SBPRA).
Bradford, Danette J. Eric & Wrinkles Meet the Bunnyworms. Bunker, Thomas, illus. 2012. 28p. pap. 24.95 (978-1-4560-4261-5(0)) America Star Bks.
Brafman, Joshua. Death Bunny! 2008. 248p. 26.95 (978-0-595-51446-5(4)); pap. 16.95 (978-0-595-52098-5(7)) iUniverse, Inc.
Brandt-Taylor, Diane. The Bunny, the Bear, the Bug & the Bee. Brandt, Michael, illus. 2005. (J). cd-rom 9.88 (978-0-9773236-0-9(9)) TaySysCo Publishing.
Bray, Sorcha. The Adventures of Powerpup & Wonderboy & the Case of the Wicked Chickens. 2010. 48p. pap. 19.75 (978-1-4490-7133-2(3)) AuthorHouse.
Brennan, Sarah. The Tale of Rhonda Rabbit. Harrison, Harry, illus. 2012. (ENG.). 32p. (J). 24.95 (978-1-937160-22-7(X)) Eliassen Creative.
Brenner, Barbara, et al. Bunny Tails. Munsinger, Lynn, illus. 2005. 32p. 15.95 (978-0-689-03925-6(5), Milk & Cookies) ibooks, Inc.
Brett, Jan. The Animals' Santa. Brett, Jan, illus. 2014. (ENG., Illus.). 32p. (J). (gr. -1-k). 17.99 (978-0-399-25784-1(5), G.P. Putnam's Sons Books for Young Readers) Penguin Young Readers Group.
—The Easter Egg. Brett, Jan, illus. (ENG., Illus.). 32p. (J). 2017. (-k). bds. 8.99 (978-0-399-54733-1(9)) 2010. (gr. -1-k). 17.99 (978-0-399-25238-9(X)) Penguin Young Readers Group. (G.P. Putnam's Sons Books for Young Readers).
Brewin, Barbara. Sidney Snail's Wonderful World of Adventure. 2009. (Illus.). 32p. pap. 14.49 (978-1-4389-4100-4(5)) AuthorHouse.
Bright, Rachel. Benjamin & the Super Spectacles (the Wonderful World of Walter & Winnie) 2015. (Wonderful World of Walter & Winnie Ser.). (ENG.). 32p. (J). 17.99 (978-0-00-758595-3(0), HarperCollins Children's Bks.) HarperCollins Pubs. Ltd. GBR. Dist: HarperCollins Pubs.
—Walter & the No-Need-To-Worry Suit (the Wonderful World of Walter & Winnie) 2015. (Wonderful World of Walter & Winnie Ser.). (ENG.). 32p. (J). 17.99 (978-0-00-758594-6(2), HarperCollins Children's Bks.) HarperCollins Pubs. Ltd. GBR. Dist: HarperCollins Pubs.
Broster, Marie. Binky Bunny's Day Out & Poems for Children. 2006. (Illus.). 60p. pap. (978-1-84401-793-5(1)) Athena Pr.
Brown, Margaret Wise. A Baby's Gift: Goodnight Moon & the Runaway Bunny, 2 vols. Hurd, Clement, illus. 2014. 70p. (J). (gr. -1 — 1). pap. 15.99 (978-0-694-01638-9(1), HarperFestival) HarperCollins Pubs.
—Boa Noite Lua. pap. 19.95 (978-85-336-0713-2(X)) Livraria Martins Editora BRA. Dist: Distribooks, Inc.
—Bonsoir Lune.Tr. of Goodnight Moon. (FRE.). (J). pap. 21.95 (978-2-211-01028-3(8)) Archimede Editions FRA. Dist: Distribooks, Inc.
—Buenas Noches Conejito. 2006. (Illus.). 24p. (J). (gr. -1-k). 12.95 (978-1-882077-63-2(6)) Sweetwater Pr.
—Buenas Noches, Luna. 2006.Tr. of Goodnight Moon. (SPA.). (J). (gr. -1-2). lib. bdg. 18.40 (978-0-613-09961-5(3), Turtleback) Turtleback Bks.
—El Conejito Andarin, 1 vol. Marcuse, Aida E., tr. Hurd, Clement, illus. 2006. (SPA.). 48p. (J). (gr. -1-2). pap. 6.99 (978-0-06-077694-7(3)) HarperCollins Pubs.
—The Golden Bunny. Weisgard, Leonard, illus. 2015. (ENG.). 32p. (J). (-k). 16.99 (978-0-385-39274-7(5), Golden Bks.) Random Hse. Children's Bks.
—The Golden Egg Book. Weisgard, Leonard, illus. 2004. (Big Little Golden Book Ser.). (ENG.). 32p. (J). (gr. -1-2). 8.99 (978-0-375-82717-4(X), Golden Bks.) Random Hse. Children's Bks.
—The Golden Egg Book. Weisgard, Leonard, illus. 2015. (Little Golden Book Ser.). (ENG.). 24p. (J). (-k). 4.99 (978-0-385-38476-6(9), Golden Bks.) Random Hse. Children's Bks.
—Good Day, Good Night. Long, Loren, illus. 2017. 40p. (J). (gr. -1-3). 18.99 **(978-0-06-238310-5(8))** HarperCollins Pubs.
—Goodnight Moon. Hurd, Clement, illus. (J). (gr. -1 — 1). 2012. (ENG.). 8p. pap. 14.99 (978-0-06-076224-7(1), HarperFestival) 2007. (ENG.). 32p. pap. 24.99

(978-0-06-111977-4(6), HarperFestival) 2005. 32p. lib. bdg. 18.89 (978-0-06-077586-5(6)) 60th anniv. ed. 2007. (ENG.). 34p. bds. 8.99 (978-0-694-00361-7(1), HarperFestival) 60th anniv. ed. 2007. (ENG.). 32p. 18.99 (978-0-06-077585-8(8)) 60th anniv. ed. 2007. (ENG.). 32p. pap. 8.99 (978-0-06-443017-3(0)) HarperCollins Pubs.
—Goodnight Moon. 2007. (J). (gr. -1-2). lib. bdg. 18.40 (978-0-8085-9386-7(2), Turtleback) Turtleback Bks.
—Goodnight Moon. Hurd, Clement, illus. (J). pap. 32.75 incl. audio. (gr. -1-3). 24.95 incl. audio Weston Woods Studios, Inc.
—Goodnight Moon 123: A Counting Book. Hurd, Clement, illus. (J). 2013. (ENG.). 30p. (gr. -1-k). bds. 9.99 (978-0-06-224405-5(1), HarperFestival) 2007. (ENG.). 32p. (gr. -1-k). 16.99 (978-0-06-112593-5(8)) 2007. 32p. (gr. -1-k). lib. bdg. 17.89 (978-0-06-112594-2(6)) 2007. (978-1-4287-4853-8(9)) HarperCollins Pubs.
—Goodnight Moon 123/Buenas Noches, Luna 123: A Counting Book/un Libro para Contar. Hurd, Clement, illus. 2007. (ENG & SPA.). 32p. (J). (gr. -1-k). 16.99 (978-0-06-117325-7(8), Rayo) HarperCollins Pubs.
—Goodnight Moon Board Book & Bunny. Hurd, Clement, illus. 2005. (ENG.). 34p. (J). (gr. -1 — 1). bds. 16.99 (978-0-06-076027-4(3), HarperFestival) HarperCollins Pubs.
—Goodnight Moon Classic Library: Contains Goodnight Moon, the Runaway Bunny, & My World. Hurd, Clement, illus. 2011. (ENG.). 32p. (J). (gr. -1-1). 14.99 (978-0-06-199823-2(0)) HarperCollins Pubs.
—Home for a Bunny. Williams, Garth, illus. (Little Golden Board Book Ser.). (ENG.). (J). 2015. 26p. (-k). bds. 7.99 (978-0-385-39093-4(9)) 2003. 32p. (gr. -1-k). reprint ed. 9.99 (978-0-307-10546-2(6)) Random Hse. Children's Bks. (Golden Bks.).
—Margaret Wise Brown's the Golden Bunny. Weisgard, Leonard, illus. 2015. (ENG.). 32p. (J). (-k). lib. bdg. 19.99 (978-0-375-97372-7(9), Golden Bks.) Random Hse. Children's Bks.
—Margaret Wise Brown's the Whispering Rabbit. 2017. (Little Golden Book Ser.). (ENG., Illus.). 24p. (J). (-k). 4.99 (978-0-399-55518-3(8), Golden Bks.) Random Hse. Children's Bks.
—Mon Petit Monde (French edition of My World) 2004. 40p. 29.95 (978-0-320-06689-4(4)) French & European Pubns., Inc.
—My World: A Companion to Goodnight Moon. Hurd, Clement, illus. (ENG.). (J). (gr. -1 — 1). 2004. 32p. pap. 6.99 (978-0-694-01660-0(8)) 2003. 36p. bds. 8.99 (978-0-694-00862-9(1), HarperFestival) HarperCollins Pubs.
—Over the Moon: Goodnight Moon, the Runaway Bunny, & My World. Hurd, Clement, illus. 2006. (ENG.). 108p. (J). (gr. -1-1). 19.99 (978-0-06-076162-2(8)) HarperCollins Pubs.
—The Runaway Bunny. Hurd, Clement, illus. (J). (gr. -1 — 1). 2017. (ENG.). 34p. bds. 8.99 (978-0-06-107429-5(2), HarperFestival) 2017. (ENG.). 36p. bds. 12.99 (978-0-694-01671-6(3), HarperFestival) 2017. (ENG.). 48p. 17.99 (978-0-06-077582-7(3)) 2017. (ENG.). 48p. pap. 7.99 (978-0-06-443018-0(9)) 2005. 48p. lib. bdg. 18.89 (978-0-06-077583-4(1)) HarperCollins Pubs.
Brown, Tiffanie & Duncan, Kathryn. Benny Builds a House. 2012. 16p. pap. 12.95 (978-1-257-93819-3(3)) Lulu Pr., Inc.
Bruna, Dick. Miffy Dances. 2004. (Illus.). 24p. pap. 4.99 (978-1-59226-010-2(1)) Big Tent Entertainment, Inc.
—Miffy Says, I Love You! 2004. (Illus.). 12p. bds. 5.99 (978-1-59226-187-1(6)) Big Tent Entertainment, Inc.
—Miffy the Artist. 2016. (ENG., Illus.). 12p. (J). (gr. -1-k). bds. 14.50 (978-1-84976-395-0(X)) Tate Publishing, Ltd. GBR. Dist: Abrams, Inc.
Bryan, Sean. A Boy & His Bunny. Murphy, Tom, illus. 2011. (ENG.). 32p. (J). (gr. -1-k). 14.95 (978-1-61145-023-1(3), 611023, Arcade Publishing) Skyhorse Publishing Co., Inc.
Bryson, Brenda. The Adventures of Roo & Winston. 2007. 78p. pap. 12.95 (978-1-4357-0145-8(3)) Lulu Pr., Inc.
—The Adventures of Roo & Winston - Crop Circles. 2009. 64p. pap. 12.43 (978-0-557-17564-2(X)) Lulu Pr., Inc.
Bunce, Margaret. Adventures with Nature: A Story about Olivia & Her Little Dog, Jake. 2011. 24p. pap. 12.95 (978-1-4567-2497-9(5)) AuthorHouse.
Bunnicula. 2005. (J). (978-1-59564-838-9(0)) Steps To Literacy, LLC.
Bunny's House. Date not set. (Illus.). (J). bds. 4.98 (978-1-4054-0785-4(9)) Parragon, Inc.
Burgess, Thornton W. The Adventures of Jimmy Skunk. 112p. 2008. per. 9.95 (978-1-60312-416-4(0)) 2007. 22.95 (978-1-60312-594-9(9)) Aegypan.
—The Adventures of Lightfoot the Deer. 2008. 108p. (gr. -1-3). 22.95 (978-1-60664-951-0(5)) Aegypan.
—The Adventures of Old Mr Toad. 2007. 140p. (gr. 4-7). 24.95 (978-1-60312-637-3(6)); per. 11.95 (978-1-60312-379-2(2)) Aegypan.
—The Adventures of Old Mr Toad. 2011. 138p. 25.95 (978-1-4638-9561-7(5)) Rodgers, Alan Bks.
—The Adventures of Paddy the Beaver. 2008. 108p. per. 9.95 (978-1-60312-502-4(7)) Aegypan.
—The Adventures of Poor Mrs Quack. 2008. 124p. (gr. 4-7). per. 10.95 (978-1-60312-417-1(9)) Aegypan.
—Big Book of Animal Stories. 2011. (Dover Children's Classics Ser.). (ENG., Illus.). 272p. (J). (gr. 3-8). 9.95 (978-0-486-41980-0(0)) Dover Pubns., Inc.
—Mrs. Peter Rabbit. (J). 18.95 (978-0-8488-0390-2(6)) Amereon Ltd.
—Mrs Peter Rabbit. 120p. (gr. -1-3). 2007. per. 10.95 (978-1-60312-005-0(X)) 2006. 22.95 (978-1-59818-464-8(4)) Aegypan.
—Mrs Peter Rabbit. 2011. 118p. 23.95 (978-1-4638-9573-0(9)) Rodgers, Alan Bks.
—Mrs. Peter Rabbit. 2004. reprint ed. pap. 1.99 (978-1-4192-3581-8(8)); pap. 15.95 (978-1-4191-3581-1(3)) Kessinger Publishing, LLC.
—Old Mother West Wind. 2008. 112p. per. 9.95 (978-1-60312-453-9(5)); 22.95 (978-1-60312-551-2(5)) Aegypan.
Burks Ii, Tony Lamair. The Tale of Imani the Bunny. 2013. 24p. pap. 14.95 (978-1-62646-460-5(X)) Booklocker.com, Inc.
Bush, Martha Faircloth. Helping Hurting Children: a Journey of Healing: Children's Workbook. 2013. 174p. pap. 19.95 (978-1-4497-8527-7(1), WestBow Pr.) Author Solutions, Inc.
Butler, Dori. The Tortoise & the Hare: An Aesop's Fable. 2006. (J). pap. (978-1-4108-6167-2(8)) Benchmark Education Co.
Butler, M. Christina. One Noisy Night. Macnaughton, Tina, illus. 2016. (ENG.). 32p. (J). (gr. -1-2). 16.99 (978-1-68010-034-1(3)) Tiger Tales.
Calvani, Mayra. Humberto, the Bookworm Hamster. Grady, Kit, illus. 2009. 20p. pap. 10.95 (978-1-935137-92-4(1)) Guardian Angel Publishing, Inc.
Cannon, Sherrill S. Peter & the Whimper-Whineys. 2010. 30p. pap. 13.00 (978-1-60911-517-3(1), Strategic Bk. Publishing) Strategic Book Publishing & Rights Agency (SBPRA).
Capobianco, Sue Murphy. Buttons the Bunny of Button Cove Lane. 2013. (ENG., Illus.). (J). 14.95 (978-1-62086-377-0(4)) Mascot Bks., Inc.
Capucilli, Alyssa Satin. Biscuit Meets the Class Pet. Schories, Pat, illus. 2009. (My First I Can Read Ser.). (ENG.). 32p. (J). (gr. -1-3). 16.99 (978-0-06-117747-7(4)); pap. 3.99 (978-0-06-117749-1(0)) HarperCollins Pubs.
—Biscuit Meets the Class Pet. 2009. (Biscuit: My First I Can Read! Ser.). (J). lib. bdg. 13.55 (978-0-606-06960-1(7), Turtleback) Turtleback Bks.
Carbone, Courtney. Somebunny Special (SpongeBob SquarePants) Golden Books Staff, illus. 2013. (Holographic Sticker Book Ser.). (ENG.). 48p. (J). (gr. -1-2). pap. 3.99 (978-0-307-98104-2(5), Golden Bks.) Random Hse. Children's Bks.
Cardarelli, Mario. Bunny, an Orphan's Story. 2008. 44p. pap. 18.99 (978-1-4389-1597-5(7)) AuthorHouse.
Cardoza, Kristina. Pinky Bunny's First Day of Kindergarten. 2011. 16p. pap. 8.75 (978-1-4634-8753-9(3)) AuthorHouse.
Carlson, Amanda. Sultenfuss Moose's Lost Slipper. 2006. 26p. 18.03 (978-1-4116-7729-6(3)) Lulu Pr., Inc.
Carlson, Nancy. Get up & Go! 2008. (ENG., Illus.). 32p. (J). (gr. -1-k). pap. 5.99 (978-0-14-241064-6(0), Puffin Books) Penguin Young Readers Group.
—Get up & Go! 2008. (Illus.). (gr. -1-3). 16.00 (978-0-7569-8922-4(1)) Perfection Learning Corp.
—Harriet & George's Christmas Treat. Carlson, Nancy, illus. 2005. (Picture Bks.). (Illus.). 32p. (J). (gr. k-2). 15.95 (978-1-57505-506-0(6)) Lerner Publishing Group.
—Harriet & George's Christmas Treat. 2003. (ENG., Illus.). 32p. (J). (gr. k-2). pap. 9.95 (978-1-57505-639-5(9)) Lerner Publishing Group.
—Harriet & the Roller Coaster. 20th anniv. ed. (Nancy Carlson's Neighborhood Ser.). (Illus.). 32p. (gr. k-2). 2005. 15.95 (978-1-57505-053-9(6)) 2003. (ENG., (J). 6.95 (978-1-57505-202-1(4)) Lerner Publishing Group.
—Loudmouth George & the Big Race. rev. ed. 2004. (Carolrhoda Picture Books Ser.). (ENG., Illus.). 32p. (J). (gr. k-2). 15.95 (978-1-57505-673-9(9)); per. 6.95 (978-1-57505-724-8(7)) Lerner Publishing Group.
—Loudmouth George & the Cornet. rev. ed. 2004. (Carolrhoda Picture Books Ser.). (ENG., Illus.). 32p. (J). (gr. k-2). pap. 9.95 (978-1-57505-725-5(5)) Lerner Publishing Group.
—Loudmouth George & the Fishing Trip. 2nd rev. ed. 2005. (ENG., Illus.). 32p. (J). (gr. k-2). pap. 9.95 (978-1-57505-733-0(6), First Avenue Editions) Lerner Publishing Group.
—Loudmouth George & the Sixth Grade Bully. 20th anniv. ed. 2005. (Nancy Carlson's Neighborhood Ser.). (Illus.). 32p. (gr. k-2). 15.95 (978-1-57505-218-2(0)) Lerner Publishing Group.
—Loudmouth George & the Sixth-Grade Bully. 20th anniv. rev. ed. 2003. (Nancy Carlson's Neighborhood Ser.). (ENG., Illus.). 32p. (J). (gr. k-2). pap. 6.95 (978-1-57505-549-7(X)) Lerner Publishing Group.
—Loudmouth George Earns His Allowance. Carlson, Nancy, illus. (ENG., Illus.). 32p. (J). (gr. k-2). 2013. 9.95 (978-1-4677-0865-4(8)) 2007. 15.95 (978-0-8225-6560-4(9)) Lerner Publishing Group. (Carolrhoda Bks.).
Carnesi, Mónica. Sleepover with Beatrice & Bear. Carnesi, Mónica, illus. 2014. (ENG., Illus.). 32p. (J). (gr. -1-k). 15.99 (978-0-399-25667-7(9), Nancy Paulsen Books) Penguin Young Readers Group.
Carrer, Chiara. Otto Carrotto. 2011. (ENG., Illus.). 26p. (YA). (gr. -1-3). 16.00 (978-0-8028-5393-6(5), Eerdmans Bks For Young Readers) Eerdmans, William B. Publishing Co.
Carroll, Kathy. Rabbit & the Amazing Hopping Contest. 2007. (Illus.). 16p. (J). 9.99 (978-0-9791401-6-7(1)) Abecedarian Bks.
Carrotblanca. Date not set. (J). 7.98 incl. audio (978-1-57042-320-8(2)) Warner Brothers Records.
Casey, Dawn. A Lullaby for Little One. Fuge, Charles, illus. 2015. (ENG.). 32p. (J). (-k). 12.99 (978-0-7636-7608-7(X), Nosy Crow) Candlewick Pr.
Cate, Annette LeBlanc. The Magic Rabbit. Cate, Annette LeBlanc, illus. 2013. (ENG., Illus.). 32p. (J). (gr. -1-3). 6.99 (978-0-7636-6685-9(8)) Candlewick Pr.
—The Magic Rabbit. 2013. lib. bdg. 17.20 (978-0-606-31601-9(9), Turtleback) Turtleback Bks.
Chaconas, Dori. Looking for Easter. Moore, Margie, illus. 2012. (J). 34.28 (978-1-61913-120-0(X)) Weigl Pubs., Inc.
Chafe, Justin. Bunny Rabbit on the Moon. 2007. (Illus.). 28p. (J). 14.95 (978-0-9787660-0-9(8)) Baboosic Enterprises, LLC.
Chambers, Dori. Princesses' Pink Pillows. 2009. 20p. pap. 10.50 (978-1-60693-431-9(7), Eloquent Bks.) Strategic Book Publishing & Rights Agency (SBPRA).
Chance, C. The Trepets Book Three Rabbit Race Day. Champion, Vanessa, illus. 2007. 112p. per. (978-0-9551289-2-9(7), Bumble Bks.) Dragonfly Bks. & Arts.
Chandler, Pauline. Mr. Rabbit the Farmer. Smith, Eric, illus. 2005. (ENG.). 24p. (J). lib. bdg. 23.65 (978-1-59646-736-1(3)) Dingles & Co.
Charles Santore. The Velveteen Rabbit (Kohl's Edition) Charles Santore, illus. 2012. (ENG., Illus.). 48p. (J). 5.00 (978-1-60464-032-8(4), Applesauce Pr.) Cider Mill Pr. Bk. Pubs., LLC.
Charles Santore & Williams, Margery. The Velveteen Rabbit Set: Or How Toys Become Real. gif. ed. 2014. (ENG.). 48p. (J). 24.95 (978-1-60433-335-0(9), Applesauce Pr.) Cider Mill Pr. Bk. Pubs., LLC.
Chase, Kit. Oliver's Tree. Chase, Kit, illus. 2014. (ENG., Illus.). 32p. (J). (gr. -1-k). 16.99 (978-0-399-25700-1(4), G.P. Putnam's Sons Books for Young Readers) Penguin Young Readers Group.
Chattin, A. K. Dust Bunnies. 1 vol. 2009. 48p. pap. 16.95 (978-1-61582-872-2(9)) America Star Bks.
Chaud, Benjamin. Farewell Floppy. 2015. (ENG., Illus.). 40p. (J). (gr. -1-k). 17.99 (978-1-4521-3734-6(X)) Chronicle Bks. LLC.
Chavez, Joe. Benny the Bunny & Jesus. 2013. 136p. (J). pap. 9.99 (978-1-62697-463-0(2)) Salem Author Services.
Child, Jeremy. Bunny. Davies, Caroline, illus. 2013. (Rock & Rattle Bks.). (ENG.). 8p. (J). (gr. -1 — 1). bds. 3.99 (978-0-7641-6589-4(5)) Barron's Educational Series, Inc.
Chin, Oliver Clyde. The Year of the Rabbit: Tales from the Chinese Zodiac. Roth, Justin, illus. 2010. (Tales from the Chinese Zodiac Ser.). (ENG.). 36p. (J). (gr. -1-3). 15.95 (978-1-59702-023-7(0)) Immedium.
The Christmas Rabbit. 2009. (J). per. 17.95 net. (978-0-9749915-2-8(X)) Sawmill Publishing.
Circle of Friends: The Camelot Rabbitry Series - Volume Three. 2006. (Camelot Rabbitry Ser.: 3). (Illus.). 98p. (J). per. 9.95 (978-0-9672375-3-4(X)) Camelot Tales.
Clare, Caitien. A Rabbit Hash Christmas. Haltermon, Becky, illus. 2012. 36p. (J). 10.00 (978-0-9816123-9-3(3)) Merlot Group, LLC, The.
Clarke, Graham. Fluffy Rabbit & Friends. 2016. (ENG.). 117p. (J). (gr. 1-2). 10.95 (978-1-78554-339-5(3), 80259502-e5fd-4c6b-93c4-99cb4e1f5c2c) Austin, Stan AUS. Dist: Bookmasters Distribution.
Clarke, Jane. Clover the Bunny. 2016. (Dr. KittyCat Ser.: 2). (ENG.). 96p. (J). (gr. 2-5). pap. 4.99 (978-0-545-87336-9(3), Scholastic Paperbacks) Scholastic, Inc.
Clymer, Susan. There's a Rabbit in My Backpack. 2007. 100p. pap. 8.50 (978-1-4303-2959-6(9)) Lulu Pr., Inc.
Cocca-Leffler, Maryann. Easter Bunny in Training. Cocca-Leffler, Maryann, illus. 2009. (Sneak a Peek Ser.). (Illus.). 16p. (J). (gr. -1-3). pap. 6.99 (978-0-06-125673-8(0)) HarperCollins Pubs.
Coe, Jara & Hardy, Donna. Jack Meets the New Baby. 2010. 32p. 12.99 (978-1-4520-7420-7(8)) AuthorHouse.
Coe, Victoria J. Fenway & Hattie & the Evil Bunny Gang. 2017. (Fenway & Hattie Ser.). (ENG.). 192p. (J). (gr. 3-7). 16.99 (978-1-101-99633-1(1), G.P. Putnam's Sons Books for Young Readers) Penguin Young Readers Group.
Coffelt, Soraya. It's Not about You Mr. Easter Bunny: A Love Letter about the True Meaning of Easter. Seroya, Tea, illus. 2017. (Love Letters Book Ser.). (ENG.). 36p. (J). pap. 8.99 (978-1-68350-063-6(6)) Morgan James Publishing.
Coll-Seck, Jayden. Roddy the Rabbit, 01 vols., 1. 2016. (Rosen REAL Readers: Social Studies Nonfiction / Fiction: Family, Community, & the World Ser.). (ENG.). 8p. (J). pap. 5.46 (978-1-5081-1833-6(7), Rosen Classroom) Rosen Publishing Group, Inc., The.
Conejito Azul: Es un Valiente Socorrista.Tr. of Little Blue Bunny: Fairy Tale Story of Bunny Rabbit to the Rescue. (SPA.). (J). 2.98 (978-970-22-0018-5(0)) Larousse, Ediciones, S. A. de C. V. MEX. Dist: Continental Bk. Co., Inc.
Conejito Azul: Salva a los Peces.Tr. of Bunny Rabbit Saves the Fish. (SPA.). (J). 2.98 (978-970-22-0021-5(0)) Larousse, Ediciones, S. A. de C. V. MEX. Dist: Continental Bk. Co., Inc.
Conejito Azul: Y la Aventura de Pap Conejo.Tr. of Bunny Rabbit-Father's Adventure. (SPA.). (J). 2.98 (978-970-22-0019-2(9)) Larousse, Ediciones, S. A. de C. V. MEX. Dist: Continental Bk. Co., Inc.
Connolly, Patrick. The Adventures of Funny, the Amazing Fish-Bunny. 2013. (ENG.). 70p. (YA). pap. 13.95 (978-1-4787-0440-9(3)) Outskirts Pr., Inc.
Conrad, Liz, illus. Little Bunny. 2009. (My Sparkling Springtime Friends Ser.). (ENG.). 10p. (J). bds. 3.95 (978-1-58117-865-4(4), Intervisual/Piggy Toes) Bendon, Inc.
Constantinople, Louise T. The Adventures of Ralph Ribbit. 2012. (ENG.). 103p. pap. 8.95 (978-1-4327-8853-7(1)) Outskirts Pr., Inc.
Conte, Paola, et al. Some Bunny to Talk To: A Story for Children about Going to Therapy. Beeke, Tiphanie, illus. 2014. (J). (978-1-4338-1649-9(0)); pap. (978-1-4338-1650-5(4)) American Psychological Assn. (Magination Pr.).
Cook, Sherry & Johnson, Terri. Ronnie Rock. 26. Kuhn, Jesse, illus. l.t. ed. 2006. (Quirkles — Exploring Phonics through Science Ser.: 18). 32p. (J). 7.99 (978-1-933815-17-6(5), Quirkles, The) Creative 3, LLC.
—Vinnie Volcano. 26. Kuhn, Jesse, illus. l.t. ed. 2006. (Quirkles — Exploring Phonics through Science Ser.: 22). 32p. (J). 7.99 (978-1-933815-21-3(3), Quirkles, The) Creative 3, LLC.
Cooper, Helen S. Tatty-Ratty. Cooper, Helen S., illus. 2004. (Illus.). 28p. (J). (gr. k-3). reprint ed. 19.00 (978-0-7567-7214-7(1)) DIANE Publishing Co.
Cooper, Robert. The Light Behind Their Eyes: The Story of Jack & Bunny Rabbit. 2005. 92p. pap. 33.75 (978-1-4184-0722-3(4)) AuthorHouse.
Cory, David. Little Jack Rabbit's Favorite Bunny Tales. Day, Maurice, illus. 2014. (ENG.). 320p. (J). (gr. 1-5). pap. 12.99 (978-0-486-78556-1(4)) Dover Pubns., Inc.
Cosgrove, Stephen. GrandPa Sam. Edelson, Wendy, illus. 2015. (Barely There Ser.). (ENG.). 32p. (J). (gr. k-4). pap. 7.95 (978-1-941437-48-3(6)) Heritage Builders, LLC.
—The Grumpling. James, Robin, illus. 2003. (Serendipity Bks.). (Orig.). (J). (gr. k-4). 12.65 (978-0-7569-5259-4(X)) Perfection Learning Corp.
Costa, Maria S. How to Find a Friend. 2017. (ENG., Illus.). 32p. (J). (gr. -1-3). 16.99 (978-0-544-92678-3(1)) Houghton Mifflin Harcourt Publishing Co.
Cotton, Katie. Dear Bunny. Gomez, Blanca, illus. 2015. (ENG.). 24p. (J). (gr. -1-1). 16.99 (978-1-84780-685-7(6), Frances Lincoln) Quarto Publishing Group UK GBR. Dist: Littlehampton Bk Services, Ltd.
—Dear Bunny... Gomez, Blanca, illus. 2016. (ENG.). 24p. (J). (gr. -1-2). 15.99 (978-1-84780-846-2(8), Frances Lincoln Children's Bks.) Quarto Publishing Group UK GBR. Dist: Hachette Bk. Group.
Coven, Wanda. Heidi Heckelbeck & the Tie-Dyed Bunny. 2014. (Heidi Heckelbeck Ser.: 10). lib. bdg. 16.00 (978-0-606-35429-5(8)) Turtleback Bks.
Covey, Sean. A Place for Everything: Habit 3. Curtis, Stacy, illus. 2010. (7 Habits of Happy Kids Ser.: 3). (ENG.). 32p. (J). (gr. -1-1). 7.99 (978-1-4169-9425-1(4), Simon & Schuster Bks. For Young Readers) Simon & Schuster Bks. For Young Readers.
Cowell, Cressida. That Rabbit Belongs to Emily Brown. Layton, Neal, illus. 2007. (ENG.). 40p. (gr. -1-3). 16.99 (978-1-4231-0645-6(8)) Hyperion Pr.
Craddock, Erik. BC Mambo. Craddock, Erik, illus. 2009. (Stone Rabbit Ser.: Bk. 1). (ENG., Illus.). 96p. (J). (gr. 3-7). pap. 6.99 (978-0-375-84360-0(4), Random Hse. Bks. for Young Readers) Random Hse. Children's Bks.
—Dragon Boogie. Craddock, Erik, illus. 2012. (Stone Rabbit Ser.: Vol. 7). (ENG., Illus.). 96p. (J). (gr. 2-5). pap. 6.99 (978-0-375-86912-9(3), Random Hse. Bks. for Young Readers) Random Hse. Children's Bks.
—Dragon Boogie. 2012. (Stone Rabbit Ser.: 7). lib. bdg. 17.20 (978-0-606-23868-7(9), Turtleback) Turtleback Bks.
—Ninja Slice. Craddock, Erik, illus. 2010. (Stone Rabbit Ser.: No. 5). (ENG., Illus.). 96p. (J). (gr. 3-7). pap. 6.99 (978-0-375-86723-1(6), Random Hse. Bks. for Young Readers) Random Hse. Children's Bks.
—Pirate Palooza. Craddock, Erik, illus. 2009. (Stone Rabbit Ser.: Bk. 2). (ENG., Illus.). 96p. (J). (gr. 3-7). pap. 6.99 (978-0-375-85660-0(9), Random Hse. Bks. for Young Readers) Random Hse. Children's Bks.
—Robot Frenzy. 2013. (Stone Rabbit Ser.: 8). lib. bdg. 17.20 (978-0-606-27004-5(3), Turtleback) Turtleback Bks.
—Stone Rabbit #6: Night of the Living Dust Bunnies. Craddock, Erik, illus. 2011. (Stone Rabbit Ser.: 6). (ENG., Illus.). 96p. (J). (gr. 3-7). pap. 6.99 (978-0-375-86724-8(4), Random Hse. Bks. for Young Readers) Random Hse. Children's Bks.
—Stone Rabbit #8: Robot Frenzy. Craddock, Erik, illus. 2013. (Stone Rabbit Ser.). (ENG., Illus.). 96p. (J). (gr. 2-5). pap. 6.99 (978-0-375-86913-6(1)); lib. bdg. 12.99 (978-0-375-96913-3(6)) Random Hse. Children's Bks. (Random Hse. Bks. for Young Readers).
Crann, Jacqueline J. Answers for Xavier: How Did I Get Here Mommy? 2010. 28p. pap. 13.99 (978-1-4490-3872-4(7)) AuthorHouse.
Creamer, Joan Klatil. The Magic Sceptre & Reginald the Rabbit. 2007. (Illus.). 32p. (J). 16.95 (978-0-9778476-5-5(9)) Silver Snowflake Publishing.
Crimi, Carolyn. Henry & the Buccaneer Bunnies. Manders, John, illus. 2009. (ENG.). 40p. (J). (gr. -1-3). pap. 7.99 (978-0-7636-4540-3(0)) Candlewick Pr.
—Henry & the Crazed Chicken Pirates. Manders, John, illus. 2010. (ENG.). 40p. (J). (gr. -1-3). pap. 7.99 (978-0-7636-4999-9(6)) Candlewick Pr.
Cronin, Doreen. Rescue Bunnies. Menchin, Scott, illus. 2010. (ENG.). 32p. (J). (gr. -1-3). 16.99 (978-0-06-112871-4(6)) HarperCollins Pubs.
Crow, Nosy. Bunny Boo Has Lost Her Teddy: A Tiny Tab Book. 2014. (Tiny Tab Ser.). (ENG.). 8p. (J). (— 1). bds. 7.99 (978-0-7636-7274-4(2), Nosy Crow) Candlewick Pr.
—Pip & Posy: the Bedtime Frog. Scheffler, Axel, illus. 2014. (Pip & Posy Ser.). (ENG.). 32p. (J). (-k). 12.99 (978-0-7636-7068-9(5), Nosy Crow) Candlewick Pr.
—Pip & Posy: the Scary Monster. Scheffler, Axel, illus. 2014. (Pip & Posy Ser.). (ENG.). 24p. (J). (-k). bds. 6.99 (978-0-7636-7231-7(9), Nosy Crow) Candlewick Pr.
Crummel, Susan Stevens. Tumbleweed Stew. Stevens, Janet, illus. 2003. (Green Light Readers Level 2 Ser.). (ENG.). 32p. (J). (gr. -1-3). pap. 3.95 (978-0-15-204830-3(8)) Houghton Mifflin Harcourt Publishing Co.
Cummins, Chris. Bigsbie - A Bunny's Tale of Surviving Cancer. 2007. 107p. pap. 15.00 (978-1-4116-5785-4(3)) Lulu Pr., Inc.
Dahl, Michael. Bunny Eats Lunch. 1 vol. Vidal, Oriol, illus. 2010. (Hello Genius Ser.). (ENG.). 20p. (gr. 1-2). bds. 7.99 (978-1-4048-5728-5(1)) Picture Window Bks.
Dale, Hannah, illus. Mr. Hare's Big Secret. 2016. (ENG.). 32p. (J). (gr. -1-2). 16.99 (978-0-553-53856-4(X), Doubleday Bks. for Young Readers) Random Hse. Children's Bks.
Davies, Katie. The Great Rabbit Rescue. Shaw, Hannah, illus. 2011. (Great Critter Capers Ser.). (ENG.). 224p. (J). (gr. 3-7). 12.99 (978-1-4424-2064-9(2), Beach Lane Bks.) Beach Lane Bks.
Davis, Chasta. The Easter Bunny & His Famous Painted Eggs. 2011. 28p. pap. 24.95 (978-1-4512-1649-3(1)) America Star Bks.
Davis, Jacky. Black Belt Bunny. Fleck, Jay, illus. 2017. (ENG.). 40p. (J). (-k). 16.99 **(978-0-525-42902-9(6)**, Dial Bks) Penguin Young Readers Group.
Davis, Nancy & Davis, Kathryn Lynn. Wake Up! Wake Up! Davis, Nancy & Davis, Kathryn Lynn, illus. 2011. (ENG., Illus.). 14p. (J). (gr. -1 — 1). bds. 5.99 (978-1-4424-1217-0(8), Little Simon) Little Simon.
De Sena, Joseph. The Butterfly & the Bunny's Tail. Anfuso, Dennis, illus. 2007. 60p. per. 19.95 (978-1-4327-0404-9(4)) Outskirts Pr., Inc.
Dean, James & Dean, Kimberly. Big Easter Adventure. Dean, James & Dean, Kimberly, illus. 2014. (Pete the Cat Ser.). (ENG., Illus.). 24p. (J). (gr. -1-3). 9.99 (978-0-06-219867-9(X)) HarperCollins Pubs.
Dean, Kim & Dean, James. Big Easter Adventure. 2014. (Pete the Cat Ser.). (Illus.). (J). (978-1-4844-1829-1(8)) HarperCollins Pubs.
Degen, Bruce. Snow Joke. Degen, Bruce, illus. 2014. (I Like to Read(r) Ser.). (ENG., Illus.). 24p. (J). (gr. -1-3). 14.95 (978-0-8234-3065-9(0)) Holiday Hse., Inc.
—Snow Joke. 2014. 24p. pap. (978-0-8234-3223-3(8)) Holiday Hse., Inc.
Delaporte, Bérengère & Leroy, Jean. Superfab Saves the Day. 2014. (ENG., Illus.). 40p. (J). (gr. -1-3). 16.95 (978-1-77147-076-6(3), Owlkids) Owlkids Bks. Inc. CAN. Dist: Publishers Group West (PGW).
Delaronde, Deborah L. The Rabbits' Race. McCoy, Virginia, illus. 2009. (Rabbit's Race Ser.). (ENG.). 50p. (gr. 4-6). 18.95 (978-1-894778-76-3(6)) Theytus Bks., Ltd. CAN. Dist: Univ. of Toronto Pr.
DeLuise, Dom & Carter, Derek. Pouch Potato. 2007. 33p. pap. 9.95 (978-0-9717952-0-4(7)) Bacchus Bks.
Denim, Sue & Pilkey, Dav. The Dumb Bunnies. 2nd ed. 2005. (Dumb Bunnies Ser.). (ENG., Illus.). 32p. (J). (gr. -1-3). pap. 6.99 (978-0-439-66944-3(8)) Scholastic, Inc.
Depken, Kristen L. Here Comes Peter Cottontail. 2012. (Step into Reading Level 2 Ser.). lib. bdg. 13.55 (978-0-606-23719-2(4), Turtleback) Turtleback Bks.
—Here Comes Peter Cottontail (Peter Cottontail) Karl, Linda, illus. 2012. (Step into Reading Ser.). (ENG.). 32p. (J). (gr. -1-1). pap. 3.99 (978-0-307-93032-3(7), Random Hse. Bks. for Young Readers) Random Hse. Children's Bks.
Depken, Kristen L. & Jackson, Kathryn. Tawny Scrawny Lion. DiCicco, Sue, illus. 2016. (Step into Reading Ser.). (ENG.).

32p. (J). (gr. -1-1). pap. 3.99 *(978-1-101-93424-1(7),* Random Hse. Bks. for Young Readers) Random Hse. Children's Bks.

DeRosier, Cher. The Plight of the Jelly Bean. Contreras, Gilbert, illus. 2005. (J). *(978-1-891685-50-7(3))* Dearborn Publishing.

deRubertis, Barbara. Jeremy Jackrabbit's Jumping Journey. Alley, R. W., illus. 2010. (Animal Antics A to Z Ser.). 32p. (J). (gr. -1-3). pap. 7.95 *(978-1-57565-314-3(1));* lib. bdg. 22.60 *(978-1-57565-321-1(4))* Kane Press, Inc.

DeVogt, Rindia M. Tommy Hare & the Color Purple, 1 vol. Trogdon, Kathryn, illus. 2009. (ENG.). 22p. pap. 24.95 *(978-1-61582-827-2(3))* America Star Bks.

Dew, Rachel. The Big Bunny Bed. 2009. 12p. pap. 11.50 *(978-1-60693-316-9(7),* Eloquent Bks.) Strategic Book Publishing & Rights Agency (SBPRA).

Dewdney, Anna. Nobunny's Perfect. (ENG.). 32p. (J). (gr. -1-k). 2012. bds. 6.99 *(978-0-670-01408-8(7),* Viking Books for Young Readers) 2010. pap. 6.99 *(978-0-14-241533-7(2),* Puffin Books) Penguin Young Readers Group.

Dharma Publishing Staff. The Rabbit Who Overcame Fear: A Story about Wise Action. 2nd ed. 2013. (ENG.). 36p. (gr. -1-7). pap. 8.95 *(978-0-89800-492-2(6))* Dharma Publishing.

DiCamillo, Kate. The Miraculous Journey of Edward Tulane. Ibatoulline, Bagram, illus. (ENG.). (J). 2015. 240p. (gr. 2-5). pap. 7.99 *(978-0-7636-8090-9(7))* 2009. 228p. (gr. 2-5). pap. 11.99 *(978-0-7636-4783-4(7))* 2006. 228p. (gr. 1-4). 19.99 *(978-0-7636-2589-4(2))* Candlewick Pr.

—The Miraculous Journey of Edward Tulane. 2012. 22.00 *(978-1-61383-813-6(1))* Perfection Learning Corp.

—The Miraculous Journey of Edward Tulane. 2015. lib. bdg. 17.20 *(978-0-606-37892-5(8))* Turtleback Bks.

—The Miraculous Journey of Edward Tulane. Ibatoulline, Bagram, illus. 2009. 198p. (gr. 8-12). 23.30 *(978-1-4178-0763-5(6),* Turtleback) Turtleback Bks.

DiCicco, Sue. Funny Bunnies: Morning, Noon, & Night. 2015. (Illus.). 32p. (J). *(978-1-4844-4595-2(3))* Scholastic, Inc.

Dicicco, Sue. Scholastic Reader Level 1: Funny Bunnies: Morning, Noon, & Night. 2014. (Scholastic Reader Level 1 Ser.). (ENG.). 32p. (J). (gr. -1-1). pap. 3.99 *(978-0-545-67631-1(2))* Scholastic, Inc.

Dinardo, Jeff. Bunny & Bird Are Best Friends: Making New Friends. Ho, Jannie, illus. 2014. (Funny Bone Readers: Being a Friend Ser.). 24p. (gr. -1-1). pap. 4.99 *(978-1-939656-02-5(8))* Red Chair Pr.

Disney Book Group. Disney Bunnies an Eggcellent Day. Disney Book Group, illus. 2017. (ENG., Illus.). 12p. (J). (gr. -1-k). bds. 7.99 *(978-1-4847-7369-7(1))* Disney Pr.

—Disney Bunnies I Love You, My Bunnies Reissue with Stickers. Disney Storybook Art Team, illus. 2017. (ENG.). 24p. (J). (gr. -1-k). pap. 4.99 *(978-1-4847-7370-3(5))* Disney Pr.

Disney Book Group Staff. Thumper Finds a Friend. Disney Storybook Artists Staff & Disney Storybook Art Team, illus. 2010. (ENG.). 32p. (J). (gr. -1-k). pap. 3.99 *(978-1-4231-2313-2(1))* Disney Pr.

Disney Book Group Staff & Driscoll, Laura. Thumper & the Noisy Ducky. Disney Storybook Art Team, illus. 2014. (ENG.). 12p. (J). (gr. -1 — 1). bds. 6.99 *(978-1-4231-8487-4(4))* Disney Pr.

Disney Press Staff & Disney Book Group Staff. Thumper's Furry Friends. 2010. (Touch-And-feel Book Ser.). (ENG.). 12p. (J). (gr. -1-k). bds. 6.99 *(978-1-4231-1840-4(5))* Disney Pr.

DiTerlizzi, Tony. Kenny & the Dragon. 2008. (Playaway Children Ser.). (J). (gr. 3-7). 39.99 *(978-1-60640-958-9(1))* Findaway World, LLC.

—Kenny & the Dragon. DiTerlizzi, Tony, illus. (ENG., Illus.). (J). (gr. 3-7). 2012. 176p. pap. 8.99 *(978-1-4424-3651-0(4))* 2008. 160p. 17.99 *(978-1-4169-3977-1(6))* Simon & Schuster Bks. For Young Readers. (Simon & Schuster Bks. For Young Readers).

—Kenny & the Dragon. DiTerlizzi, Tony, illus. 2008. (Illus.). 160p. (J). (gr. 3-7). 15.99 Simon & Schuster Children's Publishing.

Divine, Jill. Wicked Rabbit. 2011. (Illus.). 86p. pap. 12.95 *(978-1-4457-3797-3(3))* Lulu Pr., Inc.

Dixon, Bob. Holiday Bunny. 2009. 28p. pap. 13.99 *(978-1-4490-0436-1(9))* AuthorHouse.

Doan, Nicholas. Fat Rabbit Farm: Big T's Big Adventure. 2012. (ENG.). pap. 17.95 *(978-1-4675-2918-1(4))* Independent Pub.

Dockray, Tracy. My Life Story. Dockray, Tracy, illus. 2003. (Illus.). 40p. (J). lib. bdg. 15.95 *(978-1-58717-218-2(6),* SeaStar Bks.) Chronicle Bks. LLC.

Dodd, Emma. Love. Dodd, Emma, illus. 2016. (Emma Dodd's Love You Bks.). (ENG., Illus.). 24p. (J). (-k). 12.99 *(978-0-7636-8941-4(6),* Nosy Crow) Candlewick Pr.

Dodd, Emma. Spoonful for Bunny. 2017. (Illus.). 12p. (J). bds. ***(978-1-4083-3982-4(X))*** Barron's Educational Series, Inc.

Doerrfeld, Cori. Little Bunny Foo Foo: The Real Story. (ENG., Illus.). 32p. (J). 2016. (-k). pap. 8.99 *(978-1-101-99774-1(5),* Puffin Books) 2012. (gr. -1-k). 16.99 *(978-0-8037-3470-8(0),* Dial Bks) Penguin Young Readers Group.

Donaki & Rosenberry, Donald. Spectacular Journey. Rosenberry, Akiko & Rosenberry, Susan, illus. 2006. (J). per. 20.00 *(978-0-9771482-6-4(2),* Ithaca Pr.) Authors & Artists Publishers of New York, Inc.

Donaldson, Julia. The Rhyming Rabbit Sticker Book. 2017. (ENG.). 24p. (J). (gr. -1-1). pap. 9.99 ***(978-1-5098-3925-4(9))*** Pan Macmillan GBR. Dist: Independent Pubs. Group.

Dopirak, Kate. Snuggle Bunny (a StoryPlay Book) Doerrfeld, Cori, illus. 2016. (ENG.). 40p. (J). (gr. -1-k). 5.99 *(978-0-545-81536-9(3),* Cartwheel Bks.) Scholastic, Inc.

Dorling Kindersley Publishing Staff. The Adventures of Brer Rabbit & Friends. Copeland, Eric, illus. 2006. (ENG.). 64p. (J). (gr. 5-12). per. 6.99 *(978-0-7566-1813-1(4),* DK Children) Dorling Kindersley Publishing, Inc.

—Good Night, Baby Moon. 2017. (ENG.). 12p. (J). (-k). bds. 12.99 ***(978-1-4654-6307-4(0),*** DK Children) Dorling Kindersley Publishing, Inc.

Dorling Kindersley Publishing Staff. Hoppity Hop Peekaboo! 2010. (ENG.). 12p. (J). (gr. -1 — 1). bds. 9.99 *(978-0-7566-5861-8(6),* DK Children) Dorling Kindersley Publishing, Inc.

Dossantos, Laurie Staples. The Adventures of Stormy. 2009. 34p. pap. 10.50 *(978-1-60693-365-7(5),* Eloquent Bks.) Strategic Book Publishing & Rights Agency (SBPRA).

Dotlich, Rebecca Kai. The Knowing Book. Cordell, Matthew, illus. 2016. (ENG.). 32p. (J). (gr. k). 16.95 *(978-1-59078-926-1(1))* Boyds Mills Pr.

Doudna, Kelly. Las Orejas del Conejo, 1 vol. Nobens, C. A., illus. 2007. (Cuentos de Animales Ser.).Tr. of Rabbit Ears. (SPA & ENG.). 24p. (J). (gr. k-3). lib. bdg. 24.21 *(978-1-59928-669-3(6),* SandCastle) ABDO Publishing Co.

—Rabbit Ears, 1 vol. Nobens, Cheryl A., illus. 2006. (Animal Tales Ser.). (ENG.). 24p. (J). (gr. k-3). lib. bdg. 24.21 *(978-1-59679-961-5(7),* SandCastle) ABDO Publishing Co.

—Rabbit Ears. Nobens, C. A., illus. 2006. (Fact & Fiction Ser.). 24p. (J). pap. 48.42 *(978-1-59679-962-2(5))* ABDO Publishing Co.

Dougherty, Mary. Life Adventures with Fossy. 2004. 7p. (J). pap. 10.58 *(978-1-4116-1497-0(6))* Lulu Pr., Inc.

Douglas, Babette. Curly Hare Gets It Straight. Williams, Ted, illus. 2006. (Kiss a Me Teacher Creature Stories Ser.). (J). (gr. -1-3). *(978-1-890343-35-4(8))* Kiss A Me Productions, Inc.

Dove, Debra. The Fur Flew. 2010. 42p. pap. 19.99 *(978-1-60957-425-3(7))* Salem Author Services.

Driscoll, Laura. Thumper Goes A-Thumpin' Tyminski, Lori, illus. 2015. (ENG.). 12p. (J). (gr. -1 — 1). bds. 6.99 *(978-1-4847-0960-3(8))* Disney Pr.

Driscoll, Laura & Disney Book Group Staff. I Love You, My Bunnies. Tyminski, Lori et al, illus. 2008. (ENG.). 24p. (J). (gr. -1-k). pap. 3.99 *(978-1-4231-2095-7(7))* Disney Pr.

—Thumper Finds an Egg. Tyminski, Lori et al, illus. 2009. (ENG.). 24p. (J). (gr. -1-k). pap. 3.99 *(978-1-4231-1717-9(4))* Disney Pr.

—Thumper's Fluffy Tail. Tyminski, Lori & Vallorani, Giorgio, illus. rev. ed. 2008. (Touch-And-feel Book Ser.). (ENG.). 12p. (J). (gr. -1-k). bds. 6.99 *(978-1-4231-0443-8(9))* Disney Pr.

Drummond, Ree. Charlie's New Friend. 2014. (I Can Read! Level 1 Ser.). (J). lib. bdg. 13.55 *(978-0-606-35041-9(1),* Turtleback) Turtleback Bks.

Dub-u-el. Zoom-Zoom & Slo-Poke. 2005. (J). pap. 15.00 *(978-0-8059-6808-8(3))* Dorrance Publishing Co., Inc.

Dubosarsky, Ursula. The Terrible Plop. Joyner, Andrew, illus. 2009. (ENG.). 40p. (J). (gr. -1-1). 17.99 *(978-0-374-37428-0(7),* 9780374374280, Farrar, Straus & Giroux (BYR)) Farrar, Straus & Giroux.

Dudar, Judy. I Spy a Bunny (pb), 1 vol. Rudnicki, Richard, illus. 2013. (ENG.). 32p. (J). (gr. -1-3). pap. 12.95 *(978-1-55109-942-2(X))* Nimbus Publishing, Ltd. CAN. Dist: Orca Bk. Pubs. USA.

Dunbar, Joyce. Tell Me Something Happy Before I Go to Sleep. Gliori, Debi, illus. 2013. (ENG.). 24p. (J). (— 1). bds. 11.99 *(978-0-547-94059-5(9))* Houghton Mifflin Harcourt Publishing Co.

Dunn, Judy. The Little Rabbit. Dunn, Phoebe, photos by. 2016. (Step into Reading Ser.). (ENG., Illus.). 32p. (J). (gr. -1-1). pap. 3.99 *(978-0-553-53354-5(1),* Random Hse. Bks. for Young Readers) Random Hse. Children's Bks.

Dunrea, Olivier. Gideon & Otto. 2012. (Gossie & Friends Ser.). (ENG., Illus.). 32p. (J). (gr. k — 1). 9.99 *(978-0-618-43662-0(6))* Houghton Mifflin Harcourt Publishing Co.

—Gideon & Otto: Best Friends, Lost & Found. 2013. (Gossie & Friends Ser.). (ENG., Illus.). 32p. (J). (— 1). bds. 6.99 *(978-0-547-98398-1(0))* Houghton Mifflin Harcourt Publishing Co.

Durk, Jim, illus. Rabbid of the Sea. 2015. (Rabbids Invasion Ser.). (ENG.). 40p. (J). (gr. 1-3). pap. 3.99 *(978-1-4814-3545-1(0),* Simon Spotlight) Simon Spotlight.

Duvall, Deborah L. How Rabbit Lost His Tail: A Traditional Cherokee Legend. Jacob, Murv, illus. 2003. (Grandmother Stories Ser.: Vol. 3). (ENG.). 32p. (J). 16.95 *(978-0-8263-3010-9(X))* Univ. of New Mexico Pr.

—Rabbit & the Fingerbone Necklace. Jacob, Murv, illus. 2009. (ENG.). 32p. (J). (gr. 1). 19.95 *(978-0-8263-4723-7(1))* Univ. of New Mexico Pr.

—Rabbit Goes to Kansas. Jacob, Murv, illus. 2007. (ENG.). 32p. (J). (gr. 1-18). 16.95 *(978-0-8263-4181-5(0))* Univ. of New Mexico Pr.

Dyan, Penelope. There's No Business Like Bartholomew Bunny's Business. Dyan, Penelope, illus. 2009. (Illus.). 44p. pap. 11.95 *(978-1-935118-54-1(4))* Bellissima Publishing, LLC.

Dyckman, Ame. Wolfie the Bunny. OHora, Zachariah, illus. 2015. (ENG.). 40p. (J). (gr. -1-1). 17.99 *(978-0-316-22614-1(9))* Little, Brown Bks. for Young Readers.

Dyess, Hal. The Night the Rabbits Dance: An Easter Story. 2011. 20p. pap. 10.00 *(978-1-4567-3613-2(2))* AuthorHouse.

Eaddy, Susan. Poppy's Best Paper (1 Hardcover/1 CD) Bonnet, Rosalinde, illus. 2016. (ENG.). (J). (gr. 1-4). audio compact disk 29.95 *(978-1-4301-2187-9(4))* Live Oak Media.

East, Jacqueline, illus. Easter Hop. 2008. (ENG.). 16p. (gr. -1-k). bds. 5.95 *(978-1-58117-686-5(4),* Intervisual/Piggy Toes) Bendon, Inc.

Eaton, Maxwell, III. Birds vs. Bunnies. 2013. (Flying Beaver Brothers Ser.). (ENG., Illus.). 96p. (J). (gr. 1-4). pap. 7.99 *(978-0-449-81022-4(4),* Knopf Bks. for Young Readers) Random Hse. Children's Bks.

—Birds vs. Bunnies. 2013. (Flying Beaver Brothers Ser.: 4). lib. bdg. 18.40 *(978-0-606-32234-8(5),* Turtleback) Turtleback Bks.

Edgar, Amy. Bunny Surprise. Tejido, Jomike, illus. 2017. (Scholastic Reader, Level 2 Ser.). (ENG.). 32p. (J). (gr. k-2). pap. 5.99 *(978-1-338-04590-1(3))* Scholastic, Inc.

Edgeworth, Maria. Rosamond: With Other Tales. by Maria Edgeworth. 2006. 388p. per. 26.99 *(978-1-4255-4076-0(7))* Michigan Publishing.

Edmonds, Lin. Patric the Pony & the Race for Freedom. 2011. 32p. pap. 15.50 *(978-1-4670-3662-7(5))* AuthorHouse.

—Patric the Pony Finds a Friend. Connors, Mary, illus. 2009. 32p. pap. 12.99 *(978-1-4389-5167-6(1))* AuthorHouse.

Edvall, Lilian. The Rabbit Who Couldn't Find His Daddy. Gimbergsson, Sara, illus. 2006. 32p. (J). (gr. -1-3). 15.00 *(978-91-29-66429-4(2))* R & S Bks. SWE. Dist: Macmillan.

Edwards, Melvin Neal. Goodee the Rabbit. 2012. 76p. (gr. -1). 20.84 *(978-1-4669-5072-6(2));* pap. 10.84 *(978-1-4669-5070-2(6))* Trafford Publishing.

Eggleton, Jill. Rabbit & Rooster's Ride: 3-in-1 Package. Taylor, Clive, illus. (Sails Literacy Ser.). 24p. (gr. k-18). 57.00 *(978-0-7578-8617-1(5))* Rigby Education.

—Rabbit & Rooster's Ride: 6 Small Books. Taylor, Clive, illus. (Sails Literacy Ser.). 24p. (gr. k-18). 25.00 *(978-0-7578-7727-8(3))* Rigby Education.

—Rabbit & Rooster's Ride: Big Book Only. Taylor, Clive, illus. (Sails Literacy Ser.). 24p. (gr. k-18). 27.00 *(978-0-7578-6200-7(4))* Rigby Education.

Eisele, Barbara. Miss Thistle & Friends. 2009. 48p. pap. 12.99 *(978-1-4490-2007-1(0))* AuthorHouse.

Ekholm, Jan. The Little Red Rascal. 2011. 88p. pap. 30.28 *(978-1-4567-9501-6(5))* AuthorHouse.

Elliott, David. Wuv Bunnies from Outers Pace. Long, Ethan, illus. 2008. (ENG.). (J). 108p. (gr. 4-7). pap. 6.95 *(978-0-8234-2183-1(X));* 112p. (gr. 2-4). 16.95 *(978-0-8234-1902-9(9))* Holiday Hse., Inc.

Elrod, Julie. Splitting Hares. 2008. 36p. pap. 16.50 *(978-1-60693-484-5(8),* Eloquent Bks.) Strategic Book Publishing & Rights Agency (SBPRA).

Emerson, Carl. Opie the Opossum Wakes Up, 1 vol. Trover, Zachary, illus. 2007. (Animal Underdogs Ser.). (ENG.). 32p. (gr. -1-4). 28.50 *(978-1-60270-017-8(6),* Looking Glass Library) ABDO Publishing Co.

Empson, Jo. Rabbityness. Empson, Jo, illus. 2012. (Child's Play Library). (ENG., Illus.). 32p. (J). *(978-1-84643-492-1(0))* Child's Play International Ltd.

Engle, Margarita. Tiny Rabbit's Big Wish. Walker, David, illus. 2014. (ENG.). 32p. (J). (gr. -1-3). 16.99 *(978-0-547-85286-7(X),* HMH Books For Young Readers) Houghton Mifflin Harcourt Publishing Co.

Equipo Staff. Este No es Mi Conejito. 2004.Tr. of That's Not My Bunny. (SPA., Illus.). 12p. (J). (gr. -1). 7.95 *(978-0-7460-4512-1(3))* EDC Publishing.

Eriksen, Craig A. Nollie Gnome & Friends: 1. Return from Holiday. 2008. 52p. pap. 10.50 *(978-1-4092-0497-8(9))* Lulu Pr., Inc.

Escoffier, Michaël. Rabbit & the Not-So-Big-Bad Wolf. Di Giacomo, Kris, illus. 2013. (ENG.). 32p. (J). (gr. -1-3). 16.95 *(978-0-8234-2813-7(3))* Holiday Hse., Inc.

Fable, Aesop. The Tortoise & the Hare. 2012. (J). 29.99 *(978-1-61913-103-3(X))* Weigl Pubs., Inc.

Falkenstern, Lisa. A Dragon Moves In, 0 vols. 2011. (ENG.). 32p. (J). (gr. -1-3). 16.99 *(978-0-7614-5947-7(2),* 9780761459477, Amazon Children's Publishing) Amazon Publishing.

Fanger, Rolf. Benjamin Bunny Learns to Fly. 2004. (Just in Time for Easter Fun! Ser.). (Illus.). 32p. (J). 10.99 *(978-1-59384-042-6(X))* Parklane Publishing.

Faria, N. K. The Little Smart Rabbit & the Greedy Wolf: Finding Carrots. 2009. (Illus.). 24p. pap. 11.49 *(978-1-4490-1004-1(0))* AuthorHouse.

Farnsworth-Simpson, Patricia Ann. Flick the Karate Pig. 2008. 163p. pap. 16.50 *(978-1-4357-2843-1(2))* Lulu Pr., Inc.

Felton, Carol & Felton, Amanda. Where's Harley? O'Rourke, Page Eastburn, illus. 2003. (Math Matters Ser.). (ENG.). 32p. (J). pap. 5.95 *(978-1-57565-132-3(7))* Kane Press, Inc.

Ferri, Francesca. Hello Bunny. 2016. (Cuddly Book Set Ser.). (ENG.). 8p. (J). (gr. -1 — 1). 12.99 *(978-1-4380-7755-0(6))* Barron's Educational Series, Inc.

Filippis, Dina De. Mrs Nguyen's Garden. 2011. 28p. pap. 15.99 *(978-1-4568-3337-4(5))* Xlibris Corp.

Finn, Rebecca, illus. Little Bunny. (Cuddly Cuffstm Ser.). 6p. (J). 6.95 *(978-1-58925-767-2(7))* Tiger Tales.

First Bunny Stories. Date not set. (Illus.). (J). bds. 9.98 *(978-0-7525-9170-4(3))* Parragon, Inc.

Fleming, Candace. Muncha! Muncha! Muncha! Karas, G. Brian, illus. pap. 16.95 incl. audio *(978-1-59112-463-4(8));* pap. 18.95 incl. audio compact disk *(978-1-59112-923-3(0));* pap. incl. audio *(978-1-59112-465-8(4));* pap. incl. audio compact disk *(978-1-59112-925-7(7))* Live Oak Media.

—Muncha! Muncha! Muncha! 2004. (Illus.). (J). 28.95 incl. audio compact disk *(978-1-59112-924-0(9))* Live Oak Media.

—Ñam! Ñam! Ñam! Schmidt, Alejandra, tr. from ENG. Karas, G. Brian, illus. 2007. (SPA.). 32p. (J). (gr. -1-2). 15.95 *(978-1-933032-35-1(9))* Lectorum Pubns., Inc.

—Tippy-Tippy-Tippy, Hide! Karas, G. Brian, illus. 2007. (ENG.). 40p. (J). (gr. -1-3). 17.99 *(978-0-689-87479-6(0),* Atheneum Bks. for Young Readers) Simon & Schuster Children's Publishing.

—Tippy-Tippy-Tippy, Splash! Karas, G. Brian, illus. 2014. (ENG.). 40p. (J). (gr. -1-3). 16.99 *(978-1-4169-5403-3(1),* Atheneum Bks. for Young Readers) Simon & Schuster Children's Publishing.

Floppy's Friends. 2004. (J). (ENG & VIE.). *(978-1-84444-666-7(2));* (ENG & TUR.). *(978-1-84444-664-3(6));* (ENG & SPA.). *(978-1-84444-662-9(X));* (ENG & SOM.). *(978-1-84444-661-2(1));* (ENG & POR.). *(978-1-84444-660-5(3));* (ENG & PAN.). *(978-1-84444-658-2(1));* (ENG & LAO.). *(978-1-84444-657-5(3));* (ENG & HIN.). *(978-1-84444-656-8(5));* (ENG & GUJ.). *(978-1-84444-655-1(7));* (ENG & FRE.). *(978-1-84444-654-4(9));* (ENG & PER.). *(978-1-84444-653-7(0));* (CRO & ENG.). *(978-1-84444-652-0(2));* (CHI & ENG.). *(978-1-84444-651-3(4));* (ARA & ENG.). *(978-1-84444-648-3(4));* (ALB & ENG.). *(978-1-84444-647-6(6));* (ENG & TAM.). *(978-1-84444-663-6(8))* Mantra Lingua.

Flor Ada, Alma. A Surprise for Mother Rabbit. (Stories the Year 'Round Ser.). (Illus.). 28p. (J). (gr. k-3). pap. 8.95 *(978-1-58105-214-5(6))* Santillana USA Publishing Co., Inc.

The Flower Pot Bunnies Return. 2006. (J). *(978-0-9755390-2-6(7))* Fifth Ave Pr.

Floyd, Lucy. Conejo y Tortuga van a la Escuela. Flor Ada, Alma & Campoy, F. Isabel, trs. from ENG. Denise, Christopher, illus. 2010. (Green Light Readers Level 1 Ser.).Tr. of Rabbit & Turtle Go to School. (SPA & ENG.). 28p. (J). (gr. -1-3). pap. 3.99 *(978-0-547-33898-9(8))* Houghton Mifflin Harcourt Publishing Co.

Foley, James. Danny & the Blue Cloud: Coping with Childhood Depression. Ng-Benitez, Shirley, illus. 2016. 32p. (J). *(978-1-4338-2103-5(6),* Magination Pr.) American Psychological Assn.

Foley, James M. Baxter Turns down His Buzz: A Story for Little Kids about ADHD. Ng-Benitez, Shirley, illus. 2016. 32p. (J). 15.95 *(978-1-4338-2268-1(7),* Magination Pr.) American Psychological Assn.

Fontes, Justine. Clean up, Grumpy Bunny. 2006. (Illus.). *(978-0-439-68779-9(9))* Scholastic, Inc.

—Please Say Please, Grumpy Bunny! McQueen, Lucinda, illus. 2007. (J). *(978-0-439-02012-1(3))* Scholastic, Inc.

Ford, Bernette G. First Snow. Braun, Sebastien, illus. 2005. 32p. (J). *(978-0-9547373-3-7(4))* Boxer Bks., Ltd.

Ford, Bernette G. & Ford, Bernette. First Snow. Braun, Sebastien, illus. 2005. (ENG.). 32p. (J). (gr. -1-3). 16.95 *(978-0-8234-1937-1(1))* Holiday Hse., Inc.

Ford, Jessie, illus. My Bunny Puzzle Book. 2012. (ENG.). 8p. (J). (gr. -1-k). 6.95 *(978-1-4197-0205-1(X),* Abrams Appleseed) Abrams, Inc.

Forssén Ehrlin, Carl-Johan. El Conejito Que Quiere Dormirse: Una Nueva Forma de Hacer Que los Niños Se Duerman. 2015. (SPA.). 32p. (J). (gr. -1-2). 9.95 *(978-1-941999-59-2(X))* Beascoa, Ediciones S.A. ESP. Dist: Two Rivers Distribution.

—The Rabbit Who Wants to Fall Asleep: A New Way of Getting Children to Sleep. Maununen, Irina, illus. 2015. (ENG.). 32p. (J). (gr. -1-2). 15.99 *(978-0-399-55413-1(0),* Crown Books For Young Readers) Random Hse. Children's Bks.

Foster, Thelma Louise Elisher. A Brand New House. 2011. 24p. pap. 15.99 *(978-1-4568-4803-3(8))* Xlibris Corp.

Franciosa, John F. Little Johnny Lion. 2009. 24p. pap. 11.99 *(978-1-4389-8810-8(9))* AuthorHouse.

Freedman, Claire. The Monster of the Woods! Julian, Russell, illus. 2013. (ENG.). 32p. (J). pap. *(978-0-545-51571-9(8),* Cartwheel Bks.) Scholastic, Inc.

—Oops-a-Daisy! Hansen, Gaby, illus. 32p. (J). 2004. tchr. ed. 15.95 *(978-1-58925-037-6(0))* 2006. reprint ed. 6.95 *(978-1-58925-398-8(1))* Tiger Tales.

—You're My Little Bunny. Scott, Gavin, illus. 2010. (ENG.). 20p. (J). (gr. k — 1). bds. 8.99 *(978-0-545-20721-8(5),* Cartwheel Bks.) Scholastic, Inc.

Fronis, Aly. This Little Bunny. Rescek, Sanja, illus. 2016. (ENG.). 16p. (J). (gr. -1-1). bds. 5.99 *(978-1-4998-0105-7(X))* Little Bee Books Inc.

Fry, Sonali. Bang! Clang! 2005. (Ready-to-Read Ser.). (J). pap. 3.99 *(978-0-689-87419-2(7),* Simon Spotlight) Simon Spotlight.

Fuerst, Jeff. The Lion & the Rabbit: A Fable from India. 2006. (J). pap. *(978-1-4108-7156-5(8))* Benchmark Education Co.

Fuller, Suzy. Andrew Discovers A Cottontail. 2005. (Illus.). 30p. (J). per. 9.99 *(978-1-932338-77-5(2))* Lifevest Publishing, Inc.

Furnari, Eva. Fuzz Mcflops. Entrekin, Alison, tr. from POR. 2015. (ENG., Illus.). 56p. (J). (gr. k-3). pap. 12.95 *(978-1-78269-075-7(1),* Pushkin Press) Steerforth Pr.

Galbraith, Kathryn O. Boo, Bunny! Mack, Jeff, illus. 2008. (ENG.). 40p. (J). (gr. -1-2). 16.00 *(978-0-15-216246-7(1))* Houghton Mifflin Harcourt Publishing Co.

—Boo, Bunny! Board Book. Mack, Jeff, illus. 2012. (ENG.). 32p. (J). (gr. -1 — 1). bds. 5.99 *(978-0-547-81850-4(5))* Houghton Mifflin Harcourt Publishing Co.

—Two Bunny Buddies. Cepeda, Joe, illus. 2014. (ENG.). 32p. (J). (gr. -1-3). 16.99 *(978-0-544-17652-2(9),* HMH Books For Young Readers) Houghton Mifflin Harcourt Publishing Co.

Gallagher, Kristin Ellerbusch. Cottontail Rabbits. 2005. (Pull Ahead Bks.). (Illus.). 32p. (gr. k-3). lib. bdg. 22.60 *(978-0-8225-3617-8(X))* Lerner Publishing Group.

Ganz, Yaffa. Raise a Rabbit, Grow a Goose. Klineman, Harvey, illus. 2008. 30p. 14.99 *(978-1-59826-235-3(1))* Feldheim Pubs.

Gardner, Louise, illus. Five Little Easter Eggs. (ENG.). 10p. (J). 2009. (gr. -1). 5.95 *(978-1-58117-849-4(2))* 2008. 9.95 *(978-1-58117-682-7(1))* Bendon, Inc. (Intervisual/Piggy Toes).

Garis, Howard R. Bed Time Stories: Uncle Wiggily in the Woods. Wisa, Louis, illus. 2007. 160p. per. *(978-1-4065-2772-8(6))* Dodo Pr.

—Bed Time Stories: Uncle Wiggily's Adventures. Wisa, Louis, illus. 2007. 140p. per. *(978-1-4065-2773-5(4))* Dodo Pr.

—Bed Time Stories: Uncle Wiggily's Travels. Wisa, Louis, illus. 2007. 160p. per. *(978-1-4065-2774-2(2))* Dodo Pr.

—Sammie & Susie Littletail. Wisa, Louis, illus. 2007. 120p. per. *(978-1-4065-2770-4(X))* Dodo Pr.

—Uncle Wiggily & Old Mother Hubbard. 2008. 116p. 22.95 *(978-1-60664-970-1(1))* Aegypan.

—Uncle Wiggily in the Woods. 2008. 132p. 24.95 *(978-1-60664-971-8(X))* Aegypan.

—Uncle Wiggily in the Woods. 2007. 132p. pap. 18.99 *(978-1-4346-3898-4(7));* (ENG.). 138p. pap. 19.99 *(978-1-4346-3899-1(5))* Creative Media Partners, LLC.

—Uncle Wiggily's Adventures. 2008. 132p. 24.95 *(978-1-60664-905-3(1));* pap. 10.95 *(978-1-60664-024-1(0))* Aegypan.

—Uncle Wiggily's Travels. 2008. 132p. 24.95 *(978-1-60664-906-0(X));* pap. 10.95 *(978-1-60664-025-8(9))* Aegypan.

Garis, Howard Roger. Daddy Takes Us to the Garden. 2007. (Illus.). 132p. per. *(978-1-4065-2766-7(1))* Dodo Pr.

—Favorite Uncle Wiggily Animal Bedtime Stories. Kliros, Thea, illus. unabr. ed. 2011. (Dover Children's Thrift Classics Ser.). (ENG.). 64p. (J). (gr. 3-8). pap. 3.00 *(978-0-486-40101-0(4))* Dover Pubns., Inc.

—Uncle Wiggily Bedtime Stories: In Easy-to-Read Type. Kliros, Thea, illus. unabr. ed. 2011. (Dover Children's Thrift Classics Ser.). (ENG.). 80p. (J). (gr. 3-8). pap. 2.50 *(978-0-486-29372-1(6))* Dover Pubns., Inc.

—Uncle Wiggily's Travels. 2005. 26.95 *(978-1-4218-1469-8(2));* 164p. pap. 11.95 *(978-1-4218-1569-5(9))* 1st World Publishing, Inc. (1st World Library - Literary Society).

Garland, Sally Anne. Share. Garland, Sally Anne, illus. 2014. (ENG., Illus.). 32p. (J). (gr. -1-3). 17.95 *(978-1-77147-005-6(4),* Owlkids) Owlkids Bks. Inc. CAN. Dist: Publishers Group West (PGW).

Garoche, Camille. Snow Rabbit. 2015. (ENG., Illus.). 56p. (J). (gr. -1-3). 16.95 *(978-1-59270-181-0(7))* Enchanted Lion Bks., LLC.

Garrett, Christine. Dream Bunny's Tales - Saving the Land of Dreams. 2009. (Illus.). 48p. pap. 13.95

(978-1-60860-451-7(9), Eloquent Bks.) Strategic Book Publishing & Rights Agency (SBPRA).

Garrido, Felipe. El Coyote Tonto. Gonzalez, Francisco, illus. 2003. (Infantil Alfaguara Ser.).Tr. of Dumb Coyote. (SPA.). 60p. (J). (gr. 3-5). pap. 8.95 *(978-968-19-0277-3(7))* Santillana USA Publishing Co., Inc.

Gaster, Valerie Land. Jesus Loves the Easter Bunny. 2011. 20p. 14.50 *(978-1-4567-4418-2(6))* AuthorHouse.

Gay, Romney. Bonny's Wish. 2011. 36p. pap. 35.95 *(978-1-258-06495-2(2))* Literary Licensing, LLC.

Gehl, Laura & Aesop. Hare & Tortoise Race Across Israel. Goodreau, Sarah, illus. 2015. (J). 6.99 *(978-1-4677-6202-1(4)*, Kar-Ben Publishing) Lerner Publishing Group.

Gerrity, Arlene. The Tale of Chicken Noodle & Rabbit Stew Number Two. 2010. 24p. 10.99 *(978-1-4251-6258-0(4))* Trafford Publishing.

Gershator, Phillis. Time for a Bath. Walker, David, illus. 2016. (Snuggle Time Stories Ser.). (ENG.). 22p. (J). (— 1). bds. 6.95 *(978-1-4549-2069-4(6))* Sterling Publishing Co., Inc.

—Time for a Nap. Walker, David, illus. 2017. (Snuggle Time Stories Ser.). (ENG.). 32p. (J). (gr. -1-k). 9.95 *(978-1-4549-1981-0(7))* Sterling Publishing Co., Inc.

Gershator, Phillis & Green, Mim. Time for a Hug. Walker, David, illus. 2013. (Snuggle Time Stories Ser.). (ENG.). 22p. (J). (gr. -1-k). bds. 6.95 *(978-1-4549-0856-2(4))* Sterling Publishing Co., Inc.

Gershator, Phillis & Walker, David. Time for a Bath. 2014. (Snuggle Time Stories Ser.). (ENG., Illus.). 24p. (J). (gr. -1-k). 9.95 *(978-1-4549-1032-9(1))* Sterling Publishing Co., Inc.

Ghigna, Charles. Cuddle Bunny. East, Jacqueline, illus. 2015. (Tiny Tales Ser.). (ENG.). 64p. (gr. -1-2). lib. bdg. 23.99 *(978-1-4795-6528-3(8))* Tiny Tales.

Giachetti, Julia & Benchmark Education Co. Staff. A Tail for a Tail - Cherokee Trickster Tales. 2014. (Text Connections Ser.). (J). (gr. 5). *(978-1-4900-1375-6(X))* Benchmark Education Co.

Gillingham, Sara & Chronicle Books Staff. In My Meadow. Siminovich, Lorena, illus. 2009. (ENG.). 12p. (J). (gr. -1 — 1). bds. 8.99 *(978-0-8118-7338-3(2))* Chronicle Bks. LLC.

Ginoschio De Osceola, Ibrahim. Enter the Corn Bunny, Vol. 1. 2007. 56p. per. 8.95 *(978-0-595-45273-6(6))* iUniverse, Inc.

Giordano, Anne. Spencer, the Magic Rabbit. 2009. 40p. pap. 16.99 *(978-1-4490-3296-8(6))* AuthorHouse.

Glass, Calliope. Disney Bunnies All Ears. Disney Storybook Art Team, illus. 2016. (ENG.). 12p. (J). (gr. -1 — 1). bds. 7.99 *(978-1-4847-2210-7(8))* Disney Pr.

Gobo, creator. Up! Goes the Bunny! 2005. (Illus.). 10p. (J). (gr. -1-k). bds. 9.95 *(978-1-932915-11-2(7))* Sandvik Innovations, LLC.

Goertzen, Angelina. Tinsel the Christmas Tree. 2009. 32p. pap. 12.49 *(978-1-4389-8569-5(X))* AuthorHouse.

Golden Books. Here Comes Peter Cottontail Big Golden Book (Peter Cottontail) Golden Books, illus. 2017. (Big Golden Book Ser.). (ENG., Illus.). 32p. (J). (gr. -1-2). 9.99 *(978-0-399-55785-9(7)*, Golden Bks.) Random Hse. Children's Bks.

Golden Books Staff. Bunny Business. Aikins, Dave, illus. 2011. (Color Plus Flocked Stickers Ser.). (ENG.). 64p. (J). (gr. -1-2). pap. 4.99 *(978-0-375-86818-4(6)*, Golden Bks.) Random Hse. Children's Bks.

—Bunny's Garden. Golden Books Staff, illus. 2010. (Shaped Board Book Ser.). (ENG., Illus.). 12p. (J). (gr. -1 — 1). bds. 7.99 *(978-0-375-85788-1(5)*, Golden Bks.) Random Hse. Children's Bks.

—Pat the Bunny: At the Apple Orchard. Vilela, Luiz, illus. 2015. (ENG.). 24p. (J). (— 1). bds. 6.99 *(978-0-553-51205-2(6)*, Golden Bks.) Random Hse. Children's Bks.

—Sleepy Bunny. 2003. (Cloth Book Ser.). (ENG., Illus.). 8p. (J). (gr. -1 — 1). 14.99 *(978-0-375-82531-6(2)*, Golden Bks.) Random Hse. Children's Bks.

Goldhawk, Emma. Snuggle Bunny. Lambert, Jonathan, illus. 2015. (Snuggle Puppet Ser.). (ENG.). 10p. (J). bds. 14.95 *(978-1-62686-327-9(X)*, Silver Dolphin Bks.) Readerlink Distribution Services, LLC.

Gorbachev, Valeri. Christopher Counting. Gorbachev, Valeri, illus. 2008. (ENG., Illus.). 32p. (J). (gr. -1-3). 16.99 *(978-0-399-24629-6(0)*, Philomel Bks.) Penguin Young Readers Group.

Gordon, Janice Knuth. The Eager Bunny. 2009. 60p. (J). pap. 27.95 *(978-1-4327-3673-6(6))* Outskirts Pr., Inc.

Gore, Leonid. Danny's First Snow. Gore, Leonid, illus. 2007. (ENG., Illus.). 40p. (J). (gr. -1-2). 16.99 *(978-1-4169-1330-6(0)*, Atheneum Bks. for Young Readers) Simon & Schuster Children's Publishing.

Grandma's Attic. 2008. (Max & Ruby Ser.). 7p. (J). (gr. -1-k). 9.99 *(978-0-448-44895-4(5)*, Grosset & Dunlap) Penguin Publishing Group.

Grant, V. F. Stories from Grimley Forest. 2011. 48p. (gr. 1-2). pap. 19.50 *(978-1-4567-4709-1(6))* AuthorHouse.

Gravett, Emily. Bear & Hare Go Fishing. Gravett, Emily, illus. 2015. (Bear & Hare Ser.). (ENG., Illus.). 32p. (J). (gr. -1-3). 15.99 *(978-1-4814-2289-5(8)*, Simon & Schuster Bks. For Young Readers) Simon & Schuster Bks. For Young Readers.

—Bear & Hare Snow! Gravett, Emily, illus. 2015. (Bear & Hare Ser.). (ENG., Illus.). 32p. (J). (gr. -1-3). 16.99 *(978-1-4814-4514-6(6)*, Simon & Schuster Bks. For Young Readers) Simon & Schuster Bks. For Young Readers.

—The Rabbit Problem. Gravett, Emily, illus. 2010. (ENG., Illus.). 32p. (J). (gr. -1-3). 17.99 *(978-1-4424-1255-2(0)*, Simon & Schuster Bks. For Young Readers) Simon & Schuster Bks. For Young Readers.

—Where's Bear? Gravett, Emily, illus. 2016. (Bear & Hare Ser.). (ENG., Illus.). 32p. (J). (gr. -1-3). 16.99 *(978-1-4814-5615-9(6)*, Simon & Schuster Bks. For Young Readers) Simon & Schuster Bks. For Young Readers.

—Wolves. Gravett, Emily, illus. 2006. (ENG., Illus.). 40p. (J). (gr. k-3). 17.99 *(978-1-4169-1491-4(9)*, Simon & Schuster Bks. For Young Readers) Simon & Schuster Bks. For Young Readers.

Griffith, Helen V. Moonlight. Dronzek, Laura, illus. 2012. (ENG.). 32p. (J). (gr. -1-k). 16.99 *(978-0-06-203285-0(2)*, Greenwillow Bks.) HarperCollins Pubs.

Grindley, Sally, et al. Pam Mae'r Awyr Yn Las? Stori Gan Sally Grindley. 2005. (WEL., Illus.). 25p. *(978-1-85596-265-1(9))* Dref Wen.

Grist, Paul. Rabbit Hunt, Vol. 2. 2004. (ENG., Illus.). 144p. (YA). pap. 12.95 *(978-1-58240-355-7(4)*, 9781582403557) Image Comics.

Grosset and Dunlap Staff. I Would Like to Actually Keep It. 2011. (Charlie & Lola Ser.). (ENG.). 24p. (J). (gr. k-3). pap. 3.99 *(978-0-448-45678-2(8)*, Grosset & Dunlap) Penguin Young Readers Group.

Guarnieri, Rossana. Fiabe della Buonanotte. pap. 26.95 *(978-88-09-02216-4(5))* Giunti Gruppo Editoriale ITA. Dist: Distribooks, Inc.

Gulino, ViTina Corso. Peter Rabbit & My Tulips. Murariu, Lorraine, illus. 2012. 26p. (J). pap. 9.95 *(978-1-61863-275-3(2))* Bookstand Publishing.

Hagen, Oddmund. Campo Abierto (Open Field) Santos, Nuria G., tr. from NOR. Dezakin, Akin, illus. 2003. (Rosa y Manzana Ser.). (SPA.). 32p. 16.95 *(978-84-89804-42-5(7))* Lóguez Ediciones ESP. Dist: Baker & Taylor Bks.

Hailes, Ronald. The Pink Rabbit. 2009. 24p. pap. 10.96 *(978-1-4269-1456-0(3))* Trafford Publishing.

Halcomb, Suzanne. The Mcfee Family Harvest. 2012. 40p. pap. 19.75 *(978-1-4269-9647-4(0))* Trafford Publishing.

Hale, Shannon & Hale, Dean. The Princess in Black & the Hungry Bunny Horde. Pham, LeUyen, illus. 2016. (Princess in Black Ser.: 3). (ENG.). (J). (gr. k-3). 96p. pap. 6.99 *(978-0-7636-9089-2(9))*; 85p. 14.99 *(978-0-7636-6513-5(4))* Candlewick Pr.

—The Princess in Black & the Hungry Bunny Horde. Pham, LeUyen, illus. 2016. (Princess in Black Ser.: 3). (ENG.). 85p. (J). (gr. k-3). 17.20 *(978-0-606-39109-2(6))* Turtleback Bks.

Hamilton, Elizabeth L. Jeremy Rabbit's Honesty Pie. 2003. (Character Critters Ser.: No. 2). (Illus.). 32p. (J). (gr. -1-3). per. 5.95 *(978-0-9713749-5-9(3)*, Character-in-Action) Quiet Impact, Inc.

Hammock, Mary B. Msn Cpnp. Princess Reagan & the Paci Fairy. 2012. 24p. pap. 15.99 *(978-1-4797-1074-4(1))* Xlibris Corp.

Hands, Nikki. Lilly Bunny Goes to the Doctor. 2011. 28p. pap. 24.95 *(978-1-4626-3638-9(1))* America Star Bks.

Haneberg, Janet. Eggie Rabbit. 2006. 37p. (J). pap. 15.23 *(978-1-4116-4157-0(4))* Lulu Pr., Inc.

Hannigan, Katherine. Emmaline & the Bunny. Hannigan, Katherine, illus. 2009. (ENG., Illus.). 112p. (J). (gr. 2-7). 16.99 *(978-0-06-162654-8(6)*, Greenwillow Bks.) HarperCollins Pubs.

Harris, Dee. The Croaker Sack Bunny. Bohart, Lisa, illus. 2012. 24p. pap. 12.95 *(978-1-61493-043-3(0))* Peppertree Pr., The.

Harris, Donna. Dust Bunnies Do Love Donuts. 2009. 40p. pap. 16.99 *(978-1-4490-0628-0(0))* AuthorHouse.

Harris, Joel Chandler, et al. The Classic Tales of Brer Rabbit. Daily, Don, illus. 2008. (ENG.). 56p. (J). (gr. 1-17). 9.95 *(978-0-7624-3219-6(5))* Running Pr. Bk. Pubs.

Harrison, Paula. The Golden Shell. 2014. (Rescue Princesses Ser.: 12). (ENG.). 128p. (J). (gr. 2-5). pap. 4.99 *(978-0-545-66168-3(4)*, Scholastic Paperbacks) Scholastic, Inc.

—The Golden Shell. 2014. (Rescue Princesses Ser.: 12). lib. bdg. 14.75 *(978-0-606-35838-5(2))* Turtleback Bks.

Harry, Rebecca. Snow Bunny's Christmas Gift. 2015. (ENG., Illus.). 32p. (J). (gr. -1-3). 17.99 *(978-1-4998-0164-4(5))* Little Bee Books Inc.

—Snow Bunny's Christmas Wish. Harry, Rebecca, illus. 2013. (ENG., Illus.). 32p. (J). (gr. -1-3). 16.99 *(978-0-545-54103-9(4)*, Orchard Bks.) Scholastic, Inc.

Hartzell, Andy. Fox Bunny Funny. 2007. (ENG., Illus.). 104p. pap. 10.00 *(978-1-891830-97-6(X)*, 9781891830976) Top Shelf Productions.

Hattan, Ann. Jake & Bobby's Magical Christmas. 2012. (Illus.). 16p. pap. 18.30 *(978-1-4772-2748-0(2))* AuthorHouse.

Hawes, Carlin. Abigail's Bunny. 2012. 16p. pap. 12.68 *(978-1-4669-5601-8(1))* Trafford Publishing.

Hawkins, Emily. Good Night, Little Bunny: A Changing-Picture Book. Butler, John, illus. 2011. (ENG.). 14p. (J). (gr. -1-2). 12.99 *(978-0-7636-5263-0(6)*, Templar) Candlewick Pr.

Hay, Sam. Rise of the Zombie Rabbit. 2015. (Undead Pets Ser.: 5). lib. bdg. 16.00 *(978-0-606-36769-1(1))* Turtleback Bks.

—Rise of the Zombie Rabbit #5. Cooper, Simon, illus. 2015. (Undead Pets Ser.: 5). (ENG.). 112p. (J). (gr. 1-3). 5.99 *(978-0-448-47799-2(8)*, Grosset & Dunlap) Penguin Young Readers Group.

Hayes, Geoffrey. A Night-Light for Bunny. Date not set. 32p. (J). (gr. -1-3). pap. 5.99 *(978-0-06-443728-8(0))* HarperCollins Pubs.

—A Night-Light for Bunny. Hayes, Geoffrey, illus. 2004. (Illus.). 32p. (J). (gr. -1-3). 14.99 *(978-0-06-029163-1(X))* HarperCollins Pubs.

Hayes, J. B. Freddy the Frog's First Christmas. 2012. 44p. pap. 21.99 *(978-1-4772-2870-8(5))* AuthorHouse.

Henkel, Pat. Jeffrey's Great Day. Elliott, Luke, illus. 2012. 16p. pap. 24.95 *(978-1-4626-7993-5(5))* America Star Bks.

Henkes, Kevin. Little White Rabbit. Henkes, Kevin, illus. 2011. (Illus.). 40p. (J). (gr. -1-3). 17.89 *(978-0-06-200643-1(6))*; (ENG., 16.99 *(978-0-06-200642-4(8))* HarperCollins Pubs. (Greenwillow Bks.).

—Little White Rabbit Board Book. Henkes, Kevin, illus. 2014. (ENG., Illus.). 34p. (J). (gr. -1-3). bds. 7.99 *(978-0-06-231409-3(2)*, Greenwillow Bks.) HarperCollins Pubs.

—So Happy! Lobel, Anita, illus. 2005. (ENG.). 32p. (J). (gr. -1-3). 16.99 *(978-0-06-056483-4(0)*, Greenwillow Bks.) HarperCollins Pubs.

Henne, R. J. The Talking Rabbit & the Farmer. 2011. 124p. pap. 19.95 *(978-1-4560-7337-4(0))* America Star Bks.

Henry, Steve. Here Is Big Bunny. 2017. (I Like to Read(r) Ser.). (ENG.). 32p. (J). (gr. -1-3). 6.99 *(978-0-8234-3774-0(4))* Holiday Hse., Inc.

—Here Is Big Bunny. Henry, Steve, illus. 2016. (ENG., Illus.). 32p. (J). (gr. -1-3). 15.95 *(978-0-8234-3458-9(3))* Holiday Hse., Inc.

Hensley, Tana. Rosa's Rabbit: Step by Step. 2017. (Computer Science for the Real World Ser.). 8p. (gr. 5-6). pap. 6.20 ***(978-1-5383-5040-9(8)***, Rosen Classroom) Rosen Publishing Group, Inc., The.

Henson, Heather, et al. The Vampire Bunny. Mack, Jeff, tr. Mack, Jeff, illus. 2004. (Bunnicula & Friends Ser.: 1). (ENG.). 48p. (J). (gr. 1-3). 16.99 *(978-0-689-85724-9(1)*, Simon Spotlight) Simon Spotlight.

Hersh, Kristin. Toby Snax. 2016. (ENG., Illus.). 40p. (J). 14.95 *(978-1-4773-1127-1(0))* Univ. of Texas Pr.

Heyward, DuBose. The Country Bunny & the Little Gold Shoes 75th Anniversary Edition. Flack, Marjorie, illus. 2014. (ENG.). 56p. (J). (gr. -1-3). 14.99 *(978-0-544-25197-7(0)*, HMH Books For Young Readers) Houghton Mifflin Harcourt Publishing Co.

—The Country Bunny & the Little Gold Shoes Gift Edition with Charm. Flack, Marjorie, illus. 2010. (ENG.). 56p. (J). (gr. -1-3). 9.99 *(978-0-547-14418-4(0))* Houghton Mifflin Harcourt Publishing Co.

Hiebert, Elfrieda H. & Juel, Connie. Where Does the Rabbit Hop? (Little Book Practice Reader Ser.). (J). *(978-0-8136-0794-8(9))* Modern Curriculum Pr.

Hillert, Margaret. The Baby Bunny. Bond, Denny, illus. 2016. (BeginningtoRead Ser.). (ENG.). 32p. (J). (gr. -1-2). pap. 11.94 *(978-1-60357-934-6(6))*; (gr. k-2). 22.60 *(978-1-59953-793-1(1))* Norwood Hse. Pr.

—Baby Bunny. (Illus.). (J). 4.95 *(978-0-87895-653-1(0))* Modern Curriculum Pr.

Himmelman, John. Bunjitsu Bunny Jumps to the Moon. Himmelman, John, illus. 2016. (Bunjitsu Bunny Ser.). (ENG., Illus.). 128p. (J). 13.99 *(978-1-62779-732-0(7)*, 9781627797320, Holt, Henry & Co. Bks. For Young Readers) Holt, Henry & Co.

—Bunjitsu Bunny's Best Move. Himmelman, John, illus. 2015. (Bunjitsu Bunny Ser.: 2). (ENG., Illus.). 128p. (J). (gr. 1-3). 13.99 *(978-0-8050-9971-3(9)*, 9780805099713, Holt, Henry & Co. Bks. For Young Readers) Holt, Henry & Co.

—Tales of Bunjitsu Bunny. Himmelman, John. 2014. (Bunjitsu Bunny Ser.: 1). (ENG., Illus.). 128p. (J). (gr. 1-3). 13.99 *(978-0-8050-9970-6(0)*, 9780805099706, Holt, Henry & Co. Bks. For Young Readers) Holt, Henry & Co.

Hirschmann, Kris. Hello, Bunny! Hutto, Victoria, illus. 2010. (Paint Me Pals Ser.). (ENG.). 24p. (J). 9.99 *(978-1-4169-7903-6(4)*, Simon Scribbles) Simon Scribbles.

Hobbs, Constance. Bugsy's Special Event. 2008. 64p. pap. 10.50 *(978-0-9556783-7-0(4))* Hobbs, Constance GBR. Dist: Lulu Pr., Inc.

Hollar, Cheryl Faye. Billy the Bunny Goes to the State Fair. 2005. (J). pap. 7.97 *(978-0-9763826-0-7(1))* Hollar, Cheryl Public Relations.

Holloway, Jamie. Hop's Big Race. 2015. (Rosen REAL Readers: STEM & STEAM Collection). (ENG.). 8p. pap. 5.46 *(978-1-4994-9602-4(8)*, Rosen Classroom) Rosen Publishing Group, Inc., The.

Holmes, Janet A. Me & You. Rossell, Judith, illus. 2009. (ENG.). 32p. (J). (gr. -1-3). 14.95 *(978-0-7358-2250-4(6))* North-South Bks., Inc.

Honigsberg, Peter Jan. Pillow of Dreams. Morse, Tony, illus. 2004. 32p. (gr. k-4). 17.95 *(978-1-57143-076-2(8))* RDR Bks.

Hop-along Bunny. 2004. (J). per. *(978-1-57657-515-4(2))* Paradise Pr., Inc.

Hopgood, Tim. Hooray for Hoppy! 2015. (ENG., Illus.). 32p. (J). (gr. -1-k). 16.99 *(978-0-374-30129-3(8)*, 9780374301293, Farrar, Straus & Giroux (BYR)) Farrar, Straus & Giroux.

Horse, Harry. Little Rabbit Goes to School. Horse, Harry, illus. (Little Rabbit Ser.). (Illus.). 32p. (J). 2011. (gr. -1-1). pap. 7.95 *(978-1-56145-574-4(1))* 2004. (ENG., (gr. k-1). 15.95 *(978-1-56145-320-7(X))* Peachtree Pubs.

—Little Rabbit Lost. Horse, Harry, illus. 2005. (ENG., Illus.). 32p. (J). (gr. k-1). bds. 9.95 *(978-1-56145-345-0(5))* Peachtree Pubs.

—Little Rabbit Runaway. Horse, Harry, illus. 2005. (ENG., Illus.). 32p. (J). (gr. k-1). 15.95 *(978-1-56145-343-6(9))* Peachtree Pubs.

—Little Rabbit's Christmas. Horse, Harry, illus. 2007. (Illus.). 32p. (J). (gr. k-3). 15.95 *(978-1-56145-419-8(2))* Peachtree Pubs.

—Little Rabbit's New Baby, 1 vol. Horse, Harry, illus. (Little Rabbit Ser.). (Illus.). 32p. (J). 2016. (ENG.). (gr. -1-k). pap. 7.95 *(978-1-56145-915-5(1))* 2008. (gr. k-1). 16.95 *(978-1-56145-431-0(1))* Peachtree Pubs.

—Little Rabbit's New Baby / Book & Doll Package. 2008. (Illus.). 32p. (J). (gr. k-1). pap., pap. 22.90 *(978-1-56145-453-2(2))* Peachtree Pubs.

Horvath, Polly. Lord & Lady Bunny — Almost Royalty! Blackall, Sophie, illus. 2016. (ENG.). 304p. (J). (gr. 3-7). pap. 8.99 *(978-0-307-98068-7(5)*, Yearling) Random Hse. Children's Bks.

—Mr. & Mrs. Bunny: Detectives Extraordinaire! Blackall, Sophie, illus. 2012. (ENG.). 256p. (J). (gr. 3-7). 16.99 *(978-0-375-86755-2(4)*, Schwartz & Wade Bks.) Random Hse. Children's Bks.

How Rabbit Caught the Sun: Individual Title Six-Packs. (Story Steps Ser.). (gr. k-2). 32.00 *(978-0-7635-9811-2(9))* Rigby Education.

Howard, Cheryl L. Duster Dustbunny's Seven Days of the Week & Twelve Months in a Year. 2009. (Illus.). 48p. pap. 17.50 *(978-1-60860-787-7(9)*, Eloquent Bks.) Strategic Book Publishing & Rights Agency (SBPRA).

Howe, Deborah & Howe, James. Bunnicula. Daniel, Alan, illus. 2006. (Bunnicula & Friends Ser.). (ENG.). 128p. (J). (gr. 3-7). pap. 7.99 *(978-1-4169-2817-1(0)*, Atheneum Bks. for Young Readers) Simon & Schuster Children's Publishing.

—A Rabbit-Tale of Mystery. unabr. ed. 2004. (Bunnicula Ser.). 98p. (J). (gr. 3-7). pap. 29.00 incl. audio *(978-0-8072-8204-5(9)*, YYA139SP, Listening Library) Random Hse. Audio Publishing Group.

Howe, James. Bunnicula Strikes Again! 2004. (Bunnicula Ser.). 116p. (J). (gr. 3-7). pap. 29.00 incl. audio *(978-0-8072-8213-7(8)*, Listening Library) Random Hse. Audio Publishing Group.

—Bunnicula Strikes Again! Daniel, Alan, illus. 2007. (Bunnicula & Friends Ser.). (ENG.). 144p. (J). (gr. 3-7). pap. 6.99 *(978-1-4169-3968-9(7)*, Atheneum Bks. for Young Readers) Simon & Schuster Children's Publishing.

—The Celery Stalks at Midnight. unabr. ed. 2004. (Bunnicula Ser.). 111p. (J). (gr. 3-7). pap. 29.00 incl. audio *(978-0-8072-8357-8(6)*, YA173SP, Listening Library) Random Hse. Audio Publishing Group.

—The Celery Stalks at Midnight. Morrill, Leslie H., illus. 2006. (Bunnicula & Friends Ser.). (ENG.). 144p. (J). (gr. 3-7). pap. 6.99 *(978-1-4169-2814-0(6)*, Atheneum Bks. for Young Readers) Simon & Schuster Children's Publishing.

—Harold & Chester Stories. Date not set. (Bunnicula & Friends Ser.). (J). (gr. k-3). *(978-0-688-10298-2(0))*; lib. bdg. *(978-0-688-10299-9(9))* HarperCollins Pubs.

—Hot Fudge. Mack, Jeff, illus. 2006. (Bunnicula & Friends Ser.). 42p. (gr. k-4). 14.00 *(978-0-7569-7224-0(8))* Perfection Learning Corp.

—Hot Fudge. Mack, Jeff, tr. Mack, Jeff, illus. 2004. (Bunnicula & Friends Ser.: 2). (ENG.). 48p. (J). (gr. 1-3). 16.99 *(978-0-689-85725-6(X)*, Atheneum Bks. for Young Readers) Simon & Schuster Children's Publishing.

—Howliday Inn. unabr. ed. 2004. (Bunnicula Ser.). 195p. (J). (gr. 3-7). pap. 29.00 incl. audio *(978-0-8072-8382-0(7)*, YA179SP, Listening Library) Random Hse. Audio Publishing Group.

—Rabbit-Cadabra! Mack, Jeff, illus. (Bunnicula & Friends Ser.: 4). (ENG.). 48p. (J). (gr. 1-3). 2007. pap. 3.99 *(978-0-689-85752-2(7))* 2006. 16.99 *(978-0-689-85727-0(6))* Simon Spotlight. (Simon Spotlight).

—Scared Silly. Mack, Jeff, illus. 2006. (Bunnicula & Friends Ser.). 42p. (gr. 1-3). 14.00 *(978-0-7569-7225-7(6))* Perfection Learning Corp.

—Scared Silly. Mack, Jeff, illus. 2005. (Bunnicula & Friends Ser.: 3). (ENG.). 48p. (J). (gr. 1-3). 16.99 *(978-0-689-85726-3(8)*, Atheneum Bks. for Young Readers) Simon & Schuster Children's Publishing.

—Scared Silly. Mack, Jeff, illus. 2006. (Bunnicula & Friends Ser.: 3). (ENG.). 48p. (J). (gr. 1-3). pap. 3.99 *(978-0-689-85751-5(9)*, Simon Spotlight) Simon Spotlight.

—The Vampire Bunny. Mack, Jeff, illus. 2005. (Bunnicula & Friends Ser.). 41p. (J). (gr. 1-3). 11.65 *(978-0-7569-6832-8(1))* Perfection Learning Corp.

—The Vampire Bunny. Mack, Jeff, illus. 2005. (Bunnicula & Friends Ser.: 1). (ENG.). 48p. (J). (gr. 1-3). pap. 3.99 *(978-0-689-85749-2(7)*, Simon Spotlight) Simon Spotlight.

Huang, Yu-Hsuan, illus. Baby Bunny: Finger Puppet Book. 2017. (ENG.). 12p. (J). bds. 6.99 *(978-1-4521-5609-5(3))* Chronicle Bks. LLC.

Hucks, Doris. Quackie the Bunny. 2012. 42p. pap. 20.99 *(978-1-4772-9527-4(5))* AuthorHouse.

Hudson, Katy. Too Many Carrots. 2016. (ENG., Illus.). 32p. (gr. -1-1). 14.95 *(978-1-62370-638-8(6))* Capstone Young Readers of Coughlan Cos.

Hughes, Laura. We're Going on an Egg Hunt. Hughes, Laura, illus. 2017. (ENG., Illus.). 24p. (J). 17.99 *(978-1-68119-314-4(0)*, 9781681193144, Bloomsbury USA Childrens) Bloomsbury Publishing USA.

Hurrell, Dianne. Tom Burrows & Friends: Short Stories, Rhymes & Poems. 2010. (ENG., Illus.). 50p. pap. *(978-1-84748-782-7(3))* Athena Pr.

Hurt, John Washington, reader. Rabbit Ears World Tales. 2007. (J). 34.99 *(978-0-7393-7549-5(0))* Findaway World, LLC.

Hutchings, Tony, illus. A Week at the Seaside. 2014. (J). *(978-1-4351-5464-3(9))* Barnes & Noble, Inc.

Hyde, Willie. Paddles the Amazing Rabbit. 2012. pap. 8.95 *(978-0-7414-8130-6(8))* Infinity Publishing.

—Paddles the Amazing Rabbit - Color. 2012. pap. 13.95 *(978-0-7414-8131-3(6))* Infinity Publishing.

Ikeda, Daisaku. The Princess & the Moon. McCaughrean, Geraldine, tr. from JPN. Wildsmith, Brian, illus. 2013. 6.95 *(978-1-935523-58-1(9))* World Tribune Pr.

Image Books Staff & Chronicle Books Staff. Little Bunny. van der Put, Klaartje, illus. 2006. (Little Finger Puppet Board Bks.: FING). (ENG.). 12p. (J). (gr. -1 — 1). bds. 6.99 *(978-0-8118-5644-7(5))* Chronicle Bks. LLC.

Jacobs, Lily. The Littlest Bunny in Arkansas: An Easter Adventure. 2015. (ENG.). 32p. (J). (-3). 9.99 *(978-1-4926-1027-4(5)*, Sourcebooks Jabberwocky) Sourcebooks, Inc.

—The Littlest Bunny in Austin. Dunn, Robert, illus. 2016. (ENG.). 32p. (J). (-7). 9.99 *(978-1-4926-3347-1(X)*, 9781492633471, Sourcebooks Jabberwocky) Sourcebooks, Inc.

—The Littlest Bunny in Bentonville: An Easter Adventure. 2015. (ENG.). 32p. (J). (-3). 9.99 *(978-1-4926-1030-4(5)*, Sourcebooks Jabberwocky) Sourcebooks, Inc.

—The Littlest Bunny in Boise: An Easter Adventure. 2015. (ENG.). 32p. (J). (-3). 9.99 *(978-1-4926-1033-5(X)*, Sourcebooks Jabberwocky) Sourcebooks, Inc.

—The Littlest Bunny in Buffalo. Dunn, Robert, illus. 2016. (ENG.). 32p. (J). (-7). 9.99 *(978-1-4926-3346-4(1)*, 9781492633464, Sourcebooks Jabberwocky) Sourcebooks, Inc.

—The Littlest Bunny in Calgary: An Easter Adventure. Dunn, Robert, illus. 2015. (ENG.). 32p. (J). (-3). 11.99 *(978-1-4926-1039-7(9)*, Sourcebooks Jabberwocky) Sourcebooks, Inc.

—The Littlest Bunny in California: An Easter Adventure. Dunn, Robert, illus. 2015. (ENG.). 32p. (J). (-3). 9.99 *(978-1-4926-1042-7(9)*, Sourcebooks Jabberwocky) Sourcebooks, Inc.

—The Littlest Bunny in Canada: An Easter Adventure. Dunn, Robert, illus. 2015. (ENG.). 32p. (J). (-3). 11.99 *(978-1-4926-1045-8(3)*, Sourcebooks Jabberwocky) Sourcebooks, Inc.

—The Littlest Bunny in Chicago: An Easter Adventure. 2015. (ENG.). 32p. (J). (-3). 9.99 *(978-1-4926-1051-9(8)*, Sourcebooks Jabberwocky) Sourcebooks, Inc.

—The Littlest Bunny in Cleveland. Dunn, Robert, illus. 2016. (ENG.). 32p. (J). (-7). 9.99 *(978-1-4926-3353-2(4)*, 9781492633532, Sourcebooks Jabberwocky) Sourcebooks, Inc.

—The Littlest Bunny in Dallas. Dunn, Robert, illus. 2016. (ENG.). 32p. (J). (-7). 9.99 *(978-1-4926-3349-5(6)*, 9781492633495, Sourcebooks Jabberwocky) Sourcebooks, Inc.

—The Littlest Bunny in Illinois: An Easter Adventure. Dunn, Robert, illus. 2015. (ENG.). 32p. (J). (-3). 9.99 *(978-1-4926-1081-6(X)*, Sourcebooks Jabberwocky) Sourcebooks, Inc.

—The Littlest Bunny in Indiana: An Easter Adventure. Dunn, Robert, illus. 2015. (ENG.). 32p. (J). (-3). 9.99 *(978-1-4926-1084-7(4)*, Sourcebooks Jabberwocky) Sourcebooks, Inc.

—The Littlest Bunny in Nashville. Dunn, Robert, illus. 2016. (ENG.). 32p. (J). (-7). 9.99 *(978-1-4926-3351-8(8)*, 9781492633518, Sourcebooks Jabberwocky) Sourcebooks, Inc.

—The Littlest Bunny in New Orleans. Dunn, Robert, illus. 2016. (ENG.). 32p. (J). (-7). 9.99 *(978-1-4926-3350-1(X)*, 9781492633501, Sourcebooks Jabberwocky) Sourcebooks, Inc.

—The Littlest Bunny in Newfoundland. Dunn, Robert, illus. 2016. (ENG.). 32p. (J). (-7). 11.99 *(978-1-4926-3352-5(6)*, 9781492633525, Sourcebooks Jabberwocky) Sourcebooks, Inc.

—The Littlest Bunny in Ottawa: An Easter Adventure. Dunn, Robert, illus. 2015. (ENG.). 32p. (J). (-3). 11.99 *(978-1-4926-1174-5(3)*, Sourcebooks Jabberwocky) Sourcebooks, Inc.

—The Littlest Bunny in San Diego. Dunn, Robert, illus. 2016. (ENG.). 32p. (J). (-7). 9.99 *(978-1-4926-3348-8(8)*, 9781492633488, Sourcebooks Jabberwocky) Sourcebooks, Inc.

—The Littlest Bunny in Utah: An Easter Adventure. Dunn, Robert, illus. 2015. (ENG.). 32p. (J). (-3). 9.99 *(978-1-4926-1219-3(7)*, Sourcebooks Jabberwocky) Sourcebooks, Inc.

Jacques, Brian. The Long Patrol: A Tale from Redwall. Curless, Allan, illus. 2004. (Redwall Ser.). (ENG.). 368p. (J). (gr. 5-3). 8.99 *(978-0-14-240245-0(1)*, Firebird) Penguin Young Readers Group.

Jake's Big Adventure. 2008. (Jake Flocked Board Ser.). 8p. bds. *(978-1-4075-1818-3(6))* Parragon, Inc.

Jake's Perfect Day. 2008. (Jake Flocked Board Ser.). 8p. bds. *(978-1-4075-1817-6(8))* Parragon, Inc.

James, Brian. Easter Bunny's on His Way! 2005. pap. *(978-0-439-74530-7(6))* Scholastic, Inc.

James, Catherine. Bobby Cottontail's Gift. Collier, Kevin Scott, illus. 2008. 28p. pap. 10.95 *(978-1-935137-07-8(7))* 2006. 32p. (J). E-Book 9.95 incl. cd-rom *(978-1-933090-24-5(3))* Guardian Angel Publishing, Inc.

James, Helen Foster. Grandma Loves You! Brown, Petra, illus. 2013. (ENG.). 32p. (J). (gr. -1 — 1). 14.99 *(978-1-58536-836-5(9)*, 202884) Sleeping Bear Pr.

—Grandpa Loves You! Brown, Petra, illus. 2016. (ENG.). 32p. (J). (gr. -1-1). 15.99 *(978-1-58536-940-9(3)*, 204032) Sleeping Bear Pr.

James, Jake. Jake s Short Stories. 2010. 64p. pap. 10.99 *(978-1-60957-640-0(3))* Salem Author Services.

James, Rosalind. Bertie Rides Again. 2012. (Illus.). 126p. 29.99 *(978-1-4771-2272-3(9))* Xlibris Corp.

Jane, Johnson. Are You Ready for Bed? Gaby, Hansen, illus. 2010. (ENG.). 24p. (J). bds. 8.95 *(978-1-58925-806-8(1))* Tiger Tales.

Jasnoch, Dorothy. Frankie the Bunny: Mystery in the Forest. Korzeniowski, Samson O., ed. Jasnoch, Dorothy, illus. 2013. (Illus.). 32p. 17.99 *(978-1-937752-16-3(X))* Owl About Bks. Pub., Inc.

—Frankie the Bunny: The Fall Scramble Begins. Korzeniowski, Samson O., ed. Jasnoch, Dorothy, illus. 2013. (Illus.). 28p. 17.99 *(978-1-937752-19-4(4))* Owl About Bks. Pub., Inc.

—Frankie the Bunny: Wheels of Fortune. Korzeniowski, Samson O., ed. Jasnoch, Dorothy, illus. 2013. (Illus.). 28p. 17.99 *(978-1-937752-17-0(8))* Owl About Bks. Pub., Inc.

—Frankie the Bunny: Woodland Warning. Korzeniowski, Samson O., ed. Jasnoch, Dorothy, illus. 2013. (Illus.). 28p. 17.99 *(978-1-937752-18-7(6))* Owl About Bks. Pub., Inc.

—Frankie the Bunny Helping the Birds. Korzeniowski, Samson, ed. Jasnoch, Dorothy, illus. 2012. (ENG., Illus.). 28p. pap. 12.99 *(978-1-937752-05-7(4))* Owl About Bks. Pub., Inc.

—Frankie the Bunny the Fall Scramble Begins. Korzeniowski, Samson, ed. Jasnoch, Dorothy, illus. 2012. (Illus.). 28p. pap. 12.99 *(978-1-937752-04-0(6))* Owl About Bks. Pub., Inc.

Jenks, Patricia. I'm Only a Little Bunny. Lehto, Christine, illus. 2013. 34p. 15.99 *(978-1-937165-48-2(5))* Orange Hat Publishing.

Jennings, Richard W. Orwell's Luck. 2006. (ENG.). 160p. (J). (gr. 5-7). pap. 11.95 *(978-0-618-69335-1(1))* Houghton Mifflin Harcourt Publishing Co.

Jeram, Anita. Bunny My Honey. Jeram, Anita, illus. 2009. (ENG., Illus.). 22p. (J). (gr. k-k). bds. 7.99 *(978-0-7636-4645-5(8))* Candlewick Pr.

—I Love My Little Storybook. Jeram, Anita, illus. 2010. (ENG., Illus.). 32p. (J). (-k). 7.99 *(978-0-7636-4806-0(X))* Candlewick Pr.

—Me Gusta Mi Libro de Cuentos. Mlawer, Teresa, tr. (SPA.). (J). (gr. -1-k). 14.95 *(978-1-930332-29-4(7)*, LC5087) Lectorum Pubns., Inc.

Jin, Susie Lee. Mine! Jin, Susie Lee, illus. 2016. (ENG., Illus.). 40p. (J). (gr. -1-3). 16.99 *(978-1-4814-2772-2(5)*, Simon & Schuster Bks. For Young Readers) Simon & Schuster Bks. For Young Readers.

JJ Rabbit & the Monster: Level K, 6 vols. 128p. (gr. 2-3). 49.95 *(978-0-7699-0981-3(7))* Shortland Pubns. (U. S. A.) Inc.

Johannes, Avril & Branham, Jan. Bunny an Alaskan Hare. 2006. 32p. 7.95 *(978-0-9749360-3-1(0))* Icicle Falls Publishing Co.

Johanson, Rhonda. The Great Tempo Race. 2011. 32p. pap. 21.99 *(978-1-4568-5363-1(5))* Xlibris Corp.

Johnson, Gerald J. J. Buffy Bunny. Miltenberger, Jeri & Miltenberger, Dave, illus. 2011. 32p. pap. 24.95 *(978-1-4512-5292-7(7))* America Star Bks.

Johnson, Jane. Are You Ready for Bed? Hansen, Gaby, illus. (J). 2017. (ENG.). 28p. (gr. -1-k). bds. 7.99 ***(978-1-68010-513-1(2))*** 2004. 32p. tchr. ed. 14.95 *(978-1-58925-017-8(6))* Tiger Tales.

—Little Bunny's Bathtime! 2004. (Illus.). 32p. (J). tchr. ed. 15.95 *(978-1-58925-043-7(5))* Tiger Tales.

—Little Bunny's Bedtime. Hansen, Gaby, illus. 2006. Orig. Title: Are You Ready for Bed? 16p. (J). bds. 6.95 *(978-1-58925-773-3(1))* Tiger Tales.

Johnson, Kimberly P. The Adventures of the Itty Bitty Bunny. 2004. (Illus.). 24p. (gr. k-2). 14.95 *(978-1-57197-155-5(6)*, Ivy House Publishing Group) Pentland Pr., Inc.

Johnson, Regan. Little Bunny Kung Fu. Johnson, Regan, illus. 2005. (ENG., Illus.). 32p. (J). (gr. -1 — 1). 14.95 *(978-0-9769417-8-1(3))* Blooming Tree Pr.

Johnson, Shane L., illus. Attack of the Zombie Rabbids. 2016. (Rabbids Invasion Ser.). (ENG.). 40p. (J). (gr. 1-3). pap. 3.99 *(978-1-4814-6066-8(8)*, Simon Spotlight) Simon Spotlight.

—The Chickens & the Eggs. 2014. (Rabbids Invasion Ser.). (ENG.). 40p. (J). (gr. 1-3). pap. 3.99 *(978-1-4814-0042-8(8)*, Simon Spotlight) Simon Spotlight.

—The Need for Speed. 2014. (Rabbids Invasion Ser.). (ENG.). 40p. (J). (gr. 1-3). 16.99 *(978-1-4814-2292-5(8))*; pap. 3.99 *(978-1-4814-2291-8(X))* Simon Spotlight. (Simon Spotlight).

Jones, Janey Louise. Violet the Velvet Rabbit. Poh, Jennie, illus. 2016. (Superfairies Ser.). (ENG.). 56p. (gr. k-3). lib. bdg. 23.99 *(978-1-4795-8644-8(7))* Picture Window Bks.

Jones, Mary Noble. Itsy Rabbit & Friends: Itsy's First Adventure. Jones, Mary Noble, illus. 2007. (Illus.). 28p. (J). per. 15.00 *(978-0-9796209-8-0(8))* Righter Publishing Co., Inc.

Jones, Nancy. The Grandpaws. 2005. 57p. pap. 16.95 *(978-1-4137-4778-2(7))* America Star Bks.

Jordan, Apple. The Bunny Surprise. 2012. (Step into Reading Level 1 Ser.). lib. bdg. 13.55 *(978-0-606-23723-9(2)*, Turtleback) Turtleback Bks.

Josiah, Iris. Tiny Rabbit. 2012. (Illus.). 28p. (J). pap. *(978-0-9572728-0-4(4))* Tiny Island Pr.

Journey of Egg & Rabbit by Lee Grass Whitefeather. 2004. (YA). cd-rom *(978-0-9767413-5-0(0))* Wakinglion Studio.

Joyce, Melanie. I Love You Because ... Lovsin, Polona, illus. 2016. (ENG.). 24p. (J). (gr. -1-1). 16.99 *(978-1-4998-0212-2(9))* Little Bee Books Inc.

Joyce, William. E. Aster Bunnymund & the Warrior Eggs at the Earth's Core!, Bk. 2. Joyce, William, illus. 2012. (Guardians Ser.: 2). (ENG., Illus.). 272p. (J). (gr. 2-6). 15.99 *(978-1-4424-3050-1(8)*, Atheneum Bks. for Young Readers) Simon & Schuster Children's Publishing.

Just Bunny & Me: Big Book. (Pebble Soup Explorations Ser.). (SPA.). 16p. (gr. -1-18). 31.00 *(978-0-7578-1666-6(5))* Rigby Education.

Just Bunny & Me: Small Book. (Pebble Soup Explorations Ser.). (SPA.). 16p. (gr. -1-18). 5.00 *(978-0-7578-1706-9(8))* Rigby Education.

Kaplan, Michael B. Betty Bunny Didn't Do It. Jorisch, Stéphane, illus. 2013. (Betty Bunny Ser.). (ENG.). 32p. (J). (gr. -1-k). 16.99 *(978-0-8037-3858-4(7)*, Dial Bks) Penguin Young Readers Group.

—Betty Bunny Loves Chocolate Cake. Jorisch, Stéphane, illus. 2011. (Betty Bunny Ser.). (ENG.). 36p. (J). (gr. -1-k). 17.99 *(978-0-8037-3407-4(7)*, Dial Bks) Penguin Young Readers Group.

—Betty Bunny Wants a Goal. Jorisch, Stéphane, illus. 2014. (Betty Bunny Ser.). (ENG.). 32p. (J). (gr. -1-k). 16.99 *(978-0-8037-3859-1(5)*, Dial Bks) Penguin Young Readers Group.

—Betty Bunny Wants Everything. Jorisch, Stéphane, illus. 2012. (Betty Bunny Ser.). (ENG.). 32p. (J). (gr. -1-k). 17.99 *(978-0-8037-3408-1(5)*, Dial Bks) Penguin Young Readers Group.

Kapoor, Natalya. My Favorite Time of Day. 2013. 12p. pap. 12.99 *(978-1-4772-8344-8(7))* AuthorHouse.

Karlik, Danielle. The Kaylee Chronicles: First Day Fright. 2007. 20p. per. 24.95 *(978-1-4241-8346-3(4))* America Star Bks.

Karr, Lily. Easter Parade! 2013. lib. bdg. 14.75 *(978-0-606-31494-7(6)*, Turtleback) Turtleback Bks.

—My Easter Bunny! Johnson, Jay B., illus. 2012. (ENG.). 12p. (J). (gr. -1-k). bds. 4.99 *(978-0-545-37117-9(1)*, Cartwheel Bks.) Scholastic, Inc.

Kaye, Christian Thomas. Rachel the Homely Rabbit: A Story about Kindness. Albright, Audrey, illus. 2011. 30p. pap. 9.95 *(978-1-60844-763-3(4))* Dog Ear Publishing, LLC.

Kaye, Shannie. Funny Bunny. 2013. 20p. pap. 24.95 *(978-1-4241-0079-8(8))* America Star Bks.

Keilbart, L. S. One. Benson, Barbara, illus. 2007. (ENG.). 76p. (J). (gr. k-k). per. *(978-1-85756-610-9(6))* Janus Publishing Co.

Keller, Laurie. Do unto Otters: A Book about Manners. Keller, Laurie, illus. 2007. (ENG., Illus.). 40p. (J). (gr. k-3). 18.99 *(978-0-8050-7996-8(3)*, 9780805079968, Holt, Henry & Co. Bks. For Young Readers) Holt, Henry & Co.

—Do unto Otters: A Book about Manners. Keller, Laurie, illus. 2009. (ENG., Illus.). 40p. (J). (gr. k-3). pap. 7.99 *(978-0-312-58140-4(8)*, 9780312581404) Square Fish.

Kerr, Judith. Cuando Hitler Robó el Conejo Rosa.Tr. of When Hitler Stole Pink Rabbit. (SPA.). 272p. (J). 9.95 *(978-84-204-4791-9(9))* Ediciones Alfaguara ESP. Dist: Santillana USA Publishing Co., Inc.

—Cuando Hitler Robó el Conejo Rosa. 2003.Tr. of When Hitler Stole Pink Rabbit. (SPA.). (YA). (gr. 5-8). pap. *(978-84-345-8586-7(3)*, AF0202) Salvat Editores, S.A. ESP. Dist: Lectorum Pubns., Inc.

Kibuishi, Kazu. The Stonekeeper. 2008. (Amulet Ser.: 1). (ENG., Illus.). 192p. (J). (gr. 3-7). 24.99 *(978-0-439-84680-6(3))*; pap. 12.99 *(978-0-439-84681-3(1))* Scholastic, Inc. (Graphix).

Kiefer, Janet Kennedy & Barrett, Jill. Can I Play with You? Freckles Book 2. 2013. 42p. pap. *(978-1-4602-0038-4(1))* FriesenPress.

Kim, Cecil. Nicknames. Han, SooJin, illus. 2014. (MySELF Bookshelf Ser.). (ENG.). 32p. (J). (gr. k-2). pap. 11.94 *(978-1-60357-699-4(1))*; lib. bdg. 25.27 *(978-1-59953-664-4(1))* Norwood Hse. Pr.

Kim, YeShil. Tortoise & Hare. Kheiriyeh, Rashin, illus. 2014. (MySELF Bookshelf Ser.). (ENG.). 32p. (J). (gr. k-2). pap. 11.94 *(978-1-60357-700-7(9))*; lib. bdg. 25.27 *(978-1-59953-665-1(X))* Norwood Hse. Pr.

Kimura, Yuichi. On the Seesaw Bridge. Hata, Kowshiro, illus. 2011. (ENG.). 36p. (J). (gr. -1-3). 14.95 *(978-1-935654-18-6(7)*, Vertical) Vertical, Inc.

Kinder, Connie & Virden, Carole. Dash's Pause: An Adventure in Being Found. 2012. (Illus.). 40p. pap. 20.95 *(978-1-4497-6981-9(0)*, WestBow Pr.) Author Solutions, Inc.

Kintz, Elizabeth. The Magic Hose. 2012. 30p. 16.95 *(978-1-4575-1087-8(1))*; pap. 14.00 *(978-1-4575-0948-3(2))* Dog Ear Publishing, LLC.

Kirk, Daniel. Ten Things I Love about You. Kirk, Daniel, illus. 2012. (ENG., Illus.). 36p. (J). (gr. k-3). 16.99 *(978-0-399-25288-4(6)*, Nancy Paulsen Books) Penguin Young Readers Group.

Kiser, Dolores White. The Marriage of White Rabbit. 2005. (J). 10.00 net. *(978-0-976648-3-3(6))* White Kiser, Dolores.

A Kiss for Jake. 2008. (Jake Flocked Board Ser.). 8p. bds. *(978-1-4075-1816-9(X))* Parragon, Inc.

Kisseloff, Jeff & Wells, Rosemary. Ruby's Tea for Two. 2003. (Max & Ruby Ser.). (ENG.). 12p. (J). (gr. -1 — 1). bds. 6.99 *(978-0-670-03652-3(8)*, Viking Books for Young Readers) Penguin Young Readers Group.

Kline, Trish & Donev, Mary. A Scary Day in the Forest: KA Reader 5. 2007. (Illus.). 32p. (J). per. 20.00 *(978-0-9717234-8-1(6))* Ghost Hunter Productions.

Klise, Kate. Little Rabbit & the Meanest Mother on Earth. Klise, M. Sarah, illus. (ENG.). 32p. (J). (gr. -1-3). 2015. 6.99 *(978-0-544-45611-2(4)*, HMH Books For Young Readers) 2010. 17.99 *(978-0-15-206201-9(7))* Houghton Mifflin Harcourt Publishing Co.

—Shall I Knit You a Hat? A Christmas Yarn. Klise, M. Sarah, illus. 2007. (ENG.). 32p. (J). (gr. -1-2). per. 8.99 *(978-0-312-37139-5(X)*, 9780312371395) Square Fish.

—Why Do You Cry? Not a Sob Story. Klise, M. Sarah, illus. rev. ed. 2006. (ENG.). 32p. (J). (gr. -1-2). 18.99 *(978-0-8050-7319-5(1)*, 9780805073195, Holt, Henry & Co. Bks. For Young Readers) Holt, Henry & Co.

Knudsen, Michelle. Big Mean Mike. Magoon, Scott, illus. 2012. (ENG.). 40p. (J). (gr. -1-3). 15.99 *(978-0-7636-4990-6(2))* Candlewick Pr.

Knutson, Barbara. Sungura & Leopard: A Swahili Trickster Tale. Knutson, Barbara, illus. 2007. (Illus.). 26p. (J). (gr. -1-3). per. 6.95 *(978-0-8225-6801-8(2)*, First Avenue Editions) Lerner Publishing Group.

Kohake, Beverly. The Funny Bunny. 2008. 32p. pap. 16.95 *(978-1-4303-2736-3(7))* Lulu Pr., Inc.

Korman, Justine. Spring Is Here, Grumpy Bunny! McQueen, Lucinda, illus. 2008. (Clifford's Bedtime Ser.). (ENG.). 64p. (J). (gr. -1-3). pap. 4.99 *(978-0-545-03402-9(7)*, Cartwheel Bks.) Scholastic, Inc.

Kramer, Alan & Kramer, Candice. Brer Rabbit Hears a Big Noise in the Woods: An African /American Folktale. 2006. (J). pap. *(978-1-4108-7163-3(0))* Benchmark Education Co.

Krensky, Stephen. The Lion & the Hare. Reeves, Jeni, illus. 2008. (On My Own Folklore Ser.). (ENG.). 48p. (gr. 2-4). lib. bdg. 25.26 *(978-0-8225-7546-7(9)*, Millbrook Pr.) Lerner Publishing Group.

—Milo the Really Big Bunny. Suber, Melissa, illus. 2010. (ENG.). 32p. (J). (gr. -1-1). 11.99 *(978-1-4424-1434-1(0)*, Simon & Schuster Bks. For Young Readers) Simon & Schuster Bks. For Young Readers.

Krosoczka, Jarrett J. Naptastrophe! 2017. (ENG.). 40p. (J). (gr. -1-2). 17.99 ***(978-0-385-75483-5(3))***; lib. bdg. 20.99 ***(978-0-385-75484-2(1))*** Random Hse. Children's Bks. (Knopf Bks. for Young Readers).

Kumiega, Michelle. The Bunnies Who Learn Not to Bully. 2011. 24p. pap. 24.95 *(978-1-4560-6742-7(7))* America Star Bks.

—The Greedy Bunny. 2008. 28p. pap. 24.95 *(978-1-60672-966-3(7))* America Star Bks.

Kunhardt, Dorothy. Pat the Bunny. Golden Books Staff, illus. collector's deluxe ed. 2011. (Touch-And-Feel Ser.). (ENG.). 24p. (J). (gr. -1-2). 14.99 *(978-0-307-20047-1(7)*, Golden Bks.) Random Hse. Children's Bks.

—Pat the Bunny: First Books for Baby, 3 vols. 2015. (Touch-And-Feel Ser.). (ENG., Illus.). 20p. (J). (— 1). pap. 29.99 *(978-0-553-50838-3(5)*, Golden Bks.) Random Hse. Children's Bks.

Kurkosky, Tina. Bunny Brothers. 2011. 24p. pap. 24.95 *(978-1-4626-3608-2(X))* America Star Bks.

Kyrja. Rupert's Tales: Rupert Helps Clean Up, 1 vol. Osborn, Tonia Benington, illus. 2013. (ENG.). 64p. (J). 19.99 *(978-0-7643-4284-4(3)*, 9780764342844) Schiffer Publishing, Ltd.

—Rupert's Tales: The Wheel of the Year - Samhain, Yule, Imbolc, & Ostara, 1 vol. Osborn, Tonia Bennington, illus. 2012. (ENG.). 64p. (J). 19.99 *(978-0-7643-3987-5(7)*, 9780764339875) Schiffer Publishing, Ltd.

—Rupert's Tales: The Wheel of the Year Activity Book, 1 vol. Osborn, Tonia Bennington, illus. 2012. (ENG.). 40p. (J). pap. 9.99 *(978-0-7643-4020-8(4)*, 9780764340208) Schiffer Publishing, Ltd.

Kyrja, et al. Rupert's Tales: The Wheel of the Year Beltane, Litha, Lammas, & Mabon, 1 vol. 2011. (ENG., Illus.). 64p. (J). 19.99 *(978-0-7643-3689-8(4)*, 9780764336898, Schiffer Publishing Ltd) Schiffer Publishing, Ltd.

Lade, Linda. Peter Bunny: Adventures in the Kudzu Pat. 2006. 82p. pap. 16.95 *(978-1-4241-3818-0(3))* PublishAmerica, Inc.

Lamm, Drew C. Cottontail at Clover Crescent. 2005. (Smithsonian's Backyard Ser.). (ENG., Illus.). 32p. (J). (gr. -1-2). 8.95 *(978-1-59249-225-1(8)*, SC5005) Soundprints.

—Cottontail at Clover Crescent. Davis, Allen, illus. 2005. (Smithsonian's Backyard Ser.). (ENG.). 32p. (J). (gr. -1-2). pap. 6.95 *(978-1-59249-112-4(X)*, S5005) Soundprints.

Lane, W. Seth. Riley Rabbit's Quest to the Ark. 2011. 32p. (gr. -1 — 1). pap. 17.25 *(978-1-4269-6178-6(2))* Trafford Publishing.

Langen, Annette. Felix & the Flying Suitcase Adventure. Droop, Constanza, illus. 2003. 47p. (J). 14.99 *(978-1-59384-035-8(7))* Parklane Publishing.

—Felix Explores Planet Earth. Droop, Constanza, illus. 2004. (Perfect for Earth Day Promotions! Ser.). 47p. (J). 14.99 *(978-1-59384-030-3(6))* Parklane Publishing.

—Felix's Christmas Around the World. Droop, Constanza, illus. 2003. 40p. (J). 14.99 *(978-1-59384-036-5(5))* Parklane Publishing.

—Letters from Felix: A Little Rabbit on a World Tour. Droop, Constanza, illus. 2003. 47p. (J). 14.99 *(978-1-59384-034-1(9))* Parklane Publishing.

Langley, C. Kevin. Brer Rabbit Comic. 2009. 16p. pap. 9.80 *(978-0-557-11631-7(7))* Lulu Pr., Inc.

Langreuter, Jutta. So Happy Together! Dahle, Stephanie, illus. 2017. (ENG.). 32p. (J). (gr. -1-3). 17.95 *(978-0-7358-4279-3(5))* North-South Bks., Inc.

Lapytski, Serge & Lapytski, Kristina. The Heart of a Lion! E-Hare. 2011. 84p. pap. 12.84 *(978-1-4567-4281-2(7))* AuthorHouse.

Larsen, Andrew. Bella & the Bunny. Endle, Kate, illus. 2007. (ENG.). 32p. (J). (gr. -1-k). 14.95 *(978-1-55337-970-6(5))* Kids Can Pr., Ltd. CAN. Dist: Hachette Bk. Group.

Latimer, Alex. Lion vs Rabbit, 1 vol. Latimer, Alex, illus. 2013. (ENG., Illus.). 32p. (J). (gr. -1-3). 15.95 *(978-1-56145-709-0(4))* Peachtree Pubs.

Latimer, Alex. Lion vs. Rabbit, 1 vol. Latimer, Alex, illus. 2017. (ENG., Illus.). 32p. (J). (gr. -1-3). pap. 7.95 ***(978-1-56145-898-1(8))*** Peachtree Pubs.

Lauterbach, B. L. Home-Grown Experiences. 2008. 68p. pap. 7.95 *(978-1-4327-2620-1(X))* Outskirts Pr., Inc.

Lawson, Robert. Rabbit Hill. l.t. ed. (J). (gr. 4-6). reprint ed. 10.00 *(978-0-89064-076-0(9))* National Assn. for Visually Handicapped.

Leathers, Philippa. The Black Rabbit. Leathers, Philippa, illus. (ENG., Illus.). 40p. (J). (gr. -1-2). 2016. 6.99 *(978-0-7636-8879-0(7))* 2013. 14.00 *(978-0-7636-5714-7(X))* Candlewick Pr.

Leathers, Rain. Purple Mountain. 2008. 36p. pap. 20.95 *(978-1-4327-2685-0(4))* Outskirts Pr., Inc.

Lee, Carol & Bell, Donna. Saying Goodbye to Hare: A Story about Death & Dying to Be Used with Children. Ages 5-9. 2013. (ENG., Illus.). 24p. pap. 6.95 *(978-1-85741-138-6(2))* Southgate Pubs. GBR. Dist: Parkwest Pubns., Inc.

Lester, Helen. Listen, Buddy. Munsinger, Lynn, illus. 2013. (Laugh-Along Lessons Ser.). (ENG.). 32p. (J). (gr. -1-3). 8.99 *(978-0-544-00322-4(5))* Houghton Mifflin Harcourt Publishing Co.

Levy, Elizabeth. A Hare-Raising Tale. Gerstein, Mordicai, illus. unabr. ed. 2006. (First Chapter Bks.). (J). (gr. 2-4). pap. 17.95 incl. audio *(978-1-59519-704-7(4))*; pap. 20.95 incl. audio compact disk *(978-1-59519-705-4(2))* Live Oak Media.

Levy, Elizabeth & Coville, Bruce. The Dragon of Doom. Gerstein, Mordicai & Coville, Katherine, illus. 2005. 71p. (J). lib. bdg. 15.00 *(978-1-59054-903-2(1))* Fitzgerald Bks.

Lewman, David. Case File #1 First Contact. Spaziante, Patrick, illus. 2014. (Rabbids Invasion Ser.). (ENG.). 96p. (J). (gr. 2-5). pap. 4.99 *(978-1-4814-0037-4(1)*, Simon Spotlight) Simon Spotlight.

—Case File #4 Rabbids Go Viral. Spaziante, Patrick, illus. 2015. (Rabbids Invasion Ser.). (ENG.). 96p. (J). (gr. 2-5). 16.99 *(978-1-4814-2766-1(0)*, Simon Spotlight) Simon Spotlight.

—Case File #7 Red Carpet Rabbids. Johnson, Shane L., illus. 2016. (Rabbids Invasion Ser.). (ENG.). 96p. (J). (gr. 2-5). 16.99 *(978-1-4814-5253-3(3)*, Simon Spotlight) Simon Spotlight.

—New Developments, No. 2. Spaziante, Patrick, illus. 2014. (Rabbids Invasion Ser.). (ENG.). 96p. (J). (gr. 2-5). pap. 4.99 *(978-1-4814-0204-0(8)*, Simon Spotlight) Simon Spotlight.

—Red Carpet Rabbids. Johnson, Shane L., illus. 2016. (Rabbids Invasion Ser.). (ENG.). 96p. (J). (gr. 2-5). pap. 5.99 *(978-1-4814-5252-6(5)*, Simon Spotlight) Simon Spotlight.

Light, Steve. The Bunny Burrow Buyer's Book: A Tale of Rabbit Real Estate. 2016. (ENG., Illus.). 16p. (J). (gr. -1-3). 19.95 *(978-1-57687-752-4(3)*, powerHouse Bks.) powerHouse Cultural Entertainment, Inc.

The Lion & the Hare: [an East African Folktale]. 2009. (On My Own Folklore Ser.). (gr. 3-5). pap. 6.95 *(978-1-58013-849-9(7)*, First Avenue Editions) Lerner Publishing Group.

Lispector, Clarice. Misterio do Coelho Pensante. pap. 19.95 *(978-85-325-1061-7(2))* Rocco, Editora, Ltda BRA. Dist: Distribooks, Inc.

Little Bunny. 2003. (Goodnight Mr. Moon Ser.). (Illus.). (J). bds. 2.98 *(978-0-7525-4741-1(0))* Parragon, Inc.

Little Rabbit Waits for the Moon. (Picture Books... Ser.). 24p. 4.99 *(978-1-4054-9537-0(5))* Parragon, Inc.

Liv‡n, Paco. THE THING THAT HURTS MOST IN THE WORLD. 2007. (ENG., Illus.). 36p. (J). 17.95 *(978-84-96788-89-3(X))* OQO, Editora ESP. Dist: Baker & Taylor Bks.

Llama, Gram. The Bunny Fuzz Mystery. 2007. 32p. per. 24.95 *(978-1-4241-8371-5(5))* America Star Bks.

Lloyd-Jones, Sally. Bunny's First Spring, 1 vol. McPhail, David, illus. 2015. (ENG.). 32p. (J). 16.99 *(978-0-310-73386-7(3))* Zonderkidz.

—Skip to the Loo, My Darling! a Potty Book. Jeram, Anita, illus. 2016. (ENG.). 32p. (J). (-k). 11.99 *(978-0-7636-7234-8(3))* Candlewick Pr.

Lobe, Mira & Kovács, Cécile. Hoppelpopp & the Best Bunny. Kaufmann, Angelika, illus. 2015. (ENG.). 32p. (J). (gr. -1-3). 16.95 *(978-0-8234-3287-5(4))* Holiday Hse., Inc.

Lobel, Anita. 10 Hungry Rabbits. 2015. (ENG., Illus.). 20p. (J). (-k). bds. 7.99 *(978-0-553-49828-8(2)*, Knopf Bks. for Young Readers) Random Hse. Children's Bks.

—10 Hungry Rabbits: Counting & Color Concepts. Bowers, Tim, illus. 2012. (ENG.). 24p. (J). (gr. k-k). 9.99 *(978-0-375-86864-1(X)*, Knopf Bks. for Young Readers) Random Hse. Children's Bks.

Lobel, Gill. Little Bear's Special Wish. Hansen, Gaby, illus. 2004. 32p. (J). tchr. ed. 16.95 *(978-1-58925-034-5(6))* Tiger Tales.

Logan, J. Gavin. Plum Bunny. 2008. 52p. pap. 16.95 *(978-1-60563-654-2(1))* America Star Bks.

Loney, Andrea J. Bunnybear. Saldaña, Carmen, illus. 2017. (ENG.). 32p. (J). (gr. -1-3). 16.99 *(978-0-8075-0938-8(8))* Whitman, Albert & Co.

Lorenzo, Amanda. Clovis Escapes! Bks. 3: Runt Farm. Walker, Mark Evan, illus. 2009. 136p. 12.95 *(978-0-9800952-2-7(0))* BooktiMookti Pr.

Lorini, Andrea. Bunny's Easter Surprise. 2015. (ENG., Illus.). 8p. (J). (gr. -1 — 1). bds. 6.99 *(978-0-7641-6782-9(0))* Barron's Educational Series, Inc.

Lowell, Susan. The Tortoise & the Jackrabbit: La Tortuga y la Liebre. Harris, Jim, illus. 2004. (New Bilingual Picture Book Ser.). (ENG, SPA & MUL.). 32p. (J). (gr. -1-3). pap. 7.95 *(978-0-87358-869-0(X))* Cooper Square Publishing Llc.

Lowell, Susan, et al. The Tortoise & the Jackrabbit. Harris, Jim, illus. 2003. (Avenues Ser.). (ENG.). 32p. (C). (gr. -1-3). pap. 26.95 *(978-0-87358-586-6(0))* National Geographic School Publishing, Inc.

Luchesi, Dennis. Benji Rabbit. 2013. 24p. pap. 24.95 *(978-1-62709-894-6(1))* America Star Bks.

Lundquist, Mary. Cat & Bunny. Lundquist, Mary, illus. 2015. (ENG., Illus.). 32p. (J). (gr. -1-3). 17.99 *(978-0-06-228780-9(X))* HarperCollins Pubs.

Maccarone, Grace. Bunny Race! Long, Ethan, illus. 2009. (J). *(978-0-545-11290-1(7))* Scholastic, Inc.

MacDonald, Margaret Read. Pickin' Peas. Cummings, Pat, illus. 2014. (ENG.). 32p. pap. 8.95 *(978-1-939160-83-6(9))* August Hse. Pubs., Inc.

Mack, Jeff. Hippo & Rabbit. Mack, Jeff, illus. 2011. (Scholastic Reader Level 1 Ser.). (ENG., Illus.). 32p. (J). (gr. -1-2). pap. 3.99 *(978-0-545-27445-6(1)*, Cartwheel Bks.) Scholastic, Inc.
—Hippo & Rabbit in Brave Like Me. Mack, Jeff, illus. 2011. (Scholastic Reader Level 1 Ser.). (ENG., Illus.). 32p. (J). (gr. -1-2). pap. 3.99 *(978-0-545-28360-1(4)*, Cartwheel Bks.) Scholastic, Inc.
Mack, Jeff, illus. Good News, Bad News. 2012. (ENG.). 40p. (J). (gr. -1-1). 16.99 *(978-1-4521-0110-1(8))* Chronicle Bks. LLC.
MacKenzie, Emily. Wanted! Ralfy Rabbit, Book Burglar. 2016. (ENG., Illus.). 32p. (J). 16.99 *(978-1-68119-220-8(9)*, 9781681192208, Bloomsbury USA Childrens) Bloomsbury Publishing USA.
MacKinnon, Mairi, ed. The Hare & the Tortoise. Howarth, Daniel, illus. 2007. (First Reading Level 4 Ser.). 48p. (J). (gr. -1-3). 8.99 *(978-0-7945-1612-3(2)*, Usborne) EDC Publishing.
Magone, Teresa. Little Bunny Has Belly Surgery. 2012. 38p. pap. 9.50 *(978-0-615-58595-6(7))* Little Bunny Bks.
Magsamen, Sandra. Are You My Cuddle Bunny? 2017. (Heart-Felt Bks.: 4). (ENG.). 12p. (J). (— 1). 7.99 *(978-0-545-92797-0(8)*, Cartwheel Bks.) Scholastic, Inc.
—Bedtime Bunny. 2009. (Board Books with Plush Toy Ser.). (ENG., Illus.). 20p. (J). (gr. -1 — 1). bds. 7.99 *(978-0-316-00390-2(5))* Little, Brown Bks. for Young Readers.
Maillet, Kevin And Haylie. The Scruzzels: Life on the Farm. 2012. 32p. pap. 19.99 *(978-1-4772-2805-0(5))* AuthorHouse.
Malaspina, Ann. Guinea Fowl & Rabbit Get Justice: An African Folktale. Wendland, Paula, illus. 2013. (Folktales from Around the World Ser.). (ENG.). 24p. (J). (gr. k-3). 28.50 *(978-1-62323-614-4(2)*, 206381) Child's World, Inc., The.
Maloney, Brenna. Ready Rabbit Gets Ready! 2015. *(978-0-698-15065-2(1))* Penguin Publishing Group.
Mancini, Kristen Belmont. A Bunny Named Boo. 2011. 24p. pap. *(978-1-4269-7640-7(2))* Trafford Publishing (UK) Ltd.
Mandara, Melissa. Who would you Be? 2010. 32p. pap. 15.95 *(978-1-4520-1605-4(4))* AuthorHouse.
Mandy, Stanley. Bella: The Birthday Party. Mandy, Stanley, illus. 2010. (ENG., Illus.). 32p. (J). (gr. -1-k). 9.95 *(978-1-58925-850-1(9))* Tiger Tales.
—Bella: The Fairy Ball. Mandy, Stanley, illus. 2010. (ENG., Illus.). 32p. (J). (gr. -1-k). 9.95 *(978-1-58925-851-8(7))* Tiger Tales.
Marie, Barbara. Snowy & Felix Find Christmas. 2009. 24p. pap. 11.49 *(978-1-4389-7392-0(6))* AuthorHouse.
Marino, Gianna. Too Tall Houses. 2012. (ENG.). 40p. (J). (gr. -1-k). 16.99 *(978-0-670-01314-2(5)*, Viking Books for Young Readers) Penguin Young Readers Group.
Marion, L. K. Summer Holiday with Funny Bunny. 2012. 32p. pap. 17.25 *(978-1-4669-6475-4(8))* Trafford Publishing.
Marlow, Layn. Hurry up & Slow Down. 2009. (ENG., Illus.). 32p. (J). (gr. -1-3). 16.95 *(978-0-8234-2178-7(3))* Holiday Hse., Inc.
Marrone, Amanda. The Multiplying Menace. 2010. (Magic Repair Shop Ser.: 1). (ENG.). 288p. (J). (gr. 3-7). pap. 6.99 *(978-1-4169-9033-8(X)*, Aladdin) Simon & Schuster Children's Publishing.
Marshall, Denise. The Adventures of Hip Hop: Hip Hop & the Blueberry Pancakes. Champagne, Heather, illus. 2012. 36p. pap. 14.75 *(978-1-62212-331-5(X)*, Strategic Bk. Publishing) Strategic Book Publishing & Rights Agency (SBPRA).
—The Adventures of Hip Hop: Hip Hop & the Yellow Hat. Schley, Cheri & Champagne, Heather, illus. 2011. 36p. pap. 14.75 *(978-1-60976-342-8(4)*, Eloquent Bks.) Strategic Book Publishing & Rights Agency (SBPRA).
Martin, Bridgitt. Bunny & the Amazing Gift: God Cares for All His Creation. 2013. 28p. pap. 13.99 *(978-1-4908-0952-6(X)*, WestBow Pr.) Author Solutions, Inc.
Marzot, Janet. Las Liebres Blancas. (SPA.). 32p. (J). 13.95 *(978-84-261-1459-4(8))* Juventud, Editorial ESP. Dist: AIMS International Bks., Inc.
Mason, Christopher. Little Bunny Comfy Pants. 2011. 20p. pap. 24.95 *(978-1-4626-0900-0(7))* America Star Bks.
Massie, Rosemary. Rhymen the Rabbit: Meeting the Forest Ranger. 2011. 28p. pap. 13.95 *(978-1-4634-2572-2(4))* AuthorHouse.
—Rhymen the Rabbit: Save the Forest. 2011. 28p. pap. 13.95 *(978-1-4634-1597-6(4))* AuthorHouse.
Mastrangelo, Judy. What Do Bunnies Do All Day? Mastrangelo, Judy, illus. (Illus.). (J). 32p. pap. 4.95 *(978-0-8249-5370-6(3))*; 2006. (ENG.). 24p. (gr. -1-k). per. 3.95 *(978-0-8249-5532-8(3))* Worthy Publishing. (Ideal Pubns.).
Mastrangelo, Judy, illus. What Do Bunnies Do All Day? 2003. (ENG.). 24p. (J). bds. 6.95 *(978-0-8249-6520-4(5)*, Ideal Pubns.) Worthy Publishing.
Mather, Daniel, illus. Case File #3 the Accidental Accomplice. 2014. (Rabbids Invasion Ser.: 3). (ENG.). 96p. (J). (gr. 2-5). pap. 4.99 *(978-1-4814-1720-4(7)*, Simon Spotlight) Simon Spotlight.
May, Bonnie. The Tale of a Rabbit's Tail. 2008. 66p. pap. 34.50 *(978-1-4357-0313-1(8))* Lulu Pr., Inc.
May, R. B. Charlie Finds a Friend. 2010. 32p. pap. 12.99 *(978-1-4490-6913-1(4))* AuthorHouse.
Mayer, Kirsten & Auerbach, Annie, texts. Hop: The Chapter Book. 2011. (Hop Ser.). (ENG.). 80p. (J). (gr. 3-7). pap. 4.99 *(978-0-316-12900-8(3))* Little, Brown Bks. for Young Readers.
McBratney, Sam. Guess How Much I Love You. Jeram, Anita, illus. 2005. 34p. (J). bds. 19.95 *(978-0-9769313-1-7(1))* BrailleInk.
—Guess How Much I Love You. Jeram, Anita, illus. (Guess How Much I Love You Ser.). (J). 2014. (ENG.). 30p. (gr. k-4). 9.99 *(978-0-7636-7446-5(X))* 2011. (ENG.). 16p. (gr. -1-2). 19.99 *(978-0-7636-5378-1(0))* 2011. (ENG.). (gr. -1-k). bds. 9.99 *(978-0-7636-4976-0(7))* 2006. 32p. (gr. -1-3). 15.99 *(978-0-7636-3503-9(0))* Candlewick Pr.
—Guess How Much I Love You 20th Anniversary Edition. Jeram, Anita, illus. 2014. (Guess How Much I Love You Ser.). (ENG.). 40p. (J). (gr. k-12). 16.99 *(978-0-7636-7448-9(6))* Candlewick Pr.
—Guess How Much I Love You All Year Round. Jeram, Anita, illus. 2010. (Guess How Much I Love You Ser.). (ENG.). 72p. (J). (gr. -1-2). 16.99 *(978-0-7636-4654-7(7))* Candlewick Pr.
—Guess How Much I Love You: Colors. Jeram, Anita, illus. 2013. (Guess How Much I Love You Ser.). (ENG.). 14p. (J). (— 1). bds. 4.99 *(978-0-7636-6476-3(6))* Candlewick Pr.
—Guess How Much I Love You Lap-Size Board Book. Jeram, Anita, illus. 2013. (Guess How Much I Love You Ser.). (ENG.). 24p. (J). (— 1). bds. 12.99 *(978-0-7636-7006-1(5))* Candlewick Pr.
—Guess How Much I Love You: One More Tickle! Jeram, Anita, illus. 2016. (Guess How Much I Love You Ser.). (ENG.). (J). (gr. k-k). bds. 17.99 *(978-0-7636-8819-6(3))* Candlewick Pr.
—Guess How Much I Love You: One More Tickle! Tray, 3 vols. 2016. (ENG.). (J). bds. 53.97 *(978-0-7636-9127-1(5))* Candlewick Pr.
—Let's Play in the Snow. Jeram, Anita, illus. 2012. (Guess How Much I Love You Ser.). (ENG.). 24p. (J). (gr. k — 1). bds. 4.99 *(978-0-7636-6121-2(X))* Candlewick Pr.
—The Nutbrown Hare Storybook Pair. Jeram, Anita, illus. 2008. (Guess How Much I Love You Ser.). (ENG.). 48p. (J). (gr. k-k). bds. 14.99 *(978-0-7636-4265-5(7))* Candlewick Pr.
—A Surprise for the Nutbrown Hares. Jeram, Anita, illus. 2009. (J). *(978-0-7636-4903-6(1))* Candlewick Pr.
McCall, Val. Twelve Rabbits & a Turtle: Bilingual English French. 2012. 46p. pap. 9.95 *(978-1-938367-00-7(6))* Destinee Media.
McCallum, Ann. Rabbits Rabbits Everywhere: A Fibonacci Tale. Kendall, Gideon, illus. (ENG.). 32p. (J). (gr. 1-4). 2008. 16.95 *(978-1-57091-895-7(3))* 2007. per. 7.95 *(978-1-57091-896-4(1))* Charlesbridge Publishing, Inc.
McCann, Shawn, illus. Why the Owl Has Big Ears. 2005. 32p. (J). (gr. -1-3). 8.75 *(978-0-9771466-0-4(X))* Goulasche Pr.
McCarty, Peter. Bunny Dreams. McCarty, Peter, illus. 2016. (ENG., Illus.). 40p. (J). 16.99 *(978-0-8050-9687-3(6)*, 9780805096873, Holt, Henry & Co. Bks. For Young Readers) Holt, Henry & Co.
—Chloe. McCarty, Peter, illus. 2012. (Illus.). 40p. (J). (gr. -1-1). (ENG.). 16.99 *(978-0-06-114291-8(3))*; lib. bdg. 17.89 *(978-0-06-114292-5(1))* HarperCollins Pubs.
McCue, Lisa. Little Bunny. 2012. (ENG., Illus.). 20p. (J). (gr. k-k). bds. 5.99 *(978-0-375-87141-2(1)*, Random Hse. Bks. for Young Readers) Random Hse. Children's Bks.
—Quiet Bunny. (ENG., Illus.). (J). (gr. -1-1). 2015. 40p. pap. 6.95 *(978-1-4549-1577-5(3))* 2009. 32p. 14.95 *(978-1-4027-5719-8(0))* Sterling Publishing Co., Inc.
—Quiet Bunny & Noisy Puppy. (ENG., Illus.). (J). 2013. 30p. (gr. -1 — 1). bds. 7.95 *(978-1-4549-0860-9(2))* 2011. 32p. 14.95 *(978-1-4027-8559-7(3))* Sterling Publishing Co., Inc.
—Quiet Bunny's Many Colors. 2011. (ENG., Illus.). 32p. (J). (gr. -1-1). 14.95 *(978-1-4027-7209-2(2))* Sterling Publishing Co., Inc.
McCue, Lisa, illus. Busy Bunnies. 2014. (ENG.). 14p. (J). (gr. -1 — 1). bds. 5.99 *(978-0-7944-3039-9(2))* Reader's Digest Assn., Inc., The.
McCue, Lisa & Falken, L. C. Snuggle Bunnies. McCue, Lisa, illus. 2003. (Boardbooks - Board Book Ser.). (ENG., Illus.). 11p. (J). (gr. -1 — 1). bds. 6.99 *(978-0-7944-0040-8(X)*, Reader's Digest Children's Bks.) Studio Fun International.
McCully, Emily Arnold. Pete Likes Bunny. McCully, Emily Arnold, illus. 2016. (I Like to Read(r) Ser.). (ENG., Illus.). 24p. (J). (gr. -1-2). 6.99 *(978-0-8234-3687-3(X))* Holiday Hse., Inc.
—Pete Likes Bunny. 2016. (I Like to Read(r) Ser.). (ENG., Illus.). 24p. (J). (gr. -1-2). 14.95 *(978-0-8234-3653-8(5))* Holiday Hse., Inc.
McCune, Susan. Rabbit & Turtle, 01 vols., 1. 2016. (Rosen REAL Readers: STEM & STEAM Collection). (ENG.). 8p. (J). pap. 5.46 *(978-1-5081-1409-3(9)*, Rosen Classroom) Rosen Publishing Group, Inc., The.
McEnroe, Jim. The Rabbit King: Kingdom Leporidae. 2011. 32p. pap. 15.95 *(978-1-4520-9199-0(4))* AuthorHouse.
McGill, Erin. I Do Not Like Al's Hat. McGill, Erin, illus. 2017. (Illus.). 32p. (J). (gr. -1-3). 17.99 *(978-0-06-245576-5(1)*, Greenwillow Bks.) HarperCollins Pubs.
McInnes, Lisa. Evelyn's Special Eggs. Duersch, Gretchen, ed. Schlund, Mackenzie, illus. 2011. 32p. pap. *(978-1-77067-394-6(6))* FriesenPress.
McIntyre, Mel. Flutter Bunnies. Grady, Kit, illus. 2008. 24p. pap. 10.95 *(978-1-933090-68-9(5))* Guardian Angel Publishing, Inc.
McKay, Hilary. Lulu & the Rabbit Next Door. Lamont, Priscilla, illus. 2014. (Lulu Ser.: Book 4). (ENG.). 112p. (J). (gr. 1-5). 13.99 *(978-0-8075-4816-5(2))* Whitman, Albert & Co.
McKenzie, Tiffany M. The Adventures of Alan & the Man-Eating Rabbits. 2013. 24p. pap. 24.95 *(978-1-63000-143-8(0))* America Star Bks.
McLaren, Meg. Rabbit Magic. 2017. (ENG., Illus.). 40p. (J). (gr. -1-3). 16.99 *(978-0-544-78469-7(3))* Houghton Mifflin Harcourt Publishing Co.
McLeod, Cinders. Earn It! McLeod, Cinders, illus. 2017. (ENG., Illus.). 32p. (J). (-k). 16.99 ***(978-0-399-54444-6(5)***, Nancy Paulsen Books) Penguin Young Readers Group.
McMullan, Kate. One Funny Day. Alley, R. W., illus. 2012. (Pearl & Wagner Ser.: 1). (ENG.). 48p. (J). (gr. 1-3). pap. 3.99 *(978-0-448-45866-3(7)*, Penguin Young Readers) Penguin Young Readers Group.
—Pearl & Wagner: Five Days till Summer. 2014. (Penguin Young Readers Level 3 Ser.). lib. bdg. 13.55 *(978-0-606-35727-2(0))* Turtleback Bks.
—Pearl & Wagner: Three Secrets. 2013. (Penguin Young Readers Level 3 Ser.). lib. bdg. 13.55 *(978-0-606-31708-5(2)*, Turtleback) Turtleback Bks.
—Three Secrets. Alley, R. W., illus. 2013. (Pearl & Wagner Ser.: 3). (ENG.). 48p. (J). (gr. 1-3). pap. 3.99 *(978-0-448-46472-5(1)*, Penguin Young Readers) Penguin Young Readers Group.
—Two Good Friends. Alley, R. W., illus. 2011. (Pearl & Wagner Ser.: 2). (ENG.). 48p. (J). (gr. 1-3). pap. 3.99 *(978-0-448-45690-4(7)*, Penguin Young Readers) Penguin Young Readers Group.
MCP Staff. Little Bunny's Lunch: Short u; Consonants b, h; Blends br, cr; Digraphs ch, sh, th. (J). (gr. 1-2). 38.50 *(978-0-8136-1116-7(4))* Modern Curriculum Pr.
McPhail, David. Budgie & Boo. 2009. (ENG., Illus.). 32p. (J). (gr. -1-k). 15.95 *(978-0-8109-8324-3(9)*, Abrams Bks. for Young Readers) Abrams, Inc.
—Rick Is Sick. 2004. (Green Light Readers Level 1 Ser.). (ENG., Illus.). 24p. (J). (gr. -1-3). pap. 3.95 *(978-0-15-205092-4(2))* Houghton Mifflin Harcourt Publishing Co.
—Rick Is Sick. 2004. (Green Light Readers — Level 1 Ser.). 13.50 *(978-0-613-97286-4(4)*, Turtleback) Turtleback Bks.
McQueen, Todd. Bob & Rob & Corn on the Cob. McQueen, Todd, illus. 2014. (ENG., Illus.). 32p. (J). (gr. -1-k). 16.95 *(978-1-62873-591-8(0)*, Sky Pony Pr.) Skyhorse Publishing Co., Inc.
Meadows, Daisy. Bella the Bunny Fairy. Ripper, Georgie, illus. 2008. (Rainbow Magic — the Pet Fairies Ser.). 65p. (gr. 7). lib. bdg. 14.75 *(978-1-4178-2996-5(6)*, Turtleback) Turtleback Bks.
—Lucy Longwhiskers Gets Lost. 2015. (Magic Animal Friends Ser.: 1). (ENG., Illus.). 112p. (J). (gr. 2-5). pap. 4.99 *(978-0-545-68642-6(3)*, Scholastic Paperbacks) Scholastic, Inc.
Melling, David. Hugless Douglas & the Big Sleepover. 2013. (ENG., Illus.). 32p. (J). *(978-1-58925-116-8(4))* Tiger Tales.
Menard, Michele R. Who Do I Think You Are? 2013. 26p. pap. 10.95 *(978-0-9887969-5-9(3))* Four Menards, The.
Menchin, Scott. What Are You Waiting For? Phelan, Matt, illus. 2017. (ENG.). 32p. (J). 16.99 *(978-1-62672-152-4(1)*, 9781626721524) Roaring Brook Pr.
Merrick, Patrick. Easter Bunnies. 2015. (Our Holiday Symbols Ser.). (ENG.). 24p. (J). (gr. 1-4). 25.64 *(978-1-63143-743-4(7)*, 208552) Child's World, Inc., The.
Metzger, Steve. Five Little Bunnies Hopping on a Hill. 2006. (J). *(978-0-439-80382-3(9))* Scholastic, Inc.
Meyer, Matthew. Raising Hare: Welcome to Sherwood Acores. 2010. 24p. pap. 11.49 *(978-1-4490-8839-2(2))* AuthorHouse.
Meyer, Susan. Matthew & Tall Rabbit Go Camping. Huntington, Amy, illus. 2008. (ENG.). 32p. (J). (gr. -1-3). 15.95 *(978-0-89272-769-8(1))* Down East Bks.
M.H.Pruitt. The Adventures of Rexie the Bear. 2009. 16p. pap. 8.99 *(978-1-4490-4211-0(2))* AuthorHouse.
Midden, Maribeth Grubb. Rosie: The Patchwork Bunny. Techau, Ashlyn, illus. 2011. 24p. (gr. 1-2). pap. 12.99 *(978-1-4269-5671-3(1))* Trafford Publishing.
Middle, Myra. Rabi's Halloween Adventure. 2012. 28p. pap. 21.99 *(978-1-4691-5380-3(7))* Xlibris Corp.
Miller, Dorothy North. How Mr Foxy Fox Was Outfoxed. 2009. 32p. pap. 14.95 *(978-0-9825086-1-9(1))* Fiction Publishing, Inc.
Miller, Jayna. Too Much Trick or Treat. Thatch, Nancy, ed. Miller, Jayna, illus. 2005. (Illus.). 29p. (J). per. 19.95 *(978-0-933849-83-9(4))* landmark Hse., Ltd.
Miller, Jennifer. Christmas Tails. Knight, Vanessa, illus. 2009. 56p. pap. 17.26 *(978-1-4251-8987-7(3))* Trafford Publishing.
Mind Wave Inc. Strawberry Moshi's Activity Book. Mind Wave Inc., illus. 2012. (MoshiMoshiKawaii Ser.). (ENG., Illus.). 28p. (J). (gr. -1-2). pap. 4.99 *(978-0-7636-6236-3(4))* Candlewick Pr.
—Strawberry Princess Moshi's Activity Book. Mind Wave Inc., illus. 2012. (MoshiMoshiKawaii Ser.). (ENG., Illus.). 28p. (J). (gr. -1-2). pap., act. bk. ed. 4.99 *(978-0-7636-6237-0(2))* Candlewick Pr.
Minear, Jason. Jr & the Carrot Coaster. 2008. 17p. pap. 24.95 *(978-1-60563-469-2(7))* America Star Bks.
Minich, Eric. Digger & the Search for Home. 2006. 48p. pap. 16.95 *(978-1-4241-0321-8(5))* PublishAmerica, Inc.
Minor, Florence. How to Be a Bigger Bunny. Minor, Wendell, illus. 2017. 32p. (J). (gr. -1-3). 14.99 *(978-0-06-235255-2(5)*, Tegen, Katherine Bks) HarperCollins Pubs.
Miot, Ray. Alexis the Wizard Rabbit: Pascale & Alain Adventures. 2009. 36p. pap. 17.99 *(978-1-4389-3440-2(8))* AuthorHouse.
Miskimen, Cora. Mrs. Hunny Bunny's New Spring Hat. 2008. 32p. pap. 24.95 *(978-1-4241-8939-7(X))* America Star Bks.
Mitton, Tony & Parker, Ant. Super Submarines. 2014. (Amazing Machines Ser.). (ENG., Illus.). 24p. (J). (gr. -1-k). 4.99 *(978-0-7534-7208-8(2)*, 9780753472088, Kingfisher) Roaring Brook Pr.
—Super Submarines. 2014. (Amazing Machines Ser.). (J). lib. bdg. 14.75 *(978-0-606-36133-0(2))* Turtleback Bks.
Miyakoshi, Akiko. The Way Home in the Night. Miyakoshi, Akiko, illus. 2017. (ENG., Illus.). 32p. (J). (gr. -1-2). 16.95 *(978-1-77138-663-0(0))* Kids Can Pr., Ltd. CAN. Dist: Hachette Bk. Group.
Moncure, Jane Belk. Rabbits' Habits: A Book about Good Habits. DeSantis, Susan, illus. 2013. (Magic Castle Readers Ser.). (ENG.). 32p. (J). (gr. -1-2). 25.64 *(978-1-62323-569-7(3)*, 206304) Child's World, Inc., The.
Mooney, Ginger. Grandmother Rabbit's Old Red Hat. 2009. 12p. pap. 9.99 *(978-1-4490-0586-3(1))* AuthorHouse.
Morgan, Ruth. The Funny Easter Bunny. 2003. (Illus.). 22p. per. 1.95 *(978-1-932338-10-2(1))* Lifevest Publishing, Inc.
Moroney, Trace. Things I Love about Bedtime. Moroney, Trace, illus. 2012. (ENG., Illus.). 16p. (J). (gr. -1-k). bds. 8.99 *(978-0-545-29016-6(3)*, Cartwheel Bks.) Scholastic, Inc.
Morris, Jackie. Song of the Golden Hare. 2013. (ENG., Illus.). 40p. (J). (gr. k-3). 18.99 *(978-1-84780-450-1(0)*, Frances Lincoln) Quarto Publishing Group UK GBR. Dist: Hachette Bk. Group.
Morrison, Toni & Morrison, Slade. The Tortoise or the Hare. Cepeda, Joe, illus. (ENG.). 32p. (J). (gr. -1-3). 2014. 7.99 *(978-1-4169-8335-4(X))* 2010. 17.99 *(978-1-4169-8334-7(1))* Simon & Schuster/Paula Wiseman Bks. (Simon & Schuster/Paula Wiseman Bks.).
Mortimer, Anne. Bunny's Easter Egg. Mortimer, Anne, illus. 2010. (ENG., Illus.). 32p. (J). (gr. -1-2). 12.99 *(978-0-06-136664-2(1)*, Tegen, Katherine Bks) HarperCollins Pubs.
Moseley, Tabitha. Pearl's Tales a Collection of Children's Stories. 2009. 92p. pap. 17.25 *(978-1-60860-670-2(8)*, Strategic Bk. Publishing) Strategic Book Publishing & Rights Agency (SBPRA).
Motto, Bernadine. The Adventures of Fluff the Bunny. 2007. 32p. per. 11.95 *(978-1-59800-908-8(7))* Outskirts Pr., Inc.
Mühle, Jörg. Bathtime for Little Rabbit. Mühle, Jörg, illus. 2017. (ENG., Illus.). 20p. (J). (gr. -1-k). bds. 9.99 ***(978-1-77657-137-6(1))*** Gecko Pr. NZL. Dist: Lerner Publishing Group.
Murray, Alison. Hare & Tortoise. Murray, Alison, illus. 2016. (ENG., Illus.). 32p. (J). (-k). 16.99 *(978-0-7636-8721-2(9))* Candlewick Pr.
Murray, Rosalie. Bobby & Bun Bun's Afternoon Adventure. Swope, Brenda, illus. 2012. 32p. pap. 24.95 *(978-1-4560-5090-0(7))* America Star Bks.
Murrow, Marjorie. The Surprise in Grandma's Eyes. 2009. (Illus.). 16p. pap. 10.98 *(978-1-4389-8104-8(X))* AuthorHouse.
Mussenbrock, Anne. Easter Notes. 2004. 12p. (J). (gr. -1-k). 5.99 *(978-1-59384-037-2(3))* Parklane Publishing.
My Big Book of Beginner Books about Me. 2011. (Beginner Books(R) Ser.). (ENG., Illus.). 208p. (J). (gr. -1-2). 16.99 *(978-0-307-93183-2(8)*, Random Hse. Bks. for Young Readers) Random Hse. Children's Bks.
Myers, Robin. Pinky Rabbit Learns to Share. 2008. 20p. pap. 24.95 *(978-1-60703-937-2(0))* America Star Bks.
Na, Il Sung. Snow Rabbit, Spring Rabbit: A Book of Changing Seasons. 2011. (ENG.). 24p. (J). (gr. -1-2). 15.99 *(978-0-375-86786-6(4)*, Knopf Bks. for Young Readers) Random Hse. Children's Bks.
Nahorniak, Mike. Kalico Jack. 2016. (ENG., Illus.). (J). 16.95 ***(978-1-5069-0333-0(9))***; pap. 14.95 ***(978-1-5069-0290-6(1))*** First Edition Design eBook Publishing.
Nass, Marcia Shoshana. The Rabbit Who Lost His Hop: A Story about Self-Control. Gilgannon-Collins, Denise, illus. 2004. (Early Prevention Ser.: 5). (J). per. 19.95 *(978-1-58815-061-5(5)*, 66525) Childswork/Childsplay.
Nathan, Sarah. Blue-Ribbon Bunny. 2014. (Sofia the First World of Reading Ser.). (J). lib. bdg. 13.55 *(978-0-606-35264-2(3))* Turtleback Bks.
Nathan, Sarah & Disney Book Group Staff. Blue Ribbon Bunny, Level 1. Disney Storybook Art Team, illus. 2014. (World of Reading Ser.). (ENG.). 32p. (J). (gr. -1-k). pap. 3.99 *(978-1-4231-7158-4(6))* Disney Pr.
Nelson, Sean. Bungles Does the Bunny Op. 2012. 36p. pap. 16.95 *(978-1-4575-1106-6(1))* Dog Ear Publishing, LLC.
—Bungles Loses His Marbles. 2008. 36p. pap. 16.95 *(978-1-59858-605-3(X))* Dog Ear Publishing, LLC.
Nelson, Steve & Rollins, Jack. Here Comes Peter Cottontail. Rasmussen, Wendy, illus. 2005. (ENG.). 20p. (J). bds. 9.95 *(978-0-8249-6573-0(6)*, Ideal Pubns.) Worthy Publishing.
—Here Comes Peter Cottontail! Levy, Pamela R., illus. 2011. 16p. (J). bds. 10.99 *(978-0-8249-1843-9(6))* 2007. (ENG.). 26p. (gr. -1-k). bds. 12.99 *(978-0-8249-6690-4(2))* Worthy Publishing. (Ideal Pubns.).
—Here Comes Peter Cottontail, Set. Levy, Pamela R., illus. 2007. (ENG.). 26p. 16.99 *(978-0-8249-6689-8(9)*, Ideal Pubns.) Worthy Publishing.
Neutzling, Laura. Grandpa Hugs, 1 vol. 2017. (ENG., Illus.). 20p. (J). bds. 9.99 *(978-0-7180-8940-5(5))* Nelson, Thomas Inc.
Newberry, Clare Turlay. Marshmallow. Newberry, Clare Turlay, illus. 2008. (ENG., Illus.). 32p. (J). (gr. -1-1). 16.99 *(978-0-06-072486-3(2))* HarperCollins Pubs.
Nicholas, Nicki. Spring Has Sprung for Peter & Lil. 2012. 24p. pap. 15.50 *(978-1-4669-2211-2(7))* Trafford Publishing.
Nicola A Green. Pumpkin: The easter Bunny. 2010. (Illus.). 48p. pap. *(978-1-907011-10-8(2))* Esteemworld Pubns.
Niddrie, June. E. B. & the Bees. 2010. 32p. pap. 16.10 *(978-0-557-31873-5(4))* Lulu Pr., Inc.
Nieting, Sherry. Adventures in Hope Forest: Isabelle's Search for God. 2011. 24p. pap. 10.95 *(978-1-4497-2518-1(X)*, WestBow Pr.) Author Solutions, Inc.
Nolan, Allia Zobel. When God Tucks in the Day. Chung, Chi, illus. 2005. 16p. (J). 12.99 *(978-0-8254-5524-7(3))* Kregel Pubns.
Noruziaan, Bahman. The Lonely Snake: Stories of Inspector Rabbit. 2013. 20p. pap. 13.77 *(978-1-4669-8678-7(6))* Trafford Publishing.
Nosy Crow Staff. Cutie Pie Looks for the Easter Bunny: A Tiny Tab Book. Ho, Jannie, illus. 2015. (Tiny Tab Ser.). (ENG.). 8p. (J). (— 1). bds. 7.99 *(978-0-7636-7599-8(7)*, Nosy Crow) Candlewick Pr.
—Hush-A-Bye Bunny. Surplice, Holly, illus. 2017. (ENG.). 16p. (J). (-k). bds. 8.99 *(978-0-7636-9459-3(2)*, Nosy Crow) Candlewick Pr.
—Pip & Posy: the Little Puddle. Scheffler, Axel, illus. 2011. (Pip & Posy Ser.). (ENG.). 32p. (J). (gr. k-k). 12.99 *(978-0-7636-5878-6(2)*, Nosy Crow) Candlewick Pr.
—Pip & Posy: the New Friend. Scheffler, Axel, illus. 2017. (Pip & Posy Ser.). (ENG.). 32p. (J). (-k). 12.99 *(978-0-7636-9339-8(1)*, Nosy Crow) Candlewick Pr.
—Pip & Posy: the Super Scooter. Scheffler, Axel, illus. 2011. (Pip & Posy Ser.). (ENG.). 32p. (J). (gr. k-k). 12.99 *(978-0-7636-5877-9(4)*, Nosy Crow) Candlewick Pr.
Nyeu, Tao. Bunny Days. Nyeu, Tao, illus. 2010. (ENG., Illus.). 48p. (J). (gr. -1-k). 16.99 *(978-0-8037-3330-5(5)*, Dial Bks) Penguin Young Readers Group.
O'Byrne, Nicola. Use Your Imagination. O'Byrne, Nicola, illus. 2015. (ENG., Illus.). 36p. (J). (gr. -1-2). 15.99 *(978-0-7636-8001-5(X)*, Nosy Crow) Candlewick Pr.
O'connor, Jane. Fancy Nancy & the Missing Easter Bunny. 2017. (Fancy Nancy Picture Bks.). (J). lib. bdg. 14.75 ***(978-0-606-39618-9(7))*** Turtleback Bks.
Odierno, Lisa. Bunny Hide-and-Seek. 2009. (Smithsonian Baby Animals Ser.). (ENG., Illus.). 16p. (J). (gr. -1-k). 6.95 *(978-1-60727-092-8(7))* Soundprints.
Odierno, Lisa & Soundprints Staff. Bunny Hide-and-Seek. 2009. (Smithsonian Baby Animals Ser.). (ENG., Illus.). 16p. (J). (gr. -1-k). 6.95 *(978-1-60727-105-5(2))* Soundprints.
Ojo, Loyce. Bath Time. 2015. (ENG.). 35p. (J). mass mkt. 13.95 *(978-1-78554-304-3(0)*, 9fd86c2b-11cf-4b00-9409-3a9c56e1bdc5) Austin, Stan AUS. Dist: Bookmasters Distribution.
Olson, Jennifer Gray. Ninja Bunny. 2015. (ENG., Illus.). 32p. (J). (gr. -1-2). 16.99 *(978-0-385-75493-4(0)*, Knopf Bks. for Young Readers) Random Hse. Children's Bks.
—Ninja Bunny: Sister vs. Brother. 2016. (ENG., Illus.). 32p. (J). (gr. -1-2). 16.99 *(978-0-399-55074-4(7)*, Knopf Bks. for Young Readers) Random Hse. Children's Bks.
O'Neill, Rachael. Do You Want a Hug, Honey Bunny? O'Neill, Rachael, illus. 2008. (Tiger Tales Ser.). (Illus.). 12p. (J). (gr. -1-k). 8.95 *(978-1-58925-829-7(0))* Tiger Tales.
Osborn, Valerie Huffman. A Week of Bunnies. Osborn, Kimberly, ed. 2007. (ENG., Illus.). 32p. (J). 19.95 *(978-1-932278-25-5(7))* Mayhaven Publishing, Inc.
Osborne, Amber & Osborne, Dwight. Puffy Buffy Jones Jones Osborne Dadoot Da Do. Osborne, Amber, illus. 2006. (Illus.). (J). pap. 11.99 *(978-0-9786431-0-2(0))* AAO Publishing.

O'Toole-Freel, Judy. Zigzag the Rocking Roadrunner. Freel, Mirle, illus. 2012. 40p. 24.95 (978-1-4626-9970-4(7)) America Star Bks.

Ouchley, Amy Griffin. Swamper: Letters from a Louisiana Swamp Rabbit. 2013. (ENG., Illus.). 72p. (gr. 4-7). 22.50 (978-0-8071-5074-0(6), 9780807150740) Louisiana State Univ. Pr.

Oud, Pauline. Christmas with Lily & Milo. 2012. (Clavis Toddler: Language Development Ser.). (ENG.). 30p. (J). (gr. k — 1). 12.95 (978-1-60537-128-3(9)) Cobblestone Publishing Co.

—Eating with Lily & Milo. Oud, Pauline, illus. 2010. (Lily & Milo Ser.). (ENG., Illus.). 30p. (J). (gr. k — 1). 12.95 (978-1-60537-055-2(X)) Cobblestone Publishing Co.

—Getting Dressed with Lily & Milo. Oud, Pauline, illus. 2010. (Lily & Milo Ser.). (ENG., Illus.). 30p. (J). (gr. k — 1). 12.95 (978-1-60537-060-6(6)) Cobblestone Publishing Co.

—Going to the Beach with Lily & Milo. Oud, Pauline, illus. 2011. (Lily & Milo Ser.). (ENG., Illus.). 28p. (J). (gr. k — 1). 12.95 (978-1-60537-094-1(0)) Cobblestone Publishing Co.

—Going to the Zoo with Lily & Milo. Oud, Pauline, illus. 2011. (Lily & Milo Ser.). (ENG., Illus.). 28p. (J). (gr. k — 1). 12.95 (978-1-60537-093-4(2)) Cobblestone Publishing Co.

—Having a Party with Lily & Milo. Oud, Pauline, illus. 2012. (Clavis Toddler: Skills Ser.). (ENG., Illus.). 24p. (J). (— 1). 12.95 (978-1-60537-129-0(7)) Cobblestone Publishing Co.

Overington, Marcus. Lost on Bodmin Moor. 2012. (Illus.). 50p. pap. (978-1-909039-36-0(5)) Legend Pr.

The Package: KinderConcepts Individual Title Six-Packs. (Kinderstarters Ser.). 8p. (gr. -1-1). 21.00 (978-0-7635-8737-6(0)) Rigby Education.

Pagnoni, Roberta, illus. It's Easter Time. 2010. (ENG.). 10p. (J). (gr. -1-k). bds. 6.99 (978-0-7641-6334-0(5)) Barron's Educational Series, Inc.

Palatini, Margie. Goldie & the Three Hares. Davis, Jack E., illus. 2011. (ENG.). 32p. (J). (gr. -1-2). 16.99 (978-0-06-125314-0(6), Tegen, Katherine Bks) HarperCollins Pubs.

Pankiw, Mary. Ruffles Rabbit. 2013. 52p. pap. 19.39 (978-1-4669-7572-9(5)) Trafford Publishing.

Pappas, Peter. Stu the Rabbit. 2007. (J). (978-0-9801439-3-5(4)) Town & Country Reprographics.

Paquette, Ammi-Joan. Bunny Bus. Withrow, Lesley Breen, illus. 2017. (ENG.). 32p. (J). 16.99 (978-0-374-30225-2(1), 9780374302252, Farrar, Straus & Giroux (BYR)) Farrar, Straus & Giroux.

Parasciuc, Natalia. Beaverlini & Rodney Are Having Fun! 2011. 28p. pap. 12.99 (978-0-557-84882-9(2)) Lulu Pr., Inc.

Park, Barbara. Dumb Bunny. Brunkus, Denise, illus. 2007. (Junie B. Jones Ser.: No. 11). (ENG.). 128p. (J). (gr. 1-4). lib. bdg. 14.99 (978-0-375-93809-2(5), Random Hse. Bks. for Young Readers) Random Hse. Children's Bks.

Parker, Emma. Mr Grumpy Bunny. 2010. (Illus.). pap. (978-1-877561-22-1(3)) First Edition Ltd.

Parker, Vic, compiled by. The Fish & the Hare & Other Silly Stories. 2016. (Silly Stories Ser.). (ENG.). 40p. (J). (gr. 2-3). pap. 14.05 (978-1-4824-4199-4(3)) Stevens, Gareth Publishing LLLP.

—The Hare-Brained Crocodiles & Other Silly Stories. 2016. (Silly Stories Ser.). (ENG.). 40p. (J). (gr. 2-3). pap. 14.05 (978-1-4824-4202-1(7)) Stevens, Gareth Publishing LLLP.

Parunia, Des. The Quest for the Magic Funnel. 2012. (Illus.). 196p. (gr. 4-6). pap. 18.24 (978-1-4772-3508-9(6)) AuthorHouse.

Paul, Ann Whitford. Fiesta Fiasco. Long, Ethan, illus. 2009. (ENG.). 32p. (J). (gr. -1-2). pap. 6.95 (978-0-8234-2275-3(5)) Holiday Hse., Inc.

—Fiesta Fiasco. Long, Ethan, illus. 2012. pap. 18.95 (978-1-4301-1099-6(6)) Live Oak Media.

Paul, Dwain. The Fox the Hare the Wolf & the Sheep. 2011. 28p. 16.10 (978-1-4269-5573-0(1)) Trafford Publishing.

Payton-Wright, Kaye. The Secret Wood. 2010. 28p. pap. 21.99 (978-1-4535-0321-8(8)) Xlibris Corp.

PC Treasures Staff, prod. Peter Rabbit. 2007. (J). (978-1-60072-021-5(8)) PC Treasures, Inc.

Penguin Young Readers. I Am Lily. 2013. (Peter Rabbit Animation Ser.). (ENG.). 32p. (J). (gr. 1-3). 14.99 (978-0-7232-8083-5(5)); pap. 3.99 (978-0-7232-8074-3(6)) Penguin Young Readers Group. (Penguin Young Readers).

Penguin Young Readers Group Staff. I Am Peter. 2014. (Peter Rabbit Animation Ser.). (ENG.). 32p. (J). (gr. 1-3). pap. 3.99 (978-0-14-135006-6(7), Penguin Young Readers) Penguin Young Readers Group.

Perkins, Larry B. Jasper Rabbit. 2005. 33p. per. 8.95 (978-1-4116-1936-4(6)) Lulu Pr., Inc.

Peter Rabbit Books 800845, 3. 2005. (J). (978-1-59794-046-7(1)) Environments, Inc.

Peters, Andrew Fusek. Rabbit Cooks up a Cunning Plan! Robert, Bruno, illus. 2007. (Traditional Tales with a Twist Ser.). (ENG.). 32p. (J). (gr. 2-2). pap. (978-1-84643-097-8(6)) Child's Play International Ltd.

Petersen, David. Snowy Valentine. Petersen, David, illus. 2011. (ENG., Illus.). 32p. (J). (gr. -1-3). 14.99 (978-0-06-146378-5(7)) HarperCollins Pubs.

Petreman, Gwen. Caught by Rabroar. 2012. 20p. pap. 11.59 (978-1-4669-5098-6(6)) Trafford Publishing.

Pevear, Ted F. & Pevear, Linda W. Finding Little Feathers a Hub-A-Son. 2012. 24p. 24.95 (978-1-4626-5874-9(1)) America Star Bks.

Phillips, Dee & Ticktock Media, Ltd. Staff. What Do Rabbits Do? 2009. (What Do Animals Do? Ser.). (ENG.). 5p. (J). (gr. k — 1). bds. 4.95 (978-1-84696-961-4(1), TickTock Books) Octopus Publishing Group GBR. Dist: Independent Pubs. Group.

Pilkey, Dav. The Dumb Bunnies. 2007. (Dumb Bunnies Ser.). (ENG., Illus.). 32p. (J). (gr. -1-3). 12.99 (978-0-545-03938-3(X), Levine, Arthur A. Bks.) Scholastic, Inc.

—The Dumb Bunnies' Easter. 2008. (Dumb Bunnies Ser.). (ENG., Illus.). 32p. (J). (gr. -1-3). pap. 6.99 (978-0-545-00880-8(8), Scholastic Paperbacks) Scholastic, Inc.

—Dumb Bunnies' Easter. Pilkey, Dav, illus. 2009. (Dumb Bunnies Ser.). (ENG., Illus.). 32p. (J). (gr. -1-3). 16.99 (978-0-545-03946-8(0)) Scholastic, Inc.

—The Dumb Bunnies Go to the Zoo. (Dumb Bunnies Ser.). (ENG.). 32p. 2009. (J). (gr. -1-3). 16.99 (978-0-545-03937-6(1)) 2007. pap. 5.99 (978-0-439-93049-9(9)) Scholastic, Inc.

—Make Way for Dumb Bunnies. 2007. (Dumb Bunnies Ser.). (ENG., Illus.). 32p. (J). (gr. -1-3). 10.99 (978-0-545-03939-0(8), Levine, Arthur A. Bks.) Scholastic, Inc.

Pinkney, Jerry. The Tortoise & the Hare. 2013. (ENG., Illus.). 40p. (J). (gr. -1-3). 18.00 (978-0-316-18356-7(3)) Little, Brown Bks. for Young Readers.

Pinkwater, Daniel M. Bear & Bunny. Hillenbrand, Will, illus. 2015. (ENG.). 40p. (J). 15.99 (978-0-7636-7153-2(3)) Candlewick Pr.

—Bear in Love. Hillenbrand, Will, illus. 2012. (ENG.). 40p. (J). (gr. k-k). 15.99 (978-0-7636-4569-4(9)) Candlewick Pr.

Pledger, Maurice. Billy Bunny & the Butterflies. 2013. (ENG., Illus.). 16p. (J). bds. 10.95 (978-1-60710-808-5(9), Silver Dolphin Bks.) Readerlink Distribution Services, LLC.

Poehler, S. Applecheeks & the Pop E. Tree. 2012. 12p. pap. 15.99 (978-1-4772-8180-2(0)) AuthorHouse.

Ponti, Claude. En El Coche. 2003. (SPA.). 32p. 15.95 (978-84-95150-08-0(5)) Corimbo, Editorial S.L. ESP. Dist: Distribooks, Inc.

Por que el conejo tiene las orejas tan Largas? Lap Book. (Pebble Soup Exploraciones Ser.). (SPA.). 16p. (gr. -1-18). 21.00 (978-0-7578-1691-8(6)) Rigby Education.

Por que el conejo tiene las orejas tan Largas? Small Book. (Pebble Soup Exploraciones Ser.). (SPA.). 16p. (gr. -1-18). 5.00 (978-0-7578-1731-1(9)) Rigby Education.

Por que los conejos tienen las orejas Largas: Individual Title Six-Packs. (Literatura 2000 Ser.). (SPA.). (gr. 2-3). 33.00 (978-0-7635-1271-2(0)) Rigby Education.

Portis, Antoinette. Not a Box. Portis, Antoinette, illus. 2006. (Illus.). 32p. (J). (gr. -1 — 1). (ENG.). 15.99 (978-0-06-112322-1(6)); lib. bdg. 14.89 (978-0-06-112323-8(4)) HarperCollins Pubs.

—Not a Box Board Book. Portis, Antoinette, illus. 2011. (ENG., Illus.). 28p. (J). (gr. -1 — 1). bds. 7.99 (978-0-06-199442-5(1), HarperFestival) HarperCollins Pubs.

Posey, Lee. Night Rabbits, 1 vol. Montgomery, Michael, illus. 2007. (ENG.). 32p. (J). (gr. k-3). 7.95 (978-1-56145-397-9(8)) Peachtree Pubs.

Posey, Sandra Mizumoto. Rabbits with Stars in their Eyes. 2010. 32p. pap. 15.00 (978-0-557-12242-4(2)) Lulu Pr., Inc.

Posner-Sanchez, Andrea. Bunny Magic! (Disney Junior: Sofia the First) RH Disney Staff, illus. 2014. (Little Golden Book Ser.). (ENG.). 24p. (J). (-k). 4.99 (978-0-7364-3085-2(7), Golden/Disney) Random Hse. Children's Bks.

Posner, Tina. Rabbit Tricks. Corbett, Liza, illus. 2006. 8p. (J). pap. (978-0-439-73513-1(0)) Scholastic, Inc.

Potter, Beatrix. A Beatrix Potter Treasury. 2007. (Peter Rabbit Ser.). (ENG., Illus.). 192p. (J). (gr. -1-2). 19.99 (978-0-7232-5957-2(7), Warne) Penguin Young Readers Group.

—The Classic Tale of Peter Rabbit: And Other Cherished Stories. Santore, Charles, illus. 2013. (ENG.). 68p. (J). 19.95 (978-1-60433-376-3(6), Applesauce Pr.) Cider Mill Pr. Bk. Pubs., LLC.

—The Classic Tale of the Flopsy Bunnies. Santore, Charles, illus. 2015. (ENG.). 22p. (J). bds. 8.95 (978-1-60433-551-4(3), Applesauce Pr.) Cider Mill Pr. Bk. Pubs., LLC.

—Cuento - Perico el Conejo. Orig. Title: Tale of Peter Rabbit. (SPA.). 60p. (J). 8.95 (978-84-7444-725-5(9)) Debate, Editorial ESP. Dist: AIMS International Bks., Inc.

—El Gato Tomas. 2003. (Coleccion el Mundo de Peter Rabbit). (SPA., Illus.). (J). (gr. k-2). pap. (978-950-07-1722-9(0), SA30685) Editorial Sudamericana S.A. ARG. Dist: Lectorum Pubns., Inc.

—Jeremias el Pescador. 2003. (Coleccion el Mundo de Peter Rabbit). (SPA., Illus.). (J). (gr. k-2). pap. (978-950-07-1721-2(2), SA30686) Editorial Sudamericana S.A. ARG. Dist: Lectorum Pubns., Inc.

—Munch! 2009. (Peter Rabbit Naturally Better Ser.). (ENG.). 10p. (J). (gr. -1 — 1). bds. 7.99 (978-0-7232-6390-6(6), Warne) Penguin Young Readers Group.

—Mystery Thief! 2013. (Peter Rabbit Animation Ser.). (ENG.). 32p. (J). (gr. -1-k). 3.99 (978-0-7232-8041-5(X), Warne) Penguin Young Readers Group.

—La Oca Carlota. 2003. (Coleccion el Mundo de Peter Rabbit). (SPA., Illus.). (J). (gr. k-2). pap. (978-950-07-1723-6(9), SA30687) Editorial Sudamericana S.A. ARG. Dist: Lectorum Pubns., Inc.

—Peekaboo! 2009. (Peter Rabbit Naturally Better Ser.). (ENG.). 10p. (J). (gr. -1 — 1). bds. 6.99 (978-0-7232-6350-0(7), Warne) Penguin Young Readers Group.

—Peter & Friends Sticker Activity Book. 2013. (Peter Rabbit Animation Ser.). (ENG., Illus.). 16p. (J). (gr. -1-2). pap. 6.99 (978-0-7232-8042-2(8), Warne) Penguin Young Readers Group.

—Peter Rabbit. Britt, Stephanie McFetridge, illus. 2006. (ENG.). 32p. (J). (gr. -1-3). pap. 3.95 (978-0-8249-5533-5(1), Ideal Pubns.) Worthy Publishing.

—The Peter Rabbit & Friends Treasury. Potter, Beatrix, illus. 2006. (Illus.). 240p. (J). (gr. k-4). reprint ed. 20.00 (978-1-4223-5452-0(0)) DIANE Publishing Co.

—Peter Rabbit Book & Toy. 2006. (Peter Rabbit Ser.). (ENG., Illus.). 70p. (J). (gr. -1 — 1). 16.99 (978-0-7232-5356-3(0), Warne) Penguin Young Readers Group.

—Peter Rabbit Lift-the-Flap Words, Colors, & Numbers. 2007. (Potter Ser.). (ENG., Illus.). 12p. (J). (gr. -1-18). 14.99 (978-0-7232-5828-5(7), Warne) Penguin Publishing Group.

—Sgeulachd Bheniamin Coineanach. MacDonald, James, 1st, tr. from ENG. Potter, Beatrix, illus. 2008.Tr. of Tale of Benjamin Bunny. (GAE., Illus.). 64p. (J). (978-0-9552326-4-0(3)) Grace Note Pubns.

—The Story of Peter Rabbit. McCue, Lisa, illus. 2005. (Easter Ornament Bks.). (ENG.). 20p. (J). (gr. -1-1). 10.99 (978-0-7944-0527-4(4), Reader's Digest Children's Bks.) Studio Fun International.

—The Tale of Benjamin Bunny. Rasmussen, Wendy, illus. 2009. (Classic Tales by Beatrix Potter Ser.). (ENG.). 24p. (J). (gr. k-3). 28.50 (978-1-60253-292-2(3), 200118) Child's World, Inc., The.

—The Tale of Benjamin Bunny. 2007. (Illus.). 60p. per. (978-1-4065-5873-9(7)) Dodo Pr.

—The Tale of Benjamin Bunny. 2007. 60p. per. 16.95 (978-0-548-80107-9(X)) Kessinger Publishing, LLC.

—The Tale of Benjamin Bunny. 2012. (Peter Rabbit Ser.). (ENG.). (J). 32p. (gr. -1-2). mass mkt. 3.99 (978-0-7232-6836-9(3), Warne); 32p. (gr. 1-2). pap. 3.99 (978-0-7232-6814-7(2), Penguin Young Readers); 110th ed. (Illus.). 64p. (gr. -1-2). 6.99 (978-0-7232-6773-7(1), Warne) Penguin Young Readers Group.

—The Tale of Benjamin Bunny. (Illus.). 12p. 4.95 (978-1-58989-272-9(0)) Thurman Hse., LLC.

—The Tale of Peter Rabbit. 2013. 30p. pap. 12.00 (978-1-927558-35-5(2)) 2012. 26p. pap. 12.00 (978-0-9880821-2-0(8)) Birch Tree Publishing.

—The Tale of Peter Rabbit. Rasmussen, Wendy, illus. 2009. (Classic Tales by Beatrix Potter Ser.). (ENG.). 24p. (J). (gr. k-3). 28.50 (978-1-60253-295-3(8), 200121) Child's World, Inc., The.

—The Tale of Peter Rabbit. 2010. (ENG.). 30p. pap. 9.49 (978-1-4538-2670-6(X)) CreateSpace Independent Publishing Platform.

—The Tale of Peter Rabbit. Hague, Michael, illus. 2003. 29p. (J). (gr. 2-5). reprint ed. 16.00 (978-0-7567-6968-0(X)) DIANE Publishing Co.

—The Tale of Peter Rabbit, 5 vols. 110th ed. 2012. (Peter Rabbit Ser.). (ENG., Illus.). 72p. (J). (gr. -1-2). 6.99 (978-0-7232-6769-0(3), Warne) Penguin Young Readers Group.

—The Tale of Peter Rabbit. McPhail, David, illus. 2014. (ENG.). 28p. (J). (gr. -1 — 1). bds. 6.99 (978-0-545-65096-0(8), Cartwheel Bks.) Scholastic, Inc.

—The Tale of Peter Rabbit, 1 vol. Jorgensen, David, illus. 2007. (Rabbit Ears: A Classic Tale Ser.). (ENG.). 36p. (gr. -1-3). 25.65 (978-1-59961-313-0(1)) Spotlight.

—The Tale of Peter Rabbit. (Illus.). 12p. 4.95 (978-1-58989-271-2(2)) Thurman Hse., LLC.

—The Tale of Peter Rabbit. 2012. (Penguin Young Readers Level 2 Ser.). lib. bdg. 13.55 (978-0-606-23629-4(5), Turtleback) Turtleback Bks.

—The Tale of the Flopsy Bunnies. Rasmussen, Wendy, illus. 2009. (Classic Tales by Beatrix Potter Ser.). (ENG.). 24p. (J). (gr. k-3). 28.50 (978-1-60253-297-7(4), 200123) Child's World, Inc., The.

—The Tale of the Flopsy Bunnies. 2012. (Peter Rabbit Ser.). (ENG.). 58p. (J). (gr. -1-2). mass mkt. 3.99 (978-0-7232-6837-6(1), Warne) Penguin Young Readers Group.

—Tickle, Tickle, Peter! 2012. (Peter Rabbit Ser.). (ENG.). 10p. (J). (gr. -1-k). bds. 9.99 (978-0-7232-6750-8(2), Warne) Penguin Young Readers Group.

Potter, Beatrix, illus. The Tale of Peter Rabbit. 2014. (J). pap. (978-1-4677-5772-0(1), First Avenue Editions) Lerner Publishing Group.

Powell, Christine. Bootsie's Underground Adventure. 2012. 28p. pap. 24.95 (978-1-4626-7449-7(6)) America Star Bks.

Powell, Richard. Becky Bunny. Rhodes, Katie, illus. 2004. (Fuzzy Friends Ser.). 10p. (J). 7.95 (978-1-58925-723-8(5)) Tiger Tales.

Powers-Fish, Amy Rose. Ethics 4 Every Bunny. 2012. 78p. pap. 34.77 (978-1-105-50495-2(6)) Lulu Pr., Inc.

Poydar, Nancy. Bunny Business. 2003. (ENG., Illus.). 32p. (J). (gr. k-3). tchr. ed. 16.95 (978-0-8234-1771-1(9)) Holiday Hse., Inc.

Prasadam-halls, Smriti. I Love You Night & Day. Brown, Alison, illus. 2014. (ENG.). 32p. (J). (gr. -1-1). 16.99 (978-1-61963-222-6(5), 9781619632226, Bloomsbury USA Childrens) Bloomsbury Publishing USA.

Price, Mathew. Polo y Los Conejos. (SPA.). pap. 7.95 (978-950-07-1978-0(9)) Editorial Sudamericana S.A. ARG. Dist: Distribooks, Inc.

Priddy, Roger. Hide & Seek Bunnies. 2015. (Lift-The-Flap Tab Bks.). (ENG., Illus.). 16p. (J). (gr. -1 — 1). bds. 8.99 (978-0-312-51784-7(X), 9780312517847, Priddy Bks.) St. Martin's Pr.

—Little Friends: Let's Play. 2014. (Little Friends Ser.). (ENG., Illus.). 8p. (J). (gr. -1 — 1). bds. 8.99 (978-0-312-51683-3(5), 9780312516833, Priddy Bks.) St. Martin's Pr.

Prignano, Barbara. How Bunnies Got Their Cottontails. 2009. (Illus.). 20p. pap. 11.95 (978-1-60860-675-7(9), Eloquent Bks.) Strategic Book Publishing & Rights Agency (SBPRA).

Principe, Tami. The Green Rabbit: Rabbits Aren't Supposed to Be Green! 2012. 32p. pap. 10.95 (978-1-4626-7509-8(3)) America Star Bks.

Publications International Ltd. Staff, ed. Disney Bunnies. 2009. 16p. (J). bds. 9.98 (978-1-4127-1721-2(3), PIL Kids) Publications International, Ltd.

—Disney(r) Sofia the FirstShow-And-Tell Surprise. 2015. 8p. (J). bds. (978-1-4508-7560-8(2), 1450875602) Publications International, Ltd.

Puglisi, Salvatore. It's best to be Me. 2008. (ENG.). 36p. pap. 14.99 (978-1-4196-8330-5(6)) CreateSpace Independent Publishing Platform.

Pyne, Jane. Tommy's Secret. 2009. 86p. pap. 10.49 (978-1-4389-9102-3(9)) AuthorHouse.

Rabbit's Spring Adventure. 2012. (Illus.). (J). (978-1-4351-4584-9(4)) Barnes & Noble, Inc.

Rabe, Tish. Thump!/The Lost Egg (Cat in the Hat/Seuss) Ruiz, Aristides & Mathieu, Joe, illus. 2013. (Pictureback(R) Ser.). (ENG.). 32p. (J). (gr. -1-2). pap. 4.99 (978-0-307-98063-2(4), Random Hse. Bks. for Young Readers) Random Hse. Children's Bks.

Rabe, Tish & Yaccarino, Dan. Five Little Bunnies. Yaccarino, Dan, illus. 2016. (Illus.). 16p. (J). (gr. -1 — 1). bds. 6.99 (978-0-06-225339-2(5)) HarperCollins Pubs.

Ralph the Rabbit. 2003. (Chunky Animal Shaped Boards Ser.). (J). 10p. bds. 9.95 (978-0-7525-7855-2(3)); (Illus.). bds. 1.98 (978-0-7525-7776-0(X)) Parragon, Inc.

Ramsey, Byra L. Little Stick. 2009. 28p. pap. 13.99 (978-1-4490-3371-2(7)) AuthorHouse.

Rand, Betseygail & Rand, Colleen. Big Bunny. Rand, Colleen, illus. 2011. (ENG., Illus.). 32p. (J). (gr. -1-2). 14.99 (978-1-58246-376-6(X), Tricycle Pr.) Random Hse. Children's Bks.

Rand, Johnathan. Freddie Fernortner #9: Attack of the Dust Bunnies from Outer Space. 2008. 96p. (J). pap. 4.99 (978-1-893699-95-3(1)) AudioCraft Publishing, Inc.

Random House. My First Pet (Barbie) 2016. (Pictureback(R) Ser.). (ENG., Illus.). 16p. (J). (gr. -1-2). 4.99 (978-1-101-93729-7(7), Random Hse. Bks. for Young Readers) Random Hse. Children's Bks.

Random House Disney Staff. Big Trouble in Little Rodentia. Random House Disney Staff, illus. 2016. (Pictureback(R) Ser.). (ENG., Illus.). 24p. (J). (gr. -1-2). 4.99 (978-0-7364-3531-4(X), RH/Disney) Random Hse. Children's Bks.

Random House Staff. Dora's Easter Bunny Adventure (Dora the Explorer) Random House Staff, illus. 2013. (Pictureback(R) Ser.). (ENG., Illus.). 16p. (J). (gr. -1-2). pap. 3.99 (978-0-449-81442-0(4), Random Hse. Bks. for Young Readers) Random Hse. Children's Bks.

Raschka, Chris. Five for a Little One. Raschka, Chris, illus. 2006. (ENG., Illus.). 48p. (J). (gr. -1-2). 17.99 (978-0-689-84599-4(5), Atheneum/Richard Jackson Bks.) Simon & Schuster Children's Publishing.

Rath, Tom H. Donkey Oatie's Field Trip. Gaudet, Christine, illus. 2013. 26p. pap. (978-0-9918033-4-7(5)) Wood Islands Prints.

Rawlinson, Julia & Warnes, Tim. A Surprise for Rosie. 2005. (Illus.). 32p. (J). 15.95 (978-1-58925-046-8(X)) Tiger Tales.

Reader's Digest Staff. Busy Day Bunnies: A Carry along Treasury. McCue, Lisa, illus. 2011. (Carry along Bks.). (ENG.). 20p. (J). (gr. -1-k). 14.99 (978-0-7944-2168-7(7)) Reader's Digest Assn., Inc., The.

Reasoner, Charles, illus. Honey Bunny. 2015. (J). (978-1-4795-5945-9(8)) Picture Window Bks.

Redbank, Tennant. The Kitchen Catastrophe. The Disney Storybook Art Team & Batson, Alan, illus. 2016. (Disney Chapters Ser.). (ENG.). 64p. (J). (gr. 1-4). 5.99 (978-0-7364-3643-4(X), RH/Disney) Random Hse. Children's Bks.

Reitze, Glenn Logan. Ernie the Easter Hippopotamus: A Comic Adventure for Anytime. Reitze, Glenn Logan, illus. 2007. (ENG., Illus.). 48p. (J). lib. bdg. 19.95 (978-0-88265-040-1(8), Fine Art Editions) North American International.

Reitze, Glenn Logan, illus. & text. Ernie the Easter Hippotamus: A Comic Adventure for Anytime. Reitze, Glenn Logan, text. 2007. (J). pap. (978-0-88265-041-8(6)) North American International.

Renoult, Armelle. Basil Becomes a Big Brother. Frossard, Claire, illus. 2012. (My Little Picture Book Ser.). (ENG.). 32p. (J). (gr. -1). 6.95 (978-2-7338-2143-5(1)) Auzou, Philippe Editions FRA. Dist: Consortium Bk. Sales & Distribution.

Rey, H. A. & Rey, Margret. Jorge el Curioso Vuela Una Cometa. 2012. (Curious George Ser.). (ENG & SPA., Illus.). 80p. (J). (gr. -1-3). pap. 7.99 (978-0-547-69162-6(9)) Houghton Mifflin Harcourt Publishing Co.

Reynolds, Aaron. Creepy Carrots! Brown, Peter, illus. 2012. (ENG.). 40p. (J). (gr. -1-3). 17.99 (978-1-4424-0297-3(0), Simon & Schuster Bks. For Young Readers) Simon & Schuster Bks. For Young Readers.

—Creepy Pair of Underwear! Brown, Peter, illus. 2017. (ENG.). 48p. (J). (gr. -1-3). 17.99 (978-1-4424-0298-0(9), Simon & Schuster Bks. For Young Readers) Simon & Schuster Bks. For Young Readers.

—Las Zanahorias Maléficas. 2015.Tr. of Creepy Carrots. (SPA.). 40p. (J). (gr. k-3). 24.95 (978-84-16117-13-0(6)) Ediciones Obelisco ESP. Dist: Spanish Pubs., LLC.

Rhae, Sympne. My Name Is Johnson? l.t. ed. 2006. (Illus.). 53p. (J). per. 13.75 (978-0-9770043-9-3(2)) New Global Publishing.

Rice, Dona Herwick. The Tortoise & the Hare, 1 vol. 2008. (Building Fluency Through Reader's Theater Ser.). (ENG.). 24p. (J). (gr. 1-3). pap. 6.99 (978-1-4333-0290-9(X)) Teacher Created Materials, Inc.

Richard, Ramonda. Robert the Bully. 2012. 28p. pap. 24.95 (978-1-4626-7170-0(5)) America Star Bks.

Richards, Kitty & Disney Book Group Staff. Goodnight, Thumper! Tyminski, Lori & Gordon, Dean, illus. 2007. (ENG.). 16p. (J). (gr. -1-k). bds. 5.99 (978-1-4231-0077-5(8)) Disney Pr.

Rigby Education Staff. A Class Pet. (Illus.). 8p. (J). bds. 6.95 (978-0-7635-6439-1(7), 764397C99) Rigby Education.

Rigo, L., illus. Little Bunny. 2012. (Mini Look at Me Bks.). (ENG.). 10p. (J). bds. 4.99 (978-0-7641-6509-2(7)) Barron's Educational Series, Inc.

Risom, Ole. I Am a Bunny. Scarry, Richard, illus. 2004. (Golden Sturdy Book Ser.). (ENG.). 26p. (J). (gr. k — 1). bds. 7.99 (978-0-375-82778-5(1), Golden Bks.) Random Hse. Children's Bks.

Ritchie, Alison. The Tortoise & the Hare. Noj, Nahta, illus. 2015. (ENG.). 32p. (J). (-k). 15.99 (978-0-7636-7601-8(2), Templar) Candlewick Pr.

Ritchie, Joseph R. Peter Cottontail's Busy Day. Halverson, Lydia, illus. (J). 2009. 14p. (gr. -1-k). bds. 6.99 (978-0-8249-1842-2(8)) 2006. (ENG.). 26p. (gr. -1-k). 12.95 (978-0-8249-6652-2(X)) 2005. (ENG.). 16p. bds. 9.95 (978-0-8249-6571-6(X)) Worthy Publishing. (Ideal Pubns.).

—Peter Cottontail's Easter Egg Hunt. Thornburgh, Rebecca McKillip, illus. (J). 2012. 14p. bds. 6.99 (978-0-8249-1880-4(0)) 2004. (ENG.). 12p. (gr. -1-k). bds. 9.95 (978-0-8249-6522-8(1)) Worthy Publishing. (Ideal Pubns.).

—Peter Cottontail's Easter Surprise. Halverson, Lydia, illus. 2006. (ENG.). 18p. (J). (gr. -1-k). bds. 9.95 (978-0-8249-6627-0(9), Ideal Pubns.) Worthy Publishing.

Rivers-Moore, Debbie. Little Bunny's Butterflies. Fox, Lisa, illus. 2012. (Springtime Shakers Ser.). (ENG.). 8p. (J). bds. 5.99 (978-0-7641-6488-0(0)) Barron's Educational Series, Inc.

Robe, Adam D. Moving to Another Foster Home. Robe, Kim A., ed. Gavet, Nathalie, illus. 2009. 16p. pap. 11.99 (978-0-9817403-4-8(0)) Robe Communications, Inc.

—Robbie's Trail Through Adoption. Robe, Kim A., ed. Gavet, Nathalie, illus. 2010. 44p. pap. 23.99 (978-1-935831-03-7(8)) Robe Communications, Inc.

—Robbie's Trail Through Adoption — Activity Book. Robe, Kim A., ed. Gavet, Nathalie, illus. 2010. 36p. pap. 16.99 (978-1-935831-04-4(6)) Robe Communications, Inc.

—Robbie's Trail Through Adoption — Adult Guide. Robe, Kim A., ed. Gavet, Nathalie, illus. 2010. 28p. pap. 16.99 (978-1-935831-05-1(4)) Robe Communications, Inc.

—Robbie's Trail Through Foster Care. Robe, Kim A., ed. Gavet, Nathalie, illus. 2010. 40p. pap. 23.99 (978-1-935831-00-6(3)) Robe Communications, Inc.

—Robbie's Trail Through Foster Care — Activity Book. Robe, Kim A., ed. Gavet, Nathalie, illus. 2010. 36p. pap. 16.99 (978-1-935831-01-3(1)) Robe Communications, Inc.

—Robbie's Trail Through Foster Care — Adult Guide. Robe, Kim A., ed. Gavet, Nathalie, illus. 2010. 28p. pap. 16.99 (978-1-935831-02-0(X)) Robe Communications, Inc.

—Robbie's Trail Through Open Adoption. Robe, Kim A., ed. Gavet, Nathalie, illus. 2010. 44p. pap. 23.99 (978-1-935831-06-8(2)) Robe Communications, Inc.

—Wanting to Belong. Robe, Kim A., ed. Gavet, Nathalie, illus. 2009. 16p. pap. 11.99 (978-0-9817403-6-2(7)) Robe Communications, Inc.

Robe, Kim. Robbie's Trail Through Divorce. Gavet, Nathalie, illus. 2012. 40p. (-18). pap. 23.99 (978-1-935831-11-2(9)) Robe Communications, Inc.

—Robbie's Trail Through Divorce - Activity Book. Gavet, Nathalie, illus. 2012. 28p. (-18). pap. 16.99 (978-1-935831-12-9(7)) Robe Communications, Inc.

—Robbie's Trail Through Divorce - Adult Guide. Gavet, Nathalie, illus. 2012. 28p. (-18). pap. 16.99 (978-1-935831-13-6(5)) Robe Communications, Inc.

Robertson, Susan, illus. Little Bunny. 2005. (Bedtime Babies Ser.). 8p. (J). (gr. -1). per., bds. 6.99 (978-1-57755-503-2(1)) Flying Frog Publishing, Inc.

Robey, Katharine Crawford. Hare & the Big Green Lawn. MacDougall, Larry, illus. 2006. (ENG.). 32p. (J). (gr. -1-3). 15.95 (978-0-87358-889-8(4)) Cooper Square Publishing Llc.

Robinson, Jeanette. Blueberry Bunny. 2012. 32p. pap. 19.99 (978-1-4685-6410-5(2)) AuthorHouse.

Rodgers, Greg, as told by. Chukfi Rabbit's Big, Bad Bellyache: A Trickster Tale. 2014. (ENG., Illus.). 40p. (J). pap. 7.95 (978-1-935955-27-6(6)) Cinco Puntos Pr.

Rogers, Carol J. The Adventures of Buttonballs' Trails. 2012. 28p. pap. 19.99 (978-1-4772-4481-4(6)) AuthorHouse.

Rogers, Jewels. The Princess & the Rabbit. 2011. 28p. pap. 12.50 (978-1-4567-5171-5(9)) AuthorHouse.

Rogger. The Fifty-Fifth Bear & the Awkward Rabbits: An Amazing Thick Blue Wood Bear Adventure. 2009. (Illus.). 60p. pap. 21.99 (978-1-4389-1672-9(8)) AuthorHouse.

Rohmann, Eric. My Friend Rabbit. Rohmann, Eric, illus. 2011. (ENG., Illus.). 36p. (J). (gr. -1-3). bds. 7.99 (978-1-59643-641-1(7), 9781596436411) Roaring Brook Pr.

—My Friend Rabbit. Rohmann, Eric, illus. 2007. (ENG., Illus.). 32p. (J). (gr. -1-3). per. 7.99 (978-0-312-36752-7(X), 9780312367527) Square Fish.

Rohmann, Eric, creator. My Friend Rabbit & the Snow Geese. 2013. (My Readers Ser.). (ENG., Illus.). 32p. (J). (gr. -1-1). pap. 3.99 (978-1-250-01661-4(4), 9781250016614) Square Fish.

Rosenthal, Amy Krouse. Duck! Rabbit! Lichtenheld, Tom, illus. aut. ed. 2009. (J). 16.99 (978-0-8118-8332-0(9)) Chronicle Bks. LLC.

Rosie the Counting Rabbit. (J). (gr. k-2). pap. 9.90 (978-0-669-15293-7(5)); pap. 9.90 (978-0-669-15888-5(7)) Houghton Mifflin Harcourt School Pubs.

Rowe, Eva McKenzie & Hodge, Darren. Harrison Bean. 2012. 28p. pap. 24.95 (978-1-4626-6503-7(9)) America Star Bks.

Roy, Ron. February Friend. Gurney, John Steven, illus. 2009. (Calendar Mysteries Ser.: 2). (ENG.). 80p. (J). (gr. 1-4). 4.99 (978-0-375-85662-4(5), Random Hse. Bks. for Young Readers) Random Hse. Children's Bks.

Roy Windham, Windham & Windham, Roy. Uncle Fuddy-Duddy & the Big Bad Bear. 2010. 28p. 16.09 (978-1-4269-3065-2(8)) Trafford Publishing.

Rueda, Claudia. Bunny Slopes. 2016. (ENG., Illus.). 60p. (J). (gr. -1-k). 15.99 (978-1-4521-4197-8(5)) Chronicle Bks. LLC.

Rumbaugh, Melinda. Somebunny Loves You! Biscoe, Cee, illus. 2015. (ENG.). 16p. (J). 12.99 (978-0-8249-1950-4(5), Ideal Pubns.) Worthy Publishing.

Rumford, James. Beo-Bunny. 2012. 50p. pap. 14.00 (978-1-891839-09-2(8)) Manoa Pr.

Russell, Natalie. Brown Rabbit in the City. 2010. (ENG.). 40p. (J). (gr. -1-k). 16.99 (978-0-670-01234-3(3), Viking Books for Young Readers) Penguin Young Readers Group.

Russell, Rachel. How the Hare Saved the Animals of the Savanna from a Drought. 2011. 48p. pap. 21.99 (978-1-4520-7518-1(2)) AuthorHouse.

Russo, Brian. Yoga Bunny. Russo, Brian, illus. 2016. (Illus.). 40p. (J). (gr. -1-3). 17.99 (978-0-06-242952-0(3)) HarperCollins Pubs.

Russo, Marisabina. The Bunnies Are Not in Their Beds. 2013. lib. bdg. 18.40 (978-0-606-26964-3(9), Turtleback) Turtleback Bks.

—Sophie Sleeps Over. Russo, Marisabina, illus. 2014. (ENG., Illus.). 32p. (J). (gr. -1-2). 16.99 (978-1-59643-933-7(5), 9781596439337) Roaring Brook Pr.

Rutt, Preston. Tortoise vs. Hare: The Rematch. Redlich, Ben, illus. 2015. (ENG.). 24p. (J). (gr. -1-3). 7.99 (978-1-85733-722-8(0)) Lerner Publishing Group.

Rylant, Cynthia. Annie & Snowball & the Dress-Up Birthday. Stevenson, Suçie, illus. (Annie & Snowball Ser.: 1). (ENG.). 40p. (J). (gr. k-2). 2008. pap. 3.99 (978-1-4169-1459-4(5)) 2007. 16.99 (978-1-4169-0938-5(9)) Simon Spotlight. (Simon Spotlight).

—Annie & Snowball & the Dress-Up Birthday. 2008. (Annie & Snowball Ready-To-Read Ser.). lib. bdg. 13.55 (978-1-4178-1126-7(9), Turtleback) Turtleback Bks.

—Annie & Snowball & the Grandmother Night. Stevenson, Suçie, illus. (Annie & Snowball Ser.: 12). (ENG.). 40p. (J). (gr. k-2). 2013. pap. 3.99 (978-1-4169-7204-4(8)) 2012. 16.99 (978-1-4169-7203-7(X)) Simon Spotlight. (Simon Spotlight).

—Annie & Snowball & the Grandmother Night. 2013. (Annie & Snowball Ready-To-Read Ser.). lib. bdg. 13.55 (978-0-606-35183-6(3)) Turtleback Bks.

—Annie & Snowball & the Surprise Day. Stevenson, Suçie, illus. (Annie & Snowball Ser.: 11). (ENG.). 40p. (J). (gr. k-2). 2013. pap. 3.99 (978-1-4169-3948-1(2)) 2012. 16.99 (978-1-4169-3944-3(X)) Simon Spotlight. (Simon Spotlight).

—Annie & Snowball & the Teacup Club. Stevenson, Suçie, illus. (Annie & Snowball Ser.: 3). (ENG.). 40p. (J). (gr. k-2). 2009. pap. 3.99 (978-1-4169-1461-7(7)) 2008. 16.99 (978-1-4169-0940-8(0)) Simon Spotlight. (Simon Spotlight).

—Annie & Snowball & the Thankful Friends. 2012. (Annie & Snowball Ready-To-Read Ser.). lib. bdg. 13.55 (978-0-606-26917-9(7), Turtleback) Turtleback Bks.

—Annie & Snowball & the Wedding Day. Stevenson, Suçie, illus. 2014. (Annie & Snowball Ser.: 13). (ENG.). 40p. (J). (gr. k-2). 16.99 (978-1-4169-7485-7(7), Simon Spotlight) Simon Spotlight.

—Annie & Snowball & the Wedding Day: The Thirteenth Book of Their Adventures. Stevenson, Suçie, illus. 2015. (Annie & Snowball Ser.: 13). (ENG.). 40p. (J). (gr. k-2). pap. 3.99 (978-1-4169-7486-4(5), Simon Spotlight) Simon Spotlight.

—The Case of the Climbing Cat. Karas, G. Brian, illus. 2003. (High-Rise Private Eyes Ser.: No. 2). (J). (gr. -1-3). 25.96 incl. audio (978-1-59112-190-9(6)); pap. 29.95 incl. audio (978-1-59112-191-6(4)) Live Oak Media.

—The Case of the Puzzling Possum. Karas, G. Brian, illus. 2003. (High-Rise Private Eyes Ser.: No. 3). (J). (gr. -1-3). 25.95 incl. audio (978-1-59112-198-5(1)); (gr. k-3). pap. 29.95 incl. audio (978-1-59112-199-2(X)) Live Oak Media.

Sadler, Marilyn. P. J. Funnybunny's Bag of Tricks. Bollen, Roger, illus. 2005. (Step into Reading Ser.). 32p. 14.00 (978-0-7569-5405-5(3)) Perfection Learning Corp.

—P. J. Funnybunny's Bag of Tricks. Bollen, Roger, illus. 2004. (Step into Reading Ser.). (ENG.). 32p. (J). (gr. -1-1). pap. 3.99 (978-0-375-82444-9(8), Random Hse. Bks. for Young Readers) Random Hse. Children's Bks.

—P. J. Funnybunny's Bag of Tricks. 2004. (Step into Reading Level 2 Ser.). (gr. -1-2). lib. bdg. 13.55 (978-0-613-83535-0(2), Turtleback) Turtleback Bks.

Sadler, Marilyn & Bollen, Roger. Money, Money, Honey Bunny! 2006. (Bright & Early Books(R) Ser.). (ENG., Illus.). 36p. (J). (gr. -1-k). 9.99 (978-0-375-83370-0(6), Random Hse. Bks. for Young Readers) Random Hse. Children's Bks.

Sakai, Komako. The Snow Day. 2009. (J). pap. (978-0-545-01322-2(4), Levine, Arthur A. Bks.) Scholastic, Inc.

Sakai, Komako, creator. The Velveteen Rabbit. 2012. (ENG., Illus.). 40p. (J). (gr. -1). 17.95 (978-1-59270-128-5(0)) Enchanted Lion Bks., LLC.

Sakai, Stan. Usagi Yojimbo Vol. 3: Al Filo de la Vida y la Muerte. 2007. (SPA., Illus.). 200p. reprint ed. pap. 15.95 (978-1-59497-319-2(9)) Public Square Bks.

—Usagi Yojimbo Vol. 4: Estaciones. 2007. (SPA., Illus.). 200p. reprint ed. pap. 15.95 (978-1-59497-320-8(2)) Public Square Bks.

—Usagi Yojimbo Vol. 5: Segadora. 2007. (SPA., Illus.). 256p. reprint ed. pap. 17.95 (978-1-59497-321-5(0)) Public Square Bks.

—Usagi Yojimbo Vol. 6: Primeras Andanzas. 2007. (SPA., Illus.). 128p. reprint ed. pap. 12.95 (978-1-59497-322-2(9)) Public Square Bks.

—Usagi Yojimbo Vol. 7: Samurai (en Español) 2007. (SPA., Illus.). 144p. reprint ed. pap. 14.95 (978-1-59497-323-9(7)) Public Square Bks.

Samson, Lucretia. Hungry Tiger & Clever Rabbit: A Tale from Korea. Bijloo, Adrian, illus. 2016. 24p. (J). pap. (978-1-927244-58-6(7)) Clean Slate Pr. Ltd.

—Hungry Tiger & Clever Rabbit (Big Book Edition) A Tale from Korea. Bijloo, Adrian, illus. 2016. 24p. (J). pap. (978-1-927244-68-5(4)) Flying Start Bks.

San Souci, Daniel. Rabbit & the Dragon King: Based on a Korean Folk Tale. Neilan, Eujin Kim, illus. 2006. (ENG.). 32p. (J). (gr. 1-4). pap. 9.95 (978-1-59078-418-1(9)) Boyds Mills Pr.

Sandall, Ellie. Everybunny Dance! 2017. (ENG., Illus.). 32p. (J). (gr. -1-3). 17.99 (978-1-4814-9822-7(3), McElderry, Margaret K. Bks.) McElderry, Margaret K. Bks.

Sande, Hans. Snake in the Grass. Vetleseter, Tonje, tr. from NOR. Moursund, Gry, illus. 2008. 40p. (J). (gr. -1-1). 16.95 (978-0-9815761-0-7(9)) Mackenzie Smiles, LLC.

Santos, Penelope. Bird & Rabbit. 2015. (Rosen REAL Readers: STEM & STEAM Collection). (ENG.). 8p. pap. 5.46 (978-1-4994-9493-8(9), Rosen Classroom) Rosen Publishing Group, Inc., The.

Sarfatti, Esther, tr. from ENG. Berto Da la Talla. 2006. (Libro de Capitulos de Arturo Ser.). (Illus.). 55p. (J). (gr. 6-8). per. 4.99 (978-1-930332-94-2(7)) Lectorum Pubns., Inc.

Sargent, Dave & Sargent, Pat. Chrissy Cottontail: Mind Your Mama, 15 bks. Huff, Jeane, illus. 2nd rev. ed. 2003. (Animal Pride Ser.: 7). 42p. (J). 7. pap. 6.95 (978-1-56763-772-4(8)) Vol. 7. lib. bdg. 20.95 (978-1-56763-771-7(X)) Ozark Publishing.

—Fuzzy Bunny, 10 vols., Vol. 19. Robinson, Laura, illus. 2004. (Learn to Read Ser.: 10). 18p. (J). lib. bdg. 10.95 (978-1-56763-834-9(1)); lib. bdg. 20.95 (978-1-56763-833-2(3)) Ozark Publishing.

—Fuzzy Bunny/el conejito Velloso, 10 vols., Vol. 19. Robinson, Laura, illus. 2004. (Learn to Read Ser.: 10). (ENG & SPA.). 18p. (J). pap. 10.95 (978-1-56763-998-8(4)); lib. bdg. 20.95 (978-1-56763-997-1(6)) Ozark Publishing.

—Young Dawn: Friends Care! Woodword, Elaine, illus. 2005. (Young Animal Pride Ser.: 8). 24p. (J). 8. pap. 6.95 (978-1-56763-878-3(3)) Vol. 8. lib. bdg. 20.95 (978-1-56763-877-6(5)) Ozark Publishing.

—Young Dike: Teamwork! Woodward, Elaine, illus. 2003. (Young Animal Pride Ser.: 5). 24p. (J). 5. pap. 6.95 (978-1-56763-872-1(4)) Vol. 5. lib. bdg. 20.95 (978-1-56763-871-4(6)) Ozark Publishing.

—Young Sammy: I'm a Little Stinker!, Vol. 9. Woodword, Elaine, illus. 2005. (Young Animal Pride Ser.). 24p. (J). pap. 10.95 (978-1-56763-880-6(5)) Ozark Publishing.

—Young White Thunder: I'm a Leader!, Vol. 6. Woodword, Elaine, illus. 2005. (Young Animal Pride Ser.). 24p. (J). pap. 10.95 (978-1-56763-874-5(0)) Ozark Publishing.

Sargent, Dave, et al. Young Chrissy: Mind Your Mama!, Vol. 7. 2005. (Young Animal Pride Ser.). (Illus.). 24p. (J). lib. bdg. 20.95 (978-1-56763-875-2(9)) Ozark Publishing.

Sasscer, Abby. Sophie's Stuff. Cayless, Sophie, illus. 2012. 36p. pap. 9.95 (978-0-9854729-1-7(X)) Sasscer, Abby.

Savage, Doug. Laser Moose & Rabbit Boy. 2016. (ENG.). 144p. (J). pap. 9.99 (978-1-4494-7094-4(7)) Andrews McMeel Publishing.

Saxon, Victoria. Big Trouble in Little Rodentia. 2016. (Illus.). (J). **(978-1-5182-0883-6(5))** Random House Children's Books.

Sazaklis, John. The Hopping Hero, 1 vol. Baltazar, Art, illus. 2011. (DC Super-Pets Ser.). (ENG.). 56p. (gr. 2-2). pap. 4.95 (978-1-4048-6843-4(7)); lib. bdg. 23.99 (978-1-4048-6477-1(6)) Picture Window Bks. (DC Super-Pets).

Scaglione, Dapos & Maria. A Unique Bunny. 2005. 65p. pap. 19.95 (978-1-4137-9530-1(7)) America Star Bks.

Scarry, Patricia M. & Scarry, Patsy. The Bunny Book. Scarry, Richard, illus. 2005. (Little Golden Book Ser.). (ENG.). 24p. (J). (gr. -1-2). 4.99 (978-0-375-83224-6(6), Golden Bks.) Random Hse. Children's Bks.

Scarry, Patsy. The Bunny Book. Scarry, Richard, illus. 2016. (Little Golden Board Book Ser.). (ENG.). 26p. (J). (— 1). bds. 7.99 (978-0-553-53587-7(0), Random Hse. Bks. for Young Readers) Random Hse. Children's Bks.

—Richard Scarry's the Bunny Book. Scarry, Richard, illus. 2015. (Big Golden Book Ser.). (ENG.). 32p. (J). (-k). 9.99 (978-0-385-39090-3(4), Golden Bks.) Random Hse. Children's Bks.

Scarry, Richard. Best Little Board Book Ever. Random House Staff, illus. 2013. (ENG.). 24p. (J). (— 1). bds. 4.99 (978-0-449-81901-2(9), Golden Bks.) Random Hse. Children's Bks.

Scheffler, Axel & Nosy Crow Staff. Pip & Posy: the Snowy Day. Scheffler, Axel, illus. 2013. (Pip & Posy Ser.). (ENG., Illus.). 32p. (J). (-k). 12.99 (978-0-7636-6607-1(6), Nosy Crow) Candlewick Pr.

Schindel, John. Busy Bunnies. Holt, Steven, photos by. 2008. (Busy Book Ser.). (ENG., Illus.). 20p. (J). (— 1). bds. 6.99 (978-1-58246-242-4(9), Knopf Bks. for Young Readers) Random Hse. Children's Bks.

Schneider, Cheryl & Olson, Carole. Bunnaby Bunny (L) Toddler Reader. Schneider, Cheryl, illus. deluxe ed. 2006. (Illus.). 20p. (J). bds. 10.00 (978-0-9712816-5-3(3)) Third Week Bks.

Schomp, Virginia. Brer Rabbit & the Goober Patch. 2013. (American Legends & Folktales 2 Ser.). (Illus.). 32p. (J). (gr. 6-9). pap. 10.58 (978-1-62712-014-2(9)) Cavendish Square Publishing.

Schulman, Janet. 10 Easter Egg Hunters: A Holiday Counting Book. Davick, Linda, illus. (ENG.). (J). (gr. -1 — 1). 2012. 26p. bds. 6.99 (978-0-375-86637-1(X)) 2011. 32p. 8.99 (978-0-375-86787-3(2)) Random Hse. Children's Bks. (Knopf Bks. for Young Readers).

Schwartz, Amy & Marcus, Leonard S. Oscar: The Big Adventure of a Little Sock Monkey. Schwartz, Amy, illus. 2006. (Illus.). 32p. (J). (gr. -1-2). 16.99 (978-0-06-072622-5(9), Tegen, Katherine Bks) HarperCollins Pubs.

Scieszka, Jon & Barnett, Mac. Battle Bunny. Myers, Matthew, illus. 2013. (ENG.). 32p. (J). (gr. k-4). 14.99 (978-1-4424-4673-1(0), Simon & Schuster Bks. For Young Readers) Simon & Schuster Bks. For Young Readers.

Segal, John. Carrot Soup. Segal, John, illus. 2006. (ENG., Illus.). 32p. (J). (gr. -1-3). 17.99 (978-0-689-87702-5(1), McElderry, Margaret K. Bks.) McElderry, Margaret K. Bks.

—Sopa de Zanahoria. Mlawer, Teresa, tr. from ENG. 2006. (Illus.). (gr. -1-k). 12.99 (978-1-933032-13-9(8)) Lectorum Pubns., Inc.

Sena, Keiko. Gracie Meets a Ghost. 2016. (Gracie Wears Glasses Book Ser.). (ENG.). 32p. (J). (gr. -1-k). 16.99 (978-1-940842-13-4(1)) Museyon.

Seresin, Lynn & Schwartz, Betty Ann. Hop, Hop Bunny. Ng, Neiko, illus. 2015. (Follow-Along Book Ser.). (ENG.). 10p. (J). (gr. -1 — 1). bds. 9.99 (978-1-4521-2464-3(7)) Chronicle Bks. LLC.

Seuss, Dr. & Seuss. The Eye Book. abr. ed. 2016. (Big Bright & Early Board Book Ser.). (ENG., Illus.). 24p. (J). (gr. -1 — 1). bds. 6.99 (978-0-553-53631-7(1), Random Hse. Bks. for Young Readers) Random Hse. Children's Bks.

Shea, Bob. Race You to Bed. Shea, Bob, illus. 2010. (ENG., Illus.). 40p. (J). (gr. -1-2). 16.99 (978-0-06-170417-8(2), Tegen, Katherine Bks) HarperCollins Pubs.

Shepherd, Anita. Easter Rabbit's Magic. 2013. 48p. pap. 7.95 (978-0-9882368-2-0(6)) New Eden Publishing.

Shields, Gillian. The Littlest Bunny. Lovsin, Polona, illus. 2015. 32p. (J). (978-1-4351-5967-9(5)) Barnes & Noble, Inc.

—When the World Is Ready for Bed. Currey, Anna, illus. 2010. (ENG.). 26p. (J). (gr. -1 — 1). bds. 7.99 (978-1-59990-533-4(7), 9781599905334, Bloomsbury USA Childrens) Bloomsbury Publishing USA.

—When the World Was Waiting for You. Currey, Anna, illus. 2012. (ENG.). 26p. (J). (gr. -1 — 1). bds. 7.99 (978-1-59990-849-6(2), 9781599908496, Bloomsbury USA Childrens) Bloomsbury Publishing USA.

Shoshan, Beth. Little Rabbit Waits for the Moon. Peel, Stephanie, illus. 2013. (J). (978-1-4351-4802-4(9)) Barnes & Noble, Inc.

Silbaugh, Michael John. Crosseyed Puzzle. 2009. 28p. pap. 15.99 (978-1-4415-8779-4(9)) Xlibris Corp.

Sixtus, Albert. Rabbit School: A Light-Hearted Tale. Freischlad, Roland, tr. from GER. Koch-Gotha, Fritz, illus. 2009. (ENG.). 32p. (J). (gr. -1-2). 14.95 (978-1-56792-383-4(6)) Godine, David R. Pub.

Skidmore, Marlene. In Trouble Again! 2010. 24p. pap. 9.99 (978-0-9845208-9-3(9)) Faithful Life Pubs.

—Wesley's Swoo-Foo. 2008. 28p. pap. 9.99 (978-0-9821408-5-7(1)) Faithful Life Pubs.

Slater, Jean M. The Adventures of Hopper. Slater, Jean M., illus. 2003. (Illus.). 8p. (J). bds. 16.00 (978-0-9743149-3-8(5)) Slater Software. Inc.

Sledge-Yancy, Barbara. The Red Haired Hare. 2011. 40p. pap. 17.49 (978-1-4568-6647-1(8)) Xlibris Corp.

Small, Lily. Bella the Bunny. 2015. (Fairy Animals of Misty Wood Ser.: 2). (ENG., Illus.). 144p. (J). (gr. k-3). pap. 5.99 (978-1-62779-142-7(6), 9781627791427, Holt, Henry & Co. Bks. For Young Readers) Holt, Henry & Co.

Smart, Jamie. Bunny vs. Monkey. Smart, Jamie, illus. 2016. (ENG., Illus.). 64p. (J). (gr. 2-5). pap. 7.99 (978-0-545-86184-7(5), Graphix) Scholastic, Inc.

Smith, Carrie. The Lion & the Rabbit: Classic Tales Edition. Greenhead, Bill, illus. 2011. (Classic Tales Ser.). (J). (978-1-936258-65-9(X)) Benchmark Education Co.

—Tortoise & Hare Run a Race: Lap Book Edition. Berchtold, Lauren, illus. 2016. (My First Reader's Theater Tales Ser.). (J). (gr. k). (978-1-5021-5509-2(5)) Benchmark Education Co.

—Tortoise & Hare Run a Race: Small Book Edition. Berchtold, Lauren, illus. 2016. (My First Reader's Theater Tales Ser.). (J). (gr. k). (978-1-5021-5514-6(1)) Benchmark Education Co.

Smith, Kathryn & Scott, Karen. King Murray's Royal Tail: The True Story of an Easter Bunny. 2004. 59p. pap. 8.95 (978-0-595-31090-6(7)) iUniverse, Inc.

Smith, Lesley & Award Publications Staff. Brer Rabbit & Brer Fox. 2014. (ENG., Illus.). 24p. (J). pap. 6.95 (978-1-84135-962-5(9)) Award Pubns. Ltd. GBR. Dist: Parkwest Pubns., Inc.

—Brer Rabbit & the Honey Pot. 2014. (ENG., Illus.). 24p. (J). pap. 6.95 (978-1-84135-961-8(0)) Award Pubns. Ltd. GBR. Dist: Parkwest Pubns., Inc.

—Brer Rabbit & the Tar Baby. 2014. (ENG., Illus.). 24p. (J). pap. 6.95 (978-1-84135-964-9(5)) Award Pubns. Ltd. GBR. Dist: Parkwest Pubns., Inc.

Smith, Lesley, et al. Brer Rabbit & the Great Race. 2014. (ENG., Illus.). 24p. (J). pap. 6.95 (978-1-84135-963-2(7)) Award Pubns. Ltd. GBR. Dist: Parkwest Pubns., Inc.

Smith, Maggie Caldwell. Tommy Wilson, Junior Veterinarian: The Case of the Wounded Jack Rabbit. McHose, Jean, illus. 2005. 104p. (J). (gr. 3-6). pap. 7.95 (978-1-889159-14-0(X)) Magpie Pr., Pine Mountain Club, CA.

Smith, Stephanie. Snowshoe Hare's Family. Hynes, Robert, illus. 2nd ed. 2007. (Soundprints' Read-and-Discover Ser.). (ENG.). (J). (gr. 1-3). 32p. 12.95 (978-1-931465-44-1(4), PS2053); 48p. pap. 3.95 (978-1-931465-15-1(0), S2003) Soundprints.

Smith, Suzanne C. Peter Cottontail & the Easter Bunny Imposter. Brittingham, Geoffrey, illus. 24p. (J). pap. 3.25 (978-0-8249-5372-0(X), Ideal Pubns.) Worthy Publishing.

Smithem, Beth. Dust Bunny's Mission. 2010. 84p. pap. 10.49 (978-1-4520-1934-5(7)) AuthorHouse.

Smythe, Theresa. Chester's Colorful Easter Eggs. Smythe, Theresa, illus. 2013. (ENG., Illus.). 24p. (J). (gr. -1-k). 12.99 (978-0-8050-9326-1(5), 9780805093261, Holt, Henry & Co. Bks. For Young Readers) Holt, Henry & Co.

Snow Rabbit, Spring Rabbit: a Book of Changing Seasons. 2013. (ENG.). 24p. (J). (gr. -1 — 1). bds. 6.99 (978-0-307-97790-8(0), Knopf Bks. for Young Readers) Random Hse. Children's Bks.

Snyder, Betsy E. Sweet Dreams Lullaby. 2012. (ENG., Illus.). 32p. (J). (— 1). bds. 6.99 (978-0-307-98060-1(X), Random Hse. Bks. for Young Readers) Random Hse. Children's Bks.

Solomon, Chad. Adventures of Rabbit & Bear Paws: The Voyageurs. 2008. (ENG.). 32p. pap. (978-0-9739906-2-1(7)) Little Spirit Bear Productions CAN. Dist: Lone Pine Publishing.

Sommer, Carl. Miserable Millie. Vignolo, Enrique, illus. 2014. (J). pap. (978-1-57537-960-9(0)) Advance Publishing, Inc.

Soo, Kean, illus. The Baker's Run. 2015. (March Grand Prix Ser.). (ENG.). 48p. (gr. 1-3). lib. bdg. 33.32 (978-1-4342-9640-5(7)) Capstone Young Readers of Coughlan Cos.

—The Great Desert Rally. 2015. (March Grand Prix Ser.). (ENG.). 48p. (gr. 1-3). lib. bdg. 33.32 (978-1-4342-9641-2(5)) Capstone Young Readers of Coughlan Cos.

—March Grand Prix: The Fast & the Furriest. 2015. (March Grand Prix Ser.). (ENG.). 144p. (gr. 1-3). pap. 14.95 (978-1-62370-171-0(6)) Capstone Young Readers of Coughlan Cos.

—The Race at Harewood. 2015. (March Grand Prix Ser.). (ENG.). 48p. (gr. 1-3). lib. bdg. 33.32 (978-1-4342-9639-9(3)) Capstone Young Readers of Coughlan Cos.

Speed, Evelyn. Digger Rabbit & the First Easter. 2009. (Illus.). 24p. pap. 11.49 (978-1-4389-6105-7(7)) AuthorHouse.

Spelman, Cornelia. When I Feel Angry. Cote, Nancy, illus. 2012. (J). reprint ed. lib. bdg. 32.71 (978-1-61913-139-2(0)) Weigl Pubs., Inc.

Spicer, Candace. Hopper & the Happy Houses. 2012. 18.95 (978-0-7414-6863-5(8)); pap. 11.95 (978-0-7414-6862-8(X)) Infinity Publishing.

Spiegelman, Art. Jack & the Box, 1 vol. 2013. (Toon Bks). (ENG.). 36p. (J). (gr. k-1). lib. bdg. 27.07 (978-1-61479-151-5(1)) Spotlight.

Spin & Match - Kings, Cookies, & Quakers: The Cookie Man, New Clothes for the King, the Ugly Baby Duck. 2006. (ENG.). 66p. (J). 9.99 (978-1-59204-203-6(1)) Learning Wrap-Ups, Inc.

Spinelli, Eileen. A Big Boy Now. Lloyd, Megan, illus. 2012. (ENG.). 32p. (J). (gr. -1-3). 16.99 (978-0-06-008673-2(4)) HarperCollins Pubs.

Sprick, Marilyn & Lemieux, Aurora, adapted by. The Race: Read Well Level K Unit 13 Storybook. 2003. (Read Well Level K Ser.). (Illus.). 20p. (J). (978-1-57035-684-1(X), 55538) Cambium Education, Inc.

Stanley, Mandy. The Birthday Party. Stanley, Mandy, illus. 2011. (ENG., Illus.). 32p. (J). (gr. -1-k). pap. 9.95 (978-0-00-718409-5(3), HarperCollins Children's Bks.) HarperCollins Pubs. Ltd. GBR. Dist: HarperCollins Pubs.

Stapylton, K. E. The Terror of Prism Fading. 2008. 260p. pap. 15.90 (978-1-4357-5457-7(3)) Lulu Pr., Inc.

Steig, William & Steig. Which Would You Rather Be? Bliss, Harry, illus. 2005. (ENG.). 32p. (J). (gr. -1-3). reprint ed. pap. 8.99 (978-0-06-443792-9(2)) HarperCollins Pubs.

Steinkraus, Kyla. In the Doghouse. Myer, Ed, illus. 2012. (ENG.). 24p. (gr. 2-3). pap. 8.95 (978-1-61810-332-1(6)) Rourke Educational Media.

Stephenson, Alan. The Adventures of Roy & Rosie Rabbit. 2011. (Illus.). 48p. pap. 19.51 (978-1-4567-9728-7(X)) AuthorHouse.

Steve Cormey. The Brothers Foot: A Hare Raising Story. Ronda Eden, illus. 2009. 56p. pap. 21.99 (978-1-4389-4269-8(9)) AuthorHouse.

Stevens, Deon. Frankie's Kingdom: Winning in Face of Uncertainty. 2010. 218p. pap. 19.99 (978-1-4535-5409-8(2)) Xlibris Corp.

Stevens, Janet & Crummel, Susan Stevens. Tumbleweed Stew/Sopa de Matojos. Flor Ada, Alma & Campoy, F. Isabel, trs. from ENG. Stevens, Janet, illus. 2009. (Green Light Readers Level 2 Ser.). (SPA & ENG., Illus.). 36p. (J). (gr. -1-3). pap. 3.99 (978-0-547-25261-2(7)) Houghton Mifflin Harcourt Publishing Co.

Stevens, Terry. The Battle at Longshore Causeway. 2006. 64p. pap. (978-1-84401-751-5(6)) Athena Pr.

Stewart, Amber & Rankin, Laura. Rabbit Ears. Rankin, Laura, illus. 2012. (ENG., Illus.). 32p. (J). (gr. -1-1). pap. 8.99 (978-1-59990-740-6(2), 9781599907406, Bloomsbury USA Childrens) Bloomsbury Publishing USA.

Stewart, Paul. Un Regalo de Cumpleanos. Riddell, Chris, illus. (SPA.). 30p. (J). (gr. k-2). (978-84-348-6840-3(7), SM30935) SM Ediciones ESP. Dist: Lectorum Pubns., Inc.

Stewart, Paul & Stewart, Paul. Un Poquito de Invierno. Riddell, Chris, illus. 2003. (SPA.). 30p. (J). (gr. k-2). (978-84-348-6839-7(3), SM30933) SM Ediciones ESP. Dist: Lectorum Pubns., Inc.

Stiegemeyer, Julie. Seven Little Bunnies, 0 vols. Bryant, Laura J., illus. 2010. (ENG.). 24p. (J). (gr. -1-3). 15.99 (978-0-7614-5600-1(7), 9780761456001, Amazon Children's Publishing) Amazon Publishing.

Stills, Caroline & Stills-Blott, Sarcia. The House of 12 Bunnies. Rossell, Judith, illus. 2012. (ENG.). 24p. (J). 16.95 (978-0-8234-2422-1(7)) Holiday Hse., Inc.

StJohn, Amanda. How to Check Out a Book. Ostrom, Bob, illus. 2012. (Library Skills Ser.). (ENG.). 24p. (J). (gr. -1-2). 28.50 (978-1-61473-249-5(3), 204951) Child's World, Inc., The.

—How to Find a Book. Ostrom, Bob, illus. 2012. (Library Skills Ser.). (ENG.). 24p. (J). (gr. -1-2). 28.50 (978-1-61473-250-1(7), 204952) Child's World, Inc., The.

—How to Find Information Online. Ostrom, Bob, illus. 2012. (Library Skills Ser.). (ENG.). 24p. (J). (gr. -1-2). 28.50 (978-1-61473-251-8(5), 204953) Child's World, Inc., The.

—How to Treat a Book. Ostrom, Bob, illus. 2012. (Library Skills Ser.). (ENG.). 24p. (J). (gr. -1-2). 28.50 (978-1-61473-252-5(3), 204954) Child's World, Inc., The.

Stocks, David. Moon Rabbit. 2008. 276p. pap. (978-1-84747-838-2(7)) Chipmunkapublishing.

Stone, Kate & Accord Publishing Staff. Bunnies for Tea. 2013. (ENG., Illus.). 10p. (J). bds. 7.99 (978-1-4494-2887-7(8)) Andrews McMeel Publishing.

Stowell, Louie. Brer Rabbit down the Well. Muszynski, Eva, illus. 2010. (First Reading Level 2 Ser.). 32p. (J). 6.99 (978-0-7945-2674-0(8), Usborne) EDC Publishing.

Strohmenger, Marie. The Smart Bunny: A Story about Big & Small, Smart & Stupid, Winning & Losing. 2007. 24p. per. 24.95 (978-1-4241-8249-7(2)) America Star Bks.

Stroschin, Jane H. Atsa & Ga: A Story from the High Desert. Stich, Carolyn R., illus. 2005. 32p. (J). (gr. k-6). (978-1-883960-29-2(0)) Henry Quill Pr.

Stuart, Wrigley. Who'd Have Thunk It? 2014. (Amazing World of Gumball Ser.). (ENG., Illus.). 208p. (J). (gr. 3-7). pap. 9.99 (978-0-8431-8106-7(0), Price Stern Sloan) Penguin Young Readers Group.

Suen, Anastasia. Don't Forget! A Responsibility Story, 1 vol. Ebbeler, Jeff, illus. 2008. (Main Street School - Kids with Character Ser.). (ENG.). 32p. (gr. -1-4). 28.50 (978-1-60270-269-1(1), Looking Glass Library) ABDO Publishing Co.

Summers, Darien. The Mischievous Hare. 2009. (Illus.). 48p. pap. 9.95 (978-1-4327-4602-5(2)) Outskirts Pr., Inc.

Surplice, Holly. Peek-a-Boo Bunny. Surplice, Holly, illus. 2014. (ENG., Illus.). 32p. (J). (gr. -1-3). 9.99 (978-0-06-224265-5(2)) HarperCollins Pubs.

Sutherland, David. Samantha Cardigan & the Genie's Revenge. Roberts, David, illus. 2005. (Red Bananas Ser.). (ENG.). 48p. (J). lib. bdg. (978-0-7787-1070-7(X)) Crabtree Publishing Co.

—Samantha Cardigan & the Ghastly Twirling Sickness. Roberts, David, illus. 2005. (Red Bananas Ser.). (ENG.). 48p. (J). lib. bdg. (978-0-7787-1069-1(6)) Crabtree Publishing Co.

Sutherland, David & Roberts, David. Samantha Cardigan & the Genie's Revenge. 2005. (Red Bananas Ser.). (ENG., Illus.). 48p. (J). (gr. 1-3). (978-0-7787-1086-8(6)) Crabtree Publishing Co.

—Samantha Cardigan & the Ghastly Twirling Sickness. 2005. (Red Bananas Ser.). (ENG., Illus.). 48p. (J). (gr. 1-3). (978-0-7787-1085-1(8)) Crabtree Publishing Co.

Sweeney, Kimberly A. Tippy Meets the Easter Bunny! 2012. 24p. pap. 17.99 (978-1-4685-8460-8(X)) AuthorHouse.

Symes, Ruth Louise. Floppy Ears. Kenyon, Tony, illus. 2005. 32p. (J). (978-1-84255-264-3(3), Orion Children's Bks.) Hachette Children's Group.

Tanaka, Usa. Give Me That! Tanaka, Usa, illus. 2007. (ENG., Illus.). 32p. (J). 15.95 (978-0-9741319-0-0(3)) 4N Publishing LLC.

Tangerine Designs Ltd. Bobby Bunny. 2015. (Little Loves Rattle Bks.). (ENG.). 8p. (J). (gr. -1 — 1). 7.99 (978-1-4380-7562-4(6)) Barron's Educational Series, Inc.

Taplin, Sam. Easter Bunny Flap Book. 2012. (Flap Bks). 10p. (J). ring bd. 7.99 (978-0-7945-3256-7(X), Usborne) EDC Publishing.

Tardif, Elizabeth. A Bunny Named Apple. Buehrle, Jacquelyn, illus. 2011. 28p. pap. 24.95 (978-1-4560-0946-5(X)) America Star Bks.

Tatsuyama, Sayuri. Happy Happy Clover, Vol. 1. Tatsuyama, Sayuri, illus. 2009. (ENG., Illus.). 200p. (J). pap. 7.99 (978-1-4215-2656-0(5)) Viz Media.

—Happy Happy Clover, Vol. 2. Tatsuyama, Sayuri, illus. 2009. (ENG., Illus.). 192p. (J). pap. 9.99 (978-1-4215-2657-7(3)) Viz Media.

—Happy Happy Clover, Vol. 4. Tatsuyama, Sayuri, illus. 2010. (ENG., Illus.). 192p. (J). pap. 7.99 (978-1-4215-2735-2(9)) Viz Media.

Taylor, Chet. Last, but Not Least. 2007. (Illus.). 20p. (J). per. 11.99 (978-0-9797574-8-8(7)) Dragonfly Publishing, Inc.

—Last, but Not Least. Taylor, Chet, illus. l.t. ed. 2004. (Illus.). 20p. (J). 17.99 (978-0-9755888-6-4(9)); lib. bdg. 22.99 (978-0-9755888-1-9(8)) Dragonfly Publishing, Inc.

Teckentrup, Britta, illus. Busy Bunny Days: In the Town, on the Farm & at the Port. 2014. (ENG.). 56p. (J). (gr. -1-3). 17.99 (978-1-4521-1700-3(4)) Chronicle Bks. LLC.

Tegen, Katherine. The Story of the Easter Bunny. Lambert, Sally Anne, illus. (ENG.). 40p. (J). (gr. -1-3). 2007. pap. 6.99 (978-0-06-058781-9(4)) 2005. 12.99 (978-0-06-050711-4(X)) HarperCollins Pubs.

Tharlet, Eve. Happy Birthday, Davy Tuff Book. 2011. (ENG., Illus.). 28p. (J). (gr. -1-3). 6.95 (978-0-7358-4026-3(1)) North-South Bks., Inc.

Thomas Nelson Community College Staff. God's Love in My Heart, 1 vol. 2014. (ENG.). 24p. bds. 9.99 (978-0-529-11141-8(1)) Nelson, Thomas Inc.

Thompson, Carol. I Like You the Best. Thompson, Carol, illus. 2011. (ENG., Illus.). 32p. (J). (gr. -1-1). 16.95 (978-0-8234-2341-5(7)) Holiday Hse., Inc.

Thompson, Don. Bunny World: Kindness Is the Key to Happiness. 2009. 28p. pap. 14.99 (978-1-4389-5475-2(1)) AuthorHouse.

Thompson, Emma. The Further Tale of Peter Rabbit. Taylor, Eleanor, illus. 2012. (Peter Rabbit Ser.). (ENG.). 72p. (J). (gr. -1-2). 20.00 (978-0-7232-6910-6(6), Warne) Penguin Young Readers Group.

—The Spectacular Tale of Peter Rabbit. Taylor, Eleanor, illus. 2014. (Peter Rabbit Ser.). (ENG.). 72p. (J). (gr. -1-2). 20.00 (978-0-7232-7116-1(X), Warne) Penguin Young Readers Group.

Thompson, Emma, et al. Sgeulachd Eile Mu Pheader Rabaid. Taylor, Eleonor, illus. 2012.Tr. of Further Tale of Peter Rabbit. (GLA.). 80p. (J). (978-1-907676-12-3(0)) Grace Note Pubns.

Thompson, Lauren. Little Bunny. Butler, John, illus. 2013. (ENG.). 30p. (J). (gr. -1-k). bds. 5.99 (978-1-4424-5851-2(8), Little Simon) Little Simon.

—Little Chick/Little Bunny Vertical 2-Pack. Butler, John, illus. 2014. (ENG.). 60p. (J). (gr. -1-k). bds. 11.98 (978-1-4814-1876-8(9), Little Simon) Little Simon.

—Wee Little Bunny. Butler, John, illus. 2010. (Wee Little Ser.). (ENG.). 32p. (J). (gr. -1-1). 14.99 (978-1-4169-7937-1(9), Simon & Schuster Bks. For Young Readers) Simon & Schuster Bks. For Young Readers.

Thoughts Staff. Bugsy Rabbit: Furry Tales, No. 1. 2005. 13p. 8.99 (978-1-4116-3331-5(8)) Lulu Pr., Inc.

Tidhar, Lavie. Central Station, 1 vol. unabr. ed. 2017. (ENG.). 9.99 **(978-1-5436-2453-3(7)**, 9781543624533) Brilliance Publishing, Inc.

Tidholm, Anna-Clara. Knock! Knock! Bradley, MaryChris, tr. 2009. (Illus.). 32p. (J). (gr. -1). 9.95 (978-0-9815761-6-9(8)) Mackenzie Smiles, LLC.

Tillis, Doris. Rudy the Rabbit. Tillis, Carrie, illus. 2005. 32p. per. 17.95 (978-1-58961-410-9(0)) PageFree Publishing, Inc.

Tillworth, Mary. Nickelodeon 5-Minute Stories Collection. Random House, illus. 2016. (5-Minute Story Collection). (ENG.). 160p. (J). (gr. -1-2). 12.99 (978-0-399-55314-1(2), Random Hse. Bks. for Young Readers) Random Hse. Children's Bks.

Tireman, Loyd. Baby Jack & Jumping Jack Rabbit. Douglass, Ralph, illus. 2015. (Mesaland Ser.). (ENG.). 48p. (J). 12.95 (978-0-8263-5604-8(4)) Univ. of New Mexico Pr.

—Hop-a-Long: Stories. Douglass, Ralph, illus. 2015. (Mesaland Ser.). (ENG.). 48p. (J). 12.95 (978-0-8263-5608-6(7)) Univ. of New Mexico Pr.

Todd, Burt Kerr. Bun Bun & Other Tales. 2006. pap. 10.00 (978-1-4257-1857-2(4)) Xlibris Corp.

Todd, Diana. Carrotsville. 2004. 42p. per. 12.95 (978-1-932344-61-5(6)) Thornton Publishing, Inc.

Togden, Ra Chel. The Legendary Rabbit of Death - Volume One [Paperback]. 2013. 108p. pap. (978-1-898185-27-7(1)) Aro Bks. worldwide.

Tommy. Bubba & Cecil. 2009. 52p. pap. 16.95 (978-1-60836-860-0(2)) America Star Bks.

Tonatiuh, Duncan. Pancho Rabbit & the Coyote: A Migrant's Tale. 2013. (ENG., Illus.). 32p. (J). (gr. 1-4). 17.95 (978-1-4197-0583-0(0), Abrams Bks. for Young Readers) Abrams, Inc.

Tonderum, Angela. Kaycee Kangaroo Lost in Alphabet Forest: Adventures of Kaycee Kangaroo. Carlson, Christine, illus. 2008. 41p. pap. 24.95 (978-1-60672-601-3(3)) America Star Bks.

Tone, Satoe. The Very Big Carrot. 2013. (ENG., Illus.). 26p. (J). 12.00 (978-0-8028-5426-1(5), Eerdmans Bks For Young Readers) Eerdmans, William B. Publishing Co.

Torrel, Wendy. GUARDIAN of DREAMS (1st Edition) Klingbeil, Kendall, illus. l.t. ed. 2004. 32p. (J). 14.95 (978-0-9746890-0-5(9)); pap. 10.95 (978-0-9746890-1-2(7)) White Tulip Publishing.

Trasler, Janee. Mimi & Bear Make a Friend. Trasler, Janee, illus. 2017. (Mimi & Bear Ser.). (ENG., Illus.). 32p. (J). 16.99 (978-0-374-30360-0(6), 9780374303600, Farrar, Straus & Giroux (BYR)) Farrar, Straus & Giroux.

Umansky, Kaye. Sophie in Charge. Currey, Anna, illus. 2005. 30p. (J). 9.95 (978-1-56148-478-2(4), Good Bks.) Skyhorse Publishing Co., Inc.

Vainio, Pirkko. Little Bunny Finds Christmas. Vainio, Pirkko, illus. 2008. (ENG., Illus.). 32p. (J). (gr. -1-3). 16.95 (978-0-7358-2221-4(2)) North-South Bks., Inc.

van Genechten, Guido. Floppy. 2004. (Illus.). 28p. (J). (978-1-85269-517-0(X)); (ENG & POR., pap. (978-1-85269-523-1(4)); (ENG., pap. (978-1-85269-524-8(2)); (ENG & PAN., pap. (978-1-85269-522-4(6)); (ENG & TAM., pap. (978-1-85269-526-2(9)); (ENG & TUR., pap. (978-1-85269-527-9(7)); (ENG & VIE., pap. (978-1-85269-529-3(3)); (ENG & YOR., pap. (978-1-85269-530-9(7)); (ENG & GUJ., pap. (978-1-85269-520-0(X)); (ENG & ALB., pap. (978-1-85269-516-3(1)); (ENG & SOM., pap. (978-1-85269-525-5(0)) Mantra Lingua.

—Floppy's Friends. van Genechten, Guido, illus. 2004. (ENG & POL., Illus.). 28p. (J). bds. (978-1-84444-659-9(X)) Mantra Lingua.

—Floppy's Friends. 2004. (J). (BEN & ENG.). 16.95 (978-1-84444-649-0(2)); (ENG & URD.). 16.95 (978-1-84444-665-0(4)); (CHI & ENG.). 16.95 (978-1-84444-650-6(6)) Mantra Lingua GBR. Dist: Chinasprout, Inc.

—Knight Ricky. van Genechten, Guido, illus. 2010. (Ricky Ser.). (ENG., Illus.). 30p. (J). (gr. -1-k). 16.95 (978-1-60537-059-0(2)) Cobblestone Publishing Co.

—Ricky. 2008. (ENG.). 32p. (J). (gr. -1-k). 16.95 (978-1-60537-009-5(6)) Clavis ROM. Dist: Publishers Group West (PGW).

—Ricky & Annie. van Genechten, Guido, illus. 2010. (Ricky Ser.). (ENG., Illus.). 30p. (J). (gr. -1-k). 16.95 (978-1-60537-062-0(2)) Cobblestone Publishing Co.

—Ricky & the Squirrel. van Genechten, Guido, illus. 2010. (Ricky Ser.). (ENG., Illus.). 30p. (J). (gr. -1-k). 16.95 (978-1-60537-078-1(9)) Cobblestone Publishing Co.

—Ricky Is Brave. van Genechten, Guido, illus. 2011. (Ricky Ser.). (ENG., Illus.). 32p. (J). (gr. -1-k). 16.95 (978-1-60537-097-2(5)) Cobblestone Publishing Co.

van Genechten, Guido, tr. from DUT. Floppy in the Dark: Floppy Dans le Noir. 2004. (Illus.). 25p. (J). (978-1-85269-242-1(1)) Mantra Lingua.

Van Laan, Nancy. Scrubba Dub. Pons, Bernadette, illus. 2008. (ENG.). 32p. (J). (gr. -1-1). 8.99 (978-1-4169-7859-6(3), Simon & Schuster/Paula Wiseman Bks.) Simon & Schuster/Paula Wiseman Bks.

Van Leeuwen, Jean. Five Funny Bunnies: Three Bouncing Tales, 0 vols. Wilsdorf, Anne, illus. 2012. (ENG.). 40p. (J). (gr. -1-3). 17.99 (978-0-7614-6114-2(0), 9780761461142, Amazon Children's Publishing) Amazon Publishing.

Van Oss, Laura. Indigo's Gift: Does Indigo Have a Secret Gift? Wolf, Claudia, illus. 2006. 24p. (J). per. 2.99 (978-1-59958-003-6(9)) Journey Stone Creations, LLC.

Velthuijs, Max. Frog & Hare. (ENG., Illus.). 8p. (J). 6.99 (978-0-86264-995-1(1)) Andersen Pr. GBR. Dist: Trafalgar Square Publishing.

Vetter Squires, Diane. Basil's New Home: The Garden Rabbit Series - Part One. McAteer, Thomas, illus. 2009. 28p. pap. 13.99 (978-1-4490-0675-4(2)) AuthorHouse.

Vezeau, Sheila. Sky, the Blue Bunny. Ostrowski, Justin, illus. 2012. 16p. pap. 24.95 (978-1-4626-7533-3(6)) America Star Bks.

Voorheis, Tracy. Nibbles... a strawberry Tale. Voorheis, Tracy, illus. 2007. (Illus.). 60p. (J). per. 19.00 (978-0-9787113-0-6(0), Ithaca Pr.) Authors & Artists Publishers of New York, Inc.

Vulliamy, Clara. Martha Bunny Loves School. Vulliamy, Clara, illus. 2013. (ENG., Illus.). 32p. (J). (gr. -1-3). 16.99 (978-0-8075-4976-6(2)) Whitman, Albert & Co.

Waddell, Martin. Class Six & the Very Big Rabbit. Ross, Tony, illus. 2005. (Collins Big Cat Ser.). (ENG.). 80p. (J). (gr. 1-3). pap. 7.99 (978-0-00-718629-7(0)) HarperCollins Pubs. Ltd. GBR. Dist: Independent Pubs. Group.

Wade, Maryam. Bently & the Crooked Carrot. 2013. 32p. pap. 24.95 (978-1-63000-801-7(X)) America Star Bks.

—Bently & the Silver Wings. 2011. 24p. pap. 24.95 (978-1-4560-7503-3(9)) America Star Bks.

Wahl, Jan. Rabbits on Mars. Schamber, Kimberly, illus. 2005. 32p. (gr. k-2). 15.25 (978-1-57505-511-4(2)) Lerner Publishing Group.

Wahman, Wendy, illus. Rabbit Stew. 2017. (ENG.). 32p. (J). (gr. -1-2). 16.95 (978-1-62979-583-6(6)) Boyds Mills Pr.

Wakeman, Daniel. Ben's Bunny Trouble, 1 vol. Van Stralen, Dirk, illus. 2007. (ENG.). 32p. (J). (gr. -1-3). 18.95 (978-1-55143-611-1(6)) Orca Bk. Pubs. USA.

Wallace, G. Ira. Bunny Tales: The Journey Begins. 2009. 24p. pap. 12.00 (978-1-60860-869-0(7), Strategic Bk. Publishing) Strategic Book Publishing & Rights Agency (SBPRA).

Wallace, Nancy Elizabeth. Pumpkin Day, 0 vols. Wallace, Nancy Elizabeth, illus. unabr. ed. 2006. (ENG., Illus.). 32p. (J). (gr. -1-2). per. 9.99 (978-0-7614-5327-7(X), 9780761453277, Amazon Children's Publishing) Amazon Publishing.

—Recycle Every Day!, 0 vols. Wallace, Nancy Elizabeth, illus. 2006. (ENG., Illus.). 41p. (J). (gr. -1-3). pap. 9.99 (978-0-7614-5290-4(7), 9780761452904, Amazon Children's Publishing) Amazon Publishing.

—Tell-A-Bunny, 0 vols. Wallace, Nancy Elizabeth, illus. 2007. (ENG., Illus.). 36p. (J). (gr. -1-1). 7.99 (978-0-7614-5369-7(5), 9780761453697, Amazon Children's Publishing) Amazon Publishing.

—Valentine Express, 0 vols. 2008. (ENG., Illus.). 32p. (J). (gr. -1-2). pap. 9.99 (978-0-7614-5447-2(0), 9780761454472, Amazon Children's Publishing) Amazon Publishing.

Walsh, Ellen Stoll. Hop Jump. 2010. (Rise & Shine Ser.). (ENG., Illus.). 32p. (C). (gr. -1-3). pap. 11.95 (978-0-15-201375-2(X)) National Geographic School Publishing, Inc.

Walton, Rick. Bunny Christmas: A Family Celebration. Miglio, Paige, illus. 2004. 32p. (J). (ENG.). 15.99 (978-0-06-008415-8(4)); lib. bdg. 16.89 (978-0-06-008416-5(2)) HarperCollins Pubs.

Ward, Helen. Hare & Tortoise. 2005. (ALB & ENG., Illus.). 32p. (J). pap. (978-1-84444-779-4(0)) Mantra Lingua.

Ward, Helen & Aesop. Hare & Tortoise. 2005. (Illus.). 32p. (J). pap. (978-1-84444-784-8(7)) Mantra Lingua.

Warne. The Peter Rabbit Club. 2014. (Peter Rabbit Animation Ser.). (ENG.). 32p. (J). (gr. -1-k). 3.99 (978-0-14-135319-7(8), Warne) Penguin Young Readers Group.

—Peter's Favorite Places (Sticker Stories) 2014. (Peter Rabbit Animation Ser.). (ENG., Illus.). 16p. (J). (gr. -1-2). pap. 6.99 (978-0-14-135005-9(9), Warne) Penguin Young Readers Group.

—A Present for Mom. 2015. (Peter Rabbit Animation Ser.). (ENG., Illus.). 32p. (J). (gr. -1-k). 3.99 (978-0-7232-9568-6(9), Warne) Penguin Young Readers Group.

Warner, Liz. El Conejito Grande. 2007. 40p. per. 21.32 (978-1-4257-5616-1(6)) Xlibris Corp.

Warnes, Tim. Warning! Do Not Touch! Warnes, Tim, illus. 2016. (ENG., Illus.). 32p. (J). (gr. -1-2). 16.99 (978-1-68010-013-6(0)) Tiger Tales.

Washington, Donna L. Li'l Rabbit's Kwanzaa. Evans, Shane W., illus. 2010. (ENG.). 32p. (J). (gr. -1-2). 12.99 (978-0-06-072816-8(7), Tegen, Katherine Bks) HarperCollins Pubs.

Washington, Sharalee Marie Shepherd. Little Bear Rabbit Goes to London. 2012. 80p. 24.99 (978-1-4797-2677-6(X)); pap. 15.99 (978-1-4797-2676-9(1)) Xlibris Corp.

Watase, Yuu & Caselman, Lance. Alice 19th, Vol. 1, 7 vols. Watase, Yuu, illus. 2003. (ENG., Illus.). 192p. pap. 9.95 (978-1-59116-215-5(7)) Viz Media.

Watson, Richard Jesse. The Magic Rabbit. Watson, Richard Jesse, illus. 2005. (ENG., Illus.). 40p. (J). (gr. -1-3). 16.99 (978-0-590-47964-6(4), Blue Sky Pr., The) Scholastic, Inc.

Watt, Fiona. Hide-and-Seek Bunnies. Danson, Lesley, illus. 2007. (Touchy-Feely Flap Bks). 10p. (J). (gr. -1-k). bds. 16.99 (978-0-7945-1566-9(5), Usborne) EDC Publishing.

—That's Not My Bunny. Wells, Rachel, illus. 2004. (Touchy-Feely Board Bks.). (SPA & ENG.). 1p. (J). (gr. -1-18). bds. 7.99 (978-0-7460-4179-6(9)) EDC Publishing.

Watt, Mélanie. You're Finally Here! Watt, Mélanie, illus. 2011. (Illus.). 40p. (gr. -1-1). 15.99 (978-1-4231-3486-2(9)) Hyperion Pr.

Watts, Robin Queen. The Adventures of Beauty & Sam. 2009. 20p. pap. 10.50 (978-1-4269-1286-3(2)) Trafford Publishing.

Weber, Joanne M. Flabby Rabbit. 2011. 28p. pap. 15.99 (978-1-4568-9153-4(7)) Xlibris Corp.

Weber, Rebecca. A Party for Rabbit: Set Of 6. 2010. (Early Connections Ser.). (J). 33.00 net. (978-1-59000-713-6(1)) Benchmark Education Co.

Wedge, Chris. Bunny: A Picture Book Adapted from the Animated Film. Wedge, Chris, illus. 2004. (Illus.). 30p. (J). (gr. k-4). reprint ed. 19.00 (978-0-7567-7460-8(8)) DIANE Publishing Co.

Wehr, Paul. The Animated Bunny's Tail. Wehr, Julian, illus. 2005. 20p. (J). 18.95 (978-0-9748093-1-1(4)) Wehr Animations.

Weiss, Ellen. Winter Spring Summer Fall: A Touch-and-Feel Seasons Book. Bennett, Andy, illus. 2006. (PBS Kids Ser.). 8p. (J). (gr. -1-k). bds. 6.95 (978-1-57791-312-2(4)) Brighter Minds Children's Publishing.

Weiss, Flo. Little Bit Is Big Enough. 2012. 28p. pap. 16.09 (978-1-4669-4074-1(3)) Trafford Publishing.

Wejrmeijer, Annelien. Emma & Bo. van de Liejgraaf, Deborah, illus. 2013. (My Best Friend & Me Ser.). (ENG.). 10p. (J). (gr. -1 — 1). bds. 6.99 (978-0-7641-6635-8(2)) Barron's Educational Series, Inc.

Welch, Willy. Grumbly Bunnies. Lyon, Tammie Speer, illus. 2004. 32p. (J). 15.95 (978-1-58089-086-1(5)) Charlesbridge Publishing, Inc.

Welling, Peter J. Justin Potemkin & the 500-Mile Race, 1 vol. Welling, Peter J., illus. 2004. (ENG., Illus.). 32p. (J). (gr. k-3). 16.99 (978-1-58980-149-3(0)) Pelican Publishing Co., Inc.

Wellings, Chris R. Sparkles Meets the Easter Bunny: The Adventures of Sparkles. Hammersley, Karen, illus. 2011. 48p. pap. 24.95 (978-1-4560-7063-2(0)) America Star Bks.

Wells, Rosemary. Bunny Cakes. Wells, Rosemary, illus. 2014. (Max & Ruby Ser.). (ENG & SPA., Illus.). 32p. (J). (gr. -1-k). 7.99 (978-0-14-751586-5(6), Puffin Books) Penguin Young Readers Group.

—Bunny Mail. Wells, Rosemary, illus. 2004. (Max & Ruby Ser.). (ENG., Illus.). 32p. (J). (gr. -1-k). 15.99 (978-0-670-03630-1(7), Viking Books for Young Readers) Penguin Young Readers Group.

—Bunny Party. 2003. (Max & Ruby Ser.). (ENG., Illus.). 32p. (J). (gr. -1-k). pap. 6.99 (978-0-14-250162-7(X), Puffin Books) Penguin Young Readers Group.

—Emily's First 100 Days of School. Wells, Rosemary, illus. 2005. (ENG., Illus.). 64p. (J). (gr. -1-1). pap. 9.99 (978-0-7868-1354-4(7)) Hyperion Pr.

—Emily's First 100 Days of School. 2006. (Illus.). (J). (gr. -1-4). 18.95 (978-0-439-84903-6(9), WPCD654) Weston Woods Studios, Inc.

—Hungry Bunny Tales. 2012. (Max & Ruby Ser.). lib. bdg. 14.75 (978-0-606-23658-4(9), Turtleback) Turtleback Bks.

—Max & Ruby at the Warthogs' Wedding. Wells, Rosemary, illus. 2014. (Max & Ruby Ser.). (ENG., Illus.). 40p. (J). (gr. -1-k). 17.99 (978-0-670-78461-5(3), Viking Books for Young Readers) Penguin Young Readers Group.

—Max & Ruby Play School. 2003. (All Aboard Reading Ser.). (gr. -1-2). lib. bdg. 13.55 (978-0-613-64064-0(0), Turtleback) Turtleback Bks.

—Max & Ruby's Bedtime Book. 2010. (Max & Ruby Ser.). (ENG.). 48p. (J). (gr. -1-k). 17.99 (978-0-670-01141-4(X), Viking Books for Young Readers) Penguin Young Readers Group.

—Max & Ruby's Preschool Pranks. 2016. (Max & Ruby Ser.). (ENG., Illus.). 40p. (J). (-k). 17.99 (978-0-670-78462-2(1), Viking Books for Young Readers) Penguin Young Readers Group.

—Max & Ruby's Treasure Hunt. 2012. (Max & Ruby Ser.). (ENG.). 32p. (J). (gr. -1-k). 17.99 (978-0-670-06317-8(7), Viking Books for Young Readers) Penguin Young Readers Group.

—Max & the Fall Parade. 2014. (Max Ruby Ser.). lib. bdg. 13.55 (978-0-606-36192-7(8)) Turtleback Bks.

—Max's ABC. 2008. (Max & Ruby Ser.). (ENG.). 32p. (J). (gr. -1-k). pap. 6.99 (978-0-14-241172-8(8), Puffin Books) Penguin Young Readers Group.

—Max's ABC. 2008. (Max & Ruby Ser.). (Illus.). 26p. (gr. -1-k). 17.00 (978-0-7569-8924-8(8)) Perfection Learning Corp.

—Max's Breakfast. 2004. (Max & Ruby Ser.). (ENG.). 12p. (J). (gr. 1 — 1). bds. 5.99 (978-0-670-88712-5(9), Viking Books for Young Readers) Penguin Young Readers Group.

—Max's Bunny Business. 2008. (Max & Ruby Ser.). (ENG., Illus.). 32p. (J). (gr. -1-k). 15.99 (978-0-670-01105-6(3), Viking Books for Young Readers) Penguin Young Readers Group.

—Max's Christmas. 2013. (Max & Ruby Ser.). (ENG.). 32p. (J). (gr. -1-k). 8.99 (978-0-14-750947-5(5), Puffin Books) Penguin Young Readers Group.

—Max's Christmas. 2013. (Max Ruby Ser.). lib. bdg. 18.40 (978-0-606-32139-6(X), Turtleback) Turtleback Bks.

—Max's Valentine. 2003. (Max & Ruby Ser.). (ENG., Illus.). 32p. (J). (gr. -1 — 1). bds. 5.99 (978-0-670-03668-4(4), Viking Books for Young Readers) Penguin Young Readers Group.

—Read to Your Bunny. Wells, Rosemary, illus. 2003. (ENG., Illus.). 6p. (J). bds. 7.99 (978-0-439-54337-8(1), Cartwheel Bks.) Scholastic, Inc.

—Ruby's Beauty Shop. Wells, Rosemary, illus. 2004. (Max & Ruby Ser.). (ENG., Illus.). 32p. (J). (gr. -1-k). pap. 6.99 (978-0-14-240194-1(3), Puffin Books) Penguin Young Readers Group.

—Ruby's Falling Leaves. 2007. (Max & Ruby Ser.). lib. bdg. 13.55 (978-1-4177-9651-9(0), Turtleback) Turtleback Bks.

—Sporty Bunny Tales. 2014. (Max & Ruby Ser.). lib. bdg. 14.75 (978-0-606-34464-7(0), Turtleback) Turtleback Bks.

—Voyage to the Bunny Planet. 2008. (ENG., Illus.). 88p. (J). (gr. -1-2). 17.99 (978-0-670-01103-2(7), Viking Books for Young Readers) Penguin Young Readers Group.

—Voyage to the Bunny Planet. 2011. (J). (gr. -1-2). 29.95 (978-0-545-09458-0(5)) Weston Woods Studios, Inc.

Weninger, Brigitte. Davy Loves the Baby. Tharlet, Eve, illus. 2015. (ENG.). 32p. (J). 15.95 (978-0-7358-4210-6(8)) North-South Bks., Inc.

—Davy, Soccer Star! Tharlet, Eve, illus. 2010. (ENG.). 40p. (J). (gr. -1-3). pap. 7.95 (978-0-7358-2287-0(5)) North-South Bks., Inc.

Weninger, Brigitte & Tharlet, Eve. Davy Loves His Mommy. 2014. (ENG., Illus.). 32p. (J). (gr. k-3). 15.95 (978-0-7358-4164-2(0)) North-South Bks., Inc.

Werner, Janet, et al. Grandpa Bunny. Walt Disney Studios Staff & Random House Disney Staff, illus. 2007. (Little

Golden Book Ser.). (ENG.). 24p. (J). (gr. -1-2). 4.99 *(978-0-375-83930-6(5),* Golden/Disney) Random Hse. Children's Bks.

West, Colin. Helicopter Hare. (Illus.). 61p. (J). pap. 7.95 *(978-0-340-66095-9(3))* Hodder & Stoughton GBR. Dist: Trafalgar Square Publishing.

West, Tracey. Rabbit Hood: Stealing Laughs in Sherwood Forest. 2004. (Illus.). 57p. *(978-0-439-56600-1(2))* Scholastic, Inc.

Weston, Carrie. What Noise Does a Rabbit Make? Byrne, Richard, illus. 2013. (ENG.). 32p. (J). (gr. -1-3). 16.95 *(978-1-4677-2032-8(1))* Lerner Publishing Group.

Weston Woods Staff, creator. Emily's First 100 Days of School. 2011. 38.75 *(978-0-439-84892-3(X))* Weston Woods Studios, Inc.

—Goodnight Moon. 2011. 18.95 *(978-0-439-72684-9(0));* 38.75 *(978-0-439-72686-3(7));* 29.95 *(978-0-439-73472-1(X))* Weston Woods Studios, Inc.

—Morris's Disappearing. 2011. 18.95 *(978-0-439-72855-3(X))* Weston Woods Studios, Inc.

—Morris's Disappearing Bag. 2011. 38.75 *(978-0-439-72858-4(4))* Weston Woods Studios, Inc.

—Mr. Rabbit & the Lovely Present. 2011. 38.75 *(978-0-439-72860-7(6));* 18.95 *(978-0-439-72859-1(2))* Weston Woods Studios, Inc.

—Mr Rabbit & the Lovely Present. 2011. 29.95 *(978-0-439-73502-5(5))* Weston Woods Studios, Inc.

Wheelie, P. The Fishing Trip: The tales of Tommy the tortoise & Friends. 2009. (Illus.). 32p. pap. 12.99 *(978-1-4389-6414-0(5))* AuthorHouse.

White, Jenny. A Surprise for Junior. 2013. 24p. pap. 17.99 *(978-1-4817-0602-5(0))* AuthorHouse.

White, Kathryn. Snowshoe the Hare. Rivers, Ruth, illus. 2005. (Red Go Bananas Ser.). (ENG.). 48p. (J). (gr. 2-3). pap. *(978-0-7787-2699-9(1),* 1253648) Crabtree Publishing Co.

White, Rebecca. Holly's Not So Plain & Ordinary Day. 2011. 38p. pap. 13.97 *(978-1-61204-376-0(3),* Strategic Bk. Publishing) Strategic Book Publishing & Rights Agency (SBPRA).

Whitford Paul, Ann. Fiesta Fiasco. 2012. 29.95 *(978-1-4301-1100-9(3))* Live Oak Media.

Whitmore, Gary. Prince Luna & the Space Dreamers. 2011. (ENG.). 204p. pap. 8.50 *(978-1-4565-8438-2(3))* CreateSpace Independent Publishing Platform.

Widener, Leslie Stall, illus. Chukfi Rabbit's Big, Bad Bellyache: A Trickster Tale. 2014. (ENG.). 40p. (J). (gr. k-5). 16.95 *(978-1-935955-26-9(8))* Cinco Puntos Pr.

Wilce, Colin. The Rain & Blossom (Rabbit Brook Tales Volume 2) 2007. 88p. pap. 11.66 *(978-1-84728-105-0(2))* Lulu Pr., Inc.

—The Youngsters' Adventure & Thanksgiving (Rabbit Brook Tales Volume 4) 2007. 80p. pap. 17.95 *(978-1-84753-202-2(0))* Lulu Pr., Inc.

Wilhelm, Hans. Bunny Trouble Treasury. 2014. (ENG., Illus.). 128p. (J). (gr. k-3). pap. 14.99 *(978-0-486-49275-9(3))* Dover Pubns., Inc.

Willard, Nancy. A Starlit Snowfall. Pinkney, Jerry, illus. 2011. (ENG.). 32p. (J). (gr. -1-3). 6.99 *(978-0-316-18366-6(0))* Little Brown & Co.

Willems, Mo. Knuffle Bunny: A Cautionary Tale. Willems, Mo, illus. 2004. (Knuffle Bunny Ser.). (ENG., Illus.). 40p. (J). (gr. -1-k). 17.99 *(978-0-7868-1870-9(0))* Hyperion Pr.

Williams, Brenda & Lacombe, Benjamin. Lin Yi's Lantern. Lacombe, Benjamin, illus. 2012. (ENG., Illus.). 32p. (J). (gr. k-3). pap. 8.99 *(978-1-84686-793-4(2))* Barefoot Bks., Inc.

Williams, Deborah. Little Rabbit Is Sad. Gedeon, Gloria, illus. I.t. ed. 2005. (ENG.). 12p. (Orig.). (gr. k-1). pap. 7.95 *(978-1-879835-99-3(1),* Kaeden Bks.) Kaeden Corp.

Williams, Donald & Williams, Ronald. The Adventures of Wacko Rabbit. 2012. (Illus.). (J). 14.95 *(978-1-62086-058-8(9))* Mascot Bks., Inc.

Williams, Larry. The League of Clique. Williams, Larry, illus. 2007. (ENG., Illus.). 80p. per. 19.95 *(978-1-4241-5976-5(8))* America Star Bks.

Williams, Margery. The Velveteen Rabbit. 0 vols. Spirin, Gennady, illus. 2011. (ENG.). 48p. (J). (gr. 3-7). 17.99 *(978-0-7614-5848-7(4),* 9780761458487, Amazon Children's Publishing) Amazon Publishing.

—The Velveteen Rabbit. Massini, Sarah, illus. 2017. (ENG.). 64p. (J). (gr. k-4). 19.99 ***(978-0-7636-9641-2(2),*** Nosy Crow) Candlewick Pr.

—The Velveteen Rabbit. Felix, Monique, illus. 40p. 2013. (ENG.). (J). (gr. 1-3). pap. 8.99 *(978-0-89812-831-4(5),* Creative Paperbacks) 2005. pap. 8.95 *(978-0-89812-383-8(6))* Creative Co., The.

—The Velveteen Rabbit. Nicholson, William, illus. 2011. (Dover Children's Classics Ser.). (ENG.). 48p. (J). (gr. k-5). pap. 8.99 *(978-0-486-48606-2(0))* Dover Pubns., Inc.

—The Velveteen Rabbit. 2003. (J). 9.99 *(978-0-9740847-3-2(5))* GiGi Bks.

—The Velveteen Rabbit. Nicholson, William, illus. 2005. (ENG.). 96p. (J). (gr. -1-1). 9.95 *(978-0-7573-0333-3(1))* Health Communications, Inc.

—The Velveteen Rabbit. 2010. (CHI., Illus.). (J). *(978-957-762-476-5(6))* Hsin Yi Pubns.

—The Velveteen Rabbit. 2008. (Charm Book Classics Ser.). 32p. *(978-1-4075-1581-6(0))* Parragon, Inc.

—The Velveteen Rabbit. Nicholson, William, illus. 2014. (ENG.). 48p. (J). (gr. -1-2). 19.99 *(978-0-385-37566-5(2),* Doubleday Bks. for Young Readers) Random Hse. Children's Bks.

—The Velveteen Rabbit, 1 vol. Jorgensen, David, illus. 2005. (Rabbit Ears: A Classic Tale Ser.). (ENG.). 40p. (gr. 2-7). 25.65 *(978-1-59197-757-5(6))* Spotlight.

—The Velveteen Rabbit. Hague, Michael, illus. 2008. (ENG.). 48p. (J). (gr. -1-2). per. 7.99 *(978-0-312-37750-2(9),* 9780312377502) Square Fish.

—The Velveteen Rabbit. Wilson, Katherine, illus. 2006. (ENG.). 32p. (J). (gr. -1-1). per. 3.95 *(978-0-8249-5530-4(7),* Ideal Pubns.) Worthy Publishing.

—The Velveteen Rabbit. Daily, Don, illus. 2007. (ENG.). 28p. (J). (gr. -1-17). bds. 5.95 *(978-0-7624-2935-6(6),* Running Pr. Kids) Running Pr. Bk. Pubs.

—The Velveteen Rabbit. Nicholson, William, illus. 2014. (ENG.). 48p. (J). (gr. -1-k). pap. 9.99 *(978-1-4052-1054-6(0))* Egmont Bks., Ltd. GBR. Dist: Independent Pubs. Group.

—The Velveteen Rabbit: Or How Toys Become Real. Santore, Charles, illus. 2013. (Classic Edition Ser.). (ENG.). 48p. (J). 17.95 *(978-1-60433-277-3(8),* Applesauce Pr.) Cider Mill Pr. Bk. Pubs., LLC.

—The Velveteen Rabbit: Or, How Toys Become Real. Encarnacion, Liz, ed. Santore, Charles, illus. 2014. (ENG.). 24p. (J). bds. 8.95 *(978-1-60433-461-6(4),* Applesauce Pr.) Cider Mill Pr. Bk. Pubs., LLC.

—The Velveteen Rabbit & Other Stories Book & Charm. 2008. 128p. (J). (gr. 2-5). 6.99 *(978-0-06-145942-9(9),* HarperFestival) HarperCollins Pubs.

—The Velveteen Rabbit Book & Charm. Nicholson, William, illus. 2006. 40p. (J). (gr. -1-3). pap. 4.99 *(978-0-06-076067-0(2),* HarperFestival) HarperCollins Pubs.

—The Velveteen Rabbit Coloring Book. Kiiros, Thea, illus. 2013. (ENG.). 48p. (J). (gr. 2-5). pap. 4.99 *(978-0-486-25924-6(2))* Dover Pubns., Inc.

Williams, Margery & Bianco, Margery Williams. The Velveteen Rabbit. Felix, Monique, illus. 2004. (ENG.). 40p. (J). (gr. 1-3). 19.99 *(978-1-56846-217-2(4),* Creative Editions) Creative Co., The.

Williams, Sam. School Bus Bunny Bus. Trotter, Stuart, illus. 2006. (ENG.). 10p. (J). (gr. -1-1). 12.95 *(978-1-905417-17-9(9))* Boxer Bks., Ltd. GBR. Dist: Sterling Publishing Co., Inc.

Wilson, Gerrard. Alice on Top of the World. 2009. 159p. pap. 17.50 *(978-0-9561553-0-6(8))* Wilson, Gerrard IRL. Dist: Lulu Pr., Inc.

Wilson, Laurie Harman. The Treasures of Destiny. 2012. 72p. pap. 7.95 *(978-0-9848050-3-7(6),* Little Creek Bks.) Jan-Carol Publishing, INC.

Winch, John. Run, Hare, Run. 2007. (Illus.). 40p. pap. *(978-1-921049-55-2(3))* Little Hare Bks. AUS. Dist: HarperCollins Pubs. Australia.

Winget, Susan. Tucker's Apple-Dandy Day. Winget, Susan, illus. 2006. (Illus.). 40p. (J). (gr. -1-k). 13.89 *(978-0-06-054647-2(6))* HarperCollins Pubs.

—Tucker's Four-Carrot School Day. Winget, Susan, illus. 2005. (ENG., Illus.). 40p. (J). (gr. -1-k). 12.99 *(978-0-06-054642-7(5))* HarperCollins Pubs.

Winship, Daniel, illus. The Tortoise & the Hare: The Tortoise & the Hare. 2012. (SGN, ARA, BOS, CHI & FRE.). 32p. (J). pap. 19.95 incl. DVD *(978-0-9818139-2-9(5))* ASL Tales.

Witkowski, Teri. Bitty Bunny's Slipper Search. Ackley, Peggy Jo, illus. 2009. (J). *(978-1-59369-586-6(1),* American Girl) American Girl Publishing, Inc.

—Bunny & Piggy at the Beach. Ackley, Peggy Jo, illus. 2005. (J). *(978-1-58485-961-1(X))* American Girl Publishing, Inc.

Wolff, T. Hal & His Pal Al: The Easter Bunny's Helpers. 2007. (Illus.). 36p. per. 12.97 *(978-1-932344-93-6(4))* Thornton Publishing, Inc.

Wood, A. J. Slide & Play: Busy Bunny. Pledger, Maurice, illus. 2016. (Slide & Play Ser.). (ENG.). 16p. (J). (gr. -1). bds. 14.99 *(978-1-62686-573-0(6),* Silver Dolphin Bks.) Readerlink Distribution Services, LLC.

Wood, David. A Year in the Life of the Kingwood Bunnies. Floeter, Nell, illus. 2010. 54p. pap. 15.95 *(978-1-936343-07-2(X))* Peppertree Pr., The.

Wreggelsworth, Irene. The Funny, Naughty Bunny: A Bilingual Book in English & German. Piccione, Dana, illus. 2010. (ENG.). 102p. pap. 26.99 *(978-1-4537-2122-3(3))* CreateSpace Independent Publishing Platform.

Wright, Johanna. Bunnies on Ice. Wright, Johanna, illus. 2013. (ENG., Illus.). 32p. (J). (gr. -1-1). 16.99 *(978-1-59643-404-2(X),* 9781596434042) Roaring Brook Pr.

Yager, Jan. The Reading Rabbit. Lyman, Mitzi, illus. 32p. (J). 2014. (ENG.). 25.95 *(978-1-938998-00-3(6))* 2013. pap. 17.95 *(978-1-938998-01-0(4))* Hannacroix Creek Bks., Inc.

Yang, Belle. Summertime Rainbow: A Mandarin Chinese-English Bilingual Book of Colors. Yang, Belle, illus. 2012. (ENG & CHI., Illus.). 22p. (J). (gr. k — 1). bds. 6.99 *(978-0-7636-5280-7(6))* Candlewick Pr.

Yelchin, Eugene. Spring Hare. Yelchin, Eugene, illus. 2017. (ENG., Illus.). 32p. (J). 16.99 *(978-1-62779-392-6(5),* 9781627793926, Holt, Henry & Co. Bks. For Young Readers) Holt, Henry & Co.

Yontz, Barbara J. The Adventures of Baby Z & the Rabbit of Oz. 2012. 24p. pap. 15.99 *(978-1-4797-3514-3(0))* Xlibris Corp.

Yoon, Salina. Humpty Dumpty. Yoon, Salina, illus. 2012. (ENG., Illus.). 18p. (J). (gr. -1 — 1). bds. 5.99 *(978-1-4424-1411-2(1),* Little Simon) Little Simon.

Zangrillo, Marguerite Rochelle. The Bunny with the Polka Dot Nose. 2009. 28p. pap. 15.99 *(978-1-4363-8966-2(6))* Xlibris Corp.

Ziegler-Sullivan, Ursula. The Pups Save the Bunnies. 2016. (Illus.). (J). *(978-1-5182-1575-9(0))* Random Hse., Inc.

Zobel-Nolan, Allia. Bunnies Are for Kissing. East, Jacqueline, illus. 2009. 24p. (J). (gr. -1-k). 7.95 *(978-1-58925-842-6(8))* Tiger Tales.

Zondervan Staff & Lyons, P. J. Little Bunny's Bible, 1 vol. Mitchell, Melanie, illus. 2015. (ENG.). 16p. (J). bds. 15.99 *(978-0-310-74444-3(X))* Zonderkidz.

Zuckerman, Linda. A Taste for Rabbit. 2007. (J). *(978-0-439-86978-2(1),* Levine, Arthur A. Bks.) Scholastic, Inc.

RACCOON

Agusta, Autum. Rita & Rascal. 2013. 116p. (gr. 2-4). 22.25 *(978-1-4669-6973-5(3));* pap. 12.25 *(978-1-4669-6971-1(7))* Trafford Publishing.

Baicker, Karen. Raccoons. 2010. (Amazing Animals Ser.). (ENG.). 48p. (J). (gr. 2-6). pap. 10.50 *(978-1-4339-4020-0(5));* lib. bdg. 28.00 *(978-1-4339-4019-4(1))* Stevens, Gareth Publishing LLLP. (Gareth Stevens Learning Library).

—Raccoons. 2007. (J). *(978-1-59939-125-0(2),* Reader's Digest Young Families, Inc.) Studio Fun International.

Berger, Melvin & Berger, Gilda. Raccoons. 2010. (Illus.). 16p. (J). *(978-0-545-24434-3(X))* Scholastic, Inc.

Berne, Emma Carlson. Raccoons. 2014. (Scavengers: Eating Nature's Trash Ser.). (Illus.). 24p. (J). (gr. k-5). lib. bdg. 23.60 *(978-1-4777-6597-5(2),* PowerKids Pr.) Rosen Publishing Group, Inc., The.

Borgert-Spaniol, Megan. Baby Raccoons. 2017. (Super Cute! Ser.). (ENG., Illus.). 24p. (J). (gr. k-3). lib. bdg. 25.95 *(978-1-62617-545-7(4),* Blastoff! Readers) Bellwether Media.

Bowman, Chris. Raccoons. 2015. (North American Animals Ser.). (ENG., Illus.). 24p. (J). (gr. k-3). lib. bdg. 25.95 *(978-1-62617-263-0(3),* Blastoff! Readers) Bellwether Media.

Crossingham, John, et al. Les Ratons Laveurs. 2005. (Petit Monde Vivant Ser.). (FRE., Illus.). 32p. (J). pap. 9.95 *(978-2-89579-048-8(5))* Bayard Canada Livres CAN. Dist: Crabtree Publishing Co.

Doudna, Kelly. It's a Baby Raccoon!, 1 vol. 2008. (Baby Mammals Ser.). (ENG., Illus.). 24p. (J). (gr. k-3). lib. bdg. 24.21 *(978-1-60453-030-8(8))* ABDO Publishing Co.

Gagne, Tammy. Backyard Jungle Safari Raccoons: Raccoons. 2015. (ENG., Illus.). 32p. (J). 26.50 *(978-1-62469-102-7(1))* Purple Toad Publishing, Inc.

Gish, Melissa. Raccoons. 2015. (Illus.). 46p. (J). *(978-1-60818-570-2(2),* Creative Education) Creative Co., The.

—Raccoons: Living Wild. 2016. (Living Wild Ser.). (ENG.). 48p. (J). (gr. 5-9). pap. 12.00 *(978-1-62832-171-5(7),* Creative Paperbacks) Creative Co., The.

Gonzales, Doreen. Raccoons in the Dark. 2009. 24p. (YA). pap. 8.25 *(978-1-4358-3259-6(0));* (Illus.). (J). (gr. 1-3). 22.60 *(978-1-4042-8101-1(0))* Rosen Publishing Group, Inc., The.

Green, Emily. Raccoons. 2010. (Backyard Wildlife Ser.). (ENG., Illus.). 24p. (J). (gr. k-3). lib. bdg. 25.95 *(978-1-60014-444-8(6),* Blastoff! Readers) Bellwether Media.

Green, Jen. Raccoons. 2009. (Illus.). 52p. (J). *(978-0-7172-6281-6(2))* Grolier, Ltd.

Hancock, Lyn. Tabasco the Saucy Raccoon, 1 vol. Kemp, Loraine, illus. 2006. (ENG.). 168p. (J). (gr. 4-7). per. 10.95 *(978-1-55039-156-5(9))* Sono Nis Pr. CAN. Dist: Orca Bk. Pubs. USA.

Helbig-Miller, Theresa. Benny the Raccoon, 1 vol. 2008. (ENG.). 27p. per. 24.95 *(978-1-60441-214-7(3))* America Star Bks.

Hurtig, Jennifer. Raccoons. (J). 2012. *(978-1-61913-266-5(4))* 2012. *(978-1-61913-069-2(6))* 2007. (Illus.). 24p. (gr. -1-3). lib. bdg. 24.45 *(978-1-59036-669-1(7))* Weigl Pubs., Inc.

—Raccoons. Hudak, Heather C., ed. 2007. (Backyard Animals Ser.). (Illus.). 24p. (J). (gr. -1-3). pap. 8.95 *(978-1-59036-670-7(0))* Weigl Pubs., Inc.

Johnson, J. Angelique. Raccoons, 1 vol. (Nocturnal Animals Ser.). (ENG., 24p. (gr. k-1). 2011. Illus.). pap. 7.29 *(978-1-4296-6194-2(1))* 2011. pap. 41.70 *(978-1-4296-6363-2(4))* 2010. lib. bdg. 26.65 *(978-1-4296-5288-9(8))* Capstone Press of Coughlan Cos. (Pebble Plus).

Johnson, Jinny. Raccoon. 2014. (North American Mammals Ser.). 24p. (gr. 2-5). 28.50 *(978-1-62588-036-9(7))* Black Rabbit Bks.

—Raccoon. 2014. (North American Mammals Ser.). (ENG., Illus.). 24p. (J). (gr. -1-4). pap. 8.95 *(978-1-77092-171-9(0))* Saunders Bk. Co. CAN. Dist: RiverStream Publishing.

Kalman, Bobbie. Baby Raccoons. 2010. (ENG., Illus.). 24p. (J). *(978-0-7787-3963-0(5));* pap. *(978-0-7787-3982-1(1))* Crabtree Publishing Co.

—Raccoon Family Adventures. 2016. (ENG., Illus.). 32p. (J). *(978-0-7787-2230-4(9))* Crabtree Publishing Co.

Kalman, Bobbie & Crossingham, John. The Life Cycle of a Raccoon. Bedell, Barbara, illus. 2003. (Life Cycle Ser.). (ENG.). 32p. (J). (gr. 3-4). pap. *(978-0-7787-0691-5(5));* lib. bdg. *(978-0-7787-0661-8(3))* Crabtree Publishing Co.

Kissock, Heather. Raccoons. 2016. (J). ***(978-1-4896-5399-4(6))*** Weigl Pubs., Inc.

Kite, L. Patricia. Raccoons. Boucher, Jerry, illus. Boucher, Jerry, photos by. 2004. (Early Bird Nature Bks.). 47p. (J). 25.26 *(978-0-8225-3049-7(X),* Lerner Pubns.) Lerner Publishing Group.

Lake, G. G. Raccoons. 2016. (Woodland Wildlife Ser.). (ENG., Illus.). 24p. (gr. k-1). lib. bdg. 26.65 *(978-1-5157-0817-9(9),* Pebble Plus) Capstone Press of Coughlan Cos.

Landau, Elaine. Raccoons: Scavengers of the Night. 2007. (Animals after Dark Ser.). (Illus.). 32p. (J). (gr. 2-4). lib. bdg. 23.94 *(978-0-7660-2767-1(8),* Enslow Elementary) Enslow Pubs., Inc.

Magby, Meryl. Raccoons. 2013. (American Animals Ser.). (Illus.). 24p. (J). (gr. k-5). pap. 49.50 *(978-1-4777-0951-1(7));* pap. 8.25 *(978-1-4777-0950-4(9));* lib. bdg. 22.60 *(978-1-4777-0789-0(1))* Rosen Publishing Group, Inc., The. (PowerKids Pr.).

Mattern, Joanne. Raccoons Are Night Animals. 2007. (Night Animals Ser.). (Illus.). 24p. (gr. k-3). pap. 8.15 *(978-0-8368-7856-1(6));* lib. bdg. 22.00 *(978-0-8368-7849-3(3))* Stevens, Gareth Publishing LLLP. (Weekly Reader Leveled Readers).

—Raccoons Are Night Animals/Los Mapaches Son Animales Nocturnos. 2007. (Night Animals/ Animales Nocturnos Ser.). (SPA & ENG., Illus.). 24p. (gr. k-3). pap. 8.15 *(978-0-8368-8053-3(6),* Weekly Reader Leveled Readers) Stevens, Gareth Publishing LLLP.

—Raccoons (Los Mapaches) 2007. (Night Animals/ Animales Nocturnos Ser.). (SPA & ENG., Illus.). 24p. (gr. k-3). lib. bdg. 22.00 *(978-0-8368-8046-5(3),* Weekly Reader Leveled Readers) Stevens, Gareth Publishing LLLP.

McAneney, Caitie. Look Out for the Raccoon! 2015. (Surprisingly Scary! Ser.). (ENG., Illus.). 24p. (J). (gr. 2-3). pap. 8.25 *(978-1-4994-0882-9(X),* PowerKids Pr.) Rosen Publishing Group, Inc., The.

McGill, Jordan. Mapaches. 2012. (SPA.). (J). *(978-1-61913-195-8(1))* Weigl Pubs., Inc.

—Raccoons. 2011. (J). 27.13 *(978-1-61690-932-1(3))* Weigl Pubs., Inc.

MCP Staff. A Small Baby Raccoon, 6 bks., set, Level 12, Bk. 42. 2003. (J). (gr. -1-3). 33.50 *(978-0-8136-2079-4(1))* Modern Curriculum Pr.

Nelson, Kristin L. Clever Raccoons. (Pull Ahead Bks.). (Illus.). 32p. (gr. k-3). 2005. lib. bdg. 22.60 *(978-0-8225-3763-2(X))* 2003. (ENG., (J). pap. 6.95 *(978-0-8225-3644-4(7))* Lerner Publishing Group.

North, Sterling. Rascal. 2004. (Puffin Modern Classics Ser.). (ENG., Illus.). 192p. (J). (gr. 3-7). 5.99 *(978-0-14-240252-8(4),* Puffin Books) Penguin Young Readers Group.

—Rascal, Mi Tremendo Mapache. 2003. (Cuatro Vientos Ser.: Vol. 9). (SPA.). 168p. (gr. 5-12). pap. 13.99 *(978-84-279-3109-1(3),* NG3492) Lectorum Pubns., Inc.

O'Mara, Jean Claude. Raccoons in the Dark. 2012. (Creatures of the Night Ser.). (Illus.). 24p. (J). (gr. 1-3). pap. 8.15 *(978-1-4339-6378-0(7));* lib. bdg. 22.60 *(978-1-4339-6376-6(0))* Stevens, Gareth Publishing LLLP.

O'Shaughnessy, Ruth. Raccoons after Dark. 2015. (Animals of the Night Ser.). (ENG.). 32p. (J). (gr. 3-4). pap. 10.52 *(978-0-7660-6762-2(9));* (Illus.). 25.27 *(978-0-7660-6764-6(5))* Enslow Pubs., Inc.

Otfinoski, Steven. Raccoons. 2010. (Animals Animals Ser.). 48p. (gr. 3-6). 23.95 *(978-0-7614-4841-9(1))* Marshall Cavendish Corp.

Owen, Ruth. Raccoon Cubs. 2011. (Wild Baby Animals Ser.). 24p. (J). (gr. k-3). lib. bdg. 19.96 *(978-1-61772-154-0(9));* lib. bdg., E-Book 39.93 *(978-1-61772-242-4(1))* Bearport Publishing Co., Inc.

Payne, Donald. The Little Lost Raccoons. 2009. 28p. pap. 12.99 *(978-1-4389-6159-0(6))* AuthorHouse.

Petrie, Kristin. Raccoons, 1 vol. 2014. (Backyard Animals Ser.). (ENG.). 32p. (J). (gr. 3-6). 27.07 *(978-1-62403-662-0(7))* ABDO Publishing Co.

Read, Tracy C. Exploring the World of Raccoons. 2010. (Exploring the World Of Ser.). (ENG., Illus.). 24p. (J). (gr. 2-5). 16.95 *(978-1-55407-626-0(9),* 9781554076260); pap. 6.95 *(978-1-55407-617-8(X),* 9781554076178) Firefly Bks., Ltd.

Riggs, Kate. Amazing Animals: Raccoons. 2017. (Amazing Animals Ser.). (ENG.). 24p. (J). (gr. 1-3). pap. 8.99 ***(978-1-62832-365-8(5),*** Creative Paperbacks) Creative Co., The.

Riggs, Kate. Raccoons. 2017. (J). *(978-1-60818-757-7(8),* Creative Education) Creative Co., The.

Roza, Greg. Your Neighbor the Raccoon. 2011. (City Critters Ser.). (ENG., Illus.). 24p. (J). (gr. k-5). pap. 8.25 *(978-1-4488-5129-4(7));* lib. bdg. 22.60 *(978-1-4488-5000-6(2))* Windmill Bks.

Rustad, Martha E. H. Raccoons. 2013. (ENG., Illus.). 24p. (J). lib. bdg. 25.65 *(978-1-62031-072-4(4))* Jump! Inc.

Schuh, Mari C. Raccoons. 2015. (Backyard Animals Ser.). (ENG.). 24p. (gr. k-1). lib. bdg. 26.65 *(978-1-4914-2087-4(1),* Pebble Plus) Capstone Press of Coughlan Cos.

Storm, Marysa. El Mapache. 2017. (Spot Backyard Animals Ser.). (SPA & ENG.). 16p. (gr. k-3). 17.95 ***(978-1-68151-275-4(0))*** Amicus Publishing.

—Raccoons. 2017. (Spot Backyard Animals Ser.). (ENG.). 16p. (gr. k-3). 17.95 ***(978-1-68151-095-8(2))*** Amicus Publishing.

Thomas, Isabel. Raccoon: City Safari, 1 vol. 2014. (City Safari Ser.). (ENG., Illus.). 24p. (gr. 1-1). lib. bdg. 23.32 *(978-1-4329-8811-1(5),* Heinemann Read & Learn) Heinemann-Raintree.

Wegman, Marcia. Lula Belle. Wegman, Marcia, illus. 2012. (Illus.). 30p. pap. 16.00 *(978-1-932043-82-2(9))* Penfield Bks.

Whitehouse, Patricia. El Mapache, 1 vol. 2010. (¿Qué Está Despierto? Ser.).Tr. of Racoons. (ENG & SPA.). 24p. (gr. k-2). 23.32 *(978-1-4329-4202-1(6));* pap. 6.79 *(978-1-4329-4211-3(5))* Heinemann-Raintree.

RACCOON—FICTION

Appelt, Kathi. The True Blue Scouts of Sugar Man Swamp. 2014. (ENG., Illus.). 352p. (J). (gr. 3-7). pap. 8.99 *(978-1-4424-2108-0(8),* Atheneum Bks. for Young Readers) Simon & Schuster Children's Publishing.

—The True Blue Scouts of Sugar Man Swamp. Bricking, Jennifer, illus. 2013. (ENG.). 336p. (J). (gr. 3-7). 16.99 *(978-1-4424-2105-9(3))* Simon & Schuster Children's Publishing.

—The True Blue Scouts of Sugar Man Swamp. 2014. lib. bdg. 19.65 *(978-0-606-35793-7(9))* Turtleback Bks.

Arnosky, Jim. Raccoon on His Own. Arnosky, Jim, illus. 2003. (ENG., Illus.). 32p. (J). (gr. -1-k). 7.99 *(978-0-14-250071-2(2),* Puffin Books) Penguin Young Readers Group.

Baggett, Shirley Reed. Adventures of Bandit: A Little Racoon Goes into the Forbidden Forest. 2011. 16p. (gr. 1-2). pap. 9.99 *(978-1-4567-6575-0(2))* AuthorHouse.

Ballard, John. The Shining Thing, 1 vol. Hume, Jeff, illus. 2009. 35p. pap. 19.95 *(978-1-61546-655-9(X))* PublishAmerica, Inc.

Bloom, Becky. Leo & Lester. Biet, Pascal, illus. 2003. (J). 32p. 15.95 *(978-1-59034-582-5(7));* 33p. pap. *(978-1-59034-583-2(5))* Mondo Publishing.

Bluedorn, Johannah. The Story of Mr. Pippin. Bluedorn, Johannah, illus. 2004. (Illus.). 32p. (J). 12.00 *(978-0-9743616-8-0(2))* Trivium Pursuit.

Bottiglieri, Tim. Robber Raccoon, 1 vol. Bishop, John E., illus. 2009. 16p. pap. 24.95 *(978-1-61546-432-6(8))* America Star Bks.

Braymer, Donna. The Adventures of Rowdy Raccoon. 2006. (J). audio compact disk 5.99 *(978-0-9766823-8-7(9))* Sable Creek Pr. LLC.

Brightwood, Laura, illus. King Zargon Rules. Brightwood, Laura, . 2006. (J). *(978-0-9789871-0-7(1))* 3-C Institute for Social Development.

—Look What You've Done. Brightwood, Laura, . 2007. (J). DVD *(978-1-934409-03-9(0))* 3-C Institute for Social Development.

Brown, Ron. Three-Toes the Raccoon Visits the Farm. 2009. 24p. pap. 10.49 *(978-1-4389-9035-4(9))* AuthorHouse.

Burgess, Thornton W. The Adventures of Bobby Coon. (J). 18.95 *(978-0-8488-0383-4(3))* Amereon Ltd.

—The Adventures of Bobby Coon. 2006. pap. 10.95 *(978-1-59605-767-8(X),* Cosimo Classics) Cosimo, Inc.

Burkhart, Lorene. Raccoon Tales: Hip, Flip, Skip & Boo & Their Friend Stu. 2007. (Illus.). (J). 8.95 *(978-0-9790975-1-5(7))* Burkhart Bks.

—Raccoon Tales: Hip, Flip, Skip & Boo go to the Zoo. 2007. (Illus.). (J). 8.95 *(978-0-9790975-2-2(5))* Burkhart Bks.

Cope, Andrew. Raccoon Rampage. 2013. (Awesome Animals Ser.). (ENG.). 192p. (J). (gr. 2-7). pap. 6.99 *(978-1-4380-0302-3(1))* Barron's Educational Series, Inc.

Councilman, Janet H. Rocky & His Responsible Band of Cowboys, 1 vol. 2009. pap. 24.95 *(978-1-60749-384-6(5))* America Star Bks.

—Rocky the Respectful Raccoon & His Red Sunglasses. 2008. 16p. pap. 24.95 *(978-1-60813-100-6(9))* America Star Bks.

Crane, Jordan. Keep Our Secrets. 2012. (ENG., Illus.). 32p. (J). (gr. -1-4). bds. 15.95 *(978-1-936365-52-4(9))* McSweeney's Publishing.

Crenshaw, Glenda. Friends of the Enchanted Forest: How they Save Christmas. 2011. 28p. pap. 15.47 (978-1-4520-0512-6(5)) AuthorHouse.

deRubertis, Barbara. Rosie Raccoon's Rock & Roll Raft. Alley, R. W., illus. 2011. (Animal Antics A to Z Ser.). 32p. (J). pap. 45.32 (978-0-7613-7664-4(X)); lib. bdg. 22.60 (978-1-57565-339-6(7)); (gr. -1-3). pap. 7.95 (978-1-57565-330-3(3)) Kane Press, Inc.

deRubertis, Barbara & DeRubertis, Barbara. Rosie Raccoon's Rock & Roll Raft. Alley, R. W., illus. 2012. (Animal Antics A to Z Ser.). 32p. (J). (gr. 2 — 1). cd-rom 7.95 (978-1-57565-411-9(3)) Kane Press, Inc.

DiCamillo, Kate. Francine Poulet Meets the Ghost Raccoon. Van Dusen, Chris, illus. 2015. (Tales from Deckawoo Drive Ser.: Vol. 2). (ENG.). 112p. (J). (gr. 1-4). 12.99 (978-0-7636-6886-0(9)) Candlewick Pr.

—Francine Poulet Meets the Ghost Raccoon. Van Dusen, Chris, illus. 2016. (Tales from Deckawoo Drive Ser.: 2). (ENG.). 112p. (J). (gr. 1-4). 16.00 (978-0-606-39088-0(X)) Turtleback Bks.

Dillemuth, Julie. Lucy in the City: A Story about Spatial Thinking. Wood, Laura, illus. 2015. (J). pap. (978-1-4338-1928-5(7), Magination Pr.) American Psychological Assn.

Dipucchio, Kelly. Super Manny Stands Up! Graegin, Stephanie, illus. 2017. (Super Manny Ser.). (ENG.). 40p. (J). (gr. -1-3). 17.99 (978-1-4814-5960-0(0)) Simon & Schuster Children's Publishing.

Eaton, Maxwell, III. The Flying Beaver Brothers & the Crazy Critter Race. 2015. (Flying Beaver Brothers Ser.). (ENG., Illus.). 96p. (J). (gr. 1-4). pap. 7.99 (978-0-385-75469-9(8), Knopf Bks. for Young Readers) Random Hse. Children's Bks.

Elliott, Laura Malone. Hunter's Best Friend at School. Munsinger, Lynn, illus. 2005. (gr. -1-2). 17.00 (978-0-7569-5786-5(9)) Perfection Learning Corp.

Erickson, John R. Moonlight Madness. Holmes, Gerald L., illus. 2011. (Hank the Cowdog Ser.: No. 23). (ENG.). 114p. (J). (gr. 3-6). pap. 5.99 (978-1-59188-123-0(4)) Maverick Bks., Inc.

—The Secret Laundry Monster Files. Holmes, Gerald L., illus. 2011. (Hank the Cowdog Ser.). (ENG.). 128p. (J). (gr. 3-6). pap. 5.99 (978-1-59188-139-1(0)) Maverick Bks., Inc.

Friend, Catherine. Eddie the Raccoon: Brand New Readers. Yee, Wong Herbert, illus. 2004. (Brand New Readers Ser.). (ENG.). 32p. (J). (gr. -1-3). pap. 5.99 (978-0-7636-2334-0(2)) Candlewick Pr.

Hallagin, Janet. The Way of Courage. 2006. 30.99 (978-1-4257-1249-5(5)); pap. 20.99 (978-1-4257-1248-8(7)) Xlibris Corp.

Hamilton, Elizabeth L. Ricky Raccoon's Trustworthiness Tree. l.t. ed. 2005. (Character Critters Ser.: No. 11). (Illus.). 32p. (J). per. 5.95 (978-0-9754629-8-0(9), Character-in-Action) Quiet Impact, Inc.

Hanzik, Sharon. Raccoons Don't Use Spoons. 2009. 24p. pap. 17.95 (978-1-4327-2815-1(6)) Outskirts Pr., Inc.

Hesselbein, Deborah A. Tail Talks. Claycomb, Norma L., illus. 2008. 48p. per. 15.95 (978-1-59858-560-5(6)) Dog Ear Publishing, LLC.

Hill, Susan. Ruby Bakes a Cake. Moore, Margie, illus. 2004. (My First I Can Read Bks.). 32p. (J). (gr. k-3). lib. bdg. 16.89 (978-0-06-008976-4(8)) HarperCollins Pubs.

—Ruby Bakes a Cake, 1 vol. Moore, Margie, illus. 2010. (I Can Read! / Ruby Raccoon Ser.). (ENG.). 32p. (J). pap. 3.99 (978-0-310-72022-5(2)) Zonderkidz.

—Ruby's Perfect Day, 1 vol. Moore, Margie, illus. 2010. (I Can Read! / Ruby Raccoon Ser.). (ENG.). 32p. (J). pap. 3.99 (978-0-310-72024-9(9)) Zonderkidz.

Jackson, Bobby L. Boon the Raccoon & Easel the Weasel. Rodriguez, Christina, illus. 2004. 32p. (J). pap. 11.95 (978-1-884242-03-8(0), BREW2NED); 19.95 (978-1-884242-02-1(2), BREW2NED) Multicultural Pubns.

James, Shilah & James, Michael. Little Land Adventures - Little Racoon. Castles, Heather, illus. 2010. 24p. pap. (978-1-926635-36-1(1)) Adlibbed, Ltd.

Johnson, Joshua C. The Raccoon in My Room. 2010. 20p. 10.49 (978-1-4520-7273-9(6)) AuthorHouse.

Johnson, Virginia. Officer Rick & the Raccoon — a True Story. 2011. 24p. pap. 11.50 (978-1-60976-114-1(6), Eloquent Bks.) Strategic Book Publishing & Rights Agency (SBPRA).

Kelley, Khris. Ringo the Helpful Raccoon. Crisenbery, Casey, illus. 2012. 38p. (J). 14.95 (978-1-937406-70-7(9)) Mascot Bks., Inc.

Krulik, Nancy. Camp Rules! John and Wendy Staff, illus. 2007. (Katie Kazoo, Switcheroo Ser.: No. 5). (ENG.). 160p. (J). (gr. 2-4). pap. 5.99 (978-0-448-44542-7(5), Grosset & Dunlap) Penguin Young Readers Group.

London, C. Alexander. Moonlight Brigade. 2016. (Wild Ones Ser.: 2). (ENG.). 240p. (J). (gr. 3-7). 17.99 (978-0-399-17100-0(2), Philomel Bks.) Penguin Young Readers Group.

London, C. Alexander & Mack, Jeff. The Wild Ones. 2015. (Wild Ones Ser.: 1). (ENG., Illus.). 256p. (J). (gr. 3-7). bds. 17.99 (978-0-399-17099-7(5), Philomel Bks.) Penguin Young Readers Group.

Luebs, Robin. Please Pick Me up, Mama! Luebs, Robin, illus. 2009. (ENG., Illus.). 40p. (J). (gr. -1-k). 15.99 (978-1-4169-7977-7(8), Beach Lane Bks.) Beach Lane Bks.

Lyle-Soffe, Shari. The Misadventures of Rooter & Snuffle. Collier, Kevin Scott, illus. 2006. 28p. (J). E-Book 5.00 incl. cd-rom (978-1-933090-43-6(X)) Guardian Angel Publishing, Inc.

—On the Go with Rooter & Snuffle. Collier, Kevin Scott, illus. 2008. 20p. pap. 9.95 (978-1-933090-96-2(0)) Guardian Angel Publishing, Inc.

—Trouble Finds Rooter & Snuffle. Collier, Kevin Scott, illus. 2008. 20p. pap. 9.95 (978-1-933090-72-6(3)) Guardian Angel Publishing, Inc.

Macieiski, Ellen. Little Raccoon's Adventures. 2012. 56p. pap. 24.99 (978-1-4685-3854-0(3)) AuthorHouse.

Marie, Tina. Raccoon Round-Up at the Diamond R Ranch. 2012. 32p. pap. 24.95 (978-1-4626-7599-9(9)) America Star Bks.

Mattix, Tracy. Begging for Marshmallows. 2013. 44p. pap. 16.95 (978-1-63000-542-9(8)) America Star Bks.

Maxwell, Andre L. & Maxwell, Amanda L. The Great Chicken Caper. Carter, Jill, illus. 2012. 34p. (-18). 18.00 (978-0-9881811-1-3(8)) Maxwell, Andre.

McCorkle, Barbara. Bandit Raccoon. Taylor, David A., illus. l.t. ed. 2006. 39p. (J). 19.95 (978-1-59879-170-9(2)); per. 13.99 (978-1-59879-123-5(0)) Lifevest Publishing, Inc.

McPhail, David. The Searcher & Old Tree. McPhail, David, illus. 2011. (ENG., Illus.). 32p. (J). (gr. -1-2). pap. 7.95 (978-1-58089-224-7(8)) Charlesbridge Publishing, Inc.

—Waddles. 2011. (ENG., Illus.). 32p. (J). (gr. k-2). 16.95 (978-0-8109-8415-8(6), Abrams Bks. for Young Readers) Abrams, Inc.

Melton, David. The Wonder Years of Oscar the Raccoon. 2013. (ENG.). 32p. (J). 15.95 (978-1-4327-9964-9(9)) Outskirts Pr., Inc.

Michaud, Sylvie. Book of Dreams - the Ringtail Family. Michaud, Monique, illus. 2012. 24p. pap. (978-0-9782955-8-5(7)) Crafty Canuck, Inc.

—Book of Love - the Ringtail Family. Michaud, Monique, illus. 2012. 24p. pap. (978-1-927471-00-5(1)) Crafty Canuck, Inc.

—Book of Wishes - the Ringtail Family. Michaud, Monique, illus. 2012. 24p. pap. (978-0-9782955-9-2(5)) Crafty Canuck, Inc.

Nieting, Sherry. Adventures in Hope Forest: Isabelle's Search for God. 2011. 24p. pap. 10.95 (978-1-4497-2518-1(X), WestBow Pr.) Author Solutions, Inc.

Odom, Rebecca. Grandpa & the Raccoon. Tebbit, Jake, illus. 2009. 36p. pap. 24.95 (978-1-60749-912-1(6)) America Star Bks.

Opal, Paola. Rokko. 2012. (Simply Small Ser.). (ENG., Illus.). 24p. (J). (gr. -1-3). bds. 7.95 (978-1-897476-59-8(0)) Simply Read Bks. CAN. Dist: Ingram Publisher Services.

Otto, Carolyn B. Raccoon at Clear Creek Road. Trachok, Cathy, illus. 2005. (Smithsonian's Backyard Ser.). 32p. (J). (gr. -1-3). pap. 8.95 incl. audio (978-1-59249-490-3(0), SC5008); (ENG.). per. 6.95 (978-1-59249-481-1(1), S5008) Soundprints.

Penn, Audrey. Un Beso en Mi Mano. Harper, Ruth E. & Leak, Nancy M., illus. 2006. (Kissing Hand Ser.). (SPA & ENG.). 32p. (J). (gr. -1-3). 16.95 (978-1-933718-01-9(3)) Tanglewood Pr.

—Chester Raccoon & the Acorn Full of Memories. Gibson, Barbara L., illus. 2009. (Kissing Hand Ser.). (ENG.). 32p. (J). (gr. -1-3). 16.95 (978-1-933718-29-3(3)) Tanglewood Pr.

—Chester the Brave. Gibson, Barbara Leonard, illus. 2012. (Kissing Hand Ser.). (ENG.). 32p. (J). (gr. -1-3). 16.95 (978-1-933718-79-8(X)) Tanglewood Pr.

—A Color Game for Chester Raccoon. Gibson, Barbara Leonard, illus. 2012. (Kissing Hand Ser.). (ENG.). 14p. (J). (gr. -1-k). bds. 7.95 (978-1-933718-58-3(7)) Tanglewood Pr.

—The Kissing Hand. Gibson, Barbara Leonard, illus. 2014. (Kissing Hand Ser.). (ENG.). 14p. (J). (-k). bds. 7.99 (978-1-933718-77-4(3)) Tanglewood Pr.

—The Kissing Hand. Harper, Ruth E. & Leak, Nancy M., illus. 2007. (Kissing Hand Ser.). (ENG.). 32p. (J). (gr. -1-3). 28.95 (978-1-933718-07-1(2)); 12.95 (978-1-933718-10-1(2)) Tanglewood Pr.

—A Pocket Full of Kisses. Gibson, Barbara Leonard, illus. 2004. (New Child & Family Press Titles Ser.). 32p. (gr. -1-1). 16.95 (978-0-87868-894-4(3), 8943, Child & Family Pr.) Child Welfare League of America, Inc.

—A Pocket Full of Kisses. Gibson, Barbara Leonard, illus. 2006. (Kissing Hand Ser.). (ENG.). 32p. (J). (gr. -1-3). 16.95 (978-1-933718-02-6(1)) Tanglewood Pr.

Penn, Audrey, et al, illus. The Kissing Hand. 2010. 23.05 (978-0-7569-9299-6(0)) Natl Bk. Network.

Penn, Audrey & Gibson, Barbara L. Chester Raccoon & the Big Bad Bully. 2008. (Kissing Hand Ser.). (ENG., Illus.). 32p. (J). (gr. -1-3). 16.95 (978-1-933718-15-6(3)) Tanglewood Pr.

Percival, Tom. Herman's Letter. 2014. (ENG., Illus.). 32p. (J). (gr. -1-1). 17.99 (978-1-61963-423-7(6), 9781619634237, Bloomsbury USA Childrens) Bloomsbury Publishing USA.

—Herman's Vacation. 2016. (ENG., Illus.). 32p. (J). 17.99 (978-1-61963-990-4(4), 9781619639904, Bloomsbury USA Childrens) Bloomsbury Publishing USA.

Petrella, Angela, et al. Recipe. Althea, Erin & Bertino, Mike, illus. 2013. (ENG.). 48p. (J). (gr. -1-3). 17.95 (978-1-936365-84-5(7)) McSweeney's Publishing.

Phillips, Dixie. One Noble Journey. Sponaugle, Kim, illus. 2009. 16p. pap. 9.95 (978-1-935137-86-3(7)) Guardian Angel Publishing, Inc.

Pick Me up, Mama! 2014. (ENG., Illus.). 34p. (J). (gr. -1-k). bds. 5.99 (978-1-4814-1633-7(2), Little Simon) Little Simon.

Plant, David J. Hungry Roscoe. 2015. (ENG., Illus.). 40p. (J). (gr. -1-2). 17.95 (978-1-909263-53-6(2)) Flying Eye Bks. GBR. Dist: Consortium Bk. Sales & Distribution.

Qualls, Millie Marie. Miss Cooney & Her New Home. 2012. 24p. 24.95 (978-1-4626-7426-8(7)) America Star Bks.

Rankine-Van Wassenhoven, Jacqueline. Three Pumpkin Pies for Three Good Neighbors. 2009. 20p. pap. 11.00 (978-1-4389-3242-2(1)) AuthorHouse.

Rayner, Catherine. The Bear Who Shared. 2011. (ENG.). 32p. (J). (gr. -1-k). 16.99 (978-0-8037-3576-7(6), Dial Bks) Penguin Young Readers Group.

Robertson-Eletto, Joanne. Rocky: The Okeeheelee Bandit. 2013. 48p. pap. 20.99 (978-1-4808-0298-8(0)) Archway Publishing.

Roddy, Lee. The Legend of the White Raccoon. 2008. (D. J. Dillon Adventure Ser.: No. 6). (J). 7.99 (978-0-88062-270-7(9)) Mott Media.

Rubin, Adam. Fiesta Secreta de Pizza. Salmieri, Daniel, illus. 2015. (ENG & SPA.). 40p. (J). (gr. -1-k). 8.99 (978-0-14-751560-5(2), Puffin Books) Penguin Young Readers Group.

—Secret Pizza Party. Salmieri, Daniel, illus. 2013. (ENG.). 36p. (J). (gr. -1-2). 17.99 (978-0-8037-3947-5(8), Dial Bks) Penguin Young Readers Group.

Rylant, Cynthia. The Case of the Climbing Cat. Karas, G. Brian, illus. 2003. (High-Rise Private Eyes Ser.: No. 2). (J). (gr. -1-3). 25.96 incl. audio (978-1-59112-190-9(6)); pap. 29.95 incl. audio (978-1-59112-191-6(4)) Live Oak Media.

—The Case of the Puzzling Possum. Karas, G. Brian, illus. 2003. (High-Rise Private Eyes Ser.: No. 3). (J). (gr. -1-3). 25.95 incl. audio (978-1-59112-198-5(1)); (gr. k-3). pap. 29.95 incl. audio (978-1-59112-199-2(X)) Live Oak Media.

Sargent, Dave & Sargent, David, Jr. Hoot Owl: Mind Your Mamma, 19 vols., Vol. 9. Lenoir, Jane, illus. 2003. (Feather Tales Ser.: 9). 42p. (J). pap. 10.95 (978-1-56763-736-6(1)) Ozark Publishing.

Sargent, Dave & Sargent, David M., Jr. Hoot Owl: Mind Your Mamma, 20 vols., Vol. 9. Lenoir, Jane, illus. 2nd ed. 2003. (Feather Tales Ser.: 9). 42p. (J). lib. bdg. (978-1-56763-735-9(3)) Ozark Publishing.

Sargent, Dave & Sargent, Pat. Roy Raccoon: I Love Adventure, 15 vols., Vol. 1. Huff, Jeane, illus. 2nd rev. ed. 2003. (Animal Pride Ser.: 1). 42p. (J). pap. 10.95 (978-1-56763-760-1(4)); lib. bdg. 20.95 (978-1-56763-759-5(0)) Ozark Publishing.

Schachner, Judy. Dewey Bob. Schachner, Judy, illus. 2015. (ENG., Illus.). 32p. (J). (gr. k-3). 17.99 (978-0-8037-4120-1(0), Dial Bks) Penguin Young Readers Group.

Sheets, Katherine. Captured by Henrey, 1 vol. 2010. 48p. pap. 16.95 (978-1-4489-4538-2(0)) America Star Bks.

Sherry, Kevin. Remy Sneakers vs. the Robo-Rats. Sherry, Kevin, illus. 2017. (Remy Sneakers Ser.: 1). (ENG., Illus.). 128p. (J). (gr. 2-5). 9.99 **(978-1-338-03460-8(X)**, Scholastic Pr.) Scholastic, Inc.

Spurlock, Necole. Rocky & Rudy's Wild Adventure, 1 vol. 2009. 48p. pap. 16.95 (978-1-61582-600-1(9)) America Star Bks.

Trish Lynch Marquis. Pesty Neighbor. 2009. 28p. pap. 14.99 (978-1-4389-9011-8(1)) AuthorHouse.

Ulch, Virginia. I Love You Anyway. 2007. 32p. per. 18.95 (978-1-59858-433-2(2)) Dog Ear Publishing, LLC.

—Love, Bandit - a Tail of Foster Care. 2007. 36p. per. 18.95 (978-1-59858-353-3(0)) Dog Ear Publishing, LLC.

Verrett, Michael. The White Alligator Crown Quatro. 2010. 147p. pap. 13.95 (978-0-557-58121-4(4)) Lulu Pr., Inc.

Weck, Peter. Lima Bear's Halloween. DiSalvo, Len, illus. 2012. (Lima Bear Stories Ser.). 40p. (J). 15.95 (978-1-933872-16-2(0)) Lima Bear Pr LLC, The.

Young, Skottie. Rocket Raccoon & Groot, Volume 1. 2016. (J). lib. bdg. 30.60 (978-0-606-38357-8(3)) Turtleback Bks.

RACCOONS

see Raccoon

RACE

Alaskan Iditarod Adventure: Represent & Solve Problems Involving Multiplication. 2014. (Rosen Common Core Math Readers Ser.). (ENG., Illus.). 24p. (J). (gr. 3-4). pap. 8.25 (978-1-4777-4962-3(4), PowerKids Pr.) Rosen Publishing Group, Inc., The.

All about Us Interactive Packages: Here I Am. (Pebble Soup Explorations Ser.). (gr. -1-18). 52.00 (978-0-7578-5227-5(0)) Rigby Education.

All about Us Interactive Packages: Making Friends. (Pebble Soup Explorations Ser.). (gr. -1-18). 52.00 (978-0-7578-5228-2(9)) Rigby Education.

The Amazing Race, 6 vols., Pack. (Chiquilibros Ser.). (gr. k-1). 23.00 (978-0-7635-0437-3(8)) Rigby Education.

La carrera Increible: Individual Title-Six Packs. (Chiquilibros Ser.). (SPA.). (gr. k-1). 23.00 (978-0-7635-8603-4(X)) Rigby Education.

Hamilton, S. L. Iditarod. 2013. (Xtreme Races Ser.). 32p. (J). (gr. 3-9). lib. bdg. 27.07 (978-1-61783-693-0(1), Abdo & Daughters) ABDO Publishing Co.

Higgins, Melissa. Celebrating Differences. 2012. (Celebrating Differences Ser.). (ENG.). 24p. (gr. k-1). pap. 29.16 (978-1-4296-8324-1(4)); lib. bdg. 79.95 (978-1-4296-8110-0(1)) Capstone Press of Coughlan Cos. (Pebble Plus).

Nelson, David, ed. Race in John Howard Griffinrsquo's Black Like Me. 2013. (Social Issues in Literature Ser.). (ENG., Illus.). 224p. (gr. 10-12). lib. bdg. 40.95 (978-0-7377-6373-7(6)); pap. 32.00 (978-0-7377-6374-4(4)) Cengage Gale. (Greenhaven Pr., Inc.).

Robbins, Maureen. En Sus Marcas, Listos, ¡Ya! 2012.Tr. of Ready, Set, Race! (SPA & ENG.). 24p. (gr. 2-3). pap. 8.95 (978-1-61810-538-7(8)) Rourke Educational Media.

Robinson, Chuck. Critical World Issues: Racism, Vol. 16. 2016. (Critical World Issues Ser.: Vol. 16). (ENG., Illus.). 112p. (J). (gr. 7-12). 25.95 (978-1-4222-3659-8(5)) Mason Crest.

Sax, Anita. One Step at a Time. Jasuna, Aija, illus. 2013. 24p. (J). 17.95 (978-1-60131-152-8(4), Castlebridge Bks.) Big Tent Bks.

Stephens, Aarti, ed. Is Racism a Serious Problem? 2009. (At Issue Ser.). (ENG.). 128p. (gr. 10-12). pap. 27.80 (978-0-7377-4417-0(0), Greenhaven Pr., Inc.) Cengage Gale.

Stephens, Aarti D. Is Racism a Serious Problem?, No. 9. 2009. (At Issue Ser.). (ENG.). 128p. (gr. 10-12). 39.40 (978-0-7377-4416-3(2), Greenhaven Pr., Inc.) Cengage Gale.

RACE DISCRIMINATION

see also Race Relations

Anderson, Wayne. Fighting Racial Discrimination: Treating All Americans Fairly under the Law. 2009. (Progressive Movement 1900-1920: Efforts to Reform America's New Industrial Society Ser.). 32p. (gr. 3-4). 47.90 (978-1-60854-164-5(9)) Rosen Publishing Group, Inc., The.

Cushman, Clare, et al. Black, White, & Brown: The Landmark School Desegregation Case in Retrospect, 00 vols. rev. ed. 2004. (ENG., Illus.). 258p. (YA). (gr. 9-18). 65.00 (978-1-56802-911-5(X)) CQ Pr.

Esty, Amos. Plessy V. Ferguson. 2012. (Civil Rights Movement Ser.). (Illus.). 112p. (YA). (gr. 7-12). 28.95 (978-1-59935-182-7(X)) Reynolds, Morgan Inc.

Gold, Susan Dudley. The Civil Rights ACT of 1964. 2010. (Landmark Legislation Ser.). 128p. (YA). (gr. 7-12). 39.93 (978-1-60870-040-0(2)) Marshall Cavendish GBR. Dist: Marshall Cavendish Corp.

Greenhaven Press Staff, ed. Multiracial America. 2012. (Opposing Viewpoints Ser.). (ENG., Illus.). 240p. (gr. 10-12). pap. 28.90 (978-0-7377-6331-7(0)); lib. bdg. 41.70 (978-0-7377-6330-0(2)) Cengage Gale. (Greenhaven Pr., Inc.).

Grinapal, Corinne. Racial Profiling & Discrimination: Your Legal Rights. 2015. (Know Your Rights Ser.). (ENG., Illus.). 64p. (J). (gr. 6-6). pap. 12.95 (978-1-4777-8619-2(8), Rosen Young Adult) Rosen Publishing Group, Inc., The.

Grinapol, Corinne. Racial Profiling & Discrimination: Your Legal Rights. 2015. (Know Your Rights Ser.). (ENG., Illus.). 64p. (J). (gr. 6-6). 33.25 (978-1-4777-8020-6(3), Rosen Young Adult) Rosen Publishing Group, Inc., The.

Hanson-Harding, Alexandra. Are You Being Racially Profiled? 2016. (Got Issues? Ser.). (ENG., Illus.). 112p. (J). (gr. 7-8). lib. bdg. 37.27 (978-0-7660-7138-4(3)) Enslow Pubs., Inc.

Lentin, Alana. Racism & Ethnic Discrimination. 2011. (Contemporary Issues Ser.). 139p. (YA). (gr. 9-12). lib. bdg. 37.95 (978-1-4488-1861-7(3)) Rosen Publishing Group, Inc., The.

Lishak, Antony. Racism. 2007. (What's That Got to Do with Me?/Watts Ser.). (Illus.). 32p. (YA). (gr. 4-7). lib. bdg. 28.50 (978-1-59920-038-5(4)) Black Rabbit Bks.

Lo Bosco, Maryellen. Confronting Racism. 2017. pap. **(978-1-5383-8176-2(1))** Rosen Publishing Group, Inc., The.

Lüsted, Marcia Amidon. Lyndon B. Johnson & the Civil Rights ACT. 2017. (J). **(978-1-5383-8048-2(X))**; pap. **(978-1-5081-7746-3(5))** Rosen Publishing Group, Inc., The.

Open for Debate - Group 5, 4 bks., Set. Incl. National Health Care. Kowalski, Kathiann M. lib. bdg. 42.79 (978-0-7614-2943-2(3)); Political Campaigns. Naden, Corinne J. lib. bdg. 42.79 (978-0-7614-2944-9(1)); Religious Fundamentalism. Fridell, Ron. lib. bdg. 42.79 (978-0-7614-2945-6(X)); Right to Die. Stefoff, Rebecca. lib. bdg. 42.79 (978-0-7614-2948-7(4)); 128p. (gr. 7-18). (Open for Debate 5 Ser.). 2008. Set lib. bdg. 171.16 (978-0-7614-2940-1(9), Benchmark Bks.) Marshall Cavendish Corp.

Orr, Tamra. Coping with Racial Inequality. 2017. (Coping Ser.). 112p. (gr. 12-12). 37.10 **(978-1-5081-7396-0(6)**, Rosen Young Adult) Rosen Publishing Group, Inc., The.

Sanna, Ellyn. Native North American Indians. 2012. (Gallup Guides for Youth Facing Persistent Prejudice Ser.). 64p. (J). (gr. 7-8). 22.95 (978-1-4222-2469-4(4)); pap. 9.95 (978-1-4222-2478-6(3)) Mason Crest.

Seba, Jaime. Gallup Guides for Youth Facing Persistent Prejudice. 2012. (J). (978-1-4222-2462-5(7)) Mason Crest.

—Gallup Guides for Youth Facing Persistent Prejudice - The LGBT Community. 2012. (Gallup Guides for Youth Facing Persistent Prejudice Ser.). 64p. (J). (gr. 7-8). 22.95 (978-1-4222-2467-0(8)) Mason Crest.

Seba, Jaime & Sanna, Ellyn. Gallup Guides for Youth Facing Persistent Prejudice. 2012. (Gallup Guides for Youth Facing Persistent Prejudice Ser.). 64p. (J). (gr. 7-8). 22.95 (978-1-4222-2465-6(1)) Mason Crest.

Stone, Tanya Lee. Courage Has No Color - The True Story of the Triple Nickles: America's First Black Paratroopers. 2013. (ENG., Illus.). 160p. (J). (gr. 5). pap. 17.99 (978-0-7636-6548-7(7)); 24.99 (978-0-7636-5117-6(6)) Candlewick Pr.

Thomas, Pat. The Skin I'm In: A First Look at Racism. Harker, Lesley, illus. 2003. (First Look At... Ser.). (ENG.). 32p. (J). pap. 7.99 (978-0-7641-2459-4(5)) Barron's Educational Series, Inc.

Warner, Jody Nyasha. Viola Desmond Won't Be Budged, 1 vol. Rudnicki, Richard & Junaid, Bushra, illus. 2010. (ENG.). 32p. (J). (gr. k-4). 18.95 (978-0-88899-779-1(5)) Groundwood Bks. CAN. Dist: Publishers Group West (PGW).

Watson, Marilyn Myrick. Raul Castro: Arizona's First Hispanic Governor. 2007. (J). (978-0-9790826-5-8(X)); (978-0-9790826-6-5(8)) Acacia Publishing, Inc.

RACE PROBLEMS

see Race Relations

RACE RELATIONS

see also Discrimination; Emigration and Immigration; Multicultural Education

also names of countries, cities, etc. with the subdivision Race Relations, e.g. U. S.—Race Relations

Aikins, Anne Marie. Racism: Deal with It Before It Gets under Your Skin, 1 vol. Murray, Steven, illus. 2004. (Lorimer Deal with It Ser.). (ENG.). 32p. (J). (gr. 4-6). 12.95 (978-1-55028-844-5(X), 9781550288445) Lorimer, James & Co., Ltd., Pubs. CAN. Dist: Casemate Pubs. & Bk. Distributors, LLC.

Aronson, Marc. Race: A History Beyond Black & White. 2007. (ENG., Illus.). 336p. (YA). (gr. 6-12). 21.99 (978-0-689-86554-1(6), Atheneum Bks. for Young Readers) Simon & Schuster Children's Publishing.

Cline-Ransome, Lesa. Benny Goodman & Teddy Wilson: Taking the Stage As the First Black-and-White Jazz Band in History. Ransome, James E., illus. 2014. (ENG.). 32p. (J). (gr. 3-7). 16.95 (978-0-8234-2362-0(X)) Holiday Hse., Inc.

Cooper, John, Jr. Season of Rage: Hugh Burnett & the Struggle for Civil Rights. 2005. (ENG., Illus.). 80p. (J). (gr. 5-12). pap. 9.95 (978-0-88776-700-5(1), Tundra Bks.) Tundra Bks. CAN. Dist: Penguin Random Hse. LLC.

Edwards, Nicola. Racism. (Illus.). 32p. (YA). (gr. 1-18). lib. bdg. 27.10 (978-1-932333-06-0(1)) Chrysalis Education.

Fiorelli, June Estep. Fannie Lou Hamer: A Voice for Freedom. 2004. (Avisson Young Adult Ser.). (Illus.). 117p. (J). pap. 19.95 (978-1-888105-62-9(3)) Avisson Pr., Inc.

Ford, Carin T. African-American Soldiers in the Civil War: Fighting for Freedom. 2004. (Civil War Library). (Illus.). 48p. (J). (gr. 3-4). lib. bdg. 25.27 (978-0-7660-2254-6(4)) Enslow Pubs., Inc.

—The Civil War's African-American Soldiers Through Primary Sources. 2013. (Civil War Through Primary Sources Ser.). 48p. (J). (gr. 4-10). pap. 8.95 (978-1-4644-0183-1(7)); 25.27 (978-0-7660-4125-7(5)) Enslow Pubs., Inc.

Gay, Kathlyn. Cultural Diversity: Conflicts & Challenges. 2003. (It Happened to Me Ser.: 6). (ENG., Illus.). 144p. pap. 45.00 (978-0-8108-4805-4(8)) Scarecrow Pr., Inc.

Gifford, Clive. Racism. (Illus.). 64p. (YA). (gr. 5-18). lib. bdg. 29.95 (978-1-931983-83-9(6)) Chrysalis Education.

Gosman, Gillian. Rosa Parks. 2011. (Life Stories Ser.). (Illus.). 24p. (J). pap. 8.25 (978-1-4488-2757-2(4), PowerKids Pr.); (gr. 1-4). lib. bdg. 22.60 (978-1-4488-2584-4(9), PowerKids Pr.); (ENG & SPA., (gr. 1-4). lib. bdg. 22.60 (978-1-4488-3218-7(7)) Rosen Publishing Group, Inc., The.

Hanes, Richard Clay, et al. Prejudice in the Modern World. 2007. (J). (978-1-4144-0205-5(8)); (978-1-4144-0206-2(6)) Cengage Gale.

Hill, Z. B. Gallup Guides for Youth Facing Persistent Prejudice. 2012. (Gallup Guides for Youth Facing Persistent Prejudice Ser.). 64p. (J). (gr. 7-8). 22.95 (978-1-4222-2463-2(5)) Mason Crest.

Jelloun, Tahar. Racisme Explique a Ma Fille. pap. 19.95 *(978-88-7754-206-9(3))* Cideb ITA. Dist: Distribooks, Inc.
Johnson, Claudia Durst. Race in the Poetry of Langston Hughes. Greenhaven Press Editors, ed. 2013. (Social Issues in Literature Ser.). (ENG., Illus.). 224p. (gr. 10-12). pap. 32.00 *(978-0-7377-6981-4(5))*; lib. bdg. 46.40 *(978-0-7377-6980-7(7))* Cengage Gale. (Greenhaven Pr., Inc.).
Lester, Julius. Let's Talk about Race. Barbour, Karen, illus. 2008. (ENG.). 32p. (J). (gr. 1-5). pap. 6.99 *(978-0-06-446226-6(9)*, Amistad) HarperCollins Pubs.
Mancini, Candice. Racism in the Autobiography of Malcolm X. 2008. (Social Issues in Literature Ser.). (ENG., Illus.). 175p. (YA). (gr. 10-12). 28.45 *(978-0-7377-4261-9(5)*, LML02109-243175); pap. 40.95 *(978-0-7377-4260-2(7)*, LML02109-243171) Cengage Gale. (Greenhaven Pr., Inc.).
Marcovitz, Hal. Teens & Race. 2008. (Gallup Youth Survey, Major Issues & Trends Ser.). (Illus.). 112,128p. (YA). (gr. 7-9). lib. bdg. 22.95 *(978-1-59084-721-3(0))* Mason Crest.
Marsico, Katie. Racism. 2008. (21st Century Skills Library: Global Perspectives Ser.). (ENG.). 32p. (gr. 4-8). lib. bdg. 28.50 *(978-1-60279-134-3(1)*, 200107) Cherry Lake Publishing.
Miller, Jake. The Montgomery Bus Boycott: Integrating Public Buses. 2004. (Library of the Civil Rights Movement Ser.). (Illus.). 24p. (J). lib. bdg. 22.60 *(978-0-8239-6251-8(2)*, PowerKids Pr.) Rosen Publishing Group, Inc., The.
Miller, Karen. Race Relations. 2011. (Opposing Viewpoints Ser.). 240p. (ENG.). 42.95 *(978-0-7377-4986-1(5))*; pap. 29.45 *(978-0-7377-4987-8(3))* Cengage Gale. (Greenhaven Pr., Inc.).
Pederson, Charles E. Racism & Intolerance. 2008. (Man's Inhumanities Ser.). (YA). (gr. 7-12). 23.95 *(978-1-60217-976-9(X))* Erickson Pr.
Rodger, Marguerite & Rodger, Jessie. Racism & Prejudice. 2010. (Straight Talk about... Ser.). (ENG.). 48p. (J). (gr. 7-10). pap. *(978-0-7787-2136-9(1))* Crabtree Publishing Co.
Rooney, Anne. Race Hate. 2010. (Voices Ser.). (Illus.). 48p. pap. *(978-0-237-54215-3(3))* Evans Brothers, Ltd.
Schramm, Linda Anette. Don't Let the Zeiglers into the Zoo! 2004. 31p. pap. 24.95 *(978-1-4137-1541-5(9))* PublishAmerica, Inc.
Seba, Jaime. Gallup Guides for Youth Facing Persistent Prejudice: Blacks. 2012. (Gallup Guides for Youth Facing Persistent Prejudice Ser.). 64p. (J). (gr. 7-8). 22.95 *(978-1-4222-2464-9(3))* Mason Crest.
Steele, Philip. Race & Crime. 2016. (Illus.). 48p. (J). *(978-0-7787-2588-6(X))* Crabtree Publishing Co.
Supples, Kevin. Speaking Out: The Civil Rights Movement 1950-1964. 2005. (Crossroads America Ser.). (ENG., Illus.). 40p. (gr. k-3). 12.95 *(978-0-7922-8279-2(5))*; lib. bdg. 21.90 *(978-0-7922-8359-1(7))* National Geographic Society. (National Geographic Children's Bks.).
Sutherland, Jonathan & Canwell, Diane. African Americans in the Vietnam War. 2005. (American Experience in Vietnam Ser.). (Illus.). 48p. (gr. 5-12). lib. bdg. 31.00 *(978-0-8368-5772-6(0)*, Gareth Stevens Secondary Library) Stevens, Gareth Publishing LLLP.
Swan, Bill. Real Justice: Jailed for Life for Being Black: The Story of Rubin Hurricane Carter, 1 vol. 2014. (Lorimer Real Justice Ser.). (ENG., Illus.). 144p. (YA). (gr. 8-12). pap. 12.95 *(978-1-4594-0665-0(6)*, 9781459406650) Lorimer, James & Co., Ltd., Pubs. CAN. Dist: Casemate Pubs. & Bk. Distributors, LLC.
Thomson Gale Staff. Prejudice in the Modern World. Hanes, Sharon M., ed. rev. ed. 2007. (Prejudice in the Modern World Reference Library). (ENG.). 256p. (YA). 106.00 *(978-1-4144-0208-6(2)*, UXL) Cengage Gale.
—Prejudice in the Modern World - Almanac, 2.0. Hanes, Richard C. et al, eds. rev. ed. 2007. (Prejudice in the Modern World Reference Library). (ENG.). 462p. (YA). 191.00 *(978-1-4144-0204-8(X)*, UXL) Cengage Gale.
Thomson Gale Staff & Hermsen, Sarah. Prejudice in the Modern World: Biographies. Hanes, Richard C. & Rudd, Kelly, eds. rev. ed. 2007. (Prejudice in the Modern World Reference Library). (ENG.). 288p. (YA). 106.00 *(978-1-4144-0207-9(4)*, UXL) Cengage Gale.
—Prejudice in the Modern World: Cumulative Index. rev. ed. 2007. (Prejudice in the Modern World Reference Library). (ENG.). 34p. (YA). 5.00 *(978-1-4144-0209-3(0)*, UXL) Cengage Gale.
Vaughn, Wally G. & Davis, Mattie Campbell, eds. The Selma Campaign, 1963-1965: The Decisive Battle of the Civil Rights Movement. 2006. (ENG., Illus.). 244p. pap. 19.95 *(978-0-912469-44-7(7))* Majority Pr., The.
Where Did the Races Come from? 2003. (BUL.). (YA). 0.75 *(978-1-893345-13-3(0))* Answers in Genesis Ministries.
Worth, Richard. Slave Life on the Plantation: Prisons Beneath the Sun. 2004. (Slavery in American History Ser.). (Illus.). 128p. (J). lib. bdg. 27.94 *(978-0-7660-2152-5(1))* Enslow Pubs., Inc.

RACE RELATIONS—FICTION

Alexie, Sherman. The Absolutely True Diary of a Part-Time Indian. Forney, Ellen, illus. (ENG.). (YA). (gr. 7-17). 2009. 288p. pap. 15.99 *(978-0-316-01369-7(2))* 2007. 240p. 20.00 *(978-0-316-01368-0(4))* Little, Brown Bks. for Young Readers.
—The Absolutely True Diary of a Part-Time Indian. 10th anniv. ed. 2017. (ENG., Illus.). 320p. (YA). (gr. 7-17). 20.99 *(978-0-316-50404-1(1))* Little, Brown Bks. for Young Readers.
—The Absolutely True Diary of a Part-Time Indian. 2011. 10.36 *(978-0-7848-3391-9(5))* 2009. 14.44 *(978-0-7848-3800-6(3))* Marco Bk. Co. (Everbind).
—The Absolutely True Diary of a Part-Time Indian. Forney, Ellen, illus. 2008. 230p. 25.00 *(978-1-60686-072-4(0))* Perfection Learning Corp.
—The Absolutely True Diary of a Part-Time Indian. 2008. (YA). 1.25 *(978-1-4281-8291-2(8))*; 78.49 *(978-1-4361-0259-9(6))*; 57.75 *(978-1-4281-8294-3(2))*; 68.75 *(978-1-4281-8300-1(0))*; 55.75 *(978-1-4281-8296-7(9))*; 212.75 *(978-1-4281-8295-0(0))*; 70.75 *(978-1-4281-8298-1(5))* Recorded Bks., Inc.
—The Absolutely True Diary of a Part-Time Indian. Forney, Ellen, illus. l.t. ed. 2008. (Thorndike Literacy Bridge Ser.). (ENG.). 302p. (YA). (gr. 7-12). 23.95 *(978-1-4104-0499-2(4))* Thorndike Pr.
—The Absolutely True Diary of a Part-Time Indian. 2009. (YA). lib. bdg. 28.15 *(978-0-606-07296-0(9)*, Turtleback) Turtleback Bks.
Armistead, John. The Return of Gabriel. Gregory, Fran, illus. 2004. 218p. (gr. 3-8). 17.45 *(978-0-7569-3460-6(5))* Perfection Learning Corp.
Armistead, John & Gregory, Fran. The $66 Summer: A Novel of the Segregated South. 2nd ed. 2006. (Milkweed Prize for Children's Literature Ser.). (ENG., Illus.). 240p. (J). (gr. 3-8). reprint ed. per. 8.00 *(978-1-57131-663-9(9))* Milkweed Editions.
Badger, Ty. Crayons Alive. 2007. pap. 30.00 *(978-0-8059-8636-5(7))* Dorrance Publishing Co., Inc.
Bankole, Adekemi. The Rain Beat Dance. 2011. 32p. pap. 21.99 *(978-1-4568-7346-2(6))* Xlibris Corp.
Banks, Sara Harrell. The Everlasting Now, 1 vol. 2010. (ENG.). 168p. (J). (gr. 3-7). 15.95 *(978-1-56145-525-6(3)*, Peachtree Junior) Peachtree Pubs.
Beus, Bryan. Westly: A Spider's Tale. Beus, Bryan, illus. 2015. (Illus.). 171p. (J). 15.99 *(978-1-62972-068-5(2)*, Shadow Mountain) Deseret Bk. Co.
Bildner, Phil. The Soccer Fence: A Story of Friendship, Hope, & Apartheid in South Africa. Watson, Jesse Joshua, illus. 2014. (ENG.). 40p. (J). (gr. 1-3). 16.99 *(978-0-399-24790-3(4)*, G.P. Putnam's Sons Books for Young Readers) Penguin Young Readers Group.
Blackman, Malorie. Black & White. 2007. (ENG.). 512p. (YA). (gr. 9-12). pap. 12.99 *(978-1-4169-0017-7(9)*, Simon & Schuster Bks. For Young Readers) Simon & Schuster Bks. For Young Readers.
—Knife Edge. 2007. (ENG., Illus.). 368p. (YA). (gr. 9-12). 16.99 *(978-1-4169-0018-4(7)*, Simon & Schuster Bks. For Young Readers) Simon & Schuster Bks. For Young Readers.
—Naughts & Crosses. 2005. (ENG., Illus.). 400p. (YA). (gr. 9-18). 18.99 *(978-1-4169-0016-0(0)*, Simon & Schuster Bks. For Young Readers) Simon & Schuster Bks. For Young Readers.
Blume, Judy. Iggie's House. 2014. (ENG., Illus.). (J). (gr. 3-7). 160p. 17.99 *(978-1-4814-1410-4(0))*; 176p. pap. 7.99 *(978-1-4814-1104-2(7))* Simon & Schuster Children's Publishing. (Atheneum Bks. for Young Readers).
Bond, Victoria & Simon, T. R. Zora & Me. (Zora & Me Ser.). (ENG., Illus.). 192p. (J). (gr. 5). 2011. pap. 7.99 *(978-0-7636-5814-4(6))* 2010. 16.99 *(978-0-7636-4300-3(9))* Candlewick Pr.
Bowlby, Linda S. Future Hope. Helms, Dana, illus. 2008. 298p. (J). (gr. -1-3). pap. 9.95 *(978-0-9779993-6-1(X))* Red Earth Publishing.
Bradley, John Ed. Call Me by My Name. (ENG.). (YA). (gr. 7). 2015. 288p. pap. 11.99 *(978-1-4424-9794-8(7))* 2014. (Illus.). 272p. 17.99 *(978-1-4424-9793-1(9)*, Atheneum Bks. for Young Readers) Simon & Schuster Children's Publishing.
Brockenbrough, Martha. The Game of Love & Death. 2015. (ENG.). 336p. (J). (gr. 7). 17.99 *(978-0-545-66834-7(4))* Scholastic, Inc.
Brooks, Bruce. The Moves Make the Man. 2003. (ENG.). 256p. (YA). (gr. 8-18). pap. 8.99 *(978-0-06-447022-3(9)*, HarperTeen) HarperCollins Pubs.
—The Moves Make the Man. (J). pap., stu. ed. *(978-0-13-017518-2(8))*; 3rd ed. pap. 3.95 *(978-0-13-800079-0(4))* Prentice Hall (Schl. Div.).
Brouwer, Sigmund. Thunderbird Spirit, 1 vol. 2008. (Orca Sports Ser.). (ENG.). 192p. (YA). (gr. 6-10). pap. 9.95 *(978-1-55469-045-9(5))* Orca Bk. Pubs. USA.
Bundy, Tamara. Walking with Miss Millie. 2017. (ENG.). 240p. (J). (gr. 5). 16.99 ***(978-0-399-54456-9(9)***, Nancy Paulsen Books) Penguin Young Readers Group.
Burg, Shana. A Thousand Never Evers. 2009. (ENG.). 320p. (J). (gr. 3-7). 7.99 *(978-0-440-42209-9(4)*, Yearling) Random Hse. Children's Bks.
Choldenko, Gennifer. If a Tree Falls at Lunch Period. 2009. (ENG., Illus.). 224p. (J). (gr. 5-7). pap. 7.99 *(978-0-15-206644-4(6))* Houghton Mifflin Harcourt Publishing Co.
Christopher, Matt. The Basket Counts. 2008. (New Matt Christopher Sports Library). 96p. (J). (gr. 4-6). lib. bdg. 26.60 *(978-1-59953-212-7(3))* Norwood Hse. Pr.
Clements, Andrew. The Jacket. 2014. (ENG.). 96p. (J). (gr. 3-7). 10.24 *(978-1-63245-301-3(0))* Lectorum Pubns., Inc.
Coleman, Evelyn. Freedom Train. 2012. (ENG.). 160p. (J). (gr. 3-7). pap. 7.99 *(978-1-4424-3652-7(2)*, McElderry, Margaret K. Bks.) McElderry, Margaret K. Bks.
—Freedom Train. Riley, David, illus. 2008. (ENG.). 160p. (J). (gr. 3-7). 17.99 *(978-0-689-84716-5(5)*, McElderry, Margaret K. Bks.) McElderry, Margaret K. Bks.
Collier, Kristi. Jericho Walls. 2007. (ENG.). 224p. (YA). (gr. 4-9). pap. 10.99 *(978-0-8050-8184-8(4)*, 9780805081848, Holt, Henry & Co. Bks. For Young Readers) Holt, Henry & Co.
Conkling, Winifred. Sylvia & Aki. (ENG.). 160p. (J). 2013. (gr. 4-7). 6.99 *(978-1-58246-345-2(X)*, Yearling) 2011. (Illus.). (gr. 3-7). 16.99 *(978-1-58246-337-7(9)*, Tricycle Pr.) Random Hse. Children's Bks.
Crawford, Ann Fears. Keechee: The Witch of the Woods. 2005. (J). *(978-1-931823-21-0(9))* Halcyon Pr.
Crowe, Chris. Mississippi Trial 1955. 2003. (ENG.). 240p. (YA). (gr. 7-18). 5.99 *(978-0-14-250192-4(1)*, Speak) Penguin Young Readers Group.
—The Mississippi Trial 1955. 2003. (gr. 7-12). lib. bdg. 16.00 *(978-0-613-86522-7(7)*, Turtleback) Turtleback Bks.
Dal Santo, Sandy. I Live on a Colorful Street. 2009. 32p. pap. 13.49 *(978-1-4389-3978-0(7))* AuthorHouse.
De la Peña, Matt. Ball Don't Lie. 2007. (ENG.). 288p. (YA). (gr. 9-12). pap. 9.99 *(978-0-385-73425-7(5)*, Ember) Random Hse. Children's Bks.
Deborah, Wiles. Freedom Summer. 2014. (ENG.). 32p. (J). (gr. k-3). 12.24 *(978-1-63245-316-7(9))* Lectorum Pubns., Inc.
Dowell, Frances O'Roark. Trouble the Water. (ENG.). (J). (gr. 4-8). 2017. 304p. pap. 7.99 *(978-1-4814-2464-6(5))* 2016. (Illus.). 288p. 16.99 *(978-1-4814-2463-9(7))* Simon & Schuster Children's Publishing.
—Trouble the Water. 2017. lib. bdg. 18.40 ***(978-0-606-40126-5(1))*** Turtleback Bks.
Down, Heather. A Deadly Distance. 2005. (Illus.). 128p. (YA). pap. *(978-0-88878-455-1(4)*, Sandcastle Bks.) Dundurn.
Draper, Sharon M. Copper Sun. 2006. (ENG.). 320p. (YA). (gr. 8-18). 19.99 *(978-0-689-82181-3(6)*, Atheneum Bks. for Young Readers) Simon & Schuster Children's Publishing.
—Fire from the Rock. 2008. (ENG.). 240p. (YA). (gr. 7-18). 7.99 *(978-0-14-241199-5(X)*, Speak) Penguin Young Readers Group.
Dunagan, Ted M. Secret of the Satilfa. 2010. (ENG.). 208p. (J). (gr. 3-18). 21.95 *(978-1-58838-249-8(4)*, NewSouth Bks.) NewSouth, Inc.
—A Yellow Watermelon. 2014. (ENG.). 240p. (J). pap. 17.95 *(978-1-58838-301-3(6)*, NewSouth Bks.) NewSouth, Inc.
Edwards, Myrtice J. Dirty Sally. 2007. 44p. per. 18.95 *(978-1-4327-0774-3(4))* Outskirts Pr., Inc.
Ehrenberg, Pamela. Ethan, Suspended. 2009. (ENG.). 272p. (J). (gr. 6-9). pap. 8.50 *(978-0-8028-5317-2(X))* 2007. 266p. (YA). (gr. 7-18). 16.00 *(978-0-8028-5324-0(2)*, Eerdmans Bks For Young Readers) Eerdmans, William B. Publishing Co.
Elkins, Stephen. Ebony & Ivory: Discovering 10 Keys to Racial Harmony. Reisch, Jessie, illus. 2003. 32p. (J). (gr. k-18). 14.99 incl. audio compact disk *(978-0-8054-2674-8(4))* B&H Publishing Group.
Elster, Jean Alicia. Who's Jim Hines? 2008. (Great Lakes Books Ser.). (ENG., Illus.). 146p. (J). pap. 14.99 *(978-0-8143-3402-7(4)*, 2162) Wayne State Univ. Pr.
Emond, Stephen. Bright Lights, Dark Nights. 2015. (ENG., Illus.). 384p. (YA). (gr. 7). 17.99 *(978-1-62672-206-4(4))* Roaring Brook Pr.
Emory, Kb. Tyler Tales: What Is My Color/ Different Families. 2012. 36p. pap. 21.99 *(978-1-4797-2504-5(8))* Xlibris Corp.
English, Karen. Francie. 2007. (ENG.). 208p. (J). (gr. 4-8). per. 8.99 *(978-0-312-37383-2(X)*, 9780312373832) Square Fish.
—It All Comes down to This. 2017. (ENG.). 368p. (J). (gr. 5-7). 16.99 *(978-0-544-83957-1(9)*, Clarion Bks.) Houghton Mifflin Harcourt Trade & Reference Pubs.
Erskine, Kathryn. Seeing Red. 2013. (YA). *(978-0-545-57645-1(8))*; (ENG.). 352p. (J). (gr. 5-9). 16.99 *(978-0-545-46440-6(4))* Scholastic, Inc. (Scholastic Pr.).
Frank, Steven B. Armstrong & Charlie. 2017. (ENG.). 304p. (J). (gr. 5-7). 16.99 *(978-0-544-82608-3(6)*, HMH Books For Young Readers) Houghton Mifflin Harcourt Publishing Co.
Friedland, Joyce, ed. Lizzie Bright & the Buckminster Boy: Novel-Ties Study Guide. 2007. 36p. pap. 16.95 *(978-0-7675-3558-8(8))* Learning Links Inc.
Fuqua, Jonathon Scott. Darby. 2006. (ENG.). 256p. (J). (gr. 5-7). per. 7.99 *(978-0-7636-2290-9(7))* Candlewick Pr.
Gansworth, Eric L. If I Ever Get Out of Here. (ENG.). 368p. (J). (gr. 7). 2015. pap. 10.99 *(978-0-545-41731-0(7))* 2013. 17.99 *(978-0-545-41730-3(9))* Scholastic, Inc. (Levine, Arthur A. Bks.).
Garlington, William R. The Great Divide: Coloring & Activity Book. 2004. (Illus.). (J). 5.95 *(978-0-9708395-4-1(5))* Legacy Publishing Services, Inc.
—The Great Divide: The Adventures of Billy Bean & Bobby Nut. 2004. (Illus.). 127p. (J). pap. 12.95 *(978-0-9708395-2-7(9))* Legacy Publishing Services, Inc.
Going, K. L. The Liberation of Gabriel King. 2007. (ENG.). 160p. (J). (gr. 3-7). 6.99 *(978-0-14-240766-0(6)*, Puffin Books) Penguin Young Readers Group.
—The Liberation of Gabriel King. 2007. 151p. (gr. 3-7). 17.00 *(978-0-7569-7762-7(2))* Perfection Learning Corp.
Gutman, Dan. Jackie & Me. 2005. (Baseball Card Adventures Ser.). (Illus.). 145p. (YA). (gr. 4-8). reprint ed. 20.00 *(978-0-7567-9569-6(9))* DIANE Publishing Co.
—Satch & Me. (Baseball Card Adventures Ser.). (ENG.). 192p. (J). (gr. 5-9). 2009. pap. 5.99 *(978-0-06-059493-0(4))* 2006. (Illus.). 16.99 *(978-0-06-059491-6(8))* HarperCollins Pubs. (Amistad).
Hale, Marian. Dark Water Rising. 2010. (ENG.). 256p. (J). (gr. 5-9). pap. 7.99 *(978-0-312-62908-3(7)*, 9780312629083) Square Fish.
Harrington, Janice N. Going North. Lagarrigue, Jerome, illus. 2004. (ENG.). 40p. (J). (gr. k-3). 18.99 *(978-0-374-32681-4(9)*, 9780374326814, Farrar, Straus & Giroux (BYR)) Farrar, Straus & Giroux.
Harris, E. Lynn. Diaries of a Light-Skinned Colored Boy, No. 1. (Illus.). 160p. (J). (gr. 7-17). 15.99 *(978-0-7868-0632-4(X)*, Jump at the Sun) Hyperion Bks. for Children.
Haugaard, Kay. The Day the Dragon Danced. Barritt, Carolyn Reed, illus. 2004. (Day the Dragon Danced Ser.). 32p. (J). (gr. -1-3). 16.95 *(978-1-885008-30-5(9)*, Shen's Bks.) Lee & Low Bks., Inc.
Hay, Barbara. Lesson of the White Eagle. Hay, Peter, illus. 2012. (ENG.). 144p. (YA). pap. 11.99 *(978-1-937054-01-4(2))* RoadRunner Pr.
Hegedus, Bethany. Between Us Baxters. 2009. 306p. (YA). (gr. 7-9). 17.95 *(978-1-934813-02-7(8))* 2011. 9.14 *(978-1-934813-18-8(4))* Westside Bks.
Hemphill, Helen. The Adventurous Deeds of Deadwood Jones. (ENG.). 232p. (J). 2011. (gr. 6-9). pap. 7.95 *(978-1-59078-896-7(6))* 2008. (gr. 5-18). 16.95 *(978-1-59078-637-6(8)*, Front Street) Boyds Mills Pr.
Jackson, Linda. Midnight Without a Moon. 2017. (ENG.). 320p. (J). (gr. 5-7). 16.99 *(978-0-544-78510-6(X)*, HMH Books For Young Readers) Houghton Mifflin Harcourt Publishing Co.
Johnson, Allen, Jr. My Brother's Story. McMorris, Kelley, illus. 2014. (Blackwater Novels Ser.: Vol. 1). (ENG.). 191p. (J). (gr. 4-7). 14.99 *(978-1-933725-37-6(0))* Premium Pr. America.
Johnston, Tony. Bone by Bone by Bone. 2007. (ENG.). 192p. (YA). (gr. 7-12). 29.99 *(978-1-59643-113-3(X)*, 9781596431133) Roaring Brook Pr.
Jones-Cisneros, Tiffany. Blaxicana It's a ed World. 2012. 12p. pap. 15.99 *(978-1-4685-6192-0(8))* AuthorHouse.
Jones, Patrick. At the Center. 2016. (Bounce Ser.). (ENG.). 104p. (YA). (gr. 6-12). 26.65 *(978-1-5124-1122-5(1))* Lerner Publishing Group.
Jordan, Rosa. Lost Goat Lane, 1 vol. 2004. (ENG.). 192p. (J). (gr. 3-7). 14.95 *(978-1-56145-325-2(0))* Peachtree Pubs.
Ketchum, Liza. The Life Fantastic. 2017. (ENG.). 256p. (YA). 17.99 *(978-1-4405-9876-0(2)*, Simon Pulse) Simon Pulse.
Kirkpatrick, Katherine. Between Two Worlds. (ENG.). 304p. (YA). (gr. 9). 2015. pap. 9.99 *(978-0-375-87221-1(3)*, Ember) 2014. 16.99 *(978-0-385-74047-0(6)*, Lamb, Wendy Bks.) Random Hse. Children's Bks.
Krech, Bob. Rebound, 0 vols. 2009. (ENG.). 276p. (YA). (gr. 7-9). pap. 9.99 *(978-0-7614-5543-1(4)*, 9780761455431, Amazon Children's Publishing) Amazon Publishing.
Krensky, Stephen. Play Ball, Jackie! Morse, Joe, illus. 2011. (Single Titles Ser.). (ENG.). 32p. (J). (gr. 2-5). lib. bdg. 16.95 *(978-0-8225-9030-9(1)*, Millbrook Pr.) Lerner Publishing Group.
Latham, Jennifer. Dreamland Burning. 2017.Tr. of s. (ENG.). 384p. (YA). (gr. 9-17). 18.99 *(978-0-316-38493-3(3))* Little, Brown Bks. for Young Readers.
Les Becquets, Diane. The Stones of Mourning Creek, 0 vols. 2005. (ENG.). 320p. (YA). (gr. 7-9). reprint ed. pap. 9.99 *(978-0-7614-5238-6(9)*, 9780761452386, Amazon Children's Publishing) Amazon Publishing.
Levine, Kristin. The Best Bad Luck I Ever Had. 2010. (ENG.). 272p. (J). (gr. 5-18). 7.99 *(978-0-14-241648-8(7)*, Puffin Books) Penguin Young Readers Group.
—The Lions of Little Rock. (ENG.). (J). (gr. 5-9). 2013. 320p. pap. 7.99 *(978-0-14-242435-3(8)*, Puffin Books) 2012. 304p. 16.99 *(978-0-399-25644-8(X)*, G.P. Putnam's Sons Books for Young Readers) Penguin Young Readers Group.
Levy, Marilyn. Checkpoints. 2009. (ENG.). 256p. (gr. 7). pap. 14.95 *(978-0-8276-0870-2(5))* Jewish Pubn. Society.
Long, Loren & Bildner, Phil. Water, Water Everywhere. Long, Loren, illus. (Sluggers Ser.: 4). (ENG., Illus.). (J). (gr. 3-7). 2010. 288p. pap. 7.99 *(978-1-4169-1890-5(6))* 2009. 272p. 14.99 *(978-1-4169-1866-0(3))* Simon & Schuster Bks. For Young Readers. (Simon & Schuster Bks. For Young Readers).
Lorbiecki, Marybeth. Jackie's Bat. Pinkney, Brian, illus. 2006. (ENG.). 40p. (J). (gr. k-3). 17.99 *(978-0-689-84102-6(7)*, Simon & Schuster Bks. For Young Readers) Simon & Schuster Bks. For Young Readers.
Lupica, Mike. Fast Break. 2015. (ENG.). 272p. (J). (gr. 5-8). 17.99 *(978-0-399-25606-6(7)*, Philomel Bks.) Penguin Publishing Group.
—Fast Break. 2016. (ENG.). 288p. (J). (gr. 5). pap. 8.99 *(978-1-101-99783-3(4)*, Puffin Books) Penguin Young Readers Group.
—Fast Break. 2016. (ENG.). 288p. (J). (gr. 5). 19.65 *(978-0-606-39313-3(7))* Turtleback Bks.
Lyon, George Ella. Sonny's House of Spies. 2007. (ENG.). 304p. (J). (gr. 6-9). pap. 14.95 *(978-1-4169-6815-3(6)*, Simon & Schuster/Paula Wiseman Bks.) Simon & Schuster/Paula Wiseman Bks.
Maddern, Eric. The Fire Children: A West African Folk Tale. Lessac, Frané, illus. 2015. (ENG.). 32p. (J). (gr. -1-2). pap. 9.99 *(978-1-84780-652-9(X)*, Frances Lincoln) Quarto Publishing Group UK GBR. Dist: Hachette Bk. Group.
Magoon, Kekla. How It Went Down. 2014. (ENG.). 336p. (YA). (gr. 9-12). 18.99 *(978-0-8050-9869-3(0)*, 9780805098693, Holt, Henry & Co. Bks. For Young Readers) Holt, Henry & Co.
—How It Went Down. Barcellona, Christine, ed. 2015. (ENG.). 352p. (YA). (gr. 9). pap. 9.99 *(978-1-250-06823-1(1)*, 9781250068231) Square Fish.
—How It Went Down. 2015. (YA). lib. bdg. 20.85 *(978-0-606-37593-1(7))* Turtleback Bks.
—The Rock & the River. 2010. (ENG.). 304p. (J). (gr. 5-9). pap. 7.99 *(978-1-4169-7803-9(8)*, Aladdin) Simon & Schuster Children's Publishing.
Martínez, Jessica. The Vow. 2013. (ENG.). 432p. (YA). (gr. 9). 17.99 *(978-1-4424-5864-2(X)*, Simon Pulse) Simon Pulse.
Mazellan, Ron, illus. We Will Walk. 2005. 16p. (J). pap. *(978-0-7367-2919-2(4))* Zaner-Bloser, Inc.
McGuigan, Mary Ann. Morning in a Different Place. 2009. (ENG.). 195p. (YA). (gr. 7-18). 17.95 *(978-1-59078-551-5(7)*, Front Street) Boyds Mills Pr.
McKernan, Victoria. Son of Fortune. 2015. (ENG.). 448p. (YA). (gr. 7). pap. 9.99 *(978-0-375-85786-7(9)*, Ember) Random Hse. Children's Bks.
McKissack, Patricia C. A Friendship for Today. 2008. 172p. (J). pap. *(978-0-545-06563-4(1))* Scholastic, Inc.
McMullan, Margaret. When I Crossed No-Bob. 2009. (ENG.). 224p. (J). (gr. 2-5). pap. 7.99 *(978-0-547-23763-3(4))* Houghton Mifflin Harcourt Publishing Co.
Medearis, Angela Shelf. Singing for Dr. King. Hu, Ying-Hwa & Van Wright, Cornelius, illus. 2004. 32p. (J). lib. bdg. 15.00 *(978-1-4242-0237-9(X))* Fitzgerald Bks.
Meyer, Carolyn. White Lilacs. 2007. (ENG., Illus.). 256p. (J). (gr. 2-5). pap. 8.99 *(978-0-15-205851-7(6))* Houghton Mifflin Harcourt Publishing Co.
—White Lilacs. 2006. (Illus.). 242p. (gr. 4-7). 16.95 *(978-0-7569-6683-6(3))* Perfection Learning Corp.
Meyer, Susan Lynn. Skating with the Statue of Liberty. 2016. (ENG.). 320p. (J). (gr. 3-7). 19.99 *(978-0-375-99010-6(0)*, Delacorte Bks. for Young Readers) Random Hse. Children's Bks.
Mickles Sr., Robert T. S. Blood Kin, a Savannah Story. 2007. 108p. per. 9.95 *(978-0-595-45129-6(2))* iUniverse, Inc.
Milton, Nina. Tough Luck. 2013. 180p. pap. *(978-1-909734-13-5(6))* ThornBerry Publishing UK.
Mohamoud, Ashlee. Brown Is Beautiful, 1 vol. 2010. 18p. 24.95 *(978-1-4512-0064-5(1))* PublishAmerica, Inc.
Molnar, Gwen. Hate Cell: A Casey Templeton Mystery. 2009. (Casey Templeton Mystery Ser.: 1). (ENG.). 184p. (YA). (gr. 5). pap. 11.99 *(978-1-55002-850-8(2))* Dundurn CAN. Dist: Ingram Publisher Services.
Moses, Shelia P. The Legend of Buddy Bush. 2004. (ENG., Illus.). 224p. (YA). (gr. 7). 19.99 *(978-0-689-85839-0(6)*, McElderry, Margaret K. Bks.) McElderry, Margaret K. Bks.
—The Legend of Buddy Bush. 2005. (Illus.). 211p. (gr. 7-12). 17.00 *(978-0-7569-5459-8(2))* Perfection Learning Corp.
—The Legend of Buddy Bush, 3 vols. unabr. ed. 2005. (YA). (gr. 3-7). 54.75 *(978-1-4193-3575-4(8)*, 42043) Recorded Bks., Inc.
—The Return of Buddy Bush. 2005. (ENG., Illus.). 160p. (J). (gr. 7-12). 15.95 *(978-0-689-87431-4(6)*, McElderry, Margaret K. Bks.) McElderry, Margaret K. Bks.
Mullinax, Jerry. Enoree. 2009. (YA). pap. *(978-0-88092-646-1(5))* Royal Fireworks Publishing Co.
Myers, Anna. Tulsa Burning. 2004. (Illus.). 184p. (J). (gr. 3-7). 16.95 *(978-0-8027-8829-0(7))* Walker & Co.
Myers, Walter Dean. The Cruisers. (ENG.). 144p. (J). (gr. 5-9). 2015. (News Crew Ser.). pap. 6.99 *(978-0-545-82874-1(0))* 2011. (Cruisers Ser.: 1). pap. 5.99 *(978-0-439-91633-2(X))* 2010. (Cruisers Ser.: 1). 15.99 *(978-0-439-91626-4(7))* Scholastic, Inc. (Scholastic Pr.).
—Oh, Snap! 2013. (Cruisers Ser.: Bk. 4). (ENG.). 128p. (J). (gr. 5-9). 17.99 *(978-0-439-91629-5(1)*, Scholastic Pr.) Scholastic, Inc.

Napoli, Donna Jo. Alligator Bayou. 2010. (ENG.). 288p. (YA). (gr. 7). pap. 8.99 *(978-0-553-49417-4(1),* Lamb, Wendy Bks.) Random Hse. Children's Bks.

Naylor, Phyllis Reynolds. Alice in Charge. (Alice Ser.: 22). (ENG., (YA). (gr. 9). 304p. pap. 8.99 *(978-1-4169-7555-7(1))* 2010. 336p. 16.99 *(978-1-4169-7552-6(7))* Simon & Schuster Children's Publishing. (Atheneum Bks. for Young Readers).

Neil Wallace, Sandra. Muckers. 2013. (ENG.). 288p. (YA). (gr. 7). 16.99 *(978-0-375-86754-5(6),* Knopf Bks. for Young Readers) Random Hse. Children's Bks.

Noe, Katherine Schlick. Something to Hold. 2011. (ENG., Illus.). 256p. (J). (gr. 5-7). 17.99 *(978-0-547-55813-4(9))* Houghton Mifflin Harcourt Publishing Co.

Nolan, Han. A Summer of Kings. 2006. 334p. (J). *(978-1-4156-7340-9(3))* Harcourt Trade Pubs.

Olsen, Sylvia. Middle Row, 1 vol. 2008. (Orca Soundings Ser.). (ENG.). (YA). (gr. 8-12). 112p. 16.95 *(978-1-55143-901-3(8));* 136p. pap. 9.95 *(978-1-55143-899-3(2))* Orca Bk. Pubs. USA.

Pantoja, Stephen. The Amalaganimals: Eracism Sc. 2010. 33p. pap. 23.90 *(978-0-557-31722-6(3))* Lulu Pr., Inc.

Parkhurst, Liz S. Under One Flag: A Year at Rohwer. Clifton, Tom, illus. 2006. (ENG.). 32p. (J). (gr. 3-7). 16.95 *(978-0-87483-759-9(6),* 1241971) August Hse. Pubs., Inc.

Patrick, Denise Lewis. A Matter of Souls. 2014. 192p. (YA). (gr. 6-12). 16.95 *(978-0-7613-9280-4(7),* Carolrhoda Lab™) Lerner Publishing Group.

Paul, Volponi. Black & White. 2014. (ENG.). 208p. (YA). 11.24 *(978-1-63245-196-5(4))* Lectorum Pubns., Inc.

Pearsall, Shelley. Trouble Don't Last. 2003. (ENG.). 256p. (J). (gr. 3-7). reprint ed. 6.99 *(978-0-440-41811-5(9),* Yearling) Random Hse. Children's Bks.

Peck, Richard. The River Between Us. 2005. (ENG.). 176p. (J). (gr. 3-7). reprint ed. pap. 7.99 *(978-0-14-240310-5(5),* Puffin Books) Penguin Young Readers Group.

Perkins, Mitali, ed. Open Mic: Riffs on Life Between Cultures in Ten Voices. 2016. (ENG.). 144p. (J). (gr. 7). pap. 7.99 *(978-0-7636-9095-3(3))* Candlewick Pr.

Perkyns, Dorothy. Last Days in Africville. 2005. (Illus.). 144p. (YA). pap., tchr. ed. *(978-0-88878-446-9(5),* Sandcastle Bks.) Dundurn.

—Last Days in Africville. 2006. (ENG.). 120p. (J). (gr. 4-7). pap. 10.99 *(978-1-55002-630-6(5),* Dundurn Pr.) Dundurn CAN. Dist: Ingram Publisher Services.

Phillips, Lyda. Mr Touchdown. 2008. 184p. 23.95 *(978-1-4401-0976-8(1));* pap. 13.95 *(978-1-60528-029-5(1))* iUniverse, Inc. (iUniverse Star).

Pinkney, Andrea Davis. Boycott Blues: How Rosa Parks Inspired a Nation. Pinkney, Brian, illus. 2008. (ENG.). 40p. (J). (gr. k-3). 16.99 *(978-0-06-082118-0(3),* Greenwillow Bks.) HarperCollins Pubs.

Polacco, Patricia. Chicken Sunday. 2015. 32p. pap. 8.00 *(978-1-61003-527-9(5))* Center for the Collaborative Classroom.

Powell, Patricia Hruby. Loving vs. Virginia: A Documentary Novel of the Landmark Civil Rights Case. Strickland, Shadra, illus. 2017. (ENG.). 260p. (YA). (gr. 7-12). 21.99 *(978-1-4521-2590-9(2))* Chronicle Bks. LLC.

Raschka, Chris. Yo! Yes? Raschka, Chris, illus. 2007. (Scholastic Bookshelf Ser.). (ENG., Illus.). 32p. (J). (gr. -1-1). pap. 6.99 *(978-0-439-92185-5(6))* Scholastic, Inc.

Reynolds, Aaron. Back of the Bus. Cooper, Floyd, illus. 2010. (ENG.). 32p. (J). (gr. 1-3). 16.99 *(978-0-399-25091-0(3),* Philomel Bks.) Penguin Young Readers Group.

Reynolds, Jason & Brendan Kiely. All American Boys. 2017. (ENG.). (YA). lib. bdg. 20.85 *(978-0-606-39493-2(1))* Turtleback Bks.

Reynolds, Jason & Kiely, Brendan. All American Boys. 2015. (ENG., Illus.). 320p. (YA). (gr. 7). 19.99 *(978-1-4814-6333-1(0),* Atheneum/Caitlyn Dlouhy Books) Simon & Schuster Children's Publishing.

Rhodes, Jewell Parker. Sugar. 2013. (ENG.). 288p. (J). (gr. 3-7). 16.99 *(978-0-316-04305-2(2))* Little, Brown Bks. for Young Readers.

Richards, Elizabeth. Black City. 2013. (Black City Novel Ser.: 1). (ENG., Illus.). 400p. (YA). (gr. 9). pap. 9.99 *(978-0-14-242722-4(5),* Speak) Penguin Young Readers Group.

—Phoenix. 2nd ed. 2014. (Black City Novel Ser.: 2). (ENG.). 368p. (YA). (gr. 9). pap. 9.99 *(978-0-14-751137-9(2),* Speak) Penguin Young Readers Group.

Rinaldi, Ann. The Education of Mary: A Little Miss of Color, 1832. 2005. 176p. (J). pap. *(978-0-7868-1377-3(6))* Hyperion Pr.

Robinet, Harriette Gillem. Walking to the Bus-Rider Blues. 2004. (Jean Karl Bks.). 146p. (gr. 3-7). 16.00 *(978-0-7569-4265-6(9))* Perfection Learning Corp.

Robinson, Sharon. The Hero Two Doors Down: A Story of Friendship Between a Boy & a Baseball Legend. 2017. (ENG.). 208p. (J). (gr. 3-7). pap. 6.99 ***(978-0-545-80452-3(3),*** Scholastic Paperbacks) Scholastic, Inc.

Robles, Tony. Joey Gonzalez, Great American. Pryor, Jim, illus. 2008. (ENG.). (J). (gr. 2-3). 15.95 *(978-0-9767269-3-7(9))* WND Bks, Inc.

Rodman, Mary Ann. Yankee Girl. 2008. (ENG.). 240p. (J). (gr. 4-6). pap. 9.99 *(978-0-312-53576-6(7),* 9780312535766) Square Fish.

Salcedo, Betsy. Together we Can. 2006. 9.00 *(978-0-8059-9155-0(7))* Dorrance Publishing Co., Inc.

Scattergood, Augusta. Glory Be. (ENG.). 208p. (J). (gr. 3-7). 2014. pap. 6.99 *(978-0-545-33181-4(1))* 2012. 16.99 *(978-0-545-33180-7(3))* Scholastic, Inc. (Scholastic Pr.).

Schmidt, Gary D. Lizzie Bright & the Buckminster Boy. 2013. (ENG.). 224p. (J). (gr. 5-7). pap. 7.99 *(978-0-544-02279-9(3))* Houghton Mifflin Harcourt Publishing Co.

—Trouble. 2010. (ENG.). 304p. (YA). (gr. 7). pap. 8.99 *(978-0-547-33133-1(9))* Houghton Mifflin Harcourt Publishing Co.

Scholastic, Inc. Staff & Medearis, Angela Shelf. Singing for Dr. King. Van Wright, Cornelius & Hu, Ying-Hwa, illus. 2004. (Just for You Ser.). (ENG.). 32p. (gr. k-3). pap. 3.99 *(978-0-439-56855-5(2),* Teaching Resources) Scholastic, Inc.

Schraff, Anne. Freedom Knows No Color. 2008. (Passages to History Ser.). 118p. (J). lib. bdg. 13.95 *(978-0-7569-8392-5(4));* (YA). (gr. 7-12). pap. 8.50 *(978-0-7891-7567-0(3))* Perfection Learning Corp.

Schwartz, Ellen. Stealing Home. 2006. (ENG.). 224p. (J). (gr. 4-7). pap. 9.95 *(978-0-88776-765-4(6),* Tundra Bks.) Tundra Bks. CAN. Dist: Penguin Random Hse. LLC.

Scott, Lisa Ann. School of Charm. 2014. (ENG.). 304p. (J). (gr. 3-7). 16.99 *(978-0-06-220758-6(X),* Tegen, Katherine Bks) HarperCollins Pubs.

Sharenow, Robert. My Mother the Cheerleader. 2009. (ENG.). 320p. (YA). (gr. 8). pap. 9.99 *(978-0-06-114898-9(9),* HarperTeen) 2007. 304p. (J). (gr. 7-18). 16.99 *(978-0-06-114896-5(2),* Geringer, Laura Book) 2007. 304p. (J). (gr. 7-18). lib. bdg. 17.89 *(978-0-06-114897-2(0),* Geringer, Laura Book) HarperCollins Pubs.

Shaw, Marilyn Bishop. Solomon. 2006. (Florida Historical Fiction for Youth Ser.). (ENG.). 204p. (J). (gr. 4-9). 14.95 *(978-1-56164-349-3(1))* Pineapple Pr., Inc.

Smadja, Brigitte. Tarte aux Escargots. pap. 17.95 *(978-2-211-03633-7(3))* Archimede Editions FRA. Dist: Distribooks, Inc.

Smith, D. James. It Was September When We Ran Away the First Time. 2012. (ENG.). 240p. (J). (gr. 3-7). pap. 11.99 *(978-1-4169-3810-1(9),* Atheneum Bks. for Young Readers) Simon & Schuster Children's Publishing.

Smith, Sarah. The Other Side of Dark. (ENG., 320p. (YA). (gr. 7). 2011. Illus.). pap. 11.99 *(978-1-4424-0281-2(4))* 2010. 16.99 *(978-1-4424-0280-5(6))* Simon & Schuster Children's Publishing. (Atheneum Bks. for Young Readers).

Stanley, Brenda. I Am Nuchu. 2010. 334p. (YA). (gr. 9-18). 16.95 *(978-1-934813-47-8(8))* Westside Bks.

Stanley, George E. Night Fires. 2009. (ENG.). 192p. (J). (gr. 3-7). 15.99 *(978-1-4169-7559-5(4),* Simon & Schuster/Paula Wiseman Bks.) Simon & Schuster/Paula Wiseman Bks.

Stanley, George Edward. Night Fires. 2011. (ENG.). 192p. (J). (gr. 3-7). pap. 6.99 *(978-1-4169-1250-7(9),* Simon & Schuster/Paula Wiseman Bks.) Simon & Schuster/Paula Wiseman Bks.

Stephenson, Lynda. Dancing with Elvis. 2006. (ENG.). 331p. (YA). (gr. 7). per. 8.00 *(978-0-8028-5300-4(5),* Eerdmans Bks For Young Readers) Eerdmans, William B. Publishing Co.

Stiver, Joan. The Door in the Floor: An Underground Railroad Adventure. 2008. 48p. pap. 4.99 *(978-1-4343-2953-0(4))* AuthorHouse.

Swinford, Betty. Secrets. 2006. (Freestyle Fiction 12+ Ser.). (ENG.). 176p. (J). (gr. 4-7). per. 6.99 *(978-1-84550-127-3(6),* 2b7eb6f6-fcab-409d-af77-f07255764855) Christian Focus Pubns. GBR. Dist: Bookmasters Distribution.

Talley, Robin. Lies We Tell Ourselves. 2016. (ENG.). 416p. pap. 9.99 *(978-0-373-21204-0(6),* Harlequin Teen) Harlequin Enterprises, Ltd. CAN. Dist: HarperCollins Pubs.

Taschek, Karen. The Risen Horse. 2010. (ENG.). 248p. (YA). (gr. 7-18). pap. 15.95 *(978-0-8263-4837-1(8))* Univ. of New Mexico Pr.

Taylor, Mildred D. The Friendship. 2014. (ENG.). 56p. (J). (gr. 3-7). 11.24 *(978-1-63245-342-6(8))* Lectorum Pubns., Inc.

—Roll of Thunder, Hear My Cry. 40th anniv. ed. 2016. (ENG., Illus.). 304p. (J). (gr. 3-7). 19.99 *(978-1-101-99388-0(X),* Dial Bks) Penguin Young Readers Group.

Thomas, Angie. The Hate U Give. 2017. (ENG.). 464p. (YA). (gr. 9). 17.99 *(978-0-06-249853-3(3))* HarperCollins Pubs.

Thompson, Tavia. Made by God Wonderfully. 2013. 28p. pap. 24.95 *(978-1-63000-403-3(0))* America Star Bks.

Tocher, Timothy. Chief Sunrise, John McGraw, & Me. 2004. (ENG.). 168p. (J). (gr. 4-8). 16.95 *(978-0-8126-2711-4(3))* Cricket Bks.

The Troubles of Johnny Cannon. 2014. (ENG., Illus.). 304p. (J). (gr. 3-7). 16.99 *(978-1-4814-0003-9(7),* Simon & Schuster Bks. For Young Readers) Simon & Schuster Bks. For Young Readers.

Tuck, Pamela M. As Fast As Words Could Fly, 1 vol. Velasquez, Eric, illus. 2013. (ENG.). 40p. (J). 18.95 *(978-1-60060-348-8(3))* Lee & Low Bks., Inc.

Turner, Ann Warren. Sitting Bull Remembers. Minor, Wendell, illus. 2007. (ENG.). 32p. (J). (gr. 1-4). 16.99 *(978-0-06-051399-3(3))* HarperCollins Pubs.

Twain, Mark, pseud. The Adventures of Huckleberry Finn. Andreasen, Dan, illus. 2010. (Classic Starts(tm) Ser.). (ENG.). 160p. (J). (gr. 2-4). cd-rom 9.95 *(978-1-4027-7355-6(2))* Sterling Publishing Co., Inc.

—Las Aventuras de Huckleberry Finn. de Atauri, Ines & de Atauri, Juan Diaz, eds. 2006. (Clasicos Juveniles Ser.).Tr. of Adventures of Huckleberry Finn. (SPA., Illus.). 359p. pap. 17.95 *(978-84-263-5252-1(9))* Vives, Luis Editorial (Edelvives) ESP. Dist: Lectorum Pubns., Inc.

Vander Zee, Ruth. Mississippi Morning. Cooper, Floyd, illus. 2004. 32p. (J). 16.00 *(978-0-8028-5211-3(4))* Eerdmans, William B. Publishing Co.

Vaught, Susan. Things Too Huge to Fix by Saying Sorry. 2016. (ENG., Illus.). 352p. (J). (gr. 5-9). 16.99 *(978-1-4814-2279-6(0),* Simon & Schuster Bks. For Young Readers) Simon & Schuster Bks. For Young Readers.

—Things Too Huge to Fix by Saying Sorry. 2017. (ENG.). 368p. (J). (gr. 5-9). pap. 7.99 ***(978-1-4814-2280-2(4),*** Simon & Schuster/Paula Wiseman Bks.) Simon & Schuster/Paula Wiseman Bks.

Vawter, Vince. Paperboy. 2013. (ENG.). 240p. (J). (gr. 5). 16.99 *(978-0-385-74244-3(4));* lib. bdg. 19.99 *(978-0-375-99058-8(5))* Random Hse. Children's Bks. (Delacorte Bks. for Young Readers).

Volponi, Paul. Response. 2010. (ENG.). 176p. (YA). (gr. 7-18). 6.99 *(978-0-14-241603-7(7),* Speak) Penguin Young Readers Group.

—Rooftop. 2007. (ENG.). 224p. (YA). (gr. 7-18). 6.99 *(978-0-14-240844-5(1),* Puffin Books) Penguin Young Readers Group.

—Rooftop. 2007. 199p. 17.00 *(978-0-7569-7958-4(7))* Perfection Learning Corp.

Walker, Brian F. Black Boy White School. 2012. (ENG.). 256p. (YA). (gr. 9). 17.99 *(978-0-06-191483-6(5),* HarperTeen) HarperCollins Pubs.

Wallace, Jason. Out of Shadows. (ENG., Illus.). 272p. (J). (gr. 10). 2012. pap. 8.95 *(978-0-8234-2436-8(7))* 2011. 17.95 *(978-0-8234-2342-2(5))* Holiday Hse., Inc.

Walsh, Ann. Shabash! 2nd ed. 2008. (ENG.). 112p. (J). (gr. 4-8). pap. 11.99 *(978-1-55002-829-4(4),* Sandcastle Bks.) Dundurn CAN. Dist: Ingram Publisher Services.

Walvoord, Linda & Walvoord. Rosetta, Rosetta, Sit by Me!, 0 vols. Velasquez, Eric, illus. 2004. (ENG.). 80p. (J). (gr. 3-6). 14.95 *(978-0-7614-5171-6(4),* 9780761451716, Amazon Children's Publishing) Amazon Publishing.

Watkins, Steve. Down Sand Mountain. (ENG., Illus.). 336p. (YA). (gr. 7). 2011. pap. 7.99 *(978-0-7636-4835-0(3))* 2008. 16.99 *(978-0-7636-3839-9(0))* Candlewick Pr.

Watts, Jeri. Kizzy Ann Stamps. 2013. (ENG., Illus.). 192p. (J). (gr. 4-7). pap. 5.99 *(978-0-7636-6976-8(8))* Candlewick Pr.

Weatherford, Carole Boston. Freedom on the Menu: The Greensboro Sit-Ins. Lagarrigue, Jerome Lagarrigue, illus. 2007. (ENG.). 32p. (J). (gr. -1-3). pap. 5.99 *(978-0-14-240894-0(8),* Puffin Books) Penguin Young Readers Group.

Wein, Elizabeth. Black Dove, White Raven. 2015. (ENG.). 368p. (YA). (gr. 7-12). 17.99 *(978-1-4231-8310-5(X))* Hyperion Bks. for Children.

Weston Woods Staff, creator. Crow Boy. 2011. 18.95 *(978-0-545-23383-5(6));* 38.75 *(978-0-545-23384-2(4));* 29.95 *(978-0-545-23382-8(8))* Weston Woods Studios, Inc.

Wilcox, Katherine A. Let Me Be Myself. 2004. 60p. pap. 25.75 *(978-1-4140-3674-8(4))* AuthorHouse.

Wiles, Deborah. The Aurora County All-Stars. (ENG., Illus.). 256p. (J). 2009. (gr. 2-5). pap. 7.99 *(978-0-15-206626-0(8))* 2007. (gr. 5-7). 16.00 *(978-0-15-206068-8(5))* Houghton Mifflin Harcourt Publishing Co.

—Freedom Summer. Lagarrigue, Jerome, illus. 50th anniv. ed. 2014. (ENG.). 32p. (J). (gr. -1-3). 17.99 *(978-1-4814-2298-7(7),* Atheneum Bks. for Young Readers) Simon & Schuster Children's Publishing.

Woodson, Jacqueline. Feathers. (ENG.). (J). (gr. 5-18). 2010. 160p. 8.99 *(978-0-14-241550-4(2),* Speak) 2007. 128p. 16.99 *(978-0-399-23989-2(8),* G.P. Putnam's Sons Books for Young Readers) Penguin Young Readers Group.

—I Hadn't Meant to Tell You This. 2010. (ENG.). 160p. (YA). (gr. 7-18). 7.99 *(978-0-14-241704-1(1),* Puffin Books) Penguin Young Readers Group.

—I Hadn't Meant to Tell You This. 2006. 114p. (YA). (gr. 7-12). 13.65 *(978-0-7569-6730-7(9))* Perfection Learning Corp.

—If You Come Softly. 2010. (ENG.). 224p. (YA). (gr. 7-18). 7.99 *(978-0-14-241522-1(7),* Speak) Penguin Young Readers Group.

Wright, Barbara. Crow. 2013. (ENG.). 320p. (J). (gr. 5-7). pap. 7.99 *(978-0-375-87367-6(8),* Yearling) Random Hse. Children's Bks.

Yee, Paul. What Happened This Summer, 1 vol. 2006. (ENG., Illus.). 178p. (YA). (gr. 8-12). per. 10.95 *(978-1-896580-88-3(2))* Tradewind Bks. CAN. Dist: Orca Bk. Pubs. USA.

RACES OF MAN

see Ethnology

RACIAL BALANCE IN SCHOOLS

see Segregation in Education

RACIALLY MIXED PEOPLE

ABDO Publishing Company Staff & Wheeler, Jill C. Barack Obama, 1 vol. 2009. (United States Presidents Ser.). (ENG., Illus.). 40p. (YA). (gr. 3-6). 27.07 *(978-1-60453-481-8(8))* ABDO Publishing Co.

Barack Obama. 2007. (Political Profiles Ser.). (Illus.). 128p. (YA). (gr. 5-9). lib. bdg. 27.95 *(978-1-59935-045-5(9))* Reynolds, Morgan Inc.

Bourcier, Cammy S. Barack Obama. 2009. (Sharing the American Dream Ser.). (Illus.). 64p. (YA). (gr. 7-12). 22.95 *(978-1-4222-0574-7(6))* Mason Crest.

Bradley, Michael. Derek Jeter. 2004. (Benchmark All-Stars Ser.). (Illus.). 48p. (gr. 4-18). lib. bdg. 27.07 *(978-0-7614-1626-5(9),* Benchmark Bks.) Marshall Cavendish Corp.

Brill, Marlene Targ. Barack Obama: Working to Make a Difference. 2006. (J). pap. 6.95 *(978-0-8225-6056-2(9),* First Avenue Editions); (Illus.). 48p. 23.93 *(978-0-8225-3417-4(7))* Lerner Publishing Group.

—Barack Obama (Revised Edition) 2009. pap. 52.95 *(978-0-7613-5031-6(4))* Lerner Publishing Group.

Britton, Tamara L. Barack Obama, 1 vol. 2013. (United States Presidents Ser.). (ENG.). 40p. (gr. 3-6). lib. bdg. 27.07 *(978-1-61783-492-9(0),* Checkerboard Library) ABDO Publishing Co.

Brown, Jonatha A. & Raatma, Lucia. Tiger Woods. 2004. (People We Should Know Ser.). (Illus.). 24p. (gr. 1-4). pap. 8.15 *(978-0-8368-4320-0(7));* lib. bdg. 22.00 *(978-0-8368-4313-2(4))* Stevens, Gareth Publishing LLLP. (Weekly Reader Leveled Readers).

Corey, Shana. Barack Obama: Out of Many, One. Bernardin, James, illus. 2009. (Step into Reading Ser.). (ENG.). 48p. (J). (gr. k-3). pap. 3.99 *(978-0-375-86339-4(7),* Random Hse. Bks. for Young Readers) Random Hse. Children's Bks.

—Barack Obama: Out of Many, One. 2014. (Step into Reading Ser.). (ENG., Illus.). 48p. (J). (gr. k-3). lib. bdg. 12.99 *(978-0-375-97371-0(0),* Random Hse. Bks. for Young Readers) Random Hse. Children's Bks.

Davis, William Michael. Barack Obama: The Politics of Hope. 2007. (Illus.). 168p. (J). (gr. 10-18). lib. bdg. 25.95 *(978-1-59556-024-7(6));* (YA). (gr. 8-18). pap. 16.99 *(978-1-59556-032-2(7))* OTTN Publishing.

De Medeiros, Michael. Barack Obama. (J). 2013. *(978-1-62127-388-2(1))* 2008. (Illus.). 24p. (gr. 4-6). pap. 8.95 *(978-1-59036-989-0(0))* 2008. (Illus.). 24p. (gr. 4-6). lib. bdg. 24.45 *(978-1-59036-988-3(2))* Weigl Pubs., Inc.

Doeden, Matt. Tiger Woods. 2005. (Sports Heroes & Legends Ser.). (ENG., Illus.). 112p. (gr. 5-12). lib. bdg. 30.60 *(978-0-8225-3082-4(1))* Lerner Publishing Group.

Donovan, Sandy. Derek Jeter. 2008. pap. 40.95 *(978-1-58013-718-8(0))* 2004. 32p. (J). (gr. 2-5). pap. 6.95 *(978-0-8225-2038-2(9))* 2004. (Illus.). 32p. (J). (gr. 3-4). lib. bdg. 23.93 *(978-0-8225-3674-1(9))* Lerner Publishing Group.

Dunn, Joeming. Barack Obama: 44th U. S. President, 1 vol. Espinosa, Rod, illus. 2011. (Presidents of the United States Bio-Graphics Ser.). (ENG.). 32p. (YA). (gr. 3-6). 28.50 *(978-1-61641-648-5(3))* Magic Wagon.

Edwards, Roberta. Barack Obama: United States President. Call, Ken, illus. rev. exp. ed. 2009. (ENG.). 64p. (J). (gr. 1-3). mass mkt. 5.99 *(978-0-448-45234-0(0),* Grosset & Dunlap) Penguin Young Readers Group.

—Who Is Barack Obama? Harrison, Nancy & O'brien, John, illus. 2009. (Who Was? Ser.). (ENG.). 112p. (J). (gr. 3-7). pap. 5.99 *(978-0-448-45330-9(4),* Grosset & Dunlap) Penguin Young Readers Group.

Falk, Laine. Meet President Barack Obama. 2009. (Scholastic News Nonfiction Readers Ser.). (ENG.). 24p. (J). (gr. 1-2). 20.00 *(978-0-531-23403-7(7),* Children's Pr.) Scholastic Library Publishing.

Feinstein, Stephen. Barack Obama. 2008. (African-American Heroes Ser.). (Illus.). 24p. (J). (gr. 1-3). lib. bdg. 22.60 *(978-0-7660-2893-7(3),* Enslow Elementary) Enslow Pubs., Inc.

Fields, Julianna. Multiracial Families. 2010. (Changing Face of Modern Families Ser.). (Illus.). 64p. (YA). (gr. 5-18). lib. bdg. 22.95 *(978-1-4222-1494-7(X))* Mason Crest.

Goodman, Michael E. Tiger Woods. 2003. (Ovations Ser.). (Illus.). 32p. (J). *(978-1-58341-246-6(8),* Creative Education) Creative Co., The.

Gormley, Beatrice. Barack Obama: Our 44th President. 2015. (Real-Life Story Ser.). (ENG., Illus.). 272p. (J). (gr. 3-7). 17.99 *(978-1-4814-4648-8(7),* Aladdin) Simon & Schuster Children's Publishing.

Greenberg, Keith Elliot. Derek Jeter. 2005. (Sports Heroes & Legends Ser.). (Illus.). 106p. (J). (gr. 3-7). lib. bdg. 27.93 *(978-0-8225-3068-8(6),* Lerner Pubns.) Lerner Publishing Group.

Grimes, Nikki. Barack Obama: Son of Promise, Child of Hope. Collier, Bryan, illus. 2012. (ENG.). 48p. (J). (gr. k-3). pap. 9.99 *(978-1-4424-5077-6(0),* Little Simon) Little Simon.

—Barack Obama: Son of Promise, Child of Hope. Collier, Bryan, illus. (ENG.). 48p. (J). (gr. k-3). 2012. 9.99 *(978-1-4424-4092-0(9))* 2008. 16.99 *(978-1-4169-7144-3(0))* Simon & Schuster Bks. For Young Readers. (Simon & Schuster Bks. For Young Readers).

Hansen, Grace. Barack Obama. 2015. (Biografías de Los Presidentes de Los Estados Unidos Ser.). (SPA., Illus.). 24p. (gr. k-1). pap. 7.95 *(978-1-4966-0403-3(2))* Capstone Classroom.

Hoe, Susan. Rosa Parks. 2007. (Sharing the American Dream Ser.). 64p. (YA). (gr. 7-18). pap. 9.95 *(978-1-4222-0760-4(9))* Mason Crest.

Hoppe, Ludwig Augustin. Die Epiklesis Der Griechischen Und Orientalischen Liturgieen Und Der Römische Consekrationskanon (German Edition) 2010. 350p. pap. 32.75 *(978-1-142-96440-5(X))* Creative Media Partners, LLC.

Howard, Tim. The Keeper - The Unguarded Story of Tim Howard. 2015. (ENG.). 288p. (J). (gr. 3-7). pap. 6.99 *(978-0-06-238758-5(8))* HarperCollins Pubs.

Kawa, Katie. Barack Obama: First African American President. 2012. (Beginning Biographies Ser.). (ENG., Illus.). 24p. (J). (gr. 1-3). 22.60 *(978-1-4488-8595-4(7),* PowerKids Pr.) Rosen Publishing Group, Inc., The.

Klein, Adria F. Barack Obama. 2009. pap. 13.25 *(978-1-60559-055-4(X))* Hameray Publishing Group, Inc.

Kramer, Barbara. Beyoncé: Singer, Songwriter, & Actress, 1 vol. 2013. (Contemporary Lives Set 2 Ser.). (ENG.). 112p. (J). (gr. 6-12). lib. bdg. 35.64 *(978-1-61783-617-6(6),* Essential Library) ABDO Publishing Co.

Marcovitz, Hal. The Obama Family Tree. 2007. (Obamas Ser.). (Illus.). 64p. (YA). (gr. 3-6). pap. 9.95 *(978-1-4222-1488-6(5));* (gr. 4-7). lib. bdg. 19.95 *(978-1-4222-1481-7(8))* Mason Crest.

—Obama Mania. 2007. (Obamas Ser.). (Illus.). 64p. (YA). (gr. 3-6). pap. 9.95 *(978-1-4222-1489-3(3));* (gr. 4-7). lib. bdg. 19.95 *(978-1-4222-1482-4(6))* Mason Crest.

Mendell, David & Thomson, Sarah L. Obama: A Promise of Change. 2008. (ENG., Illus.). 192p. (J). (gr. 3-7). pap. 6.99 *(978-0-06-169700-5(1),* Amistad) HarperCollins Pubs.

O'Connell, Jack. Derek Jeter: The Yankee Kid. Rains, Rob, ed. 2003. (Super Star Ser.). 96p. (J). pap. 4.95 *(978-1-58261-043-6(6))* Sports Publishing, LLC.

O'Neal, Claire. What's So Great about Barack Obama. 2009. (What's So Great About... ? Ser.). 32p. (J). (gr. 2-4). lib. bdg. 25.70 *(978-1-58415-830-1(1))* Mitchell Lane Pubs., Inc.

Poole, H. W. Multiracial Families, Vol. 12. 2016. (Families Today Ser.). (Illus.). 48p. (J). (gr. 5). 20.95 *(978-1-4222-3622-2(6))* Mason Crest.

Poole, Hilary W. Military Families. 2017. (Illus.). 48p. (J). *(978-1-4222-3612-3(9))* Mason Crest.

Rappoport, Ken. Jason Kidd: Leader on the Court. 2004. (Sports Leaders Ser.). (Illus.). 104p. (J). lib. bdg. 27.94 *(978-0-7660-2214-0(5))* Enslow Pubs., Inc.

—Super Sports Star Derek Jeter. 2004. (Super Sports Star Ser.). (Illus.). 48p. (J). lib. bdg. 25.27 *(978-0-7660-2139-6(4))* Enslow Pubs., Inc.

Roberts, Russell. Alicia Keys: Singer-Songwriter, Musician, Actress, & Producer. 2012. (Transcending Race Ser.). 64p. (J). (gr. 5). 22.95 *(978-1-4222-2727-5(8))* Mason Crest.

Robinson, Tom. Barack Obama: 44th U. S. President. 2009. (J). lib. bdg. 32.79 *(978-1-60453-528-0(8),* Essential Library) ABDO Publishing Co.

Sapet, Kerrily. Halle Berry: Academy Award/Winning Actress. 2012. (Transcending Race Ser.). 64p. (J). (gr. 5). 22.95 *(978-1-4222-2729-9(4))* Mason Crest.

Savage, Jeff. Tiger Woods. (Amazing Athletes Ser.). 32p. 2005. (Illus.). (gr. 3-4). lib. bdg. 22.60 *(978-0-8225-1337-7(4))* rev. ed. 2007. (ENG., Illus.). (gr. 2-5). per. 7.95 *(978-0-8225-6890-2(X),* First Avenue Editions) 2nd rev. ed. 2009. (ENG.). (gr. 2-5). 25.26 *(978-0-7613-4921-1(9))* Lerner Publishing Group.

Schuman, Michael A. Barack Obama: We Are One People. 2008. (African-American Biography Library). (Illus.). 128p. (J). (gr. 3-7). lib. bdg. 33.27 *(978-0-7660-2891-3(7))* Enslow Pubs., Inc.

—Barack Obama: We Are One People, Revised & Expanded. rev. ed. 2009. (African-American Biography Library). (Illus.). 160p. (J). (gr. 6). lib. bdg. 33.27 *(978-0-7660-3649-9(9))* Enslow Pubs., Inc.

Sheen, Barbara. Derek Jeter. 2008. (People in the News Ser.). (ENG., Illus.). 104p. (YA). (gr. 7-12). lib. bdg. 33.95 *(978-1-4205-0089-9(9),* LML02109-242093) Cengage Gale.

Sirvaitis, Karen. Barack Obama: A Leader in a Time of Change. 2009. (USA TODAY Lifeline Biographies Ser.).

(ENG.). 112p. (gr. 6-12). lib. bdg. 34.60 *(978-0-7613-4235-9(4))* Lerner Publishing Group.

Smith, Crystal. I Am Hapa. Garcia, Michael Satoshi, photos by. 2016. (Illus.). (J). *(978-0-9973947-0-2(6))* East West Discovery Pr.

Smith, Crystal & Garcia, Michael Satoshi. I Am Hapa! 2016. (CHI, SPA & ENG., Illus.). (J). *(978-0-9913454-6-5(0))* East West Discovery Pr.

St. Stephen's Community House Staff. It's Not All Black & White: Multiracial Youth Speak Out. 2012. (ENG., Illus.). 120p. (YA). (gr. 7-12). pap. 12.95 *(978-1-55451-380-2(4),* 9781554513802) Annick Pr., Ltd. CAN. Dist: Publishers Group West (PGW).

Sutcliffe, Jane. Barack Obama. 2010. (History Maker Biographies Ser.). (ENG.). 48p. (gr. 3-6). lib. bdg. 27.93 *(978-0-7613-5205-1(8),* Lerner Pubns.) Lerner Publishing Group.

Taylor, Charlotte & Feinstein, Stephen. Barack Obama: First African-American President. 2015. (Exceptional African Americans Ser.). (ENG.). 24p. (J). (gr. 3-4). pap. 9.35 *(978-0-7660-7122-3(7));* (Illus.). 22.60 *(978-0-7660-7124-7(3))* Enslow Pubs., Inc.

Thornley, Stew. Derek Jeter: Daring to Dream. 2004. (Sports Leaders Ser.). (Illus.). 104p. (J). lib. bdg. 27.94 *(978-0-7660-2035-1(5))* Enslow Pubs., Inc.

Tieck, Sarah. Barack Obama. 1 vol. 2010. (First Biographies Set 6 Ser.). (ENG.). 32p. (J). (gr. 1-4). 27.07 *(978-1-60453-985-1(2))* ABDO Publishing Co.

Torres, John Albert. Derek Jeter. 2004. (Blue Banner Biography Ser.). (Illus.). 32p. (J). lib. bdg. 25.70 *(978-1-58415-333-7(4))* Mitchell Lane Pubs., Inc.

Wagner, Heather Lehr. Barack Obama: Politician. 2008. (Black Americans of Achievement Ser.). (Illus.). 104p. (YA). (gr. 7-12). lib. bdg. 35.00 *(978-0-7910-9716-8(1))* Facts On File, Inc.

Winter, Jonah. Barack. Ford, A. G., illus. 32p. (J). (gr. -1-2). 2010. (ENG.). pap. 7.99 *(978-0-06-170396-6(6),* Tegen, Katherine Bks) 2008. lib. bdg. 18.89 *(978-0-06-170393-5(1))* 2008. (ENG.). 17.99 *(978-0-06-170392-8(3),* Tegen, Katherine Bks) HarperCollins Pubs.

—Barack. 2 vols. 2009. (J). 38.75 *(978-1-4407-3624-7(3));* 38.75 *(978-1-4407-3620-9(0));* 40.75 *(978-1-4407-3618-6(9));* 40.75 *(978-1-4407-3622-3(7));* 1.25 *(978-1-4407-3625-4(1));* 222.75 *(978-1-4407-3619-3(7))* Recorded Bks., Inc.

Wong, Angi Ma. Barack Obama: Historymaker. 2009. (Illus.). 104p. (J). *(978-1-928753-86-5(8))* Pacific Heritage Bks.

Wong, Angi Ma, illus. Meet President Obama: America's 44th President. 2009. 32p. (J). *(978-1-928753-28-5(0))* Pacific Heritage Bks.

Zeiger, Jennifer. Barack Obama. 2012. (Cornerstones of Freedom, Third Ser.). (ENG.). 64p. (J). (gr. 4-6). pap. 8.95 *(978-0-531-28150-5(7));* lib. bdg. 30.00 *(978-0-531-23050-3(3))* Scholastic Library Publishing. (Children's Pr.).

Zumbusch, Amelie von. Barack Obama: Man of Destiny. 2010. (Making History: the Obamas Ser.). (Illus.). 24p. (J). pap. 8.25 *(978-1-4358-9866-0(4));* (gr. 2-3). lib. bdg. 22.60 *(978-1-4358-9387-0(5))* Rosen Publishing Group, Inc., The. (PowerKids Pr.).

RACIALLY MIXED PEOPLE—FICTION

Anderson, Jessica Lee. Border Crossing. 2009. (ENG.). 160p. (J). (gr. 5-10). pap. 8.00 *(978-1-57131-691-2(4))* Milkweed Editions.

Bacho, Peter. Leaving Yesler. 2010. 285p. (YA). pap. 16.00 *(978-1-929355-57-0(2))* Pleasure Boat Studio: A Literary Pr.

Bacigalupi, Paolo. Zombie Baseball Beatdown. (ENG.). (J). (gr. 3-7). 2014. 320p. pap. 7.99 *(978-0-316-22079-8(5))* 2013. 304p. 17.00 *(978-0-316-22078-1(7))* Little, Brown Bks. for Young Readers.

Ball, Jeff. Son Who Returns. 2014. (ENG.). (YA). pap. 9.95 *(978-1-939053-04-6(8),* 7th Generation) Book Publishing Co.

Barkow, Henriette. That's My Mum. Brazell, Derek, illus. 2004. (J). 24p. *(978-1-85269-604-7(4));* (ENG & TUR.). 28p. pap. *(978-1-85269-608-5(7));* (ENG & GUJ.). 28p. pap. *(978-1-85269-601-6(X));* (ENG & CZE.). 28p. pap. *(978-1-85269-628-3(1));* (ENG & SPA.). 28p. pap. *(978-1-85269-606-1(0));* (ENG & SOM.). 28p. pap. *(978-1-85269-605-4(2));* (ENG & BEN.). 28p. pap. *(978-1-85269-597-2(8));* (ENG & CHI.). 28p. pap. *(978-1-85269-598-9(6));* (ENG & PER.). 28p. pap. *(978-1-85269-599-6(4));* (ENG & POR.). 28p. pap. *(978-1-85269-603-0(6));* (ENG & PAN.). 28p. pap. *(978-1-85269-602-3(8));* (ENG & URD.). 28p. pap. *(978-1-85269-609-2(5));* (ENG & YOR.). 28p. pap. *(978-1-84444-381-9(7));* (ALB & ENG.). 28p. pap. *(978-1-85269-595-8(1));* (ENG & ITA.). 28p. pap. *(978-1-85269-804-1(7));* (GER & ENG.). 28p. pap. *(978-1-85269-803-4(9));* (ENG & VIE.). 28p. pap. *(978-1-85269-802-7(0))* Mantra Lingua.

—That's My Mum: Ajo Eshte Nena Ime. Brazell, Derek, illus. 2004. (ENG & ARA.). 28p. (J). pap. *(978-1-85269-596-5(X))* Mantra Lingua.

Benjamin, Floella. My Two Grannies. Chamberlain, Margaret, illus. 2009. (ENG.). 32p. (J). (gr. k-3). pap. 7.95 *(978-1-84780-034-3(3),* Frances Lincoln Children's Bks.) Quarto Publishing Group UK GBR. Dist: Hachette Bk. Group.

Brazell, Derek. That's My Mum: Voici Ma Mere. Barkow, Henriette, illus. 2004. (ENG & FRE.). 28p. (J). pap. *(978-1-85269-600-9(1))* Mantra Lingua.

Brown, Monica. Marisol McDonald & the Clash Bash/Marisol Mcdonald y la Fiesta Sin Igual. Palacios, Sara, illus. 2013. (Marisol Mcdonald Ser.). (ENG & SPA.). 40p. (J). 18.95 *(978-0-89239-273-5(8))* Lee & Low Bks., Inc.

—Marisol Mcdonald & the Monster: Marisol Mcdonald y el Monstruo. Palacios, Sara, illus. 2016. (Marisol Mcdonald Ser.). (ENG & SPA.). 32p. (J). (gr. k-3). 18.95 *(978-0-89239-326-8(2))* Lee & Low Bks., Inc.

—Marisol Mcdonald Doesn't Match / Marisol Mcdonald no Combina. Palacios, Sara, illus. 2013. (Marisol Mcdonald Ser.). (SPA & ENG.). 32p. (J). (gr. -1-3). 17.95 *(978-0-89239-235-3(5))* Lee & Low Bks., Inc.

Cann, Kate. Consumed. 2011. (ENG.). 336p. (J). (gr. 9-9). 16.99 *(978-0-545-26388-7(3))* Scholastic, Inc.

—Possessed. 2010. (ENG.). 336p. (J). (gr. 9-12). 16.99 *(978-0-545-12812-4(9))* Scholastic, Inc.

Carey, Janet Lee. In the Time of Dragon Moon. 2015. (ENG.). 480p. (YA). (gr. 7). 17.99 *(978-0-8037-3810-2(2),* Kathy Dawson Books) Penguin Young Readers Group.

Chan, Crystal. Bird. (ENG.). (J). (gr. 3-7). 2015. 320p. pap. 8.99 *(978-1-4424-5091-2(6))* 2014. (Illus.). 304p. 16.99 *(978-1-4424-5089-9(4),* Atheneum Bks. for Young Readers) Simon & Schuster Children's Publishing.

Chang, Margaret. Celia's Robot. 2009. (ENG.). 208p. (J). (gr. 3-7). 16.95 *(978-0-8234-2181-7(3))* Holiday Hse., Inc.

Chari, Sheela. Finding Mighty. 2017. (ENG., Illus.). 320p. (J). (gr. 5-9). 16.95 *(978-1-4197-2296-7(4),* Amulet Bks.) Abrams, Inc.

Chen, Justina. Nothing but the Truth (And a Few White Lies) 2007. (Justina Chen Novel Ser.). (ENG.). 256p. (J). (gr. 7-17). per. 9.99 *(978-0-316-01131-0(2))* Little, Brown Bks. for Young Readers.

Cheng, Andrea. Shanghai Messenger. 1 vol. Young, Ed, illus. 2005. (ENG.). 40p. (J). (gr. 3-7). 17.95 *(978-1-58430-238-4(0))* Lee & Low Bks., Inc.

Cheng, Andrea & Young, Ed. Shanghai Messenger. 2015. (ENG.). 40p. (J). pap. 10.95 *(978-1-62014-230-1(9))* Lee & Low Bks., Inc.

Cheng, Andrea, et al. Grandfather Counts. Zhang, Ange, illus. 2003. (Avenues Ser.). (ENG.). 32p. (C). pap. 11.95 *(978-1-58430-158-5(9))* National Geographic School Publishing, Inc.

Clark, Tracy. Mirage. 2016. (ENG.). 272p. (J). (gr. 9). 17.99 *(978-0-544-51790-5(3),* HMH Books For Young Readers) Houghton Mifflin Harcourt Publishing Co.

Compestine, Ying Chang. Crouching Tiger. Nascimbene, Yan, illus. 2011. (ENG.). 40p. (J). (gr. 1-4). 16.99 *(978-0-7636-4642-4(3))* Candlewick Pr.

Crutcher, Chris. Whale Talk. 2004. 224p. (J). (gr. 7-18). pap. 38.00 incl. audio *(978-0-8072-2289-8(5),* Listening Library) Random Hse. Audio Publishing Group.

Cruz, Maria Colleen. Border Crossing. 2003. 128p. (J). pap. 9.95 *(978-1-55885-405-5(3),* Piñata Books) Arte Publico Pr.

—Border Crossing. 2006. 122p. (gr. 8-12). 19.95 *(978-0-7569-6587-7(X))* Perfection Learning Corp.

Curry, Jane Louise. The Black Canary. 2005. (ENG., Illus.). 288p. (J). (gr. 5-9). 18.99 *(978-0-689-86478-0(7),* McElderry, Margaret K. Bks.) McElderry, Margaret K. Bks.

De la Peña, Matt. Mexican WhiteBoy. 2010. (ENG.). 256p. (YA). (gr. 9). pap. 9.99 *(978-0-440-23938-3(9),* Ember) Random Hse. Children's Bks.

—Mexican WhiteBoy. 2010. lib. bdg. 20.85 *(978-0-606-12316-7(4),* Turtleback) Turtleback Bks.

Dell, Pamela. Half-Breed: A Story of Two Boys During the Klondike Gold Rush. 2003. (Scrapbooks of America Ser.). (ENG., Illus.). 48p. (J). (gr. 3-6). 32.79 *(978-1-59187-044-9(5),* 200809) Child's World, Inc., The.

Diggs, Taye. Mixed Me! Evans, Shane W., illus. 2015. (ENG.). 40p. (J). (gr. -1-3). 17.99 *(978-1-250-04719-9(6),* 9781250047199) Feiwel & Friends.

Dilloway, Margaret. Momotaro Xander & the Dream Thief. Yoon, Choong, illus. 2017. (Momotaro Ser.). (ENG.). 336p. (J). (gr. 3-7). 16.99 *(978-1-4847-2488-0(7))* Hyperion Bks. for Children.

—Momotaro Xander & the Lost Island of Monsters. Yung, Choong, illus. 2016. (Momotaro Ser.). (ENG.). 310p. (J). (gr. 3-7). 16.99 *(978-1-4847-2487-3(9))* Disney Publishing Worldwide.

—Xander & the Lost Island of Monsters. 2017. (J). lib. bdg. 17.20 *(978-0-606-39503-8(2))* Turtleback Bks.

Edwards, Nicholas & White, Ellen Emerson. The Rescue. 2009. (Dog Whisperer Ser.: 1). (ENG.). 224p. (J). (gr. 3-7). pap. 9.99 *(978-0-312-36768-8(6),* 9780312367688) Square Fish.

Elliott, Kate, pseud. Court of Fives. 2015. (Court of Fives Ser.: Bk. 1). (ENG., Illus.). 448p. (YA). (gr. 7-17). 18.00 *(978-0-316-36419-5(3))* Little Brown & Co.

—Court of Fives. 2016. (Court of Fives Ser.: 1). (ENG., Illus.). 464p. (YA). (gr. 7-17). pap. 10.99 *(978-0-316-36430-0(4))* Little, Brown Bks. for Young Readers.

—Poisoned Blade. 2016. (Court of Fives Ser.: 2). (ENG., Illus.). 480p. (YA). (gr. 7-17). 17.99 *(978-0-316-34437-1(0))* Little, Brown Bks. for Young Readers.

Engle, Margarita. Lion Island: Chinese Cuba's Warrior of Words. 2017. (ENG.). 192p. (J). (gr. 5). pap. 7.99 *(978-1-4814-6113-9(3))* Simon & Schuster Children's Publishing.

—Lion Island: Cuba's Warrior of Words. 2016. (ENG., Illus.). 176p. (J). (gr. 5). 16.99 *(978-1-4814-6112-2(5),* Atheneum Bks. for Young Readers) Simon & Schuster Children's Publishing.

Farish, Terry. Either the Beginning or the End of the World. 2015. (ENG.). 200p. (YA). (gr. 8-12). 18.99 *(978-1-4677-8813-7(9),* Carolrhoda Lab™); 18.99 *(978-1-4677-7483-3(9))* Lerner Publishing Group.

Faulkner, Matt. Gaijin: American Prisoner of War. 2014. (ENG., Illus.). 144p. (J). (gr. 3-7). 19.99 *(978-1-4231-3735-1(3))* Hyperion Bks. for Children.

Ferguson, Alane & Skurzynski, Gloria. Escape from Fear: A Mystery in Virgin Islands National Park. 2008. (Mysteries in Our National Park Ser.). (ENG., Illus.). 160p. (J). (gr. 3-7). mass mkt. 4.99 *(978-1-4263-0181-0(2),* National Geographic Children's Bks.) National Geographic Society.

Finotti, M. C. The Treasure of Amelia Island. 2008. (Florida Historical Fiction for Youth Ser.). (ENG., Illus.). 97p. (J). (gr. 3-7). 14.95 *(978-1-56164-416-2(1))* Pineapple Pr., Inc.

Finotti, M. C. & National Geographic Learning Staff. The Treasure of Amelia Island. 2012. (ENG.). 108p. (C). pap. 14.95 *(978-1-56164-536-7(2))* National Geographic School Publishing, Inc.

Flint, Shamini. Ten: A Soccer Story. 2017. (ENG.). 176p. (J). (gr. 5-7). 16.99 *(978-0-544-85001-9(7),* Clarion Bks.) Houghton Mifflin Harcourt Trade & Reference Pubs.

Flood, Pansie Hart. It's Test Day, Tiger Turcotte. Wummer, Amy, tr. Wummer, Amy, illus. 2004. (Young Reader Fiction Ser.). 72p. (J). (gr. 1-4). pap. 6.95 *(978-1-57505-670-8(4));* lib. bdg. 19.93 *(978-1-57505-056-0(0),* Carolrhoda Bks.) Lerner Publishing Group.

—Tiger's Trouble with Donut Head. Wummer, Amy, illus. 2005. 71p. (J). lib. bdg. 19.93 *(978-1-57505-814-6(6),* Carolrhoda Bks.) Lerner Publishing Group.

Frazier, Sundee T. Brendan Buckley's Sixth-Grade Experiment. 2013. (ENG.). 288p. (J). (gr. 4-7). 6.99 *(978-0-385-74051-7(4),* Yearling) Random Hse. Children's Bks.

—Brendan Buckley's Universe & Everything in It. 2008. (ENG.). 208p. (J). (gr. 3-7). 6.99 *(978-0-440-42206-8(X),* Yearling) Random Hse. Children's Bks.

—Cleo Edison Oliver in Persuasion Power. 2017. (ENG.). 256p. (J). (gr. 3-7). 16.99 *(978-0-545-82239-8(4),* Levine, Arthur A. Bks.) Scholastic, Inc.

—The Other Half of My Heart. 2011. (ENG.). 304p. (J). (gr. 3-7). 7.99 *(978-0-440-24006-8(9),* Yearling) Random Hse. Children's Bks.

Garcia, Cristina. I Wanna Be Your Shoebox. 2009. (ENG.). 208p. (J). (gr. 3-7). pap. 6.99 *(978-1-4169-7904-3(2),* Simon & Schuster Bks. For Young Readers) Simon & Schuster Bks. For Young Readers.

Giles, Lamar. Endangered. 2015. (ENG.). 288p. (YA). (gr. 9). 17.99 *(978-0-06-229756-3(2),* HarperTeen) HarperCollins Pubs.

Gill, David Macinnis. Soul Enchilada. (ENG.). (YA). (gr. 9). 2010. 384p. pap. 8.99 *(978-0-06-167303-0(X))* 2009. 368p. 16.99 *(978-0-06-167301-6(3))* HarperCollins Pubs. (Greenwillow Bks.).

Graff, Lisa. Absolutely Almost. 2014. (ENG.). 304p. (J). (gr. 3-7). 16.99 *(978-0-399-16405-7(7),* Philomel Bks.) Penguin Young Readers Group.

Gurtler, Janet. If I Tell. 2011. (ENG.). 256p. (YA). (gr. 7-12). pap. 12.99 *(978-1-4022-6103-9(9))* Sourcebooks, Inc.

Haislip, Phyllis Hall. Between the Lines: A Revolutionary War Slave's Journey to Freedom. 2012. (ENG., Illus.). 190p. (J). pap. 8.95 *(978-1-57249-409-1(3),* White Mane Kids) White Mane Publishing Co., Inc.

Hale, Bruce. Ends of the Earth. Dorman, Brandon, illus. 2015. (School for Spies Novel Ser.). (ENG.). 304p. (J). (gr. 3-7). 16.99 *(978-1-4231-6852-2(6))* Disney Pr.

—School for SPIES Book 2 Thicker Than Water. Dorman, Brandon, illus. 2014. (School for Spies Novel Ser.). (ENG.). 352p. (J). (gr. 3-7). 16.99 *(978-1-4231-6851-5(8))* Hyperion Bks. for Children.

—School for SPIES Book One Playing with Fire. Dorman, Brandon, illus. 2014. (School for Spies Novel Ser.). (ENG.). 336p. (J). (gr. 3-7). pap. 6.99 *(978-1-4231-7105-8(5))* Hyperion Bks. for Children.

—School for SPIES Thicker Than Water. Dorman, Brandon, illus. 2015. (ENG.). 368p. (J). (gr. 3-7). pap. 6.99 *(978-1-4231-7106-5(3))* Hyperion Bks. for Children.

Hamilton, Virginia, et al. Plain City. (Barco de Vapor). (SPA.). 176p. (YA). (gr. 5-8). 6.95 *(978-84-348-4686-9(1),* LEC6861) SM Ediciones ESP. Dist: Continental Bk. Co., Inc.

Hearn, Julie. Hazel. 2009. (ENG.). 400p. (YA). (gr. 7-18). 17.99 *(978-1-4169-2504-0(X),* Atheneum Bks. for Young Readers) Simon & Schuster Children's Publishing.

Heathfield, Lisa. Paper Butterflies. 2017. (ENG.). 272p. (YA). (gr. 7-12). 18.99 ***(978-1-5124-8241-6(2),*** Carolrhoda Bks.) Lerner Publishing Group.

Hesse, Karen. Aleutian Sparrow. McGillivray, Kim & Zerbetz, Evon, illus. 2005. (ENG.). 160p. (J). (gr. 4-9). reprint ed. pap. 7.99 *(978-1-4169-0327-7(5),* McElderry, Margaret K. Bks.) McElderry, Margaret K. Bks.

—Aleutian Sparrow. Zerbetz, Evon, illus. 2005. 156p. (J). (gr. 5-9). 13.65 *(978-0-7569-5589-2(0))* Perfection Learning Corp.

Hilton, Marilyn. Full Cicada Moon. 2015. (ENG.). 400p. (J). (gr. 3-7). 17.99 *(978-0-525-42875-6(5),* Dial Bks) Penguin Young Readers Group.

Hiranandani, Veera. The Whole Story of Half a Girl. 2013. (ENG.). 224p. (J). (gr. 4-7). 6.99 *(978-0-375-87167-2(5),* Yearling) Random Hse. Children's Bks.

Hopkinson, Nalo. The Chaos. (ENG.). 256p. (YA). (gr. 9). 2013. Illus.). pap. 9.99 *(978-1-4424-5926-7(3))* 2012. 16.99 *(978-1-4169-5488-0(0))* McElderry, Margaret K. Bks. (McElderry, Margaret K. Bks.).

Jaffe, Michele. Bad Kitty. 2006. (Bad Kitty Ser.: Bk. 1). (ENG., Illus.). 288p. (YA). (gr. 7-12). 16.99 *(978-0-06-078108-8(4))* HarperCollins Pubs.

—Kitty Kitty. 2008. (Bad Kitty Ser.: Bk. 2). 320p. (YA). (gr. 7-18). lib. bdg. 17.89 *(978-0-06-078114-9(9),* HarperTeen) HarperCollins Pubs.

Johnson, Kristin F. Wall of Water. 2017. (Day of Disaster Ser.). (ENG.). 112p. (gr. 6-12). (J). 26.65 *(978-1-5124-2778-3(0));* (YA). 12.99 ***(978-1-5124-3516-0(3),*** Darby Creek); (YA). 39.99 ***(978-1-5124-3515-3(5),*** Darby Creek); (YA). 39.99 ***(978-1-5124-2786-8(1),*** Darby Creek) Lerner Publishing Group.

Jones, Kelly. Unusual Chickens for the Exceptional Poultry Farmer. Kath, Katie, illus. 2015. (ENG.). 224p. (J). (gr. 3-7). 16.99 *(978-0-385-75552-8(X),* Knopf Bks. for Young Readers) Random Hse. Children's Bks.

Jones, Patrick. Barrier. 2014. (Alternative Ser.). (ENG.). 104p. (YA). (gr. 6-12). pap. 7.95 *(978-1-4677-4481-2(6),* Darby Creek); lib. bdg. 27.93 *(978-1-4677-3899-6(9))* Lerner Publishing Group.

—Combat Zone. 2015. (ENG.). 96p. (YA). (gr. 6-12). pap. 7.99 *(978-1-4677-8094-0(4))* Lerner Publishing Group.

—Drift: Nissan Skyline. 2013. (Turbocharged Ser.). (ENG.). 112p. (gr. 6-12). pap. 7.95 *(978-1-4677-1474-7(7));* lib. bdg. 27.93 *(978-1-4677-1242-2(6))* Lerner Publishing Group. (Darby Creek).

—Slammed: Honda Civic. 2013. (Turbocharged Ser.). (ENG.). 96p. (gr. 6-12). pap. 7.95 *(978-1-4677-1478-5(X));* lib. bdg. 27.93 *(978-1-4677-1245-3(0))* Lerner Publishing Group. (Darby Creek).

Jubilee Jr., Thomas. The Same As James. Baker, David, illus. 2011. 28p. pap. 24.95 *(978-1-4626-0288-9(6))* America Star Bks.

Katz, Karen. The Colors of Us. Katz, Karen, illus. 2007. (ENG., Illus.). 32p. (J). (gr. -1-3). pap. 26.99 *(978-0-8050-8118-3(6),* 9780805081183, Holt, Henry & Co. Bks. For Young Readers) Holt, Henry & Co.

Keyser, Amber J. The Way Back from Broken. 2015. (ENG.). 216p. (YA). (gr. 6-12). 18.99 *(978-1-4677-8817-5(1),* Carolrhoda Lab™); 18.99 *(978-1-4677-7590-8(8))* Lerner Publishing Group.

Landman, Tanya. Hell & High Water. 2017. (ENG.). 320p. (J). (gr. 7). 17.99 *(978-0-7636-8875-2(4))* Candlewick Pr.

Lariviere, Sarah. The Bad Kid. 2016. (ENG., Illus.). 304p. (J). (gr. 3-7). 16.99 *(978-1-4814-3581-9(7),* Simon & Schuster Bks. For Young Readers) Simon & Schuster Bks. For Young Readers.

Lawrence, Caroline. P. K. Pinkerton & the Deadly Desperados. 2013. (P. K. Pinkerton Ser.: 1). (ENG.). 304p. (J). (gr. 3-7). pap. 7.99 *(978-0-14-242381-3(5),* Puffin Books) Penguin Young Readers Group.

—P. K. Pinkerton & the Pistol-Packing Widows. 2015. (P. K. Pinkerton Ser.: 3). (ENG.). 320p. (J). (gr. 3-7). 7.99 *(978-0-14-751130-0(5),* Puffin Books) Penguin Young Readers Group.

Lenzi, Christy. Stone Field. 2016. (ENG.). 320p. (YA). 17.99 *(978-1-62672-069-5(X),* 9781626720695) Roaring Brook Pr.

Lewis, Richard. The Demon Queen. 2012. (ENG.). 240p. (YA). (gr. 7). pap. 11.99 *(978-1-4169-3590-2(8),* Simon & Schuster Bks. For Young Readers) Simon & Schuster Bks. For Young Readers.

Little, Kimberley Griffiths. The Last Snake Runner. 2006. 201p. (YA). (gr. 7-10). reprint ed. 16.00 *(978-1-4223-5838-2(0))* DIANE Publishing Co.

Lowitz, Leza. Up from the Sea. 2016. (ENG.). 272p. (YA). (gr. 7). 17.99 *(978-0-553-53474-0(2),* Crown Books For Young Readers) Random Hse. Children's Bks.

Magoon, Kekla. Camo Girl. 2012. (ENG.). 224p. (J). (gr. 3-9). pap. 7.99 *(978-1-4169-7805-3(4),* Aladdin) Simon & Schuster Children's Publishing.

—Camo Girl. 2011. (ENG., Illus.). 224p. (J). (gr. 3-9). 16.99 *(978-1-4169-7804-6(6),* Simon & Schuster/Paula Wiseman Bks.) Simon & Schuster/Paula Wiseman Bks.

Maldonado, Torrey. Secret Saturdays. 2012. (ENG.). 208p. (YA). (gr. 7-18). 7.99 *(978-0-14-241747-8(5),* Puffin Books) Penguin Young Readers Group.

—Secret Saturdays. 2012. lib. bdg. 18.40 *(978-0-606-23645-4(7),* Turtleback) Turtleback Bks.

Marsden, Carolyn. Take Me with You. 2010. (ENG., Illus.). 176p. (J). (gr. 5-18). 14.99 *(978-0-7636-3739-2(4))* Candlewick Pr.

Mayer, Pamela. Chicken Soup, Chicken Soup. Melmon, Deborah, illus. 2016. (ENG.). 32p. (J). (gr. -1-3). 17.99 *(978-1-4677-8934-9(8),* Kar-Ben Publishing) Lerner Publishing Group.

McNeil, Gretchen. Possess. (ENG.). (YA). (gr. 8). 2012. 400p. pap. 9.99 *(978-0-06-206072-3(4))* 2011. 384p. 17.99 *(978-0-06-206071-6(6))* HarperCollins Pubs.

Meshon, Aaron. Take Me Out to the Yakyu. Meshon, Aaron, illus. 2013. (ENG., Illus.). 40p. (J). (gr. -1-3). 16.99 *(978-1-4424-4177-4(1),* Atheneum Bks. for Young Readers) Simon & Schuster Children's Publishing.

Meyer, Carolyn. Jubilee Journey. 2007. (ENG., Illus.). 288p. (J). (gr. 5-7). pap. 17.95 *(978-0-15-205845-6(1))* Houghton Mifflin Harcourt Publishing Co.

—Jubilee Journey. 2007. 271p. (J). (gr. 5-9). 14.60 *(978-0-7569-6682-9(5))* Perfection Learning Corp.

Monk, Isabell. Hope. Porter, Janice Lee, illus. 2004. (Carolrhoda Picture Books Ser.). 32p. (J). (gr. -1-3). 6.95 *(978-1-57505-792-7(1))* Lerner Publishing Group.

Mora, Pat & Parra, John. Gracias/Thanks. 2005. (ENG & SPA., Illus.). 32p. (J). (gr. k-5). 17.95 *(978-1-60060-258-0(4))* Lee & Low Bks., Inc.

Namioka, Lensey. Half & Half. 2005. 136p. (gr. 3-7). 16.00 *(978-0-7569-5680-6(3))* Perfection Learning Corp.

—Half & Half. 2004. (ENG.). 144p. (J). (gr. 3-7). 5.99 *(978-0-440-41890-0(9),* Yearling) Random Hse. Children's Bks.

Nelson, Marilyn. American Ace. 2016. (ENG.). 128p. (YA). (gr. 7). 17.99 *(978-0-8037-3305-3(4),* Dial Bks) Penguin Young Readers Group.

Olivas, Daniel. Benjamin & the Word: Benjamin y la Palabra. Baeza Ventura, Gabriela, tr. Dyen, Don, illus. 2011. 32p. (J). pap. 7.95 *(978-1-55885-687-5(0),* Piñata Books) Arte Publico Pr.

—Benjamin & Word Benjamin Y la Palabra. (SPA & ENG., Illus.). 32p. 15.95 *(978-1-55885-413-0(4),* Piñata Books) Arte Publico Pr.

Osborne, Mary Pope. Adaline Falling Star. unabr. ed. 2004. (Middle Grade Cassette Librariestm Ser.). 176p. (J). (gr. 3-7). pap. 29.00 incl. audio *(978-0-8072-1195-3(8),* S YA 319 SP, Listening Library) Random Hse. Audio Publishing Group.

Ostow, Micol. Emily Goldberg Learns to Salsa. 2007. (ENG.). 208p. (YA). (gr. 7-18). 8.99 *(978-1-59514-144-6(8),* Razorbill) Penguin Young Readers Group.

Parry, Rosanne. The Turn of the Tide. 2016. (ENG., Illus.). 304p. (J). (gr. 3-7). 16.99 *(978-0-375-86972-3(7),* Random Hse. Bks. for Young Readers) Random Hse. Children's Bks.

Partridge, Elizabeth. Dogtag Summer. (ENG.). 240p. (YA). (gr. 3-12). 2012. pap. 7.99 *(978-1-59990-829-8(8),* 9781599908298) 2011. 16.99 *(978-1-59990-183-1(8),* 9781599901831) Bloomsbury Publishing USA. (Bloomsbury USA Childrens).

Peck, Richard. The River Between Us. 2005. (ENG.). 176p. (J). (gr. 3-7). reprint ed. pap. 7.99 *(978-0-14-240310-5(5),* Puffin Books) Penguin Young Readers Group.

Philbrick, Rodman. Zane & the Hurricane: A Story of Katrina. (ENG.). 192p. (J). (gr. 5-9). 2015. pap. 6.99 *(978-0-545-34239-1(2))* 2014. (Illus.). 16.99 *(978-0-545-34238-4(4))* Scholastic, Inc. (Blue Sky Pr., The).

Prendergast, G. S. Zero Repeat Forever. 2017. (Nahx Invasions Ser.: 1). (ENG., Illus.). 496p. (YA). (gr. 9). 17.99 ***(978-1-4814-8184-7(3),*** Simon & Schuster Bks. For Young Readers) Simon & Schuster Bks. For Young Readers.

Prendergast, Gabrielle. Zero Repeat Forever. 2017. (YA). pap. ***(978-1-4814-8185-4(1),*** Simon & Schuster Bks. For Young Readers) Simon & Schuster Bks. For Young Readers.

Raffa, Edwina & Rigsby, Annelle. Escape to the Everglades. 2013. (Florida Historical Fiction for Youth Ser.). (ENG.). 112p. (J). pap. 9.95 *(978-1-56164-619-7(9))* Pineapple Pr., Inc.

—Escape to the Everglades Teacher's Activity Guide. 2006. (ENG., Illus.). 31p. pap., tchr. ed., act. bk. ed. 6.00 *(978-1-56164-362-2(9))* Pineapple Pr., Inc.

Resau, Laura. What the Moon Saw. 2008. (ENG.). 272p. (J). (gr. 3-7). pap. 7.99 *(978-0-440-23957-4(5),* Yearling) Random Hse. Children's Bks.

Rinaldi, Ann. The Education of Mary: A Little Miss of Color, 1832. 2005. 176p. (J). pap. *(978-0-7868-1377-3(6))* Hyperion Pr.

—Mutiny's Daughter. 2005. 218p. (J). (gr. 3-7). 13.65 *(978-0-7569-5602-8(1))* Perfection Learning Corp.
Rivers, Karen. The Encyclopedia of Me. 2012. (ENG., Illus.). 256p. (J). (gr. 4-7). 16.99 *(978-0-545-31028-4(8)*, Levine, Arthur A. Bks.) Scholastic, Inc.
Sedgwick, Julian. The Black Dragon. Moffett, Patricia, illus. 2016. (Mysterium Ser.: 1). (ENG.). 352p. (gr. 4-8). 18.99 *(978-1-4677-7567-0(3))*; 38.65 *(978-1-4677-9555-5(0))* Lerner Publishing Group. (Carolrhoda Bks.).
—The Palace of Memory. Moffett, Patricia, illus. 2017. (Mysterium Ser.: 2). (ENG.). 352p. (J). (gr. 4-8). 18.99 *(978-1-4677-7568-7(1)*, Carolrhoda Bks.) Lerner Publishing Group.
Shin, Sun Yung. Cooper's Lesson. Cogan, Kim & Paek, Min, trs. from ENG. Cogan, Kim, illus. 2004. (ENG & KOR.). 32p. (J). 16.95 *(978-0-89239-193-6(6))* Lee & Low Bks., Inc.
—Cooper's Lesson. Cogan, Kim, illus. 2015. (ENG & KOR.). 32p. (J). (gr. k-3). pap. 9.95 *(978-0-89239-361-9(0)*, Children's Book Press) Lee & Low Bks., Inc.
Shusterman, Neal. Red Rider's Hood. 2006. (Dark Fusion Ser.: 3). (ENG.). 192p. (YA). (gr. 7-18). 6.99 *(978-0-14-240678-6(3)*, Speak) Penguin Young Readers Group.
Stanley, Brenda. I Am Nuchu. 2010. 334p. (YA). (gr. 9-18). 16.95 *(978-1-934813-47-8(8))* Westside Bks.
Stauffacher, Sue. Animal Rescue Team: Gator on the Loose! Lamont, Priscilla, illus. 2011. (Animal Rescue Team Ser.). (ENG.). 160p. (J). (gr. 3-7). 5.99 *(978-0-375-85131-5(3)*, Yearling) Random Hse. Children's Bks.
—Animal Rescue Team: Hide & Seek. Lamont, Priscilla, illus. 2011. (Animal Rescue Team Ser.). (ENG.). 160p. (J). (gr. 3-7). 5.99 *(978-0-375-85133-9(X)*, Yearling) Random Hse. Children's Bks.
—Animal Rescue Team: Special Delivery! Lamont, Priscilla, illus. 2011. (Animal Rescue Team Ser.). (ENG.). 176p. (J). (gr. 3-7). 6.99 *(978-0-375-85132-2(1)*, Yearling) Random Hse. Children's Bks.
—Show Time. Lamont, Priscilla, illus. 2011. (Animal Rescue Team Ser.). (ENG.). 160p. (J). (gr. 3-7). 5.99 *(978-0-375-85134-6(8)*, Yearling) Random Hse. Children's Bks.
—Special Delivery! Lamont, Priscilla, illus. 2010. (Animal Rescue Team Ser.: No. 2). (ENG.). 176p. (J). (gr. 3-7). 12.99 *(978-0-375-85848-2(2)*, Knopf Bks. for Young Readers) Random Hse. Children's Bks.
Stehlik, Tania Duprey. Violet, 1 vol. Jovanovic, Vanja Vuleta & Second Story Press Staff, illus. 2009. (ENG.). 32p. (J). (gr. -1-2). 15.95 *(978-1-897187-60-9(2))* Second Story Pr. CAN. Dist: Orca Bk. Pubs. USA.
Stellings, Caroline. The Contest, 1 vol. 2009. (ENG.). 160p. (J). (gr. 4-7). pap. 9.95 *(978-0-9779183-5-5(1)*, 7th Generation) Book Publishing Co.
Stevenson, Sarah Jamila. The Latte Rebellion. 2011. (ENG., Illus.). 336p. (YA). (gr. 9-18). pap. 9.95 *(978-0-7387-2278-8(2)*, Flux) North Star Editions.
Sweeney, Joyce. Waiting for June, 0 vols. 2006. (ENG.). 158p. (YA). (gr. 10-12). pap. 7.99 *(978-0-7614-5329-1(6)*, 9780761453291, Amazon Children's Publishing) Amazon Publishing.
Tan, Susan. Cilla Lee-Jenkins: Future Author Extraordinaire. Wulfekotte, Dana, illus. 2017. (Cilla Lee-Jenkins Ser.). (ENG.). 256p. (J). 16.99 *(978-1-62672-551-5(9)*, 9781626725515) Roaring Brook Pr.
Thompson, Mary G. Flicker & Mist. 2017. (ENG.). 384p. (YA). (gr. 7). 17.99 *(978-0-544-64840-1(4)*, Clarion Bks.) Houghton Mifflin Harcourt Trade & Reference Pubs.
Tolcser, Sarah. Song of the Current. 2017. (ENG.). 384p. (YA). 17.99 *(978-1-68119-297-0(7)*, 9781681192970, Bloomsbury USA Childrens) Bloomsbury Publishing USA.
Tucker, Zekita. Don't Call Me N!gga. 2007. per. 0.01 net. *(978-1-60402-249-0(3))* Independent Pub.
Turner, Diane D. My Name Is Oney Judge. Massey, Cal, illus. 2010. (J). pap. *(978-0-88378-321-4(5))* Third World Press.
—My Name Is Oney Judge. Massey, Call, illus. 2010. (ENG.). 40p. (J). 19.95 *(978-0-88378-304-7(5))* Third World Press.
Wallace, Kali. Shallow Graves. (YA). (gr. 9). 2017. 384p. pap. 9.99 ***(978-0-06-236621-4(1))*** 2016. 368p. 17.99 *(978-0-06-236620-7(3))* HarperCollins Pubs. (Tegen, Katherine Bks).
Washington, Kathy. Three Colors of Katie. Farina, Kathy, illus. 2010. (J). (gr. k-2). pap. 9.95 *(978-1-932514-18-6(X))* College of DuPage Pr.
Webber, Katherine. The Heartbeats of Wing Jones. 2017. (ENG.). 336p. (YA). (gr. 7). 17.99 *(978-0-399-55502-2(1)*, Delacorte Pr.) Random Hse. Children's Bks.
Wenberg, Michael. Stringz. 2010. 216p. (YA). (gr. 6-10). 16.95 *(978-1-934813-33-1(8))* Westside Bks.
Weston, Robert Paul. Blues for Zoey. 2015. (ENG.). 312p. (YA). pap. 9.99 *(978-0-7387-4340-0(2)*, Flux) North Star Editions.
Wientge, Kristi. Karma Khullar's Mustache. 2017. (ENG., Illus.). 272p. (J). (gr. 3-7). 16.99 ***(978-1-4814-7770-3(6)***, Simon & Schuster Bks. For Young Readers) Simon & Schuster Bks. For Young Readers.
—Karma Khullar's Mustache. 2017. (J). pap. ***(978-1-4814-7771-0(4)***, Simon & Schuster Bks. For Young Readers) Simon & Schuster Bks. For Young Readers.
Williams, Julie. Drama Queens in the House. 2014. (ENG.). 432p. (YA). (gr. 7). 17.99 *(978-1-59643-735-7(9)*, 9781596437357) Roaring Brook Pr.
Willis, Meredith Sue. Billie of Fish House Lane. 2006. (J). pap. 12.95 *(978-1-932727-02-9(7))* Montemayor Pr.
Wilson, Diane Lee. Black Storm Comin' 2006. (ENG.). 240p. (J). (gr. 5-9). pap. 7.99 *(978-0-689-87138-2(4)*, McElderry, Margaret K. Bks.) McElderry, Margaret K. Bks.
—Black Storm Comin' 2006. (Illus.). 291p. (gr. 5-9). 17.00 *(978-0-7569-6908-0(5))* Perfection Learning Corp.
Winters, Cat. The Steep & Thorny Way. (ENG.). (YA). (gr. 8-17). 2017. 368p. pap. 9.99 ***(978-1-4197-2350-6(2))*** 2016. (Illus.). 352p. 17.95 *(978-1-4197-1915-8(7))* Abrams, Inc. (Amulet Bks.).
Wong, Janet S. Minn & Jake's Almost Terrible Summer. Côté, Geneviève, illus. 2008. (ENG.). 112p. (J). (gr. 2-5). 15.99 *(978-0-374-34977-6(0)*, 9780374349776, Farrar, Straus & Giroux (BYR)) Farrar, Straus & Giroux.
Woods, Brenda. Blossoming Universe of Violet Diamond. (ENG.). 240p. (J). (gr. 3-7). 2015. 7.99 *(978-0-14-751430-1(4)*, Puffin Books) 2014. 16.99 *(978-0-399-25714-8(4)*, Nancy Paulsen Books) Penguin Young Readers Group.
Woodson, Jacqueline. The House You Pass on the Way. 2010. (ENG.). 160p. (YA). (gr. 7-18). 8.99 *(978-0-14-241706-5(8)*, Puffin Books) Penguin Young Readers Group.
—Miracle's Boys. 2010. (ENG.). 176p. (YA). (gr. 7-18). 8.99 *(978-0-14-241553-5(7)*, Speak) Penguin Young Readers Group.
Yoon, Nicola. Everything, Everything. (ENG.). (YA). (gr. 7). 2017. 352p. pap. 10.99 ***(978-0-553-49667-3(0)***, Ember) 2015. (Illus.). 320p. 18.99 *(978-0-553-49664-2(6)*, Delacorte Pr.) 2017. 336p. 18.99 ***(978-1-5247-6980-2(0)***, Delacorte Pr.) Random Hse. Children's Bks.
—Everything, Everything. 2017. lib. bdg. 22.10 ***(978-0-606-40341-2(8))*** Turtleback Bks.
Young, Karen Romano. Doodlebug: A Novel in Doodles. 2012. (ENG., Illus.). 128p. (J). (gr. 3-7). pap. 7.99 *(978-1-250-01020-9(9)*, 9781250010209) Square Fish.
—Stuck in the Middle (of Middle School) A Novel in Doodles. 2013. (ENG., Illus.). 112p. (J). (gr. 3-7). 12.99 *(978-0-312-55596-2(2)*, 9780312555962) Feiwel & Friends.
—Stuck in the Middle (of Middle School) A Novel in Doodles. 2014. (ENG., Illus.). 128p. (J). (gr. 3-7). pap. 6.99 *(978-1-250-03997-2(5)*, 9781250039972) Square Fish.
Zettel, Sarah. Bad Luck Girl. 2014. (American Fairy Trilogy Ser.: Bk. 3). (ENG.). 368p. (YA). (gr. 7). 17.99 *(978-0-375-86940-2(9)*, Random Hse. Bks. for Young Readers) Random Hse. Children's Bks.
—Golden Girl. 2013. (American Fairy Trilogy Ser.: Bk. 2). (ENG.). 320p. (YA). (gr. 7). 17.99 *(978-0-375-86939-6(5)*, Random Hse. Bks. for Young Readers) Random Hse. Children's Bks.

RACKET GAMES

see also Badminton; Tennis

Salzmann, Mary Elizabeth. Bats, Sticks & Rackets, 1 vol. 2012. (Sports Gear Ser.). (ENG., Illus.). 24p. (J). (gr. k-3). lib. bdg. 24.21 *(978-1-61714-823-1(7))* ABDO Publishing Co.

RACKETEERING

Benson, Michael. Organized Crime. 2008. (Criminal Investigations Ser.). (Illus.). 120p. (C). (gr. 9-12). 35.00 *(978-0-7910-9410-5(3)*, Chelsea Hse.) Facts On File, Inc.
Black, Andy. Organized Crime, Vol. 20. Gomez, Manny, ed. 2016. (Crime & Detection Ser.). (Illus.). 96p. (J). (gr. 7). 24.95 *(978-1-4222-3483-9(5))* Mason Crest.

RACKETEERING—FICTION

Campbell, Isaiah. The Struggles of Johnny Cannon. 2015. 322p. (J). pap. *(978-1-4814-2632-9(X)*, Simon & Schuster Bks. For Young Readers) Simon & Schuster Bks. For Young Readers.
Estep, Jennifer. Bright Blaze of Magic. 2016. (Black Blade Ser.). (ENG.). 368p. (YA). (gr. 9). pap. 9.95 *(978-1-61773-828-9(X))* Kensington Publishing Corp.
Green, Tim. Deep Zone. 2012. (Football Genius Ser.: 5). (J). lib. bdg. 17.20 *(978-0-606-26854-7(5)*, Turtleback) Turtleback Bks.
Hale, Bruce. Murder, My Tweet. 2005. (Chet Gecko Mystery Ser.). (Illus.). 117p. (gr. 3-7). 16.00 *(978-0-7569-5248-8(4))* Perfection Learning Corp.
Higgins, Jack & Richards, Justin. Death Run. 2009. (Rich & Jade Ser.: Bk. 2). (ENG.). 288p. (YA). (gr. 7-18). 8.99 *(978-0-14-241475-0(1)*, Speak) Penguin Young Readers Group.
Korman, Gordon. Son of the Mob (repackage) 2017. (ENG.). 240p. (J). (gr. 5-9). pap. 8.99 ***(978-1-4847-9845-4(7))*** Hyperion Bks. for Children.
Larbalestier, Justine. Razorhurst. 2016. (ENG.). 336p. (YA). (gr. 9). pap. 10.99 *(978-1-61695-625-7(9)*, Soho Teen) Soho Pr., Inc.
Lloyd-Jones, Emily. Deceptive: An Illusive Novel. 2015. (Illusive Ser.: 2). (ENG.). 432p. (YA). (gr. 7-17). 18.00 *(978-0-316-25464-9(9))* Little Brown & Co.
Maetani, Valynne E. Ink & Ashes. 2015. (ENG.). 368p. (YA). 19.95 *(978-1-62014-211-0(2)*, Tu Bks.) Lee & Low Bks., Inc.
Maher, Allison. I, the Spy. 2006. (ENG.). 180p. (J). (gr. 4-7). per. 13.95 *(978-1-897235-04-1(6))* Thistledown Pr., Ltd. CAN. Dist: Univ. of Toronto Pr.
Martinez, Jessica. Kiss Kill Vanish. 2014. (ENG.). 432p. (YA). (gr. 9). 17.99 *(978-0-06-227449-6(X)*, Tegen, Katherine Bks) HarperCollins Pubs.
Meyer, Kai. Arcadia Awakens. 2013. (Arcadia Ser.: 1). (ENG.). 480p. (YA). (gr. 9). pap. 9.99 *(978-0-06-200607-3(X))* HarperCollins Pubs.
—Arcadia Falls. 2014. (Arcadia Ser.: 3). (ENG.). 480p. (YA). (gr. 9). 17.99 *(978-0-06-200610-3(X))* HarperCollins Pubs.
Moore, Graeme. Ruin. 2009. 240p. pap. 21.50 *(978-1-4092-8737-7(8))* Lulu Pr., Inc.
Rylander, Chris. The Fourth Stall, Pt. 3. 2014. (Fourth Stall Ser.: 3). (ENG.). 320p. (J). (gr. 3-7). pap. 6.99 *(978-0-06-212006-9(9)*, Walden Pond Pr.) HarperCollins Pubs.
Schmidt, Tiffany. Hold Me Like a Breath. (ENG.). (YA). 2016. 416p. pap. 9.99 *(978-1-61963-870-9(3)*, 9781619638709) 2015. (Once upon a Crime Family Ser.: Bk. 1). 400p. 17.99 *(978-0-8027-3782-3(X)*, 9780802737823) Bloomsbury Publishing USA. (Bloomsbury USA Childrens).
Zevin, Gabrielle. Because It Is My Blood. 2013. (Birthright Ser.: 2). (ENG.). 384p. (YA). (gr. 7). pap. 9.99 *(978-1-250-03422-9(1)*, 9781250034229) Square Fish.

RADAR

Gregory, Josh. From Bats to... Radar. 2012. (21st Century Skills Innovation Library: Innovations from Nature Ser.). (ENG.). 32p. (gr. 4-8). 28.50 *(978-1-61080-496-7(1)*, 202106); pap. 14.21 *(978-1-61080-670-1(0)*, 202280) Cherry Lake Publishing.
On the Radar: Defend & Protect: Spring 2012 New Releases. 2012. (On the Radar: Defend & Protect Ser.). 32p. (gr. 4-8). lib. bdg. 106.40 *(978-0-7613-8898-2(2)*, Lerner Pubns.) Lerner Publishing Group.
On the Radar: Street Style: Spring 2012 New Releases. 2012. (On the Radar: Street Style Ser.). 32p. (gr. 4-8). lib. bdg. 106.40 *(978-0-7613-8899-9(0)*, Lerner Pubns.) Lerner Publishing Group.
Prentzas, Scott. Radar Guns. 2009. (21st Century Skills Library: Global Products Ser.). (ENG., Illus.). 32p. (gr. 4-8). lib. bdg. 28.50 *(978-1-60279-507-5(X)*, 200322) Cherry Lake Publishing.
Zelon, Helen. The Endeavor SRTM: Mapping the Earth. 2009. (Space Missions Ser.). 24p. (gr. 3-4). 42.50 *(978-1-60853-118-9(X)*, PowerKids Pr.) Rosen Publishing Group, Inc., The.

RADIATION

see also Light; Quantum Theory; Radioactivity; Radium; Sound; X-Rays

Allman, Toney. Radiation Sickness. 2013. (Diseases & Disorders Ser.). (ENG., Illus.). 128p. (gr. 7-10). lib. bdg. 39.90 *(978-1-4205-0900-7(4)*, Lucent Bks.) Cengage Gale.
American Cancer Society Staff. Mission: Sunwise (Story Book) Sunwise (Story Book) Environmental Protection Agency (US), ed. 2010. (ENG., Illus.). 13p. (gr. 4). 4.00 *(978-0-16-085823-9(2)*, Environmental Protection Agency) United States Government Printing Office.
Gastineau, John. Nuclear Radiation with Vernier. 2008. (YA). spiral bd. 25.00 *(978-1-929075-54-6(5))* Vernier Software & Technology.
Greeley, August. Fallout: Nuclear Disasters in Our World. 2009. (Man-Made Disasters Ser.). 24p. (gr. 3-3). 42.50 *(978-1-61514-348-1(3)*, PowerKids Pr.) Rosen Publishing Group, Inc., The.
Jankowski, Connie. All about Light & Sound, 1 vol. 2007. (Science Readers Ser.). (SPA & ENG.). 32p. (J). (gr. 4-4). pap. 8.99 *(978-0-7439-0579-4(2))* Shell Educational Publishing.
Solway, Andrew. Exploring Sound, Light, & Radiation. 2007. (Exploring Physical Science Ser.). (Illus.). 48p. (YA). (gr. 5-9). lib. bdg. 29.25 *(978-1-4042-3746-9(1))* Rosen Publishing Group, Inc., The.
Woodford, Chris. Light & Radiation. 2004. (Routes of Science Ser.). (Illus.). 40p. (J). (gr. 4-7). 24.95 *(978-1-4103-0297-7(0)*, Blackbirch Pr., Inc.) Cengage Gale.

RADIATION, SOLAR

see Solar Radiation

RADIATION CHEMISTRY

see Radiochemistry

RADICALISM

see also Radicals

Merino, Noël. Extremism. 2014. (Global Viewpoints Ser.). (ENG., Illus.). 224p. 46.20 *(978-0-7377-6908-1(4)*, Greenhaven Pr., Inc.) Cengage Gale.
Perritano, John. Radical Republicans: The Struggle for Equality. 2008. (Graphic America Ser.). (ENG., Illus.). 32p. (J). (gr. 3-6). lib. bdg. *(978-0-7787-4187-9(7))* Crabtree Publishing Co.

RADICALS

see also Reformers; Revolutions; Right and Left (Political Science)

Higgins, Melissa. Julian Assange: WikiLeaks Founder, 1 vol. 2011. (Essential Lives Set 7 Ser.). (ENG., Illus.). 112p. (J). (gr. 6-12). lib. bdg. 35.64 *(978-1-61783-001-3(1))* ABDO Publishing Co.
Ni Dheirg, Iosold. The Story of Michael Collins. 2017. (ENG.). 140p. (J). pap. 10.00 ***(978-1-78117-491-3(1))*** Mercier Pr., Ltd., The IRL. Dist: Dufour Editions, Inc.
Robinson, C. L. MATH1on1 Radicals Foundation. 2006. (YA). per. 9.99 *(978-0-9786767-8-0(5))* Robinson, Consuelo.

RADIO

Bonner, Richard. Boy Inventors Radio Telephone. 2006. 27.95 *(978-1-4218-3004-9(3))*; pap. 12.95 *(978-1-4218-3104-6(X))* 1st World Publishing, Inc.
Brooks, Philip. Radio. 2008. (21st Century Skills Innovation Library: Innovation in Entertainment Ser.). (ENG., Illus.). 32p. (gr. 4-8). lib. bdg. 28.50 *(978-1-60279-217-3(8)*, 200148) Cherry Lake Publishing.
Fedunkiw, Marianne. Inventing the Radio. 2007. (Breakthrough Inventions Ser.). (ENG., Illus.). 32p. (J). (gr. 3-7). lib. bdg. 22.60 *(978-0-7787-2817-7(X))*; pap. *(978-0-7787-2839-9(0))* Crabtree Publishing Co.
Kulling, Monica. Making Contact! Marconi Goes Wireless. 2016. (Great Idea Ser.). (ENG., Illus.). 32p. (J). (gr. k-3). pap. 6.99 *(978-1-101-91842-5(X)*, Tundra Bks.) Tundra Bks. CAN. Dist: Penguin Random Hse. LLC.
—Making Contact! Marconi Goes Wireless. Rudnicki, Richard, illus. 2013. (Great Idea Ser.). (ENG.). 32p. (J). (gr. k-3). 17.95 *(978-1-77049-378-0(6)*, Tundra Bks.) Tundra Bks. CAN. Dist: Penguin Random Hse. LLC.
Mattern, Joanne. The Radio: The World Tunes In. (Technology That Changed the World Ser.). 24p. 2009. (gr. 2-3). 42.50 *(978-1-60853-277-3(1))* 2003. (Illus.). (J). lib. bdg. 22.60 *(978-0-8239-6491-8(4))* Rosen Publishing Group, Inc., The. (PowerKids Pr.).
O'Shei, Tim. Marconi & Tesla: Pioneers of Radio Communication. 2008. (Inventors Who Changed the World Ser.). (Illus.). 128p. (J). (gr. 3-7). lib. bdg. 34.60 *(978-1-59845-076-7(X)*, MyReportLinks.com Bks.) Enslow Pubs., Inc.
Radios, Phones & Telecommunications. 2005. (Inventions Ser.). (Illus.). 30p. (J). pap. 15.95 incl. audio *(978-0-9724983-4-0(6))* Jazwares Distribution, Inc.
Sherrow, Victoria. Guglielmo Marconi: Inventor of Radio & Wireless Communication. 2004. (Nobel Prize-Winning Scientists Ser.). (Illus.). 112p. (J). lib. bdg. 27.94 *(978-0-7660-2280-5(3))* Enslow Pubs., Inc.
Smibert, Angie. 12 Great Moments That Changed Radio History. 2015. (ENG., Illus.). 32p. (J). *(978-1-63235-026-8(2))* Pr. Room Editions LLC.
Spilsbury, Richard & Spilsbury, Louise. The Radio, 1 vol. 2011. (Tales of Invention Ser.). (ENG.). 32p. (gr. 3-5). pap. 8.95 *(978-1-4329-4887-0(3))*; 30.65 *(978-1-4329-4878-8(4))* Heinemann-Raintree. (NA-h).
Zannos, Susan. Guglielmo Marconi & Radio Waves. 2004. (Uncharted, Unexplored, & Unexplained Ser.). (Illus.). 48p. (J). (gr. 4-8). lib. bdg. 29.95 *(978-1-58415-265-1(6))* Mitchell Lane Pubs., Inc.

RADIO—APPARATUS AND SUPPLIES

see Radio—Equipment and Supplies

RADIO—BROADCASTING

see Radio Broadcasting

RADIO—EQUIPMENT AND SUPPLIES

Petrie, Kristin. Radios, 1 vol. 2009. (Everyday Inventions Ser.). (ENG., Illus.). 32p. (gr. 3-6). 27.07 *(978-1-60453-087-2(1)*, Checkerboard Library) ABDO Publishing Co.

RADIO—OPERATORS

see Radio Operators

RADIO ASTRONOMY

see also names of celestial radio sources, e.g. Quasars

Firestone, Mary. Seti Science. 2005. (Weird Careers in Science Ser.). (Illus.). 88p. (gr. 5-8). lib. bdg. 25.00 *(978-0-7910-8701-5(8)*, Chelsea Hse.) Facts On File, Inc.
Jefferis, David. Star Spotters: Telescopes & Observatories. 2008. (Exploring Our Solar System Ser.). (ENG., Illus.). 32p. (J). (gr. 3-8). lib. bdg. *(978-0-7787-3725-4(X))* Crabtree Publishing Co.

RADIO BROADCASTING

see also Television Broadcasting

Anniss, Matt. Dj-Ing. 2010. (Master This! Ser.). (ENG.). 32p. (J). lib. bdg. 25.25 *(978-1-61532-596-2(4)*, PowerKids Pr.) Rosen Publishing Group, Inc., The.
Connolly, Sean. Getting the Message: Television & Radio. 2010. 34.25 *(978-1-59920-350-8(2))* Black Rabbit Bks.
McCarthy, Meghan. Aliens Are Coming! The True Account of the 1938 War of the Worlds Radio Broadcast. 2009. (ENG.). 40p. (J). (gr. -1-2). pap. 7.99 *(978-0-385-73678-7(9)*, Dragonfly Bks.) Random Hse. Children's Bks.
Pelusey, Michael & Pelusey, Jane. Radio. 2005. (Media Ser.). (Illus.). 32p. (gr. 5-8). lib. bdg. 21.95 *(978-0-7910-8801-2(4)*, Chelsea Hse.) Facts On File, Inc.
Smibert, Angie. 12 Great Moments That Changed Radio History. 2015. (ENG., Illus.). 32p. (J). *(978-1-63235-026-8(2))* Pr. Room Editions LLC.
—12 Great Moments that Changed Radio History. 2015. (ENG., Illus.). 32p. (J). pap. 9.95 *(978-1-63235-086-2(6))* RiverStream Publishing.
Teitelbaum, Michael. Sports Broadcasting. 2008. (21st Century Skills Innovation Library: Innovation in Entertainment Ser.). (ENG., Illus.). 32p. (gr. 4-8). lib. bdg. 28.50 *(978-1-60279-216-6(X)*, 200147) Cherry Lake Publishing.
Walters, John. Sports Broadcasting, Vol. 10. Ferrer, Al, ed. 2015. (Careers off the Field Ser.). (Illus.). 64p. (J). (gr. 7). 23.95 *(978-1-4222-3271-2(9))* Mason Crest.

RADIO BROADCASTING—BIOGRAPHY

Pezzi, Bryan. David Suzuki: Ma Vie. Karvonen, Tanjah, tr. from ENG. 2011. (FRE., Illus.). 24p. (YA). (gr. 2-4). *(978-1-77071-429-8(4))* Weigl Educational Pubs. Ltd.

RADIO CHEMISTRY

see Radiochemistry

RADIO JOURNALISM

see Journalism; Radio Broadcasting

RADIO OPERATORS

Broderick, Kevin Joyce. The JipiJapa Hat. 2007. 124p. per. 12.95 *(978-0-595-45071-8(7))* iUniverse, Inc.

RADIO OPERATORS—FICTION

Chapman, Allen. The Radio Boys' First Wireless; or, Winning the Ferberton Prize. 2007. 100p. per. *(978-1-4068-4516-7(7))* Echo Library.

RADIOACTIVE SUBSTANCES

see Radioactivity

RADIOACTIVE WASTES

Bell, Samantha S. How Can We Reduce Nuclear Pollution? 2016. (Searchlight Books — What Can We Do about Pollution? Ser.). (ENG., Illus.). 40p. (J). (gr. 3-5). lib. bdg. 30.65 *(978-1-4677-9516-6(X))* Lerner Publishing Group.
Friedman, Lauri S. Nuclear Power. 2009. (Introducing Issues with Opposing Viewpoints Ser.). (ENG., Illus.). 144p. (gr. 10-12). 42.00 *(978-0-7377-4482-8(0))* Cengage Gale.
Jakubiak, David J. What Can We Do about Nuclear Waste? 2012. (Illus.). 24p. (J). 49.50 *(978-1-4488-5115-7(7)*, PowerKids Pr.); (J). pap. 8.25 *(978-1-4488-5114-0(9)*, PowerKids Pr.); (YA). (gr. 2-5). lib. bdg. 22.60 *(978-1-4488-4983-3(7))* Rosen Publishing Group, Inc., The.
Kiesbye, Stefan. Nuclear & Toxic Waste. 2010. (At Issue Ser.). (Illus.). 128p. (J). 34.45 *(978-0-7377-4681-5(5))*; pap. 24.45 *(978-0-7377-4682-2(3))* Cengage Gale. (Greenhaven Pr., Inc.).

RADIOACTIVITY

see also Electrons; Nuclear Physics; Radiochemistry; Radium; Uranium; X-Rays

Barton, Chris. The Day-Glo Brothers: The True Story of Bob & Joe Switzer's Bright Ideas & Brand-New Colors. Persiani, Tony, illus. 2009. (ENG.). 44p. (J). (gr. 2-5). 19.95 *(978-1-57091-673-1(X))* Charlesbridge Publishing, Inc.
Henderson, Harry. The Curie Family. 2012. (Trailblazers in Science & Technology Ser.). 136p. (gr. 6-12). 35.00 *(978-1-60413-675-3(8)*, Chelsea Hse.) Facts On File, Inc.
Jackson, Tom. Radioactive Elements. 2005. (Elements Ser.). (Illus.). 32p. (gr. 4-7). lib. bdg. 28.50 *(978-0-7614-1923-5(3)*, Benchmark Bks.) Marshall Cavendish Corp.
Jerome, Kate Boehm. Atomic Universe: The Quest to Discover Radioactivity. 2006. (Science Quest Ser.). (ENG., Illus.). 64p. (J). (gr. 5-9). 17.95 *(978-0-7922-5543-7(7)*, National Geographic Children's Bks.) National Geographic Society.
Karam, P. Andrew & Stein, Ben P. Radioactivity. 2009. (Science Foundations Ser.). (Illus.). 128p. (YA). (gr. 7-12). lib. bdg. 35.00 *(978-1-60413-016-4(4))* Facts On File, Inc.
Lin, Yoming S. The Curies & Radioactivity. 2012. (Eureka! Ser.). (Illus.). 24p. (YA). (gr. 3-6). lib. bdg. 22.60 *(978-1-4488-5033-4(9))* Rosen Publishing Group, Inc., The.
Miller, Connie Colwell. Marie Curie & Radioactivity, 1 vol. Larson, Scott & Heike, Mark, illus. 2006. (Inventions & Discovery Ser.). (ENG.). 32p. (gr. 3-4). 30.65 *(978-0-7368-6486-2(5)*, Graphic Library) Capstone Press of Coughlan Cos.
O'Quinn, Amy M. Marie Curie for Kids: Her Life & Scientific Discoveries, with 21 Activities & Experiments. 2016. (For Kids Ser.). (ENG.). 144p. (J). (gr. 4). pap. 16.99 *(978-1-61373-320-2(8))* Chicago Review Pr., Inc.
Tracy, Kathleen. Pierre & Marie Curie & the Discovery of Radium. 2004. (Uncharted, Unexplored, & Unexplained Ser.). (Illus.). 48p. (J). (gr. 4-8). lib. bdg. 29.95 *(978-1-58415-310-8(5))* Mitchell Lane Pubs., Inc.

PQR

RADIOCHEMISTRY

Jackson, Tom. Radioactive Elements. 2005. (Elements Ser.). (Illus.). 32p. (gr. 4-7). lib. bdg. 28.50 (978-0-7614-1923-5(3), Benchmark Bks.) Marshall Cavendish Corp.

RADIOGRAPHY

see X-Rays

RADISSON, PIERRE ESPRIT, APPROXIMATELY 1636-1710

Bailey, Katharine. Radisson & des Groseilliers: Fur Traders of the North. 2006. (In the Footsteps of Explorers Ser.). (ENG., Illus.). 32p. (J). (gr. 3-7). lib. bdg. (978-0-7787-2422-3(0), 1253444); (gr. 4-7). pap. (978-0-7787-2458-2(1), 1253444) Crabtree Publishing Co.

RADIUM

see also Radioactivity

Miller, Connie Colwell. Marie Curie & Radioactivity, 1 vol. Larson, Scott & Heike, Mark, illus. 2006. (Inventions & Discovery Ser.). (ENG.). 32p. (gr. 3-4). 30.65 (978-0-7368-6486-2(5), Graphic Library) Capstone Press of Coughlan Cos.

RAILROAD CONSTRUCTION

see Railroad Engineering

RAILROAD ENGINEERING

Caravantes, Peggy. The Building of the Transcontinental Railroad. 2017. (Engineering That Made America Ser.). (ENG.). 32p. (J). (gr. 3-6). lib. bdg. 28.50 (978-1-5038-1635-0(4), 211154) Child's World, Inc., The.

Kallen, Stuart. The Chunnel. 2014. (Great Idea Ser.). (ENG., Illus.). 48p. (J). (gr. 4-6). pap. 13.26 (978-1-60357-576-8(6)) Norwood Hse. Pr.

Kallen, Stuart A. The Chunnel. 2014. (Great Idea Ser.). (ENG., Illus.). 48p. (J). (gr. 4-6). lib. bdg. 26.60 (978-1-59953-596-8(3)) Norwood Hse. Pr.

Otfinoski, Steven. High-Speed Trains: From Concept to Consumer. 2015. (ENG.). 64p. (J). lib. bdg. (978-0-531-21899-0(6), Orchard Bks.) Scholastic, Inc.

RAILROAD STATIONS

Steffora, Tracey. Math at the Train Station, 1 vol. 2013. (Math on the Job Ser.). (ENG., Illus.). 24p. (gr. k-2). pap. 6.29 (978-1-4329-7161-8(1)); lib. bdg. 22.65 (978-1-4329-7154-0(9)) Heinemann-Raintree. (Acorn).

Williams, Dinah. Creepy Stations. 2013. (Scary Places Ser.). 32p. (J). (gr. 4-8). lib. bdg. 25.27 (978-1-61772-749-8(0)) Bearport Publishing Co., Inc.

Wing, Natasha. When Jackie Saved Grand Central. Boiger, Alexandra, illus. 2017. (ENG.). 48p. (J). (gr. 1-4). 17.99 (978-0-547-44921-0(6), HMH Books For Young Readers) Houghton Mifflin Harcourt Publishing Co.

RAILROADS

see also Freight and Freightage; Railroad Engineering; Subways

Ackerman, Jill & Landers, Ace. I Am a Train. Scholastic, Inc. Staff, ed. 2008. (ENG.). 8p. (J). (gr. -1 — 1). bds. 4.99 (978-0-545-07962-4(4), Cartwheel Bks.) Scholastic, Inc.

Amery, Heather & Doherty, Gillian. Wind-up Train Book. 2008. (Wind-up Bks). 14p. (J). bds. 29.99 (978-0-7945-2192-9(4), Usborne) EDC Publishing.

Balkwill, Richard. The Best Book of Trains. 2008. (Best Books Of Ser.). (ENG., Illus.). 32p. (J). (gr. -1-3). pap. 6.99 (978-0-7534-6171-6(4), 9780753461716, Kingfisher) Roaring Brook Pr.

Barker, Stephen. I Want to Be a Train Driver. 2016. (ENG., Illus.). 10p. (J). (gr. -1-k). bds. 10.99 (978-1-4052-7640-5(1)) Egmont Bks., Ltd. GBR. Dist: Independent Pubs. Group.

Bender, Lionel. Trains & Trams. 2006. (On the Move Ser.). (978-1-59389-269-2(1)) Chrysalis Education.

Biello, David. Bullet Trains: Inside & Out. 2005. (Technology: Blueprints of the Future Ser.). (Illus.). 48p. (YA). (gr. 4-8). lib. bdg. 29.25 (978-0-8239-6113-9(3)) Rosen Publishing Group, Inc., The.

Bone, Emily. Trains. 2011. (Beginner's Science Ser.). 32p. (J). ring bd. 4.99 (978-0-7945-3112-6(1), Usborne) EDC Publishing.

Bridges, Sarah. I Drive a Freight Train, 1 vol. Muehlenhardt, Amy Bailey, illus. 2006. (Working Wheels Ser.). (ENG.). 24p. (gr. -1-2). 26.65 (978-1-4048-1607-7(0)) Picture Window Bks.

Brooks, Felicity. Trains lift & Look. Litchfield, Jo, illus. 2005. 12p. (J). 9.99 (978-0-7945-0935-4(5), Usborne) EDC Publishing.

Burch, Lynda S. Wicky Wacky Things that Go! Trains 1. Burch, Lynda S., photos by. 2004. (Illus.). 16p. (J). E-Book 9.95 incl. cd-rom (978-1-933090-02-3(2)) Guardian Angel Publishing, Inc.

Carroll, Colleen. Trains. 2008. (How Artists See Jr.: Ser.). (ENG., Illus.). 18p. (J). (gr. -1-k). bds. 7.95 (978-0-7892-0971-9(3), Abbeville Kids) Abbeville Pr., Inc.

Cefrey, Holly. The Inventions of Granville Woods: The Railroad Telegraph System & the "Third Rail" 2003. (19th Century American Inventors Ser.). (Illus.). 24p. (J). lib. bdg. 22.60 (978-0-8239-6442-0(6), PowerKids Pr.) Rosen Publishing Group, Inc., The.

Chiu, David. Government Regulation of the Railroads: Fighting Unfair Trade Practices in America. (Progressive Movement, 1900-1920 — Efforts to Reform America's New Industrial Society Ser.). (Illus.). 32p. 2006. (ENG.). (gr. 4-8). pap. 10.00 (978-1-4042-0849-0(6)) 2004. (YA). (gr. 5-9). lib. bdg. 22.50 (978-1-4042-0190-3(4)) Rosen Publishing Group, Inc., The.

Clapper, Nikki Bruno. High-Speed Trains. 2015. (All Aboard! Ser.). (ENG., Illus.). 24p. (gr. k-1). lib. bdg. 26.65 (978-1-4914-6039-9(3), Pebble Plus) Capstone Press of Coughlan Cos.

Corrigan, Kathleen. Building a Nation. 2016. (Canada Through Time Ser.). (ENG., Illus.). 32p. (gr. 1-4). lib. bdg. 29.99 (978-1-4109-8120-2(7), Read Me!) Heinemann-Raintree.

Cullis, Megan. Big Book of Big Trains. 2013. (Big Bks). 16p. (J). ring bd. 14.99 (978-0-7945-3378-6(7), Usborne) EDC Publishing.

Curry, Peter, illus. Trains, Boats, & Planes. 2016. (ENG.). 12p. (J). (gr. -1 — 1). bds. 4.99 (978-1-4998-0262-7(5)) Little Bee Books Inc.

Daynes, Katie, et al. The Railway Revolution. 2016. (ENG.). 56p. (J). (gr. 4-5). pap. 9.95 (978-0-00-816395-2(2)) HarperCollins Pubs. Ltd. GBR. Dist: Independent Pubs. Group.

DiSiena, Laura Lyn & Eliot, Hannah. Trains Can Float: And Other Fun Facts. Oswald, Pete & Spurgeon, Aaron, illus. 2014. (Did You Know? Ser.). (ENG.). 32p. (J). (gr. -1-3). 17.99 (978-1-4814-0281-1(1), Little Simon) Little Simon.

Donahue, Peter. All Aboard! Trains Stained Glass Coloring Book. 2011. (Dover Stained Glass Coloring Book Ser.). (ENG., Illus.). 32p. (J). (gr. -1-2). pap. 6.99 (978-0-486-47896-8(3)) Dover Pubns., Inc.

Dorling Kindersley Publishing Staff & Colley, John. Train. 2009. (DK Eyewitness Bks.). (ENG.). 72p. (J). (gr. 3-7). 16.99 (978-0-7566-5032-2(1), DK Children) Dorling Kindersley Publishing, Inc.

Dubowski, Mark. Superfast Trains. 2005. (Ultimate Speed Ser.). (Illus.). 32p. (J). (gr. 3-6). lib. bdg. 25.27 (978-1-59716-084-1(9)) Bearport Publishing Co., Inc.

Dyan, Penelope. Steam Train! All the Way to Canterbury, England. Weigand, John D., photos by. 2011. (Illus.). 40p. pap. 11.95 (978-1-935630-75-3(X)) Bellissima Publishing, LLC.

Emberley, Ed. Ed Emberley's Drawing Book of Trucks & Trains. Emberley, Ed, illus. 2005. (ENG., Illus.). 32p. (J). (gr. 2-17). pap. 6.99 (978-0-316-78967-7(4)) Little, Brown Bks. for Young Readers.

Ganeri, Anita. Flip the Flaps: Things That Go! Humphries, Tudor, illus. 2014. (Flip the Flaps Ser.). (ENG.). 32p. (J). (gr. -1-1). pap. 6.99 (978-0-7534-7133-3(7), 9780753471333, Kingfisher) Roaring Brook Pr.

Goodman, Steve. The Train They Call the City of New Orleans. McCurdy, Michael, illus. pap. incl. audio compact disk (978-1-59112-905-9(2)); pap. incl. audio (978-1-59112-901-1(X)); pap. 18.95 incl. audio compact disk (978-1-59112-903-5(6)); pap. 16.95 incl. audio (978-1-59112-899-1(4)) Live Oak Media.

Goopar, Rocio Arvea. Ro & Otilo: The Magic Train. 2011. 36p. pap. 15.14 (978-1-4634-1665-2(2)) AuthorHouse.

Graham, Ian. On the Rails. 2008. (QEB Machines at Work Ser.). (Illus.). 36p. (YA). (gr. 4-7). 19.95 (978-1-59566-316-0(9)) QEB Publishing Inc.

Hammond Editors, ed. Trains. 2009. (Hammond Undercover Ser.). 72p. (J). (gr. 3-7). pap. 13.99 (978-0-8416-1496-3(2)) Hammond World Atlas Corp.

Hanson, Anders. Let's Go by Cable Car, 1 vol. Craig, Diane, ed. 2008. (Let's Go Ser.). (ENG., Illus.). 24p. (J). (gr. k-3). lib. bdg. 24.21 (978-1-59928-896-3(6), SandCastle) ABDO Publishing Co.

Harris, Michael & Parker, Steve. Trains - Railways; Tunnels; Signals; Diesel; Steam: With 10 Easy-to-Do Experiments & 230 Exciting Pictures. 2016. (ENG., Illus.). 64p. 12.99 (978-1-86147-489-6(X), Armadillo) Anness Publishing GBR. Dist: National Bk. Network.

Hill, Lee Sullivan. Trains on the Move. 2011. (Lightning Bolt Books Vroom-Vroom Ser.). 32p. pap. 45.32 (978-0-7613-7620-0(8)) Lerner Publishing Group.

Hill, Lee Sullivan & Hill, Lee Sullivan. Trains on the Move. 2011. (Lightning Bolt Books Vroom-Vroom Ser.). (ENG.). 32p. (gr. k-2). pap. 7.95 (978-0-7613-7109-0(5)) Lerner Publishing Group.

Hyde, Natalie. Transcontinental Railroads. 2017. 48p. (J). **(978-0-7787-3941-8(4))** Crabtree Publishing Co.

Ikids Staff. Junior Groovies: Trains (Storybook, Fun Facts & Toys) Voltz, Ralph, illus. 2011. (ENG.). 10p. (J). (gr. -1-1). 12.99 (978-1-60169-149-1(1)) Innovative Kids.

Kraft, Eric. The Transcontinental Railroad: Set Of 6. 2011. (Navigators Ser.). (J). pap. 48.00 net. (978-1-4108-0436-5(4)) Benchmark Education Co.

Langston-George, Rebecca. Orphan Trains: Taking the Rails to a New Life. 2016. (Encounter: Narrative Nonfiction Stories Ser.). (ENG., Illus.). 128p. (gr. 3-4). lib. bdg. 30.65 (978-1-4914-8551-4(5)) Capstone Press of Coughlan Cos.

—Orphan Trains: Taking the Rails to a New Life. 2016. (Encounter: Narrative Nonfiction Stories Ser.). (ENG., Illus.). 128p. (gr. 3-4). pap. 6.95 (978-1-62370-630-2(0)) Encounter Bks.

Leighton, Christina. City Trains. 2017. (Amazing Trains Ser.). (ENG., Illus.). 24p. (J). (gr. k-3). lib. bdg. 25.95 **(978-1-62617-669-0(8)**, Blastoff! Readers) Bellwether Media.

—Monorails. 2017. (Amazing Trains Ser.). (ENG., Illus.). 24p. (J). (gr. k-3). lib. bdg. 25.95 **(978-1-62617-672-0(8)**, Blastoff! Readers) Bellwether Media.

Lindeen, Mary. Trains. 2007. (Mighty Machines Ser.). (ENG., Illus.). 24p. (J). (gr. k-3). lib. bdg. 25.95 (978-1-60014-062-4(9)) Bellwether Media.

Matthews, John R. The Railroad. 2006. (Inventions That Shaped the World Ser.). (Illus.). 80p. (J). (gr. 5-8). 17.60 (978-0-7569-6861-8(5)) Perfection Learning Corp.

—The Railroad. 2006. (Inventions That Shaped the World Ser.). (ENG., Illus.). 80p. (J). (gr. 5-8). per. 9.95 (978-0-531-16745-8(3), Watts, Franklin) Scholastic Library Publishing.

Mills, Cindy, illus. Cass Railroad Fun Book. 2007. 32p. (J). pap. 2.95 (978-0-929915-74-6(7)) Headline Bks., Inc.

Murray, Julie. Trains, 1 vol. 2014. (Transportation Ser.). (ENG.). 24p. (J). (gr. 4-8). lib. bdg. 28.50 (978-1-62970-082-3(7)) ABDO Publishing Co.

National Railway Museum & Dorling Kindersley Publishing Staff. The Big Book of Trains. 2016. (ENG., Illus.). 32p. (J). (gr. k-4). 14.99 (978-1-4654-5361-7(X), DK Children) Dorling Kindersley Publishing, Inc.

Oczkus, Lori. Close Reading with Paired Texts, 1 vol. 2015. (Close Reading with Paired Texts). (ENG., Illus.). 128p. (gr. k-k). mass mkt. 19.99 (978-1-4258-1356-7(9)) Shell Educational Publishing.

Parker, Lewis K. Cornelius Vanderbilt & the Railroad Industry. (American Tycoons Ser.). 24p. 2009. (gr. 3-3). 42.50 (978-1-61511-389-7(4)) 2003. (Illus.). (J). lib. bdg. 22.60 (978-0-8239-6450-5(7)) Rosen Publishing Group, Inc., The. (PowerKids Pr.).

Peters, Elisa. Let's Ride the Streetcar! 2014. (Public Transportation Ser.). 24p. (J). (gr. k-2). pap. 49.50 (978-1-4777-6513-5(1), PowerKids Pr.) Rosen Publishing Group, Inc., The.

—¡Vamos a Tomar el Tranvía! / Let's Ride the Streetcar! de la Vega, Eida, ed. 2014. (Transporte Público / Public Transportation Ser.). (SPA & ENG.). 24p. (J). (gr. k-2). 23.60 (978-1-4777-6779-5(7), PowerKids Pr.) Rosen Publishing Group, Inc., The.

Prior, Jennifer. All Aboard! How Trains Work, 1 vol. 2nd rev. ed. 2011. (Nonfiction Readers Ser.). (ENG.). 28p. (J). (gr. 3-3). pap. 8.99 (978-1-4333-3656-0(1)) Teacher Created Materials, Inc.

Rajczak, Michael. The Transcontinental Railroad, Vol. 1. 2014. (What You Didn't Know about History Ser.). (ENG., Illus.). 24p. (J). (gr. 2-3). 22.60 (978-1-4824-0600-9(4)) Stevens, Gareth Publishing LLLP.

Rickards, Lynne. My First Train Trip. Honor Roberts, Ley, illus. 2016. (Cambridge Reading Adventures Ser.). (ENG.). 16p. pap. 6.56 (978-1-107-57594-3(X)) Cambridge Univ. Pr.

Riggs, Kate. Bullet Trains. 2010. (Now That's Fast! Ser.). 24p. (J). (gr. -1-3). 16.95 (978-1-58341-911-3(X), Creative Education) Creative Co., The.

Rogers, Hal. Trains. 2014. (Big Machines at Work Ser.). (ENG.). 24p. (J). (gr. -1-2). 25.64 (978-1-62323-972-5(9), 206747) Child's World, Inc., The.

Rottman, Gordon L. The Most Daring Raid of the Civil War: The Great Locomotive Chase. 2011. (Most Daring Raids in History Ser.). (Illus.). 64p. (YA). (gr. 7-12). 31.95 (978-1-4488-1870-9(2)) Rosen Publishing Group, Inc., The.

Roza, Greg. The Incredible Story of Trains. 2009. (Kid's Guide to Incredible Technology Ser.). 24p. (gr. 3-4). 42.50 (978-1-61511-175-6(1), PowerKids Pr.) Rosen Publishing Group, Inc., The.

Ryan, Phillip. Freight Trains. 2010. (All Aboard! Ser.). (ENG.). 24p. (J). pap. 8.25 (978-1-4488-1211-0(9)); lib. bdg. 22.60 (978-1-4488-0635-5(6)) Rosen Publishing Group, Inc., The.

—Monorails. 2010. (All Aboard! Ser.). (ENG.). 24p. (J). pap. 8.25 (978-1-4488-1217-2(8)); lib. bdg. 22.60 (978-1-4488-0638-6(0)) Rosen Publishing Group, Inc., The.

—Steam-Powered Trains. 2010. (All Aboard! Ser.). (ENG.). 24p. (J). pap. 8.25 (978-1-4488-1221-9(6)); lib. bdg. 22.60 (978-1-4488-0640-9(2)) Rosen Publishing Group, Inc., The. (PowerKids Pr.).

—Streetcars. 2010. (All Aboard! Ser.). (ENG.). 24p. (J). pap. 8.25 (978-1-4488-1219-6(4)); lib. bdg. 22.60 (978-1-4488-0639-3(9)) Rosen Publishing Group, Inc., The. (PowerKids Pr.).

Shea, Therese. Cornelius Vanderbilt & the Railroad Industry. 2016. (Great Entrepreneurs in U. S. History Ser.). (Illus.). 32p. (J). (gr. 5-5). pap. 11.75 (978-1-4994-2119-4(2), PowerKids Pr.) Rosen Publishing Group, Inc., The.

Shields, Amy. Trains. 2011. (Readers Ser.). (ENG., Illus.). 32p. (J). (gr. -1-1). pap. 3.99 (978-1-4263-0777-5(2), National Geographic Children's Bks.) National Geographic Society.

Simon, Seymour & Simon. Seymour Simon's Book of Trains. 2004. (ENG., Illus.). 40p. (J). (gr. -1-3). reprint ed. pap. 6.99 (978-0-06-446223-5(4)) HarperCollins Pubs.

Smith, A. G. Cut & Assemble an Old-Fashioned Train. 2010. (Dover Children's Activity Bks.). (ENG.). 40p. (J). (gr. 6-12). 11.95 (978-0-486-25324-4(4)) Dover Pubns., Inc.

Smithyman, Kathryn & Kalman, Bobbie. Trains on the Tracks. 2007. (Vehicles on the Move Ser.). (ENG., Illus.). 32p. (J). (gr. 3-7). lib. bdg. (978-0-7787-3045-3(X)) Crabtree Publishing Co.

Snedden, Robert. Railroads. 2016. (Engineering Eurekas Ser.). 00032p. (J). (gr. 3-4). pap. 10.00 (978-1-4994-3097-4(3), PowerKids Pr.) Rosen Publishing Group, Inc., The.

St. Louis Union Station: A City Within a City. 2003. 19.95 (978-0-9748109-0-4(8)) Market 1 Group Inc.

Stein, R. Conrad. The Incredible Transcontinental Railroad: Stories in American History. 2012. (Stories in American History Ser.). (Illus.). 128p. (J). (gr. 5-18). pap. 10.95 (978-1-4644-0026-1(1)) Enslow Pubs., Inc.

Stone, Kate, illus. ABC Train. 2013. (ENG.). 20p. (J). bds. 10.99 (978-1-4494-3157-0(7)) Andrews McMeel Publishing.

Summers, Alex. Train. 2017. (Transportation & Me! Ser.). (ENG.). (J). (gr. k-1). 28.51 **(978-1-68342-163-4(9))** Rourke Educational Media.

Taplin, Sam. First Sticker Book Trains. 2013. (First Sticker Bks). 24p. (J). pap. 6.99 (978-0-7945-3351-9(5), Usborne) EDC Publishing.

Tiner, John Hudson. Trains. (Illus.). 32p. 2004. pap. 8.95 (978-0-89812-391-3(7), Creative Paperbacks) 2003. (J). lib. bdg. 18.95 (978-1-58341-260-2(3), Creative Education) Creative Co., The.

Trains. (Color & Learn Ser.). 36p. (J). (gr. 1-5). pap. (978-1-882210-11-4(5)) Action Publishing, Inc.

Turnbull, S. Los Trenes. 2004. Orig. Title: Trains. (SPA.). (J). lib. bdg. 16.95 (978-1-58086-500-5(3), Usborne) EDC Publishing.

Wetterer, Margaret K. Kate Shelley y el Tren de Medianoche. Ritz, Karen, illus. 2005. (Yo Solo - Historia (on My Own - History) Ser.).Tr. of Kate Shelley & the Midnight Express. (SPA.). 48p. (J). (gr. 2-5). per. 6.95 (978-0-8225-3193-7(3)) Lerner Publishing Group.

—Kate Shelley y el Tren de Medianoche. Translations.com Staff, tr. Ritz, Karen, illus. 2005. (Yo Solo - Historia (on My Own - History) Ser.).Tr. of Kate Shelley & the Midnight Express. (SPA.). 48p. (gr. 2-4). lib. bdg. 25.26 (978-0-8225-3096-1(1)) Lerner Publishing Group.

Windmill Books & Windmill Books. Let's Look at Trains. 2009. (Let's Go! Ser.). (Illus.). 18p. (J). (gr. -1-k). bds. 12.75 (978-1-60754-419-7(9)) Windmill Bks.

Wittmann, Kelly. Building the Transcontinental Railroad: Race of the Railroad Companies. 2017. (Great Race: Fight to the Finish Ser.). 48p. (gr. 4-5). pap. 84.30 **(978-1-5382-0804-5(0))** Stevens, Gareth Publishing LLLP.

Zimmermann, Karl. All Aboard! Passenger Trains Around the World. Zimmermann, Karl, photos by. 2006. (ENG., Illus.). 48p. (J). (gr. 5-7). 19.95 (978-1-59078-325-2(5)) Boyds Mills Pr.

RAILROADS—FICTION

Aboutt, Corinne & Mabire, Grégoire. All Aboard. 2011. (One by One Ser.). (Illus.). 14p. bds. (978-1-84089-687-9(6)) Zero to Ten, Ltd.

Alger, Horatio. The Erie Train Boy. reprint ed. pap. 79.00 (978-1-4047-3565-1(8)) Classic Textbooks.

Amery, Heather. The Old Steam Train. Cartwright, Stephen, illus. rev. ed. 2007. (Farmyard Tales Readers Ser.). 16p. (J). (gr. -1-3). pap. 5.99 (978-0-7945-0804-3(9), Usborne) EDC Publishing.

—Rusty's Train Ride. Cartwright, Stephen, illus. rev. ed. 2007. (Farmyard Tales Readers Ser.). 16p. (J). (gr. -1-3). pap. 5.99 (978-0-7945-0802-9(2), Usborne) EDC Publishing.

Anna, Jennifer. Maxwell Dreams of Trains. Blue, Buster, illus. 2009. (ENG.). 88p. (J). 10.99 (978-1-883573-05-8(X)) Blue Forge Pr.

Appleton, Victor. Tom Swift & His Electric Locomotive. 2005. 27.95 (978-1-4218-1087-4(5)); 200p. pap. 12.95 (978-1-4218-1187-1(1)) 1st World Publishing, Inc. (1st World Library - Literary Society).

—Tom Swift & His Electric Locomotive: Or Two Miles a Minute on the Rails. 2007. (ENG.). 136p. pap. 18.99 (978-1-4346-1490-2(5)) Creative Media Partners, LLC.

—Tom Swift & His Electric Locomotive or. 2006. pap. (978-1-4065-0899-4(3)) Dodo Pr.

Armitage, Ronda. Wave the Flag & Blow the Whistle: A Railway Adventure. Gordon, Andrew, illus. 2012. (ENG.). 32p. (J). (gr. -1-k). 17.99 (978-1-4052-5339-0(8)) Egmont Bks., Ltd. GBR. Dist: Independent Pubs. Group.

Awdry, W. Animals Everywhere! Courtney, Richard, illus. 2011. (Step into Reading Ser.). (ENG.). 32p. (J). (gr. -1-1). pap. 3.99 (978-0-375-86812-2(7), Random Hse. Bks. for Young Readers) Random Hse. Children's Bks.

—Busy, Busy Thomas. Stubbs, Tommy, illus. 2013. (Nifty Lift-And-Look Ser.). (ENG.). 12p. (J). (— 1). bds. 5.99 (978-0-449-81642-4(7), Random Hse. Bks. for Young Readers) Random Hse. Children's Bks.

—Go, Go, Thomas! 2013. (Thomas & Friends 8X8 Ser.). lib. bdg. 14.75 (978-0-606-26992-6(4), Turtleback) Turtleback Bks.

—The Good Sport. Courtney, Richard, illus. 2016. 24p. (J). **(978-1-5182-1481-3(9))** Random Hse., Inc.

—Hero of the Rails. Golden Books Staff, illus. 2010. (Little Golden Book Ser.). (ENG.). 24p. (J). (gr. -1-k). 4.99 (978-0-375-85950-2(0), Golden Bks.) Random Hse. Children's Bks.

—James & the Express (Thomas & Friends) Dalby, C. Reginald, illus. 2016. (ENG.). 24p. (J). (— 1). bds. 6.99 (978-1-101-93758-7(0), Random Hse. Bks. for Young Readers) Random Hse. Children's Bks.

—The Lost Ship. Courtney, Richard, illus. 2015. (Step into Reading Ser.). (ENG.). 32p. (J). (gr. -1-1). 3.99 (978-0-553-52171-9(3)); lib. bdg. 12.99 (978-0-553-52172-6(1)) Random Hse. Children's Bks. (Random Hse. Bks. for Young Readers).

—Misty Island Rescue. Golden Books Staff, illus. 2011. (Little Golden Book Ser.). (ENG.). 24p. (J). (gr. -1-k). 4.99 (978-0-375-87212-9(4), Golden Bks.) Random Hse. Children's Bks.

—Not So Fast, Bash & Dash! 2013. (Thomas & Friends Step into Reading Ser.). lib. bdg. 13.55 (978-0-606-32228-7(0), Turtleback) Turtleback Bks.

—Rail Blazers! (Thomas & Friends) Durk, Jim, illus. 2011. (Paint Box Book Ser.). (ENG.). 48p. (J). (gr. -1-2). pap. 3.99 (978-0-375-87390-4(2), Golden Bks.) Random Hse. Children's Bks.

—The Rocket Returns. 2014. (Thomas & Friends Step into Reading Ser.). lib. bdg. 13.55 (978-0-606-35207-9(4)) Turtleback Bks.

—Runaway Engine! Stubbs, Tommy, illus. 2011. (Pictureback(R) Ser.). (ENG.). 16p. (J). (gr. -1-2). pap. 4.99 (978-0-375-87253-2(1), Random Hse. Bks. for Young Readers) Random Hse. Children's Bks.

—Santa's Little Engine. 2014. (Thomas & Friends Step into Reading Ser.). lib. bdg. 13.55 (978-0-606-36014-2(X)) Turtleback Bks.

—Secret of the Green Engine. 2012. (Thomas & Friends Step into Reading Ser.). lib. bdg. 13.55 (978-0-606-26804-2(9), Turtleback) Turtleback Bks.

—Sodor's Legend of the Lost Treasure. 2015. (Big Golden Book Ser.). (ENG., Illus.). 32p. (J). (gr. -1-2). 9.99 (978-0-553-52076-7(8), Golden Bks.) Random Hse. Children's Bks.

—Steam Team! Stubbs, Tommy, illus. 2011. (Reusable Sticker Book Ser.). (ENG.). 12p. (J). (gr. -1-2). pap. 6.99 (978-0-375-87162-7(4), Golden Bks.) Random Hse. Children's Bks.

—Thomas' 123 Book. Courtney, Richard, illus. 2013. (Pictureback(R) Ser.). (ENG.). 24p. (J). (gr. -1-2). pap. 3.99 (978-0-307-98203-2(3), Random Hse. Bks. for Young Readers) Random Hse. Children's Bks.

—Thomas' 123 Book. 2013. (Thomas & Friends 8X8 Ser.). lib. bdg. 13.55 (978-0-606-26991-9(6), Turtleback) Turtleback Bks.

—Thomas & Friends - Go, Thomas Go! 2007. (Bright & Early Playtime Bks.). (ENG., Illus.). 14p. (J). (gr. k-k). 10.99 (978-0-375-83983-2(6), Random Hse. Bks. for Young Readers) Random Hse. Children's Bks.

—Thomas & Friends: Movie Theater Storybook & Movie Projector. 2016. (Movie Theater Ser.: 1). (ENG.). 32p. (J). (gr. -1-1). 19.99 (978-0-7944-3705-3(2), Reader's Digest Children's Bks.) Studio Fun International.

—Thomas & the Monster (Thomas & Friends) 2014. (Color Plus Chunky Crayons Ser.). (ENG.). 48p. (J). (gr. -1-2). pap. 3.99 (978-0-385-38511-4(0), Golden Bks.) Random Hse. Children's Bks.

—Thomas & the Volcano. 2015. (Thomas & Friends Step into Reading Ser.). lib. bdg. 14.75 (978-0-606-36404-1(8)) Turtleback Bks.

—Thomas' Big Book of Beginner Books. Random House Staff, illus. 2013. (Beginner Books Ser.). (ENG.). 224p. (J). (gr. -1-1). 16.99 (978-0-449-81643-1(5), Random Hse. Bks. for Young Readers) Random Hse. Children's Bks.

—Thomas Saves Easter! Stubbs, Tommy, illus. 2013. (Glitter Board Book Ser.). (ENG.). 12p. (J). (-k). bds. 6.99 (978-0-307-98158-5(4), Golden Bks.) Random Hse. Children's Bks.

—Thomas Scares the Crows (Thomas & Friends) 2016. (Pictureback(R) Ser.). (ENG.). 24p. (J). (gr. -1-2). 4.99 (978-1-101-93831-7(5), Random Hse. Bks. for Young Readers) Random Hse. Children's Bks.

—Thomas the Tank Engine: the Very First Stories (Thomas & Friends) 2015. (ENG., Illus.). 40p. (J). (gr. -1-3). 16.99 (978-0-553-52335-5(X), Random Hse. Bks. for Young Readers) Random Hse. Children's Bks.

—Thomas's Christmas Delivery. Stubbs, Tommy, illus. 2004. (Sparkle Storybook Ser.). (ENG.). 32p. (J). (gr. -1-2). 8.99 (978-0-375-82877-5(X), Random Hse. Bks. for Young Readers) Random Hse. Children's Bks.

—Treasure on the Tracks. 2013. (Thomas & Friends Step into Reading Ser.). lib. bdg. 13.55 *(978-0-606-32229-4(9),* Turtleback) Turtleback Bks.

—A Valentine for Percy. 2015. (Thomas & Friends Step into Reading Ser.). lib. bdg. 14.75 *(978-0-606-38471-1(5))* Turtleback Bks.

Awdry, Wilbert V. Big Book of Engines. Golden Books Staff, illus. 2014. (Big Golden Book Ser.). (ENG.). 64p. (J). (gr. -1-2). 9.99 *(978-0-307-93131-3(5),* Golden Bks.) Random Hse. Children's Bks.

—Blue Train, Green Train. Stubbs, Tommy, illus. 2006. (Bright & Early Books(R) Ser.). (ENG.). 36p. (J). (gr. k-k). 8.99 *(978-0-375-83463-9(X),* Random Hse. Bks. for Young Readers) Random Hse. Children's Bks.

—The Close Shave. Courtney, Richard H., illus. 2008. (Step into Reading Ser.). (ENG.). 32p. (J). (gr. -1-1). pap. 3.99 *(978-0-375-85180-3(1),* Random Hse. Bks. for Young Readers) Random Hse. Children's Bks.

—Day of the Diesels. Golden Books Staff, illus. 2012. (Little Golden Book Ser.). (ENG.). 24p. (J). (gr. k-k). 4.99 *(978-0-307-92989-1(2),* Golden Bks.) Random Hse. Children's Bks.

—Easter Engines. Courtney, Richard, illus. 2012. (Step into Reading Ser.). (ENG.). 32p. (J). (gr. -1-1). pap. 3.99 *(978-0-307-92996-9(5),* Random Hse. Bks. for Young Readers) Random Hse. Children's Bks.

—Easter Engines. 2012. (Thomas & Friends Step into Reading Ser.). lib. bdg. 13.55 *(978-0-606-23717-8(8),* Turtleback) Turtleback Bks.

—Fast Train, Slow Train. Stubbs, Tommy, illus. 2009. (Bright & Early Books(R) Ser.). (ENG.). 36p. (J). (gr. -1-2). 8.99 *(978-0-375-85689-1(7),* Golden Bks.) Random Hse. Children's Bks.

—Fast Train, Slow Train (Thomas & Friends) 2014. (Big Bright & Early Board Book Ser.). (ENG., Illus.). 24p. (J). (— 1). bds. 6.99 *(978-0-385-37408-8(9),* Random Hse. Bks. for Young Readers) Random Hse. Children's Bks.

—Go, Go, Thomas! - Express Coming Through. Random House Staff, illus. 2013. (Pictureback(R) Ser.). (ENG.). 32p. (J). (gr. -1-2). pap. 4.99 *(978-0-307-98216-2(5),* Random Hse. Bks. for Young Readers) Random Hse. Children's Bks.

—Go, Train, Go! Stubbs, Tommy, illus. 2006. (Bright & Early Board Books(TM) Ser.). (ENG.). 24p. (J). (— 1). bds. 4.99 *(978-0-375-83461-5(3),* Random Hse. Bks. for Young Readers) Random Hse. Children's Bks.

—Halloween in Anopha. Courtney, Richard, illus. 2008. (Thomas in Town Ser.). (ENG.). 32p. (J). (gr. -1-2). 5.99 *(978-0-375-84413-3(9),* Random Hse. Bks. for Young Readers) Random Hse. Children's Bks.

—Henry & the Elephant. 2007. (Thomas & Friends Step into Reading Ser.). 13.55 *(978-1-4177-7088-5(0),* Turtleback) Turtleback Bks.

—The Lost Crown of Sodor. Random House Staff, illus. 2013. (Pictureback Ser.). (ENG.). 24p. (J). (gr. -1-2). 3.99 *(978-0-449-81533-5(1),* Random Hse. Bks. for Young Readers) Random Hse. Children's Bks.

—Making Tracks! (Thomas & Friends) Golden Books Staff, illus. 2012. (Write-On/Wipe-off Activity Book Ser.). (ENG.). 12p. (J). (gr. -1-2). bds. 9.99 *(978-0-307-93002-6(5),* Golden Bks.) Random Hse. Children's Bks.

—My Red Railway Book Box. Stubbs, Tommy, illus. 2008. (Bright & Early Board Books(TM) Ser.). (ENG.). 96p. (J). (— 1). bds. 14.99 *(978-0-375-84322-8(1),* Random Hse. Bks. for Young Readers) Random Hse. Children's Bks.

—Not So Fast, Bash & Dash! Courtney, Richard, illus. 2013. (Step into Reading Ser.). (ENG.). 24p. (J). (gr. -1-1). 3.99 *(978-0-449-81539-7(0),* Random Hse. Bks. for Young Readers) Random Hse. Children's Bks.

—Risky Rails! 2012. (Thomas & Friends 8X8 Ser.). lib. bdg. 13.55 *(978-0-606-26803-5(0),* Turtleback) Turtleback Bks.

—The Rocket Returns. 2014. (Step into Reading Ser.). (ENG., Illus.). 32p. (J). (gr. -1-1). lib. bdg. 12.99 *(978-0-375-97204-1(8),* Random Hse. Bks. for Young Readers) Random Hse. Children's Bks.

—Rolling on the Rails. Golden Books Staff, illus. 2011. (Thomas & Friends Ser.). (ENG.). 12p. (J). (gr. k — 1). bds. 8.99 *(978-0-375-87304-1(X),* Golden Bks.) Random Hse. Children's Bks.

—Search & Rescue! (Thomas & Friends) Random House Staff, illus. 2012. (Pictureback(R) Ser.). (ENG.). 16p. (J). (gr. -1-2). pap. 4.99 *(978-0-307-93029-3(7),* Random Hse. Bks. for Young Readers) Random Hse. Children's Bks.

—The Secret of the Mine. Durk, Jim, illus. 2013. (Glow-In-the-Dark Sticker Book Ser.). (ENG.). 48p. (J). (gr. -1-2). pap. 3.99 *(978-0-449-81711-7(3),* Golden Bks.) Random Hse. Children's Bks.

—Tales of Discovery. Golden Books Staff, illus. 2011. (Padded Board Book Ser.). (ENG.). 30p. (J). (gr. k — 1). bds. 11.99 *(978-0-375-87192-4(6),* Golden Bks.) Random Hse. Children's Bks.

—Thomas & the Shark. Courtney, Richard, illus. 2013. (Step into Reading Ser.). (ENG.). 32p. (J). (gr. -1-1). pap. 3.99 *(978-0-307-98200-1(9),* Random Hse. Bks. for Young Readers) Random Hse. Children's Bks.

—Thomas & the Shark. 2013. (Thomas & Friends Step into Reading Ser.). lib. bdg. 13.55 *(978-0-606-26996-4(7),* Turtleback) Turtleback Bks.

—Thomas in Charge. 2012. (Thomas & Friends 8X8 Ser.). lib. bdg. 14.75 *(978-0-606-26397-9(7),* Turtleback) Turtleback Bks.

—Trains, Cranes & Troublesome Trucks. Stubbs, Tommy, illus. 2008. (Beginner Books Ser.). (ENG.). 36p. (J). (gr. -1-1). 8.99 *(978-0-375-84977-0(7),* Random Hse. Bks. for Young Readers) Random Hse. Children's Bks.

Awdry, Wilbert V. & Awdry, Rev. W. Thomas' Colorful Ride (Thomas & Friends) Golden Books Staff, illus. 2011. (Deluxe Chunky Crayon Book Ser.). (ENG.). 128p. (J). (gr. -1-2). pap. 7.99 *(978-0-375-87248-8(5),* Golden Bks.) Random Hse. Children's Bks.

Awdry, Wilbert V. & Awdry, W. Blue Train, Green Train. Stubbs, Tommy, illus. 2007. (Bright & Early Board Books(TM) Ser.). (ENG.). 24p. (J). (— 1). bds. 4.99 *(978-0-375-83984-9(4),* Random Hse. Bks. for Young Readers) Random Hse. Children's Bks.

—Down at the Docks. Courtney, Richard, illus. 2003. (Pictureback Ser.). (ENG.). 24p. (J). (gr. -1-2). pap. 3.99 *(978-0-375-82592-7(4),* Random Hse. Bks. for Young Readers) Random Hse. Children's Bks.

Awdry, Wilbert V. & Random House Disney Staff. Thomas' Mixed-Up Day - Thomas Puts the Brakes On. Random House Disney Staff, illus. 2010. (Pictureback(R) Ser.). (ENG., Illus.). 32p. (J). (gr. -1-2). pap. 4.99 *(978-0-375-85919-9(5),* Random Hse. Bks. for Young Readers) Random Hse. Children's Bks.

Awdry, Wilbert V. & Random House Editors. Thomas & Percy & the Dragon. 2003. (Thomas & Friends Step into Reading Ser.). (gr. -1-2). lib. bdg. 13.55 *(978-0-613-89791-4(9),* Turtleback) Turtleback Bks.

Awdry, Wilbert Were. The Missing Christmas Tree. Stubbs, Tommy, illus. 2013. (Glitter Board Book Ser.). (ENG.). 12p. (J). (— 1). bds. 6.99 *(978-0-449-81713-1(X),* Golden Bks.) Random Hse. Children's Bks.

Bailer, Darice. The Last Rail. 2011. (ENG.). 32p. (J). 9.95 *(978-1-60727-173-4(7))* Soundprints.

—Railroad!, Level 3: A Story of the Transcontinental Railroad. Farnsworth, Bill, illus. 3rd ed. 2004. (Soundprints' Read-and-Discover Ser.). (ENG.). 48p. (J). (gr. 1-4). pap. 3.95 *(978-1-59249-017-2(4),* S2007) Soundprints.

Barnett, Mac. It Happened on a Train. Rex, Adam, illus. (Brixton Brothers Ser.: 3). (ENG.). (J). (gr. 3-7). 2012. 304p. pap. 7.99 *(978-1-4169-7820-6(8))* 2011. 288p. 17.99 *(978-1-4169-7819-0(4))* Simon & Schuster Bks. For Young Readers. (Simon & Schuster Bks. For Young Readers).

Barton, Chris. Shark vs. Train. Lichtenheld, Tom, illus. (ENG.). (J). (gr. -1 — 1). 2015. 20p. bds. 6.99 *(978-0-316-37814-7(3))* 2010. 40p. 18.99 *(978-0-316-00762-7(5))* Little, Brown Bks. for Young Readers.

Baxter, Nicola. The Trouble with Trains. Ball, Geoff, illus. 2012. (ENG.). 24p. (J). (gr. -1-k). pap. 6.99 *(978-1-84322-785-4(1),* Armadillo) Anness Publishing GBR. Dist: National Bk. Network.

Beil, Michael D. Lantern Sam & the Blue Streak Bandits. (ENG., Illus.). 288p. (J). (gr. 3-7). 2015. pap. 7.99 *(978-0-385-75320-3(9),* Yearling) 2014. 15.99 *(978-0-385-75317-3(9),* Knopf Bks. for Young Readers) Random Hse. Children's Bks.

Bently, Peter. The Cat, the Mouse, & the Runaway Train. Cox, Steve, illus. 2013. (J). *(978-1-4351-4968-7(8))* Barnes & Noble, Inc.

—Train Is on Track. Conway, Louise, illus. 2015. (Busy Wheels Ser.). (ENG.). 24p. (J). (gr. -1-k). 14.95 *(978-1-60992-790-5(7))* QEB Publishing Inc.

Benton, Ann. Ferdinand: The Engine That Went off the Rails. 2009. (Colour Bks.). (ENG., Illus.). 40p. (J). 7.99 *(978-1-84550-444-1(5),* 506364f9-0f36-4fc3-909c-1010b7b811f6) Christian Focus Pubns. GBR. Dist: Bookmasters Distribution.

Berry, Ron & Mead, David. All Aboard! Charlie the Can-Do Choo Choo. Sharp, Chris, illus. 2009. (ENG.). 8p. 12.99 *(978-0-8249-1420-2(1),* Ideal Pubns.) Worthy Publishing.

Bingham, Jane. The Story of Trains. King, Colin, illus. 2004. (Young Reading Series Two Ser.). 64p. (J). (gr. 2-18). pap. 5.95 *(978-0-7945-0737-4(9),* Usborne) EDC Publishing.

Blathwayt, Benedict, illus. Great Big Train. 2015. (J). *(978-0-553-51289-2(7))* Knopf, Alfred A. Inc.

Bleck, Linda. What's in My Train? 2016. (ENG.). 10p. (J). (— 1). 6.99 *(978-0-545-90768-2(3),* Cartwheel Bks.) Scholastic, Inc.

Boat, Patty. A Disappointing Homecoming: (A Soldier's Story), 1 vol. 2009. 158p. pap. 24.95 *(978-1-61546-997-0(4))* PublishAmerica, Inc.

Boehnert, Ernest. The Magic Christmas Train. 2010. 24p. 14.93 *(978-1-4269-4447-5(0))* Trafford Publishing.

Braun, Sebastien. Whoosh & Chug! Braun, Sebastien, illus. 2014. (Illus.). 32p. (J). (gr. -1-3). 16.99 *(978-0-06-207754-7(6))* HarperCollins Pubs.

Brown, Carron. On the Train: Shine-A-Light. Johnson, Bee, illus. 2015. (ENG.). 36p. (J). 12.99 *(978-1-61067-365-5(4))* Kane Miller.

Brown, Margaret Wise. Two Little Trains. Dillon, Leo & Dillon, Diane, illus. 2003. (ENG.). 32p. (J). (gr. -1-k). pap. 7.99 *(978-0-06-443568-0(7))* HarperCollins Pubs.

Burleigh, Robert. Night Train, Night Train. Minor, Wendell, illus. 2017. (J). lib. bdg. ***(978-1-58089-717-4(7))*** Charlesbridge Publishing, Inc.

Burt, Vicky. Eager Beavers. Lindsey, Jessica, illus. 2012. 28p. pap. 13.99 *(978-1-937129-39-2(X))* Faithful Life Pubs.

C. Larene Hall. Martha's Freedom Train. 2009. 100p. pap. 10.49 *(978-1-4389-7977-9(0))* AuthorHouse.

Candlewick Press, Candlewick. Peppa Pig & the Little Train. 2016. (Peppa Pig Ser.). (ENG., Illus.). 32p. (J). (-k). 12.99 *(978-0-7636-9044-1(9),* Candlewick Entertainment) Candlewick Pr.

Capeci, Anne. Ghost Train, 1 vol., Vol. 3. Casale, Paul, illus. 2004. (Cascade Moutain Railroad Mystery Ser.: 3). (ENG.). 144p. (J). (gr. 2-5). 12.95 *(978-1-56145-324-5(2))* Peachtree Pubs.

—Missing!, 1 vol. Casale, Paul, illus. 2005. (Cascade Mountain Railroad Mysteries Ser.). (ENG.). 144p. (J). (gr. 2-5). 12.95 *(978-1-56145-334-4(X))* Peachtree Pubs.

Cartwright, Stephen. Llittle Book of Train Stories. rev. ed. 2011. (Farmyard Tales Readers Ser.). 64p. (J). ring bd. 8.99 *(978-0-7945-3070-9(2),* Usborne) EDC Publishing.

Chatton, Julie. Trains: Safe & Sound. 2008. 24p. pap. 13.50 *(978-1-60693-307-7(8),* Eloquent Bks.) Strategic Book Publishing & Rights Agency (SBPRA).

Chin, Oliver. Timmy & Tammy's Train of Thought. McPherson, Heath, illus. 2007. (ENG.). 36p. (J). (gr. -1-3). 15.95 *(978-1-59702-008-4(7))* Immedium.

Choo Choo. 2011. (Dora the Explorer Ser.). (Illus.). 10p. (J). bds. 10.98 *(978-0-7853-8278-2(X),* 7182700) Publications International, Ltd.

Cohen, Deborah Bodin. Engineer Ari & the Hanukkah Mishap. Kober, Shahar, illus. 2011. (Hanukkah Ser.). (ENG.). 32p. (J). (gr. k-3). pap. 7.95 *(978-0-7613-5146-7(9))*; lib. bdg. 17.95 *(978-0-7613-5145-0(0))* Lerner Publishing Group. (Kar-Ben Publishing).

—Engineer Ari & the Passover Rush. Kober, Shahar, illus. 2015. (J). 6.99 *(978-1-4677-6201-4(6))*; (ENG.). 32p. lib. bdg. 17.95 *(978-1-4677-3470-7(5))* Lerner Publishing Group. (Kar-Ben Publishing).

—Engineer Ari & the Rosh Hashanah Ride. 2008. (High Holidays Ser.). (Illus.). 32p. (J). (gr. -1-3). lib. bdg. 17.95 *(978-0-8225-8648-7(7),* Kar-Ben Publishing) Lerner Publishing Group.

—Engineer Ari & the Sukkah Express. Kober, Shahar, illus. 2010. (Sukkot & Simchat Torah Ser.). (ENG.). 32p. (J). (gr. k-3). pap. 7.95 *(978-0-7613-5128-3(0))*; lib. bdg. 17.95 *(978-0-7613-5126-9(4))* Lerner Publishing Group. (Kar-Ben Publishing).

Cohen, Deborah Bodin. Engineer Arielle & the Israel Independence Day Surprise: High, Low, & on the Go. Orrelle, Yael Kimhi, illus. 2017. (ENG.). 32p. (gr. k-3). 17.99 ***(978-1-5124-2094-4(8))***; pap. 7.99 ***(978-1-5124-2095-1(6))*** Lerner Publishing Group. (Kar-Ben Publishing).

Coleman, Evelyn. Freedom Train. 2012. (ENG.). 160p. (J). (gr. 3-7). pap. 7.99 *(978-1-4424-3652-7(2),* McElderry, Margaret K. Bks.) McElderry, Margaret K. Bks.

Coombs, Charles. Railroad Stories: Young Readers. Geer, Charles H., illus. 2011. 194p. 42.95 *(978-1-258-10208-1(0))* Literary Licensing, LLC.

Cooper, Elisha. Train. 2013. (ENG., Illus.). 40p. (J). (gr. -1-3). 17.99 *(978-0-545-38495-7(8),* Orchard Bks.) Scholastic, Inc.

Courtney, Richard, illus. Reds Against Blues! 2016. 22p. (J). ***(978-1-4806-9772-0(9))*** Random Hse., Inc.

Courtney, Richard, illus. Thomas Gets a Snowplow. 2004. (Pictureback Ser.). (ENG.). 24p. (J). (gr. -1-2). 3.99 *(978-0-375-82783-9(8),* Random Hse. Bks. for Young Readers) Random Hse. Children's Bks.

Cousins, Lucy. Maisy's Train. Cousins, Lucy, illus. 2009. (Maisy Ser.). (ENG., Illus.). 16p. (J). (gr. k-k). bds. 5.99 *(978-0-7636-4251-8(7))* Candlewick Pr.

Cowley, Joy. The Bedtime Train. Odone, Jamison, illus. 2008. (ENG.). 32p. (J). (gr. k-2). 16.95 *(978-1-59078-493-8(6),* Front Street) Boyds Mills Pr.

—Mrs. WishyWashy & the Big Tub. 2009. pap. 8.25 *(978-1-60559-233-6(1))* Hameray Publishing Group, Inc.

Crabtree, Sally. Magic Train Ride. Esplugas, Sonia & Espulgas, Sonia, illus. 2007. (ENG.). 32p. (J). (gr. -1-k). 6.99 *(978-1-84686-132-1(2))* Barefoot Bks., Inc.

—Magic Train Ride. Esplugas, Sonia, illus. (Barefoot Singalongs Ser.). (J). 2007. (ENG.). 32p. (gr. -1-k). pap. 9.99 *(978-1-905236-91-6(3))* 2006. 0032p. 16.99 *(978-1-905236-52-7(2))* Barefoot Bks., Inc.

Crampton, Gertrude, et al. Little Golden Book Train Stories. Gergely, Tibor, illus. 2014. (Little Golden Book Favorites Ser.). (ENG.). 80p. (J). (-k). 7.99 *(978-0-385-37862-8(9),* Golden Bks.) Random Hse. Children's Bks.

Crebbin, June. El Viaje en Tren. Rubio, Esther, tr. Lambert, Stephen, illus. 2004. (SPA.). (J). 7.95 *(978-1-930332-76-8(9))* Lectorum Pubns., Inc.

Crews, Donald. Freight Train. Crews, Donald, illus. (Illus.). (J). 2016. 32p. (gr. -1 — 1). bds. 7.99 *(978-0-06-245708-0(X),* Greenwillow Bks.) 2008. (SPA & ENG., 24p. (gr. -1-3). pap. 7.99 *(978-0-06-056204-5(8),* Greenwillow Bks.) 2003. (SPA & ENG., 24p. lib. bdg., bds. 16.89 *(978-0-06-056203-8(X))* 2003. (SPA & ENG., 24p. (gr. -1-3). 16.99 *(978-0-06-056202-1(1),* Greenwillow Bks.) 2003. (ENG., 24p. (gr. -1-3). 16.99 *(978-0-688-80165-6(X),* Greenwillow Bks.) 2003. (ENG., 24p. (gr. -1-3). pap. 6.99 *(978-0-688-11701-6(5),* Greenwillow Bks.) HarperCollins Pubs.

Crews, Donald & Crews, D. Freight Train. 2003. (J). (gr. k-3). 17.20 *(978-0-8085-3581-2(1),* Turtleback) Turtleback Bks.

Crise, Jeff. The Little Train That Had No Bell. 2011. (ENG.). 25p. pap. 9.95 *(978-1-4327-7673-2(8))* Outskirts Pr., Inc.

Crow, Melinda Melton. Brave Fire Truck, 1 vol. Thompson, Chad, illus. 2011. (Wonder Wheels Ser.). (ENG.). 32p. (gr. -1-1). pap. 6.25 *(978-1-4342-3384-4(7))*; lib. bdg. 22.65 *(978-1-4342-3029-4(5))* Stone Arch Bks.

—Busy, Busy Train, 1 vol. Thompson, Chad, illus. 2011. (Wonder Wheels Ser.). (ENG.). 32p. (gr. -1-1). pap. 6.25 *(978-1-4342-3383-7(9))*; lib. bdg. 22.65 *(978-1-4342-3028-7(7))* Stone Arch Bks.

—The Long Train Ride, 1 vol. Thompson, Chad, illus. 2012. (Wonder Wheels Ser.). (ENG.). 32p. (gr. -1-1). pap. 6.25 *(978-1-4342-4239-6(0))*; lib. bdg. 22.65 *(978-1-4342-4018-7(5))* Stone Arch Bks.

Crunk, Tony. Railroad John & the Red Rock Run, 1 vol. Austin, Michael, illus. 2006. (ENG.). 32p. (J). (gr. k-3). 16.95 *(978-1-56145-363-4(3))* Peachtree Pubs.

Dale, Penny. Dinosaur Rescue! Dale, Penny, illus. 2016. (ENG., Illus.). 24p. (J). (-k). bds. 6.99 *(978-0-7636-8000-8(1),* Nosy Crow) Candlewick Pr.

Dallas, Sandra. The Quilt Walk. (ENG.). 216p. (J). 2013. (gr. 4-7). pap. 9.95 *(978-1-58536-799-3(0),* 202373) 2012. 18.95 *(978-1-58536-800-6(8))* Sleeping Bear Pr.

Dean, James. Pete the Cat's Train Trip. Dean, James, illus. 2015. (My First I Can Read Ser.). (ENG., Illus.). 32p. (J). (gr. -1-3). pap. 3.99 *(978-0-06-230385-1(6))* HarperCollins Pubs.

Demarest, Chris L. Train. 2017. (ENG., Illus.). 16p. (J). (— 1). bds. 6.99 *(978-0-544-87608-8(3),* HMH Books For Young Readers) Houghton Mifflin Harcourt Publishing Co.

Demers, David & Demers, Lee Ann. My Grandpa Loves Trains: A Picture Storybook for Preschoolers. Demers, David, photos by. l.t. ed. 2005. (Illus.). 76p. (J). 27.95 *(978-0-922993-36-9(X))* Marquette Bks., LLC.

—My Grandpa Loves Trains: A Storybook for Preschoolers. Demers, David, photos by. l.t. ed. 2005. (Illus.). 76p. (J). per. 19.95 *(978-0-922993-23-9(8))* Marquette Bks., LLC.

Dorfman, Craig. I Knew You Could! A Book for All the Stops in Your Life. Ong, Cristina, illus. 2003. (Little Engine That Could Ser.). (ENG.). 32p. (J). (gr. -1-2). 11.99 *(978-0-448-43148-2(3),* Grosset & Dunlap) Penguin Young Readers Group.

Douglas, Ryke Leigh. Molly the Trolley & Bud. 2008. 24p. pap. 11.95 *(978-1-4327-2207-4(7))* Outskirts Pr., Inc.

Down the Track, 6 Packs. (Story Steps Ser.). (gr. k-2). 32.00 *(978-0-7635-9804-4(6))* Rigby Education.

Durbin, William. Until the Last Spike: The Journal of Sean Sullivan, a Transcontinental Railroad Worker, Nebraska & Points West 1867. 2013. (My Name Is America Ser.). lib. bdg. 17.20 *(978-0-606-32342-0(2),* Turtleback) Turtleback Bks.

Dyer, Mary E. Secret Whispers. 2008. 99p. pap. 19.95 *(978-1-60610-261-9(3))* America Star Bks.

Eaton, Jason Carter. How to Train a Train. Rocco, John, illus. (ENG.). (J). 2016. 28p. (-k). bds. 7.99 *(978-0-7636-8899-8(1))* 2013. 48p. (gr. -1-3). 16.99 *(978-0-7636-6307-0(7))* Candlewick Pr.

Elaine & Shaun Turner. Owen's Train Ride. 2010. 24p. pap. 15.99 *(978-1-4535-0420-8(6))* Xlibris Corp.

Evans, Beryl. Charlie the Choo-Choo. Dameron, Ned, illus. 2016. (ENG.). 24p. (J). (gr. -1). 14.99 *(978-1-5344-0123-5(7),* Simon & Schuster Bks. For Young Readers) Simon & Schuster Bks. For Young Readers.

Falksen, G. D. The Transatlantic Conspiracy. Iwata, Nat, illus. (ENG.). 240p. (YA). 2017. (gr. 9). pap. 10.99 *(978-1-61695-814-5(6))* 2016. (gr. 7). 18.99 *(978-1-61695-417-8(5))* Soho Pr., Inc. (Soho Teen).

Fath, Teresa. The Train Track Trolley & the Bell Dogs. 2009. 32p. pap. 21.99 *(978-1-4415-4350-9(3))* Xlibris Corp.

Feldman, Luke & Chin, Amanda. Chaff n' Skaffs: Mai & the Lost Moskivvy. Feldman, Luke, illus. 2009. (ENG., Illus.). 36p. (J). (gr. -1-3). 15.95 *(978-1-59702-013-8(3))* Immedium.

Figorito, Marcus. Tara Takes the Train. 2006. (Neighborhood Readers Ser.). (ENG.). 16p. (gr. 1-3). pap. 6.50 *(978-1-4042-7208-8(9),* Rosen Classroom) Rosen Publishing Group, Inc., The.

Fiona Fox Staff, ed. The Railway Children. 2012. (ENG., Illus.). 64p. (J). 15.00 *(978-1-84135-840-6(1))* Award Pubns. Ltd. GBR. Dist: Parkwest Pubns., Inc.

Francis, Mayann. Mayann's Train Ride, 1 vol. Thiébaux-Heikalo, Tamara, illus. 2016. (ENG.). 32p. (J). (gr. -1-3). 19.95 *(978-1-77108-348-5(4))* Nimbus Publishing, Ltd. CAN. Dist: Orca Bk. Pubs. USA.

Frank, Hannah. The Train to Baker Street. 2008. 44p. pap. 19.49 *(978-1-4389-1026-0(6))* AuthorHouse.

Gail, Ginnie. The Great Pigeon Race. Griffin, Don, illus. 2008. 28p. per. 24.95 *(978-1-4241-9457-5(1))* America Star Bks.

Galvin, Laura Gates. I've Been Working on the Railroad. Brown, Dan, illus. 2008. (ENG.). 32p. (J). (gr. k-2). 14.95 *(978-1-59249-771-3(3))*; 8.95 *(978-1-59249-772-0(1))* Soundprints.

Gerald, Tom. Traveling by Train: Read Well Level K Unit 19 Storybook. Weber, Philip A., Jr., illus. 2003. (Read Well Level K Ser.). 20p. (J). *(978-1-57035-690-2(4),* 55597) Cambium Education, Inc.

Golden Books. Journey Beyond Sodor. Stubbs, Tommy, illus. 2017. (Little Golden Book Ser.). (ENG.). 24p. (J). (-k). 4.99 ***(978-1-5247-1653-0(7),*** Golden Bks.) Random Hse. Children's Bks.

—Thomas & Friends: Nine Favorite Tales (Thomas & Friends) A Little Golden Book Collection. 2014. (Little Golden Book Treasury Ser.). (ENG., Illus.). 224p. (J). (-k). 12.99 *(978-0-385-37644-0(8),* Golden Bks.) Random Hse. Children's Bks.

—Thomas & the Dinosaur (Thomas & Friends) Lapadula, Thomas, illus. 2015. (Little Golden Book Ser.). (ENG.). 24p. (J). (-k). 4.99 *(978-0-553-49681-9(6),* Golden Bks.) Random Hse. Children's Bks.

—Tons of Fun with Thomas (Thomas & Friends) 2016. (ENG.). 80p. (J). (gr. -1-2). pap. 6.99 *(978-1-101-93724-2(6),* Golden Bks.) Random Hse. Children's Bks.

—Trains, Cranes & Troublesome Trucks (Thomas & Friends) 2015. (Big Bright & Early Board Book Ser.). (ENG., Illus.). 24p. (J). (— 1). bds. 6.99 *(978-0-385-37393-7(7),* Random Hse. Bks. for Young Readers) Random Hse. Children's Bks.

Golden Books Staff. Friends from Sodor. Hit Entertainment Staff, illus. 2008. (Deluxe Paint Box Book Ser.). (ENG.). 128p. (J). (gr. -1-2). pap. 7.99 *(978-0-375-84292-4(6),* Golden Bks.) Random Hse. Children's Bks.

—May the Best Engine Win! Stubbs, Tommy, illus. Courtney, Richard, photos by. 2008. (Little Golden Book Ser.). (ENG.). 24p. (J). (gr. -1-2). 3.99 *(978-0-375-84381-5(7),* Golden Bks.) Random Hse. Children's Bks.

—Trainloads of Fun. Golden Books Staff, illus. 2010. (Jumbo Coloring Book Ser.). (ENG., Illus.). 224p. (J). (gr. -1-2). pap. 5.99 *(978-0-375-86363-9(X),* Golden Bks.) Random Hse. Children's Bks.

Golden Books Staff, illus. Favorites: Thomas Breaks a Promise - Thomas & the Big, Big Bridge/May the Best Engine Win! 2009. (Little Golden Book Favorites Ser.). (ENG.). 80p. (J). (gr. -1-2). 7.99 *(978-0-375-85554-2(8),* Golden Bks.) Random Hse. Children's Bks.

Greenberg, Nicki. Teddy Took the Train. Greenberg, Nicki, illus. 2015. (ENG., Illus.). 32p. (J). (gr. -1-1). 15.99 *(978-1-76011-213-4(5))* Allen & Unwin AUS. Dist: Independent Pubs. Group.

Greenburg, Dan. Secrets of Dripping Fang, Book Eight: When Bad Snakes Attack Good Children. Fischer, Scott M., illus. 2007. (Secrets of Dripping Fang Ser.: Bk. 8). (ENG.). 144p. (J). (gr. 2-5). 11.99 *(978-0-15-206056-5(1))* Houghton Mifflin Harcourt Publishing Co.

Griffiths, Robert. Adventures of Clive. 2005. 45p. (J). pap. 10.01 *(978-1-4116-5332-0(7))* Lulu Pr., Inc.

Hall, Kirsten. Toot! Alder, Charlie, illus. 2013. (ENG.). 24p. (J). (gr. -1-k). bds. 8.99 *(978-0-448-46587-6(6),* Grosset & Dunlap) Penguin Young Readers Group.

Harby, Melanie. All Aboard for Dreamland! Valério, Geraldo, illus. 2012. (ENG.). 32p. (J). (gr. -1-k). 16.99 *(978-1-4424-3091-4(5),* Simon & Schuster Bks. For Young Readers) Simon & Schuster Bks. For Young Readers.

Hasany, Syed M. Stop the Train, Monkey! 2013. 28p. pap. 16.09 *(978-1-4669-7792-1(2))* Trafford Publishing.

Hautman, Pete. Invisible. Hautman, Pete, illus. 2006. (ENG., Illus.). 160p. (YA). (gr. 7-12). reprint ed. pap. 9.99 *(978-0-689-86903-7(7),* Simon & Schuster Bks. For Young Readers) Simon & Schuster Bks. For Young Readers.

Heard, Foreman. Tales of Pinkie Posie. 2008. 76p. pap. 15.90 *(978-1-4357-3292-6(8))* Lulu Pr., Inc.

High, Linda Oatman. Tenth Avenue Cowboy. Farnsworth, Bill, illus. 2008. 32p. (J). (gr. 4-7). 17.00 *(978-0-8028-5330-1(7),* Eerdmans Bks For Young Readers) Eerdmans, William B. Publishing Co.

Hill, Susanna Leonard. Freight Train Trip! A Lift-the-Flap Adventure. Larrañaga, Ana Martín, illus. 2009. (ENG.). 12p. (J). (gr. -1-k). bds. 7.99 *(978-1-4169-7833-6(X),* Little Simon) Little Simon.

Hillert, Margaret. Little Puff. Dammer, Mike, illus. 2016. (BeginningtoRead Ser.). (ENG.). 32p. (J). (gr. -1-2). pap. 11.94 *(978-1-60357-941-4(9))*; (gr. k-2). 22.60 *(978-1-59953-800-6(8))* Norwood Hse. Pr.

Hooke, R. Schuyler. Thomas & the Jet Engine. 2009. (Step into Reading Ser.). (ENG., Illus.). 32p. (J). (gr. k-3). pap. 3.99

(978-0-375-84289-4(6), Random Hse. Bks. for Young Readers) Random Hse. Children's Bks.

—Thomas & the Treasure. Palone, Terry & Permane, Terry, photos by. 2008. (Thomas & Friends Ser.). (ENG., Illus.). 24p. (J). (gr. -1-2). pap. 3.99 (978-0-375-84287-0(X), Random Hse. Bks. for Young Readers) Random Hse. Children's Bks.

Hope, Laura Lee. Freddie & Flossie & the Train Ride. Pyle, Chuck, illus. 2005. (Bobbsey Twins Ser.). (ENG.). 32p. (J). (gr. -1-k). pap. 13.99 (978-1-4169-0269-0(4), Simon Spotlight) Simon Spotlight.

Horender, Philip M. Head West, Young Mouse: Transcontinental Railroad Traveler, 1 vol. Wolek, Guy, illus. 2013. (Maximilian P. Mouse, Time Traveler Ser.). (ENG.). 112p. (J). (gr. 3-6). lib. bdg. 27.07 (978-1-61641-959-2(8), Calico Chapter Bks) Magic Wagon.

Houghton Mifflin Harcourt Publishing Company Staff & Rey, H. A. Start Your Engines 5-Minute Stories. 2014. (5-Minute Stories Ser.). (ENG., Illus.). 224p. (J). (gr. -1-3). 12.99 (978-0-544-15881-8(4), HMH Books For Young Readers) Houghton Mifflin Harcourt Publishing Co.

Howard, Elizabeth Fitzgerald. The Train to Lulu's. Casilla, Robert, illus. 2007. (ENG.). 36p. (J). (gr. -1-3). 10.99 (978-1-4169-6161-1(5), Simon & Schuster/Paula Wiseman Bks.) Simon & Schuster/Paula Wiseman Bks.

Hubbell, Patricia. Trains: Steaming! Pulling! Huffing!, 0 vols. Addy, Sean & Halsey, Megan, illus. 2009. (ENG.). 34p. (J). (gr. -1-1). pap. 9.99 (978-0-7614-5593-6(0), 9780761455936, Amazon Children's Publishing) Amazon Publishing.

Johnson, Angela. I Dream of Trains. Long, Loren, illus. 2003. (ENG.). 32p. (J). (gr. k-2). 18.99 (978-0-689-82609-2(5), Simon & Schuster Bks. For Young Readers) Simon & Schuster Bks. For Young Readers.

Kavan, Barbara. Trainman: Gaining Acceptance ... & Friends ... Through Special Interests. 2010. (Illus.). 40p. (J). pap. 17.95 (978-1-934575-70-3(4)) Autism Asperger Publishing Co.

King, Trey. Mystery on the LEGO Express. Wang, Sean, illus. 2014. 24p. (J). (978-1-4242-6168-0(6)) Scholastic, Inc.

—Mystery on the Lego Express. 2014. (LEGO City 8X8 Ser.). (Illus.). 24p. (J). lib. bdg. 13.55 (978-0-606-36068-5(9)) Turtleback Bks.

Kivel, Lee. The Lonely Train. Tucci, Al, illus. 2005. 36p. (J). per. 14.95 (978-0-9774999-0-8(1)) Kivel, Lee.

Klein, Adria F. The Big Train. Cameron, Craig, illus. 2013. (Train Time Ser.). (ENG.). 32p. (gr. -1-1). pap. 5.95 (978-1-4342-4886-2(0)) Stone Arch Bks.

—The Big Train: Takes a Trip. Cameron, Craig, illus. 2013. (Train Time Ser.). (ENG.). 32p. (gr. -1-1). lib. bdg. 22.65 (978-1-4342-4191-7(2)) Stone Arch Bks.

—Big Train Takes a Trip. Cameron, Craig, illus. 2013. (Train Time Ser.). (ENG.). 32p. (gr. -1-1). pap. 29.70 (978-1-4342-6300-1(2)) Stone Arch Bks.

—Circus Train & the Clowns. Cameron, Craig, illus. 2013. (Train Time Ser.). (ENG.). 32p. (gr. -1-1). pap. 29.70 (978-1-4342-6303-2(7)) Stone Arch Bks.

—City Train, 1 vol. Cameron, Craig, illus. 2013. (Train Time Ser.). (ENG.). 32p. (gr. -1-1). lib. bdg. 22.65 (978-1-4342-4189-4(0)) Stone Arch Bks.

—City Train in Trouble. Cameron, Craig, illus. 2013. (Train Time Ser.). (ENG.). 32p. (gr. -1-1). pap. 29.70 (978-1-4342-6302-5(9)) Stone Arch Bks.

—Freight Train, 1 vol. Cameron, Craig, illus. 2013. (Train Time Ser.). (ENG.). 32p. (gr. -1-1). pap. 5.95 (978-1-4342-4885-5(2)); lib. bdg. 22.65 (978-1-4342-4190-0(4)) Stone Arch Bks.

—The Full Freight Train. Cameron, Craig, illus. 2013. (Train Time Ser.). (ENG.). 32p. (gr. -1-1). pap. 29.70 (978-1-4342-6301-8(0)) Stone Arch Bks.

—Train Time. 2013. (Train Time Ser.). (ENG.). 32p. (gr. -1-1). pap. 23.80 (978-1-4342-9041-0(7)) Stone Arch Bks.

—Train Time. Cameron, Craig, illus. 2013. (Train Time Ser.). (ENG.). 32p. (gr. -1-1). lib. bdg. 90.60 (978-1-4342-6055-0(0)); lib. bdg. 181.20 (978-1-4342-6056-7(9)) Stone Arch Bks.

—Train Time. 2013. (Train Time Ser.). (ENG.). 32p. (gr. -1-1). pap. 23.80 (978-1-4342-4902-9(6)) Stone Arch Bks.

Kropik, Linda Kristine. Christopher the Choo Choo Train. Haezer, Jane, illus. 2011. 24p. pap. 11.50 (978-1-60911-522-7(8), Strategic Bk. Publishing) Strategic Book Publishing & Rights Agency (SBPRA).

Lamkin, Robert J. Tommy's Train. 2008. 44p. pap. 24.95 (978-1-60672-147-6(X)) America Star Bks.

Le Guin, Ursula K. Tom Mouse. 2004. (Illus.). (J). (gr. k-3). spiral bd. (978-0-616-14584-5(5)) Canadian National Institute for the Blind/Institut National Canadien pour les Aveugles.

Lehman, Barbara. Trainstop. 2008. (ENG., Illus.). 32p. (J). (gr. -1-3). 16.99 (978-0-618-75640-7(X)) Houghton Mifflin Harcourt Publishing Co.

Light, Steve. Trains Go. 2012. (ENG., Illus.). 16p. (J). (gr. -1 — 1). bds. 9.99 (978-0-8118-7942-2(9)) Chronicle Bks. LLC.

Lukas, Catherine & Artifact Group, The. Trouble on the Train. 2007. (Backyardigans Ser.: 6). (ENG., Illus.). 24p. (J). (gr. -1-1). pap. 3.99 (978-1-4169-2818-8(9), Simon Spotlight/Nickelodeon) Simon Spotlight/Nickelodeon.

Lund, Deb. All Aboard the Dinotrain. Fine, Howard, illus. (ENG.). (J). (gr. -1 — 1). 2011. 30p. bds. 7.99 (978-0-547-55415-0(X)) 2009. 40p. pap. 7.99 (978-0-547-24825-7(3)) Houghton Mifflin Harcourt Publishing Co.

Lupa, Mary R. Stacy Takes the Train to School. Andriyevskaya, Yevgeniya, illus. 2009. 20p. (J). pap. 10.95 (978-1-4327-1609-7(3)) Outskirts Pr., Inc.

Macaulay, David. Black & White. 2005. (ENG., Illus.). 32p. (J). (gr. -1-3). 7.99 (978-0-618-63687-7(0)) Houghton Mifflin Harcourt Publishing Co.

Mack, Karen. Who Makes the Sound? 2008. 11p. pap. 24.95 (978-1-60610-852-9(2)) America Star Bks.

Mackall, Dandi Daley. Rudy Rides the Rails: A Depression Era Story. Ellison, Chris, illus. rev. ed. 2007. (Tales of Young Americans Ser.). (ENG.). 32p. (J). (gr. -1-3). 17.95 (978-1-58536-286-8(7)) Sleeping Bear Pr.

Mara, Nichole. All Aboard! Let's Ride a Train. Kolb, Andrew, illus. 2017. (ENG.). 10p. (J). (gr. -1 — 1). bds. 9.95 **(978-1-4197-2567-8(X)**, Abrams Appleseed) Abrams, Inc.

Marsh, Carole. The Mystery on Alaska's Iditarod Trail. 2009. (Real Kids, Real Places Ser.). 145p. (J). 18.99 (978-0-635-06997-9(0), Marsh, Carole Mysteries) Gallopade International.

McCaughrean, Geraldine. Stop the Train! 2003. (ENG.). 304p. (J). (gr. 5-18). 16.99 (978-0-06-050749-7(7)) HarperCollins Pubs.

McLaughlin, B. G. Reuben Rides the Rails. 2010. (Illus.). 32p. pap. 14.49 (978-1-4490-4448-0(4)) AuthorHouse.

McMullan, Kate. I'm Fast! McMullan, Jim, illus. 2012. 40p. (J). (gr. -1-3). (ENG.). 16.99 (978-0-06-192085-1(1)); lib. bdg. 17.89 (978-0-06-192086-8(X)) HarperCollins Pubs.

McPhail, J. A. Dawn of Day. Battis, Gwen, illus. 2012. 200p. 17.99 (978-0-9851196-2-1(4)) Rowe Publishing and Design.

Meister, Cari. Train Trip, 1 vol. Janovitz, Marilyn, illus. 2009. (My First Graphic Novel Ser.). (ENG.). 32p. (gr. k-2). 24.65 (978-1-4342-1616-8(0), My First Graphic Novel) Stone Arch Bks.

Meister, Cari & Stone Arch Books Staff. Train Trip, 1 vol. Janovitz, Marilyn, illus. 2010. (My First Graphic Novel Ser.). (ENG.). 32p. (gr. k-2). pap. 6.25 (978-1-4342-2289-3(6), My First Graphic Novel) Stone Arch Bks.

Metzger, Steve. The Turkey Train. Paillot, Jim, illus. 2013. (ENG.). 32p. (J). (gr. -1-k). 6.99 (978-0-545-49229-4(7), Cartwheel Bks.) Scholastic, Inc.

Miéville, China. Railsea. 2013. (ENG., Illus.). 448p. pap. 12.00 (978-0-345-52453-9(5), Del Rey) Random House Publishing Group.

Monks, Lydia. Mungo Monkey Goes on a Train. 2015. (ENG., Illus.). 14p. (J). (gr. -1-k). 13.99 (978-1-4052-6910-0(3)) Egmont Bks., Ltd. GBR. Dist: Independent Pubs. Group.

Murray, Regina Waldron. The Very Exciting Train Ride: An Adventure. 2006. (J). per. 15.95 (978-0-9664042-1-0(1)) Murray, Regina Waldron.

Nelson, Dianne Elizabeth. By Here. 2009. 32p. pap. 14.49 (978-1-4490-0366-1(4)) AuthorHouse.

Nesbit, E. The Railway Children. 2007. 236p. per. 12.95 (978-1-4218-3945-5(8)); (ENG.). (gr. 4-7). 27.95 (978-1-4218-3845-8(1)) 1st World Publishing, Inc. (1st World Library - Literary Society).

—The Railway Children. 2006. (ENG.). 228p. (gr. 4-7). per. 14.95 (978-1-59818-933-9(6)); 26.95 (978-1-59818-179-1(3)) Aegypan.

—The Railway Children. 2013. 140p. pap. (978-1-908388-94-0(3)) Aziloth Bks.

—The Railway Children. 2008. (J). 8.99 (978-1-59166-924-1(3)) BJU Pr.

—The Railway Children. Brock, C. E., illus. (YA). 14.95 (978-0-8118-4933-3(3)) Chronicle Bks. LLC.

—The Railway Children. 2012. (ENG.). 234p. pap. 14.99 (978-1-4812-4818-1(9)) CreateSpace Independent Publishing Platform.

—The Railway Children. 2008. 204p. (gr. 4-7). 24.99 (978-0-554-36009-6(8)); 27.99 (978-0-554-26706-7(3)) Creative Media Partners, LLC.

—The Railway Children. 2008. (gr. 4-7). pap. 5.99 (978-1-4209-3105-1(9)) Digireads.com Publishing.

—The Railway Children. Brock, C. E., illus. 2008. (ENG.). 248p. per. (978-1-4065-9815-5(1)) Dodo Pr.

—The Railway Children. 2007. (ENG.). 204p. per. (978-1-4065-3083-4(2)) Dodo Pr.

—The Railway Children. 2006. pap. (978-1-4068-3505-2(6)) 2005. 348p. pap. (978-1-84637-205-6(4)) Echo Library.

—The Railway Children. Brock, Charles Edmund, illus. 2012. 232p. pap. (978-1-78201-004-3(1)) Evertype.

—The Railway Children. 2010. (Illus.). 118p. pap. 19.99 (978-1-153-71841-7(3)) General Bks. LLC.

—The Railway Children. Dryhurst, Dinah, tr. Dryhurst, Dinah, illus. 2004. 184p. 18.95 (978-1-56792-261-5(9)) Godine, David R. Pub.

—The Railway Children. 2010. 184p. pap. (978-1-4076-1891-3(1)) HardPr.

—The Railway Children. (J). (978-0-340-71497-3(2)) Hodder & Stoughton.

—The Railway Children. 2010. 194p. 30.36 (978-1-169-28328-2(4)) 2010. 194p. pap. 18.36 (978-1-162-70632-0(5)) 2010. 194p. 37.95 (978-1-161-47496-1(X)) 2004. reprint ed. pap. 22.95 (978-1-4191-7972-3(1)) 2004. reprint ed. pap. 1.99 (978-1-4192-7972-0(6)) Kessinger Publishing, LLC.

—The Railway Children. 2006. (Twelve-Point Ser.). lib. bdg. 25.00 (978-1-58287-399-2(2)); lib. bdg. 26.00 (978-1-58287-890-4(0)) North Bks.

—The Railway Children. 2012. (Oxford Children's Classics Ser.). (ENG.). 240p. 9.95 (978-0-19-275819-4(5)) Oxford Univ. Pr., Inc.

—The Railway Children. unabr. ed. 2004. (Chrysalis Childrens Classics Ser.). (Illus.). 128p. (YA). pap. (978-1-84365-050-6(9), Pavilion Children's Books) Pavilion Bks.

—The Railway Children. 2nd ed. 2008. (ENG., Illus.). 48p. pap. 11.99 (978-1-4058-6964-5(X)) Pearson Education.

—The Railway Children. 2nd ed. 2011. (Puffin Classics Ser.). (ENG., Illus.). 304p. (J). (gr. 5-7). pap. 5.99 (978-0-14-132160-8(1), Puffin Books) Penguin Young Readers Group.

—The Railway Children. (ENG.). (J). (gr. 4-7). 2013. 320p. pap. 10.99 (978-0-09-957299-2(0)) 2012. 290p. 10.99 (978-0-09-957715-7(1)) Random Hse. GBR. Dist: Independent Pubs. Group.

—The Railway Children. 2010. 146p. (gr. 4-7). pap. 8.95 (978-1-61104-337-2(9)) ReadaClassic.com.

—The Railway Children. 2004. (ENG.). 580p. (978-0-9548401-2-9(7)) Shoes & Ships & Sealing Wax Ltd.

—The Railway Children. 2011. 200p. (gr. 4-7). pap. (978-3-8424-4120-0(7)) Tredition GmbH.

—The Railway Children. 2009. 156p. (gr. 4-7). pap. 6.99 (978-1-60459-698-4(8)) Wilder Pubns., Corp.

N'Leh, Anne-Claire. The Planet of Trainiacs. Elyum Studio, illus. 2013. (Little Prince Ser.: 10). (ENG.). 56p. (J). (gr. 4-8). lib. bdg. 26.60 (978-0-7613-8760-2(9), Graphic Universe™) Lerner Publishing Group.

Nolen, Jerdine. Eliza's Freedom Road: An Underground Railroad Diary. Strickland, Shadra, illus. 2011. (ENG.). 160p. (J). (gr. 3-7). 16.99 (978-1-4169-5814-7(2), Simon & Schuster/Paula Wiseman Bks.) Simon & Schuster/Paula Wiseman Bks.

O'Dell, Kathryn L. From Wagon to Train. Chalik, Chris, illus. 2017. (Text Connections Guided Close Reading Ser.). (J). (gr. 2). (978-1-4900-1854-6(9)) Benchmark Education Co.

Ogilvy, Ian. Measle & the Wrathmonk. 2004. 224p. (J). (gr. 4-6). 15.99 (978-0-06-058685-0(0)) HarperCollins Pubs.

Opie, David, illus. Monkey & the Engineer. 2007. 24p. (J). 14.95 (978-0-9793972-6-4(X)) JD Publishing.

Oppel, Kenneth. The Boundless. Tierney, Jim, illus. 2014. (ENG.). 336p. (J). (gr. 3-7). 17.99 (978-1-4424-7288-4(X), Simon & Schuster Bks. For Young Readers) Simon & Schuster Bks. For Young Readers.

Papp, Robert, illus. The Mystery of the Orphan Train. 2005. (Boxcar Children Mysteries Ser.: 105). (ENG.). 128p. (J). (gr. 1-5). lib. bdg. 14.99 (978-0-8075-5558-3(4)); per. 6.99 (978-0-8075-5559-0(2)) Whitman, Albert & Co.

Parker, Amy. Night Night, Train, 1 vol. Allyn, Virginia, illus. 2017. (Night Night Ser.). (ENG.). 20p. (J). bds. 9.99 **(978-0-7180-8932-0(4))** Nelson, Thomas Inc.

Parker, Danny & Bodman, Charlotte. Molly & Mae: A Friendship Journey. Blackwood, Freya, illus. 2017. (ENG.). 32p. (J). (gr. -1-3). 16.99 **(978-1-328-71543-2(4)**, HMH Books For Young Readers) Houghton Mifflin Harcourt Publishing Co.

Parker, Emma. All Aboard! 2010. (Illus.). 20p. pap. (978-1-877561-74-0(6)) First Edition Ltd.

Paul, Miranda. Trainbots. McG, Shane, illus. 2016. (ENG.). 32p. (J). (gr. -1-3). 16.99 (978-1-4998-0167-5(X)) Little Bee Books Inc.

Peet, Bill. The Caboose Who Got Loose, 1 vol. Peet, Bill, illus. 2008. (Read along Book & CD Ser.). (ENG., Illus.). 48p. (J). (gr. -1-3). audio compact disk 10.99 (978-0-618-95979-2(3)) Houghton Mifflin Harcourt Publishing Co.

Piper, Watty & Penguin / LeapFrog. The Little Engine That Could. Long, Loren, illus. 2008. (J). 13.99 (978-1-59319-938-8(4)) LeapFrog Enterprises, Inc.

Powell, Jillian. Are We There Yet?, 1 vol. Colnaghi, Stefania, illus. 2013. (Start Reading Ser.). (ENG.). 24p. (gr. k-1). pap. 7.95 (978-1-4765-4083-2(7)) Capstone Press of Coughlan Cos.

Priddy, Roger. Santa Express. 2013. (Shaped Board Bks.). (ENG., Illus.). 6p. (J). (gr. -1-k). bds. 6.99 (978-0-312-51619-2(3), 9780312516192, Priddy Bks.) St. Martin's Pr.

Prince, Joshua. I Saw an Ant on the Railroad Track. Pamintuan, Macky, illus. 2006. (ENG.). 24p. (J). (gr. -1-k). 14.95 (978-1-4027-2183-0(8), 1252268) Sterling Publishing Co., Inc.

Pryor, Bonnie. The Iron Dragon: The Courageous Story of Lee Chin. 2010. (Historical Fiction Adventures (HFA) Ser.). (Illus.). 160p. (J). (gr. 3-6). 29.27 (978-0-7660-3389-4(9)); (gr. 4-6). pap. 10.95 (978-1-59845-215-0(0)) Enslow Pubs., Inc.

Publications International Ltd. Staff. Chuggington Little Lift & Listen. 2011. 12p. (J). bds. 10.98 (978-1-4508-0504-9(3)) Phoenix International Publications, Inc.

Publications International Ltd. Staff, ed. Interactive Play a Sound Thomas the Tank. 2009. 24p. (J). 17.98 (978-0-7853-1360-1(5), PIL Kids) Publications International, Ltd.

—Record a Story with Thomas & Friends: Good Night, Little Engine. 2011. (Illus.). 20p. (J). bds. 25.98 (978-1-4508-1164-4(7)) Phoenix International Publications, Inc.

Pugliano-Martin, Carol. John Henry: An American Tall Tale. 2006. (J). pap. (978-1-4108-6170-2(8)) Benchmark Education Co.

Rabe, Tish. Huff & Puff. Guile, Gill, illus. 2014. (My First I Can Read Ser.). (ENG.). 24p. (J). (gr. -1-3). 16.99 (978-0-06-230502-2(6)); pap. 3.99 (978-0-06-230501-5(8)) HarperCollins Pubs.

—Huff & Puff Have Too Much Stuff! Guile, Gill, illus. 2014. (My First I Can Read Ser.). (ENG.). 24p. (J). (gr. -1-3). pap. 3.99 (978-0-06-230505-3(0)) HarperCollins Pubs.

Raffa, Edwina & Rigsby, Annelle. Kidnapped in Key West. (Florida Historical Fiction for Youth Ser.). (ENG.). (J). 2012. 138p. pap. 9.95 (978-1-56164-537-4(0)) 2008. (Illus.). 127p. (gr. 3-7). 14.95 (978-1-56164-413-1(7)) Pineapple Pr., Inc.

Ramoutar, Tagore. Trains, Engines & Locomotives: I Love Trains. 2013. 38p. pap. (978-1-907837-63-0(9)) Longshot Ventures, Ltd.

Random House. Dinos & Discoveries/Emily Saves the World, 2 bks. in 1. 2015. (Pictureback(R) Ser.). (ENG., Illus.). 24p. (J). (gr. -1-2). 4.99 (978-0-553-50870-3(9), Random Hse. Bks. for Young Readers) Random Hse. Children's Bks.

—Five Tank Engine Tales (Thomas & Friends) Courtney, Richard, illus. 2015. (Step into Reading Ser.). (ENG.). 160p. (J). (gr. -1-1). pap. 7.99 (978-0-385-38496-4(3), Random Hse. Bks. for Young Readers) Random Hse. Children's Bks.

—The Great Train Mystery. 2013. (Spongebob Squarepants Step into Reading Ser.). lib. bdg. 13.55 (978-0-606-35116-4(7)) Turtleback Bks.

—Henry in the Dark. 2017. (Step into Reading Ser.). (ENG., Illus.). 24p. (J). (gr. -1-1). pap. 4.99 (978-0-399-55862-7(4), Random Hse. Bks. for Young Readers) Random Hse. Children's Bks.

—Thomas & Friends: the Adventure Begins (Thomas & Friends) 2015. (Pictureback(R) Ser.). (ENG., Illus.). 24p. (J). (gr. -1-2). 3.99 (978-0-553-53553-2(6), Random Hse. Bks. for Young Readers) Random Hse. Children's Bks.

—Thomas & the Lost Pirate / the Sunken Treasure, 2 bks. in 1. Stubbs, Tommy, illus. 2015. (Pictureback(R) Ser.). (ENG.). 24p. (J). (gr. -1-2). 4.99 (978-0-553-52078-1(4), Random Hse. Bks. for Young Readers) Random Hse. Children's Bks.

—Thomas at the Animal Park (Thomas & Friends) Lapadula, Thomas, illus. 2014. (ENG.). 10p. (J). (— 1). 10.99 (978-0-385-38469-8(6), Random Hse. Bks. for Young Readers) Random Hse. Children's Bks.

—Thomas' Tall Friend (Thomas & Friends) 2016. (Step into Reading Ser.). (ENG., Illus.). 24p. (J). (gr. -1-1). 4.99 (978-1-101-94034-1(4), Random Hse. Bks. for Young Readers) Random Hse. Children's Bks.

—5-Minute Stories - The Sleepytime Collection. 2016. (ENG., Illus.). 160p. (J). (gr. -1-2). 12.99 (978-0-399-55207-6(3), Random Hse. Bks. for Young Readers) Random Hse. Children's Bks.

Random House Disney Staff. A Valentine for Percy (Thomas & Friends) Courtney, Richard, illus. 2015. (Step into Reading Ser.). (ENG.). 24p. (J). (gr. -1-1). 4.99 (978-1-101-93287-2(2), Random Hse. Bks. for Young Readers) Random Hse. Children's Bks.

Random House Editors. Thomas' Tall Friend. 2016. (Step into Reading Level 2 Ser.). lib. bdg. 14.75 (978-0-606-38883-2(4)) Turtleback Bks.

Random House Staff. The Great Train Mystery (SpongeBob SquarePants) Random House Staff, illus. 2013. (Step into Reading Ser.). (ENG., Illus.). 32p. (J). (gr. -1-1). pap. 3.99 (978-0-449-81441-3(6), Random Hse. Bks. for Young Readers) Random Hse. Children's Bks.

—Thomas & Friends: Percy's Chocolate Crunch & Other Thomas the Tank Engine Stories. Random House Staff, illus. Mitton, David et al, photos by. 2003. (Pictureback(R) Ser.). (ENG., Illus.). 32p. (J). (gr. -1-2). pap. 3.99 (978-0-375-81392-4(6), Random Hse. Bks. for Young Readers) Random Hse. Children's Bks.

Reader's Digest Staff. Thomas & Friends Movie Theater. HIT Entertainment Staff, illus. 2010. (Movie Theater Ser.). (ENG.). 48p. (J). (gr. -1-2). bds. 19.99 (978-0-7944-2002-4(8)) Reader's Digest Assn., Inc., The.

Rey, Margret & Rey, H. A. Takes a Train. Weston, Martha, illus. 2010. (Curious George Ser.). (ENG.). 24p. (J). (gr. -1-3). pap. 4.99 (978-0-547-50424-7(1)) Houghton Mifflin Harcourt Publishing Co.

Rice, Dona Herwick. John Henry, 1 vol. 2009. (Building Fluency Through Reader's Theater Ser.). (ENG.). 24p. (J). (gr. 2-4). pap. 6.99 (978-1-4333-0992-2(0)) Teacher Created Materials, Inc.

Richardson, Arleta. Prairie Homestead. 2016. (Beyond the Orphan Train Ser.: 3). (ENG.). 192p. (J). pap. 7.99 (978-0-7814-1357-2(5)) Cook, David C.

—Whistle-Stop West. 2016. (Beyond the Orphan Train Ser.: 2). (ENG.). 192p. (J). pap. 7.99 (978-1-4347-0956-1(6)) Cook, David C.

Richter, Bernd & Richter, Susan. When Grandma & Grandpa Rode the Alaska Train. 2008. (ENG., Illus.). 16p. (J). bds. 8.95 (978-1-931353-40-3(9)) Saddle Pal Creations, Inc.

Rinker, Sherri Duskey. Steam Train, Dream Train. Lichtenheld, Tom, illus. 2013. (ENG.). 40p. (J). (gr. -1-1). 16.99 (978-1-4521-0920-6(6)) Chronicle Bks. LLC.

—Steam Train, Dream Train Colors. Lichtenheld, Tom, illus. 2016. (ENG.). 20p. (J). (gr. -1 — 1). bds. 7.99 (978-1-4521-4915-8(1)) Chronicle Bks. LLC.

—Steam Train, Dream Train Counting. Lichtenheld, Tom, illus. 2016. (ENG.). 20p. (J). (gr. -1 — 1). bds. 7.99 (978-1-4521-4914-1(3)) Chronicle Bks. LLC.

—Steam Train, Dream Train Sound Book. Lichtenheld, Tom, illus. 2015. (ENG.). 12p. (J). (gr. -1-k). 12.99 (978-1-4521-2825-2(1)) Chronicle Bks. LLC.

Rosen, Michael. Running with Trains: A Novel in Poetry & Two Voices. 2012. (ENG.). 112p. (J). (gr. 5). 15.95 (978-1-59078-863-9(X), Wordsong) Boyds Mills Pr.

Rosenbaum, Andria Warmflash & Gill, Deirdre. Trains Don't Sleep. Rosenbaum, Andria Warmflash & Gill, Deirdre, illus. 2017. (ENG., Illus.). 40p. (J). (gr. -1-3). 16.99 (978-0-544-38074-5(6), HMH Books For Young Readers) Houghton Mifflin Harcourt Publishing Co.

Ross, Diana. The Little Red Engine & the Rocket. Wood, Leslie, illus. 2005. (Little Red Engine Ser.: 1). (ENG.). 32p. (J). (gr. k-2). pap. 8.99 (978-0-233-00146-3(8)) Andre Deutsch GBR. Dist: Independent Pubs. Group.

—The Little Red Engine Goes to Town. Wood, Leslie, illus. 2005. (Little Red Engine Ser.: 1). (ENG.). 32p. (J). (gr. k-2). pap. 8.99 (978-0-233-00151-7(4)) Andre Deutsch GBR. Dist: Independent Pubs. Group.

Roy, Ron. Capital Mysteries #13: Trapped on the D. C. Train! Bush, Timothy, illus. 2011. (Capital Mysteries Ser.). (ENG.). 96p. (J). (gr. 1-4). 4.99 (978-0-375-85926-7(8), Random Hse. Bks. for Young Readers) Random Hse. Children's Bks.

The Runaway Engine & Other Stories: Individual Title Six-Pack. (Story Steps Ser.). (gr. k-2). 48.00 (978-0-7635-9803-7(8)) Rigby Education.

Sander, Sonia. Scooby-Doo & the International Express. 2009. (Illus.). 32p. (J). pap. (978-0-545-16283-8(1)) Scholastic, Inc.

Santillo, LuAnn. The Tracks. Santillo, LuAnn, ed. 2003. (Half-Pint Kids Readers Ser.). (Illus.). 7p. (J). (gr. -1-1). pap. 1.00 (978-1-59256-080-6(6)) Half-Pint Kids, Inc.

Sayres, Brianna Caplan. Where Do Steam Trains Sleep at Night? Slade, Christian, illus. (ENG.). (J). (gr. -1 — 1). 2017. 26p. bds. 7.99 **(978-0-553-52100-9(4))** 2016. 32p. 19.99 (978-0-375-97471-7(7)) Random Hse. Children's Bks. (Random Hse. Bks. for Young Readers).

Schaefer, Nikki. The Potty Train. Schaefer, Nikki, illus. 2010. (Illus.). 24p. pap. 10.95 (978-1-61633-043-9(0)) Guardian Angel Publishing, Inc.

Selig, Josh. Ride the Potato Train. Gibbons, Cassandra, illus. 2013. 30p. (J). (978-1-4844-0420-1(3), Planet Dexter) Penguin Publishing Group.

Selznick, Brian. The Invention of Hugo Cabret. 2007. (CHI., Illus.). 534p. (J). (978-957-570-894-8(6)) Eastern Publishing Co., Ltd., The.

—The Invention of Hugo Cabret. 2008. (CHI., Illus.). 465p. (J). pap. (978-7-5448-0279-6(5)) Jieli Publishing Hse.

—The Invention of Hugo Cabret. Selznick, Brian, illus. 2007. (Illus.). (ENG.). 544p. (J). (gr. 4-7). 24.99 (978-0-439-81378-5(6), Scholastic Pr.); 534p. (978-1-4071-0348-8(2)) Scholastic, Inc.

Shepherd, David & Plummer, William K. We Were There at the Driving of the Golden Spike. 2013. (ENG., Illus.). 192p. (J). (gr. 3-8). pap. 6.99 (978-0-486-49259-9(1)) Dover Pubns., Inc.

Shortle, Stacy & Mooney, Dean J. M. A Train Ride to Grandma's (with NO Chocolate Donut!) Wulfing, Amy J., illus. 2009. 48p. (J). 18.95 (978-0-9759850-5-2(1)) Maple Leaf Ctr.

Skinner, Daphne. All Aboard! Smath, Jerry, illus. 2007. (Math Matters Ser.). (ENG.). 32p. (J). (gr. -1-3). pap. 5.95 (978-1-57565-239-9(0)) Kane Press, Inc.

Slayton, Fran. When the Whistle Blows. 2010. (ENG.). 176p. (J). (gr. 5-18). 6.99 (978-0-14-241732-4(7), Puffin Books) Penguin Young Readers Group.

Smith, B. M. Evan & Cassie Go on a Train Meet, 1 vol. Smith, Mandy M., illus. 2009. 35p. pap. 24.95 (978-1-60836-552-4(2)) America Star Bks.

Snicket, Lemony, pseud. Why Is This Night Different from All Other Nights? Seth, illus. 2015. (ENG.). 304p. (J). (gr. 3-17).

16.00 *(978-0-316-12304-4(8))* Little, Brown Bks. for Young Readers.

Sobel, June. The Goodnight Train. Huliska-Beith, Laura, illus. 2006. (ENG.). 32p. (J). (gr. -1-3). 16.99 *(978-0-15-205436-6(7))* Houghton Mifflin Harcourt Publishing Co.

Sommer, Carl. The Little Red Train. James, Kennon, illus. 2014. (J). pap. *(978-1-57537-958-6(9))* Advance Publishing, Inc.

—The Little Red Train. 2003. (Another Sommer-Time Story Ser.). (Illus.). 48p. (J). (gr. k-4). lib. bdg. 23.95 incl. audio *(978-1-57537-764-3(0))* Advance Publishing, Inc.

—The Little Red Train. James, Kennon, illus. 2003. (Another Sommer-Time Story Ser.). (ENG.). 48p. (J). (gr. k-3). 16.95 incl. audio compact disk *(978-1-57537-014-9(X))*; lib. bdg. 23.95 incl. audio compact disk *(978-1-57537-714-8(4))* Advance Publishing, Inc.

—The Little Red Train. 2003. (Another Sommer-Time Story Ser.). (Illus.). 48p. (J). (gr. 1-4). 16.95 incl. audio *(978-1-57537-563-2(X))*; 16.95 incl. audio compact disk *(978-1-57537-514-4(1))* Advance Publishing, Inc.

—The Little Red Train(El Trenecito Rojo) James, Kennon, illus. 2009. (Another Sommer-Time Story Bilingual Ser.). (SPA & ENG.). 48p. (J). lib. bdg. 16.95 *(978-1-57537-158-0(8))* Advance Publishing, Inc.

Spencer, Jamie. The Train to Maine. Reed, Rebecca, illus. 2008. (ENG.). 32p. (J). (gr. -1-3). 15.95 *(978-0-89272-767-4(5))* Down East Bks.

Stephenson, Mary. Naven's Dream. 2011. 24p. pap. 24.95 *(978-1-4626-0309-1(2))* America Star Bks.

Sterling Children's, Sterling. Railway. Finn, Rebecca, illus. 2015. (Busy Bks.). (ENG.). 10p. (J). (— 1). bds. 8.95 *(978-1-4549-1735-9(0))* Sterling Publishing Co., Inc.

Stilton, Geronimo. The Fastest Train in the West. Cooper-McGuinness, Nanette, tr. 2013. (Geronimo Stilton Graphic Novels Ser.). (ENG., Illus.). 56p. (J). (gr. 2-6). 9.99 *(978-1-59707-448-3(9)*, 9781597074483) Papercutz.

Stilton, Thea. Thea Stilton & the Mystery on the Orient Express. 2012. (Thea Stilton Ser.: 13). lib. bdg. 19.65 *(978-0-606-26757-1(3)*, Turtleback) Turtleback Bks.

Stockham, Jess, illus. Down by the Station. 2003. (Classic Books with Holes 8x8 Ser.). (ENG.). 16p. (J). *(978-0-85953-132-0(5))* Child's Play International Ltd.

Stubbs, Tommy, illus. A Crack in the Track. 2004. (Bright & Early Board Books(TM) Ser.). (ENG.). 24p. (J). (— 1). bds. 4.99 *(978-0-375-82755-6(2)*, Random Hse. Bks. for Young Readers) Random Hse. Children's Bks.

Sturges, Philemon. I Love Trains! Halpern, Shari, illus. (ENG.). (J). (gr. -1-1). 2006. 28p. bds. 6.99 *(978-0-06-083774-7(8)*, HarperFestival) 2003. 32p. pap. 6.99 *(978-0-06-443667-0(5))* HarperCollins Pubs.

Terhune, Albert Payson. Caleb Conover: Railroader. (J). 13.95 *(978-0-8488-1484-7(3))* Amereon Ltd.

—Lad: A Dog. (J). 24.95 *(978-0-8488-1485-4(1))* Amereon Ltd.

Testa, Maggie. A Ride Through the Neighborhood. Style Guide Staff, illus. 2014. (Daniel Tiger's Neighborhood Ser.). (ENG.). 12p. (J). (gr. -1-1). bds. 6.99 *(978-1-4424-9839-6(0)*, Simon Spotlight) Simon Spotlight.

Thomas The Tank Engine & Egmont Staff. Thomas & Friends. 2008. (Illus.). 140p. *(978-0-603-56338-6(4))* Egmont Bks., Ltd.

Tillworth, Mary. Triple-Track Train Race! (Bubble Guppies) Unten, Eren, illus. 2015. (Little Golden Book Ser.). (ENG.). 24p. (J). (-k). 4.99 *(978-0-553-49769-4(3)*, Golden Bks.) Random Hse. Children's Bks.

Titcomb, Gordon. The Last Train. Minor, Wendell, illus. 2010. (ENG.). 32p. (J). (gr. -1-3). 18.99 *(978-1-59643-164-5(4)*, 9781596431645) Roaring Brook Pr.

Top That, ed. Let's Play Magnetic Play Scene Trains. 2008. *(978-1-84666-557-8(4))* Top That! Publishing PLC.

Top That!, creator. ABC Train. 2007. (Jigsaw Book Ser.). (Illus.). 18p. (J). (gr. -1-3). bds. *(978-1-84666-095-5(5))* Top That! Publishing PLC.

—123 Train. 2007. (Jigsaw Book Ser.). (Illus.). 18p. (J). (gr. -1-3). bds. *(978-1-84666-097-9(1))* Top That! Publishing PLC.

Tunnell, Michael O. Mailing May. Rand, Ted, illus. 2015. 32p. pap. 7.00 *(978-1-61003-610-8(7))* Center for the Collaborative Classroom.

Twinn, A. Down by the Station. Stockham, Jess, illus. 2007. (Classic Books with Holes 8x8 with CD Ser.). (ENG.). 16p. (J). (gr. -1-1). pap. incl. audio compact disk *(978-1-904550-68-6(1))* Child's Play International Ltd.

Vago, Mike. Train: A Journey Through the Pages Book. Rockefeller, Matthew, illus. 2016. (ENG.). 14p. (J). (gr. -1-3). 22.95 *(978-0-7611-8716-5(2))* Workman Publishing Co., Inc.

Vaillard, Fabiola. Tongo: The Wish Train. 2012. 32p. pap. 13.95 *(978-1-4633-3431-4(1))* Palibrio.

Vamos, Samantha R. Alphabet Trains. O'Rourke, Ryan, illus. 2015. (ENG.). 32p. (J). (gr. -1-2). lib. bdg. 14.95 *(978-1-58089-592-7(1))* Charlesbridge Publishing, Inc.

VanArsdale, Anthony, illus. Journey on a Runaway Train. 2017. (Boxcar Children Great Adventure Ser.: 1). (ENG.). 160p. (J). (gr. 1-5). 12.99 ***(978-0-8075-0695-0(8))***; 6.99 ***(978-0-8075-0696-7(6))*** Whitman, Albert & Co.

Vanoosting, James. Walking Mary. 2005. 144p. (J). (gr. 7-18). lib. bdg. 16.89 *(978-0-06-028472-5(2))* HarperCollins Pubs.

Verne, Jules. The Adventures of a Special Correspondent. 2009. 180p. 25.95 *(978-1-60664-635-9(4))*; pap. 13.95 *(978-1-60664-377-8(0))* Rodgers, Alan Bks.

Waddell, Barbara. If I Could Catch a Train. 2009. 20p. pap. 9.15 *(978-1-4251-8667-8(X))* Trafford Publishing.

Walton, Dana E. Bo John's Train. 2012. 28p. pap. 19.99 *(978-1-4772-0818-2(6))* AuthorHouse.

Warner, Gertrude Chandler. Journey on a Runaway Train. 2017. (Boxcar Children Great Adventure Ser.: 1). (J). lib. bdg. 17.20 ***(978-0-606-40315-3(9))*** Turtleback Bks.

Warren, Bertie. Sammie's Journey to Freedom. 2006. (ENG.). 52p. per. 16.95 *(978-1-4241-5142-4(2))* America Star Bks.

Watt, Fiona. Choo Choo. 2009. (Stroller Bks). 8p. (J). 7.99 *(978-0-7945-2496-8(6)*, Usborne) EDC Publishing.

—Pull-Back Busy Train. Field, Jim, illus. 2013. (Pull-Back Bks). 10p. (J). ring bd. 24.99 *(978-0-7945-3333-5(7)*, Usborne) EDC Publishing.

—That's Not My Train. rev. ed. 2008. (Touchy-Feely Board Bks). 10p. (J). bds. 8.99 *(978-0-7945-2168-4(1)*, Usborne) EDC Publishing.

Watt, Fiona & Wells, Rachel. That's Not My Train: Its Wheels Are Too Slippery. 2004. (Touchy-Feely Board Bks.). (SPA & ENG., Illus.). 1p. (J). (gr. -1-18). bds. 7.95 *(978-0-7460-3779-9(1))* EDC Publishing.

Weakly, Chris A. Toby the Little Switch Engine. 2012. 24p. 24.95 *(978-1-4626-4884-9(3))* America Star Bks.

Webster, Christy. Get Rolling with Phonics (Thomas & Friends) 2016. (Step into Reading Ser.). (ENG., Illus.). 144p. (J). (gr. -1-2). pap. 12.99 *(978-1-101-93726-6(2)*, Random Hse. Bks. for Young Readers) Random Hse. Children's Bks.

Welch, Julie. Happy Hearts, 1 vol. 2009. 52p. pap. 16.95 *(978-1-4489-1971-0(1))* America Star Bks.

Wells, Rosemary. On the Blue Comet. Ibatoulline, Bagram, illus. (ENG.). 336p. (J). (gr. 5). 2012. pap. 8.99 *(978-0-7636-5815-1(4))* 2010. 16.99 *(978-0-7636-3722-4(X))* Candlewick Pr.

Whipple, Wayne. Radio Boys Cronies. 2004. reprint ed. pap. 15.95 *(978-1-4191-4378-6(6))* Kessinger Publishing, LLC.

Wilson, Diane Lee. Tracks. (ENG.). (J). (gr. 5-9). 2013. Illus.). 304p. pap. 6.99 *(978-1-4424-2014-4(6))* 2012. 288p. 16.99 *(978-1-4424-2013-7(8))* McElderry, Margaret K. Bks. (McElderry, Margaret K. Bks.).

Wondriska, William. Puff. 2015. (ENG., Illus.). 32p. (J). (gr. k-4). 16.95 *(978-0-7893-2911-0(5))* Universe Publishing.

Woodford, Pamela. Sid, Spark & the Signal Man. 2013. (Brighter Little Minds Ser.). (ENG., Illus.). 24p. (J). pap. 9.99 *(978-1-871305-82-1(9))* Orpen Pr. IRL. Dist: M.H. Gill & Co. U. C.

Worthington, Heather Hill. Miles of Smiles: The Story of Roxey, the Long Island Rail Road Dog. Farnsworth, Bill, illus. 2010. (J). *(978-0-9792918-4-5(4))*; pap. *(978-0-9792918-8-3(7))* Blue Marlin Pubns.

Yee, Paul. Ghost Train. Chan, Harvey, illus. 2004. 29p. (J). (gr. k-4). reprint ed. 16.00 *(978-0-7567-9083-7(2))* DIANE Publishing Co.

Yin. Coolies. Soentpiet, Chris K., illus. 2003. (ENG.). 40p. (J). (gr. 2-5). 7.99 *(978-0-14-250055-2(0)*, Puffin Books) Penguin Young Readers Group.

—Coolies. Soentpiet, Chris K., illus. 2003. (gr. k). 18.00 *(978-0-7569-1545-2(7))* Perfection Learning Corp.

Zimmerman, Andrea & Clemesha, David. Train Man. Zimmerman, Andrea & Clemesha, David, illus. 2012. (ENG., Illus.). 32p. (J). (gr. -1-k). 14.99 *(978-0-8050-7991-3(2)*, 9780805079913, Holt, Henry & Co. Bks. For Young Readers) Holt, Henry & Co.

Zullo, Germano. Line 135. Albertine, illus. 2013. (ENG.). 44p. (J). (gr. -1-1). 18.95 *(978-1-4521-1934-2(1))* Chronicle Bks. LLC.

RAILROADS—FREIGHT

see Freight and Freightage

RAILROADS—HISTORY

Argyle, Ray. The Boy in the Picture: The Craigellachie Kid & the Driving of the Last Spike. 2010. (ENG., Illus.). 152p. (YA). pap. 19.99 *(978-1-55488-787-3(9))* Dundurn CAN. Dist: Ingram Publisher Services.

Ashley, Susan. Por Tren. 2003. (Weekly Reader Early Learning Library). (SPA., Illus.). 24p. (gr. 1-4). pap. 8.15 *(978-0-8368-3842-8(4)*, Weekly Reader Leveled Readers) Stevens, Gareth Publishing LLLP.

Bankston, John. Electric Trains & Trolleys (1880-1920) 2012. (J). lib. bdg. 29.95 *(978-1-61228-291-6(1))* Mitchell Lane Pubs., Inc.

Bingham, Jane. The Story of Trains. King, Colin, illus. 2004. (Young Reading Ser.: Vol. 2). 64p. (J). (gr. 2-18). lib. bdg. 13.95 *(978-1-58086-702-3(2)*, Usborne) EDC Publishing.

Cefrey, Holly. The Inventions of Granville Woods: The Railroad Telegraph System & the Third Rail. 2009. (19th Century American Inventors Ser.). 24p. (gr. 2-3). 42.50 *(978-1-60854-952-8(6)*, PowerKids Pr.) Rosen Publishing Group, Inc., The.

Chiu, David. Government Regulation of the Railroads: Fighting Unfair Trade Practicesin America. 2009. (Progressive Movement 1900-1920: Efforts to Reform America's New Industrial Society Ser.). 32p. (gr. 3-4). 47.90 *(978-1-60854-165-2(7))* Rosen Publishing Group, Inc., The.

Clapper, Nikki Bruno. All Aboard! 2015. (All Aboard! Ser.). (ENG.). 24p. (gr. k-1). 106.60 *(978-1-4914-6923-1(4)*, Pebble Plus) Capstone Press of Coughlan Cos.

Coleman, Wim & Perrin, Pat. The Transcontinental Railroad & the Great Race to Connect the Nation. 2006. (Wild History of the American West Ser.). (Illus.). 128p. (J). (gr. 4-10). lib. bdg. 34.60 *(978-1-59845-014-9(X)*, MyReportLinks.com Bks.) Enslow Pubs., Inc.

Curlee, Lynn. Trains. Curlee, Lynn, illus. 2009. (ENG., Illus.). 48p. (J). (gr. 4-6). 19.99 *(978-1-4169-4848-3(1)*, Atheneum Bks. for Young Readers) Simon & Schuster Children's Publishing.

Dooling, Sandra. Last Spike in CPR: Defining Moments in Canadian History. 2011. (Illus.). 32p. (gr. 5-8). *(978-1-77071-689-6(0))* Weigl Educational Pubs. Ltd.

Dunn, Joeming W. Building the Transcontinental Railroad, 1 vol. Espinosa, Rod, illus. 2008. (Graphic History Ser.). (ENG.). 32p. 28.50 *(978-1-60270-180-9(6)*, Graphic Planet-Nonfiction) ABDO Publishing Co.

Dyan, Penelope. The Comeback Kids, Book 12, the Redwood Forest. Weigand, John D., photos by. 2013. (Illus.). 34p. pap. 14.95 *(978-1-61477-081-7(6))* Bellissima Publishing, LLC.

Floca, Brian. Locomotive. Floca, Brian, illus. 2013. (ENG., Illus.). 64p. (J). (gr. -1-5). 17.99 *(978-1-4169-9415-2(7)*, Atheneum/Richard Jackson Bks.) Simon & Schuster Children's Publishing.

Gibson, Karen. The Railroad Comes to America (1820-1830) 2012. (Illus.). 47p. (J). lib. bdg. 29.95 *(978-1-61228-287-9(3))* Mitchell Lane Pubs., Inc.

Gove, Bill. Sky Route to the Quarries: History of the Barre Railroad. 2003. 98p. per. 21.95 *(978-1-931271-12-7(7))* Bondcliff Bks.

Graham, Ian. You Wouldn't Want to Work on the Railroad! (Revised Edition) 2014. (You Wouldn't Want to... Ser.). (ENG.). 32p. (J). lib. bdg. 29.00 *(978-0-531-21178-6(9)*, Watts, Franklin) Scholastic Library Publishing.

Halpern, Monica. Railroad Fever: Building the Transcontinental Railroad 1830-1870. 2004. (Crossroads America Ser.). (ENG., Illus.). 40p. (J). (gr. 5-9). 12.95 *(978-0-7922-6767-6(2)*, National Geographic Children's Bks.) National Geographic Society.

—Railroad Fever: Building the Transcontinental Railroad, 1830-1870. 2004. (Crossroads America Ser.). (ENG., Illus.). 40p. (J). (gr. 5-9). 21.90 *(978-0-7922-6993-9(4)*, National Geographic Children's Bks.) National Geographic Society.

Hansen, Holly T. & Johnson, Jennifer Hunt. Memories of the Railroad, 14 vols. 2003. (Illus.). 21p. 9.95 *(978-0-9741172-3-2(4)*, CMB10) Tapis & Assocs., Inc.

Hemenway, Scott. Anthracite Collieries & Railroads of the Western Middle Field. 2008. *(978-1-931014-08-3(6))* Garrigues Hse. Pubs.

Hodge, Deborah. The Kids Book of Canada's Railway: And How the CPR Was Built. Mantha, John, illus. 2008. (Kids Book Of Ser.). (ENG.). 48p. (J). (gr. 3-7). pap. 14.95 *(978-1-55453-256-8(6))* Kids Can Pr., Ltd. CAN. Dist: Hachette Bk. Group.

Hynson, Colin. A History of Railroads. 2006. (From Past to Present Ser.). (Illus.). 36p. (gr. 3-7). lib. bdg. 26.00 *(978-0-8368-6287-4(2)*, Gareth Stevens Learning Library) Stevens, Gareth Publishing LLLP.

Jarrow, Jesse. Oil, Steel, & Railroads: America's Big Businesses in the Late 1800s. (America's Industrial Society in the 19th Century Ser.). 32p. 2009. (gr. 4-4). 47.90 *(978-1-61511-337-8(1))* 2004. (ENG., Illus.). (gr. 5-8). pap. 10.00 *(978-0-8239-4276-3(7))* Rosen Publishing Group, Inc., The.

Lewis, Norma. Connecting the Coasts: The Race to Build the Transcontinental Railroad, 1 vol. 2014. (Adventures on the American Frontier Ser.). (ENG.). 32p. (gr. 3-4). lib. bdg. 27.32 *(978-1-4914-0186-6(9))* Capstone Press of Coughlan Cos.

Lightfoot, Gordon. Canadian Railroad Trilogy, 1 vol. Wallace, Ian, illus. 2010. (ENG.). 56p. (gr. -1). 24.95 *(978-0-88899-953-5(4))* Groundwood Bks. CAN. Dist: Publishers Group West (PGW).

Lohse, Joyce B. General William Palmer: Railroad Pioneer. 2009. (Now You Know Bio Ser.: 12). (Illus.). 104p. (J). pap. 8.95 *(978-0-86541-092-3(5))* Filter Pr., LLC.

Lynette, Rachel. The Transcontinental Railroad. 2013. (Pioneer Spirit: the Westward Expansion Ser.). 24p. (J). (gr. 3-6). 22.60 *(978-1-4777-0785-2(9))*; (ENG., Illus.). pap. 8.25 *(978-1-4777-0903-0(7))* Rosen Publishing Group, Inc., The. (PowerKids Pr.).

Magram, Hannah Straus. Railroads of the West. 2004. (History of the Old West Ser.). (Illus.). 64p. (YA). (gr. 5-18). lib. bdg. 19.95 *(978-1-59084-073-3(9))* Mason Crest.

Marsh, Carole. The Transcontinental Railroad: The Big Race to the Golden Spike. 2010. (American Milestones Ser.). (Illus.). 28p. (J). pap. 6.99 *(978-0-635-07506-2(7))* Gallopade International.

Marsico, Katie. Trains. 2008. (21st Century Skills Innovation Library: Innovation in Transportation Ser.). (ENG., Illus.). 32p. (gr. 4-8). lib. bdg. 28.50 *(978-1-60279-234-0(8)*, 200164) Cherry Lake Publishing.

Mattern, Joanne. The Birth of the Locomotive (1780-1820) 2012. (Illus.). 47p. (J). (gr. 4-8). lib. bdg. 29.95 *(978-1-61228-286-2(5))* Mitchell Lane Pubs., Inc.

Morris, Neil. Trains. (Past & Present Ser.). (Illus.). 32p. lib. bdg. 24.25 *(978-1-931983-37-2(2))* Chrysalis Education.

Murdico, Suzanne J. Railroads & Steamships: Important Developments in American Transportation. (America's Industrial Society in the 19th Century Ser.). 32p. 2009. (gr. 4-4). 47.90 *(978-1-61511-340-8(1))* 2004. (ENG., Illus.). (J). (gr. 5-8). pap. 10.00 *(978-0-8239-4278-7(3))* Rosen Publishing Group, Inc., The.

Murphy, Jim. Across America on an Emigrant Train. 2003. (ENG., Illus.). 168p. (J). (gr. 5-7). pap. 10.95 *(978-0-395-76483-1(1))* Houghton Mifflin Harcourt Publishing Co.

Nardo, Don. The Golden Spike: How a Photograph Celebrated a Connected Continent. 2015. (Captured History Ser.). (ENG.). 64p. (gr. 5-7). lib. bdg. 34.65 *(978-0-7565-4991-6(4))* Compass Point Bks.

O'Mara, Jack. How Railroads Shaped America. 2009. (Real Life Readers Ser.). 32p. (gr. 4-5). pap. 10.00 *(978-1-4358-0175-2(X)*, Rosen Classroom); (gr. 4-4). 47.90 *(978-1-61511-368-2(1)*, PowerKids Pr.); (J). (gr. 3-4). lib. bdg. 25.25 *(978-1-4358-2993-0(X)*, PowerKids Pr.) Rosen Publishing Group, Inc., The.

Orr, Tamra. The Railroad & the Civil War (1860s) 2012. (J). lib. bdg. 29.95 *(978-1-61228-289-3(X))* Mitchell Lane Pubs., Inc.

Offinoski, Steven. Building the Transcontinental Railroad: An Interactive Engineering Adventure, 1 vol. 2014. (You Choose: Engineering Marvels Ser.). (ENG.). 112p. (gr. 3-4). 31.99 *(978-1-4914-0401-0(9)*, You Choose Bks.) Capstone Press of Coughlan Cos.

Pierce, Alan. Transcontinental Railroad, 1 vol. 2005. (American Moments Ser.). (ENG., Illus.). 48p. 27.07 *(978-1-59197-941-8(2)*, Abdo & Daughters) ABDO Publishing Co.

The Pullman Strike Of 1894. 2006. (American Workers Ser.). (Illus.). 144p. (J). (gr. 5-7). lib. bdg. 26.95 *(978-1-931798-89-1(3))* Reynolds, Morgan Inc.

Rajczak, Michael. The Transcontinental Railroad, Vol. 1. 2014. (What You Didn't Know about History Ser.). (Illus.). 24p. (J). (gr. 2-5). pap. 8.15 *(978-1-4824-0599-6(7))* Stevens, Gareth Publishing LLLP.

Raum, Elizabeth. Orphan Trains: An Interactive History Adventure, 1 vol. (You Choose: History Ser.). (ENG.). 112p. (gr. 3-4). 2011. pap. 6.95 *(978-1-4296-6273-4(5))* 2011. pap. 41.70 *(978-1-4296-6441-7(X))* 2010. 31.99 *(978-1-4296-5479-1(1))* Capstone Press of Coughlan Cos. (You Choose Bks.).

Renehan, Edward J., Jr. The Transcontinental Railroad: The Gateway to the West. 2007. (Milestones in American History Ser.). (Illus.). 120p. (YA). (gr. 7-12). lib. bdg. 35.00 *(978-0-7910-9351-1(4))* Facts On File, Inc.

Richter, Bernd & Richter, Susan. All Aboard the White Pass & Yukon Route Railroad. 2003. 48p. 9.95 *(978-1-931353-11-3(5))* Saddle Pal Creations, Inc.

Roberts, Russell. The Railroad Fuels Westward Expansion (1870s) 2012. (Illus.). 47p. (J). lib. bdg. 29.95 *(978-1-61228-290-9(3))* Mitchell Lane Pubs., Inc.

Shea, Therese. The Transcontinental Railroad: Using Proportions to Solve Problems. (Math for the Real World Ser.). 32p. 2009. (ENG., Illus.). (gr. 6-7). pap. 10.00 *(978-1-4042-6075-7(7))* 2009. (gr. 5-5). 47.90 *(978-1-60851-370-3(X)*, PowerKids Pr.) 2006. (Illus.). (YA). (gr. 5-9). lib. bdg. 25.25 *(978-1-4042-3361-4(X))* Rosen Publishing Group, Inc., The.

Shoup, Kate. Life As an Engineer on the First Railroads in America. 2016. (Life As... Ser.). (ENG.). 32p. (J). (gr. 3-3). pap. 63.48 *(978-1-5026-1088-1(4))* Cavendish Square Publishing.

Sís, Peter. The Train of States. Sís, Peter, illus. 2004. (Illus.). 64p. (J). (gr. 1-18). 17.99 *(978-0-06-057838-1(6))* HarperCollins Pubs.

Staunton, Ted. The Dreadful Truth: Building the Railway. Goff, Brian, illus. 2005. (Dreadful Truth Ser.). (ENG.). 80p. (J). (gr. 3-8). *(978-0-88780-690-2(2))* Formac Publishing Co., Ltd.

Stunkard, Geoff. Rail Mail: A Century of American Railroading on Picture Postcards. 2004. (Illus.). 128p. pap. 17.95 *(978-0-9748216-0-3(8)*, QMP608) Quarter Milestones Publishing.

Tracy, Kathleen. The Railroad Grows into an Industry (1840-1850) 2012. (Illus.). 47p. (J). lib. bdg. 29.95 *(978-1-61228-288-6(1))* Mitchell Lane Pubs., Inc.

The Transcontinental Railroad. 2013. (Pioneer Spirit: the Westward Expansion Ser.). 24p. (J). (gr. 3-6). pap. 49.50 *(978-1-4777-0904-7(5)*, PowerKids Pr.) Rosen Publishing Group, Inc., The.

Uschan, Michael V. The Transcontinental Railroad. 2003. (Landmark Events in American History Ser.). (Illus.). 48p. (J). (gr. 5-12). pap. 14.05 *(978-0-8368-5410-7(1)*, Gareth Stevens Secondary Library) Stevens, Gareth Publishing LLLP.

Uschan, Michael V. & Crewe, Sabrina. The Transcontinental Railroad. 2004. (Events That Shaped America Ser.). (Illus.). 32p. (gr. 3-6). lib. bdg. 26.00 *(978-0-8368-3401-7(1)*, Gareth Stevens Learning Library) Stevens, Gareth Publishing LLLP.

The World's Railroads. 2005. (World's Railroads Ser.). 64p. (gr. 6-12). 55.00 *(978-0-7910-5558-8(2)*, Chelsea Hse.) Facts On File, Inc.

Zimmermann, Karl. The Stourbridge Lion: America's First Locomotive. Walker, Steven, illus. 2012. (ENG.). 32p. (J). (gr. k). 16.95 *(978-1-59078-859-2(1))* Boyds Mills Pr.

Zollitsch, Mike. Buffalo, Rochester, & Pittsburgh Railway: In Color. 2004. (Illus.). 59.95 *(978-1-58248-092-3(3))* Morning Sun Bks., Inc.

RAILROADS—STATIONS

see Railroad Stations

RAILROADS—TRAINS

Amato, William. Bullet Trains. 2009. (High-Tech Vehicles Ser.). 24p. (gr. 2-3). 42.50 *(978-1-61513-304-8(6)*, PowerKids Pr.) Rosen Publishing Group, Inc., The.

—Trenes Bala. 2004. (Vehículos de Alta Tecnología (High-Tech Vehicles) Ser.). (SPA & ENG., Illus.). 24p. (J). (gr. 3-6). lib. bdg. 22.60 *(978-0-8239-6881-7(2)*, Editorial Buenas Letras) Rosen Publishing Group, Inc., The.

—Trenes bala (Bullet Trains) 2009. (Vehículos de alta tecnología (High-Tech Vehicles) Ser.). (SPA.). 24p. (gr. 2-3). 42.50 *(978-1-60854-722-7(1)*, Editorial Buenas Letras) Rosen Publishing Group, Inc., The.

AZ Books, creator. Talking Train. 2012. (Lively Machines Ser.). (ENG., Illus.). 10p. (J). (gr. -1-k). bds. 10.95 *(978-1-61889-325-3(4))* AZ Bks. LLC.

Bergin, Mark. Trains. 2012. (You Can Draw Ser.). (Illus.). 32p. (J). (gr. 1-3). pap. 10.50 *(978-1-4339-7478-6(9))*; lib. bdg. 26.60 *(978-1-4339-7477-9(0))* Stevens, Gareth Publishing LLLP.

Beyer, Mark. Trains of the Past. 2009. (Transportation Through the Ages Ser.). 24p. (gr. 1-1). 42.50 *(978-1-60854-591-9(1)*, PowerKids Pr.) Rosen Publishing Group, Inc., The.

—Trenes del Pasado. 2004. (Transporte Ayer y Hoy (Transportation Through the Ages) Ser.). (SPA & ENG., Illus.). 24p. (J). (gr. 3-6). lib. bdg. 22.60 *(978-0-8239-6852-7(9)*, Editorial Buenas Letras) Rosen Publishing Group, Inc., The.

—Trenes del pasado (Trains of the Past) 2009. (transporte ayer y hoy (Transportation Through the Ages) Ser.). (SPA.). 24p. (gr. 1-2). 42.50 *(978-1-61512-256-1(7)*, Editorial Buenas Letras) Rosen Publishing Group, Inc., The.

Biello, David. Bullet Trains: Inside & Out. 2009. (Technology: Blueprints of the Future Ser.). 48p. (gr. 4-4). 53.00 *(978-1-60853-282-7(8))* Rosen Publishing Group, Inc., The.

—Trenes de Alta Velocidad: Por dentro y por fuera (Bullet Trains: Inside & Out) 2009. (Tecnología: Mapas para el Futuro Ser.). (SPA.). 48p. (gr. 4-4). 53.00 *(978-1-60853-291-9(7)*, Editorial Buenas Letras) Rosen Publishing Group, Inc., The.

Bingham, Jane. The Story of Trains. King, Colin, illus. 2004. (Young Reading Ser.: Vol. 2). 64p. (J). (gr. 2-18). lib. bdg. 13.95 *(978-1-58086-702-3(2)*, Usborne) EDC Publishing.

Bowman, Chris. Trains. 2017. (Mighty Machines in Action Ser.). (ENG., Illus.). 24p. (J). (gr. k-3). lib. bdg. 25.95 *(978-1-62617-610-2(8)*, Blastoff! Readers) Bellwether Media.

Brooks, Felicity, des. Build a Picture Trains Sticker Book. 2012. (Build a Picture Sticker Bks). 24p. (J). pap. 6.99 *(978-0-7945-3261-1(6)*, Usborne) EDC Publishing.

Caravantes, Peggy. The Orphan Trains: A History Perspectives Book. 2013. (Perspectives Library). (ENG., Illus.). 32p. (J). (gr. 4-8). 28.50 *(978-1-62431-420-9(1)*, 202800); pap. 14.21 *(978-1-62431-496-4(1)*, 202802) Cherry Lake Publishing.

Carr, Aaron. Trains. 2014. (Illus.). 24p. (J). *(978-1-4896-3236-4(0))* Weigl Pubs., Inc.

Ciovacco, Justine. All about Trains. 2016. (Let's Find Out! Ser.). 32p. (J). (gr. 3-2). lib. bdg. 24.45 *(978-1-68048-446-5(X))* Rosen Publishing Group, Inc., The.

Clapper, Nikki Bruno. City Trains. 2015. (All Aboard! Ser.). (ENG., Illus.). 24p. (gr. k-1). lib. bdg. 26.65 *(978-1-4914-6037-5(7)*, Pebble Plus) Capstone Press of Coughlan Cos.

—Passenger Trains. 2015. (All Aboard! Ser.). (ENG., Illus.). 24p. (gr. k-1). lib. bdg. 26.65 *(978-1-4914-6040-5(7)*, Pebble Plus) Capstone Press of Coughlan Cos.

Clark, Willow. Trains on the Move. 2010. (Transportation Station Ser.). 24p. (J). (ENG.). pap. 8.25 *(978-1-4358-9750-2(1))*; (Illus.). (gr. 2-5). lib. bdg. 22.60 *(978-1-4358-9331-3(X))* Rosen Publishing Group, Inc., The. (PowerKids Pr.).

Crowther, Robert. Trains: A Pop-Up Railroad Book. Crowther, Robert, illus. 2016. (ENG., Illus.). 10p. (J). (gr. 1-4). 19.99 *(978-0-7636-8129-6(6))* Candlewick Pr.

P
Q
R

David West. Train. 2006. (Illus.). 32p. (J). pap. *(978-1-4109-2564-0(1))* Steck-Vaughn.

Dawson, Emily C. Trains. 2012. (ENG., Illus.). 24p. (J). lib. bdg. 25.65 *(978-1-62031-022-9(8))* Jump! Inc.

Dorling Kindersley Publishing Staff, creator. Train. 2005. (Ultimate Sticker Bks.). (ENG., Illus.). 16p. (J). (gr. k-3). pap. 6.99 *(978-0-7566-1460-7(0),* DK Children) Dorling Kindersley Publishing, Inc.

Eason, Sarah. How Does a High-Speed Train Work? 2010. (How Does It Work? Ser.). 32p. (J). (gr. 3-6). lib. bdg. 26.00 *(978-1-4339-3468-1(X));* (Illus.). pap. 10.50 *(978-1-4339-3469-8(8))* Stevens, Gareth Publishing LLLP. (Gareth Stevens Learning Library).

Editors of Kingfisher. Speedy Trains. 2016. (It's All About... Ser.). (ENG.). 32p. pap. 5.99 *(978-0-7534-7287-3(2),* 9780753472873, Kingfisher) Roaring Brook Pr.

Farndon, John. Stickmen's Guide to Trains & Automobiles. Paul de Quay, John, illus. 2016. (Stickmen's Guides to How Everything Works). (ENG.). 32p. (J). (gr. 3-6). 30.65 *(978-1-4677-9590-6(9))* Lerner Publishing Group.

Frith, Alex. Look Inside Trains. 2015. (Look Inside Board Bks.). (ENG.). 14p. (J). (gr. k-5). 14.99 *(978-0-7945-3448-6(1),* Usborne) EDC Publishing.

Goodman, Susan E. Trains! Doolittle, Michael, illus. 2012. (Step into Reading Ser.). (ENG.). 48p. (J). (gr. 1-4). pap. 3.99 *(978-0-375-86941-9(7),* Random Hse. Bks. for Young Readers) Random Hse. Children's Bks.

—Trains! 2012. (Step into Reading Level 3 Ser.). lib. bdg. 13.55 *(978-0-606-23859-5(X),* Turtleback) Turtleback Bks.

Gordon, Nick. Monster Trains. 2013. (Monster Machines Ser.). (ENG., Illus.). 24p. (J). (gr. k-3). lib. bdg. 25.95 *(978-1-60014-939-9(1),* Blastoff! Readers) Bellwether Media.

Hamilton, Robert M. On a Train. 2012. (Going Places Ser.). (ENG.). 24p. (J). (gr. k-2). pap. 8.15 *(978-1-4339-6283-7(7));* lib. bdg. 22.60 *(978-1-4339-6281-3(0))* Stevens, Gareth Publishing LLLP.

Hanson, Anders. Let's Go by Train, 1 vol. 2008. (Let's Go Ser.). (ENG., Illus.). 24p. (J). (gr. k-3). lib. bdg. 24.21 *(978-1-59928-903-8(2),* SandCastle) ABDO Publishing Co.

Hill, Lee Sullivan. Trains on the Move. 2011. (Lightning Bolt Books Vroom-Vroom Ser.). (ENG., Illus.). 32p. (gr. k-2). lib. bdg. 26.60 *(978-0-7613-3921-2(3))* Lerner Publishing Group.

Hofer, Charles. Bullet Trains. (World's Fastest Machines Ser.). 24p. 2009. (gr. 2-3). 42.50 *(978-1-60854-852-1(X))* 2008. (Illus.). (J). (gr. 3-7). lib. bdg. 22.60 *(978-1-4042-4174-9(4))* Rosen Publishing Group, Inc., The. (PowerKids Pr.).

Isbell, Hannah. Zoom in on Rail Networks. 2017. (Zoom in on Engineering Ser.). 24p. (J). (gr. 2-2). lib. bdg. 22.60 ***(978-0-7660-8709-5(3))*** Enslow Pubs., Inc.

Jacob, Ellen, et al. My Train Book. Vandenberg, Michael, photos by. 2007. (ENG., Illus.). 16p. (J). (gr. -1-k). bds. 6.99 *(978-0-06-089970-7(0),* Collins) HarperCollins Pubs.

Johnstone, Michael, et al. Trains. (ENG., Illus.). 32p. (J). mass mkt. 8.99 *(978-0-590-24654-5(2))* Scholastic, Inc.

Juettner, Bonnie. Hybrid Cars. 2009. (Great Idea Ser.). (Illus.). 48p. (J). (gr. 4-6). lib. bdg. 26.60 *(978-1-59953-193-9(3))* Norwood Hse. Pr.

Kate Shelley & the Midnight Express. 9.95 *(978-1-59112-169-5(8))* Live Oak Media.

Kluth, Paula & Kluth, Victoria. "A Is for All Aboard!", 1 vol. Littlejohn, Brad, illus. 2009. (ENG.). 32p. (J). 16.95 *(978-1-59857-071-7(4))* Brookes Publishing.

Leighton, Christina. Freight Trains. 2017. (Amazing Trains Ser.). (ENG., Illus.). 24p. (J). (gr. k-3). lib. bdg. 25.95 ***(978-1-62617-670-6(1),*** Blastoff! Readers) Bellwether Media.

—High-Speed Trains. 2017. (Amazing Trains Ser.). (ENG., Illus.). 24p. (J). (gr. k-3). lib. bdg. 25.95 ***(978-1-62617-671-3(X),*** Blastoff! Readers) Bellwether Media.

—Passenger Trains. 2017. (Amazing Trains Ser.). (ENG., Illus.). 24p. (J). (gr. k-3). lib. bdg. 25.95 ***(978-1-62617-673-7(6),*** Blastoff! Readers) Bellwether Media.

Litchfield, Jo & Brooks, F. Trains. 2004. (Chunky Board Bks.). (ENG., Illus.). 6p. (J). bds. 4.95 *(978-0-7945-0348-2(9),* Usborne) EDC Publishing.

Lock, Deborah & Dorling Kindersley Publishing Staff. Train Travel, Level 1. 2013. (DK Readers Ser.). (ENG.). 32p. (J). (gr. k-4). pap. 3.99 *(978-1-4654-0892-1(4),* DK Children) Dorling Kindersley Publishing, Inc.

MacArthur, Collin. Inside a High-Speed Train. 2014. (Life in the Fast Lane Ser.). (Illus.). 48p. (J). (gr. 4-6). 31.36 *(978-1-62713-043-1(8))* Cavendish Square Publishing.

Mara, Wil. From Kingfishers to... Bullet Trains. 2012. (21st Century Skills Innovation Library: Innovations from Nature Ser.). (ENG.). 32p. (gr. 4-8). 28.50 *(978-1-61080-498-1(8),* 202108); pap. 14.21 *(978-1-61080-672-5(7),* 202282) Cherry Lake Publishing.

Maynard, Christopher. High-Speed Trains. 2003. (Need for Speed Ser.). (Illus.). 32p. (J). (gr. 3-6). pap. 7.95 *(978-0-8225-0390-3(5))* Lerner Publishing Group.

—Trains. 2005. (Need for Speed Ser.). (Illus.). 32p. (gr. 3-5). lib. bdg. 23.93 *(978-0-8225-0387-3(5))* Lerner Publishing Group.

McMahon, Peter. Ultimate Trains. Mora, Andy, illus. 2010. (Machines of the Future Ser.). (ENG.). 40p. (J). (gr. 4-7). 16.95 *(978-1-55453-366-4(X))* Kids Can Pr., Ltd. CAN. Dist: Hachette Bk. Group.

Murray, Julie, et al. Trenes. 2015. (Medios de Transporte Ser.). (SPA.). 24p. (gr. k-1). pap. 7.95 *(978-1-4966-0495-8(4))* Capstone Classroom.

Oxlade, Chris. Trains. 2009. (Mighty Machines Ser.). (Illus.). 31p. (J). (gr. 4-7). pap. 7.95 *(978-1-59920-258-7(1))* Black Rabbit Bks.

Oxlade, Chris & Farndon, John. Stickmen's Guide to Trains & Automobiles. Pyke, Jerry & Quay, John Paul de, illus. 2016. (Stickmen's Guides to How Everything Works). (ENG.). 32p. (J). (gr. 3-6). lib. bdg. 26.65 *(978-1-4677-9360-5(4))* Lerner Publishing Group.

Peters, Elisa. Let's Take the Train! 2014. (Public Transportation Ser.). (Illus.). 24p. (J). (gr. k-2). pap. 49.50 *(978-1-4777-6514-2(X),* PowerKids Pr.) Rosen Publishing Group, Inc., The.

—¡Vamos a Tomar el Tren! / Let's Take the Train! de la Vega, Eida, ed. 2014. (Transporte Público / Public Transportation Ser.). (SPA & ENG.). 24p. (J). (gr. k-2). 23.60 *(978-1-4777-6781-8(9),* PowerKids Pr.) Rosen Publishing Group, Inc., The.

Plourde, Lynn. Storytime Stickers: Choo Choo Trains. Cerato, Mattia, illus. 2011. (Storytime Stickers Ser.). (ENG.). 16p. (J). (gr. k). pap. 5.95 *(978-1-4027-8186-5(5))* Sterling Publishing Co., Inc.

Priddy, Roger. My Big Train Book. 2015. (My Big Board Bks.). (ENG.). 10p. (J). (gr. -1 — 1). bds. 7.99 *(978-0-312-51943-8(5),* 9780312519438, Priddy Bks.) St. Martin's Pr.

Prior, Jennifer. All Aboard! How Trains Work, 1 vol. 2nd rev. ed. 2014. (TIME for KIDS(r) Nonfiction Readers Ser.). (ENG., Illus.). 28p. (J). (gr. 3-3). pap. 25.96 *(978-1-4807-1071-9(7))* Shell Educational Publishing.

Prunier, James. Trains. Grant, Donald & Prunier, James, illus. 2012. (ENG.). 34p. (J). (gr. -1-k). spiral bd. 14.99 *(978-1-85103-400-0(5))* Moonlight Publishing, Ltd. GBR. Dist: Independent Pubs. Group.

Radtke, Becky. Trains Activity Book. 2007. (Dover Little Activity Bks.). (ENG., Illus.). 64p. (J). (gr. k-3). per. 1.99 *(978-0-486-45683-6(8))* Dover Pubns., Inc.

Rau, Dana Meachen. Trains. 2009. (Bookworms Ser.). 24p. (gr. k-1). 15.95 *(978-0-7614-4081-9(X))* Marshall Cavendish Corp.

—Trains/En Trenes. 2009. (Bookworms Ser.). (SPA & ENG.). 24p. (gr. k-1). lib. bdg. 15.95 *(978-0-7614-4773-3(3))* Marshall Cavendish Corp.

Richardson, Adele D. Freight Trains in Action, 1 vol. 2011. (Transportation Zone Ser.). (ENG.). 24p. (gr. 1-2). lib. bdg. 25.32 *(978-1-4296-6828-6(8),* First Facts) Capstone Press of Coughlan Cos.

Riggs, Kate. Bullet Trains. 2015. (J). *(978-1-60818-519-1(2),* Creative Education) Creative Co., The.

—Seedlings: Bullet Trains. 2015. (Seedlings Ser.). (ENG.). 24p. (J). (gr. -1-1). pap. 7.99 *(978-1-62832-119-7(9),* Creative Paperbacks) Creative Co., The.

—Trains. 2007. (My First Look at: Vehicles Ser.). (Illus.). 24p. (J). (gr. -1-3). lib. bdg. 24.25 *(978-1-58341-529-0(7),* Creative Education) Creative Co., The.

Roza, Greg. The Incredible Story of Trains. 2004. (Kid's Guide to Incredible Technology Ser.). (Illus.). 24p. (J). lib. bdg. 22.60 *(978-0-8239-6712-4(3),* PowerKids Pr.) Rosen Publishing Group, Inc., The.

Ryan, Phillip. Passenger Trains. 2010. (All Aboard! Ser.). (ENG.). 24p. (J). pap. 8.25 *(978-1-4488-1215-8(1));* lib. bdg. 22.60 *(978-1-4488-0637-9(2))* Rosen Publishing Group, Inc., The. (PowerKids Pr.).

Schuh, Mari. Trains. 2017. (Transportation Ser.). (ENG.). 24p. (gr. k-1). pap. 6.95 ***(978-1-5157-7308-5(6),*** Pebble Bks.) Capstone Press of Coughlan Cos.

Sheffield, S. A Train on the Track: Learning the TR Sound. 2009. (PowerPhonics Ser.). 24p. (gr. 1-1). 39.90 *(978-1-60851-430-4(7),* PowerKids Pr.) Rosen Publishing Group, Inc., The.

Shields, Amy. Trains (1 Hardcover/1 CD) 2016. (National Geographic Readers: Pre-Reader Ser.). (ENG.). (J). *(978-1-4301-2120-6(3))* Live Oak Media.

—Trains (1 Paperback/1 CD) 2016. (National Geographic Readers: Pre-Reader Ser.). (ENG.). (J). pap. *(978-1-4301-2119-0(X))* Live Oak Media.

Silverman, Buffy. How Do Trains Work? 2016. (Lightning Bolt Books (tm) — How Vehicles Work Ser.). (ENG.). 32p. (J). (gr. 1-3). 26.65 *(978-1-4677-9500-5(3))* Lerner Publishing Group.

Smithyman, Kathryn & Kalman, Bobbie. Trains on the Tracks. rev. ed. 2007. (Vehicles on the Move Ser.). (ENG., Illus.). 32p. (J). (gr. 1-5). pap. *(978-0-7787-3059-0(X))* Crabtree Publishing Co.

—Trenes en las Vias. 2007. (Vehículos en Acción Ser.). (SPA & ENG., Illus.). 32p. (J). lib. bdg. *(978-0-7787-8307-7(3));* (gr. 4-7). pap. *(978-0-7787-8317-6(0))* Crabtree Publishing Co.

Spaight, Anne J. Trains on the Go. 2016. (Bumba Books (tm) — Machines That Go Ser.). (ENG., Illus.). 24p. (J). (gr. -1-1). lib. bdg. 25.32 *(978-1-5124-1447-9(6))* Lerner Publishing Group.

—Trenes en Accion. 2017. (Bumba Books (tm) en Español — Máquinas en Acción (Machines That Go) Ser.). (SPA & ENG., Illus.). 24p. (J). (gr. -1-1). pap. 6.99 ***(978-1-5124-2977-0(5))*** Lerner Publishing Group.

Spaight, Anne J. Trenes en Accion (Trains on the Go) 2017. (Bumba Books (tm) en Español — Máquinas en Acción (Machines That Go) Ser.). (SPA & ENG., Illus.). 24p. (J). (gr. -1-1). lib. bdg. 25.32 *(978-1-5124-2881-0(7))* Lerner Publishing Group.

Thomas, Mary Ann. Our Train Trip: Learning to Add Times by the Half Hour. 2009. (Math for the REAL World Ser.). 12p. (gr. 1-2). pap. 5.90 *(978-0-8239-8849-5(X),* Rosen Classroom) Rosen Publishing Group, Inc., The.

Turnbull, Stephanie. Trains. 2009. (Discovery History Ser.). 48p. (YA). (gr. 3-18). 8.99 *(978-0-7945-2246-9(7),* Usborne) EDC Publishing.

Veitch, Catherine. Big Machines Ride Rails!, 1 vol. 2014. (Big Machines Ser.). (ENG.). 24p. (gr. k-1). 23.32 *(978-1-4846-0589-9(6),* Heinemann Read & Learn) Heinemann-Raintree.

West, David. Trains. 2014. (Mechanic Mike's Machines Ser.). 24p. (gr. k-3). 28.50 *(978-1-62588-060-4(X))* Black Rabbit Bks.

RAILROADS, UNDERGROUND

see Subways

RAILROADS—VOCATIONAL GUIDANCE

Otfinoski, Steven. High-Speed Trains: From Concept to Consumer. 2015. (ENG.). 64p. (J). lib. bdg. *(978-0-531-21899-0(6),* Orchard Bks.) Scholastic, Inc.

RAILWAYS

see Railroads

RAIN AND RAINFALL

see also Floods; Meteorology; Snow; Storms

Anderson, Judith. Once There Was a Raindrop. Gordon, Mike, illus. 2010. (Nature's Miracles Ser.). (ENG.). 32p. (J). (gr. -1-2). pap. 5.99 *(978-0-7641-4495-0(2))* Barron's Educational Series, Inc.

Appleby, Alex. It's Rainy! 2013. (What's the Weather? Ser.). (Illus.). 24p. (J). (gr. k-2). pap. 48.90 *(978-1-4339-9398-5(8));* pap. 8.15 *(978-1-4339-9397-8(X));* (ENG., lib. bdg. 22.60 *(978-1-4339-9396-1(1))* Stevens, Gareth Publishing LLLP.

—It's Rainy! / Est Lloviendo! 2013. (What's the Weather? / Qu Tiempo Hace? Ser.). (SPA & ENG., Illus.). 24p. (J). (gr. k-2). 22.60 *(978-1-4339-9460-9(7))* Stevens, Gareth Publishing LLLP.

Bauer, Marion Dane & Wallace, John. Rain. Wallace, John, illus. 2004. (Weather Ready-To-Reads Ser.). (ENG., Illus.). 32p. (J). (gr. -1-1). pap. 3.99 *(978-0-689-85439-2(0),* Simon Spotlight) Simon Spotlight.

Bauman, Carey. God Controls the Storm. Bauman, Carey, tr. 2007. (Little Jewel Book Ser.). (Illus.). 24p. (J). (gr. 2). pap. 2.70 *(978-0-7399-2396-2(X))* Rod & Staff Pubs., Inc.

Berne, Emma. From River to Raindrop: The Water Cycle. 2017. (Start to Finish, Second Ser.). (ENG.). (J). (gr. k-3). pap. 6.99 ***(978-1-5124-5623-3(3))*** Lerner Publishing Group.

Berne, Emma Carlson. From River to Raindrop: The Water Cycle. 2017. (Start to Finish, Second Ser.). (ENG.). 24p. (J). (gr. k-3). 23.99 ***(978-1-5124-3442-2(6))*** Lerner Publishing Group.

Boerger, Kristin & Boyett, Suzi. Let's Read about Rain. 2007. (Let's Read about Weather Ser.). (Illus.). 12p. (gr. -1-2). lib. bdg. 15.00 *(978-0-8368-7805-9(1),* Weekly Reader Leveled Readers) Stevens, Gareth Publishing LLLP.

—Llueve. 2007. (Que tiempo hace? (Let's Read about Weather) Ser.). (Illus.). 12p. (J). (gr. -1-2). (SPA.). pap. 4.10 *(978-0-8368-8118-9(4));* (ENG & SPA., lib. bdg. 15.00 *(978-0-8368-8113-4(3))* Stevens, Gareth Publishing LLLP. (Weekly Reader Leveled Readers).

Boothroyd, Jennifer. What Is Today's Weather? 2014. (First Step Nonfiction - Let's Watch the Weather Ser.). (Illus.). 24p. (gr. k-2). pap. 6.95 *(978-1-4677-4500-0(6));* (ENG., lib. bdg. 23.93 *(978-1-4677-3916-0(2),* Lerner Pubns.) Lerner Publishing Group.

Branley, Franklyn M. Down Comes the Rain. Fraser, Mary Ann, illus. 2017. (Let's-Read-And-Find-Out Science 2 Ser.). 40p. (J). (gr. -1-3). pap. 6.99 *(978-0-06-238663-2(8))* HarperCollins Pubs.

Bundey, Nikki. Rain & People. 2005. (Science of Weather Ser.). (Illus.). 32p. (gr. 4-6). lib. bdg. 21.27 *(978-1-57505-494-0(9))* Lerner Publishing Group.

—Rain & the Earth. 2005. (Science of Weather Ser.). (Illus.). 32p. (gr. 4-6). lib. bdg. 21.27 *(978-1-57505-469-8(8))* Lerner Publishing Group.

Chambers, Catherine. Rain & Life in a Nigerian Village. 2010. (Big Picture: Climate Ser.). (ENG.). 24p. (gr. 1-2). pap. 41.70 *(978-1-4296-5825-6(8),* First Facts) Capstone Press of Coughlan Cos.

Clay, Kathryn. Rain Showers. 2016. (Celebrate Spring Ser.). (ENG., Illus.). 24p. (gr. k-1). lib. bdg. 21.99 *(978-1-4914-8303-9(2),* Pebble Bks.) Capstone Press of Coughlan Cos.

Collins, Betsy. Raindrops. Cotton, Lisa, illus. 2008. 28p. pap. 13.99 *(978-1-4343-7062-4(3))* AuthorHouse.

Coster, Patience. Rain & Floods. 2010. (Weatherwise Ser.). 32p. (ENG.). (J). pap. 10.60 *(978-1-61532-274-9(4),* PowerKids Pr.); (Illus.). (YA). (gr. 3-6). lib. bdg. 26.50 *(978-1-61532-261-9(2))* Rosen Publishing Group, Inc., The.

Cox Cannons, Helen. Rain, 1 vol. 2014. (Weather Wise Ser.). (ENG., Illus.). 24p. (gr. -1-1). pap. 5.99 *(978-1-4846-0555-4(1),* Acorn) Heinemann-Raintree.

D'Aubuisson, Elisabeth. Rainy Days. 2007. (What's the Weather? Ser.). (Illus.). 24p. (J). (gr. 3-7). lib. bdg. 22.60 *(978-1-4042-3682-0(1),* PowerKids Pr.) Rosen Publishing Group, Inc., The.

d'Aubuisson, Elisabeth. Rainy Days. 2009. (What's the Weather? Ser.). 24p. (gr. 2-3). 42.50 *(978-1-60854-775-3(2),* PowerKids Pr.) Rosen Publishing Group, Inc., The.

Doherty, Gillian. Rainy Day. 2005. (First Discovery Ser.). 24p. (J). 9.99 *(978-0-7945-0867-8(7),* Usborne) EDC Publishing.

Donnelly, Karen J. Droughts of the Past & the Future. 2003. (Earth's Changing Weather & Climate Ser.). (Illus.). 24p. (J). lib. bdg. 22.60 *(978-0-8239-6217-4(2),* PowerKids Pr.) Rosen Publishing Group, Inc., The.

Doubleday Entertainment USA - Weather Watch: Rain. 2006. (J). per. 7.95 *(978-1-59566-230-9(8));* per. 7.95 *(978-1-59566-231-6(6))* QEB Publishing Inc.

Doudna, Kelly. It Is Raining, 1 vol. 2003. (Weather Ser.). (ENG., Illus.). 24p. (J). (gr. k-3). lib. bdg. 24.21 *(978-1-57765-774-3(8),* SandCastle) ABDO Publishing Co.

Edison, Erin. Rain, 1 vol. 2011. (Weather Basics Ser.). (ENG.). 24p. (gr. k-1). pap. 7.29 *(978-1-4296-7079-1(7));* pap. 41.70 *(978-1-4296-7084-5(3));* lib. bdg. 26.65 *(978-1-4296-6055-6(4))* Capstone Press of Coughlan Cos. (Pebble Plus).

Edison, Erin & Saunders-Smith, Gail. Lluvia. Strictly Spanish LLC. Staff, tr. from ENG. 2013. (Lo Básico Sobre el Tiempo/Weather Basics Ser.).Tr. of Rain. (SPA, ENG & MUL.). 24p. (gr. k-1). lib. bdg. 26.65 *(978-1-62065-165-0(3))* Capstone Press of Coughlan Cos.

Firely, G. M. The Raindrop. Holmes, Joshua D., illus. 2004. 21p. pap. 24.95 *(978-1-4137-3388-4(3))* PublishAmerica, Inc.

Ganeri, Anita. Rain. 2004. (Weather Around You Ser.). (Illus.). 24p. (gr. 1-4). pap. 8.15 *(978-0-8368-4304-0(5));* lib. bdg. 22.00 *(978-0-8368-4299-9(5))* Stevens, Gareth Publishing LLLP. (Weekly Reader Leveled Readers).

Ghigna, Charles. Raindrops Fall All Around. Watson, Laura, illus. 2015. (Springtime Weather Wonders Ser.). (ENG.). 24p. (gr. -1-2). lib. bdg. 21.99 *(978-1-4795-6030-1(8))* Picture Window Bks.

—Springtime Weather Wonders. Watson, Laura, illus. 2015. (Springtime Weather Wonders Ser.). (ENG.). 24p. (gr. -1-2). lib. bdg. 87.96 *(978-1-4795-6045-5(6))* Picture Window Bks.

Gibbons, Gail. It's Raining! Gibbons, Gail, illus. (ENG., Illus.). 32p. (J). (gr. -1-3). 2015. 7.99 *(978-0-8234-3303-2(X))* 2014. 17.95 *(978-0-8234-2924-0(5))* Holiday Hse., Inc.

—It's Raining! (1 Hardcover/1 CD) 2016. (ENG.). (J). (gr. k-3). audio compact disk 29.95 *(978-1-4301-2179-4(3))* Live Oak Media.

—It's Raining! (1 Paperback/1 CD) 2016. (ENG.). (J). (gr. k-3). audio compact disk 19.95 *(978-1-4301-2178-7(5))* Live Oak Media.

—It's Raining! (4 Paperbacks/1 CD) 2016. (ENG.). (J). (gr. k-3). audio compact disk 44.95 *(978-1-4301-2180-0(7))* Live Oak Media.

Hansen, Grace. La Lluvia. 2016. (Clima Ser.). (SPA.). 24p. (J). (gr. 1-6). pap. 7.95 *(978-1-4966-0693-8(0))* Capstone Classroom.

—Rain, 1 vol. 2016. (ENG., Illus.). 24p. *(978-1-62970-932-1(8))* ABDO Publishing Co.

Herriges, Ann. Rain. 2006. (Rain Ser.). (Illus.). 24p. (J). (gr. k-3). pap. 6.99 *(978-0-531-17879-9(X),* Blastoff! Readers) Bellwether Media.

—Rain. 2011. (Blastoff! Readers Ser.). 24p. (J). pap. 5.95 *(978-0-531-27622-8(8),* Children's Pr.) Scholastic Library Publishing.

Higgins, Nadia. It's Raining!, 1 vol. Ward, Damian, illus. 2010. (Weather Watchers Ser.). (ENG.). 32p. (J). (gr. k-3). 28.50 *(978-1-60270-733-7(2))* Magic Wagon.

Hirschmann, Kris. It's Wet Out!, 1 vol. 2008. (What's It Like Out? Ser.). (ENG.). 32p. (gr. k-6). 27.07 *(978-1-59928-944-1(X),* Checkerboard Library) ABDO Publishing Co.

Hoffmann, Sara E. Ana & the Rainy Day. Strange, Katie, illus. 2013. (My Reading Neighborhood: First-Grade Sight Word Stories Ser.). (ENG.). 16p. (gr. -1-1). pap. 5.95 *(978-1-4677-1174-6(8))* Lerner Publishing Group.

Holden, Pam. Water from Rain. 2015. (ENG., Illus.). 16p. (-1). pap. *(978-1-77654-084-6(0),* Red Rocket Readers) Flying Start Bks.

I Feel Cold: Individual Title Six-Packs. (gr. -1-2). 23.00 *(978-0-7635-9015-4(0))* Rigby Education.

Jango-Cohen, Judith. Why Does It Rain? Feltes, Tess, illus. (On My Own Science Ser.). 2006. 47p. (J). (gr. k-3). per. 6.95 *(978-1-57505-854-2(5))* 2005. (ENG.). 48p. (gr. 2-4). lib. bdg. 25.26 *(978-1-57505-762-0(X))* Lerner Publishing Group. (Millbrook Pr.).

Jennings, Terry J. The Weather: Rain. 2004. (J). lib. bdg. 27.10 *(978-1-59389-143-5(1))* Chrysalis Education.

Kaner, Etta. Who Likes the Rain? Lafrance, Marie, illus. 2007. (Exploring the Elements Ser.). (ENG.). 32p. (J). (gr. -1-2). 14.95 *(978-1-55337-841-9(5))* Kids Can Pr., Ltd. CAN. Dist: Hachette Bk. Group.

Landman, Tanya. A Drop of Rain Green Band. Tait, Carys, illus. 2016. (Cambridge Reading Adventures Ser.). (ENG.). 16p. pap. 6.56 *(978-1-107-55060-5(2))* Cambridge Univ. Pr.

Lazo, Caroline Evensen. Frank Gehry. 2005. (First Step Nonfiction Ser.). (Illus.). 112p. (J). (gr. 3-7). lib. bdg. 29.27 *(978-0-8225-2649-0(2),* Lerner Pubns.) Lerner Publishing Group.

MacDonald, Margaret. Rain. 2011. (Learn-Abouts Ser.). (Illus.). 16p. (J). pap. 7.95 *(978-1-59920-649-3(8))* Black Rabbit Bks.

Mara, Wil. Why Does It Rain? 2009. (Tell Me Why, Tell Me How Ser.). 32p. (gr. 3-18). 29.93 *(978-0-7614-3991-2(9))* Marshall Cavendish Corp.

Nelson, Robin. El Ciclo Del Agua. 2003. (SPA.). 23p. (J). pap. 5.95 *(978-0-8225-4824-9(0),* Lerner Pubns.) Lerner Publishing Group.

—El Ciclo Del Agua (Earth's Water Cycle) 2012. (Mi Primer Paso Al Mundo Real - Descubriendo Los Ciclos de la Naturaleza (First Step Nonfiction - Discovering Nature's Cycles) Ser.) (ENG & SPA., Illus.). 24p. (gr. k-2). pap. 6.95 *(978-0-7613-9348-1(X),* Ediciones Lerner) Lerner Publishing Group.

—Un Dia Lluvioso. Translations.com Staff, tr. from ENG. 2006. (Mi Primer Paso Al Mundo Real - el Estado Del Tiempo (First Step Nonfiction - Weather) Ser.). (SPA., Illus.). 24p. (gr. k-2). lib. bdg. 23.93 *(978-0-8225-6211-5(1),* Ediciones Lerner) Lerner Publishing Group.

—Un Día lluvioso (A Rainy Day) 2006. (Mi Primer Paso al Mundo Real Ser.). (Illus.). 23p. (J). (gr. -1-3). per. 4.25 *(978-0-8225-6550-5(1),* Ediciones Lerner) Lerner Publishing Group.

—Rainy. (First Step Nonfiction - Kinds of Weather Ser.). (ENG., 8p. (gr. -1-1). 2015. Illus.). 11.99 *(978-1-5124-1037-2(3))* 2005. pap. 4.95 *(978-0-8225-5365-6(1),* Lerner Pubns.) Lerner Publishing Group.

—The Water Cycle. 2003. (First Step Nonfiction Ser.). (Illus.). 24p. (J). (gr. k-2). lib. bdg. 18.60 *(978-0-8225-4596-5(9))* Lerner Publishing Group.

Nelson, Robin & National Geographic Learning Staff. A Rainy Day. 2010. (Rise & Shine Ser.). (ENG., Illus.). 24p. (C). (gr. k-2). pap. 11.95 *(978-0-8225-1962-1(3))* National Geographic School Publishing, Inc.

O'Connell, Bailey. Earth's Rainiest Places. 2015. (Earth's Most Extreme Places Ser.). (ENG.). 24p. (J). (gr. 2-3). pap. 8.15 *(978-1-4824-1910-8(6))* Stevens, Gareth Publishing LLLP.

Perish, Patrick. What Makes It Rain? 2016. (Everyday Earth Science Ser.). (ENG.). 24p. (J). (gr. k-3). 27.07 *(978-1-5038-0795-2(9),* 210630) Child's World, Inc., The.

Plattner, Josh & Craig, Diane. Hail or Freezing Rain?, 1 vol. 2016. (This or That? Weather Ser.). (ENG., Illus.). 24p. (J). (gr. k-4). 25.65 *(978-1-62403-954-6(5))* ABDO Publishing Co.

Posner, Renee & Quinton, Sasha. Suzy Season Loves Fall. D'Argo, Laura, illus. 2003. (Be Mine Bears Ser.). (J). bds. 4.99 *(978-1-58209-352-9(0))* Bks. Are Fun, Ltd.

Purslow, Frances. Precipitation. 2015. (Illus.). 24p. (J). *(978-1-5105-0054-9(5));* pap. *(978-1-5105-0286-4(6))* SmartBook Media, Inc.

—Precipitation. 2016. (J). ***(978-1-4896-5797-8(5))*** Weigl Pubs., Inc.

Rain, Snow, & Hail: Individual Title Six-Packs. (Discovery World Ser.). 16p. (gr. 1-2). 28.00 *(978-0-7635-8466-5(5))* Rigby Education.

René, Ellen. Investigating Why It Rains. 2009. (Science Detectives Ser.). 24p. (gr. 2-3). 42.50 *(978-1-60853-016-8(7),* PowerKids Pr.); (Illus.). (J). lib. bdg. 22.60 *(978-1-4042-4483-2(2))* Rosen Publishing Group, Inc., The.

Reyes, Sonja. Looks Like Rain! What's the Problem? 2017. (Computer Science for the Real World Ser.). 8p. (gr. 5-6). pap. 6.20 ***(978-1-5383-5028-7(9),*** Rosen Classroom) Rosen Publishing Group, Inc., The.

Rustad, Martha E. H. Today Is a Rainy Day. 2017. (What Is the Weather Today? Ser.). (ENG., Illus.). 24p. (gr. k-1). lib. bdg. 21.99 *(978-1-5157-4921-9(5));* pap. 6.29 *(978-1-4966-0944-1(1))* Capstone Press of Coughlan Cos. (Pebble Bks.).

Sayre, April Pulley. Raindrops Roll. Sayre, April Pulley, photos by. 2015. (ENG., Illus.). 40p. (J). (gr. -1-3). 17.99 *(978-1-4814-2064-8(X),* Beach Lane Bks.) Beach Lane Bks.

Selwyn, Josephine. How Do You Measure Rain & Wind? 2014. (Little Books of Answers: Level F Ser.). (Illus.). 16p. (gr. k-2). pap. 7.95 *(978-1-927136-56-0(3))* Three Crows Media NZL. Dist: RiverStream Publishing.

Sévigny, Eric, illus. Caillou & the Rain. 2012. (Clubhouse Ser.). (ENG.). 24p. (J). (gr. -1-1). pap. 3.99 (978-2-89450-870-1(0)) Caillouet, Gerry.

Sherman, Josepha. Flakes & Flurries: A Book about Snow, 1 vol. Yesh, Jeff, illus. 2003. (Amazing Science: Weather Ser.). (ENG.). 24p. (gr. -1-3). per. 8.95 (978-1-4048-0342-8(4)) Picture Window Bks.

—Splish! Splash! A Book about Rain, 1 vol. Yesh, Jeff, illus. 2003. (Amazing Science: Weather Ser.). (ENG.). 24p. (gr. -1-3). per. 8.95 (978-1-4048-0339-8(4)) Picture Window Bks.

Slade, Suzanne. A Raindrop's Journey, 1 vol. Conger, Holli, illus. (Follow It! Ser.). (ENG.). 24p. (gr. 1-3). 2011. pap. 7.49 (978-1-4048-6712-3(0)) 2010. lib. bdg. 26.65 (978-1-4048-6266-1(8)) Picture Window Bks.

Solanet & Bergandi. ¿Que Hace Llover? (Coleccion Primeros Pasos en la Ciencia). (SPA., Illus.). 176p. (J). (gr. 1-3). (978-950-724-017-1(9), LMA8215) Lumen ARG. Dist: Lectorum Pubns., Inc.

Staunton, Ted & Clark, Brenda. L' Homme De Boue, Mini Bk. (FRE.). (J). pap. 3.99 (978-0-590-74821-6(1)) Scholastic, Inc.

Sterling, Kristin. It's Rainy Today. 2009. (Lightning Bolt Books — What's the Weather Like? Ser.). (ENG., Illus.). 32p. (gr. k-2). 26.60 (978-0-7613-4257-1(5), Lerner Pubns.); pap. 7.95 (978-0-7613-5020-0(9)) Lerner Publishing Group.

Stewart, Melissa. Droughts. Ceolin, Andre, illus. 2017. (Let's-Read-And-Find-Out Science 2 Ser.). 40p. (J). (gr. -1-3). pap. 6.99 **(978-0-06-238665-6(4))** HarperCollins Pubs.

Stewart, Melissa. When Rain Falls, 1 vol. Bergum, Constance R., illus. 2008. (ENG.). 32p. (J). (gr. k-3). 16.95 (978-1-56145-438-9(9)) Peachtree Pubs.

Trueit, Trudi Strain. Rainy Days. 2009. (Benchmark Rebus: Weather Watch Ser.). 24p. (gr. k-1). 15.95 (978-0-7614-4012-3(7)) Marshall Cavendish GBR. Dist: Marshall Cavendish Corp.

Vastola, P. Rain: Learning the AI Sound. 2009. (PowerPhonics Ser.). 24p. (gr. 1-1). 39.90 (978-1-60851-469-4(2), PowerKids Pr.) Rosen Publishing Group, Inc., The.

Williams, Judith. How Come It's Raining? 2015. (How Does Weather Happen? Ser.). 24p. (J). (gr. k-3). pap. 7.95 (978-0-7660-6381-5(X)); lib. bdg. 22.60 (978-0-7660-6380-8(1)) Enslow Pubs., Inc. (Enslow Elementary).

—Why Is It Raining? 2005. (I Like Weather! Ser.). (Illus.). 24p. (J). lib. bdg. 22.60 (978-0-7660-2318-5(4), Enslow Elementary) Enslow Pubs., Inc.

Wilson, Abby. What Makes Rain? 2013. (Nature's Super Secrets Ser.). 24p. (gr. 1-3). 22.60 (978-1-4339-8170-8(X)); pap. 8.15 (978-1-4339-8171-5(8)) Stevens, Gareth Publishing LLLP.

RAIN AND RAINFALL—FICTION

Abuhamda, Nasser. A Flower in the Rain. 2009. 40p. pap. 14.95 (978-1-59858-879-8(6)) Dog Ear Publishing, LLC.

Adams, Peter. Why Rain & Fire Are Enemies. 2009. 28p. pap. 21.99 (978-1-4415-4317-2(1)) Xlibris Corp.

Albert, Burton. Windsongs & Rainbows. 2008. (ENG.). 28p. (J). 11.99 (978-1-4169-7122-1(X), Simon & Schuster/Paula Wiseman Bks.) Simon & Schuster/Paula Wiseman Bks.

Alley, R. W. Clark in the Deep Sea. 2016. (ENG., Illus.). 32p. (J). (gr. -1-3). 14.99 (978-0-547-90692-8(7)) Houghton Mifflin Harcourt Publishing Co.

Alumenda, Stephen. Toko & the Lost Kittens. 2004. (Illus.). 24p. pap. (978-9966-25-170-1(7)) Heinemann Kenya, Limited (East African Educational Publishers Ltd E.A.E.P.) KEN. Dist: Michigan State Univ. Pr.

Ashman, Linda. Rain! Robinson, Christian, illus. (ENG.). (J). 2017. 30p. (— 1). bds. 7.99 (978-0-544-88037-5(4), HMH Books For Young Readers) 2013. 32p. (gr. -1-3). 16.99 (978-0-547-73395-1(X)) Houghton Mifflin Harcourt Publishing Co.

Atteberry, Kevan. Puddles!!! Atteberry, Kevan, illus. 2016. (Illus.). 32p. (J). (gr. -1-3). 14.99 (978-0-06-230784-2(3), Tegen, Katherine Bks) HarperCollins Pubs.

Austin-Lockhart, Lora. Raindrop Rewards. 2007. 88p. per. 16.95 (978-1-4241-7006-7(0)) PublishAmerica, Inc.

Barney, V. J. My Rainy Day. 2012. 32p. pap. 21.99 (978-1-4691-5162-5(6)) Xlibris Corp.

BeachHouse Publishing. Geckos Make a Rainbow. Murakami, Jon, illus. 2010. (ENG.). 28p. (J). (gr. -1-1). bds. 8.95 (978-1-933067-38-4(1)) Beachhouse Publishing, LLC.

Becker, Michele Joy. What If Marshmallows Fell from the Sky. Joslin, Irene, illus. 2009. 32p. pap. 12.99 (978-1-4389-0152-7(6)) AuthorHouse.

Benchmark Education Co., LLC. It's Raining, It's Pouring Big Book. 2014. (Shared Reading Foundations Ser.). (J). (gr. -1). (978-1-4509-9440-8(7)) Benchmark Education Co.

Bergens, Teri. Mud Trouble. 2010. 34p. pap. 11.99 (978-1-60844-302-4(7)) Dog Ear Publishing, LLC.

Bianchi, John. Here Comes the Rain. 2015. (2G Bird, Bunny & Bear Ser.). (ENG., Illus.). 16p. (J). pap. 5.99 (978-1-63437-142-1(9)) American Reading Co.

The Big Rain. 2003. (Illus.). 32p. (J). mass mkt. (978-0-9740599-2-1(7), 3) Omnibus Publishing.

Bluemle, Elizabeth. Tap Tap Boom Boom. Karas, G. Brian, illus. 2014. (ENG.). 32p. (J). (gr. -1-2). 16.99 (978-0-7636-5696-6(8)) Candlewick Pr.

Boswell, Addie & Addie, Boswell. The Rain Stomper, 0 vols. Velasquez, Eric, illus. 2008. (ENG.). 32p. (J). (gr. -1-3). 16.99 (978-0-7614-5393-2(8), 9780761453932, Amazon Children's Publishing) Amazon Publishing.

Brafman, Bonnie. Treasure in Marci's House. 2007. (J). pap. 8.00 (978-0-8059-7418-8(0)) Dorrance Publishing Co., Inc.

Brouillard, Anne. The Bathtub Prima Donna. Brouillard, Anne, illus. 2004. (Illus.). 24p. (J). (gr. k-4). reprint ed. 13.00 (978-0-7567-7755-5(0)) DIANE Publishing Co.

Carroll, Claudia. Old Dumpling & the Rainy Day. 2008. 55p. pap. 9.95 (978-0-557-01565-8(0)) Lulu Pr., Inc.

Carson, Penny & Hess, Amy. Simon's Day of Rain. 2008. 17p. 10.94 (978-1-4357-2168-5(3)) Lulu Pr., Inc.

Cavaliere, Lisa. Lainey Lemonade's Cupcake Parade. 2008. 32p. pap. 24.95 (978-1-60474-860-4(5)) America Star Bks.

Celee. The Adventures of Remmy Raindrop: Book I. 2009. 16p. pap. 8.49 (978-1-4389-3623-9(0)) AuthorHouse.

Cerullo, Claudio V. Isabella's Rainy Day with Her Friends. 2011. 16p. pap. 24.95 (978-1-4626-2463-8(4)) America Star Bks.

Chang, Grace. Jin Jin & Rain Wizard. Chang, Chong, illus. 2009. (ENG.). 48p. (J). (gr. -1-3). 16.95 (978-1-59270-086-8(1)) Enchanted Lion Bks., LLC.

Church, Caroline Jayne. Rain, Rain, Go Away. Church, Caroline Jayne, illus. 2013. (ENG., Illus.). 12p. (J). (— 1). bds. 6.99 (978-0-545-48542-5(8), Cartwheel Bks.) Scholastic, Inc.

Clark, William. Magic Raindrops. 2013. 24p. pap. 14.93 (978-1-4669-7414-2(1)) Trafford Publishing.

Colgan, Jenny. The Stormy Day. 2017. (Polly & the Puffin Ser.). (ENG., Illus.). 96p. (J). (gr. k-2). pap. 7.99 **(978-0-349-13192-4(9))** Little, Brown Bks. for Young Readers.

Connor, Naomi. Rainy Day Blues. 2012. 26p. pap. 15.99 (978-1-4685-7388-6(8)) AuthorHouse.

Costa, Nicoletta. Olga the Cloud. Costa, Nicoletta, illus. 2014. (ENG., Illus.). 32p. (J). (gr. -1-k). 16.95 (978-0-8234-3051-2(0)) Holiday Hse., Inc.

Crisp, Dan, illus. The Ants Go Marching! 2009. (Classic Books with Holes Big Book Ser.). (ENG.). 16p. (J). (gr. -1-1). (978-1-84643-207-1(3)); pap. incl. audio compact disk (978-1-84643-256-9(1)) Child's Play International Ltd.

Crow, Melinda Melton. Mud Mess, 1 vol. Rooney, Ronnie, illus. 2009. (Truck Buddies Ser.). (ENG.). 32p. (gr. -1-1). pap. 6.25 (978-1-4342-1753-0(1)) Stone Arch Bks.

DePalma, Johnny. The Raindrop Keeper. Crabapple, Molly, illus. 2006. (J). per. 8.50 (978-0-9791127-1-3(0)) Umbrelly Bks.

—The Raindrop Keeper: (Limited Edition Hardcover) Crabapple, Molly, illus. 2006. 50p. (J). 16.50 (978-0-9791127-8-2(8)) Umbrelly Bks.

Dharma Publishing Staff. The Fish King: A Story about the Power of Goodness. 2nd ed. 2013. (ENG.). 36p. (gr. -1-7). pap. 8.95 (978-0-89800-491-5(8)) Dharma Publishing.

Disney Book Group Staff & Weinberg, Jennifer Liberts. World of Reading: Doc Mcstuffins Blame It on the Rain: Level 1. Disney Storybook Artists Staff & Disney Storybook Art Team, illus. 2014. (World of Reading Ser.). (ENG.). 32p. (J). (gr. -1-k). pap. 3.99 (978-1-4847-0676-3(5)) Disney Pr.

Dragonwagon, Crescent. And Then It Rained ... And Then the Sun Came Out... Greenseid, Diane, illus. 2014. (ENG.). 40p. (J). (gr. -1-3). 19.99 (978-1-4814-2529-2(3), Atheneum Bks. for Young Readers) Simon & Schuster Children's Publishing.

Du Lac, Leo J. Dogfish on the Moon: Santa Claus & the Flying Carpet 2. Baker, David, illus. 2012. 26p. 24.95 (978-1-4560-1036-2(0)) America Star Bks.

Dunrea, Olivier. Gossie & Gertie. 2006. (Illus.). 32p. pap. (978-1-4063-0119-9(1)) Walker Bks., Ltd.

Dussling, Jennifer. El Misterio del Arco Iris. Ramirez, Alma B., tr. from ENG. Gott, Barry, illus. 2009. (Science Solves It! en Espanol Ser.). (SPA.). 32p. (J). (gr. 1-3). pap. 5.95 (978-1-57565-283-2(8)) Kane Press, Inc.

Dyan, Penelope. I Can't Stand the Rain! Dyan, Penelope, illus. 2012. (Illus.). 34p. pap. 11.95 (978-1-61477-040-4(9)) Bellissima Publishing, LLC.

Echeverria, Jessica. Dora y el Día lluvioso. Savitsky, Steven, illus. 2009. (Dora la Exploradora Ser.). Orig. Title: Dora & the Rainy Day. (SPA.). 26p. (J). (gr. -1). bds. 5.99 (978-1-4169-7186-3(6), Libros Para Ninos) Libros Para Ninos.

Ehlert, Lois. Rain Fish. Ehlert, Lois, illus. 2016. (ENG., Illus.). 40p. (J). (gr. -1-3). 17.99 (978-1-4814-6152-8(4), Beach Lane Bks.) Beach Lane Bks.

Farrell, Steve. What Do You Do on a Rainy Day? Bendoly, Lynne, illus. 2013. 48p. pap. 24.95 (978-1-4626-9685-7(6)) America Star Bks.

Feiffer, Kate. My Side of the Car. Feiffer, Jules, illus. 2011. (ENG.). 32p. (J). (gr. -1-3). 16.99 (978-0-7636-4405-5(6)) Candlewick Pr.

Fernandes, Eugenie. Kitten's Summer. Fernandes, Eugenie, illus. 2013. (ENG., Illus.). 24p. (J). (gr. -1 — 1). bds. 7.95 (978-1-55453-721-1(5)) Kids Can Pr., Ltd. CAN. Dist: Hachette Bk. Group.

Feurer, Paige. And Then It Rained on Malcolm. Farr, Rich, illus. 2015. (ENG.). 40p. (J). (gr. -1-k). 16.99 (978-1-63450-150-7(0), Sky Pony Pr.) Skyhorse Publishing Co., Inc.

Fienberg, Anna & Fienberg, Barbara. Once Tashi Met a Dragon. Gamble, Kim, illus. 2014. (Tashi Ser.). (ENG.). 34p. (J). (gr. k-2). 16.99 (978-1-74175-887-0(4)) Allen & Unwin AUS. Dist: Independent Pubs. Group.

Foster, Ron, illus. I Like Rain. 2007. 28p. (J). (gr. 1-4). (978-1-929039-39-5(5)) Ambassador Bks., Inc.

Gammell, Stephen. Mudkin. Gammell, Stephen, illus. 2011. (Carolrhoda Picture Bks.). (ENG., Illus.). 32p. (J). (gr. k-3). 16.95 (978-0-7613-5790-2(4)) Lerner Publishing Group.

Giles, Mike, illus. Spring Showers Bring Flowers. 2014. (Yo Gabba Gabba! Ser.). (ENG.). 12p. (J). (gr. -1-k). bds. 5.99 (978-1-4424-9572-2(3), Simon Spotlight) Simon Spotlight.

Gorbachev, Valeri. Catty Jane Who Hated the Rain. Gorbachev, Valeri, illus. 2012. (ENG., Illus.). 32p. (J). (gr. -1-3). 16.95 (978-1-59078-700-7(5)) Boyds Mills Pr.

—Un Dia de lluvia. Gorbachev, Valeri, illus. 2007. (SPA., Illus.). 40p. (J). (gr. -1-3). pap. 8.95 (978-958-04-7074-8(X)) Norma S.A. COL. Dist: Distribuidora Norma, Inc.

Grant, Callie. Mud Puddle Hunting Day. Magee, Melanie, illus. 2013. (ENG.). 20p. (J). bds. 8.99 (978-0-9854090-0-5(2)) Blanchard, Graham.

Gray, Joanna. The Little Raindrop. Kolanovic, Dubravka, illus. 2014. (ENG.). 32p. (J). (gr. -1-k). 16.95 (978-1-62873-821-6(9), Sky Pony Pr.) Skyhorse Publishing Co., Inc.

Groth-fleming. Professor Fergus Fahrenheit & His Wonderful Weat. 2009. (ENG.). 36p. (J). (gr. -1-3). pap. 10.99 (978-1-4424-0220-1(2), Simon & Schuster Bks. For Young Readers) Simon & Schuster Bks. For Young Readers.

Haley, Patty. William's Wet Week. Sayer, Blair, illus. 2010. (ENG.). 16p. (gr. k-2). pap. 7.95 (978-1-61181-043-1(4), Kaeden Bks.) Kaeden Corp.

—William's Wet Week (6 Pack) Sayer, Blair, illus. 2010. (ENG.). 16p. (gr. k-2). pap. (978-1-61181-044-8(2), Kaeden Bks.) Kaeden Corp.

Hergenroeder, Ernie, illus. Little Drop of Water. 2007. 24p. (J). 15.00 (978-0-9724272-4-1(4)) Katydid Publishing LLC.

Hesse, Karen. Come on, Rain! 2004. (J). (gr. k-3). 29.95 (978-1-55592-500-0(6)) Weston Woods Studios, Inc.

Higginson, Sheila Sweeny. Drip, Drop! the Rain Won't Stop! Your Turn, My Turn Reader. Yee, Josie, illus. 2010. (Playskool Ser.). (ENG.). 24p. (J). (gr. -1-k). pap. 3.99 (978-1-4169-9046-8(1), Simon Spotlight) Simon Spotlight.

Hinbest, Wendy. Frizzy Tizzy Camps In. 2011. 20p. pap. 11.95 (978-1-4583-5826-4(7)) Lulu Pr., Inc.

Hobbie, Nathaniel. Priscilla & the Pixie Princess. Hobbie, Jocelyn, illus. 2011. (ENG.). 32p. (J). (gr. -1-3). pap. 6.99 (978-0-316-08349-2(6)) Little, Brown Bks. for Young Readers.

Hodson, Debbie. A Mountain Rainbow. 2004. (Illus.). 31p. (J). per. 10.95 (978-0-9755771-0-3(7)) IvyStone Pr.

Holub, Joan. Itty Bitty Kitty & the Rainy Play Day. Burks, James, illus. 2016. 32p. (J). (gr. -1-3). 17.99 (978-0-06-232220-3(6)) HarperCollins Pubs.

Hope, Laura Lee. Bunny Brown & His Sister Sue Keeping S. 2006. 26.95 (978-1-4218-2975-3(4)); pap. 11.95 (978-1-4218-3075-9(2)) 1st World Publishing, Inc.

—Bunny Brown & His Sister Sue Keeping Store. 2007. (ENG.). 142p. pap. 18.99 (978-1-4264-5200-0(4)) 2006. 160p. pap. 21.99 (978-1-4264-5501-8(1)) Creative Media Partners, LLC.

Husted, Ursula. Making Rain. 2004. 56p. (J). per. 9.95 (978-0-9753225-0-5(8)) Atomic Fruit Pr.

Hyder, M. A. Donia: Stolen Raindrops or Honour among Thieves. 2011. (Illus.). 364p. pap. 20.53 (978-1-4567-7428-8(X)) AuthorHouse.

ImageBooks Staff. Little Zebra. Put, Klaartje van der, illus. 2013. (Little Finger Puppet Board Bks.). (ENG.). 12p. (J). (gr. -1 — 1). bds. 6.99 (978-1-4521-1252-7(5)) Chronicle Bks. LLC.

Jackson, Bridgett. The Bobos Save the Day: Book One of Tales from the Creek. 2008. 36p. pap. 14.49 (978-1-4389-2034-4(2)) AuthorHouse.

Jackson, Richard. This Beautiful Day. Lee, Suzy, illus. 2017. (ENG.). 40p. (J). (gr. -1-3). 15.99 **(978-1-4814-4139-1(6)**, Atheneum/Caitlyn Dlouhy Books) Simon & Schuster Children's Publishing.

Jasmine, Jean-Pierre. It's Raining Uber. 2013. 166p. (J). pap. 13.99 (978-1-4808-0122-6(4)) Archway Publishing.

Jennings, Arleen Naish. God Is in the Rain. 2012. 64p. (gr. 1-2). pap. 8.95 (978-1-4759-3292-8(8)) iUniverse, Inc.

Johnson, Amy Crane. Cinnamon & the April Shower. Mommaerts, Robb, illus. 2009. (ENG.). 32p. (J). (gr. -1-3). 16.95 (978-1-934960-54-7(3), Raven Tree Pr.,Csi) Continental Sales, Inc.

Kerlikowske, Elizabeth. Before the Rain. 2003. 72p. per. 15.00 (978-1-882983-90-2(4)) March Street Pr.

Khamis, Johnny. Costi & the Raindrop Adventure. Belanger, Damon, illus. 2007. 32p. (J). (gr. -1-3). 6.95 (978-1-60005-029-9(8)) Happy About.

Klein-Carroll, Theodora. Tippy & the Runaway Cloud. 2013. 28p. pap. 16.95 (978-1-4525-7390-8(5), Balboa Pr.) Author Solutions, Inc.

—Tippy the Raindrop. 2012. 30p. pap. 16.99 (978-1-4525-5725-0(X)) Balboa Pr.

Kolodny, Cynthia. We Like Puddles. Sagasti, Miriam, illus. 2004. (ENG.). 12p. (gr. k-1). pap. 7.95 (978-1-57874-040-6(1), Kaeden Bks.) Kaeden Corp.

Koontz, Robin. La Pequeña Lagartija, ¡el Cielo Se Está Cayendo! / Lizzie Little, the Sky Is Falling! 2012. (SPA & ENG.). 24p. (gr. 2-3). pap. 8.95 (978-1-61810-541-7(8)) Rourke Educational Media.

Krahn, Maria. Charity Prays for Rain. Eshbach, Ariel, illus. 2014. 32p. (J). (978-0-7399-2475-4(3)) Rod & Staff Pubs., Inc.

Ladd, Debbie. Puddles. Morejon, Tom, illus. 2006. 32p. (J). pap. 8.95 (978-0-9727615-4-3(3)) Deb on Air Bks.

Lamb, Anne. Beat Bugs: Rain. 2017. (Beat Bugs Ser.). 16p. (J). (gr. -1 — 1). bds. 6.99 (978-0-06-264073-4(9), HarperFestival) HarperCollins Pubs.

Latty, Jasmin. Oh, My Boring Toes! 2005. (J). pap. 12.00 (978-0-8059-6668-8(4)) Dorrance Publishing Co., Inc.

Lewis, Anne Margaret. Puddle Jumpers. Cote, Nancy, illus. 2016. (ENG.). 32p. (J). (gr. -1-k). 16.99 (978-1-63450-185-9(3), Sky Pony Pr.) Skyhorse Publishing Co., Inc.

Lewis, Kim. Seymour & Henry. Lewis, Kim, illus. 2009. (ENG., Illus.). 32p. (J). (gr. k-k). 15.99 (978-0-7636-4243-3(6)) Candlewick Pr.

Lichtenheld, Tom. Cloudette. Lichtenheld, Tom, illus. 2011. (ENG., Illus.). 40p. (J). (gr. -1-2). 17.99 (978-0-8050-8776-5(1), 9780805087765, Holt, Henry & Co. Bks. For Young Readers) Holt, Henry & Co.

Liniers. The Big Wet Balloon (El Globo Grande y Mojado) Liniers, illus. 2013. (ENG & SPA., Illus.). 32p. (J). (gr. -1-3). 12.95 (978-1-935179-40-5(3)) TOON Books / RAW Junior, LLC.

—The Big Wet Balloon (El Globo Grande y Mojado) Liniers, illus. 2013. (ENG & SPA., Illus.). 32p. (J). (gr. -1-3). pap. 4.99 (978-1-935179-39-9(X)) TOON Books / RAW Junior, LLC.

Liniers, Ricardo. The Big Wet Balloon. Liniers, Ricardo, illus. 2013. (ENG., Illus.). 32p. (J). (gr. -1-3). 12.95 (978-1-935179-32-0(2)) TOON Books / RAW Junior, LLC.

Magee, Kanika. Rain, Rain, Come Today. Crosson, Cierra, illus. 2004. (J). (978-0-9748834-2-7(5)) Ebenezer A.M.E. Church.

Markey, Kevin. Rainmaker. 2012. (Illus.). (J). 230p. lib. bdg. 16.89 (978-0-06-115229-0(3)); (ENG., 240p. (gr. 3-7). 15.99 (978-0-06-115228-3(5)) HarperCollins Pubs.

Martin, David. Peep & Ducky Rainy Day. Walker, David, illus. 2015. (ENG.). 32p. (J). (— 1). 14.99 (978-0-7636-6884-6(2)) Candlewick Pr.

Martin, Emily. Downpour. Shaughnessy, Mara, illus. 2013. (ENG.). 32p. (J). (gr. -1-k). 14.95 (978-1-62087-545-2(4), 620545, Sky Pony Pr.) Skyhorse Publishing Co., Inc.

Mase, Naokata. The Rainy Trip Surprise. Perry, Mia Lynn, tr. Mase, Naokata, illus. 2006. (Illus.). 24p. (J). (gr. -1-1). 19.95 incl. audio compact disk (978-1-74126-436-4(7)) R.I.C. Pubns. AUS. Dist: SCB Distributors.

Masterson, Carla Jo. What's on the Other Side of the Rainbow? The Secret of the Golden Mirror. Fochtman, Omra Jo, illus. 2006. 40p. (J). 24.95 (978-1-59975-228-0(X)) Father & Son Publishing.

Matranga, Cindy. It Never Rains in Sunny California. 2010. 32p. pap. 12.99 (978-1-4389-4816-4(6)) AuthorHouse.

McCanna, Tim. Water Song. Smythe, Richard, illus. 2017. (ENG.). 32p. (J). (gr. -1-3). 17.99 (978-1-4814-6881-7(2), Simon & Schuster/Paula Wiseman Bks.) Simon & Schuster/Paula Wiseman Bks.

McDonald, Kirsten. The Big Rain, 1 vol. Meza, Erika, illus. 2016. (Carlos & Carmen Ser.). (ENG.). 32p. (J). (gr. k-3). 27.07 (978-1-62402-137-4(9)) Magic Wagon.

McKee, David. Elmer & the Flood. McKee, David, illus. 2015. (ENG., Illus.). 32p. (J). (gr. -1-3). 17.99 (978-1-4677-9314-8(0)); 17.99 (978-1-4677-9312-4(4)) Lerner Publishing Group.

Melmed, Laura Krauss. The Rainbabies. LaMarche, Jim, illus. 2004. (ENG.). 32p. (J). (gr. -1-3). pap. 6.99 (978-0-688-15113-3(2)) HarperCollins Pubs.

Miles, Ryan. The Picnic Nightmare. 2012. 24p. pap. 24.95 (978-1-4512-7153-9(0)) America Star Bks.

Miyares, Daniel. Float. Miyares, Daniel, illus. 2015. (ENG., Illus.). 48p. (J). (gr. -1-3). 17.99 (978-1-4814-1524-8(7), Simon & Schuster Bks. For Young Readers) Simon & Schuster Bks. For Young Readers.

Moriarty, Ros. Summer Rain. Balarinji, illus. 2016. (ENG.). 24p. (J). (gr. -1-k). 9.99 (978-1-76011-211-0(9)) Allen & Unwin AUS. Dist: Independent Pubs. Group.

Moss, Lucille. The Gift Within. Uhouse, Debra, illus. l.t. ed. 2005. 19p. (J). 14.95 (978-1-59879-063-4(3)) Lifevest Publishing, Inc.

Muhammad, Renay. Daddy Why Do We Have Rain. 2004. (Illus.). (J). cd-rom (978-0-9754024-1-2(2)) Doses of Reality, Inc.

Nash, Damien K. H. & Nash, Kathy. Big Box, Little Box: The Forecast Calls for Potential Rain! Miller, Steve, illus. 2012. 80p. pap. 13.99 (978-0-9846507-1-2(7)) Faith Bks. & MORE.

Opal, Paola. Saffy Looks for Rain. 2009. (Simply Small Ser.). (ENG., Illus.). 24p. (J). (gr. k — 1). bds. 7.95 (978-1-897476-03-1(5)) Simply Read Bks. CAN. Dist: Ingram Publisher Services.

Padilla, Felix M. Smiling at the Rain. Padilla, Eren Star, illus. 32p. (J). (gr. 3-18). 16.00 (978-0-9710860-4-3(4)) Libros, Encouraging Cultural Literacy.

Pelletier, Jennifer. The Wonderful Imagination of Alish. 2011. 32p. pap. 24.95 (978-1-4626-2613-7(0)) America Star Bks.

Peyo. Rain, Rain, Smurf Away. Peyo, illus. 2012. (Smurfs Classic Ser.). (ENG., Illus.). 24p. (J). (gr. -1-3). pap. 3.99 (978-1-4424-3600-8(X), Simon Spotlight) Simon Spotlight.

Phelan, Matt. Druthers. Phelan, Matt, illus. 2014. (ENG., Illus.). 32p. (J). (-k). 15.99 (978-0-7636-5955-4(X)) Candlewick Pr.

Promitzer, Rebecca. The Pickle King. 2010. (ENG.). 416p. (J). (gr. 3-7). 17.99 (978-0-545-17087-1(7), Chicken Hse., The) Scholastic, Inc.

Quinn, Jordan. The Witch's Curse. McPhillips, Robert, illus. 2014. (Kingdom of Wrenly Ser.: 4). (ENG.). 128p. (J). (gr. k-4). pap. 5.99 (978-1-4814-0075-6(4), Little Simon) Little Simon.

A Rainbow in our Yard. 2005. (J). bds. (978-0-9761228-1-4(2)) World of Imagination.

The Rainy Day: Individual Title Two-Packs. (Chiquilibros Ser.). (gr. -1-1). 12.00 (978-0-7635-8532-7(7)) Rigby Education.

Rath, Tom H. Donkey Oatie's Field Trip. Gaudet, Christine, illus. 2013. 26p. pap. (978-0-9918033-4-7(5)) Wood Islands Prints.

Ray, Mary Lyn. Red Rubber Boot Day. Stringer, Lauren, illus. 2005. (ENG.). 32p. (J). (gr. -1-3). pap. 6.99 (978-0-15-205398-7(0)) Houghton Mifflin Harcourt Publishing Co.

Rooks, Elizabeth. Rayne: Queen Water Supplier of the World. 2012. 32p. pap. 19.99 (978-1-4772-2375-8(4)) AuthorHouse.

Rosenthal, Amy Krouse. Uni the Unicorn & the Dream Come True. Barrager, Brigette, illus. 2017. (ENG.). 40p. (J). (gr. -1-2). 17.99 **(978-1-101-93659-7(2))**; lib. bdg. 20.99 **(978-1-101-93660-3(6))** Random Hse. Children's Bks. (Random Hse. Bks. for Young Readers).

Rumford, James. Rain School. 2010. (ENG., Illus.). 32p. (J). (gr. -1-3). 17.99 (978-0-547-24307-8(3)) Houghton Mifflin Harcourt Publishing Co.

Salzano, Tammi. One Rainy Day. Wood, Hannah, illus. 2011. (ENG.). 24p. (J). (gr. -1-k). bds. 8.95 (978-1-58925-860-0(6)) Tiger Tales.

Sanders, Rob. Ruby Rose, Big Bravos. Ohi, Debbie Ridpath, illus. 2017. 40p. (J). (gr. -1-3). 15.99 **(978-0-06-223571-8(0))** HarperCollins Pubs.

Sauvageau-Smestad, Sheila. Rain, Rain, What a Pain! 2006. (Illus.). 37p. (J). per. 17.95 (978-0-9771971-6-3(6)) Brass Frog Bookworks.

Scaletta, Kurtis. Mudville. 2010. (ENG.). 272p. (J). (gr. 3-7). 8.99 (978-0-375-84472-0(4), Yearling) Random Hse. Children's Bks.

Schoeningh, Debby. Little Raindrop. Brown, Margaret, illus. 2012. 24p. pap. 9.95 (978-0-9746360-7-8(X)) Country Side Pr., The.

Scott, Jeanne Ann. Raining Worms. 2005. 160p. (J). pap. 6.99 net. (978-1-59975-218-1(2)) Independent Pub.

Scotton, Rob. The Rain Is a Pain. Scotton, Rob, illus. 2012. (I Can Read Level 1 Ser.). (ENG., Illus.). 32p. (J). (gr. -1-3). pap. 3.99 (978-0-06-209017-1(8)) HarperCollins Pubs.

—The Rain Is a Pain. 2012. (Splat the Cat: I Can Read Ser.). (J). lib. bdg. 13.55 (978-0-606-26861-5(8), Turtleback) Turtleback Bks.

—Splat the Cat - The Rain Is a Pain. Scotton, Rob, illus. 2012. (I Can Read Level 1 Ser.). (ENG., Illus.). 32p. (J). (gr. -1-3). 16.99 (978-0-06-209018-8(6)) HarperCollins Pubs.

Sendak, Jack & Sendak, J. The Happy Rain. Sendak, Maurice, illus. 2004. (Sendak Reissues Ser.). (ENG.). 48p. (J). reprint ed. 13.95 (978-0-06-028785-6(3)) HarperCollins Pubs.

Sesen, Cihan. Stop the Rain, Issue #1. 2010. 45p. pap. 12.99 (978-0-557-48426-3(X)) Lulu Pr., Inc.

Shannon, David. The Rain Came Down. 2009. (ENG.). (J). (gr. -1-3). 9.95 (978-0-545-13850-5(7)) Scholastic, Inc.

Sheth, Kashmira. Monsoon Afternoon, 1 vol. Jaeggi, Yoshiko, illus. 2008. (ENG.). 32p. (J). (gr. k-3). 16.95 (978-1-56145-455-6(9), Peachtree Junior) Peachtree Pubs.

Shollar, Leah Pearl. Shadow Play: A True Story of Tefillah. Gerber, Pesach, illus. 2006. 32p. (J). 11.95 (978-1-929628-21-6(8)) Hachai Publishing.

Shulevitz, Uri & National Geographic Learning Staff. Rain Rain Rivers. Shulevitz, Uri, illus. 2006. (ENG., Illus.). 32p. (J). (gr. -1-3). reprint ed. pap. 8.99 *(978-0-374-46195-9(3),* 9780374461959) Square Fish.

Silverman, Erica. Cowgirl Kate & Cocoa: Rain or Shine. Lewin, Betsy, illus. 2009. (Cowgirl Kate & Cocoa Ser.). (ENG.). 44p. (J). (gr. 1-4). pap. 5.99 *(978-0-15-206602-4(0))* Houghton Mifflin Harcourt Publishing Co.

Skyberg, Andrea, creator. Snickeyfritz. 2009. (ENG., Illus.). 48p. (J). 17.99 *(978-0-615-25177-6(3))* Wooden Nickel Pr.

Sonriendole a la Lluvia. (SPA.). (J). *(978-0-9710860-5-0(2))* Libros, Encouraging Cultural Literacy.

Stojic, Manya. Rain. Stojic, Manya, illus. 2009. (Rise & Shine Ser.). (ENG., Illus.). 32p. (J). (gr. -1-2). pap. 7.99 *(978-0-385-73729-6(7),* Dragonfly Bks.) Random Hse. Children's Bks.

Stranaghan, Crystal J. Then It Rained. Espadaler, Rosa, illus. 2007. 24p. (J). *(978-0-9784047-8-9(5))* Pays et Terroirs.

Strathgryffe, Alexander. The Drizzleys. 2009. (Illus.). 48p. pap. *(978-1-84748-543-4(X))* Athena Pr.

Taft, Jean & dePaola, Tomie. Worm Weather. Hunt, Matt, illus. 2015. (ENG.). 32p. (J). (-k). bds. 3.99 *(978-0-448-48740-3(3),* Grosset & Dunlap) Penguin Young Readers Group.

Talbot, Kathy. Camille's Rainy Day Adventure. 2011. 24p. pap. 8.32 *(978-1-4634-5998-7(X))* AuthorHouse.

Testa, Maggie. Olivia & the Rain Dance. 2012. (Olivia Ready-To-Read Level 1 Ser.). lib. bdg. 13.55 *(978-0-606-23688-1(0),* Turtleback) Turtleback Bks.

Thompson, Carol. Rain! 2014. (Whatever the Weather Ser.: 4). (ENG., Illus.). 12p. (J). (gr. k-k). bds. *(978-1-84643-683-3(4))* Child's Play International Ltd.

Thompson, Jan & Sharpe, Jaime. Amara's Magical Playhouse: The Adventure Begins. 2010. 108p. pap. 37.99 *(978-1-4520-8284-4(7))* AuthorHouse.

Tremblay, Carole. Floop's New Umbrella. Beshwaty, Steve, illus. 2009. (Floop Ser.). 24p. (J). (gr. -1-k). 22.60 *(978-1-60754-347-3(8));* pap. 8.15 *(978-1-60754-348-0(6))* Windmill Bks.

Tukel, Onur. Rainstack!, 0 vols. 2013. (ENG.). 64p. (J). (gr. -1-3). 17.99 *(978-1-4778-1655-4(0),* 9781477816554, Amazon Children's Publishing) Amazon Publishing.

Turcotte, Carolyn E. Little Drip Drop's Big Rainy Day. 2011. 40p. (gr. 1-2). pap. 18.46 *(978-1-4567-4873-9(4))* AuthorHouse.

Tuzee, John, text. Puffy: La Nube Que No Podia Llover. 2005. (SPA.). (J). 8.95 *(978-0-9755348-1-6(5))* Kids Life Pr.

Valent, Fred. The Tiniest Raindrop, 1 vol. 2008. (ENG.). 31p. 24.95 *(978-1-60441-393-9(X))* America Star Bks.

Van Cleve, Kathleen. Drizzle. 2011. (ENG.). 368p. (J). (gr. 3-7). 7.99 *(978-0-14-241113-1(2),* Puffin Books) Penguin Young Readers Group.

Van Straaten, Harmen. TIM & the FLYING MACHINE. 2008. (ENG.). 28p. (J). (gr. 1-7). 12.95 *(978-1-60136-003-8(7))* Audio Holdings, LLC.

Virtue, Queen Petals De. Princess & the Rain. 2012. 28p. pap. 21.99 *(978-1-4691-2744-6(X))* Xlibris Corp.

Wack, Nancy. Puddle Pirate. 2007. 40p. 20.50 *(978-0-615-16634-6(2))* Wack, Nancy.

Walker, Lisa & Coyne, Adrian. The Boy Who Brought Thunder. 2012. (Illus.). 40p. pap. 12.95 *(978-9987-08-222-3(X))* Mkuki na Nyoka Pubs. TZA. Dist: African Bks. Collective, Ltd.

Walker, Tanisha. Rainbow Tots- 10-28. 2011. 36p. pap. 19.99 *(978-0-557-80890-8(1))* Lulu Pr., Inc.

Waters, Graham. The Raindrops & the Wrong Cloud. 2009. (Illus.). 28p. pap. 15.49 *(978-1-4490-0685-3(X))* AuthorHouse.

Weaver, Griz. A Day in the Rain. 2005. 35p. (J). 12.28 *(978-1-4116-0565-7(9))* Lulu Pr., Inc.

Weinberg, Jennifer Liberts. Doc Mcstuffins: Blame It on the Rain. 2014. (World of Reading Ser.). (J). lib. bdg. 13.55 *(978-0-606-35909-2(5))* Turtleback Bks.

Wenger, Brahm & Green, Alan. Dewey Doo-It Builds a House: A Children's Story about Habitat for Humanity. 2006. (ENG., Illus.). 32p. (J). (gr. -1-2). 17.95 incl. lp *(978-0-9745143-2-1(2))* RandallFraser Publishing.

Westover, Gail. Mrs Mouse's Garden Party in Giggleswick Village. Daly, Karen Anne, illus. 2012. 26p. pap. 9.95 *(978-0-9821507-9-5(2))* Thistlewood Publishing.

Whaley, Michelle Marie. Does It Really Rain Cats & Dogs? Ortiz, Ada, illus. 2008. 36p. pap. 24.95 *(978-1-60563-233-9(3))* America Star Bks.

White, Dianne. Blue on Blue. Krommes, Beth, illus. 2014. (ENG.). 48p. (J). (gr. k-3). 17.99 *(978-1-4424-1267-5(4),* Beach Lane Bks.) Beach Lane Bks.

White, Sandi. Playing with Rain. 2010. 36p. pap. 21.99 *(978-1-4500-1534-9(4))* Xlibris Corp.

Widner, Jan. Then Came the Rains. 2013. 28p. pap. 16.95 *(978-1-4497-9456-9(4),* WestBow Pr.) Author Solutions, Inc.

Wilce, Colin. The Rain & Blossom (Rabbit Brook Tales Volume 2) 2007. 88p. pap. 11.66 *(978-1-84728-105-0(2))* Lulu Pr., Inc.

Wilhelm, Hans. I Love Rainy Days! Wilhelm, Hans, illus. 2011. (Scholastic Reader Level 1 Ser.). (ENG., Illus.). 32p. (J). (gr. -1-2). pap. 3.99 *(978-0-545-24503-6(6),* Cartwheel Bks.) Scholastic, Inc.

Williamson, Linda. Groundhog Breakfast, Soft Petals, & a Roof That Don't Leak Too Much, 1 vol. Mollett, Irene, illus. 2009. 23p. pap. 24.95 *(978-1-60749-618-2(6))* America Star Bks.

Winters, Kari-Lynn. On My Walk, 1 vol. Leist, Christina, illus. 2010. (ENG.). 32p. (J). (gr. k-1). 16.95 *(978-1-896580-61-6(0))* Tradewind Bks. CAN. Dist: Orca Bk. Pubs. USA.

Wolek, Guy, illus. OLIVIA & the Rain Dance. 2012. (Olivia TV Tie-In Ser.). (ENG.). 24p. (J). (gr. -1-1). 15.99 *(978-1-4424-3543-8(7));* pap. 3.99 *(978-1-4424-3542-1(9))* Simon Spotlight. (Simon Spotlight).

Woodford, Pamela. Watching Raindrops. 2013. (Brighter Little Minds Ser.). (ENG., Illus.). 24p. (J). pap. 9.99 *(978-1-871305-84-5(5))* Orpen Pr. IRL. Dist: M.H. Gill & Co. U. C.

Yildirim, Rabia. Wind, Rain & Snow. 2013. (ENG., Illus.). 53p. (J). (gr. k-1). pap. 9.95 *(978-1-59784-284-6(2))* Tughra Bks.

Yum, Hyewon. Puddle. 2016. (ENG., Illus.). 40p. (J). 16.99 *(978-0-374-31695-2(3),* 9780374316952, Farrar, Straus & Giroux (BYR)) Farrar, Straus & Giroux.

Zalme, Ron, illus. Rainy Day Tales. 2009. (J). *(978-1-59078-734-2(X))* Highlights for Children.

RAIN AND RAINFALL—POETRY

O'Rourke, Ryan, illus. One Big Rain: Poems for Every Season. 2014. (ENG.). 32p. (J). (gr. 2-5). pap. 7.95 *(978-1-57091-717-2(5))* Charlesbridge Publishing, Inc.

RAIN FOREST ECOLOGY

Alaina, Maria. Rainforest. 2011. (Wonder Readers Early Level Ser.). (ENG.). 16p. (gr. -1-1). pap. 35.94 *(978-1-4296-8171-1(3),* Wonder Readers) Capstone Press of Coughlan Cos.

Allaby, Michael. Tropical Forests. Garratt, Richard, illus. 2006. (Biomes of the Earth Ser.). 288p. (gr. 6-12). 39.50 *(978-0-8160-5322-3(7))* Facts On File, Inc.

Allgor, Marie. Endangered Rain Forest Animals. 2012. (Save Earth's Animals! Ser.). (ENG., Illus.). 24p. (J). (gr. k-5). pap. 8.25 *(978-1-4488-7495-8(5));* lib. bdg. 22.60 *(978-1-4488-7422-4(X))* Rosen Publishing Group, Inc., The. (PowerKids Pr.).

Aloian, Molly & Kalman, Bobbie. Cadenas Alimentarias del Bosque Tropical. 2007. (Cadenas Alimentarias Ser.). (SPA., Illus.). 32p. (J). (gr. 3-7). pap. *(978-0-7787-8549-1(1))* Crabtree Publishing Co.

—Un Hábitat de Bosque Tropical. 2007. (Introducción a Los Habitats Ser.). (SPA., Illus.). 32p. (J). (gr. 3-7). lib. bdg. *(978-0-7787-8333-6(2));* (gr. k-3). pap. *(978-0-7787-8357-2(X))* Crabtree Publishing Co.

—Rainforest Food Chains. 2006. (Food Chains Ser.). (ENG., Illus.). 32p. (J). (gr. -1-3). pap. *(978-0-7787-1997-7(9))* Crabtree Publishing Co.

—A Rainforest Habitat. 2006. (Introducing Habitats Ser.). (ENG., Illus.). 32p. (J). (gr. -1-3). pap. *(978-0-7787-2986-0(9))* Crabtree Publishing Co.

Aspen-Baxter, Linda. Rainforests. 2006. (ENG.). (J). pap. 9.95 *(978-1-59036-447-5(3))* Weigl Pubs., Inc.

Barnes, Julia. Tropical Rain Forests. 2003. (One Hundred One Facts about Our World Ser.). (Illus.). 32p. (gr. 1-4). lib. bdg. 26.00 *(978-0-8368-3710-0(X),* Gareth Stevens Learning Library) Stevens, Gareth Publishing LLLP.

Benchmark Education Co., LLC. Who Do You See? a Rain Forest Rap Big Book. 2014. (Shared Reading Foundations Ser.). (J). (gr. -1). *(978-1-4509-9444-6(X))* Benchmark Education Co.

Benoit, Peter. Tropical Rain Forests. 2011. (True Bks.). 48p. (J). (gr. 3-5). 29.00 *(978-0-531-20554-9(1),* Children's Pr.); (ENG.). pap. 6.95 *(978-0-531-28103-1(5))* Scholastic Library Publishing.

Bodden, Valerie. Rainforests. 2006. (Our World Ser.). (Illus.). 24p. (J). (gr. -1-3). lib. bdg. 16.95 *(978-1-58341-465-1(7),* Creative Education) Creative Co., The.

Brown, Carron. Secrets of the Rain Forest. Nassner, Alyssa, illus. 2015. (ENG.). 36p. (J). 12.99 *(978-1-61067-325-9(5))* Kane Miller.

Castaldo, Nancy F. Rainforests: An Activity Guide for Ages 6-9. 2003. (ENG., Illus.). 144p. (J). (gr. 2-4). pap. 14.95 *(978-1-55652-476-9(5))* Chicago Review Pr., Inc.

Champion, Neil. Tropical Rain Forests. 2006. (Caring for the Planet Ser.). (Illus.). 48p. (YA). (gr. 5-9). lib. bdg. 32.80 *(978-1-58340-508-6(9))* Black Rabbit Bks.

Cole, Melissa S. Rain Forests. 2003. (Wild America Habitats Ser.). (Illus.). 24p. (J). 21.20 *(978-1-56711-808-7(9),* Blackbirch Pr., Inc.) Cengage Gale.

Collard, Sneed B., III. In the Rain Forest Canopy. 2005. (Science Adventures Ser.). (Illus.). 44p. (J). (gr. 3-7). lib. bdg. 29.93 *(978-0-7614-1954-9(3),* Benchmark Bks.) Marshall Cavendish Corp.

De la Bédoyère, Camilla. Rainforests. 2010. (Unpredictable Nature Ser.). (Illus.). 48p. (J). (gr. 3-18). lib. bdg. 19.95 *(978-1-4222-2004-7(4))* Mason Crest.

deMarin, Layne. Amazon Adventure, 1 vol. 2011. (Wonder Readers: Science Ser.). (ENG.). (gr. -1-2). 20p. lib. bdg. 22.65 *(978-1-4296-8634-1(0));* 16p. pap. 35.94 *(978-1-4296-8069-1(5));* 32p. pap. 5.99 *(978-1-4296-7907-7(7))* Capstone Press of Coughlan Cos. (Wonder Readers).

Do You Really Want to Visit a Rainforest? 2015. (Do You Really Want to Visit... ? Ser.). (Illus.). 24p. (J). 27.10 *(978-1-60753-453-2(3))* Amicus Publishing.

Duke, Kate. In the Rainforest. Duke, Kate, illus. 2014. (Let's-Read-And-Find-Out Science 2 Ser.). (ENG., Illus.). 40p. (J). (gr. -1-3). 17.99 *(978-0-06-028259-2(2));* pap. 5.99 *(978-0-06-445197-0(6))* HarperCollins Pubs.

Dunphy, Madeleine. Here Is the Tropical Rain Forest. Rothman, Michael, illus. 2006. (Web of Life Ser.). (ENG.). 32p. (J). (gr. -1-3). 16.95 *(978-0-9773795-1-4(5))* Web of Life Children's Bks.

Editors of Kingfisher. Mysterious Rain Forests: Come Face to Face with Life in the Rain Forest. 2016. (Fast Facts Ser.). (ENG., Illus.). 32p. (J). pap. 6.99 *(978-0-7534-7248-4(1),* 9780753472484, Kingfisher) Roaring Brook Pr.

—Remarkable Rain Forests. 2016. (It's All About... Ser.). (ENG., Illus.). 32p. (J). pap. 5.99 *(978-0-7534-7263-7(5),* 9780753472637, Kingfisher) Roaring Brook Pr.

Einspruch, Andrew. Rain Forest Habitats. 2013. (Discovery Education: Habitats Ser.). 32p. (J). (gr. 3-6). 25.25 *(978-1-4777-1324-2(7));* pap. 10.00 *(978-1-4777-1483-6(9));* pap. 60.00 *(978-1-4777-1484-3(7))* Rosen Publishing Group, Inc., The. (PowerKids Pr.).

Ganeri, Anita. Exploring Rain Forests: A Benjamin Blog & His Inquisitive Dog Investigation, 1 vol. 2014. (Exploring Habitats with Benjamin Blog & His Inquisitive Dog Ser.). (ENG., Illus.). 32p. (gr. 1-3). pap. 8.95 *(978-1-4329-8786-2(0));* lib. bdg. 29.99 *(978-1-4329-8779-4(8))* Heinemann-Raintree. (NA-h).

—Rainforests. Bull, Peter, illus. 2013. (Explorers Ser.). (ENG.). 32p. (J). (gr. 2-5). 6.99 *(978-0-7534-7073-2(X),* 9780753470732, Kingfisher) Roaring Brook Pr.

Gardeski, Christina Mia. All about Rain Forests. 2017. (Habitats Ser.). (ENG.). 24p. (gr. k-1). lib. bdg. 21.99 ***(978-1-5157-7643-7(3),*** Pebble Bks.) Capstone Press of Coughlan Cos.

Gardner, Robert. Rain Forest Experiments: 10 Science Experiments in One Hour or Less. 2014. (Last Minute Science Projects with Biomes Ser.). (Illus.). 48p. (J). (gr. 5-12). lib. bdg. 25.27 *(978-0-7660-5937-5(5))* Enslow Pubs., Inc.

Gray, Leon. Tropical Rain Forests. 2015. (Amazing Biomes Ser.). (Illus.). 32p. (gr. 3-6). 31.35 *(978-1-78121-246-2(5),* 1389656) Brown Bear Bks.

Greeley, August. Fading Forests: The Destruction of Our Rainforests. 2003. (Man-Made Disasters Ser.). (Illus.). 24p. (J). lib. bdg. 22.60 *(978-0-8239-6486-4(8),* PowerKids Pr.) Rosen Publishing Group, Inc., The.

Green, Jen. Find Out about Rainforests: With 20 Projects & More Than 250 Pictures. 2013. (ENG., Illus.). 64p. (J). (gr. k-8). 9.99 *(978-1-84322-746-5(0),* Armadillo) Anness Publishing GBR. Dist: National Bk. Network.

—Rain Forest Extremes. 2008. (Extreme Nature Ser.). (ENG., Illus.). 32p. (J). (gr. 2-3). pap. *(978-0-7787-4521-1(X));* lib. bdg. *(978-0-7787-4504-4(X))* Crabtree Publishing Co.

Hantula, Richard. Rocks & Fossils. 2007. (Vital Science Earth Science Ser.). (Illus.). 48p. (gr. 5-12). lib. bdg. 27.00 *(978-0-8368-7765-6(9),* Gareth Stevens Secondary Library) Stevens, Gareth Publishing LLLP.

Hollar, Sherman. Investigating Earth's Desert, Grassland, & Rainforest Biomes. 2011. (J). lib. bdg. 31.70 *(978-1-61530-502-5(5))* Rosen Publishing Group, Inc., The.

Hunter, Rebecca. Rain Forests. 2012. (Eco Alert! Ser.). (Illus.). 32p. (gr. 4-6). lib. bdg. 28.50 *(978-1-59771-297-2(3))* Sea-To-Sea Pubns.

Jackson, Tom. Tropical Forests, 1 vol. 2nd ed. 2010. (Biomes Atlases Ser.). (ENG.). 64p. (gr. 6-9). 34.65 *(978-1-4329-4177-2(1))* Heinemann-Raintree.

Johansson, Philip. The Tropical Rain Forest: A Web of Life. 2004. (World of Biomes Ser.). (Illus.). 48p. (J). lib. bdg. 25.27 *(978-0-7660-2199-0(8))* Enslow Pubs., Inc.

—The Tropical Rain Forest: Discover This Wet Biome. 2015. (Discover the World's Biomes Ser.). 48p. (J). (gr. 3-4). 25.27 *(978-0-7660-6420-1(4));* pap. 8.95 *(978-0-7660-6421-8(2))* Enslow Pubs., Inc. (Enslow Elementary).

Johnson, Robin. Rain Forests Inside Out. 2014. (ENG.). 32p. (J). *(978-0-7787-0637-3(0))* Crabtree Publishing Co.

Kalman, Bobbie. Les Forêts Humides. 2012. (FRE.). 32p. (J). pap. 9.95 *(978-2-89579-477-6(4))* Bayard Canada CAN. Dist: Crabtree Publishing Co.

Kite, Lorien. Life in a Rain Forest. 2010. (Nature in Focus Ser.). (Illus.). 32p. (gr. 2-5). (J). pap. 10.50 *(978-1-4339-3408-7(6),* Gareth Stevens Learning Library); (YA). lib. bdg. 26.00 *(978-1-4339-3410-0(8))* Stevens, Gareth Publishing LLLP.

Kopp, Megan. What Do You Find in a Rainforest Tree? 2016. (ENG., Illus.). 24p. (J). *(978-0-7787-2261-8(9))* Crabtree Publishing Co.

Levy, Janey. Life in a Rain Forest Ecosystem. 2009. (Science Scope Ser.). 32p. (gr. 5-5). 47.90 *(978-1-60853-054-0(X),* PowerKids Pr.) Rosen Publishing Group, Inc., The.

Llewellyn, Claire & Feldman, Thea. Kingfisher Readers L2: in the Rainforest. 2014. (Kingfisher Readers Ser.). (ENG., Illus.). 32p. (J). (gr. k-3). 12.99 *(978-0-7534-7144-9(2),* 9780753471449, Kingfisher) Roaring Brook Pr.

Mason, Paul. Rainforest Research Journal. 2010. (ENG.). 32p. (J). *(978-0-7787-9903-0(4));* pap. *(978-0-7787-9924-5(7))* Crabtree Publishing Co.

McKissack, Fredrick L. & McKissack, Lisa Beringer. Counting in the Rain Forest. 2008. (Counting in the Biomes Ser.). (Illus.). 32p. (J). (gr. 1-3). lib. bdg. 23.94 *(978-0-7660-2992-7(1),* Enslow Elementary) Enslow Pubs., Inc.

McLeish, Ewan. Rain Forest Destruction. 2007. (What If We Do Nothing? Ser.). (Illus.). 48p. (gr. 5-12). pap. 14.05 *(978-0-8368-8158-5(3));* lib. bdg. 31.00 *(978-0-8368-7758-8(6))* Stevens, Gareth Publishing LLLP. (Gareth Stevens Secondary Library).

McNeil, Niki, et al. Rainforest Habitats. 2007. (In the Hands of a Child: Custom Designed Project Pack Ser.). (Illus.). 93p. spiral bd. 22.50 *(978-1-60308-095-8(3))* In the Hands of a Child.

Messner, Kate. Tree of Wonder. Mulazzani, Simona, illus. 2015. (ENG.). 36p. (J). (gr. k-3). 16.99 *(978-1-4521-1248-0(7))* Chronicle Bks. LLC.

Moore, Heidi. Rain Forest Food Chains, 1 vol. 2010. (Protecting Food Chains Ser.). (ENG., Illus.). 48p. (gr. 3-6). 33.32 *(978-1-4329-3860-4(6));* pap. 9.95 *(978-1-4329-3867-3(3))* Heinemann-Raintree. (Heinemann InfoSearch).

Morey, Allan. Rain Forest Food Chains. 2003. (What Eats What? Ser.). (J). pap. *(978-1-58417-225-3(8));* lib. bdg. *(978-1-58417-224-6(X))* Lake Street Pubs.

Murray, Aaron R. Counting in the Rain Forest 1-2-3. 2012. (All about Counting in the Biomes Ser.). (Illus.). (J). 24p. pap. 7.95 *(978-1-4644-0063-6(6));* 24p. (gr. -1-1). 22.60 *(978-0-7660-4055-7(0));* 23p. E-Book *(978-1-4645-0970-4(0))* Enslow Pubs., Inc.

O'Hare, Ted. Plants of the Rain Forest. 2004. (Rain Forest Today Discovery Library Ser.). (Illus.). 24p. (gr. 1-4). lib. bdg. 22.79 *(978-1-59515-154-4(0))* Rourke Educational Media.

—Vanishing Rain Forests. 2005. (Rain Forest Today Discovery Library Ser.). (Illus.). 24p. (gr. 1-4). 14.95 *(978-1-59515-156-8(7))* Rourke Educational Media.

Patkau, Karen. Who Needs a Jungle? 2012. (Ecosystem Ser.). (ENG., Illus.). 32p. (J). (gr. 2-5). 17.95 *(978-0-88776-992-4(6),* Tundra Bks.) Tundra Bks. CAN. Dist: Penguin Random Hse. LLC.

Pettiford, Rebecca. Rain Forest Food Chains. 2016. (Who Eats What?). 24p. (J). (gr. 2-5). lib. bdg. 25.65 *(978-1-62031-304-6(9),* Pogo) Jump! Inc.

Pratt-Serafini, Kristin Joy. A Walk in the Rainforest. Pratt-Serafini, Kristin Joy, illus. 2007. (Simply Nature Book Ser.). (Illus.). 26p. (J). (gr. -1 — 1). bds. 7.95 *(978-1-58469-088-7(7))* Dawn Pubns.

Pratt-Serafini, Kristin Joy & Crandell, Rachel. The Forever Forest: Kids Save a Tropical Treasure, 1 vol. Pratt-Serafini, Kristin Joy, illus. 2008. (ENG., Illus.). 32p. (J). (gr. k-5). 16.95 *(978-1-58469-101-3(8))* Dawn Pubns.

—The Forever Forest: Kids Save a Tropical Treasure. 2008. (Illus.). 32p. (J). (gr. k-5). pap. 8.95 *(978-1-58469-102-0(6))* Dawn Pubns.

Pyers, Greg. Biodiversity of Rain Forests. 2010. (Biodiversity Ser.). 32p. (gr. 4-18). 28.50 *(978-1-60870-073-8(9))* Marshall Cavendish Corp.

The Rain Forest, 6 Packs. (Action Packs Ser.). 128p. (gr. 3-5). 44.00 *(978-0-7635-3311-3(4))* Rigby Education.

Ranson, Erin. Rainforest Wonders. Wood, Hannah & Mahoney, Daniel J., illus. 2007. (Sparkling Slide Nature Bks.). (ENG.). 12p. (J). (gr. -1-k). 9.99 *(978-1-84666-356-7(3),* Tide Mill Pr.) Top That! Publishing PLC GBR. Dist: Independent Pubs. Group.

Read, Nicholas. A Bear's Life, 1 vol. McAllister, Ian, photos by. 2017. (My Great Bear Rainforest Ser.). (ENG., Illus.). 32p. (J). (gr. k-3). 19.95 ***(978-1-4598-1270-3(0))*** Orca Bk. Pubs. USA.

—The Sea Wolves: Living Wild in the Great Bear Rainforest, 1 vol. McAllister, Ian, photos by. 2010. (ENG., Illus.). 128p. (J). (gr. 3-7). pap. 19.95 *(978-1-55469-206-4(7))* Orca Bk. Pubs. USA.

—Wolf Island, 1 vol. McAllister, Ian, photos by. 2017. (My Great Bear Rainforest Ser.). (ENG., Illus.). 32p. (J). (gr. k-3). 19.95 *(978-1-4598-1264-2(6))* Orca Bk. Pubs. USA.

Rice, William B. Amazon Rainforest, 1 vol. 2nd rev. ed. 2013. (Nonfiction Readers Ser.). (ENG., Illus.). 32p. (J). (gr. 3-3). pap. 25.96 *(978-1-4807-1080-1(6))* Shell Educational Publishing.

Riggs, Kate. Food for Life: Rainforests. 2015. (Food for Life Ser.). (ENG.). 24p. (J). (gr. 1-3). pap. 9.99 *(978-1-62832-103-6(2),* Creative Paperbacks) Creative Co., The.

—Rainforests. 24p. (J). 2016. (Illus.). *(978-1-60818-744-7(6))* 2010. (gr. 1-4). 16.95 *(978-1-58341-829-1(6))* Creative Co., The. (Creative Education).

Roumanis, Alexis. Rainforests. 2014. (Illus.). 24p. (J). *(978-1-4896-3018-6(X))* Weigl Pubs., Inc.

Royston, Angela. Rain Forest Food Chains, 1 vol. 2014. (Food Chains & Webs Ser.). (ENG., Illus.). 32p. (gr. 1-3). 27.32 *(978-1-4846-0518-9(7),* Heinemann First Library) Heinemann-Raintree.

Schomp, Virginia. 24 Hours in a Tropical Rain Forest. 2013. (Day in an Ecosystem Ser.). 48p. (J). (gr. 4-8). pap. 12.93 *(978-1-62712-068-5(8))* Cavendish Square Publishing.

Schuetz, Kari. Life in a Tropical Rain Forest. 2016. (Biomes Alive! Ser.). (ENG., Illus.). 24p. (J). (gr. k-3). lib. bdg. 25.95 *(978-1-62617-320-0(6),* Blastoff! Readers) Bellwether Media.

Scott, Janine. Rain Forest Life, 1 vol. 2011. (Habitats Around the World Ser.). (ENG.). 24p. (gr. k-1). pap. 7.29 *(978-1-4296-7152-1(1));* pap. 41.70 *(978-1-4296-7156-9(4))* Capstone Press of Coughlan Cos. (Pebble Plus).

Senior, Kathryn. Life in a Rain Forest. 2005. (What on Earth? Ser.). (ENG., Illus.). 32p. (J). (gr. 2-4). lib. bdg. 25.50 *(978-0-516-25315-2(8),* Children's Pr.) Scholastic Library Publishing.

Senisi, Ellen B. All in a Rainforest Day. Marent, Thomas, photos by. (Illus.). (J). 2016. (ENG.). (gr. -1-3). pap. 7.95 *(978-0-9912337-1-7(9))* 2016. (gr. -1-3). 45.99 ***(978-0-9912337-2-4(7))*** 2014. (ENG., 32p. 17.95 *(978-0-9912337-0-0(0))* EdTechLens.

Smith, Kathie Billingslea. Rainforest Animals. Bonforte, Lisa, illus. 2005. 12p. (J). (gr. k-3). 6.99 *(978-1-57755-509-4(0))* Flying Frog Publishing, Inc.

Snedden, Robert. Who Eats Who in the Rainforest? 2006. (Food Chains in Action Ser.). (Illus.). 32p. (YA). (gr. 4-7). 28.50 *(978-1-58340-961-9(0))* Black Rabbit Bks.

Sobol, Richard. Breakfast in the Rainforest: A Visit with Mountain Gorillas. Sobol, Richard, photos by. 2010. (Traveling Photographer Ser.). (ENG., Illus.). 48p. (J). (gr. 1-4). pap. 7.99 *(978-0-7636-5134-3(6))* Candlewick Pr.

Sovak, Jan. Rain Forest Wildlife. 2008. (Dover Nature Stained Glass Coloring Book Ser.). (ENG., Illus.). 32p. (J). (gr. 3-8). pap. 6.99 *(978-0-486-41554-3(6))* Dover Pubns., Inc.

Stradling, Jan. Rain Forest Life: Level I, 6 vols., Vol. 2. (First Explorers Ser.). 24p. (gr. 1-2). 29.95 *(978-0-7699-1463-3(2))* Shortland Pubns. (U. S. A.) Inc.

Tarbox, A. D. Nature's Bounty: Rainforest. 2011. (ENG.). 48p. (J). (gr. 4-7). pap. 12.00 *(978-0-89812-739-3(4),* Creative Paperbacks) Creative Co., The.

—A Rain Forest Food Chain. 2008. (Nature's Bounty Ser.). (Illus.). 43p. 22.95 *(978-1-58341-601-3(3),* Creative Education) Creative Co., The.

—A Rainforest Food Chain: Nature's Bounty. 2nd ed. 2015. (Illus.). 80p. (J). *(978-1-60818-543-6(5),* Creative Education) Creative Co., The.

Vernon, Caitlyn. Nowhere Else on Earth: Standing Tall for the Great Bear Rainforest, 1 vol. 2011. (ENG., Illus.). 136p. (J). (gr. 4-12). pap. 22.95 *(978-1-55469-303-0(9))* Orca Bk. Pubs. USA.

Welsbacher, Anne. Life in a Rain Forest: The Hawaiian Islands. 2003. (Ecosystems in Action Ser.). (ENG., Illus.). 72p. (gr. 5-9). lib. bdg. 26.60 *(978-0-8225-4685-6(X))* Lerner Publishing Group.

—Protecting Earth's Rain Forests. 2009. pap. 58.95 *(978-0-7613-4697-5(X))* 2008. 72p. (YA). (gr. 4-7). lib. bdg. 30.60 *(978-0-8225-7562-7(0))* Lerner Publishing Group.

Wiley, G. D. Tropical Rain Forests. 2003. (Biomes Around the World Ser.). (J). pap. *(978-1-58417-301-4(7));* lib. bdg. *(978-1-58417-300-7(9))* Lake Street Pubs.

Wilkes, Angela, et al. Rain Forest Animals. Holmes, Steve, illus. rev. ed. 2004. (Ladders Ser.). 32p. (J). (gr. -1-3). 12.95 *(978-1-58728-606-3(8),* Two-Can Publishing) T&N Children's Publishing.

Wojahn, Rebecca Hogue & Donald. A Rain Forest Food Chain: A Who-Eats-What Adventures in South America. 2009. pap. 58.95 *(978-0-7613-4660-9(0))* Lerner Publishing Group.

Wojahn, Rebecca Hogue & Wojahn, Donald. A Rain Forest Food Chain: A Who-Eats-What Adventure in South America. 2009. (Follow That Food Chain Ser.). (ENG.). 64p. (gr. 3-5). 30.60 *(978-0-8225-7497-2(7))* Lerner Publishing Group.

Woolf, Alex. Trekking in the Congo Rainforest. 2014. (Traveling Wild Ser.). 32p. (J). (gr. 3-6). pap. 63.00 *(978-1-4824-1253-6(5))* Stevens, Gareth Publishing LLLP.

World Book, Inc Staff, contrib. by. Tropical Regions & Rain Forests. 2012. (J). *(978-0-7166-0449-5(3))* World Bk., Inc.

Worth, Bonnie. If I Ran the Rain Forest: All about Tropical Rain Forests. Ruiz, Aristides, illus. 2003. (Cat in the Hat's Learning Library). (ENG.). 48p. (J). (gr. -1-3). 9.99 *(978-0-375-81097-8(8),* Random Hse. Bks. for Young Readers) Random Hse. Children's Bks.

RAIN FORESTS

Alaina, Maria. Rainforest. 2011. (Wonder Readers Early Level Ser.). (ENG.). (gr. -1-1). 16p. pap. 35.94 *(978-1-4296-8171-1(3));* 32p. pap. 5.99 *(978-1-4296-8057-8(1))* Capstone Press of Coughlan Cos. (Wonder Readers).

Allan, Tony. Rainforests. 2003. (Illus.). lib. bdg. 28.50 (978-1-59389-124-4(5)) Chrysalis Education.

American Museum of Natural History. ABC Rainforest. 2016. (AMNH ABC Board Bks.). (ENG., Illus.). 18p. (J). (gr. -1-k). bds. 7.95 (978-1-4549-1746-5(6)) Sterling Publishing Co., Inc.

Amstutz, Lisa J. Rain Forest Animal Adaptations, 1 vol. 2011. (Amazing Animal Adaptations Ser.). (ENG.). 32p. (gr. 1-2). pap. 8.10 (978-1-4296-7034-0(7)); lib. bdg. 27.32 (978-1-4296-6028-0(7)) Capstone Press of Coughlan Cos. (Aplus Bks.).

Aspen-Baxter, Linda. Rainforests. 2011. (J). (gr. 5-8). pap. 13.95 (978-1-61690-646-7(4), AV2 by Weigl); (Illus.). 32p. (gr. 2-5). 28.55 (978-1-61690-640-5(5)) Weigl Pubs., Inc.

Bailey, Diane. Saving the Rainforests: Inside the World's Most Diverse Habitat. 2017. (Protecting the Earth's Animals Ser.). (ENG.). (J). (gr. 5-8). 23.95 **(978-1-4222-3880-6(6))** Mason Crest.

Bailey, Gerry. Tangled in the Rainforest. 2014. (ENG., Illus.). 32p. (J). (978-0-7787-0432-4(7)) Crabtree Publishing Co.

Banner, Horace. Rain Forest Adventures. 2006. (Adventure Ser.). (ENG., Illus.). 96p. (J). pap. 8.99 (978-1-85792-627-9(7), 7807b34b-fb7e-45ff-bb86-539531158470) Christian Focus Pubns. GBR. Dist: Bookmasters Distribution.

Bartholomew, Linda & Bartholomew, Al. Adventures in the Tropics. Bartholomew, Linda & Bartholomew, Al, photos by. 2005. (Illus.). 76p. (J). 15.00 (978-0-9764802-1-1(2)) Solutions for Human Services, LLC.

—The Rain Forest Book for Kids. Bartholomew, Linda & Bartholomew, Al, photos by. 2005. (Illus.). 32p. (J). 9.00 (978-0-9764802-0-4(4)) Solutions for Human Services, LLC.

Benchmark Education Company. Tropical Rain Forests (Teacher Guide) 2005. (978-1-4108-4649-5(0)) Benchmark Education Co.

Benduhn, Tea. Living in Tropical Rain Forests. 2007. (Life on the Edge Ser.). (Illus.). 24p. (gr. 1-4). pap. 8.15 (978-0-8368-8349-7(7)); lib. bdg. 22.00 (978-0-8368-8344-2(6)) Stevens, Gareth Publishing LLLP. (Weekly Reader Leveled Readers).

Benoit, Peter. Tropical Rain Forests. 2011. (True Bks.). 48p. (J). (gr. 3-5). 29.00 (978-0-531-20554-9(1), Children's Pr.); (ENG.). pap. 6.95 (978-0-531-28103-1(5)) Scholastic Library Publishing.

Berger, Gilda. Rain Forest. Date not set. (Smart Science Ser.). (Illus.). 16p. (J). (gr. 2-5). pap. 5.95 (978-1-58273-510-8(7)) Sundance/Newbridge Educational Publishing.

Bodden, Valerie. Rainforests. 2006. (Our World Ser.). (Illus.). 24p. (J). (gr. -1-3). lib. bdg. 16.95 (978-1-58341-465-1(7), Creative Education) Creative Co., The.

Bowman, Lucy. Rainforest (Level 2) - Internet Referenced. 2008. (Beginners Nature Ser.). 32p. (J). 4.99 (978-0-7945-2141-7(X), Usborne) EDC Publishing.

Brannon, Barbara. Discover Tropical Rain Forests. 2005. (J). pap. (978-1-4108-5130-7(3)) Benchmark Education Co.

Brim, Warren & Eglitis, Anna. Creatures of the Rainforest: Two Artists Explore Djabugay Country. Brim, Warren & Eglitis, Anna, illus. 2005. (ENG., Illus.). 64p. (J). (gr. k). 19.95 (978-1-875641-99-4(8)) Magabala Bks. AUS. Dist: Independent Pubs. Group.

Brown, Carron. Secrets of the Rain Forest. Nassner, Alyssa, illus. 2015. (ENG.). 36p. (J). 12.99 (978-1-61067-325-9(5)) Kane Miller.

Butterfield, Moira. Protecting Rain Forests. 2005. (Protecting Habitats Ser.). (Illus.). 32p. (gr. 4-7). lib. bdg. 26.00 (978-0-8368-4994-3(9), Gareth Stevens Learning Library) Stevens, Gareth Publishing LLLP.

Castaldo, Nancy F. Rainforests: An Activity Guide for Ages 6-9. 2003. (ENG., Illus.). 144p. (J). (gr. 2-4). pap. 14.95 (978-1-55652-476-9(5)) Chicago Review Pr., Inc.

Chambers, Jo. Tropical Rainforest. 2007. (Trackers-Math Ser.). (gr. 2-5). pap. 5.00 (978-1-59055-924-6(X)) Pacific Learning, Inc.

Channing, Margot. Rain Forest. 2014. (Closer Look At... Ser.). (Illus.). 32p. (gr. 3-6). 31.35 (978-1-904642-71-8(3)) Book Hse. GBR. Dist: Black Rabbit Bks.

Chapman, Simon. In the Jungle. Chapman, Simon, illus. 2005. (Illus.). 116p. (J). lib. bdg. 20.00 (978-1-4242-0630-8(8)) Fitzgerald Bks.

Chinery, Michael & Michael, Chinery. Las Selvas.Tr. of Rain Forests. (SPA.). 40p. (J). (gr. 3-5). 12.76 (978-84-241-2052-8(3)) Everest Editora ESP. Dist: Lectorum Pubns., Inc.

Clark Sawyer, J. Los Colores de la Selva Tropical: Hermosos y Brillantes. 2014. (Los Colores Cuentan una Historia Ser.). (SPA.). 24p. (J). (gr. -1-3). lib. bdg. 23.93 (978-1-62724-468-8(9)) Bearport Publishing Co., Inc.

—Rain Forest Colors: Bright & Beautiful. 2014. (Little Bits: Colors Tell a Story Ser.). (ENG.). 24p. (J). (gr. -1-3). lib. bdg. 23.93 (978-1-62724-326-1(7)) Bearport Publishing Co., Inc.

Clarke, Ginjer L. & dePaola, Tomie. What's up in the Amazon Rainforest. 2015. (What's Up Ser.). (ENG., Illus.). 144p. (J). (gr. 3-7). bds. 8.99 (978-0-448-48103-6(0), Grosset & Dunlap) Penguin Young Readers Group.

Clarke, Penny. Scary Creatures of the Rain Forest. 2008. (Scary Creatures Ser.). (ENG., Illus.). 32p. (J). (gr. 2-7). 27.00 (978-0-531-20544-0(4), Children's Pr.); pap. 8.95 (978-0-531-21010-9(3), Watts, Franklin) Scholastic Library Publishing.

Cole, Joanna. The Rainforest. 2014. (Magic School Bus Presents Ser.). lib. bdg. 17.20 (978-0-606-36332-7(7)) Turtleback Bks.

Cole, Joanna & Jackson, Tom. The Rainforest. Degen, Bruce & Bracken, Carolyn, illus. 2014. (Magic School Bus Presents Ser.). (ENG.). 32p. (J). (gr. 1-3). pap. 6.99 (978-0-545-68585-6(0), Scholastic Paperbacks) Scholastic, Inc.

Cole, Melissa S. Rain Forests. 2003. (Wild America Habitats Ser.). (Illus.). 24p. (J). 21.20 (978-1-56711-808-7(9), Blackbirch Pr., Inc.) Cengage Gale.

Colson, Mary. What Happens If the Rain Forests Disappear? 2015. (Unstable Earth Ser.). 32p. (J). 31.35 (978-1-62588-163-2(0)) Black Rabbit Bks.

Cooper, Jenny, illus. Rainforest to Color. 2013. (Nature Coloring Bks). 32p. (J). pap. 5.99 (978-0-7945-3306-9(X), Usborne) EDC Publishing.

Cowcher, Helen. Rainforest. (Illus.). 40p. (CHI, ENG, URD, TUR & VIE.). 16.95 (978-1-84059-017-3(3)); (VIE, ENG, URD, TUR & CHI., 16.95 (978-1-84059-022-7(X)) Milet Publishing.

Datta, Aparajita & Manjrekar, Nima. Walk the Rainforest with Niwupah. Ramaswamy, Maya, illus. 2004. (J). (978-81-89020-15-6(3)) Katha.

De la Bédoyère, Camilla. Rainforests. 2010. (Unpredictable Nature Ser.). (Illus.). 48p. (J). (gr. 3-18). lib. bdg. 19.95 (978-1-4222-2004-7(4)) Mason Crest.

Declus, Jennifer. What Might I Find in a Rainforest. Kalasea, illus. 2004. (ENG.). (J). (978-0-9743690-1-3(2)) Britt Allcroft Productions.

Delano, Marfe Ferguson. Explore My World Rain Forests. 2017. (Explore My World Ser.). (ENG.). 32p. (J). (gr. -1-2). lib. bdg. 14.90 **(978-1-4263-2829-9(X))**; (Illus.). pap. 4.99 **(978-1-4263-2828-2(1))** National Geographic Society. (National Geographic Children's Bks.).

Do You Really Want to Visit a Rainforest? 2015. (Do You Really Want to Visit... ? Ser.). (Illus.). 24p. (J). 27.10 (978-1-60753-453-2(3)) Amicus Publishing.

Dorling Kindersley Publishing Staff. The Amazon. 2015. (DK Eyewitness Bks.). (ENG., Illus.). 72p. (J). (gr. 3-7). 19.99 (978-1-4654-3567-5(0), DK Children) Dorling Kindersley Publishing, Inc.

—DK Eyewitness Books: the Amazon: The Amazon. 2015. (DK Eyewitness Bks.). (ENG., Illus.). 72p. (J). (gr. 3-7). pap. 9.99 (978-1-4654-3566-8(2), DK Children) Dorling Kindersley Publishing, Inc.

—Rain Forest. 2013. (Eye Wonder Ser.). (ENG., Illus.). 56p. (J). (gr. k-4). 10.99 (978-1-4654-0907-2(6), DK Children) Dorling Kindersley Publishing, Inc.

Dorling Kindersley Publishing Staff & Greenaway, Theresa. DK Eyewitness Books - Jungle. Dann, Geoff, illus. Dann, Geoff, photos by. 2009. (DK Eyewitness Bks.). (ENG.). 72p. (J). (gr. 3-7). 16.99 (978-0-7566-4544-1(1), DK Children) Dorling Kindersley Publishing, Inc.

Dunphy, Madeleine. Here Is the Tropical Rain Forest. Rothman, Michael, illus. 2006. (Web of Life Ser.). (ENG.). 32p. (J). (gr. -1-3). 16.95 (978-0-9773795-1-4(5)) Web of Life Children's Bks.

Dunphy, Madeleine & National Geographic Learning Staff. Here Is the Tropical Rain Forest. Rothman, Michael, illus. 2006. (Web of Life Ser.). (ENG.). 32p. (J). (gr. -1-3). pap. 9.95 (978-0-9773795-0-7(7)) Web of Life Children's Bks.

Editors of Kingfisher. Mysterious Rain Forests: Come Face to Face with Life in the Rain Forest. 2016. (Fast Facts Ser.). (ENG., Illus.). 32p. (J). pap. 6.99 (978-0-7534-7248-4(1), 9780753472484, Kingfisher) Roaring Brook Pr.

—Remarkable Rain Forests. 2016. (It's All About... Ser.). (ENG., Illus.). 32p. (J). pap. 5.99 (978-0-7534-7263-7(5), 9780753472637, Kingfisher) Roaring Brook Pr.

Esbaum, Jill & National Geographic Kids Staff. Angry Birds Playground: Rain Forest: A Forest Floor to Treetop Adventure. 2016. (ENG., Illus.). 128p. (J). (gr. -1-3). pap. 9.99 (978-1-4263-2458-1(8), National Geographic Children's Bks.) National Geographic Society.

Fabiny, Sarah. Where Is the Amazon? Colón, Daniel & Groff, David, illus. 2016. (Where Is? Ser.). (ENG.). 112p. (J). (gr. 3-7). lib. bdg. 15.99 (978-0-399-54233-6(7), Grosset & Dunlap) Penguin Young Readers Group.

Fowler, Allan & National Geographic Learning Staff. Save the Rain Forests. 2010. (Rise & Shine Ser.). (ENG., Illus.). 32p. (C). (gr. 1-2). pap. 7.95 (978-0-516-26084-6(7)) National Geographic School Publishing, Inc.

Framingham Community Charter School Grade Students. Rainforest Exhibits: How We Learned about Designing & Creating an Authentic Biome. 2003. 73p. pap. 6.25 (978-1-4116-0071-3(1)) Lulu Pr., Inc.

Franchino, Vicky. Amazon Rain Forest. 2016. (Community Connections: Getting to Know Our Planet Ser.). (ENG., Illus.). 24p. (J). (gr. 2-5). lib. bdg. 27.07 (978-1-63470-513-4(0), 207783) Cherry Lake Publishing.

Franklin, Yvonne. Las Selvas Lluviosas, 1 vol. rev. ed. 2010. (Science Readers: a Closer Look Ser.). (SPA., Illus.). 32p. (J). (gr. 2-3). pap. 8.99 (978-1-4333-2141-2(6)) Shell Educational Publishing.

Frost, Helen. Tigers [Scholastic]. 2011. (Rain Forest Animals Ser.). 24p. pap. 0.50 (978-1-4296-6311-3(1), Pebble Bks.) Capstone Press of Coughlan Cos.

Fuhr, Ute & Allaire, Caroline. Let's Look at the Rainforest. Sautai, Raoul, illus. 2012. (ENG.). 38p. (J). (gr. 1-4). pap. 11.99 (978-1-85103-360-7(2)) Moonlight Publishing, Ltd. GBR. Dist: Independent Pubs. Group.

Gaarder-Juntti, Oona. What Lives in the Rain Forest?, 1 vol. 2008. (Animal Habitats Ser.). (ENG., Illus.). 24p. (J). (gr. k-3). 25.65 (978-1-60453-177-0(0)) ABDO Publishing Co.

Ganeri, Anita. Exploring Habitats, with Benjamin Blog & His Inquisitive Dog, 1 vol. 2014. (Exploring Habitats with Benjamin Blog & His Inquisitive Dog Ser.). (ENG.). 32p. (gr. 1-3). lib. bdg. 179.94 (978-1-4329-8781-7(X), NA-h) Heinemann-Raintree.

—Exploring Rain Forests: A Benjamin Blog & His Inquisitive Dog Investigation, 1 vol. 2014. (Exploring Habitats with Benjamin Blog & His Inquisitive Dog Ser.). (ENG., Illus.). 32p. (gr. 1-3). pap. 8.95 (978-1-4329-8786-2(0)); lib. bdg. 29.99 (978-1-4329-8779-4(8)) Heinemann-Raintree. (NA-h).

—Rainforests. Bull, Peter, illus. 2013. (Explorers Ser.). (ENG.). 32p. (J). (gr. 2-5). 6.99 (978-0-7534-7073-2(X), 9780753470732, Kingfisher) Roaring Brook Pr.

Gardeski, Christina Mia. All about Rain Forests. 2017. (Habitats Ser.). (ENG.). 24p. (gr. k-1). lib. bdg. 21.99 **(978-1-5157-7643-7(3)**, Pebble Bks.) Capstone Press of Coughlan Cos.

Gardner, Robert. Rain Forest Experiments: 10 Science Experiments in One Hour or Less. 2014. (Last Minute Science Projects with Biomes Ser.). (Illus.). 48p. (J). (gr. 5-12). lib. bdg. 25.27 (978-0-7660-5937-5(5)) Enslow Pubs., Inc.

Gray, Leon. Tropical Rain Forests. 2015. (Amazing Biomes Ser.). (Illus.). 32p. (gr. 3-6). 31.35 (978-1-78121-246-2(5), 1389656) Brown Bear Bks.

Greeley, August. Fading Forests: The Destruction of Our Rainforests. (Man-Made Disasters Ser.). 24p. 2009. (gr. 3-3). 42.50 (978-1-61514-347-4(5)) 2003. (Illus.). (J). lib. bdg. 22.60 (978-0-8239-6486-4(8)) Rosen Publishing Group, Inc., The. (PowerKids Pr.).

Green, Jen. Rain Forest Extremes. 2008. (Extreme Nature Ser.). (ENG., Illus.). 32p. (J). (gr. 2-3). pap. (978-0-7787-4521-1(X)); lib. bdg. (978-0-7787-4504-4(X)) Crabtree Publishing Co.

—Rainforests at Risk. 2006. (Illus.). 32p. (YA). (gr. 4-18). lib. bdg. 27.10 (978-1-59389-116-9(4)) Chrysalis Education.

Group/McGraw-Hill, Wright. In the Rain Forest, 6 vols. (Wildcats Ser.). 32p. (gr. 2-8). (978-0-322-00599-0(X)) Wright Group/McGraw-Hill.

—Tropical Treasure: The Rain Forest, 6 vols. (Book2WebTM Ser.). (gr. 4-8). 36.50 (978-0-322-04432-6(4)) Wright Group/McGraw-Hill.

—La Vida en la Selva Tropical, 6 vols., Vol. 2. (First Explorers. Primeros Exploradores Nonfiction Sets Ser.). (SPA.). (gr. 1-2). 29.95 (978-0-7699-1487-9(X)) Shortland Pubns. (U. S. A.) Inc.

Guiberson, Brenda Z. Rain, Rain, Rain Forest. 2015. (J). lib. bdg. 18.40 (978-0-606-37341-8(1)) Turtleback Bks.

Hamilton, Jean. The Secrets of Tropical Rainforests: Hot & Humid & Teeming with Life. Leon, Vicki, ed. 2nd ed. 2005. (Jean-Michel Cousteau Presents Ser.). Orig. Title: Tropical Rainforests. (ENG., Illus.). 48p. (J). pap. 9.95 (978-0-9666490-5-5(2)) London Town Pr.

Harris, Nicholas. Rainforest. 2006. (Panoramas Ser.). (Illus.). 23p. (J). (978-0-7607-8157-9(5)) backpackbook.

Harrison, James. Rainforests. 2014. 48p. pap. 4.00 (978-1-61003-362-6(0)) Center for the Collaborative Classroom.

Heinrichs, Ann. The Amazon Rain Forest. 2009. (Nature's Wonders 2 Ser.). 96p. (gr. 6). 35.64 (978-0-7614-3932-5(3)) Marshall Cavendish Corp.

Hendra, Sue. Busy Day, Busy Night: Rain Forest. 2009. (Rookie Preschool Ser.). (ENG.). 24p. (J). (gr. -1). 23.00 (978-0-531-24407-4(5), Children's Pr.) Scholastic Library Publishing.

—Busy Day, Busy Night: Rainforest. 2009. (Rookie Preschool-NEW Ser.). (ENG.). 24p. (J). (gr. -1-k). pap. 6.95 (978-0-531-24582-8(9), Children's Pr.) Scholastic Library Publishing.

Hunter, Nick. Rain Forests: An Explorer Travel Guide, 1 vol. 2013. (Explorer Travel Guides). (ENG.). 48p. (gr. 3-6). 29.99 (978-1-4109-5432-9(3)); pap. 8.95 (978-1-4109-5439-8(0)) Heinemann-Raintree. (NA-r).

Hunter, Rebecca. Rain Forests. 2012. (Eco Alert! Ser.). (Illus.). 32p. (gr. 4-6). lib. bdg. 28.50 (978-1-59771-297-2(3)) Sea-To-Sea Pubns.

Hyde, Natalie. Amazon Rainforest Research Journal. 2017. (Illus.). 32p. (J). **(978-0-7787-3467-3(6))**; pap. **(978-0-7787-3492-5(7))** Crabtree Publishing Co.

In the Rain Forest: Level F. 16p. 31.50 (978-0-322-00376-7(8)) Wright Group/McGraw-Hill.

Iyer, Rani. Endangered Rain Forests: Investigating Rain Forests in Crisis. 2015. (Endangered Earth Ser.). (ENG.). 32p. (gr. 3-4). lib. bdg. 27.32 (978-1-4914-2039-3(1)) Capstone Press of Coughlan Cos.

Jewitt, Kathryn & Dogi, Fiametta. 3D Theater: Rainforest. 2011. (3D Theater Ser.). (ENG., Illus.). 20p. (J). (gr. -1-3). 19.99 (978-0-7534-6467-0(5), 9780753464670, Kingfisher) Roaring Brook Pr.

Johnson, Rebecca L. A Walk in the Rain Forest. Saroff, Phyllis V., illus. Braasch, Gary, photos by. 2005. (Biomes of North America Ser.). 48p. (gr. 3-6). 23.93 (978-1-57505-154-3(0)) Lerner Publishing Group.

Kainen, Dan & Wollard, Kathy. Jungle: A Photicular Book. 2016. (Photicular Ser.). (ENG., Illus.). 24p. 25.95 (978-0-7611-8953-4(X)) Workman Publishing Co., Inc.

Kalman, Bobbie. Baby Animals in Rainforest Habitats. 2011. (ENG.). 24p. (J). pap. (978-0-7787-7745-8(6)) Crabtree Publishing Co.

—Les Forêts Humides. 2012. (FRE.). 32p. (J). pap. 9.95 (978-2-89579-477-6(4)) Bayard Canada CAN. Dist: Crabtree Publishing Co.

Kenan, Tessa. Es un Camaleón! 2017. (Bumba Books (tm) en Español — Animales de la Selva Tropical (Rain Forest Animals) Ser.). (SPA., Illus.). 24p. (J). (gr. -1-1). pap. 6.99 **(978-1-5124-5408-6(7))** Lerner Publishing Group.

—Es un Chimpancé! 2017. (Bumba Books (tm) en Español — Animales de la Selva Tropical (Rain Forest Animals) Ser.). (SPA., Illus.). 24p. (J). (gr. -1-1). 25.32 **(978-1-5124-4131-4(7))** Lerner Publishing Group.

—Es un Jaguar! 2017. (Bumba Books (tm) en Español — Animales de la Selva Tropical (Rain Forest Animals) Ser.). (SPA., Illus.). 24p. (J). (gr. -1-1). 25.32 **(978-1-5124-4130-7(9))** Lerner Publishing Group.

—Es una Boa Constrictora! 2017. (Bumba Books (tm) en Español — Animales de la Selva Tropical (Rain Forest Animals) Ser.). (SPA., Illus.). 24p. (J). (gr. -1-1). 25.32 **(978-1-5124-4126-0(0))** Lerner Publishing Group.

Kenshole, Fiona. Let's Go to the Rainforest. 2010. (ENG., Illus.). 28p. 4.81 (978-0-19-440106-7(5)) Oxford Univ. Pr., Inc.

Kite, Lorien. Life in a Rain Forest. 2010. (Nature in Focus Ser.). (Illus.). 32p. (gr. 2-5). (J). pap. 10.50 (978-1-4339-3408-7(6), Gareth Stevens Learning Library); (YA). lib. bdg. 26.00 (978-1-4339-3410-0(8)) Stevens, Gareth Publishing LLLP.

Kratter, Paul. The Living Rain Forest: An Animal Alphabet. Kratter, Paul, illus. rev. ed. 2010. (ENG., Illus.). 32p. (J). (gr. 1-4). pap. 7.95 (978-1-58089-393-0(7)) Charlesbridge Publishing, Inc.

Langley, Andrew. Navigators: Rainforest. 2013. (Navigators Ser.). (ENG., Illus.). 48p. (J). (gr. 4-7). pap. 8.99 (978-0-7534-6938-5(3), 9780753469385, Kingfisher) Roaring Brook Pr.

Lawler, Janet. Rain Forest Colors. Laman, Tim, photos by. 2014. (ENG., Illus.). 32p. (J). (-k). 16.99 (978-1-4263-1733-0(6), National Geographic Children's Bks.) National Geographic Society.

Levete, Sarah. Life in the Rain Forest. 2011. (Big Picture: Homes Ser.). (ENG.). 24p. (gr. 1-2). pap. 41.70 (978-1-4296-6732-6(X), First Facts) Capstone Press of Coughlan Cos.

—Rain Forest. 2011. (ENG.). 24p. (J). pap. (978-0-7787-7865-3(7)); (gr. 3-6). (978-0-7787-7843-1(6)) Crabtree Publishing Co.

Levinson, Nancy Smiler. Rain Forests. Hearn, Diane Dawson, illus. 2008. (Holiday House Readers: Level 2 Ser.). (ENG.). 40p. (J). (gr. 3-7). 15.95 (978-0-8234-1899-2(5)) Holiday Hse., Inc.

Levy, Janey. Discovering Rain Forests. (World Habitats Ser.). 32p. 2009. (gr. 4-5). 47.90 (978-1-60854-836-1(8), PowerKids Pr.) 2007. (Illus.). (YA). (gr. 3-6). lib. bdg. 25.25 (978-1-4042-3782-7(8)) Rosen Publishing Group, Inc., The.

Lindeen, Mary & Sexton, Colleen. Rain Forests. 2007. (Learning about the Earth Ser.). (ENG., Illus.). 24p. (J). (gr. k-3). lib. bdg. 25.95 (978-1-60014-115-7(3)) Bellwether Media.

Llewellyn, Claire & Feldman, Thea. Kingfisher Readers L2: in the Rainforest. 2014. (Kingfisher Readers Ser.). (ENG., Illus.). 32p. (J). (gr. k-3). 12.99 (978-0-7534-7144-9(2), 9780753471449, Kingfisher) Roaring Brook Pr.

Lynette, Rachel. Who Lives in a Wet, Wild Rain Forest? 2010. (Exploring Habitats Ser.). (ENG.). 24p. (J). pap. 8.25 (978-1-4488-1283-7(6)); lib. bdg. 22.60 (978-1-4488-0678-2(X)) Rosen Publishing Group, Inc., The. (PowerKids Pr.).

Marianne, Berkes. Over in the Jungle: A Rainforest Rhyme. Jeanette, Canyon, illus. 2008. 26p. (J). (gr. -1). bds. 7.95 (978-1-58469-108-2(5)) Dawn Pubns.

Mattern, Joanne. Animals of the Tropical Rain Forest. (Reading Room Collection 1 Ser.). 16p. 2009. (gr. 2-3). 37.50 (978-1-60851-941-5(4)) 2006. (Illus.). (J). (gr. 3-7). lib. bdg. 17.25 (978-1-4042-3341-6(5)) Rosen Publishing Group, Inc., The. (PowerKids Pr.).

McKenzie, Precious. Rainforests. 2010. (ENG., Illus.). 24p. (gr. 3-6). pap. 8.95 (978-1-61590-555-3(3)) Rourke Educational Media.

McKissack, Fredrick L. & McKissack, Lisa Beringer. Counting in the Rain Forest. 2008. (Counting in the Biomes Ser.). (Illus.). 32p. (J). (gr. 1-3). lib. bdg. 23.94 (978-0-7660-2992-7(1), Enslow Elementary) Enslow Pubs., Inc.

McLeish, Ewan. Rain Forest Destruction. 2007. (What If We Do Nothing? Ser.). (Illus.). 48p. (gr. 5-12). pap. 14.05 (978-0-8368-8158-5(3), Gareth Stevens Secondary Library) Stevens, Gareth Publishing LLLP.

Meister, Cari. Do You Really Want to Meet a Monkey? Fabbri, Daniele, illus. 2015. (Do You Really Want to Meet... ? Ser.). 24p. (J). 27.10 (978-1-60753-456-3(8)) Amicus Publishing.

Mettler, Renè, illus. The Jungle. 2012. (ENG.). 36p. (J). (gr. -1-k). spiral bd. 12.99 (978-1-85103-399-7(8)) Moonlight Publishing, Ltd. GBR. Dist: Independent Pubs. Group.

Morey, Allan. Rain Forest Food Chains. 2003. (What Eats What? Ser.). (J). pap. (978-1-58417-225-3(8)); lib. bdg. (978-1-58417-224-6(X)) Lake Street Pubs.

Morris, Ting & Morris, Neil. Rainforest. Hulse, Gillian, illus. 2006. (Sticky Fingers Ser.). 32p. (J). lib. bdg. 28.50 (978-1-59771-028-2(8)) Sea-To-Sea Pubns.

Murphy, Alexa Gordon. Chico Mendes. 2011. (Conservation Heroes Ser.). (Illus.). 128p. (gr. 6-12). 35.00 (978-1-60413-951-8(X), Chelsea Hse.) Facts On File, Inc.

Murray, Aaron R. Counting in the Rain Forest 1-2-3. 2012. (All about Counting in the Biomes Ser.). (Illus.). (J). 24p. pap. 7.95 (978-1-4644-0063-6(6)); 24p. (gr. -1-1). 22.60 (978-0-7660-4055-7(0)); 23p. E-Book (978-1-4645-0970-4(0)) Enslow Pubs., Inc.

National Geographic Kids Staff & Esbaum, Jill. Angry Birds Playground: Rain Forest: A Forest Floor to Treetop Adventure. 2014. (ENG., Illus.). 128p. (J). (gr. -1-3). 14.95 (978-1-4263-1685-2(2), National Geographic Children's Bks.) National Geographic Society.

Newland, Sonya. Rain Forest Animals. 2011. (Saving Wildlife Ser.). 32p. (gr. 4-7). lib. bdg. 31.35 (978-1-59920-660-8(9)) Black Rabbit Bks.

O'Hare, Ted. Amazing Rain Forest. 2005. (Rain Forest Today Discovery Library Ser.). (Illus.). 24p. (gr. 1-4). 14.95 (978-1-59515-151-3(6)) Rourke Educational Media.

—Vanishing Rain Forests. 2005. (Rain Forest Today Discovery Library Ser.). (Illus.). 24p. (gr. 1-4). 14.95 (978-1-59515-156-8(7)) Rourke Educational Media.

Powell, Jillian. Projects with Rainforests. 2014. (Make & Learn Ser.). (Illus.). 32p. (J). (gr. 3-6). 27.50 (978-1-4777-7165-5(4), PowerKids Pr.) Rosen Publishing Group, Inc., The.

Prebeg, Rick. Into the Jungle. Prebeg, Rick, photos by. 2005. (Illus.). (J). (978-1-933248-05-9(X)) World Quest Learning.

Priddy, Roger. Smart Kids: Rainforest. 2014. (Smart Kids Ser.). (ENG., Illus.). 30p. (J). (gr. -1-2). 9.99 (978-0-312-51739-7(4), 9780312517397, Priddy Bks.) St. Martin's Pr.

Pyers, Greg. Biodiversity of Rain Forests. 2010. (Biodiversity Ser.). 32p. (gr. 4-18). 28.50 (978-1-60870-073-8(9)) Marshall Cavendish Corp.

Rain Forest Animals Pack [Scholastic]. 2011. (Rain Forest Animals Ser.). 24p. pap. 2.50 (978-1-4296-6316-8(2), Pebble Bks.) Capstone Press of Coughlan Cos.

Rainforest. 2003. (J). per. (978-1-57657-884-1(4)) Paradise Pr., Inc.

Read, Nicholas. Wolf Island, 1 vol. McAllister, Ian, photos by. 2017. (My Great Bear Rainforest Ser.). (ENG., Illus.). 32p. (J). (gr. k-3). 19.95 (978-1-4598-1264-2(6)) Orca Bk. Pubs. USA.

Rice, Howard. Step into the Rainforest, 1 vol. 2nd rev. ed. 2013. (Nonfiction Readers Ser.). (ENG., Illus.). 28p. (J). (gr. 2-2). pap. 23.96 (978-1-4807-1051-1(2)) Shell Educational Publishing.

—Step into the Rainforest, 1 vol. 2nd rev. ed. 2011. (Nonfiction Readers Ser.). (ENG.). 28p. (J). (gr. 2-2). pap. 6.99 (978-1-4333-3630-0(8)) Teacher Created Materials, Inc.

Rice, William & Franklin, Yvonne. Rainforests, 1 vol. 2009. (Science Readers: a Closer Look Ser.). (ENG.). 32p. (J). (gr. 3-3). pap. 8.99 (978-1-4333-0319-7(1)) Teacher Created Materials, Inc.

Rice, William B. Amazon Rainforest, 1 vol. 2nd rev. ed. 2012. (Nonfiction Readers Ser.). (ENG.). 32p. (J). (gr. 3-3). pap. 8.99 (978-1-4333-3671-3(5)) Teacher Created Materials, Inc.

Rice, William B. La Selva Amazónica. 2017. (TIME for Kids en Español - Level 3 Ser.). (SPA.). 32p. (gr. 3-3). lib. bdg. 31.99 **(978-1-5157-5178-6(3))** Capstone Press of Coughlan Cos.

Riggs, Kate. Rainforests. (Seedlings Ser.). (Illus.). 24p. (J). (gr. k-2). 2017. (ENG.). pap. 7.99 (978-1-62832-340-5(X), Creative Paperbacks) 2016. (978-1-60818-744-7(6), Creative Education) Creative Co., The.

Rissman, Rebecca. Living & Nonliving in the Rain Forest, 1 vol. 2013. (Is It Living or Nonliving? Ser.). (ENG.). 24p. (gr.

k-2). 23.32 *(978-1-4109-5382-7(3))*; pap. 6.95 *(978-1-4109-5389-6(0))* Heinemann-Raintree.

Rockett, Paul. 30 Million Different Insects in the Rain Forest. Ruffle, Mark, illus. 2015. (Big Countdown Ser.). (ENG.). 32p. (gr. 3-5). 29.99 *(978-1-4109-6876-0(6)*, Raintree Perspectives) Heinemann-Raintree.

Romero, Libby. Tropical Rain Forests. 2005. (J). pap. *(978-1-4108-4601-3(6))* Benchmark Education Co.

Ross, Suzanne. BOOST Rain Forest Activity Book. 2013. (BOOST Educational Ser.). (ENG.). 48p. (J). (gr. 1-2). pap. 5.99 *(978-0-486-49413-5(6))* Dover Pubns., Inc.

Roumanis, Alexis. Rainforests. 2014. (Illus.). 24p. (J). *(978-1-4896-3018-6(X))* Weigl Pubs., Inc.

Royston, Angela. Rain Forest Food Chains, 1 vol. 2014. (Food Chains & Webs Ser.). (ENG., Illus.). 32p. (gr. 1-3). 27.32 *(978-1-4846-0518-9(7)*, Heinemann First Library) Heinemann-Raintree.

Sadan, Dana. Animals of the Rain Forest. 2008. (Reading Rocks! Ser.). (ENG., Illus.). 32p. (J). (gr. 2-5). 28.50 *(978-1-60253-094-2(7)*, 200757) Child's World, Inc., The.

Sandler, Michael. Rain Forests: Surviving in the Amazon. 2005. (X-treme Places Ser.). (Illus.). 32p. (YA). (gr. 2-5). lib. bdg. 25.27 *(978-1-59716-089-6(X))* Bearport Publishing Co., Inc.

Schomp, Virginia. 24 Hours in a Tropical Rain Forest. 2013. 48p. (J). (gr. 4-8). 29.93 *(978-1-60870-895-6(0))* Cavendish Square Publishing.

Selvas Tropicales. (SPA.). (YA). (gr. 5-8). *(978-84-236-3191-9(5)*, ED5686) Edebé ESP. Dist: Lectorum Pubns., Inc.

Senisi, Ellen B. All in a Rainforest Day. Marent, Thomas, photos by. (Illus.). (J). 2016. (ENG.). (gr. -1-3). pap. 7.95 *(978-0-9912337-1-7(9))* 2016. (gr. -1-3). 45.99 ***(978-0-9912337-2-4(7))*** 2014. (ENG., 32p. 17.95 *(978-0-9912337-0-0(0))* EdTechLens.

Silverman, Buffy. Let's Visit the Rain Forest. 2016. (Lightning Bolt Books (tm) — Biome Explorers Ser.). (ENG.). 32p. (J). (gr. 1-3). 26.65 *(978-1-5124-1195-9(7))* Lerner Publishing Group.

Simon, Seymour. Tropical Rainforests. 2010. (ENG.). 32p. (J). (gr. k-4). 16.99 *(978-0-06-114253-6(0)*, Collins) HarperCollins Pubs.

Smith, Kathie Billingslea. Rainforest Animals. Bonforte, Lisa, illus. 2005. 12p. (J). (gr. k-3). 6.99 *(978-1-57755-509-4(0))* Flying Frog Publishing, Inc.

Spilsbury, Louise. Rain Forests. 2015. (Research on the Edge Ser.). (ENG., Illus.). 32p. (J). (gr. 3-8). 31.35 *(978-1-62588-156-4(8))* Black Rabbit Bks.

—Surviving the Rainforest. 2016. (Sole Survivor Ser.). 48p. (gr. 5-4). pap. 14.05 *(978-1-4824-5079-8(8))* Stevens, Gareth Publishing LLLP.

Spilsbury, Louise & Spilsbury, Richard. In the Rainforest. 2016. (Science on Patrol Ser.). 00048p. (J). pap. 14.05 ***(978-1-4824-5980-7(9))*** Stevens, Gareth Publishing LLLP.

Sundance/Newbridge LLC Staff. The Rain Forest. 2007. (Early Science Ser.). (gr. k-3). 18.95 *(978-1-4007-6486-0(6))*; pap. 6.10 *(978-1-4007-6482-2(3))* Sundance/Newbridge Educational Publishing.

Taylor, Barbara. Tropical Rain Forest Habitats. 2006. (Exploring Habitats Ser.). (Illus.). 36p. (gr. 3-7). lib. bdg. 26.00 *(978-0-8368-7258-3(4)*, Gareth Stevens Learning Library) Stevens, Gareth Publishing LLLP.

Taylor, Trace & Zorzi, Gina. This Is a Rainforest. 2011. (Power 100 - Ecosystems Ser.). 28p. (J). (gr. k-2). pap. 7.95 *(978-1-61541-225-9(5))* American Reading Co.

Thompson, Gare. Amazon Journey: Cruising the Rain Forest. 2006. (Science Chapters Ser.). (ENG., Illus.). 48p. (J). (gr. 1-4). lib. bdg. 17.90 *(978-0-7922-5951-0(3)*, National Geographic Children's Bks.) National Geographic Society.

Thomson, Ruth. Rain Forests. 2012. (Geography Corner Ser.). (ENG., Illus.). 24p. (J). (gr. k-3). 21.25 *(978-1-4488-6618-2(9)*, PowerKids Pr.) Rosen Publishing Group, Inc., The.

Trumbauer, Lisa. Discover the Rain Forest. 2005. (Yellow Umbrella Fluent Level Ser.). (ENG., Illus.). 16p. (gr. k-1). pap. 35.70 *(978-0-7368-5294-4(8)*, Yellow Umbrella Bks.) Capstone Press of Coughlan Cos.

Vogt, Richard C. Rain Forests. 2009. (Insiders Ser.). (ENG.). 64p. (J). (gr. 3-7). 17.99 *(978-1-4169-3866-8(4)*, Simon & Schuster Bks. For Young Readers) Simon & Schuster Bks. For Young Readers.

Watson, Galadriel Findlay. The Amazon Rain Forest: The Largest Rain Forest in the World. 2004. (Illus.). 32p. (J). lib. bdg. 26.00 *(978-1-59036-270-9(5))* Weigl Pubs., Inc.

Welsbacher, Anne. Protecting Earth's Rain Forests. (Saving Our Living Earth Ser.). 2015. (ENG., Illus.). 72p. (gr. 4-7). 30.65 *(978-1-5124-1050-1(0)*, Lerner Pubns.) 2009. pap. 58.95 *(978-0-7613-4697-5(X))* 2008. 72p. (YA). (gr. 4-7). lib. bdg. 30.60 *(978-0-8225-7562-7(0))* Lerner Publishing Group.

Williams, Judith. Explorando la Selva Tropical con una Científica. 2008. (I Like Science! Bilingual Ser.).Tr. of Exploring the Rain Forest with a Scientist. (SPA & ENG., Illus.). 24p. (J). (gr. 1-3). lib. bdg. 22.60 *(978-0-7660-2982-8(4)*, Enslow Elementary) Enslow Pubs., Inc.

—Exploring the Rain Forest Treetops with a Scientist. 2004. (I Like Science! Ser.). (Illus.). 24p. (J). lib. bdg. 22.60 *(978-0-7660-2294-2(3))* Enslow Pubs., Inc.

Woolf, Alex. Trekking in the Congo Rainforest. 2014. (Traveling Wild Ser.). 32p. (J). (gr. 3-6). pap. 63.00 *(978-1-4824-1253-6(5))* Stevens, Gareth Publishing LLLP.

World Book, Inc Staff, contrib. by. Rain Forest Animals. 2007. (J). *(978-0-7166-7729-1(6))* World Bk., Inc.

Wright, Craig, ed. Let's Go to the Rainforest. 2010. (ENG., Illus.). 14p. act. bk. ed. 4.06 *(978-0-19-440167-8(7))* Oxford Univ. Pr., Inc.

RAIN FORESTS—FICTION

Albert, Toni Diana. Saving the Rain Forest with Cammie & Cooper. Bowles, Carol, illus. l.t. ed. 2003. 32p. (J). pap. 7.95 *(978-1-929432-02-8(X)*, 800-353-2791) Trickle Creek Bks.

Allen, Nancy Kelly. On the Banks of the Amazon/en las orillas del Amazonas. de la Vega, Eida, tr. Driessen, Elizabeth, illus. 2003.Tr. of En las orillas del Amazonas. (SPA & ENG.). 32p. (J). (gr. -1-3). 16.95 *(978-0-9720192-7-9(8)*, 626999, Raven Tree Pr.,Csi) Continental Sales, Inc.

Angelo, Mary L. The Legend of the Crystal Skull. 2008. 147p. pap. 15.50 *(978-1-4357-3194-3(8))* Lulu Pr., Inc.

Arlon, Penelope. Rainforest. 2013. (Scholastic Discover More Ser.). (ENG.). 80p. (J). (gr. 2-5). 12.99 *(978-0-545-49562-2(8)*, Scholastic Reference) Scholastic, Inc.

Ballantyne, R. M. The Lighthouse. 2006. pap. *(978-1-4065-0531-3(5))* Dodo Pr.

Branch, Keith. Forest Elves: Protectors of the Rainforest. 2013. (ENG.). 42p. (J). pap. 8.95 *(978-1-4787-0650-2(3))* Outskirts Pr., Inc.

Breitrose, Prudence & Yue, Stephanie. Mousemobile: When Mice Hit the Road. 2014. (Mousenet Book Ser.). (ENG., Illus.). 288p. (J). (gr. 3-7). pap. 7.99 *(978-1-4231-7438-7(0))* Hyperion Bks. for Children.

Brett, Jan. The Umbrella. Brett, Jan, illus. 2011. (ENG., Illus.). 34p. (J). (gr. -1 — 1). bds. 7.99 *(978-0-399-25540-3(0)*, G.P. Putnam's Sons Books for Young Readers) Penguin Young Readers Group.

Bucher, Charlotte. Cecil Learns to Smile. 2010. 26p. (J). pap. 19.95 *(978-1-4327-4992-7(7))* Outskirts Pr., Inc.

Bunton, M. Catherine. The Fairy Tale Keeper. 2012. 134p. pap. 8.95 *(978-1-60594-783-9(0))* Aeon Publishing Inc.

Burke, Zoe. Charley Harper's What's in the Rain Forest? A Nature Discovery Book. Harper, Charley, illus. 2013. 34p. (J). 14.95 *(978-0-7649-6584-5(0))* Pomegranate Communications, Inc.

Burns, Ian. Possum & Python. 2005. 23p. 8.00 *(978-1-4116-5490-7(0))* Lulu Pr., Inc.

Courtney, Suzanne Gene. Rainfrog. 2011. 34p. pap. 14.50 *(978-1-61204-189-6(2)*, Eloquent Bks.) Strategic Book Publishing & Rights Agency (SBPRA).

Covey, Richard D. & Pappas, Diane H. What's Happening to the Rain Forests? 2009. (Planet Earth Patrol Ser.). (Illus.). (J). *(978-0-545-06103-2(2))* Scholastic, Inc.

Crouch, Cheryl. Troo Makes a Big Splash, 1 vol. Zimmer, Kevin, illus. 2011. (I Can Read! / Rainforest Friends Ser.). (ENG.). 32p. (J). (gr. -1-2). pap. 3.99 *(978-0-310-71810-9(4))* Zonderkidz.

—Troo's Big Climb, 1 vol. Zimmer, Kevin, illus. 2011. (I Can Read! / Rainforest Friends Ser.). (ENG.). 32p. (J). (gr. -1-2). pap. 3.99 *(978-0-310-71808-6(2))* Zonderkidz.

—Troo's Secret Clubhouse, 1 vol. Zimmer, Kevin, illus. 2011. (I Can Read! / Rainforest Friends Ser.). (ENG.). 32p. (J). (gr. -1-2). pap. 3.99 *(978-0-310-71809-3(0))* Zonderkidz.

Del Moral, Susana. Un Paseo Por la Selva. Zaidi, Nadeem, illus. 2005. (Baby Einstein: Libros de Carton Ser.). (SPA.). 10p. (J). (gr. -1). bds. *(978-970-718-306-3(3)*, Silver Dolphin en Español) Advanced Marketing, S. de R. L. de C. V.

Dey, Lorraine. The Rainforest Party / Fiesta en el bosque Tropical. 2012. (ENG.). 32p. 16.95 *(978-1-936299-28-7(3)*, Raven Tree Pr.,Csi) Continental Sales, Inc.

Earhart, Kristin. Race the Wild #1: Rain Forest Relay. 2015. (Race the Wild Ser.: 1). (ENG., Illus.). 144p. (J). (gr. 2-5). pap. 4.99 *(978-0-545-77353-9(9)*, Scholastic Paperbacks) Scholastic, Inc.

—Rain Forest Relay. 2015. (Race the Wild Ser.: 1). lib. bdg. 14.75 *(978-0-606-37042-4(0))* Turtleback Bks.

Engle, Margarita. Silver People: Voices from the Panama Canal. 2014. (ENG.). 272p. (J). (gr. 7-12). 17.99 *(978-0-544-10941-4(4)*, HMH Books For Young Readers) Houghton Mifflin Harcourt Publishing Co.

Evans, Leah Beth. A Different Kind of Hero. Gedrich, Colleen, illus. 2007. 40p. (J). per. 14.95 *(978-0-9795045-2-5(X))* Tribute Bks.

Fallon, Karla. Rainforest Moon. 2005. 102p. pap. 9.98 *(978-1-4116-3776-4(3))* Lulu Pr., Inc.

Faye, Charlet. The Chilling Adventures of Marshall McCaw. 2004. (Illus.). 60p. (J). 18.95 *(978-0-9655222-1-2(0))* FayeHouse: Pr. International.

Giancamilli, Vanessa. Gecko Gathering. Kest, Kristin, illus. 2005. (Amazing Animal Adventures Ser.). (ENG.). (J). (gr. -1-2). 36p. 2.95 *(978-1-59249-289-3(4)*, S7157); 32p. 9.95 *(978-1-59249-323-4(8)*, PS7157); 36p. 15.95 *(978-1-59249-288-6(6)*, B7107); 36p. pap. 6.95 *(978-1-59249-290-9(8)*, S7107) Soundprints.

Gilman, David. Blood Sun. 2012. (Danger Zone Ser.). (ENG.). 432p. (YA). (gr. 7). pap. 10.99 *(978-0-440-42241-9(8)*, Ember) Random Hse. Children's Bks.

Glennon, Michelle. My Big Green Teacher: Take a Deep Breath: Saving Our Rainforests. Glennon, Michelle, illus. 2008. (ENG., Illus.). 32p. (J). 19.95 *(978-0-9797952-0-6(6))* GDG Publishing.

Greenburg, J. C. In the Jungle. 2007. (Andrew Lost Ser.: 15). (ENG., Illus.). 96p. (J). (gr. 1-4). 3.99 *(978-0-375-83564-3(4)*, Random Hse. Bks. for Young Readers) Random Hse. Children's Bks.

Hammond, Jo. Home Before Dark, 1 vol. 2005. (ENG.). 144p. (YA). (gr. 7-12). per. 7.95 *(978-1-55143-340-0(0))* Orca Bk. Pubs. USA.

Harrison, Paula. The Lost Gold. 2013. (Rescue Princesses Ser.: 7). lib. bdg. 14.75 *(978-0-606-32374-1(0)*, Turtleback) Turtleback Bks.

Harvey, M. A. Attack of the Jaguar: Dare to Take the Test. 2004. (Illus.). 128p. (J). pap. *(978-1-84458-051-4(2)*, Pavilion Children's Books) Pavilion Bks.

Heer, Dusty Rhoades. The Forest That Rains Frogs. 2012. (ENG.). 58p. pap. 19.95 *(978-1-4327-9303-6(9))* Outskirts Pr., Inc.

Hill, Michelle M. Stanley. 2012. 12p. pap. 15.99 *(978-1-4772-2923-1(X))* AuthorHouse.

Hoch, Jeff. Guess Who Saves the Rain Forest? Hoch, Jeff, ed. Kiedrowski, Steve, illus. Date not set. 39p. (J). (gr. k-5). pap. 7.00 *(978-0-9650629-3-0(7))* Coulee Region Pubns., Inc.

Khoury, Jessica. Origin. 2013. (ENG., Illus.). 432p. (YA). (gr. 7). pap. 9.99 *(978-1-59514-596-3(6)*, Razorbill) Penguin Young Readers Group.

Killion, Bette. Little Lek Longtail Learns to Sleep. Vidal, Beatriz, illus. 2016. (ENG.). 28p. (J). (gr. k-3). 17.95 *(978-1-937786-63-2(3)*, Wisdom Tales) World Wisdom, Inc.

Knife & Packer, creator. Rain Forest Rumble. 2016. (Illus.). 94p. (J). pap. 6.99 *(978-1-61067-399-0(9))* Kane Miller.

Krebs, Laurie. We're Roaming in the Rainforest. Wilson, Anne, illus. 2010. 40p. (J). (ENG.). (gr. k-5). 8.99 *(978-1-84686-545-9(X))*; (SPA.). (gr. k-5). pap. 8.99 *(978-1-84686-551-0(4))*; (ENG.). (gr. -1-5). 16.99 *(978-1-84686-331-8(7))* Barefoot Bks., Inc.

Krulik, Nancy & dePaola, Tomie. Dogs Don't Have Webbed Feet. Braun, Sebastien, illus. 2015. (Magic Bone Ser.: 7). (ENG.). 128p. (J). (gr. 1-3). bds. 5.99 *(978-0-448-48096-1(4)*, Grosset & Dunlap) Penguin Young Readers Group.

Lamond, Peter. The Rainforest Family & Those Terrible Toads. Purnell, Teresa, illus. 2011. 92p. pap. 27.25 *(978-1-60976-297-1(5)*, Eloquent Bks.) Strategic Book Publishing & Rights Agency (SBPRA).

Lewis, Axel. Rain Forest Rampage, 1 vol. 2014. (Robot Racers Ser.). (ENG.). 160p. (gr. 2-4). 26.65 *(978-1-4342-6571-5(4))* Stone Arch Bks.

London, C. Alexander. We Dine with Cannibals. 2013. (Accidental Adventure Ser.: 2). (ENG.). 384p. (J). (gr. 3-7). pap. 7.99 *(978-0-14-242474-2(9)*, Puffin Books) Penguin Young Readers Group.

Long, Jan. Azule & the White Hummingbird: The Birth of the White Hummingbird. 2014. (ENG., Illus.). 84p. (J). pap. 9.95 *(978-1-63047-171-2(2))* Morgan James Publishing.

Lonsdale, Cathy. Bill the Brush Turkey. 2008. 24p. 13.95 *(978-1-4092-0414-5(6))* Lulu Pr., Inc.

Lumry, Amanda & Hurwitz, Laura. Operation Orangutan. 2007. (Adventures of Riley (Unnumbered) Ser.). (Illus.). 36p. (J). (gr. -1-3). 15.95 *(978-0-9748411-4-4(5))* Eaglemont Pr.

Marsh, Carole. The Mystery in the Amazon Rainforest: South America. (Around the World in 80 Mysteries Ser.). (Illus.). 131p. (J). 2009. lib. bdg. 18.99 *(978-0-635-07017-3(0)*, Marsh, Carole Mysteries) 2007. (gr. 3-5). 14.95 *(978-0-635-06212-3(7))* 2007. (gr. 3-5). per. 7.99 *(978-0-635-06208-6(9))* Gallopade International.

Meadows, Daisy. The Earth Fairies #5: Lily the Rain Forest Fairy. 2014. (Earth Fairies Ser.: 5). (ENG.). 80p. (J). (gr. 2-5). pap. 4.99 *(978-0-545-60528-1(8)*, Scholastic Paperbacks) Scholastic, Inc.

—Lily the Rain Forest Fairy. 2014. (Rainbow Magic — the Earth Fairies Ser.). lib. bdg. 14.75 *(978-0-606-35834-7(X))* Turtleback Bks.

Menard, Michele R. The Canopy House - Vol 2- Gus & Ester Meet the Neighbors. 2013. 34p. pap. 12.50 *(978-0-9891734-1-4(0))* Four Menards, The.

—The Canopy House - Volume 1. 2013. 38p. pap. 13.50 *(978-0-9887969-7-3(X))* Four Menards, The.

Mitchell, Susan K. The Rainforest Grew All Around, 1 vol. McLennan, Connie, illus. 2007. (ENG.). 32p. (J). (gr. -1-2). 16.95 *(978-0-9768823-6-7(1))*; pap. 8.95 *(978-0-9777423-8-7(5))* Arbordale Publishing.

Mitton, Tony. Rainforest Adventure. 2015. (Amazing Animals Ser.). (ENG., Illus.). 24p. (J). (gr. -1-1). pap. 4.99 *(978-0-7534-7227-9(9)*, 9780753472279, Kingfisher) Roaring Brook Pr.

Mitton, Tony & Parker, Ant. Rainforest Romp. 2009. (Amazing Animals Ser.). (ENG., Illus.). 24p. (J). (gr. -1-1). 9.99 *(978-0-7534-6298-0(2)*, 9780753462980, Kingfisher) Roaring Brook Pr.

Nelson, N. A. Bringing the Boy Home. 2008. (ENG.). 224p. (J). (gr. 3-7). 16.99 *(978-0-06-088698-1(6))* HarperCollins Pubs.

Osorio, Rick. The Great Adventure of Sally Rock & the Secret of Man, 1 vol. 2009. 164p. pap. 24.95 *(978-1-60813-596-7(9))* America Star Bks.

Packer. Rain Forest Rumble. Knife, illus. 2016. 94p. (J). *(978-1-61067-479-9(0))* Kane Miller.

Page, P. K. Uirapurú: Based on a Brazilian Legend. Bridgeman, Kristi, illus. 2010. (ENG.). 32p. (J). 19.95 *(978-0-88982-264-1(6))* Oolichan Bks. CAN. Dist: Univ. of Toronto Pr.

Parente, Peter. Peeper the Kinkajou. l.t. ed. 2004. (Peeper & Friends Ser.). (Illus.). 28p. (J). 15.95 *(978-0-9745052-0-6(X)*, Peeper & Friends) Tree Of Life Publishing.

Platt, Richard. The Vanishing Rainforest. van Wyk, Rupert, illus. 2007. (ENG.). 32p. (J). pap. *(978-0-7112-2170-3(7)*, Frances Lincoln) Quarto Publishing Group UK.

—The Vanishing Rainforest. van Wyk, Rupert, illus. 2003. 32p. (YA). *(978-0-7112-1960-1(5))* ReiseArt Buchhandlung GmbH.

Sandusky, Thomas & Hill, Kathy. Peter the Poison Dart Frog, Stories of the Rainforest. Johnson, Gretchen, illus. 2011. 24p. pap. 12.95 *(978-1-936343-85-0(1))* Peppertree Pr., The.

Sarago-Kendrick, Delphine. Nana's Land. Sarago-Kendrick, Delphine, illus. 2004. (Illus.). 44p. (J). pap. *(978-1-875641-90-1(4))* Magabala Bks.

Schlegl, Stacey Lynn. Little Frog. 2008. (J). per. 8.95 *(978-0-9801504-0-7(X))* Jan-Carol Publishing, INC.

Shumway, Gail. Stripey Follows His Dream. 2010. 60p. (J). 19.95 *(978-0-9824611-7-4(8))* Snow In Sarasota Publishing.

Smith, Dale. What the Orangutan Told Alice: A Rain Forest Adventure. Smith, Dale & Russon, Anne E., photos by. 2003. (Illus.). 192p. (gr. 6-12). pap. 15.95 *(978-0-9651452-8-2(X))* Deer Creek Publishing.

Stephens, Sarah Hines & Hines-Stephens, Sarah. Rumble in the Rainforest, 1 vol. Schoening, Dan, illus. (Wonder Woman Ser.). (ENG.). 56p. (gr. 2-3). 2014. pap. 4.95 *(978-1-4342-2765-2(0))* 2010. 26.65 *(978-1-4342-1992-3(5))* Stone Arch Bks. (DC Super Heroes).

Stilton, Geronimo. Rumble in the Jungle. 2013. (Geronimo Stilton Ser.: 53). lib. bdg. 18.40 *(978-0-606-31527-2(6)*, Turtleback) Turtleback Bks.

Terry, Will, illus. The Frog with the Big Mouth, 1 vol. 2008. (ENG.). 32p. (J). (gr. k-3). 16.99 *(978-0-8075-2621-7(5))* Whitman, Albert & Co.

Turner, Tracey. Lost in the Jungle of Doom. 2014. (ENG., Illus.). 128p. (J). *(978-0-7787-0727-1(X))* Crabtree Publishing Co.

What's in the Rainforest. 2003. (J). per. *(978-1-57657-933-6(6))* Paradise Pr., Inc.

Whitmore, Andrew. Beast of the Jungle. 2007. 96p. (YA). pap. *(978-1-4207-0728-1(0))* Sundance/Newbridge Educational Publishing.

Witte, Anna. The Parrot Tico Tango. 2005. (ENG., Illus.). 24p. (J). (gr. -1-3). 6.99 *(978-1-905236-11-4(5))* Barefoot Bks., Inc.

—The Parrot Tico Tango. Witte, Anna, illus. 2005. (Illus.). 24p. (J). (gr. k-3). 15.99 *(978-1-84148-243-9(9))* Barefoot Bks., Inc.

Worth, Bonnie. If I Ran the Rain Forest: All about Tropical Rain Forests. Ruiz, Aristides, illus. 2003. (Cat in the Hat's Learning Library). (ENG.). 48p. (J). (gr. -1-3). 9.99 *(978-0-375-81097-8(8)*, Random Hse. Bks. for Young Readers) Random Hse. Children's Bks.

Young, Judy. Tuki & Moka: A Tale of Two Tamarins. Madsen, Jim, illus. 2013. (ENG.). 32p. 16.99 *(978-1-58536-795-5(8))* Sleeping Bear Pr.

RAINFALL

see Rain and Rainfall

RAINFORESTS

see Rain Forests

RALEIGH, WALTER, SIR, 1552?-1618

McPherson, Stephanie Sammartino. Sir Walter Raleigh. 2005. (History Maker Bios Ser.). (Illus.). 48p. (J). (gr. 3-7). lib. bdg. 26.60 *(978-0-8225-2945-3(9)*, Lerner Pubns.) Lerner Publishing Group.

Olson, Steven P. Sir Walter Raleigh: Explorer for the Court of Queen Elizabeth. (Library of Explorers & Exploration Ser.). 112p. (gr. 5-8). 2009. 66.50 *(978-1-60853-612-2(2))* 2003. (Illus.). lib. bdg. 34.60 *(978-0-8239-3631-1(7))* Rosen Publishing Group, Inc., The. (Rosen Reference).

Petrie, Kristin. Sir Walter Raleigh, 1 vol. 2007. (Explorers Set 2 Ser.). (ENG., Illus.). 32p. (gr. 4-7). 27.07 *(978-1-59679-748-2(7)*, Checkerboard Library) ABDO Publishing Co.

Rice, Earle, Jr. The Life & Times of Sir Walter Raleigh. 2006. (Profiles in American History Ser.). (Illus.). 48p. (J). (gr. 3-7). lib. bdg. 29.95 *(978-1-58415-452-5(7))* Mitchell Lane Pubs., Inc.

Ward, Nancy. Sir Walter Raleigh: Founding the Virginia Colony. 2006. (In the Footsteps of Explorers Ser.). (ENG., Illus.). 32p. (J). (gr. 4-7). pap. *(978-0-7787-2460-5(3)*, 1253445); lib. bdg. *(978-0-7787-2424-7(7)*, 1253445) Crabtree Publishing Co.

RAMS

see Sheep

RANCH LIFE

see also Cowboys

Ancona, George. Mi Casa: My House. 2005. (Somos Latinos (We Are Latinos) Ser.). (SPA & ENG., Illus.). 32p. (J). (gr. 1-3). pap. 8.95 *(978-0-516-25065-6(5)*, Children's Pr.) Scholastic Library Publishing.

Cameron, Charles. Why Lizzie Johnson Matters to Texas. 2014. (Illus.). 32p. (J). lib. bdg. 26.25 *(978-1-4777-0908-5(8))* Rosen Publishing Group, Inc., The.

—Why Richard King Matters to Texas. 2014. (Illus.). 32p. (J). lib. bdg. 26.25 *(978-1-4777-0910-8(X))* Rosen Publishing Group, Inc., The.

Catala, Ellen. On the Ranch. 2003. (Shutterbug Bks.). (Illus.). 16p. pap. 4.10 *(978-0-7398-7641-1(4))* Steck-Vaughn.

Craats, Rennay. Ranching. 2003. (Real Life Stories Ser.). (Illus.). 24p. (J). lib. bdg. 24.45 *(978-1-59036-081-1(8))* Weigl Pubs., Inc.

Drinkard, Lawson. Riding on a Range: Western Activities for Kids. Lee, Fran, illus. 2003. (ENG.). 64p. (YA). pap. 9.99 *(978-1-58685-036-4(9))* Gibbs Smith, Publisher.

Get Inside Series. Incl. Baseball. Almonte, Paul. 80p. 14.95 *(978-1-881889-55-7(6))*; Ranch. Morgenroth, Barbara. 64p. 14.95 *(978-1-881889-56-4(4))*; (Illus.). (J). 1994. 29.90 *(978-1-881889-79-3(3))* Silver Moon Pr.

Gilkerson, Patricia. My Adventure on a Ranch. 2006. 44p. (J). 8.99 *(978-1-59092-282-8(4))* Blue Forge Pr.

Gordon, Sharon. At Home on the Ranch. 2005. (Bookworms Ser.). (SPA., Illus.). 32p. (J). (gr. 3-7). lib. bdg. *(978-0-7614-1962-4(4)*, Benchmark Bks.) Marshall Cavendish Corp.

—At Home on the Ranch/Mi Casa en el Rancho. 2006. (Bookworms Ser.). (ENG & SPA., Illus.). 32p. (gr. k-2). lib. bdg. 15.95 *(978-0-7614-2458-1(X))* Marshall Cavendish Corp.

—Mi Casa en el Rancho. 2006. (Bookworms Ser.). (SPA & ENG., Illus.). 32p. (gr. k-2). lib. bdg. 15.95 *(978-0-7614-2378-2(8))* Marshall Cavendish Corp.

James, Will. The Will James Cowboy Book, Vol. 1. rev. ed. (Illus.). 128p. (J). (gr. 4). *(978-0-87842-469-6(5)*, 816) Mountain Pr. Publishing Co., Inc.

Kalman, Bobbie. A Visual Dictionary of the Old West. 2007. (Crabtree Visual Dictionaries Ser.). (ENG., Illus.). 32p. (J). (gr. 3-7). lib. bdg. *(978-0-7787-3503-8(6))* Crabtree Publishing Co.

Keaster, Diane W. Darby - the Cow Dog, 9 vols. Page, Debbie et al, illus. l.t. ed. 2005. (ZC Horses: 9). (ENG.). 68p. (J). per. 7.95 *(978-0-9721496-8-6(6))* ZC Horses Series of Children's Bks.

Letters of a Woman Homesteader. 2003. (Our American Heritage Ser.). (J). pap. 62.00 incl. audio compact disk *(978-1-58472-527-5(3)*, In Audio) Sound Room Pubs., Inc.

Nathan, Sandy. Tecolote: The Little Horse That Could. 2011. (Illus.). 44p. (J). pap. 14.95 *(978-0-9762809-9-6(X))* Vilasa Pr.

Peppas, Lynn. Why Charles Goodnight Matters to Texas. 2014. (Illus.). 32p. (J). lib. bdg. 26.25 *(978-1-4777-0907-8(X))* Rosen Publishing Group, Inc., The.

Peterson, Cris. Amazing Grazing. Upitis, Alvis, photos by. 2011. (ENG., Illus.). 32p. (J). (gr. k-2). pap. 10.95 *(978-1-59078-868-4(0))* Boyds Mills Pr.

Rau, Dana Meachen. On the Ranch. 2007. (J). pap. 6.99 *(978-0-7614-3313-2(9))* Marshall Cavendish Corp.

Rey, Carol. Iris Wall, Cracker Cowgirl, 1 vol. Lux, Eldon, illus. 2012. (ENG.). 32p. (J). (gr. k-3). 16.99 *(978-1-4556-1525-4(0))* Pelican Publishing Co., Inc.

Sanford, William R. & Green, Carl R. Richard King: Courageous Texas Cattleman. 2012. (Courageous Heroes of the American West Ser.). (Illus.). 48p. (J). pap. 8.95 *(978-1-4644-0088-9(1))*; (gr. 5-18). 22.60 *(978-0-7660-4003-8(8))* Enslow Pubs., Inc.

Savage, Candace. Born to Be a Cowgirl: A Spirited Ride Through the Old West. 2004. (Illus.). *(978-1-55054-838-9(7))* Da Capo Pr., Inc.

Schwartz, Heather. Lizzie Johnson: Texan Cowgirl, 1 vol. 2012. (Primary Source Readers Ser.). (ENG.). 32p. (J). (gr. 3-3). pap. 8.99 *(978-1-4333-5051-1(3))* Teacher Created Materials, Inc.

Thompson, Gare. When the Mission Padre Came to the Rancho: The Early California Adventures of Rosalinda & Simon Delgado. 2004. (I Am American Ser.). (ENG., Illus.). 40p. (J). (gr. 3-7). pap. 6.99 *(978-0-7922-6945-8(4)*, National Geographic Children's Bks.) National Geographic Society.

Thompson, Gare & National Geographic Learning Staff. Missions & Ranchos. 2007. (Reading Expeditions Ser.).

(ENG., Illus.). 40p. (J). pap. 19.95 (978-0-7922-4548-3(2)) CENGAGE Learning.

Urbigkit, Cat. Cattle Kids: A Year on the Western Range. 2007. (ENG., Illus.). 32p. (J). (gr. 2-4). 16.95 (978-1-59078-508-9(8)) Boyds Mills Pr.

Wade, Mary Dodson. Henrietta King: Loving the Land. Farnsworth, Bill, illus. 2011. (ENG.). 24p. 16.95 (978-1-933979-64-9(X), dcf39346-020e-471d-9505-349b26473e11) Bright Sky Pr.

West, David. Lots of Things You Want to Know about Cowboys: ... & Some You Don't! 2015. (Lots of Things You Want to Know About Ser.). (Illus.). 24p. (J). 28.50 (978-1-62588-089-5(8)) Black Rabbit Bks.

Wheeler, Jill C. Pioneer Practices with Ree Drummond, 1 vol. 2016. (ENG., Illus.). 32p. (J). (978-1-62403-819-8(0)) ABDO Publishing Co.

Whitney, Gleaves & Whitney, Louise Doak. B Is for Buckaroo: A Cowboy Alphabet. Guy, Sue & Guy, Susan, illus. rev. ed. 2003. (Sports Ser.). (ENG.). 40p. (J). (gr. 1-4). 17.95 (978-1-58536-139-7(9), 202000) Sleeping Bear Pr.

Williams, Jack S. Townspeople & Ranchers of the California Mission Frontier. 2009. (People of the California Missions Ser.). 64p. (gr. 4-4). 58.50 (978-1-60851-161-7(8), PowerKids Pr.) Rosen Publishing Group, Inc., The.

RANCH LIFE—FICTION

Alphin, Elaine Marie. Dinosaur Hunter. Bolognese, Don, illus. 2004. (I Can Read Bks.). 48p. (gr. 2-4). 14.00 (978-0-7569-3241-1(6)) Perfection Learning Corp.

Babcock, Nona Burroughs. Little Wolf's Adventure: A Medicine Dream & Warrior Ghosts. 2008. 212p. 24.95 (978-0-595-49087-5(5)); pap. 14.95 (978-0-595-46072-4(0)) iUniverse, Inc.

Baker, Willard F. The Boy Ranchers among the Indians: Or-Trailing the Yaquis. 2007. (ENG.). 140p. pap. 18.99 (978-1-4346-3478-8(7)); 154p. pap. 21.99 (978-1-4346-3479-5(5)) Creative Media Partners, LLC.

Banks, Radine. Nochi Come Back. 2006. 112p. per. 12.20 (978-1-4120-8803-9(8)) Trafford Publishing.

Beecher, Elizabeth. Roy Rogers on the Double-R Ranch. Nordli, Ernest, illus. 2011. 78p. 37.95 (978-1-258-03590-7(1)) Literary Licensing, LLC.

Blom, Jen K. Possum Summer. Rayyan, Omar, illus. 2011. (ENG.). 256p. (J). (gr. 3-7). 17.95 (978-0-8234-2331-6(X)) Holiday Hse., Inc.

Brammer, Ethriam Cash. The Rowdy, Rowdy Ranch / Alla en el Rancho Grande. Cruz, D. Nina, illus. 2003. (ENG & SPA.). 32p. (J). 16.95 (978-1-55885-409-3(6), Piñata Books) Arte Publico Pr.

Brinegar, R. L. Ron. Pokey: The Fastest Horse on the Ranch. 2007. 33p. pap. 8.95 (978-0-7414-4078-5(4)) Infinity Publishing.

Brouwer, Sigmund. Blazer Drive, 1 vol. 2007. (Orca Sports Ser.). (ENG.). 176p. (YA). (gr. 6-10). per. 9.95 (978-1-55143-717-0(1)) Orca Bk. Pubs. USA.

Bryant, Annie. Ghost Town. 2009. (Beacon Street Girls Ser.: 11). (ENG.). 240p. (J). (gr. 4-8). pap. 7.99 (978-1-4169-6441-4(X), Aladdin) Simon & Schuster Children's Publishing.

Buchanan, Buck. Denni-Jo & Navajo. Rath, Robert & Wald, Christina, illus. 2017. (ENG.). 32p. (J). (gr. k-3). 16.99 (978-1-943328-46-8(3), West Winds Pr.) Graphic Arts Ctr. Publishing Co.

Burkhart, Kiersi & Keyser, Amber J. At Top Speed. 2017. (Quartz Creek Ranch Ser.). (ENG.). 240p. (J). (gr. 4-8). 27.99 (978-1-4677-9255-4(1)) Lerner Publishing Group.

—One Brave Summer. 2017. (Quartz Creek Ranch Ser.). (ENG.). 224p. (J). (gr. 4-8). 27.99 (978-1-4677-9254-7(3)) Lerner Publishing Group.

Burkhart, Kiersi, et al. The Long Trail Home. 2017. (Quartz Creek Ranch Ser.). (ENG.). 240p. (gr. 4-8). 6.99 (978-1-5124-3090-5(0), Darby Creek) Lerner Publishing Group.

Carkhuff Jr., Sam. The Ranch Race. Crow, Katie, illus. 2012. 36p. 16.99 (978-1-939054-03-6(6)); pap. 11.99 (978-1-939054-02-9(8)) Rowe Publishing and Design.

Carr, Annie Roe. Nan Sherwood at Rose Ranch. 2007. 124p. per. (978-1-4068-4396-5(2)) Echo Library.

—Nan Sherwood at Rose Ranch or the Old Me. 2007. pap. (978-1-4065-1295-3(8)) Dodo Pr.

Christian, Diana. The Lucky Seven. 2005. 71p. pap. 19.95 (978-1-4137-5471-1(6)) America Star Bks.

Citra, Becky. Missing, 1 vol. 2011. (ENG.). 184p. (J). (gr. 4-7). pap. 9.95 (978-1-55469-345-0(4)) Orca Bk. Pubs. USA.

Clark, Brenda. Spiro Goes West: More Adventures of Spiro the Shooting Star. 2008. 57p. pap. 16.95 (978-1-60474-770-6(6)) America Star Bks.

Compton, Dawn. Leave 'Em Standing. 2005. (Illus.). pap. 12.95 (978-1-932196-73-3(0)) WordWright.biz, Inc.

Coombs, Charles. Ranch Mystery: Young Readers. Priscilla, Louis, illus. 2011. 188p. 42.95 (978-1-258-09854-4(7)) Literary Licensing, LLC.

Cousins Camp. 2010. 32p. pap. 12.99 (978-1-4490-8387-8(0)) AuthorHouse.

Curtin, Ann. Dreamcatcher. 2015. 201p. (YA). (978-1-61271-246-8(0)) Zumaya Pubns. LLC.

Dahlstrom, S. J. Texas Grit: the Adventures of Wilder Good #2. 2014. (Adventures of Wilder Good Ser.). (ENG.). 141p. (J). (gr. 3). pap. 7.95 (978-1-58988-094-8(3)) Dry, Paul Bks., Inc.

Davis, Susan Page. Sarah's Long Ride. 2007. (Piper Ranch Ser.). 173p. (J). (gr. 3-7). per. 8.99 (978-1-59166-737-7(2)) BJU Pr.

Dembo, Jaiden. Finding Strider. 2010. 52p. pap. 15.54 (978-0-557-39981-9(5)) Lulu Pr., Inc.

Draper, Tricia. Bobby Bear Learns to Be a Cowboy. Babinski, Michael, illus. 2004. 36p. (gr. -1-3). per. 14.95 (978-1-58961-246-4(9)) PageFree Publishing, Inc.

Drummond, Ree. Charlie Plays Ball. deGroat, Diane, illus. 2015. (Charlie the Ranch Dog Ser.). (ENG.). 40p. (J). (gr. -1-3). 17.99 (978-0-06-229752-5(X)) HarperCollins Pubs.

—Charlie the Ranch Dog. deGroat, Diane, illus. 2011. (Charlie the Ranch Dog Ser.). (ENG.). 40p. (J). (gr. -1-3). 17.99 (978-0-06-199655-9(6)) HarperCollins Pubs.

—Charlie the Ranch Dog. 2013. (I Can Read! Level 1 Ser.). (J). lib. bdg. 13.55 (978-0-606-31822-8(4), Turtleback) Turtleback Bks.

—Charlie the Ranch Dog: Charlie Goes to the Doctor. deGroat, Diane, illus. 2014. (I Can Read Level 1 Ser.). (ENG.). 32p. (J). (gr. -1-3). pap. 3.99 (978-0-06-221917-6(0)) HarperCollins Pubs.

—Charlie the Ranch Dog: Charlie's New Friend. deGroat, Diane, illus. 2014. (I Can Read Level 1 Ser.). (ENG.). 32p. (J). (gr. -1-3). 16.99 (978-0-06-221915-2(4)); pap. 3.99 (978-0-06-221914-5(6)) HarperCollins Pubs.

—Charlie the Ranch Dog: Stuck in the Mud. deGroat, Diane & Whipple, Rick, illus. 2015. (I Can Read Level 1 Ser.). (ENG.). 32p. (J). (gr. -1-3). 16.99 (978-0-06-234775-6(6)); pap. 3.99 (978-0-06-234774-9(8)) HarperCollins Pubs.

—Charlie's Snow Day. 2013. (I Can Read! Level 1 Ser.). (J). lib. bdg. 13.55 (978-0-606-32161-7(6), Turtleback) Turtleback Bks.

—Little Ree. Rogers, Jacqueline, illus. 2017. (Little Ree Ser.). 40p. (J). (gr. -1-3). 17.99 (978-0-06-245318-1(1)) HarperCollins Pubs.

Edge, Laura Bufano. Wild West Dreams. 2006. (J). pap. (978-0-88092-623-2(6)); lib. bdg. (978-0-88092-622-5(8)) Royal Fireworks Publishing Co.

Enderle, Dotti. Crosswire. 2010. (ENG.). 144p. (J). (gr. 4-6). 17.95 (978-1-59078-751-9(X), Calkins Creek) Boyds Mills Pr.

Erickson, John R. The Big Question. Holmes, Gerald L., illus. 2012. 128p. (J). pap. (978-1-59188-160-5(9)) Maverick Bks.

—The Big Question. Holmes, Gerald L., illus. 2012. (Hank the Cowdog Ser.: Vol. 60). (ENG.). 128p. (J). (gr. 3-6). 15.99 (978-1-59188-260-2(5)) Maverick Bks., Inc.

—The Case of the Black-Hooded Hangmans. Holmes, Gerald L., illus. 2011. (Hank the Cowdog Ser.). (ENG.). 113p. (J). (gr. 3-6). pap. 5.99 (978-1-59188-124-7(2)) Maverick Bks., Inc.

—The Case of the Blazing Sky. Holmes, Gerald L., illus. 2011. (Hank the Cowdog Ser.). (ENG.). 129p. (J). (gr. 3-6). pap. 5.99 (978-1-59188-151-3(X)) Maverick Bks., Inc.

—The Case of the Booby-Trapped Pickup. Holmes, Gerald L., illus. 2011. (Hank the Cowdog Ser.). (ENG.). 129p. (J). (gr. 3-6). pap. 5.99 (978-1-59188-149-0(8)) Maverick Bks., Inc.

—The Case of the Car-Barkaholic Dog. Holmes, Gerald L., illus. 2011. (Hank the Cowdog Ser.). (ENG.). 115p. (J). (gr. 3-6). pap. 5.99 (978-1-59188-117-9(X)) Maverick Bks., Inc.

—The Case of the Coyote Invasion. Holmes, Gerald L., illus. 2011. (Hank the Cowdog Ser.: No. 56). (ENG.). 132p. (J). (gr. 3-6). pap. 5.99 (978-1-59188-156-8(0)) Maverick Bks., Inc.

—The Case of the Deadly Ha-Ha Game. Holmes, Gerald L., illus. 2011. (Hank the Cowdog Ser.). (ENG.). 128p. (J). (gr. 3-6). pap. 5.99 (978-1-59188-137-7(4)) Maverick Bks., Inc.

—The Case of the Dinosaur Birds. Holmes, Gerald L., illus. 2011. (Hank the Cowdog Ser.). (ENG.). 125p. (J). (gr. 3-6). pap. 5.99 (978-1-59188-154-4(4)) Maverick Bks., Inc.

—The Case of the Double Bumblebee Sting. Holmes, Gerald L., illus. 2011. (Hank the Cowdog Ser.: No. 22). (ENG.). 114p. (J). (gr. 3-6). pap. 5.99 (978-1-59188-122-3(6)) Maverick Bks., Inc.

—The Case of the Falling Sky. Holmes, Gerald L., illus. 2011. (Hank the Cowdog Ser.: No. 45). (ENG.). 129p. (J). (gr. 3-6). pap. 5.99 (978-1-59188-145-2(5)) Maverick Bks., Inc.

—The Case of the Fiddle-Playing Fox. Holmes, Gerald L., illus. 2011. (Hank the Cowdog Ser.: No. 12). (ENG.). 118p. (J). (gr. 3-6). pap. 5.99 (978-1-59188-112-4(9)) Maverick Bks., Inc.

—The Case of the Haystack Kitties. Holmes, Gerald L., illus. 2011. (Hank the Cowdog Ser.). (ENG.). 123p. (J). (gr. 3-6). pap. 5.99 (978-1-59188-130-8(7)) Maverick Bks., Inc.

—The Case of the Hooking Bull. Holmes, Gerald L., illus. 2011. (Hank the Cowdog Ser.). (ENG.). 119p. (J). (gr. 3-6). pap. 5.99 (978-1-59188-118-6(8)) Maverick Bks., Inc.

—The Case of the Kidnapped Collie. Holmes, Gerald L., illus. 2011. (Hank the Cowdog Ser.). (ENG.). 113p. (J). (gr. 3-6). pap. 5.99 (978-1-59188-126-1(9)) Maverick Bks., Inc.

—The Case of the Measled Cowboy. Holmes, Gerald L., illus. 2011. (Hank the Cowdog Ser.: No. 33). (ENG.). 126p. (J). (gr. 3-6). pap. 5.99 (978-1-59188-133-9(1)) Maverick Bks., Inc.

—The Case of the Midnight Rustler. Holmes, Gerald L., illus. 2011. (Hank the Cowdog Ser.: No. 19). (ENG.). 113p. (J). (gr. 3-6). pap. 5.99 (978-1-59188-119-3(6)) Maverick Bks., Inc.

—The Case of the Missing Bird Dog. Holmes, Gerald L., illus. 2011. (Hank the Cowdog Ser.: No. 40). (ENG.). 126p. (J). (gr. 3-6). pap. 5.99 (978-1-59188-140-7(4)) Maverick Bks., Inc.

—The Case of the Missing Cat. Holmes, Gerald L., illus. 2011. (Hank the Cowdog Ser.: No. 15). (ENG.). 114p. (J). (gr. 3-6). pap. 5.99 (978-1-59188-115-5(3)) Maverick Bks., Inc.

—The Case of the Monkey Burglar. Holmes, Gerald L., illus. 2011. (Hank the Cowdog Ser.: No. 48). (ENG.). 129p. (J). (gr. 3-6). pap. 5.99 (978-1-59188-148-3(X)) Maverick Bks., Inc.

—The Case of the Mysterious Voice. Holmes, Gerald L., illus. 2012. (Hank the Cowdog (Quality) Ser.: Vol. 58). (ENG.). 123p. (J). (gr. 3-6). pap. 5.99 (978-1-59188-158-2(7)) Maverick Bks., Inc.

—The Case of the Night-Stalking Bone Monster. Holmes, Gerald L., illus. 2011. (Hank the Cowdog Ser.). (ENG.). 115p. (J). (gr. 3-6). pap. 5.99 (978-1-59188-127-8(7)) Maverick Bks., Inc.

—The Case of the Perfect Dog. Holmes, Gerald L., illus. 2012. 127p. (J). (978-1-59188-259-6(1)) Maverick Bks.

—The Case of the Perfect Dog. Holmes, Gerald L., illus. 2012. (Hank the Cowdog (Quality) Ser.). (ENG.). 127p. (J). (gr. 3-6). pap. 5.99 (978-1-59188-159-9(5)) Maverick Bks., Inc.

—The Case of the Raging Rottweiler. Holmes, Gerald L., illus. 2011. (Hank the Cowdog Ser.). (ENG.). 131p. (J). (gr. 3-6). pap. 5.99 (978-1-59188-136-0(6)) Maverick Bks., Inc.

—The Case of the Saddle House Robbery. Holmes, Gerald L., illus. 2011. (Hank the Cowdog Ser.: No. 35). (ENG.). 125p. (J). (gr. 3-6). pap. 5.99 (978-1-59188-135-3(8)) Maverick Bks., Inc.

—The Case of the Secret Weapon. Holmes, Gerald L., illus. 2011. (Hank the Cowdog Ser.). (ENG.). 125p. (J). (gr. 3-6). pap. 5.99 (978-1-59188-155-1(2)) Maverick Bks., Inc.

—The Case of the Shipwrecked Tree. Holmes, Gerald L., illus. 2011. (Hank the Cowdog Ser.: No. 41). (ENG.). 119p. (J). (gr. 3-6). pap. 5.99 (978-1-59188-141-4(2)) Maverick Bks., Inc.

—The Case of the Swirling Killer Tornado. Holmes, Gerald L., illus. 2011. (Hank the Cowdog Ser.). (ENG.). 112p. (J). (gr. 3-6). pap. 5.99 (978-1-59188-125-4(0)) Maverick Bks., Inc.

—The Case of the Tender Cheeping Chickies. Holmes, Gerald L., illus. 2011. (Hank the Cowdog Ser.). (ENG.). 129p. (J). (gr. 3-6). pap. 5.99 (978-1-59188-147-6(1)) Maverick Bks., Inc.

—The Case of the Three Rings. Holmes, Gerald L., illus. 2014. 124p. (J). pap. (978-1-59188-164-3(1)) Maverick Bks., Inc.

—The Case of the Tricky Trap. Holmes, Gerald L., illus. 2011. (Hank the Cowdog Ser.). (ENG.). 126p. (J). (gr. 3-6). pap. 5.99 (978-1-59188-146-9(3)) Maverick Bks., Inc.

—The Case of the Twisted Kitty. Holmes, Gerald L., illus. 2004. (Hank the Cowdog Ser.: No. 43). 131p. (J). lib. bdg. 17.00 (978-1-4242-1600-0(1)) Fitzgerald Bks.

—The Case of the Twisted Kitty. Holmes, Gerald L., illus. 2011. (Hank the Cowdog Ser.). (ENG.). 131p. (J). (gr. 3-6). pap. 5.99 (978-1-59188-143-8(9)) Maverick Bks., Inc.

—The Case of the Vampire Cat. Holmes, Gerald L., illus. 2011. (Hank the Cowdog Ser.). (ENG.). 115p. (J). (gr. 3-6). pap. 5.99 (978-1-59188-121-6(8)) Maverick Bks., Inc.

—The Case of the Vampire Vacuum Sweeper. Holmes, Gerald L., illus. 2011. (Hank the Cowdog Ser.). (ENG.). 119p. (J). (gr. 3-6). pap. 5.99 (978-1-59188-129-2(3)) Maverick Bks., Inc.

—The Case of the Vanishing Fishhook. Holmes, Gerald L., illus. 2011. (Hank the Cowdog Ser.: No. 31). (ENG.). 124p. (J). (gr. 3-6). pap. 5.99 (978-1-59188-131-5(5)) Maverick Bks., Inc.

—The Disappearance of Drover. Holmes, Gerald L., illus. 2011. (Hank the Cowdog Ser.). (ENG.). 122p. (J). (gr. 3-6). pap. 5.99 (978-1-59188-157-5(9)) Maverick Bks., Inc.

—Drover's Secret Life. Holmes, Gerald L., illus. 2011. (Hank the Cowdog Ser.). (ENG.). 118p. (J). (gr. 3-6). pap. 5.99 (978-1-59188-153-7(6)) Maverick Bks., Inc.

—The Dungeon of Doom. Holmes, Gerald L., illus. 2004. (Hank the Cowdog Ser.: No. 44). 122p. (J). lib. bdg. 17.00 (978-1-4242-1601-7(X)) Fitzgerald Bks.

—The Dungeon of Doom. Holmes, Gerald L., illus. 2011. (Hank the Cowdog Ser.). (ENG.). 122p. (J). (gr. 3-6). pap. 5.99 (978-1-59188-144-5(7)) Maverick Bks., Inc.

—The Fling. Holmes, Gerald L., illus. 2011. (Hank the Cowdog Ser.). (ENG.). 126p. (J). (gr. 3-6). pap. 5.99 (978-1-59188-138-4(2)) Maverick Bks., Inc.

—The Garbage Monster from Outer Space. Holmes, Gerald L., illus. 2011. (Hank the Cowdog Ser.). (ENG.). 126p. (J). (gr. 3-6). pap. 5.99 (978-1-59188-132-2(3)) Maverick Bks., Inc.

—The Ghost of Rabbits Past. Holmes, Gerald L., illus. 2013. 128p. (J). pap. (978-1-59188-162-9(5)) Maverick Bks., Inc.

—Hank the Cowdog & Monkey Business. Holmes, Gerald L., illus. 2011. (Hank the Cowdog Ser.). (ENG.). 110p. (J). (gr. 3-6). pap. 5.99 (978-1-59188-114-8(5)) Maverick Bks., Inc.

—Lost in the Blinded Blizzard. Holmes, Gerald L., illus. 2011. (Hank the Cowdog Ser.). (ENG.). 115p. (J). (gr. 3-6). pap. 5.99 (978-1-59188-116-2(1)) Maverick Bks., Inc.

—Moonlight Madness. Holmes, Gerald L., illus. 2011. (Hank the Cowdog Ser.: No. 23). (ENG.). 114p. (J). (gr. 3-6). pap. 5.99 (978-1-59188-123-0(4)) Maverick Bks., Inc.

—The Mopwater Files. Holmes, Gerald L., illus. 2011. (Hank the Cowdog Ser.). (ENG.). 111p. (J). (gr. 3-6). pap. 5.99 (978-1-59188-128-5(5)) Maverick Bks., Inc.

—The Original Adventures of Hank the Cowdog. Holmes, Gerald L., illus. (ENG.). 127p. (J). (gr. 3-6). 2012. (Hank the Cowdog Ser.: Vol. 1). 15.99 (978-1-59188-201-5(X)) 2011. (Hank the Cowdog Ser.: No. 1). pap. 5.99 (978-1-59188-101-8(3)) Maverick Bks., Inc.

—The Phantom in the Mirror. Holmes, Gerald L., illus. 2011. (Hank the Cowdog Ser.: No. 20). (ENG.). 114p. (J). (gr. 3-6). pap. 5.99 (978-1-59188-120-9(X)) Maverick Bks., Inc.

—The Quest for the Great White Quail. Holmes, Gerald L., illus. 2011. (Hank the Cowdog Ser.). (ENG.). 123p. (J). (gr. 3-6). pap. 5.99 (978-1-59188-152-0(8)) Maverick Bks., Inc.

—The Return of the Charlie Monsters. Holmes, Gerald L., illus. 2014. 128p. (J). pap. (978-1-59188-163-6(3)) Maverick Bks., Inc.

—The Secret Laundry Monster Files. Holmes, Gerald L., illus. 2011. (Hank the Cowdog Ser.). (ENG.). 128p. (J). (gr. 3-6). pap. 5.99 (978-1-59188-139-1(0)) Maverick Bks., Inc.

—Slim's Good-Bye. Holmes, Gerald L., illus. 2011. (Hank the Cowdog Ser.). (ENG.). 132p. (J). (gr. 3-6). pap. 5.99 (978-1-59188-134-6(X)) Maverick Bks., Inc.

—The Wounded Buzzard on Christmas Eve. Holmes, Gerald L., illus. 2011. (Hank the Cowdog Ser.: No. 13). (ENG.). 112p. (J). (gr. 3-6). pap. 5.99 (978-1-59188-113-1(7)) Maverick Bks., Inc.

Erickson, John R. & Holmes, Gerald L., illus. The Case of the Prowling Bear. 2013. 126p. (J). (978-1-59188-261-9(3)); pap. (978-1-59188-161-2(7)) Maverick Bks.

Erickson, Mary Ellen. Who Jinxed the CG Ranch? 2009. 196p. 24.95 (978-1-4401-4218-5(1)); pap. 14.95 (978-1-4401-4216-1(5)) iUniverse, Inc.

Estergren, Fred B. Tale of a Dog Called Sunshine, 1 vol. 2009. 201p. pap. 24.95 (978-1-4489-2575-9(4)) America Star Bks.

Estevis, Anne. Chicken Foot Farm. 2008. 154p. (J). (gr. 6-18). pap. 10.95 (978-1-55885-505-2(X), Piñata Books) Arte Publico Pr.

Farley, Terri. Desert Dancer. 2003. (Phantom Stallion Ser.). (Illus.). 234p. (J). (gr. 5-9). 12.65 (978-0-7569-3561-0(X)) Perfection Learning Corp.

—Phantom Stallion - Wild Horse Island Bk. 2: The Shining Stallion. 2007. (Phantom Stallion: Wild Horse Island Ser.: 2). (ENG., Illus.). 224p. (J). (gr. 5-9). pap. 4.99 (978-0-06-081543-1(4)) HarperCollins Pubs.

—Rain Forest Rose Bk. 3. 2007. (Phantom Stallion: Wild Horse Island Ser.: 3). (ENG.). 224p. (J). (gr. 5-18). pap. 4.99 (978-0-06-088616-5(1)) HarperCollins Pubs.

Fleming, Bryn. Cassie & Jasper: Cattle Drive Danger. 2016. (Range Riders Ser.). (ENG.). 147p. (J). pap. 10.99 (978-1-941821-95-4(2), West Winds Pr.) Graphic Arts Ctr. Publishing Co.

—Cassie & Jasper: Kidnapped Cattle. 2016. (Range Riders Ser.). (ENG.). 147p. (J). 24.99 (978-1-943328-66-6(8), West Winds Pr.) Graphic Arts Ctr. Publishing Co.

—Cassie & Jasper to the Rescue. 2014. (Range Riders Ser.). (ENG.). 128p. (YA). (gr. 3-7). 23.99 (978-1-941821-04-6(9)); pap. 9.99 (978-0-88240-992-4(1)) Graphic Arts Ctr. Publishing Co. (West Winds Pr.).

—Jasper & Willie: Wildfire. 2015. (Range Riders Ser.). (ENG.). 130p. (J). 28.99 (978-1-941821-92-3(8)); pap. 9.99 (978-1-941821-71-8(5)) Graphic Arts Ctr. Publishing Co. (West Winds Pr.).

Gabel, Stacey. The New Blue Tractor. Neuman, Richard, illus. 2007. 24p. per. 13.95 (978-1-59858-424-0(3)) Dog Ear Publishing, LLC.

Garis, Howard R. Curlytops at Uncle Frank's Ranch. 2009. 120p. pap. 10.95 (978-1-60664-408-9(4)) Rodgers, Alan Bks.

—The Curlytops at Uncle Frank's Ranch; or, Little Folks on Ponyback. 2007. 160p. per. (978-1-4065-2763-6(7)) Dodo Pr.

Garis, Howard Roger. The Curlytops at Uncle Frank's Ranch. 2005. 26.95 (978-1-4218-1466-7(8), 1st World Library - Literary Society) 1st World Publishing, Inc.

—The Curlytops at Uncle Franks Ranch. 2005. 192p. pap. 11.95 (978-1-4218-1566-4(4), 1st World Library - Literary Society) 1st World Publishing, Inc.

—The Curlytops at Uncle Frank's Ranch. 2004. reprint ed. pap. 1.99 (978-1-4192-5842-8(7)); pap. 21.95 (978-1-4191-5842-1(2)) Kessinger Publishing, LLC.

Garst, Shannon. Silver Spurs for Cowboy Boots. Hargens, Charles, illus. 2011. 194p. 42.95 (978-1-258-08454-7(6)) Literary Licensing, LLC.

Green, D. L. Sparkling Jewel. Wallis, Emily, illus. 2015. (Silver Pony Ranch Ser.: 1). (ENG.). 96p. (J). (gr. 1-3). pap. 4.99 (978-0-545-79765-8(9)) Scholastic, Inc.

—Sweet Buttercup. Wallis, Emily, illus. 2016. (Silver Pony Ranch Ser.: 2). (ENG.). 96p. (J). (gr. 1-3). 15.99 (978-0-545-79770-2(5)) Scholastic, Inc.

Haesche, Richard, Sr. Ghost Wolf. 2007. (ENG.). 207p. (YA). 10.99 (978-0-9798536-5-4(6)) Kreative X-Pressions Pubns.

Hanes, Rosann. Diamond H Ranch: Told by: Val - Loyal Ranch Dog. 2010. 28p. pap. 13.99 (978-1-4490-7714-3(5)) AuthorHouse.

HarperCollins Publishers Ltd. Staff, ed. Home on the Range. Date not set. 40p. (J). (gr. -1-3). pap. 5.99 (978-0-06-443567-3(9)) HarperCollins Pubs.

Heimbuch, Carol Jo. Twilight Tracks. 2007. 112p. per. 10.95 (978-1-59330-466-9(8)) Aventine Pr.

Helidoniotis, Kathy. Horse Mad Western. 2008. 272p. (978-0-7322-8424-4(4)) HarperCollins Pubs. Australia.

Horseshoe Canyon. 2005. (J). 30.00 (978-1-884270-38-3(7)) Hall, Nancy Inc.

Horvath, Polly. Northward to the Moon. 2012. (ENG.). 256p. (J). (gr. 5-8). 7.99 (978-0-307-92980-8(9), Yearling) Random Hse. Children's Bks.

Hubbard, Kirsten. Watch the Sky. 2016. (ENG.). 288p. (J). (gr. 3-7). pap. 7.99 (978-1-4847-0898-9(9)) Hyperion Bks. for Children.

Isaacs, Anne. Meanwhile, Back at the Ranch. Hawkes, Kevin, illus. 2014. (ENG.). 56p. (J). (gr. k-4). 17.99 (978-0-375-86745-3(7), Schwartz & Wade Bks.) Random Hse. Children's Bks.

James, Will. Look-See with Uncle Bill. rev. ed. (Illus.). 190p. (J). (gr. 4). pap. (978-0-87842-458-0(X), 814) Mountain Pr. Publishing Co., Inc.

—My First Horse, Vol. 1. rev. ed. (Illus.). 48p. (J). (gr. 4). 16.00 (978-0-87842-488-7(1), 819) Mountain Pr. Publishing Co., Inc.

—Uncle Bill: A Tale of Two Kids & a Cowboy. rev. ed. (Tumbleweed Ser.). (Illus.). 185p. (J). (gr. 4-12). pap. 14.00 (978-0-87842-380-4(X), 694) Mountain Pr. Publishing Co., Inc.

—Young Cowboy. rev. ed. 2004. (Illus.). 88p. (J). (gr. 4-7). 15.00 (978-0-87842-419-1(9), 806) Mountain Pr. Publishing Co., Inc.

Johnston, Jeanna. My Busy Day at the Ranch. 2011. 28p. pap. 15.99 (978-1-4628-9301-0(5)) Xlibris Corp.

Kelso, Mary Jean. Andy & Spirit in Search & Rescue. Snider, Kc, illus. 2013. 28p. pap. 10.95 (978-1-61633-408-6(8)) Guardian Angel Publishing, Inc.

Kennedy, Marlane. Tornado Alley. 2014. (Disaster Strikes Ser.: 2). lib. bdg. 14.75 (978-0-606-35828-6(5)) Turtleback Bks.

Kephart, Beth. Small Damages. 2013. (ENG., Illus.). 304p. (YA). (gr. 9). pap. 8.99 (978-0-14-242641-8(5), Speak) Penguin Young Readers Group.

Ketteman, Helen. Waynetta & the Cornstalk: A Texas Fairy Tale. Greenseid, Diane, illus. 2012. (ENG.). 32p. (J). (gr. -1-3). pap. 7.99 (978-0-8075-8688-4(9)) Whitman, Albert & Co.

Keyser, Amber J. & Burkhart, Kiersi. At Top Speed. 2017. (Quartz Creek Ranch Ser.). (ENG.). 240p. (gr. 4-8). 35.99 **(978-1-5124-2697-7(0)**, Darby Creek) Lerner Publishing Group.

—The Long Trail Home. 2017. (Quartz Creek Ranch Ser.). (ENG.). 240p. (gr. 4-8). lib. bdg. 27.99 (978-1-4677-9256-1(X)); 35.99 **(978-1-5124-2698-4(9))** Lerner Publishing Group. (Darby Creek).

Keyser, Amber J. & Burkhart, Kiersi. One Brave Summer. 2017. (Quartz Creek Ranch Ser.). (ENG.). 224p. (gr. 4-8). 35.99 **(978-1-5124-0892-8(1)**, Darby Creek) Lerner Publishing Group.

Law, Ingrid. Scumble. (ENG.). (J). (gr. 3-7). 2011. 432p. 8.99 (978-0-14-241962-5(1), Puffin Books) 2010. 416p. 17.99 (978-0-8037-3307-7(0), Dial Bks) Penguin Young Readers Group.

—Scumble. l.t. ed. 2011. (Companion to the Newberry Honor Winner Savvy Ser.). (ENG.). 575p. 23.99 (978-1-4104-3531-6(8)) Thorndike Pr.

Lewis, Ali. Timber Creek Station. 2016. (ENG.). 240p. (YA). (gr. 6-12). 18.99 (978-1-4677-8117-6(7)); 35.99 (978-1-4677-8816-8(3), Carolrhoda Lab™) Lerner Publishing Group.

Marlow, Susan K. Andrea Carter & the Dangerous Decision, 1 vol. 2007. (Circle C Adventures Ser.). 144p. (J). pap. 7.99 (978-0-8254-3357-3(6)) Kregel Pubns.

—Andrea Carter & the Family Secret, 1 vol. 2008. (Circle C Adventures Ser.). 144p. (J). pap. 7.99 (978-0-8254-3365-8(7)) Kregel Pubns.

—Andrea Carter & the Price of Truth, 1 vol. 2017. (Circle C Adventures Ser.: 6). 144p. (J). pap. 8.99 **(978-0-8254-4505-7(1))** Kregel Pubns.

—Andrea Carter's Tales from the Circle C Ranch, 1 vol. 2015. (Illus.). 160p. (J). pap. 7.99 *(978-0-8254-4379-4(2))* Kregel Pubns.

—The Last Ride: An Andrea Carter Book, 1 vol. 2016. (Circle C Milestones Ser.: 3). 176p. (YA). pap. 9.99 *(978-0-8254-4369-5(5))* Kregel Pubns.

—Thick As Thieves: An Andrea Carter Book, 1 vol. 2015. (Circle C Milestones Ser.: 1). 176p. (YA). pap. 9.99 *(978-0-8254-4367-1(9))* Kregel Pubns.

Martinello, Marian L. Ready's Gifts. 2003. (Illus.). 158p. (YA). (gr. 8-18). per. 12.95 *(978-0-9724113-0-1(5))* MindCatcher Pr.

Marusak, Elaine Truly. Truly Tales: Aunt Gertie & Uncle George's Haunted House. 2007. (ENG.). 84p. per. 19.95 *(978-1-4241-5959-8(8))* America Star Bks.

Meddaugh, Susan. Martha & Skits Out West. 2011. (Martha Speaks Ser.). (ENG., Illus.). 96p. (J). (gr. 1-4). pap. 5.99 *(978-0-547-21074-2(4))* Houghton Mifflin Harcourt Publishing Co.

Miller, Paula. One-Eyed Jack. Forrest, Chris, illus. (J). 2007. (ENG.). 133p. (gr. 2-7). pap. 8.95 *(978-0-9769417-0-5(8))* 2006. 144p. 13.95 *(978-0-9718348-8-0(1))* Blooming Tree Pr.

Moen, Louise. The Devil in Ol' Rosie. 2009. (ENG.). 208p. (J). (gr. 3-6). pap. 10.99 *(978-1-4424-0202-7(4),* Atheneum Bks. for Young Readers) Simon & Schuster Children's Publishing.

Montgomery, Rutherford G. The Golden Stallion's Victory. (J). 20.95 *(978-0-8488-0133-5(4))* Amereon Ltd.

Nolan, Lucy. Home on the Range, 0 vols. Reed, Mike, illus. 2010. (Down Girl & Sit Ser.: 4). (ENG.). 64p. (J). (gr. 1-4). 14.99 *(978-0-7614-5649-0(X),* 9780761456490, Amazon Children's Publishing) Amazon Publishing.

Oldfield, Jenny. Crazy Horse. 2009. (Horses of Half Moon Ranch Ser.: 3). (ENG.). 160p. (J). (gr. 4-7). pap. 9.99 *(978-1-4022-1702-9(1),* Sourcebooks Jabberwocky) Sourcebooks, Inc.

Out of the Blue. 2014. (J). pap. *(978-0-8163-5016-2(7))* Pacific Pr. Publishing Assn.

Palmer, Catherine. Fatal Harvest. l.t. ed. 2004. (Matthew 25 Ser.). 496p. (YA). 28.95 *(978-0-7862-6259-5(1))* Thorndike Pr.

Papp, Robert, illus. A Horse Named Dragon. 2008. (Boxcar Children Mysteries Ser.: 114). (ENG.). 128p. (J). (gr. 1-5). lib. bdg. 14.99 *(978-0-8075-5571-2(1));* per. 5.99 *(978-0-8075-5572-9(X))* Whitman, Albert & Co.

Parish, Herman. Go West, Amelia Bedelia! Sweat, Lynn, illus. (I Can Read Level 2 Ser.). 64p. (J). (gr. k-4). 2012. (ENG.). pap. 3.99 *(978-0-06-084363-2(2))* 2011. (ENG.). 17.99 *(978-0-06-084361-8(6))* 2011. lib. bdg. 18.89 *(978-0-06-084362-5(4))* HarperCollins Pubs. (Greenwillow Bks.).

Parry, Rosanne. Heart of a Shepherd. 2010. (ENG.). 176p. (J). (gr. 3-7). pap. 7.99 *(978-0-375-84803-2(7),* Yearling) Random Hse. Children's Bks.

Petruck, Rebecca. Steering Toward Normal. 2014. (ENG.). 336p. (J). (gr. 3-7). 16.95 *(978-1-4197-0732-2(9),* Amulet Bks.) Abrams, Inc.

Platt, Chris. Storm Chaser, 1 vol. 2009. (ENG.). 160p. (J). (gr. 3-7). 15.95 *(978-1-56145-496-9(6))* Peachtree Pubs.

Prentice-Hall Staff. The Red Pony. 2nd ed. (J). stu. ed. *(978-0-13-717133-0(1))* Prentice Hall (Schl. Div.).

Pyke, Helen Godfrey. Julia. 2012. (J). pap. *(978-0-8163-3400-1(5))* Pacific Pr. Publishing Assn.

Roach, Joyce Gibson, tr. Cowgirl of the Rocking R. 2003. (J). *(978-0-9726573-0-3(4))* Crosswinds Bks.

Runels, Margie "B". Talon. 2009. 12p. pap. 8.49 *(978-1-4490-3248-7(6))* AuthorHouse.

Sargent, Dave & Sargent, Pat. Chick: (Chocolate Chestnut) Be Loyal, 30 vols., Vol. 16. Lenoir, Jane, illus. 2003. (Saddle up Ser.: Vol. 16). 42p. (J). pap. 10.95 *(978-1-56763-678-9(0));* lib. bdg. 23.60 *(978-1-56763-677-2(2))* Ozark Publishing.

—Lily: (Lilac Dun) A Second Chance, 30 vols., Vol. 38. Lenoir, Jane, illus. 2003. (Saddle up Ser.: Vol. 38). 42p. (J). pap. 10.95 *(978-1-56763-698-7(5));* lib. bdg. 23.60 *(978-1-56763-697-0(7))* Ozark Publishing.

Sclafani, Terry. The Thompson Twins Western Adventure. 2009. 114p. pap. 11.95 *(978-1-4327-3783-2(X))* Outskirts Pr., Inc.

Scott, Elizabeth M. It's Rodeo Time! With Mamma Scottie & the Kids. 2009. 52p. pap. 24.99 *(978-1-4490-1750-7(9))* AuthorHouse.

Shafer, Patty. Annie the Texas Ranch Dog - Danger at Lost Maples. Retzlaff, Shay, illus. 2012. (ENG.). 96p. (J). pap. 9.95 *(978-1-61899-009-9(8),* Tadpole Pr. 4 Kids) Smooth Sailing Pr., LLC.

—Annie the Texas Ranch Dog - Injured Hero. Retzlaff, Shay, illus. 2012. 96p. (J). pap. 9.95 *(978-1-61899-008-2(X),* Tadpole Pr. 4 Kids) Smooth Sailing Pr., LLC.

Simmons, Andra. What Anna Loves. Capaldi, Gina, illus. 2006. 24p. (J). (gr. -1-3). 15.95 *(978-1-59714-044-7(9))* Heyday.

Simmons, Lynn Sheffield. Sugar Lump, the Orphan Calf, 1 vol. 2003. (ENG., Illus.). 50p. (J). (gr. k-5). 12.95 *(978-1-58980-216-2(0))* Pelican Publishing Co., Inc.

Smiley, Jane. Gee Whiz. Clayton, Elaine, illus. 2013. (Horses of Oak Valley Ranch Ser.: Bk. 5). (ENG.). 272p. (J). (gr. 5). 16.99 *(978-0-375-86969-3(7),* Knopf Bks. for Young Readers) Random Hse. Children's Bks.

—The Georges & the Jewels. 2010. (Horses of Oak Valley Ranch Ser.: Bk. 1). (ENG.). 240p. (J). (gr. 5). 6.99 *(978-0-375-86228-1(5),* Yearling) Random Hse. Children's Bks.

—A Good Horse. 2011. (Horses of Oak Valley Ranch Ser.: Bk. 2). (ENG.). 256p. (J). (gr. 5). 6.99 *(978-0-375-86230-4(7),* Yearling) Random Hse. Children's Bks.

—Pie in the Sky. 2013. (Horses of Oak Valley Ranch Ser.). (ENG.). 272p. (J). (gr. 5). 6.99 *(978-0-375-87131-3(4),* Yearling) Random Hse. Children's Bks.

—True Blue. 2012. (Horses of Oak Valley Ranch Ser.: Bk. 3). (ENG.). 304p. (J). (gr. 5). 6.99 *(978-0-375-86232-8(3),* Yearling) Random Hse. Children's Bks.

Smith, Andrew. Ghost Medicine. 2010. (ENG.). 384p. (YA). (gr. 8-13). pap. 18.99 *(978-0-312-62912-0(5))* Square Fish.

Standish, Burt L. Frank Merriwell's Ranch. Rudman, Jack, ed. 2003. (Frank Merriwell Ser.). pap. 9.95 *(978-0-8373-9168-7(7))* Merriwell, Frank Inc.

Stilton, Geronimo & Stilton, Thea. Thea Stilton & the Mountain of Fire. 2009. (Thea Stilton Ser.: 2). lib. bdg. 19.65 *(978-0-606-00232-5(4),* Turtleback) Turtleback Bks.

Stites, Clara. Rosalba of Santa Juanita: A California Story. 2015. (ENG., Illus.). 100p. (J). pap. 8.95 *(978-1-56474-394-7(2),* Fithian Pr) Daniel & Daniel, Pubs., Inc.

Stone, Judith. Billie the Buffalo Goes to Town. 2008. 20p. pap. 12.95 *(978-1-4389-2877-7(7))* AuthorHouse.

Stratemeyer, Edward. Dave Porter at Star Ranch. 2007. 260p. 28.95 *(978-1-4218-4144-1(4),* 1st World Library - Literary Society) 1st World Publishing, Inc.

Sylvester, Kevin. Neil Flambé & the Duel in the Desert. Sylvester, Kevin, illus. (Neil Flambe Capers Ser.: 6). (ENG., Illus.). 304p. (J). (gr. 3-7). 2017. pap. 7.99 *(978-1-4814-1042-7(3))* 2016. 13.99 *(978-1-4814-1041-0(5))* Simon & Schuster Bks. For Young Readers. (Simon & Schuster Bks. For Young Readers).

Tripp, Valerie. Josefina Story Collection. Tibbles, Jean-Paul, illus. 2008. 420p. pap. 29.95 *(978-1-59369-453-1(9))* American Girl Publishing, Inc.

Van Slyke, Rebecca. Lexie the Word Wrangler. Hartland, Jessie, illus. 2017. (ENG.). 40p. (J). (gr. k-3). 17.99 *(978-0-399-16957-1(1),* Nancy Paulsen Books) Penguin Young Readers Group.

Van Tol, Alex. A Punta de Cuchillo, 1 vol. 2011. (Spanish Soundings Ser.). (SPA & ENG.). 136p. (YA). (gr. 8-12). pap. 9.95 *(978-1-55469-863-9(4))* Orca Bk. Pubs. USA.

Wallace, Bill. That Doggone Calf. Wallace, Carol, illus. 2010. (ENG.). 160p. (J). (gr. 3-7). pap. 6.95 *(978-0-8234-2303-3(4))* Holiday Hse., Inc.

Walter, Mildred Pitts. Justin & the Best Biscuits in the World. Stock, Catherine, illus. 2010. (ENG.). 144p. (J). (gr. 3-7). pap. 5.99 *(978-0-06-195891-5(3),* Amistad) HarperCollins Pubs.

—Justin & the Best Biscuits in the World. 2011. 8.32 *(978-0-7848-3586-9(1),* Everbind) Marco Bk. Co.

Waters, Zack C. Blood Moon Rider. 2006. (Florida Historical Fiction for Youth Ser.). (ENG.). 126p. (J). (gr. 4-9). 13.95 *(978-1-56164-350-9(5))* Pineapple Pr., Inc.

Webster, Frank V. Bob Chester's Grit. 2007. (ENG.). 180p. per. 11.95 *(978-1-4218-3327-9(1))* 1st World Publishing, Inc.

—Bob Chester's Grit: From Ranch to Riches. 2007. (ENG.). 142p. pap. 18.99 *(978-1-4346-0723-2(2));* 156p. pap. 21.99 *(978-1-4346-0783-6(6))* Creative Media Partners, LLC.

—The Boy from the Ranch: Or, Roy Bradner's City Experiences. 2007. (ENG.). 132p. pap. 18.99 *(978-1-4346-4347-6(6));* 148p. pap. 19.99 *(978-1-4346-4348-3(4))* Creative Media Partners, LLC.

—Comrades of the Saddle. 2007. 176p. 26.95 *(978-1-4218-3229-6(1),* 1st World Library - Literary Society); (ENG.). per. 11.95 *(978-1-4218-3329-3(8))* 1st World Publishing, Inc.

—Comrades of the Saddle or the Young Rough Riders of the Plains. 2004. reprint ed. pap. 1.99 *(978-1-4192-1372-4(5))* Kessinger Publishing, LLC.

Weldon, Stayton. Whitey on the Ranch. Anderson-Shorter, Susan, illus. 2010. 52p. pap. 12.95 *(978-1-4490-5474-8(9))* AuthorHouse.

Yu, Jennifer & Jenn, Lady. Texas Animal Ranch: Ricky's Secret Friends Picture Book Series, vols. 6, vol. 2. Yu, Jennifer & Jenn, Lady, illus. 2016. (Ricky's Secret Friends Picturebook Ser.: 6). (ENG & CHI., Illus.). (gr. 1-4). 29.95 *(978-0-9787591-2-4(5))* Direct World Publishing.

RANDOLPH, A. PHILIP (ASA PHILIP), 1889-1979

Miller, Calvin Craig. A. Philip Randolph & the African American Labor Movement. 2005. (Civil Rights Leaders Ser.). (Illus.). 160p. (YA). (gr. 6-12). 26.95 *(978-1-931798-50-1(8))* Reynolds, Morgan Inc.

RANK

see Social Classes

RAP (MUSIC)

Ander, Martin. The Hip Hop Board Book. 2012. (ENG., Illus.). 20p. 14.95 *(978-91-85639-53-3(2))* Dokument forlag, Fotograf Malcolm Jacobsson SWE. Dist: SCB Distributors.

Anniss, Matt. The Story of Hip-Hop. 2013. (Pop Histories Ser.). 32p. (gr. 4-7). 31.35 *(978-1-59920-965-4(9))* Black Rabbit Bks.

Baker, Soren. The History of Rap & Hip-Hop. 2006. (Music Library). (ENG., Illus.). 112p. (YA). (gr. 7-10). lib. bdg. 33.45 *(978-1-59018-739-5(3),* Lucent Bks.) Cengage Gale.

Bankston, John. Eminem. l.t. ed. 2003. (Blue Banner Biography Ser.). (Illus.). 32p. (J). (gr. 3-8). lib. bdg. 25.70 *(978-1-58415-222-4(2))* Mitchell Lane Pubs., Inc.

—Jay-Z. l.t. ed. 2004. (Blue Banner Biography Ser.). (Illus.). 32p. (J). (gr. 3-8). lib. bdg. 25.70 *(978-1-58415-223-1(0))* Mitchell Lane Pubs., Inc.

Berlatsky, Noah, ed. Rap Music. 2012. (Introducing Issues with Opposing Viewpoints Ser.). (ENG., Illus.). 144p. (gr. 7-10). lib. bdg. 36.95 *(978-0-7377-6496-3(1),* Greenhaven Pr., Inc.) Cengage Gale.

Britton, Felicity. Nicki Minaj: Conquering Hip-Hop. 2013. (USA TODAY Lifeline Biographies Ser.). (ENG., Illus.). 112p. (gr. 6-12). lib. bdg. 34.60 *(978-1-4677-0810-4(0))* Lerner Publishing Group.

Burns, Kate. Rap Music & Culture. 2008. (Current Controversies Ser.). (ENG., Illus.). (gr. 10-12). 176-240p. (J). 28.45 *(978-0-7377-3965-7(7));* 224p. 46.40 *(978-0-7377-3964-0(9))* Cengage Gale. (Greenhaven Pr., Inc.).

Carr, Aaron. Rap. 2015. (J). *(978-1-4896-3589-1(0))* Weigl Pubs., Inc.

Dagnino, Michelle. Hip Hop from A to Z: A Fresh Look at the Music, the Culture, & the Message. Baldwin, Alisa, illus. 2007. 192p. (J). (gr. 8-12). pap. *(978-1-897073-36-0(4))* Lobster Pr.

Earl, C. F. Hip-Hop: A Short History. 2012. (J). pap. *(978-1-4222-2545-5(3));* (Illus.). 48p. (gr. 3-4). 19.95 *(978-1-4222-2519-6(4))* Mason Crest.

Ellis, Carol. Landmark Hip-Hop Hits. 2012. (Illus.). 64p. (J). pap. *(978-1-4222-2134-1(2));* (gr. 4). 22.95 *(978-1-4222-2121-1(0))* Mason Crest.

Gaines, Ann Graham & Majors, Reggie. The Hip-Hop Scene: The Stars, the Fans, the Music. 2009. (Music Scene Ser.). (Illus.). 48p. (J). (gr. 5-9). lib. bdg. 25.27 *(978-0-7660-3396-2(1))* Enslow Pubs., Inc.

Garofoli, Wendy. Hip-Hop Culture, 1 vol. 2010. (Hip-Hop World Ser.). (ENG.). 48p. (gr. 3-4). lib. bdg. 31.99 *(978-1-4296-4016-9(2))* Capstone Press of Coughlan Cos.

—Hip-Hop History, 1 vol. 2010. (Hip-Hop World Ser.). (ENG.). 48p. (gr. 3-4). lib. bdg. 31.99 *(978-1-4296-4018-3(9))* Capstone Press of Coughlan Cos.

Garofoli Zamora, Wendy. Hip-Hop History [Scholastic]. 2010. (Hip-Hop World Ser.). 48p. pap. 1.00 *(978-1-4296-5979-6(3))* Capstone Press of Coughlan Cos.

Gogerly, Liz. Street Dance. 2011. (On the Radar: Dance Ser.). (ENG., Illus.). 32p. (gr. 4-8). lib. bdg. 26.60 *(978-0-7613-7761-0(1))* Lerner Publishing Group.

Greenhaven Press Editors. The History of Rap & Hip-Hop. 2012. (Music Library). (ENG., Illus.). 128p. (J). (gr. 7-10). lib. bdg. 34.45 *(978-1-4205-0822-2(9))* Cengage Gale.

Hall, Marcella Runell & Cameron, Andrea. The 10 Most Influential Hip Hop Artists. 2008. 14.99 *(978-1-55448-504-8(5))* Scholastic Library Publishing.

Harper, P. Thandi Hicks. Hip-Hop Development. 2005. *(978-1-887191-02-9(X))* Youth Popular Culture Institute, Inc.

Hatch, Thomas. A History of Hip-Hop: The Roots of Rap. 2005. (High Five Reading - Blue Ser.). (ENG., Illus.). 48p. (gr. 3-4). per. 9.00 *(978-0-7368-5750-5(8),* High Five Reading (RBL)) Capstone Press of Coughlan Cos.

Hip-Hop World, 4 vols. 2010. (Hip-Hop World Ser.). (ENG.). 48p. (gr. 3-4). lib. bdg. 127.96 *(978-1-4296-4424-2(9))* Capstone Press of Coughlan Cos.

Hip-Hop World [Capstone Sole Source]. 2010. (Hip-Hop World Ser.). 48p. lib. bdg. 122.60 *(978-1-4296-5866-9(5))* Capstone Press of Coughlan Cos.

Hoffmann, Frank. Rhythm & Blues, Rap, & Hip-Hop. 2007. (American Popular Music Ser.). (Illus.). 352p. (gr. 6-12). per. 21.95 *(978-0-8160-7341-2(4),* Checkmark Bks.) Facts On File, Inc.

Kalman, Bobbie. Reptile Rap. 2010. (My World Ser.). (ENG.). 16p. (J). (gr. k-3). *(978-0-7787-9512-4(8));* pap. *(978-0-7787-9537-7(3))* Crabtree Publishing Co.

Kenney, Karen Latchana. Cool Hip-Hop Music: Create & Appreciate What Makes Music Great!, 1 vol. 2008. (Cool Music Ser.). (ENG., Illus.). 32p. (YA). (gr. 3-6). 28.50 *(978-1-59928-971-7(7))* ABDO Publishing Co.

Mattern, Joanne. Nicki Minaj. 2013. (ENG.). 32p. (gr. 4-8). lib. bdg. 25.70 *(978-1-61228-468-2(X))* Mitchell Lane Pubs., Inc.

Merino, Noël. Rap Music. 2008. (Introducing Issues with Opposing Viewpoints Ser.). (ENG., Illus.). 112-144p. (gr. 7-10). 36.95 *(978-0-7377-3978-7(9),* Greenhaven Pr., Inc.) Cengage Gale.

Mills, Clifford W. Tupac Shakur. 2007. (Hip-Hop Stars Ser.). (Illus.). 104p. (YA). (gr. 7-12). lib. bdg. 30.00 *(978-0-7910-9495-2(2))* Facts On File, Inc.

Moore, Sarah W. The Rap Scene: The Stars, the Fans, the Music. 2009. (Music Scene Ser.). (Illus.). 48p. (J). (gr. 5-9). lib. bdg. 25.27 *(978-0-7660-3397-9(X))* Enslow Pubs., Inc.

Morse, Eric. What Is Hip-Hop? Yi, Anny, illus. 2017. (ENG.). 32p. (J). (gr. -1-2). 15.95 ***(978-1-61775-584-2(2),*** Black Sheep) Akashic Bks.

Norton, James R. Russell Simmons. 2009. (Library of Hip-Hop Biographies Ser.). 48p. (gr. 5-5). 53.00 *(978-1-60853-704-4(8))* Rosen Publishing Group, Inc., The.

Original Raps for the All Occasion Kid, 3 vols. 2003. (J). Vols. IV-VI. pap. *(978-0-9745630-1-5(3))*Vols. I, II, and III. pap. incl. audio compact disk *(978-0-9745630-0-8(5))*Vols. VII, VIII, IX. pap. *(978-0-9745630-2-2(1))* F & S Music KS Publishing Co.

Publishers, Chelsea House, creator. Hip-Hop Stars Set, 10-Volumes. 2007. (Hip-Hop Stars Ser.). (gr. 6-12). 300.00 *(978-0-7910-9736-6(6),* Chelsea Hse.) Facts On File, Inc.

Sacks, Nathan. American Hip-Hop: Rappers, Djs, & Hard Beats. 2012. (American Music Milestones Ser.). (ENG., Illus.). 64p. (gr. 5-12). lib. bdg. 30.60 *(978-0-7613-4500-8(0))* Lerner Publishing Group.

Saddleback Educational Publishing Staff. Jay-Z. 2013. (Hip-Hop Biographies (Saddleback Publishing) Ser.). (YA). lib. bdg. 23.25 *(978-0-606-31484-8(9),* Turtleback) Turtleback Bks.

Thompson, Kim Mitzo & Hilderbrand, Karen Mitzo. Multiplication Rap. 2008. (Playaway Children Ser.). (J). 44.99 *(978-1-59922-324-7(4))* Findaway World, LLC.

Thompson, Tamara. Rap & Hip-Hop. 2013. (Current Controversies Ser.). (ENG.). 224p. (gr. 10-12). pap. 32.00 *(978-0-7377-6244-0(6));* lib. bdg. 46.40 *(978-0-7377-6243-3(8))* Cengage Gale. (Greenhaven Pr., Inc.).

Vander Hook, Sue. Hip-Hop Fashion, 1 vol. 2010. (Hip-Hop World Ser.). (ENG.). 48p. (gr. 3-4). lib. bdg. 31.99 *(978-1-4296-4017-6(0))* Capstone Press of Coughlan Cos.

Walker, Ida. Around the World. 2009. (Hip-Hop Ser.). (Illus.). 64p. (YA). (gr. 4-7). pap. 7.95 *(978-1-4222-0350-7(6));* (gr. 7-12). lib. bdg. 22.95 *(978-1-4222-0293-7(3))* Mason Crest.

Waters, Rosa. Yung Joc. 2009. (Hip Hop (Mason Crest Paperback) Ser.). (Illus.). 64p. (YA). pap. 7.95 *(978-1-4222-0339-2(5))* Mason Crest.

RAP (MUSIC)—FICTION

England, Linda. 3 Kids Dreamin' Schutzer, Dena, illus. 2011. (ENG.). 32p. (J). (gr. 4-6). 6.99 *(978-1-4424-2944-4(5),* McElderry, Margaret K. Bks.) McElderry, Margaret K. Bks.

Goode, Laura. Sister Mischief. 2011. (ENG., Illus.). 384p. (YA). (gr. 9-18). 16.99 *(978-0-7636-4640-0(7))* Candlewick Pr.

Gutman, Dan. Rappy Goes to School. Bowers, Tim, illus. 2016. 40p. (J). (gr. -1-3). 17.99 *(978-0-06-229181-3(5))* HarperCollins Pubs.

—Rappy the Raptor. Bowers, Tim, illus. 2015. (ENG.). 40p. (J). (gr. -1-3). 17.99 *(978-0-06-229180-6(7))* HarperCollins Pubs.

Jenkins-Greaves, Shenita. Raptown U. S. A. Rappers. 2013. 24p. pap. 14.95 *(978-1-4669-7717-4(5))* Trafford Publishing.

Morningforest, Chris & Raymond, Rebecca. Mooseman Reindeer & Uncle Utley. 2006. 36p. (J). pap. 15.43 *(978-1-4116-8390-7(0))* Lulu Pr., Inc.

Raschka, Chris. Hip Hop Dog. Radunsky, Vladimir, illus. 2010. (ENG.). 32p. (J). (gr. -1-3). 16.99 *(978-0-06-123963-2(1))* HarperCollins Pubs.

Zephaniah, Benjamin. Gangsta Rap. 2004. (ENG.). 336p. (YA). (gr. 9-13). pap. 8.99 *(978-1-58234-886-5(3),* 9781582348865, Bloomsbury USA Childrens) Bloomsbury Publishing USA.

RAP MUSICIANS

Abrams, Dennis. Beastie Boys. 2007. (Hip-Hop Stars Ser.). (Illus.). 104p. (YA). (gr. 7-12). lib. bdg. 30.00 *(978-0-7910-9480-8(4))* Facts On File, Inc.

—Jay-Z. 2007. (Hip-Hop Stars Ser.). (Illus.). 112p. (YA). (gr. 7-12). lib. bdg. 30.00 *(978-0-7910-9551-5(7))* Facts On File, Inc.

Allen, Amy Ruth. Queen Latifah: From Jersey Girl to Superstar. 2012. (USA TODAY Lifeline Biographies Ser.). (ENG., Illus.). 112p. (gr. 6-12). lib. bdg. 34.60 *(978-0-7613-4234-2(6))* Lerner Publishing Group.

Aretha, David. Eminem: Grammy-Winning Rapper, 1 vol. 2012. (Contemporary Lives Set 1 Ser.). (ENG.). 112p. (J). (gr. 6-12). lib. bdg. 35.64 *(978-1-61783-323-6(1))* ABDO Publishing Co.

Azzarelli, Ally. Drake! Hip-Hop Celebrity. 2013. (Sizzling Celebrities Ser.). 48p. (J). (gr. 4-9). pap. 8.95 *(978-1-4644-0275-3(2));* (Illus.). 25.27 *(978-0-7660-4168-4(9))* Enslow Pubs., Inc.

Bailey, Diane. Mary J. Blige. 2009. (Library of Hip-Hop Biographies Ser.). (ENG., Illus.). 48p. (J). (gr. 7-12). pap. 11.75 *(978-1-4358-5441-3(1));* 48p. (gr. 5-5). 53.00 *(978-1-60853-694-8(7));* (J). lib. bdg. 29.25 *(978-1-4358-5055-2(6))* Rosen Publishing Group, Inc., The.

Bankston, John. Bow Wow. l.t. ed. 2004. (Blue Banner Biography Ser.). (Illus.). 32p. (J). (gr. 3-8). lib. bdg. 25.70 *(978-1-58415-220-0(6))* Mitchell Lane Pubs., Inc.

—Eminem. l.t. ed. 2003. (Blue Banner Biography Ser.). (Illus.). 32p. (J). (gr. 3-8). lib. bdg. 25.70 *(978-1-58415-222-4(2))* Mitchell Lane Pubs., Inc.

—Ja Rule. l.t. ed. 2004. (Blue Banner Biography Ser.). (Illus.). 32p. (J). (gr. 3-8). lib. bdg. 25.70 *(978-1-58415-221-7(4))* Mitchell Lane Pubs., Inc.

—Jay-Z. l.t. ed. 2004. (Blue Banner Biography Ser.). (Illus.). 32p. (J). (gr. 3-8). lib. bdg. 25.70 *(978-1-58415-223-1(0))* Mitchell Lane Pubs., Inc.

—Nelly. l.t. ed. 2003. (Blue Banner Biography Ser.). (Illus.). 32p. (J). (gr. 3-8). lib. bdg. 25.70 *(978-1-58415-218-7(4))* Mitchell Lane Pubs., Inc.

Baughan, Brian. LL Cool J. 2008. (Hip-Hop Ser.). (Illus.). 64p. (YA). (ENG.). (gr. 3-7). per. 7.95 *(978-1-4222-0271-5(2));* (gr. 7-12). lib. bdg. 22.95 *(978-1-4222-0121-3(X))* Mason Crest.

Bezdecheck, Bethany. Missy Elliott. 2009. (Library of Hip-Hop Biographies Ser.). (ENG., Illus.). 48p. (J). (gr. 7-12). pap. 11.75 *(978-1-4358-5442-0(X));* 48p. (gr. 5-5). 53.00 *(978-1-60853-697-9(1));* (J). lib. bdg. 29.25 *(978-1-4358-5056-9(4))* Rosen Publishing Group, Inc., The.

Bingham, Hettie. Will. I. Am. 2017. (Real-Life Stories Ser.). (ENG., Illus.). 32p. (J). (gr. 4-6). pap. 11.99 *(978-0-7502-8947-4(3),* Wayland) Hachette Children's Group GBR. Dist: Hachette Bk. Group.

Boone, Mary. Akon. 2007. (Blue Banner Biography Ser.). (Illus.). 32p. (J). (gr. 4-5). lib. bdg. 25.70 *(978-1-58415-630-7(9))* Mitchell Lane Pubs., Inc.

—50 Cent. 2006. (Blue Banner Biography Ser.). (Illus.). 32p. (YA). (gr. 4-7). lib. bdg. 25.70 *(978-1-58415-523-2(X),* 1259604) Mitchell Lane Pubs., Inc.

Borus, Audrey. Kanye West: Grammy-Winning Hip-Hop Artist & Producer, 1 vol. 2013. (Contemporary Lives Set 2 Ser.). (ENG.). 112p. (J). (gr. 6-12). lib. bdg. 35.64 *(978-1-61783-623-7(0),* Essential Library) ABDO Publishing Co.

Boyd, Christie Brewer. Eminem. Hillstrom, Laurie, ed. 2012. (People in the News Ser.). (ENG., Illus.). 128p. (gr. 7-10). lib. bdg. 39.40 *(978-1-4205-0753-9(2),* Lucent Bks.) Cengage Gale.

—Nicki Minaj. Greenhaven Press Staff, ed. 2012. (People in the News Ser.). (ENG., Illus.). 128p. (gr. 7-10). 39.40 *(978-1-4205-0888-8(1),* Lucent Bks.) Cengage Gale.

Bridwell, Norman. Clifford's Birthday Party. 50th anniv. ed. 2013. (Clifford 8x8 Ser.). lib. bdg. 14.75 *(978-0-606-31539-5(X),* Turtleback) Turtleback Bks.

Britton, Felicity. Nicki Minaj: Conquering Hip-Hop. 2013. (USA TODAY Lifeline Biographies Ser.). (ENG., Illus.). 112p. (gr. 6-12). lib. bdg. 34.60 *(978-1-4677-0810-4(0))* Lerner Publishing Group.

Brown, Risa. Pit Bull. 2014. (Illus.). 32p. (J). 25.70 *(978-1-61228-644-0(5))* Mitchell Lane Pubs., Inc.

Brown, Terrell. Mary J. Blige. 2008. (Hip-Hop Ser.). (Illus.). 64p. (YA). (gr. 3-7). per. 7.95 *(978-1-4222-0264-7(X));* (gr. 7-12). lib. bdg. 22.95 *(978-1-4222-0113-8(9))* Mason Crest.

—Pharell Williams. 2008. (Hip-Hop Ser.). (ENG., Illus.). 64p. (YA). (gr. 3-7). per. 7.95 *(978-1-4222-0275-3(5))* Mason Crest.

—Pharrell Williams. 2008. (Hip-Hop Ser.). (Illus.). 64p. (YA). (gr. 3-7). lib. bdg. 22.95 *(978-1-4222-0125-1(2))* Mason Crest.

—Reverend Run (Run-D. M. C.) 2008. (Hip-Hop Ser.). (Illus.). 64p. (YA). (ENG.). (gr. 3-7). per. 7.95 *(978-1-4222-0277-7(1));* (gr. 7-12). lib. bdg. 22.95 *(978-1-4222-0127-5(9))* Mason Crest.

Burlingame, Jeff. Eminem: Hip-Hop Mogul. 2014. (Hip-Hop Moguls Ser.). (Illus.). 48p. (J). (gr. 4-9). 14.95 *(978-1-62285-206-2(0))* Enslow Pubs., Inc.

—Jay-Z: A Biography of a Hip-Hop Icon. 2014. (African-American Icons Ser.). 104p. (J). lib. bdg. 27.94 *(978-0-7660-4232-2(4))* Enslow Pubs., Inc.

—Kanye West: Hip-Hop Mogul. 2014. (Hip-Hop Moguls Ser.). (Illus.). 48p. (J). (gr. 4-9). 14.95 *(978-1-62285-211-6(7))* Enslow Pubs., Inc.

—50 Cent: Hip-Hop Mogul. 2014. (Hip-Hop Moguls Ser.). (Illus.). 48p. (J). (gr. 4-9). 14.95 *(978-1-62285-201-7(X))* Enslow Pubs., Inc.

Carlson-Berne, Emma. Snoop Dogg. 2008. (Hip-Hop Ser.). (Illus.). 64p. (YA). (ENG.). (gr. 3-7). per. 7.95 *(978-1-4222-0279-1(8));* (gr. 7-12). lib. bdg. 22.95 *(978-1-4222-0129-9(5))* Mason Crest.

Collins, Tracy Brown & Chuck D. Missy Elliott. 2007. (Hip-Hop Stars Ser.). (Illus.). 100p. (YA). (gr. 7-12). lib. bdg. 30.00 *(978-0-7910-9569-0(X))* Facts On File, Inc.

Cotts, Nat. Daddy Yankee. 2009. (Hip-Hop Ser.). (Illus.). 64p. (YA). (gr. 4-7). pap. 7.95 *(978-1-4222-0342-2(5));* (gr. 7-12). lib. bdg. 22.95 *(978-1-4222-0288-3(7))* Mason Crest.

—Don Omar. 2009. (Hip Hop (Mason Crest Paperback) Ser.). (Illus.). 64p. (YA). (gr. 4-7). pap. 7.95 *(978-1-4222-0346-0(8));* (gr. 7-12). lib. bdg. 22.95 *(978-1-4222-0290-6(9))* Mason Crest.

—Pitbull. 2009. (Hip Hop (Mason Crest Paperback) Ser.). (Illus.). 64p. (YA). (gr. 4-7). pap. 7.95 *(978-1-4222-0343-9(3))*; (gr. 7-12). lib. bdg. 22.95 *(978-1-4222-0302-6(6))* Mason Crest.

—Young Jeezy. 2009. (Hip-Hop 2 Ser.). (Illus.). 64p. (YA). (gr. 7-12). lib. bdg. 22.95 *(978-1-4222-0306-4(9))* Mason Crest.

Davids, Stacy B. Hip-Hop Greats, 1 vol. 2011. (Best of the Best Ser.). (ENG.). 32p. (gr. 1-2). pap. 8.10 *(978-1-4296-7247-4(1))*; pap. 47.70 *(978-1-4296-7248-1(X))*; lib. bdg. 26.65 *(978-1-4296-6502-5(5))* Capstone Press of Coughlan Cos. (Blazers).

Doeden, Matt. Will Smith. 2007. (Illus.). 112p. (J). pap. 9.95 *(978-0-8225-7064-6(5))*; (ENG., (gr. 5-12). lib. bdg. 27.93 *(978-0-8225-6608-3(7)*, Lerner Pubns.) Lerner Publishing Group.

—Will Smith: Box Office Superstar. 2009. (USA TODAY Lifeline Biographies Ser.). (ENG., Illus.). 112p. (J). (gr. 6-12). lib. bdg. 34.60 *(978-0-7613-4265-6(6)*, 1299611) Lerner Publishing Group.

Donatelli, Jen Jones. Sean Diddy Combs: A Biography of a Music Mogul. 2014. (African-American Icons Ser.). 104p. (J). pap. 10.95 *(978-1-4644-0537-2(9))* Enslow Pubs., Inc.

Earl, C. F. Black Eyed Peas. 2012. (Superstars of Hip-Hop Ser.). 48p. (J). (gr. 3-4). pap. 9.95 *(978-1-4222-2537-0(2))*; (Illus.). 19.95 *(978-1-4222-2511-0(9))* Mason Crest.

—Dr. Dre. 2012. (J). pap. *(978-1-4222-2543-1(7))*; (Illus.). 48p. (gr. 3-4). 19.95 *(978-1-4222-2517-2(8))* Mason Crest.

—Drake. 2012. (Superstars of Hip-Hop Ser.). (Illus.). 48p. (J). (gr. 3-4). 19.95 *(978-1-4222-2516-5(X))*; pap. 9.95 *(978-1-4222-2542-4(9))* Mason Crest.

—Flo Rida. 2012. (Superstars of Hip-Hop Ser.). 48p. (J). (gr. 3-4). pap. 9.95 *(978-1-4222-2551-6(8))*; (Illus.). 19.95 *(978-1-4222-2525-7(9))* Mason Crest.

—Jay-Z. 2012. (Superstars of Hip-Hop Ser.). 48p. (J). (gr. 3-4). pap. 9.95 *(978-1-4222-2546-2(1))*; (Illus.). 19.95 *(978-1-4222-2520-2(8))* Mason Crest.

—Kanye West. 2012. (Superstars of Hip-Hop Ser.). 48p. (J). (gr. 3-4). pap. 9.95 *(978-1-4222-2559-2(3))*; (Illus.). 19.95 *(978-1-4222-2533-2(X))* Mason Crest.

—Lil' Wayne. 2012. (Superstars of Hip-Hop Ser.). 48p. (J). (gr. 3-4). pap. 9.95 *(978-1-4222-2558-5(5))*; (Illus.). 19.95 *(978-1-4222-2532-5(1))* Mason Crest.

—Ludacris. 2012. (J). pap. *(978-1-4222-2549-3(6))*; (Illus.). 48p. (gr. 3-4). 19.95 *(978-1-4222-2523-3(2))* Mason Crest.

—Superstars of Hip Hop: T-Pain. 2012. (J). *(978-1-4222-2555-4(0))* Mason Crest.

—T. I. 2012. (J). pap. *(978-1-4222-2553-0(4))* Mason Crest.

—Timbaland. 2012. (J). *(978-1-4222-2554-7(2))*; (Illus.). 48p. (gr. 3-4). 19.95 *(978-1-4222-2528-8(3))* Mason Crest.

Earl, C. F. & Hill, Z. B. Superstars of Hip Hop - T-Pain. 2012. (Superstars of Hip-Hop Ser.). (Illus.). 48p. (J). (gr. 3-4). 19.95 *(978-1-4222-2529-5(1))* Mason Crest.

Embacher, Eric. Will Smith: The Funny, Funky, & Confident Fresh Prince. 2003. (High Five Reading - Red Ser.). (ENG., Illus.). 48p. (gr. 3-4). per. 9.00 *(978-0-7368-2829-1(X)*, High Five Reading (RBL)) Capstone Press of Coughlan Cos.

Etingoff, Kim. Ivy Queen. 2009. (Hip-Hop Ser.). (Illus.). 64p. (YA). (gr. 4-7). pap. 7.95 *(978-1-4222-0349-1(2))*; (gr. 7-12). lib. bdg. 22.95 *(978-1-4222-0295-1(X))* Mason Crest.

—T. I. 2009. (Hip-Hop 2 Ser.). (Illus.). 64p. (YA). (gr. 7-12). lib. bdg. 22.95 *(978-1-4222-0303-3(4))* Mason Crest.

Feinstein, Stephen. Queen Latifah. 2008. (African-American Heroes Ser.). (Illus.). 24p. (J). (gr. 1-3). lib. bdg. 22.60 *(978-0-7660-2896-8(8))* Enslow Pubs., Inc.

—Will Smith. 2007. (African-American Heroes Ser.). (Illus.). 24p. (J). (gr. 1-3). lib. bdg. 22.60 *(978-0-7660-2765-7(1)*, Enslow Elementary) Enslow Pubs., Inc.

Ferrier, Morwenna. Lil Wayne: Takin' the Rap. 2012. (ENG., Illus.). 128p. 15.99 *(978-0-85775-279-6(0)*, 9780857752796) Flame Tree Publishing GBR. Dist: Bookmasters Distribution.

Flores, Christopher Lee. Pharrell Williams: Singer & Songwriter. 2016. (Junior Biographies Ser.). 24p. (J). pap. 9.35 *(978-0-7660-8192-5(3))* Enslow Pubs., Inc.

Forget, Thomas. Beastie Boys. 2009. (Library of Hip-Hop Biographies Ser.). 48p. (gr. 5-5). 53.00 *(978-1-60853-681-8(5))* Rosen Publishing Group, Inc., The.

Gagne, Tammy. LL Cool J. 2013. (ENG.). 32p. (gr. 4-8). lib. bdg. 25.70 *(978-1-61228-464-4(7))* Mitchell Lane Pubs., Inc.

—Will. I. am. 2012. (Illus.). 32p. (J). lib. bdg. 25.70 *(978-1-61228-318-0(7))* Mitchell Lane Pubs., Inc.

Gelfand, Dale Evva. Sean Combs. 2007. (Hip-Hop Stars Ser.). (Illus.). 104p. (YA). (gr. 7-12). lib. bdg. 30.00 *(978-0-7910-9494-5(4))* Facts On File, Inc.

Gisnash, Sahara. Salt-N-Pepa. 2009. (Library of Hip-Hop Biographies Ser.). 48p. (gr. 5-5). 53.00 *(978-1-60853-705-1(6))* Rosen Publishing Group, Inc., The.

Golus, Carrie. Tupac Shakur. (USA TODAY Lifeline Biographies Ser.). (Illus.). 112p. 2010. (ENG.). (gr. 6-12). lib. bdg. 34.60 *(978-0-7613-5473-4(5))* 2007. (J). pap. 9.95 *(978-0-8225-7063-9(7))* 2007. (ENG., (gr. 5-12). lib. bdg. 27.93 *(978-0-8225-6609-0(5))* Lerner Publishing Group.

Gordon, Stephen G. Jay-Z: CEO of Hip-Hop. 2013. (USA TODAY Lifeline Biographies Ser.). (ENG.). 112p. (gr. 6-12). lib. bdg. 34.60 *(978-1-4677-0811-1(9))* Lerner Publishing Group.

Grucella, Ethan. Kanye West. 2012. (Hip-Hop Headliners Ser.). (ENG., Illus.). 32p. (J). (gr. 4-8). pap. 10.50 *(978-1-4339-6614-9(X))*; lib. bdg. 25.25 *(978-1-4339-6612-5(3))* Stevens, Gareth Publishing LLLP.

Gunderson, Jessica. Jay-Z: Hip-Hop Icon, 1 vol. Kinsella, Pat, illus. 2012. (American Graphic Ser.). (ENG.). 32p. (gr. 3-4). pap. 8.10 *(978-1-4296-7993-0(X))*; pap. 47.70 *(978-1-4296-8475-0(5))*; lib. bdg. 30.65 *(978-1-4296-6017-4(1))* Capstone Press of Coughlan Cos. (Graphic Library).

Hamilton, Toby G. Busta Rhymes. 2009. (Hip Hop (Mason Crest Paperback) Ser.). (Illus.). 64p. (YA). (gr. 4-7). pap. 7.95 *(978-1-4222-0333-0(6))*; (gr. 7-12). lib. bdg. 22.95 *(978-1-4222-0284-5(4))* Mason Crest.

—Dmx. 2009. (Hip Hop (Mason Crest Paperback) Ser.). (Illus.). 64p. (YA). (gr. 4-7). pap. 7.95 *(978-1-4222-0340-8(9))*; (gr. 7-12). lib. bdg. 22.95 *(978-1-4222-0289-0(5))* Mason Crest.

—Fat Joe. 2009. (Hip Hop (Mason Crest Paperback) Ser.). (Illus.). 64p. (YA). (gr. 4-7). pap. 7.95 *(978-1-4222-0344-6(1))*; (gr. 7-12). lib. bdg. 22.95 *(978-1-4222-0291-3(7))* Mason Crest.

—Ice Cube. 2009. (Hip Hop 2 Ser.). (Illus.). 64p. (YA). (gr. 4-7). pap. 7.95 *(978-1-4222-0327-9(1))*; (gr. 7-12). lib. bdg. 22.95 *(978-1-4222-0294-4(1))* Mason Crest.

Harris, Ashley Rae. Tupac Shakur: Multi-Platinum Rapper, 1 vol. 2010. (Lives Cut Short Set 1 Ser.). (ENG.). 112p. (J). (gr. 6-12). lib. bdg. 35.64 *(978-1-60453-791-8(4))* ABDO Publishing Co.

Heos, Bridget. Jay-Z. 2009. (Library of Hip-Hop Biographies Ser.). (ENG., Illus.). 48p. (J). (gr. 7-12). pap. 11.75 *(978-1-4358-5438-3(1))*; 48p. (gr. 5-5). 53.00 *(978-1-60853-682-5(3))*; (J). lib. bdg. 29.25 *(978-1-4358-5052-1(1))* Rosen Publishing Group, Inc., The.

Hill, Laban Carrick. When the Beat Was Born: DJ Kool Herc & the Creation of Hip Hop. Taylor, Theodore, III, illus. 2013. (ENG.). 32p. (J). (gr. 1-5). 17.99 *(978-1-59643-540-7(2)*, 9781596435407) Roaring Brook Pr.

Hill, Z. B. Eminem. 2012. (Superstars of Hip-Hop Ser.). 48p. (J). (gr. 3-4). pap. 9.95 *(978-1-4222-2544-8(5))*; (Illus.). 19.95 *(978-1-4222-2518-9(6))* Mason Crest.

—LL Cool J. 2012. (J). *(978-1-4222-2548-6(8))*; (Illus.). 48p. (gr. 3-4). 19.95 *(978-1-4222-2522-6(4))* Mason Crest.

—Mary J. Blige. 2012. (J). pap. *(978-1-4222-2538-7(0))* Mason Crest.

—Notorious B.I.G. 2012. (J). *(978-1-4222-2550-9(X))*; (Illus.). 48p. (gr. 3-4). 19.95 *(978-1-4222-2524-0(0))* Mason Crest.

—Sean "Diddy" Combs. 2012. (J). pap. *(978-1-4222-2540-0(2))*; (Illus.). 48p. (gr. 3-4). 19.95 *(978-1-4222-2514-1(3))* Mason Crest.

—Snoop Dogg. 2012. (Superstars of Hip-Hop Ser.). (Illus.). 48p. (J). (gr. 3-4). 19.95 *(978-1-4222-2515-8(1))* Mason Crest.

—Tupac. 2012. (J). pap. *(978-1-4222-2556-1(9))*; (Illus.). 48p. (gr. 3-4). 19.95 *(978-1-4222-2530-1(5))* Mason Crest.

—50 Cent. 2012. (J). pap. *(978-1-4222-2535-6(6))*; (Illus.). 48p. (gr. 3-4). 19.95 *(978-1-4222-2509-7(7))* Mason Crest.

Hill, Z. B. & Earl, C. F. Mary J. Blige. 2012. (Superstars of Hip-Hop Ser.). (Illus.). 48p. (J). (gr. 3-4). 19.95 *(978-1-4222-2512-7(7))* Mason Crest.

Hillstrom, Laurie Collier. Jay-Z. 2009. (People in the News Ser.). (ENG., Illus.). 128p. (YA). (gr. 7-12). 33.95 *(978-1-4205-0158-2(5))* Cengage Gale.

Hip-Hop: The Complete Series, 25 bks., Set. Incl. Ashanti. Waters, Rosa. (gr. 3-7). lib. bdg. 22.95 *(978-1-4222-0111-4(2))*; LL Cool J. Baughan, Brian. (gr. 7-12). lib. bdg. 22.95 *(978-1-4222-0121-3(X))*; Ludacris. Scott, Celicia. (gr. 7-12). lib. bdg. 22.95 *(978-1-4222-0122-0(8))*; Mariah Carey. Scott, Celicia. (gr. 7-12). lib. bdg. 22.95 *(978-1-4222-0114-5(7))*; Mary J. Blige. Brown, Terrell. (gr. 7-12). lib. bdg. 22.95 *(978-1-4222-0113-8(9))*; Missy Elliot. Lawlor, Michelle. (gr. 7-12). lib. bdg. 22.95 *(978-1-4222-0117-6(1))*; Nelly. Hooper, James. (gr. 7-12). lib. bdg. 22.95 *(978-1-4222-0123-7(6))*; Pharrell Williams. Brown, Terrell. (gr. 3-7). lib. bdg. 22.95 *(978-1-4222-0125-1(2))*; Queen Latifah. Snyder, Gail. (gr. 7-12). lib. bdg. 22.95 *(978-1-4222-0126-8(0))*; Reverend Run (Run-D.M.C.) Brown, Terrell. (gr. 7-12). lib. bdg. 22.95 *(978-1-4222-0127-5(9))*; Snoop Dogg. Carlson-Berne, Emma. (gr. 7-12). lib. bdg. 22.95 *(978-1-4222-0129-9(5))*; Usher. Lord, Raymond. (gr. 7-12). lib. bdg. 22.95 *(978-1-4222-0131-2(7))*; (Illus.). 64p. (YA). 2008. 2007. 573.75 *(978-1-4222-0108-4(2))* Mason Crest.

Hip-Hop 2, 25 vols., Set. Incl. Around the World. Walker, Ida. (Illus.). lib. bdg. 22.95 *(978-1-4222-0293-7(3))*; Busta Rhymes. Hamilton, Toby G. (Illus.). lib. bdg. 22.95 *(978-1-4222-0284-5(4))*; Christina Aguilera. Lemmens, Mary Jo. lib. bdg. 22.95 *(978-1-4222-0285-2(2))*; Ciara. Simone, Jacquelyn. (Illus.). lib. bdg. 22.95 *(978-1-4222-0286-9(0))*; Cypress Hill. Lemmens, Maryjo. (Illus.). lib. bdg. 22.95 *(978-1-4222-0287-6(9))*; Daddy Yankee. Cotts, Nat. (Illus.). lib. bdg. 22.95 *(978-1-4222-0288-3(7))*; Dmx. Hamilton, Toby G. (Illus.). lib. bdg. 22.95 *(978-1-4222-0289-0(5))*; Don Omar. Cotts, Nat. (Illus.). lib. bdg. 22.95 *(978-1-4222-0290-6(9))*; Fat Joe. Hamilton, Toby G. (Illus.). lib. bdg. 22.95 *(978-1-4222-0291-3(7))*; Game. Sanna, Lindsey. (Illus.). lib. bdg. 22.95 *(978-1-4222-0292-0(5))*; Ice Cube. Hamilton, Toby G. (Illus.). lib. bdg. 22.95 *(978-1-4222-0294-4(1))*; Ivy Queen. Etingoff, Kim. (Illus.). lib. bdg. 22.95 *(978-1-4222-0295-1(X))*; Jennifer Lopez. Lemmens, Maryjo & Lemmens, Maryjo. (Illus.). lib. bdg. 22.95 *(978-1-4222-0296-8(8))*; Juelz Santana. Rockworth, Janice. (Illus.). lib. bdg. 22.95 *(978-1-4222-0297-5(6))*; Lloyd Banks. Sanna, E. J. (Illus.). lib. bdg. 22.95 *(978-1-4222-0299-9(2))*; Nas. Rockworth, Janice. (Illus.). lib. bdg. 22.95 *(978-1-4222-0300-2(X))*; Outkast. Simone, Jacquelyn. (Illus.). lib. bdg. 22.95 *(978-1-4222-0301-9(8))*; Pitbull. Cotts, Nat. (Illus.). lib. bdg. 22.95 *(978-1-4222-0302-6(6))*; T. I. Etingoff, Kim. (Illus.). lib. bdg. 22.95 *(978-1-4222-0303-3(4))*; Wu-Tang Clan. Rockworth, Janice. (Illus.). lib. bdg. 22.95 *(978-1-4222-0304-0(2))*; Xzibit. Lemmens, Maryjo. (Illus.). lib. bdg. 22.95 *(978-1-4222-0305-7(0))*; Young Jeezy. Cotts, Nat. (Illus.). lib. bdg. 22.95 *(978-1-4222-0306-4(9))*; Yung Joc. Waters, Rosa. (Illus.). lib. bdg. 22.95 *(978-1-4222-0307-1(7))*; (YA). (gr. 7-12). 2009. 64p. 2007. Set lib. bdg. 573.75 *(978-1-4222-0077-3(9))* Mason Crest.

Hip-Hop World, 4 vols. 2010. (Hip-Hop World Ser.). (ENG.). 48p. (gr. 3-4). lib. bdg. 127.96 *(978-1-4296-4424-2(9))* Capstone Press of Coughlan Cos.

Hip-Hop World [Capstone Sole Source]. 2010. (Hip-Hop World Ser.). 48p. lib. bdg. 122.60 *(978-1-4296-5866-9(5))* Capstone Press of Coughlan Cos.

Hooper, James. Nelly. 2008. (Hip-Hop Ser.). (Illus.). 64p. (YA). (ENG.). (gr. 3-7). per. 7.95 *(978-1-4222-0273-9(9))*; (gr. 7-12). lib. bdg. 22.95 *(978-1-4222-0123-7(6))* Mason Crest.

Isbell, Hannah. Drake: Actor & Rapper. 2017. (Junior Biographies Ser.). 24p. (gr. 3-4). (J). pap. 9.35 ***(978-0-7660-8789-7(1))***; lib. bdg. 22.60 ***(978-0-7660-8668-5(2))*** Enslow Pubs., Inc.

Jones, Jen. Sean "Diddy" Combs: A Biography of a Music Mogul. 2014. (African-American Icons Ser.). 104p. (J). 27.94 *(978-0-7660-4296-4(0))* Enslow Pubs., Inc.

Kampff, Joseph. Jay Z: Rapper & Businessman. 2016. (Exceptional African Americans Ser.). (ENG., Illus.). 24p. (J). (gr. 3-3). 22.60 *(978-0-7660-7254-1(1))* Enslow Pubs., Inc.

Kennedy, Robert. Drake. 2012. (Hip-Hop Headliners Ser.). (ENG., Illus.). 32p. (J). (gr. 4-8). pap. 10.50 *(978-1-4339-6606-4(9))*; lib. bdg. 25.25 *(978-1-4339-6604-0(2))* Stevens, Gareth Publishing LLLP.

Kennon, Michou. Queen Latifah. 2011. (Hip-Hop Headliners Ser.). (Illus.). 32p. (J). (gr. 3-8). lib. bdg. 25.25 *(978-1-4339-4808-4(7))* Stevens, Gareth Publishing LLLP.

Koestler-Grack, Rachel A. Queen Latifah. 2007. (Hip-Hop Stars Ser.). (Illus.). 104p. (YA). (gr. 7-12). lib. bdg. 30.00 *(978-0-7910-9498-3(7))* Facts On File, Inc.

Kowalski, Emma. The Story of Roc-A-Fella Records. 2012. (J). pap. *(978-1-4222-2132-7(6))*; 64p. (gr. 4). 22.95 *(978-1-4222-2119-8(9))* Mason Crest.

Krumenauer, Heidi. Flo-Rida. 2010. (Blue Banner Biography Ser.). (Illus.). 32p. (YA). (gr. 4-7). lib. bdg. 25.70 *(978-1-58415-906-3(5))* Mitchell Lane Pubs., Inc.

La Bella, Laura. Kanye West. 2009. (Library of Hip-Hop Biographies Ser.). (ENG., Illus.). 48p. (J). (gr. 7-12). pap. 11.75 *(978-1-4358-5439-0(X))*; 48p. (gr. 5-5). 53.00 *(978-1-60853-685-6(8))*; (J). lib. bdg. 29.25 *(978-1-4358-5053-8(X))* Rosen Publishing Group, Inc., The.

Lajiness, Katie. Pharrell Williams, 1 vol. 2016. (Big Buddy Pop Biographies Ser.). (ENG., Illus.). 32p. (J). (gr. 2-5). 28.50 *(978-1-68078-063-5(8))* ABDO Publishing Co.

Lawlor, Michelle. Missy Elliot. 2008. (Hip-Hop Ser.). (Illus.). 64p. (YA). (ENG.). (gr. 3-7). per. 7.95 *(978-1-4222-0268-5(2))*; (gr. 7-12). lib. bdg. 22.95 *(978-1-4222-0117-6(1))* Mason Crest.

Lemmens, Mary Jo. Cypress Hill. 2009. (Hip Hop (Mason Crest Paperback) Ser.). (Illus.). 64p. (YA). (gr. 4-7). pap. 7.95 *(978-1-4222-0345-3(X))* Mason Crest.

Lemmens, Maryjo. Cypress Hill. 2009. (Hip-Hop 2 Ser.). (Illus.). 64p. (YA). (gr. 7-12). lib. bdg. 22.95 *(978-1-4222-0287-6(9))* Mason Crest.

—Xzibit. 2009. (Hip Hop (Mason Crest Paperback) Ser.). (Illus.). 64p. (YA). (gr. 4-7). pap. 7.95 *(978-1-4222-0337-8(9))*; (gr. 7-12). lib. bdg. 22.95 *(978-1-4222-0305-7(0))* Mason Crest.

Llanas, Sheila Griffin. Hip-Hop Stars, 1 vol. 2010. (Hip-Hop World Ser.). (ENG.). 48p. (gr. 3-4). lib. bdg. 31.99 *(978-1-4296-4019-0(7))* Capstone Press of Coughlan Cos.

Lord, Raymond. Usher. 2008. (Hip-Hop Ser.). (Illus.). 64p. (YA). (gr. 3-7). per. 7.95 *(978-1-4222-0180-0(5))* Mason Crest.

Maimone, Sofia Z. Mary J. Blige. 2011. (Hip-Hop Headliners Ser.). (Illus.). 32p. (J). (gr. 3-8). 25.25 *(978-1-4339-4804-6(4))*; pap. 10.50 *(978-1-4339-4805-3(2))* Stevens, Gareth Publishing LLLP.

Marcovitz, Hal. Dr. Dre. 2008. (Hip-Hop Ser.). (ENG., Illus.). 64p. (YA). (gr. 3-7). per. 7.95 *(978-1-4222-0267-8(4))* Mason Crest.

—Notorious B. I. G. 2008. (Hip-Hop Ser.). (ENG., Illus.). 64p. (YA). (gr. 3-7). per. 7.95 *(978-1-4222-0274-6(7))* Mason Crest.

Mattern, Joanne. Eminem. 2008. (Hip-Hop Ser.). (Illus.). 64p. (YA). per. 7.95 *(978-1-4222-0179-4(1))* Mason Crest.

—Ludacris. 2011. (Blue Banner Biography Ser.). (Illus.). 32p. (YA). (gr. 4-7). lib. bdg. 25.70 *(978-1-61228-055-4(2))* Mitchell Lane Pubs., Inc.

—Nicki Minaj. 2013. (ENG.). 32p. (gr. 4-8). lib. bdg. 25.70 *(978-1-61228-468-2(X))* Mitchell Lane Pubs., Inc.

MattyB & Thrasher, Travis. That's a Rap. 2016. (ENG., Illus.). 272p. (J). (gr. 5-9). 19.99 *(978-1-5011-3379-4(9)*, Gallery Bks.) Gallery Bks.

Mills, Clifford W. Tupac Shakur. 2007. (Hip-Hop Stars Ser.). (Illus.). 104p. (YA). (gr. 7-12). lib. bdg. 30.00 *(978-0-7910-9495-2(2))* Facts On File, Inc.

Morgan, Kayla. Kanye West: Soul-Fired Hip-Hop. 2012. (USA TODAY Lifeline Biographies Ser.). (ENG., Illus.). 112p. (gr. 6-12). lib. bdg. 34.60 *(978-0-7613-8640-7(8))* Lerner Publishing Group.

Morreale, Marie. Pharrell Williams. 2015. (Real Bios Ser.). (ENG.). 48p. (J). lib. bdg. 29.00 *(978-0-531-21378-0(1))* Scholastic Library Publishing.

Murray, Laura K. Iggy Azalea. 2016. (J). *(978-1-60818-671-6(7)*, Creative Education) Creative Co., The.

Nacerous, Roman P. Jay-Z. 2011. (Hip-Hop Headliners Ser.). (Illus.). 32p. (J). (gr. 3-8). pap. 10.50 *(978-1-4339-4797-1(8))*; lib. bdg. 25.25 *(978-1-4339-4796-4(X))* Stevens, Gareth Publishing LLLP.

O'Neal, Claire. T. I. 2009. (Blue Banner Biography Ser.). (Illus.). 32p. (YA). (gr. 4-7). lib. bdg. 25.70 *(978-1-58415-769-4(0))* Mitchell Lane Pubs., Inc.

Orr, Tamra B. Ice Cube. 2006. (Blue Banner Biography Ser.). (Illus.). 32p. (YA). (gr. 4-7). lib. bdg. 25.70 *(978-1-58415-517-1(5))* Mitchell Lane Pubs., Inc.

O'Sorus, Roman. Eminem. 2012. (Hip-Hop Headliners Ser.). (ENG., Illus.). 32p. (J). (gr. 4-8). pap. 10.50 *(978-1-4339-6610-1(7))* Stevens, Gareth Publishing LLLP.

O'Sorus, Roman & O'sorus, Roman. Eminem. 2012. (Hip-Hop Headliners Ser.). (ENG., Illus.). 32p. (J). (gr. 4-8). lib. bdg. 25.25 *(978-1-4339-6608-8(5))* Stevens, Gareth Publishing LLLP.

Otfinoski, Steve. Drake: Actor & Hip-Hop Artist, 1 vol. 2013. (Contemporary Lives Set 2 Ser.). (ENG.). 112p. (J). (gr. 6-12). lib. bdg. 35.64 *(978-1-61783-618-3(4)*, Essential Library) ABDO Publishing Co.

Payment, Simone. Queen Latifah. (Library of Hip-Hop Biographies Ser.). 48p. 2009. (gr. 5-5). 53.00 *(978-1-60853-703-7(X))* 2006. (Illus.). (YA). (gr. 7-12). lib. bdg. 29.25 *(978-1-4042-0518-5(7)*, 1254005) Rosen Publishing Group, Inc., The.

Peppas, Lynn. Drake. 2011. (ENG.). 32p. (J). pap. *(978-0-7787-7611-6(5))* Crabtree Publishing Co.

Pettinella, Amy. Queen Latifah: Award-Winning Actress & Hip-Hop Activist. 2014. (Leading Women Ser.). 112p. (J). (gr. 7-11). lib. bdg. 39.93 *(978-1-62712-984-8(7))* Cavendish Square Publishing.

Publishers, Chelsea House, creator. Hip-Hop Stars Set, 10-Volumes. 2007. (Hip-Hop Stars Ser.). (gr. 6-12). 300.00 *(978-0-7910-9736-6(6)*, Chelsea Hse.) Facts On File, Inc.

Rockworth, Janice. Juelz Santana. 2009. (Hip Hop (Mason Crest Paperback) Ser.). (Illus.). 64p. (YA). (gr. 4-7). pap. 7.95 *(978-1-4222-0341-5(7))*; (gr. 7-12). lib. bdg. 22.95 *(978-1-4222-0297-5(6))* Mason Crest.

—Nas. 2009. (Hip-Hop 2 Ser.). (Illus.). 64p. (YA). (gr. 7-12). lib. bdg. 22.95 *(978-1-4222-0300-2(X))* Mason Crest.

—Wu-Tang Clan. 2009. (Hip-Hop Ser.). (Illus.). 64p. (YA). (gr. 4-7). pap. 7.95 *(978-1-4222-0335-4(2))*; (gr. 7-12). lib. bdg. 22.95 *(978-1-4222-0304-0(2))* Mason Crest.

Roza, Greg. OutKast. 2009. (Library of Hip-Hop Biographies Ser.). (ENG., Illus.). 48p. (J). (gr. 7-12). pap. 11.75 *(978-1-4358-5443-7(8))*; 48p. (gr. 5-5). 53.00 *(978-1-60853-700-6(5))*; (J). lib. bdg. 29.25 *(978-1-4358-5057-6(2))* Rosen Publishing Group, Inc., The.

Saddleback Educational Publishing. Chris Brown, 1 vol. 2013. (Hip-Hop Biographies Ser.). (ENG.). 48p. (YA). (gr. 9-12). 11.95 *(978-1-62250-017-8(2))* Saddleback Educational Publishing, Inc.

—Usher, 1 vol. 2013. (Hip-Hop Biographies Ser.). (ENG.). 48p. (YA). (gr. 9-12). 11.95 *(978-1-62250-009-3(1))* Saddleback Educational Publishing, Inc.

—50 Cent, 1 vol. 2013. (Hip-Hop Biographies Ser.). (ENG.). 48p. (YA). (gr. 9-12). 11.95 *(978-1-62250-008-6(3))* Saddleback Educational Publishing, Inc.

Saddleback Educational Publishing Staff. Chris Brown. 2013. (Hip-Hop Biographies (Saddleback Publishing) Ser.). (YA). lib. bdg. 23.25 *(978-0-606-31482-4(2)*, Turtleback) Turtleback Bks.

—Drake, 1 vol. 2013. (Hip-Hop Biographies Ser.). (ENG.). 48p. (YA). (gr. 9-12). 11.95 *(978-1-62250-013-0(X))* Saddleback Educational Publishing, Inc.

—Drake. 2013. (Hip-Hop Biographies (Saddleback Publishing) Ser.). (YA). lib. bdg. 23.25 *(978-0-606-31483-1(0)*, Turtleback) Turtleback Bks.

—Jay-Z, 1 vol. 2013. (Hip-Hop Biographies Ser.). (ENG.). 48p. (YA). (gr. 9-12). 11.95 *(978-1-62250-012-3(1))* Saddleback Educational Publishing, Inc.

—Kanye West, 1 vol. 2013. (Hip-Hop Biographies Ser.). (ENG.). 48p. (YA). (gr. 9-12). 11.95 *(978-1-62250-016-1(4))* Saddleback Educational Publishing, Inc.

—Kanye West. 2013. (Hip-Hop Biographies (Saddleback Publishing) Ser.). (YA). lib. bdg. 23.25 *(978-0-606-31485-5(7)*, Turtleback) Turtleback Bks.

—Lil Wayne, 1 vol. 2013. (Hip-Hop Biographies Ser.). (ENG.). 48p. (YA). (gr. 9-12). 11.95 *(978-1-62250-014-7(8))* Saddleback Educational Publishing, Inc.

—Lil Wayne. 2013. (Hip-Hop Biographies (Saddleback Publishing) Ser.). (YA). lib. bdg. 23.25 *(978-0-606-31486-2(5)*, Turtleback) Turtleback Bks.

—Nicki Minaj, 1 vol. 2013. (Hip-Hop Biographies Ser.). (ENG.). 48p. (YA). (gr. 9-12). 11.95 *(978-1-62250-010-9(5))* Saddleback Educational Publishing, Inc.

—Pitbull, 1 vol. 2013. (Hip-Hop Biographies Ser.). (ENG.). 48p. (YA). (gr. 9-12). 11.95 *(978-1-62250-015-4(6))* Saddleback Educational Publishing, Inc.

—Sean Combs, 1 vol. 2015. (Hip-Hop Biographies Ser.). (ENG.). 48p. (YA). (gr. 9-12). 11.95 *(978-1-62250-929-4(3))* Saddleback Educational Publishing, Inc.

—50 Cent. 2013. (Hip-Hop Biographies (Saddleback Publishing) Ser.). (YA). lib. bdg. 23.25 *(978-0-606-31481-7(4)*, Turtleback) Turtleback Bks.

Sanna, E. J. Lloyd Banks. 2009. (Hip Hop (Mason Crest Paperback) Ser.). (Illus.). 64p. (YA). (gr. 4-7). pap. 7.95 *(978-1-4222-0336-1(0))*; (gr. 7-12). lib. bdg. 22.95 *(978-1-4222-0299-9(2))* Mason Crest.

Sanna, Lindsey. The Game. 2009. (Hip-Hop Ser.). (Illus.). 64p. (YA). (gr. 3-7). pap. 7.95 *(978-1-4222-0329-3(8))*; (gr. 7-12). lib. bdg. 22.95 *(978-1-4222-0292-0(5))* Mason Crest.

Schuman, Michael A. Will Smith: A Biography of a Rapper Turned Movie Star. 2013. (African-American Icons Ser.). 104p. (J). (gr. 6-12). pap. 10.95 *(978-1-59845-397-3(1))* Enslow Pubs., Inc.

—Will Smith: I Like Blending a Message with Comedy. 2006. (African-American Biography Library). (Illus.). 128p. (J). (gr. 6). lib. bdg. 33.27 *(978-0-7660-2465-6(2)*, 1250489) Enslow Pubs., Inc.

Schweitzer, Karen. Soulja Boy Tell 'Em. (Role Model Entertainers Ser.). (Illus.). 64p. (YA). 2010. (gr. 7-12). 22.95 *(978-1-4222-0509-9(6))* 2007. pap. 9.95 *(978-1-4222-0796-3(X))* Mason Crest.

Scott, Celicia. Ludacris. 2008. (Hip-Hop Ser.). (Illus.). 64p. (YA). (ENG.). (gr. 3-7). per. 7.95 *(978-1-4222-0272-2(0))*; (gr. 7-12). lib. bdg. 22.95 *(978-1-4222-0122-0(8))* Mason Crest.

Shea, Kevin Pearce. Snoop Dogg. 2012. (Hip-Hop Headliners Ser.). (ENG., Illus.). 32p. (J). (gr. 4-8). pap. 10.50 *(978-1-4339-6622-4(0))*; lib. bdg. 25.25 *(978-1-4339-6620-0(4))* Stevens, Gareth Publishing LLLP.

Shea, Molly. The Black Eyed Peas. 2011. (Hip-Hop Headliners Ser.). (Illus.). 32p. (J). (gr. 3-8). pap. 10.50 *(978-1-4339-4793-3(5))*; lib. bdg. 25.25 *(978-1-4339-4792-6(7))* Stevens, Gareth Publishing LLLP.

Sheen, Barbara. Kanye West. 2009. (People in the News Ser.). (ENG.). 128p. (gr. 7-12). 39.40 *(978-1-4205-0159-9(3))* Cengage Gale.

Shekell, Dustin. LL Cool J. 2007. (Hip-Hop Stars Ser.). (Illus.). 103p. (YA). (gr. 7-12). lib. bdg. 30.00 *(978-0-7910-9519-5(3))* Facts On File, Inc.

Simone, Jacquelyn. Outkast. 2009. (Hip Hop (Mason Crest Paperback) Ser.). (Illus.). 64p. (YA). (gr. 4-7). pap. 7.95 *(978-1-4222-0328-6(X))*; (gr. 7-12). lib. bdg. 22.95 *(978-1-4222-0301-9(8))* Mason Crest.

Simons, Rae. Kanye West. 2008. (Hip-Hop Ser.). (ENG., Illus.). 64p. (YA). (gr. 3-7). per. 7.95 *(978-1-4222-0281-4(X))* Mason Crest.

Slavicek, Louise Chipley. Run-DMC. 2007. (Hip-Hop Stars Ser.). (Illus.). 104p. (YA). (gr. 7-12). lib. bdg. 30.00 *(978-0-7910-9499-0(5))* Facts On File, Inc.

Snyder, Gail. Queen Latifah. 2008. (Hip-Hop Ser.). (Illus.). 64p. (YA). (ENG.). (gr. 3-7). per. 7.95 *(978-1-4222-0276-0(3))*; (gr. 7-12). lib. bdg. 22.95 *(978-1-4222-0126-8(0))* Mason Crest.

Sol & K'naan. When I Get Older: The Story Behind Wavin' Flag. Gutierrez, Rudy, illus. 2012. (ENG.). 1p. (J). (gr. 1-4). 17.95 *(978-1-77049-302-5(6)*, Tundra Bks.) Tundra Bks. CAN. Dist: Penguin Random Hse. LLC.

Spilsbury, Richard. Jay-Z, 1 vol. 2012. (Titans of Business Ser.). (ENG.). 48p. (gr. 4-6). lib. bdg. 32.65 *(978-1-4329-6430-6(5)*, NA-h) Heinemann-Raintree.

Tieck, Sarah. Psy: Gangnam Style Rapper, 1 vol. 2013. (Big Buddy Biographies Set 10 Ser.). (ENG.). 32p. (J). (gr. 2-5). lib. bdg. 28.50 *(978-1-61783-860-6(8)*, Big Buddy Bks.) ABDO Publishing Co.

Torres, Jennifer. Eve. 2004. (Blue Banner Biography Ser.). (Illus.). 32p. (J). (gr. 3-8). lib. bdg. 25.70 *(978-1-58415-317-7(2))* Mitchell Lane Pubs., Inc.

—Mary J. Blige. 2007. (Blue Banner Biography Ser.). (Illus.). 32p. (YA). (gr. 4-7). lib. bdg. 25.70 *(978-1-58415-612-3(0))* Mitchell Lane Pubs., Inc.

P
Q
R

Torres, John A. Lil Wayne. 2009. (Blue Banner Biography Ser.). (Illus.). 32p. (YA). (gr. 4-7). lib. bdg. 25.70 *(978-1-58415-768-7(2))* Mitchell Lane Pubs., Inc.
—Timbaland. 2008. (Blue Banner Biography Ser.). (Illus.). 32p. (YA). (gr. 4-7). lib. bdg. 25.70 *(978-1-58415-671-0(6))* Mitchell Lane Pubs., Inc.
Torres, John Albert. Jay-Z: Hip-Hop Mogul. 2014. (Hip-Hop Moguls Ser.). (Illus.). 48p. (J). (gr. 4-9). 14.95 *(978-1-62285-191-1(9))* Enslow Pubs., Inc.
—Ludacris: Hip-Hop Mogul. 2014. (Hip-Hop Moguls Ser.). (Illus.). 48p. (J). (gr. 4-9). 14.95 *(978-1-62285-196-6(X))* Enslow Pubs., Inc.
—P. Diddy. 2004. (Blue Banner Biography Ser.). (Illus.). 32p. (J). (gr. 3-8). lib. bdg. 25.70 *(978-1-58415-315-3(6))* Mitchell Lane Pubs., Inc.
Tracy, Kathleen. Chris Brown. 2007. (Blue Banner Biography Ser.). (Illus.). 32p. (YA). (gr. 4-7). lib. bdg. 25.70 *(978-1-58415-617-8(1))* Mitchell Lane Pubs., Inc.
—Queen Latifah. 2004. (Blue Banner Biography Ser.). (Illus.). 32p. (J). (gr. 3-8). lib. bdg. 25.70 *(978-1-58415-313-9(X))* Mitchell Lane Pubs., Inc.
Traugh, Susan. Sean Combs. 2010. (People in the News Ser.). (ENG., Illus.). 104p. 33.95 *(978-1-4205-0237-4(9)*, Lucent Bks.) Cengage Gale.
Uschan, Michael V. Tupac Shakur. 2007. (Illus.). 104p. (J). *(978-7-81590-189-0(1)*, Lucent Bks.) Cengage Gale.
—50 Cent. 2007. (People in the News Ser.). (ENG., Illus.). 104p. (YA). (gr. 7-12). lib. bdg. 33.45 *(978-1-4205-0011-0(2))* Cengage Gale.
Uschan, Michael V. & Juettner, Bonnie. Will Smith. 2009. (People in the News Ser.). (ENG., Illus.). 128p. (gr. 7-12). lib. bdg. 39.40 *(978-1-4205-0130-8(5)*, LML02109-245444) Cengage Gale.
Waters, Rosa. Yung Joc. 2009. (Hip-Hop 2 Ser.). (Illus.). 64p. (YA). (gr. 7-12). lib. bdg. 22.95 *(978-1-4222-0307-1(7))* Mason Crest.
Watson, Stephanie. Cee lo Green: Rapper, Singer, & Record Producer, 1 vol. 2013. (Contemporary Lives Set 2 Ser.). (ENG.). 112p. (J). (gr. 6-12). lib. bdg. 35.64 *(978-1-61783-619-0(2)*, Essential Library) ABDO Publishing Co.
Weicker, Gretchen. Kanye West: Hip-Hop Star. 2009. (Hot Celebrity Biographies Ser.). (Illus.). 48p. (J). (gr. 5-9). pap. 8.95 *(978-0-7660-3629-1(4))*; lib. bdg. 25.27 *(978-0-7660-3214-9(0))* Enslow Pubs., Inc.
Wells, Peggy Sue. Kanye West. 2008. (Blue Banner Biography Ser.). (Illus.). 32p. (YA). (gr. 4-7). lib. bdg. 25.70 *(978-1-58415-677-2(5))* Mitchell Lane Pubs., Inc.
—Soulja Boy Tell 'Em. 2008. (Blue Banner Biography Ser.). (Illus.). 32p. (YA). (gr. 4-7). lib. bdg. 25.70 *(978-1-58415-676-5(7))* Mitchell Lane Pubs., Inc.
Will Smith: Actor. 2nd rev. ed. 2010. (Black Americans of Achievement Legacy Edition Ser.). (Illus.). 104p. (gr. 6-12). 35.00 *(978-1-60413-713-2(4))* Facts On File, Inc.
Wittmann, Kelly. Sean Diddy Combs. 2008. (Hip-Hop Ser.). (ENG., Illus.). 64p. (YA). (gr. 3-7). per. 7.95 *(978-1-4222-0266-1(6))* Mason Crest.
Wolny, Philip. Ludacris. 2009. (Library of Hip-Hop Biographies Ser.). (ENG., Illus.). 48p. (J). (gr. 7-12). pap. 11.75 *(978-1-4358-5440-6(3))*; 48p. (gr. 5-5). 53.00 *(978-1-60853-691-7(2))*; (J). lib. bdg. 29.25 *(978-1-4358-5054-5(8))* Rosen Publishing Group, Inc., The.
—Sean Combs. (Library of Hip-Hop Biographies Ser.). 48p. 2009. (gr. 5-5). 53.00 *(978-1-60853-706-8(4))* 2006. (Illus.). (YA). (gr. 7-12). lib. bdg. 29.25 *(978-1-4042-0516-1(0))* Rosen Publishing Group, Inc., The.

RAPE

Coppin, Cheryl Branch. Everything You Need to Know about Healing from Rape Trauma. 2005. (Need to Know Library). (Illus.). 64p. (YA). (gr. 7-12). 31.95 *(978-0-8239-3122-4(6)*, NTHERT) Rosen Publishing Group, Inc., The.
Gunton, Sharon. Date & Acquaintance Rape. 2008. (Social Issues Firsthand Ser.). (ENG., Illus.). 107p. (YA). (gr. 10-12). lib. bdg. 33.75 *(978-0-7377-4250-3(X)*, LML02109-243162, Greenhaven Pr., Inc.) Cengage Gale.
Henneberg, Susan. I Have Been Raped, Now What? 2015. (Teen Life 411 Ser.). (ENG., Illus.). 112p. (J). (gr. 6-7). 35.60 *(978-1-4994-6142-8(9)*, Rosen Young Adult) Rosen Publishing Group, Inc., The.
Hook, Sue Vander & Kamisar, Yale. Miranda v. Arizona: An Individual's Rights When under Arrest, 1 vol. 2012. (Landmark Supreme Court Cases Ser.). (ENG., Illus.). 160p. (J). (gr. 6-12). 37.07 *(978-1-61783-474-5(2))* ABDO Publishing Co.
Kaminker, Laura. Everything You Need to Know about Dealing with Sexual Assault. rev. ed. 2005. (Need to Know Library). (Illus.). 64p. (YA). (gr. 7-12). lib. bdg. 31.95 *(978-0-8239-3303-7(2))* Rosen Publishing Group, Inc., The.
Kehner, George B. Date Rape Drugs. 2004. (Drugs Ser.). (Illus.). 96p. (YA). (gr. 9-13). 30.00 *(978-0-7910-7634-7(2)*, Chelsea Hse.) Facts On File, Inc.
Landau, Elaine. Date Violence. 2005. (Life Balance Ser.). (ENG., Illus.). 80p. (J). (gr. 5-8). pap. 6.95 *(978-0-531-16613-0(9)*, Watts, Franklin) Scholastic Library Publishing.
Levy, Barrie. In Love & in Danger: A Teen's Guide to Breaking Free of Abusive Relationships. 3rd rev. ed. 2006. (ENG., Illus.). 144p. (Orig.). per. 13.00 *(978-1-58005-187-3(1))* Seal Pr.
Mooney, Carla. Everything You Need to Know about Sexual Consent. 2017. (Need to Know Library). 64p. (J). (gr. 12-11). 34.45 ***(978-1-5081-7412-7(1))***; pap. 12.95 ***(978-1-5081-7410-3(5))*** Rosen Publishing Group, Inc., The. (Rosen Young Adult).
Orr, Tamra. Frequently Asked Questions about Date Rape. (FAQ: Teen Life Ser.). 64p. 2009. (gr. 5-6). 58.50 *(978-1-61512-572-2(8))* 2006. (Illus.). (YA). (gr. 7-12). lib. bdg. 31.95 *(978-1-4042-1972-4(2))* Rosen Publishing Group, Inc., The.
Piehl, Norah, ed. Date Rape. 2012. (Issues That Concern You Ser.). (ENG., Illus.). 144p. (gr. 7-10). lib. bdg. 36.95 *(978-0-7377-6287-7(X))* Cengage Gale.
Schmermund, Elizabeth, ed. Campus Sexual Violence. 2017. (At Issue Ser.). 128p. (YA). (gr. 10-12). pap. 27.80 ***(978-1-5345-0037-2(5))***; lib. bdg. 39.40 ***(978-1-5345-0018-1(9))*** Greenhaven Publishing LLC. (Greenhaven Publishing).
Uschan, Michael V. The Scottsboro Case. 2004. (Landmark Events in American History Ser.). (Illus.). 48p. (gr. 5-12). lib. bdg. 31.00 *(978-0-8368-5388-9(1)*, Gareth Stevens Secondary Library) Stevens, Gareth Publishing LLLP.
Wilkins, Jessica. Date Rape. 2010. (Straight Talk about... Ser.). (ENG.). 48p. (J). (gr. 7-10). pap. *(978-0-7787-2135-2(3))*; lib. bdg. *(978-0-7787-2128-4(0))* Crabtree Publishing Co.

RAPE—FICTION

Almond, David. The Tightrope Walkers. 2016. (ENG.). 336p. (YA). (gr. 9). pap. 9.99 *(978-0-7636-9104-2(6))* Candlewick Pr.
Anderson, Laurie Halse. Speak. 2006. 24.50 *(978-0-8446-7292-2(0))* Smith, Peter Pub., Inc.
—Speak. 2011. (ENG.). 224p. (YA). (gr. 7-12). pap. 10.99 *(978-0-312-67439-7(2)*, 9780312674397) Square Fish.
Blakemore, Megan Frazer. Good & Gone. 2017. 304p. (YA). (gr. 8). 17.99 ***(978-0-06-234842-5(6)***, HarperTeen) HarperCollins Pubs.
Buckley, Kate. Choices: A Novel. 2009. 208p. (J). pap. 14.95 *(978-1-935359-12-8(6))* Book Pubs. Network.
Butcher, Kristin. The Trouble with Liberty, 1 vol. 2003. (Orca Soundings Ser.). (ENG.). 128p. (YA). (gr. 8-12). pap. 9.95 *(978-1-55143-274-8(9))* Orca Bk. Pubs. USA.
Deriso, Christine Hurley. Thirty Sunsets. 2014. (ENG.). 240p. (YA). pap. 9.99 *(978-0-7387-3991-5(X)*, Flux) North Star Editions.
Desir, C. Fault Line. 2013. (ENG.). 240p. (YA). (gr. 10). 16.99 *(978-1-4424-6072-0(5)*, Simon Pulse) Simon Pulse.
Downham, Jenny. You Against Me. 2012. (ENG.). 416p. (YA). (gr. 9). pap. 9.99 *(978-0-385-75266-4(0)*, Ember) Random Hse. Children's Bks.
Draper, Sharon M. Darkness Before Dawn. 2014. (Hazelwood High Trilogy Ser. 3 Ser.). (ENG.). 288p. (YA). (gr. k-k). 11.24 *(978-1-63245-162-0(X))* Lectorum Pubns., Inc.
—Darkness Before Dawn. 2013. (Hazelwood High Trilogy Ser.: 3). (ENG., Illus.). 256p. (YA). (gr. 7). pap. 9.99 *(978-1-4424-8915-8(4)*, Atheneum Bks. for Young Readers) Simon & Schuster Children's Publishing.
—Darkness Before Dawn. 2013. (Hazelwood High Trilogy Ser.: 3). lib. bdg. 20.85 *(978-0-606-32334-5(1)*, Turtleback) Turtleback Bks.
Fault Line. 2014. (ENG., Illus.). 256p. (YA). (gr. 10). pap. 11.99 *(978-1-4424-6073-7(3)*, Simon Pulse) Simon Pulse.
Geras, Adèle. Watching the Roses: The Egerton Hall Novels, Volume Two, Vol. 2. 2005. (ENG.). 192p. (YA). (gr. 7-12). pap. 11.95 *(978-0-15-205531-8(2))* Houghton Mifflin Harcourt Publishing Co.
Halbrook, Kristin. Every Last Promise. 2015. (ENG.). 288p. (YA). (gr. 8). pap. 9.99 *(978-0-06-212128-8(6)*, HarperTeen) HarperCollins Pubs.
Hamilton, Elizabeth L. Date with Responsibility. 2004. (Character-in-Action Ser.: No. 2). (Illus.). 384p. (YA). per. 19.95 *(978-0-9713749-0-4(2)*, Character-in-Action) Quiet Impact, Inc.
Hartzler, Aaron. What We Saw. 2015. 336p. (YA). (ENG.). (gr. 9). 17.99 *(978-0-06-233874-7(9)*, HarperTeen); *(978-0-06-243062-5(9))* HarperCollins Pubs.
Johnston, E. K. Exit, Pursued by a Bear. 2016. (ENG.). 256p. (YA). (gr. 9). 17.99 *(978-1-101-99458-0(4)*, Dutton Books for Young Readers) Penguin Young Readers Group.
Klein, Alina. Rape Girl. 2012. 132p. (YA). 18.95 *(978-1-60898-123-6(1))*; pap. 9.95 *(978-1-60898-124-3(X))* namelos llc.
Krossing, Karen. Punch Like a Girl, 1 vol. 2015. (ENG.). 240p. (YA). (gr. 8-12). pap. 12.95 *(978-1-4598-0828-7(2))* Orca Bk. Pubs. USA.
Levine, Ellen. In Trouble. 2011. (Carolrhoda YA Ser.). (ENG.). 208p. (YA). (gr. 9-12). 17.95 *(978-0-7613-6558-7(3)*, Carolrhoda Lab™) Lerner Publishing Group.
Lipsyte, Robert. Raiders Night. (YA). (gr. 9-12). 2007. (ENG.). 256p. pap. 9.99 *(978-0-06-059948-5(0))* 2006. 232p. 15.99 *(978-0-06-059946-1(4))* 2006. 232p. lib. bdg. 16.89 *(978-0-06-059947-8(2))* HarperCollins Pubs. (HarperTeen).
Lynch, Chris. Inexcusable. 2005. (ENG., Illus.). 176p. (YA). (gr. 7-18). 19.99 *(978-0-689-84789-9(0)*, Atheneum Bks. for Young Readers) Simon & Schuster Children's Publishing.
—Inexcusable: 10th Anniversary Edition. 10th ed. 2015. (ENG., Illus.). 192p. (YA). (gr. 8). pap. 9.99 *(978-1-4814-3202-3(8)*, Simon & Schuster Bks. For Young Readers) Simon & Schuster Bks. For Young Readers.
—Irreversible. 2016. (ENG., Illus.). 352p. (YA). (gr. 7). 17.99 *(978-1-4814-2985-6(X)*, Simon & Schuster Bks. For Young Readers) Simon & Schuster Bks. For Young Readers.
Marcus, Kimberly. Exposed. 2012. (ENG.). 272p. (YA). (gr. 9). pap. 8.99 *(978-0-375-86591-6(8)*, Ember) Random Hse. Children's Bks.
Myers, Jason. Dead End. 2011. (ENG.). 384p. (YA). (gr. 10-18). pap. 9.99 *(978-1-4424-1430-3(8)*, Simon Pulse) Simon Pulse.
Padian, Maria. Wrecked. 2016. (ENG.). 368p. (YA). (gr. 9-12). 17.95 *(978-1-61620-624-6(1))* Algonquin Bks. of Chapel Hill.
Reed, Amy Lynn. The Nowhere Girls. 2017. (YA). pap. ***(978-1-4814-8174-8(6)***, Simon Pulse) Simon Pulse.
Scoppettone, Sandra. Happy Endings Are All Alike. 2014. (ENG., Illus.). 200p. (gr. 6). pap. 12.95 *(978-1-939601-04-9(5))* Ig Publishing, Inc.
Shaw, Susan. Safe. 2007. (ENG.). 176p. (YA). (gr. 9-18). pap. 14.00 *(978-0-525-47829-4(9)*, Dutton Books for Young Readers) Penguin Young Readers Group.
Smith, Amber. The Way I Used to Be. 2017. (ENG.). 384p. (YA). (gr. 9). pap. 10.99 *(978-1-4814-4936-6(2)*, McElderry, Margaret K. Bks.) McElderry, Margaret K. Bks.
—The Way I Used to Be. Twomey, Kevin, photos by. 2016. (ENG., Illus.). 384p. (YA). (gr. 9). 17.99 *(978-1-4814-4935-9(4)*, McElderry, Margaret K. Bks.) McElderry, Margaret K. Bks.
Stratton, Allan. Leslie's Journal. rev. ed. 2008. (ENG.). 200p. (YA). (gr. 8-12). 21.95 *(978-1-55451-149-5(6)*, 9781554511495) Annick Pr., Ltd. CAN. Dist: Publishers Group West (PGW).
Summers, Courtney. All the Rage. (ENG.). 336p. (YA). 2016. pap. 10.99 *(978-1-250-06915-3(7)*, 9781250069153) 2015. (gr. 9-13). 18.99 *(978-1-250-02191-5(X)*, 9781250021915) St. Martin's Pr. (St. Martin's Griffin).
Sutton, Michelle. It's Not about Me. 2012. (Second Glances Ser.). (ENG.). 252p. pap. 12.99 *(978-0-9838836-9-2(6))* Sword of the Spirit Publishing.
Walton, K. M. Empty. 2013. (ENG., (YA). (gr. 9). Illus.). 272p. pap. 10.99 *(978-1-4424-5358-6(3))*; 256p. 16.99 *(978-1-4424-5359-3(1))* Simon Pulse. (Simon Pulse).
Yates, Marie. Reggie & Me: The First Book in the Dani Moore Trilogy. 2014. (ENG.). 183p. pap. 11.95 *(978-1-78279-723-4(8)*, Lodestone Bks.) Hunt, John Publishing Ltd. GBR. Dist: National Bk. Network.
Yates, Marie. Sammy & Me: The Second Book in the Dani Moore Trilogy. 2017. (ENG.). 184p. (YA). (gr. 8-17). pap. 11.95 ***(978-1-78535-502-8(3)***, O Bks.) Hunt, John Publishing Ltd. GBR. Dist: National Bk. Network.
York, Kelley. Modern Monsters. 2015. (Entangled Teen Ser.). (ENG.). 352p. (YA). pap. 9.99 *(978-1-63375-002-9(7)*, 9781633750029) Entangled Publishing, LLC.

RAPHAEL, 1483-1520

Klein, Adam G. Raphael, 1 vol. 2007. (Great Artists Set 2 Ser.). (ENG., Illus.). 32p. (gr. -1-3). 27.07 *(978-1-59679-734-5(7)*, Checkerboard Library) ABDO Publishing Co.
Mofford, Juliet. Raphael. 2009. (Art Profiles for Kids Ser.). (Illus.). 48p. (YA). (gr. 4-7). lib. bdg. 29.95 *(978-1-58415-745-8(3))* Mitchell Lane Pubs., Inc.

RATS

Albright, Rosie. Detection Rats. 2012. (Animal Detectives Ser.). (ENG., Illus.). 24p. (J). (gr. k-3). pap. 8.25 *(978-1-4488-6256-6(6))*; lib. bdg. 22.60 *(978-1-4488-6149-1(7))* Rosen Publishing Group, Inc., The. (PowerKids Pr.).
—Detection Rats: Ratas Detectoras. Alamán, Eduardo, tr. from ENG. 2012. (Animal Detectives / Detectives Del Reino Animal Ser.). (SPA & ENG.). 24p. (J). (gr. k-3). lib. bdg. 22.60 *(978-1-4488-6715-8(0)*, PowerKids Pr.) Rosen Publishing Group, Inc., The.
Armentrout, David & Armentrout, Patricia. The Facts on Rats. 2010. (Let's Talk about Pets Ser.). (Illus.). 24p. (J). (gr. k-4). 28.50 *(978-1-61590-247-7(3))* Rourke Educational Media.
Berne, Emma Carlson. Rats: Biting Through Concrete! 2013. (Animal Superpowers Ser.). 24p. (J). (gr. k-5). pap. 49.50 *(978-1-4777-0846-0(4))*; lib. bdg. 22.60 *(978-1-4777-0752-4(2))* Rosen Publishing Group, Inc., The. (PowerKids Pr.).
Burt, Jonathan. Rat. 2nd ed. 2006. (Animal Ser.). (ENG., Illus.). 192p. per. 19.95 *(978-1-86189-224-9(1))* Reaktion Bks., Ltd. GBR. Dist: Chicago Distribution Ctr.
Carr, Aaron. Rat. 2014. (J). *(978-1-4896-3102-2(X))* Weigl Pubs., Inc.
Chancellor, Deborah. Rats. 2009. (Extreme Pets Ser.). (YA). (gr. 4-7). 28.50 *(978-1-59920-236-5(0))* Black Rabbit Bks.
Claybourne, Anna. Rats, 1 vol. 2013. (Animal Abilities Ser.). (ENG.). 32p. (gr. 2-4). 29.99 *(978-1-4109-5241-7(X))*; pap. 8.95 *(978-1-4109-5248-6(7))* Heinemann-Raintree. (Raintree Perspectives).
Colson, Rob. Rat. 2017. (Pet to Get Ser.). (ENG., Illus.). 32p. (J). (gr. 4-6). pap. 12.99 ***(978-0-7502-8929-0(5)***, Wayland) Hachette Children's Group GBR. Dist: Hachette Bk. Group.
Coppendale, Jean. Rats. 2004. (QEB You & Your Pet Ser.). (Illus.). 32p. (J). lib. bdg. 18.95 *(978-1-59566-054-1(2))* QEB Publishing Inc.
Doudna, Kelly. Running Rats, 1 vol. 2007. (Perfect Pets Ser.). (ENG., Illus.). 24p. (J). (gr. k-3). lib. bdg. 24.21 *(978-1-59928-754-6(4)*, SandCastle) ABDO Publishing Co.
Eagen, Rachel. Rats Around Us. 2010. (Creepy Crawlies Ser.). (ENG.). 32p. (J). (gr. 3-6). *(978-0-7787-2501-5(4))*; pap. *(978-0-7787-2508-4(1))* Crabtree Publishing Co.
Fee, Deb. The Life & Times of Sir Ear Alot. 2012. 32p. pap. 19.99 *(978-1-4685-7983-3(5))* AuthorHouse.
Gravel, Elise. The Rat. (Disgusting Critters Ser.). (ENG., Illus.). 32p. (J). (gr. 1-4). 2016. pap. 5.99 *(978-1-77049-659-0(9))* 2014. 10.99 *(978-1-77049-658-3(0))* Tundra Bks. CAN. (Tundra Bks.). Dist: Penguin Random Hse. LLC.
Gregory, Josh. Rats. 2016. (Nature's Children Ser.). (ENG., Illus.). 48p. (J). pap. 6.95 *(978-0-531-22521-9(6)*, Children's Pr.) Scholastic Library Publishing.
Hansen, Grace. Rats, 1 vol. 2015. (ENG., Illus.). 24p. (J). 28.50 *(978-1-62970-896-6(8))* ABDO Publishing Co.
Herriott, Charlotte. Rat vs. Cockroach. 2015. (Bizarre Beast Battles Ser.). (ENG.). 24p. (J). (gr. 2-3). pap. 8.15 *(978-1-4824-2788-2(5))* Stevens, Gareth Publishing LLLP.
Johnson, Jinny. Rats & Mice. 2009. (Get to Know Your Pet Ser.). (J). 28.50 *(978-1-59920-091-0(0))* Black Rabbit Bks.
—Rats & Mice. 2009. (Get to Know Your Pet Ser.). (Illus.). 32p. (J). (gr. 4-7). pap. *(978-1-897563-33-5(7))* Saunders Bk. Co.
Kenney, Karen. Rat. 2015. (ENG.). 32p. (gr. 3-6). 32.79 *(978-1-63430-435-1(7))* Rourke Educational Media.
Lunde, Darrin. Dirty Rats? Gustavson, Adam, illus. 2015. (ENG.). 32p. (J). (gr. -1-2). 16.95 *(978-1-58089-566-8(2))* Charlesbridge Publishing, Inc.
Lynette, Rachel. Rats. 2013. (Monsters of the Animal Kingdom Ser.). (ENG., Illus.). 24p. (J). (gr. k-5). pap. 8.25 *(978-1-4488-9717-9(3))*; lib. bdg. 22.60 *(978-1-4488-9630-1(4))* Rosen Publishing Group, Inc., The. (PowerKids Pr.).
Markle, Sandra. Outside & Inside Rats & Mice. 2008. (ENG.). 44p. (J). (gr. k-4). 10.99 *(978-1-4169-7571-7(3)*, Simon & Schuster/Paula Wiseman Bks.) Simon & Schuster/Paula Wiseman Bks.
Marrin, Albert. Oh Rats! Mordan, C. B., illus. 2014. (ENG.). 112p. (J). (gr. 5). pap. 8.99 *(978-0-14-751281-9(6)*, Puffin Books) Penguin Young Readers Group.
—Oh, Rats! The Story of Rats & People. 2006. (ENG., Illus.). 48p. (J). (gr. 5-18). 16.99 *(978-0-525-47762-4(4)*, Dutton Books for Young Readers) Penguin Young Readers Group.
Morgan, Sally. Rats & Mice. 2012. (Pets Plus Ser.). (Illus.). 32p. (gr. 3-6). lib. bdg. 31.35 *(978-1-59920-703-2(6))* Black Rabbit Bks.
Owings, Lisa. Rat Attack. 2012. (Animal Attacks Ser.). (ENG., Illus.). 24p. (J). (gr. 3-7). lib. bdg. 25.95 *(978-1-60014-790-6(9)*, Torque Bks.) Bellwether Media.
Petrie, Kristin. Naked Mole Rats, 1 vol. 2010. (Nocturnal Animals Ser.). (ENG.). 24p. (YA). (gr. 3-6). 25.65 *(978-1-60453-738-3(8))* ABDO Publishing Co.
Quinton, Sasha. Rat-A-Tat: A Phonics Reader. 2009. (Illus.). pap. *(978-1-936199-04-4(1))* Book Shop, Ltd., The.
Rafferty, John P. Rats, Bats, & Xenarthrans. 2011. (Britannica Guide to Predators & Prey Ser.). (Illus.). 256p. (YA). (gr. 9-12). lib. bdg. 51.70 *(978-1-61530-332-8(4))* Rosen Publishing Group, Inc., The.
Rafferty, John P., ed. Rats, Bats, & Xenarthrans. 2011. (Britannica Guide to Predators & Prey Ser.). (Illus.). 256p. (YA). 103.40 *(978-1-61530-456-1(8))* Rosen Publishing Group, Inc., The.
Rayner, Matthew. Rat. Sawyer, Darren, photos by. 2007. (I Am Your Pet Ser.). (Illus.). 32p. (gr. k-4). lib. bdg. 26.00 *(978-0-8368-8386-2(1)*, Gareth Stevens Learning Library) Stevens, Gareth Publishing LLLP.
Rebman, Renee C. Rats. 2011. (Animals Animals 12 Ser.). (Illus.). 48p. (J). (gr. 3). 23.95 *(978-0-7614-4877-8(2))* Marshall Cavendish GBR. Dist: Marshall Cavendish Corp.
Savage, Stephen. Rat. 2009. (Animal Neighbors Ser.). 32p. (gr. k-5). pap. 10.60 *(978-1-4042-4568-6(5)*, Rosen Classroom); (Illus.). (J). (gr. 3-6). lib. bdg. 25.25 *(978-1-4358-4991-4(4)*, PowerKids Pr.) Rosen Publishing Group, Inc., The.
Silverstein, Alvin, et al. Rats: Cool Pets! Kelley, Gerald, illus. 2012. (Far-Out & Unusual Pets Ser.). 48p. (J). (gr. 3-4). pap. 8.95 *(978-1-4644-0127-5(6))*; 25.27 *(978-0-7660-3882-0(3))* Enslow Pubs., Inc. (Enslow Elementary).
Simon, Elizabeth. Caring for Your Rat. (Caring for Your Pet Ser.). (Illus.). 32p. (J). 2005. (gr. 4-7). per. 9.95 *(978-1-59036-217-4(9))* 2004. lib. bdg. 26.00 *(978-1-59036-197-9(0))* Weigl Pubs., Inc.
—Rat. 2010. pap. 9.95 *(978-1-61690-080-9(6))*; 32p. (J). (gr. 3-5). lib. bdg. 27.13 *(978-1-61690-079-3(2))* Weigl Pubs., Inc.
Thomas, Isabel. Rat: City Safari, 1 vol. 2014. (City Safari Ser.). (ENG., Illus.). 24p. (gr. 1-1). lib. bdg. 23.32 *(978-1-4329-8807-4(7)*, Heinemann Read & Learn) Heinemann-Raintree.
—Squeak's Guide to Caring for Your Pet Rats or Mice, 1 vol. Peterson, Rick, illus. 2014. (Pets' Guides). (ENG.). 32p. (gr. 1-3). pap. 8.29 *(978-1-4846-0271-3(4))*; 27.32 *(978-1-4846-0264-5(1))* Heinemann-Raintree. (Heinemann First Library).
Toor, Rachel. Misunderstood: A Book about Rats. 2016. (ENG., Illus.). 256p. (J). 17.99 *(978-0-374-30308-2(8)*, 9780374303082, Farrar, Straus & Giroux (BYR)) Farrar, Straus & Giroux.

RATS—FICTION

AaronG, Driftin'. Claude Henry, the Iditarod Mouse: The Adventures Begin. 2007. 108p. (J). per. 9.95 *(978-0-595-44990-3(5))* iUniverse, Inc.
Adeola, Ogechi. Jo & Skippa: I want to be You! 2011. (Illus.). 28p. 12.52 *(978-1-4567-7340-3(2))* AuthorHouse.
Angleberger, Tom. The Rat with the Human Face. 2015. (Qwikpick Papers). (ENG., Illus.). 160p. (J). (gr. 3-7). 12.95 *(978-1-4197-1489-4(9)*, Amulet Bks.) Abrams, Inc.
—The Rat with the Human Face: The Qwikpick Papers. 2016. (Qwikpick Papers). (ENG., Illus.). 176p. (J). (gr. 3-7). pap. 6.95 *(978-1-4197-1940-0(8)*, Amulet Bks.) Abrams, Inc.
Armstrong, Alan W. Whittington. Schindler, S. D., illus. 2007. 191p. (gr. 3-7). 17.00 *(978-0-7569-7768-9(1))* Perfection Learning Corp.
Avi. The Mayor of Central Park. Floca, Brian, illus. 2003. (ENG.). 208p. (J). (gr. 3-6). 15.99 *(978-0-06-000682-2(X))* HarperCollins Pubs.
—The Mayor of Central Park. Floca, Brian, illus. 2005. 193p. (J). (gr. 3-7). 13.65 *(978-0-7569-5125-2(9))* Perfection Learning Corp.
Bailer, Darice & Dominguez, Madelca. La Ratita Presumida. Curto, Rosa Maria, illus. 2007. (SPA & ENG.). 28p. (J). *(978-0-545-03031-1(5))* Scholastic, Inc.
Barkow, Henriette. The Pied Piper. Dry, Roland, illus. 2004. 32p. (J). *(978-1-85269-990-1(6))*; (PAN & ENG.). pap. *(978-1-85269-970-3(1))*; (ENG & ITA.). pap. *(978-1-85269-965-9(5))*; (ENG & GUJ.). pap. *(978-1-85269-955-0(8))*; (ENG & GER.). pap. *(978-1-85269-950-5(7))*; (FRE & ENG.). pap. *(978-1-85269-945-1(0))*; (ENG & PER.). pap. *(978-1-85269-940-6(X))*; (ENG & CZE.). pap. *(978-1-85269-935-2(3))*; (ENG & POL.). pap. *(978-1-85269-975-8(2))*; (URD & ENG.). pap. *(978-1-85269-916-1(7))*; (ENG & ALB.). pap. *(978-1-85269-915-4(9))*; (TUR & ENG.). pap. *(978-1-85269-911-6(6))*; (ENG & TAM.). pap. *(978-1-85269-906-2(X))*; (ENG & SPA.). pap. *(978-1-85269-901-7(9))*; (SOM & ENG.). pap. *(978-1-85269-995-6(7))*; (ENG & ARA.). pap. *(978-1-85269-920-8(5))*; (ENG & POR.). pap. *(978-1-85269-980-2(9))* Mantra Lingua.
Bartell, Maggie. Ratsquirrel. 2009. 41p. pap. 14.64 *(978-0-557-11816-8(6))* Lulu Pr., Inc.
Beck, W. H. Malcolm at Midnight. Lies, Brian, illus. (ENG.). 272p. (J). (gr. 2-5). 2015. pap. 7.99 *(978-0-544-33666-7(6)*, HMH Books For Young Readers) 2012. 16.99 *(978-0-547-68100-9(3))* Houghton Mifflin Harcourt Publishing Co.
Bessesen, Brooke. Zachary Z. Packrat & His Amazing Collections. Campbell, Jenney, illus. 2008. 40p. pap. 19.95 *(978-1-932082-83-8(2))* Arizona Highways.
Bethel, Ellie. Michael Recycle Meets Litterbug Doug. Colombo, Alexandra, illus. 2009. (Michael Recycle Ser.). (ENG.). 24p. (J). (gr. 2-5). 15.99 *(978-1-60010-392-6(8)*, 9781600103926) Idea & Design Works, LLC.
Blackburn, Sheila M. Stewie Scraps & the Space Racer. 2008. 68p. pap. *(978-1-903853-84-9(2))* Brilliant Pubns.
—Stewie Scraps & the Super Sleigh. 2008. 72p. pap. *(978-1-903853-89-4(3))* Brilliant Pubns.
Blacker, Terence. Ms. Wiz Smells a Rat. 2003. (ENG., Illus.). 64p. (J). pap. *(978-0-330-37466-8(4)*, Pan) Pan Macmillan.
Bootman, Colin, illus. The Steel Pan Man of Harlem. 2009. (Carolrhoda Picture Bks.). 32p. (J). (gr. 1-3). 16.95 *(978-0-8225-9026-2(3))* Lerner Publishing Group.
Brennan, Sarah. The Tale of Run Run Rat. Harrison, Harry, illus. 2012. (ENG.). 32p. (J). 24.95 *(978-1-937160-25-8(4))* Eliassen Creative.
Brown, Alan James. Incredible Journey of Walter Rat. (Illus.). 63p. (J). pap. *(978-0-340-72750-8(0))* Hodder & Stoughton.
Brown, Rosie L. Zach & Rob's Journey: The Lost Eggs. 2007. 24p. per. 24.95 *(978-1-4241-8401-9(0))* America Star Bks.
Bryant, Phoebe. What Is That in the Air? A play date with Sayde. 2009. (Illus.). 28p. pap. 12.99 *(978-1-4490-2209-9(X))* AuthorHouse.
Butterworth, Nick. The Whisperer. Butterworth, Nick, illus. 2005. (ENG., Illus.). 32p. (J). (gr. k-3). pap. 15.95

(978-0-00-712018-5(4), HarperCollins Children's Bks.) HarperCollins Pubs. Ltd. GBR. Dist: HarperCollins Pubs.

Carballeira, Paula. Paco. Barrio, Blanca, illus. 2003. 32p. (J). 14.95 (978-84-95730-38-1(3)) Kalandraka Catalunya, Edicions, S.L. ESP. Dist: Independent Pubs. Group.

Casey, Dawn. The Great Race: The Story of the Chinese Zodiac. Wilson, Anne, illus. 2008. (ENG.). 32p. (J). (gr. -1-2). 8.99 (978-1-84686-202-1(7)) Barefoot Bks., Inc.

Chichester Clark, Emma. We Are Not Fond of Rat! Chichester Clark, Emma, illus. 2006. (Collins Big Cat Phonics Ser.). (ENG., Illus.). 16p. (J). (gr. -1-1). pap. 5.99 (978-0-00-723590-2(9)) HarperCollins Pubs. Ltd. GBR. Dist: Independent Pubs. Group.

Chin, Oliver Clyde. The Year of the Rat: Tales from the Chinese Zodiac. Alcorn, Miah, illus. 2008. (Tales from the Chinese Zodiac Ser.). (ENG.). 36p. (J). (gr. -1-k). 15.95 (978-1-59702-011-4(7)) Immedium.

Coomber, Suzanne. Salt & Pepper. 2010. 24p. pap. 12.99 (978-1-4490-6311-5(X)) AuthorHouse.

Cooper, Jay. Mutant Rat Attack! 2017. (Spy Next Door Ser.: 1). (ENG.). 144p. (J). (gr. 2-5). 9.99 (978-0-545-93297-4(1), Scholastic Pr.) Scholastic, Inc.

Cooper, Velyn. Rusty the Rat. 2012. 48p. pap. 9.89 (978-1-4669-1133-8(6)) Trafford Publishing.

Cope, Clifford D. Caleb: The mouse Engineer. 2009. 24p. pap. 12.99 (978-1-4389-9877-0(5)) AuthorHouse.

Cousineau, Craig S. Skippy & Oaf: The Battle Against Oxygen Radicals. 2007. (ENG., Illus.). 48p. (J). (gr. 2-4). per. (978-1-933255-27-9(7)) DNA Pr.

Cousins, Lucy. Pina Piace Giocare. pap. 18.95 (978-88-04-48797-5(6)) Mondadori ITA. Dist: Distribooks, Inc.

Cox, Judy. The Case of the Purloined Professor, 0 vols. Rayyan, Omar, illus. 2009. (Tails of Frederick & Ishbu Ser.: 0). (ENG.). 256p. (J). (gr. 5-7). 16.99 (978-0-7614-5544-8(2), 9780761455448, Amazon Children's Publishing) Amazon Publishing.

—The Mystery of the Burmese Bandicoot, 1 vol. Rayyan, Omar, illus. 2007. (Tails of frederick & Ishbu Ser.). (ENG.). 224p. (J). (gr. 5-9). lib. bdg. 16.99 (978-0-7614-5376-5(8)) Marshall Cavendish Corp.

—The Mystery of the Burmese Bandicoot. 2012. 254p. (gr. 4-6). pap. 15.95 (978-1-4759-3838-8(1)) iUniverse, Inc.

Crangle, Claudine, illus. Priscilla the Pack Rat: Making Room for Friendship. 2017. 32p. (J). 15.95 (978-1-4338-2335-0(7), Magination Pr.) American Psychological Assn.

Crocker, Carter & Snyder, Carrie A. The Tale of the Swamp Rat. 2005. (ENG.). 240p. (J). (gr. 3-7). reprint ed. 6.99 (978-0-14-240314-3(8), Puffin Books) Penguin Young Readers Group.

Crompton, Paul. Remarkable for Short. 2005. 113p. pap. 19.95 (978-1-4241-0287-7(1)) PublishAmerica, Inc.

Dahl, Michael. Rats on the Page, 1 vol. Kendall, Bradford, illus. 2010. (Return to the Library of Doom Ser.). (ENG.). 72p. (gr. 1-3). lib. bdg. 23.99 (978-1-4342-2147-6(4), Zone Bks.) Stone Arch Bks.

Daley, Michael J. Rat Trap. 2008. (ENG.). 272p. (J). (gr. 3-7). 16.95 (978-0-8234-2093-3(0)) Holiday Hse., Inc.

—Space Station Rat. 2008. (ENG., Illus.). 181p. (J). (gr. 4-7). 6.95 (978-0-8234-2151-0(1)) Holiday Hse., Inc.

Deacon, Alexis. Cheese Belongs to You! Schwarz, Viviane, illus. 2013. (ENG.). 32p. (J). (gr. -1-1). 15.99 (978-0-7636-6608-8(4)) Candlewick Pr.

Dean, Barbara. Rattalia's Birthday Stories. 2nd ed. 2013. 132p. (978-0-9572470-4-8(4)); pap. (978-0-9572470-5-5(2)) Newpole Bks.

DeKeyser, Stacy. The Brixen Witch. Nickle, John, illus. (ENG.). 208p. (J). (gr. 3-7). 2013. pap. 6.99 (978-1-4424-3329-8(9)) 2012. 15.99 (978-1-4424-3328-1(0)) McElderry, Margaret K. Bks. (McElderry, Margaret K. Bks.).

DeMaio, Alison. Tyler, the tiniest Tiger. 2010. 21p. 12.21 (978-0-557-19780-4(5)) Lulu Pr., Inc.

Derrick, Patricia & O'Neil, Shirley. Rathbone the Rat. Martinez, J-P Loppo, illus. 2007. 32p. (J). (gr. -1-3). 18.95 incl. audio compact disk (978-1-933818-17-7(4)) Animalations.

Dessers, Rik. Rosie & Roger. Schuurmans, Hilde, illus. 2015. (ENG.). 100p. (J). pap. 16.95 (978-1-931290-09-8(1)) Tallfellow Pr.

Dodson, Emma. The Very Important Idea. Dodson, Emma, illus. 2006. (ENG., Illus.). 32p. (J). (gr. -1-k). 19.99 (978-0-340-87808-8(8)) Hachette Children's Group GBR. Dist: Hachette Bk. Group.

Donaldson, Julia. The Highway Rat. Scheffler, Axel, illus. 2013. (ENG.). 32p. (J). (gr. -1-3). 16.99 (978-0-545-47758-1(1), Levine, Arthur A. Bks.) Scholastic, Inc.

Doudna, Kelly. Pack Rat, 1 vol. Chawla, Neena, illus. 2006. (Animal Tales Ser.). 24p. (J). (gr. k-3). (ENG.). lib. bdg. 24.21 (978-1-59679-955-4(2), SandCastle); pap. 48.42 (978-1-59679-956-1(0)) ABDO Publishing Co.

—La Rata Coleccionista, 1 vol. Chawla, Neena, illus. 2007. (Cuentos de Animales Ser.).Tr. of Pack Rat. (SPA & ENG.). 24p. (J). (gr. k-3). lib. bdg. 24.21 (978-1-59928-671-6(8), SandCastle) ABDO Publishing Co.

Drachman, Eric. Bad Rats. Muscarello, James, illus. 2008. (ENG.). 32p. (J). (gr. -1-3). 18.95 incl. lp (978-0-9703809-4-4(1)) Kidwick Bks.

Egielski, Richard. Slim & Jim. Egielski, Richard, illus. 2005. (Illus.). 37p. (J). (gr. k-4). reprint ed. 16.00 (978-0-7567-8936-7(2)) DIANE Publishing Co.

Eleanor Russell Brown. Mary Warin's Rats: A Time Warp Adventure. 2009. 24p. pap. 12.99 (978-1-4389-6456-0(0)) AuthorHouse.

Eriksen, Valanee. Christmas Bells & Hero's Tails. 2015. (Illus.). vi, 90p. (J). pap. 7.99 (978-1-4621-1737-6(6)) Cedar Fort, Inc./CFI Distribution.

Escott, Jamison. The Clockmaker of Mullen. Escott, Esther, illus. 2004. 24p. (J). pap. 8.95 (978-1-57733-127-8(3), Papillon Publishing) Blue Dolphin Publishing, Inc.

Esopo. EL LEÓN Y EL RATÓN. 2004. (Caballo Alado Clásicos-Al Galope Ser.). (SPA & ENG., Illus.). 24p. (J). (gr. k-2). 7.95 (978-84-7864-784-2(8)) Combel Editorial, S.A. ESP. Dist: Independent Pubs. Group.

Ewers, Joe, illus. The Pied Piper: A Tale about Promises. 2006. (J). 6.99 (978-1-59939-004-8(3)) Cornerstone Pr.

Fairfield, J. S. Cunning Foe: Faulkil. 2009. 88p. pap. 19.95 (978-1-61546-603-0(7)) America Star Bks.

Fiedler, Lisa. Hopper's Destiny. To, Vivienne, illus. 2016. (Mouseheart Ser.: 2). (ENG.). 368p. (J). (gr. 3-7). pap. 7.99 (978-1-4814-2090-7(9), McElderry, Margaret K. Bks.) McElderry, Margaret K. Bks.

—Mouseheart. To, Vivienne, illus. (Mouseheart Ser.: 1). (ENG.). (J). (gr. 3-7). 2015. 336p. pap. 7.99 (978-1-4424-8783-3(6)) 2014. 320p. 16.99 (978-1-4424-8781-9(X)) McElderry, Margaret K. Bks. (McElderry, Margaret K. Bks.).

—Return of the Forgotten. To, Vivienne, illus. 2015. (Mouseheart Ser.: 3). (ENG.). 320p. (J). (gr. 3-7). 16.99 (978-1-4814-2092-1(5), McElderry, Margaret K. Bks.) McElderry, Margaret K. Bks.

Flor Ada, Alma & Campoy, F. Isabel. Ratoncito Prez, Cartero. Escriva, Sandra Lopez, illus. 2015. (Santillana USA Ser.).Tr. of New Job for Pérez, the Mouse. (SPA.). 32p. (J). (gr. 6-6). pap. 15.95 (978-1-63113-547-7(3), Santillana) Santillana USA Publishing Co., Inc.

Fraser, P. J. The Mouse with the Torch, 1 vol. 2009. 48p. pap. 16.95 (978-1-4489-2080-8(9)) America Star Bks.

Frederick, Heather Vogel. For Your Paws Only. 2013. (Spy Mice Ser.: 2). (ENG., Illus.). 240p. (J). (gr. 3-6). pap. 6.99 (978-1-4424-6703-3(7), Simon & Schuster Bks. For Young Readers) Simon & Schuster Bks. For Young Readers.

—For Your Paws Only. Comport, Sally Wern, illus. 2006. (Spy Mice Ser.: 2). (ENG.). 272p. (J). (gr. 3-6). pap. 5.99 (978-1-4169-4025-8(1), Simon & Schuster Bks. For Young Readers) Simon & Schuster Bks. For Young Readers.

—Goldwhiskers. 2013. (Spy Mice Ser.: 3). (ENG., Illus.). 272p. (J). (gr. -1-6). pap. 6.99 (978-1-4424-6705-7(3), Simon & Schuster Bks. For Young Readers) Simon & Schuster Bks. For Young Readers.

Furie, Matt, illus. The Night Riders. 2013. (ENG.). 48p. (J). (gr. -1-3). 8.95 (978-1-938073-72-4(X)) McSweeney's Publishing.

Geshell, Carmen. The Surf Rats of Waikiki Beach. Pagay, Jeff, illus. 2004. 24p. 10.95 (978-1-57306-226-8(X)) Bess Pr., Inc.

Grahame, Kenneth. The Wind in the Willows. Roberts, David, illus. 2013. (ENG.). 256p. (J). (gr. 5). 24.99 (978-0-7636-6526-5(6)) Candlewick Pr.

—The Wind in the Willows. Ingpen, Robert R., illus. 2012. (Sterling Illustrated Classics Ser.). (ENG.). 224p. (J). (gr. 2-8). 19.95 (978-1-4027-8283-1(7)) Sterling Publishing Co., Inc.

Green, Teri & Taylor, Sue. The Littlest Soldier, 1 vol. 2009. 94p. pap. 19.95 (978-1-4489-2714-2(5)) America Star Bks.

Griffiths, Andy. The Cat, the Rat, & the Baseball Bat. Denton, Terry, illus. 2013. (My Readers Ser.). (ENG.). 32p. (J). (gr. -1-1). pap. 3.99 (978-1-250-02774-0(8), 9781250027740) Square Fish.

Guillain, Charlotte. Ratpunzel, 1 vol. Beacon, Dawn, illus. 2014. (Animal Fairy Tales Ser.). (ENG.). 24p. (gr. 1-2). lib. bdg. 23.99 (978-1-4109-6112-9(5), NA-r) Heinemann-Raintree.

Haller, Reese. Giving & Receiving. Haller, Reese, illus. 2007. (Fred the Mouse Ser.). (Illus.). 104p. (J). (gr. 4-7). per. 4.97 (978-0-9772321-5-4(8)) Personal Power Pr.

Hanson, Mary. How to Save Your Tail: If You Are a Rat Nabbed by Cats Who Really Like Stories about Magic Spoons, Wolves with Snout-Warts, Big, Hairy Chimney Trolls ... & Cookies, Too. 2008. (ENG., Illus.). 112p. (J). (gr. 1-4). 5.99 (978-0-440-42228-0(0), Yearling) Random Hse. Children's Bks.

Harries, Tony. Zeegpaw & the Cat Cult. 2008. 304p. pap. 18.95 (978-1-4357-0754-2(0)) Lulu Pr., Inc.

Heinz, Brian J. The Barnyard Cat. l.t. ed. 2003. (Illus.). 32p. (J). pap. 6.96 (978-0-936335-07-0(6)) Ballyhoo BookWorks, Inc.

Henry, Kristina. The Rat Tank, 1 vol. Ambler, Laura & Brown, Amanda, illus. 2011. (ENG.). 40p. (J). 16.99 (978-0-7643-3842-7(0), 9780764338427, Schiffer Publishing Ltd) Schiffer Publishing, Ltd.

Herbert, James. The Rats. 2003. (Rats Ser.: Bk. 1). (ENG.). 208p. (J). 32.50 (978-0-333-76118-2(9)) Macmillan Pubs., Ltd. GBR. Dist: Trafalgar Square Publishing.

Hodder, Bridget. The Rat Prince. 2016. (ENG.). 272p. (J). 16.99 (978-0-374-30213-9(8), 9780374302139, Farrar, Straus & Giroux (BYR)) Farrar, Straus & Giroux.

Hofmeister, Alan, et al. The Bat Rat. (Reading for All Learners Ser.). (Illus.). (J). pap. (978-1-56861-119-8(6)) Swift Learning Resources.

—Mat. (Reading for All Learners Ser.). (Illus.). (J). pap. (978-1-56861-077-1(7)) Swift Learning Resources.

—Mat & the Nut. (Reading for All Learners Ser.). (Illus.). (J). pap. (978-1-56861-109-9(9)) Swift Learning Resources.

—Mat at Bat. (Reading for All Learners Ser.). (Illus.). (J). pap. (978-1-56861-118-1(8)) Swift Learning Resources.

—Mat Did It. (Reading for All Learners Ser.). (Illus.). (J). pap. (978-1-56861-102-0(1)) Swift Learning Resources.

—Mat Is Wet. (Reading for All Learners Ser.). (Illus.). (J). pap. (978-1-56861-120-4(X)) Swift Learning Resources.

—Mat the Rat. (Reading for All Learners Ser.). (Illus.). (J). pap. (978-1-56861-111-2(0)) Swift Learning Resources.

—Nat. (Reading for All Learners Ser.). (Illus.). (J). pap. (978-1-56861-093-1(9)) Swift Learning Resources.

Inkpen, Mick. Rollo & Ruff & the Little Fluffy Bird. Inkpen, Mick, illus. 2011. (ENG., Illus.). 32p. (J). (gr. k-2). pap. 9.99 (978-0-340-98959-3(9)) Hodder & Stoughton GBR. Dist: Hachette Bk. Group.

Jackson, Aaron. Milton Da Rat: A Family Barbeque. 2009. 24p. pap. 12.49 (978-1-4389-4387-9(3)) AuthorHouse.

Jennings, Patrick. Bat & Rat. Cordell, Matthew, illus. 2012. (ENG.). 40p. (J). (gr. k-2). 16.95 (978-1-4197-0160-3(6), Abrams Bks. for Young Readers) Abrams, Inc.

Jones, Rena. A Dinner Date for Dilly. Nielson, Ginger, illus. 2012. 28p. pap. 14.99 (978-0-9852661-2-7(0)) 4RV Publishing, LLC.

Jones, Rene'. A New Friend for Dilly. Nielson, Ginger, illus. 2011. 32p. pap. 14.99 (978-0-9826423-0-6(X)) 4RV Publishing, LLC.

Jukes, Carlisle E. The Rhino & the Rat: The Delightful Story of Coco & Max. 2009. 28p. pap. 13.25 (978-1-4389-6751-6(9)) AuthorHouse.

Kasza, Keiko. The Rat & the Tiger. 2007. (ENG., Illus.). 32p. (J). (gr. -1-2). pap. 6.99 (978-0-14-240900-8(6), Puffin Books) Penguin Young Readers Group.

Kellogg, Steven. The Pied Piper's Magic. Kellogg, Steven, illus. 2009. (ENG., Illus.). 40p. (J). (gr. -1-3). 16.99 (978-0-8037-2818-9(2), Dial Bks) Penguin Young Readers Group.

Kelso, Mary Jean. Rv Mouse. Snider, K. C., illus. 2010. 24p. pap. 10.95 (978-1-61633-025-5(2)) Guardian Angel Publishing, Inc.

Kondrat, Lauren. Mischievous Mort. 2010. 40p. pap. 17.91 (978-0-557-43708-5(3)) Lulu Pr., Inc.

Krensky, Stephen. Snack Attack. Curtis, Stacy, illus. 2008. (Ready-To-Reads Ser.). (ENG.). 32p. (J). (gr. -1-1). pap. 3.99 (978-1-4169-0238-6(4), Simon Spotlight) Simon Spotlight.

Kroll, Steven. Stuff! Reduce, Reuse, Recycle, 0 vols. Cox, Steve, illus. 2012. (ENG.). 32p. (J). (gr. -1-3). pap. 7.99 (978-0-7614-6237-8(6), 9780761462378, Amazon Children's Publishing) Amazon Publishing.

Ladybird. Anansi Helps a Friend, Level 1. 2016. (Ladybird Readers Ser.). (ENG.). 16p. (J). (gr. 2-4). pap., act. bk. ed. 5.99 (978-0-241-25420-2(5)) Penguin Bks., Ltd. GBR. Dist: Independent Pubs. Group.

Laks, Shan. The Tale of Brave Ritchie: Be Aware of Strangers; Beat the Bullies & Exercise Changes Health. 2012. 76p. pap. 42.05 (978-1-4797-2882-4(9)) Xlibris Corp.

LaReau, Kara. The Infamous Ratsos. Myers, Matt, illus. 2017. (Infamous Ratsos Ser.). (ENG.). (J). (gr. k-3). 96p. 14.99 **(978-0-7636-7637-7(3))**; 64p. pap. 4.99 **(978-0-7636-9875-1(X))** Candlewick Pr.

Lears, Laurie. Stay Away from Rat Boy! Hansen, Red, illus. 2009. (ENG.). 32p. (J). (gr. 2-3). 16.99 (978-0-8075-6789-0(2)) Whitman, Albert & Co.

Lee, Maxine. Pi-Rat! Lee, Maxine, illus. 2013. (ENG., Illus.). 32p. (J). (gr. -1-k). 14.99 (978-1-58925-143-4(1)) Tiger Tales.

Lewis, Jan, illus. The Pied Piper of Hamelin. 2006. (First Fairy Tales Ser.). 30p. (J). (gr. -1-3). lib. bdg. 28.50 (978-1-59771-072-5(5)) Sea-To-Sea Pubns.

Liberto, Lorenzo. Matt the Rat & His Magic Cloud / Raton Mateo y Su Nube Magica: A Day at School / un Dia de Escuela. Gomez, Rocio, ed. Torres, Irving, illus. 2003. (Matt the Rat Ser. / La Serie de Ratón Mateo). (ENG & SPA.). 32p. (J). lib. bdg. 20.00 (978-0-9743668-0-7(3)) Harvest Sun Pr., LLC.

—Matt the Rat & His Sister Maggie (Raton Mateo y Su Hermana Maggie) When I Grow Up (Cuando Yo Crezca) Gomez, Rocio, ed. Torres, Irving, illus. 2003. (Matt the Rat Ser. / La Serie de Ratón Mateo). (SPA & ENG.). 40p. (J). lib. bdg. 20.00 (978-0-9743668-1-4(1)) Harvest Sun Pr., LLC.

—Matt the Rat Fights Back / Ratón Mateo se Defiende. Gomez, Rocio, tr. from ENG. Torres, Irving, illus. 2005. (Matt the Rat Ser. / La Serie de Ratón Mateo). (ENG & SPA.). 32p. (J). lib. bdg. 20.00 (978-0-9743668-4-5(6)) Harvest Sun Pr., LLC.

—Save the Planet / Salva el Planeta. Gomez, Rocio, tr. Torres, Irving, illus. 2005. (Matt the Rat Ser. / La Serie de Ratón Mateo). (ENG & SPA.). 32p. (J). lib. bdg. 20.00 (978-0-9743668-5-2(4)) Harvest Sun Pr., LLC.

Liberto, Lorenzo, et al. Matt the Rat's Incredible Creations / Las Creaciones Increíbles de Ratón Mateo. Torres, Irving, illus. 2004. (ENG & SPA.). 32p. (J). lib. bdg. 20.00 (978-0-9743668-3-8(8)) Harvest Sun Pr., LLC.

—Practice Makes Perfect / la Práctica Hace al Maestro. Torres, Irving, illus. 2004. (ENG & SPA.). 32p. (J). lib. bdg. 20.00 (978-0-9743668-2-1(X)) Harvest Sun Pr., LLC.

Lieb, Josh. Ratscalibur. 2016. lib. bdg. 19.65 (978-0-606-38850-4(8)) Turtleback Bks.

Lyons, Maggie. Dewi & the Seeds of Doom. 2012. 70p. pap. 9.99 (978-1-61244-094-1(0)) Halo Publishing International.

Mariconda, Barbara. Sort It Out!, 1 vol. Rogers, Sherry, illus. 2008. (ENG.). 32p. (J). (gr. k-4). 16.95 (978-1-934359-11-2(4)); pap. 8.95 (978-1-934359-32-7(7)) Arbordale Publishing.

Marquez, Sofia. Pepe Perez Mexican Mouse: Pepe Perez Comes to the United States: Book 1, 1 vol. 2010. 20p. 24.95 (978-1-4489-6600-4(0)) PublishAmerica, Inc.

Mathews, Leslie. Edgar Wants to Be Alone. Dumont, Jean-françois, illus. 2015. (ENG.). 26p. (J). 16.00 (978-0-8028-5457-5(5), Eerdmans Bks For Young Readers) Eerdmans, William B. Publishing Co.

Matulewicz, Elisabeth Ann. Benny & Marshmallow. Sponaugle, Kim, illus. 2008. 31p. (J). pap. 15.00 (978-0-9786211-7-9(4), Ithaca Pr.) Authors & Artists Publishers of New York, Inc.

McDonald, Jill, illus. Ghoulish Gang. 2008. (ENG.). 12p. (J). 9.95 (978-1-58117-782-4(8), Intervisual/Piggy Toes) Bendon, Inc.

McFarlane, Brian. Coaching the River Rats. 10th ed. 2008. (Mitchell Brothers Ser.). (ENG.). 198p. (J). (gr. 3-7). pap. (978-1-55168-302-7(4)) Me to We.

McGranaghan, John. Saturn for My Birthday, 1 vol. Edelson, Wendy, illus. 2008. (ENG.). 32p. (J). (gr. -1-4). 16.95 (978-1-934359-13-6(0)); pap. 8.95 (978-1-934359-27-3(0)) Arbordale Publishing.

McPhail, David. Big Brown Bear's up & down Day. McPhail, David, illus. 2005. (Illus.). 42p. (J). (gr. -1-3). reprint ed. 16.00 (978-0-7567-8542-0(1)) DIANE Publishing Co.

Milford, Diana Viola. Fuzzum & Wuzzum, 1 vol. 2010. 34p. pap. 24.95 (978-1-4489-9168-6(4)) PublishAmerica, Inc.

Mitchell, Stan R. Oskar & Myer at the Lake. 2013. 24p. pap. 24.95 (978-1-63000-414-9(6)) America Star Bks.

Morgan, Mary Sue. Swifty. 2008. 24p. pap. 24.95 (978-1-60441-579-7(7)) America Star Bks.

Morris, Ashara. Let's Find Lucy! 2008. (Illus.). 32p. pap. 17.95 (978-1-4327-3221-9(8)) Outskirts Pr., Inc.

Nees, Susan. Class Pets. 2013. (Missy's Super Duper Royal Deluxe Ser.: 2). (ENG., Illus.). 80p. (J). (gr. k-2). pap. 4.99 (978-0-545-43852-0(7)) Scholastic, Inc.

—Class Pets. 2013. (Missy's Super Duper Royal Deluxe Ser.: 2). lib. bdg. 14.75 (978-0-606-31980-5(8), Turtleback) Turtleback Bks.

Newbigging, Robert Delford. Robert Rat Has A Problem: A Tale of Broccoli. 2010. 44p. pap. 16.99 (978-1-4520-2134-8(1)) AuthorHouse.

O'Brien, Robert C. Mrs. Frisby & the Rats of NIMH. 2006. (KOR.). 280p. (J). (gr. 4-7). **(978-89-90794-37-6(4))** Green Bks. Co., Ltd.

—Mrs. Frisby & the Rats of NIMH. (J). 2009. 73.75 (978-1-4618-3748-0(0)) 2003. 81.75 (978-1-4025-6007-1(9)) Recorded Bks., Inc.

Otitoloju/Blazing Ideas ltd, Ololade/Adewunmi, retold by. Kunkuru, Jaba Da Kurege: The Tortoise, the Rat & the Squirrel. 2008. (YOR & ENG., Illus.). 36p. 16.00 (978-0-9801243-7-8(9)) Blazing Ideas Ltd.

—Mbe, Nkapi na Osa. 2008. (YOR & ENG., Illus.). 36p. 16.00 (978-0-9801243-3-0(6)) Blazing Ideas Ltd.

Parker, Vic, ed. The Rat Catcher & Other Stories. 2015. (Scary Fairy Tales Ser.). (ENG.). 40p. (J). (gr. 3-4). pap. 14.05 (978-1-4824-3101-8(7)) Stevens, Gareth Publishing LLLP.

Parkins, Rebecca Katherine. Lilly the Little Lava Mouse. 2009. 180p. pap. 43.49 (978-1-4389-4330-5(X)) AuthorHouse.

Parsons, Tom. Pinky the Rat at the Brussels Sprout Museum. 2007. 194p. 27.76 (978-1-4303-1538-4(5)) Lulu Pr., Inc.

Pastis, Stephan. Beginning Pearls. 2013. lib. bdg. 20.85 (978-0-606-31764-1(3), Turtleback) Turtleback Bks.

A Path of Clouds: The Book off Rhymes. 2013. 50p. pap. (978-965-550-241-1(4)) Contento De Semrik.

Pauli, Lorenz. Fox in the Library. Schaerer, Kathrin, illus. 2013. (ENG.). 32p. (J). (gr. -1-3). 17.95 (978-0-7358-4150-5(0)) North-South Bks., Inc.

Pearce, Jacqueline. The Truth about Rats (and Dogs), 1 vol. 2006. (ENG.). 160p. (J). (gr. 4-7). per. 7.95 (978-1-55143-473-5(3)) Orca Bk. Pubs. USA.

Petit, Karen. The Mystery of the Stolen Stallion. 2007. (Illus.). 246p. (J). per. 14.95 (978-0-9794420-4-9(4)) Red Letter Pr.

Pratchett, Terry. The Amazing Maurice & His Educated Rodents. 2008. (Discworld Novels Ser.). 368p. (YA). (gr. 8-18). pap. 8.99 (978-0-06-001235-9(8)) HarperCollins Pubs.

—The Amazing Maurice & His Educated Rodents. 2003. (ENG.). 340p. (gr. 7). 19.00 (978-0-7569-1458-5(2)) Perfection Learning Corp.

—The Amazing Maurice & His Educated Rodents. 2008. (Discworld Ser.: 33). (YA). (gr. 5-8). 19.65 (978-0-613-65757-0(8), Turtleback) Turtleback Bks.

Publications International Ltd. Staff. Look & Find Ratatouille. 2007. 24p. (J). 7.10 (978-1-4127-6837-5(3), PIL Kids) Publications International, Ltd.

Ratatouille. 2008. (Disney Pixar Character Storybook Ser.). 48p. (978-1-4075-1739-1(2)) Parragon, Inc.

Ratatouille, Oh, Brother! Oh, Hermano! (Disney 8*8's Bilingual Ser.). 24p. pap. (978-1-4054-9388-8(7)) Parragon, Inc.

Reuker, Heidi. Queen of the Rats. 2007. 56p. per. 16.95 (978-1-4137-9801-2(2)) America Star Bks.

Richards, Kitty & RH Disney Staff. Run, Remy, Run! Disney Storybook Artists Staff, illus. 2007. (Step into Reading Ser.). (ENG.). 32p. (J). (gr. k-3). pap. 3.99 (978-0-7364-2476-9(8), RH/Disney) Random Hse. Children's Bks.

Rodgers, Ilona. Musgrove in Kensington Gardens. 2007. (ENG.). 50p. 10.95 (978-1-905299-49-2(4), Stacey International) Stacey Publishing GBR. Dist: Casemate Pubs. & Bk. Distributors, LLC.

—Musgrove There's Something in My Shoe. 2006. (ENG., Illus.). 32p. 10.95 (978-1-905299-19-5(2), Stacey International) Stacey Publishing GBR. Dist: Casemate Pubs. & Bk. Distributors, LLC.

Roudon Jr., James. The Adventures of Ratsy & Kitten: Which Way Is Home? 2007. 56p. per. 16.95 (978-1-4241-8549-8(1)) America Star Bks.

Russell Brown, Eleanor. The Ring of Rats: An Other World Dimension. 2009. 28p. pap. 12.99 (978-1-4490-0393-7(1)) AuthorHouse.

Samos (Amos Amir). Nemo the Mole Rat: Stories from the Woodland. 2011. (Illus.). 52p. pap. 23.51 (978-1-4567-8187-3(1)) AuthorHouse.

Saxon, Victoria & RH Disney Staff. Ratatouille. Tilley, Scott & Orpinas, Jean-Paul, illus. 2007. (Little Golden Book Ser.). (ENG.). 24p. (J). (gr. -1-2). 3.99 (978-0-7364-2423-3(7), RH/Disney) Random Hse. Children's Bks.

Seidler, Tor. A Rat's Tale. Marcellino, Fred, illus. 2008. (ENG.). 192p. (J). (gr. 3-7). pap. 11.99 (978-0-374-40031-6(8), 9780374400316, Farrar, Straus & Giroux (BYR)) Farrar, Straus & Giroux.

—A Rat's Tale. 186p. (J). (gr. 3-5). pap. 6.95 (978-0-8072-1514-2(7), Listening Library) Random Hse. Audio Publishing Group.

Shaskan, Trisha Speed. The Case of the Missing Mola Lisa! Shaskan, Stephen, illus. 2017. (Q & Ray Ser.: 1). (ENG.). 48p. (gr. 2-5). 26.65 (978-1-5124-1147-8(7), Graphic Universe™) Lerner Publishing Group.

Shubuck, Shella. I Love You All Year Round. Padron, Alicia, illus. 2008. (ENG.). 16p. (J). (gr. -1). 10.95 (978-1-58117-786-2(0), Intervisual/Piggy Toes) Bendon, Inc.

Smiley, Mark. A Journey Far Away. 2006. 164p. pap. 13.95 (978-1-59526-494-7(9)) Aeon Publishing Inc.

Smith, Brooke. Mimi & Maty to the Rescue! Book 1: Roger the Rat Is on the Loose! Arnold, Alli, illus. 2014. (ENG.). 88p. (J). (gr. k-4). pap. 9.95 (978-1-62914-619-5(6), Sky Pony Pr.) Skyhorse Publishing Co., Inc.

—Mimi & Maty to the Rescue! Bk. 1: Roger the Rat Is on the Loose! Arnold, Alli, illus. 2012. (ENG.). 88p. (J). (gr. 1-4). 14.95 (978-1-62087-252-9(8), 620252, Sky Pony Pr.) Skyhorse Publishing Co., Inc.

Smith, Holly C. Tyler the Monkey & Andy the Mouse. 2012. 28p. (-18). pap. 24.95 (978-1-4626-9501-0(9)) America Star Bks.

Staunton, Ted. Morgan's Pet Plot, 1 vol. Slavin, Bill & Shannon, Ben, illus. 2003. (Formac First Novels Ser.: 24). (ENG.). 64p. (J). (gr. 1-5). 4.95 (978-0-88780-587-5(6), 9780887805875) Formac Publishing Co., Ltd. CAN. Dist: Casemate Pubs. & Bk. Distributors, LLC.

—Morgan's Pet Plot. Slavin, Bill, illus. 2003. (Formac First Novels Ser.: 24). (ENG.). 64p. (J). (gr. 1-5). 14.95 (978-0-88780-588-2(4), 9780887805882) Formac Publishing Co., Ltd. CAN. Dist: Casemate Pubs. & Bk. Distributors, LLC.

Stilton, Geronimo. A Cheese-Colored Camper. 2005. (Geronimo Stilton Ser.: 16). (ENG., Illus.). 128p. (J). (gr. 2-5). pap. 7.99 (978-0-439-69139-0(7), Scholastic Paperbacks) Scholastic, Inc.

—Watch Your Whiskers, Stilton! 17th ed. 2005. (Geronimo Stilton Ser.: 17). (ENG., Illus.). 128p. (J). (gr. 2-5). pap. 7.99 (978-0-439-69140-6(0), Scholastic Paperbacks) Scholastic, Inc.

Storad, Conrad J. Desert Night Shift: A Pack Rat Story. Jensen, Nathaniel P., illus. 2006. 48p. (J). (gr. -1-3). 15.95 (978-1-891795-16-9(3)) RGU Group, The.

Strout, Morgan. Petri's Adventures. 2013. 18p. pap. 8.95 (978-1-4575-2094-5(X)) Dog Ear Publishing, LLC.

Stuart, Lisa Marie. The Little Cat, the Wonderful Witch, & the Clever Mouse. Potter, Lori, illus. 2008. 60p. pap. 21.95 *(978-1-59858-691-6(2))* Dog Ear Publishing, LLC.

Tauilili, Pemerika L. The Rat & the Bat: And Other Short Stories. 2009. 88p. pap. 16.99 *(978-1-4490-4389-6(5))*; pap. 32.49 *(978-1-4389-2700-8(2))* AuthorHouse.

Thompson, Colin. The Short & Incredibly Happy Life of Riley. Lissiat, Amy, illus. 2006. 32p. (J). *(978-0-7344-0806-8(4)*, Lothian Children's Bks.) Hachette Australia.

Tremblay, Carole. Romeo, le Rat Romantique. 2004. (FRE., Illus.). (J). (gr. -1-3). spiral bd. *(978-0-616-07266-0(X))* Canadian National Institute for the Blind/Institut National Canadien pour les Aveugles.

Velazquez, Anna. Stewart's Airplane Adventure. 2008. 40p. pap. 24.95 *(978-1-60441-486-8(3))* America Star Bks.

Velthuijs, Max. Frog & the Stranger. 2014. (ENG., Illus.). 32p. (J). (-k). pap. 12.95 *(978-1-78344-143-3(7))* Andersen Pr. GBR. Dist: Independent Pubs. Group.

Ventura, Marne. Nervous Nellie Fights First-Day Frenzy. Trinidad, Leo, illus. 2016. (Worry Warriors Ser.). (ENG.). 96p. (gr. 2-4). lib. bdg. 25.99 *(978-1-4965-3613-6(4))* Stone Arch Bks.

Vernon, Ursula. Ratpunzel. 2016. (Hamster Princess Ser.: 3). (ENG., Illus.). 240p. (J). (gr. 3-7). 12.99 *(978-0-8037-3985-7(0)*, Dial Bks) Penguin Young Readers Group.

Wagner, Hilary. Lords of Trillium: Book Iii of the Nightshade Chronicles. Rayyan, Omar, illus. 2014. (Nightshade Chronicles Ser.: 3). (ENG.). 224p. (J). (gr. 4). 17.95 *(978-0-8234-2413-9(8))* Holiday Hse., Inc.

—Lords of Trillium: Book III of the Nightshade Chronicles. Rayyan, Omar, illus. 2015. (Nightshade Chronicles Ser.: 3). (ENG.). 224p. (J). (gr. 4). pap. 7.95 *(978-0-8234-3306-3(4))* Holiday Hse., Inc.

—Nightshade City. Rayyan, Omar, illus. (Nightshade Chronicles Ser.: 1). (ENG.). 320p. (J). 2011. pap. 7.95 *(978-0-8234-2387-3(5))* 2010. (gr. 3-7). 17.95 *(978-0-8234-2285-2(2))* Holiday Hse., Inc.

—White Assassin. Rayyan, Omar, illus. 2011. (Nightshade Chronicles Ser.: 2). (ENG.). 304p. (J). (gr. 4). 17.95 *(978-0-8234-2333-0(6))* Holiday Hse., Inc.

—The White Assassin. 2012. (Nightshade Chronicles Ser.: 2). (ENG.). 304p. (J). (gr. 4). pap. 7.95 *(978-0-8234-2485-6(5))* Holiday Hse., Inc.

Wall, Layton E. Rat Fishin' with Ralphie Rat: A Bully Learns a Lesson. 2010. 28p. pap. 12.85 *(978-1-4520-4960-1(2))* AuthorHouse.

Wendling, Nathalie & Glatzmayer, Thomas. Melanie & Tommy Have Two Pet Rats & One Syndrome. 2010. 48p. pap. *(978-1-926582-67-2(5))* Insomniac Pr.

Wersba, Barbara. Walter: The Story of a Rat. Diamond, Donna, illus. 2012. (ENG.). 64p. (J). (gr. 4-6). pap. 8.95 *(978-1-59078-948-3(2))* Boyds Mills Pr.

Westen, Leah. Jack the Tooth Rat. 2009. (Illus.). 28p. pap. 12.50 *(978-1-60693-558-3(5)*, Eloquent Bks.) Strategic Book Publishing & Rights Agency (SBPRA).

Winthrop, Elizabeth. The Red-Hot Rattoons. Lewin, Betsy, illus. 2006. (ENG.). 224p. (J). (gr. 3-6). pap. 16.99 *(978-0-8050-7986-9(6)*, 9780805079869, Holt, Henry & Co. Bks. For Young Readers) Holt, Henry & Co.

Zepp, Gene W. Return of the Pied Piper of Hamelin. 2011. 48p. pap. 21.99 *(978-1-4628-7007-3(4))* Xlibris Corp.

RAVENS

Berne, Emma Carlson. Ravens. 2014. (Scavengers: Eating Nature's Trash Ser.). (Illus.). 24p. (J). (gr. k-5). lib. bdg. 23.60 *(978-1-4777-6612-5(X)*, PowerKids Pr.) Rosen Publishing Group, Inc., The.

Bradley, James V. Crows & Ravens. 2006. (Nature Walk Ser.). (Illus.). 64p. (gr. 4-6). lib. bdg. 28.00 *(978-0-7910-9115-9(5)*, Chelsea Hse.) Facts On File, Inc.

Dewey, Jennifer Owings. Clem: The Story of a Raven. Dewey, Jennifer Owings, illus. 2003. (ENG., Illus.). 128p. (J). pap. 14.95 *(978-0-8263-3023-9(1))* Univ. of New Mexico Pr.

Webster, Christine. Ravens. 2009. (Backyard Animals Ser.). (Illus.). 24p. (J). (gr. 3-5). pap. 8.95 *(978-1-60596-083-8(7))*; lib. bdg. 24.45 *(978-1-60596-082-1(9))* Weigl Pubs., Inc.

RAVENS—FICTION

Adams, Jennifer. Edgar & the Tattle-Tale Heart, 1 vol. Stucki, Ron, illus. 2014. (ENG.). 32p. (J). 16.99 *(978-1-4236-3766-0(6))* Gibbs Smith, Publisher.

—Edgar & the Treehouse of Usher: A BabyLit First Steps Book, 1 vol. Stucki, Ron, illus. 2015. (ENG.). 32p. (J). 16.99 *(978-1-4236-4043-1(8))* Gibbs Smith, Publisher.

Aiken, Joan. Arabel's Raven. Blake, Quentin, illus. 2007. (ENG.). 160p. (J). (gr. 2-5). pap. 11.95 *(978-0-15-206094-7(4))* Houghton Mifflin Harcourt Publishing Co.

Al-Ghani, K.I. Ronnie Raven Recycles, 1 vol. Al-Ghani, Haitham, illus. 2011. (ENG.). 44p. (J). 16.99 *(978-0-7643-3840-3(4)*, 9780764338403, Schiffer Publishing Ltd) Schiffer Publishing, Ltd.

Anastasio, Dina, retold by. How Raven Became Black & Owl Got Its Spots: Set Of 6. 2010. (Early Connections Ser.). (J). pap. 37.00 net. *(978-1-4108-1093-9(3))* Benchmark Education Co.

Avi. Old Wolf. Floca, Brian, illus. 2015. (ENG.). 160p. (J). (gr. 3-7). 16.99 *(978-1-4424-9921-8(4))* Simon & Schuster Children's Publishing.

Bansch, Helga. Odd Bird Out. 2011. (Gecko Press Titles Ser.). (ENG., Illus.). 32p. pap. 17.95 *(978-1-877467-08-0(1))* Gecko Pr. NZL. Dist: Lerner Publishing Group.

Bouchard, David. I am Raven. Everson, Andy, illus. 2nd ed. 2008. 28p. (J). *(978-0-9784327-0-6(3))* More Than Words Bks., Inc.

Brouillet, Chrystine. Le Corbeau. 2003. (Roman Jeunesse Ser.). (FRE.). 96p. (YA). (gr. 4-7). pap. *(978-2-89021-132-2(0))* Diffusion du livre Mirabel (DLM).

Carlstrom, Nancy White. Raven & River. Van Zyle, Jon, illus. 2011. (ENG.). 32p. pap. 11.95 *(978-1-60223-150-4(8))* Univ. of Alaska Pr.

Cotes, Gilles. OGM et Chant de Mais. Begin, Jean-Guy, illus. 2004. (FRE.). 112p. (J). *(978-2-89599-002-4(6))* Editions de la Paix CAN. Dist: World of Reading, Ltd.

Dawson, Willow. The Wolf-Birds. 2015. (ENG., Illus.). 40p. (J). (gr. k-4). 17.95 *(978-1-77147-054-4(2)*, Owlkids) Owlkids Bks. Inc. CAN. Dist: Publishers Group West (PGW).

Derubertis, Barbara. Victor Vicuna's Volcano Vacation. Alley, R. W., illus. 2011. (Animal Antics A to Z Set III Ser.). pap. 45.32 *(978-0-7613-8431-1(6))* Kane Press, Inc.

deRubertis, Barbara. Victor Vicuna's Volcano Vacation. Alley, R. W., illus. 2011. (Animal Antics A to Z Ser.). 32p. (J). (ENG.). pap. 7.95 *(978-1-57565-347-1(8))*; lib. bdg. 22.60 *(978-1-57565-355-6(9))* Kane Press, Inc.

deRubertis, Barbara & DeRubertis, Barbara. Victor Vicuna's Volcano Vacation. Alley, R. W., illus. 2012. (Animal Antics A to Z Ser.). 32p. (J). (gr. 2 — 1). cd-rom 7.95 *(978-1-57565-415-7(6))* Kane Press, Inc.

Drummond, Sarah, illus. Raven & the Red Ball. 2013. (ENG.). 28p. (J). 9.95 *(978-0-7649-6609-5(X))* Pomegranate Communications, Inc.

Galera Staff. Cuervo y la Raposa (Raven & the Fox) (SPA.). 24p. (J). 9.95 *(978-84-246-1601-4(4))* La Galera, S.A. Editorial ESP. Dist: AIMS International Bks., Inc.

George, Jean Craighead. Charlie's Raven. George, Jean Craighead, illus. 2006. (ENG., Illus.). 208p. (J). (gr. 5-18). reprint ed. 6.99 *(978-0-14-240547-5(7)*, Puffin Books) Penguin Young Readers Group.

Hagen, George. Gabriel Finley & the Raven's Riddle. Bakal, Scott, illus. 2014. (ENG.). 384p. (J). (gr. 4-7). 16.99 *(978-0-385-37103-2(9)*, Schwartz & Wade Bks.) Random Hse. Children's Bks.

Harris, Patricia. Raven & the Farmer. 2017. (Raven's Orchard Ser.). 24p. (gr. 4-6). pap. 8.25 ***(978-1-5081-6143-1(7)***, PowerKids Pr.) Rosen Publishing Group, Inc., The.

—Raven in the City. 2017. (Raven's Orchard Ser.). 24p. (gr. 4-6). pap. 8.25 ***(978-1-5081-6147-9(X)***, PowerKids Pr.) Rosen Publishing Group, Inc., The.

—Raven's Garden. 2017. (Raven's Orchard Ser.). 24p. (gr. 4-6). pap. 8.25 ***(978-1-5081-6151-6(8)***, PowerKids Pr.) Rosen Publishing Group, Inc., The.

Johannes, Avril & Branham, Jan. Eeny, Meeny, Miney, Moe, Four Alaskan Ravens. Tessama, C., illus. 2003. 32p. (J). 7.95 *(978-0-9749360-0-0(6))* Icicle Falls Publishing Co.

Lassiter, Rhiannon. Void: Hex; Shadows; Ghosts. 2011. (ENG.). 688p. (YA). (gr. 7). pap. 9.99 *(978-1-4424-2929-1(1)*, Simon Pulse) Simon Pulse.

Osborne, Mary Pope. Haunted Castle on Hallows Eve. Murdocca, Sal, illus. 2010. (Magic Tree House Merlin Mission Ser.: 2). (ENG.). 144p. (J). (gr. 2-5). pap. 5.99 *(978-0-375-86090-4(8)*, Random Hse. Bks. for Young Readers) Random Hse. Children's Bks.

—Haunted Castle on Hallows Eve. 2010. (Magic Tree House Merlin Missions Ser.: 2). lib. bdg. 16.00 *(978-0-606-13992-2(3)*, Turtleback) Turtleback Bks.

Raven's Orchard. 2017. (Raven's Orchard Ser.). 24p. (gr. 4-6). 70.80 ***(978-1-5081-6188-2(7))***; pap. 24.75 ***(978-1-5081-6190-5(9))*** Rosen Publishing Group, Inc., The. (PowerKids Pr.).

Sophia Hansen, Hansen & Hansen, Sophia. The Crow & the Raven. 2010. 20p. 9.50 *(978-1-4269-2752-2(5))* Trafford Publishing.

Stephenson, Midji. The Ravenous Raven. Gray, Steve, illus. 2015. (J). *(978-1-934656-70-9(4))* Grand Canyon Assn.

Stewart, Sharon. Raven Quest. 2005. (ENG.). 320p. (J). (gr. 4-6). 15.95 *(978-1-57505-894-8(4)*, Carolrhoda Bks.) Lerner Publishing Group.

van Keuren, Luise. Raven, Stay by Me. 2012. (ENG.). 162p. pap. *(978-1-894377-30-0(3))* Breakwater Bks., Ltd.

Woodruff, Elvira. The Ravenmaster's Secret. 2005. (Escape from the Tower of London Ser.). (Illus.). 225p. (gr. 3-7). 16.00 *(978-0-7569-4791-0(X))* Perfection Learning Corp.

RAYS, ROENTGEN

see X-Rays

RCMP

see Royal Canadian Mounted Police

REACTORS (NUCLEAR PHYSICS)

see Nuclear Reactors

READERS

Here are entered school readers in English. For readers in other languages, use the name of the language with the subdivision Readers, e.g. French Language—Readers.

see also Primers

Level I, 6 vols. (Wonder WorldTM Ser.). 16p. 29.95 *(978-0-7802-1035-6(2))* Wright Group/McGraw-Hill.

Abdo Publishing. Adventures in Extreme Reading, 1 vol. 2013. (Adventures in Extreme Reading Ser.: 6). (ENG.). 112p. (J). (gr. 3-6). lib. bdg. 162.42 *(978-1-61641-918-9(0)*, Calico Chapter Bks) Magic Wagon.

ABDO Publishing. Scooby-Doo Comic Readers. 2016. (Scooby-Doo Comic Readers Ser.: 6). (ENG.). 32p. (J). (gr. k-3). lib. bdg. 145.26 *(978-1-61479-450-9(2)*, Graphic Planet) Magic Wagon.

ABDO Publishing Company Staff. Fact & Fiction: Animal Tales: Set of 24, 1 vol. 2006. (Animal Tales Ser.: 24). (ENG.). 24p. (J). (gr. k-3). lib. bdg. 581.04 *(978-1-59679-923-3(4)*, SandCastle) ABDO Publishing Co.

—Magic Readers. 2014. (Magic Readers Ser.: 18). (ENG.). 24p. (J). (gr. 5-9). lib. bdg. 435.78 *(978-1-62402-053-7(4))* Magic Wagon.

—Sight Words. 2004. (Sight Words Ser.: 4). (ENG.). 24p. (J). (gr. k-3). lib. bdg. 96.84 *(978-1-59197-463-5(1)*, SandCastle) ABDO Publishing Co.

Abela, Donna. The Princess & the Pea Vol. 9: Band 15/Emerald. Stewart, Chantal, illus. 2007. (Collins Big Cat Ser.). (ENG.). 32p. (J). pap. 8.99 *(978-0-00-722866-9(X))* HarperCollins Pubs. Ltd. GBR. Dist: Independent Pubs. Group.

Abnett, Dan. The Battle of Gettysburg: Invasion of the North! 2007. (Graphic Battles: Civil War Ser.). (ENG., Illus.). 48p. (gr. 5-8). pap. 14.05 *(978-1-4042-6477-9(9)*, Rosen Classroom) Rosen Publishing Group, Inc., The.

Accelerated Reader. 2005. cd-rom *(978-1-59455-200-7(2))* Renaissance Learning, Inc.

Accelerated Reader RP Student Subscription. 2004. cd-rom *(978-1-59455-164-2(2))* Renaissance Learning, Inc.

Accelerated Reader RP Student Subscription Renewal. 2004. cd-rom *(978-1-59455-166-6(9))* Renaissance Learning, Inc.

Achieve Now Institute Staff. ESR Anthology, Band 3-5. 2004. pap. 24.08 *(978-0-7398-9889-5(2))* Steck-Vaughn.

ACT Reading Victory Student Textbook. 2nd ed. 2005. per. *(978-1-58894-033-9(0))* Cambridge Educational Services, Inc.

Action Packs: Complete Action Packs Add-to Pack. 492.00 *(978-0-7578-8404-7(0))* Rigby Education.

Action Words Board Books 800670, 5. 2005. (J). bds. *(978-1-59794-011-5(9))* Environments, Inc.

Activity Worksheets. 2004. (J). spiral bd. 29.95 *(978-1-886441-64-4(2))* Zoo-phonics, Inc.

Adams, Alison. Changes in the Kitchen. 2017. (Text Connections Guided Close Reading Ser.). (J). (gr. 1). *(978-1-4900-1803-4(4))* Benchmark Education Co.

Adams, Colleen. At the Toy Store. 2006. (Neighborhood Readers Ser.). (ENG.). 8p. (gr. -1-3). pap. 5.15 *(978-1-4042-5732-0(2)*, Rosen Classroom) Rosen Publishing Group, Inc., The.

—The Big Day! 2006. (Neighborhood Readers Ser.). (ENG.). 8p. (gr. -1-3). pap. 5.15 *(978-1-4042-5708-5(X)*, Rosen Classroom) Rosen Publishing Group, Inc., The.

—Jugando en la nieve (Playing in the Snow) 2007. (Lecturas del barrio (Neighborhood Readers) Ser.). (SPA.). 8p. 29.95 *(978-1-4042-7064-0(7)*, Rosen Classroom) Rosen Publishing Group, Inc., The.

—Playing in the Snow. (Neighborhood Readers Ser.). (ENG.). 8p. 2007. 29.95 *(978-1-4042-7059-6(0))* 2006. (gr. -1-3). pap. 5.15 *(978-1-4042-5657-6(1))* Rosen Publishing Group, Inc., The. (Rosen Classroom).

—School Is Cool! 2006. (Neighborhood Readers Ser.). (ENG.). 8p. (gr. -1-3). pap. 5.15 *(978-1-4042-5676-7(8)*, Rosen Classroom) Rosen Publishing Group, Inc., The.

Adams, Georgie. The Three Little Vampires. Bolam, Emily, illus. 2016. (Early Reader Ser.). (ENG.). 80p. (J). (gr. k-2). 6.99 *(978-1-4440-1147-0(2)*, Orion Children's Bks.) Hachette Children's Group GBR. Dist: Hachette Bk. Group.

Add-On Literature Set, 6 vols., Level C. (Into English! Ser.). (gr. 2-18). 47.88 *(978-1-56334-897-6(7)*, SC0201) CENGAGE Learning.

Adler, David A. Helen Keller. Wallner, John, illus. 2006. (ENG.). 32p. (J). (gr. -1-3). 4.95 *(978-0-8234-2042-1(6))* Holiday Hse., Inc.

Afzal, Uz. Dance to the Beat. Lumb, Steve, illus. 2005. (Collins Big Cat Ser.). (ENG.). 320p. (J). (gr. k-1). pap. 5.99 *(978-0-00-718576-4(6))* HarperCollins Pubs. Ltd. GBR. Dist: Independent Pubs. Group.

—Dance to the Beat. 2005. (Big Cat Ser.). (gr. k-2). pap. 6.50 *(978-1-60457-058-8(X))* Pacific Learning, Inc.

Agard, John & Nichols, Grace. Full Moon Night in Silk Cotton Tree Village: A Collection of Caribbean Folk Tales. Woods, Rosie, illus. 2016. (ENG.). 48p. (J). pap. 9.95 *(978-0-00-814724-2(8))* HarperCollins Pubs. Ltd. GBR. Dist: Independent Pubs. Group.

Agnew, Kate. Space Saver. Castle, Frances, illus. 2016. (Reading Ladder Ser.). (ENG.). 48p. (J). (gr. k-2). 7.99 *(978-1-4052-8213-0(4))* Egmont Bks., Ltd. GBR. Dist: Independent Pubs. Group.

Agnew, Leoni & Collins UK Publishing Staff. The Battle of Kupe & Te Wheke. Bianchi, Fausto, illus. 2016. (ENG.). 32p. (J). pap. 8.95 *(978-0-00-814716-7(7))* HarperCollins Pubs. Ltd. GBR. Dist: Independent Pubs. Group.

Ahearn, Dan. Time for Kids Readers. 2003. (Time for Kids Readers Ser.). (ENG.). pap. 84.96 *(978-0-15-340566-2(X))* Harcourt Schl. Pubs.

Ahmad, Kamil. Up, up, up! the Tale of a Magical Basket. 2017. (Text Connections Guided Close Reading Ser.). (J). (gr. 1). *(978-1-4900-1821-8(2))* Benchmark Education Co.

Aiken, Zora & Aiken, David. Chesapeake Play Day, 1 vol. 2015. (ENG., Illus.). 32p. (J). 14.99 *(978-0-7643-4883-9(3)*, 9780764348839) Schiffer Publishing, Ltd.

Aikins, David. The Good, the Bad, & the Krabby! 2015. (SpongeBob Squarepants 8X8 Ser.). lib. bdg. 14.75 *(978-0-606-36397-6(1))* Turtleback Bks.

Akers, Martin, et al. Fran Grabs It - Stop! It's a Frog! - the Best Nest: BuildUp Unit 3 Lap Book. Palacios, Sara & Battuz, Christine, illus. 2015. (Build up Core Phonics Ser.). (J). (gr. 1). *(978-1-4900-2602-2(9))* Benchmark Education Co.

Akinyemi, Rowena. Under the Moon, Level 1. Oxford University Press Staff & Bassett, Jennifer, eds. 3rd ed. 2008. (ENG., Illus.). 64p. 9.38 *(978-0-19-478922-6(5))* Oxford Univ. Pr., Inc.

al-Qadi, Charlotte. Arif Goes Shopping Pink a Band. Van Wyk, Rupert, illus. 2016. (Cambridge Reading Adventures Ser.). (ENG.). 16p. pap. 6.56 *(978-1-316-60810-4(7))* Cambridge Univ. Pr.

Alagna, Magdalena. Wyatt Earp: Lawman of the American West. 2009. (Primary Sources of Famous People in American History Ser.). 32p. (gr. 2-3). 47.90 *(978-1-60851-747-3(0))* Rosen Publishing Group, Inc., The.

Alaina, Maria. Wonder Readers Next Steps: Social Studies. 2013. (Wonder Readers Next Steps: Social Studies). (ENG.). 20p. (gr. -1-1). lib. bdg. 67.95 *(978-1-4765-0046-1(0)*, Wonder Readers) Capstone Press of Coughlan Cos.

The Alamo Journals. 2003. (Illus.). pap. 7.60 *(978-0-7398-7523-0(X))* Steck-Vaughn.

Alarcon, Roben. American Indians in the 1800s, 1 vol. 2005. (Primary Source Readers Ser.). (ENG., Illus.). 24p. (J). (gr. 5-5). pap. 8.99 *(978-0-7439-8913-8(9))* Shell Educational Publishing.

—The Constitution & the Bill of Rights, 1 vol. 2004. (Primary Source Readers Ser.). (ENG.). 24p. (J). (gr. 5-5). pap. 8.99 *(978-0-7439-8783-7(7))* Shell Educational Publishing.

—John Jay, 1 vol. 2004. (Primary Source Readers Ser.). (ENG.). 24p. (J). (gr. 4-4). pap. 8.99 *(978-0-7439-8784-4(5))* Shell Educational Publishing.

—Librarians Then & Now, 1 vol. 2006. (Primary Source Readers Ser.). (ENG.). 32p. (J). (gr. 1-1). pap. 8.99 *(978-0-7439-9376-0(4))* Shell Educational Publishing.

—Sitting Bull, 1 vol. 2005. (Primary Source Readers Ser.). (ENG.). 24p. (J). (gr. 4-4). pap. 8.99 *(978-0-7439-8914-5(7))* Shell Educational Publishing.

—Teachers Then & Now, 1 vol. 2006. (Primary Source Readers Ser.). (ENG.). 32p. (J). (gr. 2-2). pap. 8.99 *(978-0-7439-9375-3(6))* Shell Educational Publishing.

Albee, Jo. American Heroes, 6 vols., Set. 2003. (Phonics Readers 1-36 Ser.). (ENG.). 8p. (gr. k-1). pap. 29.70 *(978-0-7368-3205-2(X)*, Phonics Readers) Capstone Press of Coughlan Cos.

Albee, Sarah. Julius Caesar, Cleopatra. 2011. (Readers' & Writers' Genre Workshop Ser.). (YA). pap. *(978-1-4509-3023-9(9))* Benchmark Education Co.

Albee, Sarah, et al. Read Around Sesame Street (Sesame Street) Mathieu, Joe, illus. 2014. (Step into Reading Ser.). (ENG.). 160p. (J). (gr. -1-1). pap. 7.99 *(978-0-385-37411-8(9)*, Random Hse. Bks. for Young Readers) Random Hse. Children's Bks.

Alcraft, Rob. Everest Ice Climbers. 2017. (ENG.). 48p. (J). pap. 8.99 ***(978-0-00-820887-5(5))*** HarperCollins Pubs. Ltd. GBR. Dist: Independent Pubs. Group.

Alexander, Heather. Junior Groovies - Bugs! 2010. (ENG., Illus.). 10p. (J). (gr. -1-1). 15.99 *(978-1-60169-019-7(3))* Innovative Kids.

Alexander, Linda. As-Easy-As-ABC-123. 50th ed. 2003. (Illus.). (J). cd-rom *(978-0-9714299-2-5(8))* I Save A Tree.

—As-Easy-As-ABC-123 Bilingual. 2003. (SPA., Illus.). (J). cd-rom *(978-0-9714299-3-2(6))* I Save A Tree.

Alexander, Mark. Whose Toes Are Those? 2006. (Neighborhood Readers Ser.). (ENG.). 12p. (gr. 1-3). pap. 5.90 *(978-1-4042-7042-8(6)*, Rosen Classroom) Rosen Publishing Group, Inc., The.

Alexander, Richard. The Inuit: People of the North. 2013. (Rosen Readers Ser.). (ENG.). 24p. (J). (gr. 3-4). pap. 49.50 *(978-1-4777-2549-8(0))*; pap. 8.25 *(978-1-4777-2548-1(2))* Rosen Publishing Group, Inc., The. (Rosen Classroom).

Alexander's Enrichment Activties. 2006. (J). pap. 5.95 *(978-0-9742806-6-0(6))* Heart to Heart Publishing, Inc.

The Alien, 6 vols., Pack. (gr. 1-2). 25.00 *(978-0-7635-9192-2(0))* Rigby Education.

All Across America. (Guided Reading Levels Ser.). 28.56 *(978-0-7362-1060-7(1))* CENGAGE Learning.

All from a Bottle. (Early Intervention Levels Ser.). 31.86 *(978-0-7362-0662-4(0))* CENGAGE Learning.

All in the Family. 2005. (Little Celebrations Thematic Packages Ser.). (J). (gr. k-3). 133.50 *(978-0-673-75386-1(7))* Celebration Pr.

Allan, Jasper. Let's Go to the Supermarket. 2008. (Real Readers - Upper Emergent Ser.). (ENG., Illus.). 12p. (gr. 1-2). pap. 5.90 *(978-0-8239-8125-0(8))* Rosen Publishing Group, Inc., The.

Allen, Kenny. Bird Builds a House. 2006. (Neighborhood Readers Ser.). (ENG.). 8p. (gr. -1-3). pap. 5.15 *(978-1-4042-6690-2(9)*, Rosen Classroom) Rosen Publishing Group, Inc., The.

—A Great Day to Skate. 2006. (Neighborhood Readers Ser.). (ENG.). 8p. (gr. 1-3). pap. 5.15 *(978-1-4042-6819-7(7)*, Rosen Classroom) Rosen Publishing Group, Inc., The.

—My School. 2009. (Real Life Readers Ser.). 8p. (gr. k-1). pap. 5.15 *(978-1-4042-7969-8(5)*, Rosen Classroom) Rosen Publishing Group, Inc., The.

Allen, Margaret. Jingle Jangles Vol. 2256: Fun, Interactive Reading Selections for Fluency Practice. Walter, LaDawn, ed. Rojas, Mary & Vangsgard, Amy, illus. 2004. 128p. (J). (gr. k-2). pap. 14.99 *(978-1-59198-048-3(8)*, 2256) Creative Teaching Pr., Inc.

Alley, R. W., illus. The Prince's Tooth Is Loose! 2005. (I'm Going to Read(r) Ser.). (ENG.). 28p. (J). (gr. -1-k). pap. 3.95 *(978-1-4027-2721-4(6))* Sterling Publishing Co., Inc.

Almy, Judy. My Name Is Ick: A Rhyming Story of an Alaska Caribou. 2003. 9.95 *(978-1-59433-009-4(3))* Publication Consultants.

Alspach, Kate M. Farts Are Fantastic. 2012. 24p. pap. 15.99 *(978-1-4691-5589-0(3))* Xlibris Corp.

Altobello, Albert & Wadhams, Doyle. The 10 Most Important Civil Rights Decisions. 2008. 14.99 *(978-1-55448-528-4(2))* Scholastic Library Publishing.

Alvarez, Lourdes M. My First Book Things. Brooks, David, illus. 2005. (My First Book Ser.). 9p. (J). (gr. -1-1). bds. 3.95 *(978-1-933050-10-2(1))* Sweetwater Pr.

Amazing Academy Assort. 2009. (J). *(978-1-84879-339-2(1))* Make Believe Ideas.

Amelia Bedilia Book Set 800916, 3 vols. 2005. (J). pap. *(978-1-59794-081-8(X))* Environments, Inc.

American Heritage Dictionary Editors, ed. ¿Dónde Me Escondo? Zagarenski, Pamela, illus. 2005.Tr. of Where Am I Hiding? (SPA & ENG.). 8p. (J). (gr. -1 — 1). bds. 3.95 *(978-0-618-51176-1(8))* Houghton Mifflin Harcourt Publishing Co.

American Indian Crafts. 2005. (Book Treks Ser.). (J). (gr. 3-18). stu. ed. 34.95 *(978-0-673-62838-1(8))* Celebration Pr.

American Tract Society Staff, compiled by. The Tract Primer: First Lessons in Sound Doctrine for Young Children. 2007. 112p. per. 11.00 *(978-1-59925-130-1(2))* Solid Ground Christian Bks.

The American Tradition: The EMC Write-in Reader. 2nd ed. (Literature & the Language Arts Ser.). (YA). (gr. 11-18). wbk. ed. 19.99 *(978-0-8219-2918-6(6))* EMC/Paradigm Publishing.

Amerikaner, Susan. Goofy at Bat. 2013. (Mickey & Friends World of Reading Ser.). (J). lib. bdg. 13.55 *(978-0-606-27117-2(1)*, Turtleback) Turtleback Bks.

Amery, Heather. Grumpy Goat. Cartwright, Stephen, illus. 2004. 16p. (J). pap. 5.95 *(978-0-7945-0788-6(3)*, Usborne) EDC Publishing.

—Market Day. Cartwright, Stephen, illus. 2004. 16p. (J). pap. 5.95 *(978-0-7945-0783-1(2)*, Usborne) EDC Publishing.

—Runaway Tractor. Cartwright, Stephen, illus. 2004. 16p. (J). pap. 5.95 *(978-0-7945-0748-0(4)*, Usborne) EDC Publishing.

Amery, Heather, et al. First Hundred Words in Maori. 2008. (MAO., Illus.). 40p. pap. 14.00 *(978-1-86969-304-6(3))* Huia Pubs. NZL. Dist: Univ. of Hawaii Pr.

Amos, Eduardo & Pearson Education Staff. Amazon Rally. 2007. (ENG.). 24p. pap. 17.32 incl. cd-rom *(978-1-4058-5199-2(6))* Pearson Education.

Amos Fortune Free Man Student Packet. 2004. (J). 12.99 *(978-1-58130-506-7(0))* Novel Units, Inc.

Ana, Moh. Kookaburra Tales # 3: Laugh Not at Others. 2013. 16p. pap. 16.81 *(978-1-4669-3477-1(8))* Trafford Publishing.

Anastasio, Dina & Jenkins, Amanda. Jake Digs a Hole, Luke & the Bug Man. 2011. (Readers' & Writers' Genre Workshop Ser.). (YA). pap. *(978-1-4509-3022-2(0))* Benchmark Education Co.

Andersen, Hans Christian & Capstone Press Editors. La Bella y la Bestia: La Novela Grafica. Feldman, Luke, illus. 2010. (Graphic Spin en Español Ser.). (SPA.). 40p. (gr. 1-3). lib.

bdg. 25.32 *(978-1-4342-1899-5(6),* Graphic Spin en Español) Stone Arch Bks.

Andersen, Hans Christian & Capstone Press Staff. Caperucita Roja. Rivas, Victor, illus. 2010. (Graphic Spin en Español Ser.). (SPA.). 40p. (gr. 1-3). lib. bdg. 25.32 *(978-1-4342-1903-9(8),* Graphic Spin en Español) Stone Arch Bks.

—Cenicienta. Feely, Maria Luisa, tr. Timmins, Jeffrey Stewart, illus. 2010. (Graphic Spin en Español Ser.). (SPA.). 40p. (gr. 1-3). lib. bdg. 25.32 *(978-1-4342-1900-8(3),* Graphic Spin en Español) Stone Arch Bks.

—Hansel y Gretel: La Novela Grafica. Dietrich, Sean, illus. 2010. (Graphic Spin en Español Ser.). (SPA.). 40p. (gr. 1-3). lib. bdg. 25.32 *(978-1-4342-1901-5(1),* Graphic Spin en Español) Stone Arch Bks.

—Jack y los Frijoles Magicos. Tercio, Ricardo, illus. 2010. (Graphic Spin en Español Ser.). (SPA.). 40p. (gr. 1-3). lib. bdg. 25.32 *(978-1-4342-1902-2(X),* Graphic Spin en Español) Stone Arch Bks.

—Rumpelstiltskin: La Novela Grafica. Valdez Y Alanis, Erik, illus. 2010. (Graphic Spin en Español Ser.). (SPA.). 40p. (gr. 1-3). lib. bdg. 25.32 *(978-1-4342-1904-6(6),* Graphic Spin en Español) Stone Arch Bks.

Andersen, Hans Christian & Stone Arch Books Staff. La Bella y la Bestia: La Novela Grafica, 1 vol. Feldman, Luke, illus. 2010. (Graphic Spin en Español Ser.). (SPA & ENG.). 40p. (gr. 1-3). pap. 5.95 *(978-1-4342-2269-5(1),* Graphic Spin en Español) Stone Arch Bks.

—Caperucita Roja. Rivas, Victor, illus. 2010. (Graphic Spin en Español Ser.). (SPA & ENG.). 40p. (gr. 1-3). pap. 5.95 *(978-1-4342-2315-9(9),* Graphic Spin en Español) Stone Arch Bks.

—Cenicienta: La Novela Grafica. Timmins, Jeffrey Stewart, illus. 2010. (Graphic Spin en Español Ser.). (SPA & ENG.). 40p. (gr. 1-3). pap. 5.95 *(978-1-4342-2270-1(5),* Graphic Spin en Español) Stone Arch Bks.

—Hansel y Gretel: La Novela Grafica. Dietrich, Sean, illus. 2010. (Graphic Spin en Español Ser.). (SPA & ENG.). 40p. (gr. 1-3). pap. 5.95 *(978-1-4342-2271-8(3),* Graphic Spin en Español) Stone Arch Bks.

—Jack y los Frijoles Magicos. Tercio, Ricardo, illus. 2010. (Graphic Spin en Español Ser.). (SPA & ENG.). 40p. (gr. 1-3). pap. 5.95 *(978-1-4342-2272-5(1),* Graphic Spin en Español) Stone Arch Bks.

—Rumpelstiltskin: La Novela Grafica, 1 vol. Alanis, Erik Valdez Y., illus. 2010. (Graphic Spin en Español Ser.). (ENG & SPA.). 40p. (gr. 1-3). pap. 5.95 *(978-1-4342-2273-2(X),* Graphic Spin en Español) Stone Arch Bks.

Andersen, Jill. All about Ramps. 2016. (Rosen REAL Readers: STEM & STEAM Collection). 8p. (gr. 1-k). pap. 5.46 *(978-1-5081-2371-2(3),* Rosen Classroom) Rosen Publishing Group, Inc., The.

—Carlos Keeps His Cool at School. 2016. (Rosen REAL Readers: Social Studies Nonfiction / Fiction: Family, Community, & the World Ser.). 12p. (gr. 1-k). pap. 6.33 *(978-1-5081-2533-4(3),* Rosen Classroom) Rosen Publishing Group, Inc., The.

—Chanice Visits the Children's Museum. 2016. (Rosen REAL Readers: Social Studies Nonfiction / Fiction: Family, Community, & the World Ser.). 8p. (gr. 1-k). pap. 5.46 *(978-1-5081-2482-5(5),* Rosen Classroom) Rosen Publishing Group, Inc., The.

—The Greatest Gift. 2016. (Rosen REAL Readers: Social Studies Nonfiction / Fiction: Family, Community, & the World Ser.). 12p. (gr. 1-k). pap. 6.33 *(978-1-5081-2541-9(4),* Rosen Classroom) Rosen Publishing Group, Inc., The.

—The Robins in Our Yard. 2016. (Rosen REAL Readers: STEM & STEAM Collection). 8p. (gr. 1-k). pap. 5.46 *(978-1-5081-2631-7(3),* Rosen Classroom) Rosen Publishing Group, Inc., The.

—A Walk in the Mountains. 2016. (Rosen REAL Readers: STEM & STEAM Collection). 8p. (gr. 1-k). pap. 5.46 *(978-1-5081-2610-2(0),* Rosen Classroom) Rosen Publishing Group, Inc., The.

—We Are Friends of the Earth. 2016. (Rosen REAL Readers: STEM & STEAM Collection). 8p. (gr. 1-k). pap. 5.46 *(978-1-5081-2616-4(X),* Rosen Classroom) Rosen Publishing Group, Inc., The.

—We Need Air to Breathe. 2016. (Rosen REAL Readers: STEM & STEAM Collection). 8p. (gr. 1-k). pap. 5.46 *(978-1-5081-2395-8(0),* Rosen Classroom) Rosen Publishing Group, Inc., The.

—Why Birds Chirp. 2016. (Rosen REAL Readers: STEM & STEAM Collection). 8p. (gr. 1-k). pap. 5.46 *(978-1-5081-2416-0(7),* Rosen Classroom) Rosen Publishing Group, Inc., The.

Andersen, Neil. WWW: Surfing with Celebrities. 2007. (Steck-Vaughn BOLDPRINT Anthologies Ser.). (ENG., Illus.). 48p. (gr. 7-9). pap. 16.90 *(978-1-4190-4029-0(4))* Houghton Mifflin Harcourt Publishing Co.

Anderson, Al. Adventures with Bingo Borden. Agora Publications Staff, tr. Kurzyca, Krystyna Emilia, illus. 2010. 77p. (J). pap. 9.50 *(978-1-887250-46-7(8))* Agora Pubns., Inc.

Anderson, James. Around Home. rev. ed. 2011. (Mathematics Readers Ser.). (ENG.). 32p. (J). (gr. k-k). pap. 8.99 *(978-1-4333-3439-9(9))* Teacher Created Materials, Inc.

—Around Town. rev. ed. 2011. (Mathematics Readers Ser.). (ENG.). 32p. (J). (gr. k-k). pap. 8.99 *(978-1-4333-3438-2(0))* Teacher Created Materials, Inc.

Anderson, Jo Marie. If I Were a Ladybug. 2017. (I'm a Bug! Ser.). 24p. (gr. 4-6). 23.60 ***(978-1-5081-5723-6(5),*** PowerKids Pr.) Rosen Publishing Group, Inc., The.

Anderson, Kris & Pearson Education Staff. The Wrong Man. 2007. (ENG., Illus.). 24p. pap. 17.32 *(978-1-4058-5204-3(6))* Pearson Education.

Anderson, Lynne. Rocket Ship Shapes. 2011. (Early Connections Ser.). (J). *(978-1-61672-596-9(6))* Benchmark Education Co.

Anderson, Nancy. All about Mirrors. 2016. (Rosen REAL Readers: STEM & STEAM Collection). 12p. (gr. 1-k). pap. 6.33 *(978-1-5081-2437-5(X),* Rosen Classroom) Rosen Publishing Group, Inc., The.

—Building Dikes. 2016. (Rosen REAL Readers: STEM & STEAM Collection). 12p. (gr. 1-k). pap. 6.33 *(978-1-5081-2464-1(7),* Rosen Classroom) Rosen Publishing Group, Inc., The.

—Election Day with the Robinsons. 2016. (Rosen REAL Readers: Social Studies Nonfiction / Fiction: Family, Community, & the World Ser.). 12p. (gr. 1-k). pap. 6.33 *(978-1-5081-2565-5(1),* Rosen Classroom) Rosen Publishing Group, Inc., The.

—Homework Help. 2016. (Rosen REAL Readers: Social Studies Nonfiction / Fiction: Family, Community, & the World Ser.). 8p. (gr. 1-k). pap. 5.46 *(978-1-5081-2500-6(7),* Rosen Classroom) Rosen Publishing Group, Inc., The.

—The House near the Pond. 2016. (Rosen REAL Readers: STEM & STEAM Collection). 8p. (gr. 1-k). pap. 5.46 *(978-1-5081-2595-2(3),* Rosen Classroom) Rosen Publishing Group, Inc., The.

—Isaiah Has a Stomachache. 2016. (Rosen REAL Readers: Social Studies Nonfiction / Fiction: Family, Community, & the World Ser.). 8p. (gr. 1-k). pap. 5.46 *(978-1-5081-2479-5(5),* Rosen Classroom) Rosen Publishing Group, Inc., The.

—The Mirror on the Wall. 2016. (Rosen REAL Readers: STEM & STEAM Collection). 12p. (gr. 1-k). pap. 6.33 *(978-1-5081-2652-2(6),* Rosen Classroom) Rosen Publishing Group, Inc., The.

—The Rocket Express. 2016. (Rosen REAL Readers: Social Studies Nonfiction / Fiction: Family, Community, & the World Ser.). 8p. (gr. 1-k). pap. 5.46 *(978-1-5081-2494-8(9),* Rosen Classroom) Rosen Publishing Group, Inc., The.

Anderson, Peggy Perry. La Niñera Dijo: "Es Hora de Ir a la Cama" 2017. (Green Light Readers Level 1 Ser.). (ENG., Illus.). 32p. (J). (gr. -1-3). pap. 3.99 *(978-0-544-80895-9(9),* HMH Books For Young Readers) Houghton Mifflin Harcourt Publishing Co.

—Time for Bed, the Babysitter Said. 2012. (Green Light Readers Level 1 Ser.). (ENG., Illus.). 32p. (J). (gr. -1-3). pap. 3.99 *(978-0-547-85061-0(1))* Houghton Mifflin Harcourt Publishing Co.

—To the Tub. 2012. (Green Light Readers Level 1 Ser.). (ENG., Illus.). 32p. (J). (gr. -1-3). pap. 3.99 *(978-0-547-85053-5(0))* Houghton Mifflin Harcourt Publishing Co.

Anderson, Scoular. Fabulous Creatures - Are They Real? Anderson, Scoular, illus. 2005. (Collins Big Cat Ser.). (ENG., Illus.). 32p. (J). (gr. 1-3). pap. 7.99 *(978-0-00-718639-6(8))* HarperCollins Pubs. Ltd. GBR. Dist: Independent Pubs. Group.

—How to Be a Knight in 10 Easy Stages. Anderson, Scoular, illus. 2007. (Collins Big Cat Ser.). (ENG., Illus.). 36p. (J). (gr. 1-2). pap. 7.99 *(978-0-00-718675-4(4))* HarperCollins Pubs. Ltd. GBR. Dist: Independent Pubs. Group.

—How to Be a Tudor in 20 Easy Stages. Anderson, Scoular, illus. 2007. (Collins Big Cat Ser.). (ENG., Illus.). 128p. (J). (gr. 3-4). pap. 8.99 *(978-0-00-723090-7(7))* HarperCollins Pubs. Ltd. GBR. Dist: Independent Pubs. Group.

—How to Be a Viking in 13 Easy Stages. Anderson, Scoular, illus. 2007. (Collins Big Cat Ser.). (ENG., Illus.). 192p. (J). (gr. 2-4). pap. 7.99 *(978-0-00-723079-2(6))* HarperCollins Pubs. Ltd. GBR. Dist: Independent Pubs. Group.

—Sticks & Bricks & Bits of Stone White Band. 2016. (Cambridge Reading Adventures Ser.). (ENG.). 32p. pap. 7.81 *(978-1-107-56056-7(X))* Cambridge Univ. Pr.

—Where on Earth? Anderson, Scoular, illus. 2005. (Collins Big Cat Ser.). (ENG., Illus.). 32p. (J). (gr. 1-3). pap. 7.99 *(978-0-00-718633-4(9))* HarperCollins Pubs. Ltd. GBR. Dist: Independent Pubs. Group.

Anderson, Sheila. Lightning Bolt Books: Our Four Seasons, 4 vols., Set. Incl. Are You Ready for Fall? lib. bdg. 26.60 *(978-0-7613-4586-2(8));* Are You Ready for Spring? lib. bdg. 26.60 *(978-0-7613-4584-8(1));* Are You Ready for Summer? lib. bdg. 26.60 *(978-0-7613-4585-5(X));* Are You Ready for Winter? lib. bdg. 26.60 *(978-0-7613-4583-1(3));* 32p. (gr. k-2). 2010. 2009. Set lib. bdg. 101.04 *(978-0-7613-4582-4(5),* Lerner Pubns.) Lerner Publishing Group.

Anderson, W. M. Action Literacy: Elephants. 2008. (Action Literacy Upper Primary Ser.). 32p. pap. 9.95 *(978-0-86431-679-0(8))* ACER Pr. AUS. Dist: ISBS Publisher Services.

Andover, Max. Octopuses & Squid. 2011. (Illus.). 16p. (J). pap. *(978-0-545-24792-4(6))* Scholastic, Inc.

Andrews, Jane. Young Reader's Series: The seven little sisters who live on the round ball that floats in the Air. 2008. 152p. pap. 14.95 *(978-1-60444-020-1(1))* IndoEuropeanPublishing.com.

Animal Parade Books 800790, 4. 2005. (J). bds. *(978-1-59794-021-4(6))* Environments, Inc.

Animal Story Board Books 800556, 5. 2005. (J). bds. *(978-1-59794-005-4(4))* Environments, Inc.

Animal Tricks. 2004. (Jasper the Cat Set 1 Ser.). (ENG., Illus.). (J). pap. 7.33 *(978-1-58453-278-1(5))* Pioneer Valley Bks.

Ankers, Angela M. Summerbook Readers: Short a & i words, 3. l.t. ed. 2004. (Illus.). 40p. (J). 5.95 *(978-1-933055-00-8(6))* Summerbook Co.

Anthony, David H. Freedom: Life after Slavery, 1 vol. 2011. (Primary Source Readers Ser.). (ENG.). 32p. (J). (gr. 5-5). pap. 8.99 *(978-1-4333-1521-3(1))* Teacher Created Materials, Inc.

—Langston Hughes: Harlem Renaissance Writer, 1 vol. 2011. (Primary Source Readers Ser.). (ENG., Illus.). 32p. (J). (gr. 4-4). pap. 8.99 *(978-1-4333-1520-6(3))* Teacher Created Materials, Inc.

Anthony, Ross. Please Don't Step on the Ants. Anthony, Ross, illus. 2006. (ENG, CHI, SPA & JPN., Illus.). (J). per. *(978-0-9727894-4-8(8))* Arizona Blueberry Studios.

Antologia: Para leer en voz Alta: Student & Teacher Support Resources. 2003. (MacMillan/McGraw-Hill. Estudios Sociales Ser.). (ENG & SPA.). (gr. 1-18). *(978-0-02-149464-4(9));* (gr. 2-18). *(978-0-02-149465-1(7));* (gr. 3-18). *(978-0-02-149466-8(5))* Macmillan/McGraw-Hill Schl. Div.

Apodaca, Blanca. All in a Day's Work: Animator, 1 vol. 2nd rev. ed. 2013. (TIME for KIDS(r) Nonfiction Readers Ser.). (ENG.). 64p. (J). (gr. 5-5). pap. 10.99 *(978-1-4333-4907-2(8))* Teacher Created Materials, Inc.

—Behind the Canvas: An Artist's Life, 1 vol. 2nd rev. ed. 2012. (TIME for KIDS(r) Nonfiction Readers Ser.). (ENG.). 48p. (J). (gr. 4-4). pap. 9.99 *(978-1-4333-4826-6(8))* Teacher Created Materials, Inc.

Appel, Marty. Pinstripe Pride: The Inside Story of the New York Yankees. 2016. lib. bdg. 24.50 *(978-0-606-38275-5(5))* Turtleback Bks.

Appleby, Alex. Feliz Da de Accin de Gracias! / Happy Thanksgiving!, Vol. 1. 2014. (¡Felices Fiestas! / Happy Holidays! Ser.). (SPA & BYN.). 24p. (J). (gr. k-k). 22.60 *(978-1-4339-9968-0(4))* Stevens, Gareth Publishing LLLP.

Appleton-Smith, Laura. Dog Agility. White, Keinyo, illus. 2007. (ENG.). 19p. (J). pap. 8.95 *(978-1-60541-012-8(8));* Books To Remember) Flyleaf Publishing.

Apte, Sunita. The March. 2005. (Illus.). 16p. pap. *(978-0-7367-2923-9(2))* Zaner-Bloser, Inc.

Apte, Sunita, text. Moving Home. 2005. (Illus.). 16p. *(978-0-7367-2954-3(2))* Zaner-Bloser, Inc.

Archer, Anita L., et al. REWARDS Plus: Reading Excellence: Reading Strategies Applied to Science Passages. 2006. (Illus.). 200p. (gr. 6-8). pap. 11.49 *(978-1-59318-286-1(4))* Cambium Education, Inc.

Aree, Bill. The Class Vote. 2009. (Real Life Readers Ser.). 12p. (gr. 1-2). pap. 5.90 *(978-1-4042-7929-2(6),* Rosen Classroom) Rosen Publishing Group, Inc., The.

Arengo, Sue. Cinderella, Level 4. 2nd ed. 2011. (ENG., Illus.). 24p. pap. 7.94 *(978-0-19-423942-4(X))* Oxford Univ. Pr., Inc.

—Classic Tales: Thumbelina. Goulding, Celeste, illus. 2006. (ENG.). 24p. 5.50 *(978-0-19-422537-3(2))* Oxford Univ. Pr. GBR. Dist: Oxford Univ. Pr., Inc.

—Jack & the Beanstalk. Ratto, Cinzia, illus. 2006. (ENG.). 24p. 5.50 *(978-0-19-422538-0(0))* Oxford Univ. Pr. GBR. Dist: Oxford Univ. Pr., Inc.

—The Princess & the Pea. 2nd ed. 2011. (ENG., Illus.). 24p. pap. 7.94 *(978-0-19-423878-6(4))* Oxford Univ. Pr., Inc.

Armour, Cy. Earthquakes!, 1 vol. 2nd rev. ed. 2011. (Nonfiction Readers Ser.). (ENG.). 24p. (J). (gr. 2-2). pap. 6.99 *(978-1-4333-3613-3(8))* Teacher Created Materials, Inc.

—Tornadoes & Hurricanes!, 1 vol. 2nd rev. ed. 2011. (Nonfiction Readers Ser.). (ENG.). 24p. (J). (gr. 2-2). pap. 6.99 *(978-1-4333-3614-0(6))* Teacher Created Materials, Inc.

—Volcanoes!, 1 vol. 2nd rev. ed. 2011. (Nonfiction Readers Ser.). (ENG.). 24p. (J). (gr. 2-2). pap. 6.99 *(978-1-4333-3615-7(4))* Teacher Created Materials, Inc.

Arnold Lobel Book Set 800917, 3 vols. 2005. (J). pap. *(978-1-59794-082-5(8))* Environments, Inc.

Arnold, Tedd. Fly Guy Presents - The White House. Arnold, Tedd, illus. 2016. (Scholastic Reader, Level 2 Ser.). (ENG., Illus.). 32p. (J). (gr. k-2). pap. 3.99 *(978-0-545-91737-7(9))* Scholastic, Inc.

—Fly Guy Presents: Castles (Scholastic Reader, Level 2) 2017. (Scholastic Reader, Level 2 Ser.). (ENG.). 32p. (J). (gr. k-2). pap. 3.99 *(978-0-545-91738-4(7))* Scholastic, Inc.

Arnone, T. I. The Magic Kazoo. 2009. (Illus.). 50p. pap. 25.00 *(978-0-557-12017-8(9))* Lulu Pr., Inc.

Arrigan, Mary. Pa Jinglebob & the Grabble Gang. 2006. (Red Bananas Ser.). (ENG., Illus.). 48p. (J). (gr. -1-3). lib. bdg. *(978-0-7787-1074-5(2))* Crabtree Publishing Co.

Art Pen Pal. 2003. 31.95 *(978-0-673-75796-8(X))* Celebration Pr.

Ashe, Susan. Cuda of the Celts. 2005. (Yellow Go Bananas Ser.). (ENG., Illus.). 48p. (J). (gr. 3-4). *(978-0-7787-2742-2(4))* Crabtree Publishing Co.

Ashley, Michele. When Do Trees Look Different? 2014. (Little Books of Answers: Level d Ser.). (Illus.). 16p. (gr. k-2). pap. 7.95 *(978-1-927136-38-6(5))* Three Crows Media NZL. Dist: RiverStream Publishing.

—Where Is This Astronaut? 2014. (Little Books of Answers: Level a Ser.). (Illus.). 16p. (gr. k-2). pap. 7.95 *(978-1-927136-06-5(7))* Three Crows Media NZL. Dist: RiverStream Publishing.

—Who Has Ears Like These? 2014. (Little Books of Answers: Level C Ser.). (Illus.). 16p. (gr. k-2). pap. 7.95 *(978-1-927136-27-0(X))* Three Crows Media NZL. Dist: RiverStream Publishing.

—Who Is This? 2014. (Little Books of Answers: Level a Ser.). (Illus.). 16p. (gr. k-2). pap. 7.95 *(978-1-927136-00-3(8))* Three Crows Media NZL. Dist: RiverStream Publishing.

—Why Does the Moon Look Different? 2014. (Little Books of Answers: Level e Ser.). (Illus.). 16p. (gr. k-2). pap. 7.95 *(978-1-927136-46-1(6))* Three Crows Media NZL. Dist: RiverStream Publishing.

Asnong, Jocey, illus. Nuptse & Lhotse Go to Iceland. 2015. (ENG.). 40p. (J). (gr. k). *(978-1-77160-124-5(8))* RMB Rocky Mountain Bks.

Asquith, Ros. Hector & the Cello. 2005. (Big Cat Ser.). pap. 6.50 *(978-1-60457-077-9(6))* Pacific Learning, Inc.

—How to Draw Cartoons. Asquith, Ros, illus. 2006. (Collins Big Cat Ser.). (ENG., Illus.). 56p. (J). (gr. 2-2). pap. 7.99 *(978-0-00-718697-6(5))* HarperCollins Pubs. Ltd. GBR. Dist: Independent Pubs. Group.

Asthma in Action. 2005. (Book Treks Ser.). (J). (gr. 3-18). stu. ed. 34.95 *(978-0-673-62843-5(4))* Celebration Pr.

Astro, Ian. Moon School. 2006. (Neighborhood Readers Ser.). (ENG.). 16p. (gr. 1-3). pap. 6.50 *(978-1-4042-7196-8(1),* Rosen Classroom) Rosen Publishing Group, Inc., The.

Astronaut Adventure. (Early Intervention Levels Ser.). 21.30 *(978-0-7362-0378-4(8))* CENGAGE Learning.

At School. (Early Intervention Levels Ser.). 3.85 *(978-1-56334-952-2(3));* 23.10 *(978-0-7362-0000-4(2))* CENGAGE Learning.

At School Set 1. 2004. (J). *(978-1-58453-262-0(9))* Pioneer Valley Bks.

At the Fair. (Early Intervention Levels Ser.). 23.10 *(978-0-7362-0013-4(4));* Vol. 2. 3.85 *(978-1-56334-963-8(9))* CENGAGE Learning.

At the Museum. (J). *(978-0-8136-5375-4(4))* Modern Curriculum Pr.

At the Toyshop: Individual Title Six-Packs. (gr. -1-2). 23.00 *(978-0-7635-9005-5(3))* Rigby Education.

Athans, Sandra K. & Parente, Robin W. Tips & Tricks for Determining Point of View & Purpose. 2014. (Common Core Readiness Guide to Reading Ser.). 80p. (J). (gr. 5-8). 32.95 *(978-1-4777-7555-4(2),* Rosen Reference) Rosen Publishing Group, Inc., The.

—Tips & Tricks for Evaluating Multimedia Content. 2014. (Common Core Readiness Guide to Reading Ser.). 80p. (YA). (gr. 5-8). 32.95 *(978-1-4777-7563-9(3),* Rosen Reference) Rosen Publishing Group, Inc., The.

Atkins, Jill. Toad Swims for his Life! Mostyn, David, illus. 2004. (ENG.). 24p. (J). lib. bdg. 23.65 *(978-1-59646-712-5(6))* Dingles & Co.

Auch, Allison. Women Who Dared: Set Of 6. 2011. (Navigators Ser.). (J). 48.00 net. *(978-1-4108-0427-3(5))* Benchmark Education Co.

Aucoin, Lee. Weather, 1 vol. 2009. (Early Childhood Themes Ser.). (ENG., Illus.). 16p. (J). (gr. -1-2). pap. 6.99 *(978-1-4333-1456-8(8));* pap. 19.99 *(978-1-4333-1457-5(6))* Shell Educational Publishing.

Austen, Elizabeth. Living!, 1 vol. rev. ed. 2014. (Science Readers: Content & Literacy Ser.). (ENG., Illus.). 24p. (gr. k-k). pap. 8.99 *(978-1-4807-4520-9(0))* Teacher Created Materials, Inc.

—Seeds, 1 vol. rev. ed. 2014. (Science Readers: Content & Literacy Ser.). (ENG., Illus.). 24p. (gr. k-k). pap. 8.99 *(978-1-4807-4522-3(7))* Teacher Created Materials, Inc.

—What Do Living Things Need?, 1 vol. rev. ed. 2014. (Science Readers: Content & Literacy Ser.). (ENG., Illus.). 24p. (gr. k-k). pap. 8.99 *(978-1-4807-4523-0(5))* Teacher Created Materials, Inc.

Austin, Judi. How Many Cookies? Learning to Subtract 1 from One-Digit Numbers. 2009. (Math for the Real World: Early Emergent Ser.). (ENG., Illus.). 8p. (gr. k-1). pap. 5.15 *(978-0-8239-8886-0(4))* Rosen Publishing Group, Inc., The.

Avenues Language & Literacy Tests: Level D Posttest Booklet (10-Pack) (Avenues Ser.). 30.00 *(978-0-7362-2516-8(1))* CENGAGE Learning.

A Avenues Level: Little Language Book Set (11 Titles) (Avenues Ser.). (gr. k-18). 41.53 *(978-0-7362-1790-3(8))* CENGAGE Learning.

A Avenues Level: Teacher Support Pack. (Avenues Ser.). (gr. k-18). 716.47 *(978-0-7362-2200-6(6))* CENGAGE Learning.

A Avenues Level: Theme Library (10 Titles), 10 vols. (Avenues Ser.). (gr. k-18). 143.98 *(978-0-7362-2108-5(5))* CENGAGE Learning.

Avenues Level B: Leveled Books & ETools. (gr. 1-18). 377.86 *(978-0-7362-2535-9(8))* CENGAGE Learning.

Avenues Level B: Literature Anthology Set, 2 vols. (Avenues Ser.). (gr. 1-18). 41.20 *(978-0-7362-2022-4(4))* CENGAGE Learning.

Avenues Level B: Teacher Support Pack. (Avenues Ser.). (gr. 1-18). 517.25 *(978-0-7362-2202-0(2))* CENGAGE Learning.

Avenues Level B: Theme Library, 12 vols. (Avenues Ser.). (gr. 1-18). 109.16 *(978-0-7362-1842-9(4))* CENGAGE Learning.

Avenues Level C: Leveled Books & ETools. (gr. 2-18). 447.46 *(978-0-7362-2536-6(6))* CENGAGE Learning.

Avenues Level C: Teacher Support Pack. (Avenues Ser.). (gr. 2-18). 405.33 *(978-0-7362-2204-4(9))* CENGAGE Learning.

Avenues Level C: Theme Library (12 Titles), 12 vols. (Avenues Ser.). (gr. 2-18). 182.78 *(978-0-7362-1891-7(2))* CENGAGE Learning.

Avenues Level D: Leveled Books & ETools. (gr. 3-18). 553.30 *(978-0-7362-2537-3(4))* CENGAGE Learning.

Avenues Level D: Theme Library (16 Titles), 16 vols. (Avenues Ser.). (gr. 3-18). 231.85 *(978-0-7362-1684-5(7))* CENGAGE Learning.

Avenues Level E: Leveled Books & ETools. (gr. 4-18). 527.49 *(978-0-7362-2538-0(2))* CENGAGE Learning.

Avenues Level E: Theme Library (16 Titles), 16 vols. (Avenues Ser.). (gr. 4-18). 186.23 *(978-0-7362-1720-0(7))* CENGAGE Learning.

Avenues Level F: Theme Library (16 Titles), 16 vols. (Avenues Ser.). (gr. 5-18). 220.14 *(978-0-7362-1756-9(8))* CENGAGE Learning.

Avenues PreK Level. 388.57 *(978-0-7362-2469-7(6))* CENGAGE Learning.

Avion, Nicole. Un tapiz de felicidad feliz (the Happy Quilt) 2006. (Lecturas del barrio (Neighborhood Readers) Ser.). (SPA.). 16p. (gr. 1-3). pap. 6.50 *(978-1-4042-7178-4(3),* Rosen Classroom) Rosen Publishing Group, Inc., The.

Award, Anna. Hansel & Gretel. 2012. (ENG.). 24p. (J). pap. 9.95 *(978-1-84135-514-6(3))* Award Pubns. Ltd. GBR. Dist: Parkwest Pubns., Inc.

Award, Anna & Aesop. The Lion & the Mouse with the Donkey & the Lapdog. Biro, Val, illus. 2014. (ENG.). 24p. (J). pap. 6.95 *(978-1-84135-953-3(X))* Award Pubns. Ltd. GBR. Dist: Parkwest Pubns., Inc.

Award, Anna & Biro, Val. The Bear & the Travellers & the Ducks & the Tortoise. 2014. (ENG.). 24p. (J). pap. 6.95 *(978-1-84135-959-5(9))* Award Pubns. Ltd. GBR. Dist: Parkwest Pubns., Inc.

Award, Anna, et al. The Boy Who Cried Wolf & the Goose That Laid the Golden Eggs. 2014. (ENG.). 24p. (J). pap. 6.95 *(978-1-84135-957-1(2))* Award Pubns. Ltd. GBR. Dist: Parkwest Pubns., Inc.

—The Eagle & the Man with the Town Mouse & the Country Mouse. 2014. (ENG.). 24p. (J). pap. 6.95 *(978-1-84135-958-8(0))* Award Pubns. Ltd. GBR. Dist: Parkwest Pubns., Inc.

—The Farmer & His Sons & the Donkey in the Lion's Den. 2014. (ENG.). 24p. (J). pap. 6.95 *(978-1-84135-960-1(2))* Award Pubns. Ltd. GBR. Dist: Parkwest Pubns., Inc.

—The Fox & the Stork & the Man, His Son & the Donkey. 2014. (ENG.). 24p. (J). pap. 6.95 *(978-1-84135-955-7(6))* Award Pubns. Ltd. GBR. Dist: Parkwest Pubns., Inc.

—Monkey & the Fishermen & the Donkey in the Pond. 2014. (ENG.). 24p. (J). pap. 6.95 *(978-1-84135-956-4(4))* Award Pubns. Ltd. GBR. Dist: Parkwest Pubns., Inc.

—The Sick Lion & Hare & the Tortoise. 2014. (ENG.). 24p. (J). pap. 6.95 *(978-1-84135-954-0(8))* Award Pubns. Ltd. GBR. Dist: Parkwest Pubns., Inc.

Award Publications Staff. Jack & the Beanstalk. 2012. (ENG., Illus.). 24p. pap. 6.50 *(978-1-84135-537-5(2))* Award Pubns. Ltd. GBR. Dist: Parkwest Pubns., Inc.

Away from Home: Fourth Grade Guided Comprehension Level M. (On Our Way to English Ser.). (gr. 4-18). 34.50 *(978-0-7578-7155-9(0))* Rigby Education.

Awdry, Wilbert V. The Rocket Returns. 2014. (Step into Reading Ser.). (ENG., Illus.). 32p. (J). (gr. -1-1). lib. bdg. 12.99 *(978-0-375-97204-1(8),* Random Hse. Bks. for Young Readers) Random Hse. Children's Bks.

Ayder, Earl. The Longest Shortcut. McGrellis, Cynthia, illus. 2005. 40p. pap. 8.53 *(978-0-7578-9857-0(2))* Rigby Education.

Baby Animals Board Books 800849, 4 vols. 2005. (J). bds. *(978-1-59794-050-4(X))* Environments, Inc.

Baby Faces Board Books 800669, 5. 2005. (J). bds. *(978-1-59794-010-8(0))* Environments, Inc.
Baby Love Board Book Set 800703, 4. 2005. (J). bds. *(978-1-59794-012-2(7))* Environments, Inc.
Baby Play Board Book Set 800807, 2. 2005. (J). bds. *(978-1-59794-044-3(5))* Environments, Inc.
Baby's Birthday: Individual Title Six-Packs. (Literatura 2000 Ser.). (gr. k-1). 28.00 *(978-0-7635-0021-4(6))* Rigby Education.
Baby's World Board Books 800848, 4. 2005. (J). bds. *(978-1-59794-049-8(6))* Environments, Inc.
Bad Bat. 2012. (Collins Big Cat Ser.). (ENG.). 16p. (J). pap., wbk. ed. 4.99 *(978-0-00-747282-6(X))* HarperCollins Pubs. Ltd. GBR. Dist: Independent Pubs. Group.
Baer, Jill. Just One of the Princes. 2014. (Sofia the First World of Reading Ser.). (J). lib. bdg. 13.55 *(978-0-606-35263-5(5))* Turtleback Bks.
Bage, Grant. Crime & Punishment Through the Ages: Band 18/Pearl. 2017. (ENG., Illus.). 80p. (J). pap. 9.99 ***(978-0-00-820899-8(9))*** HarperCollins Pubs. Ltd. GBR. Dist: Independent Pubs. Group.
Bage, Grant & Collins UK Staff. The Story of Football. 2016. (ENG.). 56p. (J). (gr. 5-6). pap. 9.95 *(978-0-00-816398-3(7))* HarperCollins Pubs. Ltd. GBR. Dist: Independent Pubs. Group.
Baghdasaryan, Rouzanna. Moush Wants to Get Lost. Yulia, Lushnikova, illus. 2010. (ARA.). 32p. (J). pap. 16.95 *(978-1-60195-091-8(8))* International Step by Step Assn.
Bagnoli, Christine. Miguel's Family Picnic. 2006. (Neighborhood Readers Ser.). (ENG.). 16p. (gr. 1-3). pap. 6.50 *(978-1-4042-7006-0(X)*, Rosen Classroom) Rosen Publishing Group, Inc., The.
Baillie, Allan. Archie the Big Good Wolf Vol. 9: Band 15/Emerald. Ogden, Betina, illus. 2007. (Collins Big Cat Ser.). (ENG.). 32p. (J). pap. 8.99 *(978-0-00-723421-9(X))* HarperCollins Pubs. Ltd. GBR. Dist: Independent Pubs. Group.
Bains-Fort. It's Keen to Be Green. 2009. 40p. pap. 23.49 *(978-1-4389-9145-0(2))* AuthorHouse.
Baker, Chris. A Year in Barrowswold Forest: Band 15/Emerald. 2017. (ENG.). 48p. (J). pap. 8.99 ***(978-0-00-820886-8(7))*** HarperCollins Pubs. Ltd. GBR. Dist: Independent Pubs. Group.
Baker, Clara B. & Baker, Edna D. Reading for Children: First Book. Betts, George Herbert, ed. 2011. 192p. 42.95 *(978-1-258-08279-6(9))* Literary Licensing, LLC.
Baker, Keith. At the Park: A Mr. & Mrs. Green Adventure. 2016. (Green Light Readers Level 2 Ser.). (ENG., Illus.). 32p. (J). (gr. 1-4). pap. 3.99 *(978-0-544-55556-3(2)*, HMH Books For Young Readers) Houghton Mifflin Harcourt Publishing Co.
Baker, Sara, illus. Ready to Read Sleeping Beauty. 2007. (Ready to Read Ser.). 31p. (J). (gr. k-2). *(978-1-84610-441-1(6))* Make Believe Ideas.
Baldwin, James. Fifty Famous Stories Retold. 2008. 100p. pap. 9.50 *(978-1-60459-518-5(3))* Wilder Pubns., Corp.
—Old Greek Storie. 2006. (Illus.). pap. *(978-1-4065-0511-5(0))* Dodo Pr.
—Old Greek Stories. 2005. 192p. pap. 11.95 *(978-1-4218-0155-1(8)*, 1st World Library - Literary Society) 1st World Publishing, Inc.
—Old Greek Stories. 2007. (ENG.). 134p. pap. 18.99 *(978-1-4346-2275-4(4))*; pap. 19.99 *(978-1-4346-2333-1(5))* Creative Media Partners, LLC.
—Old Greek Stories. 2004. reprint ed. pap. 19.95 *(978-1-4191-3803-4(0))*; pap. 1.99 *(978-1-4192-3803-1(5))* Kessinger Publishing, LLC.
—Old Greek Stories. 2008. (Illus.). 192p. pap. 9.95 *(978-1-59915-296-7(7))* Yesterday's Classics.
Ball, Nate. Forces of Nature. 2015. (Alien in My Pocket Ser.: 6). (J). lib. bdg. 14.75 *(978-0-606-37611-2(9))* Turtleback Bks.
Ballantyne, Robert Michael. Silver Lake. 2007. (ENG.). 116p. pap. 18.99 *(978-1-4346-3759-8(X))*; 130p. pap. 19.99 *(978-1-4346-3773-4(5))* Creative Media Partners, LLC.
Bank Street College. Sacajawea: the Jacabee Readers: The Adventures of Dooley, Abby & Baldy. 2012. (ENG.). 96p. (J). (gr. 1-3). pap. 9.95 *(978-1-59687-879-2(7)*, Milk & Cookies) ibooks, Inc.
Banner, Angela. Ant & Bee. 2014. (Ant & Bee Ser.: 1). (ENG., Illus.). 112p. (Orig.). (J). (gr. -1-k). 7.99 *(978-1-4052-6671-0(6))* Egmont Bks., Ltd. GBR. Dist: Independent Pubs. Group.
—Ant & Bee & Kind Dog. 2014. (Ant & Bee Ser.). (ENG., Illus.). 112p. (J). (gr. -1-k). 7.99 *(978-1-4052-7075-5(6))* Egmont Bks., Ltd. GBR. Dist: Independent Pubs. Group.
—Ant & Bee & the ABC. 2014. (Ant & Bee Ser.). (ENG., Illus.). 96p. (J). (gr. -1-k). 7.99 *(978-1-4052-7074-8(8))* Egmont Bks., Ltd. GBR. Dist: Independent Pubs. Group.
—Ant & Bee & the Doctor. 2014. (Ant & Bee Ser.). (ENG., Illus.). 88p. (J). (gr. -1-k). 7.99 *(978-1-4052-7073-1(X))* Egmont Bks., Ltd. GBR. Dist: Independent Pubs. Group.
—Ant & Bee & the Rainbow. 2014. (Ant & Bee Ser.). (ENG., Illus.). 96p. (J). (gr. -1-k). 7.99 *(978-1-4052-6674-1(0))* Egmont Bks., Ltd. GBR. Dist: Independent Pubs. Group.
—Ant & Bee Count 123. 2015. (Ant & Bee Ser.). (ENG., Illus.). 96p. (J). (gr. -1-k). 7.99 *(978-1-4052-7513-2(8))* Egmont Bks., Ltd. GBR. Dist: Independent Pubs. Group.
—Ant & Bee Go Shopping. 2015. (Ant & Bee Ser.). (ENG., Illus.). 84p. (J). (gr. -1-k). 7.99 *(978-1-4052-7514-9(6))* Egmont Bks., Ltd. GBR. Dist: Independent Pubs. Group.
—Ant & Bee Three Story Collection. 2016. (Ant & Bee Ser.). (ENG., Illus.). 336p. (J). (gr. -1-k). 15.99 *(978-1-4052-7932-1(X))* Egmont Bks., Ltd. GBR. Dist: Independent Pubs. Group.
—Ant & Bee Time. 2015. (Ant & Bee Ser.). (ENG., Illus.). 96p. (J). (gr. -1-k). 7.99 *(978-1-4052-7516-3(2))* Egmont Bks., Ltd. GBR. Dist: Independent Pubs. Group.
—Around the World with Ant & Bee. 2014. (Ant & Bee Ser.). (ENG., Illus.). 96p. (J). (gr. -1-k). 7.99 *(978-1-4052-6676-5(7))* Egmont Bks., Ltd. GBR. Dist: Independent Pubs. Group.
—Happy Birthday with Ant & Bee. 2014. (Ant & Bee Ser.). (ENG., Illus.). 96p. (J). (gr. -1-k). 7.99 *(978-1-4052-6675-8(9))* Egmont Bks., Ltd. GBR. Dist: Independent Pubs. Group.
—Left & Right with Ant & Bee. 2016. (Ant & Bee Ser.). (ENG., Illus.). 96p. (J). (gr. -1-k). 7.99 *(978-1-4052-7929-1(X))* Egmont Bks., Ltd. GBR. Dist: Independent Pubs. Group.
—Make a Million with Ant & Bee. 2016. (Ant & Bee Ser.). (ENG., Illus.). 96p. (J). (gr. -1-k). 7.99 *(978-1-4052-7930-7(3))* Egmont Bks., Ltd. GBR. Dist: Independent Pubs. Group.
—More Ant & Bee. 2014. (Ant & Bee Ser.: 2). (ENG., Illus.). 112p. (J). (gr. -1-k). 7.99 *(978-1-4052-6672-7(4))* Egmont Bks., Ltd. GBR. Dist: Independent Pubs. Group.
Barbour Publishing Staff, compiled by. What's an Alpha-Beta-Soupa? An Indispensable Guide to College. 2005. 192p. pap. 4.97 *(978-1-59310-664-5(5))* Barbour Publishing, Inc.
Barchers, Suzanne I. A Big Job, 1 vol. 2011. (Targeted Phonics Ser.). (ENG., Illus.). 16p. (J). (gr. k-2). pap. 5.99 *(978-1-4333-2413-0(X))* Teacher Created Materials, Inc.
—A Box for Ross, 1 vol. 2011. (Targeted Phonics Ser.). (ENG., Illus.). 16p. (J). (gr. k-2). pap. 5.99 *(978-1-4333-2415-4(6))* Teacher Created Materials, Inc.
—Dad Wants a Nap, 1 vol. 2011. (Targeted Phonics Ser.). (ENG., Illus.). 16p. (J). (gr. k-2). pap. 5.99 *(978-1-4333-2407-9(5))* Teacher Created Materials, Inc.
—Fix It!, 1 vol. 2011. (Targeted Phonics Ser.). (ENG., Illus.). 16p. (J). (gr. k-2). pap. 5.99 *(978-1-4333-2423-9(7))* Teacher Created Materials, Inc.
—Get to Bed, Ren!, 1 vol. 2011. (Targeted Phonics Ser.). (ENG.). 16p. (J). (gr. k-2). pap. 5.99 *(978-1-4333-2416-1(4))* Teacher Created Materials, Inc.
—Green Peas in Cream, 1 vol. 2011. (Targeted Phonics Ser.). (ENG.). 16p. (J). (gr. k-2). pap. 5.99 *(978-1-4333-2916-6(6))* Teacher Created Materials, Inc.
—Gus in the Tub, 1 vol. 2011. (Targeted Phonics Ser.). (ENG., Illus.). 16p. (J). (gr. k-2). pap. 5.99 *(978-1-4333-2419-2(9))* Teacher Created Materials, Inc.
—How Big Is Kip?, 1 vol. 2011. (Targeted Phonics Ser.). (ENG., Illus.). 16p. (J). (gr. k-2). pap. 5.99 *(978-1-4333-2410-9(5))* Teacher Created Materials, Inc.
—Kate & Gail, 1 vol. 2011. (Targeted Phonics Ser.). (ENG., Illus.). 16p. (J). (gr. k-2). pap. 5.99 *(978-1-4333-2907-4(7))* Teacher Created Materials, Inc.
—Kip Gets Fit, 1 vol. 2011. (Targeted Phonics Ser.). (ENG.). 16p. (J). (gr. k-2). pap. 5.99 *(978-1-4333-2412-3(1))* Teacher Created Materials, Inc.
—Kip Gets Sick, 1 vol. 2011. (Targeted Phonics Ser.). (ENG., Illus.). 16p. (J). (gr. k-2). pap. 5.99 *(978-1-4333-2422-2(9))* Teacher Created Materials, Inc.
—Kip Wins!, 1 vol. 2011. (Targeted Phonics Ser.). (ENG., Illus.). 16p. (J). (gr. k-2). pap. 5.99 *(978-1-4333-2411-6(3))* Teacher Created Materials, Inc.
—Late Kate, 1 vol. 2011. (Targeted Phonics Ser.). (ENG.). 16p. (J). (gr. k-2). pap. 5.99 *(978-1-4333-2906-7(9))* Teacher Created Materials, Inc.
—Luce & Duke, 1 vol. 2011. (Targeted Phonics Ser.). (ENG., Illus.). 16p. (J). (gr. k-2). pap. 5.99 *(978-1-4333-2919-7(0))* Teacher Created Materials, Inc.
—Main Street Block Party, 1 vol. 2011. (Targeted Phonics Ser.). (ENG.). 16p. (J). (gr. k-2). pap. 5.99 *(978-1-4333-2923-4(9))* Teacher Created Materials, Inc.
—Main Street Game Day, 1 vol. 2011. (Targeted Phonics Ser.). (ENG.). 16p. (J). (gr. k-2). pap. 5.99 *(978-1-4333-2922-7(0))* Teacher Created Materials, Inc.
—Main Street Parade, 1 vol. 2011. (Targeted Phonics Ser.). (ENG.). 16p. (J). (gr. k-2). pap. 5.99 *(978-1-4333-2921-0(2))* Teacher Created Materials, Inc.
—Mike Makes up His Mind, 1 vol. 2011. (Targeted Phonics Ser.). (ENG.). 16p. (J). (gr. k-2). pap. 5.99 *(978-1-4333-2911-1(5))* Teacher Created Materials, Inc.
—On a Walk with Ren, 1 vol. 2011. (Targeted Phonics Ser.). (ENG., Illus.). 16p. (J). (gr. k-2). pap. 5.99 *(978-1-4333-2417-8(2))* Teacher Created Materials, Inc.
—On My Stoop, 1 vol. 2011. (Targeted Phonics Ser.). (ENG., Illus.). 16p. (J). (gr. k-2). pap. 5.99 *(978-1-4333-2920-3(4))* Teacher Created Materials, Inc.
—On the Road with Rose & Bose, 1 vol. 2011. (Targeted Phonics Ser.). (ENG.). 16p. (J). (gr. k-2). pap. 5.99 *(978-1-4333-2914-2(X))* Teacher Created Materials, Inc.
—Pack a Bag!, 1 vol. 2011. (Targeted Phonics Ser.). (ENG.). 16p. (J). (gr. k-2). pap. 5.99 *(978-1-4333-2409-3(1))* Teacher Created Materials, Inc.
—Pete Has Fast Feet, 1 vol. 2011. (Targeted Phonics Ser.). (ENG., Illus.). 16p. (J). (gr. k-2). pap. 5.99 *(978-1-4333-2915-9(8))* Teacher Created Materials, Inc.
—Read with Gus, 1 vol. 2011. (Targeted Phonics Ser.). (ENG.). 16p. (J). (gr. k-2). pap. 5.99 *(978-1-4333-2420-8(2))* Teacher Created Materials, Inc.
—Ren in a Mess, 1 vol. 2011. (Targeted Phonics Ser.). (ENG.). 16p. (J). (gr. k-2). pap. 5.99 *(978-1-4333-2418-5(0))* Teacher Created Materials, Inc.
—Rose & Bose, 1 vol. 2011. (Targeted Phonics Ser.). (ENG., Illus.). 16p. (J). (gr. k-2). pap. 5.99 *(978-1-4333-2913-5(1))* Teacher Created Materials, Inc.
—Rose & Dad, 1 vol. 2011. (Targeted Phonics Ser.). (ENG.). 16p. (J). (gr. k-2). pap. 5.99 *(978-1-4333-2912-8(3))* Teacher Created Materials, Inc.
—Spy It!, 1 vol. 2011. (Targeted Phonics Ser.). (ENG., Illus.). 16p. (J). (gr. k-2). pap. 5.99 *(978-1-4333-2910-4(7))* Teacher Created Materials, Inc.
—To the Dunes with Luce, 1 vol. 2011. (Targeted Phonics Ser.). (ENG., Illus.). 16p. (J). (gr. k-2). pap. 5.99 *(978-1-4333-2918-0(2))* Teacher Created Materials, Inc.
—Top That!, 1 vol. 2011. (Targeted Phonics Ser.). (ENG., Illus.). 16p. (J). (gr. k-2). pap. 5.99 *(978-1-4333-2414-7(8))* Teacher Created Materials, Inc.
—Twice as Nice: Long Vowel Storybooks, 1 vol. 2011. (Targeted Phonics Ser.). (ENG.). 16p. (J). (gr. k-2). pap. 5.99 *(978-1-4333-2909-8(3))* Teacher Created Materials, Inc.
—What Can I Read?, 1 vol. 2011. (Targeted Phonics Ser.). (ENG., Illus.). 16p. (J). (gr. k-2). pap. 5.99 *(978-1-4333-2917-3(4))* Teacher Created Materials, Inc.
—What Can San Do?, 1 vol. 2011. (Targeted Phonics Ser.). (ENG., Illus.). 16p. (J). (gr. k-2). pap. 5.99 *(978-1-4333-2408-6(3))* Teacher Created Materials, Inc.
—What Luck!, 1 vol. 2011. (Targeted Phonics Ser.). (ENG.). 16p. (J). (gr. k-2). pap. 5.99 *(978-1-4333-2421-5(0))* Teacher Created Materials, Inc.
—You Can Do It!, 1 vol. 2011. (Targeted Phonics Ser.). (ENG., Illus.). 16p. (J). (gr. k-2). pap. 5.99 *(978-1-4333-2424-6(5))* Teacher Created Materials, Inc.
Barchers, Suzanne I. & Teacher Created Materials Staff. Big Day for Kate, 1 vol. 2011. (Targeted Phonics Ser.). (ENG., Illus.). 16p. (J). (gr. k-2). pap. 5.99 *(978-1-4333-2908-1(5))* Teacher Created Materials, Inc.
Bardswich, Elizabeth & Bardswich, Miriam. Out There - Travel. 2007. (Steck-Vaughn BOLDPRINT Anthologies Ser.). (ENG., Illus.). 48p. (gr. 8-10). pap. 16.90 *(978-1-4190-4030-6(8))* Houghton Mifflin Harcourt Publishing Co.
Barella, Laura, illus. Sleeping Beauty. 2009. (Flip-Up Fairy Tales Ser.). (ENG.). 24p. (J). (gr. -1-2). audio compact disk *(978-1-84643-295-8(2))* Child's Play International Ltd.
Barker, Charles Ferguson. Under Ohio: The Story of Ohio's Rocks & Fossils. 2016. (ENG.). 56p. pap. 17.95 *(978-0-8214-2195-6(6))* Ohio Univ. Pr.
Barker, Lori. How Do They Make That? rev. ed. 2012. (Mathematics Readers Ser.). (ENG.). 32p. (J). (gr. 6-6). pap. 8.99 *(978-1-4333-3453-5(4))* Teacher Created Materials, Inc.
—Land Animals. rev. ed. 2012. (Mathematics Readers Ser.). (ENG.). 32p. (J). (gr. 6-6). pap. 8.99 *(978-1-4333-3456-6(9))* Teacher Created Materials, Inc.
—On the Road: Ratios & Proportions. rev. ed. 2012. (Mathematics Readers Ser.). (ENG.). 32p. (J). (gr. 6-6). pap. 8.99 *(978-1-4333-3450-4(X))* Teacher Created Materials, Inc.
—Our New Car. rev. ed. 2012. (Mathematics Readers Ser.). (ENG.). 32p. (J). (gr. 6-6). pap. 8.99 *(978-1-4333-3451-1(8))* Teacher Created Materials, Inc.
—Sea Creatures. rev. ed. 2012. (Mathematics Readers Ser.). (ENG.). 32p. (J). (gr. 6-6). pap. 8.99 *(978-1-4333-3457-3(7))* Teacher Created Materials, Inc.
—Watch It Grow. rev. ed. 2012. (Mathematics Readers Ser.). (ENG.). 32p. (J). (gr. 6-6). pap. 8.99 *(978-1-4333-3454-2(2))* Teacher Created Materials, Inc.
—What Did I Eat? rev. ed. 2012. (Mathematics Readers Ser.). (ENG.). 32p. (J). (gr. 6-6). pap. 8.99 *(978-1-4333-3452-8(6))* Teacher Created Materials, Inc.
—Where Germs Lurk. rev. ed. 2012. (Mathematics Readers Ser.). (ENG.). 32p. (J). (gr. 6-6). pap. 8.99 *(978-1-4333-3455-9(0))* Teacher Created Materials, Inc.
Barkley, Callie. Amy on Park Patrol. 2017. (Critter Club Ser.: 17). lib. bdg. 16.00 ***(978-0-606-40208-8(X))*** Turtleback Bks.
Barlow, Helen. Easy read with grandma Read: Book 1, Stage 1. 2008. (ENG., Illus.). 48p. per. *(978-1-84748-262-4(7))* Athena Pr.
Barnyard Board Book Set 800784, 5. 2005. (J). bds. *(978-1-59794-019-1(4))* Environments, Inc.
Baron, Jessica. Let's Make Music. 2008. (Real Readers - Upper Emergent Ser.). (ENG., Illus.). 12p. (gr. 1-2). pap. 5.90 *(978-0-8239-8193-9(2))* Rosen Publishing Group, Inc., The.
—What's in the Garden? Learning to Compare Two Sets of Objects. 2009. (Math for the Real World: Early Emergent Ser.). (ENG., Illus.). 8p. (gr. k-1). pap. 5.15 *(978-0-8239-8860-0(0))* Rosen Publishing Group, Inc., The.
Barone, Bill. So Many Scoops! 2006. (Neighborhood Readers Ser.). (ENG.). 16p. (gr. 1-3). pap. 6.50 *(978-1-4042-7164-7(3)*, Rosen Classroom) Rosen Publishing Group, Inc., The.
Barr, Brady & Curtis, Jennifer Keats. Hasta la Vista, Cocodrilo: El Diario de Alexa. Detwiler, Susan, illus. 2016. (SPA.). 32p. (J). (gr. k-3). pap. 9.95 *(978-1-62855-836-4(9))* Arbordale Publishing.
Barr, Linda. Long Road to Freedom: Journey of the Hmong, 6 vols. 2004. (High Five Reading - Purple Ser.). (ENG.). 64p. (gr. 3-4). pap. 54.00 *(978-0-7368-3870-2(8)*, High Five Reading (RBL)) Capstone Press of Coughlan Cos.
Barraclough, Sue. Farm Animals. 2009. (Me & My World Ser.). (Illus.). 24p. (J). (gr. -1-2). pap. 8.15 *(978-1-60754-060-1(6))*; lib. bdg. 22.60 *(978-1-60754-056-4(8))* Windmill Bks.
—On the Move. 2009. (Me & My World Ser.). (Illus.). 24p. (J). (gr. -1-2). pap. 8.15 *(978-1-60754-064-9(9))*; lib. bdg. 22.60 *(978-1-60754-058-8(4))* Windmill Bks.
Barrett, Jennifer. Lethal Delivery, Postage Prepaid. (Thumbprint Mysteries Ser.). 32.86 *(978-0-8092-0425-0(8))* McGraw-Hill/Contemporary.
Barretta, Gene. Dear Deer: A Book of Homophones. 2007. (J). (gr. k-3). 29.95 incl. audio compact disk *(978-0-8045-4181-7(7))*; 27.95 incl. audio *(978-0-8045-6958-3(4))* Spoken Arts, Inc.
Barrie, J. M. Peter Pan: An Illustrated Classic for Kids & Young Readers (Excellent for Bedtime & Young Readers) eMusic, Tom, ed. Friday, Arthur, illus. 2013. 38p. pap. 6.99 *(978-1-62321-067-0(4))* Tommye-music Corp. DBA Tom eMusic.
Bartch, Lea & Mangrum, Kaylea J. Tucker Goes to Kindergarten. Mangrum, Kaylea J., illus. 2013. (Illus.). 54p. pap. 14.99 *(978-0-9883009-5-8(8))* Mangrum, Kaylea J.
Barwick, Sail Main5 Weather Alert Nf. 2003. (Rigby Sails Ser.). (ENG.). 32p. (gr. 5-5). pap. 9.50 *(978-0-7578-8020-9(7))* Rigby Education.
Basic Book Set 800082, 20 vols. 2005. (J). bds. *(978-1-59794-000-9(3))* Environments, Inc.
Bassett, Jennifer. Milo, 1. 2014. (Garnet Oracle Readers Ser.). (Illus.). 40p. pap., stu. ed. 4.50 *(978-1-907575-16-7(2))* Garnet Education GBR. Dist: Garnet Publishing, Ltd.
—The Watchers, 4. 2014. (Garnet Oracle Readers Ser.). (Illus.). 32p. pap., stu. ed. 4.50 *(978-1-907575-17-4(0))* Garnet Education GBR. Dist: Garnet Publishing, Ltd.
Bassett, Jennifer, ed. Long White Cloud: Stories from New Zealand. 3rd ed. 2008. (ENG., Illus.). 80p. 10.00 *(978-0-19-479139-7(4))* Oxford Univ. Pr., Inc.
Bassett, Jennifer & Stewart, Sue. Recycling. Oxford University Press Staff & Lindop, Christine, eds. 3rd ed. 2008. (ENG., Illus.). 80p. 10.00 *(978-0-19-423389-7(8))* Oxford Univ. Pr., Inc.
Bates, Matthew. The Ways We Use Water. 2012. (InfoMax Readers Ser.). (ENG., Illus.). 24p. (J). (gr. 1-2). pap. 8.25 *(978-1-4488-9013-2(6)*, Rosen Classroom) Rosen Publishing Group, Inc., The.
Batham, Matthew. Lightsleep. 2006. 167p. pap. *(978-1-904623-39-7(5))* WritersPrintShop.
Batkhuu, Kh. The Doll That Flew Away. Myagmardorj, Enkhtungalag, illus. 2007. (ARA & ENG.). 32p. (J). pap. 12.95 *(978-1-60195-092-5(6))* International Step by Step Assn.
Bauer, David. Adding Arctic Animals, 6 vols., Set. 2003. (Yellow Umbrella Early Level Ser.). (ENG.). 16p. (gr. k-1). pap. 35.70 *(978-0-7368-2990-8(3)*, Yellow Umbrella Bks.) Capstone Press of Coughlan Cos.
Bawden, Deborah. The Ogre. 2017. (Collins Big Cat Tales Ser.). (ENG., Illus.). 32p. (J). (gr. 2-4). pap. 8.99 *(978-0-00-817936-6(0))* HarperCollins Pubs. Ltd. GBR. Dist: Independent Pubs. Group.
Bawden, Deborah & Collins UK Publishing Staff. The Honey-Guide Bird. Auriemma, Monica, illus. 2016. (ENG.). 32p. (J). pap. 8.95 *(978-0-00-814710-5(8))* HarperCollins Pubs. Ltd. GBR. Dist: Independent Pubs. Group.
Baxter, Nicola. Trouble in Space: A First Reading Adventure Book. Ball, Geoff, illus. 2015. (ENG.). 24p. pap. 6.99 *(978-1-86147-491-9(1)*, Armadillo) Anness Publishing GBR. Dist: National Bk. Network.
—Trouble in the Jungle: A First Reading Adventure Book. Ball, Geoff, illus. 2015. (ENG.). 24p. pap. 6.99 *(978-1-86147-494-0(6)*, Armadillo) Anness Publishing GBR. Dist: National Bk. Network.
—Trouble on the Ice: First Reading Books for 3-5 Year Olds. Ball, Geoff, illus. 2015. (ENG.). 24p. pap. 6.99 *(978-1-86147-492-6(X)*, Armadillo) Anness Publishing GBR. Dist: National Bk. Network.
BBB Bats Song. (Song Box Ser.). (gr. 1-2). 8.50 incl. audio *(978-0-322-00247-0(8))* Wright Group/McGraw-Hill.
BBB Bats Song Big Book. (Song Box Ser.). (gr. 1-2). 31.50 *(978-0-322-00264-7(8))* Wright Group/McGraw-Hill.
BBB Bats Song Small Books Pack of 6, 6 vols. (Song Box Ser.). (gr. 1-2). 29.50 *(978-0-322-00269-2(9))* Wright Group/McGraw-Hill.
Bear Story Board Books 800655, 5. 2005. (J). bds. *(978-1-59794-007-8(0))* Environments, Inc.
Beardsley, Sally. The 10 Bravest Everyday Heroes. 2007. 14.99 *(978-1-55448-488-1(X))* Scholastic Library Publishing.
Beaton, Clare & Blackstone, Stella. Cerdota Grandota. Beaton, Clare, illus. 2006.Tr. of How Big Is a Pig. (ENG., Illus.). 24p. (J). (gr. -1-k). bds. 6.99 *(978-1-84686-018-8(0))* Barefoot Bks., Inc.
Beatty, Ken & Pearson Education Staff. Secret Codes. 2007. (ENG.). 80p. pap. 17.32 incl. cd-rom *(978-1-4058-5222-7(4))* Pearson Education.
Beaver, Simon. Dangerous & Dirty Jobs Low Intermediate Book with Online Access. 2014. (ENG., Illus.). 28p. pap. 9.50 *(978-1-107-64567-7(0))* Cambridge Univ. Pr.
—Slice by Slice: The Story of Pizza. 2014. (ENG.). 24p. (J). pap. 9.50 *(978-1-107-65037-4(2))* Cambridge Univ. Pr.
—Traffic Jams: the Road Ahead Beginning Book with Online Access. 2014. (ENG., Illus.). 24p. (J). pap. 9.50 *(978-1-107-67468-4(9))* Cambridge Univ. Pr.
BeaverSimon. FANTASTIC CREATURES: MONSTERS, MERMAIDS, AND WILD MEN BEGINNING BOOK WITH ONLINE ACCESS. 2014. (ENG.). 24p. (J). pap. 9.50 *(978-1-107-69637-2(2))* Cambridge Univ. Pr.
—A LIGHT IN THE NIGHT: THE MOON BEGINNING BOOK WITH ONLINE ACCESS. 2014. (ENG.). 24p. (J). pap. 9.50 *(978-1-107-64756-5(8))* Cambridge Univ. Pr.
—PARIS: CITY OF LIGHT BEGINNING BOOK WITH ONLINE ACCESS. 2014. (ENG.). 24p. (J). pap. 9.50 *(978-1-107-64577-6(8))* Cambridge Univ. Pr.
—SAVED! HEROES IN EVERYDAY LIFE BEGINNING BOOK WITH ONLINE ACCESS. 2014. (ENG., Illus.). 24p. pap. 7.50 *(978-1-107-64705-3(3))* Cambridge Univ. Pr.
—SPORT, GAME OR HOBBY? LOW INTERMEDIATE BOOK WITH ONLINE ACCESS. 2014. (ENG., Illus.). 48p. (J). pap. 9.50 *(978-1-107-68658-8(X))* Cambridge Univ. Pr.
—WILD AUSTRALIA! BEGINNING BOOK WITH ONLINE ACCESS. 2014. (ENG., Illus.). 24p. (J). pap. 9.50 *(978-1-107-62165-7(8))* Cambridge Univ. Pr.
—YOUNG AND AMAZING: TEENS AT THE TOP HIGH BEGINNING BOOK WITH ONLINE ACCESS. 2014. (ENG., Illus.). 24p. pap. 9.50 *(978-1-107-62252-4(2))* Cambridge Univ. Pr.
Because I'm Little, 6 Packs. (gr. -1-2). 23.00 *(978-0-7635-8798-7(2))* Rigby Education.
Beck, Isabel L., et al. Decodable Books Collections. 2003. (Trophies Ser.). (gr. 1-18). 15.60 *(978-0-15-326719-2(4))*; (gr. 1-18). 15.60 *(978-0-15-326718-5(6))*; (gr. 1-18). 15.60 *(978-0-15-326717-8(8))*; (gr. 1-18). 15.60 *(978-0-15-326716-1(X))*; (gr. 1-18). 15.60 *(978-0-15-326715-4(1))*; (gr. 1-18). 15.60 *(978-0-15-326747-5(X))*; (gr. 1-18). 15.60 *(978-0-15-326746-8(1))*; (gr. 1-18). 15.60 *(978-0-15-326745-1(3))*; (gr. 1-18). 15.60 *(978-0-15-326743-7(7))*; (gr. 1-18). 15.60 *(978-0-15-326742-0(9))*; (gr. 1-18). 15.60 *(978-0-15-326740-6(2))*; (gr. 1-18). 15.60 *(978-0-15-327353-7(4))*; (gr. 1-18). 15.60 *(978-0-15-326737-6(2))*; (gr. 1-18). 15.60 *(978-0-15-326736-9(4))*; (gr. 1-18). 15.60 *(978-0-15-326735-2(6))*; (gr. 1-18). 15.60 *(978-0-15-326734-5(8))*; (gr. 1-18). 15.60 *(978-0-15-326731-4(3))*; (gr. 1-18). 15.60 *(978-0-15-326728-4(3))*; (gr. 1-18). 15.60 *(978-0-15-326726-0(7))*; (gr. 1-18). 15.60 *(978-0-15-326724-6(0))*; (gr. 1-18). 15.60 *(978-0-15-326723-9(2))*; (gr. 1-18). 15.60 *(978-0-15-326722-2(4))*; (gr. 1-18). 15.60 *(978-0-15-326721-5(6))*; (gr. 1-18). 15.60 *(978-0-15-326720-8(8))*; (gr. 2-18). 18.40 *(978-0-15-326773-4(9))*; (gr. 2-18). 18.40 *(978-0-15-326778-9(X))*; (gr. 2-18). 18.40 *(978-0-15-326774-1(7))* Harcourt Schl. Pubs.
Beckerman, Menucha. Welcome Home. (My Little World Ser.: Vol. 6). (Illus.). 34p. (J). (gr. k-5). 4.95 *(978-1-931681-11-7(2))* Israel Bookshop Pubns.
Beckwith, Carrie, et al. Reading Detective Beginning: Using Higher-Order Thinking to Improve Reading Comprehension. 2013. (Reading Detective Ser.). 192p. (gr. 3-4). pap. 24.99 *(978-0-89455-769-9(6))* Critical Thinking Co., The.
Beebe, Katherine & Kingsley, Nellie F. The First Year Nature Reader. 2004. reprint ed. pap. 21.95 *(978-1-4191-3072-4(2))* Kessinger Publishing, LLC.
Beech, Linda Ward. Compare & Contrast. 2005. (Reading Passages That Build Comprehension Ser.). (ENG.). 48p. (gr. 2-3). pap. 10.99 *(978-0-439-55427-5(6)*, Teaching Resources) Scholastic, Inc.
—Context Clues. 2005. (Reading Passages That Build Comprehension Ser.). (ENG.). 48p. (gr. 2-3). pap. 10.99

(978-0-439-55426-8(8), Teaching Resources) Scholastic, Inc.

—Inference. 2005. (Reading Passages That Build Comprehension Ser.). (ENG.). 48p. (gr. 2-3). pap. 10.99 (978-0-439-55424-4(1), Teaching Resources) Scholastic, Inc.

—Main Idea & Details. 2005. (Reading Passages That Build Comprehension Ser.). (ENG.). 48p. (gr. 2-3). pap. 10.99 (978-0-439-55425-1(X), Teaching Resources) Scholastic, Inc.

—Predicting. 2005. (Reading Passages That Build Comprehension Ser.). (ENG.). 48p. (gr. 2-3). pap. 10.99 (978-0-439-55423-7(3), Teaching Resources) Scholastic, Inc.

Beecroft, Simon. Pirates ... & Worse! Dorling Kindersley Publishing Staff, ed. 2009. (Star Wars: the Clone Wars DK Readers Ser.). lib. bdg. 13.55 (978-0-606-07064-5(8), Turtleback) Turtleback Bks.

—R2-D2 & Friends. 2008. (Star Wars DK Readers Level 2 Ser.). (Illus.). 32p. lib. bdg. 13.55 (978-1-4364-5044-7(6), Turtleback) Turtleback Bks.

Beecroft, Simon & Saunders, Catherine. Join the Rebels. 2010. (DK Readers Ser.). (ENG.). 32p. (J). (gr. 1-3). 3.99 (978-0-7566-6313-1(X), DK Children) Dorling Kindersley Publishing, Inc.

Being Kind to Naomi: Social/Emotional Lap Book. (Pebble Soup Explorations Ser.). (gr. -1-18). 16.00 (978-0-7635-7567-0(4)) Rigby Education.

Bel, Mooney & Mooney, Bel. Who Loves Mr. Tubs? Hellard, Susan, illus. 2016. (Reading Ladder Ser.). (ENG.). 48p. (J). (gr. k-2). pap. 7.99 (978-1-4052-8205-5(3)) Egmont Bks., Ltd. GBR. Dist: Independent Pubs. Group.

Belcher, Andrew. Motorcycles Turquoise Band. 2016. (Cambridge Reading Adventures Ser.). (ENG.). 24p. pap. 7.19 (978-1-107-57624-7(5)) Cambridge Univ. Pr.

Belcher, Andy. Life on the Reef. 2016. (Cambridge Reading Adventures Ser.). (ENG.). 24p. pap. 7.19 (978-1-107-56022-2(5)) Cambridge Univ. Pr.

Belcher, Andy & Belcher, Angie. The Baby Turtle. 2007. (Collins Big Cat Ser.). (ENG.). 16p. (J). (gr. k-1). pap. 5.99 (978-0-00-718659-4(2)) HarperCollins Pubs. Ltd. GBR. Dist: Independent Pubs. Group.

—Rally Challenge: Band 10/White. Belcher, Andy & Belcher, Angie, photos by. 2005. (Collins Big Cat Ser.). (ENG., Illus.). 32p. (J). (gr. 1-3). pap. 7.99 (978-0-00-718632-7(0)) HarperCollins Pubs. Ltd. GBR. Dist: Independent Pubs. Group.

Belcher, Angie. Storyteller Chapter Books: Fluency - 1 Each of 1 Title: Level T. 6.50 (978-0-7699-1070-3(X)) Shortland Pubns. (U. S. A.) Inc.

Belcher, Angie & Belcher, Andy. Swimming with Dolphins. 2005. (Collins Big Cat Ser.). (ENG.). 24p. (J). (gr. 1-2). pap. 7.99 (978-0-00-718623-5(1)) HarperCollins Pubs. Ltd. GBR. Dist: Independent Pubs. Group.

Belgue, Nancy. Casey Little, Yo-Yo Queen, 1 vol. 2005. (Orca Young Readers Ser.). (ENG., Illus.). 128p. (J). (gr. 3-6). per. 5.95 (978-1-55143-357-8(5)) Orca Bk. Pubs. USA.

Bell, Jessica. My Wild New Yard. 2017. (Text Connections Guided Close Reading Ser.). (J). (gr. 1). (978-1-4900-1801-0(8)) Benchmark Education Co.

Bell-Martin, Janelle. Mary Had a Little Lamb, 1 vol. 2011. (Early Childhood Themes Ser.). (ENG.). 16p. (J). (gr. -1-2). pap. 19.99 (978-1-4333-2358-4(3)); pap. 6.99 (978-1-4333-2357-7(5)) Teacher Created Materials, Inc.

Bella & Rosie Play Hide & Seek. 2003. (Bella & Rosie Set 1 Ser.). (J). 7.67 (978-1-932570-11-3(X)) Pioneer Valley Bks.

Bella & Rosie Set 1. 2003. (J). (978-1-932570-08-3(X)) Pioneer Valley Bks.

Bella Is a Bad Dog. 2003. (Bella & Rosie Set 1 Ser.). (J). 7.67 (978-1-932570-14-4(4)) Pioneer Valley Bks.

Bella's Birthday. 2003. (Bella & Rosie Set 1 Ser.). (J). 7.67 (978-1-932570-09-0(8)) Pioneer Valley Bks.

Bembibre, Cecilia, et al. La Máscara del Zorro. 2014. (SPA., Illus.). 56p. pap. 13.75 incl. audio compact disk (978-84-9848-195-2(3)) Edinumen, Editorial ESP. Dist: Cambridge Univ. Pr.

—La Niña de Tus Ojos. 2014. (SPA., Illus.). 56p. pap., stu. ed. 13.75 incl. audio compact disk (978-84-9848-379-6(4)) Edinumen, Editorial ESP. Dist: Cambridge Univ. Pr.

Ben Nighthorse Campbell, Senador Y Artista. 2003. (Notas Biograficas Ser.). pap. 48.95 (978-0-8136-5913-8(2)) Modern Curriculum Pr.

Benchmark Education Co., LLC. Sight Walk Big Book. 2014. (Shared Reading Foundations Ser.). (J). (gr. -1). (978-1-4509-9436-1(9)) Benchmark Education Co.

Benchmark Education Company, LLC Staff. Spanish/English Emergent Supplement. 2005. (BookRoom Collection Ser.). (J). spiral bd. 1685.00 (978-1-4108-5614-2(3)) Benchmark Education Co.

—SpiralUp Reading Passages. 2009. (SpiralUp Phonics Ser.). (J). cd-rom (978-1-4108-8534-0(8)) Benchmark Education Co.

Benchmark Education Company, LLC Staff, compiled by. Fluency Kits for Independent Practice. 2005. spiral bd. 4150.00 (978-1-4108-6219-8(4)); spiral bd. 3345.00 (978-1-4108-5380-6(2)) Benchmark Education Co.

—Reading First Bookroom COLL. 2005. spiral bd. 11275.00 (978-1-4108-4157-5(X)) Benchmark Education Co.

—Spanish/English Early/Fluent Supplement. 2005. (J). 2815.00 net. (978-1-4108-5662-3(3)) Benchmark Education Co.

—Spanish/English Emergent Single Copy Set. 2005. (J). pap. 283.00 net. (978-1-4108-5616-6(X)) Benchmark Education Co.

Benita's Plan: Fourth Grade Guided Comprehension Level M. (On Our Way to English Ser.). (gr. 4-18). 34.50 (978-0-7578-7159-7(3)) Rigby Education.

Benjamin, Joseph & Benchmark Education Co., LLC Staff. Ten Red Hens. 2015. (StartUp Ser.). (J). (gr. k). (978-1-4900-0698-7(2)) Benchmark Education Co.

Bennett, Leonie. Locket Out. Adams, Arlene, illus. 2004. (ENG.). 24p. (J). lib. bdg. 23.65 (978-1-59646-688-3(X)) Dingles & Co.

—No Problem! Brown, Judy, illus. 2004. (ENG.). 16p. (J). lib. bdg. 23.65 (978-1-59646-680-7(4)) Dingles & Co.

Bentley, Maria. Summer Sounds Level 1 Beginner/Elementary. 2010. (ENG.). 46p. pap. 11.00 (978-84-8323-995-7(7)) Cambridge Univ. Pr.

Benton, Allie. Inside a Factory, 6 vols., Set. 2004. (Phonics Readers Books 37-72 Ser.). (ENG.). 8p. (gr. k-1). pap. 35.70 (978-0-7368-4057-6(5), Phonics Readers) Capstone Press of Coughlan Cos.

Benton, Celia. Our Flag, 6 vols., Set. 2003. (Phonics Readers 1-36 Ser.). (ENG.). 8p. (gr. k-1). pap. 29.70 (978-0-7368-3201-4(7), Phonics Readers) Capstone Press of Coughlan Cos.

Berenstain, Jan & Berenstain, Mike. The Berenstain Bears Spring Storybook Collection. Berenstain, Mike, illus. 2017. (Berenstain Bears Ser.). (Illus.). 192p. (J). (gr. -1-3). 11.99 (978-0-06-243458-6(6)) HarperCollins Pubs.

—Safe & Sound! Berenstain, Jan & Berenstain, Mike, illus. 2009. (Berenstain Bears Ser.). (ENG., Illus.). 32p. (J). (gr. -1-3). pap. 3.99 (978-0-06-057391-1(0), HarperFestival) HarperCollins Pubs.

Berenstain, Jan & Berenstain, Stan. The Berenstain Bears' New Pup. Berenstain, Jan, illus. 2017. (I Can Read Level 1 Ser.). (Illus.). 40p. (J). (gr. -1-3). 9.99 (978-0-06-257272-1(5)) HarperCollins Pubs.

Berenstain, Jan, et al. My Favorite Dog Stories: Learning to Read Box Set. 2014. (I Can Read Level 1 Ser.). (ENG.). (J). (gr. -1-3). pap. 16.99 (978-0-06-231331-7(2)) HarperCollins Pubs.

Bergman, Mara. The Twelve Dancing Princesses. 2017. (Collins Big Cat Tales Ser.). (ENG., Illus.). 48p. (J). (gr. 2-3). pap. 8.99 (978-0-00-817938-0(7)) HarperCollins Pubs. Ltd. GBR. Dist: Independent Pubs. Group.

Berres, et al. Sea Hunt. Date not set. (J). (978-0-89064-249-8(4)) National Assn. for Visually Handicapped.

Berrios, Frank. To Protect & Serve. 2015. (Cars Step into Reading Ser.). lib. bdg. 14.75 (978-0-606-36393-8(9)) Turtleback Bks.

Bertrand, Diane Gonzales. Cecilia & Miguel Are Best Friends. Ventura, Gabriela Baeza, tr. Muraida, Thelma, illus. 2014.Tr. of Cecilia y Miguel Son Mejores Amigos. (SPA & ENG.). 32p. (J). 17.95 (978-1-55885-794-0(X)) Arte Publico Pr.

Bertrand, Diane Gonzalez. The Park Our Town Built. Bauerle, Tanja, illus. 2011. (ENG & SPA.). 32p. (gr. -1-3). lib. bdg. 16.95 (978-1-936299-14-0(3), Raven Tree Pr.,Csi) Continental Sales, Inc.

—The Park Our Town Built/El Parque Que Nuestro Pueblo Construyó. Bauerle, Tanja, illus. 2011. (ENG & SPA.). 32p. (gr. -1-3). lib. bdg. 16.95 (978-1-936299-12-6(7), Raven Tree Pr.,Csi) Continental Sales, Inc.

Betances, Brendan. Granny's Garden. 2006. (Neighborhood Readers Ser.). (ENG., Illus.). 12p. (gr. 1-3). pap. 5.90 (978-1-4042-7022-0(1), Rosen Classroom) Rosen Publishing Group, Inc., The.

Bethune, Helen. Barnaby Dell, 1 vol. 2013. (Fiction Readers Ser.). (ENG., Illus.). 24p. (J). (gr. 2-2). pap. 6.99 (978-1-4333-5523-3(X)) Shell Educational Publishing.

Betsy Ross. (Lexile Levels Ser.). 9.09 (978-1-56334-735-1(0)) CENGAGE Learning.

Bevan, Clare. The Creature in Wide-Mouth Cave, 8 vols. 2005. (QEB Readers). (Illus.). 24p. (J). (gr. -1-3). lib. bdg. 15.95 (978-1-59566-065-7(8)) QEB Publishing Inc.

—The Jolly Rascal. 2004. (QEB Start Reading Ser.). (Illus.). 24p. (J). lib. bdg. 15.95 (978-1-59566-013-8(5)) QEB Publishing Inc.

—Said Mouse to Mole. 2004. (QEB Start Reading Ser.). (Illus.). 24p. (J). lib. bdg. 15.95 (978-1-59566-014-5(3)) QEB Publishing Inc.

—The Wobbly Wand, 8 vols. 2005. (QEB Readers). (Illus.). 24p. (J). (gr. -1-3). lib. bdg. 15.95 (978-1-59566-073-2(9)) QEB Publishing Inc.

Big Book of R Carry-over Stories. 2004. per. 34.99 (978-0-9760490-4-3(X)) Say It Right.

Big Book Package, 6 bks., Set. 2004. (gr. 3-18). 218.30 (978-0-673-61079-9(9)) Addison-Wesley Educational Pubs., Inc.

Big Book Tote Bag. (gr. -1-12). 18.13 (978-0-7362-1101-7(2)) CENGAGE Learning.

Big Books, 22 bks. 2004. (Scott Foresman Reading Ser.). (gr. k-18). 654.90 (978-0-328-02950-1(5)) Addison-Wesley Educational Pubs., Inc.

Big Books. (Rosen Real Readers Big Bookstm Ser.). (J). 8p. (gr. k-1). 167.70 (978-1-4042-6291-1(1)); 2006. 12p. (gr. 1-2). pap. 160.95 (978-1-4042-6292-8(X)); 2006. 16p. (gr. 2-3). pap. 184.00 (978-1-4042-6293-5(8)) Rosen Publishing Group, Inc., The.

Big City Port. (Lexile Levels Ser.). 7.98 (978-1-56334-693-4(1)) CENGAGE Learning.

Big Idea Entertainment, LLC. Tomato Sawyer & Huckleberry Larry's Big River Rescue. Jones, Cory, illus. 2016. (VeggieTales Ser.). (ENG.). 32p. (J). (gr. -1-3). pap. 3.99 (978-1-4336-4351-4(0), B&H Kids) B&H Publishing Group.

The Big Race, Level 2. 2016. (Ladybird Readers Ser.). (ENG.). 48p. (J). (gr. 2-4). pap. 9.99 (978-0-241-25448-6(5)) Penguin Bks., Ltd. GBR. Dist: Independent Pubs. Group.

Billings, Henry, et al. In the Spotlight, Vol. 1. 2006. (Jt Hi-Lo Non-fiction Ser.). (ENG., Illus.). 112p. (gr. 6-12). per. 4.44 (978-0-07-874320-7(6), 0078743206) McGraw-Hill Cos., The.

—The Outer Edge: Danger Zone. 2005. (Jt: Non-Fiction Reading Ser.). (ENG., Illus.). 120p. (gr. 6-12). per. 25.56 (978-0-07-872905-8(X), 007872905X) McGraw-Hill Cos., The.

Biographies Classroom Library. (gr. k-2). lib. bdg. 90.95 (978-0-7368-9457-9(8)) Red Brick Learning.

Biographies Complete Unit. (gr. k-2). 520.95 (978-0-7368-9458-6(6)) Red Brick Learning.

Birch, Beverley. Turtle's Party in the Clouds. Jenny, Christine, illus. 2015. (Collins Big Cat Ser.). (ENG.). 24p. (J). (gr. 2-2). pap. 6.95 (978-0-00-759106-0(3)) HarperCollins Pubs. Ltd. GBR. Dist: Independent Pubs. Group.

Birch, Beverley. Two Animal Tales from Africa: Band 15/Emerald. 2017. (Collins Big Cat Tales Ser.). (ENG., Illus.). 48p. (J). (gr. 3-4). pap. 8.99 **(978-0-00-817942-7(5))** HarperCollins Pubs. Ltd. GBR. Dist: Independent Pubs. Group.

Bird Talk. 2005. (Book Treks Ser.). (J). (gr. 3-18). stu. ed. 34.95 (978-0-673-62846-6(9)) Celebration Pr.

Birkhead, Jennifer. Peeping Through the Low, Green Grass. 2011. 28p. pap. 12.03 (978-1-4490-5490-8(0)) AuthorHouse.

The Birthday Party. (Early Intervention Levels Ser.). 3.85 (978-1-56334-953-9(1)) CENGAGE Learning.

A Birthday Present for Spaceboy. 2003. (Spaceboy Set 1 Ser.). (J). pap. 7.33 (978-1-932570-03-8(9), Pioneer Valley Bks.) Pioneer Valley Bks.

Bishop, Celeste. Hace Sol / It's Sunny. 2016. (¿Qué Tiempo Hace? / What's the Weather Like? Ser.). (ENG & SPA., Illus.). 24p. (J). (gr. 1-1). lib. bdg. 23.60 (978-1-4994-2330-3(6), PowerKids Pr.) Rosen Publishing Group, Inc., The.

—Hace Sol (It's Sunny) 2016. (¿Qué Tiempo Hace? (What's the Weather Like?) Ser.). (ENG & SPA., Illus.). 24p. (J). (gr. 1-1). lib. bdg. 23.60 (978-1-4994-2326-6(8), PowerKids Pr.) Rosen Publishing Group, Inc., The.

—Hace Viento / It's Windy. 2016. (¿Qué Tiempo Hace? / What's the Weather Like? Ser.). (ENG & SPA., Illus.). 24p. (J). (gr. 1-1). lib. bdg. 23.60 (978-1-4994-2337-2(3), PowerKids Pr.) Rosen Publishing Group, Inc., The.

—Hace Viento (It's Windy) 2016. (¿Qué Tiempo Hace? (What's the Weather Like?) Ser.). (ENG & SPA., Illus.). 24p. (J). (gr. 1-1). lib. bdg. 23.60 (978-1-4994-2333-4(0), PowerKids Pr.) Rosen Publishing Group, Inc., The.

—¿Por Qué Las Plantas Tienen Hojas? / Why Do Plants Have Leaves?, 01 vols., 1. 2016. (Partes de la Planta / Plant Parts Ser.). (ENG & SPA., Illus.). 24p. (J). 23.60 (978-1-5081-4741-1(8), PowerKids Pr.) Rosen Publishing Group, Inc., The.

Bishop, Nic. NIC Bishop - Spiders. Bishop, Nic, photos by. 2012. (Scholastic Reader Level 2 Ser.). (ENG., Illus.). 32p. (J). (gr. k-2). pap. 3.99 (978-0-545-23757-4(2), Scholastic Paperbacks) Scholastic, Inc.

Bishop, Nic & Hughes, Jon. Is There Anybody Out There? Bishop, Nic, photos by. 2005. (Collins Big Cat Ser.). (ENG., Illus.). 352p. (J). (gr. 2-3). pap. 7.99 (978-0-00-718635-8(5)) HarperCollins Pubs. Ltd. GBR. Dist: Independent Pubs. Group.

BishopRoby, Joshua. The World of Animals, 1 vol. 2007. (Science Readers Ser.). (SPA & ENG.). 32p. (J). (gr. 4-4). pap. 8.99 (978-0-7439-0593-0(8)) Shell Educational Publishing.

Bjerregaard, Malynda. Chatter Batter: Four Stories for Speech. 2005. pap. 34.25 (978-1-4184-9768-2(1)) AuthorHouse.

BJU Staff. Reading Student Text Grd 2 If. 2004. 21.00 (978-1-57924-170-4(0)) BJU Pr.

—Reading Student Text Grd 2 Whe. 2004. 21.00 (978-1-57924-171-1(9)) BJU Pr.

—A Reading Student Text Grd 3. 2004. 21.00 (978-1-57924-172-8(7)) BJU Pr.

—Reading Student Text Grd 3 B. 2004. 21.00 (978-1-57924-173-5(5)) BJU Pr.

—Reading Student Text Grd 4. 2004. 32.00 (978-1-57924-348-7(7)) BJU Pr.

—Reading Student Text Grd 5. 2004. 32.00 (978-1-57924-371-5(1)) BJU Pr.

—Reading Student Text Grd 6. 2004. 32.00 (978-1-57924-542-9(0)) BJU Pr.

—Reading Worktext Student Grd 2. 2004. pap. 16.50 (978-1-57924-174-2(3)) BJU Pr.

—Reading Worktext Student Grd 3. 2004. pap. 16.50 (978-1-57924-175-9(1)) BJU Pr.

—Reading Worktext Student Grd 4. 2004. pap. 16.50 (978-1-57924-458-3(0)) BJU Pr.

—Reading Worktext Student Grd 5. 2004. pap. 16.50 (978-1-57924-443-9(2)) BJU Pr.

—Reading Worktext Student Grd 6. 2004. pap. 16.50 (978-1-57924-543-6(9)) BJU Pr.

Blachowicz, Camille L. Z. Reading Fluency: Reader. 2004. (JT: READING RATE & FLUENCY Ser.). (ENG.). 48p. (gr. 6-12). spiral bd. 24.64 (978-0-07-861709-6(X), 007861709X) McGraw-Hill Cos., The.

—Reading Fluency: Reader's Record. 2004. (JT: READING RATE & FLUENCY Ser.). (ENG.). 74p. (gr. 6-12). pap. 17.04 (978-0-07-861712-6(X), 007861712X) McGraw-Hill Cos., The.

Black, Amber. A Day with Miss Sassy. 2008. 16p. pap. 24.95 (978-1-60610-338-8(5)) PublishAmerica, Inc.

Blackledge, Annabel. Let's Go Riding, Level 2. 2005. (DK Readers Ser.). (ENG., Illus.). 32p. (J). (gr. 1-3). pap. 3.99 (978-0-7566-1694-6(8), DK Children) Dorling Kindersley Publishing, Inc.

Blackman, Malorie. Sinclair the Wonder Bear. Allwright, Deborah, illus. 2016. (Reading Ladder Ser.). (ENG.). 48p. (J). (gr. k-2). pap. 7.99 (978-1-4052-8203-1(7)) Egmont Bks., Ltd. GBR. Dist: Independent Pubs. Group.

Blackstone, Stella. Bear about Town (Oso en las Ciudad) Harter, Debbie, illus. 2010. (ENG, SPA & FRE.). 24p. (J). (gr. -1-1). pap. 6.99 (978-1-84686-377-6(5)) Barefoot Bks., Inc.

—Bear at Home (Oso en Casa) Harter, Debbie, illus. 2010. (ENG & SPA.). 24p. (J). (gr. -1-1). pap. 6.99 (978-1-84686-422-3(4)) Barefoot Bks., Inc.

Blackstone, Stella. Bear in a Square / Ours Dans un Carré. Harter, Debbie, illus. rev. ed. 2017. (ENG & FRE.). 24p. (J). (gr. -1-1). pap. 6.99 **(978-1-78285-330-5(8))** Barefoot Bks., Inc.

Blackstone, Stella & Meza-Riedewald, Leticia. Oso en un Cuadrado. Harter, Debbie, illus. 2009. (SPA & ENG.). 24p. (J). (gr. -1-k). pap. 6.99 (978-1-84686-387-5(2)) Barefoot Bks., Inc.

Blanche, David. A Day in My Town. 2012. (InfoMax Readers Ser.). (ENG., Illus.). 16 pp.p. (J). (gr. k-1). pap. 7.00 (978-1-4488-8977-8(4), Rosen Classroom) Rosen Publishing Group, Inc., The.

Blane, Francisco. The Little Girl with Curl. Kelley, Gerald, illus. 2009. (Reader's Theater Nursery Rhymes & Songs Set B Ser.). 48p. (J). pap. (978-1-60859-157-2(3)) Benchmark Education Co.

—Little Jack Horner Eats Pie. Price, Nick, illus. 2009. (Reader's Theater Nursery Rhymes & Songs Set B Ser.). 48p. (J). pap. (978-1-60859-158-9(1)) Benchmark Education Co.

—Looking for the Muffin Man. 2008. (Reader's Theater Nursery Rhymes & Songs Ser.). (Illus.). 48p. (J). (gr. k-1). pap. (978-1-60437-966-2(9)) Benchmark Education Co.

—My New Clothes: Lap Book. 2009. (My First Reader's Theater Set B Ser.). (J). 28.00 (978-1-935441-01-4(9)) Benchmark Education Co.

—One Raining, Pouring Morning. 2008. (Reader's Theater Nursery Rhymes & Songs Ser.). (Illus.). 48p. (J). (gr. k-1). pap. (978-1-60437-977-8(4)) Benchmark Education Co.

—People at School: Lap Book. 2009. (My First Reader's Theater Set B Ser.). (J). 28.00 (978-1-935441-00-7(0)) Benchmark Education Co.

—Stripes at the Beach: Lap Book. 2009. (My First Reader's Theater Set B Ser.). (J). 28.00 (978-1-60634-988-5(0)) Benchmark Education Co.

—Tim Rows a Boat Gently down the Stream. 2008. (Reader's Theater Nursery Rhymes & Songs Ser.). (Illus.). 48p. (J). (gr. k-1). pap. (978-1-60437-980-8(4)) Benchmark Education Co.

—Up & Down: Lap Book. 2009. (My First Reader's Theater Set B Ser.). (J). 28.00 (978-1-60634-989-2(9)) Benchmark Education Co.

—Vegetables Are Good! Lap Book. 2009. (My First Reader's Theater Set B Ser.). (J). 28.00 (978-1-60634-990-8(2)) Benchmark Education Co.

—What Will You Be? Lap Book. 2009. (My First Reader's Theater Set B Ser.). (J). 28.00 (978-1-60634-993-9(7)) Benchmark Education Co.

Blank Tabletop Pocket Chart Cards. 2004. (J). 4.95 (978-1-56911-200-7(2)) Learning Resources, Inc.

Blazeman, Christopher. Eagles up Close, 1 vol. 2nd rev. ed. 2011. (Nonfiction Readers Ser.). (ENG.). 28p. (J). (gr. 2-2). pap. 6.99 (978-1-4333-3616-4(2)) Teacher Created Materials, Inc.

—Horses up Close, 1 vol. 2nd rev. ed. 2011. (Nonfiction Readers Ser.). (ENG.). 28p. (J). (gr. 2-2). pap. 6.99 (978-1-4333-3617-1(0)) Teacher Created Materials, Inc.

—Snakes up Close, 1 vol. 2nd rev. ed. 2011. (Nonfiction Readers Ser.). (ENG.). 28p. (J). (gr. 2-2). pap. 6.99 (978-1-4333-3618-8(9)) Teacher Created Materials, Inc.

Blends & Digraphs Set: Level D. (Sing-along Songs Ser.). (gr. -1-2). 48.46 incl. audio compact disk (978-0-7362-0422-4(9)) CENGAGE Learning.

Blevins, Wiley. Can You See It?, 6 vols., Set. 2003. (Phonics Readers 1-36 Ser.). (ENG.). 8p. (gr. k-1). pap. 29.70 (978-0-7368-3191-8(6), Phonics Readers) Capstone Press of Coughlan Cos.

—Germs, 6 vols., Set. 2004. (Phonics Readers Books 37-72 Ser.). (ENG.). 8p. (gr. k-1). pap. 35.70 (978-0-7368-4055-2(9), Phonics Readers) Capstone Press of Coughlan Cos.

—Is It Hot? Is It Not?, 6 vols., Set. 2003. (Phonics Readers 1-36 Ser.). (ENG.). 8p. (gr. k-1). pap. 29.70 (978-0-7368-3186-4(X), Phonics Readers) Capstone Press of Coughlan Cos.

—Now & Long Ago, 6 vols., Set. 2003. (Phonics Readers 1-36 Ser.). (ENG.). 8p. (gr. k-1). pap. 29.70 (978-0-7368-3218-2(1), Phonics Readers) Capstone Press of Coughlan Cos.

—Parts of a Plant, 6 vols., Set C. 2003. (Phonics Readers 1-36 Ser.). (ENG.). 8p. (gr. k-1). pap. 29.70 (978-0-7368-3219-9(X), Phonics Readers) Capstone Press of Coughlan Cos.

—Phonics from A to Z. 2nd ed. 2006. (Scholastic Teaching Strategies Ser.). (ENG., Illus.). 240p. (gr. k-3). pap., instr.'s gde. ed. 25.99 (978-0-439-84511-3(4), Teaching Resources) Scholastic, Inc.

—Push or Pull?, 6 vols., Set. 2003. (Phonics Readers 1-36 Ser.). (ENG.). 8p. (gr. k-1). pap. 29.70 (978-0-7368-3212-0(2), Phonics Readers) Capstone Press of Coughlan Cos.

—Who Am I?, 6 vols., Set. 2003. (Phonics Readers 1-36 Ser.). (ENG.). 8p. (gr. k-1). pap. 29.70 (978-0-7368-3185-7(1), Phonics Readers) Capstone Press of Coughlan Cos.

Bloch, Joanne. A Few Little Lies. 2009. (Hodder African Readers Ser.). (Illus.). 96p. pap. 12.95 (978-0-340-98415-4(5)) Hodder Education Group GBR. Dist: Trans-Atlantic Pubns., Inc.

Block, Cheryl, et al. Reading Detective Rx: Using Higher-Order Thinking to Improve Reading Comprehension. 2012. (Reading Detective Ser.). 192p. (gr. 6-12). pap. 24.99 (978-0-89455-801-6(3)) Critical Thinking Co., The.

Bloomfield, Kevin. Mr. Biggs in the City. Bloomfield, Kevin, illus. 2011. (ENG & SPA., Illus.). 32p. (gr. -1-3). lib. bdg. 16.95 (978-1-936299-26-3(7), Raven Tree Pr.,Csi) Continental Sales, Inc.

Blue & Green Levels Certificate Only. (gr. k-5). 89.00 (978-0-7578-6540-4(2)) Rigby Education.

Blue, Green, Orange, Turquoise, Purple & Gold Levels Certificate Only. (gr. k-5). 89.00 (978-0-7578-6538-1(0)) Rigby Education.

Blumenfeld, Samuel L. Blumenfeld's Alpha-Phonics: A Primer for Beginning Readers. 2006. spiral bd. 29.95 (978-0-9776024-0-7(0)) Blumont Company, The.

Bluming. Hebrew Reading Homework Book: Lamer Shteigin in Ivri. 2003. (YID.). 48p. (J). (gr. 2-4). pap. 10.55 (978-0-9729232-0-0(9)) Kreizel Enterprises, Inc.

BMX Billy, 6 pack. (Literatura 2000 Ser.). (gr. 1-2). 28.00 (978-0-7635-0083-2(6)) Rigby Education.

Board Book Classics Set, 8. 2005. (J). bds. (978-1-59794-009-2(7)) Environments, Inc.

Board Books & Tapes 800865, 4 vols. 2005. (J). (978-1-59794-051-1(8)) Environments, Inc.

Boardman Moen, Christine. Instant PowerPoint Lessons & Activities: Literary Elements: 16 Model Lessons That Guide Students to Create Easy PowerPoint Presentations That Help Them Analyze Literary Elements in the Books They Read. 2012. (ENG., Illus.). 64p. (gr. 4-8). 19.99 (978-0-545-33280-4(X), Teaching Resources) Scholastic, Inc.

Body Numbers, 6 pack. (Discovery World Ser.). 16p. (gr. 1-2). 28.00 (978-0-7635-8467-2(3)) Rigby Education.

Body, Wendy. Zeebo's Numbers, 4 vols. 2005. (QEB Readers). (Illus.). 24p. (J). (gr. -1-3). lib. bdg. 15.95 (978-1-59566-103-6(4)) QEB Publishing Inc.

—Zia's Colors, 4 vols. 2005. (QEB Readers). (Illus.). 24p. (J). (gr. -1-3). lib. bdg. 15.95 (978-1-59566-105-0(0)) QEB Publishing Inc.

Body Works. (Guided Reading Levels Ser.). 32.22 (978-0-7362-1053-9(9)) CENGAGE Learning.

PQR

Bolivar, Simon. Champion of Freedom. 2007. (Read on! Special Edition: Level BA Ser.). (Illus.). 23p. pap. 18.51 (978-1-4190-3527-2(4)) Steck-Vaughn.

Bond, Janice & Fiebelkorn, Claire. Water on Earth. 2012. (InfoMax Readers Ser.). (ENG., Illus.). 24p. (J). (gr. 1-2). pap. 8.25 (978-1-4488-9034-7(9), Rosen Classroom) Rosen Publishing Group, Inc., The.

Bonnell, Kris. The Big Hungry Cat. 2006. (J). pap. 5.95 (978-1-933727-33-2(0)) Reading Reading Bks., LLC.

—Down in the Sea. 2006. (J). pap. 5.95 (978-1-933727-38-7(1)) Reading Reading Bks., LLC.

—Frog Fun. 2006. (J). pap. 5.95 (978-1-933727-39-4(X)) Reading Reading Bks., LLC.

—The Happy Moon. 2006. (J). pap. 5.95 (978-1-933727-30-1(6)) Reading Reading Bks., LLC.

—Lemonade. 2006. (J). pap. 5.95 (978-1-933727-31-8(4)) Reading Reading Bks., LLC.

—The Little Boat. 2006. (J). pap. 5.95 (978-1-933727-34-9(9)) Reading Reading Bks., LLC.

—The Little Sprout. 2007. (J). pap. 5.95 (978-1-933727-54-7(3)) Reading Reading Bks., LLC.

—Look Up! 2007. (J). pap. 5.95 (978-1-933727-48-6(9)) Reading Reading Bks., LLC.

—Mother Animals. 2007. (J). pap. 5.95 (978-1-933727-49-3(7)) Reading Reading Bks., LLC.

—Mudskipper & the Water. 2006. (J). pap. 3.95 (978-1-933727-21-9(7)) Reading Reading Bks., LLC.

—Pets for Us. 2007. (J). pap. 5.95 (978-1-933727-50-9(0)) Reading Reading Bks., LLC.

—Picking a Pumpkin. 2007. (J). pap. 5.95 (978-1-933727-51-6(9)) Reading Reading Bks., LLC.

—Pizza for Carl. 2006. (J). pap. 3.95 (978-1-933727-27-1(6)) Reading Reading Bks., LLC.

—Presents for Mom. 2007. (J). pap. 6.95 (978-1-933727-61-5(6)) Reading Reading Bks., LLC.

—Red Apples for Me. 2007. (J). pap. 5.95 (978-1-933727-52-3(7)) Reading Reading Bks., LLC.

—Robins in the Spring. 2007. (J). pap. 5.95 (978-1-933727-53-0(5)) Reading Reading Bks., LLC.

—Spring Is Coming! 2007. (J). pap. 6.95 (978-1-933727-64-6(0)) Reading Reading Bks., LLC.

—Too Big to Play. 2006. (J). pap. 5.95 (978-1-933727-35-6(7)) Reading Reading Bks., LLC.

—We Like the Beach. 2007. (J). pap. 5.95 (978-1-933727-55-4(1)) Reading Reading Bks., LLC.

—We Love Pets. 2007. (J). pap. 5.95 (978-1-933727-56-1(X)) Reading Reading Bks., LLC.

—What Tigers Do. 2006. (J). pap. 5.95 (978-1-933727-41-7(1)) Reading Reading Bks., LLC.

—Where Can Louis Sleep? 2007. (J). pap. 5.95 (978-1-933727-57-8(8)) Reading Reading Bks., LLC.

—Where Is a Bear? 2007. (J). pap. 6.95 (978-1-933727-63-9(2)) Reading Reading Bks., LLC.

—Where Is the Big Cat? 2007. (J). pap. 6.95 (978-1-933727-62-2(4)) Reading Reading Bks., LLC.

—The White, White Snow. 2007. (J). pap. 5.95 (978-1-933727-44-8(6)) Reading Reading Bks., LLC.

—Who Can Wiggle? 2006. (J). pap. 5.95 (978-1-933727-42-4(X)) Reading Reading Bks., LLC.

—Who Has a Hump? 2007. (J). pap. 5.95 (978-1-933727-58-5(6)) Reading Reading Bks., LLC.

—Yellow Flowers. 2006. (J). pap. 5.95 (978-1-933727-36-3(5)) Reading Reading Bks., LLC.

Boocock, Charles & Yu, Jennifer. The 10 Most Memorable Court Cases. 2008. 14.99 (978-1-55448-548-2(7)) Scholastic Library Publishing.

Book Builder. 2004. (Scott Foresman Reading Ser.). (gr. k-18). cd-rom 29.97 (978-0-673-64103-8(1)); (gr. 1-18). cd-rom 29.97 (978-0-673-64104-5(X)); (gr. 2-18). cd-rom 29.97 (978-0-673-64105-2(8)); (gr. 3-18). cd-rom 29.97 (978-0-673-64106-9(6)) Addison-Wesley Educational Pubs., Inc.

Booking, Walt. Teddy's Tale. 2006. (Neighborhood Readers Ser.). (ENG.). 12p. (gr. 1-3). pap. 5.90 (978-1-4042-7054-1(X), Rosen Classroom) Rosen Publishing Group, Inc., The.

Books, 6 Pack. (Chiquilibros Ser.). (gr. k-1). 23.00 (978-0-7635-0423-6(8)) Rigby Education.

BookSource Staff, compiled by. Obi-Wan Kenobi: Jedi Knight. 2012. (Star Wars DK Readers Level 3 Ser.). lib. bdg. 13.55 (978-0-606-26678-9(X), Turtleback) Turtleback Bks.

—Who Saved the Galaxy? 2012. (Star Wars DK Readers Level 1 Ser.). lib. bdg. 13.55 (978-0-606-26677-2(1), Turtleback) Turtleback Bks.

Bookweb 3 & 4 Certificate Only. (Bookweb Ser.). (gr. 4-18). 89.00 (978-0-7578-6525-1(9)) Rigby Education.

Bookweb 4 Blackline Masters Book, Vol. 4. (Bookweb Ser.). (gr. 4-18). 52.00 (978-0-7635-5937-3(7)) Rigby Education.

Bookweb 5 & 6 Certificate Only. (Bookweb Ser.). (gr. 6-18). 89.00 (978-0-7578-6526-8(7)) Rigby Education.

Bookweb 5 Blackline Masters Book, Vol. 5. (Bookweb Ser.). (gr. 5-18). 52.00 (978-0-7635-5926-7(1)) Rigby Education.

Bookweb 6 Blackline Masters Book, Vol. 6. (Bookweb Ser.). (gr. 6-18). 52.00 (978-0-7578-1653-6(3)) Rigby Education.

Boomerangs, 6 Pack. (Story Steps Ser.). (gr. k-2). 32.00 (978-0-7635-9805-1(4)) Rigby Education.

Booth, Jack. The 10 Greatest Accidental Inventions. 2007. (J). 14.99 (978-1-55448-510-9(X)) Scholastic Library Publishing.

—The 10 Most Amazing Migrations. 2008. (J). 14.99 (978-1-55448-522-2(3)) Scholastic Library Publishing.

—The 10 Most Daring Heists. 2007. (J). 14.99 (978-1-55448-486-7(3)) Scholastic Library Publishing.

—The 10 Most Gripping 20th Century War Stories. 2008. 14.99 (978-1-55448-497-3(9)) Scholastic Library Publishing.

Bot's Bits: Set A Individual Title Six-Packs. (gr. k-3). 29.00 (978-0-7635-0534-9(X)) Rigby Education.

Boundaries Washed Away: Fifth Grade Guided Comprehension Level P. (On Our Way to English Ser.). (gr. 5-18). 34.50 (978-0-7578-6608-1(5)) Rigby Education.

Bourke, Kenna. Deadly Animals High Beginning Book with Online Access. 2014. (ENG., Illus.). 24p. (J). pap. 9.50 (978-1-107-69371-5(3)) Cambridge Univ. Pr.

—So Cute! Beginning Book with Online Access. 2014. (ENG.). 24p. pap. 9.50 (978-1-107-64649-0(9)) Cambridge Univ. Pr.

BourkeKenna. JEFF CORWIN: WILD MAN BEGINNING BOOK WITH ONLINE ACCESS. 2014. (ENG.). 24p. pap. 9.50 (978-1-107-68039-5(5)) Cambridge Univ. Pr.

—LOST: THE MYSTERY OF AMELIA EARHART HIGH BEGINNING BOOK WITH ONLINE ACCESS. 2014. (ENG.). 24p. (J). pap. 9.50 (978-1-107-69335-7(7)) Cambridge Univ. Pr.

—SLIME: THE WONDERFUL WORLD OF MUCUS LOW INTERMEDIATE BOOK WITH ONLINE ACCESS. 2014. (ENG.). 24p. (J). pap. 9.50 (978-1-107-67343-4(7)) Cambridge Univ. Pr.

Bove, Candace Scobie. Calypso: A Day in the Life of a Puppy. 2012. 24p. 24.95 (978-1-4626-4122-2(9)) America Star Bks.

Bowers, Linda. Spotlight on Reading Comprehension Making Inferences & Drawing Conclusions. 2005. (Illus.). (J). per. 11.95 (978-0-7606-0585-1(8)) LinguiSystems, Inc.

Bowers, Linda, et al. Spotlight on Reading Comprehension Characters & Actions. 2005. (J). per. 11.95 (978-0-7606-0583-7(1)) LinguiSystems, Inc.

—Spotlight on Reading Comprehension Comparing & Contrasting. 2005. (Illus.). (J). per. 11.95 (978-0-7606-0581-3(5)) LinguiSystems, Inc.

—Spotlight on Reading Comprehension Figurative Language & Exclusion. 2005. (Illus.). (J). per. 11.95 (978-0-7606-0582-0(3)) LinguiSystems, Inc.

—Spotlight on Reading Comprehension Paraphrasing & Summarizing. 2005. (J). per. 11.95 (978-0-7606-0584-4(X)) LinguiSystems, Inc.

—Spotlight on Reading Comprehension Sequencing & Problem Solving. 2005. (Illus.). (J). 11.95 (978-0-7606-0580-6(7)) LinguiSystems, Inc.

Bowler, Bill. Troy. 2nd ed. 2013. (ENG., Illus.). 40p. pap. 9.38 **(978-0-19-424970-6(0))** Oxford Univ. Pr., Inc.

Bowley, Catherine. Giants of the Ocean Gold Band. 2016. (Cambridge Reading Adventures Ser.). (ENG.). 24p. pap. 7.19 (978-1-107-55165-7(X)) Cambridge Univ. Pr.

Boyd, David. Marco Polo & the Roc. Ng, Drew, illus. 2007. 48p. (J). lib. bdg. 23.08 (978-1-4242-1621-5(4)) Fitzgerald Bks.

Boyd, Nicole. Let's Brush Our Teeth. 2008. (Rosen Real Readers: Upper Emergent Ser.). (ENG., Illus.). 12p. (gr. 1-2). pap. 5.90 (978-0-8239-8133-5(9)) Rosen Publishing Group, Inc., The.

Boynton, Alice & Blevins, Wiley. Nonfiction Passages with Graphic Organizers for Independent Practice: Selections with Graphic Organizers, Assessments, & Writing Activities That Help Students Understand the Structures & Features of Nonfiction. 2005. (Nonfiction Passages with Graphic Organizers for Independent Practice Ser.). (ENG.). 128p. (gr. 2-4). pap. 18.99 (978-0-439-59018-1(3), Teaching Strategies) Scholastic, Inc.

Bradley, Kathleen. The Boy Who Cried Wolf, 1 vol. 2008. (Building Fluency Through Reader's Theater Ser.). (ENG.). 24p. (J). (gr. 1-3). pap. 6.99 (978-1-4333-0297-8(7)) Teacher Created Materials, Inc.

Bradley, Kathleen E. Making Money Grow, 1 vol. 2nd rev. ed. 2013. (Nonfiction Readers Ser.). (ENG.). 64p. (J). (gr. 5-5). pap. 10.99 (978-1-4333-4908-9(6)) Teacher Created Materials, Inc.

Bradley, Timothy. Teddy Bear, Teddy Bear, Say Good Night, 1 vol. Medina, Conni & Stark, Kristy, eds. 2009. (Early Childhood Themes Ser.). (ENG., Illus.). 16p. (J). (gr. -1-2). pap. 19.99 (978-1-4333-1472-8(X)) Shell Educational Publishing.

Bradley, Timothy J. Animal Architects, 1 vol. 2nd rev. ed. 2012. (TIME for KIDS(r) Nonfiction Readers Ser.). (ENG., Illus.). 48p. (J). (gr. 4-4). pap. 9.99 (978-1-4333-4822-8(5)) Teacher Created Materials, Inc.

—Bug Builders, 1 vol. 2nd rev. ed. 2012. (Nonfiction Readers Ser.). (ENG., Illus.). 48p. (J). (gr. 4-4). pap. 9.99 (978-1-4333-4821-1(7)) Teacher Created Materials, Inc.

—Danger in the Desert, 1 vol. 2nd rev. ed. 2013. (Nonfiction Readers Ser.). (ENG.). 64p. (J). (gr. 5-5). pap. 10.99 (978-1-4333-4897-6(7)) Teacher Created Materials, Inc.

—Demons of the Deep, 1 vol. 2nd rev. ed. 2013. (Nonfiction Readers Ser.). (ENG., Illus.). 64p. (J). (gr. 5-5). pap. 10.99 (978-1-4333-4896-9(9)) Teacher Created Materials, Inc.

—Strange but True: Bizarre Animals, 1 vol. 2nd rev. ed. 2012. (Nonfiction Readers Ser.). (ENG.). 48p. (J). (gr. 4-4). pap. 9.99 (978-1-4333-4861-7(6)) Teacher Created Materials, Inc.

—Strange but True: Gross Anatomy, 1 vol. 2nd rev. ed. 2012. (Nonfiction Readers Ser.). (ENG.). 48p. (J). (gr. 4-4). pap. 9.99 (978-1-4333-4860-0(8)) Teacher Created Materials, Inc.

—Strange but True Tiny Creatures, 1 vol. 2nd rev. ed. 2012. (Nonfiction Readers Ser.). (ENG.). 48p. (J). (gr. 4-4). pap. 9.99 (978-1-4333-4862-4(4)) Teacher Created Materials, Inc.

—Terror in the Tropics, 1 vol. 2nd rev. ed. 2013. (TIME for KIDS(r) Nonfiction Readers Ser.). (ENG.). 64p. (J). (gr. 5-5). pap. 10.99 (978-1-4333-4898-3(5)) Teacher Created Materials, Inc.

—Wild Cities, 1 vol. 2nd rev. ed. 2012. (Nonfiction Readers Ser.). (ENG.). 48p. (J). (gr. 4-4). pap. 9.99 (978-1-4333-4823-5(3)) Teacher Created Materials, Inc.

Bradman, Tom. Hall of the Bulls. 2014. (Collins Big Cat Progress Ser.). (ENG., Illus.). 32p. (J). (gr. 2-3). pap. 7.99 (978-0-00-751927-9(3)) HarperCollins Pubs. Ltd. GBR. Dist: Independent Pubs. Group.

—King Fox Purple Band. Bernstein, Galia, illus. 2016. (Cambridge Reading Adventures Ser.). (ENG.). 24p. pap. 7.19 (978-1-107-56215-8(5)) Cambridge Univ. Pr.

Bradman, Tony. Baba Yaga, Level 22. pap. (978-0-19-030001-2(9)) Oxford Univ. Pr., Inc.

—Dilly & the Goody-Goody. Hellard, Susan, illus. 2nd ed. 2016. (Reading Ladder Ser.). (ENG.). 48p. (J). (gr. k-2). pap. 7.99 (978-1-4052-8222-2(3)) Egmont Bks., Ltd. GBR. Dist: Independent Pubs. Group.

—Dilly the Dinosaur: 30th Anniversary Edition. Hellard, Susan, illus. 2nd ed. 2016. (ENG.). 64p. (J). (gr. 1-4). pap. 7.99 **(978-1-4052-8466-0(8))** Egmont Bks., Ltd. GBR. Dist: Independent Pubs. Group.

—The Frog Prince Hops to It, 1 vol. Warburton, Sarah, illus. 2009. (After Happily Ever After Ser.). (ENG.). 56p. (gr. 2-3). 25.32 (978-1-4342-1303-7(X), After Happily Ever After) Stone Arch Bks.

—Mei & the Pirate Queen White Band. Anderson, Scoular, illus. 2016. (Cambridge Reading Adventures Ser.). (ENG.). 32p. pap. 7.81 (978-1-316-50090-3(X)) Cambridge Univ. Pr.

—The Mummy Family Find Fame. 2006. (Red Bananas Ser.). (ENG., Illus.). 48p. (J). (gr. -1-3). lib. bdg. (978-0-7787-1076-9(9)) Crabtree Publishing Co.

—The Mummy Family Find Fame. Chatterton, Martin, illus. 2nd ed. 2016. (Reading Ladder Ser.). (ENG.). 48p. (J). (gr. k-2). pap. 7.99 (978-1-4052-8241-3(X)) Egmont Bks., Ltd. GBR. Dist: Independent Pubs. Group.

—Polly & the Pirates. Davies, James, illus. 2nd ed. 2016. (Reading Ladder Ser.). (ENG.). 48p. (J). (gr. k-2). 7.99 (978-1-4052-8249-9(5)) Egmont Bks., Ltd. GBR. Dist: Independent Pubs. Group.

—The Silk Road White Band. Cerisier, Emmanuel, illus. 2016. (Cambridge Reading Adventures Ser.). (ENG.). 15p. pap. 7.81 (978-1-107-56232-5(5)) Cambridge Univ. Pr.

—The Surprise Party. Chatterton, Martin, illus. 2nd ed. 2016. (Reading Ladder Ser.). (ENG.). 48p. (J). (gr. k-2). pap. 7.99 (978-1-4052-8239-0(8)) Egmont Bks., Ltd. GBR. Dist: Independent Pubs. Group.

—Yu & the Great Flood Gold Band. Hitori De, Nicola, illus. 2016. (Cambridge Reading Adventures Ser.). (ENG.). 24p. pap. 7.19 (978-1-107-56225-7(2)) Cambridge Univ. Pr.

Bradman, Tony & Bradman, Tom. The King Who Thought He Was Clever - A Folk Tale from Russia. Oliver, Juanbjuan, illus. 2017. (Collins Big Cat Tales Ser.). (ENG.). 48p. (J). (gr. 3-4). pap. 8.99 (978-0-00-817940-3(9)) HarperCollins Pubs. Ltd. GBR. Dist: Independent Pubs. Group.

Bradshaw, Georgine & Wrighton, Charlene. Basic Kit - Kindergarten. Clark, Irene, illus. 2005. Orig. Title: Basic Kit II. (J). 249.95 (978-1-886441-31-6(6)) Zoo-phonics, Inc.

—Kindergarten Zoo-per Kit. Clark, Irene, illus. 2005. (J). 499.95 (978-1-886441-34-7(0), ZOP4219) Zoo-phonics, Inc.

—Preschool Zoo-per Kit. Clark, Irene, illus. 2005. (J). 449.95 (978-1-886441-32-3(4), ZOP4218) Zoo-phonics, Inc.

Braidich, Shelby. What Is a Mountain? 2008. (Real Readers - Upper Emergent Ser.). (ENG., Illus.). 12p. (gr. 1-2). pap. 5.90 (978-0-8239-8122-9(3)) Rosen Publishing Group, Inc., The.

Braidich, Victoria. Monday with Meg. 2006. (Neighborhood Readers Ser.). (ENG.). 12p. (gr. -1-3). pap. 5.90 (978-1-4042-6459-5(0), Rosen Classroom) Rosen Publishing Group, Inc., The.

Brain, Helen. No More Secrets. 2009. (Hodder African Readers Ser.). (Illus.). 144p. pap. 12.95 (978-0-340-98419-2(8)) Hodder Education Group GBR. Dist: Trans-Atlantic Pubns., Inc.

Brand New View. (J). (gr. 2-3). pap. 9.90 (978-0-669-15290-6(0)); pap. 75.00 (978-0-669-13446-9(5)); pap. 9.90 (978-0-669-15889-2(5)) Houghton Mifflin Harcourt School Pubs.

Brasch, Nicolas. A Baseball Giant, 1 vol. rev. ed. 2013. (Fiction Readers Ser.). (ENG., Illus.). 32p. (J). (gr. 3-3). pap. 8.99 (978-1-4333-5644-5(9)) Shell Educational Publishing.

Brasch, Nicolas & Dawson, Amanda. The Chalk Circle. 2008. (Rigby Focus Forward: Level G Ser.). (Illus.). 24p. (J). (gr. 4-7). pap. (978-1-4190-3713-9(7), Rigby) Pearson Education Australia.

Brasch, Nicolas & Nickel, Adam. Dad & Dan Go Camping. 2008. (Rigby Focus Forward: Level G Ser.). (Illus.). 24p. (J). (gr. 4-7). pap. (978-1-4190-3705-4(6), Rigby) Pearson Education Australia.

—Dad & Dan Go Fishing. 2008. (Rigby Focus Forward: Level D Ser.). (Illus.). 16p. (J). (gr. 4-7). pap. (978-1-4190-3668-2(8), Rigby) Pearson Education Australia.

Brasch, Nicolas & Parton, Daron. The Riddle of the Camel Race. 2008. (Rigby Focus Forward: Level L Ser.). (Illus.). 24p. (J). (gr. -1-3). pap. (978-1-4190-3820-4(6), Rigby) Pearson Education Australia.

Brennan, Frank. Tasty Tales Level 4, 1 vol. 2009. (ENG.). 96p. pap. 16.50 incl. audio compact disk (978-84-8323-545-4(5)) Cambridge Univ. Pr.

Breslin, Theresa, et al. The Firebird: A Russian Folk Tale. Oliver, Juanbjuan, illus. 2016. (ENG.). 48p. (J). pap. 9.95 (978-0-00-814718-1(3)) HarperCollins Pubs. Ltd. GBR. Dist: Independent Pubs. Group.

Brezinova, Ivona. Dorothy & the Glasses. Llapashtica, Mentor, illus. 2007. 32p. (J). (POL & ENG.). pap. 12.95 (978-1-60195-099-4(3)); (ARA & ENG.). pap. 12.95 (978-1-60195-088-8(8)) International Step by Step Assn.

—To Have a Dog. Deisadze, Zaur, illus. 2007. (POL & ENG.). 32p. (J). pap. 12.95 (978-1-60195-106-9(X)) International Step by Step Assn.

Brian, Janeen. Maya Monkey, 1 vol. rev. ed. 2013. (Fiction Readers Ser.). (ENG., Illus.). 20p. (J). (gr. 1-1). pap. 15.96 (978-1-4807-1142-6(X)); pap. 4.99 (978-1-4333-5486-1(1)) Shell Educational Publishing.

Bridge, Chris Helene. Read to Me! Bilingual. 2016. (ENG., Illus.). 32p. (J). pap. 9.95 (978-1-942945-36-9(1), 9781942945369) Bright Sky Pr.

Bridges, Sarah. Working Wheels, 6 bks. Alderman, Derrick & Shea, Denise, illus. Incl. I Drive a Bulldozer. 26.65 (978-1-4048-0613-9(X)); I Drive a Snowplow. 26.65 (978-1-4048-0617-7(2)); (gr. -1-2). (Working Wheels Ser.). (ENG., Illus.). 24p. 2004. 159.90 o.p. (978-1-4048-0634-4(2)) Picture Window Bks.

Brinton, Margaret. 100 Little Reading Comprehension Lessons, Grade 1-4: Fun-To-Read Stories with Skill-Building Exercises. Shalansky, Len, illus. 2004. (ENG.). 112p. pap. 12.95 (978-1-57310-425-8(6)) Teaching & Learning Co.

The British Tradition: The EMC Write-in Reader. 2nd ed. (Literature & the Language Arts Ser.). (YA). (gr. 12-18). wbk. ed. 19.99 (978-0-8219-2920-9(8)) EMC/Paradigm Publishing.

Brooke, Jasmine. The Princess & the Pea: Pass the Pea Pressure Test! 2017. (Fairy Tale Fixers: Fixing Fairy Tale Problems with STEM Ser.). 32p. (gr. 3-4). pap. 63.00 **(978-1-5382-0667-6(6))** Stevens, Gareth Publishing LLLP.

Brooks, Felicity. School Look & Say. Litchfield, Jo, illus. 2005. 10p. (J). 7.95 (978-0-7945-1015-2(9), Usborne) EDC Publishing.

Brooks, Susie. A Day in the Life of T. Rex. Woodward, Jonathan, illus. 2016. (Reading Ladder Ser.). (ENG.). 32p. (J). (gr. 1-3). pap. 7.99 (978-1-4052-8040-2(9)) Egmont Bks., Ltd. GBR. Dist: Independent Pubs. Group.

Brooks, Susie. A Day in the Life of Triceratops. Woodward, Jonathan, illus. 2016. (Reading Ladder Ser.). (ENG.). 32p. (J). (gr. 1-4). pap. 6.99 **(978-1-4052-8042-6(5))** Egmont Bks., Ltd. GBR. Dist: Independent Pubs. Group.

Brooksbank, Angela, illus. My Busy Patterns. 2008. (ENG.). 10p. (J). (gr. -1-2). bds. 11.95 (978-0-230-52909-0(7), Macmillan) Pan Macmillan GBR. Dist: Trans-Atlantic Pubns., Inc.

Brown Bear Figures It Out. (Early Intervention Levels Ser.). 31.86 (978-0-7362-0667-9(1)) CENGAGE Learning.

Brown, Janet. The Gingerbread Man (Floor Book) My First Reading Book. Morton, Ken, illus. 2013. (ENG.). 24p. (J). (gr. -1-2). pap. 6.99 (978-1-84322-900-1(5), Armadillo) Anness Publishing GBR. Dist: National Bk. Network.

—Hansel & Gretel: My First Reading Book. Morton, Ken, illus. 2013. (ENG.). 24p. (J). (gr. -1-4). 5.99 (978-1-84322-737-3(1), Armadillo) Anness Publishing GBR. Dist: National Bk. Network.

—Jack & the Beanstalk: My First Reading Book. Morton, Ken, illus. 2013. (ENG.). 24p. (J). (gr. -1-4). 5.99 (978-1-84322-738-0(X), Armadillo) Anness Publishing GBR. Dist: National Bk. Network.

—Puss in Boots. Morton, Ken, illus. 2012. (ENG.). 24p. (J). (gr. -1-12). 5.99 (978-1-84322-848-6(3)) Anness Publishing GBR. Dist: National Bk. Network.

—Puss in Boots (Floor Book) My First Reading Book. Morton, Ken, illus. 2013. (ENG.). 24p. (J). (gr. -1-2). pap. 6.99 (978-1-84322-902-5(1), Armadillo) Anness Publishing GBR. Dist: National Bk. Network.

—Red Riding Hood: My First Reading Book. 2012. (ENG., Illus.). 24p. (J). (gr. -1-12). 5.99 (978-1-84322-849-3(1)) Anness Publishing GBR. Dist: National Bk. Network.

—Red Riding Hood (Floor Book) My First Reading Book. Morton, Ken, illus. 2015. (ENG.). 24p. (J). (gr. -1-1). pap. 6.99 (978-1-86147-399-8(0), Armadillo) Anness Publishing GBR. Dist: National Bk. Network.

—Snow White & the Seven Dwarves. Morton, Ken, illus. 2012. (ENG.). 24p. (J). (gr. -1-12). 5.99 (978-1-84322-850-9(5)) Anness Publishing GBR. Dist: National Bk. Network.

—Snow White & the Seven Dwarves (Floor Book) My First Reading Book. Morton, Ken, illus. 2013. (ENG.). 30p. (J). (gr. -1-2). pap. 6.99 (978-1-84322-903-2(X), Armadillo) Anness Publishing GBR. Dist: National Bk. Network.

—Three Little Pigs (Floor Book) My First Reading Book. Morton, Ken, illus. 2015. (ENG.). 24p. (J). (gr. -1-1). pap. 6.99 (978-1-86147-396-7(6), Armadillo) Anness Publishing GBR. Dist: National Bk. Network.

—The Ugly Duckling (Floor Book) My First Reading Book. Morton, Ken, illus. 2015. (ENG.). 24p. (J). (gr. -1-1). pap. 6.99 (978-1-86147-398-1(2), Armadillo) Anness Publishing GBR. Dist: National Bk. Network.

Brown, Jeff. Flat Stanley & the Firehouse. Pamintuan, Macky, illus. 2011. (I Can Read Level 2 Ser.). (ENG.). 32p. (J). (gr. -1-3). 16.99 (978-0-06-143006-0(4)); pap. 3.99 (978-0-06-143009-1(9)) HarperCollins Pubs.

—Flat Stanley & the Haunted House. Pamintuan, Macky, illus. 2010. (I Can Read Level 2 Ser.). (ENG.). 32p. (J). (gr. -1-3). 16.99 (978-0-06-143004-6(8)); pap. 3.99 (978-0-06-143005-3(6)) HarperCollins Pubs.

Brown, Kelli. Yellowstone Park. 2006. (Neighborhood Readers Ser.). (ENG.). 16p. (gr. 1-3). pap. 6.50 (978-1-4042-7132-6(5), Rosen Classroom) Rosen Publishing Group, Inc., The.

Brown, Marcy & Haley, Dennis. We Both Read Bilingual Edition-The Well-Mannered Monster/el Monstruo Debuenos Modales. Raglin, Tim, illus. 2011. (ENG & SPA.). 44p. (J). pap. 4.99 (978-1-60115-044-8(X)) Treasure Bay, Inc.

Brown, Marcy, et al. The Well-Mannered Monster: Monstruo de Buenos Modales. Raglin, Tim, illus. 2010. 41p. (J). (978-1-60115-043-1(1)) Treasure Bay, Inc.

Brown, Richard, illus. Wait for Us! 2005. (I'm Going to Read(r) Ser.). (ENG.). 28p. (J). (gr. -1-k). pap. 3.95 (978-1-4027-2506-7(X)) Sterling Publishing Co., Inc.

Brown, Vanessa. Kentucky. 2009. (Bilingual Library of the United States of America Ser.). (ENG & SPA.). 32p. (gr. 2-2). 47.90 (978-1-60853-362-6(X), Editorial Buenas Letras) Rosen Publishing Group, Inc., The.

Browne, Eileen. Wait for Me!, 8 bks. 2005. (QEB Readers). (Illus.). 24p. (J). (gr. -1-3). lib. bdg. 15.95 (978-1-59566-075-6(5)) QEB Publishing Inc.

Browne, Hetty S. & Sarah Withers. The Child s World. 2007. (ENG.). 192p. pap. 19.99 (978-1-4264-8460-5(7)); 214p. pap. 22.99 (978-1-4264-8518-3(2)) Creative Media Partners, LLC.

Brunel, Aude. Let's Go to Work. Mancek, Marjan, illus. 2007. 32p. (J). (ARA & ENG.). pap. 16.95 (978-1-60195-089-5(6)); (POL & ENG.). pap. 16.95 (978-1-60195-101-4(9)) International Step by Step Assn.

Bryant, Sheree, et al. The Glencoe Reader, Course 1. 2003. (Glencoe Literature Grade 7 Ser.). (ENG., Illus.). 340p. (gr. 6-6). stu. ed., per. 8.92 (978-0-07-845927-6(3), 0078459273) McGraw-Hill Higher Education.

—The Glencoe Reader, Course 2. 2003. (Glencoe Literature Grade 7 Ser.). (ENG., Illus.). 353p. (gr. 7-7). stu. ed., per. 8.92 (978-0-07-845928-3(1), 0078459281) McGraw-Hill Higher Education.

—The Glencoe Reader Course 4, Course 4. 2003. (ENG., Illus.). 382p. (C). (gr. 6-12). stu. ed., per. 8.28 (978-0-07-845930-6(3), 0078459303) McGraw-Hill Higher Education.

Bryson, Theresa. Costume Party. 2011. (Early Connections Ser.). (J). (978-1-61672-346-0(7)) Benchmark Education Co.

—Farm Alarm. 2011. (Early Connections Ser.). (J). (978-1-61672-350-7(5)) Benchmark Education Co.

—Farm Work. 2011. (Early Connections Ser.). (J). (978-1-61672-351-4(3)) Benchmark Education Co.

Buchanan, Fannie R. Magic Music Story Interpretations. 2006. (Illus.). pap. 21.95 (978-1-4286-5945-2(5)) Kessinger Publishing, LLC.

Buckley, Arabella. Plant Life in Field & Garden. 2008. 88p. pap. 11.95 (978-1-59915-273-8(8)) Yesterday's Classics.

Buckley, Arabella B. Wild Life in Woods & Fields (Yesterday's Classics) 2008. (Illus.). 60p. pap. 9.95 (978-1-59915-271-4(1)) Yesterday's Classics.

Buckley, James & Bader, Bonnie. The Moon. 2016. (Smithsonian Ser.). (ENG., Illus.). 48p. (J). (gr. 3-4). 3.99 (978-0-448-49020-5(X), Penguin Young Readers) Penguin Young Readers Group.

Buenas Letras Reading Room Series, Set. 2003. (Buenas Letras Reading Room Ser.). (SPA & ENG., Illus.). (J). lib. bdg. 112.50 (978-0-8239-7278-4(X), Editorial Buenas Letras) Rosen Publishing Group, Inc., The.

Buesser, Jeanne. He Talks Funny: A Heartwarming Story of Everyday Life. 2010. 28p. 12.49 (978-1-4520-2595-7(9)) AuthorHouse.

Bugs! (18), Vol. 18. (Early Intervention Levels Ser.). 5.31 *(978-0-7362-0614-3(0))* CENGAGE Learning.

Building a Doghouse: Fourth Grade Guided Comprehension Level M. (On Our Way to English Ser.). (gr. 4-18). 34.50 *(978-0-7578-7157-3(7))* Rigby Education.

Burg, Ann E. The New York Reader. Darnell, K. L., illus. 2008. (Readers Ser.). (ENG.). 96p. (J). pap. 5.95 *(978-1-58536-349-0(9))* Sleeping Bear Pr.

Burgess, Melvyn & Pearson Education Staff. Billy Elliot: 'A Writer of the Hightest Quality with Exceptional Powers of Insight' 2nd ed. 2008. (ENG., Illus.). 64p. pap. 11.99 *(978-1-4058-8176-0(3))* Pearson Education.

Burke, Anne. That's Entertainment! 2007. (Steck-Vaughn BOLDPRINT Anthologies Ser.). (ENG., Illus.). 48p. (gr. 9-12). pap., stu. ed. 16.90 *(978-1-4190-4035-1(9))* Houghton Mifflin Harcourt Publishing Co.

Burke, David, adapted by. GOLDILOCKS (English to Chinese - Level 2) Learn MANDARIN CHINESE Through Fairy Tales. 2007. (Learn Chinese Through Fairy Tales Ser.). (ENG & CHI., Illus.). (J). per. 14.95 incl. audio compact disk *(978-1-891888-85-4(4))* Slangman Publishing.

Burke, Juliet. Let's Play! 2012. (InfoMax Readers Ser.). (ENG., Illus.). 16 pp.p. (J). (gr. k-1). pap. 7.00 *(978-1-4488-8899-3(9)*, Rosen Classroom) Rosen Publishing Group, Inc., The.

Burke, Sandra & Flebotte, Morrigan. The Crusading Communicator. Flebotte, Morrigan, ed. 2004. (Illus.). 2p. (J). per. *(978-0-9735303-8-4(3))* Black Castle Industries, Inc.

—Hercules Novel Study. Flebotte, Morrigan, ed. 2004. (Illus.). (J). per. *(978-0-9735303-1-5(6))* Black Castle Industries, Inc.

Burnett, Gretel. The A-B-C Smarts: Book 2. 2009. 84p. pap. 28.99 *(978-1-4490-4575-3(8))* AuthorHouse.

Burr, Avril. Naughty Art. 2012. (Illus.). 66p. pap. *(978-1-78281-017-9(X))* Athena Pr.

Burslem, Diana & Freeman, Diana. Bee Alarm! Webb, Philip, illus. 2013. (ENG.). 24p. (gr. 3-3). pap. *(978-1-77654-020-4(4)*, Red Rocket Readers) Flying Start Bks.

Bursztyn, Dina. The Land of Lost Things: El País de las Cosas Perdidas. Bursztyn, Dina, illus. 2011. (SPA & ENG., Illus.). 32p. (J). (gr. -1-3). 16.95 *(978-1-55885-690-5(0)*, Piñata Books) Arte Publico Pr.

Burt, Judith. The 10 Most Valuable Elements. 2008. 14.99 *(978-1-55448-540-6(1))* Scholastic Library Publishing.

Burton, Margie, et al. Peaches all the Time. 2011. (Early Connections Ser.). (J). *(978-1-61672-534-1(6))* Benchmark Education Co.

Bush, John. Mr Crookodile. Paul, Korky, illus. 2016. (Reading Ladder Ser.). (ENG.). 48p. (J). (gr. k-2). pap. 7.99 *(978-1-4052-8204-8(5))* Egmont Bks., Ltd. GBR. Dist: Independent Pubs. Group.

Buster MCluster: Level G. (Wonder Worldtm Ser.). 16p. 29.95 *(978-0-7802-1033-2(6))* Wright Group/McGraw-Hill.

Buster MCluster has Chicken Pox: Level G, 6 vols. (Wonder Worldtm Ser.). 16p. 29.95 *(978-0-7802-4563-1(6))* Wright Group/McGraw-Hill.

Busy Animals Book Set 800896, 6 vols. 2005. (J). pap. *(978-1-59794-071-9(2))* Environments, Inc.

Busy Bear Book Set 800938, 4 vols. 2005. (J). bds. *(978-1-59794-097-9(6))* Environments, Inc.

Busy Bees: Cassette. (Song Box Ser.). (gr. 1-2). 8.50 incl. audio *(978-0-7802-2269-4(5))* Wright Group/McGraw-Hill.

Busy Children Book Set 800897, 6 vols. 2005. (J). pap. *(978-1-59794-072-6(0))* Environments, Inc.

Butler, Nathalie. I Love My Books! 2017. (Learning with Stories Ser.). 24p. (gr. 4-6). pap. 8.25 ***(978-1-5081-6245-2(X)***, PowerKids Pr.) Rosen Publishing Group, Inc., The.

Butterfield, Moira. The Life Cycle of the Orca: Band 16/Sapphire. 2017. (ENG., Illus.). 56p. (J). pap. 8.99 ***(978-0-00-820890-5(5))*** HarperCollins Pubs. Ltd. GBR. Dist: Independent Pubs. Group.

Butterfield, Moira. Muddypaws. Mendez, Simon, illus. 2008. (Picture Books... Ser.). 32p. (J). *(978-1-4075-1840-4(2))* Parragon, Inc.

By the Tree. (Little Book Practice Reader Ser.). (J). *(978-0-8136-0737-5(X))* Modern Curriculum Pr.

Byerly, Robbie. We Can Fix It. 2015. (1B Potato Chip Bks.). (ENG., Illus.). 16p. (J). pap. 5.99 *(978-1-63437-204-6(2))* American Reading Co.

Cain, Marie Mowery. All Eyes on You. 2013. (Big Books, Blue Ser.). (ENG & SPA., Illus.). 16p. pap. 33.00 *(978-1-59246-017-5(8))* Big Books, by George!

—Cool Places. 2013. (Big Books, Red Ser.). (ENG & SPA., Illus.). 16p. pap. 33.00 *(978-1-59246-215-5(4))* Big Books, by George!

—One by One. 2013. (Big Books, Blue Ser.). (ENG & SPA., Illus.). 16p. pap. 33.00 *(978-1-59246-020-5(8))* Big Books, by George!

The Cake: Individual Title Six-Packs. (Story Steps Ser.). (gr. k-2). 29.00 *(978-0-7635-9601-9(9))* Rigby Education.

Calfee, Pat. Issy Books Set 1, 5 bks. Gee, Isybilla, illus. 2013. 60p. (J). pap. 24.95 *(978-1-938406-13-3(3)*, Compass) Raphel Marketing, Inc.

—Issy Books Set 2, 5 bks. Gee, Isybilla, illus. 2013. 60p. (J). pap. 24.95 *(978-1-938406-14-0(1)*, Compass) Raphel Marketing, Inc.

—Issy Books Set 3, 10 books. Gee, Isybilla, illus. 2013. 120p. (J). pap. 39.95 *(978-1-938406-15-7(X)*, Compass) Raphel Marketing, Inc.

Callan, Mary Ann. Spunky Chunks. 2011. 266p. 31.99 *(978-1-4363-7523-8(1))*; pap. 21.99 *(978-1-4363-7522-1(3))* Xlibris Corp.

Called to a Cause. 2003. (Illus.). pap. 5.60 *(978-0-7398-7516-2(7))* Steck-Vaughn.

Callella, Trisha. Developing Reading Fluency, Grade 2: Using Modeled Reading, Phrasing, & Repeated Oral Reading. Fisch, Teri L., ed. Iosa, Ann W., illus. 2003. (Developing Reading Fluency Ser.). 96p. (J). (gr. 2-3). pap. 14.99 *(978-1-57471-995-6(5)*, 2248) Creative Teaching Pr., Inc.

—Developing Reading Fluency, Grade 3: Using Modeled Reading, Phrasing, & Repeated Oral Reading. Fisch, Teri L., ed. Yamada, Jane, illus. 2003. (Developing Reading Fluency Ser.). 96p. (J). (gr. 3-4). pap. 14.99 *(978-1-57471-996-3(3)*, 2240) Creative Teaching Pr., Inc.

—Developing Reading Fluency, Grade 4: Using Modeled Reading, Phrasing, & Repeated Oral Reading. Fisch, Teri L., ed. Iosa, Ann W., illus. 2003. (Developing Reading Fluency Ser.). 96p. (J). (gr. 4-5). pap. 14.99 *(978-1-57471-997-0(1)*, 2250) Creative Teaching Pr., Inc.

Callen, Sharon. Anna Goes to Zambia, 1 vol. rev. ed. 2013. (Fiction Readers Ser.). (ENG., Illus.). 20p. (J). (gr. 1-1). pap. 4.99 *(978-1-4333-5495-3(0))*; pap. 15.96 *(978-1-4807-1151-8(9))* Shell Educational Publishing.

—Boris & Bea, 1 vol. 2013. (Fiction Readers Ser.). (ENG., Illus.). 24p. (J). (gr. 2-2). pap. 6.99 *(978-1-4333-5530-1(2))* Shell Educational Publishing.

—Boris Keeps Fit, 1 vol. rev. ed. 2013. (Fiction Readers Ser.). (ENG., Illus.). 20p. (J). (gr. 1-1). pap. 4.99 *(978-1-4333-5492-2(6))*; pap. 15.96 *(978-1-4807-1148-8(9))* Shell Educational Publishing.

—Boris the Bassett, 1 vol. rev. ed. 2013. (Fiction Readers Ser.). (ENG., Illus.). 12p. (J). (gr. 1-1). pap. 4.99 *(978-1-4333-5454-0(3))*; pap. 12.96 *(978-1-4807-1133-4(0))* Shell Educational Publishing.

—Duck Pond Fun, 1 vol. rev. ed. 2013. (Fiction Readers Ser.). (ENG., Illus.). 12p. (J). (gr. 1-1). pap. 12.96 *(978-1-4807-1124-2(1))*; pap. 4.99 *(978-1-4333-5445-8(4))* Shell Educational Publishing.

—Grandpa & Me, 1 vol. rev. ed. 2013. (Fiction Readers Ser.). (ENG., Illus.). 12p. (J). (gr. 1-1). pap. 12.96 *(978-1-4807-1132-7(2))*; pap. 4.99 *(978-1-4333-5453-3(5))* Shell Educational Publishing.

—How to Be a Kitten, 1 vol. rev. ed. 2013. (Fiction Readers Ser.). (ENG., Illus.). 12p. (J). (gr. 1-1). pap. 4.99 *(978-1-4333-5457-1(8))*; pap. 12.96 *(978-1-4807-1136-5(5))* Shell Educational Publishing.

—Life at the Top, 1 vol. rev. ed. 2013. (Fiction Readers Ser.). (ENG., Illus.). 20p. (J). (gr. 1-1). pap. 15.96 *(978-1-4807-1143-3(8))*; pap. 4.99 *(978-1-4333-5487-8(X))* Shell Educational Publishing.

—Maddy's Mad Hair Day, 1 vol. rev. ed. 2013. (Fiction Readers Ser.). (ENG., Illus.). 12p. (J). (gr. 1-1). pap. 12.96 *(978-1-4807-1129-7(2))*; pap. 4.99 *(978-1-4333-5450-2(0))* Shell Educational Publishing.

—Max, 1 vol. rev. ed. 2013. (Fiction Readers Ser.). (ENG., Illus.). 12p. (J). (gr. 1-1). 4.99 *(978-1-4333-5452-6(7))*; pap. 12.96 *(978-1-4807-1131-0(4))* Shell Educational Publishing.

—My Life as a Bee, 1 vol. rev. ed. 2013. (Fiction Readers Ser.). (ENG., Illus.). 20p. (J). (gr. 1-1). pap. 15.96 *(978-1-4807-1139-6(X))*; pap. 4.99 *(978-1-4333-5483-0(7))* Shell Educational Publishing.

—Safari Camp, 1 vol. rev. ed. 2013. (Fiction Readers Ser.). (ENG., Illus.). 20p. (J). (gr. 1-1). pap. 4.99 *(978-1-4333-5494-6(2))*; pap. 15.96 *(978-1-4807-1150-1(0))* Shell Educational Publishing.

—Seb's Train, 1 vol. rev. ed. 2013. (Fiction Readers Ser.). (ENG., Illus.). 12p. (J). (gr. 1-1). pap. 12.96 *(978-1-4807-1125-9(X))*; pap. 4.99 *(978-1-4333-5446-5(2))* Shell Educational Publishing.

—Splash Down!, 1 vol. rev. ed. 2013. (Fiction Readers Ser.). (ENG., Illus.). 12p. (J). (gr. 1-1). pap. 4.99 *(978-1-4333-5456-4(X))*; pap. 12.96 *(978-1-4807-1135-8(7))* Shell Educational Publishing.

—What Can You See?, 1 vol. rev. ed. 2013. (Fiction Readers Ser.). (ENG., Illus.). 20p. (J). (gr. 1-1). pap. 15.96 *(978-1-4807-1146-4(2))*; pap. 4.99 *(978-1-4333-5490-8(X))* Shell Educational Publishing.

Callery, Sean. The Celts. 2015. (Collins Big Cat Ser.). (ENG., Illus.). 48p. (J). (gr. 3-4). pap. 9.95 *(978-0-00-812782-4(4))* HarperCollins Pubs. Ltd. GBR. Dist: Independent Pubs. Group.

Cámara, Noemí, et al. Los Fantasmas de Goya. 2014. (SPA., Illus.). 64p. pap. 13.75 incl. audio compact disk *(978-84-9848-200-3(3))* Edinumen, Editorial ESP. Dist: Cambridge Univ. Pr.

Cambridge University Press Staff. Joey's Quiet War & Other Stories. (J). pap. 8.50 *(978-0-13-177460-5(3))* Globe Fearon Educational Publishing.

Cameron, Andrea. The 10 Most Revolutionary Songs. 2008. 14.99 *(978-1-55448-493-5(6))* Scholastic Library Publishing.

Campbell, Dorthina A. Step Forward Strategies for Struggling Readers: Student Resource Guide. 2005. 59p. (J). stu. ed., per. 8.99 *(978-0-9768208-0-2(3))* Edutech Learning Resource Ctr.

Campbell, Kathy. Let's Draw a Bear with Squares. 2009. (Let's Draw with Shapes Ser.). 24p. (gr. k-k). 42.50 *(978-1-61514-202-6(9)*, PowerKids Pr.) Rosen Publishing Group, Inc., The.

—Let's Draw a Fish with Triangles. 2009. (Let's Draw with Shapes Ser.). 24p. (gr. k-k). 42.50 *(978-1-61514-207-1(X)*, PowerKids Pr.) Rosen Publishing Group, Inc., The.

—Let's Draw a Frog with Ovals. 2009. (Let's Draw with Shapes Ser.). 24p. (gr. k-k). 42.50 *(978-1-61514-208-8(8)*, PowerKids Pr.) Rosen Publishing Group, Inc., The.

Camping Out, 6 vols. (Multicultural Programs Ser.). 16p. (gr. 1-3). 24.95 *(978-0-7802-9203-1(0))* Wright Group/McGraw-Hill.

Cander, Chris. The Word Burglar. Tramonte, Katherine H., illus. 2013. (ENG.). 28p. (J). 19.95 *(978-1-936474-96-7(4)*, e4daa439-fc4a-4ff6-893d-b9aee8dc3ac7) Bright Sky Pr.

Canetti, Yanitzia. Abecedario de Profesiones y Oficios. 2009. (SPA.). 40p. (J). pap. 8.99 *(978-1-59835-122-4(2)*, BrickHouse Education) Cambridge BrickHouse, Inc.

—ABeCedario Salvaje. 2009. (SPA.). 40p. (J). (gr. -1-3). pap. 7.99 *(978-1-59835-117-0(6))* Cambridge BrickHouse, Inc.

Caple, Kathy. Termite Tales. Caple, Kathy, illus. 2009. (Brand New Readers Ser.). (ENG., Illus.). 48p. (J). (gr. -1-3). pap. 5.99 *(978-0-7636-3901-3(X))* Candlewick Pr.

Capucilli, Alyssa Satin. Biscuit & the Baby. Schories, Pat, illus. 2005. (My First I Can Read Ser.). (ENG.). 32p. (J). (gr. -1 — 1). pap. 3.99 *(978-0-06-009461-4(3))* HarperCollins Pubs.

—Biscuit Flies a Kite. Schories, Pat, illus. 2017. (My First I Can Read Ser.). 32p. (J). (gr. -1-3). pap. 3.99 *(978-0-06-223700-2(4))* HarperCollins Pubs.

—Biscuit's Day at the Farm. Schories, Pat, illus. 2007. (My First I Can Read Ser.). (ENG.). 32p. (J). (gr. -1 — 1). pap. 3.99 *(978-0-06-074169-3(4))* HarperCollins Pubs.

—Biscuit's Day at the Farm. 2007. (Biscuit: My First I Can Read! Ser.). (J). lib. bdg. 13.55 *(978-1-4177-9810-0(6)*, Turtleback) Turtleback Bks.

Carangelo, Audrey & Hess, Debra. Radiation, Rats, & Mutant Monsters! 2007. (Read on! Special Edition: Level RA Ser.). (Illus.). 23p. (J). (gr. 4-7). pap. 18.51 *(978-1-4190-3506-7(1))* Steck-Vaughn.

—Teenage Plant Food. 2007. (Read on! Special Edition: Level BA Ser.). (Illus.). 23p. (J). (gr. 4-7). pap. 18.51 *(978-1-4190-3524-1(X))* Steck-Vaughn.

Cardenas, Ernesto A. Where Does Fruit Come From? 2009. 23.95 *(978-1-60698-056-9(4))*; pap. 4.95 *(978-1-60698-054-5(8))* Milo Educational Bks. & Resources.

Carey Molter. Ate As in Skate, 1 vol. 2003. (Word Families Set 8 Ser.: Vol. 8). (ENG., Illus.). 24p. (J). (gr. k-3). lib. bdg. 24.21 *(978-1-59197-271-6(X))* ABDO Publishing Co.

Carle, Eric. The Eric Carle Ready-To-Read Collection: Have You Seen My Cat?; the Greedy Python; Pancakes, Pancakes!; Rooster Is off to See the World; a House for Hermit Crab; Walter the Baker. Carle, Eric, illus. 2014. (World of Eric Carle Ser.). (ENG., Illus.). 160p. (J). (gr. -1-2). pap. 15.99 *(978-1-4814-1632-0(4)*, Simon Spotlight) Simon Spotlight.

—Rooster Is off to See the World. 2013. (Eric Carle Ready-To-Read Ser.). lib. bdg. 13.55 *(978-0-606-32063-4(6)*, Turtleback) Turtleback Bks.

—The Very Quiet Cricket. Carle, Eric, illus. 2014. (Penguin Young Readers, Level 3 Ser.). (ENG., Illus.). 32p. (J). (gr. 1-3). pap. 3.99 *(978-0-448-48138-8(3)*, Penguin Young Readers) Penguin Young Readers Group.

Carlson, Lavelle. Can a Toucan Hoot Too? A Phonemic Awareness Tale, 10 vols. Adams, Lucas, illus. 2003. 32p. (J). (gr. -1-1). per. 16.95 *(978-0-9725803-0-4(1))* Children's Publishing.

Carlton Books UK. Science Museum. 2013. (ENG.). 24p. (J). (gr. k-2). pap., act. bk. ed. 8.99 *(978-1-78097-347-0(0))* Carlton Bks., Ltd. GBR. Dist: Independent Pubs. Group.

Carmen's Star Party. (Early Intervention Levels Ser.). 31.86 *(978-0-7362-0622-8(1))* CENGAGE Learning.

Carmen's Star Party (20), Vol. 20. (Early Intervention Levels Ser.). 5.31 *(978-0-7362-0610-5(8))* CENGAGE Learning.

Carnelos, Melissa. The 10 Most Amazing Animal Heroes. 2008. 14.99 *(978-1-55448-516-1(9))* Scholastic Library Publishing.

Carney, Elizabeth. Mummies. 2009. (Readers Ser.). (ENG., Illus.). 32p. (J). (gr. k-3). 13.90 *(978-1-4263-0529-0(X))*; pap. 3.99 *(978-1-4263-0528-3(1))* National Geographic Society. (National Geographic Children's Bks.).

—National Geographic Readers: Mars. 2014. (Readers Ser.). (ENG., Illus.). 48p. (J). (gr. 1-4). pap. 3.99 *(978-1-4263-1747-7(6)*, National Geographic Children's Bks.) National Geographic Society.

Carosella, Melissa. Dolley Madison: First Lady of the United States, 1 vol. 2011. (Primary Source Readers Ser.). (ENG.). 32p. (J). (gr. 4-4). pap. 8.99 *(978-1-4333-1504-6(1))* Teacher Created Materials, Inc.

—The Fight for Freedom: Ending Slavery in America, 1 vol. 2011. (Primary Source Readers Ser.). (ENG.). 32p. (J). (gr. 5-5). pap. 8.99 *(978-1-4333-1519-0(X))* Teacher Created Materials, Inc.

—Founding Mothers: Women Who Shaped America, 1 vol. 2011. (Primary Source Readers Ser.). (ENG.). 32p. (J). (gr. 5-5). pap. 8.99 *(978-1-4333-1505-3(X))* Teacher Created Materials, Inc.

—Frederick Douglass: Leader of the Abolitionist Movement, 1 vol. 2011. (Primary Source Readers Ser.). (ENG.). 32p. (J). (gr. 4-4). pap. 8.99 *(978-1-4333-1518-3(1))* Teacher Created Materials, Inc.

—Hillary Rodham Clinton: First Lady, Senator, & Secretary of State, 1 vol. 2011. (Primary Source Readers Ser.). (ENG.). 32p. (J). (gr. 4-4). pap. 8.99 *(978-1-4333-1508-4(4))* Teacher Created Materials, Inc.

—Still Marching Strong: Women in Modern America, 1 vol. 2011. (Primary Source Readers Ser.). (ENG.). 32p. (J). (gr. 5-5). pap. 8.99 *(978-1-4333-1509-1(2))* Teacher Created Materials, Inc.

Carr, Denis. The 10 Most Significant Medical Breakthroughs. 2008. 14.99 *(978-1-55448-491-1(X))* Scholastic Library Publishing.

Carr, Elias. Ava y el Picnic Raquitico. Garton, Michael, illus. 2016. (SPA.). (J). ***(978-1-5064-2095-0(8))*** Augsburg Fortress, Pubs.

—Hal y el Nuevo Compañero. Garton, Michael, illus. 2016. (SPA.). (J). ***(978-1-5064-2098-1(2))*** Augsburg Fortress, Pubs.

—Rufus y Su Cola Enojada. Garton, Michael, illus. 2016. (SPA.). (J). ***(978-1-5064-2096-7(6))*** Augsburg Fortress, Pubs.

Carrington, Jim. Sang Kancil & the Tiger Turquoise Band. Oliver, Juanbjuan, illus. 2016. (Cambridge Reading Adventures Ser.). (ENG.). 16p. pap. 6.56 *(978-1-107-55092-6(0))* Cambridge Univ. Pr.

Carroll. Lbd Gka Nf Fun for All Seasons. 2009. (C). pap. 8.53 *(978-1-4189-3337-1(6))* Rigby Education.

Carroll, Claudia. Missy Mouse & the Rocket Ship. 2008. 65p. pap. 9.95 *(978-0-557-01769-0(6))* Lulu Pr., Inc.

Carson-Dellosa Publishing Staff. Add & Subtract, Grade 1. 2010. (Home Workbooks Ser.). (ENG.). 64p. (gr. 1-1). pap. 4.49 *(978-1-60418-792-2(1))* Carson-Dellosa Publishing, LLC.

—Add & Subtract, Grade 2. 2010. (Home Workbooks Ser.). (ENG.). 64p. (gr. 2-2). pap. 4.49 *(978-1-60418-797-7(2))* Carson-Dellosa Publishing, LLC.

—All about Me, Grades Pk - 1. 2010. (Home Workbooks Ser.). (ENG.). 64p. (gr. -1-1). pap. 4.49 *(978-1-60418-767-0(0))* Carson-Dellosa Publishing, LLC.

—Alphabet Animals, Grades PK - K. 2010. (Home Workbooks Ser.). (ENG.). 64p. (gr. -1-k). pap. 4.49 *(978-1-60418-760-1(3))* Carson-Dellosa Publishing, LLC.

—Alphabet, Grades PK - K: Dot-to-Dot. 2010. (Home Workbooks Ser.). (ENG.). 64p. (gr. -1-k). pap. 4.49 *(978-1-60418-759-5(X))* Carson-Dellosa Publishing, LLC.

—Alphabet, Grades PK - K: Sounds & Pictures. 2010. (Home Workbooks Ser.). (ENG.). 64p. (gr. -1-k). pap. 4.49 *(978-1-60418-758-8(1))* Carson-Dellosa Publishing, LLC.

—Beginning Math, Grade 1. 2010. (Home Workbooks Ser.). (ENG.). 64p. (gr. 1-1). pap. 4.49 *(978-1-60418-790-8(5))* Carson-Dellosa Publishing, LLC.

—Beginning Math, Grade K. 2010. (Home Workbooks Ser.). (ENG.). 64p. (gr. k-k). pap. 4.49 *(978-1-60418-776-2(X))* Carson-Dellosa Publishing, LLC.

—Beginning Reading, Grade 1. 2010. (Home Workbooks Ser.). (ENG.). 64p. (gr. 1-1). pap. 4.49 *(978-1-60418-786-1(7))* Carson-Dellosa Publishing, LLC.

—Beginning Reading, Grades K. 2010. (Home Workbooks Ser.). (ENG.). 64p. (gr. k-k). pap. 4.49 *(978-1-60418-773-1(5))* Carson-Dellosa Publishing, LLC.

—Beginning Vocabulary, Grade K. 2010. (Home Workbooks Ser.). (ENG.). 64p. (gr. k-k). pap. 4.49 *(978-1-60418-775-5(1))* Carson-Dellosa Publishing, LLC.

—Colors, Grades PK - K. 2010. (Home Workbooks Ser.). (ENG.). 64p. (gr. -1-k). pap. 4.49 *(978-1-60418-765-6(4))* Carson-Dellosa Publishing, LLC.

—Cursive Practice, Grade 2-3. 2010. (Home Workbooks Ser.). (ENG.). 64p. (gr. 2-3). pap. 4.49 *(978-1-60418-801-1(4))* Carson-Dellosa Publishing, LLC.

—First Grade Skills. 2010. (Home Workbooks Ser.). (ENG.). 64p. (gr. 1-1). pap. 4.49 *(978-1-60418-784-7(0))* Carson-Dellosa Publishing, LLC.

—Kindergarten Skills. 2010. (Home Workbooks Ser.). (ENG.). 64p. (gr. k-k). pap. 4.49 *(978-1-60418-772-4(7))* Carson-Dellosa Publishing, LLC.

—Letters & Sounds, Grades K - 1. 2010. (Home Workbooks Ser.). (ENG.). 64p. (gr. k-1). pap. 4.49 *(978-1-60418-779-3(4))* Carson-Dellosa Publishing, LLC.

—Letters, Grades PK - K: Uppercase & Lowercase. 2010. (Home Workbooks Ser.). (ENG.). 64p. (gr. -1-k). pap. 4.49 *(978-1-60418-757-1(3))* Carson-Dellosa Publishing, LLC.

—Phonics for First Grade. 2010. (Home Workbooks Ser.). (ENG.). 64p. (gr. 1-1). pap. 4.49 *(978-1-60418-785-4(9))* Carson-Dellosa Publishing, LLC.

—Phonics for Kindergarten, Grade K. 2010. (Home Workbooks Ser.). (ENG.). 64p. (gr. k-k). pap. 4.49 *(978-1-60418-774-8(3))* Carson-Dellosa Publishing, LLC.

—Printing Practice for Beginners. 2010. (Home Workbooks Ser.). (ENG.). 64p. (gr. k-1). pap. 4.49 *(978-1-60418-780-9(8))* Carson-Dellosa Publishing, LLC.

—Printing Practice, Grade 2. 2010. (Home Workbooks Ser.). (ENG.). 64p. (gr. 2-2). pap. 4.49 *(978-1-60418-795-3(6))* Carson-Dellosa Publishing, LLC.

—Puzzles & Games: Word Play. 2010. (Home Workbooks Ser.). (ENG.). 64p. (gr. k-1). pap. 4.49 *(978-1-60418-782-3(4))* Carson-Dellosa Publishing, LLC.

—Puzzles & Games for Math, Grade 1. 2010. (Home Workbooks Ser.). (ENG.). 64p. (gr. 1-1). pap. 4.49 *(978-1-60418-791-5(3))* Carson-Dellosa Publishing, LLC.

—Puzzles & Games for Math, Grade 3. 2010. (Home Workbooks Ser.). (ENG.). 64p. (gr. 3-3). pap. 4.49 *(978-1-60418-803-5(0))* Carson-Dellosa Publishing, LLC.

—Puzzles & Games, Grade 1. 2010. (Home Workbooks Ser.). (ENG.). 64p. (gr. 1-1). pap. 4.49 *(978-1-60418-793-9(X))* Carson-Dellosa Publishing, LLC.

—Reading Comprehension, Grade 1. 2010. (Home Workbooks Ser.). (ENG.). 64p. (gr. 1-1). pap. 4.49 *(978-1-60418-787-8(5))* Carson-Dellosa Publishing, LLC.

—Reading Comprehension, Grade 2. 2010. (Home Workbooks Ser.). (ENG.). 64p. (gr. 2-2). pap. 4.49 *(978-1-60418-794-6(8))* Carson-Dellosa Publishing, LLC.

—Reading Comprehension, Grade 3. 2010. (Home Workbooks Ser.). (ENG.). 64p. (gr. 3-3). pap. 4.49 *(978-1-60418-800-4(6))* Carson-Dellosa Publishing, LLC.

—Scissors Skills, Grades PK - 1. 2010. (Home Workbooks Ser.). (ENG.). 64p. (gr. -1-1). pap. 4.49 *(978-1-60418-766-3(2))* Carson-Dellosa Publishing, LLC.

—Shapes, Grades PK - K. 2010. (Home Workbooks Ser.). (ENG.). 64p. (gr. -1-k). pap. 4.49 *(978-1-60418-764-9(6))* Carson-Dellosa Publishing, LLC.

—Spelling & Writing for Beginners, Grade 1. 2010. (Home Workbooks Ser.). (ENG.). 64p. (gr. 1-1). pap. 4.49 *(978-1-60418-788-5(3))* Carson-Dellosa Publishing, LLC.

—Word Play, Grades K - 1: Rhyming. 2010. (Home Workbooks Ser.). (ENG.). 64p. (gr. k-1). pap. 4.49 *(978-1-60418-781-6(6))* Carson-Dellosa Publishing, LLC.

—101 Easy Reading Games, Grade 5. 2006. (ENG.). 128p. (gr. 5-5). pap. 13.99 *(978-0-7682-3415-2(8)*, Frank Schaffer Pubns.) Carson-Dellosa Publishing, LLC.

Carson-Dellosa Publishing Staff, compiled by. Beginning Vocabulary, Grade 1. 2010. (Home Workbooks Ser.). (ENG.). 64p. (gr. 1-1). pap. 4.49 *(978-1-60418-789-2(1))* Carson-Dellosa Publishing, LLC.

—Numbers 0-10, Grades PK - K. 2010. (Home Workbooks Ser.). (ENG.). 64p. (gr. -1-k). pap. 4.49 *(978-1-60418-761-8(1))* Carson-Dellosa Publishing, LLC.

—Puzzles & Games for Beginners, Grade K. 2010. (Home Workbooks Ser.). (ENG.). 64p. (gr. k-k). pap. 4.49 *(978-1-60418-778-6(6))* Carson-Dellosa Publishing, LLC.

—Puzzles & Games for Math, Grade 2. 2010. (Home Workbooks Ser.). (ENG.). 64p. (gr. 2-2). pap. 4.49 *(978-1-60418-798-4(0))* Carson-Dellosa Publishing, LLC.

—Puzzles & Games, Grade 2. 2010. (Home Workbooks Ser.). (ENG.). 64p. (gr. 2-2). pap. 4.49 *(978-1-60418-799-1(9))* Carson-Dellosa Publishing, LLC.

—Puzzles & Games, Grade 2: Word Play. 2010. (Home Workbooks Ser.). (ENG.). 64p. (gr. 2-2). pap. 4.49 *(978-1-60418-796-0(4))* Carson-Dellosa Publishing, LLC.

Carson, Janet. Camping with Colleen. 2006. (Neighborhood Readers Ser.). (ENG.). 8p. (gr. 1-3). pap. 5.15 *(978-1-4042-6803-6(0)*, Rosen Classroom) Rosen Publishing Group, Inc., The.

Carter, Cathy. You Are My Very Best Friend: The Adventures of Mike & Gabe (in English & Spanish) 2012. 26p. 24.95 *(978-1-4626-7072-7(5))* America Star Bks.

Carthew, Mark. Hairy Toe. Lindsey, Cath, illus. 2007. (Collins Big Cat Ser.). (ENG.). 24p. (J). pap. 8.99 *(978-0-00-722867-6(8))* HarperCollins Pubs. Ltd. GBR. Dist: Independent Pubs. Group.

Cartoon Nation, Set. 2009. (Cartoon Nation Ser.). (ENG., Illus.). 32p. (gr. 3-4). lib. bdg. 61.30 *(978-1-4296-3687-2(4)*, Graphic Library) Capstone Press of Coughlan Cos.

Carus, Andre W. Flint Holds Fire, Level D. Incl. Great Beginnings. 1982. pap., wbk. ed. *(978-0-89688-292-8(6)*, 88-292); Headway Level D Real Phonics Workbook A. *(978-0-89688-294-2(2)*, 88-294); Level D. tchr.'s training gde. ed. *(978-0-89688-456-4(2)*, 88-456); Level D. pap., wbk. ed. *(978-0-89688-462-5(7)*, 88-462); Level D. suppl. ed. *(978-0-89688-468-7(6)*, 88-468); Level D. suppl. ed. (J). (gr. 2-6). *(978-0-89688-451-9(1)*, 88-451) Open Court Publishing Co.

Casey & the Nest. 2005. (Georgie Giraffe Chapter Ser.). (J). 7.67 *(978-1-932570-47-2(0))* Pioneer Valley Bks.

Casey, Dawn. Little Bear: A Folktale from Greenland. Corner, Chris, illus. 2014. (Collins Big Cat Progress Ser.). (ENG.). 32p. (J). (gr. 3-4). pap. 7.99 *(978-0-00-751925-5(7))* HarperCollins Pubs. Ltd. GBR. Dist: Independent Pubs. Group.

—Tales of Two Dragons - Collins Big Cat. Kawa, Cosei, illus. 2015. (Collins Big Cat Ser.). (ENG.). 48p. (J). (gr. 3-4). pap. 9.95 *(978-0-00-812784-8(0))* HarperCollins Pubs. Ltd. GBR. Dist: Independent Pubs. Group.

Casey, Dawn & Collins UK Publishing Staff. The White Mouse. Masukawa, Masako, illus. 2016. (ENG.). 32p. (J). pap. 9.95 *(978-0-00-814721-1(3))* HarperCollins Pubs. Ltd. GBR. Dist: Independent Pubs. Group.

Castle, Patricia. In the Garden. 2012. (InfoMax Readers Ser.). (ENG., Illus.). 16 pp.p. (J). (gr. k-1). pap. 7.00 *(978-1-4488-8944-0(8)*, Rosen Classroom) Rosen Publishing Group, Inc., The.

Castor, Harriet. The Incredible Present. Young, Norman, illus. 2004. (Usborne Young Reading: Series Two Ser.). 64p. (J). (gr. k-4). 8.99 *(978-0-7945-1785-4(4)*, Usborne) EDC Publishing.

Castor, Harriet & Collins UK Staff. Charlotte Bronte. 2016. (ENG.). 80p. (J). (gr. 5-6). pap. 9.95 *(978-0-00-816405-8(3))* HarperCollins Pubs. Ltd. GBR. Dist: Independent Pubs. Group.

Cat & Dog Play Hide & Seek. 2012. (Collins Big Cat Ser.). (ENG.). 24p. (J). (gr. -1-k). pap., wbk. ed. 4.99 *(978-0-00-747432-5(6))* HarperCollins Pubs. Ltd. GBR. Dist: Independent Pubs. Group.

The Cat-Flap Trap: Individual Title Six-Packs. (Story Steps Ser.). (gr. k-2). 32.00 *(978-0-7635-9824-2(0))* Rigby Education.

Catron, John. Stories of Many Cultures. 2008. 136p. (gr. 10-11). pap. 21.50 *(978-0-340-96629-7(7))* Hodder Education Group GBR. Dist: Trans-Atlantic Pubns., Inc.

Caulson, Kathleen. Power Reading: Games. Caulson, Kathleen, illus. 2005. (Illus.). (J). 76p. (gr. 2-4). 29.95 *(978-1-883186-98-2(6)*, PPMXG2-3); 88p. (gr. 4-5). 79.95 *(978-1-883186-99-9(4)*, PPMXG45) National Reading Styles Institute, Inc.

—Power Reading: Games/Mixed P1. 2005. (Illus.). 76p. (J). (gr. k-2). 29.95 *(978-1-883186-97-5(8)*, PPMXGP1) National Reading Styles Institute, Inc.

CD & the Giant Cat: Individual Title Six-Packs. (Action Packs Ser.). 120p. (gr. 3-5). 44.00 *(978-0-7635-8426-9(6))* Rigby Education.

Celebrating Children Set 800827, 7. 2005. (J). *(978-1-59794-024-5(0))* Environments, Inc.

Celebrations Grade Level Libraries: I Like Me! 2005. (Little Celebrations Ser.). (J). (gr. k-3). 74.50 *(978-0-673-77743-0(X))* Celebration Pr.

Celebrations Grade Level Libraries: Jamberry. 2005. (Little Celebrations Ser.). (J). (gr. k-3). 82.95 *(978-0-673-75782-1(X))* Celebration Pr.

Celebrations Grade Level Libraries: The Best Bug Parade. 2005. (Little Celebrations Ser.). (J). (gr. k-3). 82.95 *(978-0-673-77590-0(9))* Celebration Pr.

Cernek, Kim. Preschool Songs & Fingerplays: Building Language Experience Through Rhythm & Movement. 2006. (Early Learning Ser.). (Illus.). 128p. (J). (gr. -1-1). per. 13.99 *(978-1-59198-223-4(5))* Creative Teaching Pr., Inc.

Certificate Only. (gr. k-5). 89.00 *(978-0-7578-6542-8(9))*; (gr. 3-5). 89.00 *(978-0-7578-6523-7(2))*; (gr. 3-5). 89.00 *(978-0-7578-6524-4(0))*; (gr. 4-5). 89.00 *(978-0-7578-6536-7(4))*; (gr. 4-5). 89.00 *(978-0-7578-6535-0(6))* Rigby Education.

Chambers, Catherine. Draw the World Turquoise Band. 2016. (Cambridge Reading Adventures Ser.). (ENG., Illus.). 24p. pap. 7.19 *(978-1-107-57684-1(9))* Cambridge Univ. Pr.

Champman, Joan. Val's Vacation. 2006. (Neighborhood Readers Ser.). (ENG.). 16p. (gr. 1-3). pap. 6.50 *(978-1-4042-6990-3(8)*, Rosen Classroom) Rosen Publishing Group, Inc., The.

Chancellor, Deborah. The Changing Environment, Level 5. 2014. (Kingfisher Readers Ser.). (ENG., Illus.). 48p. (J). (gr. k-3). pap. 3.99 *(978-0-7534-7153-1(1)*, 9780753471531, Kingfisher) Roaring Brook Pr.

Chandler, Pauline. Mr. Rabbit the Farmer. Smith, Eric, illus. 2005. (ENG.). 24p. (J). lib. bdg. 23.65 *(978-1-59646-736-1(3))* Dingles & Co.

A Change in Plans: Fourth Grade Guided Comprehension Level M. (On Our Way to English Ser.). (gr. 4-18). 34.50 *(978-0-7578-7156-6(9))* Rigby Education.

Chapman, Cindy. Play It Safe!, 6 vols., Set. 2003. (Phonics Readers 1-36 Ser.). (ENG.). 8p. (gr. k-1). pap. 29.70 *(978-0-7368-3209-0(2)*, Phonics Readers) Capstone Press of Coughlan Cos.

—Where Is Your Home?, 6 vols., Set. 2003. (Phonics Readers 1-36 Ser.). (ENG.). 8p. (gr. k-1). pap. 29.70 *(978-0-7368-3208-3(4)*, Phonics Readers) Capstone Press of Coughlan Cos.

Chapman, Joan. A Cloud Called Cleo. 2006. (Neighborhood Readers Ser.). (ENG.). 12p. (gr. 1-3). pap. 5.90 *(978-1-4042-7050-3(7)*, Rosen Classroom) Rosen Publishing Group, Inc., The.

—Heavy & Light: Learning to Compare Weights of Objects. 2009. (Math for the Real World: Early Emergent Ser.). (ENG., Illus.). 8p. (gr. k-1). pap. 5.15 *(978-0-8239-8844-0(9))* Rosen Publishing Group, Inc., The.

—Living Things. 2008. (Real Readers - Upper Emergent Ser.). (ENG., Illus.). 12p. (gr. 1-2). pap. 5.90 *(978-0-8239-8190-8(8))* Rosen Publishing Group, Inc., The.

—The Lonely Crayon. 2006. (Neighborhood Readers Ser.). (ENG.). 16p. (gr. 1-3). pap. 6.50 *(978-1-4042-7212-5(7)*, Rosen Classroom) Rosen Publishing Group, Inc., The.

—Visiting the Police Station. 2008. (Rosen Real Readers: Upper Emergent Ser.). (ENG., Illus.). 12p. (gr. 1-2). pap. 5.90 *(978-0-8239-8124-3(X))* Rosen Publishing Group, Inc., The.

Chapman, Simon. Himalayas - Bottom to Top. 2017. (ENG., Illus.). 80p. (J). pap. 9.99 ***(978-0-00-820900-1(6))*** HarperCollins Pubs. Ltd. GBR. Dist: Independent Pubs. Group.

Charbonneau, Joelle. The Testing. 2015. (Testing Ser.: 1). lib. bdg. 20.85 *(978-0-606-36831-5(0))* Turtleback Bks.

Charlesworth, Liza. Animal Phonics Readers: A Big Collection of Exciting Informational Books That Target & Teach Key Phonics Skills. 2014. (ENG.). (-2). 129.99 *(978-0-545-57814-1(0)*, Teaching Resources) Scholastic, Inc.

—Dog & Frog: An Animal Friends Reader. Smith, Ian, illus. 2015. 16p. (J). ***(978-0-545-85962-2(X))*** Scholastic, Inc.

—Fish School: An Animal Friends Reader. Smith, Ian, illus. 2015. 16p. (J). pap. ***(978-0-545-85963-9(8))*** Scholastic, Inc.

—Introduction to Nonfiction Write-On - Wipe-Off Flip Chart: An Interactive Learning Tool That Teaches Young Learners How to Navigate Nonfiction Text Features for Reading Success. 2009. (ENG.). 22p. (gr. k-3). pap. 24.99 *(978-0-545-15660-8(2)*, Teaching Resources) Scholastic, Inc.

—Night on the Farm: An Animal Friends Reader. Smith, Ian, illus. 2015. 16p. (J). pap. ***(978-0-545-85964-6(6))*** Scholastic, Inc.

—Six Silly Chicks: An Animal Friends Reader. Smith, Ian, illus. 2015. 16p. (J). pap. ***(978-0-545-85966-0(2))*** Scholastic, Inc.

—Wake up, Rooster! An Animal Friends Reader. Smith, Ian, illus. 2015. 16p. (J). pap. ***(978-0-545-85971-4(9))*** Scholastic, Inc.

Charlesworth, Liza, ed. Life Cycles: Exciting Nonfiction Books That Build Kids' Vocabularies. 2007. (Science Vocabulary Readers Ser.). (ENG.). (gr. 1-3). 79.99 *(978-0-545-01597-4(9)*, Teaching Resources) Scholastic, Inc.

—Wild Weather: Weather!, Tornadoes!, Blizzards!, Hurricanes!, Floods!, Lightning! 2007. (Science Vocabulary Readers Ser.). (ENG., Illus.). (gr. 1-2). 69.99 *(978-0-545-01598-1(7)*, Teaching Resources) Scholastic, Inc.

Charlie & Champ. 2nd ed. 2004. (J). 4.95 *(978-0-943864-57-0(7))* Davenport, May Pubs.

Charlotte's Web Page: Individual Title Six-Packs. (Action Packs Ser.). 104p. (gr. 3-5). 44.00 *(978-0-7635-2987-1(7))* Rigby Education.

Chaud, Benjamin & Cali, Davide. Yo No Hice Mi Tarea Porque ... 2017. (ENG & SPA., Illus.). 44p. (J). 12.99 *(978-1-4521-5934-8(3))* Chronicle Bks. LLC.

Chavez, Sonia, et al. What Will He Wear? 2010. (Reach for Reading Ser.). (ENG., Illus.). 8p. (C). pap. 7.95 *(978-0-7362-7991-8(1))* CENGAGE Learning.

Cheung, Lisa. The 10 Most Destructive Ecosystem Invaders. 2008. 14.99 *(978-1-55448-489-8(8))* Scholastic Library Publishing.

Chewy Books 800779, 2. 2005. (J). *(978-1-59794-040-5(2))* Environments, Inc.

Chichester Clark, Emma. We Are Not Fond of Rat! Chichester Clark, Emma, illus. 2006. (Collins Big Cat Phonics Ser.). (ENG., Illus.). 16p. (J). (gr. -1-1). pap. 5.99 *(978-0-00-723590-2(9))* HarperCollins Pubs. Ltd. GBR. Dist: Independent Pubs. Group.

Chicken Food: 3-in-1 Package. (Sails Literacy Ser.). 24p. (gr. 2-18). 57.00 *(978-0-7578-3213-0(X))* Rigby Education.

Chicken Food: Big Book Only. (Sails Literacy Ser.). 24p. (gr. 2-18). 27.00 *(978-0-7635-6999-0(2))* Rigby Education.

Children & Families Books 800716, 10. 2005. (J). *(978-1-59794-014-6(3))* Environments, Inc.

Children's Feelings Books 800829, 14. 2005. (J). *(978-1-59794-026-9(7))* Environments, Inc.

Childrens Press Staff, ed. A Rookie Reader. 2005. (Rookie Reader Ser.). (ENG.). 96p. (J). (gr. -1-2). Set. pap. 9.95 *(978-0-516-25327-5(1))*Set 1. pap. 9.95 *(978-0-516-25326-8(3))* Scholastic Library Publishing. (Children's Pr.).

—A Rookie Reader - Level A, Set 1. 2005. (Rookie Reader Ser.). (ENG.). 72p. (J). (gr. -1-2). pap. 9.95 *(978-0-516-25325-1(5)*, Children's Pr.) Scholastic Library Publishing.

Children's World Books 800828, 10. 2005. (J). *(978-1-59794-025-2(9))* Environments, Inc.

Child's World Tapes Book Set 800912, 3 vols. 2005. (J). pap. *(978-1-59794-077-1(1))* Environments, Inc.

Chile Fever. (Lexile Levels Ser.). 9.09 *(978-1-56334-733-7(4))* CENGAGE Learning.

Chilek, Laurie. ¡Qué miedo! ¡un tobogán! (the Scary Slide) 2007. (Lecturas del barrio (Neighborhood Readers) Ser.). (SPA.). 8p. 29.95 *(978-1-4042-7291-0(7)*, Rosen Classroom) Rosen Publishing Group, Inc., The.

—The Scary Slide. (Neighborhood Readers Ser.). (ENG.). 8p. 2007. 29.95 *(978-1-4042-7290-3(9))* 2006. (gr. -1-3). pap. 5.15 *(978-1-4042-6698-8(4))* Rosen Publishing Group, Inc., The. (Rosen Classroom).

Chinery, Michael. Animales Salvajes. (Enciclopedias Everest Internacional Ser.). (SPA., Illus.). 320p. (J). (gr. 3-5). *(978-84-241-9399-7(7)*, EV1502) Everest Editora ESP. Dist: Lectorum Pubns., Inc.

Chinery, Michael & Michael, Chinery. Enciclopedia de los Animales Salvajes, 8 vols.Tr. of Wild World of Animals. (SPA.). 346p. (J). (gr. 3-5). 100.00 *(978-84-241-2059-7(0))* Everest Editora ESP. Dist: Lectorum Pubns., Inc.

Chiquilibros: Add-to Packs. (Smart Start Ser.). (gr. k-1). 37.00 *(978-0-7635-4062-3(5))*; 76.00 *(978-0-7635-4068-5(4))*; 37.00 *(978-0-7635-4064-7(1))*; 37.00 *(978-0-7635-4066-1(8))* Rigby Education.

Chiquilibros: Chiquicuentos Complete Package. (gr. -1-1). 250.00 *(978-0-7635-8570-9(X))* Rigby Education.

Chiquilibros: Chiquicuentos Grupo A Add-to Pack. (gr. -1-1). 125.00 *(978-0-7635-8566-2(1))* Rigby Education.

Chiquilibros: Chiquicuentos Grupo B Add-to Pack. (gr. -1-1). 125.00 *(978-0-7635-8567-9(X))* Rigby Education.

Chiquilibros: Cuentos listos Complete Packages. (gr. k-1). 250.00 *(978-0-7635-4067-8(6))*; 151.00 *(978-0-7635-4065-4(X))*; 151.00 *(978-0-7635-4063-0(3))*; 151.00 *(978-0-7635-4061-6(7))* Rigby Education.

Ciencias. (Enciclopedias Everest Internacional Ser.). (SPA., Illus.). (YA). (gr. 5-8). 41.95 *(978-84-241-9405-5(5)*, EV7495) Everest Editora ESP. Dist: Lectorum Pubns., Inc.

Cinderella, Level 1. 2016. (Ladybird Readers Ser.). (ENG., Illus.). 48p. (J). (gr. 2-4). pap. 9.99 *(978-0-241-25407-3(8))* Penguin Bks., Ltd. GBR. Dist: Independent Pubs. Group.

Citra, Becky. Jeremy & the Golden Fleece, 1 vol. Milne, Jessica, illus. 2007. (Orca Echoes Ser.). (ENG.). 64p. (J). (gr. 2-3). per. 6.95 *(978-1-55143-657-9(4))* Orca Bk. Pubs. USA.

—Strawberry Moon, 1 vol., Vol. 5. 2005. (Orca Young Readers Ser.: Book #5). (ENG., Illus.). 96p. (J). (gr. 3-6). per. 5.95 *(978-1-55143-367-7(2))* Orca Bk. Pubs. USA.

A City Divided. 2003. (Illus.). pap. 7.60 *(978-0-7398-7526-1(4))* Steck-Vaughn.

Civardi, Anne. The Complete Book of First Experiences. Cartwright, Stephen, illus. 2005. (Usborne First Experiences Ser.). 144p. (J). (gr. -1-3). 19.95 *(978-0-7945-1012-1(4)*, Usborne) EDC Publishing.

Clark, Julie. The 10 Greatest Breakthroughs in Space Exploration. 2008. (J). 14.99 *(978-1-55448-520-8(7))* Scholastic Library Publishing.

—The 10 Most Essential Chemical Messengers in the Body. 2008. 14.99 *(978-1-55448-541-3(X))* Scholastic Library Publishing.

Clark, Lisa. The 10 Most Revolting Parasites. 2008. (J). 14.99 *(978-1-55448-521-5(5))* Scholastic Library Publishing.

Clark, Sarah Kartchner. Doctors Then & Now, 1 vol. 2006. (Primary Source Readers Ser.). (ENG.). 32p. (J). (gr. 2-2). pap. 8.99 *(978-0-7439-9373-9(X))* Shell Educational Publishing.

—Nurses Then & Now, 1 vol. 2006. (Primary Source Readers Ser.). (ENG.). 32p. (J). (gr. 1-1). pap. 8.99 *(978-0-7439-9374-6(8))* Shell Educational Publishing.

Clarke, Catriona. The Life Cycle of a Polar Bear. 2017. (ENG., Illus.). 48p. (J). pap. 8.99 ***(978-0-00-820881-3(6))*** HarperCollins Pubs. Ltd. GBR. Dist: Independent Pubs. Group.

—Living in an Earthquake Zone. 2017. (ENG., Illus.). 32p. (J). pap. 8.99 ***(978-0-00-820878-3(6))*** HarperCollins Pubs. Ltd. GBR. Dist: Independent Pubs. Group.

Clarke, Ella. I Am So Beautiful, 1 vol. rev. ed. 2013. (Fiction Readers Ser.). (ENG., Illus.). 20p. (J). (gr. 1-1). 4.99 *(978-1-4333-5485-4(3))*; pap. 15.96 *(978-1-4807-1141-9(1))* Shell Educational Publishing.

—When I Grow Up, 1 vol. rev. ed. 2013. (Fiction Readers Ser.). (ENG., Illus.). 12p. (J). (gr. 1-1). pap. 12.96 *(978-1-4807-1127-3(6))*; pap. 4.99 *(978-1-4333-5448-9(9))* Shell Educational Publishing.

Clarke, Evelyn. Crisis. 2007. (Steck-Vaughn BOLDPRINT Anthologies Ser.). (ENG., Illus.). 48p. (gr. 9-12). pap. 16.90 *(978-1-4190-4034-4(0))* Houghton Mifflin Harcourt Publishing Co.

Clarke, Jane. The Amazing Adventures of Batbird. Schon, Nick, illus. 2005. (Collins Big Cat Ser.). (ENG.). 32p. (J). (gr. 2-3). pap. 7.99 *(978-0-00-718637-2(1))* HarperCollins Pubs. Ltd. GBR. Dist: Independent Pubs. Group.

—Chewy Hughie. McConnell, Sarah, illus. 2006. (Collins Big Cat Ser.). (ENG.). 136p. (J). (gr. 2-2). pap. 6.99 *(978-0-00-718692-1(4))* HarperCollins Pubs. Ltd. GBR. Dist: Independent Pubs. Group.

—I'm Not Wearing That! Mostyn, David, illus. 2005. (ENG.). 24p. (J). lib. bdg. 23.65 *(978-1-59646-716-3(9))* Dingles & Co.

—Prince Albert's Birthday. Chatterton, Martin, illus. 2005. 24p. (J). lib. bdg. 23.65 *(978-1-59646-748-4(7))* Dingles & Co.

Clarke, M. The Story of Troy. 2007. (Illus.). 184p. per. *(978-1-4065-1381-3(4))* Dodo Pr.

Clarke, Michael. The Story of Troy. l.t. ed. 2007. (ENG.). 202p. pap. 22.99 *(978-1-4346-0682-2(1))* Creative Media Partners, LLC.

—The Story of Troy: The Story of Troy. 2007. (ENG.). 178p. pap. 19.99 *(978-1-4346-0607-5(4))* Creative Media Partners, LLC.

Clarke, Zoë. The Modern Pentathlon. 2012. (Collins Big Cat Progress Ser.). (ENG., Illus.). 48p. (J). (gr. 4-5). pap. 6.99 *(978-0-00-742884-7(7))* HarperCollins Pubs. Ltd. GBR. Dist: Independent Pubs. Group.

Class Collection: Fourth Grade. (On Our Way to English Ser.). (gr. 4-18). cd-rom 29.95 *(978-0-7578-4368-6(9))* Rigby Education.

Classic Storytapes Book Set 800911, 3 vols. 2005. (J). pap. *(978-1-59794-076-4(3))* Environments, Inc.

Classification (Gr. 1-2) 2003. (J). *(978-1-58232-040-3(3))* ECS Learning Systems, Inc.

Clausen, Andrew. Prince Caspian. 2003. stu. ed., ring bd. 14.99 *(978-1-58609-195-8(6))* Progeny Pr.

Claybourne, Anna & Veres, Laszlo. Charles Darwin & Alfred Russel Wallace. 2014. (Collins Big Cat Ser.). (ENG.). 256p. (J). (gr. 5). pap. 9.95 *(978-0-00-753014-4(5))* HarperCollins Pubs. Ltd. GBR. Dist: Independent Pubs. Group.

Cleaning up the Park: Individual Title Six-Packs. (gr. -1-2). 23.00 *(978-0-7635-8817-5(2))* Rigby Education.

Cleary, Brian P. & Maday, Alice M. Sounds Like Reading, 8 vols., Set. Miskimins, Jason, illus. Incl. Bug in the Jug Wants a Hug: A Short Vowel Sounds Book. lib. bdg. 23.93 *(978-0-7613-9503-4(2))*; Clown in the Gown Drives the Car with the Star: A Book about Diphthongs & R-Controlled Vowel. lib. bdg. 23.93 *(978-0-8225-7637-2(6))*; Frail Snail on the Trail: Long Vowel Sounds with Consonant Blends. lib. bdg. 23.93 *(978-0-8225-7638-9(4))*; Nice Mice in the Rice: A Long Vowel Sound Book. lib. bdg. 23.93 *(978-0-8225-7628-0(7))*; Peaches on the Beaches: A Book about Inflectional Endings. lib. bdg. 23.93 *(978-0-8225-7636-5(8))*; Stop, Drop, & Flop in the Slop: A Short Vowel Sounds Book with Consonant Blends. lib. bdg. 23.93 *(978-0-8225-7635-8(X))*; Thing on the Wing Can Sing: Short Vowel Sounds & Consonant Digraphs. lib. bdg. 23.93 *(978-0-8225-7639-6(2))*; Whose Shoes Would You Choose? A Long Vowel Sounds Book with Consonant Digraphs. lib. bdg. 23.93 *(978-0-8225-7640-2(6))*; (Illus.). 32p. (gr. -1-2). 2009. lib. bdg. *(978-0-7613-9502-7(4)*, Millbrook Pr.) Lerner Publishing Group.

Clemens, Micki. The 10 Most Ingenious Fictional Detectives. 2007. (Illus.). (J). 14.99 *(978-1-55448-514-7(2))* Scholastic Library Publishing.

Clements, Jonathan, et al. Early Kings of England. 2016. (ENG., Illus.). 48p. (J). (gr. 3-4). pap. 9.95 *(978-0-00-816386-0(3))* HarperCollins Pubs. Ltd. GBR. Dist: Independent Pubs. Group.

Clendenin, Arlene M. & Clendenin, Bernard S. The Adventures of the Yellow Beak Bird & the Flying Cats: Yellow Beak Bird & the Flying Cats. 2013. 48p. pap. 11.99 *(978-0-9897662-1-0(7))* Clendenin Fine Art Concepts.

Climbing: Individual Title Six-Packs. (Literatura 2000 Ser.). (gr. k-1). 28.00 *(978-0-7635-0047-4(X))* Rigby Education.

Clish, Marian L. Fish Don't Swim in a Tree. Clish, Lori, illus. (J). (gr. k-3). pap. 7.95 *(978-1-928632-12-2(2))* Writers Marketplace:Consulting, Critiquing & Publishing.

Cloudcatcher, 6 Packs. (Action Packs Ser.). 104p. (gr. 3-5). 44.00 *(978-0-7635-8412-2(6))* Rigby Education.

Clough, Lisa. Petal & Poppy & the Spooky Halloween! Briant, Ed, illus. 2014. (Green Light Readers Level 2 Ser.). (ENG.). 32p. (J). (gr. -1-3). 12.99 *(978-0-544-33602-5(X)*, HMH Books For Young Readers) Houghton Mifflin Harcourt Publishing Co.

Clover, Louise. Bullring Kid & Country Cowboy Level 4 Intermediate. 2009. (ENG., Illus.). 96p. pap. 12.75 *(978-84-8323-495-2(5))* Cambridge Univ. Pr.

Clyne, Margaret & Griffiths, Rachel. Let's Make Music. 2004. (ENG., Illus.). 16p. (J). (gr. 1-1). pap. 10.92 *(978-0-7652-5155-8(8)*, Celebration Pr.) Pearson Schl.

Coan, Sharon. Special Me, 1 vol. 2009. (Early Childhood Themes Ser.). (ENG., Illus.). 16p. (J). (gr. -1-2). pap. 6.99 *(978-1-4333-1469-8(X))* Shell Educational Publishing.

—Yo Soy Especial, 1 vol. rev. ed. 2010. (Early Childhood Themes Ser.).Tr. of Special Me. (SPA., Illus.). 16p. (J). (gr. -1-2). pap. 19.99 *(978-1-4333-1945-7(4))*; pap. 6.99 *(978-1-4333-1944-0(6))* Shell Educational Publishing.

Cochran, Kate & Benchmark Education Co., LLC Staff. Why Mice Hide. 2015. (BuildUp Ser.). (J). (gr. 1). *(978-1-4900-0728-1(8))* Benchmark Education Co.

Cofreros, Felipe. Sam's Wish. 2007. 28p. per. 21.99 *(978-1-4257-8486-7(0))* Xlibris Corp.

Cohen, Della. Whoppers! 2005. (Illus.). 32p. (J). *(978-0-669-51412-4(8))* Great Source Education Group, Inc.

Cohn, Jessica. Hand to Earth Saving the Environment, 1 vol. 2nd rev. ed. 2012. (Nonfiction Readers Ser.). (ENG.). 48p. (J). (gr. 4-4). pap. 9.99 *(978-1-4333-4868-6(3))* Teacher Created Materials, Inc.

—Hand to Heart: Improving Communities, 1 vol. 2nd rev. ed. 2012. (Nonfiction Readers Ser.). (ENG.). 48p. (J). (gr. 4-4). pap. 9.99 *(978-1-4333-4866-2(7))* Teacher Created Materials, Inc.

—Hand to Paw - Protecting Animals, 1 vol. 2nd rev. ed. 2012. (TIME for KIDS(r) Nonfiction Readers Ser.). (ENG.). 48p. (J). (gr. 4-4). pap. 9.99 *(978-1-4333-4867-9(5))* Teacher Created Materials, Inc.

—The Medieval Islamic World, 1 vol. 2012. (Primary Source Readers Ser.). (ENG.). 32p. (J). (gr. 5-5). pap. 8.99 *(978-1-4333-5003-0(3))* Teacher Created Materials, Inc.

—Muhammad: Prophet of Islam, 1 vol. 2012. (Primary Source Readers Ser.). (ENG.). 32p. (J). (gr. 4-4). pap. 8.99 *(978-1-4333-5004-7(1))* Teacher Created Materials, Inc.

Cohn, Jessica & Kuligowski, Stephanie. Fearless! Stunt People, 1 vol. 2nd rev. ed. 2013. (Nonfiction Readers Ser.). (ENG.). 64p. (J). (gr. 5-5). pap. 10.99 *(978-1-4333-4941-6(8))* Teacher Created Materials, Inc.

—Wild Work! Animal Trainers, 1 vol. 2nd rev. ed. 2013. (Nonfiction Readers Ser.). (ENG.). 64p. (J). (gr. 5-5). pap. 10.99 *(978-1-4333-4942-3(6))* Teacher Created Materials, Inc.

Coirault, Christine. Colors. 2008. (Gymboree Play & Music Ser.). (ENG., Illus.). 24p. (J). (gr. -1). bds. *(978-1-55470-039-4(6))* Me to We.

—Numbers: Learn to Count in Five Languages (English, Spanish, French, German, Italian) 2008. (Gymboree Play & Music Ser.). (ENG., Illus.). 24p. (J). (gr. -1). bds. *(978-1-55470-032-5(9))* Magma.

Coldwell, Lamar. Baron's Book Hunt. 2016. (Rosen REAL Readers: Social Studies Nonfiction / Fiction: Family, Community, & the World Ser.). 8p. (gr. 1-k). pap. 5.46 *(978-1-5081-2476-4(0)*, Rosen Classroom) Rosen Publishing Group, Inc., The.

—Building with Strong Materials. 2016. (Rosen REAL Readers: STEM & STEAM Collection). 12p. (gr. 1-k). pap. 6.33 *(978-1-5081-2449-8(3)*, Rosen Classroom) Rosen Publishing Group, Inc., The.

—Camillia Captures el Cuco. 2016. (Rosen REAL Readers: Social Studies Nonfiction / Fiction: Family, Community, & the World Ser.). 12p. (gr. 1-k). pap. 6.33 *(978-1-5081-2556-3(2)*, Rosen Classroom) Rosen Publishing Group, Inc., The.

—Constitution Day. 2016. (Rosen REAL Readers: Social Studies Nonfiction / Fiction: Family, Community, & the World Ser.). 8p. (gr. 1-k). pap. 5.46 *(978-1-5081-2287-6(3)*, Rosen Classroom) Rosen Publishing Group, Inc., The.

—The Day My Brother Got Lost. 2016. (Rosen REAL Readers: Social Studies Nonfiction / Fiction: Family, Community, & the World Ser.). 12p. (gr. 1-k). pap. 6.33 *(978-1-5081-2530-3(9)*, Rosen Classroom) Rosen Publishing Group, Inc., The.

—A Law for People. 2016. (Rosen REAL Readers: Social Studies Nonfiction / Fiction: Family, Community, & the World Ser.). 8p. (gr. 1-k). pap. 5.46 *(978-1-5081-2503-7(1)*, Rosen Classroom) Rosen Publishing Group, Inc., The.

—A River Runs Through This Valley. 2016. (Rosen REAL Readers: Social Studies Nonfiction / Fiction: Family, Community, & the World Ser.). 8p. (gr. 1-k). pap. 5.46 *(978-1-5081-2521-1(X)*, Rosen Classroom) Rosen Publishing Group, Inc., The.

—The Stone House. 2016. (Rosen REAL Readers: STEM & STEAM Collection). 12p. (gr. 1-k). pap. 6.33 *(978-1-5081-2664-5(X)*, Rosen Classroom) Rosen Publishing Group, Inc., The.

—The Sun on Our Roof. 2016. (Rosen REAL Readers: Social Studies Nonfiction / Fiction: Family, Community, & the World Ser.). 12p. (gr. 1-k). pap. 6.33 *(978-1-5081-2574-7(0)*, Rosen Classroom) Rosen Publishing Group, Inc., The.

—The Tuning Fork. 2016. (Rosen REAL Readers: STEM & STEAM Collection). 12p. (gr. 1-k). pap. 6.33 *(978-1-5081-2428-3(0)*, Rosen Classroom) Rosen Publishing Group, Inc., The.

Cole, Bob. Power Reading: Chapter Books/Wizard of OZ. Sirrell, Terri, illus. 2004. 94p. (J). (gr. 3-4). vinyl bd. 39.95 *(978-1-883186-64-7(1)*, PPCL1) National Reading Styles Institute, Inc.

—Power Reading: Chapter/Sci-Fi/Dr. Little. Sirrell, Terri, illus. 2004. 25p. (J). (gr. 3-4). vinyl bd. 39.95 *(978-1-883186-63-0(3)*, PPSF1) National Reading Styles Institute, Inc.

—Power Reading: Chapter/Sci-Fi/Dr. Little 2. Ford, David, illus. 2005. 25p. (J). (gr. 3-4). vinyl bd. 39.95 *(978-1-883186-76-0(5)*, PPSF4) National Reading Styles Institute, Inc.

—Power Reading: Chapter/Sci-Fi/Superhero. Ford, David, illus. 2004. 25p. (J). (gr. 3-4). vinyl bd. 39.95

PQR

(978-1-883186-62-3(5), PPSF2) National Reading Styles Institute, Inc.
—Power Reading: Chapter/Sci-Fi/Time Warp. Ford, David, illus. 2004. 25p. (J). (gr. 4-18). vinyl bd. 39.95 *(978-1-883186-60-9(9)*, PPSF3) National Reading Styles Institute, Inc.
—Power Reading: Chapter/Sci-Fi/Time Warp 2. Ford, David, illus. 2005. 52p. (J). (gr. 4-18). vinyl bd. 39.95 *(978-1-883186-75-3(7)*, PPSF5) National Reading Styles Institute, Inc.
—Power Reading: Classics/Jungle Book. Connor, Robin, illus. 2004. 94p. (J). (gr. 4-18). vinyl bd. 39.95 *(978-1-883186-61-6(7)*, PPCL2) National Reading Styles Institute, Inc.
—Power Reading: Classics/Treasure Island. Lee, Joe, illus. 2004. 94p. (J). (gr. 5-6). vinyl bd. 39.95 *(978-1-883186-59-3(5)*, PPCL3) National Reading Styles Institute, Inc.
—Power Reading: Comic Book/Dr. Little. Sirrell, Terri, illus. 2005. 36p. (J). (gr. 2-4). vinyl bd. *(978-1-883186-77-7(3)*, PPSFC1) National Reading Styles Institute, Inc.
—Power Reading: Comic Book/Jungle Book. Connor, Robin, illus. 2005. 62p. (J). (gr. 3-18). vinyl bd. 39.95 *(978-1-883186-74-6(9)*, PPCLC2) National Reading Styles Institute, Inc.
—Power Reading: Comic Book/Time Warp. Ford, David, illus. 2005. 36p. (J). (gr. 3-4). vinyl bd. 29.95 *(978-1-883186-69-2(2)*, PPSFC3) National Reading Styles Institute, Inc.
—Power Reading: Comic Book/Time Warp 2. Ford, David, illus. 2005. 36p. (J). (gr. 3-4). vinyl bd. 29.95 *(978-1-933533-01-8(3)*, PPSFC3A) National Reading Styles Institute, Inc.
—Power Reading: Comic Book/Wizard of OZ. Sirrell, Terri, illus. 2005. 60p. (J). (gr. 3-4). vinyl bd. 39.95 *(978-1-883186-80-7(3)*, PPCLC1) National Reading Styles Institute, Inc.
—Power Reading: Nail-Biters! 2. Morton, Vivian, illus. 2005. 94p. (J). (gr. 6-18). vinyl bd. 89.95 *(978-1-883186-25-8(0)*, PPNB2) National Reading Styles Institute, Inc.
Cole, Bob & Sirrell, Terri. Power Reading: Comic Book/Dr. Little 2. 2005. (Illus.). 36p. (J). (gr. 2-4). vinyl bd. 29.95 *(978-1-933533-00-1(5)*, PPSFC1A) National Reading Styles Institute, Inc.
Cole, Steve. Twit Twoo: The Owl Who Was Nearly Magic Twit Twoo. Porter, Jane, illus. 2016. (Early Reader Ser.). (ENG.). 64p. (J). (gr. k-2). 6.99 *(978-1-4440-1344-3(0)*, Orion Children's Bks.) Hachette Children's Group GBR. Dist: Hachette Bk. Group.
Coleman-Smith, Charlotte. Spotlight on Brazil - Collins Big Cat. 2015. (Collins Big Cat Ser.). (ENG., Illus.). 32p. (J). (gr. 2-3). pap. 8.95 *(978-0-00-812777-0(8))* HarperCollins Pubs. Ltd. GBR. Dist: Independent Pubs. Group.
Colfer, Eoin. The Legend of Spud Murphy. McCoy, Glenn, illus. 2005. (Eoin Colfer's Legend Of... Ser.). 95p. (gr. 2-6). 16.00 *(978-0-7569-6514-3(4))* Perfection Learning Corp.
Coll-Seck, Jayden. The Class Photo, 01 vols., 1. 2016. (Rosen REAL Readers: Social Studies Nonfiction / Fiction: Family, Community, & the World Ser.). (ENG.). 8p. (J). pap. 5.46 *(978-1-5081-1851-0(5)*, Rosen Classroom) Rosen Publishing Group, Inc., The.
—Fairy Tale Food, 01 vols., 1. 2016. (Rosen REAL Readers: Social Studies Nonfiction / Fiction: Family, Community, & the World Ser.). (ENG.). 12p. (J). pap. 6.33 *(978-1-5081-1955-5(4)*, Rosen Classroom) Rosen Publishing Group, Inc., The.
—The Finger Paint Party, 01 vols., 1. 2016. (Rosen REAL Readers: STEM & STEAM Collection). (ENG.). 8p. (J). pap. 5.46 *(978-1-5081-1461-1(7)*, Rosen Classroom) Rosen Publishing Group, Inc., The.
—In Uncle Bill's Shop, 01 vols., 1. 2016. (Rosen REAL Readers: STEM & STEAM Collection). (ENG.). 12p. (J). pap. 6.33 *(978-1-5081-1542-7(7)*, Rosen Classroom) Rosen Publishing Group, Inc., The.
—Our School Motto Matters, 01 vols., 1. 2016. (Rosen REAL Readers: Social Studies Nonfiction / Fiction: Family, Community, & the World Ser.). (ENG.). 12p. (J). pap. 6.33 *(978-1-5081-1928-9(7)*, Rosen Classroom) Rosen Publishing Group, Inc., The.
—Principal for a Day, 01 vols., 1. 2016. (Rosen REAL Readers: Social Studies Nonfiction / Fiction: Family, Community, & the World Ser.). (ENG.). 12p. (J). pap. 6.33 *(978-1-5081-1979-1(1)*, Rosen Classroom) Rosen Publishing Group, Inc., The.
—The Quilt, 01 vols., 1. 2016. (Rosen REAL Readers: Social Studies Nonfiction / Fiction: Family, Community, & the World Ser.). (ENG.). 8p. (J). pap. 5.46 *(978-1-5081-1887-9(6)*, Rosen Classroom) Rosen Publishing Group, Inc., The.
—Sara Tries Again, 01 vols., 1. 2016. (Rosen REAL Readers: STEM & STEAM Collection). (ENG.). 12p. (J). pap. 6.33 *(978-1-5081-1524-3(9)*, Rosen Classroom) Rosen Publishing Group, Inc., The.
—Tanya the Chef, 01 vols., 1. 2016. (Rosen REAL Readers: Social Studies Nonfiction / Fiction: Family, Community, & the World Ser.). (ENG.). 12p. (J). pap. 6.33 *(978-1-5081-1393-5(9)*, Rosen Classroom) Rosen Publishing Group, Inc., The.
—A Tree's Tale, 01 vols., 1. 2016. (Rosen REAL Readers: STEM & STEAM Collection). (ENG.). 8p. (J). pap. 5.46 *(978-1-5081-1397-3(1)*, Rosen Classroom) Rosen Publishing Group, Inc., The.
—A Turtle for Malia, 01 vols., 1. 2016. (Rosen REAL Readers: STEM & STEAM Collection). (ENG.). 8p. (J). pap. 5.46 *(978-1-5081-1441-3(2)*, Rosen Classroom) Rosen Publishing Group, Inc., The.
—Who Are the Millers?, 01 vols., 1. 2016. (Rosen REAL Readers: Social Studies Nonfiction / Fiction: Family, Community, & the World Ser.). (ENG.). 8p. (J). pap. 5.46 *(978-1-5081-1383-6(1)*, Rosen Classroom) Rosen Publishing Group, Inc., The.
—Who Is the Man in the Photo?, 01 vols., 1. 2016. (Rosen REAL Readers: Social Studies Nonfiction / Fiction: Family, Community, & the World Ser.). (ENG.). 8p. (J). pap. 5.46 *(978-1-5081-1869-5(8)*, Rosen Classroom) Rosen Publishing Group, Inc., The.
Collection for Readers Bookshelf Collection, 6 units, Set. 2004. (Scott Foresman Reading Ser.). (gr. 3-18). 180.00 *(978-0-328-03135-1(6))*; (gr. 6-18). 180.00 *(978-0-328-03138-2(0))* Addison-Wesley Educational Pubs., Inc.
Collection for Readers Take-Home. 2004. (Scott Foresman Reading Ser.). (gr. 3-18). 48.00 *(978-0-328-02302-8(7))*; (gr. 4-18). 48.00 *(978-0-328-02684-5(0))*; (gr. 5-18). 48.00 *(978-0-328-02685-2(9))*; (gr. 6-18). 48.00 *(978-0-328-02686-9(7))* Addison-Wesley Educational Pubs., Inc.
Collins, Anne. Island for Sale. 2007. (ENG., Illus.). 22p. pap. 17.32 *(978-1-4058-5201-2(1))* Pearson Education.
Collins Staff. Amazing Composers. 2014. (Collins English Readers Ser.). (ENG.). 80p. pap. 13.95 incl. audio compact disk *(978-0-00-754502-5(9))* HarperCollins Pubs. Ltd. GBR. Dist: Independent Pubs. Group.
—Amazing Leaders (Level 4) 2014. (Collins English Readers Ser.). (ENG.). 112p. pap. 13.95 incl. audio compact disk *(978-0-00-754507-0(X))* HarperCollins Pubs. Ltd. GBR. Dist: Independent Pubs. Group.
—Amazing Philanthropists, Level 3. 2014. (Collins English Readers Ser.). (ENG.). 96p. pap. 13.95 incl. audio compact disk *(978-0-00-754504-9(5))* HarperCollins Pubs. Ltd. GBR. Dist: Independent Pubs. Group.
Collins UK. My Balcony Oasis: Level 10. 2016. (Collins Big Cat Arabic Ser.). (ENG.). 24p. (J). pap. 5.99 ***(978-0-00-818582-4(4))*** HarperCollins Pubs. Ltd. GBR. Dist: Independent Pubs. Group.
Color It My Way: Individual Title Six-Packs. (Story Steps Ser.). (gr. k-2). 32.00 *(978-0-7635-9611-8(6))* Rigby Education.
The Color Purple Student Packet. 2004. (YA). 12.99 *(978-1-58130-508-1(7))* Novel Units, Inc.
Come & Have Fun: KinderWords Individual Title Six-Packs. (Kinderstarters Ser.). 8p. (gr. -1-1). 21.00 *(978-0-7635-8701-7(X))* Rigby Education.
Come on Up: KinderWords Individual Title Six-Packs. (Kinderstarters Ser.). 8p. (gr. -1-1). 21.00 *(978-0-7635-8698-0(6))* Rigby Education.
Come to My House. (Greetings Ser.: Vol. 3). 24p. (gr. 2-3). 31.00 *(978-0-7635-5702-7(1))* Rigby Education.
Comic Book Facts. 2003. (Illus.). pap. 5.60 *(978-0-7398-7514-8(0))* Steck-Vaughn.
Como buenos Amigos: Social/Emotional Lap Book. (Pebble Soup Exploraciones Ser.). (gr. -1-18). 16.00 *(978-0-7578-1782-3(3))* Rigby Education.
Complete Add-on. 2005. (Book Treks Ser.). (J). (gr. 3-18). 152.95 *(978-0-7652-6134-2(0))*; (gr. 4-18). 157.50 *(978-0-7652-6135-9(9))*; (gr. 5-18). 157.50 *(978-0-7652-6136-6(7))* Celebration Pr.
Complete DRA Pack. (Dra Levels Ser.). 752.54 *(978-0-7362-2576-2(5))* CENGAGE Learning.
Complete Early Intervention Pack. (Early Intervention Levels Ser.). 610.07 *(978-0-7362-2557-1(9))* CENGAGE Learning.
The Complete Graphica Collection (2013) 2013. (Graphica Ser.). (ENG., Illus.). 24–48p. (gr. 3-8). 16041.10 *(978-1-4777-0643-5(7)*, Rosen Classroom) Rosen Publishing Group, Inc., The.
Complete Guided Reading Pack. (Guided Reading Levels Ser.). 752.54 *(978-0-7362-2565-6(X))* CENGAGE Learning.
Complete High Five USA Reading Program I. (gr. 4-18). 667.95 incl. audio *(978-0-7368-9580-4(9)*, High Five) Red Brick Learning.
Complete High Five USA Reading Program I, Books Only. (gr. 4-18). 599.95 *(978-0-7368-9581-1(7)*, High Five) Red Brick Learning.
Complete High Five USA Reading Program II. (gr. 4-18). 667.95 incl. audio *(978-0-7368-3859-7(7)*, High Five) Red Brick Learning.
Complete High Five USA Reading Program II, Books Only. (gr. 4-18). 599.95 *(978-0-7368-3861-0(9)*, High Five) Red Brick Learning.
Complete Letter Books Program. (gr. k-2). 409.95 *(978-0-7368-4127-6(X))* Red Brick Learning.
Complete Lexile Pack. (Lexile Levels Ser.). 967.73 *(978-0-7362-2577-9(3))* CENGAGE Learning.
Complete Pebble Reading Program. (gr. k-2). 2836.95 *(978-0-7368-1489-8(2)*, Pebble Bks.) Capstone Press of Coughlan Cos.
Comprehension Power Readers: Add-on Pack (Reading Level 1-2) 2005. (Comprehension Power Readers Ser.). (J). (gr. 1-18). 166.95 *(978-0-7652-4339-3(3))*; (gr. 2-18). 166.95 *(978-0-7652-4340-9(7))* Modern Curriculum Pr.
Comprehension Power Readers: Add-on Pack (Reading Level 3-4) 2005. (Comprehension Power Readers Ser.). (J). (gr. 3-18). 194.50 *(978-0-7652-4341-6(5))*; (gr. 4-18). 194.50 *(978-0-7652-4342-3(3))* Modern Curriculum Pr.
Comprehension Power Readers: Add-on Pack (Reading Level 5-6) 2005. (Comprehension Power Readers Ser.). (J). (gr. 5-18). 219.95 *(978-0-7652-4343-0(1))*; (gr. 6-18). 219.95 *(978-0-7652-4344-7(X))* Modern Curriculum Pr.
Comprehension Power Readers: Library (Reading Level 1-2) 2005. (Comprehension Power Readers Ser.). (J). (gr. 1-18). 1026.50 *(978-0-7652-4333-1(4))*; (gr. 2-18). 1026.50 *(978-0-7652-4334-8(2))* Modern Curriculum Pr.
Comprehension Power Readers: Library (Reading Level 3-4) 2005. (Comprehension Power Readers Ser.). (J). (gr. 3-18). 1193.50 *(978-0-7652-4335-5(0))*; (gr. 4-18). 1193.50 *(978-0-7652-4336-2(9))* Modern Curriculum Pr.
Comprehension Power Readers: Library (Reading Level 5-6) 2005. (Comprehension Power Readers Ser.). (J). (gr. 5-18). 1334.95 *(978-0-7652-4337-9(7))*; (gr. 6-18). 1334.95 *(978-0-7652-4338-6(5))* Modern Curriculum Pr.
Comprendiendo las Diferencias. 2010. (Comprendiendo Las Diferencias/Understanding Differences Ser.).Tr. of Understanding Differences. (MUL & ENG.). 24p. lib. bdg. 65.97 *(978-1-4296-4607-9(1))* Capstone Press of Coughlan Cos.
Conklin, Blane. Barack Obama: President of the United States. 2011. (Primary Source Readers Focus On Ser.). (ENG.). 32p. (J). (gr. 4-4). pap. 8.99 *(978-1-4333-1522-0(X))* Teacher Created Materials, Inc.
Conklin, Wendy. Battles of the Civil War, 1 vol. 2005. (Primary Source Readers Ser.). (ENG., Illus.). 24p. (J). (gr. 5-5). pap. 8.99 *(978-0-7439-8919-0(8))* Shell Educational Publishing.
—Benjamin Franklin, 1 vol. 2004. (Primary Source Readers Ser.). (ENG.). 24p. (J). (gr. 4-4). pap. 8.99 *(978-0-7439-8755-4(1))* Shell Educational Publishing.
—Civil Rights Movement, 1 vol. 2007. (Primary Source Readers Ser.). (ENG.). 32p. (J). (gr. 5-5). pap. 8.99 *(978-0-7439-0670-8(5))* Shell Educational Publishing.
—Civil War Leaders, 1 vol. 2005. (Primary Source Readers Ser.). (ENG.). 24p. (J). (gr. 5-5). pap. 8.99 *(978-0-7439-8917-6(1))* Shell Educational Publishing.
—The Cold War, 1 vol. 2007. (Primary Source Readers Ser.). (ENG.). 32p. (J). (gr. 5-5). pap. 8.99 *(978-0-7439-0672-2(1))* Shell Educational Publishing.
—Cold War Leaders, 1 vol. 2007. (Primary Source Readers Ser.). (ENG.). 32p. (J). (gr. 4-4). pap. 8.99 *(978-0-7439-0673-9(X))* Shell Educational Publishing.
—Early Congresses, 1 vol. 2004. (Primary Source Readers Ser.). (ENG.). 24p. (J). (gr. 5-5). pap. 8.99 *(978-0-7439-8750-9(0))* Shell Educational Publishing.
—Exploring the New World, 1 vol. 2004. (Primary Source Readers Ser.). (ENG.). 24p. (J). (gr. 5-5). 8.99 *(978-0-7439-8740-0(3))* Shell Educational Publishing.
—Moctezuma: Aztec Ruler, 1 vol. 2007. (Primary Source Readers Ser.). (ENG.). 32p. (J). (gr. 4-4). pap. 8.99 *(978-0-7439-0457-5(5))* Shell Educational Publishing.
—Robert E. Lee, 1 vol. 2005. (Primary Source Readers Ser.). (ENG.). 24p. (J). (gr. 4-4). pap. 8.99 *(978-0-7439-8918-3(X))* Shell Educational Publishing.
Conley, Jennise M. I Think There's a Monster under My Bed! 2013. 28p. 9.99 *(978-1-61061-972-1(2))* My Three Sisters Publishing.
Connect Package. 2016. (ENG.). 48p. (gr. 3-4). pap. 174.00 *(978-1-5157-1817-8(4)*, Connect) Stone Arch Bks.
Connelly, Erin. Watch Out for Wolves! 2017. (Text Connections Guided Close Reading Ser.). (J). (gr. 1). *(978-1-4900-1820-1(4))* Benchmark Education Co.
Connolly, Debbie & Danley, Laurie. Passport to Genre: A Literature Enrichment Guide. Mitchell, Judy, ed. Hillam, Corbin, illus. 2006. 64p. (J). pap. 9.95 *(978-1-57310-488-3(4))* Teaching & Learning Co.
Connolly, Ryan. Tom's Field Trip. 2012. (InfoMax Readers Ser.). (ENG., Illus.). 16 pp.p. (J). (gr. k-1). pap. 7.00 *(978-1-4488-8971-6(5)*, Rosen Classroom) Rosen Publishing Group, Inc., The.
Contemporary Biography, 7 Bks, Set. (Robbie Reader Ser.). (Illus.). (gr. 1-4). lib. bdg. *(978-1-58415-350-4(4))* Mitchell Lane Pubs., Inc.
Content Connect! (gr. 3-5). 1081.53 *(978-0-7362-2579-3(X))* CENGAGE Learning.
Content Connect! Picture It! Big Book with Pen & Teacher's Guide. (gr. 4-8). tchr. ed. 54.98 *(978-0-7362-2436-9(X))* CENGAGE Learning.
Context Clues (Gr. 1-3) 2003. (J). *(978-1-58232-080-9(2))* ECS Learning Systems, Inc.
Cook, Julia. Cheaters Never Prosper. DuFalla, Anita, illus. 2016. (ENG.). 32p. (J). pap. 10.95 ***(978-1-944882-08-2(1))*** Boys Town Pr.
Cooling, Wendy. The Camel Fair. 2005. (Collins Big Cat Ser.). (ENG.). 48p. (J). (gr. 2-3). pap. 7.99 *(978-0-00-718634-1(7))* HarperCollins Pubs. Ltd. GBR. Dist: Independent Pubs. Group.
Cooper, Terry, ed. Reading & Math. 2005. (ENG.). 320p. pap., wbk. ed. 14.99 *(978-0-439-78603-4(7)*, Teaching Resources) Scholastic, Inc.
—Reading & Math, Grade 3. 2005. (ENG.). 320p. pap., wbk. ed. 14.99 *(978-0-439-78602-7(9)*, Teaching Resources) Scholastic, Inc.
—1st Grade Reading Practice. 2006. (Practice Ser.). (ENG., Illus.). 48p. (gr. 1-1). per. 5.99 *(978-0-439-81900-8(8)*, Teaching Resources) Scholastic, Inc.
—3rd Grade Reading Practice. 2006. (Practice Ser.). (ENG., Illus.). 48p. (gr. 3-3). per. 5.99 *(978-0-439-81902-2(4)*, Teaching Resources) Scholastic, Inc.
Cooper, Terry, ed. Reading & Math. Cooper, Terry, . 2005. (ENG.). 320p. pap., wbk. ed. 14.99 *(978-0-439-78599-0(5)*, Teaching Resources) Scholastic, Inc.
Cope, Clifford D. Caleb: The mouse Engineer. 2009. 24p. pap. 12.99 *(978-1-4389-9877-0(5))* AuthorHouse.
Corey, Shana & Awdry, Wilbert V. Stuck in the Mud. Courtney, Richard, illus. 2009. (Step into Reading Ser.). (ENG.). 32p. (J). (gr. -1-1). pap. 3.99 *(978-0-375-86177-2(7)*, Random Hse. Bks. for Young Readers) Random Hse. Children's Bks.
Corner Store. (J). 21.95 *(978-0-8136-4337-3(6))*; pap. 13.15 *(978-0-8136-4336-6(8))* Modern Curriculum Pr.
Cosgrove, Stephen. Across a Stream. 2004. (Reader's Theater Ser.). (J). pap. *(978-1-4108-1142-4(5))* Benchmark Education Co.
—Columbus Meets Isabella & Ferdinand. 2004. (Reader's Theater Ser.). (J). pap. *(978-1-4108-1138-7(7))* Benchmark Education Co.
—Storybook Readers, 5 bks. Steelhammer, Ilona, illus. (J). lib. bdg. 73.75 *(978-1-56674-921-3(2))* Forest Hse. Publishing Co., Inc.
Cosgrove, Stephen & Higgins, Kathy. Under Siege. 2004. (Reader's Theater Ser.). (J). pap. *(978-1-4108-1143-1(3))* Benchmark Education Co.
Cosgrove, Stephen & Higgins, Kitty. The Golden Spike. 2004. (Reader's Theater Ser.). (J). pap. *(978-1-4108-1141-7(7))* Benchmark Education Co.
Cottringer, Anne. Hot Dog. Walker, Katherine, illus. 2005. (ENG.). 24p. (J). lib. bdg. 23.65 *(978-1-59646-738-5(X))* Dingles & Co.
Cousineau-Peiffer, Trisha. Have You Ever Heard of a Rainbow Farm. Everett-Hawkes, Bonnie, illus. 2006. 32p. (J). 12.95 *(978-0-9792084-1-6(6))* Dream Ridge Pr.
—Have You Ever Heard of a Rainbow Farm: The Missing Color Kittens. Everett-Hawkes, Bonnie, illus. 2007. 48p. (J). per. 15.95 *(978-0-9792084-2-3(4))* Dream Ridge Pr.
Coven, Wanda. Heidi Heckelbeck & the Never-Ending Day. Burris, Priscilla, illus. 2017. (Heidi Heckelbeck Ser.: 21). (ENG.). 128p. (J). (gr. k-4). 16.99 ***(978-1-4814-9525-7(9))***; pap. 5.99 ***(978-1-4814-9524-0(0))*** Little Simon. (Little Simon).
Cowley, Joy. Big Bear & Little Bear: Buttons. Lam, Amy, illus. 2013. (ENG.). 8p. pap. *(978-1-927186-33-6(1)*, Joy Cowley Club) Flying Start Bks.
—Big Bear & Little Bear: Cold Feet. Lam, Amy, illus. 2013. (ENG.). 8p. pap. *(978-1-927186-27-5(7)*, Joy Cowley Club) Flying Start Bks.
—Big Bear & Little Bear: Cookies. Lam, Amy, illus. 2013. (ENG.). 8p. pap. *(978-1-927186-29-9(3)*, Joy Cowley Club) Flying Start Bks.
—Big Bear & Little Bear: Egg. Lam, Amy, illus. 2013. (ENG.). 8p. pap. *(978-1-927186-32-9(3)*, Joy Cowley Club) Flying Start Bks.
—Big Bear & Little Bear: Ice Cream. Lam, Amy, illus. 2013. (ENG.). 8p. pap. *(978-1-927186-21-3(8)*, Joy Cowley Club) Flying Start Bks.
—Big Bear & Little Bear: Jackets. Lam, Amy, illus. 2013. (ENG.). 8p. pap. *(978-1-927186-26-8(9)*, Joy Cowley Club) Flying Start Bks.
—Big Bear & Little Bear: Lemonade. Lam, Amy, illus. 2013. (ENG.). 8p. pap. *(978-1-927186-28-2(5)*, Joy Cowley Club) Flying Start Bks.
—Big Bear & Little Bear: Lollipop. Lam, Amy, illus. 2013. (ENG.). 8p. pap. *(978-1-927186-30-5(7)*, Joy Cowley Club) Flying Start Bks.
—Big Bear & Little Bear: Puddle. Lam, Amy, illus. 2013. (ENG.). 8p. pap. *(978-1-927186-34-3(X)*, Joy Cowley Club) Flying Start Bks.
—Big Bear & Little Bear: Race. Lam, Amy, illus. 2013. (ENG.). 8p. pap. *(978-1-927186-22-0(6)*, Joy Cowley Club) Flying Start Bks.
—Big Bear & Little Bear: Singing. Lam, Amy, illus. 2013. (ENG.). 8p. pap. *(978-1-927186-25-1(0)*, Joy Cowley Club) Flying Start Bks.
—Big Bear & Little Bear: Story. Lam, Amy, illus. 2013. (ENG.). 8p. pap. *(978-1-927186-23-7(4)*, Joy Cowley Club) Flying Start Bks.
—Big Bear & Little Bear: Wind. Lam, Amy, illus. 2013. (ENG.). 8p. pap. *(978-1-927186-20-6(X)*, Joy Cowley Club) Flying Start Bks.
—The Hungry Giant's Shoe Big Book. 2010. 48.25 *(978-1-60559-250-3(1))* Hameray Publishing Group, Inc.
—Meanies in the House Big Book. 2010. 48.25 *(978-1-60559-251-0(X))* Hameray Publishing Group, Inc.
—Miss Doll & Friends: A Surprise for Miss Doll. Bordicchia, Gaia, illus. 2014. (ENG.). 8p. pap. *(978-0-927244-52-7(7)*, Joy Cowley Club) Flying Start Bks.
—Miss Doll & Friends: Tin Clown. Bordicchia, Gaia, illus. 2014. (ENG.). 8p. pap. *(978-0-927244-55-8(1)*, Joy Cowley Club) Flying Start Bks.
—Miss Doll & Friends: Tin Clown¿s Hat. Bordicchia, Gaia, illus. 2014. (ENG.). 8p. pap. *(978-0-927244-79-4(9)*, Joy Cowley Club) Flying Start Bks.
—Miss Doll & Friends: Where Is Fire Engine? Bordicchia, Gaia, illus. 2014. (ENG.). 8p. pap. *(978-0-927244-57-2(8)*, Joy Cowley Club) Flying Start Bks.
—Mrs. Wishy-Washy's Tub. (Story Box Ser.). 8p. 20.95 *(978-0-7802-9365-6(7))* Wright Group/McGraw-Hill.
—Mrs. WishyWashy & the Big Wash. 2009. pap. 8.25 *(978-1-60559-235-0(8))* Hameray Publishing Group, Inc.
—Mrs. WishyWashy & the Big Wash Big Book. 2010. 48.25 *(978-1-60559-247-3(1))* Hameray Publishing Group, Inc.
—Mud Walk. (Story Box Ser.). 16p. pap. 31.50 *(978-0-322-02463-2(3))* Wright Group/McGraw-Hill.
—Smarty Pants at the Circus Big Book. 2010. 48.25 *(978-1-60559-249-7(8))* Hameray Publishing Group, Inc.
—Space Aliens in Our School. Ming, Choo Hill, illus. 2004. (ENG.). 8p. (J). (gr. 1-1). pap. 4.67 *(978-1-56270-755-2(8)*, Dominie Elementary) Pearson Schl.
Cox, Katherine. The Missing Fox. 2015. (Scholastic Reader Level 2 Ser.). lib. bdg. 13.55 *(978-0-606-37748-5(4))* Turtleback Bks.
The Craft Stick Project: Fourth Grade Guided Comprehension Level L. (On Our Way to English Ser.). (gr. 4-18). 34.50 *(978-0-7578-7152-8(6))* Rigby Education.
Crawford, Georgina. Archie-Parchie-Piddley-Poo. 2009. (Illus.). 24p. pap. 12.99 *(978-1-4389-7307-4(1))* AuthorHouse.
Crebbin, June. A Cat for Tom. 2005. (ENG.). 32p. pap. 9.50 *(978-0-521-67471-3(9))* Cambridge Univ. Pr.
Crebbin, June. The Rat-Catcher of Hamelin: Band 14/Ruby. 2017. (Collins Big Cat Tales Ser.). (ENG., Illus.). 48p. (J). (gr. 3-4). pap. 8.99 ***(978-0-00-817937-3(9))*** HarperCollins Pubs. Ltd. GBR. Dist: Independent Pubs. Group.
Crebbin, June, et al. Spike & the Concert. 2005. (Cambridge Reading Ser.). pap. *(978-5-7107-6036-9(6))* Cambridge Univ. Pr.
Creese, Sarah. Dinosaurs: I-Explore Reader. 2013. (ENG.). 32p. (J). pap. 4.99 *(978-1-78235-156-6(6))* Make Believe Ideas GBR. Dist: Nelson, Thomas Inc.
Cregan, Elizabeth R. C. All about Mitosis & Meiosis, 1 vol. 2007. (Science Readers Ser.). (SPA & ENG.). 32p. (J). (gr. 4-4). pap. 8.99 *(978-0-7439-0585-5(7))* Shell Educational Publishing.
—Investigating Electromagnetism, 1 vol. 2007. (Science Readers Ser.). (ENG.). 32p. (J). (gr. 4-4). pap. 8.99 *(978-0-7439-0575-6(X))* Shell Educational Publishing.
—Investigating the Chemistry of Atoms, 1 vol. 2007. (Science Readers Ser.). (ENG.). 32p. (J). (gr. 4-4). pap. 8.99 *(978-0-7439-0569-5(5))* Shell Educational Publishing.
—Pioneers in Cell Biology, 1 vol. 2007. (Science Readers Ser.). (ENG.). 32p. (J). (gr. 3-3). pap. 8.99 *(978-0-7439-0586-2(5))* Shell Educational Publishing.
Crime Solvers. 2017. (Crime Solvers Ser.). 48p. (gr. 6-6). pap. 84.30 ***(978-1-5382-0611-9(0))*** Stevens, Gareth Publishing LLLP.
Crittenden, Alex. Reading for Real. 2007. (ENG., Illus.). 384p. (C). per. 106.20 *(978-0-13-150034-1(1))* Pearson Education.
Crocodile Tears. (Sails Literacy Ser.). 24p. (gr. k-18). 8.00 *(978-0-7635-7034-7(6))* Rigby Education.
Crocodile's Bag: Level J, 6 vols. 128p. (gr. 2-3). 41.95 *(978-0-7699-0992-9(2))* Shortland Pubns. (U. S. A.) Inc.
Croft, Andy. David Beckham. 3rd rev. ed. 2005. (ENG., Illus.). 32p. pap. *(978-0-340-90072-7(5))* Cambridge Univ. Pr.
Cronick, Mitch. In the Garden. Sharp, Melanie, illus. 2005. (Collins Big Cat Ser.). (ENG.). 192p. (J). (gr. -1-k). pap. 5.99 *(978-0-00-718538-2(3))* HarperCollins Pubs. Ltd. GBR. Dist: Independent Pubs. Group.
—In the Garden. 2005. (Big Cat Ser.). (gr. k-2). pap. 6.50 *(978-1-60457-007-6(5))* Pacific Learning, Inc.
Cronin, Doreen. Giggle, Giggle, Quack. 2016. (Simon & Schuster Ready-To-Read Level 2 Ser.). lib. bdg. 13.55 ***(978-0-606-39752-0(3))*** Turtleback Bks.
Crops. (Guided Reading Levels Ser.). 28.56 *(978-0-7362-1061-4(X))* CENGAGE Learning.

Cross, Gillian. Brother Aelred's Feet. Stevens, Tim, illus. 2007. (Collins Big Cat Ser.). (ENG.). 544p. (J). (gr. 3-4). pap. 8.99 *(978-0-00-723093-8(1))* HarperCollins Pubs. Ltd. GBR. Dist: Independent Pubs. Group.

—Sam Sorts It Out. Mier, Colin, illus. 2005. (ENG.). 24p. (J). lib. bdg. 23.65 *(978-1-59646-702-6(9))* Dingles & Co.

Crossley-Holland, Kevin. Storm. Marks, Alan, illus. 2nd ed. 2016. (Reading Ladder Ser.). (ENG.). 48p. (J). (gr. k-2). 7.99 *(978-1-4052-8236-9(3))* Egmont Bks., Ltd. GBR. Dist: Independent Pubs. Group.

Crowe, Sharon. Daniel & the Big Belly Button. 2009. 23p. (J). pap. 17.95 *(978-1-4327-1549-6(6))* Outskirts Pr., Inc.

Crum, Anna-Maria. Trackers of Dynamic Earth: Set Of 6. 2011. (Navigators Ser.). (J). pap. 48.00 net. *(978-1-4108-0441-9(0))* Benchmark Education Co.

Cullimore, Stan. Alien Swap. Schon, Nick, illus. 2005. (ENG.). 24p. (J). lib. bdg. 23.65 *(978-1-59646-744-6(4))* Dingles & Co.

Cundy, David. Animals Spell Love. 2016. (Illus.). 40p. (J). *(978-1-56792-586-9(3))* Godine, David R. Pub.

Currie, Robin. Tuktuk: Un Cuento Sobre la Tundra. Saroff, Phyllis, illus. 2016. (SPA.). 32p. (J). (gr. k-3). pap. 9.95 *(978-1-62855-881-4(4))* Arbordale Publishing.

Cushing, Christopher. Let's Celebrate! 2012. (InfoMax Readers Ser.). (ENG., Illus.). 16 pp.p. (J). (gr. k-1). pap. 7.00 *(978-1-4488-8962-4(6),* Rosen Classroom) Rosen Publishing Group, Inc., The.

Custureri, Mary. Happy Anderson & Connie Clam. Folmsbee, Patricia, illus. 2006. 36p. (J). spiral bd. 24.95 *(978-1-933190-00-6(0))* HighPoint Publishing, Inc.

Cutting, Robert. Falling Star. Ng, Drew, illus. 2007. 48p. (J). lib. bdg. 23.08 *(978-1-4242-1625-3(7))* Fitzgerald Bks.

—Mars Colony. Jeevan, Dhamindra, illus. 2007. 48p. (J). lib. bdg. 23.08 *(978-1-4242-1630-7(3))* Fitzgerald Bks.

—The 10 Most Revolutionary Inventions. 2007. (J). 14.99 *(978-1-55448-460-7(X))* Scholastic Library Publishing.

Cuxart, Bernardette, illus. Cuentame un Cuento, No. 4. (SPA.). 96p. (J). (gr. k-3). *(978-84-480-1602-9(5),* TM8095) Timun Mas, Editorial S.A. ESP. Dist: Lectorum Pubns., Inc.

Da Guia, Higina. Pajamas O Pijam. 2008. 32p. pap. 18.95 *(978-1-4327-2055-1(4))* Outskirts Pr., Inc.

Da Silva, Rosa. The 10 Most Uncontrollable Functions of the Body. 2008. (J). 14.99 *(978-1-55448-531-4(2))* Scholastic Library Publishing.

Dad & I, Vol. 3. (Early Intervention Levels Ser.). 3.85 *(978-1-56334-977-5(9))* CENGAGE Learning.

Dal Fuoco, Gina. Spaceship Earth, 1 vol. 2007. (Science Readers Ser.). (ENG., Illus.). 32p. (J). (gr. 4-4). pap. 8.99 *(978-0-7439-0565-7(2))* Shell Educational Publishing.

Dale, Elizabeth. My Secret Alien. Wood, Steven, illus. 2nd ed. 2016. (Reading Ladder Ser.). (ENG.). 48p. (J). (gr. k-2). pap. 7.99 *(978-1-4052-8231-4(2))* Egmont Bks., Ltd. GBR. Dist: Independent Pubs. Group.

Dale, Jay. Baby Dinosaur Can Play, 1 vol. East, Jacqueline, illus. 2012. (Engage Literacy Red Ser.). (ENG.). 32p. (gr. k-2). pap. 5.99 *(978-1-4296-8936-6(6),* Engage Literacy) Capstone Press of Coughlan Cos.

—Baby Dinosaur Is Hiding, 1 vol. East, Jacqueline, illus. 2012. (Engage Literacy Yellow Ser.). (ENG.). 32p. (gr. k-2). pap. 5.99 *(978-1-4296-8952-6(8),* Engage Literacy) Capstone Press of Coughlan Cos.

—Baby Dinosaur Is Lost, 1 vol. East, Jacqueline, illus. 2012. (Engage Literacy Blue Ser.). (ENG.). 32p. (gr. k-2). pap. 5.99 *(978-1-4296-8972-4(2),* Engage Literacy) Capstone Press of Coughlan Cos.

—Bananas in My Tummy, 1 vol. Hancock, Anna, illus. 2012. (Engage Literacy Yellow Ser.). (ENG.). 32p. (gr. k-2). pap. 5.99 *(978-1-4296-8835-2(1),* Engage Literacy) Capstone Press of Coughlan Cos.

—Big Balloon, 1 vol. Meldrum, Ned, photos by. 2012. (Engage Literacy Yellow Ser.). (ENG., Illus.). 32p. (gr. k-2). pap. 5.99 *(978-1-4296-8962-5(5),* Engage Literacy) Capstone Press of Coughlan Cos.

—Big Green Crocodile, 1 vol. Hancock, Anna, illus. 2012. (Engage Literacy Blue Ser.). (ENG.). 32p. (gr. k-2). pap. 5.99 *(978-1-4296-8984-7(6),* Engage Literacy) Capstone Press of Coughlan Cos.

—Can You See It?, 1 vol. Ball, Natalie, illus. 2012. (Engage Literacy Yellow Ser.). (ENG.). 32p. (gr. k-2). pap. 5.99 *(978-1-4296-8954-0(4),* Engage Literacy) Capstone Press of Coughlan Cos.

—In My Car, 1 vol. Kreinberg, Sylvia, photos by. 2012. (Engage Literacy Magenta Ser.). (ENG., Illus.). 32p. (gr. k-2). pap. 5.99 *(978-1-4296-8850-5(5),* Engage Literacy) Capstone Press of Coughlan Cos.

—Lazy Old Pirates, 1 vol. Diggory, Nick, illus. 2012. (Wonder Words Ser.). (ENG.). 32p. (gr. k-2). pap. 5.99 *(978-1-4296-8930-4(7),* Engage Literacy) Capstone Press of Coughlan Cos.

—Lea Is Hungry, 1 vol. Gulliver, Amanda, illus. 2012. (Engage Literacy Red Ser.). (ENG.). 32p. (gr. k-2). pap. 5.99 *(978-1-4296-8833-8(5),* Engage Literacy) Capstone Press of Coughlan Cos.

—Lea's Birthday, 1 vol. Gulliver, Amanda, illus. 2012. (Engage Literacy Yellow Ser.). (ENG.). 32p. (gr. k-2). pap. 5.99 *(978-1-4296-8964-9(1),* Engage Literacy) Capstone Press of Coughlan Cos.

—Little Sam, 1 vol. Jackson, Katy, illus. 2012. (Wonder Words Ser.). (ENG.). 32p. (gr. k-2). pap. 5.99 *(978-1-4296-8900-7(5),* Engage Literacy) Capstone Press of Coughlan Cos.

—Look at the Animals, 1 vol. Fleming, Garry, illus. 2012. (Engage Literacy Magenta Ser.). (ENG.). 32p. (gr. k-2). pap. 5.99 *(978-1-4296-8880-2(7),* Engage Literacy) Capstone Press of Coughlan Cos.

—My Little Toys, 1 vol. 2012. (Engage Literacy Magenta Ser.). (ENG.). 32p. (gr. k-2). pap. 5.99 *(978-1-4296-8876-5(9),* Engage Literacy) Capstone Press of Coughlan Cos.

—My Pets, 1 vol. Richards, Kirsten, illus. 2012. (Wonder Words Ser.). (ENG.). 32p. (gr. k-2). pap. 5.99 *(978-1-4296-8886-4(6),* Engage Literacy) Capstone Press of Coughlan Cos.

Dalton, Annie. Lilac Peabody, No. 3. Griff, illus. 2009. (ENG.). 96p. (J). pap. 5.99 *(978-0-00-713773-2(7),* HarperCollins Children's Bks.) HarperCollins Pubs. Ltd. GBR. Dist: HarperCollins Pubs.

—Lilac Peabody & Honeysuckle Hope, No. 4. Griff, illus. 2009. (ENG.). 96p. (J). (gr. 2-4). pap. 5.99 *(978-0-00-713774-9(5))* HarperCollins Pubs. Ltd. GBR. Dist: HarperCollins Pubs.

Daniel, Claire. A Winning Attitude. Winborn, Marsha, illus. 2007. 14p. pap. 4.75 *(978-0-15-377381-5(2))* Harcourt Schl. Pubs.

Daronco, Mickey & Ohanesian, Diane. Am I in It? Set Of 6. 2nd rev. ed. 2011. (BuildUp Ser.). (J). pap. 27.00 net. *(978-1-4108-0736-6(3))* Benchmark Education Co.

—The Big Band: Set Of 6. 2nd rev. ed. 2004. (BuildUp Ser.). (J). 27.00 net. *(978-1-4108-1525-5(0))* Benchmark Education Co.

—Look at Me Now! Set Of 6. 2nd rev. ed. 2004. (BuildUp Ser.). (J). pap. 27.00 net. *(978-1-4108-1528-6(5))* Benchmark Education Co.

—A Lot to Sell: Set Of 6. 2nd rev. ed. 2004. (BuildUp Ser.). (J). pap. 27.00 net. *(978-1-4108-1524-8(2))* Benchmark Education Co.

—My Big Day: Set Of 6. 2nd rev. ed. 2004. (BuildUp Ser.). (J). pap. 27.00 net. *(978-1-4108-1532-3(3))* Benchmark Education Co.

—On a Cold Day: Set Of 6. 2nd rev. ed. 2004. (BuildUp Ser.). (J). pap. 27.00 net. *(978-1-4108-1529-3(3))* Benchmark Education Co.

—Play this Game with Me. 2nd.rev. ed. 2003. (BuildUp Ser.). (J). pap. 22.00 *(978-1-4108-0759-5(2))* Benchmark Education Co.

—What Might I Spy? Set Of 6. 2nd rev. ed. 2004. (BuildUp Ser.). (J). pap. 27.00 net. *(978-1-4108-1536-1(6))* Benchmark Education Co.

—Will It Float? Set Of 6. 2nd rev. ed. 2004. (BuildUp Ser.). (J). pap. 27.00 net. *(978-1-4108-1531-6(5))* Benchmark Education Co.

Dase, Pam. Hurricane Hunters. rev. ed. 2012. (Mathematics Readers Ser.). (ENG.). 32p. (J). (gr. 6-6). pap. 8.99 *(978-1-4333-3462-7(3))* Teacher Created Materials, Inc.

—Tonight's Concert. rev. ed. 2012. (Mathematics Readers Ser.). (ENG.). 32p. (J). (gr. 6-6). pap. 8.99 *(978-1-4333-3464-1(X))* Teacher Created Materials, Inc.

—Tornado Chasers. rev. ed. 2012. (Mathematics Readers Ser.). (ENG.). 32p. (J). (gr. 6-6). pap. 8.99 *(978-1-4333-3463-4(1))* Teacher Created Materials, Inc.

David, Jack. F-14 Tomcats. 2008. (Torque Ser.). (ENG.). 24p. (J). (gr. 3-7). 20.00 *(978-0-531-21643-9(8),* Children's Pr.) Scholastic Library Publishing.

—F-15 Eagles. 2008. (Torque Ser.). (ENG.). 24p. (J). (gr. 3-7). 20.00 *(978-0-531-21644-6(6),* Children's Pr.) Scholastic Library Publishing.

Davidson, Susanna. The Musicians of Bremen. Gordon, Mike & Gordon, Carl, illus. 2007. (Usborne First Reading: Level 3 Ser.). 48p. (J). 8.99 *(978-0-7945-1911-7(3),* Usborne) EDC Publishing.

—The Story of Hanukkah. 2007. (Young Reading Series 1 Gift Bks). 48p. (J). 8.99 *(978-0-7945-1781-6(1),* Usborne) EDC Publishing.

Davies, Beth. Batman's Missions. 2015. (DK Reader Level 3 Ser.). lib. bdg. 13.55 *(978-0-606-36692-2(X))* Turtleback Bks.

Davies, Caroline & Martin, Sharon. Y Frech Goch. 2005. (WEL., Illus.). 12p. pap. *(978-1-86101-079-7(6))* Acen Limited.

Davies, Gill & Freeman, Tina. Friend for Flash. 2004. (Tales from Yellow Barn Farm Ser.). (Illus.). 24p. (J). 3.99 *(978-1-85854-324-6(X))* Brimax Books Ltd. GBR. Dist: Byeway Bks.

Davis, Ashley. The Big Storm. 2006. (Neighborhood Readers Ser.). (ENG.). 16p. (gr. 1-3). pap. 6.50 *(978-1-4042-7192-0(9),* Rosen Classroom) Rosen Publishing Group, Inc., The.

Davis, Cathy Mackey. Lucky el Perro de la Estación de Bomberos, 1 vol. rev. ed. 2007. (Building Fluency Through Reader's Theater Ser.). (SPA.). 20p. (J). (gr. 1-2). pap. 6.99 *(978-1-4333-0016-5(8))* Teacher Created Materials, Inc.

Davis, Deneena. The 10 Most Essential Natural Resources. 2008. 14.99 *(978-1-55448-549-9(5))* Scholastic Library Publishing.

Davis, Helen J. Good Times with Gregory: Birds: Rescuing a Baby Bird. Davis, Robyn L., illus. 2008. (Good Times with Gregory Ser.). 54p. (J). (gr. -1-4). 12.95 *(978-1-935122-10-4(X))* K&B Products.

Davis, Jim. Garfield y el Deporte. (SPA.). 96p. (J). 9.95 *(978-84-7419-470-8(9),* AU003) Grijalbo Mondadori, S.A.-Junior ESP. Dist: Continental Bk. Co., Inc.

Dawson, Eugene T. Little Valerie Wants to Grow Taller. 2009. 24p. pap. 14.95 *(978-1-4389-7002-8(1))* AuthorHouse.

The Day: Individual Title Six-Packs. (Sails Literacy Ser.). 16p. (gr. k-18). 27.00 *(978-0-7635-4390-7(X))* Rigby Education.

Day & Night. (J). pap. 13.15 *(978-0-8136-4306-9(6))* Modern Curriculum Pr.

The Day of the Dead, 6 packs. (Greetings Ser.: Vol. 1).Tr. of El Dia La Noche. 24p. (gr. 2-3). 31.00 *(978-0-7635-9411-4(3))* Rigby Education.

Day, Susie. The Emperor's New Clothes. 2017. (Collins Big Cat Tales Ser.). (ENG.). 32p. (J). (gr. 2-3). pap. 7.99 *(978-0-00-817930-4(1))* HarperCollins Pubs. Ltd. GBR. Dist: Independent Pubs. Group.

The Day the Class Chameleon Disappeared: Word Study: Prefixes dis-, un-, ex-, re-, Level B. 2003. ("Plaid" Phonics & Stories Libraries). (gr. 2-3). 38.50 *(978-0-8136-9154-1(0))* Modern Curriculum Pr.

Daynes, Katie. Chocolate. Larkum, Adam, illus. 2004. 48p. (J). (gr. 2-18). pap. 5.95 *(978-0-7945-0759-6(X),* Usborne) EDC Publishing.

Dia De los Veteranos, 18 vols., Set. Incl. Año Nuevo Chino. Dickmann, Nancy. (Illus.). pap. 6.29 *(978-1-4329-5399-7(0));* Día de las Elecciones. Rissman, Rebecca. (Illus.). pap. 6.29 *(978-1-4329-5412-3(1));* Diwali. Dickmann, Nancy. pap. 6.29 *(978-1-4329-5400-0(8));* Janucá. Dickmann, Nancy. pap. 6.29 *(978-1-4329-5401-7(6));* Navidad. Dickmann, Nancy. pap. 6.29 *(978-1-4329-5396-6(6));* Pascua. Dickmann, Nancy. (Illus.). pap. 6.29 *(978-1-4329-5397-3(4));* Ramadán y el Eid Al-Fitr. Dickmann, Nancy. (Illus.). pap. 6.29 *(978-1-4329-5398-0(2));* (gr. -1-1). (Fiestas Ser.). (SPA.). 24p. 2011. Set pap. 44.03 *(978-1-4329-5414-7(8),* Bellota) Heinemann-Raintree.

Deadman, Ron & Gifford, Griselda. The Goat Monster & Other Stories, 4 vols. 2014. (ENG.). 128p. pap. 46.00 *(978-0-17-402427-9(4))* Oxford Univ. Pr., Inc.

Dean, James. Pete the Cat & the Surprise Teacher. Dean, James, illus. 2017. (My First I Can Read Ser.). (Illus.). 32p. (J). (gr. -1-3). 3.99 *(978-0-06-240428-2(8))* HarperCollins Pubs.

—Pete the Cat Phonics Box. Dean, James & Dean, Josh, illus. 2017. (My First I Can Read Ser.). 144p. (J). (gr. -1-3). pap. 12.99 *(978-0-06-240452-7(0))* HarperCollins Pubs.

Dean, James, illus. Sir Pete the Brave. 2016. 32p. (J). ***(978-1-5182-0881-2(9))*** Harper & Row Ltd.

DeAnda, Diane. The Monster in the Mattress & Other Stories: El Monstruo en el Colchón y Otros Cuentos. 2011. (SPA & ENG., Illus.). 90p. (J). (gr. 3-7). pap. 9.95 *(978-1-55885-693-6(5),* Piñata Books) Arte Publico Pr.

Dear Bess, Vol. 6. (Early Intervention Levels Ser.). 3.55 *(978-0-7362-0172-8(6))* CENGAGE Learning.

Deen, Marilyn. Wonder Readers: Mathematics. (Wonder Readers: Mathematics Ser.). (ENG.). 20p. (gr. k-1). 2012. lib. bdg. 181.20 *(978-1-4296-9619-7(2))* 2012. lib. bdg. 90.60 *(978-1-4296-9618-0(4))* 2011. lib. bdg. 90.60 *(978-1-4296-8633-4(2))* Capstone Press of Coughlan Cos. (Wonder Readers).

The Deer Report. 2005. (The Fawn Chapter Ser.). (J). 7.67 *(978-1-58453-311-5(0))* Pioneer Valley Bks.

Defoe, Daniel. Robinson Crusoe, Level 4. 2009. (ENG.). 96p. pap. 12.75 *(978-84-8323-553-9(6))* Cambridge Univ. Pr.

—ROBINSON CRUSOE LEVEL 4 INTERMEDIATE BOOK WITH CD-ROM AND AUDIO CD, 1 vol. 2009. (ENG.). 96p. pap. 16.50 incl. cd-rom, audio compact disk *(978-84-8323-550-8(1))* Cambridge Univ. Pr.

Deighton, Jo, adapted by. Ali Baba & the Forty Thieves: Traditional Stories:Cinderella: The Elves & the Shoemaker. (Scheherezade Presents Ser.: No. 11). (Illus.). 48p. (J). pap. *(978-1-85964-101-9(6),* Ithaca Pr.) Garnet Publishing, Ltd.

—Bacbouc the Lazy Tailor: Traditional Stories:Beauty & the Beast: The Red Shoes. (Scheherezade Presents Ser.: No. 12). (Illus.). 48p. (J). pap. *(978-1-85964-102-6(4),* Ithaca Pr.) Garnet Publishing, Ltd.

—Codadad & His Brothers: Traditional Stories:The Grocer, the Student & the Elf: The Ugly Duckling. (Scheherezade Presents Ser.: No. 13). (Illus.). 48p. (J). pap. *(978-1-85964-103-3(2),* Ithaca Pr.) Garnet Publishing, Ltd.

—The Fisherman & the Wicked Genie: Traditional Stories:The Shepherdess & the Chimney Sweep: Seven with One Blow. (Scheherezade Presents Ser.: No. 14). (Illus.). 48p. (J). pap. *(978-1-85964-104-0(0),* Ithaca Pr.) Garnet Publishing, Ltd.

deMarin, Layne. Wonder Readers: Science. (Wonder Readers: Science Ser.). (ENG.). 20p. (gr. k-1). 2012. lib. bdg. 67.95 *(978-1-4296-9620-3(6))* 2012. lib. bdg. 158.55 *(978-1-4296-9621-0(4))* 2011. lib. bdg. 90.60 *(978-1-4296-8638-9(3))* Capstone Press of Coughlan Cos. (Wonder Readers).

The Dentist, 2 Packs. (Chiquilibros Ser.). (gr. -1-1). 12.00 *(978-0-7635-8545-7(9))* Rigby Education.

dePaola, Tomie. Strega Nona & Her Tomatoes. 2017. (Simon & Schuster Ready-To-Read Level 1 Ser.). lib. bdg. 13.55 ***(978-0-606-40214-9(4))*** Turtleback Bks.

—Strega Nona & the Twins. 2017. (Simon & Schuster Ready-To-Read Level 1 Ser.). lib. bdg. 13.55 ***(978-0-606-40215-6(2))*** Turtleback Bks.

Depken, Kristen L. I Can Be a Gymnast (Barbie) 2014. (Step into Reading Ser.). (ENG., Illus.). 32p. (J). (gr. -1-1). lib. bdg. 12.99 *(978-0-375-97347-5(8),* Random Hse. Bks. for Young Readers) Random Hse. Children's Bks.

Depree, Helen. Foundations: Upper Emergent - Upper Emergent - Complete Kit, Vol. 2. 2nd ed. (gr. 1-18). 423.95 *(978-0-322-04291-9(7))* Wright Group/McGraw-Hill.

Derby, Katy. The 10 Most Daring Escapes. 2008. 14.99 *(978-1-55448-487-4(1))* Scholastic Library Publishing.

deRubertis, Barbara. Lana Llama's Little Lamb. Alley, R. W., illus. 2011. (Animal Antics A to Z Ser.). 32p. (J). (ENG.). lib. bdg. 22.60 *(978-1-57565-333-4(8));* (gr. -1-3). pap. 7.95 *(978-1-57565-324-2(9))* Kane Press, Inc.

—Maxwell Moose's Mountain Monster. Alley, R. W., illus. 2011. (Animal Antics A to Z Ser.). (ENG.). 32p. (J). lib. bdg. 22.60 *(978-1-57565-334-1(6));* (gr. -1-3). pap. 7.95 *(978-1-57565-325-9(7))* Kane Press, Inc.

—Nina Nandu's Nervous Noggin. Alley, R. W., illus. 2011. (Animal Antics A to Z Ser.). (ENG.). 32p. (J). lib. bdg. 22.60 *(978-1-57565-335-8(4))* Kane Press, Inc.

deRubertis, Barbara & Roser, Nancy. Let's Read Together: Resource Guide. 2005. (Let's Read Together Ser.). (Illus.). 56p. pap. 12.95 *(978-1-57565-139-2(4))* Kane Press, Inc.

Dessen, Maci. Bedtime. 2016. (It's Time Ser.). 24p. (gr. 1-1). pap. 8.25 *(978-1-4994-2277-1(6),* PowerKids Pr.) Rosen Publishing Group, Inc., The.

Dhami, Narinder. Monster under the Stairs. Spoor, Mike, illus. 2005. (ENG.). 24p. (J). lib. bdg. 23.65 *(978-1-59646-718-7(5))* Dingles & Co.

—Samosa Thief. Blundell, Tony, illus. 2005. (ENG.). 24p. (J). lib. bdg. 23.65 *(978-1-59646-708-8(8))* Dingles & Co.

Di-Nsteins, The Albert. No Reading Allowed. 2012. 32p. pap. *(978-1-77093-477-1(4))* Flowerpot Children's Pr. Inc.

Día del Árbol, 18 vols., Set. Incl. Día de las Elecciones. Rissman, Rebecca. (Illus.). 22.65 *(978-1-4329-5393-5(1));* Diwali. Dickmann, Nancy. 22.65 *(978-1-4329-5381-2(8));* Janucá. Dickmann, Nancy. 22.65 *(978-1-4329-5382-9(6));* Ramadán y el Eid Al-Fitr. Dickmann, Nancy. (Illus.). 22.65 *(978-1-4329-5379-9(6));* (gr. -1-1). (Fiestas Ser.). (SPA.). Illus.). 24p. 2011. Set lib. bdg. 113.25 *(978-1-4329-5395-9(8),* Bellota) Heinemann-Raintree.

Diamond, Claudia. Children of Ancient Greece. 2006. (Rosen Real Readers Big Bookstm Ser.). (ENG.). 16p. (gr. 2-3). 37.95 *(978-1-4042-6223-2(7))* Rosen Publishing Group, Inc., The.

Diaz, Alexandra. El Unico Destino. 2016. (SPA., Illus.). 320p. (J). (gr. 3-7). 16.99 *(978-1-4814-8441-1(9),* Simon & Schuster/Paula Wiseman Bks.) Simon & Schuster/Paula Wiseman Bks.

—El único Destino (the Only Road) 2016. (SPA., Illus.). 320p. (J). (gr. 3-7). pap. 7.99 *(978-1-4814-8442-8(7),* Simon & Schuster/Paula Wiseman Bks.) Simon & Schuster/Paula Wiseman Bks.

Dibble, Traci. Bats. 2010. (1-3Y Wild Animals Ser.). (ENG.). 16p. (J). (gr. k-2). pap. 5.99 *(978-1-61541-299-0(9))* American Reading Co.

—Brown Bears. Dibble, Traci, illus. 2010. (1-3Y Animals Ser.). (ENG., Illus.). 16p. (J). (gr. k-2). pap. 5.99 *(978-1-61541-375-1(8))* American Reading Co.

—Cobras. Dibble, Traci, illus. 2010. (1-3Y Wild Animals Ser.). (ENG., Illus.). 16p. (J). (gr. k-2). pap. 5.99 *(978-1-61541-367-6(7))* American Reading Co.

Dibble, Traci & Washington, Jol. Wolves. Washington, Jol, illus. 2010. (1-3Y Animals Ser.). (ENG., Illus.). 16p. (J). (gr. k-2). pap. 5.99 *(978-1-61541-363-8(4))* American Reading Co.

Dibels. 2003. (Scott Foresman Reading Ser.). (gr. k-18). *(978-0-328-07796-0(8));* (gr. k-18). *(978-0-328-07800-4(X));* (gr. 1-18). *(978-0-328-07797-7(6));* (gr. 1-18). *(978-0-328-07801-1(8));* (gr. 2-18). *(978-0-328-07798-4(4));* (gr. 3-18). *(978-0-328-07799-1(2))* Addison-Wesley Educational Pubs., Inc. (Scott Foresman).

Dickinson, Tom. Bob's Secret Hideaway. 2014. (Collins Big Cat Ser.). (ENG., Illus.). 32p. (J). (gr. k-1). pap. 6.99 *(978-0-00-753850-8(2))* HarperCollins Pubs. Ltd. GBR. Dist: Independent Pubs. Group.

Dickmann, Nancy. ¡Mira Cómo Crece!, 11 vols., Set. Incl. Vida de la Abeja. pap. 6.29 *(978-1-4329-5282-2(X));* Vida de la Manzana. (Illus.). pap. 6.29 *(978-1-4329-5286-0(2));* Vida de la Mariposa. (Illus.). pap. 6.29 *(978-1-4329-5283-9(8));* Vida de la Rana. pap. 6.29 *(978-1-4329-5285-3(4));* Vida de la Tortuga. pap. 6.29 *(978-1-4329-5292-1(7));* Vida del Frijol. (Illus.). pap. 6.29 *(978-1-4329-5287-7(0));* Vida del Girasol. pap. 6.29 *(978-1-4329-5289-1(7));* Vida del Perro. pap. 6.29 *(978-1-4329-5290-7(0));* Vida del Pingüino. (Illus.). pap. 6.29 *(978-1-4329-5291-4(9));* Vida del Pollo. (Illus.). pap. 6.29 *(978-1-4329-5284-6(6));* Vida del Roble. pap. 6.29 *(978-1-4329-5288-4(9));* (gr. -1-1). (¡Mira Cómo Crece! Ser.). (SPA.). 24p. 2011. Set pap. 69.19 *(978-1-4329-5293-8(5));* Set lib. bdg. 203.85 *(978-1-4329-5281-5(1))* Heinemann-Raintree. (Bellota).

—El Mundo de la Granja, 6 vols., Set. Incl. Alimentos de la Granja. pap. 6.29 *(978-1-4329-5315-7(X));* Animales de la Granja. pap. 6.29 *(978-1-4329-5313-3(3));* Estaciones en la Granja. pap. 6.29 *(978-1-4329-5318-8(4));* Las Plantas de la Granja. (Illus.). pap. 6.29 *(978-1-4329-5317-1(6));* Máquinas de la Granja. pap. 6.29 *(978-1-4329-5314-0(1));* Trabajos en la Granja. pap. 6.29 *(978-1-4329-5316-4(8));* (gr. -1-1). (Mundo de la Granja Ser.). (SPA.). 24p. 2011. Set pap. 35.94 *(978-1-4329-5319-5(2),* Bellota) Heinemann-Raintree.

Dickson, Sue. Sing, Spell, Read & Write: All Aboard. rev. ed. 2005. (J). (gr. k-3). stu. ed. 12.95 *(978-0-7652-3211-3(1))* Modern Curriculum Pr.

—Sing, Spell, Read & Write: On Track. rev. ed. 2005. (J). (gr. k-3). stu. ed. 8.50 *(978-0-7652-3210-6(3))* Modern Curriculum Pr.

Did You Hear? Fourth Grade Guided Comprehension Level N. (On Our Way to English Ser.). (gr. 4-18). 34.50 *(978-0-7578-7160-3(7))* Rigby Education.

DiGugno, Josh. I Heard That! 2017. (Text Connections Guided Close Reading Ser.). (J). (gr. 1). *(978-1-4900-1829-4(8))* Benchmark Education Co.

Dill, Bonnie. Brain Quest Grade 1 Reading. 2nd rev. ed. 2007. (ENG.). 148p. (J). (gr. 1-1). 11.95 *(978-0-7611-4139-6(1),* 14139) Workman Publishing Co., Inc.

—Brain Quest Grade 2 Reading. 2nd rev. ed. 2007. (ENG., Illus.). 148p. (J). (gr. 2-2). 11.95 *(978-0-7611-4140-2(5),* 14140) Workman Publishing Co., Inc.

Ding-a-lings & Flutterbys. (Sails Literacy Ser.). 24p. (gr. k-18). 8.00 *(978-0-7635-7033-0(8))* Rigby Education.

Dining with Prunella. (J). pap. 13.75 *(978-0-8136-4640-4(5))* Modern Curriculum Pr.

Dinner Time. 2005. (Gilbert the Pig Chapter Ser.). (J). 7.67 *(978-1-58453-298-9(X))* Pioneer Valley Bks.

Dinosaur Detective: 6 Each of 1 Anthology, 6 vols. (Wildcats Ser.). 32p. (gr. 2-8). *(978-0-322-00586-0(8))* Wright Group/McGraw-Hill.

The dinosaur Hunt: Individual Title, 6 packs. (gr. 1-2). 22.00 *(978-0-7635-9185-4(8))* Rigby Education.

Dinosaurs, Level 2. 2016. (Ladybird Readers Ser.). (ENG.). (J). 48p. pap. 9.99 *(978-0-241-25447-9(7));* 16p. (gr. 2-4). pap. 5.99 *(978-0-241-25455-4(8));* 16p. (gr. 2-4). pap. 5.99 *(978-0-241-25455-4(8))* Penguin Bks., Ltd. GBR. Dist: Independent Pubs. Group.

Discover America State by State, 51 vols., Set. 2005. (Discover America State by State Ser.). (ENG., Illus.). (J). (gr. 1-3). 915.45 *(978-1-58536-294-3(8),* 202286) Sleeping Bear Pr.

Discovering Literature: The EMC Write-in Reader. 2nd ed. (Literature & the Language Arts Ser.). (J). (gr. 6-18). wbk. ed. 17.99 *(978-0-8219-2908-7(9))* EMC/Paradigm Publishing.

Disney. Big Hero 6 Step into Reading. 2014. (Step into Reading Level 3 Ser.). lib. bdg. 13.55 *(978-0-606-35996-2(6))* Turtleback Bks.

Disney Book Group. Elena of Avalor un Dia para Recordar (Spanish Edition) Disney Storybook Art Team, illus. 2017. (ENG.). 24p. (J). (gr. 1-3). pap. 5.99 ***(978-1-368-00110-6(6))*** Disney Pr.

—Trapped in the Death Star! 2016. (Star Wars: World of Reading Ser.). (J). lib. bdg. 14.75 ***(978-0-606-39174-0(6))*** Turtleback Bks.

—World of Reading: Puppy Dog Pals A. R. F. Disney Storybook Art Team & Premise Entertainment Staff, illus. 2017. (ENG.). 32p. (J). (gr. -1-k). pap. 4.99 ***(978-1-368-00417-6(2))*** Disney Pr.

—World of Reading: Elena of Avalor Isabel's School Adventure: Journey to Crystal Caverns: Level 1. Disney Storybook Art Team, illus. 2017. (World of Reading Ser.). (ENG.). 32p. (J). (gr. 1-3). pap. 4.99 *(978-1-4847-4798-8(4))* Disney Pr.

—World of Reading: Henry Hugglemonster Snow Day: Level Pre-1. Disney Storybook Art Team, illus. 2015. (ENG.). 32p. (J). (gr. -1-k). pap. 3.99 *(978-1-4847-1805-6(4))* Disney Pr.

—World of Reading: Sofia the First Clover Time: Level Pre-1. Disney Storybook Art Team, illus. 2016. (World of Reading Ser.). (ENG.). 32p. (J). (gr. -1-k). pap. 3.99 *(978-1-4847-1590-1(X))* Disney Pr.

Disney Book Group & Geron, Eric. Beauty & the Beast, Level 2: Something More. Disney Book Group, illus. 2017. (World of Reading Ser.). (ENG., Illus.). 32p. (J). (gr. 1-3). pap. 4.99 *(978-1-4847-8284-2(4))* Disney Pr.

Disney Book Group Staff. Aladdin Read-Along Storybook & CD. Disney Storybook Artists Staff, illus. 2015. (Read-Along

Storybook & CD Ser.). (ENG.). 32p. (J). (gr. -1-k). pap. 6.99 (978-1-4231-4688-9(3)) Disney Pr.
—Reading Adventures Cars Level 1 Boxed Set. Disney Storybook Artists Staff, illus. 2013. (Reading Adventures Ser.). (ENG.). 160p. (J). (gr. 1-3). pap. 9.99 (978-1-4231-6980-2(8)) Disney Pr.
Disney Book Group Staff & Gold, Gina. Minnie a Walk in the Park, Level 1. Disney Storybook Artists Staff, illus. 2014. (World of Reading Ser.). (ENG.). 32p. (J). (gr. -1-k). pap. 3.99 (978-1-4847-0678-7(1)) Disney Pr.
Disney Book Group Staff & Rusu, Meredith L. Star Wars - Rebels. 2014. (Read-Along Storybook & CD Ser.). (ENG.). 32p. (J). (gr. 1-3). pap. 6.99 (978-1-4847-0504-9(1)) Disney Pr.
Disney Book Group Staff & Weinberg, Jennifer Liberts. World of Reading: Doc Mcstuffins Blame It on the Rain: Level 1. Disney Storybook Artists Staff & Disney Storybook Art Team, illus. 2014. (World of Reading Ser.). (ENG.). 32p. (J). (gr. -1-k). pap. 3.99 (978-1-4847-0676-3(5)) Disney Pr.
Disney Editors. Big Hero 6 Deluxe Step into Reading. 2014. (Step into Reading Level 3 Ser.). lib. bdg. 14.75 (978-0-606-35997-9(4)) Turtleback Bks.
—Ocean of Color. 2016. (Step into Reading Level 1 Ser.). lib. bdg. 14.75 (978-0-606-38890-0(7)) Turtleback Bks.
Disney Editors. Pua & Heihei. 2017. (Disney Princess Step into Reading Ser.). (Illus.). 21p. (J). lib. bdg. 14.75 **(978-0-606-39854-1(6))** Turtleback Bks.
Disney Press Editors. Callie Asks for Help. 2015. (World of Reading Ser.). (J). lib. bdg. 13.55 (978-0-606-36897-1(3)) Turtleback Bks.
—Cinderella. 2015. (World of Reading Ser.). (J). lib. bdg. 13.55 (978-0-606-35918-4(4)) Turtleback Bks.
—Ewoks Join the Fight. 2015. (Star Wars: World of Reading Ser.). (J). lib. bdg. 13.55 (978-0-606-36912-1(0)) Turtleback Bks.
—Lion Guard: Bunga the Wise. 2016. (World of Reading Ser.). (J). lib. bdg. 13.55 (978-0-606-37539-9(2)) Turtleback Bks.
—Sheriff Callie's Wild West: Peck's Trail Mix Mix-Up. 2015. (World of Reading Ser.). (J). lib. bdg. 13.55 (978-0-606-35915-3(X)) Turtleback Bks.
—Use the Force! 2015. (Star Wars: World of Reading Ser.). (J). lib. bdg. 13.55 (978-0-606-35923-8(0)) Turtleback Bks.
Disney Publishing Staff. Where Is Your Home?, 15 vols. 2003. (It's Fun to Learn Ser.). (Illus.). 32p. (J). (gr. -1-3). 3.99 (978-1-57973-133-5(3)) Advance Pubs. LLC.
Disney's World of English. 2005. 899.00 incl. DVD (978-1-59172-090-4(7)); 899.00 incl. VHS (978-1-59172-098-0(2)) Lexicon Marketing, LLC.
Dixon, Dougal. Dinosaur Explorer, 8 vols. 2005. (QEB Readers). (Illus.). 24p. (J). (gr. -1-3). lib. bdg. 15.95 (978-1-59566-070-1(4)) QEB Publishing Inc.
Do That, Do This! Set B, 6 Pack. (Supersonic Phonics Ser.). (gr. k-3). 29.00 (978-0-7635-0540-0(4)) Rigby Education.
Do You Like My Pet? (Early Intervention Levels Ser.). 21.30 (978-0-7362-0369-2(9)); Vol. 2. 3.55 (978-0-7362-0090-5(8)) CENGAGE Learning.
The Doctor, 2 Pack. (Chiquilibros Ser.). (gr. -1-1). 12.00 (978-0-7635-8544-0(0)) Rigby Education.
Doeden, Matt. You Choose: Survival. 2012. (You Choose: Survival Ser.). (ENG.). 112p. (gr. 3-4). 63.98 (978-1-4296-8180-3(2)); 191.94 (978-1-4296-8181-0(0)); pap. 13.90 (978-1-4296-9514-5(5)) Capstone Press of Coughlan Cos. (You Choose Bks.).
Doerrfeld, Cori. Matilda in the Middle. 2015. (ENG., Illus.). 40p. (J). (gr. -1-3). 17.00 (978-0-316-20713-3(6)) Little, Brown Bks. for Young Readers.
Doherty, Ellen. Ellis Island. 2011. (Early Connections Ser.). (J). (978-1-61672-660-7(1)) Benchmark Education Co.
—Willliam's Journal: Set Of 6. 2011. (Early Connections Ser.). (J). pap. 39.00 net. (978-1-4108-1558-3(7)) Benchmark Education Co.
Dolan, Penny. The Great Chapatti Chase. Suad, Laura, illus. 2015. (Collins Big Cat Ser.). (ENG.). 32p. (J). (gr. 2-2). pap. 7.95 (978-0-00-759121-3(7)) HarperCollins Pubs. Ltd. GBR. Dist: Independent Pubs. Group.
—Two Ghost Stories. Tambellini, Stefano, illus. 2015. (Collins Big Cat Ser.). (ENG.). 48p. (J). (gr. 3-4). pap. 9.95 (978-0-00-812780-0(8)) HarperCollins Pubs. Ltd. GBR. Dist: Independent Pubs. Group.
Dolan, Penny & Collins UK Publishing Staff. The Tinder Box. Joaquin, Javier, illus. 2016. (ENG.). 48p. (J). pap. 9.95 (978-0-00-814723-5(X)) HarperCollins Pubs. Ltd. GBR. Dist: Independent Pubs. Group.
The Dome. 2003. (Illus.). pap. 7.60 (978-0-7398-7525-4(6)) Steck-Vaughn.
Dominguez, Angela. How Do You Say? / ¿Cómo Se Dice? Dominguez, Angela, illus. 2016. (SPA & ENG., Illus.). 32p. (J). 17.99 (978-1-62779-496-1(4), 9781627794961, Holt, Henry & Co. Bks. For Young Readers) Holt, Henry & Co.
Dominguez, Elaudy. The Mountain Mystery. 2006. (Neighborhood Readers Ser.). (ENG.). 16p. (gr. 1-3). pap. 6.50 (978-1-4042-7124-1(4), Rosen Classroom) Rosen Publishing Group, Inc., The.
Don, Lari. The House of the Nine Doors. McLellan, Stu, illus. 2015. (Collins Big Cat Ser.). (ENG.). 32p. (J). (gr. 3-3). pap. 8.95 (978-0-00-812772-5(7)) HarperCollins Pubs. Ltd. GBR. Dist: Independent Pubs. Group.
Donaldson, Julia. The Quick Brown Fox Cub. 2006. (Red Bananas Ser.). (ENG., Illus.). 48p. (J). (gr. -1-3). lib. bdg. (978-0-7787-1080-6(7)) Crabtree Publishing Co.
—Spinderella. Pichon, Liz, illus. 2nd ed. 2016. (Reading Ladder Ser.). (ENG.). 48p. (J). (gr. k-2). pap. 7.99 (978-1-4052-8202-4(9)) Egmont Bks., Ltd. GBR. Dist: Independent Pubs. Group.
Donaldson, Julia & Axworthy, Anni. The Mermaid & the Octopus. 2006. (Collins Big Cat Ser.). (ENG., Illus.). 16p. (J). (gr. 1-1). pap. 5.99 (978-0-00-718684-6(3)) HarperCollins Pubs. Ltd. GBR. Dist: Independent Pubs. Group.
Donaldson, Julia & Richards, Lucy. The Quick Brown Fox Cub. Richards, Lucy, illus. 2nd ed. 2016. (Reading Ladder Ser.). (ENG., Illus.). 48p. (J). (gr. k-2). pap. 7.99 (978-1-4052-8240-6(1)) Egmont Bks., Ltd. GBR. Dist: Independent Pubs. Group.
Donaldson, Julia & Walker, Sholto. The Pot of Gold. 2006. (Collins Big Cat Ser.). (ENG., Illus.). 24p. (J). (gr. 2-2). pap. 7.99 (978-0-00-718696-9(7)) HarperCollins Pubs. Ltd. GBR. Dist: Independent Pubs. Group.
Donbavand, Tommy & Harpercollins Staff. Our Head Teacher Is a Super-Villain. Mosedale, Julian, illus. 2015. (Collins Big Cat Ser.). (ENG.). 32p. (J). (gr. 2-2). pap. 7.95 (978-0-00-759122-0(5)) HarperCollins Pubs. Ltd. GBR. Dist: Independent Pubs. Group.
Donofrio, Antonio R. & Donofrio, Beatrice Batnag. G-String Cordilleran Revelries: Fairy Tales Retold for Centuries to Teach Life's Family Values & Basic Reading Skills with Simple Magic Tricks & I. 2009. 176p. pap. 17.99 (978-1-4490-0181-0(5)) AuthorHouse.
Donovan, Barbara A. It's All Matter, 6 vols., Set. 2004. (Phonics Readers Books 37-72 Ser.). (ENG.). 8p. (gr. k-1). pap. 35.70 (978-0-7368-4060-6(5), Phonics Readers) Capstone Press of Coughlan Cos.
—Move It!, 6 vols., Set. 2004. (Phonics Readers Books 37-72 Ser.). (ENG.). 8p. (gr. k-1). pap. 35.70 (978-0-7368-4085-9(0), Phonics Readers) Capstone Press of Coughlan Cos.
Don't Interrupt! Individual Title Six-Packs. (gr. 1-2). 25.00 (978-0-7635-9193-9(9)) Rigby Education.
Don't Splash Me!, 6 Packs. (gr. 1-2). 22.00 (978-0-7635-9160-1(2)) Rigby Education.
Dooley, Virginia & Teaching Resources Staff. Reading & Math Jumbo. Cooper, Terry, ed. 2005. (ENG.). 320p. pap., wbk. ed. 14.99 (978-0-439-78598-3(7), Teaching Resources) Scholastic, Inc.
Dorling Kindersley Publishing Staff. Ahsoka in Action! 2012. (Star Wars: the Clone Wars DK Readers Ser.). lib. bdg. 13.55 (978-0-606-31472-5(5), Turtleback) Turtleback Bks.
—Beware the Inquisitor. 2014. (DK Readers Ser.). (ENG., Illus.). 48p. (J). (gr. k-4). pap. 3.99 (978-1-4654-2845-5(3), DK Children) Dorling Kindersley Publishing, Inc.
—Blast Off!, Pre-Level 1. 2010. (DK Readers Ser.). (ENG.). 32p. (J). (gr. -1-1). pap. 3.99 (978-0-7566-6692-7(9), DK Children) Dorling Kindersley Publishing, Inc.
—Can You Spot a Jedi? 2014. (Star Wars DK Readers Pre-Level Ser.). lib. bdg. 13.55 (978-0-606-35323-6(2)) Turtleback Bks.
—DK Readers L2: Star Wars Rebels: Beware the Inquisitor: Star Wars Rebels: Beware the Inquisitor. 2014. (DK Readers Ser.). (ENG., Illus.). 48p. (J). (gr. k-4). 14.99 (978-1-4654-2844-8(5), DK Children) Dorling Kindersley Publishing, Inc.
—DK Readers L3: Real-Life Heroes. 2017. (DK Readers Ser.). (ENG.). 64p. (J). (gr. 2-4). 14.99 **(978-1-4654-6243-5(0))**; pap. 3.99 **(978-1-4654-6244-2(9))** Dorling Kindersley Publishing, Inc. (DK Children).
—Don't Wake the Zillo Beast! 2011. (DK Readers Ser.). (ENG.). 32p. (J). (gr. -1-1). 3.99 (978-0-7566-8279-8(7), DK Children) Dorling Kindersley Publishing, Inc.
—The LEGO Batman Movie. 2016. (LEGO DC Universe DK Readers Ser.). lib. bdg. 13.55 **(978-0-606-39895-4(3))** Turtleback Bks.
—Let's Go Riding! 2013. (DK Reader Level 2 Ser.). lib. bdg. 13.55 (978-0-606-31477-0(6), Turtleback) Turtleback Bks.
—Masters of the Force. 2012. (Star Wars: the Clone Wars DK Readers Ser.). lib. bdg. 13.55 (978-0-606-31473-2(3), Turtleback) Turtleback Bks.
—Meet the Rebels. 2014. (DK Readers Ser.). (ENG.). 32p. (J). (gr. 1-3). 14.99 (978-1-4654-2268-2(4)); pap. 3.99 (978-1-4654-2269-9(2)) Dorling Kindersley Publishing, Inc. (DK Children).
—OBI-Wan Kenobi Jedi Knight, Level 3. 2012. (DK Readers Ser.). (ENG.). 48p. (J). (gr. 2-4). pap. 3.99 (978-0-7566-9810-2(3), DK Children) Dorling Kindersley Publishing, Inc.
—Secret Ninja Force. 2017. (DK Readers Ser.). (ENG.). 48p. (J). (gr. k-2). pap. 3.99 **(978-1-4654-6195-7(7)**, DK Children) Dorling Kindersley Publishing, Inc.
Dorling Kindersley Publishing Staff. Who Saved the Galaxy? 2012. (DK Readers Ser.). (ENG., Illus.). 32p. (J). (gr. k-4). pap. 3.99 (978-0-7566-9808-9(1), DK Children) Dorling Kindersley Publishing, Inc.
Dorling Kindersley Publishing Staff & Beecroft, Simon. Even Droids Need Friends. 2013. (DK Readers Ser.). (ENG.). 32p. (J). (gr. -1-1). pap. 3.99 (978-1-4654-0182-3(2), DK Children) Dorling Kindersley Publishing, Inc.
—Even Droids Need Friends! 2013. (DK Readers Ser.). (ENG.). 32p. (J). (gr. -1-1). 14.99 (978-1-4654-0183-0(0), DK Children) Dorling Kindersley Publishing, Inc.
Dorling Kindersley Publishing Staff & Buckley, Jim. Spiders & Other Deadly Animals. 2016. (DK Readers Ser.). (ENG., Illus.). 96p. (J). (gr. 3-7). lib. bdg. 14.99 (978-1-4654-5211-5(7), DK Children) Dorling Kindersley Publishing, Inc.
Dorling Kindersley Publishing Staff & Buller, Laura. DK Readers L2: Amazing Dogs. 2016. (DK Readers Ser.). (ENG., Illus.). 48p. (J). (gr. k-2). pap. 3.99 (978-1-4654-4596-4(X), DK Children) Dorling Kindersley Publishing, Inc.
Dorling Kindersley Publishing Staff & Fry, Jason. Rogue One - Secret Mission. 2016. (DK Readers Ser.). (ENG.). 96p. (J). (gr. 3-7). pap. 3.99 (978-1-4654-5264-1(8), DK Children) Dorling Kindersley Publishing, Inc.
Dorling Kindersley Publishing Staff & Gersh, Camilla. Frogs & Toads. 2014. (DK Readers Ser.). (ENG.). 32p. (J). (gr. -1-1). 14.99 (978-1-4654-2011-4(8), DK Children) Dorling Kindersley Publishing, Inc.
Dorling Kindersley Publishing Staff & Hibbert, Clare. The Clone Wars - Jedi Heroes. 2010. (DK Readers Ser.). (ENG.). 48p. (J). (gr. 2-4). pap. 3.99 (978-0-7566-6689-7(9), DK Children) Dorling Kindersley Publishing, Inc.
—Tatooine Adventures, Level 1. 2011. (DK Readers Ser.). (ENG.). 48p. (J). (gr. k-4). 3.99 (978-0-7566-7128-0(0), DK Children) Dorling Kindersley Publishing, Inc.
Dorling Kindersley Publishing Staff & Hidalgo, Pablo. Rogue One - The Ultimate Visual Guide. 2016. (ENG., Illus.). 200p. (J). (gr. 4-7). 30.00 (978-1-4654-5263-4(X), DK Children) Dorling Kindersley Publishing, Inc.
Dorling Kindersley Publishing Staff & Kelly, James Floyd. DK Readers L2: Story of Coding. 2017. (DK Readers Ser.). (ENG.). 48p. (J). (gr. k-2). 14.99 **(978-1-4654-6231-2(7))**; pap. 3.99 **(978-1-4654-6242-8(2))** Dorling Kindersley Publishing, Inc. (DK Children).
Dorling Kindersley Publishing Staff & Last, Shari. Meet Unikitty! 2014. (DK Readers Ser.). (ENG., Illus.). 48p. (J). (gr. k-4). pap. 3.99 (978-1-4654-3497-5(6), DK Children) Dorling Kindersley Publishing, Inc.
Dorling Kindersley Publishing Staff & Saunders, Catherine. Let's Go Riding!, Level 2. 2013. (DK Readers Ser.). (ENG.). 32p. (J). (gr. 1-3). pap. 3.99 (978-1-4654-0261-5(6), DK Children) Dorling Kindersley Publishing, Inc.
—Summer Adventures, Level 3. 2013. (DK Readers Ser.). (ENG.). 48p. (J). (gr. 2-4). pap. 3.99 (978-1-4654-0259-2(4), DK Children) Dorling Kindersley Publishing, Inc.
Dorling Kindersley Publishing Staff & Stock, Lisa. DK Readers L2: Star Wars: Rey to the Rescue! 2017. (DK Readers Ser.). (ENG.). 48p. (J). (gr. k-2). pap. 3.99 (978-1-4654-5580-2(9), DK Children) Dorling Kindersley Publishing, Inc.
Dorling Kindersley Publishing Staff, et al. Darth Maul Sith Apprentice. 2012. (DK Readers Ser.). (ENG.). 48p. (J). (gr. 3-7). 3.99 (978-0-7566-8866-0(3), DK Children) Dorling Kindersley Publishing, Inc.
Dotson, Jacob. React & Rise Up, 1 vol. 2010. 58p. pap. 16.95 (978-1-4489-4168-1(7)) America Star Bks.
Doudna, Kelly. Any Day but Today! 2004. (Sight Words Ser.). (ENG., Illus.). 24p. (J). (gr. k-3). lib. bdg. 24.21 (978-1-59197-464-2(X)) ABDO Publishing Co.
—Et As in Jet, 1 vol. 2003. (Word Families Set 2 Ser.). (ENG.). 24p. (J). (gr. k-3). lib. bdg. 24.21 (978-1-59197-230-3(2), SandCastle) ABDO Publishing Co.
—Give It a Try! 2004. (Sight Words Ser.). (ENG., Illus.). 24p. (J). (gr. k-3). lib. bdg. 24.21 (978-1-59197-469-7(0), SandCastle) ABDO Publishing Co.
—Id As in Squid, 1 vol. 2003. (Word Families Set 3 Ser.). (ENG., Illus.). 24p. (J). (gr. k-3). lib. bdg. 24.21 (978-1-59197-235-8(3), SandCastle) ABDO Publishing Co.
—Ig As in Pig, 1 vol. Marx, Monica, ed. 2003. (Word Families Set 3 Ser.). (ENG., Illus.). 24p. (J). (gr. k-3). lib. bdg. 24.21 (978-1-59197-236-5(1), SandCastle) ABDO Publishing Co.
—Ill As in Grill, 1 vol. 2003. (Word Families Set 3 Ser.). (ENG., Illus.). 24p. (J). (gr. k-3). lib. bdg. 24.21 (978-1-59197-237-2(X), SandCastle) ABDO Publishing Co.
—In As in Twin, 1 vol. 2003. (Word Families Set 3 Ser.). (ENG., Illus.). 24p. (J). (gr. k-3). lib. bdg. 24.21 (978-1-59197-238-9(8), SandCastle) ABDO Publishing Co.
—Ip As in Ship, 1 vol. 2003. (Word Families Set 3 Ser.). (ENG., Illus.). 24p. (J). (gr. k-3). lib. bdg. 24.21 (978-1-59197-239-6(6), SandCastle) ABDO Publishing Co.
—It As in Sit, 1 vol. 2003. (Word Families Set 3 Ser.). (ENG., Illus.). 24p. (J). (gr. k-3). lib. bdg. 24.21 (978-1-59197-240-2(X), SandCastle) ABDO Publishing Co.
—Just Make Some Art! 2004. (Sight Words Ser.). (ENG., Illus.). 24p. (J). (gr. k-3). lib. bdg. 24.21 (978-1-59197-481-9(X), SandCastle) ABDO Publishing Co.
—Ow As in Crow, 1 vol. 2003. (Word Families Set 7 Ser.). (ENG., Illus.). 24p. (J). (gr. k-3). lib. bdg. 24.21 (978-1-59197-265-5(5), SandCastle) ABDO Publishing Co.
—There Are Ants down There! 2004. (Sight Words Ser.). (ENG., Illus.). 24p. (J). (gr. k-3). lib. bdg. 24.21 (978-1-59197-473-4(9), SandCastle) ABDO Publishing Co.
—Was That Fun? 2004. (Sight Words Ser.). (ENG., Illus.). 24p. (J). (gr. k-3). lib. bdg. 24.21 (978-1-59197-475-8(5), SandCastle) ABDO Publishing Co.
—When Can You Play Again? 2004. (Sight Words Ser.). (ENG., Illus.). 24p. (J). (gr. k-3). lib. bdg. 24.21 (978-1-59197-478-9(X), SandCastle) ABDO Publishing Co.
Dovey, Belinda. Alphabet Adventures. 2012. 136p. pap. 71.99 (978-1-4653-7250-5(4)) Xlibris Corp.
Dow, Suzanne. The Bike Race. 2006. (Neighborhood Readers Ser.). (ENG., Illus.). 12p. (gr. 1-3). pap. 5.90 (978-1-4042-7018-3(3), Rosen Classroom) Rosen Publishing Group, Inc., The.
Down on the Farm. 2005. (Little Celebrations Thematic Packages Ser.). (J). (gr. k-3). 133.50 (978-0-673-75377-9(8)) Celebration Pr.
Down the Hill: KinderReaders Individual Title Six-Packs. (Kinderstarters Ser.). 8p. (gr. -1-1). 21.00 (978-0-7635-8654-6(4)) Rigby Education.
Downey, Glen. Escape from East Berlin. Lingas, Leo, illus. 2007. 48p. (J). lib. bdg. 23.08 (978-1-4242-1635-2(4)) Fitzgerald Bks.
—Miracle Men. Brennan, Anthony, illus. 2007. (Timeline Ser.). 48p. pap. 8.99 (978-1-4190-4410-6(9)) Steck-Vaughn.
Downey, Glen R. The 10 Greatest Sports Showdowns. 2008. 14.99 (978-1-55448-535-2(5)) Scholastic Library Publishing.
—The 10 Most Decisive Battles. 2007. 14.99 (978-1-55448-507-9(X)) Scholastic Library Publishing.
—The 10 Most Extreme Jobs. 2008. 14.99 (978-1-55448-536-9(3)) Scholastic Library Publishing.
—The 10 Most Memorable TV Moments. 2008. 14.99 (978-1-55448-544-4(4)) Scholastic Library Publishing.
—The 10 Most Remarkable Writers. 2008. 14.99 (978-1-55448-553-6(3)) Scholastic Library Publishing.
—The 10 Most Revolutionary Military Inventions. 2008. 14.99 (978-1-55448-500-0(2)) Scholastic Library Publishing.
—The 10 Most Shocking Sports Scandals. 2007. 14.99 (978-1-55448-505-5(3)) Scholastic Library Publishing.
—The 10 Most Significant Documents in History. 2008. 14.99 (978-1-55448-547-5(9)) Scholastic Library Publishing.
—The 10 Most Unforgettable NASCAR Moments. 2008. 14.99 (978-1-55448-515-4(0)) Scholastic Library Publishing.
—The 10 Smartest Animals. 2007. 14.99 (978-1-55448-512-3(6)) Scholastic Library Publishing.
Downey, Glen R. & Cond, Sandie. The 10 Coolest Flying Machines. 2008. 14.99 (978-1-55448-530-7(4)) Scholastic Library Publishing.
Downey, Glen R. & Malara, Maria. The 10 Hottest Hollywood Cars. 2007. 14.99 (978-1-55448-526-0(6)) Scholastic Library Publishing.
Downey, Tika. The Biggest Snowball. 2006. (Neighborhood Readers Ser.). (ENG.). 16p. (gr. 1-3). pap. 6.50 (978-1-4042-7200-2(3), Rosen Classroom) Rosen Publishing Group, Inc., The.
—Tracks in the Snow. 2006. (Neighborhood Readers Ser.). (ENG.). 16p. (gr. 1-3). pap. 6.50 (978-1-4042-7180-7(5), Rosen Classroom) Rosen Publishing Group, Inc., The.
Downing, Johnette. Mumbo Jumbo, Stay Out of the Gumbo, 1 vol. Lindsley, Jennifer, illus. 2017. 32p. (J). (gr. -1-3). 16.99 (978-1-4556-2300-6(8)) Pelican Publishing Co., Inc.
Dowsett, Elizabeth & Bazaldua, Barbara. La Guia Esencial. 2017. (ENG & SPA.). 64p. (J). (gr. k-2). 12.99 (978-1-4654-6133-9(7), DK Children) Dorling Kindersley Publishing, Inc.
Doyle, Malachy. The Football Ghosts. Parsons, Garry, illus. 2nd ed. 2016. (Reading Ladder Ser.). (ENG.). 48p. (J). (gr. k-2). pap. 7.99 (978-1-4052-8243-7(6)) Egmont Bks., Ltd. GBR. Dist: Independent Pubs. Group.
—Hair Scare. Allen, Jonathan, illus. 2005. (ENG.). 24p. (J). lib. bdg. 23.65 (978-1-59646-724-8(X)) Dingles & Co.
—King Donal's Secret. Watson, Richard, illus. 2005. (ENG.). 24p. (J). lib. bdg. 23.65 (978-1-59646-740-8(1)) Dingles & Co.
—Rory's Lost His Voice. Semple, David, illus. 2005. (ENG.). 24p. (J). lib. bdg. 23.65 (978-1-59646-714-9(2)) Dingles & Co.
Dr. Seuss Book Set 800481, 4. 2005. (J). (978-1-59794-033-7(X)) Environments, Inc.
Dr. Seuss Book Set 800877, 6 vols. 2005. (J). bds. (978-1-59794-055-9(0)) Environments, Inc.
Dr. Seuss Books & Tapes Book Set 800910, 3 vols. 2005. (J). pap. (978-1-59794-075-7(5)) Environments, Inc.
The Dragon Compass: Individual Title Six-Packs. (Bookweb Ser.). 32p. (gr. 6-18). 34.00 (978-0-7578-0898-2(0)) Rigby Education.
The Dragon Inside. 2003. (Illus.). pap. 5.60 (978-0-7398-7517-9(5)) Steck-Vaughn.
Drake, Carol. The 10 Best Movies from Books. 2007. (J). 14.99 (978-1-55448-463-8(4)) Scholastic Library Publishing.
—The 10 Most Incredible Ancient Wonders. 2007. (J). 14.99 (978-1-55448-467-6(7)) Scholastic Library Publishing.
Drawing Conclusions & Inferences (Gr. 1-3) 2003. (J). (978-1-58232-079-3(9)) ECS Learning Systems, Inc.
Driesel, Amy. Why Gretchen Can't Spell. 2009. 28p. pap. 13.99 (978-1-4343-6166-0(7)) AuthorHouse.
Driscoll, Laura. El Chico del Despegue. Ramirez, Alma, tr. from ENG. Thornburgh, Rebecca McKillip, illus. 2009. (Math Matters en Espanol Ser.). (SPA.). 32p. (J). (gr. k-2). pap. 5.95 (978-1-57565-267-2(6)) Kane Press, Inc.
Duckworth, Michael. Voodoo Island. Oxford University Press Staff & Bassett, Jennifer, eds. 3rd ed. 2008. (ENG., Illus.). 64p. 10.00 (978-0-19-479075-8(4)) Oxford Univ. Pr., Inc.
DuFalla, Anita, illus. Sumac & the Magic Lake. 2004. (Reader's Theater Ser.). (J). pap. (978-1-4108-2291-8(5), A22915) Benchmark Education Co.
Dufresne, Michele. Reading Partners. 2004. (At School Ser.). (J). 7.33 (978-1-58453-267-5(X)) Pioneer Valley Bks.
Dugan, Christine. Between the Wars, 1 vol. 2007. (Primary Source Readers Ser.). (ENG.). 32p. (J). (gr. 5-5). pap. 8.99 (978-0-7439-0666-1(7)) Shell Educational Publishing.
—Defying Gravity! Rock Climbing, 1 vol. 2nd rev. ed. 2012. (TIME for KIDS(r) Nonfiction Readers Ser.). (ENG.). 48p. (J). (gr. 4-4). pap. 9.99 (978-1-4333-4830-3(6)) Teacher Created Materials, Inc.
—Final Lap! Go-Kart Racing, 1 vol. 2nd rev. ed. 2012. (TIME for KIDS(r) Nonfiction Readers Ser.). (ENG.). 48p. (J). (gr. 4-4). pap. 9.99 (978-1-4333-4832-7(2)) Teacher Created Materials, Inc.
—From Rags to Riches, 1 vol. 2nd rev. ed. 2013. (Nonfiction Readers Ser.). (ENG.). 64p. (J). (gr. 5-5). pap. 10.99 (978-1-4333-4910-2(8)) Teacher Created Materials, Inc.
—Hang Ten! Surfing, 1 vol. 2nd rev. ed. 2012. (TIME for KIDS(r) Nonfiction Readers Ser.). (ENG.). 48p. (J). (gr. 4-4). pap. 9.99 (978-1-4333-4831-0(4)) Teacher Created Materials, Inc.
—Landscape by Design. rev. ed. 2012. (Mathematics Readers Ser.). (ENG.). 32p. (J). (gr. 6-6). pap. 8.99 (978-1-4333-3459-7(3)) Teacher Created Materials, Inc.
—Living in Space, 1 vol. 2nd rev. ed. 2012. (Nonfiction Readers Ser.). (ENG.). 32p. (J). (gr. 3-3). pap. 8.99 (978-1-4333-3675-1(8)) Teacher Created Materials, Inc.
—Rome, 1 vol. 2007. (Primary Source Readers Ser.). (ENG.). 32p. (J). (gr. 5-5). pap. 8.99 (978-0-7439-0432-2(X)) Shell Educational Publishing.
—A Sense of Art. rev. ed. 2012. (Mathematics Readers Ser.). (ENG.). 32p. (J). (gr. 6-6). pap. 8.99 (978-1-4333-3458-0(5)) Teacher Created Materials, Inc.
—Space Exploration, 1 vol. 2nd rev. ed. 2012. (Nonfiction Readers Ser.). (ENG.). 32p. (J). (gr. 3-3). pap. 8.99 (978-1-4333-3674-4(X)) Teacher Created Materials, Inc.
Dugan, Christine & Lane, Chloe. Pack It Up: Surface Area & Volume. rev. ed. 2012. (Mathematics Readers Ser.). (ENG.). 32p. (J). (gr. 6-6). pap. 8.99 (978-1-4333-3461-0(5)) Teacher Created Materials, Inc.
Duncan, Cynthia L. Kids Say Such Silly Things. 2012. (Illus.). 20p. pap. 12.99 (978-1-4567-5095-4(X)) AuthorHouse.
Dunrea, Olivier. Gemma & Gus. 2017. (Gossie & Friends Ser.). (ENG., Illus.). 32p. (J). (gr. -1-3). pap. 3.99 (978-0-544-93722-2(8), HMH Books For Young Readers) Houghton Mifflin Harcourt Publishing Co.
Dupasquier, Philippe. La Obra. (Coleccion Aqui Se Trabaja). (SPA., Illus.). 22p. (J). 10.95 (978-84-207-3799-7(2), ANY762) Grupo Anaya, S.A. ESP. Dist: Continental Bk. Co., Inc.
Durant, Alan. Spider Mcdrew & the Egyptians: Band 12. Hopman, Philip, illus. 2007. (Collins Big Cat Ser.). (ENG.). 32p. (J). (gr. 2-3). pap. 7.99 (978-0-00-723076-1(1)) HarperCollins Pubs. Ltd. GBR. Dist: Independent Pubs. Group.
—The Teeth. Scratchmann, Max, illus. 2014. (Collins Big Cat Progress Ser.). (ENG.). 32p. (J). (gr. 3-4). pap. 7.99 (978-0-00-751933-0(8)) HarperCollins Pubs. Ltd. GBR. Dist: Independent Pubs. Group.
Durant, Alan & Walker, Sholto. Buzz & Bingo in the Starry Sky. 2005. (Collins Big Cat Ser.). (ENG., Illus.). 16p. (J). (gr. 1-3). pap. 7.99 (978-0-00-718630-3(4)) HarperCollins Pubs. Ltd. GBR. Dist: Independent Pubs. Group.
Duras, Marguerite. Hiroshima Mon Amour, Level B.Tr. of Hiroshima My Love. (FRE.). (YA). (gr. 7-12). 9.95 (978-0-88436-998-1(6), 40308) EMC/Paradigm Publishing.
Dussling, Jennifer. Bugs! Bugs! Bugs! 2011. (DK Readers Ser.). (ENG.). 32p. (J). (gr. 1-3). 3.99 (978-0-7566-7205-8(8), DK Children) Dorling Kindersley Publishing, Inc.
Dussling, Jennifer A. Lo Justo Es Justo! Palmisciano, Diane, illus. 2008. (Math Matters en Espanol Ser.). (SPA.). 32p. (J). (gr. -1-3). pap. 5.95 (978-1-57565-269-6(2)) Kane Press, Inc.
Dyan, Penelope. Ba-Ba-Ba-Bad — -The Story of One Mean Moose. Dyan, Penelope, illus. 2012. (Illus.). 34p. pap. 11.95 (978-1-61477-053-4(0)) Bellissima Publishing, LLC.

—Bake a Cake, Make Two — -and Let Them Eat Cake. Dyan, Penelope, illus. 2008. (Illus.). 44p. pap. 11.95 (978-1-935118-18-3(8)) Bellissima Publishing, LLC.

—The Comeback Kids — Book 10 — The American Bison. Weigand, John, photos by. 2012. (Illus.). 34p. pap. 14.95 (978-1-61477-063-3(8)) Bellissima Publishing, LLC.

—Don't Wake up the Bear! Dyan, Penelope, illus. 2013. (Illus.). 34p. pap. 11.95 (978-1-61477-094-7(8)) Bellissima Publishing, LLC.

—Fat Rat, Fat Cat — -Because Cats & Rats Are Also People. Dayn, Penelope, illus. 2008. 40p. pap. 11.95 (978-1-935118-11-4(0)) Bellissima Publishing, LLC.

—Go Far Star Car — Even Though Cars Are Not People. Dyan, Penelope, illus. 2008. (Illus.). 44p. pap. 11.95 (978-1-935118-12-1(9)) Bellissima Publishing, LLC.

—Go Run, Have Fun — -Because Everyone Likes Fun. Dyan, Penelope, illus. 2008. (Illus.). 44p. pap. 11.95 (978-1-935118-15-2(3)) Bellissima Publishing, LLC.

—Go to Rat House, Go to Cat House — Even Though Houses Are Not People. Dyan, Penelope, illus. 2008. (Illus.). 44p. pap. 11.95 (978-1-935118-14-5(5)) Bellissima Publishing, LLC.

—I Love You! Dyan, Penelope, illus. 2012. (Illus.). 34p. pap. 11.95 (978-1-61477-050-3(6)) Bellissima Publishing, LLC.

—If You Snooze! Dyan, Penelope, illus. 2012. (Illus.). 34p. pap. 11.95 (978-1-61477-059-6(X)) Bellissima Publishing, LLC.

—In Gracie's Yard! Dyan, Penelope, illus. 2012. (Illus.). 34p. pap. 11.95 (978-1-61477-067-1(0)) Bellissima Publishing, LLC.

—Jump Frog, Funny Frog — -Because Frogs Are Funny. Dyan, Penelope, illus. 2008. (Illus.). 44p. pap. 11.95 (978-1-935118-19-0(6)) Bellissima Publishing, LLC.

—Mikey & Me & the Spider — -the Continuing Story of a Girl & Her Dog. Dyan, Penelope, illus. 2010. (Illus.). 50p. pap. 14.95 (978-1-935118-95-4(1)) Bellissima Publishing, LLC.

—Molly Moose Is on the Loose. Dyan, Penelope, illus. 2012. (Illus.). 34p. pap. 11.95 (978-1-61477-025-1(5)) Bellissima Publishing, LLC.

—Olympic Gold — Because Everyone Loves a Winner! Dyan, Penelope, illus. 2008. (Illus.). 44p. pap. 11.95 (978-1-935118-20-6(X)) Bellissima Publishing, LLC.

—Respect! Dyan, Penelope, illus. 2012. (Illus.). 34p. pap. 11.95 (978-1-61477-058-9(1)) Bellissima Publishing, LLC.

—Sticks — the for Boys Only Version — Because Sticks Are Also People. Dyan, Penelope, illus. 2008. (Illus.). 52p. pap. 11.95 (978-1-935118-13-8(7)) Bellissima Publishing, LLC.

—The Sunny Side! Dyan, Penelope, illus. 2012. (Illus.). 34p. pap. 11.95 (978-1-61477-057-2(3)) Bellissima Publishing, LLC.

—Teeth! Dyan, Penelope, illus. 2012. (Illus.). 34p. pap. 11.95 (978-1-61477-060-2(3)) Bellissima Publishing, LLC.

—That Fat Elephant — -Because Everyone Likes Elephants. Dyan, Penelope, illus. 2008. (Illus.). 44p. pap. 11.95 (978-1-935118-16-9(1)) Bellissima Publishing, LLC.

—That Fat Rat Family — Because All Families Aren't Rats. Dyan, Penelope, illus. 2008. (Illus.). 44p. pap. 11.95 (978-1-935118-17-6(X)) Bellissima Publishing, LLC.

—There's a Flea in My Te. Dyan, Penelope, illus. 2012. (Illus.). 34p. pap. 11.95 (978-1-61477-047-3(6)) Bellissima Publishing, LLC.

—There's a Skunk in My Trunk. Dyan, Penelope, illus. 2012. (Illus.). 34p. pap. 11.95 (978-1-61477-045-9(X)) Bellissima Publishing, LLC.

—There's a Teddy Bear in My Heart! Dyan, Penelope, illus. 2012. (Illus.). 34p. pap. 11.95 (978-1-61477-048-0(4)) Bellissima Publishing, LLC.

—What Is a Telephant? Dyan, Penelope, illus. 2013. (Illus.). 34p. pap. 11.95 (978-1-61477-112-8(X)) Bellissima Publishing, LLC.

—Where Is Lucy? Dyan, Penelope, illus. 2013. (Illus.). 34p. pap. 11.95 (978-1-61477-120-3(0)) Bellissima Publishing, LLC.

—The White Elephant No One Wants. Dyan, Penelope, illus. 2012. (Illus.). 34p. pap. 11.95 (978-1-61477-024-4(7)) Bellissima Publishing, LLC.

—Who Cut the Cheese? a for Boys Only Book. Dyan, Penelope, illus. 2008. (Illus.). 44p. pap. 11.95 (978-1-935118-22-0(6)) Bellissima Publishing, LLC.

—Why Angels Sing! Dyan, Penelope, illus. 2012. (Illus.). 34p. pap. 11.95 (978-1-61477-065-7(4)) Bellissima Publishing, LLC.

—Work It Out! Dyan, Penelope, illus. 2012. (Illus.). 34p. pap. 11.95 (978-1-61477-056-5(5)) Bellissima Publishing, LLC.

DynaNotes Grade 9 Reading Review Guide. 2006. (YA). pap. (978-1-933854-29-8(4)) DynaStudy, Inc.

DynaNotes Grade 9 Reading Review Guide Transparency Set. 2006. (YA). trans. (978-1-933854-33-5(2)) DynaStudy, Inc.

Earle, Phil. Elsie & the Magic Biscuit Tin. Littler, Jamie, illus. 2016. (Early Reader Ser.). (ENG.). 64p. (J). (gr. k-2). 6.99 (978-1-4440-1360-3(2), Orion Children's Bks.) Hachette Children's Group GBR. Dist: Hachette Bk. Group.

Early Emergent Guided Reading, Vol. 1. (gr. k-18). 372.95 (978-0-7802-2770-5(0)) Wright Group/McGraw-Hill.

Early in the Morning. (Early Intervention Levels Ser.). 23.10 (978-0-7362-0039-4(8)); Vol. 4. 3.85 (978-1-56334-986-7(8)) CENGAGE Learning.

Early Reading Comprehension. 2004. (Reading comprehension, ERC MRC Ser.). (gr. 2-4). pap. 8.65 (978-0-8388-0621-0(X)) Educators Publishing Service, Inc.

Eastman, P. D. Are You My Mother?/¿Eres Tú Mi Mamá? 2016. (ENG & SPA., Illus.). 72p. (J). (gr. 1-4). 16.99 (978-0-553-53990-5(6), Random Hse. Bks. for Young Readers) Random Hse. Children's Bks.

—¿Eres Tú Mi Mamá? (Are You My Mother?) 2016. (Beginner Books(R) Ser.). (ENG & SPA., Illus.). 72p. (J). (gr. 1-4). 9.99 (978-0-553-53989-9(2), Random Hse. Bks. for Young Readers) Random Hse. Children's Bks.

—Go, Dog. Go! Eastman, P. D., illus. 2008. (ENG., Illus.). 64p. pap. (978-0-00-722546-0(6)) HarperCollins Pubs. Ltd.

Eclipse: Individual Title, 6 pack. (Story Steps Ser.). (gr. k-2). 32.00 (978-0-7635-9810-5(0)) Rigby Education.

Edgar Allan Poe Collection of Stories Student Packet. 2004. (YA). 12.99 (978-1-58130-510-4(9)) Novel Units, Inc.

Educational Solutions Staff & Gattegno, Caleb. Primary 3. (J). 84.00 (978-0-87825-170-4(7)); tchr. ed. 6.85 (978-0-87825-205-3(3)) Educational Solutions, Inc.

Education.com. Tell Me a Story: A Workbook of Story Pages & Activities. 2015. (ENG.). 128p. (J). (gr. 1-1). pap. 7.99 (978-0-486-80258-9(2)) Dover Pubns., Inc.

EduTax, Vol. 1. Date not set. (978-1-888042-03-0(6)); (978-1-888042-02-3(8)) Good Reading Bks.

Edwards, Amelia. Carousel Colors, 1 vol. rev. ed. 2013. (Fiction Readers Ser.). (ENG., Illus.). 12p. (J). (gr. 1-1). pap. 4.99 (978-1-4333-5447-2(0)); pap. 12.96 (978-1-4807-1126-6(8)) Shell Educational Publishing.

—It's Good Enough to Eat!, 1 vol. rev. ed. 2013. (Fiction Readers Ser.). (ENG., Illus.). 20p. (J). (gr. 1-1). pap. 4.99 (978-1-4333-5493-9(4)); pap. 15.96 (978-1-4807-1149-5(7)) Shell Educational Publishing.

—Playground Friends, 1 vol. rev. ed. 2013. (Fiction Readers Ser.). (ENG., Illus.). 12p. (J). (gr. 1-1). 4.99 (978-1-4333-5449-6(7)); pap. 12.96 (978-1-4807-1128-0(4)) Shell Educational Publishing.

Edwards-Hammond, Arlene. Keys, Please? Please Keys? 2012. 50p. pap. 15.99 (978-1-4771-0376-0(7)) Xlibris Corp.

Edwards, Jean E. Adventure Tales: For Kids Who Want to Become Better Readers. 2012. 102p. 24.99 (978-1-4771-4118-2(9)); pap. 15.99 (978-1-4771-4117-5(0)) Xlibris Corp.

Edwards, Roberta. Best Friends: The True Story of Owen & Mzee. Schwartz, Carol, illus. 2007. (All Aboard Science Reader Ser.). 32p. (gr. -1-3). 14.00 (978-0-7569-8167-9(0)) Perfection Learning Corp.

Eeles, Alex. Bedtime on the Farm Red Band. Ortu, Davide, illus. 2016. (Cambridge Reading Adventures Ser.). (ENG.). 16p. pap. 6.56 (978-1-316-50081-1(0)) Cambridge Univ. Pr.

Eggers, Casey. A Great Day in the City. 2003. (Rise & Shine Ser.). (ENG.). (C). pap. 10.95 (978-0-7362-1894-8(7)) CENGAGE Learning.

Eggleton. Sail Blu Nf Chimpanzees. 2004. (Rigby Sails Early Ser.). (ENG.). 16p. (gr. 1-2). pap. 6.95 (978-0-7578-9960-7(9)) Rigby Education.

—Sail Blu Nf Fantastic Frogs. 2004. (Rigby Sails Early Ser.). (ENG.). 16p. (gr. 1-2). pap. 6.95 (978-0-7578-9952-2(8)) Rigby Education.

Eggleton, Jill. Bertha & the Beeman. (Sails Literacy Ser.). 24p. (gr. 1-18). 27.00 (978-0-7578-6201-4(2)) Rigby Education.

—Bertha & the Beeman: 3-in-1 Package. (Sails Literacy Ser.). 24p. (gr. 1-18). 57.00 (978-0-7578-8618-8(3)) Rigby Education.

—Big Bill's Bed. Matijasevich, Astrid, illus. 2003. (Rigby Sails Early Ser.). (ENG.). 16p. (gr. 1-2). pap. 6.95 (978-0-7578-8731-4(7)) Houghton Mifflin Harcourt Publishing Co.

—Big Red Comes to Stay. Cammell, Sandra, illus. 2004. (Rigby Sails Early Ser.). (ENG.). 16p. (gr. 1-2). pap. 6.95 (978-0-7578-9303-2(1)) Houghton Mifflin Harcourt Publishing Co.

—Billy Mcbrown. Pye, Trevor, illus. (Sails Literacy Ser.). 24p. (gr. 1-18). 27.00 (978-0-7578-6202-1(0));Pack. 57.00 (978-0-7578-8620-1(5)) Rigby Education.

—A Bird Is a Bird. Chambers, Brent, illus. 2003. (Rigby Sails Early Ser.). (ENG.). 16p. (gr. 1-2). pap. 6.95 (978-0-7578-8662-1(0)) Houghton Mifflin Harcourt Publishing Co.

—Bubble Trouble: 3-in-1 Package. Webb, Philip, illus. (Sails Literacy Ser.). 24p. (gr. k-18). 57.00 (978-0-7578-8614-0(0)) Rigby Education.

—Bubble Trouble: 6 Small Books. Webb, Philip, illus. (Sails Literacy Ser.). 24p. (gr. k-18). 25.00 (978-0-7578-7726-1(5)) Rigby Education.

—Bubble Trouble: Big Book Only. Webb, Philip, illus. (Sails Literacy Ser.). 24p. (gr. k-18). 27.00 (978-0-7578-6197-0(0)) Rigby Education.

—Clown's Pants. Smith, Craig, illus. 2003. (Rigby Sails Early Ser.). (ENG.). 16p. (gr. 1-2). pap. 6.95 (978-0-7578-8723-9(6)) Houghton Mifflin Harcourt Publishing Co.

—Clown's Party. Smith, Craig, illus. 2003. (Rigby Sails Early Ser.). (ENG.). 16p. (gr. 1-2). pap. 6.95 (978-0-7578-8669-0(8)) Houghton Mifflin Harcourt Publishing Co.

—Creatures of the Extreme. 2007. (Connectors Ser.). (gr. 2-5). pap. (978-1-877453-10-6(2)) Global Education Systems Ltd.

—The Deep Ocean. 2007. (Connectors Ser.). (gr. 2-5). pap. (978-1-877453-02-1(1)) Global Education Systems Ltd.

—The Dream Catcher. (Sails Literacy Ser.). 24p. (gr. 1-18). 8.00 (978-0-7635-6983-9(6)) Rigby Education.

—The Eye of the Law. 2007. (Connectors Ser.). (gr. 2-5). pap. (978-1-877453-14-4(5)) Global Education Systems Ltd.

—Fearless Phil: 3-in-1 Package. McGrath, Raymond, illus. (Sails Literacy Ser.). 24p. (gr. 3-18). 57.00 (978-0-7578-6996-9(3)) Rigby Education.

—Fearless Phil: 6 Small Books. McGrath, Raymond, illus. (Sails Literacy Ser.). 24p. (gr. 3-18). 25.00 (978-0-7578-6988-4(2)) Rigby Education.

—Fearless Phil: Big Book Only. McGrath, Raymond, illus. (Sails Literacy Ser.). 24p. (gr. 3-18). 27.00 (978-0-7578-6980-8(7)) Rigby Education.

—The Fire. Pye, Trevor, illus. 2003. (Rigby Sails Early Ser.). (ENG.). 16p. (gr. 1-2). pap. 6.95 (978-0-7578-8663-8(9)) Houghton Mifflin Harcourt Publishing Co.

—Flea & Big Bill. Matijasevich, Astrid, illus. 2003. (Rigby Sails Early Ser.). (ENG.). 16p. (gr. 1-2). pap. 6.95 (978-0-7578-8722-2(8)) Houghton Mifflin Harcourt Publishing Co.

—Flea Goes Out! Matijasevich, Astrid, illus. 2003. (Rigby Sails Early Ser.). (ENG.). 16p. (gr. 1-2). pap. 6.95 (978-0-7578-8737-6(6)) Houghton Mifflin Harcourt Publishing Co.

—Granny Groggin: 3-in-1 Package. (Sails Literacy Ser.). 24p. (gr. 3-18). 57.00 (978-0-7578-6997-6(1)) Rigby Education.

—The Ice-Cream Machine. Pye, Trevor, illus. 2003. (Rigby Sails Early Ser.). (ENG.). 16p. (gr. 1-2). pap. 6.95 (978-0-7578-8728-4(7)) Houghton Mifflin Harcourt Publishing Co.

—Invasive Species. 2007. (Connectors Ser.). (gr. 2-5). pap. (978-1-877453-04-5(8)) Global Education Systems Ltd.

—Mickey Maloney's Missing Bag. Pye, Trevor, illus. 2004. (Rigby Sails Early Ser.). (ENG.). 16p. (gr. 1-2). pap. 6.95 (978-0-7578-9299-8(X)) Houghton Mifflin Harcourt Publishing Co.

—Mrs. Mcfee. Webb, Philip, illus. 2009. 39.95 (978-0-7664-3147-8(9)) Abrams & Co. Pubs., Inc.

—The Mystery of Missing Big Wig, 3 vols., Pack. (Sails Literacy Ser.). 24p. (gr. 3-18). 57.00 (978-0-7578-6998-3(X)) Rigby Education.

—Nomads. 2007. (Connectors Ser.). (gr. 2-5). pap. (978-1-877453-12-0(9)) Global Education Systems Ltd.

—Sailor Sam in Trouble. Storey, Jim, illus. 2004. (Rigby Sails Early Ser.). (ENG.). 16p. (gr. 1-2). pap. 6.95 (978-0-7578-9295-0(7)) Houghton Mifflin Harcourt Publishing Co.

—The Sky Bridge. (Sails Literacy Ser.). 24p. (gr. 1-18). 8.00 (978-0-7635-6982-2(8)) Rigby Education.

—Tony's Dad. Hawley, Kelvin, illus. 2003. (Rigby Sails Sailing Solo Ser.). (ENG.). 24p. (gr. 1-2). pap. 9.05 (978-0-7578-3975-7(4)) Rigby Education.

—Treasures. 2007. (Connectors Ser.). (gr. 2-5). pap. (978-1-877453-17-5(X)) Global Education Systems Ltd.

—Turtle's Trouble. Cammell, Sandra, illus. 2003. (Rigby Sails Early Ser.). (ENG.). 16p. (gr. 1-2). pap. 6.95 (978-0-7578-8672-0(8)) Houghton Mifflin Harcourt Publishing Co.

—Where Are You, Mouse? McGrath, Raymond, illus. 2003. (Rigby Sails Early Ser.). (ENG.). 16p. (gr. 1-2). pap. 6.95 (978-0-7578-8741-3(4)) Houghton Mifflin Harcourt Publishing Co.

—The Wonder of the Wind. 2007. (Connectors Ser.). (gr. 2-5). pap. (978-1-877453-19-9(6)) Global Education Systems Ltd.

El Khatiri, Basma. Momma's Song. Kala, Sabah, illus. 2016. (Stories & Fables from Around the World Ser.). (ENG.). 24p. (J). (gr. 2-1). lib. bdg. 24.60 (978-1-4777-5694-2(9), Windmill Bks.) Rosen Publishing Group, Inc., The.

Elephant Walk: Level K, 6 vols. 128p. (gr. 2-3). 40.50 (978-0-7699-0993-6(0)) Shortland Pubns. (U. S. A.) Inc.

Elizabeth, Shelby. Dabby's Pond. 2006. (Neighborhood Readers Ser.). (ENG.). 16p. (gr. 1-3). pap. 6.50 (978-1-4042-7148-7(1), Rosen Classroom) Rosen Publishing Group, Inc., The.

Elliott, Rebecca. Baxter Is Missing: a Branches Book (Owl Diaries #6) 2017. (Owl Diaries: 6). (ENG.). 80p. (J). (gr. k-2). lib. bdg. 15.99 **(978-1-338-04285-6(8))** Scholastic, Inc.

Ellis, Julie. Shark & Crab Big Book Edition. Hawley, Kelvin, illus. 2014. (ENG.). 16p. (gr. 1-1). Beta (978-1-77654-094-5(8), Red Rocket Readers) Flying Start Bks.

Ellis, Julie & Nickel, Adam. The Giant's Causeway. 2008. (Rigby Focus Forward: Level K Ser.). (Illus.). 24p. (J). (gr. -1-3). pap. (978-1-4190-3796-2(X), Rigby) Pearson Education Australia.

Ellis, Julie & Stewart, Christen. Lizzie's Hidden Message. 2008. (Rigby Focus Forward: Level N Ser.). (Illus.). 24p. (J). (gr. 4-7). pap. (978-1-4190-3839-6(7), Rigby) Pearson Education Australia.

Elson, William H. The Elson Readers, Bk. 5. l.t. ed. 2007. (ENG.). 436p. pap. 28.99 (978-1-4264-3446-4(4)) Creative Media Partners, LLC.

—The Elson Readers, Vol. 5. 2004. reprint ed. pap. 1.99 (978-1-4192-6079-7(0)) Kessinger Publishing, LLC.

—The Elson Readers, Bk. 4. 2005. (Elson Readers Ser.). (ENG., Illus.). 367p. (J). (gr. -1-12). per. 18.95 (978-1-890623-18-0(0)) Lost Classic Bks.

—The Elson Readers, Book 5. 2007. (ENG.). 372p. pap. 25.99 (978-1-4264-3396-2(4)) Creative Media Partners, LLC.

Elson, William H. & Keck, Christine M. The Elson Readers - Book V. 2007. 420p. per. (978-1-4065-2501-4(4)) Dodo Pr.

Elson, William H., et al. The Elson Readers. 2005. (Elson Readers Ser.). (ENG., (J). (gr. -1-12). Bk. 5. Illus.). 439p. per. 19.95 (978-1-890623-19-7(9))Bk. 6. 477p. tchr. ed., per. 21.95 (978-1-890623-20-3(2))Bk. 7. (Illus.). 549p. per. 22.95 (978-1-890623-21-0(0)) Lost Classic Bks.

—The Elson Readers, 9 vols. 2005. (Illus.). (J). pap. (978-1-890623-23-4(7)) Lost Classics Bk. Co.

—The Elson Readers, Book Eight, Vol. 8. 2005. (Elson Readers Ser.). (ENG.). 575p. (J). (gr. -1-12). per. 23.95 (978-1-890623-22-7(9)) Lost Classic Bks.

The Elves & the Shoemaker, Level 3. 2016. (Ladybird Readers Ser.). (ENG.). 64p. (J). (gr. 2-4). pap. 9.99 (978-0-241-25385-4(3)) Penguin Bks., Ltd. GBR. Dist: Independent Pubs. Group.

Ely, Jennifer W. Mommy Teach Me to Read: Pre-Reader Series 1. 2006. (J). 16.99 (978-0-9777150-0-8(0)) Growing Little Readers.

Embacher, Eric. Will Smith: The Funny, Funky, & Confident Fresh Prince, 6 vols., Set. 2003. (High Five Reading - Red Ser.). (ENG.). 48p. (gr. 3-4). pap. 54.00 (978-0-7368-2839-0(7), High Five Reading (RBL)) Capstone Press of Coughlan Cos.

Emerald, Ruby & Sapphire Levels Certificate Only. (gr. k-5). 89.00 (978-0-7578-6537-4(2)) Rigby Education.

Emergent: 1 Each of 8 Big Books, Vol. 3. (Sunshinetm Science Ser.). (gr. 1-2). 250.50 (978-0-7802-0571-0(5)) Wright Group/McGraw-Hill.

Emergent Vol. 3: 1 Each of 8 Student Books. (Sunshinetm Science Ser.). (gr. 1-2). 48.95 (978-0-7802-0572-7(3)) Wright Group/McGraw-Hill.

Emmett, Jonathan. Danny Dreadnought Saves the World. Chatterton, Martin, illus. (Reading Ladder Ser.). (ENG.). 48p. (J). (gr. k-2). 2016. pap. 7.99 (978-1-4052-8219-2(3)) 2015. pap. 8.99 (978-1-4052-7072-4(1)) Egmont Bks., Ltd. GBR. Dist: Independent Pubs. Group.

—The Emperor's New Clones. Chatterton, Martin, illus. 2nd ed. 2016. (Reading Ladder Ser.). (ENG.). 48p. (J). (gr. k-2). pap. 7.99 (978-1-4052-8252-9(5)) Egmont Bks., Ltd. GBR. Dist: Independent Pubs. Group.

Encounter: Narrative Nonfiction Picture Books. 2016. (Encounter: Narrative Nonfiction Picture Bks.). (ENG.). 113.27 (978-1-4914-8050-2(5)) Encounter Bks.

Ende, Michael & Michael, Ende. El Largo Camino Hacia Santa Cruz. Kehn, Regina, illus. (SPA.). 64p. (J). (gr. 3-5). 6.95 (978-84-241-3354-2(4), EV3073) Everest Editora ESP. Dist: Lectorum Pubns., Inc.

Ender's Game Student Packet. 2004. (YA). (gr. 7-8). stu. ed. 12.99 (978-1-58130-512-8(5)) Novel Units, Inc.

Endres, Hollie J. The Letter Ee Set: Things That Are Alike, 6 vols. 2004. (Letter Bks.). (ENG.). 8p. (gr. k-1). pap. 29.70 (978-0-7368-4104-7(0), Letter Bks.) Capstone Press of Coughlan Cos.

—The Letter Hh Set: Homes, 6 vols. 2004. (Letter Bks.). (ENG.). 8p. (gr. k-1). pap. 29.70 (978-0-7368-4107-8(5), Letter Bks.) Capstone Press of Coughlan Cos.

—The Letter Nn Set: At the Grocery Store, 6 vols. 2004. (Letter Bks.). (ENG.). 8p. (gr. k-1). pap. 29.70 (978-0-7368-4113-9(X), Letter Bks.) Capstone Press of Coughlan Cos.

—The Letter Xx Set: Things I Can See, 6. 2004. (Letter Bks.). (ENG.). 8p. (gr. k-1). pap. 29.70 (978-0-7368-4123-8(7), Letter Bks.) Capstone Press of Coughlan Cos.

—The Letter Yy Set: All about Me!, 6 vols. 2004. (Letter Bks.). (ENG.). 8p. (gr. k-1). pap. 29.70 (978-0-7368-4124-5(5), Letter Bks.) Capstone Press of Coughlan Cos.

—Our Red-White-and-Blue Holidays, 6 vols., Set. 2004. (Phonics Readers Books 37-72 Ser.). (ENG.). 8p. (gr. k-1). pap. 35.70 (978-0-7368-4054-5(0), Phonics Readers) Capstone Press of Coughlan Cos.

—A Trip to the Repair Shop, 6 vols., Set. 2004. (Letter Bks.). (ENG.). 8p. (gr. k-1). pap. 29.70 (978-0-7368-4111-5(3), Letter Bks.) Capstone Press of Coughlan Cos.

Energy - English Take Home Book. 2007. (Journeys Ser.). (J). pap. 20.00 (978-1-4042-9535-3(6), Rosen Classroom) Rosen Publishing Group, Inc., The.

Engelmann, Siegfried & Engelmann, Owen. Funnix Beginning Math. 2011. (J). DVD 32.00 (978-0-9714798-2-1(8)) Royal Limited Partnership.

—Funnix Beginning Math Workbook. 2011. (J). instr.'s gde. ed. 10.00 (978-0-9714798-4-5(4)) Royal Limited Partnership.

English for a Changing World Listening Comprehension Manual: Level 3, 6 vols. (Fluency Strand Ser.). (YA). 45.00 (978-1-4045-1217-7(9)) Wright Group/McGraw-Hill.

English in My Pocket: Add-to Pack of Little Books. 34.00 (978-0-7635-2931-4(1)) Rigby Education.

English in My Pocket: Add-to Pack of Manipulatives. 42.00 (978-0-7635-2932-1(X)) Rigby Education.

English-Spanish Book Set 800937, 4 vols. 2005. (J). bds. (978-1-59794-096-2(8)) Environments, Inc.

English to a Beat! (gr. 2-8). 763.19 (978-0-7362-2508-3(0)) CENGAGE Learning.

English to a Beat! Folk Tales Single-Copy Set. (gr. 2-8). 95.84 (978-0-7362-2507-6(2)) CENGAGE Learning.

Ennett, Jonathan. Clever Computers Turquoise Band. 2016. (Cambridge Reading Adventures Ser.). (ENG.). 24p. pap. 7.19 (978-1-316-50331-7(3)) Cambridge Univ. Pr.

—Town Underground. 2016. (Cambridge Reading Adventures Ser.). (ENG.). 24p. pap. 7.19 (978-1-316-50333-1(X)) Cambridge Univ. Pr.

The Enormous Turnip, Level 1. 2016. (Ladybird Readers Ser.). (ENG., Illus.). 48p. (J). pap., act. bk. ed. 9.99 (978-0-241-25408-0(6)) Penguin Bks., Ltd. GBR. Dist: Independent Pubs. Group.

The Entire World of SH & CH Book of Stories. 2004. per. 34.99 (978-0-9760490-2-9(3)) Say It Right.

Eric Carle Board Book Set 800489, 3. 2005. (J). bds. (978-1-59794-003-0(8)) Environments, Inc.

Erin, K. c. The Carnival. 2009. 60p. pap. 23.99 (978-1-4389-7048-6(X)) AuthorHouse.

Escott, John & Pearson Education Staff. Ghost of Genny Castle. 2nd ed. 2008. (ENG., Illus.). 48p. pap. 11.99 (978-1-4058-6953-9(4)) Pearson Education.

Esquivel, Rosaura. It's Time for School. 2017. (Let's Tell Time Ser.). 24p. (J). (gr. 4-6). 23.60 **(978-1-5081-5725-0(1)**, PowerKids Pr.) Rosen Publishing Group, Inc., The.

Essential Words Reading & Language Arts Activity Book (Elementary) Elementary. 2006. (J). 8.95 (978-1-933655-01-7(1)) New Leaf Educ., Inc.

ETA/Cuisenaire Staff. Ben's Bath. 2003. (SunSprouts Big Bk Ser.). (ENG.). (gr. -1-3). pap. 33.50 (978-0-7406-2018-8(5), SunSprouts) ETA hand2mind.

—I See. 2003. (SunSprouts Ser.). (ENG.). (gr. -1-3). pap. 4.95 (978-0-7406-2104-8(1), SunSprouts) ETA hand2mind.

Eubanks, Holly L. Through the Eye of the Needle. (J). stu. ed. 18.95 (978-1-56270-047-8(2)) Dominie Pr., Inc.

—Through the Eye of the Needle: Answer Key. (J). 395.00 (978-1-56270-049-2(9)) Dominie Pr., Inc.

Evan-Moor. Skill Sharpenerd Reading Grade 3. 2005. (Skill Sharpeners Ser.). (ENG., Illus.). 144p. (J). pap. 9.99 (978-1-59673-039-7(0), emc 4531) Evan-Moor Educational Pubs.

—Skill Sharpeners Reading, Grade 1. 2005. (Sharpeners Ser.). (ENG., Illus.). 144p. (J). pap. 9.99 (978-1-59673-037-3(4)) Evan-Moor Educational Pubs.

—Skill Sharpeners Reading, Grade 2. 2005. (ENG.). 144p. (J). pap. 9.99 (978-1-59673-038-0(2), emc 4530) Evan-Moor Educational Pubs.

—Skill Sharpeners Reading, Grade 4. 2005. (ENG.). 144p. (J). pap. 9.99 (978-1-59673-040-3(4), emc 4532) Evan-Moor Educational Pubs.

—Skill Sharpeners Reading, Grade 5. 2005. (ENG.). 144p. (J). pap. 9.99 (978-1-59673-041-0(2), emc 4533) Evan-Moor Educational Pubs.

—Skill Sharpeners, Reading, Grade 6. 2005. (ENG., Illus.). 144p. (J). pap. 9.99 (978-1-59673-042-7(0), emc 4534) Evan-Moor Educational Pubs.

—Skill Sharpeners, Reading, Grade K. 2005. (ENG.). 144p. (J). pap. 9.99 (978-1-59673-036-6(6), emc 4528) Evan-Moor Educational Pubs.

—Skill Sharpeners Reading, Grade PreK. 2005. (ENG.). 144p. (J). pap. 9.99 (978-1-59673-035-9(8), emc 4527) Evan-Moor Educational Pubs.

Evans, Cordelia, adapted by. Doozers Have Green Thumbs. 2015. (Doozers Ser.). (ENG., Illus.). 32p. (J). (gr. -1-1). pap. 3.99 (978-1-4814-3220-7(6), Simon Spotlight) Simon Spotlight.

Eva's Lost & Found Report: Fourth Grade Guided Comprehension Level L. (On Our Way to English Ser.). (gr. 4-18). 34.50 (978-0-7578-7150-4(X)) Rigby Education.

EventoSusan. YOUR DREAM VACATION HIGH BEGINNING BOOK WITH ONLINE ACCESS. 2014. (ENG.). 24p. (J). pap. 9.50 (978-1-107-69043-1(9)) Cambridge Univ. Pr.

Everett-Camplin, Helen. Grandad's Magic Gadgets. 2009. (ENG.). 64p. pap. 12.00 (978-84-8323-522-5(6)) Cambridge Univ. Pr.

Every Body Tells a Story: Level Q, 6 vols., Vol. 3. (Explorers Ser.). 32p. (gr. 3-6). 44.95 (978-0-7699-0621-8(4)) Shortland Pubns. (U. S. A.) Inc.

Every Morning: Lap Book. (Pebble Soup Explorations Ser.). 16p. (gr. -1-18). 21.00 (978-0-7578-1656-7(8)) Rigby Education.

Every Morning: Small Book. (Pebble Soup Explorations Ser.). 16p. (gr. -1-18). 5.00 (978-0-7578-1696-3(7)) Rigby Education.

Everyday Assessment with Reading Rods. 2004. (J). lib. bdg. 24.95 (978-1-56911-176-5(6)) Learning Resources, Inc.

Excuse Me, Sir. (J). 26.20 (978-0-8136-8396-6(3)); (gr. -1-3). 59.50 (978-0-8136-7912-9(5)) Modern Curriculum Pr.

Excuses, Excuses: 6 Small Books. (gr. k-3). 24.00 (978-0-7635-6236-6(X)) Rigby Education.

Explore! (Early Intervention Levels Ser.). 21.42 (978-0-7362-1051-5(2)) CENGAGE Learning.

The Explorer: Individual Title Six-Packs. (gr. -1-2). 27.00 (978-0-7635-9448-0(2)) Rigby Education.

Explorers: Fluency - Student Book Set - 1 Each of 12 Titles. (Explorers. Exploradores Nonfiction Sets Ser.). (gr. 3-6). 89.95 (978-0-7699-0815-1(2)) Shortland Pubns. (U. S. A.) Inc.

Exploring Literature: The EMC Write-in Reader. 2nd ed. (Literature & the Language Arts Ser.). (YA). (gr. 7-18). wbk. ed. 17.99 (978-0-8219-2910-0(0)) EMC/Paradigm Publishing.

Extensions Through the Library TAKS Reading Preparation Grades 3-5: Curriculum Connected Resources. 2004. (Region IV ESC Resources for Librarian Ser.). spiral bd. (978-1-933049-05-2(7)) Region IV Education Service Ctr.

Extensions Through the Library TAKS Reading Preparation Grades 6-8. 2005. spiral bd. (978-1-933049-46-5(4)) Region IV Education Service Ctr.

Fabregat, Antonio-Manuel. Los Cuentos de Mi Escuela. (SPA.). 64p. (J). (gr. 4). (978-84-216-1593-5(9), BU4751) Bruño, Editorial ESP. Dist: Lectorum Pubns., Inc.

La Fabrica. (Coleccion Aqui Se Trabaja). (SPA., Illus.). (J). 10.95 (978-84-207-3624-2(4), ANY765) Grupo Anaya, S.A. ESP. Dist: Continental Bk. Co., Inc.

Fabulas Fabulosas. 2006. (SPA.). (J). (978-1-933485-24-9(8)) Publicaciones Puertorriquenas, Inc.

Fabulous PH Riddles Blends/Dig. (J). pap. 18.16 (978-0-8136-0864-8(3)) Modern Curriculum Pr.

Fact & Opinion (Gr. 1-3) 2003. (J). (978-1-58232-078-6(0)) ECS Learning Systems, Inc.

Fair Weather Student Packet. 2004. (J). 12.99 (978-1-58130-514-2(1)) Novel Units, Inc.

Fakhouri, Shoua. Omar's First Day at School Pink B Band. Pérez, Moni, illus. 2016. (Cambridge Reading Adventures Ser.). (ENG.). 16p. pap. 6.56 (978-1-316-60811-1(5)) Cambridge Univ. Pr.

Falletta, Bernadette. We Love to Read Stories Coloring Book & Word Search Puzzles. 2005. 23p. (J). 10.95 (978-1-4116-6291-9(1)) Lulu Pr., Inc.

Falletta, Bernadette & Lewis, Marla. We Love to Read Stories & Songs. 2005. 27p. (J). 14.95 (978-1-4116-4734-3(3)) Lulu Pr., Inc.

The Family: Individual Title, 6 pack. (Sails Literacy Ser.). 16p. (gr. k-18). 27.00 (978-0-7635-4409-6(4)) Rigby Education.

Family Counts. (Early Intervention Levels Ser.). 23.10 (978-0-7362-0001-1(0)) CENGAGE Learning.

Family Living Board Book Set 800646, 4. 2005. (J). bds. (978-1-59794-038-2(0)) Environments, Inc.

Family Stories: Individual Packs Pack A. (gr. k-2). 15.40 (978-0-7362-0491-0(1)) CENGAGE Learning.

Family Stories: Individual Packs Pack B. (gr. k-2). 15.40 (978-0-7362-0493-4(8)) CENGAGE Learning.

Family Stories: Jumbo Packs. (gr. k-2). 157.08 (978-0-7362-0051-6(7)) CENGAGE Learning.

Famous Tales. 2016. (Famous Tales Ser.). 24p. (gr. 2-2). pap. 49.50 (978-1-5081-9273-2(1), Windmill Bks.) Rosen Publishing Group, Inc., The.

Far Away. (Early Intervention Levels Ser.). 3.85 (978-0-7362-1865-8(3)) CENGAGE Learning.

Farber, Erica. Richard Scarry's Readers (Level 3): Spooky Campout. Scarry, Huck, illus. 2015. (Richard Scarry's Great Big Schoolhouse Ser.). (ENG.). 24p. (J). (gr. 1-2). pap. 3.95 (978-1-4027-9915-0(2)) Sterling Publishing Co., Inc.

Farley, Robin. Mia & the Too Big Tutu. Ivanov, Aleksey & Ivanov, Olga, illus. 2010. (My First I Can Read Ser.). (ENG.). 32p. (J). (gr. -1-3). 16.99 (978-0-06-173302-4(4)); pap. 3.99 (978-0-06-173301-7(6)) HarperCollins Pubs.

Farmer's Market. (Early Intervention Levels Ser.). 21.30 (978-0-7362-2126-9(3)) CENGAGE Learning.

Farming. (Early Intervention Levels Ser.). 8.48 (978-0-7362-1900-6(5)); 50.88 (978-0-7362-2127-6(1)) CENGAGE Learning.

Fast Forward! 2003. (Fast Forward! Ser.). Level C. (J). (gr. 1-18). stu. ed., per. 7.95 (978-1-58830-779-8(4))Level C. (J). (gr. 1-18). stu. ed., per. 67.95 (978-1-58830-333-2(0))Level D. (J). (gr. 2-18). stu. ed., per. 7.95 (978-1-58830-780-4(8))Level D. (J). (gr. 2-18). stu. ed., per. 67.95 (978-1-58830-334-9(9))Level A. tchr. ed., per., tchr.'s training gde. ed. 39.95 (978-1-58830-783-5(2))Level A. (J). (gr. 1-18). stu. ed., per. 67.95 (978-1-58830-331-8(4))Level A. (J). (gr. 1-18). stu. ed., per. 7.95 (978-1-58830-777-4(8))Level B. tchr. ed., per., tchr.'s training gde. ed. 39.95 (978-1-58830-784-2(0))Level B. (J). (gr. 1-18). stu. ed., per. 7.95 (978-1-58830-778-1(6))Level B. (J). (gr. 1-18). stu. ed., per. 67.95 (978-1-58830-332-5(2))Level E. (J). (gr. 1-18). stu. ed., per. 7.95 (978-1-58830-781-1(6))Level E. (J). (gr. 2-18). 369.95 (978-1-58830-799-6(9))Level E. (J). (gr. 2-18). stu. ed., per. 67.95 (978-1-58830-335-6(7))Level F. (J). (gr. 2-18). 369.95 (978-1-58830-800-9(6))Level F. (J). (gr. 2-18). stu. ed., per. 7.95 (978-1-58830-782-8(4))Level F. (J). (gr. 2-18). stu. ed., per. 67.95 (978-1-58830-336-3(5)) Metropolitan Teaching & Learning Co.

FATUS SOPHIE. My Big Barefoot Book of Spanish & English Words. 2016. (ENG & SPA.). 48p. (J). (gr. -1-1). 19.99 (978-1-78285-286-5(7)) Barefoot Bks., Inc.

Faundez, Anne. A Cloak for Swallow, 4 vols. 2005. (QEB Readers). (Illus.). 24p. (J). (gr. 1-4). lib. bdg. 15.95 (978-1-59566-093-0(3)) QEB Publishing Inc.

—Imaginary Creatures, 4 vols. 2005. (QEB Readers). (Illus.). 24p. (J). (gr. -1-3). lib. bdg. 15.95 (978-1-59566-102-9(6)) QEB Publishing Inc.

—Sing a Song of Sixpence, 8 vols. 2005. (QEB Readers). (Illus.). 24p. (J). (gr. -1-3). lib. bdg. 15.95 (978-1-59566-072-5(0)) QEB Publishing Inc.

Faundez, Anne, et al. QEB Start Reading Multipack (6 Titles) Paperback, 6 vols. 2005. (QEB Start Reading Ser.). (Illus.). 144p. (J). lib. bdg. 40.00 (978-1-59566-063-3(1)) QEB Publishing Inc.

Favorite Animals Book Set 2 800893, 6 vols. 2005. (J). pap. (978-1-59794-068-9(2)) Environments, Inc.

Favorite Characters 800885, 6 vols. 2005. (J). pap. (978-1-59794-060-3(7)) Environments, Inc.

Favorite Characters No. 2 800886, 6 vols. 2005. (J). pap. (978-1-59794-061-0(5)) Environments, Inc.

The Fawn. 2005. (The Fawn Chapter Ser.). (J). 7.67 (978-1-58453-309-2(9)) Pioneer Valley Bks.

Fawn Chapter Books, Set 1. 2005. (J). (978-1-58453-308-5(0)) Pioneer Valley Bks.

The Feast: 3-in-1 Package. (Sails Literacy Ser.). 24p. (gr. 2-18). 57.00 (978-0-7578-3214-7(8)) Rigby Education.

The Feast: Big Book Only. (Sails Literacy Ser.). 24p. (gr. 2-18). 27.00 (978-0-7635-6994-5(1)) Rigby Education.

Fekany Lee, Kimberly. Cell Scientists: Discovering How Cells Work, 1 vol. 2007. (Science Readers Ser.). (ENG.). 32p. (J). (gr. 3-3). pap. 8.99 (978-0-7439-0584-8(9)) Shell Educational Publishing.

Feldman, Jean R. & Karapetkova, Holly. Arms Are for Hugging (Tune, the Girl I Left Behind Me) Lap Book. 2010. (ENG., Illus.). 12p. (gr. -1-k). 9.95 (978-1-61590-200-2(7)) Rourke Educational Media.

—Basic Needs (Lap Book) 2010. (ENG., Illus.). 12p. (gr. -1-k). 9.95 (978-1-61590-212-5(0)) Rourke Educational Media.

—Chant & Write (Tune, Sound off Cadence) Lap Book. 2010. (ENG., Illus.). 12p. (gr. -1-k). 9.95 (978-1-61590-192-0(2)) Rourke Educational Media.

—Continents Together (Tune, He's Got the Whole World in His Hands) Lap Book. 2010. (ENG., Illus.). 12p. (gr. -1-k). 9.95 (978-1-61590-194-4(9)) Rourke Educational Media.

—Deck the Room (Tune, Deck the Halls) Lap Book. 2010. (ENG., Illus.). 12p. (gr. -1-k). 9.95 (978-1-61590-184-5(1)) Rourke Educational Media.

—Earth Day (Tune, Clap Your Hands Together) Lap Book. 2010. (ENG., Illus.). 12p. (gr. -1-k). 9.95 (978-1-61590-218-7(X)) Rourke Educational Media.

—Eat Green! (Lap Book) 2010. (ENG., Illus.). 12p. (gr. -1-k). 9.95 (978-1-61590-188-3(4)) Rourke Educational Media.

—Five Senses (Lap Book) 2010. (ENG., Illus.). 12p. (gr. -1-k). 9.95 (978-1-61590-176-0(0)) Rourke Educational Media.

—Found a Penny (Tune, Found a Peanut) Lap Book. 2010. (ENG., Illus.). 16p. (gr. -1-k). 9.95 (978-1-61590-204-0(X)) Rourke Educational Media.

—Fraction Pizza (Tune, He's Got the Whole World in His Hands) 2010. (ENG., Illus.). 12p. (gr. -1-k). 9.95 (978-1-61590-222-4(8)) Rourke Educational Media.

—Good Bye, Friends (Tune, Buffalo Gal) Lap Book. 2010. (ENG., Illus.). 12p. (gr. -1-k). 9.95 (978-1-61590-220-0(1)) Rourke Educational Media.

Feldman, Thea. Kingfisher Readers L1: Tyrannosaurus. 2014. (Kingfisher Readers Ser.). (ENG., Illus.). 32p. (J). (gr. k-3). pap. 3.99 (978-0-7534-7137-1(X), 9780753471371, Kingfisher) Roaring Brook Pr.

Fentiman, David. The Force Awakens. 2015. (DK Readers Ser.). (ENG., Illus.). 48p. (J). (gr. k-2). pap. 3.99 (978-1-4654-3814-0(9), DK Children) Dorling Kindersley Publishing, Inc.

—The Force Awakens: New Adventures. 2015. (DK Readers Ser.). (ENG., Illus.). 48p. (J). (gr. k-2). 14.99 (978-1-4654-3813-3(0), DK Children) Dorling Kindersley Publishing, Inc.

—The Lego Movie. 2013. (DK Reader Level 3 Ser.). lib. bdg. 13.55 (978-0-606-35322-9(4)) Turtleback Bks.

Fentiman, David. New Adventures. 2015. (Illus.). 47p. (J). **(978-1-4806-9626-6(9))** Dorling Kindersley Publishing, Inc.

Fernandez, Joyce & Marsh, Laura. Eins Is One. 2009. 22p. 15.95 (978-0-578-00209-5(4)) My Second Language Publishing, USA.

—Eins und Zwei are One & Two. 2009. 22p. 15.95 (978-0-578-00208-8(6)) My Second Language Publishing, USA.

—Um Is One. 2009. 22p. 15.95 (978-0-557-05629-3(2)) Lulu Pr., Inc.

—Uno y Dos are One & Two. 2008. 22p. pap. 15.95 (978-0-615-26150-8(7)) My Second Language Publishing, USA.

Fetzer, Erin. The Sonday System Readers - 6a-10c, 1. Breckman, Cindy, ed. l.t. ed. 2004. (Illus.). 12p. (J). (978-1-891602-14-6(4)) Winsor Learning, Inc.

Fiction & Nonfiction Packs: Jumbo Packs. (gr. k-2). 438.19 (978-1-56334-397-1(5)) CENGAGE Learning.

Fiction Readers, 30, Set. 2013. (Fiction Readers Ser.). (SPA., Illus.). 20p. (gr. 1-1). spiral bd. 149.70 (978-1-4938-0207-4(0)) Teacher Created Materials, Inc.

Fielder, Scott. The 10 Greatest 21st Century Innovations. 2008. 14.99 (978-1-55448-550-5(9)) Scholastic Library Publishing.

Figorito, Christine. Real Facts about Rivers. 2008. (Rosen Real Readers: Upper Emergent Ser.). (ENG., Illus.). 12p. (gr. 1-2). pap. 5.90 (978-0-8239-8123-6(1)) Rosen Publishing Group, Inc., The.

Figorito, Marcus. A Dime's Busy Day. 2006. (Neighborhood Readers Ser.). (ENG.). 8p. (gr. -1-3). pap. 5.15 (978-1-4042-6710-7(7), Rosen Classroom) Rosen Publishing Group, Inc., The.

—Tara Takes the Train. 2006. (Neighborhood Readers Ser.). (ENG.). 16p. (gr. 1-3). pap. 6.50 (978-1-4042-7208-8(9), Rosen Classroom) Rosen Publishing Group, Inc., The.

Filella, Nacho, et al. Los Disfraces. 2005. (SPA.). 6p. 5.99 (978-84-272-6682-7(0)) Molino, Editorial ESP. Dist: Santillana USA Publishing Co., Inc.

Find the Sock. (Early Intervention Levels Ser.). 21.30 (978-0-7362-0394-4(X)); Vol. 6. 3.55 (978-0-7362-0174-2(2)) CENGAGE Learning.

Findley, Violet. Sea Turtles. 2011. (Illus.). 16p. (J). pap. (978-0-545-24791-7(8)) Scholastic, Inc.

Fine, Anne. Press Play. Dreidemy, Joëlle, illus. 2nd ed. 2016. (Reading Ladder Ser.). (ENG.). 48p. (J). (gr. k-2). pap. 7.99 (978-1-4052-8242-0(8)) Egmont Bks., Ltd. GBR. Dist: Independent Pubs. Group.

—Under the Bed. Robertson, Matt, illus. 2nd ed. 2016. (Reading Ladder Ser.). (ENG.). 48p. (J). (gr. k-2). pap. 7.99 (978-1-4052-8220-8(7)) Egmont Bks., Ltd. GBR. Dist: Independent Pubs. Group.

—Under the Bed: Blue Banana. Robertson, Matt, illus. 2015. (Blue Banana Ser.). (ENG.). 48p. (J). (gr. k-2). pap. 8.99 (978-1-4052-7348-0(8)) Egmont Bks., Ltd. GBR. Dist: Independent Pubs. Group.

Fine, Edith Hope & Josephson, Judith Pinkerton. Armando y la Escuela de Lona Azul. Sosa, Hernan, illus. 2015.Tr. of Armando & the Blue Tarp School. (SPA & ENG.). 32p. (J). (gr. k-4). pap. 10.95 (978-1-60060-449-2(8)) Lee & Low Bks., Inc.

Fiorella, Christina. My Boy Kyle. 2010. 20p. 13.99 (978-1-4520-6519-9(5)) AuthorHouse.

First Adventures Book Set 800918, 3 vols. 2005. (J). pap. (978-1-59794-083-2(6)) Environments, Inc.

First Chapter Book Set 2 800899, 6 vols. 2005. (J). pap. (978-1-59794-074-0(7)) Environments, Inc.

First Chapter Book Set 800898, 3 vols. 2005. (J). (978-1-59794-073-3(9)) Environments, Inc.

A First Clay Gathering (Review Multiple Meanings), Level C. 2003. ("Plaid" Phonics & Stories Libraries). 43.50 (978-0-8136-9234-0(2)) Modern Curriculum Pr.

First Fables Book Set 800915, 6 vols. 2005. (J). pap. (978-1-59794-080-1(1)) Environments, Inc.

First I can Read Set 800882, 4 vols. 2005. (J). pap. (978-1-59794-057-3(7)) Environments, Inc.

First Nature Books 800939, 4. 2005. (J). bds. (978-1-59794-030-6(5)) Environments, Inc.

The First Rainbow: Fourth Grade Guided Comprehension Level O. (On Our Way to English Ser.). (gr. 4-18). 34.50 (978-0-7578-7165-8(8)) Rigby Education.

First Stories (Gr. K-1) 2003. (J). (978-1-58232-035-9(7)) ECS Learning Systems, Inc.

First Things: Individual Title Six-Packs. (gr. -1-2). 23.00 (978-0-7635-8799-4(0)) Rigby Education.

Flaherty, Finn. The Flowerpot. 2006. (Neighborhood Readers Ser.). (ENG.). 16p. (gr. 1-3). pap. 6.50 (978-1-4042-7224-8(0), Rosen Classroom) Rosen Publishing Group, Inc., The.

Fleming, Maria. The Bug Book. Swift, Gary, illus. 2004. (Grammar Tales Ser.). (ENG.). 16p. (J). (gr. 3-7). pap. 3.25 (978-0-439-45818-4(8)) Scholastic, Inc.

Fleming, Maria & Charlesworth, Liza. Chicken in the City. Kennedy, Kelly, illus. 2004. (Grammar Tales Ser.). (ENG.). 16p. (J). (gr. 3-7). pap. 3.25 (978-0-439-45816-0(1)) Scholastic, Inc.

Flor Ada, Alma. Quiero Ayudar! Dominguez, Angela, illus. 2010.Tr. of Let Me Help! (ENG & SPA.). 32p. (J). (gr. -1-3). 16.95 (978-0-89239-232-2(0)) Lee & Low Bks., Inc.

Florie, Christine & Dalby, Danny Brooks. La Mariquita Lara. Dalby, Danny Brooks, illus. 2011. (Rookie Ready to Learn Español Ser.). (SPA., Illus.). 32p. (J). pap. 5.95 (978-0-531-26783-7(0)); lib. bdg. 23.00 (978-0-531-26115-6(8)) Scholastic Library Publishing. (Children's Pr.).

Flounders, Anne. The Corps of Discovery. Leon, Karen, illus. 2004. (Reader's Theater Ser.). (J). pap. (978-1-4108-2310-6(5), A23105) Benchmark Education Co.

The Flutey Family Fruitcake: Level L, 6 vols. 128p. (gr. 2-3). 41.95 (978-0-7699-1019-2(X)) Shortland Pubns. (U. S. A.) Inc.

The Fly: Individual Title Six-Pack. (Story Steps Ser.). (gr. k-2). 20.00 (978-0-7635-9596-8(9)) Rigby Education.

The Flying Machine: KinderConcepts Individual Title Six-Packs. (Kinderstarters Ser.). 8p. (gr. -1-1). 21.00 (978-0-7635-8719-2(2)) Rigby Education.

Flynn, Warren. Different Voices. 200p. (YA). pap. 13.95 (978-1-86368-299-2(6)) Fremantle Pr. AUS. Dist: Independent Pubs. Group.

Fogerty, Ramona. Stories That Increase Reading Fluency: Improving Word Recognition & Comprehension. 2005. (J). per. 19.95 (978-0-9759889-2-3(1)) Potenial Psychotherapy Counseling & Remedial Service.

Folklore. Two Strangers. (J). pap. 2.99 (978-0-8136-2413-6(4)) Modern Curriculum Pr.

—Two Strangers Director's Guide. (J). pap. 5.99 (978-0-8136-2438-9(X)) Modern Curriculum Pr.

Follett, Katherine. Energy Sources for the 21st Century. 2011. (Readers' & Writers' Genre Workshop Ser.). (J). pap. (978-1-4509-3029-1(8)) Benchmark Education Co.

Follow That Spy! Individual Title Six-Packs. (Action Packs Ser.). 120p. (gr. 3-5). 44.00 (978-0-7635-8419-1(3)) Rigby Education.

Follow the Leader: Individual Title Six-Packs. (gr. 1-2). 22.00 (978-0-7635-9152-6(1)) Rigby Education.

Following Directions (Gr. K-1) 2003. (J). (978-1-58232-030-4(6)) ECS Learning Systems, Inc.

Fontana, Lynn & Hoge, Patricia, eds. Education Station Reading Anthology, Volume One: A-B, Band 1-2. 2004. (Illus.). 314p. spiral bd. 48.72 (978-0-7398-9887-1(6)) Steck-Vaughn.

—Education Station Reading Anthology, Volume Two. 2004. (Illus.). Band 1-2. 274p. spiral bd. 52.36 (978-0-7398-9888-8(4))Band 3-5. 132p. spiral bd. 21.84 (978-0-7398-9890-1(6)) Steck-Vaughn.

—Education Station Reading, Volume One: C-E: Student Resource Book. 2004. (Illus.). 248p. per. 7.84 (978-0-7398-9883-3(3)) Steck-Vaughn.

—Education Station Reading, Volume One: F-H: Student Resource Book. 2004. (Illus.). 248p. per. 9.24 (978-0-7398-9885-7(X)) Steck-Vaughn.

Fontes, Justine. Cheerios Action Park Adventure. 2005. (Picture Clue Math Reader Ser.). (Illus.). 28p. (J). pap. (978-0-439-70343-7(3)) Scholastic, Inc.

For the Love of Turtles: Six-Pack. (Greetings Ser.: Vol. 1). 24p. (gr. 2-3). 31.00 (978-0-7635-9423-7(7)) Rigby Education.

Ford, Bernette G. Hurry Up! Kindert, Jennifer C., illus. 2004. (Just for You Ser.). (ENG.). 32p. (gr. k-1). pap. 3.99 (978-0-439-56849-4(8), Teaching Resources) Scholastic, Inc.

Ford, Ron. Cindy's Backyard Circus. 2006. (Neighborhood Readers Ser.). (ENG.). 16p. (gr. 1-3). pap. 6.50 (978-1-4042-7136-4(8), Rosen Classroom) Rosen Publishing Group, Inc., The.

—El circo de Cindy (Cindy's Backyard Circus) 2006. (Lecturas del barrio (Neighborhood Readers) Ser.). (SPA.). 16p. (gr. 1-3). pap. 6.50 (978-1-4042-7138-8(4), Rosen Classroom) Rosen Publishing Group, Inc., The.

—What Do You See? 2006. (Neighborhood Readers Ser.). (ENG.). 12p. (gr. 1-3). pap. 5.90 (978-1-4042-6831-9(6), Rosen Classroom) Rosen Publishing Group, Inc., The.

Forde, Patricia. Witches Do Not Like Bicycles. Dreidemy, Joëlle, illus. (Blue Banana Ser.). (ENG.). 48p. (J). 2015. pap. 7.99 (978-1-4052-7071-7(3)) 2nd ed. 2016. pap. 7.99 (978-1-4052-8218-5(5)) Egmont Bks., Ltd. GBR. Dist: Independent Pubs. Group.

Foresman, Scott. Scott Foresman Reading: Practice. 2003. (ENG.). (gr. 1-1). pap. 20.97 net. (978-0-328-07537-9(X)); (gr. 2-2). pap. 20.97 net. (978-0-328-07538-6(8)); (gr. 3-3). pap. 20.97 net. (978-0-328-07539-3(6)); (gr. 4-4). pap. 20.97 net. (978-0-328-07540-9(X)); (gr. 5-5). pap. 20.97 net. (978-0-328-07541-6(8)); (gr. 6-6). pap. 20.97 net. (978-0-328-07542-3(6)) Pearson Schl. (Scott Foresman).

The Forest Walk: Individual Title Two-Packs. (Chiquilibros Ser.). (gr. -1-1). 12.00 (978-0-7635-8527-3(0)) Rigby Education.

Forrest. Sign of Blood. (Thumbprint Mysteries Ser.). 32.86 (978-0-8092-0408-3(8)) McGraw-Hill/Contemporary.

Forte, Imogene. Ready to Learn Beginning Reading. 2003. (Illus.). 64p. per. 7.95 (978-0-86530-595-3(1)) Incentive Pubns., Inc.

Foster, John. Marathon. 2006. (Collins Big Cat Ser.). (ENG., Illus.). 24p. (J). (gr. 2-2). pap. 6.99 (978-0-00-718689-1(4)) HarperCollins Pubs. Ltd. GBR. Dist: Independent Pubs. Group.

Foster, Ruth. Nonfiction Reading Comprehension - Science. 2006. (ENG.). 144p. pap. 16.99 (978-1-4206-8026-3(9)) Teacher Created Resources, Inc.

—Nonfiction Reading Comprehension - Science, Grade 3. 2006. (ENG.). 144p. pap. 16.99 (978-1-4206-8021-8(8)) Teacher Created Resources, Inc.

—Nonfiction Reading Comprehension - Social Studies, Grades 1-2. 2006. (ENG.). 144p. pap. 16.99 (978-1-4206-8027-0(7)) Teacher Created Resources, Inc.

—Nonfiction Reading Comprehension - Social Studies, Grades 2-3. 2006. (ENG.). 144p. pap. 16.99 (978-1-4206-8023-2(4)) Teacher Created Resources, Inc.

—Social Studies, Grade 3. 2006. (Nonfiction Reading Comprehension Ser.). (ENG., Illus.). 144p. per. 16.99 (978-1-4206-8024-9(2)) Teacher Created Resources, Inc.

Four Cheerful Chipmunks. (Early Intervention Levels Ser.). 28.38 (978-0-7362-0415-6(6)) CENGAGE Learning.

Four Cheerful Chipmunks (14), Vol. 14. (Early Intervention Levels Ser.). 4.73 (978-0-7362-0240-4(4)) CENGAGE Learning.

Fowler, Will S. Shakespeare: His Life & Plays. 2nd ed. 2008. (ENG., Illus.). 72p. pap. 11.99 **(978-1-4058-8231-6(X))** Pearson Education.

The Fox in the Moon. (Lexile Levels Ser.). 9.09 (978-1-56334-705-4(9)) CENGAGE Learning.

Fox, Jennifer. Teen Titans, Go: Pizza Power. 2016. (Passport to Reading Level 2 Ser.). (J). lib. bdg. 14.75 (978-0-606-38326-4(3)) Turtleback Bks.

Foxe, Steve. Meet Blurr. 2016. (Transformers Passport to Reading Ser.). (J). lib. bdg. 13.55 (978-0-606-39191-7(6)) Turtleback Bks.

Foxley, Janet. Red Riding Hood. Bascon, Pedro, illus. 2015. (Collins Big Cat Ser.). (ENG.). 48p. (J). (gr. 3-4). pap. 9.95 (978-0-00-812779-4(4)) HarperCollins Pubs. Ltd. GBR. Dist: Independent Pubs. Group.

Francis, JennaKay. Michael's Safari. Howarth, Craig, illus. 2013. 12p. pap. 8.95 (978-1-61633-411-6(8)) Guardian Angel Publishing, Inc.

Franco, Fabiola. El Novio Robado. (SPA.). (J). pap., wbk. ed. 5.95 (978-0-8219-0034-5(X), 70654); (Illus.). stu. ed. 6.95 (978-0-8219-0033-8(1), 70278) EMC/Paradigm Publishing.

Frederiksen, Barbara. Rippen Ricky Loves the Game: A Book of Perseverance. 2011. 24p. pap. 15.99 (978-1-4628-2999-6(6)) Xlibris Corp.

Freed, Kira. Classifying Animals. 2017. (Text Connections Guided Close Reading Ser.). (J). (gr. 1). (978-1-4900-1799-0(2)) Benchmark Education Co.

—Saving Squirt. Zolotic, Aleksander, illus. 2017. (Text Connections Guided Close Reading Ser.). (J). (gr. 2). (978-1-4900-1834-8(4)) Benchmark Education Co.

Freeman, Maggie & Murray, Pat. Building High. 2005. (Collins Big Cat Ser.). (ENG.). 320p. (J). (gr. 2-3). pap. 7.99 (978-0-00-718642-6(8)) HarperCollins Pubs. Ltd. GBR. Dist: Independent Pubs. Group.

Freeman, Trudy. Shaggy Nick. 2011. 28p. pap. 15.99 (978-1-4653-4763-3(1)) Xlibris Corp.

French, Jackie. Too Many Pears! (Portuguese/English), 1 vol. 2009. (ENG., Illus.). 32p. (J). pap. 6.95 (978-1-59572-197-6(5)) Star Bright Bks., Inc.

French, Kathy. Snap, Crackle, & Flow: Set Of 6. 2011. (Navigators Ser.). (J). 48.00 net. (978-1-4108-0428-0(3)) Benchmark Education Co.

French, Moira. The Swingewood Stories. 2009. 36p. pap. 16.99 (978-1-4490-4777-1(7)) AuthorHouse.

French, Vivian. Emily Mouse's Birthday Party. Marshall, Mark, illus. 2016. (Early Reader Ser.). (ENG.). 64p. (J). (gr. k-3). 6.99 (978-1-4440-1614-7(8), Orion Children's Bks.) Hachette Children's Group GBR. Dist: Hachette Bk. Group.

—The Lion & the Mouse Green Band. Rogers, Alan, illus. 2016. (Cambridge Reading Adventures Ser.). (ENG.). 16p. pap. 6.56 (978-1-107-55038-4(6)) Cambridge Univ. Pr.

—Mountain Mona: Band 09/Gold. Fisher, Chris, illus. 2006. (Collins Big Cat Ser.). (ENG.). 24p. (J). (gr. 2-2). pap. 7.99 (978-0-00-718700-3(9)) HarperCollins Pubs. Ltd. GBR. Dist: Independent Pubs. Group.

French, Vivian, et al. Aladdin & the Genies. 2016. (ENG., Illus.). 48p. (J). pap. 9.95 (978-0-00-814720-4(5)) HarperCollins Pubs. Ltd. GBR. Dist: Independent Pubs. Group.

Freund, Lisa. The Seven Natural Wonders: Set Of 6. 2010. (Navigators Ser.). (J). pap. 44.00 net. (978-1-4108-0403-7(8)) Benchmark Education Co.

Fried, Caren Loebel. Legend of the Gourd. 2010. (HAW & ENG.). 36p. (J). 16.95 (978-1-58178-103-8(2)) Bishop Museum Pr.

P
Q
R

Friedman, Laurie. Happy Birthday, Mallory! Schmitz, Tamara, illus. 2006. (Mallory Ser.: 4). (ENG.). 160p. (J). (gr. 2-5). per. 5.95 *(978-0-8225-6502-4(1)*, First Avenue Editions) Lerner Publishing Group.

A Friend for Jasper. 2004. (Jasper the Cat Chapter Ser.). (ENG., Illus.). (J). pap. 7.67 *(978-1-58453-284-2(X))* Pioneer Valley Bks.

Friends of All Colors. (J). 26.20 *(978-0-8136-8405-5(6))*; (gr. -1-3). 59.50 *(978-0-8136-7930-3(3))* Modern Curriculum Pr.

Friends of All Colours. (J). 26.20 *(978-0-8136-8404-8(8))* Modern Curriculum Pr.

Friendship in Action: Individual Title Six-Packs. (Action Packs Ser.). 120p. (gr. 3-5). 44.00 *(978-0-7635-8390-3(1))* Rigby Education.

Frino, Michael G. Welcome to Waycool School: Where Learning Is Fun & Lessons are Learned by Everyone! 2010. 32p. pap. 17.25 *(978-1-4269-4048-4(3))* Trafford Publishing.

Frog & Toad Book Set 2 800923, 3 vols. 2005. (J). *(978-1-59794-088-7(7))* Environments, Inc.

Frog & Toad Book Set 3 800924, 6 vols. 2005. (J). pap. *(978-1-59794-089-4(5))* Environments, Inc.

Frog & Toad Book Set 800922, 3 vols. 2005. (J). pap. *(978-1-59794-087-0(9))* Environments, Inc.

From Sea to Sea, Level E. Incl. Headway: Level E from Sea to Sea. *(978-0-89688-457-1(0)*, 88-457); Level E. pap., wbk. ed. *(978-0-89688-463-2(5)*, 88-463); Level E. suppl. ed. Level E. suppl. ed. Level E. suppl. ed. *(978-0-89688-469-4(4)*, 88-469); Level E. suppl. ed. (J). (gr. 2-3). *(978-0-89688-452-6(X)*, 88-452) Open Court Publishing Co.

From Seed to Plant. (Lexile Levels Ser.). 9.09 *(978-1-56334-719-1(9))* CENGAGE Learning.

From the Lake to Your Faucet: Fourth Grade Guided Comprehension Level L. (On Our Way to English Ser.). (gr. 4-18). 34.50 *(978-0-7578-7153-5(4))* Rigby Education.

Fruchter, Jason, illus. Friends Help Each Other. 2014. (Daniel Tiger's Neighborhood Ser.). (ENG.). 32p. (J). (gr. -1-k). pap. 3.99 *(978-1-4814-0366-5(4)*, Simon Spotlight) Simon Spotlight.

Fruits & Vegetables I Like to Eat - English Take Home Book. 2007. (Journeys Ser.). (J). pap. 15.00 *(978-1-4042-5462-6(5)*, Rosen Classroom) Rosen Publishing Group, Inc., The.

Fry, Edward B. Reading Drills. 2004. pap., tchr. ed., suppl. ed. *(978-0-8092-0358-1(8))* Jamestown.

—Skimming & Scanning. 2004. pap., tchr. ed., suppl. ed. *(978-0-8092-0362-8(6))* Jamestown.

Fuerst, Jeffrey B. Baa Baa Black Sheep Sells Her Wool. 2008. (Reader's Theater Nursery Rhymes & Songs Ser.). (Illus.). 48p. (J). (gr. k-1). pap. *(978-1-60437-965-5(0))* Benchmark Education Co.

—Bear Goes over the Mountain. 2008. (Reader's Theater Nursery Rhymes & Songs Ser.). (Illus.). 48p. (J). (gr. k-1). pap. *(978-1-60437-972-3(3))* Benchmark Education Co.

—Bingo. Greenhead, Bill, illus. 2010. (Rising Readers Ser.). (J). 3.49 *(978-1-60719-687-7(5))* Newmark Learning LLC.

—Bingo, Come Home! Greenhead, Bill, illus. 2009. (Reader's Theater Nursery Rhymes & Songs Set B Ser.). 48p. (J). pap. *(978-1-60859-151-0(4))* Benchmark Education Co.

—Chuck, Woodchuck, Chuck! Greenhead, Bill, illus. 2009. (Reader's Theater Nursery Rhymes & Songs Set B Ser.). 48p. (J). pap. *(978-1-60859-152-7(2))* Benchmark Education Co.

—Going Places: Lap Book. 2009. (My First Reader's Theater Set B Ser.). (J). 28.00 *(978-1-4108-8544-9(5))* Benchmark Education Co.

—Hickory Dickory Dock; or, Go, Mouse, Go! 2008. (Reader's Theater Nursery Rhymes & Songs Ser.). (Illus.). 48p. (J). (gr. k-1). pap. *(978-1-60437-960-0(X))* Benchmark Education Co.

—Hot Cross Buns for Everyone. Abbott, Jason, illus. 2009. (Reader's Theater Nursery Rhymes & Songs Set B Ser.). 48p. (J). pap. *(978-1-60859-153-4(0))* Benchmark Education Co.

—Hunting We Will Go. 2008. (Reader's Theater Nursery Rhymes & Songs Ser.). (Illus.). 48p. (J). (gr. k-1). pap. *(978-1-60437-974-7(X))* Benchmark Education Co.

—Itsy Bitsy Spider Climbs Again. 2008. (Reader's Theater Nursery Rhymes & Songs Ser.). (Illus.). 48p. (J). (gr. k-1). pap. *(978-1-60437-968-6(5))* Benchmark Education Co.

—The Itsy Bity Spider. Collins, Daryll, illus. 2010. (Rising Readers Ser.). (J). 3.49 *(978-1-60719-689-1(1))* Newmark Learning LLC.

—Jack B. Nimble Jumps. Colby, Garry, illus. 2009. (Reader's Theater Nursery Rhymes & Songs Set B Ser.). 48p. (J). pap. *(978-1-60859-154-1(9))* Benchmark Education Co.

—Lazy Mary Gets Up. Kelley, Gerald, illus. 2009. (Reader's Theater Nursery Rhymes & Songs Set B Ser.). 48p. (J). pap. *(978-1-60859-156-5(5))* Benchmark Education Co.

—Look at it Go! Lap Book. 2009. (My First Reader's Theater Set B Ser.). (J). 28.00 *(978-1-935441-02-1(7))* Benchmark Education Co.

—Lunch with Little Miss Muffet. 2008. (Reader's Theater Nursery Rhymes & Songs Ser.). (Illus.). 48p. (J). (gr. k-1). pap. *(978-1-60437-961-7(8))* Benchmark Education Co.

—Miss Mary Mack & the Jumping Elephants. Workman, Terry, illus. 2009. (Reader's Theater Nursery Rhymes & Songs Set B Ser.). 48p. (J). pap. *(978-1-60859-161-9(1))* Benchmark Education Co.

—The Old Gray Mare IS What She Used to Be. Currant, Gary, illus. 2009. (Reader's Theater Nursery Rhymes & Songs Set B Ser.). 48p. (J). pap. *(978-1-60859-162-6(X))* Benchmark Education Co.

—Old MacDonald's Noisy Farm. 2008. (Reader's Theater Nursery Rhymes & Songs Ser.). (Illus.). (J). (gr. k-1). pap. *(978-1-60437-967-9(7))* Benchmark Education Co.

—Party Time with Old King Cole. 2008. (Reader's Theater Nursery Rhymes & Songs Ser.). (Illus.). 48p. (J). (gr. k-1). pap. *(978-1-60437-962-4(6))* Benchmark Education Co.

—Peter Piper Picks & Pickles Peppers. 2008. (Reader's Theater Nursery Rhymes & Songs Ser.). (Illus.). 48p. (J). (gr. k-1). pap. *(978-1-60437-970-9(7))* Benchmark Education Co.

—Peter Pumpkin Eater Loses His Appetite. Greenhead, Bill, illus. 2009. (Reader's Theater Nursery Rhymes & Songs Set B Ser.). 48p. (J). pap. *(978-1-60859-164-0(6))* Benchmark Education Co.

—Pies for Simple Simon. Ledger, Bill, illus. 2009. (Reader's Theater Nursery Rhymes & Songs Set B Ser.). 48p. (J). pap. *(978-1-60859-165-7(4))* Benchmark Education Co.

—Run, Three Blind Mice! Walker, Sholto, illus. 2009. (Reader's Theater Nursery Rhymes & Songs Set B Ser.). 48p. (J). pap. *(978-1-60859-168-8(9))* Benchmark Education Co.

—Sing a Song of Sixpence, the King's Special Pie. 2008. (Reader's Theater Nursery Rhymes & Songs Ser.). (Illus.). 48p. (J). (gr. k-1). pap. *(978-1-60437-979-2(0))* Benchmark Education Co.

—Sorting at My Desk: Lap Book. 2009. (My First Reader's Theater Set B Ser.). (J). 28.00 *(978-1-60634-987-8(2))* Benchmark Education Co.

—Visiting Grandma: Lap Book. 2009. (My First Reader's Theater Set B Ser.). (J). 28.00 *(978-1-60634-991-5(0))* Benchmark Education Co.

—Wishing on a Bright Star. 2008. (Reader's Theater Nursery Rhymes & Songs Ser.). (Illus.). 48p. (J). (gr. k-1). pap. *(978-1-60437-971-6(5))* Benchmark Education Co.

—The Woman Who Lived in a Shoe. Greenhead, Bill, illus. 2009. (Reader's Theater Nursery Rhymes & Songs Set B Ser.). 48p. (J). pap. *(978-1-60859-172-5(7))* Benchmark Education Co.

The Fun Bus: 3-in-1 Package. (Sails Literacy Ser.). 24p. (gr. 1-18). 57.00 *(978-0-7578-3207-9(5))* Rigby Education.

The Fun Bus: 6 Small Books. (Sails Literacy Ser.). 24p. (gr. 1-18). 25.00 *(978-0-7578-3183-6(4))* Rigby Education.

The Fun Bus: Big Book Only. (Sails Literacy Ser.). 24p. (gr. 1-18). 27.00 *(978-0-7635-5931-1(8))* Rigby Education.

Fun in the Snow. 2003. (Bella & Rosie Set 1 Ser.). (J). 7.67 *(978-1-932570-13-7(6))* Pioneer Valley Bks.

Fun with Friends. (Early Intervention Levels Ser.). 23.10 *(978-0-7362-0006-6(1))* CENGAGE Learning.

Funny Faces & Funny Places. (Little Book Practice Reader Ser.). (J). *(978-0-8136-0687-3(X))* Modern Curriculum Pr.

Furgang, Kathy. A Rainbow Party. 2011. (Early Connections Ser.). (J). *(978-1-61672-569-3(9))* Benchmark Education Co.

—A Seat on the Bus: Set Of 6. 2010. (Early Connections Ser.). (J). 37.00 net. *(978-1-4108-1084-7(4))* Benchmark Education Co.

—Shrimp Joins the Team: Set Of 6. 2010. (Early Connections Ser.). (J). pap. 37.00 net. *(978-1-4108-1368-8(1))* Benchmark Education Co.

—Wendy the Water Drop: Set Of 6. 2010. (Early Connections Ser.). (J). pap. 37.00 net. *(978-1-4108-1095-3(X))* Benchmark Education Co.

Futaba, Aoi. Level C, Vol. 4. 2005. (Illus.). 194p. pap. 9.99 *(978-1-58655-726-3(2)*, KGNOV-0539) Media Blasters, Inc.

Fyne, Olga. Jerry & Sherry. 2008. (Illus.). 24p. pap. 12.99 *(978-1-4389-3672-7(9))* AuthorHouse.

Gabolinscy, Jack. Do Not Disturb. Cashmore-Hingley, Michael, illus. 2013. (ENG.). 24p. (gr. 3-4). pap. *(978-1-77654-019-8(0)*, Red Rocket Readers) Flying Start Bks.

Gabolinscy, Jack & Harrison, Brian. Not Again. 2008. (Rigby Focus Forward: Level P Ser.). (Illus.). 24p. (J). (gr. 4-7). pap. *(978-1-4190-3859-4(1)*, Rigby) Pearson Education Australia.

Gabolinscy, Jack & Oppatt, Karen. Danny's Dream. 2008. (Rigby Focus Forward: Level O Ser.). (Illus.). 24p. pap. *(978-1-4190-3843-3(5)*, Rigby) Pearson Education Australia.

Galashan, Kathy. Robots. 2005. (ENG., Illus.). 32p. pap. 8.50 *(978-0-340-87311-3(6))* Cambridge Univ. Pr.

Galat, Joan & National Geographic Kids Staff. Cats, Level 1. 2017. (Readers Ser.). (ENG., Illus.). 48p. (J). (-k). pap. 4.99 ***(978-1-4263-2883-1(4)***, National Geographic Children's Bks.) National Geographic Society.

Gall, Chris. Meet the Dinotrux. 2015. (Passport to Reading Level 1 Ser.). (ENG., Illus.). 32p. (J). (gr. -1-3). pap. 4.99 *(978-0-316-40063-3(7))* Little, Brown Bks. for Young Readers.

Ganeri, Anita. All Kinds of Plants Blue Band. 2016. (Cambridge Reading Adventures Ser.). (ENG.). 16p. pap. 6.56 *(978-1-316-60579-0(5))* Cambridge Univ. Pr.

—The Book of World Facts Purple Band. 2016. (Cambridge Reading Adventures Ser.). (ENG.). 24p. pap. 7.19 *(978-1-316-60080-1(7))* Cambridge Univ. Pr.

—From Rags to Bags Gold Band. 2016. (Cambridge Reading Adventures Ser.). (ENG.). 16p. pap. 6.56 *(978-1-316-50086-6(1))* Cambridge Univ. Pr.

—Super Malls Orange Band. 2016. (Cambridge Reading Adventures Ser.). (ENG.). 16p. pap. 6.56 *(978-1-316-50335-5(6))* Cambridge Univ. Pr.

Garcia, Mario, et al. My Family. 2010. (Reach for Reading Ser.). (ENG., Illus.). 8p. (C). pap. 7.95 *(978-0-7362-7985-7(7))* CENGAGE Learning.

A Garden: Individual Title Six-Packs. (Sails Literacy Ser.). 16p. (gr. k-18). 27.00 *(978-0-7635-4384-6(5))* Rigby Education.

Gardner, Lindsey, et al. Pan Fydd Popi a Macs yn Fawr. 2005. (WEL., Illus.). 20p. *(978-1-902416-45-8(7))* Cymdeithas Lyfrau Ceredigion.

Garson, Cindy. Welcome to Kristy's Farm: Book I (Black & White Version) 2007. (ENG.). 56p. per. 21.80 *(978-1-84728-321-4(7))* Lulu Pr., Inc.

Gary, Romain. La Vie Devant Soi, Level C. (FRE.). (YA). (gr. 7-12). 9.99 *(978-0-8219-0869-3(3)*, 40326) EMC/Paradigm Publishing.

Garza, Sarah. Action! Making Movies, 1 vol. 2nd rev. ed. 2013. (TIME for KIDS(r) Nonfiction Readers Ser.). (ENG.). 64p. (J). (gr. 5-5). pap. 10.99 *(978-1-4333-4949-2(3))* Teacher Created Materials, Inc.

Garza, Xavier. Rooster Joe & the Bully / el Gallo Joe y el Abusón. 2016. (ENG & SPA.). 128p. (J). (gr. 5-8). pap. 9.95 *(978-1-55885-835-0(0)*, Piñata Books) Arte Publico Pr.

Garza, Xavier, illus. Maximilian & the Mystery of the Guardian Angel. 2011. (Max's Lucha Libre Adventures Ser.). (SPA & ENG.). 160p. (J). (gr. 5-8). pap. 12.95 *(978193693-98-9(3))* Cinco Puntos Pr.

Garza, Xavier & Villarroel, Carolina. Zulema & the Witch Owl/Zulema y la Bruja Lechuza. Garza, Xavier, illus. 2009. (SPA & ENG., Illus.). 32p. (J). (gr. -1-4). 16.95 *(978-1-55885-515-1(7)*, Piñata Books) Arte Publico Pr.

Gassman, Julie. Encounter: Narrative Nonfiction Picture Books. Moors, Steve, illus. 2016. (Encounter: Narrative Nonfiction Picture Bks.). (ENG.). (gr. 3-4). 140.59 *(978-1-5157-3364-5(5))* Encounter Bks.

Gates, Susan. Mole Who was Scared of the Dark. Breakespeare, Andrew, illus. 2005. (ENG.). 24p. (J). lib. bdg. 23.65 *(978-1-59646-710-1(X))* Dingles & Co.

—Pirate! Band 15. McClellan, Maddy, illus. 2007. (Collins Big Cat Ser.). (ENG.). 48p. (J). (gr. 3-4). pap. 8.99 *(978-0-00-723095-2(8))* HarperCollins Pubs. Ltd. GBR. Dist: Independent Pubs. Group.

Gaydos, Nora. Clever Critters. Sullivan, Mary & Gray, Steve, illus. 2008. (NIR! Leveled Readers Ser.). (ENG.). 128p. (J). (gr. -1-3). 16.99 *(978-1-58476-666-7(2)*, Now I'm Reading!) Random Hse. Children's Bks.

—I'M a New Big Sister. Gutierrez, Akemi, illus. 2010. (ENG.). 30p. (J). (gr. -1-17). 6.99 *(978-1-60169-009-8(6))* Innovative Kids.

—Now I'm Reading! Pre-Reader - More Word Play. Sams, B. B., illus. 2016. (NIR! Leveled Readers Ser.). (ENG.). 120p. (J). (gr. -1-2). pap. 16.99 *(978-1-101-91962-0(0)*, Now I'm Reading!) Random Hse. Children's Bks.

—Simply Science Independent Volume 1. 2006. (Now I'm Reading!: Independent Ser.). (ENG., Illus.). 74p. (J). (gr. -1-2). 16.99 *(978-1-58476-247-8(0)*, IKIDS) Innovative Kids.

Geatches, Hazel. Cities, Level 2. 2012. (ENG., Illus.). 40p. pap. 9.38 *(978-0-19-464682-6(3))* Oxford Univ. Pr., Inc.

Geatches, Hazel, contrib. by. Electricity. 2013. (ENG.). 40p. pap. 9.38 *(978-0-19-464685-7(8))* Oxford Univ. Pr., Inc.

Geatches, Hazel, ed. At the Beach. 2012. (ENG., Illus.). 32p. 9.38 *(978-0-19-464628-4(9))* Oxford Univ. Pr., Inc.

—Earth. 2012. (ENG., Illus.). 40p. pap., act. bk. ed. 10.00 *(978-0-19-464679-6(3))* Oxford Univ. Pr., Inc.

—Schools. 2012. (ENG., Illus.). 32p. pap. 10.00 *(978-0-19-464627-7(0))* Oxford Univ. Pr., Inc.

Geatches, Hazel & Spilsbury, Louise. Sunny & Rainy. 2012. (ENG., Illus.). 40p. pap. 9.38 *(978-0-19-464680-2(7))* Oxford Univ. Pr., Inc.

Geiger, Beth & Fuerst, Jeffrey B. Return to Earth. Wolk-Stanley, Jessica, illus. 2004. (Reader's Theater Ser.). (J). pap. *(978-1-4108-2306-9(7)*, A23067) Benchmark Education Co.

Geiser, Traci Ferguson & Boylan, Maureen McCourt. Leap into Literacy Fall. Cernek, Kim, ed. Mason, Mark & Willardson, David, illus. 2003. 160p. (J). (gr. k-2). pap. 17.99 *(978-1-57471-960-4(2)*, 3376) Creative Teaching Pr., Inc.

—Leap into Literacy Spring. Cernek, Kim, ed. Rojas, Mary & Willardson, David, illus. 2003. 160p. (J). (gr. k-2). pap. 17.99 *(978-1-57471-959-8(9)*, 3375) Creative Teaching Pr., Inc.

—Leap into Literacy Winter. Cernek, Kim, ed. Valko, Diane & Willardson, David, illus. 2003. 160p. (J). (gr. k-2). pap. 17.99 *(978-1-57471-958-1(0)*, 3374) Creative Teaching Pr., Inc.

Gemmen, Heather. Learn-to-Read Bible. Wilber, Peggy M., ed. 2003. (Rocket Readers Ser.). (Illus.). 448p. (J). (gr. 1-2). 16.99 *(978-0-7814-3975-6(2)*, 0781439752) Cook, David C.

Gentner, Norma L. & Young, Steve. Save a Tree for Me. (Song Box Ser.). (Illus.). 16p. (gr. 1-2). 31.50 *(978-0-7802-2264-9(4))* Wright Group/McGraw-Hill.

Geok, Wee Bee & Collins UK Publishing Staff. The Story of Nian: A Folk Tale from China. Tran, Turine, illus. 2016. (ENG.). 32p. (J). pap. 8.95 *(978-0-00-814711-2(6))* HarperCollins Pubs. Ltd. GBR. Dist: Independent Pubs. Group.

George, Chris. Big & Small. 2017. (Early Concepts Ser.). 24p. (gr. 4-6). pap. 8.25 ***(978-1-5081-6217-9(4)***, PowerKids Pr.) Rosen Publishing Group, Inc., The.

George, Jean Craighead. Goose & Duck. Lamont, Priscilla, illus. 2008. (I Can Read Level 2 Ser.). (ENG.). 48p. (J). (gr. k-3). 16.99 *(978-0-06-117076-8(3))* HarperCollins Pubs.

George, Kallie. Duck, Duck, Dinosaur & the Noise at Night. Vidal, Oriol, illus. 2017. 40p. (J). (gr. -1-3). 17.99 *(978-0-06-235317-7(9))* HarperCollins Pubs.

—Duck, Duck, Dinosaur: Perfect Pumpkin. Vidal, Oriol, illus. 2017. (My First I Can Read Ser.). 32p. (J). (gr. -1-3). 16.99 ***(978-0-06-235315-3(2))***; pap. 3.99 ***(978-0-06-235314-6(4))*** HarperCollins Pubs.

George, Kallie. Splash. Cote, Genevieve, illus. 2016. (Tiny Tails Ser.: 3). (ENG.). 44p. (J). (gr. -1-3). 12.95 *(978-1-927018-77-4(3))* Simply Read Bks. CAN. Dist: Ingram Publisher Services.

George, Lynn. The Leaf Pile. 2006. (Neighborhood Readers Ser.). (ENG.). 16p. (gr. 1-3). pap. 6.50 *(978-1-4042-7120-3(1)*, Rosen Classroom) Rosen Publishing Group, Inc., The.

—Sammy's Sunglasses. 2006. (Neighborhood Readers Ser.). (ENG.). 8p. (gr. -1-3). pap. 5.15 *(978-1-4042-5738-2(1)*, Rosen Classroom) Rosen Publishing Group, Inc., The.

—The Super Sandwich. 2006. (Neighborhood Readers Ser.). (ENG.). 16p. (gr. 1-3). pap. 6.50 *(978-1-4042-7240-8(2)*, Rosen Classroom) Rosen Publishing Group, Inc., The.

Gerber, Paul. Is It Alive? 2012. (InfoMax Readers Ser.). (ENG., Illus.). 16 pp.p. (J). (gr. k-1). pap. 7.00 *(978-1-4488-8965-5(0)*, Rosen Classroom) Rosen Publishing Group, Inc., The.

Getting Along: Social/Emotional Lap Book. (Pebble Soup Explorations Ser.). (gr. -1-18). 16.00 *(978-0-7635-7563-2(1))* Rigby Education.

Getting Dressed 800638, 3. 2005. (J). bds. *(978-1-59794-036-8(4))* Environments, Inc.

Getting Ready for Bed: KinderConcepts Individual Title Six-Packs. (Kinderstarters Ser.). 8p. (gr. -1-1). 21.00 *(978-0-7635-8729-1(X))* Rigby Education.

Getting Ready for School: KinderConcepts Individual Title Six-Packs. (Kinderstarters Ser.). 8p. (gr. -1-1). 21.00 *(978-0-7635-8730-7(3))* Rigby Education.

Getting the Sequence (Gr. 1-3) 2003. (J). *(978-1-58232-076-2(4))* ECS Learning Systems, Inc.

Getting to Know Your Neighbors: Fourth Grade Guided Comprehension Level N. (On Our Way to English Ser.). (gr. 4-18). 34.50 *(978-0-7578-7161-0(5))* Rigby Education.

Ghosts! 2003. 31.95 *(978-0-673-75801-9(X))* Celebration Pr.

Giant Games. (Early Intervention Levels Ser.). 31.86 *(978-0-7362-0665-5(5))* CENGAGE Learning.

Giant Games (18), Vol. 18. (Early Intervention Levels Ser.). 5.31 *(978-0-7362-0653-2(1))* CENGAGE Learning.

The Giant of Ginger Hill: 3-in-1 Package. (Sails Literacy Ser.). 24p. (gr. 2-18). 57.00 *(978-0-7578-3216-1(4))* Rigby Education.

The Giant of Ginger Hill: 6 Small Books. (Sails Literacy Ser.). 24p. (gr. 2-18). 25.00 *(978-0-7578-3192-8(3))* Rigby Education.

The Giant of Ginger Hill: Big Book Only. (Sails Literacy Ser.). 24p. (gr. 2-18). 27.00 *(978-0-7635-6992-1(5))* Rigby Education.

Gibbs, Maddie. Las Vacas / Cows, 1 vol. 2015. (Amigos de la Granja / Farmyard Friends Ser.). (ENG & SPA.). 24p. (J). 23.60 *(978-1-4994-0265-0(1)*, PowerKids Pr.) Rosen Publishing Group, Inc., The.

—Los Caballos / Horses, 1 vol. 2015. (Amigos de la Granja / Farmyard Friends Ser.). (ENG & SPA.). 24p. (J). 23.60 *(978-1-4994-0267-4(8)*, PowerKids Pr.) Rosen Publishing Group, Inc., The.

—Los Patos / Ducks, 1 vol. 2015. (Amigos de la Granja / Farmyard Friends Ser.). (ENG & SPA.). 24p. (J). 23.60 *(978-1-4994-0269-8(4)*, PowerKids Pr.) Rosen Publishing Group, Inc., The.

Gibson. Sail Yel Nf Colorful Animals. 2003. (Rigby Sails Early Ser.). (ENG.). 16p. (gr. 1-2). pap. 6.95 *(978-0-7578-8895-3(X))* Rigby Education.

—Sail Yel Nf Out of the Egg. 2003. (Rigby Sails Early Ser.). (ENG.). 16p. (gr. 1-2). pap. 6.95 *(978-0-7578-8892-2(5))* Rigby Education.

Gibson, Brylee. Dinosaur Discoveries. 2007. (Connectors Ser.). (gr. 2-5). pap. *(978-1-877453-13-7(7))* Global Education Systems Ltd.

—Extreme Scientists. 2007. (Connectors Ser.). (gr. 2-5). pap. *(978-1-877453-08-3(0))* Global Education Systems Ltd.

—Megacities. 2007. (Connectors Ser.). (gr. 2-5). pap. *(978-1-877453-07-6(2))* Global Education Systems Ltd.

—Scams. 2007. (Connectors Ser.). (gr. 2-5). pap. *(978-1-877453-01-4(3))* Global Education Systems Ltd.

—Tails, Tails, Tails. 2003. (Rigby Sails Early Ser.). (ENG., Illus.). 16p. (gr. 1-2). pap. 6.95 *(978-0-7578-8904-2(2))* Houghton Mifflin Harcourt Publishing Co.

—Unseen by the Eye. 2007. (Connectors Ser.). (gr. 2-5). pap. *(978-1-877453-00-7(5))* Global Education Systems Ltd.

—Wildlife Detectives. 2007. (Connectors Ser.). (gr. 2-5). pap. *(978-1-877453-18-2(8))* Global Education Systems Ltd.

—Wonders of the World Megastructures. 2007. (Connectors Ser.). (gr. 2-5). pap. *(978-1-877453-20-5(X))* Global Education Systems Ltd.

—The World Beyond Earth. 2007. (Connectors Ser.). (gr. 2-5). pap. *(978-1-877453-11-3(0))* Global Education Systems Ltd.

Gifford, Clive. Animal Survivors. Horne, Sarah, illus. 2017. (Reading Ladder Ser.). (ENG.). 32p. (J). (gr. 1-3). pap. 6.99 ***(978-1-4052-8492-9(7))*** Egmont Bks., Ltd. GBR. Dist: Independent Pubs. Group.

—The Empire Windrush. 2014. (Collins Big Cat Progress Ser.). (ENG., Illus.). 32p. (J). (gr. 3-4). pap. 7.99 *(978-0-00-751926-2(5))* HarperCollins Pubs. Ltd. GBR. Dist: Independent Pubs. Group.

Gifford, Clive. Romans. Scruton, Ben, illus. 2016. (Reading Ladder Ser.). (ENG.). 32p. (J). (gr. 1-4). pap. 6.99 ***(978-1-4052-8043-3(3))*** Egmont Bks., Ltd. GBR. Dist: Independent Pubs. Group.

Gifford, Myrna Ross. Silent E: A Read-and-Sing Book. Cooper, Frances, illus. 2005. 12p. (J). 9.95 *(978-0-9754618-0-8(X))* Action Factor, Inc.

Giglio, Judy. Dreaming of Great Ideas, 6 vols., Set. 2004. (Phonics Readers Books 37-72 Ser.). (ENG.). 8p. (gr. k-1). pap. 35.70 *(978-0-7368-4064-4(8)*, Phonics Readers) Capstone Press of Coughlan Cos.

—Sounds & How We Hear Them, 6 vols., Set. 2004. (Phonics Readers Books 37-72 Ser.). (ENG.). 8p. (gr. k-1). pap. 35.70 *(978-0-7368-4069-9(9)*, Phonics Readers) Capstone Press of Coughlan Cos.

Gikow, Louise A. I Can Read. Patience, John, illus. 2005. (My First Reader Ser.). (ENG.). 32p. (J). (gr. k-1). pap. 3.95 *(978-0-516-25114-1(7)*, Children's Pr.) Scholastic Library Publishing.

Gilbert Goes on a Picnic. 2004. (Gilbert the Pig Set 2 Ser.). (J). 7.33 *(978-1-58453-221-7(1))* Pioneer Valley Bks.

Gilbert the Pig Set 2. 2004. (J). *(978-1-58453-220-0(3))* Pioneer Valley Bks.

Gilbert the Special Pig. 2004. (Gilbert the Pig Set 2 Ser.). (J). 7.33 *(978-1-58453-223-1(8))* Pioneer Valley Bks.

Gilchrist, Cherry & Pearson Education Staff. Princess Diana. 2nd ed. 2008. (ENG., Illus.). 56p. pap. 11.99 *(978-1-4058-8201-9(8))* Pearson Education.

Gillen, Kristin M. Raspberries on Tummies. 2011. 32p. pap. 21.99 *(978-1-4568-9436-8(6))* Xlibris Corp.

Gillen, Lisa P. Spring Time. Gillen, Lisa P., illus. l.t. ed. 2006. (Illus.). 12p. (J). (gr. -1-k). pap. 10.95 *(978-1-57332-351-2(9)*, HighReach Learning, Incorporated) Carson-Dellosa Publishing, LLC.

Gillis, Jennifer Blizin. Two Nice Mice. Krejca, Gary, illus. 2006. (Reader's Clubhouse Level 2 Reader Ser.). (ENG.). 24p. (J). (gr. 1-4). pap. 3.99 *(978-0-7641-3295-7(4))* Barron's Educational Series, Inc.

Gillot, Laurence & Sebaoun, Elisabeth. Half & Half-Swimming with Dolphins. Rocco & Dorémus, Gaëtan, illus. 2010. 32p. (J). 9.95 *(978-1-60115-215-2(9))*; pap. 4.99 *(978-1-60115-216-9(7))* Treasure Bay, Inc.

The Gingerbread Man: 6 Small Books. (gr. k-1). 30.00 *(978-0-7635-6205-2(X))* Rigby Education.

The Gingerbread Man, Level 2. 2016. (Ladybird Readers Ser.). (ENG.). 48p. (J). pap. 9.99 *(978-0-241-25442-4(6))* Penguin Bks., Ltd. GBR. Dist: Independent Pubs. Group.

Giraffe's Sad Tale. (Lexile Levels Ser.). 47.88 *(978-1-56334-392-6(4))* CENGAGE Learning.

Gittings, Clare. What Are You Looking At? Band 14. 2007. (Collins Big Cat Ser.). (ENG., Illus.). 48p. (J). (gr. 3-4). pap. 8.99 *(978-0-00-723091-4(5))* HarperCollins Pubs. Ltd. GBR. Dist: Independent Pubs. Group.

Giulieri, Anne. In the Water, 1 vol. Hancock, Anna, illus. 2012. (Engage Literacy Magenta Ser.). (ENG.). 32p. (gr. k-2). pap. 5.99 *(978-1-4296-8854-3(8)*, Engage Literacy) Capstone Press of Coughlan Cos.

—My Shopping, 1 vol. 2012. (Engage Literacy Magenta Ser.). (ENG.). 32p. (gr. k-2). pap. 5.99 *(978-1-4296-8884-0(X)*, Engage Literacy) Capstone Press of Coughlan Cos.

Gleisner, Jenna Lee. Animals in Fall. 2017. (Welcome, Fall! Ser.). (ENG.). 24p. (J). (gr. -1-2). lib. bdg. 27.07 *(978-1-5038-1659-6(1)*, 211495) Child's World, Inc., The.

—Back to School! 2017. (Welcome, Fall! Ser.). (ENG.). 24p. (J). (gr. -1-2). lib. bdg. 27.07 *(978-1-5038-1666-4(4)*, 211497) Child's World, Inc., The.

—A Trip to the Pumpkin Patch. 2017. (Welcome, Fall! Ser.). (ENG.). 24p. (J). (gr. -1-2). lib. bdg. 27.07 (978-1-5038-1664-0(8), 211494) Child's World, Inc., The.

Glencoe McGraw-Hill Staff, creator. The American Vision Reading Essentials & Study Guide Student Workbook. 2nd ed. 2004. (United States History (hs) Ser.). (ENG., Illus.). 534p. (gr. 9-12). per. 16.00 (978-0-07-865439-8(4), 0078654394) McGraw-Hill Higher Education.

The Glory Field Student Packet. 2004. (YA). 12.99 (978-1-58130-516-6(8)) Novel Units, Inc.

A Gnu Named Blue. (Early Intervention Levels Ser.). 31.86 (978-0-7362-0621-1(3)) CENGAGE Learning.

Go, Red Hens! (Early Intervention Levels Ser.). 21.30 (978-0-7362-0393-7(1)); Vol. 6. 3.55 (978-0-7362-0173-5(4)) CENGAGE Learning.

Go to the Zoo, Level 1. 2016. (Ladybird Readers Ser.). (ENG., Illus.). 48p. (J). (gr. 2-4). pap. 9.99 (978-0-241-25414-1(0)) Penguin Bks., Ltd. GBR. Dist: Independent Pubs. Group.

The Goddess of the Volcano: Six-Pack, 6 packs. (Greetings Ser.: Vol. 1). (gr. 3-5). 31.00 (978-0-7635-1843-1(3)) Rigby Education.

Godfrey. Murder in the Shadows. (Thumbprint Mysteries Ser.). 32.86 (978-0-8092-0418-2(5)) McGraw-Hill/Contemporary.

Goh, Michelle. The 10 Best Cinderella Stories in Sports. 2008. 14.99 (978-1-55448-495-9(2)) Scholastic Library Publishing.

Goin, Miriam Busch. Storms (1 Hardcover/1 CD) 2016. (National Geographic Readers: Pre-Reader Ser.). (ENG.). (J). (978-1-4301-2125-1(4)) Live Oak Media.

—Storms (1 Paperback/1 CD) 2016. (National Geographic Readers: Pre-Reader Ser.). (ENG.). (J). pap. (978-1-4301-2124-4(6)) Live Oak Media.

Going Fishing. (Little Book Practice Reader). (J). 6.47 (978-0-8136-5371-6(1)) Modern Curriculum Pr.

Going Fishing. 2007. (Artic Adventures Ser.). (Illus.). 20p. (J). 7.67 (978-1-58453-314-6(5)) Pioneer Valley Bks.

Going Home: KinderConcepts Individual Title Six-Packs. (Kinderstarters Ser.). 8p. (gr. -1-1). 21.00 (978-0-7635-8724-6(9)) Rigby Education.

Going to the Park with GranDaDy: Big Book: Level F. (Visions Ser.). 8p. 20.95 (978-0-7802-9745-6(8)) Wright Group/McGraw-Hill.

Going West: Fifth Grade Newcomer Books. (On Our Way to English Ser.). (gr. 5-18). 34.50 (978-0-7578-7277-8(8)) Rigby Education.

Golden, Brenda. Celebrity. 2007. (Steck-Vaughn BOLDPRINT Anthologies Ser.). (ENG., Illus.). 48p. (gr. 8-10). pap., stu. ed. 16.90 (978-1-4190-4031-3(6)) Houghton Mifflin Harcourt Publishing Co.

The Golden Dragon: Set D Individual Title Six-Packs. (Supersonic Phonics Ser.). (gr. k-3). 29.00 (978-0-7635-0552-3(8)) Rigby Education.

Goldie's Shortcut. 12p. (J). bds. (978-2-7643-0051-0(4)) Phidal Publishing, Inc./Editions Phidal, Inc.

Goldilocks & the Three Bears: Take-Home Book. 2005. (Emergent Library: Vol. 2). (YA). (gr. -1-1). 12.60 (978-0-8215-7260-3(1)) Sadlier, William H. Inc.

Golding, Julia. Pandora's Box. 2017. (Collins Big Cat Tales Ser.). (ENG., Illus.). 48p. (J). (gr. 3-4). pap. 8.99 (978-0-00-817944-1(1)) HarperCollins Pubs. Ltd. GBR. Dist: Independent Pubs. Group.

Goldish, Meish. The Empty Pot: A Chinese Legend. Treatner, Meryle, illus. 2005. 14p. pap. 6.00 (978-0-15-350582-9(6)) Harcourt Schl. Pubs.

—Lights! Camera! Action! 2012. (Discovery Phonics Ser.). (ENG., Illus.). 14p. (J). (gr. 1-3). pap. 10.47 (978-0-8136-1154-9(7)) Modern Curriculum Pr.

Goldsmith, Ros. Who Lives near the North Pole? 2014. (Little Books of Answers: Level e Ser.). (Illus.). 16p. (gr. k-2). pap. 7.95 (978-1-927136-45-4(8)) Three Crows Media NZL. Dist: RiverStream Publishing.

Gomboli, Mario. Comer Bien, Saber Comer. (Coleccion Lobo Rojo).Tr. of Eat Well, Know What to Eat. (SPA.). 32p. (J). (gr. k-3). 6.36 (978-84-216-3458-5(5)) Bruño, Editorial ESP. Dist: Lectorum Pubns., Inc.

—Lavarse Es Divertido. (SPA.). 32p. (J). (gr. k-3). 6.36 (978-84-216-3459-2(3)) Bruño, Editorial ESP. Dist: Lectorum Pubns., Inc.

Gonzales, Felipe C. Little Folk Stories & Tales by Don Pablo: Bilingual Stories in Spanish & English = Chistes y Cuentos de Don Pablo: Cuentos Bilingües en Español e Inglés. 2010. (SPA & ENG.). (J). pap. 24.95 (978-0-86534-772-4(7)) Sunstone Pr.

Gonzalez-Jensen, Margarita. The Bird Who Ate Too Much. Wolff, Jason, illus. 2003. (Rigby on Our Way to English Ser.). (ENG.). 24p. (gr. 3-3). pap. 50.70 (978-0-7578-4208-5(9)) Rigby Education.

González, Lucía. The Storyteller's Candle: La Velita de Los Cuentos. Delacre, Lulu, illus. 2013. (ENG & SPA.). 32p. (J). pap. 9.95 (978-0-89239-237-7(1), Children's Book Press) Lee & Low Bks., Inc.

Gonzalez, Tomás, et al. Family Feelings. 2010. (Reach for Reading Ser.). (ENG., Illus.). 8p. (C). pap. 7.95 (978-0-7362-7986-4(5)) CENGAGE Learning.

Goodhart, Pippa. Cake Test. McCafferty, Jan, illus. 2nd ed. 2016. (Reading Ladder Ser.). (ENG.). 48p. (J). (gr. k-2). pap. 7.99 (978-1-4052-8223-9(1)) Egmont Bks., Ltd. GBR. Dist: Independent Pubs. Group.

—Dragon Boy. Ursell, Martin, illus. 2nd ed. 2016. (Reading Ladder Ser.). (ENG.). 48p. (J). (gr. k-2). pap. 7.99 (978-1-4052-8238-3(X)) Egmont Bks., Ltd. GBR. Dist: Independent Pubs. Group.

—House that Jack Built. Parker, Andy, illus. 2004. (ENG.). 24p. (J). lib. bdg. 23.65 (978-1-59646-700-2(2)) Dingles & Co.

Goodnight Board Books Set 800492, 3. 2005. (J). bds. (978-1-59794-004-7(6)) Environments, Inc.

Goodrum, L. E. Counting with G & Me. 2009. 20p. pap. 24.95 (978-1-60749-615-1(1)) America Star Bks.

Goodspeed, Horace. Will's Neighborhood. 2012. (InfoMax Readers Ser.). (ENG., Illus.). 16 pp.p. (J). (gr. k-1). pap. 7.00 (978-1-4488-8881-8(6), Rosen Classroom) Rosen Publishing Group, Inc., The.

The Goose Who Acted Like a Cow (18), Vol. 18. (Early Intervention Levels Ser.). 5.31 (978-0-7362-0615-0(9)) CENGAGE Learning.

Gordo, Lydia & Gordo, Françs, eds. La Celestina: Análisis y Estudio Sobre la Obra, el Autor y Su Época. 2004. (Compendios Vosgos Ser.). (SPA & ENG.). 80p. pap. 9.95 (978-84-95761-08-8(4)) Ediciones Norte, Inc.

—Lazarillode de Tormes: Análisis y Estudio Sobre la Obra, el Autor y Su Epoca. 2005. (Compendios Vosgos Ser.). (SPA & ENG.). 86p. pap. 9.95 (978-84-95761-24-8(6)) Ediciones Norte, Inc.

—Poema de Mio Cid: Análisis y Estudio Sobre la Obra, el Autor y Su Epoca. 2005. (Compendios Vosgos Ser.). (SPA & ENG.). 126p. pap. 9.95 (978-84-95761-15-6(7)) Ediciones Norte, Inc.

Gordon, Sharon. Bookworms: At Home, 6 bks., Set. Incl. At Home by the Ocean. lib. bdg. (978-0-7614-1959-4(4)); At Home in the City. lib. bdg. (978-0-7614-1960-0(8)); At Home in the Desert. lib. bdg. (978-0-7614-1963-1(2)); At Home on the Farm. lib. bdg. (978-0-7614-1958-7(6)); At Home on the Mountain. lib. bdg. (978-0-7614-1961-7(6)); At Home on the Ranch. lib. bdg. (978-0-7614-1962-4(4)); (Illus.). 32p. (J). (gr. 3-7). 2005. (978-0-7614-1957-0(8), Benchmark Bks.) Marshall Cavendish Corp.

—Bookworms: Ready for School, 6 bks., Set. Incl. We Are a Team. lib. bdg. 22.79 (978-0-7614-1994-5(2)); We Are Kind. lib. bdg. 22.79 (978-0-7614-1992-1(6)); We Listen. lib. bdg. 22.79 (978-0-7614-1991-4(8)); We Share. lib. bdg. 22.79 (978-0-7614-1993-8(4)); We Tell the Truth. lib. bdg. 22.79 (978-0-7614-1996-9(9)); (Illus.). 24p. (J). (gr. 3-7). 2005. (978-0-7614-1990-7(X), Benchmark Bks.) Marshall Cavendish Corp.

—Listos para ir a la Escuela, 6 bks., Set. Incl. Compartimos: Listos para Ir a la Escuela. lib. bdg. 15.95 (978-0-7614-2360-7(5)); Decimos la Verdad. lib. bdg. 15.95 (978-0-7614-2362-1(1)); Escuchamos. lib. bdg. 15.95 (978-0-7614-2359-1(1)); Respetamos las Reglas. lib. bdg. 15.95 (978-0-7614-2358-4(3)); Somos Amables. lib. bdg. 15.95 (978-0-7614-2356-0(7)); Somos un Equipo. lib. bdg. 15.95 (978-0-7614-2357-7(5)); (Illus.). 24p. (gr. k-1). (Bookworms — Spanish Editions: Listos para Ir a la Escuela Ser.). (SPA.). 2006. Set lib. bdg. 95.70 (978-0-7614-2354-6(0), Benchmark Bks.) Marshall Cavendish Corp.

—Ready for School (Listos para Ir a la Escuela) Incl. We Are a Team/Somos un Equipo. lib. bdg. 15.95 (978-0-7614-2436-9(9)); We Are Kind/Somos Amables. lib. bdg. 15.95 (978-0-7614-2435-2(0)); We Follow the Rules/Respetamos Las Reglas. lib. bdg. 15.95 (978-0-7614-2438-3(5)); We Listen/Escuchamos. lib. bdg. 15.95 (978-0-7614-2439-0(3)); We Share/Compartimos. lib. bdg. 15.95 (978-0-7614-2441-3(5)); We Tell the Truth/Decimos la Verdad. lib. bdg. 15.95 (978-0-7614-2442-0(3)); (Illus.). 24p. (gr. k-1). (Bookworms — Bilingual Editions: Ready for School/Listos para Ir a la Escuela Ser.). (ENG & SPA.). 2006. Set lib. bdg. 95.70 (978-0-7614-2434-5(2)) Marshall Cavendish Corp.

—We Tell the Truth. 2007. (J). pap. 6.99 (978-0-7614-3277-7(9)) Marshall Cavendish Corp.

Gorilla Games. (Early Intervention Levels Ser.). 21.30 (978-0-7362-0363-0(X)); Vol. 2. 3.55 (978-0-7362-0084-4(3)) CENGAGE Learning.

Goring, Ruth & Meza, Erika. Los Angeles de Adriana (Spanish Edition) Meza, Erika, illus. 2017. (SPA., Illus.). (J). 16.99 **(978-1-5064-2507-8(0)**, Sparkhouse Family) Augsburg Fortress, Pubs.

Gott, Barry, illus. Class Pets. 2005. (I'm Going to Read(r) Ser.). (ENG.). 48p. (J). (gr. 2-3). pap. 3.95 (978-1-4027-2709-2(7)) Sterling Publishing Co., Inc.

Gottesfeld, Jeff. Fight School, 1 vol. 2014. (Red Rhino Ser.). (ENG.). 68p. (J). (gr. 4-6). pap. 7.95 (978-1-62250-919-5(6)) Saddleback Educational Publishing, Inc.

Gould, Jane. At the Pond. rev. ed. 2011. (Mathematics Readers Ser.). (ENG.). 32p. (J). (gr. k-k). pap. 8.99 (978-1-4333-3430-6(5)) Teacher Created Materials, Inc.

—In the Garden. rev. ed. 2011. (Mathematics Readers Ser.). (ENG.). 32p. (J). (gr. k-k). pap. 8.99 (978-1-4333-3431-3(3)) Teacher Created Materials, Inc.

Gould, Robert. Dinosaurs. 2005. (Big Stuff Ser.: 7). (ENG., Illus.). 16p. (J). bds. 7.95 (978-1-929945-58-0(2)) Big Guy Bks., Inc.

—Sea Creatures. 2005. (Big Stuff Ser.: 8). (ENG., Illus.). 16p. (J). bds. 7.95 (978-1-929945-59-7(0)) Big Guy Bks., Inc.

Gould, Sloane. Jameer Blasts Off! What Will Happen? 2017. (Computer Science for the Real World Ser.). 16p. (gr. 7-8). pap. 7.95 **(978-1-5383-5210-6(9)**, Rosen Classroom) Rosen Publishing Group, Inc., The.

—Kaydra's Comrows: Over & over Again. 2017. (Computer Science for the Real World Ser.). 12p. (gr. 6-7). pap. 7.05 **(978-1-5383-5166-6(8)**, Rosen Classroom) Rosen Publishing Group, Inc., The.

Grace, Elora. Umbrellas Everywhere! 2006. (Neighborhood Readers Ser.). (ENG.). 8p. (gr. 1-3). pap. 5.15 (978-1-4042-6791-6(3), Rosen Classroom) Rosen Publishing Group, Inc., The.

Graf, Mike & Follett, Dave. Mudslide. 2008. (Rigby Focus Forward: Level M Ser.). (Illus.). 24p. (J). (gr. 4-7). pap. (978-1-4190-3828-0(1), Rigby) Pearson Education Australia.

Graf, Mike & Sakas, Anne. Dinosaur Canyon. Weston, Steve, illus. 2005. 40p. pap. 8.53 (978-0-7578-9858-7(0)) Houghton Mifflin Harcourt Supplemental Pubs.

Graf, Mike & Morden, Richard. Dirt on My Shoe. 2008. (Rigby Focus Forward: Level L Ser.). (Illus.). 24p. (J). (gr. 4-7). pap. (978-1-4190-3805-1(2), Rigby) Pearson Education Australia.

Graham, Chris. So Many Snakes. 2008. (Real Readers - Upper Emergent Ser.). (ENG., Illus.). 12p. (gr. 1-2). pap. 5.90 (978-0-8239-8197-7(5)) Rosen Publishing Group, Inc., The.

—Spiders! 2008. (Real Readers - Upper Emergent Ser.). (ENG., Illus.). 12p. (gr. 1-2). pap. 5.90 (978-0-8239-8198-4(3)) Rosen Publishing Group, Inc., The.

Graham, Elspeth. Sandwich that Jack Made. Mould, Chris, illus. 2004. (ENG.). (J). lib. bdg. 23.65 (978-1-59646-698-2(7)) Dingles & Co.

Graham, Ian. You Wouldn't Want to Climb Mount Everest! A Deadly Journey to the Top of the World. 2010. (You Wouldn't Want to... Ser.). 32p. (J). 29.00 (978-0-531-20505-1(3)); (ENG., Illus.). (gr. 3-18). pap. 9.95 (978-0-531-13785-7(6)) Scholastic Library Publishing. (Watts, Franklin).

Graham, S. Jewels for the Journey. 2004. pap. 8.99 (978-1-58158-043-3(6)) McDougal Publishing Co.

Grahame, Kenneth. The Wind in the Willows. 2004. 224p. pap. 12.95 (978-1-59540-046-8(X), 1st World Library - Literary Society) 1st World Publishing, Inc.

—The Wind in the Willows. 3rd ed. 2008. (ENG., Illus.). 80p. 10.00 (978-0-19-479137-3(8)) Oxford Univ. Pr., Inc.

Grandfather's Dream. (Lexile Levels Ser.). 9.09 (978-1-56334-707-8(5)) CENGAGE Learning.

Grandma's House. 2004. (Jasper the Cat Set 1 Ser.). (J). 7.33 (978-1-58453-277-4(7)) Pioneer Valley Bks.

Grange, Emma. Empire Strikes Back. 2014. (DK Readers Ser.). (ENG.). 32p. (J). (gr. 1-3). 14.99 (978-1-4654-2028-2(2), DK Children) Dorling Kindersley Publishing, Inc.

—A New Hope. 2014. (DK Readers Ser.). (ENG.). 32p. (J). (gr. k-4). 14.99 (978-1-4654-2026-8(6), DK Children) Dorling Kindersley Publishing, Inc.

Graves, Sue. The Messy Cake. 2012. (Espresso Story Time Ser.). (ENG., Illus.). 32p. (J). (gr. k-2). pap. 7.99 (978-1-4451-0416-4(4), Franklin Watts) Hachette Children's Group GBR. Dist: Hachette Bk. Group.

Gray, P. J. The Accident Book 2, 1 vol. 2015. (Trippin' Ser.). (ENG.). 64p. (YA). (gr. 9-12). pap. 8.95 (978-1-62250-932-4(3)) Saddleback Educational Publishing, Inc.

—The Lab, Bk. 3. 2015. (Trippin' Ser.: 3). (YA). lib. bdg. 19.60 (978-0-606-36835-3(3)) Turtleback Bks.

—Odds Are Yes [2]. 2016. (TERL Boosters Ser.). (ENG.). 49p. (YA). (gr. 9-12). 7.95 (978-1-68021-129-0(3)) Saddleback Educational Publishing, Inc.

The Great Invention: Individual Title Six-Packs. (gr. -1-2). 27.00 (978-0-7635-9452-7(0)) Rigby Education.

Greathouse, Lisa. Backstage Pass: Fashion, 1 vol. 2nd rev. ed. 2011. (TIME for KIDS(r) Nonfiction Readers Ser.). (ENG.). 32p. (J). (gr. 3-3). pap. 8.99 (978-1-4333-3661-4(8)) Teacher Created Materials, Inc.

—The Bakery. rev. ed. 2011. (Mathematics Readers Ser.). (ENG.). 32p. (J). (gr. k-k). pap. 8.99 (978-1-4333-3435-1(6)) Teacher Created Materials, Inc.

—Big Digs - Construction Site, 1 vol. 2nd rev. ed. 2011. (Nonfiction Readers Ser.). (ENG.). 32p. (J). (gr. 3-3). pap. 8.99 (978-1-4333-3662-1(6)) Teacher Created Materials, Inc.

—Count Me In! School Carnival, 1 vol. 2nd rev. ed. 2011. (TIME for KIDS(r) Nonfiction Readers Ser.). (ENG.). 28p. (J). (gr. 2-2). pap. 6.99 (978-1-4333-3637-9(5)) Teacher Created Materials, Inc.

—Count Me In! Soccer Tournament, 1 vol. 2nd rev. ed. 2011. (TIME for KIDS(r) Nonfiction Readers Ser.). (ENG.). 28p. (J). (gr. 2-2). pap. 6.99 (978-1-4333-3638-6(3)) Teacher Created Materials, Inc.

—Eat Healthy, 1 vol. 2011. (Science Readers: a Closer Look Ser.). (ENG., Illus.). 32p. (J). (gr. 3-3). pap. 8.99 (978-1-4333-3087-2(3)) Teacher Created Materials, Inc.

—Emergency! Be Prepared, 1 vol. 2011. (Science Readers: a Closer Look Ser.). (ENG., Illus.). 32p. (J). (gr. 2-2). pap. 8.99 (978-1-4333-3092-6(X)) Teacher Created Materials, Inc.

—Farm Animals: Classifying & Sorting. rev. ed. 2011. (Mathematics Readers Ser.). (ENG.). 32p. (J). (gr. k-k). pap. 8.99 (978-1-4333-3442-9(9)) Teacher Created Materials, Inc.

—Find Your Sport, 1 vol. 2011. (Science Readers: a Closer Look Ser.). (ENG., Illus.). 32p. (J). (gr. 2-2). pap. 8.99 (978-1-4333-3090-2(3)) Teacher Created Materials, Inc.

—Fun in the Sun. rev. ed. 2011. (Mathematics Readers Ser.). (ENG.). 32p. (J). (gr. k-k). pap. 8.99 (978-1-4333-3433-7(X)) Teacher Created Materials, Inc.

—Games Are Fun. rev. ed. 2011. (Mathematics Readers Ser.). (ENG.). 32p. (J). (gr. k-k). pap. 8.99 (978-1-4333-3437-5(2)) Teacher Created Materials, Inc.

—Get Moving, 1 vol. 2011. (Science Readers: a Closer Look Ser.). (ENG.). 32p. (J). (gr. 3-3). pap. 8.99 (978-1-4333-3089-6(X)) Teacher Created Materials, Inc.

—Healthy Habits, Healthy You, 1 vol. 2011. (Science Readers: a Closer Look Ser.). (ENG., Illus.). 32p. (J). (gr. 3-3). pap. 8.99 (978-1-4333-3091-9(1)) Teacher Created Materials, Inc.

—Johnny Appleseed, 1 vol. 2009. (Building Fluency Through Reader's Theater Ser.). (ENG.). 24p. (J). (gr. 2-4). pap. 6.99 (978-1-4333-0990-8(4)) Teacher Created Materials, Inc.

—Make It Healthy, 1 vol. 2011. (Science Readers: a Closer Look Ser.). (ENG.). 32p. (J). (gr. 2-2). pap. 8.99 (978-1-4333-3088-9(1)) Teacher Created Materials, Inc.

—The Pet Store. rev. ed. 2011. (Mathematics Readers Ser.). (ENG.). 32p. (J). (gr. k-k). pap. 8.99 (978-1-4333-3428-3(3)) Teacher Created Materials, Inc.

—Recess Time: Patterns. rev. ed. 2011. (Mathematics Readers Ser.). (ENG.). 32p. (J). (gr. k-k). pap. 8.99 (978-1-4333-3436-8(4)) Teacher Created Materials, Inc.

—The Snack Shop. rev. ed. 2011. (Mathematics Readers Ser.). (ENG.). 32p. (J). (gr. k-k). pap. 8.99 (978-1-4333-3434-4(8)) Teacher Created Materials, Inc.

—Sweet: Inside a Bakery, 1 vol. 2nd rev. ed. 2011. (TIME for KIDS(r) Nonfiction Readers Ser.). (ENG.). 32p. (J). (gr. 3-3). pap. 8.99 (978-1-4333-3663-8(4)) Teacher Created Materials, Inc.

—The Toy Store. rev. ed. 2011. (Mathematics Readers Ser.). (ENG.). 32p. (J). (gr. k-k). pap. 8.99 (978-1-4333-3429-0(1)) Teacher Created Materials, Inc.

—What's for Lunch?, 1 vol. 2nd rev. ed. 2011. (Nonfiction Readers Ser.). (ENG., Illus.). 28p. (J). (gr. 2-2). pap. 6.99 (978-1-4333-3639-3(1)) Teacher Created Materials, Inc.

—Wild Animals, Level K. rev. ed. 2011. (Mathematics Readers Ser.). (ENG.). 32p. (J). (gr. k-k). pap. 8.99 (978-1-4333-3443-6(7)) Teacher Created Materials, Inc.

Greathouse, Lisa & Kuligowski, Stephanie. Unsolved! Mysterious Events, 1 vol. 2nd rev. ed. 2012. (Nonfiction Readers Ser.). (ENG., Illus.). 48p. (J). (gr. 4-4). pap. 9.99 (978-1-4333-4827-3(6)) Teacher Created Materials, Inc.

—Unsolved! Mysterious Places, 1 vol. 2nd rev. ed. 2012. (Nonfiction Readers Ser.). (ENG., Illus.). 48p. (J). (gr. 4-4). pap. 9.99 (978-1-4333-4828-0(4)) Teacher Created Materials, Inc.

Greathouse, Lisa E. Astronomers Through Time, 1 vol. 2007. (Science Readers Ser.). (ENG.). 32p. (J). (gr. 4-4). pap. 8.99 (978-0-7439-0562-6(8)) Shell Educational Publishing.

Green, Dan. Doodle Book. 2016. (ENG.). 128p. (J). pap. 10.99 (978-1-4059-2652-2(X), 9781405926522) Penguin Bks., Ltd. GBR. Dist: Diamond Comic Distributors, Inc.

Green Footprints: Individual Title Six-Packs. (Literatura 2000 Ser.). (gr. 1-2). 28.00 (978-0-7635-0053-5(4)) Rigby Education.

Green, Jen. Flying High. 2016. (Collins Big Cat Ser.). (ENG.). 24p. (J). (gr. 2-2). pap. 7.99 (978-0-00-759120-6(9)) HarperCollins Pubs. Ltd. GBR. Dist: Independent Pubs. Group.

—Snow Leopards. 2014. (Collins Big Cat Progress Ser.). (ENG., Illus.). 32p. (J). (gr. 2-3). pap. 7.99 (978-0-00-751932-3(X)) HarperCollins Pubs. Ltd. GBR. Dist: Independent Pubs. Group.

Green, Ken. Not a Chance. (Thumbprint Mysteries Ser.). 32.86 (978-0-8092-0422-9(3)) McGraw-Hill/Contemporary.

Green Light Level 1 Book Set 2 800895, 5 vols. 2005. (J). pap. (978-1-59794-070-2(4)) Environments, Inc.

Green Light Level 1 Book Set 800894, 5 vols. 2005. (J). (978-1-59794-069-6(0)) Environments, Inc.

Green Light Level 2 Book Set 800914, 6 vols. 2005. (J). pap. (978-1-59794-079-5(8)) Environments, Inc.

Green, Rico. Super Animals! 2016. (Step into Reading Level 2 Ser.). lib. bdg. 14.75 (978-0-606-38487-2(1)) Turtleback Bks.

Greene, Janice. Blood & Basketball, 1 vol. unabr. ed. 2010. (Q Reads Ser.). (ENG.). 32p. (YA). (gr. 9-12). pap. 6.95 (978-1-61651-213-2(X)) Saddleback Educational Publishing, Inc.

—Breaking Point, 1 vol. unabr. ed. 2010. (Q Reads Ser.). (ENG.). 32p. (YA). (gr. 9-12). pap. 6.95 (978-1-61651-199-9(0)) Saddleback Educational Publishing, Inc.

—The Dark Lady. 2005. (Quickreads Ser.). (Illus.). 32p. (J). pap. 2.95 (978-1-56254-741-7(0), SP7410) Saddleback Educational Publishing, Inc.

—The Eye of the Hurricane, 1 vol. unabr. ed. 2010. (Q Reads Ser.). (ENG.). 32p. (YA). (gr. 9-12). pap. 6.95 (978-1-61651-191-3(5)) Saddleback Educational Publishing, Inc.

—Fat Boy, 1 vol. unabr. ed. 2010. (Q Reads Ser.). (ENG.). 32p. (YA). (gr. 9-12). pap. 6.95 (978-1-61651-201-9(6)) Saddleback Educational Publishing, Inc.

—The House on the Hill, 1 vol. unabr. ed. 2010. (Q Reads Ser.). (ENG.). 32p. (YA). (gr. 9-12). pap. 6.95 (978-1-61651-192-0(3)) Saddleback Educational Publishing, Inc.

—No Way to Run, 1 vol. unabr. ed. 2010. (Q Reads Ser.). (ENG.). 32p. (YA). (gr. 9-12). pap. 6.95 (978-1-61651-184-5(2)) Saddleback Educational Publishing, Inc.

—The Plot, 1 vol. unabr. ed. 2010. (Q Reads Ser.). (ENG.). 32p. (YA). (gr. 9-12). pap. 6.95 (978-1-61651-204-0(0)) Saddleback Educational Publishing, Inc.

—Read My Lips. 2005. (Quickreads Ser.). (Illus.). 32p. (J). pap. 2.95 (978-1-56254-742-4(9), SP7429) Saddleback Educational Publishing, Inc.

—The Ritual, 1 vol. unabr. ed. 2010. (Q Reads Ser.). (ENG.). 32p. (YA). (gr. 9-12). pap. 6.95 (978-1-61651-185-2(0)) Saddleback Educational Publishing, Inc.

—Tough Girl. 2005. (Quickreads Ser.). (Illus.). 32p. (J). pap. 2.95 (978-1-56254-746-2(1), SP7461) Saddleback Educational Publishing, Inc.

Greene, Janice & Thomas, Terri. Read My Lips, 1 vol. unabr. ed. 2010. (Q Reads Ser.). (ENG.). 32p. (YA). (gr. 9-12). pap. 6.95 (978-1-61651-216-3(4)) Saddleback Educational Publishing, Inc.

Greenley, Amanda & Evans, Linda. The Birthday Party - Ali & Sam Help Out - Well Spotted!, Bk. 1. 2005. (ENG., Illus.). 46p. (C). 23.95 (978-1-84312-152-7(2), RX4678) Fulton, David Pubs. GBR. Dist: Taylor & Francis Group.

—The Gang: Learning about the Victorians; Ali & Sam's School Trip. 2005. (ENG., Illus.). 80p. (C). 23.95 (978-1-84312-154-1(9), RX4680) Fulton, David Pubs. GBR. Dist: Taylor & Francis Group.

—Sledmere Stories Bk. 2: The Gameboy; Thanks Sophie!, Stop Thief! 2005. (ENG., Illus.). 80p. (C). 23.95 (978-1-84312-153-4(0), RX4679) Fulton, David Pubs. GBR. Dist: Taylor & Francis Group.

Greetings! Add-to Pack. 47.00 (978-0-7635-9407-7(5)) Rigby Education.

Greetings! Cluster Packages. (Saludos Ser.). (gr. 2-3). 135.00 (978-0-7635-9412-1(1)); 135.00 (978-0-7635-9408-4(3)); 135.00 (978-0-7635-9422-0(9)); 135.00 (978-0-7635-9416-9(4)) Rigby Education.

Greetings! The Earth Is Our Home Complete Package. 385.00 (978-0-7635-9420-6(2)) Rigby Education.

Gregoire, Maryellen. Escuelas Viejas y Nuevas (Old & New Schools) 2012. (Wonder Readers Spanish Emergent Ser.). (SPA.). 16p. (gr. -1-1). pap. 35.94 (978-1-62065-574-0(8)) Capstone Press of Coughlan Cos.

Gregorich, Barbara. Same or Different. deluxe ed. 2004. (ENG., Illus.). 64p. (J). pap., wbk. ed. 3.99 (978-1-58947-356-0(6), 02278) School Zone Publishing Co.

Gregory, Cam. When Do I Go to School? 2014. (Little Books of Answers: Level B Ser.). (Illus.). 16p. (gr. k-2). pap. 7.95 (978-1-927136-11-9(3)) Three Crows Media NZL. Dist: RiverStream Publishing.

—Where Can I Find A Good Friend? 2014. (Little Books of Answers: Level d Ser.). (Illus.). 16p. (gr. k-2). pap. 7.95 (978-1-927136-33-1(4)) Three Crows Media NZL. Dist: RiverStream Publishing.

—Where Do Tall Trees Grow? 2014. (Little Books of Answers: Level C Ser.). (Illus.). 16p. (gr. k-2). pap. 7.95 (978-1-927136-28-7(8)) Three Crows Media NZL. Dist: RiverStream Publishing.

—Who Lives Here? 2014. (Little Books of Answers: Level a Ser.). (Illus.). 16p. (gr. k-2). pap. 7.95 (978-1-927136-01-0(6)) Three Crows Media NZL. Dist: RiverStream Publishing.

—Who Should Follow Signs? 2014. (Little Books of Answers: Level F Ser.). (Illus.). 16p. (gr. k-2). pap. 7.95 (978-1-927136-53-9(9)) Three Crows Media NZL. Dist: RiverStream Publishing.

—Why Are Polar Bears in Danger? 2014. (Little Books of Answers: Level e Ser.). (Illus.). 16p. (gr. k-2). pap. 7.95 (978-1-927136-44-7(X)) Three Crows Media NZL. Dist: RiverStream Publishing.

Gregory, the Mean Dragon (16), Vol. 16. (Early Intervention Levels Ser.). 4.73 (978-0-7362-0234-3(X)) CENGAGE Learning.

Greve, Meg. The Birdhouse That Jack Built. Poole, Helen, illus. 2012. (ENG.). 24p. (J). (gr. k-1). pap. 8.95 *(978-1-61810-300-0(8))* Rourke Educational Media.
—Painting Party. Anglicas, Louise, illus. 2013. (ENG.). 24p. (gr. -1-1). pap. 8.95 *(978-1-62169-207-2(8))* Rourke Educational Media.
Griffin, C. R. Runt & the Two Roses. 2011. 24p. pap. 15.99 *(978-1-4628-4589-7(4))* Xlibris Corp.
Griffin, Mary. Our Needs & Wants. 2008. (Real Life Readers Ser.). 8p. (gr. k-1). pap. 5.15 *(978-1-4042-7965-0(2),* Rosen Classroom) Rosen Publishing Group, Inc., The.
Griffiths, Rachel. What's the Address? 2004. (ENG., Illus.). 16p. (J). (gr. 1-1). pap. 10.92 *(978-0-7652-5163-3(9),* Celebration Pr.) Pearson Schl.
Grimm, Jacob, et al. Hansel & Gretel. 2005. 48p. (J). (gr. 2-18). 8.95 *(978-0-7945-1053-4(1),* Usborne) EDC Publishing.
Grimm, Wilhelm K., et al. Elves & Shoemaker. 2004. 48p. (J). (gr. 2-18). pap. 5.95 *(978-0-7945-0759-9(1),* Usborne) EDC Publishing.
Grindley, Sally. Puff Flies. Fuller, Jeremy, illus. 2011. (My Phonics Readers: Level 3 Ser.). 24p. (J). (gr. -1-1). 24.25 *(978-1-84898-514-8(2))* Sea-To-Sea Pubns.
—Queen Ella's Feet. Aguilar, Sandra, illus. 2011. (My Phonics Readers: Level 3 Ser.). 24p. (J). (gr. -1-1). 24.25 *(978-1-84898-513-1(4))* Sea-To-Sea Pubns.
Gro, Wright. Matchword/Prog Set. (Fast Track Reading Ser.). (gr. k-6). 158.95 incl. cd-rom *(978-0-322-03751-9(4))* Wright Group/McGraw-Hill.
Grogan, John & Hill, Susan. Marley's Big Adventure. Cowdrey, Richard & Halverson, Lydia, illus. 2009. (I Can Read Book 2 Ser.). 32p. (J). (gr. -1-3). 16.99 *(978-0-06-185384-5(4));* (ENG.). (gr. k-3). pap. 3.99 *(978-0-06-185383-8(6))* HarperCollins Pubs.
Grosset and Dunlap Staff & Penguin Young Readers Group Staff. Go Away, Spot. 5 vols. 2003. (Dick & Jane Ser.: 5). (ENG., Illus.). 32p. (J). (gr. 1-2). mass mkt. 3.99 *(978-0-448-43404-9(0),* Penguin Young Readers) Penguin Young Readers Group.
Grosset and Dunlap Staff, et al. Fun with Dick & Jane. 2004. (Penguin Young Readers Level 2 Ser.). (gr. k-3). lib. bdg. 13.55 *(978-0-613-72512-5(3),* Turtleback) Turtleback Bks.
Group/McGraw-Hill, Wright. A Friend in the Wild: Level Q, 6 vols. (Whispering Pines Ser.). 128p. (gr. 5-18). 36.95 *(978-0-322-05905-4(4))* Wright Group/McGraw-Hill.
—Gourmet Delights, 6 vols. (Comprehension Strand Ser.). (YA). (gr. 4-8). pap. 54.00 *(978-0-322-06028-9(1))* Wright Group/McGraw-Hill.
—Legends of the Wild West: Level O, 6 vols. (Autumn Leaves Ser.). 128p. (gr. 3-6). 36.95 *(978-0-322-06732-5(4))* Wright Group/McGraw-Hill.
—Mountain Peaks: Complete Set. (Mountain Peaks Ser.). 327.95 *(978-0-322-07966-3(7))* Wright Group/McGraw-Hill.
—Raging Rivers: Classroom Library Set. (Raging Rivers Ser.). 81.50 *(978-0-322-07970-0(5))* Wright Group/McGraw-Hill.
—Raging Rivers: Complete Set. (Raging Rivers Ser.). 327.95 *(978-0-322-07964-9(0))* Wright Group/McGraw-Hill.
—Riverboat Bill: Level H, 6 vols. (Take Twostm Ser.). 16p. 29.95 *(978-0-322-08958-7(1))* Wright Group/McGraw-Hill.
—Story Box, Leveled Books. 79.95 *(978-0-322-02563-9(X))* Wright Group/McGraw-Hill.
—Storyteller: Upper Emergent - Upper Emergent-Early Fluency - Complete Kit. (Storyteller Ser.). (gr. 1-18). 565.50 *(978-1-4045-1042-5(7))* Wright Group/McGraw-Hill.
—Storyteller Chapter Books: Fluency - 1 Each of 4 Titles: Level S. 24.50 *(978-1-4045-0953-5(4))* Wright Group/McGraw-Hill.
—Sunshine: Early Fluency - Groups 1-2; 1 each of 17 titles: Level M. (Sunshine Ser.). 99.50 *(978-0-322-04312-1(3))* Wright Group/McGraw-Hill.
—Take Twos: Upper Emergent - Level H: 1 Each of 4 Lesson Plans: Level H. (Take Twostm Ser.). 31.50 *(978-1-4045-1729-5(4))* Wright Group/McGraw-Hill.
Grubnedor Press. Tuppy the Turtle Puppy. 2007. (Illus.). 32p. (J). 10.95 *(978-0-9795407-0-7(4))* Grubnedor Pr.
Grudzina, Rebecca. Baby Bumblebee. Boyer, Lyn, illus. 2010. (Rising Readers Ser.). (J). 3.49 *(978-1-60719-688-4(3))* Newmark Learning LLC.
—A Baby Bumblebee for Mommy. Boyer, Lyn, illus. 2009. (Reader's Theater Nursery Rhymes & Songs Set B Ser.). 48p. (J). pap. *(978-1-60859-149-7(2))* Benchmark Education Co.
—Pease Porridge, Please! Harrington, David, illus. 2009. (Reader's Theater Nursery Rhymes & Songs Set B Ser.). 48p. (J). pap. *(978-1-60859-163-3(8))* Benchmark Education Co.
—Red Roses, Blue Violets, And... ? Ledger, Bill, illus. 2009. (Reader's Theater Nursery Rhymes & Songs Set B Ser.). 48p. (J). pap. *(978-1-60859-167-1(0))* Benchmark Education Co.
—Tim's Swim. Piwowarski, Marcin, illus. 2017. (Text Connections Guided Close Reading Ser.). (J). (gr. k). *(978-1-4900-1766-2(6))* Benchmark Education Co.
The Grumpy Millionaire: Individual Title Six-Packs. (Bookweb Ser.). 32p. (gr. 5-18). 34.00 *(978-0-7635-3777-7(2))* Rigby Education.
Guess What! Individual Title Six-Packs. (Literatura 2000 Ser.). (gr. k-1). 28.00 *(978-0-7635-0054-2(2))* Rigby Education.
Guess Who? Individual Title Six-Packs. (gr. k-1). 23.00 *(978-0-7635-8856-4(3))* Rigby Education.
Guest, Elissa Haden. Iris & Walter: the Sleepover. Davenier, Christine, illus. alt. ed. 2012. (Green Light Readers Level 3 Ser.). (ENG.). 44p. (J). (gr. 1-4). pap. 3.99 *(978-0-547-74556-5(7))* Houghton Mifflin Harcourt Publishing Co.
—The School Play. 2015. (Iris & Walter — Green Light Reader Ser.). lib. bdg. 13.55 *(978-0-606-36558-1(3))* Turtleback Bks.
Guided Reading Levels. 25 bks., Set, Level A. (Guided Reading Levels Ser.). 92.05 *(978-0-7362-1186-4(1))* CENGAGE Learning.
Guillain, Charlotte. Extreme Animals. 2014. (Collins Big Cat Progress Ser.). (ENG., Illus.). 32p. (J). (gr. 4-5). pap. 7.99 *(978-0-00-751928-6(1))* HarperCollins Pubs. Ltd. GBR. Dist: Independent Pubs. Group.
Guillain, Charlotte & Colson, Mary. Dream It, Do It!, 1 vol. 2014. (Dream It, Do It! Ser.). (ENG.). 32p. (gr. 1-3). lib. bdg. 119.96 *(978-1-4109-6266-9(0),* Read Me!) Heinemann-Raintree.
Gunby, Shirley & Laman, Judi-Lynn. Extinct & Endangered: Big Animals Small World - Painting for Peanuts. 2007. (Steck-Vaughn BOLDPRINT Anthologies Ser.). (ENG., Illus.). 48p. (gr. 4-8). pap. 16.90 *(978-1-4190-4023-8(5))* Houghton Mifflin Harcourt Publishing Co.
Gunn, Barbara. Old MacDonald's Farm: Read Well Level K Unit 7 Storybook. Marier, Chuck, illus. 2004. (Read Well Level K Ser.). 20p. (J). *(978-1-57035-679-7(3))* Cambium Education, Inc.
Gunn, Barbara, et al. Mark & Dan Go West: Read Well Level K Unit 17 Storybook. Weber, Philip A., Jr., illus. 2003. (Read Well Level K Ser.). 20p. (J). *(978-1-57035-688-9(2),* 55571) Cambium Education, Inc.
Gura, Timothy & Lee, Charlotte. Oral Interpretation. 11th ed. 2004. 544p. (YA). pap. 78.76 *(978-0-618-30817-0(2),* 318462) CENGAGE Learning.
Gurney, Stella. Mr. Bickle & the Ghost. Raga, Silvia, illus. 2009. (Get Ready (Windmill Books) Ser.). 32p. (J). (gr. k-2). lib. bdg. 22.60 *(978-1-60754-260-5(9))* Windmill Bks.
Gutman, Dan. My Weird School, 4 bks. in 1. Pamintuan, Macky & Paillot, Jim, illus. 2016. (My Weird School Ser.). 384p. (J). (gr. 1-5). 14.99 *(978-0-06-249668-3(9))* HarperCollins Pubs.
—My Weird School Goes to the Museum. Paillot, Jim, illus. 2016. 30p. (J). ***(978-1-5182-2157-6(2))*** Harper & Row Ltd.
—Rappy Goes to the Library. Bowers, Tim, illus. 2017. (I Can Read Level 2 Ser.). 32p. (J). (gr. -1-3). pap. 3.99 *(978-0-06-225265-4(8))* HarperCollins Pubs.
—Rappy Goes to the Supermarket. Bowers, Tim, illus. 2017. (I Can Read Level 2 Ser.). 32p. (J). (gr. -1-3). 3.99 *(978-0-06-225262-3(3))* HarperCollins Pubs.
Gutner, Howard. Egypt. 2009. (True Book Ser.). (ENG.). 48p. (J). pap. 6.95 *(978-0-531-21356-8(0),* Children's Pr.) Scholastic Library Publishing.
Guy, Ginger Foglesong & Guy, Ginger F. Siesta Board Book. Moreno, Rene King, illus. 2009. (SPA & ENG.). 34p. (J). (gr. -1 — 1). bds. 7.99 *(978-0-06-168884-3(3),* Greenwillow Bks.) HarperCollins Pubs.
Gwent (Wales), Staff Development Unit Staff & Acen Staff, contrib. by. Croeso I Gartref Llew. 2005. (WEL., Illus.). 8p. pap. *(978-1-874049-34-0(3))* Acen Limited.
—Nos Da, Arthur. 2005. (WEL., Illus.). 8p. pap. *(978-1-874049-31-9(9))* Acen Limited.
Haas, Jessie. Bramble & Maggie Give & Take. Friend, Alison, illus. 2015. (Candlewick Sparks Ser.). (ENG.). 56p. (J). (gr. k-4). pap. 3.99 *(978-0-7636-7787-9(6))* Candlewick Pr.
Hager, Janet. Truly Julie. 2012. 26p. 14.95 *(978-1-4626-6121-3(1))* America Star Bks.
Haladay, Max. Max Gets Mad. 2006. (Neighborhood Readers Ser.). (ENG.). 8p. (gr. 1-3). pap. 5.15 *(978-1-4042-6811-1(1),* Rosen Classroom) Rosen Publishing Group, Inc., The.
Haley, Amanda, illus. Ready, Alice? 2005. (I'm Going to Read(r) Ser.). (ENG.). 32p. (J). (gr. k-1). per. 3.95 *(978-1-4027-2717-7(8))* Sterling Publishing Co., Inc.
Hall, Kirsten. Hide-and-Seek: All about Location. Luedecke, Bev, illus. 2005. (Beastieville Ser.). (ENG.). 32p. (J). (gr. k-1). pap. 3.95 *(978-0-516-25519-4(3),* Children's Pr.) Scholastic Library Publishing.
Hall, Marcella Runell & Cameron, Andrea. The 10 Most Influential Hip Hop Artists. 2008. 14.99 *(978-1-55448-504-8(5))* Scholastic Library Publishing.
Hallett, R. B. The 10 Most Decisive Battles on American Soil. 2008. 14.99 *(978-1-55448-538-3(X))* Scholastic Library Publishing.
Hama, Larry. The Battle of First Bull Run: The War Begins! 2007. (Graphic Battles: Civil War Ser.). (ENG., Illus.). 48p. (gr. 5-6). pap. 14.05 *(978-1-4042-6476-2(0),* Rosen Classroom) Rosen Publishing Group, Inc., The.
—The Battle of Shiloh: Surprise Attack! 2007. (Graphic Battles: Civil War Ser.). (ENG., Illus.). 48p. (gr. 5-8). pap. 14.05 *(978-1-4042-6478-6(7),* Rosen Classroom) Rosen Publishing Group, Inc., The.
Hammond, Veronica. Wash Those Hands. 2009. 20p. pap. 9.45 *(978-1-4269-1590-1(X))* Trafford Publishing.
Hank's Tank, 6 vols. 8p. (gr. k-1). 21.50 *(978-0-322-02061-0(1))* Wright Group/McGraw-Hill.
Hansel & Gretel. 2015. (ENG., Illus.). 32p. (J). (gr. -1-3). *(978-1-78393-583-3(9))* Make Believe Ideas.
Hanson, Ed. The Floodgates. 2005. (Barclay Family Adventures 2 Ser.). 64p. (J). per. 3.95 *(978-1-56254-803-2(4),* SP8034) Saddleback Educational Publishing, Inc.
—Ransom. 2005. (Barclay Family Adventures 2 Ser.). 64p. (J). per. 3.95 *(978-1-56254-808-7(5),* SP8085) Saddleback Educational Publishing, Inc.
Hanson, Sharon. The 10 Best Love Poems. 2008. 14.99 *(978-1-55448-543-7(6))* Scholastic Library Publishing.
Hapka, Catherine, pseud. Meet the Buddies! Lyon, Tammie, illus. 2013. (World of Reading Ser.). (ENG.). 32p. (J). (gr. 1-3). pap. 3.99 *(978-1-4231-6946-8(8))* Disney Pr.
—Plants vs. Zombies. 2014. (I Can Read! Level 2 Ser.). (J). lib. bdg. 13.55 *(978-0-606-35477-6(8))* Turtleback Bks.
Happy Baby Board Books 800847, 3. 2005. (J). bds. *(978-1-59794-048-1(8))* Environments, Inc.
Happy Tunes Book Set 800944, 5. 2005. (J). bds. *(978-1-59794-031-3(3))* Environments, Inc.
Harcourt Achieve, creator. Avenues. 2005. (Steck-Vaughn Read on! Go Bks.). (Illus.). 108p. (J). per. 8.95 *(978-0-7398-8970-1(2))* Steck-Vaughn.
—Images. 2005. (Steck-Vaughn Read on! Go Bks.). (Illus.). 172p. (J). per. 8.95 *(978-0-7398-8969-5(9))* Steck-Vaughn.
—People. 2005. (Steck-Vaughn Read on! Go Bks.). (Illus.). 88p. (J). per. 8.95 *(978-0-7398-8967-1(2))* Steck-Vaughn.
—Windows. 2005. (Steck-Vaughn Read on! Go Bks.). (Illus.). 152p. (J). per. 8.95 *(978-0-7398-8968-8(0))* Steck-Vaughn.
Harcourt School Publishers, creator. Earth's Changing Crust: Lessons 3-5. 2006. (ENG.). pap. 27.00 *(978-0-15-354803-1(7))* Harcourt Schl. Pubs.
—Ecosystems: Lessons 3-4. 2006. (ENG.). pap. 27.00 *(978-0-15-354818-5(5))* Harcourt Schl. Pubs.
—Energy Transfer & Weather: Lessons 2-3. 2006. (ENG.). pap. 27.00 *(978-0-15-354814-7(2))* Harcourt Schl. Pubs.
—Invisible Pull: Electricity & Magnets. 2009. (ENG., Illus.). 16p. (J). pap. 14.95 *(978-0-15-362219-9(9))* Harcourt Schl. Pubs.
Harcourt School Publishers Staff. Banner Days Level 2-2. 3rd ed. 2003. (Harcourt School Publishers Trophies Ser.). (ENG., Illus.). 448p. (gr. 2-2). pupil's gde. ed. 59.90 *(978-0-15-322475-1(4))* Harcourt Schl. Pubs.
—Horizons Big Book Collection. 2nd ed. 2003. (Illus.). (gr. 1). pap. 840.00 *(978-0-15-337573-6(6));* (gr. 2). pap. 840.00 *(978-0-15-337581-1(7))* Harcourt Schl. Pubs.
—Horizons Big Book Collection Unit 1. 2nd ed. 2003. (Illus.). pap. 140.00 *(978-0-15-337812-6(3));* pap. 140.00 *(978-0-15-337574-3(4))* Harcourt Schl. Pubs.
—Horizons Big Book Collection Unit 2. 2nd ed. 2003. (Illus.). pap. 140.00 *(978-0-15-337575-0(2));* pap. 140.00 *(978-0-15-337813-3(1))* Harcourt Schl. Pubs.
—Horizons Big Book Collection Unit 3. 2nd ed. 2003. (Illus.). pap. 140.00 *(978-0-15-337577-4(9));* pap. 140.00 *(978-0-15-337814-0(X))* Harcourt Schl. Pubs.
—Horizons Big Book Collection Unit 4. 2nd ed. 2003. (Illus.). pap. 140.00 *(978-0-15-337815-7(8));* pap. 140.00 *(978-0-15-337578-1(7))* Harcourt Schl. Pubs.
—Horizons Big Book Collection Unit 5. 2nd ed. 2003. (Illus.). pap. 140.00 *(978-0-15-337579-8(5));* (J). pap. 140.00 *(978-0-15-337816-4(6))* Harcourt Schl. Pubs.
—Horizons Big Book Collection Unit 6. 2nd ed. 2003. (Illus.). pap. 140.00 *(978-0-15-337817-1(4));* pap. 140.00 *(978-0-15-337580-4(9))* Harcourt Schl. Pubs.
—Horizons ESL Summary. 4th ed. 2004. (gr. 1). pap. 9.30 *(978-0-15-341413-8(8));* (gr. 2). pap. 9.30 *(978-0-15-341414-5(6))* Harcourt Schl. Pubs.
—Horizons ESL Summary with Ancient Civilizations. 4th ed. 2004. (gr. 3). pap. 12.40 *(978-0-15-341415-2(4))* Harcourt Schl. Pubs.
—Horizons, Grade 2: Time for Kids Readers. 3rd ed. 2003. (Harcourt Horizons Ser.). pap., tchr. ed. 51.20 *(978-0-15-334647-7(7))* Harcourt Schl. Pubs.
—Lets Visit Museum, Above Level Reader Grade K: Harcourt School Publishers Social Studies. 2005. pap. 5.60 *(978-0-15-351872-0(3))* Harcourt Schl. Pubs.
—Little Red Hen Library Book Grade K: Harcourt School Publishers Storytown. 2005. 32p. pap. 8.75 *(978-0-15-352474-5(X))* Harcourt Schl. Pubs.
—Moving into English Big Books: Leveled Library Collection. 2nd ed. 2003. (Illus.). (gr. 2). pap. 508.40 *(978-0-15-337426-5(8))* Harcourt Schl. Pubs.
—Trophies: Lead the Way. 3rd ed. 2003. (Harcourt School Publishers Trophies Ser.). (ENG., Illus.). 784p. (gr. 4-4). 82.50 *(978-0-15-339787-5(X))* Harcourt Schl. Pubs.
—Trophies: Mr. Putter & Tabby, Set 2. 2004. (Illus.). pap. 17.85 *(978-0-15-205375-8(1))* Harcourt Schl. Pubs.
—Trophies: Timeless Treasures. 3rd ed. 2003. (Harcourt School Publishers Trophies Ser.). (ENG., Illus.). 752p. (gr. 6-6). 82.50 *(978-0-15-339789-9(6))* Harcourt Schl. Pubs.
—Trophies Level 1-1: Guess Who. 3rd ed. 2003. (Harcourt School Publishers Trophies Ser.). (ENG., Illus.). 160p. (gr. 1-1). stu. ed. 37.85 *(978-0-15-339776-9(4))* Harcourt Schl. Pubs.
—Trophies Level 1-2: Catch the Dream. 3rd ed. 2003. (Harcourt School Publishers Trophies Ser.). (ENG., Illus.). 176p. (gr. 1-1). stu. ed. 37.85 *(978-0-15-339777-6(2))* Harcourt Schl. Pubs.
—Trophies Level 1-3: Here & There. 3rd ed. 2003. (Harcourt School Publishers Trophies Ser.). (ENG., Illus.). 192p. (gr. 1-1). 40.05 *(978-0-15-339778-3(0))* Harcourt Schl. Pubs.
—Trophies Level 2-2: Banner Days. 3rd ed. 2003. (Harcourt School Publishers Trophies Ser.). (ENG., Illus.). 448p. (gr. 2-2). stu. ed. 58.70 *(978-0-15-339783-7(7))* Harcourt Schl. Pubs.
—Trophies Level 3-1: Changing Patterns. 3rd ed. 2003. (Harcourt School Publishers Trophies Ser.). (ENG., Illus.). 448p. (gr. 3-3). 60.75 *(978-0-15-339784-4(5))* Harcourt Schl. Pubs.
—Trophies Level 3-2: On Your Mark. 3rd ed. 2003. (Harcourt School Publishers Trophies Ser.). (ENG., Illus.). 464p. (gr. 3-3). stu. ed. 60.75 *(978-0-15-339786-8(1))* Harcourt Schl. Pubs.
—Watch This! Level 1-5 Grade 1: Harcourt School Publishers Storytown Florida. 2005. 264p. 23.73 *(978-0-15-352170-6(8))* Harcourt Schl. Pubs.
—Your Health Reader: The Morning. 3rd ed. 2003. (Illus.). pap. 9.40 *(978-0-15-338777-7(7))* Harcourt Schl. Pubs.
Hardy, Thomas. THE MAYOR OF CASTERBRIDGE LEVEL 5 UPPER-INTERMEDIATE BOOK WITH CD-ROM AND AUDIO CDS (2) PACK, 1 vol. 2009. (ENG.). 112p. pap. 16.50 incl. cd-rom, audio compact disk *(978-84-8323-556-0(0))* Cambridge Univ. Pr.
—Plpr4: Far from the Madding Crowd RLA. 2nd ed. 2009. (ENG., Illus.). 72p. pap. 11.99 *(978-1-4058-8217-0(4))* Pearson Education.
Hargis, Alvin. Kingdom of Mystique Series: Book 1. 2007. 25p. pap. 24.95 *(978-1-4241-8635-8(8))* PublishAmerica, Inc.
Harimann, Sierra. Ice Age: Dawn of the Dinosaurs - Momma Mix-Up. 2009. (I Can Read Level 2 Ser.). (ENG.). 32p. (J). (gr. k-3). pap. 3.99 *(978-0-06-168978-9(5))* HarperCollins Pubs.
Harkness, Karen. Coralee's Best Run Yet. 2007. (Illus.). 40p. (J). per. 7.99 net. *(978-0-9800934-0-7(6))* H&W Publishing Inc.
Harmon, Dan, et al. Monster House - La Casa de los Sustos. 2014. (SPA., Illus.). 40p. pap. 13.75 incl. audio compact disk *(978-84-9848-132-7(5))* Edinumen, Editorial ESP. Dist: Cambridge Univ. Pr.
Harold First Readers 800883, 4 vols. 2005. (J). pap. *(978-1-59794-058-0(5))* Environments, Inc.
Harper, Ben. Super Friends: Going Bananas. Random House Staff, illus. 2009. (Step into Reading Ser.). (ENG.). 32p. (J). (gr. -1-1). pap. 3.99 *(978-0-375-85613-6(7),* Random Hse. Bks. for Young Readers) Random Hse. Children's Bks.
Harper, C. J. The Wilderness. 2014. (ENG.). 416p. (YA). pap. 9.99 *(978-0-85707-700-4(7),* Simon & Schuster Children's) Simon & Schuster, Ltd. GBR. Dist: Simon & Schuster, Inc.
Harper Collins & Auerbach, Annie. Meet Paddington. 2014. (Paddington — I Can Read Ser.). (J). lib. bdg. 13.55 *(978-0-606-35966-5(4))* Turtleback Bks.
Harper, Kathryn. Dressing for the Weather Green Band. Sims, Sean, illus. 2016. (Cambridge Reading Adventures Ser.). (ENG.). 16p. pap. 6.56 *(978-1-316-50324-9(0))* Cambridge Univ. Pr.
—Earthquakes White Band. Dean, Venitia, illus. 2016. (Cambridge Reading Adventures Ser.). (ENG.). 24p. pap. 7.19 *(978-1-316-50342-3(9))* Cambridge Univ. Pr.
—Leopard & His Spots Red Band. Mosedale, Julian, illus. 2016. (Cambridge Reading Adventures Ser.). (ENG.). 16p. pap. 6.56 *(978-1-316-50308-9(9))* Cambridge Univ. Pr.
—Please Stop, Sara! Pink a Band. Nicholls, Paul, illus. 2016. (Cambridge Reading Adventures Ser.). (ENG.). 16p. pap. 6.56 *(978-1-316-50313-3(5))* Cambridge Univ. Pr.
—Seagull Red Band. Villalba, Ana, illus. 2016. (Cambridge Reading Adventures Ser.). (ENG.). 16p. pap. 6.56 *(978-1-316-50310-2(0))* Cambridge Univ. Pr.
Harper, Suzanne. The 10 Most Tragic Romances. 2008. (J). 14.99 *(978-1-55448-546-8(0))* Scholastic Library Publishing.
Harper, Suzanne & Sheppard, Bonnie. The 10 Most Extreme Vacations. 2008. (J). 14.99 *(978-1-55448-534-5(7))* Scholastic Library Publishing.
Harris, Brooke. Baby Gets a Cake. Beckstrand, Jared, illus. 2009. (Reader's Theater Nursery Rhymes & Songs Set B Ser.). 48p. (J). pap. *(978-1-60859-150-3(6))* Benchmark Education Co.
—Brother John, Wake Up! 2008. (Reader's Theater Nursery Rhymes & Songs Ser.). (Illus.). 48p. (J). (gr. k-1). pap. *(978-1-60437-973-0(1))* Benchmark Education Co.
—Fun with Our Friends: Lap Book. 2009. (My First Reader's Theater Set B Ser.). (J). 28.00 *(978-1-4108-8543-2(7))* Benchmark Education Co.
—Healthy Snacks: Lap Book. 2009. (My First Reader's Theater Set B Ser.). (J). 28.00 *(978-1-4108-8545-6(3))* Benchmark Education Co.
—Jack & Jill Play on the Hill. 2008. (Reader's Theater Nursery Rhymes & Songs Ser.). (Illus.). 48p. (J). (gr. k-1). pap. *(978-1-60437-964-8(2))* Benchmark Education Co.
—Little Boy Blue, Where are You? 2008. (Reader's Theater Nursery Rhymes & Songs Ser.). (Illus.). 48p. (J). (gr. k-1). pap. *(978-1-60437-976-1(6))* Benchmark Education Co.
—London Bridge Has Fallen Down. Boyer, Lyn, illus. 2009. (Reader's Theater Nursery Rhymes & Songs Set B Ser.). 48p. (J). pap. *(978-1-60859-159-6(X))* Benchmark Education Co.
—Mary's Garden: How Does it Grow? Xin, Xiao, illus. 2009. (Reader's Theater Nursery Rhymes & Songs Set B Ser.). 48p. (J). pap. *(978-1-60859-160-2(3))* Benchmark Education Co.
—Playing at My House: Lap Book. 2009. (My First Reader's Theater Set B Ser.). (J). 28.00 *(978-1-60634-986-1(4))* Benchmark Education Co.
—The Purple Cow. Hohnstadt, Cedric, illus. 2009. (Reader's Theater Nursery Rhymes & Songs Set B Ser.). 48p. (J). pap. *(978-1-60859-166-4(2))* Benchmark Education Co.
—This Little Pig, That Little Pig. 2008. (Reader's Theater Nursery Rhymes & Songs Ser.). (Illus.). 48p. (J). (gr. k-1). pap. *(978-1-60437-969-3(3))* Benchmark Education Co.
—The Twinkling Stars. Harrington, David, illus. 2009. (Reader's Theater Nursery Rhymes & Songs Set B Ser.). 48p. (J). pap. *(978-1-60859-170-1(0))* Benchmark Education Co.
—Where Has My Little Dog Gone? 2008. (Reader's Theater Nursery Rhymes & Songs Ser.). (Illus.). 48p. (J). (gr. k-1). pap. *(978-1-60437-975-4(8))* Benchmark Education Co.
—Working on the Railroad. 2008. (Reader's Theater Nursery Rhymes & Songs Ser.). (Illus.). 48p. (J). (gr. k-1). pap. *(978-1-60437-981-5(2))* Benchmark Education Co.
Harris, Robie H. Maybe a Bear Ate It (a StoryPlay Book) Emberley, Michael, illus. 2017. (StoryPlay Ser.). (ENG.). 40p. (J). (gr. -1-k). 5.99 ***(978-1-338-16110-6(5),*** Cartwheel Bks.) Scholastic, Inc.
Harris, Trudy. Say Something, Perico. RéBora, Cecilia, illus. 2011. (Millbrook Picture Books Ser.). (ENG.). 32p. (J). (gr. -1-2). lib. bdg. 16.95 *(978-0-7613-5231-0(7),* Millbrook Pr.) Lerner Publishing Group.
HarrisNic. EMPIRE: RISE AND FALL LOW INTERMEDIATE BOOK WITH ONLINE ACCESS. 2014. (ENG., Illus.). 24p. (J). pap. 9.50 *(978-1-107-62844-1(X))* Cambridge Univ. Pr.
—THE GREATEST INVENTION OF ALL TIME LOW INTERMEDIATE BOOK WITH ONLINE ACCESS. 2014. (ENG., Illus.). 24p. (J). pap. 9.50 *(978-1-107-62161-9(5))* Cambridge Univ. Pr.
—GROWING UP: FROM BABY TO ADULT HIGH BEGINNING BOOK WITH ONLINE ACCESS. 2014. (ENG.). 24p. (J). pap. 9.50 *(978-1-107-68744-8(6))* Cambridge Univ. Pr.
—HOW COOL IS COLD! LOW INTERMEDIATE BOOK WITH ONLINE ACCESS. 2014. (ENG.). 24p. (J). pap. 9.50 *(978-1-107-65803-5(9))* Cambridge Univ. Pr.
—MEDICINE: OLD AND NEW LOW INTERMEDIATE BOOK WITH ONLINE ACCESS. 2014. (ENG., Illus.). 24p. (J). pap. 9.50 *(978-1-107-65866-0(7))* Cambridge Univ. Pr.
—THE SCIENCE OF HEAT LOW INTERMEDIATE BOOK WITH ONLINE ACCESS. 2014. (ENG., Illus.). 24p. (J). pap. 9.50 *(978-1-107-69772-0(7))* Cambridge Univ. Pr.
Harrison, David L. Paul Bunyan: My Story. Kanzler, John, illus. 2008. (Step into Reading Ser.). (ENG.). 48p. (J). (gr. k-3). 4.99 *(978-0-375-84688-5(3),* Random Hse. Bks. for Young Readers) Random Hse. Children's Bks.
Harrison, Lorraine. My Fourth of July. 2012. (InfoMax Readers Ser.). (ENG., Illus.). 24p. (J). (gr. 1-2). pap. 8.25 *(978-1-4488-9046-0(2),* Rosen Classroom) Rosen Publishing Group, Inc., The.
Harrison, Paul. Noisy Books. Fiorin, Fabiano, illus. 2009. (Get Ready (Windmill Books) Ser.). 32p. (J). (gr. k-2). lib. bdg. 22.60 *(978-1-60754-258-2(7))* Windmill Bks.
Hart, Melissa. A Guide for Using the Tale of Despereaux in the Classroom. 2005. (ENG.). 48p. pap. 9.99 *(978-1-4206-3164-7(0))* Teacher Created Resources, Inc.
Hartley, Susan. Welcome to Our School. 2004. (Shared Connections Ser.). (J). pap. *(978-1-4108-1626-9(5));* instr.'s gde. ed. 27.00 *(978-1-4108-1602-3(8))* Benchmark Education Co.
Harvey, Damian. Mr. Fox's Socks. Rescek, Sanja, illus. 2004. (ENG.). 16p. (J). lib. bdg. 23.65 *(978-1-59646-678-4(2))* Dingles & Co.
—Whizzy Witch. Dumortier, Marjorie, illus. 2008. (Reading Corner Ser.). (ENG.). 24p. (J). (gr. k-2). pap. 6.99 *(978-0-7496-7699-5(X),* Franklin Watts) Hachette Children's Group GBR. Dist: Hachette Bk. Group.
Harvey, Damien. Dinosaur Rock. Ward, Matt, illus. 2005. (Collins Big Cat Ser.). (ENG.). 56p. (J). (gr. -1-k). pap. 5.99 *(978-0-00-718540-5(5))* HarperCollins Pubs. Ltd. GBR. Dist: Independent Pubs. Group.

Harvey, John. My New Skates. 2006. (Neighborhood Readers Ser.). (ENG.). 16p. (gr. 1-3). pap. 6.50 *(978-1-4042-7172-2(4),* Rosen Classroom) Rosen Publishing Group, Inc., The.
Harvey, Ken. The Leftovers. Hermes, Mary Sue, illus. 2003. (Life in the 'Fridge Ser.). (J). *(978-1-930093-21-8(7))* Brookfield Reader, Inc., The.
Harvey, Paul & Pearson Education Staff. Surfer! 2nd ed. 2008. (ENG.). 32p. pap. 11.99 *(978-1-4058-6969-0(0))* Pearson Education.
Harvey, William C. Ingles para Ninos: English for Children. 2nd rev. ed. 2012. (SPA.). 216p. (gr. 2-6). pap. 12.99 *(978-1-4380-0001-5(4))* Barron's Educational Series, Inc.
Hatched from an Egg. (J). pap. 13.15 *(978-0-8136-4261-1(2))* Modern Curriculum Pr.
Hawes, Alison. At the Market Pink B Band. Robert, LeyHonor, illus. 2016. (Cambridge Reading Adventures Ser.). (ENG.). 16p. pap. 6.56 *(978-1-107-54993-7(0))* Cambridge Univ. Pr.
—The Enormous Watermelon. Rodriguez, Elba, illus. 2016. (Cambridge Reading Adventures Ser.). (ENG.). 16p. pap. 6.56 *(978-1-107-54924-1(8))* Cambridge Univ. Pr.
—A Hot Day Pink a Band. Lee, Maxine, illus. 2016. (Cambridge Reading Adventures Ser.). (ENG.). 16p. pap. 6.56 *(978-1-316-60069-6(6))* Cambridge Univ. Pr.
—Jamila Finds a Friend. Piwowarski, Marcin, illus. 2016. (Cambridge Reading Adventures Ser.). (ENG.). 16p. pap. 6.56 *(978-1-107-54963-0(9))* Cambridge Univ. Pr.
—The Last Lemon Pink B Band. Anegón, Tamara, illus. 2016. (Cambridge Reading Adventures Ser.). (ENG.). 16p. pap. 6.56 *(978-1-107-54909-8(4))* Cambridge Univ. Pr.
—Leela Can Skate Pink B Band. Yoshizumi, Carol, illus. 2016. (Cambridge Reading Adventures Ser.). (ENG.). 16p. pap. 6.56 *(978-1-107-57582-0(6))* Cambridge Univ. Pr.
—My Exercise Diary: Band 02B/Red B. 2006. (Collins Big Cat Ser.). (ENG., Illus.). 16p. (J). (gr. -1-k). pap. 5.99 *(978-0-00-718669-3(X))* HarperCollins Pubs. Ltd. GBR. Dist: Independent Pubs. Group.
—Packing My Bag Pink a Band. Jennings, Sarah, illus. 2016. (Cambridge Reading Adventures Ser.). (ENG.). 16p. pap. 6.56 *(978-1-316-60082-5(3))* Cambridge Univ. Pr.
—School Trip. Mould, Chris, illus. 2004. (ENG.). 24p. (J). lib. bdg. 23.65 *(978-1-59646-694-4(4))* Dingles & Co.
—Weather Report: Band 02a/Red A. Stojic, Manya, illus. 2007. (Collins Big Cat Ser.). (ENG.). 16p. (J). (gr. -1-k). pap. 5.99 *(978-0-00-718655-6(X))* HarperCollins Pubs. Ltd. GBR. Dist: Independent Pubs. Group.
—What Are You Making? Band 02b/Red B. Elworthy, Antony, illus. 2007. (Collins Big Cat Ser.). (ENG.). 16p. (J). (gr. -1-k). pap. 5.99 *(978-0-00-718657-0(6))* HarperCollins Pubs. Ltd. GBR. Dist: Independent Pubs. Group.
The Hawkers' Amazing Machines. (Early Intervention Levels Ser.). 31.86 *(978-0-7362-0661-7(2))* CENGAGE Learning.
The Hawkers' Amazing Machines (24), Vol. 24. (Early Intervention Levels Ser.). 5.31 *(978-0-7362-0649-5(3))* CENGAGE Learning.
Hawthorne, Philip & Tyler, Jenny. Who's Making That Noise? Cartwright, Stephen, illus. 2005. (Flap Books Ser.). 16p. (J). (gr. 1-18). pap. 7.95 *(978-0-7945-0432-8(9),* Usborne) EDC Publishing.
Haxhia, Miranda. Andy's Cherry Tree. Deisadze, Zaur, illus. 2007. (POL & ENG.). 32p. (J). pap. 12.95 *(978-1-60195-094-9(2))* International Step by Step Assn.
—The Dolls Nose. Kohler, Ursula, illus. 2007. 32p. (J). (ARA & ENG.). pap. 16.95 *(978-1-60195-087-1(X));* (POL & ENG.). pap. 16.95 *(978-1-60195-097-0(7))* International Step by Step Assn.
Hay, Sam. That Dog! Oelofsen, Vian, illus. 2011. (My Phonics Readers: Level 2 Ser.). 24p. (J). (gr. -1-1). 24.25 *(978-1-84898-510-0(X))* Sea-To-Sea Pubns.
—Wish Fish. May, Kate, illus. 2011. (My Phonics Readers: Level 2 Ser.). 24p. (J). (gr. -1-1). 24.25 *(978-1-84898-508-7(8))* Sea-To-Sea Pubns.
Haydon, Julie. Locust Plague, Vol. 107. 2014. (ENG.). 24p. spiral bd. 9.00 *(978-1-4085-0155-9(4))* Oxford Univ. Pr., Inc.
Haye, Lucy. ABCD & an Ant's Story. 2005. 23p. pap. 24.95 *(978-1-4137-2537-7(6))* PublishAmerica, Inc.
Haymond, Mary & Lee, Linda. Building Independent Readers - A Systematic Approach: 30 Mini-Lessons That Teach Students the Strategies They Need for Successful Sustained Independent Reading-All Year Long! 2012. (ENG.). 128p. pap. 18.99 *(978-0-545-32963-7(9),* Teaching Resources) Scholastic, Inc.
HB Staff. Alien Vacation. 97th ed. 2003. (Signatures Ser.). (gr. 1-18). pap. 19.20 *(978-0-15-308179-8(1))* Harcourt Schl. Pubs.
—The Baby. 97th ed. 2003. (First-Place Reading Ser.). (gr. 1-18). pap. 16.50 *(978-0-15-308131-6(7))* Harcourt Schl. Pubs.
—Bird's Bad Day. 97th ed. 2003. (First-Place Reading Ser.). (gr. 1-18). pap. 16.50 *(978-0-15-308132-3(5))* Harcourt Schl. Pubs.
—Help! Said Jed. 97th ed. 2003. (First-Place Reading Ser.). (gr. 1-18). pap. 16.50 *(978-0-15-308134-7(1))* Harcourt Schl. Pubs.
—Henry. 97th ed. 2003. (Signatures Ser.). (gr. 1-18). pap. 19.20 *(978-0-15-308184-2(8))* Harcourt Schl. Pubs.
—How the Sky Got It's Stars. 97th ed. 2003. (Signatures Ser.). (gr. 1-18). pap. 19.20 *(978-0-15-308180-4(5))* Harcourt Schl. Pubs.
—I Was Just about to Go to Bed. 97th ed. 2003. (First-Place Reading Ser.). (gr. 1-18). pap. 16.50 *(978-0-15-308145-3(7))* Harcourt Schl. Pubs.
—Just Like You. 97th ed. 2003. (First-Place Reading Ser.). (gr. 1-18). pap. 16.50 *(978-0-15-308127-9(9))* Harcourt Schl. Pubs.
—The King Who Loved to Dance. 97th ed. 2003. (Signatures Ser.). (gr. 1-18). pap. 16.50 *(978-0-15-308161-3(9))* Harcourt Schl. Pubs.
—The Little Chicks Sing. 97th ed. 2003. (Signatures Ser.). (gr. 1-18). pap. 16.50 *(978-0-15-308159-0(7))* Harcourt Schl. Pubs.
—Lunch in Space. 97th ed. 2003. (Signatures Ser.). (gr. 1-18). pap. 19.20 *(978-0-15-308178-1(3))* Harcourt Schl. Pubs.
—My Family Band. 97th ed. 2003. (First-Place Reading Ser.). (gr. 1-18). pap. 16.50 *(978-0-15-308142-2(2))* Harcourt Schl. Pubs.
—My Sister Is My Friend. 97th ed. 2003. (First-Place Reading Ser.). (gr. 1-18). pap., suppl. ed. 16.50 *(978-0-15-308128-6(7))* Harcourt Schl. Pubs.
—My Wild Woolly. 97th ed. 2003. (First-Place Reading Ser.). (gr. 1-18). pap. 16.50 *(978-0-15-308163-7(5))* Harcourt Schl. Pubs.
—One Little Slip. 97th ed. 2003. (First-Place Reading Ser.). (gr. 1-18). pap. 16.50 *(978-0-15-308141-5(4))* Harcourt Schl. Pubs.
—The Perfect Pet. 97th ed. 2003. (First-Place Reading Ser.). (gr. 1-18). pap. 16.50 *(978-0-15-308133-0(3))* Harcourt Schl. Pubs.
—Play Ball! 97th ed. 2003. (Signatures Ser.). (gr. 1-18). pap. 16.50 *(978-0-15-308155-2(4))* Harcourt Schl. Pubs.
—Silly Aunt Tilly. 97th ed. 2003. (Signatures Ser.). (gr. 1-18). pap. 19.20 *(978-0-15-308185-9(6))* Harcourt Schl. Pubs.
—Today Is Monday. 97th ed. 2003. (Signatures Ser.). (gr. 1-18). pap. 16.50 *(978-0-15-308169-9(4))* Harcourt Schl. Pubs.
—What a Shower! 97th ed. 2003. (First-Place Reading Ser.). (gr. 1-18). pap. 16.50 *(978-0-15-308124-8(4))* Harcourt Schl. Pubs.
—Where Babies Play. 97th ed. 2003. (First-Place Reading Ser.). (gr. 1-18). pap. 16.50 *(978-0-15-308136-1(8))* Harcourt Schl. Pubs.
Heads & Tails: Individual Title Six-Packs. (gr. 1-2). 22.00 *(978-0-7635-9154-0(8))* Rigby Education.
Heads or Tails? Fourth Grade Guided Comprehension Level Q. (On Our Way to English Ser.). (gr. 4-18). 34.50 *(978-0-7578-7177-1(1))* Rigby Education.
Heady, Heather. What's at the Beach? Storch, Ellen N., illus. l.t. ed. 2005. 10p. (J). (gr. -1-k). pap. 10.95 *(978-1-57332-355-0(1),* HighReach Learning, Incorporated) Carson-Dellosa Publishing, LLC.
Health & Safety Book Set 800840, 4. 2005. (J). *(978-1-59794-027-6(5))* Environments, Inc.
Health Care Book Set 800842, 6. 2005. (J). *(978-1-59794-028-3(3))* Environments, Inc.
Heaton, Maria. Kangaroos Say Sorry, Too. 2006. (Neighborhood Readers Ser.). (ENG.). 12p. (gr. 1-3). pap. 5.90 *(978-1-4042-7030-5(2),* Rosen Classroom) Rosen Publishing Group, Inc., The.
Heaton, Mark. Ruth Tells the Truth. 2006. (Neighborhood Readers Ser.). (ENG.). 16p. (gr. 1-3). pap. 6.50 *(978-1-4042-7264-4(X),* Rosen Classroom) Rosen Publishing Group, Inc., The.
Heddle, Becca. Plants, Pollen & Pollinators. 2016. (ENG., Illus.). 32p. (J). (gr. 2-3). pap. 8.95 *(978-0-00-816385-3(5))* HarperCollins Pubs. Ltd. GBR. Dist: Independent Pubs. Group.
Hege, Lynnita. The Little Black Hen. Keyes, Tina Misrasi, illus. 2013. 208p. (J). *(978-0-7399-2465-5(6))* Rod & Staff Pubs., Inc.
Heim, Barbara. The Hudson Beavers Build a Lodge. 2013. (ENG.). 44p. (J). 13.95 *(978-1-938586-45-3(X))* Writer's Cramp, Inc.
Helen's Job. (Early Intervention Levels Ser.). 21.30 *(978-0-7362-0360-9(5));* Vol. 2. 3.55 *(978-0-7362-0081-3(9))* CENGAGE Learning.
Helmetag Murdock, Kita. Future Flash. 2017. (ENG.). 192p. (J). (gr. 2-7). pap. 9.99 *(978-1-5107-1011-5(6),* Sky Pony Pr.) Skyhorse Publishing Co., Inc.
Help for Rosie. 2003. (Bella & Rosie Set 1 Ser.). (J). 7.67 *(978-1-932570-10-6(1))* Pioneer Valley Bks.
Help When Needed. 64p. (YA). (gr. 9-12). pap. 9.95 *(978-0-8224-7155-4(8),* 7155) Globe Fearon Educational Publishing.
A Helpful Change. (Early Intervention Levels Ser.). 31.86 *(978-0-7362-0670-9(1))* CENGAGE Learning.
Hemstock, Whitney M. The ABC's of Traffic Safety. 2010. 34p. pap. 16.95 *(978-0-557-28733-8(2))* Lulu Pr., Inc.
The Hen, the Rooster, & the Bean. (Lexile Levels Ser.). 47.88 *(978-1-56334-393-3(2))* CENGAGE Learning.
Henkes, Kevin. Crisantemo. 2017.Tr. of Chrysanthemum. (SPA.). (J). pap. ***(978-1-63245-664-9(8))*** Lectorum Pubns., Inc.
—Julius, el Rey de la Casa. 2017.Tr. of Julius, the Baby of the World. (SPA.). (J). pap. ***(978-1-63245-668-7(0))*** Lectorum Pubns., Inc.
—Lily y Su Bolso de Plastico Morado. 2017.Tr. of Lilly's Purple Plastic Purse. (SPA.). (J). pap. ***(978-1-63245-667-0(2))*** Lectorum Pubns., Inc.
—Owen. 2017. (SPA.). (J). pap. ***(978-1-63245-665-6(6))*** Lectorum Pubns., Inc.
—Prudencia Se Preocupa. 2017.Tr. of Wemberly Worried. (SPA.). (J). pap. ***(978-1-63245-666-3(4))*** Lectorum Pubns., Inc.
Henry, O. One Thousand Dollars & Other Plays, Level 2. Oxford University Press Staff & West, Clare, eds. 2nd ed. 2008. (ENG., Illus.). 64p. 9.38 *(978-0-19-423520-4(3))* Oxford Univ. Pr., Inc.
—The Ransom of Red Chief. 2nd ed. 2008. (ENG., Illus.). 48p. 9.38 *(978-0-19-423415-3(0))* Oxford Univ. Pr., Inc.
Henry, Steve. Happy Cat. Henry, Steve, illus. 2014. (I Like to Read(r) Ser.). (ENG., Illus.). 24p. (J). (gr. -1-3). 6.99 *(978-0-8234-3177-9(0))* Holiday Hse., Inc.
Henry Wilson, David. Elephants Don't Sit on Cars. Scheffler, Axel, illus. 2017. (Jeremy James Ser.: 1). (ENG.). 128p. (J). (gr. k-5). pap. 8.99 ***(978-1-5098-1876-1(6))*** Pan Macmillan GBR. Dist: Independent Pubs. Group.
Hensley, Sarah M. I Can Be. Teeple, Jackie, illus. l.t. ed. 2006. 12p. (J). (gr. -1-k). pap. 10.95 *(978-1-57332-339-0(X),* HighReach Learning, Incorporated) Carson-Dellosa Publishing, LLC.
Hensley, Sarah M. At the Park. Crowell, Knox, illus. l.t. ed. 2006. 10p. (J). (gr. -1-k). pap. 10.95 *(978-1-57332-354-3(3),* HighReach Learning, Incorporated) Carson-Dellosa Publishing, LLC.
—Water Fun. Crowell, Knox, illus. l.t. ed. 2005. (J). (gr. -1-k). pap. 10.95 *(978-1-57332-343-7(8));* pap. 10.95 *(978-1-57332-342-0(X))* Carson-Dellosa Publishing, LLC. (HighReach Learning, Incorporated).
Hensley, Tana. Keesha Counts Money: Putting Data in Order. 2017. (Computer Science for the Real World Ser.). 12p. (gr. 6-7). pap. 7.05 ***(978-1-5383-5127-7(7),*** Rosen Classroom) Rosen Publishing Group, Inc., The.
Her Story. (J). (gr. 4-6). 84.80 *(978-0-8136-6024-0(6))* Modern Curriculum Pr.
Herbst, Kailee. Lots of Clocks: Learning about Tools That Measure Time. 2009. (Math for the Real World: Early Emergent Ser.). (ENG., Illus.). 8p. (gr. k-1). pap. 5.15 *(978-0-8239-8858-7(9))* Rosen Publishing Group, Inc., The.
—Who's Short? Who's Tall? Learning to Compare Heights. 2009. (Math for the Real World: Early Emergent Ser.). (ENG., Illus.). 8p. (gr. k-1). pap. 5.15 *(978-0-8239-8856-3(2))* Rosen Publishing Group, Inc., The.
Herman, Gail. Enterrado en el Jardin. Smath, Jerry, illus. 2008. (Science Solves It! en Espanol Ser.). (SPA.). 32p. (J). (gr. -1-3). pap. 5.95 *(978-1-57565-262-7(5))* Kane Press, Inc.
—Scooby-Doo: A Scooby-Rific Reader. 2012. (Illus.). (J). *(978-1-4351-3986-2(0))* Scholastic, Inc.
Hernandez, Carlos. It's the Law! 2012. (InfoMax Readers Ser.). (ENG., Illus.). 24p. (J). (gr. 1-2). pap. 8.25 *(978-1-4488-9073-6(X),* Rosen Classroom) Rosen Publishing Group, Inc., The.
Herweck, Diana. All in a Day's Work - Police Officer, 1 vol. 2nd rev. ed. 2013. (Nonfiction Readers Ser.). (ENG.). 64p. (J). (gr. 5-5). pap. 10.99 *(978-1-4333-4905-8(1))* Teacher Created Materials, Inc.
—A Day in the Life of a Ballet Dancer, 1 vol. 2nd rev. ed. 2011. (Nonfiction Readers Ser.). (ENG.). 28p. (J). (gr. 3-3). pap. 8.99 *(978-1-4333-3650-8(2))* Teacher Created Materials, Inc.
—ER Doctor, 1 vol. 2nd rev. ed. 2013. (Nonfiction Readers Ser.). (ENG.). 64p. (J). (gr. 5-5). pap. 10.99 *(978-1-4333-4906-5(X))* Teacher Created Materials, Inc.
—In the Game - An Athlete's Life, 1 vol. 2nd rev. ed. 2012. (Nonfiction Readers Ser.). (ENG.). 48p. (J). (gr. 4-4). pap. 9.99 *(978-1-4333-4824-2(1))* Teacher Created Materials, Inc.
—On the Scene: A CSI's Life, 1 vol. 2nd rev. ed. 2012. (Nonfiction Readers Ser.). (ENG.). 48p. (J). (gr. 4-4). pap. 9.99 *(978-1-4333-4825-9(X))* Teacher Created Materials, Inc.
Herweck, Don. All about Energy, 1 vol. 2007. (Science Readers Ser.). (SPA & ENG.). 32p. (J). (gr. 4-4). pap. 8.99 *(978-0-7439-0571-8(7))* Shell Educational Publishing.
—All about Mechanical Engineering, 1 vol. 2007. (Science Readers Ser.). (ENG.). 32p. (J). (gr. 4-4). pap. 8.99 *(978-0-7439-0577-0(6))* Shell Educational Publishing.
Herweck, Dona. A Day in the Life of a Cowhand, 1 vol. 2nd rev. ed. 2011. (Nonfiction Readers Ser.). (ENG.). 28p. (J). (gr. 3-3). pap. 8.99 *(978-1-4333-3649-2(9))* Teacher Created Materials, Inc.
—A Day in the Life of a Firefighter, 1 vol. 2nd rev. ed. 2011. (Nonfiction Readers Ser.). (ENG.). 28p. (J). (gr. 3-3). pap. 8.99 *(978-1-4333-3651-5(0))* Teacher Created Materials, Inc.
—George Washington, 1 vol. 2nd rev. ed. 2011. (Nonfiction Readers Ser.). (ENG.). 28p. (J). (gr. 2-2). pap. 6.99 *(978-1-4333-3640-9(5))* Teacher Created Materials, Inc.
—Martin Luther King Jr., 1 vol. 2nd rev. ed. 2011. (TIME for KIDS(r) Nonfiction Readers Ser.). (ENG.). 28p. (J). (gr. 2-2). pap. 6.99 *(978-1-4333-3641-6(3))* Teacher Created Materials, Inc.
—Susan B. Anthony, 1 vol. 2nd rev. ed. 2011. (Nonfiction Readers Ser.). (ENG.). 28p. (J). (gr. 2-2). pap. 6.99 *(978-1-4333-3642-3(1))* Teacher Created Materials, Inc.
Herwick Rice, Dona & Bradley, Kathleen. Reconstruction: After the Civil War, 1 vol. 2009. (Building Fluency Through Reader's Theater Ser.). (ENG.). 32p. (J). (gr. 3-5). pap. 7.99 *(978-1-4333-0547-4(X))* Teacher Created Materials, Inc.
Herwick Rice, Dona & Isecke, Harriet. The Sojourner Truth Story, 1 vol. 2009. (Building Fluency Through Reader's Theater Ser.). (ENG.). 32p. (J). (gr. 3-5). pap. 7.99 *(978-1-4333-0544-3(5))* Teacher Created Materials, Inc.
Herwick Rice, Dona & Paris, Stephanie. Sal Fink, 1 vol. 2009. (Building Fluency Through Reader's Theater Ser.). (ENG.). 24p. (J). (gr. 2-4). pap. 6.99 *(978-1-4333-0995-3(5))* Teacher Created Materials, Inc.
Herwick Rice, Dona & Sugarman, Dorothy. World War I: In Flanders Fields, 1 vol. 2009. (Building Fluency Through Reader's Theater Ser.). (ENG.). 32p. (J). (gr. 3-5). pap. 7.99 *(978-1-4333-0551-1(8))* Teacher Created Materials, Inc.
Herzog, Joyce. Excursion into Reading Reader: Part of the Little Beginner's Book Series. 2005. (J). spiral bd. 15.00 *(978-1-887225-36-6(6))* Herzog, Joyce.
Heskett, Tracie. Informational Reading, Grades 1-2. 2007. (ENG.). 144p. pap. 16.99 *(978-1-4206-8861-0(8))* Teacher Created Resources, Inc.
Hess, Debra. On Trial in Rome: Cicero Versus Caesr. 2007. (Read on! Special Edition: Level AA Ser.). (Illus.). 23p. pap. 18.51 *(978-1-4190-3517-3(7))* Steck-Vaughn.
Hetty Hackett's Farm: 3-in-1 Package. (Sails Literacy Ser.). 24p. (gr. k-18). 57.00 *(978-0-7578-3197-3(4))* Rigby Education.
Hewitt, Sally. Keeping Healthy, 8 vols. 2005. (QEB Readers). (Illus.). 24p. (J). (gr. -1-3). lib. bdg. 15.95 *(978-1-59566-071-8(2))* QEB Publishing Inc.
—The Spick-and-Span Fairy, 8 vols. 2005. (QEB Readers). (Illus.). 24p. (J). (gr. -1-3). lib. bdg. 15.95 *(978-1-59566-066-4(6))* QEB Publishing Inc.
—Where's My Shirt?, 8 vols. 2005. (QEB Readers). (Illus.). 24p. (J). (gr. -1-3). lib. bdg. 15.95 *(978-1-59566-067-1(4))* QEB Publishing Inc.
Hey, Kids! (10-lesson edition All-English version) Book 1 Student's Book (with CD) English Language Teaching. 2003. (Illus.). 112p. spiral bd. incl. audio compact disk *(978-0-7428-1051-8(8))* C C L S Publishing Hse.
Hey, Kids! (10-lesson edition All-English version) Book 2 Student's Book (with CD) English Language Teaching. 2003. (Illus.). 112p. spiral bd. incl. audio compact disk *(978-0-7428-1052-5(6))* C C L S Publishing Hse.
Heyer, Sandra. True Stories Behind the Songs. 2010. (ENG.). 112p. (C). pap. 37.32 *(978-0-13-246804-6(2))* Prentice Hall, ESL Dept.
Hicks, Diana & Littlejohn, Andrew. American English Primary Colors 2. 2003. (ENG., Illus.). 68p. pap., stu. ed. 16.25 *(978-0-521-53920-3(X))* Cambridge Univ. Pr.
Hide & Seek, 6 Packs. (Chiquilibros Ser.). (gr. k-1). 23.00 *(978-0-7635-0439-7(4))* Rigby Education.
Hiebert. Ready Readers Study Guide to the Big Book Collection. (J). (gr. -1-3). Vol. 1. 314.95 *(978-0-8136-1697-1(2))* Vol. 2. 2003. 422.95 *(978-0-8136-1698-8(0))* Modern Curriculum Pr.
Hiebert, Elfrieda H. Quickreads. 2005. (J). (gr. 2-6). stu. ed. 47.50 *(978-0-7652-4420-8(9));* Vol. 2. stu. ed. 47.50 *(978-0-7652-4422-2(5));* Vol. 3. stu. ed. 47.50 *(978-0-7652-4424-6(1))* Modern Curriculum Pr.
—Quickreads: Level B Macintosh Classroom Package. 2005. (J). (gr. 2-18). 1067.50 *(978-0-7652-5115-2(9))* Modern Curriculum Pr.
—Quickreads: Level B Windows Classroom Package. 2005. (J). (gr. 2-18). 1067.50 *(978-0-7652-5112-1(4))* Modern Curriculum Pr.
—Quickreads: Level C Macintosh Classroom Package. 2005. (J). (gr. 3-18). 1067.50 *(978-0-7652-5116-9(7))* Modern Curriculum Pr.
—Quickreads: Level C Windows Classroom Package. 2005. (J). (gr. 3-18). 1067.50 *(978-0-7652-5113-8(2))* Modern Curriculum Pr.
—Quickreads: Level D Macintosh Classroom Package. 2005. (J). (gr. 4-18). 1067.50 *(978-0-7652-5117-6(5))* Modern Curriculum Pr.
—Quickreads: Level D Windows Classroom Package. 2005. (J). (gr. 4-18). 1067.50 *(978-0-7652-5114-5(0))* Modern Curriculum Pr.
—Quickreads: Level E Complete Program. 2005. (J). (gr. 5-18). 351.95 *(978-0-7652-4427-7(6))* Modern Curriculum Pr.
—Quickreads: Macintosh Classroom Program. 2005. (J). (gr. 5-18). 1067.50 *(978-0-7652-6157-1(X))* Modern Curriculum Pr.
—Quickreads: Windows Classroom Program. 2005. (J). (gr. 5-18). 1067.50 *(978-0-7652-6158-8(8))* Modern Curriculum Pr.
Hiebert, Elfrieda H. & Juel, Connie. At the Track. (J). *(978-0-8136-2062-6(7))* Modern Curriculum Pr.
—The Best Birthday Mole Ever Had. (Little Book Practice Reader Ser.). (J). *(978-0-8136-0969-0(0))* Modern Curriculum Pr.
—The Bike That Spike Likes. (Little Book Practice Reader Ser.). (J). *(978-0-8136-0963-8(1))* Modern Curriculum Pr.
—Blastoff! (Little Book Practice Reader Ser.). (J). *(978-0-8136-0825-9(2))* Modern Curriculum Pr.
—Can a Cow Hop? (Little Book Practice Reader Ser.). (J). *(978-0-8136-0796-2(5))* Modern Curriculum Pr.
—The Fourth of July. (Little Book Practice Reader Ser.). (J). *(978-0-8136-0977-5(1))* Modern Curriculum Pr.
—Haddie's Caps. (Little Book Practice Reader Ser.). (J). *(978-0-8136-0786-3(8))* Modern Curriculum Pr.
—Let's Move! (Little Book Practice Reader Ser.). (J). *(978-0-8136-0685-9(3))* Modern Curriculum Pr.
—Little Frog's Monster Story. (Little Book Practice Reader Ser.). (J). *(978-0-8136-0807-5(4))* Modern Curriculum Pr.
—Looking for Angus. (Little Book Practice Reader Ser.). (J). *(978-0-8136-0817-4(1))* Modern Curriculum Pr.
—My Hamster, Van. (Little Book Practice Reader Ser.). (J). *(978-0-8136-0790-0(6))* Modern Curriculum Pr.
—My Monster & Me. (Little Book Practice Reader). (J). *(978-0-8136-0677-4(2))* Modern Curriculum Pr.
—My Shadow. (Little Book Practice Reader Ser.). (J). *(978-0-8136-0827-3(9))* Modern Curriculum Pr.
—Nanny Goat's Nap. (Little Book Practice Reader Ser.). (J). *(978-0-8136-0692-7(6))* Modern Curriculum Pr.
—Night & Day. (Little Book Practice Reader Ser.). (J). *(978-0-8136-0813-6(9))* Modern Curriculum Pr.
—Night Animals. (Little Book Practice Reader Ser.). (J). *(978-0-8136-0744-3(2))* Modern Curriculum Pr.
—Pat's Perfect Pizza. (Little Book Practice Reader). (J). *(978-0-8136-1944-6(0));*Level 3, Bk. 14. (gr. -1-3). 24.50 *(978-0-8136-1945-3(9))* Modern Curriculum Pr.
—The River Grows. (Little Book Practice Reader Ser.). (J). *(978-0-8136-0815-0(5))* Modern Curriculum Pr.
—Sandy. (Little Book Practice Reader). (J). *(978-0-8136-1950-7(5))* Modern Curriculum Pr.
—Save That Trash. (Little Book Practice Reader Ser.). (J). *(978-0-8136-0943-0(7))* Modern Curriculum Pr.
—Six Fine Fish. (Little Book Practice Reader Ser.). (J). *(978-0-8136-0877-8(5))* Modern Curriculum Pr.
—Six Go By. (Little Book Practice Reader Ser.). (J). *(978-0-8136-0674-3(8))* Modern Curriculum Pr.
—Sparky's Bone. (Little Book Practice Reader Ser.). (J). *(978-0-8136-0839-6(2))* Modern Curriculum Pr.
—Steve's Room. (Little Book Practice Reader Ser.). (J). *(978-0-8136-0959-1(3))* Modern Curriculum Pr.
—Stop That! (Little Book Practice Reader Ser.). (J). *(978-0-8136-0784-9(1))* Modern Curriculum Pr.
—Too High. (Little Book Practice Reader Ser.). (J). *(978-0-8136-0776-4(0))* Modern Curriculum Pr.
—Too Much Ketchup. (Little Book Practice Reader Ser.). (J). *(978-0-8136-0748-1(5))* Modern Curriculum Pr.
—The Trip. (Little Book Practice Reader Ser.). (J). *(978-0-8136-0792-4(2))* Modern Curriculum Pr.
—We Are Singing. (Little Book Practice Reader Ser.). (J). 6.47 *(978-0-8136-0678-1(0))* Modern Curriculum Pr.
—When I Go See Gram. (Little Book Practice Reader Ser.). (J). *(978-0-8136-0953-9(4))* Modern Curriculum Pr.
—When We Are Big. (Little Book Practice Reader Ser.). (J). *(978-0-8136-0833-4(3))* Modern Curriculum Pr.
—Where Does the Rabbit Hop? (Little Book Practice Reader Ser.). (J). *(978-0-8136-0794-8(9))* Modern Curriculum Pr.
—Where Is the Queen? (Little Book Practice Reader Ser.). (J). *(978-0-8136-0829-7(5))* Modern Curriculum Pr.
—Who Came Out? (Little Book Practice Reader Ser.). (J). *(978-0-8136-0765-8(5))* Modern Curriculum Pr.
—Who Has a Tail? (Little Book Practice Reader Ser.). (J). *(978-0-8136-0975-1(5))* Modern Curriculum Pr.
—Who Is Ready? (Little Book Practice Reader Ser.). (J). *(978-0-8136-0683-5(7))* Modern Curriculum Pr.
Higginson, Sheila Sweeny. Diego rescata al bebé manatí (Diego's Manatee Rescue) McGee, Warner, illus. 2009. (Go, Diego, Go! Ser.). (SPA.). 24p. (J). pap. 3.99 *(978-1-4169-7983-8(2),* Libros Para Ninos) Libros Para Ninos.
High Five Reading - Purple, Set II. 2004. (High Five Reading - Purple Ser.). (ENG.). (gr. 3-4). pap. 45.00 *(978-0-7368-3864-1(3),* High Five Reading (RBL)) Capstone Press of Coughlan Cos.
High Five USA Reading, Green Level I. (gr. 4-18). 250.95 incl. audio *(978-0-7368-9570-5(1),* High Five) Red Brick Learning.

P Q R

High Five USA Reading, Green Level II. (gr. 4-18). 250.95 incl. audio (978-0-7368-2860-4(5), High Five) Red Brick Learning.

High Five USA Reading, Purple Level I. (gr. 4-18). 250.95 incl. audio (978-0-7368-9516-3(7), High Five) Red Brick Learning.

High Five USA Reading, Purple Level II. (gr. 4-18). 250.95 incl. audio (978-0-7368-3863-4(5), High Five) Red Brick Learning.

High Five USA Reading, Red Level I. (gr. 4-18). 250.95 incl. audio (978-0-7368-9544-6(2), High Five) Red Brick Learning.

High Five USA Reading, Red Level II. (gr. 4-18). 250.95 incl. audio (978-0-7368-2855-0(9), High Five) Red Brick Learning.

High Point. (High Point Ser.). (gr. 6-12). 7.52 (978-0-7362-0935-9(2)); 57.61 (978-0-7362-0969-4(7)); 7.52 (978-0-7362-0967-0(0)); tchr. ed. 33.37 (978-0-7362-0949-6(2)); tchr. ed. 33.37 (978-0-7362-0981-6(6)); suppl. ed. 57.61 (978-0-7362-0937-3(9)); tchr.'s assessmt. gde. ed. 27.50 (978-0-7362-0950-2(6)); instr.'s hndbk. ed. 27.50 (978-0-7362-0982-3(4)); tchr. ed. 14.19 (978-0-7362-0968-7(9)); tchr. ed. 14.19 (978-0-7362-0936-6(0)) CENGAGE Learning.

High Point: Decodable Stories Set, 18 vols. (Reading Basics Ser.). (gr. 3-12). 8.31 (978-0-7362-1553-4(0)) CENGAGE Learning.

High Point: Reading Basics Package. (gr. 6-12). 160.56 (978-0-7362-1286-1(8)) CENGAGE Learning.

High Point: The Basics Bookshelf, 6 vols. (gr. 6-12). 443.72 (978-0-7362-1278-6(7)); 487.59 incl. audio compact disk (978-0-7362-1279-3(5)); 531.44 incl. reel tape (978-0-7362-1280-9(9)) CENGAGE Learning.

High Point Diagnosis & Placement Inventory: Test Booklets (10-pack) 19.90 (978-0-7362-2345-4(2)) CENGAGE Learning.

A High Point Level: The Basics Bookshelf with Teacher's Guide, 6 vols. (High Point Ser.). (gr. 6-12). tchr. ed. 459.28 (978-0-7362-1281-6(7)) CENGAGE Learning.

Hileman, Jane & Pitt, Marilyn. I Love to Sleep. Bianchi, John, illus. 2009. (1G Potato Chip Bks.). (ENG.). 12p. (J). (gr. k-1). pap. 5.99 (978-1-59301-797-2(9)) American Reading Co.

—I Want a Dog. Bianchi, John, illus. 2009. (1G Potato Chip Bks.). (ENG.). 12p. (J). (gr. k-1). pap. 5.99 (978-1-59301-768-2(5)) American Reading Co.

—Time for a Bath. Bianchi, John, illus. 2009. (1G Potato Chip Bks.). (ENG.). 12p. (J). (gr. k-1). pap. 5.99 (978-1-59301-772-9(3)) American Reading Co.

—You Can't Have It! Bianchi, John, illus. 2009. (1G Potato Chip Bks.). (ENG.). 12p. (J). (gr. k-1). pap. 5.99 (978-1-59301-767-5(7)) American Reading Co.

Hill, Oriah. My Day at the Library. 2012. 16p. pap. 15.99 (978-1-4772-7954-0(7)) AuthorHouse.

Hill, Susan & Sewell, Anna. Black Beauty & the Thunderstorm. Farnsworth, Bill, illus. 2011. (My Readers Ser.). (ENG.). 48p. (J). (gr. 1-3). pap. 3.99 (978-0-312-64721-6(2), 9780312647216) Square Fish.

Hill, Susanna Leonard. Freight Train Trip! A Lift-the-Flap Adventure. Larrañaga, Ana Martín, illus. 2009. (ENG.). 12p. (J). (gr. -1-k). bds. 7.99 (978-1-4169-7833-6(X), Little Simon) Little Simon.

Hillert, Margaret. Dear Dragon Learns to Read. Pullan, Jack, illus. 2015. (BeginningtoRead Ser.). (ENG.). 32p. (J). (gr. k-2). pap. 11.94 (978-1-60357-792-2(0)) Norwood Hse. Pr.

—I Can Do It: For the Earliest Reader. Starfall Education, illus. 2006. (ENG.). 32p. (J). (978-1-59577-039-4(9)); pap. (978-1-59577-040-0(2)) Starfall Education.

—Not Too Little to Help, 5 bks. Starfall Education, illus. 2005. (ENG.). 32p. (J). 6.95 (978-1-59577-026-4(7)); pap. (978-1-59577-027-1(5)) Starfall Education.

—Penguin, Penguin: For the Earliest Reader, 5 bks. 2005. (ENG., Illus.). 32p. (J). 6.95 (978-1-59577-020-2(8)); pap. (978-1-59577-021-9(6)) Starfall Education.

—Pumpkin, Pumpkin: For the Earliest Reader. Starfall Education, photos by. 2006. (ENG., Illus.). 32p. (J). (978-1-59577-035-6(6)); pap. (978-1-59577-036-3(4)) Starfall Education.

—Three Little Plays, 5 bks. Starfall Education, illus. 2005. (ENG.). 32p. (J). 6.95 (978-1-59577-018-9(6)); pap. (978-1-59577-019-6(4)) Starfall Education.

The History Nook. (Early Intervention Levels Ser.). 31.86 (978-0-7362-0663-1(9)) CENGAGE Learning.

The History Nook (30), Vol. 30. (Early Intervention Levels Ser.). 5.31 (978-0-7362-0651-8(5)) CENGAGE Learning.

The History of Guitars: Fourth Grade Guided Comprehension Level N. (On Our Way to English Ser.). (gr. 4-18). 34.50 (978-0-7578-7164-1(X)) Rigby Education.

Hobbs, Ruth & Miller, Lester, contrib. by. A Time to Plant. 2005. (Rod & Staff's Readers Ser.). (Illus.). 256p. (gr. 5-18). 10.85 (978-0-7399-0405-3(1), 11501) Rod & Staff Pubs., Inc.

Hoberman, Mary Ann. You Read to Me, I'll Read to You: Very Short Fairy Tales to Read Together. 2012. (You Read to Me, I'll Read to You Ser.). (ENG., Illus.). 32p. (J). (gr. -1-3). pap. 6.99 (978-0-316-20744-7(6)) Little, Brown Bks. for Young Readers.

—You Read to Me, I'll Read to You: Very Short Fairy Tales to Read Together. Emberley, Michael, illus. 2004. (ENG.). 32p. (J). (gr. -1-3). 16.99 (978-0-316-14611-1(0)) Little, Brown Bks. for Young Readers.

The Hobyahs: 6 Small Books. (gr. k-1). 37.00 (978-0-7635-6246-5(7)) Rigby Education.

Hof, Marjolijn. Against the Odds, 1 vol. Prins, Johanna, tr. 2011.Tr. of Een Kleine Kans. (ENG.). 128p. (J). (gr. 3-7). pap. 8.95 (978-0-88899-950-4(X)) Groundwood Bks. CAN. Dist: Publishers Group West (PGW).

Hoff, Syd. Danny & the Dinosaur - Too Tall. Hoff, Syd, illus. 2015. (I Can Read Level 1 Ser.). (ENG., Illus.). 32p. (J). (gr. -1-3). pap. 3.99 (978-0-06-228155-5(0)) HarperCollins Pubs.

Hoffman, Mary. The Sword in the Stone. Ginevra, Dante, illus. 2014. (Collins Big Cat Progress Ser.). (ENG.). 32p. (J). (gr. 4-5). pap. 7.99 (978-0-00-751935-4(4)) HarperCollins Pubs. Ltd. GBR. Dist: Independent Pubs. Group.

Hoffman, Mary Ann. Elbert Takes a Trip. 2006. (Neighborhood Readers Ser.). (ENG., Illus.). 12p. (gr. 1-3). pap. 5.90 (978-1-4042-6847-0(2), Rosen Classroom) Rosen Publishing Group, Inc., The.

—Happy Birthday, Rita Raccoon! 2006. (Neighborhood Readers Ser.). (ENG.). 16p. (gr. 1-3). pap. 6.50 (978-1-4042-7140-1(6), Rosen Classroom) Rosen Publishing Group, Inc., The.

—The Maple Tree Mystery. (Neighborhood Readers Ser.). (ENG.). 16p. 2007. 37.95 (978-1-4042-7342-9(5)) 2006. (gr. 1-3). pap. 6.50 (978-1-4042-7220-0(8)) Rosen Publishing Group, Inc., The. (Rosen Classroom).

—The Missing Wheel. 2006. (Neighborhood Readers Ser.). (ENG.). 8p. (gr. -1-3). pap. 5.15 (978-1-4042-5668-2(7), Rosen Classroom) Rosen Publishing Group, Inc., The.

—El misterio en el árbol (the Maple Tree Mystery) 2007. (Lecturas del barrio (Neighborhood Readers) Ser.). (SPA.). 16p. 37.95 (978-1-4042-7343-6(3), Rosen Classroom) Rosen Publishing Group, Inc., The.

—Molly Makes a Milkshake. 2006. (Neighborhood Readers Ser.). (ENG.). 12p. (gr. -1-3). pap. 5.90 (978-1-4042-5768-9(3), Rosen Classroom) Rosen Publishing Group, Inc., The.

—A Parrot for Pam. 2006. (Neighborhood Readers Ser.). (ENG.). 8p. (gr. -1-3). pap. 5.15 (978-1-4042-5690-3(3), Rosen Classroom) Rosen Publishing Group, Inc., The.

—Piñata Party. 2006. (Neighborhood Readers Ser.). (ENG.). 8p. (gr. -1-3). pap. 5.15 (978-1-4042-5720-7(9), Rosen Classroom) Rosen Publishing Group, Inc., The.

Hoffman, Stephanie. Sharp Teeth, Flat Teeth. 2009. (Real Life Readers Ser.). 12p. (gr. 1-2). pap. 5.90 (978-1-4042-7917-9(2), Rosen Classroom) Rosen Publishing Group, Inc., The.

Hoffmann, Sara E. Ana & the Pet Show. Strange, Katie, illus. 2013. (My Reading Neighborhood: First-Grade Sight Word Stories Ser.). (ENG.). 16p. (gr. -1-1). pap. 5.95 (978-1-4677-1170-8(5)) Lerner Publishing Group.

—Ana & the Rainy Day. Strange, Katie, illus. 2013. (My Reading Neighborhood: First-Grade Sight Word Stories Ser.). (ENG.). 16p. (gr. -1-1). pap. 5.95 (978-1-4677-1174-6(8)) Lerner Publishing Group.

—Ben Gives a Gift. Dieterichs, Shelley, illus. 2013. (My Reading Neighborhood: Kindergarten Sight Word Stories Ser.). (ENG.). 16p. (gr. -1-1). pap. 5.95 (978-1-4677-1164-7(0)) Lerner Publishing Group.

—Fall Fun for Kit. Roraback, Robin, illus. 2013. (My Reading Neighborhood: Kindergarten Sight Word Stories Ser.). (ENG.). 16p. (gr. -1-1). pap. 5.95 (978-1-4677-1165-4(9)) Lerner Publishing Group.

—Holidays with Joe. Bueno, Lisa, illus. 2013. (My Reading Neighborhood: First-Grade Sight Word Stories Ser.). (ENG.). 16p. (gr. -1-1). pap. 5.95 (978-1-4677-1169-2(1)) Lerner Publishing Group.

—Nan Swims. Roraback, Robin, illus. 2013. (My Reading Neighborhood: Kindergarten Sight Word Stories Ser.). (ENG.). 16p. (gr. -1-1). pap. 5.95 (978-1-4677-1166-1(7)) Lerner Publishing Group.

—Nia Bakes Cookies. Strange, Katie, illus. 2013. (My Reading Neighborhood: First-Grade Sight Word Stories Ser.). (ENG.). 16p. (gr. -1-1). pap. 5.95 (978-1-4677-1172-2(1)) Lerner Publishing Group.

—A Party with Joe. Bueno, Lisa, illus. 2013. (My Reading Neighborhood: First-Grade Sight Word Stories Ser.). (ENG.). 16p. (gr. -1-1). pap. 5.95 (978-1-4677-1173-9(X)) Lerner Publishing Group.

—A Picnic with Kit. Roraback, Robin, illus. 2013. (My Reading Neighborhood: Kindergarten Sight Word Stories Ser.). (ENG.). 16p. (gr. -1-1). pap. 5.95 (978-1-4677-1168-5(3)) Lerner Publishing Group.

—School for Ken. Bueno, Lisa, illus. 2013. (My Reading Neighborhood: First-Grade Sight Word Stories Ser.). (ENG.). 16p. (gr. -1-1). pap. 5.95 (978-1-4677-1171-5(3)) Lerner Publishing Group.

Hofmeister, Alan, et al. Ann & Nan. (Reading for All Learners Ser.). (Illus.). (J). pap. (978-1-56861-085-6(8)) Swift Learning Resources.

—The Ant & the Bee. (Reading for All Learners Ser.). (Illus.). (J). pap. (978-1-56861-125-9(0)) Swift Learning Resources.

—The Bad Men. (Reading for All Learners Ser.). (Illus.). (J). pap. (978-1-56861-117-4(X)) Swift Learning Resources.

—The Bat Rat. (Reading for All Learners Ser.). (Illus.). (J). pap. (978-1-56861-119-8(6)) Swift Learning Resources.

—The Bee. (Reading for All Learners Ser.). (Illus.). (J). pap. (978-1-56861-124-2(2)) Swift Learning Resources.

—Ben the Ant. (Reading for All Learners Ser.). (Illus.). (J). pap. (978-1-56861-123-5(4)) Swift Learning Resources.

—Bud & the Tree. (Reading for All Learners Ser.). (Illus.). (J). pap. (978-1-56861-135-8(8)) Swift Learning Resources.

—The Bus. (Reading for All Learners Ser.). (Illus.). (J). pap. (978-1-56861-122-8(6)) Swift Learning Resources.

—Cartons & Clouds. (Reading for All Learners Ser.). (Illus.). (J). pap. (978-1-56861-195-2(1)) Swift Learning Resources.

—The Creatures of Loon. (Reading for All Learners Ser.). (Illus.). (J). pap. (978-1-56861-217-1(6)) Swift Learning Resources.

—Freckles & Forests. (Reading for All Learners Ser.). (Illus.). (J). pap. (978-1-56861-201-0(X)) Swift Learning Resources.

—The Fun Fish. (Reading for All Learners Ser.). (Illus.). (J). pap. (978-1-56861-121-1(8)) Swift Learning Resources.

—Fun with the Sheet. (Reading for All Learners Ser.). (Illus.). (J). pap. (978-1-56861-115-0(3)) Swift Learning Resources.

—The Hat. (Reading for All Learners Ser.). (Illus.). (J). pap. (978-1-56861-105-1(6)) Swift Learning Resources.

—I See Sam. (Reading for All Learners Ser.). (Illus.). (J). pap. (978-1-56861-073-3(4)) Swift Learning Resources.

—In a Tub. (Reading for All Learners Ser.). (Illus.). (J). pap. (978-1-56861-128-0(5)) Swift Learning Resources.

—In the Mud. (Reading for All Learners Ser.). (Illus.). (J). pap. (978-1-56861-127-3(7)) Swift Learning Resources.

—In the Tent. (Reading for All Learners Ser.). (Illus.). (J). pap. (978-1-56861-132-7(3)) Swift Learning Resources.

—It Is Ann. (Reading for All Learners Ser.). (Illus.). (J). pap. (978-1-56861-084-9(X)) Swift Learning Resources.

—The Mask. (Reading for All Learners Ser.). (Illus.). (J). pap. (978-1-56861-139-6(0)) Swift Learning Resources.

—Mat. (Reading for All Learners Ser.). (Illus.). (J). pap. (978-1-56861-077-1(7)) Swift Learning Resources.

—Mat & the Nut. (Reading for All Learners Ser.). (Illus.). (J). pap. (978-1-56861-109-9(9)) Swift Learning Resources.

—Mat at Bat. (Reading for All Learners Ser.). (Illus.). (J). pap. (978-1-56861-118-1(8)) Swift Learning Resources.

—Mat Did It. (Reading for All Learners Ser.). (Illus.). (J). pap. (978-1-56861-102-0(1)) Swift Learning Resources.

—Mat in the Hat. (Reading for All Learners Ser.). (Illus.). (J). pap. (978-1-56861-106-8(4)) Swift Learning Resources.

—Mat in the Sun. (Reading for All Learners Ser.). (Illus.). (J). pap. (978-1-56861-094-8(7)) Swift Learning Resources.

—Mat Is Wet. (Reading for All Learners Ser.). (Illus.). (J). pap. (978-1-56861-120-4(X)) Swift Learning Resources.

—Mat the Rat. (Reading for All Learners Ser.). (Illus.). (J). pap. (978-1-56861-111-2(0)) Swift Learning Resources.

—Meet Mit. (Reading for All Learners Ser.). (Illus.). (J). pap. (978-1-56861-079-5(3)) Swift Learning Resources.

—The Men. (Reading for All Learners Ser.). (Illus.). (J). pap. (978-1-56861-116-7(1)) Swift Learning Resources.

—Mit & the Weed. (Reading for All Learners Ser.). (Illus.). (J). pap. (978-1-56861-113-6(7)) Swift Learning Resources.

—Mit Is Wet. (Reading for All Learners Ser.). (Illus.). (J). pap. (978-1-56861-108-2(0)) Swift Learning Resources.

—Nan & the Man. (Reading for All Learners Ser.). (Illus.). (J). pap. (978-1-56861-086-3(6)) Swift Learning Resources.

—Nan Sits. (Reading for All Learners Ser.). (Illus.). (J). pap. (978-1-56861-092-4(0)) Swift Learning Resources.

—Nat. (Reading for All Learners Ser.). (Illus.). (J). pap. (978-1-56861-093-1(9)) Swift Learning Resources.

—Nell & Ed. (Reading for All Learners Ser.). (Illus.). (J). pap. (978-1-56861-097-9(1)) Swift Learning Resources.

—The Pond. (Reading for All Learners Ser.). (Illus.). (J). pap. (978-1-56861-131-0(5)) Swift Learning Resources.

—Ruff. (Reading for All Learners Ser.). (Illus.). (J). pap. (978-1-56861-137-2(4)) Swift Learning Resources.

—Run, Feet, Run. (Reading for All Learners Ser.). (Illus.). (J). pap. (978-1-56861-095-5(5)) Swift Learning Resources.

—Sam. (Reading for All Learners Ser.). (Illus.). (J). pap. (978-1-56861-074-0(2)) Swift Learning Resources.

—Sam Is Mad. (Reading for All Learners Ser.). (Illus.). (J). pap. (978-1-56861-087-0(4)) Swift Learning Resources.

—Sam Sat. (Reading for All Learners Ser.). (Illus.). (J). pap. (978-1-56861-083-2(1)) Swift Learning Resources.

—See It. (Reading for All Learners Ser.). (Illus.). (J). pap. (978-1-56861-080-1(7)) Swift Learning Resources.

—See Mat. (Reading for All Learners Ser.). (Illus.). (J). pap. (978-1-56861-078-8(5)) Swift Learning Resources.

—See Me. (Reading for All Learners Ser.). (Illus.). (J). pap. (978-1-56861-076-4(9)) Swift Learning Resources.

—See Sam. (Reading for All Learners Ser.). (Illus.). (J). pap. (978-1-56861-075-7(0)) Swift Learning Resources.

—See Them. (Reading for All Learners Ser.). (Illus.). (J). pap. (978-1-56861-107-5(2)) Swift Learning Resources.

—The Seed. (Reading for All Learners Ser.). (Illus.). (J). pap. (978-1-56861-112-9(9)) Swift Learning Resources.

—Sell the Shell. (Reading for All Learners Ser.). (Illus.). (J). pap. (978-1-56861-104-4(8)) Swift Learning Resources.

—The Shell. (Reading for All Learners Ser.). (Illus.). (J). pap. (978-1-56861-103-7(X)) Swift Learning Resources.

—The Ship. (Reading for All Learners Ser.). (Illus.). (J). pap. (978-1-56861-133-4(1)) Swift Learning Resources.

—Sid. (Reading for All Learners Ser.). (Illus.). (J). pap. (978-1-56861-088-7(2)) Swift Learning Resources.

—Sid & the Mess. (Reading for All Learners Ser.). (Illus.). (J). pap. (978-1-56861-090-0(4)) Swift Learning Resources.

—Sis. (Reading for All Learners Ser.). (Illus.). (J). pap. (978-1-56861-082-5(3)) Swift Learning Resources.

—Sis in a Mess. (Reading for All Learners Ser.). (Illus.). (J). pap. (978-1-56861-091-7(2)) Swift Learning Resources.

—Sis in the Well. (Reading for All Learners Ser.). (Illus.). (J). pap. (978-1-56861-098-6(X)) Swift Learning Resources.

—Sit on It. (Reading for All Learners Ser.). (Illus.). (J). pap. (978-1-56861-081-8(5)) Swift Learning Resources.

—Smash It. (Reading for All Learners Ser.). (Illus.). (J). (978-1-56861-136-5(6)) Swift Learning Resources.

—Swim with Us. (Reading for All Learners Ser.). (Illus.). (J). pap. (978-1-56861-140-2(4)) Swift Learning Resources.

—To the Den. (Reading for All Learners Ser.). (Illus.). (J). (978-1-56861-138-9(2)) Swift Learning Resources.

—A Trip. (Reading for All Learners Ser.). (Illus.). (J). pap. (978-1-56861-130-3(7)) Swift Learning Resources.

—Up the Path. (Reading for All Learners Ser.). (Illus.). (J). pap. (978-1-56861-134-1(X)) Swift Learning Resources.

—Up We Go. (Reading for All Learners Ser.). (Illus.). (J). pap. (978-1-56861-129-7(3)) Swift Learning Resources.

—Was It Wet? (Reading for All Learners Ser.). (Illus.). (J). pap. (978-1-56861-114-3(5)) Swift Learning Resources.

—We Will Run. (Reading for All Learners Ser.). (Illus.). (J). pap. (978-1-56861-099-3(8)) Swift Learning Resources.

—We Will See. (Reading for All Learners Ser.). (Illus.). (J). pap. (978-1-56861-089-4(0)) Swift Learning Resources.

—Who Am I? (Reading for All Learners Ser.). (Illus.). (J). pap. (978-1-56861-096-2(3)) Swift Learning Resources.

—Will We Win? (Reading for All Learners Ser.). (Illus.). (J). pap. (978-1-56861-110-5(2)) Swift Learning Resources.

Hohmeier, Marla. Amazingly Wonderful Things. Weber, Penny, illus. 2011. (ENG & SPA.). 32p. (J). (gr. -1-3). lib. bdg. 16.95 (978-1-936299-10-2(0), Raven Tree Pr.,Csi) Continental Sales, Inc.

Holden, Barry. The Milky Way BIG BOOK Edition. 2014. (ENG.). 16p. (gr. 2-2). Beta (978-1-77654-100-3(6), Red Rocket Readers) Flying Start Bks.

Holden, Pam. About Lighthouses. 2015. (ENG., Illus.). 16p. (-1). pap. (978-1-77654-077-8(8), Red Rocket Readers) Flying Start Bks.

—Animal Art, 6 vols. Storey, Jim, illus. 2009. (Red Rocket Readers Ser.). (ENG.). 16p. (gr. 1-1). pap. (978-1-877419-73-7(7), Red Rocket Readers) Flying Start Bks.

—Animal Defences. (ENG., Illus.). 16p. pap. **(978-1-77654-135-5(9)**, Red Rocket Readers) Flying Start Bks.

—Animal Defenses. 2015. (ENG., Illus.). 16p. (-1). pap. (978-1-77654-146-1(4), Red Rocket Readers) Flying Start Bks.

—Are You Hungry?, 6 pack. Hawley, Kelvin, illus. 2009. (Red Rocket Readers Ser.). (ENG.). 16p. (gr. -1-1). pap. (978-1-877363-23-8(5), Red Rocket Readers) Flying Start Bks.

—Baby Whale's Mistake, 6 pack. Aziz, Lamia, illus. 2009. (Red Rocket Readers Ser.). (ENG.). 16p. (gr. 2-2). pap. (978-1-877363-87-0(1)) Flying Start Bks.

—Balloons Fly By. 2015. (ENG., Illus.). 16p. (-1). pap. (978-1-77654-106-5(5), Red Rocket Readers) Flying Start Bks.

—Bear Gets Stuck. Whimp, Pauline, illus. 2015. (ENG.). 16p. (-1). pap. (978-1-77654-127-0(8), Red Rocket Readers) Flying Start Bks.

—The Big Bad Wolf, 6 pack. Hawley, Kelvin, illus. 2009. (Red Rocket Readers Ser.). (ENG.). 16p. (gr. 2-2). pap. (978-1-877363-56-6(1), Red Rocket Readers) Flying Start Bks.

—A Brave Girl. 2015. (ENG., Illus.). 16p. (-1). pap. (978-1-77654-105-8(7), Red Rocket Readers) Flying Start Bks.

—Bugs & Beetles. 2015. (ENG., Illus.). 16p. (-2). pap. (978-1-77654-137-9(5), Red Rocket Readers) Flying Start Bks.

—Caterpillar to Butterfly. 2015. (ENG., Illus.). 16p. (-1). pap. (978-1-77654-078-5(6), Red Rocket Readers) Flying Start Bks.

—Charlie to the Rescue. Hawley, Kelvin, illus. 2015. (ENG.). 16p. (-1). pap. (978-1-77654-128-7(6), Red Rocket Readers) Flying Start Bks.

—Close to Home - BIG BOOK. 2016. (ENG.). 16p. (-1). Beta (978-1-77654-161-4(8), Red Rocket Readers) Flying Start Bks.

—Cross the River. 2015. (ENG., Illus.). 16p. (-1). pap. (978-1-77654-107-2(3), Red Rocket Readers) Flying Start Bks.

—Dance, Dance, Dance!, 6 pack. 2009. (Red Rocket Readers Ser.). (ENG., Illus.). 16p. (gr. 1-1). pap. (978-1-877490-21-7(0)) Flying Start Bks.

—Dinosaur Hunters, 6 pack. Storey, Jim & Hawley, Kelvin, illus. 2009. (Red Rocket Readers Ser.). (ENG.). 16p. (gr. 2-2). pap. (978-1-877363-59-7(6), Red Rocket Readers) Flying Start Bks.

—Everyone Reads - BIG BOOK. Johnson, Deborah, illus. 2016. (ENG.). 16p. (-1). Beta (978-1-77654-162-1(6), Red Rocket Readers) Flying Start Bks.

—Farm Friends, 6 pack. Hawley, Kelvin, illus. 2009. (Red Rocket Readers Ser.). (ENG.). 16p. (gr. -1-1). pap. (978-1-877363-14-6(6), Red Rocket Readers) Flying Start Bks.

—Fire in the Jungle, 6 pack. Hatam, Samer, illus. 2009. (Red Rocket Readers Ser.). (ENG.). 16p. (gr. 2-2). pap. (978-1-877363-73-3(1)) Flying Start Bks.

—The Flying Monkey, 6 pack. East, Jacqueline, illus. 2009. (Red Rocket Readers Ser.). (ENG.). 16p. (gr. -1-1). pap. (978-1-877363-29-0(4), Red Rocket Readers) Flying Start Bks.

—From Tadpole to Frog. 2015. (ENG., Illus.). 16p. (-1). pap. (978-1-77654-142-3(1), Red Rocket Readers) Flying Start Bks.

—From Tadpole to Frog - BIG BOOK. 2016. (ENG.). 16p. (-1). Beta (978-1-77654-165-2(0), Red Rocket Readers) Flying Start Bks.

—Fruit for You, 6 pack. Cooper, Jenny, illus. 2009. (Red Rocket Readers Ser.). (ENG.). 16p. (gr. -1-1). pap. (978-1-877363-01-6(4), Red Rocket Readers) Flying Start Bks.

—Funny Races. Cashmore-Hingley, Michael, illus. 2015. (ENG.). 16p. (-2). pap. (978-1-77654-131-7(6), Red Rocket Readers) Flying Start Bks.

—The Gentle Giant, 6 pack. Hatam, Samer, illus. 2009. (Red Rocket Readers Ser.). (ENG.). 16p. (gr. 2-2). pap. (978-1-877363-81-8(2)) Flying Start Bks.

—Getting Clean. 2015. (ENG., Illus.). 16p. (-1). pap. (978-1-77654-108-9(1), Red Rocket Readers) Flying Start Bks.

—Going Up, 6 pack. Hawley, Kelvin, illus. 2009. (Red Rocket Readers Ser.). (ENG.). 16p. (gr. -1-1). pap. (978-1-877363-18-4(9), Red Rocket Readers) Flying Start Bks.

—Good Things from Trees. 2015. (ENG., Illus.). 16p. (-1). pap. (978-1-77654-079-2(4), Red Rocket Readers) Flying Start Bks.

—Greedy Gus the Pirate, 6 pack. Whimp, Pauline, illus. 2009. (Red Rocket Readers Ser.). (ENG.). 16p. (gr. 2-2). pap. (978-1-877363-74-0(X)) Flying Start Bks.

—Happy Birthday, 6 pack. Hawley, Kelvin, illus. 2009. (Red Rocket Readers Ser.). (ENG.). 16p. (gr. -1-1). pap. (978-1-877363-03-0(0), Red Rocket Readers) Flying Start Bks.

—Having Fun. 2015. (ENG., Illus.). 16p. (-1). pap. (978-1-77654-109-6(X), Red Rocket Readers) Flying Start Bks.

—How Many Legs. 2015. (ENG., Illus.). 16p. (-1). pap. (978-1-77654-110-2(3), Red Rocket Readers) Flying Start Bks.

—Huff & Puff!, 6 pack. Storey, Jim, illus. 2009. (Red Rocket Readers Ser.). (ENG.). 16p. (gr. 2-2). pap. (978-1-877363-58-0(8), Red Rocket Readers) Flying Start Bks.

—Hunting for Treasure, 6 pack. Whimp, Pauline, illus. 2009. (Red Rocket Readers Ser.). (ENG.). 16p. (gr. 2-2). pap. (978-1-877363-65-8(0), Red Rocket Readers) Flying Start Bks.

—I Like to Paint, 8, Set. 2009. (Red Rocket Readers Ser.). (ENG., Illus.). 16p. (gr. -1-1). pap. (978-1-877435-97-3(X)) Flying Start Bks.

—Jobs People Do Big Book Edition. 2014. (ENG.). 16p. (gr. 1-1). Beta (978-1-77654-046-4(8), Red Rocket Readers) Flying Start Bks.

—Keeping Safe. 2015. (ENG., Illus.). 16p. (-2). pap. (978-1-77654-139-3(1), Red Rocket Readers) Flying Start Bks.

—King of the Zoo, 6 pack. Cammell, Sandra, illus. 2009. (Red Rocket Readers Ser.). (ENG.). 16p. (gr. -1-1). pap. (978-1-877363-13-9(8), Red Rocket Readers) Flying Start Bks.

—Knock, Knock!, 6 pack. Hoit, Richard, illus. 2009. (Red Rocket Readers Ser.). (ENG.). 16p. (gr. 2-2). pap. (978-1-877363-60-3(X), Red Rocket Readers) Flying Start Bks.

—Learn about Birds. 2015. (ENG., Illus.). 16p. (-1). pap. (978-1-77654-080-8(8), Red Rocket Readers) Flying Start Bks.

—Learning to Swim. 2015. (ENG., Illus.). 16p. (-1). pap. *(978-1-77654-081-5(6)*, Red Rocket Readers) Flying Start Bks.

—Let's Play Ball, 6 pack. Webb, Philip, illus. 2009. (Red Rocket Readers Ser.). (ENG.). 16p. (gr. -1-1). pap. *(978-1-877363-17-7(0)*, Red Rocket Readers) Flying Start Bks.

—The Long, Long Ride, 6 pack. Storey, Jim, illus. 2009. (Red Rocket Readers Ser.). (ENG.). 16p. (gr. 2-2). pap. *(978-1-877363-76-4(6))* Flying Start Bks.

—Look at My Home, 6 vols. East, Jacqueline, illus. 2009. (Red Rocket Readers Ser.). (ENG.). 16p. (gr. -1-1). pap. *(978-1-877363-04-7(9)*, Red Rocket Readers) Flying Start Bks.

—Look in the Mirror. 2015. (ENG., Illus.). 16p. (-1). pap. *(978-1-77654-082-2(4)*, Red Rocket Readers) Flying Start Bks.

—Magic Stone Soup. 2015. (ENG., Illus.). 16p. (-1). pap. *(978-1-77654-075-4(1)*, Red Rocket Readers) Flying Start Bks.

—The Mailbox Man. 2015. (ENG., Illus.). 16p. (-1). pap. *(978-1-77654-071-6(9)*, Red Rocket Readers) Flying Start Bks.

—Masks, 6 pack. 2009. (Red Rocket Readers Ser.). (ENG., Illus.). 16p. (gr. 1-1). pap. *(978-1-877490-19-4(9))* Flying Start Bks.

—Max Monkey, 6 pack. East, Jacqueline, illus. 2009. (Red Rocket Readers Ser.). (ENG.). 16p. (gr. -1-1). pap. *(978-1-877363-24-5(3)*, Red Rocket Readers) Flying Start Bks.

—Message from Camp, 6 pack. Webb, Philip, illus. 2009. (Red Rocket Readers Ser.). (ENG.). 16p. (gr. 2-2). pap. *(978-1-877363-64-1(2)*, Red Rocket Readers) Flying Start Bks.

—My Hands, 6 pack. Hawley, Kelvin, illus. 2009. (Red Rocket Readers Ser.). (ENG.). 16p. (gr. -1-1). pap. *(978-1-877363-25-2(1)*, Red Rocket Readers) Flying Start Bks.

—Naughty Goldilocks, 6 pack. Hoit, Richard, illus. 2009. (Red Rocket Readers Ser.). (ENG.). 16p. (gr. -1-1). pap. *(978-1-877363-08-5(1)*, Red Rocket Readers) Flying Start Bks.

—Noisy Traffic. 2015. (ENG., Illus.). 16p. (-1). pap. *(978-1-77654-111-9(1)*, Red Rocket Readers) Flying Start Bks.

—On the Outside - BIG BOOK. 2016. (ENG.). 16p. (-1). Beta *(978-1-77654-163-8(4)*, Red Rocket Readers) Flying Start Bks.

—Our Puppet Show. 2015. (ENG., Illus.). 16p. (-1). pap. *(978-1-77654-072-3(7)*, Red Rocket Readers) Flying Start Bks.

—Paper Chains, 6 pack. 2009. (Red Rocket Readers Ser.). (ENG., Illus.). 16p. (gr. 2-2). pap. *(978-1-877435-43-0(0))* Flying Start Bks.

—The Paper Trail, 6 pack. Hawley, Kelvin, illus. 2009. (Red Rocket Readers Ser.). (ENG.). 16p. (gr. 2-2). pap. *(978-1-877363-69-6(3))* Flying Start Bks.

—Pass It On, 6 pack. Hawley, Kelvin, illus. 2009. (Red Rocket Readers Ser.). (ENG.). 16p. (gr. 2-2). pap. *(978-1-877363-66-5(9)*, Red Rocket Readers) Flying Start Bks.

—Paulo the Pilot, 6 pack. Whimp, Pauline, illus. 2009. (Red Rocket Readers Ser.). (ENG.). 16p. (gr. 2-2). pap. *(978-1-877363-67-2(7)*, Red Rocket Readers) Flying Start Bks.

—Pin the Tail on the Donkey, 6 pack. Hawley, Kelvin, illus. 2009. (Red Rocket Readers Ser.). (ENG.). 16p. pap. *(978-1-877363-78-8(2))* Flying Start Bks.

—Presents for Grace, 6 pack. Hawley, Kelvin, illus. 2009. (Red Rocket Readers Ser.). (ENG.). 16p. (gr. 2-2). pap. *(978-1-877363-61-0(8)*, Red Rocket Readers) Flying Start Bks.

—A Quick Picnic, 6 pack. Ross, Christine, illus. 2009. (Red Rocket Readers Ser.). (ENG.). 16p. (gr. -1-1). pap. *(978-1-877363-22-1(7)*, Red Rocket Readers) Flying Start Bks.

—The Rainbow Party, 6 pack. Whimp, Pauline, illus. 2009. (Red Rocket Readers Ser.). (ENG.). 16p. pap. *(978-1-877363-82-5(0))* Flying Start Bks.

—Red Riding Hood, 6 pack. Hawley, Kelvin, illus. 2009. (Red Rocket Readers Ser.). (ENG.). 16p. (gr. -1-1). pap. *(978-1-877363-09-2(X)*, Red Rocket Readers) Flying Start Bks.

—Ringing Bells. 2015. (ENG., Illus.). 16p. (-1). pap. *(978-1-77654-083-9(2)*, Red Rocket Readers) Flying Start Bks.

—Sally Snip Snap's Party, 6 pack. Storey, Jim, illus. 2009. (Red Rocket Readers Ser.). (ENG.). 16p. (gr. 2-1). pap. *(978-1-877363-57-3(X)*, Red Rocket Readers) Flying Start Bks.

—See Me Ride, 6 pack. East, Jacqueline, illus. 2009. (Red Rocket Readers Ser.). (ENG.). 16p. (gr. -1-1). pap. *(978-1-877363-30-6(8)*, Red Rocket Readers) Flying Start Bks.

—Show Me a Shape, 6 pack. Cooper, Jenny, illus. 2009. (Red Rocket Readers Ser.). (ENG.). 16p. (gr. -1-1). pap. *(978-1-877363-27-6(8)*, Red Rocket Readers) Flying Start Bks.

—Sneaky Spider, 6 pack. Storey, Jim, illus. 2009. (Red Rocket Readers Ser.). (ENG.). 16p. (gr. 2-2). pap. *(978-1-877363-83-2(9))* Flying Start Bks.

—So Fast, 6 pack. Webb, Philip, illus. 2009. (Red Rocket Readers Ser.). (ENG.). 16p. (gr. -1-1). pap. *(978-1-877363-20-7(0)*, Red Rocket Readers) Flying Start Bks.

—Stickybeak the Parrot, 6 pack. East, Jacqueline, illus. 2009. (Red Rocket Readers Ser.). (ENG.). 16p. (gr. -1-1). pap. *(978-1-877363-28-3(6)*, Red Rocket Readers) Flying Start Bks.

—Stone Soup, 6 pack. Hawley, Kelvin, illus. 2009. (Red Rocket Readers Ser.). (ENG.). 16p. (gr. 2-2). pap. *(978-1-877363-84-9(7))* Flying Start Bks.

—Surprise from the Sky, 6 pack. Whimp, Pauline, illus. 2009. (Red Rocket Readers Ser.). (ENG.). 16p. (gr. 2-1). pap. *(978-1-877363-68-9(5))* Flying Start Bks.

—The Surprise Visitor, 6 pack. Hoit, Richard, illus. 2009. (Red Rocket Readers Ser.). (ENG.). 16p. (gr. 2-2). pap. *(978-1-877363-85-6(5))* Flying Start Bks.

—Thirsty Baby Elephant. 2015. (ENG., Illus.). 16p. (-1). pap. *(978-1-77654-076-1(X)*, Red Rocket Readers) Flying Start Bks.

—Three Billy Goats Gruff, 6 pack. Hawley, Kelvin, illus. 2009. (Red Rocket Readers Ser.). (ENG.). 16p. (gr. -1-1). pap. *(978-1-877363-10-8(3)*, Red Rocket Readers) Flying Start Bks.

—Three Little Pigs, 6 pack. Storey, Jim, illus. 2009. (Red Rocket Readers Ser.). (ENG.). 16p. (gr. -1-1). pap. *(978-1-877363-11-5(1)*, Red Rocket Readers) Flying Start Bks.

—Tin Lizzy, 6 pack. Hawley, Kelvin, illus. 2009. (Red Rocket Readers Ser.). (ENG.). 16p. (gr. 2-2). pap. *(978-1-877363-86-3(3))* Flying Start Bks.

—Too Big & Heavy, 6 pack. Hatam, Samer, illus. 2009. (Red Rocket Readers Ser.). (ENG.). 16p. (gr. 2-2). pap. *(978-1-877363-70-2(7))* Flying Start Bks.

—Toys That Can Go, 6 pack. 2009. (Red Rocket Readers Ser.). (ENG., Illus.). 16p. (gr. -1-1). pap. *(978-1-877435-93-5(7))* Flying Start Bks.

—Trip, Trap!, 6 pack. Hawley, Kelvin, illus. 2009. (Red Rocket Readers Ser.). (ENG.). 16p. (gr. 2-2). pap. *(978-1-877363-62-7(6)*, Red Rocket Readers) Flying Start Bks.

—Trip Trap - BIG BOOK. 2016. (ENG.). 16p. (-2). Beta *(978-1-77654-166-9(9)*, Red Rocket Readers) Flying Start Bks.

—Turtle Is Lost. 2015. (ENG., Illus.). 16p. (-1). pap. *(978-1-77654-074-7(3)*, Red Rocket Readers) Flying Start Bks.

—Two Pirates, 6 pack. Whimp, Pauline, illus. 2009. (Red Rocket Readers Ser.). (ENG.). 16p. (gr. 2-2). pap. *(978-1-877363-71-9(5))* Flying Start Bks.

—The Ugly Troll. Hawley, Kelvin, illus. 2017. 16p. (J). pap. ***(978-1-77654-191-1(X)***, Red Rocket Readers) Flying Start Bks.

—Umbrellas Go Up. 2015. (ENG., Illus.). 16p. (-1). pap. *(978-1-77654-073-0(5)*, Red Rocket Readers) Flying Start Bks.

—Watch Me Swim, 6 pack. Hansen, Christine, illus. 2009. (Red Rocket Readers Ser.). (ENG.). 16p. (gr. -1-1). pap. *(978-1-877363-31-3(6)*, Red Rocket Readers) Flying Start Bks.

—Watch Out for Whales, 6 pack. Aziz, Lamia, illus. 2009. (Red Rocket Readers Ser.). (ENG.). 16p. (gr. 2-2). pap. *(978-1-877363-63-4(4)*, Red Rocket Readers) Flying Start Bks.

—Watch the Ball, 6 pack. Whimp, Pauline, illus. 2009. (Red Rocket Readers Ser.). (ENG.). 16p. (gr. 2-2). pap. *(978-1-877363-80-1(4))* Flying Start Bks.

—Water from Rain. 2015. (ENG., Illus.). 16p. (-1). pap. *(978-1-77654-084-6(0)*, Red Rocket Readers) Flying Start Bks.

—Whale Rescue, 6 pack. Aziz, Lamia, illus. 2009. (Red Rocket Readers Ser.). (ENG.). 16p. (gr. 2-2). pap. *(978-1-877363-79-5(0))* Flying Start Bks.

—When I Grow Up. East, Jacqueline, illus. 2009. (Red Rocket Readers Ser.). (ENG.). 16p. (gr. -1-1). pap. *(978-1-877363-06-1(5)*, Red Rocket Readers) Flying Start Bks.

—Who Swims Here. 2015. (ENG., Illus.). 16p. (-1). pap. *(978-1-77654-112-6(X)*, Red Rocket Readers) Flying Start Bks.

—Who Wins the Race? 2015. (ENG., Illus.). 16p. (-1). pap. *(978-1-77654-070-9(0)*, Red Rocket Readers) Flying Start Bks.

Holden, Pam & Aesop. Clever Crow. Hatam, Samer, illus. (ENG.). 24p. (gr. 3-3). pap. *(978-1-927197-34-9(1)*, Red Rocket Readers) Flying Start Bks.

The Hole in the Hill: Individual Title Six-Packs. (Action Packs Ser.). 104p. (gr. 3-5). 44.00 *(978-0-7635-2993-2(1))* Rigby Education.

Holland, Karen. The Garden Gang. 2010. (Illus.). 32p. pap. 12.99 *(978-1-4490-6532-4(5))* AuthorHouse.

Hollenbeck, Kathleen M. Fluency Practice Mini-Books: 15 Short, Leveled Fiction & Nonfiction Mini-Books with Research-Based Strategies to Help Students Build Word Recognition, Fluency, & Comprehension. 2005. (Best Practices in Action Ser.). (ENG., Illus.). 80p. (gr. 1). per. 12.99 *(978-0-439-55416-9(0))*; (gr. 2). per. 12.99 *(978-0-439-55417-6(9))* Scholastic, Inc. (Teaching Resources).

Holliday, Patricia. I Look in the Mirror. 2005. 17p. (J). 10.52 *(978-1-4116-4656-8(8))* Lulu Pr., Inc.

—You & me makes Two. 2008. 32p. pap. 17.35 *(978-1-4357-5321-1(6))* Lulu Pr., Inc.

Hollingsworth, Tamara. Anne Frank: A Light in the Dark, 1 vol. 2nd rev. ed. 2012. (TIME for KIDS(r) Nonfiction Readers Ser.). (ENG.). 48p. (J). (gr. 4-4). pap. 9.99 *(978-1-4333-4865-5(9))* Teacher Created Materials, Inc.

—Helen Keller: A New Vision, 1 vol. 2nd rev. ed. 2012. (Nonfiction Readers Ser.). (ENG.). 48p. (J). (gr. 4-4). pap. 9.99 *(978-1-4333-4863-1(2))* Teacher Created Materials, Inc.

—Martin Luther: A Reforming Spirit, 1 vol. 2012. (Primary Source Readers Ser.). (ENG.). 32p. (J). (gr. 4-4). pap. 8.99 *(978-1-4333-5010-8(6))* Teacher Created Materials, Inc.

—Nelson Mandela: Leading the Way, 1 vol. 2nd rev. ed. 2012. (Nonfiction Readers Ser.). (ENG., Illus.). 48p. (J). (gr. 4-4). pap. 9.99 *(978-1-4333-4864-8(0))* Teacher Created Materials, Inc.

—The Reformation: A Religious Revolution, 1 vol. 2012. (Primary Source Readers Ser.). (ENG.). 32p. (J). (gr. 5-5). pap. 8.99 *(978-1-4333-5009-2(2))* Teacher Created Materials, Inc.

—Unforgettable Catastrophes, 1 vol. 2nd rev. ed. 2013. (Nonfiction Readers Ser.). (ENG.). 64p. (J). (gr. 5-5). pap. 10.99 *(978-1-4333-4946-1(9))* Teacher Created Materials, Inc.

—Unforgettable Natural Disasters, 1 vol. 2nd rev. ed. 2013. (Nonfiction Readers Ser.). (ENG.). 64p. (J). (gr. 5-5). pap. 10.99 *(978-1-4333-4944-7(2))* Teacher Created Materials, Inc.

—Unforgettable News Reports, 1 vol. 2nd rev. ed. 2013. (TIME for KIDS(r) Nonfiction Readers Ser.). (ENG., Illus.). 64p. (J). (gr. 5-5). pap. 10.99 *(978-1-4333-4945-4(0))* Teacher Created Materials, Inc.

Holmes, Quentin. Real Street Kidz: Art of Authenticity. 2011. 92p. (gr. 3-7). pap. 10.99 *(978-1-4575-0268-2(2))* Dog Ear Publishing, LLC.

HolmesKaren. SLOW MOTION: TAKING YOUR TIME HIGH BEGINNING BOOK WITH ONLINE ACCESS. 2014. (ENG., Illus.). 24p. (J). pap. 7.50 *(978-1-107-69129-2(X))* Cambridge Univ. Pr.

Holt, Rinehart and Winston Staff. Elemental Literature - Elements of Literature. 5th ed. 2003. (Elements of Literature Ser.). (ENG., Illus.). 160p. (gr. 6-6). pap. 17.15 *(978-0-03-035709-1(8))* Houghton Mifflin Harcourt Publishing Co.

—Elements of Literature: Adapted Reader. 5th ed. 2003. (Elements of Literature Ser.). (ENG., Illus.). 168p. (gr. 10-10). pap. 17.15 *(978-0-03-035458-8(7))* Houghton Mifflin Harcourt Publishing Co.

—Elements of Literature: Holt Adapted Reader. 5th ed. 2004. (Elements of Literature Ser.). (ENG.). 184p. (gr. 7-7). pap. 17.15 *(978-0-03-035711-4(X))* Houghton Mifflin Harcourt Publishing Co.

—Elements of Literature: Holt Reader. 5th ed. 2003. (Elements of Literature Ser.). (ENG., Illus.). 424p. (gr. 9-9). pap. 17.15 *(978-0-03-068393-0(9))* Houghton Mifflin Harcourt Publishing Co.

—Elements of Literature - Adapted Reader. 5th ed. 2003. (Elements of Literature Ser.). (ENG., Illus.). 184p. (gr. 12-12). pap. 17.15 *(978-0-03-035461-8(7))* Houghton Mifflin Harcourt Publishing Co.

—Elements of Literature - Holt Adapted Reader. 5th ed. 2003. (Elements of Literature Ser.). (ENG., Illus.). 208p. (gr. 11-11). pap. 17.15 *(978-0-03-035459-5(5))*; (gr. 9-9). pap. 17.15 *(978-0-03-035454-0(4))* Houghton Mifflin Harcourt Publishing Co.

—Elements of Literature 2005 - The Holt Reader. 5th ed. 2003. (Elements of Literature Ser.). (ENG., Illus.). 400p. (gr. 11-11). pap. 17.15 *(978-0-03-068396-1(3))* Houghton Mifflin Harcourt Publishing Co.

—Holt Adapted Reader. 5th ed. 2004. (Elements of Literature Ser.). (ENG., Illus.). 224p. (gr. 8-8). pap. 17.15 *(978-0-03-035712-1(8))* Houghton Mifflin Harcourt Publishing Co.

—Holt Reader. 5th ed. 2003. (Elements of Literature Ser.). (ENG., Illus.). 392p. (gr. 12-12). pap. 17.15 *(978-0-03-068397-8(1))*; 384p. (gr. 7-7). pap. 17.15 *(978-0-03-068391-6(2))* Houghton Mifflin Harcourt Publishing Co.

—The Holt Reader. 5th ed. 2003. (Elements of Literature Ser.). (ENG., Illus.). 368p. (gr. 8-8). pap. 17.15 *(978-0-03-068392-3(0))* Houghton Mifflin Harcourt Publishing Co.

—NY Strategy & Practice for Reading 2004: Science Spectrum. 4th ed. 2004. pap. 12.80 *(978-0-03-074164-7(5))* Holt McDougal.

—OH Strategy & Practice for Reading 2004: Science Spectrum. 2004. pap. 12.80 *(978-0-03-074168-5(8))* Holt McDougal.

—Reader Fourth Course. 4th ed. 2003. (Elements of Literature Ser.). (ENG., Illus.). 408p. (gr. 10-10). pap. 17.15 *(978-0-03-068394-7(7))* Houghton Mifflin Harcourt Publishing Co.

Holt, Sharon & Proudfoot, Dean. Don't Embarrass Me, Dad! 2008. (Rigby Focus Forward: Level H Ser.). (Illus.). 24p. (J). (gr. 4-7). pap. *(978-1-4190-3735-1(8)*, Rigby) Pearson Education Australia.

Holzer, Angela. Fat Freddy. Tucker, Barclay, illus. 2009. 36p. (J). lib. bdg. 8.99 *(978-0-9821563-4-6(0))* Good Sound Publishing.

—My Dog, Eddie. Funk, Debbie, illus. 2009. 36p. (J). lib. bdg. 8.99 *(978-0-9821563-5-3(9))* Good Sound Publishing.

Homberg, Ruth. Jewels for a Princess (Disney Princess) Random House Disney Staff, illus. 2012. (Step into Reading Ser.). (ENG.). 32p. (J). (gr. -1-1). pap. 3.99 *(978-0-7364-2908-5(5)*, RH/Disney) Random Hse. Children's Bks.

A Home: Individual Title Six-Packs. (Sails Literacy Ser.). 16p. (gr. k-18). 27.00 *(978-0-7635-4387-7(X))* Rigby Education.

A Home for Nellie. 2005. (Book Treks Ser.). (J). (gr. 3-18). stu. ed. 34.95 *(978-0-673-62849-7(3))* Celebration Pr.

Homes & Places. 2005. (Little Celebrations Thematic Packages Ser.). (J). (gr. k-3). 133.50 *(978-0-673-75385-4(9))* Celebration Pr.

Homework. 2004. (J). *(978-1-58453-216-3(5))* Pioneer Valley Bks.

Honders, Jamie. Our Community Helpers. 2012. (InfoMax Readers Ser.). (ENG., Illus.). 16 pp.p. (J). (gr. k-1). pap. 7.00 *(978-1-4488-8917-4(0)*, Rosen Classroom) Rosen Publishing Group, Inc., The.

Honest Abe. (Lexile Levels Ser.). 9.09 *(978-1-56334-706-1(7))* CENGAGE Learning.

The Honey Tree, 6 Packs. (Literatura 2000 Ser.). (gr. 2-3). 33.00 *(978-0-7635-0262-1(6))* Rigby Education.

Hook, Francis. Finding the Djinn. 2009. (Hodder African Readers Ser.). (Illus.). 112p. pap. 12.95 *(978-0-340-99029-2(5))* Hodder Education Group GBR. Dist: Trans-Atlantic Pubns., Inc.

Hoop Dancers. (Early Intervention Levels Ser.). 31.86 *(978-0-7362-0660-0(4))* CENGAGE Learning.

Hope, Anthony. Prisoner of Zenda: Reader, Pack. 2nd ed. 2016. (ENG.). x, 86p. (C). pap. 10.99 incl. cd-rom ***(978-1-4082-7649-5(6))*** Pearson Education.

Hopkins, Andy & Potter, Joc. Animals in Danger, Level 1. Lindop, Christine, ed. 3rd ed. 2008. (ENG., Illus.). 64p. pap. 9.38 *(978-0-19-423379-8(0))* Oxford Univ. Pr., Inc.

Hoppey, Tim. Pedro, the Pirate. Bonder, Dianna, illus. 2012. (ENG & SPA.). 32p. (J). lib. bdg. 16.95 *(978-1-936299-18-8(6)*, Raven Tree Pr.,Csi) Continental Sales, Inc.

Hord, Colleen. Itsy Bitsy Spider. Poole, Helen, illus. 2012. (ENG.). 24p. (gr. 1-2). pap. 8.95 *(978-1-61810-310-9(5))* Rourke Educational Media.

—Keep Your Chin Up. Dufalla, Anita, illus. 2012. (ENG.). 24p. (gr. 1-2). pap. 8.95 *(978-1-61810-315-4(6))* Rourke Educational Media.

—Who's Mr. Goldfluss? Poole, Helen, illus. 2012. (ENG.). 24p. (gr. 1-2). pap. 8.95 *(978-1-61810-318-5(0))* Rourke Educational Media.

Hoshino, Felicia. Sora & the Cloud. 2012. (JPN & ENG., Illus.). 36p. (J). (gr. -1-3). 15.95 *(978-1-59702-027-5(3))* Immedium.

Hotchkins, Dewayne. Family History. 2016. (Rosen REAL Readers: Social Studies Nonfiction / Fiction: Family, Community, & the World Ser.). 8p. (gr. 1-k). pap. 5.46 *(978-1-5081-2524-2(4)*, Rosen Classroom) Rosen Publishing Group, Inc., The.

—Farmer Jack's Farm Stand. 2016. (Rosen REAL Readers: Social Studies Nonfiction / Fiction: Family, Community, & the World Ser.). 8p. (gr. 1-k). pap. 5.46 *(978-1-5081-2509-9(0)*, Rosen Classroom) Rosen Publishing Group, Inc., The.

—Jayla Wins a Flag. 2016. (Rosen REAL Readers: Social Studies Nonfiction / Fiction: Family, Community, & the World Ser.). 8p. (gr. 1-k). pap. 5.46 *(978-1-5081-2473-3(6)*, Rosen Classroom) Rosen Publishing Group, Inc., The.

—The Polar Bear & the Glacier. 2016. (Rosen REAL Readers: STEM & STEAM Collection). 12p. (gr. 1-k). pap. 6.33 *(978-1-5081-2682-9(8)*, Rosen Classroom) Rosen Publishing Group, Inc., The.

—We Buy Vegetables from Mr. Owens. 2016. (Rosen REAL Readers: Social Studies Nonfiction / Fiction: Family, Community, & the World Ser.). 8p. (gr. 1-k). pap. 5.46 *(978-1-5081-2293-7(8)*, Rosen Classroom) Rosen Publishing Group, Inc., The.

A House: Individual Title Six-Packs. (Sails Literacy Ser.). 16p. (gr. k-18). 27.00 *(978-0-7635-4425-6(6))* Rigby Education.

House, Catherine. Hanan the Peanut Seller. 2004. (Illus.). 31p. *(978-0-636-06419-5(0))* Maskew Miller Longman.

A House for Sergin: Six-Pack. (Greetings Ser.: Vol. 2). 24p. (gr. 2-3). 31.00 *(978-0-7635-9427-5(X))* Rigby Education.

Housel, Debra J. Immigration, 1 vol. 2007. (Primary Source Readers Ser.). (ENG.). 32p. (J). (gr. 5-5). pap. 8.99 *(978-0-7439-0662-3(4))* Shell Educational Publishing.

—Incredible Invertebrates, 1 vol. 2nd rev. ed. 2011. (Nonfiction Readers Ser.). (ENG.). 28p. (J). (gr. 3-3). pap. 8.99 *(978-1-4333-3660-7(X))* Teacher Created Materials, Inc.

—Industrial Giants, 1 vol. 2007. (Primary Source Readers Ser.). (ENG.). 32p. (J). (gr. 4-4). pap. 8.99 *(978-0-7439-0661-6(6))* Shell Educational Publishing.

—Industrial Revolution, 1 vol. 2007. (Primary Source Readers Ser.). (ENG.). 32p. (J). (gr. 5-5). pap. 8.99 *(978-0-7439-0660-9(8))* Shell Educational Publishing.

—Inside Ecosystems & Biomes, 1 vol. 2007. (Science Readers Ser.). (ENG., Illus.). 32p. (J). (gr. 4-4). pap. 8.99 *(978-0-7439-0591-6(1))* Shell Educational Publishing.

—Mammal Mania, 1 vol. 2nd rev. ed. 2011. (Nonfiction Readers Ser.). (ENG.). 28p. (J). (gr. 3-3). pap. 8.99 *(978-1-4333-3658-4(8))* Teacher Created Materials, Inc.

—Pioneering Ecologists, 1 vol. 2007. (Science Readers Ser.). (SPA & ENG.). 32p. (J). (gr. 3-3). pap. 8.99 *(978-0-7439-0592-3(X))* Shell Educational Publishing.

—Slithering Reptiles & Amphibians, 1 vol. 2nd rev. ed. 2011. (Nonfiction Readers Ser.). (ENG.). 28p. (J). (gr. 3-3). pap. 8.99 *(978-1-4333-3659-1(6))* Teacher Created Materials, Inc.

Housel, Debra J. & Rice, Dona Herwick. Buy It! History of Money, 1 vol. 2nd rev. ed. 2012. (Nonfiction Readers Ser.). (ENG.). 32p. (J). (gr. 3-3). pap. 8.99 *(978-1-4333-3681-2(2))* Teacher Created Materials, Inc.

How Big Is My World? (J). pap. 7.95 *(978-0-8136-0082-6(0))* Modern Curriculum Pr.

How Many Jelly Beans? (Early Intervention Levels Ser.). 21.30 *(978-0-7362-0374-6(5))*; Vol. 2. 3.55 *(978-0-7362-0095-0(9))* CENGAGE Learning.

How the Whale Got His Throat. 2017. (Picture Bks.). (ENG.). (J). 9.99 ***(978-0-7945-3869-9(X)***, Usborne) EDC Publishing.

How Things Work Interactive Packages: Looking Closer. (Pebble Soup Explorations Ser.). (gr. -1-18). 52.00 *(978-0-7578-5246-6(7))* Rigby Education.

Howell, Gill. Selkie Child. Keen, Sophie, illus. 2005. (ENG.). 24p. (J). lib. bdg. 23.65 *(978-1-59646-750-7(9))* Dingles & Co.

—Snow King. Cann, Helen, illus. 2005. (ENG.). 24p. (J). lib. bdg. 23.65 *(978-1-59646-742-2(8))* Dingles & Co.

—Tortoise & the Baboon. Woody, illus. 2004. (ENG.). 16p. (J). lib. bdg. 23.65 *(978-1-59646-686-9(3))* Dingles & Co.

Howlett, Bruce & Pitcher, Jeff, creators. Hop, Skip & Jump into Reading Software: For Six Students. 2003. (J). cd-rom *(978-0-9742485-1-6(7))* Sound Reading Solutions.

—Hop, Skip & Jump into Reading Software: For Two Students. 2003. (J). cd-rom *(978-0-9742485-0-9(9))* Sound Reading Solutions.

Howlett, Bruce, et al. Hop, Skip & Jump into Reading. Pitcher, Jeff, illus. 2003. (J). Bk. 1. 9.00 *(978-0-9704183-4-0(5))*Bk. 2. 9.00 *(978-0-9704183-3-3(7)*, Sound Reading)Bk. 3. 9.00 *(978-0-9704183-8-8(8)*, Sound Reading) Sound Reading Solutions.

HSP Staff. Band of Angels Challenge Trade Book Grade 2: Harcourt School Publishers Storytown. 2006. pap. 8.75 *(978-0-15-365114-4(8))* Harcourt Schl. Pubs.

—Eager Challenge Trade Book Grade 6: Harcourt School Publishers Storytown. 2006. pap. 8.75 *(978-0-15-365195-3(4))* Harcourt Schl. Pubs.

—Grandpa Stre Challenge Trade Book Grade 2: Harcourt School Publishers Storytown. 2006. pap. 8.75 *(978-0-15-365112-0(1))* Harcourt Schl. Pubs.

—Loser Challenge Trade Book Grade 6: Harcourt School Publishers Storytown. 2006. pap. 8.75 *(978-0-15-365187-8(3))* Harcourt Schl. Pubs.

—My Rows & Cns Challenge Trade Book Grade 2: Harcourt School Publishers Storytown. 2006. pap. 8.75 *(978-0-15-365118-2(0))* Harcourt Schl. Pubs.

Huang, SuHua. A Faithful Reading Partner: A Story from a Hakka Village. 2012. 28p. pap. 19.99 *(978-1-4685-6267-5(3))* AuthorHouse.

Hudicourt, Caroline. A Mango for Grandpa. Sainsilus, Ismer, illus. 2007. 32p. (J). (POL.). pap. 14.95 *(978-1-60195-093-2(4))*; (ARA & ENG.). pap. 14.95 *(978-1-60195-085-7(3))* International Step by Step Assn.

Hudson, Wade. The Two Tyrones. Page, Mark, illus. 2004. (Just for You Ser.). (ENG.). 32p. (gr. 2-3). pap. 3.99 *(978-0-439-56866-1(8)*, Teaching Resources) Scholastic, Inc.

Hughes, Jon. What Happened to Dinosaurs? Hughes, Jon, illus. 2007. (Collins Big Cat Ser.). (ENG., Illus.). 32p. (J). (gr.

2-4). pap. 8.99 *(978-0-00-723084-6(2))* HarperCollins Pubs. Ltd. GBR. Dist: Independent Pubs. Group.

Hughes, Mónica. The Big Turnip. Williams, Lisa, illus. 2006. (Collins Big Cat Ser.). (ENG.). 32p. (J). (gr. -1-k). pap. 5.99 *(978-0-00-718644-0(4))* HarperCollins Pubs. Ltd. GBR. Dist: Independent Pubs. Group.

—Cars. 2005. (Big Cat Ser.). (gr. k-2). pap. 6.50 *(978-1-60457-026-7(1))* Pacific Learning, Inc.

—Little Mouse Deer & the Crocodile. Moriuchi, Mique, illus. 2004. 24p. (J). lib. bdg. 23.65 *(978-1-59646-684-5(7))* Dingles & Co.

—More Little Mouse Deer Tales. Clemenston, John, illus. 2005. 24p. (J). lib. bdg. 23.65 *(978-1-59646-730-9(4))* Dingles & Co.

—Pushing & Pulling. Coote, Mark, illus. 2005. (Collins Big Cat Ser.). (ENG.). 16p. (J). (gr. -1-k). pap. 5.99 *(978-0-00-718541-2(3))* HarperCollins Pubs. Ltd. GBR. Dist: Independent Pubs. Group.

—Pushing & Pulling. 2005. (Big Cat Ser.). (gr. k-2). pap. 6.50 *(978-1-60457-025-0(3))* Pacific Learning, Inc.

—Shapes: Band 01A/Pink A. 2006. (Collins Big Cat Ser.). (ENG., Illus.). 16p. (J). (gr. -1-k). pap. 5.99 *(978-0-00-718649-5(5))* HarperCollins Pubs. Ltd. GBR. Dist: Independent Pubs. Group.

—Stripes. 2005. (Collins Big Cat Ser.). (ENG.). 16p. (J). (gr. -1-k). pap. 5.99 *(978-0-00-718534-4(0))* HarperCollins Pubs. Ltd. GBR. Dist: Independent Pubs. Group.

—Stripes. 2005. (Big Cat Ser.). (gr. k-2). pap. 6.50 *(978-1-60457-021-2(0))* Pacific Learning, Inc.

Hughes, Mónica & Zlatic, Tomislav. Lights. 2006. (Collins Big Cat Ser.). (ENG., Illus.). 136p. (J). (gr. 1-1). pap. 5.99 *(978-0-00-718680-8(0))* HarperCollins Pubs. Ltd. GBR. Dist: Independent Pubs. Group.

Hugo & Splot: Individual Title Six-Packs. (Bookweb Ser.). 32p. (gr. 3-18). 34.00 *(978-0-7635-3936-8(8))* Rigby Education.

The Hummingbirds' Gift. (Lexile Levels Ser.). 9.09 *(978-1-56334-720-7(2))* CENGAGE Learning.

Humphreys, Pauline A. Romance of the Airman. 2005. pap. 43.95 *(978-1-4191-0278-3(8))* Kessinger Publishing, LLC.

The Hungry Chickens: Individual Title Six-Packs. (Literatura 2000 Ser.). (gr. 1-2). 28.00 *(978-0-7635-0136-5(0))* Rigby Education.

Hunt, Jilly & Collins UK Staff. Great Architects. 2016. (ENG.). 32p. (J). (gr. 2-3). pap. 8.95 *(978-0-00-816378-5(2))* HarperCollins Pubs. Ltd. GBR. Dist: Independent Pubs. Group.

—Super Boats. 2016. (ENG.). 32p. (J). (gr. 2-3). pap. 8.95 *(978-0-00-816381-5(2))* HarperCollins Pubs. Ltd. GBR. Dist: Independent Pubs. Group.

Hunter, Nick & Collins UK Staff. Greatest Ashes Moments. 2017. (ENG., Illus.). 48p. (J). (gr. 3-4). pap. 9.95 *(978-0-00-816387-7(1))* HarperCollins Pubs. Ltd. GBR. Dist: Independent Pubs. Group.

Hurley, Trish. The 10 Most Enduring Fashion Trends. 2008. (J). 14.99 *(978-1-55448-524-6(X))* Scholastic Library Publishing.

—The 10 Most Outrageous Outlaws. 2008. 14.99 *(978-1-55448-506-2(1))* Scholastic Library Publishing.

Hutmacher, Kimberly M. I Want a Pet. 2012. (I Want a Pet Ser.). (ENG.). 24p. (gr. k-1). lib. bdg. 106.60 *(978-1-4296-8116-2(0)*, Pebble Plus) Capstone Press of Coughlan Cos.

I Am Six. (Early Intervention Levels Ser.). 63.00 *(978-0-7362-2112-2(3))*; 10.50 *(978-0-7362-0513-9(6))* CENGAGE Learning.

I Can Swim. (J). 14.15 *(978-0-8136-2035-0(X))* Modern Curriculum Pr.

I Love My Grandma, Vol. 6. (Early Intervention Levels Ser.). 3.85 *(978-1-56334-970-6(1))* CENGAGE Learning.

I See Tails! (Early Intervention Levels Ser.). 23.10 *(978-0-7362-0009-7(6))*; Vol. 2. 3.85 *(978-1-56334-959-1(0))* CENGAGE Learning.

Ida B Reading Group Guide. (J). *(978-0-06-074412-0(X))* HarperCollins Pubs.

Ideas of the Modern World, 8 vols., Set. 2003. 205.52 *(978-0-7398-6420-3(3))* Steck-Vaughn.

Idee, Ari. What's Your Snack? 2013. 28p. pap. 9.49 *(978-0-9798991-2-6(5))* Technology & Imagination Pr.

If I Were You. 2003. (Illus.). pap. 5.60 *(978-0-7398-7519-3(1))* Steck-Vaughn.

If You Could Be Anything. 2003. (Illus.). pap. 7.60 *(978-0-7398-7530-8(2))* Steck-Vaughn.

Iggy Iguana's Trip. (Early Intervention Levels Ser.). 21.30 *(978-0-7362-0380-7(X))*; Vol. 3. 3.55 *(978-0-7362-0101-8(7))* CENGAGE Learning.

Ignatow, Amy. The Popularity Papers: The Less-Than-Hidden Secrets & Final Revelations of Lydia Goldblatt & Julie Graham-Chang. 2015. (Popularity Papers). (ENG., Illus.). 208p. (J). (gr. 3-7). pap. 8.95 *(978-1-4197-1357-6(4)*, Amulet Bks.) Abrams, Inc.

Ikids Staff. Old MacDonald's Farm. King, Travis, illus. 2010. (ENG.). 20p. (J). (gr. -1-k). 14.99 *(978-1-60169-024-1(X))* Innovative Kids.

I'm Glad I'm Me: Individual Title Six-Packs. (gr. 1-2). 25.00 *(978-0-7635-9194-6(7))* Rigby Education.

I'm not, I'm Not: Individual Title Six-Packs. (gr. 1-2). 22.00 *(978-0-7635-9155-7(6))* Rigby Education.

ImageBooks Staff & Mulligan, Lenz. Little Polar Bear Finger Puppet Book. 2009. (Little Finger Puppet Board Bks.: FING). (ENG., Illus.). 12p. (J). (gr. -1 — 1). bds. 6.99 *(978-0-8118-6974-4(1))* Chronicle Bks. LLC.

The Imaginer: Individual Title Six-Packs. (Bookweb Ser.). 32p. (gr. 6-18). 34.00 *(978-0-7578-0900-2(6))* Rigby Education.

In the Bathroom: Individual Title, 6 Packs. (Chiquilibros Ser.). (gr. k-1). 23.00 *(978-0-7635-0452-6(1))* Rigby Education.

In the Box, Vol. 3. (Early Intervention Levels Ser.). 3.55 *(978-0-7362-0098-1(3))* CENGAGE Learning.

In the City Vol. 4: Step K, Level B. (Early Intervention Levels Ser.). 3.85 *(978-1-56334-968-3(X))* CENGAGE Learning.

In the Country: Individual Title Six-Packs. (gr. -1-2). 23.00 *(978-0-7635-8810-6(5))* Rigby Education.

In the Garden. 2012. (Collins Big Cat Ser.). (ENG., Illus.). 16p. (J). pap., wbk. ed. 4.99 *(978-0-00-747489-9(X))* HarperCollins Pubs. Ltd. GBR. Dist: Independent Pubs. Group.

In the Rain. (Little Book Practice Reader). (J). *(978-0-8136-5359-4(2))* Modern Curriculum Pr.

In the Sun. (Early Intervention Levels Ser.). 21.30 *(978-0-7362-0390-6(7))*; Vol. 4. 3.55 *(978-0-7362-0170-4(X))* CENGAGE Learning.

In the Teacup: KinderWords Individual Title, 6 Packs. (Kinderstarters Ser.). 8p. (gr. -1-1). 21.00 *(978-0-7635-8695-9(1))* Rigby Education.

In the Yard. (Early Intervention Levels Ser.). 5.34 *(978-0-7362-1694-4(4))*; 32.04 *(978-0-7362-2142-9(5))* CENGAGE Learning.

Independent Readers Bookshelf Collection, 6 bks., Set. 2004. (gr. 1-18). 99.00 *(978-0-328-00408-9(1))* Addison-Wesley Educational Pubs., Inc.

Instruc, Shurley. Shurley English 1 Kit H/S Ed. 2004. 70.00 *(978-1-58561-048-8(8))* Shurley Instructional Materials, Inc.

—Shurley English 1 Stu Workbook. 2004. pap. 12.00 *(978-1-58561-049-5(6))* Shurley Instructional Materials, Inc.

—Shurley English 2 Kit H/S Ed. 2004. pap. 70.00 *(978-1-58561-044-0(5))* Shurley Instructional Materials, Inc.

—Shurley English 2 Stu Workbook. 2004. pap. 12.00 *(978-1-58561-045-7(3))* Shurley Instructional Materials, Inc.

—Shurley English 3 Kit H/S Ed. 2004. 70.00 *(978-1-58561-040-2(2))* Shurley Instructional Materials, Inc.

—Shurley English 3 Stu Workbook. 2004. pap. 12.00 *(978-1-58561-041-9(0))* Shurley Instructional Materials, Inc.

—Shurley English 4 Kit H/S Ed. 2004. pap. 70.00 *(978-1-58561-036-5(4))* Shurley Instructional Materials, Inc.

—Shurley English 4 Stu Workbook. 2004. pap. 12.00 *(978-1-58561-037-2(2))* Shurley Instructional Materials, Inc.

—Shurley English 5 Kit H/S Ed. 2004. pap. 70.00 *(978-1-58561-032-7(1))* Shurley Instructional Materials, Inc.

—Shurley English 5 Stu Workbook. 2004. pap. 12.00 *(978-1-58561-033-4(X))* Shurley Instructional Materials, Inc.

—Shurley English 6 Stu Workbook. 2004. pap. 12.00 *(978-1-58561-029-7(1))* Shurley Instructional Materials, Inc.

Intervention Handbook. 2004. (Scott Foresman Reading Ser.). (gr. 3-18). 45.68 *(978-0-328-02600-5(X))*; (gr. 4-18). 45.68 *(978-0-328-02601-2(8))*; (gr. 5-18). 45.68 *(978-0-328-02602-9(6))*; (gr. 6-18). tchr. ed. 45.68 *(978-0-328-02603-6(4))* Addison-Wesley Educational Pubs., Inc.

Into English!, 13 vols. (Into English! Ser.). Level C. (gr. k-6). 137.49 *(978-1-56334-803-7(9)*, ES0208)Level C. (gr. 2-18). 810.14 *(978-1-56334-825-9(X)*, IN0202)Level C. (gr. 2-18). stu. ed., act. bk. ed. 5.84 *(978-1-56334-823-5(3)*, LA0201)Level D. (gr. k-6). 110.53 *(978-1-56334-804-4(7)*, ES0307)Level D. (gr. 3-18). 648.64 incl. cd-rom *(978-1-56334-843-3(8)*, IN0304)Level D. (gr. 3-18). stu. ed., act. bk. ed. 5.84 *(978-1-56334-718-4(0)*, LA0301)Level A. (gr. k-6). 116.54 *(978-1-56334-805-1(5)*, ES0007)Level B. (gr. k-6). 149.56 *(978-1-56334-802-0(0)*, ES0108)Level B. (gr. 1-18). 810.14 *(978-1-56334-807-5(1)*, IN0102)Level B. (gr. 1-18). 47.88 *(978-1-56334-896-9(9)*, SC0101)Level B. (gr. 1-18). stu. ed., act. bk. ed. 5.84 *(978-1-56334-822-8(5)*, LA0101)Level F. (gr. k-6). 112.14 *(978-1-56334-904-1(3)*, ES0507)Level F. (gr. 5-18). 45.45 *(978-1-56334-900-3(0)*, SC0503)Level F. (gr. 5-18). 648.64 incl. cd-rom *(978-1-56334-875-4(6)*, IN0504)Level F. (gr. 5-18). stu. ed., act. bk. ed. 5.84 *(978-1-56334-746-7(6)*, LA0501)Level G. (gr. k-6). 99.48 *(978-1-56334-907-2(8)*, ES0607)Level G. (gr. 6-18). 648.64 incl. cd-rom *(978-1-56334-901-0(9)*, IN0602)Level G. (gr. 6-18). 44.34 *(978-1-56334-916-4(7)*, SC0603)Level G. (gr. 6-18). 626.27 *(978-1-56334-908-9(6)*, IN0604)Level G. (gr. 6-18). stu. ed., act. bk. ed. 5.84 *(978-1-56334-756-6(3)*, LA0601) CENGAGE Learning.

Into English! Portable Packs: Level B. (Into English! Ser.). (gr. 1-5). 286.60 *(978-0-7362-1393-6(7))* CENGAGE Learning.

Into English! Portable Packs: Level C. (Into English! Ser.). (gr. 1-5). 286.60 *(978-0-7362-1394-3(5))* CENGAGE Learning.

Into English! Portable Packs: Level D. (Into English! Ser.). (gr. 1-5). 278.51 *(978-0-7362-1395-0(3))* CENGAGE Learning.

Into English! Portable Packs: Level E. (Into English! Ser.). (gr. 1-5). 278.51 *(978-0-7362-1396-7(1))* CENGAGE Learning.

Into English! Portable Packs: Level F. (Into English! Ser.). (gr. 1-5). 278.51 *(978-0-7362-1397-4(X))* CENGAGE Learning.

Iopeners: Big Book Collection, 20 vols. 2005. (J). (gr. k-18). 525.95 *(978-0-7652-4972-2(3))*; (gr. 1-18). 587.50 *(978-0-7652-4976-0(6))* Modern Curriculum Pr.

Iopeners: Classroom Library. 2005. (J). (gr. k-18). 440.50 *(978-0-7652-4969-2(3))*; (gr. 1-18). 518.50 *(978-0-7652-4973-9(1))*; (gr. 2-18). 518.50 *(978-0-7652-4977-7(4))*; (gr. 3-18). 616.50 *(978-0-7652-4980-7(4))*; (gr. 4-18). 616.50 *(978-0-7652-4983-8(9))*; (gr. 5-18). 694.50 *(978-0-7652-4986-9(3))*; (gr. 6-18). 694.50 *(978-0-7652-4989-0(8))* Modern Curriculum Pr.

Iopeners: Science Library, 10 vols. 2005. (J). (gr. k-18). 220.95 *(978-0-7652-4970-8(7))* Modern Curriculum Pr.

Iopeners: Social Studies Library, 10 vols. 2005. (J). (gr. k-18). 220.95 *(978-0-7652-4971-5(5))* Modern Curriculum Pr.

Is Jim In? Set A Individual Title Six-Packs. (Supersonic Phonics Ser.). (gr. k-3). 29.00 *(978-0-7635-0531-8(5))* Rigby Education.

Isabel, Delgado Maria. Chave's Memories / Los Recuerdos de Chave. Yvonne, Symank, illus. 2008. 32p. (J). pap. 7.95 *(978-1-55885-244-0(1)*, Piñata Books) Arte Publico Pr.

Isecke, Harriet. Finding Texas: Exploration in New Lands, 1 vol. 2012. (Primary Source Readers Ser.). (ENG.). 32p. (J). (gr. 4-4). pap. 8.99 *(978-1-4333-5042-9(4))* Teacher Created Materials, Inc.

—Lyndon B. Johnson: A Texan in the White House, 1 vol. 2012. (Primary Source Readers Ser.). (ENG.). 32p. (J). (gr. 3-3). pap. 8.99 *(978-1-4333-5052-8(1))* Teacher Created Materials, Inc.

—Stephen F. Austin: The Father of Texas, 1 vol. 2012. (Primary Source Readers Ser.). (ENG.). 32p. (J). (gr. 3-3). pap. 8.99 *(978-1-4333-5045-0(9))* Teacher Created Materials, Inc.

—Susan B. Anthony & Elizabeth Cady Stanton: Early Suffragists, 1 vol. 2011. (Primary Source Readers Ser.). (ENG., Illus.). 32p. (J). (gr. 4-4). pap. 8.99 *(978-1-4333-1506-0(8))* Teacher Created Materials, Inc.

—Texas in the 20th Century: Building Industry & Community, 1 vol. 2012. (Primary Source Readers Ser.). (ENG.). 32p. (J). (gr. 4-4). pap. 8.99 *(978-1-4333-5209-6(5))* Teacher Created Materials, Inc.

—Texas Today: Leading America into the Future, 1 vol. 2012. (Primary Source Readers Ser.). (ENG.). 32p. (J). (gr. 4-4). pap. 8.99 *(978-1-4333-5053-5(X))* Teacher Created Materials, Inc.

—Women's Suffrage: Fighting for Women's Rights, 1 vol. 2011. (Primary Source Readers Ser.). (ENG.). 32p. (J). (gr. 5-5). pap. 8.99 *(978-1-4333-1507-7(6))* Teacher Created Materials, Inc.

¡Ser Amable no Cuesta Nada! Social/Emotional Lap Book. (Pebble Soup Exploraciones Ser.). (SPA.). (gr. -1-18). 16.00 *(978-0-7578-1783-0(1))* Rigby Education.

It's Not Fair: 6 Small Books. (gr. k-3). 24.00 *(978-0-7635-6243-4(2))* Rigby Education.

Ivanoff, George & Quarmby, Toby. My Best Friend Thinks I'm a Genius. 2008. (Rigby Focus Forward Ser.). (ENG., Illus.). 24p. (gr. 3-8). pap. 11.20 *(978-1-4190-3849-5(4))* Houghton Mifflin Harcourt Publishing Co.

Iversen, Sandra. Alphabet Book Aa. 2009. (Quick60 Alphabet Bks.). (ENG., Illus.). 12p. (J). pap. *(978-1-77540-000-4(X))* Iversen Publishing Ltd.

—Alphabet Book Bb. 2009. (Quick60 Alphabet Bks.). (ENG., Illus.). 12p. (J). pap. *(978-1-77540-001-1(8))* Iversen Publishing Ltd.

—Alphabet Book Cc. 2009. (Quick60 Alphabet Bks.). (ENG., Illus.). 12p. (J). pap. *(978-1-77540-002-8(6))* Iversen Publishing Ltd.

—Alphabet Book Dd. 2009. (Quick60 Alphabet Bks.). (ENG., Illus.). 12p. (J). pap. *(978-1-77540-003-5(4))* Iversen Publishing Ltd.

—Alphabet Book Ee. 2009. (Quick60 Alphabet Bks.). (ENG., Illus.). 12p. (J). pap. *(978-1-77540-004-2(2))* Iversen Publishing Ltd.

—Alphabet Book Ff. 2009. (Quick60 Alphabet Bks.). (ENG., Illus.). 12p. (J). pap. *(978-1-77540-005-9(0))* Iversen Publishing Ltd.

—Alphabet Book Gg. 2009. (Quick60 Alphabet Bks.). (ENG., Illus.). 12p. (J). pap. *(978-1-77540-006-6(9))* Iversen Publishing Ltd.

—Alphabet Book Hh. 2009. (Quick60 Alphabet Bks.). (ENG., Illus.). 12p. (J). pap. *(978-1-77540-007-3(7))* Iversen Publishing Ltd.

—Alphabet Book Ii. 2009. (Quick60 Alphabet Bks.). (ENG., Illus.). 12p. (J). pap. *(978-1-77540-008-0(5))* Iversen Publishing Ltd.

—Alphabet Book Jj. 2009. (Quick60 Alphabet Bks.). (ENG., Illus.). 12p. (J). pap. *(978-1-77540-009-7(3))* Iversen Publishing Ltd.

—Alphabet Book Kk. 2009. (Quick60 Alphabet Bks.). (ENG., Illus.). 12p. (J). pap. *(978-1-77540-010-3(7))* Iversen Publishing Ltd.

—Alphabet Book Ll. 2009. (Quick60 Alphabet Bks.). (ENG., Illus.). 12p. (J). pap. *(978-1-77540-011-0(5))* Iversen Publishing Ltd.

—Alphabet Book Mm. 2009. (ENG., Illus.). 12p. (J). pap. *(978-1-77540-012-7(3))* Iversen Publishing Ltd.

—Alphabet Book Nn. 2009. (Quick60 Alphabet Bks.). (ENG., Illus.). 12p. (J). pap. *(978-1-77540-013-4(1))* Iversen Publishing Ltd.

—Alphabet Book Oo. 2009. (Quick60 Alphabet Bks.). (ENG., Illus.). 12p. (J). pap. *(978-1-77540-014-1(X))* Iversen Publishing Ltd.

—Alphabet Book Pp. 2009. (Quick60 Alphabet Bks.). (ENG., Illus.). 12p. (J). pap. *(978-1-77540-015-8(8))* Iversen Publishing Ltd.

—Alphabet Book Zz. 2009. (Quick60 Alphabet Bks.). (ENG., Illus.). 12p. (J). pap. *(978-1-77540-025-7(5))* Iversen Publishing Ltd.

—A Day on the Mountain. 2010. (Quick60 Factual Bks.). (ENG., Illus.). 12p. (J). pap. *(978-1-77540-220-6(7))* Iversen Publishing Ltd.

—What Is It? 2009. (ENG., Illus.). 12p. (J). pap. *(978-1-77540-046-2(8))* Iversen Publishing Ltd.

The J-Files: Individual Title, 6 Packs. (Bookweb Ser.). 32p. (gr. 3-18). 34.00 *(978-0-7635-3941-2(4))* Rigby Education.

Jack: 6 Small Books. (gr. k-2). 23.00 *(978-0-7635-8497-9(5))* Rigby Education.

Jackson, Patrick & Kimura, Rie. Potato Pals. 2005. (ENG., Illus.). 48p. act. bk. ed. 6.95 *(978-0-19-439190-0(6))* Oxford Univ. Pr., Inc.

—Potato Pals 1. 2005. (ENG., Illus.). wbk. ed. 6.95 *(978-0-19-439191-7(4))* Oxford Univ. Pr., Inc.

—Potato Pals 1 User's Guide. 2005. (ENG., Illus.). 99p. 8.95 *(978-0-19-439193-1(0))* Oxford Univ. Pr., Inc.

Jackson, Tiffany D. Allegedly. 2017. 400p. (YA). (gr. 9). 17.99 *(978-0-06-242264-4(2)*, Tegen, Katherine Bks) HarperCollins Pubs.

Jacobs, Evan. Zombies! 2014. (Red Rhino Ser.). (J). lib. bdg. 18.40 *(978-0-606-36243-6(6))* Turtleback Bks.

James, Anne. ¡Ataque de las Hormigas! Ramirez, Alma B., tr. from ENG. Lewis, Anthony, illus. 2008. (Science Solves It! en Espanol Ser.). (SPA.). 32p. (J). (gr. -1-3). pap. 5.95 *(978-1-57565-278-8(1))* Kane Press, Inc.

James Baldwin. Fifty Famous Stories Retold. 2009. (Illus.). 132p. pap. 5.95 *(978-1-60386-206-6(4)*, Merchant Bks.) Rough Draft Printing.

James, Eric. Up & Down. 2012. (InfoMax Readers Ser.). (ENG., Illus.). 16 pp.p. (J). (gr. k-1). pap. 7.00 *(978-1-4488-8878-8(6)*, Rosen Classroom) Rosen Publishing Group, Inc., The.

James Is Hiding: Individual Title, 6 Packs. (gr. 1-2). 22.00 *(978-0-7635-9162-5(9))* Rigby Education.

James, Karim. The Kids Time to Rhyme: Read & Rhyme at the same Time. 2009. 16p. pap. 14.99 *(978-1-4490-0424-8(5))* AuthorHouse.

James, Lincoln. Sal Sleeps In. 2006. (Neighborhood Readers Ser.). (ENG.). 8p. (gr. -1-3). pap. 5.15 *(978-1-4042-5780-1(2)*, Rosen Classroom) Rosen Publishing Group, Inc., The.

—The Street Fair. 2006. (Neighborhood Readers Ser.). (ENG.). 16p. (gr. 1-3). pap. 6.50 *(978-1-4042-7228-6(3)*, Rosen Classroom) Rosen Publishing Group, Inc., The.

James, M. R. OXFORD BOOKWORMS. STAGE 4: THE UNIQUE GRAVE SHORT STORIES EDITION 08. 3rd ed. 2008. (ENG., Illus.). 96p. 9.38 *(978-0-19-479191-5(2))* Oxford Univ. Pr., Inc.

—PENGUIN ACTIVE READING 1: CROWN, THE BOOK AND CD-ROM PACK. 2007. (ENG.). 48p. pap. 17.32 incl. cd-rom *(978-1-4058-5200-5(3))* Pearson Education.

James, Wayan. Chalise, Master of Maps. 2016. (Rosen REAL Readers: Social Studies Nonfiction / Fiction: Family, Community, & the World Ser.). 12p. (gr. 1-k). pap. 6.33 *(978-1-5081-2571-6(6)*, Rosen Classroom) Rosen Publishing Group, Inc., The.

—Hot Days, Cold Days. 2016. (Rosen REAL Readers: STEM & STEAM Collection). 12p. (gr. 1-k). pap. 6.33 *(978-1-5081-2419-1(1)*, Rosen Classroom) Rosen Publishing Group, Inc., The.

—The Marble Match. 2016. (Rosen REAL Readers: STEM & STEAM Collection). 8p. (gr. 1-k). pap. 5.46 *(978-1-5081-2583-9(X)*, Rosen Classroom) Rosen Publishing Group, Inc., The.

Jamiol, Paul. Bikers Are Animals: A Children's Book on Motorcycling. Habib, Linda, ed. 2009. 38p. pap. 14.95 *(978-1-60844-232-4(2))* Dog Ear Publishing, LLC.

Jankowski, Connie. All about Light & Sound, 1 vol. 2007. (Science Readers Ser.). (SPA & ENG.). 32p. (J). (gr. 4-4). pap. 8.99 *(978-0-7439-0579-4(2))* Shell Educational Publishing.

—Hippocrates: Making the Way for Medicine, 1 vol. 2007. (Science Readers Ser.). (ENG.). 32p. (J). (gr. 3-3). pap. 8.99 *(978-0-7439-0596-1(2))* Shell Educational Publishing.

—Investigating the Human Body, 1 vol. 2007. (Science Readers Ser.). (ENG., Illus.). 32p. (J). (gr. 4-4). pap. 8.99 *(978-0-7439-0595-4(4))* Shell Educational Publishing.

Janovich, Leah. Patty's Pictures. Billin-Frye, Paige, illus. 2010. 16p. (J). *(978-0-545-24820-4(5))* Scholastic, Inc.

Jarman, Julia. Molly & the Giant. Sholto, Walker, illus. 2005. (ENG.). 24p. (J). lib. bdg. 23.65 *(978-1-59646-746-0(0))* Dingles & Co.

—Stowaway? Oldroyd, Mark, illus. 2007. (Collins Big Cat Ser.). (ENG.). 48p. (J). (gr. 3-4). pap. 8.99 *(978-0-00-723088-4(5))* HarperCollins Pubs. Ltd. GBR. Dist: Independent Pubs. Group.

Jarrell, Pamela R. A Nice Cool Drink. Teeple, Jackie, illus. l.t. ed. 2005. (J). (gr. -1-k). pap. 10.95 *(978-1-57332-340-6(3))*; pap. 10.95 *(978-1-57332-341-3(1))* Carson-Dellosa Publishing, LLC. (HighReach Learning, Incorporated).

—Planting a Seed. Meier, Kerry L., illus. l.t. ed. 2006. 12p. (J). (gr. -1-k). pap. 10.95 *(978-1-57332-350-5(0)*, HighReach Learning, Incorporated) Carson-Dellosa Publishing, LLC.

Jasper & the Kitten. 2004. (Jasper the Cat Chapter Ser.). (J). 7.67 *(978-1-58453-283-5(1))* Pioneer Valley Bks.

Jasper the Cat Chapter Set 1. 2004. (J). *(978-1-58453-287-3(4))* Pioneer Valley Bks.

Jasper the Cat Set 1. 2004. (J). *(978-1-58453-282-8(3))* Pioneer Valley Bks.

Jasper the Fat Cat. 2004. (Jasper the Cat Set 1 Ser.). (J). 7.33 *(978-1-58453-276-7(9))* Pioneer Valley Bks.

Jeffries, Katherine. Plants Grow: Lap Book. 2009. (My First Reader's Theater Set B Ser.). (J). 28.00 *(978-1-60634-985-4(6))* Benchmark Education Co.

—Tim's Head, Shoulders, Knees, & Toes. Price, Nick, illus. 2009. (Reader's Theater Nursery Rhymes & Songs Set B Ser.). 48p. (J). pap. *(978-1-60859-169-5(7))* Benchmark Education Co.

Jeffus, Sharon2006, as told by. Artsy Animals: Learn to Read. 2006. (Illus.). 70p. (J). 19.95 *(978-0-9715970-9-9(X))* Visual Manna.

Jenkins, Amanda. Mere Moments A Story of Pearl Harbor, the Day the Towers Fell. 2011. (Readers' & Writers' Genre Workshop Ser.). (J). pap. *(978-1-4509-3019-2(0))* Benchmark Education Co.

—The Strong & the Weak Hammurabi's Code, Tomb Robbers! A Story of Ancient Egypt. 2011. (Readers' & Writers' Genre Workshop Ser.). (YA). pap. *(978-1-4509-3020-8(4))* Benchmark Education Co.

Jenkins, Donna. When I Grow up, I Want to Be a Builder. 2010. 16p. pap. 10.49 *(978-1-4490-6072-5(2))* AuthorHouse.

—When I Grow up, I Want to Be a Football Player. 2010. 16p. pap. 10.49 *(978-1-4490-6496-9(5))* AuthorHouse.

Jenkins, Henry A. The Adventures of Monkey Squirrel & Frogman: Sand Trap. 2009. 16p. pap. 8.49 *(978-1-4343-7827-9(6))* AuthorHouse.

Jenkins, Jacqueline. The Kangaroo Tale: Matilda. Minoza, Kersly, illus. 2013. 24p. (J). 28.03 *(978-1-4836-9159-6(4))* Xlibris Corp.

Jenkins, Jennifer Meghan. The 10 Deadliest Predators. 2008. 14.99 *(978-1-55448-502-4(9))* Scholastic Library Publishing.

Jenkins, Meghan. The 10 Most Amazing Birds. 2008. (J). 14.99 *(978-1-55448-532-1(0))* Scholastic Library Publishing.

Jenkins, Saffy. The Boy Who Cried Wolf, Bk. 2. Broadley, Leo, illus. 2013. (Collins Big Cat Ser.). (ENG.). 16p. (J). (gr. -1-k). pap. 5.99 *(978-0-00-751267-6(8))* HarperCollins Pubs. Ltd. GBR. Dist: Independent Pubs. Group.

Jennings, Sharon, et al, adapted by. Franklin's Pond Phantom. 2005. (Kids Can Read Ser.). (ENG., Illus.). 32p. (J). (gr. 1-2). 14.95 *(978-1-55337-718-4(4))* Kids Can Pr., Ltd. CAN. Dist: Hachette Bk. Group.

Jennings, Terry. Bird Watch, 8 bks. 2005. (QEB Readers). (Illus.). 24p. (J). (gr. -1-3). lib. bdg. 15.95 *(978-1-59566-078-7(X))* QEB Publishing Inc.

—Bugs & Slugs, 8 vols. 2005. (QEB Readers). (Illus.). 24p. (J). (gr. -1-3). lib. bdg. 15.95 *(978-1-59566-069-5(0))* QEB Publishing Inc.

Jennison, Nancy. Integrating Test Prep into Reading & Writing Workshops: Classroom-Tested Lessons & Activities That Teach Students the Skills They Need to Become Successful Readers & Writers-And Excel on the Tests. 2011. (ENG.). 240p. pap. 25.99 *(978-0-545-14711-8(5)*, Teaching Resources) Scholastic, Inc.

Jessup, Dylan. We're All Americans. 2012. (InfoMax Readers Ser.). (ENG., Illus.). 24p. (J). (gr. 1-2). pap. 8.25 *(978-1-4488-9079-8(9)*, Rosen Classroom) Rosen Publishing Group, Inc., The.

Jinkins, Lisa Heath. PB & J Otter Noodle Stories: Busy Day. 2005. (ENG.). 24p. (J). (gr. -1-1). pap. 3.99 *(978-0-7868-4282-7(2))* Disney Pr.

John, Louise. My Mom Can't See. Elkerton, Andy, illus. 2013. (Start Reading Ser.). (ENG.). 24p. (gr. k-1). pap. 41.94 *(978-1-4765-3226-4(5))*; pap. 7.95 *(978-1-4765-3201-1(X))* Capstone Press of Coughlan Cos.

—Small. Elkerton, Andy, illus. 2013. (Start Reading Ser.). (ENG.). 24p. (gr. k-1). pap. 41.94 *(978-1-4765-3231-8(1))*;

pap. 7.95 *(978-1-4765-3202-8(8))* Capstone Press of Coughlan Cos.
Johns, Linda & Jones, Melanie Davis. I Can Do It! I Can Bowl!/I Can Ski!/I Can Do It All. Boles, Terry, illus. 2006. (ENG.). 93p. (J). (gr. k-2). pap. 9.95 *(978-0-531-16923-0(5)*, Children's Pr.) Scholastic Library Publishing.
Johnson, Bruce. We Both Read-about Dogs. 2009. (ENG., Illus.). 44p. (J). (gr. -1-3). 9.95 *(978-1-60115-237-4(X))* Treasure Bay, Inc.
—We Both Read-About Dogs. 2009. (ENG., Illus.). 44p. (J). pap. 4.99 *(978-1-60115-238-1(8))* Treasure Bay, Inc.
Johnson, Bruce & McKay, Sindy. Zoo Day/Dia Del Zoologico: Spanish/English Bilingual Edition (We Both Read - Level 1) Johnson, Meredith, illus. 2016. (We Both Read - Level 1 Ser.). (ENG & SPA.). (J). pap. 4.99 *(978-1-60115-078-3(4))* Treasure Bay, Inc.
Johnson, D. C. & Turner, Sandra. Let's Be Friends. Johnson, D. C. & Johnson, Darnell, illus. 2007. (J). per. 9.95 *(978-1-933556-66-6(8))* Publishers' Graphics, L.L.C.
Johnson, Errol. What's That Sound? 2006. (Neighborhood Readers Ser.). (Illus.). 12p. (gr. -1-3). pap. 5.90 *(978-1-4042-6738-1(7)*, Rosen Classroom) Rosen Publishing Group, Inc., The.
Johnson, Gee. The Octopus. Johnson, Gee, illus. 2010. (2G Marine Life Ser.). (ENG., Illus.). 20p. (J). (gr. k-2). pap. 5.99 *(978-1-61541-221-1(2))* American Reading Co.
Johnson, Gee & Zorzi, Gina. Tiger Sharks. 2010. (2G Marine Life Ser.). (ENG.). 24p. (J). (gr. k-2). pap. 5.99 *(978-1-61541-167-2(4))* American Reading Co.
Johnson, Jennifer. Gettysburg: The Bloodiest Battle of the Civil War. 2009. (24/7 Goes to War Ser.). (ENG.). 64p. (J). (gr. 6-12). pap. 7.95 *(978-0-531-25453-0(4)*, Watts, Franklin) Scholastic Library Publishing.
Johnson, Jo. Grandpa Seashells. 2017. (ENG., Illus.). 32p. (C). pap. 6.95 ***(978-0-86388-997-4(2)***, Y328929) Routledge.
Johnson, Margaret. Gone! Level Starter/Beginner American English. 2010. (ENG., Illus.). 48p. pap. 12.00 *(978-0-521-14904-4(5))* Cambridge Univ. Pr.
—Gone! Starter/Beginner. 2009. (ENG.). 48p. pap. 11.00 *(978-84-8323-509-6(9))* Cambridge Univ. Pr.
—Running Wild Level 3 Lower-Intermediate. 2009. (ENG.). 80p. pap. 12.75 *(978-84-8323-501-0(3))* Cambridge Univ. Pr.
Johnson, Rebecca L. Microquests: Classroom Set. 2008. pap. 43.95 *(978-0-8225-9113-9(8))* Lerner Publishing Group.
—Microquests: Complete Set. 2008. pap. 263.95 *(978-0-8225-9377-5(7))* Lerner Publishing Group.
Johnson, Shane L., illus. The Need for Speed. 2014. (Rabbids Invasion Ser.). (ENG., Illus.). 40p. (J). (gr. 1-3). 16.99 *(978-1-4814-2292-5(8))*; pap. 3.99 *(978-1-4814-2291-8(X))* Simon Spotlight. (Simon Spotlight).
Jones, Karl. Day of the Dead Activity Book. Simpson, Steve, illus. 2013. (ENG.). 16p. (J). (gr. 1-4). 9.99 *(978-0-8431-7300-0(9)*, Price Stern Sloan) Penguin Young Readers Group.
Jones, Milo. Snow Friends. Lewis, Stephen, illus. 2010. 16p. (J). pap. *(978-0-545-24823-5(X))* Scholastic, Inc.
Jones, Shelley V. & Gunn, Barbara. Read Well Magazine Unit 20: Slanted Text. 2003. (Read Well Level K Ser.). (Illus.). 8p. (J). *(978-1-59318-104-8(3))* Cambium Education, Inc.
—Shells on the Shore: Read Well Level K Unit 14 Storybook. Jerde, Susan, illus. 2003. (Read Well Level K Ser.). 20p. (J). *(978-1-57035-685-8(8)*, 55546) Cambium Education, Inc.
Jones, Stephen Anderton. America Is Good. 2008. 60p. (gr. -1). pap. 22.50 *(978-1-4343-6321-3(X))* AuthorHouse.
Jones, Tammy. At the Shore. 2009. (Sight Word Readers Set A Ser.). (J). 3.49 net. *(978-1-60719-137-7(7))* Newmark Learning LLC.
—Big Pet, Little Pet. 2009. (Sight Word Readers Set A Ser.). (J). 3.49 net. *(978-1-60719-153-7(9))* Newmark Learning LLC.
—Count Around the Room. 2009. (Sight Word Readers Set A Ser.). (J). 3.49 net. *(978-1-60719-157-5(1))* Newmark Learning LLC.
—Count at the Baseball Field. 2009. (Sight Word Readers Set A Ser.). (J). 3.49 net. *(978-1-60719-156-8(3))* Newmark Learning LLC.
—Count on Me. 2009. (Sight Word Readers Set A Ser.). (J). *(978-1-60719-154-4(7))* Newmark Learning LLC.
—I Am Active. 2009. (Sight Word Readers Set A Ser.). (J). *(978-1-60719-139-1(3))* Newmark Learning LLC.
—I Go! 2009. (Sight Word Readers Set A Ser.). (J). 3.49 net. *(978-1-60719-143-8(1))* Newmark Learning LLC.
—I Like the Spring! 2009. (Sight Word Readers Set A Ser.). (J). 3.49 net. *(978-1-60719-138-4(5))* Newmark Learning LLC.
—I Like to Play Sports. 2009. (Sight Word Readers Set A Ser.). (J). 3.49 net. *(978-1-60719-135-3(0))* Newmark Learning LLC.
—In the Water. 2009. (Sight Word Readers Set A Ser.). (J). 3.49 net. *(978-1-60719-142-1(3))* Newmark Learning LLC.
—Jobs Around Town. 2009. (Sight Word Readers Set A Ser.). (J). 3.49 net. *(978-1-60719-158-2(X))* Newmark Learning LLC.
—Look at the Coins. 2009. (Sight Word Readers Set A Ser.). (J). 3.49 net. *(978-1-60719-155-1(5))* Newmark Learning LLC.
—Look at the Shapes. 2009. (Sight Word Readers Set A Ser.). (J). 3.49 net. *(978-1-60719-152-0(0))* Newmark Learning LLC.
—Look at the Sky. 2009. (Sight Word Readers Set A Ser.). (J). 3.49 net. *(978-1-60719-141-4(5))* Newmark Learning LLC.
—Look at the Weather. 2009. (Sight Word Readers Set A Ser.). (J). *(978-1-60719-140-7(7))* Newmark Learning LLC.
—My Family. 2009. (Sight Word Readers Set A Ser.). (J). 3.49 net. *(978-1-60719-148-3(2))* Newmark Learning LLC.
—My Home. 2009. (Sight Word Readers Set A Ser.). (J). 3.49 net. *(978-1-60719-144-5(X))* Newmark Learning LLC.
—My Pet. 2009. (Sight Word Readers Set A Ser.). (J). 3.49 net. *(978-1-60719-145-2(8))* Newmark Learning LLC.
—My Town. 2009. (Sight Word Readers Set A Ser.). (J). *(978-1-60719-147-6(4))* Newmark Learning LLC.
—We Go to School. 2009. (Sight Word Readers Set A Ser.). (J). 3.49 net. *(978-1-60719-146-9(6))* Newmark Learning LLC.
—We Have Fruit. 2009. (Sight Word Readers Set A Ser.). (J). *(978-1-60719-136-0(9))* Newmark Learning LLC.
—We Like Birthdays. 2009. (Sight Word Readers Set A Ser.). (J). 3.49 net. *(978-1-60719-149-0(0))* Newmark Learning LLC.
—What Has Stripes? 2009. (Sight Word Readers Set A Ser.). (J). 3.49 net. *(978-1-60719-151-3(2))* Newmark Learning LLC.
—What Is the Time? 2009. (Sight Word Readers Set A Ser.). (J). 3.49 net. *(978-1-60719-150-6(4))* Newmark Learning LLC.
Jon's Football Team, Level 1. 2016. (Ladybird Readers Ser.). (ENG., Illus.). 48p. (J). (gr. 2-4). pap. 9.99 *(978-0-241-25411-0(6))* Penguin Bks., Ltd. GBR. Dist: Independent Pubs. Group.
Jordan, Apple. The Right Track (Disney Frozen) RH Disney, illus. 2017. (Step into Reading Ser.). (ENG.). 24p. (J). (gr. -1-1). pap. 4.99 *(978-0-7364-3588-8(3)*, RH/Disney) Random Hse. Children's Bks.
—Star Song. 2016. (Barbie Step into Reading Level 2 Ser.). lib. bdg. 14.75 *(978-0-606-38885-6(0))* Turtleback Bks.
Jordan, Shirley J. Egypt, 1 vol. 2007. (Primary Source Readers Ser.). (ENG.). 32p. (J). (gr. 5-5). pap. 8.99 *(978-0-7439-0428-5(1))* Shell Educational Publishing.
—Hatshepsut: First Female Pharaoh, 1 vol. 2007. (Primary Source Readers Ser.). (ENG.). 32p. (J). (gr. 4-4). pap. 8.99 *(978-0-7439-0429-2(X))* Shell Educational Publishing.
The Journal: Dear Future II: Individual Title Six-Packs. (Action Packs Ser.). 104p. (gr. 3-5). 44.00 *(978-0-7635-8417-7(7))* Rigby Education.
Joven, C. C. Baseball Buzz. Shems, Ed, illus. 2017. (Sports Illustrated Kids Starting Line Readers Ser.). (ENG.). 32p. (gr. -1-1). lib. bdg. 22.65 *(978-1-4965-4252-6(5))* Capstone Press of Coughlan Cos.
—Basketball Break. Lopez, Alex, illus. 2017. (Sports Illustrated Kids Starting Line Readers Ser.). (ENG.). 32p. (gr. -1-1). lib. bdg. 22.65 *(978-1-4965-4253-3(3))* Capstone Press of Coughlan Cos.
Joyce, Jeffrey. A Week with Nate. 2012. (InfoMax Readers Ser.). (ENG., Illus.). 16 pp.p. (J). (gr. k-1). pap. 7.00 *(978-1-4488-8908-2(1)*, Rosen Classroom) Rosen Publishing Group, Inc., The.
Joyner, Michael. Na Anijoi Sigwa - the Three Pigs. 2015. (ENG & CHR., Illus.). 88p. pap. 11.99 *(978-1-329-31978-3(8))* Lulu Pr., Inc.
—Na Anijoi Wesa Anida Ale Jitaga Usdi - the Three Kittens & Chicken Little. 2016. (ENG & CHR., Illus.). 68p. pap. 10.99 *(978-1-329-93340-8(0))* Lulu Pr., Inc.
—Na Anijoi Wesa Anida Ale Jitaga Usdi / Jalagi-Yonega Didehlogwasdodi - the Three Kittens & Chicken Little / Cherokee-English Dictionary. 2016. (ENG & CHR., Illus.). 42p. pap. 9.99 *(978-1-329-93441-2(5))* Lulu Pr., Inc.
—Na Anijoi Yona - the Three Bears. 2015. (ENG & CHR., Illus.). 60p. pap. 11.99 *(978-1-329-35573-6(3))* Lulu Pr., Inc.
—Na Usdi Agigage Jitaga Agisi - the Little Red Hen. 2015. (ENG & CHR., Illus.). 82p. pap. 11.99 *(978-1-329-22721-7(2))* Lulu Pr., Inc.
Juel, Connie, et al. Ready Readers: Collection. 2005. (J). (gr. 2-18). 698.50 *(978-0-7652-6094-9(8))* Modern Curriculum Pr.
—Ready Readers: Nonfiction Favorites. 2005. (J). (gr. k-18). 699.95 *(978-0-7652-6089-5(1))*; (gr. 1-18). 469.95 *(978-0-7652-6093-2(X))* Modern Curriculum Pr.
—Ready Readers: Set 1 Collection. 2005. (J). (gr. k-18). 910.50 *(978-0-7652-6086-4(7))*; (gr. 1-18). 793.50 *(978-0-7652-6090-1(5))* Modern Curriculum Pr.
—Ready Readers: Set 2 Collection. 2005. (J). (gr. k-18). 979.95 *(978-0-7652-6087-1(5))*; (gr. 1-18). 1325.95 *(978-0-7652-6091-8(3))* Modern Curriculum Pr.
—Ready Readers: Set 3 Collection. 2005. (J). (gr. k-18). 793.50 *(978-0-7652-6088-8(3))*; (gr. 1-18). 1138.50 *(978-0-7652-6092-5(1))* Modern Curriculum Pr.
Julia, Donaldson. Follow the Swallow. Ursell, Martin, illus. 2nd ed. 2016. (Reading Ladder Ser.). (ENG.). 48p. (J). (gr. k-2). pap. 7.99 *(978-1-4052-8200-0(2))* Egmont Bks., Ltd. GBR. Dist: Independent Pubs. Group.
Jump & Thump! Individual Title Six-Packs. (gr. -1-2). 23.00 *(978-0-7635-8802-1(4))* Rigby Education.
The Jungle: Individual Title Six-Packs. (Sails Literacy Ser.). 16p. (gr. k-18). 27.00 *(978-0-7635-4388-4(8))* Rigby Education.
Jungle Fun. 2017. (Jungle Fun Ser.). 24p. (gr. 4-6). 70.80 ***(978-1-5081-6182-0(8)***, PowerKids Pr.) Rosen Publishing Group, Inc., The.
Jungman, Ann. The Footballing Frog. Burnett, Seb, illus. 2007. (Collins Big Cat Ser.). (ENG.). 80p. (J). (gr. 3-4). pap. 8.99 *(978-0-00-723087-7(7))* HarperCollins Pubs. Ltd. GBR. Dist: Independent Pubs. Group.
The junk Box 6 Packs. Individual Title. (gr. 1-2). 22.00 *(978-0-7635-9170-0(X))* Rigby Education.
The Junk-Food Files. 2003. (Illus.). pap. 5.60 *(978-0-7398-7513-1(2))* Steck-Vaughn.
Junyk, Myra. The 10 Greatest Presidents. 2007. (J). 14.99 *(978-1-55448-457-7(X))* Scholastic Library Publishing.
—The 10 Mightiest Rivers. 2008. (J). 14.99 *(978-1-55448-519-2(3))* Scholastic Library Publishing.
—The 10 Most Defining Moments of the Civil War. 2008. (J). 14.99 *(978-1-55448-518-5(5))* Scholastic Library Publishing.
Just Ducky Board Book Set 800794, 3. 2005. (J). bds. *(978-1-59794-023-8(2))* Environments, Inc.
Just My Luck! 6 Packs. Individual Title. (Literatura 2000 Ser.). (gr. 1-2). 28.00 *(978-0-7635-0139-6(5))* Rigby Education.
Just Right: KinderConcepts Individual Title Six-Packs. (Kinderstarters Ser.). 8p. (gr. -1-1). 21.00 *(978-0-7635-8738-3(9))* Rigby Education.
Just the Right Word! (gr. k-3). 106.00 *(978-0-7362-2594-6(3))* CENGAGE Learning.
Justice, Laura M. & Sofka, Amy E. Engaging Children with Print: Building Early Literacy Skills Through Quality Read-Alouds. 2010. (ENG., Illus.). 214p. 73.00 *(978-1-60623-536-2(2))*; pap. 28.00 *(978-1-60623-535-5(4))* Guilford Pubns.
K Take-Home Readers Blms Set. 2003. (Metro Reading Ser.). (gr. k). *(978-1-58120-608-1(9))* Metropolitan Teaching & Learning Co.
Kachur, Matthew. A Miracle Material: Set Of 6. 2011. (Navigators Ser.). (J). 48.00 net. *(978-1-4108-0430-3(5))* Benchmark Education Co.
Kalar, Bonnie. At Dawn. Spreen, Kathe, illus. Date not set. 8p. (J). (gr. -1-2). pap. *(978-1-891619-24-3(1))* Corona Pr.
—At the Lake. Spreen, Kathe, illus. Date not set. 12p. (J). (gr. -1-2). pap. *(978-1-891619-34-2(9))* Corona Pr.
—At the Pond. Spreen, Kathe, illus. Date not set. 8p. (J). (gr. -1-2). pap. *(978-1-891619-07-6(1))* Corona Pr.
—At the Zoo. Spreen, Kathe, illus. Date not set. 8p. (J). (gr. -1-2). pap. *(978-1-891619-18-2(7))* Corona Pr.
—Beth & Thad. Spreen, Kathe, illus. Date not set. 12p. (J). (gr. -1-2). pap. *(978-1-891619-17-5(9))* Corona Pr.
—The Bird & the Shirt. Spreen, Kathe, illus. Date not set. 12p. (J). (gr. -1-2). pap. *(978-1-891619-30-4(6))* Corona Pr.
—Burt. Spreen, Kathe, illus. Date not set. 8p. (J). (gr. -1-2). pap. *(978-1-891619-31-1(4))* Corona Pr.
—Chuck & the Chick. Spreen, Kathe, illus. Date not set. 8p. (J). (gr. -1-2). pap. *(978-1-891619-16-8(0))* Corona Pr.
—The Clown. Spreen, Kathe, illus. Date not set. 12p. (J). (gr. -1-2). pap. *(978-1-891619-22-9(5))* Corona Pr.
—The Cook & the Crook. Spreen, Kathe, illus. Date not set. 12p. (J). (gr. -1-2). pap. *(978-1-891619-29-8(2))* Corona Pr.
—The Crows. Spreen, Kathe, illus. Date not set. 8p. (J). (gr. -1-2). pap. *(978-1-891619-28-1(4))* Corona Pr.
—A Dream. Spreen, Kathe, illus. Date not set. 12p. (J). (gr. -1-2). pap. *(978-1-891619-23-6(3))* Corona Pr.
—Early Phonetic Readers - Set A, 5 bks., Set. Spreen, Kathe, illus. Incl. Bob. pap. *(978-1-891619-01-4(2))*; Cat & the Ant. pap. *(978-1-891619-02-1(0))*; Gus on the Bus. pap. *(978-1-891619-03-8(9))*; Hen & the Jet. pap. *(978-1-891619-05-2(5))*; Tim & Kim. pap. *(978-1-891619-04-5(7))*; 8p. (J). (gr. -1-2). 1998. (Illus.). 8.25 *(978-1-891619-00-7(4))* Corona Pr.
—Early Phonetic Readers - Set B, 5 bks., Set. Spreen, Kathe, illus. Incl. At the Pond. pap. *(978-1-891619-07-6(1))*; Fran & the Doll. pap. *(978-1-891619-09-0(8))*; Fred. pap. *(978-1-891619-10-6(1))*; Stan & His Sled. pap. *(978-1-891619-08-3(X))*; Trip. pap. *(978-1-891619-11-3(X))*; 8p. (J). (gr. -1-2). (Illus.). 8.25 *(978-1-891619-06-9(3))* Corona Pr.
—Early Phonetic Readers - Set C, 20 bks., Set. Spreen, Kathe, illus. Incl. At Dawn. 8p. pap. *(978-1-891619-24-3(1))*; At the Zoo. 8p. pap. *(978-1-891619-18-2(7))*; Beth & Thad. 12p. pap. *(978-1-891619-17-5(9))*; Bird & the Shirt. 12p. pap. *(978-1-891619-30-4(6))*; Bright Light. 8p. 5.25 hd *(978-1-891619-32-8(2))*; Burt. 8p. pap. *(978-1-891619-31-1(4))*; Chuck & the Chick. 8p. pap. *(978-1-891619-16-8(0))*; Clown. 12p. pap. *(978-1-891619-22-9(5))*; Cook & the Crook. 12p. pap. *(978-1-891619-29-8(2))*; Crows. 8p. pap. *(978-1-891619-28-1(4))*; Dream. 12p. pap. *(978-1-891619-23-6(3))*; Gail Sails. 12p. pap. *(978-1-891619-20-5(9))*; Gay & Jay Play. 8p. pap. *(978-1-891619-19-9(5))*; Jack. 12p. pap. *(978-1-891619-13-7(6))*; Joan's Coat. 12p. pap. *(978-1-891619-21-2(7))*; Josh & the Fish. 8p. pap. *(978-1-891619-14-4(4))*; Lew & His New Cap. 8p. pap. *(978-1-891619-27-4(6))*; Mark at the Farm. 12p. pap. *(978-1-891619-25-0(X))*; Scouts. 8p. pap. *(978-1-891619-26-7(8))*; Sheep & the Bee. 8p. pap. *(978-1-891619-15-1(2))*; (J). (gr. -1-2). (Illus.). 38.50 *(978-1-891619-12-0(8))* Corona Pr.
—Early Phonetic Readers - Set D, 3 bks., Set. Spreen, Kathe, illus. Incl. At the Lake. 12p. pap. *(978-1-891619-34-2(9))*; Mike. 8p. pap. *(978-1-891619-35-9(7))*; Rose & the Mole. 12p. pap. *(978-1-891619-36-6(5))*; (J). (gr. -1-2). (Illus.). 6.25 *(978-1-891619-33-5(0))* Corona Pr.
—Fran & the Doll. Spreen, Kathe, illus. Date not set. 8p. (J). (gr. -1-2). pap. *(978-1-891619-09-0(8))* Corona Pr.
—Fred. Spreen, Kathe, illus. Date not set. 8p. (J). (gr. -1-2). pap. *(978-1-891619-10-6(1))* Corona Pr.
—Gail Sails. Spreen, Kathe, illus. Date not set. 12p. (J). (gr. -1-2). pap. *(978-1-891619-20-5(9))* Corona Pr.
—Gay & Jay Play. Spreen, Kathe, illus. Date not set. 8p. (J). (gr. -1-2). pap. *(978-1-891619-19-9(5))* Corona Pr.
—Joan's Coat. Spreen, Kathe, illus. Date not set. 12p. (J). (gr. -1-2). pap. *(978-1-891619-21-2(7))* Corona Pr.
—Lew & His New Cap. Spreen, Kathe, illus. Date not set. 8p. (J). (gr. -1-2). pap. *(978-1-891619-27-4(6))* Corona Pr.
—Mark at the Farm. Spreen, Kathe, illus. Date not set. 12p. (J). (gr. -1-2). pap. *(978-1-891619-25-0(X))* Corona Pr.
—Mike. Spreen, Kathe, illus. Date not set. 8p. (J). (gr. -1-2). pap. *(978-1-891619-35-9(7))* Corona Pr.
—Rose & the Mole. Spreen, Kathe, illus. Date not set. 12p. (J). (gr. -1-2). pap. *(978-1-891619-36-6(5))* Corona Pr.
—The Sheep & the Bee. Spreen, Kathe, illus. Date not set. 8p. (J). (gr. -1-2). pap. *(978-1-891619-15-1(2))* Corona Pr.
—Stan & His Sled. Spreen, Kathe, illus. Date not set. 8p. (J). (gr. -1-2). pap. *(978-1-891619-08-3(X))* Corona Pr.
—The Trip. Spreen, Kathe, illus. Date not set. 8p. (J). (gr. -1-2). pap. *(978-1-891619-11-3(X))* Corona Pr.
Kalinowski, Delphine. Frog's Fruit Stand. 2006. (Neighborhood Readers Ser.). (ENG.). 8p. (gr. 1-3). pap. 5.15 *(978-1-4042-6807-4(3)*, Rosen Classroom) Rosen Publishing Group, Inc., The.
—The Weather Report. 2008. (Real Readers - Upper Emergent Ser.). (ENG., Illus.). 12p. (gr. 1-2). pap. 5.90 *(978-0-8239-8207-3(6))* Rosen Publishing Group, Inc., The.
Kammerer, Heitiare. Pa'a Pono. 2008. (ENG & HAW.). (J). lib. bdg. *(978-0-9773495-7-9(8))* Na Kamalei Koolauloa Early Education Program.
Kann, Victoria. Cherry Blossom. 2015. (Pinkalicious I Can Read Ser.). (J). lib. bdg. 13.55 *(978-0-606-36480-5(3))* Turtleback Bks.
—Pinkalicious & the Babysitter. Kann, Victoria, illus. 2017. (I Can Read Level 1 Ser.). (Illus.). 32p. (J). (gr. -1-3). pap. 3.99 ***(978-0-06-256688-1(1))*** HarperCollins Pubs.
Kann, Victoria. Story Time. 2016. (Pinkalicious I Can Read Ser.). (J). lib. bdg. 13.55 *(978-0-606-38758-3(7))* Turtleback Bks.
Katz, Ben & Nyman, Debbie. The 10 Greatest Sports Dynasties. 2008. 14.99 *(978-1-55448-525-3(8))* Scholastic Library Publishing.
Kawa, Katie. The Fearless Honey Badger. 2013. (Rosen Readers Ser.). (ENG.). 24p. (J). (gr. 3-4). pap. 8.25 *(978-1-4777-2513-9(X))*; pap. 49.50 *(978-1-4777-2514-6(8))* Rosen Publishing Group, Inc., The. (Rosen Classroom).
Kelly, Maoliosa. My Bike Ride: Band 02A/Red A. Roberts, Ley Honor, illus. 2006. (Collins Big Cat Ser.). (ENG.). 16p. (J). (gr. -1-k). pap. 5.99 *(978-0-00-718661-7(4))* HarperCollins Pubs. Ltd. GBR. Dist: Independent Pubs. Group.
—My Party. Lumb, Steve, photos by. 2005. (Collins Big Cat Ser.). (ENG., Illus.). 16p. (J). (gr. -1-k). pap. 5.99 *(978-0-00-718533-7(2))* HarperCollins Pubs. Ltd. GBR. Dist: Independent Pubs. Group.
—My Party. 2005. (Big Cat Ser.). (gr. k-2). pap. 6.50 *(978-1-60457-020-5(2))* Pacific Learning, Inc.
—What Am I? Band 00/Lilac. Blake, Beccy, illus. 2007. (Collins Big Cat Ser.). (ENG.). 16p. (J). (gr. -1-k). pap. 5.99 *(978-0-00-718679-2(7))* HarperCollins Pubs. Ltd. GBR. Dist: Independent Pubs. Group.
Kelly, Sharon L. C. M. Coco's Vineyard Vacation: Double Fun on Martha's Vineyard. Galbraith, Alison L., illus. 2005. 40p. (J). 16.95 *(978-0-9766283-0-9(9))* Secret Garden Bookworks.
Kemp, Kristin. Of Mice & Men: An Instructional Guide for Literature. 2015. (Great Works). (ENG., Illus.). 72p. (gr. 9-12). pap. 9.99 *(978-1-4807-8508-3(3))* Shell Educational Publishing.
Kennedy, J. Aday. Stella, the Fire Farting Dragon. Foster, Jack, illus. 2011. 20p. pap. 10.95 *(978-1-61633-149-8(6))* Guardian Angel Publishing, Inc.
Kennedy, Laura. Pat's Vat Goes Splat: A Lesson in Honesty. 2013. 12p. pap. 10.99 *(978-0-9836230-1-4(5))* Kennedy Enterprises, LLC.
Kennedy, Tim, compiled by. The Road Less Traveled: Seventh Grade Reader. 2004. (Reading to Learn Ser.). (Illus.). v, 265p. (J). *(978-0-87813-852-4(8))* Christian Light Pubns., Inc.
Kenrick, Joanna. Tears of a Friend. 2004. (Shades Ser.). 56p. (J). pap. *(978-0-237-52731-0(6))* Evans Brothers, Ltd.
Kenshole, Fiona. Let's Go to the Rainforest. 2010. (ENG., Illus.). 28p. 4.81 *(978-0-19-440106-7(5))* Oxford Univ. Pr., Inc.
Kernan, Elizabeth. Dolly Takes a Drive. 2006. (Neighborhood Readers Ser.). (ENG., Illus.). 12p. (gr. -1-3). pap. 5.90 *(978-1-4042-6754-1(9)*, Rosen Classroom) Rosen Publishing Group, Inc., The.
—Fred's Bread. 2006. (Neighborhood Readers Ser.). (ENG., Illus.). 16p. (gr. 1-3). pap. 6.50 *(978-1-4042-7010-7(8)*, Rosen Classroom) Rosen Publishing Group, Inc., The.
—Patty's Pictures. 2006. (Neighborhood Readers Ser.). (ENG.). 12p. (gr. -1-3). pap. 5.90 *(978-1-4042-6471-7(X)*, Rosen Classroom) Rosen Publishing Group, Inc., The.
Kerrigan, Juliet. Life & Death in a Hill Fort. 2015. (Collins Big Cat Ser.). (ENG., Illus.). 32p. (J). (gr. 3-3). pap. 8.95 *(978-0-00-812773-2(5))* HarperCollins Pubs. Ltd. GBR. Dist: Independent Pubs. Group.
—Underwater Treasure. 2016. (ENG.). 32p. (J). (gr. 2-3). pap. 8.95 *(978-0-00-816384-6(7))* HarperCollins Pubs. Ltd. GBR. Dist: Independent Pubs. Group.
Kerrin, Jessica Scott & Kerrin, Jessica. Martin Bridge: On the Lookout! Kelly, Joseph, illus. 2005. (Martin Bridge Ser.). (ENG.). 144p. (J). (gr. 2-5). 6.95 *(978-1-55337-773-3(7))* Kids Can Pr., Ltd. CAN. Dist: Hachette Bk. Group.
Kertell, Lynn Maslen. Bob Books: First Stories. Sullivan, Dana, illus. 2015. (ENG.). (J). (gr. k-2). pap. 16.99 *(978-0-545-73409-7(6))* Scholastic, Inc.
—Cupcake Surprise! 2012. (BOB Books: Scholastic Readers Level 1 Ser.). lib. bdg. 13.55 *(978-0-606-23910-3(3)*, Turtleback) Turtleback Bks.
Kerven, Rosalind. Sparrow, the Crow & the Pearl. Williamson, Melanie, illus. 2005. (ENG.). 24p. (J). lib. bdg. 23.65 *(978-1-59646-754-5(1))* Dingles & Co.
Kessler, Colleen & Benchmark Education Co. Staff. Rodrigo & the Dogs. 2014. (Text Connections Ser.). (J). (gr. 6). *(978-1-4900-1525-5(6))* Benchmark Education Co.
Khan, Sarah. Birds Lift-the-Flap. Scott, Peter, illus. 2004. (Luxury Lift-the-Flap Ser.). 16p. (J). (gr. 1-18). 11.95 *(978-0-7945-0714-5(X)*, Usborne) EDC Publishing.
Khatreja, Himani. Free the Galaxy. 2015. (LEGO Star Wars DK Reader Ser.). lib. bdg. 13.55 *(978-0-606-37410-1(8))* Turtleback Bks.
Kids Can Read Staff, ed. Franklin's Pond Phantom. 2005. (Kids Can Read Ser.). (ENG., Illus.). 32p. (J). (gr. 1-2). 3.95 *(978-1-55337-719-1(2))* Kids Can Pr., Ltd. CAN. Dist: Hachette Bk. Group.
The Kids from Quiller's Bend: Individual Title Six-Packs. (Action Packs Ser.). 120p. (gr. 3-5). 44.00 *(978-0-7635-8432-0(0))* Rigby Education.
Kij, Krysia. Becoming a Butterfly. 2008. (Real Readers - Upper Emergent Ser.). (ENG., Illus.). 12p. (gr. 1-2). pap. 5.90 *(978-0-8239-8203-5(3))* Rosen Publishing Group, Inc., The.
Kimmelman, Leslie & Shepherd, Jodie. Phonics Fun! (Sesame Street) Brannon, Tom, illus. 2017. (ENG.). 144p. (J). (gr. -1-2). pap. 12.99 *(978-1-101-93755-6(6)*, Random Hse. Bks. for Young Readers) Random Hse. Children's Bks.
Kincaid, S. J. Catalyst. 2015. (Insignia Ser.: 3). (ENG.). 432p. (YA). (gr. 8). pap. 9.99 *(978-0-06-209306-6(1)*, Tegen, Katherine Bks) HarperCollins Pubs.
Kindergarten Book Set 800084, 10. 2005. (J). bds. *(978-1-59794-002-3(X))* Environments, Inc.
Kindergarten Ell Picture Book Stories Blms. 2003. (Metro Reading Ser.). (gr. k). 35.99 *(978-1-58120-601-2(1))* Metropolitan Teaching & Learning Co.
Kindergarten Ell Practice Picture Cards Blms. 2003. (Metro Reading Ser.). (gr. k). 41.29 *(978-1-58120-602-9(X))* Metropolitan Teaching & Learning Co.
Kindergarten Ell Program Lap Book. 2003. (Metro Reading Ser.). (J). (gr. k). spiral bd. 116.55 *(978-1-58120-603-6(8))* Metropolitan Teaching & Learning Co.
Kindergarten Ell Program Teacher's Guide. 2003. (Metro Reading Ser.). (gr. k). per. 41.29 *(978-1-58120-607-4(0))* Metropolitan Teaching & Learning Co.
Kindergarten Review 1.1: Take-Home Version. 2004. (Scott Foresman Reading Ser.). (gr. 1-18). stu. ed. 48.00 *(978-0-328-02543-5(7))* Addison-Wesley Educational Pubs., Inc.
Kinderstarters: KinderStarters Complete Package. 1840.00 *(978-0-7635-8909-7(8))* Rigby Education.
King, Emmett. A Kitten Grows. 2007. (Illus.). 8p. pap. 4.75 *(978-0-15-377221-4(2))* Harcourt Schl. Pubs.
King, Germain. At the Aquarium. 2006. (Neighborhood Readers Ser.). (ENG., Illus.). 12p. (gr. -1-3). pap. 5.90 *(978-1-4042-6726-8(3)*, Rosen Classroom) Rosen Publishing Group, Inc., The.

King, Zelda. The Class Surprise. 2006. (Neighborhood Readers Ser.). (ENG.). 16p. (gr. 1-3). pap. 6.50 *(978-1-4042-6994-1(0),* Rosen Classroom) Rosen Publishing Group, Inc., The.

—The Lemonade Stand. 2006. (Neighborhood Readers Ser.). (ENG.). 12p. (gr. -1-3). pap. 5.90 *(978-1-4042-6722-0(0),* Rosen Classroom) Rosen Publishing Group, Inc., The.

—Let's Bake a Cake. 2006. (Neighborhood Readers Ser.). (ENG.). 16p. (gr. 1-3). pap. 6.50 *(978-1-4042-7260-6(7),* Rosen Classroom) Rosen Publishing Group, Inc., The.

—Where's That Cat? 2006. (Neighborhood Readers Ser.). (ENG.). 12p. (gr. 1-3). pap. 5.90 *(978-1-4042-6851-7(0),* Rosen Classroom) Rosen Publishing Group, Inc., The.

Kingdom of the Golden Dragon Bilingual Reading Group Guide. (J). *(978-0-06-072254-8(1))* HarperCollins Pubs.

The King's Cake: 3-in-1 Package. (Sails Literacy Ser.). 24p. (gr. k-18). 57.00 *(978-0-7578-3198-0(2))* Rigby Education.

The King's Cake: Big Book Only. (Sails Literacy Ser.). 24p. (gr. k-18). 27.00 *(978-0-7635-6984-6(4))* Rigby Education.

The King's Ring: KinderReaders Individual Title Six-Packs. (Kinderstarters Ser.). 8p. (gr. -1-1). 21.00 *(978-0-7635-8656-0(0))* Rigby Education.

Kinsner, Kathy. The Amazon: Set Of 6. 2010. (Early Connections Ser.). (J). pap. 39.00 net. *(978-1-4108-1549-1(8))* Benchmark Education Co.

Kirkova, Milena & Hannigan, Paula. When I'm Big. 2010. (ENG.). 12p. (J). (gr. -1-1). bds. 14.99 *(978-0-7407-9727-9(1))* Andrews McMeel Publishing.

Kirszner, Laurie G. Casebook: A Good Man Is Hard to Find. pap. 38.95 *(978-0-8384-7942-1(1))*; pap. 28.95 *(978-0-8384-7871-4(9))* Cengage Heinle.

Kita-Bradley, Linda. The Big Snore. 2003. (ENG., Illus.). 22p. pap. ***(978-1-894593-25-0(1))*** Grass Roots Pr.

—The Big Surprise. 2003. (ENG., Illus.). 28p. pap. ***(978-1-894593-24-3(3))*** Grass Roots Pr.

Kites, Vol. 3. (Early Intervention Levels Ser.). 3.55 *(978-0-7362-0089-9(4))* CENGAGE Learning.

Kithinji, Gerald, et al. Of Friends, Money & Gossip: 3 Stories & a Play. 2009. (Hodder African Readers Ser.). (Illus.). 96p. pap. 12.95 *(978-0-340-99027-8(9))* Hodder Education Group GBR. Dist: Trans-Atlantic Pubns., Inc.

Kitzmiller, Brenda. Muddy Mud — an Easy to Read Beginning Reader Book. 2005. 24p. 7.85 *(978-1-4116-2937-0(X))* Lulu Pr., Inc.

Klein, Abby. Stop That Hamster! McKinley, John, illus. 2008. (Ready, Freddy! Ser.: Bk. 12). 95p. (gr. -1-3). 16.00 *(978-0-7569-8300-0(2))* Perfection Learning Corp.

Klein, Judith Anne. Tuxedo Flyer. 2009. 28p. pap. 14.65 *(978-1-4490-0635-8(3))* AuthorHouse.

Klier, Kimberly Wagner & National Geographic Learning Staff. Firefly Friend. Garland, Michael, illus. 2010. (Rise & Shine Ser.). (ENG.). 32p. (C). (gr. k-2). pap. 7.95 *(978-0-516-26817-0(1))* National Geographic School Publishing, Inc.

Klimchuk, Karen. Manuel Makes a Map! 2013. (Rosen Readers Ser.). (ENG.). 24p. (J). (gr. 2-3). pap. 49.50 *(978-1-4777-2320-3(X))*; pap. 8.25 *(978-1-4777-2319-7(6))* Rosen Publishing Group, Inc., The. (Rosen Classroom).

Kline, Trish & Donev, Mary. Coming Home: KA Reader 8. 2007. (Illus.). 32p. (J). per. 20.00 *(978-1-934307-01-4(7))* Ghost Hunter Productions.

—Don't Frown, Clown! KA Reader 9. 2007. (Illus.). 32p. (J). per. 20.00 *(978-1-934307-02-1(5))* Ghost Hunter Productions.

—Hoops in the Coop: KA Reader 7. 2007. (Illus.). 32p. (J). per. 20.00 *(978-1-934307-00-7(9))* Ghost Hunter Productions.

Knapman, Timothy & Collins UK Staff. Leisure & Entertainment since 1900. 2016. (ENG.). 32p. (J). (gr. 2-3). pap. 8.95 *(978-0-00-816382-2(0))* HarperCollins Pubs. Ltd. GBR. Dist: Independent Pubs. Group.

Knight, Andrew. Dead Beckoning. (Thumbprint Mysteries Ser.). 32.86 *(978-0-8092-0421-2(5))* McGraw-Hill/Contemporary.

—The Monster in the Loch. (Thumbprint Mysteries Ser.). 32.86 *(978-0-8092-0411-3(8))* McGraw-Hill/Contemporary.

Knighton, Kate, retold by. Phantom of the Opera. 2008. (Young Reading Series 2 Gift Bks). 64p. (J). 8.99 *(978-0-7945-2082-3(0),* Usborne) EDC Publishing.

Knope, Liz. Carter Visits the U. S. Capitol. 2013. (Rosen Readers Ser.). (ENG.). 24p. (J). (gr. 3-4). pap. 8.25 *(978-1-4777-2531-3(8))*; pap. 49.50 *(978-1-4777-2532-0(6))* Rosen Publishing Group, Inc., The. (Rosen Classroom).

Know Zone Reading. 2004. (Scott Foresman Reading Ser.). (gr. k-1). cd-rom 29.97 *(978-0-201-68378-3(4))* Addison-Wesley Educational Pubs., Inc.

Knudsen, Michelle. El Caso de Vivian la Vampira. Wummer, Amy, illus. 2008. (Science Solves It! en Espanol Ser.). (SPA.). 32p. (J). (gr. -1-3). pap. 5.95 *(978-1-57565-277-1(3))* Kane Press, Inc.

—Fish & Frog Big Book: Brand New Readers. Petrone, Valeria, illus. 2010. (Brand New Readers Ser.). (ENG.). 48p. (J). (gr. -1-3). pap. 24.99 *(978-0-7636-4810-7(8))* Candlewick Pr.

Koch, Dorothy Clarke. When the Cows Got Out. 2016. (Illus.). 32p. (J). ***(978-0-7399-2535-5(0))*** Rod & Staff Pubs., Inc.

Koch, Dott Clarke. Jacob's House. Koch, William, ed. 2006. (J). incl. audio compact disk *(978-0-9789043-4-0(6))*; pap. *(978-0-9789043-5-7(4))* Wildot Pr.

Kocienda, Genevieve. Aliens: Is Anybody Out There? Low Intermediate Book with Online Access. 2014. (ENG.). 24p. (J). pap. 9.50 *(978-1-107-66000-7(9))* Cambridge Univ. Pr.

—Do Not Disturb: the Importance of Sleep High Beginning Book with Online Access. 2014. (ENG., Illus.). 24p. pap. 9.50 *(978-1-107-64682-7(0))* Cambridge Univ. Pr.

—Madagascar Low Intermediate Book with Online Access. 2014. (ENG., Illus.). 24p. (J). pap. 9.50 *(978-1-107-62940-0(3))* Cambridge Univ. Pr.

—On the Move: The Lives of Nomads. 2014. (ENG., Illus.). 28p. pap. 9.50 *(978-1-107-63293-6(5))* Cambridge Univ. Pr.

—Only in America Low Intermediate Book with Online Access. 2014. (ENG.). 28p. (J). pap. 9.50 *(978-1-107-63700-9(7))* Cambridge Univ. Pr.

KociendaGenevieve. BLIZZARDS: KILLER SNOWSTORM BEGINNING BOOK WITH ONLINE ACCESS. 2014. (ENG.). 24p. pap. 9.50 *(978-1-107-62164-0(X))* Cambridge Univ. Pr.

—THE MAGIC OF MUSIC LOW INTERMEDIATE BOOK WITH ONLINE ACCESS. 2014. (ENG., Illus.). 24p. (J). pap. 9.50 *(978-1-107-66558-3(2))* Cambridge Univ. Pr.

—SUSHI NATION LOW INTERMEDIATE BOOK WITH ONLINE ACCESS. 2014. (ENG., Illus.). 28p. (J). pap. 9.50 *(978-1-107-63147-2(5))* Cambridge Univ. Pr.

—THREE IN ONE: THE CHALLENGE OF THE TRIATHLON LOW INTERMEDIATE BOOK WITH ONLINE ACCESS. 2014. (ENG., Illus.). 24p. (J). pap. 9.50 *(978-1-107-62255-5(7))* Cambridge Univ. Pr.

—WATER: VITAL FOR LIFE LOW INTERMEDIATE BOOK WITH ONLINE ACCESS. 2014. (ENG., Illus.). 24p. (J). pap. 9.50 *(978-1-107-62251-7(4))* Cambridge Univ. Pr.

—WEIRD ANIMALS LOW INTERMEDIATE BOOK WITH ONLINE ACCESS. 2014. (ENG.). 24p. (J). pap. 9.50 *(978-1-107-65664-2(8))* Cambridge Univ. Pr.

—WHAT ARE THE ODDS? FROM SHARK ATTACK TO LIGHTNING STRIKE LOW INTERMEDIATE BOOK WITH ONLINE ACCESS. 2014. (ENG.). 24p. pap. 9.50 *(978-1-107-66839-3(5))* Cambridge Univ. Pr.

Koh, Frederick. The 10 Mightiest Conquerors. 2008. (J). 14.99 *(978-1-55448-517-8(7))* Scholastic Library Publishing.

—The 10 Most Compelling News Images. 2008. (J). 14.99 *(978-1-55448-533-8(9))* Scholastic Library Publishing.

—The 10 Most Fascinating Cities. 2008. (J). 14.99 *(978-1-55448-499-7(5))* Scholastic Library Publishing.

—The 10 Most Outstanding Entrepreneurs. 2008. (J). 14.99 *(978-1-55448-498-0(7))* Scholastic Library Publishing.

Kondrchek, Jamie & Rasemas, Joe. On My Way to School (De Camino a la Escuela) Vega, Eida de la, tr. Rasemas, Joe, illus. 2009. (Day in the Life Ser.). (SPA & ENG., Illus.). 32p. (J). (gr. -1-1). 25.70 *(978-1-58415-840-0(9))* Mitchell Lane Pubs., Inc.

—What Day Is It? (Que Dia Es Hoy?) Vega, Eida de la, tr. Rasemas, Joe, illus. 2009. (Day in the Life Ser.). (SPA & ENG., Illus.). 32p. (J). (gr. -1-1). 25.70 *(978-1-58415-838-7(7))* Mitchell Lane Pubs., Inc.

—What Should I Wear Today? (Que Ropa Me Pondre Hoy?) Vega, Eida de la, tr. Rasemas, Joe, illus. 2009. (Day in the Life Ser.). (ENG & SPA., Illus.). 32p. (J). (gr. -1-1). 25.70 *(978-1-58415-839-4(5))* Mitchell Lane Pubs., Inc.

Koontz, Robin. Paul Bunyan. Koontz, Robin, illus. 2012. (ENG., Illus.). 24p. (gr. 2-3). pap. 8.95 *(978-1-61810-326-0(1))* Rourke Educational Media.

—La Pequeña Lagartija, ¡el Cielo Se Está Cayendo! / Lizzie Little, the Sky Is Falling! 2012. (SPA & ENG.). 24p. (gr. 2-3). pap. 8.95 *(978-1-61810-541-7(8))* Rourke Educational Media.

—Rumpelstiltskin. Koontz, Robin, illus. 2012. (ENG., Illus.). 24p. (gr. 2-3). pap. 8.95 *(978-1-61810-327-7(X))* Rourke Educational Media.

—Run... It's a Bee! Koontz, Robin, illus. 2012. (ENG., Illus.). 24p. (gr. 2-3). pap. 8.95 *(978-1-61810-333-8(4))* Rourke Educational Media.

Koontz, Robin Michal. Robin Hood. Koontz, Robin Michal, illus. 2012. (ENG., Illus.). 24p. (gr. 2-3). pap. 8.95 *(978-1-61810-325-3(3))* Rourke Educational Media.

Koponen, Libby. Floods. 2009. (True Book Ser.). (ENG.). 48p. (J). pap. 6.95 *(978-0-531-21351-3(X),* Children's Pr.) Scholastic Library Publishing.

Korba, Joanna. Yeh-shen: A Cinderella Tale from China. 2006. (J). pap. *(978-1-4108-6162-7(7))* Benchmark Education Co.

Korky Paul: Biography of an Illustrator: Individual Title Six-Packs. (Discovery World Ser.). 24p. (gr. 1-2). 33.00 *(978-0-7635-8471-9(1))* Rigby Education.

Korman, Gordon. Everest: The Climb. 2006. pap. 8.75 *(978-0-15-365176-2(8))* Harcourt Schl. Pubs.

Korringa, Olivia. Miss Olivia Series: Lessons to Start Your Child on the Right Path of Speaking English Correctly. 2009. 28p. pap. 15.99 *(978-1-4415-8751-0(9))* Xlibris Corp.

Kovats, Moira. Tony's Deal. 2003. (ENG., Illus.). 24p. pap. ***(978-1-894593-27-4(8))*** Grass Roots Pr.

Kramer, Alan. Path from Extinction. 2004. (Reader's Theater Ser.). (J). pap. *(978-1-4108-1145-5(X))* Benchmark Education Co.

Kramer, Alan & Romer, Ruth. The Wizard of Wherever. 2004. (Reader's Theater Ser.). (J). pap. *(978-1-4108-0793-9(2))* Benchmark Education Co.

Kramer, Jennifer E. Good Luck Charlie. Moores, Jeff, illus. 2005. (Rookie Reader Skill Set Ser.). (ENG.). 32p. (J). (gr. k-2). pap. 4.95 *(978-0-516-25826-3(5),* Children's Pr.) Scholastic Library Publishing.

Kramer, Nash. What Goes Fastest? 2014. (Little Books of Answers: Level B Ser.). (Illus.). 16p. (gr. k-2). pap. 7.95 *(978-1-927136-19-5(9))* Three Crows Media NZL. Dist: RiverStream Publishing.

—Where Did My Grandparents Come From? 2014. (Little Books of Answers: Level C Ser.). (Illus.). 16p. (gr. k-2). pap. 7.95 *(978-1-927136-21-8(0))* Three Crows Media NZL. Dist: RiverStream Publishing.

—Why Do You Change in Winter? 2014. (Little Books of Answers: Level F Ser.). (Illus.). 16p. (gr. k-2). pap. 7.95 *(978-1-927136-57-7(1))* Three Crows Media NZL. Dist: RiverStream Publishing.

Kramer, S. A. Baseball's Greatest Hitters. 2016. (Step into Reading Ser.). (ENG., Illus.). 48p. (J). (gr. 2-4). 3.99 *(978-0-553-53910-3(8),* Random Hse. Bks. for Young Readers) Random Hse. Children's Bks.

Krasinski, Norma. I Am the One That Reads. 2005. (J). per. 16.99 *(978-0-9773962-1-4(5))* Marx Group, The.

—I Am Their Reading Hero. 2005. (J). per. 12.99 *(978-0-9773962-0-7(7))* Marx Group, The.

—Please, Please, Read to Me. 2005. (J). per. 14.99 *(978-0-9773962-2-1(3))* Marx Group, The.

—The Tyler Story. 2005. (J). per. 12.99 *(978-0-9773962-3-8(1))* Marx Group, The.

Krasinski, Norma & Marx, Donald. Kids Reading to Kids: The Phenomenon. 2006. per. 29.95 *(978-0-9773962-4-5(X))* Marx Group, The.

Kratky, Lada. Hello, Duck! 2003. (Rise & Shine Ser.). (ENG.). (C). pap. 7.95 *(978-0-7362-1861-0(0))* CENGAGE Learning.

Kratky, Lada, et al. Add-on Components. 2003. (Summer School Ser.). (ENG.). (C). (gr. -1-k). pap. 18.95 *(978-0-7362-2007-1(0))* CENGAGE Learning.

Kratt, Chris & Kratt, Martin. Wild Animal Babies! Random House, illus. 2016. (Step into Reading Ser.). (ENG.). 24p. (J). (gr. -1-1). 4.99 *(978-1-101-93171-4(X),* Random Hse. Bks. for Young Readers) Random Hse. Children's Bks.

—Wild Insects & Spiders! (Wild Kratts) Random House, illus. 2016. (Step into Reading Ser.). (ENG.). 24p. (J). (gr. -1-1). 4.99 *(978-1-101-93901-7(X),* Random Hse. Bks. for Young Readers) Random Hse. Children's Bks.

—Wild Kratts Step into Reading Bind-Up. Random House, illus. 2017. (Step into Reading Ser.). (ENG.). 160p. (J). (gr. -1-1). 7.99 *(978-1-101-93900-0(1),* Random Hse. Bks. for Young Readers) Random Hse. Children's Bks.

—Wild Predators (Wild Kratts) Random House, illus. 2015. (Step into Reading Ser.). (ENG.). 32p. (J). (gr. -1-1). 3.99 *(978-0-553-52472-7(0),* Random Hse. Bks. for Young Readers) Random Hse. Children's Bks.

Krebs, Laurie. We're Roaming in the Rainforest. Wilson, Anne, illus. 2010. (SPA.). 40p. (J). (gr. k-5). pap. 8.99 *(978-1-84686-551-0(4))* Barefoot Bks., Inc.

Kroll, Jennifer. The Cutting Edge: Breakthroughs in Technology, 1 vol. 2nd rev. ed. 2013. (TIME for KIDS(r) Nonfiction Readers Ser.). (ENG.). 64p. (J). (gr. 5-5). pap. 10.99 *(978-1-4333-4947-8(7))* Teacher Created Materials, Inc.

—Mighty Macros: Little Things, Big Results, 1 vol. 2nd rev. ed. 2013. (TIME for KIDS(r) Nonfiction Readers Ser.). (ENG.). 64p. (J). (gr. 5-5). pap. 10.99 *(978-1-4333-4948-5(5))* Teacher Created Materials, Inc.

Krpan, Cathy Marks. The 10 Most Phenomenal Modern Buildings. 2008. 14.99 *(978-1-55448-496-6(0))* Scholastic Library Publishing.

Kruk, Halya. The Littlest One. Morchiladze, Manana, illus. 2007. (ARA & ENG.). 32p. (J). pap. 14.95 *(978-1-60195-090-1(X))* International Step by Step Assn.

Krulik, Nancy. Crash! 2017. (Kid from Planet Z Ser.: 1). lib. bdg. 16.00 ***(978-0-606-40107-4(5))*** Turtleback Bks.

Krutop, Lee, creator. Go Out to Play. 2008. (Illus.). 10p. (J). (gr. -1-1). bds. *(978-1-74178-572-2(3))* Brimax Books Ltd.

Kubler, Annie, illus. If You're Happy & You Know It... /Si Te Sientes Bien Contento... 2009. (Baby Board Bks.). (SPA & ENG.). 12p. (J). bds. *(978-1-84643-310-8(X))* Child's Play International Ltd.

—Ten Little Fingers/Tengo Diez Deditos. 2009. (Baby Board Bks.). (SPA & ENG.). 12p. (J). bds. *(978-1-84643-312-2(6))* Child's Play International Ltd.

—This Little Piggy / Este Cochinito. 2009. (Baby Board Bks.). (SPA & ENG.). 12p. (J). bds. *(978-1-84643-313-9(4))* Child's Play International Ltd.

Kubuitsile, Lauri. Animal Homes Pink a Band. 2016. (Cambridge Reading Adventures Ser.). (ENG., Illus.). 16p. pap. 6.56 *(978-1-316-60071-9(8))* Cambridge Univ. Pr.

—For Today, for Tomorrow Orange Band. Pérez, Moni, illus. 2016. (Cambridge Reading Adventures Ser.). (ENG.). 16p. pap. 6.56 *(978-1-107-55081-0(5))* Cambridge Univ. Pr.

—Oh Bella! Yellow Band. Brown, Steve, illus. 2016. (Cambridge Reading Adventures Ser.). (ENG.). 15p. pap. 6.56 *(978-1-107-55070-4(X))* Cambridge Univ. Pr.

—Stars Yellow Band. 2016. (Cambridge Reading Adventures Ser.). (ENG.). 16p. pap. 6.56 *(978-1-316-50315-7(1))* Cambridge Univ. Pr.

—Tefo & the Lucky Football Boots Gold Band. Pérez, Moni, illus. 2016. (Cambridge Reading Adventures Ser.). (ENG.). 24p. pap. 7.19 *(978-1-107-55141-1(2))* Cambridge Univ. Pr.

Kuligowski, Stephanie. The Colonization of Texas: Missions & Settlers, 1 vol. 2012. (Primary Source Readers Ser.). (ENG.). 32p. (J). (gr. 4-4). pap. 8.99 *(978-1-4333-5044-3(0))* Teacher Created Materials, Inc.

—Leonardo Da Vinci: Renaissance Artist & Inventor, 1 vol. 2012. (Primary Source Readers Ser.). (ENG.). 32p. (J). (gr. 4-4). pap. 8.99 *(978-1-4333-5008-5(4))* Teacher Created Materials, Inc.

—The Renaissance: A Rebirth of Culture, 1 vol. 2012. (Primary Source Readers Ser.). (ENG.). 32p. (J). (gr. 5-5). pap. 8.99 *(978-1-4333-5007-8(6))* Teacher Created Materials, Inc.

—La Salle: Early Texas Explorer, 1 vol. 2012. (Primary Source Readers Ser.). (ENG.). 32p. (J). (gr. 3-3). pap. 8.99 *(978-1-4333-5043-6(2))* Teacher Created Materials, Inc.

Kumon Staff. Let's Fold!, 4 vols. 2005. (Kumon First Steps Workbooks Ser.). (Illus.). 40p. (J). (gr. -1). pap., wbk. ed. 5.95 *(978-1-933241-12-8(8))* Kumon Publishing North America, Inc.

—Let's Sticker & Paste!, 4 vols. 2005. (Kumon First Steps Workbooks Ser.). (Illus.). 40p. (J). (gr. -1). pap. 5.95 *(978-1-933241-13-5(6))* Kumon Publishing North America, Inc.

Kurtz, John & Kurtz, Sandrina. Storyland: Mr. Rodento Cleans House: A Story Coloring Book. 2015. (ENG., Illus.). 32p. (J). (gr. k-5). pap. 3.99 *(978-0-486-79391-7(5))* Dover Pubns., Inc.

Labella, Susan. Animal Survivors, 6 bks., Set. Incl. Chameleons & Other Animals with Amazing Skin. (Illus.). 24p. (J). (gr. 1-2). 2005. lib. bdg. 22.00 *(978-0-516-24925-4(8))*; (Scholastic News Nonfiction Readers Ser.). 2005. 108.00 o.p. *(978-0-516-25390-9(5),* Children's Pr.) Scholastic Library Publishing.

LaBerge, Margaret M. Sara Safety, Personal Safety: Kid's Activity Book. Lucas, Stacey L. & Lopresti, Sarah H., illus. 2004. 21p. (J). pap. *(978-0-9755561-2-2(6))* Reading Resc.

—Sara Safety, School Safety: Kid's Activity Book. Seager, Maryann et al, illus. 2004. (J). pap. *(978-0-9755561-1-5(8))* Reading Resc.

Ladybird. Anansi Helps a Friend, Level 1. 2016. (Ladybird Readers Ser.). (ENG.). 16p. (J). (gr. 2-4). pap., act. bk. ed. 5.99 *(978-0-241-25420-2(5))* Penguin Bks., Ltd. GBR. Dist: Independent Pubs. Group.

—Cars. 2016. (Read It Yourself with Ladybird Ser.). (ENG.). 32p. (J). 5.99 *(978-0-241-24444-9(7))* Penguin Bks., Ltd. GBR. Dist: Independent Pubs. Group.

—Emergency Rescue. 2016. (Read It Yourself with Ladybird Ser.). (ENG.). 32p. (J). (gr. 2-4). 5.99 *(978-0-241-24442-5(0))* Penguin Bks., Ltd. GBR. Dist: Independent Pubs. Group.

—Favourite Pets. 2016. (Read It Yourself with Ladybird Ser.). (ENG.). 32p. (J). 5.99 *(978-0-241-23734-2(3))* Penguin Bks., Ltd. GBR. Dist: Independent Pubs. Group.

—Minibeasts. 2016. (Read It Yourself with Ladybird Ser.). (ENG., Illus.). 48p. (J). 5.99 *(978-0-241-23737-3(8))* Penguin Bks., Ltd. GBR. Dist: Independent Pubs. Group.

—Our Solar System. 2016. (Read It Yourself with Ladybird Ser.). (ENG.). 48p. (J). (gr. 2-4). 5.99 *(978-0-241-23743-4(2))* Penguin Bks., Ltd. GBR. Dist: Independent Pubs. Group.

—The Pied Piper of Hamelin. 2016. (Ladybird Readers Ser.). (ENG.). 16p. (J). pap., act. bk. ed. 5.99 *(978-0-241-25373-1(X))* Penguin Bks., Ltd. GBR. Dist: Independent Pubs. Group.

—Planet Earth. 2016. (Read It Yourself with Ladybird Ser.). (ENG., Illus.). 48p. (J). 5.99 *(978-0-241-23740-3(8))* Penguin Bks., Ltd. GBR. Dist: Independent Pubs. Group.

—Sharks, Level 3. 2016. (Ladybird Readers Ser.). (ENG.). 64p. (J). (gr. 2-4). pap. 9.99 *(978-0-241-25382-3(9))* Penguin Bks., Ltd. GBR. Dist: Independent Pubs. Group.

—Space, Level 4. 2016. (Ladybird Readers Ser.). (ENG.). 16p. (J). (gr. 2-4). pap., act. bk. ed. 5.99 *(978-0-241-25377-9(2))* Penguin Bks., Ltd. GBR. Dist: Independent Pubs. Group.

Ladybird Books Staff. How to Use Ladybird Readers: A Teacher & Parent Guide. 2016. (Ladybird Readers Ser.). (ENG.). 16p. (J). pap. 5.99 *(978-0-241-26230-6(5))* Penguin Bks., Ltd. GBR. Dist: Independent Pubs. Group.

Lagonegro, Melissa. Monster Games. RH Disney Staff, illus. 2013. (Step into Reading Ser.). (ENG.). 32p. (J). (gr. -1-1). 3.99 *(978-0-7364-3106-4(3),* RH/Disney) Random Hse. Children's Bks.

Laínez, René Colato. From North to South/Del Norte Al Sur. Cepeda, Joe, illus. 2010.Tr. of Del norte al Sur. (ENG & SPA.). 32p. (J). (gr. k-3). 17.95 *(978-0-89239-231-5(2))* Lee & Low Bks., Inc.

Laird, Elizabeth & Davison, Roz. Jungle School. Sim, David, illus. 2006. (Green Bananas Ser.). (ENG.). 48p. (J). (gr. -1-3). lib. bdg. *(978-0-7787-1026-4(2))* Crabtree Publishing Co.

Lakeshore Learning Materials Staff, contrib. by. Read & Learn Nonfiction: Bold Words & Glossaries, Set of 6 Student Books. 2007. (ELX.). (J). pap. 19.95 *(978-1-59746-035-4(4))* Lakeshore Learning Materials.

—Read & Learn Nonfiction: Bold Words & Glossaries Big Book. 2007. (J). pap. 19.95 *(978-1-59746-032-3(X))* Lakeshore Learning Materials.

—Read & Learn Nonfiction: Maps, Charts, & Graphs, Set of 6 Student Books. 2007. (J). pap. 19.95 *(978-1-59746-034-7(6))* Lakeshore Learning Materials.

—Read & Learn Nonfiction: Maps, Charts, & Graphs Big Book. 2007. (J). pap. 19.95 *(978-1-59746-031-6(1))* Lakeshore Learning Materials.

—Read & Learn Nonfiction: Photos, Captions, & Diagrams, Set of 6 Student Books. 2007. (J). pap. 19.95 *(978-1-59746-033-0(8))* Lakeshore Learning Materials.

—Read & Learn Nonfiction: Photos, Captions, & Diagrams Big Book. 2007. (J). pap. 19.95 *(978-1-59746-030-9(3))* Lakeshore Learning Materials.

—Storyteller Complete Library: CD Version. 2007. (J). 99.50 incl. audio compact disk *(978-1-59746-019-4(2))* Lakeshore Learning Materials.

Lakin, Patricia. Max & Mo's Halloween Surprise. Floca, Brian, illus. 2008. (Max & Mo Ser.). (ENG.). 32p. (J). (gr. -1-1). pap. 3.99 *(978-1-4169-2539-2(2),* Simon Spotlight) Simon Spotlight.

Lakin, Patricia & Bader, Bonnie. Vroom, Zoom, Bud. Atkinson, Cale, illus. 2016. (Penguin Young Readers, Level 1 Ser.). (ENG.). 32p. (J). (gr. k-1). 3.99 *(978-0-448-48832-5(9),* Penguin Young Readers) Penguin Young Readers Group.

Lalley, Kristine. Busy Bees. 2008. (Rosen Real Readers: Upper Emergent Ser.). (ENG., Illus.). 12p. (gr. 1-2). pap. 5.90 *(978-0-8239-8132-8(0))* Rosen Publishing Group, Inc., The.

—Show & Tell. 2006. (Neighborhood Readers Ser.). (ENG.). 12p. (gr. -1-3). pap. 5.90 *(978-1-4042-6465-6(5),* Rosen Classroom) Rosen Publishing Group, Inc., The.

Laman, Judi-Lynn. The 10 Most Bizarre Animal Habits. 2008. 14.99 *(978-1-55448-542-0(8))* Scholastic Library Publishing.

Lambert, Mark John. The 10 Most Incredible Landforms. 2008. (J). 14.99 *(978-1-55448-529-1(0))* Scholastic Library Publishing.

Lambert, Nancy R. Ant-Man Game Over. 2015. (Marvel World of Reading Level 2 Ser.). (J). lib. bdg. 13.55 *(978-0-606-37536-8(8))* Turtleback Bks.

Lamplighter Staff. The Boys of Grit Who Changed. 2004. 16.00 *(978-1-58474-031-5(0))* Cornerstone Family Ministries/Lamplighter Publishing.

—Clean Your Boots Sir? 2004. 14.00 *(978-1-58474-015-5(9))* Cornerstone Family Ministries/Lamplighter Publishing.

—Fireside Readings. 2004. 16.00 *(978-1-58474-042-1(6))* Cornerstone Family Ministries/Lamplighter Publishing.

—Hidden Hand. 2004. 22.00 *(978-1-58474-107-7(4))* Cornerstone Family Ministries/Lamplighter Publishing.

—Highland Chairman. 2004. 12.00 *(978-1-58474-037-7(X))* Cornerstone Family Ministries/Lamplighter Publishing.

—Inheritance. 2004. 15.00 *(978-1-58474-009-4(4))* Cornerstone Family Ministries/Lamplighter Publishing.

—Me & Nobbles. 2004. 17.00 *(978-1-58474-102-2(3))* Cornerstone Family Ministries/Lamplighter Publishing.

—Melody the Story of a Child. 2004. 16.00 *(978-1-58474-016-2(7))* Cornerstone Family Ministries/Lamplighter Publishing.

—Nobody Loves Me. 2004. 15.00 *(978-1-58474-035-3(3))* Cornerstone Family Ministries/Lamplighter Publishing.

—Probable Sons. 2004. 15.00 *(978-1-58474-033-9(7))* Cornerstone Family Ministries/Lamplighter Publishing.

Lamson, Martha. Oliver. 2008. 28p. pap. 15.99 *(978-1-4363-5100-3(6))* Xlibris Corp.

Lancett, Peter. Escape from the Dark (Blue Series), 1 vol. 2015. (Dark Man Ser.). (ENG.). 36p. (YA). (gr. 9-12). pap. 7.95 *(978-1-68021-126-9(9))* Saddleback Educational Publishing, Inc.

—The Past Is Dark. 2008. (Dark Man Ser.). (ENG., Illus.). 48p. pap. *(978-1-84167-747-7(7))* Ransom Publishing Ltd.

—The Shadow in the Dark, 1 vol. unabr. ed. 2010. (Dark Man Ser.). (ENG.). 34p. (YA). (gr. 9-12). pap. 7.95 *(978-1-61651-021-3(8))* Saddleback Educational Publishing, Inc.

Lanchais, Aurelie, et al. Kto A? 2005. (Who Am I? What Am I? Ser.).Tr. of Who Am I? (RUS, ENG, TUR, VIE & CHI., Illus.). 16p. (J). (gr. -1-1). 9.95 *(978-1-84059-232-0(X))* Milet Publishing.

—What Am I? 2005. (Who Am I? What Am I? Ser.). (Illus.). 16p. (J). (gr. -1-1). (URD, ENG, CHI, ARA & BEN.). 9.95 *(978-1-84059-248-1(6))*; (ARA, ENG, URD, TUR & CHI., 9.95 *(978-1-84059-243-6(5))* Milet Publishing.

—Who Am I? 2005. (Who Am I? What Am I? Ser.). (CHI, ENG, VIE, GUJ & RUS., Illus.). 16p. (J). (gr. -1-1). 9.95 *(978-1-84059-229-0(X))* Milet Publishing.

Landeman, Tanya. The Little Egg. 2006. (Collins Big Cat Ser.). (ENG., Illus.). 16p. (J). (gr. 1-1). pap. 5.99 *(978-0-00-718677-8(0))* HarperCollins Pubs. Ltd. GBR. Dist: Independent Pubs. Group.

Landman, Tanya. A Drop of Rain Green Band. Tait, Carys, illus. 2016. (Cambridge Reading Adventures Ser.). (ENG.). 16p. pap. 6.56 *(978-1-107-55060-5(2))* Cambridge Univ. Pr.

Landman, Tanya. The Fisherman & His Wife: Band 12/Copper. 2017. (Collins Big Cat Tales Ser.). (ENG., Illus.). 32p. (J). (gr. 2-3). pap. 7.99 ***(978-0-00-817931-1(X))*** HarperCollins Pubs. Ltd. GBR. Dist: Independent Pubs. Group.

Landolf, Diane Wright. Thumbelina. Random House Audio Publishing Group Staff, illus. 2009. (Step into Reading Ser.). (ENG.). 32p. (J). (gr. -1-1). pap. 3.99 *(978-0-375-85690-7(0),* Random Hse. Bks. for Young Readers) Random Hse. Children's Bks.

Landolfi, Meghan Ann. Washington, D. C. 2003. (Rosen Real Readers: Upper Emergent Ser.). (ENG., Illus.). 12p. (gr. 1-2). per. 5.90 *(978-0-8239-6356-0(X))* Rosen Publishing Group, Inc., The.

Lane, Chloe. Package Design. rev. ed. 2012. (Mathematics Readers Ser.). (ENG.). 32p. (J). (gr. 6-6). pap. 8.99 *(978-1-4333-3460-3(7))* Teacher Created Materials, Inc.

Lane, Tracy & Benchmark Education Co., LLC Staff. Shade Lake. 2015. (BuildUp Ser.). (J). (gr. 1). *(978-1-4900-0725-0(3))* Benchmark Education Co.

Langford, Jane. Hero. Vince, Dawn, illus. 2005. (ENG.). 24p. (J). lib. bdg. 23.65 *(978-1-59646-720-0(7))* Dingles & Co.

—An Old Red Hat. Axworthy, Anni, illus. 2004. (ENG.). 24p. (J). lib. bdg. 23.65 *(978-1-59646-676-0(6))* Dingles & Co.

Langston-George, Rebecca, et al. Encounter: Narrative Nonfiction Stories. 2016. (Encounter: Narrative Nonfiction Stories Ser.). (ENG.). (gr. 3-4). 97.29 *(978-1-5157-3360-7(2))* Encounter Bks.

LaRose, Melinda & Disney Book Group Staff. The Croc Takes the Cake. Disney Storybook Artists Staff, illus. 2012. (World of Reading Ser.). (ENG.). 32p. (J). (gr. -1-k). pap. 3.99 *(978-1-4231-5543-0(2))* Disney Pr.

—X Marks the Croc!, Pre-Level 1. Disney Storybook Art Team, illus. 2013. (World of Reading Ser.). (ENG.). 32p. (J). (gr. -1-k). pap. 3.99 *(978-1-4231-6392-3(3))* Disney Pr.

Larsen, Becca. Buying & Selling. 2013. (Rosen Readers Ser.). (ENG.). 24p. (J). (gr. 2-3). pap. 49.50 *(978-1-4777-2261-9(0));* pap. 8.25 *(978-1-4777-2260-2(2))* Rosen Publishing Group, Inc., The. (Rosen Classroom).

Larsen, Carolyn. Little Angels Bible Storybook. Incrocci, Rick, illus. 2012. (ENG.). 432p. (J). 16.99 *(978-1-4143-7022-4(9))* Tyndale Hse. Pubs.

Larsen, Kirsten, et al. Mater & the Easter Buggy. Disney Storybook Art Team, illus. 2012. (ENG.). 48p. (J). (gr. -1-k). 12.99 *(978-1-4231-3875-4(9))* Disney Pr.

Larson, Julie, et al. Jobs in Our Community. 2010. (Reach for Reading Ser.). (ENG., Illus.). 8p. (C). pap. 7.95 *(978-0-7362-7995-6(4))* CENGAGE Learning.

—Up in the Sky. 2010. (Reach for Reading Ser.). (ENG., Illus.). 8p. (C). pap. 7.95 *(978-0-7362-7998-7(9))* CENGAGE Learning.

LaSala, Paige. Pig Kissing. Gullotti, Pat, illus. 2010. 24p. pap. 12.99 *(978-1-4520-2849-1(4))* AuthorHouse.

Last, Shari. Rebel Heroes. 2017. (Star Wars DK Readers Level 3 Ser.). lib. bdg. 13.55 ***(978-0-606-39898-5(8))*** Turtleback Bks.

Latou, Pierre. Where Do Big Machines Work? 2014. (Little Books of Answers: Level B Ser.). (Illus.). 16p. (gr. k-2). pap. 7.95 *(978-1-927136-12-6(1))* Three Crows Media NZL. Dist: RiverStream Publishing.

—Who Eats Who in A Food Chain? 2014. (Little Books of Answers: Level F Ser.). (Illus.). 16p. (gr. k-2). pap. 7.95 *(978-1-927136-58-4(X))* Three Crows Media NZL. Dist: RiverStream Publishing.

—Who Works Here? 2014. (Little Books of Answers: Level C Ser.). (Illus.). 16p. (gr. k-2). pap. 7.95 *(978-1-927136-22-5(9))* Three Crows Media NZL. Dist: RiverStream Publishing.

—Why Can Plants Grow in the Desert? 2014. (Little Books of Answers: Level e Ser.). (Illus.). 16p. (gr. k-2). pap. 7.95 *(978-1-927136-48-5(2))* Three Crows Media NZL. Dist: RiverStream Publishing.

Lavelle, Sheila. Clever Dog, Webster. 2005. *(978-1-901358-00-1(3))* CAMFA.

Lavoie, Mathieu. Toto's Apple. 2016. (ENG., Illus.). 64p. (gr. -1-k). 17.95 *(978-0-7148-7251-3(2))* Phaidon Pr., Inc.

Law, Karina, et al. Collins Primary Literacy, Bk. 1B. 2008. (Collins Primary Literacy Ser.). (ENG., Illus.). 32p. (J). (gr. 1-1). pap., stu. ed. 9.99 *(978-0-00-722694-8(2))* HarperCollins Pubs. Ltd. GBR. Dist: Independent Pubs. Group.

Lawrence, D. H. & Pearson Education Staff. British & American Short Stories. 2nd ed. 2013. (ENG.). 88p. pap. 11.99 *(978-1-4058-8239-2(5))* Pearson Education.

Leardi, Jeannette. The Brain. 2011. (Readers' & Writers' Genre Workshop Ser.). (J). pap. *(978-1-4509-3032-1(8))* Benchmark Education Co.

Learn to Read, Vol. 2. 2006. (J). per. 10.00 *(978-0-9774302-1-5(9))* Braun Pubns.

Learning Company, Inc. Staff & Houghton Mifflin Harcourt Children's Group Staff, creators. Learning with Curious George Kindergarten Reading. 2012. (Learning with Curious George Ser.). (ENG., Illus.). 64p. (J). (gr. -1-3). pap. 4.99 *(978-0-547-79096-1(1))* Houghton Mifflin Harcourt Publishing Co.

LeBaron, Cecilia. The Cap. 2007. (Illus.). 16p. (J). 5.95 *(978-0-9798869-2-8(9))* Crush Publishing.

—The Map. 2007. (Illus.). 16p. (J). 5.95 *(978-0-9798869-1-0(0))* Crush Publishing.

—Sam & Val. 2007. (Illus.). 16p. (J). 5.95 *(978-0-9798869-3-5(7))* Crush Publishing.

Leber, Nancy. Sounds All Around Us, 6 vols., Set. 2003. (Phonics Readers 1-36 Ser.). (ENG.). 8p. (gr. k-1). pap. 29.70 *(978-0-7368-3217-5(3),* Phonics Readers) Capstone Press of Coughlan Cos.

Leblanc, Denise. Mr. Blue, I Have a Question for You. 2013. 36p. pap. 15.95 *(978-1-4908-1232-8(6),* WestBow Pr.) Author Solutions, Inc.

Ledieux, Jack. The Worst Trip EVER! 2017. (Text Connections Guided Close Reading Ser.). (J). (gr. 2). *(978-1-4900-1853-9(0))* Benchmark Education Co.

Lee, April. Helping at School. 2012. (InfoMax Readers Ser.). (ENG., Illus.). 16 pp.p. (J). (gr. k-1). pap. 7.00 *(978-1-4488-8896-2(4),* Rosen Classroom) Rosen Publishing Group, Inc., The.

—How We Get Around Town. 2012. (InfoMax Readers Ser.). (ENG., Illus.). 16 pp.p. (J). (gr. k-1). pap. 7.00 *(978-1-4488-8941-9(3),* Rosen Classroom) Rosen Publishing Group, Inc., The.

Lee, Betsy B. A Funny Dolch Word Book # 1: Un Libro Comico # 1 de la Palabra de Dolch. Davis, Pollyanna S., tr. 2006. (ENG & SPA.). pap. 5.95 *(978-0-9720267-5-8(4))* Learning Abilities Bks.

Lee, David. Ellie's Family Album. 2013. (Rosen Readers Ser.). (ENG.). 24p. (J). (gr. 2-3). pap. 8.25 *(978-1-4777-2257-2(2));* pap. 49.50 *(978-1-4777-2258-9(0))* Rosen Publishing Group, Inc., The. (Rosen Classroom).

Lee, Gisela. China, 1 vol. 2007. (Primary Source Readers Ser.). (ENG.). 32p. (J). (gr. 5-5). pap. 8.99 *(978-0-7439-0436-0(2))* Shell Educational Publishing.

Lee, Kimberly Fekany. Looking Inside Cells, 1 vol. 2007. (Science Readers Ser.). (SPA & ENG.). 32p. (J). (gr. 4-4). pap. 8.99 *(978-0-7439-0583-1(0))* Shell Educational Publishing.

Lee, Quinlan B. Phonics: 12 Book Reading Program, 12 vols. 2006. (Illus.). *(978-0-439-78948-6(6)); (978-0-439-78949-3(4)); (978-0-439-78938-7(9)); (978-0-439-78939-4(7)); (978-0-439-78940-0(0)); (978-0-439-78941-7(9)); (978-0-439-78942-4(7)); (978-0-439-78943-1(5)); (978-0-439-78944-8(3)); (978-0-439-78945-5(1)); (978-0-439-78946-2(X)); (978-0-439-78947-9(8))* Scholastic, Inc.

Leech, Bonnie. The Names of Numbers: Learning How Numbers Are Represented with Words. 2009. (Math for the Real World: Early Emergent Ser.). (ENG., Illus.). 8p. (gr. k-1). pap. 5.15 *(978-0-8239-8884-6(8))* Rosen Publishing Group, Inc., The.

Lefebvre, Gail. A Week at Snug Bend. 2009. 64p. pap. 19.50 *(978-1-60693-627-6(1),* Strategic Bk. Publishing) Strategic Book Publishing & Rights Agency (SBPRA).

The Legend of the Bluebonnet: Fourth Grade Guided Comprehension Level L. (On Our Way to English Ser.). (gr. 4-18). 34.50 *(978-0-7578-7151-1(8))* Rigby Education.

Lei, Vicki. Mr Grumpy. 2011. 28p. pap. 15.99 *(978-1-4568-5587-1(5))* Xlibris Corp.

Leigh, Autumn. The Apple Tree. (Neighborhood Readers Ser.). (ENG.). 16p. 2007. 33.50 *(978-1-4042-7328-3(X))* 2006. (gr. 1-3). pap. 6.50 *(978-1-4042-7128-9(7))* Rosen Publishing Group, Inc., The. (Rosen Classroom).

—Door to Door. 2006. (Neighborhood Readers Ser.). (ENG.). 12p. (gr. -1-3). pap. 5.90 *(978-1-4042-6469-4(8),* Rosen Classroom) Rosen Publishing Group, Inc., The.

—Far-Out Friends. 2006. (Neighborhood Readers Ser.). (ENG.). 8p. (gr. -1-3). pap. 5.15 *(978-1-4042-6750-3(6),* Rosen Classroom) Rosen Publishing Group, Inc., The.

—El manzano (the Apple Tree) 2007. (Lecturas del barrio (Neighborhood Readers) Ser.). (SPA.). 16p. 33.50 *(978-1-4042-7329-0(8),* Rosen Classroom) Rosen Publishing Group, Inc., The.

—My Teacher. 2009. (Real Life Readers Ser.). 8p. (gr. k-1). pap. 5.15 *(978-1-4042-7975-9(X),* Rosen Classroom) Rosen Publishing Group, Inc., The.

—On the Ball: Learning to Identify the Place Values of Ones & Tens. 2009. (Math for the Real World: Early Emergent Ser.). (ENG., Illus.). 8p. (gr. k-1). pap. 5.15 *(978-0-8239-8859-4(7))* Rosen Publishing Group, Inc., The.

—Signs on the Road: Learning to Identify the Four Basic Geometric Shapes. 2009. (Math for the Real World: Early Emergent Ser.). (ENG., Illus.). 8p. (gr. k-1). pap. 5.15 *(978-0-8239-8857-0(0))* Rosen Publishing Group, Inc., The.

Leipe, Ulla. Lo Que los Ninos Quieren Saber. Limmer, Hannes, illus. (SPA.). 180p. (YA). 11.95 *(978-84-241-5501-8(7),* EV867) Everest Editora ESP. Dist: Continental Bk. Co., Inc.

Lemay, Didi. A Winter Solstice Celebration. Campbell, Jacquie, illus. 2008. 56p. pap. 23.99 *(978-1-4389-0998-1(5))* AuthorHouse.

Lemonade for Gilbert. 2004. (Gilbert the Pig Set 2 Ser.). (J). 7.33 *(978-1-58453-222-4(X))* Pioneer Valley Bks.

The Lemonade Stand: Individual Title Six-Packs. (gr. -1-2). 27.00 *(978-0-7635-9457-2(1))* Rigby Education.

Lend a Hand. (Early Intervention Levels Ser.). 28.38 *(978-0-7362-0413-2(X))* CENGAGE Learning.

Lend a Hand (18), Vol. 18. (Early Intervention Levels Ser.). 4.73 *(978-0-7362-0238-1(2))* CENGAGE Learning.

Leonard, M. G. Beetle Boy. 2017. lib. bdg. 17.20 ***(978-0-606-40151-7(2))*** Turtleback Bks.

Lerner Publishing Group Staff. History Speaks: Picture Books Plus Reader's Theater, 6 vols., Set. 2011. (J). (gr. 2-4). lib. bdg. 167.58 *(978-0-7613-7483-1(3))* Lerner Publishing Group.

LernerClassroom Editors. First Step Nonfiction-Animal Families Teaching Guide. 2009. pap. 7.95 *(978-0-8225-5658-9(8))* Lerner Publishing Group.

—First Step Nonfiction-Animal Homes Teaching Guide. 2009. pap. 7.95 *(978-0-8225-5672-5(3))* Lerner Publishing Group.

—First Step Nonfiction-Basic Human Needs. 2009. pap., tchr. ed. 7.95 *(978-0-8225-1747-4(7))* Lerner Publishing Group.

—On My Own History Teaching Guide. 2009. pap. 7.95 *(978-0-8225-5321-2(X))* Lerner Publishing Group.

—Pull Ahead Books-Continents Teaching Guide. 2009. pap. 7.95 *(978-0-8225-2349-9(3))* Lerner Publishing Group.

LernerClassroom Editors, ed. Microquests. 2008. pap. 7.95 *(978-0-8225-9223-5(1))* Lerner Publishing Group.

Lesespiele. (Duden-Schuelerhilfen Ser.). (GER.). 96p. (J). (gr. 3-4). *(978-3-411-02607-4(3))* Bibliographisches Institut & F. A. Brockhaus AG DEU. Dist: International Bk. Import Service, Inc.

Let's Celebrate. (Early Intervention Levels Ser.). 23.10 *(978-0-7362-0024-0(X))* CENGAGE Learning.

Let's Eat. 2005. (Little Celebrations Thematic Packages Ser.). (J). (gr. k-3). 133.50 *(978-0-673-75379-3(4))* Celebration Pr.

Let's Go Shopping! (Early Intervention Levels Ser.). 23.10 *(978-0-7362-0027-1(4));* Vol. 4. 3.85 *(978-1-56334-975-1(2))* CENGAGE Learning.

Let's Hear It for Ears! (Early Intervention Levels Ser.). 5.31 *(978-0-7362-1915-0(3));* 31.86 *(978-0-7362-2134-4(4))* CENGAGE Learning.

Let's Paint!, Vol. 4. (Early Intervention Levels Ser.). 3.85 *(978-1-56334-962-1(0))* CENGAGE Learning.

Let's Read Big Book, 3 bks., Set. (Phonics & Friends Ser.). (gr. -1-2). Level C. 14.76 *(978-0-7362-1065-2(2))*Level D. 14.76 *(978-0-7362-1066-9(0))*Level B. 14.76 *(978-0-7362-1064-5(4))* CENGAGE Learning.

Letter Clusters Big Book, 6 vols. 32p. (gr. k-3). 38.50 *(978-0-7802-7194-4(7))* Wright Group/McGraw-Hill.

Level 16 Pack: Set of 17 Titles. (Early Intervention Levels Ser.). 89.99 *(978-0-7362-2554-0(4))* CENGAGE Learning.

Level 18 Pack: Set of 13 Titles. (Early Intervention Levels Ser.). 71.47 *(978-0-7362-2555-7(2))* CENGAGE Learning.

Level 2 Book Collection 800920, 6 vols. 2005. (J). *(978-1-59794-085-6(2))* Environments, Inc.

Level 2 Pack: Set of 16 Titles. (Dra Levels Ser.). 60.09 *(978-0-7362-2566-3(8))* CENGAGE Learning.

Level 2 Paperback Book Collection 800921, 6 vols. 2005. (J). pap. *(978-1-59794-086-3(0))* Environments, Inc.

Level 3 Books & Tapes Book Set 800927, 6 vols. 2005. (J). pap. *(978-1-59794-092-4(5))* Environments, Inc.

Level 3 Pack: Set of 14 Titles. (Dra Levels Ser.). 58.15 *(978-0-7362-2567-0(6))* CENGAGE Learning.

Level 3 Pack: Set of 18 Titles. (Early Intervention Levels Ser.). 66.90 *(978-0-7362-2548-9(X))* CENGAGE Learning.

Level 3 Paperback Books Set 800928, 6 vols. 2005. (J). pap. *(978-1-59794-093-1(3))* Environments, Inc.

Level 4 Pack: Set of 24 Titles. (Dra Levels Ser.). 89.72 *(978-0-7362-2568-7(4))* CENGAGE Learning.

Level 5 Pack: Set of 19 Titles. (Early Intervention Levels Ser.). 70.45 *(978-0-7362-2549-6(8))* CENGAGE Learning.

Level 6 Pack: Set of 11 Titles. (Early Intervention Levels Ser.). 49.29 *(978-0-7362-2550-2(1))* CENGAGE Learning.

Level 6 Pack: Set of 14 Titles. (Dra Levels Ser.). 51.52 *(978-0-7362-2569-4(2))* CENGAGE Learning.

Level a Big Book Program. (Phonics & Friends Ser.). (gr. -1-2). 651.23 *(978-0-7362-0355-5(9))* CENGAGE Learning.

Level A-C Ell Program Lap Book. 2003. (Metro Reading Ser.). (J). (gr. 12). spiral bd. 116.55 *(978-1-58120-617-3(8))* Metropolitan Teaching & Learning Co.

Level A-C Ell Program Practice Picture Cards Blms. 2003. (Metro Reading Ser.). (gr. 12). 41.29 *(978-1-58120-618-0(6))* Metropolitan Teaching & Learning Co.

Level A Super Classroom Set. (Into English! Ser.). (gr. k-6). 625.88 *(978-1-56334-806-8(3))* CENGAGE Learning.

Level B Pack: Set of 26 Titles. (Guided Reading Levels Ser.). 104.04 *(978-0-7362-2558-8(7))* CENGAGE Learning.

Level D Pack: Set of 21 Titles. (Guided Reading Levels Ser.). 101.29 *(978-0-7362-2560-1(9))* CENGAGE Learning.

Level D Super Classroom Set. (Into English! Ser.). (gr. 3-18). 626.27 *(978-1-56334-849-5(7))* CENGAGE Learning.

Level E Classroom Set. (Phonics & Friends Ser.). (gr. -1-2). 682.59 *(978-0-7362-0601-3(9))* CENGAGE Learning.

Level E Let's Read Little Book Set. (Phonics & Friends Ser.). (gr. -1-2). 14.76 *(978-0-7362-1068-3(7))* CENGAGE Learning.

Level F Classroom Set. (Phonics & Friends Ser.). (gr. -1-2). 682.59 *(978-0-7362-0644-0(2))* CENGAGE Learning.

Level F Let's Read Little Book Set. (Phonics & Friends Ser.). (gr. -1-2). 14.76 *(978-0-7362-1069-0(5))* CENGAGE Learning.

Level F Super Classroom Set. (Into English! Ser.). (gr. 5-18). 626.27 *(978-1-56334-881-5(0))* CENGAGE Learning.

Level L-Set Of 6. 126.23 *(978-0-7565-0862-3(2))* Compass Point Bks.

Leveled Readers A: Easy, Bookshelf Collection, 30 bks., Set. 2004. (gr. 1-18). 495.00 *(978-0-328-01865-9(1));* (gr. 2-18). 495.00 *(978-0-328-00411-9(1));* (gr. 3-18). 495.00 *(978-0-328-00412-6(X));* (gr. 4-18). 495.00 *(978-0-328-00413-3(8));* (gr. 5-18). 495.00 *(978-0-328-00414-0(6));* (gr. 6-18). 495.00 *(978-0-328-00415-7(4))* Addison-Wesley Educational Pubs., Inc.

Leveled Readers B: On-Level, Bookshelf Collection, 30 bks., Set. 2004. (gr. 1-18). 495.00 *(978-0-328-00422-5(7));* (gr. 2-18). 495.00 *(978-0-328-00423-2(5));* (gr. 3-18). 495.00 *(978-0-328-00424-9(3));* (gr. 4-18). 495.00 *(978-0-328-00425-6(1));* (gr. 5-18). 495.00 *(978-0-328-00426-3(X));* (gr. 6-18). 495.00 *(978-0-328-00427-0(8))* Addison-Wesley Educational Pubs., Inc.

Leveled Readers C: Challenge, Bookshelf Collection, 6 units, Set. 2004. (Scott Foresman Reading Ser.). (gr. 2-18). 99.00 *(978-0-328-00435-5(9));* (gr. 6-18). 99.00 *(978-0-328-00439-3(1))* Addison-Wesley Educational Pubs., Inc.

Levels 10-12 Pack: Set of 9 Titles. (Early Intervention Levels Ser.). 46.43 *(978-0-7362-2552-6(8))* CENGAGE Learning.

Levels 12-14 Pack: Set of 10 Titles. (Dra Levels Ser.). 85.63 *(978-0-7362-2571-7(4))* CENGAGE Learning.

Levels 13-15 Pack: Set of 10 Titles. (Early Intervention Levels Ser.). 49.89 *(978-0-7362-2553-3(6))* CENGAGE Learning.

Levels 16-18 Pack: Set of 22 Titles. (Dra Levels Ser.). 115.82 *(978-0-7362-2572-4(2))* CENGAGE Learning.

Levels 20-24 Pack: Set of 12 Titles. (Dra Levels Ser.). 63.31 *(978-0-7362-2573-1(0))* CENGAGE Learning.

Levels 20-24 Pack: Set of 16 Titles. (Early Intervention Levels Ser.). 86.72 *(978-0-7362-2556-4(0))* CENGAGE Learning.

Levels 28-30 Pack: Set of 18 Titles. (Dra Levels Ser.). 114.42 *(978-0-7362-2574-8(9))* CENGAGE Learning.

Levels 38-40 Pack: Set of 14 Titles. (Dra Levels Ser.). 88.02 *(978-0-7362-2575-5(7))* CENGAGE Learning.

Levels 7-8 Pack: Set of 6 Titles. (Early Intervention Levels Ser.). 32.16 *(978-0-7362-2551-9(X))* CENGAGE Learning.

Levels 8-10 Pack: Set of 15 Titles. (Dra Levels Ser.). 85.63 *(978-0-7362-2570-0(6))* CENGAGE Learning.

Levels E-F Pack: Set of 20 Titles. (Guided Reading Levels Ser.). 97.02 *(978-0-7362-2561-8(7))* CENGAGE Learning.

Levels E-F Super Classroom Set. (Phonics & Friends Ser.). (gr. -1-2). 1204.58 *(978-0-7362-0596-2(9))* CENGAGE Learning.

Levels G-J Pack: Set of 24 Titles. (Guided Reading Levels Ser.). 118.32 *(978-0-7362-2562-5(5))* CENGAGE Learning.

Levels K-M Pack: Set of 30 Titles. (Guided Reading Levels Ser.). 172.30 *(978-0-7362-2563-2(3))* CENGAGE Learning.

Levels N-Q Pack: Set of 17 Titles. (Guided Reading Levels Ser.). 106.73 *(978-0-7362-2564-9(1))* CENGAGE Learning.

Levin, Amy. A Bear's Year, 6 vols., Set. 2003. (Phonics Readers 1-36 Ser.). (ENG.). 8p. (gr. k-1). pap. 29.70 *(978-0-7368-3200-7(9),* Phonics Readers) Capstone Press of Coughlan Cos.

—Hard Workers, 6 vols., Set. 2003. (Phonics Readers 1-36 Ser.). (ENG.). 8p. (gr. k-1). pap. 29.70 *(978-0-7368-3214-4(9),* Phonics Readers) Capstone Press of Coughlan Cos.

—The Vet, 6 vols., Set. 2003. (Phonics Readers 1-36 Ser.). (ENG.). 8p. (gr. k-1). pap. 29.70 *(978-0-7368-3193-2(2),* Phonics Readers) Capstone Press of Coughlan Cos.

Levy, Emily, rev. Strategies for Study Success: Highlighting I. 2004. 12.00 *(978-0-9772110-0-5(2))* EBL Coaching.

Levy, Janey. Edwin Visits Earth. 2006. (Neighborhood Readers Ser.). (ENG.). 16p. (gr. 1-3). pap. 6.50 *(978-1-4042-7160-9(0),* Rosen Classroom) Rosen Publishing Group, Inc., The.

—Jenny in the Jungle. 2006. (Neighborhood Readers Ser.). (ENG.). 8p. (gr. -1-3). pap. 5.15 *(978-1-4042-5702-3(0),* Rosen Classroom) Rosen Publishing Group, Inc., The.

—The Piggles Picnic. 2006. (Neighborhood Readers Ser.). (ENG.). 12p. (gr. -1-3). pap. 5.90 *(978-1-4042-6455-7(8),* Rosen Classroom) Rosen Publishing Group, Inc., The.

—Plaga: La Peste Negra (Plague: the Black Death) Sarfatti, Esther, tr. from ENG. 2015. (Desastres Ser.). (SPA., Illus.). 32p. (J). (gr. 4-5). lib. bdg. 26.60 *(978-1-4824-3248-0(X))* Stevens, Gareth Publishing LLLP.

—Play Ball! 2006. (Neighborhood Readers Ser.). (ENG.). 8p. (gr. -1-3). pap. 5.15 *(978-1-4042-5659-0(8),* Rosen Classroom) Rosen Publishing Group, Inc., The.

—What Would I Wear? 2006. (Neighborhood Readers Ser.). (ENG.). 12p. (gr. -1-3). pap. 5.90 *(978-1-4042-6682-7(8),* Rosen Classroom) Rosen Publishing Group, Inc., The.

Lewman, David. Drop the Beat! (DreamWorks Trolls) Random House et al, illus. 2017. (Step into Reading Ser.). (ENG.). 24p. (J). (gr. -1-1). pap. 4.99 ***(978-1-5247-1842-8(4));*** lib. bdg. 12.99 ***(978-1-5247-1843-5(2))*** Random Hse. Children's Bks. (Random Hse. Bks. for Young Readers).

Lewman, David. Proud to Be a Ghostbuster. 2016. (Simon & Schuster Ready-To-Read Level 3 Ser.). lib. bdg. 13.55 *(978-0-606-38994-5(6))* Turtleback Bks.

Liberts, Jennifer. Monster Phonics (Blaze & the Monster Machines) Dynamo Limited, illus. 2016. (Step into Reading Ser.). (ENG.). 144p. (J). (gr. -1-1). pap. 12.99 *(978-1-101-94026-6(3,* Random Hse. Bks. for Young Readers) Random Hse. Children's Bks.

Life Cycles Book Set 800741, 4. 2005. (J). pap. *(978-1-59794-039-9(9))* Environments, Inc.

Light, John. Neighbours Are a Nuisance! 2005. (Illus.). 24p. *(978-1-897968-22-2(1))* Photon Pr.

Lightning Bolt Books: Exploring Economics, 6 vols., Set. Incl. Do I Need It? or Do I Want It? Making Budget Choices. Larson, Jennifer S. lib. bdg. 26.60 *(978-0-7613-3914-4(0));* What Can You Do with Money? Earning, Spending, & Saving. Larson, Jennifer S. lib. bdg. 26.60 *(978-0-7613-3910-6(8));* What Do We Buy? A Look at Goods & Services. Nelson, Robin. lib. bdg. 26.60 *(978-0-7613-3913-7(2));* What Is Money, Anyway? Why Dollars & Coins Have Value. Larson, Jennifer S. lib. bdg. 26.60 *(978-0-7613-3915-1(9));* Where Do We Keep Money? How Banks Work. Larson, Jennifer S. lib. bdg. 26.60 *(978-0-7613-3911-3(6));* Who's Buying? Who's Selling? Understanding Consumers & Producers. Larson, Jennifer S. lib. bdg. 26.60 *(978-0-7613-3912-0(4));* (Illus.). 32p. (gr. k-2). 2010. 2009. Set lib. bdg. 151.56 *(978-0-7613-3909-0(4),* Lerner Pubns.) Lerner Publishing Group.

Lin, Aja, et al. What Do You See? 2010. (ENG., Illus.). 8p. (C). pap. 7.95 *(978-0-7362-7997-0(0))* CENGAGE Learning.

Lin, Joyce, tr. The frog in the Well. Caprio, Pattie, illus. 2008. (ENG & CHI.). 36p. (J). 14.95 *(978-0-9801305-1-5(4))* CE Bilingual Bks. LLC.

Lindeen, Carol K. Farm Tools over Time, 6 vols., Set. 2004. (Phonics Readers Books 37-72 Ser.). (ENG.). 8p. (gr. k-1). pap. 35.70 *(978-0-7368-4084-2(2),* Phonics Readers) Capstone Press of Coughlan Cos.

—The Sky at Night, 6 vols., Set. 2004. (Phonics Readers Books 37-72 Ser.). (ENG.). 8p. (gr. k-1). pap. 35.70 *(978-0-7368-4062-0(1),* Phonics Readers) Capstone Press of Coughlan Cos.

—What Is a Museum?, 6 vols., Set. 2004. (Phonics Readers Books 37-72 Ser.). (ENG.). 8p. (gr. k-1). pap. 35.70 *(978-0-7368-4076-7(1),* Phonics Readers) Capstone Press of Coughlan Cos.

Lindeen, Mary. Leading the Way, 1 vol. 2012. (Wonder Readers: Social Studies). (ENG.). 20p. (gr. -1-2). lib. bdg. 22.65 *(978-1-4296-9615-9(X),* Wonder Readers) Capstone Press of Coughlan Cos.

—The Letter Aa Set: Things at School, 6 vols. 2004. (Letter Bks.). (ENG.). 8p. (gr. k-1). pap. 29.70 *(978-0-7368-4100-9(8),* Letter Bks.) Capstone Press of Coughlan Cos.

—Wonder Readers. (Wonder Readers Ser.). (ENG.). 20p. (gr. k-1). 2012. lib. bdg. 249.15 *(978-1-4296-9624-1(9))* 2012. lib. bdg. 520.95 *(978-1-4296-9625-8(7))* 2011. lib. bdg. 271.80 *(978-1-4296-8644-0(8))* Capstone Press of Coughlan Cos. (Wonder Readers).

—Wonder Readers: Social Studies. (Wonder Readers: Social Studies). (ENG.). 20p. (gr. k-1). 2012. lib. bdg. 90.60 *(978-1-4296-9622-7(2))* 2012. lib. bdg. 181.20 *(978-1-4296-9623-4(0))* 2011. lib. bdg. 90.60 *(978-1-4296-8643-3(X))* Capstone Press of Coughlan Cos. (Wonder Readers).

Lindsay, Kristine. Basic Reading Series - Binder 3. 2004. (J). ring bd. 49.95 *(978-1-58804-371-9(1))* P C I Education.

Lindsey, Cameron. The 10 Best Animal Camouflages. 2008. 14.99 *(978-1-55448-492-8(8))* Scholastic Library Publishing.

—The 10 Most Dangerous Geographic Locations. 2008. 14.99 *(978-1-55448-539-0(8))* Scholastic Library Publishing.

—The 10 Most Terrifying Experiences. 2008. 14.99 *(978-1-55448-551-2(7))* Scholastic Library Publishing.

Lindstrom, Florence M. Meeting New Friends. 2nd ed. 2007. (Illus.). 185p. pap. 8.95 *(978-1-932971-00-2(9))* Christian Liberty Pr.

LinkIt Reading Sudent Resource Book, Level 3. 2006. per. *(978-0-9786500-1-8(8))* Creative Curriculum Initiatives.

Linn, Margot. The Big Red Blanket. Jacobson, David, illus. 2005. (I'm Going to Read(r) Ser.: Level 1). (ENG.). 28p. (J). (gr. -1-k). pap. 3.95 (978-1-4027-2091-8(2)) Sterling Publishing Co., Inc.

—Can You Play?, Bolam, Emily, illus. 2005. (I'm Going to Read(r) Ser.: Level 1). (ENG.). 28p. (J). (gr. -1-k). pap. 3.95 (978-1-4027-2094-9(7)) Sterling Publishing Co., Inc.

—Harry's Bath. Chwast, Seymour, illus. 2005. (I'm Going to Read(r) Ser.: Level 2). (ENG.). 32p. (J). (gr. k-1). pap. 3.95 (978-1-4027-2100-7(5)) Sterling Publishing Co., Inc.

—I Won't Go to Bed! Baruffi, Andrea, illus. 2005. (I'm Going to Read(r) Ser.: Level 3). (ENG.). 32p. (J). (gr. 1-2). pap. 3.95 (978-1-4027-2104-5(8)) Sterling Publishing Co., Inc.

—I'm Going to New York to Visit the Lions. Roitman, Tanya, illus. 2005. (I'm Going to Read(r) Ser.: Level 2). (ENG.). 32p. (J). (gr. k-1). pap. 3.95 (978-1-4027-2099-4(8)) Sterling Publishing Co., Inc.

—Pizza & Other Stinky Poems. Haley, Amanda, illus. 2005. (I'm Going to Read(r) Ser.: Level 4). (ENG.). 32p. (J). (gr. 2-3). pap. 3.95 (978-1-4027-2110-6(2)) Sterling Publishing Co., Inc.

—Silly Pig. Rader, Laura, illus. 2005. (I'm Going to Read(r) Ser.). (ENG.). 32p. (J). (gr. k-1). pap. 3.95 (978-1-4027-2097-0(1)) Sterling Publishing Co., Inc.

—Sometimes I Share. Nicklaus, Carol, illus. 2005. (I'm Going to Read(r) Ser.). (ENG.). 28p. (J). (gr. -1-k). pap. 3.95 (978-1-4027-2090-1(4)) Sterling Publishing Co., Inc.

Lion King: Simba's Hide & Seek. (My First Read Along Ser.). (J). 7.99 incl. audio (978-1-55723-747-7(6)) Walt Disney Records.

Lionni, Leo. When? 2014. (ENG., Illus.). 16p. (J). (— 1). bds. 5.99 (978-0-385-75408-8(6), Knopf Bks. for Young Readers) Random Hse. Children's Bks.

Lipson, Greta Barclay. Two Sides to Every Story. Hierstein, Judith, illus. 2004. 128p. (J). pap. 14.95 (978-1-57310-439-5(6)) Teaching & Learning Co.

Litchfield, Jo. First Words Look & Say. Litchfield, Jo, illus. 2005. (Illus.). 18p. (J). 14.99 (978-0-7945-1024-4(8), Usborne) EDC Publishing.

Little Animals Board Books Set 800975, 6. 2005. (J). bds. (978-1-59794-100-6(X)) Environments, Inc.

Little Bear Book Set 2 800890, 6 vols. 2005. (J). pap. (978-1-59794-065-8(8)) Environments, Inc.

Little Bear Book Set 800876, 3 vols. 2005. (J). bds. (978-1-59794-054-2(2)) Environments, Inc.

Little Bear Book Set 800891, 3 vols. 2005. (J). pap. (978-1-59794-066-5(6)) Environments, Inc.

Little Books Collection: Includes 30 Little Books. 2003. 127.95 (978-0-7652-0129-4(1)) Modern Curriculum Pr.

Little Dragon & the Magic Wagon. 2008. (Little Dragon Storybooks Ser.). 32p. (978-1-4075-1289-1(7)) Parragon, Inc.

Little, Jean. Forward, Shakespeare!, 1 vol. 2005. (Orca Young Readers Ser.). (ENG., Illus.). 112p. (J). (gr. 3-6). per. 5.95 (978-1-55143-339-4(7)) Orca Bk. Pubs. USA.

Little, Jean & de Vries, Maggie. Once upon a Golden Apple: 25th Anniversary Edition. Gilman, Phoebe, illus. 25th ed. 2016. (ENG.). 26p. (J). (— 1). bds. 7.99 (978-0-670-07007-7(6), Puffin Canada) Penguin Random House Canada Young Readers CAN. Dist: Penguin Random Hse. LLC.

Little Red Riding Hood. 2015. (ENG., Illus.). 32p. (J). (gr. -1-3). (978-1-78393-575-8(8)) Make Believe Ideas.

Little Red Riding Hood, Level 2. 2016. (Ladybird Readers Ser.). (ENG.). 48p. (J). (gr. 2-4). pap. 9.99 (978-0-241-25446-2(9)) Penguin Bks., Ltd. GBR. Dist: Independent Pubs. Group.

A Little Seed: Set A Individual Title Six-Packs. (Smart Start Ser.). (gr. k-1). 23.00 (978-0-7635-0411-3(4)) Rigby Education.

Littlefield, Angie & Littlefield, Jennifer. The 10 Deadliest Plants. 2007. (J). 14.99 (978-1-55448-511-6(8)) Scholastic Library Publishing.

Litz, Amanda. Sam & Pam Can & You Can Too! We Can Ride Our Bikes. Garcia, Cynthia, illus. 2011. 32p. (J). pap. 3.99 (978-0-9841496-2-9(7)) Traveler's Trunk Publishing LLC.

Live Oak Media PB/CD Readalong Collection. pap. 758.00 incl. audio compact disk (978-1-59519-235-6(2)); Vol. 3. pap. 728.00 incl. audio compact disk (978-1-59519-239-4(5)) Live Oak Media.

Live Oak Media Readalong Collection Set. 2004. cd-rom 84.00 (978-0-87499-713-2(5)); cd-rom 84.00 (978-0-87499-712-5(7)); Vol. 2. pap. 610.00 incl. audio (978-1-59519-004-8(X)) Live Oak Media.

Llewellyn, Claire. Asi Nace un Arbol. Mendez, Simon, illus. 2004. (Colección Así Nace... / Starting Life Collection Ser.). (SPA.). 24p. (gr. k-6). pap. 14.95 (978-1-59437-449-4(X)) Santillana USA Publishing Co., Inc.

—Asi Nace un Pato. Mendez, Simon, illus. 2004. (Colección Así Nace... / Starting Life Collection Ser.). (SPA.). 24p. (gr. k-6). pap. 14.95 (978-1-59437-448-7(1)) Santillana USA Publishing Co., Inc.

—Asi Nace una Rana. Mendez, Simon, illus. 2003. (Colección Así Nace... / Starting Life Collection Ser.). (SPA.). 24p. (gr. k-6). pap. 14.95 (978-1-59437-789-1(8)) Santillana USA Publishing Co., Inc.

—Big Bugs Green Band. 2016. (Cambridge Reading Adventures Ser.). (ENG.). 16p. pap. 6.56 (978-1-107-55064-3(5)) Cambridge Univ. Pr.

—Boo-Hoo, Baby! Lovsin, Polona, illus. 2013. (Start Reading Ser.). (ENG.). 24p. (gr. k-1). pap. 41.94 (978-1-4765-3208-0(7)); pap. 7.95 (978-1-4765-3182-3(X)) Capstone Press of Coughlan Cos.

—Cat Nap, 1 vol. East, Jacqueline, illus. 2013. (Start Reading Ser.). (ENG.). 24p. (gr. k-1). pap. 7.95 (978-1-4765-4087-0(X)) Capstone Press of Coughlan Cos.

—How Chocolate Is Made Turquoise Band. 2016. (Cambridge Reading Adventures Ser.). (ENG.). 24p. pap. 7.19 (978-1-107-57616-2(4)) Cambridge Univ. Pr.

—In the Sea Red Band. Belcher, Andy, photos by. 2016. (Cambridge Reading Adventures Ser.). (ENG., Illus.). 16p. pap. 6.56 (978-1-107-57578-3(8)) Cambridge Univ. Pr.

—Late for School Yellow Band. Pérez, Moni, illus. 2016. (Cambridge Reading Adventures Ser.). (ENG.). 16p. pap. 6.56 (978-1-107-57679-7(2)) Cambridge Univ. Pr.

—Looking after Animals. 2016. (Cambridge Reading Adventures Ser.). (ENG., Illus.). 16p. pap. 6.56 (978-1-316-60582-0(5)) Cambridge Univ. Pr.

—On the Track Blue Band. Ruffle, Mark, illus. 2016. (Cambridge Reading Adventures Ser.). (ENG.). 16p. pap. 6.56 (978-1-316-50322-5(4)) Cambridge Univ. Pr.

—Our Senses Red Band. 2016. (Cambridge Reading Adventures Ser.). (ENG.). 16p. pap. 6.56 (978-1-316-60568-4(X)) Cambridge Univ. Pr.

—Sand!, 1 vol. Beard, Lauren, illus. 2013. (Start Reading Ser.). (ENG.). 24p. (gr. k-1). pap. 7.95 (978-1-4765-3187-8(0)); pap. 41.94 (978-1-4765-3230-1(3)) Capstone Press of Coughlan Cos.

—The Sun Is up Pink a Band. Lopez, Ayesha, illus. 2016. (Cambridge Reading Adventures Ser.). (ENG.). 16p. pap. 6.56 (978-1-107-54987-6(6)) Cambridge Univ. Pr.

—Water Pink a Band. 2016. (Cambridge Reading Adventures Ser.). (ENG.). 16p. pap. 6.56 (978-1-107-57584-4(2)) Cambridge Univ. Pr.

—The Weather Today Red Band. Jonatronix, illus. 2016. (Cambridge Reading Adventures Ser.). (ENG.). 16p. pap. 6.56 (978-1-107-57676-6(8)) Cambridge Univ. Pr.

Llewellyn, Claire & Feldman, Thea. Kingfisher Readers L2: Amazing Animal Senses. 2014. (Kingfisher Readers Ser.). (ENG., Illus.). 32p. (J). (gr. k-3). 12.99 (978-0-7534-7173-9(6), 9780753471739, Kingfisher) Roaring Brook Pr.

Llewellyn, Claire, et al. Spiders: Deadly Predators. 7th ed. 2014. (Kingfisher Readers Ser.). (ENG., Illus.). 32p. (J). (gr. k-3). 12.99 (978-0-7534-7150-0(7), 9780753471500, Kingfisher) Roaring Brook Pr.

Llorente, Pilar Molina. Aura Gris. (SPA.). 80p. (YA). (gr. 5-8). 7.16 (978-84-216-1636-9(6)) Bruño, Editorial ESP. Dist: Lectorum Pubns., Inc.

Lloyd Jones, Rob. The Story of Spying. 2007. (Young Reading Series 3 Gift Bks). (Illus.). 62p. (J). (gr. 2-5). 8.99 (978-0-7945-1720-5(X), Usborne) EDC Publishing.

Loader, Mandy. Amazing Young Sports People, Level 1, 1 vol., Pack. 2009. (ENG.). 48p. pap. 13.25 (978-84-8323-568-3(4)) Cambridge Univ. Pr.

—Amazing Young Sports People Level 1 Beginner/Elementary. 2010. (ENG.). 48p. pap. 11.00 (978-84-8323-572-0(2)) Cambridge Univ. Pr.

Lobb, Nancy. 16 Extraordinary Native Americans. 2nd ed. 2007. (Illus.). 132p. (YA). (gr. 6-12). tchr. ed., per. 25.00 (978-0-8251-6282-4(3)) Walch Education.

—16 Extraordinary Young Americans. 2nd ed. 2007. (16 Extraordinary Ser.). (Illus.). 127p. (gr. 6-12). tchr. ed., per. 25.00 (978-0-8251-6283-1(1)) Walch Education.

Lock, Deborah. Big Trucks. 2013. (DK Reader Pre Level Ser.). lib. bdg. 13.55 (978-0-606-32459-5(3), Turtleback) Turtleback Bks.

Lock, Deborah & Dorling Kindersley Publishing Staff. Big Trucks. 2013. (DK Readers Ser.). (ENG.). 32p. (J). (gr. -1-1). pap. 3.99 (978-1-4654-0890-7(8), DK Children) Dorling Kindersley Publishing, Inc.

Lockyer, John. The Moon. 2015. (ENG., Illus.). 16p. (-2). pap. (978-1-77654-140-9(5), Red Rocket Readers) Flying Start Bks.

Lockyer, John & Holden, Pam. Making a Movie, 6 pack. 2009. (Red Rocket Readers Ser.). (ENG., Illus.). 16p. (gr. 2-2). pap. (978-1-877435-50-8(3), Red Rocket Readers) Flying Start Bks.

Lodge, Ali, illus. The Leopard & the Sky God. 2007. (Usborne First Reading: Level 3 Ser.). 48p. (J). (gr. -1-3). 8.99 (978-0-7945-1838-7(9), Usborne) EDC Publishing.

Loewen, Nancy. Farthest from the Sun: The Planet Neptune, 1 vol. Yesh, Jeff, illus. 2008. (Amazing Science: Planets Ser.). (ENG.). 24p. (gr. k-4). lib. bdg. 26.65 (978-1-4048-3955-7(0), 1278900) Picture Window Bks.

Lofting, Hugh. La Historia del Doctor Dolittle. (SPA.). 136p. 12.95 (978-84-239-9048-1(6)); (Illus.). 184p. (YA). (gr. 5-8). 11.95 (978-84-239-2733-3(4), EC2743) Espasa Calpe, S.A. ESP. Dist: Planeta Publishing Corp., Continental Bk. Co., Inc., Lectorum Pubns., Inc.

Lois, Lowry. Gooney Bird Greene Three Books in One! (Gooney Bird Greene, Gooney Bird & the Room Mother, Gooney the Fabulous) 2016. (Gooney Bird Greene Ser.). (ENG.). 384p. (J). (gr. 1-4). 13.99 (978-0-544-84824-5(1), HMH Books For Young Readers) Houghton Mifflin Harcourt Publishing Co.

London, Jack. PENGUIN ACTIVE READING 2: CALL OF THE WILD BOOK AND CD-ROM PACK. 2007. (ENG., Illus.). 60p. pap. 17.32 incl. cd-rom (978-1-4058-5207-4(0)) Pearson Education.

Long Ago Children. (J). pap. 13.15 (978-0-8136-4296-3(5)) Modern Curriculum Pr.

Long, David. War School for Dogs: Band 16/Sapphire. 2017. (ENG., Illus.). 56p. (J). pap. 8.99 **(978-0-00-820891-2(3))** HarperCollins Pubs. Ltd. GBR. Dist: Independent Pubs. Group.

Long, Ethan. Fright Club. 2016. (ENG.). 30p. (J). bds. 7.99 (978-1-68119-043-3(5), 9781681190433, Bloomsbury USA Childrens) Bloomsbury Publishing USA.

Longoria, Madelín G. Verdeazul. 2009. (J). (978-1-59835-132-3(X)) Cambridge BrickHouse, Inc.

Longstaff, Abie. Rumplestiltskin. Romanet, Caroline, illus. 2015. (Collins Big Cat Ser.). (ENG.). 24p. (J). (gr. 2-2). pap. 7.95 (978-0-00-759117-6(9)) HarperCollins Pubs. Ltd. GBR. Dist: Independent Pubs. Group.

Look & Learn. (Illus.). (J). (gr. -1-2). lib. bdg. 55.80 (978-1-56674-928-2(X)) Forest Hse. Publishing Co., Inc.

Look Out for Space Monster. 2003. (Spaceboy Set 1 Ser.). (J). 7.33 (978-1-932570-04-5(7)) Pioneer Valley Bks.

Looking for Eggs: Individual Title Six-Packs. (gr. 1-2). 22.00 (978-0-7635-9179-3(3)) Rigby Education.

Looking for Lewis. (J). pap. 13.75 (978-0-8136-4650-3(2)) Modern Curriculum Pr.

Looking for the Queen. (Early Intervention Levels Ser.). 31.86 (978-0-7362-0628-0(0)) CENGAGE Learning.

Looking for the Queen (18), Vol. 18. (Early Intervention Levels Ser.). 5.31 (978-0-7362-0616-7(7)) CENGAGE Learning.

Loose Tooth. 2005. (J). (978-1-932570-31-1(4)) Pioneer Valley Bks.

Lopez, Andre. Emily's Electricity Experiments. 2013. (Rosen Readers Ser.). (ENG.). 24p. (J). (gr. 3-4). pap. 8.25 (978-1-4777-2458-3(3)); pap. 49.50 (978-1-4777-2459-0(1)) Rosen Publishing Group, Inc., The. (Rosen Classroom).

Lopez, Juan, et al. School Tools. 2010. (Reach for Reading Ser.). (ENG., Illus.). 8p. (C). pap. 7.95 (978-0-7362-7983-3(0)) CENGAGE Learning.

Lorimer, Janet. The Bad Luck Play, 1 vol. unabr. ed. 2010. (Q Reads Ser.). (ENG.). 32p. (YA). (gr. 9-12). pap. 6.95 (978-1-61651-198-2(2)) Saddleback Educational Publishing, Inc.

—Beasts, 1 vol. unabr. ed. 2010. (Q Reads Ser.). (ENG.). 32p. (YA). (gr. 9-12). pap. 6.95 (978-1-61651-212-5(1)) Saddleback Educational Publishing, Inc.

—Ben Cody's Treasure, 1 vol. unabr. ed. 2010. (Q Reads Ser.). (ENG.). 32p. (YA). (gr. 9-12). pap. 6.95 (978-1-61651-189-0(3)) Saddleback Educational Publishing, Inc.

—Danger on Ice, 1 vol. unabr. ed. 2010. (Q Reads Ser.). (ENG.). 32p. (YA). (gr. 9-12). pap. 6.95 (978-1-61651-179-1(6)) Saddleback Educational Publishing, Inc.

—Death Grip, 1 vol. unabr. ed. 2010. (Q Reads Ser.). (ENG.). 32p. (YA). (gr. 9-12). pap. 6.95 (978-1-61651-200-2(8)) Saddleback Educational Publishing, Inc.

—Empty Eyes, 1 vol. unabr. ed. 2010. (Q Reads Ser.). (ENG.). 32p. (YA). (gr. 9-12). pap. 6.95 (978-1-61651-180-7(X)) Saddleback Educational Publishing, Inc.

—Look to the Light, 1 vol. unabr. ed. 2010. (Q Reads Ser.). (ENG.). 32p. (YA). (gr. 9-12). pap. 6.95 (978-1-61651-193-7(1)) Saddleback Educational Publishing, Inc.

—The Mystery Quilt, 1 vol. unabr. ed. 2010. (Q Reads Ser.). (ENG.). 32p. (YA). (gr. 9-12). pap. 6.95 (978-1-61651-183-8(4)) Saddleback Educational Publishing, Inc.

—No Place Like Home, 1 vol. unabr. ed. 2010. (Q Reads Ser.). (ENG.). 32p. (YA). (gr. 9-12). pap. 6.95 (978-1-61651-203-3(2)) Saddleback Educational Publishing, Inc.

—Ring of Fear, 1 vol. unabr. ed. 2010. (Q Reads Ser.). (ENG.). 32p. (YA). (gr. 9-12). pap. 6.95 (978-1-61651-194-4(X)) Saddleback Educational Publishing, Inc.

—Ruby's Terrible Secret, 1 vol. unabr. ed. 2010. (Q Reads Ser.). (ENG.). 32p. (YA). (gr. 9-12). pap. 6.95 (978-1-61651-218-7(0)) Saddleback Educational Publishing, Inc.

—Tug-of-War, 1 vol. unabr. ed. 2010. (Q Reads Ser.). (ENG.). 32p. (YA). (gr. 9-12). pap. 6.95 (978-1-61651-196-8(6)) Saddleback Educational Publishing, Inc.

Loser Student Packet. 2004. (J). 12.99 (978-1-58130-518-0(4)) Novel Units, Inc.

Lost: Individual Title, 6 Packs. (Story Steps Ser.). (gr. k-2). 23.00 (978-0-7635-9817-4(8)) Rigby Education.

Lost! Individual Title, 6 Packs. (gr. k-1). 23.00 (978-0-7635-9069-7(X)) Rigby Education.

Lost! Set D Individual Title, 6 Packs. (Smart Start Ser.). (gr. k-1). 23.00 (978-0-7635-0450-2(5)) Rigby Education.

Lost in the Woods. 2003. (Bella & Rosie Set 1 Ser.). (J). 7.67 (978-1-932570-12-0(8)) Pioneer Valley Bks.

Lovvorn, Ann R. Chocolate Puddles. Reece, James A., illus. 2010. 36p. pap. 15.49 (978-1-4520-5158-1(5)) AuthorHouse.

Low, Vicki. Cave of Secrets. Rooth, Mike, illus. 2007. (Timeline Ser.). 48p. pap. 8.99 (978-1-4190-4391-8(9)) Steck-Vaughn.

Lttle Bear Book Set 800889, 3 vols. 2005. (J). (978-1-59794-064-1(X)) Environments, Inc.

Lucas Film Book Group. World of Reading Star Wars Trouble on Tatooine (Level 2) 2017. (World of Reading Ser.). (ENG.). 32p. (J). (gr. 1-3). pap. 4.99 (978-1-4847-9934-5(8), Disney Lucasfilm Press) Disney Publishing Worldwide.

Lucas, Sally. Dancing Dinos at the Beach. 2010. (Step into Reading Level 1 Ser.). lib. bdg. 13.55 (978-0-606-14653-1(9), Turtleback) Turtleback Bks.

Lucy Meets a Dragon, 6 Packs. (Literatura 2000 Ser.). (gr. 2-3). 33.00 (978-0-7635-0177-8(8)) Rigby Education.

Luke's Adventures: Individual Title Six-Packs. (gr. -1-2). 27.00 (978-0-7635-9460-2(1)) Rigby Education.

Luna, James & Villarroel, Carolina. The Runaway Piggy/El Cochinito Fugitivo. Lacámara, Laura, illus. 2010. (SPA.). 32p. (J). (gr. -1-3). 16.95 (978-1-55885-586-1(6), Piñata Books) Arte Publico Pr.

Lunch at the Joy House Cafe. (Early Intervention Levels Ser.). 31.86 (978-0-7362-0666-2(3)) CENGAGE Learning.

Lunch at the Joy House Cafe (24), Vol. 24. (Early Intervention Levels Ser.). 5.31 (978-0-7362-0654-9(X)) CENGAGE Learning.

Lunch Orders: 6 Small Books. (gr. k-3). 24.00 (978-0-7635-6238-0(6)) Rigby Education.

The Lunchroom: Individual Title Six-Packs. (gr. -1-2). 27.00 (978-0-7635-9461-9(X)) Rigby Education.

Lundy, Kathleen Gould. In a Class of Her Own. Alward, Jeff, illus. 2007. 48p. (J). lib. bdg. 23.08 (978-1-4242-1629-1(X)) Fitzgerald Bks.

Lunis, Natalie. Making a Bug Habitat. 2011. (Early Connections Ser.). (J). (978-1-61672-561-7(3)) Benchmark Education Co.

Luton, Susan. Bilingual Beginning Skills, Grades PreK-1. 2009. (Bilingual Beginning Skills Ser.). (Illus.). 96p. (J). (gr. -1-3). pap. 14.99 (978-1-4190-9929-8(9)) Steck-Vaughn.

Lying as Still as I Can: Six-Pack. (Greetings Ser.: Vol. 3). (gr. 2-3). 31.00 (978-0-7635-9433-6(4)) Rigby Education.

MacAndrew, Richard. The Black Pearls Starter/Beginner. 2008. (Cambridge English Readers Ser.). (ENG.). 32p. pap. 8.50 (978-0-521-73289-5(1)) Cambridge Univ. Pr.

—A Little Trouble in Dublin Level 1 Beginner/Elementary. 2010. (ENG., Illus.). 46p. pap. 11.00 (978-84-8323-695-6(8)) Cambridge Univ. Pr.

—A Little Trouble in the Yorkshire Dales Level 3 Lower-Intermediate. 2009. (ENG.). 80p. pap. 12.75 (978-84-8323-584-3(6)) Cambridge Univ. Pr.

—Scotland. 2009. (ENG., Illus.). 80p. pap. 12.75 (978-84-8323-579-9(X)) Cambridge Univ. Pr.

Macaulay, David & Keenan, Sheila. Castle: How It Works. 2015. (ENG., Illus.). 32p. (J). (gr. 1-4). 17.99 (978-1-62672-208-8(0), 9781626722088, Macaulay, David Studio) Roaring Brook Pr.

Macbeth. 2014. (Collins Big Cat Ser.). (ENG., Illus.). 176p. (J). (gr. 5). pap. 9.99 (978-0-00-753013-7(7)) HarperCollins Pubs. Ltd. GBR. Dist: Independent Pubs. Group.

Macceca, Michael L. The World of Plants, 1 vol. 2007. (Science Readers Ser.). (SPA & ENG.). 32p. (J). (gr. 4-4). pap. 8.99 (978-0-7439-0589-3(X)) Shell Educational Publishing.

Macceca, Stephanie. George Washington Carver: Agriculture Pioneer, 1 vol. 2007. (Science Readers Ser.). (ENG.). 32p. (J). (gr. 3-3). pap. 8.99 (978-0-7439-0590-9(3)) Shell Educational Publishing.

Macdonald, Fiona. The Dragon's Bride & Other Dragon Stories. 2017. (Collins Big Cat Tales Ser.). (ENG., Illus.). 48p. (J). (gr. 3-4). pap. 8.99 **(978-0-00-817939-7(5))** HarperCollins Pubs. Ltd. GBR. Dist: Independent Pubs. Group.

Macdonald, Fiona. You Wouldn't Want to Work on a Medieval Cathedral! A Difficult Job That Never Ends. 2010. (You Wouldn't Want to... Ser.). 32p. (J). 29.00 (978-0-531-20504-4(5), Watts, Franklin) Scholastic Library Publishing.

MacDonald, Fiona. You Wouldn't Want to Work on a Medieval Cathedral! A Difficult Job That Never Ends. 2010. (You Wouldn't Want to... Ser.). (ENG., Illus.). 32p. (J). (gr. 3-18). pap. 9.95 (978-0-531-13784-0(8), Watts, Franklin) Scholastic Library Publishing.

MacDonald, Kimber. The Misfits, Level 3. Swain, Wilson, illus. 2006. (ENG.). 24p. (J). (gr. 1-17). per. 3.99 (978-1-58476-421-2(X), IKIDS) Innovative Kids.

MacDonald, Margaret. Animal Habitats. 2011. (Learn-Abouts: Level 10 Ser.). (Illus.). 16p. (J). pap. 7.95 (978-1-59920-598-4(X)) Black Rabbit Bks.

—Boots & Shoes. 2011. (Learn-Abouts: Level 10 Ser.). (Illus.). 16p. (J). pap. 7.95 (978-1-59920-604-2(8)) Black Rabbit Bks.

—Caves. 2011. (Learn-Abouts Ser.). (Illus.). 16p. (J). pap. 7.95 (978-1-59920-633-2(1)) Black Rabbit Bks.

—Deciduous & Evergreen Trees. 2011. (Learn-Abouts: Level 10 Ser.). (Illus.). 16p. (J). pap. 7.95 (978-1-59920-603-5(X)) Black Rabbit Bks.

—Energy from the Sun. 2011. (Learn-Abouts Ser.). (Illus.). 16p. (J). pap. 7.95 (978-1-59920-634-9(X)) Black Rabbit Bks.

—A Family Tree. 2011. (Learn-Abouts Ser.). (Illus.). 16p. (J). pap. 9.95 (978-1-59920-613-4(7)) Palgrave Macmillan.

—Fire. 2011. (Learn-Abouts Ser.). (Illus.). 16p. (J). pap. 7.95 (978-1-59920-618-9(8)) Black Rabbit Bks.

—Glass. 2011. (Learn-Abouts Ser.). (Illus.). 16p. (J). pap. 7.95 (978-1-59920-636-3(6)) Black Rabbit Bks.

—Homes of the Past. 2011. (Learn-Abouts Ser.). (Illus.). 16p. (J). pap. 7.95 (978-1-59920-645-5(5)) Black Rabbit Bks.

—How Do Plants Grow? 2011. (Learn-Abouts Ser.). (Illus.). 16p. (J). pap. 9.95 (978-1-59920-635-6(8)) Palgrave Macmillan.

—I Want to Buy a Rabbit. 2011. (Learn-Abouts Ser.). (Illus.). 16p. (J). pap. 7.95 (978-1-59920-631-8(5)) Black Rabbit Bks.

—Job Quiz. 2011. (Learn-Abouts: Level 10 Ser.). (Illus.). 16p. (J). pap. 7.95 (978-1-59920-599-1(8)) Black Rabbit Bks.

—Kitchen Machines. 2011. (Learn-Abouts: Level 10 Ser.). (Illus.). 16p. (J). pap. 7.95 (978-1-59920-602-8(1)) Black Rabbit Bks.

—Leisure in the Past. 2011. (Learn-Abouts Ser.). (Illus.). 16p. (J). pap. 7.95 (978-1-59920-629-5(3)) Black Rabbit Bks.

—Meat-Eating Plants. 2011. (Learn-Abouts Ser.). (Illus.). 16p. (J). pap. 7.95 (978-1-59920-619-6(6)) Black Rabbit Bks.

—Rain. 2011. (Learn-Abouts Ser.). (Illus.). 16p. (J). pap. 7.95 (978-1-59920-649-3(8)) Black Rabbit Bks.

—Rivers of the World. 2011. (Learn-Abouts Ser.). (Illus.). 16p. (J). pap. 7.95 (978-1-59920-646-2(3)) Black Rabbit Bks.

—Rules on the Soccer Field. 2011. (Learn-Abouts Ser.). (Illus.). 16p. (J). pap. 7.95 (978-1-59920-616-5(1)) Black Rabbit Bks.

—Scooters & Skates. 2011. (Learn-Abouts Ser.). (Illus.). 16p. (J). pap. 7.95 (978-1-59920-650-9(1)) Black Rabbit Bks.

—Toys Long Ago. 2011. (Learn-Abouts: Level 10 Ser.). (Illus.). 16p. (J). pap. 7.95 (978-1-59920-597-7(1)) Black Rabbit Bks.

—What Are Houses Made Of? 2011. (Learn-Abouts Ser.). (Illus.). 16p. (J). pap. 7.95 (978-1-59920-620-2(X)) Black Rabbit Bks.

—What Do New Clothes Cost? 2011. (Learn-Abouts Ser.). (Illus.). 16p. (J). pap. 7.95 (978-1-59920-615-8(3)) Black Rabbit Bks.

—What Do People Do in Winter? 2011. (Learn-Abouts: Level 10 Ser.). (Illus.). 16p. (J). pap. 7.95 (978-1-59920-601-1(3)) Black Rabbit Bks.

—What Does the Referee Do? 2011. (Learn-Abouts Ser.). (Illus.). 16p. (J). pap. 7.95 (978-1-59920-632-5(3)) Black Rabbit Bks.

Macdonald, Margaret. What Keeps Me Healthy? 2014. (Little Books of Answers: Level B Ser.). (Illus.). 16p. (gr. k-2). pap. 7.95 (978-1-927136-13-3(X)) Three Crows Media NZL. Dist: RiverStream Publishing.

MacDonald, Margaret. What Season Is It? 2011. (Learn-Abouts Ser.). (Illus.). 16p. (J). pap. 7.95 (978-1-59920-617-2(X)) Black Rabbit Bks.

Macdonald, Margaret. What Things Did Your Parents Play With? 2014. (Little Books of Answers: Level e Ser.). (Illus.). 16p. (gr. k-2). pap. 7.95 (978-1-927136-41-6(5)) Three Crows Media NZL. Dist: RiverStream Publishing.

MacDonald, Margaret. What to Do When You Are Lost. 2011. (Learn-Abouts: Level 10 Ser.). (Illus.). 16p. (J). pap. 7.95 (978-1-59920-600-4(5)) Black Rabbit Bks.

Macdonald, Margaret. When Does This Tree Grow Best? 2014. (Little Books of Answers: Level a Ser.). (Illus.). 16p. (gr. k-2). pap. 7.95 (978-1-927136-04-1(0)) Three Crows Media NZL. Dist: RiverStream Publishing.

—Where Am I? 2014. (Little Books of Answers: Level a Ser.). (Illus.). 16p. (gr. k-2). pap. 7.95 (978-1-927136-05-8(9)) Three Crows Media NZL. Dist: RiverStream Publishing.

—Where Can You Eat This Food? 2014. (Little Books of Answers: Level F Ser.). (Illus.). 16p. (gr. k-2). pap. 7.95 (978-1-927136-50-8(4)) Three Crows Media NZL. Dist: RiverStream Publishing.

—Who Can Save Power? 2014. (Little Books of Answers: Level B Ser.). (Illus.). 16p. (gr. k-2). pap. 7.95 (978-1-927136-14-0(8)) Three Crows Media NZL. Dist: RiverStream Publishing.

MacDonald, Margaret. Working as a Team. 2011. (Learn-Abouts Ser.). (Illus.). 16p. (J). pap. 7.95 (978-1-59920-648-6(X)) Black Rabbit Bks.

Machajewski, Sarah. Our Country's Symbols. 2012. (InfoMax Readers Ser.). (ENG., Illus.). 24p. (J). (gr. 1-2). pap. 8.25 (978-1-4488-8980-8(4), Rosen Classroom) Rosen Publishing Group, Inc., The.

Mackey Davis, Cathy. Postal Workers Then & Now, 1 vol. 2006. (Primary Source Readers Ser.). (ENG.). 32p. (J). (gr. 1-1). pap. 8.99 *(978-0-7439-9381-4(0))* Shell Educational Publishing.

MacKinnon, Mairi. Croc Gets a Shock. Blunt, Fred, illus. 2014. (Usborne Phonics Readers Ser.). (ENG.). (J). (gr. -1-3). pap. 6.99 *(978-0-7945-3395-3(7),* Usborne) EDC Publishing.

Maclaine, James. Elephants IR. 2011. (Beginner's Nature Ser.). 32p. (J). ring bd. 4.99 *(978-0-7945-3122-5(9),* Usborne) EDC Publishing.

MacPhail, Catherine. Own Goal. Philips, Mike, illus. 2015. (Collins Big Cat Ser.). (ENG.). 24p. (J). (gr. 2-2). pap. 7.95 *(978-0-00-759114-5(4))* HarperCollins Pubs. Ltd. GBR. Dist: Independent Pubs. Group.

Made in Korea: Six-Pack. (Greetings Ser.: Vol. 3). (gr. 3-5). 31.00 *(978-0-7635-1824-0(7))* Rigby Education.

La Madera. (Coleccion Conceptos de Ciencia en Big Books). (SPA., Illus.). (J). (gr. k-3). 21.95 *(978-0-8136-7426-1(3),* MD7216) Modern Curriculum Pr.

Magazine Level D. 2004. (Reading Central Ser.). (J). (gr. 2-18). 5.95 *(978-1-58830-870-2(7))* Metropolitan Teaching & Learning Co.

Magazine Level E. 2004. (Reading Central Ser.). (J). (gr. 2-18). 5.95 *(978-1-58830-871-9(5))* Metropolitan Teaching & Learning Co.

Magazine Level F. 2004. (Reading Central Ser.). (J). (gr. 2-18). 5.95 *(978-1-58830-872-6(3))* Metropolitan Teaching & Learning Co.

Magee, Wes. Little Dragon. Warburton, Sarah, illus. 2004. (ENG.). 24p. (J). lib. bdg. 23.65 *(978-1-59646-690-6(1))* Dingles & Co.

—Who Likes Pancakes?, 4 vols. 2005. (QEB Readers). (Illus.). 24p. (J). (gr. 1-4). lib. bdg. 15.95 *(978-1-59566-091-6(7))* QEB Publishing Inc.

Maggart, Kaye Wiley & Prentice Hall Staff. Shining Star, Introductory Level. 2003. (ENG., Illus.). xiv, 289p. (gr. 6-12). 73.20 *(978-0-13-111285-8(6))* Pearson ESL.

Magic Food: Individual Title-Six Packs. (Chiquilibros Ser.). (gr. k-1). 23.00 *(978-0-7635-0441-0(6))* Rigby Education.

Magic Tricks. Date not set. (Illus.). 64p. (J). 5.98 *(978-1-4054-0409-9(4))* Parragon, Inc.

Mahy, Margaret. The Gargling Gorilla. Phillips, Mike, illus. 2007. (Collins Big Cat Ser.). (ENG.). 112p. (J). (gr. 3-4). pap. 8.99 *(978-0-00-723089-1(3))* HarperCollins Pubs. Ltd. GBR. Dist: Independent Pubs. Group.

The Mail: Individual Title Two-Packs. (Chiquilibros Ser.). (gr. -1-1). 12.00 *(978-0-7635-8541-9(6))* Rigby Education.

Maile, Ruby. When Do You Sleep? 2014. (Little Books of Answers: Level e Ser.). (Illus.). 16p. (gr. k-2). pap. 7.95 *(978-1-927136-40-9(7))* Three Crows Media NZL. Dist: RiverStream Publishing.

—Why Are You Having A Party? 2014. (Little Books of Answers: Level B Ser.). (Illus.). 16p. (gr. k-2). pap. 7.95 *(978-1-927136-10-2(5))* Three Crows Media NZL. Dist: RiverStream Publishing.

—Why Do You Live Here? 2014. (Little Books of Answers: Level C Ser.). (Illus.). 16p. (gr. k-2). pap. 7.95 *(978-1-927136-25-6(3))* Three Crows Media NZL. Dist: RiverStream Publishing.

—Why Should I Eat Fruit? 2014. (Little Books of Answers: Level a Ser.). (Illus.). 16p. (gr. k-2). pap. 7.95 *(978-1-927136-03-4(2))* Three Crows Media NZL. Dist: RiverStream Publishing.

Maisy Cloth Books Set 800846, 4. 2005. (J). *(978-1-59794-047-4(X))* Environments, Inc.

Make a Tune. (Early Intervention Levels Ser.). 28.38 *(978-0-7362-0403-3(2))* CENGAGE Learning.

Make a Tune (20), Vol. 20. (Early Intervention Levels Ser.). 4.73 *(978-0-7362-0228-2(5))* CENGAGE Learning.

Make It! (Early Intervention Levels Ser.). 3.55 *(978-0-7362-0078-3(9));* 21.30 *(978-0-7362-0357-9(5))* CENGAGE Learning.

Malam, John. You Wouldn't Want to Be a Secret Agent During World War II! A Perilous Mission Behind Enemy Lines. 2010. (You Wouldn't Want to... Ser.). 32p. (J). 29.00 *(978-0-531-20474-0(X));* (ENG.). (gr. 3-18). pap. 9.95 *(978-0-531-13783-3(X))* Scholastic Library Publishing. (Watts, Franklin).

Malara, Maria. Mysterious Places. 2007. (Steck-Vaughn BOLDPRINT Anthologies Ser.). (ENG., Illus.). 48p. (gr. 4-8). pap. 16.90 *(978-1-4190-4022-1(7))* Houghton Mifflin Harcourt Publishing Co.

Man-Kong, Mary. Mariposa. 2008. (Pictureback(R) Ser.). (ENG., Illus.). 16p. (J). (gr. -1-2). pap. 3.99 *(978-0-375-84798-1(7),* Golden Bks.) Random Hse. Children's Bks.

Man on the Moon. (Guided Reading Levels Ser.). 8.48 *(978-0-7362-1692-0(8));* 50.88 *(978-0-7362-2141-2(7))* CENGAGE Learning.

Mangieri, Catherine. A Funny First Day. 2006. (Neighborhood Readers Ser.). (ENG., Illus.). 12p. (gr. 1-3). pap. 5.90 *(978-1-4042-6839-5(1),* Rosen Classroom) Rosen Publishing Group, Inc., The.

Mangieri, Catherine C. & National Geographic Learning Staff. What Is a Rainbow? 2012. (ENG., Illus.). 12p. (C). (gr. 1-2). pap. 9.95 *(978-0-8239-8135-9(5))* National Geographic School Publishing, Inc.

Mann, Rachel. Race to a Fire!, 6 vols., Set. 2003. (Phonics Readers 1-36 Ser.). (ENG.). 8p. (gr. k-1). pap. 29.70 *(978-0-7368-3194-9(0),* Phonics Readers) Capstone Press of Coughlan Cos.

—Sun & Rain, 6 vols., Set. 2003. (Phonics Readers 1-36 Ser.). (ENG.). 8p. (gr. k-1). pap. 29.70 *(978-0-7368-3192-5(4),* Phonics Readers) Capstone Press of Coughlan Cos.

Manolis, Kay. Blastoff! Readers - Body Systems, 6 vols., Set. Incl. Circulatory System. 20.00 *(978-0-531-21701-6(9));* Digestive System. 20.00 *(978-0-531-21702-3(7));* Muscular System. 20.00 *(978-0-531-21703-0(5));* Nervous System. 20.00 *(978-0-531-21704-7(3));* Respiratory System. 20.00 *(978-0-531-21705-4(1));* Skeletal System. 20.00 *(978-0-531-21706-1(X));* (Illus.). 24p. (J). (gr. k-3). 2009. 2009. Set lib. bdg. 120.00 *(978-0-531-27900-7(6),* Children's Pr.) Scholastic Library Publishing.

Mansfield, Katherine. PARTIES AND PRESENTS: THREE SHORT STORIES LEVEL 2 ELEMENTARY/LOWER-INTERMEDIATE. 2010. (ENG., Illus.). 62p. pap. 12.00 *(978-84-8323-836-3(5))* Cambridge Univ. Pr.

—PARTIES AND PRESENTS THREE SHORT STORIES LEVEL 2 ELEMENTARY/LOWER-INTERMEDIATE WITH CD-ROM/AUDIO CD, 1 vol. 2010. (ENG., Illus.). 62p. pap. 14.25 incl. cd-rom *(978-84-8323-684-0(2))* Cambridge Univ. Pr.

Manuel Reeves, Emily. Fiona Flamingo Has Lost Her Pink. 2013. 20p. pap. 10.00 *(978-0-9821506-1-0(X))* Reeves, Emily.

Mara, Wil. Trucks! 2009. (Readers Ser.). (ENG., Illus.). 32p. (J). (gr. -1-1). 13.90 *(978-1-4263-0527-6(3));* pap. 3.99 *(978-1-4263-0526-9(5))* National Geographic Society. (National Geographic Children's Bks.).

March, Julia. DK Readers L2: LEGO NEXO KNIGHTS: Meet the Knights. 2016. (DK Readers Ser.). (ENG.). 48p. (J). (gr. 1-3). 14.99 *(978-1-4654-4473-8(4),* DK Children) Dorling Kindersley Publishing, Inc.

—DK Readers L3: LEGO NEXO KNIGHTS: Monster Battles. 2016. (DK Readers Ser.). (ENG.). 64p. (J). (gr. 2-4). 14.99 *(978-1-4654-4475-2(0),* DK Children) Dorling Kindersley Publishing, Inc.

—Lego Ninjago - Ninja, Go! 2015. (DK Reader Level 2 Ser.). lib. bdg. 13.55 *(978-0-606-36924-4(4))* Turtleback Bks.

Marchessault, Sara J. Pinky the Dreamer & Her Silver Jet. 2009. 36p. pap. 15.49 *(978-1-4389-9902-9(X))* AuthorHouse.

Marion Nash Jackie Lowe Staff & Lowe, Jackie. Spirals Series - Activities for Home Books, 3 vols. 2005. (Spirals Ser.). (C). pap., pap., pap. 83.95 *(978-1-84312-412-2(2),* RU51880) Fulton, David Pubs. GBR. Dist: Taylor & Francis Group.

Markel, Michelle. The Shark That Taught Me English/El Tiburon Que Me Enseno Ingles. Kim, Bo Young, illus. 2008. 28p. (J). pap. 8.95 *(978-1-60448-003-0(3))* Lectura Bks.

—The Shark That Taught Me English/El Tiburon Que Me Enseno Ingles. Guerrero, Ernesto, tr. Kim, Bo Young, illus. 2008. (ENG & SPA.). 28p. (J). (gr. 1-2). 15.95 *(978-1-60448-002-3(5))* Lectura Bks.

Markle, Sandra. Ranger Rick: I Wish I Was an Orca. 2017. (I Can Read Level 1 Ser.). 32p. (J). (gr. -1-3). pap. 3.99 ***(978-0-06-243207-0(9))*** HarperCollins Pubs.

Markowitz-Meredith, Susan. Stump Hill: Set Of 6. 2011. (Early Connections Ser.). (J). pap. 39.00 net. *(978-1-4108-1554-5(4))* Benchmark Education Co.

Marks, Melanie. Phonics Comics: Spooky Sara - Level 3, Level 3. Ball, Victoria, illus. 2006. (ENG.). 24p. (J). (gr. 1-17). per. 3.99 *(978-1-58476-473-1(2),* IKIDS) Innovative Kids.

Marland, Michael. Ideas, Insights & Arguments: A Non-Fiction Collection. 2008. (Cambridge Collections). (ENG., Illus.). 256p. pap. 12.90 *(978-0-521-70323-9(9))* Cambridge Univ. Pr.

Marsh, Carole. I'm Reading about the Statue of Liberty. 2016. (I'm Reading About Ser.). (ENG., Illus.). (J). lib. bdg. 24.99 ***(978-0-635-12207-0(3));*** pap. 7.99 ***(978-0-635-12208-7(1))*** Gallopade International.

Marsh, Laura. Caterpillar to Butterfly. 2012. (Readers Ser.). (ENG., Illus.). 32p. (J). (gr. -1-1). pap. 3.99 *(978-1-4263-0920-5(1),* National Geographic Children's Bks.) National Geographic Society.

—Halloween. 2012. (Readers Ser.). (ENG., Illus.). 32p. (J). (gr. -1-1). pap. 3.99 *(978-1-4263-1034-8(X),* National Geographic Children's Bks.) National Geographic Society.

—Lizards. 2012. (Readers Ser.). (ENG., Illus.). 32p. (J). (gr. k-3). pap. 3.99 *(978-1-4263-0922-9(8),* National Geographic Children's Bks.) National Geographic Society.

—National Geographic Readers: Halloween. 2012. (Readers Ser.). (ENG., Illus.). 32p. (J). (gr. -1-1). lib. bdg. 13.90 *(978-1-4263-1035-5(8),* National Geographic Children's Bks.) National Geographic Society.

—Owls. 2014. (Readers Ser.). (ENG., Illus.). 32p. (J). (gr. -1-1). pap. 3.99 *(978-1-4263-1743-9(3),* National Geographic Children's Bks.) National Geographic Society.

—Ponies (1 Hardcover/1 CD) 2016. (National Geographic Readers: Pre-Reader Ser.). (ENG.). (J). *(978-1-4301-2105-3(X))* Live Oak Media.

—Sea Otters. 2014. (Readers Ser.). (ENG., Illus.). 32p. (J). (gr. -1-1). pap. 3.99 *(978-1-4263-1751-4(4),* National Geographic Children's Bks.) National Geographic Society.

Marshall, James. George & Martha No. 4: The Best of Friends Early Reader. 2011. (Green Light Readers Level 2 Ser.). (ENG., Illus.). 32p. (J). (gr. -1-3). pap. 4.99 *(978-0-547-51988-3(5))* Houghton Mifflin Harcourt Publishing Co.

—George & Martha Early Reader. 2010. (Green Light Readers Level 2 Ser.). (ENG., Illus.). 24p. (J). (gr. -1-3). pap. 4.99 *(978-0-547-40624-4(X))* Houghton Mifflin Harcourt Publishing Co.

—George & Martha Two Great Friends Early Reader. 2010. (Green Light Readers Level 2 Ser.). (ENG., Illus.). 32p. (J). (gr. -1-3). pap. 4.99 *(978-0-547-40625-1(8))* Houghton Mifflin Harcourt Publishing Co.

—Rise & Shine No. 5. 2011. (George & Martha Ser.). (ENG., Illus.). 40p. (J). (gr. -1-3). pap. 4.99 *(978-0-547-57687-9(0))* Houghton Mifflin Harcourt Publishing Co.

Marshall, Natalie. My Turn to Learn Numbers. 2013. (My Turn to Learn Ser.). (ENG., Illus.). 12p. (J). (gr. -1 — 1). bds. 6.99 *(978-0-316-25164-8(X))* Little, Brown Bks. for Young Readers.

—My Turn to Learn Opposites. 2013. (My Turn to Learn Ser.). (ENG.). 12p. (J). (gr. -1 — 1). bds. 6.99 *(978-0-316-25165-5(8))* Little, Brown Bks. for Young Readers.

—My Turn to Learn Shapes. 2013. (My Turn to Learn Ser.). (ENG., Illus.). 12p. (J). (gr. -1 — 1). bds. 6.99 *(978-0-316-25166-2(6))* Little, Brown Bks. for Young Readers.

Marsham, Liz. DK Readers L3: DC Comics Wonder Woman: Warrior for Justice! 2017. (DK Readers Ser.). (ENG.). 64p. (J). (gr. 2-4). 14.99 *(978-1-4654-6065-3(9),* DK Children) Dorling Kindersley Publishing, Inc.

Martin, Elena. Look Inside. 2003. (Shutterbug Books: Social Studies). (Illus.). 16p. pap. 4.10 *(978-0-7398-7642-8(2))* Steck-Vaughn.

Martin, Elizabeth B. I'm Not a Silly Goose. 2013. (ENG.). (J). pap. 13.00 net. *(978-0-578-12913-6(2))* Martin, Elizabeth B.

Martin, Elizabeth B., illus. I'm Not a Silly Goose. Martin, Elizabeth B., . 2014. (ENG.). (J). 9.99 *(978-0-9910543-1-2(8))* Martin, Elizabeth B.

Martin, John David. A Time to Plant: Tests. 2005. (Rod & Staff's Readers Ser.). 22p. (gr. 5-18). 1.55 *(978-0-7399-0404-6(3),* 11511) Rod & Staff Pubs., Inc.

—A Time to Plant: Workbook. 2005. (Rod & Staff's Readers Ser.). 145p. (gr. 5-18). 4.80 *(978-0-7399-0402-2(7),* 11521) Rod & Staff Pubs., Inc.

Martin, Kevin. Arnold Lobel Wrote Great Stories. 2017. (Text Connections Guided Close Reading Ser.). (J). (gr. 1). *(978-1-4900-1800-3(X))* Benchmark Education Co.

Martin, Mary. God Made Nuts. Derstine, Charlene, illus. 2012. 53p. (J). *(978-0-7399-2501-0(6))* Rod & Staff Pubs., Inc.

Martin, Mary S. Fishing with Uncle Nathan. Petre, Emily, illus. 2016. 63p. (J). ***(978-0-7399-2524-9(5))*** Rod & Staff Pubs., Inc.

Martin's mighty Hit: Individual Title Six-Packs. (gr. 1-2). 25.00 *(978-0-7635-9144-1(0))* Rigby Education.

Marvel Book Group. Iron Man Trilogy Read-Along Storybook & CD. 2017. (ENG.). 96p. (J). (gr. 1-3). pap. 9.99 ***(978-1-368-00959-1(X),*** Marvel Pr.) Disney Publishing Worldwide.

—World of Reading Listen Along. 2017. (World of Reading Ser.). (ENG.). 96p. (J). (gr. -1-k). pap. 7.99 ***(978-1-4847-9948-2(8),*** Marvel Pr.) Disney Publishing Worldwide.

Marvel Book Group & Macri, Thomas. This Is Spider-Man. 2012. (Marvel World of Reading Level 1 Ser.). (J). lib. bdg. 13.55 *(978-0-606-23787-1(9),* Turtleback) Turtleback Bks.

Marvel Book Group & West, Alexandra. This is Doctor Strange. 2016. (World of Reading Ser.). (ENG.). 32p. (J). (gr. 1-3). pap. 3.99 *(978-1-4847-8732-8(3),* Marvel Pr.) Disney Publishing Worldwide.

Marvel Book Group Editors. Thwip! You Are It! 2017. (World of Reading Ser.). (J). lib. bdg. 13.55 *(978-0-606-39507-6(5))* Turtleback Bks.

—Tricky Trouble! 2017. (World of Reading Ser.). (J). lib. bdg. 13.55 *(978-0-606-39508-3(3))* Turtleback Bks.

Marwood, Diane. Kim's Top Hat. 2012. (Espresso Phonics Ser.). (ENG., Illus.). 16p. (J). (gr. k-2). pap. 4.99 *(978-1-4451-0434-8(2),* Franklin Watts) Hachette Children's Group GBR. Dist: Hachette Bk. Group.

—The Roman Treasure. 2012. (Espresso Story Time Ser.). (ENG., Illus.). 32p. (J). (gr. k-2). pap. 5.99 *(978-1-4451-0417-1(2),* Franklin Watts) Hachette Children's Group GBR. Dist: Hachette Bk. Group.

Maryland Reading Success Grade 1. 2003. (Illus.). 32p. (J). 9.95 *(978-0-9722452-0-3(0))* New Leaf Educ., Inc.

Maryland Reading Success Grade 2, 3 vols., Vol. 2. 2003. (Illus.). 32p. (J). 9.95 *(978-0-9722452-1-0(9))* New Leaf Educ., Inc.

Maryland Reading Success Grade 3, Vol. 3. 2003. (Illus.). 32p. (J). 9.95 *(978-0-9722452-5-8(1))* New Leaf Educ., Inc.

Marzollo, Jean. I Spy Adventure: 4 Picture Riddle Books. Wick, Walter, illus. Wick, Walter, photos by. 2012. (J). *(978-1-4351-3984-8(4))* Scholastic, Inc.

—I Spy Lightning in the Sky. Wick, Walter, illus. 2005. (Scholastic Reader Level 1 Ser.). (ENG.). 32p. (J). (gr. -1-3). pap. 3.99 *(978-0-439-68052-3(2),* Cartwheel Bks.) Scholastic, Inc.

—I'm a Seed. Moffatt, Judith, illus. 2010. (Rise & Shine Ser.: Level 1). (ENG.). 32p. (C). (gr. -1-1). pap. 10.95 *(978-0-590-26586-7(5))* National Geographic School Publishing, Inc.

—A Pumpkin. Wick, Walter, illus. 2006. (Scholastic Reader Level 1 Ser.). (ENG.). 32p. (J). (gr. -1-3). pap. 3.99 *(978-0-439-73863-7(6),* Cartwheel Bks.) Scholastic, Inc.

Maslen, Bobby Lynn & Maslen. Beginning Readers, Set. 2006. (Bob Bks.). (ENG., Illus.). 12p. (J). (gr. -1-3). pap. 16.99 *(978-0-439-84500-7(9),* Scholastic Paperbacks) Scholastic, Inc.

Maslen, Bobby Lynn & Maslen, John R. Long Vowels, Set. 2006. (Bob Bks.: No. 5). (ENG.). 16p. (J). (gr. -1-3). pap. 16.99 *(978-0-439-86541-8(7),* Scholastic Paperbacks) Scholastic, Inc.

Maslen, John R. & Maslen, Bobby Lynn. Advancing Beginners, Set. 2006. (Bob Bks.). (ENG., Illus.). 16p. (J). (gr. -1-3). pap. 16.99 *(978-0-439-84502-1(5),* Scholastic Paperbacks) Scholastic, Inc.

—Compound Words, Set. Maslen, John R., illus. 2006. (Bob Bks.). (ENG., Illus.). 16p. (J). (gr. -1-3). pap. 16.99 *(978-0-439-84506-9(8),* Scholastic Paperbacks) Scholastic, Inc.

Masoliver, Juan Antonio. Historias Breves para Leer, Level 2. (SPA & ENG.). 128p. (J). 14.95 *(978-84-7143-732-7(5),* SGS4393) Sociedad General Espanola de Libreria ESP. Dist: Continental Bk. Co., Inc.

Masoliver, Juan Antonio & Masoliver, Joaquín. Historias Breves para Leer, Level 1. 9th ed. (SPA & ENG., Illus.). 150p. (J). 14.95 *(978-84-7143-825-6(9),* SGS8259) Sociedad General Espanola de Libreria ESP. Dist: Continental Bk. Co., Inc.

Mass, Wendy & Brawer, Michael. Archie's Alien Disguise. 2015. (Space Taxi Ser.: 3). (ENG., Illus.). 128p. (J). (gr. 1-5). pap. 5.99 *(978-0-316-24328-5(0))* Little, Brown Bks. for Young Readers.

The Masterpiece: Level M, 6 vols. 128p. (gr. 2-3). 41.95 *(978-0-7699-1026-0(2))* Shortland Pubns. (U. S. A.) Inc.

Matheson, Hughena. The 10 Most Historic Speeches. 2007. 14.99 *(978-1-55448-478-2(2))* Scholastic Library Publishing.

Mathis, Pamela. Sound Town the Story of Words. 2010. 32p. pap. 15.99 *(978-1-4389-9194-8(0))* AuthorHouse.

Mattern, Joanne. The Annexation of Texas: From Republic to Statehood, 1 vol. 2012. (Primary Source Readers Ser.). (ENG.). 32p. (J). (gr. 4-4). pap. 8.99 *(978-1-4333-5048-1(3))* Teacher Created Materials, Inc.

—Geoffrey Chaucer: Medieval Writer, 1 vol. 2012. (Primary Source Readers Ser.). (ENG.). 32p. (J). (gr. 4-4). pap. 8.99 *(978-1-4333-5006-1(8))* Teacher Created Materials, Inc.

—Medieval Times: England in the Middle Ages, 1 vol. 2012. (Primary Source Readers Ser.). (ENG.). 32p. (J). (gr. 5-5). pap. 8.99 *(978-1-4333-5005-4(X))* Teacher Created Materials, Inc.

—Sam Houston: A Fearless Statesman, 1 vol. 2012. (Primary Source Readers Ser.). (ENG.). 32p. (J). (gr. 3-3). pap. 8.99 *(978-1-4333-5049-8(1))* Teacher Created Materials, Inc.

Matthas, Seth. Mateo's Family Traits: Gathering Data. 2017. (Computer Science for the Real World Ser.). 16p. (gr. 7-8). pap. 7.95 ***(978-1-5383-5186-4(2),*** Rosen Classroom) Rosen Publishing Group, Inc., The.

Matthew, Anna. Goal! Heyworth, Heather, illus. 2013. (Start Reading Ser.). (ENG.). 24p. (gr. k-1). pap. 41.94 *(978-1-4765-3215-8(X));* pap. 7.95 *(978-1-4765-3203-5(6))* Capstone Press of Coughlan Cos.

—Hopscotch, 1 vol. Heyworth, Heather, illus. 2013. (Start Reading Ser.). (ENG.). 24p. (gr. k-1). pap. 7.95 *(978-1-4765-3205-9(2));* pap. 41.94 *(978-1-4765-3218-9(4))* Capstone Press of Coughlan Cos.

—Jumping Rope! Heyworth, Heather, illus. 2013. (Start Reading Ser.). (ENG.). 24p. (gr. k-1). pap. 41.94 *(978-1-4765-3222-6(2));* pap. 7.95 *(978-1-4765-3206-6(0))* Capstone Press of Coughlan Cos.

Matthews. Death in the Desert. (Thumbprint Mysteries Ser.). 32.86 *(978-0-8092-0416-8(9))* McGraw-Hill/Contemporary.

Matthews, Andrew. Gulliver's Travels. Horrocks, Steve, illus. 2014. (Collins Big Cat Progress Ser.). (ENG.). 32p. (J). (gr. 5-6). pap. 7.99 *(978-0-00-751937-8(0))* HarperCollins Pubs. Ltd. GBR. Dist: Independent Pubs. Group.

Matthews, Layla, et al. Eat at Grandma's? Kids Review a New Restaurant. 2017. (Text Connections Guided Close Reading Ser.). (J). (gr. 2). *(978-1-4900-1860-7(3))* Benchmark Education Co.

Matthews, Trisha. I Smell Pancakes! 2006. (Neighborhood Readers Ser.). (ENG., Illus.). 16p. (gr. 1-3). pap. 6.50 *(978-1-4042-7188-3(0),* Rosen Classroom) Rosen Publishing Group, Inc., The.

Maule, David. Stealing High Beginning Book with Online Access. 2014. (ENG.). 24p. (J). pap. 9.50 *(978-1-107-67774-6(2))* Cambridge Univ. Pr.

—What Makes a Place Special? Moscow, Egypt, Australia. 2014. (ENG., Illus.). 24p. (J). pap. 9.50 *(978-1-107-63317-9(6))* Cambridge Univ. Pr.

MauleDavid. ARE YOU LISTENING? THE SENSE OF HEARING HIGH BEGINNING BOOK WITH ONLINE ACCESS. 2014. (ENG.). 24p. (J). pap. 9.50 *(978-1-107-63251-6(X))* Cambridge Univ. Pr.

—GENIUS BEGINNING BOOK WITH ONLINE ACCESS. 2014. (ENG.). 24p. (J). pap. 9.50 *(978-1-107-67865-1(X))* Cambridge Univ. Pr.

Maupassant, Guy de. Mon Oncle Jules et Autres Nouvelles, Level D. (FRE., Illus.). (YA). (gr. 7-12). 9.95 *(978-0-88436-044-5(X),* 40281) EMC/Paradigm Publishing.

May I Go Out? (J). 26.20 *(978-0-8136-8428-4(5));* 26.20 *(978-0-8136-8429-1(3));* (gr. -1-3). 59.50 *(978-0-8136-7978-5(8))* Modern Curriculum Pr.

May I Stay Home Today? 6 Small Books. (gr. k-3). 24.00 *(978-0-7635-6239-7(4))* Rigby Education.

May, Paul. Elephants. 2009. (Wild Reads Ser.). (ENG., Illus.). 32p. (YA). (gr. k). pap. 4.95 *(978-0-19-911928-8(7))* Oxford Univ. Pr., Inc.

Mayer, Mercer. The Fall Festival. 2012. (Illus.). 32p. (J). *(978-1-4351-4384-5(1))* HarperCollins Pubs.

—Just a Baby Bird. 2016. (Little Critter: I Can Read! Ser.). (J). lib. bdg. 13.55 *(978-0-606-38158-1(9))* Turtleback Bks.

—Little Critter Collector's Quintet. Mayer, Mercer, illus. 2017. (My First I Can Read Ser.). (Illus.). 160p. (J). (gr. -1-3). pap. 16.99 *(978-0-06-265349-9(0))* HarperCollins Pubs.

—Snowball Soup. Mayer, Mercer, illus. 2007. (My First I Can Read Ser.). (ENG., Illus.). 32p. (J). (gr. -1-3). pap. 3.99 *(978-0-06-083543-9(5))* HarperCollins Pubs.

Mayer, Mercer & Mayer, Gina. My Family: A Big Little Critter Book. 2013. (Big Little Critter Ser.: 2). (ENG., Illus.). 98p. (J). 12.95 *(978-1-60746-810-3(7),* Premiere) FastPencil, Inc.

—On the Go. 2013. (Big Little Critter Ser.: 4). (ENG., Illus.). 96p. (J). 12.95 *(978-1-60746-983-4(9),* Premiere) FastPencil, Inc.

—Staying Well. 2013. (Big Little Critter Ser.: 5). (ENG.). 96p. (J). 12.95 *(978-1-60746-732-8(1),* Premiere) FastPencil, Inc.

Mayfield, Christine & Quinn, Kristine M. Hammurabi: Babylonian Ruler, 1 vol. 2007. (Primary Source Readers Ser.). (ENG.). 32p. (J). (gr. 4-4). pap. 8.99 *(978-0-7439-0441-4(9))* Shell Educational Publishing.

—Mesopotamia, 1 vol. 2007. (Primary Source Readers Ser.). (ENG.). 32p. (J). (gr. 5-5). pap. 8.99 *(978-0-7439-0440-7(0))* Shell Educational Publishing.

Mayfield, Sue. The Four Franks. Parsons, Garry, illus. 2005. (Blue Go Bananas Ser.). (ENG.). 48p. (J). (gr. 1-2). *(978-0-7787-2651-7(7))* Crabtree Publishing Co.

Mayhew, Jon. Blood Cave. Bacchin, Giorgio, illus. 2014. (Collins Big Cat Progress Ser.). (ENG.). 32p. (J). (gr. 4-5). pap. 7.99 *(978-0-00-751921-7(4))* HarperCollins Pubs. Ltd. GBR. Dist: Independent Pubs. Group.

Mazza, Barbara. How the Short Vowels Got Their Sound. 2007. 28p. per. 17.32 *(978-1-4257-2721-5(2))* Xlibris Corp.

McAllister, Margaret. Emily & the Lamb. Vince, Dawn, illus. 2005. (ENG.). 24p. (J). lib. bdg. 23.65 *(978-1-59646-756-9(8))* Dingles & Co.

McBratney, Sam. Henry Seamouse. 2005. *(978-1-901358-13-1(5))* CAMFA.

McCall, Val. Twelve Rabbits & a Turtle: Bilingual English French. 2012. 46p. pap. 9.95 *(978-1-938367-00-7(6))* Destinee Media.

McCallum, Rory. Li Lost His Mitten: Fixing a Problem. 2017. (Computer Science for the Real World Ser.). 8p. (gr. 5-6). pap. 6.20 ***(978-1-5383-5048-5(3),*** Rosen Classroom) Rosen Publishing Group, Inc., The.

McCarrier, Andrea, et al. Fact & Fiction 1: Reece to the Rescue; Here Comes a Thunderstorm; Garden Giant; A Sunflower Life Cycle; Mugs Indoors & Outdoors; Cats Are Hunters; Beach Days; Oceans All Around Us, 8 bks., Set. Morley, Amanda et al, illus. 2006. (ENG.). 16p. (J). pap. 120.00 *(978-1-893986-25-1(X))* Keep Bks.

McCaughrean, Geraldine & Willey, Bee. Collins Big Cat - Think Again! 2005. (Collins Big Cat Ser.). (ENG.). 32p. (J). (gr. 1-3). pap. 7.99 *(978-0-00-718643-3(6))* HarperCollins Pubs. Ltd. GBR. Dist: Independent Pubs. Group.

McClatchy, Lisa & Thompson, Kay. Eloise & the Big Parade. Lyon, Tammie, illus. 2007. (Eloise Ser.). (ENG.). 32p. (J). (gr. -1-1). pap. 3.99 *(978-1-4169-3523-0(1),* Simon Spotlight) Simon Spotlight.

McClenney, Earl H., Jr. Mamma, Is the Maid Goin' Teach? Portraits of Black Women Who Integrated the Public Schools

in Richmond, VA. 2005. spiral bd. 10.95 net. *(978-0-9618835-5-3(3))* First Associates Publishing.
McCombie, Karen & Collins UK Publishing Staff. The Black Bull. Dünzinger, Eva, illus. 2016. (ENG.). 48p. (J). pap. 8.95 *(978-0-00-814717-4(5))* HarperCollins Pubs. Ltd. GBR. Dist: Independent Pubs. Group.
McCune, Susan. At the Watering Hole, 01 vols., 1. 2016. (Rosen REAL Readers: STEM & STEAM Collection). (ENG.). 8p. (J). pap. 5.46 *(978-1-5081-1455-0(2),* Rosen Classroom) Rosen Publishing Group, Inc., The.
—Benny & Pops Have a Surprise, 01 vols., 1. 2016. (Rosen REAL Readers: STEM & STEAM Collection). (ENG.). 8p. (J). pap. 5.46 *(978-1-5081-1475-8(7),* Rosen Classroom) Rosen Publishing Group, Inc., The.
—The Choice, 01 vols., 1. 2016. (Rosen REAL Readers: Social Studies Nonfiction / Fiction: Family, Community, & the World Ser.). (ENG.). 12p. (J). pap. 6.33 *(978-1-5081-1991-3(0),* Rosen Classroom) Rosen Publishing Group, Inc., The.
—Every Penny Helps, 01 vols., 1. 2016. (Rosen REAL Readers: Social Studies Nonfiction / Fiction: Family, Community, & the World Ser.). (ENG.). 12p. (J). pap. 6.33 *(978-1-5081-1913-5(9),* Rosen Classroom) Rosen Publishing Group, Inc., The.
—A Grandmother's Story, 01 vols., 1. 2016. (Rosen REAL Readers: Social Studies Nonfiction / Fiction: Family, Community, & the World Ser.). (ENG.). 8p. (J). pap. 5.46 *(978-1-5081-1522-9(2),* Rosen Classroom) Rosen Publishing Group, Inc., The.
—Granny's Guacamole, 01 vols., 1. 2016. (Rosen REAL Readers: STEM & STEAM Collection). (ENG.). 12p. (J). pap. 6.33 *(978-1-5081-1572-4(9),* Rosen Classroom) Rosen Publishing Group, Inc., The.
—An Inch Taller, 01 vols., 1. 2016. (Rosen REAL Readers: Social Studies Nonfiction / Fiction: Family, Community, & the World Ser.). (ENG.). 8p. (J). pap. 5.46 *(978-1-5081-1863-3(9),* Rosen Classroom) Rosen Publishing Group, Inc., The.
—Our Party at the Park, 01 vols., 1. 2016. (Rosen REAL Readers: Social Studies Nonfiction / Fiction: Family, Community, & the World Ser.). (ENG.). 8p. (J). pap. 5.46 *(978-1-5081-1899-2(X),* Rosen Classroom) Rosen Publishing Group, Inc., The.
—Paul's Sneakers, 01 vols., 1. 2016. (Rosen REAL Readers: STEM & STEAM Collection). (ENG.). 8p. (J). pap. 5.46 *(978-1-5081-1514-4(1),* Rosen Classroom) Rosen Publishing Group, Inc., The.
—The Push-Up Test, 01 vols., 1. 2016. (Rosen REAL Readers: STEM & STEAM Collection). (ENG.). 12p. (J). pap. 6.33 *(978-1-5081-1554-0(0),* Rosen Classroom) Rosen Publishing Group, Inc., The.
—Space Camp, 01 vols., 1. 2016. (Rosen REAL Readers: STEM & STEAM Collection). (ENG.). 12p. (J). pap. 6.33 *(978-1-5081-1626-4(1),* Rosen Classroom) Rosen Publishing Group, Inc., The.
—Taking Turns Talking, 01 vols., 1. 2016. (Rosen REAL Readers: Social Studies Nonfiction / Fiction: Family, Community, & the World Ser.). (ENG.). 8p. (J). pap. 5.46 *(978-1-5081-1412-3(9),* Rosen Classroom) Rosen Publishing Group, Inc., The.
McCurry, Kristen. Little Scribe, 1 vol. 2014. (Little Scribe Ser.). (ENG.). 32p. (gr. 1-2). pap. 31.80 *(978-1-4765-7913-9(X),* Aplus Bks.) Capstone Press of Coughlan Cos.
McDonald, Kirsten. Carlos & Carmen. 2016. (Carlos & Carmen Ser.: 4). (ENG.). 32p. (J). (gr. k-3). lib. bdg. 108.28 *(978-1-62402-136-7(0))* Magic Wagon.
McDonnell, Ginger. Next Stop: The Caribbean, 1 vol. 2nd rev. ed. 2011. (Nonfiction Readers Ser.). (ENG.). 24p. (J). (gr. 2-2). pap. 6.99 *(978-1-4333-3612-6(X))* Teacher Created Materials, Inc.
—Next Stop - Canada, 1 vol. 2nd rev. ed. 2011. (Nonfiction Readers Ser.). (ENG.). 24p. (J). (gr. 2-2). pap. 6.99 *(978-1-4333-3611-9(1))* Teacher Created Materials, Inc.
—Next Stop - Mexico, 1 vol. 2nd rev. ed. 2011. (Nonfiction Readers Ser.). (ENG.). 24p. (J). (gr. 2-2). pap. 6.99 *(978-1-4333-3610-2(3))* Teacher Created Materials, Inc.
McEwan, Elaine K., et al. Word Analysis,Grades 4-8. 2008. (Reading Puzzle Ser.). (ENG., Illus.). 96p. (gr. 4-7). pap. 16.95 *(978-1-4129-5825-7(3),* B58257P) Corwin Pr.
McGraw-Hill Education Editors. The American Vision, StudentWorks Plus CD-ROM. 2nd ed. 2005. (United States History (hs) Ser.). (ENG.). (gr. 9-12). 152.24 *(978-0-07-865456-5(4),* 0078654564) McGraw-Hill Higher Education.
McGraw-Hill Staff. Listen!Listen!Letter Sounds in Rhymes Complt Set. (gr. k-1). 210.95 *(978-0-322-02636-0(9))* Wright Group/McGraw-Hill.
—Song Box Sets & Resources:Save the Tree for Me Cass. (Song Box Ser.). (gr. 1-2). 8.50 incl. audio *(978-0-7802-2265-6(2))* Wright Group/McGraw-Hill.
McGreevy, Joyce. The Wind Eagle. 2003. (Rise & Shine Ser.). (ENG.). (Orig.). (C). pap. 15.95 *(978-0-7362-1695-1(2))* CENGAGE Learning.
McGuffey, William H. New Mcguffey Fourth Reader. 2006. (ENG.). 204p. pap. 20.99 *(978-1-4264-0489-4(1));* pap. 22.99 *(978-1-4264-0563-1(4))* Creative Media Partners, LLC.
McHale, Scarlett. Brady Makes a Weather Graph. 2013. (InfoMax Readers Ser.). (ENG., Illus.). 24p. (J). (gr. 3-4). pap. 8.25 *(978-1-4777-2460-6(5),* Rosen Classroom) Rosen Publishing Group, Inc., The.
McKay, Hilary. The Terrible Time Without Tilly. Scott, Kimberley, illus. 2016. (Reading Ladder Ser.). (ENG.). 48p. (J). (gr. k-2). 7.99 *(978-1-4052-8248-2(7))* Egmont Bks., Ltd. GBR. Dist: Independent Pubs. Group.
—Tilly & the Trouble in the Night. Scott, Kimberley, illus. 2016. (Reading Ladder Ser.). (ENG.). 48p. (J). (gr. k-2). pap. 7.99 *(978-1-4052-8250-5(9))* Egmont Bks., Ltd. GBR. Dist: Independent Pubs. Group.
McKay, Sindy. The Frog Prince/el Principe Rana: Spanish/English (We Both Read - Level 1-2) Ulrich, George, illus. 2016. (We Both Read - Level 1-2 Ser.). (ENG & SPA.). (J). pap. 4.99 *(978-1-60115-076-9(8))* Treasure Bay, Inc.
—Too Many Cats: Demasiados Gatos. 2010. (SPA., Illus.). 41p. (J). *(978-1-60115-039-4(3))* Treasure Bay, Inc.
—We Both Read Bilingual Edition-Museum Day/Dia Del Museo. Johnson, Meredith, illus. 2015.Tr. of Dia Del Museo. (ENG & SPA.). 44p. (J). (gr. k-1). pap. 4.99 *(978-1-60115-064-6(4))* Treasure Bay, Inc.
—We Both Read Bilingual Edition-Too Many Cats/Demasiados Gatos. Johnson, Meredith, illus. 2011. (ENG & SPA.). 44p. (J). pap. 4.99 *(978-1-60115-040-0(7))* Treasure Bay, Inc.
—We Both Read-My Car Trip. Johnson, Meredith, illus. 2005. (We Both Read Ser.). 48p. (J). (gr. -1-2). lib. bdg. 7.99 *(978-1-891327-63-6(1));* per. 4.99 *(978-1-891327-64-3(X))* Treasure Bay, Inc.
—We Read Phonics-Matt & Sid. Reinhart, Larry, illus. 2010. 32p. (J). 9.95 *(978-1-60115-315-9(5));* pap. 4.99 *(978-1-60115-316-6(3))* Treasure Bay, Inc.
—We Read Phonics-Pat, Cat, & Rat. Johnson, Meredith, illus. 2010. 32p. (J). 9.95 *(978-1-60115-311-1(2));* pap. 4.99 *(978-1-60115-312-8(0))* Treasure Bay, Inc.
—We Read Phonics-the Garden Crew. Johnson, Meredith, illus. 2011. 32p. (J). 9.95 *(978-1-60115-345-6(7));* pap. 4.99 *(978-1-60115-346-3(5))* Treasure Bay, Inc.
Mckenzie, Precious. Now or Later Alligator. Snape, Jenny, illus. 2012. (ENG.). 24p. (gr. k-1). pap. 8.95 *(978-1-61810-305-5(9))* Rourke Educational Media.
McManus, Madelyn. Britney Makes a Budget. 2013. (Rosen Readers Ser.). (ENG.). 24p. (J). (gr. 3-4). pap. 8.25 *(978-1-4777-2528-3(8));* pap. 49.50 *(978-1-4777-2529-0(6))* Rosen Publishing Group, Inc., The. (Rosen Classroom).
McMillan, Dawn. Catch of the Day! Vignolo, Enrique, illus. 2013. (ENG.). 24p. (gr. 3-3). pap. *(978-1-927197-70-7(8),* Red Rocket Readers) Flying Start Bks.
McNee, I. Knights - Internet Referenced. 2005. (Beginners Ser.). 32p. (J). (gr. 1-18). pap. 4.95 *(978-0-7945-0896-8(0),* Usborne) EDC Publishing.
McOmber, Rachel B., ed. McOmber Phonics Storybooks: A Night to Celebrate. rev. ed. (Illus.). (J). *(978-0-944991-71-8(8))* Swift Learning Resources.
—McOmber Phonics Storybooks: Fizz in the Pit. rev. ed. (Illus.). (J). *(978-0-944991-12-1(2))* Swift Learning Resources.
—McOmber Phonics Storybooks: Fizz Mix. rev. ed. (Illus.). (J). *(978-0-944991-11-4(4))* Swift Learning Resources.
—McOmber Phonics Storybooks: Fizz Mud. rev. ed. (Illus.). (J). *(978-0-944991-21-3(1))* Swift Learning Resources.
MCP Staff. The Baby Who Got All the Blame. (J). (gr. 1-2). 38.50 *(978-0-8136-9136-7(2));* 38.50 *(978-0-8136-1071-9(0))* Modern Curriculum Pr.
—The Big Cat, 6 bks., set, Level 4, Bk. 2. 2003. (J). (gr. -1-3). 24.50 *(978-0-8136-2373-3(1))* Modern Curriculum Pr.
—By the Tree, Level 4, Bk. 22. (J). (gr. -1-3). 24.50 *(978-0-8136-0693-4(4))* Modern Curriculum Pr.
—Can a Cow Hop?, Level 4, Bk. 27. (J). (gr. -1-3). 24.50 *(978-0-8136-0795-5(7))* Modern Curriculum Pr.
—Cat's Trip, 6 bks., Set, Level 12, Bk. 50. (J). (gr. -1-3). pap. 33.50 *(978-0-8136-2107-4(0))* Modern Curriculum Pr.
—Fast As a Fox, Level 4, Bk. 29. (J). (gr. -1-3). 24.50 *(978-0-8136-1961-3(0))* Modern Curriculum Pr.
—Little Bunny's Lunch: Short u; Consonants b, h; Blends br, cr; Digraphs ch, sh, th. (J). (gr. 1-2). 38.50 *(978-0-8136-1116-7(4))* Modern Curriculum Pr.
—My Cat, Level 4, Bk. 13. 2003. (J). (gr. -1-3). 24.50 *(978-0-8136-0679-8(9))* Modern Curriculum Pr.
—The Name Is the Same, 6 bks., set, Level 12, Bk. 43. 2003. (J). (gr. -1-3). 33.50 *(978-0-8136-2081-7(3))* Modern Curriculum Pr.
—Nut Pie for Judy, Level 4, Bk. 43. 2003. (J). (gr. -1-3). 24.50 *(978-0-8136-1973-6(4))* Modern Curriculum Pr.
—Sandy, Level 3, Bk. 19. (J). (gr. -1-3). 24.50 *(978-0-8136-1951-4(3))* Modern Curriculum Pr.
—Six Go By, Level A. 2003. (J). (gr. -1-3). 21.95 *(978-0-8136-0672-9(1))* Modern Curriculum Pr.
—Stop That!, Level 3, Bk. 16. (J). (gr. -1-3). 24.50 *(978-0-8136-0783-2(3))* Modern Curriculum Pr.
—Terrific Shoes, Level 3, Bk. 8. (J). (gr. -1-3). 24.50 *(978-0-8136-1941-5(6))* Modern Curriculum Pr.
—True or False?, 6 bks., Set, Level 12, Bk. 47. 2003. (J). (gr. -1-3). pap. 33.50 *(978-0-8136-2105-0(4))* Modern Curriculum Pr.
—Very Big, Level 4, Bk. 45. 2003. (J). (gr. -1-3). 24.50 *(978-0-8136-1447-2(3))* Modern Curriculum Pr.
—We Are Singing, Level 2, Bk. 7. (J). (gr. -1-3). 21.95 *(978-0-8136-0673-6(X))* Modern Curriculum Pr.
—When Bob Woke up Late, 6 bks., set, Level 12, Bk. 45. 2003. (J). (gr. -1-3). 33.50 *(978-0-8136-2085-5(6))* Modern Curriculum Pr.
—Where Do They Live?, Level 3, Bk. 17. (J). (gr. -1-3). 24.50 *(978-0-8136-1949-1(1))* Modern Curriculum Pr.
—Who Said Boo? Long u; Consonants d, m; Blend dr. (J). 38.50 *(978-0-8136-1091-7(5))* Modern Curriculum Pr.
—Wilma's Wagon, Level 4, Bk. 32. (J). (gr. -1-3). 24.50 *(978-0-8136-1965-1(3))* Modern Curriculum Pr.
McRoberts, Richard. The Curious Incident of the Dog in the Night Time. 2005. (Cambridge Wizard English Student Guides). (ENG.). 64p. pap. 19.95 *(978-0-521-61379-8(5))* Cambridge Univ. Pr.
Meachen Rau, Dana. Neil Armstrong. 2014. (Rookie Biographies(r) Ser.). (ENG.). 32p. (J). lib. bdg. 23.00 *(978-0-531-21063-5(4))* Scholastic Library Publishing.
Meachen Rau, Dana & Franco-Feeney, Betsy. All about Me: My Book by Me - My Pinkie Finger - My Special Space. Meachen Rau, Dana et al, illus. 2006. (ENG.). 93p. (J). (gr. k-2). pap. 9.95 *(978-0-531-16924-7(3),* Children's Pr.) Scholastic Library Publishing.
Meadows, Daisy. Scholastic Reader Level 2: Rainbow Magic: Pet Fairies to the Rescue! Artful Doodlers Ltd Staff, illus. 2013. (Scholastic Reader Level 2 Ser.). (ENG.). 32p. (J). (gr. -1-3). pap. 3.99 *(978-0-545-46295-2(9),* Scholastic Paperbacks) Scholastic, Inc.
Meddaugh, Susan. Haunted House. 2010. (Martha Speaks Ser.). (ENG., Illus.). 24p. (J). (gr. -1-3). pap. 3.99 *(978-0-547-21073-5(6))* Houghton Mifflin Harcourt Publishing Co.
—Martha Speaks: Good Luck, Martha! (Reader) 2012. (Martha Speaks Ser.). (ENG., Illus.). 24p. (J). (gr. -1-3). 12.99 *(978-0-547-57657-2(9));* pap. 3.99 *(978-0-547-57658-9(7))* Houghton Mifflin Harcourt Publishing Co.
—Martha Speaks: Haunted House (Reader) 2010. (Martha Speaks Ser.). (ENG., Illus.). 24p. (J). (gr. -1-3). 12.99 *(978-0-547-39353-7(9))* Houghton Mifflin Harcourt Publishing Co.
—Martha Speaks: Meet Martha (Picture Reader) 2010. (Martha Speaks Ser.). (ENG., Illus.). 24p. (J). (gr. -1-3). 12.99 *(978-0-547-36904-4(2))* Houghton Mifflin Harcourt Publishing Co.
—Meet Martha. 2010. (Martha Speaks Ser.). (ENG., Illus.). 24p. (J). (gr. -1-3). pap. 3.99 *(978-0-547-21079-7(5))* Houghton Mifflin Harcourt Publishing Co.
—Toy Trouble. 2010. (Martha Speaks Ser.). (ENG., Illus.). 24p. (J). (gr. -1-3). pap. 3.99 *(978-0-547-21078-0(7))* Houghton Mifflin Harcourt Publishing Co.
Medina, Conni. Make a Chinese New Year Dragon, 1 vol. 2nd rev. ed. 2011. (Nonfiction Readers Ser.). (ENG.). 20p. (J). (gr. 1-1). pap. 4.99 *(978-1-4333-3593-8(X))* Teacher Created Materials, Inc.
—Make a Gingerbread Man, 1 vol. 2nd rev. ed. 2011. (Nonfiction Readers Ser.). (ENG.). 20p. (J). (gr. 1-1). pap. 4.99 *(978-1-4333-3594-5(8))* Teacher Created Materials, Inc.
—Make Papel Picado, 1 vol. 2nd rev. ed. 2011. (Nonfiction Readers Ser.). (ENG.). 20p. (J). (gr. 1-1). pap. 4.99 *(978-1-4333-3592-1(1))* Teacher Created Materials, Inc.
Medina, Meg. Mango, Abuela, & Me. Dominguez, Angela, illus. 2015. (ENG & SPA.). 32p. (J). (gr. k-3). 7.99 *(978-0-7636-8099-2(0))* Candlewick Pr.
Mega Jumbo ABC And 123. 2006. (J). per. 9.95 *(978-1-885920-13-3(X))* Pyramid Publishing, Inc.
Meg's Mad Magnet, 6 vols., Pack,Set C. (Supersonic Phonics Ser.). (gr. k-3). 29.00 *(978-0-7635-0542-4(0))* Rigby Education.
Meissner, David. My Neighborhood: Set Of 6. 2011. (Early Connections Ser.). (J). pap. 39.00 net. *(978-1-4108-1540-8(4))* Benchmark Education Co.
Meister, Cari. Tiny Goes to the Movies. Davis, Rich, illus. 2016. (Tiny Ser.). (ENG.). 32p. (J). (gr. k-1). pap. 3.99 *(978-0-448-48295-8(9),* Penguin Young Readers) Penguin Young Readers Group.
Meister, Cari & Bader, Bonnie. Hi-Ho, Tiny. Davis, Rich, illus. 2015. (Tiny Ser.). (ENG.). 32p. (J). (gr. k-1). 3.99 *(978-0-448-48291-0(6),* Penguin Young Readers) Penguin Young Readers Group.
—Tiny Saves the Day. Davis, Rich, illus. 2016. (Tiny Ser.). (ENG.). 32p. (J). (gr. k-1). 3.99 *(978-0-448-48293-4(2),* Penguin Young Readers) Penguin Young Readers Group.
Meister, Cari & Sirrell, Terry. Me Fascinan los árboles. Sirrell, Terry, illus. 2011. (Rookie Ready to Learn Español Ser.). (SPA., Illus.). 40p. (J). lib. bdg. 23.00 *(978-0-531-26118-7(2),* Children's Pr.) Scholastic Library Publishing.
—Me Fascinan los Árboles. Sirrell, Terry, illus. 2011. (Rookie Ready to Learn Español Ser.). (SPA., Illus.). 40p. (J). pap. 5.95 *(978-0-531-26786-8(5),* Children's Pr.) Scholastic Library Publishing.
Melinda, Luke. El perro verde (the Green Dog) 2008. (SPA.). (J). pap. 5.95 *(978-1-57565-264-1(1))* Kane Press, Inc.
Mellon, Nicole. Liam's Pets. Filipina, Monika, illus. 2017. (Text Connections Guided Close Reading Ser.). (J). (gr. 1). *(978-1-4900-1802-7(6))* Benchmark Education Co.
Mendoza, Javier, et al. El Mundo. 2008. (SPA., Illus.). 32p. (J). pap. 7.99 *(978-1-84686-209-0(4))* Barefoot Bks., Inc.
Meredith, Susan Markowitz. All Work, No Play: Set Of 6. 2010. (Early Connections Ser.). (J). pap. 37.00 net. *(978-1-4108-1072-4(0))* Benchmark Education Co.
Metal, Liana. Storytime. 2008. 33p. pap. 16.50 *(978-1-4092-2451-8(1))* Lulu Pr., Inc.
Metcalf, Calvin John. The Literary World Seventh Reader. 2007. 308p. 98.99 *(978-1-4280-7591-7(7));* per. 91.99 *(978-1-4280-7587-0(9))* IndyPublish.com.
Meyers, Terri. Shih Tzu Achoo!! 2009. 24p. pap. 12.99 *(978-1-4389-5696-1(7))* AuthorHouse.
Mi hermanita Annie. (Pebble Soup Exploraciones Ser.). 16p. (gr. -1-18). 31.00 *(978-0-7578-1670-3(3))* Rigby Education.
Mi hermanita Annie: Small Book. (Pebble Soup Exploraciones Ser.). 16p. (gr. -1-18). 5.00 *(978-0-7578-1710-6(6))* Rigby Education.
Michaels, Chris. Finding Stripes. 2010. (Sight Word Readers Ser.). (J). 3.49 *(978-1-60719-626-6(3))* Newmark Learning LLC.
Michaels, Eric. Women of Courage, 6, Set. 2004. (Phonics Readers Books 37-72 Ser.). (ENG.). 16p. (gr. k-1). pap. 35.70 *(978-0-7368-4087-3(7),* Phonics Readers) Capstone Press of Coughlan Cos.
Michele, Tracey. African Art. 2011. (Learn-Abouts Ser.). (Illus.). 16p. (J). pap. 7.95 *(978-1-59920-637-0(4))* Black Rabbit Bks.
—Big Cats, Little Cats. 2011. (Learn-Abouts Ser.). (Illus.). 16p. (J). pap. 7.95 *(978-1-59920-595-3(5))* Black Rabbit Bks.
—Bugs & Beetles. 2011. (Learn-Abouts Ser.). (Illus.). 16p. (J). pap. 7.95 *(978-1-59920-611-0(0))* Black Rabbit Bks.
—Clocks. 2011. (Learn-Abouts Ser.). (Illus.). 16p. (J). pap. 7.95 *(978-1-59920-639-4(0))* Black Rabbit Bks.
—Earth's Land & Water. 2011. (Learn-Abouts Ser.). (Illus.). 16p. (J). pap. 7.95 *(978-1-59920-593-9(9))* Black Rabbit Bks.
—Follow the Road Map. 2011. (Learn-Abouts Ser.). (Illus.). 16p. (J). pap. 7.95 *(978-1-59920-638-7(2))* Black Rabbit Bks.
—From Plan to House. 2011. (Illus.). 16p. (J). pap. 7.95 *(978-1-59920-623-3(4))* Black Rabbit Bks.
—Games Around the World. 2011. (Learn-Abouts Ser.). (Illus.). 16p. (J). pap. 7.95 *(978-1-59920-621-9(8))* Black Rabbit Bks.
—Gas & Air. 2011. (Learn-Abouts Ser.). (Illus.). 16p. (J). pap. 7.95 *(978-1-59920-644-8(7))* Black Rabbit Bks.
—Having Fun with Matter. 2011. (Learn-Abouts Ser.). (Illus.). 16p. (J). pap. 7.95 *(978-1-59920-628-8(5))* Black Rabbit Bks.
—The Life Cycle of a Frog. 2011. (Learn-Abouts Ser.). (Illus.). 16p. (J). pap. 7.95 *(978-1-59920-627-1(7))* Black Rabbit Bks.
—The Life of a River. 2011. (Learn-Abouts Ser.). (Illus.). 16p. (J). pap. 9.95 *(978-1-59920-609-7(9))* Palgrave Macmillan.
—Make a Color. 2011. (Learn-Abouts Ser.). (Illus.). 16p. (J). pap. 7.95 *(978-1-59920-596-0(3))* Black Rabbit Bks.
—Make a String Phone. 2011. (Learn-Abouts Ser.). (Illus.). 16p. (J). pap. 7.95 *(978-1-59920-607-3(2))* Black Rabbit Bks.
—Make a Treasure Map. 2011. (Illus.). 16p. (J). pap. 7.95 *(978-1-59920-606-6(4))* Black Rabbit Bks.
—Map the School. 2011. (ENG., Illus.). 16p. (J). pap. 7.95 *(978-1-59920-590-8(4))* Black Rabbit Bks.
—Measure the Weather. 2011. (Learn-Abouts Ser.). (Illus.). 16p. (J). pap. 7.95 *(978-1-59920-641-7(2))* Black Rabbit Bks.
—The Moon. 2011. (Learn-Abouts Ser.). (Illus.). 16p. (J). pap. 7.95 *(978-1-59920-625-7(0))* Black Rabbit Bks.
—Musical Instruments. 2011. (Learn-Abouts Ser.). (Illus.). 16p. (J). pap. 7.95 *(978-1-59920-642-4(0))* Black Rabbit Bks.
—My School, Your School. 2011. (Learn-Abouts Ser.). (ENG., Illus.). 16p. (J). pap. 7.95 *(978-1-59920-605-9(6))* Black Rabbit Bks.
—Old Buildings, New Buildings. 2011. (Learn-Abouts Ser.). (Illus.). 16p. (J). pap. 7.95 *(978-1-59920-591-5(2))* Black Rabbit Bks.
—People Who Help at Car Accidents. 2011. (Learn-Abouts Ser.). (Illus.). 16p. (J). pap. 7.95 *(978-1-59920-608-0(0))* Black Rabbit Bks.
—People Who Work for the City. 2011. (Learn-Abouts Ser.). (Illus.). 16p. (J). pap. 7.95 *(978-1-59920-640-0(4))* Black Rabbit Bks.
—Pumpkin Time. 2011. (Learn-Abouts Ser.). (Illus.). 16p. (J). pap. 7.95 *(978-1-59920-589-2(0))* Black Rabbit Bks.
—Riding a Bike. 2011. (Learn-Abouts Ser.). (Illus.). 16p. (J). pap. 7.95 *(978-1-59920-626-4(9))* Black Rabbit Bks.
—What Do Firefighters Do? 2011. (Learn-Abouts Ser.). (Illus.). 16p. (J). pap. 7.95 *(978-1-59920-592-2(0))* Black Rabbit Bks.
—What Is a Mammal? 2011. (Learn-Abouts Ser.). (Illus.). 16p. (J). pap. 7.95 *(978-1-59920-643-1(9))* Black Rabbit Bks.
—What Is A Natural Resource? 2014. (Little Books of Answers: Level B Ser.). (Illus.). 16p. (gr. k-2). pap. 7.95 *(978-1-927136-15-7(6))* Three Crows Media NZL. Dist: RiverStream Publishing.
—When Can A Flood Happen? 2014. (Little Books of Answers: Level d Ser.). (Illus.). 16p. (gr. k-2). pap. 7.95 *(978-1-927136-35-5(0))* Three Crows Media NZL. Dist: RiverStream Publishing.
—When Can I Help in the Classroom? 2014. (Little Books of Answers: Level C Ser.). (Illus.). 16p. (gr. k-2). pap. 7.95 *(978-1-927136-23-2(7))* Three Crows Media NZL. Dist: RiverStream Publishing.
—Where Does the Garbage Go? 2011. (Learn-Abouts Ser.). (Illus.). 16p. (J). pap. 7.95 *(978-1-59920-612-7(9))* Black Rabbit Bks.
—Why Is it Expensive? 2014. (Little Books of Answers: Level a Ser.). (Illus.). 16p. (gr. k-2). pap. 7.95 *(978-1-927136-02-7(4))* Three Crows Media NZL. Dist: RiverStream Publishing.
Midnight Rescue, 6 vols., Pack. (Action Packs Ser.). 120p. (gr. 3-5). 44.00 *(978-0-7635-8391-0(X))* Rigby Education.
A Midsummer Night's Dream. 2014. (Collins Big Cat Ser.). (ENG., Illus.). 192p. (J). (gr. 5-6). pap. 9.99 *(978-0-00-753012-0(9))* HarperCollins Pubs. Ltd. GBR. Dist: Independent Pubs. Group.
Miles, Lisa. Starting to Read. 2004. (Usborne Farmyard Tales Ser.). (ENG., Illus.). 1p. (J). (gr. -1-3). pap. 6.95 *(978-0-7460-3408-8(3))* EDC Publishing.
Milet Publishing Staff. Milet Interactive for Kids - Chinese for English Speakers. 2012. (Milet Interactive for Kids Ser.). (ENG., Illus.). 1p. (J). (gr. k-2). cd-rom 24.95 *(978-1-84059-676-2(7))* Milet Publishing.
Milford, Alison. A Finders' Guide to Rocks, Fossils & Soils. 2017. (ENG., Illus.). 32p. (J). pap. 8.99 ***(978-0-00-820877-6(8))*** HarperCollins Pubs. Ltd. GBR. Dist: Independent Pubs. Group.
Milford, Alison. The Water Cycle. 2016. (ENG., Illus.). 48p. (J). (gr. 3-4). pap. 9.95 *(978-0-00-816388-4(X))* HarperCollins Pubs. Ltd. GBR. Dist: Independent Pubs. Group.
The Mill on the Hill, 6 vols., Pack,Set B. (Supersonic Phonics Ser.). (gr. k-3). 29.00 *(978-0-7635-0536-3(6))* Rigby Education.
Miller, Heather. The 10 Most Outstanding American Symbols. 2008. 14.99 *(978-1-55448-508-6(8))* Scholastic Library Publishing.
—The 10 Most Provocative 20th Century Artworks. 2007. (J). 14.99 *(978-1-55448-483-6(9))* Scholastic Library Publishing.
Miller, Kathryn L. Abc's with Sadie: Sadie Goes to the Zoo. 2011. 32p. pap. 17.25 *(978-1-4269-5940-0(0))* Trafford Publishing.
Miller, Marie. Party Time. 2006. (Neighborhood Readers Ser.). (ENG.). 8p. (gr. -1-3). pap. 5.15 *(978-1-4042-6706-0(9),* Rosen Classroom) Rosen Publishing Group, Inc., The.
Miller, Michael. Hilde und Günter Level Two Reader, 2 books. 2003. (GER., Illus.). 53p. 6.00 *(978-0-9743522-0-6(9),* 0-9743522-0-9) Miller, Michael.
Miller, Mona. Poppy & Branch's Big Adventure. 2017. (Step into Reading Level 3 Ser.). lib. bdg. 14.75 ***(978-0-606-39851-0(1))*** Turtleback Bks.
Millett, Peter. The Great Escape White Band. Belli, Alfredo, illus. 2016. (Cambridge Reading Adventures Ser.). (ENG.). 24p. pap. 7.19 *(978-1-107-55158-9(7))* Cambridge Univ. Pr.
—Lost at Sea. Bacchin, Giorgio, illus. 2016. (Cambridge Reading Adventures Ser.). (ENG.). 26p. pap. 7.19 *(978-1-316-50344-7(5))* Cambridge Univ. Pr.
—Power Cut Turquoise Band. Daff, Russ, illus. 2016. (Cambridge Reading Adventures Ser.). (ENG.). 24p. pap. 7.19 *(978-1-316-60586-8(8))* Cambridge Univ. Pr.
—Sandstorm Purple Band. Bacchin, Giorgio, illus. 2016. (Cambridge Reading Adventures Ser.). (ENG.). 24p. pap. 7.19 *(978-1-107-57607-0(5))* Cambridge Univ. Pr.
—Take Zayan with You! Green Band. Daff, Russ, illus. 2016. (Cambridge Reading Adventures Ser.). (ENG.). 16p. pap. 6.56 *(978-1-107-57587-5(7))* Cambridge Univ. Pr.
Millett, Peter & Chambers, Mal. Goal! 2008. (Rigby Focus Forward: Level O Ser.). (Illus.). 24p. (J). (gr. 4-7). pap. *(978-1-4190-3845-7(1),* Rigby) Pearson Education Australia.
Millett, Peter & Scales, Simon. The Game. 2008. (Rigby Focus Forward: Level H Ser.). (Illus.). 24p. (J). (gr. 4-7). pap. *(978-1-4190-3723-8(4),* Rigby) Pearson Education Australia.
Millett, Peter & Texidor, Dee. On the Team. 2008. (Rigby Focus Forward: Level F Ser.). (Illus.). 24p. (J). (gr. 4-7). pap. *(978-1-4190-3698-9(X),* Rigby) Pearson Education Australia.
Millett, Peter & Wallace-Mitchell, Jane. Lions! 2008. (Rigby Focus Forward: Level G Ser.). (Illus.). 24p. (J). (gr. 4-7). pap. *(978-1-4190-3717-7(X),* Rigby) Pearson Education Australia.
Milligan, Jean F. Inferences for Young Audiences. Kennedy, Allan, illus. 2004. 96p. (J). (gr. 3-7). 14.95 *(978-0-9637825-2-6(5))* Autumn Hse. Publishing.
Mills, Nathan. Living or Nonliving? 2012. (Rosen Readers Ser.). (ENG., Illus.). 16p. (J). (gr. k-1). pap. 7.00 *(978-1-4488-8746-0(1),* Rosen Classroom) Rosen Publishing Group, Inc., The.
Mills, Nathan & Allyn, Daisy. Around My Neighborhood. 2012. (Rosen Readers Ser.). (ENG., Illus.). 16p. (J). (gr. k-1). pap. 7.00 *(978-1-4488-8646-3(5),* Rosen Classroom) Rosen Publishing Group, Inc., The.

Mills, Nathan & Baker, Rick. More or Less? 2012. (Rosen Readers Ser.). (ENG., Illus.). 16p. (J). (gr. k-1). pap. 7.00 *(978-1-4488-8649-4(X)*, Rosen Classroom) Rosen Publishing Group, Inc., The.

Mills, Nathan & Biehn, Mike. Things I Need, Things I Want. 2012. (Rosen Readers Ser.). (ENG., Illus.). 16p. (J). (gr. k-1). pap. 7.00 *(978-1-4488-8728-6(3)*, Rosen Classroom) Rosen Publishing Group, Inc., The.

Mills, Nathan & Christopher, Nick. Time for a Field Trip. 2012. (Rosen Readers Ser.). (ENG., Illus.). 16p. (J). (gr. k-1). pap. 7.00 *(978-1-4488-8752-1(6)*, Rosen Classroom) Rosen Publishing Group, Inc., The.

Mills, Nathan & Davidson, Amy. My Busy Week. 2012. (Rosen Readers Ser.). (ENG., Illus.). 16p. (J). (gr. k-1). pap. 7.00 *(978-1-4488-8689-0(9)*, Rosen Classroom) Rosen Publishing Group, Inc., The.

Mills, Nathan & Ericson, Emma. Up or Down? 2012. (Rosen Readers Ser.). (ENG., Illus.). 16p. (J). (gr. k-1). pap. 7.00 *(978-1-4488-8643-2(0)*, Rosen Classroom) Rosen Publishing Group, Inc., The.

Mills, Nathan & Faraday, Daniel. Walk, Run, Skip, & Jump! 2012. (Rosen Readers Ser.). (ENG., Illus.). 16p. (J). (gr. k-1). pap. 7.00 *(978-1-4488-8680-7(5)*, Rosen Classroom) Rosen Publishing Group, Inc., The.

Mills, Nathan & Frampton, Callie. Tools Tell the Weather. 2012. (Rosen Readers Ser.). (ENG., Illus.). 24p. (J). (gr. 1-2). pap. 8.25 *(978-1-4488-8800-9(X)*, Rosen Classroom) Rosen Publishing Group, Inc., The.

Mills, Nathan & Francis, Bill. Hannah's Four Seasons. 2012. (Rosen Readers Ser.). (ENG., Illus.). 16p. (J). (gr. k-1). pap. 7.00 *(978-1-4488-8740-8(2)*, Rosen Classroom) Rosen Publishing Group, Inc., The.

Mills, Nathan & Fudoli, Melissa. I Have One More. 2012. (Rosen Readers Ser.). (ENG., Illus.). 16p. (J). (gr. k-1). pap. 7.00 *(978-1-4488-8655-5(4)*, Rosen Classroom) Rosen Publishing Group, Inc., The.

Mills, Nathan & Goodwin, Josh. How Do I Get There? 2012. (Rosen Readers Ser.). (ENG., Illus.). 24p. (J). (gr. 1-2). pap. 8.25 *(978-1-4488-8779-8(8)*, Rosen Classroom) Rosen Publishing Group, Inc., The.

Mills, Nathan & Holtz, Mary Elizabeth. Sabrina's School. 2012. (Rosen Readers Ser.). (ENG., Illus.). 16p. (J). (gr. k-1). pap. 7.00 *(978-1-4488-8719-4(4)*, Rosen Classroom) Rosen Publishing Group, Inc., The.

Mills, Nathan & Hume, Desmond. Earth's Water. 2012. (Rosen Readers Ser.). (ENG., Illus.). 24p. (J). (gr. 1-2). pap. 8.25 *(978-1-4488-8818-4(2)*, Rosen Classroom) Rosen Publishing Group, Inc., The.

Mills, Nathan & Jamison, Linc. Getting Around Our City. 2012. (Rosen Readers Ser.). (ENG., Illus.). 16p. (J). (gr. k-1). pap. 7.00 *(978-1-4488-8722-4(4)*, Rosen Classroom) Rosen Publishing Group, Inc., The.

Mills, Nathan & Kurkowiak, Anne. Tyler's New Friend. 2012. (Rosen Readers Ser.). (ENG., Illus.). 16p. (J). (gr. k-1). pap. 7.00 *(978-1-4488-8731-6(3)*, Rosen Classroom) Rosen Publishing Group, Inc., The.

Mills, Nathan & Ludlow, Susan. From Ice to Steam. 2012. (Rosen Readers Ser.). (ENG., Illus.). 24p. (J). (gr. 1-2). pap. 8.25 *(978-1-4488-8812-2(3)*, Rosen Classroom) Rosen Publishing Group, Inc., The.

Mills, Nathan & Machajewski, Sarah. Symbols of the United States. 2012. (Rosen Readers Ser.). (ENG., Illus.). 24p. (J). (gr. 1-2). pap. 8.25 *(978-1-4488-8761-3(5)*, Rosen Classroom) Rosen Publishing Group, Inc., The.

Mills, Nathan & McCann, Margaret. How We Use Water. 2012. (Rosen Readers Ser.). (ENG., Illus.). 24p. (J). (gr. 1-2). pap. 8.25 *(978-1-4488-8794-1(1)*, Rosen Classroom) Rosen Publishing Group, Inc., The.

Mills, Nathan & Miller, Andy. Is It Cloth, Clay, or Paper? 2012. (Rosen Readers Ser.). (ENG., Illus.). 16p. (J). (gr. k-1). pap. 7.00 *(978-1-4488-8707-1(0)*, Rosen Classroom) Rosen Publishing Group, Inc., The.

Mills, Nathan & Ridolfi, Isabella. Sue Goes to the Store. 2012. (Rosen Readers Ser.). (ENG., Illus.). 16p. (J). (gr. k-1). pap. 7.00 *(978-1-4488-8737-8(2)*, Rosen Classroom) Rosen Publishing Group, Inc., The.

Mills, Nathan & Rose, Craig. Carlos Reads a Map. 2012. (Rosen Readers Ser.). (ENG., Illus.). 16p. (J). (gr. k-1). pap. 7.00 *(978-1-4488-8716-3(X)*, Rosen Classroom) Rosen Publishing Group, Inc., The.

—We Help at School. 2012. (Rosen Readers Ser.). (ENG., Illus.). 16p. (J). (gr. k-1). pap. 7.00 *(978-1-4488-8661-6(9)*, Rosen Classroom) Rosen Publishing Group, Inc., The.

Mills, Nathan & Sotherden, Nora. Our Classroom Rules. 2012. (Rosen Readers Ser.). (ENG., Illus.). 16p. (J). (gr. k-1). pap. 7.00 *(978-1-4488-8692-0(9)*, Rosen Classroom) Rosen Publishing Group, Inc., The.

Mills, Nathan & Stern, Robin. Sara's Seeds. 2012. (Rosen Readers Ser.). (ENG., Illus.). 16p. (J). (gr. k-1). pap. 7.00 *(978-1-4488-8713-2(5)*, Rosen Classroom) Rosen Publishing Group, Inc., The.

Mills, Nathan & Swan, Henry. How Animals Live & Grow. 2012. (Rosen Readers Ser.). (ENG., Illus.). 24p. (J). (gr. 1-2). pap. 8.25 *(978-1-4488-8764-4(X)*, Rosen Classroom) Rosen Publishing Group, Inc., The.

Mills, Nathan & Wesolowski, Harriet. The Songs We Sing: Honoring Our Country. 2012. (Rosen Readers Ser.). (ENG., Illus.). 24p. (J). (gr. 1-2). pap. 8.25 *(978-1-4488-8821-4(2)*, Rosen Classroom) Rosen Publishing Group, Inc., The.

Mills, Nathan & White, Ella. Months of the Year. 2012. (Rosen Readers Ser.). (ENG., Illus.). 24p. (J). (gr. 1-2). pap. 8.25 *(978-1-4488-8785-9(2)*, Rosen Classroom) Rosen Publishing Group, Inc., The.

Mills, Nathan & Wilson, Emily. Good Night, Bears: Learning about Hibernation. 2012. (Rosen Readers Ser.). (ENG., Illus.). 24p. (J). (gr. 1-2). pap. 8.25 *(978-1-4488-8776-7(3)*, Rosen Classroom) Rosen Publishing Group, Inc., The.

Mills, Nathan & Worthy, Shanya. Ana's Community Helpers. 2012. (Rosen Readers Ser.). (ENG., Illus.). 16p. (J). (gr. k-1). pap. 7.00 *(978-1-4488-8698-2(8)*, Rosen Classroom) Rosen Publishing Group, Inc., The.

Mini Plays & Folktale Plays that Build Reading Skills. 2005. (J). pap. *(978-1-60015-036-4(5))* Steps To Literacy, LLC.

Minnie & Minnie. The Science Playground: Fun with Science Concepts & Nature. 2009. 48p. pap. 24.99 *(978-1-4389-3466-2(1))* AuthorHouse.

Mis Amigos los Monstruos, 6 vols., Pack. (Literatura 2000 Ser.). (SPA.). (gr. 1-2). 28.00 *(978-0-7635-1047-3(5))* Rigby Education.

The Missing Suit. (Early Intervention Levels Ser.). 28.38 *(978-0-7362-0405-7(9))* CENGAGE Learning.

The Missing Suit (14), Vol. 14. (Early Intervention Levels Ser.). 4.73 *(978-0-7362-0230-5(7))* CENGAGE Learning.

Mitchell-Hughes, Kimberley. The 10 Most Extreme Sports. 2008. 14.99 *(978-1-55448-555-0(X))* Scholastic Library Publishing.

Mitchell, Julie & Chambers, Mal. Bertha. 2008. (Rigby Focus Forward: Level G Ser.). (Illus.). 24p. (J). (gr. 4-7). pap. *(978-1-4190-3703-0(X)*, Rigby) Pearson Education Australia.

—Vega Bay. 2008. (Rigby Focus Forward: Level K Ser.). (Illus.). 24p. pap. *(978-1-4190-3801-3(X)*, Rigby) Pearson Education Australia.

Mitchell, Julie & Konye, Paul. The Bully. 2008. (Rigby Focus Forward: Level K Ser.). (Illus.). 24p. (J). (gr. 4-7). pap. *(978-1-4190-3784-9(6)*, Rigby) Pearson Education Australia.

Mitchell, Julie & McKenzie, Heather. Metal Mouth. 2008. (Rigby Focus Forward: Level H Ser.). (Illus.). 24p. (J). (gr. 4-7). pap. *(978-1-4190-3738-2(2)*, Rigby) Pearson Education Australia.

Mitchell, Lucy Sprague. Here & Now Story Book. Van Loon, Hendrik Willem & Price, Christine, illus. 2015. (ENG.). 256p. (J). (gr. k-3). pap. 7.99 *(978-0-486-79196-8(3))* Dover Pubns., Inc.

Mitchell, Marie & Smith, Mason. Squatch Watch & Other Stories. 2013. 130p. pap. 9.95 *(978-0-692-02010-4(1))* Smith, Mason.

Mitchell, Pratima. Raju's Ride. Waterhouse, Stephen, illus. 2005. (ENG.). 24p. (J). lib. bdg. 23.65 *(978-1-59646-726-2(6))* Dingles & Co.

Modern Staff. Day at Our Dairy Farm. (J). (gr. k-1). 38.95 *(978-0-8136-1358-1(2))* Modern Curriculum Pr.

—Feather for Her Hair Big Book. (J). 22.95 *(978-0-8136-4821-7(1))* Modern Curriculum Pr.

—Positively Me!, 8 bks. (J). (gr. k-2). pap. *(978-0-8136-4801-9(7))* Modern Curriculum Pr.

—Positively Me! Big Book Collection, 8 bks., No. 1. (J). (gr. k-2). *(978-0-8136-4857-6(2))* Modern Curriculum Pr.

Molloy, Bonnie. Ms Flitter-Flutter. 2009. 24p. pap. 9.00 *(978-1-4269-1587-1(X))* Trafford Publishing.

Molly the Perfect Houseguest. Date not set. (Young Global Reader Ser.: Vol. 1). (J). *(978-1-887176-07-1(1))* Global Age Publishing/Global Academy Pr.

Molter, Carey. -Ain As in Train, 1 vol. 2003. (Word Families Set 8 Ser.). (ENG., Illus.). 24p. (J). (gr. k-3). lib. bdg. 24.21 *(978-1-59197-272-3(8))* ABDO Publishing Co.

—Ake As in Cake, 1 vol. 2003. (Word Families Set 8 Ser.). (ENG., Illus.). 24p. (J). (gr. k-3). lib. bdg. 24.21 *(978-1-59197-270-9(1))* ABDO Publishing Co.

—Eam As in Ice Cream, 1 vol. 2003. (Word Families Set 8 Ser.). (ENG., Illus.). 24p. (J). (gr. k-3). lib. bdg. 24.21 *(978-1-59197-273-0(6)*, SandCastle) ABDO Publishing Co.

—En As in Pen, 1 vol. 2003. (Word Families Set 2 Ser.). (ENG., Illus.). 24p. (J). (gr. k-3). lib. bdg. 24.21 *(978-1-59197-229-7(9)*, SandCastle) ABDO Publishing Co.

—Ide As in Tide, 1 vol. 2003. (Word Families Set 8 Ser.). (ENG., Illus.). 24p. (J). (gr. k-3). lib. bdg. 24.21 *(978-1-59197-275-4(2)*, SandCastle) ABDO Publishing Co.

—One As in Stone, 1 vol. 2003. (Word Families Set 8 Ser.). (ENG., Illus.). 24p. (J). (gr. k-3). lib. bdg. 24.21 *(978-1-59197-274-7(4)*, SandCastle) ABDO Publishing Co.

—Oon As in Spoon, 1 vol. 2003. (Word Families Set 7 Ser.). (ENG., Illus.). 24p. (J). (gr. k-3). lib. bdg. 24.21 *(978-1-59197-266-2(3)*, SandCastle) ABDO Publishing Co.

Mom & Dad Set 1. 2003. (J). *(978-1-58453-250-7(5))* Pioneer Valley Bks.

Monckeberg, Paulina. Pascualina 2006 Portuguese. 2005. (Pascualina Family of Products Ser.). (ENG.). 272p. (J). spiral bd. 16.99 *(978-956-8222-29-1(4))* Pascualina Producciones S.A.

Monster Mop. (J). *(978-0-8136-5219-1(7))* Modern Curriculum Pr.

The Monster Next Door, Level 2. 2016. (Ladybird Readers Ser.). (ENG.). 48p. (J). (gr. 2-4). pap. 9.99 *(978-0-241-25444-8(2))* Penguin Bks., Ltd. GBR. Dist: Independent Pubs. Group.

Montgomery, Anne. Nature Made, 1 vol. rev. ed. 2014. (Science Readers: Content & Literacy Ser.). (ENG., Illus.). 24p. (gr. k-k). pap. 8.99 *(978-1-4807-4528-5(6))* Teacher Created Materials, Inc.

—Tell Me about It, 1 vol. rev. ed. 2014. (Science Readers: Content & Literacy Ser.). (ENG., Illus.). 24p. (gr. k-k). pap. 8.99 *(978-1-4807-4526-1(X))* Teacher Created Materials, Inc.

Montgomery, L. PENGUIN ACTIVE READING 2: ANNE OF GREEN GABLES BOOK AND CD-ROM PACK. 2007. (ENG.). 64p. pap. 17.32 *(978-1-4058-5205-0(4))* Pearson Education.

Montgomery, Mary Sue. A Cloud Is a Cloud Is a What? You've got to be Kidding, 1 vol. 2010. 34p. 24.95 *(978-1-4489-4360-9(4))* PublishAmerica, Inc.

Moon, Cliff, ed. Balancing Acts. 2014. (Collins Big Cat Ser.). (ENG., Illus.). 576p. (J). (gr. 5-5). pap. 9.99 *(978-0-00-753010-6(2))* HarperCollins Pubs. Ltd. GBR. Dist: Independent Pubs. Group.

Moon, Nicola. Margarine & Marbles. 2005. (Red Go Bananas Ser.). (ENG., Illus.). 48p. (J). (gr. 2-3). *(978-0-7787-2698-2(3))* Crabtree Publishing Co.

Moor, Evan. Daily Reading Comprenesion, Grade 8. 2013. pap. *(978-1-60823-639-8(0))* Evan-Moor Educational Pubs.

Moore, Elizabeth & Gregory, Helen. Where Do People Work? 2011. (Wonder Readers Emergent Level Ser.). (ENG.). 16p. (gr. -1-1). pap. 35.94 *(978-1-4296-8206-0(X)*, Wonder Readers) Capstone Press of Coughlan Cos.

Moore, Inga. Raising Readers House in the Woods. 2014. (ENG.). 56p. (J). 3.40 *(978-0-7636-7913-2(5))* Candlewick Pr.

Moore, Kevin. The Road Maker. 2008. 52p. pap. 31.99 *(978-1-4363-7007-3(8))* Xlibris Corp.

Moore, Monica A. Everyday Heroes. 2006. (ENG.). 52p. per. 12.95 *(978-1-59800-563-9(4))* Outskirts Pr., Inc.

Moore, Philip. When Did American Astronauts Explore Space? 2014. (Little Books of Answers: Level C Ser.). (Illus.). 16p. (gr. k-2). pap. 7.95 *(978-1-927136-26-3(1))* Three Crows Media NZL. Dist: RiverStream Publishing.

—When Is This A Home? 2014. (Little Books of Answers: Level a Ser.). (Illus.). 16p. (gr. k-2). pap. 7.95 *(978-1-927136-07-2(5))* Three Crows Media NZL. Dist: RiverStream Publishing.

Moore, Phillip. Where Does Used Paper Go? 2014. (Little Books of Answers: Level F Ser.). (Illus.). 16p. (gr. k-2). pap. 7.95 *(978-1-927136-54-6(7))* Three Crows Media NZL. Dist: RiverStream Publishing.

Moore, Sharon. The Runaway Kite. 2006. (Neighborhood Readers Ser.). (ENG.). 8p. (gr. -1-3). pap. 5.15 *(978-1-4042-6714-5(X)*, Rosen Classroom) Rosen Publishing Group, Inc., The.

—The Starry Sky. 2006. (Neighborhood Readers Ser.). (ENG.). 16p. (gr. 1-3). pap. 6.50 *(978-1-4042-7152-4(X)*, Rosen Classroom) Rosen Publishing Group, Inc., The.

Mora, Pat. Doña Flor: A Tall Tale about a Giant Woman with a Great Big Heart. Colón, Raúl, illus. 2010. (ENG & SPA.). 32p. (J). (gr. -1-2). pap. 7.99 *(978-0-375-86144-4(0)*, Dragonfly Bks.) Random Hse. Children's Bks.

—Here, Kitty, Kitty! (Ven, Gatita, Ven!) Suarez, Maribel, illus. 2008. (My Family: Mi Familia Ser.). (SPA & ENG.). 24p. (J). (gr. 4-7). lib. bdg. 15.89 *(978-0-06-085045-6(0)*, Rayo) HarperCollins Pubs.

—Here Kitty Kitty!/Ven Gatita Ven! Suarez, Maribel, illus. 2008. (My Family: Mi Familia Ser.). (SPA & ENG.). 24p. (J). (gr. -1-1). 14.99 *(978-0-06-085044-9(2)*, Rayo) HarperCollins Pubs.

More Than a Meal. (Early Intervention Levels Ser.). 28.56 *(978-0-7362-1049-2(0))* CENGAGE Learning.

Morgan, Bernard P. Pszczelarz. Juraszek, Barbara, tr. Parekh, Rikin, illus. 2008. 28p. pap. *(978-1-904312-44-4(6))* MX Publishing, Ltd.

Morgan, Hawys. The Journey of Odysseus: Band 15/Emerald. 2017. (Collins Big Cat Tales Ser.). (ENG., Illus.). 48p. (J). (gr. 3-4). pap. 8.99 ***(978-0-00-817941-0(7))*** HarperCollins Pubs. Ltd. GBR. Dist: Independent Pubs. Group.

Morgan, Michaela. Band of Friends. Price, Nick, illus. 2005. (ENG.). 24p. (J). lib. bdg. 23.65 *(978-1-59646-734-7(7))* Dingles & Co.

—Mouse with No Name. Mikhail, Jess, illus. 2004. (ENG.). 24p. (J). lib. bdg. 23.65 *(978-1-59646-682-1(0))* Dingles & Co.

—Shy Shark. Gomez, Elena, illus. 2005. (ENG.). 24p. (J). lib. bdg. 23.65 *(978-1-59646-722-4(3))* Dingles & Co.

—Tiger's Tales. Boon, Debbie, illus. 2005. (Collins Big Cat Ser.). (ENG.). 32p. (J). (gr. 1-3). pap. 7.99 *(978-0-00-718631-0(2))* HarperCollins Pubs. Ltd. GBR. Dist: Independent Pubs. Group.

Morgan, Michaela & Phillips, Mike. Tig in the Dumps: Lime. 2005. (Collins Big Cat Ser.). (ENG., Illus.). 32p. (J). (gr. 1-3). pap. 7.99 *(978-0-00-718636-5(3))* HarperCollins Pubs. Ltd. GBR. Dist: Independent Pubs. Group.

Morgan, Ruth. Big Liam, Little Liam. Archbold, Tim, illus. 2005. (ENG.). 24p. (J). lib. bdg. 23.65 *(978-1-59646-728-6(2))* Dingles & Co.

—Jess & the Bean Root. Vagnozzi, Barbara, illus. 2005. (ENG.). 24p. (J). lib. bdg. 23.65 *(978-1-59646-732-3(0))* Dingles & Co.

Morgan, Sally. Food Chains. 2016. (ENG.). 48p. (J). pap. 9.95 *(978-0-00-816389-1(8))* HarperCollins Pubs. Ltd. GBR. Dist: Independent Pubs. Group.

—How Do We Move?, 8 bks. 2005. (QEB Readers). (Illus.). 24p. (J). (gr. -1-3). lib. bdg. 15.95 *(978-1-59566-077-0(1))* QEB Publishing Inc.

Morgan, Sally. The Incredible Life of David Attenborough, Bd. 16. 2017. (ENG.). 56p. (J). pap. 8.99 ***(978-0-00-820889-9(1))*** HarperCollins Pubs. Ltd. GBR. Dist: Independent Pubs. Group.

The Morning: Individual Title, 2 packs. (Chiquilibros Ser.). (gr. -1-1). 12.00 *(978-0-7635-8531-0(9))* Rigby Education.

Morpurgo, Michael. It's a Dog's Life. George, Hannah, illus. 2016. (Reading Ladder Ser.). (ENG.). 48p. (J). (gr. k-2). pap. 7.99 *(978-1-4052-8256-7(8))* Egmont Bks., Ltd. GBR. Dist: Independent Pubs. Group.

Morpurgo, Michael & Richards, Lucy. Mairi's Mermaid. Richards, Lucy, illus. 2nd ed. 2016. (Reading Ladder Ser.). (ENG., Illus.). 48p. (J). (gr. k-2). pap. 7.99 *(978-1-4052-8201-7(0))* Egmont Bks., Ltd. GBR. Dist: Independent Pubs. Group.

Morton, Carlene. Alpha Betti. Lucas, Margeaux, illus. 2007. (ENG.). (J). (gr. -1-3). 17.95 *(978-1-932146-69-1(5)*, Upstart Bks.) Highsmith Inc.

Morton, Ken, illus. Cinderella. 2012. (ENG.). 24p. (J). (gr. -1-12). 5.99 *(978-1-84322-803-5(3))* Anness Publishing GBR. Dist: National Bk. Network.

—The Three Billy Goats Gruff: My First Reading Book. 2013. (ENG.). 24p. 5.99 *(978-1-84322-832-5(7)*, Armadillo) Anness Publishing GBR. Dist: National Bk. Network.

Moses, Antoinette. The Girl at the Window. 2007. (Cambridge English Readers Ser.). (ENG., Illus.). 32p. pap. 8.50 *(978-0-521-70585-1(1))* Cambridge Univ. Pr.

—Vinnie's Vacation Level 1 Beginner/Elementary American English Edition. 2012. (ENG.). 48p. pap. 9.50 *(978-1-107-62130-5(5))* Cambridge Univ. Pr.

Moses, Brian. Cookie Crumbs, 4 vols. 2005. (QEB Readers). (Illus.). 24p. (J). (gr. -1-3). lib. bdg. 15.95 *(978-1-59566-099-2(2))* QEB Publishing Inc.

Moskal, Greg. Give the Band a Hand. 2006. (Neighborhood Readers Ser.). (ENG.). 12p. (gr. 1-3). pap. 5.90 *(978-1-4042-6859-3(6)*, Rosen Classroom) Rosen Publishing Group, Inc., The.

—Meet Officer Jerry. 2008. (Real Readers Series: Level Blue Ser.). (ENG., Illus.). 12p. (gr. 1-2). pap. 5.90 *(978-0-8239-8118-2(5))* Rosen Publishing Group, Inc., The.

Mother Goose Asks Why? A Family Guide Introducing Science Through Great Children's Literature. 2005. (J). spiral bd. *(978-0-9753985-6-2(3))* Mother Goose Programs.

A Mouse in the House. 2004. (Jasper the Cat Set 1 Ser.). (ENG., Illus.). (J). pap. 7.33 *(978-1-58453-281-1(5))* Pioneer Valley Bks.

Mowat, Diane. Pair of Ghostly Hands & Other Stories. 3rd ed. 2008. (ENG., Illus.). 80p. 9.38 *(978-0-19-479125-0(4))* Oxford Univ. Pr., Inc.

Mr. Putter Book Set 800926, 6 vols. 2005. (J). pap. *(978-1-59794-091-7(7))* Environments, Inc.

Mr Verdi's New Path: Individual Title Six-Packs. (gr. k-1). 23.00 *(978-0-7635-8859-5(8))* Rigby Education.

Mr. Worm. 2008. (ENG & SPA., Illus.). 64p. (J). 14.95 *(978-0-9787462-6-1(0))* Heritage Publishing Co.

Mrs Sheep's Garden. (Early Intervention Levels Ser.). 31.86 *(978-0-7362-0619-8(1))* CENGAGE Learning.

Mud Pie: Individual Title Six-Packs. (Literatura 2000 Ser.). (gr. -1-1). 28.00 *(978-0-7635-0034-4(8))* Rigby Education.

Muench-Williams, Heather. I Want a Pet. Teeple, Jackie, illus. l.t. ed. 2006. 12p. (J). (gr. -1-k). pap. 10.95 *(978-1-57332-353-6(5)*, HighReach Learning, Incorporated) Carson-Dellosa Publishing, LLC.

Muhall, Jill K. & Alarcon, Jill. Causes of the Revolution, 1 vol. 2004. (Primary Source Readers Ser.). (ENG., Illus.). 24p. (J). (gr. 5-5). pap. 8.99 *(978-0-7439-8785-1(3))* Shell Educational Publishing.

Muir, Suzanne. Animal Homes. 2007. (Steck-Vaughn BOLDPRINT Anthologies Ser.). (ENG., Illus.). 48p. (gr. 4-6). pap. 16.90 *(978-1-4190-4018-4(9))* Houghton Mifflin Harcourt Publishing Co.

Mulhall, Jill K. Declaration of Independence, 1 vol. 2004. (Primary Source Readers Ser.). (SPA & ENG.). 24p. (J). (gr. 5-5). pap. 8.99 *(978-0-7439-8746-2(2))* Shell Educational Publishing.

—Expanding the Nation, 1 vol. 2005. (Primary Source Readers Ser.). (ENG.). 24p. (J). (gr. 5-5). pap. 8.99 *(978-0-7439-8905-3(8))* Shell Educational Publishing.

—James Madison, 1 vol. 2005. (Primary Source Readers Ser.). (ENG.). 24p. (J). (gr. 4-4). pap. 8.99 *(978-0-7439-8908-4(2))* Shell Educational Publishing.

—Thomas Jefferson, 1 vol. 2004. (Primary Source Readers Ser.). (ENG.). 24p. (J). (gr. 4-4). pap. 8.99 *(978-0-7439-8747-9(0))* Shell Educational Publishing.

—The War of 1812, 1 vol. 2005. (Primary Source Readers Ser.). (ENG.). 24p. (J). (gr. 5-5). pap. 8.99 *(978-0-7439-8907-7(4))* Shell Educational Publishing.

Mullican, Jody. What Can It Be? Gray, Stacy A., illus. l.t. ed. 2006. 12p. (J). (gr. -1-k). pap. 10.95 *(978-1-57332-352-9(7)*, HighReach Learning, Incorporated) Carson-Dellosa Publishing, LLC.

Mullican, Judy. Mary & Marsha Make Cookies. Storch, Ellen N., illus. l.t. ed. 2005. 18p. (J). (gr. -1-k). pap. 10.95 *(978-1-57332-346-8(2)*, HighReach Learning, Incorporated) Carson-Dellosa Publishing, LLC.

—Someone New in the Neighborhood. Storch, Ellen N. & Gillen, Lisa P., illus. l.t. ed. 2005. 20p. (J). (gr. -1-k). pap. 10.95 *(978-1-57332-356-7(X)*, HighReach Learning, Incorporated) Carson-Dellosa Publishing, LLC.

Multicultural Book Set 800717, 10. 2005. (J). *(978-1-59794-015-3(1))* Environments, Inc.

Multicultural Celebrations II, 6 bks. (J). (gr. 2-4). pap. 34.95 *(978-0-8136-2353-5(7))* Modern Curriculum Pr.

Multicultural Nonfiction Photo Books, 6 vols. (Content Collections). (gr. k-2). 180.30 *(978-0-7362-2268-6(5))* CENGAGE Learning.

Munsch, Robert. Mud Puddle. Petricic, Dusan, illus. 3rd ed. 2012. (Munsch for Kids Ser.). (ENG.). 32p. (J). (gr. -1-2). 19.95 *(978-1-55451-427-4(4)*, 9781554514274) Annick Pr., Ltd. CAN. Dist: Publishers Group West (PGW).

Muntean, Michael. Brain Quest Grade 3 Reading. 2nd rev. ed. 2007. (ENG., Illus.). 148p. (J). (gr. 3-3). 11.95 *(978-0-7611-4141-9(3)*, 14141) Workman Publishing Co., Inc.

Murphy, Eileen. 3 Big Steps. Montgomery, Violet, illus. 2008. 25p. pap. 24.95 *(978-1-60563-310-7(0))* America Star Bks.

Murray, Helen. Awesome Adventures. 2013. (DK Readers Ser.). (ENG.). 32p. (J). (gr. 1-3). 14.99 *(978-1-4654-1696-4(X)*, DK Children) Dorling Kindersley Publishing, Inc.

—Calling All Master Builders! 2013. (DK Readers Ser.). (ENG.). 32p. (J). (gr. 2-4). 14.99 *(978-1-4654-1698-8(6)*, DK Children) Dorling Kindersley Publishing, Inc.

—The Lego Movie. 2013. (DK Reader Level 2 Ser.). lib. bdg. 13.55 *(978-0-606-35321-2(6))* Turtleback Bks.

Murray, W. We Have Fun. 2nd ed. (Series S705: No. 2). (Illus.). 30p. (J). (gr. -1-5). pap., stu. ed. 1.95 *(978-0-7214-3063-8(5)*, Dutton Juvenile) Penguin Publishing Group.

—Workbook 1: For Use with Books 1a/1b/1c. 2nd ed. (Key Words Readers Ser.: A Series, No. 641-1a). (Illus.). 30p. (J). (gr. -1-5). pap., stu. ed. 1.95 *(978-0-7214-3062-1(7)*, S705, Dutton Juvenile) Penguin Publishing Group.

—Workbook 3: To Be Used with Books 3a, 3b, 3c. 2nd ed. (Key Words Readers Ser.: A Series, No. 641-3a). (Illus.). 30p. (J). (gr. -1-5). pap., stu. ed. 1.95 *(978-0-7214-3064-5(3)*, Dutton Juvenile) Penguin Publishing Group.

—Workbook 4: To Be Used with Books 4a, 4b, 4c. 2nd ed. (Key Words Readers Ser.: A Series, No. 641-4a). (Illus.). 30p. (J). (gr. -1-5). pap., stu. ed. 1.95 *(978-0-7214-3065-2(1)*, Dutton Juvenile) Penguin Publishing Group.

—Workbook 6: To Be Used with Books 6A, 6B, 6C) 2nd ed. (Key Words Readers Ser.: Series S705, No. 6). (Illus.). 30p. (J). (gr. -1-5). pap., stu. ed. 1.95 *(978-0-7214-3067-6(8)*, Dutton Juvenile) Penguin Publishing Group.

Murtagh, Ciaran. The Making of Mozart. 2017. (ENG., Illus.). 32p. (J). pap. 7.99 ***(978-0-00-820876-9(X))*** HarperCollins Pubs. Ltd. GBR. Dist: Independent Pubs. Group.

Murtagh, Ciaran. The Stubborn Prince. 2017. (Collins Big Cat Tales Ser.). (ENG., Illus.). 48p. (J). (gr. 3-4). pap. 8.99 *(978-0-00-817943-4(3))* HarperCollins Pubs. Ltd. GBR. Dist: Independent Pubs. Group.

Murtagh, Ciaran & Collins UK Staff. Roman Life in Britain. 2016. (ENG.). 32p. (J). (gr. 2-3). pap. 8.95 *(978-0-00-816377-8(4))* HarperCollins Pubs. Ltd. GBR. Dist: Independent Pubs. Group.

My Big Buddy. (J). 52.45 *(978-0-8136-8014-9(X))*; 26.20 *(978-0-8136-8447-5(1))*; 26.20 *(978-0-8136-8446-8(3))* Modern Curriculum Pr.

My Box: Individual Title-Six Packs. (Chiquilibros Ser.). (gr. k-1). 23.00 *(978-0-7635-0435-9(1))* Rigby Education.

My Brother. (Early Intervention Levels Ser.). 23.10 *(978-0-7362-0015-8(0))*; Vol. 4. 3.85 *(978-1-56334-965-2(5))* CENGAGE Learning.

My Child's First Reading Book. 2005. per. *(978-0-9742195-2-3(5))* Den Publishing Co.

My Classroom. 2004. (At School Ser.). (J). 7.33 *(978-1-58453-266-8(1))* Pioneer Valley Bks.

My Day. (Early Intervention Levels Ser.).Tr. of Mi dia. 23.10 (978-0-7362-0014-1(2)); Vol. 3. 3.85 (978-1-56334-964-5(7)) CENGAGE Learning.

My Family Board Book Set 800645, 6. 2005. (J). bds. (978-1-59794-037-5(2)) Environments, Inc.

My Fish. (Early Intervention Levels Ser.). 21.30 (978-0-7362-0359-3(1)) CENGAGE Learning.

My Little Christmas Library. 2008. (Pocket Libraries Ser.). 5p. bds. (978-1-4075-3193-9(X)) Parragon, Inc.

My Nest, 6 vols. 8p. (gr. k-1). 21.50 (978-0-322-02063-4(8)) Wright Group/McGraw-Hill.

My Place: Individual Title Six-Pack. (Story Steps Ser.). (gr. k-2). 20.00 (978-0-7635-9572-2(1)) Rigby Education.

My Planet, 6 Packs. (Chiquilibros Ser.). (gr. k-1). 23.00 (978-0-7635-0446-5(7)) Rigby Education.

My Pony. (Early Intervention Levels Ser.). 23.10 (978-0-7362-0018-9(5)); Vol. 2. 3.85 (978-1-56334-967-6(1)) CENGAGE Learning.

My School. 2004. (At School Ser.). (J). 7.33 (978-1-58453-264-4(5)) Pioneer Valley Bks.

My Teacher. 2004. (At School Ser.). (J). 7.33 (978-1-58453-263-7(7)) Pioneer Valley Bks.

My Trip: Individual Title Six-Packs. (Sails Literacy Ser.). 16p. (gr. k-18). 27.00 (978-0-7635-4430-0(2)) Rigby Education.

My Two, Very, Special Friends, 1. 2006. (Illus.). 19p. (J). per. 4.00 (978-0-9788386-1-4(0)) Taylor, Y. H.

Mystery Clues. 2005. (YA). ring bd. 49.95 (978-1-58804-403-7(3)) P C I Education.

Myth or Mystery? Individual Title Six-Packs. (Action Packs Ser.). 104p. (gr. 3-5). 44.00 (978-0-7635-8415-3(0)) Rigby Education.

Nadin, Joanna. Snow White & Rose Red: Band 12/Copper. 2017. (Collins Big Cat Tales Ser.). (ENG., Illus.). 32p. (J). (gr. 2-8). pap. 7.99 **(978-0-00-817929-8(8))** HarperCollins Pubs. Ltd. GBR. Dist: Independent Pubs. Group.

Nadin, Joanna. The Stepmonster. Ceulemans, Eglantine, illus. 2nd ed. 2016. (Reading Ladder Ser.). (ENG.). 48p. (J). (gr. k-2). pap. 7.99 (978-1-4052-8221-5(5)) Egmont Bks., Ltd. GBR. Dist: Independent Pubs. Group.

Naidoo, Beverley. The Great Tug of War. Grobler, Piet, illus. 2006. (ENG.). 96p. (J). (gr. 2-17). per. 7.95 (978-1-84507-055-7(0), Frances Lincoln) Quarto Publishing Group UK GBR. Dist: Hachette Bk. Group.

Nap Time, 6 Packs. (Kinderstarters Ser.). 8p. (gr. -1-1). 21.00 (978-0-7635-8647-8(1)) Rigby Education.

Nap Time for Gilbert. 2004. (Gilbert the Pig Set 2 Ser.). (J). 7.33 (978-1-58453-224-8(6)) Pioneer Valley Bks.

Narváez, Concha López & Salmeron, Carmelo. Tomas Es Distinto a los Demas.Tr. of Tomas Is Different from the Others. (SPA.). 64p. (J). (gr. 2-4). (978-84-216-3432-5(1)) Bruño, Editorial ESP. Dist: Lectorum Pubns., Inc.

National Geographic Editors. Creepy Crawly Collection. 2012. lib. bdg. 18.40 (978-0-606-26822-6(7), Turtleback) Turtleback Bks.

National Geographic Kids Staff. National Geographic Readers: Planet Earth Collection: Readers That Grow with You. 2014. (ENG., Illus.). 128p. (J). (gr. k-3). pap. 7.99 (978-1-4263-1813-9(8), National Geographic Children's Bks.) National Geographic Society.

National Geographic Kids Staff & Kramer, Barbara. National Geographic Readers: Nelson Mandela. 2014. (Readers Bios Ser.). (ENG., Illus.). 48p. (J). (gr. 1-4). pap. 3.99 (978-1-4263-1763-7(8), National Geographic Children's Bks.) National Geographic Society.

National Geographic Kids Staff & Neuman, Susan B. Hop, Bunny! 2014. (Readers Ser.). (ENG., Illus.). 24p. (J). (-k). pap. 3.99 (978-1-4263-1739-2(5), National Geographic Children's Bks.) National Geographic Society.

—National Geographic Readers: Hang on Monkey! 2014. (Readers Ser.). (ENG.). 24p. (J). (-k). pap. 3.99 (978-1-4263-1755-2(7), National Geographic Children's Bks.) National Geographic Society.

National Geographic Learning, National Geographic Learning. Early Elementary Level: Student Handbook. 2003. (Avenues Ser.). (ENG.). (C). (gr. 2-3). stu. ed. 53.95 (978-0-7362-1645-6(6)) CENGAGE Learning.

—English to a Beat! Practice Book. 2004. (ENG.). (C). (gr. 2-8). pap. 11.95 (978-0-7362-2498-7(X)) CENGAGE Learning.

—Intermediate Level: Student Handbook. 2003. (Avenues Ser.). (ENG.). 416p. (C). (gr. 4-8). stu. ed. 66.95 (978-0-7362-1973-0(0)) CENGAGE Learning.

—Just the Right Word! 2004. (English at Your Command! Ser.). (ENG.). (C). (gr. k-3). pap., stu. ed. 12.95 (978-0-7362-2533-5(1)) CENGAGE Learning.

—Picture Perfect Word Book. Incl. (C). 2000. pap. 22.95 (978-0-7362-0175-9(0), P17001); Picture Perfect Word Book. (J). pap., tchr. ed. 30.00 (gr. -1-1). 48.19 (978-0-7362-0176-6(9), P17002) CENGAGE Learning.

—Welcome to Our Home. (Avenues Ser.). (ENG.). (C). 2006. pap. 65.95 (978-0-7362-2152-8(2)) 2003. pap. 10.95 (978-0-7362-1724-8(X)) CENGAGE Learning.

—What a Week! (Avenues Ser.). (ENG.). (C). 2005. pap. 87.95 (978-0-7362-2129-0(8)) 2003. pap. 14.95 (978-0-7362-1906-8(4)) CENGAGE Learning.

—What's It Worth? (Avenues Ser.). (ENG.). (C). 2005. pap. 65.95 (978-0-7362-2160-3(3)) 2003. pap. 10.95 (978-0-7362-1739-2(8)) CENGAGE Learning.

—Your Great State. (Avenues Ser.). (ENG.). (C). 2005. pap. 73.95 (978-0-7362-2159-7(X)) 2003. 16p. pap. 11.95 (978-0-7362-1737-8(1)) CENGAGE Learning.

National Geographic Learning, National Geographic Learning, et al. Early Elementary Level: Practice Book. 2003. (English at Your Command! Ser.). (ENG.). 160p. (C). (gr. 2-3). pap. 13.95 (978-0-7362-1648-7(0)) CENGAGE Learning.

—Early Elementary Level: Student Handbook. 2003. (Avenues Ser.). (ENG.). (C). (gr. 2-3). pap., stu. ed. 44.95 (978-0-7362-1646-3(4)) CENGAGE Learning.

—Intermediate Level: Practice Book. 2003. (English at Your Command! Ser.). (ENG.). 176p. (C). (gr. 4-8). pap. 13.95 (978-0-7362-1975-4(7)) CENGAGE Learning.

—Intermediate Level: Student Handbook. 2003. (Avenues Ser.). (ENG.). (C). (gr. 4-8). pap., stu. ed. 57.95 (978-0-7362-1972-3(2)) CENGAGE Learning.

Nations, Susan & Alonso, Mellissa. Primary Literacy Responses: Core Tasks for Readers & Writers. 2014. (Maupin House Ser.). (ENG.). 224p. pap. 29.95 (978-1-62521-520-8(7)) Capstone Press of Coughlan Cos.

Naughton, Diane. Bones: And the Stories They Tell. 2014. (ENG.). 28p. (J). pap. 9.50 (978-1-107-67054-9(3)) Cambridge Univ. Pr.

—Our Green Future. 2014. (ENG., Illus.). 28p. (J). pap. 9.50 (978-1-107-67286-4(4)) Cambridge Univ. Pr.

—Secrets to a Long Life Intermediate Book with Online Access. 2014. (ENG., Illus.). 28p. (J). pap. 9.50 (978-1-107-68378-5(5)) Cambridge Univ. Pr.

—True Colors Intermediate Book with Online Access, 1 vol. 2014. (ENG., Illus.). 28p. (J). pap. 9.50 (978-1-107-66068-7(8)) Cambridge Univ. Pr.

—Venice: The Floating City. 2014. (ENG., Illus.). 28p. (J). pap. 9.50 (978-1-107-62163-3(1)) Cambridge Univ. Pr.

—What Are You Afraid of? Fears & Phobias Intermediate Book with Online Access. 2014. (ENG.). 28p. (J). pap. 9.50 (978-1-107-65051-0(8)) Cambridge Univ. Pr.

Nayer, Judy. 25 Easy Bilingual Nonfiction Mini-Books: Easy-to-Read Reproducible Mini-Books in English & Spanish That Build Vocabulary & Fluency-And Support the Social Studies & Science Topics You Teach. 2005. (ENG.). 64p. (gr. k-1). pap. 11.99 (978-0-439-70544-8(4), Teaching Resources) Scholastic, Inc.

Neasi, Barbara J. & Ochoa, Ana. Muchas Veces Yo. Ochoa, Ana, illus. 2011. (Rookie Ready to Learn Español Ser.). (SPA., Illus.). 40p. (J). pap. 5.95 (978-0-531-26789-9(X)); lib. bdg. 23.00 (978-0-531-26121-7(2)) Scholastic Library Publishing. (Children's Pr.).

Necklaces. (Early Intervention Levels Ser.). 21.30 (978-0-7362-0371-5(0)); Vol. 3. 3.55 (978-0-7362-0092-9(4)) CENGAGE Learning.

Nees, Susan. School Play. 2013. (Missy's Super Duper Royal Deluxe Ser.: 3). lib. bdg. 14.75 (978-0-606-32366-6(X), Turtleback) Turtleback Bks.

Neher, Anna-Luise. A Tale from the Trunk No. 2: With Words! Words! Words! 2009. 56p. pap. 10.82 (978-1-4251-8284-7(4)) Trafford Publishing.

The Neighborhood Picnic, 6 vols. (Multicultural Programs Ser.). 16p. (gr. 1-3). 24.95 (978-0-7802-9217-8(0)) Wright Group/McGraw-Hill.

Neighborhood Soup. (J). 21.95 (978-0-8136-4267-3(1)); (gr. 2). 23.50 (978-0-8136-8830-5(2)) Modern Curriculum Pr.

Nelid, Piper. Baking Bread with Grandpa, 01 vols., 1. 2016. (Rosen REAL Readers: STEM & STEAM Collection). (ENG.). 12p. (J). pap. 6.33 (978-1-5081-1569-4(9), Rosen Classroom) Rosen Publishing Group, Inc., The.

—The Coolest Fourth of July of All Time, 01 vols., 1. 2016. (Rosen REAL Readers: Social Studies Nonfiction / Fiction: Family, Community, & the World Ser.). (ENG.). 12p. (J). pap. 6.33 (978-1-5081-1937-1(6), Rosen Classroom) Rosen Publishing Group, Inc., The.

—Emilio & the Baby Pig, 01 vols., 1. 2016. (Rosen REAL Readers: STEM & STEAM Collection). (ENG.). 8p. (J). pap. 5.46 (978-1-5081-1404-8(8), Rosen Classroom) Rosen Publishing Group, Inc., The.

—Father's Day with My Forever Dad, 01 vols., 1. 2016. (Rosen REAL Readers: Social Studies Nonfiction / Fiction: Family, Community, & the World Ser.). (ENG.). 8p. (J). pap. 5.46 (978-1-5081-1389-8(0), Rosen Classroom) Rosen Publishing Group, Inc., The.

—First Place, 01 vols., 1. 2016. (Rosen REAL Readers: Social Studies Nonfiction / Fiction: Family, Community, & the World Ser.). (ENG.). 12p. (J). pap. 6.33 (978-1-5081-1988-3(0), Rosen Classroom) Rosen Publishing Group, Inc., The.

—The Green Building, 01 vols., 1. 2016. (Rosen REAL Readers: Social Studies Nonfiction / Fiction: Family, Community, & the World Ser.). (ENG.). 8p. (J). pap. 5.46 (978-1-5081-1860-2(4), Rosen Classroom) Rosen Publishing Group, Inc., The.

—The New Kid, 01 vols., 1. 2016. (Rosen REAL Readers: Social Studies Nonfiction / Fiction: Family, Community, & the World Ser.). (ENG.). 12p. (J). pap. 6.33 (978-1-5081-1919-7(8), Rosen Classroom) Rosen Publishing Group, Inc., The.

—Racing Day, 01 vols., 1. 2016. (Rosen REAL Readers: STEM & STEAM Collection). (ENG.). 8p. (J). pap. 5.46 (978-1-5081-1472-7(2), Rosen Classroom) Rosen Publishing Group, Inc., The.

—Rick Gets a Cast, 01 vols., 1. 2016. (Rosen REAL Readers: STEM & STEAM Collection). (ENG.). 12p. (J). pap. 6.33 (978-1-5081-1551-9(6), Rosen Classroom) Rosen Publishing Group, Inc., The.

—Sarah the Great, 01 vols., 1. 2016. (Rosen REAL Readers: Social Studies Nonfiction / Fiction: Family, Community, & the World Ser.). (ENG.). 8p. (J). pap. 5.46 (978-1-5081-1842-8(6), Rosen Classroom) Rosen Publishing Group, Inc., The.

—Seesaw Fun, 01 vols., 1. 2016. (Rosen REAL Readers: STEM & STEAM Collection). (ENG.). 12p. (J). pap. 6.33 (978-1-5081-1623-3(7), Rosen Classroom) Rosen Publishing Group, Inc., The.

—A Special Dinner with My Moms, 01 vols., 1. 2016. (Rosen REAL Readers: Social Studies Nonfiction / Fiction: Family, Community, & the World Ser.). (ENG.). 8p. (J). pap. 5.46 (978-1-5081-1510-6(9), Rosen Classroom) Rosen Publishing Group, Inc., The.

Nelson, Jo & Bustamente, Martin. Copernicus, Galileo & Newton. 2014. (Collins Big Cat Ser.). (ENG.). 128p. (J). (gr. 5). pap. 9.95 (978-0-00-753017-5(X)) HarperCollins Pubs. Ltd. GBR. Dist: Independent Pubs. Group.

Nesbit, E. The Story of the Treasure Seekers: Being the Adventures of the Bastable Children in Search of A Fortune. 2006. 132p. (gr. 4-7). per. 10.95 (978-1-59818-963-6(8)); 24.95 (978-1-59818-172-2(6)) Aegypan.

Neuman, Susan B. National Geographic Readers: Jump Pup! 2014. (Readers Ser.). (ENG.). 24p. (J). (-k). pap. 3.99 (978-1-4263-1508-4(2), National Geographic Children's Bks.) National Geographic Society.

—Swim Fish! Explore the Coral Reef. 2014. (Readers Ser.). (ENG.). 24p. (J). (-k). pap. 3.99 (978-1-4263-1510-7(4), National Geographic Children's Bks.) National Geographic Society.

Never Say Never. (Little Book Practice Reader Ser.). (J). (978-0-8136-0883-9(X)) Modern Curriculum Pr.

Newcomb, Kristene. Molly Q's Trash Travels Through the Water Cycle. Paschall, Patricia, ed. Newcomb, Kristene, illus. 2007. (Illus.). 32p. (J). per. 8.00 (978-0-9760790-9-5(7)) Folsom Fallies Pr.

Newcomer, Mary Jane, et al. The Elson Readers, Bk. 4. Fitterling, Michael, illus. 2005. (ENG.). 193p. (J). (gr. -1-12). tchr. ed., per. 17.95 (978-1-890623-28-9(8)) Lost Classic Bks.

Newman, Lee. How Many Animals? 2007. (Collins Big Cat Ser.). (ENG.). 24p. (J). (gr. -1-k). pap. 5.99 (978-0-00-718647-1(9)) HarperCollins Pubs. Ltd. GBR. Dist: Independent Pubs. Group.

Newmark Learning, compiled by. Rising Readers Set A Sets Of 6. 2009. (Rising Readers Ser.). (J). (gr. -1-k). 1005.12 net. (978-1-60719-110-0(5)) Newmark Learning LLC.

—Sight Word Readers 12 copy set with Rack Set A. 2009. (Sight Word Readers Set A Ser.). (J). 1095.12 net. (978-1-60719-159-9(8)) Newmark Learning LLC.

Nicholson, Nancy. Devotional Stories for Little Folks Too. 2007. (J). per. (978-0-9771236-1-2(8)) For Little Folks.

Nielsen, Aubrie. After School. rev. ed. 2011. (Mathematics Readers Ser.). (ENG.). 32p. (J). (gr. k-k). pap. 8.99 (978-1-4333-3440-5(2)) Teacher Created Materials, Inc.

—At School. rev. ed. 2011. (Mathematics Readers Ser.). (ENG.). 32p. (J). (gr. k-k). pap. 8.99 (978-1-4333-3441-2(0)) Teacher Created Materials, Inc.

Nine Days a Queen Reading Group Guide. (J). (978-0-06-077997-9(7)) HarperCollins Pubs.

Nixon & Brush. Champagne with a Corpse. (Thumbprint Mysteries Ser.). 32.86 (978-0-8092-0420-5(7)) McGraw-Hill/Contemporary.

No Place Like Home. (Lexile Levels Ser.). 47.88 (978-1-56334-094-9(1)) CENGAGE Learning.

No Queen Today! 3-in-1 Package. (Sails Literacy Ser.). 24p. (gr. 2-18). 57.00 (978-0-7578-3217-8(2)) Rigby Education.

No Queen Today! 6 Small Books. (Sails Literacy Ser.). 24p. (gr. 2-18). 25.00 (978-0-7578-3193-5(1)) Rigby Education.

No Queen Today! Big Book Only. (Sails Literacy Ser.). 24p. (gr. 2-18). 27.00 (978-0-7635-6995-2(X)) Rigby Education.

No Secrets. 64p. (YA). (gr. 6-12). pap. (978-0-8224-2381-2(2)) Globe Fearon Educational Publishing.

No Time to Lose. 2003. (Illus.). pap. 7.60 (978-0-7398-7533-9(7)) Steck-Vaughn.

Noble, Trinka Hakes. The New Jersey Reader. Darnell, K. L., illus. 2009. (Readers Ser.). (ENG.). 96p. 12.95 (978-1-58536-438-1(X)) Sleeping Bear Pr.

—Pennsylvania Reader. Darnell, K. L., illus. rev. ed. 2007. (State Readers Ser.). (ENG.). 96p. (J). (gr. 1-5). 12.95 (978-1-58536-320-9(0)) Sleeping Bear Pr.

Noonan, Diana. On the Move, 6 vols. (Wonder Worldtm Ser.). 16p. 29.95 (978-0-7802-2014-0(5)) Wright Group/McGraw-Hill.

Northcott, Richard. In the Mountains. Geatches, Hazel, ed. 2013. (ENG.). 40p. pap. 9.38 (978-0-19-464687-1(4)) Oxford Univ. Pr., Inc.

Not Too Messy, Not Too Neat. (J). (gr. 3-5). 75.00 (978-0-669-13694-4(8)) Houghton Mifflin Harcourt School Pubs.

Not When It's Hot. (Early Intervention Levels Ser.). 21.30 (978-0-7362-0387-6(7)) CENGAGE Learning.

Novel Units, Inc. Staff, creator. Black Beauty Student Packet. 2004. (J). 12.99 (978-1-58130-852-5(3)) Novel Units, Inc.

—The Five People You Meet in Heaven Student Packet. 2004. (YA). (gr. 9-12). stu. ed. 12.99 (978-1-58130-854-9(X)) Novel Units, Inc.

—The Hound of the Baskervilles Student Packet. 2004. (YA). 12.99 (978-1-58130-856-3(6)) Novel Units, Inc.

—The Hunchback of Notre Dame Student Packet. 2004. (YA). 12.99 (978-1-58130-858-7(2)) Novel Units, Inc.

—The Magician's Nephew Student Packet. 2004. (J). 12.99 (978-1-58130-860-0(4)) Novel Units, Inc.

—Red Scarf Girl Student Packet. 2004. (J). 12.99 (978-1-58130-862-4(0)) Novel Units, Inc.

—Riding Freedom Student Packet. 2004. (J). 12.99 (978-1-58130-864-8(7)) Novel Units, Inc.

—Sideways Stories from Wayside School Student Packet. 2004. (J). 12.99 (978-1-58130-866-2(3)) Novel Units, Inc.

—Uncle Tom's Cabin Student Packet. 2004. (YA). 12.99 (978-1-58130-870-9(1)) Novel Units, Inc.

—When My Name Was Keoko Student Packet. 2004. (J). 12.99 (978-1-58130-872-3(8)) Novel Units, Inc.

—Winterdance Student Packet. 2004. (J). 12.99 (978-1-58130-874-7(4)) Novel Units, Inc.

Novelli, Joan. Phonics: 30 Instant Centers with Reproducible Templates & Activities That Help Kids Practice Important Literacy Skills-Independently! 2006. (Shoe Box Learning Centers Ser.). (ENG.). 80p. (J). pap. 12.99 (978-0-439-53796-4(7), Teaching Resources) Scholastic, Inc.

Null Petersen, Casey. Games Around the World, 1 vol. 2nd rev. ed. 2011. (Nonfiction Readers Ser.). (ENG.). 28p. (J). (gr. 3-3). pap. 8.99 (978-1-4333-3653-9(7)) Teacher Created Materials, Inc.

—Markets Around the World, 1 vol. 2nd rev. ed. 2011. (TIME for KIDS(r) Nonfiction Readers Ser.). (ENG.). 28p. (J). (gr. 3-3). pap. 8.99 (978-1-4333-3652-2(9)) Teacher Created Materials, Inc.

Null Petersen, Kathleen C. Theater Actors Then & Now, 1 vol. 2006. (Primary Source Readers Ser.). (ENG.). 32p. (J). (gr. 2-2). pap. 8.99 (978-0-7439-9379-1(9)) Shell Educational Publishing.

—Writers Then & Now, 1 vol. 2006. (Primary Source Readers Ser.). (ENG.). 32p. (J). (gr. 1-1). pap. 8.99 (978-0-7439-9380-7(2)) Shell Educational Publishing.

Nutrition Adventures with the Nutri Gang, Race Day, Issue #1: The Nutri Gang. 2007. (J). 2.99 (978-0-9792383-0-7(7)) KJ Pubns.

Nuttall, Gina. Is Lion Sick?, 4 vols. 2005. (QEB Readers). (Illus.). 24p. (J). (gr. -1-3). lib. bdg. 15.95 (978-1-59566-100-5(X)) QEB Publishing Inc.

Nyman, Debbie & Wortzman, Ricki. The 10 Best Plays. 2008. 14.99 (978-1-55448-503-1(7)) Scholastic Library Publishing.

—The 10 Most Notable Elected Female Leaders. 2008. 14.99 (978-1-55448-527-7(4)) Scholastic Library Publishing.

—The 10 Most Outstanding Women. 2007. 14.99 (978-1-55448-468-3(5)) Scholastic Library Publishing.

O'Brien, Kathryn. I'd Be Your Princess: A Royal Tale of Godly Character. Garland, Michael, illus. 2007. 28p. (J). (gr. -1-3). 6.99 (978-0-7847-1964-0(0)) Standard Publishing.

O'Brien, Renee McMullen. The Amazing Mocha & His Courageous Journey. O'Brien, Renee McMullen, illus. 2009. (Illus.). 28p. pap. 12.95 (978-1-936051-60-1(5)) Peppertree Pr., The.

O'Brien, Tim. The Billy-Goats Tough. Mancini, Robert, illus. 2007. (Collins Big Cat Ser.). (ENG.). 1p. (J). pap. 8.99 (978-0-00-722863-8(5)) HarperCollins Pubs. Ltd. GBR. Dist: Independent Pubs. Group.

Oceanak, Karla. Finicky. Spanjer, Kendra, illus. 2012. (Aldo Zelnick Comic Novel Ser.: 6). (ENG.). 160p. (J). (gr. 3-7). 12.95 (978-1-934649-24-4(4)) Bailiwick Pr.

O'Connor, Jane. Fancy Nancy's Fantastic Phonics, 12 vols. Glasser, Robin Preiss, illus. 2013. (My First I Can Read Ser.). (ENG.). 120p. (J). (gr. -1-3). pap. 12.99 (978-0-06-208633-4(2)) HarperCollins Pubs.

—It's Backward Day! 2016. (Fancy Nancy - I Can Read! Ser.). (Illus.). 32p. (J). lib. bdg. 13.55 (978-0-606-38175-8(9)) Turtleback Bks.

Oczkus, Lori. Close Reading with Paired Texts. 2015. (Close Reading with Paired Texts). (ENG., Illus.). 128p. (gr. 3-3). pap. 19.99 (978-1-4258-1359-8(3)) Shell Educational Publishing.

—Close Reading with Paired Texts, Level 5. 2015. (Close Reading with Paired Texts). (ENG., Illus.). 128p. (gr. 5-5). pap. 19.99 (978-1-4258-1361-1(5)) Shell Educational Publishing.

—Disappearing Rainforests. 2015. (Close Reading with Paired Texts). (ENG., Illus.). 128p. (gr. 2-2). pap. 19.99 (978-1-4258-1358-1(5)) Shell Educational Publishing.

O'Dea, Lori. Super Dog. Greenhead, Bill, illus. 2017. (Text Connections Guided Close Reading Ser.). (J). (gr. k). (978-1-4900-1770-9(4)) Benchmark Education Co.

O'Dell, Kathryn. Life Online: the Digital Age Low Intermediate Book with Online Access. 2014. (ENG.). 28p. (J). pap. 9.50 (978-1-107-65069-5(0)) Cambridge Univ. Pr.

O'DellKathryn. THE SCIENCE OF DARKNESS LOW INTERMEDIATE BOOK WITH ONLINE ACCESS. 2014. (ENG., Illus.). 28p. (J). pap. 9.50 (978-1-107-65493-8(9)) Cambridge Univ. Pr.

—THE SCIENCE OF LIGHT LOW INTERMEDIATE BOOK WITH ONLINE ACCESS. 2014. (ENG., Illus.). 28p. (J). pap. 9.50 (978-1-107-68198-9(7)) Cambridge Univ. Pr.

—SHARK ATTACK LOW INTERMEDIATE BOOK WITH ONLINE ACCESS. 2014. (ENG.). 28p. (J). pap. 9.50 (978-1-107-66183-7(8)) Cambridge Univ. Pr.

—SHOOT TO KILL: WHY WE HUNT HIGH BEGINNING BOOK WITH ONLINE ACCESS. 2014. (ENG., Illus.). 24p. (J). pap. 9.50 (978-1-107-62253-1(0)) Cambridge Univ. Pr.

—SURVIVAL GUIDE: LOST IN THE MOUNTAINS LOW INTERMEDIATE BOOK WITH ONLINE ACCESS. 2014. (ENG.). 28p. (J). pap. 9.50 (978-1-107-64328-4(7)) Cambridge Univ. Pr.

Odenthal, Ingrid. The Warm Heart. 2009. 20p. pap. 12.49 (978-1-4490-5188-4(X)) AuthorHouse.

O'Donnell, Kerri. A Giraffe Can Laugh. 2006. (Neighborhood Readers Ser.). (ENG.). 12p. (gr. -1-3). pap. 5.90 (978-1-4042-5762-7(4), Rosen Classroom) Rosen Publishing Group, Inc., The.

—King of the Swamp. 2006. (Neighborhood Readers Ser.). (ENG.). 16p. (gr. 1-3). pap. 6.50 (978-1-4042-7216-3(X), Rosen Classroom) Rosen Publishing Group, Inc., The.

—Sue Helps Out. 2006. (Neighborhood Readers Ser.). (ENG.). 8p. (gr. -1-3). pap. 5.15 (978-1-4042-5684-2(9), Rosen Classroom) Rosen Publishing Group, Inc., The.

—When Sue Is Sad. 2006. (Neighborhood Readers Ser.). (ENG.). 8p. (gr. -1-3). pap. 5.15 (978-1-4042-5653-8(9), Rosen Classroom) Rosen Publishing Group, Inc., The.

—Whose Hat Is That? 2006. (Neighborhood Readers Ser.). (ENG.). 8p. (gr. -1-3). pap. 5.15 (978-1-4042-5647-7(4), Rosen Classroom) Rosen Publishing Group, Inc., The.

O'Donnell, Mabel & Monro, Rona. Janet & John: Off to Play. 2007. (Janet & John Bks.). (ENG., Illus.). 40p. (J). (gr. -1-2). 9.99 (978-1-84024-615-5(4)) Summerdale Pubs. GBR. Dist: Independent Pubs. Group.

O'Donoghue, Chris. Charlie's Reading Rescue: Improve an Older Child's Reading. 2011. (Illus.). 188p. pap. 10.50 (978-1-60976-573-6(7), Eloquent Bks.) Strategic Book Publishing & Rights Agency (SBPRA).

Oe, Patricia Daly. Blue Mouse, Yellow Mouse. Oe, Patricia Daly, illus. 2007. (R. I. C. Story Chest Ser.). (Illus.). 20p. (J). (gr. -1-k). 11.95 incl. audio compact disk (978-1-74126-439-5(1)) R.I.C. Pubns. AUS. Dist: SCB Distributors.

Ofelia, Dumas Lachtman. Big Enough Bastante Grande. Enrique, Sanchez, illus. 2008. 32p. (J). pap. 7.95 (978-1-55885-239-6(5)) Arte Publico Pr.

O'Gorman, Neil. Plants & Their Environments. 2009. (Real Life Readers Ser.). 16p. (gr. 2-3). pap. 7.05 (978-1-4358-0067-0(2), Rosen Classroom) Rosen Publishing Group, Inc., The.

The Old Toad. (Early Intervention Levels Ser.). 28.38 (978-0-7362-0398-2(2)) CENGAGE Learning.

The Old Toad (8), Vol. 8. (Early Intervention Levels Ser.). 4.73 (978-0-7362-0223-7(4)) CENGAGE Learning.

Olien, Jessica. Adrift: An Odd Couple of Polar Bears. Olien, Jessica, illus. 2017. (Illus.). 40p. (J). (gr. -1-3). 17.99 (978-0-06-245177-4(4)) HarperCollins Pubs.

Olivas, John D. Endeavour's Long Journey/la Larga Travesía de Endeavour. Roski, Gayle G., illus. 2016. (SPA.). 40p. (J). 19.95 **(978-0-9973947-2-6(2))** East West Discovery Pr.

Olker, Constance. The Punctuation Pals Go to the Baseball Park. Guzman, Minerva, illus. 2005. (Punctuation Pals Ser.). 44p. (J). per. 18.95 (978-1-933449-15-9(2)) Nightengale Pr.

—The Punctuation Pals Go to the Beach. Guzman, Minerva, illus. 2005. (Punctuation Pals Ser.). 36p. (J). per. 18.95 (978-1-933449-12-8(8)) Nightengale Pr.

—The Punctuation Pals Go to the Moon. 2005. (Illus.). 64p. (J). per. 24.95 (978-1-933449-13-5(6)) Nightengale Pr.

—The Punctuation Pals Meet at School. 2005. (Illus.). 40p. (J). per. 18.95 (978-1-933449-07-4(1)) Nightengale Pr.

Olsen, Jan Z. Mat Man Opposites. Delaney, Molly, illus. 2009. (ENG.). stu. ed. 13.75 (978-1-891627-94-1(5)) Handwriting Without Tears.

O'Mara, Blanche. A Year with Carmen. 2006. (Neighborhood Readers Ser.). (ENG.). 12p. (gr. 1-3). pap. 5.90 (978-1-4042-6835-7(9), Rosen Classroom) Rosen Publishing Group, Inc., The.

On a Roll: How Communities Build State Parks. 2005. (Book Treks Ser.). (J). 37.95 *(978-0-7652-3254-0(5))* Celebration Pr.

On Our Way to English: Complete Package - Grade 4. (gr. 4-18). 2195.00 *(978-0-7578-6971-6(8))* Rigby Education.

On Our Way to English: Complete Package - Grade 5. (gr. 5-18). 2195.00 *(978-0-7578-6972-3(6))* Rigby Education.

On Our Way to English: Complete Package - Kindergarten. (gr. k-18). 1895.00 *(978-0-7578-6967-9(X))* Rigby Education.

On the Go. 2005. (Little Celebrations Thematic Packages Ser.). (J). (gr. k-3). 133.50 *(978-0-673-75383-0(2))* Celebration Pr.

On This Earth. (Early Intervention Levels Ser.). 23.10 *(978-0-7362-0037-0(1))* CENGAGE Learning.

On Your Mark: Grade 1 Reading Fluency Booklet. (gr. 1-18). 57.19 *(978-0-7362-2474-1(2))* CENGAGE Learning.

On Your Mark: Grade 2 Reading Fluency Booklet. (gr. 2-18). 57.19 *(978-0-7362-2475-8(0))* CENGAGE Learning.

On Your Mark: Grade 3 Reading Fluency Booklet. (gr. 3-18). 57.19 *(978-0-7362-2476-5(9))* CENGAGE Learning.

On Your Mark: Grade 4 Reading Fluency Booklet. (gr. 4-18). 57.19 *(978-0-7362-2477-2(7))* CENGAGE Learning.

On Your Mark: Grade 5 Reading Fluency Booklet. (gr. 5-18). 57.19 *(978-0-7362-2478-9(5))* CENGAGE Learning.

On Your Mark: Grade 6 Reading Fluency Booklet. (gr. 6-18). 57.19 *(978-0-7362-2479-6(3))* CENGAGE Learning.

On Your Mark: Grade 7 Reading Fluency Booklet. (gr. 7-18). 57.19 *(978-0-7362-2480-2(7))* CENGAGE Learning.

On Your Mark: Grade 8 Reading Fluency Booklet. (gr. 8-18). 57.19 *(978-0-7362-2481-9(5))* CENGAGE Learning.

One Afternoon. (Early Intervention Levels Ser.). 47.88 *(978-0-7362-2121-4(2))* CENGAGE Learning.

One Piece at a Time. 2003. (Illus.). pap. 5.60 *(978-0-7398-7511-7(6))* Steck-Vaughn.

One, Two, Three, Four. (Early Intervention Levels Ser.). 23.10 *(978-0-7362-0035-6(5))*; Vol. 6. 3.85 *(978-1-56334-983-6(3))* CENGAGE Learning.

O'Neill, John R. Mahatma Gandhi, Nelson Mandela. 2011. (Readers' & Writers' Genre Workshop Ser.). (YA). pap. *(978-1-4509-3024-6(7))* Benchmark Education Co.

O'Neill, Rachael, illus. My First Library: With Nine Colorful Books. (J). *(978-1-85479-804-6(9))* O'Mara, Michael Bks., Ltd.

Open Court Staff. Intermediate Think Storybook: Level 4. (J). pap. *(978-0-89688-693-3(X)*, 88693) Open Court Publishing Co.

Optometrist: Individual Title Six-Packs. (Bookweb Ser.). 32p. (gr. 3-18). 34.00 *(978-0-7635-3946-7(5))* Rigby Education.

Oral Language Flip Chart: Time to Speak & Listen. 2004. (gr. k-18). suppl. ed. 109.15 *(978-0-328-02214-4(4))* Addison-Wesley Educational Pubs., Inc.

Orange & Red Levels Certificate Only. (Discovery World Ser.). (gr. 1-2). 89.00 *(978-0-7578-6527-5(5))* Rigby Education.

Orca Book Publishers, ed. Orca Young Readers Collection, 24 vols. 2011. (Orca Young Readers Ser.). (ENG.). 128p. (J). (gr. 2-6). pap. 190.80 *(978-1-55469-387-0(X))* Orca Bk. Pubs. USA.

O'Reilly, Elaine & Pearson Education Staff. Another World, Pack. 2007.Tr. of En Annan Varld. (ENG.). pap. 17.32 incl. cd-rom *(978-1-4058-5206-7(2))* Pearson Education.

Orme, David. Blitz. 2007. (Sharp Shades Ser.). (ENG., Illus.). 64p. (J). (gr. 6-8). pap. 8.99 *(978-0-237-53444-8(4))* Evans Brothers, Ltd. GBR. Dist: Independent Pubs. Group.

—Bugs & Spiders. 2010. (Fact to Fiction Grafx Ser.). (Illus.). 36p. (J). lib. bdg. 16.95 *(978-1-60686-465-4(3))* Perfection Learning Corp.

—Bugs & Spiders. Mongiovi, Jorge, illus. 2010. (Fact to Fiction Ser.). 36p. pap. 7.45 *(978-0-7891-7990-6(3))* Perfection Learning Corp.

—Deadly Virus. 2008. (Starchasers Ser.). (ENG., Illus.). 48p. pap. *(978-1-84167-767-5(1))* Ransom Publishing Ltd.

—Death. 2007. (Trailblazers Ser.). (ENG., Illus.). 36p. pap. *(978-1-84167-591-6(1))* Ransom Publishing Ltd.

—Don't Try This at Home. 2008. (Trailblazers Ser.). (ENG., Illus.). 36p. pap. *(978-1-84167-652-4(7))* Ransom Publishing Ltd.

—Extreme Science. 2009. (Fact to Fiction Ser.). (Illus.). 36p. (J). lib. bdg. 16.95 *(978-0-7569-9279-8(6))* Perfection Learning Corp.

—Extreme Sports. 2007. (Trailblazers Ser.). (ENG., Illus.). 36p. pap. *(978-1-84167-590-9(3))* Ransom Publishing Ltd.

—Extreme Sports. 2011. (Fact to Fiction Grafx Ser.). (ENG., Illus.). 36p. (J). (gr. 4-7). lib. bdg. 17.45 *(978-1-61384-019-1(5))* Perfection Learning Corp.

—Fashion. 2008. (Trailblazers Ser.). (ENG., Illus.). 36p. pap. *(978-1-84167-650-0(0))* Ransom Publishing Ltd.

—Fear. 2011. (Fact to Fiction Grafx Ser.). (ENG., Illus.). 36p. (J). (gr. 4-7). lib. bdg. 17.45 *(978-1-61384-018-4(7))* Perfection Learning Corp.

—Great Journeys. 2008. (Trailblazers Ser.). (ENG., Illus.). 36p. pap. *(978-1-84167-653-1(5))* Ransom Publishing Ltd.

—How to Be a Pop Star. 2007. (Trailblazers Ser.). (ENG., Illus.). 36p. pap. *(978-1-84167-594-7(6))* Ransom Publishing Ltd.

—Lost Animals. Mongiovi, Jorge, illus. 2010. (Fact to Fiction Grafx Ser.). 36p. pap. 7.45 *(978-0-7891-7993-7(8))* Perfection Learning Corp.

—Manga. 2007. (Trailblazers Ser.). (ENG., Illus.). 36p. pap. *(978-1-84167-593-0(8))* Ransom Publishing Ltd.

—Plague. 2004. (Shades Ser.). (ENG.). 58p. (J). pap. 7.99 *(978-0-237-52729-7(4))* Evans Brothers, Ltd. GBR. Dist: Independent Pubs. Group.

—Plagues. 2010. (Fact to Fiction Grafx Ser.). (Illus.). 36p. (J). pap. 7.45 *(978-0-7891-7997-5(0))* Perfection Learning Corp.

—Sea Killers. 2007. (Trailblazers Ser.). (ACE & ENG., Illus.). 36p. pap. *(978-1-84167-592-3(X))* Ransom Publishing Ltd.

—Speed. 2009. (Fact to Fiction Ser.). (Illus.). 36p. (J). 16.95 *(978-0-7569-9283-5(4))* Perfection Learning Corp.

—Spies. 2010. (Fact to Fiction Grafx Ser.). (Illus.). 36p. (J). lib. bdg. 16.95 *(978-1-60686-473-9(4))* Perfection Learning Corp.

—Spies. Martin, Jan, illus. 2010. (Fact to Fiction Grafx Ser.). 36p. pap. 7.45 *(978-0-7891-7998-2(9))* Perfection Learning Corp.

—Strange Creatures. Lindblad, Stefan, illus. 2010. (Fact to Fiction Grafx Ser.). 36p. pap. 7.45 *(978-0-7891-7994-4(6))* Perfection Learning Corp.

—Weird Places. 2007. (Trailblazers Ser.). (ENG., Illus.). 36p. pap. *(978-1-84167-589-3(X))* Ransom Publishing Ltd.

Orme, David & Orme, David. Science Fiction. 2008. (Trailblazers Ser.). (ENG., Illus.). 36p. pap. *(978-1-84167-693-7(4))* Ransom Publishing Ltd.

Orme, Helen. Lost! Brett, Cathy, illus. 2007. (Siti's Sisters Ser.). (ENG.). 36p. (J). per. *(978-1-84167-598-5(9))* Ransom Publishing Ltd.

Ormiston, Rickey. My Dog Wiggles. 2010. 20p. 11.49 *(978-1-4490-9824-7(X))* AuthorHouse.

Orozco, Jose-Luis. Rin, Rin, Rin - Do, Re, Mi. Diaz, David, illus. 2005. (Lee y Seras Ser.). (ENG.). 32p. (J). (gr. -1-k). 3.99 *(978-0-439-75531-3(X)*, Orchard Bks.) Scholastic, Inc.

Orshoski, Paul. We Read Phonics-Bugs on the Bus. Noiset, Michele, illus. 2010. 32p. (J). 9.95 *(978-1-60115-325-8(2))*; pap. 4.99 *(978-1-60115-326-5(0))* Treasure Bay, Inc.

—We Read Phonics-Dad Does It All. Ebbeler, Jeffrey, illus. 2011. 32p. (J). 9.95 *(978-1-60115-341-8(4))*; (YA). pap. 4.99 *(978-1-60115-342-5(2))* Treasure Bay, Inc.

Ortells, Estela. En Africa. (Coleccion Pequeno Simon). (SPA., Illus.). 32p. (J). 7.95 *(978-84-7189-177-8(8)*, ORT342) Ortells, Alfredo Editorial S.L. ESP. Dist: Continental Bk. Co., Inc.

—En el Aire. (Coleccion Pequeno Simon). (SPA., Illus.). 32p. (J). 7.95 *(978-84-7189-173-0(5)*, ORT328) Ortells, Alfredo Editorial S.L. ESP. Dist: Continental Bk. Co., Inc.

—En el Colegio. (Coleccion Pequeno Simon). (SPA., Illus.). 32p. (J). 7.95 *(978-84-7189-170-9(0)*, ORT327) Ortells, Alfredo Editorial S.L. ESP. Dist: Continental Bk. Co., Inc.

—En el Rio. (Coleccion Pequeno Simon). (SPA., Illus.). 32p. (J). 7.95 *(978-84-7189-169-3(7)*, ORT346) Ortells, Alfredo Editorial S.L. ESP. Dist: Continental Bk. Co., Inc.

—En Japon. (Coleccion Pequeno Simon). (SPA., Illus.). 32p. (J). 7.95 *(978-84-7189-176-1(X)*, ORT331) Ortells, Alfredo Editorial S.L. ESP. Dist: Continental Bk. Co., Inc.

—En la India. (Coleccion Pequeno Simon). (SPA., Illus.). 32p. (J). 7.95 *(978-84-7189-175-4(1)*, ORT330) Ortells, Alfredo Editorial S.L. ESP. Dist: Continental Bk. Co., Inc.

—En la Montana. (Coleccion Pequeno Simon). (SPA., Illus.). 32p. (J). 7.95 *(978-84-7189-167-9(0)*, ORT343) Ortells, Alfredo Editorial S.L. ESP. Dist: Continental Bk. Co., Inc.

—En la Nieve. (Coleccion Pequeno Simon). (SPA., Illus.). 32p. (J). 7.95 *(978-84-7189-172-3(7)*, ORT344) Ortells, Alfredo Editorial S.L. ESP. Dist: Continental Bk. Co., Inc.

—En la Playa. (Coleccion Pequeno Simon). (SPA., Illus.). 32p. (J). 7.95 *(978-84-7189-168-6(9)*, ORT347) Ortells, Alfredo Editorial S.L. ESP. Dist: Continental Bk. Co., Inc.

—El Pequeno Castor. (Coleccion Pequeno Simon). (SPA., Illus.). 32p. (J). 7.95 *(978-84-7189-171-6(9)*, ORT329) Ortells, Alfredo Editorial S.L. ESP. Dist: Continental Bk. Co., Inc.

—Y los Chihuhuas. (Coleccion Pequeno Simon). (SPA., Illus.). 32p. (J). 7.95 *(978-84-7189-174-7(3)*, ORT345) Ortells, Alfredo Editorial S.L. ESP. Dist: Continental Bk. Co., Inc.

Oscar & Tatiana: Individual Title Six-Packs. (Literatura 2000 Ser.). (gr. 2-3). 33.00 *(978-0-7635-0267-6(7))* Rigby Education.

Oscar y Tatiana: Individual Title Six-Packs. (Literatura 2000 Ser.). (gr. 2-3). 33.00 *(978-0-7635-1268-2(0))* Rigby Education.

Osteen, Victoria. Unexpected Treasures. Palmisciano, Diane, illus. 2009. (ENG.). 32p. (J). (gr. -1-3). 17.99 *(978-1-4169-5550-4(X)*, Little Simon Inspirations) Little Simon Inspirations.

Otfinoski, Steve. Coin Collecting for Kids. Graham, Jack, illus. 2007. (ENG.). 12p. (J). (gr. 2-7). spiral bd. 17.99 *(978-1-58476-624-7(7)*, IKIDS) Innovative Kids.

Otfinoski, Steven & Langston-George, Rebecca. Encounter: Narrative Nonfiction Stories. 2016. (Encounter: Narrative Nonfiction Stories Ser.). (ENG.). pap. 32.80 *(978-1-5157-6564-6(4))* Encounter Bks.

Otter, Otter. (Early Intervention Levels Ser.). 21.30 *(978-0-7362-0381-4(8))*; Vol. 4. 3.55 *(978-0-7362-0102-5(5))* CENGAGE Learning.

Otter, Otter. (J). 26.20 *(978-0-8136-8416-1(1))*; (gr. -1-3). 59.50 *(978-0-8136-7954-9(0))* Modern Curriculum Pr.

Ottolenghi, Carol. La Bella Durmiente. 2009. (Keepsake Stories Ser.).Tr. of Sleeping Beauty. (SPA & ENG.). 32p. (gr. -1-2). pap. 3.99 *(978-0-7696-5862-9(8)*, Brighter Child) Carson-Dellosa Publishing, LLC.

—The Princess & the Pea. 2009. (Keepsake Stories Ser.). (ENG.). 32p. (gr. -1-3). pap. 3.99 *(978-0-7696-5869-8(5)*, Brighter Child) Carson-Dellosa Publishing, LLC.

—The Princess & the Pea (La Princesa y el Guisante) 2009. (Keepsake Stories Ser.). (ENG & SPA.). 32p. (gr. -1-2). pap. 3.99 *(978-0-7696-5865-0(2)*, Brighter Child) Carson-Dellosa Publishing, LLC.

—Puss in Boots. 2009. (Keepsake Stories Ser.). (ENG.). 32p. (gr. -1-3). pap. 3.99 *(978-0-7696-5867-4(9)*, Brighter Child) Carson-Dellosa Publishing, LLC.

—Puss in Boots (El Gato con Botas) 2009. (Keepsake Stories Ser.). (ENG & SPA.). 32p. (gr. -1-2). pap. 3.99 *(978-0-7696-5863-6(6)*, Brighter Child) Carson-Dellosa Publishing, LLC.

—Sleeping Beauty. 2009. (Keepsake Stories Ser.). (ENG.). 32p. (gr. -1-3). pap. 3.99 *(978-0-7696-5866-7(0)*, Brighter Child) Carson-Dellosa Publishing, LLC.

—The Three Billy Goats Gruff. 2009. (Keepsake Stories Ser.). (ENG.). 32p. (gr. -1-3). pap. 3.99 *(978-0-7696-5868-1(7)*, Brighter Child) Carson-Dellosa Publishing, LLC.

—The Three Billy Goats Gruff (Los Tres Chivitos) 2009. (Keepsake Stories Ser.). (ENG & SPA.). 32p. (gr. -1-2). pap. 3.99 *(978-0-7696-5864-3(4)*, Brighter Child) Carson-Dellosa Publishing, LLC.

Our Adobe House: 6 Small Books. (Greetings Ser.: Vol. 2). 24p. (gr. 2-3). 31.00 *(978-0-7635-9428-2(8))* Rigby Education.

Our Adobe House: Big Book. (Greetings Ser.: Vol. 2). 24p. (gr. 2-3). 31.00 *(978-0-7635-5860-4(5))* Rigby Education.

Our New Baby, 6 Packs. (gr. -1-2). 27.00 *(978-0-7635-9469-5(5))* Rigby Education.

Ousley, Pamala. Amy & the Pacifier. 2009. 24p. pap. 15.99 *(978-1-4415-1364-9(7))* Xlibris Corp.

Over the Edge: Magazine Anthology: Level 7, 6 vols. (Comprehension Strand Ser.). (gr. 4-8). 54.00 *(978-0-322-06043-2(5))* Wright Group/McGraw-Hill.

Owen, Anna. A Day Out. Hammond, Andy, illus. 2005. (Collins Big Cat Ser.). (ENG.). 80p. (J). (gr. -1-k). pap. 5.99 *(978-0-00-718555-9(3))* HarperCollins Pubs. Ltd. GBR. Dist: Independent Pubs. Group.

Owings, Jeff. Tiny Todd: Swooped Away. 2009. 20p. pap. 10.49 *(978-1-4490-1214-4(0))* AuthorHouse.

—Tiny Todd: Tiny Todd's First Pet. 2009. 20p. pap. 10.49 *(978-1-4490-1216-8(7))* AuthorHouse.

Oxford University Press Staff & Bassett, Jennifer, eds. Omega Files - Short Stories. 3rd ed. 2008. (ENG., Illus.). 64p. 10.00 *(978-0-19-478913-4(6))* Oxford Univ. Pr., Inc.

Oxford University Press Staff & Lindop, Christine, eds. Australia & New Zealand, Level 3. 3rd ed. 2008. (ENG., Illus.). 80p. 10.00 *(978-0-19-423390-3(1))* Oxford Univ. Pr., Inc.

Oxlade, Chris. Mighty Machines, 8bks. 2005. (QEB Readers). (Illus.). 24p. (J). (gr. -1-3). lib. bdg. 15.95 *(978-1-59566-079-4(8))* QEB Publishing Inc.

—The Mobile Continent White Band. 2016. (Cambridge Reading Adventures Ser.). (ENG.). 32p. pap. 7.81 *(978-1-316-60067-2(X))* Cambridge Univ. Pr.

Paderewski, Elliot. A Baby Brother. 2016. (Rosen REAL Readers: STEM & STEAM Collection). 12p. (gr. 1-k). pap. 6.33 *(978-1-5081-2655-3(0)*, Rosen Classroom) Rosen Publishing Group, Inc., The.

—Born on the Fourth of July. 2016. (Rosen REAL Readers: Social Studies Nonfiction / Fiction: Family, Community, & the World Ser.). 8p. (gr. 1-k). pap. 5.46 *(978-1-5081-2506-8(6)*, Rosen Classroom) Rosen Publishing Group, Inc., The.

—Children Have Basic Rights. 2016. (Rosen REAL Readers: Social Studies Nonfiction / Fiction: Family, Community, & the World Ser.). 12p. (gr. 1-k). pap. 6.33 *(978-1-5081-2320-0(9)*, Rosen Classroom) Rosen Publishing Group, Inc., The.

—Dwayne's Water Fund. 2016. (Rosen REAL Readers: Social Studies Nonfiction / Fiction: Family, Community, & the World Ser.). 12p. (gr. 1-k). pap. 6.33 *(978-1-5081-2568-6(6)*, Rosen Classroom) Rosen Publishing Group, Inc., The.

—The Mystery Plant. 2016. (Rosen REAL Readers: STEM & STEAM Collection). 12p. (gr. 1-k). pap. 6.33 *(978-1-5081-2670-6(4)*, Rosen Classroom) Rosen Publishing Group, Inc., The.

—Waterfall Power. 2016. (Rosen REAL Readers: Social Studies Nonfiction / Fiction: Family, Community, & the World Ser.). 12p. (gr. 1-k). pap. 6.33 *(978-1-5081-2577-8(5)*, Rosen Classroom) Rosen Publishing Group, Inc., The.

—Why Babies Cry. 2016. (Rosen REAL Readers: STEM & STEAM Collection). 12p. (gr. 1-k). pap. 6.33 *(978-1-5081-2440-5(X)*, Rosen Classroom) Rosen Publishing Group, Inc., The.

Paéz, Enrique. Devuelveme el Anillo, Pelo Cepillo. (SPA.). (YA). (gr. 5-8). 112p. *(978-84-216-2561-3(6)*, BU7584); 12th ed. (Illus.). 144p. *(978-84-216-1800-4(8)*, BU5113) Bruño, Editorial ESP. Dist: Lectorum Pubns., Inc.

Page, Nick. Read with Me Three Little Pigs. 2011. 32p. (J). 3.99 *(978-1-78065-013-5(2))* Make Believe Ideas GBR. Dist: Nelson, Thomas Inc.

Page, Nick & Page, Claire. The Good Samaritan. Loy, Nikki, illus. 2006. (Read with Me (Make Believe Ideas) Ser.). 31p. (J). (gr. k-2). *(978-1-84610-174-8(3))* Make Believe Ideas.

—Read with Me Jack & the Beanstalk: Sticker Activity Book. Goodberry, Jo, illus. 2006. (Read with Me (Make Believe Ideas) Ser.). 12p. (J). (gr. k-2). pap. *(978-1-84610-180-9(8))* Make Believe Ideas.

—Read with Me Jonah the Moaner: Sticker Activity Book. Loy, Nikki, illus. 2006. (Read with Me (Make Believe Ideas) Ser.). 12p. (J). (gr. k-2). pap. *(978-1-84610-183-0(2))* Make Believe Ideas.

—Read with Me Rumpelstiltskin: Sticker Activity Book. Baker, Sara, illus. 2006. (Read with Me (Make Believe Ideas) Ser.). 12p. (J). (gr. k-2). pap. *(978-1-84610-182-3(4))* Make Believe Ideas.

—Read with Me Snow White: Sticker Activity Book. Willey, Bee, illus. 2006. (Read with Me (Make Believe Ideas) Ser.). 12p. (J). (gr. k-2). pap. *(978-1-84610-179-3(4))* Make Believe Ideas.

—Read with Me the Elves & the Shoemaker: Sticker Activity Book. Baker, Sara, illus. 2006. (Read with Me (Make Believe Ideas) Ser.). 12p. (J). (gr. k-2). pap. *(978-1-84610-177-9(8))* Make Believe Ideas.

—Read with Me Three Billy Goats Gruff: Sticker Activity Book. Saunders, Katie, illus. 2006. (Read with Me (Make Believe Ideas) Ser.). 12p. (J). (gr. k-2). pap. *(978-1-84610-181-6(6))* Make Believe Ideas.

—Read W/Me 6v. 2006. (Illus.). (J). (gr. -1-3). *(978-5-558-47727-6(X))* Make Believe Ideas.

—Ready to Read Jack & the Beanstalk Sticker Activity Workbook. Goodberry, Jo, illus. 2006. (Ready-to-Read Sticker Ser.). 12p. (J). (gr. -1-3). pap., wbk. ed., act. bk. ed. *(978-1-84610-127-4(1))* Make Believe Ideas.

—The Runaway Son. Baker, Sara, illus. 2006. (Read with Me Ser.). 31p. (J). (gr. k-2). *(978-1-84610-176-2(X))* Make Believe Ideas.

Page, Nick & Claire. Noah & the Ark. 2006. (Read with Me (Make Believe Ideas) Ser.). (Illus.). 32p. (J). (gr. k-2). *(978-1-84610-168-7(9))* Make Believe Ideas.

Page, Philip & Pettit, Marilyn. Much Ado about Nothing. 2005. (ENG., Illus.). 64p. pap. *(978-0-340-88808-7(3))* Cambridge Univ. Pr.

Page, Robin. What Do You Do with a Tail Like This? Jenkins, Steve, illus. 2011. (J). (gr. -1-3). 29.95 *(978-0-545-10698-6(2))* Weston Woods Studios, Inc.

Pahn, Latosha. Come go on a Read along Ride with Me: Read along Ride. 2008. 68p. pap. 9.95 *(978-1-4184-4896-7(6))* AuthorHouse.

Palazzolo, Fran. Wise Owl's First Sounds & Sight Words. 2009. 248p. pap. 88.50 *(978-0-557-08128-8(9))* Lulu Pr., Inc.

—Wise Owl's Vowels. 2009. 290p. pap. 98.95 *(978-0-557-07812-7(1))* Lulu Pr., Inc.

Pan y Canela: Super Classroom Set. (SPA.). (gr. k-2). 1289.61 *(978-0-7362-0445-3(8))* CENGAGE Learning.

Pandora's Box: Level M, 6 vols. 128p. (gr. 2-3). 41.95 *(978-0-7699-1027-7(0))* Shortland Pubns. (U. S. A.) Inc.

Panev, Aleksandar. Queen Nzinga. Stefflbauer, Thomas, illus. 2007. 48p. (J). lib. bdg. 23.08 *(978-1-4242-1641-3(9))* Fitzgerald Bks.

Panman, Sandra & Panman, Richard. The Active Reader for Writers. Panman, Sandra, ed. 3rd rev. ed. 2004. 288p. (C). (gr. 9-12). pap. 24.95 *(978-0-912813-30-1(X))* Active Learning Corp.

Papaloizos, Theodore C. My Greek Reader. Frangouli, Rena, illus. 2004. (GRE & ENG.). 124p. (Orig.). (YA). (gr. 2). pap. *(978-0-932416-46-9(2))* Papaloizos Pubns., Inc.

The Paper Trail: Individual Title Six-Packs. (gr. 1-2). 25.00 *(978-0-7635-9137-3(8))* Rigby Education.

Paprocki, Beth. Storyland: the Marvelous Mccrittersons — Road Trip to Grandma's: A Story Coloring Book. Paprocki, Greg, illus. 2015. (ENG.). 32p. (J). (gr. k-5). pap. 3.99 *(978-0-486-79383-2(4))* Dover Pubns., Inc.

Paris, Stephanie. Drag! Friction & Resistance, 1 vol. 2nd rev. ed. 2013. (Nonfiction Readers Ser.). (ENG.). 64p. (J). (gr. 5-5). pap. 10.99 *(978-1-4333-4940-9(X))* Teacher Created Materials, Inc.

—Drugs & Alcohol, 1 vol. 2nd rev. ed. 2012. (Nonfiction Readers Ser.). (ENG., Illus.). 48p. (J). (gr. 4-4). pap. 9.99 *(978-1-4333-4859-4(4))* Teacher Created Materials, Inc.

—Engineering Feats & Failures, 1 vol. 2nd rev. ed. 2012. (Nonfiction Readers Ser.). (ENG., Illus.). 48p. (J). (gr. 4-4). pap. 9.99 *(978-1-4333-4871-6(3))* Teacher Created Materials, Inc.

—Pecos Bill & Slue-Foot Sue, 1 vol. 2009. (Building Fluency Through Reader's Theater Ser.). (ENG.). 24p. (J). (gr. 2-4). pap. 6.99 *(978-1-4333-0991-5(2))* Teacher Created Materials, Inc.

—Pop! Air & Water Pressure, 1 vol. 2nd rev. ed. 2013. (Nonfiction Readers Ser.). (ENG.). 64p. (J). (gr. 5-5). pap. 10.99 *(978-1-4333-4939-3(6))* Teacher Created Materials, Inc.

—Straight Talk: Smoking, 1 vol. 2nd rev. ed. 2012. (TIME for KIDS(r) Nonfiction Readers Ser.). (ENG., Illus.). 48p. (J). (gr. 4-4). pap. 9.99 *(978-1-4333-4858-7(6))* Teacher Created Materials, Inc.

—Straight Talk - The Truth about Food , 1 vol. 2nd rev. ed. 2012. (Nonfiction Readers Ser.). (ENG.). 48p. (J). (gr. 4-4). pap. 9.99 *(978-1-4333-4857-0(8))* Teacher Created Materials, Inc.

—Technology Feats & Failures, 1 vol. 2nd rev. ed. 2012. (Nonfiction Readers Ser.). (ENG.). 48p. (J). (gr. 4-4). pap. 9.99 *(978-1-4333-4869-3(1))* Teacher Created Materials, Inc.

—Vroom! Speed & Acceleration, 1 vol. 2nd rev. ed. 2013. (Nonfiction Readers Ser.). (ENG.). 64p. (J). (gr. 5-5). pap. 10.99 *(978-1-4333-4938-6(8))* Teacher Created Materials, Inc.

—20th Century: Race to the Moon, 1 vol. 2nd rev. ed. 2013. (Nonfiction Readers Ser.). (ENG.). 64p. (J). (gr. 5-5). pap. 10.99 *(978-1-4333-4899-0(3))* Teacher Created Materials, Inc.

Paris, Stephanie & Kuligowski, Stephanie. 22nd Century - Future of Space, 1 vol. 2nd rev. ed. 2013. (Nonfiction Readers Ser.). (ENG.). 64p. (J). (gr. 5-5). pap. 10.99 *(978-1-4333-4901-0(9))* Teacher Created Materials, Inc.

Parish, Herman. Amelia Bedelia. Avril, Lynne, illus. 2017. (I Can Read Level 1 Ser.). 160p. (J). (gr. -1-3). pap. 16.99 *(978-0-06-244357-1(7)*, Greenwillow Bks.) HarperCollins Pubs.

Parish, Peggy. Amelia Bedelia. Siebel, Fritz, illus. 2017. (I Can Read Level 2 Ser.). 72p. (J). (gr. -1-3). 9.99 ***(978-0-06-257279-0(2)***, Greenwillow Bks.) HarperCollins Pubs.

Parish, Peggy. Amelia Bedelia I Can Read, Set. Siebel, Fritz et al, illus. 2016. (I Can Read Level 2 Ser.). 320p. (J). (gr. -1-3). pap. 16.99 *(978-0-06-244356-4(9)*, Greenwillow Bks.) HarperCollins Pubs.

Parker, Christi E. Abraham Lincoln, 1 vol. 2005. (Primary Source Readers Ser.). (ENG.). 24p. (J). (gr. 4-4). pap. 8.99 *(978-0-7439-8916-9(3))* Shell Educational Publishing.

—American Revolution, 1 vol. 2004. (Primary Source Readers Ser.). (ENG.). 24p. (J). (gr. 5-5). pap. 8.99 *(978-0-7439-8748-6(9))* Shell Educational Publishing.

—Civil War Is Coming, 1 vol. 2005. (Primary Source Readers Ser.). (ENG.). 24p. (J). (gr. 5-5). pap. 8.99 *(978-0-7439-8915-2(5))* Shell Educational Publishing.

—George Washington, 1 vol. 2004. (Primary Source Readers Ser.). (ENG.). 24p. (J). (gr. 4-4). pap. 8.99 *(978-0-7439-8749-3(7))* Shell Educational Publishing.

—Pioneer Trails, 1 vol. 2005. (Primary Source Readers Ser.). (ENG.). 24p. (J). (gr. 5-5). pap. 8.99 *(978-0-7439-8909-1(0))* Shell Educational Publishing.

Parker, Helen. Weird Weapons Intermediate Book with Online Access. 2014. (ENG., Illus.). 28p. (J). pap. 9.50 *(978-1-107-65200-2(6))* Cambridge Univ. Pr.

Parker, Ian. Ride On: Bikes & Riders Who Rule. 2007. (Steck-Vaughn BOLDPRINT Anthologies Ser.). (ENG., Illus.). 48p. (gr. 6-9). pap. 16.90 *(978-1-4190-4026-9(X))* Houghton Mifflin Harcourt Publishing Co.

Parker, John. Sucked In. 2008. (Lightning Strikes Ser.). 96p. (J). pap. *(978-1-921150-62-3(9))* Walker Bks. Australia Pty, Ltd.

Parker, Richard Green. Parker's Second Reader: National Series of Selections for Reading Designe. 2007. (ENG.). 166p. pap. 19.99 *(978-1-4346-0596-2(5))*; 176p. pap. 21.99 *(978-1-4346-0671-6(6))* Creative Media Partners, LLC.

Parker, Steve & Collins UK Staff. Mega Plants. 2016. (ENG.). 32p. (J). (gr. 2-3). pap. 8.95 *(978-0-00-816379-2(0))* HarperCollins Pubs. Ltd. GBR. Dist: Independent Pubs. Group.

Parker, Tyrone, et al. Community Places. 2010. (Reach for Reading Ser.). (ENG., Illus.). 8p. (C). pap. 7.95 *(978-0-7362-7993-2(8))* CENGAGE Learning.

Parkin, Lance & Jones, Mark. Dark Matters: An Unofficial & Unauthorised Guide to Philip Pullman's Dark Materials Trilogy. 2005. (ENG.). 272p. (YA). mass mkt. *(978-0-7535-1025-4(1)*, Virgin Books Limited) Ebury Publishing GBR. Dist: Independent Pubs. Group.

Parnell, Declan. Blueprint for Pablo, 01 vols., 1. 2016. (Rosen REAL Readers: STEM & STEAM Collection). (ENG.). 12p. (J). pap. 6.33 *(978-1-5081-1575-5(3)*, Rosen Classroom) Rosen Publishing Group, Inc., The.

—Dwayne Leads the Song, 01 vols., 1. 2016. (Rosen REAL Readers: Social Studies Nonfiction / Fiction: Family, Community, & the World Ser.). (ENG.). 12p. (J). pap. 6.33 *(978-1-5081-1925-8(2)*, Rosen Classroom) Rosen Publishing Group, Inc., The.

—The Fast Canoe, 01 vols., 1. 2016. (Rosen REAL Readers: Social Studies Nonfiction / Fiction: Family, Community, & the

World Ser.). (ENG.). 8p. (J). pap. 5.46 *(978-1-5081-1830-5(2)*, Rosen Classroom) Rosen Publishing Group, Inc., The.

—Hooray for Bubbles!, 01 vols., 1. 2016. (Rosen REAL Readers: STEM & STEAM Collection). (ENG.). 12p. (J). pap. 6.33 *(978-1-5081-1593-9(1)*, Rosen Classroom) Rosen Publishing Group, Inc., The.

—Ping Cleans Her Room, 01 vols., 1. 2016. (Rosen REAL Readers: Social Studies Nonfiction / Fiction: Family, Community, & the World Ser.). (ENG.). 8p. (J). pap. 5.46 *(978-1-5081-1382-9(3)*, Rosen Classroom) Rosen Publishing Group, Inc., The.

—Sammy's Big Trip, 01 vols., 1. 2016. (Rosen REAL Readers: Social Studies Nonfiction / Fiction: Family, Community, & the World Ser.). (ENG.). 8p. (J). pap. 5.46 *(978-1-5081-1415-4(3)*, Rosen Classroom) Rosen Publishing Group, Inc., The.

—Speedy & Pete, 01 vols., 1. 2016. (Rosen REAL Readers: STEM & STEAM Collection). (ENG.). 8p. (J). pap. 5.46 *(978-1-5081-1438-3(2)*, Rosen Classroom) Rosen Publishing Group, Inc., The.

—Teresa's Construction Challenge, 01 vols., 1. 2016. (Rosen REAL Readers: STEM & STEAM Collection). (ENG.). 12p. (J). pap. 6.33 *(978-1-5081-1539-7(1)*, Rosen Classroom) Rosen Publishing Group, Inc., The.

Parr, Todd. Otto Goes to the Beach. 2014. (Passport to Reading Level 1 Ser.). (J). lib. bdg. 13.55 *(978-0-606-35303-8(8))* Turtleback Bks.

Parramón, José María. Mi Escuela. Borday, Irene, illus. (Coleccion Estoy En...).Tr. of My School. (SPA.). 32p. (J). (gr. k-3). 6.36 *(978-84-342-1004-2(5))* Parramon Ediciones S.A. ESP. Dist: Lectorum Pubns., Inc.

Parramón, José María & Bordoy, Irene. Mi Escuela.Tr. of My School. (SPA., Illus.). (J). (gr. -1-1). 6.95 *(978-958-04-1276-2(6))* Norma S.A. COL. Dist: Distribuidora Norma, Inc.

Parsons, Garry & Donaldson, Julia. The Wrong Kind of Bark. 2nd ed. 2016. (Reading Ladder Ser.). (ENG., Illus.). 48p. (J). (gr. k-2). pap. 7.99 *(978-1-4052-8237-6(1))* Egmont Bks., Ltd. GBR. Dist: Independent Pubs. Group.

Partners: Individual Title Six-Packs. (gr. -1-2). 23.00 *(978-0-7635-8820-5(2))* Rigby Education.

Party Clothes. 2004. (Jasper the Cat Set 1 Ser.). (J). 7.33 *(978-1-58453-279-8(3))* Pioneer Valley Bks.

A Party for the Alley Cats: 3-in-1 Package. (Sails Literacy Ser.). 24p. (gr. 2-18). 57.00 *(978-0-7578-6832-0(0))* Rigby Education.

A Party for the Alley Cats: 6 Small Books. (Sails Literacy Ser.). 24p. (gr. 2-18). 25.00 *(978-0-7578-6828-3(2))* Rigby Education.

A Party for the Alley Cats: Big Book Only. (Sails Literacy Ser.). 24p. (gr. 2-18). 27.00 *(978-0-7578-6820-7(7))* Rigby Education.

Pascal, Francine. Con las Riendas Firmes. Orig. Title: Lucy Takes the Reins. (SPA.). 168p. (J). 6.95 *(978-84-272-4645-4(5))* Molino, Editorial ESP. Dist: AIMS International Bks., Inc.

Pasqualin, Marcia A. Good Ozzy, Bad Bella: Sight Words for First Readers. 2010. 24p. 14.93 *(978-1-4269-4194-8(3))* Trafford Publishing.

El pastel Perfecto: Individual Title Six-Packs. (Literatura 2000 Ser.). (SPA.). (gr. k-1). 28.00 *(978-0-7635-1026-8(2))* Rigby Education.

Patchett, Fiona. Puss in Boots. 2005. 48p. (J). (gr. 2-18). 8.95 *(978-0-7945-0970-5(3)*, Usborne) EDC Publishing.

Patenaude, Jeremy, et al. Little Dolphin. 2014. (DK Readers Ser.). (ENG.). 32p. (J). (gr. k-4). pap. 3.99 *(978-1-4654-1997-2(7)*, DK Children) Dorling Kindersley Publishing, Inc.

Patricelli, Leslie. Boo! / ¡Bu! Patricelli, Leslie, illus. 2017. (Leslie Patricelli Board Bks.). (ENG & SPA., Illus.). 26p. (J). (— 1). bds. 6.99 *(978-0-7636-9314-5(6))* Candlewick Pr.

Pat's Train: KinderReaders, 6 Packs. (Kinderstarters Ser.). 8p. (gr. -1-1). 21.00 *(978-0-7635-8655-3(2))* Rigby Education.

Patterson, Marie. Early American Indian Tribes, 1 vol. 2004. (Primary Source Readers Ser.). (ENG.). 24p. (J). (gr. 5-5). pap. 8.99 *(978-0-7439-8744-8(6))* Shell Educational Publishing.

—Pocahontas, 1 vol. 2004. (Primary Source Readers Ser.). (ENG.). 24p. (J). (gr. 4-4). pap. 8.99 *(978-0-7439-8745-5(4))* Shell Educational Publishing.

Paul. Best Friends. 2012. 24p. pap. 17.99 *(978-1-4772-0755-0(4))* AuthorHouse.

Paul Ahrens-Gray & Ericka Grogan. Fish. 2005. (Illus.). 60p. (J). pap., act. bk. ed. 4.95 *(978-1-59867-001-1(8))* Global Learning, Inc.

Paul, Ann Whitford. Word Builder. Cyrus, Kurt, illus. 2009. (ENG.). 32p. (J). (gr. k-2). 18.99 *(978-1-4169-3981-8(4)*, Simon & Schuster Bks. For Young Readers) Simon & Schuster Bks. For Young Readers.

Paulo the Pilot: Individual Title Six-Packs. (gr. 1-2). 22.00 *(978-0-7635-9187-8(4))* Rigby Education.

Pavón Córdoba, María del Mar. ¡SELENA, SELEEENA! 2005. (Caballo Alado Series-Al Galope Ser.). (SPA & ENG., Illus.). 24p. (J). (gr. k-2). pap. 5.95 *(978-84-7864-885-6(2))* Combel Editorial, S.A. ESP. Dist: Independent Pubs. Group.

Pearce, Kevin. I'm Special Because... 2006. (Neighborhood Readers Ser.). (ENG.). 8p. (gr. 1-3). pap. 5.15 *(978-1-4042-6815-9(4)*, Rosen Classroom) Rosen Publishing Group, Inc., The.

Pearl, Nancy. Book Crush: For Kids & Teens - Recommended Reading for Every Mood, Moment, & Interest. 2007. (Lust Ser.). (ENG., Illus.). 304p. per. 16.95 *(978-1-57061-500-9(4))* Sasquatch Bks.

Pearson Education Staff. Room in the Tower & Other Stories. 2nd ed. 2008. (ENG., Illus.). 48p. pap. 11.99 *(978-1-4058-6962-1(3))* Pearson Education.

—Spin! Grammar, Vocabulary, & Writing. 2003. (ENG.). 112p. (C). pap., stu. ed. 22.80 *(978-0-13-041994-1(X))* Prentice Hall, ESL Dept.

—Spin!, Level E. 2003. (ENG.). 112p. (C). pap., stu. ed. 22.80 *(978-0-13-041999-6(0))* Prentice Hall, ESL Dept.

Pearson, Mary E. & Shelly, Jeff. Puedo Hacer de Todo. Shelly, Jeff, illus. 2011. (Rookie Ready to Learn Español Ser.).Tr. of I Can Do It All. (SPA., Illus.). 40p. (J). pap. 5.95 *(978-0-531-26787-5(3))*; lib. bdg. 23.00 *(978-0-531-26119-4(0))* Scholastic Library Publishing. (Children's Pr.).

Peattie, Cindy. A Cinderella Atlas. Mountford, Karl, illus. 2017. (Text Connections Guided Close Reading Ser.). (J). (gr. 1). *(978-1-4900-1819-5(0))* Benchmark Education Co.

Peattie, Cindy & Benchmark Education Co. Staff. The Secret Language of Elephants. 2014. (Text Connections Ser.). (J). (gr. 5). *(978-1-4900-1367-1(9))* Benchmark Education Co.

Pecci, Mary. Pecci Reading Series: Primer. 2008. (Pecci Reading Ser.). pap. 9.95 *(978-0-943220-16-1(5))* Pecci Educational Pubs.

Peirce, Lincoln. Big Nate on a Roll. 2015. (Big Nate Ser.: 3). (J). lib. bdg. 17.20 *(978-0-606-36958-9(9))* Turtleback Bks.

Penguin Books Staff. We Look. 2003. (Dick & Jane Ser.: 1). (ENG., Illus.). 32p. (J). (gr. k-1). pap. 3.99 *(978-0-448-43400-1(8)*, Penguin Young Readers) Penguin Young Readers Group.

Penguin Young Readers Group Staff. Dick & Jane - Go, Go, Go, 6 vols. 2003. (Dick & Jane Ser.: 6). (ENG., Illus.). 32p. (J). (gr. k-1). pap. 3.99 *(978-0-448-43405-6(9)*, Penguin Young Readers) Penguin Young Readers Group.

—Guess Who, 4 vols. 2003. (Dick & Jane Ser.: 4). (ENG., Illus.). 32p. (J). (gr. 1-2). mass mkt. 3.99 *(978-0-448-43403-2(2)*, Penguin Young Readers) Penguin Young Readers Group.

—Jump & Run, 3 vols. 2003. (Dick & Jane Ser.: 3). (ENG., Illus.). 32p. (J). (gr. k-1). pap. 3.99 *(978-0-448-43402-5(4)*, Penguin Young Readers) Penguin Young Readers Group.

—Something Funny, 2 vols. 2003. (Dick & Jane Ser.: 2). (ENG., Illus.). 32p. (J). (gr. k-1). mass mkt. 3.99 *(978-0-448-43401-8(6)*, Penguin Young Readers) Penguin Young Readers Group.

Penovi, Celina. The Clumsy Stork - la Cigüeña Despistad. 2009. 32p. pap. 17.50 *(978-1-4490-2746-9(6))* AuthorHouse.

The People, Places & Principles of English Language Skills, Chapter 1, Activities. 2003. *(978-1-928629-79-5(2))* Paradigm Accelerated Curriculum.

The People, Places & Principles of English Language Skills, Chapter 1, Text. 2003. *(978-1-928629-69-6(5))* Paradigm Accelerated Curriculum.

The People, Places & Principles of English Language Skills, Chapter 10, Activities. 2003. *(978-1-928629-88-7(1))* Paradigm Accelerated Curriculum.

The People, Places & Principles of English Language Skills, Chapter 10, Text. 2003. *(978-1-928629-78-8(4))* Paradigm Accelerated Curriculum.

The People, Places & Principles of English Language Skills, Chapter 2, Activities. 2003. *(978-1-928629-80-1(6))* Paradigm Accelerated Curriculum.

The People, Places & Principles of English Language Skills, Chapter 2, Text. 2003. *(978-1-928629-70-2(9))* Paradigm Accelerated Curriculum.

The People, Places & Principles of English Language Skills, Chapter 3, Activities. 2003. *(978-1-928629-81-8(4))* Paradigm Accelerated Curriculum.

The People, Places & Principles of English Language Skills, Chapter 3, Text. 2003. *(978-1-928629-71-9(7))* Paradigm Accelerated Curriculum.

The People, Places & Principles of English Language Skills, Chapter 4, Activities. 2003. *(978-1-928629-82-5(2))* Paradigm Accelerated Curriculum.

The People, Places & Principles of English Language Skills, Chapter 4, Text. 2003. *(978-1-928629-72-6(5))* Paradigm Accelerated Curriculum.

The People, Places & Principles of English Language Skills, Chapter 5, Activities. 2003. *(978-1-928629-83-2(0))* Paradigm Accelerated Curriculum.

The People, Places & Principles of English Language Skills, Chapter 5, Text. 2003. *(978-1-928629-73-3(3))* Paradigm Accelerated Curriculum.

The People, Places & Principles of English Language Skills, Chapter 6, Activities. 2003. *(978-1-928629-84-9(9))* Paradigm Accelerated Curriculum.

The People, Places & Principles of English Language Skills, Chapter 6, Text. 2003. *(978-1-928629-74-0(1))* Paradigm Accelerated Curriculum.

The People, Places & Principles of English Language Skills, Chapter 7, Activities. 2003. *(978-1-928629-85-6(7))* Paradigm Accelerated Curriculum.

The People, Places & Principles of English Language Skills, Chapter 7, Text. 2003. *(978-1-928629-75-7(X))* Paradigm Accelerated Curriculum.

The People, Places & Principles of English Language Skills, Chapter 8, Activities. 2003. *(978-1-928629-86-3(5))* Paradigm Accelerated Curriculum.

The People, Places & Principles of English Language Skills, Chapter 8, Text. 2003. *(978-1-928629-76-4(8))* Paradigm Accelerated Curriculum.

The People, Places & Principles of English Language Skills, Chapter 9, Activities. 2003. *(978-1-928629-87-0(3))* Paradigm Accelerated Curriculum.

Peppas, Lynn. Tractors at Work. 2010. (Vehicles on the Move Ser.). (ENG.). 32p. (J). (gr. k-3). pap. *(978-0-7787-3064-4(6))* Crabtree Publishing Co.

Peppers. (Early Intervention Levels Ser.). 23.10 *(978-0-7362-0021-9(5))*; Vol. 4. 3.85 *(978-1-56334-971-3(X))* CENGAGE Learning.

Pérez, Amada Irma. Mi Diario de Aquí Hasta Allá. Gonzalez, Maya Christina, illus. 2013.Tr. of My Diary from Here to There. (ENG & SPA.). 32p. (J). (gr. k). pap. 9.95 *(978-0-89239-230-8(4))* Lee & Low Bks., Inc.

Perritano, John. Fault Lines. 2015. (Red Rhino Nonfiction Ser.). (J). lib. bdg. 20.80 *(978-0-606-37201-5(9))* Turtleback Bks.

Perry, Daniel. The Case of the Missing Shoes. 2013. 28p. pap. 9.95 *(978-1-4787-2649-4(0))* Outskirts Pr., Inc.

Peter & the Wolf. 2016. (Ladybird Tales Ser.). (ENG., Illus.). 48p. (J). (gr. k-2). 9.99 *(978-0-7232-9448-1(8))* Penguin Bks., Ltd. GBR. Dist: Independent Pubs. Group.

Peters, Andrew, et al. Winter Olympics. 2014. (Collins Big Cat Progress Ser.). (ENG., Illus.). 32p. (YA). (gr. 7). pap. 7.99 *(978-0-00-751924-8(9))* HarperCollins Pubs. Ltd. GBR. Dist: Independent Pubs. Group.

Peters, Andrew Fusek. Free Running. 2014. (Collins Big Cat Progress Ser.). (ENG., Illus.). 32p. (J). (gr. 3-4). pap. 7.99 *(978-0-00-751934-7(6))* HarperCollins Pubs. Ltd. GBR. Dist: Independent Pubs. Group.

Peters, Elisa. It's a Bird! 2009. (Everyday Wonders Ser.). 24p. (gr. 1-1). 42.50 *(978-1-61512-321-6(0)*, PowerKids Pr.) Rosen Publishing Group, Inc., The.

—It's a Caterpillar! 2009. (Everyday Wonders Ser.). 24p. (gr. 1-1). 42.50 *(978-1-61512-322-3(9)*, PowerKids Pr.) Rosen Publishing Group, Inc., The.

—It's a Dragonfly! 2009. (Everyday Wonders Ser.). 24p. (gr. 1-1). 42.50 *(978-1-61512-323-0(7)*, PowerKids Pr.) Rosen Publishing Group, Inc., The.

—It's a Sunflower! 2009. (Everyday Wonders Ser.). 24p. (gr. 1-1). 42.50 *(978-1-61512-324-7(5)*, PowerKids Pr.) Rosen Publishing Group, Inc., The.

—It's an Apple Tree! 2009. (Everyday Wonders Ser.). 24p. (gr. 1-1). 42.50 *(978-1-61512-325-4(3)*, PowerKids Pr.) Rosen Publishing Group, Inc., The.

—It's Snow! 2009. (Everyday Wonders Ser.). 24p. (gr. 1-1). 42.50 *(978-1-61512-326-1(1)*, PowerKids Pr.) Rosen Publishing Group, Inc., The.

Petting Gilbert. 2004. (Gilbert the Pig Set 2 Ser.). (J). 7.33 *(978-1-58453-225-5(4))* Pioneer Valley Bks.

Petty, Kate. Don't Wake Stanley, 8 bks. 2005. (QEB Readers). (Illus.). 24p. (J). (gr. -1-3). lib. bdg. 15.95 *(978-1-59566-074-9(7))* QEB Publishing Inc.

Peyton, K. M. Horses. 2009. (Wild Reads Ser.). (ENG., Illus.). 32p. (YA). (gr. k). pap. 4.95 *(978-0-19-911972-1(4))* Oxford Univ. Pr., Inc.

Pfeffer, Judith, illus. We Didn't Know. 2012. 8p. (J). *(978-0-7367-2742-6(6))* Zaner-Bloser, Inc.

Phan, Sandy. American Indians in Texas: Conflict & Survival, 1 vol. 2012. (Primary Source Readers Ser.). (ENG.). 32p. (J). (gr. 4-4). pap. 8.99 *(978-1-4333-5040-5(8))* Teacher Created Materials, Inc.

—The Caddo & Comanche: American Indians Tribes in Texas, 1 vol. 2012. (Primary Source Readers Ser.). (ENG.). 32p. (J). (gr. 3-3). pap. 8.99 *(978-1-4333-5041-2(6))* Teacher Created Materials, Inc.

—Cecil Rhodes: The Man Who Expanded an Empire, 1 vol. 2012. (Primary Source Readers Ser.). (ENG.). 32p. (J). (gr. 4-4). pap. 8.99 *(978-1-4333-5016-0(5))* Teacher Created Materials, Inc.

—Imperialism: Expanding Empires, 1 vol. 2012. (Primary Source Readers Ser.). (ENG.). 32p. (J). (gr. 5-5). pap. 8.99 *(978-1-4333-5015-3(7))* Teacher Created Materials, Inc.

Phelps, Bonnie. Story Time with Our Librarian. 2016. (Community Helpers Ser.). 00024p. (J). (gr. 1-1). pap. 8.25 *(978-1-4994-2708-0(5)*, PowerKids Pr.) Rosen Publishing Group, Inc., The.

Phonemic Awareness Pack. (Phonemic Awareness Pack Ser.). (gr. -1-k). 523.57 incl. audio compact disk *(978-0-7362-0899-4(2))* CENGAGE Learning.

Phonemic Awareness Pack with Tapes. (Phonemic Awareness Pack Ser.). (gr. -1-k). 538.88 *(978-0-7362-0900-7(X))* CENGAGE Learning.

Phonics Decodable Reader 1. 2004. (Scott Foresman Reading Ser.). (gr. 1-18). suppl. ed. 3.35 *(978-0-673-65172-3(X))* Addison-Wesley Educational Pubs., Inc.

Phonics Decodable Reader 2. 2004. (Scott Foresman Reading Ser.). (gr. 1-18). suppl. ed. 3.35 *(978-0-673-65173-0(8))* Addison-Wesley Educational Pubs., Inc.

Phonics Decodable Reader 3. 2004. (Scott Foresman Reading Ser.). (gr. 1-18). suppl. ed. 3.35 *(978-0-673-65174-7(6))* Addison-Wesley Educational Pubs., Inc.

Phonics Decodable Reader 33-41. 2004. (Scott Foresman Reading Ser.). (gr. 1-18). suppl. ed. 7.75 *(978-0-673-65180-8(0))* Addison-Wesley Educational Pubs., Inc.

Phonics Decodable Reader 4. 2004. (Scott Foresman Reading Ser.). (gr. 1-18). suppl. ed. 3.35 *(978-0-673-65175-4(4))* Addison-Wesley Educational Pubs., Inc.

Phonics Decodable Reader 42-50. 2004. (Scott Foresman Reading Ser.). (gr. 1-18). suppl. ed. 7.75 *(978-0-673-65181-5(9))* Addison-Wesley Educational Pubs., Inc.

Phonics Decodable Reader 5. 2004. (Scott Foresman Reading Ser.). (gr. 1-18). suppl. ed. 3.35 *(978-0-673-65176-1(2))* Addison-Wesley Educational Pubs., Inc.

Phonics Practice Book. (De Canciones A Cuentos Ser.). (SPA.). (gr. 1-18). 9.13 *(978-1-56334-895-2(0))* CENGAGE Learning.

Phonics Readers, Bks. 37-72. (Phonics Readers Ser.). (gr. k-2). 932.95 *(978-0-7368-4096-5(6))* Red Brick Learning.

Phonics Readers Big Books. 2005. (J). pap. 95.00 *(978-1-58970-687-3(0))* Lakeshore Learning Materials.

Phonics Readers Bookshelf Collection, 36 bks., Set. 2004. (gr. 1-18). 594.00 *(978-0-328-00401-0(4))*; (gr. 2-18). 495.00 *(978-0-328-00402-7(2))*; (gr. 3-18). 495.00 *(978-0-328-00403-4(0))* Addison-Wesley Educational Pubs., Inc.

Phonics Readers Student Books. 2005. (J). pap. 29.95 *(978-1-58970-685-9(4))* Lakeshore Learning Materials.

Phonics Take-Home Readers. 2004. (Scott Foresman Reading Ser.). (gr. 3-18). 48.00 *(978-0-673-61260-1(0))* Addison-Wesley Educational Pubs., Inc.

Pick a Pet. 2005. (Little Celebrations Thematic Packages Ser.). (J). (gr. k-3). 133.50 *(978-0-673-75387-8(5))* Celebration Pr.

Picou, Lin. Who's Right. Dufalla, Anita, illus. 2012. (ENG.). 24p. (gr. 2-3). pap. 8.95 *(978-1-61810-323-9(7))* Rourke Educational Media.

Picture Perfect Word Book. (gr. -1-2). pap. 206.58 *(978-0-7362-2547-2(1))* CENGAGE Learning.

Pie Day. (Early Intervention Levels Ser.). 28.38 *(978-0-7362-0406-4(7))*; Vol. 12. 4.73 *(978-0-7362-0231-2(5))* CENGAGE Learning.

Piercy, Jennifer. Ellie's Math Adventure. 2013. 28p. pap. 16.09 *(978-1-4669-1909-9(4))* Trafford Publishing.

Pin It! Fix It! (Early Intervention Levels Ser.). 21.30 *(978-0-7362-0389-0(3))*; Vol. 6. 3.55 *(978-0-7362-0169-8(6))* CENGAGE Learning.

Pimot, Karen Hutchins. Night Traveler. Pimot, Karen Hutchins, illus. 2007. (Illus.). 24p. per. 12.95 *(978-1-934246-97-9(2))* Peppertree Pr., The.

Pirotta, Saviour. George & the Dragon - Collins Big Cat. Peluso, Martina, illus. 2015. (Collins Big Cat Ser.). (ENG.). 32p. (J). (gr. 2-3). pap. 8.95 *(978-0-00-812776-3(X))* HarperCollins Pubs. Ltd. GBR. Dist: Independent Pubs. Group.

Pirotta, Saviour. The Talking Bird: Band 13/Topaz. 2017. (Collins Big Cat Tales Ser.). (ENG., Illus.). 32p. (J). (gr. 3-4). pap. 8.99 ***(978-0-00-817935-9(2))*** HarperCollins Pubs. Ltd. GBR. Dist: Independent Pubs. Group.

Pitt, Marilyn & Hileman, Jane. I Like My Stuff. Bianchi, John, illus. 2009. (1G Potato Chip Bks.). (ENG.). 12p. (J). (gr. k-1). pap. 5.99 *(978-1-59301-769-9(3))* American Reading Co.

—Where Is My Boy? Bianchi, John, illus. 2009. (1G Potato Chip Bks.). (ENG.). 12p. (J). (gr. k-1). pap. 5.99 *(978-1-59301-766-8(9))* American Reading Co.

—Where Is That Dog? Bianchi, John, illus. 2009. (1G Potato Chip Bks.). (ENG.). 12p. (J). (gr. k-1). pap. 5.99 *(978-1-59301-770-5(7))* American Reading Co.

Pitt, Marilyn & Sanchez, Lucia M. La Nevada: Snow Dog. Bianchi, John, illus. 2011. (poder de 50 - Libros papas fritas Ser.). (SPA.). 12p. pap. 33.92 *(978-1-61541-439-0(8))* American Reading Co.

—Perro en Apuros: Let Me In. Bianchi, John, illus. 2011. (poder de 50 - Libros papas fritas Ser.). (SPA.). 12p. pap. 33.92 *(978-1-61541-165-8(8))* American Reading Co.

Pitt, Marilyn & Sánchez, Lucia M. Solos en Casa. Bianchi, John, illus. 2011. (1G Libros Papas Fritas Ser.).Tr. of Home Alone. (SPA.). 12p. (J). (gr. k-1). pap. 6.99 *(978-1-61541-409-3(6))* American Reading Co.

Pitt, Marilyn & Sanchez, Lucia M. La Tormenta: The Storm. Bianchi, John, illus. 2011. (poder de 50 - Libros papas fritas Ser.). (SPA.). 12p. pap. 33.92 *(978-1-61541-441-3(X))* American Reading Co.

Pittis, Arthur M. As My Heart Awakes: A Waldorf Reader for Early Third Grade. Mitchell, David S., ed. Peacock, Ausa M., illus. 2005. (J). bds. 10.00 *(978-1-888365-62-7(5))* Waldorf Publications.

—Fee Fi Fo Fum: A Waldorf Reader for Late Second Grade. Mitchell, David S., ed. Peacock, Ausa M., illus. 2005. (J). bds. 10.00 *(978-1-888365-63-4(3))* Waldorf Publications.

—Sun So Hot I Froze to Death: A Waldorf Reader for Advanced Fourth Grade. Mitchell, David S., ed. Peacock, Ausa M., illus. 2005. (ENG.). (J). bds. 12.00 *(978-1-888365-65-8(X))* Waldorf Publications.

—When I Hear My Heart Wonder: A Waldorf Reader for Late Third Grade. Mitchell, David S., ed. Peacock, Ausa M., illus. 2005. (J). bds. 10.00 *(978-1-888365-66-5(8))* Waldorf Publications.

The Pizza Shop, 2 Packs. (Chiquilibros Ser.). (gr. -1-1). 12.00 *(978-0-7635-8535-8(1))* Rigby Education.

Places: KinderFacts Individual Title Six-Packs. (Kinderstarters Ser.). 8p. (gr. -1-1). 21.00 *(978-0-7635-8746-8(X))* Rigby Education.

Places in My Community. 2016. (Places in My Community Ser.). 00024p. (J). (gr. 1-1). 94.40 *(978-1-4994-2659-5(3)*, PowerKids Pr.) Rosen Publishing Group, Inc., The.

El Planeta de los Cuentos.Tr. of Planet of Storybook Tales. (SPA.). (J). *(978-84-7773-630-1(8))* Grafalco, S.A.

Platt, Richard. The Golden Age of Baghdad. 2017. (ENG.). 56p. (J). pap. 8.99 ***(978-0-00-820895-0(6))*** HarperCollins Pubs. Ltd. GBR. Dist: Independent Pubs. Group.

Platt, Richard. The Maya. 2015. (Collins Big Cat Ser.). (ENG., Illus.). 80p. (J). (gr. 5). pap. 9.95 *(978-0-00-812797-8(2))* HarperCollins Pubs. Ltd. GBR. Dist: Independent Pubs. Group.

Platt, Richard & Lawrie, Robin. Palaces, Peasants & Plagues: England in the 14th Century. 2014. (Collins Big Cat Ser.). (ENG.). 576p. (J). (gr. 5). pap. 9.95 *(978-0-00-753016-8(1))* HarperCollins Pubs. Ltd. GBR. Dist: Independent Pubs. Group.

Play the Game You Know. 2005. (Book Treks Ser.). (J). 37.95 *(978-0-7652-3258-8(8))* Celebration Pr.

Pobst, Sandy. Scientific Discovery in the Renaissance: Text Pairs. 2008. (Bridges/Navigators Ser.). (J). (gr. 6). 89.00 *(978-1-4108-8448-0(1))* Benchmark Education Co.

Pocket Chart. (gr. -1-12). 26.27 *(978-0-7362-1100-0(4))* CENGAGE Learning.

Poe, Edgar Allen. TALES OF TERROR LEVEL 3 LOWER-INTERMEDIATE. 2009. (ENG., Illus.). 80p. pap. 12.75 *(978-84-8323-532-4(3))* Cambridge Univ. Pr.

Police Work. 2005. (Book Treks Ser.). (J). (gr. 3-18). stu. ed. 34.95 *(978-0-673-62839-8(6))* Celebration Pr.

Pollack, Pam & Belviso, Meg. Gallinas de Aqui para Alla. Adams, Lynn, illus. 2008. (Math Matters en Espanol Ser.). (SPA.). 32p. (J). (gr. -1-3). pap. 5.95 *(978-1-57565-268-9(4))* Kane Press, Inc.

Popcorn: KinderFacts, 6 Packs. (Kinderstarters Ser.). 8p. (gr. -1-1). 21.00 *(978-0-7635-8747-5(8))* Rigby Education.

Popper, Lisa. Bunny Bop. 2004. (Illus.). (J). pap. *(978-0-9708947-0-0(8))* Northern Speech Services.

—Danny Dragon. 2004. (Illus.). 16p. (J). pap. *(978-0-9708947-6-2(7))* Northern Speech Services.

—Hanna Hippo. 2004. (Illus.). 16p. (J). pap. *(978-0-9708947-5-5(9))* Northern Speech Services.

—Len & Lil. 2004. (J). pap. *(978-0-9761967-2-3(7))* Northern Speech Services.

—Let' Make Music. 2004. (J). pap. *(978-0-9761967-1-6(9))* Northern Speech Services.

—My Rad Dad. 2005. (ENG.). (J). pap. 69.00 *(978-0-9765497-2-7(7))* Northern Speech Services.

—Nifty Noodle. 2004. (Illus.). 16p. (J). pap. *(978-0-9708947-4-8(0))* Northern Speech Services.

—Patty the Pink Pig. 2004. (J). pap. *(978-0-9761967-0-9(0))* Northern Speech Services.

—Rat Rap. 2004. 16p. (J). pap. *(978-0-9708947-9-3(1))* Northern Speech Services.

—Sammy. 2004. 16p. (J). pap. *(978-0-9708947-8-6(3))* Northern Speech Services.

—Timmy Turtle. 2004. 16p. (J). pap. *(978-0-9708947-7-9(5))* Northern Speech Services.

Posada, Jorge. Sí, Puedes. Colón, Raúl, illus. 2010.Tr. of Play Ball! (SPA.). 32p. (J). (gr. 1-5). 6.99 *(978-1-4169-9826-6(8)*, Simon & Schuster/Paula Wiseman Bks.) Simon & Schuster/Paula Wiseman Bks.

Posner-Sanchez, Andrea. Hello, Olaf! 2015. (Disney Princess Step into Reading Ser.). lib. bdg. 14.75 *(978-0-606-36663-2(6))* Turtleback Bks.

Povey, Jeff. Shift. 2017. (ENG.). 368p. (J). pap. 9.99 *(978-1-4711-1868-5(1),* Simon & Schuster Children's) Simon & Schuster, Ltd. GBR. Dist: Simon & Schuster, Inc.

Powell, Jillian. Caribbean Carnival. 2016. (ENG., Illus.). 32p. (J). (gr. 2-3). pap. 8.95 *(978-0-00-816383-9(9))* HarperCollins Pubs. Ltd. GBR. Dist: Independent Pubs. Group.

—The First World War. 2014. (Collins Big Cat Progress Ser.). (ENG., Illus.). 32p. (J). (gr. 4-5). pap. 7.99 *(978-0-00-751936-1(2))* HarperCollins Pubs. Ltd. GBR. Dist: Independent Pubs. Group.

—Olympic Heroes. 2012. (Collins Big Cat Ser.). (ENG., Illus.). 24p. (J). (gr. k-1). pap. 6.99 *(978-0-00-746190-5(9))* HarperCollins Pubs. Ltd. GBR. Dist: Independent Pubs. Group.

—Oops! Gulliver, Amanda, illus. 2013. (Start Reading Ser.). (ENG.). 24p. (gr. k-1). pap. 41.94 *(978-1-4765-3227-1(3));* pap. 7.95 *(978-1-4765-3190-8(0))* Capstone Press of Coughlan Cos.

—War Art. 2014. (Collins Big Cat Progress Ser.). (ENG., Illus.). 32p. (J). (gr. 5-6). pap. 7.99 *(978-0-00-751930-9(3))* HarperCollins Pubs. Ltd. GBR. Dist: Independent Pubs. Group.

Power Out. (Early Intervention Levels Ser.). 21.42 *(978-0-7362-1056-0(3))* CENGAGE Learning.

Power Reading, 26 vols. 2003. (Illus.). (gr. k-9). vinyl bd. incl. audio *(978-1-883186-37-1(4),* PPS 25); vinyl bd. incl. audio *(978-1-883186-35-7(8),* PPS 25) National Reading Styles Institute, Inc.

Power Reading: Power PAK. 2005. (Illus.). 80p. (J). (gr. 2-4). vinyl bd. 129.95 *(978-1-883186-73-9(0),* PPMX2-3); (gr. 4-5). vinyl bd. 129.95 *(978-1-883186-72-2(2),* PPMX4-5) National Reading Styles Institute, Inc.

Power Reading: Power PAK 4C. 2005. (Illus.). 80p. (J). (gr. 4-5). vinyl bd. 129.95 *(978-1-883186-70-8(6),* PPO4C) National Reading Styles Institute, Inc.

Prasadam-Halls, Smriti. Norman the Naughty Knight. Smith, Ian, illus. 2016. (Reading Ladder Ser.). (ENG.). 48p. (J). (gr. k-2). pap. 7.99 *(978-1-4052-8214-7(2))* Egmont Bks., Ltd. GBR. Dist: Independent Pubs. Group.

Prasadam-Halls, Smriti. Norman the Naughty Knight & the Flying Horse. Smith, Ian, illus. 2017. (Reading Ladder Ser.). (ENG.). 48p. (J). (gr. k-2). pap. 7.99 ***(978-1-4052-8453-0(6))*** Egmont Bks., Ltd. GBR. Dist: Independent Pubs. Group.

Pre-K Literacy Library. 2003. 430.50 *(978-0-7652-2478-1(X))* Modern Curriculum Pr.

Preece, Phil. Nightmare Park. 2004. (Shades Ser.). 52p. (J). pap. *(978-0-237-52730-3(8))* Evans Brothers, Ltd.

Prentice-Hall Staff. Bridge to Terabithia. 2nd ed. (J). stu. ed. *(978-0-13-717109-5(9))* Prentice Hall (Schl. Div.).

Prereading Activities (K) 2003. (J). *(978-1-58232-045-8(4))* ECS Learning Systems, Inc.

Preschool Books 800083, 10. 2005. (J). bds. *(978-1-59794-001-6(1))* Environments, Inc.

PRESS, Celebration. America's Secret Weapon: The Navajo Code Talkers of World War II. 2003. (ENG.). (J). (gr. 6-8). pap. 37.95 *(978-0-7652-3246-5(4),* Celebration Pr.) Pearson Schl.

—Blast Zone: The Eruption & Recovery of Mount St. Helens. 2003. (ENG.). (J). (gr. 6-8). pap. 37.95 *(978-0-7652-3245-8(6),* Celebration Pr.) Pearson Schl.

—The Case of the Missing Planet. 2003. (ENG.). (J). (gr. 2-5). pap., stu. ed. 34.95 *(978-0-673-62845-9(0),* Celebration Pr.) Pearson Schl.

—Communicating with Animals. 2003. (ENG.). (J). (gr. 6-8). pap. 37.95 *(978-0-7652-3247-2(2),* Celebration Pr.) Pearson Schl.

—Hanging Around Bats. 2003. (ENG.). (J). (gr. 2-5). pap., stu. ed. 34.95 *(978-0-673-62834-3(5),* Celebration Pr.) Pearson Schl.

—The Hot Shots. 2003. (ENG.). (J). (gr. 6-8). pap. 37.95 *(978-0-7652-3257-1(X),* Celebration Pr.) Pearson Schl.

—Hunting Crocodiles with Steve Irwin. 2003. (ENG.). (J). (gr. 2-5). pap., stu. ed. 34.95 *(978-0-673-62080-4(8),* Celebration Pr.) Pearson Schl.

—Looking at Lizards. 2003. (ENG.). (J). (gr. 2-5). pap., stu. ed. 34.95 *(978-0-673-62835-0(3),* Celebration Pr.) Pearson Schl.

—Remarkable Robots. 2003. (ENG.). (J). (gr. 6-8). pap. 37.95 *(978-0-7652-3243-4(X),* Celebration Pr.) Pearson Schl.

—The Renaissance Kids. 2003. (ENG.). (J). (gr. 6-8). pap. 37.95 *(978-0-7652-3255-7(3),* Celebration Pr.) Pearson Schl.

—Scream Machines: All about Roller Coasters. 2003. (ENG.). (J). (gr. 6-8). pap. 37.95 *(978-0-7652-3244-1(8),* Celebration Pr.) Pearson Schl.

PRESS, Modern Curriculum. Sing, Spell, Read & Write Summer School Intervention Kit: Level 1 Student Pack. 2003. (ENG.). (J). (gr. 1-1). 32.95 *(978-0-7652-3233-5(2),* Modern Curriculum Pr.) Pearson Schl.

—Sing, Spell, Read & Write Summer School Intervention Kit: Off We Go. 2003. (ENG.). (J). (gr. 1-1). pap., stu. ed. 8.50 *(978-0-7652-3173-4(5),* Modern Curriculum Pr.) Pearson Schl.

—Sing, Spell, Read & Write Summer School Intervention Kit: Raceway. 2003. (ENG.). (J). (gr. 1-1). pap., stu. ed. 12.95 *(978-0-7652-3174-1(3),* Modern Curriculum Pr.) Pearson Schl.

Price, Sean Stewart & Price, Sean. Attila the Hun: Leader of the Barbarian Hordes. 2009. (Wicked History Ser.). (ENG.). 128p. (J). (gr. 6-12). pap. 5.95 *(978-0-531-20737-6(4),* Watts, Franklin) Scholastic Library Publishing.

Price, Stern, Sloan Publishing Staff & Merrell, Billy. Bob's Burgers Mad Libs. 2015. (Mad Libs Ser.). (ENG.). 48p. (J). (gr. 3-7). bds. 4.99 *(978-0-8431-8294-1(6),* Mad Libs) Penguin Young Readers Group.

Priddy, Roger. Treasure Hunt for Boys. 2010. (ENG.). 22p. (J). (gr. k-3). bds. 9.99 *(978-0-312-50818-0(2),* 9780312508180, Priddy Bks.) St. Martin's Pr.

Prime Time History, 4 vols., Set. Incl. Crusades: The Two Hundred Years War: The Clash Between the Cross & the Crescent in the Middle East 1096-1291. Harpur, James. 118p. lib. bdg. 42.60 *(978-1-4042-1367-8(8));* Troy: The Myth & Reality Behind the Epic Legend. McCarty, Nick. 122p. lib. bdg. 42.60 *(978-1-4042-1365-4(1));* (Illus.). (YA). (gr. 9-12). 2008. 2008. Set lib. bdg. 159.80 *(978-1-4042-1487-3(9))* Rosen Publishing Group, Inc., The.

The Princess & the Pea. 2015. (ENG., Illus.). 32p. (J). (gr. -1-3). *(978-1-78393-576-5(6))* Make Believe Ideas.

Prior, Jennifer. All Aboard! How Trains Work, 1 vol. 2nd rev. ed. 2011. (Nonfiction Readers Ser.). (ENG.). 28p. (J). (gr. 3-3). pap. 8.99 *(978-1-4333-3656-0(1))* Teacher Created Materials, Inc.

—The Digestive System, 1 vol. 2nd rev. ed. 2012. (Nonfiction Readers Ser.). (ENG.). 32p. (J). (gr. 3-3). pap. 8.99 *(978-1-4333-3677-5(4))* Teacher Created Materials, Inc.

—The Five Senses, 1 vol. 2nd rev. ed. 2012. (Nonfiction Readers Ser.). (ENG.). 32p. (J). (gr. 3-3). pap. 8.99 *(978-1-4333-3676-8(6))* Teacher Created Materials, Inc.

—The Human Life Cycle, 1 vol. 2nd rev. ed. 2012. (Nonfiction Readers Ser.). (ENG.). 32p. (J). (gr. 3-3). pap. 8.99 *(978-1-4333-3678-2(2))* Teacher Created Materials, Inc.

—Take Off! All about Airplanes, 1 vol. 2nd rev. ed. 2011. (Nonfiction Readers Ser.). (ENG.). 28p. (J). (gr. 3-3). pap. 8.99 *(978-1-4333-3655-3(3))* Teacher Created Materials, Inc.

—Zoom! How Cars Move, 1 vol. 2nd rev. ed. 2011. (Nonfiction Readers Ser.). (ENG.). 28p. (J). (gr. 3-3). pap. 8.99 *(978-1-4333-3657-7(X))* Teacher Created Materials, Inc.

Pritchard, Gabby. The Great Inventor. Gallego, Pablo, illus. 2016. (Cambridge Reading Adventures Ser.). (ENG.). 16p. pap. 6.56 *(978-1-316-50083-5(7))* Cambridge Univ. Pr.

—The Great Jewelled Egg Mystery Turquoise Band. Franco, Paula, illus. 2016. (Cambridge Reading Adventures Ser.). (ENG.). 16p. pap. 6.56 *(978-1-107-57614-8(8))* Cambridge Univ. Pr.

—Look! It's Baby Duck Red Band. Boden, Lucy, illus. 2016. (Cambridge Reading Adventures Ser.). (ENG.). 16p. pap. 6.56 *(978-1-107-54957-9(4))* Cambridge Univ. Pr.

—Lost! Blue Band. Stuart, Jon, illus. 2016. (Cambridge Reading Adventures Ser.). (ENG.). 16p. pap. 6.56 *(978-1-316-60078-8(5))* Cambridge Univ. Pr.

—Omar in Trouble Orange Band. Pérez, Moni, illus. 2016. (Cambridge Reading Adventures Ser.). (ENG.). 16p. pap. 6.56 *(978-1-316-50329-4(1))* Cambridge Univ. Pr.

—Our Den. Girasole, Alessia, illus. 2016. (Cambridge Reading Adventures Ser.). (ENG.). 16p. pap. 6.56 *(978-1-316-50078-1(0))* Cambridge Univ. Pr.

—Turtle Is a Hero Green Band. Di Baldo, Fabrizio, illus. 2016. (Cambridge Reading Adventures Ser.). (ENG.). 16p. pap. 6.56 *(978-1-107-55046-9(7))* Cambridge Univ. Pr.

Protobunker Studio Staff & Wells, H. G. La Guerra de los Mundos. Ruiz, Alfonso, illus. 2010. (Classic Fiction Ser.). (SPA.). 72p. (gr. 2-3). 27.99 *(978-1-4342-2322-7(1),* Graphic Revolve en Español) Stone Arch Bks.

Prue, Sally. Big Bad Troll. Knight, Tom, illus. 2017. (Reading Ladder Ser.). (ENG.). 48p. (J). (gr. k-2). pap. 7.99 ***(978-1-4052-7825-6(0))*** Egmont Bks., Ltd. GBR. Dist: Independent Pubs. Group.

Publications International Ltd. Staff, ed. Baby Einstein. 2007. (J). 10.98 *(978-1-4127-7467-3(5))* Publications International, Ltd.

—Disney Pixar Cars: Cuentos de Miedo (Little English Spanish Sound Book) 2011. 12p. (J). bds. 10.98 *(978-1-4508-1401-0(8))* Phoenix International Publications, Inc.

—Disney Pixar Cars 2 - World Tour. 2011. 14p. (J). 17.98 *(978-1-4508-1473-7(5))* Phoenix International Publications, Inc.

—Disney Pixar Cars 2 (Look & Find Soft Cover) 2011. 20p. (J). pap. 5.98 *(978-1-4508-1457-7(3))* Publications International, Ltd.

—Disney Pixar Cars 2 Play-a-Sound Book. 2011. 24p. (J). 12.98 *(978-1-4508-0569-8(8))* Phoenix International Publications, Inc.

—Disney Pixar Cars Story Reader 2. 0 Unit. 2011. (J). 30.98 *(978-1-4508-0588-9(4))* Publications International, Ltd.

—Disney Princess Storybook & Magic Bracelet. 2010. 12p. (J). bds. 12.98 *(978-1-4127-9912-6(0))* Phoenix International Publications, Inc.

—Early Learning: My First Library. 2010. 10p. (J). bds. *(978-0-7853-7919-5(3),* 0785379193) Phoenix International Publications, Inc.

—Handy Manny: Fiesta Fun. 2008. (J). bds. 10.98 *(978-1-4127-8867-0(6))* Publications International, Ltd.

—Padded Treasury 160 Spa Sesame Street. 2009. 160p. 12.98 *(978-1-4127-9548-7(6))* Phoenix International Publications, Inc.

—Ring-a-Ling! A Friend Is Here. 2010. 12p. (J). 9.98 *(978-1-4127-7939-5(1))* Phoenix International Publications, Inc.

Publishers, Chelsea House, creator. Scientific American Set, 8-Volumes. 2007. (Scientific American Ser.). (gr. 5-8). 240.00 *(978-0-7910-9811-0(7),* Chelsea Hse.) Facts On File, Inc.

PuffFlashBang! (Lexile Levels Ser.). 9.09 *(978-1-56334-703-0(2))* CENGAGE Learning.

Pug & Chug: Set C Individual Title Six-Packs. (Supersonic Phonics Ser.). (gr. k-3). 29.00 *(978-0-7635-0544-8(7))* Rigby Education.

Pugliano-Martin, Carol. The Day I Followed the Pickle. Beckes, Shirley, illus. 2004. (Reader's Theater Ser.). (J). pap. *(978-1-4108-2297-0(4),* A22974) Benchmark Education Co.

—The Earth on Turtle's Back: Set Of 6. 2011. (Early Connections Ser.). (J). pap. 39.00 net. *(978-1-4108-1555-2(2))* Benchmark Education Co.

—Famous Americans: Fluency-Building Plays with Activities That Expand Vocabulary & Content Knowledge. 2009. (15 Plays for Beginning Readers Ser.). (ENG.). 48p. pap. 11.99 *(978-0-545-11082-2(3),* Teaching Resources) Scholastic, Inc.

—Why Spiders Have Small Waists. 2004. (Shared Connections Ser.). (J). pap. *(978-1-4108-1645-0(1));* instr.'s gde. ed. 27.00 *(978-1-4108-1621-4(4))* Benchmark Education Co.

Punter, Russell. Cow Takes a Bow. Blunt, Fred, illus. 2014. (Usborne Phonics Readers Ser.). (ENG.). (J). pap. 6.99 *(978-0-7945-3368-7(X),* Usborne) EDC Publishing.

—Underpants for Ants. Blunt, Fred, illus. 2014. (Usborne Phonics Readers Ser.). (ENG.). (J). (gr. -1-3). pap. 6.99 *(978-0-7945-3396-0(5),* Usborne) EDC Publishing.

Punter, Russell & MacKinnon, Mairi. Snail Brings the Mail. Blunt, Fred, illus. 2014. (Usborne Phonics Readers Ser.). (ENG.). (J). pap. 6.99 *(978-0-7945-3369-4(8),* Usborne) EDC Publishing.

Puri, Devi. Sydney Works at the School Store. 2013. (InfoMax Readers Ser.). (ENG.). 24p. (J). (gr. 3-4). pap. 49.50 *(978-1-4777-2589-4(X));* (Illus.). pap. 8.25 *(978-1-4777-2588-7(1))* Rosen Publishing Group, Inc., The. (Rosen Classroom).

Purple & Gold Levels Certificate Only. (gr. k-5). 89.00 *(978-0-7578-6541-1(0))* Rigby Education.

Puss in Boots. 2015. (ENG., Illus.). 32p. (J). (gr. -1-3). *(978-1-78393-578-9(2))* Make Believe Ideas.

Pyers. Sail Main5 Monkeys, Diverse Animals. 2003. (Rigby Sails Ser.). (ENG.). 32p. (gr. 5-5). pap. 9.50 *(978-0-7578-8019-3(3))* Rigby Education.

Pym, Tasha. Have You Ever? Elworthy, Antony, illus. 2007. (Collins Big Cat Ser.). (ENG.). 24p. (J). (gr. -1-k). pap. 5.99 *(978-0-00-718654-9(1))* HarperCollins Pubs. Ltd. GBR. Dist: Independent Pubs. Group.

—Monster Mess. Villet, Olivia, illus. 2007. (Collins Big Cat Ser.). (ENG.). 16p. (J). (gr. -1-k). pap. 5.99 *(978-0-00-718650-1(9))* HarperCollins Pubs. Ltd. GBR. Dist: Independent Pubs. Group.

—Super Sculptures. Elworthy, Antony, photos by. 2006. (Collins Big Cat Ser.). (ENG., Illus.). 24p. (J). (gr. 1-1). pap. 6.99 *(978-0-00-718686-0(X))* HarperCollins Pubs. Ltd. GBR. Dist: Independent Pubs. Group.

Pym, Tasha & Pichon, Liz. Colour Bears. 2006. (Collins Big Cat Ser.). (ENG., Illus.). 56p. (J). (gr. -1-k). pap. 5.99 *(978-0-00-718652-5(5))* HarperCollins Pubs. Ltd. GBR. Dist: Independent Pubs. Group.

QEB Start Reading & Writing National Book Stores Edition: Little Red Riding Hood. 2006. (J). per. *(978-1-59566-267-5(7))* QEB Publishing Inc.

QEB Start Reading Set. 2006. (J). per. *(978-1-59566-334-4(7))* QEB Publishing Inc.

Quality Time Easy Readers, 5 bks. (Illus.). (J). lib. bdg. 64.75 *(978-1-56674-925-1(5))* Forest Hse. Publishing Co., Inc.

Quan-D'Eramo, Sandra. The 10 Best TV Game Shows. 2008. 14.99 *(978-1-55448-494-2(4))* Scholastic Library Publishing.

—The 10 Most Amazing Animated Movies. 2007. (J). 14.99 *(978-1-55448-513-0(4))* Scholastic Library Publishing.

Quasar Kids. (J). (gr. 3-5). 75.00 *(978-0-669-13453-7(8))* Houghton Mifflin Harcourt School Pubs.

Queen of the Bean: Individual Title Six-Packs. (Action Packs Ser.). 104p. (gr. 3-5). 44.00 *(978-0-7635-2983-3(4))* Rigby Education.

Queen on a Quilt. (J). *(978-0-8136-5372-3(X))* Modern Curriculum Pr.

Quible, Rennie G. Upepo the Rainmaker. 2008. 44p. pap. 17.49 *(978-1-4363-8454-4(0))* Xlibris Corp.

Quick & Quiet. (Early Intervention Levels Ser.). 21.30 *(978-0-7362-0376-0(1));* Vol. 3. 3.55 *(978-0-7362-0097-4(5))* CENGAGE Learning.

Quinley, Elliot & Greene, Janice. Read Reflect Respond 2, 1 vol. 2015. (Read Reflect Respond Ser.). (ENG.). (J). (gr. 5-12). 44.95 *(978-1-68021-002-6(5))* Saddleback Educational Publishing, Inc.

Quintana, Juan. Farmer's Market. 2003. (Rise & Shine Ser.). (ENG.). (C). pap. 7.95 *(978-0-7362-1898-6(X))* CENGAGE Learning.

Qusar Kids. (J). (gr. 3-5). pap. 9.90 *(978-0-669-15294-4(3))* Houghton Mifflin Harcourt School Pubs.

Rabe, Tish. Big Snowman, Little Snowman. Random House Disney Staff, illus. 2013. (Step into Reading Ser.). (ENG.). 32p. (J). (gr. -1-1). 3.99 *(978-0-7364-3119-4(5),* RH/Disney) Random Hse. Children's Bks.

—Have No Fear! Halloween Is Here!(Dr. Seuss/Cat in the Hat) Brannon, Tom, illus. 2016. (Step into Reading Ser.). (ENG.). 24p. (J). (gr. -1-1). 4.99 *(978-1-101-93492-0(1),* Random Hse. Bks. for Young Readers) Random Hse. Children's Bks.

—Innovative Kids Readers: Milly's Silly Suitcase - Level 1. Janovitz, Marilyn, illus. 2006. (J). (gr. -1-1). 6.99 *(978-1-58476-493-9(7))* Innovative Kids.

Rabley, Stephen. Marcel & Mona Lisa Book, Pack. 2nd ed. 2016. (ENG., Illus.). 16p. pap. 14.65 incl. audio compact disk ***(978-1-4058-8064-0(3))*** Pearson Education.

Rabley, Stephen. Red Rock/Roca Roja. Rabley, Stephen & Ursell, Martin, illus. 2009. (Let's Read! Bks.). (FRE & ENG.). 32p. (J). (gr. 3-7). pap. 4.99 *(978-0-7641-4360-1(3))* Barron's Educational Series, Inc.

Rabley, Stephen & Pearson Education Staff. Maisie & the Dolphin. 2nd ed. 2009. (ENG.). 20p. pap. 11.99 *(978-1-4058-6954-6(2))* Pearson Education.

Raby, Charlotte. City Tours. 2017. (ENG., Illus.). 48p. (J). pap. 8.99 ***(978-0-00-820882-0(4))*** HarperCollins Pubs. Ltd. GBR. Dist: Independent Pubs. Group.

The Race: Individual Title Six-Packs. (gr. 1-2). 22.00 *(978-0-7635-9165-6(3))* Rigby Education.

Radlauer, Edward. More Readers, 3 bks. (Illus.). (J). (gr. -1-4). lib. bdg. 38.85 *(978-1-56674-922-0(0))* Forest Hse. Publishing Co., Inc.

Ragbag: Set A Individual Title Six-Packs. (Supersonic Phonics Ser.). (gr. k-3). 29.00 *(978-0-7635-0529-5(3))* Rigby Education.

Rainbow Fish Readers 800884, 4 vols. 2005. (J). pap. *(978-1-59794-059-7(3))* Environments, Inc.

Raise a Reader: Language Learning System Level 1. 2006. (SPA.). (J). bds. incl. DVD *(978-0-9785744-0-6(0))* LTL Media LLC.

Ralphs, Matt. Space Jump. 2014. (Collins Big Cat Progress Ser.). (ENG., Illus.). 32p. (J). (gr. 5-6). pap. 7.99 *(978-0-00-751938-5(9))* HarperCollins Pubs. Ltd. GBR. Dist: Independent Pubs. Group.

Ramirez, Iz. Bob the Lizard, 1 vol. Swope, Brenda, illus. 2009. 26p. pap. 24.95 *(978-1-60749-232-0(6))* America Star Bks.

Ramirez, Lasean. Jamal's Wagon. 2016. (Rosen REAL Readers: STEM & STEAM Collection). 8p. (gr. 1-k). pap. 5.46 *(978-1-5081-2580-8(5),* Rosen Classroom) Rosen Publishing Group, Inc., The.

Randolph, Joanne. Electricity in My World. 2007. (Journeys Ser.). (ENG.). 24p. (gr. k-8). pap. 7.05 *(978-1-4042-8418-0(4),* Rosen Classroom) Rosen Publishing Group, Inc., The.

—Let's Draw a Butterfly with Circles. 2009. (Let's Draw with Shapes Ser.). 24p. (gr. k-k). 42.50 *(978-1-61514-204-0(5),* PowerKids Pr.) Rosen Publishing Group, Inc., The.

—Let's Draw a Horse with Rectangles. 2009. (Let's Draw with Shapes Ser.). 24p. (gr. k-k). 42.50 *(978-1-61514-209-5(6),* PowerKids Pr.) Rosen Publishing Group, Inc., The.

—Let's Draw a Truck with Shapes. 2009. (Let's Draw with Shapes Ser.). 24p. (gr. k-k). 42.50 *(978-1-61514-212-5(6),* PowerKids Pr.) Rosen Publishing Group, Inc., The.

Random House. All about the Troll. Random House, illus. 2016. (Step into Reading Ser.). (ENG., Illus.). 32p. (J). (gr. -1-2). pap. 4.99 *(978-0-399-55903-7(5),* Random Hse. Bks. for Young Readers) Random Hse. Children's Bks.

—Barbie Dreamtopia Step into Reading (Barbie) 2017. (Step into Reading Ser.). (ENG.). 24p. (J). (gr. -1-1). lib. bdg. 12.99 ***(978-1-5247-1639-4(1));*** (Illus.). pap. 4.99 ***(978-1-5247-1638-7(3))*** Random Hse. Children's Bks. (Random Hse. Bks. for Young Readers).

—Farm Alarm! (Team Umizoomi) Fruchter, Jason, illus. 2014. (Step into Reading Ser.). (ENG.). 24p. (J). (gr. -1-1). pap. 3.99 *(978-0-385-38508-4(0),* Random Hse. Bks. for Young Readers) Random Hse. Children's Bks.

—Henry in the Dark. 2017. (Step into Reading Ser.). (ENG., Illus.). 24p. (J). (gr. -1-1). pap. 4.99 *(978-0-399-55862-7(4),* Random Hse. Bks. for Young Readers) Random Hse. Children's Bks.

Random House. Meet Rusty Rivets! (Rusty Rivets) Cassity, Donald, illus. 2017. (Step into Reading Ser.). (ENG.). 24p. (J). (gr. -1-1). pap. 4.99 ***(978-1-5247-1686-8(3));*** lib. bdg. 12.99 ***(978-1-5247-1687-5(1))*** Random Hse. Children's Bks. (Random Hse. Bks. for Young Readers).

Random House, illus. Five Puptacular Tales! (PAW Patrol) 2016. (Step into Reading Ser.). (ENG.). 144p. (J). (gr. -1-1). 7.99 *(978-0-399-55300-4(2),* Random Hse. Bks. for Young Readers) Random Hse. Children's Bks.

Random House Disney Staff. Five Tales from the Road (Disney/Pixar Cars) Random House Disney Staff, illus. 2013. (Step into Reading Ser.). (ENG., Illus.). 160p. (J). (gr. -1-1). pap. 7.99 *(978-0-7364-3108-8(X),* RH/Disney) Random Hse. Children's Bks.

—Race Team. Random House Disney Staff, illus. 2008. (Step into Reading Ser.). (ENG., Illus.). 32p. (J). (gr. k-3). pap. 3.99 *(978-0-7364-2571-1(3),* RH/Disney) Random Hse. Children's Bks.

—Trolls. Random House Disney Staff & Matta, Gabriella, illus. 2016. (Step into Reading Ser.). (ENG.). 32p. (J). (gr. -1-2). lib. bdg. 12.99 *(978-0-399-55907-5(8),* Random Hse. Bks. for Young Readers) Random Hse. Children's Bks.

Random House Disney Staff, illus. Five Classic Tales (Disney Classics) 2014. (Step into Reading Ser.). (ENG.). 160p. (J). (gr. -1-1). 7.99 *(978-0-7364-3180-4(2),* RH/Disney) Random Hse. Children's Bks.

—Five Disney/Pixar Tales (Disney/Pixar) 2014. (Step into Reading Ser.). (ENG.). 160p. (J). (gr. -1-1). pap. 7.99 *(978-0-7364-3171-2(3),* RH/Disney) Random Hse. Children's Bks.

—Five Toy Tales (Disney/Pixar Toy Story) 2012. (Step into Reading Ser.). (ENG.). 160p. (J). (gr. -1-1). pap. 7.99 *(978-0-7364-2845-3(3),* RH/Disney) Random Hse. Children's Bks.

Random House Disney Staff & Liberts, Jennifer. Race for the Stars. 2017. (Step into Reading Ser.). (ENG., Illus.). 24p. (J). (gr. -1-1). pap. 4.99 *(978-0-399-55858-0(6),* Random Hse. Bks. for Young Readers) Random Hse. Children's Bks.

Random House Staff. Big Truck Show! Jackson, Mike, illus. 2013. (Step into Reading Ser.). (ENG.). 32p. (J). (gr. -1-1). 3.99 *(978-0-449-81896-1(9),* Random Hse. Bks. for Young Readers) Random Hse. Children's Bks.

—Dora's Puppy, Perrito! (Dora the Explorer) Aikins, David, illus. 2013. (Step into Reading Ser.). (ENG.). 32p. (J). (gr. -1-1). 3.99 *(978-0-449-81857-2(8),* Random Hse. Bks. for Young Readers) Random Hse. Children's Bks.

—Mission PAW (PAW Patrol) Random House Staff & Lovett, Nate, illus. 2017. (Step into Reading Ser.). (ENG.). 24p. (J). (gr. -1-1). pap. 4.99 *(978-1-5247-6413-5(2),* Random Hse. Bks. for Young Readers) Random Hse. Children's Bks.

—Railway Adventures. Random House Staff, illus. 2010. (Step into Reading Ser.). (ENG., Illus.). 160p. (J). (gr. -1-1). pap. 7.99 *(978-0-375-86653-1(1),* Random Hse. Bks. for Young Readers) Random Hse. Children's Bks.

—The Spring Chicken! (Bubble Guppies) Random House Staff & Trover, Zachary, illus. 2013. (Step into Reading Ser.). (ENG.). 24p. (J). (gr. -1-1). pap. 3.99 *(978-0-449-81440-6(8),* Random Hse. Bks. for Young Readers) Random Hse. Children's Bks.

Random House Staff, illus. Barbie Fairytale Collection. 2011. (Step into Reading Ser.). (ENG.). 160p. (J). (gr. -1-1). pap. 7.99 *(978-0-375-87255-6(8),* Random Hse. Bks. for Young Readers) Random Hse. Children's Bks.

—I Can Be... Story Collection (Barbie) 2013. (Step into Reading Ser.). (ENG.). 160p. (J). (gr. -1-2). 7.99 *(978-0-449-81666-0(4),* Random Hse. Bks. for Young Readers) Random Hse. Children's Bks.

Random House Staff & Holtz, Thomas R. T. Rex: Hunter or Scavenger? (Jurassic World) Random House Staff, illus. 2015. (Step into Reading Ser.). (ENG., Illus.). 48p. (J). (gr. 2-4). lib. bdg. 12.99 *(978-1-101-93409-8(3),* Random Hse. Bks. for Young Readers) Random Hse. Children's Bks.

Random House Staff & Posner-Sanchez, Andrea. Dog Days. Random House Staff, illus. 2016. (Step into Reading Ser.). (ENG., Illus.). 24p. (J). (gr. -1-2). 4.99 *(978-0-399-55497-1(1),* Random Hse. Bks. for Young Readers) Random Hse. Children's Bks.

Rao, Lisa. Iron Man: I Am Iron Man! Guidi, Guido, illus. 2008. (I Can Read Bks.). 32p. (J). (gr. -1-2). pap. 3.99 *(978-0-06-082193-7(0),* Harper Trophy) HarperCollins Pubs.

Rasinski, Timothy. Reader's Theater Scripts: Texas History, 1 vol. rev. ed. 2014. (Reader's Theater Scripts Ser.). (ENG., Illus.). 176p. (gr. 4-7). pap. 19.99 *(978-1-4258-1009-2(8))* Shell Educational Publishing.

Rasinski, Timothy V. 100 Reproducible Word Study Lessons That Help Kids Boost Reading, Vocabulary, Spelling & Phonics Skills — Independently! 2005. (Daily Word Ladders Ser.). (ENG., Illus.). 112p. (gr. 2-3). pap. 15.99 *(978-0-439-51383-8(9),* Teaching Resources) Scholastic, Inc.

Ratcliff, Charline. The Princess, the Toad & the Whale. 2012. (ENG.). 36p. (J). (-18). pap. 12.95 *(978-1-4787-1672-3(X))* Outskirts Pr., Inc.

Rau, Dana Meachen. Corn Aplenty. Iwai, Melissa, illus. 2009. (Step into Reading Ser.). (ENG.). 32p. (J). (gr. -1-1). 3.99 *(978-0-375-85575-7(0),* Random Hse. Bks. for Young Readers) Random Hse. Children's Bks.

P
Q
R

—?Que Es un Banco? 2010. (Dinero y los Bancos (Money & Banks) Ser.). (SPA., Illus.). 24p. (J). (gr. 2-5). lib. bdg. 22.00 *(978-1-4339-3726-2(3))* Stevens, Gareth Publishing LLLP.
Raum, Elizabeth & Collins, Terry. You Choose: Historical Eras, 1 vol. 2012. (You Choose: Historical Eras Ser.). (ENG.). 112p. (gr. 3-4). pap. 13.90 *(978-1-4296-9492-6(0))*; pap. 333.60 *(978-1-4296-9477-3(7))* Capstone Press of Coughlan Cos. (You Choose Bks.).
Raum, Elizabeth, et al. You Choose: Historical Eras. 2012. (You Choose: Historical Eras Ser.). (ENG.). 112p. (gr. 3-4). 63.98 *(978-1-4296-4782-3(5)*, You Choose Bks.) Capstone Press of Coughlan Cos.
Rawsthorne, Paul, et al. Little Women. Selivanova, Elena, illus. 2016. (ENG.). 80p. (J). pap. 9.95 *(978-0-00-814737-2(X))* HarperCollins Pubs. Ltd. GBR. Dist: Independent Pubs. Group.
Ray, Hannah. The Great Big Friend Hunt. 2004. (QEB Start Reading Ser.). (Illus.). 24p. (J). lib. bdg. 15.95 *(978-1-59566-012-1(7))* QEB Publishing Inc.
—Katie's Mom Is a Mermaid, 4 vols. 2005. (QEB Readers). (Illus.). 24p. (J). (gr. -1-3). lib. bdg. 15.95 *(978-1-59566-101-2(8))* QEB Publishing Inc.
Ray, Liz. One Land, Many Cultures, 6 vols., Set. 2004. (Phonics Readers Books 37-72 Ser.). (ENG.). 8p. (gr. k-1). pap. 35.70 *(978-0-7368-4079-8(6)*, Phonics Readers) Capstone Press of Coughlan Cos.
Ray, Nan. Meet the People. 2004. 66p. (J). per. 8.95 *(978-0-9760280-0-0(X))* You're On!, Inc.
Rayner, Shoo. Cat & Dog Play Hide & Seek. 2005. (Big Cat Ser.). (gr. k-2). pap. 6.50 *(978-1-60457-014-4(8))* Pacific Learning, Inc.
Rayner, Shoo, concept. Cat & Dog Play Hide & Seek. 2006. (Collins Big Cat Ser.). (ENG., Illus.). 80p. (J). (gr. -1-k). pap. 5.99 *(978-0-00-718660-0(6))* HarperCollins Pubs. Ltd. GBR. Dist: Independent Pubs. Group.
Rayner, Shoo, illus. The Big, Bad City. 2015. (Collins Big Cat Ser.). (ENG.). 24p. (J). (gr. 2-2). pap. 6.95 *(978-0-00-759109-1(8))* HarperCollins Pubs. Ltd. GBR. Dist: Independent Pubs. Group.
Rea, Lynn. Tug of War. 2006. (Neighborhood Readers Ser.). (ENG.). 16p. (gr. 1-3). pap. 6.50 *(978-1-4042-7272-9(0)*, Rosen Classroom) Rosen Publishing Group, Inc., The.
Rea, Thelma. Taking Care of Our World. 2003. (Rosen Real Readers: Upper Emergent Ser.). (ENG., Illus.). 12p. (gr. 1-2). pap. 5.90 *(978-0-8239-6368-3(3))* Rosen Publishing Group, Inc., The.
Reaching Higher Additional Resources: English Books (55 Titles) (Reach for Reading Ser.). (gr. 3-5). 260.00 *(978-0-7635-3747-0(0))* Rigby Education.
Reaching Higher Additional Workstations: Without Books. (Reach for Reading Ser.). (gr. 3-5). 285.00 *(978-0-7578-6847-4(9))* Rigby Education.
Reaching up Additional Resources: English Books (75 Titles) (Reach for Reading Ser.). (gr. 1-3). 205.00 *(978-0-7635-3748-7(9))* Rigby Education.
Reaching up Additional Workstations: With Books. (Reach for Reading Ser.). (gr. 1-3). 390.00 *(978-0-7635-3698-5(9))* Rigby Education.
Reaching up Additional Workstations: Without Books. (Reach for Reading Ser.). (gr. 1-3). 285.00 *(978-0-7578-3536-0(8))* Rigby Education.
Read & Spell with Zoo-phonics. 2004. (J). cd-rom 29.95 *(978-1-886441-46-0(4))* Zoo-phonics, Inc.
Read & Spell with Zoo=Phonics Guide for CD-ROM. 2004. (J). 14.95 *(978-1-886441-45-3(6))* Zoo-phonics, Inc.
Read & Write. 2005. (J). pap. 3.99 *(978-1-933200-18-7(9))* Family Bks. at Home.
Read-at-Home Book, Books 1-36. (Phonics Readers Ser.). (gr. k-2). 29.95 *(978-0-7368-3239-7(4))* Red Brick Learning.
Read-at-Home Book, Books 37-72. (Phonics Readers Ser.). (gr. k-2). 29.95 *(978-0-7368-4089-7(3))* Red Brick Learning.
Read-It! Chapter Books - Swat, 8 bks., Set. 2006. (Read-It! Chapter Books: SWAT Ser.). (ENG.). (gr. 2-4). 149.24 *(978-1-4048-1710-4(7))* Picture Window Bks.
Read-It! Readers. 2005. (Read-It! Readers: Gus the Hedgehog Ser.). (ENG.). 32p. (gr. k-3). 99.95 *(978-1-4048-1526-1(0))*; (Illus.). 100.61 *(978-1-4048-0998-7(8))* Picture Window Bks.
Read-It! Readers - Gus the Hedgehog. 2005. (Read-It! Readers: Gus the Hedgehog Ser.). (ENG., Illus.). 32p. (gr. k-3). 79.96 *(978-1-4048-0995-6(3))* Picture Window Bks.
Read It! Readers: Folk Tales, 6 vols. 2005. (Read-It! Readers: Folk Tales Ser.). (ENG., Illus.). 32p. (gr. k-3). 59.97 *(978-1-4048-0999-4(6))* Picture Window Bks.
Read-It! Readers en Espanol. 2006. (Read-It! Readers en Español: Story Collection). (SPA.). (gr. -1-3). lib. bdg. 106.60 *(978-1-4048-1813-2(8)*, Easy Readers) Picture Window Bks.
Read-It! Readers en Español. 2006. (Read-It! Readers en Español: Story Collection). (SPA.). lib. bdg. 234.52 *(978-1-4048-1812-5(X)*, Easy Readers) Picture Window Bks.
Read, Lorna. The Lies They Tell. Date not set. (Sky Bks.). 232p. pap. 54.75 *(978-0-582-08109-3(2))* Addison-Wesley Longman, Ltd. GBR. Dist: Trans-Atlantic Pubns., Inc.
Read on Target Grade 4. 2005. (J). stu. ed., per. 10.95 *(978-1-59230-127-0(4))* Englefield & Assocs., Inc.
Read on Target Grade 5. 2006. (J). pap., stu. ed. 10.95 *(978-1-59230-155-3(X))* Englefield & Assocs., Inc.
Read on Target Grade 6. 2006. (J). stu. ed., per. 10.95 *(978-1-59230-153-9(3))* Englefield & Assocs., Inc.
Reading 2000 Leveled Readers C: Challenge, Bookshelf Collection, 5 units. 2004. (gr. 1-18). 82.50 *(978-0-328-00434-8(0))*;Set. (gr. 3-18). 99.00 *(978-0-328-00436-2(7))*;Set. (gr. 4-18). 99.00 *(978-0-328-00437-9(5)*, Scott Foresman);Set. (gr. 5-18). 99.00 *(978-0-328-00438-6(3))* Addison-Wesley Educational Pubs., Inc.
Reading 2000 Trade Book Library Resource Guide. 2004. (Trade Book Library Resource Guide Ser.). (gr. 6-18). 48.00 *(978-0-673-63003-2(X))* Addison-Wesley Educational Pubs., Inc.
Reading 2002 Big Book Grade Level Package Grade 1.1, 3 bks., Set. 2004. (gr. 1-18). 109.15 *(978-0-328-02951-8(3))* Addison-Wesley Educational Pubs., Inc.
Reading 2002 Collection For Readers Bookshelf Collection. 2004. (gr. 5-18). 180.00 *(978-0-328-03137-5(2))*;Units 1-6. (gr. 4-18). 180.00 *(978-0-328-03136-8(4))* Addison-Wesley Educational Pubs., Inc.
Reading 2002 Independent Reader Bookshelf Collection, 36 bks. 2004. (gr. k-18). 594.00 *(978-0-328-02901-3(7))* Addison-Wesley Educational Pubs., Inc.
Reading 2002 Kindergarten Reader Bookshelf Collection, 36 bks. 2004. (gr. k-18). 594.00 *(978-0-328-02903-7(3)*, Scott Foresman) Addison-Wesley Educational Pubs., Inc.
Reading 2002 Wordless Story Bookshelf Collection, 36 bks. 2004. (gr. k-18). 594.00 *(978-0-328-02940-2(8))* Addison-Wesley Educational Pubs., Inc.
Reading 2004 Comprehensive Kindergarten Program 2004. 2004. (gr. k-18). *(978-0-328-05065-9(2)*, Scott Foresman) Addison-Wesley Educational Pubs., Inc.
Reading 2004 Pupil Edition Grade 1.2. 2004. (gr. 1-18). stu. ed. *(978-0-328-03928-9(4)*, Scott Foresman) Addison-Wesley Educational Pubs., Inc.
Reading 2004 Pupil Edition Grade 1.3. 2004. (gr. 1-18). *(978-0-328-03929-6(2)*, Scott Foresman) Addison-Wesley Educational Pubs., Inc.
Reading 2004 Pupil Edition Grade 1.4. 2004. (gr. 1-18). *(978-0-328-03930-2(6)*, Scott Foresman) Addison-Wesley Educational Pubs., Inc.
Reading 2004 Pupil Edition Grade 2.2. 2nd ed. 2004. (gr. 2-18). stu. ed. *(978-0-328-03934-0(9)*, Scott Foresman) Addison-Wesley Educational Pubs., Inc.
Reading at Home: Easy Reading Combo. (gr. k-2). 145.50 *(978-1-56334-413-8(0))* CENGAGE Learning.
Reading at Home: Jumbo Pack. (gr. k-2). 1235.86 *(978-0-7362-1399-8(6))* CENGAGE Learning.
Reading at Home: Phonics Grade 1 Combo. (gr. 1-18). 517.92 *(978-0-7362-1401-8(1))* CENGAGE Learning.
Reading at Home: Sound & Letter Combo. (gr. k-2). 341.12 *(978-0-7362-1400-1(3))* CENGAGE Learning.
Reading Central Level a Kit with 4/C Readers. 2004. (Reading Central Ser.). (J). (gr. 1-18). 299.95 *(978-1-58830-855-9(3))* Metropolitan Teaching & Learning Co.
Reading Central Level a Kit with Paperbks. 2004. (Reading Central Ser.). (J). (gr. 1-18). 364.95 *(978-1-58830-861-0(8))* Metropolitan Teaching & Learning Co.
Reading Central Level a Sh. 2004. (Reading Central Ser.). (J). (gr. 1-18). per. 67.95 *(978-1-58830-168-0(0))* Metropolitan Teaching & Learning Co.
Reading Central Level a Student Handbook. 2004. (Reading Central Ser.). (J). (gr. 1-18). per. 7.95 *(978-1-58830-891-7(X))* Metropolitan Teaching & Learning Co.
Reading Central Level B Kit with 4/C Readers. 2004. (Reading Central Ser.). (J). (gr. 1-18). 299.95 *(978-1-58830-856-6(1))* Metropolitan Teaching & Learning Co.
Reading Central Level B Kit with Paperbks. 2004. (Reading Central Ser.). (J). (gr. 1-18). 364.95 *(978-1-58830-862-7(6))* Metropolitan Teaching & Learning Co.
Reading Central Level B Sh. 2004. (Reading Central Ser.). (J). (gr. 1-18). per. 67.95 *(978-1-58830-169-7(9))* Metropolitan Teaching & Learning Co.
Reading Central Level B Student Handbook. 2004. (Reading Central Ser.). (J). (gr. 1-18). per. 7.95 *(978-1-58830-892-4(8))* Metropolitan Teaching & Learning Co.
Reading Central Level C Kit with 4/C Readers. 2004. (Reading Central Ser.). (J). (gr. 1-18). 299.95 *(978-1-58830-857-3(X))* Metropolitan Teaching & Learning Co.
Reading Central Level C Kit with Paperbks. 2004. (Reading Central Ser.). (J). (gr. 1-18). 364.95 *(978-1-58830-863-4(4))* Metropolitan Teaching & Learning Co.
Reading Central Level C Sh. 2004. (Reading Central Ser.). (J). (gr. 1-18). per. 67.95 *(978-1-58830-192-5(3))* Metropolitan Teaching & Learning Co.
Reading Central Level C Student Handbook. 2004. (Reading Central Ser.). (J). (gr. 1-18). per. 7.95 *(978-1-58830-893-1(6))* Metropolitan Teaching & Learning Co.
Reading Central Level D Kit with 4/C Readers. 2004. (Reading Central Ser.). (J). (gr. 2-18). 299.95 *(978-1-58830-858-0(8))* Metropolitan Teaching & Learning Co.
Reading Central Level D Kit with Paperbks. 2004. (Reading Central Ser.). (J). (gr. 2-18). 369.95 *(978-1-58830-864-1(2))* Metropolitan Teaching & Learning Co.
Reading Central Level D Sh. 2004. (Reading Central Ser.). (J). (gr. 2-18). per. 67.95 *(978-1-58830-193-2(1))* Metropolitan Teaching & Learning Co.
Reading Central Level D Student Handbook. 2004. (Reading Central Ser.). (J). (gr. 2-18). per. 7.95 *(978-1-58830-894-8(4))* Metropolitan Teaching & Learning Co.
Reading Central Level E Kit with 4/C Readers. 2004. (Reading Central Ser.). (J). (gr. 2-18). 299.95 *(978-1-58830-859-7(6))* Metropolitan Teaching & Learning Co.
Reading Central Level E Kit with Paperbks. 2004. (Reading Central Ser.). (J). (gr. 2-18). 369.95 *(978-1-58830-865-8(0))* Metropolitan Teaching & Learning Co.
Reading Central Level E Sh. 2004. (Reading Central Ser.). (J). (gr. 2-18). per. 67.95 *(978-1-58830-194-9(X))* Metropolitan Teaching & Learning Co.
Reading Central Level E Student Handbook. 2004. (Reading Central Ser.). (J). (gr. 2-18). per. 7.95 *(978-1-58830-895-5(2))* Metropolitan Teaching & Learning Co.
Reading Central Level F Kit with 4/C Readers. 2004. (Reading Central Ser.). (J). (gr. 2-18). 299.95 *(978-1-58830-860-3(X))* Metropolitan Teaching & Learning Co.
Reading Central Level F Kit with Paperbks. 2004. (Reading Central Ser.). (J). (gr. 2-18). 369.95 *(978-1-58830-866-5(9))* Metropolitan Teaching & Learning Co.
Reading Central Level F Sh. 2004. (Reading Central Ser.). (J). (gr. 2-18). per. 67.95 *(978-1-58830-196-3(6))* Metropolitan Teaching & Learning Co.
Reading Central Level F Student Handbook. 2004. (Reading Central Ser.). (J). (gr. 2-18). per. 39.95 *(978-1-58830-896-2(0))* Metropolitan Teaching & Learning Co.
Reading First Through Science Grade 4. 2005. (ENG., Illus.). *(978-0-9766802-6-0(2))* Educational Tools, Inc.
Reading Friends Staff. Witches Single. (J). *(978-0-8136-3823-2(2))* Modern Curriculum Pr.
Reading Remedies. 352p. (gr. 1-4). 23.99 *(978-0-513-02100-6(0)*, TSD21000) Denison, T. S. & Co., Inc.
Reading Together Intermediate Phase II&III Tutor's Guide Book. 2004. (J). pap. *(978-1-931840-70-5(9))* Learning Together.
Reading Together Tutors Guidebook Phase II&III Grade 3. 2004. (J). pap. *(978-1-931840-66-8(0))* Learning Together.
Reading Worktext Grade 1, Book 2. 2004. 10.50 *(978-0-89084-472-4(0))* BJU Pr.
Ready, Dee. Our Community Helpers. 2013. (Our Community Helpers Ser.). (ENG.). 24p. (gr. k-1). pap. 35.70 *(978-1-62065-853-6(4))*; pap. 214.20 *(978-1-62065-854-3(2))*; lib. bdg. 131.94 *(978-1-62065-085-1(1))* Capstone Press of Coughlan Cos. (Pebble Bks.).
Ready Reader Staff. Apple Farm, Level 8, Bk. 49. (J). (gr. -1-3). pap. 33.50 *(978-0-8136-0799-3(X))* Modern Curriculum Pr.
—The Best Place, 6 bks., set , Level 4, Bk. 4. (J). (gr. -1-3). pap. 24.50 *(978-0-8136-2011-4(2))* Modern Curriculum Pr.
Ready, Set, Read (Gr. K-1) 2003. (J). *(978-1-58232-033-5(0))* ECS Learning Systems, Inc.
Reaume, Christopher J. The 10 Greatest Threats to Earth. 2008. 14.99 *(978-1-55448-501-7(0))* Scholastic Library Publishing.
Red Egg & Ginger, 6 Pack. (Greetings Ser.: Vol. 1). 24p. (gr. 2-3). 31.00 *(978-0-7635-9409-1(1))* Rigby Education.
The Red Knight, Level 3. 2016. (Ladybird Readers Ser.). (ENG.). 64p. (J). (gr. 2-4). pap. 9.99 *(978-0-241-25384-7(5))* Penguin Bks., Ltd. GBR. Dist: Independent Pubs. Group.
Red, Yellow, Blue & Green Levels Certificate Only. (Sails Literacy Ser.). (gr. 1-6). 89.00 *(978-0-7578-6555-8(0))* Rigby Education.
Redmond, Diane & Mould, Chris. Hercules - Superhero. 2005. (Collins Big Cat Ser.). (ENG.). 288p. (J). (gr. 1-3). pap. 7.99 *(978-0-00-718638-9(X))* HarperCollins Pubs. Ltd. GBR. Dist: Independent Pubs. Group.
Redondo, Kurt. Treasure Map. 2006. (Neighborhood Readers Ser.). (ENG.). 12p. (gr. -1-3). pap. 5.90 *(978-1-4042-6463-2(9)*, Rosen Classroom) Rosen Publishing Group, Inc., The.
Rees, Celia & Bacchin, Giorgio. The Tear Jar. 2014. (Collins Big Cat Ser.). (ENG., Illus.). 320p. (J). (gr. 5-6). pap. 9.99 *(978-0-00-753011-3(0))* HarperCollins Pubs. Ltd. GBR. Dist: Independent Pubs. Group.
Reeve, Elizabeth. Sassy: the short stories of being a service Dog. 2010. 35p. pap. 17.00 *(978-0-557-39319-0(1))* Lulu Pr., Inc.
Reeve, Philip, et al. The Legend of Blackbeard. Kravets, Ivan, illus. 2016. (ENG.). 48p. (J). pap. 9.95 *(978-0-00-814725-9(6))* HarperCollins Pubs. Ltd. GBR. Dist: Independent Pubs. Group.
Reher, Matt. Are You in My Family? 2017. (1G Science Ser.). (ENG.). 28p. pap. 5.99 ***(978-1-63437-842-0(3))*** American Reading Co.
—Dan Gets a Call. 2015. (1B Fiction Ser.). (ENG., Illus.). 12p. (J). pap. 5.99 *(978-1-63437-177-3(1))* American Reading Co.
—What's So Good about Matt? 2015. (1B Fiction Ser.). (ENG., Illus.). 16p. (J). pap. 5.99 *(978-1-63437-200-8(X))* American Reading Co.
—Who Can I Call? 2015. (1B Fiction Ser.). (ENG., Illus.). 12p. (J). pap. 5.99 *(978-1-63437-048-6(1))* American Reading Co.
Reid, James. Across the Sea, 1 vol. rev. ed. 2013. (Fiction Readers Ser.). (ENG., Illus.). 12p. (J). (gr. 1-1). pap. 12.96 *(978-1-4807-1130-3(6))*; pap. 4.99 *(978-1-4333-5451-9(9))* Shell Educational Publishing.
—Dinosaur House, 1 vol. rev. ed. 2013. (Fiction Readers Ser.). (ENG., Illus.). 12p. (J). (gr. 1-1). pap. 4.99 *(978-1-4333-5459-5(4))*; pap. 12.96 *(978-1-4807-1138-9(1))* Shell Educational Publishing.
—Edward the Explorer, 1 vol. rev. ed. 2013. (Fiction Readers Ser.). (ENG., Illus.). 12p. (J). (gr. 1-1). 4.99 *(978-1-4333-5455-7(1))*; pap. 12.96 *(978-1-4807-1134-1(9))* Shell Educational Publishing.
—Ready, Set, Go!, 1 vol. rev. ed. 2013. (Fiction Readers Ser.). (ENG., Illus.). 20p. (J). (gr. 1-1). 4.99 *(978-1-4333-5488-5(8))*; pap. 15.96 *(978-1-4807-1144-0(6))* Shell Educational Publishing.
—This Is My Story by Frederick G. Frog, 1 vol. rev. ed. 2013. (Fiction Readers Ser.). (ENG., Illus.). 20p. (J). (gr. 1-1). pap. 15.96 *(978-1-4807-1140-2(3))*; pap. 4.99 *(978-1-4333-5484-7(5))* Shell Educational Publishing.
Reid, Rob. Storytime Slam: 15 Lesson Plans for Preschool & Primary Story Programs. 2006. (Illus.). 85p. per. 16.95 *(978-1-932146-52-3(0)*, Upstart Bks.) Highsmith Inc.
Reid, Stef & Bannister, Philip. Against the Odds. 2014. (Collins Big Cat Ser.). (ENG.). 448p. (J). (gr. 5). pap. 9.95 *(978-0-00-753015-1(3))* HarperCollins Pubs. Ltd. GBR. Dist: Independent Pubs. Group.
Reid, Stephanie. My Body, 1 vol. 2011. (Early Childhood Themes Ser.). (ENG.). 16p. (J). (gr. -1-2). pap. 19.99 *(978-1-4333-2368-3(0))*; pap. 6.99 *(978-1-4333-2367-6(2))* Teacher Created Materials, Inc.
—My Country, 1 vol. 2011. (Early Childhood Themes Ser.). (ENG.). 16p. (J). (gr. -1-2). pap. 19.99 *(978-1-4333-2361-4(3))*; pap. 6.99 *(978-1-4333-2360-7(5))* Teacher Created Materials, Inc.
—School, 1 vol. 2011. (Early Childhood Themes Ser.). (ENG.). 16p. (J). (gr. -1-2). pap. 6.99 *(978-1-4333-2353-9(2))*; pap. 19.99 *(978-1-4333-2354-6(0))* Teacher Created Materials, Inc.
Reilly, Carmel. Making Headlines, Vol. 83. 2014. (ENG.). 24p. spiral bd. 8.00 *(978-1-4085-0149-8(X))* Oxford Univ. Pr., Inc.
Reilly, Carmel & Ashforth, Kate. A Night Out. 2008. (Rigby Focus Forward: Level E Ser.). (Illus.). 24p. (J). (gr. 4-7). pap. *(978-1-4190-3678-1(5)*, Rigby) Pearson Education Australia.
Reilly, Carmel & Culic, Ned. Ben Fox Saves the Day. 2008. (Rigby Focus Forward: Level D Ser.). (Illus.). 24p. (J). (gr. 4-7). pap. *(978-1-4190-3665-1(3)*, Rigby) Pearson Education Australia.
Reilly, Carmel & Hopkinson, Courtney. Magic Tricks. 2008. (Rigby Focus Forward: Level F Ser.). (Illus.). 24p. (J). (gr. 4-7). pap. *(978-1-4190-3697-2(1)*, Rigby) Pearson Education Australia.
—New Tricks. 2008. (Rigby Focus Forward: Level J Ser.). (Illus.). 24p. (J). (gr. 4-7). pap. *(978-1-4190-3766-5(8)*, Rigby) Pearson Education Australia.
Reilly, Carmel & Orsini, Cheryl. Everything Is Changing. 2008. (Rigby Focus Forward: Level I Ser.). (Illus.). 24p. (J). (gr. 4-7). pap. *(978-1-4190-3753-5(6)*, Rigby) Pearson Education Australia.
—Saying Goodbye. 2008. (Rigby Focus Forward: Level G Ser.). (Illus.). 24p. (J). (gr. 4-7). pap. *(978-1-4190-3719-1(6)*, Rigby) Pearson Education Australia.
Reilly, Carmel & Stewart, Christen. More Like Home. 2008. (Rigby Focus Forward: Level P Ser.). (Illus.). 24p. (J). (gr. 4-7). pap. *(978-1-4190-3854-9(0)*, Rigby) Pearson Education Australia.
Reilly, Carmel & Wallace-Mitchell, Jane. Harry Helps Out. 2008. (Rigby Focus Forward: Level E Ser.). (Illus.). 24p. (J). (gr. 4-7). pap. *(978-1-4190-3673-6(4)*, Rigby) Pearson Education Australia.
—Mercury & the Woodcutter. 2008. (Rigby Focus Forward: Level J Ser.). (Illus.). 24p. (J). (gr. 4-7). pap. *(978-1-4190-3765-8(X)*, Rigby) Pearson Education Australia.
Reilly, Carmel & Young, Karen. Anna Goes to the Zoo. 2008. (Rigby Focus Forward: Level D Ser.). (Illus.). 24p. (J). (gr. 4-7). pap. *(978-1-4190-3663-7(7)*, Rigby) Pearson Education Australia.
—Buzz & Zip Get Lost. 2008. (Rigby Focus Forward: Level G Ser.). (Illus.). 24p. (J). (gr. 4-7). pap. *(978-1-4190-3704-7(8)*, Rigby) Pearson Education Australia.
—Taking Off. 2008. (Rigby Focus Forward: Level F Ser.). (Illus.). 24p. (J). (gr. 4-7). pap. *(978-1-4190-3690-3(4)*, Rigby) Pearson Education Australia.
Reilly, Carmel, et al. Shipwreck. 2008. (Rigby Focus Forward: Level O Ser.). (Illus.). 24p. (J). (gr. 4-7). pap. *(978-1-4190-3850-1(8)*, Rigby) Pearson Education Australia.
Renert, Gerry. Nathan Saves Summer/Nathan Rescata el Verano. Bradshaw, Carrie Anne, illus. 2010. (ENG & SPA.). 32p. (J). (gr. -1-3). 16.95 *(978-1-934960-74-5(8)*, Raven Tree Pr.,Csi) Continental Sales, Inc.
Responding to Literature: The EMC Write-in Reader. 2nd ed. (Literature & the Language Arts Ser.). (YA). (gr. 8-18). wbk. ed. 17.99 *(978-0-8219-2912-4(7))* EMC/Paradigm Publishing.
The Responsible Dr Bones: Social/Emotional Lap Book. (Pebble Soup Explorations Ser.). (gr. -1-18). 16.00 *(978-0-7635-7566-3(6))* Rigby Education.
Rey, H. A. Builds an Igloo. 2013. (Curious George Ser.). (ENG., Illus.). 24p. (J). (gr. -1-3). pap. 3.99 *(978-0-544-09666-0(5))* Houghton Mifflin Harcourt Publishing Co.
—Curious George at the Baseball Game (Jorge el Curioso en el Partido de Beisbol) 2011. (Curious George Ser.). (SPA & ENG., Illus.). 24p. (J). (gr. -1-3). pap. 4.99 *(978-0-547-51500-7(6))* Houghton Mifflin Harcourt Publishing Co.
—Curious George Builds a Tree House (CGTV Reader) 2017. (Curious George Ser.). (ENG., Illus.). 24p. (J). (gr. -1-3). pap. 3.99 *(978-0-544-86704-8(1)*, HMH Books For Young Readers) Houghton Mifflin Harcourt Publishing Co.
—Jorge el Curioso en el Partido de Beisbol. 2011. (Curious George Ser.).Tr. of Curious George at the Baseball Game. (SPA & ENG., Illus.). 24p. (J). (gr. -1-3). 12.99 *(978-0-547-54746-6(3))* Houghton Mifflin Harcourt Publishing Co.
—Race Day. 2010. (Curious George Ser.). (ENG., Illus.). 24p. (J). (gr. -1-3). pap. 3.99 *(978-0-547-39361-2(X))* Houghton Mifflin Harcourt Publishing Co.
—Sight Words. 2017. (Curious George Ser.). (ENG., Illus.). 160p. (J). (gr. -1-k). 14.99 *(978-0-544-89824-0(9)*, HMH Books For Young Readers) Houghton Mifflin Harcourt Publishing Co.
—Storybook Collection. 2010. (Curious George Ser.). (ENG., Illus.). 208p. (J). (gr. -1-3). 10.99 *(978-0-547-39631-6(7))* Houghton Mifflin Harcourt Publishing Co.
—A Treasury of Curious George (Coleccion de Oro Jorge el Curioso) 2011. (Curious George Ser.). (ENG & SPA., Illus.). 208p. (J). (gr. -1-3). 11.99 *(978-0-547-52310-1(6))* Houghton Mifflin Harcourt Publishing Co.
Rey, H. A. & Rey, Margret. Home Run. 2012. (Curious George TV Tie-In Early Reader Ser.). lib. bdg. 13.55 *(978-0-606-23985-1(5)*, Turtleback) Turtleback Bks.
—Shapes. 2008. (Curious George Ser.). (ENG., Illus.). 10p. (J). (gr. k — 1). bds. 6.99 *(978-0-618-89198-6(6))* Houghton Mifflin Harcourt Publishing Co.
—Takes a Trip. 2007. (Curious George Ser.). (ENG., Illus.). 24p. (J). (gr. -1-3). pap. 3.99 *(978-0-618-88403-2(3))* Houghton Mifflin Harcourt Publishing Co.
Rey, Margret & Rey, H. A. Curious about Phonics. 2008. (Curious George Ser.). (ENG., Illus.). 192p. (J). (gr. -1-3). 12.95 *(978-0-618-95670-8(0))* Houghton Mifflin Harcourt Publishing Co.
Reyes, Gabrielle. Winter Friends. 2013. (Illus.). 30p. (J). pap. *(978-0-545-59210-9(0))* Scholastic, Inc.
RH Disney. Belle - Discovery. RH Disney, illus. 2017. (Stepping Stone Book(TM) Ser.). (ENG., Illus.). 128p. (J). (gr. 1-4). 6.99 *(978-0-7364-3579-6(4)*, RH/Disney) Random Hse. Children's Bks.
—Moana Deluxe Step into Reading #1 (Disney Moana) RH Disney, illus. 2016. (Step into Reading Ser.). (ENG., Illus.). 24p. (J). (gr. -1-1). pap. 4.99 *(978-0-7364-3644-1(8)*, RH/Disney) Random Hse. Children's Bks.
—Mulan Is Loyal/Merida Is Brave (Disney Princess) RH Disney, illus. 2017. (Step into Reading Ser.). (ENG., Illus.). 48p. (J). (gr. -1-1). lib. bdg. 12.99 ***(978-0-7364-9017-7(5)***, RH/Disney) Random Hse. Children's Bks.
—Pua & Heihei. RH Disney, illus. 2017. (Step into Reading Ser.). (ENG., Illus.). 24p. (J). (gr. -1-1). pap. 4.99 *(978-0-7364-3684-7(7)*, RH/Disney) Random Hse. Children's Bks.
—Quest for the Heart. RH Disney, illus. 2016. (Step into Reading Ser.). (ENG., Illus.). 32p. (J). (gr. -1-1). pap. 4.99 *(978-0-7364-3646-5(4)*, RH/Disney) Random Hse. Children's Bks.
RH Disney Staff. Toy Story. RH Disney Staff, illus. 2009. (Little Golden Book Ser.). (ENG., Illus.). 24p. (J). (gr. -1-2). 4.99 *(978-0-7364-2596-4(9)*, Golden/Disney) Random Hse. Children's Bks.
RH Disney Staff & Rabe, Tish. Frozen - Big Snowman, Little Snowman. RH Disney Staff, illus. 2013. (Step into Reading Ser.). (ENG., Illus.). 32p. (J). (gr. -1-1). lib. bdg. 12.99 *(978-0-7364-8130-4(3)*, RH/Disney) Random Hse. Children's Bks.

RH Disney Staff & Redbank, Tennant. Toy to Toy. RH Disney Staff et al, illus. 2010. (Step into Reading Ser.). (ENG.). 32p. (J). (gr. k-3). pap. 3.99 *(978-0-7364-2665-7(5),* RH/Disney) Random Hse. Children's Bks.

Rhoades, Jacqueline. Rhoades to Reading Level II. 4th ed. 2004. 102p. (YA). spiral bd., wbk. ed. 19.95 *(978-1-930006-53-9(5))* Rhoades & Assocs.

—Rhoades to Reading Level III. 4th ed. 2004. 286p. (YA). spiral bd., wbk. ed. 29.95 *(978-1-930006-55-3(1))* Rhoades & Assocs.

—Rhoades to Reading Level IV. 4th ed. 2004. 166p. spiral bd., wbk. ed. 19.95 *(978-1-930006-57-7(8),* 1008) Rhoades & Assocs.

—Rhoades to Reading Level V. 4th ed. 2004. 80p. (YA). spiral bd., wbk. ed. 14.95 *(978-1-930006-59-1(4))* Rhoades & Assocs.

Rhoades, Jacquelline. Rhoades to Reading Level I. 4th ed. 2004. 134p. (YA). spiral bd., wbk. ed. 19.95 *(978-1-930006-51-5(9),* 1002) Rhoades & Assocs.

Rhodes, Karen. 7 Sensational Stories. 2005. (J). pap. 1.79 *(978-1-59317-084-4(X))* Warner Pr., Inc.

Rhyme Time. 2005. (Little Celebrations Thematic Packages Ser.). (J). (gr. k-3). 133.50 *(978-0-673-75380-9(8))* Celebration Pr.

The Ribbon. (Early Intervention Levels Ser.). 23.10 *(978-0-7362-0016-5(9));* Vol. 3. 3.85 *(978-1-56334-966-9(3))* CENGAGE Learning.

Rice, D. M. A Visit to a Car Factory, 1 vol. 2nd rev. ed. 2011. (Nonfiction Readers Ser.). (ENG.). 24p. (J). (gr. 2-2). pap. 6.99 *(978-1-4333-3607-2(3))* Teacher Created Materials, Inc.

—A Visit to a Farm, 1 vol. 2nd rev. ed. 2011. (Nonfiction Readers Ser.). (ENG.). 24p. (J). (gr. 2-2). pap. 6.99 *(978-1-4333-3608-9(1))* Teacher Created Materials, Inc.

Rice, Dona. Growing Up, 1 vol. rev. ed. 2014. (Science Readers: Content & Literacy Ser.). (ENG., Illus.). 24p. (gr. k-k). pap. 8.99 *(978-1-4807-4524-7(3))* Teacher Created Materials, Inc.

—Here Comes the Sun, 1 vol. (Science Readers: Content & Literacy Ser.). (ENG., Illus.). 24p. (gr. k-k). 2015. (J). 22.96 *(978-1-4938-1139-7(8))* 2014. pap. 8.99 *(978-1-4807-4529-2(4))* Teacher Created Materials, Inc.

—Mohandas Gandhi, 1 vol. 2nd rev. ed. 2012. (Nonfiction Readers Ser.). (ENG.). 32p. (J). (gr. 3-3). pap. 8.99 *(978-1-4333-3682-9(0))* Teacher Created Materials, Inc.

—Roberto Clemente, 1 vol. 2nd rev. ed. 2012. (Nonfiction Readers Ser.). (ENG.). 32p. (J). (gr. 3-3). pap. 8.99 *(978-1-4333-3683-6(9))* Teacher Created Materials, Inc.

—Sort It!, 1 vol. rev. ed. 2014. (Science Readers: Content & Literacy Ser.). (ENG., Illus.). 24p. (gr. k-k). pap. 8.99 *(978-1-4807-4535-3(9))* Teacher Created Materials, Inc.

—Too Much Trash!, 1 vol. rev. ed. 2014. (Science Readers: Content & Literacy Ser.). (ENG., Illus.). 24p. (gr. k-k). pap. 8.99 *(978-1-4807-4534-6(0))* Teacher Created Materials, Inc.

—What Kind of Weather?, 1 vol. 2009. (Early Childhood Themes Ser.). (ENG., Illus.). 16p. (J). (gr. -1-2). pap. 19.99 *(978-1-4333-1459-9(2))* Shell Educational Publishing.

Rice, Dona & Petersen, Casey Null. School Around the World, 1 vol. 2nd rev. ed. 2011. (Nonfiction Readers Ser.). (ENG.). 28p. (J). (gr. 3-3). pap. 8.99 *(978-1-4333-3654-6(5))* Teacher Created Materials, Inc.

Rice, Dona Herweck. American Through & Through, 1 vol. 2011. (Early Childhood Themes Ser.). (ENG.). 16p. (J). (gr. -1-2). pap. 6.99 *(978-1-4333-2362-1(1))* Teacher Created Materials, Inc.

—American Through & Through Lap Book, 1 vol. 2011. (Early Childhood Themes Ser.). (ENG.). 16p. (J). (gr. -1-2). pap. 19.99 *(978-1-4333-2363-8(X))* Teacher Created Materials, Inc.

—Animal Eyes, 1 vol. 2nd rev. ed. 2011. (TIME for KIDS(r) Nonfiction Readers Ser.). (ENG.). 12p. (J). (gr. 1-1). 4.99 *(978-1-4333-3578-5(6))* Teacher Created Materials, Inc.

—Animal Mothers & Babies, 1 vol. 2nd rev. ed. 2011. (Nonfiction Readers Ser.). (ENG.). 12p. (J). (gr. 1-1). pap. 4.99 *(978-1-4333-3579-2(4))* Teacher Created Materials, Inc.

—Bad Guys & Gals of the Ancient World, 1 vol. 2nd rev. ed. 2013. (Nonfiction Readers Ser.). (ENG.). 64p. (J). (gr. 5-5). pap. 10.99 *(978-1-4333-4904-1(3))* Teacher Created Materials, Inc.

—Bad Guys & Gals of the Wild West, 1 vol. 2nd rev. ed. 2013. (Nonfiction Readers Ser.). (ENG.). 64p. (J). (gr. 5-5). pap. 10.99 *(978-1-4333-4903-4(5))* Teacher Created Materials, Inc.

—Bad Guys & Gals on the High Seas, 1 vol. 2nd rev. ed. 2013. (TIME for KIDS(r) Nonfiction Readers Ser.). (ENG.). 64p. (J). (gr. 5-5). pap. 10.99 *(978-1-4333-4902-7(7))* Teacher Created Materials, Inc.

—Batter Up! History of Baseball, 1 vol. 2nd rev. ed. 2012. (TIME for KIDS(r) Nonfiction Readers Ser.). (ENG.). 32p. (J). (gr. 3-3). pap. 8.99 *(978-1-4333-3679-9(0))* Teacher Created Materials, Inc.

—A Bee's Life, 1 vol. 2nd rev. ed. 2011. (Nonfiction Readers Ser.). (ENG.). 20p. (J). (gr. 1-1). pap. 4.99 *(978-1-4333-3588-4(3))* Teacher Created Materials, Inc.

—Big & Little, 1 vol. 2nd rev. ed. 2011. (Nonfiction Readers Ser.). (ENG.). 12p. (J). (gr. 1-1). pap. 4.99 *(978-1-4333-3565-5(4))* Teacher Created Materials, Inc.

—Big Kid School, 1 vol. 2011. (Early Childhood Themes Ser.). (ENG.). 16p. (J). (gr. -1-2). pap. 6.99 *(978-1-4333-2355-3(9));* pap. 19.99 *(978-1-4333-2356-0(7))* Teacher Created Materials, Inc.

—A Butterfly's Life, 1 vol. 2nd rev. ed. 2011. (TIME for KIDS(r) Nonfiction Readers Ser.). (ENG.). 20p. (J). (gr. 1-1). 4.99 *(978-1-4333-3587-7(5))* Teacher Created Materials, Inc.

—Colors, 1 vol. 2nd rev. ed. 2011. (Nonfiction Readers Ser.). (ENG.). 12p. (J). (gr. 1-1). pap. 4.99 *(978-1-4333-3566-2(2))* Teacher Created Materials, Inc.

—Delicious & Nutritious, 1 vol. 2011. (Early Childhood Themes Ser.). (ENG.). 16p. (J). (gr. -1-2). pap. 6.99 *(978-1-4333-2369-0(9));* pap. 19.99 *(978-1-4333-2370-6(2))* Teacher Created Materials, Inc.

—A Frog's Life, 1 vol. 2nd rev. ed. 2011. (TIME for KIDS(r) Nonfiction Readers Ser.). (ENG.). 20p. (J). (gr. 1-1). 4.99 *(978-1-4333-3586-0(7))* Teacher Created Materials, Inc.

—Going Buggy!, 1 vol. 2nd rev. ed. 2011. (Nonfiction Readers Ser.). (ENG.). 20p. (J). (gr. 1-1). pap. 4.99 *(978-1-4333-3591-4(3))* Teacher Created Materials, Inc.

—Hit It! - History of Tools, 1 vol. 2nd rev. ed. 2012. (Nonfiction Readers Ser.). (ENG.). 32p. (J). (gr. 3-3). pap. 8.99 *(978-1-4333-3680-5(4))* Teacher Created Materials, Inc.

—Homes Around the World, 1 vol. 2nd rev. ed. 2011. (Nonfiction Readers Ser.). (ENG.). 20p. (J). (gr. 1-1). pap. 4.99 *(978-1-4333-3598-3(0))* Teacher Created Materials, Inc.

—How Plants Grow, 1 vol. 2nd rev. ed. 2011. (Nonfiction Readers Ser.). (ENG.). 12p. (J). (gr. 1-1). pap. 4.99 *(978-1-4333-3577-8(8))* Teacher Created Materials, Inc.

—I Can, 1 vol. 2nd rev. ed. 2011. (Nonfiction Readers Ser.). (ENG.). 12p. (J). (gr. 1-1). pap. 4.99 *(978-1-4333-3569-3(7))* Teacher Created Materials, Inc.

—I Can Be Anything, 1 vol. 2009. (Early Childhood Themes Ser.). (ENG., Illus.). 16p. (J). (gr. -1-2). pap. 6.99 *(978-1-4333-1475-9(4))* Shell Educational Publishing.

—Keeping Fit with Sports, 1 vol. 2nd rev. ed. 2011. (TIME for KIDS(r) Nonfiction Readers Ser.). (ENG.). 20p. (J). (gr. 1-1). 4.99 *(978-1-4333-3596-9(4))* Teacher Created Materials, Inc.

—Kids Around the World, 1 vol. 2nd rev. ed. 2014. (TIME for KIDS(r) Nonfiction Readers Ser.). (ENG., Illus.). 20p. (J). (gr. 1-1). pap. 19.96 *(978-1-4807-1032-0(6))* Shell Educational Publishing.

—Kids Around the World, 1 vol. 2nd rev. ed. 2011. (TIME for KIDS(r) Nonfiction Readers Ser.). (ENG.). 20p. (J). (gr. 1-1). 4.99 *(978-1-4333-3599-0(9))* Teacher Created Materials, Inc.

—Land, 1 vol. 2nd rev. ed. 2013. (Nonfiction Readers Ser.). (ENG., Illus.). 12p. (J). (gr. 1-1). pap. 15.96 *(978-1-4807-1013-9(X))* Shell Educational Publishing.

—Land, 1 vol. 2nd rev. ed. 2011. (Nonfiction Readers Ser.). (ENG.). 12p. (J). (gr. 1-1). pap. 4.99 *(978-1-4333-3574-7(3))* Teacher Created Materials, Inc.

—My Big Family, 1 vol. 2nd rev. ed. 2011. (Nonfiction Readers Ser.). (ENG.). 12p. (J). (gr. 1-1). pap. 4.99 *(978-1-4333-3570-9(0))* Teacher Created Materials, Inc.

—On the Go, 1 vol. 2nd rev. ed. 2011. (Nonfiction Readers Ser.). (ENG.). 12p. (J). (gr. 1-1). pap. 4.99 *(978-1-4333-3571-6(9))* Teacher Created Materials, Inc.

—Physical Feats & Failures, 1 vol. 2nd rev. ed. 2012. (TIME for KIDS(r) Nonfiction Readers Ser.). (ENG.). 48p. (J). (gr. 4-4). pap. 9.99 *(978-1-4333-4870-9(5))* Teacher Created Materials, Inc.

—Places Around the World, 1 vol. 2nd rev. ed. 2011. (Nonfiction Readers Ser.). (ENG., Illus.). 20p. (gr. 1-1). pap. 7.96 *(978-1-4333-3600-3(6))* Shell Educational Publishing.

—Places to Go, 1 vol. 2nd rev. ed. 2011. (Nonfiction Readers Ser.). (ENG.). 12p. (J). (gr. 1-1). pap. 4.99 *(978-1-4333-3573-0(5))* Teacher Created Materials, Inc.

—Sea Life, 1 vol. 2nd rev. ed. 2011. (Nonfiction Readers Ser.). (ENG.). 20p. (J). (gr. 1-1). pap. 4.99 *(978-1-4333-3590-7(5))* Teacher Created Materials, Inc.

—Shapes, 1 vol. 2nd rev. ed. 2011. (Nonfiction Readers Ser.). (ENG.). 12p. (J). (gr. 1-1). pap. 4.99 *(978-1-4333-3567-9(0))* Teacher Created Materials, Inc.

—Staying Healthy, 1 vol. 2nd rev. ed. 2011. (Nonfiction Readers Ser.). (ENG.). 20p. (J). (gr. 1-1). pap. 4.99 *(978-1-4333-3595-2(6))* Teacher Created Materials, Inc.

—Things with Wings, 1 vol. 2nd rev. ed. 2011. (Nonfiction Readers Ser.). (ENG.). 20p. (J). (gr. 1-1). pap. 4.99 *(978-1-4333-3589-1(1))* Teacher Created Materials, Inc.

—This Is Me, 1 vol. 2nd rev. ed. 2011. (Nonfiction Readers Ser.). (ENG.). 12p. (J). (gr. 1-1). pap. 4.99 *(978-1-4333-3568-6(9))* Teacher Created Materials, Inc.

—Unsolved! History's Mysteries, 1 vol. 2nd rev. ed. 2012. (TIME for KIDS(r) Nonfiction Readers Ser.). (ENG.). 48p. (J). (gr. 4-4). pap. 9.99 *(978-1-4333-4829-7(2))* Teacher Created Materials, Inc.

—Water, 1 vol. 2nd rev. ed. 2011. (Nonfiction Readers Ser.). (ENG.). 12p. (J). (gr. 1-1). pap. 4.99 *(978-1-4333-3576-1(X))* Teacher Created Materials, Inc.

—Weather, 1 vol. 2nd rev. ed. 2011. (Nonfiction Readers Ser.). (ENG.). 12p. (J). (gr. 1-1). pap. 4.99 *(978-1-4333-3575-4(1))* Teacher Created Materials, Inc.

—Workers, 1 vol. 2nd rev. ed. 2011. (TIME for KIDS(r) Nonfiction Readers Ser.). (ENG.). 12p. (gr. 1-1). 4.99 *(978-1-4333-3572-3(7))* Teacher Created Materials, Inc.

Rice, Dona Herweck & Aucoin, Lee. All about Me, 1 vol. 2009. (Early Childhood Themes Ser.). (ENG., Illus.). 16p. (J). (gr. -1-2). pap. 19.99 *(978-1-4333-1468-1(1))* Shell Educational Publishing.

Rice, Dona Herweck & Coan, Sharon. Special Me, 1 vol. 2009. (Early Childhood Themes Ser.). (ENG., Illus.). 16p. (J). (gr. -1-2). pap. 19.99 *(978-1-4333-1470-4(3))* Shell Educational Publishing.

Rice, Dona Herweck & Thompson, Chad. Old Mother Hubbard, 1 vol. 2009. (Early Childhood Themes Ser.). (ENG., Illus.). 16p. (J). (gr. -1-2). pap. 19.99 *(978-1-4333-1478-0(9))* Shell Educational Publishing.

Rice, Dona Herwick. Eating Right, 1 vol. 2nd rev. ed. 2011. (Nonfiction Readers Ser.). (ENG.). 20p. (J). (gr. 1-1). pap. 4.99 *(978-1-4333-3597-6(2))* Teacher Created Materials, Inc.

—The Fox & the Crow, 1 vol. 2008. (Building Fluency Through Reader's Theater Ser.). (ENG.). 24p. (J). (gr. 1-3). pap. 6.99 *(978-1-4333-0295-4(0))* Teacher Created Materials, Inc.

—John Henry, 1 vol. 2009. (Building Fluency Through Reader's Theater Ser.). (ENG.). 24p. (J). (gr. 2-4). pap. 6.99 *(978-1-4333-0992-2(0))* Teacher Created Materials, Inc.

—The Lion & the Mouse, 1 vol. 2008. (Building Fluency Through Reader's Theater Ser.). (ENG.). 24p. (J). (gr. 1-3). pap. 6.99 *(978-1-4333-0293-0(4))* Teacher Created Materials, Inc.

—The North Wind & the Sun, 1 vol. 2008. (Building Fluency Through Reader's Theater Ser.). (ENG.). 24p. (J). (gr. 1-3). pap. 6.99 *(978-1-4333-0296-1(9))* Teacher Created Materials, Inc.

—Paul Bunyan, 1 vol. 2009. (Building Fluency Through Reader's Theater Ser.). (ENG.). 24p. (J). (gr. 2-4). pap. 6.99 *(978-1-4333-0994-6(7))* Teacher Created Materials, Inc.

—The Tortoise & the Hare, 1 vol. 2008. (Building Fluency Through Reader's Theater Ser.). (ENG.). 24p. (J). (gr. 1-3). pap. 6.99 *(978-1-4333-0290-9(X))* Teacher Created Materials, Inc.

Rice, Dona Herwick & Bradley, Kathleen. Chief Joseph & the Nez Perce, 1 vol. 2009. (Building Fluency Through Reader's Theater Ser.). (ENG., Illus.). 32p. (J). (gr. 3-5). pap. 7.99 *(978-1-4333-0543-6(7))* Teacher Created Materials, Inc.

—The Goose That Laid the Golden Eggs, 1 vol. 2008. (Building Fluency Through Reader's Theater Ser.). (ENG., Illus.). 24p. (J). (gr. 1-3). pap. 6.99 *(978-1-4333-0291-6(8))* Teacher Created Materials, Inc.

—Lewis & Clark, 1 vol. 2009. (Building Fluency Through Reader's Theater Ser.). (ENG., Illus.). 32p. (J). (gr. 3-5). pap. 7.99 *(978-1-4333-0540-5(2))* Teacher Created Materials, Inc.

—Molly Pitcher, 1 vol. 2009. (Building Fluency Through Reader's Theater Ser.). (ENG., Illus.). 24p. (J). (gr. 2-4). pap. 6.99 *(978-1-4333-0993-9(9))* Teacher Created Materials, Inc.

Rice, Dona Herwick & Housel, Debra. The Grasshopper & the Ants, 1 vol. 2008. (Building Fluency Through Reader's Theater Ser.). (ENG., Illus.). 24p. (J). (gr. 1-3). pap. 6.99 *(978-1-4333-0292-3(6))* Teacher Created Materials, Inc.

—The Town Mouse & the Country Mouse, 1 vol. 2008. (Building Fluency Through Reader's Theater Ser.). (ENG., Illus.). 24p. (J). (gr. 1-3). pap. 6.99 *(978-1-4333-0294-7(2))* Teacher Created Materials, Inc.

Rice, Dona Herwick & Isecke, Harriet. Child Labor & the Industrial Revolution, 1 vol. 2009. (Building Fluency Through Reader's Theater Ser.). (ENG., Illus.). 32p. (J). (gr. 3-5). pap. 7.99 *(978-1-4333-0548-1(8))* Teacher Created Materials, Inc.

—Remember the Alamo, 1 vol. 2009. (Building Fluency Through Reader's Theater Ser.). (ENG., Illus.). 32p. (J). (gr. 3-5). pap. 7.99 *(978-1-4333-0541-2(0))* Teacher Created Materials, Inc.

Rice, Dona Herwick & Shannon, Catherine. Narcissa Whitman & the Westward Movement, 1 vol. 2009. (Building Fluency Through Reader's Theater Ser.). (ENG., Illus.). 32p. (J). (gr. 3-5). pap. 7.99 *(978-1-4333-0542-9(9))* Teacher Created Materials, Inc.

Rice, Dona Herwick & Sugarman, Dorothy. Women's Suffrage, 1 vol. 2009. (Building Fluency Through Reader's Theater Ser.). (ENG., Illus.). 32p. (J). (gr. 3-5). pap. 7.99 *(978-1-4333-0550-4(X))* Teacher Created Materials, Inc.

—World War II: Battle of Normandy, 1 vol. 2009. (Building Fluency Through Reader's Theater Ser.). (ENG., Illus.). 32p. (J). (gr. 3-5). pap. 7.99 *(978-1-4333-0553-5(4))* Teacher Created Materials, Inc.

Rice, Donna Herweck. I Can Be Anything, 1 vol. 2009. (Early Childhood Themes Ser.). (ENG., Illus.). 16p. (J). (gr. -1-2). pap. 19.99 *(978-1-4333-1476-6(2))* Shell Educational Publishing.

Rice, Howard. Step into the Desert, 1 vol. 2nd rev. ed. 2011. (Nonfiction Readers Ser.). (ENG.). 28p. (J). (gr. 2-2). pap. 6.99 *(978-1-4333-3629-4(4))* Teacher Created Materials, Inc.

—Step into the Forest, 1 vol. 2nd rev. ed. 2011. (Nonfiction Readers Ser.). (ENG.). 28p. (J). (gr. 2-2). pap. 6.99 *(978-1-4333-3628-7(6))* Teacher Created Materials, Inc.

—Step into the Rainforest, 1 vol. 2nd rev. ed. 2011. (Nonfiction Readers Ser.). (ENG.). 28p. (J). (gr. 2-2). pap. 6.99 *(978-1-4333-3630-0(8))* Teacher Created Materials, Inc.

Rice, Katelyn & Kuligowski, Stephanie. Dangerous Catch! Deep Sea Fishers, 1 vol. 2nd rev. ed. 2013. (Nonfiction Readers Ser.). (ENG.). 64p. (J). (gr. 5-5). pap. 10.99 *(978-1-4333-4943-0(4))* Teacher Created Materials, Inc.

Rice, William B. African Grasslands, 1 vol. 2nd rev. ed. 2012. (Nonfiction Readers Ser.). (ENG.). 32p. (J). (gr. 3-3). pap. 8.99 *(978-1-4333-3670-6(7))* Teacher Created Materials, Inc.

—Amazon Rainforest, 1 vol. 2nd rev. ed. 2012. (Nonfiction Readers Ser.). (ENG.). 32p. (J). (gr. 3-3). pap. 8.99 *(978-1-4333-3671-3(5))* Teacher Created Materials, Inc.

—Death Valley Desert, 1 vol. 2nd rev. ed. 2012. (Nonfiction Readers Ser.). (ENG.). 32p. (J). (gr. 3-3). pap. 8.99 *(978-1-4333-3672-0(3))* Teacher Created Materials, Inc.

—Endangered Animals of the Desert, 1 vol. 2nd rev. ed. 2013. (Nonfiction Readers Ser.). (ENG.). 64p. (J). (gr. 5-5). pap. 10.99 *(978-1-4333-4936-2(1))* Teacher Created Materials, Inc.

—Endangered Animals of the Jungle, 1 vol. 2nd rev. ed. 2013. (Nonfiction Readers Ser.). (ENG.). 64p. (J). (gr. 5-5). pap. 10.99 *(978-1-4333-4937-9(X))* Teacher Created Materials, Inc.

—Endangered Animals of the Sea, 1 vol. 2nd rev. ed. 2013. (Nonfiction Readers Ser.). (ENG.). 64p. (J). (gr. 5-5). pap. 10.99 *(978-1-4333-4935-5(3))* Teacher Created Materials, Inc.

—The First Geologists, 1 vol. 2007. (Science Readers Ser.). (ENG.). 32p. (J). (gr. 3-3). pap. 8.99 *(978-0-7439-0554-1(7))* Shell Educational Publishing.

—Jane Goodall, 1 vol. 2nd rev. ed. 2012. (TIME for KIDS(r) Nonfiction Readers Ser.). (ENG.). 32p. (J). (gr. 3-3). pap. 8.99 *(978-1-4333-3684-3(7))* Teacher Created Materials, Inc.

—Survival! Desert, 1 vol. 2nd rev. ed. 2012. (Nonfiction Readers Ser.). (ENG., Illus.). 48p. (J). (gr. 4-4). pap. 9.99 *(978-1-4333-4818-1(7))* Teacher Created Materials, Inc.

—Survival! Jungle, 1 vol. 2nd rev. ed. 2012. (Nonfiction Readers Ser.). (ENG., Illus.). 48p. (J). (gr. 4-4). pap. 9.99 *(978-1-4333-4820-4(9))* Teacher Created Materials, Inc.

—Survival! Ocean, 1 vol. 2nd rev. ed. 2012. (Nonfiction Readers Ser.). (ENG., Illus.). 48p. (J). (gr. 4-4). pap. 9.99 *(978-1-4333-4819-8(5))* Teacher Created Materials, Inc.

—The World of Rocks & Minerals, 1 vol. 2007. (Science Readers Ser.). (ENG., Illus.). 32p. (J). (gr. 4-4). pap. 8.99 *(978-0-7439-0553-4(9))* Shell Educational Publishing.

Rice, William B. & Wolfe, Hillary. Blast off to Space Camp, 1 vol. 2nd rev. ed. 2012. (Nonfiction Readers Ser.). (ENG.). 32p. (J). (gr. 3-3). pap. 8.99 *(978-1-4333-3673-7(1))* Teacher Created Materials, Inc.

Richards, Cassandra. I Help in the Kitchen. Aguilera, Aurora, illus. 2017. (Ways I Help Ser.). 24p. (J). (gr. 4-6). 23.60 ***(978-1-5081-5739-7(1),*** PowerKids Pr.) Rosen Publishing Group, Inc., The.

Richards, Kitty. Meet the Sparkplugs, Level 3. Simard, Remy, illus. 2006. (ENG.). 24p. (J). (gr. 1-17). per. 3.99 *(978-1-58476-419-9(8),* IKIDS) Innovative Kids.

—Phonics Comics: Twisted Tales - Level 3, Level 3. Juarez, Fernando, illus. 2006. (ENG.). 24p. (J). (gr. 1-17). per. 3.99 *(978-1-58476-514-1(3),* IKIDS) Innovative Kids.

Richie's Rocket. (Lexile Levels Ser.). 9.09 *(978-1-56334-736-8(9))* CENGAGE Learning.

Richter, Abigail. I See a Horse! 2006. (Neighborhood Readers Ser.). (ENG.). 16p. (gr. 1-3). pap. 6.50 *(978-1-4042-7248-4(8),* Rosen Classroom) Rosen Publishing Group, Inc., The.

—Mike the Bike. 2006. (Neighborhood Readers Ser.). (ENG.). 16p. (gr. 1-3). pap. 6.50 *(978-1-4042-7168-5(6),* Rosen Classroom) Rosen Publishing Group, Inc., The.

—Money: Saving & Spending. 2008. (Real Readers - Upper Emergent Ser.). (ENG., Illus.). 12p. (gr. 1-2). pap. 5.90 *(978-0-8239-8194-6(0))* Rosen Publishing Group, Inc., The.

Rick & Rosie. (Early Intervention Levels Ser.). 21.30 *(978-0-7362-0365-4(6));* Vol. 2. 3.55 *(978-0-7362-0086-8(X))* CENGAGE Learning.

Rickards, Lynne. Baking Bread Green Band. 2016. (Cambridge Reading Adventures Ser.). (ENG.). 17p. pap. 6.56 *(978-1-316-50327-0(5))* Cambridge Univ. Pr.

—Games Pink a Band. 2016. (Cambridge Reading Adventures Ser.). (ENG.). 16p. pap. 6.56 *(978-1-316-60084-9(X))* Cambridge Univ. Pr.

—Hide & Seek Green Band. Pérez, Moni, illus. 2016. (Cambridge Reading Adventures Ser.). (ENG.). 16p. pap. 6.56 *(978-1-107-57599-8(0))* Cambridge Univ. Pr.

—Houses & Homes Red Band. 2016. (Cambridge Reading Adventures Ser.). (ENG.). 16p. pap. 6.56 *(978-1-107-54949-4(3))* Cambridge Univ. Pr.

—My Dad Is a Builder Pink B Band. Hustache, Timothy, illus. 2016. (Cambridge Reading Adventures Ser.). (ENG.). 16p. pap. 6.56 *(978-1-107-54973-9(6))* Cambridge Univ. Pr.

—My First Train Trip. Honor Roberts, Ley, illus. 2016. (Cambridge Reading Adventures Ser.). (ENG.). 16p. pap. 6.56 *(978-1-107-57594-3(X))* Cambridge Univ. Pr.

—Omar Can Help Red Band. Pérez, Moni, illus. 2016. (Cambridge Reading Adventures Ser.). (ENG.). 16p. pap. 6.56 *(978-1-107-57572-1(9))* Cambridge Univ. Pr.

—One Potato. Rowland, Andy, illus. 2015. (Collins Big Cat Ser.). (ENG.). 24p. (J). (gr. 1-1). pap. 6.95 *(978-0-00-759102-2(0))* HarperCollins Pubs. Ltd. GBR. Dist: Independent Pubs. Group.

—Playgrounds Yellow Band. 2016. (Cambridge Reading Adventures Ser.). (ENG.). 16p. pap. 6.56 *(978-1-316-50318-8(6))* Cambridge Univ. Pr.

Riddell, Chris. The Emperor of Absurdia. 2013. (Let's Read! Ser.). (ENG., Illus.). 32p. (J). (gr. k-3). pap. 8.99 *(978-1-4472-3535-4(5))* Pan Macmillan GBR. Dist: Independent Pubs. Group.

Rider, Cynthia. Chatterbox Turtle. Petrlik, Andrea, illus. 2004. (ENG.). 24p. (J). lib. bdg. 23.65 *(978-1-59646-696-8(0))* Dingles & Co.

—The Explorers. Aguilar, Sandra, illus. 2013. (Start Reading Ser.). (ENG.). 24p. (gr. k-1). pap. 7.95 *(978-1-4765-4097-9(7))* Capstone Press of Coughlan Cos.

—A Sunny Day. Evans, Nicola, illus. 2013. (Start Reading Ser.). (ENG.). 24p. (gr. k-1). pap. 41.94 *(978-1-4765-3233-2(8));* pap. 7.95 *(978-1-4765-3197-7(8))* Capstone Press of Coughlan Cos.

RIGBY. American Journeys: Fourth Grade Class Collection Books. 2003. (Rigby on Our Way to English Ser.). (ENG.). 32p. (gr. 4-4). pap. 50.70 *(978-0-7578-4337-2(9))* Rigby Education.

—Are We There Yet? Second Grade Big Books. 2003. (Rigby on Our Way to English Ser.). (ENG.). 24p. (gr. 2-2). pap. 50.70 *(978-0-7578-1415-0(8))* Rigby Education.

—By the People: Fifth Grade Class Collection Books. 2003. (Rigby on Our Way to English Ser.). (ENG.). 32p. (gr. 5-5). pap. 50.70 *(978-0-7578-4468-3(5))* Rigby Education.

—Can You Help Me Find My Puppy? Kindergarten Big Books. 2003. (Rigby on Our Way to English Ser.). (ENG.). 16p. (gr. k-k). pap. 50.70 *(978-0-7578-1618-5(5))* Rigby Education.

—Diego Saves the Planet! Third Grade Big Books. 2003. (Rigby on Our Way to English Ser.). (ENG.). 24p. (gr. 3-3). pap. 50.70 *(978-0-7578-4212-2(7))* Rigby Education.

—The Early Americas: Fourth Grade Class Collection Books. 2003. (Rigby on Our Way to English Ser.). (ENG.). 32p. (gr. 4-4). pap. 50.70 *(978-0-7578-4341-9(7))* Rigby Education.

—Earth, Moon, & Sun: Fifth Grade Class Collection Books. 2003. (Rigby on Our Way to English Ser.). (ENG.). 32p. (gr. 5-5). pap. 48.75 *(978-0-7578-4473-7(1))* Rigby Education.

—Future Space Explorers: Third Grade Big Books. 2003. (Rigby on Our Way to English Ser.). (ENG.). 24p. (gr. 3-3). pap. 50.70 *(978-0-7578-4211-5(9))* Rigby Education.

—Getting Ready: Kindergarten Big Books. 2003. (Rigby on Our Way to English Ser.). (ENG.). 16p. (gr. k-k). pap. 50.70 *(978-0-7578-1616-1(9))* Rigby Education.

—Golden Opportunities: Fourth Grade Class Collection Books. 2003. (Rigby on Our Way to English Ser.). (ENG.). 32p. (gr. 4-4). pap. 50.70 *(978-0-7578-4343-3(3))* Rigby Education.

—Good News: First Grade Big Books. 2003. (Rigby on Our Way to English Ser.). (ENG.). 16p. (gr. 1-1). pap. 50.70 *(978-0-7578-1505-8(7))* Rigby Education.

—A Growing Nation: Fifth Grade Class Collection Books. 2009. (Rigby on Our Way to English Ser.). (ENG.). 32p. (gr. 5-5). pap. 50.70 *(978-0-7578-4471-3(5))* Rigby Education.

—Ibis & Jaguar's Dinner: Second Grade Big Books. 2003. (Rigby on Our Way to English Ser.). (ENG.). 24p. (gr. 2-2). pap. 50.70 *(978-0-7578-1427-3(1))* Rigby Education.

—In the Deep: Fifth Grade Class Collection Books. 2003. (Rigby on Our Way to English Ser.). (ENG.). 32p. (gr. 5-5). pap. 48.75 *(978-0-7578-4470-6(7))* Rigby Education.

—Just Like Me! First Grade. 2003. (Rigby on Our Way to English Ser.). (ENG.). 24p. (gr. 1-1). pap. 50.70 *(978-0-7578-1513-3(8))* Rigby Education.

—Making a Difference: Third Grade Big Books. 2003. (Rigby on Our Way to English Ser.). (ENG.). 24p. (gr. 3-3). pap. 52.80 *(978-0-7578-4213-9(5))* Rigby Education.

—My Rooster Speaks Korean: Kindergarten Big Books. 2003. (Rigby on Our Way to English Ser.). (ENG.). 16p. (gr. k-k). pap. 50.70 *(978-0-7578-1622-2(3))* Rigby Education.

—Now Hear This! Fifth Grade Class Collection Books. 2003. (Rigby on Our Way to English Ser.). (ENG.). 32p. (gr. 5-5). pap. 50.70 *(978-0-7578-4469-0(3))* Rigby Education.

—Picture Cards: Package of 100 Cards First Grade. 2003. (Rigby on Our Way to English Ser.). (ENG.). 100p. (gr. 1-1). 215.25 *(978-0-7578-1598-0(7))* Rigby Education.

—Picture Cards: Package of 100 Cards Kindergarten. 2003. (Rigby on Our Way to English Ser.). (ENG.). 100p. (gr. k-k). 215.25 *(978-0-7578-1611-6(8))* Rigby Education.

—Picture Cards: Package of 100 Cards Second Grade. 2003. (Rigby on Our Way to English Ser.). (ENG.). 100p. (gr. 2-2). 215.25 *(978-0-7578-1410-5(7))* Rigby Education.

—Picture Cards: Package of 100 Cards Third Grade. 2003. (Rigby on Our Way to English Ser.). (ENG.). 101p. (gr. 3-3). 215.25 *(978-0-7578-4233-7(X))* Rigby Education.

—A Pocketful of Opossums: Second Grade Big Books. 2003. (Rigby on Our Way to English Ser.). (ENG.). 24p. (gr. 2-2). pap. 48.75 (978-0-7578-1417-4(4)) Rigby Education.

—Pulse of Life: Fifth Grade Class Collection Books. 2003. (Rigby on Our Way to English Ser.). (ENG.). 32p. (gr. 5-5). pap. 48.75 (978-0-7578-4474-4(X)) Rigby Education.

—Rice All Day: Kindergarten Big Books. 2003. (Rigby on Our Way to English Ser.). (ENG.). 16p. (gr. k-k). pap. 50.70 (978-0-7578-1620-8(7)) Rigby Education.

—Road to Freedom: Fifth Grade Class Collection Books. 2003. (Rigby on Our Way to English Ser.). (ENG.). 32p. (gr. 5-5). pap. 48.75 (978-0-7578-4467-6(7)) Rigby Education.

—Rosita's Robot: Third Grade Big Books. 2003. (Rigby on Our Way to English Ser.). (ENG.). 24p. (gr. 3-3). pap. 50.70 (978-0-7578-4210-8(0)) Rigby Education.

—Tran & the Beautiful Tree: First Grade Big Books. 2003. (Rigby on Our Way to English Ser.). (ENG.). 24p. (gr. 1-1). pap. 50.70 (978-0-7578-1515-7(4)) Rigby Education.

—Under the Canopy: Fourth Grade Class Collection Books. 2009. (Rigby on Our Way to English Ser.). (ENG.). 32p. (gr. 4-4). pap. 50.70 (978-0-7578-4342-6(5)) Rigby Education.

—Unearthing the Past: Fourth Grade Class Collection Books. 2003. (Rigby on Our Way to English Ser.). (ENG.). 32p. (gr. 4-4). pap. 48.75 (978-0-7578-4340-2(9)) Rigby Education.

—Water Detective: Second Grade. 2003. (Rigby on Our Way to English Ser.). (ENG.). 24p. (gr. 2-2). pap. 50.70 (978-0-7578-1421-1(2)) Rigby Education.

—What Are the Seasons Like? Kindergarten Big Books. 2003. (Rigby on Our Way to English Ser.). (ENG.). 16p. (gr. k-k). pap. 50.70 (978-0-7578-1624-6(X)) Rigby Education.

—When I Grow Up: Kindergarten Big Books. 2003. (Rigby on Our Way to English Ser.). (ENG.). 16p. (gr. k-k). pap. 50.70 (978-0-7578-1626-0(6)) Rigby Education.

—Word Wall Starters: Package of 100 Cards Third Grade. 2003. (Rigby on Our Way to English Ser.). (ENG.). 99p. (gr. 3-3). 44.95 (978-0-7578-4286-3(0)) Rigby Education.

—Word Wall Starters: Package of 115 Cards First Grade. 2003. (Rigby on Our Way to English Ser.). (ENG.). 115p. (gr. 1-1). 51.15 (978-0-7578-1474-7(3)) Rigby Education.

—Word Wall Starters: Package of 124 Cards Second Grade. 2003. (Rigby on Our Way to English Ser.). (ENG.). 124p. (gr. 2-2). 55.95 (978-0-7578-1386-3(0)) Rigby Education.

—Word Wall Starters: Package of 65 Cards Kindergarten. 2003. (Rigby on Our Way to English Ser.). (ENG.). 65p. (gr. k-k). 31.00 (978-0-7578-1562-1(6)) Rigby Education.

Rigby Education Staff. Activity Guide. (Illus.). (gr. k-1). tchr. ed. 18.00 (978-0-7635-2006-9(3)); tchr. ed. 18.00 (978-0-7635-2005-2(5)); tchr. ed. 18.00 (978-0-7635-2008-3(X)); tchr. ed. 18.00 (978-0-7635-2007-6(1)) Rigby Education.

—A Day on the Farm. (Illus.). 8p. (J). bds. 3.95 (978-0-7635-6463-6(X), 764639C99) Rigby Education.

—Discovery World Org Where Does. (Discovery World Ser.). (Illus.). 12p. (gr. 1-2). 27.00 (978-0-7635-2698-6(3)) Rigby Education.

—Discovery World Red Biography III. (Discovery World Ser.). 12p. (gr. 1-2). 31.00 (978-0-7635-2703-7(3)) Rigby Education.

—Everything Changes Big Book: Little Red Riding Hood. (Pebble Soup Explorations Ser.). 16p. (gr. -1-18). 21.00 (978-0-7635-6482-7(6)) Rigby Education.

—Follow the Paw Prints. (Pebble Soup Explorations Ser.). (Illus.). 16p. (gr. -1-18). 31.00 (978-0-7635-6446-9(X), 764469C99) Rigby Education.

—Jack Big Book. (gr. k-2). 21.00 (978-0-7635-2409-8(3)) Rigby Education.

—Jumbled Tumble Little Miss. (gr. k-2). 21.00 (978-0-7635-2415-9(8)) Rigby Education.

—Jumbled Tumble Little Tom. (gr. k-2). 21.00 (978-0-7635-2414-2(X)) Rigby Education.

—Max. (Sails Literacy Ser.). (Illus.). 16p. (gr. 1-2). 27.00 (978-0-7635-9906-5(9), 699069C99) Rigby Education.

—Roger's Best Friend. (Illus.). 16p. (J). pap. 30.00 (978-0-7635-6434-6(6), 764346C99) Rigby Education.

—Stage 1 Components. (gr. k-3). 57.00 (978-0-7635-9245-5(5)) Rigby Education.

—Tom Sawyer: Jumbled Tumble. (gr. k-2). 26.00 (978-0-7635-2424-1(7)) Rigby Education.

—Touching the Moon. (Illus.). 16p. (J). pap. 30.00 (978-0-7635-6498-8(2), 764982C99) Rigby Education.

—Two Eyes That See. (Illus.). 16p. (J). pap. 3.95 (978-0-7635-7037-8(0), 764265C99) Rigby Education.

—Who Works in Your Neighborhood? (Illus.). (J). suppl. ed. 20.00 (978-0-7635-6453-7(2), 764532C99) Rigby Education.

—William Tell. (gr. k-2). 21.00 (978-0-7635-2426-5(3)) Rigby Education.

Rigby, Robert & Cámara, Noemí. Gol II: Viviendo el Sueño. 2014. (SPA & ENG., Illus.). 40p. pap. 13.75 incl. audio compact disk (978-84-9848-130-3(9)) Edinumen, Editorial ESP. Dist: Cambridge Univ. Pr.

Rigol, Francesc, illus. Dan & Din Learn Numbers. 2009. (Learning with Dan & Din Ser.). 12p. (J). (gr. -1-k). bds. 11.40 (978-1-60754-402-9(4)) Windmill Bks.

—Dan & Din Learn Shapes. 2009. (Learning with Dan & Din Ser.). 12p. (J). (gr. -1-k). bds. 11.40 (978-1-60754-400-5(8)) Windmill Bks.

Rigolo 1 Puppet Set, 2. 2014. 1p. 110.00 (978-0-7487-8351-9(2)) Oxford Univ. Pr., Inc.

Riley, Cooper. Absolutely Awesome Island Animals. 2009. 24p. pap. 9.95 (978-0-9740582-4-5(6)) Tiki Tales.

Riley, Kana. The Princess & the Wise Woman. Williams, Jenny, illus. 2012. (Ready Readers: Stage 5 Ser.). (ENG.). 24p. (J). (gr. k-2). pap. 6.97 (978-0-8136-2371-9(5)) Modern Curriculum Pr.

Rimes with Ball 6 Packs. KinderRimes. (Kinderstarters Ser.). (gr. -1-1). 21.00 (978-0-7635-8667-6(6)) Rigby Education.

Rimes with Cake 6 Packs. KinderRimes. (Kinderstarters Ser.). (gr. -1-1). 21.00 (978-0-7635-8668-3(4)) Rigby Education.

Rimes with Cap 6 Packs. KinderRimes. (Kinderstarters Ser.). (gr. -1-1). 21.00 (978-0-7635-8669-0(2)) Rigby Education.

Rimes with Cat 6 Packs. KinderRimes. (Kinderstarters Ser.). (gr. -1-1). 21.00 (978-0-7635-8670-6(6)) Rigby Education.

Rimes with Clock 6 Packs. KinderRimes. (Kinderstarters Ser.). (gr. -1-1). 21.00 (978-0-7635-8671-3(4)) Rigby Education.

Rimes with Clown 6 Packs. KinderRimes. (Kinderstarters Ser.). (gr. -1-1). 21.00 (978-0-7635-8672-0(2)) Rigby Education.

Rimes with Drink 6 Packs. KinderRimes. (Kinderstarters Ser.). (gr. -1-1). 21.00 (978-0-7635-8673-7(0)) Rigby Education.

Rimes with Goat 6 Packs. KinderRimes. (Kinderstarters Ser.). (gr. -1-1). 21.00 (978-0-7635-8674-4(9)) Rigby Education.

Rimes with Hay 6 Packs. KinderRimes. (Kinderstarters Ser.). (gr. -1-1). 21.00 (978-0-7635-8675-1(7)) Rigby Education.

Rimes with Hill 6 Packs. KinderRimes. (Kinderstarters Ser.). (gr. -1-1). 21.00 (978-0-7635-8676-8(5)) Rigby Education.

Rimes with Jump 6 Packs. KinderRimes. (Kinderstarters Ser.). (gr. -1-1). 21.00 (978-0-7635-8677-5(3)) Rigby Education.

Rimes with Kick 6 Packs. KinderRimes. (Kinderstarters Ser.). (gr. -1-1). 21.00 (978-0-7635-8678-2(1)) Rigby Education.

Rimes with King 6 Packs. KinderRimes. (Kinderstarters Ser.). (gr. -1-1). 21.00 (978-0-7635-8679-9(X)) Rigby Education.

Rimes with Man 6 Packs. KinderRimes. (Kinderstarters Ser.). (gr. -1-1). 21.00 (978-0-7635-8680-5(3)) Rigby Education.

Rimes with Mice 6 Packs. KinderRimes. (Kinderstarters Ser.). (gr. -1-1). 21.00 (978-0-7635-8681-2(1)) Rigby Education.

Rimes with Net 6 Packs. KinderRimes. (Kinderstarters Ser.). (gr. -1-1). 21.00 (978-0-7635-8682-9(X)) Rigby Education.

Rimes with Pig 6 Packs. KinderRimes. (Kinderstarters Ser.). (gr. -1-1). 21.00 (978-0-7635-8683-6(8)) Rigby Education.

Rimes with Ram 6 Packs. KinderRimes. (Kinderstarters Ser.). (gr. -1-1). 21.00 (978-0-7635-8684-3(6)) Rigby Education.

Rimes with Ship 6 Packs. KinderRimes. (Kinderstarters Ser.). (gr. -1-1). 21.00 (978-0-7635-8686-7(2)) Rigby Education.

Rimes with Skate 6 Packs. KinderRimes. (Kinderstarters Ser.). (gr. -1-1). 21.00 (978-0-7635-8687-4(0)) Rigby Education.

Rimes with Snail 6 Packs. KinderRimes. (Kinderstarters Ser.). (gr. -1-1). 21.00 (978-0-7635-8688-1(9)) Rigby Education.

Rimes with Track 6 Packs. KinderRimes. (Kinderstarters Ser.). (gr. -1-1). 21.00 (978-0-7635-8689-8(7)) Rigby Education.

Rimes with Train 6 Packs. KinderRimes. (Kinderstarters Ser.). (gr. -1-1). 21.00 (978-0-7635-8690-4(0)) Rigby Education.

Ripley, Catherine. Great Math Ideas. 2007. (ENG., Illus.). 16p. (J). (gr. 2-2). pap. 9.47 net. (978-0-7652-8598-0(3), Celebration Pr.) Pearson Schl.

Rissman, Rebecca. Say What You See. 2013. (Say What You See Ser.). (ENG.). 24p. (gr. -1-1). pap. 27.96 (978-1-4109-5055-0(7)); lib. bdg. 90.60 (978-1-4109-5050-5(6)) Heinemann-Raintree.

The River. (Pebble Soup Explorations Ser.). 16p. (gr. -1-18). 31.00 (978-0-7578-1660-4(6)) Rigby Education.

The River: Small Book. (Pebble Soup Explorations Ser.). 16p. (gr. -1-18). 5.00 (978-0-7578-1700-7(9)) Rigby Education.

A River Ran Wild. (Lexile Levels Ser.). 9.09 (978-1-56334-737-5(7)) CENGAGE Learning.

RiverStream Readers - Pre-1. 2013. (RiverStream Readers Ser.: PK). 124p. (gr. -1-2). 11.49 (978-1-62588-900-3(3)) Black Rabbit Bks.

Robb, Anina. Graphic Organizers & Strategy Sheets: That Scaffold Writing from Paragraphs to Essays - Student Packets with Guided Lessons, Writing Models, Graphic Organizers, & Planning Sheets. 2007. (Teaching Strategies Ser.). (ENG., Illus.). 112p. pap. 17.99 (978-0-439-82772-0(8), Teaching Resources) Scholastic, Inc.

A Robbie Reader Series, 12 Bks, Set. 2004. (Illus.). (gr. 1-4). lib. bdg. 203.40 (978-1-58415-319-1(9)) Mitchell Lane Pubs., Inc.

Robbins, Eliza. The Popcorn Surprise. 2006. (Neighborhood Readers Ser.). (ENG.). 16p. (gr. 1-3). pap. 6.50 (978-1-4042-7232-3(1), Rosen Classroom) Rosen Publishing Group, Inc., The.

—Which Holds More? Learning to Compare Volume. (Math for the Real World: Early Emergent Ser.). (ENG., Illus.). 8p. (gr. k-1). 2009. pap. 5.15 (978-0-8239-8845-7(7)) 2004. 29.95 (978-0-8239-7631-7(9)) Rosen Publishing Group, Inc., The.

Robbins, Eliza & National Geographic Learning Staff. Nana's New Room. 2010. (Rise & Shine Ser.). (ENG.). 12p. (C). (gr. -1-3). pap. 9.95 (978-1-4042-6734-3(4)) National Geographic School Publishing, Inc.

Robbins, Maureen. El Hábitat de los Murciélagos. 2012. Tr. of Habitat for Bats. (SPA & ENG.). 24p. (gr. 2-3). pap. 8.95 (978-1-61810-546-2(9)) Rourke Educational Media.

Robbins, Trina & Hess, Debra. Native Princess: Sarah Winnemucca. 2007. (Read on! Special Edition: Level AA Ser.). (Illus.). 23p. pap. 4.84 (978-1-4190-3515-9(0)) Steck-Vaughn.

Roberto Clemente: Fourth Grade Guided Comprehension Level N. (On Our Way to English Ser.). (gr. 4-18). 34.50 (978-0-7578-7162-7(3)) Rigby Education.

Robertson, Charmaine. All about Data. 2016. (Rosen REAL Readers: STEM & STEAM Collection). 8p. (gr. 1-k). pap. 5.46 (978-1-5081-2404-7(3), Rosen Classroom) Rosen Publishing Group, Inc., The.

—Bend but Don't Break. 2016. (Rosen REAL Readers: STEM & STEAM Collection). 12p. (gr. 1-k). pap. 6.33 (978-1-5081-2667-6(4), Rosen Classroom) Rosen Publishing Group, Inc., The.

—Building with Flexible Materials. 2016. (Rosen REAL Readers: STEM & STEAM Collection). 12p. (gr. 1-k). pap. 6.33 (978-1-5081-2452-8(3), Rosen Classroom) Rosen Publishing Group, Inc., The.

—Hot Rocks. 2016. (Rosen REAL Readers: STEM & STEAM Collection). 8p. (gr. 1-k). pap. 5.46 (978-1-5081-2625-6(9), Rosen Classroom) Rosen Publishing Group, Inc., The.

—The Landslide. 2016. (Rosen REAL Readers: STEM & STEAM Collection). 12p. (gr. 1-k). pap. 6.33 (978-1-5081-2676-8(3), Rosen Classroom) Rosen Publishing Group, Inc., The.

Robertson, Jean. Monkey Business. Dufalla, Anita, illus. 2012. (ENG.). 24p. (gr. 2-3). pap. 8.95 (978-1-61810-322-2(9)) Rourke Educational Media.

—My Name Is Not... Dufalla, Anita, illus. 2012. (ENG.). 24p. (gr. 1-2). pap. 8.95 (978-1-61810-320-8(2)) Rourke Educational Media.

Robes, Ruth & Almendro, Herminio. Habia una Vez: Libro Segundo de Lectura. (SPA.). (J). pap. 12.95 (978-84-357-0109-9(3), CPR30) Ediciones y Distribuciones Codice, S.A. ESP. Dist: Continental Bk. Co., Inc.

Robins E. Be Fair. 2005. (Carter High Chronicles Senior Year Ser.). (Illus.). 48p. (J). per. 3.95 (978-1-56254-768-4(2), SP7682) Saddleback Educational Publishing, Inc.

Robins, Eleanor. Boy of Their Dreams. 2004. (Carter High Chronicles (High-Interest Readers) Ser.). (Illus.). 48p. (J). per. 3.95 (978-1-56254-679-3(1), SP6791) Saddleback Educational Publishing, Inc.

—Time to Move On. 2005. (Carter High Chronicles Senior Year Ser.). (Illus.). 48p. (J). per. 3.95 (978-1-56254-778-3(X), SP778X) Saddleback Educational Publishing, Inc.

—Worst Year Ever. 2005. (Carter High Chronicles Senior Year Ser.). (Illus.). 48p. (J). per. 3.95 (978-1-56254-780-6(1), SP7801) Saddleback Educational Publishing, Inc.

—The Wrong Way. 2005. (Carter High Chronicles Senior Year Ser.). (Illus.). 48p. (YA). per. 4.95 (978-1-56254-782-0(8), SP7828) Saddleback Educational Publishing, Inc.

Robins, Maureen Picard. One Land, Many Cultures. 2012. (ENG.). 24p. (gr. k-2). pap. 8.95 (978-1-61810-276-8(1)) Rourke Educational Media.

Robinson, Hilary. Beauty & the Pea. Sanfilippo, Simona, illus. 2013. (ENG.). 32p. (J). pap. (978-0-7787-1159-9(5)) Crabtree Publishing Co.

—Cinderella & the Beanstalk. Sanfilippo, Simona, illus. 2013. (ENG.). 32p. (J). pap. (978-0-7787-1161-2(7)) Crabtree Publishing Co.

—Hansel, Gretel, & the Ugly Duckling. Sanfilippo, Simona, illus. 2013. (ENG.). 32p. (J). pap. (978-0-7787-1166-7(8)) Crabtree Publishing Co.

—Rapunzel & the Billy Goats. Sanfilippo, Simona, illus. 2013. (ENG.). 32p. (J). pap. (978-0-7787-1158-2(7)) Crabtree Publishing Co.

Rodgers, Kelly. The Byzantine Empire: A Society That Shaped the World, 1 vol. 2012. (Primary Source Readers Ser.). (ENG.). 32p. (J). (gr. 5-5). pap. 8.99 (978-1-4333-5001-6(7)) Teacher Created Materials, Inc.

—Justinian I: Byzantine Emperor, 1 vol. 2012. (Primary Source Readers Ser.). (ENG.). 32p. (J). (gr. 4-4). pap. 8.99 (978-1-4333-5002-3(5)) Teacher Created Materials, Inc.

—Leaders in the Texas Revolution: United for a Cause, 1 vol. 2012. (Primary Source Readers Ser.). (ENG.). 32p. (J). (gr. 3-3). pap. 8.99 (978-1-4333-5047-4(5)) Teacher Created Materials, Inc.

—The Texas Revolution: Fighting for Independence, 1 vol. 2012. (Primary Source Readers Ser.). (ENG.). 32p. (J). (gr. 4-4). pap. 8.99 (978-1-4333-5046-7(7)) Teacher Created Materials, Inc.

Roesser, Griffin. Digger Makes a Friend. 2006. (Neighborhood Readers Ser.). (ENG.). 8p. (gr. -1-3). pap. 5.15 (978-1-4042-5774-0(8), Rosen Classroom) Rosen Publishing Group, Inc., The.

—Who Ate the Turkey? 2006. (Neighborhood Readers Ser.). (ENG.). 12p. (gr. -1-3). pap. 5.90 (978-1-4042-6457-1(4), Rosen Classroom) Rosen Publishing Group, Inc., The.

Rog, Lori Jamison. Guided Reading Basics: Organizing, Managing, & Implementing a Balanced Literacy Program in K-3. 2003. (ENG., Illus.). 128p. (C). (gr. k-3). pap. 28.67 (978-1-57110-383-3(X)) Pembroke Pubs., Ltd. CAN. Dist: Stenhouse Pubs.

Rogers, Jane & Benchmark Education Co., LLC Staff. The Best Nest. 2015. (BuildUp Ser.). (J). (gr. 1). (978-1-4900-0721-2(0)) Benchmark Education Co.

Rollason, Jane. Freddie's War Level 6 Advanced. 2010. (ENG.). 128p. pap. 14.50 (978-84-8323-909-4(4)) Cambridge Univ. Pr.

—Freddie's War Level 6 Advanced Book with CD-ROM & Audio CDs (3), 1 vol. 2010. (ENG.). 128p. cd-rom, audio compact disk 18.25 (978-84-8323-662-8(1)) Cambridge Univ. Pr.

—Killer Bees. 2009. (ENG.). 64p. pap. 12.00 (978-84-8323-503-4(X)) Cambridge Univ. Pr.

Rollason, Jane & Pearson Education Staff. Gandhi. 2nd ed. 2008. (ENG., Illus.). 32p. pap. 11.99 (978-1-4058-7693-3(X)) Pearson Education.

The Roller Coaster: KinderWords Individual Title Six-Packs. (Kinderstarters Ser.). 8p. (gr. -1-1). 21.00 (978-0-7635-8708-6(7)) Rigby Education.

Roman, Edward. My Busy Year. 2012. (InfoMax Readers Ser.). (ENG., Illus.). 24p. (J). (gr. 1-2). pap. 8.25 (978-1-4488-9004-0(7), Rosen Classroom) Rosen Publishing Group, Inc., The.

Romer, Ruth. Jill Gets Fit. 2004. (Reader's Theater Ser.). (J). pap. (978-1-4108-0791-5(6)) Benchmark Education Co.

—Pet Care Kids. 2004. (Reader's Theater Ser.). (J). pap. (978-1-4108-1146-2(8)) Benchmark Education Co.

Rondeau, Amanda. Ed As in Bed, 1 vol. 2003. (Word Families Set 2 Ser.). (ENG., Illus.). 24p. (J). (gr. k-3). lib. bdg. 24.21 (978-1-59197-228-0(0), SandCastle) ABDO Publishing Co.

—Ob As in Knob, 1 vol. 2003. (Word Families Set 5 Ser.). (ENG., Illus.). 24p. (J). (gr. k-3). lib. bdg. 24.21 (978-1-59197-249-5(3), SandCastle) ABDO Publishing Co.

—Ock As in Block, 1 vol. 2003. (Word Families Set 5 Ser.). (ENG., Illus.). 24p. (J). (gr. k-3). lib. bdg. 24.21 (978-1-59197-250-1(7), SandCastle) ABDO Publishing Co.

—Og As in Dog, 1 vol. 2003. (Word Families Set 5 Ser.). (ENG., Illus.). 24p. (J). (gr. k-3). lib. bdg. 24.21 (978-1-59197-251-8(5), SandCastle) ABDO Publishing Co.

—Op As in Top, 1 vol. 2003. (Word Families Set 5 Ser.). (ENG., Illus.). 24p. (J). (gr. k-3). lib. bdg. 24.21 (978-1-59197-252-5(3), SandCastle) ABDO Publishing Co.

—Ore As in Core, 1 vol. 2003. (Word Families Set 7 Ser.). (ENG., Illus.). 24p. (J). (gr. k-3). lib. bdg. 24.21 (978-1-59197-267-9(1), SandCastle) ABDO Publishing Co.

—Ot As in Knot, 1 vol. 2003. (Word Families Set 5 Ser.). (ENG., Illus.). 24p. (J). (gr. k-3). lib. bdg. 24.21 (978-1-59197-253-2(1), SandCastle) ABDO Publishing Co.

—Ow As in Cow, 1 vol. 2003. (Word Families Set 5 Ser.). (ENG., Illus.). 24p. (J). (gr. k-3). lib. bdg. 24.21 (978-1-59197-254-9(X), SandCastle) ABDO Publishing Co.

Rondina, Catherine. The 10 Worst Things about Internet. 2008. 14.99 (978-1-55448-556-7(8)) Scholastic Library Publishing.

Rooney, Anne. No Wobbly Teeth, 1 vol. Fiorin, Fabiano, illus. 2013. (Start Reading Ser.). (ENG.). 24p. (gr. k-1). pap. 7.95 (978-1-4765-4125-9(6)) Capstone Press of Coughlan Cos.

Rooney, Rachel. Sleeping Beauty. 2015. (Collins Big Cat Ser.). (ENG.). 32p. (J). (gr. 3-3). pap. 8.95 (978-0-00-812771-8(9)) HarperCollins Pubs. Ltd. GBR. Dist: Independent Pubs. Group.

Rosa-Mendoza, Gladys. My Body/Mi Cuerpo. Butler, Chris, illus. 2007. (English Spanish Foundations Ser.). (ENG & SPA.). 20p. (gr. -1-2). pap. 19.95 (978-1-931398-85-5(2)) Me+Mi Publishing.

Rosado, Maribel. Little Red Hen Is a Good Hen. 2017. (Text Connections Guided Close Reading Ser.). (J). (gr. 1). (978-1-4900-1804-1(2)) Benchmark Education Co.

Rose, Emma. Energy Every Day, 6 vols., Set. 2004. (Phonics Readers Books 37-72 Ser.). (ENG.). 8p. (gr. k-1). pap. 35.70 (978-0-7368-4086-6(9), Phonics Readers) Capstone Press of Coughlan Cos.

—Our Natural Resources, 6 vols., Set. 2004. (Phonics Readers Books 37-72 Ser.). (ENG.). 16p. (gr. k-1). pap. 35.70 (978-0-7368-4070-5(2), Phonics Readers) Capstone Press of Coughlan Cos.

Rose, Malcolm. The Water Cycle. Sims, Sean, illus. 2017. (Reading Ladder Ser.). (ENG.). 32p. (J). (gr. 1-3). pap. 7.99 **(978-1-4052-8493-6(5))** Egmont Bks., Ltd. GBR. Dist: Independent Pubs. Group.

Rose, Mary. My Family. 2010. (ENG., Illus.). 20p. 4.81 (978-0-19-440079-4(4)) Oxford Univ. Pr., Inc.

Rosen Common Core Math Readers: Levels a - D. 2013. (Rosen Common Core Math Readers Ser.). 16p. (J). (gr. k-1). pap. 280.50 (978-1-4777-2213-8(0)); pap. 1683.00 (978-1-4777-2214-5(9)) Rosen Publishing Group, Inc., The. (Rosen Classroom).

Rosen Common Core Math Readers: Levels d - I. 2013. (Rosen Common Core Math Readers Ser.). 24p. (J). (gr. 1-2). pap. 1534.50 (978-1-4777-2219-0(X)); pap. 255.75 (978-1-4777-2220-6(3)) Rosen Publishing Group, Inc., The. (Rosen Classroom).

Rosen, Lucy & Sazaklis, John. Meet High Tide. 2015. (Transformers Passport to Reading Ser.). (J). lib. bdg. 13.55 (978-0-606-37513-9(9)) Turtleback Bks.

Rosen, Lucy, et al. The Squeakquel: Meet the 'Munks. 2009. (I Can Read Level 2 Ser.). (ENG., Illus.). 32p. (J). (gr. k-3). pap. 3.99 (978-0-06-184566-6(3)) HarperCollins Pubs.

Rosen Publishing Staff. The Britannica Common Core Library: Set 2, 1 vol. 2015. (Britannica Common Core Library). (ENG.). 32p. (J). 117.25 (978-1-62275-676-6(2), Britannica Educational Publishing) Rosen Publishing Group, Inc., The.

Rosen, Rachel & Benchmark Education Co., LLC Staff. Rob, Ron, & I. 2015. (StartUp Ser.). (J). (gr. k). (978-1-4900-0697-0(4)) Benchmark Education Co.

—Sit, Sit, Sit. 2015. (StartUp Ser.). (J). (gr. k). (978-1-4900-0689-5(3)) Benchmark Education Co.

Rosen Real Readers Big Books. 855.90 (978-1-4042-6227-0(X)) Rosen Publishing Group, Inc., The.

Rosenthal, Amy Krouse. Cookies: Bite-Size Life Lessons. Dyer, Jane, illus. 2016. 36p. (J). (gr. -1 — 1). bds. 7.99 (978-0-06-242739-7(3), HarperFestival) HarperCollins Pubs.

Roses Sing on New Snow. (Lexile Levels Ser.). 9.09 (978-1-56334-721-4(0)) CENGAGE Learning.

Ross, Dev. We Both Read Bilingual Edition-Frank & the Giant/Sapi y el Globo. Reinhart, Larry, illus. 2011. (ENG & SPA.). 44p. (J). pap. 4.99 (978-1-60115-042-4(3)) Treasure Bay, Inc.

Ross, Dev & Canetti, Yanitzia. Frank & the Balloon: Sapi y el Globo. Reinhart, Larry, illus. 2010. (SPA & ENG.). 41p. (J). (978-1-60115-041-7(5)) Treasure Bay, Inc.

Rosselson, Leon. Tom the Whistling Wonder. Haslam, John, illus. 2005. (ENG.). 24p. (J). lib. bdg. 23.65 (978-1-59646-758-3(4)) Dingles & Co.

Rossi, Rich, illus. Pillow Fight. 2005. (I'm Going to Read(r) Ser.). (ENG.). 32p. (J). (gr. k-1). per. 3.95 (978-1-4027-2719-1(4)) Sterling Publishing Co., Inc.

Round: Individual Title Six-Packs. (gr. 1-2). 22.00 (978-0-7635-9180-9(7)) Rigby Education.

Roxbee Cox, Phil. Phonics Stories for Young Readers, Vol. 2. 2009. (Phonics Readers Ser.). 96p. (J). 14.99 (978-0-7945-1887-5(7), Usborne) EDC Publishing.

Roy, Alene Adele. The Legend of Dragonfly Pond: Book Three. 2010. 60p. pap. 23.99 (978-1-4490-0834-5(8)) AuthorHouse.

Roy G Biv: Level G. Group 2. (Story Box Ser.). 16p. 31.50 (978-0-322-00333-0(4)) Wright Group/McGraw-Hill.

Roy, James. Queasy Rider. 2008. (Lightning Strikes Ser.). 96p. (J). pap. (978-1-921150-57-9(2)) Walker Bks. Australia Pty, Ltd.

Roza, Greg. A Day for Dad. 2006. (Neighborhood Readers Ser.). (ENG.). 16p. (gr. 1-3). pap. 6.50 (978-1-4042-7268-2(2), Rosen Classroom) Rosen Publishing Group, Inc., The.

—El Día de San Valentín (Valentines for Vinnie) 2007. (Lecturas del barrio (Neighborhood Readers) Ser.). (SPA.). 12p. 33.50 (978-1-4042-7301-6(8), Rosen Classroom) Rosen Publishing Group, Inc., The.

—Goal! 2006. (Neighborhood Readers Ser.). (ENG.). 16p. (gr. 1-3). pap. 6.50 (978-1-4042-7046-6(9), Rosen Classroom) Rosen Publishing Group, Inc., The.

—Happy New Year! 2006. (Neighborhood Readers Ser.). (ENG., Illus.). 16p. (gr. 1-3). pap. 6.50 (978-1-4042-7026-8(4), Rosen Classroom) Rosen Publishing Group, Inc., The.

—Lucy's Lunch. 2006. (Neighborhood Readers Ser.). (ENG.). 16p. (gr. -1-3). pap. 5.15 (978-1-4042-5649-1(0), Rosen Classroom) Rosen Publishing Group, Inc., The.

—Out & About. 2006. (Neighborhood Readers Ser.). (ENG.). 8p. (gr. -1-3). pap. 5.15 (978-1-4042-5680-4(6), Rosen Classroom) Rosen Publishing Group, Inc., The.

—The Peanut Butter Party. 2006. (Neighborhood Readers Ser.). (ENG., Illus.). 12p. (gr. 1-3). pap. 5.90 (978-1-4042-6827-2(8), Rosen Classroom) Rosen Publishing Group, Inc., The.

—A Piggy Bank for Pedro. 2006. (Neighborhood Readers Ser.). (ENG.). 8p. (gr. -1-3). pap. 5.15 (978-1-4042-5714-6(4), Rosen Classroom) Rosen Publishing Group, Inc., The.

—Valentines for Vinnie. (Neighborhood Readers Ser.). (ENG.). 12p. 2007. 33.50 (978-1-4042-7300-9(X)) 2006. (gr. 1-3). pap. 5.90 (978-1-4042-6799-2(9)) Rosen Publishing Group, Inc., The. (Rosen Classroom).

—Where's the Spaghetti? 2006. (Neighborhood Readers Ser.). (ENG.). 8p. (gr. -1-3). pap. 5.15 (978-1-4042-5655-2(5), Rosen Classroom) Rosen Publishing Group, Inc., The.

Rucker, Jeffrey A. A Trip to the Fire Station. 2008. (Rosen Real Readers: Upper Emergent Ser.). (ENG., Illus.). 12p. (gr. 1-2). pap. 5.90 (978-0-8239-8131-1(2)) Rosen Publishing Group, Inc., The.

P
Q
R

Ruffell, Ann & Orme, David. Treachery by Night. 2004. (Shades Ser.). (ENG.). 62p. (J). pap. *(978-0-237-52728-0(6))* Evans Brothers, Ltd.

Ruiz-Flores, Lupe. The Battle of the Snow Cones/La Guerra de las Raspas. 2010. (SPA.). 32p. (J). (gr. -1-3). 16.95 *(978-1-55885-575-5(0),* Piñata Books) Arte Publico Pr.

A Rumble & a Grumble: 3-in-1 Package. (Sails Literacy Ser.). 24p. (gr. 1-18). 57.00 *(978-0-7578-3210-9(5))* Rigby Education.

Russell, Marcia. A Visit to a Marine Base, 1 vol. 2nd rev. ed. 2011. (Nonfiction Readers Ser.). (ENG.). 24p. (J). (gr. 2-2). pap. 6.99 *(978-1-4333-3609-6(X))* Teacher Created Materials, Inc.

Ruth, Annie. I Can Read. Ruth, Annie, illus. l.t. ed. 2005. (Illus.). 32p. (J). (gr. -1-3). pap. 10.00 *(978-0-9656306-7-2(6))* Ruth, A. Creations.

Ryan. Lost: Big Book: Level Q. Group 1. (Take-Twostm Ser.). 32p. 38.95 *(978-0-322-04485-2(5))* Wright Group/McGraw-Hill.

Ryan, Ann Marie. The Best Gift. Denis, Florencia, illus. 2011. (My Phonics Readers: Level 1 Ser.). 24p. (J). (gr. -1-1). 24.25 *(978-1-84898-507-0(X))* Sea-To-Sea Pubns.

Rylant, Cynthia. Henry & Mudge & a Very Merry Christmas. Stevenson, Suçie, illus. 2005. (Henry & Mudge Ser.). 40p. (gr. -1-3). 14.00 *(978-0-7569-5816-9(4))* Perfection Learning Corp.

—Poppleton Se Divierte. Teague, Mark, illus. 2006. (Poppleton Ser.). (SPA.). 48p. pap. 11.73 *(978-0-15-356487-1(3))* Harcourt Children's Bks.

Sabo, J. Train Wrecker. 2011. 28p. pap. 24.95 *(978-1-4626-4379-0(5))* America Star Bks.

Saddleback Educational Publishing Staff, creator. Barclay Family Adventures Resource Guide. 2003. (Barclay Family Adventure Ser.). 48p. tchr. ed., per. 9.95 *(978-1-56254-560-4(4),* SP 5604) Saddleback Educational Publishing, Inc.

Saffiedine, Amanda. I Don't Understand. 2009. 32p. pap. 12.99 *(978-1-4490-1310-3(4))* AuthorHouse.

Sage, Alison. Going on a Plane Purple Band. 2016. (Cambridge Reading Adventures Ser.). (ENG.). 24p. pap. 7.19 *(978-1-316-50088-0(8))* Cambridge Univ. Pr.

Said Mouse to Mole. 2005. (J). per. 8.95 *(978-1-59566-139-5(5))* QEB Publishing Inc.

Saltzberg, Barney. I Love Cats. 2006. 20p. pap. 8.99 *(978-0-7636-3318-9(6))* Four Blocks.

Salzmann, Mary Elizabeth. -Ad As in Dad, 1 vol. 2003. (Word Families Set 1 Ser.). (ENG., Illus.). 24p. (J). (gr. k-3). lib. bdg. 24.21 *(978-1-59197-226-6(4))* ABDO Publishing Co.

—Ag As in Flag, 1 vol. 2003. (Word Families Set 1 Ser.). (ENG., Illus.). 24p. (J). (gr. k-3). lib. bdg. 24.21 *(978-1-59197-225-9(6))* ABDO Publishing Co.

—Am As in Ham, 1 vol. 2003. (Word Families Set 1 Ser.). (ENG., Illus.). 24p. (J). (gr. k-3). lib. bdg. 24.21 *(978-1-59197-223-5(X))* ABDO Publishing Co.

—Ap As in Cap, 1 vol. 2003. (Word Families Set 1 Ser.). (ENG., Illus.). 24p. (J). (gr. k-3). lib. bdg. 24.21 *(978-1-59197-224-2(8))* ABDO Publishing Co.

—An As in Fan. 2003. (Word Families Set 1 Ser.). (ENG., Illus.). 24p. (J). (gr. k-3). lib. bdg. 24.21 *(978-1-59197-222-8(1))* ABDO Publishing Co.

—At As in Cat, 1 vol. 2003. (Word Families Set 1 Ser.). (ENG., Illus.). 24p. (J). (gr. k-3). lib. bdg. 24.21 *(978-1-59197-221-1(3),* SandCastle) ABDO Publishing Co.

—Ay As in Clay, 1 vol. 2003. (Word Families Set 7 Ser.). (ENG., Illus.). 24p. (J). (gr. k-3). lib. bdg. 24.21 *(978-1-59197-264-8(7))* ABDO Publishing Co.

—Come Home with Me! 2004. (Sight Words Ser.). (ENG., Illus.). 24p. (J). (gr. k-3). lib. bdg. 24.21 *(978-1-59197-465-9(8))* ABDO Publishing Co.

—Did You See One Jump? 2004. (Sight Words Ser.). (ENG., Illus.). 24p. (J). (gr. k-3). lib. bdg. 24.21 *(978-1-59197-466-6(6),* SandCastle) ABDO Publishing Co.

—Ell As in Well, 1 vol. 2003. (Word Families Set 2 Ser.). (ENG., Illus.). 24p. (J). (gr. k-3). lib. bdg. 24.21 *(978-1-59197-231-0(0),* SandCastle) ABDO Publishing Co.

—I Had a Great Time! 2004. (Sight Words Ser.). (ENG., Illus.). 24p. (J). (gr. k-3). lib. bdg. 24.21 *(978-1-59197-477-2(1),* SandCastle) ABDO Publishing Co.

—It's Not Good, It's Great! 2003. (Sight Words Ser.). (ENG., Illus.). 24p. (J). (gr. k-3). lib. bdg. 24.21 *(978-1-59197-479-6(8),* SandCastle) ABDO Publishing Co.

—No Pigs on the Farm! 2004. (Sight Words Ser.). (ENG., Illus.). 24p. (J). (gr. k-3). lib. bdg. 24.21 *(978-1-59197-471-0(2),* SandCastle) ABDO Publishing Co.

—Out for the Summer! 2004. (Sight Words Ser.). (ENG., Illus.). 24p. (J). (gr. k-3). lib. bdg. 24.21 *(978-1-59197-472-7(0),* SandCastle) ABDO Publishing Co.

—Snow & More Snow! 2004. (Sight Words Ser.). (ENG., Illus.). 24p. (J). (gr. k-3). lib. bdg. 24.21 *(978-1-59197-470-3(4),* SandCastle) ABDO Publishing Co.

—They Are the Best! 2004. (Sight Words Ser.). (ENG., Illus.). 24p. (J). (gr. k-3). lib. bdg. 24.21 *(978-1-59197-474-1(7),* SandCastle) ABDO Publishing Co.

—Way to Go! 2004. (Sight Words Ser.). (ENG., Illus.). 24p. (J). (gr. k-3). lib. bdg. 24.21 *(978-1-59197-468-0(2),* SandCastle) ABDO Publishing Co.

—We All Like It! 2004. (Sight Words Ser.). (ENG., Illus.). 24p. (J). (gr. k-3). lib. bdg. 24.21 *(978-1-59197-467-3(4),* SandCastle) ABDO Publishing Co.

—What a Day in the Park! 2004. (Sight Words Ser.). (ENG., Illus.). 24p. (J). (gr. k-3). lib. bdg. 24.21 *(978-1-59197-476-5(3),* SandCastle) ABDO Publishing Co.

—Who Is This at the Beach? 2004. (Sight Words Ser.). (ENG., Illus.). 24p. (J). (gr. k-3). lib. bdg. 24.21 *(978-1-59197-480-2(1),* SandCastle) ABDO Publishing Co.

Sam & the Robots. 2016. (Ladybird Readers Ser.). (ENG.). 16p. (J). pap., act. bk. ed. 5.99 *(978-0-241-25376-2(4))* Penguin Bks., Ltd. GBR. Dist: Independent Pubs. Group.

Sam's big Clean-up: Individual Title Six-Packs. (gr. 1-2). 25.00 *(978-0-7635-9145-8(9))* Rigby Education.

Sam's Dad: Level M, 6 vols. 128p. (gr. 2-3). 41.95 *(978-0-7699-1029-1(7))* Shortland Pubns. (U. S. A.) Inc.

Samson, Tess. Snack Time. 2010. (Sight Word Readers Ser.). (J). 3.49 *(978-1-60719-618-1(2))* Newmark Learning LLC.

—What Goes Up? 2010. (Sight Word Readers Ser.). (J). 3.49 *(978-1-60719-617-4(4))* Newmark Learning LLC.

Samuel, Adele. Wild World of Sports. 2007. (Steck-Vaughn BOLDPRINT Anthologies Ser.). (ENG., Illus.). 48p. (gr. 4-7). pap. 16.90 *(978-1-4190-4020-7(0))* Houghton Mifflin Harcourt Publishing Co.

Samuel, Nigel. Creatures of the Deep. 2007. (Steck-Vaughn BOLDPRINT Anthologies Ser.). (ENG., Illus.). 48p. (gr. 4-7). pap. 16.90 *(978-1-4190-4021-4(9))* Houghton Mifflin Harcourt Publishing Co.

—The 10 Coolest Wonders of the Universe. 2008. (Illus.). (J). 14.99 *(978-1-55448-490-4(1))* Scholastic Library Publishing.

—The 10 Mightiest Mountains. 2007. (Illus.). (J). 14.99 *(978-1-55448-509-3(6))* Scholastic Library Publishing.

San Vicente, Luis, illus. The Festival of Bones / el Festival de Las Calaveras. 2014. (ENG.). 32p. (J). 7.95 *(978-1-941026-03-8(6))* Cinco Puntos Pr.

Sand Castles: Level I, 6 vols. (Wonder Worldtm Ser.). 16p. 29.95 *(978-0-7802-4597-6(0))* Wright Group/McGraw-Hill.

Sandage, Charley. ALL AROUND ARKANSAS Big Book. 2005. (Illus.). (J). pap. *(978-0-9794044-2-9(8))* Archeological Assessments, Inc.

Sander, Sonia. All Aboard! 2010. (Lego City Ser.). (ENG.). 32p. (J). (gr. -1-k). pap. 3.99 *(978-0-545-17764-1(2))* Scholastic, Inc.

—Werewolf Watch. 2012. (Scooby Doo Reader Ser.). lib. bdg. 13.55 *(978-0-606-23961-5(8),* Turtleback) Turtleback Bks.

Sanders, Nancy I. Cut & Paste Mini-Books: Math: 15 Fun, Interactive Mini-Books That Reinforce Key Math Concepts & Boost Reading Skills. 2010. (ENG.). 128p. (gr. k-1). pap. 16.99 *(978-0-439-60630-1(6),* Teaching Resources) Scholastic, Inc.

Sandler, Michael & Hess, Debra. Checkered Flag! 2007. (Read on! Special Edition: Level AA Ser.). (Illus.). 23p. (J). (gr. 4-7). pap. 4.84 *(978-1-4190-3516-6(9))* Steck-Vaughn.

Sandoval, Migs, illus. Beauty & the Beast: Level 3: Learn Chinese Mandarin Through Fairy Tales. 2006. (Learn Chinese Through Fairy Tales Ser.). (ENG & CHI.). 29p. (J). (gr. -1-3). pap. 14.95 incl. audio compact disk *(978-1-891888-91-5(9))* Slangman Publishing.

Sands, Nora. Crunch & Munch. 2007. (Collins Big Cat Ser.). (ENG., Illus.). 48p. (J). (gr. k-1). pap. 6.99 *(978-0-00-718665-5(7))* HarperCollins Pubs. Ltd. GBR. Dist: Independent Pubs. Group.

A Sandwich Person: Level H, 6 vols. (Wonder Worldtm Ser.). 16p. 29.95 *(978-0-7802-2028-7(5))* Wright Group/McGraw-Hill.

Sanfilippo, Simona, illus. Rapunzel. 2009. (Flip-Up Fairy Tales Ser.). (ENG.). 24p. (J). (gr. -1-2). audio compact disk *(978-1-84643-292-7(8))* Child's Play International Ltd.

Santiago Baca, Jimmy. En Suelo Firme: El Nacimiento de un Poeta. Berástegui, Manu, tr. 2005. (SPA., Illus.). 360p. pap. 25.95 *(978-84-204-6424-4(4),* Alfaguara) Santillana USA Publishing Co., Inc.

Santiano, Carlos, et al. Where Is He? 2010. (Reach for Reading Ser.). (ENG., Illus.). 8p. (C). pap. 7.95 *(978-0-7362-7994-9(6))* CENGAGE Learning.

Sargemt, Dave & Sargent, Pat. Batley Needs Glasses, 10 vols., Vol. 12. Robinson, Laura, illus. 2004. (Learn to Read Ser.: 10). 18p. (J). lib. bdg. 20.95 *(978-1-56763-819-6(8))* Ozark Publishing.

Sargent, Brian. Altruism: What's in It for Me? 2014. (ENG., Illus.). 32p. (J). pap. 9.50 *(978-1-107-62262-3(X))* Cambridge Univ. Pr.

—Life on the Edge. 2014. (ENG.). 28p. (J). pap. 9.50 *(978-1-107-63028-4(2))* Cambridge Univ. Pr.

—Losing It: The Meaning of Loss. 2014. (ENG., Illus.). 28p. (J). pap. 9.50 *(978-1-107-68191-0(X))* Cambridge Univ. Pr.

—Mark Your Territory Intermediate Book with Online Access. 2014. (ENG., Illus.). 28p. pap. 9.50 *(978-1-107-65895-0(0))* Cambridge Univ. Pr.

Sargent, Dave & Sargent, Pat. Batley Needs Glasses, 10 vols., Vol. 12. Robinson, Laura, illus. 2004. (Learn to Read Ser.: 10).Tr. of Batley Necesita Anteojos. 18p. (J). pap. 10.95 *(978-1-56763-820-2(1))* Ozark Publishing.

SargentBrian. LIFE IN MUMBAI HIGH BEGINNING BOOK WITH ONLINE ACCESS. 2014. (ENG., Illus.). 24p. pap. 9.50 *(978-1-107-62167-1(4))* Cambridge Univ. Pr.

—THE TRADITIONS OF DEATH INTERMEDIATE BOOK WITH ONLINE ACCESS. 2014. (ENG.). 28p. (J). pap. 9.50 *(978-1-107-63578-4(0))* Cambridge Univ. Pr.

The Saturday Club. (Early Intervention Levels Ser.). 31.86 *(978-0-7362-0623-5(X))* CENGAGE Learning.

The Saturday Club (18), Vol. 18. (Early Intervention Levels Ser.). 5.31 *(978-0-7362-0611-2(6))* CENGAGE Learning.

Saviola, Erin. Airplane Jane. 2006. (Neighborhood Readers Ser.). (ENG., Illus.). 16p. (gr. 1-3). pap. 6.50 *(978-1-4042-7236-1(4),* Rosen Classroom) Rosen Publishing Group, Inc., The.

—The Biggest Fish. 2006. (Neighborhood Readers Ser.). (ENG.). 8p. (gr. -1-3). pap. 5.15 *(978-1-4042-6453-3(1),* Rosen Classroom) Rosen Publishing Group, Inc., The.

Saxby, Karen. Storyfun for Flyers Student's Book. 2010. (ENG., Illus.). 96p. pap. 17.50 *(978-0-521-13410-1(2))* Cambridge Univ. Pr.

Say Hello! (Early Intervention Levels Ser.). 3.85 *(978-1-56334-955-3(8));* 23.10 *(978-0-7362-0004-2(5))* CENGAGE Learning.

Sayles, Alayne. Alphie & the Alphabets: A Fun Way to Learn to Read. Platt, Greg, illus. 2005. 44p. (J). spiral bd. 79.95 incl. audio compact disk *(978-0-9767506-0-4(0))* Reading Studio Pr.

Saylor-Marchant, Linda. Hip Hop into Reading Series: It's easy to read & rap/read & rap like the President. 2009. (Illus.). (J). pap. 19.95 *(978-0-615-24951-3(5))* 44 Enterprises.

Sazaklis, John. Day of Doom. 2013. (Justice League Classic: I Can Read! Ser.). (J). lib. bdg. 13.55 *(978-0-606-32162-4(4),* Turtleback) Turtleback Bks.

Scaglione, Joanne & Small, Gail. Life's Little Lessons: An Inch-by-Inch Tale of Success. 2006. (ENG., Illus.). 64p. pap. 21.00 *(978-1-57886-336-5(8))* Rowman & Littlefield Publishers, Inc.

Scanlon, Jack. Rainbow Zoo. 2006. (Neighborhood Readers Ser.). (ENG., Illus.). 8p. (gr. -1-3). pap. 5.15 *(978-1-4042-6686-5(0),* Rosen Classroom) Rosen Publishing Group, Inc., The.

A Scare in the City. (Early Intervention Levels Ser.). 31.86 *(978-0-7362-0625-9(6))* CENGAGE Learning.

Scarry, Richard & Farber, Erica. Cake Soup. Scarry, Huck, illus. 2011. (Richard Scarry's Great Big Schoolhouse Ser.). (ENG.). 24p. (J). (gr. -1-k). pap. 3.95 *(978-1-4027-7317-4(X))* Sterling Publishing Co., Inc.

Schaefer, Elizabeth. Rey Meets BB-8. 2015. (Star Wars: World of Reading Ser.). (J). lib. bdg. 13.55 *(978-0-606-38312-7(3))* Turtleback Bks.

Schecter, Deborah. Sight Word Manipulatives for Reading Success: Wheels, Pull-Throughs, Puzzles, & Dozens of Other Easy-to-Make Manipulatives That Help Kids Read, Write, & Really Learn High-Frequency Words. 2005. (ENG.). 144p. (gr. k-2). pap. 17.99 *(978-0-439-54259-3(6),* Teaching Resources) Scholastic, Inc.

—25 Reproducible Mini-Books in English & Spanish That Give Kids a Great Start in Reading. 2005. (My First Bilingual Little Readers Ser.). (ENG.). 64p. (gr. k-1). pap. 11.99 *(978-0-439-70069-6(8),* Teaching Resources) Scholastic, Inc.

Scherm, Deedra. Cinco Panes y un Par de Peces: Una Historia de la Fe y de Dar. Dreyer, Laura, illus. 2008. (SPA.). 20p. (J). (gr. -1-3). bds. 7.99 *(978-1-934789-06-3(2))* Lemon Vision Productions.

—Solo uno Como Yo: Una Rima Dulce y Pequenita para Ayudar Hacer Brillar Tu Lucecita. Dreyer, Laura, illus. 2008. (SPA.). 22p. (J). (gr. -1-3). 7.99 *(978-1-934789-05-6(4))* Lemon Vision Productions.

Scheunemann, Pam. -Ack As in Snack, 1 vol. 2003. (Word Families Set 6 Ser.). (ENG., Illus.). 24p. (J). (gr. k-3). lib. bdg. 24.21 *(978-1-59197-261-7(2))* ABDO Publishing Co.

—Ash As in Trash, 1 vol. 2003. (Word Families Set 6 Ser.). (ENG., Illus.). 24p. (J). (gr. k-3). lib. bdg. 24.21 *(978-1-59197-260-0(4))* ABDO Publishing Co.

—Aw As in Paw, 1 vol. 2003. (Word Families Set 7 Ser.). (ENG., Illus.). 24p. (J). (gr. k-3). lib. bdg. 24.21 *(978-1-59197-263-1(9))* ABDO Publishing Co.

—Ent As in Cent, 1 vol. 2003. (Word Families Set 2 Ser.). (ENG., Illus.). 24p. (J). (gr. k-3). lib. bdg. 24.21 *(978-1-59197-233-4(7),* SandCastle) ABDO Publishing Co.

—Ick As in Kick, 1 vol. 2003. (Word Families Set 6 Ser.). (ENG., Illus.). 24p. (J). (gr. k-3). lib. bdg. 24.21 *(978-1-59197-258-7(2),* SandCastle) ABDO Publishing Co.

—Ing As in King, 1 vol. 2003. (Word Families Set 6 Ser.). (ENG., Illus.). 24p. (J). (gr. k-3). lib. bdg. 24.21 *(978-1-59197-256-3(6),* SandCastle) ABDO Publishing Co.

—Ink As in Drink, 1 vol. 2003. (Word Families Set 6 Ser.). (ENG., Illus.). 24p. (J). (gr. k-3). lib. bdg. 24.21 *(978-1-59197-257-0(4),* SandCastle) ABDO Publishing Co.

—Unk As in Skunk, 1 vol. 2003. (Word Families Set 6 Ser.). (ENG., Illus.). 24p. (J). (gr. k-3). lib. bdg. 24.21 *(978-1-59197-259-4(0),* SandCastle) ABDO Publishing Co.

Schifini, Alfredo, et al. Avenues Level C: Literature Anthology. 2003. (Avenues Ser.). (ENG.). (C). (gr. 2-18). 91.95 *(978-0-7362-1876-4(9))* CENGAGE Learning.

—Avenues Level D: Literature Anthology. 2003. (Avenues Ser.). (ENG.). 504p. (C). (gr. 3-18). 91.95 *(978-0-7362-1673-9(1))* CENGAGE Learning.

—Avenues Level E: Literature Anthology. 2003. (Avenues Ser.). (ENG.). 504p. (C). (gr. 4-18). 91.95 *(978-0-7362-1709-5(6))* CENGAGE Learning.

—Avenues Level F: Literature Anthology. 2003. (Avenues Ser.). (ENG.). (C). (gr. 5-18). 91.95 *(978-0-7362-1745-3(2))* CENGAGE Learning.

Schmauss, Judy Kentor, et al. Reader's Clubhouse Long Vowels Level 2 Valu-Pak, 6 vols. 2006. (Reader's Clubhouse Ser.). (ENG., Illus.). 120p. (J). (gr. -1-1). pap. 15.96 *(978-0-7641-7969-3(1))* Barron's Educational Series, Inc.

Scholastic & Schmidt, Rebecca L. Movie Magic. Scholastic, Inc. Staff, illus. 2016. (LEGO NEXO Knights Ser.). (ENG.). 32p. (J). (gr. 2-5). pap. 3.99 *(978-1-338-03802-6(8))* Scholastic, Inc.

Scholastic Editors. The Rescue Mission. 2015. (Ninjago Readers Ser.: 11). lib. bdg. 13.55 *(978-0-606-36373-0(4))* Turtleback Bks.

Scholastic Editors & Howard, Kate. Return of the Djinn. 2016. (Lego Ninjago Ser.). (ENG.). 32p. (J). (gr. 1-3). pap. 3.99 *(978-0-545-92553-2(3))* Scholastic, Inc.

Scholastic Inc, contrib. by. All Around Me. 2017. (Words Are Fun Ser.). (ENG.). 12p. (J). bds. 8.95 *(978-0-531-23724-3(9),* Children's Pr.) Scholastic Library Publishing.

Scholastic Inc. (US) Staff, contrib. by. All about Me/ Todo Sobre Mí. 2017. (Words Are Fun/ Diverpalabras (Bilingual) Ser.). (ENG.). 12p. (J). bds. 8.95 *(978-0-531-23071-8(6),* Children's Pr.) Scholastic Library Publishing.

Scholastic, Inc. Staff. Always in Style. 2016. (Shopkins Ser.). (ENG.). 32p. (J). (gr. -1-3). pap. 5.99 *(978-0-545-94059-7(1))* Scholastic, Inc.

—Mi Primera Biblia. 2015. (ENG & SPA.). 147p. (J). (gr. -1-k). bds. 9.99 *(978-0-545-05656-4(X),* Scholastic en Espanol) Scholastic, Inc.

Scholastic, Inc. Staff, contrib. by. Adventures in LEGO City, Set. 2nd ed. 2015. (Lego City Ser.). (ENG.). (J). (gr. -1-3). pap. 24.99 *(978-0-545-80861-3(8))* Scholastic, Inc.

Scholastic, Inc. Staff & Barnes, Derrick D. Low-Down Bad-Day Blues. Boyd, Aaron, illus. 2004. (Just for You Ser.). (ENG.). 32p. (gr. k-1). pap. 3.99 *(978-0-439-56867-8(6),* Teaching Resources) Scholastic, Inc.

—Stop, Drop, & Chill. Phillips-Duke, Barbara Jean & Duke, Barbara, illus. 2004. (Just for You Ser.). (ENG.). 32p. pap. 3.99 *(978-0-439-56870-8(6),* Teaching Resources) Scholastic, Inc.

Scholastic, Inc. Staff & Bermiss, Aamir Lee. I Hate to Be Sick! Wilson-Max, Ken, illus. 2004. (Just for You Ser.). (ENG.). 32p. (gr. k-3). pap. 3.99 *(978-0-439-56877-7(3),* Teaching Resources) Scholastic, Inc.

Scholastic, Inc. Staff & Black, Sonia. Jumping the Broom. Hu, Ying-Hwa & Van Wright, Cornelius, illus. 2004. (Just for You Ser.). (ENG.). 32p. pap. 3.99 *(978-0-439-56878-4(1),* Teaching Resources) Scholastic, Inc.

Scholastic, Inc. Staff & Chapman, Cindy. Baby Animals, 6 vols., Set. 2003. (Phonics Readers 1-36 Ser.). (ENG.). 8p. (gr. k-1). pap. 29.70 *(978-0-7368-3188-8(6),* Phonics Readers) Capstone Press of Coughlan Cos.

Scholastic, Inc. Staff & Ford, Juwanda G. Shop Talk. Hoston, Jim, illus. 2004. (Just for You Ser.). (ENG.). 32p. (gr. k-3). pap. 3.99 *(978-0-439-56873-9(0),* Teaching Resources) Scholastic, Inc.

Scholastic, Inc. Staff & George, Olivia. The Bravest Girls in the World. DuBurke, Randy, illus. 2004. (Just for You Ser.). (ENG.). 32p. pap. 3.99 *(978-0-439-56875-3(7),* Teaching Resources) Scholastic, Inc.

Scholastic, Inc. Staff & Hooks, Gwendolyn. The Mystery of the Missing Dog. Devard, Nancy, illus. 2004. (Just for You Ser.). (ENG.). 32p. (gr. k-3). pap. 3.99 *(978-0-439-56864-7(1),* Teaching Resources) Scholastic, Inc.

—Three's a Crowd. Walker, Sylvia, illus. 2004. (Just for You Ser.). (ENG.). 32p. (gr. k-3). pap. 3.99 *(978-0-439-56865-4(X),* Teaching Resources) Scholastic, Inc.

Scholastic, Inc. Staff & Medearis, Angela Shelf. Singing for Dr. King. Van Wright, Cornelius & Hu, Ying-Hwa, illus. 2004. (Just for You Ser.). (ENG.). 32p. (gr. k-3). pap. 3.99 *(978-0-439-56855-5(2),* Teaching Resources) Scholastic, Inc.

Scholastic, Inc. Staff & Roberson, Karla. My Shoelaces Are Hard to Tie! Holley, Vanessa, illus. 2004. (Just for You Ser.). (ENG.). 32p. pap. 3.99 *(978-0-439-56869-2(2),* Teaching Resources) Scholastic, Inc.

Scholastic, Inc. Staff, et al. Sunday Best. Bootman, Colin, illus. 2004. (Just for You Ser.). (ENG.). 32p. pap. 3.99 *(978-0-439-56854-8(4),* Teaching Resources) Scholastic, Inc.

Scholastic News Nonfiction Readers: Kids Like Me (Global Awareness), 5 vols., Set. Incl. This Is the Way We Dress. Behrens, Janice. lib. bdg. 22.00 *(978-0-531-21338-4(2));* This Is the Way We Eat Our Food. Falk, Laine. lib. bdg. 22.00 *(978-0-531-21339-1(0));* This Is the Way We Go to School. Falk, Laine. lib. bdg. 22.00 *(978-0-531-21341-4(2));* This Is the Way We Help at Home. Miller, Amanda. lib. bdg. 22.00 *(978-0-531-21340-7(4));* This Is the Way We Play. Miller, Amanda. lib. bdg. 22.00 *(978-0-531-21342-1(0));* 24p. (J). (gr. 1-2). 2009. Set lib. bdg. 110.00 *(978-0-531-21035-2(9),* Children's Pr.) Scholastic Library Publishing.

The School Day, 2, Pack. (Chiquilibros Ser.). (gr. -1-1). 12.00 *(978-0-7635-8542-6(4))* Rigby Education.

School Lunch. (J). 6.47 *(978-0-8136-5338-9(X))* Modern Curriculum Pr.

The School Story Student Packet. 2004. (J). 12.99 *(978-1-58130-520-3(6))* Novel Units, Inc.

School Zone. Wonder Words Flash Action Software. 2007. 128p. pap. 15.99 *(978-1-58947-112-2(1))* School Zone Publishing Co.

School Zone Publishing Company Staff. Beginning Reading 1-2. deluxe ed. 2005. (ENG.). 64p. (J). pap., wbk. ed. 3.99 *(978-1-58947-337-9(X))* School Zone Publishing Co.

School Zone Staff. Readiness. 2005. (ENG.). 56p. (J). 2.79 *(978-1-58947-479-6(1))* School Zone Publishing Co.

Schorr, Titus. Backyard Fun, 01 vols., 1. 2016. (Rosen REAL Readers: STEM & STEAM Collection). (ENG.). 12p. (J). pap. 6.33 *(978-1-5081-1566-3(4),* Rosen Classroom) Rosen Publishing Group, Inc., The.

—A Big Change, 01 vols., 1. 2016. (Rosen REAL Readers: STEM & STEAM Collection). (ENG.). 12p. (J). pap. 6.33 *(978-1-5081-1584-7(2),* Rosen Classroom) Rosen Publishing Group, Inc., The.

—Doing Homework with Dad, 01 vols., 1. 2016. (Rosen REAL Readers: STEM & STEAM Collection). (ENG.). 8p. (J). pap. 5.46 *(978-1-5081-1507-6(9),* Rosen Classroom) Rosen Publishing Group, Inc., The.

—Field Trip Day, 01 vols., 1. 2016. (Rosen REAL Readers: STEM & STEAM Collection). (ENG.). 8p. (J). pap. 5.46 *(978-1-5081-1489-5(7),* Rosen Classroom) Rosen Publishing Group, Inc., The.

—The Gift, 01 vols., 1. 2016. (Rosen REAL Readers: Social Studies Nonfiction / Fiction: Family, Community, & the World Ser.). (ENG.). 8p. (J). pap. 5.46 *(978-1-5081-1875-6(2),* Rosen Classroom) Rosen Publishing Group, Inc., The.

—The Package, 01 vols., 1. 2016. (Rosen REAL Readers: Social Studies Nonfiction / Fiction: Family, Community, & the World Ser.). (ENG.). 12p. (J). pap. 6.33 *(978-1-5081-1922-7(8),* Rosen Classroom) Rosen Publishing Group, Inc., The.

—The Spelling Bee, 01 vols., 1. 2016. (Rosen REAL Readers: Social Studies Nonfiction / Fiction: Family, Community, & the World Ser.). (ENG.). 8p. (J). pap. 5.46 *(978-1-5081-1839-8(6),* Rosen Classroom) Rosen Publishing Group, Inc., The.

—Star Watch, 01 vols., 1. 2016. (Rosen REAL Readers: STEM & STEAM Collection). (ENG.). 12p. (J). pap. 6.33 *(978-1-5081-1548-9(6),* Rosen Classroom) Rosen Publishing Group, Inc., The.

—Wings, 01 vols., 1. 2016. (Rosen REAL Readers: Social Studies Nonfiction / Fiction: Family, Community, & the World Ser.). (ENG.). 12p. (J). pap. 6.33 *(978-1-5081-1907-4(4),* Rosen Classroom) Rosen Publishing Group, Inc., The.

Schraff, Anne. The Accuser, 1 vol. unabr. ed. 2010. (Q Reads Ser.). (ENG.). 32p. (YA). (gr. 9-12). pap. 6.95 *(978-1-61651-188-3(5))* Saddleback Educational Publishing, Inc.

—And We Will Be No More. 2008. (Passages to History Ser.). 127p. (J). (gr. 4-6). lib. bdg. 13.95 *(978-0-7569-8395-6(9))* Perfection Learning Corp.

—Black Widow Beauty, 1 vol. unabr. ed. 2010. (Q Reads Ser.). (ENG.). 32p. (YA). (gr. 9-12). pap. 6.95 *(978-1-61651-178-4(8))* Saddleback Educational Publishing, Inc.

—Blackout, 1 vol. unabr. ed. 2010. (Q Reads Ser.). (ENG.). 32p. (YA). (gr. 9-12). pap. 6.95 *(978-1-61651-190-6(7))* Saddleback Educational Publishing, Inc.

—The Darkest Secret. 2008. (Passages Ser.). 114p. (YA). (gr. 7-9). lib. bdg. 13.95 *(978-0-7569-8376-5(2))* Perfection Learning Corp.

—The Experiment, 1 vol. unabr. ed. 2010. (Q Reads Ser.). (ENG.). 32p. (YA). (gr. 9-12). pap. 6.95 *(978-1-61651-181-4(8))* Saddleback Educational Publishing, Inc.

—The Haunting of Hawthorne. 2008. (Passages Ser.). 125p. (YA). (gr. 7-9). lib. bdg. 13.95 *(978-0-7569-8379-6(7))* Perfection Learning Corp.

—The Shadow Man. 2008. (Passages Ser.). 134p. (YA). (gr. 7-9). lib. bdg. 13.95 *(978-0-7569-8382-6(7))* Perfection Learning Corp.

—The Shining Mark. 2008. (Passages Ser.). 109p. (J). lib. bdg. 13.95 (978-0-7569-8383-3(5)) Perfection Learning Corp.

—To Be a Man, 1 vol. unabr. ed. 2011. (Urban Underground Ser.). (ENG.). 181p. (YA). (gr. 9-12). pap. 9.95 (978-1-61651-008-4(0)) Saddleback Educational Publishing, Inc.

—To Be Somebody. 2008. (Passages Ser.). 120p. (J). (gr. 4-6). lib. bdg. 13.95 (978-0-7569-8390-1(8)) Perfection Learning Corp.

—Under the Mushroom Cloud. 2008. (Passages to Adventure Ser.). 115p. (J). (gr. 4-6). lib. bdg. 13.95 (978-0-7569-8399-4(1)) Perfection Learning Corp.

Schreyer, Karmel. Turtles: Ancient Symbol/Modern Survivor Upper Intermediate Book with Online Access. 2014. (ENG.). 28p. (J). pap. 9.50 (978-1-107-66057-1(2)) Cambridge Univ. Pr.

SchreyerKarmel. TRAGEDY ON THE SLOPES UPPER INTERMEDIATE BOOK WITH ONLINE ACCESS. 2014. (ENG., Illus.). 28p. pap. 9.50 (978-1-107-62159-6(3)) Cambridge Univ. Pr.

—Water Power: The Greatest Force on Earth. 2014. (ENG., Illus.). 28p. (J). pap. 9.50 (978-1-107-68897-1(3)) Cambridge Univ. Pr.

Schulz. Buon San Valentino Dolce. pap. 19.95 (978-88-451-2996-4(9)) Fabbri Editori - RCS Libri ITA. Dist: Distribooks, Inc.

—Tutti qui Biscotti. pap. 19.95 (978-88-451-2810-3(5)) Fabbri Editori - RCS Libri ITA. Dist: Distribooks, Inc.

Schulz, Kathy. Necesito una Ayudita. Iosa, Ann, illus. 2011. (Rookie Ready to Learn Español Ser.). (SPA.). 32p. (J). pap. 5.95 (978-0-531-26782-0(2)); lib. bdg. 23.00 (978-0-531-26114-9(X)) Scholastic Library Publishing. (Children's Pr.).

Schwartz, Heather. The French Revolution: Terror & Triumph, 1 vol. 2012. (Primary Source Readers Ser.). (ENG.). 32p. (J). (gr. 5-5). pap. 8.99 (978-1-4333-5011-5(4)) Teacher Created Materials, Inc.

—Lizzie Johnson: Texan Cowgirl, 1 vol. 2012. (Primary Source Readers Ser.). (ENG.). 32p. (J). (gr. 3-3). pap. 8.99 (978-1-4333-5051-1(3)) Teacher Created Materials, Inc.

—Marie Antoinette: The Controversial Queen of France, 1 vol. 2012. (Primary Source Readers Ser.). (ENG.). 32p. (J). (gr. 4-4). pap. 8.99 (978-1-4333-5012-2(2)) Teacher Created Materials, Inc.

Science Fun. 2005. (Little Celebrations Thematic Packages Ser.). (J). (gr. k-3). 133.50 (978-0-673-75382-3(4)) Celebration Pr.

Science Readers Staff & Van Gorp, Lynn. The World of Genetics, 1 vol. 2007. (Science Readers Ser.). (ENG., Illus.). 32p. (J). (gr. 4-4). pap. 8.99 (978-0-7439-0597-8(0)) Shell Educational Publishing.

Scollon, William & Disney Book Group Staff. The Key to Skull Rock, Level 1. Disney Storybook Art Team, illus. 2013. (World of Reading Ser.). (ENG.). 32p. (J). (gr. -1-k). pap. 3.99 (978-1-4231-6397-8(4)) Disney Pr.

Scott, Caitlin. Treasure Hunting Set: Looking for Lost Riches, 6 vols. 2003. (High Five Reading - Red Ser.). (ENG.). 48p. (gr. 3-4). pap. 54.00 (978-0-7368-2835-2(4), High Five Reading (RBL)) Capstone Press of Coughlan Cos.

Scott, Foresman and Company Staff. Read with Dick & Jane, 12 vols. 2004. (Read with Dick & Jane Ser.: 11). (Illus.). 32p. (J). (gr. -1-2). 250.58 (978-1-59197-628-8(6)) Spotlight.

Scott Foresman Early Reading Intervention. 2003. (gr. k-1). (978-0-328-03826-8(1), Scott Foresman) Addison-Wesley Educational Pubs., Inc.

Scott Foresman Family Reading Guide. 2004. (gr. 6-18). 13.50 (978-0-673-63400-9(0)) Addison-Wesley Educational Pubs., Inc.

Scott Foresman Reading: Additional Resources. 2004. (Scott Foresman Reading Ser.). (gr. 1-18). (978-0-328-04085-8(1), Scott Foresman) Addison-Wesley Educational Pubs., Inc.

Scott Foresman Reading: Links to Reading First. 2004. (gr. k-18). (978-0-328-07612-3(0)); (gr. k-18). (978-0-328-05801-3(7)); (gr. 1-18). (978-0-328-07613-0(9)); (gr. 1-18). (978-0-328-05802-0(5)); (gr. 2-18). (978-0-328-05803-7(3)); (gr. 2-18). (978-0-328-07614-7(7)); (gr. 3-18). (978-0-328-07615-4(5)); (gr. 3-18). (978-0-328-05804-4(1)) Addison-Wesley Educational Pubs., Inc. (Scott Foresman).

Scott Foresman Reading: Technology. 2004. (Fluency Coach Ser.). (gr. 4-18). cd-rom (978-0-328-09376-2(9), Scott Foresman) Addison-Wesley Educational Pubs., Inc.

Scott, Fred & Southworth, Gordon. English for the Thoughtful Child Vol 2, Vol. 2. 2003. (ENG., Illus.). 128p. (J). pap. 18.95 (978-1-882514-44-1(0)) Greenleaf Pr.

Scott, Johnathan & Scott, Angela. Big Cat Babies. Scott, Jonathan, illus. 2005. (Collins Big Cat Ser.). (ENG.). 48p. (J). (gr. k-1). pap. 6.99 (978-0-00-718594-8(4)) HarperCollins Pubs. Ltd. GBR. Dist: Independent Pubs. Group.

Scott, Jonathan & Scott, Angela. Africa's Big Three. Scott, Jonathan & Scott, Angela, illus. 2006. (Collins Big Cat Ser.). (ENG., Illus.). 56p. (J). (gr. 2-2). pap. 6.99 (978-0-00-718693-8(2)) HarperCollins Pubs. Ltd. GBR. Dist: Independent Pubs. Group.

—Antarctica: Land of the Penguins. 2005. (Collins Big Cat Ser.). (ENG., Illus.). 32p. (J). (gr. 1-3). pap. 7.99 (978-0-00-718640-2(1)) HarperCollins Pubs. Ltd. GBR. Dist: Independent Pubs. Group.

—The Great Migration White Band. 2016. (Cambridge Reading Adventures Ser.). (ENG.). 32p. pap. 7.81 (978-1-107-56065-9(9)) Cambridge Univ. Pr.

—Living Dinosaurs. Scott, Jonathan & Scott, Angela, illus. 2007. (Collins Big Cat Ser.). (ENG., Illus.). 48p. (J). (gr. k-1). pap. 6.99 (978-0-00-718673-0(8)) HarperCollins Pubs. Ltd. GBR. Dist: Independent Pubs. Group.

—The Masai: Tribe of Warriors. Scott, Jonathan & Scott, Angela, illus. 2007. (Collins Big Cat Ser.). (ENG., Illus.). 48p. (J). (gr. 3-4). pap. 8.99 (978-0-00-723097-6(4)) HarperCollins Pubs. Ltd. GBR. Dist: Independent Pubs. Group.

—Scarface: the Real Lion King Gold Band. 2016. (Cambridge Reading Adventures Ser.). (ENG.). 24p. pap. 7.19 (978-1-107-56047-5(0)) Cambridge Univ. Pr.

Scott-Royce, Brenda, et al. Early Adventures, Level 1. 2015. (Smithsonian Readers Ser.). (ENG., Illus.). 200p. (J). (gr. -1). 14.95 (978-1-62686-451-1(9), Silver Dolphin Bks.) Readerlink Distribution Services, LLC.

—Endless Explorations, Level 4. 2015. (Smithsonian Readers Ser.). (ENG., Illus.). 200p. (J). (gr. k). 14.95 (978-1-62686-454-2(3), Silver Dolphin Bks.) Readerlink Distribution Services, LLC.

—Smithsonian Readers - Seriously Amazing, Level 2. 2015. (Smithsonian Readers Ser.). (ENG., Illus.). 200p. (J). (gr. k). 14.95 (978-1-62686-452-8(7), Silver Dolphin Bks.) Readerlink Distribution Services, LLC.

—World of Wonder, Level 3. 2015. (Smithsonian Readers Ser.). (ENG., Illus.). 200p. (J). (gr. k). 14.95 (978-1-62686-453-5(5), Silver Dolphin Bks.) Readerlink Distribution Services, LLC.

Scott, Sally. Time for Tea. 2006. (Neighborhood Readers Ser.). (ENG.). 12p. (gr. 1-3). pap. 5.90 (978-1-4042-6867-8(7), Rosen Classroom) Rosen Publishing Group, Inc., The.

Scrapbook of ME: Individual Title Six-Packs. (Story Steps Ser.). (gr. k-2). 32.00 (978-0-7635-9814-3(3)) Rigby Education.

Scremin, Lauren. The 10 Most Amazing Skyscrapers. 2007. (J). 14.99 (978-1-55448-480-5(4)) Scholastic Library Publishing.

Sean amables con Naomi: Social/Emotional Lap Book. (Pebble Soup Exploraciones Ser.). (SPA.). (gr. -1-18). 16.00 (978-0-7578-1787-8(4)) Rigby Education.

A Second Birthday: 6 Small Books. (Greetings Ser.: Vol. 2). 24p. (gr. 2-3). 31.00 (978-0-7635-9414-5(8)) Rigby Education.

A Second Birthday: Big Book. (Greetings Ser.: Vol. 2). 24p. (gr. 2-3). 31.00 (978-0-7635-5698-3(X)) Rigby Education.

Second Mrs. Gianconda. (J). pap., stu. ed. (978-0-13-017583-0(8)) Prentice Hall (Schl. Div.).

See & Say Vinyl Books 800844, 3. 2005. (J). (978-1-59794-045-0(3)) Environments, Inc.

The Seed: Level A, 6 vols. (Wonder Worldtm Ser.). 16p. 24.95 (978-0-7802-1048-6(4)) Wright Group/McGraw-Hill.

Seed, Andy. On the Track. 2017. (ENG., Illus.). 32p. (J). pap. 7.99 (978-0-00-820875-2(1)) HarperCollins Pubs. Ltd. GBR. Dist: Independent Pubs. Group.

Sefchovich, Sara. Vivir la Vida. 2005.Tr. of Living Life. (SPA., Illus.). 243p. pap. 14.95 (978-968-19-0803-4(1)) Aguilar, Altea, Taurus, Alfaguara, S.A. de C.V MEX. Dist: Santillana USA Publishing Co., Inc.

Selleck, Richelle. Little Red Riding Hood. Myer, Ed, illus. 2012. (ENG.). 24p. (gr. 2-3). pap. 8.95 (978-1-61810-324-6(5)) Rourke Educational Media.

Selwyn, Josephine. What Holidays Do You Have? 2014. (Little Books of Answers: Level d Ser.). (Illus.). 16p. (gr. k-2). pap. 7.95 (978-1-927136-30-0(X)) Three Crows Media NZL. Dist: RiverStream Publishing.

—When Does Water Turn into Ice? 2014. (Little Books of Answers: Level F Ser.). (Illus.). 16p. (gr. k-2). pap. 7.95 (978-1-927136-59-1(8)) Three Crows Media NZL. Dist: RiverStream Publishing.

—Who Uses This Machine? 2014. (Little Books of Answers: Level C Ser.). (Illus.). 16p. (gr. k-2). pap. 7.95 (978-1-927136-29-4(6)) Three Crows Media NZL. Dist: RiverStream Publishing.

Sending Messages: Level B, 6 vols. (Wonder Worldtm Ser.). 16p. 24.95 (978-0-7802-4599-0(7)) Wright Group/McGraw-Hill.

Senior, Kathryn. You Wouldn't Want to Be a Nurse During the American Civil War! A Job That's Not for the Squeamish. 2010. (You Wouldn't Want to... Ser.). 32p. (J). 29.00 (978-0-531-20506-8(1)); (ENG., Illus.). (gr. 3-18). pap. 9.95 (978-0-531-13786-4(4)) Scholastic Library Publishing. (Watts, Franklin).

Set of 10 Big Book Favorites 800714, 10. 2005. (J). bds. (978-1-59794-013-9(5)) Environments, Inc.

Set of 17 Titles, Vol. 2. (Early Intervention Levels Ser.). 62.45 (978-0-7362-0998-4(0)) CENGAGE Learning.

Set of 5 Titles. (Early Intervention Levels Ser.). 18.95 (978-0-7362-0997-7(2)) CENGAGE Learning.

Set of 9 Titles, Vol. 4. (Early Intervention Levels Ser.). 33.15 (978-0-7362-1000-3(8)) CENGAGE Learning.

Settle, Melissa A. Firefighters Then & Now, 1 vol. 2006. (Primary Source Readers Ser.). (ENG.). 32p. (J). (gr. 1-1). pap. 8.99 (978-0-7439-9371-5(3)) Shell Educational Publishing.

—Police Then & Now , 1 vol. 2006. (Primary Source Readers Ser.). (ENG., Illus.). 32p. (J). (gr. 2-2). pap. 8.99 (978-0-7439-9372-2(1)) Shell Educational Publishing.

Seuss, Dr. The Big Green Book of Beginner Books. Stevenson, James et al, illus. 2009. (Beginner Books(R) Ser.). (ENG.). 256p. (J). (gr. -1-2). 16.99 (978-0-375-85807-9(5), Random Hse. Bks. for Young Readers) Random Hse. Children's Bks.

—Dr. Seuss's ABC Book & CD, 1 vol. 2005. (Book & CD Ser.). (ENG., Illus.). 64p. (J). (gr. -1-2). 9.95 (978-0-375-83496-7(6), Random Hse. Bks. for Young Readers) Random Hse. Children's Bks.

—Les Oeufs Verts Au Jambon: The French Edition of Green Eggs & Ham. 2009. (FRE & ENG., Illus.). 64p. (J). (gr. -1-3). 12.95 (978-1-56975-688-1(0)) Ulysses Pr.

Sexton, Colleen. Angelfish. 2009. (Blastoff! Readers Ser.). (ENG., Illus.). 24p. (J). (gr. k-3). 20.00 (978-0-531-21711-5(6), Children's Pr.) Scholastic Library Publishing.

—Frogfish. 2009. (Blastoff! Readers Ser.). (ENG., Illus.). 24p. (J). (gr. k-3). 20.00 (978-0-531-21712-2(4), Children's Pr.) Scholastic Library Publishing.

Shackleton, Caroline. Deep Blue: Discovering the Sea Intermediate Book with Online Access. 2014. (ENG., Illus.). 28p. (J). pap. 9.50 (978-1-107-69705-8(0)) Cambridge Univ. Pr.

—Down to Earth Intermediate Book with Online Access. 2014. (ENG., Illus.). 28p. pap. 9.50 (978-1-107-66117-2(X)) Cambridge Univ. Pr.

—Get Smart: Our Amazing Brain Intermediate Book with Online Access. 2014. (ENG., Illus.). 28p. (J). pap. 9.50 (978-1-107-65063-3(1)) Cambridge Univ. Pr.

ShackletonCaroline. AVALANCHE! HIGH INTERMEDIATE BOOK WITH ONLINE ACCESS, 1 vol. 2014. (ENG., Illus.). 28p. pap. 9.50 (978-1-107-62157-2(7)) Cambridge Univ. Pr.

—LIFT OFF: EXPLORING THE UNIVERSE HIGH INTERMEDIATE BOOK WITH ONLINE ACCESS. 2014. (ENG., Illus.). 28p. (J). pap. 9.50 (978-1-107-69249-7(0)) Cambridge Univ. Pr.

—MONEY TREE: THE BUSINESS OF ORGANICS HIGH INTERMEDIATE BOOK WITH ONLINE ACCESS, 1 vol. 2014. (ENG., Illus.). 28p. (J). pap. 9.50 (978-1-107-63678-1(7)) Cambridge Univ. Pr.

—POISON: MEDICINE, MURDER, AND MYSTERY HIGH INTERMEDIATE BOOK WITH ONLINE ACCESS. 2014. (ENG., Illus.). 28p. (J). pap. 9.50 (978-1-107-62260-9(3)) Cambridge Univ. Pr.

—ROBOTS: THE NEXT GENERATION? HIGH INTERMEDIATE BOOK WITH ONLINE ACCESS. 2014. (ENG., Illus.). 28p. pap. 9.50 (978-1-107-67762-3(9)) Cambridge Univ. Pr.

—SKIN UPPER INTERMEDIATE BOOK WITH ONLINE ACCESS. 2014. (ENG.). 28p. (J). pap. 9.50 (978-1-107-64189-1(6)) Cambridge Univ. Pr.

—TRAPPED! THE ARON RALSTON STORY HIGH INTERMEDIATE BOOK WITH ONLINE ACCESS. 2014. (ENG., Illus.). 28p. (J). pap. 9.50 (978-1-107-66998-7(7)) Cambridge Univ. Pr.

—UP IN THE AIR: OUR FIGHT AGAINST GRAVITY INTERMEDIATE BOOK WITH ONLINE ACCESS. 2014. (ENG.). 28p. (J). pap. 9.50 (978-1-107-63470-1(9)) Cambridge Univ. Pr.

—THE WHEEL LOW INTERMEDIATE BOOK WITH ONLINE ACCESS. 2014. (ENG.). 28p. (J). pap. 9.50 (978-1-107-66739-6(9)) Cambridge Univ. Pr.

Shadows: Level H, 6 vols. (Wonder Worldtm Ser.). 16p. 29.95 (978-0-7802-1049-3(2)) Wright Group/McGraw-Hill.

Shah, Nupur. Let's Go Camping. rev. ed. 2011. (1-3Y in My World Ser.). (ENG., Illus.). 16p. (J). (gr. k-1). pap. 5.99 (978-1-61541-415-4(0)) American Reading Co.

Shaka: King of the Zulus. (Lexile Levels Ser.). 9.09 (978-1-56334-749-8(0)) CENGAGE Learning.

Shakespeare, William. The Merchant of Venice. 2004. (Saddleback Classics Ser.). (Illus.). 48p. (J). per. 17.95 (978-1-56254-634-2(1), SP6341) Saddleback Educational Publishing, Inc.

—The Tempest Study Guide. 2004. (Shakespeare Classics Ser.). (Illus.). 48p. (J). (gr. 4-7). per. 17.95 (978-1-56254-639-7(2), SP6392) Saddleback Educational Publishing, Inc.

—Three Great Plays of Shakespeare, Pack. 2007. (ENG., Illus.). 80p. pap. 17.32 incl. cd-rom (978-1-4058-5221-0(6)) Pearson Education.

Shane & Ned, 6 Packs. (gr. 1-2). 22.00 (978-0-7635-9171-7(8)) Rigby Education.

Shank, Cathy, et al. Collaborations Literacy. pap., stu. ed. 50.95 (978-0-8384-9660-2(1)) Cengage Heinle.

Shark Rescue: Level T. Group 2, 6 vols. (Sunshine Ser.). 48p. 44.95 (978-0-7802-4174-9(6)) Wright Group/McGraw-Hill.

Sharp, Paul. Pablo el Lanzador. Sharp, Paul, illus. 2011. (Rookie Ready to Learn Español Ser.). (SPA., Illus.). 40p. (J). pap. 5.95 (978-0-531-26781-3(4)); lib. bdg. 23.00 (978-0-531-26113-2(1)) Scholastic Library Publishing. (Children's Pr.).

Shava, Ryder. At Work with My Dads, 01 vols., 1. 2016. (Rosen REAL Readers: STEM & STEAM Collection). (ENG.). 12p. (J). pap. 6.33 (978-1-5081-1581-6(8), Rosen Classroom) Rosen Publishing Group, Inc., The.

—Bear Wakes Up, 01 vols., 1. 2016. (Rosen REAL Readers: STEM & STEAM Collection). (ENG.). 8p. (J). pap. 5.46 (978-1-5081-1504-5(4), Rosen Classroom) Rosen Publishing Group, Inc., The.

—The Big Cookout, 01 vols., 1. 2016. (Rosen REAL Readers: Social Studies Nonfiction / Fiction: Family, Community, & the World Ser.). (ENG.). 8p. (J). pap. 5.46 (978-1-5081-1442-0(0), Rosen Classroom) Rosen Publishing Group, Inc., The.

—Blue Sky Day, 01 vols., 1. 2016. (Rosen REAL Readers: STEM & STEAM Collection). (ENG.). 8p. (J). pap. 5.46 (978-1-5081-1446-8(3), Rosen Classroom) Rosen Publishing Group, Inc., The.

—Bo's Sand Castle, 01 vols., 1. 2016. (Rosen REAL Readers: STEM & STEAM Collection). (ENG.). 8p. (J). pap. 5.46 (978-1-5081-1465-9(X), Rosen Classroom) Rosen Publishing Group, Inc., The.

—Button Eyes, Carrot Nose, 01 vols., 1. 2016. (Rosen REAL Readers: STEM & STEAM Collection). (ENG.). 8p. (J). pap. 5.46 (978-1-5081-1486-4(2), Rosen Classroom) Rosen Publishing Group, Inc., The.

—The Can Drive, 01 vols., 1. 2016. (Rosen REAL Readers: Social Studies Nonfiction / Fiction: Family, Community, & the World Ser.). (ENG.). 12p. (J). pap. 6.33 (978-1-5081-1982-1(1), Rosen Classroom) Rosen Publishing Group, Inc., The.

—Clara & the Ladybug, 01 vols., 1. 2016. (Rosen REAL Readers: STEM & STEAM Collection). (ENG.). 8p. (J). pap. 5.46 (978-1-5081-1399-7(8), Rosen Classroom) Rosen Publishing Group, Inc., The.

—Hair Cut Day, 01 vols., 1. 2016. (Rosen REAL Readers: Social Studies Nonfiction / Fiction: Family, Community, & the World Ser.). (ENG.). 8p. (J). pap. 5.46 (978-1-5081-1385-0(8), Rosen Classroom) Rosen Publishing Group, Inc., The.

—The Lesson, 01 vols., 1. 2016. (Rosen REAL Readers: Social Studies Nonfiction / Fiction: Family, Community, & the World Ser.). (ENG.). 8p. (J). pap. 5.46 (978-1-5081-1890-9(6), Rosen Classroom) Rosen Publishing Group, Inc., The.

—Show & Tell, 01 vols., 1. 2016. (Rosen REAL Readers: Social Studies Nonfiction / Fiction: Family, Community, & the World Ser.). (ENG.). 12p. (J). pap. 6.33 (978-1-5081-1952-4(X), Rosen Classroom) Rosen Publishing Group, Inc., The.

—Story Time, 01 vols., 1. 2016. (Rosen REAL Readers: Social Studies Nonfiction / Fiction: Family, Community, & the World Ser.). (ENG.). 12p. (J). pap. 6.33 (978-1-5081-1949-4(X), Rosen Classroom) Rosen Publishing Group, Inc., The.

—The Talent Show, 01 vols., 1. 2016. (Rosen REAL Readers: Social Studies Nonfiction / Fiction: Family, Community, & the World Ser.). (ENG.). 8p. (J). pap. 5.46 (978-1-5081-1854-1(X), Rosen Classroom) Rosen Publishing Group, Inc., The.

—A Watery World, 01 vols., 1. 2016. (Rosen REAL Readers: STEM & STEAM Collection). (ENG.). 12p. (J). pap. 6.33 (978-1-5081-1527-4(3), Rosen Classroom) Rosen Publishing Group, Inc., The.

—When I Sat in Lincoln's Lap, 01 vols., 1. 2016. (Rosen REAL Readers: Social Studies Nonfiction / Fiction: Family, Community, & the World Ser.). (ENG.). 12p. (J). pap. 6.33 (978-1-5081-2003-2(X), Rosen Classroom) Rosen Publishing Group, Inc., The.

Shaw, Gina & Bader, Bonnie. Welcome, Bao Bao. 2015. (Smithsonian Ser.). (ENG., Illus.). 48p. (J). (gr. 3-4). 3.99 (978-0-448-48225-5(8), Penguin Young Readers) Penguin Young Readers Group.

She Said. (Little Book Practice Reader). (J). (978-0-8136-5376-1(2)) Modern Curriculum Pr.

Shea, Therese. At the Luau. 2006. (Neighborhood Readers Ser.). (ENG.). 16p. (gr. 1-3). pap. 6.50 (978-1-4042-7002-2(7), Rosen Classroom) Rosen Publishing Group, Inc., The.

—Bear Likes to Share. 2006. (Neighborhood Readers Ser.). (ENG.). 8p. (gr. -1-3). pap. 5.15 (978-1-4042-5696-5(2), Rosen Classroom) Rosen Publishing Group, Inc., The.

—Carmen's Photo Album. 2006. (Neighborhood Readers Ser.). (ENG.). 12p. (gr. 1-3). pap. 5.90 (978-1-4042-6795-4(6), Rosen Classroom) Rosen Publishing Group, Inc., The.

—Digger Has a Bath. 2006. (Neighborhood Readers Ser.). (ENG.). 12p. (gr. -1-3). pap. 5.90 (978-1-4042-6467-0(1), Rosen Classroom) Rosen Publishing Group, Inc., The.

—Flag Day. 2006. (Neighborhood Readers Ser.). (ENG.). 16p. (gr. 1-3). pap. 6.50 (978-1-4042-7144-9(9), Rosen Classroom) Rosen Publishing Group, Inc., The.

—Flags & Fireworks. 2006. (Neighborhood Readers Ser.). (ENG.). 8p. (gr. -1-3). pap. 5.15 (978-1-4042-5726-9(8), Rosen Classroom) Rosen Publishing Group, Inc., The.

—A Fuss on the Bus. (Neighborhood Readers Ser.). 12p. 2007. (SPA.). 33.50 (978-1-4042-7080-0(9)) 2006. (ENG.). (gr. -1-3). pap. 5.90 (978-1-4042-5744-3(6)) Rosen Publishing Group, Inc., The. (Rosen Classroom).

—A House for Mouse. 2006. (Neighborhood Readers Ser.). (ENG.). 8p. (gr. -1-3). pap. 5.15 (978-1-4042-5672-9(5), Rosen Classroom) Rosen Publishing Group, Inc., The.

—The Kwanzaa Surprise. 2006. (Neighborhood Readers Ser.). (ENG.). 12p. (gr. -1-3). pap. 5.90 (978-1-4042-6746-6(8), Rosen Classroom) Rosen Publishing Group, Inc., The.

—The Lunch Bunch. (Neighborhood Readers Ser.). (ENG.). 12p. 2007. 33.50 (978-1-4042-7322-1(0)) 2006. (Illus.). (gr. 1-3). pap. 5.90 (978-1-4042-7038-1(8)) Rosen Publishing Group, Inc., The. (Rosen Classroom).

—Un lunch muy especial (the Lunch Bunch) 2007. (Lecturas del barrio (Neighborhood Readers) Ser.). (SPA.). 12p. 33.50 (978-1-4042-7323-8(9), Rosen Classroom) Rosen Publishing Group, Inc., The.

—One More Floor! 2006. (Neighborhood Readers Ser.). (ENG.). 16p. (gr. 1-3). pap. 6.50 (978-1-4042-7244-6(5), Rosen Classroom) Rosen Publishing Group, Inc., The.

—Sam's New Shoes. 2006. (Neighborhood Readers Ser.). (ENG.). 8p. (gr. -1-3). pap. 5.15 (978-1-4042-5651-4(2), Rosen Classroom) Rosen Publishing Group, Inc., The.

—The School Bus Mystery. 2006. (Neighborhood Readers Ser.). (ENG.). 16p. (gr. 1-3). pap. 6.50 (978-1-4042-6982-8(7), Rosen Classroom) Rosen Publishing Group, Inc., The.

—The Summer Job. 2006. (Neighborhood Readers Ser.). (ENG., Illus.). 12p. (gr. 1-3). pap. 5.90 (978-1-4042-6855-5(3), Rosen Classroom) Rosen Publishing Group, Inc., The.

—A Trip to the White House. 2006. (Neighborhood Readers Ser.). (ENG.). 16p. (gr. 1-3). pap. 6.50 (978-1-4042-7204-0(6), Rosen Classroom) Rosen Publishing Group, Inc., The.

Sheehan, P. J. Gabby's Big Game. 2006. (Neighborhood Readers Ser.). (ENG.). 12p. (gr. -1-3). pap. 5.90 (978-1-4042-6758-9(1), Rosen Classroom) Rosen Publishing Group, Inc., The.

Sheinmel, Courtney. Stella Batts: A Case of the Meanies. Bell, Jennifer A., illus. 2012. (Stella Batts Ser.: 4). (ENG.). 168p. (J). (gr. 1-3). 9.99 (978-1-58536-198-4(4), 202252); pap. 5.99 (978-1-58536-199-1(2), 202257) Sleeping Bear Pr.

Shepherd Boy & the Giant Color. 2004. pap. 1.50 (978-0-87162-913-5(5)) Warner Pr., Inc.

Sheppard, Bonnie. The 10 Greatest Art Forgers. 2007. (J). 14.99 (978-1-55448-473-7(1)) Scholastic Library Publishing.

Sherman, Patrice. The Enlightenment: A Revolution in Reason, 1 vol. 2012. (Primary Source Readers Ser.). (ENG.). 32p. (J). (gr. 5-5). pap. 8.99 (978-1-4333-5013-9(0)) Teacher Created Materials, Inc.

—George W. Bush: Gobernado de Texas y Presidente de los Estados Unidos / George W. Bush - Texan Governor & U. S. President. 2013. (Primary Source Readers Ser.). (SPA.). lib. bdg. 19.65 (978-0-606-31875-4(5), Turtleback) Turtleback Bks.

—George W. Bush: Texan Governor & U. S. President, 1 vol. 2012. (Primary Source Readers Ser.). (ENG.). 32p. (J). (gr. 3-3). pap. 8.99 (978-1-4333-5054-2(8)) Teacher Created Materials, Inc.

—John Locke: Philosopher of the Enlightenment, 1 vol. 2012. (Primary Source Readers Ser.). (ENG.). 32p. (J). (gr. 4-4). pap. 8.99 (978-1-4333-5014-6(9)) Teacher Created Materials, Inc.

Shimizu, Michio. Ding Dong. McLaughlin, Sako, tr. Yamamoto, Matsuko, illus. 2009. 32p. 14.95 (978-1-74126-440-1(5)) R.I.C. Pubns. AUS. Dist: SCB Distributors.

Shipton, Paul. Clown School. Blake, Beccy, illus. 2005. (ENG.). 24p. (J). lib. bdg. 23.65 (978-1-59646-752-1(5)) Dingles & Co.

—The Guinea Pigs. Dunton, Trevor, illus. 2006. (Collins Big Cat Ser.). (ENG.). 48p. (J). (gr. -1-k). pap. 5.99 (978-0-00-718648-8(7)) HarperCollins Pubs. Ltd. GBR. Dist: Independent Pubs. Group.

—I Can Do It! Elworthy, Antony, illus. 2007. (Collins Big Cat Ser.). (ENG.). 48p. (J). (gr. -1-k). pap. 5.99 (978-0-00-718651-8(7)) HarperCollins Pubs. Ltd. GBR. Dist: Independent Pubs. Group.

—In the Boat. Dunton, Trevor, illus. 2007. (Collins Big Cat Ser.). (ENG.). 24p. (J). (gr. -1-k). pap. 5.99 (978-0-00-718646-4(0)) HarperCollins Pubs. Ltd. GBR. Dist: Independent Pubs. Group.

—What's for Breakfast? Stuart, Jon, illus. 2006. (Collins Big Cat Ser.). (ENG.). 16p. (J). (gr. -1-k). pap. 5.99

(978-0-00-718668-6(1)) HarperCollins Pubs. Ltd. GBR. Dist: Independent Pubs. Group.
Shoes, Shoes, Shoes. (Lexile Levels Ser.). 7.98 *(978-1-56334-670-5(2))* CENGAGE Learning.
Shore, Diane Z. How to Drive Your Sister Crazy. Rankin, Laura, illus. 2008. (I Can Read Level 2 Ser.). (ENG.). 48p. (J). (gr. k-3). 16.99 *(978-0-06-052762-4(5))* HarperCollins Pubs.
Short, Deborah J., et al. Avenues Language & Literacy Tests: Level C Posttest Booklet (10-Pack) 2004. (Avenues Ser.). (ENG.). (C). pap. 66.95 *(978-0-7362-2514-4(5))* CENGAGE Learning.
—Avenues Language & Literacy Tests: Level D Pretest Booklet (10-Pack) 2004. (Avenues Ser.). (ENG.). (C). pap. 66.95 *(978-0-7362-2515-1(3))* CENGAGE Learning.
—Avenues Language & Literacy Tests: Level E Posttest Booklet (10-Pack) 2004. (Avenues Ser.). (ENG.). (C). pap. 66.95 *(978-0-7362-2518-2(8))* CENGAGE Learning.
—Avenues Language & Literacy Tests: Level E Pretest Booklet (10-Pack) 2004. (Avenues Ser.). (ENG.). (C). pap. 66.95 *(978-0-7362-2517-5(X))* CENGAGE Learning.
—Avenues Language & Literacy Tests: Level F Posttest Booklet (10-Pack) 2004. (Avenues Ser.). (ENG.). (C). pap. 66.95 *(978-0-7362-2520-5(X))* CENGAGE Learning.
—Avenues Language & Literacy Tests: Level F Pretest Booklet (10-Pack) 2004. (Avenues Ser.). (ENG.). (C). pap. 66.95 *(978-0-7362-2519-9(6))* CENGAGE Learning.
—A Avenues Level. 2003. (Alphachant Phonics Ser.). (ENG.). (C). (gr. k-18). pap. 2919.95 *(978-0-7362-2541-0(2))* CENGAGE Learning.
—A Avenues Level: Practice Book. 2003. (Alphachant Phonics Ser.). (ENG.). 96p. (C). (gr. k-18). pap. 18.95 *(978-0-7362-1786-6(X))* CENGAGE Learning.
—Avenues Level B. 2003. (Avenues Ser.). (ENG.). (C). (gr. 1-18). pap. 2485.95 *(978-0-7362-2542-7(0))* CENGAGE Learning.
—Avenues Level B: Practice Book. 2003. (Avenues Ser.). (ENG.). 112p. (C). (gr. 1-18). pap. 18.95 *(978-0-7362-1835-1(1))* CENGAGE Learning.
—Avenues Level C: Practice Book. 2003. (Avenues Ser.). (ENG.). 136p. (C). (gr. 2-18). pap. 13.95 *(978-0-7362-1884-9(X))* CENGAGE Learning.
—Avenues Level D. 2003. (Avenues Ser.). (ENG.). (C). (gr. 3-18). pap. 1117.95 *(978-0-7362-2544-1(7))* CENGAGE Learning.
—Avenues Level D: Practice Book. 2003. (Avenues Ser.). (ENG.). 136p. (C). (gr. 3-18). pap. 13.95 *(978-0-7362-1678-4(2))* CENGAGE Learning.
—Avenues Level E. 2008. (Avenues Ser.). (ENG.). (C). (gr. 4-18). pap. 1117.95 *(978-0-7362-2545-8(5))* CENGAGE Learning.
—Avenues Level E: Practice Book. 2003. (Avenues Ser.). (ENG.). 136p. (C). (gr. 4-18). pap. 13.95 *(978-0-7362-1714-9(2))* CENGAGE Learning.
—Avenues Level F. 2008. (Avenues Ser.). (ENG.). (C). (gr. 5-18). pap. 1117.95 *(978-0-7362-2546-5(3))* CENGAGE Learning.
—Avenues Level F: Leveled Books & ETools. 2004. (Avenues Ser.). (ENG.). (C). (gr. 5-18). pap. 1495.95 *(978-0-7362-2539-7(0))* CENGAGE Learning.
—Avenues Level F: Practice Book. 2003. (Avenues Ser.). (ENG.). 144p. (C). (gr. 5-18). pap. 13.95 *(978-0-7362-1750-7(9))* CENGAGE Learning.
—Avenues Unit Progress Tests: Level A Progress Test Booklets (10-Pack) 2004. (Avenues Ser.). (ENG.). (C). (gr. k-18). pap. 86.95 *(978-0-7362-2227-3(8))* CENGAGE Learning.
—Avenues Unit Progress Tests: Level B Progress Test Booklets (10-Pack) 2004. (Avenues Ser.). (ENG.). (C). (gr. 1-18). pap. 162.95 *(978-0-7362-2230-3(8))* CENGAGE Learning.
—Avenues Unit Progress Tests: Level C Progress Test Booklets - Advanced (10-Pack) 2004. (Avenues Ser.). (ENG.). (C). (gr. 2-18). pap. 162.95 *(978-0-7362-2241-9(3))* CENGAGE Learning.
—Avenues Unit Progress Tests: Level C Progress Test Booklets - Beginning (10-Pack) 2004. (Avenues Ser.). (ENG.). (C). (gr. 2-18). pap. 162.95 *(978-0-7362-2235-8(9))* CENGAGE Learning.
—Avenues Unit Progress Tests: Level C Progress Test Booklets - Intermediate (10-Pack) 2004. (Avenues Ser.). (ENG.). (C). (gr. 2-18). pap. 162.95 *(978-0-7362-2238-9(3))* CENGAGE Learning.
—Avenues Unit Progress Tests: Level D Progress Test Booklets - Advanced (10-Pack) 2004. (Avenues Ser.). (ENG.). (C). (gr. 3-18). pap. 162.95 *(978-0-7362-2252-5(9))* CENGAGE Learning.
—Avenues Unit Progress Tests: Level D Progress Test Booklets - Beginning (10-Pack) 2004. (Avenues Ser.). (ENG.). (C). (gr. 3-18). pap. 162.95 *(978-0-7362-2246-4(4))* CENGAGE Learning.
—Avenues Unit Progress Tests: Level D Progress Test Booklets - Intermediate (10-Pack) 2004. (Avenues Ser.). (ENG.). (C). (gr. 3-18). pap. 162.95 *(978-0-7362-2249-5(9))* CENGAGE Learning.
—Avenues Unit Progress Tests: Level E Progress Test Booklets - Advanced (10-Pack) 2004. (Avenues Ser.). (ENG.). (C). (gr. 4-18). pap. 162.95 *(978-0-7362-2263-1(4))* CENGAGE Learning.
—Avenues Unit Progress Tests: Level E Progress Test Booklets - Beginning (10-Pack) 2004. (Avenues Ser.). (ENG.). (C). (gr. 4-18). pap. 162.95 *(978-0-7362-2257-0(X))* CENGAGE Learning.
—Avenues Unit Progress Tests: Level E Progress Test Booklets - Intermediate (10-Pack) 2004. (Avenues Ser.). (ENG.). (C). (gr. 4-18). pap. 162.95 *(978-0-7362-2260-0(X))* CENGAGE Learning.
—Avenues Unit Progress Tests: Level F Progress Test Booklets - Advanced (10-Pack) 2004. (Avenues Ser.). (ENG.). (C). (gr. 5-18). pap. 162.95 *(978-0-7362-2284-6(7))* CENGAGE Learning.
—Avenues Unit Progress Tests: Level F Progress Test Booklets - Beginning (10-Pack) 2004. (Avenues Ser.). (ENG.). (C). (gr. 5-18). pap. 162.95 *(978-0-7362-2278-5(2))* CENGAGE Learning.
—Avenues Unit Progress Tests: Level F Progress Test Booklets - Intermediate (10-Pack) 2004. (Avenues Ser.). (ENG.). (C). (gr. 5-18). pap. 162.95 *(978-0-7362-2281-5(2))* CENGAGE Learning.
—The Birth of an Island. (Avenues Ser.). (ENG.). (C). 2004. pap. 65.95 *(978-0-7362-2167-2(0))* 2003. 16p. pap. 10.95 *(978-0-7362-1760-6(6))* CENGAGE Learning.
—Hawaii & Alaska. 2003. (Avenues Ser.). (ENG.). (C). pap. 61.95 *(978-0-7362-2158-0(1))*; pap. 9.95 *(978-0-7362-1736-1(3))* CENGAGE Learning.
—Lakeside Elementary: Add-on Components. 2003. (Avenues Ser.). (ENG.). (C). (gr. 2-5). pap., stu. ed. 11.95 *(978-0-7362-1821-4(1))* CENGAGE Learning.
—The Midnight Ride. 2004. (Avenues Ser.). (ENG.). (C). pap. 65.95 *(978-0-7362-2170-2(0))* CENGAGE Learning.
—A Nation of Immigrants. (Avenues Ser.). (ENG.). (C). 2004. pap. 65.95 *(978-0-7362-2145-0(X))* 2003. pap. 10.95 *(978-0-7362-1700-2(2))* CENGAGE Learning.
—An Old Family Recipe. (Avenues Ser.). (ENG.). (C). 2004. pap. 65.95 *(978-0-7362-2165-8(4))* 2003. pap. 10.95 *(978-0-7362-1757-6(6))* CENGAGE Learning.
—Picture Perfect Word Book: My Little Word Books. 2004. (Avenues Ser.). (ENG.). 44p. (C). (gr. -1-2). pap. 11.95 *(978-0-7362-2392-8(4))* CENGAGE Learning.
Short Vowels Set: Level B. (Sing-along Songs Ser.). (gr. -1-2). 48.46 incl. audio compact disk *(978-0-7362-0420-0(2))* CENGAGE Learning.
Show Me a Snake Hold (16), Vol. 16. (Early Intervention Levels Ser.). 4.73 *(978-0-7362-0241-1(2))* CENGAGE Learning.
Show Me a Snake Hole. (Early Intervention Levels Ser.). 28.38 *(978-0-7362-0416-3(4))* CENGAGE Learning.
Show What You Know Publishing, ed. Show What You Know on the CSAP 7, Reading/Writing Student Workbook. 2007. (J). per. 13.95 *(978-1-59230-246-8(7))* Englefield & Assocs., Inc.
—Show What You Know on the CSAP for Grade 5, Student Workbook. 2007. (J). per. 13.95 *(978-1-59230-217-8(3))* Englefield & Assocs., Inc.
—Show What You Know on the CSAP for Grade 9 Reading Student Self-Study Workbook. 2007. (YA). per. 18.95 *(978-1-59230-256-7(4))* Englefield & Assocs., Inc.
—Show What You Know on the CSAP Reading & Writing for Grade 6, Student Workbook. 2007. (J). per. 13.95 *(978-1-59230-240-6(8))* Englefield & Assocs., Inc.
Shuert, Randy. Randy Ray & Easy Jay: Court Day Adventure. 2011. 28p. pap. 21.99 *(978-1-4568-8393-5(3))* Xlibris Corp.
—Randy Ray & Easy Jay: The Wood House Adventure. 2011. 28p. pap. 21.99 *(978-1-4568-8395-9(X))* Xlibris Corp.
Shulman, Lisa. The Library, 6 vols., Set. 2004. (Phonics Readers Books 37-72 Ser.). (ENG.). 8p. (gr. k-1). pap. 35.70 *(978-0-7368-4056-9(7)*, Phonics Readers) Capstone Press of Coughlan Cos.
Shurley English 1 H/S/ Ed. 2004. pap. 8.00 *(978-1-58561-052-5(6))* Shurley Instructional Materials, Inc.
Shurley English 2 H/S Ed. 2004. pap. 8.00 *(978-1-58561-053-2(4))*; pap. 30.00 *(978-1-58561-059-4(3))* Shurley Instructional Materials, Inc.
Shurley English 3 H/S Ed. 2004. pap. 8.00 *(978-1-58561-054-9(2))* Shurley Instructional Materials, Inc.
Si estas Contento, 6 vols., Pack. (Literatura 2000 Ser.). (SPA.). (gr. 1-2). 28.00 *(978-0-7635-1078-7(5))* Rigby Education.
Siebert, Anne & Clark, Raymond C. All Around America: The Time Traveler's Talk Show. 2004. (gr. 6-12). pap., wbk. ed. 39.00 incl. cd-rom *(978-0-86647-186-2(3))* Pro Lingua Assocs., Inc.
—All Around America Activities: The Time Traveler's Talk Show. 2004. 76p. (gr. 6-12). pap., stu. ed., wbk. ed. 16.50 *(978-0-86647-184-8(7))* Pro Lingua Assocs., Inc.
Siegel, Elizabeth. Dinosaurs. 2007. (Steck-Vaughn BOLDPRINT Anthologies Ser.). (ENG., Illus.). 48p. (gr. 4-6). pap. 16.90 *(978-1-4190-4019-1(7))* Houghton Mifflin Harcourt Publishing Co.
Sight Word Reproducible Stories. 2005. (J). pap. 9.99 *(978-1-58970-702-3(8))* Lakeshore Learning Materials.
Sight Words with Samson. 2006. (J). cd-rom *(978-0-9766680-2-2(5))* Knowledge Wand, LLC.
Sigue las Huellas: Big Book. (Pebble Soup Exploraciones Ser.). (SPA.). 16p. (gr. -1-18). 31.00 *(978-0-7578-1675-8(4))* Rigby Education.
Sigue las Huellas: Small Book. (Pebble Soup Exploraciones Ser.). (SPA.). 16p. (gr. -1-18). 5.00 *(978-0-7578-1715-1(7))* Rigby Education.
Silencio! Individual Title-Six Packs. (Chiquilibros Ser.). (SPA.). (gr. k-1). 23.00 *(978-0-7635-8609-6(9))* Rigby Education.
Silver, Connie. A Story Book for Beginning Readers. 2007. 124p. per. 10.95 *(978-0-595-46524-8(2))* iUniverse, Inc.
Silver, Rhonda Graff. Graphic Organizer Booklets for Reading Response: Guided Response Packets for Any Fiction or Nonfiction Book That Boost Students' Comprehension - And Help You Manage Independent Reading. 2007. (Graphic Organizer Booklets for Reading Response Ser.). (ENG., Illus.). 64p. pap. 11.99 *(978-0-439-65612-2(5)*, Teaching Resources) Scholastic, Inc.
Silverman, Buffy. Lightning Bolt Books: Meet the Animal Groups, 6 vols., Set. Incl. Do You Know about Amphibians? (Illus.). lib. bdg. 26.60 *(978-0-8225-7543-6(4))*; Do You Know about Birds? (Illus.). lib. bdg. 26.60 *(978-0-8225-7541-2(8))*; Do You Know about Fish? (J). 25.26 *(978-0-8225-7540-5(X))*; Do You Know about Insects? (Illus.). lib. bdg. 26.60 *(978-0-8225-7544-3(2))*; Do You Know about Mammals? (Illus.). 26.60 *(978-0-8225-7539-9(6))*; Do You Know about Reptiles? (Illus.). 26.60 *(978-0-8225-7542-9(6))*; 32p. (gr. k-2). 2009. Set lib. bdg. 151.56 *(978-0-8225-7538-2(8)*, Lerner Pubns.) Lerner Publishing Group.
Silverstone, Michael. Paramedics to the Rescue: When Every Second Counts, 6 vols. 2004. (High Five Reading - Purple Ser.). (ENG.). 64p. (gr. 3-4). pap. 54.00 *(978-0-7368-3867-2(8)*, High Five Reading (RBL)) Capstone Press of Coughlan Cos.
Simms, Rosie. Read, Think, & Write about It - Binder 1. 2004. (YA). ring bd. 59.95 *(978-1-58804-356-6(8))* P C I Education.
—Read, Think, & Write about It - Binder 2. 2004. (YA). ring bd. 59.95 *(978-1-58804-357-3(6))* P C I Education.
Simon, Francesca. Look at Me. Bolam, Emily, illus. 2013. (ENG.). 80p. (J). (gr. -1-k). 7.99 *(978-1-4440-0468-7(9)*, Orion Children's Bks.) Hachette Children's Group GBR. Dist: Hachette Bk. Group.
Simon, Jenne. Lalaloopsy: Chasing Rainbows. 2014. (Scholastic Reader Level 2 Ser.). lib. bdg. 13.55 *(978-0-606-35402-8(6))* Turtleback Bks.
Simon, Mary. Oh Oh. 2004. (SPA.). 32p. (J). 2.75 *(978-0-570-05186-2(X))* Concordia Publishing Hse.
Simons, Joseph. Under a Living Sky, 1 vol. 2005. (Orca Young Readers Ser.). (ENG., Illus.). 112p. (J). (gr. 3-6). per. 5.95 *(978-1-55143-355-4(9))* Orca Bk. Pubs. USA.
Simpson, Louie. My Mom Votes! 2012. (InfoMax Readers Ser.). (ENG., Illus.). 24p. (J). (gr. 1-2). pap. 8.25 *(978-1-4488-9055-2(1)*, Rosen Classroom) Rosen Publishing Group, Inc., The.
Sims, Lesley. Midsummer Night's Drem. 2005. (Illus.). 48p. (J). (gr. 2-18). 8.95 *(978-0-7945-1077-0(9)*, Usborne) EDC Publishing.
—Snow white & the seven Dwarfs. 2005. (Illus.). 64p. (J). (gr. 2-18). 8.95 *(978-0-7945-1072-5(8)*, Usborne) EDC Publishing.
Sing a Song of People. (Early Intervention Levels Ser.). 5.34 *(978-0-7362-1895-5(5))*; 32.04 *(978-0-7362-2125-2(5))* CENGAGE Learning.
Singleton, Sarah. Century. 2008. 224p. (gr. 10-11). pap. 21.50 *(978-0-340-96628-0(9))* Hodder Education Group GBR. Dist: Trans-Atlantic Pubns., Inc.
Sink or Float? KinderFacts Individual Title Six-Packs. (Kinderstarters Ser.). 8p. (gr. -1-1). 21.00 *(978-0-7635-8749-9(4))* Rigby Education.
SIPPS Beginning Hand-held Sound Cards. 2004. *(978-1-57621-455-8(9))* Center for the Collaborative Classroom.
Sirett, Dawn & Dorling Kindersley Publishing Staff. All about Me! 6 Fun Flaps to Flap. 2008. (Fun Flaps Ser.). (ENG., Illus.). 14p. (J). (gr. -1-k). bds. 4.99 *(978-0-7566-3438-4(5)*, DK Children) Dorling Kindersley Publishing, Inc.
Six Fish in a Mix. (Early Intervention Levels Ser.). 21.30 *(978-0-7362-0388-3(5))* CENGAGE Learning.
Skittles & Skullbone, 6 Pack, Set D. (gr. k-3). 29.00 *(978-0-7635-0547-9(1))* Rigby Education.
The Sky Is Falling. 2004. (Folk Tales Set 1 Ser.). (J). 5.33 *(978-1-58453-273-6(4))* Pioneer Valley Bks.
Sky Time. (Early Intervention Levels Ser.). 28.38 *(978-0-7362-0402-6(4))* CENGAGE Learning.
Sky Time (10), Vol. 10. (Early Intervention Levels Ser.). 4.73 *(978-0-7362-0227-5(7))* CENGAGE Learning.
Sky Watch: Level O, 6 vols. (Explorers Ser.). 32p. (gr. 3-6). mac hd 44.95 *(978-0-7699-0595-2(1))* Shortland Pubns. (U. S. A.) Inc.
The Sled Ride: Individual Title Two-Packs. (Chiquilibros Ser.). (gr. -1-1). 12.00 *(978-0-7635-8526-6(2))* Rigby Education.
Sleep Tight Spaceboy. 2003. (Spaceboy Set 1 Ser.). (J). 7.33 *(978-1-932570-02-1(0))* Pioneer Valley Bks.
Slip & Slide (12), Vol. 12. (Early Intervention Levels Ser.). 4.73 *(978-0-7362-0233-6(1))* CENGAGE Learning.
Sly Fox & Red Hen, Level 2. 2016. (Ladybird Readers Ser.). (ENG.). 48p. (J). (gr. 2-4). pap. 9.99 *(978-0-241-25443-1(4))* Penguin Bks., Ltd. GBR. Dist: Independent Pubs. Group.
Small Steps, the Year I Got Polio Student Packet. 2004. (Small Steps Ser.). (J). 12.99 *(978-1-58130-522-7(2))* Novel Units, Inc.
Smallman, Steve. Super Ben. Smallman, Steve, illus. 2007. (Collins Big Cat Ser.). (ENG., Illus.). 16p. (J). (gr. -1-k). pap. 5.99 *(978-0-00-718656-3(8))* HarperCollins Pubs. Ltd. GBR. Dist: Independent Pubs. Group.
The Smartest One in Class: Individual Title Six-Packs. (gr. -1-2). 27.00 *(978-0-7635-9474-9(1))* Rigby Education.
Smith, Aimee & Johnston, Deon. My Hometown Is the Best Place to Visit. 2017. (Text Connections Guided Close Reading Ser.). (J). (gr. 1). *(978-1-4900-1824-9(7))* Benchmark Education Co.
Smith, Ben. What Makes the Air Dirty? 2014. (Little Books of Answers: Level C Ser.). (Illus.). 16p. (gr. k-2). pap. 7.95 *(978-1-927136-24-9(5))* Three Crows Media NZL. Dist: RiverStream Publishing.
—Where Can You Find Hard & Soft Things? 2014. (Little Books of Answers: Level e Ser.). (Illus.). 16p. (gr. k-2). pap. 7.95 *(978-1-927136-49-2(0))* Three Crows Media NZL. Dist: RiverStream Publishing.
—Where Do Big Cats Live? 2014. (Little Books of Answers: Level B Ser.). (Illus.). 16p. (gr. k-2). pap. 7.95 *(978-1-927136-17-1(2))* Three Crows Media NZL. Dist: RiverStream Publishing.
—Who Listens to the Weather Forecast? 2014. (Little Books of Answers: Level d Ser.). (Illus.). 16p. (gr. k-2). pap. 7.95 *(978-1-927136-36-2(9))* Three Crows Media NZL. Dist: RiverStream Publishing.
—Why Do We Celebrate? 2014. (Little Books of Answers: Level d Ser.). (Illus.). 16p. (gr. k-2). pap. 7.95 *(978-1-927136-31-7(8))* Three Crows Media NZL. Dist: RiverStream Publishing.
—Why Does This Float? 2014. (Little Books of Answers: Level d Ser.). (Illus.). 16p. (gr. k-2). pap. 7.95 *(978-1-927136-39-3(3))* Three Crows Media NZL. Dist: RiverStream Publishing.
Smith, Bernard & Pearson Education Staff. The Blue Cat Club. 2007. (ENG., Illus.). 22p. pap. 17.32 incl. cd-rom *(978-1-4058-5196-1(1))* Pearson Education.
Smith, Carrie. Finding Shapes: Lap Book. 2009. (My First Reader's Theater Set B Ser.). (J). 28.00 *(978-1-4108-8542-5(9))* Benchmark Education Co.
—Humpty Dumpty's Fall. 2008. (Reader's Theater Nursery Rhymes & Songs Ser.). (Illus.). 48p. (J). (gr. k-1). pap. *(978-1-60437-958-7(8))* Benchmark Education Co.
—The Jumping Monkeys. Harpster, Steve, illus. 2009. (Reader's Theater Nursery Rhymes & Songs Set B Ser.). 48p. (J). pap. *(978-1-60859-155-8(7))* Benchmark Education Co.
—Mary Has a Little Lamb. 2008. (Reader's Theater Nursery Rhymes & Songs Ser.). (Illus.). 48p. (J). (gr. k-1). pap. *(978-1-60437-978-5(2))* Benchmark Education Co.
—One Silly Hey Diddle Day. 2008. (Reader's Theater Nursery Rhymes & Songs Ser.). (Illus.). 48p. (J). (gr. k-1). pap. *(978-1-60437-963-1(4))* Benchmark Education Co.
—We See with Our Eyes: Lap Book. 2009. (My First Reader's Theater Set B Ser.). (J). 28.00 *(978-1-60634-992-2(9))* Benchmark Education Co.
—Where Are Bo Peep's Sheep? Abbott, Jason, illus. 2009. (Reader's Theater Nursery Rhymes & Songs Set B Ser.). 48p. (J). pap. *(978-1-60859-171-8(9))* Benchmark Education Co.
Smith, David. Nature's Garden. 2009. 132p. 22.50 *(978-1-60693-169-1(5)*, Eloquent Bks.) Strategic Book Publishing & Rights Agency (SBPRA).
Smith, Emily R. Life in the Colonies, 1 vol. 2004. (Primary Source Readers Ser.). (ENG.). 24p. (J). (gr. 5-5). pap. 8.99 *(978-0-7439-8742-4(X))* Shell Educational Publishing.
—Phillis Wheatley, 1 vol. 2004. (Primary Source Readers Ser.). (ENG.). 24p. (J). (gr. 4-4). pap. 8.99 *(978-0-7439-8743-1(8))* Shell Educational Publishing.
Smith Ford, Deborah. The Little Apple. 2009. 32p. pap. 14.62 *(978-1-4251-8806-1(0))* Trafford Publishing.
Smith, Jodene. The Day the Crayons Quit. 2015. (Great Works). (ENG., Illus.). 72p. (gr. k-3). pap. 9.99 *(978-1-4807-8506-9(7))* Shell Educational Publishing.
Smith, Kathy. Helping Hannah. 2010. (Rise & Shine Ser.). (ENG.). 12p. (C). (gr. -1-3). pap. 9.95 *(978-1-4042-6730-5(1))* National Geographic School Publishing, Inc.
Smith, Kathy & National Geographic Learning Staff. Let's Go to the Bank. 2010. (Rise & Shine Ser.). (ENG., Illus.). 12p. (C). (gr. 1-2). pap. 9.95 *(978-0-8239-8119-9(3))* National Geographic School Publishing, Inc.
Smith, Lesley & Award Publications Staff. Brer Rabbit & Brer Fox. 2014. (ENG., Illus.). 24p. (J). pap. 6.95 *(978-1-84135-962-5(9))* Award Pubns. Ltd. GBR. Dist: Parkwest Pubns., Inc.
—Brer Rabbit & the Honey Pot. 2014. (ENG., Illus.). 24p. (J). pap. 6.95 *(978-1-84135-961-8(0))* Award Pubns. Ltd. GBR. Dist: Parkwest Pubns., Inc.
—Brer Rabbit & the Tar Baby. 2014. (ENG., Illus.). 24p. (J). pap. 6.95 *(978-1-84135-964-9(5))* Award Pubns. Ltd. GBR. Dist: Parkwest Pubns., Inc.
Smith, Lesley, et al. Brer Rabbit & the Great Race. 2014. (ENG., Illus.). 24p. (J). pap. 6.95 *(978-1-84135-963-2(7))* Award Pubns. Ltd. GBR. Dist: Parkwest Pubns., Inc.
Smith, Maudie. All the King's Tights. Pye, Ali, illus. 2016. (Early Reader Ser.). (ENG.). 64p. (J). (gr. k-2). 6.99 *(978-1-4440-1425-9(0)*, Orion Children's Bks.) Hachette Children's Group GBR. Dist: Hachette Bk. Group.
Smith, Sian. Opposites, 1 vol. 2014. (Opposites Ser.). (ENG.). 24p. (gr. -1-1). pap. 35.94 *(978-1-4846-0338-3(9)*, Acorn) Heinemann-Raintree.
—Opposites Big Book, 1 vol. 2014. (Opposites Ser.). (ENG., Illus.). 24p. (gr. -1-1). 26.00 *(978-1-4846-0339-0(7)*, Acorn) Heinemann-Raintree.
Smythe, E. Louise. A Primary Reader: Old Time Stories, Fairy Tales & Myths Retold by Children. 2004. reprint ed. pap. 15.95 *(978-1-4191-0287-5(7))*; pap. 1.99 *(978-1-4192-0287-2(1))* Kessinger Publishing, LLC.
Snick Snack Sniffle-Nose: Set C Individual Title Six-Packs. (Supersonic Phonics Ser.). (gr. k-3). 29.00 *(978-0-7635-0543-1(9))* Rigby Education.
Snider, Brandon T. Meet Quickshadow. 2017. (Transformers Passport to Reading Ser.). (J). lib. bdg. 14.75 ***(978-0-606-39910-4(0))*** Turtleback Bks.
Snowbound! 2003. (Illus.). pap. 7.60 *(978-0-7398-7527-8(2))* Steck-Vaughn.
Snyder, Jane. Days of the Week: Learning Ordinal Numbers. 2009. (Math for the REAL World Ser.). 12p. (gr. 1-2). pap. 5.90 *(978-0-8239-8913-3(5)*, Rosen Classroom) Rosen Publishing Group, Inc., The.
So Many Things to Do, 6 vols., Pack. (gr. -1-2). 23.00 *(978-0-7635-9017-8(7))* Rigby Education.
So, Patty. So Simple Sightwords, 3 vols., 3 discs. 2004. Orig. Title: So Simple Learning: Sightwords. 222p. (J). DVD 189.90 *(978-0-9772158-0-5(6))* So Simple Learning.
Socks. (Little Book Practice Reader). (J). *(978-0-8136-5346-4(0))* Modern Curriculum Pr.
Socks: Individual Title Six-Packs. (Chiquilibros Ser.). (gr. k-1). 23.00 *(978-0-7635-0427-4(0))* Rigby Education.
Soft Cloth Books 800406, 4. 2005. (J). *(978-1-59794-032-0(1))* Environments, Inc.
SOft Touch Books 800780, 3. 2005. (J). *(978-1-59794-041-2(0))* Environments, Inc.
Solve This! Level J, 6 vols. 128p. (gr. 2-3). 41.95 *(978-0-7699-1025-3(1))* Shortland Pubns. (U. S. A.) Inc.
Someone to Count On. 2005. (Carter High Chronicles Senior Year Ser.). (Illus.). 48p. (J). per. 3.95 *(978-1-56254-776-9(3)*, SP7763) Saddleback Educational Publishing, Inc.
Sometimes: Individual Title Six-Packs. (gr. -1-2). 23.00 *(978-0-7635-8803-8(2))*; 27.00 *(978-0-7635-9476-3(8))* Rigby Education.
Sometimes We're Happy, Sometimes We're Sad: Social/Emotional Lap Book. (Pebble Soup Explorations Ser.). (gr. -1-18). 16.00 *(978-0-7635-7574-8(7))* Rigby Education.
Sommer, Cindy. Salvando Las Flores de Camelia, 1 vol. Klein, Laurie Allen, illus. 2016. (SPA.). 32p. (J). (gr. k-3). pap. 9.95 *(978-1-62855-872-2(5))* Arbordale Publishing.
Sows don't Pounce: Decodable Books, 6 vols. (Fast Track Reading Ser.). 24p. (gr. 4-8). 40.95 *(978-0-322-05988-7(7))* Wright Group/McGraw-Hill.
Soy Artista: Individual Title Six-Packs. (Literatura 2000 Ser.). (SPA.). (gr. 2-3). 33.00 *(978-0-7635-1251-4(6))* Rigby Education.
Soy Chef: Individual Title Six-Packs. (Literatura 2000 Ser.). (SPA.). (gr. 2-3). 33.00 *(978-0-7635-1648-2(1))* Rigby Education.
Space Fort. 2005. (J). *(978-1-932570-33-5(0))* Pioneer Valley Bks.
Spaceboy Finds a Friend. 2003. (Spaceboy Set 1 Ser.). (J). 7.33 *(978-1-932570-01-4(2))* Pioneer Valley Bks.
Spaceboy Plays Hide & Seek. 2003. (Spaceboy Set 1 Ser.). (J). 7.33 *(978-1-932570-05-2(5))* Pioneer Valley Bks.
Spaceboy Set 1. 2003. (J). *(978-1-932570-00-7(4))* Pioneer Valley Bks.
Spanish TAKS MASTER Reading, Gr. 5. 2004. (J). *(978-1-57022-472-0(2))* ECS Learning Systems, Inc.
Spanish TAKS MASTER Reading, Gr. 6. 2004. (J). *(978-1-57022-500-0(1))* ECS Learning Systems, Inc.
Speaking Out. 2003. (Illus.). pap. 7.60 *(978-0-7398-7522-3(1))* Steck-Vaughn.
Speechmark. What Is It? (ENG.). 48p. *(978-0-86388-511-2(X)*, 001-4093, Routledge) Taylor & Francis Group.

PQR

—What's Wrong? 48p. *(978-0-86388-512-9(8)*, 001-1725, Routledge) Taylor & Francis Group.

Speedsters Series. (Illus.). (J). (gr. 2-5). *(978-0-525-44950-8(7)*, Dutton Juvenile) Penguin Publishing Group.

Spider Night! (16), Vol. 16. (Early Intervention Levels Ser.). 4.73 *(978-0-7362-0236-7(6))* CENGAGE Learning.

Spielman, Madison. Build It: Skyscrapers, 1 vol. 2nd rev. ed. 2011. (Nonfiction Readers Ser.). (ENG.). 28p. (J). (gr. 2-2). pap. 6.99 *(978-1-4333-3620-1(0))* Teacher Created Materials, Inc.

—Craft It: Hand-Blown Glass, 1 vol. 2nd rev. ed. 2011. (Nonfiction Readers Ser.). (ENG.). 28p. (J). (gr. 2-2). pap. 6.99 *(978-1-4333-3619-5(7))* Teacher Created Materials, Inc.

—Make It - Chocolate, 1 vol. 2nd rev. ed. 2011. (Nonfiction Readers Ser.). (ENG.). 28p. (J). (gr. 2-2). pap. 6.99 *(978-1-4333-3621-8(9))* Teacher Created Materials, Inc.

Spielvogel, Jackson J. & McGraw-Hill Education Editors. Journey Across Time: The Early Ages. 2004. (MS World History Ser.). (ENG., Illus.). 794p. (gr. 6-9). stu. ed. 106.68 *(978-0-07-824133-8(2)*, 0078241332) McGraw-Hill Education.

Spin & Match - Kings, Cookies, & Quakers: The Cookie Man, New Clothes for the King, the Ugly Baby Duck. 2006. (ENG.). 66p. (J). 9.99 *(978-1-59204-203-6(1))* Learning Wrap-Ups, Inc.

Spin & Match - Tell Me a Story: The Grasshopper & the Ants, the Fox & the Grapes, the Turtle & the Rabbit. 2006. (ENG.). 66p. (J). 9.99 *(978-1-59204-202-9(3))* Learning Wrap-Ups, Inc.

Splawn, "E". Planting Fruitful Seeds. 2011. 32p. pap. 12.77 *(978-1-4567-3896-9(8))* AuthorHouse.

Spots, 6 vols., Set C,Pack. (Smart Start Ser.). (gr. k-1). 23.00 *(978-0-7635-0436-6(X))* Rigby Education.

Spremulli, Pam. Letter Birds. 2010. (ENG., Illus.). 40p. (J). (gr. k-4). pap. 14.00 *(978-1-935557-56-2(4))* PublishingWorks.

Sprick, Jessica. Kangaroos: Read Well Level K Unit 15 Storybook. Crum, Anna-Maria, illus. 2003. (Read Well Level K Ser.). 20p. (J). *(978-1-57035-686-5(6)*, 55554) Cambium Education, Inc.

Sprick, Marilyn. Monkey Business: Read Well Level K Unit 3 Storybook. Nolte, Larry, illus. 2003. (Read Well Level K Ser.). 20p. (J). *(978-1-57035-675-9(0))* Cambium Education, Inc.

Sprick, Marilyn, et al. Man's Best Friend: Read Well Level K Unit 5 Storybook. Zilis, Tom, illus. 2003. (Read Well Level K Ser.). 20p. (J). *(978-1-57035-677-3(7))* Cambium Education, Inc.

—Read Well K Magazine Prelude F: Plain Text. 2003. (Read Well Level K Ser.). (Illus.). 12p. (J). *(978-1-57035-731-2(5))* Cambium Education, Inc.

—Read Well Magazine Prelude A: Plain Text. 2003. (Read Well Level K Ser.). (Illus.). 12p. (J). *(978-1-57035-725-1(0))* Cambium Education, Inc.

—Read Well Magazine Prelude A: Slanted Text. 2003. (Read Well Level K Ser.). (Illus.). 12p. (J). *(978-1-57035-776-3(5))* Cambium Education, Inc.

—Read Well Magazine Prelude B: Plain Text. 2003. (Read Well Level K Ser.). (Illus.). 12p. (J). *(978-1-57035-727-5(7))* Cambium Education, Inc.

—Read Well Magazine Prelude B: Slanted Text. 2003. (Read Well Level K Ser.). (Illus.). 12p. (J). *(978-1-57035-777-0(3))* Cambium Education, Inc.

—Read Well Magazine Prelude C: Plain Text. 2004. (Read Well Level K Ser.). (Illus.). 12p. (J). *(978-1-57035-728-2(5))* Cambium Education, Inc.

—Read Well Magazine Prelude C: Slanted Text. 2003. (Read Well Level K Ser.). (Illus.). 12p. (J). *(978-1-57035-692-6(0))* Cambium Education, Inc.

—Read Well Magazine Prelude D: Plain Text. 2003. (Read Well Level K Ser.). (Illus.). 12p. (J). *(978-1-57035-729-9(3))* Cambium Education, Inc.

—Read Well Magazine Prelude D: Slanted Text. 2003. (Read Well Level K Ser.). (Illus.). 12p. (J). *(978-1-57035-693-3(9))* Cambium Education, Inc.

—Read Well Magazine Prelude E: Plain Text. 2003. (Read Well Level K Ser.). (Illus.). 12p. (J). *(978-1-57035-730-5(7))* Cambium Education, Inc.

—Read Well Magazine Prelude E: Slanted Text. 2003. (Read Well Level K Ser.). (Illus.). 12p. (J). *(978-1-57035-694-0(7))* Cambium Education, Inc.

—Read Well Magazine Preude F: Slanted Text. 2003. (Read Well Level K Ser.). (Illus.). 12p. (J). *(978-1-57035-695-7(5))* Cambium Education, Inc.

—Read Well Magazine Unit 1: Plain Text. 2003. (Read Well Level K Ser.). (Illus.). 8p. (J). *(978-1-57035-735-0(8))* Cambium Education, Inc.

—Read Well Magazine Unit 1: Slanted Text. 2004. (Read Well Level K Ser.). (Illus.). 8p. (J). *(978-1-57035-782-4(X))* Cambium Education, Inc.

—Read Well Magazine Unit 10: Plain Text. 2003. (Read Well Level K Ser.). (Illus.). 8p. (J). *(978-1-57035-740-4(4))* Cambium Education, Inc.

—Read Well Magazine Unit 10: Slanted Text. 2003. (Read Well Level K Ser.). (Illus.). 8p. (J). *(978-1-57035-791-6(9))* Cambium Education, Inc.

—Read Well Magazine Unit 11: Plain Text. 2003. (Read Well Level K Ser.). (Illus.). 8p. (J). *(978-1-57035-741-1(2))* Cambium Education, Inc.

—Read Well Magazine Unit 11: Slanted Text. 2003. (Read Well Level K Ser.). (Illus.). 8p. (J). *(978-1-57035-792-3(7))* Cambium Education, Inc.

—Read Well Magazine Unit 12: Plain Text. 2004. (Read Well Level K Ser.). (Illus.). 8p. (J). *(978-1-57035-742-8(0))* Cambium Education, Inc.

—Read Well Magazine Unit 12: Slanted Text. 2003. (Read Well Level K Ser.). (Illus.). 8p. (J). *(978-1-57035-793-0(5))* Cambium Education, Inc.

—Read Well Magazine Unit 14: Plain Text. 2003. (Read Well Level K Ser.). (Illus.). 8p. (J). *(978-1-57035-744-2(7))* Cambium Education, Inc.

—Read Well Magazine Unit 15: Plain Text. 2003. (Read Well Level K Ser.). (Illus.). 8p. (J). *(978-1-57035-745-9(5))* Cambium Education, Inc.

—Read Well Magazine Unit 15: Slanted Text. 2003. (Read Well Level K Ser.). (Illus.). 8p. (J). *(978-1-59318-099-7(3))* Cambium Education, Inc.

—Read Well Magazine Unit 16. 2003. (Read Well Level K Ser.). (Illus.). 8p. (J). *(978-1-59318-100-0(0))* Cambium Education, Inc.

—Read Well Magazine Unit 17: Plain Text. 2003. (Read Well Level K Ser.). (Illus.). 8p. (J). *(978-1-57035-747-3(1))* Cambium Education, Inc.

—Read Well Magazine Unit 18: Slanted Text. 2003. (Read Well Level K Ser.). (Illus.). 8p. (J). *(978-1-59318-102-4(7))* Cambium Education, Inc.

—Read Well Magazine Unit 19: Plain Text. 2003. (Read Well Level K Ser.). (Illus.). 8p. (J). *(978-1-57035-749-7(8))* Cambium Education, Inc.

—Read Well Magazine Unit 19: Slanted Text. 2003. (Read Well Level K Ser.). (Illus.). 8p. (J). *(978-1-59318-103-1(5))* Cambium Education, Inc.

—Read Well Magazine Unit 2: Plain Text. 2003. (Read Well Level K Ser.). (Illus.). 8p. (J). *(978-1-57035-733-6(1))* Cambium Education, Inc.

—Read Well Magazine Unit 2: Slanted Text. 2003. (Read Well Level K Ser.). (Illus.). 8p. (J). *(978-1-57035-783-1(8))* Cambium Education, Inc.

—Read Well Magazine Unit 20: Plain Text. 2003. (Read Well Level K Ser.). (Illus.). 8p. (J). *(978-1-57035-775-6(7))* Cambium Education, Inc.

—Read Well Magazine Unit 3: Plain Text. 2003. (Read Well Level K Ser.). (Illus.). 8p. (J). *(978-1-57035-734-3(X))* Cambium Education, Inc.

—Read Well Magazine Unit 3: Slanted Text. 2003. (Read Well Level K Ser.). (Illus.). 8p. (J). *(978-1-57035-784-8(6))* Cambium Education, Inc.

—Read Well Magazine Unit 4: Plain Text. 2003. (Read Well Level K Ser.). (Illus.). 8p. (J). *(978-1-57035-732-9(3))* Cambium Education, Inc.

—Read Well Magazine Unit 4: Slanted Text. 2003. (Read Well Level K Ser.). (Illus.). 8p. (J). *(978-1-57035-785-5(4))* Cambium Education, Inc.

—Read Well Magazine Unit 5: Plain Text. 2003. (Read Well Level K Ser.). (Illus.). 8p. (J). *(978-1-57035-736-7(6))* Cambium Education, Inc.

—Read Well Magazine Unit 6: Plain Text. 2003. (Read Well Level K Ser.). (Illus.). 8p. (J). *(978-1-57035-737-4(4))* Cambium Education, Inc.

—Read Well Magazine Unit 6: Slanted Text. 2003. (Read Well Level K Ser.). (Illus.). 8p. (J). *(978-1-57035-787-9(0))* Cambium Education, Inc.

—Read Well Magazine Unit 7: Plain Text. 2003. (Read Well Level K Ser.). (Illus.). 8p. (J). *(978-1-57035-738-1(2))* Cambium Education, Inc.

—Read Well Magazine Unit 8: Plain Text. 2003. (Read Well Level K Ser.). (Illus.). 8p. (J). *(978-1-57035-726-8(9))* Cambium Education, Inc.

—Read Well Magazine Unit 8: Slanted Text. 2003. (Read Well Level K Ser.). (Illus.). 8p. (J). *(978-1-57035-789-3(7))* Cambium Education, Inc.

—Read Well Magazine Unit 9: Plain Text. 2003. (Read Well Level K Ser.). (Illus.). 8p. (J). *(978-1-57035-739-8(0))* Cambium Education, Inc.

—Read Well Magazine Unit 9: Slanted Text. 2003. (Read Well Level K Ser.). (Illus.). 8p. (J). *(978-1-57035-790-9(0))* Cambium Education, Inc.

—Rescue Workers: Read Well Level K Unit 11 Storybook. Zilis, Tom, illus. 2003. (Read Well Level K Ser.). 20p. (J). *(978-1-57035-682-7(3)*, 55511) Cambium Education, Inc.

—Spiders: Read Well Level K Unit 1 Storybook. Shupe, Bobbi & Crum, Anna-Maria, illus. 2003. (Read Well Level K Ser.). 20p. (J). *(978-1-57035-673-5(4))* Cambium Education, Inc.

—Spiders: Unit 1 Read Well Level K Teacher's Storybook. Shupe, Bobbi & Crum, Anna-Maria, illus. 2003. (Read Well Level K Ser.). 20p. (J). *(978-1-57035-696-4(3))* Cambium Education, Inc.

—Student Workbook 1 (Plain Text) Units 1-9 Plus Review Unit. 2003. (Read Well Level K Ser.). (Illus.). 104p. (J). *(978-1-59318-166-6(3))* Cambium Education, Inc.

—Student Workbook 1 (Slant Text) Units 1-9 Plus Review Unit. 2003. (Read Well Level K Ser.). (Illus.). 104p. (J). *(978-1-59318-169-7(8))* Cambium Education, Inc.

—Student Workbook 2 (Plain Text) Units 10-18 Plus Review Unit. 2003. (Read Well Level K Ser.). (Illus.). 104p. (J). *(978-1-59318-167-3(1))* Cambium Education, Inc.

—Student Workbook 2 (Slant Text) Units 10-18 Plus Review Unit. 2003. (Read Well Level K Ser.). (Illus.). 104p. (J). *(978-1-59318-170-3(1))* Cambium Education, Inc.

—Student Workbook 3 (Plain Text) Unit 19 through Vowel Review Unit. 2003. (Read Well Level K Ser.). (J). *(978-1-59318-168-0(X))* Cambium Education, Inc.

Spring to Success on the PSSA Grade 5: Test Prep & Skills Practice READING. 2004. 112p. (J). per. 8.00 *(978-0-9722452-6-5(X))* New Leaf Educ., Inc.

Spring to Success on the PSSA Grade 8: Test Prep & Skills Practice READING. 2004. 112p. (YA). per. 8.00 *(978-0-9722452-2-7(7))* New Leaf Educ., Inc.

The Spy Meeting. (Sails Literacy Ser.). 24p. (gr. 2-18). 27.00 *(978-0-7635-6998-3(4))*;Pack. 57.00 *(978-0-7578-3218-5(0))* Rigby Education.

Spyri, Johanna & Ladybird Books Staff. Ladybird Classics Heidi. Peluso, Martina, illus. 2015. (Ladybird Classics Ser.). (ENG.). 72p. (J). (gr. k-3). 8.99 *(978-1-4093-1357-1(3))* Penguin Bks., Ltd. GBR. Dist: Independent Pubs. Group.

Squiggles & Strokes, 6 vols., Pack. (Bookweb Ser.). 32p. (gr. 5-18). 34.00 *(978-0-7635-3795-1(0))* Rigby Education.

Stamp, Jeffrey. Red & Slim: One Hot Day. Bohrer, Joe, illus. 2008. 40p. (J). 16.99 *(978-0-9794543-0-1(1))* Syllabets, LLC.

Stamper Bauer, Judith & Ross Keyes, Joan. Library Pack. 2005. (Oxford Picture Dictionary for Kids Ser.). (ENG., Illus.). 49.95 *(978-0-19-430939-4(8))* Oxford Univ. Pr., Inc.

Stamper, Judith Bauer & Keyes, Joan Ross. Diego's Big Day. 2004. (Oxford Picture Dictionary for Kids Ser.). (ENG., Illus.). 16p. 6.94 *(978-0-19-430931-8(2))* Oxford Univ. Pr., Inc.

—Fun on the Farm. Springer, Sally, illus. 2005. (Oxford Picture Dictionary for Kids Ser.). (ENG.). 16p. 6.94 *(978-0-19-430935-6(5))* Oxford Univ. Pr., Inc.

—Monster Parade. 2004. (Oxford Picture Dictionary for Kids Ser.). (ENG., Illus.). 16p. 6.94 *(978-0-19-430929-5(0))* Oxford Univ. Pr., Inc.

—Out the Window! 2004. (Oxford Picture Dictionary for Kids Ser.). (ENG., Illus.). 16p. 6.94 *(978-0-19-430927-1(4))* Oxford Univ. Pr., Inc.

—Snow Tracks. 2004. (Oxford Picture Dictionary for Kids Ser.). (ENG., Illus.). 16p. 6.94 *(978-0-19-430928-8(2))* Oxford Univ. Pr., Inc.

—A Sweet Surprise. 2005. (Oxford Picture Dictionary for Kids Ser.). (ENG., Illus.). 16p. 6.94 *(978-0-19-430933-2(9))* Oxford Univ. Pr., Inc.

—What's for Breakfast? Springer, Sally, illus. 2005. (Oxford Picture Dictionary for Kids Ser.). (ENG.). 16p. 6.94 *(978-0-19-430934-9(7))* Oxford Univ. Pr., Inc.

Stamper, Judith Bauer & Ross Keyes, Joan. Hop, Hop, Jump! 2005. (Oxford Picture Dictionary for Kids Ser.). (ENG., Illus.). 16p. 6.94 *(978-0-19-430932-5(0))* Oxford Univ. Pr., Inc.

Stamper, Judith Bauer, et al. Trip to Toy Town. 2004. (Oxford Picture Dictionary for Kids Ser.). (ENG., Illus.). 16p. 6.94 *(978-0-19-430930-1(4))* Oxford Univ. Pr., Inc.

Standfield, Robert. The Little Tacker's Guide to Opposites. 2012. 28p. pap. 32.70 *(978-1-4691-5763-4(2))* Xlibris Corp.

Stanek, Robert, pseud. Break Their Bad Habits. deluxe ed. 2009. (Bugville Critters Ser.: No. 9). (Illus.). 24p. 9.99 *(978-1-57545-213-5(8)*, Reagent Pr. Bks. for Young Readers) RP Media.

—Break Their Bad Habits: (the Bugville Critters, Lass's Adventures Series #2) 2009. (Bugville Critters Ser.: No. 9). (Illus.). 52p. (J). pap. 14.95 *(978-1-57545-205-0(7)*, Reagent Pr. Bks. for Young Readers) RP Media.

—Buster Bee's Adventures with Letters & Words. 2008. (ENG., Illus.). 52p. (J). per. 19.95 *(978-1-57545-169-5(7))* RP Media.

—Go to Camp. 2010. 34p. pap. 8.99 *(978-1-57545-178-7(6)*, Reagent Pr. Bks. for Young Readers) RP Media.

—Save Their Allowance. 2010. 32p. pap. 8.99 *(978-1-57545-175-6(1)*, Reagent Pr. Bks. for Young Readers) RP Media.

—Stay after School. 2009. (Bugville Critters Ser.: No. 10). (ENG., Illus.). 52p. (J). 14.95 *(978-1-57545-206-7(5)*, Reagent Pr. Bks. for Young Readers) RP Media.

—Visit City Hall. 2009. (Bugville Critters Ser.: No. 12). (ENG., Illus.). 52p. (J). 14.95 *(978-1-57545-208-1(1)*, Reagent Pr. Bks. for Young Readers) RP Media.

Stango, Diane. Too Many Tomatoes. 2006. (Neighborhood Readers Ser.). (ENG.). 12p. (gr. -1-3). pap. 5.90 *(978-1-4042-6718-3(2)*, Rosen Classroom) Rosen Publishing Group, Inc., The.

—Vicky's Vegetables. 2006. (Neighborhood Readers Ser.). (ENG.). 16p. (gr. 1-3). pap. 6.50 *(978-1-4042-7156-2(2)*, Rosen Classroom) Rosen Publishing Group, Inc., The.

Stango, Diane E. City Life. 2006. (Rosen Real Readers Big Bookstm Ser.). (ENG.). 8p. (gr. k-1). 29.95 *(978-1-4042-6210-2(5))* Rosen Publishing Group, Inc., The.

STAR Early Literacy RP Student Subscription. 2004. cd-rom *(978-1-59455-175-8(8))* Renaissance Learning, Inc.

STAR Early Literacy RP Student Subscription Renewal. 2004. cd-rom *(978-1-59455-176-5(6))* Renaissance Learning, Inc.

STAR Early Literacy RP Subscription Package. 2004. cd-rom *(978-1-59455-173-4(1))* Renaissance Learning, Inc.

Star, Ian. Breakfast at the Farm. 2006. (Neighborhood Readers Ser.). (ENG.). 12p. (gr. -1-3). pap. 5.90 *(978-1-4042-6473-1(6)*, Rosen Classroom) Rosen Publishing Group, Inc., The.

STAR Reading RP Norms Upgrade. 2004. cd-rom 599.00 *(978-1-59455-172-7(3))* Renaissance Learning, Inc.

STAR Reading RP Student Subscription. 2004. cd-rom 0.99 *(978-1-59455-169-7(3))* Renaissance Learning, Inc.

STAR Reading RP Student Subscription Renewal. 2004. cd-rom *(978-1-59455-170-3(7))* Renaissance Learning, Inc.

STAR Reading RP Subscription Package. 2004. cd-rom *(978-1-59455-168-0(5))* Renaissance Learning, Inc.

Starfall Education. Gus the Duck. Starfall Education, ed. 2004. (ENG., Illus.). 8p. (J). pap. *(978-1-59577-005-9(4))* Starfall Education.

—Level I Reading & Writing Journal - Block Print: WK201b. Starfall Education, ed. 2011. (ENG., Illus.). 96p. (J). *(978-1-59577-045-5(3))* Starfall Education.

—My Horse Glory. Starfall Education, ed. 2004. (ENG., Illus.). 8p. (J). pap. *(978-1-59577-013-4(5))* Starfall Education.

—Peg the Hen. Starfall Education, ed. 2004. (ENG., Illus.). 8p. (J). pap. *(978-1-59577-002-8(X))* Starfall Education.

—Pete's Sheep. Starfall Education, ed. 2004. (ENG., Illus.). 8p. (J). pap. *(978-1-59577-007-3(0))* Starfall Education.

—Robot & Mr. Mole. Starfall Education, ed. 2004. (ENG., Illus.). 8p. (J). pap. *(978-1-59577-009-7(7))* Starfall Education.

—Sky Ride. Starfall Education, ed. 2004. (ENG., Illus.). 8p. (J). pap. *(978-1-59577-008-0(9))* Starfall Education.

—Soap Boat. Starfall Education, ed. 2004. (ENG., Illus.). 8p. (J). pap. *(978-1-59577-011-0(9))* Starfall Education.

Starfall Education, creator. Level II Reading & Writing Journal: Second Edition. 2010. (ENG., Illus.). 96p. (J). 1.95 *(978-1-59577-130-8(1))* Starfall Education.

Stark, Barbara. Blue Dinosaur's Friends. l.t. ed. 2006. (Illus.). 24p. (J). E-Book 9.95 incl. cd-rom *(978-1-933090-20-7(0))* Guardian Angel Publishing, Inc.

Start It Up! (Early Intervention Levels Ser.). 21.30 *(978-0-7362-0391-3(5))*; Vol. 6. 3.55 *(978-0-7362-0171-1(8))* CENGAGE Learning.

Start Reading. 2013. (Start Reading Ser.). (ENG.). 24p. (gr. k-1). pap. 230.67 *(978-1-62065-765-2(1))*; pap. 174.75 *(978-1-4765-3332-2(6))* Capstone Press of Coughlan Cos.

Start Reading Classroom Collection. 2013. (Start Reading Ser.). (ENG.). 24p. (gr. k-1). pap. 1048.50 *(978-1-4765-3333-9(4))* Capstone Press of Coughlan Cos.

Starters Two, Red, & Yellow Levels Certificate Only. (gr. k-5). 89.00 *(978-0-7578-6539-8(9))* Rigby Education.

Stckvagn. AC Reading for Today. 2004. pap. *(978-0-7398-9859-8(0))* Harcourt Schl. Pubs.

Steck-Vaughn, creator. Using Information Resources, Grade 2. 2009. (Using Information Resources Ser.). (Illus.). 64p. pap. 9.99 *(978-1-4190-9937-3(X))* Steck-Vaughn.

—Using Information Resources, Grade 3. 2009. (Using Information Resources Ser.). (Illus.). 64p. pap. 9.99 *(978-1-4190-9938-0(8))* Steck-Vaughn.

Steck-Vaughn Staff. Cycles Go Bk. FA: Quests. 2004. (Illus.). pap. 8.95 *(978-0-7398-8972-5(9))* Steck-Vaughn.

—Cycles Go Bk. GA: Choices. 2004. (Illus.). pap. 8.95 *(978-0-7398-8973-2(7))* Steck-Vaughn.

—Cycles Go Bk. HA: Visions. 2004. (Illus.). pap. 8.95 *(978-0-7398-8974-9(5))* Steck-Vaughn.

—Cycles Go - Reflections. 2004. (Illus.). pap. 8.95 *(978-0-7398-8975-6(3))* Steck-Vaughn.

—Early Reading Program: Professional Development. 2004. pap. 45.00 *(978-0-7398-9948-9(1))* Harcourt Schl. Pubs.

—Exactly the Right Egg. 2003. pap. 4.10 *(978-0-7398-7631-2(7))* Steck-Vaughn.

—Fact Family Fun. 2003. pap. 4.10 *(978-0-7398-7662-6(7))* Steck-Vaughn.

—Language Art & Spelling, 8, Pack. 2004. pap. 68.00 *(978-0-7398-9933-5(3))* Harcourt Schl. Pubs.

—Language Arts & Spelling. 2004. pap. 8.50 *(978-0-7398-9848-2(5))*; pap. 68.00 *(978-0-7398-9929-8(5))*; pap., tchr. ed. 10.00 *(978-0-7398-9904-5(X))* Harcourt Schl. Pubs.

—Nonfiction Comprehension. 2005. (gr. 3). pap. 12.99 *(978-0-7398-8947-3(8))*; (gr. 5). pap. 12.99 *(978-0-7398-8948-0(6))* Harcourt Schl. Pubs.

—Nonfiction Comprehension, Middle School. 2005. pap. 12.99 *(978-0-7398-8949-7(4))* Harcourt Schl. Pubs.

—Primary Grades, Grades 1-3. 2004. (Reader's Theater Ser.). (ENG., Illus.). 160p. (gr. 1-3). pap. 16.99 *(978-0-7398-9309-8(2))* Houghton Mifflin Harcourt Publishing Co.

—Reading & Language Arts. 2004. pap. 8.50 *(978-0-7398-9845-1(0))* Harcourt Schl. Pubs.

—Reading & Language Arts 8-Pack. 2004. pap. 68.00 *(978-0-7398-9926-7(0))* Harcourt Schl. Pubs.

—Reading Comprehension: Building Vocabulary & Measurement. 2003. (Steck-Vaughn Reading Comprehension Ser.). (ENG.). 56p. (gr. k-k). pap., tchr. ed. 33.70 *(978-0-7398-8356-3(9))* Houghton Mifflin Harcourt Publishing Co.

—Reading Intermediate, 8, Pack. 2004. pap. 68.00 *(978-0-7398-9928-1(7))* Harcourt Schl. Pubs.

—Stuck on You. 2003. pap. 4.10 *(978-0-7398-7634-3(1))* Steck-Vaughn.

Steck-Vaughn Staff, creator. Test Fundamentals: Reading: Basic, 8, Pack. 2004. pap., pap. 68.00 *(978-0-7398-9932-8(5))* Harcourt Schl. Pubs.

Steele, Philip. Kingfisher Readers L3: Vikings. 2014. (Kingfisher Readers Ser.). (ENG., Illus.). 32p. (J). (gr. k-3). 12.99 *(978-0-7534-7148-7(5)*, 9780753471487, Kingfisher) Roaring Brook Pr.

Steinberg, Jon L. "Eye" See My Alphabet. 2012. 60p. (-18). pap. 24.99 *(978-1-4797-1135-2(7))* Xlibris Corp.

Steiner. Murder Takes a Fast Track. (Thumbprint Mysteries Ser.). 32.86 *(978-0-8092-0417-5(7))* McGraw-Hill/Contemporary.

Steiner, Rudolf. Fun Days. (J). pap. 2.75 *(978-0-87895-956-3(4))* Modern Curriculum Pr.

Steinkraus, Kyla. Los Problemas Del Intercambio. 2012. (SPA & ENG.). 24p. (gr. 2-3). pap. 8.95 *(978-1-61810-543-1(4))* Rourke Educational Media.

—¡Paren de Discutir! 2012.Tr. of Stop Arguing. (SPA & ENG.). 24p. (gr. 2-3). pap. 8.95 *(978-1-61810-542-4(6))* Rourke Educational Media.

Stephens, Monique Z. Fantastic Four: The Fantastic Four Versus Doctor Doom. 2005. (Festival Reader Ser.). (Illus.). 32p. (J). (gr. -1-2). 14.99 *(978-0-06-082245-3(7)*, HarperFestival) HarperCollins Pubs.

Sterling, Kristin. Lightning Bolt Books: Colors Everywhere, 12 vols., Set. Incl. Black Everywhere. lib. bdg. 26.60 *(978-0-7613-4591-6(4))*; Blue Everywhere. lib. bdg. 26.60 *(978-0-7613-4588-6(4))*; Brown Everywhere. lib. bdg. 26.60 *(978-0-7613-5438-3(7))*; Gray Everywhere. lib. bdg. 26.60 *(978-0-7613-5439-0(5))*; Green Everywhere. lib. bdg. 26.60 *(978-0-7613-5436-9(0))*; Orange Everywhere. lib. bdg. 26.60 *(978-0-7613-5435-2(2))*; Pink Everywhere. lib. bdg. 26.60 *(978-0-7613-5440-6(9))*; Purple Everywhere. lib. bdg. 26.60 *(978-0-7613-5437-6(9))*; Red Everywhere. lib. bdg. 26.60 *(978-0-7613-4590-9(6))*; Silver & Gold Everywhere. lib. bdg. 26.60 *(978-0-7613-4593-0(0))*; White Everywhere. lib. bdg. 26.60 *(978-0-7613-4592-3(2))*; Yellow Everywhere. lib. bdg. 26.60 *(978-0-7613-4589-3(2))*; (Illus.). 32p. (gr. k-2). 2010. 2009. Set lib. bdg. 303.12 *(978-0-7613-4587-9(6)*, Lerner Pubns.) Lerner Publishing Group.

Stevens, Janet & Crummel, Susan Stevens. Tumbleweed Stew/Sopa de Matojos. Flor Ada, Alma & Campoy, F. Isabel, trs. from ENG. Stevens, Janet, illus. 2009. (Green Light Readers Level 2 Ser.). (SPA & ENG., Illus.). 36p. (J). (gr. -1-3). pap. 3.99 *(978-0-547-25261-2(7))* Houghton Mifflin Harcourt Publishing Co.

Stevenson, May. Brilliant Activities for Reading Non-Fiction: Comprehension Activities for 7-11 Year Olds. 2006. (Illus.). 128p. pap. *(978-1-903853-46-7(X))* Brilliant Pubns.

Stevenson, Robert Louis. Kidnapped. 2016. (ENG., Illus.). (J). 25.95 **(978-1-359-73690-1(5))** Creative Media Partners, LLC.

—Kidnapped. 2017. (ENG., Illus.). (J). 30.99 **(978-1-366-54862-7(0))** Blurb, Inc.

—Kidnapped. 2017. (ENG., Illus.). (J). 24.95 **(978-1-374-96355-9(0))**; pap. 14.95 **(978-1-374-96354-2(2))** Capital Communications, Inc.

Stevenson-Spurgon, Barbara J. Have You Ever Made Mud Pies on a Hot Summer Day? This Is a Bitty Book. Ruffin, Aurzella, illus. 2006. 36p. (J). (gr. -1-4). per. 19.95 *(978-1-60002-234-0(0)*, 4073) Mountain Valley Publishing, LLC.

Stewart, Melissa. Water. 2014. (Readers Ser.). (ENG., Illus.). 48p. (J). (gr. 1-4). pap. 3.99 *(978-1-4263-1474-2(4)*, National Geographic Children's Bks.) National Geographic Society.

Stewart, Paul & Riddell, Chris. Mind Warp. unabr. ed. 2017. (Scavenger Ser.: 3). (ENG., Illus.). 256p. (J). (gr. 4-7). pap. 9.99 *(978-1-4472-3445-6(6))* Pan Macmillan GBR. Dist: Independent Pubs. Group.

Stiles, Amanda. The Runaway Soccer Ball. Torrey, Rich, illus. 2010. 16p. (J). pap. *(978-0-545-24819-8(1))* Scholastic, Inc.

StJohn, Amanda. How an e-Book Works. Ostrom, Bob, illus. 2012. (Library Skills Ser.). (ENG.). 24p. (J). (gr. -1-2). 28.50 *(978-1-61473-248-8(5)*, 204950) Child's World, Inc., The.

Stockton, Frank Richard, et al. Simply Suspense. 2nd ed. 2008. (ENG., Illus.). 56p. pap. 11.99 *(978-1-4058-6948-5(8))* Pearson Education.

Stoeke, Janet Morgan. Pip's Trip. Stoeke, Janet Morgan, illus. 2014. (Loopy Coop Hens Ser.). (ENG., Illus.). 32p. (J). (gr. 1-2). pap. 3.99 *(978-0-448-48133-3(2)*, Penguin Young Readers) Penguin Young Readers Group.

Stones, Brenda & Feldman, Thea. Kingfisher Readers L2 What We Eat. 2014. (Kingfisher Readers Ser.). (ENG., Illus.). 32p. (J). (gr. k-3). 12.99 *(978-0-7534-7120-3(5),* 9780753471203, Kingfisher) Roaring Brook Pr.
Stontz, Karen & Malone, Kelly. Autism & PDD Concepts How Does Becca Bunny Feel? 2004. (J). spiral bd. *(978-0-7606-0594-3(7))* LinguiSystems, Inc.
Stop That Noise! KinderWords Individual Title Six-Packs. (Kinderstarters Ser.). 8p. (gr. -1-1). 21.00 *(978-0-7635-8694-2(3))* Rigby Education.
Stories & More. 2005. (Little Celebrations Thematic Packages Ser.). (J). (gr. k-3). 133.50 *(978-0-673-75376-2(X))* Celebration Pr.
Stories from Many Lands. (J). 3.70 *(978-0-8136-2402-0(9));* tchr. ed. 9.30 *(978-0-8136-2427-3(4))* Modern Curriculum Pr.
Storm Warning: KinderConcepts Individual Title Six-Packs. (Kinderstarters Ser.). 8p. (gr. -1-1). 21.00 *(978-0-7635-8734-5(6))* Rigby Education.
Stormer, Kate. The Rescue of Little Red. Lowes, Tom, illus. 2005. 91p. (J). (gr. 3-5). per. 5.99 *(978-0-9765872-0-0(3))* Caseys World Bks.
Story Box. (gr. 2-18). 8.50 *(978-0-7802-3064-4(7))* Wright Group/McGraw-Hill.
Story Center. 2005. (YA). (gr. -1-3). 19.95 *(978-0-8215-7557-4(0))* Sadlier, William H. Inc.
Story Center Guide. 2005. (YA). (gr. -1-3). 6.00 *(978-0-8215-7558-1(9))* Sadlier, William H. Inc.
The Story of Dona Chila: Six-Pack. (Greetings Ser.: Vol. 3). (gr. 3-5). 31.00 *(978-0-7635-1775-5(5))* Rigby Education.
The Story of Jeans, 6 Pack. (Discovery World Ser.). 24p. (gr. 1-2). 33.00 *(978-0-7635-8483-2(5))* Rigby Education.
Storytapes Set 800866, 3. 2005. (J). *(978-1-59794-029-0(1))* Environments, Inc.
Stowell, Louie. Samurai. Engle, Jason, illus. 2007. (Young Reading Series 3 Gift Bks). 58p. (J). (gr. 2-5). 8.99 *(978-0-7945-1719-9(6),* Usborne) EDC Publishing.
The Streetsweeper, 6 packs. (Bookweb Ser.). 32p. (gr. 3-18). 34.00 *(978-0-7635-3943-6(0))* Rigby Education.
String Performers: Individual Title Six-Packs. (gr. k-1). 23.00 *(978-0-7635-9029-1(0))* Rigby Education.
Strings, Ropes & Cables, 6 Packs. (gr. k-1). 23.00 *(978-0-7635-9024-6(X))* Rigby Education.
Stripland, Rubye Weldon. Lucy Bell, Queen of the Pasture. 2008. 92p. pap. 10.95 *(978-1-4357-1472-4(5))* Lulu Pr., Inc.
—Lucy Bell, Queen of the Pasture Book Two. 2008. 100p. pap. 10.95 *(978-1-4357-1895-1(X))* Lulu Pr., Inc.
Strong, Jeremy. Bungleman. Mosedale, Julian, illus. 2007. (Collins Big Cat Ser.). (ENG.). 96p. (J). (gr. 2-3). pap. 8.99 *(978-0-00-723083-9(4))* HarperCollins Pubs. Ltd. GBR. Dist: Independent Pubs. Group.
—The Sneezles. Blundell, Tony, illus. 2005. (Collins Big Cat Ser.). (ENG.). 32p. (J). (gr. 1-3). pap. 7.99 *(978-0-00-718628-0(2))* HarperCollins Pubs. Ltd. GBR. Dist: Independent Pubs. Group.
Stuart, Carrie. Chinese New Year. 2006. (Neighborhood Readers Ser.). (ENG.). 12p. (gr. -1-3). pap. 5.90 *(978-1-4042-6461-8(2),* Rosen Classroom) Rosen Publishing Group, Inc., The.
—How Flowers Grow. 2008. (Rosen Real Readers: Upper Emergent Ser.). (ENG., Illus.). 12p. (gr. 1-2). pap. 5.90 *(978-0-8239-8129-8(0))* Rosen Publishing Group, Inc., The.
—Lenore's Chores. 2006. (Neighborhood Readers Ser.). (ENG.). 8p. (gr. 1-3). pap. 5.15 *(978-1-4042-6823-4(5),* Rosen Classroom) Rosen Publishing Group, Inc., The.
Stuart, Phillip. Stage Fright. 2005. (Young Reading Series 2 Ser.). 64p. (J). (gr. 2-18). pap. 5.95 *(978-0-7945-0927-9(4),* Usborne) EDC Publishing.
Sturgeon, Kristi. Freckle Juice: An Instructional Guide for Literature. 2015. (Great Works). (ENG., Illus.). 72p. (gr. 3-5). pap. 9.99 *(978-1-4807-6993-9(2))* Shell Educational Publishing.
Styles, Walker. The Case of the Missing Tiger's Eye. 2016. (Rider Woofson Ser.: 1). lib. bdg. 16.00 *(978-0-606-38262-5(3))* Turtleback Bks.
Suchanek, David. The 10 Most Inspiring Speeches. 2008. 14.99 *(978-1-55448-537-6(1))* Scholastic Library Publishing.
Sugar & Spice & All Things Nice: Level M, 6 vols. 128p. (gr. 2-3). 40.50 *(978-0-7699-0998-1(1))* Shortland Pubns. (U. S. A.) Inc.
The Sugar Bush: 6 Small Books. (Greetings Ser.: Vol. 1). 24p. (gr. 2-3). 31.00 *(978-0-7635-9424-4(5))* Rigby Education.
The Sugar Bush: Big Book. (Greetings Ser.: Vol. 1). 24p. (gr. 2-3). 31.00 *(978-0-7635-5706-5(4))* Rigby Education.
Sulky Simon, 6 Packs. (gr. 1-2). 25.00 *(978-0-7635-9146-5(7))* Rigby Education.
Sundance/Newbridge LLC Staff. The Abominable Snowman. 2005. (Choose Your Own Adventure Ser.). (gr. 4-8). pap. 5.50 *(978-0-7608-9693-8(3))* Sundance/Newbridge Educational Publishing.
—Amazing Water. 2007. (Early Science Ser.). (gr. k-3). 18.95 *(978-1-4007-6296-5(0));* pap. 6.10 *(978-1-4007-6292-7(8))* Sundance/Newbridge Educational Publishing.
—Animals & Their Babies. 2007. (Early Science Ser.). (gr. k-3). 18.95 *(978-1-4007-6215-6(4));* pap. 6.10 *(978-1-4007-6211-8(1))* Sundance/Newbridge Educational Publishing.
—Animals in Hiding. 2007. (Early Science Ser.). (gr. k-3). 18.95 *(978-1-4007-6350-4(9))* Sundance/Newbridge Educational Publishing.
—An Apple a Day. 2007. (Early Science Ser.). (gr. k-3). 18.95 *(978-1-4007-6359-7(2));* pap. 6.10 *(978-1-4007-6355-9(X))* Sundance/Newbridge Educational Publishing.
—Being Human. 2007. (Early Science Ser.). (gr. k-3). 18.95 *(978-1-4007-6513-3(7));* pap. 6.10 *(978-1-4007-6509-6(9))* Sundance/Newbridge Educational Publishing.
—Birds, Birds, Birds. 2004. (Reading PowerWorks Ser.). (gr. 1-3). pap. 6.10 *(978-0-7608-9784-3(0))* Sundance/Newbridge Educational Publishing.
—Bubbles, Bubbles Everywhere. 2007. (Early Science Ser.). (gr. k-3). 18.95 *(978-1-4007-6206-4(5));* pap. 6.10 *(978-1-4007-6202-6(2))* Sundance/Newbridge Educational Publishing.
—Busy As a Bee. 2007. (Early Science Ser.). (gr. k-3). 18.95 *(978-1-4007-6594-2(3));* pap. 6.10 *(978-1-4007-6590-4(0))* Sundance/Newbridge Educational Publishing.
—A Butterfly Is Born. 2007. (Early Science Ser.). (gr. k-3). 18.95 *(978-1-4007-6224-8(3));* pap. 6.10 *(978-1-4007-6220-0(0))* Sundance/Newbridge Educational Publishing.
—Design It! Build It! 2007. (Early Science Ser.). (gr. k-3). 18.95 *(978-1-4007-6603-1(6));* pap. 6.10 *(978-1-4007-6599-7(4))* Sundance/Newbridge Educational Publishing.
—Dollars & Cents. 2004. (Reading PowerWorks Ser.). (gr. 1-3). 37.50 *(978-0-7608-8964-0(3));* pap. 6.10 *(978-0-7608-8965-7(1))* Sundance/Newbridge Educational Publishing.
—Energy. 2007. (Early Science Ser.). (gr. k-3). 18.95 *(978-1-4007-6549-2(8));* pap. 6.10 *(978-1-4007-6545-4(5))* Sundance/Newbridge Educational Publishing.
—Exploring Our Oceans. 2004. (Reading PowerWorks Ser.). (gr. 1-3). pap. 6.10 *(978-0-7608-9760-7(3))* Sundance/Newbridge Educational Publishing.
—The Fact Families. 2004. (Reading PowerWorks Ser.). (gr. 1-3). 37.50 *(978-0-7608-9305-0(5));* pap. 6.10 *(978-0-7608-9306-7(3))* Sundance/Newbridge Educational Publishing.
—Follow the River. 2007. (Early Science Ser.). (gr. k-3). 18.95 *(978-1-4007-6558-4(7));* pap. 6.10 *(978-1-4007-6554-6(4))* Sundance/Newbridge Educational Publishing.
—For Your Information. 2007. (Early Science Ser.). (gr. k-3). 18.95 *(978-1-4007-6567-6(6));* pap. 6.10 *(978-1-4007-6563-8(3))* Sundance/Newbridge Educational Publishing.
—From Circles to Cubes. 2004. (Reading PowerWorks Ser.). (gr. 1-3). 37.50 *(978-0-7608-7839-2(0));* pap. 6.10 *(978-0-7608-7840-8(4))* Sundance/Newbridge Educational Publishing.
—From Peanuts to Peanut Butter. 2007. (Early Science Ser.). (gr. k-3). 18.95 *(978-1-4007-6170-8(0));* pap. 6.10 *(978-1-4007-6166-1(2))* Sundance/Newbridge Educational Publishing.
—Gravity. 2007. (Early Science Ser.). (gr. k-3). 18.95 *(978-1-4007-6468-6(8));* pap. 6.10 *(978-1-4007-6464-8(5))* Sundance/Newbridge Educational Publishing.
—Growing Pumpkins. 2007. (Early Science Ser.). (gr. k-3). 18.95 *(978-1-4007-6179-1(4));* pap. 6.10 *(978-1-4007-6175-3(1))* Sundance/Newbridge Educational Publishing.
—How We Use Electricity. 2007. (Early Science Ser.). (gr. k-3). 18.95 *(978-1-4007-6368-9(1));* pap. 6.10 *(978-1-4007-6364-1(9))* Sundance/Newbridge Educational Publishing.
—Inventions. 2007. (Early Science Ser.). (gr. k-3). 18.95 *(978-1-4007-6630-7(3));* pap. 6.10 *(978-1-4007-6626-0(5))* Sundance/Newbridge Educational Publishing.
—Is It Alive? 2007. (Early Science Ser.). (gr. k-3). 18.95 *(978-1-4007-6152-4(2));* pap. 6.10 *(978-1-4007-6148-7(4))* Sundance/Newbridge Educational Publishing.
—Kids for the Earth. 2007. (Early Science Ser.). (gr. k-3). 18.95 *(978-1-4007-6188-3(3));* pap. 6.10 *(978-1-4007-6184-5(0))* Sundance/Newbridge Educational Publishing.
—Leaping Frogs. 2007. (Early Science Ser.). (gr. k-3). 18.95 *(978-1-4007-6305-4(3));* pap. 6.10 *(978-1-4007-6301-6(0))* Sundance/Newbridge Educational Publishing.
—Life in a Pond. 2007. (Early Science Ser.). (gr. k-3). 18.95 *(978-1-4007-6377-1(0));* pap. 6.10 *(978-1-4007-6373-3(8))* Sundance/Newbridge Educational Publishing.
—Life in a Tree. 2007. (Early Science Ser.). (gr. k-3). 18.95 *(978-1-4007-6459-4(9));* pap. 6.10 *(978-1-4007-6455-6(6))* Sundance/Newbridge Educational Publishing.
—Light. 2007. (Early Science Ser.). (gr. k-3). 18.95 *(978-1-4007-6314-6(2));* pap. 6.10 *(978-1-4007-6310-8(X))* Sundance/Newbridge Educational Publishing.
—The Lost Jewels of Nafouti. 2005. (Choose Your Own Adventure Ser.). (gr. 4-8). pap. 5.50 *(978-0-7608-9691-4(7))* Sundance/Newbridge Educational Publishing.
—Make Mine Ice Cream. 2007. (Early Science Ser.). (gr. k-3). 18.95 *(978-1-4007-6522-5(6));* pap. 6.10 *(978-1-4007-6518-8(8))* Sundance/Newbridge Educational Publishing.
—Matter Is Everything. 2004. (Reading PowerWorks Ser.). (gr. 1-3). 37.50 *(978-0-7608-8900-8(7));* pap. 6.10 *(978-0-7608-8901-5(5))* Sundance/Newbridge Educational Publishing.
—Mystery of the Maya. 2005. (Choose Your Own Adventure Ser.). (gr. 4-8). pap. 5.50 *(978-0-7608-9692-1(5))* Sundance/Newbridge Educational Publishing.
—One World, Many Cultures. 2004. (Reading PowerWorks Ser.). (gr. 1-3). 37.50 *(978-0-7608-8952-7(X));* pap. 6.10 *(978-0-7608-8953-4(8))* Sundance/Newbridge Educational Publishing.
—Our American Folklore. 2004. (Reading PowerWorks Ser.). (gr. 1-3). 37.50 *(978-0-7608-9795-9(6));* pap. 6.10 *(978-0-7608-9796-6(4))* Sundance/Newbridge Educational Publishing.
—Our Natural Resources. 2004. (Reading PowerWorks Ser.). (gr. 1-3). 37.50 *(978-0-7608-9221-3(0));* pap. 6.10 *(978-0-7608-9222-0(9))* Sundance/Newbridge Educational Publishing.
—Our Sun, Our Weather. 2007. (Early Science Ser.). (gr. k-3). 18.95 *(978-1-4007-6531-7(5));* pap. 6.10 *(978-1-4007-6527-0(7))* Sundance/Newbridge Educational Publishing.
—Out in Space. 2007. (Early Science Ser.). (gr. k-3). 18.95 *(978-1-4007-6422-8(X));* pap. 6.10 *(978-1-4007-6418-1(1))* Sundance/Newbridge Educational Publishing.
—Pasta, Please! 2007. (Early Science Ser.). (gr. k-3). 18.95 *(978-1-4007-6332-0(0));* pap. 6.10 *(978-1-4007-6328-3(2))* Sundance/Newbridge Educational Publishing.
—Predators & Prey. 2007. (Early Science Ser.). (gr. k-3). 18.95 *(978-1-4007-6540-9(4));* pap. 6.10 *(978-1-4007-6536-2(6))* Sundance/Newbridge Educational Publishing.
—Predicting the Weather. 2004. (Reading PowerWorks Ser.). (gr. 1-3). 37.50 *(978-0-7608-9245-9(8))* Sundance/Newbridge Educational Publishing.
—Properties of Materials. 2007. (Early Science Ser.). (gr. k-3). 18.95 *(978-1-4007-6576-8(5));* pap. 6.10 *(978-1-4007-6572-0(2))* Sundance/Newbridge Educational Publishing.
—Push & Pull. 2007. (Early Science Ser.). (gr. k-3). 18.95 *(978-1-4007-6134-0(4));* pap. 6.10 *(978-1-4007-6130-2(1))* Sundance/Newbridge Educational Publishing.
—Rocks & Soil. 2007. (Early Science Ser.). (gr. k-3). 18.95 *(978-1-4007-6441-9(6));* pap. 6.10 *(978-1-4007-6437-2(8))* Sundance/Newbridge Educational Publishing.
—See, Hear, Touch, Taste, Smell. 2007. (Early Science Ser.). (gr. k-3). 18.95 *(978-1-4007-6197-5(2));* pap. 6.10 *(978-1-4007-6193-7(X))* Sundance/Newbridge Educational Publishing.
—Seeds Get Around. 2007. (Early Science Ser.). (gr. k-3). 18.95 *(978-1-4007-6341-2(X));* pap. 6.10 *(978-1-4007-6337-5(1))* Sundance/Newbridge Educational Publishing.
—Simple Machines. 2007. (Early Science Ser.). (gr. k-3). 18.95 *(978-1-4007-6612-3(5));* pap. 6.10 *(978-1-4007-6608-6(7))* Sundance/Newbridge Educational Publishing.
—Sink or Float? 2007. (Early Science Ser.). (gr. k-3). 18.95 *(978-1-4007-6269-9(3));* pap. 6.10 *(978-1-4007-6265-1(0))* Sundance/Newbridge Educational Publishing.
—Six Simple Machines. 2004. (Reading PowerWorks Ser.). (gr. 1-3). 37.50 *(978-0-7608-9735-5(2));* pap. 6.10 *(978-0-7608-9736-2(0))* Sundance/Newbridge Educational Publishing.
—Sound. 2007. (Early Science Ser.). (gr. k-3). 18.95 *(978-1-4007-6395-5(9));* pap. 6.10 *(978-1-4007-6391-7(6))* Sundance/Newbridge Educational Publishing.
—Spinning a Web. 2007. (Early Science Ser.). (gr. k-3). 18.95 *(978-1-4007-6233-0(2));* pap. 6.10 *(978-1-4007-6229-3(4))* Sundance/Newbridge Educational Publishing.
—Symbols of America. 2004. (Reading PowerWorks Ser.). (gr. 1-3). 37.50 *(978-0-7608-9257-2(1))* Sundance/Newbridge Educational Publishing.
—Wants & Needs. 2004. (Reading PowerWorks Ser.). (gr. 1-3). 37.50 *(978-0-7608-9819-2(7));* pap. 6.10 *(978-0-7608-9820-8(0))* Sundance/Newbridge Educational Publishing.
—What's That Sound? 2004. (Reading PowerWorks Ser.). (gr. 1-3). 37.50 *(978-0-7608-9807-9(3));* pap. 6.10 *(978-0-7608-9808-6(1))* Sundance/Newbridge Educational Publishing.
—A World of Tools. 2007. (Early Science Ser.). (gr. k-3). 18.95 *(978-1-4007-6504-1(8));* pap. 6.10 *(978-1-4007-6500-3(5))* Sundance/Newbridge Educational Publishing.
Sunflower. (Lexile Levels Ser.). 7.98 *(978-1-56334-672-9(9))* CENGAGE Learning.
The Super Supermarket Plan: Individual Title Six-Packs. (gr. k-1). 23.00 *(978-0-7635-8844-1(X))* Rigby Education.
Surfing 6 Packs. KinderConcepts. (Kinderstarters Ser.). 8p. (gr. -1-1). 21.00 *(978-0-7635-8726-0(5))* Rigby Education.
A Surprise for Monica, 6 Packs. (Greetings Ser.: Vol. 2). (gr. 3-5). 31.00 *(978-0-7635-1810-3(7))* Rigby Education.
A Surprise for Mrs O'Malley. (Sails Literacy Ser.). 24p. (gr. 2-18). 27.00 *(978-0-7578-6821-4(5))* Rigby Education.
A Surprise for Mrs O'Malley: 3-in-1 Package. (Sails Literacy Ser.). 24p. (gr. 2-18). 57.00 *(978-0-7578-6833-7(9))* Rigby Education.
Surprise from the Sky, 6 Packs. (gr. 1-2). 25.00 *(978-0-7635-9138-0(6))* Rigby Education.
Suter, Joanne & Greene, Janice. Read Reflect Respond 1, 1 vol. 2015. (Read Reflect Respond Ser.). (ENG.). (J). (gr. 5-12). pap. 44.95 *(978-1-68021-001-9(7))* Saddleback Educational Publishing, Inc.
Swann, Tammy & Benchmark Education Co., LLC Staff. Roy Makes a Choice. 2015. (BuildUp Ser.). (J). (gr. 1). *(978-1-4900-0738-0(5))* Benchmark Education Co.
Swanson Sateren, Shelley. Adventures at Hound Hotel. Melmon, Deborah, illus. 2016. (Adventures at Hound Hotel Ser.). (ENG.). 72p. (gr. 2-3). 202.56 *(978-1-5158-0078-1(4),* Adventures at Hound Hotel) Picture Window Bks.
Swartz, Larry & Margolin, Indrani. The 10 Coolest Dance Crazes. 2008. 14.99 *(978-1-55448-523-9(1))* Scholastic Library Publishing.
Swedeen, Staci. The Rumor Report, the Big Jump. 2011. (Readers' & Writers' Genre Workshop Ser.). (YA). pap. *(978-1-4509-3013-0(1))* Benchmark Education Co.
Sweeney, Bernadette. Monster Machines. 2007. (Steck-Vaughn BOLDPRINT Anthologies Ser.). (ENG., Illus.). 48p. (gr. 5-8). pap. 16.90 *(978-1-4190-4024-5(3))* Houghton Mifflin Harcourt Publishing Co.
Sweet, Melissa. Ants (1 Hardcover/1 CD) 2016. (National Geographic Readers: Pre-Reader Ser.). (ENG.). (J). *(978-1-4301-2115-2(7))* Live Oak Media.
—Ants (1 Paperback/1 CD) 2016. (National Geographic Readers: Pre-Reader Ser.). (ENG.). (J). pap. *(978-1-4301-2114-5(9))* Live Oak Media.
Swigert, Nancy B. Early Intervention Kit Activities Book. 2004. (J). per. *(978-0-7606-0597-4(1))* LinguiSystems, Inc.
Swimming in the Sand. (J). pap. 13.75 *(978-0-8136-3404-3(0))* Modern Curriculum Pr.
Swimow, Linda. Take on Yellowstone! 2011. 32p. pap. 12.99 *(978-1-4490-2219-8(7))* AuthorHouse.
—What's New at the Zoo? A PhotoPhOnics (c)Reader. 2009. 32p. pap. 12.99 *(978-1-4490-2218-1(9))* AuthorHouse.
Syed, Hafsa N. Piggy Wanted to Learn. 2012. 44p. pap. 11.25 *(978-1-61170-067-1(1))* Robertson Publishing.
Symbols of Our Country. 2016. (Symbols of Our Country Ser.). 00024p. (J). (gr. 1-1). 94.40 *(978-1-4994-2693-9(3),* PowerKids Pr.) Rosen Publishing Group, Inc., The.
Symington, Martha M. Global Heart Warming: Dream Believe Achieve Series. Sanderson, Jessica B., illus. 2009. 36p. pap. *(978-1-897435-34-2(7))* Agio Publishing Hse.
Szarka, Balazs. European Folk Tales. 2009. 60p. pap. 22.00 *(978-1-60860-432-6(2),* Eloquent Bks.) Strategic Book Publishing & Rights Agency (SBPRA).
Tabletop Easel. (gr. -1-12). 81.69 *(978-0-7362-0851-2(8))* CENGAGE Learning.
Take a Look at My Family. (Early Intervention Levels Ser.). 28.38 *(978-0-7362-0395-1(6))* CENGAGE Learning.
Take a Look at My Family (8), Vol. 8. (Early Intervention Levels Ser.). 4.73 *(978-0-7362-0220-6(X))* CENGAGE Learning.
Take-Home Books Collection. 2005. (YA). (gr. -1-3). 225.00 *(978-0-8215-7290-0(3))* Sadlier, William H. Inc.
TAKS MASTER Learning with Graphic Organizers, Gr. 3. 2005. (J). *(978-1-57022-550-5(8))* ECS Learning Systems, Inc.
TAKS MASTER Learning with Graphic Organizers, Gr. 4. 2005. (J). *(978-1-57022-551-2(6))* ECS Learning Systems, Inc.
TAKS MASTER Learning with Graphic Organizers, Gr. 5. 2005. (J). *(978-1-57022-552-9(4))* ECS Learning Systems, Inc.
TAKS MASTER Learning with Graphic Organizers, Gr. 6. 2005. (J). *(978-1-57022-553-6(2))* ECS Learning Systems, Inc.
TAKS MASTER Learning with Graphic Organizers, Gr. 7. 2005. (J). *(978-1-57022-554-3(0))* ECS Learning Systems, Inc.
TAKS MASTER Learning with Graphic Organizers, Gr. 8. 2005. (YA). *(978-1-57022-555-0(9))* ECS Learning Systems, Inc.
TAKS MASTER Power Practice, Reading Gr. 3. 2004. (J). *(978-1-57022-541-3(9))* ECS Learning Systems, Inc.
TAKS MASTER Power Practice, Reading Gr. 4. 2004. (J). *(978-1-57022-542-0(7))* ECS Learning Systems, Inc.
TAKS MASTER Power Practice, Reading Gr. 5. 2004. (J). *(978-1-57022-543-7(5))* ECS Learning Systems, Inc.
TAKS MASTER Power Practice, Reading Gr. 6. 2004. (J). *(978-1-57022-544-4(3))* ECS Learning Systems, Inc.
TAKS MASTER Power Practice, Reading Gr. 7. 2004. (J). *(978-1-57022-545-1(1))* ECS Learning Systems, Inc.
TAKS MASTER Power Practice, Reading Gr. 8. 2004. (YA). *(978-1-57022-546-8(X))* ECS Learning Systems, Inc.
TAKS MASTER Practice Test Reading, Gr. 3. 2004. (J). *(978-1-57022-475-1(7))* ECS Learning Systems, Inc.
TAKS MASTER Practice Test Reading, Gr. 4. 2004. (J). *(978-1-57022-528-4(1))* ECS Learning Systems, Inc.
TAKS MASTER Practice Test Reading, Gr. 5. 2004. (J). *(978-1-57022-529-1(X))* ECS Learning Systems, Inc.
TAKS MASTER Practice Test Reading, Gr. 6. 2004. (J). *(978-1-57022-530-7(3))* ECS Learning Systems, Inc.
TAKS MASTER Practice Test Reading, Gr. 7. 2004. (J). *(978-1-57022-531-4(1))* ECS Learning Systems, Inc.
TAKS MASTER Practice Test Reading, Gr. 8. 2004. (YA). *(978-1-57022-532-1(X))* ECS Learning Systems, Inc.
TAKS Open-Ended Reading Response Guide, Grades 9-11 Exit. 2004. (Region IV ESC Resources for Mathematics, Science, Social Studies & Reading Ser.). spiral bd. *(978-1-932797-19-0(X))* Region IV Education Service Ctr.
TAKS Reading Accelerated Curriculum for Grade 5. 2005. (Region IV ESC Resources for Reading Ser.). spiral bd. *(978-1-933049-06-9(5))* Region IV Education Service Ctr.
TAKS Reading Accelerated Curriculum Middle School (Volume 1) 2006. spiral bd. *(978-1-933049-18-2(9))* Region IV Education Service Ctr.
TAKS Reading Preparation Grade 10 - Student Workbook. 2003. (Region IV ESC Resources for Reading Ser.). stu. ed., per. *(978-1-932524-48-2(7))* Region IV Education Service Ctr.
TAKS Reading Preparation Grade 11 Exit. 2003. (Region IV ESC Resources for Reading Ser.). stu. ed., per., wbk. ed. *(978-1-932524-49-9(5))* Region IV Education Service Ctr.
TAKS Reading Preparation Grade 4. 2003. (Region IV ESC Resources for Reading Ser.). stu. ed., per., wbk. ed. *(978-1-932524-42-0(8))* Region IV Education Service Ctr.
TAKS Reading Preparation Grade 5. 2003. (Region IV ESC Resources for Reading Ser.). stu. ed., per., wbk. ed. *(978-1-932524-43-7(6))* Region IV Education Service Ctr.
TAKS Reading Preparation Grade 6. 2003. (Region IV ESC Resources for Reading Ser.). stu. ed., per., wbk. ed. *(978-1-932524-44-4(4))* Region IV Education Service Ctr.
TAKS Reading Preparation Grade 8. 2003. (Region IV ESC Resources for Reading Ser.). stu. ed., per., wbk. ed. *(978-1-932524-46-8(0))* Region IV Education Service Ctr.
TAKS Reading Preparation Grade 9. 2003. (Region IV ESC Resources for Reading Ser.). stu. ed., per., wbk. ed. *(978-1-932524-47-5(9))* Region IV Education Service Ctr.
TAKS Reading Preparaton Grade 7. 2003. (Region IV ESC Resources for Reading Ser.). stu. ed., per., wbk. ed. *(978-1-932524-45-1(2))* Region IV Education Service Ctr.
TAKS Readng Preparation Grade 3. 2003. (Region IV ESC Resources for Reading Ser.). stu. ed., per., wbk. ed. *(978-1-932524-41-3(X))* Region IV Education Service Ctr.
The Tale of the Golden Goose. (Early Intervention Levels Ser.). 31.86 *(978-0-7362-0617-4(5))* CENGAGE Learning.
The Tale of the Golden Goose (18), Vol. 18. (Early Intervention Levels Ser.). 5.31 *(978-0-7362-0605-1(1))* CENGAGE Learning.
Tali Drives His Car. (Pebble Soup Explorations Ser.). 16p. (gr. -1-18). 31.00 *(978-0-7578-1663-5(0))* Rigby Education.
Tali Drives His Car: Small Book. (Pebble Soup Explorations Ser.). 16p. (gr. -1-18). 5.00 *(978-0-7578-1703-8(3))* Rigby Education.
Tali Pasea en su Auto. (Pebble Soup Exploraciones Ser.). (SPA.). 16p. (gr. -1-18). 31.00 *(978-0-7578-1687-1(8))* Rigby Education.
Tali pasea en su Auto: Small Book. (Pebble Soup Exploraciones Ser.). (SPA.). 16p. (gr. -1-18). 5.00 *(978-0-7578-1727-4(0))* Rigby Education.
Tall Talk. (Sails Literacy Ser.). 24p. (gr. 2-3). 8.00 *(978-0-7635-7036-1(2))* Rigby Education.
Tarpley, Natasha Anastasia. I Love My Haircut! Lewis, E. B., illus. 2017. (ENG.). 22p. (J). (gr. -1 — 1). bds. 6.99 *(978-0-316-27606-1(5))* Little, Brown Bks. for Young Readers.
Tatchell, Judy. Bugs & Slugs Lift-the-Flap. 2004. (Luxury Lift-the-Flap Ser.). 16p. (J). (gr. 1-18). 11.95 *(978-0-7945-0762-6(X),* Usborne) EDC Publishing.
Tavadze, Olesya. Bursunsul & Paskualina. Ivanov, Evgueni, illus. 2007. (POL & ENG.). 32p. (J). pap. 16.95 *(978-1-60195-095-6(0))* International Step by Step Assn.
Taylor, Chad. Drums Save the Day. 2016. (Rosen REAL Readers: STEM & STEAM Collection). 12p. (gr. 1-k). pap. 6.33 *(978-1-5081-2649-2(6),* Rosen Classroom) Rosen Publishing Group, Inc., The.
—Drums Send a Signal. 2016. (Rosen REAL Readers: STEM & STEAM Collection). 12p. (gr. 1-k). pap. 6.33 *(978-1-5081-2434-4(5),* Rosen Classroom) Rosen Publishing Group, Inc., The.
—Equal under the Law. 2016. (Rosen REAL Readers: Social Studies Nonfiction / Fiction: Family, Community, & the World Ser.). 12p. (gr. 1-k). pap. 6.33 *(978-1-5081-2544-0(9),* Rosen Classroom) Rosen Publishing Group, Inc., The.
—We Catch Butterflies. 2016. (Rosen REAL Readers: STEM & STEAM Collection). 8p. (gr. 1-k). pap. 5.46

P Q R

(978-1-5081-2607-2(0), Rosen Classroom) Rosen Publishing Group, Inc., The.
—When the Ground Shook. 2016. (Rosen REAL Readers: STEM & STEAM Collection). 12p. (gr. 1-k). pap. 6.33 *(978-1-5081-2685-0(2),* Rosen Classroom) Rosen Publishing Group, Inc., The.
Taylor, Mary Ellen. Maniac Magee. 2015. (Great Works). (ENG., Illus.). 72p. (gr. 4-8). pap. 9.99 *(978-1-4258-8983-8(2))* Shell Educational Publishing.
Taylor, Nancy & Pearson Longman Staff. Michael Jordan. 2nd ed. 2008. (ENG., Illus.). 20p. pap. 11.99 *(978-1-4058-8151-7(8))* Pearson Education.
Taylor, Nancy & Taylor, Nancy. Michael Jordan, Pack. 2nd ed. 2015. (ENG., Illus.). 16p. pap. 14.65 incl. audio compact disk ***(978-1-4058-7812-8(6))*** Pearson Education.
Taylor, Nicole & Watts, Michael. SpongeBob Squarepants: Wormy. 2014. 32p. (J). pap. incl. audio compact disk *(978-1-909221-71-0(6))* Glasgow, Mary Pubns.
Taylor, Sean. Mojo & Weeza & the New Hat: Band 04/Blue. Mosedale, Julian, illus. 2007. (Collins Big Cat Ser.). (ENG.). 16p. (J). (gr. -1-1). pap. 5.99 *(978-0-00-718662-4(2))* HarperCollins Pubs. Ltd. GBR. Dist: Independent Pubs. Group.
Taylor, Steve. Fruit Facts. 2008. (Rosen Real Readers: Upper Emergent Ser.). (ENG., Illus.). 12p. (gr. 1-2). pap. 5.90 *(978-0-8239-8134-2(7))* Rosen Publishing Group, Inc., The.
Taylor, Susan. Blast Off! 2006. (Neighborhood Readers Ser.). (ENG.). 16p. (gr. 1-3). pap. 6.50 *(978-1-4042-6978-1(9),* Rosen Classroom) Rosen Publishing Group, Inc., The.
Taylor, Trace. B. 2010. pap. 39.62 *(978-1-61541-090-3(2))* American Reading Co.
—C. 2010. pap. 39.62 *(978-1-61541-102-3(X))* American Reading Co.
—Cats. 2010. pap. 39.62 *(978-1-61541-094-1(5))* American Reading Co.
—China. 2010. pap. 39.62 *(978-1-61541-129-0(1))* American Reading Co.
—D. 2010. pap. 39.62 *(978-1-61541-097-2(X))* American Reading Co.
—Dogs. 2010. pap. 39.62 *(978-1-61541-095-8(3))* American Reading Co.
—F. 2010. pap. 39.62 *(978-1-61541-105-4(4))* American Reading Co.
—G. 2010. pap. 39.62 *(978-1-61541-107-8(0))* American Reading Co.
—H. 2010. pap. 39.62 *(978-1-61541-109-2(7))* American Reading Co.
—J. 2010. pap. 39.62 *(978-1-61541-111-5(9))* American Reading Co.
—K. 2010. pap. 39.62 *(978-1-61541-113-9(5))* American Reading Co.
—L. 2010. pap. 39.62 *(978-1-61541-096-5(1))* American Reading Co.
—M. 2010. pap. 39.62 *(978-1-61541-091-0(0))* American Reading Co.
—N. 2010. pap. 39.62 *(978-1-61541-115-3(1))* American Reading Co.
—P. 2010. pap. 39.62 *(978-1-61541-117-7(8))* American Reading Co.
—R. 2010. pap. 39.62 *(978-1-61541-119-1(4))* American Reading Co.
—S. 2010. pap. 39.62 *(978-1-61541-099-6(6))* American Reading Co.
—T. 2010. pap. 39.62 *(978-1-61541-103-0(8))* American Reading Co.
Taylor, Trace & SáNchez, LucíA M. BáSquetbol (Basketball) 2011. (ARC Press / el poder de 100 - Deportes (Power 100 - Sports) Ser.). (SPA.). pap. 33.92 *(978-1-61541-468-0(1))* American Reading Co.
—Bélsbol (Baseball) 2011. (ARC Press / el poder de 100 - Deportes (Power 100 - Sports) Ser.). (SPA.). pap. 33.92 *(978-1-61541-470-3(3))* American Reading Co.
—China. 2010. pap. 39.62 *(978-1-61541-152-8(6))* American Reading Co.
Taylor, Trace & Sanchez, Lucia M. Delfines (Dolphins) 2011. (poder de 100 - Animales marinos Ser.). (SPA.). 12p. pap. 39.62 *(978-1-61541-283-9(2))* American Reading Co.
—En el bosque (in the Woods) 2011. (Lugares adonde voy Ser.). (SPA.). 16p. pap. 39.62 *(978-1-61541-457-4(6))* American Reading Co.
Taylor, Trace & Sánchez, Lucía M. Escarabajos: Beetles. 2011. (2G - Bichos Ser.). (SPA.). 12p. (J). (gr. k-2). pap. 6.99 *(978-1-61541-422-2(3))* American Reading Co.
Taylor, Trace & Zorzi, Gina. This Is a Desert. 2010. (2G Ecosystems Ser.). (ENG.). 36p. (J). (gr. k-2). pap. 5.99 *(978-1-61541-219-8(0))* American Reading Co.
Taylor, Trace, et al. En el Bosque. 2011. (2Y Lugares Adonde Voy Ser.).Tr. of In the Woods. (SPA.). 12p. (J). (gr. k-2). pap. 6.99 *(978-1-61541-456-7(8))* American Reading Co.
—In the Ocean. Reese, Jonathan, illus. 2006. (1-3Y Ecosystems Ser.). (ENG.). 16p. (J). (gr. k-1). pap. 5.99 *(978-1-59301-438-4(4))* American Reading Co.
Te invito a mi Casa: 6 Small Books. (Saludos Ser.: Vol. 3). (SPA.). 24p. (gr. 2-3). 31.00 *(978-0-7635-9529-6(2))* Rigby Education.
Teacher Created Materials. Early America, Set. rev. ed. 2009. (Teacher Created Materials Library). (ENG., Illus.). (J). (gr. 4-6). spiral bd. 55.92 *(978-1-4333-1895-5(4))* Shell Educational Publishing.
—Time for Kids(r) Nonfiction Readers Challenging, 15 bks., Set. rev. ed. 2013. (Teacher Created Materials Library). (ENG., Illus.). (J). (gr. 5-5). spiral bd. 479.40 *(978-1-4333-7498-2(6))* Teacher Created Materials, Inc.
Teacher Created Materials Staff, ed. Kids Learn! Grade PreK-K. 2008. (Kids Learn Ser.). 120p. pap. 9.99 *(978-1-4333-0414-9(7))* Teacher Created Materials, Inc.
—Life Science: Themed Classroom Reader Set. 2007. (Themed Reader Sets Ser.). pap. 909.99 *(978-1-4333-0155-1(5))* Teacher Created Materials, Inc.
—The 20th Century Add-on Pack: Primary Source Readers. 2008. (Primary Source Readers Ser.). 89.99 *(978-1-4333-0049-3(4))* Teacher Created Materials, Inc.
Teagarden, Janine. A Dog Named Opposite. Kennedy, Kelly, illus. 2010. 16p. (J). *(978-0-545-24821-1(3))* Scholastic, Inc.
Teddy's Colorful World. 2017. (Teddy's Colorful World Ser.). 24p. (gr. 4-6). 70.80 ***(978-1-5081-6194-3(1))***; pap. 24.75 ***(978-1-5081-6196-7(8))*** Rosen Publishing Group, Inc., The. (PowerKids Pr.).
Ted's Red Ball: Set B Individual Title, 6 packs. (Supersonic Phonics Ser.). (gr. k-3). 29.00 *(978-0-7635-0538-7(2))* Rigby Education.
Tell Me How You Feel: Big Book. (Pebble Soup Explorations Ser.). 16p. (gr. -1-18). 31.00 *(978-0-7578-1661-1(4))* Rigby Education.
Tell Me How You Feel: Small Book. (Pebble Soup Explorations Ser.). 16p. (gr. -1-18). 5.00 *(978-0-7578-1701-4(7))* Rigby Education.
Terp, Gail. Alex Morgan. 2017. (Women Who Rock Ser.). (ENG., Illus.). 32p. (J). (gr. 3-7). 31.35 ***(978-1-68072-067-9(8))*** Black Rabbit Bks.
Testa, Maggie. Olivia & the Rain Dance. 2012. (Olivia Ready-To-Read Level 1 Ser.). lib. bdg. 13.55 *(978-0-606-23688-1(0),* Turtleback) Turtleback Bks.
Textures: KinderFacts Individual Title Six-Packs. (Kinderstarters Ser.). 8p. (gr. -1-1). 21.00 *(978-0-7635-8750-5(8))* Rigby Education.
Thaler, Mike. The Class Trip from the Black Lagoon. Lee, Jared, illus. 2004. (Black Lagoon Adventures Ser.: 1). (ENG.). 64p. (J). (gr. 2-5). pap. 3.99 *(978-0-439-42927-6(7),* Scholastic Paperbacks) Scholastic, Inc.
—The Talent Show from the Black Lagoon. Lee, Jared, illus. 2004. (Black Lagoon Adventures Ser.: 2). (ENG.). 64p. (J). (gr. 2-5). 4.99 *(978-0-439-43894-0(2),* Scholastic Paperbacks) Scholastic, Inc.
Than, Ker. Earthquakes. 2009. (True Book Ser.). (ENG., Illus.). 48p. (J). (gr. 3-5). pap. 6.95 *(978-0-531-21350-6(1),* Children's Pr.) Scholastic Library Publishing.
A Theft in Time: Timedetectors II, 6 Pack. (Action Packs Ser.). 120p. (gr. 3-5). 44.00 *(978-0-7635-8425-2(8))* Rigby Education.
Theme Packs for ELL: Complete Set. (gr. k-6). 203.00 *(978-0-7635-2865-2(X))* Rigby Education.
Theme Packs for ELL: Early Fluent/Fluent Complete Set. (gr. k-6). 252.00 *(978-0-7635-2862-1(5))*; 218.00 *(978-0-7635-2853-9(6))*; 184.00 *(978-0-7635-9999-7(9))*; 262.00 *(978-0-7635-2857-7(9))*; 184.00 *(978-0-7635-9991-1(3))*; 262.00 *(978-0-7635-9995-9(6))* Rigby Education.
Theme Packs for ELL: Early Fluent/Fluent Core Set. (gr. k-6). 175.00 *(978-0-7635-2868-3(4))*; 175.00 *(978-0-7635-9987-4(5))*; 175.00 *(978-0-7635-9994-2(8))*; 175.00 *(978-0-7635-2852-2(8))*; 175.00 *(978-0-7635-2861-4(7))*; 175.00 *(978-0-7635-2856-0(0))* Rigby Education.
Theme Packs for ELL: Early to Fluent Core Set. (gr. k-6). 164.00 *(978-0-7635-2864-5(1))* Rigby Education.
Theme Packs for ELL: Emergent to Early Fluent Core Set. (gr. k-6). 153.00 *(978-0-7635-2866-9(8))* Rigby Education.
Theme Packs for ELL: Emergent/Early Complete Set. (gr. k-6). 186.00 *(978-0-7635-9986-7(7))*; 218.00 *(978-0-7635-9990-4(5))*; 148.00 *(978-0-7635-9993-5(X))*; 186.00 *(978-0-7635-9998-0(0))*; 148.00 *(978-0-7635-2851-5(X))*; 186.00 *(978-0-7635-2860-7(9))* Rigby Education.
Theme Packs for ELL: Emergent/Early Core Set. (gr. k-6). 142.00 *(978-0-7635-9997-3(2))*; 142.00 *(978-0-7635-9989-8(1))*; 142.00 *(978-0-7635-9985-0(9))*; 142.00 *(978-0-7635-2855-3(2))*; 142.00 *(978-0-7635-2859-1(5))* Rigby Education.
Theme Packs for ELL: Theme Pack Complete Set. (gr. k-6). 301.00 *(978-0-7635-2869-0(2))*; 197.00 *(978-0-7635-2867-6(6))* Rigby Education.
Theme Packs for ELL: Theme Pack Super Set. (gr. k-6). 383.00 *(978-0-7635-2858-4(7))*; 344.00 *(978-0-7635-9988-1(3))*; 383.00 *(978-0-7635-9992-8(1))*; 383.00 *(978-0-7635-9996-6(4))*; 349.00 *(978-0-7635-2850-8(1))*; 415.00 *(978-0-7635-2863-8(3))*; 349.00 *(978-0-7635-2854-6(4))* Rigby Education.
Then & Now, 6 Pack. (Discovery World Ser.). 16p. (gr. 1-2). 28.00 *(978-0-7635-8463-4(0))* Rigby Education.
Theobald, Joseph. When Arthur Wouldn't Sleep. Theobald, Joseph, illus. 2006. (Collins Big Cat Ser.). (ENG., Illus.). 24p. (J). (gr. 2-2). pap. 6.99 *(978-0-00-718688-4(6))* HarperCollins Pubs. Ltd. GBR. Dist: Independent Pubs. Group.
There Is No Water! Individual Title Six-Packs. (gr. k-1). 23.00 *(978-0-7635-8849-6(0))* Rigby Education.
There's a Rainbow in the River: Individual Title Six-Packs. (gr. k-1). 23.00 *(978-0-7635-8850-2(4))* Rigby Education.
Theurer, Heather, illus. Thaddeus Macdonald III: Aka the Boss. 2011. (ENG.). 64p. (gr. -1). 16.95 *(978-0-9826137-8-8(4),* Channel Kids) Channel Photographics.
The Things I Learn. 2016. (Things I Learn Ser.). 24p. (gr. 1-1). 141.60 *(978-1-4994-2439-3(6))*; pap. 49.50 *(978-1-4994-2492-8(2))* Rosen Publishing Group, Inc., The. (PowerKids Pr.).
Things to Do. 2005. (Little Celebrations Thematic Packages Ser.). (J). (gr. k-3). 133.50 *(978-0-673-75388-5(3))* Celebration Pr.
Think Twice, Be Nice: Social/Emotional Lap Book. (Pebble Soup Explorations Ser.). (gr. -1-18). 16.00 *(978-0-7578-7570-0(4))* Rigby Education.
This & That, 6 Packs. (gr. -1-2). 23.00 *(978-0-7635-8812-0(1))* Rigby Education.
Thomas, Christine. Language Development Inquiry Research. 2004. (BrainBuilders Ser.). (ENG.). 48p. (gr. k-4). pap. 5.25 *(978-1-4042-8527-9(X))* Rosen Publishing Group, Inc., The.
—Language Development Variety Text. 2004. (BrainBuilders Ser.). (ENG.). 48p. (gr. k-4). pap. 5.25 *(978-1-4042-8525-5(3))* Rosen Publishing Group, Inc., The.
Thomas, Isabel. Micro-Organisms. 2015. (Collins Big Cat Ser.). (ENG., Illus.). 80p. (J). (gr. 5). pap. 9.95 *(978-0-00-812798-5(0))* HarperCollins Pubs. Ltd. GBR. Dist: Independent Pubs. Group.
Thomas, Isabel & Collins UK Staff. How to Build a House. 2016. (ENG.). 56p. (J). (gr. 4-5). pap. 9.95 *(978-0-00-816394-5(4))* HarperCollins Pubs. Ltd. GBR. Dist: Independent Pubs. Group.
Thomas, Maribel. Party in the Sky. 2009. 20p. pap. 13.50 *(978-1-60693-364-0(7),* Eloquent Bks.) Strategic Book Publishing & Rights Agency (SBPRA).
Thomas, Mary Ann. The New Neighbors. 2006. (Neighborhood Readers Ser.). (ENG.). 8p. (gr. -1-3). pap. 5.15 *(978-1-4042-6694-0(1),* Rosen Classroom) Rosen Publishing Group, Inc., The.
Thomas Nelson. Rumpelstiltskin. 2015. (ENG., Illus.). 32p. (J). (gr. 1-3). pap. *(978-1-78393-582-6(0))* Make Believe Ideas.
Thomas, Teri. Bus 99. 2005. (Quickreads Ser.). (Illus.). 32p. (J). pap. 2.95 *(978-1-56254-740-0(2),* SP7402) Saddleback Educational Publishing, Inc.
—Dimes to Dollars. 2005. (Quickreads Ser.). (Illus.). 32p. (J). pap. 2.95 *(978-1-56254-743-1(7),* SP7437) Saddleback Educational Publishing, Inc.
Thomas, Terri. The Barge Ghost, 1 vol. unabr. ed. 2010. (Q Reads Ser.). (ENG.). 32p. (YA). (gr. 9-12). pap. 6.95 *(978-1-61651-211-8(3))* Saddleback Educational Publishing, Inc.
—Bus 99, 1 vol. unabr. ed. 2010. (Q Reads Ser.). (ENG.). 32p. (YA). (gr. 9-12). pap. 6.95 *(978-1-61651-214-9(8))* Saddleback Educational Publishing, Inc.
Thomas, Terri & Greene, Janice. Dimes to Dollars, 1 vol. unabr. ed. 2010. (Q Reads Ser.). (ENG.). 32p. (YA). (gr. 9-12). pap. 6.95 *(978-1-61651-217-0(2))* Saddleback Educational Publishing, Inc.
Thompson, Chad. The Itsy Bitsy Spider, 1 vol. 2009. (Early Childhood Themes Ser.). (ENG., Illus.). 16p. (J). (gr. -1-2). pap. 19.99 *(978-1-4333-1455-1(X))* Shell Educational Publishing.
—The Itsy Bitsy Spider, 1 vol. 2009. (Early Childhood Themes Ser.). (ENG., Illus.). 16p. (J). (gr. -1-2). pap. 6.99 *(978-1-4333-1454-4(1))* Teacher Created Materials, Inc.
—Yankee Doodle, 1 vol. 2011. (Early Childhood Themes Ser.). (ENG.). 16p. (J). (gr. -1-2). pap. 19.99 *(978-1-4333-2365-2(6))*; pap. 6.99 *(978-1-4333-2364-5(8))* Teacher Created Materials, Inc.
Thompson, Gare. Shaping the Constitution: Text Pairs. 2008. (Bridges/Navigators Ser.). (J). (gr. 5). 89.00 *(978-1-4108-8422-0(8))* Benchmark Education Co.
Thompson, Lauren. Little Quack's Opposites. Anderson, Derek, illus. 2010. (Super Chubbies Ser.). (ENG.). 26p. (J). (gr. -1 — 1). bds. 5.99 *(978-1-4169-6092-8(9),* Little Simon) Little Simon.
Thompson, Lesley. Zombie Attack! 2nd ed. 2013. (ENG., Illus.). 40p. pap. 9.38 *(978-0-19-424986-7(7))* Oxford Univ. Pr., Inc.
Thompson, Louise. Cold Weather Readers. 2010. 206p. pap. 21.95 *(978-0-557-38162-3(2))* Lulu Pr., Inc.
Thomson, Ruth. Leaves. 2005. (Little Hands (Chrysalis Education) Ser.). (Illus.). 24p. (J). (gr. 1-4). lib. bdg. 22.80 *(978-1-59389-211-1(X))* Chrysalis Education.
—Mountains. 2012. (Geography Corner Ser.). (ENG., Illus.). 24p. (J). (gr. k-3). 21.25 *(978-1-4488-6617-5(0),* PowerKids Pr.) Rosen Publishing Group, Inc., The.
Thomson, Sarah L. Amazing Tigers! 2005. (I Can Read Level 2 Ser.). (ENG., Illus.). 32p. (J). (gr. k-3). pap. 3.99 *(978-0-06-054452-2(X))* HarperCollins Pubs.
Those Amazingly Useful Ears. (Early Intervention Levels Ser.). 31.86 *(978-0-7362-0669-3(8))* CENGAGE Learning.
Three: KinderFacts Individual Title Six-Packs. (Kinderstarters Ser.). 8p. (gr. -1-1). 21.00 *(978-0-7635-8751-2(6))* Rigby Education.
The Three Billy Goats Gruff. 2004. (Folk Tales Set 1 Ser.). (J). 5.33 *(978-1-58453-274-3(2))* Pioneer Valley Bks.
Thurlby, Paul. Paul Thurlby's Alphabet. Thurlby, Paul, illus. 2013. (ENG., Illus.). 26p. (J). (-k). bds. 9.99 *(978-0-7636-6618-7(1),* Templar) Candlewick Pr.
Tillworth, Mary. Cupcake Challenge! 2015. (Barbie Step into Reading Level 3 Ser.). lib. bdg. 13.55 *(978-0-606-36381-5(5))* Turtleback Bks.
—Zeg & the Egg (Blaze & the Monster Machines) Foley, Niki, illus. 2016. (Step into Reading Ser.). (ENG.). 24p. (J). (gr. -1-1). 4.99 *(978-0-553-53935-6(3),* Random Hse. Bks. for Young Readers) Random Hse. Children's Bks.
Time Capsule, 6 Packs. (Bookweb Ser.). 32p. (gr. 5-18). 34.00 *(978-0-7635-3780-7(2))* Rigby Education.
Time for Lunch. (J). 6.47 *(978-0-8136-5355-6(X))* Modern Curriculum Pr.
Time for School. 2004. (At School Ser.). (J). 7.33 *(978-1-58453-265-1(3))* Pioneer Valley Bks.
Time Goes By, 8 vols., Set. Incl. Day at a Zoo. Harrison, Sarah. (J). lib. bdg. 22.60 *(978-1-58013-554-2(4))*; Day at an Airport. Harrison, Sarah. (J). lib. bdg. 22.60 *(978-1-58013-551-1(X))*; Day in a City. Harris, Nicholas. (J). lib. bdg. 22.60 *(978-1-58013-552-8(8))*; Year at a Construction Site. Harris, Nicholas. (J). lib. bdg. 22.60 *(978-1-58013-549-8(8))*; Year at a Farm. Harris, Nicholas. lib. bdg. 22.60 *(978-1-58013-553-5(6))*; Year in a Castle. Coombs, Rachel. (J). lib. bdg. 22.60 *(978-1-58013-550-4(1))*; Year in the World of Dinosaurs. Havercroft, Elizabeth. lib. bdg. 22.60 *(978-1-58013-548-1(X))*; Year on a Pirate Ship. Havercroft, Elizabeth. lib. bdg. 22.60 *(978-1-58013-547-4(1))*; (Illus.). 24p. (gr. k-3). 2008. (Time Goes By Ser.). (ENG.). 2008. Set lib. bdg. 113.00 *(978-1-58013-546-7(3))* Lerner Publishing Group.
The Time Machine Student Packet. 2004. (J). 12.99 *(978-1-58130-526-5(5))* Novel Units, Inc.
Timmy: Individual Title Six-Packs. (Literatura 2000 Ser.). (gr. 1-2). 28.00 *(978-0-7635-0067-2(4))* Rigby Education.
Tim's Bedtime: Set D Individual Title Six-Packs. (gr. k-3). 29.00 *(978-0-7635-0548-6(X))* Rigby Education.
Tim's Paintings: Individual Title-Six Packs. (Chiquilibros Ser.). (gr. k-1). 23.00 *(978-0-7635-0430-4(0))* Rigby Education.
Tim's Pumpkin: Individual Title Six-Packs. (gr. k-1). 23.00 *(978-0-7635-9040-6(1))* Rigby Education.
Tin Lizzy: Individual Title Six-Packs. (gr. 1-2). 25.00 *(978-0-7635-9147-2(5))* Rigby Education.
Tina Likes Tools: Lap Book. (Pebble Soup Explorations Ser.). 16p. (gr. -1-18). 21.00 *(978-0-7578-1662-8(2))* Rigby Education.
Tina Likes Tools: Small Book. (Pebble Soup Explorations Ser.). 16p. (gr. -1-18). 5.00 *(978-0-7578-1702-1(5))* Rigby Education.
TJ's Tree, 6 Packs. (Literatura 2000 Ser.). (gr. 1-2). 28.00 *(978-0-7635-0116-7(6))* Rigby Education.
To Begin Again: Six-Pack. (Greetings Ser.: Vol. 3). (gr. 3-5). 31.00 *(978-0-7635-2073-1(X))* Rigby Education.
Todoro, Carlie. Is It Rough? Is It Smooth? 2008. (Rosen Real Readers: Upper Emergent Ser.). (ENG., Illus.). 12p. (gr. 1-2). pap. 5.90 *(978-0-8239-8206-6(8))* Rosen Publishing Group, Inc., The.
—Let's Draw! 2003. (Real Readers - Upper Emergent Ser.). (ENG., Illus.). 12p. (gr. 1-2). pap. 5.90 *(978-0-8239-6359-1(4))* Rosen Publishing Group, Inc., The.
Toliver, K. S. Pam Brown Is Picture Perfect!! 2008. 28p. pap. 12.95 *(978-1-4327-2058-2(9))* Outskirts Pr., Inc.
Tom Sawyer: 6 Small Books. (gr. k-2). 23.00 *(978-0-7635-8507-5(6))* Rigby Education.
Tomblin, Mark. The Itchy-Scratchy Caterpillar. Jones, Doug, illus. 2010. 16p. (J). *(978-0-545-24822-8(1))* Scholastic, Inc.
Tommy's Treasure: Individual Title Six-Packs. (Literatura 2000 Ser.). (gr. 2-3). 33.00 *(978-0-7635-0189-1(1))* Rigby Education.
Tommy's Tummy Ache: Individual Title Six-Packs. (Literatura 2000 Ser.). (gr. -1-1). 28.00 *(978-0-7635-0015-3(1))* Rigby Education.
Tongues: Early Level Satellite Individual Title Six-Packs. (Sails Literacy Ser.). 16p. (gr. 1-2). 27.00 *(978-0-7578-3161-4(3))* Rigby Education.
Top Hat Big Bargains, 21 bks. (J). (gr. 1-6). 500.00 incl. cd-rom *(978-0-8136-4015-0(6))*; 250.00 *(978-0-8136-4014-3(8))*; 275.00 *(978-0-8136-4013-6(X))* Modern Curriculum Pr.
Top That Publishing Staff, ed. What's My Job. 2005. 12p. bds. *(978-1-84510-070-4(0))* Top That! Publishing PLC.
The Tortilla Factory. (Lexile Levels Ser.). 7.98 *(978-1-56334-687-3(7))* CENGAGE Learning.
Touching Spirit Bear Student Packet. 2004. (J). 12.99 *(978-1-58130-528-9(1))* Novel Units, Inc.
Toy. 2004. (J). per. *(978-1-57657-474-4(1))* Paradise Pr., Inc.
Tracking Wildlife with Frank Craighead. 2005. (Book Treks Ser.). (J). 37.95 *(978-0-7652-3252-6(9))* Celebration Pr.
Trade Book Library, 12 bks., Set. 2004. (Trade Book Library). (gr. 6-18). 112.90 *(978-0-673-60781-2(X))* Addison-Wesley Educational Pubs., Inc.
Trade Book Library Grade Level Package, 12 bks., Set. 2004. (Trade Book Library). (gr. 1-18). 112.90 *(978-0-673-60776-8(3))*; (gr. 2-18). 112.90 *(978-0-673-60777-5(1))*; (gr. 3-18). 112.90 *(978-0-673-60778-2(X))*; (gr. 4-18). 112.90 *(978-0-673-60779-9(8))*; (gr. 5-18). 112.90 *(978-0-673-60780-5(1))* Addison-Wesley Educational Pubs., Inc.
Train Time. (Early Intervention Levels Ser.). 31.86 *(978-0-7362-0618-1(3))* CENGAGE Learning.
Travelers & Traders: Level P, 6 vols., Vol. 2. (Explorers Ser.). 32p. (gr. 3-6). 44.95 *(978-0-7699-0611-9(7))* Shortland Pubns. (U. S. A.) Inc.
Traveling in America: Fourth Grade Guided Comprehension Level L. (On Our Way to English Ser.). (gr. 4-18). 34.50 *(978-0-7578-7154-2(2))* Rigby Education.
Treadwell, Harriette Taylor & Free, Margaret. A Furst Readin Book in Ulster Scot. 2011. (Illus.). 124p. pap. *(978-1-904808-68-8(9))* Evertype.
—The Primer. 2009. (Illus.). 118p. pap. *(978-1-904808-26-8(3))* Evertype.
—Reading-Literature: First Reader. Carroll, Sheila, ed. 2012. 150p. pap. 9.95 *(978-0-9818093-9-7(1))* Living Bks. Pr.
—Reading-Literature Second Reader. Richardson, Frederick, illus. 2008. 200p. pap. 9.95 *(978-1-59915-266-0(5))* Yesterday's Classics.
—Reading-Literature Third Reader. Richardson, Frederick, illus. 2008. 264p. pap. 10.95 *(978-1-59915-267-7(3))* Yesterday's Classics.
The Treasure on Fraser Street: Individual Title Six-Packs. (gr. k-1). 23.00 *(978-0-7635-9068-0(1))* Rigby Education.
Trip to Mini Town. (J). pap. 13.15 *(978-0-8136-4331-1(7))* Modern Curriculum Pr.
Trouble for Jasper. 2004. (Jasper the Cat Chapter Ser.). (ACE.). (J). 7.67 *(978-1-58453-286-6(6))* Pioneer Valley Bks.
Trowell, Michelle. Magnetic My First Words Day's Out. 2008. *(978-1-84666-586-8(8))* Top That! Publishing PLC.
Truman, Dennay H. The Happy Endings. 2007. 65p. per. 8.95 *(978-1-59824-435-9(3))* E-BookTime LLC.
Trumbauer, Lisa & Gray, Steve. Un Diente Está Flojo. Gray, Steve, illus. 2011. (Rookie Ready to Learn Español Ser.). (SPA., Illus.). 32p. (J). pap. 5.95 *(978-0-531-26785-1(7))*; lib. bdg. 23.00 *(978-0-531-26117-0(4))* Scholastic Library Publishing. (Children's Pr.).
Trussell-Cullen, Alan. Animal Disguises, Vol. 17. 2014. (ENG.). 16p. spiral bd. 8.00 *(978-1-4085-0071-2(X))* Oxford Univ. Pr., Inc.
—Animal Groups, Vol. 4. 2014. (ENG.). 16p. spiral bd. 8.00 *(978-1-4085-0058-3(2))* Oxford Univ. Pr., Inc.
—Animal Travellers, Vol. 82. 2014. (ENG.). 24p. spiral bd. 9.00 *(978-1-4085-0137-5(6))* Oxford Univ. Pr., Inc.
The Truth about Red Allen. 2003. (Illus.). pap. 7.60 *(978-0-7398-7521-6(3))* Steck-Vaughn.
Tuchman, Gail & Buckley, James, Jr. Dolphin Dive. 2014. (Scholastic Discover More Readers Ser.). (ENG.). 32p. (J). (gr. 1-2). pap. 3.99 *(978-0-545-63632-2(9),* Scholastic Reference) Scholastic, Inc.
Tuminelly, Nancy. -Est As in Nest, 1 vol. 2003. (Word Families Set 2 Ser.). (ENG., Illus.). 24p. (J). (gr. k-3). lib. bdg. 24.21 *(978-1-59197-232-7(9),* SandCastle) ABDO Publishing Co.
—Ook As in Hook, 1 vol. 2003. (Word Families Set 7 Ser.). (ENG., Illus.). 24p. (J). (gr. k-3). lib. bdg. 24.21 *(978-1-59197-268-6(X),* SandCastle) ABDO Publishing Co.
—Ub As in Tub, 1 vol. 2003. (Word Families Set 4 Ser.). (ENG., Illus.). 24p. (J). (gr. k-3). lib. bdg. 24.21 *(978-1-59197-242-6(6),* SandCastle) ABDO Publishing Co.
—Uck As in Duck, 1 vol. 2003. (Word Families Set 4 Ser.). (ENG., Illus.). 24p. (J). (gr. k-3). lib. bdg. 24.21 *(978-1-59197-247-1(7),* SandCastle) ABDO Publishing Co.
—Uff As in Cuff, 1 vol. 2003. (Word Families Set 4 Ser.). (ENG., Illus.). 24p. (J). (gr. k-3). lib. bdg. 24.21 *(978-1-59197-246-4(9),* SandCastle) ABDO Publishing Co.
—Ug As in Bug, 1 vol. 2003. (Word Families Set 4 Ser.). (ENG., Illus.). 24p. (J). (gr. k-3). lib. bdg. 24.21 *(978-1-59197-243-3(4),* SandCastle) ABDO Publishing Co.
—Um As in Drum, 1 vol. Marx, Monica, ed. 2003. (Word Families Set 4 Ser.). (ENG., Illus.). 24p. (J). (gr. k-3). lib. bdg. 24.21 *(978-1-59197-244-0(2),* SandCastle) ABDO Publishing Co.
—Ump As in Jump, 1 vol. 2003. (Word Families Set 4 Ser.). (ENG., Illus.). 24p. (J). (gr. k-3). lib. bdg. 24.21 *(978-1-59197-245-7(0),* SandCastle) ABDO Publishing Co.
The Tune of the Hickory Stick. 2004. (YA). per. 10.92 *(978-1-56870-503-3(4))* Hewell Publishing.

Turhan, Sedat. Milet Flashwords English. Hagin, Sally, illus. 2005. (Milet Flashwords Ser.). (ENG.). 60p. (J). (gr. 4-7). 8.95 *(978-1-84059-455-3(1))* Milet Publishing.
Turquoise, Purple & Gold Levels Certificate Only. (Sails Literacy Ser.). (gr. 1-6). 89.00 *(978-0-7578-6556-5(9))* Rigby Education.
Tuxworth, Nicola. Puppies. 2013. (ENG.). 12p. (J). (gr. -1-12). bds. 6.99 *(978-0-7548-2210-3(9))* Anness Publishing GBR. Dist: National Bk. Network.
—Splish Splash. 2013. (ENG.). 12p. (J). (gr. -1 — 1). bds. 6.99 *(978-0-7548-2211-0(7))* Anness Publishing GBR. Dist: National Bk. Network.
Twain, Mark, pseud. A Song for Aunt Polly. Bates, Amy, illus. 2004. (Adventures of Tom Sawyer Ser.: Vol. 1). 32p. (J). *(978-0-7607-3963-1(3))* Barnes & Noble, Inc.
Twin Sisters(r) Staff. Learning with Elmo: Animals. 2010. (J). (gr. k-2). 9.99 *(978-1-59922-402-2(X))* Twin Sisters IP, LLC.
Twine, Alice. Cats of the Wild. 2009. (Baby Animals Ser.). 24p. (gr. 1-1). 42.50 *(978-1-61511-488-7(2),* PowerKids Pr.) Rosen Publishing Group, Inc., The.
Twisters & Drenchers: Magazine Anthology: Level 5, 6 vols. (Comprehension Strand Ser.). (gr. 4-8). 54.00 *(978-0-322-06038-8(9))* Wright Group/McGraw-Hill.
Tyler, Jenny. Baby's Very First Getting Dressed. 2009. (Baby's Very First Board Bks). 10p. (J). (gr. -1). bds. 6.99 *(978-0-7945-2609-2(8),* Usborne) EDC Publishing.
—Baby's Very First Mealtime Book. 2009. (Baby's Very First Board Bks). 10p. (J). (gr. -1). bds. 6.99 *(978-0-7945-2607-8(1),* Usborne) EDC Publishing.
UC Publishing Staff & Murphy, Sally. Action Numeracy: Who Wants to be a Millionaire? 2008. (Action Numeracy Upper Primary Ser.). 32p. pap. 9.95 *(978-0-86431-791-9(3))* ACER Pr. AUS. Dist: ISBS Publisher Services.
Unbelievable! (Early Intervention Levels Ser.). 31.86 *(978-0-7362-0671-6(X))* CENGAGE Learning.
Uncle Jim: Individual Title Six-Packs. (gr. 1-2). 25.00 *(978-0-7635-9196-0(3))* Rigby Education.
Understanding Literature: The EMC Write-in Reader. 2nd ed. (Literature & the Language Arts Ser.). (YA). (gr. 10-18). wbk. ed. 17.99 *(978-0-8219-2916-2(X))* EMC/Paradigm Publishing.
Unifix Cubes & Flip Books Set 800913, 2 vols. 2005. (J). pap. *(978-1-59794-078-8(X))* Environments, Inc.
Unit Activity Books: 2-Book Set; Consumable Kindergarten. (On Our Way to English Ser.). (gr. k-18). 15.00 *(978-0-7578-6766-8(9))* Rigby Education.
Up & Away: Level P, 6 vols., Vol. 2. (Explorers Ser.). 32p. (gr. 3-6). 44.95 *(978-0-7699-0607-2(9))* Shortland Pubns. (U. S. A.) Inc.
Upper Emergent Guided Reading, Vol. 3. (gr. 1-18). 435.50 *(978-0-7802-9342-7(8))* Wright Group/McGraw-Hill.
Urban, William. Wyatt Earp: The O. K. Corral & the Law of the American West. 2009. (Library of American Lives & Times Ser.). 112p. (gr. 5-5). 69.20 *(978-1-60853-512-5(6))* Rosen Publishing Group, Inc., The.
USA Today's Debate Set: Voices & Perspectives, 8 vols. Incl. Legalized Gambling: Revenue Boom or Social Bust? Doeden, Matt. (Illus.). lib. bdg. 35.93 *(978-0-7613-5114-6(0));* Legalizing Drugs: Crime Stopper or Social Risk? Goldstein, Margaret J. lib. bdg. 35.93 *(978-0-7613-5116-0(7));* 160p. (gr. 9-12). (USA TODAY's Debate: Voices & Perspectives Ser.). (ENG., Illus.). 2010. Set lib. bdg. 431.16 *(978-0-7613-4078-2(5),* Twenty-First Century Bks.) Lerner Publishing Group.
Use Your Head: Social/Emotional Lap Book. (Pebble Soup Explorations Ser.). (gr. -1-18). 16.00 *(978-0-7635-7571-7(2))* Rigby Education.
A Vacation Journal: Individual Title Six-Packs. (Discovery World Ser.). 24p. (gr. 1-2). 33.00 *(978-0-7635-8469-6(X))* Rigby Education.
Vale, Janice. Going Fast. 2007. (Collins Big Cat Ser.). (ENG.). 16p. (J). (gr. 1-2). pap. 6.99 *(978-0-00-718671-6(1))* HarperCollins Pubs. Ltd. GBR. Dist: Independent Pubs. Group.
—True Life Survival. Wademan, Spike, illus. 2007. (Collins Big Cat Ser.). (ENG.). 32p. (J). (gr. 2-4). pap. 7.99 *(978-0-00-723078-5(8))* HarperCollins Pubs. Ltd. GBR. Dist: Independent Pubs. Group.
—Where Do You Live? Band 15. 2007. (Collins Big Cat Ser.). (ENG., Illus.). 48p. (J). (gr. 3-4). pap. 8.99 *(978-0-00-723098-3(2))* HarperCollins Pubs. Ltd. GBR. Dist: Independent Pubs. Group.
Valentine, Sophie. Zoo Hullabaloo, 1 vol. rev. ed. 2013. (Fiction Readers Ser.). (ENG., Illus.). 12p. (J). (gr. 1-1). pap. 4.99 *(978-1-4333-5458-8(6));* pap. 12.96 *(978-1-4807-1137-2(3))* Shell Educational Publishing.
Vallejo, Fernando. El Desbarrancadero. 2005. (SPA.). 197p. pap. 18.95 *(978-958-8061-62-7(8),* Alfaguara) Santillana USA Publishing Co., Inc.
The Van. (Early Intervention Levels Ser.). 21.30 *(978-0-7362-0372-2(9));* Vol. 4. 3.55 *(978-0-7362-0093-6(2))* CENGAGE Learning.
Van Dixhorn, Brenda. The Pigeon Books: An Instructional Guide for Literature. 2015. (Great Works). (ENG., Illus.). 72p. (gr. k-3). pap. 9.99 *(978-1-4807-6992-2(4))* Shell Educational Publishing.
Van Gorp, Lynn. Gregor Mendel: Genetics Pioneer, 1 vol. 2007. (Science Readers Ser.). (ENG.). 32p. (J). (gr. 3-3). pap. 8.99 *(978-0-7439-0598-5(9))* Shell Educational Publishing.
—The World of Elements & Their Properties, 1 vol. 2007. (Science Readers Ser.). (ENG.). 32p. (J). (gr. 4-4). pap. 8.99 *(978-0-7439-0581-7(4))* Shell Educational Publishing.
Van Leeuwen, Jean. Amanda Pig, First Grader. Schweninger, Ann, illus. 2009. (Oliver & Amanda Ser.). (ENG.). 48p. (J). (gr. 1-3). mass mkt. 3.99 *(978-0-14-241276-3(7),* Penguin Young Readers) Penguin Young Readers Group.
Van Lemon, M. Champions of the Garden Games: Winter Fun for Everyone. 2009. 48p. pap. 20.95 *(978-1-4490-3580-8(9))* AuthorHouse.
VanLeeuwen. Reading Connection Grade 4. 2003. (Reading Connection Ser.). 96p. (gr. 4-18). 8.95 *(978-1-932210-19-4(9))* Rainbow Bridge Publishing.
—Reading Connection Grade 5. 2003. (Reading Connection Ser.). 96p. (gr. 5-18). 8.95 *(978-1-932210-20-0(2))* Rainbow Bridge Publishing.
—Reading Connection Grade 6. 2003. (Reading Connection Ser.). 96p. (gr. 6-18). 8.95 *(978-1-932210-21-7(0))* Rainbow Bridge Publishing.
Vargas Llosa, Mario. Historia de Mayta. 2005. (SPA., Illus.). 376p. pap. 19.95 *(978-84-204-8415-0(6),* Alfaguara) Santillana USA Publishing Co., Inc.
Vargo, Sharon, illus. Sugar & Shadow. 2012. 8p. (J). *(978-0-7367-2726-6(4))* Zaner-Bloser, Inc.
Various. I Can Read, Set. 50th anniv. ed. 2007. (I Can Read Level 1 Ser.). (J). (gr. k-3). pap. 14.99 *(978-0-06-123469-9(9))* HarperCollins Pubs.
Vasiliu, Michelle & Orsini, Cheryl. Fire Ready. 2008. (Rigby Focus Forward: Level P Ser.). (Illus.). 24p. (J). (gr. 4-7). pap. *(978-1-4190-3855-6(9),* Rigby) Pearson Education Australia.
Vaughan, Susan. Let's Eat Lunch: Learning about Picture Graphs. 2009. (Math for the Real World: Early Emergent Ser.). (ENG., Illus.). 8p. (gr. k-1). pap. 5.15 *(978-0-8239-8885-3(6))* Rosen Publishing Group, Inc., The.
Veness, Coleen Degnan & Pearson Education Staff. King Kong. 2007. (ENG.). 64p. pap. 17.32 incl. cd-rom *(978-1-4058-5208-1(9))* Pearson Education.
Venezia, Mike. Getting to Know the World's Greatest Inventors & Scientists, 4 vols., Set. Venezia, Mike, illus. Incl. Charles Drew: Doctor Who Got the World Pumped up to Donate Blood. 28.00 *(978-0-531-23725-0(7));* Henry Ford: Big Wheel in the Auto Industry. 28.00 *(978-0-531-23726-7(5));* Mary Leakey - Archaeologist Who Really Dug Her Work. 28.00 *(978-0-531-23727-4(3));* Stephen Hawking: Cosmologist Who Gets a Big Bang Out of the Universe. 28.00 *(978-0-531-23728-1(1));* 32p. (J). (gr. 2-5). 2009. (Illus.). 2009. Set lib. bdg. 112.00 *(978-0-531-26130-9(1),* Watts, Franklin) Scholastic Library Publishing.
Venturini, Claudia, illus. Ali Baba & the Forty Thieves. 2009. (Flip-Up Fairy Tales Ser.). (ENG.). 24p. (J). (gr. -1-2). audio compact disk *(978-1-84643-294-1(4))* Child's Play International Ltd.
Verderosa, Laura. At Grandma's House. 2010. (Sight Word Readers Ser.). (J). 3.49 *(978-1-60719-607-5(7))* Newmark Learning LLC.
—At My School. 2010. (Sight Word Readers Ser.). (J). 3.49 *(978-1-60719-606-8(9))* Newmark Learning LLC.
—Dad Likes New Clothes. 2010. (Sight Word Readers Ser.). (J). 3.49 *(978-1-60719-605-1(0))* Newmark Learning LLC.
—In the Band. 2010. (Sight Word Readers Ser.). (J). 3.49 *(978-1-60719-612-9(3))* Newmark Learning LLC.
Vicary, Tim. Grace Darling. Oxford University Press Staff & Bassett, Jennifer, eds. 3rd ed. 2008. (ENG., Illus.). 64p. 10.00 *(978-0-19-479061-1(4))* Oxford Univ. Pr., Inc.
Vicente, Alidis. The Case of the Three Kings / el Caso de Los Reyes Magos: The Flaca Files / Los Expedientes de Flaca. 2016. (Flaca Files / Los Expedientes de Flaca Ser.). (MUL, ENG & SPA., Illus.). 96p. (J). (gr. 3-6). pap. 9.95 *(978-1-55885-822-0(9),* Piñata Books) Arte Publico Pr.
Vicente, Alidis. The Shameless Shenanigans of Mister Malo / Las Terribles Travesuras de Mister Malo: The Mister Malo Series / Serie Mister Malo. 2017. (ENG & SPA.). 115p. (J). (gr. 4-8). pap. 9.95 ***(978-1-55885-853-4(9),*** Piñata Books) Arte Publico Pr.
Vicuna, Claudio Orrego. The Surprising Adventures of Balthazar. 2011. (Peace, Justice, Human Rights, & Freedom in Latin America Ser.). (SPA & ENG.). 160p. 15.00 *(978-1-58966-218-6(0))* Univ. of Scranton Pr.
Villafane-Leon, Ines. A Story for All Seasons: Un Cuento Para Cada Estacion: Immigration of One. 2004. (ENG & SPA.). xiii, 367p. (YA). pap. 22.95 *(978-1-882897-78-0(1))* Lost Coast Pr.
Villegas, Corrina, et al. What Will I Be? 2010. (Reach for Reading Ser.). (ENG., Illus.). 8p. (C). pap. 7.95 *(978-0-7362-7996-3(2))* CENGAGE Learning.
Viney, Brigit & Pearson Education Staff. Kim's Choice. 2007. (ENG.). pap. 17.32 incl. cd-rom *(978-1-4058-5197-8(X))* Pearson Education.
Viney, Peter. The Case of the Dead Batsman, 7. 2013. (Garnet Oracle Readers Ser.). (Illus.). 40p. pap., stu. ed. 4.50 *(978-1-907575-21-1(9))* Garnet Education GBR. Dist: Garnet Publishing, Ltd.
—The Collector, 16. 2014. (Garnet Oracle Readers Ser.). (Illus.). 32p. pap., stu. ed. 4.50 *(978-1-907575-31-0(6))* Garnet Education GBR. Dist: Garnet Publishing, Ltd.
—Space Romance, 8. 2014. (Garnet Oracle Readers Ser.). (Illus.). 40p. pap., stu. ed. 4.50 *(978-1-907575-22-8(7))* Garnet Education GBR. Dist: Garnet Publishing, Ltd.
—Strawberry & the Sensations, 13. 2014. (Garnet Oracle Readers Ser.). (Illus.). 32p. pap., stu. ed. 4.50 *(978-1-907575-28-0(6))* Garnet Education GBR. Dist: Garnet Publishing, Ltd.
—Sunnyvista City, 9. 2014. (Garnet Oracle Readers Ser.). (Illus.). 40p. pap., stu. ed. 4.50 *(978-1-907575-24-2(3))* Garnet Education GBR. Dist: Garnet Publishing, Ltd.
—A Tidy Ghost, 17. 2013. (Garnet Oracle Readers Ser.). (Illus.). 40p. pap., stu. ed. 4.50 *(978-1-907575-23-5(5))* Garnet Education GBR. Dist: Garnet Publishing, Ltd.
—Underground, 12. 2014. (Garnet Oracle Readers Ser.). (Illus.). 32p. pap., stu. ed. 4.50 *(978-1-907575-27-3(8))* Garnet Education GBR. Dist: Garnet Publishing, Ltd.
Vizoso Veiga, Xoán Antón. The READING LESSON: Adventures of Huckleberry Finn. 2008. 72p. pap. 13.50 *(978-1-4092-0361-2(1))* Lulu Pr., Inc.
von Bissing, Ronimund. La Tierra del Oro Ardiente. (SPA.). *(978-84-216-1631-4(5),* BU4764) Bruño, Editorial ESP. Dist: Lectorum Pubns., Inc.
Vonthron, Satanta C. Marsy's Perfect Eyesight. Teeple, Jackie, illus. l.t. ed. 2005. (J). (gr. -1-k). pap. 10.95 *(978-1-57332-344-6(9));* pap. 10.95 *(978-1-57332-345-1(4))* Carson-Dellosa Publishing, LLC. (HighReach Learning, Incorporated).
Voskoboinikov, Valery & Linnamagi, Anne. The Icicle. 2007. (POL & ENG., Illus.). 32p. (J). pap. 16.95 *(978-1-60195-100-7(0))* International Step by Step Assn.
Waddell, Martin. Class Six & the Very Big Rabbit. Ross, Tony, illus. 2005. (Collins Big Cat Ser.). (ENG.). 80p. (J). (gr. 1-3). pap. 7.99 *(978-0-00-718629-7(0))* HarperCollins Pubs. Ltd. GBR. Dist: Independent Pubs. Group.
—Something So Big. Canty, Charlotte, illus. 2004. (ENG.). 24p. (J). lib. bdg. 23.65 *(978-1-59646-706-4(1))* Dingles & Co.
Wagner, Michael & Vanzet, Gaston. The Mess. 2008. (Rigby Focus Forward: Level E Ser.). (Illus.). 24p. (J). (gr. 4-7). pap. *(978-1-4190-3677-4(7),* Rigby) Pearson Education Australia.
Wagner, Sy. Brownie Math. 2003. (Rosen Real Readers: Upper Emergent Ser.). (ENG., Illus.). 12p. (gr. 1-2). pap. 5.90 *(978-0-8239-6366-9(7))* Rosen Publishing Group, Inc., The.
Waiting in Line: Individual Title Six-Packs. (gr. -1-2). 27.00 *(978-0-7635-9480-0(6))* Rigby Education.
Walbruck, Rita M. Auf Heiber Spur, Erlebnisse in Deutschland: Das Ratsel vom Waldsee, Reader 2. (Auf Heisser Spur, Erlebnisse in Deutschland Ser.). (GER., Illus.). 40p. (J). 3.95 *(978-0-88436-851-9(3),* 45255) EMC/Paradigm Publishing.
Walch Publishing Staff. Assessment Strategies for Reading. 2003. 86p. 24.99 *(978-0-8251-4477-6(9))* Walch Education.
A Walk at the Farm. 2005. (Gilbert the Pig Chapter Ser.). (ENG.). (J). pap. 7.67 *(978-1-58453-300-9(5))* Pioneer Valley Bks.
A Walk for Jasper. 2004. (Jasper the Cat Set 1 Ser.). (ENG.). (J). pap. 7.33 *(978-1-58453-280-4(7))* Pioneer Valley Bks.
Walker, Colin, et al. Explorando el Espacio. (Coleccion Conceptos de Ciencia en Big Books). (SPA., Illus.). (J). (gr. k-3). 12.00 *(978-0-8136-6756-0(9),* MD7215) Modern Curriculum Pr.
—La Tierra Cambia. (Coleccion Conceptos de Ciencia en Big Books). (SPA., Illus.). (J). (gr. k-3). 12.00 *(978-0-8136-6729-4(1),* MD7205) Modern Curriculum Pr.
Walker, Lois. Gigantic Turnip Tug. Guthridge, Bettina, illus. 2007. (Collins Big Cat Ser.). (ENG.). 1p. (J). pap. 7.99 *(978-0-00-722873-7(2))* HarperCollins Pubs. Ltd. GBR. Dist: Independent Pubs. Group.
Walker, Nan. Day Camp. 2011. (Early Connections Ser.). (J). *(978-1-61672-347-7(5))* Benchmark Education Co.
Walker, Rachel. Book Art. 2015. (ENG., Illus.). 16p. (-2). pap. *(978-1-77654-136-2(7),* Red Rocket Readers) Flying Start Bks.
—Help Our Oceans. 2015. (ENG., Illus.). 16p. (-2). pap. *(978-1-77654-138-6(3),* Red Rocket Readers) Flying Start Bks.
—Polar Bear Survival. 2015. (ENG., Illus.). 16p. (-2). pap. *(978-1-77654-141-6(3),* Red Rocket Readers) Flying Start Bks.
Walker, Theo. Swing, Slither, Swim Low Intermediate Book with Online Access. 2014. (ENG., Illus.). 24p. pap. 9.50 *(978-1-107-69242-8(3))* Cambridge Univ. Pr.
WalkerTheo. THE CITY EXPERIMENT: REBUILDING GREENSBURG, KANSAS LOW INTERMEDIATE BOOK WITH ONLINE ACCESS. 2014. (ENG., Illus.). 24p. (J). pap. 9.50 *(978-1-107-62256-2(5))* Cambridge Univ. Pr.
—EAT UP! BEGINNING BOOK WITH ONLINE ACCESS. 2014. (ENG.). 24p. (J). pap. 9.50 *(978-1-107-68962-6(7))* Cambridge Univ. Pr.
—SUGAR: OUR GUILTY PLEASURE LOW INTERMEDIATE BOOK WITH ONLINE ACCESS. 2014. (ENG., Illus.). 28p. (J). pap. 9.50 *(978-1-107-68146-0(4))* Cambridge Univ. Pr.
Walkley, Andrew & Dellar, Hugh. Innovations Elementary. 2005. (ENG.). 96p. (C). pap., wbk. ed. 18.95 *(978-1-4130-1271-2(X))* Cengage Heinle.
Wall, Julia & McKenzie, Heather. Nico's List. 2008. (Rigby Focus Forward: Level M Ser.). (Illus.). 24p. (J). (gr. 4-7). pap. *(978-1-4190-3829-7(X),* Rigby) Pearson Education Australia.
Wall, Julia & Nickel, Adam. Bruno's Tea. 2008. (Rigby Focus Forward: Level N Ser.). (Illus.). 24p. (J). (gr. 4-7). pap. *(978-1-4190-3833-4(8),* Rigby) Pearson Education Australia.
Wallace, Clinton. H. The Adventures of Roger Eldemire. 2013. 28p. pap. 9.95 *(978-1-4787-2493-3(5))* Outskirts Pr., Inc.
Wallace, Karen. Crias del Mundo Animal. 2005. (DK Readers Ser.). (SPA., Illus.). 32p. (J). (gr. k-2). per. 3.99 *(978-0-7566-1197-2(0),* DK Children) Dorling Kindersley Publishing, Inc.
—Dragon Hunt, 1 vol. Baines, Nigel, illus. 2013. (Start Reading Ser.). (ENG.). 24p. (gr. k-1). pap. 7.95 *(978-1-4765-4095-5(0))* Capstone Press of Coughlan Cos.
—Flash Harriet & the Loch Ness Monster. Nayler, Sarah, illus. 2007. (Collins Big Cat Ser.). (ENG.). 160p. (J). (gr. 2-4). pap. 8.99 *(978-0-00-723082-2(6))* HarperCollins Pubs. Ltd. GBR. Dist: Independent Pubs. Group.
—Stinky Giant. Brett, Cathy, illus. 2013. (Start Reading Ser.). (ENG.). 24p. (gr. k-1). pap. 7.95 *(978-1-4765-4139-6(6))* Capstone Press of Coughlan Cos.
—Wolves. 2009. (Wild Reads Ser.). (ENG., Illus.). 32p. (YA). (gr. k). pap. 4.95 *(978-0-19-911935-6(X))* Oxford Univ. Pr., Inc.
Waller, Stephen & Pearson Education Staff. Run for Your Life, Level 1. 2nd ed. 2009. (ENG., Illus.). 32p. pap. 11.99 *(978-1-4058-6970-6(4))* Pearson Education.
Walsh, Kenneth. Our Earth, 1 vol. 2nd rev. ed. 2011. (Nonfiction Readers Ser.). (ENG.). 28p. (J). (gr. 2-2). pap. 6.99 *(978-1-4333-3631-7(6))* Teacher Created Materials, Inc.
—Outer Space, 1 vol. 2nd rev. ed. 2011. (Nonfiction Readers Ser.). (ENG.). 28p. (J). (gr. 2-2). pap. 6.99 *(978-1-4333-3632-4(4))* Teacher Created Materials, Inc.
—The Solar System, 1 vol. 2nd rev. ed. 2011. (TIME for KIDS(r) Nonfiction Readers Ser.). (ENG.). 28p. (J). (gr. 2-2). pap. 6.99 *(978-1-4333-3633-1(2))* Teacher Created Materials, Inc.
Walter Dragons. (Investigating Ancient Civilizations Ser.). (J). 16.80 *(978-0-8136-6342-5(3))* Modern Curriculum Pr.
Walter, Jackie. The Ants & the Grasshopper. 2017. (Must Know Stories: Level 1 Ser.). (ENG., Illus.). 32p. (J). (gr. k-2). 4.99 ***(978-1-4451-4454-2(9),*** Franklin Watts) Hachette Children's Group GBR. Dist: Hachette Bk. Group.
Walter, Jackie. The Magic Porridge Pot. 2017. (Must Know Stories: Level 1 Ser.). (ENG., Illus.). 32p. (J). (gr. k-2). 4.99 *(978-1-4451-4450-4(6),* Franklin Watts) Hachette Children's Group GBR. Dist: Hachette Bk. Group.
Walton, Ann. Something to Do. Hinrichsen, Natalie, illus. 2010. (ENG.). 24p. (J). (gr. k-2). pap. 6.00 *(978-1-77009-706-3(6))* Jacana Media ZAF. Dist: Independent Pubs. Group.
Wang, Holman & Wang, Jack. Jane Austen's Pride & Prejudice. 2016. (ENG., Illus.). 24p. (J). (gr. -1 — 1). bds. 9.95 *(978-1-4521-5244-8(6))* Chronicle Bks. LLC.
Wang, Jack & Wang, Holman. Herman Melville's Moby Dick. 2016. (ENG., Illus.). 24p. (J). (gr. -1 — 1). bds. 9.95 *(978-1-4521-5246-2(2))* Chronicle Bks. LLC.
—Leo Tolstoy's War & Peace. 2016. (ENG., Illus.). 24p. (J). (gr. -1 — 1). bds. 9.95 *(978-1-4521-5245-5(4))* Chronicle Bks. LLC.
Wang, Jack, et al. E.T.A. Hoffman's the Nutcracker. 2016. (ENG., Illus.). 24p. (J). (gr. -1 — 1). bds. 9.95 *(978-1-4521-5248-6(9))* Chronicle Bks. LLC.
—Victor Hugo's les Misérables. 2016. (ENG., Illus.). 24p. (J). (gr. -1 — 1). bds. 9.95 *(978-1-4521-5251-6(9))* Chronicle Bks. LLC.
Wang, Michael. A Stray. 2016. (ENG.). 40p. 10.00 *(978-981-4751-30-8(8))* Marshall Cavendish International (Asia) Private Ltd. SGP. Dist: National Bk. Network.
The War Shirt: Six-Pack. (Greetings Ser.: Vol. 2). 24p. (gr. 2-3). 31.00 *(978-0-7635-9413-8(X))* Rigby Education.
War Torn. 2003. (Illus.). pap. 5.60 *(978-0-7398-7515-5(9))* Steck-Vaughn.
Waring, Jamall & National Geographic Editors. Saving the Pandas. 2008. (Footprint Reading Library). (ENG., Illus.). 24p. cd-rom 16.95 ***(978-1-4240-2348-6(3))*** Cengage Heinle.
Waring, Rob. Cupid the Dolphin (US) 2008. (Footprint Reading Library: Level 4 Ser.). (ENG.). 32p. (C). pap. 15.95 *(978-1-4240-4463-4(4))* Cengage Heinle.
Warren, Celia. Ready for a Picnic. 2004. (QEB Start Reading Ser.). (Illus.). 24p. (J). lib. bdg. 15.95 *(978-1-59566-015-2(1))* QEB Publishing Inc.
Wasson, Dawn K. T. Kuu Tutu. 2008. (ENG & HAW., Illus.). (J). lib. bdg. *(978-0-9773495-8-6(6))* Na Kamalei Koolauloa Early Education Program.
Watch me Zoom: Individual Title Six-Packs. (gr. 1-2). 22.00 *(978-0-7635-9172-4(6))* Rigby Education.
The Water Caller. 2003. (Illus.). pap. 7.60 *(978-0-7398-7529-2(9))* Steck-Vaughn.
Watermelon. (Early Intervention Levels Ser.). 23.10 *(978-0-7362-0038-7(X))* CENGAGE Learning.
Waters, Kate. Monarch Butterflies. 2009. (Growing Reader Level 3 Ser.). (Illus.). 32p. (J). pap. *(978-0-545-07234-2(4))* Scholastic, Inc.
Watt, Fiona. Fairies. Cartwright, Stephen & Bird, Glen, illus. 2004. 10p. (J). (gr. -1 — 1). per. 15.95 *(978-0-7945-0811-1(1),* Usborne) EDC Publishing.
—That's Not My Fairy. Wells, Rachel, illus. 2004. 10p. (J). 9.99 *(978-0-7945-0793-0(X),* Usborne) EDC Publishing.
—Ya Se Hacer Lazos. Cartwright, Stephen, illus. 2005. (SPA.). 10p. (J). 7.95 *(978-0-7460-6626-3(0),* Usborne) EDC Publishing.
Wax, Wendy. Sugar & Spice. Perrett, Lisa, illus. 2007. (ENG.). 24p. (J). (gr. 1-4). per. 3.99 *(978-1-58476-614-8(X),* IKIDS) Innovative Kids.
We Both Read-About Bats. 2014. (Illus.). 44p. (J). 9.95 *(978-1-60115-267-1(1))* Treasure Bay, Inc.
We Both Read-Museum Day. 2014. (Illus.). 44p. (J). 9.95 *(978-1-60115-265-7(5));* pap. 4.99 *(978-1-60115-266-4(3))* Treasure Bay, Inc.
We Can: KinderWords Individual Title Six-Packs. (Kinderstarters Ser.). 8p. (gr. -1-1). 21.00 *(978-0-7635-8710-9(9))* Rigby Education.
We Clean Up!, 6 Packs. (gr. -1-2). 23.00 *(978-0-7635-8813-7(X))* Rigby Education.
Weather Report. 2012. (Collins Big Cat Ser.). (ENG., Illus.). 16p. (J). pap., wbk. ed. 4.99 *(978-0-00-747290-1(0))* HarperCollins Pubs. Ltd. GBR. Dist: Independent Pubs. Group.
Weaver, Jo. Paul Bunyan: A Very Tall Tale, 1 vol. rev. ed. 2013. (Fiction Readers Ser.). (ENG., Illus.). 20p. (J). (gr. 1-1). pap. 15.96 *(978-1-4807-1153-2(5));* pap. 4.99 *(978-1-4333-5497-7(7))* Shell Educational Publishing.
Weaver, Kimberley & Murphy, Allyson. Pack Your Bags.... Go U. S. A. Holdren, Maria K., illus. 2005. (J). 15.99 *(978-0-9767351-0-6(5))* Sorella Bks.
Weber, Rebecca. Telling Time Through the Ages: Set Of 6. 2011. (Navigators Ser.). (J). pap. 44.00 net. *(978-1-4108-0409-9(7))* Benchmark Education Co.
Webley, Ann. Homework, Bk. 4. 2008. (Collins Primary Literacy Ser.). (ENG.). 16p. (J). (gr. 4-4). pap. 5.99 *(978-0-00-722717-4(5))* HarperCollins Pubs. Ltd. GBR. Dist: Independent Pubs. Group.
Webster, Christy. Big Fish, Little Fish. 2016. (Illus.). 24p. (J). E-Book ***(978-0-7364-3705-9(3))*** Random Hse., Inc.
Webster, Christy. Toy Box Heroes! RH Disney Staff, illus. 2014. (Step into Reading Ser.). (ENG.). 32p. (J). (gr. -1-1). 4.99 *(978-0-7364-3270-2(1),* RH/Disney) Random Hse. Children's Bks.
Webster, Grace & Golden, Emily. The Elephant's Ears. 2014. (Collins Big Cat Ser.). (ENG., Illus.). 512p. (J). (gr. k-1). pap. 6.95 *(978-0-00-753849-2(9))* HarperCollins Pubs. Ltd. GBR. Dist: Independent Pubs. Group.
Wee Whopper: Individual Title Six-Packs. (gr. 1-2). 25.00 *(978-0-7635-9139-7(4))* Rigby Education.
Weiland, Peter. So Big yet So Small. Coffey, Kevin, illus. 2012. (J). 14.95 *(978-1-937406-16-5(4))* Mascot Bks., Inc.
Weinberg, Jennifer Liberts. Happy Birthday, Mike! (Disney/Pixar Monsters, Inc.) RH Disney Staff, illus. 2014. (Step into Reading Ser.). (ENG.). 32p. (J). (gr. -1-1). 3.99 *(978-0-7364-3198-9(5),* RH/Disney) Random Hse. Children's Bks.
Weir, Jane. Inside the World of Matter, 1 vol. 2007. (Science Readers Ser.). (ENG.). 32p. (J). (gr. 4-4). pap. 8.99 *(978-0-7439-0567-1(9))* Shell Educational Publishing.
—Investigating Forces & Motion, 1 vol. 2007. (Science Readers Ser.). (ENG.). 32p. (J). (gr. 4-4). pap. 8.99 *(978-0-7439-0573-2(3))* Shell Educational Publishing.
Weiss, Bobbi & Weiss, David. Hiro: Dragon Warrior: Level 2. Short, Robbie, illus. 2007. (ENG.). 24p. (J). (gr. 1-4). per. 3.99 *(978-1-58476-616-2(6),* IKIDS) Innovative Kids.
Weldon-Owe. Shifting Sands. 2003. (Rigby InfoQuest Ser.). (ENG.). 24p. (gr. 4-4). pap. 9.50 *(978-0-7578-5718-8(3))* Rigby Education.
Wells, H. G. The Island of Dr Moreau. 2007. (ENG., Illus.). 64p. (C). pap. 11.99 *(978-1-4058-4999-9(1))* Pearson Education.
Wells, James. Stuffy, the Short-Neck Giraffe Who Liked Peanut Butter. 2006. 9.00 *(978-0-8059-9174-1(3))* Dorrance Publishing Co., Inc.
Welsh Books Staff. Llyfr Lliwio Sali Mali. 2nd ed. 2005. (WEL., Illus.). 24p. pap. *(978-1-902416-88-5(0))* Cymdeithas Lyfrau Ceredigion.
Wendorff, Anne. Bear Cubs. 2009. (Blastoff! Readers Ser.). (ENG., Illus.). 24p. (J). (gr. k-3). 20.00 *(978-0-531-21626-2(8),* Children's Pr.) Scholastic Library Publishing.

P
Q
R

—Blastoff! Readers - Watch Animals Grow, 4 vols., Set. Incl. Bear Cubs. 20.00 *(978-0-531-21626-2(8))*; Eaglets. 20.00 *(978-0-531-21627-9(6))*; Fawns. 20.00 *(978-0-531-21628-6(4))*; Lambs. 20.00 *(978-0-531-21629-3(2))*. (Illus.). 24p. (J). (gr. k-3). 2009. (Blastoff! Readers Ser.). 2009. Set lib. bdg. 80.00 *(978-0-531-26129-3(8)*, Children's Pr.) Scholastic Library Publishing.

—Eaglets. 2009. (Blastoff! Readers Ser.). (ENG., Illus.). 24p. (J). (gr. k-3). 20.00 *(978-0-531-21627-9(6)*, Children's Pr.) Scholastic Library Publishing.

—Fawns. 2009. (Blastoff! Readers Ser.). (ENG., Illus.). 24p. (J). (gr. k-3). 20.00 *(978-0-531-21628-6(4)*, Children's Pr.) Scholastic Library Publishing.

—Lambs. 2009. (Blastoff! Readers Ser.). (ENG., Illus.). 24p. (J). (gr. k-3). 20.00 *(978-0-531-21629-3(2)*, Children's Pr.) Scholastic Library Publishing.

Wendy Lee Jungling; Illustrated By My Fa. Who Do You Want to Be? 2012. 28p. 24.95 *(978-1-4626-6873-1(9))* America Star Bks.

Wernham, Sara. The Bird House, 4 Bks., Pack. Stephen, Lib, illus. 2008. (Jolly Readers, Complete Set Level 4 (pack Of 18) Ser.). (ENG.). 16p. (J). pap. 14.00 *(978-1-84414-054-1(7))* Jolly Learning, Ltd. GBR. Dist: American International Distribution Corp.

—The Enormous Turnip, 6 Bks., Pack. Stephen, Lib & Maddison, Kevin, illus. 2008. (Jolly Phonics Readers, Complete Set Level 4 Ser.). (ENG.). (J). pap. 14.00 *(978-1-84414-061-9(X)*, Jolly Learning) Jolly Learning, Ltd. GBR. Dist: American International Distribution Corp.

—Phonic; Rainforests; Monster Party, 18 vols., Pack, Set. Stephen, Lib & Maddison, Kevin, illus. 2003. (ENG.). (J). pap. 37.50 *(978-1-84414-091-6(1)*, Jolly Learning) Jolly Learning, Ltd. GBR. Dist: American International Distribution Corp.

—Snakes; the Tree That Blinked; the Tree Billy Goats Gruff, 18 Bks., Pack. Maddison, Kevin & Stephen, Lib, illus. 2004. (ENG.). (J). pap. 42.00 *(978-1-84414-090-9(3)*, Jolly Learning) Jolly Learning, Ltd. GBR. Dist: American International Distribution Corp.

—Soccer, 6 Bks., Set. Stephen, Lib & Maddison, Kevin, illus. 2008. (Jolly Phonics Readers, Complete Set Level 4 Ser.). (ENG.). (J). pap. 14.00 *(978-1-84414-068-8(7)*, Jolly Learning) Jolly Learning, Ltd. GBR. Dist: American International Distribution Corp.

—The Tree That Blinked, 6 Bks., Vol. 3. Stephen, Lib, illus. 2004. (Jolly Phonics Readers, Complete Set Level 3 Ser.). (ENG.). (J). pap. 14.00 *(978-1-84414-008-4(3)*, Jolly Learning) Jolly Learning, Ltd. GBR. Dist: American International Distribution Corp.

Wesson, André. Mrs. Applebee & the Sunshine Band, Book 1: Meet the Class! 2007. 48p. pap. 18.50 *(978-0-615-14849-6(2))* Se7enth Swan Publishing Group, LLC.

West, Colin. Have You Seen the Crocodile? Read & Share. West, Colin, illus. 2003. (Reading & Math Together Ser.). (ENG., Illus.). 32p. (J). (gr. -1-3). pap. 3.99 *(978-0-7636-0862-0(9))* Candlewick Pr.

West, Tracey. The Golden Weapons. 2012. (Lego Ninjago Ser.). (ENG.). 32p. (J). (gr. 2-5). pap. 3.99 *(978-0-545-40115-9(1))* Scholastic, Inc.

—I'M Batgirl! 2017. (LEGO Batman Movie Ser.: 2). (ENG.). 32p. (J). (gr. 1-3). pap. 4.99 *(978-1-338-11815-5(3))* Scholastic, Inc.

—Titanium Ninja. 2014. (Ninjago Readers Ser.: 10). lib. bdg. 13.55 *(978-0-606-36372-3(6))* Turtleback Bks.

West, William. All about Ants. 2008. (Real Readers - Upper Emergent Ser.). (ENG., Illus.). 12p. (gr. 1-2). pap. 5.90 *(978-0-8239-8120-5(7))* Rosen Publishing Group, Inc., The.

Weston Woods Staff, creator. Brave Irene. 2011. 29.95 *(978-0-439-73468-4(1))*; 18.95 *(978-0-439-72665-8(4))*; 38.75 *(978-0-439-72666-5(2))* Weston Woods Studios, Inc.

—Caps for Sale. 2011. 38.75 *(978-0-439-72925-3(4))*; 18.95 *(978-0-439-72924-6(6))* Weston Woods Studios, Inc.

Wetterwald, Florence. Peekaboo, Pierre (a Blabla Book) Wetterwald, Florence, illus. 2016. (ENG., Illus.). 24p. (J). (—1). bds. 7.99 *(978-0-553-51347-9(8)*, Random Hse. Bks. for Young Readers) Random Hse. Children's Bks.

What a Mess!, 6, Pack. (Chiquilibros Ser.). (gr. k-1). 23.00 *(978-0-7635-0410-6(6))* Rigby Education.

What Am I? Individual Title Six-Packs. (Story Steps Ser.). (gr. k-2). 29.00 *(978-0-7635-9593-7(4))* Rigby Education.

What are We Doing? KinderWords Individual Title Six-Packs. (Kinderstarters Ser.). 8p. (gr. -1-1). 21.00 *(978-0-7635-8697-3(8))* Rigby Education.

What Can Float? (Little Book Practice Reader). (J). *(978-0-8136-5354-9(1))* Modern Curriculum Pr.

What can Hurt?, 6 Packs. (gr. 1-2). 22.00 *(978-0-7635-9088-8(6))* Rigby Education.

What Can I Do?, 6 Packs. (Greetings Ser.: Vol. 1). (gr. 2-3). 31.00 *(978-0-7635-9425-1(3))* Rigby Education.

What can Jump?, 6, Pack. (gr. 1-2). 22.00 *(978-0-7635-9114-4(9))* Rigby Education.

What Can Swim?, 6, Pack. (gr. 1-2). 22.00 *(978-0-7635-9089-5(4))* Rigby Education.

What Can We Smell?, 6, Pack. (gr. 1-2). 22.00 *(978-0-7635-9115-1(7))* Rigby Education.

What Can You Do with a Ball of String?, 6, Pack. (gr. k-1). 23.00 *(978-0-7635-9027-7(4))* Rigby Education.

What Can You Make? (J). *(978-0-8136-5373-0(8))* Modern Curriculum Pr.

What Can You Taste?, 6, Pack. (gr. 1-2). 22.00 *(978-0-7635-9116-8(5))* Rigby Education.

What Could It Be? Big Book. (Pebble Soup Explorations Ser.). 16p. (gr. -1-18). 31.00 *(978-0-7578-1665-9(7))* Rigby Education.

What Could It Be? Small Book. (Pebble Soup Explorations Ser.). 16p. (gr. -1-18). 5.00 *(978-0-7578-1705-2(X))* Rigby Education.

What Did Ben Want?, 6, Pack. (Chiquilibros Ser.). (gr. k-1). 23.00 *(978-0-7635-0444-1(0))* Rigby Education.

What Did I Use?, 6, Pack. (Discovery World Ser.). 12p. (gr. k-1). 28.00 *(978-0-7635-8448-1(7))* Rigby Education.

What Did They Want?, 6, Pack. (Chiquilibros Ser.). (gr. k-1). 23.00 *(978-0-7635-0445-8(9))* Rigby Education.

What Did You Bring? (J). *(978-0-8136-5367-9(3))* Modern Curriculum Pr.

What Do We Have to Get? (Little Book Practice Reader). (J). *(978-0-8136-2374-0(X))* Modern Curriculum Pr.

What do you Hear? Individual Title Six-Packs. (gr. 1-2). 22.00 *(978-0-7635-9173-1(4))* Rigby Education.

What do you Hear? Individual Title Six-Packs. (gr. 1-2). 22.00 *(978-0-7635-9117-5(3))* Rigby Education.

What do you See? Individual Title Six-Packs. (gr. 1-2). 22.00 *(978-0-7635-9100-7(9))* Rigby Education.

What Do You See by the Sea? Take-Home Book. 2005. (Emergent Library: Vol. 2). (YA). (gr. -1-1). 12.60 *(978-0-8215-7252-8(0))* Sadlier, William H. Inc.

What do you Touch? Individual Title Six-Packs. (gr. 1-2). 22.00 *(978-0-7635-9118-2(1))* Rigby Education.

What Does Lucy Like? Take-Home Book. 2005. (Emergent Library: Vol. 2). (YA). (gr. -1-1). 12.60 *(978-0-8215-7256-6(3))* Sadlier, William H. Inc.

What feels Cold?, 6 Packs. (gr. 1-2). 22.00 *(978-0-7635-9101-4(7))* Rigby Education.

What feels Hot?, 6 Packs. (gr. 1-2). 22.00 *(978-0-7635-9102-1(5))* Rigby Education.

What feels Sticky?, 6 Packs. (gr. 1-2). 22.00 *(978-0-7635-9103-8(3))* Rigby Education.

What Gives You Goose Bumps?, 6 Packs. (gr. k-1). 23.00 *(978-0-7635-9044-4(4))* Rigby Education.

What Goes Around & Around?, 6 Packs. (gr. 1-2). 22.00 *(978-0-7635-9119-9(X))* Rigby Education.

What Goes in the Bathtub?, 6 Packs. (Literatura 2000 Ser.). (gr. k-1). 28.00 *(978-0-7635-0017-7(8))* Rigby Education.

What Goes into a Salad? Individual Title Six-Packs. (gr. -1-2). 23.00 *(978-0-7635-8993-6(4))* Rigby Education.

What Goes up & Down?, 6 Packs. (gr. 1-2). 22.00 *(978-0-7635-9120-5(3))* Rigby Education.

What Goes up High?, 6 Packs. (gr. 1-2). 22.00 *(978-0-7635-9090-1(8))* Rigby Education.

What Happens When You Recycle? Individual Title Six-Packs. (Discovery World Ser.). 16p. (gr. 1-2). 28.00 *(978-0-7635-8464-1(9))* Rigby Education.

What I Know: Set 2. 2017. (What I Know Ser.). 24p. (gr. k-k). pap. 48.90 ***(978-1-5382-0232-6(8))***; lib. bdg. 135.60 ***(978-1-5382-0231-9(X))*** Stevens, Gareth Publishing LLLP.

What Is at the Top? (J). *(978-0-8136-2018-3(X))* Modern Curriculum Pr.

What Is Enormous?, 6 Packs. (gr. 1-2). 22.00 *(978-0-7635-9092-5(4))* Rigby Education.

What Is Fast?, 6 Packs. (gr. 1-2). 22.00 *(978-0-7635-9104-5(1))* Rigby Education.

What Is Fierce?, 6 Packs. (gr. 1-2). 22.00 *(978-0-7635-9093-2(2))* Rigby Education.

What Is He Looking For? KinderWords Individual Title Six-Packs. (Kinderstarters Ser.). 8p. (gr. -1-1). 21.00 *(978-0-7635-8711-6(7))* Rigby Education.

What Is It? (Guided Reading Levels Ser.). 21.42 *(978-0-7362-1047-8(4))* CENGAGE Learning.

What Is Little? (Early Intervention Levels Ser.). 23.10 *(978-0-7362-0003-5(7))* CENGAGE Learning.

What Is Old? Individual Title Six-Packs. (gr. 1-2). 22.00 *(978-0-7635-9096-3(7))* Rigby Education.

What Is Slippery?, 6 Packs. (gr. 1-2). 22.00 *(978-0-7635-9097-0(5))* Rigby Education.

What Is Slow? Individual Title Six-Packs. (gr. 1-2). 22.00 *(978-0-7635-9106-9(8))* Rigby Education.

What Is Soft?, 6 Packs. (gr. 1-2). 22.00 *(978-0-7635-9107-6(6))* Rigby Education.

What Is Tall?, 6 Packs. (gr. 1-2). 22.00 *(978-0-7635-9108-3(4))* Rigby Education.

What Is This? KinderWords, 6 Packs. (Kinderstarters Ser.). 8p. (gr. -1-1). 21.00 *(978-0-7635-8699-7(4))* Rigby Education.

What Is under the Hat? (J). *(978-0-8136-5363-1(0))* Modern Curriculum Pr.

What Is Young?, 6 Packs. (gr. 1-2). 22.00 *(978-0-7635-9109-0(2))* Rigby Education.

What Should You Say? What Should You Do? Social/Emotional Lap Book. (Pebble Soup Explorations Ser.). (gr. -1-18). 16.00 *(978-0-7635-7569-4(0))* Rigby Education.

What Smells Good? Individual Title Six-Packs. (gr. 1-2). 22.00 *(978-0-7635-9121-2(1))* Rigby Education.

What Some People Will Do. 2003. (Illus.). pap. 7.60 *(978-0-7398-7535-3(3))* Steck-Vaughn.

What's Around the Corner? Individual Title Six-Packs. (Literatura 2000 Ser.). (gr. 1-2). 28.00 *(978-0-7635-0153-2(0))* Rigby Education.

What's for Lunch? (Peek A Boo Pockets Ser.). 12p. (J). bds. *(978-2-89393-879-0(5))* Phidal Publishing, Inc./Editions Phidal, Inc.

What's in the Castle? (Let's Read about... Ser.). 10p. (J). *(978-2-7643-0073-2(5))* Phidal Publishing, Inc./Editions Phidal, Inc.

What's in the Dollhouse? (Let's Read about... Ser.). 10p. (J). *(978-2-7643-0195-1(2))* Phidal Publishing, Inc./Editions Phidal, Inc.

What's in the Garage? (Let's Read about... Ser.). 10p. (J). *(978-2-7643-0194-4(4))* Phidal Publishing, Inc./Editions Phidal, Inc.

What's on My Farm? (Early Intervention Levels Ser.). 23.10 *(978-0-7362-0007-3(X))* CENGAGE Learning.

What's on the Farm? (Let's Read about Ser.). 10p. (J). *(978-2-7643-0163-0(4))* Phidal Publishing, Inc./Editions Phidal, Inc.

What's Underneath? Individual Title Six-Packs. (Discovery World Ser.). 16p. (gr. 1-2). 28.00 *(978-0-7635-8465-8(7))* Rigby Education.

Wheels Board Book Set 800789, 3. 2005. (J). bds. *(978-1-59794-042-9(9))* Environments, Inc.

When I Grow Up. (Early Intervention Levels Ser.). 23.10 *(978-0-7362-0025-7(8))* CENGAGE Learning.

When It Snowed: Individual Title, 6 packs. (gr. -1-2). 23.00 *(978-0-7635-9018-5(5))* Rigby Education.

When Lana Was Absent: 6 Small Books. (gr. k-3). 24.00 *(978-0-7635-6240-3(8))* Rigby Education.

When Mr Quinn Snored: Take-Home Book. 2005. (Emergent Library: Vol. 2). (YA). (gr. -1-1). 12.60 *(978-0-8215-7266-5(0))* Sadlier, William H. Inc.

Where are the Baby Chicks? 2004. (Gilbert the Pig Set 2 Ser.). (J). 7.33 *(978-1-58453-226-2(2))* Pioneer Valley Bks.

Where are the car Keys? Individual Title Six-Packs. (gr. 1-2). 22.00 *(978-0-7635-9156-4(4))* Rigby Education.

Where Are We Going? (J). 26.20 *(978-0-8136-8393-5(9))*; 26.20 *(978-0-8136-8392-8(0))*; (gr. -1-3). 59.50 *(978-0-8136-7906-8(0))* Modern Curriculum Pr.

Where Are You Going? KinderWords Individual Title Six-Packs. (Kinderstarters Ser.). 8p. (gr. -1-1). 21.00 *(978-0-7635-8712-3(5))* Rigby Education.

Where Does Breakfast Come From?, 6 Packs. (Discovery World Ser.). 16p. (gr. 1-2). 28.00 *(978-0-7635-8454-2(1))* Rigby Education.

Where Is It? (J). *(978-0-8136-5347-1(9))* Modern Curriculum Pr.

Where Is the Treasure? KinderConcepts Individual Title Six-Packs. (Kinderstarters Ser.). 8p. (gr. -1-1). 21.00 *(978-0-7635-8721-5(4))* Rigby Education.

Where We Live Interactive Packages: In My Neighborhood. (Pebble Soup Explorations Ser.). (gr. -1-18). 52.00 *(978-0-7578-5232-9(7))* Rigby Education.

Where We Live Interactive Packages: What People Do. (Pebble Soup Explorations Ser.). (gr. -1-18). 52.00 *(978-0-7578-5234-3(3))* Rigby Education.

Which Egg Is Mine? (Early Intervention Levels Ser.). 23.10 *(978-0-7362-0034-9(7))* CENGAGE Learning.

Which Way, Jack? Individual Title Six-Packs. (Action Packs Ser.). 104p. (gr. 3-5). 44.00 *(978-0-7635-8407-8(X))* Rigby Education.

White, Marco. Freddy's Fishbowl. 2006. (Neighborhood Readers Ser.). (ENG.). 8p. (gr. -1-3). pap. 5.15 *(978-1-4042-6702-2(6)*, Rosen Classroom) Rosen Publishing Group, Inc., The.

White, N.m. Unlock Level 1 Listening & Speaking Skills Student's Book & Online Workbook, 1 vol. 2014. (Cambridge Discovery Education Skills Ser.). (ENG.). 224p. pap. 50.50 *(978-1-107-67810-1(2))* Cambridge Univ. Pr.

White Paw, Black Paw: KinderReaders Individual Title Six-Packs. (Kinderstarters Ser.). 8p. (gr. -1-1). 21.00 *(978-0-7635-8648-5(X))* Rigby Education.

Whiteford, Rhona & Hachette Children's Group. Complete English, 3 bks. in 1. (Illus.). 96p. (YA). pap. 15.99 *(978-0-340-71582-6(0))* Hodder & Stoughton GBR. Dist: Trafalgar Square Publishing.

Whiteford, Rhona, et al. Complete English, 4 bks. in 1. (Illus.). 96p. (YA). pap. 15.99 *(978-0-340-71580-2(4))* Hodder & Stoughton GBR. Dist: Trafalgar Square Publishing.

Who Are We?, 6 Packs. (gr. -1-2). 23.00 *(978-0-7635-8805-2(9))* Rigby Education.

Who Came by Here? (Early Intervention Levels Ser.). 23.10 *(978-0-7362-0031-8(2))* CENGAGE Learning.

Who Lives on a Farm? Individual Title, 6 packs. (Story Steps Ser.). (gr. k-2). 29.00 *(978-0-7635-9570-8(5))* Rigby Education.

Who Looks after Our World? Individual Title Six-Packs. (gr. -1-2). 23.00 *(978-0-7635-8814-4(8))* Rigby Education.

Who Painted the Porcupine. (J). 23.50 *(978-0-8136-3967-3(0))* Modern Curriculum Pr.

Who Will Help Me? Individual Title Six-Packs. (gr. -1-2). 23.00 *(978-0-7635-8795-6(8))* Rigby Education.

Who Will Look Out for Danny? Individual Title Six-Packs. (Action Packs Ser.). 120p. (gr. 3-5). 44.00 *(978-0-7635-8420-7(7))* Rigby Education.

Whoops! Set D Individual Title, 6 packs. (gr. k-3). 29.00 *(978-0-7635-0551-6(X))* Rigby Education.

Who's at the Zoo? (Let's Read about Ser.). 10p. (J). *(978-2-7643-0162-3(6))* Phidal Publishing, Inc./Editions Phidal, Inc.

Who's Coming for a Ride? Individual Title, 6 packs. (Literatura 2000 Ser.). (gr. -1-1). 28.00 *(978-0-7635-0019-1(4))* Rigby Education.

Who's the Boss. 2004. (Jasper the Cat Chapter Ser.). (J). 7.67 *(978-1-58453-285-9(8))* Pioneer Valley Bks.

Whose Egg Is This? Individual Title Six-Packs. (Story Steps Ser.). (gr. k-2). 32.00 *(978-0-7635-9607-1(8))* Rigby Education.

Why the Sea Is Salty: Individual Title Six-Packs. (Literatura 2000 Ser.). (gr. 2-3). 33.00 *(978-0-7635-0246-1(4))* Rigby Education.

Whybrow, Ian. The Best Little Bullfrog in the Forest Orange Band. Smillie, Natalie, illus. 2016. (Cambridge Reading Adventures Ser.). (ENG.). 16p. pap. 7.19 *(978-1-107-56018-5(7))* Cambridge Univ. Pr.

—It's Much Too Early! Watson, Laura, illus. 2016. (Cambridge Reading Adventures Ser.). (ENG.). 16p. pap. 6.56 *(978-1-107-56032-1(2))* Cambridge Univ. Pr.

—Sinbad & the Roc Purple Band. Schon, Nick, illus. 2016. (Cambridge Reading Adventures Ser.). (ENG.). 24p. pap. 7.19 *(978-1-316-50340-9(2))* Cambridge Univ. Pr.

—Sinbad Goes to Sea Turquoise Band. Schon, Nick, illus. 2016. (Cambridge Reading Adventures Ser.). (ENG.). 16p. pap. 6.56 *(978-1-316-50338-6(0))* Cambridge Univ. Pr.

Wiedemer & Steel, Abigail. Africa. 2013. (Collins Big Cat Phonics Progress Ser.). (ENG., Illus.). 16p. (J). (gr. 1-2). pap. 6.95 *(978-0-00-751634-6(7))* HarperCollins Pubs. Ltd. GBR. Dist: Independent Pubs. Group.

Wiggin, Kate Douglas. Rebecca of Sunnybrook Farm. 2008. (Bring the Classics to Life Ser.). (Illus.). 72p. (gr. 1-12). pap., act. bk. ed. 10.95 *(978-1-55576-046-5(5)*, EDCTR-102B) EDCON Publishing Group.

Wignell, Edel. Bendelomena. Goss, Mini, illus. 2007. (Collins Big Cat Ser.). (ENG.). 1p. (J). pap. 8.99 *(978-0-00-722868-3(6))* HarperCollins Pubs. Ltd. GBR. Dist: Independent Pubs. Group.

Wilbur's Wild Ride & Other Stories: Individual Title Six-Pack. (Story Steps Ser.). (gr. k-2). 42.00 *(978-0-7635-9598-2(5))* Rigby Education.

Wilcox. The Hidden Men. (Thumbprint Mysteries Ser.). 32.86 *(978-0-8092-0415-1(0))* McGraw-Hill/Contemporary.

Wild Animal Board Book Set 800785, 5. 2005. (J). bds. *(978-1-59794-020-7(8))* Environments, Inc.

Wild Animals, Level 2. 2016. (Ladybird Readers Ser.). (ENG.). 48p. (J). (gr. 2-4). pap. 9.99 *(978-0-241-25445-5(0))* Penguin Bks., Ltd. GBR. Dist: Independent Pubs. Group.

Wild Critters. 2005. (Little Celebrations Thematic Packages Ser.). (J). (gr. k-3). 133.50 *(978-0-673-75384-7(0))* Celebration Pr.

Wild Easts Wild West: Level K, 6 vols. 128p. (gr. 2-3). 49.95 *(978-0-7699-0988-2(4))* Shortland Pubns. (U. S. A.) Inc.

Wilde, Kim. Harry's Garden. 2006. (Collins Big Cat Ser.). (ENG., Illus.). 96p. (J). (gr. 1-1). pap. 5.99 *(978-0-00-718676-1(2))* HarperCollins Pubs. Ltd. GBR. Dist: Independent Pubs. Group.

—How to Make a Scarecrow: Band 00/Lilac. 2006. (Collins Big Cat Ser.). (ENG., Illus.). 16p. (J). (gr. -1-k). pap. 5.99 *(978-0-00-718645-7(2))* HarperCollins Pubs. Ltd. GBR. Dist: Independent Pubs. Group.

Wilder, Nellie. Changing Weather, 1 vol. rev. ed. 2014. (Science Readers: Content & Literacy Ser.). (ENG., Illus.). 24p. (gr. k-k). pap. 8.99 *(978-1-4807-4531-5(6))* Teacher Created Materials, Inc.

—On Land, 1 vol. rev. ed. 2014. (Science Readers: Content & Literacy Ser.). (ENG., Illus.). 24p. (gr. k-k). pap. 8.99 *(978-1-4807-4532-2(4))* Teacher Created Materials, Inc.

—What Is the Weather?, 1 vol. rev. ed. 2014. (Science Readers: Content & Literacy Ser.). (ENG., Illus.). 24p. (gr. k-k). pap. 8.99 *(978-1-4807-4530-8(8))* Teacher Created Materials, Inc.

Wilhelm, Hans. No Kisses, Please! 2004. (Hello Reader! Ser.). (Illus.). (J). pap. *(978-0-439-56420-5(4))* Scholastic, Inc.

Wilhelm, Peggy Jo. The 10 Most Innovative Bands. 2008. 14.99 *(978-1-55448-554-3(1))* Scholastic Library Publishing.

Will, Rebel. Who Lives/Twgn/C. 8p. 20.95 *(978-0-322-00347-7(4))* Wright Group/McGraw-Hill.

Willems, Mo & Campoy, F. Isabel. ¡Hoy Volaré! Willems, Mo, illus. 2015. (Elephant & Piggie Book Ser.). (SPA., Illus.). 64p. (J). (gr. 1-3). 9.99 *(978-1-4847-2287-9(6))* Disney Publishing Worldwide.

—¡Un Tipo Grande Se Llevó Mi Pelota! Willems, Mo, illus. 2015. (Elephant & Piggie Book Ser.). (SPA., Illus.). 64p. (J). (gr. 1-3). 9.99 *(978-1-4847-2285-5(X))* Disney Publishing Worldwide.

William H. Sadlier Staff. Nice Vine, Quite Fine, Vol. 2. 2005. (Early Library). (gr. k-2). 24.00 net. *(978-0-8215-8946-5(6))* Sadlier, William H. Inc.

—Niles Likes to Smile, Vol. 2. 2005. (Early Library). (gr. k-2). 24.00 net. *(978-0-8215-8956-4(3))* Sadlier, William H. Inc.

—What Bear Cubs Like to Do. 2005. (Early Library). (gr. k-2). 24.00 net. *(978-0-8215-8953-3(9))* Sadlier, William H. Inc.

—What Do You See by the Sea? 2005. (Emergent Library: Vol. 2). (gr. -1-1). 24.00 net. *(978-0-8215-8922-9(9))* Sadlier, William H. Inc.

—What Does Lucy Like? 2005. (Emergent Library: Vol. 2). (gr. -1-1). 24.00 net. *(978-0-8215-8926-7(1))* Sadlier, William H. Inc.

—What Does Sam Sell? 2005. (Emergent Library: Vol. 1). (gr. -1-1). 24.00 net. *(978-0-8215-8902-1(4))* Sadlier, William H. Inc.

—When Mr Quinn Snored. 2005. (Emergent Library: Vol. 2). (gr. -1-1). 24.00 net. *(978-0-8215-8936-6(9))* Sadlier, William H. Inc.

—Who Can Run Fast? 2005. (Early Library). (gr. k-2). 24.00 net. *(978-0-8215-8940-3(7))* Sadlier, William H. Inc.

—Who Has Four Feet? Big Book. 2005. (Emergent Library: Vol. 1). (gr. -1-1). 24.00 net. *(978-0-8215-8900-7(8))* Sadlier, William H. Inc.

—Who Is My Mom? 2005. (Emergent Library: Vol. 1). (gr. -1-1). 24.00 net. *(978-0-8215-8901-4(6))* Sadlier, William H. Inc.

—Who Works Here? 2005. (Emergent/Early (Prek-2) Social Studies Package Ser.). 12p. (gr. -1-1). 25.20 *(978-0-8215-7833-9(2))* Sadlier, William H. Inc.

—Why Coyote Howls at Night. 2005. (Fluent Library). (gr. 1-3). 29.34 *(978-0-8215-8960-1(1))* Sadlier, William H. Inc.

—Writing a Research Paper: A Student Guide to Writing a Research Paper. 2005. (Writign a Resrch Paper Ser.). (gr. 7-12). stu. ed. 10.00 net. *(978-0-8215-0761-2(3))* Sadlier, William H. Inc.

William Tell: 6 Small Books. (gr. k-2). 23.00 *(978-0-7635-8506-8(8))* Rigby Education.

Williams, Ben. Look Inside: Your Heart & Lungs, 1 vol. 2nd rev. ed. 2011. (Nonfiction Readers Ser.). (ENG.). 28p. (J). (gr. 2-2). pap. 6.99 *(978-1-4333-3636-2(7))* Teacher Created Materials, Inc.

—Look Inside - Your Brain, 1 vol. 2nd rev. ed. 2011. (Nonfiction Readers Ser.). (ENG., Illus.). 28p. (J). (gr. 2-2). pap. 6.99 *(978-1-4333-3634-8(0))* Teacher Created Materials, Inc.

—Your Skeleton & Muscles, 1 vol. 2nd rev. ed. 2011. (Nonfiction Readers Ser.). (ENG.). 28p. (J). (gr. 2-2). pap. 6.99 *(978-1-4333-3635-5(9))* Teacher Created Materials, Inc.

Williams, Brian. People & Places. 2010. (What About... Ser.). (Illus.). 40p. (J). (gr. 6-8). lib. bdg. 19.95 *(978-1-4222-1563-0(6))* Mason Crest.

Williams, Carolea, ed. Ending Consonants Instant Learning Centers, Vol. 2196. 2004. (Illus.). 32p. (J). (gr. k-2). pap. 9.99 *(978-1-59198-056-8(9)*, CTP 2196) Creative Teaching Pr., Inc.

Williams, Laura E. Father Damien. Kofsky, Kristen, illus. 2009. (ENG.). 60p. (J). (gr. 4). pap. *(978-1-59700-757-3(9))* Island Heritage Publishing.

Williams, Rozanne Lanczak. The Ants & the Grasshopper, Vol. 4262. Adnet, Bernard, illus. 2005. (Reading for Fluency Ser.). 16p. (J). pap. 3.49 *(978-1-59198-162-6(X))* Creative Teaching Pr., Inc.

—Are We There Yet? Leary, Catherine, illus. 2005. (Science Mini Units Ser.). 8p. (J). pap. 2.49 *(978-1-59198-151-0(4)*, 4251) Creative Teaching Pr., Inc.

—The Big Hungry Bear. Hockerman, Dennis, illus. 2005. (Reading for Fluency Ser.). 8p. (J). pap. 3.49 *(978-1-59198-146-6(8)*, 4246) Creative Teaching Pr., Inc.

—Creepy, Crawly Bugs. Harris, Jennifer Beck, illus. 2005. (Reading for Fluency Ser.). 8p. (J). pap. 3.49 *(978-1-59198-149-7(2)*, 4249) Creative Teaching Pr., Inc.

—Fairy Tale Rock. Christensen, David & Leary, Catherine, illus. 2005. (Reading for Fluency Ser.). 16p. (J). pap. 3.49 *(978-1-59198-153-4(0)*, 4252) Creative Teaching Pr., Inc.

—Here Comes Coco. Banta, Susan, illus. 2005. (Reading for Fluency Ser.). 8p. (J). pap. 3.49 *(978-1-59198-145-9(X)*, 4245) Creative Teaching Pr., Inc.

—Hide & Seek Monsters. Dunne, Kathleen, illus. 2005. (Reading for Fluency Ser.). 16p. (J). pap. 3.49 *(978-1-59198-154-1(9)*, 4254) Creative Teaching Pr., Inc.

—How to Make a Friend. Nobens, Cheryl, illus. 2005. (Reading for Fluency Ser.). 16p. (J). pap. 3.49 *(978-1-59198-155-8(7)*, 4255) Creative Teaching Pr., Inc.

—I Love Mud! Twinem, Neecy, illus. 2005. (Reading for Fluency Ser.). 8p. (J). pap. 3.49 *(978-1-59198-141-1(7)*, 4241) Creative Teaching Pr., Inc.

—Look Closer. Vangsgard, Amy, illus. 2005. (Reading for Fluency Ser.). 8p. (J). pap. 3.49 *(978-1-59198-147-3(6),* 4247) Creative Teaching Pr., Inc.
—The Mouse Who Cried Cat, Vol. 4263. Mahan, Benton, illus. 2005. (Reading for Fluency Ser.). 16p. (J). pap. 3.49 *(978-1-59198-163-3(8),* 4263) Creative Teaching Pr., Inc.
—My Pink Piggy Bank. Fletcher, Rusty, illus. 2005. (Reading for Fluency Ser.). 8p. (J). pap. 2.49 *(978-1-59198-144-2(1),* 4244) Creative Teaching Pr., Inc.
—Pirates Coming Through, 24 vols., Vol. 4257. Pamintuan, Macky, illus. 2005. (Reading for Fluency Ser.). 16p. (J). pap. 3.49 *(978-1-59198-157-2(3),* 4257) Creative Teaching Pr., Inc.
—Slow & Steady Wins the Race, Vol. 4260. Edwards, Karl, illus. 2005. (Reading for Fluency Ser.). 16p. (J). pap. 3.49 *(978-1-59198-158-9(1),* 4260) Creative Teaching Pr., Inc.
—Space Trip. Burnett, Lindy, illus. 2005. (Reading for Fluency Ser.). 80p. (J). pap. 32.49 *(978-1-59198-142-8(5),* 4242) Creative Teaching Pr., Inc.
—The Swim Lesson. Burris, Priscilla, illus. 2005. (Reading for Fluency Ser.). 8p. (J). pap. 3.49 *(978-1-59198-148-0(4),* 4248) Creative Teaching Pr., Inc.
—The Teacher with the Alligator Purse, Vol. 4259. Richard, Ilene, illus. 2005. (Reading for Fluency Ser.). 16p. (J). pap. 3.49 *(978-1-59198-159-6(X))* Creative Teaching Pr., Inc.
—Today Is Somebody's Birthday. Mahan, Benton, illus. 2005. (Reading for Fluency Ser.). 8p. (J). pap. 2.49 *(978-1-59198-140-4(9),* 4240) Creative Teaching Pr., Inc.
—What Is the Best Pet?, Vol. 4258. Briles, Patty, illus. 2005. 16p. (J). pap. 3.49 *(978-1-59198-160-2(3),* 4258) Creative Teaching Pr., Inc.
—What's So Bad about the Big Bad Wolf?, 24 vols. Catalano, Dominic, illus. 2005. (Reading for Fluency Ser.). 8p. (J). pap. 2.49 *(978-1-59198-143-5(3),* 4243) Creative Teaching Pr., Inc.
—You Can't Catch Me. Edwards, Karl, illus. 2005. (Reading for Fluency Ser.). 8p. (J). pap. 3.49 *(978-1-59198-150-3(6),* 4250) Creative Teaching Pr., Inc.
Williams, Sam. It's My Turn. Dufalla, Anita, illus. 2012. (ENG.). 24p. (gr. k-1). pap. 8.95 *(978-1-61810-296-6(6))* Rourke Educational Media.
Williams, Zachary. Lions at the Library? 2006. (Neighborhood Readers Ser.). (ENG.). 12p. (gr. 1-3). pap. 5.90 *(978-1-4042-6863-0(4),* Rosen Classroom) Rosen Publishing Group, Inc., The.
—The Lost Nickel. 2006. (Neighborhood Readers Ser.). (ENG.). 8p. (gr. -1-3). pap. 5.15 *(978-1-4042-5786-3(1),* Rosen Classroom) Rosen Publishing Group, Inc., The.
—What Will It Be? 2006. (Neighborhood Readers Ser.). (ENG.). 16p. (gr. 1-3). pap. 6.50 *(978-1-4042-7252-1(6),* Rosen Classroom) Rosen Publishing Group, Inc., The.
Williamson, Jan. A Special Day in May. 2006. (Neighborhood Readers Ser.). (ENG.). 16p. (gr. 1-3). pap. 6.50 *(978-1-4042-7276-7(3),* Rosen Classroom) Rosen Publishing Group, Inc., The.
Williamson, Melanie, illus. Las Ruedas Del Autobús. 2017. (SPA.). 24p. (J). (gr. -1-1). pap. 9.99 incl. audio compact disk ***(978-1-84686-789-7(4))*** Barefoot Bks., Inc.
Willians, Rozanne Lanczak. Sing & Read with Greg & Steve All-in-One Pack. 2009. pap. 58.86 *(978-1-60689-164-3(2))* Youngheart Music.
Wilson, Anna & Collins UK Publishing Staff. Puss in Boots. Martynets, Denis, illus. 2016. (ENG.). 32p. (J). pap. 8.95 *(978-0-00-814713-6(2))* HarperCollins Pubs. Ltd. GBR. Dist: Independent Pubs. Group.
Wilson, Anne, illus. My First Box of Books: 1 2 3 Colours Animals, 3 vols. 2016. (ENG.). 72p. (J). (gr. -1-2). bds. 9.99 *(978-1-86147-416-2(4),* Armadillo) Anness Publishing GBR. Dist: National Bk. Network.
Wilson, CeCe. Micah Learns to Read. 2015. (Rosen REAL Readers: STEM & STEAM Collection). (ENG.). 8p. pap. 5.46 *(978-1-4994-9583-6(8),* Rosen Classroom) Rosen Publishing Group, Inc., The.
Wilson, Hannah. Kingfisher Readers L2: Sun, Moon, & Stars. Feldman, Thea, ed. 2014. (Kingfisher Readers Ser.). (ENG., Illus.). 32p. (J). (gr. k-3). 12.99 *(978-0-7534-7146-3(9),* 9780753471463, Kingfisher) Roaring Brook Pr.
Wilson, Jacqueline. Monster Eyeballs. Lewis, Stephen, illus. 2nd ed. 2016. (Reading Ladder Ser.). (ENG.). 48p. (J). (gr. k-2). pap. 7.99 *(978-1-4052-8199-7(5))* Egmont Bks., Ltd. GBR. Dist: Independent Pubs. Group.
—My Brother Bernadette. Roberts, David, illus. 2nd ed. 2016. (Reading Ladder Ser.). (ENG.). 48p. (J). (gr. k-2). pap. 7.99 *(978-1-4052-8235-2(5))* Egmont Bks., Ltd. GBR. Dist: Independent Pubs. Group.
Wilson, Karma & Chapman, Jane. Bear Snores On. 2009. 34p. pap. 8.50 *(978-0-15-352483-7(9))* Harcourt Schl. Pubs.
Wilson, Mike. The Williams Sisters: Venus & Serena. 2005. (ENG., Illus.). 32p. pap. 8.50 *(978-0-340-84876-0(6))* Cambridge Univ. Pr.
Wilson, Pip & Long, Ian. Blob Feelings Ball. 2017. (Blobs Ser.). (ENG.). 2p. (C). pap. 20.95 ***(978-0-86388-893-9(3),*** Y329884) Routledge.
Wilson, Zachary. Un Circulo en el Cielo. Adinolfi, JoAnn, illus. 2011. (Rookie Ready to Learn Español Ser.). (SPA.). 40p. (J). pap. 5.95 *(978-0-531-26791-2(1),* Children's Pr.) Scholastic Library Publishing.
Wilson, Zachary & Adinolfi, JoAnn. Un Circulo en el Cielo. Adinolfi, JoAnn, illus. 2011. (Rookie Ready to Learn Español Ser.). (SPA., Illus.). 40p. (J). lib. bdg. 23.00 *(978-0-531-26123-1(9),* Children's Pr.) Scholastic Library Publishing.
The Wind Eagle. (Guided Reading Levels Ser.). 42.96 *(978-0-7362-2143-6(3))* CENGAGE Learning.
The Wind That Would Not Blow. (Early Intervention Levels Ser.). 31.86 *(978-0-7362-0620-4(5))* CENGAGE Learning.
The Wind That Would Not Blow (28), Vol. 28. (Early Intervention Levels Ser.). 5.31 *(978-0-7362-0608-2(6))* CENGAGE Learning.
Windham, Ryder. Journey Through Space. 2015. (DK Readers Ser.). (ENG.). 48p. (J). (gr. 1-3). 14.99 *(978-1-4654-3389-3(9),* DK Children) Dorling Kindersley Publishing, Inc.
Windsor. Sail Main4 Comets Nf. 2003. (Rigby Sails Ser.). (ENG.). 32p. (gr. 4-4). pap. 9.50 *(978-0-7578-8507-5(1))* Rigby Education.
Windsor, Herbert C. The Colour Monster. 2009. (Illus.). 32p. pap. 12.99 *(978-1-4490-1056-0(3))* AuthorHouse.
Windsor, Jo. A Long Time Ago: Early Level Satellite Individual Title Six-Packs. (Sails Literacy Ser.). 16p. (gr. 1-2). 27.00 *(978-0-7578-3163-8(X))* Rigby Education.
Wings: KinderWords Individual Title Six-Packs. (Kinderstarters Ser.). 8p. (gr. -1-1). 21.00 *(978-0-7635-8691-1(9))* Rigby Education.
Winter, Barbara. Fight for Rights. Kostic, Dimitri, illus. 2007. 48p. (J). lib. bdg. 23.08 *(978-1-4242-1636-9(2))* Fitzgerald Bks.
—The 10 Most Endangered Animals. 2008. 14.99 *(978-1-55448-552-9(5))* Scholastic Library Publishing.
Wise-Douglas, Terri. The Wonderful World of Cupcakes. Duckworth, Jeffrey, illus. 2011. 28p. pap. 24.95 *(978-1-4626-3570-2(9))* America Star Bks.
The Wise Old Woman. (Lexile Levels Ser.). 9.09 *(978-1-56334-747-4(4))* CENGAGE Learning.
Wood, Alexander. Our Jobs. 2009. (Real Life Readers Ser.). 8p. (gr. k-1). pap. 5.15 *(978-1-4042-8011-3(1),* Rosen Classroom) Rosen Publishing Group, Inc., The.
Wood, Cary D. Davis & Pop Go Hiking. Turner, Cecilia, illus. 2014. (ENG.). 30p. (gr. -1-4). 34.95 *(978-1-63047-217-7(4))* Morgan James Publishing.
Wood, D. K. Nightmare at Indian Cave. 2006. pap. 10.00 *(978-1-4257-1640-0(7))* Xlibris Corp.
Wood, Ira. The Fourth of July. 2008. (Real Readers - Upper Emergent Ser.). (ENG., Illus.). 12p. (gr. 1-2). pap. 5.90 *(978-0-8239-8199-1(1))* Rosen Publishing Group, Inc., The.
—The Sandcastle. 2006. (Neighborhood Readers Ser.). (ENG.). 16p. (gr. 1-3). pap. 6.50 *(978-1-4042-6986-6(X),* Rosen Classroom) Rosen Publishing Group, Inc., The.
—Water, Ice, & Steam. 2003. (Real Readers Series: Level Blue Ser.). (ENG., Illus.). 12p. (gr. 1-2). pap. 5.90 *(978-0-8239-6353-9(5))* Rosen Publishing Group, Inc., The.
Wood, Lisa. The Human Hotel. 2010. 36p. pap. 15.49 *(978-1-4389-7466-8(3))* AuthorHouse.
Woodcock, Sandra, et al. Being a Model. 2005. (ENG., Illus.). 32p. pap. *(978-0-340-74716-2(1))* Cambridge Univ. Pr.
Woods, Lin. Kenny Can: "Don't Judge Me" 2011. 24p. pap. 15.99 *(978-1-4568-9958-5(9))* Xlibris Corp.
Woods, Sadie. I Help at the Store. Aguilera, Aurora, illus. 2017. (Ways I Help Ser.). 24p. (J). (gr. 4-6). pap. 8.25 ***(978-1-5081-5678-9(6),*** PowerKids Pr.) Rosen Publishing Group, Inc., The.
Woolly, Woolly: Individual Title Six-Packs. (Literatura 2000 Ser.). (gr. 1-2). 28.00 *(978-0-7635-0159-4(X))* Rigby Education.
Wordless Story Book: In My Own Words. 2004. (In My Own Words Reproducible Wordless Story Book Ser.). (gr. -1-k). 29.95 *(978-0-673-65205-8(X))* Addison-Wesley Educational Pubs., Inc.
Wordless Story Books: Take-Home Version. 2004. (gr. k-18). 48.00 *(978-0-328-02301-1(9))* Addison-Wesley Educational Pubs., Inc.
Workers: KinderWords Individual Title Six-Packs. (Kinderstarters Ser.). 8p. (gr. -1-1). 21.00 *(978-0-7635-8714-7(1))* Rigby Education.
World of Football. 2012. (Collins Big Cat Ser.). (ENG.). 16p. (J). pap., wbk. ed. 4.99 *(978-0-00-747286-4(2))* HarperCollins Pubs. Ltd. GBR. Dist: Independent Pubs. Group.
World of Language Book Set 800930, 5 vols. 2005. (J). pap. *(978-1-59794-094-8(1))* Environments, Inc.
Wright, Craig. Double Trouble. 2010. (ENG., Illus.). 14p. act. bk. ed. 4.06 *(978-0-19-440152-4(9))* Oxford Univ. Pr., Inc.
—Matt's Mistake. 2010. (ENG., Illus.). 14p. act. bk. ed. 4.06 *(978-0-19-440157-9(X))* Oxford Univ. Pr., Inc.
—Meet Molly, Level 1. 2010. (ENG., Illus.). 14p. act. bk. ed. 4.06 *(978-0-19-440144-9(8))* Oxford Univ. Pr., Inc.
Wright, Craig, ed. City Girl, Country Boy. 2010. (ENG., Illus.). 16p. act. bk. ed. 4.06 *(978-0-19-440173-9(1))* Oxford Univ. Pr., Inc.
—In the Ocean. 2010. (ENG., Illus.). 16p. act. bk. ed. 4.06 *(978-0-19-440174-6(X))* Oxford Univ. Pr., Inc.
—Just Like Mine. 2010. (ENG., Illus.). 14p. act. bk. ed. 4.06 *(978-0-19-440164-7(2))* Oxford Univ. Pr., Inc.
—Let's Go to the Rainforest. 2010. (ENG., Illus.). 14p. act. bk. ed. 4.06 *(978-0-19-440167-8(7))* Oxford Univ. Pr., Inc.
—My Family. 2010. (ENG.). 16p. act. bk. ed. 4.06 *(978-0-19-440138-8(3))* Oxford Univ. Pr., Inc.
—New Girl in School, Level 3. 2010. (ENG., Illus.). 14p. act. bk. ed. 4.06 *(978-0-19-440162-3(6))* Oxford Univ. Pr., Inc.
—Students in Space, Level 3. 2010. (ENG., Illus.). 14p. act. bk. ed. 4.06 *(978-0-19-440160-9(X))* Oxford Univ. Pr., Inc.
—Things That Fly. 2010. (ENG., Illus.). 14p. act. bk. ed. 4.06 *(978-0-19-440166-1(9))* Oxford Univ. Pr., Inc.
—What Did You Do Yesterday? 2010. (ENG., Illus.). 14p. pap., act. bk. ed. 4.06 *(978-0-19-440161-6(8))* Oxford Univ. Pr., Inc.
—Yesterday, Today, & Tomorrow, Level 4. 2010. (ENG., Illus.). 16p. act. bk. ed. 4.06 *(978-0-19-440169-2(3))* Oxford Univ. Pr., Inc.
Wright Group. Early Emergent Guided Reading. 2nd ed. 2004. (Wright Group Literacy Ser.). (gr. k-18). 423.95 *(978-0-322-04287-2(9))* Wright Group/McGraw-Hill.
Wright, Holly. Sunflower. 2004. (J). *(978-0-9743690-5-1(5))* Britt Allcroft Productions.
Wrighton, Charlene & Bradshaw, Georgine. Basic Kit - Preschool. Clark, Irene, illus. 2005. Orig. Title: Basis Kit I. (J). 249.95 *(978-1-886441-30-9(8))* Zoo-phonics, Inc.
Wu, Nicholas. The Bears' Story by Baldwin B. Bear, 1 vol. rev. ed. 2013. (Fiction Readers Ser.). (ENG., Illus.). 20p. (J). (gr. 1-1). pap. 15.96 *(978-1-4807-1147-1(0));* pap. 4.99 *(978-1-4333-5491-5(8))* Shell Educational Publishing.
—The Princess & the Pea, 1 vol. rev. ed. 2013. (Fiction Readers Ser.). (ENG., Illus.). 20p. (J). (gr. 1-1). pap. 4.99 *(978-1-4333-5489-2(6))* Shell Educational Publishing.
—The Princess & the Pea: A Retelling of Hans Christian Andersen's Story, 1 vol. rev. ed. 2013. (Fiction Readers Ser.). (ENG., Illus.). 20p. (J). (gr. 1-1). pap. 15.96 *(978-1-4807-1145-7(4))* Shell Educational Publishing.
Wuest, Marcia. Twelve Things to Do at Age 12. 2009. (ENG.). 26p. pap. 7.25 *(978-0-521-73733-3(8))* Cambridge Univ. Pr.
Wyatt, Chris. This Is Ant-Man. 2015. (Marvel World of Reading Level 1 Ser.). (J). lib. bdg. 13.55 *(978-0-606-36906-0(6))* Turtleback Bks.
Yang, Gene Luen. Paths & Portals. Holmes, Mike, illus. 2016. (Secret Coders Ser.: 2). (ENG.). 96p. (J). pap. 10.99 *(978-1-62672-076-3(2),* 9781626720763, First Second Bks.) Roaring Brook Pr.
Yang, Maya, et al. Let's Grow! 2010. (Reach for Reading Ser.). (ENG., Illus.). 8p. (C). pap. 7.95 *(978-0-7362-7990-1(3))* CENGAGE Learning.
Yeager, Anne H. American Tall Tales. 2017. (Text Connections Guided Close Reading Ser.). (J). (gr. 2). *(978-1-4900-1839-3(5))* Benchmark Education Co.
A Year Without Rain. (Early Intervention Levels Ser.). 21.42 *(978-0-7362-1048-5(2))* CENGAGE Learning.
Yee, Soo, et al. School Places. 2010. (Reach for Reading Ser.). (ENG., Illus.). 8p. (C). pap. 7.95 *(978-0-7362-7984-0(9))* CENGAGE Learning.
Yellow Overalls: Individual Title Six-Packs. (Literatura 2000 Ser.). (gr. 2-3). 33.00 *(978-0-7635-0247-8(2))* Rigby Education.
Yellow Umbrella, Early Level. (gr. k-2). 999.95 *(978-0-7368-3056-0(1),* Yellow Umbrella Bks.) Capstone Press of Coughlan Cos.
Yes I Can. (Little Book Practice Reader Ser.). (J). *(978-0-8136-0771-9(X))* Modern Curriculum Pr.
Yip & Yap: Consonant y: Level A, 6 vols. (Wright Skills Ser.). 12p. (gr. k-3). 17.95 *(978-0-322-03120-3(6))* Wright Group/McGraw-Hill.
Yolen, Jane. How Do Dinosaurs Laugh Out Loud? Teague, Mark, illus. 2010. (How Do Dinosaurs... Ser.). (ENG.). 16p. (J). (gr. -1-k). bds. 7.99 *(978-0-545-23652-2(5),* Cartwheel Bks.) Scholastic, Inc.
Yolonda's Genius Student Packet. 2004. (J). stu. ed. 12.99 *(978-1-58130-530-2(3))* Novel Units, Inc.
Yomtov, Nel. Adventures in Science. O'Neill, Sean et al, illus. 2012. (Adventures in Science Ser.). (ENG.). 32p. (gr. 3-4). pap. 31.80 *(978-1-4296-8469-9(0));* pap. 190.80 *(978-1-4296-8470-5(4))* Capstone Press of Coughlan Cos. (Graphic Library).
Yomtov, Nel, et al. Adventures in Science. O'Neill, Sean et al, illus. 2012. (Adventures in Science Ser.). (ENG.). 32p. (gr. 3-4). lib. bdg. 91.95 *(978-1-4296-8172-8(1),* Graphic Library) Capstone Press of Coughlan Cos.
Yoon, Salina. Penguin Gets Ready for Bed! Yoon, Salina, illus. 2010. (Illus.). 10p. bds. 7.95 *(978-1-60747-751-8(3),* Pickwick Pr.) Phoenix Bks., Inc.
—Pinwheel. 2013. (ENG., Illus.). 16p. (J). (gr. -1-1). bds. 14.99 *(978-0-316-22176-4(7))* Little, Brown Bks. for Young Readers.
You do ride Well: Individual Title Six-Packs. (gr. 1-2). 25.00 *(978-0-7635-9197-7(1))* Rigby Education.
Young, Annemarie. At the Park. Redshaw, Louise, illus. 2013. (Start Reading Ser.). (ENG.). 24p. (gr. k-1). pap. 41.94 *(978-1-4765-3207-3(9));* pap. 7.95 *(978-1-4765-3191-5(9))* Capstone Press of Coughlan Cos.
—Let's Go Out. Redshaw, Louise, illus. 2013. (Start Reading Ser.). (ENG.). 24p. (gr. k-1). pap. 41.94 *(978-1-4765-3223-3(0));* pap. 7.95 *(978-1-4765-3193-9(5))* Capstone Press of Coughlan Cos.
—Our Castle, 1 vol. Redshaw, Louise, illus. 2013. (Start Reading Ser.). (ENG.). 24p. (gr. k-1). pap. 7.95 *(978-1-4765-3194-6(3));* pap. 41.94 *(978-1-4765-3228-8(1))* Capstone Press of Coughlan Cos.
Young, Caroline, et al, des. First Picture Word Book. 2004. (First Picture Word Book Ser.). (ENG., Illus.). 16p. (J). bds. 11.95 *(978-0-7945-0645-2(3),* Usborne) EDC Publishing.
Young Eagles Take to the Sky. 2005. (Book Treks Ser.). (J). (gr. 3-18). stu. ed. 34.95 *(978-0-673-62842-8(6))* Celebration Pr.
Young Explorers in Science. (J). 105.00 *(978-0-8136-4363-2(5))* Modern Curriculum Pr.
Young, Judy. Digger et Daisy Vont Au Docteur (Digger & Daisy Go to the Doctor) Sullivan, Dana, illus. 2016. (I AM a READER: Digger & Daisy Ser.). (FRE & ENG.). 32p. (J). (gr. k-2). 12.95 *(978-1-62753-949-4(2),* 204172) Sleeping Bear Pr.
—Digger y Daisy Van a la Ciudad (Digger & Daisy Go to the City) Sullivan, Dana, illus. 2016. (I AM a READER: Digger & Daisy Ser.). (SPA & ENG.). 32p. (J). (gr. k-2). 9.99 *(978-1-62753-954-8(9),* 204177) Sleeping Bear Pr.
—Digger y Daisy Van Al Médico (Digger & Daisy Go to the Doctor) Sullivan, Dana, illus. 2016. (I AM a READER: Digger & Daisy Ser.). (SPA & ENG.). 32p. (J). (gr. k-2). 9.99 *(978-1-62753-953-1(0),* 204176) Sleeping Bear Pr.
—Digger y Daisy Van Al Zoológico (Digger & Daisy Go to the Zoo) Sullivan, Dana, illus. 2016. (I AM a READER: Digger & Daisy Ser.). (SPA & ENG.). 32p. (J). (gr. k-2). 9.99 *(978-1-62753-951-7(4),* 204174) Sleeping Bear Pr.
—Digger y Daisy Van de Picnic (Digger & Daisy Go on a Picnic) Sullivan, Dana, illus. 2016. (I AM a READER: Digger & Daisy Ser.). (SPA & ENG.). 32p. (J). (gr. k-2). 9.99 *(978-1-62753-952-4(2),* 204175) Sleeping Bear Pr.
Young, Judy Dockrey. The Missouri Reader. Darnell, Kate, illus. 2010. (Readers Ser.). (ENG.). 96p. (J). 12.95 *(978-1-58536-437-4(1))* Sleeping Bear Pr.
Young Reader Series, 9 bks., Set. (Illus.). (J). (gr. 3-6). lib. bdg. 121.05 *(978-1-56674-914-5(X))* Forest Hse. Publishing Co., Inc.
Yoyo. Learning Words. 2005. 40p. bds. *(978-90-5843-887-4(2))* YoYo Bks.
Yuen, Kevin. The 10 Most Intense College Football Rivalries. 2008. 14.99 *(978-1-55448-545-1(2))* Scholastic Library Publishing.
Yun's Visit: Fourth Grade Guided Comprehension Level K. (On Our Way to English Ser.). (gr. 4-18). 34.50 *(978-0-7578-7146-7(1))* Rigby Education.
Zamosky, Lisa. Fishers Then & Now, 1 vol. 2006. (Primary Source Readers Ser.). (ENG.). 32p. (J). (gr. 1-1). pap. 8.99 *(978-0-7439-9378-4(0))* Shell Educational Publishing.
—Government Leaders Then & Now, 1 vol. 2006. (Primary Source Readers Ser.). (ENG.). 32p. (J). (gr. 2-2). pap. 8.99 *(978-0-7439-9386-9(1))* Shell Educational Publishing.
—Greece, 1 vol. 2007. (Primary Source Readers Ser.). (ENG.). 32p. (J). (gr. 5-5). pap. 8.99 *(978-0-7439-0434-6(6))* Shell Educational Publishing.
—India, 1 vol. 2007. (Primary Source Readers Ser.). (ENG.). 32p. (J). (gr. 5-5). pap. 8.99 *(978-0-7439-0430-8(3))* Shell Educational Publishing.
—Investigating Simple Organisms, 1 vol. 2007. (Science Readers Ser.). (ENG., Illus.). 32p. (J). (gr. 4-4). pap. 8.99 *(978-0-7439-0587-9(3))* Shell Educational Publishing.
—Mansa Musa: Leader of Mali, 1 vol. 2007. (Primary Source Readers Ser.). (ENG.). 32p. (J). (gr. 4-4). pap. 8.99 *(978-0-7439-0439-1(7))* Shell Educational Publishing.
—Sanitation Workers Then & Now, 1 vol. 2006. (Primary Source Readers Ser.). (ENG.). 32p. (J). (gr. 2-2). pap. 8.99 *(978-0-7439-9382-1(9))* Shell Educational Publishing.
—Sub-Saharan Africa, 1 vol. 2007. (Primary Source Readers Ser.). (ENG.). 32p. (J). (gr. 5-5). pap. 8.99 *(978-0-7439-0438-4(9))* Shell Educational Publishing.
—World War I, 1 vol. 2007. (Primary Source Readers Ser.). (ENG.). 32p. (J). (gr. 5-5). pap. 8.99 *(978-0-7439-0664-7(0))* Shell Educational Publishing.
Zamosky, Lisa & Conklin, Wendy. World War II, 1 vol. 2007. (Primary Source Readers Ser.). (ENG.). 32p. (J). (gr. 5-5). pap. 8.99 *(978-0-7439-0668-5(3))* Shell Educational Publishing.
Zamosky, Lisa & National Geographic Learning Staff. Farmers Then & Now. 2010. (ENG., Illus.). 32p. (C). (gr. 2-2). pap. 14.95 *(978-0-7439-9377-7(2))* National Geographic School Publishing, Inc.
Zemke, Deborah. The Curse of Einstein's Pencil. 2017. (Bea Garcia Ser.: 2). lib. bdg. 18.40 ***(978-0-606-40084-8(2))*** Turtleback Bks.
Zepeda, Gwendolyn. I Kick the Ball: Pateo el Balón. Ventura, Gabriela Baeza, tr. Torrecilla, Pablo, illus. 2011. (SPA & ENG.). 32p. (J). (gr. -1-3). 16.95 *(978-1-55885-688-2(9),* Piñata Books) Arte Publico Pr.
Zephaniah, Benjamin. Being Cool. Bellemare, Paule Trudel, illus. 2014. (Collins Big Cat Progress Ser.). (ENG.). 32p. (J). (gr. 5-6). pap. 7.99 *(978-0-00-751929-3(X))* HarperCollins Pubs. Ltd. GBR. Dist: Independent Pubs. Group.
Zepp, Gene W. Return of the Pied Piper of Hamelin. 2011. 48p. pap. 21.99 *(978-1-4628-7007-3(4))* Xlibris Corp.
Ziefert, Harriet. Rhyming Words. Kido, Yukiko, illus. 2007. (I'm Going to Read(r) Ser.). (ENG.). 64p. (J). (gr. -1-1). pap. 5.95 *(978-1-4027-5059-5(5))* Sterling Publishing Co., Inc.
Ziefert, Harriet & National Geographic Learning Staff. I'm Going to Washington to Visit the President. Roitman, Tanya, illus. 2010. (Rise & Shine Ser.). (ENG.). 24p. (C). (gr. -1-k). pap. 6.95 *(978-1-4027-3408-3(5))* National Geographic School Publishing, Inc.
Zobel, Derek. Bucket Trucks. 2009. (Blastoff! Readers Ser.). (ENG., Illus.). 24p. (J). (gr. k-3). 20.00 *(978-0-531-21707-8(8),* Children's Pr.) Scholastic Library Publishing.
—Diggers. 2009. (Blastoff! Readers Ser.). (ENG., Illus.). 24p. (J). (gr. k-3). 20.00 *(978-0-531-21708-5(6),* Children's Pr.) Scholastic Library Publishing.
—F-22 Raptors. 2008. (Torque Ser.). (ENG.). 24p. (J). (gr. 3-7). 20.00 *(978-0-531-21645-3(4),* Children's Pr.) Scholastic Library Publishing.
Zoehfeld, Kathleen Weidner. Dinosaurs (1 Hardcover/1 CD) 2016. (National Geographic Readers: Pre-Reader Ser.). (ENG.). (J). *(978-1-4301-2110-7(6))* Live Oak Media.
—Dinosaurs (1 Paperback/1 CD) 2016. (National Geographic Readers: Pre-Reader Ser.). (ENG.). (J). pap. *(978-1-4301-2109-1(2))* Live Oak Media.
Zoo-phonics Quick Tests for the Classroom. 2004. cd-rom *(978-1-886441-41-5(3))* Zoo-phonics, Inc.
Zoom In! Level M, 6 vols. 128p. (gr. 2-3). 40.50 *(978-0-7699-1032-1(7))* Shortland Pubns. (U. S. A.) Inc.
The Zoomer: KinderWords Individual Title Six-Packs. (Kinderstarters Ser.). 8p. (gr. -1-1). 21.00 *(978-0-7635-8709-3(5))* Rigby Education.
Zorzi, Gina & Sánchez, Lucía M. Desiertos: This Is a Desert. 2011. (2G Ecosistemas Ser.). (SPA.). 36p. (J). (gr. k-2). pap. 6.99 *(978-1-61541-424-6(X))* American Reading Co.
1 Potato, 2 Potato: Individual Title Six-Packs. (Literatura 2000 Ser.). (gr. 2-3). 33.00 *(978-0-7635-0266-9(9))* Rigby Education.
21st Century Debates, 24 bks. 2004. 650.88 *(978-0-7398-6472-2(6))* Harcourt Schl. Pubs.

READING

Here are entered books on methods of teaching reading and general books on the art of reading. Works on teaching retarded readers are entered under Reading—Remedial Teaching. books on the cultural aspects of reading and general discussions of books to read are entered under Books and Reading.

see also Books and Reading

ABDO Publishing Company Staff. Rhyme Time. 2005. (Rhyme Time Ser.: 46). (ENG.). 24p. (J). (gr. k-3). lib. bdg. 1113.66 *(978-1-59197-773-5(8),* SandCastle) ABDO Publishing Co.
Acid Rain: Level M, 6 vols. (Wonder Worldtm Ser.). 16p. 34.95 *(978-0-7802-2887-0(1))* Wright Group/McGraw-Hill.
Action Sports, 12 vols. 2005. (Action Sports Ser.). (Illus.). 32p. (gr. 4-6). 308.00 *(978-0-7910-7532-6(X),* Chelsea Hse.) Facts On File, Inc.
Adding English/ESL Support. 2004. (Scott Foresman Reading Ser.). (gr. 2-18). 109.15 *(978-0-328-03065-1(1));* (gr. 3-18). 109.50 *(978-0-328-03066-8(X));* (gr. 4-18). 109.50 *(978-0-328-03067-5(8));* (gr. 5-18). 109.50 *(978-0-328-03068-2(6))* Addison-Wesley Educational Pubs., Inc.
The Adventures of Tutankhamen: Level T, Group 2, 6 vols. (Sunshine Ser.). 48p. 44.95 *(978-0-7802-4175-6(4))* Wright Group/McGraw-Hill.
Afflerbach, Peter. Seeing Is Believing. l.t. ed. 2004. (gr. 4-18). 70.40 *(978-0-328-03937-1(3),* Scott Foresman) Addison-Wesley Educational Pubs., Inc.
After the Dinosaurs: Level P, 6 vols. (Wonder Worldtm Ser.). 48p. 39.95 *(978-0-7802-7084-8(3))* Wright Group/McGraw-Hill.
Against the Odds, 6 vols. (Wildcats Ser.). 32p. (gr. 2-8). *(978-0-322-02443-4(9))* Wright Group/McGraw-Hill.
Alien Monchers: Level 4, 6 vols. (Fluency Strand Ser.). (gr. 4-8). 45.00 *(978-1-4045-1222-1(5))* Wright Group/McGraw-Hill.
All about Ants, 6 vols. (Book2WebTM Ser.). (gr. 4-8). 36.50 *(978-0-322-02977-4(5))* Wright Group/McGraw-Hill.
All about Maps: Level R, 6 vols. (Wonder Worldtm Ser.). 48p. 44.95 *(978-0-7802-7074-9(6))* Wright Group/McGraw-Hill.
All Kinds of Bears, 6 vols. (Book2WebTM Ser.). (gr. 4-8). 36.50 *(978-0-322-02972-9(4))* Wright Group/McGraw-Hill.

PQR

All Through the Year, 6 vols. (Multicultural Programs Ser.). 16p. (gr. 1-3). 24.95 *(978-0-7802-9202-4(2))* Wright Group/McGraw-Hill.
Alligator Alley, 6 vols., Vol. 3. (Woodland Mysteriestm Ser.). 133p. (gr. 3-7). 42.50 *(978-0-322-02372-7(6))* Wright Group/McGraw-Hill.
Alliteration Configuration. 2006. (Illus.). 60p. (J). 24.99 *(978-0-9790434-0-6(9))* Jamiram Publishing.
Amaze Us!, 6 vols. (Wildcats Ser.). 32p. (gr. 2-8). *(978-0-322-02442-7(0))* Wright Group/McGraw-Hill.
Amazing Maps: Level Q, 6 vols. (Wonder Worldtm Ser.). 48p. 39.95 *(978-0-7802-2945-7(2))* Wright Group/McGraw-Hill.
American Literature. 2004. (gr. 11-18). cd-rom *(978-0-618-30390-8(1), 2-04295)* Holt McDougal.
American Literature: EEdition Plus Online (1 Year License) 2004. (gr. 11-18). *(978-0-618-31043-2(6), 2-04463)* Holt McDougal.
American Literature: EEdition Plus Online (6 Year License) 2004. (gr. 11-18). *(978-0-618-30836-1(9), 2-04342)* Holt McDougal.
American Literature: The InterActive Reader Plus. 2004. (Language of Literature Ser.). (gr. 11-18). *(978-0-618-30990-0(X), 2-04430)* Holt McDougal.
American Literature: The InterActive Reader Plus for English Learners. 2004. (gr. 11-18). *(978-0-618-31022-7(3), 2-04444)* Holt McDougal.
American Literature: The InterActive Reader Plus with Additional Support. 2004. (Language of Literature Ser.). (gr. 11-18). *(978-0-618-31007-4(X), 2-04437)* Holt McDougal.
And I Mean It, Stanley. 2003. 22.95 *(978-0-673-75905-4(9))* Celebration Pr.
Anderson, Neil J. Active Skills for Reading, Bk. 3. pap. 31.95 *(978-0-8384-7048-0(3))* Cengage Heinle.
Angela's Ashes: Response Journal. 2003. 40p. (YA). *(978-1-58049-991-0(0), RJ91)* Prestwick Hse., Inc.
Animal Sounds: Big Book: Level C. (Visions Ser.). 8p. 20.95 *(978-0-322-00308-8(3))* Wright Group/McGraw-Hill.
Animal Tracks: Level C, 6 vols. (Wonder Worldtm Ser.). 16p. 24.95 *(978-0-7802-1211-4(8))* Wright Group/McGraw-Hill.
Animals Grow: Level J. (Wonder Worldtm Ser.). 16p. 26.50 *(978-0-7802-3472-7(3))*; 29.95 *(978-0-7802-1191-9(X))* Wright Group/McGraw-Hill.
The Ants & the Grasshopper: R-Controlled Review: Level C, 6 vols. (Wright Skills Ser.). 16p. (gr. k-3). 26.50 *(978-0-322-01501-2(4))* Wright Group/McGraw-Hill.
Appleton-Smith, Laura & Blackaby, Susan. Butterfly Life Cycle. 2014. (Book to Remember Ser.). (ENG., Illus.). 26p. (J). pap. 8.95 *(978-1-60541-153-8(1), Books To Remember)* Flyleaf Publishing.
Appointment with Action: 6 Each of 1 Anthology, 6 vols. (Wildcats Ser.). 32p. (gr. 2-8). *(978-0-322-00597-6(3))* Wright Group/McGraw-Hill.
Are they here Yet? Short Vowel e: Level A, 6 vols. (Wright Skills Ser.). 12p. (gr. k-3). 17.95 *(978-0-322-03121-0(4))* Wright Group/McGraw-Hill.
Are You a Ladybug?, 6 vols. (Sunshinetm Ser.). 16p. (gr. k-18). 29.50 *(978-0-7802-5430-5(9))* Wright Group/McGraw-Hill.
Around the World in Eighty Days: Response Journal. 2003. 40p. (YA). *(978-1-58049-987-3(2), RJ87)* Prestwick Hse., Inc.
Ashton, Christine. The Genie of the Bike Lamp: Level P, 6 vols. (Mountain Peaks Ser.). 128p. (gr. 6-18). 36.95 *(978-0-322-05892-7(9))* Wright Group/McGraw-Hill.
At Camp with Gramps: Final Blends -mp, -st: Level B, 6 vols. (Wright Skills Ser.). 16p. (gr. k-3). 17.95 *(978-0-322-01463-3(8))* Wright Group/McGraw-Hill.
Athans, Sandra K. & Parente, Robin W. The Common Core Readiness Guide to Reading. 2014. (Common Core Readiness Guide to Reading Ser.). 80p. (YA). (gr. 5-8). 263.60 *(978-1-4777-7599-8(4), Rosen Reference)* Rosen Publishing Group, Inc., The.
Au, Kathryn. Super Qar for Test-Wise Students: Grade 1, 5-Pack, 5 vols. (gr. 1-8). 36.95 *(978-0-322-09107-8(1))* Wright Group/McGraw-Hill.
—Super Qar for Test-Wise Students: Grade 2 5-Pack, 5 vols. (gr. 1-8). 36.95 *(978-0-322-09108-5(X))* Wright Group/McGraw-Hill.
—Super Qar for Test-Wise Students: Grade 4 5-Pack, 5 vols. (gr. 1-8). 36.95 *(978-0-322-09111-5(X))* Wright Group/McGraw-Hill.
—Super Qar for Test-Wise Students: Grade 5 5-Pack, 5 vols. (gr. 1-8). 36.95 *(978-0-322-09112-2(8))* Wright Group/McGraw-Hill.
—Super Qar for Test-Wise Students: Grade 6 5-Pack, 5 vols. (gr. 1-8). 36.95 *(978-0-322-09113-9(6))* Wright Group/McGraw-Hill.
—Super Qar for Test-Wise Students: Grade 7 5-Pack, 5 vols. (gr. 1-8). 36.95 *(978-0-322-09114-6(4))* Wright Group/McGraw-Hill.
—Super Qar for Test-Wise Students: Grade 8 5-Pack, 5 vols. (gr. 1-8). 36.95 *(978-0-322-09115-3(2))* Wright Group/McGraw-Hill.
—Super Qar for Test-Wise Students: Grade 8 Kit. (gr. 1-8). 264.95 *(978-0-322-09222-8(1))* Wright Group/McGraw-Hill.
Auntie Dot's Pot, 6 vols. 8p. (gr. k-1). 21.50 *(978-0-322-02082-5(4))* Wright Group/McGraw-Hill.
Auntie Jan's Plan, 6 vols. 8p. (gr. k-1). 21.50 *(978-0-322-02084-9(0))* Wright Group/McGraw-Hill.
Baby Animals at Home: Level F. 16p. 31.50 *(978-0-322-00372-9(5))* Wright Group/McGraw-Hill.
A Bad Job? Consonant b: Level A, 6 vols. (Wright Skills Ser.). 12p. (gr. k-3). 17.95 *(978-0-322-03113-5(3))* Wright Group/McGraw-Hill.
Barlow, Helen. Easy Read with Grandma Read: Book 1, Stage 3. 2009. (Illus.). 48p. pap. *(978-1-84748-507-6(3))* Athena Pr.
Barney's Horse. 2003. 22.95 *(978-0-673-75907-8(5))* Celebration Pr.
The Baseball Heroes, 6 vols. (Woodland Mysteriestm Ser.). 133p. (gr. 3-7). 42.50 *(978-0-7802-7931-5(X))* Wright Group/McGraw-Hill.
A Basket Full of Surprises: Take-Home Book. 2005. (Emergent Library: Vol. 2). (J). (gr. -1-1). 12.60 *(978-0-8215-7255-9(5))* Sadlier, William H. Inc.
Basketball: Level A, 6 vols. (Wonder Worldtm Ser.). 16p. 24.95 *(978-0-7802-1029-5(8))* Wright Group/McGraw-Hill.
The Bath. (Little Book Practice Reader). (J). *(978-0-8136-5340-2(1))* Modern Curriculum Pr.
Bath Time: Level A, 6 vols. (Wonder Worldtm Ser.). 16p. 24.95 *(978-0-7802-1195-7(2))* Wright Group/McGraw-Hill.
The Battle of Bowling Street: Level 4, 6 vols. (Fluency Strand Ser.). (gr. 4-8). 45.00 *(978-1-4045-1224-5(1))* Wright Group/McGraw-Hill.
Be a Plant Scientist: Level L, 6 vols. (Take-Twostm Ser.). 16p. 36.95 *(978-0-322-03403-7(5))* Wright Group/McGraw-Hill.
Be Quiet!, 6 Packs. (Chiquilibros Ser.). (gr. k-1). 23.00 *(978-0-7635-0429-8(7))* Rigby Education.
Beautiful Flowers: Level B, 6 vols. (Wonder Worldtm Ser.). 16p. 24.95 *(978-0-7802-1980-9(5))* Wright Group/McGraw-Hill.
Beck, Isabel L., et al. Julian's Glorious Summer. 2003. (Trophies Ser.). (gr. 3-18). 50.40 *(978-0-15-319277-7(1))* Harcourt Schl. Pubs.
The Bee & the Bug, 6 vols. 8p. (gr. k-1). 21.50 *(978-0-322-02076-4(X))* Wright Group/McGraw-Hill.
The Bee Sting: Digraphs -ck, -ng: Level B, 6 vols. (Wright Skills Ser.). 16p. (gr. k-3). 17.95 *(978-0-322-01476-3(X))* Wright Group/McGraw-Hill.
Behind the Rocks: Level E, 6 vols. (Wonder Worldtm Ser.). 16p. 24.95 *(978-0-7802-1030-1(1))* Wright Group/McGraw-Hill.
Bell, Megan. Brody the Reading Tutor. 2013. 34p. 16.95 *(978-0-9889775-0-1(8))* Bell, Megan.
Benchmark Education Co., LLC. Up in the Sky Big Book. 2014. (Shared Reading Foundations Ser.). (J). (gr. -1). *(978-1-4509-9446-0(6))* Benchmark Education Co.
—We Need a Seed Big Book. 2014. (Shared Reading Foundations Ser.). (J). (gr. -1). *(978-1-4509-9449-1(0))* Benchmark Education Co.
—What Can We Share? Big Book. 2014. (Shared Reading Foundations Ser.). (J). (gr. -1). *(978-1-4509-9424-8(5))* Benchmark Education Co.
—What Do Bears Eat? Big Book. 2014. (Shared Reading Foundations Ser.). (J). (gr. -1). *(978-1-4509-9433-0(4))* Benchmark Education Co.
—What Is That Sound? Big Book. 2014. (Shared Reading Foundations Ser.). (J). (gr. -1). *(978-1-4509-9437-8(7))* Benchmark Education Co.
Benchmark Education Company, LLC Staff. SpiralUp Reading Passages. 2009. (SpiralUp Phonics Ser.). (J). cd-rom *(978-1-4108-8534-0(8))* Benchmark Education Co.
Benchmark Education Company, LLC Staff, compiled by. Comprehension Strategy Posters. 2008. (Comprehension Strategy Posters Ser.). (J). (gr. 3-5). 199.00 *(978-1-4108-8451-0(1))* Benchmark Education Co.
The Best Children in the World: Big Book: Level H. Group 1. (Story Box Ser.). 16p. 31.50 *(978-0-322-00324-8(5))* Wright Group/McGraw-Hill.
Betty Bline, 6 vols. 8p. (gr. k-1). 21.50 *(978-0-322-02069-6(7))* Wright Group/McGraw-Hill.
Between the Tides: Level F, 6 vols. (Wonder Worldtm Ser.). 16p. 29.95 *(978-0-7802-1982-3(1))* Wright Group/McGraw-Hill.
Bevan, Clare. The Great Big Book of Reading Kindergarten Costco. 2008. (J). pap. *(978-1-59566-622-2(2))* QEB Publishing Inc.
Beyond the Beyond, 6 vols. (Wildcats Ser.). 32p. (gr. 2-8). *(978-0-322-02444-1(7))* Wright Group/McGraw-Hill.
Bickel, Karla. The Reading Machine. Bickel, Karla, illus. l.t. ed. 2004. (Illus.). 16p. (J). (gr. -1-6). pap. 5.00 *(978-1-891452-15-4(0), 9)* Heart Arbor Bks.
Big & Green: Level A, 6 vols. (Wonder Worldtm Ser.). 16p. 24.95 *(978-0-7802-1031-8(X))* Wright Group/McGraw-Hill.
Big & Little: Level C. Group 1. (Sunshine Ser.). 8p. 20.95 *(978-0-7802-5720-7(0))* Wright Group/McGraw-Hill.
The Big Bigfoot Debate. 2004. (Literacy Think-Togethers Ser.). 16-24p. (gr. 2-3). pap. 39.50 *(978-0-322-06381-5(7))* Wright Group/McGraw-Hill.
Big Blank Piece of Paper. (J). (gr. 2). pap. 12.79 *(978-0-673-80022-0(9), Scott Foresman)* Addison Wesley Schl.
Big Enough: Level F. (Visions Ser.). 8p. 20.95 *(978-0-322-00312-5(1))* Wright Group/McGraw-Hill.
The Big, Fun Hat: Review of Consonants, Short Vowels, Word Families: Level A, 6 vols. (Wright Skills Ser.). 12p. (gr. k-3). 17.95 *(978-0-322-03125-8(7))* Wright Group/McGraw-Hill.
The Big Round Up: Big Book: Level I. (Wonder Worldtm Ser.). 16p. 26.50 *(978-0-7802-3477-2(4))* Wright Group/McGraw-Hill.
The Big Roundup: Level I, 6 vols. (Wonder Worldtm Ser.). 16p. 29.95 *(978-0-7802-1245-9(2))* Wright Group/McGraw-Hill.
The Big Tan Rat: Short Vowel Word Family Review: Level B, 6 vols. (Wright Skills Ser.). 16p. (gr. k-3). 17.95 *(978-0-322-01458-9(1))* Wright Group/McGraw-Hill.
Bigger & Bigger: Big Book: Level C. 8p. 20.95 *(978-0-322-00355-2(5))* Wright Group/McGraw-Hill.
A Bigger Barger: Level I. Group 1. (Story Box Ser.). 16p. 31.50 *(978-0-322-02464-9(1))* Wright Group/McGraw-Hill.
Bilingual Take-Home Books Collection. 2005. (YA). (gr. -1-1). 113.40 *(978-0-8215-1209-8(9))* Sadlier, William H. Inc.
Billy Drake's Cake, 6 vols. 8p. (gr. k-1). 21.50 *(978-0-322-02085-6(9))* Wright Group/McGraw-Hill.
Bird Beaks: Big Book: Level K. (Wonder Worldtm Ser.). 16p. 26.50 *(978-0-7802-3473-4(1))* Wright Group/McGraw-Hill.
Bird Beaks: Level K, 6 vols. (Wonder Worldtm Ser.). 16p. 34.95 *(978-0-7802-1197-1(9))* Wright Group/McGraw-Hill.
Blachowicz, Camille L. Z. Reading Fluency. 2003. (JT: READING RATE & FLUENCY Ser.). (ENG.). (gr. 6-12). 80p. spiral bd. 24.64 *(978-0-07-830908-3(5), 0078309085)*; 160p. per. 17.04 *(978-0-07-845706-7(8), 0078457068)* McGraw-Hill Education.
—Reading Fluency: Reader. 2003. (JT: READING RATE & FLUENCY Ser.). (ENG.). 74p. (gr. 6-12). pap. 24.64 *(978-0-07-830910-6(7), 0078309107)* McGraw-Hill Cos., The.
—Reading Fluency: Reader. 2003. (JT: READING RATE & FLUENCY Ser.). (ENG.). 74p. (gr. 6-12). pap. 24.64 *(978-0-07-830909-0(3), 0078309093)* McGraw-Hill Education.
—Reading Fluency: Reader. 2003. (JT: READING RATE & FLUENCY Ser.). (ENG.). 80p. (gr. 6-12). spiral bd. 24.64 *(978-0-07-845698-5(3), 0078456983)* SRA/McGraw-Hill.
—Reading Fluency: Reader's Record. 2003. (JT: READING RATE & FLUENCY Ser.). (ENG.). 160p. (gr. 6-12). per. 17.04 *(978-0-07-845702-9(5), 0078457025)* McGraw-Hill Education.
—Reading Fluency, Level C: Reader's Record. 2003. (JT: READING RATE & FLUENCY Ser.). (ENG.). 160p. (gr. 6-12). per. 17.04 *(978-0-07-845700-5(9), 0078457009)* McGraw-Hill Education.
—Reading Fluency, Level F. 2003. (JT: READING RATE & FLUENCY Ser.). (ENG.). 80p. (gr. 6-12). spiral bd. 24.64 *(978-0-07-830911-3(5), 0078309115)* McGraw-Hill Education.
—Reading Fluency, Level G. 2003. (JT: READING RATE & FLUENCY Ser.). (ENG.). 160p. (gr. 6-12). per. 17.04 *(978-0-07-845705-0(X), 007845705X)* McGraw-Hill Education.
—Reading Fluency, Level G: Reader. 2003. (JT: READING RATE & FLUENCY Ser.). (ENG.). 74p. (gr. 6-12). spiral bd. 24.64 *(978-0-07-845699-2(1), 0078456991)* McGraw-Hill Education.
Blanche, Lynn. What Makes It Go? 2005. (IOpeners Ser.). (Illus.). 8p. (J). pap. 7.56 *(978-0-7652-5138-1(8))* Celebration Pr.
The Blue Fruit Pie: Digraphs ie, ue: Level B, 6 vols. (Wright Skills Ser.). 16p. (gr. k-3). 17.95 *(978-0-322-01481-7(6))* Wright Group/McGraw-Hill.
Bobby Fling, 6 vols. 8p. (gr. k-1). 21.50 *(978-0-322-02068-9(9))* Wright Group/McGraw-Hill.
Boehm, Richard G., et al. Reading Support & Test Preparation: A Child's Place. 2003. (Harcourt Brace Social Studies). (gr. k-7). 27.00 *(978-0-15-312374-0(5))* Harcourt Schl. Pubs.
Boggywooga: Level I. Group 1. (Sunshine Ser.). 16p. 31.50 *(978-0-7802-5754-2(5))* Wright Group/McGraw-Hill.
Bogle's Feet: Level L. Group 1, 6 vols. (Sunshine Ser.). 16p. 36.50 *(978-0-7802-5790-0(1))* Wright Group/McGraw-Hill.
Bonnell, Kris. Clouds Tell the Weather. 2007. (J). pap. 5.95 *(978-1-933727-47-9(0))* Reading Reading Bks., LLC.
—A Friend for Jellyfish. 2006. (J). pap. 3.95 *(978-1-933727-28-8(4))* Reading Reading Bks., LLC.
—A Garden Is Fun. 2006. (J). pap. 5.95 *(978-1-933727-37-0(3))* Reading Reading Bks., LLC.
—A House for Squirrel. 2007. (J). pap. 5.95 *(978-1-933727-46-2(2))* Reading Reading Bks., LLC.
—A Walk with Dad. 2006. (J). pap. 5.95 *(978-1-933727-43-1(8))* Reading Reading Bks., LLC.
Book Treks Add-on Pack, Vol. 4. 2005. (Book Treks Ser.). (J). (gr. 4-8). 100.95 *(978-0-673-61956-3(7))* Modern Curriculum Pr.
Books Only Package. 2005. (Little Celebrations Picture/Text & Literacy Cards Ser.). (J). (gr. k-3). 510.95 *(978-0-673-77194-0(6))*; 551.95 *(978-0-673-77195-7(4))*; 633.50 *(978-0-673-77865-9(7))* Celebration Pr.
Boten, Wallace. From Farm to Store, 6 vols., Set. 2003. (Phonics Readers 1-36 Ser.). (ENG.). 8p. (gr. k-1). pap. 29.70 *(978-0-7368-3216-8(5), Phonics Readers)* Capstone Press of Coughlan Cos.
A Bottle Garden: Level F, 6 vols. (Wonder Worldtm Ser.). 16p. 29.95 *(978-0-7802-1984-7(8))* Wright Group/McGraw-Hill.
Boyd, Amanda. A Trip Around Town: Learning to Add 3 One-Digit Numbers. 2009. (Math for the REAL World Ser.). 12p. (gr. 1-2). pap. 5.90 *(978-0-8239-8915-7(1), Rosen Classroom)* Rosen Publishing Group, Inc., The.
Bozo: Level I, 6 vols. (Wonder Worldtm Ser.). 16p. 29.95 *(978-0-7802-4561-7(X))* Wright Group/McGraw-Hill.
Braun, Cheskel. Learn to Read, Vol. 1. 2006. (YID.). (J). per. 12.00 *(978-0-9774302-0-8(0))* Braun Pubns.
Bread Sets: 1 Each of 3 Big Books. (Sunshinetm Science Ser.). (gr. 1-2). 111.50 *(978-0-7802-2808-5(1))* Wright Group/McGraw-Hill.
Bread Sets: 1 Each of 3 Student Books. (Sunshinetm Science Ser.). (gr. 1-2). 20.95 *(978-0-7802-2809-2(X))* Wright Group/McGraw-Hill.
The Bridge: Level B. Group 2. (Story Box Ser.). 8p. 20.95 *(978-0-7802-9364-9(9))* Wright Group/McGraw-Hill.
Bridge, Chris. Read to Me! 2015. (ENG., Illus.). 32p. (J). 19.95 *(978-1-931721-12-7(2), 9781931721127)* Bright Sky Pr.
Bridges: 6 Each of 1 Anthology, 6 vols. (Wildcats Ser.). 32p. (gr. 2-8). *(978-0-322-02425-0(0))* Wright Group/McGraw-Hill.
Bridges-Across the Gap: Level O, 6 vols. (Wonder Worldtm Ser.). 48p. 39.95 *(978-0-7802-2963-1(0))* Wright Group/McGraw-Hill.
Bright & Beyond - Reading. 2004. (J). *(978-0-9726170-8-6(6))* Pal Toys, LLC.
Brocker, Susan. Across the Oregon Trail: Level R, 6 vols. (Mountain Peaks Ser.). 128p. (gr. 6-18). 36.95 *(978-0-322-05890-3(2))* Wright Group/McGraw-Hill.
Broken Bones, 6 vols. (Sunshinetm Science Ser.). 24p. (gr. 1-2). 31.50 *(978-0-7802-0300-6(3))*; 36.95 *(978-0-7802-0551-2(0))* Wright Group/McGraw-Hill.
Brooks, Bearl. Jumbo Reading Yearbook: Kindergarten. (Jumbo Reading Ser.). 96p. (J). 15.95 *(978-0-8209-0011-7(7), B-JECR-R)* ESP, Inc.
Brotherly Love Little Book: Early Reading Fluency, Level A. 2004. (ENG.). pap. 6.00 *(978-0-7398-8158-3(2))* Steck-Vaughn.
Bryan, Lynn. Where Do Plants Grow? 2005. (IOpeners Ser.). (Illus.). 8p. (J). pap. 7.56 *(978-0-7652-5145-9(0))* Celebration Pr.
Bryant, Sheree, et al. The Glencoe Reader World Literature. 2003. (Glencoe Literature Grade 7 Ser.). (ENG., Illus.). 300p. (gr. 10-12). stu. ed., per. 8.92 *(978-0-07-845934-4(6), 0078459346)* McGraw-Hill Higher Education.
A Bug in a Rug: Consonants c, l, r; Short Vowel u word families: Level A, 6 vols. (Wright Skills Ser.). 12p. (gr. k-3). 17.95 *(978-0-322-01452-7(2))* Wright Group/McGraw-Hill.
Bug-Watching: Big Book: Level B, 6 vols. 8p. 20.95 *(978-0-7802-9744-9(X))* Wright Group/McGraw-Hill.
Building Dreams, Grade 3: American Readers. (J). tchr. ed., wbk. ed. *(978-0-669-05019-6(9))*; wbk. ed. *(978-0-669-05018-9(0))* Houghton Mifflin Harcourt School Pubs.
Building Dreams Reading Kit: American Readers. (J). (gr. 3). *(978-0-669-05026-4(1))* Houghton Mifflin Harcourt School Pubs.
Building Things, 6 vols. (Sunshinetm Ser.). 16p. (gr. k-18). 29.50 *(978-0-7802-5420-6(1))* Wright Group/McGraw-Hill.
Built for Speed Classroom Library. (gr. 4-18). lib. bdg. 24.95 *(978-0-7368-8949-0(3))* Red Brick Learning.
Bump! Bump! Bump!, 6 vols. 8p. (gr. k-1). 21.50 *(978-0-322-02086-3(7))* Wright Group/McGraw-Hill.
The Burglars' Ball: Level Q, 6 vols. (Wonder Worldtm Ser.). 48p. 39.95 *(978-0-7802-2961-7(4))* Wright Group/McGraw-Hill.
The Bush Telegraph: Level T. Group 2, 6 vols. (Sunshine Ser.). 48p. 44.95 *(978-0-7802-4178-7(9))* Wright Group/McGraw-Hill.
Buster: Level E. 8p. 20.95 *(978-0-7802-9742-5(3))* Wright Group/McGraw-Hill.
Buster MCluster: Level G. (Wonder Worldtm Ser.). 16p. 26.50 *(978-0-7802-2828-3(6))* Wright Group/McGraw-Hill.
Busy Bees: 1 Big Book, 6 Each of 1 Student Book, & 1 Cassette. (Song Box Ser.). (gr. 1-2). 68.95 *(978-0-7802-3203-7(8))* Wright Group/McGraw-Hill.
Butler, Heather, ed. Reading for Fluency Resource Guide: Learning to Read Text Accurately & Quickly. 2005. (Reading for Fluency Ser.). (Illus.). 64p. (J). pap. 12.99 *(978-1-59198-166-4(2), 4239)* Creative Teaching Pr., Inc.
The Buzz in the Box: Consonant z: Level A, 6 vols. (Wright Skills Ser.). 12p. (gr. k-3). 17.95 *(978-0-322-03124-1(9))* Wright Group/McGraw-Hill.
Buzzing Files: Level C. Group 1. (Sunshine Ser.). 8p. 20.95 *(978-0-7802-5721-4(9))* Wright Group/McGraw-Hill.
By the Pond: Open Vowel Pattern, Words Ending in y with Long i Sound, Ending in o, Ending in e: Level B, 6 vols. (Wright Skills Ser.). 16p. (gr. k-3). 26.50 *(978-0-322-01470-1(0))* Wright Group/McGraw-Hill.
Can I have a Cat? Consonant c: Level A, 6 vols. (Wright Skills Ser.). 12p. (gr. k-3). 17.95 *(978-0-322-03117-3(6))* Wright Group/McGraw-Hill.
Can Kim & Kip Play? Consonant k: Level A, 6 vols. (Wright Skills Ser.). 12p. (gr. k-3). 17.95 *(978-0-322-03132-6(X))* Wright Group/McGraw-Hill.
Carbo Recorded Books: Primary/Intermediate. 2003. (Illus.). (J). (gr. 2-5). pap. 729.00 incl. audio *(978-1-883186-30-2(7), NPIS9)* National Reading Styles Institute, Inc.
Carey Molter. Ate As in Skate, 1 vol. 2003. (Word Families Set 8 Ser.: Vol. 8). (ENG., Illus.). 24p. (J). (gr. k-3). lib. bdg. 24.21 *(978-1-59197-271-6(X))* ABDO Publishing Co.
Carson-Dellosa Publishing Staff. Reading Comprehension, Grade 1. 2010. (Home Workbooks Ser.). (ENG.). 64p. (gr. 1-1). pap. 4.49 *(978-1-60418-787-8(5))* Carson-Dellosa Publishing, LLC.
—Reading Comprehension, Grade 2. 2010. (Home Workbooks Ser.). (ENG.). 64p. (gr. 2-2). pap. 4.49 *(978-1-60418-794-6(8))* Carson-Dellosa Publishing, LLC.
—Reading Comprehension, Grade 3. 2010. (Home Workbooks Ser.). (ENG.). 64p. (gr. 3-3). pap. 4.49 *(978-1-60418-800-4(6))* Carson-Dellosa Publishing, LLC.
Carson, J. You Can Do It! Learning the Y Sound. 2009. (PowerPhonics Ser.). 24p. (gr. 1-1). 39.90 *(978-1-60851-481-6(1), PowerKids Pr.)* Rosen Publishing Group, Inc., The.
Castellano Boyum, Marie. More Simply Super Storytimes: Programming Ideas for Ages 3-6. 2006. (Illus.). 172p. (J). (gr. -1-1). per. 16.95 *(978-1-932146-29-5(6), Upstart Bks.)* Highsmith Inc.
Catching Glimpses: American Readers. (J). (gr. 3). *(978-0-669-05028-8(8))*; *(978-0-669-05027-1(X))*; wbk. ed. *(978-0-669-05032-5(6))* Houghton Mifflin Harcourt School Pubs.
Cats: Level F, 6 vols. (Wonder Worldtm Ser.). 16p. 29.95 *(978-0-7802-2889-4(8))* Wright Group/McGraw-Hill.
A Cat's Day: Level A, 6 vols. 8p. 20.95 *(978-0-322-00356-9(3))* Wright Group/McGraw-Hill.
Celebrate Reading! (J). pap., stu. ed. 21.29 *(978-0-673-80011-4(3))*; (J). (gr. 1). pap., stu. ed. 21.29 *(978-0-673-80014-5(8))*; (J). (gr. 1). pap., stu. ed. 21.29 *(978-0-673-80013-8(X))*; (J). (gr. 1). pap., stu. ed. 21.29 *(978-0-673-80012-1(1))*; (J). (gr. 1). pap., stu. ed. 21.29 *(978-0-673-80015-2(6))*; (J). (gr. 1). pap., stu. ed. 21.29 *(978-0-673-80016-9(4))*; (J). (gr. 2). pap., stu. ed. 12.79 *(978-0-673-80021-3(0))*;Bk. C. (J). (gr. 2). pap., stu. ed. 12.79 *(978-0-673-80023-7(7))*;Bk. C. (J). (gr. 3). pap., stu. ed. 13.73 *(978-0-673-80033-6(4))*;Bk. C. (J). (gr. 4). pap., stu. ed. 8.98 *(978-0-673-80043-5(1))*;Bk. C. (J). (gr. 5). pap., stu. ed. 8.98 *(978-0-673-80053-4(9))*;Bk. C. (J). (gr. 5). pap., stu. ed. 8.98 *(978-0-673-80063-3(6))*;Bk. C. (YA). (gr. 7). pap., stu. ed. 14.71 *(978-0-673-80075-6(X))*;Bk. D. (J). (gr. 2). pap., stu. ed. 12.79 *(978-0-673-80024-4(5))*;Bk. D. (J). (gr. 3). pap., stu. ed. 13.73 *(978-0-673-80034-3(2))*;Bk. D. (J). (gr. 4). pap., stu. ed. 8.98 *(978-0-673-80044-2(X))*;Bk. D. (J). (gr. 5). pap., stu. ed. 8.98 *(978-0-673-80054-1(7))*;Bk. D. (J). (gr. 5). pap., stu. ed. 8.98 *(978-0-673-80064-0(4))*;Bk. A. (J). (gr. 3). pap., stu. ed. 13.73 *(978-0-673-80031-2(8))*;Bk. A. (J). (gr. 4). pap., stu. ed. 8.98 *(978-0-673-80051-0(2))*;Bk. A. (J). (gr. 4). pap., stu. ed. 8.98 *(978-0-673-80041-1(5))*;Bk. A. (J). (gr. 5). pap., stu. ed. 8.98 *(978-0-673-80061-9(X))*;Bk. B. (J). (gr. 3). pap., stu. ed. 13.73 *(978-0-673-80032-9(6))*;Bk. B. (J). (gr. 4). pap., stu. ed. 8.98 *(978-0-673-80042-8(3))*;Bk. B. (J). (gr. 5). pap., stu. ed. 8.98 *(978-0-673-80062-6(8))*;Bk. B. (J). (gr. 5). pap., stu. ed. 8.98 *(978-0-673-80052-7(0))*;Bk. E. (J). (gr. 2). pap., stu. ed. 12.79 *(978-0-673-80025-1(3))*;Bk. E. (J). (gr. 3). pap., stu. ed. 13.73 *(978-0-673-80035-0(0))*;Bk. E. (J). (gr. 4). pap., stu. ed. 8.98 *(978-0-673-80045-9(8))*;Bk. E. (J). (gr. 5). pap., stu. ed. 8.98 *(978-0-673-80055-8(5))*;Bk. E. (J). (gr. 5). pap., stu. ed. 8.98 *(978-0-673-80065-7(2))*;Bk. F. (J). (gr. 2). pap., stu. ed. 12.79 *(978-0-673-80026-8(1))*;Bk. F. (J). (gr. 3). pap., stu. ed. 13.73 *(978-0-673-80036-7(9))*;Bk. F. (J). (gr. 4). pap., stu. ed. 8.98 *(978-0-673-80046-6(6))*;Bk. F. (J). (gr. 5). pap., stu. ed. 8.98 *(978-0-673-80066-4(0))*;Bk. F. (J). (gr. 5). pap., stu. ed. 8.98 *(978-0-673-80056-5(3))*;Unit 7A, Bk. A. (YA). (gr. 7). pap., stu. ed. 14.71 *(978-0-673-80071-8(7))*;Unit 7B, Bk. B. (YA). (gr. 7). pap., stu. ed. 14.71 *(978-0-673-80072-5(5))*;Unit 7D, Bk. D. (YA). (gr. 7). pap., stu. ed. 14.71 *(978-0-673-80076-3(8))*;Unit 8A, Bk. A. (YA). (gr. 8). pap., stu. ed. 14.71 *(978-0-673-80081-7(4))*;Unit 8B, Bk. B. (YA). (gr. 8). pap., stu. ed. 14.71 *(978-0-673-80083-1(0))*;Unit 8C, Bk. C. (YA). (gr. 8). pap., stu. ed. 14.71 *(978-0-673-80084-8(9))*;Unit 8D, Bk. D. (YA). (gr. 8). pap., stu. ed. 14.71 *(978-0-673-80085-5(7))* Addison Wesley Schl. (Scott Foresman).
Chad Is the Champ: Digraph ch: Level B, 6 vols. (Wright Skills Ser.). 16p. (gr. k-3). 17.95 *(978-0-322-01472-5(7))* Wright Group/McGraw-Hill.

Challenges Set. 2005. (Challenges Ser.: Vol. 2). (J). (gr. 3-5). tchr. ed. 198.95 (978-0-7652-2129-2(2)) Modern Curriculum Pr.

Change of Heart: Level 2, 6 vols. (Fluency Strand Ser.). (gr. 4-8). 45.00 (978-1-4045-1214-6(4)) Wright Group/McGraw-Hill.

Changing Views: American Readers. (J). (gr. 7). (978-0-669-05084-4(9)); (978-0-669-05086-8(5)); wbk. ed. (978-0-669-05087-5(3)) Houghton Mifflin Harcourt School Pubs.

Charlesworth, Liza & Schecter, Deborah. The Big Collection of Mini-Books for Guided Reading: 75 Reproducible Mini-Books for Levels A, B & C That Give Kids a Great Start in Reading. 2012. (ENG.). 240p. (gr. k-k). pap. 24.99 (978-0-545-43521-5(8), Teaching Resources) Scholastic, Inc.

Charlie the Pancake Pirate: Level O, 6 vols. (Wonder Worldtm Ser.). 48p. 39.95 (978-0-7802-2949-5(5)) Wright Group/McGraw-Hill.

Chicchelly, Dana. Preparing for FCAT Reading/ Grade 6. 2007. (J). pap. (978-1-56765-156-0(9), R029W) AMSCO Schl. Pubns., Inc.

Chris's Diary: Level 3, 6 vols. (Fluency Strand Ser.). (gr. 4-8). 45.00 (978-1-4045-1216-0(0)) Wright Group/McGraw-Hill.

Cinderella. 2015. (ENG., Illus.). 32p. (J). (gr. -1-3). (978-1-78393-579-6(0)) Make Believe Ideas.

The Circus: Level D, 6 vols. (Wonder Worldtm Ser.). 16p. 24.95 (978-0-7802-1034-9(4)) Wright Group/McGraw-Hill.

Claire, Elizabeth. Hi! (Illus.). (J). wbk. ed. (978-0-8056-0122-0(8)) Minerva Bks., Ltd.

Classical Learning Universe. Reading Success: Foundations Student Book: Effective Comprehension Strategies. 2004. (978-0-9763376-0-7(6)) Classical Learning Universe, LLC.

—Reading Success: Student Book: Effective Comprehension Strategies Level C. 2004. (978-0-9721733-7-7(4)) Classical Learning Universe, LLC.

Classroom Complete Press, creator. High Frequency Picture Words, Grades PK-2. 2011. (Literacy Skills Ser.). (ENG.). 39.95 (978-1-55319-514-6(0), Classroom Complete Pr.) Rainbow Horizons Publishing, Inc.

—High Frequency Sight Words, Grades PK-2. 2011. (Literacy Skills Ser.). (ENG.). 39.95 (978-1-55319-513-9(2), Classroom Complete Pr.) Rainbow Horizons Publishing, Inc.

—Sight & Picture Words, Grades PK-2. 2011. (Literacy Skills Ser.). (ENG.). 54.95 (978-1-55319-515-3(9), Classroom Complete Pr.) Rainbow Horizons Publishing, Inc.

Clearing Paths: American Readers. (J). (gr. 4). (978-0-669-05040-0(7)) Houghton Mifflin Harcourt School Pubs.

Clearing Paths Reading Kit: American Readers. (J). (gr. 4). (978-0-669-05053-0(9)) Houghton Mifflin Harcourt School Pubs.

Clearing Paths Workbook: American Readers. (J). (gr. 4). wbk. ed. (978-0-669-05048-6(2)) Houghton Mifflin Harcourt School Pubs.

Cleary, Brian P. The Bug in the Jug Wants a Hug. Miskimins, Jason, illus. 2009. (Sounds Like Reading (r) Ser.: 1). (ENG.). (gr. -1-2). pap. 39.62 (978-0-7613-4700-2(3)) Lerner Publishing Group.

—The Clown in the Gown Drives the Car with the Star. Miskimins, Jason, illus. 2009. (Sounds Like Reading (r) Ser.: 8). (ENG.). (gr. -1-2). pap. 39.62 (978-0-7613-4707-1(0)) Lerner Publishing Group.

—The Frail Snail on the Trail. Miskimins, Jason, illus. 2009. (Sounds Like Reading (r) Ser.: 4). (ENG.). (gr. -1-2). pap. 39.62 (978-0-7613-4703-3(8)) Lerner Publishing Group.

—The Nice Mice in the Rice. Miskimins, Jason, illus. 2009. (Sounds Like Reading (r) Ser.: 3). (ENG.). (gr. -1-2). pap. 39.62 (978-0-7613-4702-6(X)) Lerner Publishing Group.

—The Peaches on the Beaches. Miskimins, Jason, illus. 2009. (Sounds Like Reading (r) Ser.: 7). (ENG.). (gr. -1-2). pap. 39.62 (978-0-7613-4706-4(2)) Lerner Publishing Group.

—Stop, Drop, & Flop in the Slop. Miskimins, Jason, illus. 2009. (Sounds Like Reading (r) Ser.: 2). (ENG.). (gr. -1-2). pap. 39.62 (978-0-7613-4701-9(1)) Lerner Publishing Group.

—The Thing on the Wing Can Sing. Miskimins, Jason, illus. 2009. (Sounds Like Reading (r) Ser.: 5). (ENG.). (gr. -1-2). pap. 39.62 (978-0-7613-4704-0(6)) Lerner Publishing Group.

—Whose Shoes Would You Choose. Miskimins, Jason, illus. 2009. (Sounds Like Reading (r) Ser.: 6). (ENG.). (gr. -1-2). pap. 39.62 (978-0-7613-4705-7(4)) Lerner Publishing Group.

Cleary, Brian P. & Maday, Alice M. The Bug in the Jug Wants a Hug: A Short Vowel Sounds Book. Miskimins, Jason, illus. 2009. (Sounds Like Reading (r) Ser.: 1). (ENG.). 32p. (gr. -1-2). lib. bdg. 23.93 (978-0-7613-9503-4(2)) Lerner Publishing Group.

—The Clown in the Gown Drives the Car with the Star: A Book about Diphthongs & R-Controlled Vowel. Miskimins, Jason, illus. 2009. (Sounds Like Reading (r) Ser.: 8). (ENG.). 32p. (gr. -1-2). lib. bdg. 23.93 (978-0-8225-7637-2(6)) Lerner Publishing Group.

—The Frail Snail on the Trail: Long Vowel Sounds with Consonant Blends. Miskimins, Jason, illus. 2009. (Sounds Like Reading (r) Ser.: 4). (ENG.). 32p. (gr. -1-2). lib. bdg. 23.93 (978-0-8225-7638-9(4)) Lerner Publishing Group.

—The Nice Mice in the Rice: A Long Vowel Sound Book. Miskimins, Jason, illus. 2009. (Sounds Like Reading (r) Ser.: 3). (ENG.). 32p. (gr. -1-2). lib. bdg. 23.93 (978-0-8225-7628-0(7)) Lerner Publishing Group.

—The Peaches on the Beaches: A Book about Inflectional Endings. Miskimins, Jason, illus. 2009. (Sounds Like Reading (r) Ser.: 7). (ENG.). 32p. (gr. -1-2). lib. bdg. 23.93 (978-0-8225-7636-5(8)) Lerner Publishing Group.

—Stop, Drop, & Flop in the Slop: A Short Vowel Sounds Book with Consonant Blends. Miskimins, Jason, illus. 2009. (Sounds Like Reading (r) Ser.: 2). (ENG.). 32p. (gr. -1-2). lib. bdg. 23.93 (978-0-8225-7635-8(X)) Lerner Publishing Group.

—The Thing on the Wing Can Sing: Short Vowel Sounds & Consonant Digraphs. Miskimins, Jason, illus. 2009. (Sounds Like Reading (r) Ser.: 5). (ENG.). 32p. (gr. -1-2). lib. bdg. 23.93 (978-0-8225-7639-6(2)) Lerner Publishing Group.

—Whose Shoes Would You Choose? A Long Vowel Sounds Book with Consonant Digraphs. Miskimins, Jason, illus. 2009. (Sounds Like Reading (r) Ser.: 6). (ENG.). 32p. (gr. -1-2). lib. bdg. 23.93 (978-0-8225-7640-2(6)) Lerner Publishing Group.

Climbing Up: American Readers. (J). (gr. 1). (978-0-669-04965-7(4)) Houghton Mifflin Harcourt School Pubs.

The Climbing Wall: Level 7, 6 vols. (Fluency Strand Ser.). (gr. 4-8). 45.00 (978-1-4045-1244-3(6)) Wright Group/McGraw-Hill.

The Closet in the Hall: Level G, 6 vols. (Wonder Worldtm Ser.). 16p. 29.95 (978-0-7802-1247-3(9)) Wright Group/McGraw-Hill.

Clothes: Level N, 6 vols. (Wonder Worldtm Ser.). 48p. 34.95 (978-0-7802-2892-4(8)) Wright Group/McGraw-Hill.

The Coach & the Kid: Level 5, 6 vols. (Fluency Strand Ser.). (gr. 4-8). 45.00 (978-1-4045-1233-7(0)) Wright Group/McGraw-Hill.

Collecting Cones: Level K, 6 vols. (Wonder Worldtm Ser.). 16p. 34.95 (978-0-7802-4565-5(2)) Wright Group/McGraw-Hill.

Collins Big Cat Staff. Independent Reading at Home. 2015. (Big Cat Reading Lions Ser.). (ENG.). 1p. (J). (gr. 3-4). 38.95 (978-0-00-812641-4(0)) HarperCollins Pubs. Ltd. GBR. Dist: Independent Pubs. Group.

Collins Easy Learning Staff, et al. Phonics Ages 5-6. 2015. (Collins Easy Learning Ser.). (ENG.). 32p. (J). (gr. k-1). pap. 6.95 (978-0-00-813435-8(9)) HarperCollins Pubs. Ltd. GBR. Dist: Independent Pubs. Group.

Colors at the Zoo: Take-Home Book. 2005. (Emergent Library: Vol. 2). (YA). (gr. -1-1). 12.60 (978-0-8215-7269-6(5)) Sadlier, William H. Inc.

Come Back, Amelia Bedelia. 2003. 22.95 (978-0-673-75911-5(3)) Celebration Pr.

Common Core Staff, creator. Higher Scores on Reading & Language Arts Standardized Tests, Grade 4. 2012. (Steck-Vaughn Higher Scores on Reading Standardized Tests Ser.). (ENG., Illus.). 137p. (J). pap. 19.99 (978-0-547-89849-0(5)) Heinemann-Raintree.

Communities: Level F, 6 vols. (Wonder Worldtm Ser.). 16p. 29.95 (978-0-7802-1986-1(4)) Wright Group/McGraw-Hill.

Cosmo the ACountant: Level O, 6 vols. (Wonder Worldtm Ser.). 48p. 39.95 (978-0-7802-2962-4(2)) Wright Group/McGraw-Hill.

Count with Me: Take-Home Book. 2005. (Emergent Library: Vol. 2). (YA). (gr. -1-1). 12.60 (978-0-8215-7258-0(X)) Sadlier, William H. Inc.

Cousin. My Friend at School: Big Book: Level C. (Visions Ser.). 8p. 20.95 (978-0-7802-9746-3(6)) Wright Group/McGraw-Hill.

Cox, Phil Roxbee & Cartwright, Stephen. Hen's Pens. 2004. (Phonics Board Bks.). (Illus.). 10p. (J). 4.95 (978-0-7945-0303-1(9), Usborne) EDC Publishing.

Crackles: Level P, 6 vols. (Wonder Worldtm Ser.). 48p. 39.95 (978-0-7802-7072-5(X)) Wright Group/McGraw-Hill.

Crawford, Sheryl Ann & Harris, Lauren. Human Body: 20 Short, Reproducible Plays That Teach Key Concepts, Expand Vocabulary, & Build Fluency. 2009. (ENG.). 64p. (gr. 1-2). pap. 11.99 (978-0-545-15430-7(8), Teaching Resources) Scholastic, Inc.

Cronkite, Walter, frwd. Great American Presidents, 12 vols. 2005. (Great American Presidents Ser.). (Illus.). 112p. (gr. 5-8). 210.00 (978-0-7910-7595-1(8), Chelsea Hse.) Facts On File, Inc.

The Crook by the Brook: Variant Vowel oo: Level B, 6 vols. (Wright Skills Ser.). 16p. (gr. k-3). 26.50 (978-0-322-01483-1(2)) Wright Group/McGraw-Hill.

Crossing Boundaries: American Readers. (J). (978-0-669-05064-6(4)); (gr. 5). (978-0-669-05054-7(7)); (gr. 5). wbk. ed. (978-0-669-05060-8(1)) Houghton Mifflin Harcourt School Pubs.

The Crypto Files: Level 6, 6 vols. (Fluency Strand Ser.). (gr. 4-8). 45.00 (978-1-4045-1236-8(5)) Wright Group/McGraw-Hill.

Cuando el senor Rey ronco: When Mr Quinn Snored. 2005. (Take-Home Bks.). (SPA.). (YA). (gr. -1-3). 15.75 (978-0-8215-1207-4(2)) Sadlier, William H. Inc.

Cuando el senor Rey ronco/When Mr Quinn Snored. 2005. (Libros en Espanol Para Ninos Ser.). (SPA.). (YA). (gr. -1-1). 11.97 (978-0-8215-0997-5(7)) Sadlier, William H. Inc.

Cuidando a los animales: Keeping Baby Animals Safe. 2005. (Take-Home Bks.). (SPA.). (YA). (gr. -1-3). 15.75 (978-0-8215-1206-7(4)) Sadlier, William H. Inc.

Cuidando a los animales/Keeping Baby Animals Safe. 2005. (Libros en Espanol Para Ninos Ser.). (SPA.). (YA). (gr. -1-1). 11.97 (978-0-8215-0996-8(9)) Sadlier, William H. Inc.

A Cup for a Cub: Consonants c, l, r; Short Vowel u word families: Level A, 6 vols. (Wright Skills Ser.). 12p. (gr. k-3). 17.95 (978-0-322-01453-4(0)) Wright Group/McGraw-Hill.

Custard: Level F, 6 vols. (Wonder Worldtm Ser.). 16p. 29.95 (978-0-7802-2894-8(4)) Wright Group/McGraw-Hill.

Cyberspace, 6 vols. (Wildcats Ser.). 32p. (gr. 2-8). (978-0-322-00600-3(7)) Wright Group/McGraw-Hill.

Czernecki, Stefan. How a Baby Begins. Date not set. 40p. (YA). (gr. 5-9). 15.99 (978-0-06-025412-4(2)) HarperCollins Pubs.

—Wild Queen. Date not set. 80p. (J). (gr. k-4). 13.99 (978-0-06-026263-1(X)); lib. bdg. 14.89 (978-0-06-026264-8(8)) HarperCollins Pubs.

Daley, Patrick & Allen, Janet. Riveting Read-Alouds for Middle School. 2017. (ENG., Illus.). 192p. (J). (gr. 5-12). pap. 21.99 (978-0-545-09600-3(6), Teaching Strategies) Scholastic, Inc.

Dan Gets Dressed: Level C. Group 2. (Story Box Ser.). 16p. 20.95 (978-0-7802-9366-3(5)) Wright Group/McGraw-Hill.

Dance My Dance: Level M, 6 vols. (Take-Twostm Ser.). 32p. 36.95 (978-0-322-03401-3(9)) Wright Group/McGraw-Hill.

Dangerous Jobs: Level T. Group 1, 6 vols. (Sunshine Ser.). 48p. 44.95 (978-0-7802-6094-8(5)) Wright Group/McGraw-Hill.

Daniel, Claire. Are You Scared, Jacob? Lap Book. Poole, Helen, illus. 2014. (MySELF Ser.). (J). (gr. -1-k). 27.00 (978-1-4788-0501-4(3)) Newmark Learning LLC.

—Dylan's Questions Lap Book. Evans, Antony, illus. 2014. (MySELF Ser.). (J). (gr. -1-k). 27.00 (978-1-4788-0519-9(6)) Newmark Learning LLC.

—I Can Stay Calm. Patton, Julia, illus. 2014. (J). (gr. -1). 3.99 (978-1-4788-0474-1(2)) Newmark Learning LLC.

—I Can Stay Calm Lap Book. Patton, Julia, illus. 2014. (MySELF Ser.). (J). (gr. -1-k). 27.00 (978-1-4788-0511-3(0)) Newmark Learning LLC.

Day & Night Little Book: Early Reading Fluency, Level A. 2004. pap. 6.00 (978-0-7398-8170-5(1)) Steck-Vaughn.

Day & Night Little Book, Grade 1: Early Reading Fluency: Teaching Edition, Level A. 2004. pap. 7.50 (978-0-7398-8206-1(6)) Steck-Vaughn.

de Lambana, Martha Lucia Martinez. Grafias 1 1: Escritura Asociativa Script: Afianzamiento. (SPA.). (J). (gr. k-6). 12.00 (978-958-04-5317-8(9)) Norma S.A. COL. Dist: Distribuidora Norma, Inc.

—Grafias 2 2: Escritura Asociativa Script: Transicion. (SPA.). (J). (gr. k-6). 12.00 (978-958-04-5327-7(6)) Norma S.A. COL. Dist: Distribuidora Norma, Inc.

—Grafias 3 3: Escritura Asociativa Script: Afianzamiento. (SPA.). (J). (gr. k-6). 12.00 (978-958-04-5328-4(4)) Norma S.A. COL. Dist: Distribuidora Norma, Inc.

Deadbeat: Level O, 6 vols. (Wonder Worldtm Ser.). 48p. 39.95 (978-0-7802-2947-1(9)) Wright Group/McGraw-Hill.

Dear Pop: Level O, 6 vols. (Wonder Worldtm Ser.). 48p. 39.95 (978-0-7802-2948-8(7)) Wright Group/McGraw-Hill.

Dear Tom: Level J, 6 vols. (Wonder Worldtm Ser.). 16p. 29.95 (978-0-7802-4567-9(9)) Wright Group/McGraw-Hill.

Den of Thieves: Level 6, 6 vols. (Fluency Strand Ser.). (gr. 4-8). 45.00 (978-1-4045-1238-2(1)) Wright Group/McGraw-Hill.

Desert Day: Level B. 8p. 20.95 (978-0-322-00358-3(X)); 24.95 (978-0-7802-8916-1(1)) Wright Group/McGraw-Hill.

Did You Know? Big Book: Level L. Group 1. (Sunshine Ser.). 24p. 36.50 (978-0-322-00334-7(2)) Wright Group/McGraw-Hill.

Disney Publishing Staff. I Spy Shapes, 15 vols. 2003. (It's Fun to Learn Ser.). (Illus.). 32p. (J). (gr. -1-3). 3.99 (978-1-57973-131-1(7)) Advance Pubs. LLC.

The Divers: Level C, 6 vols. (Wonder Worldtm Ser.). 16p. 24.95 (978-0-7802-1249-7(5)) Wright Group/McGraw-Hill.

Do you Like Rice?, 6 vols. 8p. (gr. k-1). 21.50 (978-0-322-02058-0(1)) Wright Group/McGraw-Hill.

Do you Remember When?, 6 vols. (Multicultural Programs Ser.). 16p. (gr. 1-3). 24.95 (978-0-7802-9206-2(5)) Wright Group/McGraw-Hill.

Dolly Fin & Friends: Level 4, 6 vols. (Fluency Strand Ser.). (gr. 4-8). 45.00 (978-1-4045-1227-6(6)) Wright Group/McGraw-Hill.

Dolphin. 2003. 22.95 (978-0-673-75914-6(8)) Celebration Pr.

Don't be Late, 6 vols. 8p. (gr. k-1). 21.50 (978-0-322-02059-7(X)) Wright Group/McGraw-Hill.

Don't Throw it Away: Level G, 6 vols. (Wonder Worldtm Ser.). 16p. 29.95 (978-0-7802-2896-2(0)) Wright Group/McGraw-Hill.

Dorling Kindersley Publishing Staff. Bathtime. 2009. (Baby Touch & Feel Ser.). (ENG., Illus.). 14p. (J). (gr. -1 — 1). bds. 5.99 (978-0-7566-5149-7(2), DK Children) Dorling Kindersley Publishing, Inc.

—Language Arts: Learn & Explore. 2014. (ENG.). 60p. (J). (gr. -1-1). pap. 6.99 (978-1-4654-1737-4(0), DK Children) Dorling Kindersley Publishing, Inc.

—Language Arts - Learn & Explore. 2014. (ENG.). 60p. (J). (gr. 1-3). pap. 6.99 (978-1-4654-1739-8(7), DK Children) Dorling Kindersley Publishing, Inc.

—Language Arts, First Grade. 2014. (ENG.). 60p. (J). (gr. k-4). pap. 6.99 (978-1-4654-1738-1(9), DK Children) Dorling Kindersley Publishing, Inc.

—Language Arts, Grade Pre-K. 2014. (ENG.). 60p. (J). (gr. -1-k). pap. 6.99 (978-1-4654-1736-7(2), DK Children) Dorling Kindersley Publishing, Inc.

Dorling Kindersley Publishing Staff & Last, Shari. DK Readers L1: the LEGO Movie: Meet Unikitty! The LEGO Movie: Meet Unikitty! 2014. (DK Readers Ser.). (ENG., Illus.). 48p. (J). (gr. k-4). 14.99 (978-1-4654-3498-2(4), DK Children) Dorling Kindersley Publishing, Inc.

Doudna, Kelly. Any Day but Today! 2004. (Sight Words Ser.). (ENG., Illus.). 24p. (J). (gr. k-3). lib. bdg. 24.21 (978-1-59197-464-2(X)) ABDO Publishing Co.

—Et As in Jet, 1 vol. 2003. (Word Families Set 2 Ser.). (ENG.). 24p. (J). (gr. k-3). lib. bdg. 24.21 (978-1-59197-230-3(2), SandCastle) ABDO Publishing Co.

—Give It a Try! 2004. (Sight Words Ser.). (ENG., Illus.). 24p. (J). (gr. k-3). lib. bdg. 24.21 (978-1-59197-469-7(0), SandCastle) ABDO Publishing Co.

—Id As in Squid, 1 vol. 2003. (Word Families Set 3 Ser.). (ENG., Illus.). 24p. (J). (gr. k-3). lib. bdg. 24.21 (978-1-59197-235-8(3), SandCastle) ABDO Publishing Co.

—Ig As in Pig, 1 vol. Marx, Monica, ed. 2003. (Word Families Set 3 Ser.). (ENG., Illus.). 24p. (J). (gr. k-3). lib. bdg. 24.21 (978-1-59197-236-5(1), SandCastle) ABDO Publishing Co.

—Ill As in Grill, 1 vol. 2003. (Word Families Set 3 Ser.). (ENG., Illus.). 24p. (J). (gr. k-3). lib. bdg. 24.21 (978-1-59197-237-2(X), SandCastle) ABDO Publishing Co.

—In As in Twin, 1 vol. 2003. (Word Families Set 3 Ser.). (ENG., Illus.). 24p. (J). (gr. k-3). lib. bdg. 24.21 (978-1-59197-238-9(8), SandCastle) ABDO Publishing Co.

—Ip As in Ship, 1 vol. 2003. (Word Families Set 3 Ser.). (ENG., Illus.). 24p. (J). (gr. k-3). lib. bdg. 24.21 (978-1-59197-239-6(6), SandCastle) ABDO Publishing Co.

—It As in Sit, 1 vol. 2003. (Word Families Set 3 Ser.). (ENG., Illus.). 24p. (J). (gr. k-3). lib. bdg. 24.21 (978-1-59197-240-2(X), SandCastle) ABDO Publishing Co.

—Just Make Some Art! 2004. (Sight Words Ser.). (ENG., Illus.). 24p. (J). (gr. k-3). lib. bdg. 24.21 (978-1-59197-481-9(X), SandCastle) ABDO Publishing Co.

—Ow As in Crow, 1 vol. 2003. (Word Families Set 7 Ser.). (ENG., Illus.). 24p. (J). (gr. k-3). lib. bdg. 24.21 (978-1-59197-265-5(5), SandCastle) ABDO Publishing Co.

—There Are Ants down There! 2004. (Sight Words Ser.). (ENG., Illus.). 24p. (J). (gr. k-3). lib. bdg. 24.21 (978-1-59197-473-4(9), SandCastle) ABDO Publishing Co.

—Was That Fun? 2004. (Sight Words Ser.). (ENG., Illus.). 24p. (J). (gr. k-3). lib. bdg. 24.21 (978-1-59197-475-8(5), SandCastle) ABDO Publishing Co.

—When Can You Play Again? 2004. (Sight Words Ser.). (ENG., Illus.). 24p. (J). (gr. k-3). lib. bdg. 24.21 (978-1-59197-478-9(X), SandCastle) ABDO Publishing Co.

Douglas. Reading Explorer. 4th ed. 2010. (ENG., Illus.). 224p. (J). pap., stu. ed. incl. cd-rom (978-1-4240-2939-6(2)) Cengage Heinle.

Down by the Pond: Level H. Group 2. (Story Box Ser.). 16p. 31.50 (978-0-322-02458-8(7)) Wright Group/McGraw-Hill.

Down to Town: Big Book: Level A. Group 1. (Sunshine Ser.). 8p. 20.95 (978-0-7802-5705-4(7)) Wright Group/McGraw-Hill.

Dragon! Level F, 6 vols. (Wonder Worldtm Ser.). 16p. 29.95 (978-0-7802-1199-5(5)) Wright Group/McGraw-Hill.

The Dragon Who Came to Dinner: Schwa Sound: Level C, 6 vols. (Wright Skills Ser.). 16p. (gr. k-3). 26.50 (978-0-322-01505-0(7)) Wright Group/McGraw-Hill.

Dragon with a Cold: Big Book: Level K. Group 1. (Sunshine Ser.). 16p. 36.50 (978-0-7802-5792-4(8)) Wright Group/McGraw-Hill.

Dragons Galore: 6 Each of 1 Anthology, 6 vols. (Wildcats Ser.). 32p. (gr. 2-8). (978-0-322-00582-2(5)) Wright Group/McGraw-Hill.

Ducks: Big Book: Level F. Group 2. (Story Box Ser.). 16p. 20.95 (978-0-7802-9370-0(3)) Wright Group/McGraw-Hill.

Duke, Nell K. & Bennett-Armistead, V. Susan. Reading & Writing Informational Text in the Primary Grades: Research-Based Practices. 2003. (ENG., Illus.). 272p. (gr. k-3). pap. 27.99 (978-0-439-53123-8(3)) Scholastic, Inc.

Duke, Nell K., et al. Beyond Bedtime Stories: A Parent's Guide to Promoting Reading Writing, & Other Literacy Skills from Birth to 5. 2nd ed. 2014. (ENG., Illus.). 208p. pap. 23.99 (978-0-545-65530-9(7), Teaching Resources) Scholastic, Inc.

Dupuis, Lynda. Au Pied de la Lettre: Manuel de Lecture de Vocabulaire d'Expression Orale et Ecrite. rev. ed. 2010. (ENG.). 232p. 70.00 (978-0-7575-7461-0(0)) Kendall Hunt Publishing Co.

Dwyer, Judy. Novel Activities. 100p. (J). (gr. 2-6). (978-1-876367-02-2(4)) Wizard Bks.

Dyan, Penelope. Changes! Dyan, Penelope, illus. 2013. (Illus.). 34p. (J). pap. 11.95 (978-1-61477-097-8(2)) Bellissima Publishing, LLC.

—Gettin' Dirty! for Boys Only R. Dyan, Penelope, illus. 2013. (Illus.). 34p. pap. 11.95 (978-1-61477-083-1(2)) Bellissima Publishing, LLC.

—Good Luck Chuck! Dyan, Penelope, illus. 2013. (Illus.). 34p. pap. 11.95 (978-1-61477-098-5(0)) Bellissima Publishing, LLC.

—Good Night! Dyan, Penelope, illus. 2013. (Illus.). 34p. pap. 11.95 (978-1-61477-089-3(1)) Bellissima Publishing, LLC.

—Hello Doctor! Dyan, Penelope, illus. 2013. (Illus.). 34p. pap. 11.95 (978-1-61477-096-1(4)) Bellissima Publishing, LLC.

—Life Is a Dream! Dyan, Penelope, illus. 2013. (Illus.). 34p. pap. 11.95 (978-1-61477-091-6(3)) Bellissima Publishing, LLC.

Early 1 Package. 2005. (Little Celebrations Emergent & Early Packages Ser.). (J). (gr. k-3). 48.95 (978-0-673-75373-1(5)) Celebration Pr.

Early 2 Package. 2005. (Little Celebrations Emergent & Early Packages Ser.). (J). (gr. k-3). 50.95 (978-0-673-75374-8(3)) Celebration Pr.

Early Fluency. (Foundation Ser.). (gr. k-3). 26.50 (978-0-322-01620-0(7)) Wright Group/McGraw-Hill.

Early Fluency Set 1: 1 Each of 8 Student Books. (Sunshinetm Science Ser.). (gr. 1-2). 55.95 (978-0-7802-1762-1(4)) Wright Group/McGraw-Hill.

Early Library. 2005. (YA). (gr. -1-3). 239.40 (978-0-8215-8885-7(0)); Vol. 2. 239.40 (978-0-8215-8886-4(9)) Sadlier, William H. Inc.

Early Stage 2. 2005. (Little Celebrations Picture/Text & Literacy Cards Ser.). (J). (gr. k-3). 128.50 (978-0-673-75273-4(9)) Celebration Pr.

Earthquake! Level F, 6 vols. (Wonder Worldtm Ser.). 16p. 29.95 (978-0-7802-1201-5(0)) Wright Group/McGraw-Hill.

The Earthworm: Level I, 6 vols. (Wonder Worldtm Ser.). 16p. 29.95 (978-0-7802-1988-5(0)) Wright Group/McGraw-Hill.

The Education of Little Tree: A Student Response Journal. 2003. 40p. (YA). (978-1-58049-978-1(3), RJ78) Prestwick Hse., Inc.

Emergent Library, Vol. 2. 2005. (YA). (gr. -1-1). 239.40 (978-0-8215-8878-9(8)); 239.40 (978-0-8215-8879-6(6)); 239.40 (978-0-8215-8877-2(X)); 239.40 (978-0-8215-8876-5(1)) Sadlier, William H. Inc.

Emergent Package. 2005. (Little Celebrations Emergent & Early Packages Ser.). (J). (gr. k-3). 49.95 (978-0-673-75372-4(7)) Celebration Pr.

Emergent Stage 1. 2005. (Little Celebrations Picture/Text & Literacy Cards Ser.). (J). (gr. k-3). 128.50 (978-0-673-75224-6(0)) Celebration Pr.

Emergent Super Big Book Package. 2005. (YA). (gr. -1-3). 900.00 (978-0-8215-8858-1(3)) Sadlier, William H. Inc.

Emergent Super Little Book. 2005. (YA). (gr. -1-3). 957.60 (978-0-8215-8857-4(5)) Sadlier, William H. Inc.

Emergent Super Little Book Package. 2005. (YA). (gr. -1-3). 183.00 (978-0-8215-8856-7(7)) Sadlier, William H. Inc.

Erickson, Karen. MEville to WEville Unit 1: Unit 1 ME, 2 Bks., manual and children's Bk. 2004. 292p. 75.00 (978-0-9666667-5-5(5)) AbleNet, Inc.

Eruption: 6 Each of 1 Anthology, 6 vols. (Wildcats Ser.). 32p. (gr. 2-8). (978-0-322-00584-6(1)) Wright Group/McGraw-Hill.

Essential Words Reading & Language Arts Activity Book (Intermediate) Intermediate/Middle School. 2005. (Illus.). 50p. (J). 8.95 (978-0-9722452-3-4(5)) New Leaf Educ., Inc.

Evaluacion del Desarrollo de la Lectura Leveled Libraries: Extending Stage, Level 40. 2003. (SPA.). tchr. ed. 43.50 (978-0-7652-2389-0(9)) Modern Curriculum Pr.

Evan-Moor Educational Publishers, creator. Reading Informational Text, Grade 2: Common Core Mastery. 2014. (Reading Informational Text: Common Core Mastery Ser.). (ENG., Illus.). 118p. (J). (gr. 2). pap. 21.99 (978-1-61368-990-5(X)) Evan-Moor Educational Pubs.

—Reading Informational Text, Grade 5. 2014. (ENG.). 116p. (J). (gr. 5). pap. 21.99 (978-1-61368-993-6(4)) Evan-Moor Educational Pubs.

—Reading Paired Text, Grade 4: Common Core Mastery. 2014. (Reading Paired Text: Common Core Mastery Ser.). (ENG., Illus.). 176p. (J). (gr. 4). pap. 21.99 (978-1-61368-986-8(1)) Evan-Moor Educational Pubs.

Explorers: Fluency - Student Book Set - 1 Each of 12 Titles. (Explorers. Exploradores Nonfiction Sets Ser.). (gr. 3-6). Vol. 2. 89.95 (978-0-7699-0817-5(9)) Vol. 3. 89.95 (978-0-7699-0819-9(5)) Shortland Pubns. (U. S. A.) Inc.

Explorers Exploradores Set 1: English - 1 Each of 12 Student Books, 1 Teacher's Resource Book. (Explorers. Exploradores Nonfiction Sets Ser.). (gr. 3-6). 137.95 (978-0-7699-0576-1(5)) Shortland Pubns. (U. S. A.) Inc.

Explorers Exploradores Set 1: English - 6 Each of 12 Student Books, 1 Teacher's Resource Book. (Explorers.

Exploradores Nonfiction Sets Ser.). (gr. 3-6). 558.50 *(978-0-7699-0583-9(8))* Shortland Pubns. (U. S. A.) Inc.

Explorers Exploradores Set 1: Spanish - 1 Each of 12 Student Books. (Explorers. Exploradores Nonfiction Sets Ser.). (gr. 3-6). 89.95 *(978-0-7699-0816-8(0))* Shortland Pubns. (U. S. A.) Inc.

Explorers Exploradores Set 1: Spanish - 6 Each of 12 Student Books, 1 Teacher's Resource Book. (Explorers. Exploradores Nonfiction Sets Ser.). (ENG & SPA.). (gr. 3-6). 558.50 *(978-0-7699-0584-6(6))* Shortland Pubns. (U. S. A.) Inc.

Explorers Exploradores Set 2: English - 1 Each of 12 Student Books, 1 Teacher's Resource Book. (Explorers. Exploradores Nonfiction Sets Ser.). (gr. 3-6). 137.95 *(978-0-7699-0578-5(1))* Shortland Pubns. (U. S. A.) Inc.

Explorers Exploradores Set 2: English - 6 Each of 12 Student Books, 1 Teacher's Resource Book. (Explorers. Exploradores Nonfiction Sets Ser.). (gr. 3-6). 558.50 *(978-0-7699-0585-3(4))* Shortland Pubns. (U. S. A.) Inc.

Explorers Exploradores Set 2: Spanish - 1 Each of 12 Student Books. (Explorers. Exploradores Nonfiction Sets Ser.). (gr. 3-6). 89.95 *(978-0-7699-0818-2(7))* Shortland Pubns. (U. S. A.) Inc.

Explorers Exploradores Set 2: Spanish - 1 Each of 12 Student Books, 1 Teacher's Resource Book. (Explorers. Exploradores Nonfiction Sets Ser.). (gr. 3-6). 137.95 *(978-0-7699-0579-2(X))* Shortland Pubns. (U. S. A.) Inc.

Explorers Exploradores Set 2: Spanish - 6 Each of 12 Student Books, 1 Teacher's Resource Book. (Explorers. Exploradores Nonfiction Sets Ser.). (ENG & SPA.). (gr. 3-6). 558.50 *(978-0-7699-0586-0(2))* Shortland Pubns. (U. S. A.) Inc.

Explorers Exploradores Set 3: English - 1 Each of 12 Student Books, 1 Teacher's Resource Book. (Explorers. Exploradores Nonfiction Sets Ser.). (gr. 3-6). 137.95 *(978-0-7699-0580-8(3))* Shortland Pubns. (U. S. A.) Inc.

Explorers Exploradores Set 3: English - 6 Each of 12 Student Books, 1 Teacher's Resource Book. (Explorers. Exploradores Nonfiction Sets Ser.). (gr. 3-6). 558.50 *(978-0-7699-0587-7(0))* Shortland Pubns. (U. S. A.) Inc.

Explorers Exploradores Set 3: Spanish - 1 Each of 12 Student Books. (Explorers. Exploradores Nonfiction Sets Ser.). (gr. 3-6). 89.95 *(978-0-7699-0820-5(9))* Shortland Pubns. (U. S. A.) Inc.

Explorers Exploradores Set 3: Spanish - 1 Each of 12 Student Books, 1 Teacher's Resource Book. (Explorers. Exploradores Nonfiction Sets Ser.). (gr. 3-6). 137.95 *(978-0-7699-0581-5(1))* Shortland Pubns. (U. S. A.) Inc.

Explorers Exploradores Set 3: Spanish - 6 Each of 12 Student Books, 1 Teacher's Resource Book. (Explorers. Exploradores Nonfiction Sets Ser.). (ENG & SPA.). (gr. 3-6). 558.50 *(978-0-7699-0588-4(9))* Shortland Pubns. (U. S. A.) Inc.

Explorers Exploradores Sets 1,3: English - 1 Each of 36 Student Books, 3 Teacher's Resource Books. (Explorers. Exploradores Nonfiction Sets Ser.). (gr. 3-6). 413.95 *(978-0-7699-0574-7(9))* Shortland Pubns. (U. S. A.) Inc.

Explorers Exploradores Sets 1,3: English - 6 Each of 36 Student Books, 3 Teacher's Resource Books. (Explorers. Exploradores Nonfiction Sets Ser.). (gr. 3-6). 1587.50 *(978-0-7699-0813-7(6))* Shortland Pubns. (U. S. A.) Inc.

Explorers Exploradores Sets 1,3: Spanish - 1 Each of 36 Student Books, 3 Teacher's Resource Books. (Explorers. Exploradores Nonfiction Sets Ser.). (gr. 3-6). 413.95 *(978-0-7699-0575-4(7))* Shortland Pubns. (U. S. A.) Inc.

Explorers Exploradores Sets 1,3: Spanish - 6 Each of 36 Student Books, 3 Teacher's Resource Books. (Explorers. Exploradores Nonfiction Sets Ser.). (SPA.). (gr. 3-6). 1587.50 *(978-0-7699-0814-4(4))* Shortland Pubns. (U. S. A.) Inc.

The Explosive Trek: Level 6, 6 vols. (Fluency Strand Ser.). (gr. 4-8). 45.00 *(978-1-4045-1234-4(9))* Wright Group/McGraw-Hill.

Eyes: Level C, 6 vols. (Wonder Worldtm Ser.). 16p. 24.95 *(978-0-7802-1992-2(9))* Wright Group/McGraw-Hill.

Eyes & Ears Sets: 1 Each of 3 Big Books. (Sunshinetm Science Ser.). (gr. 1-2). 111.50 *(978-0-7802-1445-3(5))* Wright Group/McGraw-Hill.

Eyes & Ears Sets: 1 Each of 3 Student Books. (Sunshinetm Science Ser.). (gr. 1-2). 20.95 *(978-0-7802-1747-8(0))* Wright Group/McGraw-Hill.

Face Painting: Level H, 6 vols. (Wonder Worldtm Ser.). 16p. 29.95 *(978-0-7802-2897-9(9))* Wright Group/McGraw-Hill.

Families, Families: Take-Home Book. 2005. (Lee Bennett Hopkins Worlds of Poetry Classroom Library). (YA). (gr. k-3). 13.50 *(978-0-8215-0566-3(1))* Sadlier, William H. Inc.

Families, Families: Teacher's Theme Resource Folder. 2005. (Lee Bennett Hopkins Worlds of Poetry Classroom Library). (YA). (gr. k-3). 12.00 *(978-0-8215-0515-1(7))* Sadlier, William H. Inc.

Family Reunion, 6 vols. (Multicultural Programs Ser.). 16p. (gr. 1-3). 24.95 *(978-0-7802-9213-0(8))* Wright Group/McGraw-Hill.

Fans: Consonant f: Level A, 6 vols. (Wright Skills Ser.). 12p. (gr. k-3). 17.95 *(978-0-322-03107-4(9))* Wright Group/McGraw-Hill.

The Farm. (Little Book Practice Reader). (J). *(978-0-8136-5348-8(7))* Modern Curriculum Pr.

The Farm Party: R-Controlled a: Level B, 6 vols. (Wright Skills Ser.). 16p. (gr. k-3). 26.50 *(978-0-322-01486-2(7))* Wright Group/McGraw-Hill.

Faster, Higher, Stronger: The Olympics, 6 vols. (Book2WebTM Ser.). (gr. 4-8). 36.50 *(978-0-322-02984-2(8))* Wright Group/McGraw-Hill.

Fay & Kay by the Bay: Long a Digraphs: Level B, 6 vols. (Wright Skills Ser.). 16p. (gr. k-3). 26.50 *(978-0-322-01478-7(6))* Wright Group/McGraw-Hill.

Feelings Little Book: Early Reading Fluency, Level A. 2004. (gr. 1). pap. 6.00 *(978-0-7398-8159-0(0))* Steck-Vaughn.

Feldman, Jean. Dr Jean Variety Pack. 2007. (J). (gr. -1-3). pap. 56.87 incl. audio compact disk *(978-1-59198-719-2(9))* Creative Teaching Pr., Inc.

Feldman, Reynold & Rumi, M. Jan. WisingUp: A Youth Guide to Good Living. 2004. 192p. (YA). *(978-1-932590-02-9(1))* Wisdom Foundation Publishing.

Felix, the Very Hungry Fish: Take-Home Bk. 2005. (Emergent Library: Vol. 2). (YA). (gr. -1-1). 12.60 *(978-0-8215-7250-4(4))* Sadlier, William H. Inc.

Fences. 2003. 44p. (YA). tchr. ed., ring bd. *(978-1-58049-468-7(4),* TU224) Prestwick Hse., Inc.

Ferguson, Walter F. Speed Learning: The Quest for Excellence. 2004. cd-rom 59.95 *(978-0-9745333-0-8(0))* Mystique International, Ltd.

Fernandez, Cesar. El bibliobus Magico. Torres, Marina, illus. 2004. 88p. pap. 10.00 *(978-84-931888-1-8(6))* Editorial Brief ESP. Dist: Independent Pubs. Group.

Festival Fun: 6 Each of 1 Anthology, 6 vols. (Wildcats Ser.). 32p. (gr. 2-8). *(978-0-322-02424-3(2))* Wright Group/McGraw-Hill.

Fight Deck: Level D, 6 vols. (Wonder Worldtm Ser.). 16p. 24.95 *(978-0-7802-1203-9(7))* Wright Group/McGraw-Hill.

Find It!: a Big Book of Seek & Find Adventures. 2015. (ENG.). 176p. (J). (gr. -1-3). pap. *(978-1-78393-828-5(5))* Make Believe Ideas.

Find Yourself a Friend, 6 vols. (Multicultural Programs Ser.). 16p. (gr. 1-3). 24.95 *(978-0-7802-9210-9(3))* Wright Group/McGraw-Hill.

Finding Places, Grade 1: American Readers. (J). (gr. 1). *(978-0-669-04936-7(0))*; wbk. ed. *(978-0-669-04942-8(5))* Houghton Mifflin Harcourt School Pubs.

Fire! Fire! 6 Each of 1 Anthology, 6 vols. (Wildcats Ser.). 32p. (gr. 2-8). *(978-0-322-00581-5(7))* Wright Group/McGraw-Hill.

First Explorers Primeros Exploradores Set 1: English - 1 Each of 12 Student Books, 1 Each of 12 Lesson Plans. (First Explorers. Primeros Exploradores Nonfiction Sets Ser.). (gr. 1-2). 107.95 *(978-0-7699-1360-5(1))* Shortland Pubns. (U. S. A.) Inc.

First Explorers Primeros Exploradores Set 1: English - 6 Each of 12 Student Books, 1 Each of 12 Lesson Plans: Set 1. (First Explorers. Primeros Exploradores Nonfiction Sets Ser.). (gr. 1-2). 407.50 *(978-0-7699-1364-3(4))* Shortland Pubns. (U. S. A.) Inc.

First Explorers Primeros Exploradores Set 2: English - 6 Each of 12 Student Books, 1 Each of 12 Lesson Plans. (First Explorers. Primeros Exploradores Nonfiction Sets Ser.). (gr. 1-2). 452.50 *(978-0-7699-1365-0(2))* Shortland Pubns. (U. S. A.) Inc.

First Explorers Primeros Exploradores Set. 3: English - 1 Each of 12 Student Books, 1 Each of 12 Lesson Plans. (First Explorers. Primeros Exploradores Nonfiction Sets Ser.). (gr. 1-2). 115.50 *(978-0-7699-1361-2(X))* Shortland Pubns. (U. S. A.) Inc.

First Explorers Primeros Exploradores Sets 1-2: English - 1 Each of 24 Student Books, 1 Each of 24 Lesson Plans. (First Explorers. Primeros Exploradores Nonfiction Sets Ser.). (gr. 1-2). 223.50 *(978-0-7699-1366-7(0))* Shortland Pubns. (U. S. A.) Inc.

First Explorers Primeros Exploradores Sets 1-2: English - 6 Each of 24 Student Books, 1 Each of 24 Lesson Plans. (First Explorers. Primeros Exploradores Nonfiction Sets Ser.). (gr. 1-2). 816.95 *(978-0-7699-1359-9(8))* Shortland Pubns. (U. S. A.) Inc.

Fish: Level E, 6 vols. (Wonder Worldtm Ser.). 16p. 29.95 *(978-0-7802-1994-6(5))*; 26.50 *(978-0-7802-7004-6(5))* Wright Group/McGraw-Hill.

Fishing: Level F, 6 vols. (Wonder Worldtm Ser.). 16p. 29.95 *(978-0-7802-1996-0(1))* Wright Group/McGraw-Hill.

The Five Senses: Big Book: Level I. Group 1. (Story Box Ser.). 16p. 31.50 *(978-0-322-02459-5(5))* Wright Group/McGraw-Hill.

Flash Kids Editors, ed. Main Idea: Grade 3 (Flash Skills) 2010. (Flash Skills Ser.). (ENG.). 64p. (J). pap. 3.95 *(978-1-4114-3442-4(0),* Spark Publishing Group) Sterling Publishing Co., Inc.

—Reading Comprehension: Grade 2 (Flash Skills) 2010. (Flash Skills Ser.). (ENG.). 64p. (J). pap. 3.95 *(978-1-4114-3472-1(2),* Spark Publishing Group) Sterling Publishing Co., Inc.

—Reading Comprehension: Grade 3 (Flash Skills) 2010. (Flash Skills Ser.). (ENG.). 64p. (J). pap. 3.95 *(978-1-4114-3446-2(3),* Spark Publishing Group) Sterling Publishing Co., Inc.

—Reading Comprehension: Grade 4 (Flash Skills) 2010. (Flash Skills Ser.). (ENG.). 64p. (J). pap. 3.95 *(978-1-4114-3440-0(4),* Spark Publishing Group) Sterling Publishing Co., Inc.

—Reading Comprehension: Grade 5 (Flash Skills) 2010. (Flash Skills Ser.). (ENG.). 64p. (J). pap. 3.95 *(978-1-4114-3476-9(5),* Spark Publishing Group) Sterling Publishing Co., Inc.

—Reading Comprehension: Grade 6 (Flash Skills) 2010. (Flash Skills Ser.). (ENG.). 64p. (J). pap. 3.95 *(978-1-4114-3477-6(3),* Spark Publishing Group) Sterling Publishing Co., Inc.

Flash Kids Editors, Flash Kids, ed. Summer Study, Grade 3. 2016. (Summer Study Ser.). (ENG., Illus.). 160p. (J). (gr. 3-3). pap. 9.95 *(978-1-4114-7859-6(2),* Spark Publishing Group) Sterling Publishing Co., Inc.

—Summer Study, Grade 4. 2016. (Summer Study Ser.). (ENG., Illus.). 160p. (J). (gr. 4-4). pap. 9.95 *(978-1-4114-7860-2(6),* Spark Publishing Group) Sterling Publishing Co., Inc.

—Summer Study, Grade 5. 2016. (Summer Study Ser.). (ENG., Illus.). 160p. (J). (gr. 5-5). pap. 9.95 *(978-1-4114-7861-9(4),* Spark Publishing Group) Sterling Publishing Co., Inc.

—Summer Study, Kindergarten. 2016. (Summer Study Ser.). (ENG., Illus.). 160p. (J). (gr. k-k). pap. 9.95 *(978-1-4114-7862-6(2),* Spark Publishing Group) Sterling Publishing Co., Inc.

Flea Treat Little Book: Early Reading Fluency, Level C. 2004. (gr. 3). pap. 6.00 *(978-0-7398-8290-0(2))* Steck-Vaughn.

Fletcher, Barbara. A Rose on the River: Level U, 6 vols. (Mountain Peaks Ser.). 128p. (gr. 6-18). 36.95 *(978-0-322-05888-0(0))* Wright Group/McGraw-Hill.

Flip, Flap, & Fluff: Family Blends: Level B, 6 vols. (Wright Skills Ser.). 16p. (gr. k-3). 17.95 *(978-0-322-01459-6(X))* Wright Group/McGraw-Hill.

The Flood: Level K, 6 vols. (Wonder Worldtm Ser.). 16p. 34.95 *(978-0-7802-4571-6(7))* Wright Group/McGraw-Hill.

Flor Ada, Alma, tr. Take-Home Package: Complete Package. 2003. (Dejame Leer Ser.). (J). 124.95 *(978-0-673-58720-6(7))* Celebration Pr.

Flor Ada, Alma & Campoy, F. Isabel. Colecciones de Libros de la Biblioteca: El Coraje de Sarah Noble. 2003. (Trofeos Ser.). (SPA.). (gr. 6-18). 135.90 *(978-0-15-322124-8(0))* Harcourt Schl. Pubs.

—Colecciones de Libros de la Biblioteca: El Papalote. 2003. (Trofeos Ser.). (SPA.). (gr. 1-18). 81.60 *(978-0-15-319393-4(X))* Harcourt Schl. Pubs.

—Colecciones de Libros de la Biblioteca: Lucita Regresa a Oaxaca. 2003. (Trofeos Ser.). (SPA.). (gr. 3-18). 44.00 *(978-0-15-322094-4(5))* Harcourt Schl. Pubs.

Flores, Debra, et al. Reading Comprehension 1-3: Activities for Understanding. Jennett, Pamela, ed. Grayson, Rick & Iosa, Ann, illus. 2004. 96p. (J). pap. 1.99 *(978-1-59198-045-2(3),* 3384) Creative Teaching Pr., Inc.

—Reading Comprehension 4-6: Activities for Understanding. Jennett, Pamela, ed. Grayson, Rick & Iosa, Ann, illus. 2004. 96p. (J). pap. 12.99 *(978-1-59198-046-9(1),* 3385) Creative Teaching Pr., Inc.

Flour: Level M, 6 vols. (Wonder Worldtm Ser.). 16p. 34.95 *(978-0-7802-1998-4(8))* Wright Group/McGraw-Hill.

Fluency Skills Guide. (Sunshine Skills Guides). 25.95 *(978-0-7802-9858-3(6))* Wright Group/McGraw-Hill.

Fluent Library. 2005. (YA). (gr. -1-3). 119.70 *(978-0-8215-8990-8(3))*; Vol. 2. 119.70 *(978-0-8215-8991-5(1))* Sadlier, William H. Inc.

Fluent Stage 3. 2005. (Little Celebrations Picture/Text & Literacy Cards Ser.). (J). (gr. k-3). 128.50 *(978-0-673-77359-3(0))* Celebration Pr.

Fly Away Home: Level K, 6 vols. (Wonder Worldtm Ser.). 16p. 34.95 *(978-0-7802-1205-3(3))* Wright Group/McGraw-Hill.

Follow the Map, 6 vols. 8p. (gr. k-1). 21.50 *(978-0-322-02067-2(0))* Wright Group/McGraw-Hill.

Food Trappers: Level K, 6 vols. (Wonder Worldtm Ser.). 16p. 34.95 *(978-0-7802-1209-1(6))* Wright Group/McGraw-Hill.

Foods of the World, 6 vols. (Book2WebTM Ser.). (gr. 4-8). 36.50 *(978-0-322-02985-9(6))* Wright Group/McGraw-Hill.

Foster, Kelli C. & Erickson, Gina Clegg. Get Ready... Get Set... Read!, 5 sets (35 bks.) Russell, Kerri G., illus. (J). lib. bdg. 418.25Set. lib. bdg. 418.25 *(978-1-56674-920-6(4))* Forest Hse. Publishing Co., Inc.

Foundations: Early Emergent-Upper Emergent - 1 Each of 25 Student Books: Level E. 124.95 *(978-0-322-02722-0(5))* Wright Group/McGraw-Hill.

The Four A's: 6 Each of 1 Anthology, 6 vols. (Wildcats Ser.). 32p. (gr. 2-8). *(978-0-322-00595-2(7))* Wright Group/McGraw-Hill.

The Fox: Consonants q, x, z; -ack, -ick, -ill word families: Level A, 6 vols. (Wright Skills Ser.). 12p. (gr. k-3). 17.95 *(978-0-322-01456-5(5))* Wright Group/McGraw-Hill.

Francis, Andre. Cultural Instruments: Big Book: Level R. Group 1. (Take-Twostm Ser.). 32p. 38.95 *(978-0-322-04490-6(1))* Wright Group/McGraw-Hill.

Fredericks, Anthony D. & Lynott, Vicky. Write to Comprehend: Using Writing as a Tool to Build Reading Comprehension. 2007. (Illus.). 138p. per. 19.95 *(978-1-59647-120-7(4))* Good Year Bks.

Frog & Toad All Year. 2003. 31.95 *(978-0-673-75800-2(1))* Celebration Pr.

Frog on a Log: 1 Big Book, 6 Each of 1 Student Book, & 1 Cassette. (Song Box Ser.). (gr. 1-2). 68.95 *(978-0-7802-3204-4(6))* Wright Group/McGraw-Hill.

Frog on a Log: Big Book. (Song Box Ser.). (gr. 1-2). 31.50 *(978-0-7802-2256-4(3))* Wright Group/McGraw-Hill.

From Rocks to Sand: Level L, 6 vols. (Wonder Worldtm Ser.). 16p. 34.95 *(978-0-7802-4575-4(X))* Wright Group/McGraw-Hill.

From the Air: Level F, 6 vols. (Wonder Worldtm Ser.). 16p. 29.95 *(978-0-7802-2000-3(5))* Wright Group/McGraw-Hill.

Fruit Salad: Level D, 6 vols. (Wonder Worldtm Ser.). 16p. 24.95 *(978-0-7802-1241-1(X))* Wright Group/McGraw-Hill.

Fry, Ron. Surefire Tips to Improve Your Reading Skills, 01 vols., 1. 2016. (Surefire Study Success Ser.). (ENG.). 128p. (YA). 35.60 *(978-1-5081-7094-5(0),* Rosen Young Adult) Rosen Publishing Group, Inc., The.

Fuerst, Jeffrey B. A-Hunting We Will Go. Greenhead, Bill, illus. 2010. (Rising Readers Ser.). (J). 3.49 *(978-1-60719-684-6(0))* Newmark Learning LLC.

—Jack Be Nimble. Colby, Garry, illus. 2010. (Rising Readers Ser.). (J). 3.49 *(978-1-60719-698-3(0))* Newmark Learning LLC.

—Lazy Mary. Kelley, Gerald, illus. 2010. (Rising Readers Ser.). (J). 3.49 *(978-1-60719-699-0(9))* Newmark Learning LLC.

Furgang, Kathy. Reading Fundamentals: Grade 4: Nonfiction Activities to Build Reading Comprehension Skills. 2016. (Flash Kids Fundamentals Ser.). (ENG., Illus.). 96p. (J). (gr. 4-4). pap. 7.95 *(978-1-4114-7884-8(3),* Spark Publishing Group) Sterling Publishing Co., Inc.

Gallinella Rossa. pap. 14.95 *(978-88-04-46594-2(8))* Mondadori ITA. Dist: Distribooks, Inc.

Gant, Linda G. Readers Are Leaders. Gant, Linda G., illus. Date not set. (Illus.). (J). (gr. -1-3). *(978-0-9673625-0-2(4))* Readers Are Leaders.

Gant, Robert, illus. My Big Box of Reading. gif. ed. 2005. 64p. (J). cd-rom 24.95 *(978-1-57791-195-1(4))* Brighter Minds Children's Publishing.

Garbage: Big Book: Level D. (Wonder Worldtm Ser.). 16p. 26.50 *(978-0-7802-7007-7(X))* Wright Group/McGraw-Hill.

Garbage: Level D, 6 vols. (Wonder Worldtm Ser.). 16p. 24.95 *(978-0-7802-2026-3(9))* Wright Group/McGraw-Hill.

Garcia, Ellen. Are You Listening, Jack? Patton, Julia, illus. 2014. (J). (gr. -1). 3.99 *(978-1-4788-0472-7(6))* Newmark Learning LLC.

—Are You Listening, Jack? Lap Book. Patton, Julia, illus. 2014. (MySELF Ser.). (J). (gr. -1-k). 27.00 *(978-1-4788-0509-0(9))* Newmark Learning LLC.

—Be Honest, Jess Lap Book. Mones, Marc, illus. 2014. (MySELF Ser.). (J). (gr. -1-k). 27.00 *(978-1-4788-0508-3(0))* Newmark Learning LLC.

—Be Patient, Maddie Lap Book. Patton, Julia, illus. 2014. (MySELF Ser.). (J). (gr. -1-k). 27.00 *(978-1-4788-0512-0(9))* Newmark Learning LLC.

—Charlie Is Responsible Lap Book. Mones, Marc, illus. 2014. (MySELF Ser.). (J). (gr. -1-k). 27.00 *(978-1-4788-0507-6(2))* Newmark Learning LLC.

—I Am a Star! Lap Book. Evans, Antony, illus. 2014. (MySELF Ser.). (J). (gr. -1-k). 27.00 *(978-1-4788-0516-8(1))* Newmark Learning LLC.

—I Can Make a Plan. Evans, Antony, illus. 2014. (J). (gr. -1). 3.99 *(978-1-4788-0478-9(5))* Newmark Learning LLC.

—I Can Make a Plan Lap Book. Evans, Antony, illus. 2014. (MySELF Ser.). (J). (gr. -1-k). 27.00 *(978-1-4788-0515-1(3))* Newmark Learning LLC.

Gatto con gli Stivali. pap. 14.95 *(978-88-04-44207-3(7))* Mondadori ITA. Dist: Distribooks, Inc.

Gaydos, Nora. Look Around! Sams, B. B., illus. 2003. (NIR! Leveled Readers Ser.). (ENG.). 128p. (J). (gr. -1-2). 16.99 *(978-1-58476-167-9(9),* Now I'm Reading!) Random Hse. Children's Bks.

—My World. Sams, B. B., illus. 2004. (NIR! Leveled Readers Ser.). (ENG.). 128p. (J). (gr. -1-2). 16.99 *(978-1-58476-263-8(2),* Now I'm Reading!) Random Hse. Children's Bks.

Geimer, Allan F. I Can Read, You Can Read: Basic Reading Teaching Guide. 140p. (J). pap. 12.95 *(978-1-886358-02-7(8))* Cellular Publishing.

Get Me Out of Here Little Book: Early Reading Fluency, Level C. 2004. pap. 6.00 *(978-0-7398-8296-2(1))* Steck-Vaughn.

Get Smart Skills Staff. HSPT Reading: New Jersey High School Proficiency Test. 2004. 192p. (gr. 11-18). pap. 14.95 *(978-1-932635-31-7(9))* Webster House Publishing LLC.

—PSSA Reading: Pennsylvania System of School Assessment. 2004. 192p. (gr. 11-18). pap. 14.95 *(978-1-932635-28-7(9))* Webster House Publishing LLC.

Getting FIT: Level A, 6 vols. (Wonder Worldtm Ser.). 16p. 24.95 *(978-0-7802-1036-3(0))* Wright Group/McGraw-Hill.

Getting Glasses: Level I, 6 vols. (Wonder Worldtm Ser.). 16p. 29.95 *(978-0-7802-2002-7(1))* Wright Group/McGraw-Hill.

Getting the Sequence (Gr. 4-5) 2004. (J). *(978-1-58232-131-8(0))* ECS Learning Systems, Inc.

Getting There: Level B, 6 vols. (Wonder Worldtm Ser.). 16p. 24.95 *(978-0-7802-1037-0(9))* Wright Group/McGraw-Hill.

Giachetti, Julia. Don't Give up! Lap Book. Evans, Antony, illus. 2014. (MySELF Ser.). (J). (gr. -1-k). 27.00 *(978-1-4788-0517-5(X))* Newmark Learning LLC.

—I Was So Mad. Poole, Helen, illus. 2014. (J). (gr. -1). 3.99 *(978-1-4788-0462-8(9))* Newmark Learning LLC.

—I Was So Mad Lap Book. Poole, Helen, illus. 2014. (MySELF Ser.). (J). (gr. -1-k). 27.00 *(978-1-4788-0499-4(8))* Newmark Learning LLC.

—My Happy Day. Poole, Helen, illus. 2014. (J). (gr. -1). 3.99 *(978-1-4788-0460-4(2))* Newmark Learning LLC.

—My Happy Day Lap Book. Poole, Helen, illus. 2014. (MySELF Ser.). (J). (gr. -1-k). 27.00 *(978-1-4788-0497-0(1))* Newmark Learning LLC.

—Thanks for Sharing, Tommy. Mones, Marc, illus. 2014. (J). (gr. -1). 3.99 *(978-1-4788-0466-6(1))* Newmark Learning LLC.

—Thanks for Sharing, Tommy Lap Book. Mones, Marc, illus. 2014. (MySELF Ser.). (J). (gr. -1-k). 27.00 *(978-1-4788-0503-8(X))* Newmark Learning LLC.

A Giant-Size Hamburger: Level D, 6 vols. (Wonder Worldtm Ser.). 16p. 24.95 *(978-0-7802-1028-8(X))* Wright Group/McGraw-Hill.

Giants in the City: Hard & Soft c & g: Level B, 6 vols. (Wright Skills Ser.). 16p. (gr. k-3). 26.50 *(978-0-322-01489-3(1))* Wright Group/McGraw-Hill.

Giddyoocha! Big Book: Level J. Group 1. (Story Box Ser.). 16p. 31.50 *(978-0-322-02468-7(4))* Wright Group/McGraw-Hill.

The Gig: Level 4, 6 vols. (Fluency Strand Ser.). (gr. 4-8). 45.00 *(978-1-4045-1229-0(2))* Wright Group/McGraw-Hill.

Ginger's War: Level T. Group 3, 6 vols. (Sunshine Ser.). 48p. 44.95 *(978-0-322-01939-3(7))* Wright Group/McGraw-Hill.

Girl Saves Giant: Level P, 6 vols. (Wonder Worldtm Ser.). 48p. 39.95 *(978-0-7802-7070-1(3))* Wright Group/McGraw-Hill.

Glencoe McGraw-Hill Staff, creator. Timed Readings Plus in Social Studies. 2003. (Timed Readings Plus Ser.). 118p. (J). Bk. 1. per. 17.32 *(978-0-07-845799-9(8),* 9780078457999) Vol. 8. per. 17.32 *(978-0-07-845806-4(4),* 9780078458064) Jamestown.

—Timed Readings Plus in Social Studies Book 10, Vol. 10. 2003. (Timed Readings Plus Ser.). 118p. (J). per. 17.32 *(978-0-07-845808-8(0),* 9780078458088) Jamestown.

—Timed Readings Plus in Social Studies Book 4, Vol. 4. 2003. (Timed Readings Plus Ser.). 118p. (J). (gr. 4-7). per. 17.32 *(978-0-07-845802-6(1),* 9780078458026) Jamestown.

—Timed Readings Plus in Social Studies Book 5, Vol. 5. 2003. (Timed Readings Plus Ser.). 118p. (J). (gr. 4-7). per. 17.32 *(978-0-07-845803-3(X),* 9780078458033) Jamestown.

—Timed Readings Plus in Social Studies Book 6, Vol. 6. 2003. (Timed Readings Plus Ser.). 118p. (J). (gr. 4-7). per. 17.32 *(978-0-07-845804-0(8),* 9780078458040) Jamestown.

Going Far: American Readers. (J). (gr. 1). *(978-0-669-04964-0(6))* Houghton Mifflin Harcourt School Pubs.

Going on a Field Trip, 6 vols. (Multicultural Programs Ser.). 16p. (gr. 1-3). 24.95 *(978-0-7802-9216-1(2))* Wright Group/McGraw-Hill.

Goober Peas: 1 Big Book, 6 Each of 1 Student Book, & 1 Cassette. (Song Box Ser.). (gr. 1-2). 68.95 *(978-0-7802-0943-5(5))* Wright Group/McGraw-Hill.

Good Girl! (Little Book Practice Reader). (J). 6.47 *(978-0-8136-5351-8(7))* Modern Curriculum Pr.

Good Night, Little Bug. (Little Book Practice Reader). (J). *(978-0-8136-1970-5(X))* Modern Curriculum Pr.

The Gotcha Box: Big Book: Level B. Group 2. (Story Box Ser.). 8p. 20.95 *(978-0-322-00328-6(8))* Wright Group/McGraw-Hill.

Grandma's at the Lake. 2003. 22.95 *(978-0-673-75917-7(2))* Celebration Pr.

Grandma's Heart: Level J, 6 vols. (Wonder Worldtm Ser.). 16p. 29.95 *(978-0-7802-1213-8(4))* Wright Group/McGraw-Hill.

Grandpa Knits Hats: Level E. (Wonder Worldtm Ser.). 16p. 29.95 *(978-0-7802-1038-7(7))* Wright Group/McGraw-Hill.

Great Art & Artists, 6 vols. (Book2WebTM Ser.). (gr. 4-8). 36.50 *(978-0-322-02987-3(2))* Wright Group/McGraw-Hill.

Great Battles Through the Ages, 6 vols. 2005. (Great Battles Through the Ages Ser.). (Illus.). 112p. (gr. 6-12). 180.00 *(978-0-7910-7434-3(X),* Chelsea Hse.) Facts On File, Inc.

The Great Big Book of Reading Preschool Costco Edition. 2008. (J). pap. *(978-1-59566-623-9(0))* QEB Publishing Inc.

The Great Monsieur Vertelli: Level R, 6 vols. (Wonder Worldtm Ser.). 48p. 44.95 *(978-0-7802-7083-1(5))* Wright Group/McGraw-Hill.

Grizzly & the Bumble-bee: Big Book: Level K. Group 1. (Sunshine Ser.). 16p. 36.50 *(978-0-7802-5789-4(8))* Wright Group/McGraw-Hill.

Group/McGraw-Hill, Wright. Abraham Lincoln: The Civil War President, 6 vols. (Book2WebTM Ser.). (gr. 4-8). 36.50 *(978-0-322-04462-3(6))* Wright Group/McGraw-Hill.
—Africa: Rich in Land & History, 6 vols. (Book2WebTM Ser.). (gr. 4-8). 36.50 *(978-0-322-04439-5(1))* Wright Group/McGraw-Hill.
—African Art: Level E, 6 vols. (Take Twostm Ser.). 16p. 29.95 *(978-0-322-08988-4(3))* Wright Group/McGraw-Hill.
—Against the Odds: Magazine Anthology - Level 3, 6 vols. (Comprehension Strand Ser.). (gr. 4-8). 54.00 *(978-0-322-06031-9(1))* Wright Group/McGraw-Hill.
—All's Well that End Well: Level N, 6 vols. (Autumn Leaves Ser.). 128p. (gr. 3-6). 36.95 *(978-0-322-06728-8(6))* Wright Group/McGraw-Hill.
—Animal Advocates, 6 vols. (Wildcats Ser.). 32p. (gr. 2-8). *(978-0-322-05861-3(9))* Wright Group/McGraw-Hill.
—Animal Mysteries, 6 vols. (Wildcats Ser.). 32p. (gr. 2-8). *(978-0-322-05859-0(7))* Wright Group/McGraw-Hill.
—Animals Go Mad: Level 2, 6 vols. (Fluency Strand Ser.). (gr. 4-8). 194.95 *(978-1-4045-1292-4(6))* Wright Group/McGraw-Hill.
—Art Show, 6 vols. (D-Man Beans Ser.). 47p. (gr. 4-6). 42.50 *(978-0-322-06262-7(4))* Wright Group/McGraw-Hill.
—Autumn Leaves: Classroom Library Set. (Autumn Leaves Ser.). 81.50 *(978-0-322-07969-4(1))* Wright Group/McGraw-Hill.
—Autumn Leaves: Complete Set. (Autumn Leaves Ser.). 327.95 *(978-0-322-07967-0(5))* Wright Group/McGraw-Hill.
—The Aztec People: Level I, 6 vols. (Take Twostm Ser.). 16p. 29.95 *(978-0-322-08995-2(6))* Wright Group/McGraw-Hill.
—Bad News Good News: Level N, 6 vols. (Autumn Leaves Ser.). 128p. (gr. 3-6). 36.95 *(978-0-322-06733-2(2))* Wright Group/McGraw-Hill.
—Bats about Bats! Level M, 6 vols. (Summer Skies Ser.). 128p. (gr. 3-6). 36.95 *(978-0-322-06724-0(3))* Wright Group/McGraw-Hill.
—Black Tooth the Pirate: Level G, 6 vols. (Take Twostm Ser.). 16p. 29.95 *(978-0-322-08969-3(7))* Wright Group/McGraw-Hill.
—Blow your Top: Magazine Anthology: Level 6, 6 vols. (Comprehension Strand Ser.). (gr. 4-8). 54.00 *(978-0-322-06041-8(9))* Wright Group/McGraw-Hill.
—Bobcat Level: Adventure Journal Set. (Wildcats Ser.). (gr. 2-8). 31.95 *(978-0-322-05791-3(4))* Wright Group/McGraw-Hill.
—Bobcat Level: Lesson Plan Set. (Wildcats Ser.). (gr. 2-8). 96.50 *(978-0-322-06676-2(X))* Wright Group/McGraw-Hill.
—Bobcat Level: Wildcats Bobcat Complete Kit. (Wildcats Ser.). (gr. 2-8). 599.95 *(978-0-322-06484-3(8))* Wright Group/McGraw-Hill.
—Building the Railroads, 6 vols. (Book2WebTM Ser.). (gr. 4-8). 36.50 *(978-0-322-04448-7(0))* Wright Group/McGraw-Hill.
—Burned: Magazine Anthology: Level 7, 6 vols. (Comprehension Strand Ser.). (gr. 4-8). 54.00 *(978-0-322-06044-9(3))* Wright Group/McGraw-Hill.
—Buttons: Collection 1. (Storyteller Interactive Writing Cards Ser.). (gr. k-3). *(978-0-322-09362-1(7))* Wright Group/McGraw-Hill.
—Buzz the Beekeeper: Level 6, 6 vols. (Fluency Strand Ser.). (gr. 4-8). 194.95 *(978-1-4045-1296-2(9))* Wright Group/McGraw-Hill.
—The C & P Pies: Level H, 6 vols. (Take Twostm Ser.). 16p. 29.95 *(978-0-322-08973-0(5))* Wright Group/McGraw-Hill.
—The Calendar: Level G, 6 vols. (Take Twostm Ser.). 16p. 29.95 *(978-0-322-08981-5(6))* Wright Group/McGraw-Hill.
—Celebrating the New Year: Level I, 6 vols. (Take Twostm Ser.). 16p. 29.95 *(978-0-322-08974-7(3))* Wright Group/McGraw-Hill.
—The Chinampa: Level I, 6 vols. (Take Twostm Ser.). 16p. 29.95 *(978-0-322-08996-9(4))* Wright Group/McGraw-Hill.
—Complete Level Sets: Level 3 Complete Set. 2003. (Intervention Ser.). (ENG.). (gr. 3-8). pap. 1785.80 *(978-1-4045-0396-0(X)*, 140450396X) Wright Group/McGraw-Hill.
—Complete Level Sets: Level 4 Complete Set. 2003. (Intervention Ser.). (ENG.). (gr. 3-8). pap. 1785.80 *(978-1-4045-0397-7(8)*, 1404503978) Wright Group/McGraw-Hill.
—Complete Level Sets: Level 5 Complete Set. 2003. (Intervention Ser.). (ENG.). (gr. 3-8). pap. 1785.80 *(978-1-4045-0398-4(6)*, 1404503986) Wright Group/McGraw-Hill.
—Complete Level Sets: Level 6 Complete Set. 2003. (Intervention Ser.). (ENG.). (gr. 3-8). pap. 1785.80 *(978-1-4045-0399-1(4)*, 1404503994) Wright Group/McGraw-Hill.
—Complete Level Sets: Level 7 Complete Set. 2003. (Intervention Ser.). (ENG.). (gr. 3-8). pap. 1785.80 *(978-1-4045-0400-4(1)*, 1404504001) Wright Group/McGraw-Hill.
—Complete Level Sets: Levels 1-2 Complete Set. (Fast Track Reading Ser.). (gr. 4-8). 763.00 *(978-1-4045-0395-3(1))* Wright Group/McGraw-Hill.
—Complete Program Set. 2003. (Intervention Ser.). (ENG.). (gr. 3-8). pap. 12749.16 *(978-1-4045-0404-2(4)*, 1404504044) Wright Group/McGraw-Hill.
—Complete Program Set: Comprehension Strand. (Fast Track Reading Ser.). (gr. 4-8). 2435.00 *(978-1-4045-0406-6(0))* Wright Group/McGraw-Hill.
—Complete Program Set: Fluency Strand. (Fast Track Reading Ser.). (gr. 4-8). 1445.00 *(978-1-4045-0408-0(7))* Wright Group/McGraw-Hill.
—Complete Program Set: Word Work Strand. (Fast Track Reading Ser.). (gr. 4-8). 1299.00 *(978-0-322-07226-8(3))* Wright Group/McGraw-Hill.
—A Day to Remember: Level I, 6 vols. (Take Twostm Ser.). 16p. 29.95 *(978-0-322-08975-4(1))* Wright Group/McGraw-Hill.
—Dog-Sled Racer: Level 5, 6 vols. (Fluency Strand Ser.). (gr. 4-8). 194.95 *(978-1-4045-1295-5(0))* Wright Group/McGraw-Hill.
—Dom's Dragon: Level E, 6 vols. (Take Twostm Ser.). 16p. 29.95 *(978-0-322-08977-8(8))* Wright Group/McGraw-Hill.
—Don't Go Out: Level F, 6 vols. (Take Twostm Ser.). 16p. 29.95 *(978-0-322-08954-9(9))* Wright Group/McGraw-Hill.
—Double Dare., 6 vols. (D-Man Beans Ser.). 47p. (gr. 4-6). 42.50 *(978-0-322-06265-8(9))* Wright Group/McGraw-Hill.
—E-search: Level O, 6 vols. (Autumn Leaves Ser.). 128p. (gr. 3-6). 36.95 *(978-0-322-06730-1(8))* Wright Group/McGraw-Hill.
—Early Emergent Guided Reading Kit 1: Complete Kit. (gr. k-18). 435.96 *(978-1-4045-2057-8(0))* Wright Group/McGraw-Hill.
—Early Emergent Guided Reading Kit 1: Lesson Plans. (gr. k-18). 127.95 *(978-1-4045-2071-4(6))* Wright Group/McGraw-Hill.
—Early Emergent Guided Reading Kit 1: Student Books. 2003. (Gear Up Ser.). (ENG.). (gr. k-k). pap. 159.16 *(978-1-4045-2065-3(1)*, 1404520651) Wright Group/McGraw-Hill.
—Early Fluency-Fluency Writing Kit. 2004. (Wright Group Literacy Ser.). (gr. k-3). 132.50 *(978-0-322-07021-9(X))* Wright Group/McGraw-Hill.
—Early Fluency Guided Reading Kit 1: Student Books. (Sunshine Ser.). (gr. 2-18). 93.50 *(978-0-322-04217-9(8))* Wright Group/McGraw-Hill.
—Early Fluency Guided Reading Kit 5: Student Books, Vol. 5. (gr. 2-18). 93.50 *(978-0-322-04750-1(1))* Wright Group/McGraw-Hill.
—Early Fluency Kit 1: Complete Kit. (gr. 2-18). 536.95 *(978-1-4045-2062-2(7))* Wright Group/McGraw-Hill.
—Early Fluency Kit 1: Student Books. (gr. 2-18). 94.95 *(978-1-4045-2070-7(8))* Wright Group/McGraw-Hill.
—Explorers: Fluency - Complete Kit. (gr. 3-6). 547.95 *(978-0-322-09171-9(3))* Wright Group/McGraw-Hill.
—Explorers Fluency Complete Kit 2, Vol. 2. (gr. 3-4). 547.95 *(978-0-322-09170-2(5))* Wright Group/McGraw-Hill.
—Explorers Fluency Complete Kit 3, Vol. 3. (gr. 3-4). 547.95 *(978-0-322-09169-6(1))* Wright Group/McGraw-Hill.
—Famous Shipwrecks, 6 vols. (Book2WebTM Ser.). (gr. 4-8). 36.50 *(978-0-322-04458-6(8))* Wright Group/McGraw-Hill.
—FDR & Eleanor: Triumphs & Tragedies, 6 vols. (Book2WebTM Ser.). (gr. 4-8). 36.50 *(978-0-322-04463-0(4))* Wright Group/McGraw-Hill.
—Fibonacci's Cows: Level O, 6 vols. (Mountain Peaks Ser.). 128p. (gr. 6-18). 36.95 *(978-0-322-06737-0(5))* Wright Group/McGraw-Hill.
—Fire at the Museum: Decodable Books, 6 vols. 22nd ed. (Fast Track Reading Ser.). 24p. (gr. 4-8). 40.95 *(978-0-322-05977-1(1))* Wright Group/McGraw-Hill.
—Fire at the Museum Play 11: Decodable Plays, 6 vols. (Fast Track Reading Ser.). 24p. (gr. 4-8). 40.95 *(978-0-322-05991-7(7))* Wright Group/McGraw-Hill.
—First Explorers: Upper Emergent - Complete Kit. (gr. 1-18). 386.50 *(978-0-322-09168-9(3))* Wright Group/McGraw-Hill.
—First Explorers: Upper Emergent - Lesson Plan Set - 1 Each of 12 Lesson Plans. (gr. 1-18). 47.95 *(978-0-322-08418-6(0))* Wright Group/McGraw-Hill.
—First Explorers: Upper Emergent-Early Fluency - Complete Kit. (gr. 1-2). 426.50 *(978-0-322-09167-2(5))* Wright Group/McGraw-Hill.
—First Explorers: Upper Emergent-Early Fluency - Lesson Plan Set - 1 Each of 12 Lesson Plans. (gr. 1-2). 47.95 *(978-0-322-08419-3(9))* Wright Group/McGraw-Hill.
—First Explorers: Upper Emergent-Early Fluency - Student Book Set - 1 Each of 12 Titles. (First Explorers. Primeros Exploradores Nonfiction Sets Ser.). (gr. 1-2). 67.50 *(978-0-7699-1362-9(8))* Shortland Pubns. (U. S. A.) Inc.
—Fluency Guided Reading Kit 3 Vol. 3: Student Books, (gr. 3-6). 112.50 *(978-0-322-04751-8(X))* Wright Group/McGraw-Hill.
—Fossils Reveal Clues about Ancient Life, 6 vols. (Book2WebTM Ser.). (gr. 4-8). 36.50 *(978-0-322-04431-9(6))* Wright Group/McGraw-Hill.
—Found & Lost, 6 vols. (D-Man Beans Ser.). 47p. (gr. 4-6). 42.50 *(978-0-322-06268-9(3))* Wright Group/McGraw-Hill.
—From Plan to House: Level H, 6 vols. (Take Twostm Ser.). 16p. 29.95 *(978-0-322-08999-0(9))* Wright Group/McGraw-Hill.
—Gear Up! Early Emergent - 1 Each of 8 Student Books: Level A. 35.95 *(978-1-4045-2041-7(4))* Wright Group/McGraw-Hill.
—Gear Up! Early Emergent - 1 Each of 8 Student Books: Level B. 35.95 *(978-1-4045-2042-4(2))* Wright Group/McGraw-Hill.
—Gear Up! Early Emergent - 1 Each of 8 Student Books: Level C. 35.95 *(978-1-4045-2043-1(0))* Wright Group/McGraw-Hill.
—Gear Up! Early Emergent - 1 Each of 8 Student Books: Level D. 35.95 *(978-1-4045-2044-8(9))* Wright Group/McGraw-Hill.
—Gear Up! Early Emergent - Complete Kit, Vol. 2. (gr. k-1). 435.95 *(978-1-4045-2058-5(9))* Wright Group/McGraw-Hill.
—Gear Up! Early Emergent - Student Book Set - 1 Each of 16 Titles, Vol. 2. 2003. (Gear Up Ser.). (ENG.). (gr. k-k). pap. 159.16 *(978-1-4045-2066-0(X)*, 140452066X) Wright Group/McGraw-Hill.
—Gear Up! Early Fluency - Complete Kit, Vol. 2. (Early Fluency Ser.). (gr. 2-18). 536.95 *(978-1-4045-2064-6(3))* Wright Group/McGraw-Hill.
—Gear Up! Upper Emergent- Student Book Each of 16 Titles. 2003. (Gear Up Ser.). (ENG.). (gr. 1-1). pap. 184.40 *(978-1-4045-2067-7(8)*, 1404520678) Wright Group/McGraw-Hill.
—Gear Up! Upper Emergent-Early Fluency - 1 Each of 8 Student Books: Level J. 39.50 *(978-1-4045-2051-6(1))* Wright Group/McGraw-Hill.
—Gear Up! Upper Emergent-Early Fluency - 1 Each of 8 Student Books: Level K. (Early Fluency Ser.). 47.50 *(978-1-4045-2052-3(X))* Wright Group/McGraw-Hill.
—Gear Up! Upper Emergent-Early Fluency - 1 Each of 8 Student Books: Level L. (Early Fluency Ser.). 47.50 *(978-1-4045-2053-0(8))* Wright Group/McGraw-Hill.
—Gear Up! Upper Emergent-Early Fluency - 1 Each of 8 Student Books: Level M. (Early Fluency Ser.). 47.50 *(978-1-4045-2054-7(6))* Wright Group/McGraw-Hill.
—Gear Up! Upper Emergent-Early Fluency - 1 Each of 8 Student Books: Level N. (Early Fluency Ser.). 47.50 *(978-1-4045-2056-1(2))* Wright Group/McGraw-Hill.
—Gear Up! Vol. 2: Early Emergent - Gear up! for Guided Reading. (gr. 2-18). 19.50 incl. DVD *(978-1-4045-2079-0(1))* Wright Group/McGraw-Hill.
—Gear Up! Vol. 2: Early Emergent - Gear up! Guided Reading Overview. (gr. 2-18). 19.50 *(978-1-4045-1950-3(5))* Wright Group/McGraw-Hill.
—Gear Up! Vol. 2: Early Fluency - Student Book Set - 1 Each of 16 Titles. (Early Fluency Ser.). (gr. 2-18). 71.95 *(978-1-4045-2072-1(4))* Wright Group/McGraw-Hill.
—Gear Up! Vol. 3: Upper Emergent - Complete Kit. (gr. 1-18). 499.95 *(978-1-4045-2061-5(9))* Wright Group/McGraw-Hill.
—Gear Up! Vol. 3: Upper Emergent - Student Book Set - 1 Each of 16 Titles. (gr. 1-18). 78.95 *(978-1-4045-2069-1(4))* Wright Group/McGraw-Hill.
—Ger Up! Upper Emergent - 1 Each of 8 Student Books: Level E. 39.50 *(978-1-4045-2045-5(7))* Wright Group/McGraw-Hill.
—Ger Up! Upper Emergent - 1 Each of 8 Student Books: Level F. 39.50 *(978-1-4045-2046-2(5))* Wright Group/McGraw-Hill.
—Ger Up! Upper Emergent - 1 Each of 8 Student Books: Level G. 39.50 *(978-1-4045-2048-6(1))* Wright Group/McGraw-Hill.
—Ger Up! Upper Emergent - 1 Each of 8 Student Books: Level H. 39.50 *(978-1-4045-2049-3(X))* Wright Group/McGraw-Hill.
—Ger Up! Upper Emergent - 1 Each of 8 Student Books: Level I. 39.50 *(978-1-4045-2050-9(3))* Wright Group/McGraw-Hill.
—Guided Reading Kits: Upper Emergent Kit 1 (Student Books) (gr. 1-18). 79.95 *(978-0-322-04339-8(5))* Wright Group/McGraw-Hill.
—Guided Reading Kits: Early Emergent Kit 2 Vol. 2: Student Books. (gr. k-18). 66.95 *(978-0-322-04350-3(6))* Wright Group/McGraw-Hill.
—Guided Reading Kits: Early Emergent Kit 4 Vol. 4: Student Books. (gr. k-18). 66.95 *(978-0-322-04348-0(4))* Wright Group/McGraw-Hill.
—Guided Reading Kits: Upper Emergent Kit 1: Student Books. (gr. 1-18). 79.95 *(978-0-322-04347-3(6))* Wright Group/McGraw-Hill.
—Guided Reading Kits: Upper Emergent Kit 2 Vol. 2: Student Books. (gr. 1-18). 79.95 *(978-0-322-04346-6(8))* Wright Group/McGraw-Hill.
—Guided Reading Kits: Upper Emergent Kit 3 Vol. 3: Student Books. (gr. 1-18). 79.95 *(978-0-322-04345-9(X))* Wright Group/McGraw-Hill.
—Helen Keller: Level 3, 6 vols. (Fluency Strand Ser.). (gr. 4-8). 194.95 *(978-1-4045-1293-1(4))* Wright Group/McGraw-Hill.
—I Want Some Honey: Level E, 6 vols. (Take Twostm Ser.). 16p. 29.95 *(978-0-322-08956-3(5))* Wright Group/McGraw-Hill.
—In the Rain Forest, 6 vols. (Wildcats Ser.). 32p. (gr. 2-8). *(978-0-322-00599-0(X))* Wright Group/McGraw-Hill.
—The Lazy Moon: Level G, 6 vols. (Take Twostm Ser.). 16p. 29.95 *(978-0-322-08982-2(4))* Wright Group/McGraw-Hill.
—Magnificent Masks: 6 Each of 1 Anthology, 6 vols. (Wildcats Ser.). 32p. (gr. 2-8). *(978-0-322-05624-4(1))* Wright Group/McGraw-Hill.
—Make a Raft: Level E, 6 vols. (Take Twostm Ser.). 16p. 29.95 *(978-0-322-08976-1(X))* Wright Group/McGraw-Hill.
—Make me Laugh! 6 Each of 1 Anthology, 6 vols. (Wildcats Ser.). 32p. (gr. 2-8). *(978-0-322-05628-2(4))* Wright Group/McGraw-Hill.
—Maps: Level I, 6 vols. (Take Twostm Ser.). 16p. 29.95 *(978-0-322-08966-2(2))* Wright Group/McGraw-Hill.
—Mira Hacia el Cielo, 6 vols. (First Explorers. Primeros Exploradores Nonfiction Sets Ser.). (SPA.). (gr. 1-2). 29.95 *(978-0-7699-1471-8(3))* Shortland Pubns. (U. S. A.) Inc.
—Mischief & Mayhem: Level O, 6 vols. (Autumn Leaves Ser.). 128p. (gr. 3-6). 36.95 *(978-0-322-06727-1(8))* Wright Group/McGraw-Hill.
—Mosquito Attack: Level 4, 6 vols. (Fluency Strand Ser.). (gr. 4-8). 194.95 *(978-1-4045-1294-8(2))* Wright Group/McGraw-Hill.
—Move it & Shake It! 6 Each of 1 Anthology, 6 vols. (Wildcats Ser.). 32p. (gr. 2-8). *(978-0-322-05621-3(7))* Wright Group/McGraw-Hill.
—Movie Magic, 6 vols. (Wildcats Ser.). 32p. (gr. 2-8). *(978-0-322-05630-5(6))* Wright Group/McGraw-Hill.
—The Music Scene, 6 vols. (Wildcats Ser.). 32p. (gr. 2-8). *(978-0-322-05631-2(4))* Wright Group/McGraw-Hill.
—My Word! what a Bird! Collection 4. (Storyteller Interactive Writing Cards Ser.). (gr. k-3). *(978-0-322-09325-6(2))* Wright Group/McGraw-Hill.
—No Hay Nadie Como Tu, 6 vols. (First Explorers. Primeros Exploradores Nonfiction Sets Ser.). (SPA.). (gr. 1-2). 29.95 *(978-0-7699-1478-7(0))* Shortland Pubns. (U. S. A.) Inc.
—No Room, New Rules, 6 vols. (D-Man Beans Ser.). 47p. (gr. 4-6). 42.50 *(978-0-322-06263-4(2))* Wright Group/McGraw-Hill.
—On the Prowl: 6 Each of 1 Anthology, 6 vols. (Wildcats Ser.). 32p. (gr. 2-8). *(978-0-322-05852-1(X))* Wright Group/McGraw-Hill.
—Outback School: Level E, 6 vols. (Take Twostm Ser.). 16p. 29.95 *(978-0-322-08949-5(2))* Wright Group/McGraw-Hill.
—Panther Level: Wildcats Panther Complete Kit. (Wildcats Ser.). (gr. 2-8). 599.95 *(978-0-322-06490-4(2))* Wright Group/McGraw-Hill.
—Paper Capers: Level N, 6 vols. (Raging Rivers Ser.). 128p. (gr. 3-6). 36.95 *(978-0-322-06726-4(X))* Wright Group/McGraw-Hill.
—Pat's Picture: Level E, 6 vols. (Take Twostm Ser.). 16p. 29.95 *(978-0-322-08989-1(1))* Wright Group/McGraw-Hill.
—Phonics & Word Study Complete Kits: Phonics & Word Study: Level B. (gr. k-3). 429.50 *(978-0-322-03872-1(3))* Wright Group/McGraw-Hill.
—Picture This! 6 Each of 1 Anthology, 6 vols. (Wildcats Ser.). 32p. (gr. 2-8). *(978-0-322-05627-5(6))* Wright Group/McGraw-Hill.
—Pigeon Princess: Level O, 6 vols. (Autumn Leaves Ser.). 128p. (gr. 3-6). 36.95 *(978-0-322-06729-5(4))* Wright Group/McGraw-Hill.
—Pixels & Paint, 6 vols. (Wildcats Ser.). 32p. (gr. 2-8). *(978-0-322-05625-1(X))* Wright Group/McGraw-Hill.
—Plagues: Magazine Anthology: Level 7, 6 vols. (Comprehension Strand Ser.). (gr. 4-8). 54.00 *(978-0-322-09863-3(7))* Wright Group/McGraw-Hill.
—Reading Recovery Kits: Reading Recovery Complete Set. (Reading Recovery Ser.). (J). (gr. k-6). 2754.50 *(978-0-322-04770-9(6))* Wright Group/McGraw-Hill.
—River Wild: 6 Each of 1 Anthology, 6 vols. (Wildcats Ser.). 32p. (gr. 2-8). *(978-0-322-05857-6(0))* Wright Group/McGraw-Hill.
—Rollers & Blades: Level H, 6 vols. (Take Twostm Ser.). 16p. 29.95 *(978-0-322-08964-8(6))* Wright Group/McGraw-Hill.
—The Secret Socer Ball Maker: Level G, 6 vols. (Take Twostm Ser.). 16p. 29.95 *(978-0-322-08991-4(3))* Wright Group/McGraw-Hill.
—Set 1: Los Alimentos, 6 vols. (First Explorers. Primeros Exploradores Nonfiction Sets Ser.). (SPA.). (gr. 1-2). 29.95 *(978-0-7699-1469-5(1))* Shortland Pubns. (U. S. A.) Inc.
—Set 2: Los Dinosaurios, 6 vols., Vol. 2. (First Explorers. Primeros Exploradores Nonfiction Sets Ser.). (SPA.). (gr. 1-2). 34.95 *(978-0-7699-1484-8(5))* Shortland Pubns. (U. S. A.) Inc.
—Slimed! 6 Each of 1 Anthology, 6 vols. (Wildcats Ser.). 32p. (gr. 2-8). *(978-0-322-05853-8(8))* Wright Group/McGraw-Hill.
—So You Want this Job, do You? Magazine Anthology: Level 6, 6 vols. (Comprehension Strand Ser.). (gr. 4-8). 54.00 *(978-0-322-06042-5(7))* Wright Group/McGraw-Hill.
—Stories on Stage, 6 vols. (Wildcats Ser.). 32p. (gr. 2-8). *(978-0-322-05622-0(5))* Wright Group/McGraw-Hill.
—The Story Box: Early Fluency - Student Book Set - 1 Each of 16 Titles. 2nd ed. (gr. 2-18). 98.50 *(978-0-322-04052-6(3))* Wright Group/McGraw-Hill.
—The Story Box Vol. 3: Early Emergent Kit 3- Lesson Plan Set - 1 Each of 16 Lesson Plans. (gr. k-18). 63.95 *(978-0-322-05929-0(1))* Wright Group/McGraw-Hill.
—Storyteller: Early Emergent - 1 Each of 16 Student Books: Level D. 78.95 *(978-1-4045-1977-0(7))* Wright Group/McGraw-Hill.
—Storyteller: Early Emergent - 1 Each of 3 Student Books: Level A. 14.50 *(978-1-4045-1954-1(8))* Wright Group/McGraw-Hill.
—Storyteller: Early Emergent - 1 Each of 6 Student Books: Level B. 29.50 *(978-1-4045-1962-6(9))* Wright Group/McGraw-Hill.
—Storyteller: Early Emergent - 1 Each of 7 Student Books: Level C. 34.50 *(978-1-4045-1970-1(X))* Wright Group/McGraw-Hill.
—Storyteller: Early Emergent - Student Book Set - 1 Each of 16 Fiction & Nonfiction Titles. (Storyteller Ser.). (gr. k-18). 79.95 *(978-1-4045-1051-7(6))* Wright Group/McGraw-Hill.
—Storyteller: Upper Emergent - 1 Each of 14 Student Books: Level G. 82.95 *(978-1-4045-1983-1(1))* Wright Group/McGraw-Hill.
—Storyteller: Upper Emergent - 1 Each of 15 Student Books: Level E. 88.95 *(978-1-4045-1981-7(5))* Wright Group/McGraw-Hill.
—Storyteller: Upper Emergent - 1 Each of 15 Student Books: Level F. 112.95 *(978-1-4045-1982-4(3))* Wright Group/McGraw-Hill.
—Storyteller: Upper Emergent - 1 Each of 15 Student Books: Level H. 88.95 *(978-1-4045-1984-8(X))* Wright Group/McGraw-Hill.
—Storyteller: Upper Emergent - Complete Kit, Vol. 5. (Storyteller Ser.). (gr. 1-18). 549.50 *(978-1-4045-1041-8(9))* Wright Group/McGraw-Hill.
—Storyteller: Upper Emergent - Lesson Plan Set - 1 Each of 16 Lesson Plans. (Storyteller Ser.). (gr. 1-18). 127.95 *(978-1-4045-1074-6(5))* Wright Group/McGraw-Hill.
—Storyteller: Upper Emergent - Student Book Set - 1 Each of 16 Fiction & Nonfiction Titles. (Storyteller Ser.). (gr. 1-18). 96.50 *(978-1-4045-1058-6(3))* Wright Group/McGraw-Hill.
—Storyteller: Upper Emergent-Early Fluency - 1 Each of 14 Student Books: Level I. 82.95 *(978-1-4045-1985-5(8))* Wright Group/McGraw-Hill.
—Storyteller: Upper Emergent-Early Fluency - 1 Each of 15 Student Books: Level J. 88.95 *(978-1-4045-1986-2(6))* Wright Group/McGraw-Hill.
—Storyteller: Upper Emergent-Early Fluency - 1 Each of 4 Student Books: Level K. 27.50 *(978-1-4045-1987-9(4))* Wright Group/McGraw-Hill.
—Storyteller Vol. 2: Early Emergent - Complete Kit. (Storyteller Ser.). (gr. k-18). 485.50 *(978-1-4045-1036-4(2))* Wright Group/McGraw-Hill.
—Storyteller Chapter Books: Early Fluency-Fluency - 1 Each of 10 Titles: Level O. 61.50 *(978-1-4045-0949-8(6))* Wright Group/McGraw-Hill.
—Storyteller Chapter Books: Early Fluency-Fluency - 1 Each of 11 Titles: Level N. 69.50 *(978-1-4045-0948-1(8))* Wright Group/McGraw-Hill.
—Storyteller Chapter Books: Early Fluency-Fluency - 1 Each of 4 Titles: Level P. 24.50 *(978-1-4045-0950-4(X))* Wright Group/McGraw-Hill.
—Storyteller Chapter Books: Early Fluency-Fluency - 1 Each of 4 Titles: Level Q. 24.50 *(978-1-4045-0951-1(8))* Wright Group/McGraw-Hill.
—Storyteller Chapter Books: Fluency - 1 Each of 2 Title: Level U. 11.95 *(978-1-4045-0955-9(0))* Wright Group/McGraw-Hill.
—Storyteller Chapter Books: Fluency - 1 Each of 2 Titles: Level R. 11.95 *(978-1-4045-0952-8(6))* Wright Group/McGraw-Hill.
—Storyteller Chapter Books: Upper Emergent-Early Fluency - 1 Each of 18 Titles: Level M. 130.95 *(978-1-4045-0947-4(X))* Wright Group/McGraw-Hill.
—Storyteller Chapter Books: Upper Emergent-Early Fluency - 1 Each of 4 Titles: Level J. 27.95 *(978-1-4045-0944-3(5))* Wright Group/McGraw-Hill.
—Storyteller Chapter Books: Upper Emergent-Early Fluency - 1 Each of 8 Titles: Level K. 57.50 *(978-1-4045-0945-0(3))* Wright Group/McGraw-Hill.
—Storyteller Chapter Books: Upper Emergent-Early Fluency - 1 Each of 8 Titles: Level L. 55.50 *(978-1-4045-0946-7(1))* Wright Group/McGraw-Hill.
—Storyteller Upper Emergent Guided Reading Complete Kit 1. (Storyteller Ser.). (gr. 1-18). 549.50 *(978-1-4045-1037-1(0))* Wright Group/McGraw-Hill.
—Storyteller Upper Emergent Guided Reading Complete Kit 2, Vol. 2. (Storyteller Ser.). (gr. 1-18). 549.50 *(978-1-4045-1038-8(9))* Wright Group/McGraw-Hill.
—Storyteller Upper Emergent Guided Reading Complete Kit 3, Vol. 3. (Storyteller Ser.). (gr. 1-18). 549.50 *(978-1-4045-1039-5(7))* Wright Group/McGraw-Hill.

—Storyteller Upper Emergent Guided Reading Kit, Set. (Storyteller Ser.). (gr. 1-18). 93.50 *(978-1-4045-1056-2(7))* Wright Group/McGraw-Hill.
—Storyteller Upper Emergent Guided Reading Kit 3, Set. (Storyteller Ser.). (gr. 1-18). 93.50 *(978-1-4045-1055-5(9))* Wright Group/McGraw-Hill.
—Storyteller Upper Emergent Guided Reading Kit 5, Set. (Storyteller Ser.). (gr. 1-18). 93.50 *(978-1-4045-1057-9(5))* Wright Group/McGraw-Hill.
—Stranger Than Fiction: 6 Each of 1 Anthology, 6 vols. (Wildcats Ser.). 32p. (gr. 2-8). *(978-0-322-05855-2(4))* Wright Group/McGraw-Hill.
—Summer Skies: Classroom Library Set. (Summer Skies Ser.). 81.50 *(978-0-322-07968-7(3))* Wright Group/McGraw-Hill.
—Summer Skies: Complete Set. (Summer Skies Ser.). 327.95 *(978-0-322-07963-2(2))* Wright Group/McGraw-Hill.
—Sunshine: Early Emergent - Group 3: 1 Each of 4 Student Books: Level A. (Sunshine Ser.). 16.95 *(978-0-322-03707-6(7))* Wright Group/McGraw-Hill.
—Sunshine: Early Emergent - Group 3: 1 Each of 4 Student Books: Level C. (Sunshine Ser.). 16.95 *(978-0-322-03709-0(3))* Wright Group/McGraw-Hill.
—Sunshine: Early Emergent - Group 3: 1 Each of 4 Student Books: Level D. (Sunshine Ser.). 16.95 *(978-0-322-03710-6(7))* Wright Group/McGraw-Hill.
—Sunshine: Early Emergent - Group 3:1 Each of 4 Student Books: Level B. (Sunshine Ser.). 16.95 *(978-0-322-03708-3(5))* Wright Group/McGraw-Hill.
—Sunshine: Early Emergent-Upper Emergent - Group 2: 1 Each of 8 Student Books: Level E. (Sunshine Ser.). 39.95 *(978-0-322-04317-6(4))* Wright Group/McGraw-Hill.
—Sunshine: Early Emergent-Upper Emergent - Group 3: 1 Each of 5 Student Books: Level E. (Sunshine Ser.). 24.95 *(978-0-322-03711-3(5))* Wright Group/McGraw-Hill.
—Sunshine: Early Emergent-Upper Emergent - Groups 1-2: 1 Each of 16 Student Books: Level E. (Sunshine Ser.). 79.95 *(978-0-322-04316-9(6))* Wright Group/McGraw-Hill.
—Sunshine: Early Fluency - Enrichment Library: 1 each of 12 titles: Level L. 69.95 *(978-0-322-04025-0(6))* Wright Group/McGraw-Hill.
—Sunshine: Early Fluency - Enrichment Library: 1 each of 5 titles: Level N. (Sunshine Ser.). 29.50 *(978-0-322-04028-1(0))* Wright Group/McGraw-Hill.
—Sunshine: Early Fluency - Enrichment Library, Groups 1-2: 1 each of 11 titles: Level K. (Sunshine Ser.). 69.95 *(978-0-322-04024-3(8))* Wright Group/McGraw-Hill.
—Sunshine: Early Fluency - Group 1: 1 each of 11 titles: Level K. (Sunshine Ser.). 64.50 *(978-0-322-04308-4(5))* Wright Group/McGraw-Hill.
—Sunshine: Early Fluency - Group 1: 1 each of 11 titles: Level L. (Sunshine Ser.). 64.50 *(978-0-322-04311-4(5))* Wright Group/McGraw-Hill.
—Sunshine: Early Fluency - Group 1; 1 each of 11 titles: Level M. (Sunshine Ser.). 64.50 *(978-0-322-04313-8(1))* Wright Group/McGraw-Hill.
—Sunshine: Early Fluency - Group 3: 1 each of 11 Titles: Level N. 64.50 *(978-0-322-05241-3(6))* Wright Group/McGraw-Hill.
—Sunshine: Early Fluency - Group 3: 1 each of 8 Titles: Level K. 46.95 *(978-0-322-05238-3(6))* Wright Group/McGraw-Hill.
—Sunshine: Early Fluency - Groups 1-2: 1 each of 17 titles: Level K. (Sunshine Ser.). 99.50 *(978-0-322-04307-7(7))* Wright Group/McGraw-Hill.
—Sunshine: Early Fluency - Groups 1-2: 1 each of 17 titles: Level L. (Sunshine Ser.). 99.50 *(978-0-322-04309-1(3))* Wright Group/McGraw-Hill.
—Sunshine: Early Fluency-Enrichment Library; 1 each of 7 titles: Level M. (Sunshine Ser.). 40.95 *(978-0-322-04027-4(2))* Wright Group/McGraw-Hill.
—Sunshine: Early Fluency-Group 1; 1 each of 11 titles: Level N. (Sunshine Ser.). 64.50 *(978-0-322-04315-2(8))* Wright Group/McGraw-Hill.
—Sunshine: Early Fluency-Group 3: 1 each of 8 Titles: Level L. 46.95 *(978-0-322-05239-0(4))* Wright Group/McGraw-Hill.
—Sunshine: Early Fluency-Group 3; 1 each of 8 Titles: Level M. 46.95 *(978-0-322-05240-6(8))* Wright Group/McGraw-Hill.
—Sunshine: Early Fluency-Groups 1-2; 1 each of 17 titles: Level N. (Sunshine Ser.). 99.50 *(978-0-322-04314-5(X))* Wright Group/McGraw-Hill.
—Sunshine: Fluency - Group 3: 1 Each of 4 Titles: Level S. (Sunshine Ser.). 29.95 *(978-0-322-05247-5(5))* Wright Group/McGraw-Hill.
—Sunshine: Fluency - Group 3: 1 Each of 4 Titles: Level T. (Sunshine Ser.). 29.95 *(978-0-322-05248-2(3))* Wright Group/McGraw-Hill.
—Sunshine: Fluency - Group 3: 1 each of 6 Titles: Level O. 39.95 *(978-0-322-05242-0(4))* Wright Group/McGraw-Hill.
—Sunshine: Fluency - Group 3: 1 Each of 6 Titles: Level R. (Sunshine Ser.). 44.95 *(978-0-322-05246-8(7))* Wright Group/McGraw-Hill.
—Sunshine: Fluency-Group 3: 1 each of 6 Titles: Level P. 39.95 *(978-0-322-05244-4(0))* Wright Group/McGraw-Hill.
—Sunshine: Fluency-Group 3: 1 each of 6 Titles: Level Q. 39.95 *(978-0-322-05245-1(9))* Wright Group/McGraw-Hill.
—Sunshine: Upper Emergent - Group 1:1 Each of 8 Student Books: Level G. Group 1. (Sunshine Ser.). 39.95 *(978-0-322-04321-3(2))* Wright Group/McGraw-Hill.
—Sunshine: Upper Emergent - Group 1:1 Each of 8 Student Books: Level H. Group 1. (Sunshine Ser.). 39.95 *(978-0-322-04324-4(7))* Wright Group/McGraw-Hill.
—Sunshine: Upper Emergent - Group 2: 1 Each of 8 Student Books: Level G. Group 1. (Sunshine Ser.). 39.95 *(978-0-322-04322-0(0))* Wright Group/McGraw-Hill.
—Sunshine: Upper Emergent - Group 2:1 Each of 7 Student Books: Level F. Group 2. (Sunshine Ser.). 34.95 *(978-0-322-04319-0(0))* Wright Group/McGraw-Hill.
—Sunshine: Upper Emergent - Group 2:1 Each of 9 Student Books: Level H. Group 2. (Sunshine Ser.). 44.95 *(978-0-322-04325-1(5))* Wright Group/McGraw-Hill.
—Sunshine: Upper Emergent - Group 3:1 Each of 12 Student Books: Level H. 59.95 *(978-0-322-03716-8(6))* Wright Group/McGraw-Hill.
—Sunshine: Upper Emergent - Group 3:1 Each of 6 Student Books: Level G. 29.95 *(978-0-322-03714-4(X))* Wright Group/McGraw-Hill.
—Sunshine: Upper Emergent - Group 3:1 Each of 8 Student Books: Level F. Group 3. 24.95 *(978-0-322-03713-7(1))* Wright Group/McGraw-Hill.
—Sunshine: Upper Emergent - Groups 1-2:1 Each of 15 Student Books: Level F. (Sunshine Ser.). 74.95 *(978-0-322-04318-3(2))* Wright Group/McGraw-Hill.
—Sunshine: Upper Emergent - Groups 1-2:1 Each of 16 Student Books: Level G. (Sunshine Ser.). 79.95 *(978-0-322-04320-6(4))* Wright Group/McGraw-Hill.
—Sunshine: Upper Emergent - Nonfiction:1 Each of 3 Student Books: Level G. (Sunshine Ser.). 14.95 *(978-0-322-04304-6(2))* Wright Group/McGraw-Hill.
—Sunshine: Upper Emergent-Enrichment Library: 1 each of 5 student books: Level J. (Sunshine Ser.). 24.95 *(978-0-322-04023-6(X))* Wright Group/McGraw-Hill.
—Sunshine: Upper Emergent-Group 2: 1 each of 5 student books: Level J. 24.95 *(978-0-322-03715-1(8))* Wright Group/McGraw-Hill.
—Sunshine: Upper Emergent-Group 3: 1 each of 10 student books: Level I. 49.95 *(978-0-322-03717-5(4))* Wright Group/McGraw-Hill.
—Sunshine: Upper Emergent-Groups 1-2: 1 each of 16 student books: Level I. (Sunshine Ser.). 79.95 *(978-0-322-04326-8(3))* Wright Group/McGraw-Hill.
—Sunshine: Upper Emergent-Nonfiction: 1 each of 3 student books: Level H. (Sunshine Ser.). 14.95 *(978-0-322-04305-3(0))* Wright Group/McGraw-Hill.
—Sunshine: Upper Emergent-Nonfiction: 1 each of 5 student books: Level I. (Sunshine Ser.). 24.95 *(978-0-322-04306-0(9))* Wright Group/McGraw-Hill.
—Sunshine: Upper Emergent-Nonfiction: 1 each of 5 student books: Level J. (Sunshine Ser.). 24.95 *(978-0-322-04329-9(8))* Wright Group/McGraw-Hill.
—SUNSHINE Early Fluency Guided Reading Kit 5, Vol. 5. 2004. (Wright Group Literacy Ser.). (gr. 2-18). 524.95 *(978-0-322-02746-4(3))* Wright Group/McGraw-Hill.
—Take-Twos: Fluency - 1 each of 12 Titles: Level O. 79.95 *(978-0-322-04576-7(2))* Wright Group/McGraw-Hill.
—Take Twos: Fluency - 1 Each of 4 Titles: Level S. (Take Twostm Ser.). 29.95 *(978-1-4045-0737-1(X))* Wright Group/McGraw-Hill.
—Take Twos: Fluency - 1 Each of 4Ttitles: Level T. (Take Twostm Ser.). 29.95 *(978-1-4045-0738-8(8))* Wright Group/McGraw-Hill.
—Take-Twos: Fluency - Group 1; 1 each of 12 Titles: Level P. 79.95 *(978-0-322-04577-4(0))* Wright Group/McGraw-Hill.
—Take-Twos: Fluency - Group 1; 1 each of 12 Titles: Level Q. 79.95 *(978-0-322-04578-1(9))* Wright Group/McGraw-Hill.
—Take Twos: Fluency - Group 1: 1 each of 12 Titles: Level R. 89.95 *(978-0-322-04579-8(7))* Wright Group/McGraw-Hill.
—Take Twos: Fluency - Group 1: 1 each of 6 Lesson Plans: Level R. 47.95 *(978-0-322-04573-6(8))* Wright Group/McGraw-Hill.
—Take-Twos: Fluency - Group 2; 1 Each of 4 (New) Titles: Level P. (Take Twostm Ser.). 26.95 *(978-1-4045-0731-9(0))* Wright Group/McGraw-Hill.
—Take-Twos: Fluency - Group 2; 1 Each of 4 (New) Titles: Level Q. (Take Twostm Ser.). 26.95 *(978-1-4045-0733-3(7))* Wright Group/McGraw-Hill.
—Take Twos: Fluency - Group 2: 1 Each of 8 (New) Titles: Level R. (Take Twostm Ser.). 59.95 *(978-1-4045-0735-7(3))* Wright Group/McGraw-Hill.
—Take-Twos: Fluency - Groups 1 & 2; 1 Each of 16 Titles: Level P. (Take Twostm Ser.). 106.95 *(978-1-4045-0732-6(9))* Wright Group/McGraw-Hill.
—Take-Twos: Fluency - Groups 1 & 2; 1 Each of 16 Titles: Level Q. (Take Twostm Ser.). 106.95 *(978-1-4045-0734-0(5))* Wright Group/McGraw-Hill.
—Take-Twos: Upper Emergent - 1 Each of 10 Titles: Level J. (Take Twostm Ser.). 49.95 *(978-1-4045-0744-9(2))* Wright Group/McGraw-Hill.
—Take Twos: Upper Emergent - 1 Each of 8 Titles: Level E. (Take Twostm Ser.). 39.95 *(978-1-4045-0739-5(6))* Wright Group/McGraw-Hill.
—Take Twos: Upper Emergent - 1 Each of 8 Titles: Level F. (Take Twostm Ser.). 39.95 *(978-1-4045-0740-1(X))* Wright Group/McGraw-Hill.
—Take Twos: Upper Emergent - 1 Each of 8 Titles: Level H. (Take Twostm Ser.). 39.95 *(978-1-4045-0742-5(6))* Wright Group/McGraw-Hill.
—Take Twos: Upper Emergent - 1 Each of 8 Titles: Level I. (Take Twostm Ser.). 39.95 *(978-1-4045-0743-2(4))* Wright Group/McGraw-Hill.
—Take-Twos Adventure Vol. 3: Fluency - Complete Kit. (gr. 3-4). 492.50 *(978-0-322-09178-8(0))* Wright Group/McGraw-Hill.
—Take-Twos Adventure Vol. 3: Fluency - Student Book Set - 1 Each of 12 Titles. (gr. 3-4). 83.50 *(978-0-322-09306-5(6))* Wright Group/McGraw-Hill.
—Take-Twos Circles & Cycles Vol. 2: Upper Emergent - Student Book Set - 1 Each of 12 Titles. (gr. 1-18). 59.50 *(978-0-322-09314-0(7))* Wright Group/McGraw-Hill.
—Take-Twos Circles & Cycles Vol. 2: Upper Emergent - Upper Emergent - Complete Kit. (gr. 1-18). 366.95 *(978-0-322-09280-8(9))* Wright Group/McGraw-Hill.
—Take-Twos Cultures: Upper Emergent - Complete Kit. (gr. 1-18). 366.95 *(978-0-322-09279-2(5))* Wright Group/McGraw-Hill.
—Take-Twos Cultures: Upper Emergent - Student Book Set - 1 Each of 12 Titles. (Take-Twostm Ser.). (gr. 1-18). 59.50 *(978-0-322-09312-6(0))* Wright Group/McGraw-Hill.
—Take-Twos Earth Links Vol. 3: Upper Emergent - Complete Kit. (gr. 1-18). 366.95 *(978-0-322-09282-2(5))* Wright Group/McGraw-Hill.
—Take-Twos Earth Links Vol. 3: Upper Emergent - Student Book Set - 1 Each of 12 Titles. (Take-Twostm Ser.). (gr. 1-18). 59.50 *(978-0-322-09316-4(3))* Wright Group/McGraw-Hill.
—Take-Twos Finding Out Vol. 6: Fluency - Complete Kit. (gr. 4-6). 501.50 *(978-0-322-09181-8(0))* Wright Group/McGraw-Hill.
—Take-Twos Finding Out Vol. 6: Fluency - Student Book Set - 1 Each of 12 Titles. (Take-Twostm Ser.). (gr. 4-6). 84.95 *(978-0-322-09309-6(0))* Wright Group/McGraw-Hill.
—Take-Twos Land & Air: Early Fluency - Complete Kit. (gr. 2-18). 420.50 *(978-0-322-09172-6(1))* Wright Group/McGraw-Hill.
—Take-Twos Land & Air: Early Fluency - Student Book Set - 1 Each of 12 Titles. (gr. 2-18). 69.95 *(978-0-322-09300-3(7))* Wright Group/McGraw-Hill.
—Take-Twos Making Things Vol. 3: Early Fluency - Complete Kit. (gr. 2-18). 420.50 *(978-0-322-09174-0(8))* Wright Group/McGraw-Hill.
—Take-Twos Making Things Vol. 3: Early Fluency - Student Book Set - 1 Each of 12 Titles. (gr. 2-18). 69.95 *(978-0-322-09302-7(3))* Wright Group/McGraw-Hill.
—Take-Twos Old to New Vol. 4: Fluency - Complete Kit. (gr. 3-4). 492.50 *(978-0-322-09179-5(9))* Wright Group/McGraw-Hill.
—Take-Twos Old to New Vol. 4: Fluency - Student Book Set - 1 Each of 12 Titles. (gr. 3-4). 83.50 *(978-0-322-09307-2(4))* Wright Group/McGraw-Hill.
—Take-Twos Play Time Vol. 4: Upper Emergent - Student Book Set - 1 Each of 12 Titles. (Take-Twostm Ser.). (gr. 1-18). 59.50 *(978-0-322-09318-8(X))* Wright Group/McGraw-Hill.
—Take-Twos Play Time Vol. 4: Upper Emergent - Upper Emergent - Complete Kit. (gr. 1-18). 366.95 *(978-0-322-09283-9(3))* Wright Group/McGraw-Hill.
—Take-Twos Slither, Swim, & Soar: Fluency - Complete Kit. (gr. 3-4). 483.50 *(978-0-322-09176-4(4))* Wright Group/McGraw-Hill.
—Take-Twos Slither, Swim, & Soar: Fluency - Student Book Set - 1 Each of 12 Titles. (gr. 3-4). 81.95 *(978-0-322-09304-1(X))* Wright Group/McGraw-Hill.
—Take-Twos Stories & Legends Vol. 5: Fluency - Complete Kit. (gr. 4-6). 519.50 *(978-0-322-09180-1(2))* Wright Group/McGraw-Hill.
—Take-Twos Stories & Legends Vol. 5: Fluency - Student Book Set - 1 Each of 12 Titles. (Take-Twostm Ser.). (gr. 4-6). 88.50 *(978-0-322-09308-9(2))* Wright Group/McGraw-Hill.
—Teeth: Level G, 6 vols. (Take Twostm Ser.). 16p. 29.95 *(978-0-322-08968-6(9))* Wright Group/McGraw-Hill.
—Tiger Level: Adventure Journal Set. (Wildcats Ser.). (gr. 2-8). 31.95 *(978-0-322-05790-6(6))* Wright Group/McGraw-Hill.
—Tiger Level: Lesson Plan Set. (Wildcats Ser.). (gr. 2-8). 96.50 *(978-0-322-06677-9(8))* Wright Group/McGraw-Hill.
—Tiger Level: Wildcats Tiger Complete Kit. (Wildcats Ser.). (gr. 2-8). 599.95 *(978-0-322-06483-6(X))* Wright Group/McGraw-Hill.
—Tv Times: 6 Each of 1 Anthology, 6 vols. (Wildcats Ser.). 32p. (gr. 2-8). *(978-0-322-05629-9(2))* Wright Group/McGraw-Hill.
—Twig Books: Early Emergent - 1 each of 16 student books: Level A. (Twig Ser.). 66.95 *(978-0-322-04330-5(1))* Wright Group/McGraw-Hill.
—Twig Books: Early Emergent - 1 each of 16 student books: Level B. (Twig Ser.). 66.95 *(978-0-322-04331-2(X))* Wright Group/McGraw-Hill.
—Twig Books: Early Emergent - 1 each of 16 student books: Level C. (Twig Ser.). 66.95 *(978-0-322-04332-9(8))* Wright Group/McGraw-Hill.
—Twig Books: Early Emergent - Upper Emergent - 1 each of 16 student books: Level D. (Twig Ser.). 66.95 *(978-0-322-04333-6(6))* Wright Group/McGraw-Hill.
—Twig Books: Early Emergent - Upper Emergent - 1 each of 16 student books: Level E. (Twig Ser.). 79.95 *(978-0-322-04334-3(4))* Wright Group/McGraw-Hill.
—Twig Books: Student Book Set - 1 Each of 16 Titles. (gr. k-18). 66.95 *(978-0-322-04351-0(4))* Wright Group/McGraw-Hill.
—Twig Books: Upper Emergent - 1 each of 16 student books: Level F. (Twig Ser.). 79.95 *(978-0-322-04335-0(2))* Wright Group/McGraw-Hill.
—Twig Books: Upper Emergent - 1 each of 16 student books: Level G. (Twig Ser.). 79.95 *(978-0-322-04337-4(9))* Wright Group/McGraw-Hill.
—Twig Books: Upper Emergent - 1 each of 16 student books: Level H. (Twig Ser.). 77.95 *(978-0-322-04338-1(7))* Wright Group/McGraw-Hill.
—Twig Books Vol. 3: Early Emergent - Student Book Set - 1 Each of 16 Titles. (gr. k-18). 66.95 *(978-0-322-04349-7(2))* Wright Group/McGraw-Hill.
—Twig Books Vol. 4: Upper Emergent - Student Book Set -1 Each of 16 Titles. (gr. 1-18). 79.95 *(978-0-322-04343-5(3))* Wright Group/McGraw-Hill.
—Upper Emergent Guided Reading Complete Kit 1. (Sunshine Ser.). (gr. 1-18). 486.50 *(978-0-322-04210-0(0))* Wright Group/McGraw-Hill.
—Upper Emergent Guided Reading Kit 5 Vol. 5: Student Books, (gr. 1-18). 79.95 *(978-0-322-03883-7(9))* Wright Group/McGraw-Hill.
—Upper Emergent Guided Reading Kit 6 Vol. 6: Student Books, (gr. 1-18). 79.95 *(978-0-322-03884-4(7))* Wright Group/McGraw-Hill.
—Upper Emergent Kit 1: Complete Kit. (gr. k-1). 499.95 *(978-1-4045-2059-2(7))* Wright Group/McGraw-Hill.
—Upper Emergent Kit 2 Vol. 2: Complete Kit, (gr. 1-18). 499.95 *(978-1-4045-2060-8(0))* Wright Group/McGraw-Hill.
—Upper Emergent Kit 2 Vol. 2: Student Books, 2003. (Gear Up Ser.). (ENG.). (gr. 1-1). pap. 184.40 *(978-1-4045-2068-4(6),* 1404520686) Wright Group/McGraw-Hill.
—Vegetarians: Level H, 6 vols. (Take Twostm Ser.). 16p. 29.95 *(978-0-322-08972-3(7))* Wright Group/McGraw-Hill.
—Wear your Art: 6 Each of 1 Anthology, 6 vols. (Wildcats Ser.). 32p. (gr. 2-8). *(978-0-322-05623-7(3))* Wright Group/McGraw-Hill.
—Whispering Pines: Classroom Library Set. (Whispering Pines Ser.). 81.50 *(978-0-322-07971-7(3))* Wright Group/McGraw-Hill.
—Whispering Pines: Complete Set. (Whispering Pines Ser.). 327.95 *(978-0-322-07965-6(9))* Wright Group/McGraw-Hill.
—Wildcats Strand Kits: Animals & Nature Strand. (Wildcats Ser.). (gr. 2-8). 589.95 *(978-0-322-06535-2(6))* Wright Group/McGraw-Hill.
—Wildcats Strand Kits: Arts & Entertainment Strand. (Wildcats Ser.). (gr. 2-8). 589.95 *(978-0-322-06534-5(8))* Wright Group/McGraw-Hill.
—Wildcats Strand Kits: Myths & Misconceptions Strand. (Wildcats Ser.). (gr. 2-8). 589.95 *(978-0-322-06532-1(1))* Wright Group/McGraw-Hill.
—Wildcats Strand Kits: People & Places Strand. (Wildcats Ser.). (gr. 2-8). 589.95 *(978-0-322-06528-4(3))* Wright Group/McGraw-Hill.
—Wildcats Strand Kits: Science & Technology Strand. (Wildcats Ser.). (gr. 2-8). 589.95 *(978-0-322-06529-1(1))* Wright Group/McGraw-Hill.
—Wildcats Strand Kits: Sports & Action Strand. (Wildcats Ser.). (gr. 2-8). 589.95 *(978-0-322-06531-4(3))* Wright Group/McGraw-Hill.
—Wonder World: Early Emergent - Student Book Set - 1 Each of 16 Titles. (gr. k-18). 66.95 *(978-0-322-04341-1(7))* Wright Group/McGraw-Hill.
—Wonder World: Early Fluency - Student Book Set - 1 Each of 16 Titles. (gr. 1-2). 93.50 *(978-0-322-04342-8(5))* Wright Group/McGraw-Hill.
—Wonder World: Upper Emergent - Student Book Set - 1 Each of 16 Titles, Vol. 2. (gr. 1-18). 79.95 *(978-0-322-04340-4(9))* Wright Group/McGraw-Hill.
—Working Like a Dog: 6 Each of 1 Anthology, 6 vols. (Wildcats Ser.). 32p. (gr. 2-8). *(978-0-322-05854-5(6))* Wright Group/McGraw-Hill.
—The Worm Farm: Level E, 6 vols. (Take Twostm Ser.). 16p. 29.95 *(978-0-322-08961-7(1))* Wright Group/McGraw-Hill.
—The Wright Skills: Level A Sets - Short Vowels only: 1 Each of 19 Titles. (Wright Skills Ser.). (gr. k-3). 56.95 *(978-0-322-06473-7(2))* Wright Group/McGraw-Hill.
—The Wright Skills: Level B Sets - 1 Each of 40 Titles (includes long Vowels) (Wright Skills Ser.). (gr. k-3). 143.95 *(978-0-322-03878-3(2))* Wright Group/McGraw-Hill.
—The Wright Skills: Level B Sets - 6 Each of 40 Titles (includes long Vowels) (gr. k-3). 860.50 *(978-0-322-03880-6(4))* Wright Group/McGraw-Hill.
—Young & Wild: 6 Each of 1 Anthology, 6 vols. (Wildcats Ser.). 32p. (gr. 2-8). *(978-0-322-05851-4(1))* Wright Group/McGraw-Hill.
—Zoo Tales: 6 Each of 1 Anthology, 6 vols. (Wildcats Ser.). 32p. (gr. 2-8). *(978-0-322-05856-9(2))* Wright Group/McGraw-Hill.
—The 13th Floor: Level O, 6 vols. (Autumn Leaves Ser.). 128p. (gr. 3-6). 36.95 *(978-0-322-06731-8(6))* Wright Group/McGraw-Hill.
Gruver, Sara. Reading Skills Mini-Lessons. 2003. (ENG.). 96p. pap., tchr. ed. 13.99 *(978-0-7439-3288-2(9))* Teacher Created Resources, Inc.
Guardians of the Garden: Level 3, 6 vols. (Fluency Strand Ser.). (gr. 4-8). 45.00 *(978-1-4045-1218-4(7))* Wright Group/McGraw-Hill.
Guess Who - Group 2, 6 Bks, Set. 2004. (J). 136.71 *(978-0-7614-1762-0(1))* Marshall Cavendish Corp.
Guinea Pig, 6 vols. 8p. (gr. k-1). 21.50 *(978-0-322-02060-3(3))* Wright Group/McGraw-Hill.
Gunn, Barbara. Inuit Tales: Read Well Level K Unit 10 Storybook. Jerde, Susan, illus. 2003. (Read Well Level K Ser.). 20p. (J). *(978-1-57035-681-0(5))* Cambium Education, Inc.
Haddon, Jean. Words: A Computer Lesson. Vargo, Sharon Hawkins, illus. 2003. (Silly Millies Ser.). 32p. (J). (gr. -1-1). pap. 4.99 *(978-0-7613-1797-5(X))*; lib. bdg. 17.90 *(978-0-7613-2870-4(X))* Lerner Publishing Group. (Millbrook Pr.).
Hairem Scarem Little Books: Early Reading Fluency, Level C. 2004. pap. 6.00 *(978-0-7398-8293-1(7))* Steck-Vaughn.
Hand Tools: Level N, 6 vols. (Wonder Worldtm Ser.). 48p. 34.95 *(978-0-7802-4577-8(6))* Wright Group/McGraw-Hill.
Haney Perez, Jessica. My First 100 Words Book: A Lift-the-Flap, Pull-Tab Learning Book. March, Chloe, illus. 2005. (Learn to Read Ser.). 10p. (J). 10.95 *(978-1-58117-210-2(9),* Intervisual/Piggy Toes) Bendon, Inc.
Hanrahan, Abigail & McSweeny, Catherine. 50 Quick Play Reading Games. 2004. (J). per. 34.95 *(978-0-7606-0535-6(1))* LinguiSystems, Inc.
Hansen, Jane, et al. The Prek-2 Writing Classroom: Growing Confident Writers. 2011. (ENG.). 128p. (gr. -1-2). pap. 18.99 *(978-0-545-20868-0(8),* Teaching Resources) Scholastic, Inc.
Harcourt School Publishers Staff. Assessment & Information Instruction, Grades K-6: Professional Development in Reading - Participant's Guide. 2nd ed. 2003. (Harcourt School Publishers Reading Professional Development Ser.). (ENG.). 40p. (gr. 6-6). pap. 13.90 *(978-0-15-338365-6(8))* Harcourt Schl. Pubs.
—Assessment & Information Instructions, Grades K-6: Professional Development for Reading: Guide to Video. 2nd ed. 2003. pap., tchr. ed. 54.90 *(978-0-15-337406-7(3))* Harcourt Schl. Pubs.
—Be Active!, Grade 3-6: Resource Binder Tabs. 4th ed. 2004. 45.60 *(978-0-15-341284-4(4))* Harcourt Schl. Pubs.
—Be Active!, Grade K-2: Resource Binder Tabs. 4th ed. 2004. 45.60 *(978-0-15-341283-7(6))* Harcourt Schl. Pubs.
—Collections: Phonics Activity Book. 2003. (First-Place Reading Ser.). (Illus.). (gr. k-6). 6.90 *(978-0-15-313423-4(2))* Harcourt Schl. Pubs.
—Flower Garden Lap Book. 3rd ed. 2004. (Trophies Reading Program Ser.). (Illus.). pap. 11.50 *(978-0-15-341029-1(9))* Harcourt Schl. Pubs.
—Herman the Helper Lap Book. 3rd ed. 2003. (Harcourt School Publishers Trophies Ser.). (ENG., Illus.). 32p. (gr. -1 — 1). pap. 14.10 *(978-0-15-340970-7(3))* Harcourt Schl. Pubs.
—Library Package. 2003. (Illus.). (J). (gr. -1). 151.95 *(978-0-15-216666-3(1))*; (J). (gr. k-2). 160.95 *(978-0-15-216672-4(6))*; (J). (gr. 3-4). 158.00 *(978-0-15-216678-6(5))*; (J). (gr. 5-6). 158.00 *(978-0-15-216684-7(X))*; (YA). (gr. 7-8). 145.00 *(978-0-15-216690-8(4))* Harcourt Schl. Pubs.
—The Little Quack Lap Book. 3rd ed. 2004. (Trophies Reading Program Ser.). (Illus.). pap. 11.50 *(978-0-15-340969-1(X))* Harcourt Schl. Pubs.
—The Little Red Hen Lap Book. 3rd ed. 2004. (Trophies Reading Program Ser.). (Illus.). pap. 11.50 *(978-0-15-340968-4(1))* Harcourt Schl. Pubs.
—The Months of School. 3rd ed. 2004. (Trophies Reading Program Ser.). (Illus.). (gr. -1). pap. 11.50 *(978-0-15-340896-0(0))* Harcourt Schl. Pubs.
—Trophies. 3rd ed. 2003. (Trophies Ser.). (gr. 1-18). Grade 1-1. tchr. ed. 115.50 *(978-0-15-325022-4(4))*Grade 1-2. tchr. ed. 115.50 *(978-0-15-325023-1(2))*Grade 1-3. tchr. ed.

120.20 *(978-0-15-325024-8(0))*Grade 1-4. tchr. ed. 120.20 *(978-0-15-325025-5(9))*Grade 1-5. tchr. ed. 124.80 *(978-0-15-325026-2(7))* Harcourt Schl. Pubs.

—Trophies Theme 1, Theme 1. 3rd ed. 2003. (Trophies Ser.). (gr. 2-18). tchr. ed. 65.50 *(978-0-15-325027-9(5))*; (gr. 2-18). tchr. ed. 65.50 *(978-0-15-325030-9(5))*; (gr. 3-18). tchr. ed. 65.50 *(978-0-15-325036-1(4))*; (gr. 3-18). tchr. ed. 65.50 *(978-0-15-325033-0(X))*; (gr. 4-18). tchr. ed. 69.90 *(978-0-15-325039-2(9))*; (gr. 5-18). tchr. ed. 69.90 *(978-0-15-325045-3(3))*; (gr. 6-18). tchr. ed. 72.70 *(978-0-15-325051-4(8))* Harcourt Schl. Pubs.

—Trophies Theme 2, Theme 2. 3rd ed. 2003. (Trophies Ser.). (gr. 2-18). tchr. ed. 65.50 *(978-0-15-325028-6(3))*; (gr. 2-18). tchr. ed. 65.50 *(978-0-15-325031-6(3))*; (gr. 3-18). tchr. ed. 65.50 *(978-0-15-325034-7(8))*; (gr. 3-18). tchr. ed. 65.50 *(978-0-15-325037-8(2))*; (gr. 4-18). tchr. ed. 69.90 *(978-0-15-325040-8(2))*; (gr. 5-18). tchr. ed. 69.90 *(978-0-15-325046-0(1))*; (gr. 6-18). tchr. ed. 72.70 *(978-0-15-325052-1(6))* Harcourt Schl. Pubs.

—Trophies Theme 3, Theme 3. 3rd ed. 2003. (Trophies Ser.). (gr. 2-18). tchr. ed. 65.50 *(978-0-15-325032-3(1))*; (gr. 2-18). tchr. ed. 65.50 *(978-0-15-325029-3(1))*; (gr. 3-18). tchr. ed. 65.50 *(978-0-15-325035-4(6))*; (gr. 3-18). tchr. ed. 65.50 *(978-0-15-325038-5(0))*; (gr. 4-18). tchr. ed. 69.90 *(978-0-15-325041-5(0))*; (gr. 5-18). tchr. ed. 69.90 *(978-0-15-325047-7(X))*; (gr. 6-18). tchr. ed. 72.70 *(978-0-15-325053-8(4))* Harcourt Schl. Pubs.

—Trophies Theme 4, Theme 4. 3rd ed. 2003. (Trophies Ser.). (gr. 4-18). tchr. ed. 69.90 *(978-0-15-325042-2(9))*; (gr. 5-18). tchr. ed. 69.90 *(978-0-15-325048-4(8))*; (gr. 6-18). tchr. ed. 72.70 *(978-0-15-325054-5(2))* Harcourt Schl. Pubs.

—Trophies Theme 5, Theme 5. 3rd ed. 2003. (Trophies Ser.). (gr. 4-18). tchr. ed. 69.90 *(978-0-15-325043-9(7))*; (gr. 5-18). tchr. ed. 69.90 *(978-0-15-325049-1(6))*; (gr. 6-18). tchr. ed. 72.70 *(978-0-15-325055-2(0))* Harcourt Schl. Pubs.

—Trophies Theme 6, Theme 6. 3rd ed. 2003. (Trophies Ser.). (gr. 4-18). tchr. ed. 69.90 *(978-0-15-325044-6(5))*; (gr. 5-18). tchr. ed. 69.90 *(978-0-15-325050-7(X))*; (gr. 6-18). tchr. ed. 72.70 *(978-0-15-325056-9(9))* Harcourt Schl. Pubs.

—Trophies Reading Program, Grade K. 3rd ed. 2003. tchr. ed. 135.30 *(978-0-15-339730-1(6))* Harcourt Schl. Pubs.

—Writing Express Espanol, Grade 1. 2nd ed. 2003. (Trofeos Ser.). (SPA.). (gr. 1-18). tchr. ed. 10.10 incl. cd-rom *(978-0-15-324608-1(1))* Harcourt Schl. Pubs.

—1st Place Reading: Title 1 Program Kit. 2nd ed. 2003. (Harcourt Title I Reading Programs Ser.). (gr. 5-18). tchr. ed. 1006.70 *(978-0-15-338009-9(8))* Harcourt Schl. Pubs.

Harner, Jennifer L. Reading & Learning from Informational Text. Petelinsek, Kathleen, illus. 2013. (Explorer Junior Library: Information Explorer Junior Ser.). (ENG.). 24p. (J). (gr. 1-4). 28.50 *(978-1-62431-134-5(2)*, 202856); pap. 12.79 *(978-1-62431-266-3(7)*, 202858) Cherry Lake Publishing.

Harpster, Steve, illus. First Word Search: Easy First Words. 2011. (First Word Search Ser.). (ENG.). 64p. (J). (gr. -1-1). pap. 4.95 *(978-1-4027-7808-7(2))* Sterling Publishing Co., Inc.

—First Word Search: Fun First Phonics. 2011. (First Word Search Ser.). (ENG.). 64p. (J). pap. 4.95 *(978-1-4027-7806-3(6))* Sterling Publishing Co., Inc.

—First Word Search: Reading Made Easy. 2011. (First Word Search Ser.). (ENG.). 64p. (J). (gr. -1-1). pap. 4.95 *(978-1-4027-7802-5(3))* Sterling Publishing Co., Inc.

Harris, Nancy & Rissman, Rebecca. Be the Best at Reading. 1 vol. 2012. (Top Tips Ser.). (ENG.). 32p. (gr. 1-3). 29.99 *(978-1-4109-4768-0(8)*, Read Me!) Heinemann-Raintree.

Harrison, Vanessa. Activities: 101 Ideas for Children & Adults. 128p. pap. *(978-0-86388-551-8(9)*, 002-5296, Routledge) Taylor & Francis Group.

Harry's Hat: Take-Home Book. 2005. (Emergent Library: Vol. 2). (YA). (gr. -1-1). 12.60 *(978-0-8215-7254-2(7))* Sadlier, William H. Inc.

Harvey, Bev. Animal Families, 6 vols. 2005. (Animal Families Ser.). (Illus.). 32p. (gr. 2-4). 138.00 *(978-0-7910-7539-5(7)*, Chelsea Hse.) Facts On File, Inc.

A Hat for Nan: Consonants b, w; Short Vowel i word families: Level A, 6 vols. (Wright Skills Ser.). 12p. (gr. k-3). 17.95 *(978-0-322-01451-0(4))* Wright Group/McGraw-Hill.

Hats: Big Book: Level B. 8p. 20.95 *(978-0-322-00359-0(8))* Wright Group/McGraw-Hill.

Hats: Level B. 8p. 24.95 *(978-0-7802-8919-2(6))* Wright Group/McGraw-Hill.

Hats: Level G, 6 vols. (Wonder Worldtm Ser.). 16p. 29.95 *(978-0-7802-4579-2(2))* Wright Group/McGraw-Hill.

The Haunted, 6 vols. (Ragged Island Mysteriestm Ser.). 161p. (gr. 5-7). 42.50 *(978-0-322-01652-1(5))* Wright Group/McGraw-Hill.

Hay Making: Level H, 6 vols. (Wonder Worldtm Ser.). 16p. 29.95 *(978-0-7802-1215-2(0))* Wright Group/McGraw-Hill.

HB Staff. All Fall Down. 97th ed. 2003. (First-Place Reading Ser.). (gr. 1-18). pap. 16.50 *(978-0-15-308126-2(0))* Harcourt Schl. Pubs.

Hello: Big Book: Level D. Group 1. (Story Box Ser.). 16p. 20.95 *(978-0-322-00632-4(5))* Wright Group/McGraw-Hill.

Hercules & Other Greek Legends: 6 Each of 1 Anthology, 6 vols. (Wildcats Ser.). 32p. (gr. 2-8). *(978-0-322-00590-7(6))* Wright Group/McGraw-Hill.

Here Comes the Rain! Take-Home Book. 2005. (Emergent Library: Vol. 2). (YA). (gr. -1-1). 12.60 *(978-0-8215-7263-4(6))* Sadlier, William H. Inc.

Heroes: 6 Each of 1 Anthology, 6 vols. (Wildcats Ser.). 32p. (gr. 2-8). *(978-0-322-00579-2(5))* Wright Group/McGraw-Hill.

Hide & Seek: Big Book: Level K. (Wonder Worldtm Ser.). 16p. 26.50 *(978-0-7802-3474-1(X))* Wright Group/McGraw-Hill.

Hide & Seek: Level K, 6 vols. (Wonder Worldtm Ser.). 16p. 34.95 *(978-0-7802-1217-6(7))* Wright Group/McGraw-Hill.

Hiebert, Elfrieda H. Eyes Are Everywhere. (Little Book Practice Reader Ser.). (J). *(978-0-8136-0811-2(2))* Modern Curriculum Pr.

—Humpback Whales. (Little Book Practice Reader Ser.). (J). *(978-0-8136-0809-9(0))* Modern Curriculum Pr.

Hiebert, Elfrieda H. & Juel, Connie. Blue Sue. (Little Book Practice Reader). (J). *(978-0-8136-2375-7(8))* Modern Curriculum Pr.

—Dee & Me. (Little Book Practice Reader). (J). *(978-0-8136-2112-8(7))* Modern Curriculum Pr.

—The Doctor Has the Flu. (Little Book Practice Reader). (J). *(978-0-8136-2158-6(5))* Modern Curriculum Pr.

—Eight Friends in All. (Little Book Practice Reader Ser.). (J). *(978-0-8136-0773-3(6))* Modern Curriculum Pr.

—A Fun Place to Eat. (Little Book Practice Reader). (J). *(978-0-8136-2058-9(9))* Modern Curriculum Pr.

—Goose Chase. (Little Book Practice Reader). (J). *(978-0-8136-2068-8(6))* Modern Curriculum Pr.

—The Hiccups Would Not Stop. (Little Book Practice Reader). (J). *(978-0-8136-2168-5(2))* Modern Curriculum Pr.

—A Hunt for Clues. (Little Book Practice Reader). (J). *(978-0-8136-2148-7(8))* Modern Curriculum Pr.

—Jump Right In. (Little Book Practice Reader Ser.). (J). *(978-0-8136-0746-7(9))* Modern Curriculum Pr.

—Kangaroo in the Kitchen. (Little Book Practice Reader Ser.). (J). 9.90 *(978-0-8136-0742-9(6))* Modern Curriculum Pr.

—Lobster Fishing at Dawn. (Little Book Practice Reader). (J). *(978-0-8136-2194-4(1))* Modern Curriculum Pr.

—A Mess. (Little Book Practice Reader). (J). *(978-0-8136-1934-7(3))* Modern Curriculum Pr.

—My Clock Is Sick. (Little Book Practice Reader). (J). *(978-0-8136-1974-3(2))* Modern Curriculum Pr.

—My Lost Top. (Little Book Practice Reader). (J). *(978-0-8136-2047-3(3))* Modern Curriculum Pr.

—A Nut Pie for Jud. (Little Book Practice Reader). (J). *(978-0-8136-1972-9(6))* Modern Curriculum Pr.

—Polly's Shop. (Little Book Practice Reader). (J). *(978-0-8136-2029-9(5))* Modern Curriculum Pr.

—Pop Pops the Popcorn. (J). *(978-0-8136-2008-4(2))* Modern Curriculum Pr.

—Rush, Rush, Rush. (Little Book Practice Reader). (J). *(978-0-8136-2074-9(0))* Modern Curriculum Pr.

—Sally's Spaceship. (Little Book Practice Reader). (Illus.). (J). *(978-0-8136-2045-9(7))* Modern Curriculum Pr.

—That Fly. (Little Book Practice Reader). (J). *(978-0-8136-1942-2(4))* Modern Curriculum Pr.

—True Or False? (Little Book Practice Reader). (J). *(978-0-8136-2086-2(4))* Modern Curriculum Pr.

—Very Big, Bk. 45. (Little Book Practice Reader). (J). *(978-0-8136-1457-1(0))* Modern Curriculum Pr.

—Vultures on Vacation. (Little Book Practice Reader). (J). *(978-0-8136-1938-5(6))* Modern Curriculum Pr.

—When Bob Woke Up Late. (Little Book Practice Reader). (J). *(978-0-8136-2084-8(8))* Modern Curriculum Pr.

—Where Do They Live? (Little Book Practice Reader). (J). *(978-0-8136-1948-4(3))* Modern Curriculum Pr.

—Wilma's Wagon. (J). *(978-0-8136-1964-4(5))* Modern Curriculum Pr.

High Tide: Level 7, 6 vols. (Fluency Strand Ser.). (gr. 4-8). 45.00 *(978-1-4045-1242-9(X))* Wright Group/McGraw-Hill.

A Hike in the Trees: Long e Digraphs: Level B, 6 vols. (Wright Skills Ser.). 16p. (gr. k-3). 26.50 *(978-0-322-01479-4(4))* Wright Group/McGraw-Hill.

Hiking with Dad: Level I, 6 vols. (Wonder Worldtm Ser.). 16p. 29.95 *(978-0-7802-2036-2(6))* Wright Group/McGraw-Hill.

Hill, Cheryl E. R Is for Reading Books. Pierce, Dave G., illus. 2012. 56p. pap. 17.99 *(978-0-9859770-0-9(0))* N.O.A.H Bks.

Hocus Pocus: 6 Each of 1 Anthology, 6 vols. (Wildcats Ser.). 32p. (gr. 2-8). *(978-0-322-02423-6(4))* Wright Group/McGraw-Hill.

Hohenthal, K. D., creator. The Reading & Writing Connection Journal with Herman the Crab No. 1: What Is the Story About? 2003. 70p. (J). spiral bd. 15.95 *(978-0-9716907-5-2(8)*, Ridgewood Publishing) Ridgewood Group, The.

—The Reading & Writing Connection with Herman the Crab No. 2: Story Problem & Solution. 2003. 70p. (J). spiral bd., wbk. ed. 15.95 *(978-0-9716907-6-9(6)*, Ridgewood Publishing) Ridgewood Group, The.

—The Reading & Writing Connection with Herman the Crab No. 3: Story Beginning, Middle, End. 2003. 70p. (J). spiral bd., wbk. ed. 15.95 *(978-0-9716907-8-3(2)*, Ridgewood Publishing) Ridgewood Group, The.

—The Reading & Writing Connection with Herman the Crab No. 4: Story Problem, Solution, Beginning, Middle, End. 2003. 70p. (J). spiral bd., wbk. ed. 15.95 *(978-0-9716907-9-0(0)*, Ridgewood Publishing) Ridgewood Group, The.

Holt, Rinehart and Winston Staff. Elements of Literature: Assessment: Literature, Reading & Vocabulary. 2003. 4th ed. pap. 40.20 *(978-0-03-068518-7(4))* 5th ed. pap. 40.20 *(978-0-03-068517-0(6))* 5th ed. pap. 40.20 *(978-0-03-068519-4(2))* Holt McDougal.

—Holt Reader. 4th ed. 2003. (Elements of Literature Ser.). (ENG., Illus.). 384p. (gr. 6-6). pap. 17.15 *(978-0-03-068389-3(0))* Houghton Mifflin Harcourt Publishing Co.

—Holt Science & Technology: Directed Reading Answer Key. 4th ed. 2004. (Illus.). pap. 11.20 *(978-0-03-037018-2(3))* Holt McDougal.

—Holt Science & Technology: Directed Reading Worksheets. 4th ed. 2004. pap. 15.00 *(978-0-03-036994-0(0))*; pap. 15.00 *(978-0-03-036993-3(2))*; pap. 15.00 *(978-0-03-036992-6(4))* Holt McDougal.

Holzer, Angela. My Dog, Eddie. Funk, Debbie, illus. 2009. 36p. (J). lib. bdg. 8.99 *(978-0-9821563-5-3(9))* Good Sound Publishing.

Home Pack Collection. 2005. (Nursery Rhymes Build Literacy Ser.). (YA). (gr. -1-3). 48.60 *(978-0-8215-0560-1(2))*; (gr. k-3). 48.60 *(978-0-8215-0569-4(6))* Sadlier, William H. Inc.

Hooks, Earnest. Let's go see Mother Wilkerson's Farm. 2011. 72p. pap. 27.08 *(978-1-4389-5072-3(1))* AuthorHouse.

HOP, LLC. Hooked on Phonics Reading Comprehension. 2006. 64p. 3.79 *(978-1-933863-94-8(3))* HOP, LLC.

A House for Me: Big Book: Level F. 16p. 31.50 *(978-0-322-00375-0(X))* Wright Group/McGraw-Hill.

The House on the Hill: Level 5, 6 vols. (Fluency Strand Ser.). (gr. 4-8). 45.00 *(978-1-4045-1228-3(4))* Wright Group/McGraw-Hill.

Houses: Big Book: Level D. Group 1. (Story Box Ser.). 16p. 20.95 *(978-0-7802-7637-6(X))* Wright Group/McGraw-Hill.

Houses: Level M, 6 vols. (Wonder Worldtm Ser.). 16p. 34.95 *(978-0-7802-1219-0(3))* Wright Group/McGraw-Hill.

How a Volcano Is Formed: Level M, 6 vols. (Wonder Worldtm Ser.). 16p. 34.95 *(978-0-7802-2913-6(4))* Wright Group/McGraw-Hill.

How Animals Hide: Level G, 6 vols. (Wonder Worldtm Ser.). 16p. 29.95 *(978-0-7802-4581-5(4))* Wright Group/McGraw-Hill.

How Ants Live, 6 vols. (Sunshinetm Science Ser.). 24p. (gr. 1-2). 31.50 *(978-0-7802-0288-7(0))*; 36.95 *(978-0-7802-0539-0(1))* Wright Group/McGraw-Hill.

How the Chick Tricked the Fox. (Little Book Practice Reader Ser.). (J). *(978-0-8136-0821-1(X))* Modern Curriculum Pr.

How to Make a Hen House. (J). *(978-0-8136-5360-0(6))* Modern Curriculum Pr.

Howe, Alan, et al. Core English Ks3 - Real Progress in Reading. 2014. 192p. pap. 36.50 *(978-1-4441-6895-2(9))* Hodder Education Group GBR. Dist: Trans-Atlantic Pubns., Inc.

A Hug Is Warm: Big Book: Level D. Group 1. (Sunshine Ser.). 8p. 20.95 *(978-0-7802-5729-0(4))* Wright Group/McGraw-Hill.

Huggles Can Jungle: Level A. Group 1. (Sunshine Ser.). 8p. 20.95 *(978-0-7802-5707-8(3))* Wright Group/McGraw-Hill.

Huggles Goes Away: Level A. Group 1. (Sunshine Ser.). 8p. 20.95 *(978-0-7802-5708-5(1))* Wright Group/McGraw-Hill.

Hults, Alaska, ed. American History Reader's Theater Vol. 2244: Develop Reading Fluency & Text Comprehension Skills. Hillam, Corbin & Vangsgard, Amy, illus. 2004. 96p. (J). pap. 14.99 *(978-1-59198-039-1(9)*, 2244) Creative Teaching Pr., Inc.

—Philosophers to Astronauts Reader's Theater Vol. 2243: Develop Reading Fluency & Text Comprehension Skills. Hillam, Corbin & Vangsgard, Amy, illus. 2004. 96p. (J). pap. 12.99 *(978-1-59198-038-4(0)*, 2243) Creative Teaching Pr., Inc.

I am a Book Worm: Big Book: Level C. Group 1. (Sunshine Ser.). 8p. 20.95 *(978-0-7802-5722-1(7))* Wright Group/McGraw-Hill.

I am a Twin, 6 vols. 8p. (gr. k-1). 21.50 *(978-0-322-02083-2(2))* Wright Group/McGraw-Hill.

I Cannot Fit!, 6 vols. 8p. (gr. k-1). 21.50 *(978-0-322-02071-9(9))* Wright Group/McGraw-Hill.

I Could not Keep Silent: Level T. Group 3, 6 vols. (Sunshine Ser.). 48p. 44.95 *(978-0-322-04601-6(7))* Wright Group/McGraw-Hill.

I Love My Family: Big Book: Level C. Group 1. (Sunshine Ser.). 8p. 20.95 *(978-0-7802-5723-8(5))* Wright Group/McGraw-Hill.

I See You: Level E. 8p. 20.95 *(978-0-322-00342-2(3))* Wright Group/McGraw-Hill.

I Wonder, 6 vols. (Sunshinetm Ser.). 16p. (gr. k-18). 29.50 *(978-0-7802-5423-7(6))* Wright Group/McGraw-Hill.

I Wonder Why? Level G, 6 vols. (Wonder Worldtm Ser.). 16p. 29.95 *(978-0-7802-2016-4(1))* Wright Group/McGraw-Hill.

If I Had a Piece of String. (J). 26.20 *(978-0-8136-8426-0(9))*; (gr. -1-3). 59.50 *(978-0-8136-7972-3(9))* Modern Curriculum Pr.

If I Were a Fish. (J). 26.20 *(978-0-8136-8443-7(9))*; (gr. -1-3). 59.50 *(978-0-8136-8008-8(5))* Modern Curriculum Pr.

In the Graveyard: Decodable Books, 6 vols. (Fast Track Reading Ser.). 24p. (gr. 4-8). 40.95 *(978-0-322-05986-3(0))* Wright Group/McGraw-Hill.

In the Graveyard Play 12: Decodable Plays, 6 vols. (Fast Track Reading Ser.). 24p. (gr. 4-8). 40.95 *(978-0-322-06000-5(1))* Wright Group/McGraw-Hill.

In the Mirror: Big Book: Level A. Group 1. (Story Box Ser.). 8p. 20.95 *(978-0-7802-7625-3(6))* Wright Group/McGraw-Hill.

In the News, 6 vols. (Wildcats Ser.). 32p. (gr. 2-8). *(978-0-322-02437-3(4))* Wright Group/McGraw-Hill.

In the News, 6 vols., Set 2. Incl. Climate Change. Brezina, Corona. (YA). lib. bdg. 31.95 *(978-1-4042-1913-7(7))*; Darfur: African Genocide. Xavier, John. (YA). lib. bdg. 31.95 *(978-1-4042-1912-0(9))*; Doping: Athletes & Drugs. Porterfield, Jason. (J). lib. bdg. 29.25 *(978-1-4042-1917-5(X))*; Green Technology: Earth-Friendly Innovations. Sobha, Geeta. (YA). lib. bdg. 31.95 *(978-1-4042-1914-4(5))*; Nukes: The Spread of Nuclear Weapons. Minneus, Steve. (YA). lib. bdg. 31.95 *(978-1-4042-1916-8(1))*; Oil: The Economics of Fuel. Jovinelly, Joann. (YA). lib. bdg. 31.95 *(978-1-4042-1915-1(3))*; (Illus.). 64p. (gr. 7-12). 2007. 2007. Set lib. bdg. 175.50 *(978-1-4042-1112-4(8))* Rosen Publishing Group, Inc., The.

In the News: Level O, 6 vols. (Wonder Worldtm Ser.). 48p. 39.95 *(978-0-7802-2959-4(2))* Wright Group/McGraw-Hill.

Incredible Places: 6 Each of 1 Anthology, 6 vols. (Wildcats Ser.). 32p. (gr. 2-8). *(978-0-322-00587-7(6))* Wright Group/McGraw-Hill.

Inventions of Ancient Civilization Collection, 4 pkgs., Set. (J). (gr. 3-6). 327.00 *(978-0-8136-6355-5(5))* Modern Curriculum Pr.

Iris la Bonga & the Helpful Taxi Driver: Level T. Group 1, 6 vols. (Sunshine Ser.). 48p. 44.95 *(978-0-7802-5598-2(4))* Wright Group/McGraw-Hill.

It Takes Time to Grow, 6 vols. (Sunshinetm Ser.). 16p. (gr. k-18). 29.50 *(978-0-7802-5434-3(1))* Wright Group/McGraw-Hill.

It's Noisy at Night: Level F, 6 vols. (Wonder Worldtm Ser.). 16p. 29.95 *(978-0-7802-1039-4(5))* Wright Group/McGraw-Hill.

I've Been Working on the Railroad. (Song Box Ser.). (gr. 1-2). 31.50 *(978-0-7802-0936-7(2))*; 8.50 incl. audio *(978-0-7802-0938-1(9))* Wright Group/McGraw-Hill.

I've Been Working on the Railroad: 1 Big Book, 6 Each of 1 Student Book, & 1 Cassette. (Song Box Ser.). (gr. 1-2). 68.95 *(978-0-7802-0939-8(7))* Wright Group/McGraw-Hill.

I've Been Working on the Railroad: 6 Each of 1 Student Book, 6 vols. (Song Box Ser.). (gr. 1-2). 29.50 *(978-0-7802-0937-4(0))* Wright Group/McGraw-Hill.

Jack de Pert at the Supermarket: Level J, 6 vols. (Wonder Worldtm Ser.). 16p. 29.95 *(978-0-7802-1040-0(9))* Wright Group/McGraw-Hill.

Jackman, John. Comprehension. 2011. (Collins Primary Focus Ser.). (ENG., Illus.). 128p. (J). (gr. 2-2). pap., stu. ed. 14.99 *(978-0-00-741059-0(X))* HarperCollins Pubs. Ltd. GBR. Dist: Independent Pubs. Group.

—Comprehension - Pupil Book, Bk. 2. 2011. (Collins Primary Focus Ser.). (ENG., Illus.). 48p. (J). (gr. 4-4). pap. 14.99 *(978-0-00-741061-3(1))* HarperCollins Pubs. Ltd. GBR. Dist: Independent Pubs. Group.

Jake's Big Day: Long Vowel a, CVCe Pattern: Level B, 6 vols. (Wright Skills Ser.). 16p. (gr. k-3). 17.95 *(978-0-322-01465-7(4))* Wright Group/McGraw-Hill.

Jan Can Juggle. (Little Book Practice Reader). (J). *(978-0-8136-5362-4(2))* Modern Curriculum Pr.

Janet & Donald: Decodable Books, 6 vols. (Fast Track Reading Ser.). 24p. (gr. 4-8). 40.95 *(978-0-322-05984-9(4))* Wright Group/McGraw-Hill.

Janet & Donald Play 7: Decodable Plays, 6 vols. (Fast Track Reading Ser.). 24p. (gr. 4-8). 40.95 *(978-0-322-05998-6(4))* Wright Group/McGraw-Hill.

Jean Batter Pioneer of the Sky: Level R, 6 vols. (Wonder Worldtm Ser.). 48p. 44.95 *(978-0-7802-7079-4(7))* Wright Group/McGraw-Hill.

Jen & the Pets: Consonants k, v, y; Short Vowel e Word Families: Level A, 6 vols. (Wright Skills Ser.). 12p. (gr. k-3). 17.95 *(978-0-322-01454-1(9))* Wright Group/McGraw-Hill.

Jennett, Pamela. Discoverers & Inventors Reader's Theater Vol. 2245: Develop Reading Fluency & Test Comprehension Skills. Hults, Alaska, ed. Hilliam, Corbin & Vangsgard, Amy, illus. 2004. 96p. (J). pap. 12.99 *(978-1-59198-040-7(2)*, 2245) Creative Teaching Pr., Inc.

Jennison, Nancy. Integrating Test Prep into Reading & Writing Workshops: Classroom-Tested Lessons & Activities That Teach Students the Skills They Need to Become Successful Readers & Writers-And Excel on the Tests. 2011. (ENG.). 240p. pap. 25.99 *(978-0-545-14711-8(5)*, Teaching Resources) Scholastic, Inc.

Jim Pig Is Mad: Short Vowel i: Level A, 6 vols. (Wright Skills Ser.). 12p. (gr. k-3). 17.95 *(978-0-322-03115-9(X))* Wright Group/McGraw-Hill.

Jim's Trumpet: Level K. Group 1. (Sunshine Ser.). 16p. 36.50 *(978-0-7802-5793-1(6))* Wright Group/McGraw-Hill.

Joe's Toe: Long o Digraphs: Level B, 6 vols. (Wright Skills Ser.). 16p. (gr. k-3). 26.50 *(978-0-322-01480-0(8))* Wright Group/McGraw-Hill.

Jog to the Dam: Consonants g, h, j; Short Vowel o word families: Level A, 6 vols. (Wright Skills Ser.). 12p. (gr. k-3). 17.95 *(978-0-322-01448-0(4))* Wright Group/McGraw-Hill.

Joyce, William. Santa Calls Stationery Set. Date not set. (J). 11.95 *(978-0-694-00806-3(0))* HarperCollins Pubs.

Kalar, Bonnie. Early Phonetic Readers - Set E, 7 bks., set. Spreen, Kathe, illus. Incl. Ann Paints & Plays. pap. *(978-1-891619-40-3(3))*; Clair at Home. pap. *(978-1-891619-44-1(6))*; Good Day. pap. *(978-1-891619-41-0(1))*; Kirk & the Deer. pap. *(978-1-891619-43-4(8))*; Miss Lane's Class. pap. *(978-1-891619-38-0(1))*; Neal Camps Out. pap. *(978-1-891619-39-7(X))*; Trip to the Beach. pap. *(978-1-891619-42-7(X))*; 12p. (J). (gr. -1-2). (Illus.). Set pap. 14.50 *(978-1-891619-37-3(3))* Corona Pr.

Kalman, Bobbie. What Is It? 2011. (ENG., Illus.). 16p. (J). pap. *(978-0-7787-9572-8(1))*; lib. bdg. *(978-0-7787-9547-6(0))* Crabtree Publishing Co.

Kauzlarich, David. Sociological Classics: A Prentice Hall Pocket Reader. 2004. (ENG.). 144p. (C). pap. 29.00 *(978-0-13-191806-1(0)*, Prentice Hall) Prentice Hall PTR.

Keeping Baby Animals Safe: Take-Home Book. 2005. (Emergent Library: Vol. 2). (YA). (gr. -1-1). 12.60 *(978-0-8215-7264-1(4))* Sadlier, William H. Inc.

Keller, Ellen & Schifini, Alfredo. Kids Manage Money. 2007. (Rise & Shine Ser.). (ENG., Illus.). 32p. (J). pap. 17.95 *(978-0-7922-8694-3(4))* CENGAGE Learning.

Kertell, Lynn Maslen. Pre-Reading Skills. Hendra, Sue & Maslen, John R., illus. 2008. (Bob Bks.). (ENG.). 144p. (J). (gr. -1-k). pap. 16.99 *(978-0-545-01922-4(2)*, Cartwheel Bks.) Scholastic, Inc.

Keys. (J). *(978-0-8136-5369-3(X))* Modern Curriculum Pr.

Kids Can Learn Franklin Staff. ed. Early Reading. 2004. 32p. pap. *(978-1-55337-604-0(8))* Kids Can Pr., Ltd.

Kids Can Press Staff. Measurement. 2003. (Kids Can Learn with Franklin Ser.). (ENG., Illus.). 32p. (J). (gr. k-1). 3.95 *(978-1-55337-595-1(5))* Kids Can Pr., Ltd. CAN. Dist: Hachette Bk. Group.

Kids Can Press Staff & Shannon, Rosemarie. Alphabet Mazes. 2003. (Kids Can Learn with Franklin Ser.). (ENG., Illus.). 32p. (J). (gr. -1-1). pap. 3.95 *(978-1-55337-592-0(0))* Kids Can Pr., Ltd. CAN. Dist: Hachette Bk. Group.

Kimmelman, Leslie. Ben Lost a Tooth. 2005. (IOpeners Ser.). (Illus.). 8p. (J). pap. 7.56 *(978-0-7652-5132-9(9))* Celebration Pr.

—A Dog Named Honey. 2005. (IOpeners Ser.). (Illus.). 8p. (J). pap. 7.56 *(978-0-7652-5144-2(2))* Celebration Pr.

—Star Pictures. 2005. (IOpeners Ser.). (Illus.). 8p. (J). pap. 7.56 *(978-0-7652-5134-3(5))* Celebration Pr.

The King Who Could Knit: Initial Silent Consonants: Level C, 6 vols. (Wright Skills Ser.). 16p. (gr. k-3). 26.50 *(978-0-322-01502-9(2))* Wright Group/McGraw-Hill.

King, Zelda. Try it with Triangles: Learning to Put Triangles Together to Form Other Shapes. 2004. (Math Big Bookstm Ser.). (ENG.). 16p. (gr. 2-3). 37.95 *(978-0-8239-7641-6(6))* Rosen Publishing Group, Inc., The.

The Kitty: Long Vowels e, y, CVCe & Final y Patterns: Level B, 6 vols. (Wright Skills Ser.). 16p. (gr. k-3). 17.95 *(978-0-322-03130-2(3))* Wright Group/McGraw-Hill.

Klees, Amy. 100 Ways I Love to Read. 2008. 24p. pap. 15.99 *(978-1-4363-9383-6(3))* Xlibris Corp.

Koch, Kamla Devi, et al. Teen Stories: Personal Stories for Students Who Are Beginning to Read. (J). tchr. ed. 8.95 *(978-0-916591-20-5(4))*; stu. ed. 8.95 *(978-0-916591-19-9(0))* Linmore Publishing, Inc.

Kratky, Lada Josefa. Alfarrimas: Guia Del Maestro. 2005. (Alfarrimas Ser.). (SPA & ENG., Illus.). 8p. (C). pap. 36.95 *(978-0-7362-2659-2(1))* CENGAGE Learning.

L Omino di Panpepato. pap. 14.95 *(978-88-04-44206-6(9))* Mondadori ITA. Dist: Distribooks, Inc.

LaCoste, Gary, illus. First Word Search: Phonics Word Search. 2011. (First Word Search Ser.). (ENG.). 64p. (J). (gr. -1-1). pap. 4.95 *(978-1-4027-7801-8(5))* Sterling Publishing Co., Inc.

Lalley, Kristine. How Many Legs? Learning to Multiply Using Repeated Addition. 2009. (PowerMath: Beginning Ser.). 16p. (gr. 2-2). 37.50 *(978-1-60851-373-4(4)*, PowerKids Pr.) Rosen Publishing Group, Inc., The.

Language Works Rhyme Time. 8p. (J). *(978-0-8136-3519-4(5))* Modern Curriculum Pr.

Language Works Staff. Message of the Dance. (J). 28.08 *(978-0-8136-3504-0(7))* Modern Curriculum Pr.

Last-Minute Rescue Little Book: Early Reading Fluency, Level C. 2004. pap. 6.00 *(978-0-7398-8300-6(3))* Steck-Vaughn.

Laurence, Jo. How to Be a Wizard at Nursery Rhymes. Ford, Kate, illus. 48p. (J). (gr. 1-3). pap. *(978-1-876367-28-2(8))* Wizard Bks.

Leaf, Munro. How to Be: How to Grow up to Be Healthy, Wealthy, & Wise. 2015. (Rizzoli Classics Ser.). (ENG., Illus.). 104p. (J). (-k). 19.95 *(978-0-7893-3109-0(8))* Universe Publishing.

—Reading Can Be Fun. 2004. (ENG., Illus.). 56p. (J). (gr. k-4). 14.95 *(978-0-7893-1203-7(4))* Universe Publishing.

LeapFrog Schoolhouse Staff. Read-It-All Books. 2003. (YA). (gr. 3-18). tchr. ed., spiral bd. 19.95 *(978-1-59319-017-0(4),* LeapFrog Schl. Hse.) LeapFrog Enterprises, Inc.

LeapFrog Staff. Sing-along Read-along: Early Reading Set. 2008. (J). pap. 19.99 incl. DVD *(978-1-59319-992-0(9))* LeapFrog Enterprises, Inc.

Learning Co Bks Staff. Best Gift Ever. 2005. (Learn to Read Library). pap. 3.99 *(978-0-7630-8030-3(6))* Houghton Mifflin Harcourt Learning Technology.

—Lucky for Us! 2005. (Learn to Read Library). pap. 3.99 *(978-0-7630-8037-2(3))* Houghton Mifflin Harcourt Learning Technology.

—New Friend. 2005. (Learn to Read Library). pap. 3.99 *(978-0-7630-8032-7(2))* Houghton Mifflin Harcourt Learning Technology.

—Night Noises. 2005. (Learn to Read Library). pap. 3.99 *(978-0-7630-8031-0(4))* Houghton Mifflin Harcourt Learning Technology.

—Starry, Starry Night. 2005. (Learn to Read Library). pap. 3.99 *(978-0-7630-8028-0(4))* Houghton Mifflin Harcourt Learning Technology.

Learning Company Books Staff, ed. Reader Rabbit: Reading Comprehension. 2003. (Illus.). 32p. (J). pap., wbk. ed. *(978-0-7630-7643-6(0))* Magma.

Lee, Martin & Miller, Marcia. 20 Reading Selections with Text-Marking Exercises. 2016. (Literary Passages: Close Reading Ser.). (ENG., Illus.). 64p. (gr. 1-1). pap. 11.99 *(978-0-545-79384-1(X),* Teaching Resources) Scholastic, Inc.

Legler, Caroline. Super Words Early Reading Program, 10 vols. 2005. (Illus.). (J). 16.95 *(978-0-9771233-0-8(8))* Legler, Caroline.

Legs: Big Book: Level C. 8p. 20.95 *(978-0-322-00343-9(1))* Wright Group/McGraw-Hill.

Legs: Level C, 6 vols. 8p. 24.95 *(978-0-7802-9120-1(4))* Wright Group/McGraw-Hill.

Legs, Legs, Legs: Big Book: Level B. (Wonder Worldtm Ser.). 16p. 26.50 *(978-0-7802-2829-0(4))* Wright Group/McGraw-Hill.

Legs, Legs, Legs: Level B, 6 vols. (Wonder Worldtm Ser.). 16p. 24.95 *(978-0-7802-1087-5(5))* Wright Group/McGraw-Hill.

Let's Meet Biographies, 6 vols. 2005. (Let's Meet Biographies Ser.). (Illus.). 32p. (gr. 2-4). 138.00 *(978-0-7910-7317-9(3),* Chelsea Hse.) Facts On File, Inc.

Letter Cluster Books Reproducibles. (Foundation Ser.). 64p. (gr. k-3). 26.50 *(978-0-322-01549-4(9))* Wright Group/McGraw-Hill.

Letter Clusters Student Book: 6 Each of 1 Student Book. 32p. (gr. k-3). 31.95 *(978-0-7802-9033-4(X))* Wright Group/McGraw-Hill.

Level C, Vol. 2. (J). 5.99 *(978-0-8136-1703-9(0))* Modern Curriculum Pr.

Levinson, Nancy Smiler. Prairie Friends. Schuett, Stacey, illus. 2003. (I Can Read Bks.). 64p. (J). (gr. k-3). 16.89 *(978-0-06-028002-4(6))* HarperCollins Pubs.

Linde, Barbara M. I Show Respect. Mones, Marc, illus. 2014. (J). (gr. -1). 3.99 *(978-1-4788-0468-0(8))* Newmark Learning LLC.

—I Show Respect Lap Book. Mones, Marc, illus. 2014. (MySELF Ser.). (J). (gr. -1-k). 27.00 *(978-1-4788-0505-2(6))* Newmark Learning LLC.

—I Take Turns. Patton, Julia, illus. 2014. (J). (gr. -1). 3.99 *(978-1-4788-0476-5(9))* Newmark Learning LLC.

—I Take Turns Lap Book. Patton, Julia, illus. 2014. (MySELF Ser.). (J). (gr. -1-k). 27.00 *(978-1-4788-0513-7(7))* Newmark Learning LLC.

—I Will Find a Way. Evans, Antony, illus. 2014. (J). (gr. -1). 3.99 *(978-1-4788-0483-3(1))* Newmark Learning LLC.

—I Will Find a Way Lap Book. Evans, Antony, illus. 2014. (MySELF Ser.). (J). (gr. -1-k). 27.00 *(978-1-4788-0520-5(X))* Newmark Learning LLC.

—Jealous of Josie. Poole, Helen, illus. 2014. (J). (gr. -1). 3.99 *(978-1-4788-0465-9(3))* Newmark Learning LLC.

—Jealous of Josie Lap Book. Poole, Helen, illus. 2014. (MySELF Ser.). (J). (gr. -1-k). 27.00 *(978-1-4788-0502-1(1))* Newmark Learning LLC.

—A Shopping Trip: Learning to Add Dollars & Cents up to $10.00 Without Regrouping. 2009. (Math for the REAL World Ser.). 16p. (gr. 2-3). pap. 7.05 *(978-0-8239-8900-3(3),* Rosen Classroom) Rosen Publishing Group, Inc., The.

Lindeen, Carol K. From Coast to Coast, 6 vols., Set. 2004. (Phonics Readers Books 37-72 Ser.). (ENG.). 8p. (gr. k-1). pap. 35.70 *(978-0-7368-4061-3(3),* Phonics Readers) Capstone Press of Coughlan Cos.

Linder, Don. Where Do Things Go When I Close My Eyes? 2012. (SPA.). (J). pap. 10.00 *(978-1-4675-5390-2(5))* Independent Pub.

Listen: Big Book: Level D. (Visions Ser.). 8p. 20.95 *(978-0-322-00309-5(1))* Wright Group/McGraw-Hill.

Literature Connections English: Fallen Angels. 2004. (gr. 6-12). *(978-0-395-83360-5(4),* 2-70783) Holt McDougal.

Literature Connections English: Jane Eyre. 2004. (gr. 6-12). *(978-0-395-77557-8(4),* 2-80126) Holt McDougal.

Literature Connections English: Julius Caesar. 2004. (gr. 6-12). *(978-0-395-77542-4(6),* 2-80111) Holt McDougal.

Literature Connections English: My Antonia. 2004. (gr. 6-12). *(978-0-395-77539-4(6),* 2-80108) Holt McDougal.

Literature Connections English: Nervous Conditions. 2004. (gr. 6-12). *(978-0-395-77560-8(4),* 2-80129) Holt McDougal.

Little Bear's Friend. 2003. 31.95 *(978-0-673-75802-6(8))* Celebration Pr.

Lizards: Level N, 6 vols. (Wonder Worldtm Ser.). 48p. 34.95 *(978-0-7802-4583-9(0))* Wright Group/McGraw-Hill.

Llueve, Truena y Relampaguea, 6 vols. (Explorers. Exploradores Nonfiction Sets Ser.). (SPA.). 32p. (gr. 3-6). 44.95 *(978-0-7699-0632-4(X))* Shortland Pubns. (U. S. A.) Inc.

Log Man: Level 5, 6 vols. (Fluency Strand Ser.). (gr. 4-8). 45.00 *(978-1-4045-1232-0(2))* Wright Group/McGraw-Hill.

London, S. Keith & Osleeb, Rebecca. Defined Mind Vocabulary Accelerator: Music-Driven Vocabulary & Comprehension Tools for School / Test / SAT Prep, 1. 2004. 416p. (YA). pap. 25.00 *(978-0-9763767-0-5(9))* Defined Mind, Inc.

Long Ago & Far Away: 6 Each of 1 Anthology, 6 vols. (Wildcats Ser.). 32p. (gr. 2-8). *(978-0-322-00583-9(3))* Wright Group/McGraw-Hill.

Look Closer. (J). *(978-0-8136-5364-8(9))* Modern Curriculum Pr.

Look Here! Level D, 6 vols. (Wonder Worldtm Ser.). 16p. 24.95 *(978-0-7802-1221-3(5))* Wright Group/McGraw-Hill.

Look Out, Dan! Big Book: Level C. Group 2. (Story Box Ser.). 16p. 20.95 *(978-0-7802-9367-0(3))* Wright Group/McGraw-Hill.

Looking for Crabs: Big Books Packages. 2005. (J). (gr. k-3). 75.95 *(978-0-673-77117-9(2))* Celebration Pr.

Looking Out, Climbing up, Going Far Grade 1: American Readers. (J). (gr. 1). wbk. ed. *(978-0-669-04968-8(9))* Houghton Mifflin Harcourt School Pubs.

Loves, June. Pets, 6 vols. 2005. (Pets Ser.). (Illus.). 32p. (gr. 2-4). 138.00 *(978-0-7910-7546-3(X),* Chelsea Hse.) Facts On File, Inc.

Ma, Karin & Taylor, Nicole. Differentiating Assessment in the Reading Workshop: Templates, Checklists, How-To'S, & Student Samples to Streamline Ongoing Assessments So You Can Plan & Teach More Effectively. 2009. (ENG.). 144p. pap. 24.99 *(978-0-545-05397-6(8),* Teaching Resources) Scholastic, Inc.

Madu, Abraham. The Road to take to School Is the Phonics Way: Companion Book for Students. 2003. 98p. pap. 11.95 *(978-0-595-27748-3(9))* iUniverse, Inc.

Magic! Big Book: Level C. 8p. 20.95 *(978-0-322-00623-2(6))* Wright Group/McGraw-Hill.

Magic! Level C, 6 vols. 8p. 24.95 *(978-0-7802-9122-5(0))* Wright Group/McGraw-Hill.

Mai. Many Hands. 2012. 24p. pap. 15.99 *(978-1-4771-4246-2(0))* Xlibris Corp.

Mairi, Mackinnon. Phonics Workbook 1. 2012. (Very First Reading Workbooks Ser.). 36p. (J). pap. 7.99 *(978-0-7945-3115-7(6),* Usborne) EDC Publishing.

—Phonics Workbook 2. 2012. (Very First Reading Workbooks Ser.). 36p. (J). pap. 7.99 *(978-0-7945-3116-4(4),* Usborne) EDC Publishing.

Mai's Big Surprise: Consonant review: Level C, 6 vols. (Wright Skills Ser.). 16p. (gr. k-3). 26.50 *(978-0-322-01490-9(5))* Wright Group/McGraw-Hill.

Major Jump: Big Book: Level B. Group 1. (Sunshine Ser.). 8p. 20.95 *(978-0-7802-5713-9(8))* Wright Group/McGraw-Hill.

Making a TV Documentary: Level R, 6 vols. (Wonder Worldtm Ser.). 48p. 44.95 *(978-0-7802-7082-4(7))* Wright Group/McGraw-Hill.

Making Choices: American Readers. (J). (gr. 6). *(978-0-669-05069-1(5));* wbk. ed. *(978-0-669-05071-4(7))* Houghton Mifflin Harcourt School Pubs.

Making Music: Level B, 6 vols. (Wonder Worldtm Ser.). 16p. 24.95 *(978-0-7802-2008-9(0))* Wright Group/McGraw-Hill.

Mama Goes to School: Big Book: Level D. (Visions Ser.). 8p. 20.95 *(978-0-322-00310-1(5))* Wright Group/McGraw-Hill.

Los Mamíferos Del Mar, 6 vols. (Explorers. Exploradores Nonfiction Sets Ser.). (SPA.). 32p. (gr. 3-6). 44.95 *(978-0-7699-0629-4(X))* Shortland Pubns. (U. S. A.) Inc.

Manners, Jane. Clouds. 2004. (ENG., Illus.). 16p. (J). (gr. 1-1). pap. 10.92 *(978-0-7652-5153-4(1),* Celebration Pr.) Pearson Schl.

Los Mapas Del Mundo, 6 vols., Vol. 2. (Explorers. Exploradores Nonfiction Sets Ser.). (SPA.). 32p. (gr. 3-6). 44.95 *(978-0-7699-0646-1(X))* Shortland Pubns. (U. S. A.) Inc.

Marching Along: American Readers. (J). (gr. 2). *(978-0-669-04984-8(0));* wbk. ed. *(978-0-669-04991-6(3))* Houghton Mifflin Harcourt School Pubs.

Maria's Diary: Level R, 6 vols. (Wonder Worldtm Ser.). 48p. 44.95 *(978-0-7802-7067-1(3))* Wright Group/McGraw-Hill.

Mario Mixwell: Level L, 6 vols. (Take-Twostm Ser.). 16p. 36.95 *(978-0-322-03404-4(3))* Wright Group/McGraw-Hill.

The Marketplace: Big Book: Level G. (Visions Ser.). 16p. 20.95 *(978-0-322-00628-7(7))* Wright Group/McGraw-Hill.

Martinez, Jeny. A Walk in the Park. 2011. 32p. pap. 21.99 *(978-1-4568-5229-0(9))* Xlibris Corp.

Marzollo, Jean & Wick, Walter. I Spy a Dinosaur's Eye. 2003. (I Spy — Scholastic Readers Level 1 Ser.). (gr. -1-2). lib. bdg. 13.55 *(978-0-613-72243-8(4),* Turtleback) Turtleback Bks.

Masks: Level E, 6 vols. (Wonder Worldtm Ser.). 16p. 29.95 *(978-0-7802-2010-2(2))* Wright Group/McGraw-Hill.

Mattern, Joanne. At the Football Game: Learning the Symbols +, And = 2009. (Math for the REAL World Ser.). 16p. (gr. 2-3). pap. 7.05 *(978-0-8239-8875-4(9),* Rosen Classroom) Rosen Publishing Group, Inc., The.

Max Is Sick: Consonants q, x, z; -ack, -ick, -ill word families: Level A, 6 vols. (Wright Skills Ser.). 12p. (gr. k-3). 17.95 *(978-0-322-01457-2(3))* Wright Group/McGraw-Hill.

Mayers, Shareen. Spelling & Phonics Age 5-6. 2013. (Letts Monster Practice Ser.). (ENG., Illus.). 48p. (J). (gr. k-1). pap. 6.99 *(978-1-84419-749-1(2))* HarperCollins Pubs. Ltd. GBR. Dist: Independent Pubs. Group.

—Spelling & Phonics Age 6-7. 2013. (Letts Monster Practice Ser.). (ENG., Illus.). 16p. (J). (gr. 1-2). pap. 6.99 *(978-1-84419-750-7(6))* HarperCollins Pubs. Ltd. GBR. Dist: Independent Pubs. Group.

McCollum, Betty, intro. Women in the Arts. 2005. (Women in the Arts Ser.). (Illus.). 112p. (gr. 6-12). 150.00 *(978-0-7910-7454-1(4),* Chelsea Hse.) Facts On File, Inc.

McDonnell, Flora. Splash. 2004. (CHI & ENG., Illus.). 28p. (J). pap. *(978-1-85269-549-1(8))* Mantra Lingua.

McDougal-Littell Publishing Staff. Literature Connections English: A Place Where the Sea Remembers. 2004. (McDougal Littell Literature Connections Ser.). (ENG.). 208p. (gr. 10-10). 16.25 *(978-0-395-83361-2(2),* 2-70784) Great Source Education Group, Inc.

McDougal-Littell Publishing Staff, creator. Picture Bride & Related Readings. 2006. (Literature Connections Ser.). 314p. (gr. 6-12). *(978-0-395-77540-0(X),* 2-80109) Holt McDougal.

—1984: And Related Readings. 2006. (Literature Connections Ser.). 428p. (YA). (gr. 8-12). *(978-0-395-87471-4(8),* 2-70831) Holt McDougal.

McGraw-Hill - Jamestown Education Staff. Timed Readings Plus in Social Studies, Vol. 3. 2003. pap. 17.32 *(978-0-07-845801-9(3),* 9780078458019) Jamestown.

—Timed Readings Plus in Social Studies Bk. 3, Vol. 9. 2003. pap. 17.32 *(978-0-07-845807-1(2),* 9780078458071) Jamestown.

McGraw-Hill Education Editors. Timed Readings Plus in Social Studies, Vol. 7. 2003. (JT: READING RATE & FLUENCY Ser.). (ENG.). 120p. (gr. 6-12). per. 25.60 *(978-0-07-845805-7(6),* 0078458056) Jamestown.

—Timed Readings Plus in Social Studies Bk. 3, Vol. 2. 2003. (JT: READING RATE & FLUENCY Ser.). (ENG.). 120p. (gr. 6-12). pap. 25.60 *(978-0-07-845800-2(5),* 0078458005) Jamestown.

McGraw-Hill Staff. Jo Tries: And Other Selections, 6 vols. (Fast Track Reading Ser.). 24p. (gr. 4-8). 40.95 *(978-0-322-05983-2(6))* Wright Group/McGraw-Hill.

McGraw-Hill, Wright. Treacherous Ice, 6 vols. (Comprehension Strand Ser.). (gr. 4-8). 54.00 *(978-0-322-06032-6(X))* Wright Group/McGraw-Hill.

McKay, Sindy. We Read Phonics-Magic Tricks. Johnson, Meredith, illus. 2011. (We Read Phonics Ser.). 32p. (J). (gr. 1-3). 9.95 *(978-1-60115-337-1(6));* pap. 4.99 *(978-1-60115-338-8(4))* Treasure Bay, Inc.

—We Read Phonics-Matt & Sid. Reinhart, Larry, illus. 2010. 32p. (J). 9.95 *(978-1-60115-315-9(5));* pap. 4.99 *(978-1-60115-316-6(3))* Treasure Bay, Inc.

McMahon, Philip & Collins UK Staff. 11+ Comprehension Results Booster for the CEM Tests. 2016. (Letts 11+ Success Ser.). (ENG.). 80p. (J). (gr. 5-6). pap. 14.95 *(978-1-84419-901-3(0))* HarperCollins Pubs. Ltd. GBR. Dist: Independent Pubs. Group.

McNeil, Niki, et al. HOCPP 1118 Beginning Reading. 2006. spiral bd. 30.00 *(978-1-60308-118-4(6))* In the Hands of a Child.

MCP Staff. My Monster & Me, Level 2, Bk. 6. (J). (gr. -1-3). 24.50 *(978-0-8136-0675-0(6))* Modern Curriculum Pr.

—Night Animals, Level 4, Bk. 30. (J). (gr. -1-3). 24.50 *(978-0-8136-0743-6(4))* Modern Curriculum Pr.

—One Bee Got on the Bus, Level 3, Bk. 9. (J). (gr. -1-3). 21.95 *(978-0-8136-0739-9(6))* Modern Curriculum Pr.

—The Party, Level 4, Bk. 4. (J). (gr. -1-3). 24.50 *(978-0-8136-1937-8(8))* Modern Curriculum Pr.

—Shell Shopping, 6 bks., set, Level A. 2003. (J). (gr. -1-3). 33.50 *(978-0-8136-0797-9(3))* Modern Curriculum Pr.

—Ted's Red Sled, Level 4, Bk. 40. (J). (gr. -1-3). 24.50 *(978-0-8136-1969-9(6))* Modern Curriculum Pr.

—Too High!, Level 4, Bk. 37. 2003. (J). (gr. -1-3). 24.50 *(978-0-8136-0774-0(4))* Modern Curriculum Pr.

—Vulture on Vacation, Level 3, Bk. 5. (J). (gr. -1-3). 24.50 *(978-0-8136-1939-2(4))* Modern Curriculum Pr.

—What Rhymes with Cat?, Level A, Bk. 2. (J). *(978-0-8136-1933-0(5))* Modern Curriculum Pr.

Meeting Challenges: American Readers. (J). (gr. 8). *(978-0-669-05093-6(8)); (978-0-669-05099-8(7))* Houghton Mifflin Harcourt School Pubs.

Meow-Meow Gets Out: Diphthongs ou, ow: Level B, 6 vols. (Wright Skills Ser.). 16p. (gr. k-3). 26.50 *(978-0-322-01484-8(0))* Wright Group/McGraw-Hill.

Mike & His Bride, 6 vols. 8p. (gr. k-1). 21.50 *(978-0-322-02062-7(X))* Wright Group/McGraw-Hill.

Milking: Level H, 6 vols. (Wonder Worldtm Ser.). 16p. 29.95 *(978-0-7802-1207-7(X))* Wright Group/McGraw-Hill.

Mixed-Up Wishing Well Little Book: Early Reading Fluency, Level C. 2004. pap. 6.00 *(978-0-7398-8297-9(X))* Steck-Vaughn.

Modern Staff. Discovery Phonics I: Lively Tales Unlock the Mystery of Long & Short Vowels. 2003. (J). 333.95 *(978-0-8136-1122-8(9))* Modern Curriculum Pr.

Molter, Carey. -Ain As in Train, 1 vol. 2003. (Word Families Set 8 Ser.). (ENG., Illus.). 24p. (J). (gr. k-3). lib. bdg. 24.21 *(978-1-59197-272-3(8))* ABDO Publishing Co.

—Ake As in Cake, 1 vol. 2003. (Word Families Set 8 Ser.). (ENG., Illus.). 24p. (J). (gr. k-3). lib. bdg. 24.21 *(978-1-59197-270-9(1))* ABDO Publishing Co.

—Eam As in Ice Cream, 1 vol. 2003. (Word Families Set 8 Ser.). (ENG., Illus.). 24p. (J). (gr. k-3). lib. bdg. 24.21 *(978-1-59197-273-0(6),* SandCastle) ABDO Publishing Co.

—En As in Pen, 1 vol. 2003. (Word Families Set 2 Ser.). (ENG., Illus.). 24p. (J). (gr. k-3). lib. bdg. 24.21 *(978-1-59197-229-7(9),* SandCastle) ABDO Publishing Co.

—Ide As in Tide, 1 vol. 2003. (Word Families Set 8 Ser.). (ENG., Illus.). 24p. (J). (gr. k-3). lib. bdg. 24.21 *(978-1-59197-275-4(2),* SandCastle) ABDO Publishing Co.

—One As in Stone, 1 vol. 2003. (Word Families Set 8 Ser.). (ENG., Illus.). 24p. (J). (gr. k-3). lib. bdg. 24.21 *(978-1-59197-274-7(4),* SandCastle) ABDO Publishing Co.

—Oon As in Spoon, 1 vol. 2003. (Word Families Set 7 Ser.). (ENG., Illus.). 24p. (J). (gr. k-3). lib. bdg. 24.21 *(978-1-59197-266-2(3),* SandCastle) ABDO Publishing Co.

Montoya, Martha, creator. Huevos o Pollitos: Take-Home. 2005. (Los Kitos Ser.). (SPA.). (YA). (gr. 1-3). 15.00 *(978-0-8215-8814-7(1))* Sadlier, William H. Inc.

Moon Stars. 2003. 31.95 *(978-0-673-75807-1(9))* Celebration Pr.

Moore, David W. The Good Reader's Guide: Read for Real. 2007. (Good Reader's Kit Ser.). (ENG., Illus.). 480p. (C). pap. 49.95 *(978-0-7362-3410-8(1))* CENGAGE Learning.

Moore, Sheila. Abadaba Alphabet: Learning Letter Sounds. Holsinger, Carol, illus. 2006. 31p. (gr. -1-3). 19.95 *(978-0-9789473-0-9(4))* Abadaba Reading LLC.

Morss, Martha. Advantage Reading Grade 3, Vol. 8114. Hamaguchi, Carla, ed. Tom, Darcy, illus. 2004. (Advantage Workbook Ser.). 112p. 8.99 *(978-1-59198-024-7(0),* CTP 8114) Creative Teaching Pr., Inc.

Moskal, G. I Like Winter: Learning the ER Sound. 2009. (PowerPhonics Ser.). 24p. (gr. 1-1). 39.90 *(978-1-60851-451-9(X),* PowerKids Pr.) Rosen Publishing Group, Inc., The.

Motorbike Racer: Level P, 6 vols. (Wonder Worldtm Ser.). 48p. 39.95 *(978-0-7802-7071-8(1))* Wright Group/McGraw-Hill.

Mountain Gorillas: Level N, 6 vols. (Wonder Worldtm Ser.). 48p. 34.95 *(978-0-7802-2899-3(5))* Wright Group/McGraw-Hill.

Mouse Soup. 2003. 31.95 *(978-0-673-75804-0(4))* Celebration Pr.

Mouse Tales. 2003. 31.95 *(978-0-673-75805-7(2))* Celebration Pr.

Mouse Train: Big Book: Level C. Group 2. (Story Box Ser.). 16p. 20.95 *(978-0-322-00332-3(6))* Wright Group/McGraw-Hill.

Move It: Level E, 6 vols. (Wonder Worldtm Ser.). 16p. 29.95 *(978-0-7802-1223-7(1))* Wright Group/McGraw-Hill.

Moving On: American Readers. (J). (gr. 1). *(978-0-669-04950-3(6));* wbk. ed. *(978-0-669-04956-5(5))* Houghton Mifflin Harcourt School Pubs.

Mrs Grindy's Shoes: Level I. Group 1. (Sunshine Ser.). 16p. 31.50 *(978-0-7802-5756-6(1))* Wright Group/McGraw-Hill.

Murphy, Patricia J. Counting with an Abacus: Learning the Place Values of Ones, Tens, & Hundreds. 2009. (Math for the REAL World Ser.). 16p. (gr. 2-3). pap. 7.05 *(978-0-8239-8880-8(5),* Rosen Classroom) Rosen Publishing Group, Inc., The.

My Computer: Level H, 6 vols. (Wonder Worldtm Ser.). 16p. 29.95 *(978-0-7802-1225-1(8))* Wright Group/McGraw-Hill.

My Dad has Asthma: Level L, 6 vols. (Wonder Worldtm Ser.). 16p. 34.95 *(978-0-7802-4587-7(3))* Wright Group/McGraw-Hill.

My Friend Jess: Level H, 6 vols. (Wonder Worldtm Ser.). 16p. 29.95 *(978-0-7802-1227-5(4))* Wright Group/McGraw-Hill.

My Story: Level A, 6 vols. (Wonder Worldtm Ser.). 16p. 24.95 *(978-0-7802-2901-3(0))* Wright Group/McGraw-Hill.

Mythmakers, 6 vols. (Wildcats Ser.). 32p. (gr. 2-8). *(978-0-322-02440-3(4))* Wright Group/McGraw-Hill.

Nana's Sweet Potato Pie, 6 vols. (Multicultural Programs Ser.). 16p. (gr. 1-3). 24.95 *(978-0-7802-9211-6(1))* Wright Group/McGraw-Hill.

A Nap Is not Fun: Short Vowel u: Level A, 6 vols. (Wright Skills Ser.). 12p. (gr. k-3). 17.95 *(978-0-322-03131-9(1))* Wright Group/McGraw-Hill.

National Geographic Learning, National Geographic Learning. The Good Reader's Guide: Read for Real. 2007. (Good Reader's Kit Ser.). (ENG., Illus.). 480p. (C). pap. 59.95 *(978-0-7362-3411-5(X))* CENGAGE Learning.

Native Americans: Level O, 6 vols. (Explorers Ser.). 32p. (gr. 3-6). 44.95 *(978-0-7699-0600-3(1))* Shortland Pubns. (U. S. A.) Inc.

The Neighborhood Clubhouse, 6 vols. (Multicultural Programs Ser.). 16p. (gr. 1-3). 24.95 *(978-0-7802-9212-3(X))* Wright Group/McGraw-Hill.

Nelson. Finding Places: American Readers. (J). *(978-0-669-04947-3(6))* Houghton Mifflin Harcourt School Pubs.

—Looking Out, Climbing Up, Going Far: American Readers. (J). *(978-0-669-04973-2(5))* Houghton Mifflin Harcourt School Pubs.

—Marching Along: American Readers. (J). *(978-0-669-04993-0(X))* Houghton Mifflin Harcourt School Pubs.

—Moving On: American Readers. (J). *(978-0-669-04961-9(1))* Houghton Mifflin Harcourt School Pubs.

—Turning Corners: American Readers. (J). *(978-0-669-05008-0(3))* Houghton Mifflin Harcourt School Pubs.

Nelson, Robin. What Do Pliers Do? 2012. (First Step Nonfiction - Tools at Work Ser.). (ENG., Illus.). 24p. (gr. k-2). pap. 6.95 *(978-1-58013-949-6(3))* Lerner Publishing Group.

Nests: Level A, 6 vols. (Wonder Worldtm Ser.). 16p. 24.95 *(978-0-7802-1041-7(7))* Wright Group/McGraw-Hill.

The New Building, 6 vols. (Sunshinetm Ser.). 16p. (gr. k-18). 29.50 *(978-0-7802-5424-4(4))* Wright Group/McGraw-Hill.

New Shoes: Level C, 6 vols. (Wonder Worldtm Ser.). 16p. 24.95 *(978-0-7802-1231-2(2))* Wright Group/McGraw-Hill.

Next Chapters Starter Set. 2005. (J). (gr. 3-5). tchr. ed. 119.95 *(978-0-7652-2126-1(8))* Modern Curriculum Pr.

Nighttime: Big Book: Level C. Group 1. (Story Box Ser.). 8p. 20.95 *(978-0-322-00636-2(8))* Wright Group/McGraw-Hill.

No Space to Waste: Level L, 6 vols. 128p. (gr. 2-3). 41.95 *(978-0-7699-1025-3(4))* Shortland Pubns. (U. S. A.) Inc.

No Sweat! Short e Digraph: Level B, 6 vols. (Wright Skills Ser.). 16p. (gr. k-3). 26.50 *(978-0-322-01477-0(8))* Wright Group/McGraw-Hill.

Not what it Seems, 6 vols. (Wildcats Ser.). 32p. (gr. 2-8). *(978-0-322-00602-7(3))* Wright Group/McGraw-Hill.

Notorious Nigel: Level Q, 6 vols. (Wonder Worldtm Ser.). 48p. 39.95 *(978-0-7802-2960-0(6))* Wright Group/McGraw-Hill.

Nowark, Jennifer. At the Flower Shop: Learning Simple Division by Forming Equal Groups. 2009. (Math for the REAL World Ser.). 16p. (gr. 2-3). pap. 7.05 *(978-0-8239-8930-0(5),* Rosen Classroom) Rosen Publishing Group, Inc., The.

Oatmeal: Level H, 6 vols. (Wonder Worldtm Ser.). 16p. 29.95 *(978-0-7802-1042-4(5))* Wright Group/McGraw-Hill.

Odgers, Sally. Glory Gate: Level Q, 6 vols. (Mountain Peaks Ser.). 128p. (gr. 6-18). 36.95 *(978-0-322-05889-7(9))* Wright Group/McGraw-Hill.

Olivia Agnew's Wild Imagination: Level O, 6 vols. (Wonder Worldtm Ser.). 48p. 39.95 *(978-0-7802-2957-0(6))* Wright Group/McGraw-Hill.

On & off the Road: 6 Each of 1 Anthology, 6 vols. (Wildcats Ser.). 32p. (gr. 2-8). *(978-0-322-02421-2(8))* Wright Group/McGraw-Hill.

On My Street, 6 vols. (Multicultural Programs Ser.). 16p. (gr. 1-3). 24.95 *(978-0-7802-9205-5(7))* Wright Group/McGraw-Hill.

On the Air: Level P, 6 vols. (Wonder Worldtm Ser.). 48p. 39.95 *(978-0-7802-7081-7(9))* Wright Group/McGraw-Hill.

Once I Was a Baby Little Book: Early Reading Fluency, Level A, Bk. 3. 2004. (ENG.). (gr. 1). pap. 6.00 *(978-0-7398-8156-9(6))* Steck-Vaughn.

Oppenheim, Joanne F. & Oppenheim, Stephanie. A Leer y Jugar! con Bebés y Niños Pequeños. Auclair, Joan, illus. 2006.Tr. of Read It! Play It! with Babies & Toddlers. (SPA.). 102p. pap. 10.00 *(978-0-9721050-5-7(0))* Oppenheim Toy Portfolio, Inc.

—Read It! Play It! Auclair, Joan, illus. 2005. 176p. pap. 10.00 *(978-0-9721050-1-9(8))* Oppenheim Toy Portfolio, Inc.

—Read It! Play It! with Babies & Toddlers. 2006. (Illus.). pap. 10.00 *(978-0-9721050-4-0(2))* Oppenheim Toy Portfolio, Inc.

Ornelas, Lourdes. So Can I. 2013. 32p. 25.99 (978-1-4808-0189-9(5)); pap. 16.99 (978-1-4808-0187-5(9)) Archway Publishing.
Orphan Train: Medial Digraphs: Level C, 6 vols. (Wright Skills Ser.). 16p. (gr. k-3). 26.50 (978-0-322-01498-5(0)) Wright Group/McGraw-Hill.
Orshoski, Paul. We Read Phonics-Ant in Her Pants. Ebbeler, Jeffrey, illus. 2010. (ENG.). 32p. (J). pap. 4.99 (978-1-60115-328-9(7)) Treasure Bay, Inc.
—We Read Phonics-Ants in Her Pants. Ebbeler, Jeffrey, illus. 2010. (ENG.). 32p. (J). 9.95 (978-1-60115-327-2(9)) Treasure Bay, Inc.
—We Read Phonics-Bugs on the Bus. Noiset, Michele, illus. 2010. 32p. (J). 9.95 (978-1-60115-325-8(2)); pap. 4.99 (978-1-60115-326-5(0)) Treasure Bay, Inc.
—We Read Phonics-Sports Dream. Ebbeler, Jeffrey, illus. 2011. (We Read Phonics Ser.). 32p. (J). (gr. 1-3). 9.95 (978-1-60115-335-7(X)); pap. 4.99 (978-1-60115-336-4(8)) Treasure Bay, Inc.
—We Read Phonics-Talent Night. Kulka, Joe, illus. 2011. (We Read Phonics Ser.). 32p. (J). (gr. 1-3). 9.95 (978-1-60115-339-5(2)); pap. 4.99 (978-1-60115-340-1(6)) Treasure Bay, Inc.
Osakawa. Hiking in the Wilds: Level Q. Group 1. (Take-Twostm Ser.). 32p. 38.95 (978-0-322-04488-3(X)) Wright Group/McGraw-Hill.
Ottaway, Jacqueline. Riddle of the Seaplanes (Level S), 6 vols. (Mountain Peaks Ser.). 128p. (gr. 6-18). 36.95 (978-0-322-05891-0(0)) Wright Group/McGraw-Hill.
Our Granny: Level B. Group 1. (Sunshine Ser.). 8p. 20.95 (978-0-7802-5715-3(4)) Wright Group/McGraw-Hill.
Out of Luck!, 6 vols. 8p. (gr. k-1). 21.50 (978-0-322-02081-8(6)) Wright Group/McGraw-Hill.
Out of the Computer: Level 6, 6 vols. (Fluency Strand Ser.). (gr. 4-8). 45.00 (978-1-4045-1235-1(7)) Wright Group/McGraw-Hill.
Out of the Sunless Land: Level T. Group 2, 6 vols. (Sunshine Ser.). 48p. 44.95 (978-0-7802-4186-2(X)) Wright Group/McGraw-Hill.
The Ox in the Pit: Consonant x: Level A, 6 vols. (Wright Skills Ser.). 12p. (gr. k-3). 17.95 (978-0-322-03123-4(0)) Wright Group/McGraw-Hill.
Pacholski, Robert, creator. Aperturas a Lectura. 2003. (SPA., Illus.). (gr. k-3). 78p. stu. ed., wbk. ed. 7.95 (978-0-9745220-1-2(5)); 9p. tchr. ed. 3.95 (978-0-9745220-3-6(1)) Aperturas Foundation.
A Pan for Pam: Consonant p: Level A, 6 vols. (Wright Skills Ser.). 12p. (gr. k-3). 17.95 (978-0-322-03108-1(7)) Wright Group/McGraw-Hill.
A Pan of Jam: Consonant j: Level A, 6 vols. (Wright Skills Ser.). 12p. (gr. k-3). 17.95 (978-0-322-03109-8(5)) Wright Group/McGraw-Hill.
Papil: Level T. Group 1, 6 vols. (Sunshine Ser.). 48p. 44.95 (978-0-7802-5600-2(X)) Wright Group/McGraw-Hill.
Paris, Susan. High Noon: Level P, 6 vols. (Raging Rivers Ser.). 128p. (gr. 3-6). 36.95 (978-0-322-05894-1(5)) Wright Group/McGraw-Hill.
Parr, Tom. Reading Makes You Feel Good. 2014. 32p. pap. 7.00 (978-1-61003-382-4(5)) Center for the Collaborative Classroom.
Partner, Daniel. Bible Devotions for Bedtime. 2004. (Bedtime Bible Stories Ser.). (ENG.). 256p. (J). pap. 5.99 (978-1-59310-358-3(1), Barbour Bks.) Barbour Publishing, Inc.
A Party: Level A. Group 1. (Story Box Ser.). 8p. 20.95 (978-0-322-00634-8(1)) Wright Group/McGraw-Hill.
Peek, Patsy. Reading Comprehension Practice: Grades 2-8 Practice Worksheets Featuring Story Webs, Newspaper Ads, Fliers. 2012. 64p. (gr. 2-4). pap. 13.95 (978-1-4772-4933-8(8)) AuthorHouse.
People Dance: Level F, 6 vols. (Wonder Worldtm Ser.). 16p. 29.95 (978-0-7802-2018-8(8)) Wright Group/McGraw-Hill.
Perritano, John. Mummies in the Library: Divide the Pages. 2013. (IMath Ser.). (ENG., Illus.). 32p. (J). (gr. 3-4). lib. bdg. 22.60 (978-1-59953-558-6(0)) Norwood Hse. Pr.
Peter Paper Clip, 6 vols. 8p. (gr. k-1). 21.50 (978-0-322-02065-8(4)) Wright Group/McGraw-Hill.
Phonics & Word Study Complete Kits: Phonics & Word Study: Level C. (gr. k-3). 333.95 (978-0-322-01644-6(4)) Wright Group/McGraw-Hill.
Phonics & Word Study Core Kits: Phonics & Word Study: Level A. (gr. k-3). 153.50 (978-0-322-01641-5(X)) Wright Group/McGraw-Hill.
Phonics & Word Study Core Kits: Phonics & Word Study: Level B. (gr. k-3). 185.50 (978-0-322-01643-9(6)) Wright Group/McGraw-Hill.
Phonics & Word Study Core Kits: Phonics & Word Study: Level C. (gr. k-3). 153.50 (978-0-322-01645-3(2)) Wright Group/McGraw-Hill.
Phonics Plus Staff. Phonics Plus, Bk. F. 2nd ed. (J). 9.55 (978-0-8136-0396-4(X)) Modern Curriculum Pr.
Photos, Photos: 6 Each of 1 Anthology, 6 vols. (Wildcats Ser.). 32p. (gr. 2-8). (978-0-322-00580-8(9)) Wright Group/McGraw-Hill.
Picture & Thematic Dictionary Activity Book. (Foundation Ser.). 58p. (gr. k-3). 20.95 (978-0-322-01561-6(8)) Wright Group/McGraw-Hill.
Pigs & Dogs Play Ball: Consonants b, w; Short Vowel i word families: Level A, 6 vols. (Wright Skills Ser.). 12p. (gr. k-3). 17.95 (978-0-322-01450-3(6)) Wright Group/McGraw-Hill.
The Pink Tent: Final Blends -nd, -nk, -nt: Level B, 6 vols. (Wright Skills Ser.). 16p. (gr. k-3). 17.95 (978-0-322-01462-6(X)) Wright Group/McGraw-Hill.
Places to Visit, Places to See: Take-Home Book. 2005. (Lee Bennett Hopkins Worlds of Poetry Classroom Library). (YA). (gr. k-3). 13.50 (978-0-8215-0568-7(8)) Sadlier, William H. Inc.
Los Planetas, 6 vols., Vol. 2. (Explorers. Exploradores Nonfiction Sets Ser.). (SPA.). 32p. (gr. 3-6). 44.95 (978-0-7699-0642-3(7)) Shortland Pubns. (U. S. A.) Inc.
Pop, 6 vols. 8p. (gr. k-1). 21.50 (978-0-322-02073-3(5)) Wright Group/McGraw-Hill.
A Porcupine: Big Book: Level C. (Wonder Worldtm Ser.). 16p. 26.50 (978-0-7802-3471-0(5)) Wright Group/McGraw-Hill.
A Porcupine: Level C, 6 vols. (Wonder Worldtm Ser.). 16p. 24.95 (978-0-7802-1189-6(8)) Wright Group/McGraw-Hill.
Potok, Chaim. The Chosen: And Related Readings. 2006. (McDougal Littell Literature Connections Ser.). (ENG.). 416p. (gr. 6-8). 18.50 (978-0-395-88145-3(5), 2-70858) Great Source Education Group, Inc.
Potts, Steve, et al. North American Animals. 2012. (North American Animals Ser.). (ENG.). 24p. (gr. k-1). pap. 41.70 (978-1-4296-8362-3(7)); lib. bdg. 159.90 (978-1-4296-8142-1(X)) Capstone Press of Coughlan Cos. (Pebble Plus).
PowerPhonics Skill Set I: Includes Animals I, Self I & Growing Things, 18 bks. (Illus.). (J). (gr. 1). lib. bdg. 324.00 (978-0-8239-7204-3(6), PowerKids Pr.) Rosen Publishing Group, Inc., The.
The Predator. (Song Box Ser.). (gr. 1-2). 8.50 incl. audio (978-0-7802-2261-8(X)) Wright Group/McGraw-Hill.
The Predator: 1 Big Book, 6 Each of 1 Student Book, & 1 Cassette. (Song Box Ser.). (gr. 1-2). 68.95 (978-0-7802-3205-1(4)) Wright Group/McGraw-Hill.
The Predator: Big Book. (Song Box Ser.). (gr. 1-2). 31.50 (978-0-7802-2260-1(1)) Wright Group/McGraw-Hill.
Pressnall, Debra Olson. Colorful File Folder Games: Skill-Building Center Activities for Language Arts & Math. 2006. (ENG., Illus.). 160p. (gr. -1 — 1). per. 22.99 (978-0-88724-268-7(5), CD-104047) Carson-Dellosa Publishing, LLC.
Proof of Magic, 6 vols. (Ragged Island Mysteriestm Ser.). 161p. (gr. 5-7). 42.50 (978-0-322-01649-1(5)) Wright Group/McGraw-Hill.
Publ, Griffin. Easy Olympic Sports Reader, 6 Bks, Set. 2004. (U. S. Olympic Committee Easy Olympic Sports Readers Ser.). (Illus.). 16p. (J). pap. 17.95 (978-1-58000-116-8(5)) Griffin Publishing Group.
Publications International Ltd. Staff, ed. Disney Pixar Cars: Story Reader 2. 0 3 Storybook Library. 2011. (J). 19.98 (978-1-4508-0606-0(6)) Publications International, Ltd.
—Disney Princess: My Own Carriage. 2014. 12p. (J). bds. 12.98 (978-1-4508-7381-9(2), 66a3c624-31ec-4290-ae22-6fd5a90376b3) Phoenix International Publications, Inc.
—Let's Learn to Read! 2010. 24p. (J). 16.98 (978-1-60553-361-2(0)) Publications International, Ltd.
—Preschool Reading & Math Activities. 2010. 128p. 11.98 (978-1-60553-180-9(4)) Publications International, Ltd.
Pulse- Fun with Reading & Writing. 2006. cd-rom 4.99 (978-1-60245-040-0(4)) GDL Multimedia, LLC.
Quack! Quack! Quack!, 6 vols. 8p. (gr. k-1). 21.50 (978-0-322-02074-0(3)) Wright Group/McGraw-Hill.
Que vemos en el mar? What Do You See by the Sea? 2005. (Take-Home Bks.). (SPA.). (YA). (gr. -1-3). 15.75 (978-0-8215-1202-9(1)) Sadlier, William H. Inc.
Que vemos en el mar?/What Do You See by the Sea? 2005. (Libros en Espanol Para Ninos Ser.). (SPA.). (YA). (gr. -1-1). 11.97 (978-0-8215-0992-0(6)) Sadlier, William H. Inc.
Queen Jelly Bean: Vowel Digraph Review: Level C, 6 vols. (Wright Skills Ser.). 16p. (gr. k-3). 26.50 (978-0-322-01499-2(9)) Wright Group/McGraw-Hill.
Queen of the Trail: Decodable Books, 6 vols. (Fast Track Reading Ser.). 24p. (gr. 4-8). 40.95 (978-0-322-05985-6(2)) Wright Group/McGraw-Hill.
A Quilt for Kristy: Consonant blend review: Level C, 6 vols. (Wright Skills Ser.). 16p. (gr. k-3). 26.50 (978-0-322-01493-0(X)) Wright Group/McGraw-Hill.
Quinton, Sasha. I-Spy: A Phonics Reader. 2009. (Illus.). (978-1-936199-06-8(8)) Book Shop, Ltd., The.
—Rat-A-Tat: A Phonics Reader. 2009. (Illus.). pap. (978-1-936199-04-4(1)) Book Shop, Ltd., The.
—Ring-A-Ding: A Phonics Reader. 2009. (Illus.). pap. (978-1-936199-00-6(9)) Book Shop, Ltd., The.
—Root-A-Toot: A Phonics Reader. 2009. (Illus.). pap. (978-1-936199-01-3(7)) Book Shop, Ltd., The.
—Rub-A-Dub: A Phonics Reader. 2009. (Illus.). (978-1-936199-03-7(3)) Book Shop, Ltd., The.
—Yay-Hooray: A Phonics Reader. 2009. (Illus.). pap. (978-1-936199-07-5(6)) Book Shop, Ltd., The.
Quit It! Consonant q: Level A, 6 vols. (Wright Skills Ser.). 12p. (gr. k-3). 17.95 (978-0-322-03122-7(2)) Wright Group/McGraw-Hill.
The Race: Level D. Group 1. (Sunshine Ser.). 8p. 20.95 (978-0-7802-5733-7(2)) Wright Group/McGraw-Hill.
A Rag for Miss Rat: Consonant r: Level A, 6 vols. (Wright Skills Ser.). 12p. (gr. k-3). 17.95 (978-0-322-03128-9(1)) Wright Group/McGraw-Hill.
Rasinski, Timothy V. Daily Word Ladders: 80+ Word Study Activities That Target Key Phonics Skills to Boost Young Learners' Reading, Writing & Spelling Confidence. 2012. (ENG.). 64p. (gr. k-1). pap. 14.99 (978-0-545-22379-9(2), Teaching Resources) Scholastic, Inc.
—Daily Word Ladders, Grades 1-2: 150+ Word Study Activities That Help Kids Boost Reading, Vocabulary, Spelling & Phonics Skills. 2012. (ENG., Illus.). 176p. (gr. 1-2). 27.99 (978-0-545-37486-6(3), Teaching Resources) Scholastic, Inc.
—Daily Word Ladders, Grades 4-6: 100 Word Study Activities That Help Kids Boost Reading, Vocabulary, Spelling & Phonics Skills. 2012. (ENG., Illus.). 112p. (gr. 4-6). 27.99 (978-0-545-37488-0(X), Teaching Resources) Scholastic, Inc.
—Daily Word Ladders, Grades K-1: 80+ Word Study Activities That Target Key Phonics Skills to Boost Young Learners' Reading, Writing & Spelling Confidence. 2012. (ENG., Illus.). 96p. (gr. k-1). 27.99 (978-0-545-37485-9(5), Teaching Resources) Scholastic, Inc.
Rasinski, Timothy V., et al. The Fluent Reader in Action, Grades 5 & Up: A Rich Collection of Research-Based, Classroom-Tested Lessons & Strategies for Improving Fluency & Comprehension. 2011. (ENG.). 128p. (gr. 5-5). pap. 18.99 (978-0-439-63340-6(0), Teaching Resources) Scholastic, Inc.
—The Fluent Reader in Action, Grades Prek-4: A Rich Collection of Research-Based, Classroom-Tested Lessons & Strategies for Improving Fluency & Comprehension. 2011. (ENG.). 128p. (gr. -1-4). pap. 18.99 (978-0-439-63341-3(9), Teaching Resources) Scholastic, Inc.
Rat Princess Little Book: Early Reading Fluency, Level C. 2004. pap. 6.00 (978-0-7398-8299-3(6)) Steck-Vaughn.
Rawson, Christopher. Stories of Giants. Cartwright, Stephen, illus. 2004. (Young Reading Ser.: Vol. 1). 48p. (J). (gr. 2-18). lib. bdg. 13.95 (978-1-58086-614-9(X), Usborne) EDC Publishing.
Reach for Reading: Reaching Higher Self-Training Package. (gr. 3-5). 725.00 (978-0-7578-5931-1(3)) Rigby Education.
Reach for Reading: Reaching up Self-Training Package. (gr. 1-3). 675.00 (978-0-7578-5932-8(1)) Rigby Education.
Reaching Higher Additional Workstations: With Books. (Reach for Reading Ser.). (gr. 3-5). 425.00 (978-0-7635-3700-5(4)) Rigby Education.
Read, Write & Publish. (J). (gr. 5). 125.25 (978-0-669-17767-1(9)) Houghton Mifflin Harcourt School Pubs.
Reader's Theater Program Levels (F-U) Set A, 24 vols - 144 Bks. 2004. (J). pap. 375.00 (978-1-4108-1512-5(9)) Benchmark Education Co.
Reading & Writing. 2004. (Help with Homework Ser.). 32p. (J). (gr. k-2). wbk. ed. 3.99 (978-1-904586-24-1(4)); (gr. 1-4). wbk. ed. 3.99 (978-1-904586-20-3(1)) Byeway Bks.
Reading Fluency Grades K-2. 2005. (J). pap. (978-1-60015-039-5(X)) Steps To Literacy, LLC.
Reading Is Everywhere, 6 vols. (Sunshinetm Ser.). 16p. (gr. k-18). 29.50 (978-0-7802-5425-1(2)) Wright Group/McGraw-Hill.
Reading Recovery Kits: Reading Recovery Starter Kit. (Reading Recovery Ser.). (gr. k-6). 367.95 (978-0-322-00641-6(4)) Wright Group/McGraw-Hill.
Reading Rods Phonemic Awareness Activity Book. 2003. (J). pap. 4.95 (978-1-56911-117-8(0)) Learning Resources, Inc.
Reading Rods Phonemic Awareness Activity Cards, Set 2. 2003. (J). 19.95 (978-1-56911-113-0(8)) Learning Resources, Inc.
Reading Rods Prefixes & Suffixes Activity Cards, Set 2. 2003. (J). pap. 19.95 (978-1-56911-109-3(X)) Learning Resources, Inc.
Reading Rods Readers: Advanced Vowel Mastery Set. 2004. (J). per. 44.95 (978-1-56911-532-9(X)) Learning Resources, Inc.
Reading Rods Readers: Advanced Vowel Mastery Set Classpack. 2004. (J). per. 249.95 (978-1-56911-574-9(5)) Learning Resources, Inc.
Reading Rods Readers: Long Vowel Mastery Set Classpack. 2004. (J). per. 184.95 (978-1-56911-549-7(4)) Learning Resources, Inc.
Reading Rods Readers: Phonics Foundation 1 Classpack. 2003. (J). per. 249.95 (978-1-56911-575-6(3)) Learning Resources, Inc.
Reading Rods Readers: Phonics Foundation 2 Classpack. 2003. (J). per. 249.95 (978-1-56911-576-3(1)) Learning Resources, Inc.
Reading Rods Readers: Phonics Foundation Set 1. 2003. (J). pap. 44.95 (978-1-56911-121-5(9)) Learning Resources, Inc.
Reading Rods Readers: Phonics Foundation Set 2. 2003. (J). pap. 44.95 (978-1-56911-122-2(7)) Learning Resources, Inc.
Reading Rods Readers: Short Vowel Mastery Set Classpack. 2004. (J). per. 184.95 (978-1-56911-548-0(6)) Learning Resources, Inc.
Reading Rods Readers: Word Families Foundation Set. 2004. (J). per. 39.95 (978-1-56911-533-6(8)) Learning Resources, Inc.
Reading Rods Readers: Word Families Foundation Set Classpack. 2004. (J). per. 249.95 (978-1-56911-573-2(7)) Learning Resources, Inc.
Reading Rods Simple Sentences Activity Cards, Set 2. 2003. (J). pap. 19.95 (978-1-56911-112-3(X)) Learning Resources, Inc.
Reading Rods Simple Sentences Instruction & Activity Book. 2003. (J). pap. 12.95 (978-1-56911-110-9(3)) Learning Resources, Inc.
Reading Rods Word Building Activity Book. 2003. (J). pap. 4.95 (978-1-56911-119-2(7)) Learning Resources, Inc.
Reading Rods Word Building Activity Cards, Set 2. 2003. (J). 19.95 (978-1-56911-115-4(4)) Learning Resources, Inc.
Reading Rods Word Families Activity Book. 2003. (J). pap. 4.95 (978-1-56911-118-5(9)) Learning Resources, Inc.
Reading Rods Word Families Activity Cards, Set 2. 2003. (J). 19.95 (978-1-56911-114-7(6)) Learning Resources, Inc.
Red Fox Cub: Review of Consonants, Short Vowels, Word Families: Level A, 6 vols. (Wright Skills Ser.). 12p. (gr. k-3). 17.95 (978-0-322-03126-5(5)) Wright Group/McGraw-Hill.
Red Or Blue. (Little Book Practice Reader). (J). (978-0-8136-5341-9(X)) Modern Curriculum Pr.
Reeder. Animals of the Arctic & Antarctic: Level O, 6 vols. (Take-Twostm Ser.). 32p. 38.95 (978-0-322-04489-0(8)) Wright Group/McGraw-Hill.
Rhodes, Immacula A. Word Families, Grades K-2: 30 Easy-to-Make, Self-Checking Manipulatives That Teach Key Word Families & Put Kids on the Path to Reading Success. 2011. (Fun Flaps Ser.). (ENG.). 48p. (gr. k-2). pap. 10.99 (978-0-545-28078-5(8), Teaching Resources) Scholastic, Inc.
Rice, Earle, Jr., ed. Great Military Leaders of the 20th Century, 6 vols. 2005. (Great Military Leaders of the 20th Century Ser.). (Illus.). 320p. (gr. 6-12). 120.00 (978-0-7910-7401-5(3), Chelsea Hse.) Facts On File, Inc.
Richardson, Ellis. Common Short Vowel Syllables Level 9: Brown Sequence. rev. ed. Date not set. (Linguistic Pattern Ser.). (Illus.). 64p. (YA). pap. (978-1-56775-081-2(8)) I S M Teaching Systems, Inc.
—The Sound of Short A Level 4: Green Sequence. rev. ed. Date not set. (Linguistic Pattern Ser.). (Illus.). 64p. (YA). pap. (978-1-56775-079-9(6)) I S M Teaching Systems, Inc.
—The Sound of Short U Level 8: Brown Sequence. rev. ed. Date not set. (Linguistic Pattern Ser.). (Illus.). 64p. (YA). pap. (978-1-56775-080-5(X)) I S M Teaching Systems, Inc.
RIGBY. Reading Strategy Cards: Complete Set of 40 Cards (K-5) 2003. (Rigby on Our Way to English Ser.). (ENG.). (gr. 5-5). 83.15 (978-0-7578-4543-7(6)) Rigby Education.
Rigby Education Staff. Where Do People Live? (Illus.). (J). suppl. ed. 20.00 (978-0-7635-6445-2(1), 764451C99) Rigby Education.
Rigg, Diana. Teach a Child to READ in... 3 Simple Steps. Walter, Deborah, illus. 2012. (J). (gr. -1-2). (978-1-921560-88-0(6)) PLD Organisation Pty. Ltd.
Right or Wrong? 6 Each of 1 Anthology, 6 vols. (Wildcats Ser.). 32p. (gr. 2-8). (978-0-322-00598-3(1)) Wright Group/McGraw-Hill.
Ristuccia, Christine & Ristuccia, James. The Entire World of S & Z Instructional Workbook: A Comprehensive Approach to Remediate Frontal & Lateral Lisps. l.t. ed. 2003. (Illus.). 208p. (J). per. 34.99 (978-0-9723457-4-3(4)) Say It Right.
Roberto's Smile: Big Book: Level F. Group 2. (Story Box Ser.). 16p. 20.95 (978-0-322-00318-7(0)) Wright Group/McGraw-Hill.
Rondeau, Amanda. Ed As in Bed, 1 vol. 2003. (Word Families Set 2 Ser.). (ENG., Illus.). 24p. (J). (gr. k-3). lib. bdg. 24.21 (978-1-59197-228-0(0), SandCastle) ABDO Publishing Co.
—Ob As in Knob, 1 vol. 2003. (Word Families Set 5 Ser.). (ENG., Illus.). 24p. (J). (gr. k-3). lib. bdg. 24.21 (978-1-59197-249-5(3), SandCastle) ABDO Publishing Co.
—Ock As in Block, 1 vol. 2003. (Word Families Set 5 Ser.). (ENG., Illus.). 24p. (J). (gr. k-3). lib. bdg. 24.21 (978-1-59197-250-1(7), SandCastle) ABDO Publishing Co.
—Og As in Dog, 1 vol. 2003. (Word Families Set 5 Ser.). (ENG., Illus.). 24p. (J). (gr. k-3). lib. bdg. 24.21 (978-1-59197-251-8(5), SandCastle) ABDO Publishing Co.
—Op As in Top, 1 vol. 2003. (Word Families Set 5 Ser.). (ENG., Illus.). 24p. (J). (gr. k-3). lib. bdg. 24.21 (978-1-59197-252-5(3), SandCastle) ABDO Publishing Co.
—Ore As in Core, 1 vol. 2003. (Word Families Set 7 Ser.). (ENG., Illus.). 24p. (J). (gr. k-3). lib. bdg. 24.21 (978-1-59197-267-9(1), SandCastle) ABDO Publishing Co.
—Ot As in Knot, 1 vol. 2003. (Word Families Set 5 Ser.). (ENG., Illus.). 24p. (J). (gr. k-3). lib. bdg. 24.21 (978-1-59197-253-2(1), SandCastle) ABDO Publishing Co.
—Ow As in Cow, 1 vol. 2003. (Word Families Set 5 Ser.). (ENG., Illus.). 24p. (J). (gr. k-3). lib. bdg. 24.21 (978-1-59197-254-9(X), SandCastle) ABDO Publishing Co.
Rose, Mary. Reading Comprehension & Fluency, Grade 1: 30 Reproducible High-Interest Readings for Kids to Read Aloud at Home - With Companion Activities. 2004. (Week-By-Week Homework for Building Reading Comprehension & Fluency Ser.). (ENG.). 96p. (gr. 1-1). pap. 16.99 (978-0-439-61656-0(5), Teaching Resources) Scholastic, Inc.
—Reading Comprehension & Fluency, Grades 2-3: 30 Reproducible High-Interest Passages for Kids to Read Aloud at Home - With Companion Activities. 2004. (Week-By-Week Homework for Building Reading Comprehension & Fluency Ser.). (ENG.). 96p. (gr. 2-3). pap. 16.99 (978-0-439-51779-9(6), Teaching Resources) Scholastic, Inc.
Ross, Val. You Can't Read This: Forbidden Books, Lost Writing, Mistranslations, & Codes. 2006. (ENG., Illus.). 152p. (J). (gr. 5-7). 19.95 (978-0-88776-732-6(X), Tundra Bks.) Tundra Bks. CAN. Dist: Penguin Random Hse. LLC.
A Royal Deal: Diphthongs oi, oy: Level B, 6 vols. (Wright Skills Ser.). 16p. (gr. k-3). 26.50 (978-0-322-01485-5(9)) Wright Group/McGraw-Hill.
Rude Luke: Long Vowel u, CVCe Pattern: Level B, 6 vols. (Wright Skills Ser.). 16p. (gr. k-3). 17.95 (978-0-322-03103-6(6)) Wright Group/McGraw-Hill.
Ruffenach, Jessie E., et al. Learn along with Ashkii: First Grade Level 2. Whitethorne, Bahe, Jr., illus. 2003. (NAV & ENG.). 16p. (J). (gr. -1-3). pap. 7.95 (978-1-893354-42-5(3)) Salina Bookshelf Inc.
—Learn along with Ashkii: Second Grade Level 1. Whitethorne, Bahe, Jr., illus. 2003. (ENG & NAV.). 16p. (J). (gr. -1-3). pap. 7.95 (978-1-893354-43-2(1)) Salina Bookshelf Inc.
—Learn along with Ashkii: Second Grade Level 2. Whitethorne, Bahe, Jr., illus. 2003. (NAV & ENG.). 16p. (J). (gr. -1-3). pap. 7.95 (978-1-893354-44-9(X)) Salina Bookshelf Inc.
—Learn along with Ashkii: Third Grade Level 1. Whitethorne, Bahe, Jr., illus. 2003. (NAV & ENG.). 16p. (J). (gr. 4-7). pap. 7.95 (978-1-893354-45-6(8)) Salina Bookshelf Inc.
Rumblefish: Response Journal. 2003. 32p. (J). (gr. 7-12). (978-1-58049-980-4(5), RJ80) Prestwick Hse., Inc.
Runaway Hank: Final Blends -ft, -lt: Level C, 6 vols. (Wright Skills Ser.). 16p. (gr. k-3). 26.50 (978-0-322-01495-4(6)) Wright Group/McGraw-Hill.
Running, 6 vols. (Multicultural Programs Ser.). 16p. (gr. 1-3). 24.95 (978-0-7802-9215-4(4)) Wright Group/McGraw-Hill.
Saddleback Educational Publishing Staff, ed. Quickreads, Vol. 4. 2010. (Q Reads Ser.). (ENG.). 48p. (YA). (gr. 9-12). tchr. ed. 12.95 incl. cd-rom (978-1-61651-221-7(0)) Saddleback Educational Publishing, Inc.
Sally & the Elephant: Level B, 6 vols. (Wonder Worldtm Ser.). 16p. 24.95 (978-0-7802-1047-9(6)) Wright Group/McGraw-Hill.
Salzmann, Mary Elizabeth. -Ad As in Dad, 1 vol. 2003. (Word Families Set 1 Ser.). (ENG., Illus.). 24p. (J). (gr. k-3). lib. bdg. 24.21 (978-1-59197-226-6(4)) ABDO Publishing Co.
—Ag As in Flag, 1 vol. 2003. (Word Families Set 1 Ser.). (ENG., Illus.). 24p. (J). (gr. k-3). lib. bdg. 24.21 (978-1-59197-225-9(6)) ABDO Publishing Co.
—Am As in Ham, 1 vol. 2003. (Word Families Set 1 Ser.). (ENG., Illus.). 24p. (J). (gr. k-3). lib. bdg. 24.21 (978-1-59197-223-5(X)) ABDO Publishing Co.
—Ap As in Cap, 1 vol. 2003. (Word Families Set 1 Ser.). (ENG., Illus.). 24p. (J). (gr. k-3). lib. bdg. 24.21 (978-1-59197-224-2(8)) ABDO Publishing Co.
—An As in Fan. 2003. (Word Families Set 1 Ser.). (ENG., Illus.). 24p. (J). (gr. k-3). lib. bdg. 24.21 (978-1-59197-222-8(1)) ABDO Publishing Co.
—At As in Cat, 1 vol. 2003. (Word Families Set 1 Ser.). (ENG., Illus.). 24p. (J). (gr. k-3). lib. bdg. 24.21 (978-1-59197-221-1(3), SandCastle) ABDO Publishing Co.
—Ay As in Clay, 1 vol. 2003. (Word Families Set 7 Ser.). (ENG., Illus.). 24p. (J). (gr. k-3). lib. bdg. 24.21 (978-1-59197-264-8(7)) ABDO Publishing Co.
—Come Home with Me! 2004. (Sight Words Ser.). (ENG., Illus.). 24p. (J). (gr. k-3). lib. bdg. 24.21 (978-1-59197-465-9(8)) ABDO Publishing Co.
—Did You See One Jump? 2004. (Sight Words Ser.). (ENG., Illus.). 24p. (J). (gr. k-3). lib. bdg. 24.21 (978-1-59197-466-6(6), SandCastle) ABDO Publishing Co.
—Ell As in Well, 1 vol. 2003. (Word Families Set 2 Ser.). (ENG., Illus.). 24p. (J). (gr. k-3). lib. bdg. 24.21 (978-1-59197-231-0(0), SandCastle) ABDO Publishing Co.
—It's Not Good, It's Great! 2003. (Sight Words Ser.). (ENG., Illus.). 24p. (J). (gr. k-3). lib. bdg. 24.21 (978-1-59197-479-6(8), SandCastle) ABDO Publishing Co.

P
Q
R

—No Pigs on the Farm! 2004. (Sight Words Ser.). (ENG., Illus.). 24p. (J). (gr. k-3). lib. bdg. 24.21 *(978-1-59197-471-0(2)*, SandCastle) ABDO Publishing Co.

—Out for the Summer! 2004. (Sight Words Ser.). (ENG., Illus.). 24p. (J). (gr. k-3). lib. bdg. 24.21 *(978-1-59197-472-7(0)*, SandCastle) ABDO Publishing Co.

—Snow & More Snow! 2004. (Sight Words Ser.). (ENG., Illus.). 24p. (J). (gr. k-3). lib. bdg. 24.21 *(978-1-59197-470-3(4)*, SandCastle) ABDO Publishing Co.

—They Are the Best! 2004. (Sight Words Ser.). (ENG., Illus.). 24p. (J). (gr. k-3). lib. bdg. 24.21 *(978-1-59197-474-1(7)*, SandCastle) ABDO Publishing Co.

—Way to Go! 2004. (Sight Words Ser.). (ENG., Illus.). 24p. (J). (gr. k-3). lib. bdg. 24.21 *(978-1-59197-468-0(2)*, SandCastle) ABDO Publishing Co.

—We All Like It! 2004. (Sight Words Ser.). (ENG., Illus.). 24p. (J). (gr. k-3). lib. bdg. 24.21 *(978-1-59197-467-3(4)*, SandCastle) ABDO Publishing Co.

—What a Day in the Park! 2004. (Sight Words Ser.). (ENG., Illus.). 24p. (J). (gr. k-3). lib. bdg. 24.21 *(978-1-59197-476-5(3)*, SandCastle) ABDO Publishing Co.

—Who Is This at the Beach? 2004. (Sight Words Ser.). (ENG., Illus.). 24p. (J). (gr. k-3). lib. bdg. 24.21 *(978-1-59197-480-2(1)*, SandCastle) ABDO Publishing Co.

Sam & Nan: Consonants d, f, n, p; Short Vowel a word families: Level A, 6 vols. (Wright Skills Ser.). 12p. (gr. k-3). 17.95 *(978-0-322-01447-3(6))* Wright Group/McGraw-Hill.

Sam & Tat: Consonants m, s, t; Short Vowel a; -am, -at word families: Level A, 6 vols. (Wright Skills Ser.). 12p. (gr. k-3). 17.95 *(978-0-322-01444-2(1))* Wright Group/McGraw-Hill.

Sam Sat: Consonants m, s, t; Short Vowel a: Level A, 6 vols. (Wright Skills Ser.). 12p. (gr. k-3). 17.95 *(978-0-322-03104-3(4))* Wright Group/McGraw-Hill.

Samson, Tess. Going up & Down. 2010. (Sight Word Readers Ser.). (J). 3.49 *(978-1-60719-613-6(1))* Newmark Learning LLC.

Sanseri, Wanda. Play by the Sea. 2003. (J). 5.00 *(978-1-880045-26-8(5))* Back Home Industries.

—SWR Chart Pack. 2003. (J). pap. 9.95 *(978-1-880045-30-5(3))* Back Home Industries.

Sanvageau, Juan. Stories, Fables & Poems for You, Vol. 2.Tr. of Cuentos, Fabulas y Poemas Para Ti. (ENG & SPA., Illus.). 89p. (J). (gr. 3-5). pap. 9.95 *(978-1-893493-01-8(6))* National Educational Systems, Inc.

Saving the Florida Panther, 6 vols., Vol. 4. 2005. (Book Treks Ser.). (Illus.). (J). (gr. 4-8). stu. ed. 35.95 *(978-0-673-61777-4(7))* Celebration Pr.

Scat! Said the Cat: Big Book: Level D. Group 1. (Sunshine Ser.). 8p. 20.95 *(978-0-7802-5734-4(0))* Wright Group/McGraw-Hill.

Scheunemann, Pam. -Ack As in Snack, 1 vol. 2003. (Word Families Set 6 Ser.). (ENG., Illus.). 24p. (J). (gr. k-3). lib. bdg. 24.21 *(978-1-59197-261-7(2))* ABDO Publishing Co.

—Ape Cape, 1 vol. 2004. (Rhyming Riddles Ser.). (ENG., Illus.). 24p. (J). (gr. k-3). lib. bdg. 24.21 *(978-1-59197-457-4(7)*, SandCastle) ABDO Publishing Co.

—Ash As in Trash, 1 vol. 2003. (Word Families Set 6 Ser.). (ENG., Illus.). 24p. (J). (gr. k-3). lib. bdg. 24.21 *(978-1-59197-260-0(4))* ABDO Publishing Co.

—Aw As in Paw, 1 vol. 2003. (Word Families Set 7 Ser.). (ENG., Illus.). 24p. (J). (gr. k-3). lib. bdg. 24.21 *(978-1-59197-263-1(9))* ABDO Publishing Co.

—Chipper Flipper, 1 vol. 2004. (Rhyming Riddles Ser.). (ENG., Illus.). 24p. (J). (gr. k-3). lib. bdg. 24.21 *(978-1-59197-458-1(5)*, SandCastle) ABDO Publishing Co.

—Cooler Ruler, 1 vol. 2004. (Rhyming Riddles Ser.). (ENG., Illus.). 24p. (J). (gr. k-3). lib. bdg. 24.21 *(978-1-59197-459-8(3)*, SandCastle) ABDO Publishing Co.

—Dill Spill, 1 vol. 2004. (Rhyming Riddles Ser.). (ENG., Illus.). 24p. (J). (gr. k-3). lib. bdg. 24.21 *(978-1-59197-460-4(7)*, SandCastle) ABDO Publishing Co.

—Ent As in Cent, 1 vol. 2003. (Word Families Set 2 Ser.). (ENG., Illus.). 24p. (J). (gr. k-3). lib. bdg. 24.21 *(978-1-59197-233-4(7)*, SandCastle) ABDO Publishing Co.

—Ick As in Kick, 1 vol. 2003. (Word Families Set 6 Ser.). (ENG., Illus.). 24p. (J). (gr. k-3). lib. bdg. 24.21 *(978-1-59197-258-7(2)*, SandCastle) ABDO Publishing Co.

—Ing As in King, 1 vol. 2003. (Word Families Set 6 Ser.). (ENG., Illus.). 24p. (J). (gr. k-3). lib. bdg. 24.21 *(978-1-59197-256-3(6)*, SandCastle) ABDO Publishing Co.

—Ink As in Drink, 1 vol. 2003. (Word Families Set 6 Ser.). (ENG., Illus.). 24p. (J). (gr. k-3). lib. bdg. 24.21 *(978-1-59197-257-0(4)*, SandCastle) ABDO Publishing Co.

—Loud Crowd, 1 vol. 2004. (Rhyming Riddles Ser.). (ENG., Illus.). 24p. (J). (gr. k-3). lib. bdg. 24.21 *(978-1-59197-461-1(5)*, SandCastle) ABDO Publishing Co.

—Overdue Kangaroo, 1 vol. 2004. (Rhyming Riddles Ser.). (ENG., Illus.). 24p. (J). (gr. k-3). lib. bdg. 24.21 *(978-1-59197-462-8(3)*, SandCastle) ABDO Publishing Co.

—Unk As in Skunk, 1 vol. 2003. (Word Families Set 6 Ser.). (ENG., Illus.). 24p. (J). (gr. k-3). lib. bdg. 24.21 *(978-1-59197-259-4(0)*, SandCastle) ABDO Publishing Co.

Scholastic Clubs US Start Readers Non-Fiction (2 Set) Start Reading. 2006. (J). 27.89 *(978-1-59566-326-9(6))* QEB Publishing Inc.

Scholastic, Inc. Staff. Brain Play 1st-3rd. 2008. (J). 29.99 *(978-0-545-05207-8(6))* Scholastic, Inc.

—Brain Play Preschool-1st. 2008. (J). 29.99 *(978-0-439-81350-1(6))* Scholastic, Inc.

Scholastic, Inc. Staff, contrib. by. Entering Pre-K. 2004. (Jumpstart Ser.). (ENG., Illus.). 96p. (J). (gr. -1-k). pap. 6.99 *(978-0-439-38232-8(7))* Scholastic, Inc.

School Zone Publishing. Reading Readiness. 2003. (ENG.). (J). cd-rom 19.99 *(978-1-58947-916-6(5))* School Zone Publishing Co.

School Zone Publishing Company Staff. Reading Comprehension 1. (Illus.). (J). 19.99 incl. audio compact disk *(978-0-88743-942-1(X))* School Zone Publishing Co.

—Reading Skills-1: And Language Activities. (Illus.). (J). 19.99 incl. audio compact disk *(978-0-88743-941-4(1))* School Zone Publishing Co.

Schulz, Charles. Where Did Woodstock Go? Date not set. (ENG.). 100p. (J). 5.95 *(978-0-694-00959-6(8))* HarperCollins Pubs.

Scott, Foresman and Company Staff. Fun with Dick & Jane. 2004. (Read with Dick & Jane Ser.). 32p. (J). (gr. -1-2). 21.35 *(978-1-59197-630-1(8))* Spotlight.

Scott, James. The Indian in the Cupboard: Response Journal. 2003. 36p. (YA). *(978-1-58049-976-7(7)*, RJ76) Prestwick Hse., Inc.

—Jane Eyre: A Student Response Journal. 2003. 48p. (YA). *(978-1-58049-984-2(8)*, RJ84) Prestwick Hse., Inc.

Set 3, 4 bks. Incl. Fishing. Yukish, Joseph. Palmer, Kate S., illus. 16p. 2001. pap. 7.95 *(978-1-879835-16-0(9))*; Guess What Kind of Ball. Urmston, Kathleen & Evans, Karen. Kaeden Corp. Staff, ed. Gedeon, Gloria, illus. 16p. 1992. pap. 7.95 *(978-1-879835-15-3(0))*; Lunch. Urmston, Kathleen & Evans, Karen. Kaeden Corp. Staff, ed. Gedeon, Gloria, illus. 12p. 2002. pap. 7.95 *(978-1-879835-14-6(2))*; Our Garage. Urmston, Kathleen. Evans, Karen & Kaeden Corp. Staff, eds. Dragony, Barbara, illus. 12p. 2001. pap. 7.95 *(978-1-879835-17-7(7))*; (gr. k-2)., Kaeden Bks. Set pap. 17.50 o.p. *(978-1-879835-18-4(5))* Kaeden Corp.

Shadows, 6 vols. (Multicultural Programs Ser.). 16p. (gr. 1-3). 24.95 *(978-0-7802-9214-7(6))* Wright Group/McGraw-Hill.

Shake, Rattle, & Roll: Magazine Anthology: Level 4, 6 vols. (Comprehension Strand Ser.). (gr. 4-8). 54.00 *(978-0-322-06034-0(6))* Wright Group/McGraw-Hill.

Shelly's Shell: Digraph sh: Level B, 6 vols. (Wright Skills Ser.). 16p. (gr. k-3). 17.95 *(978-0-322-01471-8(9))* Wright Group/McGraw-Hill.

Shoo! Level C. Group 1. (Sunshine Ser.). 8p. 20.95 *(978-0-7802-5725-2(1))* Wright Group/McGraw-Hill.

Shopping: Big Book: Level A. (Sunshine Ser.). 8p. 20.95 *(978-0-7802-5710-8(3))* Wright Group/McGraw-Hill.

Shortland. Busy Bees. (Song Box Ser.). (gr. 1-2). pap. 31.50 *(978-0-7802-2268-7(7))* Wright Group/McGraw-Hill.

Show & Tell. 2003. (J). per. *(978-1-57657-813-1(5))* Paradise Pr., Inc.

Show & Tell, 6 vols. 8p. (gr. k-1). 21.50 *(978-0-322-02075-7(1))* Wright Group/McGraw-Hill.

Show & Tell: Take-Home Book. 2005. (Emergent Library: Vol. 2). (YA). (gr. -1-1). 12.60 *(978-0-8215-7253-5(9))* Sadlier, William H. Inc.

Sigmond Slitherforth: Level R, 6 vols. (Wonder Worldtm Ser.). 48p. 44.95 *(978-0-7802-7073-2(8))* Wright Group/McGraw-Hill.

The Silly Supper: Medial Consonants: Level C, 6 vols. (Wright Skills Ser.). 16p. (gr. k-3). 26.50 *(978-0-322-01491-6(3))* Wright Group/McGraw-Hill.

Skin, Skin: Level E, 6 vols. (Wonder Worldtm Ser.). 16p. 29.95 *(978-0-7802-1235-0(5))* Wright Group/McGraw-Hill.

Skunk in the Trunk, 6 vols. 8p. (gr. k-1). 21.50 *(978-0-322-02080-1(8))* Wright Group/McGraw-Hill.

The Sky's the Limit, 6 vols. (Wildcats Ser.). 32p. (gr. 2-8). *(978-0-322-00603-4(1))* Wright Group/McGraw-Hill.

Slater, Jean M. Mixed up Morning. Slater, Jean M., illus. 2003. (Illus.). 13p. (J). bds. 16.00 *(978-0-9743149-2-1(7))* Slater Software. Inc.

Slater, Teddy. 75 Sing-Along e-Songs That Teach Essential Early Reading Skills. 2014. (ENG., Illus.). 96p. (-2). 99.99 *(978-0-545-65262-9(6)*, Teaching Resources) Scholastic, Inc.

Sleeping,Dreaming: Level Q, 6 vols. (Wonder Worldtm Ser.). 48p. 39.95 *(978-0-7802-2951-8(7))* Wright Group/McGraw-Hill.

Sloppy Tiger Bedtime: Big Book: Level M. Group 1. (Sunshine Ser.). 24p. 36.50 *(978-0-7802-5791-7(X))* Wright Group/McGraw-Hill.

Slowpoke, 6 vols. 8p. (gr. k-1). 21.50 *(978-0-322-02070-2(0))* Wright Group/McGraw-Hill.

Slug Makes a House Little Book: Early Reading Fluency, Level A. 2004. pap. 6.00 *(978-0-7398-8160-6(4))* Steck-Vaughn.

The Slumber Party Organizer: Level T. Group 1, 6 vols. (Sunshine Ser.). 48p. 44.95 *(978-0-7802-6097-9(X))* Wright Group/McGraw-Hill.

Smelly Armor: Big Book: Level J. Group 2. (Story Box Ser.). 16p. 31.50 *(978-0-322-02470-0(6))* Wright Group/McGraw-Hill.

Smiles, 6 vols. (Multicultural Programs Ser.). 16p. (gr. 1-3). 24.95 *(978-0-7802-9204-8(9))* Wright Group/McGraw-Hill.

Smith, Molly. Don't Worry, Mason. Poole, Helen, illus. 2014. (J). (gr. -1). 3.99 *(978-1-4788-0463-5(7))* Newmark Learning LLC.

—Don't Worry, Mason Lap Book. Poole, Helen, illus. 2014. (MySELF Ser.). (J). (gr. -1-k). 27.00 *(978-1-4788-0500-7(5))* Newmark Learning LLC.

Snake at the Lake: Long Vowel Review: Level C, 6 vols. (Wright Skills Ser.). 16p. (gr. k-3). 26.50 *(978-0-322-01496-1(4))* Wright Group/McGraw-Hill.

Snap Happy Little Book: Early Reading Fluency, Level A, Bk. 1. 2004. pap. 6.00 *(978-0-7398-8157-6(4))* Steck-Vaughn.

Snowball Fight: Level B, 6 vols. (Wonder Worldtm Ser.). 16p. 24.95 *(978-0-7802-1051-6(4))* Wright Group/McGraw-Hill.

Snowman: Level A. Group 2. (Story Box Ser.). 8p. 20.95 *(978-0-322-00320-0(2))* Wright Group/McGraw-Hill.

So, Patty. So Simple at-Home A Month of Ideas: 31 Fun & Simple Activities to Reinforce Your Child's Reading Success! 2007. 36p. (J). spiral bd. *(978-0-9772158-5-0(7))* So Simple Learning.

Sometimes: Level A, 6 vols. (Wonder Worldtm Ser.). 16p. 24.95 *(978-0-7802-2907-5(X))* Wright Group/McGraw-Hill.

Sommer, Carl. Noise! Noise! Noise! Read-along 2003. (Another Sommer-Time Story Ser.). (Illus.). 48p. (J). lib. bdg. 23.95 incl. audio *(978-1-57537-769-8(1))* Advance Publishing, Inc.

Soper, Sandra. Reading & Writing, Bk. 3. rev. ed. (ENG., Illus.). 32p. (J). pap. 5.99 *(978-0-330-32075-7(0)*, Pan) Pan Macmillan GBR. Dist: Trafalgar Square Publishing.

Soup can Telephone: Level K, 6 vols. (Wonder Worldtm Ser.). 16p. 34.95 *(978-0-7802-2912-9(6))* Wright Group/McGraw-Hill.

Southall, Margo. Differentiated Small-Group Reading Lessons: Scaffolded & Engaging Lessons for Word Recognition, Fluency, & Comprehension That Help Every Reader Grow. 2009. (ENG.). 160p. pap. 20.99 *(978-0-439-83920-4(3)*, Teaching Resources) Scholastic, Inc.

Spanish Little Book, 6 vols., Pack. 2005. (Libros en Espanol Para Ninos Ser.). (SPA.). (YA). (gr. -1-1). 71.82 *(978-0-8215-0990-6(X))* Sadlier, William H. Inc.

Sparks, Stacey. Clean up, Everybody Lap Book. Patton, Julia, illus. 2014. (MySELF Ser.). (J). (gr. -1-k). 27.00 *(978-1-4788-0514-4(5))* Newmark Learning LLC.

—Let's Get It Started. Evans, Antony, illus. 2014. (J). (gr. -1). 3.99 *(978-1-4788-0481-9(5))* Newmark Learning LLC.

—Let's Get It Started Lap Book. Evans, Antony, illus. 2014. (MySELF Ser.). (J). (gr. -1-k). 27.00 *(978-1-4788-0518-2(8))* Newmark Learning LLC.

A Spider Web: Level M, 6 vols. (Wonder Worldtm Ser.). 16p. 34.95 *(978-0-7802-4603-4(9))* Wright Group/McGraw-Hill.

The Sport of Reading: Read Fast, Read Smart, Boost Your Grades. (Illus.). 24p. (J). (gr. 4-18). *(978-0-930251-01-7(6))* BlueChip Pubs.

Spot that Cat! Big Book: Level I. Group 2. (Story Box Ser.). 16p. 31.50 *(978-0-322-02460-1(9))* Wright Group/McGraw-Hill.

Spreading the Word, 6 vols. (Wildcats Ser.). 32p. (gr. 2-8). *(978-0-322-00604-1(X))* Wright Group/McGraw-Hill.

Sprick, Marilyn & Sprick, Jessica. Hey Diddle Diddle: Read Well Level K Unit 16 Storybook. Clark, Steve, illus. 2003. (Read Well Level K Ser.). 20p. (J). *(978-1-57035-687-2(4)*, 55562) Cambium Education, Inc.

Spring to Success on the PSSA Grade 3: Test Prep & Skills Practice READING. 2005. (Illus.). 80p. (J). per. 8.00 *(978-0-9722452-4-1(3))* New Leaf Educ., Inc.

Stamps: Level H, 6 vols. (Wonder Worldtm Ser.). 16p. 29.95 *(978-0-7802-2032-4(3))* Wright Group/McGraw-Hill.

Standish, Russell R. & Standish, Ella. Gwanpa & Nanny's Home. 2003. (Illus.). 128p. (J). pap. 14.95 *(978-0-923309-89-3(6))* Hartland Pubns.

Stanley Stooks: Super Stuntman: Level 7, 6 vols. (Fluency Strand Ser.). (gr. 4-8). 45.00 *(978-1-4045-1245-0(4))* Wright Group/McGraw-Hill.

Starting Off: American Readers. (J). *(978-0-669-04930-5(1))* Houghton Mifflin Harcourt School Pubs.

Steck-Vaughn Staff. Access Reading. 2004. (Steck-Vaughn Access Ser.). (ENG.). 32p. (gr. 9-12). pap., tchr. ed. 8.70 *(978-0-7398-8934-3(6))* Houghton Mifflin Harcourt Publishing Co.

—At-Home Workbooks: Reading. 2004. (Illus.). (gr. 1). pap., wbk. ed. *(978-0-7398-8524-6(3))*; (gr. 2). pap., wbk. ed. *(978-0-7398-8525-3(1))*; (gr. 4). pap., wbk. ed. 5.99 *(978-0-7398-8527-7(8))* Steck-Vaughn.

—Shutterbug: Add to Package. 2004. Level A-I. pap. 141.11 *(978-0-7398-9431-6(5))*Level E-I. pap. 191.90 *(978-0-7398-9432-3(3))*Level H-M. pap. 141.11 *(978-0-7398-9433-0(1))*Level J-M. pap. 191.90 *(978-0-7398-9434-7(X))* Steck-Vaughn.

Stella, Heather & Lima, Athena Anna. Get Ready for First Grade: Spelling, Writing & Reading. 2012. (Get Ready for School Ser.). (ENG., Illus.). 320p. (J). (gr. -1-17). 17.95 *(978-1-57912-896-8(3)*, 81896, Black Dog & Leventhal Pubs. Inc.) Hachette Bks.

Stingrays: Level L, 6 vols. (Wonder Worldtm Ser.). 16p. 34.95 *(978-0-7802-4605-8(5))* Wright Group/McGraw-Hill.

Stone Works: Level M, 6 vols. (Wonder Worldtm Ser.). 16p. 34.95 *(978-0-7802-2909-9(6))* Wright Group/McGraw-Hill.

Stoneman, Sonya. First Aid in Reading. (Illus.). 68p. (J). pap., act. bk. ed. *(978-1-876367-37-4(7))* Wizard Bks.

—First Aid in Reading: Program Book. (Illus.). 180p. (J). pap. *(978-1-876367-24-4(5))* Wizard Bks.

Stop! Big Book: Level E. Group 1. (Story Box Ser.). 16p. 31.50 *(978-0-7802-7638-3(8))* Wright Group/McGraw-Hill.

Stop: Level C. (Wonder Worldtm Ser.). 16p. 24.95 *(978-0-7802-2910-5(X))* Wright Group/McGraw-Hill.

The Story Box: Early Emergent - Group 1:1 Each of 8 Student Books: Level A. 33.50 *(978-1-55911-125-6(9))* Wright Group/McGraw-Hill.

The Story Box: Early Emergent - Group 1:1 Each of 8 Student Books: Level B. 33.50 *(978-1-55911-134-8(8))* Wright Group/McGraw-Hill.

The Story Box: Early Emergent - Group 1:1 Each of 8 Student Books: Level C. 33.50 *(978-1-55911-143-0(7))* Wright Group/McGraw-Hill.

The Story Box: Early Emergent - Group 2:1 Each of 8 Student Books: Level A. 33.50 *(978-0-7802-9927-6(2))* Wright Group/McGraw-Hill.

The Story Box: Early Emergent - Group 2:1 Each of 8 Student Books: Level B. 33.50 *(978-0-7802-9928-3(0))* Wright Group/McGraw-Hill.

The Story Box: Early Emergent - Student Book Set - 1 Each of 16 Titles. (gr. k-18). 66.95 *(978-0-322-03142-5(7))*; Vol. 2. 66.95 *(978-0-7802-9530-8(7))*; Vol. 3. 66.95 *(978-0-7802-9531-5(5))* Wright Group/McGraw-Hill.

The Story Box: Early Emergent-Upper Emergent - Group 1: 1 Each of 8 Student Books: Level D. 33.50 *(978-1-55911-152-2(6))* Wright Group/McGraw-Hill.

The Story Box: Early Emergent-Upper Emergent - Group 1: 1 Each of 8 Student Books: Level E. 39.95 *(978-1-55911-161-4(5))* Wright Group/McGraw-Hill.

The Story Box: Early Emergent-Upper Emergent - Group 2: 1 Each of 8 Student Books: Level C. 33.50 *(978-0-7802-9931-3(0))* Wright Group/McGraw-Hill.

The Story Box: Early Emergent-Upper Emergent - Group 2: 1 Each of 8 Student Books: Level D. 33.50 *(978-0-7802-9932-0(9))* Wright Group/McGraw-Hill.

The Story Box: Early Emergent-Upper Emergent - Group 2: 1 Each of 8 Student Books: Level E. 39.95 *(978-0-7802-9929-0(9))* Wright Group/McGraw-Hill.

The Story Box: Early Fluency - Complete Kit. (gr. 2-18). 537.95 *(978-0-7802-2772-9(7))* Wright Group/McGraw-Hill.

The Story Box: Upper Emergent - Complete Kit. (gr. 1-18). 435.50 *(978-0-7802-2771-2(9))*; Vol. 2. 435.50 *(978-0-7802-9341-0(X))*; Vol. 4. 435.50 *(978-0-322-02574-5(5))*; Vol. 5. 435.50 *(978-0-322-02575-2(3))* Wright Group/McGraw-Hill.

The Story Box: Upper Emergent - Group 1: 1 Each of 8 Student Books: Level I. (Story Box Ser.). 39.95 *(978-0-322-02566-0(4))* Wright Group/McGraw-Hill.

The Story Box: Upper Emergent - Group 1: 1 Each of 8 Student Books: Level J. (Story Box Ser.). 39.95 *(978-0-322-02569-1(9))* Wright Group/McGraw-Hill.

The Story Box: Upper Emergent - Group 1-2: 1 Each of 16 Student Books: Level J. (Story Box Ser.). 79.95 *(978-0-322-02568-4(0))* Wright Group/McGraw-Hill.

The Story Box: Upper Emergent - Group 2: 1 Each of 8 Student Books: Level H. (Story Box Ser.). 39.95 *(978-0-322-02564-6(8))* Wright Group/McGraw-Hill.

The Story Box: Upper Emergent - Group 2: 1 Each of 8 Student Books: Level I. (Story Box Ser.). 39.95 *(978-0-322-02567-7(2))* Wright Group/McGraw-Hill.

The Story Box: Upper Emergent - Group 2: 1 Each of 8 Student Books: Level J. 39.95 *(978-0-322-02571-4(0))* Wright Group/McGraw-Hill.

The Story Box: Upper Emergent - Groups 1: 1 Each of 8 Student Books: Level F. 39.95 *(978-1-55911-170-6(4))* Wright Group/McGraw-Hill.

The Story Box: Upper Emergent - Groups 1: 1 Each of 8 Student Books: Level G. 39.95 *(978-1-55911-179-9(8))* Wright Group/McGraw-Hill.

The Story Box: Upper Emergent - Groups 2: 1 Each of 8 Student Books: Level F. 39.95 *(978-0-7802-9930-6(2))* Wright Group/McGraw-Hill.

The Story Box: Upper Emergent - Groups 2: 1 Each of 8 Student Books: Level G. 39.95 *(978-0-7802-9933-7(7))* Wright Group/McGraw-Hill.

The Story Box: Upper Emergent - Student Book Set - 1 Each of 16 Titles. (gr. 1-18). 79.95 *(978-0-322-03141-8(9))*; Vol. 2. 79.95 *(978-0-7802-9532-2(3))*; Vol. 3. 79.95 *(978-0-7802-9533-9(1))*; Vol. 4. 79.95 *(978-0-322-03139-5(7))*; Vol. 5. 79.95 *(978-0-322-03140-1(0))* Wright Group/McGraw-Hill.

The Story Box Vol. 2: Early Emergent - Early Emergent - Complete Kit. (gr. k-18). 372.95 *(978-0-7802-9339-7(8))* Wright Group/McGraw-Hill.

The Story of My Life: Response Journal. 2003. 40p. (YA). *(978-1-58049-990-3(2)*, RJ90) Prestwick Hse., Inc.

Story Time. (Little Book Practice Reader). (J). *(978-0-8136-5358-7(4))* Modern Curriculum Pr.

Story Vine: 1 Each of 12 Student Books. (Story Vinestm Ser.). (gr. 3-6). 88.95 *(978-0-7802-9413-4(0))* Wright Group/McGraw-Hill.

Story Vine: 6 Each of 12 Student Books. (Story Vinestm Ser.). (gr. 3-6). 434.50 *(978-0-7802-9414-1(9))* Wright Group/McGraw-Hill.

Stott, Jon C. Gerald McDermott & You, 1 vol. McDermott, Gerald, illus. 2004. (Author & YOU Ser.). 128p. (C). pap. 35.00 *(978-1-59158-175-8(3)*, LU1753, Greenwood) ABC-CLIO, LLC.

Stradling, Jan. Lights On: Level K, 6 vols., Vol. 2. (First Explorers Ser.). 24p. (gr. 1-2). 34.95 *(978-0-7699-1461-9(6))* Shortland Pubns. (U. S. A.) Inc.

—Look Up: Level I, 6 vols. (First Explorers Ser.). 24p. (gr. 1-2). 29.95 *(978-0-7699-1447-3(0))* Shortland Pubns. (U. S. A.) Inc.

Strange Days: Level 7, 6 vols. (Fluency Strand Ser.). (gr. 4-8). 45.00 *(978-1-4045-1241-2(1))* Wright Group/McGraw-Hill.

The Stranger from the Sea: Level T. Group 1, 6 vols. (Sunshine Ser.). 48p. 44.95 *(978-0-7802-5601-9(8))* Wright Group/McGraw-Hill.

Strauss, Elizabeth. Beginning Reading 1-2. 2008. (ENG.). 32p. (J). pap. 2.99 *(978-0-88743-756-4(7))* School Zone Publishing Co.

Street Action: 6 Each of 1 Anthology, 6 vols. (Wildcats Ser.). 32p. (gr. 2-8). *(978-0-322-00577-8(9))* Wright Group/McGraw-Hill.

The Strength of Georgia Mills: Level 2, 6 vols. (Fluency Strand Ser.). (gr. 4-8). 45.00 *(978-1-4045-1215-3(2))* Wright Group/McGraw-Hill.

The Summer Mermaid: R-Controlled e, i, u: Level B, 6 vols. (Wright Skills Ser.). 16p. (gr. k-3). 26.50 *(978-0-322-01488-6(3))* Wright Group/McGraw-Hill.

Summer Trips, 6 vols. (Multicultural Programs Ser.). 16p. (gr. 1-3). 24.95 *(978-0-7802-9219-2(7))* Wright Group/McGraw-Hill.

Sunshine: Early Emergent - 1 Each of 32 Big Books: Level A-D. (Sunshine Ser.). 628.50 *(978-0-7802-6775-6(3))* Wright Group/McGraw-Hill.

Sunshine: Early Emergent - 1 Each of 4 Big Books: Level A-D. (Sunshine Ser.). 82.95 *(978-0-7802-6772-5(9))* Wright Group/McGraw-Hill.

Sunshine: Early Emergent - Group 1: 1 Each of 8 Student Books: Level A. (Sunshine Ser.). 33.50 *(978-0-7802-7118-0(1))* Wright Group/McGraw-Hill.

Sunshine: Early Emergent - Group 1: 1 Each of 8 Student Books: Level D. (Sunshine Ser.). 33.50 *(978-0-7802-7124-1(6))* Wright Group/McGraw-Hill.

Sunshine: Early Emergent - Group 1:1 Each of 8 Student Books: Level C. (Sunshine Ser.). 33.50 *(978-0-7802-7122-7(X))* Wright Group/McGraw-Hill.

Sunshine: Early Emergent - Group 2: 1 Each of 8 Student Books: Level A. (Sunshine Ser.). 33.50 *(978-0-7802-7119-7(X))* Wright Group/McGraw-Hill.

Sunshine: Early Emergent - Group 2:1 Each of 8 Student Books: Level B. (Sunshine Ser.). 33.50 *(978-0-7802-7121-0(1))* Wright Group/McGraw-Hill.

Sunshine: Early Emergent - Group 2:1 Each of 8 Student Books: Level C. (Sunshine Ser.). 33.50 *(978-0-7802-7123-4(8))* Wright Group/McGraw-Hill.

Sunshine: Early Emergent - Nonfiction 1: 1 Each of 4 Student Books: Level A. (Sunshine Ser.). 16.95 *(978-0-7802-3763-6(3))* Wright Group/McGraw-Hill.

Sunshine: Early Emergent - Nonfiction: 1 Each of 4 Student Books: Level C. (Sunshine Ser.). 16.95 *(978-0-7802-3781-0(1))* Wright Group/McGraw-Hill.

Sunshine: Early Emergent - Nonfiction:1 Each of 4 Student Books: Level A. 16.95 *(978-0-7802-3772-8(2))* Wright Group/McGraw-Hill.

Sunshine: Early Emergent - Student Book Set - 1 Each of 16 Titles, Vol. 3. (Wright Group Literacy Ser.). (gr. k-18). 66.95 *(978-0-322-02487-8(0))* Wright Group/McGraw-Hill.

Sunshine: Early Emergent: 1 Each of 8 Student Books: Level B. (Sunshine Ser.). 24.95 *(978-0-7802-7120-3(3))* Wright Group/McGraw-Hill.

Sunshine: Early Emergent-Upper Emergent - 1 Each of 60 Big Books: Level A-J,A-D. (Sunshine Ser.). 1345.50 *(978-0-7802-6779-4(6))* Wright Group/McGraw-Hill.

Sunshine: Early Emergent-Upper Emergent - Group 1: 1 Each of 8 Student Books: Level E. (Sunshine Ser.). 39.95 *(978-0-7802-7126-5(2))* Wright Group/McGraw-Hill.

Sunshine: Early Emergent-Upper Emergent - Nonfiction: 1 Each of 4 Student Books: Level D. (Sunshine Ser.). 16.95 *(978-0-7802-3790-2(0))* Wright Group/McGraw-Hill.

Sunshine: Early Emergent-Upper Emergent - Nonfiction: 1 Each of 4 Student Books: Level E. (Sunshine Ser.). 19.95 *(978-0-7802-6791-6(5))* Wright Group/McGraw-Hill.
Sunshine: Early Fluency - Chapter books, Group 2: 1 each of 2 titles: Level K. 11.95 *(978-0-7802-6852-4(0))* Wright Group/McGraw-Hill.
Sunshine: Early Fluency - Chapter books, Group 2: 1 each of 2 titles: Level L. 11.95 *(978-0-7802-6853-1(9))* Wright Group/McGraw-Hill.
Sunshine: Early Fluency - Chapter Books, Group 2; 1 each of 2 titles: Level M. 11.95 *(978-0-7802-6854-8(7))* Wright Group/McGraw-Hill.
Sunshine: Early Fluency - Fact & Fantasy, Group 1; 1 each of 8 titles: Level L. 46.95 *(978-0-7802-8354-1(6))* Wright Group/McGraw-Hill.
Sunshine: Early Fluency - Fact & Fantasy, Group 2; 1 each of 2 titles: Level L. 11.95 *(978-0-7802-7876-9(3))* Wright Group/McGraw-Hill.
Sunshine: Early Fluency - Fact & Fantasy, Groups 1-2; 1 each of 10 titles: Level L. 58.50 *(978-0-7802-6849-4(0))* Wright Group/McGraw-Hill.
Sunshine: Early Fluency - Group 2: 1 each of 6 titles: Level K. (Sunshine Ser.). 34.95 *(978-0-7802-7138-8(6))* Wright Group/McGraw-Hill.
Sunshine: Early Fluency - Group 2; 1 each of 6 titles: Level M. 34.95 *(978-0-7802-7140-1(8))* Wright Group/McGraw-Hill.
Sunshine: Early Fluency - Nonfiction, Group 1: 1 each of 8 titles: Level K. 46.95 *(978-0-7802-8353-4(8))* Wright Group/McGraw-Hill.
Sunshine: Early Fluency - Nonfiction, Group 2: 1 each of 2 titles: Level K. (Sunshine Ser.). 11.95 *(978-0-7802-7875-2(5))* Wright Group/McGraw-Hill.
Sunshine: Early Fluency - Nonfiction, Groups 1-2: 1 each of 10 titles: Level K. 58.50 *(978-0-7802-6848-7(2))* Wright Group/McGraw-Hill.
Sunshine: Early Fluency - Student Book Set - 1 Each of 16 Titles. (Wright Group Literacy Ser.). (gr. 2-18). Vol. 2. 93.50 *(978-0-322-02491-5(9))* Vol. 3. 93.50 *(978-0-322-02492-2(7))* Vol. 4. 93.50 *(978-0-322-02493-9(5))* Wright Group/McGraw-Hill.
Sunshine: Early Fluency Fiction. 32p. (gr. 1-5). 46.95 *(978-0-7802-6856-2(3))* Wright Group/McGraw-Hill.
Sunshine: Early Fluency-Nonfiction, Group 1; 1 each of 8 titles: Level M. 46.95 *(978-0-7802-8355-8(4))* Wright Group/McGraw-Hill.
Sunshine: Early Fluency-Nonfiction, Group 2; 1 each of 2 titles: Level M. 11.95 *(978-0-7802-7877-6(1))* Wright Group/McGraw-Hill.
Sunshine: Early Fluency-Nonfiction, Groups 1-2; 1 each of 10 titles: Level M. 58.50 *(978-0-7802-6850-0(4))* Wright Group/McGraw-Hill.
Sunshine: Enrichment Library. (Sunshine Ser.). 24p. (gr. 1-5). 91.95 *(978-0-7802-9382-3(7))* Wright Group/McGraw-Hill.
Sunshine: Fact & Fantasy, Group 1: 1 each of 8 titles: Level N. 46.95 *(978-0-7802-8356-5(2))* Wright Group/McGraw-Hill.
Sunshine: Fact & Fantasy, Group 2: 1 each of 2 titles: Level N. 11.95 *(978-0-7802-7878-3(X))* Wright Group/McGraw-Hill.
Sunshine: Fact & Fantasy, Groups 1-2: 1 each of 10 titles: Level N. 58.50 *(978-0-7802-6851-7(2))* Wright Group/McGraw-Hill.
Sunshine: Fluency - Chapter books, Group 2: 1 each of 2 titles: Level O. (Sunshine Ser.). 13.50 *(978-0-7802-6876-0(8))* Wright Group/McGraw-Hill.
Sunshine: Fluency - Chapter Books, Group 2: 1 Each of 2 Titles: Level R. (Sunshine Ser.). 14.95 *(978-0-7802-6879-1(2))* Wright Group/McGraw-Hill.
Sunshine: Fluency - Chapter Books, Group 2: 1 Each of 2 Titles: Level S. (Sunshine Ser.). 14.95 *(978-0-7802-6880-7(6))* Wright Group/McGraw-Hill.
Sunshine: Fluency - Chapter Books, Group 2: 1 Each of 2 Titles: Level T. (Sunshine Ser.). 14.95 *(978-0-7802-6881-4(4))* Wright Group/McGraw-Hill.
Sunshine: Fluency - Fact & Fantasy, Group 1: 1 each of 8 titles: Level O. 53.50 *(978-0-7802-8357-2(0))* Wright Group/McGraw-Hill.
Sunshine: Fluency - Fact & Fantasy, Group 2: 1 each of 2 titles: Level O. 13.50 *(978-0-7802-7879-0(8))* Wright Group/McGraw-Hill.
Sunshine: Fluency - Fact & Fantasy, Groups 1-2: 1 each of 10 titles: Level O. (Sunshine Ser.). 66.95 *(978-0-7802-6867-8(9))* Wright Group/McGraw-Hill.
Sunshine: Fluency - Group 2: 1 each of 6 titles: Level O. 39.95 *(978-0-7802-7143-2(2))* Wright Group/McGraw-Hill.
Sunshine: Fluency - Group 2: 1 Each of 6 Titles: Level R. (Sunshine Ser.). 44.95 *(978-0-7802-7220-0(X))* Wright Group/McGraw-Hill.
Sunshine: Fluency - Group 2: 1 Each of 6 Titles: Level S. (Sunshine Ser.). 44.95 *(978-0-7802-7222-4(6))* Wright Group/McGraw-Hill.
Sunshine: Fluency - Group 2: 1 Each of 6 Titles: Level T. 44.95 *(978-0-7802-7224-8(2))* Wright Group/McGraw-Hill.
Sunshine: Fluency - Nonfiction, Group 1: 1 Each of 8 Titles: Level R. 59.95 *(978-0-7802-8360-2(0))* Wright Group/McGraw-Hill.
Sunshine: Fluency - Nonfiction, Group 1: 1 Each of 8 Titles: Level T. (Sunshine Ser.). 59.95 *(978-0-7802-8362-6(7))* Wright Group/McGraw-Hill.
Sunshine: Fluency - Nonfiction, Group 2: 1 Each of 2 Titles: Level R. (Sunshine Ser.). 14.95 *(978-0-7802-7882-0(8))* Wright Group/McGraw-Hill.
Sunshine: Fluency - Nonfiction, Group 2: 1 Each of 2 Titles: Level T. (Sunshine Ser.). 14.95 *(978-0-7802-7884-4(4))* Wright Group/McGraw-Hill.
Sunshine: Fluency - Nonfiction, Groups 1-2: 1 Each of 10 Titles: Level R. (Sunshine Ser.). 74.95 *(978-0-7802-6871-5(7))* Wright Group/McGraw-Hill.
Sunshine: Fluency - Nonfiction, Groups 1-2: 1 Each of 10 Titles: Level S. (Sunshine Ser.). 74.95 *(978-0-7802-6873-9(3))* Wright Group/McGraw-Hill.
Sunshine: Fluency - Nonfiction, Groups 1-2: 1 Each of 10 Titles: Level T. (Sunshine Ser.). 74.95 *(978-0-7802-6874-6(1))* Wright Group/McGraw-Hill.
Sunshine: Fluency - Nonfiction, Groups 2: 1 Each of 2 Titles: Level S. (Sunshine Ser.). 14.95 *(978-0-7802-7883-7(6))* Wright Group/McGraw-Hill.
Sunshine: Fluency - Student Book Set - 1 Each of 16 Titles. (Wright Group Literacy Ser.). (gr. 3-6). 112.50 *(978-0-322-02494-6(3))*; Vol. 2. 112.50 *(978-0-322-02495-3(1))* Wright Group/McGraw-Hill.
Sunshine: Fluency-Chapter books, Group 2: 1 each of 2 titles: Level P. (Sunshine Ser.). 13.50 *(978-0-7802-6877-7(6))* Wright Group/McGraw-Hill.
Sunshine: Fluency-Chapter books, Groups 2: 1 each of 2 titles: Level Q. (Sunshine Ser.). 13.50 *(978-0-7802-6878-4(4))* Wright Group/McGraw-Hill.
Sunshine: Fluency-Fact & Fantasy, Group 1: 1 each of 8 titles: Level P. 53.50 *(978-0-7802-8358-9(9))* Wright Group/McGraw-Hill.
Sunshine: Fluency-Fact & Fantasy, Group 2: 1 each of 2 titles: Level P. 13.50 *(978-0-7802-7880-6(1))* Wright Group/McGraw-Hill.
Sunshine: Fluency-Fact & Fantasy, Groups 1-2: 1 each of 10 titles: Level P. (Sunshine Ser.). 66.95 *(978-0-7802-6868-5(7))* Wright Group/McGraw-Hill.
Sunshine: Fluency Fiction. (Sunshine Ser.). 72p. (gr. 1-5). 84.95 *(978-0-7802-6882-1(2))* Wright Group/McGraw-Hill.
Sunshine: Fluency-Group 2: 1 each of 6 titles: Level P. 39.95 *(978-0-7802-7145-6(9))* Wright Group/McGraw-Hill.
Sunshine: Fluency-Group 2: 1 each of 6 titles: Level Q. 39.95 *(978-0-7802-7218-7(8))* Wright Group/McGraw-Hill.
Sunshine: Fluency-Nonfiction, Group 1: 1 each of 10 titles: Level Q. (Sunshine Ser.). 66.95 *(978-0-7802-6870-8(9))* Wright Group/McGraw-Hill.
Sunshine: Fluency-Nonfiction, Group 1: 1 each of 2 titles: Level Q. 13.50 *(978-0-7802-7881-3(X))* Wright Group/McGraw-Hill.
Sunshine: Fluency-Nonfiction, Group 1: 1 each of 8 titles: Level Q. 53.50 *(978-0-7802-8359-6(7))* Wright Group/McGraw-Hill.
Sunshine: Upper Emergent - Complete Kit, Vol. 3. (Wright Group Literacy Ser.). (gr. 1-18). 486.50 *(978-0-322-02479-3(X))* Wright Group/McGraw-Hill.
Sunshine: Upper Emergent - Group 1:1 Each of 8 Student Books: Level F. Group 1. (Sunshine Ser.). 39.95 *(978-0-7802-7128-9(9))* Wright Group/McGraw-Hill.
Sunshine: Upper Emergent - Nonfiction:1 Each of 4 Student Books: Level F. Group 1. (Sunshine Ser.). 19.95 *(978-0-7802-6792-3(3))* Wright Group/McGraw-Hill.
Sunshine: Upper Emergent - Student Book Set - 1 Each of 16 Titles, Vol. 3. (Wright Group Literacy Ser.). (gr. 1-18). 79.95 *(978-0-322-02488-5(9))* Wright Group/McGraw-Hill.
Sunshine: Upper Emergent-Group 1: 1 each of 8 student books: Level I. (Sunshine Ser.). 39.95 *(978-0-7802-7134-0(3))* Wright Group/McGraw-Hill.
Sunshine: Upper Emergent-Group 1: 1 each of 8 student books: Level J. (Sunshine Ser.). 39.95 *(978-0-7802-7136-4(X))* Wright Group/McGraw-Hill.
Sunshine: Upper Emergent-Group 2: 1 each of 8 student books: Level J. (Sunshine Ser.). 39.95 *(978-0-7802-7137-1(8))* Wright Group/McGraw-Hill.
Sunshine Fact & Fantasy Sets: Complete Set - 1 Each of 24 students Books. (Sunshine Ser.). 115.95 *(978-0-7802-6785-5(0))* Wright Group/McGraw-Hill.
SUNSHINE Fluency Guided Reading Kit 1. 2004. (Wright Group Literacy Ser.). (gr. 3-6). 604.95 *(978-0-322-02624-7(5))* Wright Group/McGraw-Hill.
Sunshine Language Skills Books: 1 Each of 16 Big Books Set 2. (gr. k-1). 474.95 *(978-0-7802-8956-7(0))* Wright Group/McGraw-Hill.
Sunshine Language Skills Books: 1 Each of 16 Student Books Set 2. (Sunshine Ser.). (gr. k-1). 91.95 *(978-0-7802-8510-1(7))* Wright Group/McGraw-Hill.
Sunshine Language Skills Books: 1 Each of 20 Big Books Sets 1-2. (gr. k-1). 594.50 *(978-0-7802-9624-4(9))* Wright Group/McGraw-Hill.
Sunshine Language Skills Books: 1 Each of 20 Student Books Set 1. (gr. k-1). 114.50 *(978-0-7802-9623-7(0))* Wright Group/McGraw-Hill.
Sunshine Language Skills Books: 1 Each of 4 Big Books Set 1. (gr. k-1). 125.50 *(978-0-7802-8955-0(2))* Wright Group/McGraw-Hill.
Sunshine Language Skills Books: 1 Each of 4 Student Books Set 2. (Sunshine Ser.). (gr. k-1). 22.95 *(978-0-7802-6823-4(7))* Wright Group/McGraw-Hill.
Sunshine Language Skills Books: 6 Each of 20 Student Books Sets 1-2. (gr. k-1). 652.50 *(978-0-7802-9657-2(5))* Wright Group/McGraw-Hill.
Sunshine Street, 6 vols. (Sunshinetm Ser.). 16p. (gr. k-18). 29.50 *(978-0-7802-5443-5(0))* Wright Group/McGraw-Hill.
Surfing: Level J, 6 vols. (Wonder Worldtm Ser.). 16p. 29.95 *(978-0-7802-4609-6(8))* Wright Group/McGraw-Hill.
Surfs Up, 6 vols. (Wildcats Ser.). 32p. (gr. 2-8). *(978-0-322-00601-0(5))* Wright Group/McGraw-Hill.
Survive!, 6 vols. (Wildcats Ser.). 32p. (gr. 2-8). *(978-0-322-02439-7(0))* Wright Group/McGraw-Hill.
Suter, Joanne. Reading Comprehension Nonfiction 1. Saddleback Educational Publishing Staff, ed. 2013. (Reading Comprehension Nonfiction Ser.). (ENG.). 100p. (gr. 5-12). pap. 44.95 *(978-1-62250-030-7(X))* Saddleback Educational Publishing, Inc.
—Reading Comprehension Nonfiction 2. Saddleback Educational Publishing Staff, ed. 2013. (Reading Comprehension Nonfiction Ser.). (ENG.). 100p. (gr. 5-12). pap. 44.95 *(978-1-62250-031-4(8))* Saddleback Educational Publishing, Inc.
The Swimming Pool: Big Book: Level G. (Visions Ser.). 16p. 20.95 *(978-0-322-00631-7(7))* Wright Group/McGraw-Hill.
Tails: Level C, 6 vols. (Wonder Worldtm Ser.). 16p. 24.95 *(978-0-7802-1052-3(2))* Wright Group/McGraw-Hill.
Tails & Claws: Level E, 6 vols. (Wonder Worldtm Ser.). 16p. 29.95 *(978-0-7802-1243-5(6))*; 26.50 *(978-0-7802-3478-9(2))* Wright Group/McGraw-Hill.
Tails can Tell: Level K, 6 vols. (Wonder Worldtm Ser.). 16p. 34.95 *(978-0-7802-2911-2(8))* Wright Group/McGraw-Hill.
Take a Look: 6 Each of 1 Anthology, 6 vols. (Wildcats Ser.). 32p. (gr. 2-8). *(978-0-322-02420-5(X))* Wright Group/McGraw-Hill.
Take-Twos: Early Fluency - 1 each of 12 titles: Level K. (Take Twostm Ser.). 69.95 *(978-0-322-02642-1(3))* Wright Group/McGraw-Hill.
Take-Twos: Early Fluency - 1 each of 12 titles: Level L. (Take Twostm Ser.). 69.95 *(978-0-322-02645-2(8))* Wright Group/McGraw-Hill.
Take-Twos: Early Fluency - 1 each of 12 titles: Level M. (Take Twostm Ser.). 69.95 *(978-0-322-02646-9(6))* Wright Group/McGraw-Hill.
Take-Twos: Early Fluency - 1 each of 12 titles: Level N. (Take Twostm Ser.). 69.95 *(978-0-322-02644-5(X))* Wright Group/McGraw-Hill.
Taking Care of our World, 6 vols. (Multicultural Programs Ser.). 16p. (gr. 1-3). 24.95 *(978-0-7802-9220-8(0))* Wright Group/McGraw-Hill.
TAKS MASTER Student Practice Book, Reading, Grade 2. 2004. (J). *(978-1-57022-468-3(4))* ECS Learning Systems, Inc.
Taylor, Trace. N. 2010. (ICP Beginning Letter Ser.). (ENG.). 16p. (J). (gr. k-1). pap. 5.99 *(978-1-61541-114-6(3))* American Reading Co.
—P. 2010. (ICP Beginning Letter Ser.). (ENG.). 16p. (J). (gr. k-1). pap. 5.99 *(978-1-61541-116-0(X))* American Reading Co.
—R. 2010. (ICP Beginning Letter Ser.). (ENG.). 16p. (J). (gr. k-1). pap. 5.99 *(978-1-61541-118-4(6))* American Reading Co.
—S. 2010. (ICP Beginning Letter Ser.). (ENG.). 16p. (J). (gr. k-1). pap. 5.99 *(978-1-61541-098-9(8))* American Reading Co.
—T. 2010. (ICP Beginning Letter Ser.). (ENG.). 16p. (J). (gr. k-1). pap. 5.99 *(978-1-61541-100-9(3))* American Reading Co.
Tea: Level M, 6 vols. (Wonder Worldtm Ser.). 16p. 34.95 *(978-0-7802-4611-9(X))* Wright Group/McGraw-Hill.
Teeth: Big Book: Level G. Group 2. (Story Box Ser.). 16p. 20.95 *(978-0-322-00321-7(0))* Wright Group/McGraw-Hill.
Teeth: Level B, 6 vols. (Wonder Worldtm Ser.). 16p. 24.95 *(978-0-7802-1053-0(0))* Wright Group/McGraw-Hill.
Teeth: Level R, 6 vols. (Wonder Worldtm Ser.). 48p. 44.95 *(978-0-7802-7075-6(4))* Wright Group/McGraw-Hill.
Tell Me No Lies, 6 vols. (Ragged Island Mysteriestm Ser.). 161p. (gr. 5-7). 42.50 *(978-0-322-01654-5(1))* Wright Group/McGraw-Hill.
Telling Stories Through Art: Level L, 6 vols. (Take-Twostm Ser.). 16p. 36.95 *(978-0-322-03398-6(5))* Wright Group/McGraw-Hill.
Terror Bear Canyon: Level 5, 6 vols. (Fluency Strand Ser.). (gr. 4-8). 45.00 *(978-1-4045-1225-2(X))* Wright Group/McGraw-Hill.
Tesoros de Lata: 6 Small Books. (Saludos Ser.: Vol. 3). (SPA.). 24p. (gr. 2-3). 31.00 *(978-0-7635-9530-2(6))* Rigby Education.
This Mouth: Level D, 6 vols. (Wonder Worldtm Ser.). 16p. 24.95 *(978-0-7802-2034-8(X))* Wright Group/McGraw-Hill.
Thompson, Deanna T. What's So Great about Silent E? The Thoughts of Sunnie Rae. Thompson, Sunnie R., illus. 2010. 28p. pap. 13.99 *(978-1-4490-9274-0(8))* AuthorHouse.
Thrills at the Fair: 3-letter blends: Level C, 6 vols. (Wright Skills Ser.). 16p. (gr. k-3). 26.50 *(978-0-322-01494-7(8))* Wright Group/McGraw-Hill.
Through the Looking Glass: Response Journal. 2003. 32p. (YA). *(978-1-58049-989-7(9)*, RJ89) Prestwick Hse., Inc.
Thud! Thump! Thud! Digraph th: Level B, 6 vols. (Wright Skills Ser.). 16p. (gr. k-3). 17.95 *(978-0-322-01473-2(5))* Wright Group/McGraw-Hill.
Tick-Tock: Big Book: Level D. Group 2. (Story Box Ser.). 16p. 24.95 *(978-0-322-00323-1(7))* Wright Group/McGraw-Hill.
Tides: Level L, 6 vols. (Wonder Worldtm Ser.). 16p. 34.95 *(978-0-7802-4613-3(6))* Wright Group/McGraw-Hill.
Time Warp: Level T. Group 1, 6 vols. (Sunshine Ser.). 48p. 44.95 *(978-0-7802-5602-6(6))* Wright Group/McGraw-Hill.
Tiny Creatures Little Book: Early Reading Fluency, Level C. 2004. pap. 6.00 *(978-0-7398-8291-7(0))* Steck-Vaughn.
To Catch a Thief: Level 3, 6 vols. (Fluency Strand Ser.). (gr. 4-8). 45.00 *(978-1-4045-1219-1(5))* Wright Group/McGraw-Hill.
To New York: Big Book: Level D. Group 1. (Story Box Ser.). 16p. 20.95 *(978-0-322-00637-9(6))* Wright Group/McGraw-Hill.
To the Moon & Beyond: Level T. Group 3, 6 vols. (Sunshine Ser.). 48p. 44.95 *(978-0-322-01835-8(8))* Wright Group/McGraw-Hill.
Tofte, Mavis. Doogie Dork's Wish. Tofte, Mavis, illus. 2003. (Illus.). (J). per. 5.75 *(978-0-9709906-2-4(6))* Creative Quill Publishing, Inc.
Together, 6 vols. (Sunshinetm Ser.). 16p. (gr. k-18). 29.50 *(978-0-7802-5426-8(0))* Wright Group/McGraw-Hill.
Tomato: Level 4, 6 vols. (Fluency Strand Ser.). (gr. 4-8). 45.00 *(978-1-4045-1223-8(3))* Wright Group/McGraw-Hill.
Too Many Graphs: Digraph ph: Level B, 6 vols. (Wright Skills Ser.). 16p. (gr. k-3). 17.95 *(978-0-322-01475-6(1))* Wright Group/McGraw-Hill.
A Too-Tight Shoes Set, 6 vols. 32p. (gr. 1-3). 26.50 *(978-0-7802-8042-7(3))* Wright Group/McGraw-Hill.
Toombs, Robert. Dottie the Bus Driver in Bicycle Safety. Barnett, Linda, illus. 2013. 24p. pap. 9.99 *(978-0-9885180-6-3(6))* Mindstir Media.
Touch: Big Book: Level E. 8p. 20.95 *(978-0-322-00369-9(5))* Wright Group/McGraw-Hill.
Tracks: Big Book: Level F. 16p. 31.50 *(978-0-322-00350-7(4))* Wright Group/McGraw-Hill.
Traffic Light Sandwich: Level J, 6 vols. (Wonder Worldtm Ser.). 16p. 29.95 *(978-0-7802-4615-7(2))* Wright Group/McGraw-Hill.
The Tram Ride, 6 vols. 8p. (gr. k-1). 21.50 *(978-0-322-02072-6(7))* Wright Group/McGraw-Hill.
The Tree House: Level B. Group 1. (Story Box Ser.). 8p. 20.95 *(978-0-7802-7629-1(9))* Wright Group/McGraw-Hill.
Trelease, Jim. Read Aloud Handbook. 5th ed. 2004. 28.25 *(978-0-8446-7234-2(3))* Smith, Peter Pub., Inc.
A Truckload of Chocolate: Level 7, 6 vols. (Fluency Strand Ser.). (gr. 4-8). 45.00 *(978-1-4045-1243-6(8))* Wright Group/McGraw-Hill.
Tuba Trouble. 2004. (Literacy Think-Togethers Ser.). 16-24p. (gr. 2-3). pap. 39.50 *(978-0-322-06368-6(X))* Wright Group/McGraw-Hill.
Tuminelly, Nancy. -Est As in Nest, 1 vol. 2003. (Word Families Set 2 Ser.). (ENG., Illus.). 24p. (J). (gr. k-3). lib. bdg. 24.21 *(978-1-59197-232-7(9)*, SandCastle) ABDO Publishing Co.
—Ook As in Hook, 1 vol. 2003. (Word Families Set 7 Ser.). (ENG., Illus.). 24p. (J). (gr. k-3). lib. bdg. 24.21 *(978-1-59197-268-6(X)*, SandCastle) ABDO Publishing Co.
—Ub As in Tub, 1 vol. 2003. (Word Families Set 4 Ser.). (ENG., Illus.). 24p. (J). (gr. k-3). lib. bdg. 24.21 *(978-1-59197-242-6(6)*, SandCastle) ABDO Publishing Co.
—Uck As in Duck, 1 vol. 2003. (Word Families Set 4 Ser.). (ENG., Illus.). 24p. (J). (gr. k-3). lib. bdg. 24.21 *(978-1-59197-247-1(7)*, SandCastle) ABDO Publishing Co.
—Uff As in Cuff, 1 vol. 2003. (Word Families Set 4 Ser.). (ENG., Illus.). 24p. (J). (gr. k-3). lib. bdg. 24.21 *(978-1-59197-246-4(9)*, SandCastle) ABDO Publishing Co.
—Ug As in Bug, 1 vol. 2003. (Word Families Set 4 Ser.). (ENG., Illus.). 24p. (J). (gr. k-3). lib. bdg. 24.21 *(978-1-59197-243-3(4)*, SandCastle) ABDO Publishing Co.
—Um As in Drum, 1 vol. Marx, Monica, ed. 2003. (Word Families Set 4 Ser.). (ENG., Illus.). 24p. (J). (gr. k-3). lib. bdg. 24.21 *(978-1-59197-244-0(2)*, SandCastle) ABDO Publishing Co.
—Ump As in Jump, 1 vol. 2003. (Word Families Set 4 Ser.). (ENG., Illus.). 24p. (J). (gr. k-3). lib. bdg. 24.21 *(978-1-59197-245-7(0)*, SandCastle) ABDO Publishing Co.
Tunes for June: Long Vowel u: Level B, 6 vols. (Wright Skills Ser.). 16p. (gr. k-3). 17.95 *(978-0-322-01468-8(9))* Wright Group/McGraw-Hill.
Turning Corners: American Readers. (J). (gr. 2). *(978-0-669-04999-2(9))* Houghton Mifflin Harcourt School Pubs.
Turning Corners: American Readers 2-2. (J). (gr. 2). wbk. ed. *(978-0-669-05004-2(0))* Houghton Mifflin Harcourt School Pubs.
Twain, Mark, pseud. The Prince & the Pauper: Response Journal. 2003. 35p. 19.95 *(978-1-58049-986-6(4)*, RJ86) Prestwick Hse., Inc.
Twig Books: Early Emergent - 1 each of 59 Big Books: Levels A-F Big Books. 1335.95 *(978-0-322-00744-4(5))* Wright Group/McGraw-Hill.
Twig Books: Upper Emergent - 1 each of 16 student books: Level I. (gr. 1-2). 79.95 *(978-0-322-02653-7(9))* Wright Group/McGraw-Hill.
Twig Books: Upper Emergent - 1 each of 16 student books: Level J. (gr. 1-2). 79.95 *(978-0-322-02654-4(7))* Wright Group/McGraw-Hill.
Twig Books: Upper Emergent - Lesson Plan Set - 1 Each of 16 Lesson Plans, Vol. 6. (Twig Ser.). (gr. 1-18). 127.95 *(978-0-322-02814-2(0))* Wright Group/McGraw-Hill.
Twig Books: Upper Emergent - Student Book Set - 1 Each of 16 Titles. (Twig Ser.). (gr. 1-18). Vol. 5. 79.95 *(978-0-322-02958-3(9))* Vol. 6. 79.95 *(978-0-322-02957-6(0))* Wright Group/McGraw-Hill.
Twisters & Other Wind Storms: 6 Each of 1 Anthology, 6 vols. (Wildcats Ser.). 32p. (gr. 2-8). *(978-0-322-00591-4(4))* Wright Group/McGraw-Hill.
The Two Runaways, 6 vols., Vol. 2. (Woodland Mysteriestm Ser.). 133p. (gr. 3-7). 42.50 *(978-0-7802-7941-4(7))* Wright Group/McGraw-Hill.
Tyler, Jenny & Gee, R. Ready for Reading. 2004. (First Learning Ser.). (ENG., Illus.). 1p. (J). pap., act. bk. ed. 4.99 *(978-0-7460-3519-1(5))* EDC Publishing.
Uncle Bill Is Feeling Iii, 6 vols. 8p. (gr. k-1). 21.50 *(978-0-322-02078-8(6))* Wright Group/McGraw-Hill.
Uncle Mort's: Level T. Group 3, 6 vols. (Sunshine Ser.). 48p. 44.95 *(978-0-322-04600-9(9))* Wright Group/McGraw-Hill.
Under the Clock, 6 vols. 8p. (gr. k-1). 21.50 *(978-0-322-02064-1(6))* Wright Group/McGraw-Hill.
Underwater Journey, 6 vols. (Sunshinetm Ser.). 16p. (gr. k-18). 29.50 *(978-0-7802-5437-4(6))* Wright Group/McGraw-Hill.
Unidad 1 Superlibro: Comunidades: Vivimos Juntos: Superlibros. 2003. (MacMillan/McGraw-Hill. Estudios Sociales Ser.). (ENG & SPA.). (gr. 2-18). *(978-0-02-149441-5(X))* Macmillan/McGraw-Hill Schl. Div.
Up High in the Mountains: 6 Each of 1 Anthology, 6 vols. (Wildcats Ser.). 32p. (gr. 2-8). *(978-0-322-02426-7(9))* Wright Group/McGraw-Hill.
Up in a Tree: Level D. Group 1. (Sunshine Ser.). 8p. 20.95 *(978-0-7802-5736-8(7))* Wright Group/McGraw-Hill.
Up They Go. (Little Book Practice Reader). (J). 6.47 *(978-0-8136-5361-7(4))* Modern Curriculum Pr.
Upper Emergent Skills Guide. (Sunshine Skills Guides). 25.95 *(978-0-7802-9810-1(1))* Wright Group/McGraw-Hill.
Using the Library: Level N, 6 vols. (Wonder Worldtm Ser.). 48p. 34.95 *(978-0-7802-4617-1(9))* Wright Group/McGraw-Hill.
Valentine's Checkup: Take-Home Book. 2005. (Emergent Library: Vol. 2). (YA). (gr. -1-1). 12.60 *(978-0-8215-7267-2(9))* Sadlier, William H. Inc.
A Van in the Mud: Consonant v: Level A, 6 vols. (Wright Skills Ser.). 12p. (gr. k-3). 17.95 *(978-0-322-03118-0(4))* Wright Group/McGraw-Hill.
Van Ravenswaay, Susan. Reading Is So Easy. 2013. 60p. pap. 19.95 *(978-0-9849214-4-7(3))* Mariner Publishing.
Vastola, P. What I Think: Learning the TH Sound. 2009. (PowerPhonics Ser.). 24p. (gr. 1-1). 39.90 *(978-1-60851-479-3(X)*, PowerKids Pr.) Rosen Publishing Group, Inc., The.
Vaughan, Marcia. Story Teller Quilts: Level S, 6 vols. (Raging Rivers Ser.). 128p. (gr. 3-6). 36.95 *(978-0-322-05899-6(6))* Wright Group/McGraw-Hill.
A Very Fine Time: Long Vowel i, CVCe Pattern: Level B, 6 vols. (Wright Skills Ser.). 16p. (gr. k-3). 17.95 *(978-0-322-01467-1(0))* Wright Group/McGraw-Hill.
Vicary, Tim. The Elephant Man, Level 1. 2006. (Illus.). 56p. (gr. 4-7). pap. 10.00 *(978-0-19-423743-7(5))* Oxford Univ. Pr., Inc.
Visions: Early Emergent - 1 each of 12 Big Books: Levels A-G Big Books. 248.50 *(978-0-322-00748-2(8))* Wright Group/McGraw-Hill.
Visions: Early Emergent - 1 Each of 12 Student Books: Level A. (Visions Ser.). 49.95 *(978-0-7802-9448-6(3))* Wright Group/McGraw-Hill.
Visions: Early Emergent - 1 Each of 13 Student Books: Level B. (Visions Ser.). 54.50 *(978-0-7802-9449-3(1))* Wright Group/McGraw-Hill.
Visions: Early Emergent - 1 Each of 13 Student Books: Level C. 54.50 *(978-0-7802-9450-9(5))* Wright Group/McGraw-Hill.
Visions: Early Emergent - Complete Kit. (Visions Ser.). (gr. k-18). 319.50 *(978-0-7802-9397-7(5))* Wright Group/McGraw-Hill.
Visions: Early Emergent-Upper Emergent - 1 Each of 12 Student Books: Level D. (Visions Ser.). 49.95 *(978-0-7802-9451-6(3))* Wright Group/McGraw-Hill.
Visions: Early Emergent-Upper Emergent - 1 Each of 12 Student Books: Level E. (Visions Ser.). 59.95 *(978-0-7802-9452-3(1))* Wright Group/McGraw-Hill.

Visions: Early Emergent-Upper Emergent - 1 Each of 13 Student Books: Level F. (Visions Ser.). 64.95 (978-0-7802-9453-0(X)) Wright Group/McGraw-Hill.

Visions: Upper Emergent - 1 Each of 12 Student Books: Level H. 59.95 (978-0-7802-9454-7(8)) Wright Group/McGraw-Hill.

Visions: Upper Emergent - 1 Each of 13 Student Books: Level G. 64.95 (978-0-7802-9455-4(6)) Wright Group/McGraw-Hill.

Visions: Upper Emergent - Complete Kit. (Visions Ser.). (gr. 1-18). 383.50 (978-0-7802-9398-4(3)) Wright Group/McGraw-Hill.

Visions Enrichment Library: 1 Each of 20 Student Books. (Multicultural Programs Ser.). (gr. 1-3). 83.50 (978-0-7802-9447-9(5)) Wright Group/McGraw-Hill..

The Voyage of the Clowns: Diphthong Review: Level C, 6 vols. (Wright Skills Ser.). 16p. (gr. k-3). 26.50 (978-0-322-01500-5(6)) Wright Group/McGraw-Hill.

Walker, Richard. Your Amazing Body. 2004. (Literacy Think-Togethers Ser.). 16-24p. (gr. 2-3). pap. 39.50 (978-0-322-06376-1(0)) Wright Group/McGraw-Hill.

Warm & Cool Sets: 1 Each of 3 Big Books. (Sunshinetm Science Ser.). (gr. 1-2). 111.50 (978-0-7802-1450-7(1)) Wright Group/McGraw-Hill.

Warming Up: American Readers. (J). (978-0-669-04913-8(1)); (978-0-669-04915-2(8)) Houghton Mifflin Harcourt School Pubs.

Water: Level J, 6 vols. (Wonder Worldtm Ser.). 16p. 29.95 (978-0-7802-2914-3(2)) Wright Group/McGraw-Hill.

Watson, Joy. The Birthday Flood: Level O, 6 vols. (Raging Rivers Ser.). 128p. (gr. 3-6). 36.95 (978-0-322-05896-5(1)) Wright Group/McGraw-Hill.

Waves: Level L, 6 vols. (Wonder Worldtm Ser.). 16p. 34.95 (978-0-7802-4619-5(5)) Wright Group/McGraw-Hill.

We Care for our School: Level K, 6 vols. (Wonder Worldtm Ser.). 16p. 34.95 (978-0-7802-4621-8(7)); 26.50 (978-0-7802-7009-1(6)) Wright Group/McGraw-Hill.

We Look the Same, 6 vols. 8p. (gr. k-1). 21.50 (978-0-322-02079-5(4)) Wright Group/McGraw-Hill.

The Week That Was: Level 3, 6 vols. (Fluency Strand Ser.). (gr. 4-8). 45.00 (978-1-4045-1221-4(7)) Wright Group/McGraw-Hill.

Weeks, Sarah. What Is a Kiss? Date not set. 32p. (J). (gr. -1-2). 15.89 (978-0-06-026256-3(7)) HarperCollins Pubs.

Weintraub, Aileen. Reading Fundamentals: Grade 5: Nonfiction Activities to Build Reading Comprehension Skills. 2016. (Flash Kids Fundamentals Ser.). (ENG., Illus.). 96p. (J). (gr. 5-5). pap. 7.95 (978-1-4114-7885-5(1), Spark Publishing Group) Sterling Publishing Co., Inc.

—Reading Fundamentals: Grade 6: Nonfiction Activities to Build Reading Comprehension Skills. 2016. (Flash Kids Fundamentals Ser.). (ENG., Illus.). 96p. (J). (gr. 6-6). pap. 7.95 (978-1-4114-7886-2(X), Spark Publishing Group) Sterling Publishing Co., Inc.

Wells, Rosemary & Rosemary, Wells. Listos para Leer. Fernandez, Leire Amigo, tr. Koelsch, Michael, illus. 2004. (SPA.). 32p. (J). (gr. k-1). 14.99 (978-84-241-8712-5(1)) Everest Editora ESP. Dist: Lectorum Pubns., Inc.

Wernham, Sara & Lloyd, Sue. Jolly Phonics Activity Book 4: Ai, J, Oa, Ie, Ee, Or, 7 vols. Stephen, Lib, illus. 2010. (ENG.). 7p. (J). pap. (978-1-84414-156-2(X)) Jolly Learning, Ltd.

Whale Watch. (Little Book Practice Reader). (J). (978-0-8136-5380-8(0)) Modern Curriculum Pr.

What do I See in the Garden: Big Book: Level F. (Wonder Worldtm Ser.). 16p. 29.95 (978-0-7802-2830-6(8)) Wright Group/McGraw-Hill.

What do I See in the Garden: Level F, 6 vols. (Wonder Worldtm Ser.). 16p. 29.95 (978-0-7802-1054-7(9)) Wright Group/McGraw-Hill.

What Do You Think? 6 Pack. (Wildcats Ser.). 32p. (gr. 2-8). (978-0-322-00578-5(7)) Wright Group/McGraw-Hill.

What Else?, 6 vols. (Sunshinetm Ser.). 16p. (gr. k-18). 29.50 (978-0-7802-5439-8(2)) Wright Group/McGraw-Hill.

What Makes a Dinosaur Sore? (J). (gr. 2-3). 75.00 (978-0-669-13452-0(X)); pap. 9.90 (978-0-669-15894-6(1)); pap. 9.90 (978-0-669-15291-3(9)) Houghton Mifflin Harcourt School Pubs.

What Season Is This? Level A, 6 vols. (Wonder Worldtm Ser.). 16p. 24.95 (978-0-7802-1055-4(7)) Wright Group/McGraw-Hill.

What was This? Level G, 6 vols. (Wonder Worldtm Ser.). 16p. 29.95 (978-0-7802-2038-6(2)) Wright Group/McGraw-Hill.

What Will You Pack? (Little Book Practice Reader). (J). 6.47 (978-0-8136-5357-0(6)) Modern Curriculum Pr.

What's for Dinner? Level T. Group 1, 6 vols. (Sunshine Ser.). 48p. 44.95 (978-0-7802-6099-3(6)) Wright Group/McGraw-Hill.

What's in the Bag?, 6 vols. (Multicultural Programs Ser.). 16p. (gr. 1-3). 24.95 (978-0-7802-9218-5(9)) Wright Group/McGraw-Hill.

What's Inside? Level M, 6 vols. (Wonder Worldtm Ser.). 16p. 34.95 (978-0-7802-2916-7(9)) Wright Group/McGraw-Hill.

When the Sun Goes Down: Level H, 6 vols. (Wonder Worldtm Ser.). 16p. 29.95 (978-0-7802-2040-9(4)) Wright Group/McGraw-Hill.

Where Can a Hippo Hide? (Little Book Practice Reader). (J). (978-0-8136-1967-5(X)) Modern Curriculum Pr.

Where Did My Toothbrush Go? (J). (gr. 2-3). 75.00 (978-0-669-13698-2(0)) Houghton Mifflin Harcourt School Pubs.

Where do all the Birds Go? Level Q, 6 vols. (Wonder Worldtm Ser.). 48p. 39.95 (978-0-7802-2955-6(X)) Wright Group/McGraw-Hill.

Where do I Sleep? Level Q, 6 vols. (Wonder Worldtm Ser.). 48p. 39.95 (978-0-7802-2956-3(8)) Wright Group/McGraw-Hill.

Where Do We Go? (Little Book Practice Reader). (J). 6.47 (978-0-8136-5352-5(5)) Modern Curriculum Pr.

Where Is My Caterpillar? Level J, 6 vols. (Wonder Worldtm Ser.). 16p. 29.95 (978-0-7802-1056-1(5)) Wright Group/McGraw-Hill.

Where's Sylvester's Bed? Level G, 6 vols. (Wonder Worldtm Ser.). 16p. 29.95 (978-0-7802-1251-0(7)) Wright Group/McGraw-Hill.

Whiskers: Level A, 6 vols. (Wonder Worldtm Ser.). 16p. 24.95 (978-0-7802-2917-4(7)) Wright Group/McGraw-Hill.

Who Is Quick? Benchmark Assessment for Level A: Level A, 6 vols. (Wright Skills Ser.). 12p. (gr. k-3). 17.95 (978-0-322-03127-2(3)) Wright Group/McGraw-Hill.

Why do I Need to Know When?, 6 vols. (Multicultural Programs Ser.). 16p. (gr. 1-3). 24.95 (978-0-7802-9221-5(9)) Wright Group/McGraw-Hill.

The Wigglewaggle-Yipperlick. 2004. (Literacy Think-Togethers Ser.). 16-24p. (gr. 2-3). pap. 31.50 (978-0-322-06356-3(6)) Wright Group/McGraw-Hill.

Wild Cats: Level P, 6 vols. (Wonder Worldtm Ser.). 48p. 39.95 (978-0-7802-7069-5(X)) Wright Group/McGraw-Hill.

The Wild Wind: Big Book: Level I. Group 2. (Story Box Ser.). 16p. 31.50 (978-0-322-02467-0(6)) Wright Group/McGraw-Hill.

Wildlife Watching: Level R, 6 vols. (Wonder Worldtm Ser.). 48p. 44.95 (978-0-7802-7076-3(2)) Wright Group/McGraw-Hill.

Will Eve Win? Long Vowels e, y, CVCe & Final y Patterns: Level B, 6 vols. (Wright Skills Ser.). 16p. (gr. k-3). 17.95 (978-0-322-01469-5(7)) Wright Group/McGraw-Hill.

Will it Rain on the Parade? Level J, 6 vols. (Wonder Worldtm Ser.). 16p. 29.95 (978-0-7802-4623-2(3)) Wright Group/McGraw-Hill.

William H. Sadlier Staff. Ah-choo! 2005. (Fluent Library). (gr. 1-3). 29.34 (978-0-8215-8962-5(8)) Sadlier, William H. Inc.

—All Mixed Up. 2005. (Early Library). (gr. k-2). 24.00 net. (978-0-8215-8951-9(2)) Sadlier, William H. Inc.

—A Basket Full of Surprises. 2005. (Emergent Library: Vol. 2). (gr. -1-1). 24.00 net. (978-0-8215-8925-0(3)) Sadlier, William H. Inc.

—The Best Place. 2005. (Early Library). (gr. k-2). 24.00 net. (978-0-8215-8944-1(X)) Sadlier, William H. Inc.

—The Best Ride: Big Book, Vol. 2. 2005. (Emergent Library: Vol. 1). (gr. -1-1). 24.00 net. (978-0-8215-8905-2(9)) Sadlier, William H. Inc.

—Brush, Brush, Brush! 2005. (Emergent (Prek-2) Health Package Ser.). 12p. (gr. -1-1). 25.20 (978-0-8215-7849-0(9)) Sadlier, William H. Inc.

—The Cheerful King, Vol. 2. 2005. (Fluent Library). (gr. 1-3). 29.34 (978-0-8215-8967-0(9)) Sadlier, William H. Inc.

—Come Meet Some Seals, Vol. 2. 2005. (Early Library). (gr. k-2). 24.00 net. (978-0-8215-8959-5(8)) Sadlier, William H. Inc.

—Content Area Readers Library: Early (K-2) 2005. (Content Area Readers Ser.). (gr. -1-2). 465.00 (978-0-8215-7809-4(X)) Sadlier, William H. Inc.

—Content Area Readers Library: Emergent (PreK-1) 2005. (Content Area Readers Ser.). (gr. -1-2). 498.00 (978-0-8215-7885-8(5)) Sadlier, William H. Inc.

—Did You Know?, Vol. 2. 2005. (Early Library). (gr. k-2). 24.00 net. (978-0-8215-8947-2(4)) Sadlier, William H. Inc.

—Discovering Dinosaurs, Vol. 2. 2005. (Fluent Library). (gr. 1-3). 29.34 (978-0-8215-8966-3(0)) Sadlier, William H. Inc.

—Do You See a Dozen? Big Book, Vol. 2. 2005. (Emergent Library: Vol. 1). (gr. -1-1). 24.00 net. (978-0-8215-8907-6(5)) Sadlier, William H. Inc.

—Don't Tell! 2005. (Early Library). (gr. k-2). 24.00 net. (978-0-8215-8954-0(7)) Sadlier, William H. Inc.

—Emergent Library. 2005. (Little Books & Big Books Ser.). (gr. -1-1). 573.00 (978-0-8215-8861-1(3)); Vol. 2. 573.00 (978-0-8215-8871-0(0)) Sadlier, William H. Inc.

—Emergent Library I Big Book Package. 2005. (Little Books & Big Books Ser.). (gr. -1-1). 450.00 (978-0-8215-8864-2(8)) Sadlier, William H. Inc.

—Emergent Library I Little Book. 2005. (Little Books & Big Books Ser.). (gr. -1-1). 479.00 net. (978-0-8215-8863-5(X)) Sadlier, William H. Inc.

—Emergent Super Libraries, 2 vols. 2005. (Emergent Libraries Ser.). (gr. -1-1). 1749.00 (978-0-8215-8855-0(9)) Sadlier, William H. Inc.

—Felix, the Very Hungry Fish. 2005. (Emergent Library: Vol. 2). (gr. -1-1). 24.00 net. (978-0-8215-8920-5(2)) Sadlier, William H. Inc.

—Good Food. 2005. (Emergent (Prek-2) Health Package Ser.). 12p. (gr. -1-1). 25.20 (978-0-8215-7847-6(2)) Sadlier, William H. Inc.

—Harry's Hat. 2005. (Emergent Library: Vol. 2). (gr. -1-1). 24.00 net. (978-0-8215-8924-3(5)) Sadlier, William H. Inc.

—Here Comes the Rain! 2005. (Emergent Library: Vol. 2). (gr. -1-1). 24.00 net. (978-0-8215-8933-5(4)) Sadlier, William H. Inc.

—How Many Are Here? Big Book. 2005. (Emergent Library: Vol. 1). (gr. -1-1). 24.00 net. (978-0-8215-8904-5(0)) Sadlier, William H. Inc.

—I Have a Question Vol. 4: Big Book. 2005. (Emergent Library: Vol. 1). (gr. -1-1). 24.00 net. (978-0-8215-8916-8(4)) Sadlier, William H. Inc.

—I Love to Read, Vol. 3. 2005. (Emergent Library: Vol. 1). (gr. -1-1). 24.00 net. (978-0-8215-8913-7(X)) Sadlier, William H. Inc.

—In January & June, Vol. 4. 2005. (Emergent Library: Vol. 1). (gr. -1-1). 24.00 net. (978-0-8215-8915-1(6)) Sadlier, William H. Inc.

—Joey's Rowboat, Vol. 2. 2005. (Early Library). (gr. k-2). 24.00 net. (978-0-8215-8957-1(1)) Sadlier, William H. Inc.

—Keeping Baby Animals Safe. 2005. (Emergent Library: Vol. 2). (gr. -1-1). 24.00 net. (978-0-8215-8934-2(2)) Sadlier, William H. Inc.

—Look at the Pictures. 2005. (Early Library). (gr. k-2). 24.00 net. (978-0-8215-8941-0(5)) Sadlier, William H. Inc.

—A Party for Nine: Big Book, Vol. 2. 2005. (Emergent Library: Vol. 1). (gr. -1-1). 24.00 net. (978-0-8215-8909-0(1)) Sadlier, William H. Inc.

—Show & Tell. 2005. (Emergent Library: Vol. 2). (gr. -1-1). 24.00 net. (978-0-8215-8923-6(7)) Sadlier, William H. Inc.

—The Tongue Twister Prize. 2005. (Fluent Library). (gr. 1-3). 29.34 (978-0-8215-8961-8(X)) Sadlier, William H. Inc.

—Too Small Jill, Vol. 2. 2005. (Fluent Library). (gr. 1-3). 29.34 (978-0-8215-8965-6(2)) Sadlier, William H. Inc.

—The Trash Can Band. 2005. (Fluent Library). (gr. 1-3). 29.34 (978-0-8215-8964-9(4)) Sadlier, William H. Inc.

—Ultra-Saver Library Emergent, Early, & Fluent. 2005. (Little Books & Big Books Ser.). (gr. -1-3). 2727.00 (978-0-8215-8850-5(8)) Sadlier, William H. Inc.

—Valentine's Checkup. 2005. (Emergent Library: Vol. 2). (gr. -1-1). 24.00 net. (978-0-8215-8937-3(7)) Sadlier, William H. Inc.

—Violets & Vegetables Vol. 4: Big Book. 2005. (Emergent Library: Vol. 1). (gr. -1-1). 24.00 net. (978-0-8215-8917-5(2)) Sadlier, William H. Inc.

—Weather Wise, Vol. 3. 2005. (Emergent Library: Vol. 1). (gr. -1-1). 24.00 net. (978-0-8215-8911-3(3)) Sadlier, William H. Inc.

—Zack Can Fix It! Vol. 4: Big Book. 2005. (Emergent Library: Vol. 1). (gr. -1-1). 24.00 net. (978-0-8215-8919-9(9)) Sadlier, William H. Inc.

Williams, Dinah. I Can Be Kind Lap Book. Mones, Marc, illus. 2014. (MySELF Ser.). (J). (gr. -1-k). 27.00 (978-1-4788-0504-5(8)) Newmark Learning LLC.

—I Can Follow the Rules. Patton, Julia, illus. 2014. (J). (gr. -1). 3.99 (978-1-4788-0473-4(4)) Newmark Learning LLC.

—I Can Follow the Rules Lap Book. Patton, Julia, illus. 2014. (MySELF Ser.). (J). (gr. -1-k). 27.00 (978-1-4788-0510-6(2)) Newmark Learning LLC.

Williams, Rozanne Lanczak. Mice Are Nice. Moore, Margie, illus. 2005. (Reading for Fluency Ser.). 16p. (J). pap. 3.49 (978-1-59198-156-5(5), 4256) Creative Teaching Pr., Inc.

—Old MacDonald's Funny Farm, Vol. 4261. Starr Taylor, Bridget, illus. 2005. (Reading for Fluency Ser.). 16p. (J). pap. 3.49 (978-1-59198-161-9(1), 4261) Creative Teaching Pr., Inc.

The Witch of Blackbird Pond: Response Journal. 2003. 36p. (YA). (978-1-58049-993-4(7), RJ93) Prestwick Hse., Inc.

Wolf Tracks, 6 vols. (Book2WebTM Ser.). (gr. 4-8). 36.50 (978-0-322-02971-2(6)) Wright Group/McGraw-Hill.

Wonder World: Early Emergent - 1 Each of 10 Student Books: Level A. 41.95 (978-0-7802-8265-0(5)) Wright Group/McGraw-Hill.

Wonder World: Early Emergent - 1 Each of 10 Student Books: Level B. 41.95 (978-0-7802-8266-7(3)) Wright Group/McGraw-Hill.

Wonder World: Early Emergent - 1 Each of 10 Student Books: Level C. 41.95 (978-0-7802-8267-4(1)) Wright Group/McGraw-Hill.

Wonder World: Early Emergent - 1 Each of 10 Student Books: Level D. 41.95 (978-0-7802-8268-1(X)) Wright Group/McGraw-Hill.

Wonder World: Early Emergent - 1 Each of 19 Big Books: Levels A-N. 476.95 (978-0-7802-8530-9(1)) Wright Group/McGraw-Hill.

Wonder World: Early Emergent - Complete Kit. (gr. k-18). 353.50 (978-0-7802-9042-6(9)) Wright Group/McGraw-Hill.

Wonder World: Early Fluency - 1 Each of 12 Student Books: Level K. 69.95 (978-0-7802-8275-9(2)) Wright Group/McGraw-Hill.

Wonder World: Early Fluency - 1 Each of 12 Student Books: Level L. 69.95 (978-0-7802-8276-6(0)) Wright Group/McGraw-Hill.

Wonder World: Early Fluency - 1 Each of 12 Student Books: Level M. 69.95 (978-0-7802-8277-3(9)) Wright Group/McGraw-Hill.

Wonder World: Early Fluency - Complete Kit. (gr. 1-2). 540.95 (978-0-7802-9044-0(5)) Wright Group/McGraw-Hill.

Wonder World: Fluency-1 Each of 10 Chapter Books: Level O. (Wonder Worldtm Ser.). (gr. 2-3). 66.95 (978-0-7802-8279-7(5)) Wright Group/McGraw-Hill.

Wonder World: Fluency-1 Each of 10 Chapter Books: Level P. (Wonder Worldtm Ser.). (gr. 2-3). 66.95 (978-0-7802-8280-3(9)) Wright Group/McGraw-Hill.

Wonder World: Fluency-1 Each of 10 Chapter Books: Level Q. (Wonder Worldtm Ser.). (gr. 2-3). 66.95 (978-0-7802-8281-0(7)) Wright Group/McGraw-Hill.

Wonder World: Fluency-1 Each of 10 Chapter Books: Level R. (Wonder Worldtm Ser.). (gr. 2-3). 74.95 (978-0-7802-8282-7(5)) Wright Group/McGraw-Hill.

Wonder World: Fluency-1 Each of 12 Student Books: Level N. 69.95 (978-0-7802-8278-0(7)) Wright Group/McGraw-Hill.

Wonder World: Levels O-R. (Wonder Worldtm Ser.). (gr. 2-3). 275.95 (978-0-7802-8283-4(3)) Wright Group/McGraw-Hill.

Wonder World: Upper Emergent - 1 Each of 12 Student Books: Level E. 59.95 (978-0-7802-8269-8(8)) Wright Group/McGraw-Hill.

Wonder World: Upper Emergent - 1 Each of 12 Student Books: Level F. 59.95 (978-0-7802-8270-4(1)) Wright Group/McGraw-Hill.

Wonder World: Upper Emergent - 1 Each of 12 Student Books: Level G. 59.95 (978-0-7802-8271-1(X)) Wright Group/McGraw-Hill.

Wonder World: Upper Emergent - Complete Kit. (gr. 1-18). 396.95 (978-0-7802-9043-3(7)) Wright Group/McGraw-Hill.

Wonder World: Upper Emergent - Upper Emergent - Complete Kit, Vol. 2. (gr. 1-18). 396.95 (978-0-7802-9041-9(0)) Wright Group/McGraw-Hill.

Wonder World: Upper Emergent-1 Each of 12 Student Books: Level H. 59.95 (978-0-7802-8272-8(8)) Wright Group/McGraw-Hill.

Wonder World: Upper Emergent-1 Each of 12 Student Books: Level I. 59.95 (978-0-7802-8273-5(6)) Wright Group/McGraw-Hill.

Wonder World: Upper Emergent-1 Each of 12 Student Books: Level J. 59.95 (978-0-7802-8274-2(4)) Wright Group/McGraw-Hill.

Woodland Mysteries. (gr. 3-7). Set 1. 424.95 (978-0-7802-7245-3(5))Set 2. 424.95 (978-0-7802-8002-1(4))Set 3. 479.95 (978-0-322-02629-2(6)) Wright Group/McGraw-Hill.

Woodland Mysteries: Classroom Library Set. (gr. 3-7). 313.95 (978-0-322-02628-5(8)) Wright Group/McGraw-Hill.

Woodland Mysteries: Complete Boxed Set. (gr. 3-7). 1238.95 (978-0-322-02625-4(3)) Wright Group/McGraw-Hill.

The Woodlanders Begin, 6 vols., Vol. 3. (Woodland Mysteriestm Ser.). 133p. (gr. 3-7). 42.50 (978-0-322-02368-0(8)) Wright Group/McGraw-Hill.

Woods, Irons, & Greens: 6 Each of 1 Anthology, 6 vols. (Wildcats Ser.). 32p. (gr. 2-8). (978-0-322-00589-1(2)) Wright Group/McGraw-Hill.

Word Work Assessment Guide. (Fast Track Reading Ser.). (gr. 4-8). 29.50 (978-0-322-05948-1(8)) Wright Group/McGraw-Hill.

A World Worth Keeping: Level T. Group 1, 6 vols. (Sunshine Ser.). 48p. 44.95 (978-0-7802-6092-4(9)) Wright Group/McGraw-Hill.

The Wrecks: Level T. Group 2, 6 vols. (Sunshine Ser.). 48p. 44.95 (978-0-7802-4177-0(0)) Wright Group/McGraw-Hill.

Wrestle Mania: Magazine Anthology: Level 5, 6 vols. (Comprehension Strand Ser.). (gr. 4-8). 54.00 (978-0-322-06036-4(2)) Wright Group/McGraw-Hill.

Wright Group, Incorporated Staff. Brice & the Whale: Decodable Books, 6 vols. (Fast Track Reading Ser.). 24p. (gr. 4-8). 40.95 (978-0-322-05981-8(X)) Wright Group/McGraw-Hill.

The Wright Skills: Level B Sets - Long vowels only: 1 Each of 6 Titles. (gr. k-3). 17.95 (978-0-322-01934-8(6)) Wright Group/McGraw-Hill.

The Wright Skills: Level B Sets - Long vowels only: 6 Each of 6 Titles. (gr. k-3). 109.50 (978-0-322-01935-5(4)) Wright Group/McGraw-Hill.

The Wright Skills: Level C Sets - 1 Each of 16 Titles. (gr. k-3). 69.95 (978-0-322-00734-5(8)) Wright Group/McGraw-Hill.

The Wright Skills: Level C Sets - 6 Each of 16 Titles. (gr. k-3). 322.95 (978-0-322-00813-7(1)) Wright Group/McGraw-Hill.

A Writer's Work: Level N, 6 vols. (Wonder Worldtm Ser.). 48p. 34.95 (978-0-7802-2918-1(5)) Wright Group/McGraw-Hill.

Yates, Irene. How to Be a Wizard at Reading. 48p. (J). (gr. 2-6). pap. (978-1-875739-66-0(1)) Wizard Bks.

The Zebra's Yellow Van. (Little Book Practice Reader). (J). (978-0-8136-5374-7(6)) Modern Curriculum Pr.

Zeros & Ones, 6 vols. (Wildcats Ser.). 32p. (gr. 2-8). (978-0-322-02438-0(2)) Wright Group/McGraw-Hill.

Zone Zoomers: Level 2, 6 vols. (Fluency Strand Ser.). (gr. 4-8). 45.00 (978-1-4045-1213-9(6)) Wright Group/McGraw-Hill.

The Zoo: Big Book: Level B. (Wonder Worldtm Ser.). 16p. 26.50 (978-0-7802-2832-0(4)) Wright Group/McGraw-Hill.

The Zoo: Level B, 6 vols. (Wonder Worldtm Ser.). 16p. 24.95 (978-0-7802-1058-5(1)) Wright Group/McGraw-Hill.

READING—FICTION

Alexander, Kwame. Booked. 2016. (ENG.). 320p. (J). (gr. 5-7). 16.99 (978-0-544-57098-6(7), HMH Books For Young Readers) Houghton Mifflin Harcourt Publishing Co.

—Booked. 2016. lib. bdg. 29.40 (978-0-606-37992-2(4)) Turtleback Bks.

—Surf's Up. Miyares, Daniel, illus. 2016. (ENG.). 32p. (J). 17.95 (978-0-7358-4220-5(5)) North-South Bks., Inc.

Auch, Mary Jane. Souperchicken. Auch, Herm, illus. 2004. (ENG.). 32p. (J). (gr. -1-3). reprint ed. pap. 6.95 (978-0-8234-1829-9(4)) Holiday Hse., Inc.

Banks, Kate. The Bear in the Book, 1 vol. Hallensleben, Georg, illus. 2012. (ENG.). 36p. (J). (gr. -1-1). 16.99 (978-0-374-30591-8(9), 9780374305918, Farrar, Straus & Giroux (BYR)) Farrar, Straus & Giroux.

Bender, Esther. Elisabeth & the Windmill. 2003. (ENG.). 112p. (J). (gr. 3-7). pap. 6.99 (978-0-8361-9204-9(4)) Herald Pr.

Bertram, Debbie & Bloom, Susan. The Best Place to Read. 2007. lib. bdg. 18.40 (978-1-4177-9097-5(0), Turtleback) Turtleback Bks.

Biery, Martha. Words Aren't Fair. 2009. 46p. pap. 15.75 (978-1-60860-793-8(3), Eloquent Bks.) Strategic Book Publishing & Rights Agency (SBPRA).

Bloom, Susan & Bertram, Debbie. The Best Place to Read. Garland, Michael, illus. 2007. (ENG.). 32p. (J). (gr. -1-2). pap. 7.99 (978-0-375-83757-9(4), Dragonfly Bks.) Random Hse. Children's Bks.

Blum, Denise. Anything Is Possible: The Ben Carson Story. Rea, Nathan, illus. 2015. (ENG.). 28p. (J). pap. 10.00 (978-0-9899479-1-6(2)) Mainstay Publishing.

Brown, Marc. Arthur's Reading Trick. 2009. (Step into Reading Ser.). (ENG., Illus.). 24p. (J). (gr. k-3). pap. 3.99 (978-0-375-82977-2(6), Random Hse. Bks. for Young Readers) Random Hse. Children's Bks.

Calvani, Mayra. Humberto, the Bookworm Hamster. Grady, Kit, illus. 2009. 20p. pap. 10.95 (978-1-935137-92-4(1)) Guardian Angel Publishing, Inc.

Capucilli, Alyssa Satin. Biscuit Loves the Library. Schories, Pat, illus. 2014. (My First I Can Read Ser.). (ENG.). 32p. (J). (gr. -1-3). 16.99 (978-0-06-193507-7(7)); pap. 3.99 (978-0-06-193506-0(9)) HarperCollins Pubs.

—Biscuit Phonics Fun. Schories, Pat, illus. 2008. (My First I Can Read Ser.). (ENG.). 100p. (J). (gr. -1 — 1). pap. 12.99 (978-0-06-143204-0(0)) HarperCollins Pubs.

Carlson, Nancy. I Don't Like to Read! Carlson, Nancy & Carlson, illus. 2009. (ENG.). 32p. (J). (gr. k-2). pap. 6.99 (978-0-14-241451-4(4), Puffin Books) Penguin Young Readers Group.

Chichester Clark, Emma. Bears Don't Read! Chichester Clark, Emma, illus. 2016. (Illus.). 32p. (J). 12.99 (978-1-61067-366-2(2)) Kane Miller.

Cline-Ransome, Lesa. Light in the Darkness: A Story about How Slaves Learned in Secret. Ransome, James E., illus. 2013. (ENG.). 40p. (J). (gr. k-3). 16.99 (978-1-4231-3495-4(8), Jump at the Sun) Hyperion Bks. for Children.

Cordoza, Sandra Sandlin. Smarticus & the Abc's. 2010. 24p. pap. 11.50 (978-1-60860-407-4(1), Eloquent Bks.) Strategic Book Publishing & Rights Agency (SBPRA).

Coulton, Mia. Danny & Heather Share. Coulton, Mia, photos by. 2003. (ENG., Illus.). 16p. pap. 5.35 (978-0-9720295-8-2(3)) Maryruth Bks., Inc.

Cuyler, Margery. Hooray for Reading Day! Howard, Arthur, illus. 2008. (Jessica Worries Ser.). (ENG.). 32p. (J). (gr. k-3). 17.99 (978-0-689-86188-8(5), Simon & Schuster Bks. For Young Readers) Simon & Schuster Bks. For Young Readers.

Dail, Maggie. Getting to First Base - Chris Struggles to Read. 2006. 157p. pap. 13.95 (978-1-4116-8125-5(8)) Lulu Pr., Inc.

Damschroder, Scott. Pinky's Rainy Day: Pinky Padooka takes a trip to Imaginationville. Faust, Laurie, illus. 2004. 36p. (J). lib. bdg. 19.95 (978-0-9754728-0-4(1)) Big Ransom Studio.

Danziger, Paula. It's a Fair Day, Amber Brown. Ross, Tony, illus. 2003. (Readalongs for Beginning Readers Ser.). (J). 25.95 incl. audio (978-1-59112-246-3(5)); pap. 29.95 incl. audio (978-1-59112-247-0(3)) Live Oak Media.

DeClements, Barthe & Declements, Barthe. Sixth Grade Can Really Kill You. 2008. (ENG.). 160p. (J). (gr. 3-7). 5.99 (978-0-14-241380-7(1), Puffin Books) Penguin Young Readers Group.

Friden, Chris & Rodríguez Braojos, Alberto. Storytime with Paige. Jaraiz, David, illus. 2008. (J). (978-0-9758785-8-3(1)); (978-0-9801849-4-5(0)) Haydenburn Lane.

Fyne, Olga. My Shadow Is a Copycat. 2009. 56p. pap. 21.99 (978-1-4389-3671-0(0)) AuthorHouse.

Garson, Cindy. Welcome to Kristy's Farm, Book 2 (Black & White Version) 2007. 104p. pap. 14.00 (978-1-4303-0366-4(2)) Lulu Pr., Inc.

—Welcome to Kristy's Farm, Book 4. 2007. 104p. pap. 19.50 *(978-1-4303-1000-6(6))* Lulu Pr., Inc.

Gaydos, Nora. Playful Pals, Level 1. Sams, B. B., illus. 2003. (Now I'm Reading!). 128p. (J). (gr. -1-2). 14.99 *(978-1-58476-243-0(8))* Innovative Kids.

—Playful Pals. Sams, B. B., illus. 2003. (NIR! Leveled Readers Ser.). (ENG.). 128p. (J). (gr. -1-3). 16.99 *(978-1-58476-203-4(9),* Now I'm Reading!) Random Hse. Children's Bks.

Giff, Patricia Reilly. Eleven. 2009. (ENG.). 176p. (J). (gr. 3-7). 7.99 *(978-0-440-23802-7(1),* Yearling) Random Hse. Children's Bks.

Gikow, Louise. I Can Read. Patience, John, illus. 2004. (My First Reader Ser.). 31p. (J). 18.50 *(978-0-516-24678-9(X),* Children's Pr.) Scholastic Library Publishing.

Gutman, Dan. Miss Klute Is a Hoot! Paillot, Jim, illus. 2014. (My Weirder School Ser.: 11). 112p. (J). (gr. 1-5). 15.89 *(978-0-06-219845-7(9));* (ENG.). pap. 4.99 *(978-0-06-219844-0(0))* HarperCollins Pubs.

—Miss Klute Is a Hoot! 2014. (My Weirder School Ser.: 11). (J). lib. bdg. 14.75 *(978-0-606-35503-2(0))* Turtleback Bks.

Hardinge, Frances. Fly by Night. 2006. 487p. (J). (gr. 5-9). 16.99 *(978-0-06-087627-2(1))* HarperCollins Pubs.

Hillert, Margaret. Dear Dragon Learns to Read. Pullan, Jack, illus. 2015. (BeginningtoRead Ser.). (ENG.). 32p. (J). (gr. k-2). lib. bdg. 22.60 *(978-1-59953-707-8(9))* Norwood Hse. Pr.

Hills, Tad. How Rocket Learned to Read. Hills, Tad, illus. 2010. (ENG., Illus.). 40p. (J). (gr. -1-2). 17.99 *(978-0-375-85899-4(7),* Schwartz & Wade Bks.) Random Hse. Children's Bks.

—Rocket's Learning Box, 2 vols. Hills, Tad, illus. 2012. (ENG., Illus.). 40p. (J). (gr. -1-3). 35.98 *(978-0-307-98235-3(1),* Schwartz & Wade Bks.) Random Hse. Children's Bks.

Homberg, Ruth. The Little Mermaid Step into Reading (Disney Princess) RH Disney Staff, illus. 2013. (Step into Reading Ser.). (ENG.). 32p. (J). (gr. -1-1). 3.99 *(978-0-7364-8128-1(1),* RH/Disney) Random Hse. Children's Bks.

Hunsaker, Debbie. Reading Rug. 2012. 28p. pap. 19.99 *(978-1-4678-7018-4(8))* AuthorHouse.

Hunt, Lynda Mullaly. COMO PEZ EN EL ÁRBOL: UNA NOVELA SOBRE LA DISLEXIA. 2016. (SPA.). 240p. (J). (gr. 4). pap. 13.95 *(978-84-15594-69-7(0),* Nube De Tinta) Penguin Random House Grupo Editorial ESP. Dist: Two Rivers Distribution.

—Fish in a Tree. (ENG.). (J). (gr. 5). 2017. 304p. 8.99 *(978-0-14-242642-5(3),* Puffin Books) 2015. 288p. 16.99 *(978-0-399-16259-6(3),* Nancy Paulsen Books) Penguin Young Readers Group.

—Fish in a Tree. 2017. lib. bdg. 19.65 ***(978-0-606-39991-3(7))*** Turtleback Bks.

Kamins, Julie Firstenberg. Why Am I at the Red Table? Long, Carlos, illus. 2008. 32p. (J). 13.95 *(978-0-9771566-9-6(9))* Librujas.

Kaniecki, Larry. Ho Ho the Elf. 2011. 44p. pap. 21.99 *(978-1-4628-6807-0(X))* Xlibris Corp.

Kemnitz, Dianna. Sing with Jack. 2012. 38p. 24.95 *(978-1-4626-5656-1(0))* America Star Bks.

Kertell, Lynn Maslen. Alphabet. Maslen, John R. & Hendra, Sue, illus. 2008. (Bob Bks.). (ENG.). 144p. (J). (gr. -1-3). pap. 16.99 *(978-0-545-01921-7(4),* Cartwheel Bks.) Scholastic, Inc.

Lee, Quinlan B. The Circus Comes to Town. 2005. (Illus.). (J). *(978-0-439-77931-9(6))* Scholastic, Inc.

—A Great Day for Soccer. 2005. (Illus.). (J). *(978-0-439-77921-0(9))* Scholastic, Inc.

—Sail Away. 2005. (Illus.). (J). *(978-0-439-77933-3(2))* Scholastic, Inc.

—Super Spies. 2005. (Illus.). (J). *(978-0-439-77923-4(5))* Scholastic, Inc.

Lorton, Sylvia. Johnny's Wish. 2013. 24p. pap. 24.95 *(978-1-63004-228-8(5))* America Star Bks.

Maltby, Robert I. Diquan & the Book Monster, 1 vol. 2009. 39p. pap. 24.95 *(978-1-61546-964-2(8))* America Star Bks.

Marcotte, Danielle. Mom, Dad, Our Books, & Me. Bisaillon, Josée, illus. 2016. (ENG.). 32p. (J). (gr. -1-3). 16.95 *(978-1-77147-201-2(4),* Owlkids) Owlkids Bks. Inc. CAN. Dist: Publishers Group West (PGW).

Mazurak, Tena. Harley Hits a Homer. 2010. 24p. pap. 12.99 *(978-1-4490-9977-0(7))* AuthorHouse.

Mcghee, Alison. Julia Gillian (and the Dream of the Dog) Kozjan, Drazen, illus. (Julia Gillian Ser.). (ENG.). 336p. (J). (gr. 3-7). 2011. pap. 6.99 *(978-0-545-03353-4(5))* 2010. 16.99 *(978-0-545-03351-0(9))* Scholastic, Inc. (Scholastic Pr.).

Nez, John. One Smart Cookie. Nez, John, illus. 2006. (ENG., Illus.). 32p. (J). (gr. k-3). lib. bdg. 16.99 *(978-0-8075-6099-0(5))* Whitman, Albert & Co.

Papp, Lisa. Madeline Finn & the Library Dog, 1 vol. Papp, Lisa, illus. 2016. (ENG., Illus.). 32p. (J). (gr. -1-3). 16.95 *(978-1-56145-910-0(0))* Peachtree Pubs.

Parsons, Corey. I Can Read. 2005. 29p. (J). 9.98 *(978-1-4116-6101-1(X))* Lulu Pr., Inc.

Paterson, Katherine. Marvin One Too Many. Clark Brown, Jane, illus. 2003. 28.95 incl. audio compact disk *(978-1-59112-635-5(5));* 25.95 incl. audio *(978-1-59112-254-8(6));* pap. 31.95 incl. audio compact disk *(978-1-59112-636-2(3));* (J). pap. 29.95 incl. audio *(978-1-59112-255-5(4))* Live Oak Media.

Paul, Sherry. Finn the Foolish Fish: Trouble with Bubbles, Set. Miller, Bob, illus. (See How I Read Ser.). 32p. (Orig.). (J). (gr. -1-2). pap. 14.10 *(978-0-675-01084-9(5))* CPI Publishing, Inc.

—Two-B & the Rock 'n' Roll Band, Set. Murphy, Bob, illus. (See How I Read Ser.). 32p. (Orig.). (J). (gr. -1-2). pap. 14.10 *(978-0-675-01082-5(9))* CPI Publishing, Inc.

Pearson, Susan. How to Teach a Slug to Read, 0 vols. Slonim, David, illus. 2011. (ENG.). 32p. (J). (gr. k-3). 16.99 *(978-0-7614-5805-0(0),* 9780761458050, Two Lions) Amazon Publishing.

Play, Laugh, & Learn All Year Long. 2007. (ENG., Illus.). 28p. (J). (gr. -1-1). 16.99 *(978-1-59069-503-6(8),* 1P1000) Studio Mouse LLC.

Polacco, Patricia. Gracias, Senor Falker. 2006. (SPA., Illus.). 34p. (J). (gr. 2-3). per. 7.99 *(978-1-933032-02-3(2),* LC34004) Lectorum Pubns., Inc.

—Thank You, Mr. Falker. Polacco, Patricia, illus. 2012. (ENG., Illus.). 40p. (J). (gr. k-3). 12.99 *(978-0-399-25762-9(4),* Philomel Bks.) Penguin Young Readers Group.

R. N., Lavanya. The Bookworm. Suleman, Shilo Shiv, illus. 2013. (ENG.). 32p. (J). (gr. k). pap. 9.95 *(978-81-8190-180-4(0))* Karadi Tales Co. Pvt, Ltd. IND. Dist: Consortium Bk. Sales & Distribution.

Radlauer. Molly at the Library. 2007. (ENG.). 32p. (J). (gr. -1-2). 8.99 *(978-1-4169-6835-1(0),* Simon & Schuster/Paula Wiseman Bks.) Simon & Schuster/Paula Wiseman Bks.

RH Disney Staff. Scaring Lessons. RH Disney Staff, illus. 2013. (Step into Reading Ser.). (ENG., Illus.). 32p. (J). (gr. -1-1). 3.99 *(978-0-7364-3035-7(0),* RH/Disney) Random Hse. Children's Bks.

Schubert, Leda. Reading to Peanut. Haley, Amanda, illus. 2011. (ENG.). 32p. (J). 16.95 *(978-0-8234-2339-2(5))* Holiday Hse., Inc.

Shaw, Nancy. Elena's Story. 2012. (Tales of the World Ser.). (ENG., Illus.). 32p. (J). (gr. 1-5). 16.95 *(978-1-58536-528-9(9))* Sleeping Bear Pr.

Sierra, Judy. Born to Read. Brown, Marc, illus. 2008. (ENG.). 40p. (J). (gr. -1-2). 16.99 *(978-0-375-84687-8(5),* Knopf Bks. for Young Readers) Random Hse. Children's Bks.

Spurling, Wesley. Books for Jacob. 2009. 24p. pap. 14.79 *(978-1-4389-2231-7(0))* AuthorHouse.

Toles-Stotts, LaShunda. When I Learned to Read. Stotts, Jasmyn & Jayda, illus. l.t. ed. 2005. 36p. (J). per. 11.99 *(978-1-59879-071-9(4))* Lifevest Publishing, Inc.

Walker, Kate. I Hate Books! Cox, David, illus. 2007. (ENG.). 88p. (J). (gr. 1-4). 16.95 *(978-0-8126-2745-9(8))* Cricket Bks.

Wallace, Suzanne. When I Was a Baby, What Did I Do? What Did I Do? 2012. 28p. pap. 21.99 *(978-1-4771-2144-3(7))* Xlibris Corp.

Walter, Mildred Pitts. Alec's Primer. Johnson, Larry, illus. 2005. (ENG.). 32p. (J). (gr. -1-3). 15.95 *(978-0-916718-20-6(4))* Vermont Folklife Ctr.

Wang, Adria. My World: My Busy Day. Nicholls, Paul, illus. 2005. 10p. (J). 4.95 *(978-1-58117-251-5(6),* Intervisual/Piggy Toes) Bendon, Inc.

Williams, Tova. The Boy Who Did Not Want to Read, 1 vol. Suggs, Aisha, illus. 2010. 36p. pap. 24.95 *(978-1-4489-5705-7(2))* PublishAmerica, Inc.

Yager, Jan. The Reading Rabbit. Lyman, Mitzi, illus. 32p. (J). 2014. (ENG.). 25.95 *(978-1-938998-00-3(6))* 2013. pap. 17.95 *(978-1-938998-01-0(4))* Hannacroix Creek Bks., Inc.

READING—REMEDIAL TEACHING

Sandviks HOP, Inc. Staff. Hooked on English. 2007. 199.99 *(978-1-60143-752-5(8))* HOP, LLC.

READING—STUDY AND TEACHING

see Reading

READING CLINICS

see Reading—Remedial Teaching

READING INTERESTS

see Books and Reading

READING INTERESTS OF CHILDREN

see Children—Books and Reading

REAGAN, RONALD, 1911-2004

Allen, Susan. The Remarkable Ronald Reagan: Cowboy & Commander in Chief. Harrington, Leslie, illus. 2013. (ENG.). 36p. (J). (gr. 1). 16.95 *(978-1-62157-038-7(X))* Regnery Publishing, Inc., An Eagle Publishing Co.

Anderson, Michael, contrib. by. Ronald Reagan. 2012. (Pivotal Presidents: Profiles in Leadership Ser.). (ENG., Illus.). 80p. (YA). (gr. 7-12). 65.80 *(978-1-61530-958-0(6));* lib. bdg. 32.90 *(978-1-61530-944-3(6))* Rosen Publishing Group, Inc., The.

Benge, Janet & Benge, Geoff. Ronald Reagan: Destiny at His Side. 2010. (ENG.). (YA). pap. 9.99 *(978-1-932096-65-1(5))* Emerald Bks.

Benson, Michael. Ronald Reagan. 2004. (Presidential Leaders Ser.). (Illus.). 112p. (J). 29.27 *(978-0-8225-0815-1(X),* Lerner Pubns.) Lerner Publishing Group.

Boshier, Rosa. Ronald Reagan: 40th US President, 1 vol. 2013. (Essential Lives Set 8 Ser.). (ENG.). 112p. (J). (gr. 6-12). lib. bdg. 35.64 *(978-1-61783-895-8(0),* Essential Library) ABDO Publishing Co.

Brill, Marlene Targ. America in the 1980s. 2009. (Decades of Twentieth-Century America Ser.). (ENG.). 144p. (gr. 5-12). lib. bdg. 38.60 *(978-0-8225-7602-0(3))* Lerner Publishing Group.

Britton, Tamara L. Ronald Reagan, 1 vol. 2009. (United States Presidents Ser.). (ENG., Illus.). 40p. (YA). (gr. 3-6). 27.07 *(978-1-60453-471-9(0))* ABDO Publishing Co.

Burgan, Michael. Ronald Reagan. 2011. 128p. pap. 14.99 *(978-0-7566-7739-8(4))* Dorling Kindersley Publishing, Inc.

—Ronald Reagan: A Photographic Story of a Life. 2010. (DK Biography Ser.). (ENG., Illus.). 128p. (J). (gr. 5-12). 6.99 *(978-0-7566-7074-0(8),* DK Children) Dorling Kindersley Publishing, Inc.

Camardella, Michele L. America in The 1980s. 2005. (Decades of American History Ser.). (Illus.). 128p. (gr. 5-8). per. 35.00 *(978-0-8160-5644-6(7))* Facts On File, Inc.

Duffield, Katy S. Ronald Reagan. 2016. (Premier Presidents Ser.). (ENG.). 24p. (J). (gr. 1-4). 27.07 *(978-1-5038-0874-4(2),* 210724) Child's World, Inc., The.

Dunn, Joeming & Dunn, Ben. Ronald Reagan: 40th U. S. President, 1 vol. 2011. (Presidents of the United States Bio-Graphics Ser.). (ENG., Illus.). 32p. (YA). (gr. 3-6). 28.50 *(978-1-61641-649-2(1))* Magic Wagon.

Edwards, Roberta. Hail to the Chiefs, 5 vols. 2013. (Who Was? Ser.). (ENG.). 560p. (J). (gr. 3-7). pap. 24.95 *(978-0-448-48122-7(7),* Grosset & Dunlap) Penguin Young Readers Group.

Gigliotti, Jim. Ronald Reagan, the 40th President. 2016. (First Look at America's Presidents Ser.). (ENG.). 24p. (J). (gr. -1-3). lib. bdg. 17.95 *(978-1-944102-69-2(8))* Bearport Publishing Co., Inc.

Hinkle, Donald. Ronald Reagan: A MyReportLinks.com Book. 2003. (Presidents Ser.). (Illus.). 48p. (J). (gr. 4-10). lib. bdg. 25.26 *(978-0-7660-5112-6(9),* MyReportLinks.com Bks.) Enslow Pubs., Inc.

Mara, Wil. Ronald Reagan. 2010. (Presidents & Their Times 4 Ser.). 96p. (gr. 6). 34.21 *(978-0-7614-4814-3(4))* Marshall Cavendish Corp.

Margaret, Amy. Ronald Reagan Presidential Library. (Presidential Libraries Ser.). 24p. 2009. (gr. 3-3). 42.50 *(978-1-60851-488-5(9))* 2004. (Illus.). (J). lib. bdg. 22.60 *(978-0-8239-6272-3(5))* Rosen Publishing Group, Inc., The. (PowerKids Pr.).

Mattern, Joanne. Nancy Reagan, 1 vol. 2008. (First Ladies Set 1 Ser.). (ENG., Illus.). 32p. (J). (gr. 1-4). 27.07 *(978-1-59928-799-7(4))* ABDO Publishing Co.

Milton, Joyce. Who Was Ronald Reagan? Wolf, Elizabeth & Harrison, Nancy, illus. 2004. (Who Was? Ser.). (ENG.). 112p. (J). (gr. 3-7). pap. 5.99 *(978-0-448-43344-8(3),* Grosset & Dunlap) Penguin Young Readers Group.

Mis, M. S. How to Draw the Life & Times of Ronald Reagan. 2009. (Kid's Guide to Drawing the Presidents of the United States of America Ser.). 32p. (gr. 4-4). 50.50 *(978-1-61511-158-9(1),* PowerKids Pr.) Rosen Publishing Group, Inc., The.

Mis, Melody S. How to Draw the Life & Times of Ronald Reagan. 2007. (Kid's Guide to Drawing the Presidents of the United States of America Ser.). (Illus.). 32p. (YA). (gr. 2-5). 26.50 *(978-1-4042-3016-3(5))* Rosen Publishing Group, Inc., The.

O'Reilly, Bill. The Day the President Was Shot: The Secret Service, the FBI, a Would-Be Killer, & the Attempted Assassination of Ronald Reagan. 2016. (ENG., Illus.). 256p. (J). (gr. 5-9). 19.99 *(978-1-62779-699-6(1),* 9781627796996, Holt, Henry & Co. Bks. For Young Readers) Holt, Henry & Co.

Orr, Tamra. Ronald Reagan. 2004. (Childhoods of the Presidents Ser.). (Illus.). 48p. (J). (gr. 4-18). lib. bdg. 17.95 *(978-1-59084-280-5(4))* Mason Crest.

Patrick, Denise Lewis. Ronald Reagan: From Silver Screen to Oval Office. 2006. 44p. (J). lib. bdg. 15.00 *(978-1-4242-0852-4(1))* Fitzgerald Bks.

Pingry, Patricia A. The Story of Ronald Reagan. Mahan, Ben, illus. 2006. (ENG.). 26p. (J). (gr. -1-k). bds. 7.69 *(978-0-8249-6621-8(X),* Ideal Pubns.) Worthy Publishing.

Ronald Reagan. annuals Date not set. (Starlog Movie Ser.). (YA). pap. *(978-0-934551-04-5(9))* Profile Entertainment, Inc.

Sutcliffe, Jane. Ronald Reagan. 2009. pap. 52.95 *(978-0-7613-4958-7(8))* 2008. (ENG.). 48p. (gr. 3-6). 27.93 *(978-0-8225-8894-8(3),* Lerner Pubns.) Lerner Publishing Group.

Sutherland, James B. Ronald Reagan: Political Star. 2008. (Up Close Ser.). (ENG.). 256p. (YA). (gr. 7-18). 16.99 *(978-0-670-06345-1(2),* Viking Books for Young Readers) Penguin Young Readers Group.

Time for Kids Editors. Time for Kids: Ronald Reagan: From Silver Screen to Oval Office. 2005. (Time for Kids Ser.). (ENG., Illus.). 48p. (J). (gr. 2-4). per. 3.99 *(978-0-06-057626-4(X))* HarperCollins Pubs.

Tucker, Rosalyn. Ronald Reagan, 1 vol. 2014. (Presidential Biographies Ser.). (ENG.). 24p. (gr. k-1). lib. bdg. 26.65 *(978-1-4765-9613-6(1),* Pebble Plus) Capstone Press of Coughlan Cos.

Venezia, Mike. Ronald Reagan: Fortieth President, 1981-1989. Venezia, Mike, illus. 2007. (Getting to Know the U. S. Presidents Ser.). (ENG., Illus.). 32p. (J). (gr. 3-4). 28.00 *(978-0-516-22644-6(4),* Children's Pr.) Scholastic Library Publishing.

Young, Jeff C. Great Communicator: The Story of Ronald Reagan. 2004. (Twentieth Century Leaders Ser.). (Illus.). 128p. (YA). (gr. 6-12). 23.95 *(978-1-931798-10-5(9))* Reynolds, Morgan Inc.

REAL ESTATE

see Real Property

REAL ESTATE BUSINESS

Clark, Betty. Choosing a Career in Real Estate. (World of Work Ser.). 64p. 2009. (gr. 5-5). 58.50 *(978-1-60854-335-9(8))* 2005. (Illus.). (YA). (gr. 7-12). lib. bdg. 31.95 *(978-0-8239-3246-7(X),* WWREES) Rosen Publishing Group, Inc., The.

REAL PROPERTY

Here are entered general works on real property in the legal sense i.e., ownership of land and buildings (immovable property) as opposed to personal property. Works limited to the buying and selling of real property are entered under Real Estate Business. General works on land without the ownership aspect are entered under Land Ue.

see also Farms; Real Estate Business

Boye, B. D. Our New Home. Boye, B. D., illus. l.t. ed. 2005. (Illus.). 18p. (J). per. 4.99 *(978-0-9768078-2-7(3))* Innerchild Publishing, Inc.

Troisi-Paton, Kimberly. Property Rights. 2006. (Bill of Rights Ser.). (ENG., Illus.). 144p. (gr. 10-12). lib. bdg. 43.20 *(978-0-7377-3543-7(0),* Greenhaven Pr., Inc.) Cengage Gale.

Wooten, Sara McIntosh. Donald Trump: From Real Estate to Reality TV. 2008. (People to Know Today Ser.). (Illus.). 128p. (J). (gr. k-6). lib. bdg. 33.27 *(978-0-7660-2890-6(9))* Enslow Pubs., Inc.

REALTY

see Real Property

REASONING

see also Intellect; Logic

Beck, Esther & Doudna, Kelly. You'll Cause a Stir When You Infer!, 1 vol. 2007. (Science Made Simple Ser.). (ENG., Illus.). 24p. (J). (gr. k-3). lib. bdg. 24.21 *(978-1-59928-626-6(2),* SandCastle) ABDO Publishing Co.

Blackwood, Melissa, et al. Maths - Problem Solving & Reasoning Age 7-9. 2015. (Letts Wild about Learning Ser.). (ENG.). 48p. (gr. 2-4). pap. 8.95 *(978-1-84419-788-0(3))* HarperCollins Pubs. Ltd. GBR. Dist: Independent Pubs. Group.

Boardworks Learning Centers: Figure It Out. 2006. (J). bds. *(978-0-9755252-4-1(7))* Evergreen Pr. of Brainerd, LLC.

Bowers, Linda, et al. No Glamour Language & Reasoning. 2003. (J). per. 41.95 *(978-0-7606-0500-4(9))* LinguiSystems, Inc.

Brown, Robin. Practice Papers: Advanced Non-Verbal Reasoning. 2nd ed. (Illus.). 32p. (YA). pap. 6.99 *(978-0-340-72686-0(5))* Hodder & Stoughton GBR. Dist: Trafalgar Square Publishing.

Carr, Mary Ann. More One-Hour Mysteries. 2005. (One-Hour Mysteries Ser.: 0). (ENG.). 64p. (gr. 4-8). pap. 13.95 *(978-1-59363-109-3(X),* 9781593631093) Prufrock Pr.

Gillham, Bill, et al. Essential Skills, 4 bks. (Illus.). 128p. (YA). pap. 15.99 *(978-0-340-71583-3(9))* Hodder & Stoughton GBR. Dist: Trafalgar Square Publishing.

Head, Alison. Verbal Reasoning, Age 8-10. 2016. 64p. pap., wbk. ed. 34.50 *(978-1-4718-4931-2(7))* Hodder Education Group GBR. Dist: Trans-Atlantic Pubns., Inc.

Head, Alison & Pearse, Chris. Verbal Reasoning, Age 9-11. 2016. 64p. pap., wbk. ed. 34.50 *(978-1-4718-4932-9(5))* Hodder Education Group GBR. Dist: Trans-Atlantic Pubns., Inc.

Letts 11+, Letts. 11+ Practice Test Papers. 2017. (Letts 11+ Success Ser.). (ENG.). 104p. (J). (gr. 4). pap. 15.99 ***(978-1-84419-896-2(0))*** HarperCollins Pubs. Ltd. GBR. Dist: Independent Pubs. Group.

MacAllister, Carol L. The Wisdom Tree & the Red Swing: Thinking Outside the Box for Preteens. 2009. (Wisdom Tree & the Red Swing Ser.). (ENG.). 116p. (J). pap. 3.99 *(978-0-9815818-4-2(6),* 9780981581842) Take Charge Bks.

McMahon, Philip, et al. Non-Verbal Reasoning. 2016. (Letts 11+ Success Ser.). (ENG.). 80p. (J). (gr. 4-5). pap. 11.95 *(978-1-84419-892-4(8))* HarperCollins Pubs. Ltd. GBR. Dist: Independent Pubs. Group.

—Verbal Reasoning. 2016. (Letts 11+ Success Ser.). (ENG.). 80p. (J). (gr. 4-5). pap. 11.95 *(978-1-84419-891-7(X))* HarperCollins Pubs. Ltd. GBR. Dist: Independent Pubs. Group.

Primrose, Alison. Verbal Reasoning, Age 10-12. 2016. 64p. pap., wbk. ed. 34.50 *(978-1-4718-4933-6(3))* Hodder Education Group GBR. Dist: Trans-Atlantic Pubns., Inc.

Walch Publishing Staff. Daily Warm-Ups: Analogies. 2007. (gr. 9-12). tchr. ed., spiral bd. 18.99 *(978-0-8251-6255-8(6))* Walch Education.

REBUSES

see Riddles

RECLAMATION OF LAND

Here are entered general works on reclamation, including drainage and irrigation.

see also Irrigation; Marshes; Sand

Bjornlund, Lydia D. Deforestation. 2009. (Compact Research Ser.). (YA). (gr. 7-12). 25.95 *(978-1-60152-075-3(1))* ReferencePoint Pr., Inc.

Brezina, Corona. Disappearing Forests: Deforestation, Desertification, & Drought. 2009. (Extreme Environmental Threats Ser.). (ENG., Illus.). 64p. (J). (gr. 7-12). pap. 12.95 *(978-1-4358-5374-4(1),* 1291449); (YA). (gr. 5-9). lib. bdg. 31.95 *(978-1-4358-5018-7(1))* Rosen Publishing Group, Inc., The.

Linde, Barbara M. Deforestation & Desertification: Text Pairs. 2008. (Bridges/Navigators Ser.). (J). (gr. 6). 94.00 *(978-1-4108-8432-9(5))* Benchmark Education Co.

RECLAMATION OF LAND—FICTION

Austin, Mike. Junkyard. Austin, Mike, illus. 2014. (ENG., Illus.). 40p. (J). (gr. -1-3). 16.99 *(978-1-4424-5961-8(1),* Beach Lane Bks.) Beach Lane Bks.

Ward, Helen. The Tin Forest. Anderson, Wayne, illus. 2003. (Rise & Shine Ser.). (ENG.). 32p. (J). (gr. -1-2). 7.99 *(978-0-14-250156-6(5),* Puffin Books) Penguin Young Readers Group.

RECOMMENDED BOOKS

see Best Books

RECONSTRUCTION (U.S. HISTORY, 1865-1877)

Here are entered works dealing with reconstruction in the United States following the Civil War.

Anderson, Dale. The Aftermath of the Civil War. 2004. (World Almanac Library of the Civil War). (Illus.). 48p. (gr. 5-12). pap. 14.05 *(978-0-8368-5597-5(3));* lib. bdg. 31.00 *(978-0-8368-5588-3(4))* Stevens, Gareth Publishing LLLP. (Gareth Stevens Secondary Library).

Baptiste, Tracey. The Civil War & Reconstruction Eras. 2015. (African American Experience: from Slavery to the Presidency Ser.). (ENG., Illus.). 80p. (J). (gr. 7-8). 32.90 *(978-1-68048-039-9(1),* Britannica Educational Publishing) Rosen Publishing Group, Inc., The.

Baptiste, Tracey, ed. The Civil War & Reconstruction Eras. 2015. (African American Experience: from Slavery to the Presidency Ser.). (ENG.). 80p. (YA). (gr. 7-8). 65.80 *(978-1-68048-040-5(5),* Britannica Educational Publishing) Rosen Publishing Group, Inc., The.

Cooke, Tim. After the War. 2012. (American Civil War: the Right Answer Ser.). (Illus.). 48p. (J). (gr. 6-8). 31.95 *(978-1-4339-7531-8(9));* pap. 14.05 *(978-1-4339-7532-5(7))* Stevens, Gareth Publishing LLLP. (Gareth Stevens Secondary Library).

Cosson, Jody. Civil War & Reconstruction: 1850-1877. 2007. (Presidents of the United States Ser.). (Illus.). (J). (gr. 4-7). 47p. lib. bdg. 29.05 *(978-1-59036-743-8(X));* 48p. per. 10.95 *(978-1-59036-744-5(8))* Weigl Pubs., Inc.

Crompton, Sam. Georgia During Reconstruction. 2017. (Spotlight on Georgia Ser.). 32p. (gr. 9-10). pap. 11.75 ***(978-1-5081-5981-0(5),*** PowerKids Pr.) Rosen Publishing Group, Inc., The.

Dudley, William. Reconstruction. 2003. (At Issue in History Ser.). (ENG., Illus.). 144p. (gr. 10-12). pap. 30.60 *(978-0-7377-1357-2(7),* Greenhaven Pr., Inc.) Cengage Gale.

Flanagan, Timothy. Reconstruction: A Primary Source History of the Struggle to Unite the North & South after the Civil War. 2005. (Primary Sources in American History Ser.). (Illus.). 64p. (J). (gr. 5-8). lib. bdg. 31.95 *(978-1-4042-0177-4(7))* Rosen Publishing Group, Inc., The.

Globe Fearon American History Vol. 1: Prehistory Through Reconstruction. 2003. (American History Ser.). 542p. (YA). (gr. 6-12). 50.95 *(978-0-13-024400-0(7))* Globe Fearon Educational Publishing.

Greene, Meg & Malvasi, Meg Greene. Into the Land of Freedom: African Americans in Reconstruction. 2004. (People's History Ser.). (ENG., Illus.). 96p. (gr. 5-12). lib. bdg. 33.26 *(978-0-8225-4690-0(6))* Lerner Publishing Group.

Grumet, Bridget Hall & Baker, Lawrence W. Primary Sources - Reconstruction Era. 2004. (Reconstruction Era Reference Library). (ENG., Illus.). 256p. (J). lib. bdg. 106.00 *(978-0-7876-9219-3(0))* Cengage Gale.

Hakim, Joy. Reconstructing America, 1865-1890. (History of US Ser.: 7). (ENG., Illus.). 208p. (gr. 4-7). 3rd rev. ed. 2006. 24.95 *(978-0-19-518900-1(0))*Bk. 7. 2nd rev. ed. 2007. per. 15.95 *(978-0-19-532721-2(7))* Oxford Univ. Pr., Inc.

Hale, Sarah Elder, ed. Rebuilding a Nation: Picking up the Pieces. 2005. (ENG., Illus.). 48p. (J). (gr. 3-9). 17.95 *(978-0-8126-7909-0(1))* Cobblestone Publishing Co.

Harkrader, Lisa. Reconstruction & Aftermath of the Civil War: A MyReportLinks. com Book. 2004. (American Civil War Ser.). (Illus.). 48p. (J). lib. bdg. 25.26 *(978-0-7660-5265-9(6),* MyReportLinks.com Bks.) Enslow Pubs., Inc.

Howell, Brian. The US Civil War & Reconstruction. 2011. (Explorer Library: Language Arts Explorer Ser.). (ENG.). 32p. (gr. 4-8). lib. bdg. 28.50 *(978-1-61080-201-7(2),* 201178) Cherry Lake Publishing.

—The U.S. Civil War & Reconstruction. 2011. (Explorer Library: Language Arts Explorer Ser.). (ENG.). 32p. (gr. 4-8). pap. 14.21 *(978-1-61080-289-5(6),* 201212) Cherry Lake Publishing.

Howes, Kelly King & Baker, Lawrence W. Almanac, Reconstruction Era. 2004. (Reconstruction Era Reference Library). (ENG., Illus.). 272p. (J). lib. bdg. 106.00 *(978-0-7876-9217-9(4),* UXL) Cengage Gale.

Howse, Jennifer. Reconstruction. 2013. (J). *(978-1-62127-194-9(3))* 2013. (J). pap. *(978-1-62127-200-7(1))* 2008. (Illus.). 48p. (YA). (gr. 5-8). pap. 10.95 *(978-1-59036-879-4(7))* 2008. (Illus.). 48p. (YA). (gr. 5-8). lib. bdg. 29.05 *(978-1-59036-878-7(9))* Weigl Pubs., Inc.

Kissock, Heather. Civil War & Reconstruction. 2016. (Illus.). 48p. (J). *(978-1-5105-1280-1(2))* SmartBook Media, Inc.

Latta, Susan M. Reconstruction Era, 1 vol. 2014. (African-American History Ser.). (ENG.). 48p. (gr. 8-12). lib. bdg. 32.79 *(978-1-62403-147-2(1))* ABDO Publishing Co.

Maloof, Torrey. Reconstruction: Freedom Delayed. 2017. (Primary Source Readers Ser.). (Illus.). 32p. (J). (gr. 4-5). pap. 8.99 *(978-1-4938-3806-6(7))* Teacher Created Materials, Inc.

Matuz, Roger & Baker, Lawrence W. Reconstruction Era: Biographies. 2004. (Reconstruction Era Reference Library). (ENG., Illus.). 272p. (J). lib. bdg. 106.00 *(978-0-7876-9218-6(2),* UXL) Cengage Gale.

McNeese, Tim. Reconstruction. 2009. (Civil War: A Nation Divided Ser.). 144p. (gr. 6-12). 35.00 *(978-1-60413-035-5(0),* Chelsea Hse.) Facts On File, Inc.

Miller, Reagan & Cocca, Lisa Colozza. Reconstruction & the Aftermath of the Civil War. 2011. (ENG.). 48p. (J). pap. *(978-0-7787-5358-2(1))*; lib. bdg. *(978-0-7787-5341-4(7))* Crabtree Publishing Co.

Nelson, Sheila. Americans Divided: The Civil War. 2006. (How America Became America Ser.). (Illus.). 96p. (YA). lib. bdg. 22.95 *(978-1-59084-908-8(6))* Mason Crest.

The New South & the Old West, 1866-1890. 2010. (Discovering U. S. History Ser.). (Illus.). 136p. (gr. 5-8). 35.00 *(978-1-60413-354-7(6),* Chelsea Hse.) Facts On File, Inc.

Osborne, Linda Barrett. Traveling the Freedom Road: From Slavery & the Civil War Through Reconstruction. 2009. (ENG., Illus.). 128p. (J). (gr. 3-7). 25.95 *(978-0-8109-8338-0(9),* Abrams Bks. for Young Readers) Abrams, Inc.

Paris, Stephanie Herweck. Jonathan Clarkson Gibbs: Reconstruction Revolutionary. 2016. (Primary Source Readers Ser.). 32p. (J). (gr. 4-4). pap. 8.99 *(978-1-4938-3540-9(8))* Teacher Created Materials, Inc.

The Reconstruction of the South after the Civil War in United States History. 2014. (In United States History Ser.). (Illus.). 96p. (J). (gr. 5-12). 27.94 *(978-0-7660-6063-0(2))* Enslow Pubs., Inc.

Rodgers, Kelly. Civil War & Reconstruction in Florida. 2016. (Primary Source Readers Ser.). 32p. (J). (gr. 4-4). pap. 8.99 *(978-1-4938-3539-3(4))* Teacher Created Materials, Inc.

Ruggiero, Adriane. Reconstruction. 2006. (American Voices Ser.). (Illus.). 103p. (J). (gr. 3-7). lib. bdg. 37.07 *(978-0-7614-2168-9(8),* Benchmark Bks.) Marshall Cavendish Corp.

Streissguth, Thomas. Perspectives on Reconstruction. 2018. (ENG.). 32p. (gr. 3-6). ***(978-1-63235-403-7(9)***, 12-Story Library) Pr. Room Editions LLC.

Stroud, Bettye. The Reconstruction Era. 2006. (Drama of African-American History Ser.). (Illus.). 80p. (gr. 6-7). lib. bdg. 35.64 *(978-0-7614-2181-8(5),* Benchmark Bks.) Marshall Cavendish Corp.

Sutherland, Jonathan. Civil War Victory & the Costly Aftermath. 2017. (Civil War Ser.: Vol. 5). (ENG.). (YA). (gr. 7-12). 24.95 ***(978-1-4222-3886-8(5))*** Mason Crest.

Swartz, Ellen. Reconstruction: Moving Toward Democracy: People of African Descent Define Freedom after the Civil War. 2007. (Illus.). 24p. (J). pap. *(978-1-929768-09-7(5))* R T A Pr.

Wittman, Susan S. Reconstruction: Outcomes of the Civil War, 1 vol. 2014. (Story of the Civil War Ser.). (ENG.). 32p. (gr. 3-4). pap. 7.95 *(978-1-4914-0728-8(X))* Capstone Press of Coughlan Cos.

Worth, Richard. African Americans During Reconstruction. Schwarz, Philip, ed. 2006. (Slavery in the Americas Ser.). (Illus.). 112p. (gr. 5-8). 35.00 *(978-0-8160-6139-6(4))* Facts On File, Inc.

Ziff, Marsha. The Reconstruction of the South after the Civil War in United States History. 2014. (In United States History Ser.). (Illus.). 96p. (J). (gr. 5-12). pap. 10.95 *(978-0-7660-6064-7(0))* Enslow Pubs., Inc.

RECONSTRUCTION (U.S. HISTORY, 1865-1877)—FICTION

Asim, Jabari. The Road to Freedom: A Story of the Reconstruction. 2004. 131p. (J). lib. bdg. 16.92 *(978-1-4242-0765-7(7))* Fitzgerald Bks.

LaFaye, A. Stella Stands Alone. 2010. (ENG.). 256p. (YA). (gr. 7). pap. 7.99 *(978-1-4169-8647-8(2),* Simon & Schuster Bks. For Young Readers) Simon & Schuster Bks. For Young Readers.

Lyons, Kelly Starling. Ellen's Broom. Minter, Daniel, illus. 2012. (ENG.). 32p. (J). (gr. k-3). 16.99 *(978-0-399-25003-3(4),* G.P. Putnam's Sons Books for Young Readers) Penguin Young Readers Group.

Osborne, Mary Pope, et al. A Time to Dance: Virginia's Civil War Diary. 2003. (My America Ser.). (ENG.). 112p. (J). 12.95 *(978-0-439-44341-8(5))* Scholastic, Inc.

Rhodes, Jewell Parker. Sugar. 2013. (ENG.). 288p. (J). (gr. 3-7). 16.99 *(978-0-316-04305-2(2))* Little, Brown Bks. for Young Readers.

Shaw, Marilyn Bishop. Solomon. 2006. (Florida Historical Fiction for Youth Ser.). (ENG.). 204p. (J). (gr. 4-9). 14.95 *(978-1-56164-349-3(1))* Pineapple Pr., Inc.

Westrick, A. B. Brotherhood. 2014. (ENG.). 384p. (J). (gr. 5). pap. 8.99 *(978-0-14-242237-3(1),* Puffin Books) Penguin Young Readers Group.

RECORD PLAYERS

see Phonograph

RECREATION

Here are entered works on the psychological and social aspects of recreation and works on organized recreational projects.

see also Amusements; Games; Hobbies; Play; Playgrounds; Sports

Abramson, Beverley. Off We Go! 2010. (ENG.). 16p. (J). (gr. -1-k). bds. 7.95 *(978-0-88776-994-8(2),* Tundra Bks.) Tundra Bks. CAN. Dist: Penguin Random Hse. LLC.

Amery, Heather. What's Happening at the Seaside? Cartwright, Stephen, illus. rev. ed. 2006. (What's Happening Ser.). 16p. (J). (gr. -1-3). 5.99 *(978-0-7945-1290-3(9),* Usborne) EDC Publishing.

Benedetti, Debra. Season of Play. Teets, Ashley, illus. 2011. 32p. (J). *(978-0-929915-99-9(2))* Headline Bks., Inc.

Beylon, Cathy. At the Amusement Park. 2004. (Dover Coloring Bks.). (ENG., Illus.). 32p. (J). (gr. -1-2). pap. 2.95 *(978-0-486-43322-6(6))* Dover Pubns., Inc.

Braun, Eric. The Guys' Guide to Making the Outdoors More Awesome, 1 vol. 2014. (Guys' Guides). (ENG.). 32p. (gr. 3-4). lib. bdg. 27.99 *(978-1-4765-3922-5(7),* Edge Bks.) Capstone Press of Coughlan Cos.

Brennan, Lara. The Adventurous Girl's Handbook - For Ages 9 to 99. Brennan, Stephen & Brennan, Lara, eds. 2nd ed. 2011. (ENG., Illus.). 208p. (J). (gr. 2-5). pap. 12.95 *(978-1-61608-164-5(3),* 608164) Skyhorse Publishing Co., Inc.

Butler, Erin K. Extreme Land Sports. 2017. (Sports to the Extreme Ser.). (ENG.). 32p. (gr. 3-4). lib. bdg. 27.99 ***(978-1-5157-7860-8(6)***, Edge Bks.) Capstone Press of Coughlan Cos.

Celebrations. 2016. (Celebrations Ser.). 00024p. (J). (gr. 1-1). 94.40 *(978-1-4994-2627-4(5),* PowerKids Pr.) Rosen Publishing Group, Inc., The.

Chissick, Michael. Ladybird's Remarkable Relaxation: How Children (And Frogs, Dogs, Flamingos & Dragons) Can Use Yoga Relaxation to Help Deal with Stress, Grief, Bullying & Lack of Confidence. Peacock, Sarah, illus. 2013. (ENG.). 48p. (J). 19.95 *(978-1-84819-146-4(4),* 2259, Singing Dragon) Kingsley, Jessica Pubs. GBR. Dist: Macmillan Distribution Ltd.

Cloutier, Toni Lynn. Word Search USA. 2010. (ENG., Illus.). 128p. (J). (gr. 3-6). spiral bd. 6.95 *(978-1-4027-6905-4(9))* Sterling Publishing Co., Inc.

Corwin, Jeff. A Whale of a Time! 2010. (Jeff Corwin Ser.). 112p. (J). (gr. 1-3). 4.99 *(978-0-14-241646-4(0),* Puffin) Penguin Publishing Group.

Cox, Catherine. Go-Carts, Catapults & Midnight Feasts: 101 Vintage Pastimes for Modern Kids. 2015. (ENG., Illus.). 224p. (J). (gr. k-5). pap. 14.99 *(978-0-7509-6429-6(4))* History Pr. Ltd.,The GBR. Dist: Independent Pubs. Group.

Danks, Fiona & Schofield, Jo. The Wild Weather Book: Loads of Things to Do Outdoors in Rain, Wind & Snow. 2013. (Going Wild Ser.). (ENG., Illus.). 128p. pap. 14.95 *(978-0-7112-3255-6(5),* 0711232555, Frances Lincoln) Quarto Publishing Group UK GBR. Dist: Hachette Bk. Group.

Deady, Kathleen W. Wild Rides!, 8 bks., Set. Incl. BMX Bikes. (ENG., Illus.). 32p. (gr. 3-4). 2001. 27.32 *(978-0-7368-0925-2(2),* Edge Bks.); (Wild Rides! Ser.). (ENG.). Illus.). 32p. 2003. Set lib. bdg. 273.20 o.p. *(978-0-7368-1524-6(4),* Edge Bks.) Capstone Press of Coughlan Cos.

Fancy Friendship Bracelets. 2009. (ENG., Illus.). 60p. (J). (gr. 3). spiral bd. 19.95 *(978-1-59174-692-8(2))* Klutz.

Florian, Melanie. A Day with Mommy. Florian, Melanie, illus. 2010. (Sticker Stories Ser.). (ENG., Illus.). 16p. (J). (gr. -1-2). pap. 5.99 *(978-0-448-45342-2(8),* Grosset & Dunlap) Penguin Young Readers Group.

Fuerst, Jeffrey B. Going Places: Lap Book. 2009. (My First Reader's Theater Set B Ser.). (J). 28.00 *(978-1-4108-8544-9(5))* Benchmark Education Co.

George, Mike. You Can Relax & Avoid Stress. 2017. (Be Your Best Self Ser.). 158p. (gr. 12-14). 44.60 ***(978-1-4994-6665-2(X)***, Rosen Young Adult) Rosen Publishing Group, Inc., The.

Glenn, Joshua & Larsen, Elizabeth Foy. Unbored Games: Serious Fun for Everyone. Leone, Tony et al, illus. 2014. (ENG.). 176p. pap. 16.00 *(978-1-62040-706-6(X),* 9781620407066) Bloomsbury Publishing USA.

Groenendyk, Doretta. Step Outside, 1 vol. 2014. (ENG., Illus.). 24p. (J). (gr. -1-3). 19.95 *(978-1-927502-19-8(5))* Acorn Pr., The CAN. Dist: Orca Bk. Pubs. USA.

Hengel, Katherine. Cool Parks & Trails: Great Things to Do in the Great Outdoors, 1 vol. 2016. (ENG., Illus.). 32p. (J). *(978-1-62403-698-9(8))* ABDO Publishing Co.

Hicks, Kelli. Zip Lines. 2009. (Illus.). 24p. (J). lib. bdg. 27.07 *(978-1-60694-359-5(6))* Rourke Educational Media.

Hip-Hop World, 4 vols. 2010. (Hip-Hop World Ser.). (ENG.). 48p. (gr. 3-4). lib. bdg. 127.96 *(978-1-4296-4424-2(9))* Capstone Press of Coughlan Cos.

Hip-Hop World [Capstone Sole Source]. 2010. (Hip-Hop World Ser.). 48p. lib. bdg. 122.60 *(978-1-4296-5866-9(5))* Capstone Press of Coughlan Cos.

Honovich, Nancy. Ultimate Explorer Guide: Explore, Discover, & Create Your Own Adventures with Real National Geographic Explorers As Your Guides! 2017. (ENG.). 160p. (J). (gr. 3-7). pap. 14.99 *(978-1-4263-2709-4(9),* National Geographic Children's Bks.) National Geographic Society.

Kessler, Colleen. The Coolest, Dirtiest, Creepy-Crawliest Backyard Activites for Kids: 100 Fun Science Games & Experiments to Become an Expert on Bugs, Beetles, Worms, Frogs, Snakes, Birds, Plants & More in Your Backyard. 2017. (ENG., Illus.). 208p. (J). pap. 19.99 *(978-1-62414-373-1(3),* 9781624143731) Page Street Publishing Co.

Klutz Editors. The Encyclopedia of Immaturity, Vol. 2. 2009. (ENG., Illus.). 200p. (J). (gr. 3). 19.95 *(978-1-59174-689-8(2))* Klutz.

—The Encyclopedia of Immaturity: How to Never Grow Up. 2007. (ENG., Illus.). 412p. (J). (gr. 3-7). 19.95 *(978-1-59174-427-6(X))* Klutz.

Kuskowski, Alex. Cool Outdoor Arts & Crafts: Great Things to Do in the Great Outdoors, 1 vol. 2016. (ENG.). 32p. *(978-1-62403-697-2(X))* ABDO Publishing Co.

—Cool Relaxing: Healthy & Fun Ways to Chill Out, 1 vol. 2012. (Cool Health & Fitness Ser.). (ENG.). 32p. (J). (gr. 3-6). lib. bdg. 27.07 *(978-1-61783-428-8(9),* Checkerboard Library) ABDO Publishing Co.

Lacey, Saskia. Surprising Things We Do for Fun. 2017. (Time for Kids Nonfiction Readers Ser.). lib. bdg. 22.10 ***(978-0-606-40280-4(2))*** Turtleback Bks.

Larsen, Elizabeth Foy & Glenn, Joshua. Unbored: The Essential Field Guide to Serious Fun. Leone, Tony et al, illus. 2012. (ENG.). 352p. 28.00 *(978-1-60819-641-8(0),* 9781608196418) Bloomsbury Publishing USA.

Mableton, Barry & Ching, Jacqueline. Camping, 01 vols., 1. 2016. (Outdoor Life Ser.). (ENG.). 64p. (J). 32.95 *(978-1-4994-6227-2(1),* Rosen Young Adult) Rosen Publishing Group, Inc., The.

MacDonald, Margaret. Leisure in the Past. 2011. (Learn-Abouts Ser.). (Illus.). 16p. (J). pap. 7.95 *(978-1-59920-629-5(3))* Black Rabbit Bks.

Martin, Bobi. Theme Parks, 01 vols., 1. 2016. (Role-Playing for Fun & Profit Ser.). (ENG.). 48p. (J). pap. 11.75 *(978-1-4994-3732-4(3),* Rosen Central) Rosen Publishing Group, Inc., The.

Myers, Edward. Let's Build a Playground. 2012. (ENG., Illus.). 48p. (J). (gr. 2-3). pap. 9.50 *(978-0-7652-0882-8(2),* Modern Curriculum Pr.) Pearson Schl.

Omoth, Tyler. Busting in the Great Outdoors. 2017. (Boredom Busters Ser.). (ENG.). 32p. (gr. 3-4). lib. bdg. 27.99 *(978-1-5157-4703-1(4),* Edge Bks.) Capstone Press of Coughlan Cos.

Rice, Dona Herweck. Places to Go, 1 vol. 2nd rev. ed. 2013. (Nonfiction Readers Ser.). (ENG., Illus.). 12p. (J). (gr. 1-1). pap. 15.96 *(978-1-4807-1012-2(1))* Shell Educational Publishing.

Rissman, Rebecca. Counting at the Park, 1 vol. 2012. (I Can Count! Ser.). (ENG.). 24p. (gr. -1-k). pap. 9.95 *(978-1-4329-6700-0(2))*; lib. bdg. 25.32 *(978-1-4329-6695-9(2))* Heinemann-Raintree.

—Going to a Stadium, 1 vol. 2012. (World of Field Trips Ser.). (ENG.). 24p. (gr. -1-1). lib. bdg. 22.65 *(978-1-4329-6069-8(5),* Acorn) Heinemann-Raintree.

Rosen, Michael J. Balls! Round 2. Margeson, John, illus. 2008. (Darby Creek Exceptional Titles Ser.). (ENG.). 80p. (gr. 4-8). 18.95 *(978-1-58196-066-2(2),* Darby Creek) Lerner Publishing Group.

Salzmann, Mary Elizabeth. Taking Time to Relax. 2004. (Healthy Habits Ser.). (ENG., Illus.). 24p. (J). (gr. k-3). lib. bdg. 24.21 *(978-1-59197-555-7(7),* SandCastle) ABDO Publishing Co.

Samuel, Charlie. Entertainment in Colonial America. 2003. (Primary Sources of Everyday Life in Colonial America Ser.). (Illus.). 24p. (J). lib. bdg. 22.60 *(978-0-8239-6600-4(3),* PowerKids Pr.) Rosen Publishing Group, Inc., The.

Scholastic, Inc. Staff & Campbell, Guy. The Boys' Book of Survival: How to Survive Anything, Anywhere. 2009. (Best at Everything Ser.). (ENG., Illus.). 128p. (J). (gr. 3-7). 10.99 *(978-0-545-08536-6(5))* Scholastic, Inc.

Scott, Steph & Akers, Katie. Let's Go Outside: Imaginative Outdoor Games & Projects for Kids. 2015. (ENG., Illus.). 144p. (J). (gr. -1-2). 12.95 *(978-1-84994-276-8(5),* Batsford) Pavilion Bks. GBR. Dist: Sterling Publishing Co., Inc.

Shava, Ryder. Camping with My Cousins, 01 vols., 1. 2016. (Rosen REAL Readers: Social Studies Nonfiction / Fiction: Family, Community, & the World Ser.). (ENG.). 8p. (J). pap. 5.46 *(978-1-5081-1641-7(5),* Rosen Classroom) Rosen Publishing Group, Inc., The.

Simon, Mary Manz. My Picnic Basket: And How God Is Always Near. Fenimore, Kristina, illus. 2013. (ENG.). 14p. (J). (gr. -1-k). bds. 9.99 *(978-0-7847-3699-9(5),* B&H Kids) B&H Publishing Group.

Son, John. Relaxation & Yoga. 2016. (True Book(tm), A — Health Ser.). (ENG., Illus.). 48p. (J). lib. bdg. 31.00 *(978-0-531-22847-0(9),* Children's Pr.) Scholastic Library Publishing.

Thomas, M. Summer at the Beach: Learning the EA Sound. 2009. (PowerPhonics Ser.). 24p. (gr. 1-1). 39.90 *(978-1-60851-472-4(2),* PowerKids Pr.) Rosen Publishing Group, Inc., The.

Tomio, Stacy & Keffer, Ken. The Kids' Outdoor Adventure Book: 448 Great Things to Do in Nature Before You Grow Up. 2013. (ENG., Illus.). 224p. pap. 18.95 *(978-0-7627-8352-6(4),* Falcon Guides) Globe Pequot Pr., The.

Usilton, Theresa A. Let's Go team: Cheer, Dance, & March, 12 vols., Set. 2003. (Let's Go Team Ser.). (Illus.). 64p. (YA). (gr. 5-18). lib. bdg. *(978-1-59084-529-5(3))* Mason Crest.

Verdick, Elizabeth. Calm-Down Time. Heinlen, Marieka, illus. 2010. (Toddler Tools Ser.). (ENG.). 24p. (J). (gr. -1). 7.95 *(978-1-57542-316-6(2))* Free Spirit Publishing, Inc.

Walsh, Liza Gardner. Muddy Boots: Outdoor Activities for Children. 2015. (ENG., Illus.). 136p. (J). (gr. -1-5). 16.95 *(978-1-60893-370-9(9),* 1388618) Down East Bks.

Webster, Dawn & Yost, Emily. Yellowstone for Kids: A Kid's Guide to Yellowstone National Park. 2016. (Illus.). (J). *(978-0-934948-40-1(2))* Yellowstone Forever.

RECREATIONAL VEHICLES

see Automobiles—Trailers

RECREATIONS, MATHEMATICAL

see Mathematical Recreations

RECREATIONS, SCIENTIFIC

see Scientific Recreations

RECTORS

see Clergy

RECYCLING (WASTE, ETC.)

Here are entered works on the processing of waste paper, cans, bottles, etc. .

Allen, Heather. Earth Day Is Every Day! 2011. (Dover Children's Activity Bks.). (ENG.). 48p. (J). (gr. 1-5). pap. 4.99 *(978-0-486-47765-7(7))* Dover Pubns., Inc.

Allman, Toney. Recycled Tires. 2009. (Great Idea Ser.). (ENG., Illus.). 48p. (J). (gr. 4-6). lib. bdg. 26.60 *(978-1-59953-197-7(6))* Norwood Hse. Pr.

Aloian, Molly. Going Green at School. 2013. (ENG., Illus.). 24p. (J). *(978-0-7787-0264-1(2))*; pap. *(978-0-7787-0283-2(9))* Crabtree Publishing Co.

ALVARADO, Claudia. The plastic Bottle. 2010. 32p. pap. 27.20 *(978-1-4461-2250-1(6))* Lulu Pr., Inc.

Asriningtyas, Visi. What Can We Do with Garbage? Sampah Bisa Diapakan Ya? 2009. (IND & ENG., Illus.). 40p. pap. 16.99 *(978-1-4389-9470-3(2))* AuthorHouse.

Barker, Geoff. How Recycling Works. 2013. (EcoWorks Ser.). 32p. (J). (gr. 3-5). 26.60 *(978-1-4339-9564-4(6))*; pap. 63.00 *(978-1-4339-9566-8(2))*; pap. 10.50 *(978-1-4339-9565-1(4))* Stevens, Gareth Publishing LLLP.

Barnham, Kay. Recycle. 2007. (Environment Action Ser.). (ENG., Illus.). 32p. (J). (gr. 3-7). pap. *(978-0-7787-3669-1(5))* Crabtree Publishing Co.

Barraclough, Sue. Recycling Materials. 2007. (Making a Difference Ser.). (Illus.). 30p. (J). (gr. -1-3). lib. bdg. 27.10 *(978-1-59771-108-1(X))* Sea-To-Sea Pubns.

Bassett, Jennifer & Stewart, Sue. Recycling. Oxford University Press Staff & Lindop, Christine, eds. 3rd ed. 2008. (ENG., Illus.). 80p. 10.00 *(978-0-19-423389-7(8))* Oxford Univ. Pr., Inc.

Bethea, Nikole Brooks. Engineering an Awesome Recycling Center with Max Axiom, Super Scientist, 1 vol. Pop Art Studios Staff, illus. 2013. (Graphic Science & Engineering in Action Ser.). (ENG.). 32p. (gr. 3-4). pap. 8.10 *(978-1-62065-699-0(X))*; lib. bdg. 30.65 *(978-1-4296-9934-1(5))* Capstone Press of Coughlan Cos. (Graphic Library).

Blake, Susannah. Crafts for Accessorizing That Look. 2013. (Eco Chic Ser.). 32p. (J). lib. bdg. 23.94 *(978-0-7660-4313-8(4))* Enslow Pubs., Inc.

Boekhoff, P. M. & Kallen, Stuart A. Recycling. 2004. (Our Environment Ser.). (ENG., Illus.). 48p. (J). (gr. 4-7). 29.15 *(978-0-7377-1517-0(0),* Kidhaven) Cengage Gale.

Bolte, Mari. Eco Gifts: Upcycled Gifts You Can Make. 2015. (Make It, Gift It Ser.). (ENG., Illus.). 32p. (gr. 3-4). lib. bdg. 27.99 *(978-1-4914-5202-8(1),* Snap Bks.) Capstone Press of Coughlan Cos.

Bone, Emily & Pratt, Leonie. Recycling Things to Make & Do. 2010. (Activity Book Ser.). 32p. (J). pap. 6.99 *(978-0-7945-2675-7(6),* Usborne) EDC Publishing.

Brager, Bruce L. How You Can Use Waste Energy to Heat & Light Your Home. 2009. (Tell Your Parents Ser.). (J). (gr. 4-7). 29.95 *(978-1-58415-765-6(8))* Mitchell Lane Pubs., Inc.

Bullard, Lisa. Choose to Reuse. Thomas, Wes, illus. 2011. (Planet Protectors Ser.). pap. 39.62 *(978-0-7613-8651-3(3))*; (ENG.). 24p. pap. 6.95 *(978-0-7613-8511-0(8))* Lerner Publishing Group. (Millbrook Pr.).

—Choose to Reuse. Thomas, Wes & Thomas, John, Jr., illus. 2011. (Cloverleaf Books (tm) — Planet Protectors Ser.). (ENG.). 24p. (gr. k-2). lib. bdg. 23.93 *(978-0-7613-6104-6(9))* Lerner Publishing Group.

—Rally for Recycling. Thomas, Wes, illus. 2011. (Planet Protectors Ser.). pap. 39.62 *(978-0-7613-8656-8(4),* Millbrook Pr.); (ENG.). 24p. pap. 6.95 *(978-0-7613-8516-5(9),* Millbrook Pr.); (ENG.). 24p. lib. bdg. 23.93 *(978-0-7613-6103-9(0))* Lerner Publishing Group.

Burton, Margie, et al. Reduce, Reuse, & Recycle. 2011. (Early Connections Ser.). (J). *(978-1-61672-503-7(6))* Benchmark Education Co.

Capstone Press. Green Crafts. 2010. (Green Crafts Ser.). (ENG.). 32p. lib. bdg. 159.90 *(978-1-4296-5940-6(8),* Snap Bks.) Capstone Press of Coughlan Cos.

Chambers, Catherine. How Effective Is Recycling? 2015. (Earth Debates Ser.). (ENG., Illus.). 48p. (gr. 4-6). 33.32 *(978-1-4846-0996-5(4),* Heinemann InfoSearch) Heinemann-Raintree.

Chapman, Gillian & Robson, Pam. Making Art with Fabric. 2007. (Everyday Art Ser.). (Illus.). 32p. (YA). (gr. 4-7). lib. bdg. 26.50 *(978-1-4042-3722-3(4))* Rosen Publishing Group, Inc., The.

—Making Art with Packaging. 2007. (Everyday Art Ser.). (Illus.). 32p. (YA). (gr. 4-7). lib. bdg. 26.50 *(978-1-4042-3724-7(0))* Rosen Publishing Group, Inc., The.

—Making Art with Rocks & Shells. 2007. (Everyday Art Ser.). (Illus.). 32p. (YA). (gr. 4-7). lib. bdg. 26.50 *(978-1-4042-3727-8(5))* Rosen Publishing Group, Inc., The.

—Making Art with Sand & Earth. 2007. (Everyday Art Ser.). (Illus.). 32p. (YA). (gr. 4-7). lib. bdg. 26.50 *(978-1-4042-3723-0(2))* Rosen Publishing Group, Inc., The.

—Making Art with Wood. 2007. (Everyday Art Ser.). (Illus.). 32p. (YA). (gr. 4-7). lib. bdg. 26.50 *(978-1-4042-3726-1(7))* Rosen Publishing Group, Inc., The.

Clausen-Grace, Nicki. What Can You Make? 2006. (Science about Me Ser.). (Illus.). 8p. (J). (gr. 3-7). pap. 5.95 *(978-1-59515-932-8(0))* Rourke Educational Media.

Close, Edward. What Do We Do with Trash? 2012. (Discovery Education: the Environment Ser.). (ENG., Illus.). 32p. (J). (gr. 3-6). pap. 10.00 *(978-1-4488-7982-3(5))*; lib. bdg. 25.25 *(978-1-4488-7894-9(2))* Rosen Publishing Group, Inc., The. (PowerKids Pr.).

David, Sarah B. Reducing Your Carbon Footprint at Home. 2009. (Your Carbon Footprint Ser.). 48p. (gr. 5-5). 53.00 *(978-1-60854-910-8(0),* Rosen Reference) Rosen Publishing Group, Inc., The.

Davidson, Simon & Gardner, Julia. What Is Waste? Inquiry Box. 2011. (PYP Springboard Ser.). (Illus.). (gr. -1 — 1). 375.00 *(978-1-4441-4733-9(1))* Hodder Education Group GBR. Dist: Trans-Atlantic Pubns., Inc.

D'Cruz, Anna-Marie. Make Your Own Masks. 2009. (Do It Yourself Projects! Ser.). 24p. (J). (gr. 3-5). (ENG.). pap. 9.40 *(978-1-4358-2923-7(9))*; lib. bdg. 25.25 *(978-1-4358-2853-7(4))* Rosen Publishing Group, Inc., The. (PowerKids Pr.).

—Make Your Own Puppets. 2009. (Do It Yourself Projects! Ser.). 24p. (J). (gr. 3-5). (ENG.). pap. 9.40 *(978-1-4358-2919-0(0))*; lib. bdg. 25.25 *(978-1-4358-2851-3(8))* Rosen Publishing Group, Inc., The. (PowerKids Pr.).

—Make Your Own Purses & Bags. 2009. (Do It Yourself Projects! Ser.). 24p. (J). (gr. 3-5). (ENG.). pap. 9.40 *(978-1-4358-2929-9(8))*; lib. bdg. 25.25

(978-1-4358-2856-8(9)) Rosen Publishing Group, Inc., The. (PowerKids Pr.).
—Make Your Own Shoes & Slippers. 2009. (Do It Yourself Projects! Ser.). (J). (ENG.). 24p. (gr. 3-5). pap. 9.40 *(978-1-4358-2921-3(2))*; lib. bdg. 25.25 *(978-1-4358-2852-0(6))* Rosen Publishing Group, Inc., The. (PowerKids Pr.).
Dutton, Michael. Amazing Carbon Footprint Facts. 2010. (Dover Nature Coloring Book Ser.). (ENG., Illus.). 32p. (J). (gr. 2-5). pap. 3.99 *(978-0-486-47552-3(2))* Dover Pubns., Inc.
Edison, Erin. Shred It!, 1 vol. 2013. (Destruction Ser.). (ENG., Illus.). 12p. (gr. k-1). bds. 9.99 *(978-1-4765-3529-6(9)*, Pebble Plus) Capstone Press of Coughlan Cos.
Enz, Tammy. Awesome Craft Stick Science. 2016. (Recycled Science Ser.). (ENG., Illus.). 32p. (gr. 3-4). lib. bdg. 27.99 *(978-1-5157-0861-2(6))* Capstone Press of Coughlan Cos.
—Repurpose It: Invent New Uses for Old Stuff, 1 vol. 2012. (Invent It Ser.). (ENG.). 32p. (gr. 3-4). pap. 8.10 *(978-1-4296-7983-1(2))*; pap. 47.70 *(978-1-4296-8457-6(7))*; lib. bdg. 27.32 *(978-1-4296-7636-6(1))* Capstone Press of Coughlan Cos. (Fact Finders).
Enz, Tammy & Wheeler-Toppen, Jodi. Whizzy Science with Recyclables: Bring Out Your Science Genius with Soda Bottles, Potato Chip Bags & More Unexpected Stuff. 2016. (Recycled Science Ser.). (ENG.). 112p. (gr. 3-4). pap. 9.95 *(978-1-62370-697-5(1))* Capstone Press of Coughlan Cos.
Fix, Alexandra. Plastic. 2016. (Reduce, Reuse, Recycle Ser.). (ENG.). 32p. (gr. 1-3). pap. 8.29 *(978-1-4846-3590-2(6)*, Heinemann First Library) Heinemann-Raintree.
Flounders, Anne. Reducing Waste. 2014. (Our Green Earth Ser.). (Illus.). 32p. (gr. 2-4). pap. 8.95 *(978-1-939656-34-6(6))* Red Chair Pr.
Friday, Megan. Green Crafts: Become an Earth-Friendly Craft Star, Step by Easy Step! 2012. (Craft Star Ser.). (Illus.). 64p. (gr. 2-4). 32.80 *(978-1-936309-38-2(6))* Quarto Publishing Group USA.
Friedman, Lauri S. Garbage & Recycling. 2009. (Introducing Issues with Opposing Viewpoints Ser.). (ENG., Illus.). 144p. (J). (gr. 7-10). 36.95 *(978-0-7377-4337-1(9)*, Greenhaven Pr., Inc.) Cengage Gale.
—Recycling. 2010. (Writing the Critical Essay: an Opposing Viewpoints Guide Ser.). (Illus.). 128p. 33.75 *(978-0-7377-4803-1(6)*, Greenhaven Pr., Inc.) Cengage Gale.
Fulcher, Roz. Science Around the House: Simple Projects Using Household Recyclables. 2010. (Dover Children's Science Bks.). (ENG., Illus.). 80p. (J). (gr. 3-5). pap. 6.99 *(978-0-486-47645-2(6))* Dover Pubns., Inc.
Fun Fabrics. 2013. (From Trash to Treasure Ser.). 32p. (J). (gr. 3-6). pap. 70.50 *(978-1-4777-1363-1(8)*, PowerKids Pr.) Rosen Publishing Group, Inc., The.
Ganeri, Anita. From Rags to Bags Gold Band. 2016. (Cambridge Reading Adventures Ser.). (ENG.). 16p. pap. 6.56 *(978-1-316-50086-6(1))* Cambridge Univ. Pr.
Gardner, Robert. Recycle: Green Science Projects for a Sustainable Planet. 2011. (Team Green Science Projects Ser.). (Illus.). 128p. (J). (gr. 5-9). lib. bdg. 33.27 *(978-0-7660-3648-2(0))* Enslow Pubs., Inc.
Gay, Kathlyn. Buried: Too Much Garbage. 2016. (End of Life As We Know It Ser.). (ENG., Illus.). 144p. (J). (gr. 7-8). lib. bdg. 37.27 *(978-0-7660-7276-3(2))* Enslow Pubs., Inc.
Goldsmith, Mike. Recycling. 2009. (Now We Know About... Ser.). (ENG., Illus.). 24p. (J). (gr. k-3). pap. *(978-0-7787-4739-0(5))*; lib. bdg. *(978-0-7787-4722-2(0))* Crabtree Publishing Co.
Goldstein, Monica. Children Go Green: Bus trip to Little Stars Elementary. 2010. 23p. (J). pap. 14.95 *(978-1-4327-2528-0(9))* Outskirts Pr., Inc.
Gordon, Jo. Reciclar (Recycling) (SPA., Illus.). 32p. (J). 10.95 *(978-84-348-3988-5(1))* SM Ediciones ESP. Dist: AIMS International Bks., Inc.
Gould, Roberta. The Kid's Book of Incredibly Fun Crafts. Martin Jourdenais, Norma Jean, illus. 2004. (Williamson's Kids Can! Ser.). 128p. (J). pap. 14.95 *(978-1-885593-85-6(6)*, Ideal Pubns.) Worthy Publishing.
Green Crafts. 2010. (Green Crafts Ser.). (ENG.). 32p. (gr. 3-4). lib. bdg. 167.94 *(978-1-4296-5460-9(0))*; lib. bdg. 55.98 *(978-1-4296-5459-3(7))*; lib. bdg. 111.96 *(978-1-4296-4768-7(X))*; lib. bdg. 55.98 *(978-1-4296-4769-4(8))* Capstone Press of Coughlan Cos. (Snap Bks.).
Green, Jen. Garbage & Litter. 2010. (J). pap. 10.60 *(978-1-61532-243-5(4)*, PowerKids Pr.); 32p. (J). (gr. 1-5). E-Book 50.50 *(978-1-4488-0365-1(9))*; (Illus.). 32p. (YA). (gr. 2-5). lib. bdg. 26.50 *(978-1-61532-234-3(5))* Rosen Publishing Group, Inc., The.
—Reducing & Recycling Waste. 2011. (Sherlock Bones Looks at the Environment Ser.). (ENG., Illus.). 32p. (YA). (gr. 3-6). lib. bdg. 25.25 *(978-1-61533-382-0(7))* Windmill Bks.
—Why Should I Recycle? Gordon, Mike, illus. 2005. (Why Should I? Bks.). (ENG.). 32p. (J). pap. 7.99 *(978-0-7641-3155-4(9))* Barron's Educational Series, Inc.
Green, Robert. From Waste to Energy. 2009. (21st Century Skills Library: Power Up! Ser.). (ENG.). 32p. (gr. 4-8). lib. bdg. 28.50 *(978-1-60279-509-9(6)*, 200324) Cherry Lake Publishing.
Greenhaven Press Editors, ed. Garbage & Recycling. 2011. (Opposing Viewpoints Ser.). (Illus.). 240p. (YA). (gr. 9-12). 42.95 *(978-0-7377-5428-5(1))* Cengage Gale.
Grier, Paul. Recycling Paper. 2013. (InfoMax Readers Ser.). (ENG.). 24p. (J). (gr. 2-3). pap. 49.50 *(978-1-4777-2275-6(0))*; (Illus.). pap. 8.25 *(978-1-4777-2274-9(2))* Rosen Publishing Group, Inc., The. (Rosen Classroom).
Heos, Bridget. Follow That Bottle! A Plastic Recycling Journey. Westgate, Alex, illus. 2016. (Keeping Cities Clean Ser.). (ENG.). 24p. (J). (gr. k-3). 20.95 *(978-1-60753-964-3(0))* Amicus Publishing.
—Follow That Garbage! A Journey to the Landfill. Westgate, Alex, illus. 2016. (Keeping Cities Clean Ser.). (ENG.). 24p. (J). (gr. k-3). 20.95 *(978-1-60753-963-6(2))* Amicus Publishing.
—Follow That Paper! A Paper Recycling Journey. Westgate, Alex, illus. 2016. (Keeping Cities Clean Ser.). (ENG.). 24p. (J). (gr. k-3). 20.95 *(978-1-60753-965-0(9))* Amicus Publishing.
Hewitt, Sally. Reduce & Reuse. 2008. (Rise & Shine Ser.). (ENG., Illus.). 32p. (J). (gr. 3-7). pap. *(978-0-7787-4102-2(8))* Crabtree Publishing Co.
—Waste & Recycling. 2008. (Rise & Shine Ser.). (ENG., Illus.). 32p. (J). (gr. 3-7). pap. *(978-0-7787-4105-3(2))*; lib. bdg. *(978-0-7787-4098-8(6))* Crabtree Publishing Co.
Hock, Peggy. Making Less Trash. 2008. (ENG.). 24p. (J). (gr. 1-2). pap. 6.95 *(978-0-531-20434-4(0)*, Children's Pr.) Scholastic Library Publishing.
Holland, Gini. Paper Crafts. 2013. (From Trash to Treasure Ser.). 32p. (J). (gr. 3-6). 26.50 *(978-1-4777-1282-5(8))*; pap. 11.75 *(978-1-4777-1358-7(1))* Rosen Publishing Group, Inc., The. (PowerKids Pr.).
Hunter, Rebecca. Waste & Recycling. 2012. (Eco Alert! Ser.). (Illus.). 32p. (gr. 4-6). lib. bdg. 28.50 *(978-1-59771-299-6(X))* Sea-To-Sea Pubns.
Icanberry, Mark. LooLeDo. 96p. Bk. 1. 2010. (Illus.). 12.95 *(978-1-893327-12-2(4))*Bk. 2. 2011. 14.95 *(978-1-893327-11-5(6))*Bk. 3. 2011. 14.95 *(978-1-893327-10-8(8))* Look, Learn & Do Pubns.
Ikids Staff. Why Do We Recycle? Science Made Simple! Pérez, Sara Rojo, illus. 2009. (ENG.). 22p. (J). (gr. -1-1). 9.99 *(978-1-58476-935-4(1))* Innovative Kids.
Inskipp, Carol. Reducing & Recycling Waste. 2005. (Improving Our Environment Ser.). (Illus.). 32p. (gr. 3-6). lib. bdg. 26.00 *(978-0-8368-4429-0(7)*, Gareth Stevens Learning Library) Stevens, Gareth Publishing LLLP.
Jackson, Steve. How Is Paper Recycled? 2013. (Rosen Readers Ser.). (ENG.). 24p. (J). (gr. 2-3). pap. 49.50 *(978-1-4777-2255-8(6))*; pap. 8.25 *(978-1-4777-2254-1(8))* Rosen Publishing Group, Inc., The. (Rosen Classroom).
James, Lincoln. Where Does the Garbage Go? 2012. (Everyday Mysteries Ser.). (ENG., Illus.). 24p. (J). (gr. 2-4). pap. 8.15 *(978-1-4339-6327-8(2))*; lib. bdg. 22.60 *(978-1-4339-6325-4(6))* Stevens, Gareth Publishing LLLP.
Jewelry. 2013. (From Trash to Treasure Ser.). 32p. (J). (gr. 3-6). pap. 70.50 *(978-1-4777-1361-7(1)*, PowerKids Pr.) Rosen Publishing Group, Inc., The.
Jones, Jen. Cool Crafts with Flowers, Leaves, & Twigs: Green Projects for Resourceful Kids, 1 vol. 2010. (Green Crafts Ser.). (ENG.). 32p. (gr. 3-4). lib. bdg. 27.99 *(978-1-4296-4766-3(3)*, Snap Bks.) Capstone Press of Coughlan Cos.
—Cool Crafts with Seeds, Beans, & Cones: Green Projects for Resourceful Kids, 1 vol. 2010. (Green Crafts Ser.). (ENG.). 32p. (gr. 3-4). lib. bdg. 27.99 *(978-1-4296-4767-0(1)*, Snap Bks.) Capstone Press of Coughlan Cos.
Jones, Jen & Sirrine, Carol. Re-Craft: Unique Projects That Look Great (And Save the Planet) 2011. (Craft It Yourself Ser.). (ENG.). 112p. (gr. 3-4). pap. 12.95 *(978-1-4296-6637-4(4))* Capstone Young Readers of Coughlan Cos.
Kemarskaya, Oksana. Planet Earth Projects. 2011. (Dover Children's Activity Bks.). (ENG., Illus.). 64p. (J). (gr. 3-5). pap. 6.99 *(978-0-486-47923-1(4))* Dover Pubns., Inc.
Kings, Gary & Ginger, Richard. Funky Junk: Recycle Rubbish into Art! Green, Barry, illus. 2012. (Dover Children's Activity Bks.). (ENG.). 64p. (J). (gr. 3-5). pap. 9.99 *(978-0-486-49022-9(X))* Dover Pubns., Inc.
Kishel, Ann-Marie. Recycle. 2006. (First Step Nonfiction - Conservation Ser.). (ENG., Illus.). 8p. (gr. -1-1). pap. 4.95 *(978-0-8225-5676-3(6)*, Lerner Pubns.) Lerner Publishing Group.
—Reduce. 2006. (First Step Nonfiction - Conservation Ser.). (ENG., Illus.). 8p. (gr. -1-1). pap. 4.95 *(978-0-8225-5677-0(4)*, Lerner Pubns.) Lerner Publishing Group.
Kondonassis, Yolanda. Our House Is Round: A Kid's Book about Why Protecting Our Earth Matters. Brush, Joan, illus. 2012. (ENG.). 48p. (J). (gr. k-3). 16.95 *(978-1-61608-588-9(6)*, 608588, Sky Pony Pr.) Skyhorse Publishing Co., Inc.
Kutner, Laura, et al. The Soda Bottle School: A True Story of Recycling & the Power of an Idea, 1 vol. 2016. (ENG., Illus.). 32p. (gr. 1-7). pap. 8.95 *(978-0-88448-372-4(X)*, 884372) Tilbury Hse. Pubs.
Lanz, Helen. Reduce, Reuse, Recycle. 2012. (Go Green Ser.). (Illus.). (gr. 3-6). lib. bdg. 28.50 *(978-1-59771-303-0(1))* Sea-To-Sea Pubns.
Lawrence, Ellen. Garbage Galore. 2014. (Science Slam: Green World, Clean World Ser.). 24p. (J). (gr. -1-3). lib. bdg. 23.93 *(978-1-62724-102-1(7))* Bearport Publishing Co., Inc.
Lepetit, Angie. Trash Magic: A Book about Recycling a Plastic Bottle. 2013. (Earth Matters Ser.). (ENG.). 32p. (gr. 1-2). pap. 47.70 *(978-1-62065-744-7(9))*; pap. 8.10 *(978-1-62065-743-0(0))*; lib. bdg. 27.32 *(978-1-62065-049-3(5))* Capstone Press of Coughlan Cos. (Aplus Bks.).
Lindeen, Mary. Reduce, Reuse, Recycle. 2017. (BeginningtoRead Ser.). (ENG.). 32p. (J). (-2). 22.60 ***(978-1-59953-876-1(8))***; pap. 11.94 ***(978-1-68404-095-7(7))*** Norwood Hse. Pr.
Llewellyn, Claire. Let's Recycle. 2005. (Illus.). 32p. (YA). (gr. 1-18). lib. bdg. 27.10 *(978-1-932333-22-0(3))* Chrysalis Education.
Limós, Anna. Easy Earth-Friendly Crafts in 5 Steps. 2008. (Easy Crafts in 5 Steps Ser.). (Illus.). 32p. (J). (gr. 3-7). lib. bdg. 23.94 *(978-0-7660-3086-2(5)*, Enslow Elementary) Enslow Pubs., Inc.
—Easy Earth-Friendly Crafts in 5 Steps. 2010. (Easy Crafts in 5 Steps Ser.). (Illus.). 32p. (J). pap. 7.95 *(978-0-7660-3761-8(4)*, Enslow Elementary) Enslow Pubs., Inc.
Lord, Michelle. La Naturaleza Recicla¿lo Haces Tú?, 1 vol. Morrison, Cathy, illus. 2013. (ENG & SPA.). 32p. (J). (gr. -1-4). 17.95 *(978-1-60718-711-0(6))* Arbordale Publishing.
—Nature Recycles: How about You?, 1 vol. Morrison, Cathy, illus. 2013. (ENG.). 32p. (J). (gr. -1-4). 17.95 *(978-1-60718-615-1(2))*; pap. 9.95 *(978-1-60718-627-4(6))* Arbordale Publishing.
Lundquist, Jean M. Recycling, Step by Step, 1 vol. 2011. (Step-By-Step Stories Ser.). (ENG.). 32p. (gr. 1-2). lib. bdg. 27.32 *(978-1-4296-6026-6(0)*, Aplus Bks.) Capstone Press of Coughlan Cos.
Macdonald, Margaret. How Can You Re-Use an Egg Carton? 2014. (Little Books of Answers: Level d Ser.). (Illus.). 16p. (gr. k-2). pap. 7.95 *(978-1-927136-34-8(2))* Three Crows Media NZL. Dist: RiverStream Publishing.
MacGregor, Cynthia. Recycling a Can. 2009. (Reading Room Collection 2 Ser.). 24p. (gr. 3-4). 42.50 *(978-1-60851-984-2(8)*, PowerKids Pr.) Rosen Publishing Group, Inc., The.
Maloof, Torrey. We Recycle, 1 vol. (Science Readers: Content & Literacy Ser.). (ENG., Illus.). 24p. (gr. 1-1). 2015. (J). 22.96 *(978-1-4938-1160-1(6))* 2014. pap. 8.99 *(978-1-4807-4573-5(1))* Teacher Created Materials, Inc.
Malue, Jenna. Recycling Plastic: Understand Place Value. 2014. (Math Masters: Number & Operations in Base Ten Ser.). (Illus.). 24p. (J). (gr. 2-3). 23.60 *(978-1-4777-6427-5(5))*; (ENG., pap. 8.25 *(978-1-4777-4651-6(X))* Rosen Publishing Group, Inc., The. (Rosen Classroom).
Mancini, Candice. Garbage & Recycling. 2010. (Global Viewpoints Ser.). (ENG.). 224p. 40.45 *(978-0-7377-5081-2(2))*; (Illus.). pap. 27.95 *(978-0-7377-5082-9(0))* Cengage Gale. (Greenhaven Pr., Inc.).
Martin, Laura C. Recycled Crafts Box: Sock Puppets, Cardboard Castles, Bottle Bugs & 37 More Earth-Friendly Projects & Activities You Can Create. 2004. (ENG., Illus.). 96p. (J). (gr. 3-8). pap. 10.95 *(978-1-58017-522-7(8)*, 67522) Storey Publishing, LLC.
McMullen, Gemma. Recycling Materials. 2017. (Environmental Issues Ser.). 24p. (J). (gr. 2-3). pap. 8.25 ***(978-1-5345-2049-3(X))***; lib. bdg. 24.60 ***(978-1-5345-2051-6(1))*** Greenhaven Publishing LLC. (KidHaven Publishing).
Meissner, David. Where Does Your Garbage Go? 2011. (Early Connections Ser.). (J). *(978-1-61672-608-9(3))* Benchmark Education Co.
Meredith, Susan. Why Should I Recycle? 2010. (What's Happening Ser.). 48p. (J). pap. 6.99 *(978-0-7945-2785-3(X)*, Usborne) EDC Publishing.
Metz, Lorijo. What Can We Do about Trash & Recycling? 2009. (Protecting Our Planet Ser.). (Illus.). 24p. (ENG.). (J). pap. 8.25 *(978-1-4358-2483-6(0)*, PowerKids Pr.); (YA). (gr. 2-5). lib. bdg. 22.60 *(978-1-4042-8082-3(0))* Rosen Publishing Group, Inc., The.
Miller, Heather. Nifty Thrifty Art Crafts. Ponte, June, illus. 2007. (Nifty Thrifty Crafts for Kids Ser.). 32p. (J). (gr. 3-7). lib. bdg. 23.94 *(978-0-7660-2780-0(5)*, Enslow Elementary) Enslow Pubs., Inc.
Milner, Sara. A Trip to the Recycling Center. 2016. (PowerKids Readers: My Community Ser.). 00024p. (J). (gr. k-k). pap. 8.25 *(978-1-4994-2778-3(6)*, PowerKids Pr.) Rosen Publishing Group, Inc., The.
Minden, Cecilia. Kids Can Clean up Trash. 2010. (21st Century Basic Skills Library: Kids Can Ser.). (ENG.). 24p. (gr. k-3). lib. bdg. 22.79 *(978-1-60279-870-0(2)*, 200606) Cherry Lake Publishing.
—Kids Can Recycle. 2010. (21st Century Basic Skills Library: Kids Can Ser.). (ENG.). 24p. (gr. k-3). lib. bdg. 22.79 *(978-1-60279-867-0(2)*, 200600) Cherry Lake Publishing.
—Kids Can Reuse. 2010. (21st Century Basic Skills Library: Kids Can Ser.). (ENG.). 24p. (gr. k-3). lib. bdg. 22.79 *(978-1-60279-868-7(0)*, 200602) Cherry Lake Publishing.
—Save the Planet: Reduce, Reuse, & Recycle. 2010. (Explorer Library: Language Arts Explorer Ser.). (ENG.). 32p. (gr. 4-8). pap. 14.21 *(978-1-60279-671-3(8)*, 200918); lib. bdg. 28.50 *(978-1-60279-662-1(9)*, 200355) Cherry Lake Publishing.
Mooney, Carla. Recycling. rev. ed. 2014. (Matters of Opinion Ser.). (ENG.). 64p. (J). (gr. 4-6). pap. 14.60 *(978-1-60357-583-6(9))*; (Illus.). lib. bdg. 27.93 *(978-1-59953-603-3(X))* Norwood Hse. Pr.
Moore, Phillip. Where Does Used Paper Go? 2014. (Little Books of Answers: Level F Ser.). (Illus.). 16p. (gr. k-2). pap. 7.95 *(978-1-927136-54-6(7))* Three Crows Media NZL. Dist: RiverStream Publishing.
Morgan, Sally. Old Clothes. 2007. (Dealing with Waste/Watts Ser.). (Illus.). 30p. (J). (gr. 4-7). lib. bdg. 28.50 *(978-1-59920-011-8(2))* Black Rabbit Bks.
Moser, Elise. What Milly Did: The Remarkable Pioneer of Plastics Recycling, 1 vol. Ritchie, Scot, illus. 2016. (ENG.). 48p. (J). (gr. 2-6). pap. 9.95 *(978-1-55498-893-8(4))* Groundwood Bks. CAN. Dist: Publishers Group West (PGW).
National Geographic Learning Staff. Taking Care of Earth, Level 3. 2011. (World Windows Ser.). (ENG., Illus.). 16p. (J). stu. ed. 9.95 *(978-1-133-56615-1(4))* Cengage Heinle.
—Why Should I Recycle Garbage? 2010. (ENG., Illus.). 32p. (C). (gr. -1-3). pap. 15.95 *(978-1-897563-47-2(7))* National Geographic School Publishing, Inc.
Nelson, Robin. How I Reduce, Reuse, & Recycle. 2014. (First Step Nonfiction - Responsibility in Action Ser.). (ENG., Illus.). 24p. (gr. k-2). lib. bdg. 23.93 *(978-1-4677-3636-7(8)*, Lerner Pubns.) Lerner Publishing Group.
Nunn, Daniel. Paper, 1 vol. 2011. (From Trash to Treasures Ser.). (ENG.). 24p. (gr. k-2). 23.32 *(978-1-4329-5151-1(3)*, Heinemann Read & Learn) Heinemann-Raintree.
—Plastic, 1 vol. 2011. (From Trash to Treasures Ser.). (ENG.). 24p. (gr. k-2). 23.32 *(978-1-4329-5148-1(3)*, Heinemann Read & Learn) Heinemann-Raintree.
Orme, Helen. Garbage & Recycling. 2008. (Earth in Danger Ser.). (Illus.). 32p. (YA). (gr. 3-6). lib. bdg. 25.27 *(978-1-59716-726-0(6)*, 1284325) Bearport Publishing Co., Inc.
Otfinoski, Steven. Recycling & Upcycling: Science, Technology, Engineering. 2016. (Calling All Innovators: a Career for You Ser.). (ENG., Illus.). 64p. (J). lib. bdg. 32.00 *(978-0-531-23002-2(3)*, Children's Pr.) Scholastic Library Publishing.
Owen, Ruth. Fun Fabrics. 2013. (From Trash to Treasure Ser.). 32p. (J). (gr. 3-6). 26.50 *(978-1-4777-1284-9(4))*; pap. 11.75 *(978-1-4777-1362-4(X))* Rosen Publishing Group, Inc., The. (PowerKids Pr.).
—Gifts. 2013. (From Trash to Treasure Ser.). 32p. (J). (gr. 3-6). 26.50 *(978-1-4777-1287-0(9))*; pap. 11.75 *(978-1-4777-1368-6(9))*; pap. 70.50 *(978-1-4777-1369-3(7))* Rosen Publishing Group, Inc., The. (PowerKids Pr.).
—Jewelry. 2013. 32p. (J). (gr. 3-6). 26.50 *(978-1-4777-1283-2(6))*; pap. 11.75 *(978-1-4777-1360-0(3))* Rosen Publishing Group, Inc., The. (PowerKids Pr.).
—Nature Crafts. 2013. (From Trash to Treasure Ser.). 32p. (J). (gr. 3-6). 26.50 *(978-1-4777-1285-6(2))*; pap. 11.75 *(978-1-4777-1364-8(6))*; pap. 70.50 *(978-1-4777-1365-5(4))* Rosen Publishing Group, Inc., The. (PowerKids Pr.).
—Paper Crafts. 2013. (From Trash to Treasure Ser.). 32p. (J). (gr. 3-6). pap. 70.50 *(978-1-4777-1359-4(X)*, PowerKids Pr.) Rosen Publishing Group, Inc., The.
Oxlade, Chris. Garbage & Recycling, 1 vol. 2012. (How Does My Home Work? Ser.). (ENG.). 24p. (gr. k-1). pap. 6.79 *(978-1-4329-6571-6(9))*; lib. bdg. 23.32 *(978-1-4329-6566-2(2))* Heinemann-Raintree. (Heinemann Read & Learn).
Palmer, Erin. Recycling, Yes or No. 2015. (ENG.). 24p. (gr. k-3). 28.50 *(978-1-63430-347-7(4))* Rourke Educational Media.
Parks, Peggy J. Garbage & Recycling. 2008. (Ripped from the Headlines Ser.). (YA). (gr. 7-12). 23.95 *(978-1-60217-023-0(1))* Erickson Pr.
—Garbage & Recycling. 2010. (Compact Research Ser.). (YA). (gr. 7-12). 26.95 *(978-1-60152-121-7(9))* ReferencePoint Pr., Inc.
Parramon's Editorial Team Staff. Recyclables. Parramon's Editorial Team Staff, photos by. 2004. (Let's Create! Ser.). (Illus.). 32p. (gr. 1-4). lib. bdg. 26.00 *(978-0-8368-4018-6(6)*, Gareth Stevens Learning Library) Stevens, Gareth Publishing LLLP.
Paul, Miranda. One Plastic Bag: Isatou Ceesay & the Recycling Women of the Gambia. Zunon, Elizabeth, illus. 2015. (ENG.). 32p. (J). (gr. k-3). lib. bdg. 19.99 *(978-1-4677-1608-6(1))* Lerner Publishing Group.
Pohl, Kathleen. What Happens at a Recycling Center? 2006. (Where People Work Ser.). (Illus.). 24p. (gr. -1-3). pap. 8.15 *(978-0-8368-6895-1(1))*; lib. bdg. 22.00 *(978-0-8368-6888-3(9))* Stevens, Gareth Publishing LLLP. (Weekly Reader Leveled Readers).
—What Happens at a Recycling Center? (Que Pasa En Un Centro De Reciclaje?) 2006. (Where People Work/Dónde Trabaja la Gente? Ser.). (SPA., Illus.). 24p. (gr. -1-3). pap. 8.15 *(978-0-8368-7396-2(3)*, Weekly Reader Leveled Readers) Stevens, Gareth Publishing LLLP.
—What Happens at a Recycling Center?/Qué Pasa en un Centro de Reciclaje? 2006. (Where People Work/Dónde Trabaja la Gente? Ser.). (ENG & SPA., Illus.). 24p. (J). (gr. -1-3). lib. bdg. 22.00 *(978-0-8368-7389-4(0)*, Weekly Reader Leveled Readers) Stevens, Gareth Publishing LLLP.
Pratt, Mary K. How Can We Reduce Household Waste? 2016. (Searchlight Books — What Can We Do about Pollution? Ser.). (ENG., Illus.). 40p. (J). (gr. 3-5). 30.65 *(978-1-4677-9517-3(8)*, Lerner Pubns.) Lerner Publishing Group.
Puri, Devi. Recycling, Reusing, & Conserving. 2016. (Global Guardians Ser.). 00024p. (J). (gr. 3-3). pap. 8.25 *(978-1-4994-2755-4(7)*, PowerKids Pr.) Rosen Publishing Group, Inc., The.
Rabe, Tish. How to Help the Earth-By the LORAX. Ruiz, Aristides et al, illus. 2012. (Step into Reading Ser.). (ENG.). 48p. (J). (gr. k-3). pap. 3.99 *(978-0-375-86977-8(8)*, Random Hse. Bks. for Young Readers) Random Hse. Children's Bks.
—How to Help the Earth-By the Lorax. 2012. (Step into Reading Level 3 Ser.). lib. bdg. 13.55 *(978-0-606-23848-9(4)*, Turtleback) Turtleback Bks.
Rau, Dana Meachen. Crafting with Recyclables. Petelinsek, Kathleen, illus. 2013. (How-To Library). (ENG.). 32p. (J). (gr. 3-6). 28.50 *(978-1-62431-146-8(6)*, 202904); pap. 14.21 *(978-1-62431-278-6(0)*, 202906) Cherry Lake Publishing.
—Crafting with Recyclables: Even More Projects. Petelinsek, Kathleen, illus. 2016. (How-To Library). (ENG.). 32p. (J). (gr. 3-6). lib. bdg. 29.93 *(978-1-63471-419-8(9)*, 208455) Cherry Lake Publishing.
Reynolds, Alison. Let's Use It Again. Hopgood, Andrew, illus. 2009. (Save Our Planet! Ser.). 12p. (J). (gr. -1-3). bds. 11.40 *(978-1-60754-415-9(6))* Windmill Bks.
Rhatigan, Joe. Get a Job at the Garbage Dump. 2016. (Bright Futures Press: Get a Job Ser.). (ENG.). 32p. (J). (gr. 4-6). 29.93 *(978-1-63471-905-6(0)*, 208941) Cherry Lake Publishing.
Riachi, Ghassan Diab & Mitchell, Anna B. L. I. B. B. Y. The Green Dog. RJI Publishing, ed. Ritzmann, Mary B., illus. 2011.Tr. of L. I. B. B. Y. , el Perro Verde. 32p. (J). mass mkt. 9.95 *(978-1-885184-11-5(5))* RJI Publishing.
Rice, Dona. Too Much Trash!, 1 vol. (Science Readers: Content & Literacy Ser.). (ENG., Illus.). 24p. (gr. k-k). 2015. (J). 22.96 *(978-1-4938-1144-1(4))* 2014. pap. 8.99 *(978-1-4807-4534-6(0))* Teacher Created Materials, Inc.
Richmond, Benjamin. Where Do Garbage Trucks Go? 2016. (Good Question! Ser.). (ENG., Illus.). 32p. (J). (gr. 1). pap. 5.95 *(978-1-4549-1625-3(7))* Sterling Publishing Co., Inc.
—Where Do Garbage Trucks Go? And Other Questions about Trash & Recycling. 2016. (Good Question! Ser.). (ENG., Illus.). 40p. (J). (gr. 1). 12.95 *(978-1-4549-1624-6(9))* Sterling Publishing Co., Inc.
Riley, Karen. Agarranderas Plasticas y Otras Cosas: Plastic Rings & Other Things. 2003. (ENG & SPA., Illus.). 16p. (J). (gr. 2-5). pap. 4.50 *(978-0-9708135-2-7(X))* S.C.R.A.P. Gallery.
Roca, Nuria. The Three R's: Reuse, Reduce, Recycle. Curto, Rosa Maria, illus. 2007. (What Do You Know about? Bks.). (ENG.). 36p. (J). (gr. -1-1). pap. 6.99 *(978-0-7641-3581-1(3))* Barron's Educational Series, Inc.
Rodger, Ellen. Recycling Waste. 2008. (Saving Our World Ser.). 32p. (gr. 4-18). lib. bdg. 28.50 *(978-0-7614-3222-7(1)*, Benchmark Bks.) Marshall Cavendish Corp.
Ross, Kathy. Earth-Friendly Crafts: Clever Ways to Reuse Everyday Items. Malépart, Céline, illus. (ENG.). 48p. (gr. 2-5). 2011. pap. 7.95 *(978-0-7613-7409-1(4))* 2009. 26.60 *(978-0-8225-9099-6(9))* Lerner Publishing Group. (Millbrook Pr.).
Ross, Michael Elsohn. Re-Cycles. Moore, Gustav, illus. 2003. (Cycles Ser.). (ENG.). 32p. (gr. 2-4). pap. 7.95 *(978-0-7613-1949-8(2)*, First Avenue Editions) Lerner Publishing Group.
Scheunemann, Pam. Cool Metal Projects: Creative Ways to Upcycle Your Trash into Treasure, 1 vol. 2012. (Cool Trash to Treasure Ser.). (ENG., Illus.). 32p. (J). (gr. 3-6). lib. bdg. 27.07 *(978-1-61783-434-9(3)*, Checkerboard Library) ABDO Publishing Co.

P
Q
R

Sévigny, Eric, illus. As Good as New. 2012. (Ecology Club Ser.). (ENG.). 24p. (J). (gr. -1-1). pap. 5.99 *(978-2-89450-832-9(8))* Caillouet, Gerry.
—Caillou - Learns to Recycle. 2013. (Ecology Club Ser.). (ENG.). 24p. (J). (gr. -1-1). 5.95 *(978-2-89718-027-0(7))* Caillouet, Gerry.
Shea, Jerry. Where Does the Recycling Go? 2012. (Everyday Mysteries Ser.). (ENG., Illus.). 24p. (J). (gr. 2-4). 22.60 *(978-1-4339-6333-9(7))*; pap. 8.15 *(978-1-4339-6335-3(3))* Stevens, Gareth Publishing LLLP.
Shores, Erika L. How Garbage Gets from Trash Cans to Landfills. 2016. (Here to There Ser.). (ENG., Illus.). 24p. (gr. k-1). lib. bdg. 26.65 *(978-1-4914-8433-3(0)*, Pebble Plus) Capstone Press of Coughlan Cos.
Slade, Suzanne, et al. The Soda Bottle School: A True Story about Recycling, Teamwork, & One Crazy Idea. 2014. (ENG., Illus.). 32p. (gr. 1-7). 16.95 *(978-0-88448-371-7(1)*, 884371) Tilbury Hse. Pubs.
Solway, Andrew. Waste Disposal. 2010. (World at Risk Ser.). (YA). (gr. 5-9). 34.25 *(978-1-59920-380-5(4))* Black Rabbit Bks.
Spilsbury, Louise. Projects with Recycling & Reusing. 2014. (Make & Learn Ser.). 32p. (J). (gr. 3-6). lib. bdg. 27.50 *(978-1-4777-7169-3(7)*, PowerKids Pr.) Rosen Publishing Group, Inc., The.
—Waste & Recycling Challenges. 2009. (Illus.). 48p. (J). 70.50 *(978-1-4358-5487-1(X)*, Rosen Reference); (ENG., pap. 11.75 *(978-1-4358-5486-4(1)*, Rosen Reference); (ENG., (gr. 5-9). lib. bdg. 29.25 *(978-1-4358-5355-3(5))* Rosen Publishing Group, Inc., The.
Stamper, Judith Bauer. Sam Helps Recycle. 2010. (J). *(978-1-60617-138-7(0))* Teaching Strategies, LLC.
Sundance/Newbridge LLC Staff. Where Does All the Garbage Go? 2007. (Early Science Ser.). (gr. k-3). 18.95 *(978-1-4007-6260-6(X))*; pap. 6.10 *(978-1-4007-6256-9(1))* Sundance/Newbridge Educational Publishing.
Thomas, Elizabeth. Reduce, Reuse, Recycle. 2011. (Go Green! Ser.). (ENG., Illus.). 32p. (J). (gr. 1-4). lib. bdg. 28.50 *(978-1-60973-176-2(X)*, 201155) Child's World, Inc., The.
Troupe, Thomas Kingsley. Shred It!, 1 vol. 2013. (Destruction Ser.). (ENG.). 24p. (gr. k-1). 26.65 *(978-1-4765-2089-6(5)*, Pebble Plus) Capstone Press of Coughlan Cos.
Turnbull, Stephanie. Trash & Recycling. 2006. (Beginners Science Ser.). (Illus.). 32p. (J). (gr. 4-7). lib. bdg. 12.99 *(978-1-58086-948-5(3)*, Usborne) EDC Publishing.
—Trash & Recycling. Fox, Christyan, illus. 2006. (Beginners Science: Level 2 Ser.). 32p. (J). (gr. 1-3). 4.99 *(978-0-7945-1400-6(6)*, Usborne) EDC Publishing.
Ventura, Marne. Amazing Recycled Projects You Can Create. 2015. (Imagine It, Build It Ser.). (ENG., Illus.). 32p. (gr. 3-4). lib. bdg. 27.99 *(978-1-4914-4292-0(1))* Capstone Press of Coughlan Cos.
—Fun Things to Do with Milk Jugs, 1 vol. 2014. (10 Things to Do Ser.). (ENG.). 32p. (gr. 1-2). 27.32 *(978-1-4765-9894-9(0))* Capstone Press of Coughlan Cos.
Walker, Kate. Food & Garden Waste. 2010. (Recycling Ser.). 32p. (gr. 1). 28.50 *(978-1-60870-129-2(8))* Marshall Cavendish Corp.
Watson, Stephanie. Making Good Choices about Recycling & Reuse. 2009. (J). 77.70 *(978-1-4358-5607-3(4)*, Rosen Reference); (ENG.). 64p. (YA). pap. 12.95 *(978-1-4358-5606-6(6)*, Rosen Reference); (Illus.). 64p. (YA). (gr. 5-9). lib. bdg. 31.95 *(978-1-4358-5312-6(1))* Rosen Publishing Group, Inc., The.
Webb, Barb. What Does Green Mean? 2011. (ENG., Illus.). 24p. (gr. k-2). pap. 8.95 *(978-1-61741-973-7(7))* Rourke Educational Media.
Weber, Rebecca. Time to Recycle, 1 vol. 2011. (Earth & Space Science Ser.). (ENG.). 24p. (gr. k-1). pap. 7.29 *(978-1-4296-7140-8(8))*; pap. 41.70 *(978-1-4296-7145-3(9))* Capstone Press of Coughlan Cos. (Pebble Plus).
Weitzman, Elizabeth. 10 Cosas Que Puedes Hacer para Reducir,reciclar y Reutilizar. 2017. (Rookie Star — Make a Difference (Spanish Translation) Ser.). (SPA.). 32p. (J). pap. 5.95 ***(978-1-338-18781-6(3))***; lib. bdg. 25.00 ***(978-0-531-22860-9(6))*** Scholastic Library Publishing. (Children's Pr.).
Weitzman, Elizabeth. 10 Things You Can Do to Reduce, Reuse, Recycle. 2016. (Rookie Star — Make a Difference Ser.). (ENG., Illus.). 32p. (J). lib. bdg. 25.00 *(978-0-531-22654-4(9)*, Children's Pr.) Scholastic Library Publishing.
Wheeler-Toppen, Jodi. Amazing Cardboard Tube Science. 2016. (Recycled Science Ser.). (ENG., Illus.). 32p. (gr. 3-4). lib. bdg. 27.99 *(978-1-5157-0860-5(8))* Capstone Press of Coughlan Cos.
Whittaker, Helen. Waste. 2011. (Living Green Ser.). 32p. (gr. 3). 28.50 *(978-1-60870-577-1(3))* Marshall Cavendish Corp.
Wilcox, Charlotte. Earth-Friendly Waste Management. 2009. pap. 58.95 *(978-0-7613-4691-3(0))* 2008. (Illus.). 72p. (YA). (gr. 4-7). lib. bdg. 30.60 *(978-0-8225-7560-3(4))* Lerner Publishing Group.
—Recycling. 2008. pap. 52.95 *(978-0-8225-9329-4(7))* 2007. (ENG., Illus.). 48p. (gr. 4-8). lib. bdg. 27.93 *(978-0-8225-6768-4(7))* Lerner Publishing Group.
Williams, Nancy Noel. Don't Lose It, Reuse It. 2010. *(978-1-60617-134-9(8))* Teaching Strategies, LLC.
Williams, Zachary. Cleaning up the Park: Learning to Count by Fives. 2009. (Math for the REAL World Ser.). 12p. (gr. 1-2). pap. 5.90 *(978-0-8239-8892-1(9)*, Rosen Classroom) Rosen Publishing Group, Inc., The.
Winnick, Nick. Reduce Waste. 2010. (Being Green Ser.). (Illus.). 32p. (YA). (gr. 3-6). lib. bdg. 27.13 *(978-1-61690-100-4(4))*; (J). (gr. 4-6). pap. 12.95 *(978-1-61690-101-1(2))* Weigl Pubs., Inc.
Yanish, Brian. ScrapKins: Junk Re-Thunk: Amazing Creations You Can Build from Junk. Yanish, Brian, illus. 2016. (ENG., Illus.). 80p. (J). pap. 12.99 *(978-1-62779-133-5(7)*, 9781627791335, Holt, Henry & Co. Bks. For Young Readers) Holt, Henry & Co.
Youngs, Clare & Young, Clare. Explorar y Crear. 2012. (SPA.). 128p. (gr. 13-13). pap. 20.99 *(978-84-261-3887-3(X))* Juventud, Editorial ESP. Dist: Lectorum Pubns., Inc.
Your Carbon Footprint, 6 vols., Set. Incl. On the Move: Green Transportation. Furgang, Kathy & Furgang, Adam. lib. bdg. 29.25 *(978-1-4042-1773-7(8))*; Reducing Your Carbon Footprint at Home. Ganchy, Sally. lib. bdg. 29.25 *(978-1-4042-1772-0(X)*, 1284463); Reducing Your Carbon Footprint at School. Nagle, Jeanne. lib. bdg. 29.25 *(978-1-4042-1774-4(6)*, 1284467); Reducing Your Carbon Footprint in the Kitchen. Hall, Linley Erin. lib. bdg. 29.25 *(978-1-4042-1776-8(2))*; Reducing Your Carbon Footprint on Vacation. Roza, Greg. lib. bdg. 29.25 *(978-1-4042-1777-5(0)*, 1284472); Smart Shopping: Shopping Green. Nagle, Jeanne. lib. bdg. 29.25 *(978-1-4042-1775-1(4)*, 1284468); (Illus.). 48p. (YA). (gr. 5-9). 2008. 2008. Set lib. bdg. 159.00 *(978-1-4042-1880-2(7))* Rosen Publishing Group, Inc., The.
Zahn, Peter. Let's Recycle. 2013. (Rosen Math Readers Ser.). (ENG.). 24p. (J). (gr. 1-2). pap. 8.25 *(978-1-4777-2109-4(6)*, Rosen Classroom) Rosen Publishing Group, Inc., The.
—Let's Recycle: Represent & Solve Addition Problems. 2013. (Core Math Skills: Operations & Algebraic Thinking Ser.). 24p. (J). (gr. 1-2). lib. bdg. 22.60 *(978-1-4777-2207-7(6)*, PowerKids Pr.) Rosen Publishing Group, Inc., The.

RECYCLING (WASTE, ETC.)—FICTION

A Boy And His Dog & Bozak, Jon. Demo: The Story of the Junkyard Dog. 2007. 56p. (J). 19.99 *(978-0-9794769-1-4(7))* Adibooks.com.
Bacigalupi, Paolo. Ship Breaker. 2011. (ENG.). 352p. (YA). (gr. 10-17). pap. 10.99 *(978-0-316-05619-9(7))* Little, Brown Bks. for Young Readers.
Belford, Bibi. Canned & Crushed. 2015. (ENG.). 192p. (J). (gr. 2-7). 14.99 *(978-1-63220-435-6(5)*, Sky Pony Pr.) Skyhorse Publishing Co., Inc.
Berenstain, Jan & Berenstain, Mike. The Berenstain Bears Go Green. 2013. (Berenstain Bears Ser.). (Illus.). (J). lib. bdg. 13.55 *(978-0-606-27142-4(2)*, Turtleback) Turtleback Bks.
Bergen, Lara. Don't Throw That Away! A Lift-the-Flap Book about Recycling & Reusing. Snyder, Betsy E., illus. 2009. (Little Green Bks.). (ENG.). 14p. (J). (gr. -1-1). bds. 7.99 *(978-1-4169-7517-5(9)*, Little Simon) Little Simon.
Berthold, Joy. Peter on Patrol. 2011. 16p. 8.49 *(978-1-4567-1247-1(0))* AuthorHouse.
Bethel, Ellie. Michael Recycle. Colombo, Alexandra, illus. 2008. (Michael Recycle Ser.). (ENG.). 28p. (J). (gr. 2-5). 15.99 *(978-1-60010-224-0(7)*, 9781600102240) Idea & Design Works, LLC.
—Michael Recycle. 2008. (Illus.). (J). 23p. *(978-1-84539-282-6(5))*; *(978-1-84539-281-9(7))* Idea & Design Works, LLC.
—Michael Recycle Meets Litterbug Doug. Colombo, Alexandra, illus. 2009. (Michael Recycle Ser.). (ENG.). 24p. (J). (gr. 2-5). 15.99 *(978-1-60010-392-6(8)*, 9781600103926) Idea & Design Works, LLC.
—Michael Recycle Saves Christmas. Colombo, Alexandra, illus. 2010. (Michael Recycle Ser.). (ENG.). 32p. (J). (gr. 2-5). 15.99 *(978-1-60010-843-3(1)*, 9781600108433) Idea & Design Works, LLC.
Bewley, Elizabeth. Choose to Recycle. Latimer, Miriam, illus. 2009. 10p. 7.95 *(978-1-58117-904-0(9)*, Intervisual/Piggy Toes) Bendon, Inc.
Brouwer, Sigmund. Justine McKeen, Bottle Throttle, 1 vol. Whamond, Dave, illus. 2016. (Orca Echoes Ser.). (ENG.). 80p. (J). (gr. 2-3). pap. 6.95 *(978-1-4598-0731-0(6))* Orca Bk. Pubs. USA.
Brown, Monica & Dominguez, Adriana. Maya's Blanket, 1 vol. Diaz, David, illus. 2015. (SPA & ENG.). 32p. (J). 17.95 *(978-0-89239-292-6(4))* Lee & Low Bks., Inc.
Cook, Sherry & Johnson, Terri. X. E. Ecology. 26. Kuhn, Jesse, illus. l.t. ed. 2006. (Quirkles — Exploring Phonics through Science Ser.: 24). 32p. (J). 7.99 *(978-1-933815-23-7(X)*, Quirkles, The) Creative 3, LLC.
Criswell, Ginger. Recycle Michael. 2012. (Illus.). 24p. 12.99 *(978-1-60010-906-5(3))* Idea & Design Works, LLC.
Dyan, Penelope. Eileen Green the Recycling Queen. Dyan, Penwlope, illus. 2009. 44p. pap. 11.95 *(978-1-935118-51-0(X))* Bellissima Publishing, LLC.
Gall, Chris. Awesome Dawson. 2013. (ENG., Illus.). 40p. (J). (gr. -1-3). 17.99 *(978-0-316-21330-1(6))* Little, Brown Bks. for Young Readers.
Ghigna, Charles. Recycling Is Fun, 1 vol. Jatkowska, Ag, illus. 2012. (My Little Planet Ser.). (ENG.). 24p. (gr. -1 — 1). 6.95 *(978-1-4048-7229-5(9))*; lib. bdg. 22.65 *(978-1-4048-6791-8(0))* Picture Window Bks. (My Little Planet).
Gilbert, Nikki Murphy. Gilbert Green. 2009. 32p. pap. 14.99 *(978-1-4490-4377-3(1))* AuthorHouse.
Glennon, Michelle. My Big Green Teacher: Please Turn off the Lights. Glennon, Michelle, illus. 2008. (ENG., Illus.). 32p. (J). 19.95 *(978-0-9796625-3-9(2))* GDG Publishing.
—My Big Green Teacher: Seven Generations from Now. Glennon, Michelle, illus. 2008. (Illus.). (J). 19.95 *(978-0-9797952-1-3(4))* GDG Publishing.
—My Big Green Teacher: Taking the Green Road. Glennon, Michelle, illus. 2008. (Illus.). 32p. (J). 19.95 *(978-0-9796625-7-7(5))* GDG Publishing.
—My Big Green Teacher: Recycling: It's Easy Being Green. Glennon, Michelle, illus. 2007. (Illus.). 32p. (J). 19.95 *(978-0-9796625-6-0(7))* GDG Publishing.
Handy, Femida & Carpenter, Carole H. Sandy's Incredible Shrinking Footprint, 1 vol. Steele-Card, Adrianna & Second Story Press Staff, illus. 2010. (ENG.). 24p. (J). (gr. 3 — 1). 15.95 *(978-1-897187-69-2(6))* Second Story Pr. CAN. Dist: Orca Bk. Pubs. USA.
Harp, Susan. Evie Goes Clean & Green. Siau, Jon, illus. 2013. 24p. (J). lib. bdg. 14.95 *(978-1-938730-09-2(7))* M.T. Publishing Co., Inc.
Harper, Charise Mericle. Just Grace Goes Green. 2009. (Just Grace Ser.: 4). (ENG., Illus.). 192p. (J). (gr. 1-4). pap. 5.99 *(978-0-547-24821-9(0))* Houghton Mifflin Harcourt Publishing Co.
Hasting, Lori A. Green with N. V. 2012. (ENG.). pap. 14.95 *(978-1-4675-4195-4(8))* Independent Pub.
Inches, Alison. The Adventures of a Plastic Bottle: A Story about Recycling. Whitehead, Pete, illus. 2009. (Little Green Bks.). (ENG.). 24p. (J). (gr. -1-1). pap. 3.99 *(978-1-4169-6788-0(5)*, Little Simon) Little Simon.
—The Adventures of an Aluminum Can: A Story about Recycling. Whitehead, Pete & Chambers, Mark L., illus. 2009. (Little Green Bks.). (ENG.). 24p. (J). (gr. -1-1). pap. 3.99 *(978-1-4169-7221-1(8)*, Little Simon) Little Simon.
Janelle, Nicole & Cholette, Daniel. Naby Recycles. 2012. 32p. pap. 14.60 *(978-1-105-53454-6(5))* Lulu Pr., Inc.
Kann, Victoria. Emeraldalicious. Kann, Victoria, illus. 2013. (Illus.). 40p. (J). (gr. -1-3). (ENG.). 17.99 *(978-0-06-178126-1(6))*; lib. bdg. 18.89 *(978-0-06-178127-8(4))* HarperCollins Pubs.
Klein, Adria F. Max Goes to the Recycling Center, 1 vol. Gallagher-Cole, Mernie, illus. 2009. (Read-It! Readers: the Life of Max Ser.). (ENG.). 24p. (J). (gr. -1-2). 21.32 *(978-1-4048-5272-3(7)*, Easy Readers) Picture Window Bks.
Klepeis, Alicia & Ventura, Gabriela Baeza. Francisco's Kites. Undercuffler, Gary, illus. 2015. (SPA & ENG.). (J). 17.95 *(978-1-55885-804-6(0)*, Piñata Books) Arte Publico Pr.
Kroll, Steven. Stuff! Reduce, Reuse, Recycle, 0 vols. Cox, Steve, illus. 2012. (ENG.). 32p. (J). (gr. -1-3). pap. 7.99 *(978-0-7614-6237-8(6)*, 9780761462378, Amazon Children's Publishing) Amazon Publishing.
Kyrja. Rupert's Tales: Rupert Helps Clean Up, 1 vol. Osborn, Tonia Benington, illus. 2013. (ENG.). 64p. (J). 19.99 *(978-0-7643-4284-4(3)*, 9780764342844) Schiffer Publishing, Ltd.
Lawson, Lela. Robin Recycles: Sharing & Reusing. 2017. (Computer Science for the Real World Ser.). 16p. (gr. 7-8). pap. 7.95 ***(978-1-5383-5220-5(6)***, Rosen Classroom) Rosen Publishing Group, Inc., The.
Lightburn, Ron. Frankenstink! A Cautionary Tale. 2015. (ENG., Illus.). 32p. (J). (gr. -1-3). 17.99 *(978-1-77049-694-1(7)*, Tundra Bks.) Tundra Bks. CAN. Dist: Penguin Random Hse. LLC.
Marshall, Linda Elovitz. Rainbow Weaver/Tejedora del Arcoíris. Chavarri, Elisa, illus. 2016. (ENG & SPA.). 40p. (J). (gr. 1-4). 18.95 *(978-0-89239-374-9(2))* Lee & Low Bks., Inc.
Meissner, David. The Race to Recycle: Set Of 6. 2010. (Early Connections Ser.). (J). pap. 37.00 net. *(978-1-4108-1361-9(4))* Benchmark Education Co.
Messner, Kate. Marty McGuire Digs Worms! Floca, Brian, illus. 2012. (ENG.). 176p. (J). (gr. -1-3). pap. 5.99 *(978-0-545-14247-2(4)*, Scholastic Pr.) Scholastic, Inc.
Miller, Edward. Recycling Day. Miller, Edward, illus. 2014. (ENG., Illus.). 32p. (J). (gr. -1-3). 16.95 *(978-0-8234-2419-1(7))* Holiday Hse., Inc.
Mommy, Tell Me a Story about What Daddy Does. 2nd ed. 2013. 32p. pap. 13.99 *(978-0-9855699-6-9(4))* Richer Life, LLC.
Montgomery, R. A. Your Very Own Robot Goes Cuckoo Bananas. 2009. (Illus.). 80p. (J). pap. 7.99 *(978-1-933390-39-0(5))* Chooseco LLC.
Noll, Tom. The Bicycle Fence. Fall, Brandon & Nishio, Kimiyo, illus. 2014. (Trash to Treasure Ser.: 1). (ENG.). 32p. (J). lib. bdg. 17.99 *(978-1-939377-50-0(1))* Green Kids Pr., LLC.
Ocampo, L. A. The Cardboard Sisters Save the World: An Activity Storybook. 2014. (ENG.). 48p. (J). (gr. -1-3). pap. 7.99 *(978-0-486-49346-6(6))* Dover Pubns., Inc.
O'Leary, Sara. This Is Sadie. Morstad, Julie, illus. 2015. (Sadie Mac Ser.). (ENG.). 32p. (J). (gr. -1-2). 17.99 *(978-1-77049-532-6(0)*, Tundra Bks.) Tundra Bks. CAN. Dist: Penguin Random Hse. LLC.
Ormand, Kate & Louise, Kate. Pierre the French Bulldog Recycles. Straker, Bethany, illus. 2015. (ENG.). 32p. (J). (gr. -1-k). 14.99 *(978-1-63220-411-0(8)*, Sky Pony Pr.) Skyhorse Publishing Co., Inc.
Pace, Marisa. My Community Project: Sharing & Reusing. 2017. (Computer Science for the Real World Ser.). 12p. (gr. 6-7). pap. 7.05 ***(978-1-5383-5170-3(6)***, Rosen Classroom) Rosen Publishing Group, Inc., The.
Papp, Robert, illus. The Clue in the Recycling Bin. 2011. (Boxcar Children Mysteries Ser.: 126). (ENG.). 128p. (J). (gr. 1-5). pap. 6.99 *(978-0-8075-1209-8(5))* Whitman, Albert & Co.
Patterson, Ellie. Michael Recycle & the Tree Top Cops. Colombo, Alexandra, illus. 2012. (Michael Recycle Ser.). (ENG.). 24p. (J). (gr. 2-5). 15.99 *(978-1-61377-161-7(4)*, 9781613771617) Idea & Design Works, LLC.
Perera, Oleene. Timmy Tangelo Goes Green. 2010. 20p. 12.50 *(978-0-557-41286-0(2))* Lulu Pr., Inc.
Readman, Jo. George Saves the World by Lunchtime. Roberts, Ley Honor, illus. 2006. (ENG.). 32p. (J). (gr. k-2). pap. 15.99 *(978-1-903919-50-7(9))* Transworld Publishers Ltd. GBR. Dist: Independent Pubs. Group.
Rey, H. A. Curious George Discovers Recycling. 2017. (Curious George Discovers Ser.). (ENG.). (J). (gr. -1-3). lib. bdg. 17.20 ***(978-0-606-39822-0(8))*** Turtleback Bks.
Rey, H. A. Curious George Plants a Tree. Wilcox, Mary, ed. 2010. (Curious George Ser.). (ENG., Illus.). 24p. (J). (gr. -1-3). pap. 4.99 *(978-0-547-29776-7(9))* Houghton Mifflin Harcourt Publishing Co.
—Curious George Plants a Tree. 2009. (Curious George Ser.). (ENG., Illus.). 32p. (J). (gr. -1-3). 14.99 *(978-0-547-15087-1(3))* Houghton Mifflin Harcourt Publishing Co.
Reynolds, Paul A. Sydney & Simon: Going Green! Reynolds, Paul A. & Reynolds, Peter H., illus. 2015. (Sydney & Simon Ser.). (ENG.). 48p. (J). (gr. 1-4). lib. bdg. 12.95 *(978-1-58089-677-1(4))* Charlesbridge Publishing, Inc.
Ross, Joel. The Fog Diver. 2015. (Fog Diver Ser.: 1). (ENG.). 336p. (J). (gr. 3-7). 16.99 *(978-0-06-235293-4(8))* HarperCollins Pubs.
Ross, Joel. The Lost Compass. (Fog Diver Ser.: 2). (J). (gr. 3-7). 2017. 368p. pap. 6.99 ***(978-0-06-235309-2(8))*** 2016. 352p. 16.99 *(978-0-06-235297-2(0))* HarperCollins Pubs.
—The Lost Compass. 2017. (Fog Diver Ser.: Vol. 2). (ENG.). (J). (gr. 3-7). lib. bdg. 17.20 ***(978-0-606-40052-7(4))*** Turtleback Bks.
Scotto, Michael. Builda the Re-Bicycler. Gabriel, Evette, illus. 2009. (J). *(978-1-935193-22-7(8))* National Network of Digital Schls.
Sensel, Joni. The Garbage Monster. Bivins, Christopher, illus. 2003. 24p. (J). (gr. -1-18). 14.95 *(978-0-9701195-2-0(6))* Dream Factory Bks.
Silverman, Toby. The Garbage Grandma. Strapec, Amy, illus. 2005. 23p. (J). 9.50 *(978-0-9793475-0-4(5))* Silverman, Toby.
Sterrett, Nicole. 1-2 Recycling's for You! 2008. 12p. pap. 24.95 *(978-1-60610-223-7(0))* America Star Bks.
Stockham, Jess, illus. Recycling! 2011. (Helping Hands Ser.). (ENG.). 24p. (J). *(978-1-84643-415-0(7))* Child's Play International Ltd.
Trantham, Cary Gordon. The Saving of Sophi: El Rescate de Sofia. 2012. 28p. pap. 19.99 *(978-1-4772-0799-4(6))* AuthorHouse.
Trice, Linda. Kenya's Art. Mitchell, Hazel, illus. 2016. (ENG.). 32p. (J). (gr. -1-3). 16.95 *(978-1-57091-848-3(1))* Charlesbridge Publishing, Inc.
Wallace, Nancy Elizabeth. Recycle Every Day!, 0 vols. Wallace, Nancy Elizabeth, illus. 2006. (ENG., Illus.). 41p. (J). (gr. -1-3). pap. 9.99 *(978-0-7614-5290-4(7)*, 9780761452904, Amazon Children's Publishing) Amazon Publishing.
Warmus, Paul J. Sue's Zoo & the Magic Garden. 2012. pap. 11.95 *(978-0-7414-7200-7(7))* Infinity Publishing.
Weihs, Sally. Big Blue Goes Green. 2012. 24p. pap. 17.99 *(978-1-4685-5587-5(1))* AuthorHouse.
Yee, Wong Herbert. A Brand-New Day with Mouse & Mole. (Mouse & Mole Story Ser.). (ENG., Illus.). 48p. (J). (gr. 1-4). 2012. pap. 3.99 *(978-0-547-72209-2(5))* 2008. 15.00 *(978-0-618-96676-9(5))* Houghton Mifflin Harcourt Publishing Co.
—A Brand-New Day with Mouse & Mole. 2012. (Green Light Readers — Level 3 Ser.). lib. bdg. 13.55 *(978-0-606-24437-4(9)*, Turtleback) Turtleback Bks.

RED CHINA

see China

RED CLOUD, 1822-1909

Drury, Bob & Clavin, Tom. The Heart of Everything That Is: Young Readers Edition. 2017. (ENG., Illus.). 320p. (J). (gr. 5). 16.99 *(978-1-4814-6460-4(4)*, McElderry, Margaret K. Bks.) McElderry, Margaret K. Bks.
Goble, Paul. Red Cloud's War: Brave Eagle's Account of the Fetterman Fight. 2015. (ENG., Illus.). 48p. (J). (gr. 3-7). 16.95 *(978-1-937786-38-0(2)*, Wisdom Tales) World Wisdom, Inc.
Higgins, Nadia. Defending the Land: Causes & Effects of Red Cloud's War. 2015. (Cause & Effect: American Indian History Ser.). (ENG.). 32p. (gr. 3-4). pap. 7.95 *(978-1-4914-2210-6(6))* Capstone Press of Coughlan Cos.
Nelson, S. D. Red Cloud: A Lakota Story of War & Surrender. 2017. (ENG., Illus.). 64p. (J). (gr. 3-7). 19.95 *(978-1-4197-2313-1(8)*, Abrams Bks. for Young Readers) Abrams, Inc.
Sanford, William R. Oglala Lakota Chief Red Cloud. 2013. (Native American Chiefs & Warriors Ser.). 48p. (J). (gr. 5-18). 22.60 *(978-0-7660-4096-0(8))*; pap. 8.95 *(978-1-4644-0259-3(0))* Enslow Pubs., Inc.

RED CROSS

see also American National Red Cross

Connolly, Sean. The International Red Cross. 2009. (Global Organizations Ser.). (Illus.). 46p. (J). (gr. 4-7). pap. *(978-1-897563-35-9(3))* Saunders Bk. Co.
Faulkner, Georgene. Red Cross Stories for Children. 2004. reprint ed. pap. 15.95 *(978-1-4179-9875-3(X))* Kessinger Publishing, LLC.
Mara, Wil. Clara Barton. 2003. (Rookie Biographies Ser.). (ENG., Illus.). 32p. (J). (gr. 1-2). pap. 4.95 *(978-0-516-27339-6(6)*, Children's Pr.) Scholastic Library Publishing.
Marsico, Katie. The Red Cross. 2014. (Community Connections: How Do They Help? Ser.). (ENG.). 24p. (J). (gr. 2-5). 25.64 *(978-1-63188-028-5(4)*, 205519) Cherry Lake Publishing.
McLuskey, Krista. The Red Cross. 2003. (International Organizations Ser.). (Illus.). 32p. (J). (gr. 4-7). lib. bdg. 26.00 *(978-1-59036-019-4(2))* Weigl Pubs., Inc.
Ransom, Candice. Clara Barton. 2003. (History Maker Bios Ser.). (Illus.). 48p. (J). (gr. 3-5). lib. bdg. 26.60 *(978-0-8225-4677-1(9))* Lerner Publishing Group.
Suen, Anastasia. La Cruz Roja. 2004. (Organizaciones de Ayuda (Helping Organizations) Ser.). (SPA & ENG., Illus.). 24p. (J). (gr. 2-4). lib. bdg. 22.60 *(978-0-8239-6856-5(1))* Rosen Publishing Group, Inc., The.
—La Cruz Roja (the Red Cross) 2009. (Organizaciones de ayuda (Helping Organizations) Ser.). (SPA.). 24p. (gr. 2-2). 42.50 *(978-1-60851-146-4(4)*, Editorial Buenas Letras) Rosen Publishing Group, Inc., The.
—The Red Cross. 2009. (Helping Organizations Ser.). 24p. (gr. 2-2). 42.50 *(978-1-61513-262-1(7)*, PowerKids Pr.) Rosen Publishing Group, Inc., The.
Wheeler, Jill C. Red Cross Volunteers, 1 vol. 2003. (Everyday Heroes Ser.). (ENG., Illus.). 32p. (gr. k-6). 27.07 *(978-1-57765-857-3(4)*, Checkerboard Library) ABDO Publishing Co.

REDUCING

see Weight Control

REDWALL ABBEY (IMAGINARY PLACE)—FICTION

Jacques, Brian. Doomwyte. 2008. (Redwall Ser.). (ENG., Illus.). 384p. (J). (gr. 5-18). 23.99 *(978-0-399-24544-2(8)*, Philomel Bks.) Penguin Young Readers Group.
—Mariel of Redwall. Chalk, Gary, illus. 2003. (Redwall Ser.). (ENG.). 400p. (J). (gr. 5-5). pap. 9.99 *(978-0-14-230239-2(2)*, Firebird) Penguin Young Readers Group.
—Marlfox: A Tale from Redwall. 2005. (Redwall Ser.). (ENG.). 400p. (J). (gr. 5-5). reprint ed. 8.99 *(978-0-14-250108-5(5)*, Firebird) Penguin Young Readers Group.
—Martin the Warrior. Chalk, Gary, illus. 2004. (Redwall Ser.). (ENG.). 384p. (J). (gr. 5-18). pap. 9.99 *(978-0-14-240055-5(6)*, Firebird) Penguin Young Readers Group.
—Martin the Warrior: The Prisoner & the Tyrant; Actors & Searchers; The Battle of Marshank. unabr. ed. 2004. (Redwall Radio Play Ser.: Bks. 1-3). (J). (gr. 4-7). 10p. pap. 50.00 incl. audio *(978-0-8072-8177-2(8)*, YA124CX); 376p. pap. 58.00 incl. audio *(978-0-8072-8178-9(6)*, YA124SP) Random Hse. Audio Publishing Group. (Listening Library).
—Mattimeo. Chalk, Gary, illus. 2003. (Redwall Ser.). (ENG.). 448p. (J). (gr. 5-7). pap. 9.99 *(978-0-14-230240-8(6)*, Firebird) Penguin Young Readers Group.
—Salamandastron. Chalk, Gary, illus. 2003. (Redwall Ser.). (ENG.). 400p. (J). (gr. 5-3). pap. 9.99 *(978-0-14-250152-8(2)*, Firebird) Penguin Young Readers Group.
—Seven Strange & Ghostly Tales. 144p. (J). (gr. 3-5). pap. 5.99 *(978-0-8072-1486-2(8)*, Listening Library) Random Hse. Audio Publishing Group.

—Taggerung. Standley, Peter & Chalk, Gary, illus. 2003. (Redwall Ser.). (ENG.). 448p. (J). (gr. 5-18). pap. 8.99 *(978-0-14-250154-2(9)*, Firebird) Penguin Young Readers Group.

REDWOOD

Halter, Loretta. A Voice for the Redwoods. Bartczak, Peter, illus. 2010. (ENG.). 64p. (J). 18.95 *(978-0-9822942-0-8(4))* Nature's Hopes & Heroes.

Weaver, Harriett E. There Stand the Giants: The Story of the Redwood Trees. 2011. 70p. 36.95 *(978-1-258-01221-2(9))* Literary Licensing, LLC.

REED, HENRY (FICTITIOUS CHARACTER)—FICTION

Robertson, Keith. Henry Reed, Inc. abr. ed. (J). (gr. 4-7). pap. 15.95 incl. audio *(978-0-670-36801-3(6))* Live Oak Media.

—Henry Reed, Inc., Set. McCloskey, Robert, illus. abr. ed. (J). (gr. 4-7). 24.95 incl. audio *(978-0-670-36800-6(8))* Live Oak Media.

REFERENCE BOOKS

see also Encyclopedias and Dictionaries

Bodden, Valerie. Print & Subscription Sources. 2012. (Research for Writing Ser.). 48p. (gr. 5-12). 23.95 *(978-1-60818-205-3(3)*, Creative Education) Creative Co., The.

Brown, Liz. Reference Materials. 2007. (Social Studies Essential Skills Ser.). (Illus.). 24p. (J). (gr. 4-7). lib. bdg. 24.45 *(978-1-59036-757-5(X))*; per. 8.95 *(978-1-59036-758-2(8))* Weigl Pubs., Inc.

Child Horizons, 10 vols, Set. Incl. Bible Story Hour. Johnson, Louisa M. (gr. k-4). 1996. 22.95 *(978-0-87392-002-5(3))*; Parade of Stories. Neigoff, Anne, ed. (gr. k-4). 1996. 22.95 *(978-0-87392-005-6(8))*; Plant & Animal Ways. Murphy, Margaret. (gr. 4-6). 1996. 22.95 *(978-0-87392-114-5(3))*; Questions Children Ask. Bonhivert, Edith & Bonhivert, Ernest. (gr. 2-4). 1997. 22.95 *(978-0-87392-010-0(4))*; Story Hour. Bjoland, Ester M. (gr. k-4). 1996. 22.95 *(978-0-87392-003-2(1))*; Words to Know. Bricker, Harry & Beckwith, Yvonne. (gr. k-3). 1997. 22.95 *(978-0-87392-011-7(2))*; (J). 200.00 *(978-0-87392-500-6(9)*, Ferguson Publishing Co.) Facts On File, Inc.

Dumont, Thora & Malone, Janet. Nemeth Reference Sheets. 2003. spiral bd. 14.95 *(978-0-939173-56-3(5))* National Braille Pr.

Hamilton, John. Libraries & Reference Materials, 1 vol. 2005. (Straight to the Source Ser.). (ENG.). 32p. (gr. k-6). 27.07 *(978-1-59197-545-8(X)*, Checkerboard Library) ABDO Publishing Co.

Helbrough, Emma. Book of Knowledge. 2004. 208p. (J). lib. bdg. 27.95 *(978-1-58086-612-5(3)*, Usborne) EDC Publishing.

—The Usborne Internet-Linked Book of Knowledge. 2004. (ENG., Illus.). 208p. (J). 19.99 *(978-0-7945-0594-3(5))* EDC Publishing.

Howell, Sara. How to Gather Information, Take Notes, & Sort Evidence, 1 vol., 1. 2014. (Core Writing Skills Ser.). (ENG.). 24p. (J). (gr. 3-4). 23.60 *(978-1-4777-2909-0(7)*, PowerKids Pr.) Rosen Publishing Group, Inc., The.

O'Laughlin, Michael C. By Mac & 'O' You'll Always Know, Mac, Mc, & 'O' Names in Ireland, Scotland & America: With Census Records from the 17th to 20th Century. 2003. (Illus.). 60p. spiral bd. 25.00 net. *(978-0-940134-60-7(8))* Irish Genealogical Foundation.

Rabbat, Suzy. Super Smart Information Strategies: Hit the Books. 2010. (Explorer Library: Information Explorer Ser.). (ENG.). 32p. (gr. 4-8). pap. 14.21 *(978-1-61080-258-1(6)*, 200906); lib. bdg. 28.50 *(978-1-60279-641-6(6)*, 200344) Cherry Lake Publishing.

Top That Publishing Staff, ed. Survival. 2004. (I-Quest Ser.). (Illus.). 48p. (J). per. *(978-1-84510-176-3(6))* Top That! Publishing PLC.

Watson, Carol. My First Book of Facts. (Illus.). (J). pap. 18.95 *(978-0-590-74341-9(4))* Scholastic, Inc.

REFORM, SOCIAL

see Social Problems

REFORM OF CRIMINALS

see Crime

REFORMATION

see also Europe—History—1492-1789; Protestantism

Carr, Simonetta. John Calvin. Taglietti, Emanuele, illus. 2008. (ENG.). 63p. (J). 18.00 *(978-1-60178-055-3(9))* Reformation Heritage Bks.

—John Knox. Abraxas, Matt, illus. 2014. (ENG.). 64p. (J). 18.00 *(978-1-60178-289-2(6))* Reformation Heritage Bks.

Chibi, Andrew A. The English Reformation: The Effect on a Nation. 2003. (Studymates Ser.). (Illus.). 98p. pap. *(978-1-84285-024-4(5))* GLMP Ltd.

Davis, Thomas J. John Calvin. 2004. (Spiritual Leaders & Thinkers Ser.). (Illus.). 120p. (C). (gr. 9-13). 30.00 *(978-0-7910-8100-6(1)*, Chelsea Hse.) Facts On File, Inc.

Flatt, Lizann. Religion in the Renaissance. 2009. (ENG., Illus.). 32p. (J). (gr. 5-7). *(978-0-7787-4597-6(X))*; (gr. 6-9). pap. *(978-0-7787-4617-1(8))* Crabtree Publishing Co.

George, Enzo. The Reformation. 2016. (Primary Sources in World History Ser.). (ENG.). 48p. (YA). (gr. 6-6). 31.36 *(978-1-5026-2016-3(2))* Cavendish Square Publishing.

Havemeyer, Janie. Catherine de' Medici: "The Black Queen" Malone, Peter, illus. 2011. (Thinking Girl's Treasury of Dastardly Dames Ser.). (ENG.). 32p. (J). (gr. 3-8). 18.95 *(978-0-9834256-3-2(9))* Goosebottom Bks. LLC.

Hollingsworth, Tamara. The Reformation: A Religious Revolution, 1 vol. 2012. (Primary Source Readers Ser.). (ENG.). 32p. (J). (gr. 5-5). pap. 8.99 *(978-1-4333-5009-2(2))* Teacher Created Materials, Inc.

MacKenzie, Catherine. What Is the Truth? 2013. (Little Lights Ser.). (ENG., Illus.). 24p. (J). 7.99 *(978-1-84550-560-8(3)*, 281bfc81-447c-4f63-85f8-daa6919a36b7) Christian Focus Pubns. GBR. Dist: Bookmasters Distribution.

—What Should I Do? 2013. (Little Lights Ser.). (ENG., Illus.). 24p. (J). 7.99 *(978-1-84550-561-5(1)*, 9781845505615) Christian Focus Pubns. GBR. Dist: Bookmasters Distribution.

Nichols, Stephen J. Reformation ABCs: The People, Places, & Things of the Reformation-From a to Z. Bustard, Ned, illus. 2017. 56p. 16.99 *(978-1-4335-5282-3(5))* Crossway.

Reformation: PowerPoint Presentation in World History. 2005. cd-rom 49.95 net. *(978-1-56004-216-7(8))* Social Studies Schl. Service.

Reformation DBA. 2003. spiral bd. 16.95 *(978-1-56004-167-2(6))* Social Studies Schl. Service.

Rijswijk, Cor van. John Is Not Afraid. 2004. (Illus.). 43p. (J). *(978-1-894666-81-7(X))* Inheritance Pubns.

—Martin Shows the Way. 2004. (Illus.). 43p. (J). *(978-1-894666-80-0(1))* Inheritance Pubns.

Roth-Beck, Meike. The Life & Times of Martin Luther. Ensikat, Klaus, illus. 2017. (ENG.). 44p. (J). ***(978-0-8028-5495-7(8)***, Eerdmans Bks For Young Readers) Eerdmans, William B. Publishing Co.

Sengele, Mark. Inside the Reformation. 2012. (J). 16.99 *(978-0-7586-3120-6(0))* Concordia Publishing Hse.

Withrow, Brandon & Withrow, Mindy. Hearts & Hands: Chronicles of the Awakening Church. 2007. (History Lives Ser.). (ENG., Illus.). 224p. (J). (gr. 4-9). per. 9.99 *(978-1-84550-288-1(4)*, 9781845502881) Christian Focus Pubns. GBR. Dist: Bookmasters Distribution.

Withrow, Mindy & Withrow, Brandon. Courage & Conviction: Chronicles of the Reformation Church, Vol. 3. 2009. (History Lives Ser.). (ENG., Illus.). 256p. (J). per. 9.99 *(978-1-84550-222-5(1)*, 9781845502225) Christian Focus Pubns. GBR. Dist: Bookmasters Distribution.

REFORMATION—FICTION

Alcock, Deborah. The King's Service: A Story of the Thirty Years' War. 2008. (YA). *(978-1-894666-06-0(2))* Inheritance Pubns.

Basye, Dale E. Rapacia. Dob, Bob, illus. 2010. (Heck Ser.). (ENG.). 384p. (J). (gr. 3-7). pap. 6.99 *(978-0-375-84078-4(8)*, Yearling) Random Hse. Children's Bks.

Farenhorst, Christine. Wings Like a Dove: The Courage of Queen Jeanne D'Albret. 2006. (Chosen Daughters Ser.). 207p. (YA). (gr. 7). per. 11.99 *(978-0-87552-642-3(X))* P & R Publishing.

Marston, Hope Irvin. Against the Tide: The Valor of Margaret Wilson. 2007. (Chosen Daughters Ser.). 219p. (J). (gr. 3-7). per. 11.99 *(978-1-59638-061-5(6))* P & R Publishing.

Van Halsema, Thea B. This Was John Calvin. 2011. 184p. (gr. 3-7). 42.95 *(978-1-258-05962-0(2))* Literary Licensing, LLC.

Walshe, Elizabeth Hely. Under the Inquisition: A Story of the Reformation in Italy. 2009. (Illus.). 315p. *(978-1-894666-30-5(5))* Inheritance Pubns.

Weinberger, Justin. Reformed. 2017. (ENG.). 208p. (J). (gr. 3-7). 16.99 *(978-0-545-90252-6(5)*, Scholastic Pr.) Scholastic, Inc.

REFORMERS

Archer, Jules. The Unpopular Ones: Fifteen American Men & Women Who Stood up for What They Believed In. 2016. (Jules Archer History for Young Readers Ser.). (ENG., Illus.). 208p. (J). (gr. 6). 16.99 *(978-1-63450-200-9(0)*, Sky Pony Pr.) Skyhorse Publishing Co., Inc.

Butler, Mary. Sojourner Truth: From Slave to Activist for Freedom. 2009. (Library of American Lives & Times Ser.). 112p. (gr. 5-5). 69.20 *(978-1-60853-505-7(3))* Rosen Publishing Group, Inc., The.

Butler, Mary G. Sojourner Truth: From Slave to Activist for Freedom. 2005. (Library of American Lives & Times). (Illus.). 112p. (YA). (gr. 4-8). lib. bdg. 34.60 *(978-0-8239-5736-1(5))* Rosen Publishing Group, Inc., The.

Collins, Kathleen. Sojourner Truth: Defensora de los derechos civiles (Sojourner Truth: Equal Rights Advocate) 2009. (Grandes personajes en la historia de los Estados Unidos (Famous People in American History) Ser.). (SPA.). 32p. (gr. 2-3). 47.90 *(978-1-61512-808-2(5)*, Editorial Buenas Letras) Rosen Publishing Group, Inc., The.

—Sojourner Truth: Equal Rights Advocate. (Primary Sources of Famous People in American History Ser.). 32p. 2009. (gr. 2-3). 47.90 *(978-1-60851-727-5(6))* 2004. (ENG., Illus.). (gr. 4-8). pap. 10.00 *(978-0-8239-4193-3(0))* Rosen Publishing Group, Inc., The.

—Sojourner Truth: Equal Rights Advocate / Defensora de los derechos Civiles. 2009. (Famous People in American History/Grandes personajes en la historia de los Estados Unidos Ser.). (ENG & SPA.). 32p. (gr. 2-3). 47.90 *(978-1-61512-556-2(6)*, Editorial Buenas Letras) Rosen Publishing Group, Inc., The.

Cox, Vicki. Margaret Sanger. 2004. (Women in Medicine Ser.). (Illus.). 112p. (gr. 6-12). 30.00 *(978-0-7910-8030-6(7)*, Chelsea Hse.) Facts On File, Inc.

Hally, Ashleigh. Lugenia Burns Hope. 2012. (Illus.). 24p. (J). lib. bdg. *(978-1-935884-76-7(X))* State Standards Publishing, LLC.

Hirsch, E. D., Jr., ed. Civil Rights Leaders. 2003. tchr. ed. 9.95 *(978-0-7690-5053-9(0))*; stu. ed. 49.95 *(978-0-7690-2958-0(2))* Pearson Learning.

Kann, Bob. Belle & Bob la Follette: Partners in Politics. 2008. (Badger Biographies Ser.). (ENG., Illus.). 144p. (J). (gr. 3-7). pap. 12.95 *(978-0-87020-407-4(6))* Wisconsin Historical Society.

Kent, Deborah. Elizabeth Cady Stanton: Woman Knows the Cost of Life. 2010. (Americans—the Spirit of a Nation Ser.). (Illus.). 128p. (J). lib. bdg. 33.27 *(978-0-7660-3357-3(0))* Enslow Pubs., Inc.

Kishel, Ann-Marie. Jane Addams: A Life of Cooperation. 2007. (Pull Ahead Books-Biographies Ser.). (ENG.). 32p. (gr. k-3). pap. 7.95 *(978-0-8225-6436-2(X))* Lerner Publishing Group.

Krass. Sojourner Truth. 2004. (Black Americans of Achievement Ser.). (Illus.). 112p. (gr. 6-12). 35.00 *(978-0-7910-8165-5(6)*, Chelsea Hse.) Facts On File, Inc.

Kudlinski, Kathleen. Sojourner Truth: Voice for Freedom. Wooden, Lenny, illus. 2003. (Childhood of Famous Americans Ser.). (ENG.). 160p. (Orig.). (J). (gr. 3-7). mass mkt. 7.99 *(978-0-689-85274-9(6)*, Simon & Schuster/Paula Wiseman Bks.) Simon & Schuster/Paula Wiseman Bks.

Mattern, Joanne. Sojourner Truth: Early Abolitionist. (Women Who Shaped History Ser.). 24p. 2009. (gr. 2-3). 42.50 *(978-1-60854-821-7(X))* 2003. (Illus.). (J). lib. bdg. 22.60 *(978-0-8239-6502-1(3))* Rosen Publishing Group, Inc., The. (PowerKids Pr.).

McKissack, Patricia C. & McKissack, Fredrick, Jr. Sojourner Truth: Ain't I a Woman? 2003. (Illus.). 186p. (gr. 4-7). 17.20 *(978-0-7857-2515-2(6)*, Turtleback) Turtleback Bks.

Osial, Heather L. Californians Who Made a Difference. 2017. (Primary Source Readers Ser.). 32p. (gr. 4-4). 9.99 ***(978-1-4258-3247-6(4))*** Teacher Created Materials, Inc.

Pinkney, Andrea Davis. Peace Warriors. 2013. (Profiles Ser.: 6). (ENG.). 144p. (J). (gr. 5-9). pap. 6.99 *(978-0-545-51857-4(1)*, Scholastic Paperbacks) Scholastic, Inc.

Rappaport, Doreen. Eleanor, Quiet No More. Kelley, Gary, illus. 2009. (ENG.). 48p. (J). (gr. 1-3). 16.99 *(978-0-7868-5141-6(4))* Hyperion Pr.

Ruffin, Frances E. Sojourner Truth: Early Abolitionist. 2009. (American Legends Ser.). 24p. (gr. 3-3). 42.50 *(978-1-61511-387-3(8)*, PowerKids Pr.) Rosen Publishing Group, Inc., The.

—Unsinkable Molly Brown. 2009. (American Legends Ser.). 24p. (gr. 3-3). 42.50 *(978-1-61511-377-4(0)*, PowerKids Pr.) Rosen Publishing Group, Inc., The.

Scandiffio, Laura. People Who Said No: Courage Against Oppression. 2nd ed. 2012. (ENG., Illus.). 172p. (J). (gr. 5-7). 24.95 *(978-1-55451-383-3(9)*, 9781554513833); pap. 14.95 *(978-1-55451-382-6(0)*, 9781554513826) Annick Pr., Ltd. CAN. Dist: Publishers Group West (PGW).

Shaw, Maura D. Dorothy Day: A Catholic Life of Action. Marchesi, Stephen, illus. 2004. (ENG.). 32p. (J). 12.99 *(978-1-59473-011-5(3)*, 9781594730115, Skylight Paths Publishing) LongHill Partners, Inc.

Shetterly, Robert. Americans Who Tell the Truth. 2008. (Illus.). 46p. (gr. 4-6). 18.00 *(978-0-7569-8912-5(4))* Perfection Learning Corp.

Steele, Philip. Activists. 2011. (20th Century Lives Ser.). (Illus.). 32p. (YA). (gr. 3-6). 26.50 *(978-1-4488-3292-7(6))* Rosen Publishing Group, Inc., The.

Stone, Tanya Lee. Elizabeth Leads the Way: Elizabeth Cady Stanton & the Right to Vote. Gibbon, Rebecca, illus. 2010. (ENG.). 32p. (J). (gr. 1-5). pap. 8.99 *(978-0-312-60236-9(7)*, 9780312602369) Square Fish.

Swain, Gwenyth. Sojourner Truth. Archambault, Matthew, illus. 2005. (On My Own Biography Ser.). 48p. (J). (gr. 1-3). pap. 6.95 *(978-1-57505-827-6(8))* Lerner Publishing Group.

—Sojourner Truth. 2005. (On My Own Biography Ser.). (Illus.). 48p. (J). 25.26 *(978-1-57505-651-7(8)*, Carolrhoda Bks.) Lerner Publishing Group.

Wilson, Janet. Our Heroes: How Kids Are Making a Difference, 1 vol. 2014. (ENG., Illus.). 32p. (J). (gr. 3-8). 18.95 *(978-1-927583-41-8(1))* Second Story Pr. CAN. Dist: Orca Bk. Pubs. USA.

—Our Rights: How Kids Are Changing the World, 1 vol. 2013. (ENG., Illus.). 32p. (J). (gr. 4-6). lib. bdg. 18.95 *(978-1-926920-95-5(3))* Second Story Pr. CAN. Dist: Orca Bk. Pubs. USA.

REFRIGERATION AND REFRIGERATING MACHINERY

Plumbing, Heating, Air Conditioning & Refrigeration Student Activity. 2004. (YA). cd-rom *(978-1-57078-954-0(1)*, CEV60033) C E V Multimedia, Ltd.

REFUGEES

Altman, Linda Jacobs. Escape-Teens on the Run: Primary Sources from the Holocaust. 2010. (True Stories of Teens in the Holocaust Ser.). (Illus.). 128p. (YA). (gr. 9-12). 33.27 *(978-0-7660-3270-5(1))* Enslow Pubs., Inc.

Aykroyd, Clarissa. Refugees. 2005. (Changing Face of North America Ser.). (Illus.). 112p. (YA). lib. bdg. 24.95 *(978-1-59084-692-6(3))* Mason Crest.

Barghoorn, Linda. A Refugee's Journey from Colombia. 2017. 32p. (J). ***(978-0-7787-3672-1(5))*** Crabtree Publishing Co.

—A Refugee's Journey from Somalia. 2017. 32p. (J). ***(978-0-7787-3675-2(X))*** Crabtree Publishing Co.

Barr, Linda. Long Road to Freedom: Journey of the Hmong. 2004. (High Five Reading - Purple Ser.). (ENG., Illus.). 64p. (gr. 3-4). per. 9.00 *(978-0-7368-3852-8(X)*, High Five Reading (RBL)) Capstone Press of Coughlan Cos.

Borden, Louise & Borden, Louise W. The Journey That Saved Curious George: The True Wartime Escape of Margret & H. A. Rey. Drummond, Allan, illus. 2005. (Curious George Ser.). (ENG.). 80p. (J). (gr. 2-5). 17.99 *(978-0-618-33924-2(8))* Houghton Mifflin Harcourt Publishing Co.

Borden, Louise W. The Journey That Saved Curious George: The True Wartime Escape of Margret & H. A. Rey. Drummond, Allan, illus. 2010. (Curious George Ser.). (ENG.). 80p. (J). (gr. 2-5). pap. 8.99 *(978-0-547-41746-2(2))* Houghton Mifflin Harcourt Publishing Co.

Bryan, Nichol. Jewish Americans, 1 vol. 2004. (One Nation Set 1 Ser.). (ENG.). 32p. (gr. k-6). 27.07 *(978-1-57765-986-0(4)*, Checkerboard Library) ABDO Publishing Co.

—Somali Americans, 1 vol. 2004. (One Nation Set 1 Ser.). (ENG.). 32p. (gr. k-6). 27.07 *(978-1-57765-989-1(9)*, Checkerboard Library) ABDO Publishing Co.

Bui, Nam. Fish over Diamond. 2012. 138p. 30.99 *(978-1-4691-9624-4(7))* Xlibris Corp.

Cohen, Sheila & Terman Cohen, Sheila. Mai Ya's Long Journey. 2005. (Badger Biographies Ser.). (ENG., Illus.). 96p. (J). (gr. 3-7). per. 12.95 *(978-0-87020-365-7(7))* Wisconsin Historical Society.

Coleman, Lori. Vietnamese in America. 2005. (In America Ser.). (Illus.). 80p. (J). (gr. 5-8). lib. bdg. 27.93 *(978-0-8225-3951-3(9))* Lerner Publishing Group.

Dau, John Bul. Lost Boy Lost Girl: Escaping Civil War in Sudan. 2010. (ENG., Illus.). 160p. (YA). (gr. 7-18). 23.90 *(978-1-4263-0709-6(8)*, National Geographic Children's Bks.) National Geographic Society.

Dau, John Bul & Akech, Martha Arual. Lost Boy, Lost Girl: Escaping Civil War in Sudan. 2010. (ENG., Illus.). 160p. (YA). (gr. 7-18). 15.95 *(978-1-4263-0708-9(X)*, National Geographic Children's Bks.) National Geographic Society.

DePietro, Frank. Central American Immigrants. 2012. (J). pap. *(978-1-4222-2334-5(5))* Mason Crest.

—Central American Immigrants. Limón, José E., ed. 2012. (Hispanic Americans: Major Minority Ser.). 64p. (J). (gr. 4). 22.95 *(978-1-4222-2317-8(5))* Mason Crest.

Dolphin, Laurie. Our Journey from Tibet. Johnson, Nancy Jo, photos by. 2006. (Illus.). 40p. (J). (gr. k-4). 16.00 *(978-0-7567-9812-3(4))* DIANE Publishing Co.

Ellis, Deborah. Children of War: Voices of Iraqi Refugees, 1 vol. 2010. (ENG., Illus.). 128p. (J). (gr. 6-9). pap. 9.95 *(978-0-88899-908-5(9))* Groundwood Bks. CAN. Dist: Publishers Group West (PGW).

Glynne, Andy. Ali's Story: A Real-Life Account of His Journey from Afghanistan. 2017. (Seeking Refuge Ser.). (ENG.). 32p. (gr. 3-4). 27.32 ***(978-1-5158-1412-2(2))*** Picture Window Bks.

—Hamid's Story: A Real-Life Account of His Journey from Eritrea. 2017. (Seeking Refuge Ser.). (ENG.). 32p. (gr. 3-4). 27.32 ***(978-1-5158-1413-9(0))*** Picture Window Bks.

—Juliane's Story: A Real-Life Account of Her Journey from Zimbabwe. 2017. (Seeking Refuge Ser.). (ENG.). 32p. (gr. 3-4). 27.32 ***(978-1-5158-1414-6(9))*** Picture Window Bks.

—Navid's Story: A Real-Life Account of His Journey from Iran. 2017. (Seeking Refuge Ser.). (ENG.). 32p. (gr. 3-4). 27.32 ***(978-1-5158-1415-3(7))*** Picture Window Bks.

—Rachel's Story: A Real-Life Account of Her Journey from Eurasia. 2017. (Seeking Refuge Ser.). (ENG.). 32p. (gr. 3-4). 27.32 ***(978-1-5158-1416-0(5))*** Picture Window Bks.

Golabek, Mona, et al. The Children of Willesden Lane: A True Story of Hope & Survival During World War II. 2017. (Illus.). 213p. (J). ***(978-0-316-55489-3(8))*** Little Brown & Co.

Hodge, Deborah. Rescuing the Children: The Story of the Kindertransport. 2012. (ENG., Illus.). 62p. (J). (gr. 5). 17.95 *(978-1-77049-256-1(9)*, Tundra Bks.) Tundra Bks. CAN. Dist: Penguin Random Hse. LLC.

Hudak, Heather C. A Refugee's Journey from Guatemala. 2017. 32p. (J). ***(978-0-7787-3673-8(3))*** Crabtree Publishing Co.

—A Refugee's Journey from Yemen. 2017. 32p. (J). ***(978-0-7787-3677-6(6))*** Crabtree Publishing Co.

Jal, David. David's Journey: The Story of David Jal, One of the Lost Boys of Sudan. Bezesky, Tracy, illus. 2012. 32p. 20.00 *(978-1-934478-30-1(X))* Sunray Publishing.

Kacer, Kathy. To Hope & Back: The Journey of the St. Louis, 1 vol. 2011. (Holocaust Remembrance Ser.). (ENG., Illus.). 200p. (J). (gr. 6-8). pap. 14.95 *(978-1-897187-96-8(3))* Second Story Pr. CAN. Dist: Orca Bk. Pubs. USA.

Kalman, Bobbie. Refugee Child: My Memories of the 1956 Hungarian Revolution. Bedell, Barbara, illus. 2006. (ENG.). 224p. (J). (gr. 3-7). lib. bdg. *(978-0-7787-2760-6(2))* Crabtree Publishing Co.

—Refugee Child Activity Guide. 2006. (ENG., Illus.). 32p. (J). (gr. 3-7). bds. *(978-0-7787-2759-0(9))* Crabtree Publishing Co.

Keat, Nawuth & Kendall, Martha. Alive in the Killing Fields: Surviving the Khmer Rouge Genocide. 2009. (ENG., Illus.). 128p. (J). (gr. 7). 23.90 *(978-1-4263-0516-0(8))*; 15.95 *(978-1-4263-0515-3(X))* National Geographic Society. (National Geographic Children's Bks.).

Kent, Deborah. Middle Eastern Migration, 1 vol. 2011. (Children's True Stories: Migration Ser.). (ENG.). 32p. (gr. 3-3). 30.65 *(978-1-4109-4073-5(X)*, Raintree Perspectives) Heinemann-Raintree.

Knight, Margy Burns. Who Belongs Here? An American Story. O'Brien, Anne Sibley, illus. 2004. 32p. 19.45 *(978-0-7569-2426-3(X))* Perfection Learning Corp.

—Who Belongs Here? An American Story, 1 vol. O'Brien, Anne Sibley, illus. 2nd ed. 2003. (SPA & ENG.). 40p. (gr. 2-6). 8.95 *(978-0-88448-169-0(7)*, 884169) Tilbury Hse. Pubs.

Knight, Margy Burns, et al. Who Belongs Here? An American Story. 2nd ed. 2004. (Illus.). 40p. (gr. 3-8). 16.95 *(978-0-88448-110-2(7))* Tilbury Hse. Pubs.

Kuntz, Doug & Shrodes, Amy. Lost & Found Cat: The True Story of Kunkush's Incredible Journey. Cornelison, Sue, illus. 2017. (ENG.). 48p. (J). (gr. -1-3). lib. bdg. 20.99 *(978-1-5247-1548-9(4)*, Crown Books For Young Readers) Random Hse. Children's Bks.

Leatherdale, Mary Beth. Stormy Seas: Stories of Young Boat Refugees. Shakespeare, Eleanor, illus. 2017. (ENG.). 64p. (gr. 4). pap. 12.95 *(978-1-55451-895-1(4))* Annick Pr., Ltd. CAN. Dist: Publishers Group West (PGW).

Levy, Janey. Refugee Workers. (Extreme Careers Ser.). 64p. (gr. 5-5). 2009. 58.50 *(978-1-61512-403-9(9)*, Rosen Reference) 2006. (Illus.). (J). lib. bdg. 31.95 *(978-1-4042-0960-2(3))* Rosen Publishing Group, Inc., The.

Marshall Cavendish. The Khmer Rouge. 2011. (Great Escapes Ser.). (Illus.). 80p. (J). (gr. 6). 34.21 *(978-1-60870-474-3(2))* Marshall Cavendish Corp.

—The Lost Boys of Sudan. 2011. (Great Escapes Ser.). 80p. (gr. 6). 34.21 *(978-1-60870-475-0(0))* Marshall Cavendish Corp.

Mason, Helen. A Refugee's Journey from Afghanistan. 2017. (Leaving My Homeland Ser.). (ENG., Illus.). 32p. (J). ***(978-0-7787-3125-2(1))***; pap. ***(978-0-7787-3129-0(4))*** Crabtree Publishing Co.

—A Refugee's Journey from Syria. 2017. (Leaving My Homeland Ser.). (ENG., Illus.). 32p. (J). ***(978-0-7787-3128-3(6))***; pap. ***(978-0-7787-3184-9(7))*** Crabtree Publishing Co.

Matthews, Jenny. Children Growing up with War. Matthews, Jenny, photos by. 2014. (ENG., Illus.). 48p. (J). (gr. 5). 17.99 *(978-0-7636-6942-3(3))* Candlewick Pr.

McCarney, Rosemary. Where Will I Live?, 1 vol. United Nations High Commissioner for Refugees (Islamabad, Pakistan) Staff, photos by. 2017. (ENG., Illus.). 24p. (J). (gr. 1-5). 19.95 *(978-1-77260-028-5(8))* Second Story Pr. CAN. Dist: Orca Bk. Pubs. USA.

Naidoo, Beverley. Making It Home: Real-Life Stories from Children Forced to Flee. 2005. (Illus.). 117p. (gr. 3-7). 17.00 *(978-0-7569-5823-7(7))* Perfection Learning Corp.

Parker, Lewis K. Why Vietnamese Immigrants Came to America. 2009. (Coming to America Ser.). 24p. (gr. 2-3). 42.50 *(978-1-61511-888-5(8)*, PowerKids Pr.) Rosen Publishing Group, Inc., The.

Perritano, John. The Making of the Modern World: 1945 to the Present: Migration & Refugees, Vol. 9. van Dijk, Ruud, ed. 2016. (Making of the Modern World: 1945 to the Present Ser.: Vol. 9). (ENG.). 64p. (J). (gr. 7-12). 23.95 *(978-1-4222-3640-6(4))* Mason Crest.

Roberts, Ceri. Refugees & Migrants. Kai, Hanane, illus. 2017. (Children in Our World Ser.). (ENG.). 32p. (J). (gr. 1-4). 9.99 ***(978-1-4380-5020-1(8))*** Barron's Educational Series, Inc.

Rodger, Ellen. A Refugee's Journey from Iraq. 2017. (Leaving My Homeland Ser.). (ENG., Illus.). 32p. (J). ***(978-0-7787-3127-6(8))***; pap. ***(978-0-7787-3157-3(X))*** Crabtree Publishing Co.

—A Refugee's Journey from Myanmar. 2017. 32p. (J). ***(978-0-7787-3674-5(1))*** Crabtree Publishing Co.

—A Refugee's Journey from South Sudan. 2017. 32p. (J). ***(978-0-7787-3676-9(8))*** Crabtree Publishing Co.

—A Refugee's Journey from the Democratic Republic of the Congo. 2017. (Leaving My Homeland Ser.). (ENG., Illus.). 32p. (J). ***(978-0-7787-3126-9(X))***; pap. ***(978-0-7787-3156-6(1))*** Crabtree Publishing Co.

Schwartz, Eric. Central American Immigrants to the United States: Refugees from Unrest. 2007. (Hispanic Heritage Ser.). (Illus.). 112p. (YA). (gr. 4-7). lib. bdg. 22.95 (978-1-59084-929-3(9)) Mason Crest.
Senker, Cath & Hachette Children's Group. Refugees. 2011. (Global Issues Ser.). (Illus.). 48p. (YA). (gr. 5-8). lib. bdg. 29.25 (978-1-4488-1880-8(X), Rosen Reference) Rosen Publishing Group, Inc., The.
Skrypuch, Marsha Forchuk. Adrift at Sea: A Vietnamese Boy's Story of Survival. Deines, Brian, illus. 2016. (ENG.). 40p. (J). (gr. 1-4). 18.95 (978-1-77278-005-5(7)) Pajama Pr. CAN. Dist: Ingram Publisher Services.
St. John, Warren. Outcasts United: The Story of a Refugee Soccer Team That Changed a Town. 2013. (ENG.). 240p. (YA). (gr. 7). pap. 9.99 (978-0-385-74195-8(2), Ember) Random Hse. Children's Bks.
Staeger, Rob. Asylees. 2005. (Changing Face of North America Ser.). (Illus.). 112p. (YA). lib. bdg. 24.95 (978-1-59084-685-8(0)) Mason Crest.
Teenage Refugees Speak Out. 2005. (Illus.). (gr. 7-12). lib. bdg. 344.50 (978-0-8239-9331-4(0)) Rosen Publishing Group, Inc., The.
Uschan, Michael V. Human Rights in Focus: Refugees. 2017. (ENG.). 80p. (YA). (gr. 5-12). **(978-1-68282-233-3(8))** ReferencePoint Pr., Inc.
Uwiringiyimana, Sandra & Pesta, Abigail. How Dare the Sun Rise: Memoirs of a War Child. 2017. 304p. (YA). (gr. 8). 19.99 (978-0-06-247014-0(0), Tegen, Katherine Bks) HarperCollins Pubs.

REFUGEES—FICTION

Abdel-Fattah, Randa. The Lines We Cross. 2017. (ENG.). 400p. (J). (gr. 7-7). 18.99 **(978-1-338-11866-7(8)**, Scholastic Pr.) Scholastic, Inc.
Agosín, Marjorie. I Lived on Butterfly Hill. White, Lee, illus. 2014. (ENG.). 464p. (J). (gr. 5-9). 18.99 (978-1-4169-5344-9(2), Atheneum Bks. for Young Readers) Simon & Schuster Children's Publishing.
Anderson, Natalie C. City of Saints & Thieves. 2017. (ENG.). 432p. (YA). (gr. 7). 18.99 (978-0-399-54758-4(4), G.P. Putnam's Sons Books for Young Readers) Penguin Young Readers Group.
Appelfeld, Aharon. Adam & Thomas. Green, Jeffrey M., tr. from HEB. Dumas, Philippe, illus. 2017. (ENG.). 160p. (J). (gr. 3-7). pap. 14.95 (978-1-60980-744-3(8), Triangle Square) Seven Stories Pr.
Aslan, Austin. The Islands at the End of the World. 2015. (ENG., Illus.). 384p. (YA). (gr. 7). pap. 9.99 (978-0-385-74403-4(X), Ember) Random Hse. Children's Bks.
Bennett, Sophia. Sequins, Secrets, & Silver Linings. 2011. (ENG.). 304p. (J). (gr. 7-11). 16.99 (978-0-545-24241-7(X), Chicken Hse., The) Scholastic, Inc.
Bondoux, Anne-Laure. A Time of Miracles. Maudet, Y., tr. from FRE. 2012. (ENG., Illus.). 192p. (YA). (gr. 7). pap. 7.99 (978-0-375-86036-2(3), Ember) Random Hse. Children's Bks.
Booth, Anne. Refuge. Usher, Sam, illus. 2016. (ENG.). 32p. (J). (gr. -1-3). 15.99 (978-0-316-36172-9(0)) Little, Brown Bks. for Young Readers.
Bouwman, H. M. A Crack in the Sea. 2017. (ENG., Illus.). 368p. (J). (gr. 5). 16.99 (978-0-399-54519-1(0), G.P. Putnam's Sons Books for Young Readers) Penguin Young Readers Group.
Boyce, Frank Cottrell. The Unforgotten Coat. Hunter, Carl & Heney, Clare, illus. Hunter, Carl & Heney, Clare, photos by. 2011. (ENG.). 112p. (J). (gr. 3-7). 16.99 (978-0-7636-5729-1(8)) Candlewick Pr.
—The Unforgotten Coat. 2011. (Playaway Children Ser.). (ENG.). (J). (gr. 4-7). 39.99 (978-1-4558-4539-2(6)) Findaway World, LLC.
Brashares, Ann. The Here & Now. 2014. 242p. (YA). (978-0-385-39008-8(4), Delacorte Pr) Random House Publishing Group.
—The Here & Now. (ENG.). 256p. (YA). (gr. 7). 2015. pap. 10.99 (978-0-385-73683-1(5), Ember) 2014. 18.99 (978-0-385-73680-0(0), Delacorte Pr.) Random Hse. Children's Bks.
Burchett, Jan & Vogler, Sara. Rainforest Rescue, 1 vol. Le Feyer, Diane, illus. 2012. (Wild Rescue Ser.). (ENG.). 152p. (gr. 3-6). lib. bdg. 25.32 (978-1-4342-3768-2(0)) Stone Arch Bks.
Burg, Ann. Rebekkah's Journey: A World War II Refugee Story. Iskowitz, Joel, illus. 2006. (Tales of Young Americans Ser.). (ENG.). 32p. (J). (gr. 3-7). 17.95 (978-1-58536-275-2(1)) Sleeping Bear Pr.
Casanova, Mary. The Klipfish Code. 2012. (ENG.). 240p. (J). (gr. 5-7). pap. 6.99 (978-0-547-74447-6(1)) Houghton Mifflin Harcourt Publishing Co.
Chapman, Fern Schumer. Is It Night or Day? 2010. (ENG.). 224p. (J). (gr. 5-9). 17.99 (978-0-374-17744-7(9), 9780374177447, Farrar, Straus & Giroux (BYR)) Farrar, Straus & Giroux.
Choyce, Lesley. Refuge Cove. 2004. (Orca Soundings Ser.). 89p. 19.95 (978-0-7569-4325-7(6)) Perfection Learning Corp.
Cooney, Caroline B. Diamonds in the Shadow. 2009. (ENG.). 240p. (YA). 9.99 (978-1-4000-7424-2(X), WaterBrook Pr.) Crown Publishing Group.
—Diamonds in the Shadow. 2009. (ENG.). 240p. (YA). (gr. 7). pap. 9.99 (978-0-385-73262-8(7), Delacorte Bks. for Young Readers) Random Hse. Children's Bks.
Cooper, Michelle. The FitzOsbornes at War. 2013. (Montmaray Journals). (ENG.). 560p. (YA). (gr. 7). pap. 10.99 (978-0-307-93058-3(0), Ember) Random Hse. Children's Bks.
—The FitzOsbornes in Exile. 2012. (Montmaray Journals). (ENG.). 464p. (YA). (gr. 7). pap. 10.99 (978-0-375-85155-1(0), Ember) Random Hse. Children's Bks.
Cornwell, Nicki. Armel's Revenge. Pal, Erika, illus. 2012. (ENG.). 96p. (J). (gr. 3-6). pap. 8.99 (978-1-84780-224-8(9), Frances Lincoln) Quarto Publishing Group UK GBR. Dist: Hachette Bk. Group.
Cremer, Andrea. The Inventor's Secret. (Inventor's Secret Ser.). (ENG.). (YA). (gr. 7). 2015. 416p. pap. 10.99 (978-0-14-751438-7(X), Speak) 2014. 336p. 18.99 (978-0-399-15962-6(2), Philomel Bks.) Penguin Young Readers Group.
Cross, Gillian. Where I Belong. 2011. (ENG., Illus.). 256p. (J). (gr. 5-18). 17.95 (978-0-8234-2332-3(8)) Holiday Hse., Inc.
Del Rizzo, Suzanne. My Beautiful Birds. Del Rizzo, Suzane, illus. 2017. (ENG.). 32p. (J). (gr. 1-3). 17.95 (978-1-77278-010-9(3)) Pajama Pr. CAN. Dist: Ingram Publisher Services.
Diaz, Alexandra. The Only Road. 2016. (ENG., Illus.). 320p. (J). (gr. 3-7). 16.99 (978-1-4814-5750-7(0), Simon & Schuster/Paula Wiseman Bks.) Simon & Schuster/Paula Wiseman Bks.
—El Unico Destino. 2016. (SPA., Illus.). 320p. (J). (gr. 3-7). 16.99 (978-1-4814-8441-1(9), Simon & Schuster/Paula Wiseman Bks.) Simon & Schuster/Paula Wiseman Bks.
—El único Destino (the Only Road) 2016. (SPA., Illus.). 320p. (J). (gr. 3-7). pap. 7.99 (978-1-4814-8442-8(7), Simon & Schuster/Paula Wiseman Bks.) Simon & Schuster/Paula Wiseman Bks.
Ehrmantraut, Brenda. Hope Weavers. Magnuson, Diana, illus. 2009. (J). (978-0-9729833-8-9(4)) Bubble Gum Pr.
Elizabeth's Story 1848. 2014. (Secrets of the Manor Ser.: 3). (ENG., Illus.). 160p. (J). (gr. 3-7). pap. 6.99 (978-1-4814-1840-9(8), Simon Spotlight) Simon Spotlight.
Ellis, Deborah. Mud City, 1 vol. 2015. (Breadwinner Ser.). (ENG., Illus.). 168p. (J). (gr. 4-9). pap. 9.95 (978-1-55498-773-3(3)) Groundwood Bks. CAN. Dist: Publishers Group West (PGW).
—Mud City. 2013. 156p. pap. (978-1-4596-6445-6(0)) ReadHowYouWant.com, Ltd.
—Parvana's Journey. 2013. 184p. pap. (978-1-4596-6476-0(0)) ReadHowYouWant.com, Ltd.
Engle, Margarita. Tropical Secrets: Holocaust Refugees in Cuba. 2009. (ENG.). 208p. (YA). (gr. 7-12). 23.99 (978-0-8050-8936-3(5), 9780805089363, Holt, Henry & Co. Bks. For Young Readers) Holt, Henry & Co.
Etienne, Sara Wilson. Lotus & Thorn. 2016. (ENG., Illus.). 464p. (YA). (gr. 9). 17.99 (978-0-399-25669-1(5), G.P. Putnam's Sons Books for Young Readers) Penguin Young Readers Group.
Farish, Terry. The Good Braider, 0 vols. 2014. (ENG.). 224p. (YA). (gr. 9-12). pap. 9.99 (978-1-4778-1628-8(3), 9781477816288, Amazon Children's Publishing) Amazon Publishing.
Flores-Galbis, Enrique. 90 Miles to Havana. 2010. (ENG.). 304p. (J). (gr. 4-7). 18.99 (978-1-59643-168-3(7), 9781596431683) Roaring Brook Pr.
—90 Miles to Havana. 2012. (ENG.). 304p. (J). (gr. 4-7). pap. 7.99 (978-1-250-00559-5(0), 9781250005595) Square Fish.
Fraillon, Zana. The Bone Sparrow. 2016. (ENG.). 240p. (J). (gr. 4-7). 16.99 (978-1-4847-8151-7(1)) Hyperion Bks. for Children.
Garland, Sarah. Azzi in Between. 2016. (ENG., Illus.). 40p. (J). (gr. 2-6). pap. 9.99 (978-1-84780-651-2(1), Frances Lincoln) Quarto Publishing Group UK GBR. Dist: Littlehampton Bk Services, Ltd.
Goring, Ruth. Adriana's Angels. Meza, Erika, illus. 2017. (J). 16.99 **(978-1-5064-1832-2(5)**, Sparkhouse Family) Augsburg Fortress, Pubs.
Goring, Ruth & Meza, Erika. Los Angeles de Adriana (Spanish Edition) Meza, Erika, illus. 2017. (SPA., Illus.). (J). 16.99 **(978-1-5064-2507-8(0)**, Sparkhouse Family) Augsburg Fortress, Pubs.
Greene, Janice. No Exit, 1 vol. unabr. ed. 2010. (Q Reads Ser.). (ENG.). 32p. (YA). (gr. 9-12). pap. 6.95 (978-1-61651-202-6(4)) Saddleback Educational Publishing, Inc.
Hager, Mandy. Into the Wilderness. 2014. (Blood of the Lamb Ser.). (ENG.). 335p. (YA). (gr. 9). 17.99 (978-1-61614-863-8(2)) Prometheus Bks., Pubs.
Halahmy, Miriam. Hidden. 2016. (ENG.). 224p. (J). 16.95 (978-0-8234-3694-1(2)) Holiday Hse., Inc.
Harris, Christine. The Silver Path. (Illus.). (J). (ENG & VIE.). 26p. (978-1-85430-327-1(9), 93381); (CHI & ENG., 32p. (978-1-85430-323-3(6), 93425) Little Tiger Pr. Group.
Hilmo, Tess. Cinnamon Moon. 2016. (ENG.). 256p. (J). 16.99 (978-0-374-30282-5(0), 9780374302825, Farrar, Straus & Giroux (BYR)) Farrar, Straus & Giroux.
Holm, Anne. I Am David. Kingsland, L. W., tr. from DAN. 2004. (ENG.). 256p. (J). (gr. 2-5). pap. 7.99 (978-0-15-205160-0(0)) Houghton Mifflin Harcourt Publishing Co.
Howard, Ellen. Different Kind of Courage. 2007. (ENG.). 184p. (J). (gr. 3-7). pap. 10.95 (978-1-4169-6730-9(3), Simon & Schuster/Paula Wiseman Bks.) Simon & Schuster/Paula Wiseman Bks.
Hyde, Heidi Smith. Shanghai Sukkah. Tsong, Jing Jing, illus. 2015. (ENG.). 32p. (J). (gr. k-4). 17.99 (978-1-4677-3474-5(8)); pap. 7.99 (978-1-4677-3475-2(6)) Lerner Publishing Group. (Kar-Ben Publishing).
Kazerooni, Abbas. The Boy with Two Lives. 2016. (ENG.). 256p. (YA). (gr. 7). 12.99 (978-1-74331-483-8(3)) Allen & Unwin AUS. Dist: Independent Pubs. Group.
Keily, Kevin. A Horse Called el Dorado. 2005. (ENG.). 144p. (J). pap. 10.95 (978-0-86278-907-7(9)) O'Brien Pr., Ltd., The IRL. Dist: Dufour Editions, Inc.
Krumwiede, Lana. Archon. 2015. (Psi Chronicles Ser.). (ENG.). 320p. (J). (gr. 5). pap. 7.99 (978-0-7636-7659-9(4)) Candlewick Pr.
—Freakling. 2014. (Psi Chronicles Ser.). (ENG.). 320p. (J). (gr. 5). pap. 7.99 (978-0-7636-6938-6(5)) Candlewick Pr.
Laird, Elizabeth. Welcome to Nowhere. 2017. (ENG., Illus.). 352p. (J). (gr. 4-9). 9.99 **(978-1-5098-4047-2(8))** Pan Macmillan GBR. Dist: Independent Pubs. Group.
Lantigua, Lizette M. Mission Libertad. 2012. (ENG.). 192p. (YA). pap. 9.95 (978-0-8198-4900-7(6)) Pauline Bks. & Media.
Lasenby, Jack. Taur. (Travellers Ser.: No. 2). (Illus.). 160p. (YA). (gr. 8-18). pap. (978-1-877135-18-7(6), Longacre Pr.) Random Hse. New Zealand.
Lombard, Jenny. Drita, My Homegirl. 2008. (ENG.). 144p. (J). (gr. 3-7). 5.99 (978-0-14-240905-3(7), Puffin Books) Penguin Young Readers Group.
—Drita, My Homegirl. 2008. 135p. (J). (gr. 4-6). 13.65 (978-0-7569-8919-4(1)) Perfection Learning Corp.
Manivong, Laura. Escaping the Tiger. 2010. (ENG.). 224p. (J). (gr. 5-18). 15.99 (978-0-06-166177-8(5)) HarperCollins Pubs.
Matthews, L. S. Fish. 2006. 183p. (gr. 5-9). 16.50 (978-0-7569-6626-3(4)) Perfection Learning Corp.
Mazer, Norma Fox. Good Night, Maman. 2010. (ENG., Illus.). 192p. (J). (gr. 5-7). pap. 12.95 (978-0-15-206173-9(8)) Houghton Mifflin Harcourt Publishing Co.
McDougall, Sophia. Mars Evacuees. (J). (gr. 3-7). 2016. 432p. pap. 7.99 (978-0-06-229400-5(8)) 2015. 416p. 16.99 (978-0-06-229399-2(0)) HarperCollins Pubs.
Mead, Alice. Year of No Rain. 2005. (Illus.). 129p. (gr. 4-7). 15.50 (978-0-7569-5158-0(5)) Perfection Learning Corp.
Meyer, Susan Lynn. Skating with the Statue of Liberty. 2016. (ENG.). 320p. (J). (gr. 3-7). 19.99 (978-0-375-99010-6(0), Delacorte Bks. for Young Readers) Random Hse. Children's Bks.
Mikaelsen, Ben. Tree Girl. 2005. (ENG.). 240p. (YA). (gr. 8). pap. 9.99 (978-0-06-009006-7(5), HarperTeen) HarperCollins Pubs.
Millard, Glenda. A Small Free Kiss in the Dark. 2010. (ENG.). 192p. (YA). (gr. 7-18). pap. 16.95 (978-0-8234-2264-7(X)) Holiday Hse., Inc.
Mohammed, Khadra & Williams, Karen Lynn. My Name Is Sangoel. Stock, Catherine, illus. 2009. (ENG.). 36p. (J). (gr. 1-5). 17.00 (978-0-8028-5307-3(2), Eerdmans Bks For Young Readers) Eerdmans, William B. Publishing Co.
Moon, Young Sook. Across the Tumen: A North Korean Kkotjebi Boy's Quest. 2013.Tr. of 꽃제비 영대: 죽음을 넘어 희망을 찾아간 소년. (ENG.). 344p. (J). pap. 16.99 (978-1-62412-009-1(1)) Seoul Selection.
Morano, John. Makoona. 2nd rev. ed. 2005. (Morano Eco-Adventure Ser.: 2). 236p. (YA). (gr. 8-12). per. 14.99 (978-1-59092-111-1(9)) Blue Forge Pr.
Morpurgo, Michael. Shadow. 2014. (ENG.). 208p. (J). (gr. 5-9). pap. 6.99 (978-1-250-03996-5(7), 9781250039965) Square Fish.
Naidoo, Beverley. The Other Side of Truth. 2008. 252p. (gr. 5-9). 17.00 (978-0-7569-8941-5(8)) Perfection Learning Corp.
O'Brien, Anne Sibley. A Path of Stars. O'Brien, Anne Sibley, illus. 2012. (ENG., Illus.). 40p. (J). (gr. k-3). 15.95 (978-1-57091-735-6(3)) Charlesbridge Publishing, Inc.
Osborne, William. Hitler's Secret. 2013. (Illus.). 333p. (YA). (978-0-545-51533-7(5)); (ENG., 352p. (J). (gr. 7). 17.99 (978-0-545-49646-9(2)) Scholastic, Inc. (Chicken Hse., The).
Padian, Maria. Out of Nowhere. (ENG.). 352p. (YA). (gr. 7). 2015. pap. 9.99 (978-0-375-86562-6(4), Ember) 2013. 16.99 (978-0-375-86580-0(2), Knopf Bks. for Young Readers) Random Hse. Children's Bks.
Park, Frances & Park, Ginger. My Freedom Trip: A Child's Escape from North Korea. Jenkins, Debra Reid, illus. 2010. (ENG.). 32p. (J). pap. 11.95 (978-1-59078-826-4(5)) Boyds Mills Pr.
Park, Linda Sue. A Long Walk to Water: Based on a True Story. (ENG., 128p. (J). (gr. 5-7). 2011. Illus.). pap. 7.99 (978-0-547-57731-9(1)) 2010. 17.99 (978-0-547-25127-1(0)) Houghton Mifflin Harcourt Publishing Co.
—A Long Walk to Water: Based on a True Story. 2009. 8.32 (978-0-7848-3885-3(2), Everbind) Marco Bk. Co.
—A Long Walk to Water: Based on a True Story. 2011. 18.00 (978-1-61383-124-3(2)) Perfection Learning Corp.
—A Long Walk to Water: Based on a True Story. 2011. lib. bdg. 18.40 (978-0-606-23406-1(3), Turtleback) Turtleback Bks.
Paterson, Katherine. The Day of the Pelican. 2010. (ENG.). 160p. (J). (gr. 5-7). pap. 7.99 (978-0-547-40627-5(4)) Houghton Mifflin Harcourt Publishing Co.
Perl, Lila. Isabel's War. 2014. (ENG.). 224p. (J). (gr. 2-7). pap. 12.95 (978-1-939601-27-8(4)) Ig Publishing, Inc.
Pinkney, Andrea Davis. The Red Pencil. Evans, Shane W., illus. 2014. (ENG.). 336p. (J). (gr. 4-17). 17.99 (978-0-316-24780-1(4)) Little, Brown Bks. for Young Readers.
Prins, Piet. The Grim Reaper. 2006. (Illus.). 130p. (J). pap. (978-1-894666-74-9(7)) Inheritance Pubns.
—Hideout in the Swamp. 2006. (Illus.). 136p. (J). pap. (978-1-894666-73-2(9)) Inheritance Pubns.
Pung, Alice. Marly & the Goat, Bk. 3. Masciullo, Lucia, illus. 3rd ed. 2016. (Our Australian Girl Ser.: 3). (ENG.). 144p. (J). (gr. 3-7). 7.99 (978-0-14-330851-5(3)) Penguin Books Australia AUS. Dist: Independent Pubs. Group.
Ross, Susan. Kiki & Jacques. 2015. (ENG.). 128p. (J). (gr. 3-7). 16.95 (978-0-8234-3427-5(3)) Holiday Hse., Inc.
Sanna, Francesca. The Journey. Sanna, Francesca, illus. 2016. (ENG., Illus.). 48p. (J). (gr. -1-2). 17.95 (978-1-909263-99-4(0)) Flying Eye Bks. GBR. Dist: Consortium Bk. Sales & Distribution.
Senzai, N. H. Shooting Kabul. (Kabul Chronicles Ser.). (ENG.). (J). (gr. 3-7). 2011. 288p. pap. 7.99 (978-1-4424-0195-2(8)) 2010. 272p. 18.99 (978-1-4424-0194-5(X)) Simon & Schuster/Paula Wiseman Bks. (Simon & Schuster/Paula Wiseman Bks.).
Sepetys, Ruta. Salt to the Sea. l.t. ed. 2016. (ENG.). 500p. 24.99 (978-1-4104-9287-6(7)) Cengage Gale.
—Salt to the Sea, 9 vols. (ENG.). (YA). 2017. pap. 98.91 **(978-0-525-48681-7(X)**, Penguin Books) 2017. 448p. (gr. 7). pap. 10.99 **(978-0-14-242362-2(9)**, Penguin Books) 2016. (Illus.). 400p. (gr. 7-12). 18.99 (978-0-399-16030-1(2), Philomel Bks.) Penguin Young Readers Group.
—Salt to the Sea. 2017. lib. bdg. 22.10 **(978-0-606-40492-1(9))** Turtleback Bks.
Shulevitz, Uri. How I Learned Geography. Shulevitz, Uri, illus. 2008. (ENG., Illus.). 32p. (J). (gr. -1-3). 17.99 (978-0-374-33499-4(4), 9780374334994, Farrar, Straus & Giroux (BYR)) Farrar, Straus & Giroux.
Simon, Tanya & Simon, Richard. Oskar & the Eight Blessings. Siegel, Mark, illus. 2015. (ENG.). 40p. (J). (gr. -1-3). 17.99 (978-1-59643-949-8(1), 9781596439498) Roaring Brook Pr.
Staples, Suzanne Fisher. Under the Persimmon Tree. 2008. (Illus.). 281p. (gr. 7-12). 20.00 (978-0-7569-9004-6(1)) Perfection Learning Corp.
—Under the Persimmon Tree. 2008. (ENG., Illus.). 304p. (YA). (gr. 7-12). pap. 9.99 (978-0-312-37776-2(2), 9780312377762) Square Fish.
Stein, R. Conrad. Someone Talked! 2011. (ENG.). 146p. (J). pap. 8.95 (978-1-935178-17-0(2), ChironBooks) Coleman/Perrin.
Swindells, Robert. Ruby Tanya. 2005. (ENG.). 256p. (J). (gr. 7). per. 15.99 (978-0-440-86398-4(8)) Transworld Publishers Ltd. GBR. Dist: Independent Pubs. Group.
Taylor, Marilyn. 17 Martin Street. 2012. (ENG.). 208p. (J). pap. 12.95 (978-1-84717-286-0(5)) O'Brien Pr., Ltd., The IRL. Dist: Dufour Editions, Inc.
TenNapel, Doug. Escape from the Lizzarks. 2015. (Nnewts Ser.: 1). (ENG., Illus.). 192p. (J). (gr. 3-7). pap. 10.99 (978-0-545-67646-5(0), Graphix) Scholastic, Inc.
—The Rise of Herk. 2016. (Nnewts Ser.: 2). (ENG.). 208p. (J). (gr. 3-7). 19.99 (978-0-545-67652-6(5), Graphix) Scholastic, Inc.
Thor, Annika. A Faraway Island. Schenck, Linda, tr. 2011. (ENG.). 256p. (J). (gr. 3-7). 6.99 (978-0-375-84495-9(3), Yearling) Random Hse. Children's Bks.
—The Lily Pond. Schenck, Linda, tr. 2012. (ENG.). 224p. (J). (gr. 4-7). 7.99 (978-0-385-74040-1(9), Yearling) Random Hse. Children's Bks.
Thor, Annika & Schenck, Linda. Deep Sea. 2015. (ENG.). 240p. (YA). (gr. 9). 20.99 (978-0-375-99132-5(8), Delacorte Pr.) Random Hse. Children's Bks.
Walter, Jon. Close to the Wind. 2015. (ENG.). 304p. (J). (gr. 5-9). 17.99 (978-0-545-81662-5(9)) Scholastic, Inc.
Walters, Eric. Walking Home. 2014. (ENG.). 304p. (J). (gr. 5). pap. 10.99 (978-0-385-68157-5(7), Doubleday Canada) Penguin Random House Canada Young Readers CAN. Dist: Penguin Random Hse. LLC.
Weber, Judith Eichler. Seeking Safety. Martin, John F., illus. 2006. (Adventures in America Ser.). (J). (978-1-893110-46-5(X)) Silver Moon Pr.
Whitman, Sylvia. The Milk of Birds. (ENG., Illus.). 384p. (YA). (gr. 9). 2014. pap. 10.99 (978-1-4424-4683-0(8)) 2013. 16.99 (978-1-4424-4682-3(X), Atheneum Bks. for Young Readers) Simon & Schuster Children's Publishing.
Whitney, Kim Ablon. The Other Half of Life. 2010. (ENG.). 256p. (YA). (gr. 7). mass mkt. 7.99 (978-0-375-84422-5(8), Laurel Leaf) Random Hse. Children's Bks.
Williams, Mary. Brothers in Hope: The Story of the Lost Boys of Sudan, 1 vol. Christie, R. Gregory, illus. 2013. (ENG.). 32p. (J). 18.95 (978-1-58430-232-2(1)) Lee & Low Bks., Inc.
Williams, Michael. Now Is the Time for Running. 2013. (ENG.). 240p. (YA). (gr. 7-17). pap. 10.99 (978-0-316-07788-0(7)) Little, Brown Bks. for Young Readers.
Wiseman, Eva. Kanada. 2006. (ENG., Illus.). 264p. (YA). (gr. 5). pap. 9.95 (978-0-88776-729-6(X), Tundra Bks.) Tundra Bks. CAN. Dist: Penguin Random Hse. LLC.
Zeiss, Joyce Burns. Out of the Dragon's Mouth. 2015. (ENG., Illus.). 240p. (YA). pap. 11.99 (978-0-7387-4196-3(5), Flux) North Star Editions.

REFUSE AND REFUSE DISPOSAL

see also Hazardous Wastes; Pollution; Sewage Disposal; Waste Products; Water—Pollution

Addison, D. R. Garbage Trucks at Work. 2009. (Big Trucks Ser.). 24p. (gr. 1-1). 42.50 (978-1-61511-585-3(4), PowerKids Pr.) Rosen Publishing Group, Inc., The.
Alexander, Richard. Que Hacen Los Recolectores de Basura? / What Do Garbage Collectors Do? 2015. (Ayudantes de la Comunidad / Helping the Community Ser.). (ENG & SPA.). 24p. (J). (gr. 1-1). 23.60 (978-1-4994-0611-5(8), PowerKids Pr.) Rosen Publishing Group, Inc., The.
—What Do Garbage Collectors Do? 2015. (Helping the Community Ser.). (ENG., Illus.). 24p. (J). (gr. 1-1). pap. 8.25 (978-1-4994-0631-3(2), PowerKids Pr.) Rosen Publishing Group, Inc., The.
Barnham, Kay. Recycle. 2007. (Environment Action Ser.). (ENG., Illus.). 32p. (J). (gr. 3-7). pap. (978-0-7787-3669-1(5)) Crabtree Publishing Co.
Barraclough, Sue. Recycling Materials. 2007. (Making a Difference Ser.). (Illus.). 30p. (J). (gr. -1-3). lib. bdg. 27.10 (978-1-59771-108-1(X)) Sea-To-Sea Pubns.
Bellamy, Rufus. Waste & Pollution. 2010. (Sustaining Our Environment Ser.). 48p. (J). 35.65 (978-1-60753-139-5(9)) Amicus Publishing.
Bodden, Valerie. The War on Waste. 2010. (Earth Issues Ser.). 48p. (YA). (gr. 5-18). 23.95 (978-1-58341-985-4(3), Creative Education) Creative Co., The.
Bourgeois, Paulette. Garbage Collectors. LaFave, Kim, illus. 2004. 32p. (J). lib. bdg. 15.38 (978-1-4242-1190-6(5)) Fitzgerald Bks.
Bullard, Lisa. Look Out for Litter. Xin, Xiao, illus. 2011. (Planet Protectors Ser.). pap. 39.62 (978-0-7613-8654-4(8), Millbrook Pr.) Lerner Publishing Group.
—Look Out for Litter. Xin, Xiao & Zheng, Xin, illus. 2011. (Cloverleaf Books (tm) — Planet Protectors Ser.). (ENG.). 24p. (gr. k-2). pap. 6.95 (978-0-7613-8514-1(2), Millbrook Pr.); lib. bdg. 23.93 (978-0-7613-6105-3(7)) Lerner Publishing Group.
—Rally for Recycling. Thomas, Wes, illus. 2011. (Planet Protectors Ser.). pap. 39.62 (978-0-7613-8656-8(4), Millbrook Pr.); (ENG.). 24p. pap. 6.95 (978-0-7613-8516-5(9), Millbrook Pr.); (ENG.). 24p. lib. bdg. 23.93 (978-0-7613-6103-9(0)) Lerner Publishing Group.
Burton, Margie, et al. Clean Beaches & Playas Limpias: 6 English, 6 Spanish Adaptations. 2011. (J). spiral bd. 75.00 net. (978-1-4108-5625-8(9)) Benchmark Education Co.
Carlson Berne, Emma. Scavengers: Eating Nature's Trash. 2014. (Scavengers: Eating Nature's Trash Ser.). 24p. (J). (gr. k-5). 141.60 (978-1-4777-6617-0(0), PowerKids Pr.) Rosen Publishing Group, Inc., The.
Carr, Aaron. Garbage Trucks. 2014. (Illus.). 24p. (J). (978-1-4896-3224-1(7)) Weigl Pubs., Inc.
Chambers, Catherine. How Effective Is Recycling? 2015. (Earth Debates Ser.). (ENG., Illus.). 48p. (gr. 4-6). 33.32 (978-1-4846-0996-5(4), Heinemann InfoSearch) Heinemann-Raintree.
Close, Edward. What Do We Do with Trash? 2012. (Discovery Education: the Environment Ser.). (ENG., Illus.). 32p. (J). (gr. 3-6). pap. 10.00 (978-1-4488-7982-3(5)); lib. bdg. 25.25 (978-1-4488-7894-9(2)) Rosen Publishing Group, Inc., The. (PowerKids Pr.).

Daynes, Katie. The Stinking Story of Garbage. Mayer, Uwe, illus. (Usborne Young Reading: Series Two Ser.). (J). 2006. 64p. (gr. 4-7). per. 5.99 *(978-0-7945-1247-7(X))* 2007. 62p. (gr. -1-3). 8.99 *(978-0-7945-1750-2(1))* EDC Publishing. (Usborne).

Dayton, Connor. Garbage Trucks. 2012. (Illus.). 24p. (J). 49.50 *(978-1-4488-5067-9(3))*; pap. 8.25 *(978-1-4488-5066-2(5))*; lib. bdg. 22.60 *(978-1-4488-4958-1(6))* Rosen Publishing Group, Inc., The. (PowerKids Pr.).

Dorion, Christiane. Earth's Garbage Crisis. 2007. (What If We Do Nothing? Ser.). (Illus.). 48p. (gr. 5-12). lib. bdg. 31.00 *(978-0-8368-7753-3(5)*, Gareth Stevens Secondary Library) Stevens, Gareth Publishing LLLP.

Earner, Claire. What a Waste: Where Does Garbage Go? Edlund, Bambi, illus. 2017. (ENG.). 92p. (J). (gr. 3-7). pap. 12.95 *(978-1-55451-918-7(7))* Annick Pr., Ltd. CAN. Dist: Publishers Group West (PGW).

Elliot, Marion. Recycled Craft Projects for Kids: 50 Fantastic Things to Make from Junk, Shown. 2014. (ENG., Illus.). 96p. (J). (gr. 2-7). 13.99 *(978-1-84322-891-2(2)*, Armadillo) Anness Publishing GBR. Dist: National Bk. Network.

Enz, Tammy. Repurpose It: Invent New Uses for Old Stuff, 1 vol. 2012. (Invent It Ser.). (ENG.). 32p. (gr. 3-4). pap. 8.10 *(978-1-4296-7983-1(2))*; pap. 47.70 *(978-1-4296-8457-6(7))*; lib. bdg. 27.32 *(978-1-4296-7636-6(1))* Capstone Press of Coughlan Cos. (Fact Finders).

Flynn, Sarah Wassner & National Geographic Kids Staff. This Book Stinks! Gross Garbage, Rotten Rubbish, & the Science of Trash. 2017. (ENG.). 128p. (J). (gr. 3-7). pap. 14.99 *(978-1-4263-2730-8(7)*, National Geographic Children's Bks.) National Geographic Society.

Forest, Anne. Sanitation Workers, 01 vols., 1. 2016. (Hands-On Jobs Ser.). (ENG., Illus.). 24p. (J). pap. 8.25 *(978-1-5081-4371-0(4)*, PowerKids Pr.) Rosen Publishing Group, Inc., The.

Friedman, Lauri S. Garbage & Recycling. 2009. (Introducing Issues with Opposing Viewpoints Ser.). (Illus.). 144p. (J). (gr. 7-10). 36.95 *(978-0-7377-4337-1(9)*, Greenhaven Pr., Inc.) Cengage Gale.

Furgang, Kathy. Where Does Your Garbage Go? & ¿Adónde va la Basura? 6 English, 6 Spanish Adaptations. 2011. (ENG & SPA.). (J). 75.00 net. *(978-1-4108-5635-7(6))* Benchmark Education Co.

Green, Jen. Garbage & Litter. 2010. (J). pap. 10.60 *(978-1-61532-243-5(4)*, PowerKids Pr.); 32p. (J). (gr. 1-5). E-Book 50.50 *(978-1-4488-0365-1(9))*; (Illus.). 32p. (YA). (gr. 2-5). lib. bdg. 26.50 *(978-1-61532-234-3(5))* Rosen Publishing Group, Inc., The.

—Water. 2010. (J). pap. 10.60 *(978-1-61532-246-6(9)*, PowerKids Pr.); 32p. (gr. 1-5). E-Book 50.50 *(978-1-4488-0368-2(3))*; (Illus.). 32p. (gr. 2-5). lib. bdg. 26.50 *(978-1-61532-235-0(3))* Rosen Publishing Group, Inc., The.

Greenhaven Press Editors, ed. Garbage & Recycling. 2011. (Opposing Viewpoints Ser.). (Illus.). 240p. (YA). (gr. 9-12). 42.95 *(978-0-7377-5428-5(1))* Cengage Gale.

Harmon, Daniel E. Jobs in Environmental Cleanup & Emergency Hazmat Response. 2010. (Green Careers Ser.). (Illus.). 80p. (YA). (gr. 7-12). lib. bdg. 33.25 *(978-1-4358-3570-2(0))* Rosen Publishing Group, Inc., The.

Harrison, Scott & Ross, Allison J. Choosing a Career in Waste Management. 2005. (World of Work Ser.). (Illus.). 64p. (YA). (gr. 7-12). lib. bdg. 31.95 *(978-0-8239-3240-5(0)*, WWVAMA) Rosen Publishing Group, Inc., The.

Heos, Bridget. Follow That Bottle! A Plastic Recycling Journey. Westgate, Alex, illus. 2016. (Keeping Cities Clean Ser.). (ENG.). 24p. (J). (gr. k-3). 20.95 *(978-1-60753-964-3(0))* Amicus Publishing.

—Follow That Garbage! A Journey to the Landfill. Westgate, Alex, illus. 2016. (Keeping Cities Clean Ser.). (ENG.). 24p. (J). (gr. k-3). 20.95 *(978-1-60753-963-6(2))* Amicus Publishing.

—Follow That Paper! A Paper Recycling Journey. Westgate, Alex, illus. 2016. (Keeping Cities Clean Ser.). (ENG.). 24p. (J). (gr. k-3). 20.95 *(978-1-60753-965-0(9))* Amicus Publishing.

Hepplewhite, Peter. Loos, Poos, & Number Twos: A Disgusting Journey Through the Bowels of History! 2015. (Awfully Ancient Ser.). (ENG., Illus.). 32p. (J). (gr. 5-5). pap. 10.50 *(978-1-4824-3117-9(3))* Stevens, Gareth Publishing LLLP.

Hewitt, Sally. Waste & Recycling. 2008. (Rise & Shine Ser.). (ENG., Illus.). 32p. (J). (gr. 3-7). pap. *(978-0-7787-4105-3(2))*; lib. bdg. *(978-0-7787-4098-8(6))* Crabtree Publishing Co.

Horn, Geoffrey M. Sewer Inspector. 2010. (Benchmark Rockets: Dirty & Dangerous Jobs Ser.). 32p. (J). (gr. 3-6). 28.50 *(978-1-60870-178-0(6))* Marshall Cavendish Corp.

Inskipp, Carol. Reducing & Recycling Waste. 2005. (Improving Our Environment Ser.). (Illus.). 32p. (gr. 3-6). lib. bdg. 26.00 *(978-0-8368-4429-0(7)*, Gareth Stevens Learning Library) Stevens, Gareth Publishing LLLP.

Jakab, Cheryl. Waste Management. 2010. (Environment in Focus Ser.). 32p. (gr. 4). 28.50 *(978-1-60870-093-6(3))* Marshall Cavendish Corp.

James, Lincoln. Where Does the Garbage Go? 2012. (Everyday Mysteries Ser.). (ENG., Illus.). 24p. (J). (gr. 2-4). pap. 8.15 *(978-1-4339-6327-8(2))*; lib. bdg. 22.60 *(978-1-4339-6325-4(6))* Stevens, Gareth Publishing LLLP.

Kallen, Stuart A. Trashing the Planet: Examining Our Global Garbage Glut. 2017. (ENG.). 104p. (YA). (gr. 8-12). 37.32 *(978-1-5124-1314-4(3)*, Twenty-First Century Bks.) Lerner Publishing Group.

Kenan, Tessa. Hooray for Garbage Collectors! 2017. (Bumba Books (tm) — Hooray for Community Helpers! Ser.). (ENG.). 24p. (J). (gr. -1-1). pap. 6.99 ***(978-1-5124-5552-6(0))***; (Illus.). 25.32 ***(978-1-5124-3352-4(7)*** Lerner Pubns.) Lerner Publishing Group.

Knight, M. J. Why Shouldn't I Drop Litter? 2009. (One Small Step Ser.). (YA). (gr. 2-5). 28.50 *(978-1-59920-265-5(4))* Black Rabbit Bks.

Knight M J. Why Shouldn't I Drop Litter? 2009. (One Small Step Ser.). (Illus.). 32p. (J). (gr. -1-3). pap. *(978-1-897563-51-9(5))* Saunders Bk. Co.

Landers, Ace & Cartwheel Editors. I Am a Garbage Truck. Scholastic, Inc. Staff, ed. 2008. (ENG.). 8p. (J). (gr. -1 — 1). bds. 4.99 *(978-0-545-07963-1(2)*, Cartwheel Bks.) Scholastic, Inc.

Latham, Donna. Garbage: Investigate What Happens When You Throw It Out with 25 Projects. Hetland, Beth, illus. 2011. (Build It Yourself Ser.). (ENG.). 128p. (J). (gr. 3-7). 21.95 *(978-1-936313-47-1(2))* Open City Bks.

Lawrence, Ellen. Garbage Galore. 2014. (Science Slam: Green World, Clean World Ser.). 24p. (J). (gr. -1-3). lib. bdg. 23.93 *(978-1-62724-102-1(7))* Bearport Publishing Co., Inc.

Linde, Barbara M. Pollution. 2014. (Illus.). 32p. (J). lib. bdg. *(978-1-4339-9926-0(9))* Stevens, Gareth Publishing LLLP.

Lindeen, Mary. Garbage Trucks. 2007. (Mighty Machines Ser.). (ENG., Illus.). 24p. (J). (gr. k-3). lib. bdg. 25.95 *(978-1-60014-117-1(X))* Bellwether Media.

Macken, JoAnn Early. Sanitation Workers. 2010. (People in My Community Ser.). (ENG.). 24p. (J). (gr. k-3). pap. 8.15 *(978-1-4339-3810-8(3))*; lib. bdg. 22.60 *(978-1-4339-3809-2(X))* Stevens, Gareth Publishing LLLP.

Mancini, Candice. Garbage & Recycling. 2010. (Global Viewpoints Ser.). (ENG.). 224p. 40.45 *(978-0-7377-5081-2(2))*; (Illus.). pap. 27.95 *(978-0-7377-5082-9(0))* Cengage Gale. (Greenhaven Pr., Inc.).

McKissick, Katie. The Hidden World of Garbage: Multi-Digit Numbers (Grade 4) 2017. (Mathematics Readers Ser.). (Illus.). 32p. (J). (gr. 4-4). pap. 8.99 ***(978-1-4258-5546-8(6))*** Teacher Created Materials, Inc.

Meissner, David. Where Does Your Garbage Go? 2011. (Early Connections Ser.). (J). *(978-1-61672-608-9(3))* Benchmark Education Co.

—Where Does Your Garbage Go? Set Of 6. 2011. (Early Connections Ser.). (J). pap. 37.00 net. *(978-1-4108-1077-9(1))* Benchmark Education Co.

Meister, Cari. Garbage Trucks. 2013. (ENG., Illus.). 24p. (J). lib. bdg. 25.65 *(978-1-62031-045-8(7))* Jump! Inc.

Meyer, Susan. Getting a Job in Sanitation. 2013. 80p. (YA). (gr. 9-12). 33.25 *(978-1-4488-9607-3(X))* Rosen Publishing Group, Inc., The.

Michele, Tracey. Where Does the Garbage Go? 2011. (Learn-Abouts Ser.). (Illus.). 16p. (J). pap. 7.95 *(978-1-59920-612-7(9))* Black Rabbit Bks.

Miller, Heather. Lo Que Hacen los Trabajadores Sanitarios. 2007. (What Does a Community Helper Do? Bilingual Ser.). (ENG & SPA., Illus.). 24p. (J). (gr. 1-3). lib. bdg. 22.60 *(978-0-7660-2829-6(1)*, Enslow Elementary) Enslow Pubs., Inc.

—What Does a Sanitation Worker Do? 2005. (What Does a Community Helper Do? Ser.). (Illus.). 24p. (J). lib. bdg. 22.60 *(978-0-7660-2543-1(8)*, Enslow Elementary) Enslow Pubs., Inc.

Miller, Mirella S. Compost Center Operator. 2015. (Gross Jobs Ser.). (ENG.). 24p. (J). (gr. 2-5). 27.07 *(978-1-63143-685-7(6)*, 208520) Child's World, Inc., The.

Minden, Cecilia. Kids Can Clean up Trash. 2010. (21st Century Basic Skills Library: Kids Can Ser.). (ENG.). 24p. (gr. k-3). lib. bdg. 22.79 *(978-1-60279-870-0(2)*, 200606) Cherry Lake Publishing.

Mulder, Michelle. Trash Talk: Moving Toward a Zero-Waste World, 1 vol. 2015. (Orca Footprints Ser.). (ENG., Illus.). 48p. (J). (gr. 3-7). 19.95 *(978-1-4598-0692-4(1))* Orca Bk. Pubs. USA.

Murray, Aaron R. Sanitation Workers Help Us. (Illus.). (J). 2013. 23p. E-Book *(978-1-4645-0965-0(4))* 2012. 24p. pap. 7.95 *(978-1-4644-0058-2(X))* 2012. 24p. (gr. -1-1). 22.60 *(978-0-7660-4049-6(6))* Enslow Pubs., Inc. (Enslow Elementary).

Nevins, Debbie & Foran, Jill. Waste Management. 2017. (J). ***(978-1-5105-2231-2(X))*** SmartBook Media, Inc.

Newman, Barbara Johansen, illus. Glamorous Garbage. 2015. (ENG.). 40p. (J). (gr. k-3). 16.95 *(978-1-62091-626-1(6))* Boyds Mills Pr.

Orme, Helen. Garbage & Recycling. 2008. (Earth in Danger Ser.). (Illus.). 32p. (YA). (gr. 3-6). lib. bdg. 25.27 *(978-1-59716-726-0(6)*, 1284325) Bearport Publishing Co., Inc.

Ostopowich, Melanie. Waste. 2009. (Science Q & A Ser.). (Illus.). 48p. (YA). (gr. 5-8). pap. 10.95 *(978-1-60596-065-4(9))*; lib. bdg. 29.05 *(978-1-60596-064-7(0))* Weigl Pubs., Inc.

Owings, Lisa. From Garbage to Compost. 2016. (Start to Finish, Second Ser.). (ENG., Illus.). 24p. (J). (gr. k-3). 23.99 *(978-1-5124-0911-6(1))* Lerner Publishing Group.

Oxlade, Chris. Garbage & Recycling, 1 vol. 2012. (How Does My Home Work? Ser.). (ENG.). 24p. (gr. k-1). pap. 6.79 *(978-1-4329-6571-6(9))*; lib. bdg. 23.32 *(978-1-4329-6566-2(2))* Heinemann-Raintree. (Heinemann Read & Learn).

Parker, Russ. Waste Management Crisis. 2009. (Planet in Crisis Ser.). 32p. (gr. 5-8). (ENG., Illus.). (J). pap. 10.00 *(978-1-4358-0683-2(2))*; (YA). lib. bdg. 25.25 *(978-1-4358-5253-2(2))* Rosen Publishing Group, Inc., The. (Rosen Reference).

Parks, Peggy J. Garbage. 2011. (J). *(978-1-60217-031-5(2))* Erickson Pr.

—Garbage & Recycling. 2008. (Ripped from the Headlines Ser.). (YA). (gr. 7-12). 23.95 *(978-1-60217-023-0(1))* Erickson Pr.

—Garbage & Recycling. 2010. (Compact Research Ser.). (YA). (gr. 7-12). 26.95 *(978-1-60152-121-7(9))* ReferencePoint Pr., Inc.

Pettiford, Rebecca. Garbage Collectors. 2015. (J). lib. bdg. 25.65 *(978-1-62031-157-8(7)*, Bullfrog Bks.) Jump! Inc.

Piehl, Janet. Sanitation Workers. 2005. (Pull Ahead Books: Community Helpers Ser.). (ENG., Illus.). 32p. (gr. k-3). lib. bdg. 22.60 *(978-0-8225-2847-0(9))* Lerner Publishing Group.

Pratt, Mary K. How Can We Reduce Household Waste? 2016. (Searchlight Books — What Can We Do about Pollution? Ser.). (ENG., Illus.). 40p. (J). (gr. 3-5). 30.65 *(978-1-4677-9517-3(8)*, Lerner Pubns.) Lerner Publishing Group.

Rabe, Tish. How to Help the Earth-By the LORAX. Ruiz, Aristides et al, illus. 2012. (Step into Reading Ser.). (ENG.). 48p. (J). (gr. k-3). pap. 3.99 *(978-0-375-86977-8(8)*, Random Hse. Bks. for Young Readers) Random Hse. Children's Bks.

—How to Help the Earth-By the Lorax. 2012. (Step into Reading Level 3 Ser.). lib. bdg. 13.55 *(978-0-606-23848-9(4)*, Turtleback) Turtleback Bks.

Reynolds, Alison. Let's Use It Again. Hopgood, Andrew, illus. 2009. (Save Our Planet! Ser.). 12p. (J). (gr. -1-3). bds. 11.40 *(978-1-60754-415-9(6))* Windmill Bks.

Rhatigan, Joe. Get a Job at the Garbage Dump. 2016. (Bright Futures Press: Get a Job Ser.). (ENG.). 32p. (J). (gr. 4-6). 29.93 *(978-1-63471-905-6(0)*, 208941) Cherry Lake Publishing.

Richmond, Benjamin. Where Do Garbage Trucks Go? 2016. (Good Question! Ser.). (ENG., Illus.). 32p. (J). (gr. 1). pap. 5.95 *(978-1-4549-1625-3(7))* Sterling Publishing Co., Inc.

—Where Do Garbage Trucks Go? And Other Questions about Trash & Recycling. 2016. (Good Question! Ser.). (ENG., Illus.). 40p. (J). (gr. 1). 12.95 *(978-1-4549-1624-6(9))* Sterling Publishing Co., Inc.

Riley, Karen. Don't Trash My Planet. 2004. (Illus.). 20p. (J). (gr. k-5). pap. 10.00 *(978-0-9708135-4-1(6)*, "5,000") S.C.R.A.P. Gallery.

Ringstad, Arnold. Garbage Collector. 2015. (Gross Jobs Ser.). (ENG.). 24p. (J). (gr. 2-5). 27.07 *(978-1-63143-686-4(4)*, 208521) Child's World, Inc., The.

Rodger, Ellen. Recycling Waste. 2008. (Saving Our World Ser.). 32p. (gr. 4-18). lib. bdg. 28.50 *(978-0-7614-3222-7(1)*, Benchmark Bks.) Marshall Cavendish Corp.

Roza, Greg. Landfills: Habitat Havoc. 2014. (Illus.). 32p. (J). *(978-1-4339-9921-5(8))* Stevens, Gareth Publishing LLLP.

Sévigny, Eric, illus. As Good as New. 2012. (Ecology Club Ser.). (ENG.). 24p. (J). (gr. -1-1). pap. 5.99 *(978-2-89450-832-9(8))* Caillouet, Gerry.

Shores, Erika L. How Garbage Gets from Trash Cans to Landfills. 2016. (Here to There Ser.). (ENG., Illus.). 24p. (gr. k-1). lib. bdg. 26.65 *(978-1-4914-8433-3(0)*, Pebble Plus) Capstone Press of Coughlan Cos.

Showers, Paul. Where Does the Garbage Go? Chewning, Randy, illus. 2015. (Let's-Read-And-Find-Out Science 2 Ser.). (ENG.). 32p. (J). (gr. -1-3). pap. 6.99 *(978-0-06-238200-9(4))* HarperCollins Pubs.

Solway, Andrew. Waste Disposal. 2010. (World at Risk Ser.). (YA). (gr. 5-9). 34.25 *(978-1-59920-380-5(4))* Black Rabbit Bks.

Spilsbury, Louise. Garbage Can. Hanna, Gary, illus. 2013. (Look Inside Ser.). (ENG.). 32p. (gr. 1-3). 27.32 *(978-1-4329-7195-3(6))*; pap. 8.29 *(978-1-4329-7202-8(2))* Heinemann-Raintree. (Heinemann First Library).

Sundance/Newbridge LLC Staff. Where Does All the Garbage Go? 2007. (Early Science Ser.). (gr. k-3). 18.95 *(978-1-4007-6260-6(X))*; pap. 6.10 *(978-1-4007-6256-9(1))* Sundance/Newbridge Educational Publishing.

Tilmont, Amy. Trash Talk: What You Throw Away. 2011. (Second Nature Ser.). 48p. (J). (gr. 5-8). lib. bdg. 26.60 *(978-1-59953-459-6(2))* Norwood Hse. Pr.

Turnbull, Stephanie. Collecting. 2015. (Try This! Ser.). (ENG., Illus.). 24p. (J). (gr. 2-6). 27.10 *(978-1-62588-371-1(4))* Black Rabbit Bks.

—Trash & Recycling. 2006. (Beginners Science Ser.). (Illus.). 32p. (J). (gr. 4-7). lib. bdg. 12.99 *(978-1-58086-948-5(3)*, Usborne) EDC Publishing.

—Trash & Recycling. Fox, Christyan, illus. 2006. (Beginners Science: Level 2 Ser.). 32p. (J). (gr. 1-3). 4.99 *(978-0-7945-1400-6(6)*, Usborne) EDC Publishing.

Walker, Kate. Clothing. 2010. (Recycling Ser.). 32p. (gr. 1). 28.50 *(978-1-60870-128-5(X))* Marshall Cavendish GBR. Dist: Marshall Cavendish Corp.

—Food & Garden Waste. 2010. (Recycling Ser.). 32p. (gr. 1). 28.50 *(978-1-60870-129-2(8))* Marshall Cavendish Corp.

Walsh, Melanie. 10 Things I Can Do to Help My World. Walsh, Melanie, illus. 2012. (ENG., Illus.). 40p. (J). (gr. -1-2). pap. 8.99 *(978-0-7636-5919-6(3))* Candlewick Pr.

Ward, D. J. What Happens to Our Trash? Meisel, Paul, illus. 2012. (Let's-Read-And-Find-Out Science 2 Ser.). (ENG.). 40p. (J). (gr. -1-3). 16.99 *(978-0-06-168756-3(1))*; pap. 5.99 *(978-0-06-168755-6(3))* HarperCollins Pubs. (Collins).

Watts, Franklin & Blount, Rachel. Refuse Collector. 2016. (Here to Help Ser.). (ENG., Illus.). 24p. (J). (gr. k-2). 16.99 *(978-1-4451-4030-8(6)*, Franklin Watts) Hachette Children's Group GBR. Dist: Hachette Bk. Group.

Weitzman, Elizabeth. 10 Cosas Que Puedes Hacer para Reducir,reciclar y Reutilizar. 2017. (Rookie Star — Make a Difference (Spanish Translation) Ser.). (SPA.). 32p. (J). pap. 5.95 ***(978-1-338-18781-6(3))***; lib. bdg. 25.00 ***(978-0-531-22860-9(6))*** Scholastic Library Publishing. (Children's Pr.).

Weitzman, Elizabeth. 10 Things You Can Do to Reduce, Reuse, Recycle. 2016. (Rookie Star — Make a Difference Ser.). (ENG., Illus.). 32p. (J). lib. bdg. 25.00 *(978-0-531-22654-4(9)*, Children's Pr.) Scholastic Library Publishing.

Wilcox, Charlotte. Earth-Friendly Waste Management. 2009. pap. 58.95 *(978-0-7613-4691-3(0))* 2008. (Illus.). 72p. (YA). (gr. 4-7). lib. bdg. 30.60 *(978-0-8225-7560-3(4))* Lerner Publishing Group.

Winnick, Nick. Reducing Waste. 2016. (J). ***(978-1-5105-2221-3(2))*** SmartBook Media, Inc.

REFUSE AND REFUSE DISPOSAL—FICTION

Angleberger, Tom. Poop Fountain! 2014. (Qwikpick Papers). (ENG., Illus.). 144p. (J). (gr. 3-7). 12.95 *(978-1-4197-0425-3(7)*, Amulet Bks.) Abrams, Inc.

Artifact Group, The. The Trash Planet. 2009. (Backyardigans Ser.: 12). (ENG.). 24p. (J). pap. 3.99 *(978-1-4169-6868-9(7)*, Simon Spotlight/Nickelodeon) Simon Spotlight/Nickelodeon.

Auerbach, Annie. Junkyard Dig! Building from A to Z. Shannon, David et al, illus. 2010. (Jon Scieszka's Trucktown Ser.). (ENG.). 26p. (J). (gr. -1-k). bds. 5.99 *(978-1-4169-4187-3(8)*, Little Simon) Little Simon.

Bildner, Phil. Marvelous Cornelius: Hurricane Katrina & the Spirit of New Orleans. Parra, John, illus. 2015. (ENG.). 44p. (J). (gr. k-3). 16.99 *(978-1-4521-2578-7(3))* Chronicle Bks. LLC.

Brimner, Larry Dane. Trash Trouble. Tripp, Christine, illus. 2003. (Rookie Choices Ser.). (ENG.). 32p. (gr. 1-2). pap. 5.95 *(978-0-516-27837-7(1)*, Children's Pr.) Scholastic Library Publishing.

Brooklyn. The Adventures of the Earth Saver Girl: Don't be a Litterbug. 2010. (Illus.). 24p. pap. 8.49 *(978-0-9822822-4-3(9))* Wright Bk. Publishing.

Carey, Edward. Foulsham: The Iremonger Trilogy: Book 2. 2015. (Iremonger Trilogy Ser.: 0). (ENG., Illus.). 336p. (gr. 5-17). 16.99 *(978-1-4683-0954-6(4)*, 460954) Overlook Pr., The.

—Foulsham: The Iremonger Trilogy: Book Two. 2015. (Iremonger Trilogy Ser.: 0). (ENG.). 336p. (gr. 5-9). pap. 10.99 *(978-1-4683-1178-5(6)*, 461178) Overlook Pr., The.

—Lungdon: The Iremonger Trilogy: Book Three. 2015. (Iremonger Trilogy Ser.: 0). (ENG., Illus.). 512p. (gr. 5-12). 17.99 *(978-1-4683-0955-3(2)*, 460955) Overlook Pr., The.

Covey, Richard D. & Pappas, Diane H. Ugh! Don't Be a Litterbug! 2009. (Illus.). (J). pap. *(978-0-545-06102-5(4))* Scholastic, Inc.

Driscoll, Laura & Random House Disney Staff. Smash Trash! Cortes, Mario et al, illus. 2008. (Step into Reading Ser.). (ENG.). 32p. (J). (gr. k-3). pap. 3.99 *(978-0-7364-2515-5(2)*, RH/Disney) Random Hse. Children's Bks.

Gnoske, Alexandra. Loui Saves the Earth. 2010. 16p. 9.49 *(978-1-4520-0034-3(4))* AuthorHouse.

Harp, Susan. Retrieving with Evie. Siau, John, illus. 2007. (ENG.). 24p. (J). lib. bdg. 12.95 *(978-1-932439-67-0(6))* M.T. Publishing Co., Inc.

Keene, Carolyn. California Schemin' 2011. (Nancy Drew (All New) Girl Detective Ser.: 45). (ENG.). 160p. (J). (gr. 3-7). pap. 5.99 *(978-1-4424-2295-7(5)*, Aladdin) Simon & Schuster Children's Publishing.

Lee, Newman. Creepy Kitchen. Elizabeth, Neering, ed. Dan, Houser, illus. 2012. 40p. (J). pap. 10.00 *(978-1-62314-873-7(1))* Fisticuff Publishing.

McMullan, Kate. I Stink! McMullan, Jim, illus. (ENG.). (J). (gr. -1-k). 2005. 34p. bds. 7.99 *(978-0-06-074592-9(4)*, HarperFestival) 2006. 40p. reprint ed. pap. 6.99 *(978-0-06-443836-0(8))* HarperCollins Pubs.

Morris, Garvin. Dump Dog. Morris, Garvin, illus. (Illus.). (J). 2008. 32p. pap. 6.95 *(978-1-60108-022-6(0))* 2007. 40p. (gr. -1-2). 15.95 *(978-1-60108-012-7(3))* Red Cygnet Pr.

Mulligan, Andy. Trash. 2011. (ENG., Illus.). 240p. (YA). (gr. 7). pap. 9.99 *(978-0-385-75216-9(4)*, Ember) Random Hse. Children's Bks.

Odanaka, Barbara. Smash! Mash! Crash! There Goes the Trash! Hillenbrand, Will, illus. 2006. (ENG.). 32p. (J). (gr. -1-3). 18.99 *(978-0-689-85160-5(X)*, McElderry, Margaret K. Bks.) McElderry, Margaret K. Bks.

Plourde, Lynn. The Dump Man's Treasures. Owens, Mary Beth, illus. 2008. (ENG.). 32p. (J). (gr. -1-3). 15.95 *(978-0-89272-725-4(X))* Down East Bks.

Reynolds, Paul A. Sydney & Simon: Going Green! Reynolds, Paul A. & Reynolds, Peter H., illus. 2015. (Sydney & Simon Ser.). (ENG.). 48p. (J). (gr. 1-4). lib. bdg. 12.95 *(978-1-58089-677-1(4))* Charlesbridge Publishing, Inc.

Sander, Sonia & Scieszka, Jon. Smash That Trash! Shannon, David et al, illus. 2009. (Jon Scieszka's Trucktown Ser.). (ENG.). 14p. (J). (gr. -1-k). 7.99 *(978-1-4169-4180-4(0)*, Little Simon) Little Simon.

Sensel, Joni. The Garbage Monster. Bivins, Christopher, illus. 2003. 24p. (J). (gr. -1-18). 14.95 *(978-0-9701195-2-0(6))* Dream Factory Bks.

Stewart, Nancy. Bella Saves the Beach. Bell, Samantha, illus. 2013. 24p. 19.95 *(978-1-61633-370-6(7))*; pap. 11.95 *(978-1-61633-371-3(5))* Guardian Angel Publishing, Inc.

Wallace, Nancy Elizabeth. Recycle Every Day!, 0 vols. Wallace, Nancy Elizabeth, illus. 2006. (ENG., Illus.). 41p. (J). (gr. -1-3). pap. 9.99 *(978-0-7614-5290-4(7)*, 9780761452904, Amazon Children's Publishing) Amazon Publishing.

Ward, Helen. The Tin Forest. Anderson, Wayne, illus. 2003. (Rise & Shine Ser.). (ENG.). 32p. (J). (gr. -1-2). 7.99 *(978-0-14-250156-6(5)*, Puffin Books) Penguin Young Readers Group.

Weston Woods Staff, creator. I Stink! 2011. 38.75 *(978-0-439-02724-3(1))*; 18.95 *(978-0-439-02722-9(5))* Weston Woods Studios, Inc.

REGATTAS

see Rowing; Yachts and Yachting

REIGN OF TERROR

see France—History—Revolution, 1789-1799

REINDEER

Ariel, A. D. Land of Reindeer. 2016. (Spring Forward Ser.). (J). (gr. 2). *(978-1-4900-9462-5(8))* Benchmark Education Co.

Bauer, Jeff. Renos Asombrosos. 2007. (SPA., Illus.). 24p. (J). pap. *(978-0-545-02281-1(9))* Scholastic, Inc.

Markovics, Joyce L. Caribou: And Reindeer, Too. 2011. (Built for Cold Ser.). 32p. (YA). (gr. 1-4). lib. bdg. 25.27 *(978-1-61772-130-4(1))*; (J). (gr. 4-5). lib. bdg., E-Book 49.22 *(978-1-61772-220-2(0))* Bearport Publishing Co., Inc.

Marsico, Katie. Reindeer, 1 vol. 2011. (Day in the Life: Polar Animals Ser.). (ENG.). 24p. (gr. k-2). pap. 6.79 *(978-1-4329-5337-9(0))*; 23.32 *(978-1-4329-5330-0(3))* Heinemann-Raintree. (Heinemann Read & Learn).

Phillips, Dee. Reindeer. 2015. (Arctic Animals: Life Outside the Igloo Ser.). (ENG.). 24p. (J). (gr. -1-3). lib. bdg. 23.93 *(978-1-62724-529-6(4))* Bearport Publishing Co., Inc.

Publications International Ltd. Staff, ed. Rudolph the Red-Nosed Reindeer: My First Library. 2010. 10p. (J). bds. 12.98 *(978-1-60553-819-8(1))* Phoenix International Publications, Inc.

—Rudolph the Red-Nosed Reindeer: Book & Cuddly Rudolph. 2010. (J). 5.98 *(978-1-60553-750-4(0))* Phoenix International Publications, Inc.

—Rudolph the Red-Nosed Reindeer (Look & Find) 2010. 24p. (J). 7.98 *(978-1-60553-958-4(9))* Phoenix International Publications, Inc.

Sandler, Martin W. The Impossible Rescue: The True Story of an Amazing Arctic Adventure. 2014. (ENG.). 176p. (J). (gr. 5). pap. 15.99 *(978-0-7636-7093-1(6))* Candlewick Pr.

Watt, Fiona. That's Not My Reindeer... Wells, Rachel, illus. 2014. (Usborne Touchy-Feely Bks.). (ENG.). 10p. (gr. -1). bds. 9.99 *(978-0-7945-3390-8(6)*, Usborne) EDC Publishing.

REINDEER—FICTION

Anderson, Derek. How the Easter Bunny Saved Christmas. Anderson, Derek, illus. 2006. (ENG., Illus.). 40p. (J). (gr. -1-3). 17.99 *(978-0-689-87634-9(3)*, Simon & Schuster Bks. For Young Readers) Simon & Schuster Bks. For Young Readers.

Anonymous. Rudolph Saves the Day. 2014. (J). lib. bdg. 14.75 *(978-0-606-36126-2(X))* Turtleback Bks.

—Rudolph the Red-Nosed Reindeer: Rudolph Saves the Day. 2014. (Rudolph the Red-Nosed Reindeer Ser.: 2). (ENG.,

P
Q
R

Illus.). 24p. (J). (gr. -1-2). 4.99 *(978-1-250-05049-6(9),* 9781250050496) Square Fish.

Bass, William E. Santa Revisits His Secret Little Helper. Salazar, Vivian, illus. 2012. 26p. 24.95 *(978-1-4626-5396-6(0))* America Star Bks.

Baugh, Helen. Rudy's Windy Christmas. Mantle, Ben, illus. 2015. (ENG.). 32p. (J). (gr. -1-3). 16.99 *(978-0-8075-7173-6(3))* Whitman, Albert & Co.

Baum, L. Frank. A Kidnapped Santa Claus. 2011. 24p. 12.95 *(978-1-4638-9603-4(4))*; pap. 6.95 *(978-1-4638-0070-3(3))* Rodgers, Alan Bks.

Berger, Samantha. Santa's Reindeer Games. Manders, John, illus. 2011. (J). *(978-0-545-36866-7(9))* Scholastic, Inc.

Blondin, John & Blondin, George. The Legend of Caribou Boy. Sundberg, Mary Rose, tr. McSwain, Ray, illus. 2009. (Legend of Caribou Boy Ser.). (ENG & DGR.). 40p. pap. 19.95 *(978-1-894778-71-8(5))* Theytus Bks., Ltd. CAN. Dist: Univ. of Toronto Pr.

Burgess, Thornton W. The Christmas Reindeer. Chase, Rhoda, illus. 2013. (Dover Children's Classics Ser.). (ENG.). 160p. (J). (gr. k-3). pap. 5.99 *(978-0-486-49153-0(6))* Dover Pubns., Inc.

Cereghino, Sandy. Oscar: The Short Legged Reindeer. 2006. (ENG., Illus.). 48p. (J). 24.95 *(978-1-59299-248-5(X))* Inkwater Pr.

Chandler, Bill & Chandler, Marie. The Reindeer That Couldn't Fly. Kling, Leslie, illus. 2009. 48p. pap. 19.99 *(978-1-933817-40-8(2))* Profits Publishing.

Chronicle Books Staff, et al. Little Reindeer. 2006. (Little Finger Puppet Board Bks.: FING). (ENG., Illus.). 12p. (J). (gr. -1 — 1). bds. 6.99 *(978-0-8118-5457-3(4))* Chronicle Bks. LLC.

Crisp, Dan. Santa's Missing Reindeer. Crisp, Dan, illus. 2011. (ENG., Illus.). 12p. (J). (gr. -1-k). 12.99 *(978-0-230-71291-1(6))* Macmillan Pubs., Ltd. GBR. Dist: Independent Pubs. Group.

Curry, Kenneth. Priscilla & the Reindeer. 2007. (Illus.). 22p. (J). 10.95 *(978-0-9798364-5-9(X))* Curry Brothers Publishing Group.

Cuthbert, R M. Reindeer. Cuthbert, R M & Vincent, Allison, illus. 2006. 30p. (J). 12.95 *(978-1-56167-908-9(9))* American Literary Pr.

Daley-Prado, M. The Super Heroes Save Christmas! 2007. 24p. per. 24.95 *(978-1-4241-9123-9(8))* America Star Bks.

Depken, Kristen L. Rudolph the Red-Nosed Reindeer. Karl, Linda, illus. 2014. (My Readers Ser.). (ENG.). 32p. (J). (gr. k-2). 15.99 *(978-1-250-05044-1(8),* 9781250050441) Square Fish.

Disney Book Group. Frozen Reindeers Are Better Than People. Disney Storybook Art Team, illus. 2015. (ENG.). 12p. (J). (gr. -1-k). bds. 6.99 *(978-1-4847-2469-9(0))* Disney Pr.

Eight Jolly Reindeer. 2014. (ENG., Illus.). 16p. (J). (gr. -1 — 1). bds. 6.99 *(978-0-545-65145-5(X),* Cartwheel Bks.) Scholastic, Inc.

Encarnacion, Elizabeth. Rudolph, the Red-Nosed Reindeer. 2007. (Miniature Editions Ser.). (ENG., Illus.). 128p. (gr. 1-17). 5.95 *(978-0-7624-3098-7(2))* Running Pr. Bk. Pubs.

Eubank, Patricia Reeder. Countdown to Christmas. 2003. (ENG., Illus.). 14p. (J). (gr. -1-k). bds. 9.95 *(978-0-8249-6505-1(1),* Ideal Pubns.) Worthy Publishing.

Evert, Lori. The Reindeer Wish. Breiehagen, Per, illus. Breiehagen, Per, photos by. 2015. (ENG.). 48p. (J). (gr. -1-2). 20.99 *(978-0-375-97335-2(4),* Random Hse. Bks. for Young Readers) Random Hse. Children's Bks.

Falk, Barbara Bustetter & Hyman, Helen Kandel. Don't Park on the Roof. 2007. 36p. per. 21.32 *(978-1-4257-7096-9(7))* Xlibris Corp.

Feldman, Thea. Rudolph the Red-Nosed Reindeer. Madrid, Erwin, illus. 2016. (ENG.). 22p. (J). bds. 10.99 *(978-1-250-12323-7(2),* 9781250123237, Holt, Henry & Co. Bks. For Young Readers) Holt, Henry & Co.

—Rudolph the Red-Nosed Reindeer - The Classic Story. Madrid, Erwin, illus. 50th ed. 2014. (Rudolph the Red-Nosed Reindeer Ser.). (ENG.). 40p. (J). (gr. -1-3). 12.99 *(978-1-250-04760-1(9),* 9781250047601) Square Fish.

Greenberg, Nicki. The Naughtiest Reindeer. Greenberg, Nicki, illus. 2014. (ENG., Illus.). 32p. (J). (gr. -1-k). 14.99 *(978-1-74331-304-6(7))* Allen & Unwin AUS. Dist: Independent Pubs. Group.

Greenberg, Nicki. The Naughtiest Reindeer Goes South. 2017. (Naughtiest Reindeer Ser.: 3). (ENG.). 32p. (J). (gr. -1-1). 12.99 ***(978-1-76029-311-6(3))*** Allen & Unwin AUS. Dist: Independent Pubs. Group.

Hansen, Eric. Ian, Ceo, North Pole. 2008. 108p. pap. 9.95 *(978-1-60693-554-5(2),* Eloquent Bks.) Strategic Book Publishing & Rights Agency (SBPRA).

Holt, Gretta Scott. The Reindeer Who Was Afraid to Fly. 2008. 24p. pap. 11.49 *(978-1-4389-1709-2(0))* AuthorHouse.

Huang, Yu-Hsuan, illus. Baby Reindeer. 2016. (ENG.). 12p. (J). (gr. -1 — 1). 6.99 *(978-1-4521-4661-4(6))* Chronicle Bks. LLC.

Inger's Promise: Evaluation Guide. 2006. (J). *(978-1-55942-409-7(5))* Witcher Productions.

Jacobson, Ryan. The Case of the Florida Freeze, 1 vol. Belkholm, Erica, illus. l.t. ed. 2005. (Santa Claus: Super Spy Ser.). (ENG.). 80p. (J). per. 4.99 *(978-0-9774122-0-4(2),* Getchu Bks.) Lake 7 Creative, LLC.

Jones, Christianne C. The Reindeer Dance. Randall, Emma, illus. 2015. (Holiday Jingles Ser.). (ENG.). 20p. (gr. -1 — 1). bds. 5.99 *(978-1-4795-6496-5(6))* Picture Window Bks.

Julius, Jessica. A New Reindeer Friend. 2015. lib. bdg. 13.55 *(978-0-606-36680-9(6))* Turtleback Bks.

—A New Reindeer Friend (Disney Frozen) RH Disney Staff, illus. 2015. (Little Golden Book Ser.). (ENG.). 24p. (J). (-k). 4.99 *(978-0-7364-3351-8(1),* Golden/Disney) Random Hse. Children's Bks.

Killen, Nicola. The Little Reindeer. Killen, Nicola, illus. 2017. (ENG., Illus.). 32p. (J). (gr. -1-3). 15.99 *(978-1-4814-8686-6(1),* Simon & Schuster/Paula Wiseman Bks.) Simon & Schuster/Paula Wiseman Bks.

Lambert, Lydia. Scrub-A-Dub Reindeer: Bath Mitt & Bath Book Set. Jones, Anna, illus. 2015. (Scrub-A-Dub Bath Mitt & Bath Book Sets Ser.). (ENG.). 8p. (J). (gr. -1 — 1). 9.99 *(978-1-4380-7584-6(7))* Barron's Educational Series, Inc.

Lester, Vivian. Wee-Dolph, the Tiniest Reindeer. Wiggs, Sue, illus. 22p. (J). (gr. -1-3). pap. 4.00 *(978-1-929785-01-8(1))* Connexions Unlimited.

Levine, Whitney Joy. The Tiniest Reindeer. 2008. 24p. pap. 12.99 *(978-1-4389-3102-9(6))* AuthorHouse.

Madaras, Diana. Kitty Humbug's Christmas Tail. Madaras, Diana & Nielsen, Ric, illus. 2009. 24p. 17.99 *(978-1-892344-56-4(4))* Palomino Publishing.

Magsamen, Sandra. Our Little Deer (Made with Love) Magsamen, Sandra, illus. 2016. (ENG., Illus.). 12p. (J). bds. 7.99 *(978-1-338-11081-4(0),* Cartwheel Bks.) Scholastic, Inc.

Marsoli, Lisa Ann. Rudolph the Red-Nosed Reindeer Pop-Up Book. Finch, Keith Andrew, illus. 2014. (ENG.). 12p. (J). (gr. -1). 19.95 *(978-1-62686-197-8(8),* Silver Dolphin Bks.) Readerlink Distribution Services, LLC.

May, Robert L. Rudolph Shines Again. Caparo, Antonio Javier, illus. 2015. (ENG.). 40p. (J). (gr. -1-1). 17.99 *(978-1-4424-7498-7(X),* Little Simon) Little Simon.

Miceli, Robert L. The Adventures of Twilight. 2008. 80p. pap. 22.50 *(978-1-60693-241-4(1),* Strategic Bk. Publishing) Strategic Book Publishing & Rights Agency (SBPRA).

Mlynowski, Sarah. Cold As Ice. 2015. (Whatever After Ser.: 6). (ENG.). 176p. (J). (gr. 3-7). pap. 5.99 *(978-0-545-62736-8(2),* Scholastic Pr.) Scholastic, Inc.

—Cold as Ice. 2014. (Whatever After Ser.: 6). (ENG.). 176p. (J). (gr. 3-7). 14.99 *(978-0-545-62734-4(6),* Scholastic Pr.) Scholastic, Inc.

Morningforest, Chris & Raymond, Rebecca. Mooseman Reindeer & Uncle Utley. 2006. 36p. (J). pap. 15.43 *(978-1-4116-8390-7(0))* Lulu Pr., Inc.

Moulton, Mark Kimball. Reindeer Christmas. Good, Karen Hillard, illus. 2008. (ENG.). 40p. (J). (gr. -1-3). 15.99 *(978-1-4169-6108-6(9),* Simon & Schuster/Paula Wiseman Bks.) Simon & Schuster/Paula Wiseman Bks.

O., Lila. Lulabelle's Jewels: The Christmas Wish of Mrs. Claus. 2008. 20p. pap. 12.49 *(978-1-4389-3189-0(1))* AuthorHouse.

Pelham, David. Here Comes Santa: A Mini Holiday Pop-Up. Pelham, David, illus. 2008. (ENG., Illus.). 18p. (J). 11.99 *(978-1-4169-5440-8(6),* Little Simon) Little Simon.

Penny, Anne. Scraper. 2006. (Illus.). 56p. pap. *(978-1-84401-921-2(7))* Athena Pr.

Priddy, Roger. Rudolph the Red-Nosed Reindeer Lift-the-Flap Tab. 2014. (Lift-The-Flap Tab Bks.). (ENG., Illus.). 16p. (J). (gr. -1 — 1). bds. 8.99 *(978-0-312-51749-6(1),* 9780312517496, Priddy Bks.) St. Martin's Pr.

—Rudolph the Red-Nosed Reindeer Slide & Find. 2014. (Slide & Find Ser.). (ENG., Illus.). 10p. (J). (gr. -1 — 1). bds. 7.99 *(978-0-312-51750-2(5),* 9780312517502, Priddy Bks.) St. Martin's Pr.

Publications International Ltd. Staff, ed. Rudolph the Red-Nosed Reindeer(r): A Flashlight Adventure Sound Book. 2014. 14p. (J). *(978-1-4508-9047-2(4),* 1450890474) Publications International, Ltd.

—Rudolph the Red-Nosed Reindeer (Book & Plush) 2011. 8p. (J). bds. 11.98 *(978-1-4508-2170-4(7))* Publications International, Ltd.

Rasmussen, Liz, illus. Too Fat to Fly. 2007. 32p. (J). 16.95 *(978-0-9793517-0-9(7))* Silver Bells Publishing Hse.

Reasoner, Charles & Wood, Hannah. Peek-A-Boo Reindeer, 1 vol. Reasoner, Charles, illus. 2014. (Charles Reasoner Peek-A-Boo Bks.). (ENG., Illus.). 10p. (gr. -1 — 1). bds. 12.99 *(978-1-4795-5179-8(1))* Picture Window Bks.

Rees, Douglas. Jeannette Claus Saves Christmas. Latyk, Olivier, illus. 2010. (ENG.). 40p. (J). (gr. k-3). 16.99 *(978-1-4169-2686-3(0),* McElderry, Margaret K. Bks.) McElderry, Margaret K. Bks.

Reindeer. 2003. (Shaped Board Books Ser.). 14p. (J). (gr. -1-k). bds. 9.95 *(978-0-7525-8850-6(8))* Parragon, Inc.

The Reindeer's Big Night. 2003. (J). per. *(978-1-57657-926-8(3))* Paradise Pr., Inc.

Repchuck, Caroline. The Little Reindeer. 2005. (ENG., Illus.). 20p. (J). *(978-1-55168-294-5(X))* Fenn, H. B. & Co., Ltd.

Rigo, L. Little Reindeer. 2011. (Look at Me Bks.). (ENG., Illus.). 10p. (J). bds. 7.99 *(978-0-7641-6450-7(3))* Barron's Educational Series, Inc.

Rigo, L., illus. Little Reindeer. 2014. (Mini People Shape Bks.). (ENG.). 10p. (J). (gr. -1-2). bds. 4.99 *(978-0-7641-6736-2(7))* Barron's Educational Series, Inc.

Rivers-Moore, Debbie. Five Christmas Reindeer. Everitt-Stewart, Andrew, illus. 2015. (ENG.). 10p. (J). (gr. -1 — 1). bds. 8.99 *(978-1-4998-0169-9(6))* Little Bee Books Inc.

Rowland, Teresa. Blusher's First Christmas. 2012. 64p. (-18). pap. 20.95 *(978-1-4525-0718-7(X))* Balboa Pr.

Rudolph the Red-Nosed Reindeer. 2004. 4p. (J). 3.95 *(978-0-634-09040-0(2))* Leonard, Hal Corp.

Rudolph the Red-Nosed Reindeer. 2014. (ENG., Illus.). 40p. (J). (gr. -1-1). 17.99 *(978-1-4424-7495-6(5),* Little Simon) Little Simon.

Saunders, Katie, illus. Little Reindeer. 2012. 10p. (J). *(978-1-4351-4314-2(0))* Barnes & Noble, Inc.

Sharp, Rhonda Winchell. The Nine Most Famous Reindeer of All. Vandewater, Rena, illus. 2004. 40p. (J). pap. 15.99 *(978-0-9748047-8-1(9))* Hickory Bark Productions.

Smallman, Steve. Santa Is Coming to Cleveland. Dunn, Robert, illus. 2014. (ENG.). 32p. (J). (-3). 9.99 *(978-1-4926-0703-8(7),* Sourcebooks Jabberwocky) Sourcebooks, Inc.

—Santa Is Coming to Connecticut. Dunn, Robert, illus. 2014. (ENG.). 32p. (J). (-3). 9.99 *(978-1-4926-0670-3(7),* Sourcebooks Jabberwocky) Sourcebooks, Inc.

—Santa Is Coming to the Jersey Shore. Dunn, Robert, illus. 2014. (ENG.). 32p. (J). (-3). 9.99 *(978-1-4926-0691-8(X),* Sourcebooks Jabberwocky) Sourcebooks, Inc.

—Santa Is Coming to Wyoming. Dunn, Robert, illus. 2014. (ENG.). 32p. (J). (-3). 9.99 *(978-1-4926-0679-6(0),* Sourcebooks Jabberwocky) Sourcebooks, Inc.

Sonneborn, Scott. The Reindeer Games. Lozano, Omar, illus. 2015. (North Police Ser.). (ENG.). 32p. (gr. k-2). lib. bdg. 21.32 *(978-1-4795-6487-3(7))* Picture Window Bks.

Sorenson, E. Randy. The First Reindeer Couldn't Fly. 2007. (Illus.). 32p. (J). 17.99 *(978-0-615-16939-2(2))* Sorenson, E. Randy.

Stainton, Sue. Christmas Magic. Melhuish, Eva, illus. 2007. 32p. (J). (gr. -1-1). lib. bdg. 16.89 *(978-0-06-078572-7(1),* Tegen, Katherine Bks) HarperCollins Pubs.

Stepp, Shirley. Santa Lost His Cell Phone. 2012. 24p. 24.95 *(978-1-4626-5479-6(7))* America Star Bks.

Sullivan, E. J. Bubba the Redneck Reindeer. Eldredge, Ernie, illus. 2007. 32p. (J). (gr. 4-7). 12.95 *(978-1-60261-008-8(8))* Cliff Road Bks.

Thomas Nelson. Touch & Feel Robbie Reindeer's Snowy Adventure. 2016. (ENG.). 12p. (gr. -1). bds. *(978-1-78598-437-2(3))* Make Believe Ideas.

Tyrell, Melissa. The Little Reindeer. Brooks, Nan, illus. enl. ed. 2005. (ENG.). 10p. (J). (gr. -1-3). 4.95 *(978-1-58117-119-8(6),* Intervisual/Piggy Toes) Bendon, Inc.

Wallace, R. Mike. Saunter. 2009. 36p. pap. 10.75 *(978-1-60693-994-9(7),* Strategic Bk. Publishing) Strategic Book Publishing & Rights Agency (SBPRA).

Watt, Fiona. That's Not My Reindeer: Its Body Is Too Furry. Wells, Rachel, illus. 2008. (Usborne Touchy-Feely Board Bks.). 10p. (J). (gr. -1-k). bds. 9.99 *(978-0-7945-1890-5(7),* Usborne) EDC Publishing.

Wheeler, Lisa. Uncles & Antlers. Floca, Brian, illus. 2014. (ENG.). 40p. (J). (gr. -1-3). 17.99 *(978-1-4814-3018-0(1),* Atheneum Bks. for Young Readers) Simon & Schuster Children's Publishing.

Woolf, Julia, illus. Reindeer Run. 2008. (ENG.). 10p. (J). bds. 4.95 *(978-1-58117-813-5(1),* Intervisual/Piggy Toes) Bendon, Inc.

RELATIVITY (PHYSICS)

see also Quantum Theory

Kook, Ima. Einstein's Theory of Relativity: Go Too Fast & Strange Things Happen. 2008. (As Dreamed by Itsy Ser.). (Illus.). 24p. (J). pap. 12.00 *(978-1-892298-23-2(6))* Abique Pub.

Manning, Phillip. Theory of Relativity. 2011. (Science Foundations Ser.). (Illus.). 128p. (gr. 6-12). lib. bdg. 35.00 *(978-1-60413-294-6(9),* Chelsea Hse.) Facts On File, Inc.

Morton, Alan. Einstein's Theories of Relativity. 2005. (Milestones in Modern Science Ser.). 48p. (gr. 6-12). pap. 14.05 *(978-0-8368-5860-0(3))*; (Illus.). lib. bdg. 31.00 *(978-0-8368-5853-2(0))* Stevens, Gareth Publishing LLLP. (Gareth Stevens Secondary Library).

Novelli, Luca. Einstein & the Time Machine. 2017. (Flashes of Genius Ser.). (ENG., Illus.). 112p. (J). (gr. 3). pap. 9.99 ***(978-1-61373-865-8(X))*** Chicago Review Pr., Inc.

Parker, Katie. The Theory of Relativity. 2009. (Big Ideas in Science Ser.). (Illus.). 48p. (gr. 5-8). 31.36 *(978-0-7614-4398-8(3))* Marshall Cavendish Corp.

Pohlen, Jerome. Albert Einstein & Relativity for Kids: His Life & Ideas with 21 Activities & Thought Experiments. 2012. (For Kids Ser.). (ENG., Illus.). 144p. (J). (gr. 4). pap. 16.95 *(978-1-61374-028-6(X))* Chicago Review Pr., Inc.

Rooney, Anne. Albert Einstein & His Theory of Relativity. 2012. (Miracle Makers Ser.). (ENG.). 48p. (YA). (gr. 5-8). 27.95 *(978-1-4488-6038-8(5),* Rosen Reference) Rosen Publishing Group, Inc., The.

Scientific American Staff. Beyond Extreme Physics. 2009. (Scientific American Cutting-Edge Science Ser.). 160p. (gr. 9-9). 63.90 *(978-1-60853-073-1(6))* Rosen Publishing Group, Inc., The.

Whiting, Jim. Mysteries of the Universe: Space & Time. 2013. (Mysteries of the Universe Ser.). (ENG., Illus.). 48p. (J). (gr. 4-7). pap. 12.00 *(978-0-89812-917-5(6),* Creative Paperbacks) Creative Co., The.

—Space & Time. 2012. (Mysteries of the Universe Ser.). (Illus.). 48p. (J). (gr. 5-12). 23.95 *(978-1-60818-192-6(8),* Creative Education) Creative Co., The.

Winterberg, Jenna. Conservation of Mass. 2015. (Science Readers: Content & Literacy Ser.). 32p. (J). (gr. 5-5). pap. 8.99 *(978-1-4807-4722-7(X))* Teacher Created Materials, Inc.

RELAXATION

see Recreation

RELIGION

see also Belief and Doubt; Faith; God; Indians of North America—Religion; Mythology; Religions; Spiritual Life; Superstition; Theology; Worship

Ajmera, Maya, et al. Faith. 2009. (ENG., Illus.). 48p. (J). (gr. -1-3). 16.95 *(978-1-58089-177-6(2))*; pap. 8.95 *(978-1-58089-178-3(0))* Charlesbridge Publishing, Inc.

Alexander, Audrey. Angels, Demons, & Religious Rituals. 2015. (J). *(978-1-61900-065-0(2))* Eldorado Ink.

Atique, Quazi M. Zahid. The Path of Peace: The Complete Code of Life. 2004. 497p. (YA). pap. 30.00 *(978-0-9766702-0-9(8))* Path of Peace Inc., The.

Attinger, Billy, illus. Baby's First Little Book of Prayers. gif. ed. 2003. (Wee Witness Ser.). 32p. (J). 7.99 *(978-0-7369-1185-6(5))* Harvest Hse. Pubs.

Bahr, Ann Marie B., ed. Religions of the World. (Illus.). (gr. 9-13). pap. 83.65 *(978-0-7910-8392-5(6))*; lib. bdg. 188.65 *(978-0-7910-8467-0(1))* Facts On File, Inc. (Chelsea Hse.).

Center for Learning Network Staff. Sexuality: Connecting Mind, Body, & Spirit — Minicourse. 2003. (Religion Ser.). 119p. (YA). tchr. ed., spiral bd. 12.95 *(978-1-56077-745-8(1))* Center for Learning, The.

The Challenge of Choices. 2003. (YA). tchr. ed. *(978-0-9706117-3-4(0))*; stu. ed. *(978-0-9706117-2-7(2))* Riverstone Group Publishing.

The Challenge of Choices Strategic Planner. 2003. *(978-0-9706117-4-1(9))* Riverstone Group Publishing.

Clarke, Steve. Themes to Inspire, Bk. 1. 2011. (Dynamic Learning Ser.). (Illus.). 96p. pap. 39.50 *(978-1-4441-2205-3(3))* Hodder Education Group GBR. Dist: Trans-Atlantic Pubns., Inc.

—Themes to Inspire for KS3, Bk. 3. 2013. (Illus.). 96p. pap. 42.50 *(978-1-4441-2211-4(8))* Hodder Education Group GBR. Dist: Trans-Atlantic Pubns., Inc.

Crosby, Jim. Devotions for the Armchair Quarterback. 2004. 109p. per. 12.95 *(978-1-932338-33-1(0))* Lifevest Publishing, Inc.

Damon, Emma. All Kinds of Beliefs. 2004. (J). *(978-1-84444-163-1(6))*; (ARA & ENG.). *(978-1-84444-160-0(1))* Mantra Lingua.

—All Kinds of Beliefs. 2003. (J). (CHI & ENG.). 17.95 *(978-1-84444-162-4(8))*; (ENG & URD.). 17.95 *(978-1-84444-164-8(4))*; (BEN & ENG., Illus.). 17.95 *(978-1-84444-161-7(X))* Mantra Lingua GBR. Dist: Chinasprout, Inc.

Dobson, Shirley. God's Ten Best Coloring Book 50-Unit Merch. 2004. 16p. 64.50 *(978-0-8307-3117-6(2),* Gospel Light) Gospel Light Pubns.

Dolan, Sean. Everything You Need to Know about Cults. 2005. (Need to Know Library). (Illus.). 64p. (YA). (gr. 7-12). 31.95 *(978-0-8239-3230-6(3),* NTCLT) Rosen Publishing Group, Inc., The.

Downey, Michael. Digging Deep: Fostering the Spirituality of Young Men. 2003. 96p. (YA). per. 27.25 *(978-0-88489-803-0(2))* St. Mary's Pr. of MN.

Dunning, Lisa. Restless Spirits-Utah's Small Town Ghosts. 2010. 256p. (J). pap. 16.99 *(978-1-59955-371-9(6),* Cedar Fort, Inc.) Cedar Fort, Inc./CFI Distribution.

Encyclopaedia Britannica Publishers, Inc. Staff, contrib. by. Religions Around the World. 2003. (Britannica Learning Library). (Illus.). 64p. (gr. 2-5). 14.95 *(978-1-59339-007-5(6),* 049908-EN-REF) Encyclopaedia Britannica, Inc.

Eugster, Rachel & Whiting, Jim. The Role of Religion in the Early Islamic World. 2012. (Life in the Early Islamic World Ser.). (ENG., Illus.). 48p. (J). pap. *(978-0-7787-2176-5(0))*; lib. bdg. *(978-0-7787-2169-7(8))* Crabtree Publishing Co.

Freeman, Lisa Show. The Colors of God. 2010. 28p. 16.95 *(978-1-4269-3063-8(1))* Trafford Publishing.

Fridell, Ron. Religious Fundamentalism. 2008. (Open for Debate Ser.). 128p. (gr. 7-18). lib. bdg. 42.79 *(978-0-7614-2945-6(X),* Benchmark Bks.) Marshall Cavendish Corp.

Friedenthal, Lora & Kavanaugh, Dorothy. Religions of Africa. Ojakorotu, Victor & Rotberg, Robert I., eds. 2013. (Africa: Progress & Problems Ser.: 13). (Illus.). 112p. (J). (gr. 7-18). 24.95 *(978-1-4222-2947-7(5))* Mason Crest.

Fruit of the Spirit Poster Pack. 2004. (gr. 1-6). 19.99 *(978-0-8307-2581-6(4),* Gospel Light) Gospel Light Pubns.

Gallery, Philip D. & Harlow, Janet L. Can You Find Followers of Jesus? Introducing Your Child to the Disciples. 2003. (Illus.). 40p. *(978-2-89507-120-4(9))* Novalis Publishing.

Gerner, Katy. Religions Around the World, 6 bks., Set. Incl. Buddhism. lib. bdg. 18.56 *(978-0-7614-3164-0(0))*; Catholicism. lib. bdg. 18.56 *(978-0-7614-3165-7(9))*; Hinduism. lib. bdg. 18.56 *(978-0-7614-3166-4(7))*; Islam. lib. bdg. 18.56 *(978-0-7614-3167-1(5))*; Judaism. 18.56 *(978-0-7614-3170-1(5))*; Protestantism. lib. bdg. 18.56 *(978-0-7614-3173-2(X))*; 32p. (gr. 3-18). (Religions Around the World Ser.). 2008. Set lib. bdg. 111.36 *(978-0-7614-3162-6(4),* Benchmark Bks.) Marshall Cavendish Corp.

Gervais, Josephine. Mommies Are Protecting Their Children. 2013. 20p. pap. 24.95 *(978-1-62709-538-9(1))* America Star Bks.

—Mommies Are Special People. 2013. 24p. pap. 24.95 *(978-1-62709-537-2(3))* America Star Bks.

Green, Edna. My Special Thoughts: Designed for African-American Children. 2004. (J). (gr. -1-5). 10.00 *(978-0-9743019-1-4(4))* My Special Thoughts.

Grenfell, Susan. Religious Studies for Common Entrance. 2nd rev. ed. 2011. (Illus.). 168p. pap. 42.50 *(978-1-4441-2425-5(0))* Hodder Education Group GBR. Dist: Trans-Atlantic Pubns., Inc.

Habitat For Humanity Of The Chesapeake, ed. Peace by Piece: Illustrations by Christian, Jewish & Muslim Children Ages 5-17. 2012. 100p. (J). pap. 24.95 *(978-1-934074-74-9(8))* Apprentice Hse.

Hossler, Margaret. Spenser Rose Is Born. 2003. 32p. 12.99 *(978-0-9650491-4-6(0))* Send The Light Distribution LLC.

Kallen, Stuart A. Voodoo. 2005. (Mystery Library). (Illus.). 112p. (YA). (gr. 7-10). lib. bdg. 29.95 *(978-1-59018-630-5(3),* Lucent Bks.) Cengage Gale.

Kalman, Bobbie. What Is Religion? 2009. (Our Multicultural World Ser.). (ENG., Illus.). 32p. (J). (gr. 1-4). pap. *(978-0-7787-4651-5(8))*; lib. bdg. *(978-0-7787-4636-2(4))* Crabtree Publishing Co.

Kaplan, Leslie C. Art & Religion in Ancient Egypt. 2004. (Primary Sources of Ancient Civilizations Ser.). (ENG.). 24p. (gr. 4-8). pap. 8.25 *(978-0-8239-8932-4(1),* PowerKids Pr.) Rosen Publishing Group, Inc., The.

Killcoyne, Hope Lourie & Wolny, Philip, eds. The 100 Most Influential Religious Leaders of All Time, 1 vol., 1. 2016. (Britannica Guide to the World's Most Influential People Ser.). (ENG.). 224p. (J). (gr. 10-10). 54.00 *(978-1-68048-277-5(7),* Britannica Educational Publishing) Rosen Publishing Group, Inc., The.

Labosh, Kathy. The Child with Autism Learns the Faith: The Sunday School Guide. 2007. per. 14.00 *(978-0-9744341-4-8(0))* Labosh Publishing.

Langley, Myrtle & Dorling Kindersley Publishing Staff. Religion. 2012. (DK Eyewitness Bks.). (ENG.). 72p. (J). (gr. 3-7). 16.99 *(978-0-7566-9079-3(X),* DK Children) Dorling Kindersley Publishing, Inc.

Martin, Oscar, Jr., creator. The Creation Story l.t. ed. 2003. (Illus.). 25p. (J). E-Book 19.95 incl. cd-rom *(978-0-9748416-0-1(9))* Build Your Story.

McNeil, Niki, et al. HOCPP 1126 the Pilgrims. 2006. spiral bd. 16.00 *(978-1-60308-126-9(7))* In the Hands of a Child.

Meisels, Dovid. Shabbos Secrets: The Mysteries Revealed. 2003. 365p. 25.95 *(978-1-931681-43-8(0))* Israel Bookshop Pubns.

Miller, Debra A. Politics & Religion. Greenhaven Press Editors, ed. 2013. (Current Controversies Ser.). (ENG., Illus.). 224p. (gr. 10-12). pap. 32.00 *(978-0-7377-6885-5(1))*; lib. bdg. 46.40 *(978-0-7377-6884-8(3))* Cengage Gale. (Greenhaven Pr., Inc.).

Moehlenpah, Arlo. Creation Versus Evolution: Scientific & Religious Considerations. 2003. 36p. (YA). *(978-0-9667054-6-1(7))* Doing Good Ministries.

Nguyen, Hy Thi. Challenges. 2013. 260p. (gr. 10-12). pap. 16.55 *(978-1-4817-2404-3(5))* AuthorHouse.

Olsen, Debi W. My Very Own Book about Religious Science. 2004. 32p. (J). 10.95 *(978-1-931947-11-4(2))* Ink & Scribe.

Place, Robert M. Shamanism. 2008. (Mysteries, Legends, & Unexplained Phenomena Ser.). (Illus.). 120p. (YA). (gr. 7-12). lib. bdg. 29.95 *(978-0-7910-9396-2(4))* Facts On File, Inc.

Pochocki, Ethel. Around the Year Once Upon a Time Saints. Hatke, Ben, illus. 2009. 211p. (YA). (gr. 5). pap. 14.95 *(978-1-932350-26-5(8))* Bethlehem Bks.

Prindle, Twyla D. Can I Have Some Money Please? Hansen, Lorie, illus. 2004. 20p. (J). (gr. k-4). 7.95 *(978-0-9759527-2-6(2))* Prindle Hse. Publishing Co.

—Deception: The Devil Hears Your Prayers Too. 2004. 184p. (YA). pap. 14.95 (978-0-9759527-1-9(4)) Prindle Hse. Publishing Co.

—Teacher's Lounge. 2004. 184p. (YA). 19.95 (978-0-9759527-0-2(6)) Prindle Hse. Publishing Co.

Pundit Baraiya, Gopaldasji. Primer of Jain Principles. Gosalia, Kirit, tr. 2004. 210p. pap. 10.00 (978-0-9748681-0-3(8)) Songadh, Jain Swadhyay Mandir.

Rabbi Schneur Zalman of Liadi. Shulchan Aruch: Hilchot Rosh Hashana thru Lulav -New Edition. 2003. (HEB.). 192p. per. 4.95 (978-0-8266-5189-1(5)) Kehot Pubn. Society.

Religion & Modern Culture: Spiritual Beliefs That Influence North America Today, 13 vols., Set. Incl. Controversial World of Biblical Archaeology: Tomb Raiders, Fakes, & Scholars. McIntosh, Kenneth. (gr. 7-18). lib. bdg. 22.95 (978-1-59084-983-5(3)); Grail, the Shroud, & Other Religious Relics: Secrets & Ancient Mysteries. McIntosh, Kenneth. (gr. 3-7). lib. bdg. 22.95 (978-1-59084-978-1(7), 1248067); Growth of North American Religious Beliefs: Spiritual Diversity. McIntosh, Jonathan S. & McIntosh, Kenneth R. (gr. 7-18). lib. bdg. 22.95 (978-1-59084-975-0(2)); Issues of Church, State, & Religious Liberties: Whose Freedom, Whose Faith? McIntosh, Kenneth & McIntosh, Marsha. (gr. 8-12). lib. bdg. 22.95 (978-1-59084-973-6(6)); Prophecies & End-Time Speculations: The Shape of Things to Come. McIntosh, Kenneth. (gr. 3-7). lib. bdg. 22.95 (978-1-59084-979-8(5), 1248068); Women & Religion: Reinterpreting Scriptures to Find the Sacred Feminine. McIntosh, Kenneth R. (gr. 3-7). lib. bdg. 22.95 (978-1-59084-977-4(9)); (YA). 2007. (Illus.). 112p. 2006. Set lib. bdg. 298.35 (978-1-59084-970-5(1), 1248067) Mason Crest.

Religions of Humanity, Set. 2005. (Religions of Humanity Ser.). 32p. (gr. 6-12). 219.50 (978-0-7910-6621-8(5), Chelsea Hse.) Facts On File, Inc.

SL Resources Staff, prod. Inhabit Student Book. 2010. 47p. (YA). 3.99 (978-1-935040-77-4(4)) SL Resources.

—SEQUENCE Student Work Book. 2009. 47p. (YA). 3.99 (978-1-935040-74-3(X)) SL Resources.

Sonnier, Suzanne. Shinto, Spirits, & Shrines: Religion in Japan. 2007. (Lucent Library of Historical Eras:Twentieth-Century Japan Ser.). (ENG., Illus.). 96p. (J). (gr. 4-7). lib. bdg. 34.80 (978-1-4205-0029-5(5), Lucent Bks.) Cengage Gale.

Staeger, Rob. Native American Religions. Johnson, Troy, ed. 2013. (Native American Life Ser.: 15). 64p. (J). (gr. 5-18). 19.95 (978-1-4222-2974-3(2)) Mason Crest.

Strobel, Lee. The Case for Faith for Kids, 1 vol. enl. ed. 2010. (Case for... Series for Kids Ser.). (ENG.). 144p. (J). pap. 7.99 (978-0-310-71991-5(7)) Zonderkidz.

Whitbread, Henry. Lives of the Great Spiritual Leaders: 20 Inspirational Tales. 2011. (ENG., Illus.). 96p. (J). (gr. 4-7). 19.95 (978-0-500-51578-5(6), 551578) Thames & Hudson.

White, Bender Richardson. Shinto. 3rd rev. ed. 2009. (World Religions Ser.). (Illus.). 144p. (gr. 6-12). 40.00 (978-1-60413-113-0(6), Chelsea Hse.) Facts On File, Inc.

White, Bender Richardson, et al. Zoroastrianism. 3rd rev. ed. 2009. (World Religions Ser.). (Illus.). 144p. (J). (gr. 6-12). 40.00 (978-1-60413-116-1(0), Chelsea Hse.) Facts On File, Inc.

RELIGION—PHILOSOPHY

Crispin, Gerald W. God Speaks Through Dreams: But Who's Listening?, No. 1. Crispin, Gerald W. & Crispin, Vera G., eds. unabr. ed. 2003. (Illus.). 160p. (gr. 10-18). reprint ed. pap. 19.95 (978-0-9744015-1-5(X)) Benchmark Book Craft.

RELIGION—STUDY AND TEACHING

see Religious Education

RELIGION AND SCIENCE

see also Creation; Evolution; Human Beings—Origin

Answers to Evolution Wall Chart. 2004. (978-1-890947-87-3(3)) Rose Publishing.

Derr, Louise Barrett. Experiencing Bible Science. 2007. 128p. per. 16.95 (978-1-59919-025-9(7)) Elim Publishing.

Engdahl, Sharon & Engdahl, Terry. The Evolution of Creation: A Children's Primer on the Evolution of God's Creation, 1 vol. 2010. 30p. 24.95 (978-1-4489-4228-2(4)) PublishAmerica, Inc.

Gonzalez, David J. There Are No Space Aliens! 12 Biblical Points Disproving Space Aliens. l.t. ed. 2003. 48p. 9.95 (978-0-9741561-0-1(8)) Gonzalez, David J. Ministries.

Science & Living in God's World. (J). 10.00 (978-1-931555-49-4(4));Bk. 1. (J). 10.00 (978-1-931555-50-0(8));Bk. 2. (J). 20.00 (978-1-931555-51-7(6));Bk. 3. (J). 22.00 (978-1-931555-52-4(4));Bk. 4. (J). 16.00 (978-1-931555-53-1(2));Bk. 5. (YA). 12.00 (978-1-931555-54-8(0));Bk. 6. (YA). 20.00 (978-1-931555-55-5(9));Bk. 7. (YA). 20.00 (978-1-931555-56-2(7));Bk. 8. (YA). 20.00 (978-1-931555-57-9(5)) Our Lady of Victory Schl.

Syed, Ibrahim. Quranic Inspirations. 2007. 688p. (YA). per. 37.95 (978-0-595-45003-9(2)) iUniverse, Inc.

Walker, Joe. Belief & Science. 2009. (Illus.). 208p. pap., tchr. ed. 43.50 (978-0-340-97302-8(1)) Hodder Education Group GBR. Dist: Trans-Atlantic Pubns., Inc.

Waunsch, John. My Very, Very First Weather Book. 2013. 56p. 23.99 (978-1-62697-903-1(0)); pap. 12.99 (978-1-62697-764-8(X)) Salem Author Services.

RELIGION AND STATE

see Church and State

RELIGIONS

see also Bahai Faith; Buddhism; Christianity; Confucianism; Hinduism; Judaism; Mythology; Religion; Sects

Adams, Simon. The History of World Religions: Explore the Great Faiths That Shaped Our Civilization. 2016. (ENG., Illus.). 64p. (J). (gr. -1-11). 12.99 (978-1-86147-752-1(X), Armadillo) Anness Publishing GBR. Dist: National Bk. Network.

Ahmedi, Waqar, et al. World Religions: Judaism, Christianity & Islam. 2017. (ENG.). 120p. (J). (gr. 6-9). pap. 29.99 **(978-0-00-822768-5(3))** HarperCollins Pubs. Ltd. GBR. Dist: Independent Pubs. Group.

Ajmera, Maya, et al. Faith. 2009. (ENG., Illus.). 48p. (J). (gr. -1-3). 16.95 (978-1-58089-177-6(2)); pap. 8.95 (978-1-58089-178-3(0)) Charlesbridge Publishing, Inc.

Altson, John & Miliotis, Patti Rae. What Happened to Grandpa? A Child Views the Hereafter Through the World's Major Religions. 2009. 36p. pap. 16.99 (978-1-4343-6743-3(6)) AuthorHouse.

Anderson, Dale. Churches & Religion in the Middle Ages. 2005. (World Almanac Library of the Middle Ages). (Illus.). 48p. (gr. 5-12). lib. bdg. 31.00 (978-0-8368-5892-1(1), Gareth Stevens Secondary Library) Stevens, Gareth Publishing LLLP.

Atkin, Pippa. Flexi-RE Evaluation, Bk. 3. 2003. (ENG., Illus.). 128p. pap., stu. ed. 15.95 (978-0-7487-6354-2(6)) Nelson Thornes Ltd. GBR. Dist: Trans-Atlantic Pubns., Inc.

Boersma, Heather. Dream Big: 30 Days to Life Beyond All You Could Ask or Imagine. 2012. ix, 119p. (978-1-77069-453-8(6)) Word Alive Pr.

Britannica, Learning Library. Religions Around the World. 2003. (Illus.). 64p. 14.95 (978-1-59339-038-9(6)) Encyclopaedia Britannica, Inc.

Bullard, Lisa. My Religion, Your Religion. Conger, Holli, illus. 2015. (Cloverleaf Books (tm) — Alike & Different Ser.). (ENG.). 24p. (gr. k-2). (J). lib. bdg. 23.99 (978-1-4677-4905-3(2)); pap. 6.99 (978-1-4677-6033-1(1)) Lerner Publishing Group. (Millbrook Pr.).

Cavell-Clarke, Steffi. Celebrating Different Beliefs. 2017. (Illus.). 24p. (J). **(978-0-7787-3261-7(4))** Crabtree Publishing Co.

Ceanadach, Siusaidh. Let's Talk about Elements & the Pagan Wheel. 2013. (ENG.). 73p. pap. 9.95 (978-1-78099-561-8(X), Moon Bks.) Hunt, John Publishing Ltd. GBR. Dist: National Bk. Network.

Clarke, Steve. Themes to Inspire, Bk. 1. 2011. (Dynamic Learning Ser.). (Illus.). 96p. pap. 39.50 (978-1-4441-2205-3(3)) Hodder Education Group GBR. Dist: Trans-Atlantic Pubns., Inc.

—Themes to Inspire for KS3, Bk. 3. 2013. (Illus.). 96p. pap. 42.50 (978-1-4441-2211-4(8)) Hodder Education Group GBR. Dist: Trans-Atlantic Pubns., Inc.

Dorling Kindersley Publishing Staff. What Do You Believe? 2016. (Big Questions Ser.). (ENG.). 96p. (J). (gr. 2-5). pap. 9.99 (978-1-4654-4386-1(X), DK Children) Dorling Kindersley Publishing, Inc.

Doudna, Kelly. Religions Around the World, 1 vol. 2004. (Around the World Ser.). (ENG., Illus.). 24p. (J). (gr. k-3). lib. bdg. 24.21 (978-1-59197-568-7(9), SandCastle) ABDO Publishing Co.

Eastwood, Kay. Places of Worship in the Middle Ages. 2003. (Medieval World Ser.). (ENG., Illus.). 32p. (J). (gr. 5). lib. bdg. (978-0-7787-1347-0(4)) Crabtree Publishing Co.

Glossop, Jennifer. The Kids Book of World Religions. Mantha, John, illus. 2013. (Kids Book Of Ser.). (ENG.). 64p. (J). (gr. 3-7). pap. 14.95 (978-1-55453-981-9(1)) Kids Can Pr., Ltd. CAN. Dist: Hachette Bk. Group.

Green, Connie R. & Oldendorf, Sandra Brenneman. Religious Diversity & Children's Literature: Strategies & Resources. 2011. E-Book (978-1-61735-398-7(1)) Information Age Publishing, Inc.

Gunderson, Cory Gideon. Religions of the Middle East. 2003. (World in Conflict-the Middle East Ser.). 32p. (gr. 4-8). 27.07 (978-1-59197-412-3(7), Abdo & Daughters) ABDO Publishing Co.

Hakowski, Maryann. Vine & Branches, ol. 3. Price, Carolyn, illus. 2003. (Resources for Youth Retreats Ser.: Vol. 3). 176p. (J). (gr. 6-7). pap. 24.95 (978-0-88489-323-3(5)) St. Mary's Pr. of MN.

Haywood, John. Through the Ages: Gods, Beliefs & Ceremonies. 2008. (ENG., Illus.). 64p. (J). (gr. 4-7). pap. 12.99 (978-1-84476-601-7(2)) Anness Publishing GBR. Dist: National Bk. Network.

Hickman, Clare & Meredith, Sue. The Usborne Encyclopedia of World Religions: Internet-Linked. Rogers, Kirsteen, ed. Rolland, Leonard Le, illus. rev. ed. 2006. (Usborne Encyclopedia of World Religions Ser.). 128p. (J). (gr. 5-9). per. 14.95 (978-0-7945-1059-6(0), Usborne) EDC Publishing.

Kallen, Stuart A. Communication with the Dead. 2009. (Library of Ghosts & Hauntings Ser.). (YA). (gr. 7-12). 26.95 (978-1-60152-089-0(1)) ReferencePoint Pr., Inc.

Kalman, Bobbie. What Is Religion? 2009. (Our Multicultural World Ser.). (ENG., Illus.). 32p. (J). (gr. 1-4). lib. bdg. (978-0-7787-4636-2(4)) Crabtree Publishing Co.

Langley, Myrtle & Dorling Kindersley Publishing Staff. Religion. 2012. (DK Eyewitness Bks.). (ENG.). 72p. (J). (gr. 3-7). 16.99 (978-0-7566-9079-3(X), DK Children) Dorling Kindersley Publishing, Inc.

Lugira, Aloysius M. & Palmer, Martin. World Religions, 14 vols., Set. 2009. (World Religions Ser.). (gr. 6-12). 560.00 (978-1-60413-649-4(9), Chelsea Hse.) Facts On File, Inc.

Major, Gail Baccelli. What Do You See in Me I am Who I am. Major, Rebekah, illus. 2013. (ENG.). 32p. (J). pap. 9.95 (978-1-939289-22-3(X), Little Creek Bks.) Jan-Carol Publishing, INC.

Mayled, Jon & Ahluwalia, Libby. Philosophy & Ethics. 2003. (ENG., Illus.). 208p. pap. (978-0-7487-7157-8(3)) Nelson Thornes Ltd.

McFarlane, Marilyn. Sacred Stories: Wisdom from World Religions. Berg, Caroline O., illus. 2012. (ENG.). 192p. (J). (gr. 4-9). 17.99 (978-1-58270-334-3(5)) Aladdin/Beyond Words.

Mead, Jean. What religions are in our Neighbourhood? 2013. (Step up Religion Ser.). (ENG., Illus.). 32p. (J). pap. 12.99 (978-0-237-54379-2(6)) Evans Brothers, Ltd. GBR. Dist: Independent Pubs. Group.

Meredith, Susan. The Usborne Book of World Religions. Evans, Cheryl, ed. Hewetson, Nicholas J., illus. 2006. (World Religions (Usborne) Ser.). 64p. (J). (gr. 5). lib. bdg. 17.99 (978-1-58086-908-9(4), Usborne) EDC Publishing.

—The Usborne Book of World Religions. Evans, Cheryl, ed. Hewetson, Nicholas J. & Gower, Jeremy, illus. rev. ed. 2006. (World Cultures Ser.). 64p. (J). (gr. 5). pap. 9.99 (978-0-7945-1027-5(2)) EDC Publishing.

Meredith, Susan & Hickman, Claire. Encyclopedia of World Religions. rev. ed. 2012. (World Cultures Ser.). 128p. (J). pap. 14.99 (978-0-7945-2753-2(1), Usborne) EDC Publishing.

Mooney, Carla. Comparative Religion: Investigate the World Through Religious Tradition. Chandhok, Lena, illus. 2015. (Inquire & Investigate Ser.). (ENG.). 128p. (gr. 6-10). 22.95 (978-1-61930-301-0(9)) Open City Bks.

Palmer, Martin, et al. Religions of the World: The Illustrated Guide to Origins, Beliefs, Traditions & Festivals. 2nd rev. ed. 2005. (Illustrated Guide to Customs & Beliefs Ser.). (Illus.). 160p. (gr. 6-12). 29.95 (978-0-8160-6258-4(7), Checkmark Bks.) Facts On File, Inc.

Raushenbush, Paul. Teen Spirit: One World, Many Paths. 2004. (ENG., Illus.). 252p. (YA). pap. 11.95 (978-0-7573-0119-3(3), HCI Teens) Health Communications, Inc.

Rogers, Kirsteen & Hickman, Clare. Religiones Del Mundo - Internet Linked. 2005. (Titles in Spanish Ser.). (SPA.). 128p. (J). 19.95 (978-0-7460-5093-4(3), Usborne) EDC Publishing.

Rotner, Shelley & Kelly, Sheila M. Many Ways: How Families Practice Their Beliefs & Religions. Rotner, Shelley, photos by. (Shelley Rotner's Early Childhood Library Ser.). (ENG., Illus.). 32p. (gr. k-3). 2010. pap. 7.95 (978-0-7613-6531-0(1)) 2005. lib. bdg. 22.60 (978-0-7613-2873-5(4), Millbrook Pr.) Lerner Publishing Group.

Schomp, Virginia & Firdawsi. The Ancient Persians. 2009. (Myths of the World Ser.). 96p. (gr. 6-7). 34.21 (978-0-7614-4218-9(9)) Marshall Cavendish Corp.

Shanddaramon. Pagan Sabbats of the Northern Hemisphere. 2008. 39p. 18.95 (978-0-615-18601-6(7)) Astor Pr.

Steckel, Richard & Steckel, Michele. Faith. Steckel, Richard & Steckel, Michele, illus. 2012. (ENG., Illus.). 36p. (J). (gr. 3-7). 17.95 (978-1-55453-750-1(9)) Kids Can Pr., Ltd. CAN. Dist: Hachette Bk. Group.

Stockstill, Gloria McQueen. To the Town of Bethlehem. Durrell, Julie, illus. 2004. 20p. (J). bds. 5.49 (978-0-7586-0051-6(8)) Concordia Publishing Hse.

Teen Spirit Guide to Modern Shamanism: A Beginner's Map Charting an Ancient Path. 2014. (ENG.). 147p. (YA). (gr. 8-17). pap. 16.95 (978-1-78279-433-2(6), Soul Rocks Bks.) Hunt, John Publishing Ltd. GBR. Dist: National Bk. Network.

Wallace, Ann Hamilton. The Messenger: Revelations from an Unlikely Prophet. 2003. (ENG., Illus.). 150p. (gr. 9-12). 22.95 (978-0-9724458-0-1(3)) Sonrise Publishing.

What Is Faith? 2006. (Faith Discovery Ser.). (Illus.). 24p. (J). bds. 6.99 (978-0-7847-1396-9(0), 04056) Standard Publishing.

White, Bender Richardson, et al. Confucianism. 3rd rev. ed. 2009. (World Religions Ser.). (Illus.). 144p. (J). (gr. 6-12). 40.00 (978-1-60413-107-9(1), Chelsea Hse.) Facts On File, Inc.

World Religions, 6 bks., Set. Incl. Buddhism. Young, Serinity. (gr. 7-18). lib. bdg. 42.79 (978-0-7614-2114-6(9), Benchmark Bks.); Hinduism. Young, Serinity. (gr. 7-7). lib. bdg. 42.79 (978-0-7614-2116-0(5), Benchmark Bks.); Islam. Alkouatli, Claire. (J). (gr. 3-7). lib. bdg. 39.93 (978-0-7614-2120-7(3)); Judaism. Wool, Daniel. (gr. 7-18). lib. bdg. 42.79 (978-0-7614-2118-4(1), Benchmark Bks.); Protestantism. Eppehimer, Trevor. (gr. 7-18). lib. bdg. 42.79 (978-0-7614-2117-7(3), Benchmark Bks.); Roman Catholicism. Otfinoski, Steven. (gr. 7-18). lib. bdg. 42.79 (978-0-7614-2119-1(X), Benchmark Bks.); (Illus.). 144p. 2006. 2007. Set lib. bdg. 239.57 (978-0-7614-2113-9(0), Benchmark Bks.) Marshall Cavendish Corp.

York Lumbard, Alexis. Everyone Prays: Celebrating Faith Around the World. Sadeghian, Alireza, illus. 2014. (ENG.). 28p. (J). (gr. -1-3). 17.95 (978-1-937786-19-9(6), Wisdom Tales) World Wisdom, Inc.

RELIGIONS—BIOGRAPHY

Here are entered collections of biographies of religious leaders not limited to the Christian religion.

see also Christian Biography

Carr, Simonetta. Marie Durand: Christian Biographies for Young Readers. Abraxas, Matt, illus. 2015. (ENG.). 60p. (J). 18.00 (978-1-60178-390-5(6)) Reformation Heritage Bks.

Grant, Myrna. Gladys Aylward - No Mountain Too High. 2013. (Trailblazers Ser.). (ENG.). 176p. (J). mass mkt. 8.99 (978-1-85792-594-4(7), 9781857925944, CF4Kids) Christian Focus Pubns. GBR. Dist: Bookmasters Distribution.

Kwiatkowski, Gerhard & Lanczkowski, Günter. Religionen: Von Alten Naturreligionen bis zu Modernen Sekten, Ursprung und Geschichte aller Religionen, 1 vol. (Duden-Schuelerduden Ser.). (GER & ENG., Illus.). 467p. (YA). 27.95 (978-3-411-01369-2(9)) Bibliographisches Institut & F. A. Brockhaus AG DEU. Dist: Continental Bk. Co., Inc.

Marty, Martin E., intro. Spiritual Leaders & Thinkers. (Illus.). (gr. 9-13). lib. bdg. 252.45 (978-0-7910-8413-7(2), Chelsea Hse.) Facts On File, Inc.

Nardo, Don. Founders of Faiths. 2011. (World Religions & Beliefs Ser.). 159p. (gr. 7-12). 28.95 (978-1-59935-147-6(1)) Reynolds, Morgan Inc.

Touger, Malka. A Door That's Never Locked. 2011. (ENG.). 64p. (J). 14.95 (978-0-8266-0131-5(6)) Kehot Pubn. Society.

RELIGIONS—FICTION

Abraham, Michelle Shapiro. Where Is Grandpa Dennis? Fried, Janice, illus. 2009. (J). (978-0-8074-1083-7(7)) URJ Pr.

Adahan, Miriam. Torah Tigers. 2009. 48p. 17.99 (978-1-59826-308-4(0)) Feldheim Pubs.

Alberti, Robert. Mitlanyal: The Gods of Change, Vol. 2. 10th ed. 2004. (Illus.). 184p. (YA). pap. 19.95 (978-0-9725880-3-4(5), mit2) Zottola Publishing, Inc.

Arnold, Edward Ronny. Rashida. 2003. 110p. (YA). pap. 7.99 (978-0-9721216-6-8(8), 0972121668) Computer Classics (R).

Barash, Chris. Is It Sukkot Yet? Psacharopulo, Alessandra, illus. 2016. (ENG.). 32p. (J). (gr. -1-3). 16.99 (978-0-8075-3388-8(2)) Whitman, Albert & Co.

Barricks, Jerim. I Want to Know??? 2003. (Illus.). 26p. (J). 10.00 (978-0-9743512-0-9(2)) Barricks, Jeri Ministry.

Bell, Shirley. Boys on the Make. 2007. 54p. 16.95 (978-1-4241-6575-9(X)) America Star Bks.

Benenfeld, Rikki. I Go Visiting. 2007. (Toddler Experience Ser.). (Illus.). 32p. (J). (gr. -1-k). 10.95 (978-1-929628-33-9(1)) Hachai Publishing.

Berry, Julie. The Passion of Dolssa. 2016. (ENG.). 496p. (YA). (gr. 7). 18.99 (978-0-451-46992-2(5), Viking Books for Young Readers) Penguin Young Readers Group.

Billiot, Christopher. And Heaven Stood Silent. Geist, Hans, illus. 2009. 36p. pap. 15.49 (978-1-4389-5894-1(3)) AuthorHouse.

Black, Joe. Afikomen Mambo. Brown, Richard E. & Prater, Linda, illus. 2011. (Passover Ser.). (ENG.). 24p. (J). (gr. -1 — 1). lib. bdg. 17.95 (978-0-7613-5638-7(X), Kar-Ben Publishing) Lerner Publishing Group.

Blume, Judy. Are You There God? It's Me, Margaret. 149p. (J). (gr. 4-6). pap. 3.50 (978-0-8072-1421-3(3)); (YA). (gr. 5-18). pap. 4.99 (978-0-8072-1508-1(2)) Random Hse. Audio Publishing Group. (Listening Library).

Brooks, Grace. The Asquinn Twins & Grant. 2010. 111p. pap. 9.94 (978-0-557-26972-3(5)) Lulu Pr., Inc.

Bunce, Elizabeth C. StarCrossed. 2011. (ENG.). 368p. (YA). pap. 9.99 (978-0-545-13606-8(7), Levine, Arthur A. Bks.) Scholastic, Inc.

Chancellor, Deborah. The Christmas Story. Downing, Julie, illus. 12p. (J). (gr. -1-18). bds. 6.95 (978-0-8294-1480-6(0)) Loyola Pr.

Chopra, Deepak. You with the Stars in Your Eyes: A Little Girl's Glimpse at Cosmic Consciousness. Zaboski, Dave, illus. 2010. (ENG & ABK.). 32p. 14.95 (978-1-4019-2711-0(4)) Hay Hse., Inc.

Chrisagis, Brian. Who & What Am I? Good News Gang. Chrisagis, Shawn, illus. 2006. 24p. (J). 9.99 (978-1-59958-014-2(4)) Journey Stone Creations, LLC.

Chrisagis, Shawn & Chrisagis, Brian. Prejudice in Mandi's Garden: Seeds of Kindness. 2006. 24p. (J). pap. 2.99 (978-1-59958-009-8(8)) Journey Stone Creations, LLC.

Cobb, Judith A. The First Gift. Cowper-Thomas, Wendy, illus. 2008. (J). pap. (978-0-87743-708-6(4)) Baha'i Publishing Trust, U.S.

Cohen, Deborah Bodin. Papa Jethro. Dippold, Jane, illus. 2007. (Jewish Identity Ser.). (ENG.). 32p. (J). (gr. -1-1). 9.95 (978-1-58013-250-3(2)); per. 7.95 (978-1-58013-252-7(9)) Lerner Publishing Group. (Kar-Ben Publishing).

Cowper-Thomas, Wendy, illus. Something Important. 2010. (J). (978-0-87743-711-6(4)) Baha'i Publishing Trust, U.S.

Coyle, Katie. Vivian Apple at the End of the World. (ENG.). (YA). (gr. 7). 2016. 288p. pap. 8.99 (978-0-544-66867-6(7)) 2015. 272p. 17.99 (978-0-544-34011-4(6)) Houghton Mifflin Harcourt Publishing Co. (HMH Books For Young Readers).

—Vivian Apple Needs a Miracle. 2015. (ENG.). 304p. (YA). (gr. 7). 17.99 (978-0-544-39042-3(3), HMH Books For Young Readers) Houghton Mifflin Harcourt Publishing Co.

Dillon, Sally Pierson. Exile of the Chosen: God's Heroes from Solomon to Malachi. 2003. (Pathfinder Junior Book Club Ser.). 223p. (J). pap. 10.99 (978-0-8280-1703-9(4), 58-710) Review & Herald Publishing Assn.

Douglas, Babette. Rosebud. 2004. (J). 9.99 (978-1-890343-12-5(9)) Kiss A Me Productions, Inc.

Finley, Martha. Christmas with Grandma Elsie, Vol. 14. 320p. (gr. 4-7). pap. 5.95 (978-1-58182-108-6(5), Cumberland Hse.) Sourcebooks, Inc.

—Elsie & the Raymonds, Vol. 15. 320p. (gr. 4-7). pap. 5.95 (978-1-58182-110-9(7), Cumberland Hse.) Sourcebooks, Inc.

—Elsie Yachting with the Raymonds, Vol. 16. 320p. (gr. 4-7). pap. 5.95 (978-1-58182-111-6(5), Cumberland Hse.) Sourcebooks, Inc.

—Elsie's Friends at Woodburn, Vol. 13. 320p. (gr. 4-7). pap. 5.95 (978-1-58182-107-9(7), Cumberland Hse.) Sourcebooks, Inc.

Finney, Ruth. A Prayer for Momma. 2007. 38p. pap. 8.00 (978-0-8059-7483-6(0)) Dorrance Publishing Co., Inc.

Fleischman, Sid. The Entertainer & the Dybbuk. 2009. (ENG.). 192p. (J). (gr. 4-9). pap. 6.99 (978-0-06-177140-8(6), Greenwillow Bks.) HarperCollins Pubs.

Goldin, Barbara Diamond. Cakes & Miracles: A Purim Tale, 0 vols. Zollars, Jaime, illus. 2010. (ENG.). 32p. (J). (gr. k-3). 17.99 (978-0-7614-5701-5(1), 9780761457015, Amazon Children's Publishing) Amazon Publishing.

Gould, M&R. What Would Jesus Do? Purity of Intention. 2008. 35p. pap. 24.95 (978-1-60672-675-4(7)) America Star Bks.

Gregory, Philippa. Stormbringers. van Deelen, Fred, illus. 2013. (Order of Darkness Ser.: 2). (ENG.). 336p. (YA). (gr. 9). pap. 9.99 (978-1-4424-7688-2(5)); 17.99 (978-1-4424-7687-5(7)) Simon Pulse. (Simon Pulse).

Hatcher, John. Ali's Dream. 2014. 310p. (J). (978-1-61851-068-6(1)) Baha'i Publishing.

Hauser, Lisa Kay. 1-2-3, & God Made Me! 2004. (Illus.). 32p. 15.95 (978-1-886864-03-0(9)) Golden Anchor Pr.

—1-2-3, Special Like Me! 2004. (Illus.). 32p. (J). 15.95 (978-1-886864-17-7(9), 1231325) Golden Anchor Pr.

Hautman, Pete. The Cydonian Pyramid. (Klaatu Diskos Ser.). (ENG.). 368p. (YA). (gr. 7). 2014. pap. 8.99 (978-0-7636-6933-1(4)) 2013. 16.99 (978-0-7636-5404-7(3)) Candlewick Pr.

—Godless. (ENG.). 208p. (YA). (gr. 7-12). 2005. pap. 11.99 (978-1-4169-0816-6(1)) 2004. (Illus.). 18.99 (978-0-689-86278-6(4)) Simon & Schuster Bks. For Young Readers. (Simon & Schuster Bks. For Young Readers).

—The Obsidian Blade. 2012. (Klaatu Diskos Ser.). (ENG., Illus.). 320p. (YA). (gr. 7). 16.99 (978-0-7636-5403-0(5)) Candlewick Pr.

Hawkins, Wanda. Geronimo Discovers Faith. 2007. (Illus.). 24p. (J). per. 12.99 (978-1-59879-336-9(5)) Lifevest Publishing, Inc.

Hawxhurst, Joan C. Bubbe & Gram: My Two Grandmothers. Bynum-Nwulu, Jane, illus. 2003. 32p. (J). (gr. -1-2). 12.95 (978-0-9651284-2-1(3)) Dovetail Publishing.

Hennesy, Carolyn. Pandora Gets Jealous. 2009. (Mythic Misadventures Ser.). (ENG., Illus.). 288p. (YA). (gr. 3-6). pap. 7.99 (978-1-59990-291-3(5), 9781599902913, Bloomsbury USA Childrens) Bloomsbury Publishing USA.

Hocknell, Barbara. The Mouse Who Attended the Last Supper: And Other Stories. 2007. (Illus.). 48p. per. (978-1-84748-200-6(7)) Athena Pr.

Hodakov, Levi. I Go to the Ohel. Rosenfeld, D. L. & Leverton, Yossi, eds. Benenfeld, Rikki, illus. 2011. (Toddler Experience Ser.). 32p. (J). 10.95 (978-1-929628-61-2(7)) Hachai Publishing.

Holmes, Andy. If You Give a Boy a Bible. 2004. 32p. (J). 10.99 (978-0-8254-5513-1(8)) Kregel Pubns.

Hünermann, Wilhelm. A Crucified Heart: A Novel of St. Herman Joseph. Szanto, Hubert, tr. from GER. 2004. Orig. Title: Der Moench Vom Steinfeld. (Illus.). 176p. (YA). (978-0-9742298-1-2(4)) St. Michael's Abbey.

Jaskwhich, Cynthia Sheperd. Mema Says Good-Bye. Mazibuko, Luthando, illus. 2010. (J). (978-0-87743-710-9(6)) Baha'i Publishing Trust, U.S.

Jenkins, Jerry B. & LaHaye, Tim. The Mark of the Beast: Witness Behind Bars. 2003. (Left Behind Ser.). 146p. (J). 13.65 *(978-0-7569-3532-0(6))* Perfection Learning Corp.
Koffsky, Ann D., illus. Shabbat Shalom, Hey! 2015. (ENG.). 24p. (J). (gr. -1-k). lib. bdg. 16.95 *(978-1-4677-4917-6(6),* Kar-Ben Publishing) Lerner Publishing Group.
Lepard, Jenina. Diamonds in the Rough. 2009. (J). pap. *(978-0-87743-713-0(0))* Baha'i Publishing Trust, U.S.
Lieberman, Leanne. Gravity, 1 vol. 2008. (ENG.). 280p. (YA). (gr. 7-12). pap. 12.95 *(978-1-55469-049-7(8))* Orca Bk. Pubs. USA.
Littman, Sarah Darer. Confessions of a Closet Catholic. 2006. (ENG.). 208p. (J). (gr. 5-18). reprint ed. 7.99 *(978-0-14-240597-0(3),* Puffin Books) Penguin Young Readers Group.
Luedke, Robert James. Eye Witness: A Fictional Tale of Absolute Truth. 2005. (Eye Witness Ser.). (ENG., Illus.). 96p. pap. 13.99 *(978-0-9758924-0-4(1));* lib. bdg. 24.99 *(978-0-9758924-1-1(X))* Head Pr. Publishing.
Madison, Ron. Ned & the World's Religions: As Seen Through the Eyes of Children. Covolo, David, illus. 2008. 36p. (J). 14.95 *(978-1-887206-26-6(4))* Ned's Head Productions.
Mahr, Aryeh. Mysteries of the Aleph Beis. 2008. 54p. 17.99 *(978-1-59826-211-7(4))* Feldheim Pubs.
Martin, W. Lyon. An Ordinary Girl, A Magical Child. Martin, W. Lyon, illus. 2008. (ENG., Illus.). 48p. (J). lib. bdg. 16.95 *(978-0-9796834-3-5(2),* Magical Child Bks.) Shades of White.
McO-Campbell, Adrian. The Wildness Within & the Tree of Eyes. 2010. 80p. pap. 38.95 *(978-1-4457-1664-0(X))* Lulu Pr., Inc.
Messner, Kate. Hide & Seek. 2013. (ENG., Illus.). 256p. (J). (gr. 3-7). 16.99 *(978-0-545-41975-8(1),* Scholastic Pr.) Scholastic, Inc.
Mills, Samuel. The Demon Slayer. 2009. 192p. (YA). pap. 15.00 *(978-0-88010-701-3(4))* SteinerBooks, Inc.
—The Fire Bringer. 2009. 128p. (J). pap. 15.00 *(978-0-88010-700-6(6))* SteinerBooks, Inc.
Morley, Farah, illus. The Spider & the Doves: The Story of the Hijra. 2012. (ENG.). 30p. (J). (gr. -1-2). 8.95 *(978-0-86037-449-7(1))* Kube Publishing Ltd. GBR. Dist: Consortium Bk. Sales & Distribution.
Naibantsky, Danail. Bludnia Sin (the Prodigal Son) Guetov, Dimitar, ed. 2nd unabr. ed. 2004. (BUL.). 228p. per. 9.99 *(978-0-9753970-3-9(6))* Capricorn Publishing.
Naughty Krishna. 2003. (J). 2.99 *(978-0-9748285-1-0(3))* Anar Bks. LLC.
Oppenheim, Shulamith. I Bis: An Islamic Tale. Young, Ed, illus. 2004. 29p. (J). (gr. k-4). reprint ed. 16.00 *(978-0-7567-7575-9(2))* DIANE Publishing Co.
Padgett, Anthony. Divinityland. 2010. (Illus.). 20p. 21.50 *(978-0-9561587-1-0(4))* Auditors of God, The GBR. Dist: Lulu Pr., Inc.
Parker, Amy Christine. Gated. 2013. (ENG.). 352p. (YA). (gr. 9). 17.99 *(978-0-449-81597-7(8),* Random Hse. Bks. for Young Readers) Random Hse. Children's Bks.
Pelletier, Cynthia L. & Rabin, Shri. She Who Walks with Tigers, 1 vol. 2010. 80p. pap. 19.95 *(978-1-4512-8767-7(4))* America Star Bks.
Peretti, Frank E. The Tombs of Anak, Vol. 3. 2004. (Cooper Kids Adventure Ser.: 3). 144p. (J). (gr. 3-6). pap. 6.99 *(978-1-58134-620-6(4))* Crossway.
Powers, Emily. Wendell Has a Cracked Shell. Moody, Jason, illus. 2008. 32p. (gr. -1-18). pap. 14.95 *(978-0-9801357-6-3(1))* Tree of Life Publishing Hse.
Rapp, Pat. Noisy Nativity. 2008. 24p. per. 24.95 *(978-1-4241-9866-5(6))* America Star Bks.
Rennie-Pattison, Caroline. The Law of Three. 2007. (ENG.). 232p. (YA). (gr. 6). pap. 10.99 *(978-1-55002-733-4(6),* Boardwalk Bks.) Dundurn CAN. Dist: Ingram Publisher Services.
Rose, Robert. Godintoxicated Becoming Paranoid. 2007. 260p. pap. 29.95 *(978-1-4327-0041-6(3))* Outskirts Pr., Inc.
Rouss, Sylvia A. Sammy Spider's First Day of School. Kahn, Katherine Janus, illus. 2009. (Kar-Ben Favorites Ser.). (ENG.). 32p. (J). (gr. -1-2). pap. 7.95 *(978-0-8225-8584-8(7),* Kar-Ben Publishing) Lerner Publishing Group.
Rupp, Rebecca. Octavia Boone's Big Questions about Life, the Universe & Everything. 2010. (ENG., Illus.). 192p. (J). (gr. 4-7). 15.99 *(978-0-7636-4491-8(9))* Candlewick Pr.
Sawyer, Ruth. The Primrose Ring. 2007. (ENG.). 106p. pap. 18.99 *(978-1-4346-4247-9(X))* Creative Media Partners, LLC.
Sawyers, Carol. Trapped At 13. 2005. 220p. (YA). pap. 14.00 *(978-0-9767778-4-7(3),* 704-724-1683) Alpha & Omega Publishing.
Shulimson, Sarene. Lights Out Shabbat. Ebbeler, Jeff, illus. 2012. (Shabbat Ser.). (ENG.). 32p. (J). (gr. -1-2). pap. 7.95 *(978-0-7613-7565-4(1),* Kar-Ben Publishing) Lerner Publishing Group.
Singer, Marilyn. Brushes with Religion. Date not set. 192p. (YA). (gr. 7-18). mass mkt. 5.99 *(978-0-06-440789-2(6))* HarperCollins Pubs.
St. John, Patricia. The Victor. 2003. 176p. 6.49 *(978-0-86201-139-0(6))* Scripture Union GBR. Dist: Gabriel Resources.
Steedman, Amy. In God's Garden (Yesterday's Classics) 2006. (J). per. 9.95 *(978-1-59915-032-1(8))* Yesterday's Classics.
Stephens, Dawn. The Little Pot. 2009. (Illus.). (J). (gr. -1-3). 17.95 *(978-1-933982-11-3(X),* bPlus Bks.) Bumble Bee Publishing.
Stevens, Noel. Tin Gods. 2008. 116p. pap. 10.95 *(978-0-595-53046-5(X))* iUniverse, Inc.
Taylor, Yvonne. Hartlie: The Streak. Taylor, Yvonne, ed. (Hartlie: Vol. 1). (Illus.). 32p. (J). 10.99 *(978-0-9709187-0-3(4))* Peaceable Productions.
Thompson, James A., Jr. The Amarna Experiment. 2003. 128p. (YA). 21.95 *(978-0-595-65753-7(2));* pap. 11.95 *(978-0-595-28296-8(2))* iUniverse, Inc.
Tika. Baby Love. Standish, Joyce, ed. Burroughs, Derrie, illus. I.t. ed. 2006. 18p. (J). (gr. 1-5). pap. 15.00 *(978-0-9716244-1-2(0))* TLS Publishing.
Townsend, Diana. He Saw Their Faith. 2007. 25p. 21.50 *(978-0-615-16214-0(2))* Townsend, Diana.
Underwood, Kathie L. Sarah & the Sand Dollar. 2004. (Illus.). 36p. (J). pap. 11.95 *(978-0-9672585-7-7(X))* CyPress Pubns.
Van Ryk, Laverne. A Garland of Emeralds. 2006. (Illus.). 305p. 31.50 *(978-1-4122-0156-8(X))* Trafford Publishing.
Von Schmid. Stolen Child. 2004. 13.00 *(978-1-58474-022-3(1))* Cornerstone Family Ministries/Lamplighter Publishing.
Warner, Susan. Daisy. 2007. 316p. pap. 14.99 *(978-1-4264-9407-9(6));* 356p. pap. 20.99 *(978-1-4264-9788-9(1))* Creative Media Partners, LLC.
Wasserman, Sand. The Sun's Special Blessing: Happens Only Once in 28 Years - French Flap. Koffsky, Ann, illus. 2009. 36p. 12.95 *(978-1-934440-76-6(0),* Pitspopany Pr.) Simcha Media Group.
—The Sun's Special Blessing: Happens Only Once in 28 Years - HC. Koffsky, Ann, illus. 2009. 36p. 17.95 *(978-1-934440-92-6(2),* Pitspopany Pr.) Simcha Media Group.
White, Ruth. A Month of Sundays. 2013. (ENG.). 192p. (YA). (gr. 5-9). pap. 6.99 *(978-1-250-02730-6(6),* 9781250027306) Square Fish.
Wiles, Patricia. My Mom's a Mortician: A Novel. 2004. 249p. (J). *(978-1-59156-433-1(6))* Covenant Communications.
Williston, Teresa Peirce. Hindu Tales. Squire, Maud Hunt, illus. 2011. 86p. 37.95 *(978-1-258-02582-3(5))* Literary Licensing, LLC.
Wittlinger, Ellen. Blind Faith. 2007. (ENG.). 304p. (YA). (gr. 7-12). pap. 9.99 *(978-1-4169-4906-0(2),* Simon & Schuster Bks. For Young Readers) Simon & Schuster Bks. For Young Readers.
Woodson, Jacqueline. Feathers. (ENG.). (J). (gr. 5-18). 2010. 160p. 8.99 *(978-0-14-241550-4(2),* Speak) 2007. 128p. 16.99 *(978-0-399-23989-2(8),* G.P. Putnam's Sons Books for Young Readers) Penguin Young Readers Group.
Zeldin, Danny. The Cholent Man. 2011. 32p. pap. 14.95 *(978-1-4567-5137-1(9))* AuthorHouse.

RELIGIOUS ART

see Art, Medieval; Christian Art and Symbolism; Church Architecture

RELIGIOUS BELIEF

see Belief and Doubt; Faith

RELIGIOUS BIOGRAPHY

see Christian Biography; Religions—Biography

RELIGIOUS CEREMONIES

see Rites and Ceremonies

RELIGIOUS DENOMINATIONS

see Sects

RELIGIOUS EDUCATION

see also Bible—Study; Moral Education

Abingdon. By the Waters: Preschool Kit. 2003. (Bible Zone Live Ser.). 79.99 *(978-0-687-08127-1(0))* Abingdon Pr.
—By the Waters: Younger Elementary Kit. 2003. (Bible Zone Live Ser.). (gr. 1-3). 79.99 *(978-0-687-08137-0(8))* Abingdon Pr.
Arthur, Kay & Arndt, Janna. Fast-Forward to the Future: Daniel 7-12. 2008. (ENG., Illus.). 192p. (J). per. 11.99 *(978-0-7369-2285-2(7))* Harvest Hse. Pubs.
Arthur, Kay & Domeij, Scoti. Wrong Way, Jonah! Leite, Eleni, tr. 2003. (Discover-4-Yourself for Kids Ser.). (POR., Illus.). 93p. (J). pap. 8.99 *(978-1-888655-71-1(2))* Precept Ministries.
The Ascension. (Illus.). (gr. 1-4). 3.00 *(978-0-570-05525-9(3),* 54-1035) Concordia Publishing Hse.
Barnabas Fund. Brothers & Sisters: Loving Our Persecuted Family. 2012. (ENG., Illus.). 38p. pap. 10.00 *(978-0-9853109-7-4(9))* Isaac Publishing.
Beller, Dyan. Creative Bible Crafts: Reproducible Activities. 2004. (Illus.). 64p. (J). (gr. 5-6). pap. 9.95 *(978-1-885358-15-8(6),* B36240) Rainbow Pubs. & Legacy Pr.
Biffi, Inos. An Illustrated Catechism: The Apostles' Creed, the Sacraments, the Ten Commandments, Prayer. Vignazia, Franco, illus. 2007. 141p. (J). (gr. 3). per. 19.95 *(978-1-56854-612-4(2))* Liturgy Training Pubns.
Bishop, Jennie. Jesus Must Be Really Special. Wummer, Amy, illus. 2006. (Heritage Builders Ser.). 32p. (J). 14.99 *(978-0-7847-1379-2(0),* 04029) Standard Publishing.
Boston, Vicki & Stroh, Debbie. Christ's Kids Create: Volume 2; Favorite Seasonal Craft Ideas, Vol. 2. 2nd ed. 2006. (CPH Teaching Resource Ser.). (Illus.). 64p. pap. 10.99 *(978-0-7586-1109-3(9))* Concordia Publishing Hse.
Brosiavick, Chris & Pichler, Tony. Totally Lent: A Teen's Journey to Easter 2006. Cannizzo, Karen A., ed. 2005. (Illus.). 64p. (J). 5.95 *(978-1-933178-24-0(8),* 3566) Pflaum Publishing Group.
Burchett, Author Walter, BA. Christian children's fill in the blank Revised. 2009. 37p. pap. 14.48 *(978-0-557-08184-4(X))* Lulu Pr., Inc.
—Christian children's questions & answers abraham & keturah to israel & rachel Volume 2. 2009. 32p. pap. 14.28 *(978-0-557-08256-8(0))* Lulu Pr., Inc.
—Christian children's questions & answers adam & eve to abraham & sarah Volume 1. 2009. 36p. pap. 14.44 *(978-0-557-08219-3(6))* Lulu Pr., Inc.
—Christian children's questions & answers joseph (coat of many colors) Volume 3. 2009. 32p. pap. 14.28 *(978-0-557-08276-6(5))* Lulu Pr., Inc.
—Christian children's questions & answers resurrection of christ Volume 7. 2009. 32p. pap. 14.28 *(978-0-557-08245-2(5))* Lulu Pr., Inc.
Cannizzo, Karen & Schippe, Cullen, eds. The Church Welcomes Me: Grade 2, 6 books. 2005. (Faith Activities for Catholic Kids Ser.). (Illus.). 32p. (J). (gr. -1-3). pap. 6.95 *(978-1-933178-16-5(7),* 2802) Pflaum Publishing Group.
—Jesus Loves Me: Grade 1, 6 books. 2005. (Faith Activities for Catholic Kids Ser.). (Illus.). 32p. (J). (gr. k-2). pap. 6.95 *(978-1-933178-15-8(9),* 2801) Pflaum Publishing Group.
—Learning the Way: Grade 3, 6 books. 2005. (Faith Activities for Catholic Kids Ser.). (Illus.). 32p. (J). (gr. 2-4). pap. 6.95 *(978-1-933178-17-2(5),* 2803) Pflaum Publishing Group.
Cannizzo, Karen & Schippe, Cullen W., eds. Discovering the Story of God's People: Grade 6, 6 bks. 2005. (Faith Activities for Catholic Kids Ser.). (Illus.). 32p. pap. 6.95 *(978-1-933178-20-2(5),* 2806) Pflaum Publishing Group.
—Learning to Celebrate: Grade 5, 6 bks. 2005. (Faith Activities for Catholic Kids Ser.). (Illus.). 32p. pap. 6.95 *(978-1-933178-19-6(1),* 2805) Pflaum Publishing Group.
Christian, Judy, et al. Scribble, Dribble, & Glue: Bible Art Projects for Kids. 2007. (Illus.). 64p. pap. 10.99 *(978-0-7586-1308-0(3))* Concordia Publishing Hse.
Complete 5 Subject Set. 2004. (Switched on Schoolhouse Ser.). (YA). (gr. 8). cd-rom 299.95 *(978-0-7403-0591-7(3))* Alpha Omega Pubns., Inc.
CrossTown. (gr. 1-18). stu. ed. 11.25 *(978-0-570-00766-1(6),* 22-2880); (gr. 3-18). stu. ed. 11.25 *(978-0-570-00770-8(4),* 22-2884) Concordia Publishing Hse.
David C. Cook Publishing Company Staff, creator. Full Tilt Wacky Games. 2008. (Bible Fun Stuff for Middle School Ser.). (Illus.). 112p. (J). (gr. 6-8). pap. 19.99 *(978-1-4347-6855-1(4))* Cook, David C.
—Fun Science That Teaches God's Word for Tweeners. 2008. (BFS Ser.). (Illus.). 120p. (gr. 4-6). per. 19.99 *(978-0-7814-4558-0(2))* Cook, David C.
—Stick'em up Bible Crafts. 2008. (Bible Fun Stuff for Preschool Ser.). (Illus.). 112p. (J). (gr. -1-k). pap. 19.99 *(978-1-4347-6864-3(3))* Cook, David C.
—Through-the-Bible Crafts. 2008. (Bible Fun Stuff for K-1 Ser.). (Illus.). 112p. (J). (gr. k-1). pap. 19.99 *(978-1-4347-6862-9(7))* Cook, David C.
Day by Day. 2004. (gr. k-1). Vol. 1. 50.00 *(978-1-58095-847-9(8),* WB001) Vol. 2. 50.00 *(978-1-58095-848-6(6),* WB002) Vol. 3. 50.00 *(978-1-58095-849-3(4),* WB003) Vol. 4. 50.00 *(978-1-58095-850-9(8),* WB004) Vol. 5. 50.00 *(978-1-58095-851-6(6),* WB005) Alpha Omega Pubns., Inc. (Weaver).
Dennis, Rainey. Passport 2 Purity. 2004. 29.99 *(978-1-57229-656-5(9))* FamilyLife.
Diagnostic Tests: Student Testing Kit, 5 bks., Set. 2004. (J). (gr. 1-8). suppl. ed. 19.95 *(978-0-7403-0096-7(2),* AS9922) Alpha Omega Pubns., Inc.
Dios Elige a Su Pueblo: Quarter 1, Level 3. (Caminando con Jesus (Walking with Jesus) Series B).Tr. of God Chooses His People. (SPA.). (J). (gr. 3-4). stu. ed. 3.50 *(978-0-570-05152-7(5),* 16-3911) Concordia Publishing Hse.
Dios Me Da Su Palabra: Quarter 1, Level 2. (Caminando con Jesus (Walking with Jesus) Series A).Tr. of God Gives Me His Word. (SPA.). (J). (gr. 1-2). stu. ed. 3.50 *(978-0-570-05132-9(0),* 16-2811) Concordia Publishing Hse.
Dios Me Dio Relaciones: Quarter 3, Level 1. (Caminando con Jesus (Walking with Jesus) Series B).Tr. of God Gave Me Relationships. (SPA.). (J). (gr. -1-k). stu. ed. 3.50 *(978-0-570-05112-1(6),* 16-1913) Concordia Publishing Hse.
Dios Me Dio un Cuerpo: Quarter 2, Level 1. (Caminando con Jesus (Walking with Jesus) Series B).Tr. of God Gave Me a Body. (SPA.). (J). (gr. -1-k). stu. ed. 3.50 *(978-0-570-05111-4(8),* 16-1912) Concordia Publishing Hse.
Dios Me Dio un Mundo: Quarter 1, Level 1. (Caminando con Jesus (Walking with Jesus) Series B).Tr. of God Gave Me a World. (SPA.). (J). (gr. -1-k). stu. ed. 3.50 *(978-0-570-05110-7(X),* 16-1911) Concordia Publishing Hse.
Dios Prepara a Su Pueblo: Quarter 2, Level 3. (Caminando con Jesus (Walking with Jesus) Series B).Tr. of God Prepares His People. (SPA.). (J). (gr. 3-4). stu. ed. 3.50 *(978-0-570-05153-4(3),* 16-3912) Concordia Publishing Hse.
Ellis, Colette. Credo: I Believe. Avakoff, Caroline, ed. Pelicano, Christopher J., illus. 2009. (Faith & Life Ser.). 121p. (J). pap. 7.95 *(978-0-89870-898-1(2))* Ignatius Pr.
El Espiritu Santo (The Holy Spirit) Quarter 1, Level 3. (Caminando con Jesus (Walking with Jesus) Series A). (SPA.). (J). (gr. 3-4). stu. ed. 3.50 *(978-0-570-05149-7(5),* 16-3811) Concordia Publishing Hse.
Evans, Gwydion, et al. Ar Dim Duw: Cyfres o Sesiynau Sydd Yn Defnyddio Byd Chwaraeon I Son Am y Ffydd Gristnogol. 2005. (WEL., Illus.). 24p. pap. *(978-1-85994-036-5(6))* Cyhoeddiadau'r Gair.
Faith First Development Team, creator. Faith First Grade 6. 2006. (Illus.). 336p. per. 12.50 *(978-0-7829-0928-9(0))* RCL Benziger Publishing.
Fears, Melissa. Thank God It's Sunday. 2004. (J). per. 6.95 *(978-0-89315-413-4(X))* Lambert Bk. Hse., Inc.
Fischer, Carl. Days of Faith: Student Planner & Assignment Book 2004-2005. Connelly, Gwen & Holmberg, Ansgar, illus. 2004. 108p. (J). spiral bd. 3.25 *(978-0-89837-199-4(6),* 9805) Pflaum Publishing Group.
Fogg, Paul. I Know That God Loves Me. 2008. (Illus.). 32p. pap. 9.95 *(978-0-9814878-3-0(1))* Little Hands Bk. Co., LLC.
Forsyth-Vail, Gail. Love & Help. 2016. (J). pap. ***(978-1-55896-788-5(5))*** Unitarian Universalist Assn.
Gallery, Philip D. Can You Find Saints? Introducing Your Child to Holy Men & Women. Harlow, Janet L., tr. Harlow, Janet L., illus. 2003. (J). (ENG.). 41p. (gr. 2-4). 16.99 *(978-0-86716-487-9(5));* 40p. *(978-2-89507-437-3(2))* Franciscan Media.
God Is Creator. 2.99 *(978-0-7847-0851-4(7))* Standard Publishing.
God Is Eternal. 2.99 *(978-0-7847-0854-5(1))* Standard Publishing.
God Is Ever-Present. 2.99 *(978-0-7847-0855-2(X))* Standard Publishing.
Gold Mine of Crafts for Kids C. 2004. pap. 16.99 *(978-0-8307-2626-4(8))* Gospel Light Pubns.
Gosselin, Suzanne Hadley. Faithgirlz Handbook, Updated & Expanded: How to Let Your Faith Shine Through, 1 vol. 2016. (Faithgirlz Ser.). (ENG.). 144p. (J). pap. 7.99 *(978-0-310-75440-4(2))* Zonderkidz.
Grebing, Diane J. & Haas, Jane Elling. Bible Craft Potpourri: 50 Clever Bible Craft Projects. 2007. (Illus.). 62p. pap. 10.99 *(978-0-7586-1309-7(1))* Concordia Publishing Hse.
Hakowski, Maryann. Vine & Branches. St. George, Carolyn, illus. 2003. (Resources for Youth Retreats Ser.: Vol. 1). 160p. (YA). (gr. 7-12). spiral bd. 24.95 *(978-0-88489-255-7(7))* St. Mary's Pr. of MN.
—Vine & Branches, Vol. 2. Stamschror, Robert P., ed. St. George, Carolyn, illus. 2003. (Resources for Youth Retreats Ser.: Vol. 2). 168p. (YA). (gr. 7-12). spiral bd. 24.95 *(978-0-88489-278-6(6))* St. Mary's Pr. of MN.
Hatfield, Tyrel & Hatfield, Justin. Righteous Roundup: Wanted: Righteous children of God. Hatfield, Tyrel, illus. 2008. (Illus.). (J). cd-rom 99.00 *(978-0-9766703-6-0(4))* Little Acorn LLC.
Holford, Karen. I Miss Grandpa: A Story to Help Your Child Understand Death — & Eternal Life. 2004. (Illus.). 32p. (J). 4.97 *(978-0-8163-2030-1(6))* Pacific Pr. Publishing Assn.
Hosch, Jenifer. 50 Bible Activities for Creative Minds. 2004. 64p. (gr. 3-6). 10.99 *(978-0-7586-0129-2(8))* Concordia Publishing Hse.
Hunt, Jeanne. Celebrating Saints & Seasons: Hundreds of Activities for Catholic Children. 2010. (ENG.). 192p. pap. 12.99 *(978-0-86716-959-1(1))* Franciscan Media.
James, Steven. 24 Tandem Bible Hero Story Scripts for Children's Ministry. 2006. (Illus.). 96p. (YA). pap. 10.99 *(978-0-7847-1321-1(9),* 04312) Standard Publishing.
—24 Tandem Bible Story Scripts for Children's Ministry. 2006. 96p. (YA). pap. 15.99 *(978-0-7847-1320-4(0),* 42038) Standard Publishing.
Jarrell, Jane & Saathoff, Deborah. Off to Work We Go. 2004. 50p. (gr. -1-18). pap., act. bk. ed. 6.99 *(978-0-8054-0823-2(1))* B&H Publishing Group.
Julio, Susan & Schooler, Cindy. Interactive Bible Bulletin Boards: Winter. 2004. 128p. (J). pap. 13.95 *(978-1-885358-33-2(4),* RB36712) Rainbow Pubs. & Legacy Pr.
Karyn, Henley. I Learn about God. 2004. pap. 2.99 *(978-0-7847-0651-0(4))* Standard Publishing.
Kawasaki, Shauna Mooney, illus. My Family Can Be Forever: Sharing Time Activities. 2003. 62p. (J). pap. *(978-1-59038-232-5(3))* Deseret Bk. Co.
Kennedy, Nancy B. Make It, Shake It, Mix It Up: 44 Bible Stories Brought to Life with Science. Cannell, Jon, illus. 2008. 61p. pap. 10.99 *(978-0-7586-1334-9(2))* Concordia Publishing Hse.
Larkin, Jean, ed. Celebrate with Jesus: A Child's Book of the Sacraments. Swisher, Elizabeth et al, illus. 2007. 32p. pap. 3.95 *(978-1-933178-67-7(1))* Pflaum Publishing Group.
Lewis, Carole. First Place Group Starter Kit. 2004. 179.99 *(978-0-8307-3369-9(8),* Gospel Light) Gospel Light Pubns.
Little KidsTime 1: Bible Story Pictures. 2004. 104p. 19.99 *(978-0-8307-2773-5(6),* Gospel Light) Gospel Light Pubns.
McMickle, Marvin Andrew. Profiles in Black: Phat Facts for Teens. Elster, Jean Alicia, ed. 2008. (Illus.). 176p. (J). pap. 22.00 *(978-0-8170-1508-4(6))* Judson Pr.
Meloche, Renee Taft. Heroes for Young Readers Activity Guide for Books 1-4: Educational & Character-Building Lessons for Children. 2006. (Heroes for Young Readers Ser.). (Illus.). 90p. per. 12.99 *(978-1-57658-367-8(8))* YWAM Publishing.
Millett, Melanie. Teeny Tiny Talks: Junior Primary: I Will Follow God's Plan for Me, Vol. 1. Millett, Melanie, illus. 2004. (Illus.). (J). per. 12.95 *(978-1-55517-778-2(6),* Cedar Fort, Inc.) Cedar Fort, Inc./CFI Distribution.
Mitzo Thompson, Kim, et al. Bible ABCs Fun Activity Book. 2017. (ENG.). 32p. (J). pap. 4.99 ***(978-1-68322-194-4(X))*** Barbour Publishing, Inc.
National Consultants for Education, creator. The Treasure of My Catholic Faith: 2nd Grade. 2004. (Treasure of My Catholic Faith Ser.: No. 2). (Illus.). 240p. pap. 14.95 *(978-0-9743661-4-2(5))* Circle Pr.
—The Treasure of My Catholic Faith: 4th Grade. 2004. (Treasure of My Catholic Faith Ser.: No. 4). (Illus.). 272p. pap. 14.95 *(978-0-9743661-6-6(1))* Circle Pr.
—The Treasure of My Catholic Faith: 5th Grade. 2004. (Treasure of My Catholic Faith Ser.: No. 5). (Illus.). 295p. pap. 14.95 *(978-0-9743661-7-3(X))* Circle Pr.
—The Treasure of My Catholic Faith: 6th Grade. 2004. (Treasure of My Catholic Faith Ser.: No. 6). (Illus.). 295p. pap. 14.95 *(978-0-9743661-8-0(8))* Circle Pr.
Noonan, Joseph. What Is My Vocation? Student Edition. 2005. 7.00 net. *(978-0-9774733-0-4(9))* Univ. St. Mary of the Lake, Mundelein Seminary.
Nystrom, Jennifer. Favorite Bible Children: Grades 1 & 2. 2004. (Illus.). 96p. (J). (gr. 1-2). pap. 11.95 *(978-1-885358-77-6(6))* Rainbow Pubs. & Legacy Pr.
—Favorite Bible Children: Grades 3 & 4. 2004. (Illus.). 96p. (J). (gr. 3-4). pap. 11.95 *(978-1-885358-78-3(4))* Rainbow Pubs. & Legacy Pr.
Olla, Debbie. Confirmation Certificate. 2004. (Illus.). (J). pap. 9.95 *(978-0-937997-76-5(5),* 504510) Pflaum Publishing Group.
Pearson, Mary R. Bible Learning Games: Reproducible Activities. 2004. (Illus.). 64p. (J). pap. 9.95 *(978-0-937282-72-4(3),* RB36251); (gr. -1-k). pap. 9.95 *(978-0-937282-73-1(1),* RB36252); (gr. 1-2). pap. 9.95 *(978-0-937282-74-8(X),* RB36253); (gr. 3-4). pap. 9.95 *(978-0-937282-75-5(8),* RB36254) Rainbow Pubs. & Legacy Pr.
El Pecado (Sin) Quarter 1, Level 2. (Caminando con Jesus (Walking with Jesus) Series B). (SPA.). (J). (gr. 1-2). stu. ed. 3.50 *(978-0-570-05135-0(5),* 16-2911) Concordia Publishing Hse.
Pitcher, Amy B. The Big Book of Bible Lessons for Crafty Kids. 2015. (Big Bks.). (ENG., Illus.). 224p. (J). (gr. 1-6). pap. 29.99 *(978-0-8307-4400-8(2))* Gospel Light Pubns.
Plum, Joan Ensor & Plum, Paul S. I Am Special: Jesus Is Our Friend. Most, Andee, illus. 5th ed. 2007. 112p. (J). (gr. k-1). per. 11.95 *(978-1-59276-296-5(4))* Our Sunday Visitor, Publishing Div.
Plum, Paul & Plum, Joanensor. Ias 3 Year Old Religious Education Program. 2005. (J). bds. 13.95 *(978-1-59276-087-9(2))* Our Sunday Visitor, Publishing Div.
Power Twins Handbook Volume One. 2006. (J). spiral bd. *(978-0-9742355-1-6(2))* Brda, Tracy.
Rainbow Publishers Staff. Bible Explorer: 52 Week Bible Study. 2004. (Illus.). 64p. (J). (gr. 1-3). pap. 9.95 *(978-0-937282-76-2(6),* RB36181) Rainbow Pubs. & Legacy Pr.
—Coloring Plus Activities: God's Promises. 2004. (Illus.). 64p. (J). (gr. -1-3). pap. 9.95 *(978-0-937282-49-6(9),* RB37165) Rainbow Pubs. & Legacy Pr.
—Coloring Plus Activities: Heroes of the Bible. 2004. (Illus.). 64p. (J). (gr. -1-3). pap. 9.95 *(978-0-937282-47-2(2),* RB37163) Rainbow Pubs. & Legacy Pr.
—Learning Adventures! Summer. 2004. (Learning Adventures! Ser.). (Illus.). 64p. (J). pap. 9.95 *(978-1-885358-14-1(8),* RB36314) Rainbow Pubs. & Legacy Pr.
—Learning Adventures! Winter. 2004. (Learning Adventures! Ser.). (Illus.). 64p. (J). pap. 9.95 *(978-1-885358-12-7(1),* RB36312) Rainbow Pubs. & Legacy Pr.
Rashad, Girmen. How Does God See Me? David, Amor, illus. 2008. (Little Christian Ser.). 24p. 9.99 *(978-0-9819100-0-0(9))* Elkarez Publishing Co.

Rhydderch, Gwyn, et al. Iesu'r Ffrind: 16 Sesiwn Yn Cyflwyno Bywyd Iesu Ar Gyfer Plant Cynradd Yn Seiliedig Ar Efengyl Luc. 2005. (WEL., Illus.). 120p. pap. *(978-1-85994-007-5(2))* Cyhoeddiadau'r Gair.
Roberts, Catrin, et al. Mawredd Mawr Moses! 16 Sesiwn Beiblaidd Ar Gyfer Clwb Plant Neu'r Ysgol Sul. 2005. (WEL., Illus.). 76p. pap. *(978-1-85994-034-1(X))* Cyhoeddiadau'r Gair.
Rock, Lois, et al. Beibl y Plant Lleiaf. 2005. (WEL., Illus.). 230p. *(978-1-85994-514-8(7))* Cyhoeddiadau'r Gair.
Rossel, Seymour. Torah Portion-by-Portion. 2007. (Illus.). 368p. (J). pap. 15.95 *(978-1-891662-94-2(5))* Torah Aura Productions.
Rostrom, Laura Lee. My First Book of Mormon Activity Book. 2012. pap. 3.99 *(978-1-59955-958-2(7))* Cedar Fort, Inc./CFI Distribution.
Savitskas, Margaret. Totally Lent! A Kid's Journey to Easter 2006. Larkin, Jean K., ed. 2005. (Illus.). 64p. (J). 5.95 *(978-1-933178-25-7(6),* 3576) Pflaum Publishing Group.
Savitskas, Margaret & Behe, Mary. Totally Lent! A Child's Journey to Easter 2006. Larkin, Jean K., ed. 2005. (Illus.). 64p. (J). 5.95 *(978-1-933178-26-4(4),* 3586) Pflaum Publishing Group.
Schippe, Cullen & Cannizzo, Karen, eds. Learning How to Live: Grade 4, 6 bks. 2005. (Faith Activities for Catholic Kids Ser.). (Illus.). 32p. (J). (gr. 3-5). pap. 6.95 *(978-1-933178-18-9(3),* 2804) Pflaum Publishing Group.
Schlegl, William. Bible Alphabet Puzzles. 2006. (Illus.). 64p. pap. 10.99 *(978-0-7586-1300-4(8))* Concordia Publishing Hse.
School of the Bible for Kids: The Most High God. 2003. (ENG & GER.). 238p. ring bd. 79.95 *(978-0-9767647-3-1(3))* Kids in Ministry International.
Sewell, Elisabeth. Bible Activity Book. 2010. (ENG., Illus.). 38p. (J). pap. 8.00 *(978-0-7152-0907-3(8))* Saint Andrew Pr., Ltd. GBR. Dist: Westminster John Knox Pr.
Shanddaramon. A Pagan Book of ABCs. 2009. 60p. pap. 24.95 *(978-0-557-09532-2(8))* Lulu Pr., Inc.
Sharer, Avigail. Here, There, Everywhere: Kids' True Stories about Finding Hashem in Their Lives. 2012. 159p. (J). *(978-1-4226-1179-1(5))* Mesorah Pubns., Ltd.
Silverstru, Emil. The Cave Book. 2008. 80p. (J). 15.99 *(978-0-89051-496-2(8))* Master Bks.
Sonharvest County Fair Starter. 2004. pap. 49.99 *(978-0-8307-3008-7(7))* Gospel Light Pubns.
Soul Survivor Guide to Service Projects. 2004. 96p. 19.99 *(978-0-8307-3529-7(1),* Gospel Light) Gospel Light Pubns.
Soul Survivor Guide to Youth Ministry. 2004. 96p. 19.99 *(978-0-8307-3530-3(5),* Gospel Light) Gospel Light Pubns.
Soul Survivor Prayer Ministry How to Pray for Others. 2004. 72p. 5.99 *(978-0-8307-3527-3(5),* Gospel Light) Gospel Light Pubns.
Stobaugh, James. Skills for Literary Analysis Student: Encouraging Thoughtful Christians to be World Changers. 2005. (Broadman & Holman Literature Ser.). 272p. stu. ed. 24.99 *(978-0-8054-5897-8(2))* B&H Publishing Group.
Stohs, Anita Reith. Praise God with Paper Cups: 45 Easy Bible Crafts; Grades 1-5. Koehler, Ed, illus. 2005. (CPH Teaching Resource Ser.). 64p. pap. 10.99 *(978-0-7586-0842-0(X))* Concordia Publishing Hse.
Story Cards - Year 1. 2003. (Story Hour Ser.). (Illus.). 5.95 *(978-1-56212-346-8(7),* 001655) Faith Alive Christian Resources.
Story Cards - Year 2. 2003. (Story Hour Ser.). (Illus.). 5.95 *(978-1-56212-409-0(9),* 001665) Faith Alive Christian Resources.
Stroh, Debbie & Boston, Vicki. Christ's Kids Create: Volume 1. 2006. (CPH Teaching Resource Ser.). (Illus.). 64p. pap. 10.99 *(978-0-7586-1106-2(4))* Concordia Publishing Hse.
Sunflower Education Staff. A Golden Thread. 2012. 54p. pap. 11.95 *(978-1-937166-13-7(9))* Sunflower Education.
Thompson, Kim Mitzo, et al. My First Bible Color & Trace Book. 2014. (I'm Learning the Bible Activity Book Ser.). (ENG.). 96p. (J). pap. 12.99 *(978-1-63058-444-3(4))* Barbour Publishing, Inc.
—My First Bible Cut & Glue Book. 2014. (I'm Learning the Bible Activity Book Ser.). (ENG.). 96p. (J). pap. 12.99 *(978-1-63058-445-0(2))* Barbour Publishing, Inc.
Thurman, Debbie. Sheer Faith: A Teen's Journey to Godly Growth. 2004. 112p. pap. 10.95 *(978-0-9676289-3-6(8))* Cedar Hse. Pubs.
Trammell, Fredi. Journey Through the Bible for Kids. 2009. (J). pap. *(978-1-61623-151-4(3))* Independent Pub.
Tyrtania, Joachim & Hemrich-Skomer, Denise. Together Time: Cycle A. 2007. (Illus.). 80p. per. 10.95 *(978-0-9787087-2-6(5))* Bound by Grace Pr., LLC.
Vacation Bible School - Look & Do Stories. 2004. (Vacation Bible School Ser.). (Illus.). 64p. (J). 9.95 *(978-1-885358-02-8(4))* Rainbow Pubs. & Legacy Pr.
Vaisey, Gill & Lewis, Siân. William Booth: Cristion Arbennig Iawn. 2005. (WEL., Illus.). 28p. pap. *(978-1-85644-620-4(4))* CAA.
Washington, Linda & Dall, Jeanette. Favorite Bible Children: Ages 2 & 3. 2004. (Illus.). 96p. (J). pap. 11.95 *(978-1-885358-75-2(X))* Rainbow Pubs. & Legacy Pr.
—Favorite Bible Children: Ages 4 & 5. 2004. (Illus.). 96p. (J). pap. 11.95 *(978-1-885358-76-9(8))* Rainbow Pubs. & Legacy Pr.
Wean, Sarah. Teach Them to Your Children: An Alphabet of Biblical Poems, Verses, & Stories. Sanford, Lori Hood, illus. 2006. 56p. (J). 17.00 *(978-0-9787559-5-9(2))* Vision Forum, Inc., The.
Williamson, Nancy. 52 Ideas for Special Days. 2004. (Fifty-Two Ways Ser.). (Illus.). 64p. (J). (gr. -1-7). pap. 9.95 *(978-0-937282-01-4(4),* RB36108) Rainbow Pubs. & Legacy Pr.
Williamson, Nancy. 52 Bible Drills & Quizzes. 2004. (Fifty-Two Ways Ser.). (Illus.). 64p. (J). (gr. -1-7). pap. 9.95 *(978-0-937282-66-3(9),* RB36168) Rainbow Pubs. & Legacy Pr.
—52 Games That Teach the Bible. 2004. (Fifty-Two Ways Ser.). (Illus.). 64p. (J). (gr. -1-7). pap. 9.95 *(978-0-937282-64-9(2),* RB36166) Rainbow Pubs. & Legacy Pr.
—52 Ways to Teach Bible Reading. 2004. (Fifty-Two Ways Ser.). (Illus.). 64p. (J). (gr. -1-7). pap. 9.95 *(978-0-937282-63-2(4),* RB36106) Rainbow Pubs. & Legacy Pr.
—52 Ways to Teach Missions. 2004. (Fifty-Two Ways Ser.). (Illus.). 64p. (J). (gr. -1-7). pap. 9.95 *(978-0-937282-67-0(7),* RB36169) Rainbow Pubs. & Legacy Pr.
—52 Ways to Teach Stewardship. 2004. (Fifty-Two Ways Ser.). (Illus.). 64p. (J). (gr. -1-7). pap. 9.95 *(978-1-885358-16-5(4),* RB36170) Rainbow Pubs. & Legacy Pr.
Wonderfully Made: God's Plan for Growing Up. (J). (gr. 2-3). 6.99 *(978-1-57153-301-2(X))* Curriculum Publishing, Presbyterian Church (U. S. A.).
Woodfield, Elaine. Stories of the Saints V1, 4 vols. Staggenborg, Kim, illus. 2009. (J). pap. 13.95 *(978-0-9788376-8-6(1))* Catholic Heritage Curricula.
—Stories of the Saints V2, 4 vols. Staggenborg, Kim, illus. 2009. (J). pap. 0.00 *(978-0-9788376-9-3(X))* Catholic Heritage Curricula.
Zondervan Bibles Staff. The Story Trading Cards - For Preschool: Pre-K Through Grade 2, 1 vol. 2011. (Story Ser.). (ENG.). 32p. (J). 4.99 *(978-0-310-72025-6(7))* Zonderkidz.

RELIGIOUS FESTIVALS
see Fasts and Feasts

RELIGIOUS FREEDOM
see Freedom of Religion

RELIGIOUS HISTORY
see Church History

RELIGIOUS LIBERTY
see Freedom of Religion

RELIGIOUS LITERATURE
see also Bible As Literature; Catholic Literature
Attinger, Billy, illus. Baby's First Little Book of Prayers. gif. ed. 2003. (Wee Witness Ser.). 32p. (J). 7.99 *(978-0-7369-1185-6(5))* Harvest Hse. Pubs.
Joslin, Mary. Bible Promises for a Little Boy. Mhasane, Ruchi, illus. 2014. (ENG.). 32p. (J). (gr. -1-2). 9.99 *(978-0-7459-6404-1(4))* Lion Hudson PLC GBR. Dist: Independent Pubs. Group.
—Bible Promises for a Little Girl. Mhasane, Ruchi, illus. 2014. (ENG.). 32p. (J). (gr. -1-2). 9.99 *(978-0-7459-6405-8(2))* Lion Hudson PLC GBR. Dist: Independent Pubs. Group.
McLaughlin, Edith M. & Curtis, T. Adrian, eds. American Cardinal Readers Book One, bk. 1. 2014. (American Cardinal Reader Ser.: 1). (ENG., Illus.). 184p. (J). (gr. k-2). reprint ed. 16.95 *(978-0-911845-36-5(4),* Neumann Pr.) TAN Bks.
—American Cardinal Readers Book Three, Bk. 3. 2014. (American Cardinal Reader Ser.: 3). (ENG., Illus.). 256p. (J). (gr. 1-3). reprint ed. 19.95 *(978-0-911845-38-9(0),* Neumann Pr.) TAN Bks.
—American Cardinal Readers Book Two, Bk. 2. 2014. (American Cardinal Reader Ser.: 2). (ENG., Illus.). 224p. (J). (gr. k-2). reprint ed. 18.95 *(978-0-911845-37-2(2),* Neumann Pr.) TAN Bks.
—American Cardinal Readers Primer: Primer. 2014. (ENG., Illus.). 104p. (J). (gr. k-1). reprint ed. 16.95 *(978-0-911845-52-5(6),* Neumann Pr.) TAN Bks.

RELIGIOUS MUSIC
see Church Music

RELIGIOUS ORDERS
see Monasticism and Religious Orders

RELIGIOUS PAINTING
see Christian Art and Symbolism

RELIGIOUS POETRY
see also Carols; Hymns
Appelt, Kathi. I See the Moon. Jenkins, Reid Debra, illus. 2009. (ENG.). 12p. (J). (gr. -1). 8.00 *(978-0-8028-5358-5(7),* Eerdmans Bks For Young Readers) Eerdmans, William B. Publishing Co.
—I See the Moon. Jenkins, Debra Reid, illus. 2004. 24p. (J). (gr. -1-2). 15.00 *(978-0-8028-5118-5(5))* Eerdmans, William B. Publishing Co.
Bartlett, Irene. The Old Testament: Bible Poems for Children. 2007. (Illus.). 92p. per. *(978-1-84748-204-4(X))* Athena Pr.
Busch, Melinda Kay. The Fiery Furnace. Koehler, Ed, illus. 2004. (Arch Bks.). 16p. (J). (gr. k-4). 1.99 *(978-0-7586-0479-8(3))* Concordia Publishing Hse.
Cotner, June. House Blessings: Prayers, Poems, & Toasts Celebrating Home & Family. 2005. (ENG., Illus.). 164p. (gr. 8-17). 15.95 *(978-0-9748486-0-0(3))* becker&mayer! books.
Draper, Diane E. Expressions from the Experience: Christian Poetry & Short Inspirations. 2003. 87p. (YA). pap. 9.95 *(978-0-7414-1482-3(1))* Infinity Publishing.
Fbs: 1ST & 2ND GRADERS' MEMORY VERSES. (J). (gr. 1-2). *(978-0-633-00372-2(7))* LifeWay Christian Resources.
Fulton, Stephen (Abdul-Hakeem). 110 Islamic Poems for Children. 2007. 41p. pap. 8.95 *(978-0-7414-3963-5(8))* Infinity Publishing.
Krug, Christine Sugultan. Favorite Action Bible Verses. 2003. (Illus.). 48p. (gr. -1-k). 10.99 *(978-0-7586-0228-2(6))* Concordia Publishing Hse.
McCauley, Marlene. Song of Kateri: Princess of the Eucharist. McCauley, R. Allan, ed. McCauley, Marlene & Children's Art-Friends of Kateri, illus. unabr. ed. 2005. 300p. (YA). (gr. 4-7). per. 14.95 *(978-0-9633633-2-9(8))* Grace Hse. Publishing.
Paterson, Katherine. Giving Thanks: Poems, Prayers, & Praise Songs of Thanksgiving. Dalton, Pamela, illus. 2013. (ENG.). 56p. (J). (gr. k-17). 18.99 *(978-1-4521-1339-5(4))* Chronicle Bks. LLC.
Reese, Amy, illus. Illustrated Psalms of Praise: Psalmos de Alabanza Ilustrados. 2005. (SPA & ENG.). 64p. (J). 16.95 *(978-1-56854-561-5(4))* Liturgy Training Pubns.
Weisheit, Eldon. 150 Psalms for Teens. 2003. 160p. (YA). 9.49 *(978-0-7586-0120-9(4))* Concordia Publishing Hse.

REMBRANDT HARMENSZOON VAN RIJN, 1606-1669
Bailer, Darice. Rembrandt. Morrow, J. T., illus. 2014. (World's Greatest Artists Ser.). (ENG.). 24p. (J). (gr. 2-5). 28.50 *(978-1-62687-354-4(2),* 207194) Child's World, Inc., The.
Blaisdell, Molly. Rembrandt & the Boy Who Drew Dogs: A Story about Rembrandt van Rijn. Lane, Nancy, illus. 2008. (ENG.). 32p. (J). (gr. k-3). 14.99 *(978-0-7641-6097-4(4))* Barron's Educational Series, Inc.
Dunn, Mary. My Adventure with Rembrandt. 2006. 44p. (J). 8.99 *(978-1-59092-463-1(0))* Blue Forge Pr.
Klein, Adam G. Rembrandt, 1 vol. 2007. (Great Artists Set 2 Ser.). (ENG., Illus.). 32p. (gr. -1-3). 27.07 *(978-1-59679-735-2(5),* Checkerboard Library) ABDO Publishing Co.
Mason, Antony & Rembrandt Harmenszoon van Rijn. Rembrandt. 2004. (Lives of the Artists Ser.). (Illus.). 48p. (gr. 5-12). lib. bdg. 31.00 *(978-0-8368-5651-4(1),* 1233346, Gareth Stevens Secondary Library) Stevens, Gareth Publishing LLLP.
Mis, Melody S. Rembrandt. 2009. (Meet the Artist Ser.). 24p. (gr. 2-3). 42.50 *(978-1-61514-632-1(6),* PowerKids Pr.) Rosen Publishing Group, Inc., The.
Pescio, Claudio. Rembrandt. 2008. (Art Masters Ser.). 64p. (YA). (gr. 6-18). lib. bdg. 24.95 net. *(978-1-934545-02-7(3))* Oliver Pr., Inc.
Roberts, Russell. Rembrandt. 2008. (Art Profiles for Kids Ser.). (Illus.). 48p. (YA). (gr. 4-7). lib. bdg. 29.95 *(978-1-58415-710-6(0))* Mitchell Lane Pubs., Inc.
Venezia, Mike. Rembrandt. Venezia, Mike, illus. rev. ed. 2015. (Getting to Know the World's Greatest Artists Ser.). (ENG., Illus.). 40p. (J). pap. 7.95 *(978-0-531-21290-5(4))* Scholastic Library Publishing.

REMEDIAL READING
see Reading—Remedial Teaching

REMINGTON, FREDERIC, 1861-1909
Mattern, Joanne. Frederic Remington, 1 vol. 2005. (Great Artists Set 1 Ser.). (ENG., Illus.). 32p. (gr. k-6). 27.07 *(978-1-59197-848-0(3),* Checkerboard Library) ABDO Publishing Co.
Osmundson, Linda L. Frederic Remington's Art, 1 vol. 2012. (How the West Was Drawn Ser.). (ENG., Illus.). 32p. (J). (gr. k-7). 16.99 *(978-1-4556-1506-3(4))* Pelican Publishing Co., Inc.
Plain, Nancy. Frederic Remington: Artist of the American West. 2003. (Historical American Biographies Ser.). (Illus.). 160p. (J). (gr. 6-12). lib. bdg. 27.94 *(978-0-7660-1975-1(6))* Enslow Pubs., Inc.
Venezia, Mike. Frederic Remington. Venezia, Mike, illus. 2003. (Getting to Know the World's Greatest Artists Ser.). (ENG., Illus.). 32p. (J). (gr. 3-4). pap. 6.95 *(978-0-516-27812-4(6),* Children's Pr.) Scholastic Library Publishing.

REMUS, UNCLE (FICTITIOUS CHARACTER)—FICTION
Cloke, Rene. My Best Brer Rabbit Stories. 2012. (ENG., Illus.). 80p. 15.00 *(978-1-84135-806-2(1))* Award Pubns. Ltd. GBR. Dist: Parkwest Pubns., Inc.
Harris, Joel Chandler. Nights with Uncle Remus. 2008. 288p. 29.95 *(978-1-60664-915-2(9));* pap. 15.95 *(978-1-60664-035-7(6))* Aegypan.
—Uncle Remus: His Songs & His Sayings. 265p. (J). 18.00 *(978-0-9645990-0-0(7))* Historic Pr.-South.

RENAISSANCE
see also Art, Renaissance; Civilization, Medieval; Humanism; Literature, Medieval; Middle Ages
Benchmark Education Company, LLC Staff, compiled by. The Renaissance: Theme Set. 2006. (J). 135.00 *(978-1-4108-7142-8(8))* Benchmark Education Co.
Boekhoff, P. M. & Kallen, Stuart A. The Italian Renaissance. 2003. (History of the World Ser.). (Illus.). 48p. (J). (gr. 3-5). 23.70 *(978-0-7377-1036-6(5),* Kidhaven) Cengage Gale.
Carr, Simonetta. Michelangelo for Kids: His Life & Ideas, with 21 Activities. 2016. (For Kids Ser.). (ENG., Illus.). 144p. (J). (gr. 4). pap. 18.99 *(978-1-61373-193-2(0))* Chicago Review Pr., Inc.
Currie, Stephen. The Renaissance. 2012. (Illus.). 96p. (YA). lib. bdg. *(978-1-60152-189-7(8))* ReferencePoint Pr., Inc.
Day, Nancy. Your Travel Guide to Renaissance Europe. 2005. (Passport to History Ser.). (Illus.). 96p. (gr. 5-8). lib. bdg. 26.50 *(978-0-8225-3080-0(5))* Lerner Publishing Group.
Elliott, Lynne. Exploration in the Renaissance. 2009. (Renaissance World Ser.). (ENG., Illus.). 32p. (J). (gr. 5-8). pap. *(978-0-7787-4613-3(5));* lib. bdg. *(978-0-7787-4593-8(7))* Crabtree Publishing Co.
—The Renaissance in Europe. 2009. (Renaissance World Ser.). (ENG., Illus.). 32p. (J). (gr. 5-8). pap. *(978-0-7787-4611-9(9));* lib. bdg. *(978-0-7787-4591-4(0))* Crabtree Publishing Co.
Flatt, Lizann. Cities & Statecraft in the Renaissance. 2009. (Renaissance World Ser.). (ENG.). 32p. (J). (gr. 6-9). pap. *(978-0-7787-4615-7(1));* (Illus.). (gr. 5-7). *(978-0-7787-4595-2(3))* Crabtree Publishing Co.
—Religion in the Renaissance. 2009. (ENG., Illus.). 32p. (J). (gr. 5-7). *(978-0-7787-4597-6(X));* (gr. 6-9). pap. *(978-0-7787-4617-1(8))* Crabtree Publishing Co.
George, Enzo. The Renaissance. 2016. (Primary Sources in World History Ser.). (ENG.). 48p. (YA). (gr. 6-6). 31.36 *(978-1-5026-1809-2(5))* Cavendish Square Publishing.
Hancock, Lee. Lorenzo de' Medici: Florence's Great Leader & Patron of the Arts. (Rulers, Scholars, & Artists of the Renaissance Ser.). 112p. 2009. (gr. 5-8). 66.50 *(978-1-60852-942-1(8),* Rosen Reference) 2004. (Illus.). (J). lib. bdg. 34.60 *(978-1-4042-0315-0(X))* Rosen Publishing Group, Inc., The.
Herold, Vickey. Science During the Renaissance. 2006. (J). pap. *(978-1-4108-6464-2(2))* Benchmark Education Co.
Hinds, Kathryn. The Countryside. 2004. (Life in the Roman Empire Ser.). (Illus.). 80p. (gr. 6). 34.21 *(978-0-7614-1656-2(0),* Benchmark Bks.) Marshall Cavendish Corp.
—Everyday Life in the Renaissance. 2009. (Everyday Life in... Ser.). 336p. (gr. 6-18). 42.79 *(978-0-7614-4483-1(1))* Marshall Cavendish Corp.
Hirsch, E. D., Jr., ed. The Renaissance, Level 5. 2003. tchr. ed. 9.95 *(978-0-7690-5074-4(3));* stu. ed. 49.95 *(978-0-7690-2853-8(5))* Pearson Learning.
Huntley, Theresa. Women in the Renaissance. 2009. (ENG., Illus.). 32p. (J). (gr. 5-7). *(978-0-7787-4598-3(8));* (gr. 6-9). pap. *(978-0-7787-4618-8(6))* Crabtree Publishing Co.
Kubesh, Katie & Belletto, Kimm. HOCPP 1056 Renaissance. 2006. spiral bd. 18.50 *(978-1-60308-056-9(2))* In the Hands of a Child.
Kuligowski, Stephanie. The Renaissance: A Rebirth of Culture, 1 vol. 2012. (Primary Source Readers Ser.). (ENG.). 32p. (J). (gr. 5-5). pap. 8.99 *(978-1-4333-5007-8(6))* Teacher Created Materials, Inc.
MacDonald, Fiona. You Wouldn't Want to Be a Crusader! A War You'd Rather Not Fight. Bergin, Mark, illus. 2005. (You Wouldn't Want to... Ser.). (ENG.). 32p. (J). (gr. 2-5). 29.00 *(978-0-531-12412-3(6));* pap. 9.95 *(978-0-531-12392-8(8))* Scholastic Library Publishing. (Watts, Franklin).
Morris, Neil. Everyday Life in the Renaissance. 2008. (Uncovering History Ser.). (ENG., Illus.). 48p. (J). (gr. 2-7). 19.95 *(978-88-89272-58-9(9))* McRae Bks. Srl ITA. Dist: Independent Pubs. Group.
Murphy, Lauren. Art & Culture of the Renaissance World. 2010. (Ancient Art & Cultures Ser.). 40p. (YA). (gr. 5-8). lib. bdg., E-Book 53.00 *(978-1-61532-967-0(6))* Rosen Publishing Group, Inc., The.
Murphy, Lauren & Matthews, Rupert. Art & Culture of the Renaissance World. 2010. (Ancient Art & Cultures Ser.). (Illus.). 40p. (J). pap. 11.75 *(978-1-61532-889-5(0));* (YA). (gr. 5-8). lib. bdg. 26.50 *(978-1-4358-3593-1(X))* Rosen Publishing Group, Inc., The. (Rosen Reference).
Phillips, John & National Geographic Kids Staff. Leonardo Da Vinci: The Genius Who Defined the Renaissance. 2008. (National Geographic World History Biographies Ser.). (ENG., Illus.). 64p. (J). (gr. 3-7). pap. 7.99 *(978-1-4263-0248-0(7),* National Geographic Children's Bks.) National Geographic Society.
Platt, Richard. In the Renaissance. Lawrence, David, illus. 2011. (How They Made Things Work! Ser.). 32p. (YA). (gr. 2-5). lib. bdg. 28.50 *(978-1-59771-289-7(2))* Sea-To-Sea Pubns.
Rajczak, Kristen. Renaissance Fairs, 01 vols., 1. 2016. (Role-Playing for Fun & Profit Ser.). (ENG.). 48p. (J). pap. 11.75 *(978-1-4994-3720-1(X),* Rosen Reference) Rosen Publishing Group, Inc., The.
The Renaissance, 1300-1600. 2004. (Stories in History Ser.). (Illus.). 190p. (gr. 6-12). 13.32 *(978-0-618-14224-8(X),* 2-00244) Holt McDougal.
Romanek, Trudee. Great Ideas of the Renaissance. 2009. (Renaissance World Ser.). (ENG., Illus.). 32p. (J). (gr. 5-7). *(978-0-7787-4596-9(1));* (gr. 6-9). pap. *(978-0-7787-4616-4(X))* Crabtree Publishing Co.
Roscoe, Kelly. The Italian & Northern Renaissance. 2017. (Power & Religion in Medieval & Renaissance Times Ser.). 112p. (gr. 14-15). 36.25 ***(978-1-68048-627-8(6),*** Britannica Educational Publishing) Rosen Publishing Group, Inc., The.
Rossi, Renzo. In Renaissance Florence with Leonardo. Baldanzi, Alessandro, illus. 2008. (Come See My City Ser.). 48p. (gr. 4-8). lib. bdg. 28.50 *(978-0-7614-4329-2(0),* Benchmark Bks.) Marshall Cavendish Corp.
Samuels, Charlie. Timeline of the Renaissance. 2010. (History Highlights: A Gareth Stevens Timeline Ser.). (Illus.). 48p. (gr. 6-8). (J). pap. 14.05 *(978-1-4339-3487-2(6));* (YA). lib. bdg. 31.95 *(978-1-4339-3486-5(8))* Stevens, Gareth Publishing LLLP. (Gareth Stevens Secondary Library).
Simpson, Kathleen. Women in the Renaissance: Text Pairs. 2008. (Bridges/Navigators Ser.). (J). (gr. 6). 89.00 *(978-1-4108-8449-7(X))* Benchmark Education Co.
Thomson, Melissa & Dean, Ruth. Women of the Renaissance. 2004. (Women in History Ser.). (ENG., Illus.). 128p. (YA). (gr. 7-10). lib. bdg. 33.45 *(978-1-59018-473-8(4),* Lucent Bks.) Cengage Gale.
Wagner, Heather Lehr. Machiavelli: Renaissance Political Analyst & Author. 2005. (Makers of the Middle Ages & Renaissance Ser.). (Illus.). 136p. (gr. 5-8). lib. bdg. 32.95 *(978-0-7910-8629-2(1),* Chelsea Hse.) Facts On File, Inc.

RENAISSANCE—FICTION
Avi. Murder at Midnight. (ENG.). (J). (gr. 3-7). 2011. 256p. pap. 6.99 *(978-0-545-08091-0(6),* Scholastic Paperbacks) 2009. 272p. 17.99 *(978-0-545-08090-3(8),* Scholastic Pr.) Scholastic, Inc.
Bolognese, Don. The Warhorse. Bolognese, Don, illus. 2010. (ENG., Illus.). 176p. (J). (gr. 5-9). pap. 9.99 *(978-1-4424-2942-0(9),* Simon & Schuster Bks. For Young Readers) Simon & Schuster Bks. For Young Readers.
Cokal, Susann. The Kingdom of Little Wounds. 2013. (ENG., Illus.). 576p. (YA). (gr. 11). 22.99 *(978-0-7636-6694-1(7))* Candlewick Pr.
Grey, Christopher Peter & Grey, Christopher. Leonardo's Shadow: Or, My Astonishing Life As Leonardo Da Vinci's Servant. 2008. (ENG.). 400p. (YA). (gr. 7). pap. 12.99 *(978-1-4169-0544-8(8),* Atheneum Bks. for Young Readers) Simon & Schuster Children's Publishing.
Hoffman, Mary. City of Secrets. (Stravaganza Ser.). (ENG.). (YA). 2010. 416p. (gr. 7). pap. 8.99 *(978-1-59990-451-1(9),* 9781599904511) 2008. 400p. (gr. 5-18). 17.99 *(978-1-59990-202-9(8),* 9781599902029) Bloomsbury Publishing USA. (Bloomsbury USA Childrens).
—City of Ships. 2010. (Stravaganza Ser.). (ENG.). 368p. (YA). (gr. 7-18). 17.99 *(978-1-59990-491-7(8),* 9781599904917, Bloomsbury USA Childrens) Bloomsbury Publishing USA.
—The Falconer's Knot: A Story of Friars, Flirtation & Foul Play. (ENG., Illus.). 304p. (YA). (gr. 7). 2008. pap. 7.99 *(978-1-59990-229-6(X),* 9781599902296) 2007. 16.95 *(978-1-59990-056-8(4),* 9781599900568) Bloomsbury Publishing USA. (Bloomsbury USA Childrens).
—Stravaganza: City of Swords. 2012. (Stravaganza Ser.). (ENG.). 368p. (YA). (gr. 7-12). 18.99 *(978-1-59990-842-7(5),* 9781599908427, Bloomsbury USA Childrens) Bloomsbury Publishing USA.
Marsh, Katherine. Jepp, Who Defied the Stars. 2013. (ENG.). 400p. (J). (gr. 5-9). pap. 9.99 *(978-1-4231-3786-3(8))* Hyperion Pr.
Napoli, Donna Jo. The Smile. 2009. (ENG.). 272p. (YA). (gr. 7-18). 7.99 *(978-0-14-241492-7(1),* Speak) Penguin Young Readers Group.
Osborne, Mary A. Nonna's Book of Mysteries. 2010. (ENG., Illus.). 352p. (gr. 8-17). pap. 16.95 *(978-1-936181-16-2(9))* Lake Street Pr.
Wettersten, Laura. My Faire Lady. 2014. (ENG., Illus.). 352p. (YA). (gr. 7). 17.99 *(978-1-4424-8933-2(2),* Simon & Schuster Bks. For Young Readers) Simon & Schuster Bks. For Young Readers.

RENOIR, AUGUSTE, 1841-1919
Boutan, Mila. Renoir & Me. 2010. (ENG., Illus.). 48p. (J). (gr. 3-7). pap. 17.95 *(978-1-4081-2384-3(3),* 9781408123843, A&C Black) Bloomsbury Publishing Plc GBR. Dist: Macmillan.
Hyde, Margaret E., ed. Renoir for Kids, 1 vol. 2003. (Great Art for Kids Ser.). (ENG., Illus.). 10p. (J). (gr. -1 — 1). bds. 8.95 *(978-1-58980-206-3(3))* Pelican Publishing Co., Inc.

PQR

Kelley, True. Pierre-Auguste Renoir - Paintings That Smile. 2005. (Smart about Art Ser.). (ENG., Illus.). 32p. (J). (gr. k-4). mass mkt. 5.99 (978-0-448-43371-4(0), Grosset & Dunlap) Penguin Young Readers Group.

Klein, Adam G. Pierre-Auguste Renoir, 1 vol. 2007. (Great Artists Set 2 Ser.). (ENG., Illus.). 32p. (gr. -1-3). 27.07 (978-1-59679-736-9(3), Checkerboard Library) ABDO Publishing Co.

Miller, Sabine. Renoir, Vol. 7. 2015. (Great Artists Collection). 64p. (J). (gr. 7). lib. bdg. 23.95 (978-1-4222-3262-0(X)) Mason Crest.

Nichols, Catherine. Pierre-Auguste Renoir. (Primary Source Library of Famous Artists Ser.). 32p. 2009. (gr. 3-4). 42.50 (978-1-60854-104-1(5)) 2006. (Illus.). (J). (gr. -1-3). lib. bdg. 23.95 (978-1-4042-2765-1(2)) Rosen Publishing Group, Inc., The. (PowerKids Pr.).

Sellier, Marie. Renoir's Colors. 2010. (ENG., Illus.). 40p. (J). (gr. -1-k). 16.95 (978-1-60606-003-2(1)) Getty Pubns.

Somervill, Barbara A. Pierre-Auguste Renoir. 2007. (Art Profiles for Kids Ser.). (Illus.). 48p. (YA). (gr. 4-7). lib. bdg. 29.95 (978-1-58415-566-9(3)) Mitchell Lane Pubs., Inc.

Spence, David. The Impressionists: Monet, Cezanne, Renoir, Degas. 2010. (ENG.). 128p. (J). (gr. 4-7). pap. 12.95 (978-1-84696-217-2(X), TickTock Books) Octopus Publishing Group GBR. Dist: Independent Pubs. Group.

—Renoir. 2010. (Great Artists & Their World Ser.). 48p. 32.80 (978-1-84898-317-5(4)) Black Rabbit Bks.

—Renoir: Color y Naturaleza. (Coleccion Grandes Artistas).Tr. of Renoir: Colot & Nature. (SPA.). (YA). (gr. 5-8). 12.76 (978-84-8211-137-7(X)) Celeste Ediciones, S.A. ESP. Dist: Lectorum Pubns., Inc.

Venezia, Mike. Pierre Auguste Renoir. 2016. (Getting to Know the World's Greatest Artists Ser.). (ENG.). 40p. (J). pap. 7.95 (978-0-531-22107-5(5), Children's Pr.) Scholastic Library Publishing.

—Pierre Auguste Renoir (Revised Edition) 2016. (Getting to Know the World's Greatest Artists Ser.). (ENG.). 40p. (J). lib. bdg. 29.00 (978-0-531-21668-2(3), Children's Pr.) Scholastic Library Publishing.

REPAIRING

see also Building—Repair and Reconstruction

Lüsted, Marcia Amidon. For People Who Love to Fix Things. 2016. (Cool Careers Without College Ser.). 00104p. (J). (gr. 7-7). 38.45 (978-1-5081-7284-0(6)) Rosen Publishing Group, Inc., The.

Van Slyke, Marge. Furniture Refinishing in A Class by Yourself. Lambert, Barbara, ed. van der Sterre, Johanna, illus. 2004. 91p. per. 9.95 (978-0-9755548-0-7(8)) Log Cabin Bks.

REPORT WRITING

Abraham, Philip. Language Development Writing Process. 2004. (BrainBuilders Ser.). (ENG.). 48p. (gr. k-4). pap. 5.25 (978-1-4042-8520-0(2)) Rosen Publishing Group, Inc., The.

Arnone, Marilyn P. & Coatney, Sharon. Mac, Information Detective, in ... the Curious Kids & Why Dolphins Visit Curiosity Creek: A Storybook Approach to Introducing Research Skills Picture Book & Educator's Guide Set, 2 vols. 2008. (Illus.). 128p. (C). pap. 40.00 (978-1-59158-498-8(1), LU4981, Libraries Unlimited) ABC-CLIO, LLC.

Asselin, Kristine Carlson. Smart Research Strategies: Finding the Right Sources, 1 vol. 2013. (Research Tool Kit Ser.). (ENG.). 32p. (gr. 3-4). pap. 8.10 (978-1-62065-790-4(2)); pap. 47.70 (978-1-62065-791-1(0)); lib. bdg. 27.32 (978-1-4296-9950-1(7)) Capstone Press of Coughlan Cos. (Fact Finders).

—Think for Yourself: Avoiding Plagiarism. 2013. (Research Tool Kit Ser.). (ENG.). 32p. (gr. 3-4). pap. 47.70 (978-1-62065-793-5(7), Fact Finders); pap. 8.10 (978-1-62065-792-8(9), Fact Finders); lib. bdg. 27.32 (978-1-4296-9951-8(5)) Capstone Press of Coughlan Cos.

Asselin, Kristine Carlson, et al. Research Tool Kit. 2013. (Research Tool Kit Ser.). (ENG.). 32p. (gr. 3-4). pap. 31.80 (978-1-62065-794-2(5)); pap. 190.80 (978-1-62065-795-9(3)); lib. bdg. 109.28 (978-1-4296-9952-5(3)) Capstone Press of Coughlan Cos. (Fact Finders).

Becnel, Kim E. Bloom's How to Write about F. Scott Fitzgerald. 2007. (Bloom's How to Write about Literature Ser.). 232p. (C). (gr. 9-18). 45.00 (978-0-7910-9482-2(0), Chelsea Hse.) Facts On File, Inc.

Bentley, Nancy. Don't Be a Copycat! Write a Great Report Without Plagiarizing. 2008. (Prime (Elementary) Ser.). (Illus.). 64p. (J). (gr. 3-7). lib. bdg. 29.27 (978-0-7660-2860-9(7)) Enslow Pubs., Inc.

Bodden, Valerie. Analyze & Define the Assignment. 2015. (Info Wise Ser.). (ENG.). 40p. (gr. 4-6). pap. 8.99 (978-1-4677-7578-6(9)); (Illus.). 30.65 (978-1-4677-5223-7(1)) Lerner Publishing Group. (Lerner Pubns.).

—Giving a Presentation. Williams, Nate, illus. 2015. (Classroom How-To Ser.). (ENG.). 48p. (J). (gr. 5-8). pap. 12.00 (978-0-89812-986-1(9), Creative Paperbacks) Creative Co., The.

—Giving a Presentation. 2014. (J). (978-1-60818-280-0(0), Creative Education) Creative Co., The.

—Research & Synthesize Your Facts. 2015. (Info Wise Ser.). (ENG., Illus.). 40p. (J). (gr. 4-6). lib. bdg. 30.65 (978-1-4677-5224-4(X), Lerner Pubns.) Lerner Publishing Group.

—Write & Revise Your Project. 2015. (Info Wise Ser.). (ENG., Illus.). 40p. (gr. 4-6). lib. bdg. 30.65 (978-1-4677-5225-1(8), Lerner Pubns.) Lerner Publishing Group.

—Writing a Research Paper. Williams, Nate, illus. 2015. (Classroom How-To Ser.). (ENG.). 48p. (J). (gr. 5-8). pap. 12.00 (978-0-89812-989-2(3), Creative Paperbacks) Creative Co., The.

—Writing a Research Paper. 2014. (J). (978-1-60818-283-1(5), Creative Education) Creative Co., The.

Buzzeo, Toni. R Is for Research. Wong, Nicole, illus. 2008. 17.95 (978-1-60213-032-6(9)); (J). (gr. 2-4). 17.95 (978-1-60213-030-2(2)) Highsmith Inc. (Upstart Bks.).

Cefrey, Holly. Researching People, Places, & Events. 2009. (Digital & Information Literacy Ser.). (Illus.). 48p. (YA). (gr. 5-8). lib. bdg. 29.25 (978-1-4358-5317-1(2), Rosen Reference) Rosen Publishing Group, Inc., The.

Checkmark Books, creator. Research & Information Management. 2nd rev. ed. 2007. (Mastering Career Skills Ser.). (Illus.). 128p. per. 12.95 (978-0-8160-7118-0(7), Checkmark Bks.) Facts On File, Inc.

Coleman, Kelly. Choose It! Finding the Right Research Topic. Petelinsek, Kathleen, illus. 2015. (Explorer Junior Library: Information Explorer Junior Ser.). (ENG.). 24p. (J). (gr. 1-4). 29.93 (978-1-63188-862-5(5), 206028) Cherry Lake Publishing.

Coleman, Miriam. Present It: Understanding Contexts & Audiences. 2012. (Core Skills Ser.). (ENG., Illus.). 32p. (J). (gr. 3-6). 25.25 (978-1-4488-7455-2(6)); pap. 10.00 (978-1-4488-7527-6(7)) Rosen Publishing Group, Inc., The. (PowerKids Pr.).

—Prove It: Gathering Evidence & Integrating Information. 2012. (Core Skills Ser.). (ENG., Illus.). 32p. (J). (gr. 3-6). 25.25 (978-1-4488-7453-8(X)); pap. 10.00 (978-1-4488-7525-2(0)) Rosen Publishing Group, Inc., The. (PowerKids Pr.).

Cornwall, Phyllis. Super Smart Information Strategies: Put It All Together. 2010. (Explorer Library: Information Explorer Ser.). (ENG.). 32p. (gr. 4-8). pap. 14.21 (978-1-61080-262-8(4), 200908); lib. bdg. 28.50 (978-1-60279-643-0(2), 200346) Cherry Lake Publishing.

Creating Book Reports with Cool New Digital Tools. 2013. (Way Beyond PowerPoint: Making 21st Century Presentations Ser.). 48p. (J). (gr. 5-8). pap. 70.50 (978-1-4777-1846-9(X), Rosen Reference) Rosen Publishing Group, Inc., The.

Digital Photo Activity Kit Deluxe Vivitar 3700 series Lab-10. 2005. (J). cd-rom 1790.00 (978-1-933229-02-7(0)) APTE, Inc.

Digital Photo Activity Kit Deluxe Vivitar 3700 series Lab-15. 2005. (J). cd-rom 2610.00 (978-1-933229-03-4(9)) APTE, Inc.

Digital Photo Activity Kit Deluxe Vivitar 3700 series Lab-20. 2005. (J). 3260.00 (978-1-933229-04-1(7)) APTE, Inc.

Digital Photo Activity Kit Deluxe Vivitar 3700 series Lab-25. 2005. (J). 3924.00 (978-1-933229-05-8(5)) APTE, Inc.

Digital Photo Activity Kit Deluxe Vivitar 3700 series Lab-30. 2005. (J). 4585.00 (978-1-933229-06-5(3)) APTE, Inc.

Digital Photo Activity Kit Deluxe Vivitar 3700 series Lab-35. 2005. (J). 5239.00 (978-1-933229-07-2(1)) APTE, Inc.

Digital Photo Activity Kit Deluxe Vivitar 3700 series Lab-5. 2005. (J). cd-rom 648.95 (978-1-933229-01-0(2)) APTE, Inc.

Digital Photo Activity Kit Deluxe Vivitar 3700 Series school Version. 2005. (J). cd-rom 133.95 (978-1-933229-00-3(4)) APTE, Inc.

Digital Photo Activity Kit Deluxe Vivitar 5300 series Lab- 2005. (J). 1759.95 (978-1-933229-09-6(8)) APTE, Inc.

Digital Photo Activity Kit Deluxe Vivitar 5300 series Lab-10. 2005. (J). 3469.99 (978-1-933229-10-2(1)) APTE, Inc.

Digital Photo Activity Kit Deluxe Vivitar 5300 series Lab-15. 2005. (J). 5129.95 (978-1-933229-11-9(X)) APTE, Inc.

Digital Photo Activity Kit Deluxe Vivitar 5300 series Lab-25. 2005. (J). 8123.90 (978-1-933229-12-6(8)) APTE, Inc.

Digital Photo Activity Kit Deluxe Vivitar 5300 series Lab-30. 2005. (J). 9624.95 (978-1-933229-14-0(4)) APTE, Inc.

Digital Photo Activity Kit Deluxe Vivitar 5300 series Lab-35. 2005. (J). 11119.95 (978-1-933229-15-7(2)) APTE, Inc.

Digital Photo Activity Kit Deluxe Vivitar 5300 series Single. 2005. (J). 359.99 (978-1-933229-08-9(X)) APTE, Inc.

Don't Panic: The Procrastinator's Guide to Writing an Effective Term Paper. 2004. 64p. (YA). per. 9.95 (978-0-9632123-5-1(4)) Crystal Pr.

DynaNotes Grade 4 Writing TAKS Review Guide Transparency Set. 2006. (J). trans. (978-1-933854-42-7(1)) DynaStudy, Inc.

DynaNotes Grade 7 Writing TAKS Review Guide. 2006. (J). pap. (978-1-933854-39-7(1)) DynaStudy, Inc.

DynaNotes Grade 7 Writing TAKS Review Guide Transparency Set. 2006. (J). trans. (978-1-933854-40-3(5)) DynaStudy, Inc.

Evan-Moor. Easy File Folder Reports Grades 3-6. 2004. (ENG.). 240p. (J). pap. 21.99 (978-1-55799-963-4(5), EMC 6001) Evan-Moor Educational Pubs.

Evergreen: a Guide to Writing with Readings. 7th ed. 2003. (YA). (gr. 6-12). stu. ed. 3.96 incl. cd-rom (978-0-618-27389-8(1), 315696) CENGAGE Learning.

Facts on File, Inc. Staff. Career Skills Library: Research & Information Management, Third Edition. 3rd rev. ed. 2009. (Career Skills Library). (Illus.). 168p. (gr. 6-12). 25.95 (978-0-8160-7777-9(0), Ferguson Publishing Co.) Facts On File, Inc.

Fandel, Jennifer. Collect Your Thoughts: Organizing Information, 1 vol. 2013. (Research Tool Kit Ser.). (ENG.). 32p. (gr. 3-4). pap. 8.10 (978-1-62065-786-7(4)); pap. 47.70 (978-1-62065-787-4(2)); lib. bdg. 27.32 (978-1-4296-9948-8(5)) Capstone Press of Coughlan Cos. (Fact Finders).

—Picture Yourself Writing Nonfiction: Using Photos to Inspire Writing. 2011. (See It, Write It Ser.). (ENG.). 32p. (gr. 3-4). pap. 47.70 (978-1-4296-7208-5(0), Fact Finders) Capstone Press of Coughlan Cos.

Fields, Jan. You Can Write Excellent Reports, 1 vol. 2012. (You Can Write Ser.). (ENG., 24p. (gr. 1-2). Illus.). pap. 7.29 (978-1-4296-7962-6(X)); pap. 41.70 (978-1-4296-8384-5(8)); (Illus.). lib. bdg. 25.32 (978-1-4296-7614-4(0)) Capstone Press of Coughlan Cos. (First Facts).

Fontichiaro, Kristin. Review It! Helping Peers Create Their Best Work. Petelinsek, Kathleen, illus. 2015. (Explorer Junior Library: Information Explorer Junior Ser.). (ENG.). 24p. (J). (gr. 1-4). 29.93 (978-1-63188-865-6(X), 206040) Cherry Lake Publishing.

Forest, Christopher. Present What You Know: Sharing Information. 2013. (Research Tool Kit Ser.). (ENG.). 32p. (gr. 3-4). pap. 47.70 (978-1-62065-789-8(9)); pap. 8.10 (978-1-62065-788-1(0)); lib. bdg. 27.32 (978-1-4296-9949-5(3)) Capstone Press of Coughlan Cos. (Fact Finders).

Gallion, Sue Lowell. Rick & Rachel Build a Research Report. Chung, Chi, illus. 2014. (Writing Builders Ser.). (ENG.). 32p. (J). (gr. 2-4). pap. 11.94 (978-1-60357-557-7(X)); lib. bdg. 25.27 (978-1-59953-583-8(1)) Norwood Hse. Pr.

Ganeri, Anita. I Can Write Instructions, 1 vol. 2013. (I Can Write Ser.). (ENG., Illus.). 32p. (gr. 1-3). pap. 8.29 (978-1-4329-6941-7(2)); lib. bdg. 27.32 (978-1-4329-6934-9(X)) Heinemann-Raintree. (Heinemann First Library).

—I Can Write Reports, 1 vol. 2013. (I Can Write Ser.). (ENG.). 32p. (gr. 1-3). lib. bdg. 27.32 (978-1-4329-6937-0(4), Heinemann First Library) Heinemann-Raintree.

—Reports. 2013. (I Can Write Ser.). (ENG.). 32p. (gr. 1-3). pap. 8.29 (978-1-4329-6944-8(7), Heinemann First Library) Heinemann-Raintree.

Gleed, Paul. Bloom's How to Write about William Shakespeare. 2007. (Bloom's How to Write about Literature Ser.). 244p. (C). (gr. 9-18). 45.00 (978-0-7910-9484-6(7), Chelsea Hse.) Facts On File, Inc.

Graff, Rhonda. Instant Nonfiction Writing Frames: Reproducible Templates & Easy How-To's That Guide Children to Research & Write Successful Reports on the Topics You Teach. 2011. (ENG.). 64p. pap. 11.99 (978-0-545-22416-1(0), Teaching Resources) Scholastic, Inc.

Greek, Joseph. Writing Term Papers with Cool New Digital Tools. 2013. (Way Beyond PowerPoint: Making 21st Century Presentations Ser.). (Illus.). 48p. (J). (gr. 5-8). 29.95 (978-1-4777-1835-3(4)); pap. 11.75 (978-1-4777-1853-7(2)) Rosen Publishing Group, Inc., The. (Rosen Reference).

Green, Julie. Super Smart Information Strategies: Write It Down. 2010. (Explorer Library: Information Explorer Ser.). (ENG.). 32p. (gr. 4-8). lib. bdg. 28.50 (978-1-60279-645-4(9), 200348) Cherry Lake Publishing.

Green, Lyric & Bullard, Lisa. Future Ready Oral & Multimedia Presentations. 2017. (Future Ready Project Skills Ser.). 48p. (J). (gr. 3-4). pap. 11.70 **(978-0-7660-8771-2(9))**; lib. bdg. 27.93 **(978-0-7660-8659-3(3))** Enslow Pubs., Inc.

Green, Lyric & Graham Gaines, Ann. Future Ready Research Papers. 2017. (Future Ready Project Skills Ser.). 48p. (J). (gr. 3-4). pap. 11.70 **(978-0-7660-8773-6(5))**; lib. bdg. 27.93 **(978-0-7660-8661-6(5))** Enslow Pubs., Inc.

Greve, Meg. Writing an Opinion Paper. 2014. (ENG.). 24p. (gr. 3-5). 28.50 (978-1-62717-693-4(4)) Rourke Educational Media.

Guillain, Charlotte. What Is Informational Writing? 2015. (Connect with Text Ser.). (ENG., Illus.). 32p. (gr. 2-4). 30.65 (978-1-4109-8035-9(9)) Heinemann-Raintree.

Hagler, Gina. Creating Book Reports with Cool New Digital Tools. 2013. (Way Beyond PowerPoint: Making 21st Century Presentations Ser.). 48p. (J). (gr. 5-8). 29.95 (978-1-4777-1834-6(6)); pap. 11.75 (978-1-4777-1845-2(1)) Rosen Publishing Group, Inc., The. (Rosen Reference).

Hamilton, John. Primary & Secondary Sources, 1 vol. 2005. (Straight to the Source Ser.). (ENG.). 32p. (gr. k-6). 27.07 (978-1-59197-548-9(4), Checkerboard Library) ABDO Publishing Co.

Herman, Gail. Make-a-Splash Writing Rules. 2009. (Grammar All-Stars: Writing Tools Ser.). 32p. (J). (gr. 2-5). (ENG.). pap. 10.50 (978-1-4339-2136-0(7)); lib. bdg. 26.00 (978-1-4339-1943-5(5)) Stevens, Gareth Publishing LLLP. (Gareth Stevens Learning Library).

Hook, Sue Vander. Writing Intriguing Informational Pieces. 2015. (ENG., Illus.). 56p. (gr. 6-8). 33.32 (978-1-4677-7907-4(5), Lerner Pubns.) Lerner Publishing Group.

Hord, Colleen. Writing a Research Paper. 2014. (ENG.). 24p. (gr. 3-5). 28.50 (978-1-62717-694-1(2)) Rourke Educational Media.

Houghton, Peggy M., et al. Houghton & Houghton Manual of Style: A Guide to Writing Research Papers. 2009. (J). (978-0-923568-97-9(2)) Baker College Publishing Co.

Howell, Sara. How to Plan, Revise, & Edit Your Text, 1 vol., 1. 2014. (Core Writing Skills Ser.). (ENG.). 24p. (J). (gr. 3-4). 23.60 (978-1-4777-2910-6(0), PowerKids Pr.) Rosen Publishing Group, Inc., The.

—How to Write an Explanatory Text, 1 vol., 1. 2014. (Core Writing Skills Ser.). (ENG.). 24p. (J). (gr. 3-4). 23.60 (978-1-4777-2907-6(0), PowerKids Pr.) Rosen Publishing Group, Inc., The.

Jensen, Eric. Student Success Secrets. 5th ed. 2003. (ENG., Illus.). 256p. pap. 10.99 (978-0-7641-2007-7(7)) Barron's Educational Series, Inc.

Kemmerer, Susan. Research in Increments. 2nd ed. 2004. 75p. pap. 12.95 (978-0-9758543-1-0(3)) Schoolhouse Publishing.

Kerr, Christine. Bloom's How to Write about J. D. Salinger. 2007. (Bloom's How to Write about Literature Ser.). 280p. (C). (gr. 9-12). 45.00 (978-0-7910-9483-9(9), Chelsea Hse.) Facts On File, Inc.

Langley, Andrew. Every Place Has a History, 1 vol. 2014. (Everything Has a History Ser.). (ENG.). 64p. (gr. 7-8). lib. bdg. 35.99 (978-1-4329-9585-0(5)) Heinemann-Raintree.

Levy, Janey. Language Development Writing Process. 2004. (BrainBuilders Ser.). (ENG.). 48p. (gr. k-4). pap. 5.25 (978-1-4042-8569-9(5)) Rosen Publishing Group, Inc., The.

Loewen, Nancy. Just the Facts: Writing Your Own Research Report, 1 vol. Beacon, Dawn & Lyles, Christopher, illus. 2009. (Writer's Toolbox Ser.). (ENG.). 32p. (gr. 2-4). pap. 8.95 (978-1-4048-5702-5(8)) Picture Window Bks.

—Just the Facts: Writing Your Own Research Report, 1 vol. Beacon, Dawn, illus. 2009. (Writer's Toolbox Ser.). (ENG.). 32p. (gr. 2-4). lib. bdg. 27.32 (978-1-4048-5519-9(X)) Picture Window Bks.

—Just the Facts [Scholastic]: Writing Your Own Research Report. Beacon, Dawn, illus. 2010. (Writer's Toolbox Ser.). 32p. pap. 0.50 (978-1-4048-6171-8(8), Nonfiction Picture Bks.) Picture Window Bks.

Marlow, Herb. A Student's Guide to Successful Writing. 2005. (J). 24.95 (978-1-893595-53-8(6)) Four Seasons Bks., Inc.

McCurry, Kristen. Pick a Picture, Write a Report!, 1 vol. 2014. (Little Scribe Ser.). (ENG.). 32p. (gr. 1-2). lib. bdg. 27.32 (978-1-4765-4239-3(2), Aplus Bks.) Capstone Press of Coughlan Cos.

McDougal-Littell Publishing Staff, creator. Writing Research Reports. 2006. (Illus.). 103p. (gr. 6-12). per. (978-0-618-05272-1(0), 2-22379) Holt McDougal.

McGuinness, Denis E. & Spencer, Lauren. Writing to Describe. 2011. (Illus.). 64p. (J). 77.70 (978-1-4488-4744-0(3), Rosen Reference); (J). pap. 12.95 (978-1-4488-4686-3(2), Rosen Reference); (YA). (gr. 5-9). lib. bdg. 31.95 (978-1-4488-4680-1(3)) Rosen Publishing Group, Inc., The.

Milton, Bess. Language Development Writing Process. 2004. (BrainBuilders Ser.). (ENG.). 48p. (gr. k-4). pap. 5.25 (978-1-4042-8559-0(8)) Rosen Publishing Group, Inc., The.

Minden, Cecilia & Roth, Kate. How to Write a Report. 2011. (Explorer Junior Library: Language Arts Explorer Junior Ser.). (ENG.). 24p. (gr. 1-4). lib. bdg. 25.64 (978-1-61080-105-8(9), 201112) Cherry Lake Publishing.

Morkane, Sue. Original Writing. 2004. (Routledge a Level English Guides). (ENG., Illus.). 112p. (C). 95.00 (978-0-415-31911-9(0)); per. 28.95 (978-0-415-31912-6(9)) Routledge.

Nash, Kimberley. Book Reports: A one-year writing Course. 2006. (ENG., Illus.). 192p. spiral bd., wbk. ed. 33.00 (978-0-9710950-6-9(X), 13030) Resurrection Resources LLC.

—Essays & Research Reports - Level A Level A: A one year writing Course. 2007. (ENG., Illus.). 181p. (gr. 5-7). spiral bd., wbk. ed. 33.00 (978-0-9653723-6-7(7), #12010) Resurrection Resources LLC.

—Essays & Research Reports - Level B: A one year writing Course. 2007. (ENG., Illus.). 247p. spiral bd., wbk. ed. 35.00 (978-0-9710950-2-1(7), 12020) Resurrection Resources LLC.

—Lab Reports: 10 Experiments. 2007. (ENG., Illus.). 140p. spiral bd., wbk. ed. 20.00 (978-0-9710950-8-3(6)) Resurrection Resources LLC.

Nelson, G. Lynn. Writing & Being: Embracing Your Life Through Creative Journaling. 2nd rev. ed. 2004. (ENG., Illus.). 176p. pap. 16.95 (978-1-880913-61-1(5)) New World Library.

Owings, Lisa. Do Your Research. 2013. (Library Smarts Ser.). (ENG., Illus.). 24p. (gr. -1-2). lib. bdg. 23.93 (978-1-4677-1503-4(4), Lerner Pubns.) Lerner Publishing Group.

—Share Your Book Report. 2013. (Library Smarts Ser.). (ENG., Illus.). 24p. (gr. -1-2). lib. bdg. 23.93 (978-1-4677-1504-1(2), Lerner Pubns.) Lerner Publishing Group.

Priddy, Anna. Bloom's How to Write about Emily Dickinson. 2007. (Bloom's How to Write about Literature Ser.). 262p. (C). (gr. 9-18). 45.00 (978-0-7910-9492-1(8), Chelsea Hse.) Facts On File, Inc.

Proudfit, Benjamin. Writing Book Reports. 2014. (Write Right! Ser.). 24p. (J). (gr. 2-5). 22.60 (978-1-4824-0804-1(X)) Stevens, Gareth Publishing LLLP.

—Writing Research Papers. 2014. (Write Right! Ser.). 24p. (J). (gr. 2-5). 22.60 (978-1-4824-1120-1(2)) Stevens, Gareth Publishing LLLP.

Range, Ellen. Take Note! Taking & Organizing Notes. 2014. (Explorer Junior Library: Information Explorer Junior Ser.). (ENG., Illus.). 24p. (J). (gr. 1-4). 28.50 (978-1-63137-788-4(4), 205395) Cherry Lake Publishing.

Rasinski, Timothy V. 100 Reproducible Word Study Lessons That Help Kids Boost Reading, Vocabulary, Spelling & Phonics Skills — Independently! 2005. (Daily Word Ladders Ser.). (ENG., Illus.). 112p. (gr. 2-3). pap. 15.99 (978-0-439-51383-8(9), Teaching Resources) Scholastic, Inc.

Rollins, Brenda. How to Write a Book Report: 80 Interactive Screen Pages. 2011. (Writing Skills Ser.). (J). (gr. 3-8). pap. 39.95 (978-1-55319-506-1(X), Classroom Complete Pr.) Rainbow Horizons Publishing, Inc.

—How to Write an Essay: 80 Interactive Screen Pages. 2011. (Writing Skills Ser.). (J). (gr. 3-8). pap. 39.95 (978-1-55319-507-8(8), Classroom Complete Pr.) Rainbow Horizons Publishing, Inc.

Roy, Jennifer Rozines. Sharpen Your Report Writing Skills. 2011. (Sharpen Your Writing Skills Ser.). (Illus.). 64p. (J). (gr. 6-18). pap. 8.95 (978-1-59845-338-6(6)); lib. bdg. 29.27 (978-0-7660-3905-6(6)) Enslow Pubs., Inc.

—Sharpen Your Story or Narrative Writing Skills. 2011. (Sharpen Your Writing Skills Ser.). (Illus.). 64p. (J). (gr. 6-18). pap. 8.95 (978-1-59845-340-9(8)); lib. bdg. 29.27 (978-0-7660-3901-8(3)) Enslow Pubs., Inc.

—You Can Write a Report. 2003. (You Can Write Ser.). (Illus.). 64p. (J). (gr. 6-12). lib. bdg. 23.94 (978-0-7660-2086-3(X)) Enslow Pubs., Inc.

Rustad, Martha E. H. Learning about Nonfiction, 1 vol. 2014. (Language Arts Ser.). (ENG.). 24p. (gr. k-1). 26.65 (978-1-4914-0579-6(1), Pebble Plus) Capstone Press of Coughlan Cos.

Sharkawy, Azza. Share It! 2014. (ENG., Illus.). 24p. (J). (978-0-7787-0781-3(4)) Crabtree Publishing Co.

Shearer, Cynthia & Washington, George. Handwriting by George 28-55: Rules of Civility & Decent Behaviour in Company & Conversation: Rules 28-53 to Draw & Write, 4 vols., Vol. 2. 2009. (ENG.). 62p. (J). pap. 9.95 (978-1-882514-37-3(8)) Greenleaf Pr.

Silate, Jennifer. Language Development Writing Process. 2004. (BrainBuilders Ser.). (ENG.). 48p. (gr. k-4). pap. 5.25 (978-1-4042-8564-4(4)) Rosen Publishing Group, Inc., The.

SIRS Discoverer. 2005. (J). mass mkt. (978-0-89777-566-3(X)) SIRS Publishing, Inc.

SIRS Discoverer: Getting Started Manual Spring 2004. 2003. (YA). cd-rom 1425.00 (978-0-89777-542-7(2)) SIRS Publishing, Inc.

Sloan, Megan S. Teaching Young Writers to Elaborate: Mini-Lessons & Strategies That Help Students Find Topics & Learn to Tell More. 2008. (ENG.). 144p. pap. 19.99 (978-0-545-03298-8(9), Teaching Resources) Scholastic, Inc.

Souter, Gerry, et al. Creating e-Reports & Online Presentations. 2003. (Internet Library). (Illus.). 64p. (J). (gr. 4-12). lib. bdg. 23.94 (978-0-7660-2080-1(0)) Enslow Pubs., Inc.

Spencer, Lauren. A Step-by-Step Guide to Informative Writing. 2009. (Library of Writing Skills Ser.). 48p. (gr. 5-8). 53.00 (978-1-60853-978-9(4), Rosen Reference) Rosen Publishing Group, Inc., The.

Sterling, Laurie A. Bloom's How to Write about Nathaniel Hawthorne. 2007. (Bloom's How to Write about Literature Ser.). 344p. (C). (gr. 9-18). 45.00 (978-0-7910-9481-5(2), Chelsea Hse.) Facts On File, Inc.

Stiles, Mary & Mills, Barbara. A Rookie's Guide to Research. 3rd ed. 2003. 92p. (YA). spiral bd. 10.95 (978-0-9721404-1-6(7)) Union Creek Communications, Inc.

Tribble. Word for Word. Date not set. (Illus.). 80p. pap. 28.75 (978-0-582-01663-7(0)) Addison-Wesley Longman, Ltd. GBR. Dist: Trans-Atlantic Pubns., Inc.

Vickers, Rebecca. Making Better Sentences: The Power of Structure & Meaning, 1 vol. 2013. (Find Your Way with Words Ser.). (ENG.). 56p. (gr. 6-7). 34.65 *(978-1-4329-7654-5(0))*; pap. 9.95 *(978-1-4329-7659-0(1))* Heinemann-Raintree.

Write on Target for Grade 5. 2006. (J). stu. ed., per., wbk. ed. 16.95 *(978-1-59230-159-1(2))* Englefield & Assocs., Inc.

Write on Target Grade 3: Student Workbook. 2005. (J). stu. ed., per. 10.95 *(978-1-59230-151-5(7))* Englefield & Assocs., Inc.

Write on Target Grade 4: Student Workbook. 2005. (J). stu. ed., per. 10.95 *(978-1-59230-149-2(5))* Englefield & Assocs., Inc.

Write on Target Grade 6: Student Workbook. 2005. (J). pap., stu. ed. 10.95 *(978-1-59230-157-7(6))* Englefield & Assocs., Inc.

Writing Term Papers with Cool New Digital Tools. 2013. (Way Beyond PowerPoint: Making 21st Century Presentations Ser.). (Illus.). 48p. (J). (gr. 5-8). pap. 70.50 *(978-1-4777-1854-4(0)*, Rosen Reference) Rosen Publishing Group, Inc., The.

Yomtov, Nel. How to Write a Lab Report. Petelinsek, Kathleen, illus. 2013. (Explorer Junior Library: How to Write Ser.). (ENG.). 24p. (J). (gr. 1-4). 25.64 *(978-1-62431-185-7(7)*, 203064); pap. 12.79 *(978-1-62431-317-2(5)*, 203066) Cherry Lake Publishing.

Zaroulis, Christina. Tackling Your High School Term Paper. 2003. (Students Helping Students Ser.). 80p. (gr. 9-12). pap. 8.95 *(978-0-9719392-1-9(7))* Natavi Guides.

REPORTERS AND REPORTING

see also Journalism

Boomhower, Ray E. The Soldier's Friend: A Life of Ernie Pyle. 2006. (Illus.). 134p. 17.95 *(978-0-87195-200-4(9))* Indiana Historical Society.

Colin Macfarlane. Hit the Headlines: Exciting Journalism Activities for Improving Writing & Thinking Skills. 2012. (ENG., Illus.). 192p. (C). pap. 50.95 *(978-0-415-69511-4(2)*, 0415695112) Routledge.

Cooper, Candy J. Reporting from Iraq: On the Ground in Fallujah. 2012. pap. *(978-0-545-32799-2(7))* Scholastic, Inc.

Hamilton, John. Real-Time Reporting. 2004. (War in Iraq Ser.). (Illus.). 48p. (gr. 4-8). 27.07 *(978-1-59197-497-0(6)*, Abdo & Daughters) ABDO Publishing Co.

Hollingsworth, Tamara. Noticias Que Marcaron la Historia. 2016. (TIME for Kids en Español - Level 5 Ser.). (SPA.). 64p. (gr. 5-5). lib. bdg. 31.99 *(978-1-5157-2943-3(5))* Time for Kids Inc AUS. Dist: Capstone Pub.

Johnson, Jennifer Hunt & Hansen, Holly T. Father Remembers, 615 vols., Vol. 6. 2003. (Illus.). 30p. 9.95 *(978-0-9729610-5-9(4)*, CMB06) Tapis & Assocs., Inc.

—Grandma Remembers, 315 vols., Vol. 3. 2003. (Illus.). 30p. 9.95 *(978-0-9729610-2-8(X)*, CMB03) Tapis & Assocs., Inc.

—Grandpa Remembers, 415 vols., Vol. 4. 2003. (Illus.). 30p. 9.95 *(978-0-9729610-3-5(8)*, CMB04) Tapis & Assocs., Inc.

—Mother Remembers, 515 vols., Vol. 5. 2003. (Illus.). 30p. 9.95 *(978-0-9729610-4-2(6)*, CMB05) Tapis & Assocs., Inc.

—My Memories, 115 vols., Vol. 1. 2003. (Illus.). 29p. 9.95 *(978-0-9729610-0-4(3)*, CMB01) Tapis & Assocs., Inc.

—Remembering Grandma, 1115 vols., Vol. 11. 2003. (Illus.). 28p. 9.95 *(978-0-9729610-6-6(2)*, CMB12) Tapis & Assocs., Inc.

—Remembering Grandpa, 1215 vols., Vol. 12. 2003. (Illus.). 28p. 9.95 *(978-0-9729610-7-3(0)*, CMB12) Tapis & Assocs., Inc.

—Your Memories, 215 vols., Vol. 2. 2003. (Illus.). 29p. 9.95 *(978-0-9729610-1-1(1)*, CMB02) Tapis & Assocs., Inc.

Loveless, Antony & Crewe, Sabrina. War Correspondents. 2012. (ENG.). 32p. (J). lib. bdg. *(978-0-7787-5103-8(1))*; (The World's Most Dangerous Jobs Ser.: No. 10). pap. *(978-0-7787-5117-5(1))* Crabtree Publishing Co.

Mahoney, Ellen. Nellie Bly & Investigative Journalism for Kids: Mighty Muckrakers from the Golden Age to Today, with 21 Activities. 2015. (For Kids Ser.). (ENG., Illus.). 144p. (J). (gr. 4). pap. 16.95 *(978-1-61374-997-5(X))* Chicago Review Pr., Inc.

Minden, Cecilia & Roth, Kate. How to Write an Interview. 2011. (Explorer Junior Library: Language Arts Explorer Junior Ser.). (ENG.). 24p. (gr. 1-4). lib. bdg. 25.64 *(978-1-60279-996-7(2)*, 200992) Cherry Lake Publishing.

Mooney, Carla. Asking Questions about How the News Is Created. 2015. (21st Century Skills Library: Asking Questions about Media Ser.). (ENG., Illus.). 32p. (J). (gr. 4-8). 29.93 *(978-1-63362-489-4(7)*, 206864) Cherry Lake Publishing.

Palser, Barb. Choosing News: What Gets Reported & Why, 1 vol. 2012. (Exploring Media Literacy Ser.). (ENG., Illus.). 80p. (gr. 6-7). pap. 9.10 *(978-0-7565-4537-6(4))*; lib. bdg. 34.65 *(978-0-7565-4517-8(X))* Compass Point Bks. (CPB Grades 4-8).

Pettiford, Rebecca. Reporters. 2015. (Illus.). 24p. (J). lib. bdg. 25.65 *(978-1-62031-159-2(3)*, Bullfrog Bks.) Jump! Inc.

Rhatigan, Joe. People You Gotta Meet Before You Grow Up: Get to Know the Movers & Shakers, Heroes & Hotshots in Your Hometown. 2014. (ENG., Illus.). 128p. (J). (gr. 2-5). 14.95 *(978-1-62354-004-3(6))* Charlesbridge Publishing, Inc.

Robinson, Tom. The Evolution of News Reporting, 1 vol. 2010. (Essential Viewpoints Set 5 Ser.). (ENG.). 112p. (J). (gr. 6-12). lib. bdg. 35.64 *(978-1-61613-521-8(2)*, Essential Library) ABDO Publishing Co.

Saenger, Diana. Everyone Wants My Job! The ABCs of Entertainment Writing. Fife, Bruce, ed. unabr. ed. 2003. (Writing & Publishing Ser.). (Illus.). 159p. (YA). (gr. 8-12). pap. 15.00 *(978-0-941599-53-5(1))* Piccadilly Bks., Ltd.

Shone, Rob. War Correspondents. 2009. (Graphic Careers Ser.). (ENG.). 48p. (YA). (gr. 5-5). 58.50 *(978-1-61512-894-5(8)*, Rosen Reference) Rosen Publishing Group, Inc., The.

—War Correspondents. Forsey, Chris, illus. 2008. (Graphic Careers Ser.). (ENG.). 48p. (J). (gr. 5-8). lib. bdg. 31.95 *(978-1-4042-1449-1(6))*; per. 14.05 *(978-1-4042-1450-7(X))* Rosen Publishing Group, Inc., The.

Wilson, Julius & Benchmark Education Co. Staff. I Was a 21st Century Civil War Reporter. 2014. (Text Connections Ser.). (J). (gr. 5). *(978-1-4900-1378-7(4))* Benchmark Education Co.

REPORTERS AND REPORTING—FICTION

Ace Reporter, 6, Pack. (Bookweb Ser.). 32p. (gr. 3-18). 34.00 *(978-0-7635-3940-5(6))* Rigby Education.

Barrow, Randi. Saving Zasha. 2013. (ENG.). 256p. (J). (gr. 3-7). pap. 6.99 *(978-0-545-20633-4(2)*, Scholastic Paperbacks) Scholastic, Inc.

Bauer, Joan. Peeled. 2009. (ENG.). 256p. (YA). (gr. 7-18). 8.99 *(978-0-14-241430-9(1)*, Speak) Penguin Young Readers Group.

Blackwood, Gary. Around the World in 100 Days. 2011. (ENG.). 368p. (J). (gr. 5-18). 7.99 *(978-0-14-241963-2(X)*, Puffin Books) Penguin Young Readers Group.

Bond, Gwenda. Fallout. 2015. (Lois Lane Ser.). (ENG.). 304p. (gr. 9-12). 16.95 *(978-1-63079-005-9(2))* Switch Pr.

Cirrone, Dorian. The Big Scoop, 1 vol. Woodruff, Liza, illus. 2006. (Marshall Cavendish Chapter Book Ser.). (ENG.). 74p. (J). (gr. 2-5). 14.99 *(978-0-7614-5323-9(7))* Marshall Cavendish Corp.

Cirrone, Dorian & Cirrone. The Missing Silver Dollar, 1 vol. Woodruff, Liza, illus. 2006. (Lindy Blues Ser.). (ENG.). 32p. (J). (gr. -1-3). 14.95 *(978-0-7614-5284-3(2))* Marshall Cavendish Corp.

Clark, Sherryl. Kim's Fake Cake Bake. McKenzie, Heath, illus. 2015. (J). pap. *(978-1-4966-0256-5(0))* Capstone Classroom.

—Kim's Pet Scoop. McKenzie, Heath, illus. 2015. (J). pap. *(978-1-4966-0238-1(2))* Capstone Classroom.

Daneshvari, Gitty. The Final Exam. (School of Fear Ser.: 3). (ENG.). (J). (gr. 3-7). 2012. 352p. pap. 8.99 *(978-0-316-18285-0(0))* 2011. 336p. 16.99 *(978-0-316-18287-4(7))* Little, Brown Bks. for Young Readers.

Davis, Christy. Newshounds. 2010. 156p. pap. 12.50 *(978-1-4389-7869-7(3))* AuthorHouse.

Dirkes, Craig. Sucktown, Alaska. 2017. (ENG.). 352p. (gr. 9-12). 17.95 *(978-1-63079-055-4(9))* Switch Pr.

Eaton, Walter Pricha. Peanut Cub Reporter: A Boy Scout's Life. 2005. pap. 28.95 *(978-1-885529-74-9(0))* Stevens Publishing.

Ellison, Joy D. Carol & Connie. 2008. 28p. per. 24.95 *(978-1-4241-9276-2(5))* America Star Bks.

Fantaskey, Beth. Isabel Feeney, Star Reporter. 2017. (ENG.). 352p. (J). (gr. 5-7). pap. 7.99 *(978-0-544-93696-6(5)*, HMH Books For Young Readers) Houghton Mifflin Harcourt Publishing Co.

—Isabel Feeney, Star Reporter. 2017. (ENG.). (J). (gr. 5-7). lib. bdg. 18.40 ***(978-0-606-39809-1(0))*** Turtleback Bks.

Fontes, Justine & Fontes, Ron. Casebook: Bigfoot. 2009. (Top Secret Graphica Mysteries Ser.). (Illus.). 48p. (YA). (gr. 2-6). 29.25 *(978-1-60754-594-1(2))*; pap. 11.75 *(978-1-60754-595-8(0))* Windmill Bks.

Garis, Howard Roger. Larry Dexter's Great Search or, the Hunt for the Missing Millionaire. 2007. 196p. per. *(978-1-4065-2768-1(8))* Dodo Pr.

Green, Tim. Football Champ. (Football Genius Ser.: 3). (ENG.). (J). (gr. 3-7). 2010. 304p. pap. 6.99 *(978-0-06-162691-3(0))* 2009. (Illus.). 288p. 16.99 *(978-0-06-162689-0(9))* HarperCollins Pubs.

Greene, Janice. The Ritual, 1 vol. unabr. ed. 2010. (Q Reads Ser.). (ENG.). 32p. (YA). (gr. 9-12). pap. 6.95 *(978-1-61651-185-2(0))* Saddleback Educational Publishing, Inc.

Hautman, Pete & Logue, Mary. Skullduggery. 2007. (Bloodwater Mysteries Ser.). (ENG.). 192p. (J). (gr. 5-18). 16.99 *(978-0-399-24378-3(X)*, G.P. Putnam's Sons Books for Young Readers) Penguin Young Readers Group.

Hergé. The Shooting Star. 2012. (Adventures of Tintin: Young Readers Edition Ser.). (ENG., Illus.). 96p. (J). (gr. 3-7). pap. 8.99 *(978-0-316-19875-2(7))* Little, Brown Bks. for Young Readers.

Judge, Malcolm. Jonny Jakes Investigates the Hamburgers of Doom. Brown, Alan, illus. 2016. (Middle-Grade Novels Ser.). (ENG.). 240p. (gr. 4-7). lib. bdg. 26.65 *(978-1-4965-2678-6(3))* Stone Arch Bks.

—Jonny Jakes Investigates the Old School Ghoul. Brown, Alan, illus. 2016. (Middle-Grade Novels Ser.). (ENG.). 240p. (gr. 4-7). lib. bdg. 25.99 *(978-1-4965-2829-2(8))* Stone Arch Bks.

Karre, Elizabeth. The Campaign. (Opportunity Ser.). (ENG.). 104p. (YA). (gr. 6-12). 2015. 34.65 *(978-1-4677-6013-3(7)*, Lerner Digital) 2013. pap. 7.95 *(978-1-4677-1498-3(4)*, Darby Creek) 2013. lib. bdg. 27.93 *(978-1-4677-1374-0(0)*, Darby Creek) Lerner Publishing Group.

Krulik, Nancy. What's Black & White & Stinks All Over? Blecha, Aaron, illus. 2011. (George Brown, Class Clown Ser.: 4). (ENG.). 128p. (J). (gr. 2-4). pap. 5.99 *(978-0-448-45370-5(3)*, Grosset & Dunlap) Penguin Young Readers Group.

Larson, Kirby. Hattie Ever After. 2014. (ENG.). 256p. (YA). (gr. 7). pap. 8.99 *(978-0-375-85090-5(2)*, Ember) Random Hse. Children's Bks.

Law, Ingrid. Scumble. (ENG.). (J). (gr. 3-7). 2011. 432p. 8.99 *(978-0-14-241962-5(1)*, Puffin Books) 2010. 416p. 17.99 *(978-0-8037-3307-7(0)*, Dial Bks) Penguin Young Readers Group.

—Scumble. l.t. ed. 2011. (Companion to the Newberry Honor Winner Savvy Ser.). (ENG.). 575p. 23.99 *(978-1-4104-3531-6(8))* Thorndike Pr.

LeSourd, Nancy. Attack at Pearl Harbor, 1 vol. 2008. (Liberty Letters Ser.). (ENG.). 224p. (J). pap. 7.99 *(978-0-310-71389-0(7))* Zonderkidz.

Lysiak, Hilde & Lysiak, Matthew. Hero Dog! Lew-Vriethoff, Joanne, illus. 2017. (Hilde Cracks the Case Ser.: 1). (ENG.). 96p. (J). (gr. 1-3). pap. 4.99 ***(978-1-338-14155-9(4))*** Scholastic, Inc.

Mackall, Dandi Daley. The Secrets of Tree Taylor. 2014. (ENG.). 288p. (J). (gr. 5). 16.99 *(978-0-375-86897-9(6)*, Knopf Bks. for Young Readers) Random Hse. Children's Bks.

MacLachlan, Patricia. Just Dance. 2017. (ENG., Illus.). 128p. (J). (gr. 2). 15.99 ***(978-1-4814-7252-4(6)***, McElderry, Margaret K. Bks.) McElderry, Margaret K. Bks.

McDonald, Megan. Amy Namey in Ace Reporter. Madrid, Erwin, illus. 2014. (Judy Moody Ser.: 3). (ENG.). 64p. (J). (gr. -1-1). 12.99 *(978-0-7636-5715-4(8))* Candlewick Pr.

Mercer, Sienna. Fangtastic! 2007. (My Sister the Vampire Ser.: 2). (ENG.). 208p. (J). (gr. 3-7). per. 6.99 *(978-0-06-087115-4(6))* HarperCollins Pubs.

Morrison, Harry Steele. The Adventures of A Boy Reporter. 2004. reprint ed. pap. 1.99 *(978-1-4192-5137-5(6))*; pap. 20.95 *(978-1-4191-5137-8(1))* Kessinger Publishing, LLC.

Parish, Herman. Amelia Bedelia, Cub Reporter. Sweat, Lynn, illus. 2012. (I Can Read Level 2 Ser.). (ENG.). 64p. (J). (gr. -1-3). 16.99 *(978-0-06-209510-7(2))*; pap. 3.99 *(978-0-06-209509-1(9))* HarperCollins Pubs. (Greenwillow Bks.).

Schindler, Holly. Feral. 2014. (ENG.). 432p. (YA). (gr. 8). 17.99 *(978-0-06-222020-2(9)*, HarperTeen) HarperCollins Pubs.

Schmidt, Annie M. G. The Cat Who Came in off the Roof. Colmer, David, tr. from DUT. 2016. (ENG.). 160p. (J). (gr. 5). 14.99 *(978-0-553-53500-6(5)*, Delacorte Bks. for Young Readers) Random Hse. Children's Bks.

Siegal, Ida. Big News! 2015. (Emma Is on the Air Ser.: 1). (ENG., Illus.). 128p. (J). (gr. 2-5). pap. 4.99 *(978-0-545-68692-1(X)*, Scholastic Paperbacks) Scholastic, Inc.

—Undercover! (Emma Is on the Air #4) 2016. (Emma Is on the Air Ser.: 4). (ENG.). 128p. (J). (gr. 2-5). pap. 4.99 *(978-0-545-68710-2(1)*, Scholastic Paperbacks) Scholastic, Inc.

Swallow, Pamela Curtis & Swallow, Pamela C. Groundhog Gets a Say. Bunkus, Denise, illus. 2007. (ENG.). 40p. (J). (gr. k-3). pap. 6.99 *(978-0-14-240896-4(4)*, Puffin Books) Penguin Young Readers Group.

Wallace, Rich. Curveball, No. 9. 2008. (Winning Season Ser.). (ENG.). 128p. (J). (gr. 3-7). 5.99 *(978-0-14-241092-9(6)*, Puffin Books) Penguin Young Readers Group.

Wise, Rachel. Breaking News. 2013. (Dear Know-It-All Ser.: 10). (ENG., Illus.). 160p. (J). (gr. 3-7). 15.99 *(978-1-4424-8965-3(0))*; pap. 6.99 *(978-1-4424-8964-6(2))* Simon Spotlight. (Simon Spotlight).

—Cast Your Ballot! 2013. (Dear Know-It-All Ser.: 9). (ENG., Illus.). 160p. (J). (gr. 3-7). 15.99 *(978-1-4424-8793-2(3))*; pap. 5.99 *(978-1-4424-8792-5(5))* Simon Spotlight. (Simon Spotlight).

REPRODUCTION

see also Cells; Embryology; Pregnancy; Sex

Ballard, Carol. Understanding Reproduction. 2010. (Understanding the Human Body Ser.). (Illus.). 48p. (YA). pap. 11.75 *(978-1-4358-9688-8(2))*; 46p. (J). 70.50 *(978-1-4358-9699-4(8))*; 48p. (YA). (gr. 5-8). lib. bdg. 29.25 *(978-1-4358-9682-6(3))* Rosen Publishing Group, Inc., The. (Rosen Reference).

Brynie, Faith Hickman. 101 Questions about Reproduction: Or How 1 + 1 = 3 or 4 or More. Holm, Sharon, illus. 2005. (101 Questions... Ser.). (ENG.). 176p. (gr. 7-12). 30.60 *(978-0-7613-2311-2(2))* Lerner Publishing Group.

The Endocrine System, the Reproductive System, Human Development. 2006. (World Book's Human Body Works). (Illus.). 48p. (J). *(978-0-7166-4431-6(2))* World Bk., Inc.

Green, Jen. Inheritance & Reproduction, 1 vol. 2013. (Essential Life Science Ser.). (ENG.). 48p. (gr. 4-6). 33.32 *(978-1-4329-7808-2(X)*, Heinemann InfoSearch) Heinemann-Raintree.

Harris, Robie H. It's So Amazing! A Book about Eggs, Sperm, Birth, Babies, & Families. Emberley, Michael, illus. 2014. (Family Library). (ENG.). 88p. (J). (gr. 2-5). 22.99 *(978-0-7636-6873-0(7))* Candlewick Pr.

—What's in There? All about Before You Were Born. Emberley, Michael & Westcott, Nadine Bernard, illus. 2013. (Let's Talk about You & Me Ser.). (ENG.). 40p. (J). (-k). 15.99 *(978-0-7636-3630-2(4))* Candlewick Pr.

Heller, Ruth. Chickens Aren't the Only Ones. l.t. ed. (FRE., Illus.). (J). rng bd. 29.95 *(978-0-590-73732-6(5))* Scholastic, Inc.

Holt, Rinehart and Winston Staff. Holt Science & Technology Chapter 26: Life Science: Reproduction & Development. 5th ed. 2004. (Illus.). pap. 12.86 *(978-0-03-030251-0(X))* Holt McDougal.

Jones, Phill. Reproduction & Cloning. 2nd rev. ed. 2012. (Science Foundations Ser.). 136p. (gr. 6-12). 35.00 *(978-1-61753-025-8(5)*, Chelsea Hse.) Facts On File, Inc.

Jones, Stan & Jones, Brenna. The Story of Me. Spector, Joel, illus. 2007. (God's Design for Sex Ser.: 1). (ENG.). 48p. (Orig.). pap. 10.99 *(978-1-60006-013-7(7))* NavPress Publishing Group.

Kim, Melissa L. The Endocrine & Reproductive Systems. 2003. (Human Body Library). (Illus.). 48p. (J). (gr. 4-10). lib. bdg. 25.27 *(978-0-7660-2020-7(7))* Enslow Pubs., Inc.

—Learning about the Endocrine & Reproductive Systems. 2013. (Learning about the Human Body Systems Ser.). 48p. (J). (gr. 5-12). pap. 8.95 *(978-1-4644-0237-1(X))* Enslow Pubs., Inc.

Klosterman, Lorrie. The Reproductive System. 2009. (Amazing Human Body 2 Ser.). 80p. (gr. 5). 34.21 *(978-0-7614-4041-3(0))* Marshall Cavendish Corp.

Krohmer, Randolph W. The Reproductive System. 2009. (Human Body: How It Works Ser.). (Illus.). 160p. (C). (gr. 9-18). 35.00 *(978-1-60413-373-8(2)*, Chelsea Hse.) Facts On File, Inc.

Loper, Ami M. The Miracle of Life. Loper, Carol J., illus. 2007. (J). *(978-0-9678798-1-9(7))* Biblical Standards Pubns.

Lowery, Zoe & Bringle, Jennifer. Reproductive Health & Women's Rights. 2017. (Women in the World Ser.). 112p. (J). (gr. 12-11). 37.10 ***(978-1-5081-7445-5(8)***, Rosen Young Adult) Rosen Publishing Group, Inc., The.

Milbourne, Anna. Where Do Baby Animals Come From? 2012. (Picture Bks). 24p. (J). bds. 10.99 *(978-0-7945-3284-0(5)*, Usborne) EDC Publishing.

Morley, Margaret Warner. A Song of Life 1922. Forsyth, Robert, illus. 2004. reprint ed. pap. 21.95 *(978-1-4179-7842-7(2))* Kessinger Publishing, LLC.

Saltz, Gail. Amazing You! Getting Smart about Your Private Parts. Cravath, Lynne Avril, illus. 2008. (ENG.). 32p. (J). (gr. -1-2). pap. 6.99 *(978-0-14-241058-5(5)*, Puffin Books) Penguin Young Readers Group.

Wanjie, Anne, ed. The Basics of Reproduction. 2013. (Core Concepts Ser.). (ENG., Illus.). 96p. (YA). (gr. 7-12). lib. bdg. 34.60 *(978-1-4777-0549-0(X)*, Rosen Classroom) Rosen Publishing Group, Inc., The.

Williams, Kara. Fertility Technology: The Baby Debate. (Focus on Science & Society Ser.). 64p. 2009. (gr. 5-6). 58.50 *(978-1-61512-622-4(8))* 2003. (Illus.). (J). lib. bdg. 31.95 *(978-0-8239-3762-2(3))* 2003. (Illus.). (YA). (gr. 4-6). lib. bdg. 26.50 *(978-0-8239-3210-8(9)*, FSFETE) Rosen Publishing Group, Inc., The.

REPTILES

see also Crocodiles; Lizards; Snakes; Turtles

ABDO Publishing Company Staff. Amazing Reptiles. 2014. (Amazing Reptiles Ser.: 8). (ENG.). 48p. (gr. 8-12). lib. bdg. 262.32 *(978-1-62403-367-4(9))* ABDO Publishing Co.

ABDO Publishing Company Staff & Hansen, Grace. Reptiles. 2014. (Reptiles Ser.: 6). (ENG.). 24p. (J). (gr. 4-8). lib. bdg. 171.00 *(978-1-62970-056-4(8))* ABDO Publishing Co.

Abramson, Andra Serlin & Ross, Paula Kovacs. Kids Meet the Reptiles. 2013. (Kids Meet Ser.: 1). (ENG.). 96p. (J). 12.95 *(978-1-60433-344-2(8)*, Applesauce Pr.) Cider Mill Pr. Bk. Pubs., LLC.

Allison, Pamela S. Emerald's Journal: A summer with Hatchlings. Cepeda, Joseph C., photos by. 2007. (Illus.). 24p. (J). lib. bdg. 16.95 *(978-0-9793474-1-2(6))* Sand Sage Pr.

Amphibians & Reptiles. 2005. (World of Animals Ser.: Vols. 41-50). (J). 499.00 *(978-0-7172-5916-8(1))* Scholastic Library Publishing.

Amstutz, Lisa J. Thorny Devil Lizards & Other Extreme Reptile Adaptations, 1 vol. 2014. (Extreme Adaptations Ser.). (ENG.). 32p. (gr. 3-4). lib. bdg. 27.32 *(978-1-4914-0168-2(0))* Capstone Press of Coughlan Cos.

Arlon, Penelope. Reptiles. (Scholastic Explora Tu Mundo Ser.). (ENG & SPA.). 80p. (J). (gr. 2-5). 2014. 12.99 *(978-0-545-62817-4(2))* 2013. 12.99 *(978-0-545-50509-3(7)*, Scholastic Reference) Scholastic, Inc.

Arnold, Tedd, illus. Fly Guy Presents: Snakes. 2016. (J). *(978-1-5182-0352-7(3))* Scholastic, Inc.

Arnosky, Jim. Slither & Crawl: Eye to Eye with Reptiles. 2015. (ENG., Illus.). 32p. (J). (gr. 1-5). pap. 6.95 *(978-1-4549-1471-6(8))* Sterling Publishing Co., Inc.

Barraclough, Susan. Snakes & Reptiles: The Scariest Cold-Blooded Creatures on Earth. 2008. (Illus.). 192p. (J). *(978-1-4351-0774-8(8))* Barnes & Noble, Inc.

Basic Domestic Reptiles & Amphibians. 2005. (Basic Domestic Reptiles & Amphibians Ser.). 64p. (gr. 6-12). 137.50 *(978-0-7910-8062-7(5)*, Chelsea Hse.) Facts On File, Inc.

Baxter, Bethany. Caimans, Gharials, Alligators, & Crocodiles. 2013. (Awesome Armored Animals Ser.). 24p. (J). (gr. k-5). 22.60 *(978-1-4777-0798-2(0))*; pap. 8.25 *(978-1-4777-0968-9(1))* Rosen Publishing Group, Inc., The. (PowerKids Pr.).

Beaumont, Holly & Lewis, Clare. Why Do Snakes & Other Animals Have Scales? 2015. (Animal Body Coverings Ser.). (ENG., Illus.). 24p. (J). (gr. 1-3). pap. 6.99 *(978-1-4846-2540-8(4)*, Heinemann Read & Learn) Heinemann-Raintree.

Bell, Samantha S. 12 Reptiles Back from the Brink. 2014. (ENG., Illus.). 32p. (J). *(978-1-63235-005-3(X))* Pr. Room Editions LLC.

Berger, Melvin & Berger, Gilda. Reptiles. 2008. (Scholastic True or False Ser.: 3). (ENG.). 48p. (J). (gr. 2-5). pap. 4.99 *(978-0-545-00393-3(8)*, Scholastic Reference) Scholastic, Inc.

Betances, Roberto. Lizard Blood. 2015. (Nature's Grossest Ser.). (ENG., Illus.). 24p. (J). (gr. 1-2). 22.60 *(978-1-4824-1843-9(6))* Stevens, Gareth Publishing LLLP.

Boothroyd, Jennifer. Endangered & Extinct Reptiles. 2014. (Lightning Bolt Books Animals in Danger Ser.). (ENG., Illus.). 32p. (gr. k-2). pap. 7.95 *(978-1-4677-2373-2(8))*; lib. bdg. 26.60 *(978-1-4677-1334-4(1)*, Lerner Pubns.) Lerner Publishing Group.

—Scales. 2011. (First Step Nonfiction / Body Coverings Ser.). pap. 33.92 *(978-0-7613-8609-4(2))*; (ENG.). 24p. pap. 6.95 *(978-0-7613-7829-7(4))*; (ENG., Illus.). 24p. lib. bdg. 23.93 *(978-0-7613-5787-2(4))* Lerner Publishing Group.

Bredeson, Carmen. Flying Geckos & Other Weird Reptiles. 2009. (I Like Weird Animals! Ser.). (Illus.). 24p. (J). (gr. 1-3). lib. bdg. 22.60 *(978-0-7660-3126-5(8)*, Enslow Elementary) Enslow Pubs., Inc.

Brett, Flora. Get to Know Reptiles. 2015. (Get to Know Reptiles Ser.). (ENG.). 24p. (gr. 1-2). lib. bdg. 101.28 *(978-1-4914-2507-7(5)*, First Facts) Capstone Press of Coughlan Cos.

—A Reptile's View of the World. 2015. (Pet Perspectives Ser.). (ENG., Illus.). 24p. (gr. 1-2). lib. bdg. 25.32 *(978-1-4914-5051-2(7))* Capstone Press of Coughlan Cos.

Brookes, Olivia. The Rise of the Reptiles. 2012. (Dinosaur Files Ser.). (ENG.). 32p. (J). (gr. 1-5). pap. 10.00 *(978-1-61533-526-8(9))*; lib. bdg. 25.25 *(978-1-61533-519-0(6))* Windmill Bks.

Buckingham, Suzanne. Meet the Bearded Dragon. 2009. (Scales & Tails Ser.). 24p. (gr. 2-3). 42.50 *(978-1-60852-980-3(0))*; (Illus.). (J). lib. bdg. 22.60 *(978-1-4042-4500-6(6))* Rosen Publishing Group, Inc., The. (PowerKids Pr.).

—Meet the Iguana. 2009. (Scales & Tails Ser.). 24p. (gr. 2-3). 42.50 *(978-1-60852-983-4(5)*, PowerKids Pr.) Rosen Publishing Group, Inc., The.

Bulletpoints Reptiles & Amphibians. 2005. (Illus.). (J). per. 4.99 *(978-1-933581-05-7(0))* Byeway Bks.

Bumstead, Pat & Worsley, Norman H. Canadian Skin & Scales. 2003. (Illus.). 168p. (YA). (gr. 5-6). pap. *(978-0-9689278-1-6(5))* Simply Wild Pubns., Inc.

Caimans, Gharials, Alligators, & Crocodiles. 2013. (Awesome Armored Animals Ser.). 24p. (J). (gr. k-5). pap. 49.50 *(978-1-4777-0969-6(X)*, PowerKids Pr.) Rosen Publishing Group, Inc., The.

Campbell, Jonathan A. & Lamar, William W. The Venomous Reptiles of the Western Hemisphere, 2 vols. 2004. (Comstock Books in Herpetology). (ENG., Illus.). 976p. 180.00 *(978-0-8014-4141-7(2)*, 80140100664830) Cornell Univ. Pr.

Caputo, Christine A. Reptiles & Amphibians. 2012. (Illus.). 32p. (J). *(978-0-545-46701-8(2))* Scholastic, Inc.

Cavell-Clarke, Steffi. Reptiles. 2017. (Animal Classification Ser.). 32p. (J). (gr. 3-4). pap. 10.50 ***(978-1-5345-2021-9(X))***; lib. bdg. 27.25 ***(978-1-5345-2023-3(6))*** Greenhaven Publishing LLC. (KidHaven Publishing).

Clarke, Catriona. Reptiles: Internet-Referenced. 2009. (Beginner's Nature Ser.). 32p. (J). 4.99 *(978-0-7945-2490-6(7)*, Usborne) EDC Publishing.

P
Q
R

Cleary, Brian P. Tortoise, Tree Snake, Gator, & Sea Snake: What Is a Reptile? Goneau, Martin, illus. 2012. (Animal Groups Are CATegorical (tm) Ser.). (ENG.). 32p. (gr. k-3). pap. 7.95 (978-1-4677-0341-3(9)); lib. bdg. 26.60 (978-0-7613-6210-4(X)) Lerner Publishing Group. (Millbrook Pr.).

Cleave, Andrew. Snakes & Reptiles - Pb: A Portrait of the Animal World. 2013. (Portrait of the Animal World Ser.). (Illus.). 80p. pap. 9.95 (978-1-59764-318-4(1)) New Line Bks.

Costain, Meredith. Reptiles: Cold-Blooded Creatures. 2014. (Discovery Education: Animals Ser.). 32p. (J). (gr. 3-6). 26.25 (978-1-4777-6936-2(6)); pap. 10.00 (978-1-4777-6937-9(4)) Rosen Publishing Group, Inc., The. (PowerKids Pr.).

Crump, Marty. Amphibians & Reptiles: An Introduction to Their Natural History & Conservation, 1 vol. 2011. (ENG., Illus.). 272p. (J). 29.95 (978-1-935778-20-2(X)) McDonald & Woodward Publishing Co., The.

Dennard, Deborah. Reptiles: Explore the Fascinating Worlds of Alligators & Crocodiles, Lizards, Snakes, Turtles. Dewey, Jennifer Owings, tr. Dewey, Jennifer Owings, illus. 2004. (Our Wild World Ser.). (ENG.). 192p. (J). (gr. 3-6). 16.95 (978-1-55971-880-6(3)) Cooper Square Publishing Llc.

Dorling Kindersley Publishing Staff. DK Eyewitness Books: Reptile. 2017. (DK Eyewitness Bks.). (ENG.). 72p. (J). (gr. 3-7). pap. 9.99 **(978-1-4654-6249-7(X)**, DK Children) Dorling Kindersley Publishing, Inc.

—DK Findout! Reptiles & Amphibians. 2017. (DK Find Out! Ser.). (ENG.). 64p. (J). (gr. 1-4). pap. 10.99 **(978-1-4654-6310-4(0)**, DK Children) Dorling Kindersley Publishing, Inc.

—Everything You Need to Know about Snakes. 2013. (Everything You Need to Know Ser.). (ENG.). 80p. (J). (gr. 2-5). 15.99 (978-1-4654-0246-2(2), DK Children) Dorling Kindersley Publishing, Inc.

—Reptile. 2017. (DK Eyewitness Bks.). (ENG.). 72p. (J). (gr. 3-7). lib. bdg. 19.99 **(978-1-4654-6252-7(X)**, DK Children) Dorling Kindersley Publishing, Inc.

Dorling Kindersley Publishing Staff. Reptiles. 2013. (Eye Wonder Ser.). (ENG., Illus.). 56p. (J). (gr. k-4). 10.99 (978-1-4654-0908-9(4), DK Children) Dorling Kindersley Publishing, Inc.

Dorling Kindersley Publishing Staff, creator. Reptile. 2005. (Ultimate Sticker Bks.). (ENG., Illus.). 16p. (J). (gr. k-3). pap. 6.99 (978-0-7566-0977-1(1), DK Children) Dorling Kindersley Publishing, Inc.

Dowling, Lucy. Why Why Why... Do Lizards Stick to Walls? 2010. (Why Why Why Ser.). 32p. (J). (gr. 1-3). lib. bdg. 18.95 (978-1-4222-1582-1(2)) Mason Crest.

Duke, Shirley Smith. Reptiles & Amphibians Explained. 2016. (Distinctions in Nature Ser.). 32p. (J). (gr. 3-3). 28.50 (978-1-5026-1746-0(3)) Cavendish Square Publishing.

Encyclopaedia Britannica, Inc. Staff, compiled by. Britannica Illustrated Science Library: Reptiles & Dinosaurs, 16 vols. 2008. (Illus.). (J). 29.95 (978-1-59339-395-3(4)) Encyclopaedia Britannica, Inc.

—My First Britannica: Birds, Insects, Reptiles, & Aquatic Life. 2008. (gr. 7-12). (978-1-59339-411-0(X)) Encyclopaedia Britannica, Inc.

Encyclopedia Britannica Staff, creator. Reptiles & Dinosaurs. 2011. (Britannica Illustrated Science Library Ser.). (J). 37.44 (978-1-61535-464-1(6)) Encyclopaedia Britannica, Inc.

Fact Atlas: Reptiles. 2009. (FACT ATLAS Ser.). 72p. (J). 14.95 (978-0-8416-1096-5(7)) Hammond World Atlas Corp.

Fisher, Diana. Reptiles & Amphibians: Step by Step Intsructions for 29 Reptiles & Amphibians. 2006. (Learn to Draw Ser.). (ENG., Illus.). 40p. (J). (gr. 1-17). per. 4.95 (978-1-56010-994-5(7), 1560109947) Quarto Publishing Group USA.

Fisher, Diana & Shelly, Jeff, illus. All about Dinosaurs & Reptiles. 2010. (All about Drawing Ser.). 80p. (J). 34.25 (978-1-936309-07-8(6)) Quarto Publishing Group USA.

Fletcher, Patricia. Why Do Thorny Devils Have Two Heads? And Other Curious Reptile Adaptations. 2017. (Odd Adaptations Ser.). 32p. (J). (gr. 3-4). pap. 10.50 **(978-1-5382-0405-4(3))** Stevens, Gareth Publishing LLLP.

Gagne, Tammy. Crocodile, 1 vol. 2013. (Great Predators Ser.). (ENG., Illus.). 48p. (J). (gr. 3-6). lib. bdg. 32.79 (978-1-61783-946-7(9)) ABDO Publishing Co.

Gaines, Ann. Kids Top 10 Pet Reptiles & Amphibians. 2015. (American Humane Association Top 10 Pets for Kids Ser.). 48p. (J). (gr. 3-4). 25.27 (978-0-7660-6645-8(2)) Enslow Pubs., Inc.

Gaines, Ann Graham. Kids Top 10 Pet Reptiles & Amphibians. 2015. (American Humane Association Top 10 Pets for Kids Ser.). 48p. (J). (gr. 3-4). pap. 8.95 (978-0-7660-6646-5(0), Enslow Elementary) Enslow Pubs., Inc.

—Top 10 Reptiles & Amphibians for Kids. 2008. (Top Pets for Kids with American Humane Ser.). (Illus.). 48p. (J). (gr. 2-5). lib. bdg. 25.27 (978-0-7660-3074-9(1)) Enslow Pubs., Inc.

Ganeri, Anita. Discover the Komodo Dragon. 2016. (Fabulous Animals Ser.). (ENG., Illus.). 32p. (gr. 1-3). lib. bdg. 27.32 (978-1-4846-2711-2(3), Heinemann First Library) Heinemann-Raintree.

Gingold, Janet. My Adventure with Reptiles: Advanced My Adventure. 2009. (ENG.). 72p. (J). pap. 9.99 (978-1-59092-464-8(9)) Blue Forge Pr.

Gish, Melissa. Alligators. 2017. (J). **(978-1-60818-817-8(5)**, Creative Education) Creative Co., The.

Green, Ken. Reptiles - Weird Wildlife, 6 bks., Set. 2003. (Illus.). pap. 48.30 (978-1-4109-0299-3(4)) Harcourt Schl. Pubs.

Greve, Tom. Reptiles. 2014. 24p. pap. 8.00 (978-1-61003-376-3(0)) Center for the Collaborative Classroom.

Hall, Julie. Reptiles & Amphibians: Grades 2 & 3. (Illus.). (J). pap., wbk. ed. 4.99 (978-0-88743-964-3(0)) School Zone Publishing Co.

Hall, Katharine. Amphibians & Reptiles, 1 vol. 2015. (Compare & Contrast Ser.). (ENG., Illus.). 32p. (J). (gr. k-3). pap. 9.95 (978-1-62855-560-8(2)) Arbordale Publishing.

—Amphibians & Reptiles: A Compare & Contrast Book, 1 vol. 2015. (SPA & ENG.). 32p. (J). (gr. k-3). pap. 9.95 (978-1-62855-569-1(6)) Arbordale Publishing.

Hamilton, S. L. Reptiles. 2013. (Xtreme Pets Ser.). (Illus.). 32p. (J). (gr. 3-9). lib. bdg. 27.07 (978-1-61783-974-0(4), Abdo & Daughters) ABDO Publishing Co.

Hansen, Grace. Komodo Dragons, 1 vol. 2014. (Reptiles Ser.). (ENG.). 24p. (J). (gr. 4-8). lib. bdg. 28.50 (978-1-62970-060-1(6)) ABDO Publishing Co.

Harrington, Jane. Extreme Pets. 2007. (ENG., Illus.). 164p. (J). (gr. 2-5). pap., instr.'s hndbk. ed. 12.99 (978-0-439-82948-9(8)) Scholastic, Inc.

Harris, Tim, ed. Reptiles & Amphibians. 2011. (FAYFT: Endangered Animals Ser.). 64p. (gr. 4-10). lib. bdg. 39.95 (978-1-936333-36-3(8)) Brown Bear Bks.

Harrison, Paul. Reptiles. (Up Close Ser.). 24p. (gr. 3-3). 2009. 47.90 (978-1-60854-700-5(0)) 2007. (Illus.). (J). lib. bdg. 25.25 (978-1-4042-3763-6(1)) Rosen Publishing Group, Inc., The. (PowerKids Pr.).

Harvey, Bev. Reptiles. (Eyes on Nature Ser.). 32p. (J). (gr. 1). pap. (978-1-882210-54-1(9)) Action Publishing, Inc.

Herrington, Lisa M. Remarkable Reptiles. 2016. (Rookie Read-About Science(tm): Strange Animals Ser.). (ENG., Illus.). 32p. (J). lib. bdg. 25.00 (978-0-531-22603-2(4), Children's Pr.) Scholastic Library Publishing.

Himmelman, John. Basic Illustrated Guide to Frogs, Snakes, Bugs, & Slugs. 2013. (Basic Illustrated Ser.). (ENG., Illus.). 104p. pap. 10.95 (978-0-7627-8259-8(5), Falcon Guides) Globe Pequot Pr., The.

Hirsch, Rebecca E. Boa Constrictors: Prey-Crushing Reptiles. 2015. (ENG., Illus.). 32p. (J). (gr. 2-4). 26.65 (978-1-4677-7981-4(4), Lerner Pubns.) Lerner Publishing Group.

—Tuataras: Dinosaur-Era Reptiles. 2015. (ENG., Illus.). 32p. (J). (gr. 2-4). 26.65 (978-1-4677-7979-1(2), Lerner Pubns.) Lerner Publishing Group.

Hirschmann, Kris. Deadliest Reptiles. 2016. (ENG.). 80p. (J). (gr. 5-12). lib. bdg. (978-1-68282-052-0(1)) ReferencePoint Pr., Inc.

Hofmann, Kate. Ranger Rick's Amazing Animals: Reptiles. 2016. (Ranger Rick: Amazing Animals Ser.). (ENG., Illus.). 40p. (J). (gr. 2-7). pap. 7.95 (978-1-63076-202-5(4)) Muddy Boots Pr.

Holt, Rinehart and Winston Staff. Holt Science & Technology Chapter 16: Life Science: Fishes, Amphibians, & Reptiles. 5th ed. 2004. (Illus.). pap. 12.86 (978-0-03-030221-3(8)) Holt McDougal.

Holub, Joan. Why Do Snakes Hiss? And Other Questions about Snakes, Lizards, & Turtles. DiVito, Anna, illus. 2004. (Penguin Young Readers, Level 3 Ser.). (ENG.). 48p. (J). (gr. 1-3). mass mkt. 3.99 (978-0-14-240105-7(6), Penguin Young Readers) Penguin Young Readers Group.

Housel, Debra J. Reptiles y Anfibios Reptantes. 2017. (TIME for Kids en Español - Level 3 Ser.). (SPA & ENG.). 32p. (gr. 3-3). lib. bdg. 31.99 **(978-1-5157-5172-4(4))** Time for Kids Inc AUS. Dist: Capstone Pub.

Housel, Debra J. Slithering Reptiles & Amphibians, 1 vol. 2nd rev. ed. 2013. (Nonfiction Readers Ser.). (ENG., Illus.). 28p. (J). (gr. 3-3). pap. 25.96 (978-1-4807-1074-0(1)) Shell Educational Publishing.

—Slithering Reptiles & Amphibians, 1 vol. 2nd rev. ed. 2011. (Nonfiction Readers Ser.). (ENG.). 28p. (J). (gr. 3-3). pap. 8.99 (978-1-4333-3659-1(6)) Teacher Created Materials, Inc.

Howell, Catherine Herbert. Ultimate Explorer Field Guide: Reptiles & Amphibians: Find Adventure! Go Outside! Have Fun! Be a Backyard Ranger & Amphibian Adventurer. 2016. (ENG., Illus.). 160p. (J). (gr. 3-7). pap. 12.99 (978-1-4263-2544-1(4), National Geographic Children's Bks.) National Geographic Society.

—Ultimate Explorer Field Guide: Reptiles & Amphibians: Find Adventure! Go Outside! Have Fun! Be a Backyard Ranger & Amphibian Adventurer! 2016. (ENG., Illus.). 160p. (J). (gr. 3-7). lib. bdg. 22.90 (978-1-4263-2545-8(2), National Geographic Children's Bks.) National Geographic Society.

Hudak, Heather C. Reptiles & Amphibians. (Animal Facts Ser.). (Illus.). 24p. (J). 2005. (gr. 2-3). per. 8.95 (978-1-59036-246-4(2)) 2004. lib. bdg. 24.45 (978-1-59036-204-4(7)) Weigl Pubs., Inc.

Hughes, Jon. Pterosaur! Purple Band. 2016. (Cambridge Reading Adventures Ser.). (ENG.). 24p. pap. 7.19 (978-1-107-55108-4(0)) Cambridge Univ. Pr.

Hughes, Sarah Anne. Reptiles & Amphibians. Peterson, Roger Tory, ed. Hughes, Sarah Anne, illus. 2nd ed. 2013. (Peterson Field Guide Color-In Bks.). (ENG., Illus.). 64p. (J). 8.95 (978-0-544-02695-7(0)) Houghton Mifflin Harcourt Publishing Co.

Hunt, Santana. Name That Reptile! 2016. (Guess That Animal! Ser.). (Illus.). 24p. (J). (gr. 2-1). lib. bdg. 22.60 (978-1-4824-4747-7(9)) Stevens, Gareth Publishing LLLP.

Hutchinson, Mark. Reptiles. 2011. (Insiders Ser.). (ENG.). 64p. (J). (gr. 3-7). 17.99 (978-1-4424-3276-5(4), Simon & Schuster Bks. For Young Readers) Simon & Schuster Bks. For Young Readers.

Iguanas & Reptiles. 2007. (Illus.). (J). cd-rom 9.99 (978-0-9795190-5-5(5)) Color & Learn.

Jackson, Tom. Reptiles. 2016. (Animal Mechanicals Ser.). 32p. (gr. 3-3). pap. 10.00 (978-1-4994-2250-4(4), PowerKids Pr.) Rosen Publishing Group, Inc., The.

Jacobs, Pat. Why Do Reptiles Have Scales? And Other Questions about Evolution & Classification. 2016. (Wildlife Wonders Ser.). 00032p. (J). (gr. 3-3). pap. 10.00 (978-1-4994-3209-1(7), PowerKids Pr.) Rosen Publishing Group, Inc., The.

Jango-Cohen, Judith. Desert Iguanas. (Pull Ahead Bks.). (Illus.). 32p. (gr. k-3). 2005. lib. bdg. 22.60 (978-0-8225-3635-2(8)) 2003. (J). pap. 5.95 (978-0-8225-3642-0(0)) Lerner Publishing Group.

Jankowski, Matt. Attack of the Burmese Pythons. 2016. (Animal Invaders: Destroying Native Habitats Ser.). 00024p. (J). pap. 8.15 **(978-1-4824-5659-2(1))** Stevens, Gareth Publishing LLLP.

Johnson, Jinny. Pteranodon & Other Flying Reptiles. Rosewarne, Graham, illus. 2007. (Dinosaurs Alive! Ser.). 32p. (J). (gr. 4-7). lib. bdg. 28.50 (978-1-59920-068-2(6)) Black Rabbit Bks.

Kalman, Bobbie. Baby Reptiles. 2008. (It's Fun to Learn about Baby Animals Ser.). (ENG., Illus.). 24p. (J). (gr. k-3). pap. (978-0-7787-3973-9(2)) Crabtree Publishing Co.

—¿Qué Son los Reptiles? 2005. (Serie la Ciencia de los Seres Vivos Ser.). (SPA., Illus.). 32p. (J). (gr. 3-4). lib. bdg. (978-0-7787-8762-4(1)) Crabtree Publishing Co.

—?Qué Son los Reptiles? 2005. (Ciencia de los Seres Vivos Ser.). (SPA., Illus.). 32p. (J). (gr. 3-4). pap. (978-0-7787-8808-9(3)) Crabtree Publishing Co.

—Reptile Rap. 2010. (My World Ser.). (ENG.). 16p. (J). (gr. k-3). (978-0-7787-9512-4(8)); pap. (978-0-7787-9537-7(3)) Crabtree Publishing Co.

—Les Reptiles. 2011. (FRE., Illus.). 32p. (J). pap. 9.95 (978-2-89579-394-6(8)) Bayard Canada CAN. Dist: Crabtree Publishing Co.

Kaminski, Mary. Raising Reptiles: Divide Within 100. 2014. (Rosen Common Core Math Readers Ser.). (ENG., Illus.). 24p. (J). (gr. 3-4). pap. 8.25 (978-1-4777-4949-4(7), PowerKids Pr.) Rosen Publishing Group, Inc., The.

Kaspar, Anna. What's a Reptile? 2012. (All about Animals Ser.). (ENG.). 24p. (J). (gr. k-3). pap. 8.25 (978-1-4488-6226-9(4)); lib. bdg. 22.60 (978-1-4488-6134-7(9)) Rosen Publishing Group, Inc., The. (PowerKids Pr.).

—What's a Reptile? Qué Es un Reptil? 2012. (All about Animals / Todo sobre los animales Ser.). (SPA & ENG., Illus.). 24p. (J). (gr. k-3). lib. bdg. 22.60 (978-1-4488-6700-4(2), PowerKids Pr.) Rosen Publishing Group, Inc., The.

Kenney, Karen Latchana. Flying Dragons. 2017. (Weird & Unusual Animals Ser.). (ENG.). 24p. (gr. 1-4). 20.95 **(978-1-68151-156-6(8))** Amicus Publishing.

Kessler, Colleen. A Project Guide to Reptiles & Birds. 2010. (Life Science Projects for Kids Ser.). (Illus.). 48p. (J). (gr. 4-8). lib. bdg. 29.95 (978-1-58415-874-5(3)) Mitchell Lane Pubs., Inc.

Kratt, Chris & Kratt, Martin. Wild Reptiles: Snakes, Crocodiles, Lizards, & Turtles. Random House, illus. 2015. (Step into Reading Ser.). (ENG.). 32p. (J). (gr. k-4). 4.99 (978-0-553-50775-1(3), Random Hse. Bks. for Young Readers) Random Hse. Children's Bks.

Kuskowski, Alex. Miniature Reptiles, 1 vol. 2014. (Mini Animal Marvels Ser.). (ENG., Illus.). 24p. (J). (gr. -1-3). 24.21 (978-1-62403-069-7(6)) ABDO Publishing Co.

Lee, Celeste & Herndon, Ryan, compiled by. Guinness World Records, Top 10. 2007. (Illus.). 29p. (J). pap. (978-0-439-87417-5(3)) Scholastic, Inc.

Levine, Michelle. Reptiles. 2015. (Illus.). 32p. (J). lib. bdg. 28.50 (978-1-60753-476-1(2)) Amicus Publishing.

Lewis, Clare. Reptile Body Parts. 2015. (Animal Body Parts Ser.). (ENG., Illus.). 24p. (gr. k-2). 23.32 (978-1-4846-2554-5(4)) Heinemann-Raintree.

Little & Large Sticker Activity - Reptiles & Amphibians. 2006. (J). 3.99 (978-1-933581-35-4(2)) Byeway Bks.

Loxton, Daniel. Plesiosaur Peril, 0 vols. Loxton, Daniel & Smith, Jim W. W., illus. 2014. (Tales of Prehistoric Life Ser.). (ENG.). 32p. (J). (gr. -1-2). 16.95 (978-1-55453-633-7(2)) Kids Can Pr., Ltd. CAN. Dist: Hachette Bk. Group.

MacAulay, Kelley & Kalman, Bobbie. Reptiles de Todo Tipo. 2005. (Que Tipo de Animal Es? Ser.). (SPA., Illus.). 32p. (J). (gr. 3-7). pap. (978-0-7787-8871-3(7)); lib. bdg. (978-0-7787-8835-5(0)) Crabtree Publishing Co.

—Reptiles of All Kinds. 2005. (What Kind of Animal Is It? Ser.). (ENG., Illus.). 32p. (J). lib. bdg. (978-0-7787-2158-1(2)); pap. (978-0-7787-2216-8(3)) Crabtree Publishing Co.

Macgregor, Eloise. Sidewinder. 2015. (Desert Animals Searchin' for Shade Ser.). (ENG.). 24p. (J). (gr. -1-3). lib. bdg. 23.93 (978-1-62724-534-0(0)) Bearport Publishing Co., Inc.

Martin, Isabel. Reptiles: A Question & Answer Book, 1 vol. 2014. (Animal Kingdom Questions & Answers Ser.). (ENG.). 24p. (gr. k-1). 26.65 (978-1-4914-0565-9(1)); (Illus.). pap. 6.95 (978-1-4914-0633-5(X)) Capstone Press of Coughlan Cos. (Pebble Plus).

Mathewson, Robert F. The How & Why Wonder Book of Reptiles & Amphibians. Sweet, Darrell & Allen, Douglas, illus. 2011. 48p. pap. 35.95 (978-1-258-09940-4(3)) Literary Licensing, LLC.

Mattern, Joanne. Reptiles & Amphibians. 2009. (Reading Room Collection 2 Ser.). 24p. (gr. 3-4). 42.50 (978-1-60851-986-6(4), PowerKids Pr.) Rosen Publishing Group, Inc., The.

—Reptiles y anfibios (Reptiles & Amphibians) 2009. (Reading Room Collection: Spanish Ser.). (SPA.). 24p. (gr. 3-4). 42.50 (978-1-60854-179-9(7), Editorial Buenas Letras) Rosen Publishing Group, Inc., The.

Mattison, Christopher. Reptiles & Amphibians. 2007. (Facts at Your Fingertips Ser.). (Illus.). 64p. (YA). (gr. 7-12). lib. bdg. 35.65 (978-1-933834-04-7(8)) Brown Bear Books.

McNab, Chris. Endangered Reptiles. 2006. (Nature's Monsters Ser.). (Illus.). 32p. (gr. 2-6). lib. bdg. 26.00 (978-0-8368-6171-6(X), Gareth Stevens Learning Library) Stevens, Gareth Publishing LLLP.

Mertz, Leslie A., et al. Grzimek's Student Animal Life Resource, 2 vols. 2005. (Illus.). xxxix, 427p. (J). (978-0-7876-9405-0(3)); (978-0-7876-9406-7(1)) Cengage Gale. (UXL).

Miller, Jake. The Bearded Dragon. (Lizard Library). 24p. 2009. (gr. 3-3). 42.50 (978-1-60854-009-9(X)) 2003. (Illus.). (J). lib. bdg. 21.25 (978-0-8239-6412-3(4)) Rosen Publishing Group, Inc., The. (PowerKids Pr.).

Miller, Mirella S. Sea Turtles Are Awesome. 2018. (ENG.). 32p. (gr. 3-6). 31.35 **(978-1-63235-437-2(3)**, 12-Story Library) Pr. Room Editions LLC.

Mitchell, Susan K. Biggest vs. Smallest Slimy, Scaly Creatures. 2010. (Biggest vs. Smallest Animals Ser.). (Illus.). 24p. (J). 22.60 (978-0-7660-3579-9(4), Enslow Elementary) Enslow Pubs., Inc.

Mugford, Simon & Priddy, Roger. Reptiles & Other Scaly Friends. 2007. (Smart Kids Ser.). (ENG., Illus.). 32p. (J). (gr. -1-2). bds. 9.99 (978-0-312-49921-1(3), 9780312499211, Priddy Bks.) St. Martin's Pr.

Munro, Alice. Friend of My Youth. 2012. (Vintage International Ser.). (ENG., Illus.). 288p. E-Book (978-0-307-81459-3(9), Vintage) Knopf Doubleday Publishing Group.

National Geographic Editors. Creepy, Crawly Collection. 2012. (Readers Ser.). (ENG., Illus.). 128p. (J). (gr. -1-1). pap. 7.99 (978-1-4263-1197-0(4), National Geographic Children's Bks.) National Geographic Society.

National Geographic Kids. National Geographic Kids Reptiles & Amphibians Sticker Activity Book. 2017. (NG Sticker Activity Bks.). (ENG.). 56p. (J). (gr. -1-3). pap. 6.99 (978-1-4263-2777-3(3), National Geographic Children's Bks.) National Geographic Society.

National Geographic Kids & Hoena, Blake. National Geographic Kids Everything Reptiles. 2016. (National Geographic Kids Everything Ser.). (ENG., Illus.). 64p. (J). (gr. 3-7). pap. 12.99 (978-1-4263-2526-7(6), National Geographic Children's Bks.) National Geographic Society.

Niven, Felicia Lowenstein & Library Association Staff. Learning to Care for Reptiles & Amphibians. 2010. (Beginning Pet Care with American Humane Ser.). 48p. (J). 25.27 (978-0-7660-3194-4(2), Enslow Elementary) Enslow Pubs., Inc.

O'Donnell, Kerri. Komodo Dragons. 2009. (Ugly Animals Ser.). 24p. (gr. 2-3). 42.50 (978-1-60854-600-8(4), PowerKids Pr.) Rosen Publishing Group, Inc., The.

O'Neill, Amanda. I Wonder Why Snakes Shed Their Skin. 2011. (I Wonder Why Ser.). (ENG., Illus.). 32p. (J). (gr. k-3). pap. 6.99 (978-0-7534-6531-8(0), 9780753465318, Kingfisher) Roaring Brook Pr.

O'Reilly, Wenda. GO FISH WILDLIFE REPTILES & AMPHIBIANS. 2007. n/ap. pap. 119.40 (978-1-59960-018-5(8)) Birdcage Pr.

Osborne, Mary Pope & Boyce, Natalie Pope. Snakes & Other Reptiles: A Nonfiction Companion to a Crazy Day with Cobras. Murdocca, Sal, illus. 2011. (Magic Tree House - Fact Tracker Ser.: 23). (ENG.). 128p. (J). (gr. 2-5). 6.99 (978-0-375-86011-9(8), Random Hse. Bks. for Young Readers) Random Hse. Children's Bks.

Parker, Janice. Reptiles. 2007. (Life Science (Weigl Hardcover) Ser.). (Illus.). 32p. (J). (gr. 4-7). lib. bdg. 26.00 (978-1-59036-711-7(1)); per. 8.95 (978-1-59036-712-4(X)) Weigl Pubs., Inc.

Parker, Steve. 50 Things You Should Know about Fierce Creatures. Marshall, Anne, ed. 2004. (50 Things You Should Know Ser.). (Illus.). 112p. (J). 14.99 (978-1-84236-301-0(8)) Miles Kelly Publishing, Ltd. GBR. Dist: Independent Pubs. Group.

Parker, Steven. See-Through Reptiles. 2004. 32p. 15.95 (978-0-7624-2290-6(4)) Running Pr. Bk. Pubs.

Peterson, Megan C. & Marx, Mandy R. Reptiles. 2016. (Reptiles Ser.). (ENG.). 24p. (gr. k-1). lib. bdg. 133.25 (978-1-5157-4036-0(6), Pebble Plus) Capstone Press of Coughlan Cos.

Peterson, Megan Cooley & Rustad, Martha E. H. Show Me Reptiles: My First Picture Encyclopedia, 1 vol. (My First Picture Encyclopedias Ser.). (ENG., Illus.). 32p. (gr. 1-2). 2013. 7.95 (978-1-62065-928-1(X), Aplus Bks.) 2012. lib. bdg. 27.32 (978-1-4296-8571-9(9)) Capstone Press of Coughlan Cos.

Peterson, Megan Cooley, et al. Reptiles. 2012. (Reptiles Ser.). (ENG.). 24p. (gr. k-1). lib. bdg. 53.30 (978-1-4296-8122-3(5), Pebble Plus) Capstone Press of Coughlan Cos.

Phillips, Dee. Reptiles & Amphibians. 2006. (Blue Zoo Guides). (ENG., Illus.). 96p. (J). (gr. -1-2). 18.95 (978-1-58728-561-5(4)) Cooper Square Publishing Llc.

Rabe, Tish. Miles & Miles of Reptiles: All about Reptiles. Ruiz, Aristides & Mathieu, Joe, illus. 2009. (Cat in the Hat's Learning Library). (ENG.). 48p. (J). (gr. -1-3). 9.99 (978-0-375-82884-3(2), Random Hse. Bks. for Young Readers) Random Hse. Children's Bks.

Rake, Matthew. Prehistoric Sea Beasts. Mendez, Simon, illus. 2017. (If Extinct Beasts Came to Life Ser.). (ENG.). 32p. (J). (gr. 3-6). 7.99 (978-1-5124-1158-4(2)); 7.99 **(978-1-5124-3618-1(6))**; 39.99 **(978-1-5124-3617-4(8))**; 39.99 **(978-1-5124-0909-3(X))** Lerner Publishing Group.

—Scaly, Slippery Creatures. Mendez, Simon, illus. 2015. (Real-Life Monsters Ser.). (ENG.). 32p. (J). (gr. 3-6). pap. 7.99 (978-1-4677-7645-5(9), Lerner Pubns.) Lerner Publishing Group.

Reference, Brown. Exploring the World of Reptiles & Amphibians, 6-Volume Set, 6 vols. 2009. (Exploring the World of Reptiles & Amphibians Ser.). (Illus.). 480p. (gr. 5-8). 210.00 (978-1-60413-256-4(6), Chelsea Hse.) Facts On File, Inc.

Reptiles. Date not set. (Question & Answers of the Natural World Ser.). 32p. 4.98 (978-0-7525-4321-5(0)) Parragon, Inc.

Reptiles & Amphibians. 2014. (Animal Q & A Ser.). (Illus.). 24p. (J). (gr. k-3). lib. bdg. 23.60 (978-1-4777-9194-3(9)) Windmill Bks.

Reptiles & Amphibians: Level P, 6 vols., Vol. 3. (Explorers Ser.). 32p. (gr. 3-6). 44.95 (978-0-7699-0614-0(1)) Shortland Pubns. (U. S. A.) Inc.

Los Reptiles Y Los Anfibios, 6 vols., Vol. 3. (Explorers. Exploradores Nonfiction Sets Ser.). (SPA.). (gr. 3-6). (978-0-7699-0650-8(8)) Shortland Pubns. (U. S. A.) Inc.

Richardson, Joy. Reptiles. 2005. (Variety of Life Ser.). (Illus.). 32p. (gr. 1-4). lib. bdg. 26.00 (978-0-8368-4508-2(0), Gareth Stevens Learning Library) Stevens, Gareth Publishing LLLP.

Riehecky, Janet. Reptiles. 2017. (My First Animal Kingdom Encyclopedias Ser.). (ENG., Illus.). 32p. (gr. 1-2). lib. bdg. 27.32 (978-1-5157-3928-9(7), Aplus Bks.) Capstone Press of Coughlan Cos.

Riggs, Kate. Pterodactylse. 2011. (ENG., Illus.). 24p. (J). 8.95 (978-1-77092-104-7(4)) Saunders Bk. Co. CAN. Dist: Creative Co., The.

Ringstad, Arnold. Totally Amazing Facts about Reptiles. 2017. (Mind Benders Ser.). (ENG.). 112p. (gr. 1-3). lib. bdg. 23.32 **(978-1-5157-6974-3(7))** Capstone Press of Coughlan Cos.

Ripley's Believe It Or Not! Staff, compiled by. Ripley Twists: Snakes & Reptiles. 2015. (Twist Ser.: 13). (ENG., Illus.). 48p. (J). 12.95 (978-1-60991-141-6(5)) Ripley Entertainment, Inc.

Ritchey, Richard I. True Adventures of the Reptileman. 2007. 60p. per. 10.95 (978-0-595-45020-6(2)) iUniverse, Inc.

Rodriguez, Ana Maria. Secret of the Puking Penguins ... & More! 2008. (Animal Secrets Revealed! Ser.). (Illus.). 48p. (J). (gr. 5-9). lib. bdg. 25.27 (978-0-7660-2955-2(7)) Enslow Pubs., Inc.

Rodriguez, Ana Maria. The Secret of the Squiggly Green Bombers... & More! 2017. (Animal Secrets Revealed! Ser.). 48p. (gr. 4-4). lib. bdg. 27.93 **(978-0-7660-8631-9(3))** Enslow Pubs., Inc.

Royston, Angela. Reptiles. (Illus.). 32p. (YA). (gr. 2-18). lib. bdg. 27.10 (978-1-932333-38-1(X)) Chrysalis Education.

—Reptiles. 2015. (Animal Classifications Ser.). (ENG., Illus.). 32p. (gr. 1-3). 27.32 (978-1-4846-0754-1(6), Heinemann First Library) Heinemann-Raintree.

Salzmann, Mary Elizabeth. What Has a Shell?, 1 vol. 2007. (Creature Features Ser.). (ENG., Illus.). 24p. (gr. -1-3). 25.65

(978-1-59928-871-0(0), Super SandCastle) ABDO Publishing Co.
—What Has Scales?, 1 vol. 2007. (Creature Features Ser.). (ENG., Illus.). 24p. (gr. -1-3). 25.65 (978-1-59928-870-3(2), Super SandCastle) ABDO Publishing Co.
Savage, Stephen. Focus on Reptiles. 2011. (Animal Watch Ser.). 32p. (YA). (gr. 3-6). lib. bdg. 26.60 (978-1-4339-5993-6(3)) Stevens, Gareth Publishing LLLP.
Scaly Things: Level N, 6 vols. (Explorers Ser.). 32p. (gr. 3-6). 44.95 (978-0-7699-0594-5(3)) Shortland Pubns. (U. S. A.) Inc.
Schafer, Susan. Invasive Reptiles & Amphibians. 2016. (Invasive Species Ser.). 48p. (J). (gr. 4-4). 31.36 (978-1-5026-1830-6(3)) Cavendish Square Publishing.
School Zone Publishing Company Staff. Reptiles & Amphibians. (Illus.). (J). 19.99 incl. audio compact disk (978-0-88743-978-0(0)) School Zone Publishing Co.
Schuetz, Kari. Reptiles. 2012. (Animal Classes Ser.). (ENG., Illus.). 24p. (J). (gr. k-3). lib. bdg. 25.95 (978-1-60014-776-0(3), Blastoff! Readers) Bellwether Media.
Schuh, Mari. The World's Biggest Reptiles. 2015. (Illus.). 24p. (J). lib. bdg. 25.65 (978-1-62031-205-6(0)) Jump! Inc.
Shaffer, Jody Jensen. Bearded Dragons, 1 vol. 2014. (Amazing Reptiles Ser.). (ENG.). 48p. (gr. 8-12). lib. bdg. 32.79 (978-1-62403-369-8(5)) ABDO Publishing Co.
Shea, Therese. Creepy Reptiles. 2012. (Nature's Creepiest Creatures Ser.). (ENG., Illus.). 24p. (J). (gr. 2-5). pap. 8.15 (978-1-4339-6499-2(6)); lib. bdg. 22.60 (978-1-4339-6497-8(X)) Stevens, Gareth Publishing LLLP. (Gareth Stevens Learning Library).
—Really Strange Reptiles. 2016. (Really Strange Adaptations Ser.). 00032p. (J). (gr. 5-5). pap. 10.00 (978-1-4994-2792-9(1), PowerKids Pr.) Rosen Publishing Group, Inc., The.
Sill, Cathryn. About Reptiles/Sobre Los Reptiles: A Guide for Children/una Guía para Niños, 1 vol. Sill, John, illus. 2016. (About... Ser.). (ENG & SPA.). 40p. (J). (gr. -1-2). pap. 8.95 (978-1-56145-909-4(7)) Peachtree Pubs.
Sill, Cathryn P. & Sill, Cathryn. About Reptiles: A Guide for Children, 1 vol. Sill, John, illus. 2003. (About...Ser.). (ENG.). 40p. (J). (gr. k-3). pap. 7.95 (978-1-56145-233-0(5)) Peachtree Pubs.
Silverman, Buffy. Do You Know about Reptiles? 2009. (Lightning Bolt Books — Meet the Animal Groups Ser.). (ENG., Illus.). 32p. (gr. k-2). 26.60 (978-0-8225-7542-9(6), Lerner Pubns.); pap. 7.95 (978-1-58013-861-1(6)) Lerner Publishing Group.
—¿Sabes Algo Sobre Reptiles? (Do You Know about Reptiles?) 2012. (Libros Rayo — Conoce Los Grupos de Animales (Lightning Bolt Books — Meet the Animal Groups) Ser.). (Illus.). 32p. (gr. k-2). (ENG & SPA.). pap. 7.95 (978-0-7613-9378-8(1)); (SPA., lib. bdg. 26.60 (978-0-7613-9332-0(3)) Lerner Publishing Group. (Ediciones Lerner).
Simon, Elizabeth. Caring for Your Iguana. 2005. (Caring for Your Pet Ser.). (Illus.). 32p. (J). per. 9.95 (978-1-59036-215-0(2)); (gr. 4-7). lib. bdg. 26.00 (978-1-59036-195-5(4)) Weigl Pubs., Inc.
Snedden, Robert. Reptiles. (Living Things Ser.). (Illus.). 32p. 2009. (J). (gr. 4-7). pap. 7.95 (978-1-59920-199-3(2)) 2007. (YA). (gr. 3-6). lib. bdg. 28.50 (978-1-59920-082-8(1)) Black Rabbit Bks.
Somervill, Barbara. Monitor Lizard. 2010. (21st Century Skills Library: Animal Invaders Ser.). (ENG.). 32p. (gr. 4-8). lib. bdg. 28.50 (978-1-60279-627-0(0), 200334) Cherry Lake Publishing.
Spilsbury, Louise. Superstar Reptiles. 2014. (Nature's Got Talent Ser.). (Illus.). 32p. (J). (gr. k-5). lib. bdg. 26.25 (978-1-4777-7056-6(9), PowerKids Pr.) Rosen Publishing Group, Inc., The.
Spirn, Michele. Ripley's Cold-Blooded Creatures. 2004. (Illus.). 60p. (J). (978-0-439-63362-8(1)) Scholastic, Inc.
Squire, Ann O. Reptiles. 2013. (True Book(tm), a — Animal Kingdom Ser.). (ENG.). 48p. (J). 31.00 (978-0-531-21755-9(8)); pap. 6.95 (978-0-531-22340-6(X)) Scholastic Library Publishing.
Stille, Darlene R. The Life Cycle of Reptiles, 1 vol. 2011. (Life Cycles Ser.). (ENG.). 48p. (gr. 3-5). pap. 9.95 (978-1-4329-4989-1(6)); 33.32 (978-1-4329-4982-2(9)) Heinemann-Raintree. (Heinemann InfoSearch).
Sullivan, Courtney. Reptiles at the Zoo: Divide Within 100, 1 vol. 2015. (InfoMax Common Core Math Readers Ser.). (ENG.). 24p. (J). pap. 8.25 (978-1-4777-4690-5(0), Rosen Classroom) Rosen Publishing Group, Inc., The.
Taylor, Barbara & Green, Jen. Explore the Deadly World of Bugs, Snakes, Spiders, Crocodiles: The Dramatic Lives & Conflicts of the World's Strangest Creatures Shown in 1500 Amazing Close-Up Photographs. 2013. (ENG., Illus.). 512p. (J). (gr. -1-12). pap. 17.99 (978-1-84322-840-0(8), Armadillo) Anness Publishing GBR. Dist: National Bk. Network.
Taylor, Barbara & O'Shea, Mark. The Ultimate Book of Snakes & Reptiles: Discover the Amazing World of Snakes, Crocodiles, Lizards & Turtles. 2015. (ENG., Illus.). 256p. pap. 13.99 (978-1-86147-459-9(8), Armadillo) Anness Publishing GBR. Dist: National Bk. Network.
Taylor, Barbara, et al. The Deadly World of Bugs, Snakes, Spiders, Crocodiles: And Hundreds of Other Amazing Reptiles & Insects. 2008. (ENG., Illus.). 512p. (J). (gr. 4-7). 29.99 (978-0-7548-1781-9(4)) Anness Publishing GBR. Dist: National Bk. Network.
Thomas, Isabel. Remarkable Reptiles, 1 vol. 2012. (Extreme Animals Ser.). (ENG.). 32p. (gr. 1-3). pap. 8.29 (978-1-4109-4688-1(6)); lib. bdg. 29.99 (978-1-4109-4682-9(7)) Heinemann-Raintree. (Read Me!).
Top That Publishing Staff, ed. How to Draw Monster Reptiles. 2005. (Illus.). 48p. pap. (978-1-84510-745-1(4)) Top That! Publishing PLC.
Twist, Clint. Reptiles & Amphibians Dictionary. 2005. (Illus.). 64p. (J). pap. (978-0-439-66828-6(X)) Scholastic, Inc.
Underwood, Gary. Reptiles. 2010. (Weird, Wild, & Wonderful Ser.). (Illus.). 24p. (J). (gr. 2-5). lib. bdg. 22.00 (978-1-4339-3572-5(4), Gareth Stevens Learning Library) Stevens, Gareth Publishing LLLP.
Uttridge, Sarah. Snakes & Reptiles Around the World. 2014. (Animals Around the World Ser.). (Illus.). 32p. (gr. 2-5). 31.35 (978-1-62588-197-7(5)) Black Rabbit Bks.
Veitch, Catherine. Reptile Babies. 2013. (Animal Babies Ser.). (ENG.). 24p. (gr. -1-1). pap. 35.94 (978-1-4329-8428-1(4)); (Illus.). 22.65 (978-1-4329-7496-1(3)); (Illus.). pap. 6.95 (978-1-4329-8421-2(7)) Heinemann-Raintree. (Acorn).
Weber, Belinda. Discover Science: Reptiles. 2014. (Discover Science Ser.). (ENG., Illus.). 56p. (J). (gr. k-3). 7.99 (978-0-7534-6782-4(8), 9780753467824, Kingfisher) Roaring Brook Pr.
—Kingfisher Young Knowledge - Reptiles. 2011. 48p. 11.99 (978-84-96609-99-0(5)) Edilupa Ediciones, S.L. ESP. Dist: Lectorum Pubns., Inc.
West, David. Pteranodon: Giant of the Sky. Riley, Terry & Ball, Geoff, illus. 2007. (Graphic Dinosaurs Ser.). (ENG.). 32p. (J). (gr. 2-5). lib. bdg. 26.50 (978-1-4042-3895-4(6)) Rosen Publishing Group, Inc., The.
Who's Hiding Inside? Reptiles. 2005. (Who's Hiding Inside Ser.). 12p. (J). bds. 7.95 (978-1-58117-307-9(5), Intervisual/Piggy Toes) Bendon, Inc.
Wild about Snakes. (Wild about Snakes Ser.). (ENG.). 32p. (gr. 3-4). 2011. pap. 190.80 (978-1-4296-6427-1(4)) 2010. lib. bdg. 111.96 (978-1-4296-5435-7(X)) Capstone Press of Coughlan Cos. (Edge Bks.).
Williams, Brian. Amazing Reptiles & Amphibians. 2008. (Amazing Life Cycles Ser.). (Illus.). 32p. (gr. 2-6). lib. bdg. 26.00 (978-0-8368-8898-0(7), Gareth Stevens Learning Library) Stevens, Gareth Publishing LLLP.
Wilsdon, Christina. Ultimate Reptileopedia: The Most Complete Reptile Reference Ever. 2015. (ENG., Illus.). 272p. (J). (gr. 2-5). 24.99 (978-1-4263-2102-3(3), National Geographic Children's Bks.) National Geographic Society.
Winner, Cherie. Everything Reptile. 2014. 64p. pap. 8.00 (978-1-61003-326-8(4)) Center for the Collaborative Classroom.
—Everything Reptile: What Kids Really Want to Know about Reptiles. 2004. (Kids Faqs Ser.). (ENG., Illus.). 64p. (J). (gr. 3-6). pap. 7.95 (978-1-55971-164-7(7)) Cooper Square Publishing Llc.
World Book, Inc. Staff, contrib. by. Amphibians & Reptiles of the United States & Canada. 2004. (World Book's Science & Nature Guides Ser.). (Illus.). 80p. (J). (978-0-7166-4209-1(3)) World Bk., Inc.
World Book, Inc Staff, contrib. by. Reptiles. 2009. (J). (978-0-7166-0408-2(6)) World Bk., Inc.
Zabludoff, Marc. The Reptile Class. 2005. (Family Trees Ser.). (Illus.). 96p. (gr. 6-7). lib. bdg. 34.21 (978-0-7614-1820-7(2), Benchmark Bks.) Marshall Cavendish Corp.
Zayarny, Jack. Reptiles. 2016. (J). (978-1-5105-1118-7(0)) SmartBook Media, Inc.
Zondervan Staff & Schriemer, Peter. Ocean Adventures, Volume 3: Winged Creatures, Waterfalls, & Wild Reptiles, 1 vol. 2013. (Nature of God Ser.). (ENG.). (J). 7.99 (978-0-310-88833-8(6)) Zonderkidz.

REPTILES—FICTION

Busby, Deehna R. Father's Precious Creations Series: Things That Crawl. 2012. 64p. pap. 24.99 (978-1-4685-5030-6(6)) AuthorHouse.
Down, Dale. The Adventures of Dennis the Dimetrodon. 2009. (Illus.). 48p. pap. (978-1-84748-463-5(8)) Athena Pr.
Hale, Bruce. Farewell, My Lunchbag. 2009. (Chet Gecko Ser.: 3). (ENG., Illus.). 128p. (J). (gr. 2-5). pap. 6.99 (978-0-15-202629-5(0)) Houghton Mifflin Harcourt Publishing Co.
Hambleton, Laura. Chameleon Races, 13 vols. 2005. (Chameleon Ser.). (Illus.). 16p. (J). (ENG & MUL.). (gr. 5). 7.95 (978-1-84059-422-5(5)); (MUL, URD & ENG., (gr. -1). 8.95 (978-1-84059-433-1(0)) Milet Publishing.
—Chameleon Swims, 13 vols. 2005. (Chameleon Ser.). (ENG, URD & MUL., Illus.). 16p. (J). (gr. -1). 8.95 (978-1-84059-446-1(2)) Milet Publishing.
—Chameleon Swims, 13 vols. Choudhury, Dorbesh, tr. from ENG. 2005. (Chameleon Ser.). (BEN, ENG & MUL., Illus.). 16p. (J). (gr. -1). 8.95 (978-1-84059-437-9(3)) Milet Publishing.
Irwin, Bindi & Kunz, Chris. Trouble at the Zoo. 2011. (Bindi's Wildlife Adventures Ser.: 1). (ENG.). 112p. (gr. 3-6). pap. 5.99 (978-1-4022-5514-4(4), Sourcebooks Jabberwocky) Sourcebooks, Inc.
Julie, Aunt. State Symbols of Texas - Paddleduck #8. 2012. 50p. pap. 5.95 (978-1-105-91163-7(2)) Lulu Pr., Inc.
Krulik, Nancy. Free the Worms! John and Wendy Staff, illus. 2008. (Katie Kazoo, Switcheroo Ser.: 28). (ENG.). 80p. (J). (gr. 2-4). pap. 3.99 (978-0-448-44675-2(8), Grosset & Dunlap) Penguin Young Readers Group.
—Free the Worms! John & Wendy, illus. 2008. (Katie Kazoo, Switcheroo Ser.). 78p. (J). 11.65 (978-0-7569-8807-4(1)) Perfection Learning Corp.
Lionni, Leo. Su Propio Color. Mlawer, Teresa, tr. from ENG. 2007. (SPA., Illus.). 32p. (J). (gr. k-2). 12.99 (978-1-933032-14-6(6)) Lectorum Pubns., Inc.
MacHado, Ana Maria. Tirinica, Jararaca y Perereca. Faria, Rosana, illus. 2003. 28p. pap. (978-980-257-283-0(7)) Ekare, Ediciones.
Mohler, Marie. Leonard's Song. 2008. 32p. 18.95 (978-1-4357-1372-7(9)) Lulu Pr., Inc.
O'Ryan, Ray. The Prehistoric Planet. Jack, Colin, illus. 2013. (Galaxy Zack Ser.: 3). (ENG.). 128p. (J). (gr. k-4). 16.99 (978-1-4424-6716-3(9)); pap. 5.99 (978-1-4424-6715-6(0)) Little Simon. (Little Simon).
Rand, Johnathan. American Chillers #27 Kentucky Komodo Dragons. 2009. 208p. (J). pap. 5.99 (978-1-893699-90-8(0)) AudioCraft Publishing, Inc.
Reasoner, Charles. Reptiles. 2009. (Learning Tab Board Bks.). (Illus.). 10p. (J). (gr. -1-k). bds. 9.99 (978-1-934650-80-6(3)) Just For Kids Pr., LLC.
Sydor, Colleen & Constantin, Pascale. Camilla Chameleon. Constantin, Pascale, illus. 2007. (ENG., Illus.). 32p. (J). (gr. -1-3). pap. 6.95 (978-1-55453-164-6(0)) Kids Can Pr., Ltd. CAN. Dist: Hachette Bk. Group.
TenNapel, Doug. Battle for Amphibopolis. 2017. (Nnewts Ser.: 3). (ENG.). 224p. (J). (gr. 3-7). 19.99 **(978-0-545-67664-9(9))**; pap. 10.99 **(978-0-545-67670-0(3))** Scholastic, Inc. (Graphix).
Townsend, Wendy. Lizard Love. 2013. 198p. 18.95 (978-1-60898-151-9(7)) namelos llc.
Vernon, Ursula. Attack of the Ninja Frogs. 2nd ed. (Dragonbreath Ser.: 2). (ENG.). 208p. (J). (gr. 3-7). 2012. pap. 6.99 (978-0-14-242066-9(2), Puffin Books) 2010. 12.99 (978-0-8037-3365-7(8), Dial Bks) Penguin Young Readers Group.
—Attack of the Ninja Frogs. 2012. (Dragonbreath Ser.: 2). lib. bdg. 17.20 (978-0-606-26666-6(6), Turtleback) Turtleback Bks.
Wrecks, Billy. Reptile Rumble! 2014. (Step into Reading Level 2 Ser.). lib. bdg. 13.55 (978-0-606-35541-4(3)) Turtleback Bks.

REPTILES, FOSSIL

see also Dinosaurs

Beaumont, Steve. Drawing Pteranodon & Other Flying Reptiles. 2010. (Drawing Dinosaurs Ser.). (Illus.). 32p. (J). pap. 11.75 (978-1-4488-0428-3(0)); (gr. 2-5). lib. bdg. 26.50 (978-1-61531-904-6(2)) Rosen Publishing Group, Inc., The.
Brown, Charlotte Lewis & Brown, Charlotte L. Beyond the Dinosaurs: Monsters of the Air & Sea. Wilson, Phil, illus. (I Can Read Level 2 Ser.). (ENG.). 32p. (J). (gr. -1-3). 2008. pap. 3.99 (978-0-06-053058-7(8)) 2007. 15.99 (978-0-06-053056-3(1)) HarperCollins Pubs.
Connors, Kathleen. Dinosaur Fossils. 2012. (Fossilized! Ser.). (Illus.). 24p. (J). (gr. 2-5). pap. 8.15 (978-1-4339-6410-7(4)); lib. bdg. 22.60 (978-1-4339-6408-4(2)) Stevens, Gareth Publishing LLLP.
Dodson, Peter. Pterosaurs up Close: Flying Reptiles. Bindon, John, illus. 2010. (Zoom in on Dinosaurs! Ser.). 24p. (J). (gr. k-3). 22.60 (978-0-7660-3332-0(5)) Enslow Pubs., Inc.
Gregory, Josh. Ichthyosaur. 2013. (21st Century Junior Library: Dinosaurs Ser.). (ENG., Illus.). 24p. (J). (gr. 2-5). pap. 12.79 (978-1-62431-298-4(5), 202986); lib. bdg. 25.64 (978-1-62431-166-6(0), 202984) Cherry Lake Publishing.
Hughes, Mónica. Swimming Giants. 2007. (I Love Reading Ser.). (Illus.). 24p. (J). (gr. -1-2). lib. bdg. 19.96 (978-1-59716-542-6(5)) Bearport Publishing Co., Inc.
Jeffrey, Gary. Elasmosaurus: The Long-Necked Swimmer. Riley, Terry, illus. 2009. (Graphic Dinosaurs Ser.). (ENG.). 32p. (gr. 2-5). pap. 12.30 (978-1-4042-7715-1(3), PowerKids Pr.) Rosen Publishing Group, Inc., The.
Johnson, Jinny. Flying Reptiles. 2014. (Discovering Dinosaurs Ser.). (Illus.). 24p. (J). (gr. 3-6). 28.50 (978-1-62588-014-7(6)) Black Rabbit Bks.
—Pteranodon & Other Flying Reptiles. Rosewarne, Graham, illus. 2009. (Dinosaurs Alive! Ser.). 32p. (J). (gr. 4-7). pap. 7.95 (978-1-59920-185-6(2)) Black Rabbit Bks.
Kelly, Harold G. How the Dinosaurs Disappeared. (Reading Room Collection 1 Ser.). 16p. 2009. (gr. 2-3). 37.50 (978-1-60851-945-3(7)) 2006. (Illus.). (J). (gr. 3-7). lib. bdg. 17.25 (978-1-4042-3340-9(7)) Rosen Publishing Group, Inc., The. (PowerKids Pr.).
Lunis, Natalie. Ocean Monsters. 2008. (Dino Times Trivia Ser.). (Illus.). 24p. (J). (gr. k-3). lib. bdg. 21.28 (978-1-59716-713-0(4), 1284318) Bearport Publishing Co., Inc.
—Sky Terrors. 2008. (Dino Times Trivia Ser.). (Illus.). 24p. (J). (gr. k-3). lib. bdg. 21.28 (978-1-59716-714-7(2), 1284317) Bearport Publishing Co., Inc.
MacLeod, Elizabeth. Monster Fliers: From the Time of the Dinosaurs. Bindon, John, illus. 2010. (ENG.). 32p. (J). (gr. k-4). 16.95 (978-1-55453-199-8(3)) Kids Can Pr., Ltd. CAN. Dist: Hachette Bk. Group.
Miles, Liz. Flying Monsters. 2012. (Illus.). 32p. (J). (978-1-84858-567-6(5)) Arcturus Pubs., Inc.
Myers, Tim. If You Give a T-Rex a Bone. Hovemann, Anisa Claire, illus. 2007. (Sharing Nature with Children Book Ser.). 32p. (J). (gr. -1-5). 16.95 (978-1-58469-097-6(9)); (ENG.). 8.95 (978-1-58469-098-6(4)) Dawn Pubns.
Parker, Steve. Did Dinosaurs Lay Eggs? And Other Questions & Answers about Prehistoric Reptiles. Rosewarne, Graham, illus. 2016. (ENG.). 32p. 7.99 (978-1-86147-481-0(4), Armadillo) Anness Publishing GBR. Dist: National Bk. Network.
Peterson, Sheryl. Pterodactyl. 2011. (Age of Dinosaurs Ser.). (ENG.). 48p. (J). (gr. 4-7). pap. 9.99 (978-0-89812-540-5(5), Creative Education) Creative Co., The.
Riggs, Kate. Pterodactyls. 2012. (J). 25.65 (978-1-60818-117-9(0), Creative Education) Creative Co., The.
Roberts, Russell. Where Did All the Dinosaurs Go? 2005. (Natural Disasters Ser.). (Illus.). 32p. (J). (gr. 1-4). lib. bdg. 25.70 (978-1-58415-420-4(9)) Mitchell Lane Pubs., Inc.
Rockwood, Leigh. Plesiosaurus. 2012. (J). 49.50 (978-1-4488-5091-4(6)); pap. 8.25 (978-1-4488-5090-7(8)); (Illus.). 24p. lib. bdg. 22.60 (978-1-4488-4970-3(5), 1329102) Rosen Publishing Group, Inc., The. (PowerKids Pr.).
—Pteranodon. 2012. (Illus.). 24p. (J). 49.50 (978-1-4488-5081-5(9), 1329103); pap. 8.25 (978-1-4488-5080-8(0), 1329103); lib. bdg. 22.60 (978-1-4488-4965-9(9), 1329103) Rosen Publishing Group, Inc., The. (PowerKids Pr.).
Staunton, Joseph. Dinosaurs in the Sky. 2010. (Discover the Dinosaurs Ser.). 32p. (J). (gr. 2-5). 28.50 (978-1-60753-108-1(9)) Amicus Publishing.
Staunton, Joseph & Hynson, Colin. Dinosaurs in the Sky. 2011. (Inside Crime Ser.). 48p. (YA). (gr. 5-9). lib. bdg. 34.25 (978-1-59920-394-2(4)) Black Rabbit Bks.
Thomson, Sarah L. & Plant, Andrew. Plesiosaur. 2017. (ENG., Illus.). 32p. (J). (gr. 1-4). lib. bdg. 12.99 (978-1-58089-542-2(5)) Charlesbridge Publishing, Inc.
Wagner, Karen. Mosasaurus: Mighty Ruler of the Sea. 2008. (ENG., Illus.). 36p. (J). (gr. k-2). pap. 6.95 (978-1-59249-781-2(0)) Soundprints.
—Mosasaurus: Mighty Ruler of the Sea. Carr, Karen, illus. 2008. (ENG.). 36p. (J). (gr. k-2). 9.95 (978-1-59249-784-3(5)); 8.95 (978-1-59249-782-9(9)); 2.95 (978-1-59249-783-6(7)); 14.95 (978-1-59249-780-5(2)) Soundprints.
West, David. Allosaurus & Other Dinosaurs & Reptiles from the Upper Jurassic. 2012. (Dinosaurs! Ser.). (ENG., Illus.). 32p. (J). (gr. 3-6). 26.60 (978-1-4339-6704-7(9)); pap. 10.50 (978-1-4339-6705-4(7)) Stevens, Gareth Publishing LLLP. (Gareth Stevens Learning Library).
—Lesothosaurus & Other Dinosaurs & Reptiles from the Lower Jurassic. West, David, illus. 2012. (Dinosaurs! Ser.). (ENG., Illus.). 32p. (J). (gr. 3-6). pap. 10.50 (978-1-4339-6717-7(0)); lib. bdg. 26.60 (978-1-4339-6715-3(4)) Stevens, Gareth Publishing LLLP. (Gareth Stevens Learning Library).
—Prehistoric Sea Reptiles, 01 vols., 1. 2016. (Prehistoric Animals Ser.). (ENG., Illus.). 24p. (J). pap. 8.25 (978-1-5081-9045-5(3), 1397681, Windmill Bks.) Rosen Publishing Group, Inc., The.
—Spinosaurus & Other Dinosaurs & Reptiles from the Upper Cretaceous. 2012. (Dinosaurs! Ser.). (ENG., Illus.). 32p. (J). (gr. 3-6). 26.60 (978-1-4339-6719-1(7)); pap. 10.50 (978-1-4339-6721-4(9)) Stevens, Gareth Publishing LLLP. (Gareth Stevens Learning Library).
—Utahraptor & Other Dinosaurs & Reptiles from the Lower Cretaceous. 2012. (Dinosaurs! Ser.). (ENG., Illus.). 32p. (J). (gr. 3-6). 26.60 (978-1-4339-6723-8(5)); pap. 10.50 (978-1-4339-6725-2(1)) Stevens, Gareth Publishing LLLP. (Gareth Stevens Learning Library).
Zabludoff, Marc. Kronosaurus. Bollinger, Peter, illus. 2010. (Prehistoric Beasts 2 Ser.). 32p. (J). (gr. 2). 29.93 (978-1-60870-035-6(6)) Marshall Cavendish Corp.

RESCUE WORK

see also First Aid

ABDO Publishing Company Staff. Emergency Workers. 2012. (Emergency Workers Ser.: 6). (ENG.). 32p. (J). (gr. 5-9). lib. bdg. 162.42 (978-1-61783-511-7(0), Abdo & Daughters) ABDO Publishing Co.
Alberti, Frances C. Finding Rover. Gremillion, Barry, illus. 2006. (J). per. (978-0-9785937-1-1(5)) Open Pages Publishing.
Allman, Toney. Jaws of Life. 2008. (Great Idea Ser.). (Illus.). 48p. (J). (gr. 4-6). lib. bdg. 26.60 (978-1-59953-191-5(7)) Norwood Hse. Pr.
Animal Rescue. 2014. (Animal Rescue Ser.). 32p. (J). (gr. 3-6). pap. 40.00 (978-1-4777-7213-3(8), PowerKids Pr.) Rosen Publishing Group, Inc., The.
Auerbach, Annie. Meet Boulder the Construction-Bot. 2013. (Transformers Passport to Reading Ser.). (J). lib. bdg. 13.55 (978-0-606-32274-4(4), Turtleback) Turtleback Bks.
Basner, Shannon. Mojo's Magical Ride: True Story of Courage, Transformation & Love; an Alaskan Dog Rescue Story. 2013. 40p. pap. 24.95 (978-1-4626-6154-1(8)) America Star Bks.
Best, B. J. Rescue Helicopters. 2017. (J). **(978-1-5026-2558-8(X))** Cavendish Square Publishing.
Blake, Kevin. Air-Sea Rescue Officers. 2016. (Police: Search & Rescue! Ser.: 6). (ENG., Illus.). 32p. (J). (gr. 2-7). lib. bdg. 19.95 (978-1-943553-12-9(2)) Bearport Publishing Co., Inc.
—City Cops. 2016. (Police: Search & Rescue! Ser.). (ENG., Illus.). 32p. (J). (gr. 2-7). 19.95 (978-1-943553-11-2(4)) Bearport Publishing Co., Inc.
Bodden, Valerie. Rescue Boats. 2011. (Rescue Vehicles Ser.). (ENG.). 24p. (J). (gr. 1-3). pap. 6.99 (978-0-89812-578-8(2), Creative Paperbacks) Creative Co., The.
Bow, James. Rescue Missions. 2008. (Science Solves It Ser.). (ENG., Illus.). 32p. (J). (gr. 3-7). pap. (978-0-7787-4176-3(1), 1286290); lib. bdg. (978-0-7787-4169-5(9), 1286290) Crabtree Publishing Co.
Bozzo, Linda & Library Association Staff. Search & Rescue Dog Heroes. 2010. (Amazing Working Dogs with American Humane Ser.). (Illus.). 48p. (J). (gr. 2-5). 25.27 (978-0-7660-3201-9(9)) Enslow Pubs., Inc.
Braun, Eric. Trapped Behind Enemy Lines: The Story of the U. S. Army Air Force 807th Medical Evacuation Squadron. 2016. (Encounter: Narrative Nonfiction Stories Ser.). (ENG., Illus.). 224p. (gr. 4-6). lib. bdg. 32.65 (978-1-4914-8042-7(4), 1400082) Encounter Bks.
Brown, Mike. Rescue Services. 2004. (Twentieth-Century Developments in Fashion & Costume Ser.). (Illus.). 64p. (YA). (gr. 7-18). lib. bdg. 19.95 (978-1-59084-428-1(9)) Mason Crest.
Burgan, Michael. Total Devastation: The Story of Hurricane Katrina. 2016. (Tangled History Ser.). (ENG., Illus.). 112p. (gr. 3-4). lib. bdg. 31.99 (978-1-4914-8452-4(7)) Capstone Press of Coughlan Cos.
Careers in Search & Rescue Operations. 2005. (Illus.). (gr. 5-8). lib. bdg. 159.00 (978-0-8239-4049-3(7)) Rosen Publishing Group, Inc., The.
Carlson Berne, Emma. Search & Rescue: Imminent Danger. 2014. (ENG.). 32p. (gr. 4-8). 32.79 (978-1-62717-655-2(1)) Rourke Educational Media.
Chancellor, Deborah. Sea Rescue. 2013. (Emergency Vehicles Ser.). (Illus.). 24p. (gr. k-3). lib. bdg. 28.50 (978-1-59920-891-6(1)) Black Rabbit Bks.
Demarest, Chris L. Mayday! Mayday! A Coast Guard Rescue. Demarest, Chris L., illus. 2004. (ENG., Illus.). 40p. (J). (gr. -1-5). 17.99 (978-0-689-85161-2(8), McElderry, Margaret K. Bks.) McElderry, Margaret K. Bks.
Doman, Mary Kate. Rescue Vehicles. 2011. (All about Big Machines Ser.). (Illus.). 24p. (J). (gr. -1-18). pap. 7.95 (978-1-59845-244-0(4), Enslow Elementary); (gr. k-3). lib. bdg. 22.60 (978-0-7660-3934-6(X)) Enslow Pubs., Inc.
Dorling Kindersley Publishing Staff & Gersh, Camilla. Emergency Rescuers & Crime Fighters. 2016. (DK Readers Ser.). (ENG., Illus.). 64p. (J). (gr. 2-4). 14.99 (978-1-4654-4500-1(5), DK Children) Dorling Kindersley Publishing, Inc.
Fortuna, Lois. Rescue Boats. 2016. (To the Rescue! Ser.). (Illus.). 24p. (J). (gr. k-k). 22.60 (978-1-4824-4662-3(6)) Stevens, Gareth Publishing LLLP.
Freedman, Jeri. Careers in Emergency Medical Response Teams' Search & Rescue Units. 2009. (Careers in Search & Rescue Operations Ser.). 64p. (gr. 5-8). 58.50 (978-1-61511-805-2(5), Rosen Reference) Rosen Publishing Group, Inc., The.
Ganeri, Anita. Survival in the Jungle. 2011. (ENG.). 24p. (J). pap. (978-0-7787-7880-6(0)); (gr. 3-6). (978-0-7787-7858-5(4)) Crabtree Publishing Co.
Gersh, Camilla. Emergency Rescue. 2016. (Illus.). 64p. (J). **(978-1-4806-9867-3(9))** Dorling Kindersley Publishing, Inc.
Gilpin, Daniel & Pang, Alex. Rescue Vehicles. 2010. (Machines Close-Up Ser.). 32p. (J). (gr. 4-7). 28.50 (978-1-60870-111-7(5)) Marshall Cavendish Corp.
Goldish, Meish. Firefighters to the Rescue. 2011. (Work of Heroes: First Responders in Action Ser.). 32p. (YA). (gr. 1-4). lib. bdg. 25.27 (978-1-61772-284-4(7)) Bearport Publishing Co., Inc.
—State Troopers. 2016. (Police: Search & Rescue! Ser.). (ENG., Illus.). 32p. (J). (gr. 2-7). 19.95 (978-1-943553-15-0(7)) Bearport Publishing Co., Inc.

Gonzalez, Lissette. Search & Rescue Specialists. (Dangerous Jobs Ser.). 24p. 2009. (gr. 2-3). 42.50 (978-1-61512-135-9(8)) 2007. (Illus.). (J). (gr. -1-3). lib. bdg. 22.60 (978-1-4042-3779-7(8)) Rosen Publishing Group, Inc., The. (PowerKids Pr.).

Gray, Susan H. Emergency Care. 2008. (21st Century Skills Innovation Library: Innovation in Medicine Ser.). (ENG., Illus.). 32p. (gr. 4-8). lib. bdg. 28.50 (978-1-60279-230-2(5), 200161) Cherry Lake Publishing.

Green, Sara. Snow Search Dogs. 2013. (Dogs to the Rescue! Ser.). (ENG., Illus.). 24p. (J). (gr. 3-8). lib. bdg. 25.95 (978-1-60014-959-7(6), Pilot Bks.) Bellwether Media.

Greene, Meg. Careers in the National Guards' Search & Rescue Units. 2005. (Careers in Search & Rescue Operations Ser.). (Illus.). 64p. (YA). (gr. 5-8). lib. bdg. 31.95 (978-0-8239-3836-0(0)) Rosen Publishing Group, Inc., The.

Gregory, Josh. What Does It Do? Ambulance. 2011. (Community Connections: What Does It Do? Ser.). (ENG.). 24p. (gr. 2-5). lib. bdg. 25.64 (978-1-60279-969-1(5), 200970) Cherry Lake Publishing.

Hamilton, S. L. Search & Rescue. 2015. (Illus.). 32p. (J). pap. 27.07 (978-1-62403-759-7(3), 1391390) ABDO Publishing Co.

Harasymiw, M. Alexander. Pararescuemen. 2012. (US Special Forces Ser.). (ENG., Illus.). 32p. (J). (gr. 3-6). pap. 10.50 (978-1-4339-6571-5(2)); lib. bdg. 26.60 (978-1-4339-6569-2(0)) Stevens, Gareth Publishing LLLP. (Gareth Stevens Learning Library).

Henningfeld, Diane Andrews & Haugen, David. Hurricane Katrina. 2010. (At Issue Ser.). (ENG.). 128p. (gr. 10-12). 39.40 (978-0-7377-4882-6(0)); pap. 27.80 (978-0-7377-4883-3(4)) Cengage Gale. (Greenhaven Pr., Inc.).

Hoffman, Mary Ann. Hurricane Katrina. (Nature in the News Ser.). 32p. 2009. (gr. 3-4). 42.50 (978-1-61514-821-9(3), PowerKids Pr.) 2007. (Illus.). (YA). (gr. 2-5). lib. bdg. 21.25 (978-1-4042-3537-3(X)) Rosen Publishing Group, Inc., The.

Jankowski, Susan & Library. True Ocean Rescue Stories. 2010. (True Rescue Stories Ser.). 48p. (J). lib. bdg. 22.60 (978-0-7660-3665-9(0)) Enslow Pubs., Inc.

—True Wilderness Rescue Stories. 2010. (True Rescue Stories Ser.). 48p. (J). lib. bdg. 22.60 (978-0-7660-3666-6(9)) Enslow Pubs., Inc.

Johnson, Linda Carlson & Johnson, Keri. 9.11 Helping the Heroes: A Salvation Army Story. 2011. (Illus.). (J). (978-0-89216-130-0(2)) Salvation Army.

Kalman, Bobbie. Bomberos Al Rescate. 2006. (Mi Communidad y Quienes Contribuyen a Ella Ser.). (ENG & SPA., Illus.). 32p. (J). (gr. 3-7). pap. (978-0-7787-8442-5(8)); lib. bdg. (978-0-7787-8428-9(2)) Crabtree Publishing Co.

—Emergency Workers Are on Their Way! 2004. (My Community & Its Helpers Ser.). (ENG., Illus.). 32p. (J). pap. (978-0-7787-2122-2(1)); lib. bdg. (978-0-7787-2094-2(2)) Crabtree Publishing Co.

—Firefighters to the Rescue! 2004. (My Community & Its Helpers Ser.). (ENG., Illus.). 32p. (J). pap. (978-0-7787-2124-6(8)) Crabtree Publishing Co.

Kast, Edie. Heroic Animals. 2005. (Illus.). 24p. (J). (978-0-328-13606-3(9), Scott Foresman) Addison-Wesley Educational Pubs., Inc.

Katz, Samuel M. Against All Odds: Counterterrorist Hostage Rescues. 2004. (Terrorist Dossiers Ser.). (Illus.). 72p. (J). (gr. 4-7). lib. bdg. 26.60 (978-0-8225-1567-8(9)) Lerner Publishing Group.

La Bella, Laura. Search & Rescue Swimmers. 2008. (Extreme Careers Ser.). (Illus.). 64p. (YA). (gr. 5-9). lib. bdg. 31.95 (978-1-4042-1786-7(X)) Rosen Publishing Group, Inc., The.

—Search-and-rescue Swimmers. 2009. (Extreme Careers Ser.). 64p. (gr. 5-5). 58.50 (978-1-61512-405-3(5), Rosen Reference) Rosen Publishing Group, Inc., The.

Ladybird. Emergency Rescue. 2016. (Read It Yourself with Ladybird Ser.). (ENG.). 32p. (J). (gr. 2-4). 5.99 (978-0-241-24442-5(0)) Penguin Bks., Ltd. GBR. Dist: Independent Pubs. Group.

—Emergency Rescue, Level 2. 2016. (Read It Yourself with Ladybird Ser.). (ENG.). 32p. (J). pap. 9.99 (978-0-241-24441-8(2)) Penguin Bks., Ltd. GBR. Dist: Independent Pubs. Group.

Lewis, Brenda Ralph. Hostage Rescue with the FBI. 2004. (Rescue & Prevention Ser.). (Illus.). 96p. (YA). (gr. 7-18). lib. bdg. 22.95 (978-1-59084-403-8(3)) Mason Crest.

—Rescuing Hostages: The FBI. 2017. (J). **(978-1-4222-3770-0(2))** Mason Crest.

Lewis, Brenda Ralph. Wilderness Rescue with the U. S. Search & Rescue Task Force. 2004. (Rescue & Prevention Ser.). (Illus.). 96p. (YA). (gr. 7-18). lib. bdg. 22.95 (978-1-59084-404-5(1)) Mason Crest.

Litchfield, J. & Brooks, F. Rescue Vehicles. 2004. (ENG., Illus.). 10p. (J). bds. 4.99 (978-0-7945-0589-9(9)) EDC Publishing.

Mattern, Joanne. Emt. 2009. (Working Together Ser.). 24p. (gr. 1-2). 42.50 (978-1-60854-830-9(9), PowerKids Pr.) Rosen Publishing Group, Inc., The.

Matthews, Carolyn. True Stories of Rescue & Survival: Canada's Unknown Heroes. 2008. (ENG., Illus.). 176p. (YA). (gr. 6-18). pap. 19.99 (978-1-55002-851-5(0)) Dundurn CAN. Dist: Ingram Publisher Services.

McNab, Chris. Surviving Hostage Rescue Missions. Carney, John, ed. 2014. (Extreme Survival in the Military Ser.: 12). 64p. (J). (gr. 7-18). lib. bdg. 23.95 (978-1-4222-3090-9(2)) Mason Crest.

Miller, Mara. Hurricane Katrina Strikes the Gulf Coast: Disaster & Survival. 2006. (Deadly Disasters Ser.). (Illus.). 48p. (J). (gr. 4-10). lib. bdg. 25.27 (978-0-7660-2803-6(8), 1251895) Enslow Pubs., Inc.

Moran, Lisa & Hawley, Mary. Making a Difference SB2 to the Rescue. 2010. (Connect to Literacy Ser.). 8p. pap. (978-1-4334-0504-4(0)) Millmark Education.

Murray, Aaron R. Firefighters Help Us. 2012. (All about Community Helpers Ser.). (Illus.). 24p. (J). pap. 7.95 (978-1-4644-0053-7(9)); (gr. -1-1). 22.60 (978-0-7660-4047-2(X)) Enslow Pubs., Inc. (Enslow Elementary).

Murray, Julie. Search-and-Rescue Animals, 1 vol. 2009. (Going to Work:Animal Edition Ser.). (ENG., Illus.). 32p. (J). (gr. 2-5). 27.07 (978-1-60453-563-1(6)) ABDO Publishing Co.

National Geographic Kids Staff. 125 Pet Rescues: From Pound to Palace: Homeless Pets Made Happy. 2017. (ENG.). 112p. (J). (gr. 3-7). pap. 12.99 (978-1-4263-2736-0(6), National Geographic Children's Bks.) National Geographic Society.

Newcomb, Tim. Search & Rescue Team, Vol. 12. 2015. (On a Mission Ser.). (Illus.). 48p. (J). (gr. 5). 20.95 (978-1-4222-3399-3(5)) Mason Crest.

Ollhoff, Jim. Search & Rescue. 2012. (Emergency Workers Ser.). 32p. (J). (gr. 5-9). lib. bdg. 27.07 (978-1-61783-516-2(1), Abdo & Daughters) ABDO Publishing Co.

Oxlade, Chris. Rescue at Sea, 1 vol. 2012. (Heroic Jobs Ser.). (ENG., Illus.). 32p. (gr. 1-2). lib. bdg. 29.99 (978-1-4109-4360-6(7), Read Me!) Heinemann-Raintree.

Peppas, Lynn. Superstorm Sandy. 2013. (ENG., Illus.). 48p. (J). (978-0-7787-1193-3(5)); pap. (978-0-7787-1195-7(1)) Crabtree Publishing Co.

Perish, Patrick. Wilderness Rescue Pilot. 2015. (Dangerous Jobs Ser.). (ENG., Illus.). 24p. (J). (gr. 3-7). lib. bdg. 25.95 (978-1-62617-199-2(8), Torque Bks.) Bellwether Media.

Perry, Phyllis Jean. Sherlock Hounds: Our Heroic Search & Rescue Dogs. 2006. (Illus.). 32p. (J). pap. (978-1-59336-728-2(7)) Mondo Publishing.

Petersen, Justin. Emergency! 2016. (Emergency! Ser.). (ENG.). 32p. (gr. 3-4). 111.96 (978-1-4914-8672-6(4), Edge Bks.) Capstone Press of Coughlan Cos.

—Search & Rescue Teams: Saving People in Danger. 2016. (Emergency! Ser.). (ENG.). 32p. (gr. 3-4). lib. bdg. 27.99 (978-1-4914-8031-1(9), Edge Bks.) Capstone Press of Coughlan Cos.

Phidal Publishing Staff, ed. Rescue Squad. (Cool Cars Ser.). (J). 16p. (978-2-7643-0132-6(4)); 2004. (Illus.). 10p. (978-2-7643-0209-5(6)) Phidal Publishing, Inc./Editions Phidal, Inc.

Pipe, Jim. Rescue Squad: Saving Lives. 2012. (Mission Impossible Ser.). 32p. (gr. 4-8). lib. bdg. 31.35 (978-1-936333-28-8(7)) Brown Bear Bks.

Poolos, Jamie. Hostage Rescuers. (Extreme Careers Ser.). 64p. (gr. 5-5). 2009. 58.50 (978-1-61512-399-5(7), Rosen Reference) 2007. (Illus.). lib. bdg. 31.95 (978-1-4042-0941-1(7)) Rosen Publishing Group, Inc., The.

Priddy, Roger. My Big Rescue Book. 2004. (Illus.). 10p. (J). (978-1-84332-215-3(3)) St. Martin's Pr.

Randolph, Joanne. Emergency Helicopters. (To the Rescue! Ser.). 24p. 2009. (gr. 1-1). 42.50 (978-1-60854-396-0(X)) 2008. (Illus.). (J). (gr. 3-7). lib. bdg. 22.60 (978-1-4042-4151-0(5)) Rosen Publishing Group, Inc., The. (PowerKids Pr.).

—Emergency Helicopters/Helicopteros de Emergencia. 2009. (To the Rescue! / ¡Al rescate! Ser.). (ENG & SPA.). 24p. (gr. 1-1). 42.50 (978-1-60854-402-8(8), Editorial Buenas Letras) Rosen Publishing Group, Inc., The.

—Emergency Helicopters/Helicopteros de Emergencia. Alaman, Eduardo, tr. from ENG. 2008. (To the Rescue! / ¡Al Rescate! Ser.). (Illus.). 24p. (J). (gr. -1-3). lib. bdg. 22.60 (978-1-4042-7672-7(6), Editorial Buenas Letras) Rosen Publishing Group, Inc., The.

Ready, Dee. Firefighters Help. 2013. (Our Community Helpers Ser.). (ENG.). 24p. (gr. k-1). pap. 35.70 (978-1-62065-846-8(1)); pap. 6.29 (978-1-62065-845-1(3)); lib. bdg. 21.99 (978-1-62065-082-0(7)) Capstone Press of Coughlan Cos. (Pebble Bks.).

Rescue! 6 Each of 1 Anthology, 6 vols. (Wildcats Ser.). 32p. (gr. 2-8). (978-0-322-00585-3(X)) Wright Group/McGraw-Hill.

Rettung in Not. (Illus.). 40p. (J). (978-3-411-08181-3(3)) Bibliographisches Institut & F. A. Brockhaus AG DEU. Dist: i. b. d., Ltd.

Riggs, Kate. Rescue Boats: Seedlings. 2016. (Seedlings Ser.). (ENG.). 24p. (J). (gr. k-2). pap. 7.99 (978-1-62832-188-3(1), Creative Paperbacks) Creative Co., The.

—To the Rescue! Williams, Nate, illus. 2016. (ENG.). 14p. (J). (gr. -1 — 1). bds. 7.99 (978-1-56846-288-2(3), Creative Editions) Creative Co., The.

Roleff, Tamara L., ed. The World Trade Center Attack. 2003. (History Firsthand Ser.). (Illus.). 202p. (YA). (gr. 7-10). pap. 21.20 (978-0-7377-1469-2(7), Greenhaven Pr., Inc.) Cengage Gale.

Roza, Greg. Careers in the Coast Guard's Search & Rescue Units. 2009. (Careers in Search & Rescue Operations Ser.). 64p. (gr. 5-8). 58.50 (978-1-61511-808-3(X), Rosen Reference) Rosen Publishing Group, Inc., The.

Sandler, Martin W. The Impossible Rescue: The True Story of an Amazing Arctic Adventure. (ENG.). 176p. (J). (gr. 5). 2014. pap. 15.99 (978-0-7636-7093-1(6)) 2012. (Illus.). 22.99 (978-0-7636-5080-3(3)) Candlewick Pr.

Sandler, Michael. Pararescuemen in Action. 2008. (Special Ops Ser.). (Illus.). 32p. (J). (gr. 3-6). lib. bdg. 25.27 (978-1-59716-633-1(2)) Bearport Publishing Co., Inc.

Somervill, Barbara A. First Response - By Air. 2007. (High Interest Bks.). (ENG., Illus.). 48p. (J). (gr. 4-7). pap. 6.95 (978-0-531-18718-0(7)) Scholastic Library Publishing.

Somerville, Louisa. Rescue Vehicles. Jensen, Hans, illus. (J). mass mkt. 8.99 (978-0-590-24557-9(0)) Scholastic, Inc.

Staniford, Linda. Firefighters to the Rescue Around the World. 2016. (To the Rescue! Ser.). (ENG.). 24p. (gr. k-2). lib. bdg. 23.32 (978-1-4846-2751-8(2), Heinemann Read & Learn) Heinemann-Raintree.

—Police to the Rescue Around the World. 2016. (To the Rescue! Ser.). (ENG., Illus.). 24p. (gr. k-2). lib. bdg. 23.32 (978-1-4846-2750-1(4), Heinemann Read & Learn) Heinemann-Raintree.

—Rescue at Sea Around the World. 2016. (To the Rescue! Ser.). (ENG., Illus.). 24p. (gr. k-2). lib. bdg. 23.32 (978-1-4846-2753-2(9), Heinemann Read & Learn) Heinemann-Raintree.

—To the Rescue! 2016. (To the Rescue! Ser.). (ENG.). 24p. (gr. k-2). 93.28 (978-1-4846-2766-2(0), Heinemann Read & Learn) Heinemann-Raintree.

Thomas, William. Wilderness Rescue Pilot. 2010. (Benchmark Rockets: Dirty & Dangerous Jobs Ser.). 32p. (J). (gr. 3-6). 28.50 (978-1-60870-180-3(8)) Marshall Cavendish Corp.

Torres, John Albert. Disaster in the Indian Ocean, Tsunami 2004. 2005. (Monumental Milestones Ser.). (Illus.). 48p. (YA). (gr. 4-7). lib. bdg. 29.95 (978-1-58415-344-3(X)) Mitchell Lane Pubs., Inc.

Tougias, Michael J. A Storm Too Soon: A Remarkable True Survival Story in 80-Foot Seas. 2016. (True Storm Rescues Ser.). (ENG., Illus.). 240p. (J). 17.99 (978-1-62779-281-3(3), 9781627792813, Holt, Henry & Co. Bks. For Young Readers) Holt, Henry & Co.

Whiting, Jim. FBI Hostage Rescue & Swat Teams. 2014. (U. S. Special Forces Ser.). (ENG., Illus.). 48p. (J). (gr. 5-8). lib. bdg. 35.65 (978-1-60818-462-0(5), Creative Education) Creative Co., The.

Wilcox, Christine. Careers in Emergency Response. 2017. (ENG.). 80p. (J). (gr. 5-12). lib. bdg. **(978-1-68282-104-6(8))** ReferencePoint Pr., Inc.

Williams, Christopher. One Incredible Dog! Kizzy. Friedman, Judith, illus. 2006. (One Incredible Dog! Ser.). (ENG.). 32p. (J). (gr. -1-3). lib. bdg. 15.95 (978-0-9766805-5-0(6)) Keene Publishing.

Yomtov, Nel. Rescue. 2016. (Military Missions Ser.). (ENG., Illus.). 24p. (J). (gr. 3-7). 25.95 (978-1-62617-438-2(5), Epic Bks.) Bellwether Media.

Young, Jeff C. True Underground Rescue Stories. 2010. (True Rescue Stories Ser.). 48p. (J). 22.60 (978-0-7660-3676-5(6)) Enslow Pubs., Inc.

Zullo, Allan. Heroes of 9/11. 2011. (Illus.). 181p. (J). pap. (978-0-545-25506-6(6)) Scholastic, Inc.

RESCUE WORK—FICTION

AMEET Studio. R2-D2 to the Rescue! 2016. (LEGO Star Wars Chapter Bks.: 4). (ENG.). 64p. (J). (gr. 2-5). lib. bdg. 14.75 (978-0-606-39152-8(5)) Turtleback Bks.

Anderson, Laurie Halse. Storm Rescue. 2008. (Vet Volunteers Ser.: 6). (ENG.). 144p. (J). (gr. 3-7). 6.99 (978-0-14-241101-8(9), Puffin Books) Penguin Young Readers Group.

Appleton, Victor. Into the Abyss. 2007. (Tom Swift, Young Inventor Ser.). (ENG.). 160p. (gr. 3-7). 27.07 (978-1-59961-350-5(6)) Spotlight.

Archer, Colleen Rutherford. Collie Rescue. Umana, Maria Gomez, illus. 2004. 112p. (J). pap. (978-1-894131-67-4(3), Virago Press) Penumbra Pr.

Arnett, Dee. Gifted. 2008. 240p. pap. 18.95 (978-1-4092-0442-8(1)) Lulu Pr., Inc.

Atchison, David C. The Adventures of Black Bart: an Encounter with Regret. 2008. 84p. pap. 7.94 (978-0-615-23723-7(1)) Black Bart Bks.

Auerbach, Annie. Meet Boulder the Construction-Bot. 2013. (Transformers Passport to Reading Ser.). (J). lib. bdg. 13.55 (978-0-606-32274-4(4), Turtleback) Turtleback Bks.

Austin, Mike. Rescue Squad No. 9. (ENG., Illus.). 40p. (J). 2017. (— 1). bds. 8.99 **(978-1-101-93665-8(7))** 2016. (gr. -1-2). 16.99 (978-1-101-93662-7(2)) Random Hse. Children's Bks. (Random Hse. Bks. for Young Readers).

Baccalario, Pierdomenico & McGuinness, Nanette. The Thief of Mirrors. Pernigotti, Chiara, tr. from ITA. Bruno, Iacopo, illus. 2015. (Enchanted Emporium Ser.). (ENG.). 240p. (gr. 4-8). lib. bdg. 26.65 (978-1-4965-0516-3(6)) Stone Arch Bks.

Bailey, Kevin. Anthony Meets the Playground Bully. 2009. 20p. pap. 13.50 (978-1-60860-072-4(6), Eloquent Bks.) Strategic Book Publishing & Rights Agency (SBPRA).

Bailey, Mary R. Vhan Zeely & the Time Prevaricators. 2009. 188p. pap. 12.95 (978-1-60911-003-1(X), Eloquent Bks.) Strategic Book Publishing & Rights Agency (SBPRA).

Ballantyne, R. M. The Lighthouse. 2006. pap. (978-1-4065-0531-3(5)) Dodo Pr.

—Saved by the Lifeboat. 2004. reprint ed. pap. 1.99 (978-1-4192-4624-1(0)) Kessinger Publishing, LLC.

Ballock-Dixon, Saige J. & Medina, Sylvia M. Chilean Mines. Eagle, Joy, illus. 2013. 36p. pap. 11.49 (978-1-939871-00-8(X)) Green Kids Club, Inc.

Baltazar, Armand. Diego & the Rangers of the Vastlantic. Baltazar, Armand, illus. 2017. (Timeless Ser.: 1). (Illus.). 624p. (J). (gr. 3-7). 19.99 (978-0-06-240236-3(6), Tegen, Katherine Bks) HarperCollins Pubs.

Barnum, P. T. Dick Broadhead: A Story of Perilous Adve. 2006. pap. 30.95 (978-1-4286-1959-3(3)) Kessinger Publishing, LLC.

Bass, Guy. The Spider's Lair. Williamson, Pete, illus. 2015. (Stitch Head Ser.). (ENG.). 208p. (gr. 3-4). 10.95 (978-1-62370-192-5(9)) Capstone Young Readers of Coughlan Cos.

Bauer, Joan. Tell Me. 2014. (ENG.). 272p. (J). (gr. 5). 16.99 (978-0-451-47033-1(8), Viking Books for Young Readers) Penguin Young Readers Group.

Beck, Andrea. Elliot's Fire Truck, 1 vol. Beck, Andrea, illus. 2010. (ENG., Illus.). 32p. (J). (gr. -1-3). 19.95 (978-1-55469-143-2(5)) Orca Bk. Pubs. USA.

Bell, Michele Ashman. Rescue: A Jungle Adventure. 2006. 246p. (J). pap. (978-1-59811-093-7(4)) Covenant Communications.

Bellis, Jill. The Return of the Magnificent Six: A Christmas Adventure. Farmer, Zoe, illus. 2008. (The Magnificent Six: Vol. 2). 62p. pap. 14.00 (978-1-58690-073-1(0)) Players Pr., Inc.

Beresford, Elisabeth. Tomsk to the Rescue. (Illus.). 15p. (J). (gr. k-6). pap. (978-0-340-73581-7(3)) Hodder & Stoughton.

Bishop, Debbie. Black Tide: Enter the Game. 2003. (Black Tide Rising Ser.: Vol. 1). (ENG., Illus.). 157p. (J). (gr. -1-12). pap. 7.95 (978-0-9664737-3-5(6)) Left Field Angel Gate.

Blabey, Aaron. Mission Unpluckable. 2017. (Bad Guys Ser.: 2). lib. bdg. 16.00 **(978-0-606-40154-8(7))** Turtleback Bks.

Blackburn, Sheila M. Stewie Scraps & the Trolley Cart. 2008. 72p. pap. (978-1-903853-88-7(5)) Brilliant Pubns.

Blake, Quentin & Blake, Quentin. Loveykins. 2016. (ENG., Illus.). 32p. (J). (gr. -1-3). pap. 7.95 (978-1-56145-760-1(4)) Peachtree Pubs.

Blazin' Hot Picture Book (English) 8x8. 2006. (J). 5.99 (978-1-933934-29-7(8)) Mighty Kids Media.

Blazin' Hot Picture Book (English) 2005. (Illus.). (J). 5.99 (978-0-9765953-9-7(7)) Mighty Kids Media.

Botha, Si. Goosala Goop. 2009. 48p. pap. 16.50 (978-1-60860-124-0(2), Strategic Bk. Publishing) Strategic Book Publishing & Rights Agency (SBPRA).

Bowen, Carl & Fuentes, Benny. Guardian Angel. Tortosa, Wilson, illus. 2015. (Shadow Squadron Ser.). (ENG.). 112p. (gr. 4-8). lib. bdg. 26.65 (978-1-4965-0382-4(1)) Stone Arch Bks.

Bracken, Beth & Fraser, Kay. Believe, 1 vol. Sawyer, Odessa, illus. 2014. (Faerieground Ser.). (ENG.). 288p. (gr. 4-8). 12.95 (978-1-62370-113-0(9)) Capstone Young Readers of Coughlan Cos.

—The Shadows, 1 vol. Sawyer, Odessa, illus. 2012. (Faerieground Ser.). (ENG.). 96p. (gr. 1-3). lib. bdg. 23.99 (978-1-4342-3306-6(5), Faerieground) Stone Arch Bks.

—The Willow Queen's Gate, 1 vol. Sawyer, Odessa, illus. 2012. (Faerieground Ser.). (ENG.). 96p. (gr. 1-3). lib. bdg. 23.99 (978-1-4342-3304-2(9), Faerieground) Stone Arch Bks.

Brightwood, Laura, illus. Ka-ulu the Strong. Brightwood, Laura, . 2006. (J). (978-0-9789871-3-8(6)) 3-C Institute for Social Development.

Brouwer, Sigmund. Ambush. 2009. (Robot Wars Ser.: 3). (ENG.). 304p. (YA). pap. 7.99 (978-1-4143-2311-4(5), Tyndale Kids) Tyndale Hse. Pubs.

Brown, Elizabeth Rhea. Sweet Maneuvers. 2013. 36p. pap. 24.95 (978-1-4626-8977-4(9)) America Star Bks.

Butler, M. Christina. One Snowy Rescue. Macnaughton, Tina, illus. 2015. (ENG.). 32p. (J). (gr. -1-3). 16.99 (978-1-58925-196-0(2)) Tiger Tales.

Butterworth, Nick. The Rescue Party. Butterworth, Nick, illus. 2011. (Tales from Percy's Park Ser.). (ENG., Illus.). 32p. (J). (gr. k-2). pap. 11.00 (978-0-00-715516-3(6), HarperCollins Children's Bks.) HarperCollins Pubs. Ltd. GBR. Dist: HarperCollins Pubs.

Cafaro, Phyllis C. Captain Mcfinn & Friends Encounter the Bully Bunker. 2012. (ENG., Illus.). 24p. (J). 17.99 (978-0-9859482-2-1(1), 9780985948221); pap. 9.99 (978-0-9859482-3-8(X), 9780985948238) Cold River Pubns.

Carlson, Claudia, illus. Avi the Ambulance Goes to School. 2015. (J). (978-1-68115-503-6(6)) Behrman Hse., Inc.

Carlson, Claudia & Koffsky, Ann D. Avi the Ambulance & the Snowy Day. Decker, C. B., illus. 2017. (J). (978-1-68115-528-9(1)) Behrman Hse., Inc.

Caron, Eleonore. Gizmo & Ellen Mysteries: The Case of the Missing Boy. 2012. 24p. pap. 24.95 (978-1-4626-6747-5(3)) America Star Bks.

Carter, Anne Laurel. Under a Prairie Sky, 1 vol. Daniel, Alan & Daniel, Lea, illus. 2004. (ENG.). 32p. (J). (gr. -1-3). pap. 7.95 (978-1-55143-282-3(X)) Orca Bk. Pubs. USA.

Cartwheel: A Sequel to Double Eagle. 2013. (ENG.). 252p. (YA). 17.00 (978-0-9844460-3-2(6)) Bucking Horse Bks.

Castillo, Ina. Red the Super Wiener. 2008. 24p. pap. 24.95 (978-1-60474-897-0(4)) America Star Bks.

Chandler, Jeff. The New Kitten: A Story about a Foster Puppy, 1 vol. 2009. 48p. pap. 24.95 (978-1-61546-176-9(0)) America Star Bks.

Charles L. Wilson. The Search Is On: The Wild Adventures of Lester & Dora. 2009. 200p. 24.99 (978-1-4269-1813-1(5)); pap. 14.99 (978-1-4269-1812-4(7)) Trafford Publishing.

Chick, Bryan. The Secret Zoo: Raids & Rescues. 2013. (Secret Zoo Ser.: 5). (ENG.). 272p. (J). (gr. 3-7). 16.99 (978-0-06-219228-8(0), Greenwillow Bks.) HarperCollins Pubs.

Clover, Peter. Rescue Riders: Fire Alert. Lt. ed. 2007. 108p. per. (978-1-905665-30-3(X)) Pollinger In Print.

Cohen, Alana. Heroes! White, David A., illus. 2011. (Lego City Ser.). (ENG.). 10p. (J). (gr. -1-k). bds. 9.99 (978-0-545-27439-5(7)) Scholastic, Inc.

Coleman, Claudia. Yo Yo & the Great Flood. 2008. 100p. pap. 22.95 (978-1-60145-606-9(9)) Booklocker.com, Inc.

Collier, Kevin Scott. Journeys of Hope, Pearl of Wisdom. Collier, Kevin Scott, illus. 2006. (Illus.). 28p. (J). E-Book 9.95 incl. cd-rom (978-1-933090-31-3(6)) Guardian Angel Publishing, Inc.

Copeland, Cynthia L. Elin's Island. 2003. (Single Titles Ser.: up). (ENG.). 144p. (YA). (gr. 6-12). lib. bdg. 22.60 (978-0-7613-2522-2(0), Millbrook Pr.) Lerner Publishing Group.

Cox, Renee K. Sammie Jane Saves Charlie: Cougar's Rescue. 2009. (Illus.). 56p. pap. 11.95 (978-1-4327-3129-8(7)) Outskirts Pr., Inc.

Cronin, Doreen. The Legend of Diamond Lil. Cornell, Kevin, illus. 2012. 144p. (J). (gr. 1-5). (ENG.). 14.99 (978-0-06-177996-1(2)); lib. bdg. 15.89 (978-0-06-198578-2(3)) HarperCollins Pubs.

—Rescue Bunnies. Menchin, Scott, illus. 2010. (ENG.). 32p. (J). (gr. -1-3). 16.99 (978-0-06-112871-4(6)) HarperCollins Pubs.

Cronshaw, Joseph. Podge & Dodge. 2009. 32p. pap. 13.50 (978-1-60693-868-3(1), Strategic Bk. Publishing) Strategic Book Publishing & Rights Agency (SBPRA).

Curtis, Jennifer Keats. Osprey Adventure, 1 vol. Ramsey, Marcy Dunn, illus. 2009. (ENG.). 30p. (gr. 3-7). 13.95 (978-0-87033-593-8(6), 9780870335938, Cornell Maritime Pr./Tidewater Pubs.) Schiffer Publishing, Ltd.

Dahlstrom, Kathryn. Peppy's Rescue. Date not set. (Good News Club Ser.). (J). (gr. 4-11). pap. 4.99 (978-1-55976-826-9(6)) CEF Pr.

Dale, Penny. Dinosaur Rescue! Dale, Penny, illus. 2016. (ENG., Illus.). 24p. (J). (-k). bds. 6.99 (978-0-7636-8000-8(1), Nosy Crow) Candlewick Pr.

Dalmatian Press Staff. To the Rescue! 2008. (ENG.). 6p. bds. 4.95 (978-1-58117-724-4(0), Intervisual/Piggy Toes) Bendon, Inc.

Darke, J. A. Attack of the Mud Creatures. Evergreen, Nelson, illus. 2015. (Spine Shivers Ser.). (ENG.). 128p. (gr. 3-4). lib. bdg. 26.65 (978-1-4965-0220-9(5)) Stone Arch Bks.

David, Erica. Extreme Rescue: Crocodile Mission. McGee, Warner, illus. 2009. (Go, Diego, Go! Ser.). (ENG.). 24p. (J). pap. 3.99 (978-1-4169-8515-0(8), Simon Spotlight/Nickelodeon) Simon Spotlight/Nickelodeon.

Davies, Beth & Ripley, Esther. DK Readers L2: LEGO City: Heroes to the Rescue. 2016. (DK Readers Ser.). (ENG., Illus.). 48p. (J). (gr. k-2). pap. 3.99 (978-1-4654-5189-7(7), DK Children) Dorling Kindersley Publishing, Inc.

Davis, Helen J. Good Times with Gregory: Birds: Rescuing a Baby Bird. Davis, Robyn L., illus. 2008. (Good Times with Gregory Ser.). 54p. (J). (gr. -1-4). 12.95 (978-1-935122-10-4(X)) K&B Products.

Depken, Kristen L. Chase's Space Case (Paw Patrol) Jackson, Mike, illus. 2016. (Step into Reading Ser.). (ENG.). 24p. (J). (gr. -1-1). 4.99 (978-0-553-53886-1(1), Random Hse. Bks. for Young Readers) Random Hse. Children's Bks.

—Rubble to the Rescue! (Paw Patrol) Jackson, Mike, illus. 2015. (Step into Reading Ser.). (ENG.). 24p. (J). (gr. -1-1).

4.99 (978-0-553-52290-7(6), Random Hse. Bks. for Young Readers) Random Hse. Children's Bks.

Devine, Ginger. The Missing Goose Egg: A Sam the Lamb Mystery. 2009. 32p. pap. 14.95 (978-1-4389-8839-9(7)) AuthorHouse.

DiCicco, Sue & Mawhinney, Art, illus. Diego y los Dinosaurios. 2008. (Go, Diego, Go! Ser.). Orig. Title: Diego's Great Dinosaur Rescue. (SPA & ENG.). 24p. (J). (gr. -1-2). pap. 3.99 (978-1-4169-5871-0(1), Libros Para Ninos) Libros Para Ninos.

—Diego's Great Dinosaur Rescue. 2008. (Go, Diego, Go! Ser.). (ENG.). 24p. (J). (gr. -1-2). pap. 3.99 (978-1-4169-5867-3(3), Simon Spotlight/Nickelodeon) Simon Spotlight/Nickelodeon.

Disney Press Editors. Awesome Guy to the Rescue! / Bella's Big Break. 2015. (Doc Mcstuffins 8X8 Ser.). (J). lib. bdg. 16.00 (978-0-606-36899-5(X)) Turtleback Bks.

—Rescue from Jabba's Palace. 2015. (Star Wars: World of Reading Ser.). (J). lib. bdg. 13.55 (978-0-606-35930-6(3)) Turtleback Bks.

Dixon, Virginia. What Happened to Willie? Thomas, Tim, illus. 2007. 32p. (J). 16.00 (978-0-9795386-0-5(2)) Grand Productions.

Dormer, Frank W. Firefighter Duckies! Dormer, Frank W., illus. 2017. (ENG., Illus.). 40p. (J). (gr. -1-3). 17.99 (978-1-4814-6090-3(0), Atheneum Bks. for Young Readers) Simon & Schuster Children's Publishing.

Dreyer, Ellen. Starfishers to the Rescue. 2012. (First Chapters: Set 2 Ser.: Vol. 10). (ENG., Illus.). 64p. (J). (gr. 2-3). pap. 9.50 (978-0-7652-0886-6(5)) Modern Curriculum Pr.

Dyan, Penelope. Vita Mccafee Mckay, Cat Rescuer. Dyan, Penelope, illus. 2009. (Illus.). 44p. pap. 11.95 (978-1-935118-53-4(6)) Bellissima Publishing, LLC.

Ehlin, Gina. Emma & Friends; Emma Rescues Cali. Ayzenberg, Nina, illus. l.t. ed. 2006. 24p. (J). 17.99 (978-1-59879-113-6(3)); per. 10.99 (978-1-59879-112-9(5)) Lifevest Publishing, Inc.

Eichler, Ken. Swift Eagle's Odyssey with the Buffalo. 2007. 59p. pap. 16.95 (978-1-60474-199-5(6)) America Star Bks.

Engle, Margarita. When You Wander: A Search-and-Rescue Dog Story. Morgan, Mary, illus. 2013. (ENG.). 32p. (J). (gr. -1-3). 16.99 (978-0-8050-9312-4(5), 9780805093124, Holt, Henry & Co. Bks. For Young Readers) Holt, Henry & Co.

Falkner, Brian. Northwood, 1 vol. 2013. (ENG.). 32p. (J). pap. (978-1-4342-8666-6(5)) Stone Arch Bks.

Filbin, Sandra A. The Enchanted World: A Tooth Fairy's Tale. 2010. 158p. pap. 14.50 (978-1-60860-379-4(2), Strategic Bk. Publishing) Strategic Book Publishing & Rights Agency (SBPRA).

Free Wheelin' Coloring/Activity Book (English) 2005. (Illus.). (J). 2.99 (978-0-9770455-7-0(9)) Mighty Kids Media.

Gallagher, Diana G. The Doggone Dog, 1 vol. Juarez, Adriana & Puglisi, Adriana, illus. 2013. (Pet Friends Forever Ser.). (ENG.). 88p. (gr. 1-3). pap. 5.95 (978-1-4795-1865-4(4)); lib. bdg. 25.32 (978-1-4048-7502-9(6)) Picture Window Bks.

—The Great Kitten Challenge, 1 vol. Juarez, Adriana & Puglisi, Adriana, illus. 2013. (Pet Friends Forever Ser.). (ENG.). 88p. (gr. 1-3). pap. 5.95 (978-1-4795-1864-7(6)); lib. bdg. 25.32 (978-1-4048-7501-2(8)) Picture Window Bks.

Garis, Howard R. The Curlytops & Their Pets. 2009. 120p. pap. 10.95 (978-1-60664-341-9(X)) Rodgers, Alan Bks.

Gayton, Sam. Lilliput, 1 vol. Ratterree, Alice, illus. 256p. (J). (gr. 3-6). 2017. (ENG.). pap. 8.95 **(978-1-68263-006-8(4))** 2016. (SPA & ENG.). 16.95 (978-1-56145-806-6(6)) Peachtree Pubs.

Getsinger, Mary. A Dream Come True. 2009. 20p. pap. 9.50 (978-1-4251-8885-6(0)) Trafford Publishing.

Golden Books. The Pups Save Christmas! (Paw Patrol) Moore, Harry, illus. 2015. (Big Golden Book Ser.). (ENG.). 48p. (J). (gr. -1-2). 9.99 (978-0-553-52391-1(0), Golden Bks.) Random Hse. Children's Bks.

Golden Books Staff. Pirate Pups! (Paw Patrol) Petrossi, Fabrizio, illus. 2016. (Little Golden Book Ser.). (ENG.). 24p. (J). (gr. -1-k). 4.99 (978-0-553-53888-5(8), Golden Bks.) Random Hse. Children's Bks.

Graham, Bob. How to Heal a Broken Wing. Graham, Bob, illus. 2008. (ENG., Illus.). 40p. (J). (gr. -1-2). 16.99 (978-0-7636-3903-7(6)) Candlewick Pr.

Graham, Bob. How to Heal a Broken Wing. Graham, Bob, illus. 2017. (ENG., Illus.). 40p. (J). (gr. -1-2). 7.99 **(978-0-7636-9841-6(5))** Candlewick Pr.

Gurtler, Janet. Shyanna's Wish. Wood, Katie, illus. 2015. (Mermaid Kingdom Ser.). (ENG.). 96p. (gr. 3-5). 23.99 (978-1-4342-9696-2(2)) Stone Arch Bks.

Haddix, Margaret Peterson. Among the Brave. 2004. (Shadow Children Ser.: Bk. 5). 132p. (J). lib. bdg. 20.00 (978-1-4242-0392-5(9)) Fitzgerald Bks.

Hall, Marjory. The Gold-Lined Box. 2003. 224p. 11.95 (978-0-9714612-6-0(0)) Green Mansion Pr. LLC.

Hamilton, Kersten & Wells, Rosemary. Yellow Copter. Petrone, Valeria, illus. 2015. (ENG.). 32p. (J). (-k). bds. 16.99 (978-0-451-46991-5(7), Viking Books for Young Readers) Penguin Young Readers Group.

Hansen, Amelia, illus. It's Raining Pups & Dogs! 2013. (Sit! Stay! Read! Ser.). (ENG.). 24p. (J). (gr. k). 16.95 (978-0-940719-16-3(9)) Gryphon Pr., The.

Harley, Stephen. The Christmastime Dog Rescue. 2013. 24p. pap. 10.95 (978-1-4624-0774-3(9), Inspiring Voices) Author Solutions, Inc.

Harpan, Gaile. The Ballad of Omar the Cat. Reddy, Sneha, illus. 2008. 28p. pap. 12.95 (978-0-9820479-1-0(6)) Peppertree Pr., The.

Harrison, Paula. The Moonlight Mystery. 2013. (Rescue Princesses Ser.: 3). (ENG., Illus.). 128p. (J). (gr. 2-5). pap. 4.99 (978-0-545-50915-2(7), Scholastic Paperbacks) Scholastic, Inc.

Hart, Alison. Whirlwind. 2010. (ENG.). 272p. (YA). (gr. 7-8). pap. 8.99 (978-0-375-86005-8(3), Laurel Leaf) Random Hse. Children's Bks.

Haslett, Katherine A. The Day Amy Met the Prime Minister & Mrs. Blair. 2007. (Illus.). 32p. (J). pap. 8.00 (978-0-8059-7353-2(2)) Dorrance Publishing Co., Inc.

Henson, Jim & Martin, Craig. Doozers. 2015. (Illus.). (J). (978-1-4806-9271-8(9), Simon Spotlight) Simon Spotlight.

Higginson, Sheila Sweeny. Diego rescata al bebé manatí (Diego's Manatee Rescue) McGee, Warner, illus. 2009. (Go, Diego, Go! Ser.). (SPA.). 24p. (J). pap. 3.99 (978-1-4169-7983-8(2), Libros Para Ninos) Libros Para Ninos.

Hilburn, L. M. Little Princesses to the Rescue. 2008. 24p. pap. 24.95 (978-1-60672-783-6(4)) America Star Bks.

Hilgenberg, Bob & Muir, Roberto. Tinker Bell & the Great Fairy Rescue. Storino, Sara & Zanotta, Roberta, illus. movie tie-in ed. 2010. (Disney Fairies Ser.). (ENG.). 56p. (J). (gr. 1-6). 9.99 (978-1-59707-232-8(X), 9781597072328) Papercutz.

Holden, Pam. Baby Whale's Mistake, 6 pack. Aziz, Lamia, illus. 2009. (Red Rocket Readers Ser.). (ENG.). 16p. (gr. 2-2). pap. (978-1-877363-87-0(1)) Flying Start Bks.

Holsather, Kent /Wilson. Sara's Moon. 2007. (Illus.). 176p. (YA). per. 12.95 (978-0-9729101-3-2(1)) Lonejack Mountain Pr.

Howard, A. G. Ensnared. 2015. (Splintered Ser.: 3). (J). lib. bdg. 19.60 (978-0-606-37434-7(5)) Turtleback Bks.

Howard, Cheryl L. Mikhael the Mighty: Be True to Who You Are & You Can Never Go Wrong. 2009. 52p. pap. 18.50 (978-1-60860-760-0(7), Strategic Bk. Publishing) Strategic Book Publishing & Rights Agency (SBPRA).

Hughes, Shirley. Alfie Gets in First. Hughes, Shirley, illus. 2009. (Alfie Ser.). (ENG., Illus.). 32p. (J). (gr. -1-k). pap. 9.99 (978-1-86230-783-4(0), Red Fox) Random House Children's Books GBR. Dist: Independent Pubs. Group.

Hugo, Victor. Les Misérables. Flores, Catty, illus. adapted ed. 2014. (ENG.). 64p. pap. 6.95 (978-1-906230-79-1(X)) Real Reads Ltd. GBR. Dist: Casemate Pubs. & Bk. Distributors, LLC.

Hulk to the Rescue. 2003. (J). per. (978-1-57657-811-7(9)) Paradise Pr., Inc.

Hunt, Bonnie. The Missing Chimp: A Grayson Twins Adventures, 1 vol. 2009. 100p. pap. 19.95 (978-1-60813-481-6(4)) America Star Bks.

Hurtado, Patricia. The Magical Feline & the White Haven. 2009. 142p. pap. 10.95 (978-1-60594-325-1(8), Llumina Pr.) Aeon Publishing Inc.

Inches, Alison. I Can Save the Earth! One Little Monster Learns to Reduce, Reuse, & Recycle. Garofoli, Viviana, illus. 2008. (Little Green Bks.). (ENG.). 24p. (J). (gr. -1-1). pap. 3.99 (978-1-4169-6789-7(3), Little Simon) Little Simon.

Jackson, Maureen. You Count Too. 2012. 20p. pap. 17.99 (978-1-4772-1241-7(8)) AuthorHouse.

Jennings, Sharon. Batnapped. (978-1-897039-30-4(1)) High Interest Publishing (HIP).

Johnson, Gerald J. J. Ellie Saves the Day, 1 vol. Funke, Peggy, illus. 2009. 12p. pap. 24.95 (978-1-60836-709-2(6)) America Star Bks.

Johnson, Sandi & Fefie, Flora. Zemo to the Rescue: Dorp 7 Rock Band. l.t. ed. 2003. (Illus.). 15p. (J). (gr. k-5). spiral bd. 4.99 (978-1-929063-25-3(3), 327) Moons & Stars Publishing For Children.

Jones, Janey Louise. Martha the Little Mouse. Poh, Jennie, illus. 2016. (Superfairies Ser.). (ENG.). 56p. (gr. k-3). lib. bdg. 23.99 (978-1-4795-8643-1(9)) Picture Window Bks.

Keene, Carolyn. The Bungalow Mystery, No. 3. 2014. (Nancy Drew Ser.: 3). (ENG.). 192p. (J). (gr. 3-7). 7.99 (978-0-448-47971-2(0), Grosset & Dunlap) Penguin Young Readers Group.

—The Hidden Staircase, No. 2. 2014. (Nancy Drew Ser.: 2). (ENG.). 192p. (J). (gr. 3-7). 7.99 (978-0-448-47970-5(2), Grosset & Dunlap) Penguin Young Readers Group.

—The Mystery at Lilac Inn. 2014. (Nancy Drew Ser.: 4). (ENG.). 192p. (J). (gr. 3-7). 7.99 (978-0-448-47972-9(9), Grosset & Dunlap) Penguin Young Readers Group.

—The Secret of the Old Clock, Bk. 1. 2014. (Nancy Drew Ser.: 1). (ENG.). 192p. (J). (gr. 3-7). 7.99 (978-0-448-47969-9(9), Grosset & Dunlap) Penguin Young Readers Group.

Kennedy, Marlane. Earthquake Shock. 2014. (Disaster Strikes Ser.: 1). lib. bdg. 14.75 (978-0-606-35827-9(7)) Turtleback Bks.

Kent, Jennifer McGrath. Chocolate River Rescue, 1 vol. 2007. (ENG.). 112p. (J). (gr. 2-5). pap. 8.95 (978-1-55109-600-1(5)) Nimbus Publishing, Ltd. CAN. Dist: Orca Bk. Pubs. USA.

Kipling, Rudyard. Captains Courageous. 2008. (Bring the Classics to Life Ser.). (ENG., Illus.). 72p. (gr. 4-12). pap., act. bk. ed. 10.95 (978-0-931334-66-5(7), EDCTR-401B) EDCON Publishing Group.

Korman, Gordon. Escape. 2008. (Island (Playaway Audio) Ser.). (J). 34.99 (978-1-60514-854-0(7)) Findaway World, LLC.

—Zoobreak. 2009. 230p. (J). (978-0-545-20027-1(X), Scholastic Pr.) Scholastic, Inc.

Larson, Sara B. Endure. 2016. (Defy Trilogy: Bk. 3). (ENG.). 320p. (J). (gr. 7). pap. 9.99 (978-1-338-09552-4(8)) Scholastic, Inc.

Lawson, Tanya. Pawpaw Harry & the Baby Squirrel. 2011. 24p. pap. 12.00 (978-1-4567-4616-2(2)) AuthorHouse.

Lego, et al. Fire Truck to the Rescue!, No. 1. 2009. (Lego City Ser.). (ENG.). 32p. (J). (gr. -1-k). pap. 3.99 (978-0-545-11543-8(4)) Scholastic, Inc.

Lester, Alison. The Snow Pony. 2006. (ENG.). 208p. (J). (gr. 5-7). pap. 12.95 (978-0-618-77125-7(5)) Houghton Mifflin Harcourt Publishing Co.

Little Airplane Productions & Fogarty, Alexandria, illus. Baby Beaver Rescue. 2009. (Wonder Pets! Ser.). (ENG.). 24p. (J). (gr. -1-2). pap. 3.99 (978-1-4169-8499-3(2), Simon Spotlight/Nickelodeon) Simon Spotlight/Nickelodeon.

Lively, Deborah Dreher. Hateya Sam. 2009. 32p. pap. 13.75 (978-1-60860-029-8(7), Eloquent Bks.) Strategic Book Publishing & Rights Agency (SBPRA).

Lush, Nella. Gracie & Belle Never Again! 2007. 20p. per. 24.95 (978-1-4241-8373-9(1)) America Star Bks.

Lyle-Soffe, Shari. On the Go with Rooter & Snuffle. Collier, Kevin Scott, illus. 2008. 20p. pap. 9.95 (978-1-933090-96-2(0)) Guardian Angel Publishing, Inc.

Lynch, Chris. Cyberia. 2008. (Cyberia Ser.: 1). (ENG.). 160p. (J). (gr. 3-7). 16.99 (978-0-545-02793-9(4), Scholastic Pr.) Scholastic, Inc.

M. F Feierabend, J. Olivia Ponty & Friends to the Rescue. 2012. 32p. pap. 32.70 (978-1-4771-1081-2(X)) Xlibris Corp.

Macdangereuse, T. T. The Untamed Scoundrel. 2014. (Epic Tales from Adventure Time Ser.). lib. bdg. 17.20 (978-0-606-35718-0(1)) Turtleback Bks.

Mackall, Dandi Daley. Dark Horse. 2009. (Starlight Animal Rescue Ser.: 4). (ENG.). 224p. (J). (gr. 3-7). mass mkt. 5.99 (978-1-4143-1271-2(7), Tyndale Kids) Tyndale Hse. Pubs.

Maher, Alex, illus. El Safari de Diego. 2007. (Go, Diego, Go! Ser.).Tr. of Diego's Safari Rescue. (SPA.). 24p. (J). (gr. -1-2). pap. 3.99 (978-1-4169-5998-4(X), Libros Para Ninos) Libros Para Ninos.

Maher, Allison. I, the Spy. 2006. (ENG.). 180p. (J). (gr. 4-7). per. 13.95 (978-1-897235-04-1(6)) Thistledown Pr., Ltd. CAN. Dist: Univ. of Toronto Pr.

Manning, Matthew K. U.S. Special Forces: Ghosts of the Night. Enecio, Jeremy, illus. 2016. (U. S. Special Ops Ser.). (ENG.). 96p. (gr. 3-4). E-Book 26.65 (978-1-4965-3477-4(8), Connect) Stone Arch Bks.

Mawhinney, Art, illus. Diego's Arctic Rescue. 2009. (Go, Diego, Go! Ser.). (ENG.). 24p. (J). (gr. -1-2). pap. 3.99 (978-1-4169-8504-4(2), Simon Spotlight/Nickelodeon) Simon Spotlight/Nickelodeon.

—Dora & Diego to the Rescue! 2010. (Go, Diego, Go! Ser.). (ENG.). 48p. (J). pap. 5.99 (978-1-4424-0660-5(7), Simon Spotlight/Nickelodeon) Simon Spotlight/Nickelodeon.

Mayer, Mercer. To the Rescue! Mayer, Mercer, illus. 2008. (My First I Can Read Bks.). (ENG., Illus.). 32p. (J). (gr. -1-3). 16.99 (978-0-06-083548-4(6)); pap. 3.99 (978-0-06-083547-7(8)) HarperCollins Pubs.

McDavid-Jones, Elizabeth. Ghost Light on Graveyard Shoal. 2009. (Mysteries Through Time Ser.). 144 - 176p. (YA). (gr. 4-8). 31.95 (978-1-60754-443-2(1)); pap. 15.25 (978-1-60754-444-9(X)) Windmill Bks.

McKee, David. Elmer & Butterfly. McKee, David, illus. 2015. (ENG., Illus.). 32p. (J). (gr. -1-3). 16.99 (978-1-4677-6326-4(8)) Lerner Publishing Group.

McKendry, Sam. To the Rescue! 2007. 6p. 9.95 (978-1-58117-562-2(0), Intervisual/Piggy Toes) Bendon, Inc.

McKimmie, Chris. Lara of Newtown. 2016. (ENG.). 32p. (J). (gr. -1-3). 19.99 (978-1-76011-232-5(1)) Allen & Unwin AUS. Dist: Independent Pubs. Group.

Meintjes, Chris. Angel's Flight. 2009. 156p. 25.99 (978-1-4269-0843-9(1)); pap. 15.99 (978-1-4269-0842-2(3)) Trafford Publishing.

Meister, Cari. The Clever Dolphin, 1 vol. Harpster, Steve, illus. 2012. (Ocean Tales Ser.). (ENG.). 32p. (gr. 2-4). pap. 6.25 (978-1-4342-4229-7(3)) Stone Arch Bks.

—The Stranded Orca, 1 vol. Harpster, Steve, illus. 2012. (Ocean Tales Ser.). (ENG.). 32p. (gr. 2-4). pap. 6.25 (978-1-4342-4232-7(3)); lib. bdg. 22.65 (978-1-4342-4026-2(6)) Stone Arch Bks.

Miles, Ellen. Bear. 2009. (Puppy Place Ser.: 14). lib. bdg. 14.75 (978-0-606-04427-1(2), Turtleback) Turtleback Bks.

—Mocha. 2013. (Puppy Place Ser.: 29). lib. bdg. 14.75 (978-0-606-32384-0(8), Turtleback) Turtleback Bks.

—Oscar. 2013. (Puppy Place Ser.). (ENG.). 96p. (J). (gr. 2-5). pap. 4.99 (978-0-545-46241-9(X), Scholastic Paperbacks) Scholastic, Inc.

Miller, Jeff. The Nerdy Dozen. 2015. (Nerdy Dozen Ser.: 1). (ENG.). 320p. (J). (gr. 3-7). pap. 6.99 (978-0-06-227263-8(2)) HarperCollins Pubs.

Miyazaki, Hayao. Ponyo Film Comic, Vol. 1. Miyazaki, Hayao, illus. movie tie-in ed. 2009. (ENG., Illus.). 172p. (J). pap. 9.99 (978-1-4215-3077-2(5)) Viz Media.

—Ponyo Film Comic, Vol. 2. Miyazaki, Hayao, illus. movie tie-in ed. 2009. (ENG., Illus.). 172p. (J). pap. 9.99 (978-1-4215-3078-9(3)) Viz Media.

—Ponyo Film Comic, Vol. 3. Miyazaki, Hayao, illus. movie tie-in ed. 2009. (ENG., Illus.). 172p. (J). pap. 9.99 (978-1-4215-3079-6(1)) Viz Media.

Moore, Eva. Lucky Ducklings. Carpenter, Nancy, illus. 2013. (ENG.). 32p. (J). (gr. k-2). 16.99 (978-0-439-44861-1(1), Orchard Bks.) Scholastic, Inc.

Morgan, Michaela. Shy Shark. Gomez, Elena, illus. 2005. (ENG.). 24p. (J). lib. bdg. 23.65 (978-1-59646-722-4(3)) Dingles & Co.

Morris, J. & J. Little Black Pearl. 2010. 80p. pap. (978-1-905553-51-8(X)) BookPublishingWorld.

Morris, Kim. Tinker Bell & the Great Fairy Rescue. 2010. (ENG.). 32p. 12.99 (978-1-4231-2925-7(3)) Disney Pr.

Mors, Peter D. & Mors, Terry M. L D the Littlest Dragster. Weiss, Tracy, illus. 2009. 36p. pap. 16.99 (978-1-4389-7445-3(0)) AuthorHouse.

Moscovich, Rotem, et al. Curious George Snowy Day. 2007. (Curious George Ser.). (ENG., Illus.). 24p. (J). (gr. -1-3). 3.99 (978-0-618-80043-8(3)) Houghton Mifflin Harcourt Publishing Co.

Myhre, J. A. A Bird, a Girl, & a Rescue. 2016. (Illus.). ix, 133p. (J). pap. 15.99 (978-1-942572-69-5(7)) New Growth Pr.

Nelson, James Gary. Smileytooth & Bushwack Plaque. Bumstead, Debbie, illus. 2009. 16p. pap. 9.95 (978-1-61633-009-5(0)) Guardian Angel Publishing, Inc.

Nickelodeon. PAW Patrol: Pawsome Teamwork. 2016. (ENG.). 12p. (J). (gr. -1-k). bds. 9.99 (978-0-7944-3759-6(1)) Studio Fun International.

Noland, Charles. The Adventures of Drew & Ellie: The Daring Rescue. Moyer, Tom, illus. 2nd ed. 2006. 92p. (J). per. 7.95 (978-0-9789297-2-5(1)) TMD Enterprises.

Northrop, Michael. Surrounded by Sharks. 2014. (ENG.). 224p. (J). (gr. 4-7). 17.99 (978-0-545-61545-7(3), Scholastic Pr.) Scholastic, Inc.

Oakes, Cory Putman. Dinosaur Boy Saves Mars. 2016. (Dinosaur Boy Ser.: 2). (ENG., Illus.). 224p. (J). (gr. 3-7). 12.99 (978-1-4926-0540-9(9), 9781492605409, Sourcebooks Jabberwocky) Sourcebooks, Inc.

O'Donnell, Liam & O'Donnell, Laura. Duncan: A Brave Rescue. Hynes, Robert, illus. 2004. (Pet Tales Ser.). (ENG.). 32p. (J). (gr. -1-3). 4.95 (978-1-59249-291-6(6), 1B001) Soundprints.

—Duncan: A Brave Rescue. Hynes, Robert, illus. 2005. (Pet Tales Ser.). (ENG.). 32p. (J). (gr. -1-2). 2.95 (978-1-59249-292-3(4), 1B003) Soundprints.

Parker, Danny. The Silk Lakes Rescue. Shield, Guy, illus. 2017. (Lola's Toy Box Ser.: 7). (ENG.). 96p. (J). (gr. k-2). pap. 9.99 **(978-1-76012-686-5(1))** Hardie Grant Egmont Pty, Ltd. AUS. Dist: Independent Pubs. Group.

Parker, John. Chaos Mountain. 2007. 96p. (YA). pap. (978-1-4207-0734-2(5)) Sundance/Newbridge Educational Publishing.

Patron, Susan. Lucky Breaks. Phelan, Matt, illus. 2009. (ENG.). 192p. (J). (gr. 3-7). 16.99 (978-1-4169-3998-6(9), Atheneum Bks. for Young Readers) Simon & Schuster Children's Publishing.

Patterson, James. Maximum Ride. 2010. (ENG.). 1392p. (YA). (gr. 5-17). pap., pap. 29.99 (978-0-316-12825-4(2), Jimmy Patterson) Little Brown & Co.

PAW Patrol, P. A. W. PAW Patrol: Chase to the Rescue. 2016. (ENG.). 24p. (J). (gr. -1 — 1). 18.99 (978-0-7944-3801-2(6), Reader's Digest Children's Bks.) Studio Fun International.

Paw Patrol, Paw. Paw Patrol: Pups Save the Day - A Slide Surprise Book. 2015. (Sliding Surprise Ser.: 4). (ENG.). 12p. (J). (gr. -1-k). bds. 10.99 (978-0-7944-3558-5(0), Reader's Digest Children's Bks.) Studio Fun International.

Peters, Tony. Kids on a Case: The Case of the Ten Grand Kidnapping. 2008. 84p. pap. 9.95 (978-1-60693-173-8(3), Eloquent Bks.) Strategic Book Publishing & Rights Agency (SBPRA).

Pickett, Anola. Whisper Island. 2013. (ENG.). 235p. (J). (gr. 3-7). pap. 14.99 (978-1-4621-1167-1(X), Sweetwater Bks.) Cedar Fort, Inc./CFI Distribution.

Pippin, Sheila C. Katrina: Through Mango's Eyes. Pippin, Kristin A. & Pippin, Sheila C., illus. 2007. (J). (gr. -1-5). pap. 12.95 (978-1-56167-956-0(9)) American Literary Pr.

Publications International Ltd. Staff, ed. Look & Find Wolverine & X Men. 2009. 24p. (J). 7.98 (978-1-4127-3592-6(0), PIL Kids) Publications International, Ltd.

Random House. High-Flying Skye (PAW Patrol) MJ Illustrations, illus. 2016. (Book & CD Ser.). (ENG.). 24p. (J). (gr. -1-2). pap. 6.99 (978-1-101-93686-3(X), Random Hse. Bks. for Young Readers) Random Hse. Children's Bks.

—PAW Patrol Deluxe Step into Reading (PAW Patrol) Random House, illus. 2016. (Step into Reading Ser.). (ENG., Illus.). 24p. (J). (gr. -1-1). pap. 4.99 (978-0-553-52288-4(4), Random Hse. Bks. for Young Readers) Random Hse. Children's Bks.

—A Paw Patrol Treasury (PAW Patrol) Random House, illus. 2016. (Padded Board Book Ser.). (ENG., Illus.). 30p. (J). (— 1). bds. 11.99 (978-1-101-93957-4(5), Random Hse. Bks. for Young Readers) Random Hse. Children's Bks.

Ransom, Candice. The Underground Adventure of Arly Dunbar, Cave Explorer. Hammond, Ted & Carbajal, Richard Pimentel, illus. 2011. (History's Kid Heroes Set III Ser.). pap. 51.02 (978-0-7613-7640-8(2), Graphic Universe™) Lerner Publishing Group.

—The Underground Adventure of Arly Dunbar, Cave Explorer. Hammond, Ted & Carbajal, Richard, illus. 2011. (History's Kid Heroes Ser.). (ENG.). 32p. (gr. 3-5). (J). 26.60 (978-0-7613-6182-4(0)); pap. 8.95 (978-0-7613-7074-1(9), Graphic Universe™) Lerner Publishing Group.

Rees, Douglas. Uncle Pirate to the Rescue. Auth, Tony, illus. 2010. (ENG.). 112p. (J). (gr. 2-5). pap. 6.99 (978-1-4169-7505-2(5), McElderry, Margaret K. Bks.) McElderry, Margaret K. Bks.

Rey, H. A. & Rey, Margret. Curious George to the Rescue. 2007. (Curious George Ser.). (ENG., Illus.). 12p. (J). (gr. -1-3). 8.99 (978-0-618-72401-7(X)) Houghton Mifflin Harcourt Publishing Co.

Richards, Pat. Bardolph Bedivere Wolf Returns. Richards, Charles, illus. 2007. 42p. (J). (978-0-9790796-4-1(0)) PJR Assocs., Ltd.

Rigby. Golden Lasso. (gr. k-1). 23.00 (978-0-7635-9021-5(5)) Rigby Education.

Riner, Kendall F. The Rescue Adventures of Fireman Frank. 2006. (Illus.). 52p. (J). pap. 12.00 (978-0-9786369-1-3(0)) Warwick Hse. Publishing.

Ripley, Esther. Heroes to the Rescue. 2016. (DK Reader Level 2 Ser.). lib. bdg. 13.55 (978-0-606-38711-8(0)) Turtleback Bks.

Rocha, K. E. Hidden Rock Rescue (Secrets of Bearhaven #3) 2016. (Secrets of Bearhaven Ser.: 3). (ENG.). 224p. (J). (gr. 3-7). 14.99 (978-0-545-81305-1(0), Scholastic Pr.) Scholastic, Inc.

Roddy, Lee. The Legend of Fire. 2006. (Ladd Family Adventure Ser.: Vol. 2). (Illus.). 133p. (J). (gr. 3-7). per. 7.99 (978-0-88062-251-6(2)) Mott Media.

Rogers, Bud & Krueger, Jim. Secret Alliance, 1 vol. Padilla, Ariel, illus. 2008. (Z Graphic Novels / Tomo Ser.). (ENG.). 160p. (J). pap. 6.99 (978-0-310-71304-3(8)) Zondervan.

Rogers, Wanda Gayle. Miss Bean & the Great Tricycle Rescue: The Great Tricycle Rescue. 2007. (J). 7.95 (978-1-59872-735-7(4)) Instant Pub.

Rooney, Anne. Muffin. Julian, Sean, illus. 2009. (Go! Readers Ser.). 48p. (J). (gr. 2-5). pap. 12.85 (978-1-60754-270-4(6)); lib. bdg. 29.25 (978-1-60754-269-8(2)) Windmill Bks.

Rosen, Lucy. Blast Off! 2015. (Transformers 8x8 Ser.). (J). lib. bdg. 13.55 (978-0-606-37228-2(8)) Turtleback Bks.

Rosen, Michael J. The Tale of Rescue. Fellows, Stan, illus. 2015. (ENG.). 112p. (J). (gr. 5). 14.99 (978-0-7636-7167-9(3)) Candlewick Pr.

Ross, Richard. Arctic Airlift. 2005. (Illus.). 36p. (J). 17.00 (978-0-9763119-0-4(9)) Blue Fox Pr.

Sagerman, Evan. Giraffe Rescue Company. Chou, Joey, illus. 2016. (J). (978-1-4424-1366-5(2)) Simon & Schuster Children's Publishing.

Sanders, Gaye Lynn. Chameleon Girl. 2008. 60p. pap. 16.95 (978-1-60703-643-2(6)) America Star Bks.

Sanders, Stephanie & Pauling, Galen T. Q. T. Pie's Rescue Adventure. 2003. (Illus.). 36p. (J). (gr. -1-6). mass mkt. 4.99 (978-0-9670875-3-5(8), 313-533-7383) SanPaul Group, LLC, The.

Sazaklis, John. Rocket to the Rescue! Atiyeh, Michael & Borkowski, Michael, illus. 2017. (Little Golden Book Ser.). (ENG.). 24p. (J). (-k). 4.99 (978-0-399-55849-8(7), Golden Bks.) Random Hse. Children's Bks.

Scribner, Don. Bennie & Thomas & the Rescue at Razor's Edge: Volume I. Scribner, Peter, illus. 2012. 44p. pap. 24.95 (978-1-4626-8957-6(4)) America Star Bks.

—Bennie & Thomas & the Rescue at Razor's Edge: Volume II. Scribner, Peter, illus. 2012. 48p. pap. 24.95 (978-1-4626-9472-3(1)) America Star Bks.

Sharp, Lydia. Whenever I'm with You. 2017. (ENG.). 304p. (J). (gr. 7). 17.99 (978-1-338-04749-3(3), Scholastic Pr.) Scholastic, Inc.

Shaw, Natalie, adapted by. Doozers Stick with It. 2015. (Doozers Ser.). (ENG., Illus.). 32p. (J). (gr. -1-1). pap. 3.99 (978-1-4814-3217-7(6), Simon Spotlight) Simon Spotlight.

Shotz, Jennifer Li. Hurricane Rescue. 2017. (Hero Ser.: 2). lib. bdg. 18.40 **(978-0-606-40134-0(2))** Turtleback Bks.

Simon Spotlight, creator. Dora & Diego's Adventures! 2007. (Dora the Explorer Ser.). (ENG., Illus.). 80p. (J). (gr. -1-2).

7.99 *(978-1-4169-3532-2(0)*, Simon Spotlight/Nickelodeon) Simon Spotlight/Nickelodeon.
Sina-Atanda, Moyin. The Phenomenal Four: Four on a Mission to Save the Animals. 2013. 52p. (gr. 4-6). pap. 10.03 *(978-1-4669-7291-9(2))* Trafford Publishing.
Slack, Michael. Turtle Tug to the Rescue. Slack, Michael, illus. 2017. (ENG., Illus.). 40p. (J). 16.99 *(978-1-62779-194-6(9)*, 9781627791946, Holt, Henry & Co. Bks. For Young Readers) Holt, Henry & Co.
Smith, Claude Clayton. The Gull That Lost the Sea. Cathcart, Sharyn, illus. 2008. (ENG.). 34p. pap. 5.95 *(978-0-9667359-7-0(8)*, BeanPole Bks.) Harren Communications, LLC.
Smith, Dan. Boy X. 2017. (ENG.). 288p. (J). (gr. 3-7). 16.99 *(978-1-338-06564-0(5)*, Chicken Hse., The) Scholastic, Inc.
Smith, L. J. The Passion. 2008. (Dark Visions Ser.: Bk. 3). (ENG.). 224p. (YA). (gr. 7). pap. 10.99 *(978-1-4169-8483-2(6)*, Simon Pulse) Simon Pulse.
Smith, Lee A. Dobee the Littlest Dragon. 2008. 24p. per. 24.95 *(978-1-60441-165-2(1))* America Star Bks.
Smith, Roland. Jack's Run. 2007. (ENG.). 256p. (J). (gr. 5-17). pap. 6.99 *(978-1-4231-0407-0(2))* Hyperion Pr.
Snider, Brandon T. Dangerous Rescue. 2016. (Transformers 8x8 Ser.). (J). lib. bdg. 13.55 *(978-0-606-37515-3(5))* Turtleback Bks.
Snyder, Maria V. Storm Watcher. 2013. 228p. (gr. 4-8). pap. 9.99 *(978-1-61603-033-9(X))* Leap Bks.
Stainton, Sue. The Lighthouse Cat. Mortimer, Anne, illus. 2004. (ENG.). 32p. (J). (gr. -1-2). 16.99 *(978-0-06-009604-5(7)*, Tegen, Katherine Bks) HarperCollins Pubs.
Stewart, E. J. The Wayfaring Dolphin. 2010. 298p. pap. 16.95 *(978-0-557-33701-9(1))* Lulu Pr., Inc.
Stewart, Whitney. Marshall: A Nantucket Sea Rescue. Lyall, Dennis, illus. 2008. (ENG.). 32p. (J). (gr. -1-2). 10.95 *(978-1-59249-857-4(4))*; 6.95 *(978-1-59249-855-0(8))*; 2.95 *(978-1-59249-856-7(6))* Soundprints.
Szymanski, Lois K. A Pony to the Rescue. 2007. (Charming Ponies Ser.). 96p. (J). (gr. 2-5). pap. 4.99 *(978-0-06-128869-2(1)*, HarperFestival) HarperCollins Pubs.
Tabares, Veronica. Monkeys on an Island. Tabares, Bridgitt, illus. 2012. 32p. (J). pap. 14.50 *(978-1-60916-005-0(3))* Sun Break Publishing.
tbd. Paw Patrol - Here to Help! 2016. (ENG.). 10p. (J). (gr. -1 — 1). bds. 8.99 *(978-0-7944-3585-1(8)*, Reader's Digest Children's Bks.) Studio Fun International.
Thomas, Blair L. The Sabatini Prophecy. 2008. (ENG.). 496p. (YA). 8.99 *(978-0-9760237-4-6(1))* Axiom Hse.
Tilert, Heather R. Ming-Ming Saves the Day: Follow the Reader Level 1. 2008. (Wonder Pets! Ser.). (ENG.). 24p. (J). 24.99 *(978-1-4169-6459-9(2)*, Simon Scribbles) Simon Scribbles.
Top That Publishing Staff, ed. Rescue Helicopter. Dronsfield, Paul, illus. 2007. (Story Book Ser.). (ENG.). 33p. (J). (gr. -1). bds. *(978-1-84666-179-2(X)*, Tide Mill Pr.) Top That! Publishing PLC.
Truax, Lois. Grandmothers Are Magic. 2010. 28p. pap. 5.95 *(978-1-935355-01-4(5))* New Shelves Bks.
Ursu, Anne. Breadcrumbs. McGuire, Erin, illus. 2013. (ENG.). 336p. (J). (gr. 3-7). pap. 6.99 *(978-0-06-201506-8(0)*, Waldon Pond Pr.) HarperCollins Pubs.
Velle, Tori. Jake the Snake. 2009. 40p. pap. 16.99 *(978-1-4490-4431-2(X))* AuthorHouse.
Verba, Joan Marie. Action Alert. 2008. 176p. (YA). pap. 15.95 *(978-0-9653575-8-6(9))* FTL Pubns.
Verne, Jules. The English at the North Pole. 2009. 160p. 24.95 *(978-1-60664-684-7(2))*; pap. 13.95 *(978-1-60664-313-6(4))* Rodgers, Alan Bks.
Waldron, Douglas E. Cody Sackett of Montana: Tales of Adventure. 2008. 188p. per. 24.95 *(978-1-4241-9781-1(3))* America Star Bks.
Wallace, Bill. Skinny-Dipping at Monster Lake. 2004. 212p. (gr. 3-7). 16.00 *(978-0-7569-3486-6(9))* Perfection Learning Corp.
—Skinny-Dipping at Monster Lake. 2004. (ENG., Illus.). 224p. (J). (gr. 3-7). pap. 6.99 *(978-0-689-85151-3(0)*, Simon & Schuster/Paula Wiseman Bks.) Simon & Schuster/Paula Wiseman Bks.
Wallace, Bill & Wallace, Carol. That Doggone Calf. 2009. (ENG.). 160p. (J). (gr. 3-7). 16.95 *(978-0-8234-2228-9(3))* Holiday Hse., Inc.
Waters, Michael. Tommy & his Flying Saucer of Milk. 2009. 32p. pap. 16.95 *(978-1-4357-4802-6(6))* Lulu Pr., Inc.
Watson, Jude. Underworld. 2005. (Star Wars Ser.: No. 3). 137p. (J). lib. bdg. 20.00 *(978-1-4242-0776-3(2))* Fitzgerald Bks.
Watt, Fiona. Busy Helicopter Book. 2012. (Pull-Back Bks). 10p. (J). ring bd. 24.99 *(978-0-7945-3203-1(9)*, Usborne) EDC Publishing.
Wax, Wendy. Diego & Papi to the Rescue. Hom, John, illus. 2007. (Go, Diego, Go! Ser.: 3). (ENG.). 24p. (J). pap. 3.99 *(978-1-4169-2781-5(6)*, Simon Spotlight/Nickelodeon) Simon Spotlight/Nickelodeon.
—Diego y Papi al Rescate. Ziegler, Argentina Palacios, tr. Hom, John, illus. 2008. (Go, Diego, Go! Ser.).Tr. of Diego & Papi to the Rescue. (SPA.). 24p. (J). (gr. -1-2). pap. 3.99 *(978-1-4169-5044-8(3)*, Libros Para Ninos) Libros Para Ninos.
Whitmore, Andrew. Beast of the Jungle. 2007. 96p. (YA). pap. *(978-1-4207-0728-1(0))* Sundance/Newbridge Educational Publishing.
Williams, Geoffrey T. Manatees & Mermaids. 2010. (ENG., Illus.). 64p. (J). (gr. 3-7). 8.95 *(978-0-9800444-3-0(X))* Save Our Seas, Ltd.
Williams, Kelly Ann. Pye. 2010. 36p. pap. 11.50 *(978-1-4452-8438-5(3))* Lulu Pr., Inc.
Wilson, Mark A. The Amazing Gift from the Woods. 2008. 48p. pap. 16.95 *(978-1-60563-056-4(X))* America Star Bks.
Wojtowycz, David, illus. Elephant Joe, Brave Firefighter! 2015. (Step into Reading Ser.). (ENG.). 32p. (J). (gr. -1-1). 12.99 *(978-0-375-97203-4(X)*, Random Hse. Bks. for Young Readers) Random Hse. Children's Bks.
Wood, Audrey. Alphabet Rescue. Wood, Bruce, illus. 2006. (ENG.). 40p. (J). (gr. -1-k). 17.99 *(978-0-439-85316-3(8)*, Blue Sky Pr., The) Scholastic, Inc.
Wood, Audrey & Wood, Bruce Robert, illus. Alphabet Rescue. 2006. (J). *(978-0-439-88927-8(8))* Scholastic, Inc.
Wooster, Devin Ann. Barbie Fall 2016 Holiday Movie Deluxe Step into Reading (Barbie) 2016. (Step into Reading Ser.). (ENG., Illus.). 24p. (J). (gr. -1-1). pap. 4.99 *(978-1-101-93995-6(8)*, Random Hse. Bks. for Young Readers) Random Hse. Children's Bks.
Wooten, Arthur. Wise Bear William: A New Beginning. Santora, Bud, illus. 2012. 44p. pap. 12.99 *(978-0-9850529-1-1(0))* Galaxias Productions.
Young, Judy. Minnow & Rose: An Oregon Trail Story. Farnsworth, Bill, illus. 2009. (Tales of Young Americans Ser.). (ENG.). 32p. (J). (gr. 1-5). 17.95 *(978-1-58536-421-3(5))* Sleeping Bear Pr.
Ziegler-Sullivan, Ursula. Pirate Pups! Petrossi, Fabrizio, illus. 2016. (J). *(978-1-4806-9717-1(6)*, Golden Bks.) Random Hse. Children's Bks.

RESEARCH

see also Discoveries in Science; Learning and Scholarship

also subjects with the subdivision Research, e.g. Agriculture—Research; Medicine—Research

Aboff, Marcie. Analyzing Doggie Data. 2011. (Data Mania Ser.). (ENG.). 24p. (gr. 1-2). pap. 41.70 *(978-1-4296-6465-3(7)*, First Facts) Capstone Press of Coughlan Cos.
Albee, Michael J. Elements of Research: The Student's Guide to Avoiding Plagiarism in the Information Age. 2003. (Illus.). 140p. per. *(978-0-9745405-0-4(1))* Albee, Michael.
Arnone, Marilyn P. & Coatney, Sharon. Mac, Information Detective, in ... the Curious Kids & Why Dolphins Visit Curiosity Creek: A Storybook Approach to Introducing Research Skills Picture Book & Educator's Guide Set, 2 vols. 2008. (Illus.). 128p. (C). pap. 40.00 *(978-1-59158-498-8(1)*, LU4981, Libraries Unlimited) ABC-CLIO, LLC.
—Mac, Information Detective, in the Case Of— Curious Kids & the Squiggly Question, 2 vols. 2005. 32p. (C). 35.00 *(978-1-59158-189-5(3)*, LU1893, Libraries Unlimited) ABC-CLIO, LLC.
Asselin, Kristine Carlson. Smart Research Strategies: Finding the Right Sources. 2013. (Research Tool Kit Ser.). (ENG.). 32p. (gr. 3-4). pap. 47.70 *(978-1-62065-791-1(0))*; pap. 8.10 *(978-1-62065-790-4(2))*; lib. bdg. 27.32 *(978-1-4296-9950-1(7))* Capstone Press of Coughlan Cos. (Fact Finders).
—Think for Yourself: Avoiding Plagiarism. 2013. (Research Tool Kit Ser.). (ENG.). 32p. (gr. 3-4). pap. 47.70 *(978-1-62065-793-5(7)*, Fact Finders); pap. 8.10 *(978-1-62065-792-8(9)*, Fact Finders); lib. bdg. 27.32 *(978-1-4296-9951-8(5))* Capstone Press of Coughlan Cos.
Asselin, Kristine Carlson, et al. Research Tool Kit. 2013. (Research Tool Kit Ser.). (ENG.). 32p. (gr. 3-4). pap. 31.80 *(978-1-62065-794-2(5))*; pap. 190.80 *(978-1-62065-795-9(3))*; lib. bdg. 109.28 *(978-1-4296-9952-5(3))* Capstone Press of Coughlan Cos. (Fact Finders).
Bodden, Valerie. Analyze & Define the Assignment. 2015. (Info Wise Ser.). (ENG.). 40p. (gr. 4-6). pap. 8.99 *(978-1-4677-7578-6(9))*; (Illus.). 30.65 *(978-1-4677-5223-7(1))* Lerner Publishing Group. (Lerner Pubns.).
—Assess & Select Your Sources. 2015. (Info Wise Ser.). (ENG., Illus.). 40p. (gr. 4-6). 30.65 *(978-1-4677-5222-0(3)*, Lerner Pubns.) Lerner Publishing Group.
—Doing Primary Research. 2012. (Research for Writing Ser.). 48p. (gr. 5-12). 23.95 *(978-1-60818-204-6(5)*, Creative Education) Creative Co., The.
—Research & Synthesize Your Facts. 2015. (Info Wise Ser.). (ENG., Illus.). 40p. (J). (gr. 4-6). lib. bdg. 30.65 *(978-1-4677-5224-4(X)*, Lerner Pubns.) Lerner Publishing Group.
—Writing a Research Paper. Williams, Nate, illus. 2015. (Classroom How-To Ser.). (ENG.). 48p. (J). (gr. 5-8). pap. 12.00 *(978-0-89812-989-2(3)*, Creative Paperbacks) Creative Co., The.
—Writing a Research Paper. 2014. (J). *(978-1-60818-283-1(5)*, Creative Education) Creative Co., The.
Brinkerhoff, Shirley. Research Scientist. Riggs, Ernestine G. & Gholar, Cheryl, eds. 2013. (Careers with Character Ser.: 18). 96p. (J). (gr. 7-18). 22.95 *(978-1-4222-2765-7(0))* Mason Crest.
Britton, Arthur K. Life at a Polar Research Station. 2013. (Extreme Jobs in Extreme Places Ser.). (Illus.). 32p. (J). (gr. 3-6). pap. 10.50 *(978-1-4339-8483-9(0))*; lib. bdg. 26.60 *(978-1-4339-8482-2(2))* Stevens, Gareth Publishing LLLP.
Carlson Berne, Emma. Answer! Analyze Your Data. 2014. (Scientific Method in Action Ser.). (Illus.). 24p. (J). (gr. 3-6). 23.60 *(978-1-4777-2930-4(5))*; pap. 49.50 *(978-1-4777-3088-1(5))*; pap. 8.25 *(978-1-4777-3017-1(6))* Rosen Publishing Group, Inc., The. (PowerKids Pr.).
—Share! Present Your Findings. 2014. (Scientific Method in Action Ser.). (Illus.). 24p. (J). (gr. 3-6). pap. 49.50 *(978-1-4777-3089-8(3)*, PowerKids Pr.) Rosen Publishing Group, Inc., The.
Cefrey, Holly. Researching People, Places, & Events. 2009. (Digital & Information Literacy Ser.). (Illus.). 48p. (YA). (gr. 5-8). lib. bdg. 29.25 *(978-1-4358-5317-1(2)*, Rosen Reference) Rosen Publishing Group, Inc., The.
Chappell, Rachel. Solving Science Questions: A Book about the Scientific Process. 2007. (Big Ideas for Young Scientists Ser.). (Illus.). 24p. (J). (gr. 2-5). lib. bdg. *(978-1-60044-542-2(X))* Rourke Educational Media.
Coleman, Kelly. Choose It! Finding the Right Research Topic. Petelinsek, Kathleen, illus. 2015. (Explorer Junior Library: Information Explorer Junior Ser.). (ENG.). 24p. (J). (gr. 1-4). 29.93 *(978-1-63188-862-5(5)*, 206028) Cherry Lake Publishing.
Coleman, Miriam. Find It: Searching for Information. 2012. (Core Skills Ser.). (ENG., Illus.). 32p. (J). (gr. 3-6). 25.25 *(978-1-4488-7451-4(3))*; pap. 10.00 *(978-1-4488-7536-8(6))* Rosen Publishing Group, Inc., The. (PowerKids Pr.).
—Prove It: Gathering Evidence & Integrating Information. 2012. (Core Skills Ser.). (ENG., Illus.). 32p. (J). (gr. 3-6). 25.25 *(978-1-4488-7453-8(X))*; pap. 10.00 *(978-1-4488-7525-2(0))* Rosen Publishing Group, Inc., The. (PowerKids Pr.).
Digital Research. 2010. (Digital World Ser.). (Illus.). 120p. (J). (gr. 6-12). 40.00 *(978-0-8160-6790-9(2)*, Chelsea Hse.) Facts On File, Inc.
Doudna, Kelly. I'll Use Information for My Explanation!, 1 vol. 2007. (Science Made Simple Ser.). (ENG., Illus.). 24p. (J). (gr. k-3). lib. bdg. 24.21 *(978-1-59928-588-7(6)*, SandCastle) ABDO Publishing Co.
Facts on File, Inc. Staff. Career Skills Library: Research & Information Management, Third Edition. 3rd rev. ed. 2009. (Career Skills Library). (Illus.). 168p. (gr. 6-12). 25.95 *(978-0-8160-7777-9(0)*, Ferguson Publishing Co.) Facts On File, Inc.
Fandel, Jennifer. Collect Your Thoughts: Organizing Information, 1 vol. 2013. (Research Tool Kit Ser.). (ENG.). 32p. (gr. 3-4). pap. 8.10 *(978-1-62065-786-7(4))*; pap. 47.70 *(978-1-62065-787-4(2))*; lib. bdg. 27.32 *(978-1-4296-9948-8(5))* Capstone Press of Coughlan Cos. (Fact Finders).
Flatt, Lizann. Collecting Data. 2016. (Get Graphing! Building Data Literacy Skills Ser.). (ENG., Illus.). 24p. (J). (gr. k-3). *(978-0-7787-2633-3(9))* Crabtree Publishing Co.
Fontichiaro, Kristin. Find Out Firsthand: Using Primary Sources. 2012. (Explorer Junior Library: Information Explorer Junior Ser.). (ENG.). 24p. (gr. 1-4). 28.50 *(978-1-61080-487-5(2)*, 202097); pap. 12.79 *(978-1-61080-661-9(1)*, 202271) Cherry Lake Publishing.
—Super Smart Information Strategies: Go Straight to the Source. 2010. (Explorer Library: Information Explorer Ser.). (ENG.). 32p. (gr. 4-8). pap. 14.21 *(978-1-61080-257-4(8)*, 200905); lib. bdg. 28.50 *(978-1-60279-640-9(8)*, 200343) Cherry Lake Publishing.
—Watch It! Researching with Videos. Petelinsek, Kathleen, illus. 2015. (Explorer Junior Library: Information Explorer Junior Ser.). (ENG.). 24p. (J). (gr. 1-4). 29.93 *(978-1-63188-863-2(3)*, 206032) Cherry Lake Publishing.
Forest, Christopher. Present What You Know: Sharing Information. 2013. (Research Tool Kit Ser.). (ENG.). 32p. (gr. 3-4). pap. 47.70 *(978-1-62065-789-8(9))*; pap. 8.10 *(978-1-62065-788-1(0))*; lib. bdg. 27.32 *(978-1-4296-9949-5(3))* Capstone Press of Coughlan Cos. (Fact Finders).
Furgang, Adam. Searching Online for Image, Audio, & Video Files. 2009. (Digital & Information Literacy Ser.). (Illus.). 48p. (YA). (gr. 5-8). lib. bdg. 29.25 *(978-1-4358-5318-8(0))* Rosen Publishing Group, Inc., The.
Gaines, Ann Graham. Master the Library & Media Center. 2009. (Ace It! Information Literacy Ser.). (Illus.). 48p. (J). (gr. 2-5). lib. bdg. 25.27 *(978-0-7660-3393-1(7))* Enslow Pubs., Inc.
Graff, Rhonda. Instant Nonfiction Writing Frames: Reproducible Templates & Easy How-To's That Guide Children to Research & Write Successful Reports on the Topics You Teach. 2011. (ENG.). 64p. pap. 11.99 *(978-0-545-22416-1(0)*, Teaching Resources) Scholastic, Inc.
Green, Lyric & Graham Gaines, Ann. Future Ready Research Papers. 2017. (Future Ready Project Skills Ser.). 48p. (J). (gr. 3-4). pap. 11.70 ***(978-0-7660-8773-6(5))***; lib. bdg. 27.93 ***(978-0-7660-8661-6(5))*** Enslow Pubs., Inc.
Greve, Meg. Writing an Opinion Paper. 2014. (ENG.). 24p. (gr. 3-5). 28.50 *(978-1-62717-693-4(4))* Rourke Educational Media.
Hamilton, John. Newspapers, 1 vol. 2005. (Straight to the Source Ser.). (ENG., Illus.). 32p. (gr. k-6). 27.07 *(978-1-59197-547-2(6)*, Checkerboard Library) ABDO Publishing Co.
—Primary & Secondary Sources, 1 vol. 2005. (Straight to the Source Ser.). (ENG.). 32p. (gr. k-6). 27.07 *(978-1-59197-548-9(4)*, Checkerboard Library) ABDO Publishing Co.
Harbo, Christopher L. Frankenstein's Monster & Scientific Methods, 1 vol. Aón, Carlos, illus. 2013. (Monster Science Ser.). (ENG.). 32p. (gr. 3-4). pap. 8.10 *(978-1-62065-816-1(X)*, Graphic Library) Capstone Press of Coughlan Cos.
—Frankenstein's Monster & Scientific Methods. An, Carlos, illus. 2013. (Monster Science Ser.). (ENG.). 32p. (gr. 3-4). pap. 47.70 *(978-1-62065-817-8(8)*, Graphic Library) Capstone Press of Coughlan Cos.
—Frankenstein's Monster & Scientific Methods, 1 vol. Aón, Carlos, illus. 2013. (Monster Science Ser.). (ENG.). 32p. (gr. 3-4). lib. bdg. 30.65 *(978-1-4296-9931-0(0)*, Graphic Library) Capstone Press of Coughlan Cos.
Harper, Leslie. Cómo Manteneres Informado. 2014. (Sé un líder de la Comunidad (Be a Community Leader) Ser.). (SPA.). 32p. (J). (gr. 4-6). pap. 60.00 *(978-1-4777-6923-2(4)*, PowerKids Pr.) Rosen Publishing Group, Inc., The.
—Cómo Manteneres Informados. 2014. (Sé un líder de la Comunidad (Be a Community Leader) Ser.). (SPA.). 32p. (J). (gr. 4-6). lib. bdg. 26.25 *(978-1-4777-6921-8(8)*, PowerKids Pr.) Rosen Publishing Group, Inc., The.
Hord, Colleen. Writing a Research Paper. 2014. (ENG.). 24p. (gr. 3-5). 28.50 *(978-1-62717-694-1(2))* Rourke Educational Media.
Howell, Sara. How to Gather Information, Take Notes, & Sort Evidence, 1 vol., 1. 2014. (Core Writing Skills Ser.). (ENG.). 24p. (J). (gr. 3-4). 23.60 *(978-1-4777-2909-0(7)*, PowerKids Pr.) Rosen Publishing Group, Inc., The.
Jakubiak, David J. A Smart Kid's Guide to Doing Internet Research. (Illus.). 24p. (J). 2010. pap. 8.25 *(978-1-4358-3352-4(X))* 2009. (gr. 2-6). lib. bdg. 22.60 *(978-1-4042-8116-5(9))* Rosen Publishing Group, Inc., The. (PowerKids Pr.).
Johnson, Emily & Fontichiaro, Kristin. Know What to Ask: Forming Great Research Questions. 2012. (Explorer Library: Information Explorer Ser.). (ENG.). 32p. (gr. 4-8). 28.50 *(978-1-61080-483-7(X)*, 202093); pap. 14.21 *(978-1-61080-657-2(3)*, 202267) Cherry Lake Publishing.
Klein, Rebecca T. & Asselin, Janelle. Cool Careers Without College for People Who Love Reading & Research. 2017. (Cool Careers Without College Ser.). 112p. (gr. 12-12). 38.45 ***(978-1-5081-7542-1(X)***, Rosen Young Adult) Rosen Publishing Group, Inc., The.
Kovacs, Vic. Get into Citizen Science. 2017. 32p. (J). ***(978-0-7787-3636-3(9))*** Crabtree Publishing Co.
Langley, Andrew. Every Place Has a History, 1 vol. 2014. (Everything Has a History Ser.). (ENG.). 64p. (gr. 7-8). lib. bdg. 35.99 *(978-1-4329-9585-0(5))* Heinemann-Raintree.
—World War II, 1 vol. 2010. (Research It! Ser.). (ENG., Illus.). 56p. (gr. 6-9). lib. bdg. 34.65 *(978-1-4329-3493-4(7)*, NA-h) Heinemann-Raintree.
Larson, Kirsten. Tools of the Trade: Using Scientific Equipment. 2016. (Let's Explore Science Ser.). (ENG.). 48p. (gr. 5-8). 35.64 *(978-1-68191-400-8(X))* Rourke Educational Media.
Linde, Barbara. Cyberspace Research. 2012. (Cyberspace Survival Guide Ser.). (Illus.). 32p. (J). (gr. 3-6). 26.60 *(978-1-4339-7216-4(6))*; pap. 10.50 *(978-1-4339-7217-1(4))* Stevens, Gareth Publishing LLLP. (Gareth Stevens Learning Library).
McKenzie, Precious. Library Skills & Internet Research. 2014. (ENG.). 24p. (gr. 3-5). 28.50 *(978-1-62717-687-3(X))* Rourke Educational Media.
—Writing an Informational Essay. 2014. (ENG.). 24p. (gr. 3-5). 28.50 *(978-1-62717-692-7(6))* Rourke Educational Media.
Michalski, Pete & Lily, Henrietta M. Research Project Success Using Digital Tools, 01 vols., 1. 2016. (Digital & Information Literacy Ser.). (ENG.). 48p. (J). 30.25 *(978-1-4994-3787-4(0))*; pap. 11.75 *(978-1-4994-3785-0(4))* Rosen Publishing Group, Inc., The. (Rosen Central).
Morse, Virginia & Nottage, Cindy. Iim: Independent Investigation Method Teacher Manual with Companion CD. 2005. spiral bd. 59.95 incl. cd-rom *(978-1-57652-024-6(2))* Active Learning Systems, LLC.
Nottage, Cindy & Morse, Virginia. Iim: Teaching Research Skills - Grades K-12. 2012. (ENG.). 232p. (-12). pap. 49.95 *(978-1-57652-059-8(5)*, 9781576520598) Prufrock Pr.
Owings, Lisa. Do Your Research. 2013. (Library Smarts Ser.). (ENG., Illus.). 24p. (gr. -1-2). lib. bdg. 23.93 *(978-1-4677-1503-4(4)*, Lerner Pubns.) Lerner Publishing Group.
Pascaretti, Vicki & Wilkie, Sara. Super Smart Information Strategies: Team up Online. 2010. (Explorer Library: Information Explorer Ser.). (ENG.). 32p. (gr. 4-8). lib. bdg. 28.50 *(978-1-60279-644-7(0)*, 200347) Cherry Lake Publishing.
—Super Smart Information Strategies: Team Up Online. 2010. (Explorer Library: Information Explorer Ser.). (ENG.). 32p. (gr. 4-8). pap. 14.21 *(978-1-61080-264-2(0)*, 200909) Cherry Lake Publishing.
Rabbat, Suzy. Super Smart Information Strategies: Hit the Books. 2010. (Explorer Library: Information Explorer Ser.). (ENG.). 32p. (gr. 4-8). pap. 14.21 *(978-1-61080-258-1(6)*, 200906); lib. bdg. 28.50 *(978-1-60279-641-6(6)*, 200344) Cherry Lake Publishing.
Research Tools You Can Use. 2014. (Research Tools You Can Use Ser.). 32p. (J). (gr. 3-6). 281.40 *(978-1-62275-759-6(9))* Rosen Publishing Group, Inc., The.
Rosenzweig, Charlotte, et al. The Path to Research. 2005. (Illus.). 95p. (YA). (gr. 8-18). pap. 8.95 *(978-0-9677925-2-1(5))* Long Beach City Schl. District.
Roslund, Samantha. Join Forces: Teaming up Online. 2012. (Explorer Junior Library: Information Explorer Junior Ser.). (ENG., Illus.). 24p. (J). (gr. 1-4). 28.50 *(978-1-61080-486-8(4)*, 202096) Cherry Lake Publishing.
Ross, Stewart. World War I, 1 vol. 2010. (Research It! Ser.). (ENG., Illus.). 56p. (gr. 6-9). lib. bdg. 34.65 *(978-1-4329-3494-1(5)*, NA-h) Heinemann-Raintree.
Smith, Paula. Plan & Investigate It! 2015. (ENG., Illus.). 24p. (J). pap. *(978-0-7787-1546-7(9))* Crabtree Publishing Co.
Somervill, Barbara A. Sorting It Out: Evaluating Data. 24p. 2009. (Think Like a Scientist Ser.). (gr. 2-3). 42.50 *(978-1-60854-357-1(9)*, PowerKids Pr.) 2007. (gr. 3-5). pap. 8.25 *(978-1-4358-2682-3(5)*, Rosen Classroom) 2006. (Think Like a Scientist Ser.: Vol. 3). (Illus.). (YA). (gr. 2-5). lib. bdg. 22.60 *(978-1-4042-3487-1(X))* Rosen Publishing Group, Inc., The.
—What Are the Facts? Collecting Information. 2006. (Think Like a Scientist Ser.). (Illus.). 24p. (YA). (gr. 2-5). lib. bdg. 22.60 *(978-1-4042-3484-0(5))* Rosen Publishing Group, Inc., The.
—What Are the Facts? Collecting Information. (Think Like a Scientist Ser.). 24p. 2009. (gr. 2-3). 42.50 *(978-1-60854-358-8(7)*, PowerKids Pr.) 2007. (gr. 3-5). pap. 8.25 *(978-1-4358-2683-0(3)*, Rosen Classroom) Rosen Publishing Group, Inc., The.
Souter, Gerry, et al. Researching on the Internet Using Search Engines, Bulletin Boards, & Listservs. 2003. (Internet Library). (Illus.). 64p. (J). (gr. 4-12). lib. bdg. 23.94 *(978-0-7660-2081-8(9))* Enslow Pubs., Inc.
Spilsbury, Louise. The Student's Toolbox: Tips for Better Researching. 2016. (Student's Toolbox Ser.). (ENG., Illus.). 32p. (J). (gr. 4-6). 17.99 *(978-0-7502-9100-2(1)*, Wayland) Hachette Children's Group GBR. Dist: Hachette Bk. Group.
Squire, Ann O. Extreme Laboratories. 2014. (True Book(tm), a — Extreme Science Ser.). (ENG.). 48p. (J). lib. bdg. 31.00 *(978-0-531-20741-3(2))* Scholastic Library Publishing.
Truesdell, Ann. Fire Away: Asking Great Interview Questions. 2012. (Explorer Library: Information Explorer Ser.). (ENG.). 32p. (gr. 4-8). 28.50 *(978-1-61080-481-3(3)*, 202091); pap. 14.21 *(978-1-61080-655-8(7)*, 202265) Cherry Lake Publishing.
Vickers, Rebecca. Every Person Has a History, 1 vol. 2014. (Everything Has a History Ser.). (ENG., Illus.). 64p. (gr. 7-8). pap. 10.95 *(978-1-4329-9589-8(8))*; lib. bdg. 35.99 *(978-1-4329-9584-3(7))* Heinemann-Raintree.
Vickers, Rebecca & Langley, Andrew. Everything Has a History, 1 vol. 2014. (Everything Has a History Ser.). (ENG.). 64p. (gr. 7-8). lib. bdg. 143.96 *(978-1-4329-9587-4(1))* Heinemann-Raintree.
Whitley, Peggy, et al. 99 Jumpstarts for Kids: Getting Started in Research, 1 vol. 2003. 240p. (C). pap. 37.00 *(978-1-56308-956-5(4)*, LU9564, Libraries Unlimited) ABC-CLIO, LLC.
Whitley, Peggy J. & Goodwin, Susan Williams. 99 Jumpstarts for Kids' Science Research, 1 vol. 2005. (Illus.). 264p. (C). per. 37.00 *(978-1-59158-261-8(X)*, LU261X, Libraries Unlimited) ABC-CLIO, LLC.
Wolny, Philip. Strengthening Research Paper Skills. 2017. (Skills for Success Ser.). 64p. (J). (gr. 12-12). 34.45 ***(978-1-5081-7572-8(1)***, Rosen Young Adult) Rosen Publishing Group, Inc., The.

RESEARCH—VOCATIONAL GUIDANCE

Checkmark Books, creator. Research & Information Management. 2nd rev. ed. 2007. (Mastering Career Skills

Ser.). (Illus.). 128p. per. 12.95 (978-0-8160-7118-0(7), Checkmark Bks.) Facts On File, Inc.

Guillain, Charlotte. Reading & Writing, 1 vol. 2012. (Jobs If You Like... Ser.). (ENG.). 32p. (gr. 1-3). pap. 8.29 (978-1-4329-6821-2(1)); lib. bdg. 27.32 (978-1-4329-6810-6(6)) Heinemann-Raintree. (Heinemann First Library).

Latta, Sara L. Ice Scientist: Careers in the Frozen Antarctic. 2009. (Wild Science Careers Ser.). (Illus.). 128p. (J). (gr. 5-9). lib. bdg. 33.27 (978-0-7660-3048-0(2)) Enslow Pubs., Inc.

RESIDENCES

see Architecture, Domestic; Houses

RESOURCES

see Marine Resources

RESPIRATION

Andrews, Barbara. Discover the Respiratory System. 2006. (J). pap. (978-1-4108-6514-4(2)) Benchmark Education Co.

Aparato Respiratorio Soplo de Vida. (Coleccion Mundo Invisible).Tr. of Respiratory System. (SPA.). (YA). (gr. 5-8). pap. 8.00 (978-958-04-3224-1(4)) Norma S.A. COL. Dist: Distribuidora Norma, Inc.

Aparato respiratorio soplo de Vida. (SPA.). (J). 10.00 (978-84-342-1909-0(3)) Parramon Ediciones S.A. ESP. Dist: Distribuidora Norma, Inc.

Bailey, Jacqui. What Happens When You Breathe? (gr. k-5). 2009. 32p. pap. 10.60 (978-1-4358-2618-2(3), Rosen Classroom) 2008. (Illus.). 30p. (J). lib. bdg. 26.50 (978-1-4042-4428-3(X), PowerKids Pr.) Rosen Publishing Group, Inc., The.

Ballard, Carol. What Is an Asthma Attack? Respiration, 1 vol. 2011. (Inside My Body Ser.). (ENG.). 32p. (gr. 3-5). 30.65 (978-1-4109-4012-4(8), NA-r) Heinemann-Raintree.

Burstein, John. The Remarkable Respiratory System: How Do My Lungs Work? 2009. (Slim Goodbody's Body Buddies Ser.). (ENG., Illus.). 32p. (J). (gr. 3-5). pap. (978-0-7787-4430-6(2)); lib. bdg. (978-0-7787-4416-0(7)) Crabtree Publishing Co.

Caster, Shannon. Lungs. 2010. (Body Works Ser.). (Illus.). 24p. (J). pap. 8.25 (978-1-4358-9830-1(3), PowerKids Pr.); (YA). (gr. 2-5). lib. bdg. 22.60 (978-1-4358-9371-9(9)) Rosen Publishing Group, Inc., The.

Concord, Parker & Hayhurst, Chris. The Lungs in 3D. 2015. (Human Body In 3D Ser.). (ENG., Illus.). 64p. (J). (gr. 5-6). 32.95 (978-1-4994-3605-1(X), Rosen Central) Rosen Publishing Group, Inc., The.

Donavan, Barbara A. Body Systems: Set of 6: Respiratory & Circulatory. 2011. (Navigators Ser.). (J). 48.00 net. (978-1-4108-5084-3(6)) Benchmark Education Co.

Donovan, Barbara A. Body Systems: Respiratory & Circulatory: Text Pairs. 2008. (Bridges/Navigators Ser.). (J). (gr. 5). 89.00 (978-1-4108-8407-7(4)) Benchmark Education Co.

Figorito, Christine. The Lungs in Your Body, 1 vol. 2015. (ENG.). 32p. (J). 23.45 (978-1-62275-628-5(2), Britannica Educational Publishing) Rosen Publishing Group, Inc., The.

Furgang, Kathy. My Lungs. 2009. (My Body Ser.). 24p. (gr. 3-3). 42.50 (978-1-61514-690-1(3), PowerKids Pr.) Rosen Publishing Group, Inc., The.

Gold, Susan Dudley. The Respiratory System. 2003. (Human Body Library). (Illus.). 48p. (J). (gr. 4-10). lib. bdg. 25.27 (978-0-7660-2021-4(5)) Enslow Pubs., Inc.

Gray, Susan H. The Respiratory System. 2014. (Human Body Ser.). (ENG.). 24p. (J). (gr. 2-5). 28.50 (978-1-62687-338-4(0), 207178) Child's World, Inc., The.

Green, Emily & Manolis, Kay. The Respiratory System. 2009. (Body Systems Ser.). (ENG., Illus.). 24p. (J). (gr. 2-5). lib. bdg. 25.95 (978-1-60014-246-8(X)) Bellwether Media.

Guillain, Charlotte. Our Lungs, 1 vol. 2010. (Our Bodies Ser.). (ENG.). 24p. (gr. -1-1). pap. 6.29 (978-1-4329-3603-7(4), Acorn) Heinemann-Raintree.

Halvorson, Karin. Inside the Lungs, 1 vol. 2013. (Super Simple Your Body Ser.). (ENG.). 32p. (J). (gr. k-4). lib. bdg. 27.07 (978-1-61783-613-8(3), Super SandCastle) ABDO Publishing Co.

Hayhurst, Chris. The Lungs: Learning How We Breathe. 2009. (3-D Library of the Human Body Ser.). 48p. (gr. 5-8). 55.90 (978-1-60853-325-1(5), Rosen Reference) Rosen Publishing Group, Inc., The.

Holt, Rinehart and Winston Staff. Holt Science & Technology Chapter 23: Life Science: Circulation & Respiration. 5th ed. 2004. (Illus.). pap. 12.86 (978-0-03-030239-8(0)) Holt McDougal.

Houghton, Gillian. Breath: The Respiratory System. 2009. (Body Works Ser.). 24p. (gr. 2-3). 42.50 (978-1-61511-643-0(5), PowerKids Pr.) Rosen Publishing Group, Inc., The.

—Breath: the Respiratory System. 2006. (Body Works Ser.). (Illus.). 24p. (J). (gr. 2-5). lib. bdg. 22.60 (978-1-4042-3471-0(3)) Rosen Publishing Group, Inc., The.

—The Respiratory System. 2007. (How Your Body Works). (ENG., Illus.). 24p. (gr. 3-5). pap. 7.05 (978-1-4042-2180-2(8), PowerKids Pr.) Rosen Publishing Group, Inc., The.

How Does It Breathe?, 6 Packs. (gr. k-1). 23.00 (978-0-7635-9036-9(3)) Rigby Education.

Jango-Cohen, Judith. El Aparato Respiratorio. Translations.com Staff, tr. 2006. (Libros Sobre el Cuerpo Humano para Madrugadores Ser.). (ENG & SPA., Illus.). 48p. (gr. 2-4). lib. bdg. 26.60 (978-0-8225-6256-6(1)) Lerner Publishing Group.

—The Respiratory System. 2004. (Early Bird Body Systems Ser.). (ENG., Illus.). 48p. (gr. 2-5). lib. bdg. 26.60 (978-0-8225-1250-9(5)) Lerner Publishing Group.

—Your Respiratory System. 2012. (Searchlight Books — How Does Your Body Work? Ser.). (ENG., Illus.). 40p. (gr. 3-5). pap. 8.95 (978-1-58013-963-2(9)); lib. bdg. 27.93 (978-0-7613-7451-0(5), Lerner Pubns.) Lerner Publishing Group.

Jordan, Apple & Rau, Dana Meachen. My Lungs. 2nd ed. 2013. 24p. (gr. 1-3). 21.36 (978-1-60870-435-4(1)) Cavendish Square Publishing.

Kolpin, Molly. Why Do I Yawn? 2015. (My Silly Body Ser.). (ENG.). 24p. (gr. k-1). lib. bdg. 26.65 (978-1-4914-2107-9(X), Pebble Plus) Capstone Press of Coughlan Cos.

Latham, Donna. Respiration & Photosynthesis. 2016. (Sci-Hi: Life Science Ser.). (ENG.). 48p. (gr. 4-4). pap. 8.99 (978-1-4109-8632-0(2), Sci-Hi) Heinemann-Raintree.

Lee, Justin. The Respiratory System. 2009. (Insider's Guide to the Body Ser.). 48p. (gr. 5-8). 53.00 (978-1-61513-585-1(5), Rosen Reference) Rosen Publishing Group, Inc., The.

Macdonald, Fiona. The Science of Snot & Phlegm. 2017. (Science of the Body Ser.). (ENG.). 32p. (J). pap. 9.95 **(978-0-531-23239-2(5)**, Watts, Franklin) Scholastic Library Publishing.

—The Science of Snot & Phlegm: The Slimy Truth about Breathing. 2017. (Science of the Body Ser.). (ENG.). 32p. (J). lib. bdg. 29.00 **(978-0-531-23144-9(5)**, Watts, Franklin) Scholastic Library Publishing.

Nunn, Daniel. Air, 1 vol. 2012. (Why Living Things Need Ser.). (ENG.). 24p. (gr. -1-1). pap. 6.29 (978-1-4329-5919-7(0)); lib. bdg. 22.65 (978-1-4329-5913-5(1)) Heinemann-Raintree. (Acorn).

Orr, Tamra B. Super Cool Science Experiments: Respiration. 2009. (Explorer Library: Science Explorer Ser.). (ENG., Illus.). 32p. (gr. 4-8). lib. bdg. 28.50 (978-1-60279-519-8(3), 200292) Cherry Lake Publishing.

Peterson, Judy Monroe. Breathe: Keeping Your Lungs Healthy. 2012. (Healthy Habits Ser.). (ENG., Illus.). 64p. (J). (gr. 5-8). lib. bdg. 31.95 (978-1-4488-6951-0(X), Rosen Reference) Rosen Publishing Group, Inc., The.

Petrie, Kristin. The Respiratory System, 1 vol. 2007. (Human Body Ser.). (ENG., Illus.). 32p. (gr. 4-7). 27.07 (978-1-59679-713-0(4), Checkerboard Library) ABDO Publishing Co.

Rau, Dana Meachen. My Lungs. 2013. (Bookworms Fluent — My Body Ser.). 24p. (gr. 1-3). pap. 8.22 (978-1-62712-035-7(1)) Cavendish Square Publishing.

Reina, Mary. A Tour of Your Respiratory System. Jones, Chris B., illus. 2012. (First Graphics: Body Systems Ser.). (ENG.). 24p. (gr. 1-2). pap. 35.70 (978-1-4296-9331-8(2)) Capstone Press of Coughlan Cos.

Rose, Simon. Respiratory System. 2014. (J). (978-1-4896-1178-9(9)) Weigl Pubs., Inc.

Schwinn, Aleaha. What Happens When I Yawn? 2013. (My Body Does Strange Stuff! Ser.). (ENG., Illus.). 24p. (J). (gr. 1-3). pap. 8.15 (978-1-4339-9358-9(9)); lib. bdg. 22.60 (978-1-4339-9357-2(0)) Stevens, Gareth Publishing LLLP.

Shea, John. The Respiratory System. 2012. (Human Body Ser.). (ENG., Illus.). 32p. (J). (gr. 4-6). pap. 10.50 (978-1-4339-6594-4(1), Gareth Stevens Learning Library); 26.60 (978-1-4339-6592-0(5)) Stevens, Gareth Publishing LLLP.

Simon, Seymour. Lungs: Your Respiratory System. 2007. (ENG., Illus.). 32p. (J). (gr. k-4). 16.99 (978-0-06-054654-0(9), Collins) HarperCollins Pubs.

Stewart, Melissa. Blasts of Gas: The Secrets of Breathing, Burping, & Farting. 2009. (Gross & Goofy Body Ser.). 48p. (gr. 3-18). 29.93 (978-0-7614-4155-7(7)) Marshall Cavendish Corp.

Taylor-Butler, Christine. The Respiratory System. 2008. (True Bks.). (ENG.). 48p. (J). pap. 6.95 (978-0-531-20736-9(6), Children's Pr.) Scholastic Library Publishing.

—The Respitory System. 2008. (True Book(tm), a — Health & the Human Body Ser.). (ENG., Illus.). 48p. (J). (gr. 3-7). 31.00 (978-0-531-16862-2(X), Children's Pr.) Scholastic Library Publishing.

Tieck, Sarah. Respiratory System, 1 vol. 2011. (Body Systems Ser.). (ENG., Illus.). 32p. (J). (gr. 2-5). lib. bdg. 27.07 (978-1-61613-501-0(8)) ABDO Publishing Co.

Waldron, Melanie. Your Respiration & Circulation: Understand Them with Numbers, 1 vol. 2014. (Your Body by Numbers Ser.). (ENG.). 48p. (gr. 3-5). lib. bdg. 32.65 (978-1-4109-5983-6(X)) Heinemann-Raintree.

What Happens When I Yawn? 2013. (My Body Does Strange Stuff! Ser.). 24p. (J). (gr. 1-3). pap. 48.90 (978-1-4339-9359-6(7)) Stevens, Gareth Publishing LLLP.

Whittemore, Susan. The Respiratory System. 2009. (Human Body: How It Works Ser.). (Illus.). 112p. (C). (gr. 9-18). 35.00 (978-1-60413-375-2(9), Chelsea Hse.) Facts On File, Inc.

World Book, Inc Staff, contrib. by. The Respiratory System. 2013. (Illus.). 32p. (J). (978-0-7166-1847-8(8)) World Bk., Inc.

RESTAURANTS

Ancona, George. Let's Eat. 2003. (J). (978-0-7636-1805-6(5)) Candlewick Pr.

Cohn, Jessica. On the Job in a Restaurant. Scheuer, Lauren, illus. 2016. (Core Content Social Studies — on the Job Ser.). (ENG.). 32p. (J). (gr. 2-5). lib. bdg. 26.65 (978-1-63440-110-4(7)) Red Chair Pr.

Colby, Jennifer. Restaurant. 2016. (21st Century Junior Library: Explore a Workplace Ser.). (ENG.). 24p. (J). (gr. 2-5). 27.07 (978-1-63471-077-0(0), 208387) Cherry Lake Publishing.

Doering Tourville, Amanda. Manners in the Lunchroom. Lensch, Chris, illus. 2009. (Way to Be!: Manners Ser.). 24p. (gr. -1-2). pap. 2.76 (978-1-4048-6051-3(7), Nonfiction Picture Bks.) Picture Window Bks.

Etingoff, Kim. Eating Out: How to Order in Restaurants. Borus, Joshua, ed. 2013. (Understanding Nutrition: a Gateway to Physical & Mental Health Ser.: 11). (Illus.). 48p. (J). (gr. 5-18). 19.95 (978-1-4222-2877-7(0)) Mason Crest.

Frisch, Aaron & Gilbert, Sara. The Story of McDonald's. 2008. (Built for Success Ser.). (Illus.). 46p. (YA). (gr. 5-9). 22.95 (978-1-58341-606-8(4)) Creative Co., The.

Gilbert, Sara. The Story of McDonald's. 2011. (ENG., Illus.). 48p. (J). (gr. 5-17). pap. (978-1-897563-04-5(3)) Saunders Bk. Co.

—The Story of McDonald's - Built for Success. 2011. (Built for Success Ser.). (ENG., Illus.). 48p. (J). (gr. 4-7). pap. 12.00 (978-0-89812-756-0(4), Creative Paperbacks) Creative Co., The.

Green, Sara. Dairy Queen. 2016. (Brands We Know Ser.). (ENG., Illus.). 24p. (J). (gr. 3-8). 25.95 (978-1-62617-407-8(5), Pilot Bks.) Bellwether Media.

—McDonald's. 2015. (Brands We Know Ser.). (ENG., Illus.). 24p. (J). (gr. 3-8). lib. bdg. 25.95 (978-1-62617-209-8(9), Pilot Bks.) Bellwether Media.

Harvey, Joanna & Crabtree, Marc. Meet My Neighbor, the Restaurant Owner. 2010. (ENG., Illus.). 24p. (J). pap. (978-0-7787-4586-0(4)); lib. bdg. (978-0-7787-4576-1(7)) Crabtree Publishing Co.

Hord, Colleen. From Farm to Restaurant. 2015. (ENG.). 24p. (gr. k-2). 28.50 (978-1-63430-057-5(2)) Rourke Educational Media.

Kishel, Ann-Marie & Rivera, Sheila. Server. 2007. (First Step Nonfiction - Work People Do Ser.). (ENG.). 8p. (gr. -1-1). pap. 4.95 (978-0-8225-6847-6(0)) Lerner Publishing Group.

Llanas, Sheila Griffin. Colonel Harland Sanders: KFC Creator, 1 vol. 2014. (Food Dudes Set 2 Ser.). (ENG.). 32p. (gr. 8-12). 27.07 (978-1-62403-318-6(0)) ABDO Publishing Co.

—Dave Thomas: Wendy's Founder, 1 vol. 2014. (Food Dudes Set 2 Ser.). (ENG.). 32p. (J). (gr. 8-12). 27.07 (978-1-62403-319-3(9)) ABDO Publishing Co.

—Tom Monaghan: Domino's Pizza Innovator, 1 vol. 2014. (Food Dudes Set 2 Ser.). (ENG.). 32p. (gr. 8-12). 27.07 (978-1-62403-316-2(4)) ABDO Publishing Co.

Machajewski, Sarah. Cool Careers Without College for People Who Love to Cook & Eat. 2013. (New Cool Careers Without College Ser.). (Illus.). 144p. (J). (gr. 7-12). 35.95 (978-1-4777-1820-9(6)) Rosen Publishing Group, Inc., The.

—Discovering STEM at the Restaurant. 2015. (STEM in the Real World Ser.). (ENG., Illus.). 24p. (J). (gr. 2-3). pap. 8.25 (978-1-4994-0924-6(9), PowerKids Pr.) Rosen Publishing Group, Inc., The.

Marsico, Katie. Good Manners in a Restaurant, 1 vol. Haslam, John, illus. 2009. (Good Manners Matter! Ser.). (ENG.). 32p. (J). (gr. -1-2). 28.50 (978-1-60270-609-5(3)) Magic Wagon.

—Working at a Restaurant. 2008. (21st Century Junior Library: Careers Ser.). (ENG., Illus.). 24p. (gr. 2-5). lib. bdg. 25.64 (978-1-60279-269-2(0), 200174) Cherry Lake Publishing.

Matthews, Layla, et al. Eat at Grandma's? Kids Review a New Restaurant. 2017. (Text Connections Guided Close Reading Ser.). (J). (gr. 2). (978-1-4900-1860-7(3)) Benchmark Education Co.

Minden, Cecilia. Restaurants by the Numbers. 2007. (21st Century Skills Library: Real World Math Ser.). (ENG.). 32p. (gr. 4-8). lib. bdg. 28.50 (978-1-60279-009-4(4), 200067) Cherry Lake Publishing.

Payment, Simone. Careers in Restaurants. 2013. (Essential Careers Ser.). (ENG., Illus.). 80p. (YA). (gr. 7-12). lib. bdg. 33.25 (978-1-4488-9475-8(1), Rosen Classroom) Rosen Publishing Group, Inc., The.

Ready Reader Staff. A Fun Place to Eat, 6 bks., set, Level 6, Bk. 27. 2003. (J). (gr. -1-3). pap. 30.95 (978-0-8136-2059-6(7)) Modern Curriculum Pr.

Scherer, Lauri S. Fast Food. Greenhaven Press Editors, ed. 2013. (Introducing Issues with Opposing Viewpoints Ser.). (ENG.). 144p. (gr. 10-12). lib. bdg. 42.00 (978-0-7377-6922-7(X), Greenhaven Pr., Inc.) Cengage Gale.

Schlosser, Eric. Chew on This: Everything You Don't Want to Know about Fast Food. 2007. lib. bdg. 20.85 (978-1-4177-7657-3(9), Turtleback) Turtleback Bks.

Senker, Cath. McDonald's: The Business Behind the Golden Arches. 2016. (Big Brands Ser.). (ENG., Illus.). 32p. (J). (gr. 4-6). 39.99 (978-1-5124-0593-4(0), Lerner Pubns.) Lerner Publishing Group.

Watt, F. Vamos a Comer! 2004.Tr. of Baby's Mealtime. (SPA., Illus.). 16p. (J). (gr. -1). pap. 4.95 (978-0-7460-4540-4(9)) EDC Publishing.

RESTAURANTS—FICTION

Adinolfi, Joanne. Tina's Diner. Adinolfi, Joanne, illus. 2014. (ENG., Illus.). 32p. (J). (gr. -1-3). 13.99 (978-1-4814-4459-0(X), Simon & Schuster Bks. For Young Readers) Simon & Schuster Bks. For Young Readers.

Akin, Sara Laux. Three Scoops & a Fig, 1 vol. Hartung, Susan Kathleen, illus. 2010. (ENG.). 32p. (J). (gr. -1-3). 15.95 (978-1-56145-522-5(9)) Peachtree Pubs.

Alger, Horatio. Joe's Luck. 2005. 28.95 (978-1-4218-1455-1(2)); 264p. pap. 13.95 (978-1-4218-1555-8(9)) 1st World Publishing, Inc. (1st World Library - Literary Society).

—Joe's Luck: Or, Always Wide Awake. 2006. (ENG.). 176p. pap. 19.99 (978-1-4264-0883-0(8)) 2006. (ENG.). 172p. pap. 19.99 (978-1-4264-6426-3(6)) 2007. 186p. pap. 21.99 (978-1-4264-6500-0(9)) 2006. (ENG.). 170p. pap. 21.99 (978-1-4264-0864-9(1)) Creative Media Partners, LLC.

—Joe's Luck: Or, Always Wide Awake. 2006. pap. (978-1-4065-0713-3(X)) Dodo Pr.

Anderson, M. T. Burger Wuss. 2008. (ENG., Illus.). 192p. (YA). (gr. 9). per. 8.99 (978-0-7636-3178-9(7)) Candlewick Pr.

Anderson, Peggy Perry. Out to Lunch. 2015. (Green Light Readers Level 1 Ser.). (ENG., Illus.). 32p. (J). (gr. 1-4). pap. 3.99 (978-0-544-52858-1(1), HMH Books For Young Readers) Houghton Mifflin Harcourt Publishing Co.

Argueta, Jorge. La Fiesta de Las Tortillas: The Fiesta of the Tortillas. Hayes, Joe & Franco, Sharon, trs. from SPA. Alvarez, Maria Jesus, illus. 2006. (Bilingual Bks). (ENG & SPA.). 32p. (gr. 3-5). 15.95 (978-1-59820-094-2(1), Alfaguara) Santillana USA Publishing Co., Inc.

Arnold, Tedd. There's a Fly Guy in My Soup. 2012. (Fly Guy Ser.: 12). (ENG.). 32p. (J). (gr. -1-3). 6.99 (978-0-545-31284-4(1), Cartwheel Bks.) Scholastic, Inc.

—There's a Fly Guy in My Soup. 2012. (Fly Guy Ser.: 12). lib. bdg. 17.20 (978-0-606-26533-1(3), Turtleback) Turtleback Bks.

Askew, Kim & Helmes, Amy. Anyone but You. 2014. (Twisted Lit Ser.). (ENG.). 224p. (YA). 17.99 (978-1-4405-7001-8(9), Simon Pulse) Simon Pulse.

Balaban, Mariah. Scooby-Doo! & the Haunted Diner. 2010. (Illus.). 31p. (J). (978-0-545-20882-6(3)) Scholastic, Inc.

Barbour, Karen. Little Nino's Pizzeria Big Book. 2015. (ENG., Illus.). 32p. (J). (gr. -1-3). 26.99 (978-0-544-45608-2(4), HMH Books For Young Readers) Houghton Mifflin Harcourt Publishing Co.

Bee, William. Stanley's Diner, 1 vol. Bee, William, illus. 2015. (Stanley Ser.). (ENG., Illus.). 32p. (J). (gr. -1-2). 14.95 (978-1-56145-802-8(3)) Peachtree Pubs.

Berenstain, Jan & Berenstain, Mike. The Berenstain Bears Go Out to Eat. 2009. (Berenstain Bears Ser.). (J). lib. bdg. 13.55 (978-0-606-09291-3(9), Turtleback) Turtleback Bks.

Burach, Ross. There's a Giraffe in My Soup. Burach, Ross, illus. 2016. (Illus.). 32p. (J). (gr. -1-3). 17.99 (978-0-06-236014-4(0)) HarperCollins Pubs.

Caletti, Deb. The Fortunes of Indigo Skye. (ENG.). (YA). (gr. 7). 2009. 320p. pap. 9.99 (978-1-4169-1008-4(5)) 2008. 304p. 15.99 (978-1-4169-1007-7(7)) Simon Pulse. (Simon Pulse).

Callaghan, Cindy. Lost in Rome. 2015. (ENG., Illus.). 208p. (J). (gr. 4-8). 17.99 (978-1-4814-4282-4(1), Aladdin) Simon & Schuster Children's Publishing.

Callen, Sharon. The Curious Café, 1 vol. rev. ed. 2013. (Fiction Readers Ser.). (ENG., Illus.). 32p. (J). (gr. 3-3). pap. 8.99 (978-1-4333-5609-4(0)) Shell Educational Publishing.

—The Curious Café. rev. ed. 2013. (Fiction Readers Ser.). (ENG., Illus.). 32p. (gr. 3-3). pap. 19.96 (978-1-4807-1731-2(2)) Teacher Created Materials, Inc.

Cheva, Cherry. She's So Money. 2009. (ENG.). 304p. (YA). (gr. 8). pap. 8.99 (978-0-06-128853-1(5), HarperTeen) HarperCollins Pubs.

Dairman, Tara. Stars So Sweet. 2016. (All Four Stars Ser.: Bk. 3). (ENG.). 288p. (J). (gr. 3-7). 16.99 (978-1-101-99648-5(X), G.P. Putnam's Sons Books for Young Readers) Penguin Young Readers Group.

Day, Alexandra. Frank & Ernest. 2010. (ENG., Illus.). 40p. (J). 15.95 (978-1-59583-424-9(9), 9781595834249, Green Tiger Pr.) Laughing Elephant.

Destiny, A. & Helms, Rhonda. Never Too Late. 2015. (Flirt Ser.). (ENG., Illus.). 224p. (YA). (gr. 7). pap. 9.99 (978-1-4814-5188-8(X), Simon Pulse) Simon Pulse.

Devlin, Wende. Old Black Witch! Devlin, Harry, illus. 2012. (ENG.). 32p. (J). (gr. -1-3). 18.95 (978-1-930900-62-2(7)) Purple Hse. Pr.

Dobkin, Bonnie. Crazy Pizza Day. Dey, Romi, illus. 2010. (J). (978-1-60617-150-9(X)) Teaching Strategies, LLC.

Dodds, Dayle Ann. Minnie's Diner: A Multiplying Menu. Manders, John, illus. 2007. (ENG.). 40p. (J). (gr. k-3). pap. 6.99 (978-0-7636-3313-4(5)) Candlewick Pr.

Doudna, Kelly. Penguin Suit, 1 vol. Chawla, Neena, illus. 2006. (Animal Tales Ser.). 24p. (J). (gr. k-3). (ENG.). lib. bdg. 24.21 (978-1-59679-957-8(9), SandCastle); pap. 48.42 (978-1-59679-958-5(7)) ABDO Publishing Co.

Dubisch, Mike, illus. The Pizza Mystery. 2010. (Boxcar Children Graphic Novels Ser.: 11). (ENG.). 32p. (J). (gr. 1-5). pap. 6.99 (978-0-8075-6537-7(7)) Whitman, Albert & Co.

Durand, Hallie. Dessert First. Davenier, Christine, illus. (ENG.). (J). (gr. 2-5). 2010. 176p. pap. 5.99 (978-1-4169-6386-8(3)) 2009. 160p. 14.99 (978-1-4169-6385-1(5)) Simon & Schuster Children's Publishing. (Atheneum Bks. for Young Readers).

—Just Desserts. Davenier, Christine, illus. (ENG.). (J). (gr. 2-5). 2011. 224p. pap. 5.99 (978-1-4169-6388-2(X)) 2010. 208p. 15.99 (978-1-4169-6387-5(1)) Simon & Schuster Children's Publishing. (Atheneum Bks. for Young Readers).

—No Room for Dessert. Davenier, Christine, illus. (ENG.). 192p. (J). (gr. 2-5). 2012. pap. 6.99 (978-1-4424-0361-1(6)) 2011. 15.99 (978-1-4424-0360-4(8)) Simon & Schuster Children's Publishing. (Atheneum Bks. for Young Readers).

Else, Barbara. The Traveling Restaurant: Jasper's Voyage in Three Parts. 2012. (Gecko Press Titles Ser.). (ENG.). 304p. (J). (gr. 5-8). 17.95 (978-1-877579-03-5(3)) Gecko Pr. NZL. Dist: Lerner Publishing Group.

Fischer, Ellen. If an Armadillo Went to a Restaurant. Wood, Laura, illus. 2014. (ENG.). 32p. (J). (-2). 14.95 (978-1-938063-39-8(2), Mighty Media Kids) Mighty Media Pr.

Ganeshram, Ramin. Stir It Up! 2011. (J). (978-0-545-16583-9(0)); (ENG.). 176p. (gr. 5-9). 16.99 (978-0-545-16582-2(2), Scholastic Pr.) Scholastic, Inc.

Gelsey, James & Duendes Del Sur Staff. Scooby-Doo & the Karate Caper, 1 vol. 2011. (Scooby-Doo Mysteries Ser.). (ENG., Illus.). 64p. (J). (gr. 3-6). 24.21 (978-1-59961-891-3(5)) Spotlight.

Goldsmann, Henri. Secret Agent Spanky Sheep in the mystery of: the Pooperous Pizza Plunderer. 2006. 140p. pap. 11.99 (978-1-4116-8094-4(4)) Lulu Pr., Inc.

Grogan, John. Thanks, Mom & Dad! Cowdrey, Richard, illus. 2011. (Marley Ser.). (ENG.). 24p. (J). (gr. -1-2). pap. 3.99 (978-0-06-185381-4(X), HarperFestival) HarperCollins Pubs.

Guess, Catherine Ritch. Rudy el Puerco Rojo. 2006. (SPA & ENG., Illus.). 32p. 14.95 (978-1-933341-21-7(1)) CRM.

—Rudy the Red Pig. Haynes, Jason & Oke, Rachel, illus. 2006. (ENG.). 32p. (J). 13.95 (978-1-933341-13-2(0)) CRM.

Inspector Grub & the Gourmet Mystery: Individual Title Six-Packs. (Bookweb Ser.). 32p. (gr. 4-18). 34.00 (978-0-7635-3726-5(8)) Rigby Education.

Isadora, Rachel. Happy Belly, Happy Smile. Isadora, Rachel, illus. 2009. (ENG., Illus.). 32p. (J). (gr. -1-3). 16.00 (978-0-15-206546-1(6)) Houghton Mifflin Harcourt Publishing Co.

Jakubowski, Michele. Tour of Trouble. Pinelli, Amerigo, illus. 2016. (Sleuths of Somerville Ser.). (ENG.). 144p. (gr. 4-6). lib. bdg. 25.99 (978-1-4965-3176-6(0)) Stone Arch Bks.

Kennedy, Claire. After Hours. 2015. (ENG., Illus.). 256p. (YA). (gr. 9). 17.99 (978-1-4814-3016-6(5), Simon Pulse) Simon Pulse.

Killeen, James. Top of the Class! Martinez, Heather, illus. 2011. (Little Golden Book Ser.). (ENG.). 24p. (J). (gr. -1-2). 3.99 (978-0-375-86568-8(3), Golden Bks.) Random Hse. Children's Bks.

Kingfisher, Rupert. Madame Pamplemousse & Her Incredible Edibles. Hellard, Sue, illus. 2008. (ENG.). 144p. (YA). (gr. 3-6). 15.99 (978-1-59990-306-4(7), 9781599903064, Bloomsbury USA Childrens) Bloomsbury Publishing USA.

Knowles, Jo. See You at Harry's. 2012. (ENG., Illus.). 310p. (J). (gr. 5). 16.99 (978-0-7636-5407-8(8)) Candlewick Pr.

Lee, Day's. The Fragrant Garden. Bellemare, Josee, illus. 2005. (ENG.). 32p. (J). (gr. -1-7). per. 11.95 (978-1-894917-26-1(X), Napoleon & Co.) Dundurn CAN. Dist: Ingram Publisher Services.

Leonard, Julia Platt. Cold Case. 2012. (ENG.). 288p. (J). (gr. 3-7). pap. 5.99 (978-1-4424-2010-6(3), Simon & Schuster/Paula Wiseman Bks.) Simon & Schuster/Paula Wiseman Bks.

—Cold Case. Mauro, Tony, illus. 2011. (ENG.). 288p. (J). (gr. 3-7). 15.99 (978-1-4424-2009-0(X), Simon & Schuster/Paula Wiseman Bks.) Simon & Schuster/Paula Wiseman Bks.

Lin, Grace. Dim Sum for Everyone! Lin, Grace, illus. 2014. (ENG., Illus.). 24p. (J). (gr. -1-2). bds. 6.99 (978-0-385-75488-0(4), Knopf Bks. for Young Readers) Random Hse. Children's Bks.

London, Jonathan. Froggy Eats Out. 2004. (Illus.). (J). (gr. -1-18). spiral bd. (978-0-616-11117-8(7)); spiral bd. (978-0-616-11118-5(5)) Canadian National Institute for the Blind/Institut National Canadien pour les Aveugles.

—Froggy Eats Out. Remkiewicz, Frank, illus. 2003. (Froggy Ser.). (ENG.). 32p. (J). (gr. -1-k). pap. 6.99 *(978-0-14-250061-3(5),* Puffin Books) Penguin Young Readers Group.

—Froggy Eats Out. Remkiewicz, Frank, illus. 2003. (Froggy Ser.). 13.65 *(978-0-7569-1464-6(7))* Perfection Learning Corp.

—Froggy Eats Out. 2003. (Froggy Ser.). (gr. k-3). lib. bdg. 17.20 *(978-0-613-67453-9(7),* Turtleback) Turtleback Bks.

McGuirk, Leslie & Von Bidder, Alex. Wiggens Learns His Manners at the Four Seasons Restaurant. McGuirk, Leslie, illus. 2009. (ENG., Illus.). 32p. (J). (gr. -1-2). 16.99 *(978-0-7636-4014-9(X))* Candlewick Pr.

McMann, Lisa. Crash. 2013. (Visions Ser.: 1). (ENG.). 256p. (YA). (gr. 9). 16.99 *(978-1-4424-0391-8(8),* Simon Pulse) Simon Pulse.

Menotti, Andrea. Operation Fowl Play. Kennedy, Kelly, illus. 2004. (Spy Five Ser.). 92p. (J). *(978-0-439-70349-9(2))* Scholastic, Inc.

—Operation Master Mole. Kennedy, Kelly, illus. 2004. (Spy Five Ser.). 93p. (J). *(978-0-439-70351-2(4))* Scholastic, Inc.

Miyazawa, Kenji. The Restaurant of Many Colors. Sato, Kunio, illus. 2005. 31p. (J). 17.95 *(978-4-902216-24-0(8))* R.I.C. Publications Asia Co, Inc. JPN. Dist: Continental Enterprises Group, Inc. (CEG).

Morimoto, Sango. Taro & the Terror of Eats Street. Morimoto, Sango, illus. 2011. (Adventures of Taro Ser.). (ENG., Illus.). 96p. (J). (gr. 1-4). pap. 7.99 *(978-1-4215-3525-8(4))* Viz Media.

Newman, Samantha. Sammy Skizzors & the Rainbow Knight. 2010. 32p. 14.99 *(978-1-4520-9976-7(6))* AuthorHouse.

Newton, Robert. The Punjabi Pappadum. 2003. 160p. (J). pap. *(978-0-7022-3363-0(3))* Univ. of Queensland Pr.

Ockler, Sarah. Bittersweet. 2012. (ENG.). (YA). (gr. 9). 400p. pap. 9.99 *(978-1-4424-3036-5(2));* 384p. 16.99 *(978-1-4424-3035-8(4))* Simon Pulse. (Simon Pulse).

Oxenbury, Helen. En El Restaurante de Mis Tios. (SPA.). 16p. (J). 7.50 *(978-84-261-1944-5(1))* Juventud, Editorial ESP. Dist: AIMS International Bks., Inc.

Patron, Susan. Lucky for Good. McGuire, Erin, illus. 2012. (ENG.). 224p. (J). (gr. 3-7). pap. 6.99 *(978-1-4169-9059-8(3),* Atheneum Bks. for Young Readers) Simon & Schuster Children's Publishing.

—Lucky for Good. McGuire, Erin K., illus. 2011. (ENG.). 224p. (J). (gr. 3-7). 16.99 *(978-1-4169-9058-1(5),* Atheneum Bks. for Young Readers) Simon & Schuster Children's Publishing.

Perelman, Helen & Studio IBOIX. Tiana: The Grand Opening, 1 vol. 2012. (Disney Princess Ser.). (ENG., Illus.). 96p. (J). (gr. 2-5). 24.21 *(978-1-59961-880-7(X))* Spotlight.

Potter, Ellen. Pish Posh. 2011. (ENG.). 176p. (J). (gr. 3-7). 6.99 *(978-0-14-241906-9(0),* Puffin Books) Penguin Young Readers Group.

Random House Dictionary Staff. You're Fired! (SpongeBob SquarePants) Random House Dictionary Staff & Aikins, Dave, illus. 2014. (Pictureback(R) Ser.). (ENG.). 24p. (J). (gr. -1-2). 3.99 *(978-0-385-37431-6(3),* Random Hse. Bks. for Young Readers) Random Hse. Children's Bks.

Random House Staff. You're Fired! 2014. (SpongeBob Squarepants 8X8 Ser.). lib. bdg. 13.55 *(978-0-606-35204-8(X))* Turtleback Bks.

Rosen, Michael. Happy Harry's Cafe. Holland, Richard, illus. 2012. (ENG.). 32p. (J). (gr. -1-2). 16.99 *(978-0-7636-6239-4(9))* Candlewick Pr.

Rosenberg, Aaron. Case of the Secret Sauce, Vol. 1. Harrington, David, illus. 2011. (Pete & Penny's Pizza Puzzles Ser.: 1). (ENG.). 64p. (J). (gr. 1-3). pap. 3.99 *(978-0-8431-9928-4(8),* Price Stern Sloan) Penguin Young Readers Group.

Rylant, Cynthia. The Case of the Missing Monkey. Karas, G. Brian, illus. 2003. (High-Rise Private Eyes Ser.: No. 1). (J). 25.95 incl. audio *(978-1-59112-194-7(9));* pap. 29.95 incl. audio *(978-1-59112-195-4(7))* Live Oak Media.

—The Case of the Missing Monkey. Karas, G. Brian, illus. 2003. (High-Rise Private Eyes Ser.: 1). 46p. (J). (gr. 1-17). 13.55 *(978-0-613-44194-0(X),* Turtleback) Turtleback Bks.

—The Van Gogh Cafe. 2006. (ENG., Illus.). 64p. (J). (gr. 2-5). pap. 6.99 *(978-0-15-205750-3(1))* Houghton Mifflin Harcourt Publishing Co.

—The Van Gogh Café. 2015. 64p. pap. 7.00 *(978-1-61003-500-2(3))* Center for the Collaborative Classroom.

Sateren, Shelley Swanson. The Lunchroom Fight. Sullivan, Mary, illus. 2013. (Max & Zoe Ser.). (ENG.). 32p. (gr. k-2). lib. bdg. 21.32 *(978-1-4048-7199-1(3),* Max & Zoe) Picture Window Bks.

Saunders, Zina, illus. Trouble at the Krusty Krab! 2004. (SpongeBob SquarePants Ser.). (ENG.). 32p. (J). pap. 3.99 *(978-0-689-86838-2(3),* Simon Spotlight/Nickelodeon) Simon Spotlight/Nickelodeon.

Scott, Elaine. Secrets of the Cirque Medrano. 2008. (ENG., Illus.). 216p. (J). (gr. 5-9). 15.95 *(978-1-57091-712-7(4))* Charlesbridge Publishing, Inc.

—The Spanish Web: An Encounter with Picasso. 2004. (Art Encounters Ser.). (J). 15.95 *(978-0-8230-0410-2(4));* pap. 6.99 *(978-0-8230-0413-3(9))* Watson-Guptill Pubns., Inc.

Scott, Janine. Café Cosmos. Wood, Hannah, illus. 2009. (Treasure Chest Readers Ser.). 24p. (J). (gr. -1-2). pap. 8.15 *(978-1-60754-674-0(4));* lib. bdg. 22.60 *(978-1-60754-673-3(6))* Windmill Bks.

Sherrard, Valerie. Chasing Shadows. 2004. (ENG.). 216p. (YA). pap. 9.99 *(978-1-55002-502-6(3))* Dundurn CAN. Dist: Ingram Publisher Services.

Slippery, Sloppery Spaghetti: Individual Title Six-Packs. (gr. k-1). 23.00 *(978-0-7635-9025-3(8))* Rigby Education.

Smith, Cynthia Leitich. Blessed. (Tantalize Ser.). (ENG., Illus.). (YA). (gr. 9). 2012. 464p. pap. 8.99 *(978-0-7636-5479-5(5))* 2011. 480p. 17.99 *(978-0-7636-4326-3(2))* Candlewick Pr.

—Tantalize. 2007. (Tantalize Ser.). (ENG., Illus.). 336p. (YA). (gr. 9-12). 16.99 *(978-0-7636-2791-1(7))* Candlewick Pr.

Smith, J. D. The Best Mariachi in the World/El Mejor Mariachi del Mundo. de la Vega, Eida, tr. Jones, Dani, illus. 2008. (ENG & SPA.). 32p. (J). (gr. 4-7). lib. bdg. 16.95 *(978-0-9770906-1-7(2),* Raven Tree Pr.,Csi) Continental Sales, Inc.

Sobel, M., et al. Poison Plate, 1 vol. Cunningham, Kelley, illus. 2006. (Vortex Bks.). (ENG.). 112p. (gr. 2-3). per. 7.19 *(978-1-59889-280-2(0),* Vortex Bks.) Stone Arch Bks.

Sorenson, Margo. Spaghetti Smiles, 1 vol. Harrington, David, illus. 2014. (ENG.). 32p. (J). (gr. k-3). 16.99 *(978-1-4556-1922-1(1))* Pelican Publishing Co., Inc.

Spinelli, Eileen. The Dancing Pancake. Lew-Vriethoff, Joanne, illus. 2011. (ENG.). 256p. (J). (gr. 3-7). 6.99 *(978-0-375-85348-7(0),* Yearling) Random Hse. Children's Bks.

Springstubb, Tricia. Mo Wren, Lost & Found. Ross, Heather, illus. 2011. (Fox Street Ser.: 2). (ENG.). 256p. (J). (gr. 3-7). 15.99 *(978-0-06-199039-7(6))* HarperCollins Pubs.

Stalcup. La Loncheria. Arroyo, illus. 2008. (SPA & ENG.). 28p. (J). pap. 8.95 *(978-1-60448-006-1(8))* Lectura Bks.

Stamper, Judith Bauer. Breakfast at Danny's Diner: A Book about Multiplication. Demarest, Chris L., illus. 2003. (All Aboard Math Reader Ser.). 48p. (J). (gr. 2-4). 11.65 *(978-0-7569-1695-4(X))* Perfection Learning Corp.

Stilton, Thea. Big Trouble in the Big Apple. 2011. (Thea Stilton Ser.: 8). (ENG., Illus.). 176p. (J). (gr. 2-5). pap. 8.99 *(978-0-545-22775-9(5),* Scholastic Paperbacks) Scholastic, Inc.

Sylvester, Kevin. Neil Flambé & the Crusader's Curse. Sylvester, Kevin, illus. (Neil Flambe Capers Ser.: 3). (ENG., Illus.). (J). (gr. 3-7). 2014. 320p. pap. 7.99 *(978-1-4424-4287-0(5))* 2012. 304p. 13.99 *(978-1-4424-4286-3(7))* Simon & Schuster Bks. For Young Readers. (Simon & Schuster Bks. For Young Readers).

—Neil Flambé & the Marco Polo Murders. 2010. (Neil Flambé Capers Ser.: No. 1). (Illus.). 304p. (YA). (gr. 5-9). *(978-1-55470-266-4(6))* Me to We.

—Neil Flambé & the Marco Polo Murders. Sylvester, Kevin, illus. 2012. (Neil Flambe Capers Ser.: 1). (ENG., Illus.). 304p. (J). (gr. 3-7). 14.99 *(978-1-4424-4604-5(8),* Simon & Schuster Bks. For Young Readers) Simon & Schuster Bks. For Young Readers.

—Neil Flambé & the Tokyo Treasure. Sylvester, Kevin, illus. (Neil Flambe Capers Ser.: 4). (ENG., Illus.). (J). (gr. 3-7). 2014. 368p. pap. 7.99 *(978-1-4424-4289-4(1))* 2012. 352p. 13.99 *(978-1-4424-4288-7(3))* Simon & Schuster Bks. For Young Readers. (Simon & Schuster Bks. For Young Readers).

Tate, Cynthia Wagoner. Gordy's Grimy but Groovy Adventure. 2006. 24p. 12.98 *(978-1-4116-6297-1(0))* Lulu Pr., Inc.

Taylor, Trace. Dogtown Diner. 2010. pap. 39.62 *(978-1-61541-088-0(0))* American Reading Co.

—Dogtown's Got Talent. 2010. pap. 39.62 *(978-1-61541-137-5(2))* American Reading Co.

—Flying over Dogtown. 2010. pap. 39.62 *(978-1-61541-141-2(0))* American Reading Co.

—Hair Day in Dogtown. 2010. pap. 39.62 *(978-1-61541-143-6(7))* American Reading Co.

—Wedding Day in Dogtown. 2010. pap. 39.62 *(978-1-61541-145-0(3))* American Reading Co.

Terrell, Brandon. Limbo's Diner. 2015. (Tartan House Ser.). (ENG., Illus.). 96p. (J). (gr. 5-12). *(978-1-63235-164-7(1),* 12-Story Library) Pr. Room Editions LLC.

Turnage, Sheila. Three Times Lucky. (ENG.). (J). (gr. 5). 2013. 336p. pap. 7.99 *(978-0-14-242605-0(9),* Puffin Books) 2012. 314p. 16.99 *(978-0-8037-3670-2(3),* Dial Bks) Penguin Young Readers Group.

—Three Times Lucky. 2013. lib. bdg. 18.40 *(978-0-606-34168-4(4),* Turtleback) Turtleback Bks.

Vinopol, Corinne & Bednarczyk, Angela. ASL Tales & Games for Kids - Biscuit Blvd: Computer Software in American Sign Language. 2004. (J). cd-rom 34.95 *(978-0-9667589-9-3(4))* Institute for Disabilities Research & Training, Inc.

Walters, Eric. A Reventar: (Stuffed), 1 vol. 2011. (Spanish Soundings Ser.). (SPA.). 144p. (YA). (gr. 8-12). pap. 9.95 *(978-1-55469-861-5(8))* Orca Bk. Pubs. USA.

Watts, Julia. Free Spirits. 2009. (ENG.). 176p. (J). (gr. 1). pap. 8.95 *(978-0-9667359-2-5(7),* BeanPole Bks.) Harren Communications, LLC.

Weeks, Sarah. Two Eggs, Please. Lewin, Betsy, illus. 2007. (ENG.). 32p. (J). (gr. -1-1). reprint ed. 7.99 *(978-1-4169-2714-3(X),* Atheneum Bks. for Young Readers) Simon & Schuster Children's Publishing.

Wellington, Monica. Pizza at Sally's. Wellington, Monica, illus. 2006. (ENG., Illus.). 32p. (J). (gr. -1-2). 15.99 *(978-0-525-47715-0(2),* Dutton Books for Young Readers) Penguin Young Readers Group.

Whelan, Gloria. The Boy Who Wanted to Cook. Adams, Steve, illus. 2011. (Tales of the World Ser.). (ENG.). 40p. (gr. k-5). lib. bdg. 16.95 *(978-1-58536-534-0(3))* Sleeping Bear Pr.

Williams, Kathryn. Pizza, Love, & Other Stuff That Made Me Famous. 2013. (ENG.). 256p. (YA). (gr. 7-12). pap. 11.99 *(978-1-250-02745-0(4),* 9781250027450) Square Fish.

Wynne-Jones, Tim. Lord of the Fries. (Illus.). pap. 6.95 *(978-0-88899-384-7(6))* Groundwood Bks. CAN. Dist: Publishers Group West (PGW).

Yee, Wong Herbert. Hamburger Heaven. 2005. (ENG., Illus.). 32p. (J). (gr. -1-3). reprint ed. 5.95 *(978-0-618-54885-9(8))* Houghton Mifflin Harcourt Publishing Co.

RETAIL TRADE

see also Advertising; Department Stores; Sales Personnel; Supermarkets

Caraccilo, Dominic. E-Tailing: Careers Selling over the Web. 2009. (Library of E-Commerce & Internet Careers Ser.). 64p. (gr. 5-5). 58.50 *(978-1-60853-587-3(8))* Rosen Publishing Group, Inc., The.

Enz, Tammy. Hidden Worlds, 4 vols., Set. Incl. Behind the Racks: Exploring the Secrets of a Shopping Mall. lib. bdg. 26.65 *(978-1-4296-3386-4(7));* Beyond the Bars: Exploring the Secrets of a Police Station. lib. bdg. 26.65 *(978-1-4296-3377-2(8));* Under the Lights: Exploring the Secrets of a Sports Stadium. lib. bdg. 26.65 *(978-1-4296-3376-5(X));* (gr. 1-2). (Hidden Worlds Ser.). (ENG.). 32p. 2010. Set lib. bdg. 79.95 *(978-1-4296-3777-0(3),* Blazers) Capstone Press of Coughlan Cos.

Gilbert, Sara. The Story of Target. 2014. (Illus.). 46p. (J). *(978-1-60818-397-5(1),* Creative Education) Creative Co., The.

—The Story of Wal-Mart. (Built for Success Ser.). (Illus.). 48p. (J). 2012. (ENG.). (gr. 4-7). pap. 12.00 *(978-0-89812-662-4(2))* 2011. (gr. 5-9). 34.25 *(978-1-60818-064-6(6))* Creative Co., The.

Glaser, Jason. Careers in Online Retailing. 2013. 80p. (YA). (gr. 9-12). 33.25 *(978-1-4488-9595-3(2))* Rosen Publishing Group, Inc., The.

Hidden Worlds [Capstone Sole Source]. 2010. (Hidden Worlds Ser.). 32p. lib. bdg. 101.28 *(978-1-4296-5865-2(7),* Blazers) Capstone Press of Coughlan Cos.

Krieg, Katherine. Sam Walton: Founder of the Walmart Empire, 1 vol. 2013. (Essential Lives Set 8 Ser.). (ENG., Illus.). 112p. (J). (gr. 6-12). lib. bdg. 35.64 *(978-1-61783-898-9(5),* Essential Library) ABDO Publishing Co.

La Bella, Laura. Getting a Job in the Retail Industry. 2016. (Job Basics: Getting the Job You Need Ser.). 80p. (J). (gr. 8-8). 35.75 *(978-1-4777-8558-4(2))* Rosen Publishing Group, Inc., The.

Lee, Sally. Sam Walton: Business Genius of Wal-Mart. 2007. (People to Know Today Ser.). (Illus.). 112p. (J). (gr. 3-7). lib. bdg. 33.27 *(978-0-7660-2692-6(2))* Enslow Pubs., Inc.

Meachen Rau, Dana. Grocer. 2007. (Jobs in Town Ser.). (SPA., Illus.). 24p. (gr. k-1). lib. bdg. 15.95 *(978-0-7614-2720-9(1),* Benchmark Bks.) Marshall Cavendish Corp.

Reeves, Diane Lindsey. Get a Job at the Shoping Mall. 2016. (Bright Futures Press: Get a Job Ser.). (ENG., Illus.). 32p. (J). (gr. 4-6). 29.93 *(978-1-63471-908-7(5),* 208953) Cherry Lake Publishing.

Rissman, Rebecca. ABCs at the Store, 1 vol. 2012. (Everyday Alphabet Ser.). (ENG., Illus.). 32p. (gr. -1-k). pap. 9.95 *(978-1-4109-4734-5(3));* lib. bdg. 25.32 *(978-1-4109-4729-1(7))* Heinemann-Raintree.

Shores, Erika L. Sam Walton, 1 vol. 2014. (Business Leaders Ser.). (ENG.). 24p. (gr. k-1). lib. bdg. 21.99 *(978-1-4765-9642-6(5),* Pebble Bks.) Capstone Press of Coughlan Cos.

Sourcebooks, Inc Staff. Easter Bunny Coupons. 2012. (ENG.). 48p. (J). (-4). pap. 5.99 *(978-1-4022-6821-2(1))* Sourcebooks, Inc.

RETAIL TRADE—VOCATIONAL GUIDANCE

Avitan, Amos. Your Life in Trade: A Contractor's Guide to Success. 2003. (Illus.). 300p. (YA). per. *(978-0-9689715-2-9(0))* Amos Avitan, Inc.

Endsaff, Najoud & Rooney, Anne. Retail Careers. 2010. (In the Workplace Ser.). 48p. (J). 35.65 *(978-1-60753-093-0(7))* Amicus Publishing.

Ensaff, Najoud, et al. Retail Careers. 2011. (Been There! Ser.). 32p. (gr. 3-6). lib. bdg. 31.35 *(978-1-59920-473-4(8))* Black Rabbit Bks.

Ferguson. Careers in Focus: Retail. 3rd rev. ed. 2007. (Careers in Focus Ser.). (Illus.). 192p. (gr. 6-12). 32.95 *(978-0-8160-6593-6(4),* Ferguson Publishing Co.) Facts On File, Inc.

Mooney, Carla. Using Computer Science in Online Retail Careers. 2017. (Coding Your Passion Ser.). 80p. (J). (gr. 12-12). 35.75 ***(978-1-5081-7519-3(5)**,* Rosen Young Adult) Rosen Publishing Group, Inc., The.

Santos, Edson. People Who Love to Buy Things. 2006. (Cool Careers Without College Ser.). (Illus.). 144p. (YA). (gr. 7-12). lib. bdg. 35.95 *(978-1-4042-0751-6(1))* Rosen Publishing Group, Inc., The.

RETARDED PERSONS

see People with Mental Disabilities

REVERE, PAUL, 1735-1818

Brandt, Keith & Macken, JoAnn Early. Paul Revere, Son of Liberty. Livingston, Francis, illus. 2007. 50p. (J). *(978-0-439-02017-6(4))* Scholastic, Inc.

Draper, Allison Stark. The Start of the American Revolutionary War: Paul Revere Rides at Midnight. 2009. (Headlines from History Ser.). 24p. (gr. 3-3). 42.50 *(978-1-61513-247-8(3),* PowerKids Pr.) Rosen Publishing Group, Inc., The.

Edwards, Roberta. Who Was Paul Revere? Harrison, Nancy & O'brien, John, illus. 2011. (Who Was? Ser.). (ENG.). 112p. (J). (gr. 3-7). pap. 5.99 *(978-0-448-45715-4(6),* Grosset & Dunlap) Penguin Young Readers Group.

Ford, Barbara. Paul Revere: American Patriot. 2015. (Legendary American Biographies Ser.). 96p. (J). (gr. 6-12). 27.94 *(978-0-7660-6485-0(9));* pap. 10.95 *(978-0-7660-6486-7(7))* Enslow Pubs., Inc.

Ford, Carin T. Paul Revere: Patriot. 2003. (Heroes of American History Ser.). (Illus.). 32p. (J). (gr. 1-4). lib. bdg. 23.94 *(978-0-7660-2001-6(0))* Enslow Pubs., Inc.

Goddu, Krystyna Poray. What's Your Story, Paul Revere? 2016. (Cub Reporter Meets Famous Americans Ser.). (ENG., Illus.). 32p. (J). (gr. k-3). pap. 8.99 *(978-1-4677-9641-5(7),* Lerner Pubns.) Lerner Publishing Group.

Golden, Nancy. The British Are Coming! The Midnight Ride of Paul Revere. 2009. (Great Moments in American History Ser.). 32p. (gr. 3-3). 47.90 *(978-1-61513-136-5(1))* Rosen Publishing Group, Inc., The.

Hicks, Dwayne. Paul Revere: American Patriot. 2012. (Beginning Biographies Ser.). (ENG., Illus.). 24p. (J). (gr. 1-3). 22.60 *(978-1-4488-8599-2(X),* PowerKids Pr.) Rosen Publishing Group, Inc., The.

Ingram, Scott. Paul Revere. 2003. (Triangle History of the American Revolution Ser.). (Illus.). 104p. (J). 28.70 *(978-1-56711-780-6(5),* Blackbirch Pr., Inc.) Cengage Gale.

Jeffrey, Gary. Paul Revere & His Midnight Ride. 2011. (Graphic Heroes of the American Revolution Ser.). 24p. (J). (gr. 3-6). lib. bdg. 23.95 *(978-1-4339-6019-2(2));* pap. 8.15 *(978-1-4339-6020-8(6),* Gareth Stevens Learning Library) Stevens, Gareth Publishing LLLP.

Kallio, Jamie. 12 Questions about Paul Revere's Ride. 2016. (Examining Primary Sources Ser.). (ENG., Illus.). 32p. (J). pap. 9.95 *(978-1-63235-336-8(9),* 12-Story Library) Pr. Room Editions LLC.

—12 Questions about "Paul Revere's Ride" 2017. (Examining Primary Sources Ser.). (ENG., Illus.). 32p. (J). (gr. 3-6). 21.95 *(978-1-63235-286-6(9))* Pr. Room Editions LLC.

Keller, Susanna. The True Story of Paul Revere's Ride. 2013. (What Really Happened? Ser.). (ENG., Illus.). 24p. (J). (gr. 3-6). pap. 8.25 *(978-1-4488-9838-1(2));* lib. bdg. 22.60 *(978-1-4488-9690-5(8))* Rosen Publishing Group, Inc., The. (PowerKids Pr.).

Mack, Molly. The Life of Paul Revere. 2012. (InfoMax Readers Ser.). (ENG., Illus.). 24p. (J). (gr. 1-2). pap. 8.25 *(978-1-4488-9049-1(7),* Rosen Classroom) Rosen Publishing Group, Inc., The.

Mara, Wil. Paul Revere. (Rookie Biographies(r) Ser.). (ENG., Illus.). 32p. (J). 2015. pap. 5.95 *(978-0-531-20597-6(5))* 2005. (gr. 1-2). pap. 4.95 *(978-0-516-25820-1(6))* Scholastic Library Publishing. (Children's Pr.).

McCarthy, Rose. Paul Revere: Freedom Rider. (Primary Sources of Famous People in American History Ser.). 32p. 2009. (gr. 2-3). 47.90 *(978-1-60851-714-5(4))* 2004. (ENG., Illus.). (gr. 4-8). pap. 10.00 *(978-0-8239-4190-2(6))* Rosen Publishing Group, Inc., The.

—Paul Revere: Freedom Rider / Jinete de la causa Revolucionaria. 2009. (Famous People in American History/Grandes personajes en la historia de los Estados Unidos Ser.). (ENG & SPA.). 32p. (gr. 2-3). 47.90 *(978-1-61512-553-1(1),* Editorial Buenas Letras) Rosen Publishing Group, Inc., The.

—Paul Revere: Jinete de la causa revolucionaria (Paul Revere: Freedom Rider) 2009. (Grandes personajes en la historia de los Estados Unidos (Famous People in American History) Ser.). (SPA.). 32p. (gr. 2-3). 47.90 *(978-1-61512-806-8(9),* Editorial Buenas Letras) Rosen Publishing Group, Inc., The.

—Paul Revere: Jinete de la guerra de Independencia. 2004. (Grandes personajes en la historia de los Estados Unidos Ser.). (SPA.). 32p. (gr. 3-6). pap. 10.00 *(978-0-8239-4236-7(8),* Rosen Classroom) Rosen Publishing Group, Inc., The.

Mills, Nathan & Hicks, Dwayne. Paul Revere: American Patriot. 2012. (Rosen Readers Ser.). (ENG., Illus.). 24p. (J). (gr. 1-2). pap. 8.25 *(978-1-4488-8836-8(0),* Rosen Classroom) Rosen Publishing Group, Inc., The.

Min, Ellen. The Midnight Ride of Paul Revere: One If by Land, Two If by Sea. 2015. (Spotlight on American History Ser.). (ENG., Illus.). 24p. (J). (gr. 4-6). pap. 10.00 *(978-1-4994-1734-0(9),* PowerKids Pr.) Rosen Publishing Group, Inc., The.

Nelson, Maria. The Life of Paul Revere. 2012. (Famous Lives Ser.). (ENG.). 24p. (J). (gr. k-3). lib. bdg. 22.60 *(978-1-4339-6353-7(1));* (gr. 1-4). pap. 8.15 *(978-1-4339-6355-1(8))* Stevens, Gareth Publishing LLLP.

—The Life of Paul Revere / la Vida de Paul Revere. 2012. (Famous Lives / Vidas extraordinarias Ser.). (ENG & SPA., Illus.). 24p. (J). (gr. k-3). 22.60 *(978-1-4339-6657-6(3))* Stevens, Gareth Publishing LLLP.

Niz, Xavier & Niz, Xavier W. Paul Revere's Ride. Bascle, Brian, illus. 2005. (Graphic History Ser.). (ENG.). 32p. (gr. 3-4). 30.65 *(978-0-7368-4965-4(3),* Graphic Library) Capstone Press of Coughlan Cos.

Roop, Peter & Roop, Connie. Let's Ride, Paul Revere! 2004. (Before I Made History Ser.). (Illus.). 60p. (J). pap. *(978-0-439-67623-6(1))* Scholastic, Inc.

Smith, Andrea P. A Day in the Life of Colonial Silversmith Paul Revere. 2012. (Illus.). 24p. (J). 63.60 *(978-1-4488-5217-8(X));* pap. 10.60 *(978-1-4488-5216-1(1));* lib. bdg. 25.25 *(978-1-4488-5189-8(0))* Rosen Publishing Group, Inc., The. (PowerKids Pr.).

Tieck, Sarah. Paul Revere, 1 vol. 2006. (First Biographies Ser.). (ENG., Illus.). 32p. (gr. -1-3). 27.07 *(978-1-59679-787-1(8),* Buddy Bks.) ABDO Publishing Co.

Wagner, Heather Lehr. Paul Revere: Messenger for Freedom. 2005. (Leaders of the American Revolution Ser.). (Illus.). 128p. (gr. 5-8). lib. bdg. 30.00 *(978-0-7910-8624-7(0))* Facts On File, Inc.

Weston Woods Staff, creator. And Then What Happened, Paul Revere? 2011. 29.95 *(978-0-439-73467-7(3));* 38.75 *(978-0-439-72663-4(8));* 18.95 *(978-0-439-72661-0(1))* Weston Woods Studios, Inc.

Whiting, Jim. The Life & Times of Paul Revere. 2006. (Profiles in American History Ser.). (Illus.). 48p. (J). (gr. 3-7). lib. bdg. 29.95 *(978-1-58415-441-9(1))* Mitchell Lane Pubs., Inc.

Winter, Jonah. Paul Revere & the Bell Ringers. Dodson, Bert, illus. 2005. 32p. (J). lib. bdg. 15.00 *(978-1-59054-952-0(X))* Fitzgerald Bks.

—Paul Revere & the Bell Ringers. Dodson, Bert, illus. 2003. (Ready-To-read COFA Ser.). (ENG.). 32p. (J). (gr. k-2). pap. 3.99 *(978-0-689-85635-8(0),* Simon Spotlight) Simon Spotlight.

REVERE, PAUL, 1735-1818—FICTION

Hardman, Ron & Hardman, Jessica. Shadow Fox: Sons of Liberty. Barnecut, Suzanne, ed. Harrigan, Mike, illus. 2010. (Shadow Fox Ser.). 186p. (J). (gr. 4-8). 22.99 *(978-0-9819607-1-5(5))* Fox Run Pr., LLC.

—Shadow Fox: Sons of Liberty. Barnecut, Suzanne, ed. Harrigan, Mike, illus. 2010. (Shadow Fox Ser.). 186p. (J). (gr. 4-8). pap. 11.99 *(978-0-9819607-0-8(7))* Fox Run Pr., LLC.

—Shadow Fox: Sons of Liberty Teacher's Edition. Barnecutt, Suzanne, ed. Harrigan, Mike, illus. 2010. (Shadow Fox Ser.: 1). 186p. (J). 34.99 *(978-0-9819607-2-2(3))* Fox Run Pr., LLC.

Lawson, Robert. Mr. Revere & I. 2003. (J). (gr. 4-8). 22.75 *(978-0-8446-7258-8(0))* Smith, Peter Pub., Inc.

Rinaldi, Ann. The Secret of Sarah Revere. 2003. (Great Episodes Ser.). (ENG.). 336p. (J). (gr. 5-7). pap. 8.99 *(978-0-15-204684-2(4))* Houghton Mifflin Harcourt Publishing Co.

REVERE, PAUL, 1735-1818—POETRY

Longfellow, Henry Wadsworth. Paul Revere's Ride: The Landlord's Tale. Santore, Charles, illus. 2003. 40p. (J). lib. bdg. 17.89 *(978-0-06-623747-3(5))* HarperCollins Pubs.

Longfellow, Henry Wadsworth & Revere, Paul. Paul Revere's Ride. 2010. (Little Books of Wisdom Ser.). (ENG.). 32p. 9.95 *(978-1-55709-072-0(6))* Applewood Bks.

REVIEWS

see Book Reviews

REVIVAL OF LETTERS

see Renaissance

REVOLUTION, AMERICAN

see United States—History—Revolution, 1775-1783

REVOLUTION, FRENCH

see France—History—Revolution, 1789-1799

REVOLUTIONS

see also France—History—Revolution, 1789-1799; Hungary—History—Revolution, 1956; Social Conflict; United States—History—Revolution, 1775-1783

The Age of Revolution. 2015. (Age of Revolution Ser.). (ENG.). 128p. (YA). (gr. 9-10). 352.50 *(978-1-68048-201-0(7),* Britannica Educational Publishing) Rosen Publishing Group, Inc., The.

Arruda, Suzanne Middendorf. Freedom's Martyr: The Story of Jose Rizal, National Hero of the Philippines. 2003. (Avisson Young Adult Ser.). (Illus.). 106p. (J). pap. 19.95 *(978-1-888105-55-1(0))* Avisson Pr., Inc.

Croce, Nicholas, ed. Anarchism, Revolution, & Terrorism. 2014. (Political & Economic Systems Ser.). 312p. (J). (gr. 9-12). 45.00 *(978-1-62275-353-6(4))* Rosen Publishing Group, Inc., The.

Fabiny, Sarah. Who Was Fidel Castro? Hammond, Ted, illus. 2017. (Who Was? Ser.). (ENG.). 112p. (J). (gr. 3-7). 5.99 ***(978-0-451-53333-3(X))***; lib. bdg. 15.99 ***(978-0-451-53335-7(6))*** Penguin Young Readers Group. (Penguin Workshop).

Gay, Kathlyn. The Aftermath of the Chinese Nationalist Revolution. 2008. (Aftermath of History Ser.). (ENG., Illus.). 160p. (J). (gr. 9-12). lib. bdg. 38.60 *(978-0-8225-7601-3(5))* Lerner Publishing Group.

Hughes, Christopher. Cuba. 2003. (Nations in Conflict Ser.). 48p. (J). 26.19 *(978-1-56711-511-6(X),* Blackbirch Pr., Inc.) Cengage Gale.

MacCurtain, Fionnuala. The Story of Tomás Mac Curtáin. 2011. (Irish Heros for Children Ser.). (ENG.). 128p. (J). 16.95 *(978-1-85635-716-6(3))* Mercier Pr., Ltd., The IRL. Dist: Dufour Editions, Inc.

Malaspina, Ann. Mao Zedong & the Chinese Revolution. 2016. (People & Events That Changed the World Ser.). (ENG., Illus.). 128p. (J). (gr. 7-8). lib. bdg. 37.27 *(978-0-7660-7292-3(4))* Enslow Pubs., Inc.

Schmermund, Elizabeth & McGowan, Tom. Maximilien Robespierre & the French Revolution. 2016. (People & Events That Changed the World Ser.). (ENG., Illus.). 128p. (J). (gr. 7-8). lib. bdg. 37.27 *(978-0-7660-7294-7(0))* Enslow Pubs., Inc.

Steele, Philip. Uprisings in the Middle East & North Africa. 2016. (Illus.). 48p. (J). *(978-0-7787-2589-3(8))* Crabtree Publishing Co.

World Book, Inc Staff, contrib. by. The Chinese Revolution. 2010. (J). *(978-0-7166-1503-3(7))* World Bk., Inc.

REVOLUTIONS—FICTION

Alvarez, Julia. Antes de Ser Libres. Valenzuela, Liliana, tr. 2004.Tr. of Before We Were Free. (SPA.). 192p. (YA). (gr. 7). mass mkt. 6.99 *(978-0-375-81545-4(7),* Laurel Leaf) Random Hse. Children's Bks.

—Antes de Ser Libres. 2004.Tr. of Before We Were Free. (SPA.). (gr. 7-12). lib. bdg. 17.20 *(978-0-613-71931-5(X),* Turtleback) Turtleback Bks.

—Before We Were Free. 2004. 192p. (J). (gr. 7-18). pap. 38.00 incl. audio *(978-1-4000-9017-4(2),* Listening Library) Random Hse. Audio Publishing Group.

—Before We Were Free. 2004. (ENG.). 192p. (YA). (gr. 7). reprint ed. mass mkt. 6.99 *(978-0-440-23784-6(X),* Laurel Leaf) Random Hse. Children's Bks.

—Before We Were Free. 2004. (gr. 7-12). lib. bdg. 17.20 *(978-0-613-72269-8(8),* Turtleback) Turtleback Bks.

Braswell, Liz. A Whole New World: A Twisted Tale. 2015. (Twisted Tale Ser.). (ENG.). 384p. (YA). (gr. 7-12). 17.99 *(978-1-4847-0729-6(X))* Disney Pr.

Brennan, Sarah Rees. Tell the Wind & Fire. (ENG.). 368p. (YA). (gr. 7). 2017. pap. 9.99 *(978-0-544-93887-8(9),* HMH Books For Young Readers) 2016. 17.99 *(978-0-544-31817-5(X))* Houghton Mifflin Harcourt Publishing Co.

Clark, Marian. Benji's Sicarii Sword. 2007. 156p. per. 13.99 *(978-1-60266-022-9(0))* Salem Author Services.

De Pauw, Linda Grant. In Search of Molly Pitcher. 2008. 164p. pap. 12.00 *(978-1-4357-0607-1(2))* Lulu Pr., Inc.

dos Santos, Steven. The Culling. 2013. (Torch Keeper Ser.: 1). (ENG.). 432p. (YA). pap. 9.99 *(978-0-7387-3537-5(X),* Flux) North Star Editions.

Ellis, M. Henderson. Petra K & the Blackhearts: A Novel. 2014. (Young Europe Bks.). (ENG., Illus.). 202p. (J). (gr. 9). pap. 11.99 *(978-0-9850623-8-5(X))* New Europe Bks.

Fine, Sarah. Of Dreams & Rust. 2016. (ENG.). 304p. (YA). (gr. 9). pap. 11.99 *(978-1-4424-8362-0(8),* McElderry, Margaret K. Bks.) McElderry, Margaret K. Bks.

Gunderson, J. Ropes of Revolution: The Boston Tea Party, 1 vol. Schoonover, Brent, illus. 2008. (Historical Fiction Ser.). (ENG.). 56p. (gr. 2-3). pap. 6.25 *(978-1-4342-0492-9(8),* Graphic Flash) Stone Arch Bks.

Ifans, Rhiannon. Owain Glyndwr: Prince of Wales. Jones, Margaret, illus. 2003. (WEL & ENG.). 96p. (J). pap. 13.95 *(978-0-86243-544-8(7))* Y Lolfa GBR. Dist: Dufour Editions, Inc.

Julia, Alvarez. Before We Were Free. 2014. (ENG.). 192p. (YA). 11.24 *(978-1-63245-139-2(5))* Lectorum Pubns., Inc.

Mac, Carrie. Storm. 2009. (ENG.). 304p. (J). (gr. k-12). 14.00 *(978-0-14-305115-2(6),* Puffin Canada) Penguin Random House Canada Young Readers CAN. Dist: Penguin Random Hse. LLC.

Marsden, Carolyn. My Own Revolution. 2012. (ENG., Illus.). 192p. (YA). (gr. 7-9). 16.99 *(978-0-7636-5395-8(0))* Candlewick Pr.

Miller, Sarah. The Lost Crown. (ENG., Illus.). 448p. (gr. 7). 2012. (YA). pap. 9.99 *(978-1-4169-8341-5(4))* 2011. (J). 17.99 *(978-1-4169-8340-8(6))* Simon & Schuster Children's Publishing. (Atheneum Bks. for Young Readers).

Mull, Brandon. Chasing the Prophecy. (Beyonders Ser.: 3). (ENG.). (J). (gr. 3-7). 2014. 528p. pap. 8.99 *(978-1-4169-9797-9(0))* 2013. 512p. 19.99 *(978-1-4169-9796-2(2))* Simon & Schuster Children's Publishing. (Aladdin).

—Seeds of Rebellion. (Beyonders Ser.: 2). (ENG., Illus.). (J). (gr. 3-7). 2013. 528p. pap. 8.99 *(978-1-4169-9795-5(4))* 2012. 512p. 19.99 *(978-1-4169-9794-8(6))* Simon & Schuster Children's Publishing. (Aladdin).

—Seeds of Rebellion. 2012. (Beyonders Ser.: Bk. 2). (ENG., Illus.). 512p. (J). pap. 10.99 *(978-1-4424-4965-7(9),* Simon & Schuster/Paula Wiseman Bks.) Simon & Schuster/Paula Wiseman Bks.

—Seeds of Rebellion. 2013. (Beyonders Ser.: 2). lib. bdg. 19.65 *(978-0-606-27030-4(2),* Turtleback) Turtleback Bks.

—A World Without Heroes. (J). 2011. (Beyonders Ser.: 1). 1.25 *(978-1-4640-0920-4(1))* (Beyonders Ser.: 1). 92.75 *(978-1-4618-0338-6(1))* 2011. (Beyonders Ser.: 1). 124.75 *(978-1-4618-0353-9(5))* 2011. 122.75 *(978-1-4618-0363-8(2))* Recorded Bks., Inc.

—A World Without Heroes. (Beyonders Ser.: 1). (ENG.). (J). (gr. 3-7). 2012. 496p. pap. 8.99 *(978-1-4169-9793-1(8))* 2011. 464p. 19.99 *(978-1-4169-9792-4(X))* Simon & Schuster Children's Publishing. (Aladdin).

—A World Without Heroes. 2011. (Beyonders Ser.: Bk. 1). (ENG.). 464p. (J). pap. 10.99 *(978-1-4424-3530-8(5),* Simon & Schuster/Paula Wiseman Bks.) Simon & Schuster/Paula Wiseman Bks.

—A World Without Heroes. 2012. (Beyonders Ser.: 1). lib. bdg. 19.65 *(978-0-606-23675-1(9),* Turtleback) Turtleback Bks.

—A World Without Heroes; Seeds of Rebellion; Chasing the Prophecy. Set. 2013. (Beyonders Ser.). (ENG., Illus.). 1456p. (J). (gr. 3-7). 59.99 *(978-1-4424-8593-8(0),* Aladdin) Simon & Schuster Children's Publishing.

North, Phoebe. Starglass. 2013. (Starglass Sequence Ser.). (ENG., Illus.). 448p. (YA). (gr. 7). 17.99 *(978-1-4424-5953-3(0),* Simon & Schuster Bks. For Young Readers) Simon & Schuster Bks. For Young Readers.

Purdie, Kathryn. Crystal Blade. 2017. (Burning Glass Ser.: 2). 368p. (YA). (gr. 9). 17.99 *(978-0-06-241239-3(6),* Tegen, Katherine Bks) HarperCollins Pubs.

Rinaldi, Ann. Cast Two Shadows: The American Revolution in the South. 2004. (Great Episodes Ser.). (ENG., Illus.). 304p. (YA). (gr. 7-8). pap. 7.99 *(978-0-15-205077-1(9))* Houghton Mifflin Harcourt Publishing Co.

Stasse, Lisa M. The Defiant. 2015. (ENG., Illus.). 352p. (YA). (gr. 7). pap. 10.99 *(978-1-4424-3272-7(1))* Simon & Schuster Children's Publishing.

—The Defiant: The Forsaken Trilogy. 2014. (ENG., Illus.). 352p. (YA). (gr. 7). 17.99 *(978-1-4424-3271-0(3),* Simon & Schuster Bks. For Young Readers) Simon & Schuster Bks. For Young Readers.

—The Uprising: The Forsaken Trilogy. 2013. (ENG.). 384p. (YA). (gr. 7). 16.99 *(978-1-4424-3268-0(3),* Simon & Schuster Bks. For Young Readers) Simon & Schuster Bks. For Young Readers.

Thomas, Rhiannon. A Wicked Thing. 2015. (ENG.). 352p. (YA). (gr. 9). 17.99 *(978-0-06-230353-0(8),* HarperTeen) HarperCollins Pubs.

Weyn, Suzanne. Faces of the Dead. 2014. (ENG.). 208p. (J). (gr. 7). 17.99 *(978-0-545-42531-5(X),* Scholastic Pr.) Scholastic, Inc.

Whelan, Gloria. Angel on the Square. 2003. (Russian Saga Ser.: 1). (ENG.). 304p. (J). (gr. 5-9). pap. 9.99 *(978-0-06-440879-0(5))* HarperCollins Pubs.

—Angel on the Square. 2004. 288p. (gr. 5-9). 20.00 *(978-0-7569-4062-1(1))* Perfection Learning Corp.

RHETORIC

see also Criticism; Debates and Debating; Letter Writing; Punctuation; Satire; Style, Literary

Abraham, Philip. Language Development Writing Process. 2004. (BrainBuilders Ser.). (ENG.). 48p. (gr. k-4). pap. 5.25 *(978-1-4042-8520-0(2))* Rosen Publishing Group, Inc., The.

Allen, Susan & Lindaman, Jane. Written Anything Good Lately? Enright, Vicky, illus. (J). 2010. (ENG.). 32p. (gr. k-3). pap. 6.95 *(978-0-7613-5477-2(8),* First Avenue Editions) 2006. 31p. (gr. 3-7). lib. bdg. 15.95 *(978-0-7613-2426-3(7),* Millbrook Pr.) Lerner Publishing Group.

Atlee, Nancy. The Absolutely Essential Writing Guide. 2004. (J). per. 13.95 *(978-1-883055-68-4(7))* Dandy Lion Pubns.

Barnard, Roger & Zemach, Dorothy E. Writing for the Real World, Level 1: An Introduction to General Writing. 2005. (ENG., Illus.). 138p. stu. ed., spiral bd. 20.50 *(978-0-19-453814-5(1))* Oxford Univ. Pr., Inc.

Basher, Simon & Budzik, Mary. Basher Basics: Creative Writing. Basher, Simon, illus. 2013. (Basher Basics Ser.). (ENG., Illus.). 64p. (J). (gr. 3-7). 12.99 *(978-0-7534-7054-1(3),* 9780753470541, Kingfisher) Roaring Brook Pr.

Beers. Elements of Literature: Enhanced Online Edition. 5th ed. 2004. (J). (gr. k). 19.93 *(978-0-03-037277-3(1));* (J). (gr. 2). 19.93 *(978-0-03-037279-7(8));* (J). (gr. 3). 19.93 *(978-0-03-037281-0(X));* (J). (gr. 4). 19.93 *(978-0-03-037282-7(8));* (gr. 5). 19.93 *(978-0-03-037283-4(6));* (gr. 6). 19.93 *(978-0-03-037284-1(4))* Holt McDougal.

Benke, Karen. Rip the Page! Adventures in Creative Writing. 2010. (ENG., Illus.). 256p. (J). (gr. 4-7). pap. 16.95 *(978-1-59030-812-7(3),* Roost Books) Shambhala Pubns., Inc.

Beutel, Roger & Spencer, Lauren. Writing a Narrative. 2011. 77.70 *(978-1-4488-4747-1(8),* Rosen Reference); pap. 12.95 *(978-1-4488-4689-4(7),* Rosen Reference); (YA). (gr. 5-9). lib. bdg. 31.95 *(978-1-4488-4683-2(8))* Rosen Publishing Group, Inc., The.

Bevan, Clare. The Wonderful Gift. 2004. (QEB Start Writing Ser.). (Illus.). 24p. (J). lib. bdg. 15.95 *(978-1-59566-022-0(4))* QEB Publishing Inc.

BJU Press, creator. Worktext for K5: For Christian Schools. 2004. (Illus.). 392p. per. 30.00 *(978-1-57924-845-1(4))* BJU Pr.

BJU Staff. American Republic Activity S 8. 2004. pap. 14.50 *(978-1-57924-333-3(9))* BJU Pr.

—American Republic Student Grd8. 2004. 32.00 *(978-1-57924-312-8(6))* BJU Pr.

—Beginnings Write Now Grd K5. 2004. pap. 5.00 *(978-1-57924-846-8(2))* BJU Pr.

Bodden, Valerie. Imagery & Description. 2017. (Odysseys in Prose Ser.). (ENG., Illus.). 80p. (J). (gr. 7-11). pap. 14.99 *(978-1-62832-324-5(8),* Creative Paperbacks) Creative Co., The.

—Narration & Point of View. 2017. (Odysseys in Prose Ser.). (ENG., Illus.). 80p. (J). (gr. 7-11). pap. 14.99 *(978-1-62832-325-2(6),* Creative Paperbacks) Creative Co., The.

Bracey, Ronay. Writing ... Take Small Steps: Improve Students' Writing Skills. 2003. spiral bd. *(978-1-933570-84-6(9))* Aardvark Global Publishing.

Brown Conroy, Erin. Writing Skillbuilders Bk. 2: A Fun-Filled Activity Book to Build Strong Handwriting Skills. 2004. (J). spiral bd. 14.95 *(978-0-9740981-7-3(5))* Celtic Cross Communications.

—Writing Skillbuilders Bk. 3: A Fun-Filled Activity Book for Beautiful Cursive Handwriting. 2004. (J). spiral bd. 14.95 *(978-0-9740981-8-0(3))* Celtic Cross Communications.

Bush, Valerie Chow, et al. Jump Write In! Creative Writing Exercises for Diverse Communities, Grades 6-12, Grd. 6-12. Tannenbaum, Judith, ed. 2005. (ENG., Illus.). 176p. per. 28.00 *(978-0-7879-7777-1(2),* Jossey-Bass) Wiley, John & Sons, Inc.

Campbell-Rush, Peggy. Ready to Write! 100 Tips & Strategies for Developing Fine-Motor Skills to Help Young Students Build a Strong Foundation for Handwriting. 2014. (ENG.). 64p. (-2). 11.99 *(978-0-545-56582-0(0),* Teaching Resources) Scholastic, Inc.

Cannon Hackett, Teresa. Creative Writing: Using Fairy Tales to Enrich Writing Skills. 2005. 42p. 14.95 *(978-1-59363-025-6(5))* Prufrock Pr.

Carroll, Joyce Armstrong, et al. Writing & Grammar: Communication in Action, 3 vols. 2003. (ENG.). 988p. (YA). (gr. 9-9). 494.00 *(978-0-13-037494-3(6),* Prentice Hall) Pearson Schl.

—Writing & Grammar: Communication in Action, Bronze Level, 3 vols. 2003. (ENG.). 812p. (YA). (gr. 7-7). 406.00 *(978-0-13-037492-9(X))* Prentice Hall Pr.

—Writing & Grammar: Communication in Action, Platinum Level, 3 vols. 2004. 992p. (YA). (gr. 10-18). 496.00 *(978-0-13-116634-9(4))* Prentice Hall Pr.

Chin, Beverly. Grammar for Writing 2007: Level Orange, Consumable. 2007. (Grammar for Writing Ser.). (gr. 10). pap. 17.00 net. *(978-0-8215-0220-4(4))* Sadlier, William H. Inc.

Cleary, Brian P. Skin Like Milk, Hair of Silk: What Are Similes & Metaphors? Gable, Brian, illus. (Words Are CATegorical (r) Ser.). (ENG.). (gr. 2-5). 2011. 32p. pap. 6.95 *(978-0-7613-3945-8(0))* 2007. pap. 39.62 *(978-0-7613-8361-1(1))* Lerner Publishing Group. (Millbrook Pr.).

Collins Easy Learning, Collins Easy. First Words - Wipe Clean: Bed Six Cat. 2017. (Collins Easy Learning Preschool Ser.). (ENG.). 24p. (J). (gr. -1-k). 7.95 ***(978-0-00-821293-3(7))*** HarperCollins Pubs. Ltd. GBR. Dist: Independent Pubs. Group.

Cooper, Terry, ed. Cursive Handwriting Practice. 2006. (Practice Ser.). (ENG., Illus.). 48p. (gr. 3-3). per. 5.99 *(978-0-439-81897-1(4),* Teaching Resources) Scholastic, Inc.

—Manuscript Handwriting Practice. 2006. (Practice Ser.). (ENG., Illus.). 48p. (gr. 1-1). per. 5.99 *(978-0-439-81895-7(8),* Teaching Resources) Scholastic, Inc.

—Writing Practice. 2006. (Practice Ser.). (ENG., Illus.). 48p. (gr. 2-2). per. 5.99 *(978-0-439-81911-4(3),* Teaching Resources) Scholastic, Inc.

—Writing Practice. 2006. (Practice Ser.). (ENG., Illus.). 48p. (gr. 1-1). per. 5.99 *(978-0-439-81910-7(5),* Teaching Resources) Scholastic, Inc.

Culham, Ruth. The Complete Guide for the Primary Grades. 2005. (6+1 Traits of Writing Ser.). (ENG., Illus.). 304p. (gr. k-2). pap. 29.99 *(978-0-439-57412-9(9))* Scholastic, Inc.

Davidson, Kay. Becoming a Better Writer Using the Simple 6: Grades 3rd - 6th. 2007. pap. 28.95 *(978-1-931334-98-3(6))* Pieces of Learning.

—The Simple 6 for K-2 Writers. 2007. pap. 28.95 *(978-1-931334-97-6(8))* Pieces of Learning.

Diamond, Mark. 6 Tricks to Student Narrative Writing Success: An Easy Guide for Students, Teachers & Parents. l.t. ed. 2005. (ENG., Illus.). 96p. per. 14.95 *(978-0-9771470-0-7(2))* Anyone Can Write bks.

Digital Photo Activity Kit Deluxe Vivitar 3700 series Lab-10. 2005. (J). cd-rom 1790.00 *(978-1-933229-02-7(0))* APTE, Inc.

Digital Photo Activity Kit Deluxe Vivitar 3700 series Lab-15. 2005. (J). cd-rom 2610.00 *(978-1-933229-03-4(9))* APTE, Inc.

Digital Photo Activity Kit Deluxe Vivitar 3700 series Lab-20. 2005. (J). 3260.00 *(978-1-933229-04-1(7))* APTE, Inc.

Digital Photo Activity Kit Deluxe Vivitar 3700 series Lab-25. 2005. (J). 3924.00 *(978-1-933229-05-8(5))* APTE, Inc.

Digital Photo Activity Kit Deluxe Vivitar 3700 series Lab-30. 2005. (J). 4585.00 *(978-1-933229-06-5(3))* APTE, Inc.

Digital Photo Activity Kit Deluxe Vivitar 3700 series Lab-35. 2005. (J). 5239.00 *(978-1-933229-07-2(1))* APTE, Inc.

Digital Photo Activity Kit Deluxe Vivitar 3700 series Lab-5. 2005. (J). cd-rom 648.95 *(978-1-933229-01-0(2))* APTE, Inc.

Digital Photo Activity Kit Deluxe Vivitar 3700 Series school Version. 2005. (J). cd-rom 133.95 *(978-1-933229-00-3(4))* APTE, Inc.

Digital Photo Activity Kit Deluxe Vivitar 5300 series Lab- 2005. (J). 1759.95 *(978-1-933229-09-6(8))* APTE, Inc.

Digital Photo Activity Kit Deluxe Vivitar 5300 series Lab-10. 2005. (J). 3469.99 *(978-1-933229-10-2(1))* APTE, Inc.

Digital Photo Activity Kit Deluxe Vivitar 5300 series Lab-15. 2005. (J). 5129.95 *(978-1-933229-11-9(X))* APTE, Inc.

Digital Photo Activity Kit Deluxe Vivitar 5300 series Lab-25. 2005. (J). 8123.90 *(978-1-933229-12-6(8))* APTE, Inc.

Digital Photo Activity Kit Deluxe Vivitar 5300 series Lab-30. 2005. (J). 9624.95 *(978-1-933229-14-0(4))* APTE, Inc.

Digital Photo Activity Kit Deluxe Vivitar 5300 series Lab-35. 2005. (J). 11119.95 *(978-1-933229-15-7(2))* APTE, Inc.

Digital Photo Activity Kit Deluxe Vivitar 5300 series Single. 2005. (J). 359.99 *(978-1-933229-08-9(X))* APTE, Inc.

DynaNotes Grade 4 Writing TAKS Review Guide. 2006. (J). pap. *(978-1-933854-41-0(3))* DynaStudy, Inc.

DynaNotes Grade 4 Writing TAKS Review Guide Transparency Set. 2006. (J). trans. *(978-1-933854-42-7(1))* DynaStudy, Inc.

DynaNotes Grade 7 Writing TAKS Review Guide. 2006. (J). pap. *(978-1-933854-39-7(1))* DynaStudy, Inc.

DynaNotes Grade 7 Writing TAKS Review Guide Transparency Set. 2006. (J). trans. *(978-1-933854-40-3(5))* DynaStudy, Inc.

Education.com. Write Away: A Workbook of Creative & Narrative Writing Prompts. 2015. (ENG.). 112p. (J). (gr. 3-3). pap. 7.99 *(978-0-486-80267-1(1))* Dover Pubns., Inc.

EMC-Paradigm Publishing Staff. Discovering Literature: Resource. (J). (gr. 6). Unit 8. pap., tchr. ed. *(978-0-8219-2039-8(1))*Unit 9. pap. *(978-0-8219-2040-4(5))*Unit 10. pap., tchr. ed. *(978-0-8219-2041-1(3))*Unit 11. pap., tchr. ed. *(978-0-8219-2042-8(1))*Unit 12. pap. *(978-0-8219-2043-5(X))* EMC/Paradigm Publishing.

Evan-Moor. Skill Sharpeners, Spell & Write, Grade 1. 2005. (ENG., Illus.). 144p. (J). pap. 9.99 *(978-1-59673-045-8(5),* emc 4537) Evan-Moor Educational Pubs.

—Skill Sharpeners Spell & Write, Grade 2. 2005. (ENG.). 144p. (J). pap. 9.99 *(978-1-59673-046-5(3),* emc 4538) Evan-Moor Educational Pubs.

—Skill Sharpeners, Spell & Write, Grade 3. 2005. (ENG.). 144p. (J). pap. 9.99 *(978-1-59673-047-2(1),* emc 4539) Evan-Moor Educational Pubs.

—Skill Sharpeners, Spell & Write, Grade 4. 2005. (ENG.). 144p. (J). pap. 9.99 *(978-1-59673-048-9(X),* emc 4540) Evan-Moor Educational Pubs.

—Skill Sharpeners, Spell & Write, Grade 5. 2005. (ENG., Illus.). 144p. (J). pap. 9.99 *(978-1-59673-049-6(8),* emc 4542) Evan-Moor Educational Pubs.

—Skill Sharpeners, Spell & Write, Grade 6. 2005. (ENG., Illus.). 144p. (J). pap. 9.99 *(978-1-59673-050-2(1),* emc 4542) Evan-Moor Educational Pubs.

—Skill Sharpeners Spell & Write Grade PreK. 2005. (Skill Sharpeners Ser.). (ENG., Illus.). 144p. (J). pap. 9.99 *(978-1-59673-043-4(9),* emc 4535) Evan-Moor Educational Pubs.

—Writing Centers, Grades 1-2. 2007. (Take It to Your Seat Ser.). (ENG., Illus.). 192p. (J). pap. 24.99 *(978-1-59673-078-6(1),* EMC 6002) Evan-Moor Educational Pubs.

—Writing Centers Grades 2-3. 2007. (Take It to Your Seat Ser.). (ENG., Illus.). 192p. (J). pap. 24.99 *(978-1-59673-079-3(X),* EMC 6003) Evan-Moor Educational Pubs.

—Writing Centers, Grades 3-4. 2007. (Take It to Your Seat Ser.). (ENG., Illus.). 192p. (J). pap. 24.99 *(978-1-59673-080-9(3),* EMC 6004) Evan-Moor Educational Pubs.

—Writing Centers, Grades 4-5. 2007. (Take It to Your Seat Ser.). (ENG., Illus.). 192p. (J). pap. 24.99 *(978-1-59673-081-6(1),* EMC 6005) Evan-Moor Educational Pubs.

—Writing Centers, Grades 5-6. 2007. (Take It to Your Seat Ser.). (ENG., Illus.). 192p. (J). pap. 24.99 *(978-1-59673-082-3(X),* EMC 6006) Evan-Moor Educational Pubs.

Evergreen: a Guide to Writing with Readings. 7th ed. 2003. (YA). (gr. 6-12). stu. ed. 3.96 incl. cd-rom *(978-0-618-27389-8(1),* 315696) CENGAGE Learning.

Fandel, Jennifer & Bodden, Valerie. Dialogue & Characterization. 2017. (Odysseys in Prose Ser.). (ENG., Illus.). 80p. (J). (gr. 7-11). pap. 14.99 *(978-1-62832-323-8(X),* Creative Paperbacks) Creative Co., The.

Festival Fun: 6 Each of 1 Anthology, 6 vols. (Wildcats Ser.). 32p. (gr. 2-8). *(978-0-322-02424-3(2))* Wright Group/McGraw-Hill.

Fire! Fire! 6 Each of 1 Anthology, 6 vols. (Wildcats Ser.). 32p. (gr. 2-8). *(978-0-322-00581-5(7))* Wright Group/McGraw-Hill.

Ford, Jeanne Marie. 12 Great Tips on Writing to Inform. 2017. (Great Tips on Writing Ser.). (ENG., Illus.). 32p. (J). (gr. 3-6). 21.95 *(978-1-63235-278-1(8))* Pr. Room Editions LLC.

Giants in the City: Hard & Soft c & g: Level B, 6 vols. (Wright Skills Ser.). 16p. (gr. k-3). 26.50 *(978-0-322-01489-3(1))* Wright Group/McGraw-Hill.

Gould, Judith S. & Gould, Evan Jay. Four Square: A Companion to the Four Square Writing Method: Writing in the Content Areas for Grades 1-4. Mitchell, Judy, ed. Radtke, Becky J., illus. 2004. 112p. (J). pap. 11.95 *(978-1-57310-421-0(3))* Teaching & Learning Co.

—Four Square: A Companion to the Four Square Writing Method: Writing in the Content Areas for Grades 5-9. Mitchell, Judy, ed. Wheeler, Ron, illus. 2004. 112p. (J). pap. 11.95 *(978-1-57310-422-7(1))* Teaching & Learning Co.

Greve, Meg. Writing an Opinion Paper. 2014. (ENG.). 24p. (gr. 3-5). 28.50 *(978-1-62717-693-4(4))* Rourke Educational Media.

Group/McGraw-Hill, Wright. Early Fluency-Fluency Writing Kit. 2004. (Wright Group Literacy Ser.). (gr. k-3). 132.50 *(978-0-322-07021-9(X))* Wright Group/McGraw-Hill.

—Emergent Writing Kit. 2004. (Wright Group Literacy Ser.). (gr. k-3). 79.50 *(978-0-322-06615-1(8))* Wright Group/McGraw-Hill.

—Five Little Frogs: Collection 1. (Storyteller Interactive Writing Cards Ser.). (J). (gr. k-3). *(978-0-322-09363-8(5))* Wright Group/McGraw-Hill.

—Holly's Birthday Cake: Collection 2. (Storyteller Interactive Writing Cards Ser.). (gr. k-3). *(978-0-322-09336-2(8))* Wright Group/McGraw-Hill.

—In the Rain Forest, 6 vols. (Wildcats Ser.). 32p. (gr. 2-8). *(978-0-322-00599-0(X))* Wright Group/McGraw-Hill.

—My Word! what a Bird! Collection 4. (Storyteller Interactive Writing Cards Ser.). (gr. k-3). *(978-0-322-09325-6(2))* Wright Group/McGraw-Hill.

—Ready, Set, Pop! Collection 3. (Storyteller Interactive Writing Cards Ser.). (gr. k-3). *(978-0-322-09348-5(1))* Wright Group/McGraw-Hill.

—River Wild: 6 Each of 1 Anthology, 6 vols. (Wildcats Ser.). 32p. (gr. 2-8). *(978-0-322-05857-6(0))* Wright Group/McGraw-Hill.

—Sand: Collection 3. (Storyteller Interactive Writing Cards Ser.). (gr. k-3). *(978-0-322-09349-2(X))* Wright Group/McGraw-Hill.

Guillain, Charlotte. What Is Persuasive Writing? 2015. (Connect with Text Ser.). (ENG., Illus.). 32p. (gr. 2-4). 30.65 *(978-1-4109-8036-6(7))* Heinemann-Raintree.

Hennessy, Brendan. Essay to Write? 2nd ed. 2004. 93p. pap. *(978-1-85703-835-4(5),* How To Books) Little, Brown Book Group Ltd.

Hercules & Other Greek Legends: 6 Each of 1 Anthology, 6 vols. (Wildcats Ser.). 32p. (gr. 2-8). *(978-0-322-00590-7(6))* Wright Group/McGraw-Hill.

Heroes: 6 Each of 1 Anthology, 6 vols. (Wildcats Ser.). 32p. (gr. 2-8). *(978-0-322-00579-2(5))* Wright Group/McGraw-Hill.

Herzog, Joyce. Budding Authors: Adventures in Writing. 2005. (J). spiral bd. 10.00 *(978-1-887225-52-6(8))* Herzog, Joyce.

—Budding Authors: Step into Writing. 2005. (J). spiral bd. 10.00 *(978-1-887225-51-9(X))* Herzog, Joyce.

—Budding Authors: Then & Now. 2005. (J). spiral bd. 10.00 *(978-1-887225-53-3(6))* Herzog, Joyce.

—Budding Authors: Twirling Around. Sinclair, Angie et al, eds. 2005. (J). spiral bd. 10.00 *(978-1-887225-56-4(0))* Herzog, Joyce.

—Budding Authors: Writing U. S. History. 2005. (J). spiral bd. 12.00 *(978-1-887225-55-7(2))* Herzog, Joyce.

—Budding Authors: Zooming Ahead. 2005. (J). spiral bd. 10.00 *(978-1-887225-54-0(4))* Herzog, Joyce.

—Draw & Write 2. 2004. (J). spiral bd. 12.00 *(978-1-887225-32-8(3))* Herzog, Joyce.

—Draw & Write I. 2004. (J). spiral bd. 12.00 *(978-1-887225-31-1(5))* Herzog, Joyce.

Higa, Ryan. Ryan Higa's How to Write Good. 2017. (ENG.). 208p. (YA). (gr. 7-17). 19.99 ***(978-0-316-46407-9(4)***, Poppy) Little, Brown Bks. for Young Readers.

Hohlt, Janie. Basic Writing 2. 2005. (J). ring bd. 49.95 *(978-1-58804-388-7(6))* P C I Education.

—Basic Writing Binder 2. 2005. (J). ring bd. 49.95 *(978-1-58804-400-6(9))* P C I Education.

Hook, Sue Vander. Writing Intriguing Informational Pieces. 2015. (ENG., Illus.). 56p. (gr. 6-8). 33.32 *(978-1-4677-7907-4(5)*, Lerner Pubns.) Lerner Publishing Group.

Hop, Jog, & Tap: Consonants g, h, j; Short Vowel o word families: Level A, 6 vols. (Wright Skills Ser.). 12p. (gr. k-3). 17.95 *(978-0-322-01449-7(2))* Wright Group/McGraw-Hill.

Howell, Sara. How to Write an Opinion Piece, 1 vol., 1. 2014. (Core Writing Skills Ser.). (ENG.). 24p. (J). (gr. 3-4). 23.60 *(978-1-4777-2906-9(2))*; pap. 8.25 *(978-1-4777-2995-3(X))* Rosen Publishing Group, Inc., The. (PowerKids Pr.).

Hutchinson, Emily. Descriptive Writing, 1 vol. Saddleback Educational Publishing Staff, ed. 2013. (Writing 4 Ser.). (ENG.). 64p. (gr. 6-12). pap. 32.95 *(978-1-62250-024-6(5))* Saddleback Educational Publishing, Inc.

—Expository Writing, 1 vol. Saddleback Educational Publishing Staff, ed. 2013. (Writing 4 Ser.). (ENG.). 64p. (gr. 6-12). pap. 32.95 *(978-1-62250-025-3(3))* Saddleback Educational Publishing, Inc.

—Narrative Writing, 1 vol. Saddleback Educational Publishing Staff, ed. 2013. (Writing 4 Ser.). (ENG.). 64p. (gr. 6-12). pap. 32.95 *(978-1-62250-026-0(1))* Saddleback Educational Publishing, Inc.

Hutson-Nechkash, Peg. Help Me Write: Frames & Rubrics for Classroom Writing Success. 2003. (Illus.). (J). 34.95 *(978-1-932054-12-5(X))* Super Duper Pubns.

In the News, 6 vols. (Wildcats Ser.). 32p. (gr. 2-8). *(978-0-322-02437-3(4))* Wright Group/McGraw-Hill.

In the News, 6 vols., Set 2. Incl. Climate Change. Brezina, Corona. (YA). lib. bdg. 31.95 *(978-1-4042-1913-7(7))*; Darfur: African Genocide. Xavier, John. (YA). lib. bdg. 31.95 *(978-1-4042-1912-0(9))*; Doping: Athletes & Drugs. Porterfield, Jason. (J). lib. bdg. 29.25 *(978-1-4042-1917-5(X))*; Green Technology: Earth-Friendly Innovations. Sobha, Geeta. (YA). lib. bdg. 31.95 *(978-1-4042-1914-4(5))*; Nukes: The Spread of Nuclear Weapons. Minneus, Steve. (YA). lib. bdg. 31.95 *(978-1-4042-1916-8(1))*; Oil: The Economics of Fuel. Jovinelly, Joann. (YA). lib. bdg. 31.95 *(978-1-4042-1915-1(3))*; (Illus.). 64p. (gr. 7-12). 2007. 2007. Set lib. bdg. 175.50 *(978-1-4042-1112-4(8))* Rosen Publishing Group, Inc., The.

Incredible Places: 6 Each of 1 Anthology, 6 vols. (Wildcats Ser.). 32p. (gr. 2-8). *(978-0-322-00587-7(6))* Wright Group/McGraw-Hill.

Jarnow, Jill. Writing to Instruct. 2009. (Write Now: A Kid's Guide to Nonfiction Writing Ser.). 24p. (gr. 3-4). 42.50 *(978-1-60854-896-5(1)*, PowerKids Pr.) Rosen Publishing Group, Inc., The.

Jones, Molly. 12 Great Tips on Writing to Persuade. 2017. (Great Tips on Writing Ser.). (ENG., Illus.). 32p. (J). (gr. 3-6). 21.95 *(978-1-63235-279-8(6))* Pr. Room Editions LLC.

Khan, Hena. How to Say What You Mean, Mean What You Say, & Get What You Want. 2004. (Illus.). 80p. (J). *(978-0-439-57904-9(X))* Scholastic, Inc.

Lawlor, Laurie. Muddy as a Duck Puddle & Other American Similes. Long, Ethan, illus. 2011. (ENG.). 32p. (J). pap. 7.95 *(978-0-8234-2389-7(1))* Holiday Hse., Inc.

Levy, Janey. Language Development Writing Process. 2004. (BrainBuilders Ser.). (ENG.). 48p. (gr. k-4). pap. 5.25 *(978-1-4042-8569-5(9))* Rosen Publishing Group, Inc., The.

The Library of Writing Skills. 2005. (Illus.). 48p. (gr. 5-8). lib. bdg. 159.00 *(978-1-4042-0349-5(4))* Rosen Publishing Group, Inc., The.

Liverman, Debra, ed. Daily Journal Prompts. 2005. 112p. (gr. 1-3). 14.95 *(978-1-56234-625-6(3))*; (gr. 4-6). 14.95 *(978-1-56234-626-3(1))* Education Ctr., Inc. (Mailbox Bks., The).

Loewen, Nancy. Stubborn as a Mule & Other Silly Similes. Watkins, Adam, illus. (Ways to Say It Ser.). (ENG.). 24p. (gr. 3-5). 2011. pap. 7.49 *(978-1-4048-6715-4(5))* 2010. lib. bdg. 27.99 *(978-1-4048-6271-5(4))* Picture Window Bks.

—Writing Powerful Persuasive Pieces. 2015. (ENG., Illus.). 56p. (J). (gr. 6-8). 33.32 *(978-1-4677-7906-7(7))* Lerner Publishing Group.

—You're Toast & Other Metaphors We Adore, 1 vol. Wu, Donald, illus. (Ways to Say It Ser.). (ENG.). 24p. (gr. 3-5). 2011. pap. 7.49 *(978-1-4048-6717-8(1))* 2010. lib. bdg. 27.99 *(978-1-4048-6270-8(6))* Picture Window Bks.

Magee, Wes. Pet the Cat. 2004. (QEB Start Writing Ser.). (Illus.). 24p. (J). lib. bdg. 15.95 *(978-1-59566-023-7(2))* QEB Publishing Inc.

Marlow, Herb. A Student's Guide to Successful Writing. 2005. (J). 24.95 *(978-1-893595-53-8(6))* Four Seasons Bks., Inc.

McCarty, Diane Bischoff. Copywork for Children: For Grades 1-3. 2004. (Illus.). 63p. (J). *(978-0-9712124-1-1(4))* Angel Heart Children's Pr.

McCurry, Kristen. Pick a Picture, Write an Opinion!, 1 vol. 2014. (Little Scribe Ser.). (ENG.). 32p. (gr. 1-2). lib. bdg. 27.32 *(978-1-4765-4240-9(6)*, Aplus Bks.) Capstone Press of Coughlan Cos.

McKenzie, Precious. Writing an Informational Essay. 2014. (ENG.). 24p. (gr. 3-5). 28.50 *(978-1-62717-692-7(6))* Rourke Educational Media.

Mechanech Publications Staff. Writing Better with Every Letter: My Handwriting Practice Book. 2004. (Illus.). (J). 112p. (gr. 1-18). pap. *(978-0-9702861-2-3(0))*; Vol. 2. 96p. (gr. 2-18). pap. 10.00 *(978-0-9702861-4-7(7))* Mechanech Pubns.

Milton, Bess. Language Development Writing Process. 2004. (BrainBuilders Ser.). (ENG.). 48p. (gr. k-4). pap. 5.25 *(978-1-4042-8559-6(8))* Rosen Publishing Group, Inc., The.

Minden, Cecilia & Roth, Kate. How to Write a News Article. 2012. (Explorer Junior Library: Language Arts Explorer Junior Ser.). (ENG., Illus.). 24p. (gr. 1-4). lib. bdg. 25.64 *(978-1-61080-308-3(6)*, 201276) Cherry Lake Publishing.

Minden, Cecilia, et al. How to Write a News Article. 2012. (Explorer Junior Library: Language Arts Explorer Junior Ser.). (ENG., Illus.). 24p. (gr. 1-4). pap. 12.79 *(978-1-61080-318-2(3)*, 201278) Cherry Lake Publishing.

Morkane, Sue. Original Writing. 2004. (Routledge a Level English Guides). (ENG., Illus.). 112p. (C). 95.00 *(978-0-415-31911-9(0))*; per. 28.95 *(978-0-415-31912-6(9))* Routledge.

Mythmakers, 6 vols. (Wildcats Ser.). 32p. (gr. 2-8). *(978-0-322-02440-3(4))* Wright Group/McGraw-Hill.

Nelson, Linda & Logie, Daniel. Writing Sourcebook: Foundations for Writing. 2004. 80p. 6.95 *(978-1-931181-38-9(1))* Universal Publishing.

Nolan, Chris & Spencer, Lauren. Writing to Persuade. 2011. (Illus.). 63p. (J). 77.70 *(978-1-4488-4749-5(4)*, Rosen Reference); (J). pap. 12.95 *(978-1-4488-4691-7(9)*, Rosen Reference); (YA). (gr. 5-9). lib. bdg. 31.95 *(978-1-4488-4685-6(4))* Rosen Publishing Group, Inc., The.

Olsen, Jan Z. Mat Man Shapes. Delaney, Molly, illus. 2007. (ENG.). 32p. stu. ed. 13.75 *(978-1-891627-92-7(9))* Handwriting Without Tears.

Orehovec, Barbara & Alley, Marybeth. Revisiting the Writing Workshop: Management, Assessment, & Mini-Lessons. 2007. (ENG., Illus.). 160p. (gr. 17). pap. 20.99 *(978-0-439-92643-0(2))* Scholastic, Inc.

Parker, Helen. Wipe Clean Phonics. 2007. (Wipe Clean Ser.). (Illus.). 12p. (J). bds. *(978-1-84610-583-8(8))* Make Believe Ideas.

Perkins, Sally J. & Stoner, Mark R. Making Sense of Messages: A Critical Apprenticeship in Rhetorical Criticism. 2006. (Illus.). 320p. (YA). pap. 67.56 *(978-0-618-14488-4(9)*, 351240) CENGAGE Learning.

Peter Pauper Press, Inc., creator. Handwriting: Learn Cursive! 2015. (ENG., Illus.). 96p. (J). pap. 5.99 *(978-1-4413-1815-2(1)*, 9781441318152) Peter Pauper Pr. Inc.

Proudfit, Benjamin. Writing Opinion Papers. 2014. (Write Right! Ser.). 24p. (J). (gr. 2-5). 22.60 *(978-1-4824-1128-7(8))* Stevens, Gareth Publishing LLLP.

Purslow, Frances. Expository Paragraphs. 2007. (Learning to Write Ser.). (Illus.). 24p. (J). (gr. 4-7). lib. bdg. 24.45 *(978-1-59036-735-3(9))*; per. 8.95 *(978-1-59036-736-0(7))* Weigl Pubs., Inc.

—Narrative Paragraphs. 2007. (Learning to Write Ser.). (Illus.). 24p. (J). (gr. 4-7). lib. bdg. 24.45 *(978-1-59036-733-9(2))*; per. 8.95 *(978-1-59036-734-6(0))* Weigl Pubs., Inc.

—Persuasive Paragraphs. 2007. (Learning to Write Ser.). (Illus.). 24p. (J). (gr. 4-6). lib. bdg. 24.45 *(978-1-59036-731-5(6))*; per. 8.95 *(978-1-59036-732-2(4))* Weigl Pubs., Inc.

Read & Write. 2005. (J). pap. 3.99 *(978-1-933200-18-7(9))* Family Bks. at Home.

Real-World Writing. 2005. (YA). ring bd. 69.95 *(978-1-58804-389-4(4))* P C I Education.

Right or Wrong? 6 Each of 1 Anthology, 6 vols. (Wildcats Ser.). 32p. (gr. 2-8). *(978-0-322-00598-3(1))* Wright Group/McGraw-Hill.

Rollins, Brenda. Master Writing: 240 Interactive Screen Pages Big Box. 2011. (Writing Skills Ser.). (J). (gr. 3-8). pap. 79.95 incl. cd-rom *(978-1-55319-508-5(6)*, Classroom Complete Pr.) Rainbow Horizons Publishing, Inc.

Rondina, Catherine. Don't Touch That Toad & Other Strange Things Adults Tell You. Sylvester, Kevin, illus. (ENG.). 96p. (J). (gr. 2-5). 2014. pap. 8.95 *(978-1-55453-455-5(0))* 2010. 14.95 *(978-1-55453-454-8(2))* Kids Can Pr., Ltd. CAN. Dist: Hachette Bk. Group.

Roy, Jennifer Rozines. Sharpen Your Story or Narrative Writing Skills. 2011. (Sharpen Your Writing Skills Ser.). (Illus.). 64p. (J). (gr. 6-18). pap. 8.95 *(978-1-59845-340-9(8))*; lib. bdg. 29.27 *(978-0-7660-3901-8(3))* Enslow Pubs., Inc.

Scardamalia, Marlene, et al. Writing for Results. xiii, 167p. (J). (gr. 4-12). *(978-0-89688-184-6(9)*, 88-184) Open Court Publishing Co.

Scholastic, Inc. Staff. First 100 Words. 2016. (Scholastic Early Learners Ser.). (ENG.). 12p. (J). (gr. -1 — 1). bds. 6.99 *(978-0-545-90330-1(0)*, Cartwheel Bks.) Scholastic, Inc.

Scholastic, Inc. Staff, contrib. by. Contemporary Cursive, Grades 2-4. 2010. (Scholastic Success with Ser.). (ENG.). 48p. (gr. 2-4). pap. 5.99 *(978-0-545-20091-2(1)*, Teaching Resources) Scholastic, Inc.

Shearer, Cynthia & Washington, George. Handwriting by George 28-55: Rules of Civility & Decent Behaviour in Company & Conversation: Rules 28-53 to Draw & Write, 4 vols., Vol. 2. 2009. (ENG.). 62p. (J). pap. 9.95 *(978-1-882514-37-3(8))* Greenleaf Pr.

Show What You Know Publishing, ed. Show What You Know on the CSAP 7, Reading/Writing Student Workbook. 2007. (J). per. 13.95 *(978-1-59230-246-8(7))* Englefield & Assocs., Inc.

—Show What You Know on the CSAP for Grade 5, Student Workbook. 2007. (J). per. 13.95 *(978-1-59230-217-8(3))* Englefield & Assocs., Inc.

—Show What You Know on the CSAP for Grade 9 Writing Student Self-Study Workbook. 2007. (YA). per. 18.95 *(978-1-59230-293-2(9))* Englefield & Assocs., Inc.

—Show What You Know on the CSAP Reading & Writing for Grade 6, Student Workbook. 2007. (J). per. 13.95 *(978-1-59230-240-6(8))* Englefield & Assocs., Inc.

Silate, Jennifer. Language Development Writing Process. 2004. (BrainBuilders Ser.). (ENG.). 48p. (gr. k-4). pap. 5.25 *(978-1-4042-8564-4(4))* Rosen Publishing Group, Inc., The.

Spencer, Lauren. A Step-by-Step Guide to Informative Writing. 2009. (Library of Writing Skills Ser.). 48p. (gr. 5-8). 53.00 *(978-1-60853-978-9(4)*, Rosen Reference) Rosen Publishing Group, Inc., The.

Spilsbury, Louise. Tips for Better Writing. 2016. (Student's Toolbox Ser.). (ENG., Illus.). 32p. (J). (gr. 4-6). 17.99 *(978-0-7502-9103-3(6)*, Wayland) Hachette Children's Group GBR. Dist: Hachette Bk. Group.

Starfall Education. Level I Reading & Writing Journal - Block Print: WK201b. Starfall Education, ed. 2011. (ENG., Illus.). 96p. (J). *(978-1-59577-045-5(3))* Starfall Education.

Starfall Education, creator. Level II Reading & Writing Journal: Second Edition. 2010. (ENG., Illus.). 96p. (J). 1.95 *(978-1-59577-130-8(1))* Starfall Education.

Stella, Heather. Get Ready for School Writing Skills. 2017. (Get Ready for School Ser.). (ENG., Illus.). 128p. (J). (gr. 1-4). spiral bd. 12.99 *(978-0-316-50255-9(3)*, Black Dog & Leventhal Pubs. Inc.) Hachette Bks.

Stobaugh, James. Skills for Rhetoric: Encouraging Thoughtful Christians to Be World Changers. 2003. (YA). 30.50 *(978-0-9725890-4-8(X))* For Such A Time As This Ministries.

—Skills for Rhetoric Student. 2005. (Broadman & Holman Literature Ser.). 272p. stu. ed. 24.99 *(978-0-8054-5898-5(0))* B&H Publishing Group.

Street, Pat & Brace, Eric. You're Pulling My Leg! 400 Human-Body Sayings from Head to Toe. Brace, Eric, illus. 2016. (ENG., Illus.). 48p. (J). (gr. 1-5). 18.95 *(978-0-8234-2135-0(X))* Holiday Hse., Inc.

TAKS MASTER Power Practice, Writing Gr. 4. 2005. (J). per. *(978-1-57022-547-5(8))* ECS Learning Systems, Inc.

TAKS MASTER Power Practice, Writing, Gr. 7. 2005. (J). per. *(978-1-57022-548-2(6))* ECS Learning Systems, Inc.

TAKS MASTER Practice Test, Writing Gr. 4. 2004. (J). *(978-1-57022-533-8(8))* ECS Learning Systems, Inc.

TAKS MASTER Practice Test, Writing Gr. 7. 2004. (J). *(978-1-57022-534-5(6))* ECS Learning Systems, Inc.

Top That Publishing, creator. Writing My First Words: Early Days Magic Writing Book. 2007. (Illus.). 8p. (gr. -1-k). bds. *(978-1-84666-340-6(7))* Top That! Publishing PLC.

Vickers, Rebecca. Making Better Sentences: The Power of Structure & Meaning, 1 vol. 2013. (Find Your Way with Words Ser.). (ENG.). 56p. (gr. 6-7). 34.65 *(978-1-4329-7654-5(0))*; pap. 9.95 *(978-1-4329-7659-0(1))* Heinemann-Raintree.

—Punctuation & Spelling: Rules That Make Things Clear, 1 vol. 2013. (Find Your Way with Words Ser.). (ENG.). 56p. (gr. 6-7). 34.65 *(978-1-4329-7655-2(9))* Heinemann-Raintree.

Voyages in English: Writing & Grammar. 2004. (gr. 1-18). tchr. ed. *(978-0-8294-0980-2(7))*; (gr. 1-18). tchr. ed., wbk. ed. *(978-0-8294-1383-0(9))*; (gr. 1-18). stu. ed. *(978-0-8294-0981-9(5))*; (gr. 1-18). stu. ed., wbk. ed. *(978-0-8294-1382-3(0))*; (gr. 2-18). tchr. ed. *(978-0-8294-0982-6(3))*; (gr. 2-18). tchr. ed., wbk. ed. *(978-0-8294-1385-4(5))*; (gr. 2-18). stu. ed. *(978-0-8294-0983-3(1))*; (gr. 2-18). stu. ed., wbk. ed. *(978-0-8294-1384-7(7))*; (gr. 3-18). *(978-0-8294-1303-8(0))*; (gr. 3-18). tchr. ed. *(978-0-8294-0985-7(8))*; (gr. 3-18). tchr. ed., wbk. ed. *(978-0-8294-1319-9(7))*; (gr. 3-18). stu. ed. *(978-0-8294-0986-4(6))*; (gr. 3-18). stu. ed., wbk. ed. *(978-0-8294-1318-2(9))*; (gr. 4-18). tchr. ed., wbk. ed. *(978-0-8294-1321-2(9))*; (gr. 4-18). stu. ed. *(978-0-8294-0988-8(2))* Loyola Pr.

Wach, Martin. An Adventure in Writing. 2007. (Illus.). 32p. (J). (gr. -1-3). per. 14.95 *(978-0-929915-54-8(2))* Headline Bks., Inc.

Wasylyk, Thomas M. Second Edition Handwriting: A Self-Improvement Workbook. 2006. (ENG.). 80p. 7.95 *(978-1-931181-66-2(7)*, Item #139) Universal Publishing.

—Second Edition Handwriting: Beginning Cursive Writing. 2006. (ENG.). 80p. 7.95 *(978-1-931181-62-4(4)*, Item # 135) Universal Publishing.

—Second Edition Handwriting: Improving Cursive Writing. 2006. (ENG.). 80p. 7.95 *(978-1-931181-63-1(2)*, Item # 136) Universal Publishing.

—Second Edition Handwriting: Introduction to Cursive. 2006. 80p. 7.95 *(978-1-931181-61-7(6)*, Item # 134) Universal Publishing.

—Second Edition Handwriting: Manuscript Review & Enrichment. 2006. 7.95 *(978-1-931181-60-0(8)*, Item # 133) Universal Publishing.

—Second Edition Handwriting: Manuscript Writing. 2006. 80p. 7.95 *(978-1-931181-59-4(4)*, Item # 132) Universal Publishing.

—Second Edition Handwriting: Reading & Writing Readiness Skills. 2006. 80p. 7.95 *(978-1-931181-57-0(8)*, Item #130) Universal Publishing.

—Second Edition Handwriting: Writing for Learning. 2006. (ENG.). 80p. 7.95 *(978-1-931181-65-5(9)*, Item # 138) Universal Publishing.

—Second Edition Handwriting: Writing in Cursive. 2006. (ENG.). 80p. 7.95 *(978-1-931181-64-8(0)*, Item # 137) Universal Publishing.

—Second Edition Handwriting: Writing the Manuscript Letters. 2nd ed. 2006. 80p. 7.95 *(978-1-931181-58-7(6)*, Item #131) Universal Publishing.

Watson, Sharon. Jump in, A Workbook for Reluctant Writers: 2-book Set. Wile, Kathleen J., ed. 2006. per. 40.00 *(978-1-932012-76-7(1))* Apologia Educational Ministries, Inc.

—Jump in, A Workbook for Reluctant Writers: Student Text. Wile, Kathleen J., ed. 2006. per., wbk. ed. 30.00 *(978-1-932012-74-3(5))* Apologia Educational Ministries, Inc.

West, Penelope Pelham. Once upon a Time Nobody Could Read. 2009. pap. 9.00 *(978-1-61623-531-4(4))* Independent Pub.

Write on Target for Grade 5. 2006. (J). stu. ed., per., wbk. ed. 16.95 *(978-1-59230-159-1(2))* Englefield & Assocs., Inc.

Write on Target Grade 3: Student Workbook. 2005. (J). stu. ed., per. 10.95 *(978-1-59230-151-5(7))* Englefield & Assocs., Inc.

Write on Target Grade 4: Student Workbook. 2005. (J). stu. ed., per. 10.95 *(978-1-59230-149-2(5))* Englefield & Assocs., Inc.

Write on Target Grade 6: Student Workbook. 2005. (J). pap., stu. ed. 10.95 *(978-1-59230-157-7(6))* Englefield & Assocs., Inc.

Write on, Wipe off Writing. 2007. (Early Days: Copy & Learn Ser.). (Illus.). 40p. *(978-1-84666-390-1(3))* Top That! Publishing PLC.

Writing Handbook. (J). 15.00 *(978-1-931555-02-9(8))* Our Lady of Victory Schl.

Writing Paragraphs (Gr. 3-4) 2003. (J). *(978-1-58232-128-8(0))* ECS Learning Systems, Inc.

Writing Resource Book. (J). (gr. 2-9). *(978-0-89688-110-5(5)*, 88-110) Open Court Publishing Co.

Writing Sentences (Gr. 2-3) 2003. (J). *(978-1-58232-127-1(2))* ECS Learning Systems, Inc.

Writing Works with NC Wordcrafter & Joey: Grade 3+ 2004. 28.00 *(978-0-9790796-0-3(8))* PJR Assocs., Ltd.

Writing Works with NC Wordcrafter & Joey: Grade 4+ 2004. 28.00 *(978-0-9790796-1-0(6))* PJR Assocs., Ltd.

Writing Works with NC Wordcrafter & Joey: Grade 5+ 2004. 28.00 *(978-0-9790796-2-7(4))* PJR Assocs., Ltd.

RHINE RIVER AND VALLEY

Leavitt, Amie Jane. The Rhine River. 2012. (J). lib. bdg. 29.95 *(978-1-61228-297-8(0))* Mitchell Lane Pubs., Inc.

Miller, Gary. The Rhine: Europe's River Highway. 2010. (Rivers Around the World Ser.). (ENG., Illus.). 32p. (J). (gr. 5-8). lib. bdg. *(978-0-7787-7446-4(5))* Crabtree Publishing Co.

Miller, Gary G. & Miller, Gary. The Rhine: Europe's River Highway. 2010. (Rivers Around the World Ser.). (ENG., Illus.). 32p. (J). (gr. 5-8). pap. *(978-0-7787-7469-3(4))* Crabtree Publishing Co.

The Rhine. 2011. (River Journey Ser.). (ENG.). 48p. (YA). (gr. 5-8). 27.95 *(978-1-4488-6013-5(X)*, Rosen Reference) Rosen Publishing Group, Inc., The.

RHINE RIVER AND VALLEY—FICTION

Brabourne, Edward Hugessen Knatchbull-Hugessen. River Legends of the Thames & Rhine. Doré, Gustave, illus. 2005. (J). pap. *(978-0-486-44372-0(8))* Dover Pubns., Inc.

RHINOCEROSES

Arnold, Quinn M. Rhinoceroses. 2016. (Illus.). 24p. (J). *(978-1-60818-797-3(7)*, Creative Education) Creative Co., The.

Baxter, Bethany. Indian Rhinoceroses. 2013. (Awesome Armored Animals Ser.). 24p. (J). (gr. k-5). pap. 8.25 *(978-1-4777-0960-3(6))*; pap. 49.50 *(978-1-4777-0961-0(4))*; lib. bdg. 22.60 *(978-1-4777-0794-4(8))* Rosen Publishing Group, Inc., The. (PowerKids Pr.).

Bergeron, Alain M., et al. Les Rhinocéros. 2010. (FRE., Illus.). 64p. (J). pap. 8.95 *(978-2-89435-500-8(9))* Quintin Pubs./Editions Michel Quintin CAN. Dist: Crabtree Publishing Co.

Bodden, Valerie. Amazing Animals: Rhinoceroses. 2013. (Amazing Animals Ser.). (ENG.). 24p. (J). (gr. 1-3). pap. 8.99 *(978-0-89812-792-8(0)*, Creative Paperbacks) Creative Co., The.

—Rhinoceroses. 2013. (Illus.). 24p. (J). 25.65 *(978-1-60818-090-5(5)*, Creative Education) Creative Co., The.

Borgert-Spaniol, Megan. Baby Rhinos. 2017. (Super Cute! Ser.). (ENG., Illus.). 24p. (J). (gr. k-3). lib. bdg. 25.95 *(978-1-62617-546-4(2)*, Blastoff! Readers) Bellwether Media.

Carr, Aaron. Rhino. 2014. (Illus.). 24p. (J). *(978-1-62127-285-4(0))* Weigl Pubs., Inc.

Carson, Mary Kay. Emi & the Rhino Scientist. Uhlman, Tom, photos by. 2010. (Scientists in the Field Ser.). (ENG., Illus.). 64p. (J). (gr. 5-7). pap. 9.99 *(978-0-547-40850-7(1))* Houghton Mifflin Harcourt Publishing Co.

Ciovacco, Justine. Rhinoceroses. 2010. (Amazing Animals Ser.). (ENG.). 48p. (J). (gr. 2-6). pap. 10.50 *(978-1-4339-4023-1(X))*; lib. bdg. 28.00 *(978-1-4339-4022-4(1))* Stevens, Gareth Publishing LLLP. (Gareth Stevens Learning Library).

—Rhinoceroses. 2007. (J). *(978-1-59939-122-9(8)*, Reader's Digest Young Families, Inc.) Studio Fun International.

Claybourne, Anna. Rhino. 2012. (Animals on the Edge Ser.). (ENG., Illus.). 48p. (gr. 3-8). pap. 12.00 *(978-1-4081-4956-0(7)*, 9781408149560, Bloomsbury USA Childrens) Bloomsbury Publishing USA.

Czech, Jan M. The Rhino: A MyReportLinks. com Book. 2005. (Endangered & Threatened Animals Ser.). (Illus.). 48p. (J). lib. bdg. 25.26 *(978-0-7660-5062-4(9)*, MyReportLinks.com Bks.) Enslow Pubs., Inc.

Doudna, Kelly. It's a Baby Rhinoceros!, 1 vol. 2009. (Baby African Animals Ser.). (ENG., Illus.). 24p. (J). (gr. k-3). lib. bdg. 24.21 *(978-1-60453-158-9(4)*, SandCastle) ABDO Publishing Co.

Firestone, Mary. Top 50 Reasons to Care about Rhinos: Animals in Peril. 2010. (Top 50 Reasons to Care about Endangered Animals Ser.). (Illus.). 104p. (J). (gr. 5-9). 33.27 *(978-0-7660-3457-0(7))* Enslow Pubs., Inc.

Gish, Melissa. Rhinoceroses. (Living Wild Ser.). (Illus.). (J). 2012. (ENG.). 48p. (gr. 4-7). pap. 12.00 *(978-0-89812-675-4(4)*, Creative Paperbacks) 2011. 46p. 35.65 *(978-1-60818-083-7(2)*, Creative Education) Creative Co., The.

Goecke, Michael P. Giant Rhino, 1 vol. 2003. (Prehistoric Animals Ser.). (ENG.). 24p. (gr. k-4). 25.65 *(978-1-57765-969-3(4)*, Buddy Bks.) ABDO Publishing Co.

—Woolly Rhinoceros, 1 vol. 2003. (Prehistoric Animals Set II Ser.). (ENG.). 24p. (gr. k-4). 25.65 *(978-1-57765-978-5(3)*, Buddy Bks.) ABDO Publishing Co.

Green, Jen. Rhinoceros. 2009. (Illus.). 52p. (J). *(978-0-7172-8034-6(9))* Grolier, Ltd.

Grucella, Ethan. Rhinoceroses. 2010. (Animals That Live in the Grasslands Ser.). (ENG.). 24p. (J). (gr. -1-3). pap. 8.15 *(978-1-4339-3882-5(0))*; lib. bdg. 22.60 *(978-1-4339-3881-8(2))* Stevens, Gareth Publishing LLLP.

Hamilton, Garry. Rhino Rescue: Changing the Future for Endangered Wildlife. 2006. (Firefly Animal Rescue Ser.). (ENG., Illus.). 64p. (J). (gr. 5-12). 19.95 *(978-1-55297-912-9(1)*, 9781552979129); pap. 9.95 *(978-1-55297-910-5(5)*, 9781552979105) Firefly Bks., Ltd.

Jones, Jack. Chizi's Tale. Taylor, Jacqui, illus. 2nd ed. 2016. (ENG.). 28p. (J). (gr. k-2). pap. 3.99 *(978-1-943154-00-5(7))* Peek-A-Boo Publishing.

Kalman, Bobbie. Endangered Rhinoceros. 2004. (Earth's Endangered Animals Ser.). (ENG., Illus.). 32p. (J). pap. *(978-0-7787-1898-7(0))* Crabtree Publishing Co.

Katirgis, Jane & Czech, Jan M. Endangered Rhinos. 2015. (Wildlife at Risk Ser.). (ENG.). 48p. (J). (gr. 6-6). pap. 11.70 *(978-0-7660-6900-8(1))*; (Illus.). 27.93 *(978-0-7660-6902-2(8))* Enslow Pubs., Inc.

Kirk, Daniel. Rhino in the House: The Story of Saving Samia. 2017. (ENG., Illus.). 40p. (J). (gr. -1-3). 17.95 *(978-1-4197-2316-2(2)*, Abrams Bks. for Young Readers) Abrams, Inc.

Kopp, Megan. Rhinos. 2014. (Illus.). 48p. (J). *(978-1-62127-228-1(1))* Weigl Pubs., Inc.

Latta, Jan. Rudy el Rinoceronte. 2007. (Familias de animales salvajes (Wild Animal Families) Ser.). (SPA., Illus.). 24p. (gr. 1-4). lib. bdg. 24.00 *(978-0-8368-7970-4(8),* Gareth Stevens Learning Library) Stevens, Gareth Publishing LLLP.
—Rudy the Rhinoceros. 2007. (Wild Animal Families Ser.). (Illus.). 24p. (gr. 1-4). pap. 8.15 *(978-0-8368-7778-6(0));* lib. bdg. 24.00 *(978-0-8368-7771-7(3))* Stevens, Gareth Publishing LLLP. (Gareth Stevens Learning Library).
Macheske, Felicia. Hefty Hulks: Rhinoceros. 2017. (Guess What Ser.). (ENG., Illus.). 24p. (J). (gr. k-2). lib. bdg. 28.50 *(978-1-63472-169-1(1),* 209248) Cherry Lake Publishing.
Marsico, Katie. Rhinos. 2017. (True Book(tm) — The Most Endangered Ser.). (ENG., Illus.). 48p. (J). lib. bdg. 31.00 *(978-0-531-22729-9(4),* Children's Pr.) Scholastic Library Publishing.
Mattern, Joanne. Rhinoceroses, 1 vol. 2010. (Asian Animals Ser.). (ENG.). 24p. (gr. k-1). pap. 7.29 *(978-1-4296-4846-2(5));* pap. 41.70 *(978-1-4296-5201-8(2))* Capstone Press of Coughlan Cos. (Pebble Plus).
Meeker, Clare Hodgson. Rhino Airlift! And More True Stories of Saving Animals. 2016. (NGK Chapters Ser.). (ENG., Illus.). 112p. (J). (gr. 2-5). pap. 5.99 *(978-1-4263-2311-9(5),* National Geographic Children's Bks.) National Geographic Society.
—Rhino Rescue! And More True Stories of Saving Animals. 2016. (NGK Chapters Ser.). (ENG., Illus.). 112p. (J). (gr. 2-5). lib. bdg. 15.90 *(978-1-4263-2312-6(3),* National Geographic Children's Bks.) National Geographic Society.
Morey, Allan. Rhinoceroses Are Awesome! 2015. (Awesome Asian Animals Ser.). (ENG., Illus.). 32p. (gr. 1-2). lib. bdg. 27.32 *(978-1-4914-3908-1(4))* Capstone Press of Coughlan Cos.
Nelson, Kristin L. African Rhinos. 2005. (Pull Ahead Bks.). (Illus.). 32p. (J). 22.60 *(978-0-8225-2423-6(6),* Lerner Pubns.); (ENG., per. 7.95 *(978-0-8225-2442-7(2))* Lerner Publishing Group.
Orme, Helen. Rhinos in Danger. 2006. (Wildlife Survival Ser.). (Illus.). 32p. (J). (gr. 2-5). lib. bdg. 25.27 *(978-1-59716-265-4(5))* Bearport Publishing Co., Inc.
Owen, Ruth. Rhinoceroses. 2012. (Dr. Bob's Amazing World of Animals Ser.). (Illus.). 32p. (J). (gr. k-5). pap. 11.75 *(978-1-61533-560-2(9));* lib. bdg. 26.50 *(978-1-61533-550-3(1))* Windmill Bks.
Pelusey, Michael & Pelusey, Jane. Rhinoceroses & Hippopotamuses. 2008. (Zoo Animals Ser.). 32p. (gr. 2-3). lib. bdg. 18.56 *(978-0-7614-3150-3(0),* Benchmark Bks.) Marshall Cavendish Corp.
Pohl, Kathleen. Rhinos. 2007. (Animals I See at the Zoo Ser.). 24p. (gr. k-3). pap. 8.15 *(978-0-8368-8229-2(6));* (Illus.). lib. bdg. 22.00 *(978-0-8368-8222-3(9))* Stevens, Gareth Publishing LLLP. (Weekly Reader Leveled Readers).
—Rhinos/Rinocerontes. 2007. (Animals I See at the Zoo/Animales que Veo en el Zoológico Ser.). (SPA & ENG., Illus.). 24p. (gr. k-3). lib. bdg. 22.00 *(978-0-8368-8236-0(9),* Weekly Reader Leveled Readers) Stevens, Gareth Publishing LLLP.
Pope, Kristen. Black Rhinos. 2015. (Endangered Animals Ser.). (ENG.). 24p. (J). (gr. 1-4). 27.07 *(978-1-63143-964-3(2),* 208799) Child's World, Inc., The.
Riggs, Kate & Arnold, Quinn M. Rhinoceroses. 2017. (Seedlings Ser.). (ENG., Illus.). 24p. (J). (gr. k-2). pap. 7.99 *(978-1-62832-350-4(7),* Creative Paperbacks) Creative Co., The.
Schuetz, Kari. Rhinoceroses. 2012. (Animal Safari Ser.). (ENG., Illus.). 24p. (J). (gr. k-3). lib. bdg. 25.95 *(978-1-60014-719-7(4),* Blastoff! Readers) Bellwether Media.
Scott, Jonathan & Scott, Angela. Africa's Big Three. Scott, Jonathan & Scott, Angela, illus. 2006. (Collins Big Cat Ser.). (ENG., Illus.). 56p. (J). (gr. 2-2). pap. 6.99 *(978-0-00-718693-8(2))* HarperCollins Pubs. Ltd. GBR. Dist: Independent Pubs. Group.
Snyder, Lydia. Rhinos in Danger. 2013. (Animals at Risk Ser.). 24p. (J). (gr. 2-5). pap. 8.15 *(978-1-4339-9160-8(8));* pap. 48.90 *(978-1-4339-9161-5(6));* (ENG., Illus.). lib. bdg. 22.60 *(978-1-4339-9159-2(4))* Stevens, Gareth Publishing LLLP.
Soundprints, creator. Rhinoceros's Bathtime. 2011. (Let's Go to the Zoo! Ser.). (ENG., Illus.). 16p. (gr. -1). 5.95 *(978-1-60727-457-5(4))* Soundprints.
Stone, Tanya Lee. Rhinos. 2003. (Wild Wild World Ser.). 24p. (YA). 24.94 *(978-1-56711-821-6(6),* Blackbirch Pr., Inc.) Cengage Gale.
Tait, Leia. Emi the Sumatran Rhino. 2008. (Inspiring Animals Ser.). (Illus.). 24p. (J). (gr. 2-4). pap. 8.95 *(978-1-59036-857-2(6));* lib. bdg. 24.45 *(978-1-59036-856-5(8))* Weigl Pubs., Inc.
Thomas, Isabel. Elephant vs. Rhinoceros. 2017. (Animal Rivals Ser.). (ENG.). 24p. (gr. k-2). lib. bdg. 23.32 ***(978-1-4846-4072-2(1),*** Heinemann Read & Learn) Heinemann-Raintree.
Walden, Katherine. Rhinoceroses. 2009. (Safari Animals Ser.). 24p. (Illus.). (J). (gr. k-3). pap. 8.25 *(978-1-4358-3061-5(X));* (gr. 1-1). 42.50 *(978-1-60852-960-5(6));* (J). (gr. -1-2). lib. bdg. 22.60 *(978-1-4358-2687-8(6))* Rosen Publishing Group, Inc., The. (PowerKids Pr.).
Walker, Sally M. Rhinos. rev. ed. 2007. (Nature Watch Ser.). (ENG., Illus.). 48p. (gr. 4-8). lib. bdg. 27.93 *(978-0-8225-6600-7(1),* Lerner Pubns.) Lerner Publishing Group.
Zane, Dory. How to Track a Rhinoceros, 1. 2014. (Scatalog: a Kid's Field Guide to Animal Poop Ser.). (ENG.). 24p. (J). (gr. k-5). 23.60 *(978-1-61533-886-3(1),* Windmill Bks.) Rosen Publishing Group, Inc., The.

RHINOCEROSES—FICTION

Anholt, Laurence. A Kiss Like This. Anholt, Catherine, illus. 2009. (ENG.). 32p. (J). (gr. -1-1). pap. 7.95 *(978-1-84507-862-1(4),* Frances Lincoln) Quarto Publishing Group UK GBR. Dist: Hachette Bk. Group.
Blecker, Lisa. The Good in Me from a to Z by Dottie. Blecker, Lisa, illus. 2006. (Illus.). bds. 20.00 *(978-1-931492-21-8(2))* Discover Writing Pr.
Borgeson, Grace. Douwlina: A Rhino's Story. 2012. (ENG., Illus.). 32p. 19.95 *(978-1-936474-63-9(8),* 87298107-73d6-41ce-8918-67bd7c8ae307) Bright Sky Pr.
Butler, Dori. How the Rhino Got Wrinkly Skin: An Adaptation of a Rudyard Kipling Story. 2006. (J). pap. *(978-1-4108-7162-6(2))* Benchmark Education Co.
Cazet, Denys. Minnie & Moo & the Seven Wonders of the World. Cazet, Denys, illus. 2003. (ENG., Illus.). 144p. (J). (gr. 2-5). 19.99 *(978-0-689-85330-2(0),* Atheneum/Richard Jackson Bks.) Simon & Schuster Children's Publishing.
Clough, Lisa. Petal & Poppy. Briant, Ed, illus. 2014. (Green Light Readers Level 2 Ser.). (ENG.). 32p. (J). (gr. -1-3). pap. 3.99 *(978-0-544-11380-0(2),* HMH Books For Young Readers) Houghton Mifflin Harcourt Publishing Co.
—Petal & Poppy & the Penguin. Briant, Ed, illus. 2014. (Green Light Readers Level 2 Ser.). (ENG.). 32p. (J). (gr. -1-3). 12.99 *(978-0-544-13770-7(1));* pap. 3.99 *(978-0-544-13330-3(7))* Houghton Mifflin Harcourt Publishing Co. (HMH Books For Young Readers).
Corderoy, Tracey. More! Warnes, Tim, illus. 2015. (ENG.). 32p. (J). (gr. -1-3). 16.99 *(978-1-58925-193-9(8))* Tiger Tales.
—No! Warnes, Tim, illus. 2015. (ENG.). 28p. (J). (gr. -1-2). bds. 7.99 *(978-1-58925-208-0(X))* Tiger Tales.
Damjan, Mischa. Big Red Squirrel & the Little Rhinoceros. Steadman, Ralph, illus. 2010. (ENG.). 32p. (J). (gr. -1-k). 15.99 *(978-1-84365-130-7(0),* Pavilion) Pavilion Bks. GBR. Dist: Independent Pubs. Group.
de Brunhoff, Laurent. Babar & the Wully-Wully. 2012. (ENG., Illus.). 40p. (J). (gr. k-2). 15.95 *(978-1-4197-0381-2(1),* Abrams Bks. for Young Readers) Abrams, Inc.
Derrick, Patricia. Riley the Rhinoceros. Martinez, J-P Loppo, illus. 2007. 32p. (J). 18.95 incl. audio compact disk *(978-1-933818-15-3(8))* Animalations.
Ende, Michael. Norberto Nucagorda, Level 5.5. Wittenberg, Stella, illus. 2003. (SPA.). 32p. (J). (gr. 3-5). pap. 8.95 *(978-84-204-3719-4(0),* AF1328) Santillana USA Publishing Co., Inc.
Eubank, Patti Reeder, illus. Just Where You Belong. 2004. 32p. (J). 8.95 *(978-0-8249-5481-9(5),* Ideal Pubns.) Worthy Publishing.
Gibbs, Stuart. Big Game. 2015. (FunJungle Ser.). (ENG.). 352p. (J). (gr. 3-7). 17.99 *(978-1-4814-2333-5(9),* Simon & Schuster Bks. For Young Readers) Simon & Schuster Bks. For Young Readers.
Gilligan, Alison. Search for the Black Rhino. 2011. (Illus.). 144p. (J). pap. 6.99 *(978-1-937133-01-6(X))* Chooseco LLC.
Green, Kim. Rinny Rhino Wants Pink Pearls & a Polka Dotted Penguin. 2013. 46p. pap. 14.99 *(978-1-61863-530-3(1))* Bookstand Publishing.
Grey, Chelsea Gillian. Ema the Rhinoceros. 2004. (African Wildlife Foundation Kids Ser.). (ENG., Illus.). 36p. (J). (gr. -1-2). 8.95 *(978-1-59249-202-2(9),* SD6500) Soundprints.
Hanson, Anders. Rhino Horns, 1 vol. Nobens, Cheryl A., illus. 2006. (Animal Tales Ser.). (ENG.). 24p. (J). (gr. k-3). lib. bdg. 24.21 *(978-1-59679-963-9(3),* SandCastle) ABDO Publishing Co.
—Rhino Horns. Nobens, C. A., illus. 2006. (Fact & Fiction Ser.). 24p. (J). pap. 48.42 *(978-1-59679-964-6(1))* ABDO Publishing Co.
—La Tuba Del Rinoceronte. Nobens, C. A., illus. 2006. (Realidad y Ficción Ser.). (SPA.). 24p. (J). 48.42 *(978-1-59928-666-2(1))* ABDO Publishing Co.
—La Tuba del Rinoceronte, 1 vol. Nobens, C. A., illus. 2007. (Cuentos de Animales Ser.). (SPA & ENG.). 24p. (J). (gr. k-3). lib. bdg. 24.21 *(978-1-59928-665-5(3),* SandCastle) ABDO Publishing Co.
Harrison, Kevin. I Know a Rhino. Blue, Buster, illus. 2nd rev. ed. 2006. 37p. (J). (gr. -1-3). per. 10.99 *(978-1-59092-223-1(9))* Blue Forge Pr.
Howard, Ryan & Howard, Krystle. The Away Game (Little Rhino #5) Madrid, Erwin, illus. 2017. (Little Rhino Ser.: 5). (ENG.). 112p. (J). (gr. 2-5). pap. 5.99 *(978-1-338-05234-3(9),* Scholastic Paperbacks) Scholastic, Inc.
Hughes, Fox Carlton. Rainbow Rhino. Hughes, Fox Carlton, illus. 2007. (ENG., Illus.). 36p. (J). (gr. -1-3). 16.95 *(978-0-9790275-3-6(5))* Ovation Bks.
Iadonisi, Carmin & Word, Amanda. Whiny Whiny Rhino. Iadonisi, Carmin & Word, Amanda, illus. 2014. (ENG., Illus.). 32p. (J). 16.99 *(978-0-9903623-0-2(2))* Blue Blanket Publishing.
Jahn-Clough, Lisa, et al. Petal & Poppy & the Mystery Valentine. Briant, Ed, illus. 2015. (Green Light Readers Level 2 Ser.). (ENG.). 32p. (J). (gr. 1-4). pap. 3.99 *(978-0-544-55549-5(X),* HMH Books For Young Readers) Houghton Mifflin Harcourt Publishing Co.
Jones, Stella J. Glitter. Abbot, Judi, illus. 2017. (ENG.). 32p. (J). (gr. -1-2). 16.99 ***(978-1-68010-039-6(4))*** Tiger Tales.
Kemp, Anna. Rhinos Don't Eat Pancakes. Ogilvie, Sara, illus. 2015. (ENG.). 32p. (J). (gr. -1-3). 17.99 *(978-1-4814-3845-2(X),* Simon & Schuster/Paula Wiseman Bks.) Simon & Schuster/Paula Wiseman Bks.
Kipling, Rudyard. How the Rhinoceros Got His Skin, 1 vol. Raglin, Tim, illus. 2005. (Rabbit Ears: A Classic Tale Ser.). (ENG.). 28p. (gr. 2-7). 25.65 *(978-1-59197-750-6(9))* Spotlight.
—How the Rhinoceros Got His Skin: The Graphic Novel, 1 vol. Rodriguez, Pedro, illus. 2012. (Graphic Spin Ser.). (ENG.). 40p. (gr. 1-3). pap. 5.95 *(978-1-4342-3882-5(2),* Graphic Revolve) Stone Arch Bks.
—How the Rhinoceros Got His Skin: The Graphic Novel, 1 vol. Rodriguez, Pedro, illus. 2012. (Graphic Spin Ser.). (ENG.). 40p. (gr. 1-3). lib. bdg. 23.99 *(978-1-4342-3025-6(2),* Graphic Revolve) Stone Arch Bks.
Lester, Helen. A Porcupine Named Fluffy. Munsinger, Lynn, illus. 2013. (Laugh-Along Lessons Ser.). (ENG.). 32p. (J). (gr. -1-3). 8.99 *(978-0-544-00319-4(5))* Houghton Mifflin Harcourt Publishing Co.
Low-DuMond, Sabrina. Weakling Willie. 2008. 28p. pap. 24.95 *(978-1-60474-258-9(5))* America Star Bks.
Mammano, Julie. Rhinos Who Play Baseball. Mammano, Julie, illus. 2006. (Illus.). 24p. (J). (gr. k-4). reprint ed. 14.00 *(978-0-7567-9995-3(3))* DIANE Publishing Co.
—Rhinos Who Rescue. 2007. (Rhinos Ser.: RHIN). (ENG., Illus.). 32p. (J). (gr. -1-1). 13.95 *(978-0-8118-5419-1(1))* Chronicle Bks. LLC.
McCully, Emily Arnold. Clara: The (Mostly) True Story of the Rhinoceros Who Dazzled Kings, Inspired Artists, & Won the Hearts of Everyone . . . While She Ate Her Way up & down a Continent! McCully, Emily Arnold, illus. 2016. (ENG., Illus.). 48p. (J). (gr. -1-3). 17.99 *(978-0-553-52246-4(9),* Schwartz & Wade Bks.) Random Hse. Children's Bks.
Milgrim, David. See Otto. Milgrim, David, illus. 2016. (Adventures of Otto Ser.). (ENG., Illus.). 32p. (J). (gr. -1-k). pap. 3.99 *(978-1-4814-6796-4(4),* Simon Spotlight) Simon Spotlight.
O'Brien, Timothy J. Rheemer the Rhymer Rhinoceros. 2009. *(978-1-61584-106-6(7))* Independent Pub.
Olsen, Grant Orrin. Rhino Trouble. Carpenter, Mike, illus. 2015. (J). 14.99 *(978-1-4621-1665-2(5))* Cedar Fort, Inc./CFI Distribution.
O'Malley, Kevin. Bruno, You're Late for School! 2012. (ENG.). 32p. (J). (gr. -1-3). 16.95 *(978-1-59687-397-1(3),* Milk & Cookies) ibooks, Inc.
Pennington, Beverly A. Jonathan's Discovery. Pennington, Beverly A., illus. 2006. (Illus.). 29p. (J). (gr. -1-3). pap. 12.95 *(978-1-56167-920-1(8))* American Literary Pr.
Powers, John. Seymour & the Big Red Rhino. Colavecchio, Alan, illus. 2005. 32p. (J). (gr. -1-3). 14.95 *(978-1-929039-21-0(2))* Ambassador Bks., Inc.
Prose, Francine. Rhino, Rhino, Sweet Potato. Armstrong, Matthew S., illus. 2009. 32p. (J). (gr. -1-1). lib. bdg. 18.89 *(978-0-06-008079-2(5))* HarperCollins Pubs.
Puttock, Simon. Who's the Boss Rhinoceros? Busby, Ailie, illus. 32p. (J). pap. 8.99 *(978-0-7497-4354-3(9))* Egmont Bks., Ltd. GBR. Dist: Trafalgar Square Publishing.
Raúl, III, illus. Otto Es un Rinoceronte. 2003. (SPA.). 102p. (J). (gr. 3-5). pap. 12.95 *(978-958-24-0179-5(6))* Santillana USA Publishing Co., Inc.
Remkiewicz, Frank. Gus Grows a Plant. 2012. (Illus.). (J). pap. *(978-0-545-34052-6(7))* Scholastic, Inc.
Rieback, Milton. The Adventures of Webb Ellis, a Tale from the Heart of Africa: The Return of the Protectors. Crowley, Cheryl, illus. 2006. (J). lib. bdg. 19.95 *(978-0-9777440-0-8(0))* Inyati Press.
Ross, Tony, illus. Rita's Rhino. 2015. (J). 17.32 *(978-1-4677-6319-6(5))* Lerner Publishing Group.
Shriver, Chelsea & Grey, Chelsea Gillian. Ema the Rhinoceros. Leeper, Christopher, illus. 2005. (African Wildlife Foundation Kids Ser.). (ENG.). 36p. (J). (gr. -1-2). 9.95 *(978-1-59249-180-3(4),* PS6550) Soundprints.
—Ema the Rhinoceros. 2005. (African Wildlife Foundation Kids Ser.). (ENG., Illus.). 36p. (J). (gr. -1-2). 2.95 *(978-1-59249-179-7(0),* S6550) Soundprints.
—Ema the Rhinoceros. Leeper, Christopher J., tr. Leeper, Christopher J., illus. 2005. (African Wildlife Foundation Ser.). (ENG.). 36p. (J). (gr. -1-2). 14.95 *(978-1-59249-177-3(4),* H6500); pap. 6.95 *(978-1-59249-178-0(2),* S6500) Soundprints.
Silverstein, Shel. Who Wants a Cheap Rhinoceros? Silverstein, Shel, illus. 50th anniv. ed. 2014. (ENG., Illus.). 64p. (J). (gr. -1-3). 17.99 *(978-1-4814-1593-4(X),* Simon & Schuster Bks. For Young Readers) Simon & Schuster Bks. For Young Readers.
Stockland, Patricia M. Stop the Grassfires!, 1 vol. Haugen, Ryan, illus. 2008. (Safari Friends Ser.). (ENG.). 32p. (gr. -1-3). 28.50 *(978-1-60270-086-4(9),* Looking Glass Library) ABDO Publishing Co.
Summy, Barrie. I So Don't Do Mysteries. 2009. (ENG.). 288p. (J). (gr. 3-7). 6.99 *(978-0-385-73603-9(7),* Yearling) Random Hse. Children's Bks.
Terry, Michael. Rhinos Horns. 2003. (Illus.). (J). *(978-1-58234-796-7(4),* Bloomsbury USA Childrens) Bloomsbury Publishing USA.
Ulick, Michael Ackerman. Romeo the Rhino's Rocky Romance: A Cautionary Tale about Differences. Guy, Will, illus. 32p. (J). 15.95 *(978-0-9679813-0-7(1))* Footprints Pr.
Willis, Jeanne. The Really Rude Rhino. Ross, Tony, illus. 2007. (ENG.). 32p. (J). (gr. -1-k). per. 12.99 *(978-1-84270-571-1(7))* Andersen Pr. GBR. Dist: Independent Pubs. Group.
You Should Try That with a Rhino: Individual Title Six-Packs. (gr. -1-2). 23.00 *(978-0-7635-8822-9(9))* Rigby Education.

RHODE ISLAND

Allio, Mark R. R Is for Rhode Island Red: A Rhode Island Alphabet. Begin, Mary Jane, illus. 2005. (Discover America State by State Ser.). (ENG.). 40p. (J). (gr. k-5). 17.95 *(978-1-58536-149-6(6))* Sleeping Bear Pr.
Feinstein, Stephen. Rhode Island: A MyReportLinks.com Book. 2003. (States Ser.). (Illus.). 48p. (J). (gr. 4-10). lib. bdg. 25.26 *(978-0-7660-5028-0(9),* MyReportLinks.com Bks.) Enslow Pubs., Inc.
Gamble, Adam. Good Night Rhode Island. Rosen, Anne, illus. 2008. (Good Night Our World Ser.). (ENG.). 20p. (J). (gr. k — 1). bds. 9.95 *(978-1-60219-024-5(0))* Good Night Bks.
Hallinan, Val. Rhode Island. 2008. (ENG.). 80p. (J). pap. 7.95 *(978-0-531-20812-0(5),* Children's Pr.) Scholastic Library Publishing.
Klein, Ted. Rhode Island. 2nd rev. ed. 2007. (Celebrate the States Ser.). 144p. (gr. 6). lib. bdg. 42.79 *(978-0-7614-2560-1(8),* Benchmark Bks.) Marshall Cavendish Corp.
Koontz, Robin Michal. Rhode Island: The Ocean State. 2010. (Our Amazing States Ser.). (Illus.). 24p. (J). pap. 8.25 *(978-1-4488-0732-1(8),* PowerKids Pr.) Rosen Publishing Group, Inc., The.
Labella, Susan. Rhode Island. 2006. (Rookie Read-About Geography Ser.). (ENG., Illus.). 32p. (J). (gr. 1-2). lib. bdg. 20.50 *(978-0-516-25388-6(3))* Scholastic Library Publishing.
Maine, Tyler. Rhode Island. 2016. (States Ser.). (ENG., Illus.). 32p. (gr. 3-4). lib. bdg. 27.32 *(978-1-5157-0427-0(0))* Next Page Pr., The.
Marsh, Carole. Rhode Island Current Events Projects: 30 Cool, Activities, Crafts, Experiments & More for Kids to Do to Learn about Your State! 2003. (Rhode Island Experience Ser.). 32p. (gr. k-8). pap. 5.95 *(978-0-635-02058-1(0),* Marsh, Carole Bks.) Gallopade International.
—Rhode Island Geography Projects: 30 Cool, Activities, Crafts, Experiments & More for Kids to Do to Learn about Your State! 2003. (Rhode Island Experience Ser.). 32p. (gr. k-5). pap. 5.95 *(978-0-635-01858-8(6),* Marsh, Carole Bks.) Gallopade International.
—Rhode Island Government Projects: 30 Cool, Activities, Crafts, Experiments & More for Kids to Do to Learn about Your State! 2003. (Rhode Island Experience Ser.). 32p. (gr. k-5). pap. 5.95 *(978-0-635-01958-5(2),* Marsh, Carole Bks.) Gallopade International.
—Rhode Island History Projects: 30 Cool, Activities, Crafts, Experiments & More for Kids to Do to Learn about Your State! 2003. (Rhode Island Experience Ser.). 32p. (gr. k-5). pap. 5.95 *(978-0-635-01808-3(X),* Marsh, Carole Bks.) Gallopade International.
—Rhode Island People Projects: 30 Cool, Activities, Crafts, Experiments & More for Kids to Do to Learn about Your State! 2003. (Rhode Island Experience Ser.). 32p. (gr. k-5). pap. 5.95 *(978-0-635-02008-6(4),* Marsh, Carole Bks.) Gallopade International.
—Rhode Island Symbols & Facts Projects: 30 Cool, Activities, Crafts, Experiments & More for Kids to Do to Learn about Your State! 2003. (Rhode Island Experience Ser.). 32p. (gr. k-5). pap. 5.95 *(978-0-635-01908-0(6),* Marsh, Carole Bks.) Gallopade International.
Mattern, Joanne. Rhode Island: The Ocean State. 2003. (World Almanac Library of the States). (Illus.). 48p. (gr. 4-9). pap. 14.05 *(978-0-8368-5330-8(X));* lib. bdg. 31.00 *(978-0-8368-5159-5(5))* Stevens, Gareth Publishing LLLP. (Gareth Stevens Learning Library).
Murray, Julie. Rhode Island, 1 vol. 2006. (United States Ser.). (ENG., Illus.). 32p. (gr. 2-4). 27.07 *(978-1-59197-698-1(7),* Buddy Bks.) ABDO Publishing Co.
Petreycik, Rick. Rhode Island. 2005. (It's My State! Ser.). (Illus.). 80p. (J). (gr. 4-7). lib. bdg. 27.07 *(978-0-7614-1859-7(8),* Benchmark Bks.) Marshall Cavendish Corp.
Petreyick, Rick. Rhode Island. 2013. (It's My State 2nd Ed 5 Ser.). 80p. (J). (gr. 4-8). pap. 17.64 *(978-1-62712-103-3(X))* Cavendish Square Publishing.
Severin, Carol. Rhode Island. 2006. (Portraits of the States Ser.). 32p. (gr. 2-6). pap. 10.50 *(978-0-8368-4724-6(5));* (Illus.). lib. bdg. 26.00 *(978-0-8368-4707-9(5))* Stevens, Gareth Publishing LLLP. (Gareth Stevens Learning Library).
Warner, J. F. Rhode Island. 2012. lib. bdg. 25.26 *(978-0-7613-4555-8(8),* Lerner Pubns.) Lerner Publishing Group.
Way, Jennifer. Rhode Island. 2009. (Bilingual Library of the United States of America Ser.). (ENG & SPA.). 32p. (gr. 2-2). 47.90 *(978-1-60853-384-8(0),* Editorial Buenas Letras) Rosen Publishing Group, Inc., The.
—Rhode Island. Brusca, Maria Cristina, tr. from ENG. 2006. (Bilingual Library of the United States of America Ser.: Set 2). (ENG & SPA., Illus.). 32p. (J). (gr. 3-6). lib. bdg. 25.25 *(978-1-4042-3105-4(6))* Rosen Publishing Group, Inc., The.
Weintraub, A. How to Draw Rhode Island's Sights & Symbols. 2009. (Kid's Guide to Drawing America Ser.). 32p. (gr. k-k). 50.50 *(978-1-61511-093-3(3),* PowerKids Pr.) Rosen Publishing Group, Inc., The.

RHODE ISLAND—FICTION

Ashton, Kenneth. Gale's Gold Ring: The Legend of Lincoln's Lost Gold. Ashton-Briggs, Shelley, illus. 2012. (ENG.). 198p. pap. 14.95 *(978-1-4327-8224-5(X))* Outskirts Pr., Inc.
Bruchac, Joseph. Whisper in the Dark. Comport, Sally Wern, illus. 2009. (ENG.). 192p. (J). (gr. 5). pap. 6.99 *(978-0-06-058089-6(5))* HarperCollins Pubs.
Castlemon, Harry. No Moss; or, the Career of a Rolling Stone, by Harry Castlemon [Pseud.]. 2006. 328p. per. 23.99 *(978-1-4255-3290-1(X))* Michigan Publishing.
Ciocca, Gina. Last Year's Mistake. 2015. (ENG., Illus.). 320p. (YA). (gr. 9). 17.99 *(978-1-4814-3223-8(0),* Simon Pulse) Simon Pulse.
Cullen, Sean. Hamish X Goes to Providence Rhode Island. 2009. (ENG.). 288p. (J). (gr. 7-18). 9.99 *(978-0-14-316920-8(3),* Puffin Canada) Penguin Random House Canada Young Readers CAN. Dist: Penguin Random Hse. LLC.
Curtis, Alice. A Little Maid of Newport. Price, Hattie Longstreet, illus. 2006. (Little Maid Ser.). (ENG.). 212p. (J). (gr. 4-7). pap. 12.95 *(978-1-55709-339-4(3))* Applewood Bks.
Dunn, Robert, illus. The Littlest Bunny in Rhode Island: An Easter Adventure. 2015. (ENG.). 32p. (J). (-3). 9.99 *(978-1-4926-1189-9(1),* Sourcebooks Jabberwocky) Sourcebooks, Inc.
Ferrari, Michael. Born to Fly. 2011. (ENG.). 224p. (J). (gr. 3-7). 6.99 *(978-0-375-84607-6(7),* Yearling) Random Hse. Children's Bks.
Fine, Sarah. Fractured, 0 vols. 2013. (Guards of the Shadowlands Ser.: 2). (ENG.). 448p. (YA). (gr. 9-12). pap. 9.99 *(978-1-4778-1691-2(7),* 9781477816912, Amazon Children's Publishing) Amazon Publishing.
Freitas, Donna. Gold Medal Summer. (ENG.). 240p. (J). 2014. (gr. 5-9). pap. 6.99 *(978-0-545-32789-3(X))* 2012. (gr. 4-7). 16.99 *(978-0-545-32788-6(1))* Scholastic, Inc. (Levine, Arthur A. Bks.).
Gray, Claudia. Spellcaster. 2013. (Spellcaster Ser.: 1). (ENG.). 400p. (YA). (gr. 8). 17.99 *(978-0-06-196120-5(5),* HarperTeen) HarperCollins Pubs.
—Steadfast. (Spellcaster Ser.: 2). (ENG.). (YA). (gr. 8). 2015. 368p. pap. 9.99 *(978-0-06-196123-6(X))* 2014. 352p. 17.99 *(978-0-06-196122-9(1))* HarperCollins Pubs. (HarperTeen).
Griffin, Adele. Tighter. (ENG.). (YA). (gr. 7). 2012. 240p. pap. 8.99 *(978-0-375-85933-5(0),* Ember) 2011. 224p. 16.99 *(978-0-375-86645-6(0),* Knopf Bks. for Young Readers) Random Hse. Children's Bks.
—Where I Want to Be. 2007. (ENG.). 176p. (YA). (gr. 7-18). 7.99 *(978-0-14-240948-0(0),* Speak) Penguin Young Readers Group.
Hood, Ann. Clara Barton: Angel of the Battlefield. Kwasney, Karl et al, illus. 2012. (Treasure Chest Ser.: 1). (ENG.). 208p. (J). (gr. 3-7). pap. 6.99 *(978-0-448-45467-2(X),* Grosset & Dunlap) Penguin Young Readers Group.
—Jewel of the East. Kwasny, Karl et al, illus. 2012. (Treasure Chest Ser.: 3). (ENG.). 208p. (J). (gr. 3-7). 15.99 *(978-0-448-45473-3(4));* pap. 6.99 *(978-0-448-45469-6(6))* Penguin Young Readers Group. (Grosset & Dunlap).
Hood, Ann & Altmann, Scott. Angel of the Battlefield. Kwasney, Karl & Zilber, Denis, illus. 2012. (Treasure Chest Ser.: 1). (ENG.). 240p. (J). (gr. 3-7). 15.99 *(978-0-448-45471-9(8),* Grosset & Dunlap) Penguin Young Readers Group.
James, Eric. A Halloween Scare in Rhode Island. Le Ray, Marina, illus. 2015. (ENG.). 32p. (J). (-5). 9.99 *(978-1-4926-2398-4(9),* 9781492623984, Sourcebooks Jabberwocky) Sourcebooks, Inc.
—Santa's Sleigh Is on Its Way to Rhode Island: A Christmas Adventure. Dunn, Robert, illus. 2016. (ENG.). 32p. (J). (-2). 12.99 *(978-1-4926-4353-1(X),* 9781492643531, Sourcebooks Jabberwocky) Sourcebooks, Inc.

Johnson, Maureen. Devilish. 2013. (ENG.). 304p. (YA). (gr. 7). pap. 9.99 *(978-0-14-750855-3(X),* Speak) Penguin Young Readers Group.

Johnson, Peter. The Amazing Adventures of John Smith, Jr. Aka Houdini. 2012. (ENG.). 176p. (J). (gr. 3-7). 16.99 *(978-0-06-198890-5(1))* HarperCollins Pubs.

—The Amazing Adventures of John Smith, Jr. AKA Houdini. 2014. (ENG.). 192p. (J). (gr. 3-7). pap. 6.99 *(978-0-06-198891-2(X))* HarperCollins Pubs.

Katherine's Story 1848. 2014. (Secrets of the Manor Ser.: 4). (ENG., Illus.). 160p. (J). (gr. 3-7). pap. 6.99 *(978-1-4814-1843-0(2),* Simon Spotlight) Simon Spotlight.

Lisle, Janet Taylor. Black Duck. 2007. (ENG.). 256p. (J). (gr. 5-18). 7.99 *(978-0-14-240902-2(2),* Puffin Books) Penguin Young Readers Group.

—The Crying Rocks. 2005. 281p. (YA). (gr. 7-12). 14.65 *(978-0-7569-5507-6(6))* Perfection Learning Corp.

Livsey, John. '38: The Great Hurricane in Quonochontaug, Rhode Island. 2004. 288p. (YA). per. 15.49 *(978-0-9754979-2-0(8))* Big Wave Bks.

Metz, Melinda. Raven's Point. 2005. pap. *(978-0-06-052373-2(5))* HarperCollins Canada, Ltd.

O'Neill, Elizabeth. Alfred Visits Rhode Island. 2007. (Illus.). 24p. (J). pap. 12.00 *(978-0-9790240-6-1(4))* Global Business Information Strategies, Inc.

Silvano, Wendi. Love Is All Around Rhode Island. Czernichowska, Joanna, illus. 2016. (ENG.). 32p. (J). (-6). 12.99 *(978-1-4926-2958-0(8),* Sourcebooks Jabberwocky) Sourcebooks, Inc.

Smallman, Steve. Santa Is Coming to Rhode Island. Dunn, Robert, illus. 2014. (ENG.). 32p. (J). (-3). 9.99 *(978-1-4926-0727-4(4),* Sourcebooks Jabberwocky) Sourcebooks, Inc.

Swanberg, Arvon & Spicer, Carolyn. The Big, Blue, Overstuffed Chair. 2013. 46p. pap. 17.99 *(978-1-4808-0432-6(0))* Archway Publishing.

Wilson, J. M. & Zolkowski, Cathy A. Blue: Adventures of a Gymnast. 2004. 150p. (YA). per. 11.95 *(978-0-9667037-5-7(8))* Verona (Bk.) Publishing, Inc.

Zschock, Martha Day. Hello, Rhode Island! 2011. (Hello! Ser.). (ENG., Illus.). 16p. (J). (gr. -1-k). bds. 9.95 *(978-1-933212-62-3(4),* Commonwealth Editions) Applewood Bks.

RHODE ISLAND—HISTORY

Axelrod-Contrada, Joan. A Primary Source History of the Colony of Rhode Island. (Primary Sources of the Thirteen Colonies & the Lost Colony Ser.). 64p. 2009. (gr. 5-8). 58.50 *(978-1-60851-888-3(4))* 2006. (Illus.). (YA). (gr. 4-7). lib. bdg. 31.95 *(978-1-4042-0434-8(2))* 2006. (ENG., Illus.). (gr. 4-8). per. 12.95 *(978-1-4042-0675-5(2))* Rosen Publishing Group, Inc., The.

Burgan, Michael. Rhode Island (Revised Edition) 2014. (America the Beautiful, Third Ser. (Revised Edition) Ser.). (ENG.). 144p. (J). lib. bdg. 40.00 *(978-0-531-28291-5(0))* Scholastic Library Publishing.

Cunningham, Kevin. The Rhode Island Colony. 2011. (True Bk Ser.). (ENG., Illus.). 48p. (J). pap. 6.95 *(978-0-531-26610-6(9));* lib. bdg. 29.00 *(978-0-531-25397-7(X))* Scholastic Library Publishing. (Children's Pr.).

Davidson, Tish. Southern New England: Connecticut, Massachusetts, Rhode Island, Vol. 19. 2015. (Let's Explore the States Ser.). (Illus.). 64p. (J). (gr. 5). 23.95 *(978-1-4222-3333-7(2))* Mason Crest.

Doak, Robin S. Exploring the Rhode Island Colony. 2016. (Exploring the 13 Colonies Ser.). (ENG., Illus.). 48p. (gr. 3-4). lib. bdg. 31.99 *(978-1-5157-2231-1(7))* Capstone Press of Coughlan Cos.

Doherty, Craig A. & Doherty, Katherine M. Rhode Island. 2005. (Thirteen Colonies Ser.). (Illus.). 144p. (gr. 5-8). 35.00 *(978-0-8160-5415-2(0))* Facts On File, Inc.

Felix, Rebecca. What's Great about Rhode Island? 2015. (Our Great States Ser.). (ENG., Illus.). 32p. (J). (gr. 2-5). lib. bdg. 26.60 *(978-1-4677-3856-9(5),* Lerner Pubns.) Lerner Publishing Group.

Friesen, Helen Lepp. Rhode Island: The Ocean State. 2012. (J). *(978-1-61913-399-0(7));* pap. *(978-1-61913-400-3(4))* Weigl Pubs., Inc.

Furgang, Adam. Rhode Island: Past & Present. 2010. (United States: Past & Present Ser.). (ENG.). 48p. (YA). pap. 11.75 *(978-1-4358-9521-8(5));* lib. bdg. 29.25 *(978-1-4358-9494-5(4))* Rosen Publishing Group, Inc., The. (Rosen Reference).

Jensen, Niels R. Rhode Island. 1 vol. 2009. (United States Ser.). (ENG., Illus.). 48p. (YA). (gr. 2-5). 27.07 *(978-1-60453-675-1(6))* ABDO Publishing Co.

Kleinmartin, Hex, et al. Rhode Island. 2015. lib. bdg. *(978-1-62713-219-0(8))* Cavendish Square Publishing.

Koontz, Robin Michal. Rhode Island: The Ocean State. 2010. (Our Amazing States Ser.). (ENG.). 24p. (J). 22.60 *(978-1-4488-0650-8(X),* PowerKids Pr.) Rosen Publishing Group, Inc., The.

Laine, Grannie. Good Night, Block Island. 2010. 24p. 12.00 *(978-1-4520-0753-3(5))* AuthorHouse.

Marsh, Carole. Exploring Rhode Island Through Project-Based Learning: Geography, History, Government, Economics & More. 2016. (Rhode Island Experience Ser.). (ENG.). (J). pap. 9.99 *(978-0-635-12363-3(0))* Gallopade International.

McDermott, Jesse. Rhode Island, 1636-1776. 2006. (National Geographic Voices from ColonialAmerica Ser.). (ENG., Illus.). 112p. (J). (gr. 5-9). 21.95 *(978-0-7922-6410-1(X),* National Geographic Children's Bks.) National Geographic Society.

McDermott, Jesse John. Rhode Island, 1636-1776. 2006. (National Geographic Voices from ColonialAmerica Ser.). (ENG., Illus.). 112p. (J). (gr. 5-9). lib. bdg. 32.90 *(978-0-7922-6868-0(7),* National Geographic Children's Bks.) National Geographic Society.

Miller, Jake. The Colony of Rhode Island: A Primary Source History. (Primary Source Library of the Thirteen Colonies & the Lost Colony Ser.). 24p. (gr. 3-4). 2009. 42.50 *(978-1-60854-156-0(8))* 2006. (Illus.). (J). lib. bdg. 22.60 *(978-1-4042-3032-3(7))* Rosen Publishing Group, Inc., The. (PowerKids Pr.).

Petreycik, Rick & Herrington, Lisa M. Rhode Island. 2013. (It's My State! Ser.). 80p. (J). (gr. 4-8). 31.36 *(978-0-7614-8002-0(1))* Cavendish Square Publishing.

Tieck, Sarah. Rhode Island. 1 vol. 2012. (Explore the United States Ser.). (ENG.). 32p. (J). (gr. 2-5). lib. bdg. 28.50 *(978-1-61783-378-6(9),* Big Buddy Bks.) ABDO Publishing Co.

Wilson, James, ed. Rhode Island Treasures. 2003. (Illus.). 112p. per. 15.00 *(978-0-615-12390-5(2))* Narragansett Graphics.

Wimmer, Teresa. Rhode Island. 2009. (This Land Called America Ser.). 32p. (YA). (gr. 3-6). 19.95 *(978-1-58341-792-8(3))* Creative Co., The.

Winans, Jay D. Rhode Island. 2011. (Guide to American States Ser.). (J). (Illus.). 48p. (gr. 3-6). 29.99 *(978-1-61690-812-6(2));* 29.99 *(978-1-61690-488-3(7))* Weigl Pubs., Inc.

—Rhode Island: The Ocean State. 2016. (J). *(978-1-4896-4935-5(2))* Weigl Pubs., Inc.

RHODES, CECIL, 1853-1902

Phan, Sandy. Cecil Rhodes: The Man Who Expanded an Empire. 1 vol. 2012. (Primary Source Readers Ser.). (ENG.). 32p. (J). (gr. 4-4). pap. 8.99 *(978-1-4333-5016-0(5))* Teacher Created Materials, Inc.

RHODESIA, SOUTHERN

see Zimbabwe

RHYMES

see Limericks; Nonsense Verses; Nursery Rhymes; Poetry—Collections

RHYTHM

see also Versification

Bodden, Valerie. Wording & Tone. (Odysseys in Prose Ser.). (Illus.). 80p. (J). 2017. (ENG.). (gr. 7-11). pap. 14.99 *(978-1-62832-326-9(4),* Creative Paperbacks) 2016. *(978-1-60818-730-0(6),* Creative Education) Creative Co., The.

Simon, Seymour. The Secret Clocks: Time Senses of Living Things. Brett, Jan, illus. 2012. (Dover Children's Science Bks.). (ENG.). 80p. (J). (gr. 3-5). pap. 5.99 *(978-0-486-48866-0(7))* Dover Pubns., Inc.

RICE, CONDOLEEZZA, 1954-

Banting, Erinn. Condoleeza Rice. 2007. (Remarkable People Ser.). (Illus.). 24p. (J). (gr. 3-7). lib. bdg. 24.45 *(978-1-59036-639-4(5))* Weigl Pubs., Inc.

—Condoleeza Rice. 2007. (Remarkable People Ser.). (Illus.). 24p. (J). (gr. 3-7). pap. 8.95 *(978-1-59036-640-0(9))* Weigl Pubs., Inc.

Blakely, Gloria. Condoleezza Rice. 2003. (African American Leaders Ser.). (Illus.). 112p. (gr. 6-12). 30.00 *(978-0-7910-7683-5(0),* Chelsea Hse.) Facts On File, Inc.

Cunningham, Kevin. Condoleezza Rice. 2009. (Journey to Freedom Ser.). (ENG., Illus.). 32p. (J). (gr. 4-7). 29.93 *(978-1-60253-120-8(X),* 200386) Child's World, Inc., The.

Ditchfield, Christin. Condoleezza Rice: America's Leading Stateswoman. 2006. (Great Life Stories Ser.). (ENG., Illus.). 112p. (J). (gr. 6-8). lib. bdg. 30.50 *(978-0-531-13874-8(7),* Watts, Franklin) Scholastic Library Publishing.

Hubbard-Brown, Janet. Condoleezza Rice: Stateswoman. 2008. (Black Americans of Achievement Ser.). (Illus.). 113p. (gr. 6-12). lib. bdg. 35.00 *(978-0-7910-9715-1(3),* Chelsea Hse.) Facts On File, Inc.

Marsh, Carole. Condoleezza Rice. 2003. 12p. (gr. k-4). 2.95 *(978-0-635-02385-8(7))* Gallopade International.

Mckenzie, Precious. Condoleezza Rice. 2013. (ENG.). 24p. (gr. k-3). pap. 8.95 *(978-1-62169-234-8(5))* Rourke Educational Media.

Rice, Condoleezza. Condoleezza Rice: A Memoir of My Extraordinary, Ordinary Family & Me. 2012. (ENG.). 336p. (J). (gr. 5). pap. 8.99 *(978-0-385-73880-4(3),* Ember) Random Hse. Children's Bks.

Wade, Linda R. Condoleezza Rice. 2004. (Illus.). 32p. (J). lib. bdg. 25.70 *(978-1-58415-332-0(6))* Mitchell Lane Pubs., Inc.

Wade, Mary Dodson. Condoleezza Rice. rev. ed. 2005. (Gateway Biography Ser.). (Illus.). 48p. (J). (gr. 4-7). pap. 8.95 *(978-0-7613-9549-2(0),* First Avenue Editions) Lerner Publishing Group.

—Condoleezza Rice: Being the Best. 2003. (Gateway Biography Ser.: 4). 48p. lib. bdg. 23.90 *(978-0-7613-2619-9(7));* (Illus.). (gr. 2-4). pap. 8.95 *(978-0-7613-1927-6(1))* Lerner Publishing Group. (Millbrook Pr.).

RICE

Brannon, Cecelia H. Rice. 2017. (All about Food Crops Ser.). 24p. (gr. k-1). lib. bdg. 22.60 ***(978-0-7660-8583-1(X))*** Enslow Pubs., Inc.

Martineau, Susan & James, Hel. Bread, Rice, & Pasta. 2012. (Healthy Eating Ser.). (Illus.). 32p. (gr. 2-6). pap. 8.95 *(978-1-59920-242-6(5))* Black Rabbit Bks.

Reynolds, Jan. Cycle of Rice, Cycle of Life: A Story of Sustainable Farming. Reynolds, Jan, photos by. 2009. (ENG., Illus.). 48p. (J). (gr. 2-7). 19.95 *(978-1-60060-254-2(1))* Lee & Low Bks., Inc.

Singer, Jane E. Rice. 2013. (Feeding the World Ser.: 8). (Illus.). 48p. (J). (gr. 4-18). 19.95 *(978-1-4222-2747-3(2))* Mason Crest.

Staniford, Linda. Where Do Grains Come From? 2016. (From Farm to Fork: Where Does My Food Come From? Ser.). (ENG.). 24p. (gr. k-2). lib. bdg. 23.99 *(978-1-4846-3349-6(0))* Capstone Press of Coughlan Cos.

Williams, Nancy Noel. Rice Is Nice. 2010. (J). *(978-1-60617-144-8(5))* Teaching Strategies, LLC.

Zronik, John Paul & Zronik, John. The Biography of Rice. 2005. (How did That Get There? Ser.). (ENG., Illus.). 32p. (J). (gr. 4-5). pap. *(978-0-7787-2518-3(9));* lib. bdg. *(978-0-7787-2482-7(4))* Crabtree Publishing Co.

RICE—FICTION

Sherer, Mary (Huston). Ho Fills the Rice Barrel. Greenwood, Marion, illus. 2012. 128p. 40.95 *(978-1-258-25056-0(X));* pap. 25.95 *(978-1-258-25732-3(7))* Literary Licensing, LLC.

Takayama, Sandi. The Musubi Baby. Hall, Pat, illus. 2007. 32p. (J). (gr. -1-3). 10.95 *(978-1-57306-272-5(3))* Bess Pr., Inc.

RICHARD I, KING OF ENGLAND, 1157-1199

Abbott, Jacob. History of King Richard the First of England. 2003. 336p. 99.00 *(978-0-7950-3593-7(4))* New Library Press LLC.

Crompton, Samuel Willard. The Third Crusade: Richard the Lionhearted vs. Saladin. 2003. (Great Battles Through the Ages Ser.). (Illus.). 112p. (J). (gr. 6-12). 30.00 *(978-0-7910-7437-4(4),* Chelsea Hse.) Facts On File, Inc.

Harkins, Susan Sales & Harkins, William H. The Life & Times of Richard the Lionheart. 2008. (Biography from Ancient Civilizations Ser.). (Illus.). 48p. (J). (gr. 4-8). lib. bdg. 29.95 *(978-1-58415-699-4(6))* Mitchell Lane Pubs., Inc.

Hilliam, David. Richard the Lionheart & the Third Crusade: The English King Confronts Saladin in AD 1191. 2009. (Library of the Middle Ages Ser.). 64p. (gr. 5-8). 58.50 *(978-1-60853-902-4(4),* Rosen Reference) Rosen Publishing Group, Inc., The.

—Richard the Lionheart & the Third Crusade: The English King Confronts Saladin, AD 1191. 2004. (Library of the Middle Ages Ser.). (Illus.). 64p. (YA). (gr. 5-8). lib. bdg. 31.95 *(978-0-8239-4213-8(9),* Rosen Reference) Rosen Publishing Group, Inc., The.

Streissguth, Tom. Richard the Lionheart: Crusader King of England. 2007. (Rulers of the Middle Ages Ser.). (Illus.). 160p. (YA). (gr. 6-12). lib. bdg. 35.94 *(978-0-7660-2714-5(7))* Enslow Pubs., Inc.

West, David. Richard the Lionheart: The Life of a King & Crusader. 2009. (Graphic Nonfiction Biographies Ser.). (Illus.). 48p. (YA). (gr. 4-5). 58.50 *(978-1-61513-025-2(X),* Rosen Reference) Rosen Publishing Group, Inc., The.

West, David & Gaff, Jackie. Richard the Lionheart: The Life of a King & Crusader. 2005. (Graphic Nonfiction Biographies Ser.). (ENG., Illus.). 48p. (YA). (gr. 4-7). lib. bdg. 31.95 *(978-1-4042-0241-2(2))* Rosen Publishing Group, Inc., The.

RICHARD I, KING OF ENGLAND, 1157-1199—FICTION

Harris, Mark W., et al. Ivanhoe. Scott, Walter, ed. (Classics Illustrated Ser.). (Illus.). 52p. (YA). pap. 4.95 *(978-1-57209-023-1(5))* Classics International Entertainment, Inc.

RICHARD II, KING OF ENGLAND, 1367-1400

Abbott, Jacob. History of King Richard the Second of England. 2003. 347p. 99.00 *(978-0-7950-3594-4(2))* New Library Press LLC.

RICHARD III, KING OF ENGLAND, 1452-1485—FICTION

Haddix, Margaret Peterson. Sent. (Missing Ser.: 2). (YA). 2011. 82.75 *(978-1-4407-2678-1(7))* 2009. 218.75 *(978-1-4407-2670-5(1))* 2009. 1.25 *(978-1-4407-2679-8(5))* 2009. 98.75 *(978-1-4407-2675-0(2))* Recorded Bks., Inc.

—Sent. (Missing Ser.: 2). (ENG.). (J). (gr. 3-7). 2010. 336p. pap. 7.99 *(978-1-4169-5423-1(6))* 2009. 320p. 16.99 *(978-1-4169-5422-4(8))* Simon & Schuster Bks. For Young Readers. (Simon & Schuster Bks. For Young Readers).

—Sent. abr. ed. 2009. *(978-1-4424-0767-1(0))* Simon & Schuster Children's Publishing.

—Sent. l.t. ed. 2010. (Missing Ser.: Bk. 2). (ENG.). 346p. 23.99 *(978-1-4104-3245-2(9))* Thorndike Pr.

—Sent. 2010. (Missing Ser.: 2). lib. bdg. 18.40 *(978-0-606-14699-9(7),* Turtleback) Turtleback Bks.

Rose, Simon. The Sorcerer's Letterbox. 1 vol. 2004. (ENG., Illus.). 114p. (J). (gr. 4-6). per. 7.95 *(978-1-896580-52-4(1))* Tradewind Bks. CAN. Dist: Orca Bk. Pubs. USA.

Stevenson, Robert Louis. The Black Arrow. l.t. ed. 2005. 448p. pap. *(978-1-84637-164-6(3))* Echo Library.

RICHTHOFEN, MANFRED ALBRECHT, FREIHERR VON, 1892-1918

Vansant, Wayne. The Red Baron: The Graphic History of Richthofen's Flying Circus & the Air War in WWI. Vansant, Wayne, illus. 2015. (Graphic Histories Ser.). (ENG., Illus.). 104p. (J). (gr. 8-12). 34.65 *(978-1-939581-80-8(X))* Quarto Publishing Group USA.

—The Red Baron: The Graphic History of Richthofen's Flying Circus & the Air War in WWI. 2014. (Zenith Graphic Histories Ser.). (ENG., Illus.). 104p. pap. 19.99 *(978-0-7603-4602-0(X),* 076034602X, Zenith Pr.) Quarto Publishing Group USA.

RICKEY, BRANCH, 1881-1965

Frystak, Timothy D. Jackie Robinson: With Profiles of Satchel Paige & & Branch Rickey. 2006. (Biographical Connections Ser.). (Illus.). 112p. (J). *(978-0-7166-1828-7(1))* World Bk., Inc.

RICOTTA, RICKY (FICTITIOUS CHARACTER)—FICTION

Pilkey, Dav. Mighty Robot vs. the Mecha-Monkeys from Mars. Santat, Dan, illus. 2014. (Ricky Ricotta Ser.: 4). (ENG.). 144p. (J). (gr. -1-3). pap. 5.99 *(978-0-545-63012-2(6))* Scholastic, Inc.

—Mighty Robot vs. the Mutant Mosquitoes from Mercury. Santat, Dan, illus. 2014. (Ricky Ricotta Ser.: 2). (ENG.). 128p. (J). (gr. -1-3). pap. 5.99 *(978-0-545-63010-8(X))* Scholastic, Inc.

—Mighty Robot vs. the Naughty Nightcrawlers from Neptune. Santat, Dan, illus. 2016. (Ricky Ricotta Ser.: 8). (ENG.). 128p. (J). (gr. -1-3). 15.99 *(978-0-439-37708-9(0))* Scholastic, Inc.

—Ricky Ricotta's Mighty Robot. 2014. (Ricky Ricotta's Mighty Robot Ser.: 1). lib. bdg. 16.00 *(978-0-606-35799-9(8))* Turtleback Bks.

—Ricky Ricotta's Mighty Robot vs. the Jurassic Jackrabbits from Jupiter. Santat, Dan, illus. 2014. (Ricky Ricotta Ser.: 5). (ENG.). 128p. (J). (gr. -1-3). pap. 5.99 *(978-0-545-63013-9(4))* Scholastic, Inc.

—Ricky Ricotta's Mighty Robot vs. the Naughty Nightcrawlers from Neptune. Santat, Dan, illus. 2016. (Ricky Ricotta Ser.: 8). (ENG.). 128p. (J). (gr. -1-3). pap. 5.99 *(978-0-439-37709-6(9))* Scholastic, Inc.

—Ricky Ricotta's Mighty Robot vs. the Unpleasant Penguins from Pluto. Santat, Dan, illus. 2016. (Ricky Ricotta's Mighty Robot Ser.: 9). (ENG.). 128p. (J). (gr. -1-3). 15.99 *(978-0-545-63016-0(9))* Scholastic, Inc.

—Uranium Unicorns from Uranus., Bk. 7. 2015. (Ricky Ricotta Ser.: 7). (ENG., Illus.). 128p. (J). (gr. -1-3). pap. 5.99 *(978-0-545-63015-3(0))* Scholastic, Inc.

—The Voodoo Vultures from Venus. Santat, Dan, illus. 2014. (Ricky Ricotta Ser.: 3). (ENG.). 128p. (J). (gr. -1-3). pap. 5.99 *(978-0-545-63011-5(8))* Scholastic, Inc.

Santat, Dan, illus. Mighty Robot vs. the Stupid Stinkbugs from Saturn. 2015. (Ricky Ricotta Ser.: 6). (ENG.). 128p. (J). (gr. -1-3). 15.99 *(978-0-545-63121-1(1))* Scholastic, Inc.

—Stupid Stinkbugs from Saturn. 2015. (Ricky Ricotta Ser.: 6). (ENG.). 128p. (J). (gr. -1-3). pap. 5.99 *(978-0-545-63014-6(2))* Scholastic, Inc.

RIDDLES

see also Puzzles

Anderson, Dee. Reading Is Funny! Motivating Kids to Read with Riddles. 2008. (Illus.). 216p. 40.00 *(978-0-8389-0957-7(4))* American Library Assn.

Anholt, Catherine & Anholt, Laurence. Can You Guess? A Lift-the-Flap Birthday Party Book. 2003. (Illus.). 16p. pap. 7.95 *(978-0-7112-2214-4(2))* Fleming, Randall.

Bathroom Readers' Institute Staff. The Grossest Joke Book Ever! 2016. (ENG., Illus.). 128p. (J). (gr. 1). pap. 4.99 *(978-1-62686-585-3(X),* Portable Pr.) Readerlink Distribution Services, LLC.

Berne, Emma Carlson. World's Best (and Worst) Animal Jokes. 2017. (J). ***(978-1-5124-8351-2(6))*** Lerner Publishing Group.

A Book of Silly Jokes! 2003. (Illus.). (J). *(978-0-439-39056-9(7))* Scholastic, Inc.

Brennan-Nelson, Denise. Little Colorado. Urban, Helle, illus. 2011. (My Little State Ser.). (ENG.). 22p. (J). 9.95 *(978-1-58536-530-2(0))* Sleeping Bear Pr.

—Little Michigan. Monroe, Michael Glenn, illus. 2010. (My Little State Ser.). (ENG.). 22p. (J). 9.95 *(978-1-58536-479-4(7))* Sleeping Bear Pr.

Brett, Jeannie. Little Maine. Brett, Jeannie, illus. 2010. (My Little State Ser.). (ENG., Illus.). 22p. (J). 9.95 *(978-1-58536-497-8(5))* Sleeping Bear Pr.

Brown, Peggy. The Little Golden Book of Jokes & Riddles. Sheldon, David, illus. 2013. (Little Golden Book Ser.). (ENG.). 24p. (J). (-k). 4.99 *(978-0-307-97916-2(4),* Golden Bks.) Random Hse. Children's Bks.

Burns, Diane L. Horsing Around: Jokes to Make Ewe Smile. Gable, Brian, illus. 2005. (Make Me Laugh! Ser.). 32p. (J). (gr. k-3). lib. bdg. 19.93 *(978-1-57505-662-3(3))* Lerner Publishing Group.

Burns, Diane L. & Scholten, Dan. Horsing Around: Jokes to Make Ewe Smile. Gable, Brian, illus. 2004. (Make Me Laugh! Ser.). 32p. (J). (gr. -1-3). per. 4.95 *(978-1-57505-737-8(9))* Lerner Publishing Group.

Cerrillo, et al. Adivina Quien Soy. 2004. (SPA., Illus.). 30p. (J). 6.50 *(978-84-348-7753-5(8))* SM Ediciones ESP. Dist: Lectorum Pubns., Inc.

Chirp Magazine Editors. Joking Around with Chirp: More Than 130 Feather-Ruffling Jokes, Riddles, & Tongue Twisters! Kain, Bob & Owlkids Books Inc. Staff, illus. 2013. (ENG.). 96p. (J). (gr. -1-3). pap. 8.95 *(978-1-926973-65-4(8))* Owlkids Bks. Inc. CAN. Dist: Publishers Group West (PGW).

Christopher, Ciara. Animal Jokes, Riddles, & Games. 2016. (ENG., Illus.). 32p. (J). *(978-0-7787-2387-5(9))* Crabtree Publishing Co.

Cliff Road Books Staff & Sweetwater Press Staff, contrib. by. Jokes & Riddles for Kids of All Ages, 3 vols. 2004. (Illus.). *(978-1-58173-313-6(5)); (978-1-58173-312-9(7)); (978-0-60261-115-3(7))* Cliff Road Bks.

Cole, Joanna & Calmenson, Stephanie, eds. Tons of Fun: Over 300 Action Rhymes, Old & New Riddles, Tongue Twisters, & Play Rhymes. Tiegren, Alan, illus. 2004. 229p. (J). (gr. k-4). reprint ed. pap. 15.00 *(978-0-7567-8222-1(8))* DIANE Publishing Co.

Conley, Erin, ed. Zany Riddles. 2005. (Made You Laugh for Kids). (ENG., Illus.). 96p. pap. 5.95 *(978-1-57528-930-4(X))* Univ. Games.

Connolly, Sean. The Fun on the Farm Joke Book. 2013. (Laugh Out Loud Ser.). (ENG., Illus.). 32p. (J). (gr. 1-5). pap. 11.75 *(978-1-61533-654-8(0));* lib. bdg. 26.50 *(978-1-61533-644-9(3))* Windmill Bks.

—The Hysterical History Joke Book. 2013. (Laugh Out Loud Ser.). (ENG., Illus.). 32p. (gr. 1-5). pap. 11.75 *(978-1-61533-656-2(7));* lib. bdg. 26.50 *(978-1-61533-645-6(1))* Windmill Bks.

—The Jolly Jungle Joke Book. 2013. (Laugh Out Loud Ser.). (ENG., Illus.). 32p. (J). (gr. 1-5). pap. 11.75 *(978-1-61533-658-6(3));* lib. bdg. 26.50 *(978-1-61533-646-3(X))* Windmill Bks.

—Laugh Out Loud: The Silly Spells Joke Book. 2013. (Laugh Out Loud Ser.). (ENG., Illus.). 32p. (J). (gr. 1-5). pap. 11.75 *(978-1-61533-662-3(1));* lib. bdg. 26.50 *(978-1-61533-648-7(6))* Windmill Bks.

—The Out to Sea Joke Book. 2013. (Laugh Out Loud Ser.). (ENG., Illus.). 32p. (J). (gr. 1-5). pap. 11.75 *(978-1-61533-660-9(5));* lib. bdg. 26.50 *(978-1-61533-647-0(8))* Windmill Bks.

Connolly, Sean & Harris, Joe. The Crazy Computers Joke Book. 2013. (Laugh Out Loud Ser.). (ENG., Illus.). 32p. (J). (gr. 1-5). pap. 11.75 *(978-1-61533-652-4(4));* lib. bdg. 26.50 *(978-1-61533-643-2(5))* Windmill Bks.

Crane, Carol. Little Florida. Monroe, Michael Glenn, illus. 2010. (My Little State Ser.). (ENG.). 22p. (J). 9.95 *(978-1-58536-487-9(8))* Sleeping Bear Pr.

—Little Georgia. Knorr, Laura, illus. 2013. (Little State Ser.). (ENG.). 20p. (J). (gr. -1-k). 9.95 *(978-1-58536-203-5(4),* 202355) Sleeping Bear Pr.

—Little North Carolina. Brett, Jeannie, illus. 2011. (My Little State Ser.). (ENG.). 20p. 9.95 *(978-1-58536-545-6(9))* Sleeping Bear Pr.

—Little South Carolina. Monroe, Michael Glenn & Tsairis, Jeannie Brett, illus. 2011. (My Little State Ser.). (ENG.). 22p. (J). 9.95 *(978-1-58536-486-2(X))* Sleeping Bear Pr.

—Little Texas. Monroe, Michael Glenn, illus. 2010. (My Little State Ser.). (ENG.). 22p. (J). 9.95 *(978-1-58536-488-6(6))* Sleeping Bear Pr.

Dahl, Michael. Scooby-Doo's Laugh-Out-Loud Jokes! Jeralds, Scott, illus. 2015. (Scooby-Doo Joke Bks.). (ENG.). 224p. (gr. 2-3). pap. 9.95 *(978-1-62370-182-6(1))* Capstone Press of Coughlan Cos.

Dahl, Michael, et al. Wise Crackers: Riddles & Jokes about Numbers, Names, Letters, & Silly Words. 1 vol. Haugen, Ryan et al, illus. 2010. (Michael Dahl Presents Super Funny Joke Bks.). (ENG.). 80p. (gr. k-3). 25.32 *(978-1-4048-6102-2(5))* Picture Window Bks.

Doering, Jennie Spray. Beach Riddles. Pica, Steve, illus. 2006. (Silly Millies Ser.). 32p. (J). (gr. 2). per. 5.95 *(978-0-8225-6471-3(8),* First Avenue Editions); (ENG.). (gr. 1-3). lib. bdg. 21.27 *(978-0-7613-2885-8(8),* Millbrook Pr.) Lerner Publishing Group.

Doolittle, John H. Dr. DooRiddles A2: Associative Reasoning Activities. 2005. (Dr. DooRiddles & Spelling DooRiddles

Ser.). 48p. (gr. -1-2). pap. 9.99 *(978-0-89455-877-1(3))* Critical Thinking Co., The.
—Dr. DooRiddles A3: Associative Reasoning Activities. 2012. (Dr. DooRiddles & Spelling DooRiddles Ser.). 48p. (gr. 2-3). pap. 9.99 *(978-0-89455-878-8(1))* Critical Thinking Co., The.
Doolittle, John H. & Doolittle, Tracy A. Dr. DooRiddles B2: Associative Reasoning Activities. 2011. (Dr. DooRiddles & Spelling DooRiddles Ser.). 64p. (gr. 4-7). pap. 9.99 *(978-0-89455-879-5(X))* Critical Thinking Co., The.
Dussling, Jennifer. In a Dark, Dark House. Jones, Davy, illus. Date not set. (All Aboard Reading Ser.). 32p. (J). (gr. -1-k). pap. *(978-0-448-40974-0(7)*, Grosset & Dunlap) Penguin Publishing Group.
Editorial, Equipo. Mis 365 Mejores Adivinanzas. Aubert, Elena G., illus. 2003. (SPA.). *(978-84-7630-904-9(X)*, LA30439) Editorial Libsa, S.A. ESP. Dist: Lectorum Pubns., Inc.
En Movimiento, 6 bks., Set. Incl. Conducir! Meachen Rau, Dana, ed. lib. bdg. 15.95 *(978-0-7614-2422-2(9))*; Flotar. Meachen Rau, Dana. lib. bdg. 15.95 *(978-0-7614-2420-8(2))*; Montar! Meachen Rau, Dana. lib. bdg. 15.95 *(978-0-7614-2423-9(7))*; Rodar! Meachen Rau, Dana. lib. bdg. 15.95 *(978-0-7614-2419-2(9))*; Trepar! Meachen Rau, Dana. lib. bdg. 15.95 *(978-0-7614-2424-6(5))*; Volar! Vargus, Nanci R. lib. bdg. 15.95 *(978-0-7614-2425-3(3))*; (Illus.). 24p. (gr. k-1). (Benchmark Rebus: en Movimiento Ser.). (SPA.). 2006. Set lib. bdg. 95.70 *(978-0-7614-2417-8(2)*, Benchmark Bks.) Marshall Cavendish Corp.
Engelman Berner, Beth. Finding Fairyland: A Picture Riddle Book. Riggs, Jenna, illus. 2005. 12p. (J). 9.95 *(978-1-58117-386-4(5)*, Intervisual/Piggy Toes) Bendon, Inc.
Everest. Adivina, Adivinanza. Quesada, Maria Fe, illus. (SPA.). (J). pap. 5.56 *(978-84-241-8037-9(2))* Everest Editora ESP. Dist: Lectorum Pubns., Inc.
Fabulous PH Riddles Blends/Dig. (J). pap. 18.16 *(978-0-8136-0864-8(3))* Modern Curriculum Pr.
Fixx, John. Things That Aren't: Things You Can't Always Touch, See, or Hear. Can You Guess What They Are? Carter, Abby, illus. 2016. (ENG.). 112p. (J). (gr. 2-7). 12.95 *(978-1-63322-176-5(8)*, Walter Foster Jr) Quarto Publishing Group USA.
Fontes, Justine. Cheerios Action Park Adventure. 2005. (Picture Clue Math Reader Ser.). (Illus.). 28p. (J). pap. *(978-0-439-70343-7(3))* Scholastic, Inc.
Foster James, Helen. Little America. 2011. (My Little State Ser.). (ENG., Illus.). 22p. (J). 7.95 *(978-1-58536-179-3(8))* Sleeping Bear Pr.
Free Spirit Publishing Staff & Stein, Deborah Jiang. Math. 2009. (In a Jar(r) Ser.). (ENG.). (J). 9.99 *(978-1-57542-937-3(3))* Free Spirit Publishing, Inc.
Gagliano, Eugene M. Little Wyoming. Urban, Helle, illus. 2010. (My Little State Ser.). (ENG.). 22p. (J). 9.95 *(978-1-58536-544-9(0))* Sleeping Bear Pr.
Garrett, Ann & Higney, Gene-Michael. Fins & Flippers, Scales & Nippers. 2003. (Illus.). 32p. (J). pap. *(978-1-59034-871-0(0))*; 15.95 *(978-1-59034-869-7(9))* Mondo Publishing.
Gilbert Square Books. The Fun of Rhyme Square Pears. 2005. (Illus.). 40p. (J). 2.50 *(978-0-9745308-3-3(2))* Gilbert Square Bks.
Gómez Yebra, Antonio. ADIVINA ADIVINANZAS: ADIVINANZAS DE HOY PARA NIÑOS. 2003. (SPA.). *(978-84-348-7336-0(2)*, SM31231) SM Ediciones ESP. Dist: Lectorum Pubns., Inc.
Gowan, Barbara. Little Arizona. 2012. (My Little State Ser.). (ENG., Illus.). 20p. (J). (gr. k-3). 9.95 *(978-1-58536-208-0(5))* Sleeping Bear Pr.
Granfield, Linda. What Am I? Herbert, Jennifer, illus. 2007. (ENG.). 32p. (J). (gr. k-k). 15.95 *(978-0-88776-812-5(1)*, Tundra Bks.) Tundra Bks. CAN. Dist: Penguin Random Hse. LLC.
Group/McGraw-Hill, Wright. Aunt Victoria's Monster: Level P, 6 vols. (Whispering Pines Ser.). 128p. (gr. 5-18). 36.95 *(978-0-322-05903-0(8))* Wright Group/McGraw-Hill.
Helmer, Marilyn. Funtime Riddles. Kurisu, Jane, illus. 2004. 31p. (J). lib. bdg. 15.38 *(978-1-4242-1184-5(0))* Fitzgerald Bks.
Hentley, Sheila Rose. Nursery Rhymes & Nursery Riddles for All Ages. 2007. 28p. per. 21.99 *(978-1-4257-9011-0(9))* Xlibris Corp.
Hershenhorn, Esther. Little Illinois. Monroe, Michael Glenn, illus. 2011. (My Little State Ser.). (ENG.). 22p. (J). 9.95 *(978-1-58536-537-1(8))* Sleeping Bear Pr.
Hillert, Margaret. What Am I? Mukuc, Lucy, illus. 2016. (BeginningtoRead Ser.). (ENG.). 32p. (J). (gr. -1-2). pap. 11.94 *(978-1-60357-982-7(6))*; (gr. 3-2). 22.60 *(978-1-59953-820-4(2))* Norwood Hse. Pr.
Hughes, Emily C. Plants vs. Zombies - Brain Busters. 2013. (Plants vs. Zombies Ser.). (ENG.). 224p. (J). (gr. 1-5). 10.99 *(978-0-06-222844-4(7)*, HarperFestival) HarperCollins Pubs.
Ideals Children's Books Staff, creator. Hands-on Highlights Riddles: A Summer of Laughs. 2007. (Hands-on Ser.). (ENG., Illus.). 32p. (J). (gr. k-3). 16.99 *(978-0-8249-1500-1(3)*, Ideal Pubns.) Worthy Publishing.
James, Helen Foster & Wilbur, Helen L. Little California. Urban, Helle, illus. 2011. (My Little State Ser.). (ENG.). 22p. (J). 9.95 *(978-1-58536-538-8(6))* Sleeping Bear Pr.
Joyce, Susan. ABC Nature Riddles. DuBosque, Doug, illus. 2004. (ABC Riddles Ser.). 32p. (J). (gr. -1-k). 13.95 *(978-0-939217-53-3(8))* Peel Productions, Inc.
Klutz Editors, ed. Carabiners: Weird Facts; Random Riddles; Really Dumb Jokes. 2004. (ENG., Illus.). 40p. (J). 3.95 *(978-1-59174-295-1(1))* Klutz.
Kowitt, Holly. Too Funny! 234 Laugh-Out-Loud Jokes. 2008. (Illus.). 63p. (J). pap. *(978-0-439-67172-9(8))* Scholastic, Inc.
Laffin, Ima. Monster Jokes, 1 vol. 2004. (Jokes Ser.). (ENG.). 24p. (gr. k-4). 25.65 *(978-1-59197-623-5(5)*, Buddy Bks.) ABDO Publishing Co.
—More Monster Jokes, 1 vol. 2005. (More Jokes! Ser.). (ENG., Illus.). 24p. (gr. k-4). 25.65 *(978-1-59197-874-9(2)*, Buddy Bks.) ABDO Publishing Co.
Lanchais, Aurelie, et al. I Can Fly, What Am I? 2005. (Who Am I? What Am I? Ser.). (Illus.). 16p. (J). (gr. -1-1). (ARA, ENG, URD, CHI & BEN.). 9.95 *(978-1-84059-250-4(8))*; (URD, ENG, CHI, ARA & BEN., 9.95 *(978-1-84059-255-9(9))* Milet Publishing.
—Kto A? 2005. (Who Am I? What Am I? Ser.).Tr. of Who Am I? (RUS, ENG, TUR, VIE & CHI., Illus.). 16p. (J). (gr. -1-1). 9.95 *(978-1-84059-232-0(X))* Milet Publishing.
—What Am I? 2005. (Who Am I? What Am I? Ser.). (Illus.). 16p. (J). (gr. -1-1). (ARA, ENG, URD, TUR & CHI.). 9.95 *(978-1-84059-243-6(5))*; (URD, ENG, CHI, ARA & BEN., 9.95 *(978-1-84059-248-1(6))* Milet Publishing.
—Who Am I? 2005. (Who Am I? What Am I? Ser.). (CHI, ENG, VIE, GUJ & RUS., Illus.). 16p. (J). (gr. -1-1). 9.95 *(978-1-84059-229-0(X))* Milet Publishing.
LeCompte, David & Padrick, Kendell. Eugene Stillwell Wants to Know!, Pt. 2. 2009. (Eugene Stillwell Wants to Know! Ser.). (ENG.). 96p. (J). (gr. 4-6). pap. 4.95 *(978-1-929945-74-0(4))* Big Guy Bks., Inc.
—Eugene Stillwell Wants to Know! Part III. 2009. (Eugene Stillwell Wants to Know! Ser.). (ENG.). 96p. (J). (gr. 4-6). pap. 4.95 *(978-1-929945-91-7(4))* Big Guy Bks., Inc.
Lee, Cyl. More Ridiculous Riddles, 1 vol. 2005. (More Jokes! Ser.). (ENG., Illus.). 24p. (gr. k-4). 25.65 *(978-1-59197-876-3(9)*, Buddy Bks.) ABDO Publishing Co.
—Really Silly Jokes, 1 vol. 2004. (Jokes Ser.). (ENG.). 24p. (gr. k-4). 25.65 *(978-1-59197-624-0(3)*, Buddy Bks.) ABDO Publishing Co.
—Ridiculous Riddles, 1 vol. 2004. (Jokes Ser.). (ENG.). 24p. (gr. k-4). 25.65 *(978-1-59197-625-7(1)*, Buddy Bks.) ABDO Publishing Co.
Lewis, J. Patrick. Just Joking Animal Riddles. 2015. (ENG., Illus.). 208p. (J). (gr. 2-5). pap. 7.99 *(978-1-4263-1869-6(3)*, National Geographic Children's Bks.) National Geographic Society.
Libal, Autumn. Folk Proverbs & Riddles. 2004. (North American Folklore Ser.). (Illus.). 112p. (YA). (gr. 7-18). lib. bdg. 22.95 *(978-1-59084-343-7(6))* Mason Crest.
El Libro de los Acertijos Historicos. (Coleccion Acertijos). (SPA.). (YA). (gr. 5-8). pap. *(978-950-724-249-6(X)*, LMA8235) Lumen ARG. Dist: Lectorum Pubns., Inc.
Lome, Emilio Angel. Lottery of Riddles. Martinez, Enrique, illus. 2011. 46p. (gr. 2-5). pap. 6.95 *(978-968-19-0663-4(2))* Aguilar, Altea, Taurus, Alfaguara, S.A. de C.V MEX. Dist: Santillana USA Publishing Co., Inc.
Lupton, Hugh. Riddle Me This! Riddles & Stories to Challenge Your Mind. Fatus, Sophie, illus. 2003. 64p. (J). 19.99 *(978-1-84148-169-2(6))* Barefoot Bks., Inc.
—Riddle Me This! Riddles & Stories to Sharpen Your Wits. Fatus, Sophie, illus. 2007. (ENG.). 64p. (J). pap. 12.99 *(978-1-905236-92-3(1))* Barefoot Bks., Inc.
Macari, Mario Duilio, ed. & illus. Funny Riddles for Kids: Squeaky Clean Easy Kid Riddles Drawn As Funny Kid's Cartoons in A Cool Comicbook Style. Macari, Mario Duilio, illus. 2007. 104p. (J). per. 10.00 *(978-0-9766755-0-1(1))* Cartoonmario.com.
Martin, Jannelle. ABC Math Riddles. Levin, Freddie, illus. 2003. (ABC Riddles Ser.). 32p. (J). 13.95 *(978-0-939217-57-1(0))* Peel Productions, Inc.
Martin, Norma. Don Martin Brain Games for Kids. 2007. 68p. pap. 3.95 *(978-1-4343-2848-9(1))* AuthorHouse.
Marzollo, Jean & Wick, Walter. I Spy a Dinosaur's Eye. 2003. (I Spy — Scholastic Readers Level 1 Ser.). (gr. -1-2). lib. bdg. 13.55 *(978-0-613-72243-8(4)*, Turtleback) Turtleback Bks.
—School Bus. 2003. (I Spy — Scholastic Readers Level 1 Ser.). (gr. -1-2). lib. bdg. 13.55 *(978-0-613-72246-9(9)*, Turtleback) Turtleback Bks.
Meachen Rau, Dana. At the Zoo. 2007. (Fun Time Ser.). (Illus.). 24p. (gr. k-1). lib. bdg. 15.95 *(978-0-7614-2610-3(8)*, Benchmark Bks.) Marshall Cavendish Corp.
—Baker. 2007. (Jobs in Town Ser.). (SPA., Illus.). 24p. (gr. k-1). lib. bdg. 15.95 *(978-0-7614-2623-3(X)*, Benchmark Bks.) Marshall Cavendish Corp.
—Un Bombero. 2007. (En el Trabajo Ser.). (SPA., Illus.). 24p. (gr. k-1). lib. bdg. 15.95 *(978-0-7614-2782-7(1)*, Benchmark Bks.) Marshall Cavendish Corp.
—Driving. 2006. (On the Move Ser.). (ENG & SPA., Illus.). 24p. (gr. k-1). lib. bdg. 15.95 *(978-0-7614-2316-4(8)*, Benchmark Bks.) Marshall Cavendish Corp.
—En el Picnic. 2007. (¡A Divertimos! Ser.). (SPA., Illus.). 24p. (gr. k-1). lib. bdg. 15.95 *(978-0-7614-2779-7(1)*, Benchmark Bks.) Marshall Cavendish Corp.
—Firefighter. 2007. (Jobs in Town Ser.). (SPA., Illus.). 24p. (gr. k-1). lib. bdg. 15.95 *(978-0-7614-2617-2(5)*, Benchmark Bks.) Marshall Cavendish Corp.
—Librarian. 2007. (J). *(978-0-7614-2621-9(3))* Marshall Cavendish.
—On a Farm. 2007. (Fun Time Ser.). (Illus.). 24p. (gr. k-1). lib. bdg. 15.95 *(978-0-7614-2605-9(1)*, Benchmark Bks.) Marshall Cavendish Corp.
—Un Panadero. 2007. (En el Trabajo Ser.). (SPA., Illus.). 24p. (gr. k-1). lib. bdg. 15.95 *(978-0-7614-2781-0(3)*, Benchmark Bks.) Marshall Cavendish Corp.
—Riding. 2006. (On the Move Ser.). (Illus.). 24p. (gr. k-1). lib. bdg. 15.95 *(978-0-7614-2317-1(6))* Marshall Cavendish Corp.
Menotti, Andrea. How to Tackle Puzzles, Unravel Riddles, Crack Codes, & Other Ways to Bend Your Brain. 2004. (Illus.). 80p. (J). *(978-0-439-57905-6(8))* Scholastic, Inc.
Miller, Shane, illus. Riddles, Riddles, Riddles: Enigmas & Anagrams, Puns & Puzzles, Quizzes & Conundrums! 2014. (ENG.). 256p. (J). (gr. 3-8). pap. 9.99 *(978-0-486-78186-0(0))* Dover Pubns., Inc.
Moore, Hugh. Bug Jokes, 1 vol. 2005. (More Jokes! Ser.). (ENG., Illus.). 24p. (gr. k-4). 25.65 *(978-1-59197-870-1(X)*, Buddy Bks.) ABDO Publishing Co.
—Food Jokes, 1 vol. 2005. (More Jokes! Ser.). (ENG., Illus.). 24p. (gr. k-4). 25.65 *(978-1-59197-871-8(8)*, Buddy Bks.) ABDO Publishing Co.
Morrison, Lillian. Guess Again! Riddle Poems. Hale, Christy, illus. 2006. (ENG.). 48p. (J). (gr. 1-4). 16.95 *(978-0-87483-730-8(8))* August Hse. Pubs., Inc.
Murray, Carol. ABC Art Riddles. Levin, Freddie, illus. 2005. (ABC Riddles Ser.). 32p. (J). (gr. -1-3). 13.95 *(978-0-939217-58-8(9))* Peel Productions, Inc.
Napier, Matt. Little Canada. 2012. (Little Country Ser.). (ENG., Illus.). 22p. (J). (gr. k-3). 9.95 *(978-1-58536-178-6(X))* Sleeping Bear Pr.
Nature Riddles [Capstone Sole Source]. 2010. (Nature Riddles Ser.). 32p. lib. bdg. 103.96 *(978-1-4296-5873-7(8)*, Aplus Bks.) Capstone Press of Coughlan Cos.
Nelson, Esther & Hirsch, Davida. Riggeldy Jiggeldy Joggeldy Jam: Can You Guess Who I Am? Ellis, Libby, illus. 2003. (J). bds. 5.95 *(978-0-7607-3278-6(7))* Barnes & Noble, Inc.
Noble, Trinka Hakes. Little New Jersey. Brett, Jeannie, illus. 2012. (My Little State Ser.). (ENG.). 20p. (J). bds. 9.95 *(978-1-58536-786-3(9))* Sleeping Bear Pr.
—Little Pennsylvania Board Book. Brett, Jeannie, illus. 2010. (My Little State Ser.). (ENG.). 22p. (J). 9.95 *(978-1-58536-506-7(8))* Sleeping Bear Pr.
O'Hare, J. The Highlights Big Book of Fun: An Amazing Collection of Jokes, Riddles, Puzzles, & More! 2003. (ENG., Illus.). 96p. (YA). (gr. k-7). pap., act. bk. ed. 9.95 *(978-1-59078-006-0(X))* Boyds Mills Pr.
Paletta, Emilio. Squire Dumpty. 2009. 28p. pap. 15.49 *(978-1-4389-4533-0(7))* AuthorHouse.
Peterson, Scott K. Let the Fun Begin: Nifty Knock-Knocks, Playful Puns, & More. Gable, Brian, illus. 2005. (Make Me Laugh! Ser.). 32p. (J). (gr. k-3). lib. bdg. 19.93 *(978-1-57505-661-6(5))* Lerner Publishing Group.
Phillips, Bob. All-Time Awesome Collection of Good Clean Jokes for Kids. 2006. (Illus.). 366p. (J). (gr. 3-12). per. 10.99 *(978-0-7369-1777-3(2))* Harvest Hse. Pubs.
Phunny, U. R. Animal Jokes, 1 vol. 2004. (Jokes Ser.). (ENG.). 24p. (gr. k-4). 25.65 *(978-1-59197-620-2(0)*, Buddy Bks.) ABDO Publishing Co.
—Dinosaur Jokes, 1 vol. 2004. (Jokes Ser.). (ENG.). 24p. (gr. k-4). 25.65 *(978-1-59197-621-9(9)*, Buddy Bks.) ABDO Publishing Co.
—More Animal Jokes, 1 vol. 2005. (More Jokes! Ser.). (ENG., Illus.). 24p. (gr. k-4). 25.65 *(978-1-59197-872-5(6)*, Buddy Bks.) ABDO Publishing Co.
Prieto, Anita C. Little Louisiana. Knorr, Laura, illus. 2011. (My Little State Ser.). (ENG.). 20p. 9.95 *(978-1-58536-184-7(4))* Sleeping Bear Pr.
Rechin, Kevin, illus. Guess Again! 1,001 Rib-Tickling Riddles from Highlights. 2012. (Laugh Attack! Ser.). (ENG.). 256p. (J). (gr. k). pap. 5.95 *(978-1-59078-919-3(9))* Boyds Mills Pr.
Regan, Lisa. Animal Riddles. 2014. (Riddle Me This! Ser.). 32p. (J). (gr. 1-5). lib. bdg. 27.50 *(978-1-4777-9157-8(4))* Windmill Bks.
—Farmyard Riddles. 2014. (Riddle Me This! Ser.). 32p. (J). (gr. 1-5). lib. bdg. 27.50 *(978-1-4777-9161-5(2))* Windmill Bks.
Richards, Kitty. Phineas & Ferb Laughapalooza Joke Book. 2011. (ENG., Illus.). (J). (-3). pap. *(978-1-4075-8486-7(3))* Parragon Bk. Service Ltd.
Riddle Me This! 2014. (Riddle Me This! Ser.). 32p. (J). (gr. 1-5). 165.00 *(978-1-4777-9181-3(7))* Windmill Bks.
Robleda, Margarita. Quien Soy? Adivinanzas Animales. Gurovich, Natalia, illus. 2003. (SPA.). 32p. (J). 12.95 *(978-970-690-805-6(6))* Planeta Mexicana Editorial S. A. de C. V. MEX. Dist: Lectorum Pubns., Inc.
Rodger, Anne-Marie. Sports Jokes, Riddles, & Games. 2016. (ENG., Illus.). 32p. (J). *(978-0-7787-2390-5(9))* Crabtree Publishing Co.
Rodger, Ellen. Monster & Creepy-Crawly Jokes, Riddles, & Games. 2016. (ENG., Illus.). 32p. (J). *(978-0-7787-2389-9(5))* Crabtree Publishing Co.
Rodger, Marguerite. Around the World in Jokes, Riddles, & Games. 2016. (ENG., Illus.). 32p. (J). *(978-0-7787-2388-2(7))* Crabtree Publishing Co.
Rosenbloom, Joseph. Jokes. Hoffman, Sanford, illus. 2007. (ENG.). 352p. (J). (gr. 2-5). pap. 6.95 *(978-1-4027-4973-5(2))* Sterling Publishing Co., Inc.
—Riddles. Hoffman, Sanford, illus. 2007. (ENG.). 352p. (J). (gr. 2-5). pap. 6.95 *(978-1-4027-4972-8(4))* Sterling Publishing Co., Inc.
Saffer, Barbara. ABC Science Riddles. Johnson, Jennifer, illus. 2004. (ABC Riddles Ser.). 32p. (J). (gr. -1-3). 13.95 *(978-0-939217-55-7(4))* Peel Productions, Inc.
Sawyers, William. What Am I? Book. 2005. 44p. pap. 8.95 *(978-1-4116-2899-1(3))* Lulu Pr., Inc.
—What Am I? Bugs. 2005. 65p. (J). pap. 16.01 *(978-1-4116-3402-2(0))* Lulu Pr., Inc.
Scheunemann, Pam. Ape Cape, 1 vol. 2004. (Rhyming Riddles Ser.). (ENG., Illus.). 24p. (J). (gr. k-3). lib. bdg. 24.21 *(978-1-59197-457-4(7)*, SandCastle) ABDO Publishing Co.
—Chipper Flipper, 1 vol. 2004. (Rhyming Riddles Ser.). (ENG., Illus.). 24p. (J). (gr. k-3). lib. bdg. 24.21 *(978-1-59197-458-1(5)*, SandCastle) ABDO Publishing Co.
—Cooler Ruler, 1 vol. 2004. (Rhyming Riddles Ser.). (ENG., Illus.). 24p. (J). (gr. k-3). lib. bdg. 24.21 *(978-1-59197-459-8(3)*, SandCastle) ABDO Publishing Co.
—Dill Spill, 1 vol. 2004. (Rhyming Riddles Ser.). (ENG., Illus.). 24p. (J). (gr. k-3). lib. bdg. 24.21 *(978-1-59197-460-4(7)*, SandCastle) ABDO Publishing Co.
—Loud Crowd, 1 vol. 2004. (Rhyming Riddles Ser.). (ENG., Illus.). 24p. (J). (gr. k-3). lib. bdg. 24.21 *(978-1-59197-461-1(5)*, SandCastle) ABDO Publishing Co.
—Overdue Kangaroo, 1 vol. 2004. (Rhyming Riddles Ser.). (ENG., Illus.). 24p. (J). (gr. k-3). lib. bdg. 24.21 *(978-1-59197-462-8(3)*, SandCastle) ABDO Publishing Co.
Scheunemann, Pam & ABDO Publishing Company Staff. Rhyming Riddles. 2004. (Rhyming Riddles Ser.: 6). (ENG.). (J). (gr. k-3). lib. bdg. 145.26 *(978-1-59197-456-7(9)*, SandCastle) ABDO Publishing Co.
Scholastic, Inc. Staff. Corny Jokes & Riddles. 2016. (Shopkins Ser.). (ENG.). 48p. (J). (gr. -1-3). pap. 4.99 *(978-0-545-94049-8(4))* Scholastic, Inc.
—I Spy Fantasy. 2008. 29.99 *(978-0-439-82065-3(0))* Scholastic, Inc.
—I Spy Riddle Master. 2008. 29.99 *(978-0-439-93519-7(9))* Scholastic, Inc.
Schonberg, Marcia. Little Ohio. Monroe, Michael Glenn, illus. 2011. (My Little State Ser.). (ENG.). 20p. (J). 9.95 *(978-1-58536-527-2(0))* Sleeping Bear Pr.
Shannon, George. Red All Over. Date not set. (J). (gr. 3-7). pap. 4.99 *(978-0-380-80072-8(1))* HarperCollins Pubs.
Sharpe, Angeles. Quiz Spinners: Book #1: Fun-Filled Facts & Brain-Teasers! 2015. (Quiz Spinners Ser.). (ENG.). 60p. (J). (gr. -1-1). 5.99 *(978-0-7641-6755-3(3))* Barron's Educational Series, Inc.
—Quiz Spinners: Book #2: Fun-Filled Facts & Brain-Teasers! 2015. (Quiz Spinners Ser.). (ENG.). 60p. (J). (gr. -1-1). 5.99 *(978-0-7641-6756-0(1))* Barron's Educational Series, Inc.
Sky Pony Editors, Sky Pony. Belly Laugh Jokes for Kids. Straker, Bethany, illus. 2015. (ENG.). 144p. (J). (gr. k). 9.99 *(978-1-63450-156-9(X)*, Sky Pony Pr.) Skyhorse Publishing Co., Inc.
Smith, Shuford. ABC All-American Riddles. 2003. (Illus.). (J). 13.95 *(978-0-939217-56-4(2))* Peel Productions, Inc.
Snedeker, Gus. An Apple a Day: Folk Proverbs & Riddles. 2013. (Illus.). 48p. (J). pap. *(978-1-4222-2504-2(6))* Mason Crest.
—An Apple a Day: Folk Proverbs & Riddles. Jabbour, Alan, ed. 2012. (North American Folklore for Youth Ser.). (Illus.). 48p. (J). (gr. 4). 19.95 *(978-1-4222-2493-9(7))* Mason Crest.
Speirs, John. Best Halloween Hunt Ever. Speirs, John, illus. 2008. (ENG., Illus.). 32p. (J). (gr. -1-3). pap. 4.99 *(978-0-545-06867-3(3)*, Cartwheel Bks.) Scholastic, Inc.
Stemen, Jeffrey, illus. Critter Giggles. 2006. (J). *(978-1-58987-035-2(2))* Kindermusik International.
Stewart, Trenton Lee. Mr. Benedict's Book of Perplexing Puzzles, Elusive Enigmas, & Curious Conundrums. Sudyka, Diana, illus. 2011. (Mysterious Benedict Society Ser.). (ENG.). 176p. (J). (gr. 3-7). 15.99 *(978-0-316-18193-8(5))* Little, Brown Bks. for Young Readers.
Super Giggles: Knock-Knocks, Jokes, & Tongue-Twisters. 2005. (Illus.). 176p. pap. *(978-0-7607-6782-5(3))* Barnes & Noble, Inc.
Tait, Chris, et al. Super Silliest Riddles. 2007. (ENG., Illus.). 352p. (J). (gr. 3-7). pap. 6.95 *(978-1-4027-4992-6(9))* Sterling Publishing Co., Inc.
Terban, Marvin. The Dove Dove: Funny Homograph Riddles. Huffman, Tom, illus. 2008. (ENG.). 64p. (J). (gr. 5-7). pap. 6.95 *(978-0-547-03186-6(6))* Houghton Mifflin Harcourt Publishing Co.
—Eight Ate: A Feast of Homonym Riddles. Maestro, Giulio, illus. 2007. (ENG.). 64p. (J). (gr. -1-3). pap. 7.99 *(978-0-618-76676-5(6))* Houghton Mifflin Harcourt Publishing Co.
—Too Hot to Hoot: Funny Palindrome Riddles. Maestro, Giulio, illus. 2008. (ENG.). 64p. (J). (gr. 2-5). pap. 8.95 *(978-0-618-19165-9(8))* Houghton Mifflin Harcourt Publishing Co.
Trueit, Trudi Strain. Christmas. 2010. (Benchmark Rebus Ser.). 24p. (gr. k-1). 15.95 *(978-0-7614-4885-3(3))* Marshall Cavendish Corp.
—Halloween. 2010. (Benchmark Rebus: Holiday Fun Ser.). 24p. (gr. k-1). 15.95 *(978-0-7614-4886-0(1))* Marshall Cavendish Corp.
—Hanukkah. 2010. (Benchmark Rebus Ser.). 24p. (gr. k-1). 15.95 *(978-0-7614-4884-6(5))* Marshall Cavendish Corp.
—Jellyfish. 2010. (Benchmark Rebus: Ocean Life Ser.). 24p. (gr. k-1). 15.95 *(978-0-7614-4891-4(8))* Marshall Cavendish Corp.
—Octopuses. 2010. (Benchmark Rebus: Ocean Life Ser.). 24p. (gr. k-1). 15.95 *(978-0-7614-4892-1(6))* Marshall Cavendish GBR. Dist: Marshall Cavendish Corp.
—Thanksgiving. 2010. (Benchmark Rebus: Holiday Fun Ser.). 24p. (gr. k-1). 15.95 *(978-0-7614-4888-4(8))* Marshall Cavendish Corp.
—Valentine's Day. 2010. (Benchmark Rebus: Holiday Fun Ser.). 24p. (gr. k-1). 15.95 *(978-0-7614-4889-1(6))* Marshall Cavendish Corp.
Vaicikonis, Kris. Puzzle Me-Brain Twisters. 2012. (Illus.). 32p. (J). pap. 4.99 *(978-1-62267-006-2(X))* Bright Connections Media.
Vidro, Kenn. Square Pears Three: Hey Diddle Riddle. 2005. (ENG., Illus.). 100p. (J). spiral bd. 9.95 *(978-0-9745308-2-6(4))* Gilbert Square Bks.
—Square Pears Two: The Equal Sequel. Vidro, Kenn, illus. 2004. (ENG., Illus.). 100p. (J). spiral bd. 9.95 *(978-0-9745308-1-9(6))* Gilbert Square Bks.
Walton, Rick & Walton, Ann. Foul Play: Sports Jokes That Won't Strike Out. Gable, Brian, illus. 2005. (Make Me Laugh! Ser.). 32p. (J). (gr. k-3). lib. bdg. 19.93 *(978-1-57505-666-1(6))* Lerner Publishing Group.
—Magical Mischief: Jokes That Shock & Amaze. Gable, Brian, illus. 2005. (Make Me Laugh! Ser.). 32p. (J). (gr. k-3). lib. bdg. 19.93 *(978-1-57505-664-7(X))* Lerner Publishing Group.
Walton, Rick, et al. Real Classy: Silly School Jokes. Gable, Brian, illus. 2005. (Make Me Laugh! Ser.). 32p. (J). (gr. k-3). lib. bdg. 19.93 *(978-1-57505-665-4(8))* Lerner Publishing Group.
Wargin, Kathy-jo. Little Minnesota. Urban, Helle, illus. 2011. (My Little State Ser.). (ENG.). 22p. (J). 9.95 *(978-1-58536-174-8(7))* Sleeping Bear Pr.
—Little Wisconsin. 2012. (My Little State Ser.). (ENG., Illus.). 20p. (J). (gr. k-3). 9.95 *(978-1-58536-209-7(3))* Sleeping Bear Pr.
West, Tracey & Nolls, Katherine. Challenge. 2008. (Pokemon Ser.). (ENG., Illus.). 64p. (J). (gr. 2-5). pap. 4.99 *(978-0-439-53052-1(0))* Scholastic, Inc.
Wilbur, Helen. Little New York. Brett, Jeannie, illus. 2010. (My Little State Ser.). (ENG.). 22p. (J). 9.95 *(978-1-58536-491-6(6))* Sleeping Bear Pr.
William H. Sadlier Staff. Buggy Riddles, Vol. 2. 2005. (Fluent Library). (gr. 1-3). 29.34 *(978-0-8215-8969-4(5))* Sadlier, William H. Inc.
Young, Judy & Wargin, Kathy-jo. Little Missouri. Urban, Helle, illus. 2012. (My Little State Ser.). (ENG.). 20p. (J). bds. 9.95 *(978-1-58536-206-6(9))* Sleeping Bear Pr.

RIDE, SALLY, 1951-2012

Anderson, AnnMarie. When I Grow up - Sally Ride. Kelley, Gerald, illus. 2015. (Scholastic Reader Level 3 Ser.). (ENG.). 32p. (J). (gr. 1-2). pap. 3.99 *(978-0-545-60983-8(6)*, Scholastic Paperbacks) Scholastic, Inc.
Bindi, Paulo. Sally Ride: The Sky's the Limit. 2013. (InfoMax Readers Ser.). (ENG.). 24p. (J). (gr. 2-3). pap. 49.50 *(978-1-4777-2452-1(4))*; (Illus.). pap. 8.25 *(978-1-4777-2451-4(6))* Rosen Publishing Group, Inc., The. (Rosen Classroom).
Edison, Erin. Sally Ride, 1 vol. 2014. (Great Women in History Ser.). (ENG.). 24p. (gr. k-1). lib. bdg. 21.99 *(978-1-4765-4215-7(5)*, Pebble Bks.) Capstone Press of Coughlan Cos.
Gomez, Rebecca. Sally Ride, 1 vol. 2003. (First Biographies Ser.). (ENG., Illus.). 32p. (gr. k-4). 27.07 *(978-1-57765-948-8(1)*, Buddy Bks.) ABDO Publishing Co.
Mattern, Joanne. Sally Ride: Astronaut. 2005. (Ferguson Career Biographies Ser.). (Illus.). 122p. (gr. 6-12). 25.00

(978-0-8160-5892-1(X), Ferguson Publishing Co.) Facts On File, Inc.

Murphy, Sage. Sally Ride: Female Astronaut. 2013. (Rosen Readers Ser.). (ENG.). 24p. (J). (gr. 2-3). pap. 8.25 (978-1-4777-2306-7(4)); pap. 49.50 (978-1-4777-2307-4(2)) Rosen Publishing Group, Inc., The. (Rosen Classroom).

Nettleton, Pamela Hill. Sally Ride: Astronaut, Scientist, Teacher. Yesh, Jeff & Nichols, Garry, illus. 2003. (Biographies Ser.). (ENG.). 24p. (gr. k-3). 26.65 (978-1-4048-0189-9(8)) Picture Window Bks.

O'Shaughnessy, Tam. Sally Ride: A Photobiography of America's Pioneering Woman in Space. 2015. (ENG., Illus.). 160p. (J). (gr. 5-8). 19.99 (978-1-59643-994-8(7), 9781596439948) Roaring Brook Pr.

Riddolls, Tom. Sally Ride: The First American Woman in Space. 2010. (Crabtree Groundbreaker Biographies Ser.). (ENG., Illus.). 112p. (J). pap. (978-0-7787-2550-3(2)); (gr. 5-8). lib. bdg. (978-0-7787-2541-1(3)) Crabtree Publishing Co.

Sally Ride: Life on a Mission. 2014. (Real-Life Story Ser.). (ENG., Illus.). 160p. (J). (gr. 3-7). 18.99 (978-1-4424-8854-0(9), Aladdin) Simon & Schuster Children's Publishing.

Stine, Megan. Who Was Sally Ride? 2013. (Who Was? Ser.). (ENG.). 112p. (J). (gr. 3-7). pap. 5.99 (978-0-448-46687-3(2), Grosset & Dunlap) Penguin Young Readers Group.

—Who Was Sally Ride? 2013. (Who Was... ? Ser.). lib. bdg. 16.00 (978-0-606-31683-5(3), Turtleback) Turtleback Bks.

RIDER, ALEX (FICTITIOUS CHARACTER)—FICTION

Horowitz, Anthony. Ark Angel. (Alex Rider Ser.: Bk. 6). (ENG.). (J). (gr. 5-18). 2007. 352p. 8.99 (978-0-14-240738-7(0), Puffin Books) 2006. 336p. 17.99 (978-0-399-24152-9(3), Philomel Bks.) Penguin Young Readers Group.

—Crocodile Tears. (Alex Rider Ser.: Bk. 8). (ENG.). (J). (gr. 5-18). 2010. 416p. 8.99 (978-0-14-241719-5(X), Puffin Books) 2009. 400p. 18.99 (978-0-399-25056-9(5), Philomel Bks.) Penguin Young Readers Group.

—Crocodile Tears, 9 vols. 2010. (Alex Rider Adventure Ser.: 8). (J). 81.75 (978-1-4407-5451-7(9)); 102.75 (978-1-4407-5456-2(X)); 79.75 (978-1-4407-5453-1(5)); 1.25 (978-1-4407-5459-3(4)); 100.75 (978-1-4407-5458-6(6)) Recorded Bks., Inc.

—Crocodile Tears. 2010. (Alex Rider Ser.: 8). lib. bdg. 19.65 (978-0-606-23639-3(2), Turtleback) Turtleback Bks.

—Eagle Strike. (Alex Rider Ser.). (ENG.). (J). (gr. 5-18). 2006. 368p. 8.99 (978-0-14-240613-7(9), Puffin Books) 2004. (Illus.). 272p. 17.99 (978-0-399-23979-3(0), Philomel Bks.) Penguin Young Readers Group.

—Point Blanc. 2004. (Alex Rider Ser.: Bk. 2). (SPA.). 264p. pap. 7.95 (978-84-414-1410-5(6)) Editorial Edaf, S.L. ESP. Dist: Spanish Pubs., LLC.

—Point Blank. 2006. (Alex Rider Ser.). (ENG.). 320p. (J). (gr. 5-18). 8.99 (978-0-14-240612-0(0), Puffin Books) Penguin Young Readers Group.

—Russian Roulette: The Story of an Assassin. 2013. (Alex Rider Ser.). (ENG.). 384p. (J). (gr. 6-9). 17.99 (978-0-399-25441-3(2), Philomel Bks.) Penguin Publishing Group.

—Scorpia. (Alex Rider Ser.). (ENG.). (J). (gr. 5-18). 2006. 416p. pap. 8.99 (978-0-14-240578-9(7), Puffin Books) 2005. 336p. 17.99 (978-0-399-24151-2(5), Philomel Bks.) Penguin Young Readers Group.

—Scorpia Rising. (Alex Rider Ser.). (ENG.). (J). (gr. 5-18). 2012. 432p. 8.99 (978-0-14-241985-4(0), Puffin Books) 2011. 416p. 17.99 (978-0-399-25057-6(3), Philomel Bks.) Penguin Young Readers Group.

—Scorpia Rising. (J). 2012. 1.25 (978-1-4640-0577-0(X)) 2012. 256.75 (978-1-4561-3362-7(4)) 2012. 90.75 (978-1-4561-3363-4(2)) 2011. 122.75 (978-1-4561-3365-8(9)) 2011. 120.75 (978-1-4561-3367-2(5)) Recorded Bks., Inc.

—Scorpia Rising. 2012. (Alex Rider Ser.: 9). lib. bdg. 19.65 (978-0-606-23638-6(4), Turtleback) Turtleback Bks.

—Skeleton Key. (Alex Rider Ser.: Bk. 3). (ENG.). (J). (gr. 5-18). 2006. 368p. 8.99 (978-0-14-240614-4(7), Puffin Books) 2003. 240p. 17.99 (978-0-399-23777-5(1), Philomel Bks.) Penguin Young Readers Group.

—Stormbreaker. Damerum, Kanako et al, illus. 2006. (Alex Rider Ser.). (ENG.). 144p. (J). (gr. 5-18). pap. 14.99 (978-0-399-24633-3(9), Philomel Bks.) Penguin Young Readers Group.

—Stormbreaker. 2006. (Alex Rider Ser.: Bk. 1). (ENG.). 304p. (J). (gr. 5-18). 8.99 (978-0-14-240611-3(2), Puffin Books) Penguin Young Readers Group.

—Stormbreaker. 2004. (Alex Rider Ser.: Bk. 1). 208p. (J). (gr. 4-7). pap. 38.00 incl. audio (978-0-8072-2277-5(1), Listening Library) Random Hse. Audio Publishing Group.

RIDING

see Horsemanship

RIEL REBELLION, 1885—FICTION

Bayle, B. J. Battle Cry at Batoche. 2008. (ENG.). 160p. (J). (gr. 7). pap. 11.99 (978-1-55002-717-4(4), Sandcastle Bks.) Dundurn CAN. Dist: Ingram Publisher Services.

RIFLES

Crompton, Samuel Willard. The Repeating Rifle. 2003. (Transforming Power of Technology Ser.). (Illus.). 112p. (J). (gr. 9-13). 30.00 (978-0-7910-7452-7(8), Chelsea Hse.) Facts On File, Inc.

Hemstock, Annie Wendt. Hunting with Rifles. 2014. (Open Season Ser.). 32p. (J). (gr. 4-6). lib. bdg. 26.25 (978-1-4777-6710-8(X), PowerKids Pr.) Rosen Publishing Group, Inc., The.

Kiland, Taylor Baldwin & Souter, Gerry. Military Rifles: Combat Ready. 2015. (Military Engineering in Action Ser.). (ENG.). 48p. (J). (gr. 6-6). pap. 11.70 (978-0-7660-7067-7(0)); (Illus.). 27.93 (978-0-7660-6916-9(8)) Enslow Pubs., Inc.

Souter, Gerry. Military Rifles: Fierce Firepower. 2006. (Mighty Military Machines Ser.). (Illus.). 48p. (J). (gr. 4-10). lib. bdg. 25.27 (978-0-7660-2662-9(0)) Enslow Pubs., Inc.

RIGHT (POLITICAL SCIENCE)

see Right and Left (Political Science)

RIGHT AND LEFT (POLITICAL SCIENCE)

see also Conservatism

Cunningham, Jesse G., ed. The McCarthy Hearings. 2003. (At Issue in History Ser.). (Illus.). 144p. (YA). (gr. 7-10). pap. 18.70 (978-0-7377-1347-3(X), Greenhaven Pr., Inc.) Cengage Gale.

RIGHT OF ASSEMBLY

see Assembly, Right of

RIGHT OF PRIVACY

see Privacy, Right of

RIGHT TO DIE

Donnelly, Karen J. Cruzan v. Missouri: The Right to Die. 2004. (Supreme Court Cases Through Primary Sources Ser.). (Illus.). 64p. (YA). (gr. 5-9). lib. bdg. 31.95 (978-0-8239-4014-1(4)) Rosen Publishing Group, Inc., The.

Ferguson, John E. & Ferguson, John E., Jr. The Right to Die. 2007. (Point/Counterpoint Ser.). (Illus.). 109p. (YA). (gr. 9-12). lib. bdg. 35.00 (978-0-7910-9287-3(9)) Facts On File, Inc.

Harris, Nancy. The Right to Die. annot. ed. 2005. (At Issue Ser.). (ENG.). 94p. (YA). (gr. 10-12). pap. 31.80 (978-0-7377-3439-3(6), Greenhaven Pr., Inc.) Cengage Gale.

Perl, Lila. Cruzan V. Missouri: The Right to Die. 2007. (Supreme Court Milestones Ser.). (Illus.). 128p. (gr. 7-7). lib. bdg. 42.79 (978-0-7614-2581-6(0), Benchmark Bks.) Marshall Cavendish Corp.

Stefoff, Rebecca. The Right to Die. 2008. (Open for Debate Ser.). 128p. (gr. 7-18). lib. bdg. 42.79 (978-0-7614-2948-7(4), Benchmark Bks.) Marshall Cavendish Corp.

Thompson, Tamara. The Right to Die. Gale, G., ed. 2014. (At Issue Ser.). (ENG.). 128p. (gr. 10-12). lib. bdg. 39.40 (978-0-7377-6850-3(9), Greenhaven Pr., Inc.) Cengage Gale.

Woodward, John. The Right to Die. annot. ed. 2004. (At Issue Ser.). (ENG.). 94p. (YA). (gr. 10-12). 22.50 (978-0-7377-3440-9(X), Greenhaven Pr., Inc.) Cengage Gale.

Yount, Lisa. Right to Die & Euthanasia. 2nd rev. ed. 2007. (Library in a Book). (Illus.). 320p. (C). (gr. 9-18). 45.00 (978-0-8160-6275-1(7)) Facts On File, Inc.

RIGHT TO WORK

see Discrimination in Employment

RIGHTS, CIVIL

see Civil Rights

RIIS, JACOB A. (JACOB AUGUST), 1849-1914—FICTION

Kroll, Steven. Sweet America: An Immigrant's Story. 2004. 172p. (J). lib. bdg. 16.92 (978-1-4242-0773-2(8)) Fitzgerald Bks.

RINGLING BROTHERS

Apps, Jerry. Tents, Tigers & the Ringling Brothers. 2006. (Badger Biographies Ser.). (ENG., Illus.). 128p. (J). (gr. 3-7). per. 12.95 (978-0-87020-374-9(6)) Wisconsin Historical Society.

RINGLING BROTHERS AND BARNUM AND BAILEY CIRCUS

Woollett, Laura A. Big Top Burning: The True Story of an Arsonist, a Missing Girl, & the Greatest Show on Earth. 2015. (ENG.). 176p. (J). (gr. 5). 18.95 (978-1-61373-114-7(0)) Chicago Review Pr., Inc.

RIO DE JANEIRO (BRAZIL)

Candlewick Press Staff. Rio de Janeiro: a 3D Keepsake Cityscape. Krauss, Trisha, illus. 2014. (Panorama Pops Ser.). (ENG.). 30p. (J). (gr. k-4). 8.99 (978-0-7636-7029-0(4)) Candlewick Pr.

Morrison, Marion. Rio de Janeiro. 2004. (Great Cities of the World Ser.). (Illus.). 48p. (gr. 5-12). lib. bdg. 31.00 (978-0-8368-5031-4(9), Gareth Stevens Secondary Library) Stevens, Gareth Publishing LLLP.

Scoones, Simon. Rio de Janeiro. Parker, Edward, photos by. 2006. (Global Cities Ser.). (Illus.). 61p. (gr. 5-8). 30.00 (978-0-7910-8857-9(X), Chelsea Hse.) Facts On File, Inc.

RIO GRANDE RIVER AND VALLEY

Fahey, Kathleen. The Rio Grande. 2003. (Rivers of North America Ser.). (Illus.). 32p. (gr. 2-6). lib. bdg. 26.00 (978-0-8368-3760-5(6), Gareth Stevens Learning Library) Stevens, Gareth Publishing LLLP.

Marsico, Katie. The Rio Grande. 2013. (Explorer Library: Social Studies Explorer Ser.). (ENG.). 32p. (J). (gr. 4-8). 28.50 (978-1-62431-012-6(5), 202499); pap. 14.21 (978-1-62431-036-2(2), 202501) Cherry Lake Publishing.

McNeese, Tim. The Rio Grande. 2004. (Rivers in World History Ser.). (Illus.). 120p. (C). (gr. 9-13). 32.50 (978-0-7910-8244-7(X), Chelsea Hse.) Facts On File, Inc.

RIOTS

Archer, Jules. Rage in the Streets: A History of American Riots. 2016. (Jules Archer History for Young Readers Ser.). (ENG., Illus.). 200p. (J). (gr. 6). 16.99 (978-1-63450-186-6(1), Sky Pony Pr.) Skyhorse Publishing Co., Inc.

Arevalo, Luis Paquime. L. A. 's Riots. 2004. (YA). per. 12.99 (978-0-9748598-0-4(X)) L. A. Eng Bks.

Buckley, A. M. Racism, 1 vol. 2011. (Essential Issues Set 2 Ser.). (ENG., Illus.). 112p. (J). (gr. 6-12). lib. bdg. 35.64 (978-1-61714-777-7(X), Essential Library) ABDO Publishing Co.

Fradin, Dennis Brindell. The Stamp Act of 1765. 2009. (Turning Points in U. S. History Ser.). (Illus.). 48p. (J). (gr. 3-18). 31.36 (978-0-7614-4260-8(X)) Marshall Cavendish Corp.

Gerdes, Louise I. 1992 Los Angeles Riots. Greenhaven Press Editors, ed. 2014. (Perspectives on Modern World History Ser.). (ENG., Illus.). 224p. (gr. 10-12). lib. bdg. 47.80 (978-0-7377-7008-7(2), Greenhaven Pr., Inc.) Cengage Gale.

McGowen, Tom. The 1968 Democratic Convention. 2003. (Cornerstones of Freedom Ser.). (ENG., Illus.). 48p. (YA). (gr. 4-7). 26.00 (978-0-516-24220-0(2)) Scholastic Library Publishing.

Wilson, Sean Michael & Dickson, Benjamin. Fight the Power! A Visual History of Protest among the English Speaking Peoples. Emerson, Hunt et al, illus. 2013. (ENG.). 192p. pap. 19.95 (978-1-60980-492-3(9)) Seven Stories Pr.

RIOTS—FICTION

Edwards, Meinir Wyn. Dic Penderyn. Wade, Gini, illus. 2008. (ENG.). 24p. (J). pap. 4.95 (978-1-84771-022-2(0)) Y Lolfa GBR. Dist: Dufour Editions, Inc.

English, Karen. It All Comes down to This. 2017. (ENG.). 368p. (J). (gr. 5-7). 16.99 (978-0-544-83957-1(9), Clarion Bks.) Houghton Mifflin Harcourt Trade & Reference Pubs.

Fletcher, Susan E. A Little in Love. 2015. (ENG.). 288p. (J). (gr. 7). 17.99 (978-0-545-82960-1(7), Chicken Hse., The) Scholastic, Inc.

Henty, George Alfred. At Agincourt: A Tale of the White Hoods of Paris. 2011. 332p. pap. 19.95 (978-1-61179-111-2(1)) Fireship Pr.

Latham, Jennifer. Dreamland Burning. 2017.Tr. of s. (ENG.). 384p. (YA). (gr. 9-17). 18.99 (978-0-316-38493-3(3)) Little, Brown Bks. for Young Readers.

Myers, Anna. Tulsa Burning. 2004. (Illus.). 184p. (J). (gr. 3-7). 16.95 (978-0-8027-8829-0(7)) Walker & Co.

Ostlere, Cathy. Karma. 2012. (ENG.). 544p. (YA). (gr. 7-18). 9.99 (978-1-59514-384-6(X), Razorbill) Penguin Young Readers Group.

Salkey, Andrew. Riot. 2011. (Caribbean Modern Classics Ser.). (ENG., Illus.). 176p. (J). (gr. 7). pap. 14.95 (978-1-84523-181-1(3)) Peepal Tree Pr., Ltd. GBR. Dist: Independent Pubs. Group.

Tullson, Diane. Riot Act, 1 vol. 2012. (Orca Soundings Ser.). (ENG.). 128p. (YA). (gr. 8-12). 16.95 (978-1-4598-0140-0(7)); pap. 9.95 (978-1-4598-0139-4(3)) Orca Bk. Pubs. USA.

RITES AND CEREMONIES

see also Baptism; Fasts and Feasts; Funeral Rites and Ceremonies; Manners and Customs; Marriage Customs and Rites

also classes of people and ethnic groups with the subdivision Rites and Ceremonies, e.g. Jews—Rites and Ceremonies

Barr, J. Bennett. Saying Goodbye. 2009. 20p. pap. 10.49 (978-1-4490-0000-4(2)) AuthorHouse.

Beker, Jeanne. The Big Night Out. Dion, Nathalie, illus. 2005. (ENG.). 80p. (J). (gr. 4-7). pap. 15.95 (978-0-88776-719-7(2), Tundra Bks.) Tundra Bks. CAN. Dist: Penguin Random Hse. LLC.

Harris, Carol & Brown, Mike. Ceremonial Costumes. 2004. (Twentieth-Century Developments in Fashion & Costume Ser.). (Illus.). 64p. (YA). (gr. 7-18). lib. bdg. 19.95 (978-1-59084-424-3(6)) Mason Crest.

Haywood, John. Through the Ages: Gods, Beliefs & Ceremonies. 2008. (ENG., Illus.). 64p. (J). (gr. 4-7). pap. 12.99 (978-1-84476-601-7(2)) Anness Publishing GBR. Dist: National Bk. Network.

Jenkins, Diana R. Goodness Graces! Ten Short Stories about the Sacraments. 2010. (J). (gr. 3-6). pap. 7.95 (978-0-8198-3110-1(7)) Pauline Bks. & Media.

MacDonald, Fiona. The Amazing History of Mummies & Tombs: Uncover the Secrets of the Egyptian Pyramids & Other Ancient Burial Sites, Shown in over 350 Exciting Pictures. 2016. (ENG., Illus.). 64p. (J). (gr. -1-12). 12.99 (978-1-86147-735-4(X), Armadillo) Anness Publishing GBR. Dist: National Bk. Network.

Mahon, Elaine. Preparing for First Reconciliation: A Guide for Families. 2013. (ENG., Illus.). 32p. (J). pap. 8.95 (978-1-84730-400-1(1)) Veritas Pubns. IRL. Dist: Dufour Editions, Inc.

Matters, Print & Montillo, Roseanne. Halloween & Commemorations of the Dead. 2009. (Holidays & Celebration Ser.). (Illus.). 104p. (gr. 5-8). 40.00 (978-1-60413-097-3(0), Chelsea Hse.) Facts On File, Inc.

McGahey, Suzanne. Winter Guard. 2009. (Team Spirit! Ser.). 64p. (gr. 6-6). 53.00 (978-1-60853-274-2(7)) Rosen Publishing Group, Inc., The.

Moore Niver, Heather. Executions & Sacrifices. 2014. (Digging up the Dead Ser.). 32p. (J). (gr. 4-6). pap. 63.00 (978-1-4824-1230-7(6)) Stevens, Gareth Publishing LLLP.

Murphy, Charles. Celebrations Around the World. 2016. (Adventures in Culture Ser.). 00024p. (J). pap. 8.15 **(978-1-4824-5575-5(7))** Stevens, Gareth Publishing LLLP.

Myers, Jack & Jack Myers Ministries. Flowing in the Anointing: Understanding the Anointing of God. 2004. 90p. pap. 7.95 (978-0-9720928-1-4(1)) Myers, Jack Ministries, Inc.

Onyefulu, Ifeoma. Welcome Dede! An African Naming Ceremony. 2004. (Illus.). 32p. (J). (978-1-84507-267-4(7)) ReiseArt Buchhandlung GmbH.

—Your Name Is Dede: An African Baby's Naming Ceremony. 2003. (Illus.). 32p. (J). (978-0-7112-1938-0(9)) ReiseArt Buchhandlung GmbH.

Post, John R., compiled by. NPKA Book of Blotar Bk. 1: Catalog of Blots & Rituals of Wotanism. num. ed. 2003. (Illus.). 421p. 35.00 (978-0-9749416-0-8(3)) Himminbjorg Publishing, Inc.

Senker, Cath. Christianity: Signs, Symbols, Stories. 2009. (Religious Signs, Symbols, & Stories Ser.). (Illus.). 32p. (J). (ENG.). pap. 10.00 (978-1-4358-3045-5(8)); lib. bdg. 25.25 (978-1-4358-3037-0(7)) Rosen Publishing Group, Inc., The. (PowerKids Pr.).

Wood, Alix. Human Sacrifice. Wood, Alix, illus. 2013. (Why'd They Do That? Strange Customs of the Past Ser.). (Illus.). 32p. (J). (gr. 4-6). pap. 10.50 (978-1-4339-9585-9(9)); pap. 63.00 (978-1-4339-9586-6(7)) Stevens, Gareth Publishing LLLP.

—Human Sacrifice. 2013. (Why'd They Do That? Strange Customs of the Past Ser.). (ENG., Illus.). 32p. (J). (gr. 4-6). lib. bdg. 26.60 (978-1-4339-9584-2(0)) Stevens, Gareth Publishing LLLP.

World Book, Inc Staff, contrib. by. Birth & Growing up Celebrations. 2009. (Illus.). 46p. (J). (978-0-7166-5044-7(4)) World Bk., Inc.

—Cumulative Glossary & Index. 46p. (J). 2009. (978-0-7166-5051-5(7)) 2003. (978-0-7166-5017-1(7)) World Bk., Inc.

World Book, Inc. Staff, contrib. by. Everyday Celebrations & Rituals. 2003. (World Book's Celebrations & Rituals Around the World Ser.). (Illus.). 46p. (J). (978-0-7166-5016-4(9)) World Bk., Inc.

World Book, Inc Staff, contrib. by. Everyday Celebrations & Rituals. 2009. (Illus.). 46p. (J). (978-0-7166-5050-8(9)) World Bk., Inc.

RITUAL

see Rites and Ceremonies

RIVERA, DIEGO, 1886-1957

Bankston, John. Diego Rivera. 2003. (Latinos in American History Ser.). (Illus.). 56p. (J). (gr. 4-8). lib. bdg. 29.95 (978-1-58415-208-8(7)) Mitchell Lane Pubs., Inc.

Bernier-Grand, Carmen. Diego: Bigger Than Life, 0 vols. Diaz, David, illus. 2009. (ENG.). 64p. (J). (gr. 8-13). 18.99 (978-0-7614-5383-3(0), 9780761453833, Amazon Children's Publishing) Amazon Publishing.

Foard, Sheila Wood. Diego Rivera. 2nd rev. ed. 2010. (Great Hispanic Heritage Ser.). (Illus.). 120p. (gr. 6-12). 35.00 (978-1-60413-845-0(9), Chelsea Hse.) Facts On File, Inc.

Guzmán, Lila & Guzmán, Rick. Diego Rivera: Artist of Mexico. 2006. (Famous Latinos Ser.). (Illus.). 32p. (J). (gr. 3-4). lib. bdg. 23.94 (978-0-7660-2641-4(8), Enslow Elementary) Enslow Pubs., Inc.

—Diego Rivera: Artista de Mexico. 2007. (Latinos Famosos Ser.). (SPA., Illus.). 32p. (J). (gr. 3-4). lib. bdg. 23.94 (978-0-7660-2676-6(0), Enslow Elementary) Enslow Pubs., Inc.

Hillstrom, Laurie & Hillstrom, Kevin. Diego Rivera, Muralist. 2008. (Twentieth Century's Most Influential Hispanics Ser.). (ENG., Illus.). 110p. (gr. 7-12). 39.40 (978-1-4205-0018-9(X)) Cengage Gale.

Jauregui, Diego. Libros de Arte para Ninos: Diego Rivera.Tr. of Art Books for Children: Diego Rivera. (SPA., Illus.). 73p. (YA). (gr. 5-8). pap. (978-968-494-026-0(2)) Centro de Informacion y Desarrollo de la Comunicacion y la Literatura.

Kent, Deborah. Diego Rivera: Painting Mexico. 2005. (Proud Heritage: the Hispanic Library). (ENG., Illus.). 40p. (J). (gr. 3-6). 29.93 (978-1-59296-384-3(6), 200006) Child's World, Inc., The.

Litwin, Laura Baskes. Diego Rivera: Legendary Mexican Painter. 2005. (Latino Biography Library). (Illus.). 128p. (J). (gr. 6-13). lib. bdg. 33.27 (978-0-7660-2486-1(5)) Enslow Pubs., Inc.

Marín, Guadalupe Rivera. My Papá Diego & Me (Mi Papa Diego y Yo) Memories of My Father & His Art (Recuerdos de Mi Padre y Su Arte) Rivera, Diego, illus. 2013. (SPA & ENG.). 32p. (J). (gr. k-5). 18.95 (978-0-89239-228-5(2)) Lee & Low Bks., Inc.

Marsh, Carole. Diego Rivera: Acclaimed Mural Painter: Acclaimed Mural Painter. 2003. 12p. (gr. k-4). 2.95 (978-0-635-02137-3(4)) Gallopade International.

Mattern, Joanne. Diego Rivera, 1 vol. 2005. (Great Artists Set 1 Ser.). (ENG., Illus.). 32p. (gr. k-6). 27.07 (978-1-59197-849-7(1), Checkerboard Library) ABDO Publishing Co.

Reef, Catherine. Frida & Diego: Art, Love, Life. 2014. (ENG., Illus.). 176p. (J). (gr. 7-12). 18.99 (978-0-547-82184-9(0), Clarion Bks.) Houghton Mifflin Harcourt Publishing Co.

Rubin, Susan Goldman. Diego Rivera: An Artist for the People. 2013. (ENG., Illus.). 56p. (J). (gr. 3-7). 22.95 (978-0-8109-8411-0(3), Abrams Bks. for Young Readers) Abrams, Inc.

Sabbeth, Carol. Frida Kahlo & Diego Rivera: Their Lives & Ideas, 24 Activities. 2005. (For Kids Ser.). (ENG., Illus.). 160p. (J). (gr. 4). pap. 17.95 (978-1-55652-569-8(9), 1241061) Chicago Review Pr., Inc.

Tieck, Sarah. Diego Rivera, 1 vol. 2006. (First Biographies Ser.). (ENG., Illus.). 32p. (gr. -1-3). 27.07 (978-1-59679-785-7(1), Buddy Bks.) ABDO Publishing Co.

Venezia, Mike. Diego Rivera. Venezia, Mike, illus. 2015. (Getting to Know the World's Greatest Artists Ser.). (ENG., Illus.). 40p. (J). lib. bdg. 29.00 (978-0-531-21261-5(0), Children's Pr.) Scholastic Library Publishing.

RIVERS

see also Dams; Floods; Hydraulic Engineering; Water—Pollution; Water Power

also names of rivers

Aloian, Molly. The Yangtze: China's Majestic River. 2010. (Rivers Around the World Ser.). (ENG., Illus.). 32p. (J). (gr. 5-8). pap. (978-0-7787-7472-3(4)); lib. bdg. (978-0-7787-7449-5(X)) Crabtree Publishing Co.

Barnes, Julia. 101 Facts about Rivers. 2003. (One Hundred One Facts about Our World Ser.). (Illus.). 32p. (gr. 1-4). lib. bdg. 26.00 (978-0-8368-3711-7(8), Gareth Stevens Learning Library) Stevens, Gareth Publishing LLLP.

Bellamy, David & Dow, Jill. Our Changing World: The River. 2004. (Illus.). 32p. (J). pap. (978-1-84507-218-6(9)) ReiseArt Buchhandlung GmbH.

Benker, Kaily. Great U. S. Rivers. 2013. (Rosen Readers Ser.). (ENG.). 24p. (J). (gr. 3-4). pap. 49.50 (978-1-4777-2563-4(6)); pap. 8.25 (978-1-4777-2562-7(8)) Rosen Publishing Group, Inc., The. (Rosen Classroom).

Best, B. J. How Are Rivers Formed? 2017. pap. 16.95 **(978-1-5026-2541-0(5))** Cavendish Square Publishing.

Brocker, Susan. Rivers of the World. 2009. (Our Planet Ser.). (YA). (gr. 3-6). lib. bdg. 25.25 (978-1-4358-2816-2(X)) Rosen Publishing Group, Inc., The.

Bulletpoints Oceans & Rivers. 2005. (Illus.). (J). per. 4.99 (978-1-933581-01-9(8)) Byeway Bks.

Burnham & Laurie. Rivers. 2007. (Extreme Earth Ser.). (Illus.). 176p. (YA). (gr. 7-12). 35.00 (978-0-8160-5916-4(0)) Facts On File, Inc.

Day, Trevor. Lakes & Rivers. Garratt, Richard, illus. 2006. (Biomes of the Earth Ser.). 272p. (gr. 6-12). 39.50 (978-0-8160-5328-5(6)) Facts On File, Inc.

La Defensa de los Rios y Lagos. (Colección Biblioteca Juvenil de Ecología). (SPA., Illus.). (YA). (gr. 5-8). pap. (978-958-04-2672-1(4), 80426721) Norma S.A. COL. Dist: Lectorum Pubns., Inc.

Editors of Kingfisher. Rushing Rivers. 2016. (It's All About... Ser.). (ENG., Illus.). 32p. (J). pap. 5.99 (978-0-7534-7264-4(3), 9780753472644, Kingfisher) Roaring Brook Pr.

Figorito, Christine. Real Facts about Rivers. 2008. (Rosen Real Readers: Upper Emergent Ser.). (ENG., Illus.). 12p. (gr. 1-2). pap. 5.90 (978-0-8239-8123-6(1)) Rosen Publishing Group, Inc., The.

Frisch, Aaron. Rivers. 2008. (Our World Ser.). (Illus.). 24p. (J). (gr. -1-3). lib. bdg. 24.25 (978-1-58341-573-3(4), Creative Education) Creative Co., The.

Gaarder-Juntti, Oona. What Lives in Streams & Rivers?, 1 vol. 2008. (Animal Habitats Ser.). (ENG., Illus.). 24p. (J). (gr. k-3). 25.65 (978-1-60453-171-8(1)) ABDO Publishing Co.

Ganeri, Anita. Exploring Habitats, with Benjamin Blog & His Inquisitive Dog, 1 vol. 2014. (Exploring Habitats with

Benjamin Blog & His Inquisitive Dog Ser.). (ENG.). 32p. (gr. 1-3). lib. bdg. 179.94 *(978-1-4329-8781-7(X)*, NA-h) Heinemann-Raintree.
—Exploring Rivers: A Benjamin Blog & His Inquisitive Dog Investigation, 1 vol. 2014. (Exploring Habitats with Benjamin Blog & His Inquisitive Dog Ser.). (ENG., Illus.). 32p. (gr. 1-3). lib. bdg. 29.99 *(978-1-4329-8775-6(5)*, NA-h) Heinemann-Raintree.
Gray, Leon. The Missouri River. 2003. (Rivers of North America Ser.). (Illus.). 32p. (gr. 2-6). lib. bdg. 26.00 *(978-0-8368-3758-2(4)*, Gareth Stevens Learning Library) Stevens, Gareth Publishing LLLP.
—Rivers. 2011. (Geography Wise Ser.). (Illus.). 32p. (YA). (gr. 2-5). lib. bdg. 26.50 *(978-1-4488-3282-8(9))* Rosen Publishing Group, Inc., The.
—Rivers & Lakes. 2015. (Amazing Biomes Ser.). (Illus.). 32p. (gr. 3-6). 31.35 *(978-1-78121-244-8(9)*, 1389646) Brown Bear Bks.
Green, Emily K. Rivers. 2011. (Blastoff! Readers Ser.). 24p. (J). pap. 5.95 *(978-0-531-26036-4(4)*, Children's Pr.) Scholastic Library Publishing.
Green, Jen. Mighty Rivers. 2009. (Amazing Planet Earth Ser.). 32p. (gr. 4-7). 31.35 *(978-1-59920-371-3(5))* Black Rabbit Bks.
Green, Mary. Rivers in Action. 2004. (Earth's Changing Landscape Ser.). (Illus.). 46p. (YA). (gr. 7-12). lib. bdg. 28.50 *(978-1-58340-477-5(5))* Black Rabbit Bks.
Group/McGraw-Hill, Wright. Rivers: From Beginning to End, 6 vols. (Book2WebTM Ser.). (gr. 4-8). 36.50 *(978-0-322-04441-8(3))* Wright Group/McGraw-Hill.
—Rivers: Level H, 6 vols. (Take Twostm Ser.). 16p. 29.95 *(978-0-322-08957-0(3))* Wright Group/McGraw-Hill.
Harrison, David L. Rivers: Nature's Wondrous Waterways. Nathan, Cheryl, illus. 2003. (Earthworks Ser.). (ENG.). 32p. (J). (gr. k-2). 15.95 *(978-1-56397-968-2(3))* Boyds Mills Pr.
Hawkes, Steve. The Tennessee River. 2003. (Rivers of North America Ser.). (Illus.). 32p. (gr. 2-6). lib. bdg. 26.00 *(978-0-8368-3763-6(0)*, Gareth Stevens Learning Library) Stevens, Gareth Publishing LLLP.
Hegarty, Patricia. The River. Clulow, Hanako, illus. 2016. (J). 12.99 *(978-1-61067-468-3(5))* Kane Miller.
Hewitt, Sally. Project Geography - Rivers. 2010. (Starting Geography Ser.). 32p. (J). (gr. 2-5). 28.50 *(978-1-60753-128-9(3))* Amicus Publishing.
—Project Geography - Rivers. 2012. (Map Smart Ser.). (Illus.). 32p. (gr. 2-6). lib. bdg. 27.10 *(978-1-59920-414-7(2))* Black Rabbit Bks.
Howard, Fran. Rivers & Streams, 1 vol. 2006. (Habitats Ser.). (ENG., Illus.). 32p. (J). (gr. -1-3). lib. bdg. 27.07 *(978-1-59679-782-6(7)*, Buddy Bks.) ABDO Publishing Co.
Iyer, Rani. Endangered Rivers: Investigating Rivers in Crisis. 2015. (Endangered Earth Ser.). (ENG.). 32p. (gr. 3-4). lib. bdg. 27.32 *(978-1-4914-2040-9(5)*, Fact Finders) Capstone Press of Coughlan Cos.
Jackson, Tom. The Arkansas River. 2003. (Rivers of North America Ser.). (Illus.). 32p. (gr. 2-6). lib. bdg. 26.00 *(978-0-8368-3752-0(5)*, Gareth Stevens Learning Library) Stevens, Gareth Publishing LLLP.
—The Ohio River. 2003. (Rivers of North America Ser.). (Illus.). 32p. (gr. 2-6). lib. bdg. 26.00 *(978-0-8368-3759-9(2)*, Gareth Stevens Learning Library) Stevens, Gareth Publishing LLLP.
Johnson, Rebecca L. A Journey into a River. Saroff, Phyllis V., illus. 2004. (Biomes of North America Ser.). (J). pap. 8.95 *(978-0-8225-2044-3(3))*; 48p. (gr. 3-6). 23.93 *(978-1-57505-595-4(3))* Lerner Publishing Group.
Junyk, Myra. The 10 Mightiest Rivers. 2008. (J). 14.99 *(978-1-55448-519-2(3))* Scholastic Library Publishing.
Kalman, Bobbie. Earth's Rivers. 2008. (Looking at Earth Ser.). (ENG., Illus.). 32p. (J). (gr. 1-4). pap. *(978-0-7787-3218-1(5))*; lib. bdg. *(978-0-7787-3208-2(8))* Crabtree Publishing Co.
—Los Ríos de la Tierra. 2009. (SPA.). 32p. (J). *(978-0-7787-8239-1(5))*; pap. *(978-0-7787-8256-8(5))* Crabtree Publishing Co.
—Where on Earth Are Rivers? 2014. (ENG., Illus.). 32p. (J). *(978-0-7787-0502-4(1))* Crabtree Publishing Co.
Labrecque, Ellen. Living Beside a River. 2015. (Places We Live Ser.). (ENG., Illus.). 32p. (gr. 1-3). 27.32 *(978-1-4846-0801-2(1)*, Heinemann First Library) Heinemann-Raintree.
Leake, Diyan. Rivers & Streams, 1 vol. 2014. (Water, Water Everywhere! Ser.). (ENG., Illus.). 24p. (gr. -1-1). 22.65 *(978-1-4846-0448-9(2)*, Acorn) Heinemann-Raintree.
Llewellyn, Claire & Feldman, Thea. Kingfisher Readers L4: Rivers. 2014. (Kingfisher Readers Ser.). (ENG., Illus.). 32p. (J). (gr. k-3). 12.99 *(978-0-7534-7124-1(8)*, 9780753471241, Kingfisher) Roaring Brook Pr.
Looye, Juliette, text. I Live near a River. 2004. (Illus.). 16p. (J). pap. *(978-0-7367-1932-2(6))* Zaner-Bloser, Inc.
MacDonald, Margaret. Rivers of the World. 2011. (Learn-Abouts Ser.). (Illus.). 16p. (J). pap. 7.95 *(978-1-59920-646-2(3))* Black Rabbit Bks.
Macken, JoAnn Early. Ríos. 2006. (Conoces la Tierra? Geografía del mundo (Where on Earth? World Geography) Ser.). (SPA., Illus.). 24p. (gr. 1-4). pap. 8.15 *(978-0-8368-6554-7(5)*, Weekly Reader Leveled Readers) Stevens, Gareth Publishing LLLP.
—Ríos (Rivers) 2006. (Conoces la Tierra? Geografía del mundo (Where on Earth? World Geography) Ser.). (ENG & SPA., Illus.). 24p. (gr. 1-4). lib. bdg. 22.00 *(978-0-8368-6547-9(2)*, Weekly Reader Leveled Readers) Stevens, Gareth Publishing LLLP.
—Rivers. (Where on Earth? World Geography Ser.). (Illus.). 24p. 2006. (gr. 1-4). pap. 8.15 *(978-0-8368-6404-5(2))* 2006. (gr. 1-4). lib. bdg. 22.00 *(978-0-8368-6397-0(6))* 2005. (gr. k-3). pap. 8.15 *(978-0-8368-4893-9(4))* 2005. (gr. k-3). lib. bdg. 22.00 *(978-0-8368-4886-1(1))* Stevens, Gareth Publishing LLLP. (Weekly Reader Leveled Readers).
—Rivers: Ríos. 2005. (Water Habitats/ Habitats acuáticos Ser.). (SPA.). 24p. (gr. k-3). pap. 8.15 *(978-0-8368-6038-2(1)*, Weekly Reader Leveled Readers) Stevens, Gareth Publishing LLLP.
Macken, JoAnn Early & Early Macken, JoAnn. Rivers/Ríos. 2005. (Water Habitats/ Habitats acuáticos Ser.). (ENG & SPA., Illus.). 24p. (gr. k-3). lib. bdg. 22.00 *(978-0-8368-6031-3(4)*, Weekly Reader Leveled Readers) Stevens, Gareth Publishing LLLP.
Make It Work Geography, 4 vol. set. 2003. (gr. 4-8). 59.00 *(978-0-7166-5124-6(6))* World Bk., Inc.
Marsico, Katie. The Missouri River. 2013. (Explorer Library: Social Studies Explorer Ser.). (ENG.). 32p. (J). (gr. 4-8). 28.50 *(978-1-62431-010-2(9)*, 202491); pap. 14.21 *(978-1-62431-034-8(6)*, 202493) Cherry Lake Publishing.
McNeese, Tim, ed. Rivers in American Life & Times. 2005. (Rivers in American Life & Times Ser.). (Illus.). 120p. (C). (gr. 9-13). 195.00 *(978-0-7910-7722-1(5)*, Chelsea Hse.) Facts On File, Inc.
—Rivers in World History. 2005. (Rivers in World History Ser.). (Illus.). 120p. (C). (gr. 9-13). 195.00 *(978-0-7910-8473-1(6)*, Chelsea Hse.) Facts On File, Inc.
Michele, Tracey. The Life of a River. 2011. (Learn-Abouts Ser.). (Illus.). 16p. (J). pap. 9.95 *(978-1-59920-609-7(9))* Palgrave Macmillan.
Miller, Mirella S. Life in Rivers. 2014. (Life in Water Biomes Ser.). (ENG.). 24p. (J). (gr. 2-5). 28.50 *(978-1-62687-299-8(6)*, 207140) Child's World, Inc., The.
Minden, Cecilia. Rivers. 2010. (21st Century Basic Skills Library: the World Around Us Ser.). (ENG.). 24p. (gr. k-3). lib. bdg. 22.79 *(978-1-60279-861-8(3)*, 200588) Cherry Lake Publishing.
Morley, Catherine Weyerhaeuser. Where Do Rivers Go, Momma? 2016. (Illus.). (J). *(978-0-87842-656-0(6))* Mountain Pr. Publishing Co., Inc.
Nadeau, Isaac. Water in Rivers & Lakes. (Water Cycle Ser.). 24p. 2009. (gr. 4-4). 42.50 *(978-1-60854-271-0(8))* 2003. (Illus.). (J). lib. bdg. 22.60 *(978-0-8239-6266-2(0))* Rosen Publishing Group, Inc., The. (PowerKids Pr.).
Nardo, Don. Early River Civilizations. 2011. (World History Ser.). (Illus.). 112p. (J). 28.95 *(978-1-59935-140-7(4))* Reynolds, Morgan Inc.
Nemeth, Jason D. Rivers, Lakes, & Oceans. 2012. (Our Changing Earth Ser.). (ENG.). 24p. (J). (gr. 3-6). pap. 8.25 *(978-1-4488-6300-6(7)*, PowerKids Pr.); lib. bdg. 22.60 *(978-1-4488-6171-2(3))* Rosen Publishing Group, Inc., The.
Nestor, John. Rivers. 2009. (21st Century Skills Library: Real World Math Ser.). (ENG.). 32p. (gr. 4-8). lib. bdg. 28.50 *(978-1-60279-497-9(9)*, 200319) Cherry Lake Publishing.
Ostopowich, Melanie. Oceans, Lakes, & Rivers. 2015. (Illus.). 24p. (J). *(978-1-5105-0052-5(9))* SmartBook Media, Inc.
—Oceans, Lakes, & Rivers. 2010. (Water Science Ser.). (Illus.). 24p. (gr. 3-5). (J). pap. 11.95 *(978-1-61690-007-6(5))*; (YA). lib. bdg. 25.70 *(978-1-61690-001-4(6))* Weigl Pubs., Inc.
—Oceans, Rivers, & Lakes. 2005. (Science Matters Ser.). (Illus.). 24p. (J). (gr. 3-7). lib. bdg. 24.45 *(978-1-59036-304-1(3))* Weigl Pubs., Inc.
Peters, Marilee. 10 Rivers That Shaped the World. Rosen, Kim, illus. 2015. (World of Tens Ser.). (ENG.). 136p. (J). (gr. 4-7). pap. 14.95 *(978-1-55451-738-1(9)*, 9781554517381) Annick Pr., Ltd. CAN. Dist: Publishers Group West (PGW).
Pollard, Michael. Great Rivers of Britain: The Clyde, Mersey, Severn, Tees, Thames, Trent. (Illus.). 45p. *(978-0-237-51829-5(5))* Evans Brothers, Ltd.
—Rivers of Britain & Ireland: The Avon, Yorkshire Ouse, Tyne, Wye, Forth, Liffey, Lagan. (Illus.). 46p. (J). *(978-0-237-51805-9(8))* Evans Brothers, Ltd.
Puncel, Maria. El Prado del Tio Pedro.Tr. of Uncle Peter's Pasture. (SPA.). 32p. (J). 12.95 *(978-84-348-1226-0(6))* SM Ediciones ESP. Dist: AIMS International Bks., Inc.
Pyers, Greg. Biodiversity of Rivers. 2011. (Biodiversity 2 Ser.). 32p. (gr. 4). 28.50 *(978-1-60870-531-3(5))* Marshall Cavendish Corp.
Rivers, Lakes, & Oceans. 2008. (Restless Earth Ser.). 112p. (YA). (gr. 5-9). 35.00 *(978-0-7910-9797-7(8))* Facts On File, Inc.
Rose, Simon. Estuaries. 2017. (J). ***(978-1-5105-2171-1(2))*** SmartBook Media, Inc.
Ross, Mandy. Rivers. 2004. (Geography Fact Files Ser.). (J). lib. bdg. 28.50 *(978-1-58340-429-4(5))* Black Rabbit Bks.
Royston, Angela. River Food Chains, 1 vol. 2014. (Food Chains & Webs Ser.). (ENG., Illus.). 32p. (gr. 1-3). 27.32 *(978-1-4846-0520-2(9)*, Heinemann First Library) Heinemann-Raintree.
Schuh, Mari. Waterfalls, 1 vol. 2010. (Natural Wonders Ser.). (ENG., 24p. (gr. k-1). Illus.). pap. 7.29 *(978-1-4296-5586-6(0))*; pap. 41.70 *(978-1-4296-5587-3(9))* Capstone Press of Coughlan Cos. (Pebble Plus).
Schuh, Mari C. Waterfalls, 1 vol. 2010. (Natural Wonders Ser.). (ENG.). 24p. (gr. k-1). lib. bdg. 26.65 *(978-1-4296-5002-1(8)*, Pebble Plus) Capstone Press of Coughlan Cos.
Smith, Farhanna. Rivers of the United States. 2013. (InfoMax Readers Ser.). (ENG.). 24p. (J). (gr. 3-4). pap. 49.50 *(978-1-4777-2627-3(6))*; (Illus.). pap. 8.25 *(978-1-4777-2626-6(8))* Rosen Publishing Group, Inc., The. (Rosen Classroom).
Smith-Llera, Danielle. River Communities Past & Present, 1 vol. 2014. (Who Lived Here? Ser.). (ENG.). 24p. (gr. 1-2). lib. bdg. 25.32 *(978-1-4765-4058-0(6)*, First Facts) Capstone Press of Coughlan Cos.
Spilsbury, Louise. Surviving the River. 2016. (Sole Survivor Ser.). 48p. (gr. 5-4). pap. 14.05 *(978-1-4824-5075-0(5))* Stevens, Gareth Publishing LLLP.
Spilsbury, Richard & Spilsbury, Louise. At Home in Rivers & Lakes, 01 vols., 1. 2016. (Home in the Biome Ser.). (ENG.). 32p. (J). pap. 10.00 *(978-1-5081-4556-1(3)*, PowerKids Pr.) Rosen Publishing Group, Inc., The.
Stradling, Jan. Ponds & Rivers: Level I, 6 vols. (First Explorers Ser.). 24p. (gr. 1-2). 29.95 *(978-0-7699-1451-0(9))* Shortland Pubns. (U. S. A.) Inc.
Sullivan, Laura L. 24 Hours in an Estuary. 2017. (J). ***(978-1-5026-2486-4(9))*** Cavendish Square Publishing.
Sundance/Newbridge LLC Staff. Follow the River. 2007. (Early Science Ser.). (gr. k-3). 18.95 *(978-1-4007-6558-4(7))*; pap. 6.10 *(978-1-4007-6554-6(4))* Sundance/Newbridge Educational Publishing.
Sweeney, Alyse. Rivers, 1 vol. 2010. (Natural Wonders Ser.). (ENG., 24p. (gr. k-1). Illus.). pap. 7.29 *(978-1-4296-5584-2(4))*; pap. 41.70 *(978-1-4296-5585-9(2))*; lib. bdg. 26.65 *(978-1-4296-5001-4(X))* Capstone Press of Coughlan Cos. (Pebble Plus).
Taylor, Barbara. Rivers. 2004. (Make It Work! Geography Ser.). (Illus.). 48p. (J). (gr. 3-6). 12.95 *(978-1-58728-256-0(9)*, Two-Can Publishing) T&N Children's Publishing.
Thomson, Ruth. Rivers. 2012. (Geography Corner Ser.). (ENG., Illus.). 24p. (J). (gr. k-3). 21.25 *(978-1-4488-6625-0(1)*, PowerKids Pr.) Rosen Publishing Group, Inc., The.
Tull, Mary. Rivers & Lakes. 2007. (Rise & Shine Ser.). (ENG., Illus.). 32p. (J). pap. 17.95 *(978-0-7922-4561-2(X))* CENGAGE Learning.
Van Zandt, Steve. River Song: With the Banana Slug String Band. Zecca, Katherine, illus. 2007. (Sharing Nature with Children Book Ser.). 32p. (J). (gr. -1-5). pap. 9.95 incl. audio compact disk *(978-1-58469-094-8(1)*, 1268621) Dawn Pubns.
—River Song: With the Banana Slug String Band (Includes Music CD) Zecca, Katherine, illus. 2007. 32p. (J). (gr. k-4). 17.95 *(978-1-58469-093-1(3)*, 1268621) Dawn Pubns.
Waldron, Melanie. Rivers, 1 vol. 2012. (Habitat Survival Ser.). (ENG.). 32p. (gr. 2-4). pap. 8.29 *(978-1-4109-4609-6(6))*; lib. bdg. 30.65 *(978-1-4109-4600-3(2))* Heinemann-Raintree. (Raintree Perspectives).
Woods, Michael & Woods, Mary B. Seven Natural Wonders of Central & South America. 2009. (Seven Wonders Ser.). (Illus.). 80p. (YA). (gr. 5-9). lib. bdg. 33.26 *(978-0-8225-9070-5(0))* Twenty First Century Bks.

RIVERS—FICTION

Anthony, Fortuna. Tim Tim the River Crayfish. 2011. 40p. (gr. -1). pap. 19.99 *(978-1-4269-6068-0(9))* Trafford Publishing.
Anthony, Mike. The Adventures of Henry the Patchwork Whale, 1 vol. 2010. 20p. 24.95 *(978-1-60813-076-4(2))* PublishAmerica, Inc.
Arnosky, Jim. Babies in the Bayou. Arnosky, Jim, illus. 2010. (ENG., Illus.). 32p. (J). (gr. -1-k). pap. 6.99 *(978-0-14-241463-7(8)*, Puffin Books) Penguin Young Readers Group.
Arrington, Linda. Ugly Trees. Arrington, Linda, photos by. 2012. (Illus.). 24p. pap. 24.95 *(978-1-4626-8925-5(6))* America Star Bks.
Bickta, Brenda L. Tad's Life in the Lily Pond. 2008. 74p. pap. 19.95 *(978-1-60672-647-1(1))* America Star Bks.
Bingamon-Haller, Mary. The Stillwater River. Burns, Sandra, illus. 2013. 24p. pap. 8.99 *(978-1-938768-30-9(2))* Gypsy Pubns.
Bishop, Michael. By the River Bank, 4 vols. Cloke, Rene, illus. 2012. (ENG.). 30p. (J). 4.95 *(978-1-84135-784-3(7))* Award Pubns. Ltd. GBR. Dist: Parkwest Pubns., Inc.
Boucher, Julie. Small Fry on the Magnetawan. 2009. 24p. pap. 14.95 *(978-0-9819727-4-9(8))* Fiction Publishing, Inc.
Byars, Betsy. Trouble River. 158p. (J). (gr. 3-5). pap. 4.99 *(978-0-8072-1388-9(8)*, Listening Library) Random Hse. Audio Publishing Group.
Caduto, Michael J. & Pastuchiv, Olga. Riparia's River, 1 vol. 2011. (ENG., Illus.). 32p. (gr. 4-7). 16.95 *(978-0-88448-327-4(4)*, 884327) Tilbury Hse. Pubs.
Carlstrom, Nancy White. Raven & River. Van Zyle, Jon, illus. 2011. (ENG.). 32p. pap. 11.95 *(978-1-60223-150-4(8))* Univ. of Alaska Pr.
Cerullo, Jillian. The Danger of the River. 2005. 36p. pap. 14.99 *(978-1-4116-6988-8(6))* Lulu Pr., Inc.
Corentin, Philippe. El Ogro, el Lobo, la Niña y el Pastel. 2004. (SPA.). 32p. (J). (gr. k-2). 19.99 *(978-84-8470-157-6(3))* Corimbo, Editorial S.L. ESP. Dist: Lectorum Pubns., Inc.
Corey's Web: Down in the Dumps. 2003. (J). per. *(978-0-9716567-9-6(7))* Book Web Publishing, Limited.
Corwin, Katherine. The River of Glass. Jasuna, Aija, illus. 2009. 24p. (J). 14.95 *(978-1-60131-002-6(1)*, Castlebridge Bks.) Big Tent Bks.
Dale, Jay. Little Zebra, 1 vol. East, Jacqueline, illus. 2012. (Wonder Words Ser.). (ENG.). 32p. (gr. k-2). pap. 5.99 *(978-1-4296-8906-9(4)*, Engage Literacy) Capstone Press of Coughlan Cos.
Downing, Johnette. Why the Crawfish Lives in the Mud, 1 vol. Downing, Johnette, illus. 2009. (ENG., Illus.). 32p. (J). (gr. k-3). 16.99 *(978-1-58980-678-8(6))* Pelican Publishing Co., Inc.
Falk, Elsa. Fire Canoe. Frankenberg, Robert, illus. 2012. 188p. 42.95 *(978-1-258-23680-9(X))*; pap. 27.95 *(978-1-258-24375-3(X))* Literary Licensing, LLC.
Fontenot, Mary Alice. Clovis Crawfish & His Friends, 1 vol. Graves, Keith, illus. 2009. (Clovis Crawfish Ser.). (ENG.). 32p. (J). (gr. k-3). 16.99 *(978-1-58980-762-4(6))* Pelican Publishing Co., Inc.
Gillingham, Sara. In My Pond. Siminovich, Lorena, illus. 2009. (ENG.). 12p. (J). (gr. -1 — 1). bds. 8.99 *(978-0-8118-6556-2(8))* Chronicle Bks. LLC.
Gonzalez, Maya Christina. Yo Se Que el Rio Me Ama. 2009.Tr. of I Know the River Loves Me. (SPA & ENG., Illus.). 24p. (J). (gr. -1-3). 16.95 *(978-0-89239-233-9(9))* Lee & Low Bks., Inc.
Grahame, Kenneth. The Wind in the Willows. Ingpen, Robert R., illus. 2012. (Sterling Illustrated Classics Ser.). (ENG.). 224p. (J). (gr. 2-8). 19.95 *(978-1-4027-8283-1(7))* Sterling Publishing Co., Inc.
Gray, Grandpa. The Land of the Three Elves Vol. 1: Beginnings. 2012. (ENG.). 317p. pap. 14.95 *(978-1-4327-9551-1(1))* Outskirts Pr., Inc.
Harvey, Roland. On the River. 2016. (ENG.). 32p. (J). (gr. k-3). 17.99 *(978-1-76011-245-5(3))* Allen & Unwin AUS. Dist: Independent Pubs. Group.
Hay, Jerry M. & Pollema-Cahill, Phyllis. A Goose Named Gilligan. 2004. (ENG., Illus.). 32p. (J). 15.95 *(978-1-932073-09-6(4))* Kramer, H.J. Inc.
Higginson, Sheila Sweeny. Diego rescata al bebé manatí (Diego's Manatee Rescue) McGee, Warner, illus. 2009. (Go, Diego, Go! Ser.). (SPA.). 24p. (J). pap. 3.99 *(978-1-4169-7983-8(2)*, Libros Para Ninos) Libros Para Ninos.
Holman, Doris Anne. Come with Me to the Pond. 2004. (Illus.). 26p. (J). (gr. k-5). pap. 11.00 *(978-0-9667192-8-4(X))* Holman, Doris Anne.
—Oscar, the River Offer. 2003. (gr. 1-5). pap. 11.00 *(978-0-9667192-9-1(8))* Holman, Doris Anne.
Hooper, Meredith. River Story. Willey, Bee, illus. 2015. (ENG.). 32p. (J). (gr. k-3). 6.99 *(978-0-7636-7646-9(2))* Candlewick Pr.
Horton, Jim. The Foot Log Incident. 2008. 30p. pap. 24.95 *(978-1-60610-706-5(2))* America Star Bks.
Johnson, Gwen. The Story of Two-Toed Sam or How the Outer Banks Were Formed. 2006. (J). 8.95 *(978-0-9795860-9-5(7))* Fish Tales Publishing.
Karwoski, Gail Langer. River Beds: Sleeping in the World's Rivers, 1 vol. McLennan, Connie, illus. 2008. (ENG.). 32p. (J). (gr. -1-3). 16.95 *(978-0-9777423-4-9(2))*; pap. 8.95 *(978-1-934359-31-0(9))* Arbordale Publishing.
Lancaster, Susan. Hell's Gate. 2004. 200p. pap. *(978-0-9730350-2-5(1))* Snosrap Publishing.
Lee, WonKyeong. Green River. Yang, HyeWon, illus. 2014. (MySELF Bookshelf Ser.). (ENG.). 32p. (J). (gr. k-2). pap. 11.94 *(978-1-60357-695-6(9))*; lib. bdg. 25.27 *(978-1-59953-660-6(9))* Norwood Hse. Pr.
Martin, Marc. A River. 2017. (ENG., Illus.). 44p. (J). 17.99 *(978-1-4521-5423-7(6))* Chronicle Bks. LLC.
Meadows, Daisy. Milly the River Fairy. 2014. (Rainbow Magic — the Earth Fairies Ser.). lib. bdg. 14.75 *(978-0-606-35835-4(8))* Turtleback Bks.
Moore, Wendy Leptien. Eaglet & the River. 2011. 108p. 21.92 *(978-1-4269-5478-8(6))*; pap. 11.92 *(978-1-4269-5477-1(8))* Trafford Publishing.
Newberry, Geoffrey C. The Cape Don Adventure. 2011. 48p. pap. 6.99 *(978-1-61667-262-1(5))* Raider Publishing International.
Nickel, Scott. Race on the River, 1 vol. Harpster, Steve, illus. 2011. (My First Graphic Novel Ser.). (ENG.). 32p. (gr. k-2). pap. 6.25 *(978-1-4342-3061-4(9))*; lib. bdg. 24.65 *(978-1-4342-2521-4(6))* Stone Arch Bks. (My First Graphic Novel).
Niland, Kilmeny. The Gingerbread Man. 2006. (Illus.). 16p. *(978-1-921049-49-1(9))* Little Hare Bks. AUS. Dist: HarperCollins Pubs. Australia.
Oguneye, Kunle. Sikulu & Harambe by the Zambezi River: An African Vversion of the Good Samaritan Story. McCorkindale, Bruce & Youtsey, Scott, illus. 2008. 32p. (J). (gr. -1-5). 14.99 *(978-0-9777382-4-3(8))* Blue Brush Media.
O'Neil-Andrews, Milly. Bandolines & Bubbles. 2011. 88p. pap. 11.25 *(978-1-4269-3089-8(5))* Trafford Publishing.
Papp, Robert, illus. The Ghost of the Chattering Bones. 2007. (Boxcar Children Ser.). 120p. 15.00 *(978-0-7569-7611-8(1))* Perfection Learning Corp.
—The Ghost of the Chattering Bones. 2005. (Boxcar Children Mysteries Ser.: 102). (ENG.). 128p. (J). (gr. 1-5). pap. 5.99 *(978-0-8075-0874-9(8))* Whitman, Albert & Co.
Perkins, R., illus. Earth Whispers. 32p. (J). (gr. 3-18). 16.00 *(978-0-9710860-2-9(8))* Libros, Encouraging Cultural Literacy.
River, Fawn. Sophy & the River. 2012. 24p. pap. 17.99 *(978-1-4772-0272-2(2))* AuthorHouse.
Röder, Marlene. In the River Darkness. 2014. (Illus.). 224p. (YA). (gr. 9-12). pap. 10.95 *(978-1-62324-011-0(5))* Enslow Pubs., Inc.
Sanders, Scott Russell. Floating House. Cogancherry, Helen, illus. 2011. 40p. (J). lib. bdg. 18.00 *(978-1-59098-425-3(0))* Wooster Bk. Co., The.
Sargent, Dave, et al. On the Banks of the Wallowa River: (Nez Perce) Use Your Talent, 20 vols., Vol. 13. Lenoir, Jane, illus. l.t. ed. 2004. (Story Keeper Ser.: 13). 48p. (J). pap. 10.95 *(978-1-56763-928-5(3))* Ozark Publishing.
Schaaf, Ron. BearClaw: Finding Courage Within. 2007. (J). *(978-0-9787555-1-5(0))* Hickory Tales Publishing.
Starkoff, Vanina. Along the River, 1 vol. Springer, Jane, tr. from POR. Starkoff, Vanina, illus. 2017. (ENG., Illus.). 32p. (J). (gr. -1). 17.95 *(978-1-55498-977-5(9))* Groundwood Bks. CAN. Dist: Publishers Group West (PGW).
Susurros de la Tierra. (SPA.). (J). *(978-0-9710860-3-6(6))* Libros, Encouraging Cultural Literacy.
Trimoglie, Mario. The Rivers. Swope, Brenda, illus. 2012. 26p. 24.95 *(978-1-4560-3907-3(5))* America Star Bks.
Walsh, Ellen Stoll. Dot & Jabber & the Mystery of the Missing Stream. 2016. (Green Light Readers Level 2 Ser.). (ENG., Illus.). 32p. (J). (gr. -1-3). 12.99 *(978-0-544-79166-4(5)*, HMH Books For Young Readers) Houghton Mifflin Harcourt Publishing Co.
Weston Woods Staff, creator. In the Small, Small Pond. 2011. 38.75 *(978-0-439-84578-6(5))* Weston Woods Studios, Inc.
Wiggin, Kate Douglas. Homespun Tales. 2007. 240p. 26.95 *(978-1-60312-668-7(6))*; per. 14.95 *(978-1-60312-410-2(1))* Aegypan.
Williamson, Peggy. Who Was Here First? 2006. (J). per. 12.00 *(978-1-59571-155-7(4))* Word Association Pubs.
Wilsdon, Christina. A New York Sailing Adventure. Hockerman, Dennis, illus. 2006. 26p. (J). 7.99 *(978-1-59939-014-7(0))* Cornerstone Pr.
Wilson, Elaine Moody. Fisherman Jack Meets the River Creatures, 1 vol. Ducker Signs Plus, illus. 2009. 40p. pap. 24.95 *(978-1-60836-967-6(6))* PublishAmerica, Inc.
Wright, Holly. River. 2004. (Illus.). (J). *(978-0-9743690-8-2(X))* Britt Allcroft Productions.
Zackery, Gary D. & Borgstedt, John. Stephen. 2011. 108p. 22.45 *(978-1-4567-2712-3(5))* AuthorHouse.

RIVERS—POLLUTION

see Water—Pollution

RIZAL Y ALONSO, JOSE, 1861-1896

Arruda, Suzanne Middendorf. Freedom's Martyr: The Story of Jose Rizal, National Hero of the Philippines. 2003. (Avisson Young Adult Ser.). (Illus.). 106p. (J). pap. 19.95 *(978-1-888105-55-1(0))* Avisson Pr., Inc.

ROAD CONSTRUCTION

see Roads

ROAD SIGNS

see Signs and Signboards

ROADRUNNER

Borgert-Spaniol, Megan. Roadrunners. 2014. (Backyard Wildlife Ser.). (ENG., Illus.). 24p. (J). (gr. k-3). lib. bdg. 25.95 *(978-1-62617-061-2(4)*, Blastoff! Readers) Bellwether Media.
Ganeri, Anita. Roadrunner, 1 vol. 2011. (Day in the Life: Desert Animals Ser.). (ENG., Illus.). 24p. (gr. k-2). pap. 6.49 *(978-1-4329-4784-2(2)*, Heinemann Read & Learn) Heinemann-Raintree.
Macgregor, Eloise. Roadrunner. 2015. (Desert Animals Searchin' for Shade Ser.). (ENG.). 24p. (J). (gr. -1-3). lib. bdg. 23.93 *(978-1-62724-533-3(2))* Bearport Publishing Co., Inc.
Macken, JoAnn Early. Roadrunners. 2nd rev. ed. 2009. (Animals That Live in the Desert Ser.). (ENG.). 24p. (J). (gr. -1-3). pap. 8.15 *(978-1-4339-2452-1(8))*; lib. bdg. 22.60

P
Q
R

(978-1-4339-2391-3(2)) Stevens, Gareth Publishing LLLP. (Weekly Reader Leveled Readers).
—Roadrunners;Correcaminos. 2nd rev. ed. 2009. (Animals That Live in the Desert/Animales del desierto Ser.). (SPA & ENG.). 24p. (J). (gr. -1-3). pap. 8.15 *(978-1-4339-2460-6(9))*; lib. bdg. 22.60 *(978-1-4339-2423-1(4))* Stevens, Gareth Publishing LLLP. (Weekly Reader Leveled Readers).

ROADS

see also Streets

Canfield, Michael. Ice Roads. 2016. (Technology Takes on Nature Ser.). 00032p. (J). pap. 10.50 ***(978-1-4824-5771-1(7))*** Stevens, Gareth Publishing LLLP.
Furgang, Kathy. Zoom in on Superhighways. 2017. (Zoom in on Engineering Ser.). 24p. (J). (gr. 2-2). lib. bdg. 22.60 ***(978-0-7660-8725-5(5))*** Enslow Pubs., Inc.
Geography Collective Staff. Mission: Explore on the Road. Morgan-Jones, Tom, illus. 2011. (Mission Explore Ser.). (ENG.). 96p. (J). (gr. 4-7). pap. 7.99 *(978-1-904872-38-2(7)*, Can of Worms Kids Pr.) Can of Worms Pr. GBR. Dist: Independent Pubs. Group.
Die Geschichte einer Strasse. (GER., Illus.). 32p. *(978-3-411-07401-3(9))* Bibliographisches Institut & F. A. Brockhaus AG DEU. Dist: i. b. d., Ltd.
Kupperberg, Paul. The Alaska Highway. 2009. (Building America Ser.). (Illus.). 144p. (gr. 5-8). 35.00 *(978-1-60413-074-4(1)*, Chelsea Hse.) Facts On File, Inc.
Mahaney, Ian F. Road Maps. (Map It! Ser.). 24p. 2009. (gr. 3-4). 42.50 *(978-1-61514-357-3(2)*, PowerKids Pr.) 2006. (Illus.). (YA). (gr. 2-5). lib. bdg. 22.60 *(978-1-4042-3056-9(4))* Rosen Publishing Group, Inc., The.
Maurer, Tracy Nelson. Using Road Maps & GPS. 2016. (Searchlight Books (tm) — What Do You Know about Maps? Ser.). (ENG., Illus.). 40p. (J). (gr. 3-5). 30.65 *(978-1-5124-0952-9(9))* Lerner Publishing Group.
Nardo, Don. Roman Roads & Aqueducts. 2014. (History's Great Structures). (ENG., Illus.). 80p. (J). lib. bdg. *(978-1-60152-634-2(2))* ReferencePoint Pr., Inc.
Nittinger, Sharon. How Did They Build That? Road. 2009. (Community Connections: How Did They Build That? Ser.). (ENG.). 24p. (gr. 2-5). lib. bdg. 25.64 *(978-1-60279-482-5(0)*, 200256) Cherry Lake Publishing.
Rand McNally Staff. Kids' Road Atlas. (Backseat Bks.). 80p. (J). pap. 3.95 *(978-0-528-96544-9(1))* Rand McNally.
Richardson, Gillian. 10 Routes That Crossed the World. Rosen, Kim, illus. 2017. (ENG.). 164p. (J). (gr. 3-7). pap. 12.95 *(978-1-55451-875-3(X))* Annick Pr., Ltd. CAN. Dist: Publishers Group West (PGW).
Roza, Greg. America's First Highway. 2009. 32p. (Illus.). (J). (gr. 5-6). pap. 10.00 *(978-1-4358-0199-8(7)*, Rosen Classroom); (gr. 5-5). 47.90 *(978-1-61511-372-9(X)*, PowerKids Pr.); (J). (gr. 4-6). lib. bdg. 25.25 *(978-1-4358-3014-1(8)*, PowerKids Pr.) Rosen Publishing Group, Inc., The.
Schaefer, Ted. Machines Large & Small. 2007. (ENG., Illus.). 16p. (gr. k-2). 28.50 *(978-1-60472-109-6(X))* Rourke Educational Media.
Snedden, Robert. Roads. 2016. (Engineering Eurekas Ser.). 00032p. (J). (gr. 3-4). pap. 10.00 *(978-1-4994-3101-8(5)*, PowerKids Pr.) Rosen Publishing Group, Inc., The.
Stefoff, Rebecca. Building Roads. 2015. (Great Engineering Ser.). (ENG.). 32p. (J). (gr. 3-4). pap. 10.58 *(978-1-5026-0603-7(8))* Cavendish Square Publishing.
Sutton, Sally. Roadwork. Lovelock, Brian, illus. 2011. (ENG.). 28p. (J). (gr. k-k). bds. 6.99 *(978-0-7636-4653-0(9))* Candlewick Pr.
Wooldridge, Connie Nordhielm. Just Fine the Way They Are: From Dirt Roads to Rail Roads to Interstates. Walz, Richard, illus. 2011. (ENG.). 32p. (J). (gr. 3-18). 17.95 *(978-1-59078-710-6(2)*, Calkins Creek) Boyds Mills Pr.

ROADS—FICTION

Barchers, Suzanne I. On the Road with Rose & Bose, 1 vol. 2011. (Targeted Phonics Ser.). (ENG.). 16p. (J). (gr. k-2). pap. 5.99 *(978-1-4333-2914-2(X))* Teacher Created Materials, Inc.
Best, Cari. When We Go Walking, 0 vols. Brooker, Kyrsten, illus. 2013. (ENG.). 32p. (J). (gr. -1-3). 17.99 *(978-1-4778-1648-6(8)*, 9781477816486, Amazon Children's Publishing) Amazon Publishing.
Doyle, Brian. Hey, Dad!, 1 vol. 3rd ed. 2006. (ENG.). 112p. (J). (gr. 4-8). pap. 6.95 *(978-0-88899-708-1(6))* Groundwood Bks. CAN. Dist: Publishers Group West (PGW).
Eames, Marion. Baner Beca. 2005. (WEL.). 80p. pap. *(978-0-86243-729-9(6))* Y Lolfa.
Educational Adventures, creator. Free Wheelin' Coloring/Activity Book (English) w/ Snipe. 2007. (J). 2.99 *(978-1-933934-52-5(2))* Mighty Kids Media.
—Street Smarts: Coloring/Activity Book (Spanish) w/ Snipe. 2006. (Illus.). (J). 2.99 *(978-1-933934-19-8(0))* Mighty Kids Media.
—Street Smarts: Picture Book (Spanish) 9x9. 2007. (Illus.). (J). per. 5.99 *(978-1-933934-77-8(8))* Mighty Kids Media.
Estes, Eleanor. The Alley. Ardizzone, Edward, illus. 2004. (Odyssey/Harcourt Young Classic Ser.). 283p. 15.95 *(978-0-7569-3475-0(3))* Perfection Learning Corp.
Feiffer, Jules. By the Side of the Road. 2005. (Illus.). 59p. (J). (gr. k-4). reprint ed. 16.00 *(978-0-7567-9371-5(8))* DIANE Publishing Co.
Ford, Robert. Adventures of Hit the Road Jack. l.t. ed. 2003. (Illus.). 40p. per. 10.00 *(978-1-932338-11-9(X))* Lifevest Publishing, Inc.
Free Wheelin' Picture Book (English) NL 9x9 with Snipe. 2007. (J). 5.99 *(978-1-933934-48-8(4))* Mighty Kids Media.
Gerhardt, Barbara. I Am of Scram. 2007. (Illus.). pap. 12.95 *(978-1-934246-15-3(8))* Peppertree Pr., The.
Horvath, James. Work, Dogs, Work: A Highway Tail. Horvath, James, illus. 2014. (ENG., Illus.). 40p. (J). (gr. -1-3). 15.99 *(978-0-06-218970-7(0))* HarperCollins Pubs.
Root, Phyllis. Rattletrap Car Big Book. Barton, Jill, illus. 2009. (ENG.). 40p. (J). (gr. -1-3). pap. 24.99 *(978-0-7636-4139-9(1))* Candlewick Pr.
Sabatino, Nick. Paint Stripes Stop Traffic Dead, 1 vol. 2010. 44p. 24.95 *(978-1-4489-5139-0(9))* PublishAmerica, Inc.
Sargent, Dave & Sargent, David M. Bob White: Use Good Judgement, 20 vols., Vol. 3. Lenoir, Jane, illus. 2003. (Feather Tales Ser.: No. 3). 42p. (J). pap. 10.95 *(978-1-56763-724-3(8))* Ozark Publishing.
Sargent, David M. Bob White: Use Good Judgement, 20 vols., Vol. 3. Lenoir, Jane, illus. 2003. (Feather Tales Ser.: No. 3). 42p. (J). lib. bdg. 20.95 *(978-1-56763-723-6(X))* Ozark Publishing.
Sharp, Euan. Diggedy Dozer in Treetop Troubles. 2008. 34p. 15.95 *(978-1-4357-0982-9(9))* Lulu Pr., Inc.
Slanina, Anne Maro. Annie Mouse's Route 66 Adventure: A Photo Journal, vols. 6, vol. 5. Collins, Kelsey, illus. 2011. (ENG.). 48p. (J). pap. 14.99 *(978-0-9793379-6-3(8))* Annie Mouse Bks.
Stegall, Kim. Rodney Robbins & the Rainy-Day Pond. Day, Bruce, illus. 2010. 29p. (J). *(978-1-60682-058-2(3))* BJU Pr.
Street Smarts: Coloring/Activity Book (English) Incl. Stickers. 2006. (Illus.). (J). 2.99 *(978-1-933934-18-1(2))* Mighty Kids Media.
Street Smarts: Picture Book 9x9 with Snipe. 2006. (Illus.). (J). 5.99 *(978-1-933934-17-4(4))* Mighty Kids Media.
Street Smarts: Picture Book (English) 8x8. 2006. (Illus.). (J). 5.99 *(978-1-933934-16-7(6))* Mighty Kids Media.
Sutton, Sally. Construction. Lovelock, Brian, illus. 2014. (ENG.). 34p. (J). (gr. -1-2). 15.99 *(978-0-7636-7325-3(0))* Candlewick Pr.
—Construir una Carretera (Roadwork) Lovelock, Brian, illus. 2013. (SPA.). 28p. (J). (-k). bds. 6.99 *(978-0-7636-6494-7(4))* Candlewick Pr.

ROANOKE ISLAND (N.C.)

Belval, Brian. A Primary Source History of the Lost Colony of Roanoke. (Primary Sources of the Thirteen Colonies & the Lost Colony Ser.). 64p. 2009. (gr. 5-8). 58.50 *(978-1-60851-891-3(4))* 2006. (Illus.). (YA). (gr. 4-7). lib. bdg. 31.95 *(978-1-4042-0435-5(0))* 2006. (ENG., Illus.). (gr. 4-8). per. 12.95 *(978-1-4042-0669-4(8))* Rosen Publishing Group, Inc., The.
Blake, Kevin. Roanoke Island: The Town That Vanished. 2015. (Abandoned: Towns Without People Ser.). (ENG.). 32p. (J). (gr. 2-7). lib. bdg. 26.60 *(978-1-62724-521-0(9))* Bearport Publishing Co., Inc.
Fritz, Jean. The Lost Colony of Roanoke. Talbott, Hudson, illus. 2004. (ENG.). 64p. (J). (gr. 2-5). 18.99 *(978-0-399-24027-0(6)*, G.P. Putnam's Sons Books for Young Readers) Penguin Young Readers Group.
Huey, Lois Miner. American Archaeology Uncovers the Earliest English Colonies. 2009. (American Archaeology Ser.). 64p. (gr. 5-6). 31.36 *(978-0-7614-4264-6(2))* Marshall Cavendish Corp.
Kent, Zachary. The Mysterious Disappearance of Roanoke Colony in American History. 2004. (In American History Ser.). (Illus.). 128p. (J). lib. bdg. 26.60 *(978-0-7660-2147-1(5))* Enslow Pubs., Inc.
McAneney, Caitlin. The Lost Colony of Roanoke. 2015. (Spotlight on the 13 Colonies Ser.). (ENG., Illus.). 24p. (J). (gr. 4-5). pap. 8.25 *(978-1-4994-0596-5(0)*, PowerKids Pr.) Rosen Publishing Group, Inc., The.
Miller, Jake. The Lost Colony of Roanoke: A Primary Source History. 2009. (Primary Source Library of the Thirteen Colonies & the Lost Colony Ser.). 24p. (gr. 3-4). 42.50 *(978-1-60854-163-8(0)*, PowerKids Pr.) Rosen Publishing Group, Inc., The.
Prentzas, G. S. Roanoke. 2011. (Lost Worlds & Mysterious Civilizations Ser.). (Illus.). 104p. (gr. 6-12). 35.00 *(978-1-60413-970-9(6)*, Chelsea Hse.) Facts On File, Inc.
Schuetz, Kari. Roanoke: The Lost Colony. 2017. (Abandoned Places Ser.). (ENG., Illus.). 24p. (J). (gr. 3-7). lib. bdg. 25.95 ***(978-1-62617-698-0(1)*** , Torque Bks.) Bellwether Media.
Simmons, Alex. Mysteries of the Past: A Chapter Book. 2005. (True Tales Ser.). (ENG., Illus.). 48p. (J). (gr. 2-4). lib. bdg. 22.50 *(978-0-516-25184-4(8)*, Children's Pr.) Scholastic Library Publishing.
Smith, Andrea P. The Mystery of Roanoke, the Lost Colony. 2012. (Illus.). 24p. (J). 63.60 *(978-1-4488-5209-3(9))*; pap. 10.60 *(978-1-4488-5208-6(0))*; lib. bdg. 25.25 *(978-1-4488-5185-0(8))* Rosen Publishing Group, Inc., The. (PowerKids Pr.).

ROBBERS AND OUTLAWS

Billy the Kid. 2010. (Legends of the Wild West Ser.). (Illus.). 104p. (gr. 6-12). 35.00 *(978-1-60413-596-1(4)*, Chelsea Hse.) Facts On File, Inc.
Bryant, Jill. John Henry Holliday. 2003. (Folk Heroes Ser.). (Illus.). 24p. (J). lib. bdg. 24.45 *(978-1-59036-077-4(X))* Weigl Pubs., Inc.
Callery, Sean. The Dark History of America's Old West. 2010. (Dark Histories Ser.). 64p. (gr. 5). 32.79 *(978-1-60870-086-8(0))* Marshall Cavendish Corp.
Collins, Kathleen. Jesse James: Bank Robber of the American West. 2009. (Primary Sources of Famous People in American History Ser.). 32p. (gr. 2-3). 47.90 *(978-1-60851-690-2(3))* Rosen Publishing Group, Inc., The.
—Jesse James: Bank Robber of the American West / Legendario bandido del oeste Americano. 2009. (Famous People in American History/Grandes personajes en la historia de los Estados Unidos Ser.). (ENG & SPA.). 32p. (gr. 2-3). 47.90 *(978-1-61512-547-0(7)*, Editorial Buenas Letras) Rosen Publishing Group, Inc., The.
—Jesse James: Legendario Bandido del Oeste Americano. 2004. (Grandes personajes en la historia de los Estados Unidos Ser.). (SPA.). 32p. (gr. 3-6). pap. 10.00 *(978-0-8239-4230-5(9)*, Rosen Classroom) Rosen Publishing Group, Inc., The.
—Jesse James: Legendario bandido del oeste americano (Jesse James: Bank Robber of the American West) 2009. (Grandes personajes en la historia de los Estados Unidos (Famous People in American History) Ser.). (SPA.). 32p. (gr. 2-3). 47.90 *(978-1-61512-801-3(8)*, Editorial Buenas Letras) Rosen Publishing Group, Inc., The.
Cooke, Tim. Billy the Kid: A Notorious Gunfighter of the Wild West. 2016. (Wanted! Famous Outlaws Ser.). (ENG., Illus.). 48p. (J). (gr. 6-8). pap. 14.05 *(978-1-4824-4243-4(4))* Stevens, Gareth Publishing LLLP.
—Butch Cassidy & the Sundance Kid: Notorious Outlaws of the West. 2016. (Wanted! Famous Outlaws Ser.). (ENG., Illus.). 48p. (J). (gr. 6-8). pap. 14.05 *(978-1-4824-4255-7(8))* Stevens, Gareth Publishing LLLP.
—Jesse James: A Notorious Bank Robber of the Wild West. 2016. (Wanted! Famous Outlaws Ser.). (ENG., Illus.). 48p. (J). (gr. 6-8). pap. 14.05 *(978-1-4824-4259-5(0))* Stevens, Gareth Publishing LLLP.
—Ned Kelly: A Notorious Bandit of the Australian Outback. 2016. (Wanted! Famous Outlaws Ser.). (ENG., Illus.). 48p. (J). (gr. 6-8). 31.95 *(978-1-4824-4262-5(0))* Stevens, Gareth Publishing LLLP.
Cunningham, Meghan Engsberg. Jesse James. Lapegüe, Matías, illus. 2016. (American Legends & Folktales Ser.). 32p. (J). 28.50 *(978-1-5026-2197-9(5))* Cavendish Square Publishing.
Elborough, Travis. Highwayman, Outlaws & Bandits of London. 2004. (... of London Ser.). (ENG., Illus.). 96p. pap. 8.99 *(978-1-904153-13-9(5))* Watling St., Ltd. GBR. Dist: Trafalgar Square Publishing.
Fenn, George Manvill. Young Robin Hood. 2004. reprint ed. pap. 15.95 *(978-1-4191-9534-1(4))* Kessinger Publishing, LLC.
Frisch, Aaron. Jesse James. 2005. (Legends of the West (Creative Education) Ser.). (Illus.). 48p. (J). (gr. 5-9). lib. bdg. 21.95 *(978-1-58341-338-8(3)*, Creative Education) Creative Co., The.
Green, Carl R. & Sanford, William R. Belle Starr. rev. ed. 2008. (Outlaws & Lawmen of the Wild West, Revised Edition Ser.). (Illus.). 48p. (J). (gr. 5-18). lib. bdg. 25.27 *(978-0-7660-3176-0(4))* Enslow Pubs., Inc.
—Billy the Kid. rev. ed. 2008. (Outlaws & Lawmen of the Wild West, Revised Edition Ser.). (Illus.). 48p. (J). (gr. 5-18). lib. bdg. 25.27 *(978-0-7660-3173-9(X))* Enslow Pubs., Inc.
—Butch Cassidy. rev. ed. 2008. (Outlaws & Lawmen of the Wild West, Revised Edition Ser.). (Illus.). 48p. (J). (gr. 5-18). lib. bdg. 25.27 *(978-0-7660-3175-3(6))* Enslow Pubs., Inc.
—Jesse James. rev. ed. 2008. (Outlaws & Lawmen of the Wild West, Revised Edition Ser.). (Illus.). 48p. (J). (gr. 5-18). lib. bdg. 25.27 *(978-0-7660-3172-2(1))* Enslow Pubs., Inc.
Hurley, Trish. The 10 Most Outrageous Outlaws. 2008. 14.99 *(978-1-55448-506-2(1))* Scholastic Library Publishing.
Jesse James. 2010. (Legends of the Wild West Ser.). (Illus.). 128p. (gr. 6-12). 35.00 *(978-1-60413-598-5(0)*, Chelsea Hse.) Facts On File, Inc.
Kovacs, Vic. Outlaws & Sheriffs. 2015. (True History of the Wild West Ser.). (ENG., Illus.). 32p. (J). (gr. 5-5). pap. 10.00 *(978-1-4994-1178-2(2)*, PowerKids Pr.) Rosen Publishing Group, Inc., The.
Landau, Elaine. Billy the Kid: Wild West Outlaw. 2004. (Best of the West Biographies Ser.). (Illus.). 48p. (J). lib. bdg. 25.27 *(978-0-7660-2207-2(2))* Enslow Pubs., Inc.
McDonnell, Julia. The Legend of Robin Hood. 2015. (Famous Legends Ser.). (ENG., Illus.). 32p. (J). (gr. 2-3). pap. 10.50 *(978-1-4824-2748-6(6))* Stevens, Gareth Publishing LLLP.
McIntosh, Kenneth. Outlaws & Lawmen: Crime & Punishment in the 1800s. 2009. (Daily Life in America in the 1800s Ser.). 64p. (YA). (gr. 7-18). pap. 9.95 *(978-1-4222-1857-0(0))*; lib. bdg. 22.95 *(978-1-4222-1784-9(1))* Mason Crest.
Moody, Ralph. Wells Fargo. Mays, Victor, illus. 2005. (ENG.). 186p. pap. 13.95 *(978-0-8032-8303-9(2)*, MOOWEX, Bison Bks.) Univ. of Nebraska Pr.
Nelson, Vaunda Micheaux. Bad News for Outlaws: The Remarkable Life of Bass Reeves, Deputy U. S. Marshall. Christie, R. Gregory, illus. 2009. (Exceptional Social Studies Titles for Intermediate Grades). (ENG.). 40p. (J). (gr. 3-6). lib. bdg. 17.95 *(978-0-8225-6764-6(4))* Lerner Publishing Group.
Newton, Michael. Bank Robbery. 2008. (Criminal Investigations Ser.). (Illus.). 120p. (C). (gr. 9-12). 35.00 *(978-0-7910-9401-3(4)*, Chelsea Hse.) Facts On File, Inc.
Nolan, Frederick W. Outlaws & Rebels. 2015. (Wild West Ser.). (Illus.). 64p. (J). (gr. 9-12). 39.95 *(978-1-78404-080-2(0))* Arcturus Publishing GBR. Dist: Black Rabbit Bks.
Pipe, Jim. Top 10 Worst Vicious Villains. Antram, David, illus. 2012. (Top 10 Worst Ser.). (ENG.). 32p. (J). (gr. 3-6). pap. 10.50 *(978-1-4339-6698-9(0))*; lib. bdg. 26.60 *(978-1-4339-6697-2(2))* Stevens, Gareth Publishing LLLP. (Gareth Stevens Learning Library).
Randolph, Ryan. A Bank Robber's End: The Death of Jesse James. 2009. (Great Moments in American History Ser.). 32p. (gr. 3-3). 47.90 *(978-1-61513-138-9(8))* Rosen Publishing Group, Inc., The.
Randolph, Ryan P. Wild West Lawmen & Outlaws. (Library of the Westward Expansion Ser.). 24p. 2009. (gr. 3-4). 42.50 *(978-1-60853-944-4(X))* 2003. (Illus.). (J). lib. bdg. 22.60 *(978-0-8239-6293-8(8))* Rosen Publishing Group, Inc., The. (PowerKids Pr.).
Rice, Dona. Chicas y Chicos Malos Del Lejano Oeste. 2016. (TIME for Kids en Español - Level 5 Ser.). (SPA.). 64p. (gr. 5-5). lib. bdg. 31.99 *(978-1-5157-2954-9(0))* Time for Kids Inc AUS. Dist: Capstone Pub.
Rice, Dona Herweck. Bad Guys & Gals of the Wild West, 1 vol. 2nd rev. ed. 2013. (Nonfiction Readers Ser.). (ENG., Illus.). 64p. (J). (gr. 5-5). pap. 31.96 *(978-1-4333-7426-5(9))* Teacher Created Materials, Inc.
Sanford, Carl R. & Sanford, William R. Outlaws & Lawmen of the Wild West, 10 bks., Set. (Illus.). (YA). (gr. 4-10). lib. bdg. 169.50 *(978-0-89490-391-5(8))* Enslow Pubs., Inc.
Savage, Jeff. Quick-Draw Gunfighters: True Tales of the Wild West. 2012. (True Tales of the Wild West Ser.). (Illus.). 48p. (J). (gr. 5-18). pap. 8.95 *(978-1-4644-0029-2(6))*; lib. bdg. 22.60 *(978-0-7660-4021-2(6))* Enslow Pubs., Inc.
Schwartz, Heather E. Outlaws, Gunslingers, & Thieves. (ShockZone (tm) — Villains Ser.). (ENG., 32p. (gr. 5-8). 2015. Illus.). 21.32 *(978-1-4677-6004-1(6)*, Lerner Digital) 2013. lib. bdg. 26.60 *(978-1-4677-0605-6(1)*, Lerner Pubns.) 2013. (Illus.). pap. 8.95 *(978-1-4677-0899-9(2))* Lerner Publishing Group.
Smith, Neil. Robin Hood, 1 vol. 2015. (ENG., Illus.). 80p. (J). 35.60 *(978-1-4777-8139-5(0)*, Rosen Young Adult) Rosen Publishing Group, Inc., The.
Thompson, Paul B. Billy the Kid: It Was a Game of Two & I Got There First. 2010. (Americans—the Spirit of a Nation Ser.). (Illus.). 128p. (J). lib. bdg. 33.27 *(978-0-7660-3480-8(1))* Enslow Pubs., Inc.
Waldman, Scott. Gunfight at the O. K. Corral: Wyatt Earp Upholds the Law. 2009. (Great Moments in American History Ser.). 32p. (gr. 3-3). 47.90 *(978-1-61513-143-3(4))* Rosen Publishing Group, Inc., The.
Woog, Adam & Triplett, Frank. Jesse James: The Wild West for Kids. 2014. (ENG., Illus.). 128p. (J). (gr. 2-7). pap. 12.95 *(978-1-62636-160-7(6)*, 263160, Sky Pony Pr.) Skyhorse Publishing Co., Inc.

ROBBERS AND OUTLAWS—FICTION

Adler, David A. Cam Jansen & the Catnapping Mystery. Natti, Susanna, illus. 2005. (Cam Jansen Ser.). 58p. (gr. 2-5). 14.00 *(978-0-7569-5045-3(7))* Perfection Learning Corp.
Alfonsi, Alice. The Almost Invisible Cases. Harrington, Rich, illus. 2007. 96p. (J). *(978-0-545-01585-1(5))* Scholastic, Inc.
—The Code Red Cases. Harrington, Rich, illus. 2006. 96p. (J). *(978-0-439-91447-5(7))* Scholastic, Inc.
—The Playing Card Cases. Harrington, Rich, illus. 2007. 96p. (J). *(978-0-545-01087-0(X))* Scholastic, Inc.
Alger, Horatio. Joe's Luck. 2005. 28.95 *(978-1-4218-1455-1(2))*; 264p. pap. 13.95 *(978-1-4218-1555-8(9))* 1st World Publishing, Inc. (1st World Library - Literary Society).
—Joe's Luck: Or, Always Wide Awake. 2006. (ENG.). 176p. pap. 19.99 *(978-1-4264-0883-0(8))* 2006. (ENG.). 172p. pap. 19.99 *(978-1-4264-6426-3(6))* 2007. 186p. pap. 21.99 *(978-1-4264-6500-0(9))* 2006. (ENG.). 170p. pap. 21.99 *(978-1-4264-0864-9(1))* Creative Media Partners, LLC.
—Joe's Luck: Or, Always Wide Awake. 2006. pap. *(978-1-4065-0713-3(X))* Dodo Pr.
—Struggling Upward: Or, Luke Larkin's Luck. 2006. pap. *(978-1-4065-0723-2(7))* Dodo Pr.
—Struggling Upward; or, Luck Larkin's Luck. 2008. 104p. pap. 7.99 *(978-1-4209-3044-3(3))* Digireads.com Publishing.
Amato, Mary. Sniff a Skunk!, Bk. 3. Jenkins, Ward, illus. 2015. (Good Crooks Ser.: Bk. 3). (ENG.). 128p. (gr. 2-4). 14.99 *(978-1-60684-598-1(5)*, Darby Creek) Lerner Publishing Group.
Andersen, C. B. The Book of Mormon Sleuth Vol. 3: The Hidden Path. 2003. ix, 214p. (J). pap. *(978-1-57008-988-6(4))* Deseret Bk. Co.
Angleberger, Tom. Fake Mustache: Or, How Jodie O'Rodeo & Her Wonder Horse (and Some Nerdy Kid) Saved the U. S. Presidential Election from a Mad Genius Criminal Mastermind. 2013. (ENG.). 208p. (J). (gr. 3-7). pap. 7.95 *(978-1-4197-1163-3(6)*, Amulet Bks.) Abrams, Inc.
Ausona, Roberto de. Robin Hood. (SPA., Illus.). 156p. (YA). 11.95 *(978-84-7281-110-2(7)*, AF1110) Auriga, Ediciones S.A. ESP. Dist: Continental Bk. Co., Inc.
Auxier, Jonathan. Peter Nimble & His Fantastic Eyes. (ENG.). 400p. (J). (gr. 3-7). 2012. pap. 9.95 *(978-1-4197-0421-5(4))* 2011. 19.95 *(978-1-4197-0025-5(1))* Abrams, Inc. (Amulet Bks.).
Avi. The End of Time. 2011. (ENG.). 240p. (J). (gr. 5). pap. 6.99 *(978-0-06-174083-1(7))* HarperCollins Pubs.
Baglio, Ben M. Max Is Missing. 2005. (Pet Finders Club Ser.: Vol. 2). (Illus.). 126p. (J). pap. *(978-0-439-68884-0(1))* Scholastic, Inc.
Balasubramanian, Lalitha. The Twins at the Ancient Villa, 1 vol. 2009. 48p. pap. 16.95 *(978-1-61582-601-8(7))* America Star Bks.
Bardugo, Leigh. Six of Crows. 2015. (Illus.). (YA). pap. *(978-1-62779-509-8(X))* Holt, Henry & Co.
—Six of Crows. Stein, Erin, ed. 2015. (Six of Crows Ser.: 1). (ENG., Illus.). 480p. (YA). (gr. 7-17). 18.99 *(978-1-62779-212-7(0)*, 9781627792127, Holt, Henry & Co. Bks. For Young Readers) Holt, Henry & Co.
—Six of Crows. 2018. (Six of Crows Ser.: 1). (YA). lib. bdg. 22.10 ***(978-0-606-39944-9(5))*** Turtleback Bks.
Barrett, Mac. It Happened on a Train. Rex, Adam, illus. (Brixton Brothers Ser.: 3). (ENG.). (J). (gr. 3-7). 2012. 304p. pap. 7.99 *(978-1-4169-7820-6(8))* 2011. 288p. 17.99 *(978-1-4169-7819-0(4))* Simon & Schuster Bks. For Young Readers. (Simon & Schuster Bks. For Young Readers).
Barnhill, Kelly. The Witch's Boy. 2014. (ENG.). 384p. (J). (gr. 4). 17.95 *(978-1-61620-351-1(X)*, 73351) Algonquin Bks. of Chapel Hill.
Beck, Ian & Beck, Ian. The Teddy Robber. 2005. (ENG., Illus.). 32p. (J). pap. 9.99 *(978-0-552-55319-3(0))* Transworld Publishers Ltd. GBR. Dist: Independent Pubs. Group.
Bell, Hilari. Shield of Stars, No. 1. 2008. (Shield, Sword, & Crown Ser.: 1). (ENG.). 288p. (J). (gr. 3-7). pap. 13.99 *(978-1-4169-0595-0(2)*, Simon & Schuster/Paula Wiseman Bks.) Simon & Schuster/Paula Wiseman Bks.
Bell, William. The Blue Helmet. 2009. (ENG.). 224p. mass mkt. 6.99 *(978-0-7704-3002-3(3)*, Seal Bks) Random Hse. of Canada CAN. Dist: Random Hse., Inc.
Berlin, Eric. The Puzzler's Mansion: The Puzzling World of Winston Breen. (Puzzling World of Winston Breen Ser.: 3). (ENG.). (J). (gr. 3-7). 2013. 272p. pap. 7.99 *(978-0-14-242643-2(1)*, Puffin Books) 2012. 256p. 16.99 *(978-0-399-25697-4(0)*, G.P. Putnam's Sons Books for Young Readers) Penguin Young Readers Group.
Bessen, Luc. Arthur & the Minimoys. Sowchek, Ellen, tr. from FRE. 2005. (ENG.). 240p. (J). 15.99 *(978-0-06-059623-1(6))* HarperCollins Pubs.
Besson, Luc. Arthur & the Minimoys. 2005. (Illus.). 240p. (J). lib. bdg. 16.89 *(978-0-06-059624-8(4))* HarperCollins Pubs.
Black, Peter Jay. Urban Outlaws. 2015. (Urban Outlaws Ser.: 1). (ENG.). 304p. (YA). (gr. 5-8). pap. 7.99 *(978-1-61963-572-2(0)*, 9781619635722, Bloomsbury USA Childrens) Bloomsbury Publishing USA.
Blackburne, Livia. Midnight Thief. (Midnight Thief Ser.). (ENG., Illus.). (YA). (gr. 7-12). 2014. 380p. 16.99 *(978-1-4231-7638-1(3))*Bk. 1. 2015. 394p. pap. 9.99 *(978-1-4231-9461-3(6))* Hyperion Bks. for Children.
Bossley, Michele Martin. Swiped, 1 vol. 2006. (Orca Currents Ser.). (ENG.). 136p. (J). (gr. 5-9). per. 9.95 *(978-1-55143-646-3(9))* Orca Bk. Pubs. USA.
Bottiglieri, Tim. Robber Raccoon, 1 vol. Bishop, John E., illus. 2009. 16p. pap. 24.95 *(978-1-61546-432-6(8))* America Star Bks.
Brezenoff, Steve. Alley of Shadows, 1 vol. Martin, Cynthia, illus. 2008. (Vortex Bks.). (ENG.). 112p. (gr. 2-3). pap. 7.19 *(978-1-59889-922-1(8)*, Vortex Bks.) Stone Arch Bks.
Bromley, Anne C. & Casilla, Robert. The Lunch Thief, 1 vol. 2010. (ENG., Illus.). 32p. (gr. 3-7). 16.95 *(978-0-88448-311-3(8)*, 884311) Tilbury Hse. Pubs.
Buckley-Archer, Linda. The Time Quake. (Gideon Trilogy Ser.: 3). (ENG.). 464p. (J). (gr. 5-9). 2010. pap. 9.99 *(978-1-4169-1530-0(3))* 2009. 17.99 *(978-1-4169-1529-4(X))* Simon & Schuster Bks. For Young Readers. (Simon & Schuster Bks. For Young Readers).
—The Time Thief. 2008. (Gideon Trilogy Ser.: 2). (ENG.). 512p. (J). (gr. 5-9). pap. 9.99 *(978-1-4169-1528-7(1)*, Simon

& Schuster Bks. For Young Readers) Simon & Schuster Bks. For Young Readers.
—The Time Travelers. 2012. (Gideon Trilogy Ser.: 1). (ENG.). 416p. (J). (gr. 5-9). 17.99 *(978-1-4424-6551-0(4)*, Simon & Schuster Bks. For Young Readers) Simon & Schuster Bks. For Young Readers.
Bunce, Elizabeth C. Liar's Moon. 2011. (YA). pap. *(978-0-545-13607-5(5))*; (ENG.). 368p. (J). (gr. 7-7). 17.99 *(978-0-545-13608-2(3))* Scholastic, Inc. (Levine, Arthur A. Bks.).
—StarCrossed. 2011. (ENG.). 368p. (YA). pap. 9.99 *(978-0-545-13606-8(7)*, Levine, Arthur A. Bks.) Scholastic, Inc.
Burnett, Frances Hodgson. Editha's Burglar. Sandham, Henry, illus. 2005. reprint ed. pap. 15.95 *(978-1-4179-0135-7(7))* Kessinger Publishing, LLC.
Calcutt, David. Robin Hood. Baker-Smith, Grahame, illus. 2012. (ENG.). 176p. (J). (gr. 4-6). pap. 12.99 *(978-1-84686-799-6(1))* Barefoot Bks., Inc.
Capeci, Anne. Ghost Train, 1 vol., Vol. 3. Casale, Paul, illus. 2004. (Cascade Moutain Railroad Mystery Ser.: 3). (ENG.). 144p. (J). (gr. 2-5). 12.95 *(978-1-56145-324-5(2))* Peachtree Pubs.
—Missing!, 1 vol. Casale, Paul, illus. 2005. (Cascade Mountain Railroad Mysteries Ser.). (ENG.). 144p. (J). (gr. 2-5). 12.95 *(978-1-56145-334-4(X))* Peachtree Pubs.
Casanova, Mary. The Day Dirk Yeller Came to Town. Hoyt, Ard, illus. 2011. (ENG.). 36p. (J). (gr. -1-3). 16.99 *(978-0-374-31742-3(9)*, 9780374317423, Farrar, Straus & Giroux (BYR)) Farrar, Straus & Giroux.
Cazet, Denys. Wanted Dead or Alive. Cazet, Denys, illus. 2007. (I Can Read Level 3 Ser.). (ENG., Illus.). 48p. (J). (gr. k-3). pap. 3.99 *(978-0-06-073012-3(9))* HarperCollins Pubs.
—Wanted Dead or Alive. Cazet, Denys, illus. 2008. (Minnie & Moo Ser.). (Illus.). (J). (gr. -1-3). pap. 16.95 incl. audio *(978-1-4301-0471-1(6))* Live Oak Media.
—Wanted Dead or Alive. 2008. (Minnie & Moo Ser.). (J). (gr. k-2). 25.95 incl. audio *(978-1-4301-0472-8(4))* Live Oak Media.
Chee, Traci. The Reader. (Sea of Ink & Gold Ser.: 1). (ENG.). 464p. (YA). (gr. 7). 2017. pap. 10.99 ***(978-0-14-751805-7(9)***, Speak)Bk. 1. 2016. 19.99 *(978-0-399-17677-7(2)*, G.P. Putnam's Sons Books for Young Readers) Penguin Young Readers Group.
—The Reader. 2017. (Sea of Ink & Gold Ser.: 1). lib. bdg. 22.10 ***(978-0-606-40001-5(X))*** Turtleback Bks.
Cherry, Alison. The Classy Crooks Club. 2016. (ENG., Illus.). 336p. (J). (gr. 3-7). 16.99 *(978-1-4814-4637-2(1)*, Aladdin) Simon & Schuster Children's Publishing.
Child, Lauren. Ruby Redfort Feel the Fear. Child, Lauren, illus. 2016. (Ruby Redfort Ser.). (ENG., Illus.). 528p. (J). (gr. 5-9). 16.99 *(978-0-7636-5470-2(1))* Candlewick Pr.
Choyce, Lesley. Running the Risk, 1 vol. 2009. (Orca Soundings Ser.). (ENG.). (YA). (gr. 8-12). 112p. 16.95 *(978-1-55469-026-8(9))*; 144p. pap. 9.95 *(978-1-55469-025-1(0))* Orca Bk. Pubs. USA.
Cody, Matthew. Will in Scarlet. 2014. (ENG., Illus.). 272p. (J). (gr. 5). pap. 6.99 *(978-0-375-87292-1(2)*, Yearling) Random Hse. Children's Bks.
Cole, Burton. Bash & the Chocolate Milk Cows. Lewis, Buddy, illus. 2015. (ENG.). 224p. (J). (gr. 3-7). pap. 8.99 *(978-1-4336-8530-9(2)*, B&H Kids) B&H Publishing Group.
Corderoy, Tracey. Shifty Mcgifty & Slippery Sam. Lenton, Steven, illus. 2013. (ENG.). 32p. (J). (gr. -1-3). 14.99 *(978-0-7636-6838-9(9)*, Nosy Crow) Candlewick Pr.
Coren, Alan. Arthur the Kid. 2004. (Illus.). 64p. *(978-0-903895-76-7(5)*, Robson Bks. Ltd.) Pavilion Bks.
—Buffalo Arthur. 2004. (Illus.). 64p. *(978-0-903895-75-0(7)*, Robson Bks. Ltd.) Pavilion Bks.
—Railroad Arthur. 2004. (Illus.). 64p. *(978-0-903895-92-7(7)*, Robson Bks. Ltd.) Pavilion Bks.
Couloumbis, Audrey. Maude March on the Run! Or Trouble Is Her Middle Name. 2008. (Maude March Ser.). (ENG., Illus.). 320p. (J). (gr. 3-7). pap. 7.99 *(978-0-375-83248-2(3)*, Yearling) Random Hse. Children's Bks.
—The Misadventures of Maude March: Or Trouble Rides a Fast Horse. 2007. (Illus.). 295p. (gr. 3-7). 18.00 *(978-0-7569-7770-2(3))* Perfection Learning Corp.
Crain, Kira. SEK Statton. 2009. (GER.). 136p. 29.95 *(978-1-4092-6127-8(1))* Lulu Pr., Inc.
Croall, Marie P. Ali Baba: Fooling the Forty Thieves: an Arabian Tale. 2008. (Graphic Myths & Legends Ser.). (Illus.). 48p. (J). (gr. 3-7). lib. bdg. 26.60 *(978-0-8225-7525-2(6)*, Graphic Universe™) Lerner Publishing Group.
Curtis, Christopher Paul & Paul, Curtis Christopher. Elias de Buxton. 2008. (SPA.). 368p. (gr. 6-12). pap. 12.99 *(978-84-441-4101-5(1))* Everest Editora ESP. Dist: Lectorum Pubns., Inc.
Dahl, Michael. The Sea of Lost Books, 1 vol. Kendall, Bradford, illus. 2010. (Return to the Library of Doom Ser.). (ENG.). 72p. (gr. 1-3). lib. bdg. 23.99 *(978-1-4342-2142-1(3)*, Zone Bks.) Stone Arch Bks.
—Tome Raider. Evergreen, Nelson, illus. 2015. (Library of Doom: the Final Chapters Ser.). (ENG.). 40p. (gr. 1-3). 23.99 *(978-1-4342-9677-1(6))* Stone Arch Bks.
Dailey, Reid. Ross the Reader & the Adventure of the Pirate's Treasure. Edgerley, Ross, illus. 2009. 44p. pap. 16.95 *(978-1-59858-900-9(8))* Dog Ear Publishing, LLC.
Daneshvari, Gitty. Class Is Not Dismissed! 2011. (School of Fear Ser.: 2). (ENG.). 336p. (J). (gr. 3-7). pap. 8.99 *(978-0-316-03329-9(4))* Little, Brown Bks. for Young Readers.
Daniels, J. M. The Secret of the Little Dutch Doll. 2009. 68p. pap. 25.49 *(978-1-4343-9356-2(9))* AuthorHouse.
Dare, Will. How to Catch a Dino Thief. 2017. (Dino Riders Ser.: 4). (ENG.). 128p. (J). (gr. 2-5). pap. 5.99 ***(978-1-4926-3623-6(1)***, Sourcebooks Jabberwocky) Sourcebooks, Inc.
Davis, Kent. A Riddle in Ruby. 2016. (Riddle in Ruby Ser.: Vol. 1). (ENG.). 432p. (J). (gr. 3-7). 18.40 *(978-0-606-39257-0(2))* Turtleback Bks.
De Campi, Alex. Kat & Mouse Vol. 1: Teacher Torture, 1 vol. Manfredi, Federica, illus. 2009. (Tokyopop Ser.). (ENG.). 96p. (gr. 2-6). 25.65 *(978-1-59961-564-6(9))* Spotlight.
—Kat & Mouse Vol. 2: Tripped, 1 vol. Manfredi, Federica, illus. 2009. (Tokyopop Ser.). (ENG.). 96p. (gr. 2-6). 25.65 *(978-1-59961-565-3(7))* Spotlight.
—Kat & Mouse Vol. 3: The Ice Storm, 1 vol. Manfredi, Federica, illus. 2009. (Tokyopop Ser.). (ENG.). 96p. (gr. 2-6). 25.65 *(978-1-59961-566-0(5))* Spotlight.
Deas, Stephen. The Thief-Taker's Apprentice: With a Sword, Comes Blood... 2011. (ENG.). 320p. (gr. 13-17). 14.99 *(978-0-575-09449-9(4)*, Gollancz) Orion Publishing Group, Ltd. GBR. Dist: Hachette Bk. Group.
Derby, Sally & Derby. Two Fools & a Horse: An Orginal Tale, 1 vol. Rayevsky, Robert, illus. 2003. (ENG.). 32p. (J). (gr. k-3). 16.95 *(978-0-7614-5119-8(6))* Marshall Cavendish Corp.
Deshpande, Shashi. 3 Novels. 2006. 379p. *(978-0-14-333511-5(1)*, Puffin) Penguin Publishing Group.
Dickens, Charles. Oliver Twist, 1 vol. McWilliam, Howard, illus. 2011. (Calico Illustrated Classics Ser.: No. 3). (ENG.). 112p. (J). (gr. 3-6). 27.07 *(978-1-61641-106-0(6))* Magic Wagon.
—Oliver Twist. abr. ed. Date not set. (Nelson Readers Ser.). (J). pap. *(978-0-17-557020-1(5))* Addison-Wesley Longman, Inc.
—Oliver Twist. 2008. (Bring the Classics to Life Ser.). (ENG., Illus.). 72p. (gr. 2-12). pap., act. bk. ed. 10.95 *(978-1-55576-325-1(1)*, EDCTR-308B) EDCON Publishing Group.
—Oliver Twist. abr. ed. (J). 9.95 *(978-1-56156-372-2(2))* Kidsbooks, LLC.
—Oliver Twist: With a Discussion of Honesty. 2003. (Values in Action Illustrated Classics Ser.). (J). *(978-1-59203-051-4(3))* Learning Challenge, Inc.
Disney Book Group. World of Reading: Sheriff Callie's Wild West Callie Asks for Help: Level Pre-1. Disney Storybook Art Team, illus. 2015. (World of Reading Ser.). (ENG.). 32p. (J). (gr. -1-k). pap. 3.99 *(978-1-4847-1631-1(0))* Disney Pr.
Disney Book Group Staff. Sheriff Callie's Wild West - The Cat Who Tamed the West. Disney Storybook Art Team, illus. 2015. (ENG.). 40p. (J). (gr. -1-k). 8.99 *(978-1-4847-1495-9(4))* Disney Pr.
Donaldson, Julia. The Highway Rat. Scheffler, Axel, illus. 2013. (ENG.). 32p. (J). (gr. -1-3). 16.99 *(978-0-545-47758-1(1)*, Levine, Arthur A. Bks.) Scholastic, Inc.
—What the Ladybug Heard. Monks, Lydia, illus. 2010. (ENG.). 32p. (J). (gr. -1-1). 18.99 *(978-0-8050-9028-4(2)*, 9780805090284, Holt, Henry & Co. Bks. For Young Readers) Holt, Henry & Co.
Dunagan, Ted M. Secret of the Satilfa. 2010. (ENG.). 208p. (J). (gr. 3-18). 21.95 *(978-1-58838-249-8(4)*, NewSouth Bks.) NewSouth, Inc.
Durell, Charles Pend. Lights off Shore or Sam & the Outlaws. 2005. pap. 28.95 *(978-1-4179-9422-9(3))* Kessinger Publishing, LLC.
Enderle, Dotti. Crosswire. 2010. (ENG.). 144p. (J). (gr. 4-6). 17.95 *(978-1-59078-751-9(X)*, Calkins Creek) Boyds Mills Pr.
Erickson, John R. The Case of the Monkey Burglar. Holmes, Gerald L., illus. 2011. (Hank the Cowdog Ser.: No. 48). (ENG.). 129p. (J). (gr. 3-6). pap. 5.99 *(978-1-59188-148-3(X))* Maverick Bks., Inc.
Erickson, Mary Ellen. Who Jinxed the CG Ranch? 2009. 196p. 24.95 *(978-1-4401-4218-5(1))*; pap. 14.95 *(978-1-4401-4216-1(5))* iUniverse, Inc.
Everett, F. The Burglar's Breakfast. 2004. (Young Reading Ser.: Vol. 1). (Illus.). 48p. (J). (gr. 2-18). pap. 5.95 *(978-0-7945-0221-8(0)*, Usborne) EDC Publishing.
Everett-Green, Evelyn. Tom Tufton's Travels. 2007. 196p. per. *(978-1-4065-3395-8(5))* Dodo Pr.
Falls, Kat. Dark Life. (Dark Life Ser.: 1). (ENG.). 304p. (J). (gr. 3-7). 2011. pap. 7.99 *(978-0-545-17815-0(0))* 2010. 16.99 *(978-0-545-17814-3(2))* Scholastic, Inc. (Scholastic Pr.).
—Rip Tide. 2011. (J). (Dark Life Ser.: 2). (ENG.). 320p. (gr. 3-7). 16.99 *(978-0-545-17843-3(6))*; 314p. pap. *(978-0-545-43175-0(1))* Scholastic, Inc. (Scholastic Pr.).
Fenn, G. Manville. Young Robin Hood. 2011. 56p. pap. 7.99 *(978-1-61203-082-1(3))* Bottom of the Hill Publishing.
Feutl, Rita. The Bike Thief, 1 vol. 2014. (Orca Soundings Ser.). (ENG.). 136p. (YA). (gr. 8-12). pap. 9.95 *(978-1-4598-0569-9(0))* Orca Bk. Pubs. USA.
Fischel, Ana. The Twelve Quests - Book 5, a Firebird's Feather. 2009. 158p. pap. *(978-1-84923-877-9(4))* YouWriteOn.
Fleischman, Sid. Bandit's Moon. Smith, Jos. A., illus. 2008. (ENG.). 192p. (J). (gr. 3-7). pap. 6.99 *(978-0-06-145096-9(0)*, Greenwillow Bks.) HarperCollins Pubs.
—The Whipping Boy. 2011. 7.52 *(978-0-7848-3459-6(8)*, Everbind) Marco Bk. Co.
—The Whipping Boy. 2003. (J). 17.20 *(978-0-613-69320-2(5)*, Turtleback) Turtleback Bks.
Franquin, André. The Marsupilami Thieves. 2013. (Spirou & Fantasio Ser.: 5). (ENG., Illus.). 64p. (J). (gr. 3-12). pap. 15.95 *(978-1-84918-167-9(5))* CineBook GBR. Dist: National Bk. Network.
Frederick, Heather Vogel. Once upon a Toad. (ENG., Illus.). (J). (gr. 5-9). 2013. 288p. pap. 6.99 *(978-1-4169-8479-5(8))* 2012. 272p. 16.99 *(978-1-4169-8478-8(X))* Simon & Schuster Bks. For Young Readers. (Simon & Schuster Bks. For Young Readers).
Funke, Cornelia. The Thief Lord. 2004.Tr. of Herr der Diebe. 376p. (J). (gr. 5-18). pap. 44.00 incl. audio *(978-0-8072-2278-2(X)*, Listening Library) Random Hse. Audio Publishing Group.
—Thief Lord. Birmingham, Christian, illus. 2010. (ENG.). 376p. (J). (gr. 3-7). 7.99 *(978-0-545-22770-4(4)*, Chicken Hse., The) Scholastic, Inc.
—The Thief Lord. 2003.Tr. of Herr der Diebe. (gr. 3-6). 18.40 *(978-0-613-84572-4(2)*, Turtleback) Turtleback Bks.
Galindo, Renata. The Cherry Thief. Galindo, Renata, illus. 2014. (Child's Play Library). (ENG., Illus.). 32p. (J). *(978-1-84643-652-9(4))* Child's Play International Ltd.
Garfield, Leon. Smith - The Story of a Pickpocket. 2013. (ENG.). 216p. (J). (gr. 4-7). 15.95 *(978-1-59017-675-7(8)*, NYR Children's Collection) New York Review of Bks., Inc., The.
George, Jessica Day. Princess of the Silver Woods. (Twelve Dancing Princesses Ser.). (ENG.). (YA). (gr. 7). 2013. 352p. pap. 9.99 *(978-1-61963-126-7(1)*, 9781619631267) 2012. 336p. 16.99 *(978-1-59990-646-1(5)*, 9781599906461) Bloomsbury Publishing USA. (Bloomsbury USA Childrens).
Gilbert, David D. Feodor Fitz: Journey to Harmony Ville. 2012. 40p. pap. 17.57 *(978-1-4772-1983-6(8))*; pap. 20.99 *(978-1-4685-8122-5(8))* AuthorHouse.
Goodwin, John. Robin Hood. Date not set. (Nelson Readers Ser.). (Illus.). 36p. (J). pap. *(978-0-17-557050-8(7))* Addison-Wesley Longman, Inc.
Goscinny, René, et al. Lucky Luke: The Dashing White Cowboy. 2008. (ENG.). 48p. (J). (gr. 2-4). pap. *(978-81-8386-014-7(1))* India Research Pr. IND. Dist: Independent Pubs. Group.
—Lucky Luke - Jesse James. 2008. (ENG.). 48p. (J). (gr. 2-4). pap. *(978-81-8386-016-1(8))* India Research Pr. IND. Dist: Independent Pubs. Group.
—Lucky Luke - Ma Dalton. 2008. (ENG.). 48p. (J). (gr. 2-4). pap. *(978-81-8386-015-4(X))* India Research Pr. IND. Dist: Independent Pubs. Group.
—Lucky Luke - the Tender Foot. 2008. (ENG.). 48p. (J). (gr. 2-4). pap. *(978-81-8386-017-8(6))* India Research Pr. IND. Dist: Independent Pubs. Group.
Gosling, Sharon. The Diamond Thief. 2014. (Diamond Thief Ser.). (ENG.). 336p. (gr. 9-12). 16.95 *(978-1-63079-002-8(8))* Switch Pr.
Grabenstein, Chris. Riley Mack & the Other Known Troublemakers. 2012. (Riley Mack Ser.: 1). (ENG.). 272p. (J). (gr. 3-7). 16.99 *(978-0-06-202620-0(8))* HarperCollins Pubs.
Graceffa, Joey. Children of Eden: A Novel. (ENG.). 288p. (gr. 7-12). 2017. pap. 12.99 ***(978-1-5011-4990-0(3))*** 2016. 18.99 *(978-1-5011-4655-8(6))* Simon & Schuster. (Atria Bks.).
Graves, Judith. Exposed, 1 vol. 2015. (Retribution Ser.). (ENG.). 144p. (YA). (gr. 8-12). pap. 9.95 *(978-1-4598-0722-8(7))* Orca Bk. Pubs. USA.
Greene, Janice. No Way to Run, 1 vol. unabr. ed. 2010. (Q Reads Ser.). (ENG.). 32p. (YA). (gr. 9-12). pap. 6.95 *(978-1-61651-184-5(2))* Saddleback Educational Publishing, Inc.
Guest, Jacqueline. Outcasts of River Falls, 1 vol. Peetoom, Laura, ed. 2012. (ENG.). 248p. (J). (gr. 4-7). pap. 9.95 *(978-1-55050-480-4(0))* Coteau Bks. CAN. Dist: Orca Bk. Pubs. USA.
Hancock, H. Irving. The Young Engineers in Arizona. rev. ed. 2006. 216p. 27.95 *(978-1-4218-1751-4(9))*; pap. 12.95 *(978-1-4218-1851-1(5))* 1st World Publishing, Inc. (1st World Library - Literary Society).
—The Young Engineers in Arizona. 2004. reprint ed. pap. 21.95 *(978-1-4191-8913-5(1))* Kessinger Publishing, LLC.
—The Young Engineers in Colorado. rev. ed. 2006. 212p. 27.95 *(978-1-4218-1744-6(6))*; pap. 12.95 *(978-1-4218-1844-3(2))* 1st World Publishing, Inc. (1st World Library - Literary Society).
—The Young Engineers in Mexico. rev. ed. 2006. 208p. 27.95 *(978-1-4218-1738-5(1))*; pap. 12.95 *(978-1-4218-1838-2(8))* 1st World Publishing, Inc. (1st World Library - Literary Society).
—The Young Engineers in Nevada. rev. ed. 2006. 220p. 27.95 *(978-1-4218-1754-5(3))*; pap. 12.95 *(978-1-4218-1854-2(X))* 1st World Publishing, Inc. (1st World Library - Literary Society).
—The Young Engineers on the Gulf. rev. ed. 2006. 216p. 27.95 *(978-1-4218-1752-1(7))*; pap. 12.95 *(978-1-4218-1852-8(3))* 1st World Publishing, Inc. (1st World Library - Literary Society).
Hanzik, Sharon. Raccoons Don't Use Spoons. 2009. 24p. pap. 17.95 *(978-1-4327-2815-1(6))* Outskirts Pr., Inc.
Harrison, Charles C. Dick Turpin. 2003. (Historias de Siempre Ser.). (SPA., Illus.). 92p. (J). (gr. 5-8). pap. 12.95 *(978-84-204-5701-7(9))* Santillana USA Publishing Co., Inc.
Harvey, Pam & Panckridge, Michael. Into the Fire. 2008. 192p. (J). *(978-0-207-20061-8(0))* HarperCollins Pubs. Australia.
Heath, Jack. Money Run. 2013. (ENG.). 256p. (J). (gr. 7). 17.99 *(978-0-545-51266-4(2))* Scholastic, Inc.
Heimerl, Kristen. Inspector Dewey. 2015. (ENG., Illus.). (J). 19.99 *(978-1-939710-27-7(8))* Orange Frazer Pr.
Hendry, Frances. Quest for a Queen: The Jackdaw. 2006. pap. *(978-1-905665-05-1(9))* Pollinger In Print.
Heneghan, James & Charles, Norma M. Bank Job, 1 vol. 2009. (ENG.). 176p. (J). (gr. 4-8). pap. 14.95 *(978-1-55143-855-9(0))* Orca Bk. Pubs. USA.
Higginson, Sheryl. Dilbert's Pets, 1 vol. 2010. 94p. pap. 19.95 *(978-1-4489-5757-6(5))* America Star Bks.
Hillerman, Tony. Buster Mesquite's Cowboy Band. 2006. (J). reprint ed. lib. bdg. 14.95 *(978-0-914001-12-6(4))* Sidewinder Publishing LLC.
Horsfall, S. J. Jodie & Lilly... & the Fake Mansion. 2009. 58p. pap. 7.50 *(978-0-557-12474-9(3))* Lulu Pr., Inc.
Houts, Richard. A Thief's Journey. 2008. 128p. pap. 15.99 *(978-0-557-02192-5(8))* Lulu Pr., Inc.
Howard, Jeremy. The Countdown: The Adventures of Starforce. 2005. 114p. 23.45 *(978-1-4208-2398-1(1))*; pap. 11.95 *(978-1-4208-2397-4(3))* AuthorHouse.
Imbernón, Maite & Dickens, Charles. Oliver Twist. 2003. (Timeless Classics Ser.). (SPA., Illus.). 92p. (J). pap. 10.95 *(978-84-204-5750-5(7))* Santillana USA Publishing Co., Inc.
Jacobson, Rick. The Mona Lisa Caper. Jacobson, Rick & Fernandez, Laura, illus. 2005. (ENG.). 24p. (J). (gr. k-3). 16.99 *(978-0-88776-726-5(5)*, Tundra Bks.) Tundra Bks. CAN. Dist: Penguin Random Hse. LLC.
Jakobsen, Lars. The Red Ruby. Jakobsen, Lars, illus. 2013. (Mortensen's Escapades Ser.: 3). (ENG., Illus.). 48p. (gr. 6-12). pap. 6.95 *(978-1-4677-0729-9(5)*, Graphic Universe™) Lerner Publishing Group.
Jakobsen, Lars & Chapman, Robyn. The Red Ruby. Jakobsen, Lars, illus. 2013. (Mortensen's Escapades Ser.: 3). (ENG., Illus.). 48p. (gr. 6-12). lib. bdg. 27.93 *(978-0-7613-7914-0(2)*, Graphic Universe™) Lerner Publishing Group.
Jenkins, Jerry B. & Fabry, Chris. Canyon Echoes. 2005. (Red Rock Mysteries Ser.: 8). (ENG.). 234p. (YA). pap. 6.99 *(978-1-4143-0147-1(2)*, Tyndale Kids) Tyndale Hse. Pubs.
Johnson, Gillian. Thora & the Green Sea-Unicorn. Johnson, Gillian, illus. 2005. (Illus.). 272p. *(978-0-207-20016-8(5))* HarperCollins Pubs. Australia.
Jones, Rob Lloyd. The Story of Robin Hood. Marks, Alan, illus. 2010. (Picture Book Classics Ser.). 24p. (J). 9.99 *(978-0-7945-2859-1(7)*, Usborne) EDC Publishing.
Jones, T. Llew. Storiau Cwm-Pen-Llo. 2005. (WEL., Illus.). 100p. pap. *(978-0-86381-750-2(5))* Gwasg Carreg Gwalch.
Jordan, Rosa. Wild Spirits. 2010. (ENG.). 272p. (J). (gr. 6). pap. 12.99 *(978-1-55488-729-3(1))* Dundurn CAN. Dist: Ingram Publisher Services.
Keene, Carolyn. The Apple Bandit. Jones, Jan Naimo, illus. 2005. (Nancy Drew Notebooks). 74p. (J). (gr. 1-4). 11.65 *(978-0-7569-6505-1(5))* Perfection Learning Corp.
Kennedy, Robert F., Jr. Robert Smalls: The Boat Thief. Faricy, Patrick, illus. 2008. (Robert F. Kennedy, Jr.'s American Heroes Ser.). (ENG.). 48p. (gr. 5-8). 16.99 *(978-1-4231-0802-3(7))* Hyperion Pr.
King, Trey. Detective Chase McCain: Save That Cargo! 2013. (LEGO City 8X8 Ser.). lib. bdg. 13.55 *(978-0-606-32393-2(7)*, Turtleback) Turtleback Bks.
—Detective Chase McCain- Save That Cargo! Primeau, Chuck, illus. 2013. (Lego City Ser.). (ENG.). 24p. (J). (gr. -1-3). 3.99 *(978-0-545-51573-3(4))* Scholastic, Inc.
King, Trey & Kiernan, Kenny. Cops, Crocs, & Crooks! 2015. (Lego City Ser.). (ENG., Illus.). 24p. (J). (gr. -1-3). pap. 3.99 *(978-0-545-78525-9(1))* Scholastic, Inc.
Krause, Ute. Nick & the Nasty Knight. 2012. (ENG., Illus.). 32p. (J). (gr. -1-3). 17.95 *(978-0-7358-4091-1(1))* North-South Bks., Inc.
Krawitz, Susan. Viva, Rose! 2017. (ENG.). 240p. (J). (gr. 5). 16.95 *(978-0-8234-3756-6(6))* Holiday Hse., Inc.
Larry, H. I. Zac's Bank Bust. 2014. (Zac Power Test Drive Ser.: 7). (ENG.). 56p. (J). (gr. k-2). 7.99 *(978-1-921502-09-5(6))* Hardie Grant Egmont Pty, Ltd. AUS. Dist: Independent Pubs. Group.
Lekich, John. The Prisoner of Snowflake Falls, 1 vol. 2012. (ENG.). 280p. (YA). (gr. 8-12). pap. 12.95 *(978-1-55469-978-0(9))* Orca Bk. Pubs. USA.
Leslie, Emma. For Merrie England: A Tale of the Weavers of Norfolk. Taylor, R., illus. 2010. 168p. 20.95 *(978-1-934671-38-2(X))*; pap. 10.95 *(978-1-934671-39-9(8))* Salem Ridge Press LLC.
Lewis, Gill. Scout & the Sausage Thief. Home, Sarah, illus. 2016. (Puppy Academy Ser.). (ENG.). 128p. (J). 16.99 *(978-1-62779-794-8(7)*, 9781627797948, Holt, Henry & Co. Bks. For Young Readers) Holt, Henry & Co.
Lloyd-Jones, Emily. Deceptive: An Illusive Novel. 2015. (Illusive Ser.: 2). (ENG.). 432p. (YA). (gr. 7-17). 18.00 *(978-0-316-25464-9(9))* Little Brown & Co.
Lloyd Jones, Rob, retold by. Robin Hood. 2008. (Young Reading Series 2 Gift Bks). 64p. (J). 8.99 *(978-0-7945-2090-8(1)*, Usborne) EDC Publishing.
MacAndrew, Richard. The Black Pearls Starter/Beginner. 2008. (Cambridge English Readers Ser.). (ENG.). 32p. pap. 8.50 *(978-0-521-73289-5(1))* Cambridge Univ. Pr.
Mack, Jeff. Clueless Mcgee. Mack, Jeff, illus. 2012. (Clueless Mcgee Ser.: 1). (ENG., Illus.). 240p. (J). (gr. 3-7). 12.99 *(978-0-399-25749-0(7)*, Philomel Bks.) Penguin Young Readers Group.
—Clueless McGee & the Inflatable Pants, Bk. 2. Mack, Jeff, illus. 2013. (Clueless Mcgee Ser.: 2). (ENG., Illus.). 256p. (J). (gr. 3-7). 12.99 *(978-0-399-25750-6(0)*, Philomel Bks.) Penguin Young Readers Group.
Magaziner, Lauren. Pilfer Academy: A School So Bad It's Criminal. 2016. (ENG.). 272p. (J). (gr. 3-7). 16.99 *(978-0-8037-3919-2(2)*, Dial Bks) Penguin Young Readers Group.
Magoon, Kekla. Rebellion of Thieves. 2016. (Robyn Hoodlum Adventure Ser.). (ENG.). 256p. (J). 16.99 *(978-1-61963-655-2(7)*, 9781619636552, Bloomsbury USA Childrens) Bloomsbury Publishing USA.
—Rebellion of Thieves. 2017. (Robyn Hoodlum Ser.: 2). (J). lib. bdg. 18.40 ***(978-0-606-40596-6(8))*** Turtleback Bks.
Magoon, Kekla. Shadows of Sherwood. (Robyn Hoodlum Adventure Ser.). (ENG.). 368p. 2016. (J). pap. 7.99 *(978-1-68119-023-5(0)*, 9781681190235) 2015. (YA). (gr. 3-6). 16.99 *(978-1-61963-634-7(4)*, 9781619636347) Bloomsbury Publishing USA. (Bloomsbury USA Childrens).
—Shadows of Sherwood. 2016. (Robyn Hoodlum Ser.: 1). (ENG.). 355p. (J). (gr. 3-6). 18.40 *(978-0-606-39281-5(5))* Turtleback Bks.
Makura, Sho. Panda Man vs. Chiwanda. Kato, Haruhi, illus. 2011. (ENG.). 96p. (J). (gr. 1-4). pap. 7.99 *(978-1-4215-3522-7(X))* Viz Media.
Manion, Denaé. Sock Stealing Thieves! 2011. 16p. (gr. 1-2). pap. 12.50 *(978-1-4567-5733-5(4))* AuthorHouse.
Marlow, Susan K. Andrea Carter & the Family Secret, 1 vol. 2008. (Circle C Adventures Ser.). 144p. (J). pap. 7.99 *(978-0-8254-3365-8(7))* Kregel Pubns.
—Heartbreak Trail: An Andrea Carter Book, 1 vol. 2015. (Circle C Milestones Ser.: 2). 168p. (YA). pap. 9.99 *(978-0-8254-4368-8(7))* Kregel Pubns.
—Thick As Thieves: An Andrea Carter Book, 1 vol. 2015. (Circle C Milestones Ser.: 1). 176p. (YA). pap. 9.99 *(978-0-8254-4367-1(9))* Kregel Pubns.
Marmell, Ari. Covenant's End: A Widdershins Adventure. 2015. (ENG.). 271p. (YA). (gr. 7). 17.99 *(978-1-61614-986-4(8)*, Pyr Bks.) Prometheus Bks., Pubs.
Marsh, Carole. The Mystery of the Ancient Pyramid: Cairo, Egypt. 2006. (Around the World in 80 Mysteries Ser.). (Illus.). 128p. (J). (gr. 4-7). 14.95 *(978-0-635-03473-1(5))* Gallopade International.
Matheny, Bill, et al. Catwoman Gets Busted by the Batman, 1 vol. 2014. (Batman Strikes! Ser.). (ENG., Illus.). 32p. (gr. 2-3). 22.60 *(978-1-4342-9211-7(8))* Stone Arch Bks.
Mawter, J. A. Launched! 2007. 256p. *(978-0-207-20073-1(4))* HarperCollins Pubs. Australia.
Mccarthy, Rebecca L. Save This Christmas! 2012. (LEGO City 8X8 Ser.). lib. bdg. 13.55 *(978-0-606-26767-0(0)*, Turtleback) Turtleback Bks.
McClintock, Norah. Tell, 1 vol. 2006. (Orca Soundings Ser.). (ENG.). 128p. (YA). (gr. 8-12). per. 9.95 *(978-1-55143-511-4(X))* Orca Bk. Pubs. USA.
McLean, Hope. Battle of the Brightest. 2013. 140p. (J). *(978-0-545-48292-9(5))* Scholastic, Inc.
—Jewel Society #4: Battle of the Brightest. 2013. (Jewel Society Ser.: 4). (ENG.). 144p. (J). (gr. 3-7). pap. 5.99 *(978-0-545-60765-0(5)*, Scholastic Paperbacks) Scholastic, Inc.
Messner, Kate. Capture the Flag. (ENG.). 240p. (J). (gr. 3-7). 2013. pap. 6.99 *(978-0-545-41974-1(3)*, Scholastic Paperbacks) 2012. 16.99 *(978-0-545-39539-7(9)*, Scholastic Pr.) Scholastic, Inc.
Methods, Bryan. The Shanghai Incident. 2017. (Master Diplexito & Mr. Scant Ser.). (ENG.). 264p. (J). (gr. 5-8). 17.99 ***(978-1-5124-0580-4(9)***, Carolrhoda Bks.) Lerner Publishing Group.

Methods, Bryan. The Thief's Apprentice. 2016. (Master Diplexito & Mr. Scant Ser.: 1). (ENG.). 272p. (gr. 5-8). (J). 17.99 (978-1-5124-0579-8(5)); 35.99 (978-1-5124-0891-1(3)) Lerner Publishing Group. (Carolrhoda Bks.).

Meyer, L. A. The Mark of the Golden Dragon: Being an Account of the Further Adventures of Jacky Faber, Jewel of the East, Vexation of the West & Pearl of the South China Sea. (Bloody Jack Adventures Ser.: 9). (ENG.). (YA). (gr. 9). 2013. 400p. pap. 9.99 (978-0-544-00328-6(4)) 2011. 384p. 16.99 (978-0-547-51764-3(5)) Houghton Mifflin Harcourt Publishing Co.

Michaelis, Antonia. Tiger Moon. 2009. (ENG.). 480p. (YA). (gr. 7-11). pap. 9.95 (978-0-8109-4499-2(5), Amulet Bks.) Abrams, Inc.

Miguel Carbonell. King Tut's Tomb Robbers. 2010. 180p. 23.95 (978-1-4502-1638-8(2)); pap. 13.95 (978-1-4502-1637-1(4)) iUniverse, Inc.

Miller, Christopher & Miller, Allan. The Legend of Gid the Kid & the Black Bean Bandits, 2 bks., Bk.1. Miller, Christopher & Miller, Allan, illus. 2007. (Heroes of Promise Ser.). (ENG., Illus.). 32p. (J). (gr. 1-5). 12.99 (978-1-59317-202-2(8)) Warner Pr., Inc.

Mills, Charles. The Bandit of Benson Park. 2003. (Honors Club Story Ser.: Vol. 1). 127p. (J). (978-0-8163-1977-0(4)) Pacific Pr. Pubns.

—The Great Sleepy-Time Stew Rescue. 2004. (Honors Club Story Ser.: Vol. 4). (Illus.). 127p. (J). 7.99 (978-0-8163-2009-7(8)) Pacific Pr. Publishing Assn.

Mone, Gregory. Dangerous Waters: An Adventure on Titanic. 2012. (ENG.). 240p. (J). (gr. 4-7). 16.99 (978-1-59643-673-2(5), 9781596436732) Roaring Brook Pr.

—Dangerous Waters: An Adventure on Titanic. 2013. (ENG.). 256p. (J). (gr. 4-7). pap. 7.99 (978-1-250-01671-3(1), 9781250016713) Square Fish.

Morgan, Nicola. The Highwayman's Curse. 2007. 368p. (YA). pap. (978-1-4063-0312-4(7)) Walker Bks., Ltd.

Morrison, Megan. Grounded: The Tale of Rapunzel. 2015. (Illus.). 374p. (J). (978-0-545-75468-2(2)) Scholastic, Inc.

Nell Nugget & the Cow Caper. 2008. (Illus.). 32p. (J). pap. 14.95 (978-0-9792820-2-7(0)) Toe The Line.

Nesbø, Jo. The Magical Fruit. 2014. (Doctor Proctor's Fart Powder Ser.). (ENG., Illus.). 320p. (J). (gr. 3-7). pap. 7.99 (978-1-4424-9343-8(7), Aladdin) Simon & Schuster Children's Publishing.

—The Magical Fruit. Chace, Tara F., tr. from NOR. Lowery, Mike, illus. 2013. (Doctor Proctor's Fart Powder Ser.). (ENG.). 320p. (J). (gr. 3-7). 17.99 (978-1-4424-9342-1(9), Aladdin) Simon & Schuster Children's Publishing.

Noyes, Alfred. The Highwayman. Kimber, Murray, illus. 2005. (Visions in Poetry Ser.). (ENG.). 48p. (J). (gr. 5-9). 17.95 (978-1-55337-425-1(8)) Kids Can Pr., Ltd. CAN. Dist: Hachette Bk. Group.

Odgers, Darrel & Odgers, Sally. The Sausage Situation. Dawson, Janine, illus. 2007. (Jack Russell: Dog Detective Ser.: 6). 96p. (J). (gr. 1-6). pap. 4.99 (978-1-933605-54-8(5)) Kane Miller.

—The Sausage Situation. 2006. (Jack Russell, Dog Detective Ser.: Bk. 6). (Illus.). 78p. (J). pap. (978-0-439-92197-8(X)) Scholastic, Inc.

Olswanger, Anna. Shlemiel Crooks. Goodman Koz, Paula, illus. 2008. 36p. (J). pap. 11.95 (978-1-58838-236-8(2), Junebug Bks.) NewSouth, Inc.

Osborne, Mary Pope. Pirates Past Noon. unabr. ed. 2004. (Magic Tree House Ser.: No. 4). 67p. (J). (gr. k-3). pap. 17.00 incl. audio (978-0-8072-0333-0(5), Listening Library) Random Hse. Audio Publishing Group.

Papp, Robert, illus. The Clue in the Recycling Bin. 2011. (Boxcar Children Mysteries Ser.: 126). (ENG.). 128p. (J). (gr. 1-5). pap. 6.99 (978-0-8075-1209-8(5)) Whitman, Albert & Co.

—The Clue in the Recycling Bin. 2011. (Boxcar Children Mysteries Ser.: 126). (ENG.). 128p. (J). (gr. 1-5). lib. bdg. 14.99 (978-0-8075-1208-1(7)) Whitman, Albert & Co.

—The Rock 'n' Roll Mystery. 2006. (Boxcar Children Mysteries Ser.: 109). (ENG.). 128p. (J). (gr. 1-5). lib. bdg. 14.99 (978-0-8075-7089-0(3)); per. 5.99 (978-0-8075-7090-6(7)) Whitman, Albert & Co.

Papp, Robert L., illus. The Dog-Gone Mystery. 2009. (Boxcar Children Mysteries Ser.: 119). (ENG.). 128p. (J). (gr. 1-5). pap. 5.99 (978-0-8075-1657-7(0)) Whitman, Albert & Co.

Patron, Susan. Behind the Masks: The Diary of Angeline Reddy - Bodie, California 1880. 2012. (Dear America Ser.). (ENG.). 304p. (J). (gr. 3-7). 12.99 (978-0-545-30437-5(7)) Scholastic, Inc.

Pau Pau. Bird Bandit, 1 vol. 2010. 56p. pap. 16.95 (978-1-4489-3991-6(7)) America Star Bks.

Perelman, Helen. Rapunzel: A Day to Remember, 1 vol. Studio IBOIX, illus. 2012. (Disney Princesses Set 2 Ser.). (ENG.). 96p. (J). (gr. 2-6). lib. bdg. 24.21 (978-1-59961-183-9(X)) Spotlight.

Petit, Karen. The Mystery of the Stolen Stallion. 2007. (Illus.). 246p. (J). per. 14.95 (978-0-9794420-4-9(4)) Red Letter Pr.

Petrucha, Stefan & Kinney, Sarah. What Goes Up... 2009. (Nancy Drew Graphic Novels: Girl Detective Ser.: 16). (ENG., Illus.). 96p. (J). (gr. 3-7). 12.95 (978-1-59707-135-2(8), 9781597071352) Papercutz.

Pflugfelder, Bob & Hockensmith, Steve. Nick & Tesla's High-Voltage Danger Lab: A Mystery with Electromagnets, Burglar Alarms, & Other Gadgets You Can Build Yourself. 2013. (Nick & Tesla Ser.: 1). (ENG., Illus.). 240p. (J). (gr. 4-7). 12.95 (978-1-59474-648-2(6)) Quirk Bks.

Polan, Alex. Catching the Jigglypuff Thief. 2016. (Unofficial Adventures for Pokemon GO Players Ser.: 1). lib. bdg. 18.40 **(978-0-606-39657-8(8))** Turtleback Bks.

Polan, Alex. Catching the Jigglypuff Thief: PokéStop Stories, Book One. 2016. (ENG.). 112p. (J). (gr. 1-7). pap. 7.99 (978-1-5107-2157-9(6), Sky Pony Pr.) Skyhorse Publishing Co., Inc.

Poon, Janice. Claire & the Bakery Thief. Poon, Janice, illus. 2008. (ENG., Illus.). 104p. (J). (gr. 2-5). 15.95 (978-1-55453-286-5(8)); pap. 7.95 (978-1-55453-245-2(0)) Kids Can Pr., Ltd. CAN. Dist: Hachette Bk. Group.

Potter, Beatrix. Mystery Thief! 2013. (Peter Rabbit Animation Ser.). (ENG.). 32p. (J). (gr. -1-k). 3.99 (978-0-7232-8041-5(X), Warne) Penguin Young Readers Group.

Proud, Amy. Izzy the Very Bad Burglar. 2016. (ENG., Illus.). 32p. (J). (gr. -1-k). 16.99 (978-1-63450-174-3(8), Sky Pony Pr.) Skyhorse Publishing Co., Inc.

Pryor, Bonnie. Mr. Munday & the Rustlers. 2013. (ENG.). 32p. (J). (gr. -1-3). 16.99 (978-1-4424-8876-2(X), Atheneum Bks. for Young Readers) Simon & Schuster Children's Publishing.

Raffa, Edwina & Rigsby, Annelle. Kidnapped in Key West. (Florida Historical Fiction for Youth Ser.). (ENG.). (J). 2012. 138p. pap. 9.95 (978-1-56164-537-4(0)) 2008. (Illus.). 127p. (gr. 3-7). 14.95 (978-1-56164-413-1(7)) Pineapple Pr., Inc.

Random House. Speed Lights! (Blaze & the Monster Machines) Random House & Dynamo Limited Staff, illus. 2016. (Step into Reading Ser.). (ENG.). 24p. (J). (gr. -1-1). pap. 4.99 (978-0-399-55692-0(3), Random Hse. Bks. for Young Readers) Random Hse. Children's Bks.

Rayes, Michael. Bank Robbery! 2007. (J). per. 13.95 (978-0-9779628-0-8(6)) Rafka Pr. LLC.

Rees, Celia. Sovay. 2010. (ENG.). 432p. (YA). (gr. 7). pap. 9.99 (978-1-59990-483-2(7), 9781599904832, Bloomsbury USA Childrens) Bloomsbury Publishing USA.

—Sovay. 2009. 1.00 (978-1-4074-4516-8(2)) Recorded Bks., Inc.

Reeve, Philip. Black Light Express. 2017. (ENG.). 352p. (gr. 9-12). 17.95 **(978-1-63079-096-7(6))** Switch Pr.

Reeve, Philip. Railhead. 2016. (ENG.). 352p. (gr. 9-12). 16.95 (978-1-63079-048-6(6)) Switch Pr.

Reilly, Carmel & Ashforth, Kate. The Jewelry Story Robbery. 2008. (Rigby Focus Forward: Level F Ser.). (Illus.). 24p. (J). (gr. 4-7). pap. (978-1-4190-3685-9(8), Rigby) Pearson Education Australia.

Rey, H. A. Curious George & the Dump Truck. 2010. (Curious George Ser.). (ENG., Illus.). 24p. (J). (gr. -1-3). pap. 4.99 (978-0-547-50425-4(X)) Houghton Mifflin Harcourt Publishing Co.

—Curious George's Dump Truck. 2014. (Curious George Ser.). (ENG., Illus.). 12p. (J). (— 1). bds. 8.99 (978-0-544-14686-0(7), HMH Books For Young Readers) Houghton Mifflin Harcourt Publishing Co.

Reynolds, Aaron. The Dung Beetle Bandits, 1 vol. Lervold, Erik, illus. 2007. (Tiger Moth Ser.). (ENG.). 40p. (gr. 1-3). lib. bdg. 23.99 (978-1-59889-317-5(3), Graphic Sparks) Stone Arch Bks.

—The Dung Beetle Bandits: Tiger Moth. Lervold, Erik, illus. 2007. (Graphic Sparks Ser.). (ENG.). 40p. (gr. 1-3). pap. 5.95 (978-1-59889-412-7(9), Graphic Sparks) Stone Arch Bks.

Richard, Laurent. The Championship! Gauvin, Edward, tr. Ryser, Nicolas, illus. 2014. (ENG.). 64p. (J). (gr. 2-5). pap. 6.95 (978-1-4677-4459-1(X)); (Tao, the Little Samurai Ser.: 4). lib. bdg. 29.27 (978-1-4677-2097-7(6)) Lerner Publishing Group. (Graphic Universe™).

The Robber: Individual Title-Six Packs. (Chiquilibros Ser.). (gr. k-1). 23.00 (978-0-7635-0433-5(5)) Rigby Education.

Roberts, Willo Davis. Hostage. 2016. (ENG., Illus.). 176p. (J). (gr. 3-7). pap. 6.99 (978-1-4814-5788-0(8), Aladdin) Simon & Schuster Children's Publishing.

—Hostage. 2016. (ENG., Illus.). 176p. (J). (gr. 3-7). 17.99 (978-1-4814-5789-7(6), Simon & Schuster/Paula Wiseman Bks.) Simon & Schuster/Paula Wiseman Bks.

Robin Hood. (Coleccion Estrella). (SPA., Illus.). 64p. (J). 14.95 (978-950-11-0014-3(6), SGM014) Sigmar ARG. Dist: Continental Bk. Co., Inc.

Rodman, Sean. Final Crossing, 1 vol. 2014. (Orca Soundings Ser.). (ENG.). 112p. (YA). (gr. 8-12). pap. 9.95 (978-1-4598-0552-1(6)) Orca Bk. Pubs. USA.

Rowe, W. W. The Robber Chief: A Tale of Vengeance & Compassion. Banigan, Chris, illus. 2003. (ENG.). 48p. (gr. 1-18). 12.95 (978-1-55939-186-3(3), Snow Lion Publications, Inc,) Shambhala Pubns., Inc.

Roy, Pat & Roy, Sandy. Jonathan Park: Return to the Hidden Cave. 2013. (Jonathan Park Adventure Fiction Ser.: Vol. 3). (ENG.). 171p. (J). (gr. 4-7). pap. 10.00 (978-1-937460-61-7(4)) Vision Forum, Inc., The.

Roy, Ron. A to Z Mysteries Collection, No. 1. Gurney, John Steven, illus. 2010. (to Z Mysteries Ser.: Nos. 1-4). (ENG.). 384p. (J). (gr. 1-4). 9.99 (978-0-375-85946-5(2), Random Hse. Bks. for Young Readers) Random Hse. Children's Bks.

—The Castle Crime. 2014. (to Z Mysteries Ser.: 32). lib. bdg. 16.00 (978-0-606-35190-4(6)) Turtleback Bks.

—The Ghost at Camp David. Bush, Timothy, illus. 2010. (Capital Mysteries Ser.: 12). (ENG.). 96p. (J). (gr. 1-4). pap. 4.99 (978-0-375-85925-0(X), Random Hse. Bks. for Young Readers) Random Hse. Children's Bks.

—The Ghost at Camp David. 2010. (Capital Mysteries Ser.: 12). lib. bdg. 14.75 (978-0-606-14010-2(7), Turtleback) Turtleback Bks.

—Mystery at the Washington Monument. Bush, Timothy, illus. 2007. (Capital Mysteries Ser.: No. 8). 87p. (gr. 1-4). 15.00 (978-0-7569-7845-7(9)) Perfection Learning Corp.

—The New Year Dragon Dilemma. Gurney, John Steven, illus. 2011. (to Z Mysteries Ser.). (ENG.). 144p. (J). (gr. 1-4). 5.99 (978-0-375-86880-1(1), Random Hse. Bks. for Young Readers) Random Hse. Children's Bks.

—Sleepy Hollow Sleepover. Gurney, John Steven, illus. 4th ed. 2010. (to Z Mysteries Ser.: 4). (ENG.). 144p. (J). (gr. 1-4). pap. 5.99 (978-0-375-86669-2(8), Random Hse. Bks. for Young Readers) Random Hse. Children's Bks.

—Sleepy Hollow Sleepover. 4th ed. 2010. (to Z Mysteries Ser.: 30). lib. bdg. 16.00 (978-0-606-14007-2(7), Turtleback) Turtleback Bks.

—The Talking T. Rex. Gurney, John Steven, illus. 2003. (to Z Mysteries Ser.: 20). (ENG.). 96p. (J). (gr. 1-4). pap. 4.99 (978-0-375-81369-6(1), Random Hse. Bks. for Young Readers) Random Hse. Children's Bks.

—The White Wolf. Gurney, John Steven, tr. Gurney, John Steven, illus. 2004. (to Z Mysteries Ser.: No. 23). (ENG.). 96p. (J). (gr. 1-4). pap. 4.99 (978-0-375-82480-7(4), Random Hse. Bks. for Young Readers) Random Hse. Children's Bks.

—The X'ed-Out X-Ray. Gurney, John Steven, illus. 2005. (to Z Mysteries Ser.: No. 24). (ENG.). 96p. (J). (gr. 1-4). 4.99 (978-0-375-82481-4(2), Random Hse. Bks. for Young Readers) Random Hse. Children's Bks.

Rushford, Patricia H. Secrets of Ghost Island. 2007. (J). (978-88-02-46255-4(0)) Moody Pubs.

Russell, Christopher & Russell, Christine. The Quest of the Warrior Sheep. 2011. (ENG.). 224p. (gr. 5-8). pap. 6.99 (978-1-4022-5511-3(X), Sourcebooks Jabberwocky) Sourcebooks, Inc.

Russell, Rachel Renée. Middle School Mayhem. Russell, Rachel Renée, illus. 2017. (Misadventures of Max Crumbly Ser.: 2). (ENG., Illus.). 240p. (J). (gr. 4-8). 13.99 **(978-1-4814-6003-3(X)**, Aladdin) Simon & Schuster Children's Publishing.

Sander, Sonia. Calling All Cars! 2010. (Lego City Ser.). (ENG.). 32p. (J). (gr. -1-k). pap. 3.99 (978-0-545-15523-6(1)) Scholastic, Inc.

—Calling All Cars! 2010. (LEGO City Adventures Scholastic Readers Level 1 Ser.: 3). lib. bdg. 13.55 (978-0-606-07120-8(2), Turtleback) Turtleback Bks.

Santillo, LuAnn. Jim & the Thug. Santillo, LuAnn, ed. 2003. (Half-Pint Kids Readers Ser.). (Illus.). 7p. (J). (gr. -1-1). pap. 1.00 (978-1-59256-078-3(4)) Half-Pint Kids, Inc.

Sargent, Dave & Sargent, Pat. Nick: (Linebacked Claybank Dun) Crime Does Not Pay, 30 vols., Vol. 42. Lenoir, Jane, illus. 2003. (Saddle up Ser.: Vol. 42). 42p. (J). pap. 10.95 (978-1-56763-702-1(7)); lib. bdg. 23.60 (978-1-56763-701-4(9)) Ozark Publishing.

Scarry, Richard. Richard Scarry's the Great Steamboat Mystery. 2014. (ENG., Illus.). 34p. (J). (gr. 1-2). 4.95 (978-1-4549-1010-7(0)) Sterling Publishing Co., Inc.

—Richard Scarry's the Supermarket Mystery. 2014. (ENG., Illus.). 34p. (J). (gr. 1-2). 4.95 (978-1-4549-1011-4(9)) Sterling Publishing Co., Inc.

Schachner, Judy. The Great Bean Caper. 2009. (Skippyjon Jones Ser.). (ENG.). 32p. (J). (gr. -1-k). mass mkt. 3.99 (978-0-448-45167-1(0), Grosset & Dunlap) Penguin Young Readers Group.

Schnetzler, Pattie L. Fast 'n Snappy. Manning, Jane K., tr. Manning, Jane K., illus. 2004. (Carolrhoda Picture Books Ser.). 32p. (J). (gr. k-3). 16.95 (978-1-57505-539-8(2)) Lerner Publishing Group.

Scholastic Editors. Stop That Heist! 2013. (LEGO City Scholastic Readers Level 1 Ser.). lib. bdg. 13.55 (978-0-606-31540-1(3), Turtleback) Turtleback Bks.

Scholastic, Inc. Staff & King, Trey. Detective Chase McCain - Stop That Heist! Kiernan, Kenny, illus. 2013. (Lego City Ser.). (ENG.). 32p. (J). (gr. -1-3). pap. 3.99 (978-0-545-49596-7(2)) Scholastic, Inc.

Schultz, Jan Neubert. Horse Sense: The Story of Will Sasse, His Horse Star & the Outlaw Jesse James. 2005. (Adventures in Time Ser.). (Illus.). 180p. (J). (gr. 4-8). 15.95 (978-1-57505-998-3(3)) Lerner Publishing Group.

Scieszka, Jon. Hey Kid, Want to Buy a Bridge? McCauley, Adam, illus. 2004. (Time Warp Trio Ser.: 11). (ENG.). 80p. (J). (gr. 2-4). pap. 5.99 (978-0-14-240089-0(0), Puffin Books) Penguin Young Readers Group.

Scott, Elizabeth. Stealing Heaven. 2009. (ENG.). 336p. (YA). (gr. 8). pap. 8.99 (978-0-06-112282-8(3), HarperTeen) HarperCollins Pubs.

Shannon, R. J. Rita Rain & the Shadow Apprentice: Book 1. 2012. 472p. 29.95 (978-1-4626-7390-2(2)) America Star Bks.

Shea, Bob. Kid Sheriff & the Terrible Toads. Smith, Lane, illus. 2014. (ENG.). 32p. (J). (gr. -1-3). 17.99 (978-1-59643-975-7(0), 9781596439757) Roaring Brook Pr.

Shire, Poppy. Jewel the Midnight Pony. Berg, Ron, illus. 2008. (Magic Pony Carousel Ser.: 4). (ENG.). 96p. (J). (gr. 2-5). pap. 3.99 (978-0-06-083788-4(8)) HarperCollins Pubs.

Sid, Fleischman. The Whipping Boy. 2014. (HarperClassics Ser.). (ENG.). 96p. (J). (gr. 3-8). 10.24 (978-1-63245-335-8(5)) Lectorum Pubns., Inc.

Skelton, Vonda Skinner. Bitsy & the Mystery at Hilton Head Island. 2008. 192p. (J). (gr. 4-7). pap. 8.95 (978-1-57072-325-4(7)) Overmountain Pr.

Sleiman, Dina L. Dauntless. 2015. (Valiant Hearts Ser.: 1). (ENG.). 368p. (YA). pap. 13.99 (978-0-7642-1312-0(1)) Bethany Hse. Pubs.

Smith, Justine. Zak Zoo & the Baffled Burglar. Elsom, Clare, illus. 2013. (ENG.). 32p. (J). (gr. k-2). pap. 7.99 (978-1-4083-1342-8(1)) Hodder & Stoughton GBR. Dist: Hachette Bk. Group.

Song, Amira. Horse Lovers Forever. 2012. 64p. pap. (978-1-4602-0144-2(2)) FriesenPress.

St. George, Victoria. Barnyard Bandits. 2011. 28p. pap. 12.99 (978-1-4567-3040-6(1)) AuthorHouse.

Steig, William. The Real Thief. 2007. (SPA.). (J). 1.25 (978-1-4193-9992-3(6)) Recorded Bks., Inc.

—The Real Thief. Steig, William, illus. 2007. (ENG., Illus.). 64p. (J). (gr. 2-5). per. 7.99 (978-0-312-37145-6(4), 9780312371456) Square Fish.

Steiner, Barbara. Mystery at Chilkoot Pass. 2009. (Mysteries Through Time Ser.). 144 - 176p. (YA). (gr. 4-8). 31.95 (978-1-60754-435-7(0)); pap. 15.25 (978-1-60754-434-0(2)) Windmill Bks.

Stern, D. G. Disappearing Diamonds: An Upton Charles Adventure. Bartlett, Rebecca, illus. 2008. (ENG.). 126p. (J). pap. 9.99 (978-0-9754676-9-5(7)) Yeoman Hse.

Stilton, Geronimo. The Peculiar Pumpkin Thief. 2010. (Geronimo Stilton Ser.: 42). (ENG.). 128p. (J). (gr. 2-5). 7.99 (978-0-545-10372-5(X), Scholastic Paperbacks) Scholastic, Inc.

Stilton, Thea. Thea Stilton & the Mystery on the Orient Express. 2012. (Thea Stilton Ser.: 13). lib. bdg. 19.65 (978-0-606-26757-1(3), Turtleback) Turtleback Bks.

Stone, David Lee. The Shadewell Shenanigans. 2006. (Illus.). 308p. (J). (978-1-4156-8147-3(3)) Hyperion Bks. for Children.

Sumerak, Marc. Ororo: Before the Storm. Barberi, Carlo, illus. 2012. (Ororo: Before the Storm Ser.). 24p. (J). (gr. 2-6). lib. bdg. 24.21 (978-1-61479-024-2(8)); lib. bdg. 24.21 (978-1-61479-026-6(4)); lib. bdg. 24.21 (978-1-61479-025-9(6)); lib. bdg. 24.21 (978-1-61479-027-3(2)) Spotlight.

Sutcliffe, William. Circus of Thieves on the Rampage. Tazzyman, David, illus. 2017. (ENG.). 288p. (J). pap. 7.99 (978-1-4711-2025-1(2), Simon & Schuster Children's) Simon & Schuster, Ltd. GBR. Dist: Simon & Schuster, Inc.

Sutton, Margaret. The Riddle of the Double Ring, No. 10. Doane, Pelagie, illus. 2008. (Judy Bolton Mysteries Ser.). (ENG.). 236p. (J). (gr. 4-7). pap. 14.95 (978-1-4290-9030-8(8)) Applewood Bks.

Sutton, Rosalind, et al. Robin Hood. Rowe, Eric F., tr. 4th ed. (Coleccion Clasicos en Accion). (SPA., Illus.). 80p. (YA). (gr. 5-8). 15.95 (978-84-241-5782-1(6), EV1455) Everest Editora ESP. Dist: Lectorum Pubns., Inc.

Swift, Carolyn. Robbers in the House. (Illus.). 96p. 2.95 (978-0-900068-59-1(0)) Penguin Publishing Group.

Tanner, Lian. Museum of Thieves. (Keepers Ser.: Bk. 1). (ENG.). 320p. (J). (gr. 3-7). 2011. 8.99 (978-0-375-85978-6(0), Yearling) 2010. 16.99 (978-0-385-73905-4(2), Delacorte Bks. for Young Readers) Random Hse. Children's Bks.

—Path of Beasts. 2013. (Keepers Trilogy: Bk. 3). (ENG.). 352p. (J). (gr. 4-7). 8.99 (978-0-375-85980-9(2), Yearling) Random Hse. Children's Bks.

Taylor, G. P. The Great Mogul Diamond. 2011. (Dopple Ganger Chronicles Ser.: 3). (ENG.). 304p. (J). (gr. 3-7). 19.99 (978-1-4143-1949-0(5), SaltRiver) Tyndale Hse. Pubs.

—The Secret of Indigo Moon. 2009. (Dopple Ganger Chronicles Ser.: 2). (ENG., Illus.). 304p. (J). (gr. 3-7). 19.99 (978-1-4143-1948-3(7), SaltRiver) Tyndale Hse. Pubs.

Taylor, Sean. The World-Famous Cheese Shop Break-In. Shaw, Hannah, illus. 2015. (ENG.). 32p. (J). (gr. -1-2). 17.99 (978-1-84780-430-3(6), Frances Lincoln) Quarto Publishing Group UK GBR. Dist: Hachette Bk. Group.

Tenbeth, Kate. Burly & Grum & the Birthday Surprise. Jones, Rob, illus. 2012. 108p. pap. (978-0-9572119-9-5(6)) Magic Toy Bks.

Thompson, J. E. Disappearance at Hangman's Bluff. (Felony Bay Mysteries Ser.: 2). (ENG.). 336p. (J). (gr. 3-7). 2015. pap. 6.99 (978-0-06-210450-2(0)) 2014. (Illus.). 16.99 (978-0-06-210449-6(7)) HarperCollins Pubs. (Waldon Pond Pr.).

Thompson, Kate. Highway Robbery. Dress, Robert & Duddle, Johnny, illus. 2009. (ENG.). 128p. (J). (gr. 5-18). 15.99 (978-0-06-173034-4(3), Greenwillow Bks.) HarperCollins Pubs.

Trine, Greg. Wyatt Burp Rides Again. Dormer, Frank W., illus. 2014. (Adventures of Jo Schmo Ser.: 2). (ENG.). 112p. (J). (gr. 1-4). pap. 5.99 (978-0-544-01899-0(0), HMH Books For Young Readers) Houghton Mifflin Harcourt Publishing Co.

Tripp, Ben. The Accidental Highwayman: Being the Tale of Kit Bristol, His Horse Midnight, a Mysterious Princess, & Sundry Magical Persons Besides. 2014. (ENG., Illus.). 304p. (YA). (gr. 6). 17.99 (978-0-7653-3549-4(2), Tor Teen) Doherty, Tom Assocs., LLC.

Turner, Megan Whalen. The King of Attolia. (Queen's Thief Ser.: 3). (ENG.). (YA). (gr. 8). 2017. 432p. pap. 9.99 (978-0-06-264298-1(7)) 2007. 432p. pap. 7.99 (978-0-06-083579-8(6)) 2006. 400p. 17.99 (978-0-06-083577-4(X)) HarperCollins Pubs. (Greenwillow Bks.).

—The King of Attolia. 2007. (Queen's Thief Ser.: BK.3). 387p. (YA). 18.00 (978-0-7569-8106-8(9)) Perfection Learning Corp.

—The King of Attolia. (YA). 2008. (Queen's Thief Ser.: BK.3). (ENG.). 84.49 (978-1-4281-8027-7(3)) 2007. (Attolia Ser.: 3). 119.75 (978-1-4281-1722-8(9)) 2007. (Queen's Thief Ser.: BK.3). (ENG.). 92.75 (978-1-4281-1716-7(4)) 2006. (Queen's Thief Ser.: BK.3). (ENG.). 90.75 (978-1-4281-1718-1(0)) 2006. (Queen's Thief Ser.: BK.3). (ENG.). 122.75 (978-1-4281-1720-4(2)) 2006. (Queen's Thief Ser.: BK.3). 281.75 (978-1-4281-1721-1(0)) 2006. (Queen's Thief Ser.: BK.3). (ENG.). 1.25 (978-1-4281-1713-6(X)) 2006. (Queen's Thief Ser.: BK.3). (ENG.). 251.75 (978-1-4281-1717-4(2)) Recorded Bks., Inc.

—The Queen of Attolia. (Queen's Thief Ser.: 2). (ENG.). (YA). (gr. 8). 2017. 416p. pap. 9.99 (978-0-06-264297-4(9)) 2006. 368p. pap. 6.99 (978-0-06-084182-9(6)) HarperCollins Pubs. (Greenwillow Bks.).

—The Queen of Attolia, 8 vols. (Attolia Ser.: 2). (J). 2013. 188.75 (978-1-4281-5237-3(7)) 2009. 73.75 (978-1-4361-6574-7(1)) 2008. 104.75 (978-1-4281-5236-6(9)) 2008. 75.75 (978-1-4281-5234-2(2)) 2007. 78.75 (978-1-4281-5232-8(6)) 2007. 101.75 (978-1-4281-5238-0(5)) 2007. 1.25 (978-1-4281-5229-8(6)) 2007. 162.75 (978-1-4281-5233-5(4)) Recorded Bks., Inc.

—The Queen of Attolia. 2017. (Queen's Thief Ser.: BK.2). (ENG.). (YA). lib. bdg. 20.85 **(978-0-606-40331-3(0))** Turtleback Bks.

Turner, Megan Whalen. The Thief. (Queen's Thief Ser.: 1). (ENG.). (YA). 2017. 320p. (gr. 8). pap. 9.99 (978-0-06-264296-7(0)) 2005. 304p. (gr. 5). reprint ed. pap. 8.99 (978-0-06-082497-6(2)) HarperCollins Pubs. (Greenwillow Bks.).

—The Thief. 2009. (Queen's Thief Ser.: BK.1). (ENG.). (YA). 9.00 (978-0-7848-3718-4(X)); 8.32 (978-0-7848-3065-9(7)) Marco Bk. Co. (Everbind).

—The Thief, 7 vols. (Queen's Thief Ser.: BK.1). (ENG.). (YA). 2005. 169.75 (978-1-4025-5458-2(3)) 2004. 92.75 (978-1-4025-5457-5(5)) Recorded Bks., Inc.

—The Thief. (Queen's Thief Ser.: BK.1). (ENG.). 2017. (YA). lib. bdg. 20.85 **(978-0-606-40328-3(0))** 2005. (J). lib. bdg. 17.20 (978-1-4177-4836-5(2), Turtleback) Turtleback Bks.

Ungerer, Tomi. The Three Robbers. 2009. (ENG., Illus.). 40p. (gr. -1-3). 16.95 (978-0-7148-4877-8(8)) Phaidon Pr., Inc.

Updale, Eleanor. Montmorency's Revenge. 2007. 289p. (J). 25.66 (978-1-4287-3312-1(4), Follettbound) Follett School Solutions.

—Thief, Liar, Gentleman? 2005. (Montmorency Ser.). 232p. (J). (gr. 4-7). 14.65 (978-0-7569-6316-3(8)) Perfection Learning Corp.

Van Draanen, Wendelin. The Greatest Power. Gilpin, Stephen, illus. 2011. (Gecko & Sticky Ser.: Bk. 1). (ENG.). 208p. (J). (gr. 3-7). 7.99 (978-0-440-42243-3(4), Yearling) Random Hse. Children's Bks.

—Sammy Keyes & the Hotel Thief. 2008. (Sammy Keyes Ser.: Bk. 1). (J). 54.99 (978-1-60640-642-7(6)) Findaway World, LLC.

Van Leeuwen, Jean. The Great Cheese Conspiracy, 0 vols. 2011. (ENG.). 96p. (J). (gr. 1-4). 15.99 (978-0-7614-5972-9(3), 9780761459729, Amazon Children's Publishing) Amazon Publishing.

Van Lieshout, Elle & Van Os, Erik. Lovey & Dovey. Van Hout, Mies, illus. 2009. (ENG.). 32p. (J). (gr. k-2). 16.95 (978-1-59078-660-4(2), Lemniscaat) Boyds Mills Pr.

Vande Velde, Vivian. Ghost of a Hanged Man, 1 vol. 2003. (ENG.). 32p. (J). (gr. 5). pap. 5.95 (978-0-7614-5154-9(4)) Marshall Cavendish Corp.

—23 Minutes. 2016. (ENG.). 176p. (J). (gr. 6-10). 16.95 *(978-1-62979-441-9(4))* Boyds Mills Pr.
VanRiper, Gary & VanRiper, Justin. The Great Train Robbery. 2004. (Adirondack Kids Ser.: Vol. 4). (Illus.). 82p. (J). (gr. 2-7). pap. 9.95 *(978-0-9707044-3-6(7))* Adirondack Kids Pr.
Vaught, Susan. Super Max & the Mystery of Thornwood's Revenge. 2017. (ENG., Illus.). 352p. (J). (gr. 3-7). 16.99 ***(978-1-4814-8683-5(7)***, Simon & Schuster/Paula Wiseman Bks.) Simon & Schuster/Paula Wiseman Bks.
Verne, Jules. The Adventures of a Special Correspondent. 2009. 180p. 25.95 *(978-1-60664-635-9(4))*; pap. 13.95 *(978-1-60664-377-8(0))* Rodgers, Alan Bks.
Verral, Charles Spain. Rin Tin Tin & the Outlaw. Crawford, Mel, illus. 2011. 28p. pap. 35.95 *(978-1-258-04034-5(4))* Literary Licensing, LLC.
Warner, Penny. The Mystery of the Missing Mustangs. 2012. 107p. (J). *(978-0-88166-411-9(1))* Meadowbrook Pr.
Watson, Jude. Loot. (ENG.). 272p. (J). (gr. 3-7). 2015. pap. 6.99 *(978-0-545-46803-9(5)*, Scholastic Paperbacks) 2014. 17.99 *(978-0-545-46802-2(7)*, Scholastic Pr.) Scholastic, Inc.
—Sting. 2016. (ENG.). 272p. (J). (gr. 3-7). 16.99 *(978-0-545-86346-9(5)*, Scholastic Pr.) Scholastic, Inc.
Watson, Tom. Stick Cat: Two Catch a Thief. Long, Ethan, illus. 2017. (Stick Cat Ser.: 3). 240p. (J). (gr. 3-7). 12.99 ***(978-0-06-241104-4(7))*** HarperCollins Pubs.
Wells, Carolyn & E. C. CASWELL. Two Little Women on a Holiday. l.t. ed. 2006. 178p. pap. 21.99 *(978-1-4264-2807-4(3))* Creative Media Partners, LLC.
Wells, Helen. Cherry Ames, Camp Nurse. 2007. (Cherry Ames Nurse Stories Ser.). 224p. (YA). (gr. 7-12). 14.95 *(978-0-8261-0417-5(7))* Springer Publishing Co., Inc.
—Cherry Ames, Department Store Nurse. 2007. (Cherry Ames Nurse Stories Ser.). 224p. (YA). (gr. 8-12). 14.95 *(978-0-8261-0415-1(0))* Springer Publishing Co., Inc.
West, Tracey. The Audio Files. Harrington, Rich, illus. 2006. 96p. (J). pap. *(978-0-439-90719-4(5))* Scholastic, Inc.
—The Fingerprint Files. Harrington, Rich, illus. 2007. 96p. (J). *(978-0-439-91451-2(5))* Scholastic, Inc.
—The Teeny Tiny Cases. Harrington, Rich, illus. 2007. 96p. (J). *(978-0-439-91450-5(7))* Scholastic, Inc.
White, Lia. Alkis. 2010. (ENG., Illus.). 106p. pap. *(978-1-84748-715-5(7))* Athena Pr.
Widmark, Martin. The Cafe Mystery. Willis, Helena, illus. 2015. (Whodunit Detective Agency Ser.: 4). (ENG.). 80p. (J). (gr. 2-4). 13.99 *(978-0-448-48073-2(5)*, Grosset & Dunlap) Penguin Young Readers Group.
Wilson, Bob. Stanley Bagshaw & the Mafeking Square Cheese Robbery. 2006. (Stanley Bagshaw Ser.). (Illus.). 32p. (J). (gr. k-2). pap. 6.95 *(978-1-903015-31-5(6))* Barn Owl Bks, London GBR. Dist: Independent Pubs. Group.
Wood, Audrey. Twenty-Four Robbers. 2004. (Child's Play Library). (ENG., Illus.). 32p. (J). (gr. 1-1). *(978-1-904550-35-8(5))* Child's Play International Ltd.
Worley, Brandi. Crumb Snatchers, Part I. 2009. 160p. pap. 14.95 *(978-0-557-06521-9(6))* Lulu Pr., Inc.
Wyatt, Ellen. Sheriff Buzzy Bullet & the Bank Robbers. 2009. 28p. pap. 12.25 *(978-1-60860-391-6(1)*, Eloquent Bks.) Strategic Book Publishing & Rights Agency (SBPRA).
Zacharias, Ravi. The Merchant & the Thief: A Folktale from India, 1 vol. Fournier, Laure, illus. 2012. (ENG.). 32p. (J). 15.99 *(978-0-310-71636-5(5))* Zonderkidz.

ROBERT I, KING OF SCOTS, 1274-1329

Burnett, Allan. Robert the Bruce. Anderson, Scoular, illus. 2006. (ENG.). 105p. pap. *(978-1-84158-497-3(5))* Birlinn, Ltd.

ROBERT I, KING OF SCOTS, 1274-1329—FICTION

Henty, George Alfred. In Freedom's Cause: A Tale of Wallace & Bruce. 2011. 372p. pap. 19.95 *(978-1-61179-152-5(9))* Fireship Pr.

ROBESON, PAUL, 1898-1976

Belton, Sandra. The Tallest Tree. 2008. (Illus.). 160p. (J). (gr. 3-7). 16.99 *(978-0-06-052749-5(8)*, Greenwillow Bks.) HarperCollins Pubs.
Ford, Carin T. Paul Robeson: I Want to Make Freedom Ring. 2007. (African-American Biography Library). (Illus.). 128p. (J). (gr. 3-7). lib. bdg. 33.27 *(978-0-7660-2703-9(1))* Enslow Pubs., Inc.
McKissack, Patricia C. & McKissack, Fredrick L. Paul Robeson: A Voice for Change. 2013. (Famous African Americans Ser.). 24p. (J). (gr. k-3). pap. 7.95 *(978-1-4644-0205-0(1))*; (Illus.). 22.60 *(978-0-7660-4107-3(7))* Enslow Pubs., Inc. (Enslow Elementary).
Slavicek, Louise Chipley. Paul Robeson. 2011. (Black Americans of Achievement Legacy Edition Ser.). 120p. (YA). (gr. 6-12). 35.00 *(978-1-60413-843-6(2))* Facts On File, Inc.
Wright, David K. The Life of Paul Robeson: Actor, Singer, Political Activist. 2014. (Legendary African Americans Ser.). 96p. (J). (gr. 6-12). 27.94 *(978-0-7660-6157-6(4))*; (Illus.). pap. 10.95 *(978-0-7660-6158-3(2))* Enslow Pubs., Inc.

ROBIN HOOD (LEGENDARY CHARACTER)

Calcutt, David. Robin Hood. Baker-Smith, Grahame, illus. 2012. (ENG.). 112p. (J). 24.99 *(978-1-84686-357-8(0))* Barefoot Bks., Inc.
Creswick, Paul & Wyeth, N. C. Robin Hood. 2003. (Scribner Storybook Classics Ser.: Vol. 4). (ENG., Illus.). 64p. (J). (gr. 3-7). 19.99 *(978-0-689-85467-5(6)*, Atheneum Bks. for Young Readers) Simon & Schuster Children's Publishing.
Fenn, G. Manville. Young Robin Hood. 2007. 52p. per. *(978-1-4065-2352-2(6))* Dodo Pr.
Fenn, George Manvill. Young Robin Hood. 2004. reprint ed. pap. 15.95 *(978-1-4191-9534-1(4))* Kessinger Publishing, LLC.
McDonnell, Julia. The Legend of Robin Hood. 2015. (Famous Legends Ser.). (ENG., Illus.). 32p. (J). (gr. 2-3). pap. 10.50 *(978-1-4824-2748-6(6))* Stevens, Gareth Publishing LLLP.
McSpadden, J. Walker. Robin Hood. 2004. reprint ed. pap. 22.95 *(978-1-4191-4516-2(9))*; pap. 1.99 *(978-1-4192-4516-9(3))* Kessinger Publishing, LLC.
Miles, Bernard. Robin Hood: His Life & Legend. Ambrus, Victor G., illus. 128p. (J). (gr. 4-18). 12.95 *(978-1-56288-412-3(3))* Checkerboard Pr., Inc.
Pyle, Howard. The Merry Adventures of Robin Hood. (Young Collector's Illustrated Classics Ser.). (Illus.). 192p. (J). (gr. 3-7). 9.95 *(978-1-56156-454-5(0))* Kidsbooks, LLC.
—The Merry Adventures of Robin Hood. l.t. ed. 2004. (Large Print Ser.). 518p. 26.00 *(978-1-58287-684-9(3))* North Bks.
Smith, Neil. Robin Hood, 1 vol. 2015. (ENG., Illus.). 80p. (J). 35.60 *(978-1-4777-8139-5(0)*, Rosen Young Adult) Rosen Publishing Group, Inc., The.
Storrie, Paul D. Robin Hood. 2008. pap. 52.95 *(978-0-8225-9463-5(3))* Lerner Publishing Group.
—Robin Hood: Outlaw of Sherwood Forest, an English Legend. Yeates, Thomas, illus. 2008. (Graphic Myths & Legends Ser.). 48p. (J). (gr. 3-7). per. 8.95 *(978-0-8225-6572-7(2))* Lerner Publishing Group.

ROBIN HOOD (LEGENDARY CHARACTER)—FICTION

Ausona, Roberto de. Robin Hood. (SPA., Illus.). 156p. (YA). 11.95 *(978-84-7281-110-2(7)*, AF1110) Auriga, Ediciones S.A. ESP. Dist: Continental Bk. Co., Inc.
Bernstein, Nina. Magic by the Book, 4 vols. unabr. ed. 2005. (J). 65.75 *(978-1-4193-3607-2(X)*, 42048) Recorded Bks., Inc.
Calcutt, David. Robin Hood. Baker-Smith, Grahame, illus. 2012. (ENG.). 176p. (J). (gr. 4-6). pap. 12.99 *(978-1-84686-799-6(1))* Barefoot Bks., Inc.
Cody, Matthew. Will in Scarlet. 2014. (ENG., Illus.). 272p. (J). (gr. 5). pap. 6.99 *(978-0-375-87292-1(2)*, Yearling) Random Hse. Children's Bks.
Côté, Denis. La Forêt aux Mille et un Périls, Tome 2. Poulin, Stephane, illus. 2004. (Roman Jeunesse Ser.). (FRE.). 96p. (J). (gr. 4-7). pap. *(978-2-89021-696-9(9))* Diffusion du livre Mirabel (DLM).
Dunkerley, Desmond & Ladybird Books Staff. Robin Hood. 2016. (Ladybird Classics Ser.). (ENG., Illus.). 72p. (J). (gr. k-3). 11.99 *(978-0-7232-9559-4(X))* Penguin Bks., Ltd. GBR. Dist: Independent Pubs. Group.
Fenn, G. Manville. Young Robin Hood. 2011. 56p. pap. 7.99 *(978-1-61203-082-1(3))* Bottom of the Hill Publishing.
Gaughen, A. C. Lady Thief. 2015. (Scarlet Ser.: No. 2). (ENG.). 336p. (YA). (gr. 7). pap. 9.99 *(978-0-8027-3788-5(9)*, 9780802737885, Bloomsbury USA Childrens) Bloomsbury Publishing USA.
—Lion Heart. 2015. (Scarlet Trilogy: No. 3). (ENG.). 352p. (YA). 17.99 *(978-0-8027-3616-1(5)*, 9780802736161, Bloomsbury USA Childrens) Bloomsbury Publishing USA.
—Lion Heart: A Scarlet Novel. 2016. (Scarlet Ser.). (ENG.). 352p. (YA). pap. 9.99 *(978-1-61963-928-7(9)*, 9781619639287, Bloomsbury USA Childrens) Bloomsbury Publishing USA.
—Scarlet. 2013. (Scarlet Ser.: 1). (ENG.). 304p. (YA). (gr. 7-12). pap. 9.99 *(978-0-8027-3424-2(3)*, 9780802734242, Bloomsbury USA Childrens) Bloomsbury Publishing USA.
Goodwin, John. Robin Hood. Date not set. (Nelson Readers Ser.). (Illus.). 36p. (J). pap. *(978-0-17-557050-8(7))* Addison-Wesley Longman, Inc.
Green, Roger Lancelyn. The Adventures of Robin Hood. Hall, Arthur, illus. 2010. (Puffin Classics Ser.). (ENG.). 320p. (J). (gr. 5-7). pap. 5.99 *(978-0-14-132938-3(6)*, Puffin Books) Penguin Young Readers Group.
Green, Roger Lancelyn & Green, Richard. Adventures of Robin Hood. Hall, Arthur & Terrazzini, Daniela Jaglenka, illus. 2010. (Puffin Classics Ser.). (ENG.). 320p. (J). (gr. 5-7). 16.99 *(978-0-14-133489-9(4)*, Puffin Books) Penguin Young Readers Group.
Hall, Tim. Shadow of the Wolf. 2016. (ENG.). 480p. (J). (gr. 9). pap. 9.99 *(978-1-338-03250-5(X))* Scholastic, Inc.
Hall, Tim K. Shadow of the Wolf. 2015. (ENG.). 480p. (J). (gr. 9). 18.99 *(978-0-545-81664-9(5))* Scholastic, Inc.
Harvey, Damian & Remphry, Martin. Robin & the Friar. 2009. (Hopscotch Adventures Ser.). (Illus.). 31p. (J). (gr. 1). lib. bdg. 25.65 *(978-1-59771-177-7(2))* Sea-To-Sea Pubns.
—Robin & the Monk. 2009. (Hopscotch Adventures Ser.). (Illus.). 31p. (J). (gr. 1). lib. bdg. 25.65 *(978-1-59771-179-1(9))* Sea-To-Sea Pubns.
Howard, Eva. League of Archers. 2016. (League of Archers Ser.: 1). (ENG., Illus.). 288p. (J). (gr. 4-8). 16.99 *(978-1-4814-6037-8(4)*, Aladdin) Simon & Schuster Children's Publishing.
Jackson, Bert, illus. The Adventures of Robin Hood: An English Legend. 2004. (ENG.). 24p. (J). (gr. 3-3). pap. 6.47 net. *(978-0-7685-2125-2(4)*, Dominie Elementary) Pearson Schl.
Jones, Rob Lloyd. The Story of Robin Hood. Marks, Alan, illus. 2010. (Picture Book Classics Ser.). 24p. (J). 9.99 *(978-0-7945-2859-1(7)*, Usborne) EDC Publishing.
Koontz, Robin Michal. Robin Hood. Koontz, Robin Michal, illus. 2012. (ENG., Illus.). 24p. (gr. 2-3). pap. 8.95 *(978-1-61810-325-3(3))* Rourke Educational Media.
Lasky, Kathryn. Hawksmaid: The Untold Story of Robin Hood & Maid Marian. 2011. (ENG.). 320p. (J). (gr. 5). pap. 6.99 *(978-0-06-000072-1(4))* HarperCollins Pubs.
Lloyd Jones, Rob, retold by. Robin Hood. 2008. (Young Reading Series 2 Gift Bks). 64p. (J). 8.99 *(978-0-7945-2090-8(1)*, Usborne) EDC Publishing.
McFadden, Deanna. Robin Hood. Calo, Marcos, illus. 2013. (Silver Penny Stories Ser.). (ENG.). 48p. (J). (gr. -1-1). 4.95 *(978-1-4027-8339-5(6))* Sterling Publishing Co., Inc.
Picture Window Books Staff. Robin Hood & the Golden Arrow, 1 vol. Yilmaz, Necdet, illus. 2008. (Read-It! Readers: Legends Ser.). (ENG.). 32p. (gr. k-3). 21.32 *(978-1-4048-4843-6(6)*, Easy Readers) Picture Window Bks.
Pyle, Howard. The Adventures of Robin Hood. 2014. (ENG.). 416p. 17.50 *(978-1-78270-045-6(5))* Award Pubns. Ltd. GBR. Dist: Parkwest Pubns., Inc.
—The Merry Adventures of Robin Hood. McKowen, Scott, illus. 2004. (Sterling Unabridged Classics Ser.). (ENG.). 344p. (J). (gr. 5). 14.95 *(978-1-4027-1456-6(4))* Sterling Publishing Co., Inc.
—The Merry Adventures of Robin Hood, 1 vol. Simon, Ute, illus. 2011. (Calico Illustrated Classics Ser.: No. 3). (ENG.). 112p. (J). (gr. 3-6). 27.07 *(978-1-61641-107-7(4))* Magic Wagon.
—The Merry Adventures of Robin Hood. 2016. (Word Cloud Classics Ser.). (ENG., Illus.). 320p. (gr. 6). pap. 14.99 *(978-1-62686-608-9(2)*, Thunder Bay Pr.) Readerlink Distribution Services, LLC.
Pyle, Howard, illus. The Merry Adventures of Robin Hood. 2015. (J). 13.32 *(978-1-4677-5841-3(8)*, First Avenue Editions) Lerner Publishing Group.
Pyle, Robert. The Merry Adventures of Robin Hood. 2009. 284p. (J). pap. 14.99 *(978-1-934941-61-4(1))* Red & Black Pubs.
Robin Hood. (Coleccion Estrella). (SPA., Illus.). 64p. (J). 14.95 *(978-950-11-0014-3(6)*, SGM014) Sigmar ARG. Dist: Continental Bk. Co., Inc.
Sanderson, Jeanette. Robin Hood Shoots for the Queen: A Legend from England. 2006. (J). pap. *(978-1-4108-7167-1(3))* Benchmark Education Co.
Springer, Nancy. Wild Boy. 2005. (Tales of Rowan Hood Ser.). 115p. (J). (gr. 3). 13.65 *(978-0-7569-5490-1(8))* Perfection Learning Corp.
Stone Arch Books Staff. Robin Hood, 1 vol. Tobon, Sara, tr. Tanner, Jennifer, illus. 2010. (Classic Fiction Ser.). (ENG & SPA.). 72p. (gr. 2-3). pap. 7.15 *(978-1-4342-2275-6(6)*, Graphic Revolve en Español) Stone Arch Bks.
Storrie, Paul D. Robin Hood: Outlaw of Sherwood Forest. Yeates, Thomas, illus. 2007. (Graphic Myths & Legends Ser.). (ENG.). 48p. (J). (gr. 4-8). lib. bdg. 27.93 *(978-0-8225-5964-1(1))* Lerner Publishing Group.
Sutton, Rosalind, et al. Robin Hood. Rowe, Eric F., tr. 4th ed. (Coleccion Clasicos en Accion). (SPA., Illus.). 80p. (YA). (gr. 5-8). 15.95 *(978-84-241-5782-1(6)*, EV1455) Everest Editora ESP. Dist: Lectorum Pubns., Inc.
Tanner, Jennifer, illus. Robin Hood. 2010. (Classic Fiction Ser.). 72p. lib. bdg. 4.95 *(978-1-4342-2604-4(2)*, Graphic Revolve) Stone Arch Bks.

ROBINS

Bechard, Clem. Mrs. Robinson Finds a Home. 2008. 24p. per. 24.95 *(978-1-4241-9692-0(2))* America Star Bks.
Berger, Melvin & Berger, Gilda. A Robin Grows Up. 2008. (Illus.). 32p. (J). *(978-0-439-02525-6(7))* Scholastic, Inc.
Borgert-Spaniol, Megan. American Robins. 2016. (North American Animals Ser.). (ENG., Illus.). 24p. (J). (gr. k-3). 25.95 *(978-1-62617-400-9(8)*, Blastoff! Readers) Bellwether Media.
Christelow, Eileen. Robins! How They Grow Up. 2017. (ENG., Illus.). 48p. (J). (gr. 1-4). 16.99 *(978-0-544-44289-4(X)*, Clarion Bks.) Houghton Mifflin Harcourt Trade & Reference Pubs.
Gillespie, Katie. Robins. 2017. (Illus.). 24p. (J). ***(978-1-4896-4507-4(1))*** Weigl Pubs., Inc.
Hudak, Heather C. Robins: Watch Them Grow. 2010. pap. 9.95 *(978-1-60596-923-7(0))*; 24p. (J). (gr. 2-4). lib. bdg. 25.70 *(978-1-60596-922-0(2))* Weigl Pubs., Inc.
Jenkins, Priscilla Belz. A Nest Full of Eggs. Rockwell, Lizzy, illus. 2015. (Let's-Read-And-Find-Out Science 1 Ser.). (ENG.). 32p. (J). (gr. -1-3). pap. 6.99 *(978-0-06-238193-4(8))* HarperCollins Pubs.
Kalz, Jill. Robins. 2003. (Birds Ser.). (Illus.). 24p. (J). lib. bdg. 21.35 *(978-1-58340-131-6(8))* Black Rabbit Bks.
Mara, Wil. Robins. 2014. (Backyard Safari Ser.). 32p. (J). (gr. 3-5). 28.50 *(978-1-62712-825-4(5))* Cavendish Square Publishing.
Meachen Rau, Dana. El Robin en el Arbol. Vargus, Nanci R., ed. 2006. (Naturaleza Ser.). (SPA., Illus.). 24p. (gr. k-1). lib. bdg. 15.95 *(978-0-7614-2410-9(5)*, Benchmark Bks.) Marshall Cavendish Corp.
—The Robin in the Tree. 2006. (Nature Ser.). (SPA., Illus.). 24p. (gr. k-1). lib. bdg. 15.95 *(978-0-7614-2304-1(4)*, Benchmark Bks.) Marshall Cavendish Corp.
Nelson, Robin. Robins. 2009. pap. 34.95 *(978-0-7613-4113-0(7))*; (ENG.). 24p. 23.93 *(978-0-7613-4068-3(8)*, Lerner Pubns.) Lerner Publishing Group.
Peterson, Megan Cooley & Rustad, Martha E. H. Look Inside a Robin's Nest, 1 vol. 2011. (Look Inside Animal Homes Ser.). (ENG.). 24p. (gr. k-1). 26.65 *(978-1-4296-6077-8(5)*, Pebble Plus) Capstone Press of Coughlan Cos.
Posada, Mia, tr. & illus. Robins: Songbirds of Spring. Posada, Mia, illus. 2004. (Carolrhoda Picture Books Ser.). 32p. (J). (gr. k-3). 15.95 *(978-1-57505-615-9(1))* Lerner Publishing Group.
Riggs, Kate. Robins. (In My Backyard Ser.). (Illus.). 24p. (J). 2017. (ENG.). (gr. 1-3). pap. 8.99 *(978-1-62832-297-2(7)*, Creative Paperbacks) 2016. *(978-1-60818-701-0(2)*, Creative Education) Creative Co., The.

ROBINS—FICTION

Bentley, Sue. Double Trouble. 2009. (Magic Kitten Ser.: 4). lib. bdg. 16.00 *(978-0-606-06004-2(9)*, Turtleback) Turtleback Bks.
Bonnell, Kris. Robins in the Spring. 2007. (J). pap. 5.95 *(978-1-933727-53-0(5))* Reading Reading Bks., LLC.
Collins, Stephan. The Chronicles of Timothy Tabbis. 2009. 45p. pap. 8.55 *(978-0-557-09266-6(3))* Lulu Pr., Inc.
Dell, Bella. Rosie the Robin. 2013. 24p. pap. 24.95 *(978-1-63000-892-5(3))* America Star Bks.
Dhade, Sukhdev Kaur. Robin with the Red Hat, 1 vol. 2010. 24p. pap. 24.95 *(978-1-4489-7235-7(3))* PublishAmerica, Inc.
Hocknell, Barbara. The Robins & the Bell. 2007. (Illus.). 52p. per. *(978-1-84748-132-0(9))* Athena Pr.
Jorgensen, Norman. In Flanders Fields. Harrison-Lever, Brian, illus. 2003. (ENG.). 32p. (J). (gr. -1-3). 16.95 *(978-1-894965-01-9(9))* Simply Read Bks. CAN. Dist: Ingram Publisher Services.
Jorgensen, Norman & Harrison-Lever, Brian. In Flanders Fields. 2004. (Illus.). 32p. pap. 13.50 *(978-1-920731-03-8(2))* Fremantle Pr. AUS. Dist: Independent Pubs. Group.
Mackall, Dandi Daley. The Story of the Easter Robin, 1 vol. Vojtech, Anna, illus. 2010. (ENG.). 32p. (J). (gr. -1-2). 15.99 *(978-0-310-71331-9(5))* Zonderkidz.
March, El. Captain Leopold. 2010. 64p. pap. 25.56 *(978-0-557-32169-8(7))* Lulu Pr., Inc.
Parish, Herman. Amelia Bedelia Is for the Birds. Avril, Lynne, illus. 2015. (I Can Read Level 1 Ser.). (ENG.). 32p. (J). (gr. -1-3). pap. 3.99 *(978-0-06-233424-4(7)*, Greenwillow Bks.) HarperCollins Pubs.
River, Fawn. Sophy & the River. 2012. 24p. pap. 17.99 *(978-1-4772-0272-2(2))* AuthorHouse.
Salzmann, Mary Elizabeth. Robin Hoods, 1 vol. Haberstroh, Anne, illus. 2007. (Critter Chronicles Ser.). (ENG.). 24p. (J). (gr. k-3). lib. bdg. 24.21 *(978-1-59928-466-8(9)*, SandCastle) ABDO Publishing Co.
Sawyers, William. The Nest That Could Fly. 2005. 43p. (J). pap. 17.96 *(978-1-4116-5446-4(3))* Lulu Pr., Inc.
Sazaklis, John. Candy Store Caper, 1 vol. Baltazar, Art, illus. 2012. (DC Super-Pets Ser.). (ENG.). 56p. (gr. 2-2). pap. 4.95 *(978-1-4048-7214-1(0))*; lib. bdg. 23.99 *(978-1-4048-6484-9(9))* Picture Window Bks. (DC Super-Pets).
Speed, Bryan W. Little Bent Cedar. Todd, Sheri, illus. 2007. (ENG.). 24p. (J). (gr. 2-4). per. *(978-1-933255-38-5(2))* DNA Pr.
Talbott, Shawn M. Springtime Robins. 2006. (J). lib. bdg. 19.95 *(978-1-933732-05-3(9))* Big Ransom Studio.
Wolf, Sallie & Bornstein, Micah. The Robin Makes a Laughing Sound: A Birder's Journal. 2010. (ENG., Illus.). 48p. (J). (gr. 4-7). 11.95 *(978-1-58089-318-3(X))* Charlesbridge Publishing, Inc.
Wyss, Johann. The Swiss Family Robinson. 2009. (Puffin Classics Ser.). (ENG.). 496p. (J). (gr. 5-7). pap. 5.99 *(978-0-14-132530-9(5)*, Puffin Books) Penguin Young Readers Group.

ROBINSON, FRANK, 1935-

Skipper, John C. Frank Robinson: A Baseball Biography, 1 vol. 2014. (ENG., Illus.). 220p. pap. 25.00 *(978-0-7864-7561-2(7)*, efd5081f-d54f-4da6-bb69-aad22ed14bb9) McFarland & Co., Inc. Pubs.

ROBINSON, JACKIE, 1919-1972

Auster, Michael A. They Led the Way. 2005. (Yellow Umbrella Fluent Level Ser.). (ENG.). 16p. (gr. k-1). pap. 35.70 *(978-0-7368-5315-6(4)*, Yellow Umbrella Bks.) Capstone Press of Coughlan Cos.
Bailey, Budd. Jackie Robinson: Breaking Baseball's Color Barrier. 2016. (Game-Changing Athletes Ser.). (ENG.). 112p. (J). (gr. 9-9). lib. bdg. 42.79 *(978-1-5026-1056-0(6))* Cavendish Square Publishing.
Benjamin, Lisa. Jackie Robinson: Changing the Game. 2005. (Voices Reading Ser.). (Illus.). 32p. (J). *(978-0-7367-2937-6(2))* Zaner-Bloser, Inc.
Bennett, Doraine. Jackie Robinson. 2008. (J). pap. *(978-1-935077-11-4(2))*; (ENG., Illus.). 24p. lib. bdg. 19.93 *(978-1-935077-04-6(X))* State Standards Publishing, LLC.
Berne, Emma Carlson. What's Your Story, Jackie Robinson? 2015. (ENG., Illus.). 32p. (J). (gr. k-3). 26.65 *(978-1-4677-7964-7(4))* Lerner Publishing Group.
Brown, Jonatha A. Jackie Robinson. Acosta, Tatiana & Gutierrez, Guillermo, trs. 2004. (Gente Que Hay Que Conocer Ser.). (SPA., Illus.). 24p. (gr. 1-4). lib. bdg. 22.00 *(978-0-8368-4353-8(3)*, Weekly Reader Leveled Readers) Stevens, Gareth Publishing LLLP.
Brown, Jonatha A. & Raatma, Lucia. Jackie Robinson. 2004. (People We Should Know Ser.). (Illus.). 24p. (gr. 1-4). pap. 8.15 *(978-0-8368-4318-7(5))*; lib. bdg. 22.00 *(978-0-8368-4311-8(8))* Stevens, Gareth Publishing LLLP. (Weekly Reader Leveled Readers).
Burgan, Michael. Daring Play: How a Courageous Jackie Robinson Transformed Baseball. 2016. (Captured History Sports Ser.). (ENG.). 64p. (gr. 5-7). lib. bdg. 34.65 *(978-0-7565-5291-6(5)*, CPB Grades 4-8) Compass Point Bks.
Burleigh, Robert. Stealing Home: Jackie Robinson: Against the Odds. Wimmer, Mike, illus. 2007. (ENG.). 32p. (J). (gr. 1-4). 17.99 *(978-0-689-86276-2(8)*, Simon & Schuster/Paula Wiseman Bks.) Simon & Schuster/Paula Wiseman Bks.
Crisp, Victor. Jackie Robinson: Breaking Barriers. 2013. (InfoMax Readers Ser.). (ENG.). 24p. (J). (gr. 3-4). pap. 49.50 *(978-1-4777-2632-7(2))*; (Illus.). pap. 8.25 *(978-1-4777-2631-0(4))* Rosen Publishing Group, Inc., The. (Rosen Classroom).
Darraj, Susan Muaddi. Jackie Robinson. 2007. (Baseball Superstars Ser.). (Illus.). 122p. (YA). (gr. 7-12). lib. bdg. 30.00 *(978-0-7910-9442-6(1))* Facts On File, Inc.
De Marco, Tony. Jackie Robinson. 2009. (Journey to Freedom Ser.). (ENG., Illus.). 32p. (J). (gr. 4-7). 29.93 *(978-1-60253-125-3(0)*, 200391) Child's World, Inc., The.
Dunn, Joe. Jackie Robinson, 1 vol. Espinosa, Rod, illus. 2007. (Bio-Graphics Ser.). (ENG.). 32p. (gr. 3-6). 28.50 *(978-1-60270-068-0(0)*, Graphic Planet- Nonfiction) ABDO Publishing Co.
Elish, Dan. Jackie Robinson. 2005. (Cornerstones of Freedom Ser.). (ENG., Illus.). 48p. (YA). (gr. 4-7). lib. bdg. 26.00 *(978-0-516-23635-3(0))* Scholastic Library Publishing.
Feinstein, Stephen. Read about Jackie Robinson. 2005. (I Like Biographies! Ser.). (Illus.). 24p. (J). lib. bdg. 22.60 *(978-0-7660-2592-9(6)*, Enslow Elementary) Enslow Pubs., Inc.
Fishman, Cathy Goldberg. When Jackie & Hank Met, 0 vols. Elliott, Mark, illus. 2012. (ENG.). 40p. (J). (gr. 2-5). 17.99 *(978-0-7614-6140-1(X)*, 9780761461401, Amazon Children's Publishing) Amazon Publishing.
Ford, Carin T. Jackie Robinson: All I Ask Is That You Respect Me as a Human Being. 2005. (African-American Biography Library). (Illus.). 128p. (J). (gr. 6-12). lib. bdg. 33.27 *(978-0-7660-2461-8(X))* Enslow Pubs., Inc.
—Jackie Robinson: Hero of Baseball. 2006. (Heroes of American History Ser.). (Illus.). 32p. (J). (gr. -1-3). lib. bdg. 23.94 *(978-0-7660-2600-1(0)*, Enslow Elementary) Enslow Pubs., Inc.
Frystak, Timothy D. Jackie Robinson: With Profiles of Satchel Paige & & Branch Rickey. 2006. (Biographical Connections Ser.). (Illus.). 112p. (J). *(978-0-7166-1828-7(1))* World Bk., Inc.
Glaser, Jason. Jackie Robinson: Baseball's Great Pioneer, 1 vol. Lentz, Bob et al, illus. 2005. (Graphic Biographies Ser.). (ENG.). 32p. (gr. 3-4). 30.65 *(978-0-7368-4633-2(6)*, Graphic Library) Capstone Press of Coughlan Cos.
—Jackie Robinson: Gran Pionero del Béisbol. Lentz, Bob, illus. 2006. (Biografías Gráficas Ser.). (ENG & SPA.). 32p. (gr. 3-4). 30.65 *(978-0-7368-6602-6(7))* Capstone Press of Coughlan Cos.
Gomez, Rebecca. Jackie Robinson, 1 vol. 2003. (First Biographies Ser.). (ENG., Illus.). 32p. (gr. k-4). 27.07 *(978-1-57765-949-5(X)*, Buddy Bks.) ABDO Publishing Co.
Gregory, Josh. Jackie Robinson. 2015. (ENG., Illus.). 48p. (J). lib. bdg. *(978-0-531-21598-2(9))* Children's Pr., Ltd.
—Jackie Robinson. 2015. (True Book(tm) — Biographies Ser.). (ENG.). 48p. (J). pap. 6.95 *(978-0-531-21760-3(4)*, Children's Pr.) Scholastic Library Publishing.

Gutman, Dan. Jackie Robinson & the Big Game. Garvin, Elaine, illus. 2006. 32p. (J). lib. bdg. 15.00 *(978-1-4242-0957-6(9))* Fitzgerald Bks.

—Jackie Robinson & the Big Game. Garvin, Elaine, illus. 2006. (Ready-To-read COFA Ser.). (ENG.). 32p. (J). (gr. k-2). pap. 3.99 *(978-0-689-86239-7(3)*, Simon & Schuster/Paula Wiseman Bks.) Simon & Schuster/Paula Wiseman Bks.

Haldy, Emma E. Jackie Robinson. Bane, Jeff, illus. 2016. (My Early Library: My Itty-Bitty Bio Ser.). (ENG.). 24p. (J). (gr. k-1). 28.50 *(978-1-63471-021-3(5)*, 208164) Cherry Lake Publishing.

Hanft, J. & Zukowski/Faust, Jean. Jackie Robinson. 2006. (Heinle Reading Library: Biography Collection). (ENG.). 240p. pap. 16.95 ***(978-1-4240-0564-2(7))*** Cengage Heinle.

Hanft, Joshua E. Jackie Robinson. Marcos, Pablo, illus. 2005. (Heroes of America Ser.). 238p. (gr. 3-8). 27.07 *(978-1-59679-259-3(0)*, Abdo & Daughters) ABDO Publishing Co.

Hansen, Grace. Jackie Robinson: Baseball Legend, 1 vol. 2014. (History Maker Biographies Ser.). (ENG., Illus.). 24p. (J). (gr. 2-4). lib. bdg. 28.50 *(978-1-62970-701-3(5))* ABDO Publishing Co.

Herman, Gail. Who Was Jackie Robinson? Harrison, Nancy & O'brien, John, illus. 2010. (Who Was? Ser.). (ENG.). 112p. (J). (gr. 3-7). pap. 5.99 *(978-0-448-45557-0(9)*, Grosset & Dunlap) Penguin Young Readers Group.

Hillstrom & Hillstrom, Laurie C. Jackie Robinson & the Integration of Baseball. 2013. 248p. lib. bdg. 55.00 *(978-0-7808-1327-4(8))* Omnigraphics, Inc.

Mara, Wil. Jackie Robinson. 2014. (Rookie Biographies(r) Ser.). (ENG.). 32p. (J). lib. bdg. 23.00 *(978-0-531-21062-8(6))* Scholastic Library Publishing.

Martin, Isabel. Jackie Robinson, 1 vol. 2014. (Great African-Americans Ser.). (ENG., Illus.). 24p. (gr. k-1). pap. 5.95 *(978-1-4914-0508-6(2)*, Pebble Bks.) Capstone Press of Coughlan Cos.

McPherson, Stephanie Sammartino. Jackie Robinson. 2010. (J). lib. bdg. 27.93 *(978-0-7613-5207-5(4)*, Lerner Pubns.) Lerner Publishing Group.

Meltzer, Brad. I Am Jackie Robinson. Eliopoulos, Christopher, illus. 2015. (Ordinary People Change the World Ser.). (ENG.). 40p. (J). (gr. k-3). 14.99 *(978-0-8037-4086-0(7)*, Dial Bks) Penguin Young Readers Group.

O'Hern, Kerri & Raatma, Lucia. Jackie Robinson. 2006. (Graphic Biographies Ser.). (Illus.). 32p. (gr. 5-8). pap. 10.50 *(978-0-8368-6250-8(3))* Stevens, Gareth Publishing LLLP.

O'Sullivan, Robyn. Jackie Robinson Plays Ball. 2007. (History Chapters Ser.). (ENG., Illus.). 48p. (J). (gr. 1-4). lib. bdg. 17.90 *(978-1-4263-0190-2(1)*, National Geographic Children's Bks.) National Geographic Society.

Patrick, Denise Lewis. Jackie Robinson Strong Inside & Out. 2005. 44p. (J). lib. bdg. 15.00 *(978-1-4242-0850-0(5))* Fitzgerald Bks.

Patrick, Denise Lewis & Time for Kids Editors. Jackie Robinson - Strong Inside & Out. 2005. (Time for Kids Ser.). (ENG., Illus.). 48p. (J). (gr. 2-4). pap. 3.99 *(978-0-06-057600-4(6))* HarperCollins Pubs.

Prince, April Jones. Jackie Robinson - He Led the Way. Casilla, Robert, illus. 2007. (Penguin Young Readers, Level 3 Ser.). (ENG.). 48p. (J). (gr. 1-3). mass mkt. 3.99 *(978-0-448-44721-6(5)*, Penguin Young Readers) Penguin Young Readers Group.

Raatma, Lucia & O'Hern, Kerri. Jackie Robinson. Campbell, Alex & Spay, Anthony, illus. (Biografias Graficas (Graphic Biographies) Ser.). 32p. (gr. 5-8). 2007. (SPA.). pap. 10.50 *(978-0-8368-7889-9(2))* 2007. (SPA.). lib. bdg. 27.00 *(978-0-8368-7882-0(5))* 2006. lib. bdg. 27.00 *(978-0-8368-6198-3(1))* Stevens, Gareth Publishing LLLP.

Rice, Dona. Jackie Robinson: Hometown Hero. 2016. (Primary Source Readers Ser.). (Illus.). 32p. (gr. 2-2). 8.99 *(978-1-4938-2560-8(7))* Teacher Created Materials, Inc.

Robinson, Sharon. Jackie Robinson: American Hero. 2013. (ENG.). 48p. (J). (gr. -1-3). pap. 4.99 *(978-0-545-54006-3(2)*, Scholastic Paperbacks) Scholastic, Inc.

—Promises to Keep: How Jackie Robinson Changed America. 2004. (ENG., Illus.). 64p. (J). (gr. 3-7). 17.99 *(978-0-439-42592-6(1))* Scholastic, Inc.

Rodriguez, Tia. Jackie Robinson: Baseball Legend. 2013. (Rosen Readers Ser.). (ENG.). 24p. (J). (gr. 3-4). pap. 49.50 *(978-1-4777-2569-6(5))*; pap. 8.25 *(978-1-4777-2568-9(7))* Rosen Publishing Group, Inc., The. (Rosen Classroom).

Saddleback Educational Publishing Staff, ed. Jackie Robinson, 1 vol. unabr. ed. 2008. (Graphic Biographies Ser.). (ENG., Illus.). 25p. (YA). (gr. 9-12). pap. 7.95 *(978-1-59905-225-0(3))* Saddleback Educational Publishing, Inc.

Sexton, Colleen. Jackie Robinson: A Life of Determination. 2007. (People of Character Ser.). (ENG., Illus.). 24p. (J). (gr. 2-5). lib. bdg. 25.95 *(978-1-60014-089-1(0))* Bellwether Media.

Simmons, Matt J. Jackie Robinson: Breaking the Color Line in Baseball. 2014. (ENG., Illus.). 112p. (J). *(978-0-7787-1242-8(7))* Crabtree Publishing Co.

Smolka, Bo. Jackie Robinson Breaks the Color Barrier, 1 vol. 2014. (Greatest Events in Sports History Ser.). (ENG.). 48p. (gr. 3-6). lib. bdg. 32.79 *(978-1-62403-594-4(9)*, SportsZone) ABDO Publishing Co.

Stille, Darlene R. Jackie Robinson: Amazing Athlete & Activist, 1 vol. Stergulz, Richard, illus. 2013. (Beginner Biographies Set 2 Ser.). (ENG.). 32p. (J). (gr. -1-4). 28.50 *(978-1-61641-940-0(7))* Magic Wagon.

Stout, Glenn & Christopher, Matt. Jackie Robinson: Legends in Sports. 2006. (ENG., Illus.). 128p. (J). (gr. 5-8). per. 15.99 *(978-0-316-10826-3(X))* Little, Brown Bks. for Young Readers.

Teitelbaum, Michael. Jackie Robinson: Champion for Equality. 2010. (Sterling Biographies(r) Ser.). (ENG., Illus.). 128p. (J). (gr. 5-18). pap. 5.95 *(978-1-4027-6362-5(X))* Sterling Publishing Co., Inc.

Trussell-Cullen, Alan. Jackie Robinson. 2009. pap. 13.25 *(978-1-60559-063-9(0))* Hameray Publishing Group, Inc.

Walker, Sally M. Jackie Robinson. Translations.com Staff, tr. Pate, Rodney S., illus. 2005. (Yo Solo: Biografías (on My Own Biographies) Ser.). (SPA & ENG.). 48p. (gr. 2-4). lib. bdg. 25.26 *(978-0-8225-3126-5(7)*, Ediciones Lerner) Lerner Publishing Group.

Wheeler, Jill C. Jackie Robinson. 2003. (Breaking Barriers Ser.). 64p. (gr. 3-8). 27.07 *(978-1-57765-739-2(X)*, Abdo & Daughters) ABDO Publishing Co.

Wilmore, Kathy. Jackie Robinson: With a Discussion of Respect. 2004. (Values in Action Ser.). (J). *(978-1-59203-071-2(8))* Learning Challenge, Inc.

Wukovits, John F. Jackie Robinson & the Integration of Baseball. 2005. (Lucent Library of Black History). (ENG., Illus.). 104p. (J). (gr. 3-7). lib. bdg. 33.45 *(978-1-59018-913-9(2)*, Lucent Bks.) Cengage Gale.

ROBINSON, JACKIE, 1919-1972—FICTION

Grossinger, Tania. Jackie & Me: A Very Special Friendship. Esperanza, Charles George, illus. 2013. (ENG.). 32p. (J). (gr. -1-3). 16.95 *(978-1-62087-683-1(3)*, 620683, Sky Pony Pr.) Skyhorse Publishing Co., Inc.

Gutman, Dan. Jackie & Me. 2005. (Baseball Card Adventures Ser.). (Illus.). 145p. (YA). (gr. 4-8). reprint ed. 20.00 *(978-0-7567-9569-6(9))* DIANE Publishing Co.

Krensky, Stephen. Play Ball, Jackie! Morse, Joe, illus. 2011. (Single Titles Ser.). (ENG.). 32p. (J). (gr. 2-5). lib. bdg. 16.95 *(978-0-8225-9030-9(1)*, Millbrook Pr.) Lerner Publishing Group.

Lorbiecki, Marybeth. Jackie's Bat. Pinkney, Brian, illus. 2006. (ENG.). 40p. (J). (gr. k-3). 17.99 *(978-0-689-84102-6(7)*, Simon & Schuster Bks. For Young Readers) Simon & Schuster Bks. For Young Readers.

Robinson, Sharon. Testing the Ice: A True Story about Jackie Robinson. Nelson, Kadir, illus. 2009. (ENG.). 40p. (J). (gr. 2-5). 18.99 *(978-0-545-05251-1(3)*, Scholastic Pr.) Scholastic, Inc.

Russell, Nancy L. M., et al. So Long, Jackie Robinson. rev. ed. 2007. (ENG.). 224p. (J). (gr. 4-7). 7.95 *(978-1-55263-863-7(4))* Leaf Storm Pr.

Uhlberg, Myron. Dad, Jackie, & Me, 1 vol. Bootman, Colin, illus. (ENG.). 32p. (J). 2010. pap. 8.95 *(978-1-56145-531-7(8))* 2005. 16.95 *(978-1-56145-329-0(3))* Peachtree Pubs.

ROBINSON, JOHN ROOSEVELT, 1919-1972

see Robinson, Jackie, 1919-1972

ROBOTS

Abramovitz, Melissa & Alpert, Barbara. Military Machines. 2012. (Military Machines Ser.). (ENG.). 24p. (gr. k-1). pap. 250.20 *(978-1-4296-8319-7(8)*, Pebble Plus) Capstone Press of Coughlan Cos.

Allman, Toney. From Insect Wings to Flying Robots. 2006. (Imitating Nature Ser.). (ENG., Illus.). 32p. (J). (gr. 3-7). lib. bdg. 26.20 *(978-0-7377-3488-1(4)*, Kidhaven) Cengage Gale.

—Jaws of Life. 2008. (Great Idea Ser.). (Illus.). 48p. (J). (gr. 4-6). lib. bdg. 26.60 *(978-1-59953-191-5(7))* Norwood Hse. Pr.

—The Nexi Robot. 2009. (Great Idea Ser.). (Illus.). 48p. (J). (gr. 4-6). lib. bdg. 26.60 *(978-1-59953-342-1(1))* Norwood Hse. Pr.

Alpert, Barbara. Military Robots. 2012. (Military Machines Ser.). (ENG.). 24p. (gr. k-1). pap. 41.70 *(978-1-4296-8315-9(5))*; lib. bdg. 26.65 *(978-1-4296-7573-4(X))* Capstone Press of Coughlan Cos. (Pebble Plus).

—U. S. Military Robots, 1 vol. 2012. (U. S. Military Technology Ser.). (ENG., Illus.). 32p. (gr. 1-2). lib. bdg. 26.65 *(978-1-4296-8438-5(0))* Capstone Press of Coughlan Cos.

Alpert, Barbara & Abramovitz, Melissa. Military Machines. 2012. (Military Machines Ser.). (ENG.). 24p. (gr. k-1). lib. bdg. 159.90 *(978-1-4296-8112-4(8)*, Pebble Plus) Capstone Press of Coughlan Cos.

Amazing Robot. 2008. (Build it now Ser.). 16p. pap. *(978-1-4075-2247-0(7))* Parragon, Inc.

Amazing Robots. 2015. (Amazing Robots Ser.). (ENG.). 48p. (J). (gr. 4-5). 191.70 *(978-1-4824-2556-7(4))*; pap., pap., pap. 505.80 *(978-1-4824-3431-6(8))*; pap., pap., pap. 84.30 *(978-1-4824-3432-3(6))* Stevens, Gareth Publishing LLLP.

Amstutz, Lisa J. All about Robots. 2017. (Cutting-Edge Technology (hardcover) Ser.). (ENG., Illus.). 32p. (J). (gr. 4-7). lib. bdg. 28.50 ***(978-1-63517-014-6(1)***, Focus Readers) North Star Editions.

Andrysek, Jan & Mihailidis, Alex. New Hands, New Life: Robots, Prostheses & Innovation. 2017. (ENG., Illus.). 64p. (J). (gr. 4-7). 19.95 ***(978-1-77085-969-2(1)***, 9781770859692); pap. 9.95 ***(978-1-77085-991-3(8)***, 9781770859913) Firefly Bks., Ltd.

Arcturus Publishing Staff. Build a Robot. 2013. (ENG.). 10p. (J). 9.95 *(978-1-78212-241-8(9))* Arcturus Publishing GBR. Dist: Bookmasters Distribution.

Arlon, Penelope & Hayes, Susan. Really? Robots. 2015. (ENG., Illus.). 64p. (J). (gr. 1-3). pap. 8.99 *(978-0-545-83345-5(0)*, Scholastic Nonfiction) Scholastic, Inc.

Baker, John R. Astonishing Robot Competitions. 2017. (Cool Competitions Ser.). (ENG.). 32p. (gr. 1-2). lib. bdg. 26.65 ***(978-1-5157-7352-8(3)***, Blazers) Capstone Press of Coughlan Cos.

Bergin, Mark. Robots. 2009. (How to Draw Ser.). (Illus.). 32p. (J). (ENG.). (gr. 4-6). pap. 11.75 *(978-1-4358-2650-2(7))*; lib. bdg. 26.50 *(978-1-4358-2521-5(7))* Rosen Publishing Group, Inc., The. (PowerKids Pr.).

Biskup, Agnieszka. The Remarkable World of Robots: Max Axiom STEM Adventures. 2017. (STEM Adventures Ser.). (ENG.). 32p. (gr. 3-4). lib. bdg. 30.65 ***(978-1-5157-7391-7(4)***, Graphic Library) Capstone Press of Coughlan Cos.

Bow, James. Maker Projects for Kids Who Love Robotics. 2016. (ENG., Illus.). 32p. (J). *(978-0-7787-2254-0(6))* Crabtree Publishing Co.

Brasch, Nicolas. Robots of the Future. 2012. (Discovery Education: Technology Ser.). (ENG., Illus.). 32p. (J). (gr. 3-6). 25.25 *(978-1-4488-7885-7(3))*; pap. 10.00 *(978-1-4488-7967-0(1))* Rosen Publishing Group, Inc., The. (PowerKids Pr.).

Bridgman, Roger & Dorling Kindersley Publishing Staff. DK Eyewitness Books - Robot. 2004. (DK Eyewitness Bks.). (ENG., Illus.). 64p. (J). (gr. 3-7). 16.99 *(978-0-7566-0254-3(8)*, DK Children) Dorling Kindersley Publishing, Inc.

Brown, Jordan D. Robo World: The Story of Robot Designer Cynthia Breazeal. 2006. (ENG., Illus.). 128p. (gr. 7-9). per. 19.95 *(978-0-309-09556-3(5)*, Joseph Henry Pr.) National Academies Pr.

Cassriel, Betsy R. Robot Builders!, Vol. 10. 2015. (Scientists in Action Ser.). (Illus.). 48p. (J). (gr. 5). 20.95 *(978-1-4222-3426-6(6))* Mason Crest.

Chaffee, Joel. How to Build a Prize-Winning Robot. 2011. (Robotics Ser.). (Illus.). 48p. (YA). (gr. 5-9). lib. bdg. 29.25 *(978-1-4488-1238-7(0))* Rosen Publishing Group, Inc., The.

Chow-Miller, Ian. Sensors & the Environment. 2016. (Robotics Ser.). (ENG., Illus.). 128p. (J). (gr. 9-12). 45.64 *(978-1-5026-1938-9(5))* Cavendish Square Publishing.

Clay, Kathryn & Shores, Erika L. Cool Robots, 1 vol. 2014. (Cool Robots Ser.). (ENG.). 24p. (gr. k-1). 106.60 *(978-1-4914-0686-1(0)*, Pebble Plus) Capstone Press of Coughlan Cos.

Clay, Kathryn & Vonne, Mira. Battling for Victory: The Coolest Robot Competitions, 1 vol. 2014. (World of Robots Ser.). (ENG.). 32p. (gr. 1-2). lib. bdg. 26.65 *(978-1-4765-3974-4(X)*, Blazers) Capstone Press of Coughlan Cos.

—Humanoid Robots: Running into the Future, 1 vol. 2014. (World of Robots Ser.). (ENG.). 32p. (gr. 1-2). lib. bdg. 26.65 *(978-1-4765-3975-1(8)*, Blazers) Capstone Press of Coughlan Cos.

—My First Guide to Robots. 2015. (My First Guides). (ENG.). 24p. (gr. 1-2). lib. bdg. 25.32 *(978-1-4914-2049-2(9))* Capstone Press of Coughlan Cos.

—Robots at Your Service: From the Factory to Your Home, 1 vol. 2014. (World of Robots Ser.). (ENG.). 32p. (gr. 1-2). lib. bdg. 26.65 *(978-1-4765-3973-7(1)*, Blazers) Capstone Press of Coughlan Cos.

—Robots in Risky Jobs: On the Battlefield & Beyond, 1 vol. 2014. (World of Robots Ser.). (ENG.). 32p. (gr. 1-2). lib. bdg. 26.65 *(978-1-4765-3972-0(3)*, Blazers) Capstone Press of Coughlan Cos.

—The World of Robots, 1 vol. 2014. (World of Robots Ser.). (ENG.). 32p. (gr. 1-2). lib. bdg. 106.60 *(978-1-4765-7844-6(3)*, Blazers) Capstone Press of Coughlan Cos.

Cohen, Jacob. Getting the Most Out of Makerspaces to Build Robots. 2014. (Makerspaces Ser.). 64p. (J). (gr. 6-12). 32.95 *(978-1-4777-7819-7(5))* Rosen Publishing Group, Inc., The.

Crane, Cody. Robots. 2017. (True Book — Behind the Scenes Ser.). (ENG.). 48p. (J). lib. bdg. 31.00 ***(978-0-531-23501-0(7)***, Children's Pr.) Scholastic Library Publishing.

Cunningham, Kevin. Robot Scientist. 2015. (21st Century Skills Library: Cool STEAM Careers Ser.). (ENG., Illus.). 32p. (J). (gr. 4-7). 29.93 *(978-1-63362-562-4(1)*, 206432) Cherry Lake Publishing.

Derrington, Louise. How to Build Robots. 2017. (Illus.). 32p. (J). ***(978-0-7787-3394-2(7))*** Crabtree Publishing Co.

Faust, Daniel R. Building Robots: Robotic Engineers, 01 vols., 1. 2016. (Engineers Rule Ser.). (ENG., Illus.). 32p. (J). pap. 11.75 *(978-1-5081-4540-0(7)*, PowerKids Pr.) Rosen Publishing Group, Inc., The.

—Manufacturing Robots. 2016. (Robots & Robotics Ser.). 32p. (J). (gr. 5-5). pap. 11.75 *(978-1-4994-2171-2(0)*, PowerKids Pr.) Rosen Publishing Group, Inc., The.

—Medical Robots. 2016. (Robots & Robotics Ser.). 32p. (J). (gr. 5-5). pap. 11.75 *(978-1-4994-2175-0(3)*, PowerKids Pr.) Rosen Publishing Group, Inc., The.

—Military & Police Robots. 2016. (Robots & Robotics Ser.). (Illus.). 32p. (J). (gr. 5-5). pap. 11.75 *(978-1-4994-2178-1(8)*, PowerKids Pr.) Rosen Publishing Group, Inc., The.

—Underwater Robots. 2016. (Robots & Robotics Ser.). 32p. (J). (gr. 5-5). pap. 11.75 *(978-1-4994-2186-6(9)*, PowerKids Pr.) Rosen Publishing Group, Inc., The.

Fliess, Sue. Robots, Robots Everywhere! Staake, Bob, illus. 2013. (Little Golden Book Ser.). (ENG.). 24p. (J). (-k). 4.99 *(978-0-449-81079-8(8)*, Golden Bks.) Random Hse. Children's Bks.

Flynn, Liam & McCombs, Kevin. Locomotion & Mechanics. 2016. (Robotics Ser.). (ENG.). 128p. (J). (gr. 9-12). 45.64 *(978-1-5026-2026-2(X))* Cavendish Square Publishing.

Forest, Christopher. Robot Competitions. 2013. (Robots Ser.). (ENG.). 32p. (gr. 3-4). pap. 47.70 *(978-1-62065-783-6(X))*; lib. bdg. 27.99 *(978-1-4296-9920-4(5))*; (Illus.). pap. 8.29 *(978-1-62065-782-9(1))* Capstone Press of Coughlan Cos. (Edge Bks.).

—Robots in Space, 1 vol. 2011. (Solar System & Beyond Ser.). (ENG.). 32p. (gr. 3-4). pap. 8.10 *(978-1-4296-7229-0(3))*; pap. 47.70 *(978-1-4296-7230-6(7))* Capstone Press of Coughlan Cos. (Fact Finders).

Forest, Christopher, et al. Robots. 2013. (Robots Ser.). (ENG.). 32p. (gr. 3-4). pap. 190.80 *(978-1-62065-785-0(6))*; pap. 31.80 *(978-1-62065-784-3(8))*; lib. bdg. 111.96 *(978-1-4296-9921-1(3))* Capstone Press of Coughlan Cos. (Edge Bks.).

Freedman, Jeri. Robots Through History. 2011. (Robotics Ser.). (Illus.). 48p. (YA). (gr. 5-9). 29.25 *(978-1-4488-1236-3(4))* Rosen Publishing Group, Inc., The.

Fretland VanVoorst, Jenny. Robots in the Factory. 2015. (Illus.). 24p. (J). lib. bdg. 25.65 *(978-1-62031-218-6(2))* Jump! Inc.

Fritz, Sandy. Robotics & Artificial Intelligence. 2003. (Hot Science Ser.). (J). lib. bdg. 28.50 *(978-1-58340-364-8(7))* Black Rabbit Bks.

Furstinger, Nancy. Helper Robots. 2014. (Lightning Bolt Books Robots Everywhere! Ser.). (Illus.). 32p. (gr. k-2). (J). lib. bdg. 26.60 *(978-1-4677-4053-1(5)*, Lerner Pubns.); pap. 7.95 *(978-1-4677-4508-6(1))* Lerner Publishing Group.

—Robots in Space. 2014. (Lightning Bolt Books Robots Everywhere! Ser.). (Illus.). 32p. (gr. k-2). (J). lib. bdg. 26.60 *(978-1-4677-4055-5(1)*, Lerner Pubns.); pap. 7.95 *(978-1-4677-4510-9(3))* Lerner Publishing Group.

Galashan, Kathy. Robots. 2005. (ENG., Illus.). 32p. pap. 8.50 *(978-0-340-87311-3(6))* Cambridge Univ. Pr.

Gendell, Megan. Rocking & Roving: Everything You Wanted to Know about Rockets, Rovers, & Robots. 2008. (Illus.). 31p. (J). *(978-0-545-04460-8(X))* Scholastic, Inc.

Gerdes, Louise I. Robotic Technology. Greenhaven Press Editors, ed. 2014. (Opposing Viewpoints Ser.). (ENG.). 224p. (gr. 10-12). pap. 33.80 *(978-0-7377-6339-3(6))*; lib. bdg. 48.80 *(978-0-7377-6338-6(8))* Cengage Gale. (Greenhaven Pr., Inc.).

Gifford, Clive. Robots. 2005. (Technology All Around Us Ser.). (Illus.). 32p. (YA). (gr. 4-7). lib. bdg. 27.10 *(978-1-58340-752-3(9))* Black Rabbit Bks.

—Robots. 2011. 48p. 11.99 *(978-84-96252-41-7(8))* Edilupa Ediciones, S.L. ESP. Dist: Lectorum Pubns., Inc.

—Robots. Picini, Frank, illus. 2008. (ENG.). 32p. (J). (gr. 3-9). 21.99 *(978-1-4169-6414-8(2)*, Atheneum Bks. for Young Readers) Simon & Schuster Children's Publishing.

Giulieri, Anne. Here Is a Robot, 1 vol. Kreinberg, Sylvia, photos by. 2012. (Engage Literacy Magenta Ser.). (ENG., Illus.). 32p. (gr. k-2). pap. 5.99 *(978-1-4296-8848-2(3)*, Engage Literacy) Capstone Press of Coughlan Cos.

Graham, Ian. Robot Technology. 2010. (New Technology Ser.). (ENG., Illus.). 48p. (J). 23.99 *(978-0-237-54075-3(4))* Evans Brothers, Ltd. GBR. Dist: Independent Pubs. Group.

Gray, Peter C. Robots. 2006. (Drawing Manga Ser.). (Illus.). 32p. (YA). (gr. 3-6). lib. bdg. 26.50 *(978-1-4042-3332-4(6))* Rosen Publishing Group, Inc., The.

Hamilton, John. Robots & Androids, 1 vol. 2006. (World of Science Fiction Ser.). (ENG., Illus.). 32p. (J). (gr. 4-7). lib. bdg. 27.07 *(978-1-59679-993-6(5)*, Abdo & Daughter) ABDO Publishing Co.

Hayes, Susan & Gordon-Harris, Tory. Really? Robots. 2015. lib. bdg. 19.65 *(978-0-606-37754-6(9))* Turtleback Bks.

Higgins, Nadia. Factory Robots. 2017. (Robotics in Our World Ser.). (ENG.). 32p. (gr. 1-4). 20.95 *(978-1-68151-141-2(X))* Amicus Publishing.

—Medical Robots. 2017. (Robotics in Our World Ser.). (ENG.). 32p. (gr. 1-4). 20.95 *(978-1-68151-143-6(6))* Amicus Publishing.

—Robots at Home. 2017. (Robotics in Our World Ser.). (ENG.). 32p. (gr. 1-4). 20.95 ***(978-1-68151-145-0(2))*** Amicus Publishing.

—Robots in Fiction. 2017. (Robotics in Our World Ser.). (ENG.). 32p. (gr. 1-4). 20.95 ***(978-1-68151-146-7(0))*** Amicus Publishing.

Holzweiss, Kristina. Amazing Makerspace DIY Basic Machines. 2017. (True Book — MakerSpace Projects Ser.). (ENG.). 48p. (J). lib. bdg. 31.00 ***(978-0-531-23844-8(X))*** Scholastic Library Publishing.

Holzweiss, Kristina & Barth, Amy. I Can Make Remarkable Robots. 2017. (Rookie Star — MakerSpace Projects Ser.). (ENG.). 32p. (J). pap. 5.95 ***(978-0-531-23879-0(2))***; lib. bdg. 25.00 ***(978-0-531-23410-5(X))*** Scholastic Library Publishing. (Children's Pr.).

How to Build a Prize-Winning Robot. 2011. (Robotics Ser.). (ENG.). 32p. (YA). pap. 11.75 *(978-1-4488-2252-2(1))* Rosen Publishing Group, Inc., The.

Howard, Ayanna. On the Job with an Engineer. 2003. (Adventures in Science Ser.). (J). pap. *(978-1-58417-122-5(7))*; lib. bdg. *(978-1-58417-059-4(X))* Lake Street Pubs.

Hulick, Kathryn. Robotics Engineer. 2017. (ENG.). 64p. (YA). (gr. 5-12). ***(978-1-68282-186-2(2))*** ReferencePoint Pr., Inc.

Hustad, Douglas. Discover Robotics. 2016. (Searchlight Books (tm) — What's Cool about Science? Ser.). (ENG., Illus.). 40p. (J). (gr. 3-5). 30.65 *(978-1-5124-0809-6(3))* Lerner Publishing Group.

Ithaca, Sciencenter, NY. Is That Robot Real? 2009. 44p. 17.20 *(978-0-578-00196-8(9))* Sciencenter.

Jefferis, David. Robot Brains. 2006. (Robozones Ser.). (ENG., Illus.). 32p. (J). (gr. 3-7). pap. *(978-0-7787-2900-6(1))*; (gr. 4-7). lib. bdg. *(978-0-7787-2886-3(2))* Crabtree Publishing Co.

—Robot Voyagers. 2006. (Robozones Ser.). (ENG., Illus.). 32p. (J). (gr. 4-7). pap. *(978-0-7787-2898-6(6))*; lib. bdg. *(978-0-7787-2884-9(6))* Crabtree Publishing Co.

—Robot Warriors. 2006. (Robozones Ser.). (ENG., Illus.). 32p. (J). (gr. 3-7). pap. *(978-0-7787-2901-3(X))* Crabtree Publishing Co.

—Robot Workers. 2006. (Robozones Ser.). (ENG., Illus.). 32p. (J). (gr. 3-7). lib. bdg. *(978-0-7787-2885-6(4))* Crabtree Publishing Co.

Johnson, Stephen T. My Little Blue Robot. Johnson, Stephen T., illus. 2012. (ENG., Illus.). 16p. (J). (gr. -1-3). 19.99 *(978-1-4424-5416-3(4)*, Simon & Schuster/Paula Wiseman Bks.) Simon & Schuster/Paula Wiseman Bks.

Kenney, Sean. Cool Robots. Kenney, Sean, illus. 2010. (ENG., Illus.). 32p. (J). (gr. -1-3). 14.99 *(978-0-8050-8763-5(X)*, 9780805087635, Holt, Henry & Co. Bks. For Young Readers) Holt, Henry & Co.

Kids Can Press Staff & Becker, Helaine. Zoobots: Wild Robots Inspired by Real Animals, 0 vols. Ries, Alex, illus. 2014. (ENG.). 32p. (J). (gr. 3-7). 17.95 *(978-1-55453-971-0(4))* Kids Can Pr., Ltd. CAN. Dist: Hachette Bk. Group.

Kops, Deborah. Exploring Space Robots. 2011. (Searchlight Books Whats Amazing about Space Ser.). (ENG., Illus.). (gr. 3-5). pap. 51.01 *(978-0-7613-8417-5(0))*; 40p. pap. 8.95 *(978-0-7613-7880-8(4))*; 40p. lib. bdg. 27.93 *(978-0-7613-5445-1(X))* Lerner Publishing Group.

Lacey, Saskia. STEM Careers. 2017. (TIME for KIDS(r) Nonfiction Readers Ser.). 48p. (J). (gr. 7-7). pap. 9.99 *(978-1-4938-3623-9(4))* Teacher Created Materials, Inc.

Lacey, Saskia. STEM Careers: Reinventing Robotics. 2017. (Time for Kids Nonfiction Readers Ser.). lib. bdg. 20.85 ***(978-0-606-40279-8(9))*** Turtleback Bks.

Larson, Kirsten W. Hobby Robots. 2017. (Robotics in Our World Ser.). (ENG.). 32p. (gr. 1-4). 20.95 *(978-1-68151-142-9(8))* Amicus Publishing.

—Military Robots. 2017. (Robotics in Our World Ser.). (ENG.). 32p. (gr. 1-4). 20.95 *(978-1-68151-144-3(4))* Amicus Publishing.

Larson, Kirsten W. Space Robots. 2017. (Robotics in Our World Ser.). (ENG.). 32p. (gr. 1-4). 20.95 ***(978-1-68151-147-4(9))*** Amicus Publishing.

Latta, Sara L. Zoom in on Medical Robots. 2017. (J). ***(978-0-7660-9228-0(3))*** Enslow Pubs., Inc.

Leider, Rick Allen. Robots: Explore the World of Robots & How They Work for Us. 2015. (Fact Atlas Ser.). (ENG., Illus.). 72p. (J). (gr. 2-7). 14.99 *(978-1-63220-439-4(8)*, Sky Pony Pr.) Skyhorse Publishing Co., Inc.

Lindeen, Mary. Humanoid Robots. 2017. (Cutting-Edge Robotics Ser.). (ENG.). 32p. (J). (gr. 3-6). 27.99 ***(978-1-5124-4012-6(4))*** Lerner Publishing Group.

—Law Enforcement Robots. 2017. (Cutting-Edge Robotics Ser.). (ENG.). 32p. (J). (gr. 3-6). 27.99 ***(978-1-5124-4011-9(6))*** Lerner Publishing Group.

—Robot Competitions. 2017. (Cutting-Edge Robotics Ser.). (ENG.). 32p. (J). (gr. 3-6). 27.99 ***(978-1-5124-4010-2(8))*** Lerner Publishing Group.

Littlewood, Peter. Rain Forest Destruction. 2012. (Mapping Global Issues Ser.). 48p. (J). (gr. 7-9). lib. bdg. 34.25 (978-1-59920-512-0(2)) Black Rabbit Bks.

Lovett, Amber. Controlling an Ozobot. 2017. (21st Century Skills Innovation Library: Makers As Innovators Junior Ser.). (ENG., Illus.). 24p. (J). (gr. 2-5). lib. bdg. 28.50 (978-1-63472-187-5(X), 209320) Cherry Lake Publishing.

Manatt, Kathleen G. Robot Scientist. 2007. (21st Century Skills Library: Cool Science Careers Ser.). (ENG., Illus.). 32p. (gr. 4-8). lib. bdg. 28.50 (978-1-60279-051-3(5), 200016) Cherry Lake Publishing.

Masiello, Ralph. Ralph Masiello's Robot Drawing Book. Masiello, Ralph, illus. 2011. (ENG., Illus.). 32p. (J). (gr. 1-4). 16.95 (978-1-57091-535-2(0)) Charlesbridge Publishing, Inc.

McCarthy, Cecilia Pinto. Military Robots. 2017. (Tech Bytes Ser.). (ENG.). 48p. (J). (gr. 4-6). 26.60 **(978-1-59953-888-4(1))**; pap. 13.26 **(978-1-68404-119-0(8))** Norwood Hse. Pr.

McComb, Gordon. Building Your Own Robots. 2016. (Dummies Junior Ser.). (ENG.). 128p. (YA). (gr. 1-5). pap. 9.99 **(978-1-119-30243-8(9)**, For Dummies) Wiley, John & Sons, Inc.

Mercer, Bobby. The Robot Book: Build & Control 20 Electric Gizmos, Moving Machines, & Hacked Toys. 2014. (Science in Motion Ser.). (ENG., Illus.). 208p. (J). (gr. 4). pap. 14.95 (978-1-55652-407-3(2)) Chicago Review Pr., Inc.

Miller, Ron. Robot Explorers. 2007. (Space Innovations Ser.). (ENG., Illus.). 112p. (gr. 6-8). lib. bdg. 31.93 (978-0-8225-7152-0(8)) Lerner Publishing Group.

Mooney, Carla. Awesome Military Robots, 1 vol. 2014. (Ready for Military Action Ser.). (ENG.). 48p. (gr. 3-6). lib. bdg. 32.79 (978-1-62403-649-1(X)) ABDO Publishing Co.

Morey, Allan. Robonauts. 2017. (Space Tech Ser.). (ENG., Illus.). 24p. (J). (gr. 3-7). lib. bdg. 25.95 **(978-1-62617-704-8(X)**, Epic Bks.) Bellwether Media.

Moss, Jenny. How Robots Work. 2013. (Robots Ser.). (ENG.). 32p. (gr. 3-4). pap. 47.70 (978-1-62065-781-2(3), Edge Bks.); lib. bdg. 27.99 (978-1-4296-9919-8(1)); (Illus.). pap. 8.29 (978-1-62065-780-5(5), Edge Bks.) Capstone Press of Coughlan Cos.

Murphy, Maggie. High-Tech DIY Projects with Robotics. 2014. (Maker Kids Ser.). (Illus.). 32p. (J). (gr. 3-6). 27.50 (978-1-4777-6669-9(3)); pap. 11.75 (978-1-4777-6675-0(8)); pap. 70.50 (978-1-4777-6656-9(1)) Rosen Publishing Group, Inc., The. (PowerKids Pr.).

Nagelhout, Ryan. Fighting Robots. 2016. (Robots & Robotics Ser.). (Illus.). 32p. (J). (gr. 5-5). pap. 11.75 (978-1-4994-2163-7(X), PowerKids Pr.) Rosen Publishing Group, Inc., The.

National Geographic Kids Staff. Robots - National Geographic Kids. 2014. (ENG., Illus.). 32p. (J). pap. (978-1-4263-1805-4(7)) National Geographic Society.

Noll, Elizabeth. Factory Robots. 2017. (World of Robots Ser.). (ENG., Illus.). 32p. (J). (gr. 3-8). 26.95 **(978-1-62617-687-4(6)**, Blastoff! Discovery) Bellwether Media.

—Medical Robots. 2017. (World of Robots Ser.). (ENG., Illus.). 32p. (J). (gr. 3-8). lib. bdg. 26.95 **(978-1-62617-689-8(2)**, Blastoff! Discovery) Bellwether Media.

—Military Robots. 2017. (World of Robots Ser.). (ENG., Illus.). 32p. (J). (gr. 3-8). lib. bdg. 26.95 **(978-1-62617-690-4(6)**, Blastoff! Readers) Bellwether Media.

—Police Robots. 2017. (World of Robots Ser.). (ENG., Illus.). 32p. (J). (gr. 3-8). lib. bdg. 26.95 **(978-1-62617-691-1(4)**, Blastoff! Discovery) Bellwether Media.

—Space Robots. 2017. (World of Robots Ser.). (ENG., Illus.). 32p. (J). (gr. 3-8). lib. bdg. 26.95 **(978-1-62617-692-8(2)**, Blastoff! Discovery) Bellwether Media.

Otfinoski, Steven. Making Robots: Science, Technology, & Engineering. 2016. (Calling All Innovators: a Career for You Ser.). (ENG., Illus.). 64p. (J). lib. bdg. 32.00 (978-0-531-21867-9(8), Children's Pr.) Scholastic Library Publishing.

Owen, Ruth. Exploring Distant Worlds As a Space Robot Engineer. 2015. (Get to Work with Science & Technology Ser.). (ENG.). 32p. (J). (gr. 2-7). lib. bdg. 26.60 (978-1-910549-38-4(X)) Bearport Publishing Co., Inc.

Oxlade, Chris. The History of Robots. 2017. (History of Technology Ser.). (ENG.). 32p. (gr. 2-5). lib. bdg. 27.32 **(978-1-4846-4036-4(5)**, Heinemann First Library) Heinemann-Raintree.

Oxlade, Chris. Readers L3: Robots. 2017. (Kingfisher Readers Ser.). (ENG.). 32p. (J). 12.99 (978-0-7534-7343-6(7), 9780753473436, Kingfisher) Roaring Brook Pr.

Parker, Andy. Mekanimals: Robotic Reef, Spanish-Language Edition. 2005. (Mekanimals Ser.). (SPA., Illus.). 8p. (J). bds. (978-970-718-321-6(7), Silver Dolphin en Español) Advanced Marketing, S. de R. L. de C. V.

Parker, Steve. Build the Robot. 2016. (Build It Ser.). (ENG., Illus.). 32p. (J). (gr. 1). 19.95 (978-1-62686-488-7(8), Silver Dolphin Bks.) Readerlink Distribution Services, LLC.

—Robots for Work & Fun. 2010. (Robot World Ser.). 32p. (J). 28.50 (978-1-60753-071-8(6)) Amicus Publishing.

—Robots in Dangerous Places. 2010. (Robot World Ser.). 32p. (J). 28.50 (978-1-60753-072-5(4)) Amicus Publishing.

—Robots in Fiction & Films. 2010. (Robot World Ser.). 32p. (J). 28.50 (978-1-60753-073-2(2)) Amicus Publishing.

—Robots in Science & Medicine. 2010. (Robot World Ser.). (Illus.). 32p. (J). lib. bdg. 28.50 (978-1-60753-074-9(0)) Amicus Publishing.

—Robots in Space. 2010. (Robot World Ser.). 32p. (J). 28.50 (978-1-60753-075-6(9)) Amicus Publishing.

—Robots on the Move. 2010. (Robot World Ser.). 32p. (J). 28.50 (978-1-60753-076-3(7)) Amicus Publishing.

Parker, Steve & Bingham, Jane. Robots in Space. 2011. (On the Edge Ser.). 32p. (YA). (gr. 3-6). lib. bdg. 28.50 (978-1-59920-514-4(9)) Black Rabbit Bks.

Parker, Steve & Pipe, Jim. Robots in Dangerous Places. 2011. (On the Edge Ser.). 32p. (YA). (gr. 3-6). lib. bdg. 28.50 (978-1-59920-516-8(5)) Black Rabbit Bks.

—Robots in Fiction & Films. 2011. (On the Edge Ser.). 32p. (YA). (gr. 3-6). lib. bdg. 28.50 (978-1-59920-515-1(7)) Black Rabbit Bks.

—Robots in Science & Medicine. 2011. (On the Edge Ser.). 32p. (YA). (gr. 3-6). lib. bdg. 28.50 (978-1-59920-513-7(0)) Black Rabbit Bks.

Payment, Simone. Robotics Careers: Preparing for the Future. 2011. (Robotics Ser.). (Illus.). 48p. (YA). (gr. 5-9). 29.25 (978-1-4488-1239-4(9)) Rosen Publishing Group, Inc., The.

Peppas, Lynn. Robotics. 2014. (ENG., Illus.). 48p. (J). (978-0-7787-1369-2(5)) Crabtree Publishing Co.

PRESS, Celebration. Remarkable Robots. 2003. (ENG.). (J). (gr. 6-8). pap. 37.95 (978-0-7652-3243-4(X), Celebration Pr.) Pearson Schl.

Price, Sean Stewart. Amazing Military Robots. 2013. (Robots Ser.). (ENG.). 32p. (gr. 3-4). pap. 47.70 (978-1-62065-777-5(5), Edge Bks.); (Illus.). pap. 8.29 (978-1-62065-776-8(7)) Capstone Press of Coughlan Cos.

—Amazing Military Robots, 1 vol. 2013. (Robots Ser.). (ENG.). 32p. (gr. 3-4). lib. bdg. 27.99 (978-1-4296-9917-4(5)) Capstone Press of Coughlan Cos.

Punter, Russell. Robots. Hamilton, Andrew, illus. 2004. 48p. (J). (gr. 2-18). pap. 5.95 (978-0-7945-0760-2(3), Usborne) EDC Publishing.

Rakos, Lynnda. Let's Color Together — Robots. 2014. (ENG., Illus.). 64p. (J). (gr. -1-3). pap. 3.99 (978-0-486-77977-5(7)) Dover Pubns., Inc.

Rechlin, Ted. Build Your Own Giant Robots Super Sticker Book. 2011. (Dover Sticker Bks.). (ENG., Illus.). 6p. (J). (gr. k-6). 7.99 (978-0-486-48276-7(6)) Dover Pubns., Inc.

Rechlin, Ted & Stickers. Mecha Robot Stickers. 2011. (Dover Little Activity Books Stickers Ser.). (ENG.). 4p. (J). (gr. k-3). pap. 1.50 (978-0-486-48275-0(8)) Dover Pubns., Inc.

Reeve, Tim. Action Robots: A Pop-up Book Showing How They Work. MacLeod, Gavin, illus. 2004. 14p. (YA). (gr. 4-10). reprint ed. 17.00 (978-0-7567-7284-0(2)) DIANE Publishing Co.

Regan, Lisa. Micro Model Battle Bots. 2004. (Illus.). (978-0-439-68926-7(0)) Scholastic, Inc.

Richardson, Erik & Chow-Miller, Ian. Integrated Robotics. 2016. (Robotics Ser.). (ENG., Illus.). 128p. (J). (gr. 9-12). 45.64 (978-1-5026-1936-5(9)) Cavendish Square Publishing.

Robotics. 2016. (Robotics Ser.). 128p. (YA). lib. bdg. 273.84 (978-1-5026-1999-0(7)) Cavendish Square Publishing.

Robotics, 4 vols., Set. Incl. How to Build a Prize-Winning Robot. Chaffee, Joel. lib. bdg. 29.25 (978-1-4488-1238-7(0)); Robotics Careers: Preparing for the Future. Payment, Simone. 29.25 (978-1-4488-1239-4(9)); Robotics Club: Teaming up to Build Robots. Shea, Therese. lib. bdg. 29.25 (978-1-4488-1237-0(2)); Robots Through History. Freedman, Jeri. 29.25 (978-1-4488-1236-3(4)); (YA). (gr. 5-9). 2011. (Robotics Ser.). (Illus.). 48p. 2011. Set lib. bdg. 106.00 (978-1-4488-1392-6(1), Rosen Reference) Rosen Publishing Group, Inc., The.

Robotics Careers: Preparing for the Future. 2011. (Robotics Ser.). (Illus.). 32p. (YA). pap. 11.75 (978-1-4488-2253-9(X), Rosen Reference) Rosen Publishing Group, Inc., The.

The Robotics Club: Teaming up to Build Robots. 2011. (Robotics Ser.). (Illus.). 32p. (YA). pap. 11.75 (978-1-4488-2251-5(3)) Rosen Publishing Group, Inc., The.

Robots & Robotics. 2016. (Robots & Robotics Ser.). 32p. (gr. 5-5). 183.75 (978-1-5081-4903-3(8)); pap. 82.25 (978-1-4994-2456-0(6)) Rosen Publishing Group, Inc., The. (PowerKids Pr.).

Robots Through History. 2011. (Robotics Ser.). (Illus.). 32p. (YA). pap. 11.75 (978-1-4488-2250-8(5), Rosen Reference) Rosen Publishing Group, Inc., The.

Saunders-Smith, Gail. Animal Robots, 1 vol. 2014. (Cool Robots Ser.). (ENG., Illus.). 24p. (gr. k-1). 26.65 (978-1-4914-0588-8(0), Pebble Plus) Capstone Press of Coughlan Cos.

—Robots in Space, 1 vol. 2014. (Cool Robots Ser.). (ENG., Illus.). 24p. (gr. k-1). 26.65 (978-1-4914-0585-7(6), Pebble Plus) Capstone Press of Coughlan Cos.

—Robots on the Job, 1 vol. 2014. (Cool Robots Ser.). (ENG.). 24p. (gr. k-1). 26.65 (978-1-4914-0586-4(4), Pebble Plus) Capstone Press of Coughlan Cos.

Scrace, Carolyn. Drawing Robots. 2016. (Art Works). 32p. (gr. 2-6). 31.35 (978-1-62588-347-6(1), Smart Apple Media) Black Rabbit Bks.

Senker, Cath. Poverty & Hunger. 2012. (Mapping Global Issues Ser.). 48p. (J). (gr. 7-9). lib. bdg. 34.25 (978-1-59920-511-3(4)) Black Rabbit Bks.

ShackletonCaroline. ROBOTS: THE NEXT GENERATION? HIGH INTERMEDIATE BOOK WITH ONLINE ACCESS. 2014. (ENG., Illus.). 28p. pap. 9.50 (978-1-107-67762-3(9)) Cambridge Univ. Pr.

Shaw-Russell, Susan. Robots Activity Book. 2009. (Dover Little Activity Bks.). (ENG., Illus.). 64p. (J). (gr. k-3). pap. 1.99 (978-0-486-47227-0(2)) Dover Pubns., Inc.

Shea, Therese. Getting to Know Lego Mindstorms. 2014. (Code Power: a Teen Programmer's Guide Ser.). (Illus.). 64p. (J). (gr. 5-8). pap. 77.70 (978-1-4777-7704-6(0), Rosen Reference) Rosen Publishing Group, Inc., The.

—The Robotics Club: Teaming up to Build Robots. 2011. (Robotics Ser.). (Illus.). 48p. (YA). (gr. 5-9). lib. bdg. 29.25 (978-1-4488-1237-0(2)) Rosen Publishing Group, Inc., The.

Sherman, Jill. Zoom in on Caregiving Robots. 2017. (J). **(978-0-7660-9229-7(1))** Enslow Pubs., Inc.

Shields, Amy & Stewart, Melissa. National Geographic Readers: Robots. 2014. (Readers Ser.). (ENG.). 48p. (J). (gr. 1-4). pap. 3.99 (978-1-4263-1344-8(6), National Geographic Children's Bks.) National Geographic Society.

Smith, Aubrey. How to Build a Robot (With Your Dad) 20 Easy-to-Build Robotic Projects. 2013. (ENG., Illus.). 168p. (gr. 2-4). pap. 19.99 (978-1-84317-878-1(8)) O'Mara, Michael Bks., Ltd. GBR. Dist: Independent Pubs. Group.

Sobey, Ed. Build Your Own Robot Science Fair Project. 2015. (Prize-Winning Science Fair Projects Ser.). (ENG.). 128p. (J). (gr. 7-7). lib. bdg. 37.27 (978-0-7660-7018-9(2)) Enslow Pubs., Inc.

Sobey, Ed, ed. Robot Experiments. 2011. (Cool Science Projects with Technology Ser.). (Illus.). 128p. (J). (gr. 5-18). lib. bdg. 33.27 (978-0-7660-3303-0(1)) Enslow Pubs., Inc.

Spilsbury, Louise & Spilsbury, Richard. Robots in Industry. 2015. (Amazing Robots Ser.). (ENG.). 48p. (J). (gr. 4-5). pap. 14.05 (978-1-4824-3001-1(0)) Stevens, Gareth Publishing LLLP.

—Robots in Law Enforcement. 2015. (Amazing Robots Ser.). (ENG.). 48p. (J). (gr. 4-5). pap. 14.05 (978-1-4824-3005-9(3)) Stevens, Gareth Publishing LLLP.

—Robots in Medicine. 2015. (Amazing Robots Ser.). (ENG.). 48p. (J). (gr. 4-5). pap. 14.05 (978-1-4824-3009-7(6)) Stevens, Gareth Publishing LLLP.

—Robots in Space. 2015. (Amazing Robots Ser.). (ENG.). 48p. (J). (gr. 4-5). pap. 14.05 (978-1-4824-3013-4(4)) Stevens, Gareth Publishing LLLP.

—Robots in the Military. 2015. (Amazing Robots Ser.). (ENG.). 48p. (J). (gr. 4-5). pap. 14.05 (978-1-4824-3017-2(7)) Stevens, Gareth Publishing LLLP.

—Robots Underwater. 2015. (Amazing Robots Ser.). (ENG.). 48p. (J). (gr. 4-5). pap. 14.05 (978-1-4824-3021-9(5)) Stevens, Gareth Publishing LLLP.

Squishy, Fishy Robot Explorers: Meet NASA Inventor Mason Peck & His Team's. 2017. (J). **(978-0-7166-6156-6(X))** World Bk., Inc.

Stark, William N. Mighty Military Robots. 2016. (Military Machines on Duty Ser.). (ENG.). 24p. (gr. 1-2). lib. bdg. 25.32 (978-1-4914-8847-8(6), First Facts) Capstone Press of Coughlan Cos.

Strom, Laura Layton. From Bugbots to Humanoids: Robotics. 2007. (Shockwave: Technology & Manufacturing Ser.). (ENG., Illus.). 36p. (J). (gr. 4-6). lib. bdg. 25.00 (978-0-531-17585-9(5), Children's Pr.) Scholastic Library Publishing.

Suen, Anastasia. Remarkable Robots. 2003. (ENG., Illus.). 32p. (J). (gr. 6-8). pap. 7.97 net. (978-0-7652-3263-2(4), Celebration Pr.) Pearson Schl.

Swanson, Jennifer. Everything Robotics: All the Robotic Photos, Facts, & Fun! 2016. (National Geographic Kids Everything Ser.). (ENG., Illus.). 64p. (J). (gr. 3-7). pap. 12.99 (978-1-4263-2331-7(X), National Geographic Children's Bks.) National Geographic Society.

Tuchman, Gail. Robots. (Illus.). 32p. (J). 2016. **(978-1-5182-0083-0(4))** 2015. (ENG., (gr. 1-3). pap. 3.99 (978-0-545-89138-7(8)) Scholastic, Inc.

Ventura, Marne. Google Glass & Robotics Innovator Sebastian Thrun. 2014. (STEM Trailblazer Bios Ser.). (ENG., Illus.). 32p. (gr. 2-5). lib. bdg. 26.60 (978-1-4677-2459-3(9), Lerner Pubns.) Lerner Publishing Group.

—The 12 Biggest Breakthroughs in Robot Technology. 2014. (ENG., Illus.). 32p. (J). (978-1-63235-016-9(5)) Pr. Room Editions LLC.

Weakland, Mark. Do-4U the Robot Experiences Forces & Motion. Moran, Mike, illus. 2012. (In the Science Lab Ser.). (ENG.). 24p. (gr. 2-3). pap. 9.95 (978-1-4048-7239-4(6)) Picture Window Bks.

—Do-4U the Robot Experiences Forces & Motion. Moran, Michael & Moran, Mike, illus. 2012. (In the Science Lab Ser.). (ENG.). 24p. (gr. 2-3). lib. bdg. 26.65 (978-1-4048-7145-8(4)) Picture Window Bks.

Woog, Adam. SCRATCHbot. 2010. (Great Idea Ser.). 48p. (J). (gr. 4-6). lib. bdg. 26.60 (978-1-59953-380-3(4)) Norwood Hse. Pr.

Yes Magazine Editors. Robots: From Everyday to Out of This World. 2008. (ENG., Illus.). 48p. (J). (gr. 3-7). 16.95 (978-1-55453-203-2(5)) Kids Can Pr., Ltd. CAN. Dist: Hachette Bk. Group.

Yes Magazine Editors, ed. Robots: From Everyday to Out of This World. Woo, Howie, illus. 2008. (ENG.). 48p. (J). (gr. 3-7). pap. 8.95 (978-1-55453-204-9(3)) Kids Can Pr., Ltd. CAN. Dist: Hachette Bk. Group.

Zuchora-Walske, Christine. Robots at Home. 2014. (Lightning Bolt Books Robots Everywhere! Ser.). (Illus.). 32p. (gr. k-2). (J). lib. bdg. 26.60 (978-1-4677-4054-8(3), Lerner Pubns.); pap. 7.95 (978-1-4677-4509-3(X)) Lerner Publishing Group.

—Weather Robots. 2014. (Lightning Bolt Books Robots Everywhere! Ser.). (Illus.). 32p. (gr. k-2). pap. 7.95 (978-1-4677-4511-6(1)) Lerner Publishing Group.

ROBOTS—FICTION

All Aboard! Softi's Adventures. 2003. (J). mass mkt. (978-1-932233-36-0(9)) Aurora Libris Corp.

Alpert, Mark. The Siege. 2016. (Six Ser.: 2). (ENG.). 288p. (J). (gr. 6-12). 17.99 (978-1-4926-3170-5(1), 9781492631705) Sourcebooks, Inc.

—The Six. 2015. (Six Ser.: 1). (ENG.). 368p. (J). (gr. 6-12). 16.99 (978-1-4926-1529-3(3), 9781492615293) Sourcebooks, Inc.

Ameet Studio Staff, illus. The Tournament of Elements. 2015. (LEGO Ninjago Ser.). (ENG.). 32p. (J). (gr. 1-3). pap., act. bk. ed. 8.99 (978-0-545-80540-7(6)) Scholastic, Inc.

Angleberger, Tom & Dellinger, Paul. Fuzzy. 2016. (ENG.). 272p. (J). (gr. 3-7). 14.95 (978-1-4197-2122-9(4), Amulet Bks.) Abrams, Inc.

The Annoying Crush. 2014. (Galaxy Zack Ser.: 9). (ENG., Illus.). 128p. (J). (gr. k-4). 16.99 (978-1-4424-9364-3(X)); pap. 5.99 (978-1-4424-9363-6(1)) Little Simon. (Little Simon).

Appleton, Victor. The Robot Olympics. 2006. (Tom Swift, Young Inventor Ser.: 2). (ENG.). 176p. (J). (gr. 3-7). pap. 4.99 (978-1-4169-1361-0(0), Aladdin) Simon & Schuster Children's Publishing.

—The Robot Olympics. 2007. (Tom Swift, Young Inventor Ser.). (ENG.). 160p. (gr. 4-7). 27.07 (978-1-59961-351-2(4)) Spotlight.

—The Space Hotel. 2007. (Tom Swift, Young Inventor Ser.). (ENG.). 160p. (gr. 4-7). 27.07 (978-1-59961-353-6(0)) Spotlight.

Ariga, Hitoshi. Mega Man Gigamix, 2 vols., Vol. 3. 2011. (ENG., Illus.). 224p. (J). pap. 13.95 (978-1-926778-31-0(6), 9781926778310) URON Entertainment Corp. CAN. Dist: Diamond Comic Distributors, Inc.

Arnold, Tedd. Fix This Mess! Arnold, Tedd, illus. (I Like to Read(r) Ser.). (ENG., Illus.). 24p. (J). (gr. -1-3). 2015. 6.99 (978-0-8234-3301-8(3)) 2014. 14.95 (978-0-8234-2942-4(3)) Holiday Hse., Inc.

Artifact Group, The & Shepherd, Jodie. Robot Rampage! 2009. (Backyardigans Ser.). (ENG.). 24p. (J). (gr. -1-1). pap. 3.99 (978-1-4169-9013-0(5), Simon Spotlight/Nickelodeon) Simon Spotlight/Nickelodeon.

Asimov, Isaac & Asimov, Janet. Norby's Other Secret. 2010. (Dover Children's Classics Ser.). (ENG.). 144p. (J). (gr. 3-12). pap. 6.99 (978-0-486-47244-7(2)) Dover Pubns., Inc.

Asimov, Janet & Asimov, Isaac. Norby the Mixed-Up Robot. 2010. (Dover Children's Classics Ser.). (ENG.). 96p. (J). (gr. 3-12). pap. 5.99 (978-0-486-47243-0(4)) Dover Pubns., Inc.

Atkins, Jill. Mom's Robot, 1 vol. Leftheri, Eleftheria-Garyfallia, illus. 2013. (Start Reading Ser.). (ENG.). 24p. (gr. k-1). pap. 7.95 (978-1-4765-4119-8(1)) Capstone Press of Coughlan Cos.

Atticus, C. J. Stranded in Space: The Stellar Life of Jpeg the Robot Dog. Domschke, Angelika, illus. 2013. 119p. (J). pap. 6.95 (978-0-9887780-2-3(5)) Atticus, C. J.

Auerbach, Annie. Transformers: Rescue Bots: Meet Boulder the Construction-Bot. 2013. (Passport to Reading Level 1 Ser.). (ENG., Illus.). 32p. (J). (gr. -1-3). 4.99 (978-0-316-22831-2(1)) Little, Brown Bks. for Young Readers.

Aureliani, Franco. Dino-Mike & the Jurassic Portal. Aureliani, Franco, illus. 2015. (Dino-Mike! Ser.). (ENG., Illus.). 128p. (gr. 1-3). lib. bdg. 25.32 (978-1-4342-9630-6(X)) Stone Arch Bks.

Austin, Mike. Junkyard. Austin, Mike, illus. 2014. (ENG., Illus.). 40p. (J). (gr. -1-3). 16.99 (978-1-4424-5961-8(1), Beach Lane Bks.) Beach Lane Bks.

Backer, Charles. Fireclaw. 2010. 288p. pap. 15.49 (978-1-4520-1229-2(6)) AuthorHouse.

Balaban, Mariah. Scooby-Doo & the Rotten Robot, 1 vol. Duendes Del Sur Staff, illus. 2012. (Scooby-Doo! Set 2 Ser.: No. 2). (ENG.). 24p. (J). (gr. k-3). lib. bdg. 24.21 (978-1-59961-868-5(0)) Spotlight.

Balchin, Lance. Mechanica. 2016. (ENG., Illus.). 40p. (J). (gr. 3-7). 17.99 (978-1-4998-0343-3(5)) Little Bee Books Inc.

Bardhan-Quallen, Sudipta. Brobot Bedtime. Campbell, Scott, illus. 2017. (ENG.). 32p. (J). (gr. k-2). 16.95 (978-1-4197-2290-5(5), Abrams Bks. for Young Readers) Abrams, Inc.

Barnes, Phil. My Teacher's a Robot! 2015. (ENG.). 63p. (J). (gr. 1-2). mass mkt. 8.95 (978-1-78455-935-9(0), e0384285-e807-49f7-959d-e33332f5b2d5) Austin, Stan AUS. Dist: Bookmasters Distribution.

Barnett, Mac. Oh No! Or How My Science Project Destroyed the World. Santat, Dan, illus. 2010. (ENG.). 40p. (J). (gr. -1-2). 16.99 (978-1-4231-2312-5(3)) Hyperion Pr.

Barr, Lester. Robots Land at Manchester Airport. 2012. (Illus.). 80p. pap. 13.66 (978-1-4772-2248-5(0)) AuthorHouse.

Bauman, Amy. Everyone Is Special! 2010. 12p. (J). (gr. -1). 9.95 (978-1-60747-719-8(X), Pickwick Pr.) Phoenix Bks., Inc.

Beal, Scott, ed. The Chameleon Toothbrush: New Stories from the Neutral Zone. 2008. (Illus.). 100p. (YA). per. 12.00 (978-0-9779289-4-1(2)) 826michigan.

Bedford, David. Soccer Camp. Brumpton, Keith, illus. 3rd ed. 2004. 80p. (978-1-877003-45-5(X)) Little Hare Bks. AUS. Dist: HarperCollins Pubs. Australia.

Beecroft, Simon. R2-D2 & Friends. 2008. (Star Wars DK Readers Level 2 Ser.). (Illus.). 32p. lib. bdg. 13.55 (978-1-4364-5044-7(6), Turtleback) Turtleback Bks.

Bell, Cece. Rabbit & Robot. 2014. (Candlewick Sparks Ser.). lib. bdg. 13.55 (978-0-606-35169-0(8)) Turtleback Bks.

—Rabbit & Robot: The Sleepover. Bell, Cece, illus. 2012. (ENG., Illus.). 56p. (J). (gr. k-4). 14.99 (978-0-7636-5475-7(2)) Candlewick Pr.

—Rabbit & Robot - The Sleepover. Bell, Cece, illus. 2014. (Candlewick Sparks Ser.). (ENG., Illus.). 56p. (J). (gr. k-4). pap. 3.99 (978-0-7636-6875-4(3)) Candlewick Pr.

—Rabbit & Robot & Ribbit. Bell, Cece, illus. 2016. (ENG., Illus.). 48p. (J). (gr. k-4). 14.99 (978-0-7636-7935-4(6)) Candlewick Pr.

Bellairs, John. The Eyes of the Killer Robot (A Johnny Dixon Mystery: Book Five) 2011. 126p. pap. 14.95 (978-1-61756-340-9(4)) Open Road Integrated Media, Inc.

Benjamin, A. H. Shamwood. 2006. 140p. pap. 24.95 (978-1-4137-9193-8(X)) PublishAmerica, Inc.

Bennett, Chris. Robots & Dinosaurs. 2012. (ENG.). 127p. (J). pap. 16.99 (978-1-926780-26-9(4)) Key Publishing Hse., Inc., The CAN. Dist: Bookmasters Distribution.

Benton, Jim. The Fran with Four Brains, 1 vol. Benton, Jim, illus. 2011. (Franny K. Stein, Mad Scientist Ser.). (ENG., Illus.). 112p. (gr. 3-6). 24.21 (978-1-59961-822-7(2)) Spotlight.

—The Fran with Four Brains. 2007. (Franny K. Stein, Mad Scientist Ser.: 6). lib. bdg. 16.00 (978-1-4177-9038-8(5), Turtleback) Turtleback Bks.

—The Invisible Fran. Benton, Jim, illus. 2004. (Franny K. Stein, Mad Scientist Ser.: 3). (ENG., Illus.). 112p. (J). (gr. 2-5). 17.99 (978-0-689-86293-9(8), Simon & Schuster Bks. For Young Readers) Simon & Schuster Bks. For Young Readers.

—The Invisible Fran, 1 vol. Benton, Jim, illus. 2011. (Franny K. Stein, Mad Scientist Ser.). (ENG., Illus.). 112p. (gr. 3-6). 24.21 (978-1-59961-819-7(2)) Spotlight.

Benz, Derek & Lewis, J. S. The Brimstone Key. 2011. (Grey Griffins: the Clockwork Chronicles Ser.: 1). (ENG.). 400p. (J). (gr. 3-7). pap. 22.99 (978-0-316-04521-6(7)) Little, Brown Bks. for Young Readers.

—The Brimstone Key Bk. 1. 2010. (Grey Griffins: the Clockwork Chronicles Ser.: 1). (ENG., Illus.). 384p. (J). (gr. 3-7). 15.99 (978-0-316-04522-3(5)) Little, Brown Bks. for Young Readers.

—The Relic Hunters: Even Heroes Have to Go to School. 2012. (Grey Griffins: the Clockwork Chronicles Ser.: 2). (ENG.). 384p. (J). (gr. 3-7). pap. 7.99 (978-0-316-04520-9(9)) Little, Brown Bks. for Young Readers.

Black, Jake & Meredith Books Staff. Robo Monster. Stewart, Scott, illus. 2008. 22p. (J). pap. 3.99 (978-0-696-23957-1(4)) Meredith Bks.

Blackwood, Gary. Curiosity. 2015. (ENG.). 336p. (J). (gr. 4-7). 8.99 (978-0-14-242448-3(X), Puffin Books) Penguin Young Readers Group.

Bowen, Carl. Jak & the Magic Nano-Beans: a Graphic Novel. Lozano, Omar, illus. 2016. (Far Out Fairy Tales Ser.). (ENG.). 40p. (gr. 3-4). lib. bdg. 25.32 (978-1-4965-2510-9(8), Far Out Fairy Tales) Stone Arch Bks.

Boyle, Bob. Rosie & Rex: A Nose for Fun! Boyle, Bob, illus. 2014. (ENG., Illus.). 40p. (J). (gr. -1-3). 15.99 (978-0-06-221131-6(5)) HarperCollins Pubs.

Broad, Michael. Zombie Cows! Broad, Michael, illus. 2011. (Agent Amelia Ser.: 2). (ENG., Illus.). 144p. (J). (gr. 2-5). pap. 5.95 (978-0-7613-8066-5(3), Darby Creek);No. 2. lib. bdg. 22.60 (978-0-7613-8057-3(4)) Lerner Publishing Group.

—#2 Zombie Cows! 2011. (Agent Amelia Ser.). pap. 33.92 (978-0-7613-8342-0(5), Darby Creek) Lerner Publishing Group.

Brooks, Kevin. Being. 2008. (ENG.). 352p. (J). (gr. 9). pap. 9.99 *(978-0-439-90342-4(4))*, PUSH) Scholastic, Inc.

Brouwer, Sigmund. Counterattack. 2009. (Robot Wars Ser.: 4). (ENG.). 304p. (YA). pap. 6.99 *(978-1-4143-2312-1(3))*, Tyndale Kids) Tyndale Hse. Pubs.

—Death Trap. 2009. (Robot Wars Ser.: 1). (ENG.). 288p. (YA). pap. 7.99 *(978-1-4143-2309-1(3))*, Tyndale Kids) Tyndale Hse. Pubs.

—Final Battle. 2009. (Robot Wars Ser.: 5). (ENG.). 320p. (YA). pap. 7.99 *(978-1-4143-2313-8(1))*, Tyndale Kids) Tyndale Hse. Pubs.

Brown, Heather. The Robot Book. Brown, Heather, illus. 2010. (ENG., Illus.). 12p. (J). bds. 16.99 *(978-0-7407-9725-5(5))* Andrews McMeel Publishing.

Brown, Jennifer. How Lunchbox Jones Saved Me from Robots, Traitors, & Missy the Cruel. (ENG.). 2017. 256p. (J). pap. 7.99 *(978-1-68119-441-7(4))*, 9781681194417) 2015. 240p. (YA). (gr. 3-6). 16.99 *(978-1-61963-454-1(6))*, 9781619634541) Bloomsbury Publishing USA. (Bloomsbury USA Childrens).

Brown, Judy. Petbots: The Great Escape. 2014. (Petbots Ser.: 1). (ENG., Illus.). 192p. (J). (gr. k-3). pap. 9.99 *(978-1-84812-348-9(5))* Bonnier Publishing GBR. Dist: Independent Pubs. Group.

—School Shutdown. Brown, Judy, illus. 2014. (Petbots Ser.: 2). (ENG., Illus.). 192p. (J). (gr. k-3). pap. 9.99 *(978-1-84812-411-0(2))* Bonnier Publishing GBR. Dist: Independent Pubs. Group.

Brown, Peter. The Wild Robot. 2016. (ENG., Illus.). 288p. (J). (gr. 3-7). 16.99 *(978-0-316-38199-4(3))* Little, Brown Bks. for Young Readers.

Brown, Sam. Sometimes I Forget You're a Robot. 2013. (ENG., Illus.). 32p. (J). (gr. -1-k). 16.99 *(978-0-8037-3825-6(0))*, Dial Bks) Penguin Young Readers Group.

Bunting, Eve. My Robot. Fehlau, Dagmar, illus. 2006. (Green Light Readers Level 2 Ser.). (ENG.). 24p. (J). (gr. -1-3). pap. 3.95 *(978-0-15-205617-9(3))* Houghton Mifflin Harcourt Publishing Co.

—My Robot. Fehlau, Dagmar, illus. 2006. (Green Light Readers Level 2 Ser.). (gr. k-2). lib. bdg. 13.95 *(978-0-7569-7211-0(6))* Perfection Learning Corp.

Burks, James. Beep & Bah. Burks, James, illus. 2012. (Carolrhoda Picture Bks.). (ENG., Illus.). 32p. (J). (gr. k-3). lib. bdg. 16.95 *(978-0-7613-6567-9(2))* Lerner Publishing Group.

Burns, Dal. The Adventures of Phoo. 2006. 148p. pap. 24.95 *(978-1-4241-1773-4(9))* PublishAmerica, Inc.

Burroughs, Scott, illus. Robot Rumble. 2013. (Hardy Boys: the Secret Files Ser.: 11). (ENG.). 96p. (J). (gr. 1-4). pap. 5.99 *(978-1-4424-5367-8(2))*, Aladdin) Simon & Schuster Children's Publishing.

Byrne, Bob. Robots Don't Cry. 2006. (Flyers Ser.: 15). (ENG., Illus.). 64p. (J). pap. 9.95 *(978-1-84717-005-7(6))* O'Brien Pr., Ltd., The IRL. Dist: Dufour Editions, Inc.

Capetta, Amy Rose. Entangled. (ENG.). (YA). (gr. 9). 2014. 352p. pap. 9.99 *(978-0-544-33624-7(0))*, HMH Books For Young Readers) 2013. 336p. 17.99 *(978-0-544-08744-6(5))* Houghton Mifflin Harcourt Publishing Co.

Carbone, Courtney. High-Stakes Heist! Atiyeh, Michael & Borkowski, Michael, illus. 2016. (Little Golden Book Ser.). (ENG.). 24p. (J). (-k). 4.99 *(978-0-385-37426-2(7))*, Golden Bks.) Random Hse. Children's Bks.

Carlson, Bryce. Wall- E: Out There. Luthi, Morgan, illus. 2010. (ENG.). 112p. (J). (gr. 3-6). pap. 9.99 *(978-1-60886-568-0(1))* Boom! Studios.

Carrick, Paul. Watch Out for Wolfgang. Carrick, Paul, illus. 2009. (ENG., Illus.). 32p. (J). (gr. -1-3). 16.95 *(978-1-57091-689-2(6))* Charlesbridge Publishing, Inc.

Carriger, Gail. Curtsies & Conspiracies. (Finishing School Ser.: 2). (ENG.). (YA). (gr. 7-17). 2014. 336p. pap. 10.00 *(978-0-316-19020-6(9))* 2013. 320p. 18.00 *(978-0-316-19011-4(X))* Little, Brown Bks. for Young Readers.

—Etiquette & Espionage. 2013. (Finishing School Ser.: 1). (ENG.). 320p. (YA). (gr. 7-17). 18.99 *(978-0-316-19008-4(X))* Little Brown & Co.

—Etiquette & Espionage. 2013. (Finishing School Ser.: 1). (ENG.). 336p. (YA). (gr. 7-17). pap. 10.99 *(978-0-316-19010-7(1))* Little, Brown Bks. for Young Readers.

Catalanotto, Peter. Monkey & Robot. Catalanotto, Peter, illus. (ENG., Illus.). 64p. (J). (gr. 1-4). 2014. pap. 5.99 *(978-1-4424-2979-6(8))*, Atheneum Bks. for Young Readers) 2013. 12.99 *(978-1-4424-2978-9(X))*, Atheneum/Richard Jackson Bks.) Simon & Schuster Children's Publishing.

—More of Monkey & Robot. Catalanotto, Peter, illus. 2014. (ENG., Illus.). 64p. (J). (gr. 1-4). 15.99 *(978-1-4424-5251-0(X))*, Atheneum/Richard Jackson Bks.) Simon & Schuster Children's Publishing.

Cawthon, Scott & Breed-Wrisley, Kira. The Silver Eyes. 2016. (Five Nights at Freddy's Ser.: 1). (ENG.). 400p. (J). (gr. 7-7). pap. 9.99 *(978-1-338-13437-7(X))* Scholastic, Inc.

Cawthon, Scott & Breed-Wrisley, Kira. The Silver Eyes. 2016. (Five Nights at Freddy's Ser.: bk.1). (YA). lib. bdg. 20.85 ***(978-0-606-39982-1(8))*** Turtleback Bks.

Chang, Margaret. Celia's Robot. 2009. (ENG.). 208p. (J). (gr. 3-7). 16.95 *(978-0-8234-2181-7(3))* Holiday Hse., Inc.

Chiaramonti, Gregory. Probie: the Space Probe, Mission One: the Ocean of Europa. 2007. 32p. (J). 16.72 *(978-0-615-13848-0(9))* Chiaramonti, Gregory.

Clark, Kent & Snider, Brandon T. Peter Powers & the Rowdy Robot Raiders. Bardin, Dave, illus. 2017. (Peter Powers Ser.: 2). (ENG.). 128p. (J). (gr. 1-5). pap. 5.99 *(978-0-316-35938-2(6))* Little, Brown Bks. for Young Readers.

—Peter Powers & the Rowdy Robot Raiders! Bardin, Dave, illus. 2016. (Peter Powers Ser.: 2). (ENG.). 128p. (J). (gr. 1-5). 15.99 *(978-0-316-35941-2(6))* Little, Brown Bks. for Young Readers.

Clements, Richmond. Turning Tiger Special Edition. Finbow, Alexander, ed. 2012. (Illus.). 56p. pap. 7.99 *(978-1-926914-87-9(2))* Arcana Studio, Inc.

Collicutt, Paul. Rust Attack! Collicutt, Paul, illus. 2009. (Robot City Ser.: 2). (ENG., Illus.). 48p. (J). (gr. 3-7). pap. 8.99 *(978-0-7636-4594-6(X))*, Templar) Candlewick Pr.

Cornwell, Betsy. Mechanica. 2016. lib. bdg. 19.65 *(978-0-606-37999-1(1))* Turtleback Bks.

Courtenay, L. A. Space Penguins Star Attack! Davies, James, illus. 2015. (Space Penguins Ser.). (ENG.). 112p. (J). (gr. 2-3). lib. bdg. 22.65 *(978-1-4342-9784-6(5))* Stone Arch Bks.

Craddock, Erik. Robot Frenzy. 2013. (Stone Rabbit Ser.: 8). lib. bdg. 17.20 *(978-0-606-27004-5(3))*, Turtleback) Turtleback Bks.

—Stone Rabbit #8: Robot Frenzy. Craddock, Erik, illus. 2013. (Stone Rabbit Ser.). (ENG., Illus.). 96p. (J). (gr. 2-5). pap. 6.99 *(978-0-375-86913-6(1))*; lib. bdg. 12.99 *(978-0-375-96913-3(6))* Random Hse. Children's Bks. (Random Hse. Bks. for Young Readers).

Craig, Joe. Jimmy Coates: Assassin? 2005. 224p. (J). (gr. 5-18). 15.99 *(978-0-06-077263-5(8))* HarperCollins Pubs.

—Jimmy Coates: Assassin? 2006. 218p. (J). (gr. 5-9). per. 5.99 *(978-0-06-077265-9(4))*, Harper Trophy) HarperCollins Pubs.

Curtis, Simon. Boy Robot. 2016. (ENG., Illus.). 432p. (YA). (gr. 9). 17.99 *(978-1-4814-5929-7(5))*, Simon Pulse) Simon Pulse.

Cushman, Doug. Space Cat. Cushman, Doug, illus. 2006. (I Can Read Level 1 Ser.). (ENG., Illus.). 32p. (J). (gr. -1-3). pap. 3.99 *(978-0-06-008967-2(9))* HarperCollins Pubs.

—Space Cat. Cushman, Doug, illus. 2006. (I Can Read Bks.). (Illus.). 32p. (J). (gr. -1-3). 14.00 *(978-0-7569-6977-6(8))* Perfection Learning Corp.

Cusick, John M. Girl Parts. (ENG., Illus.). 240p. (YA). (gr. 9). 2012. pap. 7.99 *(978-0-7636-5644-7(5))* 2010. 16.99 *(978-0-7636-4930-2(9))* Candlewick Pr.

Dahl, Michael. Dino Death-Trap. Vecchio, Luciano, illus. 2016. (Batman Tales of the Batcave Ser.). (ENG.). 40p. (gr. 1-3). lib. bdg. 24.65 *(978-1-4965-4015-7(8))*, DC Super Heroes) Stone Arch Bks.

—The Robot That Barked. Levins, Tim & Vecchio, Luciano, illus. 2017. (Superman Tales of the Fortress of Solitude Ser.). (ENG.). 40p. (gr. 1-3). lib. bdg. 24.65 *(978-1-4965-4397-4(1))*, DC Super Heroes) Stone Arch Bks.

Dean, James. Pete the Cat - Robo-Pete. Dean, James, illus. 2015. (Pete the Cat Ser.). (ENG., Illus.). 24p. (J). (gr. -1-3). pap. 4.99 *(978-0-06-230427-8(5))*, HarperFestival) HarperCollins Pubs.

Derdowski, Chad. All Robots Must Die: Nacho-Geddon. 2013. 187p. (J). pap. 7.99 *(978-1-933925-50-9(7))*, Agent of Danger) Komikwerks, LLC.

Dinardo, Jeff. Klink & Klank: Accepting Differences. Paillot, Jim, illus. 2014. (Funny Bone Readers: Being a Friend Ser.). 24p. (gr. -1-1). pap. 4.99 *(978-1-939656-04-9(4))* Red Chair Pr.

Dipucchio, Kelly. Clink. Myers, Matthew, illus. 2011. (ENG.). 32p. (J). (gr. -1-2). 16.99 *(978-0-06-192928-1(X))* HarperCollins Pubs.

Disney Book Group. Miles from Tomorrowland Mighty Merc. Disney Storybook Art Team, illus. 2015. (ENG.). 24p. (J). (gr. -1-k). pap. 3.99 *(978-1-4847-1552-9(7))* Disney Pr.

Disney Book Group Staff & Schaefer, Elizabeth A. Hera's Phantom Flight, Level 2. 2015. (World of Reading Ser.). (ENG.). 32p. (J). (gr. 1-3). pap. 3.99 *(978-1-4847-0465-3(7))*, Disney Lucasfilm Press) Disney Publishing Worldwide.

Disney Press Editors. Star Wars: Escape from Darth Vader. 2014. (Star Wars: World of Reading Ser.). (J). lib. bdg. 13.55 *(978-0-606-35924-5(9))* Turtleback Bks.

Dolamore, Jaclyn. Magic under Glass. (Magic under Glass Ser.). (ENG.). (YA). (gr. 7). 2011. 256p. pap. 8.99 *(978-1-59990-587-7(6))*, 9781599905877) 2010. 240p. 16.99 *(978-1-59990-430-6(6))*, 9781599904306) Bloomsbury Publishing USA. (Bloomsbury USA Childrens).

—Magic under Stone. 2012. (Magic under Glass Ser.). (ENG.). 304p. (YA). 16.99 *(978-1-59990-643-0(0))*, 9781599906430, Bloomsbury USA Childrens) Bloomsbury Publishing USA.

Donahue, Peter & Coloring Books Staff. Robot Buddies Stained Glass Coloring Book. 2012. (Dover Stained Glass Coloring Book Ser.). (ENG., Illus.). 32p. (J). (gr. k-5). pap. 6.99 *(978-0-486-48673-4(7))* Dover Pubns., Inc.

Dorling Kindersley Publishing Staff. The Adventures of C-3PO. 2014. (Star Wars DK Readers Level 2 Ser.). lib. bdg. 13.55 *(978-0-606-35324-3(0))* Turtleback Bks.

—Big Hero 6. 2014. (ENG.). 64p. (J). (gr. k-4). 12.99 *(978-1-4654-2270-5(6))*, DK Children) Dorling Kindersley Publishing, Inc.

—Blast Off! 2010. (DK Readers Ser.). (ENG.). 32p. (J). (gr. -1-1). 14.99 *(978-0-7566-6879-2(4))*, DK Children) Dorling Kindersley Publishing, Inc.

—The Brain Wars. 2013. (DK Reader Level 3 Ser.). lib. bdg. 13.55 *(978-0-606-32114-3(4))*, Turtleback) Turtleback Bks.

Dorling Kindersley Publishing Staff & Last, Shari. The Adventures of C-3PO. 2014. (DK Readers Ser.). (ENG.). 32p. (J). (gr. 1-3). pap. 3.99 *(978-1-4654-1682-7(X))*, DK Children) Dorling Kindersley Publishing, Inc.

Dower, Laura. They Came from Planet Q. Schlafman, Dave, illus. 2010. (Monster Squad Ser.: 4). (ENG.). 144p. (J). (gr. 2-4). pap. 5.99 *(978-0-448-44915-9(3))*, Grosset & Dunlap) Penguin Young Readers Group.

Driscoll, Laura & Random House Disney Staff. Smash Trash! Cortes, Mario et al, illus. 2008. (Step into Reading Ser.). (ENG.). 32p. (J). (gr. k-3). pap. 3.99 *(978-0-7364-2515-5(2))*, RH/Disney) Random Hse. Children's Bks.

Driza, Debra. Mila 2.0. 2013. (Mila 2. 0 Ser.: 1). (ENG.). 480p. (YA). (gr. 8). 17.99 *(978-0-06-209036-2(4))*, Tegen, Katherine Bks) HarperCollins Pubs.

—Mila 2.0: Redemption. 2016. (Mila 2. 0 Ser.: 3). (ENG.). 416p. (YA). (gr. 8). 17.99 *(978-0-06-209042-3(9))*, Tegen, Katherine Bks) HarperCollins Pubs.

Duffett-Smith, James. A Curious Robot on Mars! Straker, Bethany, illus. 2013. (ENG.). 32p. (J). (gr. -1-k). 14.95 *(978-1-62087-994-8(8))*, 620994, Sky Pony Pr.) Skyhorse Publishing Co., Inc.

Dunkle, Clare B. The Walls Have Eyes. 2009. (ENG.). 240p. (YA). (gr. 7). 16.99 *(978-1-4169-5379-1(5))*, Atheneum Bks. for Young Readers) Simon & Schuster Children's Publishing.

Dyckman, Ame. Boy & Bot. Yaccarino, Dan, illus. (ENG.). (J). (-k). 2016. 24p. bds. 7.99 *(978-1-101-93688-7(5))* 2012. 32p. E-Book *(978-0-375-98724-3(X))* 2012. 32p. 16.99 *(978-0-375-86756-9(2))* Random Hse. Children's Bks. (Knopf Bks. for Young Readers).

Dyckman, Ame. Girl + Bot. Yaccarino, Dan, illus. 2017. (J). ***(978-1-5247-0072-0(X))*** Knopf, Alfred A. Inc.

Eliopoulis, Chris, text. Franklin Richards: Son of a Genius Ultimate Collection - Book 1. 2010. (ENG., Illus.). 208p. (J). (gr. -1-17). pap., pap. 19.99 *(978-0-7851-4924-8(4))* Marvel Worldwide, Inc.

Elson, Maya Mackowiak. The Mystery of the Pirate Bell. 2013. (Transformers 8x8 Ser.). (J). lib. bdg. 13.55 *(978-0-606-32273-7(6))*, Turtleback) Turtleback Bks.

Emberley, Rebecca. Spare Parts. Emberley, Ed, illus. 2015. (ENG.). 32p. (J). (gr. -1-2). 17.99 *(978-1-59643-723-4(5))*, 9781596437234) Roaring Brook Pr.

Evans, D. L. & Sinclair, Valerie. How Rolly Robot Saved the Starbabies, 1 vol. 2012. (ENG., Illus.). 32p. (J). *(978-1-55455-201-6(X))* Fitzhenry & Whiteside, Ltd.

Evans, Dustin, illus. Raging Robots, 1 vol. 2013. (Mystical Pencil Ser.). (ENG.). 32p. (J). (gr. 3-6). 28.50 *(978-1-61641-929-5(6))* Magic Wagon.

Fee, J. M. The Amazing Adventures of Phineas Screwdriver. 2012. 64p. pap. 20.95 *(978-1-4497-7236-9(6))*, WestBow Pr.) Author Solutions, Inc.

Fentiman, David. The Adventures of BB-8. 2016. (Star Wars DK Readers Level 2 Ser.). lib. bdg. 13.55 *(978-0-606-38709-5(9))* Turtleback Bks.

Fickling, Phillip. Fillmore & Geary Take Off! Shulman, Mark, illus. 2003. 40p. (J). lib. bdg. *(978-1-58717-258-8(5))*, SeaStar Bks.) Chronicle Bks. LLC.

Fisch, Sholly, et al. Manhandled by Manhunters! 2015. (All-New Batman: the Brave & the Bold Ser.). (ENG., Illus.). 32p. (gr. 2-3). lib. bdg. 22.60 *(978-1-4342-9662-7(8))* Stone Arch Bks.

Fliess, Sue. Robots, Robots Everywhere. Staake, Bob, illus. 2014. (Little Golden Board Book Ser.). (ENG.). 26p. (J). (-k). bds. 7.99 *(978-0-385-38924-2(8))*, Random Hse. Bks. for Young Readers) Random Hse. Children's Bks.

Fox, Helen. Eager. 2006. (ENG.). 288p. (J). (gr. 3-7). 6.99 *(978-0-553-48795-4(7))*, Yearling) Random Hse. Children's Bks.

Fox, Jennifer. Meet Optimus Prime. 2015. (Passport to Reading Level 1 Ser.). (ENG., Illus.). 32p. (J). (gr. -1-3). pap. 3.99 *(978-0-316-40558-4(2))* Little, Brown Bks. for Young Readers.

—Meet Optimus Prime. 2015. (Transformers Passport to Reading Ser.). (J). lib. bdg. 13.55 *(978-0-606-35938-2(9))* Turtleback Bks.

Foxe, Steve. Decepticon Island! 2017. (Transformers Passport to Reading Ser.). (J). lib. bdg. 14.75 ***(978-0-606-39908-1(9))*** Turtleback Bks.

Frampton, Otis. Red Riding Hood, Superhero. Frampton, Otis, illus. 2015. (Far Out Fairy Tales Ser.). (ENG., Illus.). 40p. (gr. 3-4). lib. bdg. 25.32 *(978-1-4342-9650-4(4))* Stone Arch Bks.

Gabolinscy, Jack. Do Not Disturb. Cashmore-Hingley, Michael, illus. 2013. (ENG.). 24p. (gr. 3-4). pap. *(978-1-77654-019-8(0))*, Red Rocket Readers) Flying Start Bks.

Gage, Brian. The Saddest Little Robot. Otoshi, Kathryn, tr. Otoshi, Kathryn, illus. 2004. (ENG.). 90p. (J). 16.95 *(978-1-932360-05-9(0))* Cricket Bks.

Gall, Chris, illus. NanoBots. 2016. (ENG.). 40p. (J). (gr. -1-3). 16.99 *(978-0-316-37552-8(7))* Little Brown & Co.

Gelsey, James & Duendes Del Sur Staff. Scooby-Doo & the Runaway Robot, 1 vol. 2011. (Scooby-Doo Mysteries Ser.). (ENG., Illus.). 64p. (J). (gr. 3-6). 24.21 *(978-1-59961-892-0(3))* Spotlight.

Golden Books. Fix It up! (Rusty Rivets) Lovett, Nate, illus. 2017. (Deluxe Paint Box Book Ser.). (ENG.). 128p. (J). (gr. -1-2). pap. 7.99 ***(978-1-5247-1674-5(X))***, Golden Bks.) Random Hse. Children's Bks.

—I Am a Droid (Star Wars) Kennett, Chris, illus. 2016. (Little Golden Book Ser.). (ENG.). 24p. (J). (-k). 4.99 *(978-0-7364-3489-8(5))*, Golden Bks.) Random Hse. Children's Bks.

—I Am a Sith (Star Wars) Kennett, Chris, illus. 2016. (Little Golden Book Ser.). (ENG.). 24p. (J). (-k). 4.99 *(978-0-7364-3607-6(3))*, Golden Bks.) Random Hse. Children's Bks.

Golden Books. Rusty's Robot Rescue (Rusty Rivets) Dynamo Limited, illus. 2017. (Color Plus Crayons & Sticker Ser.). (ENG.). 48p. (J). (gr. -1-2). pap. 4.99 ***(978-1-5247-1675-2(8))***, Golden Bks.) Random Hse. Children's Bks.

Golden Books Staff. Follow the Ninja! Golden Books Staff & Lambe, Steve, illus. 2015. (Little Golden Book Ser.). (ENG.). 24p. (J). (-k). 4.99 *(978-0-553-51204-5(8))*, Golden Bks.) Random Hse. Children's Bks.

Grant, Gavin J. & Link, Kelly, eds. Steampunk! an Anthology of Fantastically Rich & Strange Stories. 2013. (ENG.). 432p. (YA). (gr. 9). pap. 16.99 *(978-0-7636-5797-0(2))* Candlewick Pr.

Gray, Claudia. Defy the Stars. 2017. (Defy the Stars Ser.: 1). (ENG.). 512p. (YA). (gr. 10-17). 17.99 *(978-0-316-39403-1(3))* Little, Brown Bks. for Young Readers.

Grecian, Alexander. Rocketbots: Trouble in Time: Trouble in Time. 2010. 48p. (YA). 12.99 *(978-1-60706-183-0(X))* Image Comics.

Greenburg, J. C. In the Desert. Gerardi, Jan, illus. 2008. (Andrew Lost Ser.: 17). (ENG.). 96p. (J). (gr. 1-4). per. 3.99 *(978-0-375-84667-0(0))*, Random Hse. Bks. for Young Readers) Random Hse. Children's Bks.

—In the Jungle. 2007. (Andrew Lost Ser.: 15). (ENG., Illus.). 96p. (J). (gr. 1-4). 3.99 *(978-0-375-83564-3(4))*, Random Hse. Bks. for Young Readers) Random Hse. Children's Bks.

Gritton, Steve. The Trouble with Sisters & Robots. 2012. (J). 34.28 *(978-1-61913-150-7(1))* Weigl Pubs., Inc.

Haddix, Margaret Peterson. In over Their Heads. 2017. (Under Their Skin Ser.: 2). (ENG., Illus.). 320p. (J). (gr. 3-7). 16.99 *(978-1-4814-1761-7(4))*, Simon & Schuster Bks. For Young Readers) Simon & Schuster Bks. For Young Readers.

—Under Their Skin. 2016. (Under Their Skin Ser.: 1). (ENG.). 320p. (J). (gr. 3-7). 16.99 *(978-1-4814-1758-7(4))*, Simon & Schuster Bks. For Young Readers) Simon & Schuster Bks. For Young Readers.

Hale, Bruce. Murder, My Tweet. 2005. (Chet Gecko Mystery Ser.). (Illus.). 117p. (gr. 3-7). 16.00 *(978-0-7569-5248-8(4))* Perfection Learning Corp.

Hale, Nathan. One Trick Pony. 2017. (ENG., Illus.). 128p. (J). (gr. 3-7). 14.95 *(978-1-4197-2128-1(3))*, Amulet Bks.) Abrams, Inc.

Hall, Susan, illus. Robot Repairman to the Rescue! 2009. (Backyardigans Ser.). (ENG.). 24p. (J). (gr. -1-2). pap. 3.99 *(978-1-4169-9012-3(7))*, Simon Spotlight/Nickelodeon) Simon Spotlight/Nickelodeon.

Hamilton, Kersten. The Ire of Iron Claw. Hamilton, James, illus. (Gadgets & Gears Ser.: 2). (ENG.). (J). (gr. 2-5). 2016. 192p. pap. 6.99 *(978-0-544-66854-6(5))*, HMH Books For Young Readers) 2015. 176p. 16.99 *(978-0-544-22502-2(3))* Houghton Mifflin Harcourt Publishing Co.

Harrison, Zac. Galactic Battle, 1 vol. 2014. (Hyperspace High Ser.). (ENG., Illus.). 288p. (gr. 4-8). 27.32 *(978-1-4342-6569-2(2))* Stone Arch Bks.

Hasbro. Transformers Rescue Bots: Reading Adventures: Passport to Reading Level 1. 2015. (Passport to Reading Level 1 Ser.). (ENG., Illus.). 192p. (J). (gr. -1-1). pap. 7.99 *(978-0-316-28627-5(3))* Little, Brown Bks. for Young Readers.

Hatke, Ben. Legends of Zita the Spacegirl. Hatke, Ben, illus. 2012. (Zita the Spacegirl Ser.: 2). (ENG., Illus.). 224p. (J). (gr. 3-7). 19.99 *(978-1-59643-806-4(1))*, 9781596438064); pap. 12.99 *(978-1-59643-447-9(3))*, 9781596434479) Roaring Brook Pr. (First Second Bks.).

—Legends of Zita the Spacegirl. 2012. (Zita the Spacegirl Ser.: 2). (J). lib. bdg. 24.50 *(978-0-606-26708-3(5))*, Turtleback) Turtleback Bks.

Hench, Larry. Boing-Boing the Bionic Cat & the Jewel Thief. Steed, Tobias, ed. Lear, Ruth, illus. 2004. (Boing-Boing the Bionic Cat Ser.: 2). (ENG.). 60p. (J). (gr. 2-4). pap. 7.99 *(978-1-904872-01-6(8))*, Can of Worms Kids Pr.) Can of Worms Pr. GBR. Dist: Independent Pubs. Group.

—Boing-Boing the Bionic Cat & the Space Station. Morgan-Jones, Tom, illus. 2011. (Boing-Boing the Bionic Cat Ser.: 5). (ENG.). 96p. (J). (gr. 2-4). pap. 8.99 *(978-1-904872-07-8(7))*, Can of Worms Kids Pr.) Can of Worms Pr. GBR. Dist: Independent Pubs. Group.

Hodgson, Karen J. The Robot Who Couldn't Cry. Dina, Madalina, illus. 2010. (ENG.). 32p. (J). (gr. -1-2). pap. 9.99 *(978-1-907432-01-9(9))* Hogs Back Bks. GBR. Dist: Independent Pubs. Group.

Holmes, Kimberly. Digibots Classroom Adventures. Lawson, Devin, illus. 2004. (J). *(978-0-9755725-0-4(4))*, 1238415) Digibots Corp.

Hopper, Ada. Robots Rule the School. Ricks, Sam, illus. 2016. (DATA Set Ser.: bk.4). (ENG.). 128p. (J). (gr. k-4). pap. 5.99 *(978-1-4814-6312-6(8))*, Little Simon) Little Simon.

Howard, Lee. Scooby-Doo & the High Tech House of the Future, 1 vol. 2016. (Scooby-Doo Comic Readers Ser.). (ENG.). 32p. (J). (gr. k-3). lib. bdg. 24.21 *(978-1-61479-452-3(9))*, Graphic Planet) Magic Wagon.

Huddleston, Courtney & Zirkel, Scott. A Bit Haywire. Huddleston, Courtney, illus. 2006. (Illus.). 112p. per. 11.95 *(978-0-9777883-5-4(0))* Viper Comics.

Irvine, Alexander C. & Preiss, Byron. Have Robot, Will Travel. 2013. 222p. pap. 19.95 *(978-1-59687-959-1(9))* ibooks, Inc.

JibJab Bros Studios. Trucks Are Terrific! (StoryBots) JibJab Bros Studios, illus. 2017. (ENG., Illus.). 24p. (J). (— 1). bds. 7.99 ***(978-1-5247-1825-1(4))***, Random Hse. Bks. for Young Readers) Random Hse. Children's Bks.

Jung, Mike. Geeks, Girls, & Secret Identities. Maihack, Mike, illus. 2012. (J). (ENG.). 320p. (gr. 3-7). 16.99 *(978-0-545-33548-5(5))*; pap. *(978-0-545-33549-2(3))* Scholastic, Inc. (Levine, Arthur A. Bks.).

Kade, J. V. The Meta-Rise. 2nd ed. 2014. (Bot Wars Ser.). (ENG., Illus.). 304p. (J). (gr. 5). 17.99 *(978-0-8037-3861-4(7))*, Dial Bks) Penguin Young Readers Group.

Kazenbroot, Nelly. Over the Rainbow with Googol & Googolplex, 1 vol. 2006. (Orca Echoes Ser.). (ENG., Illus.). 64p. (J). (gr. 2-3). per. 4.99 *(978-1-55143-469-8(5))* Orca Bk. Pubs. USA.

—Under the Sea with Googol & Googolplex. 2005. 63p. (J). lib. bdg. 20.00 *(978-1-4242-1263-7(4))* Fitzgerald Bks.

—Under the Sea with Googol & Googolplex, 1 vol. 2005. (Orca Echoes Ser.). (ENG., Illus.). 64p. (J). (gr. 2-3). per. 6.95 *(978-1-55143-366-0(4))* Orca Bk. Pubs. USA.

Keats, Israel. Alien Invasion. 2017. (Level Up Ser.). (ENG.). (J). (gr. 6-12). 120p. pap. 7.99 ***(978-1-5124-5356-0(0))***; lib. bdg. 26.65 ***(978-1-5124-3984-7(3))*** Lerner Publishing Group. (Darby Creek).

Kessler, MacKenzie. Murphy the Lonely Robot/Cecil the Lonely Pterodactyl. 2010. 52p. pap. 14.00 *(978-0-557-22226-1(5))* Lulu Pr., Inc.

Kibuishi, Kazu. Escape from Lucien. 2014. (Amulet Ser.: 6). lib. bdg. 24.50 *(978-0-606-36039-5(5))* Turtleback Bks.

Korman, Gordon. Ungifted. 288p. (J). (gr. 5). 2014. pap. 7.99 *(978-0-06-174267-5(8))* 2012. 16.99 *(978-0-06-174266-8(X))* 2012. lib. bdg. 17.89 *(978-0-06-174268-2(6))* HarperCollins Pubs.

Kozlowsky, M. P. Frost. 2016. (ENG.). 352p. (J). (gr. 9). 17.99 *(978-0-545-83191-8(1))*, Scholastic Pr.) Scholastic, Inc.

Krosoczka, Jarrett J. Lunch Lady & the Cyborg Substitute. 2009. (Lunch Lady Ser.). (ENG.). 96p. (J). (gr. 3-7). pap. 6.99 *(978-0-375-84683-0(2))*; lib. bdg. 12.99 *(978-0-375-94683-7(7))* Random Hse. Children's Bks. (Knopf Bks. for Young Readers).

Krulik, Nancy & Burwasser, Amanda Elizabeth. Science No Fair! Project Droid #1. Moran, Mike, illus. 2016. (Project Droid Ser.). (ENG.). 112p. (J). (gr. 1-4). 13.99 *(978-1-5107-1018-4(3))*, Sky Pony Pr.) Skyhorse Publishing Co., Inc.

—Soccer Shocker! Moran, Mike, illus. 2016. (Project Droid Ser.). (ENG.). 104p. (J). (gr. 1-4). pap. 4.99 *(978-1-5107-1029-0(9))*, Sky Pony Pr.) Skyhorse Publishing Co., Inc.

Kuhlman, Evan. Brother from a Box. Bruno, Iacopo, illus. (ENG.). 288p. (J). (gr. 4-7). 2013. pap. 6.99 *(978-1-4424-2659-7(4))* 2012. 16.99 *(978-1-4424-2658-0(6))* Simon & Schuster Children's Publishing. (Atheneum Bks. for Young Readers).

Kurtz, Rob. Meet the Robots. 2011. 20p. pap. 5.99 *(978-1-60010-512-8(2))* Idea & Design Works, LLC.

—Robots to the Rescue! 2011. 32p. pap. 3.99 *(978-1-60010-513-5(0))* Idea & Design Works, LLC.

Layne, Steven L. Paradise Lost, 1 vol. (ENG.). 312p. (YA). (gr. 7-12). 2013. pap. 8.95 *(978-1-4556-1775-3(X))* 2011. 15.99 *(978-1-58980-590-3(9))* Pelican Publishing Co., Inc.

Lemke, Amy J. Snorkeling with Sea-Bots, 1 vol. Bradley, Jessica, illus. 2013. (Comics Land Ser.). (ENG.). 32p. (gr. k-2). 7.95 *(978-1-4342-4271-6(4))*; lib. bdg. 25.32 *(978-1-4342-4030-9(4))* Stone Arch Bks.

Lemke, Amy J. & Lemke, Donald B. My Little Bro-Bot, 1 vol. Bradley, Jessica, illus. 2013. (Comics Land Ser.). (ENG.). 32p. (gr. k-2). 7.95 *(978-1-4342-6285-1(5))*; lib. bdg. 25.32 *(978-1-4342-4989-0(1))* Stone Arch Bks.

Lemke, Donald. Coldfinger: Zinc Alloy. Holgate, Douglas, illus. 2010. (Graphic Sparks Ser.). (ENG.). 40p. (gr. 1-3). pap. 5.95 *(978-1-4342-2314-2(0)*, Graphic Sparks) Stone Arch Bks.

—Revealed!, 1 vol. Holgate, Douglas, illus. 2008. (Zinc Alloy Ser.). (ENG.). 40p. (gr. 1-3). 23.99 *(978-1-4342-0763-0(3)*, Graphic Sparks) Stone Arch Bks.

—Revealed! Zinc Alloy, 1 vol. Holgate, Douglas, illus. 2008. (Graphic Sparks Ser.). (ENG.). 40p. (gr. 1-3). pap. 5.95 *(978-1-4342-0859-0(1)*, Graphic Sparks) Stone Arch Bks.

—Super Zero, 1 vol. Holgate, Douglas, illus. 2008. (Zinc Alloy Ser.). (ENG.). 40p. (gr. 1-3). 23.99 *(978-1-4342-0762-3(5))*; pap. 5.95 *(978-1-4342-0858-3(3))* Stone Arch Bks. (Graphic Sparks).

Lemke, Donald B. Coldfinger, 1 vol. Holgate, Douglas, illus. 2009. (Zinc Alloy Ser.). (ENG.). 40p. (gr. 1-3). lib. bdg. 23.99 *(978-1-4342-1586-4(5)*, Graphic Sparks) Stone Arch Bks.

—The Invincible Boy-Bot. 2012. (Zinc Alloy Ser.). (ENG.). 128p. (gr. 1-3). pap. 8.95 *(978-1-4342-4597-7(7))* Stone Arch Bks.

—Zinc Alloy vs Frankenstein, 1 vol. Holgate, Douglas, illus. (Graphic Sparks Ser.). (ENG.). 40p. (gr. 1-3). 2010. pap. 5.95 *(978-1-4342-1391-4(9))* 2009. lib. bdg. 23.99 *(978-1-4342-1188-0(6))* Stone Arch Bks. (Graphic Sparks).

Lester, Helen. Wodney Wat's Wobot. Munsinger, Lynn, illus. 2011. (ENG.). 32p. (J). (gr. -1-3). 16.99 *(978-0-547-36756-9(2))* Houghton Mifflin Harcourt Publishing Co.

Lewis, Axel. Canyon Chaos, 1 vol. 2014. (Robot Racers Ser.). (ENG., Illus.). 160p. (gr. 2-4). pap. 6.95 *(978-1-4342-7936-1(7))* Stone Arch Bks.

—Desert Disaster, 1 vol. 2014. (Robot Racers Ser.). (ENG., Illus.). 160p. (gr. 2-4). pap. 6.95 *(978-1-4342-7939-2(1))* Stone Arch Bks.

—Rain Forest Rampage. 2014. (Robot Racers Ser.). (ENG., 160p. (gr. 2-4). Illus.). pap. 6.95 *(978-1-4342-7937-8(5))*; 26.65 *(978-1-4342-6571-5(4))* Stone Arch Bks.

—Robot Races, 1 vol. 2014. (Robot Racers Ser.). (ENG.). 160p. (gr. 2-4). 106.60 *(978-1-4342-8931-5(1))* Stone Arch Bks.

Lewis, R. C. Stitching Snow. 2014. (ENG., Illus.). 332p. (YA). (gr. 9-17). 17.99 *(978-1-4231-8507-9(2))* Hyperion Bks. for Children.

Lofficier, Randy & Lofficier, Jean-Marc. Robonocchio. Martiniere, Stephan, illus. 2004. (FRE.). 128p. (YA). per. 14.95 *(978-1-932983-04-3(X)*, Black Coat Pr.) HollywoodComics.com, LLC.

Long, Ethan. Clara & Clem in Outer Space. 2013. (Penguin Young Readers, Level 1 Ser.). (ENG.). 32p. (J). (gr. k-1). 14.99 *(978-0-448-46722-1(4))*; pap. 3.99 *(978-0-448-46721-4(6))* Penguin Young Readers Group. (Penguin Young Readers).

Look at the Robot: Individual Title Six-Packs. (Sails Literacy Ser.). 16p. (gr. k-18). 27.00 *(978-0-7635-4421-8(3))* Rigby Education.

Lowery, Mike. The Rise of the Rusty Robo-Cat! 2017. (Doodle Adventures Ser.). (ENG., Illus.). 112p. (J). (gr. 2). 12.95 *(978-0-7611-8721-9(9))* Workman Publishing Co., Inc.

Lucas, David. The Robot & the Bluebird. Lucas, David, illus. 2008. (ENG., Illus.). 32p. (J). (gr. -1-3). 19.99 *(978-0-374-36330-7(7)*, 9780374363307, Farrar, Straus & Giroux (BYR)) Farrar, Straus & Giroux.

Luthardt, Kevin. When Edgar Met Cecil, 1 vol. Luthardt, Kevin, illus. 2013. (ENG., Illus.). 32p. (J). (gr. -1-3). 15.95 *(978-1-56145-706-9(X))* Peachtree Pubs.

Mackowiak Elson, Maya. Transformers: Rescue Bots: the Mystery of the Pirate Bell. 2013. (Transformers Rescue Bots Ser.). (ENG., Illus.). 24p. (J). (gr. -1-3). 3.99 *(978-0-316-22833-6(8))* Little, Brown Bks. for Young Readers.

McCanna, Tim. Bitty Bot. Carpenter, Tad, illus. 2016. (Bitty Bot Ser.). (ENG.). 32p. (J). (gr. -1-3). 16.99 *(978-1-4814-4929-8(X)*, Simon & Schuster Bks. For Young Readers) Simon & Schuster Bks. For Young Readers.

McCLOUD, Scott. Distant Thunder, 1 vol. Burchett, Rick & Austin, Terry, illus. 2012. (Superman Adventures Ser.). (ENG.). 32p. (gr. 2-3). 22.60 *(978-1-4342-4551-9(9))* Stone Arch Bks.

McGeddon, R. Robots! 2017. (Disaster Diaries: 4). (ENG., Illus.). 192p. (J). 9.99 *(978-1-250-13562-9(1)*, 9781250135629) Imprint IND. Dist: Macmillan.

McNamara, Margaret. The Three Little Aliens & the Big Bad Robot. Fearing, Mark, illus. 2011. (ENG.). 40p. (J). (gr. -1-3). 16.99 *(978-0-375-86689-0(2)*, Schwartz & Wade Bks.) Random Hse. Children's Bks.

Metz, Melinda. The Droid of Doom. McKenzie, Heath, illus. 2016. (S. M. A. R. T. S. Ser.). (ENG.). 128p. (gr. 3-6). pap. 9.95 *(978-1-4965-3017-2(9))* Stone Arch Bks.

—S. M. A. R. T. S. & the Droid of Doom. McKenzie, Heath, illus. 2016. (S. M. A. R. T. S. Ser.). (ENG.). 128p. (gr. 3-6). lib. bdg. 22.65 *(978-1-4965-3015-8(2))* S.M.A.R.T.S. Learning System.

—S. M. A. R. T. S. & the Invisible Robot. McKenzie, Heath, illus. 2015. (S. M. A. R. T. S. Ser.). (ENG.). 128p. (gr. 3-6). 22.65 *(978-1-4965-0463-0(1))* S.M.A.R.T.S. Learning System.

Milgrim, David. Go, Otto, Go! Milgrim, David, illus. 2016. (Adventures of Otto Ser.). (ENG., Illus.). 32p. (J). (gr. -1-k). pap. 3.99 *(978-1-4814-6723-0(9)*, Simon Spotlight) Simon Spotlight.

—Ride, Otto, Ride! Milgrim, David, illus. 2016. (Adventures of Otto Ser.). (ENG., Illus.). 32p. (J). (gr. -1-k). pap. 3.99 *(978-1-4814-6793-3(X)*, Simon Spotlight) Simon Spotlight.

—See Otto. Milgrim, David, illus. 2016. (Adventures of Otto Ser.). (ENG., Illus.). 32p. (J). (gr. -1-k). pap. 3.99 *(978-1-4814-6796-4(4)*, Simon Spotlight) Simon Spotlight.

—See Pip Point. Milgrim, David, illus. 2016. (Adventures of Otto Ser.). (ENG., Illus.). 32p. (J). (gr. -1-k). pap. 3.99 *(978-1-4814-6784-1(0)*, Simon Spotlight) Simon Spotlight.

—See Santa Nap. Milgrim, David, illus. 2016. (Adventures of Otto Ser.). (ENG., Illus.). 32p. (J). (gr. -1-k). pap. 3.99 *(978-1-4814-6787-2(5)*, Simon Spotlight) Simon Spotlight.

—Swing Otto Swing! Milgrim, David, illus. 2005. (Ready-to-Read Ser.). (Illus.). (J). (gr. -1-k). 11.65 *(978-0-7569-6497-9(0))* Perfection Learning Corp.

Mohr, L. C. Krumbuckets. Musheno, Erica, illus. 2007. (ENG.). 144p. (J). (gr. 2-7). 13.95 *(978-0-9769417-6-7(7))* Blooming Tree Pr.

Montgomery, R. A. Your Very Own Robot Goes Cuckoo Bananas. 2009. (Illus.). 80p. (J). pap. 7.99 *(978-1-933390-39-0(5))* Chooseco LLC.

Morris, J. S. The Jewel. 2007. 204p. pap. 22.95 *(978-1-4357-0140-3(2))* Lulu Pr., Inc.

Moulton, Erin E. Chasing the Milky Way. 2014. (ENG.). 288p. (J). (gr. 3-7). 16.99 *(978-0-399-16449-1(9)*, Philomel Bks.) Penguin Young Readers Group.

Musical Robot. If You're a Robot & You Know It. Carter, David A., illus. 2015. (ENG.). 14p. (J). (gr. -1-k). bds. 16.99 *(978-0-545-81980-0(6)*, Cartwheel Bks.) Scholastic, Inc.

Myklusch, Matt. The Accidental Hero. 2011. (Jack Blank Adventure Ser.: 1). (ENG., Illus.). 496p. (J). (gr. 3-7). pap. 7.99 *(978-1-4169-9562-3(5)*, Aladdin) Simon & Schuster Children's Publishing.

—Jack Blank & the Imagine Nation. 2010. (Jack Blank Adventure Ser.: Bk. 1). (ENG., Illus.). 480p. (J). (gr. 3-7). 16.99 *(978-1-4169-9561-6(7)*, Aladdin) Simon & Schuster Children's Publishing.

Nat'l Children's Book & Literacy Alliance. The Exquisite Corpse Adventure. 2011. (ENG., Illus.). 288p. (J). (gr. 4-7). pap. 7.99 *(978-0-7636-5773-4(5))* Candlewick Pr.

Nickel, Scott. Robot Rampage: A Buzz Beaker Brainstorm. Smith, Andy J., illus. 2006. (Graphic Sparks Ser.). (ENG.). 40p. (gr. 1-3). per. 5.95 *(978-1-59889-227-7(4)*, Graphic Sparks) Stone Arch Bks.

—T. Rex vs Robo-Dog 3000. Corts, Enrique, illus. 2008. (Graphic Sparks Ser.). (ENG.). 40p. (gr. 1-3). pap. 5.95 *(978-1-4342-0857-6(5)*, Graphic Sparks) Stone Arch Bks.

Nolen, Jerdine. Block Party Surprise. Henninger, Michelle, illus. 2015. 41p. (J). *(978-1-4806-8574-1(7))* Harcourt.

—Bradford Street Buddies: Block Party Surprise. Henninger, Michelle, illus. 2015. (Green Light Readers Level 3 Ser.). (ENG.). 48p. (J). (gr. 1-4). pap. 3.99 *(978-0-544-35863-8(5)*, HMH Books For Young Readers) Houghton Mifflin Harcourt Publishing Co.

Norman, Kim. The Bot That Scott Built. Baruzzi, Agnese, illus. 2016. (ENG.). 32p. (J). (gr. -1-2). 14.95 *(978-1-4549-1064-0(X))* Sterling Publishing Co., Inc.

North, Laura. The Big Bad Wolf & the Robot Pig. 2014. (ENG., Illus.). 32p. (J). *(978-0-7787-1291-6(5))* Crabtree Publishing Co.

Nye, Barry. Hannah & the Magic Blanket - Land of the Robots. 2009. 40p. pap. 18.50 *(978-0-557-06602-5(6))* Lulu Pr., Inc.

O'Connor, Grandma. Rodney the Robot: Why Rodney Rebels. 2008. 52p. pap. 8.95 *(978-0-595-51055-9(8))* iUniverse, Inc.

O'Donnell, Liam. Tank & Fizz: the Case of the Battling Bots, 1 vol. Deas, Mike, illus. 2016. (Tank & Fizz Ser.: 2). (ENG.). 176p. (J). (gr. 3-6). pap. 9.95 *(978-1-4598-0813-3(4))* Orca Bk. Pubs. USA.

Olander, Johan. My Robots: The Robotic Genius of Lady Regina Bonquers III, 0 vols. 2012. (ENG.). 64p. (J). (gr. 3-7). 16.99 *(978-0-7614-6173-9(6)*, 9780761461739, Amazon Children's Publishing) Amazon Publishing.

O'Ryan, Ray. The Annoying Crush. 2014. (Galaxy Zack Ser.: 9). lib. bdg. 16.00 *(978-0-606-36093-7(X))* Turtleback Bks.

Parker, Emma. Robot Tim. 2010. (Illus.). 20p. pap. *(978-1-877561-54-2(1))* First Edition Ltd.

Parker, Jake. Little Bot & Sparrow. Parker, Jake, illus. 2016. (ENG., Illus.). 40p. (J). 17.99 *(978-1-62672-367-2(2)*, 9781626723672) Roaring Brook Pr.

Patterson, James. House of Robots: Robot Revolution. Neufeld, Juliana, illus. 2017. (House of Robots Ser.: 3). (ENG.). 336p. (J). (gr. 3-7). 13.99 *(978-0-316-34958-1(5)*, Jimmy Patterson) Little Brown & Co.

Patterson, James & Grabenstein, Chris. House of Robots. Neufeld, Juliana, illus. (House of Robots Ser.: 1). (ENG.). (J). (gr. 3-7). 2015. 336p. pap. 7.99 *(978-0-316-34679-5(9))* 2014. 352p. 13.99 *(978-0-316-40591-1(4))* Little Brown & Co. (Jimmy Patterson).

—House of Robots. 2015. (J). lib. bdg. 18.40 *(978-0-606-37527-6(9))* Turtleback Bks.

—Robots Go Wild. Neufeld, Juliana, illus. 2015. (House of Robots Ser.: 2). (ENG.). 336p. (J). (gr. 3-7). 13.99 *(978-0-316-28479-0(3)*, Jimmy Patterson) Little Brown & Co.

Paul, Miranda. Trainbots. McG, Shane, illus. 2016. (ENG.). 32p. (J). (gr. -1-3). 16.99 *(978-1-4998-0167-5(X))* Little Bee Books Inc.

Perritano, John. Battle of the Bots, 1 vol. 2014. (Kid Squad Saves the World Ser.). (ENG.). 112p. (J). (gr. 8-12). lib. bdg. 27.07 *(978-1-62402-037-7(2)*, Calico Chapter Bks.) Magic Wagon.

Perry, Fred & Dlin, Doug. Gold Digger Tech Manual. 2011. (ENG.). 352p. (YA). pap., pap. 19.99 *(978-0-9844879-7-4(2)*, 9780984487974) Antarctic Pr., Inc.

Pilkey, Dav. Mighty Robot vs. the Mecha-Monkeys from Mars. Santat, Dan, illus. 2014. (Ricky Ricotta Ser.: 4). (ENG.). 144p. (J). (gr. -1-3). pap. 5.99 *(978-0-545-63012-2(6))* Scholastic, Inc.

—Mighty Robot vs. the Mutant Mosquitoes from Mercury. Santat, Dan, illus. 2014. (Ricky Ricotta Ser.: 2). (ENG.). 128p. (J). (gr. -1-3). pap. 5.99 *(978-0-545-63010-8(X))* Scholastic, Inc.

—Mighty Robot vs. the Naughty Nightcrawlers from Neptune. Santat, Dan, illus. 2016. (Ricky Ricotta Ser.: 8). (ENG.). 128p. (J). (gr. -1-3). 15.99 *(978-0-439-37708-9(0))* Scholastic, Inc.

—Ricky Ricotta's Mighty Robot. Santat, Dan, illus. 2014. (Ricky Ricotta Ser.: 1). (ENG.). 112p. (J). (gr. -1-3). pap. 5.99 *(978-0-545-63009-2(6))*; lib. bdg. 15.99 *(978-0-545-63106-8(8))* Scholastic, Inc.

—Ricky Ricotta's Mighty Robot. 2014. (Ricky Ricotta's Mighty Robot Ser.: 1). lib. bdg. 16.00 *(978-0-606-35799-9(8))* Turtleback Bks.

—Ricky Ricotta's Mighty Robot vs. the Jurassic Jackrabbits from Jupiter. Santat, Dan, illus. 2014. (Ricky Ricotta Ser.: 5). (ENG.). 128p. (J). (gr. -1-3). pap. 5.99 *(978-0-545-63013-9(4))* Scholastic, Inc.

—Ricky Ricotta's Mighty Robot vs. the Naughty Nightcrawlers from Neptune. Santat, Dan, illus. 2016. (Ricky Ricotta Ser.: 8). (ENG.). 128p. (J). (gr. -1-3). pap. 5.99 *(978-0-439-37709-6(9))* Scholastic, Inc.

—Ricky Ricotta's Mighty Robot vs. the Unpleasant Penguins from Pluto. Santat, Dan, illus. 2016. (Ricky Ricotta's Mighty Robot Ser.: 9). (ENG.). 128p. (J). (gr. -1-3). 15.99 *(978-0-545-63016-0(9))* Scholastic, Inc.

—Uranium Unicorns from Uranus., Bk. 7. 2015. (Ricky Ricotta Ser.: 7). (ENG., Illus.). 128p. (J). (gr. -1-3). pap. 5.99 *(978-0-545-63015-3(0))* Scholastic, Inc.

—The Voodoo Vultures from Venus. Santat, Dan, illus. 2014. (Ricky Ricotta Ser.: 3). (ENG.). 128p. (J). (gr. -1-3). pap. 5.99 *(978-0-545-63011-5(8))* Scholastic, Inc.

Pollack, Pamela. Spy Cats: Revenge of the Robot Rats. 2004. (Illus.). 57p. *(978-0-439-56603-2(7))* Scholastic, Inc.

Posner-Sanchez, Andrea & Weinberg, Jennifer Liberts. Bow-Bot Robot (Disney Junior: Minnie's Bow Toons) RH Disney Staff, illus. 2014. (Little Golden Book Ser.). (ENG.). 24p. (J). (-k). 4.99 *(978-0-7364-3078-4(4)*, Golden/Disney) Random Hse. Children's Bks.

Press, J. Robots Don't Clean Toilets. Kline, Michael, illus. 2013. (Doodles of Sam Dibble Ser.: 3). (ENG.). 128p. (J). (gr. 1-3). pap. 4.99 *(978-0-448-46109-0(9)*, Grosset & Dunlap) Penguin Young Readers Group.

Publications International Ltd. Staff. Wall E Large Sound BK. 2008. 24p. (J). 17.98 *(978-1-4127-8991-2(5)*, PIL Kids) Publications International, Ltd.

Rafter, Dan. Gearz. 2010. (ENG., Illus.). 96p. (YA). pap. 17.99 *(978-1-61623-929-9(8))* Bluewater Productions, Inc.

Ralph, Brian. Reggie-12. 2013. (ENG., Illus.). 96p. (YA). 21.95 *(978-1-77046-132-1(9)*, 9781770461321) Drawn & Quarterly Pubns. CAN. Dist: Macmillan.

Random House Disney Staff. Big Hero 6. Random House Disney Staff, illus. 2014. (Little Golden Book Ser.). (ENG., Illus.). 24p. (J). (-k). 4.99 *(978-0-7364-3168-2(3)*, Golden Bks.) Random Hse. Children's Bks.

—Big Hero 6 Big Golden Book (Disney Big Hero 6) Random House Disney Staff, illus. 2014. (Big Golden Book Ser.). (ENG., Illus.). 48p. (J). (gr. k-4). 9.99 *(978-0-7364-3186-6(1)*, Golden Bks.) Random Hse. Children's Bks.

—Hiro to the Rescue! Random House Disney Staff, illus. 2014. (Stepping Stone Book(TM) Ser.). (ENG., Illus.). 80p. (J). (gr. 1-4). lib. bdg. 12.99 *(978-0-7364-8154-0(0)*, RH/Disney) Random Hse. Children's Bks.

Random House Staff. I Am Baymax. 2015. (Step into Reading Level 2 Ser.). lib. bdg. 14.75 *(978-0-606-36383-9(1))* Turtleback Bks.

Random House Staff & Webster, Christy. Robot Rampage! (Teenage Mutant Ninja Turtles) Random House Staff & Spaziante, Patrick, illus. 2013. (Step into Reading Ser.). (ENG.). 48p. (J). (gr. k-3). pap. 3.99 *(978-0-307-98212-4(2)*, Random Hse. Bks. for Young Readers) Random Hse. Children's Bks.

Rau, Dana Meachen. Go Bot, Robot! Jung, Wook Jin, illus. 2013. (Step into Reading Ser.). (ENG.). 32p. (J). (gr. -1-1). 3.99 *(978-0-375-87083-5(0)*, Random Hse. Bks. for Young Readers) Random Hse. Children's Bks.

—Go Bot, Robot! Jung, Wook Jin, illus. 2013. 32p. (J). *(978-0-449-81429-1(7))* Random Hse., Inc.

—Robot, Go Bot! 2013. (Step into Reading Level 1 Ser.). lib. bdg. 13.55 *(978-0-606-31935-5(2)*, Turtleback) Turtleback Bks.

Rau, Zachary. Autobots Versus Zombies. 2012. (Transformers 8x8 Ser.). (J). lib. bdg. 13.55 *(978-0-606-26687-1(9)*, Turtleback) Turtleback Bks.

Readler, Blaine C. Under the Radar: The Spy Drone Adventure. 2006. (ENG.). 248p. (J). (gr. 7-12). per. *(978-1-933255-18-7(8))* DNA Pr.

Rechlin, Ted & Paper Dolls. Robot Battle Paper Action Figures. 2012. (Dover Paper Dolls Ser.). (ENG.). 32p. (J). (gr. 3-5). pap. 9.99 *(978-0-486-48781-6(4))* Dover Pubns., Inc.

RH Disney Staff. The Big Battle. RH Disney Staff, illus. 2014. (Step into Reading Ser.). (ENG., Illus.). 32p. (J). (gr. k-3). 4.99 *(978-0-7364-3245-0(0)*, RH/Disney) Random Hse. Children's Bks.

—Love at First Beep. 2008. (Step into Reading Ser.). (ENG., Illus.). 32p. (J). (gr. k-3). pap. 3.99 *(978-0-7364-2514-8(4)*, RH/Disney) Random Hse. Children's Bks.

RH Disney Staff & Scollon, Bill. Fight to the Finish! RH Disney Staff & Disney Storybook Art Team, illus. 2014. (Step into Reading Ser.). (ENG.). 48p. (J). (gr. k-3). 3.99 *(978-0-7364-3189-7(6)*, RH/Disney) Random Hse. Children's Bks.

Ricahrdson, Larry. Metal Mike. Ricahrdson, Brittany, illus. 2010. 24p. (J). pap. 9.95 *(978-1-935706-26-7(8))* Wiggles Pr.

Richards, Barnaby. Blip! Toon Level 1. 2016. (ENG., Illus.). 40p. (J). (gr. -1-k). 12.95 *(978-1-935179-98-6(5))* TOON Books / RAW Junior, LLC.

Richards, C. J. Battle of the Bots. Fujita, Goro, illus. (Robots Rule Ser.: 3). (ENG.). 240p. (J). (gr. 2-5). 2017. pap. 6.99 *(978-0-544-93524-2(1))* 2015. 13.99 *(978-0-544-33932-3(0))* Houghton Mifflin Harcourt Publishing Co. (HMH Books For Young Readers).

—Battle of the Bots. 2017. (Robots Rule Ser.: 3). (ENG.). (J). (gr. 2-5). lib. bdg. 17.20 ***(978-0-606-39811-4(2))*** Turtleback Bks.

—The Junkyard Bot, Bk. 7. Fujita, Goro, illus. 2014. (Robots Rule Ser.: 1). (ENG.). 208p. (J). (gr. 5-7). 13.99 *(978-0-544-33936-1(3)*, HMH Books For Young Readers) Houghton Mifflin Harcourt Publishing Co.

—The Junkyard Bot: Robots Rule, Book 1. Fujita, Goro, illus. 2016. (Robots Rule Ser.). (ENG.). 208p. (J). (gr. 5-7). pap. 6.99 *(978-0-544-66843-0(X)*, HMH Books For Young Readers) Houghton Mifflin Harcourt Publishing Co.

—Lots of Bots. Fujita, Goro, illus. (Robots Rule Ser.: 2). (ENG.). 224p. (J). (gr. 2-5). 2016. pap. 6.99 *(978-0-544-81082-2(1))* 2015. 13.99 *(978-0-544-33934-7(7))* Houghton Mifflin Harcourt Publishing Co. (HMH Books For Young Readers).

Richards, Kitty. Meet the Sparkplugs, Level 3. Simard, Remy, illus. 2006. (ENG.). 24p. (J). (gr. 1-17). per. 3.99 *(978-1-58476-419-9(8)*, IKIDS) Innovative Kids.

Richardson, Larry. Metal Mike. 2010. (Illus.). 32p. (J). pap. 9.95 *(978-1-935706-33-5(0))* Wiggles Pr.

Roberts, Daniel. Harrison & His Dinosaur Robot. 2009. (Illus.). 32p. pap. 14.95 *(978-1-4389-2846-3(7))* AuthorHouse.

—Harrison & His Dinosaur Robot & the Super-Fast Race Car. 2009. (Illus.). 32p. pap. 14.95 *(978-1-4389-2847-0(5))* AuthorHouse.

Robinson, Michelle. And the Robot Went ... Ruzzier, Sergio, illus. 2017. (ENG.). 32p. (J). (gr. -1-3). 16.99 *(978-0-544-58652-9(2)*, Clarion Bks.) Houghton Mifflin Harcourt Trade & Reference Pubs.

The Robot, 6, Pack. (Chiquilibros Ser.). (gr. k-1). 23.00 *(978-0-7635-0442-7(4))* Rigby Education.

Ronan, Amanda. The Decision. Radka, Sara, illus. 2015. (My Brother Is a Robot Ser.: 6). (ENG.). 64p. (J). (gr. 3-8). 27.99 *(978-1-62920-509-0(5))* Scobre Pr. Corp.

—The Discovery. Radka, Sara, illus. 2015. (My Brother Is a Robot Ser.: 5). (ENG.). 64p. (J). (gr. 3-8). 27.99 *(978-1-62920-506-9(0))* Scobre Pr. Corp.

—The Experiment. Radka, Sara, illus. 2015. (My Brother Is a Robot Ser.: 1). (ENG.). 64p. (J). (gr. 3-8). 27.99 *(978-1-62920-494-9(3))* Scobre Pr. Corp.

—The Fight. Radka, Sara, illus. 2015. (My Brother Is a Robot Ser.: 4). (ENG.). 64p. (J). (gr. 3-8). 27.99 *(978-1-62920-503-8(6))* Scobre Pr. Corp.

—The Master Plan. Radka, Sara, illus. 2015. (My Brother Is a Robot Ser.: 2). (ENG.). 64p. (J). (gr. 3-8). 27.99 *(978-1-62920-497-0(8))* Scobre Pr. Corp.

—The Switch. Radka, Sara, illus. 2015. (My Brother Is a Robot Ser.: 3). (ENG.). 64p. (J). (gr. 3-8). 27.99 *(978-1-62920-500-7(1))* Scobre Pr. Corp.

Rosen, Lucy. Blast Off! 2015. (Transformers 8x8 Ser.). (J). lib. bdg. 13.55 *(978-0-606-37228-2(8))* Turtleback Bks.

Rosenblum, Gregg. City 1. 2015. (Revolution 19 Ser.: 3). (ENG.). 288p. (YA). (gr. 8). 17.99 *(978-0-06-212601-6(6)*, HarperTeen) HarperCollins Pubs.

—Fugitive X. 2014. (Revolution 19 Ser.: 2). (ENG.). 272p. (YA). (gr. 8). 17.99 *(978-0-06-212597-2(4)*, HarperTeen) HarperCollins Pubs.

—Revolution 19. 2013. (Revolution 19 Ser.: 1). (ENG.). 272p. (YA). (gr. 8). 17.99 *(978-0-06-212595-8(8)*, HarperTeen) HarperCollins Pubs.

Rosenthal, Marc. One Robot Lost His Head. 2015. (ENG., Illus.). 16p. (J). (-k). 17.95 *(978-1-57687-749-4(3)*, powerHouse Bks.) powerHouse Cultural Entertainment, Inc.

Rossell, Judith. Sam & the Killer Robot. 2007. 176p. pap. *(978-1-921272-10-3(4))* Little Hare Bks. AUS. Dist: HarperCollins Pubs. Australia.

Roza, Greg. The Messy Robot. 2006. (Neighborhood Readers Ser.). (ENG., Illus.). 16p. (gr. 1-3). pap. 6.50 *(978-1-4042-7184-5(8)*, Rosen Classroom) Rosen Publishing Group, Inc., The.

Rubin, Adam. Robo-Sauce. Salmieri, Daniel, illus. 2015. (ENG.). 48p. (J). (gr. -1-3). 18.99 *(978-0-525-42887-9(9)*, Dial Bks) Penguin Young Readers Group.

Rudnick, Elizabeth. Iron Man Is Born, 1 vol. Marvel Illustrators, illus. 2012. (Avengers: Earth's Mightiest Heroes! Ser.). (ENG.). 24p. (J). (gr. -1-4). lib. bdg. 24.21 *(978-1-61479-003-7(5))* Spotlight.

Sam & the Robots. 2016. (Ladybird Readers Ser.). (ENG.). 16p. (J). pap., act. bk. ed. 5.99 *(978-0-241-25376-2(4))* Penguin Bks., Ltd. GBR. Dist: Independent Pubs. Group.

Santat, Dan, illus. Mighty Robot vs. the Stupid Stinkbugs from Saturn. 2015. (Ricky Ricotta Ser.: 6). (ENG.). 128p. (J). (gr. -1-3). 15.99 *(978-0-545-63121-1(1))* Scholastic, Inc.

—Stupid Stinkbugs from Saturn. 2015. (Ricky Ricotta Ser.: 6). (ENG.). 128p. (J). (gr. -1-3). pap. 5.99 *(978-0-545-63014-6(2))* Scholastic, Inc.

Santillo, LuAnn. Buzz. Santillo, LuAnn, ed. 2003. (Half-Pint Kids Readers Ser.). (Illus.). 7p. (J). (gr. -1-1). pap. 1.00 *(978-1-59256-046-2(6))* Half-Pint Kids, Inc.

Savage, J. Scott. Fires of Invention. 2015. (Mysteries of Cove Ser.: Bk. 1). 312p. (J). 17.99 *(978-1-62972-092-0(5)*, Shadow Mountain) Deseret Bk. Co.

Sazaklis, John. Optimus Prime Versus Predaking. 2013. (Transformers 8x8 Ser.). (J). lib. bdg. 13.55 *(978-0-606-32272-0(8)*, Turtleback) Turtleback Bks.

—Salamander Smackdown. Baltazar, Art, illus. 2011. (DC Super-Pets Ser.). (ENG.). 56p. (gr. 2-2). pap. 4.95 *(978-1-4048-6844-1(5)*, DC Super-Pets) Picture Window Bks.

—Salamander Smackdown!, 1 vol. Baltazar, Art, illus. 2011. (DC Super-Pets Ser.). (ENG.). 56p. (gr. 2-2). lib. bdg. 23.99 *(978-1-4048-6478-8(4)*, DC Super-Pets) Picture Window Bks.

—Transformers: Rescue Bots: the Ghosts of Griffin Rock. 2014. (ENG., Illus.). 24p. (J). (gr. -1-3). pap. 3.99 *(978-0-316-27704-4(5))* Little, Brown Bks. for Young Readers.

Sazaklis, John & Foxe, Steve. Transformers Robots in Disguise: Chapter Book #3. 2015. (ENG.). 144p. (J). (gr. 3-7). pap. 5.99 *(978-0-316-30192-3(2))* Little, Brown Bks. for Young Readers.

Scholastic, Inc. Staff & Rusu, Meredith. Ratchet & Clank: Hero Time. 2016. (ENG., Illus.). 48p. (J). (gr. -1-3). pap. 4.99 *(978-1-338-03042-6(6))* Scholastic, Inc.

Schorr, Titus. My Robot, 01 vols., 1. 2016. (Rosen REAL Readers: STEM & STEAM Collection). (ENG.). 12p. (J). pap. 6.33 *(978-1-5081-1620-2(2)*, Rosen Classroom) Rosen Publishing Group, Inc., The.

Scieszka, Jon. The Brain Turbo. Biggs, Brian, illus. 2015. (Frank Einstein Ser.). (ENG.). 192p. (J). (gr. 3-7). 13.95 *(978-1-4197-1643-0(3)*, Amulet Bks.) Abrams, Inc.

—Frank Einstein & the Antimatter Motor. Biggs, Brian, illus. 2014. (Frank Einstein Ser.: 1). (ENG.). 192p. (J). (gr. 2-6). 13.95 *(978-1-4197-1218-0(7)*, Amulet Bks.) Abrams, Inc.

—Frank Einstein & the Antimatter Motor. 2017. (Frank Einstein Ser.: 1). (J). lib. bdg. 18.40 ***(978-0-606-39683-7(7))*** Turtleback Bks.

—Frank Einstein & the Antimatter Motor (Frank Einstein Series #1) Book One. Biggs, Brian, illus. 2017. (Frank Einstein Ser.). (ENG.). 208p. (J). (gr. 3-7). pap. 7.95 *(978-1-4197-2492-3(4)*, Amulet Bks.) Abrams, Inc.

—Frank Einstein & the Electro-Finger. Biggs, Brian, illus. 2015. (Frank Einstein Ser.: 2). (ENG.). 176p. (J). (gr. 3-7). 13.95 *(978-1-4197-1483-2(X)*, Amulet Bks.) Abrams, Inc.

—Frank Einstein & the Electro-Finger (Frank Einstein Series #2) Book Two. Biggs, Brian, illus. 2017. (Frank Einstein Ser.). (ENG.). 192p. (J). (gr. 3-7). pap. 7.95 *(978-1-4197-2493-0(2)*, Amulet Bks.) Abrams, Inc.

—Frank Einstein & the EvoBlaster Belt (Frank Einstein Series #4) Book Four. Biggs, Brian, illus. 2016. (Frank Einstein Ser.). (ENG.). 208p. (J). (gr. 3-7). 13.95 *(978-1-4197-1887-8(8),* Amulet Bks.) Abrams, Inc.
—Frank Einstein & the EvoBlaster Belt (Frank Einstein Series #4) Book Four. Biggs, Brian, illus. 2017. (Frank Einstein Ser.). (ENG.). 224p. (J). (gr. 3-7). pap. 7.99 *(978-1-4197-2736-8(2),* Amulet Bks.) Abrams, Inc.
Scieszka, Jon. Robot Zot! Shannon, David, illus. 2009. (ENG.). 40p. (J). (gr. -1-2). 17.99 *(978-1-4169-6394-3(4),* Simon & Schuster Bks. For Young Readers) Simon & Schuster Bks. For Young Readers.
—Robot Zot! Shannon, David, illus. 2011. (J). (gr. -1-2). 29.95 *(978-0-545-32739-8(3))* Weston Woods Studios, Inc.
Scieszka, Jon & Brian Biggs. Frank Einstein & the Electro-Finger. 2017. (Frank Einstein Ser.: 2). (J). lib. bdg. 18.40 ***(978-0-606-39684-4(5))*** Turtleback Bks.
Segal, Andrew. Roberto the Robot. Scott, Peter & JessT, Grant, illus. 2007. 32p. per. *(978-1-905823-26-0(6))* Panoma Pr. Ltd.
Selznick, Brian. The Invention of Hugo Cabret. 2007. (CHI., Illus.). 534p. (J). *(978-957-570-894-8(6))* Eastern Publishing Co., Ltd., The.
—The Invention of Hugo Cabret. 2008. (CHI., Illus.). 465p. (J). pap. *(978-7-5448-0279-6(5))* Jieli Publishing Hse.
—The Invention of Hugo Cabret. Selznick, Brian, illus. 2007. (Illus.). (ENG.). 544p. (J). (gr. 4-7). 24.99 *(978-0-439-81378-5(6),* Scholastic Pr.); 534p. *(978-1-4071-0348-8(2))* Scholastic, Inc.
SFX Fantasy. Tween Tales - Robots, Dragons & the Interworld Machine. 2007. 131p. pap. 12.99 *(978-1-4303-2546-8(1))* Lulu Pr., Inc.
Shea, Lisa. Meet Heatwave the Fire-Bot. 2013. (Transformers Passport to Reading Ser.). (J). lib. bdg. 14.75 *(978-0-606-31737-5(6),* Turtleback) Turtleback Bks.
Sheehan, Anna. A Long, Long Sleep. 2011. (ENG., Illus.). 352p. (YA). (gr. 9). 16.99 *(978-0-7636-5260-9(1))* Candlewick Pr.
Shen, Prudence. Nothing Can Possibly Go Wrong. Hicks, Faith Erin, illus. 2013. (ENG.). 288p. (YA). (gr. 7). pap. 17.99 *(978-1-59643-659-6(X),* 9781596436596, First Second Bks.) Roaring Brook Pr.
Shepard, Aaron. Timothy Tolliver & the Bully Basher. 2005. 48p. (J). pap. 2.99 *(978-0-938497-24-0(3));* lib. bdg. 15.00 *(978-0-938497-23-3(5))* Shepard Pubns. (Skyhook Pr.).
Sherry, Kevin. Remy Sneakers vs. the Robo-Rats. Sherry, Kevin, illus. 2017. (Remy Sneakers Ser.: 1). (ENG., Illus.). 128p. (J). (gr. 2-5). 9.99 ***(978-1-338-03460-8(X),*** Scholastic Pr.) Scholastic, Inc.
Shulman, Mark. Fillmore & Geary Take Off! The Adventures of a Robot Boy & a Boy Boy. Fickling, Phillip, illus. 2004. (ENG.). 40p. (J). (gr. -1-7). 14.95 *(978-1-58717-256-4(9),* SeaStar Bks.) Chronicle Bks. LLC.
Siems, Thomas F. The Dangerous Pet. 2009. 48p. pap. 21.99 *(978-1-4415-3454-5(7))* Xlibris Corp.
Simon, Annette. Robot Zombie Frankenstein! Simon, Annette, illus. 2012. (ENG., Illus.). 40p. (J). (gr. -1-3). 16.99 *(978-0-7636-5124-4(9))* Candlewick Pr.
Simonson, Louise. Snow White & the Seven Robots. Sanchez, Jimena, illus. 2015. (Far Out Fairy Tales Ser.). (ENG.). 40p. (gr. 3-4). lib. bdg. 25.32 *(978-1-4342-9648-1(2))* Stone Arch Bks.
Smiley, Mark. A Journey Far Away. 2006. 164p. pap. 13.95 *(978-1-59526-494-7(9))* Aeon Publishing Inc.
Smith, Jim. Future Ratboy & the Attack of the Killer Robot Grannies. 2017. (Future Ratboy Ser.: 1). (ENG., Illus.). 256p. (J). (gr. 2-4). pap. 9.99 ***(978-1-4052-6913-1(8))*** Egmont Bks., Ltd. GBR. Dist: Independent Pubs. Group.
Smith, Joseph K. The Substitute Kid. 2008. 54p. pap. 16.95 *(978-1-60672-272-5(7))* America Star Bks.
Snider, Brandon T. Transformers Rescue Bots: The Attack of the Humungado. 2015. (ENG., Illus.). 24p. (J). (gr. -1-3). pap. 4.99 *(978-0-316-30171-8(X))* Little, Brown Bks. for Young Readers.
Sonishi, Kenji. Leave It to PET!, Vol. 2. Sonishi, Kenji, illus. 2009. (ENG., Illus.). 196p. (J). pap. 7.99 *(978-1-4215-2650-8(6))* Viz Media.
—Leave It to PET!, Vol. 4. Sonishi, Kenji, illus. 2010. (ENG., Illus.). 192p. (J). pap. 7.99 *(978-1-4215-2652-2(2))* Viz Media.
Staniszewski, Anna. Power down, Little Robot. Zeltner, Tim, illus. 2015. (ENG.). 32p. (J). (gr. -1-1). 16.99 *(978-1-62779-125-0(6),* 9781627791250, Holt, Henry & Co. Bks. For Young Readers) Holt, Henry & Co.
Starfall Education. Robot & Mr. Mole. Starfall Education, ed. 2004. (ENG., Illus.). 8p. (J). pap. *(978-1-59577-009-7(7))* Starfall Education.
Steele, Michael A. High-Tech Terror, 1 vol. Schoening, Dan, illus. 2011. (Green Lantern Ser.). (ENG.). 56p. (gr. 2-3). pap. 4.95 *(978-1-4342-3084-3(8));* lib. bdg. 26.65 *(978-1-4342-2609-9(3))* Stone Arch Bks. (DC Super Heroes).
Stephens, Sarah Hines. Superpowered Pony, 1 vol. Baltazar, Art, illus. 2011. (DC Super-Pets Ser.). (ENG.). 56p. (gr. 2-2). pap. 4.95 *(978-1-4048-6846-5(1));* lib. bdg. 23.99 *(978-1-4048-6479-5(2))* Picture Window Bks. (DC Super-Pets).
Stevenson, Robin. Ben's Robot, 1 vol. Parkins, David, illus. 2010. (Orca Echoes Ser.). (ENG.). 64p. (J). (gr. 2-3). pap. 6.95 *(978-1-55469-153-1(2))* Orca Bk. Pubs. USA.
Stilton, Geronimo, et al. Robot Attack. Usai, Luca & Verzini, Daniele, illus. 2015. 117p. (J). *(978-0-545-86796-2(7))* Scholastic, Inc.
Stine, R. L. Frankenstein's Dog. 2013. (Goosebumps Most Wanted Ser.: 4). (ENG.). 160p. (J). (gr. 3-7). pap. 6.99 *(978-0-545-41801-0(1),* Scholastic Paperbacks) Scholastic, Inc.
—Frankenstein's Dog. 2013. (Goosebumps Most Wanted Ser.: 4). 136p. (J). lib. bdg. 17.20 *(978-0-606-32006-1(7),* Turtleback) Turtleback Bks.
Stratford, Ann. Tara Toad Meets Roman the Robot Soldier. 2005. (ENG., Illus.). pap. *(978-1-84401-465-1(7))* Athena Pr.
Suen, Anastasia. The Big Catch: A Robot & Rico Story, 1 vol. Laughead, Mike, illus. 2009. (Robot & Rico Ser.). (ENG.). 32p. (gr. 1-2). 22.65 *(978-1-4342-1626-7(8));* pap. 6.25 *(978-1-4342-1751-6(5))* Stone Arch Bks.
—Dino Hunt: A Robot & Rico Story. Laughead, Mike, illus. 2010. (Robot & Rico Ser.). (ENG.). 32p. (gr. 1-2). pap. 6.25 *(978-1-4342-2300-5(0))* Stone Arch Bks.
—La Noche de Terror. Heck, Claudia M., tr. from ENG. Laughead, Mike, illus. 2012. (Robot y Rico/Robot & Rico Ser.).Tr. of Scary Night. (MUL, SPA & ENG.). 32p. (gr. 1-2). pap. 5.05 *(978-1-4342-3918-1(7));* lib. bdg. 22.65 *(978-1-4342-3779-8(6))* Stone Arch Bks. (Bilingual Stone Arch Readers).
—The Pirate Map: A Robot & Rico Story. Laughead, Mike, illus. 2010. (Robot & Rico Ser.). (ENG.). 32p. (gr. 1-2). pap. 6.25 *(978-1-4342-2301-2(9))* Stone Arch Bks.
—Un Premio Adentro. Heck, Claudia M., tr. from ENG. Laughead, Mike, illus. 2012. (Robot y Rico/Robot & Rico Ser.).Tr. of Prize Inside. (MUL, SPA & ENG.). 32p. (gr. 1-2). pap. 5.05 *(978-1-4342-3919-8(5));* lib. bdg. 22.65 *(978-1-4342-3780-4(X))* Stone Arch Bks. (Bilingual Stone Arch Readers).
—A Prize Inside: A Robot & Rico Story, 1 vol. Laughead, Mike, illus. 2009. (Robot & Rico Ser.). (ENG.). 32p. (gr. 1-2). 22.65 *(978-1-4342-1627-4(6))* Stone Arch Bks.
—The Scary Night: A Robot & Rico Story, 1 vol. Laughead, Mike, illus. 2009. (Robot & Rico Ser.). (ENG.). 32p. (gr. 1-2). 22.65 *(978-1-4342-1628-1(4));* pap. 6.25 *(978-1-4342-1752-3(3))* Stone Arch Bks.
—Snow Games: A Robot & Rico Story. Laughead, Mike, illus. 2010. (Robot & Rico Ser.). (ENG.). 32p. (gr. 1-2). pap. 6.25 *(978-1-4342-2302-9(7));* lib. bdg. 22.65 *(978-1-4342-1869-8(4))* Stone Arch Bks.
—Test Drive: A Robot & Rico Story. Laughead, Mike, illus. 2010. (Robot & Rico Ser.). (ENG.). 32p. (gr. 1-2). pap. 6.25 *(978-1-4342-2303-6(5))* Stone Arch Bks.
—Trucos en la Patineta. Heck, Claudia M., tr. from ENG. Laughead, Mike, illus. 2012. (Robot y Rico/Robot & Rico Ser.).Tr. of Skate Trick. (MUL & SPA.). 32p. (gr. 1-2). pap. 5.05 *(978-1-4342-3917-4(9));* lib. bdg. 21.32 *(978-1-4342-3778-1(8))* Stone Arch Bks. (Bilingual Stone Arch Readers).
Suen, Anastasia & Heck, Claudia M. La Gran Pesca. Laughead, Mike, illus. 2012. (Robot y Rico/Robot & Rico Ser.).Tr. of Big Catch. (MUL, SPA & ENG.). 32p. (gr. 1-2). pap. 5.05 *(978-1-4342-3920-4(9));* lib. bdg. 22.65 *(978-1-4342-3781-1(8))* Stone Arch Bks. (Bilingual Stone Arch Readers).
Sutton, Laurie S. Batman Battles the Penguin. Style Guide, illus. 2016. (Batman Unlimited Ser.). (ENG.). 64p. (J). (gr. k-4). 16.00 *(978-0-606-39248-8(3))* Turtleback Bks.
Sutton, Laurie S., et al. Gorilla Warfare, 1 vol. Doescher, Erik, illus. 2011. (Flash Ser.). (ENG.). 56p. (gr. 2-3). pap. 4.95 *(978-1-4342-3087-4(2),* DC Super Heroes) Stone Arch Bks.
Tanguay, Dave. Come Together! Vaughns, Byron, illus. 2015. (Billy Batson & the Magic of Shazam! Ser.). (ENG.). 32p. (gr. 2-3). lib. bdg. 22.60 *(978-1-4342-9744-0(6))* Stone Arch Bks.
—Deception Reception! Vaughns, Byron, illus. 2015. (Billy Batson & the Magic of Shazam! Ser.). (ENG.). 32p. (gr. 2-3). lib. bdg. 22.60 *(978-1-4342-9742-6(X))* Stone Arch Bks.
—Fire Fire Everywhere! Vaughns, Byron, illus. 2015. (Billy Batson & the Magic of Shazam! Ser.). (ENG.). 32p. (gr. 2-3). lib. bdg. 22.60 *(978-1-4342-9745-7(4))* Stone Arch Bks.
Testa, Maggie. Play with Plex. Zdanowicz, Paul, illus. 2010. (Yo Gabba Gabba! Ser.). (ENG.). 14p. (J). (gr. -1-1). bds. 8.99 *(978-1-4169-9740-5(7),* Simon Spotlight) Simon Spotlight.
Thornton, D. S. Scrap City. Bowater, Charlie, illus. 2015. (Middle-Grade Novels Ser.). (ENG.). 352p. (gr. 4-7). lib. bdg. 27.99 *(978-1-4965-0475-3(5))* Stone Arch Bks.
Tiger Tales, ed. & compiled by. Stories for Boys. Tiger Tales, compiled by. 2015. (ENG.). 176p. (J). (gr. -1-3). 12.99 *(978-1-58925-535-7(6))* Tiger Tales.
Tillworth, Mary. Rusty Rocks! (Rusty Rivets) Aikins, Dave, illus. 2017. (Pictureback(R) Ser.). (ENG.). 24p. (J). (gr. -1-2). pap. 5.99 ***(978-1-5247-1721-6(5),*** Random Hse. Bks. for Young Readers) Random Hse. Children's Bks.
Timmers, Leo. Franky. Timmers, Leo, illus. 2016. (ENG., Illus.). 40p. (gr. -1-2). 16.99 *(978-1-927271-93-3(2));* 33.32 *(978-1-77657-054-6(5));* 33.32 *(978-1-77657-053-9(7))* Gecko Pr. NZL. Dist: Lerner Publishing Group.
Torres, Mario J. The Incredible Adventures of Kaplan & Dylan: Book One: Present, 1 vol. 2009. 159p. pap. 24.95 *(978-1-4489-9513-4(2))* PublishAmerica, Inc.
Toufexis, George. MONSTER MASH-Up — Robots' Revenge. 2014. (ENG., Illus.). 48p. (J). (gr. 4). pap. 4.99 *(978-0-486-49225-4(7))* Dover Pubns., Inc.
Tougas, Chris. Mechanimals, 1 vol. 2012. (ENG.). 32p. (J). (gr. -1-3). 9.95 *(978-1-55469-0273-5(X))* Orca Bk. Pubs. USA.
Transformers: Rescue Bots: Team of Heroes. 2014. (Passport to Reading Level 1 Ser.). (ENG., Illus.). 32p. (J). (gr. -1-3). pap. 3.99 *(978-0-316-40557-7(4))* Little, Brown Bks. for Young Readers.
Trimble, Marcia J. Marsby & the Martian Detectives. Hayden, Jennifer H., illus. 2004. 56p. (J). per. 9.95 *(978-1-891577-52-9(2),* SAN299-4844) Images Pr.
Tucker, Jasmine. Robbie the Robot. 2013. 20p. pap. 24.95 *(978-1-63004-493-0(8))* America Star Bks.
Valentine, Madeline. The Bad Birthday Idea. 2013. (ENG., Illus.). 40p. (J). (gr. -1-2). 17.99 *(978-0-449-81331-7(2),* Knopf Bks. for Young Readers) Random Hse. Children's Bks.
Van Dusen, Chris. Randy Riley's Really Big Hit. Van Dusen, Chris, illus. (ENG., Illus.). (J). (gr. -1-3). 2016. 7.99 *(978-0-7636-8774-8(X))* 2012. 32p. 15.99 *(978-0-7636-4946-3(5))* Candlewick Pr.
Van Eekhout, Greg. The Boy at the End of the World. 2012. (ENG.). 240p. (YA). (gr. 5-8). pap. 8.99 *(978-1-59990-918-9(9),* 9781599909189, Bloomsbury USA Childrens) Bloomsbury Publishing USA.
Varon, Sara. Robot Dreams. Varon, Sara, illus. 2007. (ENG., Illus.). 208p. (J). (gr. 3-7). pap. 17.99 *(978-1-59643-108-9(3),* 9781596431089, First Second Bks.) Roaring Brook Pr.
Venditti, Robert. Rise of the Robot Army. Higgins, Dusty, illus. 2016. (Miles Taylor & the Golden Cape Ser.: 2). (ENG.). 304p. (J). (gr. 4-7). 16.99 *(978-1-4814-0557-7(8),* Simon & Schuster Bks. For Young Readers) Simon & Schuster Bks. For Young Readers.
Vick-E & Random House Disney Staff. Wall-E. Orpinas, Jean-Paul et al, illus. 2008. (Little Golden Book Ser.). (ENG.). 24p. (J). (gr. -1-2). 3.99 *(978-0-7364-2422-6(9),* RH/Disney) Random Hse. Children's Bks.
Villeneuve, Kevin J. The Adventures of Nick the Ecologist & His Robot O-Zone: The Mystery of the Missing Trees. 2007. 96p. per. 9.95 *(978-0-595-42362-0(0))* iUniverse, Inc.
Watson, Paul. The Robot. 2011. (ENG.). 272p. (YA). (gr. 7). E-Book *(978-1-101-54326-9(4),* Razorbill) Penguin Young Readers Group.
Weber, Erec-Michael Ollier. Bryce & the Blood Ninjas. Harvey II, Alvin, illus. 2013. 38p. pap. 20.00 *(978-0-9716481-9-7(0))* Kila Springs Pr.
Webster, Christy. Green Team! 2012. (Step into Reading Level 4 Ser.). lib. bdg. 13.55 *(978-0-606-26801-1(4),* Turtleback) Turtleback Bks.
—Robot Rampage! 2013. (Step into Reading Level 4 Ser.). lib. bdg. 13.55 *(978-0-606-26985-8(1),* Turtleback) Turtleback Bks.
Weigel, Jeff. Atomic Ace & the Robot Rampage. Weigel, Jeff, illus. 2006. (ENG., Illus.). 32p. (J). (gr. 1-5). 6.95 *(978-0-8075-0485-7(8));* 15.95 *(978-0-8075-0484-0(X))* Whitman, Albert & Co.
Weisman, Greg, et al. Wonderland, 1 vol. Jones, Christopher, illus. 2013. (Young Justice Ser.). (ENG.). 32p. (gr. 2-3). 22.60 *(978-1-4342-6040-6(2))* Stone Arch Bks.
Wells, Dan. Fragments. 2013. (Partials Sequence Ser.: 2). (ENG.). 576p. (YA). (gr. 9). 17.99 *(978-0-06-207107-1(6))* HarperCollins Pubs.
—Partials. (ENG.). (YA). 2013. (Partials Sequence Ser.: 1). 528p. (gr. 9). pap. 9.99 *(978-0-06-207105-7(X))* 2012. (Partials Sequence Ser.: 1). 480p. (gr. 9). 17.99 *(978-0-06-207104-0(1))* 2012. 496p. pap. 9.99 *(978-0-06-213669-8(4))* HarperCollins Pubs.
Wells, Robison. Feedback. (ENG.). (YA). 2013. (Variant Ser.: 2). 336p. (gr. 8). pap. 9.99 *(978-0-06-202611-8(9))* 2012. 320p. pap. 9.99 *(978-0-06-222830-7(7))* HarperCollins Pubs. (HarperTeen).
West, Tracey. Me & My Robot. Revell, Cindy, illus. 2003. (Penguin Young Readers, Level 2 Ser.). (ENG.). 32p. (J). (gr. 1-2). mass mkt. 3.99 *(978-0-448-42895-6(4),* Penguin Young Readers) Penguin Young Readers Group.
—Me & My Robot No.2: The Show-and-Tell Show-Off. 2003. (Penguin Young Readers Level 2 Ser.). (gr. k-3). lib. bdg. 13.55 *(978-0-613-64065-7(9),* Turtleback) Turtleback Bks.
West, Tracey, adapted by. Robotic Fish Gone Wild! 2005. (Illus.). 30p. (J). pap. *(978-0-439-76833-7(0))* Scholastic, Inc.
Wheeler, Shannon & Torres, J. Wall E Vol. 1: Recharge. Luthi, Morgan, illus. 2010. (ENG.). 112p. (J). 24.99 *(978-1-60886-554-3(1))* Boom! Studios.
Wheeler, Shannon, et al. Wall-E Vol. 1: Recharge. Luthi, Morgan & Barks, Carl, illus. 2010. (ENG.). 112p. (J). pap. 9.99 *(978-1-60886-512-3(6))* Boom! Studios.
Wilson, Daniel H. A Boy & His Bot. 2011. (ENG., Illus.). 192p. (YA). (gr. 3-7). 16.99 *(978-1-59990-280-7(X),* 9781599902807, Bloomsbury USA Childrens) Bloomsbury Publishing USA.
Winick, Judd. The Boy Who Crashed to Earth. 2015. (Hilo Ser.: 1). (ENG., Illus.). 208p. (J). (gr. 3-7). 16.99 *(978-0-385-38618-0(4),* Random Hse. Bks. for Young Readers) Random Hse. Children's Bks.
—Saving the Whole Wide World. 2016. (Hilo Ser.: 2). (ENG., Illus.). 208p. (J). (gr. 3-7). 16.99 *(978-0-385-38624-1(9));*Bk. 2. 13.99 *(978-0-385-38623-4(0))* Random Hse. Children's Bks. (Random Hse. Bks. for Young Readers).
Yaccarino, Dan. Doug Unplugged. (ENG.). 40p. (J). (gr. k-4). 2016. 7.99 *(978-0-375-85921-2(7),* Dragonfly Bks.) 2013. (Illus.). 16.99 *(978-0-375-86643-2(4),* Knopf Bks. for Young Readers) Random Hse. Children's Bks.
—Zorgoochi Intergalactic Pizza: Delivery of Doom. Yaccarino, Dan, illus. 2014. (ENG., Illus.). 336p. (J). (gr. 3-7). 16.99 *(978-1-250-00844-2(1),* 9781250008442) Feiwel & Friends.
Your Very Own Robot. 2007. (Choose Your Own Adventure Ser.). (Illus.). 80p. (J). (gr. 4-7). pap. 7.99 *(978-1-933390-52-9(2))* Chooseco LLC.
Zafón, Carlos Ruiz. The Watcher in the Shadows. (ENG.). (YA). (gr. 7-17). 2014. 288p. pap. 10.99 *(978-0-316-04475-2(X))* 2013. 272p. 18.00 *(978-0-316-04476-9(8))* Little, Brown Bks. for Young Readers.
Zuchora-Walske, Christine. Weather Robots. 2014. (Lightning Bolt Books Robots Everywhere! Ser.). (ENG., Illus.). 32p. (gr. k-2). lib. bdg. 26.60 *(978-1-4677-4057-9(8),* Lerner Pubns.) Lerner Publishing Group.

ROCK CLIMBING

see Mountaineering

ROCK MUSIC

Aberback, Brian. Black Sabbath: Pioneers of Heavy Metal. 2010. (Rebels of Rock Ser.). (Illus.). 112p. (J). (gr. 7-12). 33.27 *(978-0-7660-3379-5(1))* Enslow Pubs., Inc.
Alagna, Magdalena. Elvis Presley. 2009. (Rock & Roll Hall of Famers Ser.). 112p. (gr. 5-8). 63.90 *(978-1-60852-474-7(4),* Rosen Reference) Rosen Publishing Group, Inc., The.
Altmann, Scott. Guitar Rock Star Sticker Activity Book. 2008. (Dover Little Activity Bks.). (ENG.). 4p. (J). (gr. -1-5). pap. 1.50 *(978-0-486-46790-0(2))* Dover Pubns., Inc.
Anderson, Jennifer Joline. How to Analyze the Music of Michael Jackson, 1 vol. 2011. (Essential Critiques Set 2 Ser.). (ENG., Illus.). 112p. (J). (gr. 6-12). lib. bdg. 35.64 *(978-1-61783-091-4(7))* ABDO Publishing Co.
Anderson, Tom. Top 40 Fun Facts: Rock & Roll. 2003. (ENG.). 64p. pap. 24.99 *(978-0-634-06552-1(1),* 0634065521) Leonard, Hal Corp.
Anniss, Matt. Music, Fashion, & Style. 2015. (Music Scene Ser.). (J). lib. bdg. 37.10 *(978-1-59920-912-8(8))* Black Rabbit Bks.
—Performing Live. 2015. (Music Scene Ser.). (J). lib. bdg. 37.10 *(978-1-59920-913-5(6))* Black Rabbit Bks.
—The Story of Punk & Indie. 2013. (Pop Histories Ser.). 32p. (gr. 4-7). 31.35 *(978-1-59920-968-5(3))* Black Rabbit Bks.
—The Story of Rock Music. 2013. (Pop Histories Ser.). 32p. (gr. 4-9). 28.50 *(978-1-59920-969-2(1))* Black Rabbit Bks.
Anniss, Matthew. Music, Fashion & Style. 2016. (ENG., Illus.). 48p. (J). (gr. 5-9). pap. 12.99 *(978-1-4451-3940-1(5),* Franklin Watts) Hachette Children's Group GBR. Dist: Hachette Bk. Group.
—The Music Scene - Performing Live. 2016. (Music Scene Ser.). (ENG., Illus.). 48p. (J). (gr. 5-9). pap. 12.99 *(978-1-4451-3941-8(3),* Franklin Watts) Hachette Children's Group GBR. Dist: Hachette Bk. Group.
—Recording & Promoting Your Music, 1 vol. 2014. (I'm in the Band Ser.). (ENG.). 48p. (gr. 6-6). 33.32 *(978-1-4109-6726-8(3))* Heinemann-Raintree.
Barbo, Maria S. Rock Star! Gonzales, Chuck, illus. 2009. (ENG.). 128p. (J). (gr. 2-6). pap. 16.99 *(978-0-312-59606-4(5),* 9780312596064) Feiwel & Friends.
Beyer, Mark. Stevie Wonder. 2006. (Rock & Roll Hall of Famers Ser.). (Illus.). 112p. (YA). (gr. 5-8). lib. bdg. 34.60 *(978-0-8239-3525-3(6))* Rosen Publishing Group, Inc., The.
Bidini, Dave. For Those about to Rock: A Road Map to Being in a Band. 2004. (ENG.). 144p. (J). (gr. 5). pap. 8.95 *(978-0-88776-653-4(6),* Tundra Bks.) Tundra Bks. CAN. Dist: Penguin Random Hse. LLC.
Bowe, Brian J. The Clash: Punk Rock Band. 2010. (Rebels of Rock Ser.). (Illus.). 112p. (J). (gr. 7-12). 33.27 *(978-0-7660-3232-3(9))* Enslow Pubs., Inc.
—Judas Priest: Metal Gods. 2009. (Rebels of Rock Ser.). (Illus.). 112p. (J). (gr. 7-12). lib. bdg. 33.27 *(978-0-7660-3029-9(6))* Enslow Pubs., Inc.
—The Ramones: American Punk Rock Band. 2010. (Rebels of Rock Ser.). (Illus.). 128p. (J). (gr. 7-12). 33.27 *(978-0-7660-3233-0(7))* Enslow Pubs., Inc.
Boynton, Sandra. Dog Train: A Wild Ride on the Rock-and-Roll Side. Boynton, Sandra, illus. 2005. (ENG., Illus.). 64p. (J). (gr. -1-k). 17.95 *(978-0-7611-3966-9(4),* 13966) Workman Publishing Co., Inc.
Breguet, Amy. Yellowcard. 2009. (Contemporary Musicians & Their Music Ser.). 48p. (gr. 6-6). 53.00 *(978-1-61511-948-6(5))* Rosen Publishing Group, Inc., The.
Broadbent, Paul. Rock Stars. 2007. (Trackers-Math Ser.). (gr. 2-5). pap. 5.00 *(978-1-59055-939-0(8))* Pacific Learning, Inc.
Burlingame, Jeff. Aerosmith: Hard Rock Superstars. 2010. (Rebels of Rock Ser.). (Illus.). 112p. (J). (gr. 7-12). 33.27 *(978-0-7660-3236-1(1))* Enslow Pubs., Inc.
Carr, Aaron. Rock. 2015. (J). *(978-1-4896-3593-8(9))* Weigl Pubs., Inc.
Clayton, Marie. Elvis Presley: Unseen Archives. (Unseen Archives Ser.). (Illus.). 384p. *(978-0-7525-8335-8(2))* Parragon, Inc.
Corporate Contributor Staff & Perl, Sheri. The Economics of a Rock Concert. 2013. (ENG.). 48p. (J). *(978-0-7787-7969-8(6));* pap. *(978-0-7787-7974-2(2))* Crabtree Publishing Co.
Croft, Malcolm & Besley, Preston. 5 Seconds of Summer Confidential: Over 100 Amazing Photographs of the World's Hottest Boy Band. 2015. (ENG., Illus.). 96p. (YA). (gr. 3-11). pap. 9.99 *(978-1-4380-0716-8(7))* Barron's Educational Series, Inc.
Dakers, Diane. The Beatles: Leading the British Invasion. 2013. (ENG., Illus.). 112p. (J). *(978-0-7787-1035-6(1))* Crabtree Publishing Co.
Doeden, Matt. Green Day: Keeping Their Edge. 2007. (Gateway Biography Ser.). (Illus.). 48p. (J). (gr. 4-8). pap. 8.95 *(978-0-8225-6429-4(7))* Lerner Publishing Group.
Doll, Susan. Elvis Presley: With Profiles of Muddy Waters & Mick Jagger. 2006. (Biographical Connections Ser.). (Illus.). 112p. (J). *(978-0-7166-1823-2(0))* World Bk., Inc.
Edgers, Geoff. Who Were the Beatles? Tageau, Jerry, illus. 2006. (Who Was... ? Ser.). 106p. (J). *(978-0-448-43907-5(7),* Grosset & Dunlap) Penguin Publishing Group.
—Who Were the Beatles? Tugeau, Jeremy, illus. 2006. (Who Was? Ser.). (ENG.). 112p. (J). (gr. 3-7). pap. 5.99 *(978-0-448-43906-8(9),* Grosset & Dunlap) Penguin Young Readers Group.
Edward, Herman. Pink Floyd. 2007. (Popular Rock Superstars of Yesterday & Today Ser.). (Illus.). 64p. (YA). (gr. 3-7). pap. 7.95 *(978-1-4222-0313-2(1))* Mason Crest.
Faber, Nancy, et al. ShowTime Rock 'n Roll: Level 2A. 2012. (ENG.). 24p. pap. 5.99 *(978-1-61677-632-9(3),* 1616776323) Faber Piano Adventures(r).
Farseth, Erik. American Rock: Guitar Heroes, Punks, & Metalheads. 2012. (American Music Milestones Ser.). (ENG., Illus.). 64p. (gr. 5-12). lib. bdg. 30.60 *(978-0-7613-4503-9(5))* Lerner Publishing Group.
Flynn, Noa. The Who. 2007. (Popular Rock Superstars of Yesterday & Today Ser.). (Illus.). 64p. (YA). (gr. 3-7). pap. 7.95 *(978-1-4222-0323-1(8))* Mason Crest.
Forget, Thomas. The Rolling Stones. 2009. (Rock & Roll Hall of Famers Ser.). 112p. (gr. 5-8). 63.90 *(978-1-60852-478-5(7),* Rosen Reference) Rosen Publishing Group, Inc., The.
Gillie, Brian. A Guide to the Best Vocal Harmonies of Rock 'n' Roll: 1955 - 1985. 2004. 225p. 27.00 *(978-0-9760837-1-9(X));* per. 35.00 *(978-0-9760837-0-2(1))* Keysquake Music.
Golio, Gary. Jimi: Sounds Like a Rainbow - A Story of the Young Jimi Hendrix. Steptoe, Javaka, illus. 2010. (ENG.). 32p. (J). (gr. 1-4). 17.99 *(978-0-618-85279-6(4))* Houghton Mifflin Harcourt Publishing Co.
Gregory, Peter. The Allman Brothers Band. 2007. (Popular Rock Superstars of Yesterday & Today Ser.). (Illus.). 64p. (YA). (gr. 3-7). pap. 7.95 *(978-1-4222-0310-1(7))* Mason Crest.
—Queen. 2007. (Popular Rock Superstars of Yesterday & Today Ser.). (Illus.). 64p. (YA). (gr. 4-7). pap. 7.95 *(978-1-4222-0318-7(2))* Mason Crest.
Guillain, Charlotte. Punk: Music, Fashion, Attitude! 2010. (Culture in Action Ser.). (ENG.). 32p. (gr. 3-6). 30.65 *(978-1-4109-3916-6(2),* NA-r) Heinemann-Raintree.
Handyside, Chris. A History of Rock & Roll. 2006. (J). *(978-1-4109-1815-4(7))* Steck-Vaughn.
Harmon, Daniel E. How to Start Your Own Band. 2011. (Garage Bands Ser.). (ENG.). 64p. (YA). (gr. 5-8). pap. 12.95 *(978-1-4488-5661-9(2));* lib. bdg. 31.95 *(978-1-4488-5657-2(4))* Rosen Publishing Group, Inc., The. (Rosen Reference).
—Managing Your Band. 2011. (Garage Bands Ser.). (ENG.). 64p. (YA). (gr. 5-8). pap. 12.95 *(978-1-4488-5663-3(9));* lib. bdg. 31.95 *(978-1-4488-5659-6(0))* Rosen Publishing Group, Inc., The.
Holcomb, Mark. The Beach Boys. 2006. (Rock & Roll Hall of Famers Ser.). (Illus.). 112p. (YA). (gr. 5-8). lib. bdg. 34.60 *(978-0-8239-3643-4(0))* Rosen Publishing Group, Inc., The.
Hollow, Michele C. Grateful Dead: What a Long, Strange Trip It's Been. 2009. (Rebels of Rock Ser.). (Illus.). 104p. (J). (gr. 7-12). lib. bdg. 33.27 *(978-0-7660-3028-2(8))* Enslow Pubs., Inc.

Holub, Joan. What Was Woodstock? Copeland, Gregory & McVeigh, Kevin, illus. 2016. (What Was? Ser.). (ENG.). 112p. (J). (gr. 3-7). 5.99 *(978-0-448-48696-3(2),* Grosset & Dunlap) Penguin Young Readers Group.

—What Was Woodstock? 2016. (What Was... ? Ser.). lib. bdg. 16.00 *(978-0-606-38414-8(6))* Turtleback Bks.

Jay, Aye. Punk Rock Fun Time Activity Book. 2009. (ENG., Illus.). 48p. pap. *(978-1-55022-872-4(2))* Filmer Ltd.

Johnson, Robin. The Jonas Brothers. 2010. (Superstars! Ser.). (ENG.). 32p. (J). pap. *(978-0-7787-7256-9(X))* Crabtree Publishing Co.

Juzwiak, Rich. Lifehouse. 2009. (Contemporary Musicians & Their Music Ser.). 48p. (gr. 6-6). 53.00 *(978-1-61511-941-7(8))* Rosen Publishing Group, Inc., The.

Juzwiak, Richard. Lifehouse. 2006. (Contemporary Musicians & Their Music Ser.). (Illus.). 48p. (YA). (gr. 5-9). lib. bdg. 29.25 *(978-1-4042-0710-3(4))* Rosen Publishing Group, Inc., The.

Kallen, Stuart A. Bono. (Role Model Entertainers Ser.). (Illus.). 64p. (YA). 2010. (gr. 7-12). 22.95 *(978-1-4222-0499-3(5))* 2007. pap. 9.95 *(978-1-4222-0786-4(2))* Mason Crest.

Kallen, Stuart A., ed. Alternative Rock. 2012. (Music Library). (ENG., Illus.). 128p. (J). (gr. 7-10). lib. bdg. 34.45 *(978-1-4205-0738-6(9))* Cengage Gale.

—The History of Rock & Roll. 2012. (Music Library). (Illus.). 128p. (J). (gr. 7-10). lib. bdg. 34.45 *(978-1-4205-0694-5(3))* Cengage Gale.

Kenney, Karen Latchana. Cool Rock Music: Create & Appreciate What Makes Music Great!, 1 vol. 2008. (Cool Music Ser.). (ENG., Illus.). 32p. (YA). (gr. 3-6). 28.50 *(978-1-59928-974-8(1))* ABDO Publishing Co.

La Bella, Laura. My Chemical Romance. 2008. (Contemporary Musicians & Their Music Ser.). (Illus.). 48p. (J). lib. bdg. 29.25 *(978-1-4042-1818-5(1))* Rosen Publishing Group, Inc., The.

Marcovitz, Hal. Rock 'n Roll. 2004. (American Symbols & Their Meanings Ser.). (Illus.). 48p. (J). (gr. 4-18). lib. bdg. 19.95 *(978-1-59084-036-8(4))* Mason Crest.

—Rock 'N' Roll: Voice of American Youth. Moreno, Barry, ed. 2014. (Patriotic Symbols of America Ser.: 20). (Illus.). 48p. (J). (gr. 4-18). lib. bdg. 20.95 *(978-1-4222-3129-6(1))* Mason Crest.

Markel, Rita J. Jimi Hendrix. (Biography Ser.). (Illus.). 112p. (gr. 6-12). 2005. (J). lib. bdg. 27.93 *(978-0-8225-4990-1(5))* 2003. (YA). pap. 7.95 *(978-0-8225-9697-4(0),* Carolrhoda Bks.) Lerner Publishing Group.

Markel, Rita J. & Poole, Rebecca. Jimi Hendrix. 2006. (Just the Facts Biographies Ser.). (ENG., Illus.). 112p. (gr. 5-12). 27.93 *(978-0-8225-3532-4(7),* Lerner Pubns.) Lerner Publishing Group.

Masar, Brenden. The History of Punk Rock. 2006. (Music Library). (ENG., Illus.). 104p. (J). (gr. 3-7). lib. bdg. 33.45 *(978-1-59018-738-8(5),* Lucent Bks.) Cengage Gale.

Mattern, Joanne. Jonas Brothers. 2008. (Robbie Reader Ser.). (Illus.). 32p. (YA). (gr. 2-5). lib. bdg. 25.70 *(978-1-58415-721-2(6))* Mitchell Lane Pubs., Inc.

McIntosh, Kenneth. The Grateful Dead. 2007. (Popular Rock Superstars of Yesterday & Today Ser.). (Illus.). 64p. (YA). (gr. 4-7). pap. 7.95 *(978-1-4222-0314-9(X))* Mason Crest.

—U2. 2007. (Popular Rock Superstars of Yesterday & Today Ser.). (Illus.). 64p. (YA). (gr. 4-7). pap. 7.95 *(978-1-4222-0322-4(0))* Mason Crest.

Mead, Wendy. The Alternative Rock Scene: The Stars, the Fans, the Music. 2009. (Music Scene Ser.). (Illus.). 48p. (J). (gr. 5-9). lib. bdg. 25.27 *(978-0-7660-3401-3(1))* Enslow Pubs., Inc.

Miles Kelly Staff. Rock & Pop. 2003. (Flip Quiz Ser.). (Illus.). 152p. (J). spiral bd. 12.95 *(978-1-84236-145-0(7))* Miles Kelly Publishing, Ltd. GBR. Dist: Independent Pubs. Group.

Miller, Adam. Finding a Music Style, 1 vol. 2014. (I'm in the Band Ser.). (ENG.). 48p. (gr. 6-6). 33.32 *(978-1-4109-6725-1(5))* Heinemann-Raintree.

Morreale, Marie. Ross Lynch. 2015. (ENG., Illus.). 48p. (J). lib. bdg. *(978-0-531-21573-9(3))* Children's Pr., Ltd.

Morse, Eric. What Is Punk? Yi, Anny, illus. 2015. (ENG.). 32p. (J). 15.95 *(978-1-61775-392-3(0),* Black Sheep) Akashic Bks.

O'Connor, Jim. What Is Rock & Roll? Copeland, Gregory, illus. 2017. (What Was? Ser.). (ENG.). 112p. (J). (gr. 3-7). 5.99 ***(978-0-451-53381-4(X))***; lib. bdg. 15.99 ***(978-0-451-53383-8(6))*** Penguin Young Readers Group. (Grosset & Dunlap).

Okun, Milton, ed. Great Rock Ballads. 104p. (YA). pap. 15.95 *(978-0-89524-936-4(7),* 02502173) Cherry Lane Music Co.

—Shawn Colvin - Cover Girl. 32p. (Orig.). (YA). pap. 12.95 *(978-0-89524-867-1(0),* 02506918) Cherry Lane Music Co.

O'Mahony, John. Elton John. 2003. (World Musicmakers Ser.). (Illus.). 64p. (J). 26.20 *(978-1-56711-972-5(7),* Blackbirch Pr., Inc.) Cengage Gale.

One Direction Staff. One Direction: Behind the Scenes. 2012. (Illus.). 64p. (J). (gr. 3-7). pap. 10.99 *(978-0-06-222315-9(1))* HarperCollins Pubs.

Overbey, Theresa. Michael Jackson. l.t. ed. 2003. (Blue Banner Biography Ser.). (Illus.). 32p. (J). (gr. 3-8). lib. bdg. 25.70 *(978-1-58415-216-3(8))* Mitchell Lane Pubs., Inc.

Owen, Ruth. I Can Start a Band! 2017. (Kids Can Do It! Ser.). 32p. (gr. 8-8). 28.50 ***(978-1-4994-8347-5(3),*** Windmill Bks.) Rosen Publishing Group, Inc., The.

Plantz, Connie. Elvis Presley: Music Legend, Movie Star, the King. 2004. (People to Know Ser.). (Illus.). 128p. (J). lib. bdg. 26.60 *(978-0-7660-2103-7(3))* Enslow Pubs., Inc.

Polark, Kelly. Rockabet: Classic Edition. Little, Kelli Ann, illus. 2013. 32p. pap. 10.49 *(978-0-9888462-0-3(9))* Big Smile Pr., LLC.

Pop Rock: Popular Rock Superstars of Yesterday & Today, 17 vols., Set. Incl. AC/DC. Schlesinger, Ethan. (gr. 3-7). lib. bdg. 22.95 *(978-1-4222-0183-1(X));* Aerosmith. Schlesinger, Ethan. (gr. 3-7). lib. bdg. 22.95 *(978-1-4222-0184-8(8));* Allman Brothers. Gregory, Peter. (gr. 3-7). lib. bdg. 22.95 *(978-1-4222-0188-6(0));* Beatles. Gallagher, James. (gr. 4-7). lib. bdg. 22.95 *(978-1-4222-0186-2(4));* Billy Joel. Schlesinger, Ethan. (gr. 3-7). lib. bdg. 22.95 *(978-1-4222-0185-5(6));* Bob Marley & the Wailers. Waters, Rosa. (gr. 7-18). lib. bdg. 22.95 *(978-1-4222-0192-3(9));* Bruce Springsteen. Simons, Rae. (gr. 4-7). lib. bdg. 22.95 *(978-1-4222-0187-9(2));* Doors. Simons, Rae. (gr. 3-7). lib. bdg. 22.95 *(978-1-4222-0190-9(2));* Elton John. Schlesinger, Ethan. (gr. 3-7). lib. bdg. 22.95 *(978-1-4222-0189-3(9));* Grateful Dead. McIntosh, Kenneth. (gr. 4-7). lib. bdg. 22.95 *(978-1-4222-0191-6(0));* Led Zeppelin. Schlesinger, Ethan. (gr. 3-7). lib. bdg. 22.95 *(978-1-4222-0212-8(7));* Lynyrd Skynrd. Walker, Ida. (gr. 4-7). lib. bdg. 22.95 *(978-1-4222-0213-5(5));* Pink Floyd. Edward, Herman. (gr. 3-7). lib. bdg. 22.95 *(978-1-4222-0214-2(3));* Queen. Gregory, Peter. (gr. 4-7). lib. bdg. 22.95 *(978-1-4222-0193-0(7));* Rolling Stones. Schlesinger, Ethan. (gr. 3-7). lib. bdg. 22.95 *(978-1-4222-0194-7(5));* Who. Flynn, Noa. (gr. 3-7). lib. bdg. 22.95 *(978-1-4222-0196-1(1));* (Illus.). 64p. (YA). 2008. 2007. Set lib. bdg. 390.15 *(978-1-4222-0182-4(1))* Mason Crest.

Rau, Dana Meachen. Who Are the Rolling Stones? 2017. (Who Is... ? Ser.). lib. bdg. 16.00 ***(978-0-606-39778-0(7))*** Turtleback Bks.

Raymer, Miles. How to Analyze the Music of Paul McCartney, 1 vol. 2010. (Essential Critiques Set 1 Ser.). (ENG.). 112p. (J). (gr. 6-12). lib. bdg. 35.64 *(978-1-61613-531-7(X),* Essential Library) ABDO Publishing Co.

Reisfeld, Randi. This Is the Sound: The Best of Alternative Rock. 2011. (ENG.). 144p. (YA). (gr. 9). pap. 8.99 *(978-1-4424-3098-3(2),* Simon Pulse) Simon Pulse.

Riggs, Kate. Rock 'n' Roll Music. 2008. (World of Music Ser.). (Illus.). 24p. (J). (gr. -1). lib. bdg. 24.25 *(978-1-58341-569-6(6),* Creative Education) Creative Co., The.

Rivera, Ursula. The Supremes. 2009. (Rock & Roll Hall of Famers Ser.). 112p. (gr. 5-8). 63.90 *(978-1-60852-479-2(5),* Rosen Reference) Rosen Publishing Group, Inc., The.

Roberts, Jeremy. The Beatles. (Biography Ser.). (Illus.). 112p. (J). (gr. 6-12). 2005. lib. bdg. 27.93 *(978-0-8225-4998-7(0))* 2003. pap. 7.95 *(978-0-8225-5002-0(4))* Lerner Publishing Group.

—Bob Dylan: Voice of a Generation. 128p. (J). (gr. 6-18). 18.95 *(978-1-58013-155-1(7),* Kar-Ben Publishing); 2005. (ENG., Illus.). 27.93 *(978-0-8225-1368-1(4),* Lerner Pubns.) Lerner Publishing Group.

Robison, Greg. Christian Rock Festivals. (Monster Music Festivals Ser.). 48p. 2009. (gr. 5-8). pap. 11.75 *(978-1-4358-5122-1(6),* Rosen Reference) 2009. (gr. 5-6). 53.00 *(978-1-61514-650-5(4),* Rosen Reference) 2008. (Illus.). (J). lib. bdg. 29.25 *(978-1-4042-1764-3(3))* Rosen Publishing Group, Inc., The.

—Coachella. (Monster Music Festivals Ser.). 48p. 2009. (gr. 5-8). pap. 11.75 *(978-1-4358-5120-7(X),* Rosen Classroom) 2008. (Illus.). (J). lib. bdg. 29.25 *(978-1-4042-1755-3(X))* Rosen Publishing Group, Inc., The.

—Ozzfest. (Monster Music Festivals Ser.). 48p. 2009. (gr. 5-6). 53.00 *(978-1-61514-656-7(3),* Rosen Reference) 2008. (Illus.). (J). lib. bdg. 29.25 *(978-1-4042-1756-0(8))* Rosen Publishing Group, Inc., The.

—Vans Warped Tour. (Monster Music Festivals Ser.). 48p. 2009. (gr. 5-8). pap. 11.75 *(978-1-4358-5119-1(6),* Rosen Classroom) 2009. (gr. 5-6). 53.00 *(978-1-61514-659-8(8),* Rosen Reference) 2008. (Illus.). (J). lib. bdg. 29.25 *(978-1-4042-1754-6(1))* Rosen Publishing Group, Inc., The.

Robson, David. Prince: Singer-Songwriter, Musician, & Record Producer. (Transcending Race in America Ser.). 64p. (YA). 2010. (Illus.). (gr. 4-8). lib. bdg. 22.95 *(978-1-4222-1614-9(4))* 2009. (gr. 5-18). pap. 9.95 *(978-1-4222-1628-6(4))* Mason Crest.

Rock & Roll Hall of Famers. 2006. (Illus.). 112p. (gr. 5-8). lib. bdg. 263.40 *(978-0-8239-3916-9(2))* Rosen Publishing Group, Inc., The.

Rock & Roll Hall of Famers: Set 1, 6 bks. Incl. Beatles. Wentzel, Jim. lib. bdg. 34.60 *(978-0-8239-3526-0(4));* Elvis Presley. Alagna, Magdalena. lib. bdg. 34.60 *(978-0-8239-3524-6(8));* Stevie Wonder. Beyer, Mark. lib. bdg. 34.60 *(978-0-8239-3525-3(6));* Supremes. Rivera, Ursula. lib. bdg. 34.60 *(978-0-8239-3527-7(2));* 112p. (YA). (gr. 5-8). (Illus.). 2006. Set lib. bdg. 175.50 *(978-0-8239-9692-6(1))* Rosen Publishing Group, Inc., The.

Rosen, Steven & Steventon, John. History of Rock. 2009. (Crabtree Contact Ser.). (ENG., Illus.). 32p. (J). (gr. 6-8). pap. *(978-0-7787-3844-2(2));* lib. bdg. *(978-0-7787-3823-7(X))* Crabtree Publishing Co.

Saulmon, Greg. Linkin Park. (Contemporary Musicians & Their Music Ser.). 48p. 2009. (gr. 6-6). 53.00 *(978-1-61511-942-4(6))* 2006. (Illus.). (YA). (gr. 5-9). lib. bdg. 26.50 *(978-1-4042-0713-4(9))* Rosen Publishing Group, Inc., The.

Schaffer, David. Bono. 2003. (Illus.). 112p. (J). 32.45 *(978-1-59018-274-1(X),* Lucent Bks.) Cengage Gale.

Schlesinger, Ethan. AC/DC. 2008. (Pop Rock Ser.). (Illus.). 64p. (YA). (gr. 3-7). lib. bdg. 22.95 *(978-1-4222-0183-1(X))* Mason Crest.

—Aerosmith. (Pop Rock Ser.). (Illus.). 64p. (YA). (gr. 3-7). 2008. lib. bdg. 22.95 *(978-1-4222-0184-8(8))* 2007. pap. 7.95 *(978-1-4222-0309-5(3))* Mason Crest.

—Billy Joel. 2007. (Popular Rock Superstars of Yesterday & Today Ser.). (Illus.). 64p. (YA). (gr. 3-7). pap. 7.95 *(978-1-4222-0315-6(8))* Mason Crest.

—Led Zeppelin. 2008. (Pop Rock Ser.). (Illus.). 64p. (YA). (gr. 3-7). lib. bdg. 22.95 *(978-1-4222-0212-8(7))* Mason Crest.

—The Rolling Stones. 2007. (Popular Rock Superstars of Yesterday & Today Ser.). (Illus.). 64p. (YA). (gr. 3-7). pap. 7.95 *(978-1-4222-0319-4(0))* Mason Crest.

Schuman, Michael. Bob Dylan. 2017. (J). ***(978-0-7660-9206-8(2))*** Enslow Pubs., Inc.

Schuman, Michael A. Bob Dylan: The Life & Times of an American Icon. 2003. (People to Know Ser.). (Illus.). 112p. (J). lib. bdg. 26.60 *(978-0-7660-2108-2(4))* Enslow Pubs., Inc.

Simons, Rae. The Doors. 2007. (Popular Rock Superstars of Yesterday & Today Ser.). (Illus.). 64p. (YA). (gr. 3-7). pap. 7.95 *(978-1-4222-0312-5(3))* Mason Crest.

Skancke, Jennifer. The History of Indie Rock. 2007. (Music Library). (ENG., Illus.). 104p. (J). (gr. 3-7). lib. bdg. 34.45 *(978-1-59018-736-4(9),* Lucent Bks.) Cengage Gale.

Slavicek, Louise Chipley. Carlos Santana. 2006. (Great Hispanic Heritage Ser.). (Illus.). 112p. (gr. 6-12). lib. bdg. 35.00 *(978-0-7910-8844-9(8),* Chelsea Hse.) Facts On File, Inc.

Spilsbury, Richard. Forming a Band, 1 vol. 2014. (I'm in the Band Ser.). (ENG.). 48p. (gr. 6-6). 33.32 *(978-1-4109-6723-7(9))* Heinemann-Raintree.

—Performing Live, 1 vol. 2014. (I'm in the Band Ser.). (ENG.). 48p. (gr. 6-6). 33.32 *(978-1-4109-6724-4(7))* Heinemann-Raintree.

Tieck, Sarah. Jonas Brothers: Singing Sensations, 1 vol. 2009. (Big Buddy Biographies Set 2 Ser.). (ENG., Illus.). 32p. (J). (gr. 2-5). 28.50 *(978-1-60453-549-5(0))* ABDO Publishing Co.

—Nat & Alex Wolff: Stars of Nickelodeon's the Naked Brothers Band, 1 vol. 2008. (Big Buddy Biographies Ser.). (ENG.). 32p. (J). (gr. 2-5). 28.50 *(978-1-60453-126-8(6))* ABDO Publishing Co.

Tracy, Kathleen. Chris Daughtry. 2007. (Blue Banner Biography Ser.). (Illus.). 32p. (YA). (gr. 4-7). lib. bdg. 25.70 *(978-1-58415-629-1(5))* Mitchell Lane Pubs., Inc.

Vance, Vince. The Vince Vance Rock & Roll Reader: Bedtime Stories, Poems, Songs, Jokes, Pictures & Other Real Cool Stuff for Kids of All Ages. Pennington, Carole, ed. Looney, Bill, illus. Rice, Bob, photos by. 2003. 182p. (J). (gr. 3-8). per. *(978-0-9652918-0-4(4))* Fullerton Bks., Inc.

Wallenfeldt, Jeff, ed. The Birth of Rock & Roll: Music in the 1950s Through the 1960s. 2012. (Popular Music Through the Decades Ser.). (ENG., Illus.). 240p. (J). (gr. 9-12). lib. bdg. 45.00 *(978-1-61530-906-1(3))* Rosen Publishing Group, Inc., The.

—The Birth of Rock & Roll: Music in the 1950S Through The 1960S. 2012. (Popular Music Through the Decades Ser.). (ENG., Illus.). 240p. (YA). (gr. 9-12). 90.00 *(978-1-61530-915-3(2))* Rosen Publishing Group, Inc., The.

Webster, Christine. The Jonas Brothers. 2009. (Remarkable People Ser.). (Illus.). 24p. (J). (gr. 4-6). pap. 8.95 *(978-1-60596-627-4(4));* lib. bdg. 24.45 *(978-1-60596-626-7(6))* Weigl Pubs., Inc.

Weintraub, Aileen. Kiss: I Wanna Rock & Roll All Night. 2009. (Rebels of Rock Ser.). (Illus.). 112p. (J). (gr. 7-12). lib. bdg. 33.27 *(978-0-7660-3027-5(X))* Enslow Pubs., Inc.

Wentzel, Jim. The Beatles. (Rock & Roll Hall of Famers Ser.). 112p. (gr. 5-8). 2009. 63.90 *(978-1-60852-477-8(9),* Rosen Reference) 2006. (Illus.). (YA). lib. bdg. 34.60 *(978-0-8239-3526-0(4))* Rosen Publishing Group, Inc., The.

White, Katherine. Elton John. 2009. (Rock & Roll Hall of Famers Ser.). 112p. (gr. 5-8). 63.90 *(978-1-60852-473-0(6),* Rosen Reference) Rosen Publishing Group, Inc., The.

Wilhelm, Peggy Jo. The 10 Most Innovative Bands. 2008. 14.99 *(978-1-55448-554-3(1))* Scholastic Library Publishing.

Willett, Edward. Janis Joplin: Take Another Little Piece of My Heart. 2008. (American Rebels Ser.). (Illus.). 152p. (YA). (gr. 3-7). lib. bdg. 35.94 *(978-0-7660-2837-1(2))* Enslow Pubs., Inc.

Wimmer, Teresa. The Beatles' Sgt. Pepper's Lonely Hearts Club Band. 2008. (What in the World? Ser.). 22.95 *(978-1-58341-651-8(X),* Creative Education) Creative Co., The.

Winckelmann, Thom & Abushanab, Lynn. Bono: Rock Star & Humanitarian, 1 vol. 2009. (Essential Lives Set 4 Ser.). (ENG., Illus.). 112p. (J). (gr. 6-12). lib. bdg. 35.64 *(978-1-60453-698-0(5))* ABDO Publishing Co.

Witmer, Scott. Bookings & Gigs, 1 vol. 2009. (Rock Band Ser.). (ENG., Illus.). 32p. (YA). (gr. 4-7). 27.07 *(978-1-60453-689-8(6))* ABDO Publishing Co.

—Drums, Keyboards, & Other Instruments, 1 vol. 2009. (Rock Band Ser.). (ENG., Illus.). 32p. (YA). (gr. 4-7). 27.07 *(978-1-60453-690-4(X))* ABDO Publishing Co.

—History of Rock Bands, 1 vol. 2009. (Rock Band Ser.). (ENG., Illus.). 32p. (YA). (gr. 4-7). 27.07 *(978-1-60453-692-8(6))* ABDO Publishing Co.

—Managing Your Band, 1 vol. 2009. (Rock Band Ser.). (ENG., Illus.). 32p. (YA). (gr. 4-7). 27.07 *(978-1-60453-693-5(4))* ABDO Publishing Co.

—Recording, 1 vol. 2009. (Rock Band Ser.). (ENG., Illus.). 32p. (YA). (gr. 4-7). 27.07 *(978-1-60453-694-2(2))* ABDO Publishing Co.

—The Show, 1 vol. 2009. (Rock Band Ser.). (ENG., Illus.). 32p. (YA). (gr. 4-7). 27.07 *(978-1-60453-695-9(0))* ABDO Publishing Co.

Zimmerman, Robert. Switchfoot. 2009. (Contemporary Musicians & Their Music Ser.). 48p. (gr. 6-6). 53.00 *(978-1-61511-946-2(9))* Rosen Publishing Group, Inc., The.

Zimmerman, Robert K. Switchfoot. 2006. (Contemporary Musicians & Their Music Ser.). (Illus.). 48p. (YA). (gr. 5-9). lib. bdg. 29.25 *(978-1-4042-0709-7(0))* Rosen Publishing Group, Inc., The.

ROCK MUSIC—FICTION

Alvin & the Chipmunks. 2009. 64p. 4.99 *(978-0-06-184568-0(X))* HarperCollins Pubs.

Auerbach, Annie. The Squeakquel: Battle of the Bands. 2009. (Alvin & the Chipmunks Ser.). (ENG., Illus.). 24p. (J). (gr. -1-2). pap. 3.99 *(978-0-06-184565-9(5),* HarperFestival) HarperCollins Pubs.

Auseon, Andrew. Jo-Jo & the Fiendish Lot. 2009. 473p. (YA). lib. bdg. 18.89 *(978-0-06-113924-6(6),* HarperTeen) HarperCollins Pubs.

Brooks, Kevin. Naked '76. 2016. (ENG.). 424p. (gr. 9-12). 18.99 *(978-1-5124-0418-0(7),* Carolrhoda Bks.) Lerner Publishing Group.

Burian, Natalka. Welcome to the Slipstream. 2017. (ENG., Illus.). 272p. (YA). (gr. 9-12). 17.99 *(978-1-5072-0075-9(7),* Simon Pulse) Simon Pulse.

Camp Rock: Second Session: Super Special: under the Mistletoe (Camp Rock: Second Session) 2009. 256p. pap. 6.99 *(978-1-4231-2222-7(4))* Disney Pr.

Carlisle, Kelly. My Mommy Is A Rocker. 2007. (Illus.). 21p. (J). lib. bdg. *(978-0-9795046-2-4(7))* Kwist, Karla.

Castellucci, Cecil. Beige. (ENG., 320p. (YA). 2009. Illus.). (gr. 9). pap. 8.99 *(978-0-7636-4232-7(0))* 2007. 25.66 *(978-1-4287-4767-8(2))* Candlewick Pr.

Chipponeri, Kelli. SpongeBob Rocks! Martinez, Heather, illus. 2006. (SpongeBob SquarePants Ser.: 9). (ENG.). 32p. (J). (gr. -1-3). pap. 3.99 *(978-1-4169-1314-6(9),* Simon Spotlight/Nickelodeon) Simon Spotlight/Nickelodeon.

Cohn, Rachel & Levithan, David. Nick & Norah's Infinite Playlist. 2009. 10.54 *(978-0-7848-2769-7(9),* Everbind) Marco Bk. Co.

—Nick & Norah's Infinite Playlist. 2007. 183p. (gr. 9-12). 19.00 *(978-0-7569-7949-2(8))* Perfection Learning Corp.

—Nick & Norah's Infinite Playlist. (ENG.). 208p. (YA). (gr. 9-12). 2007. pap. 9.99 *(978-0-375-83533-9(4))* 2008. (Illus.). pap. 9.99 *(978-0-375-84614-4(X))* Random Hse. Children's Bks. (Ember).

Collins, Amberly & Collins, Brandilyn. Final Touch, 1 vol. 2010. (Rayne Tour Ser.). (ENG.). 224p. (YA). (gr. 8-11). pap. 9.99 *(978-0-310-71933-5(X))* Zondervan.

Colman, Michelle Sinclair. Rocker Babies Wear Jeans. Dion, Nathalie, illus. 2009. (Urban Babies Wear Black Book Ser.). (ENG.). 9p. (J). (gr. -1 — 1). bds. 6.99 *(978-1-58246-291-2(7),* Tricycle Pr.) Random Hse. Children's Bks.

Donbavand, Tommy. Flesh of the Zombie, Bk. 4. Cartoon Saloon Staff, illus. 2010. (Scream Street Ser.: 4). (ENG.). 128p. (J). (gr. 3-7). pap. 5.99 *(978-0-7636-4637-0(7))* Candlewick Pr.

Edwards, Garth. The Blue Wizard. Stasyuk, Max, illus. 2011. (Adventures of Titch & Mitch Ser.). (J). pap. *(978-0-9567449-9-9(0))* Inside Pocket Publishing, Ltd.

—The King of the Castle. Stasyuk, Max, illus. 2011. (Adventures of Titch & Mitch Ser.). (J). pap. *(978-0-9567449-7-5(4))* Inside Pocket Publishing, Ltd.

—The Magic Boots. Stasyuk, Max, illus. 2011. (Adventures of Titch & Mitch Ser.). (J). pap. *(978-0-9567449-8-2(2))* Inside Pocket Publishing, Ltd.

—The Trolls of Sugar Loaf Wood. Stasyuk, Max, illus. 2011. (Adventures of Titch & Mitch Ser.). (J). pap. *(978-0-9567449-6-8(6))* Inside Pocket Publishing, Ltd.

—The #02 Trolls of Sugar Loaf Wood. Stasyuk, Max, illus. 2011. (Adventures of Titch & Mitch, the Ser.). (J). pap. *(978-0-7613-8422-9(7))* Inside Pocket Publishing, Ltd.

—The #03 King of the Castle. Stasyuk, Max, illus. 2011. (Adventures of Titch & Mitch, the Ser.). (J). pap. *(978-0-7613-8423-6(5))* Inside Pocket Publishing, Ltd.

—The #04 Magic Boots. Stasyuk, Max, illus. 2011. (Adventures of Titch & Mitch, the Ser.). (J). pap. *(978-0-7613-8424-3(3))* Inside Pocket Publishing, Ltd.

—The #05 Blue Wizard. Stasyuk, Max, illus. 2011. (Adventures of Titch & Mitch, the Ser.). (J). pap. *(978-0-7613-8425-0(1))* Inside Pocket Publishing, Ltd.

Emerson, Kevin. Breakout. 2015. (ENG.). 304p. (YA). (gr. 7). 17.99 *(978-0-385-39112-2(9),* Crown Books For Young Readers) Random Hse. Children's Bks.

FableVision Studios Staff. Zebrafish. FableVision Studios Staff & Reynolds, Peter H., illus. 2010. (Zebrafish Ser.). (ENG.). 128p. (J). (gr. 5-9). 16.99 *(978-1-4169-9525-8(0),* Atheneum Bks. for Young Readers) Simon & Schuster Children's Publishing.

Finn, Perdita & HarperCollins Publishers Ltd. Staff. Alvin & the Chipmunks - The Squeakuel. 2009. (Alvin & the Chipmunks Ser.). (ENG., Illus.). 144p. (J). (gr. 3-7). pap. 5.99 *(978-0-06-184569-7(8),* HarperFestival) HarperCollins Pubs.

Forman, Gayle. Sisters in Sanity. (YA). 2016. (ENG.). 304p. (gr. 8). pap. 9.99 *(978-0-06-088749-0(4))* 2007. 290p. (gr. 7-12). lib. bdg. 17.89 *(978-0-06-088748-3(6))* 2007. (ENG.). 304p. (gr. 7-18). 16.99 *(978-0-06-088747-6(8))* HarperCollins Pubs. (HarperTeen).

—Where She Went. l.t. ed. 2015. (If I Stay Ser.: BK.2). (ENG.). 288p. (YA). 23.99 *(978-1-4104-7562-6(X))* Cengage Gale.

—Where She Went. (If I Stay Ser.: BK.2). (ENG.). (YA). (gr. 9-18). 2012. 304p. 10.99 *(978-0-14-242089-8(1),* Speak) 2011. 272p. 17.99 *(978-0-525-42294-5(3),* Dutton Books for Young Readers) Penguin Young Readers Group.

—Where She Went. 2012. (If I Stay Ser.: BK.2). (YA). 21.00 *(978-1-61383-394-0(6))* Perfection Learning Corp.

—Where She Went. l.t. ed. 2015. (If I Stay Ser.: BK.2). (ENG.). 286p. (YA). pap. 12.99 *(978-1-59413-855-3(9),* Large Print Pr.) Thorndike Pr.

—Where She Went. 2012. (If I Stay Ser.: BK.2). (YA). lib. bdg. 22.10 *(978-0-606-23644-7(9),* Turtleback) Turtleback Bks.

Garcia, Kami & Stohl, Margaret. Dangerous Creatures. 2015. (ENG.). 400p. (J). (gr. 7-17). pap. 12.99 *(978-0-316-37032-5(0))* 2014. 327p. (YA). *(978-0-316-37626-6(4))* 2014. (Dangerous Creatures Ser.: Bk. 1). (ENG.). 384p. (YA). (gr. 7-17). 19.00 *(978-0-316-37031-8(2))* Little, Brown Bks. for Young Readers.

Goetze, Jutta. Luna-C. 2004. (ENG.). 324p. (J). (gr. 9). pap. 13.95 *(978-1-86508-443-5(3))* Allen & Unwin AUS. Dist: Independent Pubs. Group.

Gonzalez, Gabriela & Triana, Gaby. Backstage Pass. 2004. (Illus.). 224p. (J). (gr. 7-18). 15.99 *(978-0-06-056017-1(7));* lib. bdg. 16.89 *(978-0-06-056018-8(5))* HarperCollins Pubs.

Gownley, Jim. Amelia in What Makes You Happy: #6, 1 vol. Gownley, Jim, illus. 2011. (Amelia Rules! Ser.). (ENG., Illus.). 36p. 24.21 *(978-1-59961-792-3(7))* Spotlight.

Gownley, Jimmy. What Makes You Happy. Gownley, Jimmy, illus. 2011. (Amelia Rules! Ser.). (ENG., Illus.). 176p. (J). (gr. 2-7). 19.99 *(978-1-4424-4539-0(4),* Atheneum Bks. for Young Readers) Simon & Schuster Children's Publishing.

Graham, Hilary Weisman. Reunited. 2012. (ENG.). 336p. (YA). (gr. 7). 16.99 *(978-1-4424-3984-9(X),* Simon & Schuster Bks. For Young Readers) Simon & Schuster Bks. For Young Readers.

Gran, Meredeth. Marceline & the Scream Queens. Gran, Meredith, illus. 2013. (Adventure Time Ser.). (ENG., Illus.). 128p. (J). (gr. 4). pap. 19.99 *(978-1-60886-313-6(1))* Boom! Studios.

Greenwald, Tommy. Katie Friedman Gives up Texting! And Lives to Tell about It. Coovert, J. P., illus. 2015. (ENG.). 240p. (J). (gr. 4-7). 13.99 *(978-1-59643-837-8(1),* 9781596438378) Roaring Brook Pr.

Hopkins, Cathy. The Princess of Pop. 2012. (Truth or Dare Ser.). (ENG.). 224p. (YA). (gr. 7). pap. 10.99 *(978-1-4424-6057-7(1),* Simon Pulse) Simon Pulse.

Huston, Donna. Vincent Rocks. 2006. (Illus.). 30p. (J). spiral bd. 19.99 *(978-0-9771192-0-2(3))* Shayne Publishing.

Jonas. JONAS #5: about Face. 5th ed. 2010. 128p. pap. 4.99 *(978-1-4231-1773-5(5))* Disney Pr.

—Three's a Crowd. 6th ed. 2010. 128p. pap. 4.99 *(978-1-4231-2282-1(8))* Disney Pr.

JONAS #8: Prep School Party. 2010. 128p. pap. 4.99 *(978-1-4231-2673-7(4))* Disney Pr.

Krosoczka, Jarrett J. Punk Farm. (ENG.). 40p. (J). (gr. -1-2). 2010. pap. 7.99 *(978-0-440-41793-4(7),* Dragonfly Bks.) 2005. (Illus.). 15.95 *(978-0-375-82429-6(4),* Knopf Bks. for Young Readers) Random Hse. Children's Bks.

—Punk Farm on Tour. 2007. (ENG., Illus.). 40p. (J). (gr. -1-2). 15.99 (978-0-375-83343-4(9), Knopf Bks. for Young Readers) Random Hse. Children's Bks.
Lane, Dakota. Orpheus Obsession. 2005. (Illus.). 288p. (J). lib. bdg. 17.89 (978-0-06-074174-7(0), HarperTeen) HarperCollins Pubs.
—The Orpheus Obsession. 2008. (ENG., Illus.). 288p. (YA). (gr. 9). pap. 8.99 (978-0-06-074175-4(9), HarperTeen) HarperCollins Pubs.
Leveen, Tom. Zero. 2013. (ENG.). 320p. (YA). (gr. 9). pap. 9.99 (978-0-375-87337-9(6), Ember) Random Hse. Children's Bks.
Meadows, Daisy. Destiny the Rock Star Fairy. 2011. (Rainbow Magic Ser.). (ENG., Illus.). 176p. (J). (gr. 2-5). pap. 6.99 (978-0-545-27056-4(1), Scholastic Paperbacks) Scholastic, Inc.
Moore, B. Clay, et al. Put the Book Back on the Shelf: A Belle & Sebastian Anthology. 2006. (ENG., Illus.). 144p. (YA). pap. 19.99 (978-1-58240-600-8(6), 9781582406008) Image Comics.
Nova, Jacy & Nova, Nick. City of the Lost Souls. 2008. (ENG., Illus.). 224p. (YA). (gr. 8-12). 9.99 (978-0-7582-2528-3(8), K-Teen) Kensington Publishing Corp.
Pérez, Celia C. The First Rule of Punk. 2017. (ENG., Illus.). 336p. (J). (gr. 4-7). 16.99 **(978-0-425-29040-8(9)**, Viking Books for Young Readers) Penguin Young Readers Group.
Phillips, Dee. Scout, 1 vol. unabr. ed. 2011. (Right Now! Ser.). (ENG., Illus.). 45p. (YA). (gr. 9-12). pap. 8.95 (978-1-61651-252-1(0)) Saddleback Educational Publishing, Inc.
Pollock, Hal. Meet the Brittles: In Monstermania. 2009. (ENG.). 32p. (J). (gr. -1-3). 15.95 (978-1-59687-858-7(4)) IBks., Inc.
Powell, Randy. Tribute to Another Dead Rock Star. 2003. (ENG.). 224p. (YA). (gr. 7-12). pap. 14.99 (978-0-374-47968-8(2), Sunburst) Farrar, Straus & Giroux.
Pratt, Non. Remix. 2017. (ENG.). 320p. (YA). (gr. 9). pap. 10.99 (978-1-4424-9776-4(9)) Simon & Schuster Children's Publishing.
Prendergast, Gabrielle. The Frail Days, 1 vol. 2015. (Orca Limelights Ser.). (ENG.). 128p. (J). (gr. 6-9). pap. 9.95 (978-1-4598-0464-7(3)) Orca Bk. Pubs. USA.
Raskin, Joyce. My Misadventures As a Teenage Rock Star. Chu, Carol, illus. 2011. (ENG.). 112p. (YA). (gr. 7-18). pap. 8.99 (978-0-547-39311-7(3)) Houghton Mifflin Harcourt Publishing Co.
Rich, Jamie S. Love the Way You Love. Ellerby, Marc, illus. 2006. (J). (978-1-932664-52-2(1)) Oni Pr., Inc.
Rubens, Michael. The Bad Decisions Playlist. (ENG.). 304p. (YA). (gr. 9). 2017. pap. 9.99 **(978-1-328-74208-7(3)**, HMH Books For Young Readers) 2016. 17.99 (978-0-544-09667-7(3)) Houghton Mifflin Harcourt Publishing Co.
Scarsbrook, Richard. Featherless Bipeds. 2006. (ENG.). 224p. per. 15.95 (978-1-897235-05-8(4)) Thistledown Pr., Ltd. CAN. Dist: Univ. of Toronto Pr.
Scotton, Rob. Splat the Cat with a Bang & a Clang. 2013. (Splat the Cat: I Can Read Ser.). (J). lib. bdg. 13.55 (978-0-606-27148-6(1), Turtleback) Turtleback Bks.
Simon, Francesca. Horrid Henry Rocks. Ross, Tony, illus. 2011. (Horrid Henry Ser.: 0). (ENG.). 112p. (J). (gr. 2-5). pap. 7.99 (978-1-4022-5674-5(4), 9781402256745, Sourcebooks Jabberwocky) Sourcebooks, Inc.
—Horrid Henry Rocks, 1 vol. Ross, Tony, illus. 2012. (Horrid Henry Ser.). (ENG.). 112p. (J). (gr. 2-5). lib. bdg. 24.21 (978-1-59961-190-7(2)) Spotlight.
Skuse, C. J. Rockoholic. 2012. (YA). (978-0-545-44251-0(6)); (ENG.). 368p. (J). (gr. 9). 18.99 (978-0-545-42960-3(9)) Scholastic, Inc.
Stanton, Angie. Rock & a Hard Place. 2013. (Jamieson Brothers Ser.: 1). (ENG.). 304p. (YA). (gr. 9). pap. 9.99 (978-0-06-227254-6(3), HarperTeen) HarperCollins Pubs.
—Snapshot. 2013. (Jamieson Brothers Ser.: 2). (ENG.). 416p. (YA). (gr. 9). pap. 9.99 (978-0-06-227256-0(X), HarperTeen) HarperCollins Pubs.
Stern, A. J. Rocking Out! Marts, Doreen Mulryan, illus. 2012. (Frankly, Frannie Ser.: 8). (ENG.). 128p. (J). (gr. 1-3). 12.99 (978-0-448-45751-2(2)); pap. 4.99 (978-0-448-45750-5(4)) Penguin Young Readers Group. (Grosset & Dunlap).
Stevens, R. Diesel Sweeties: I'M a Rocker, I Rock Out. 2013. (ENG., Illus.). 136p. (YA). pap. 19.99 (978-1-62010-090-5(8), 9781620100905) Oni Pr., Inc.
Styles, Walker. Undercover in the Bow-Wow Club. Whitehouse, Ben, illus. 2016. (Rider Woofson Ser.: 3). (ENG.). 128p. (J). (gr. k-4). pap. 5.99 (978-1-4814-6303-4(9), Little Simon) Little Simon.
Sutherland, Suzanne. When We Were Good, 1 vol. 2013. (ENG.). 240p. (YA). (gr. 9-12). pap. (978-1-927513-11-8(1), Sumach Pr.) Canadian Scholars.
Tashjian, Janet. For What It's Worth. 2012. (ENG.). 288p. (YA). (gr. 7-12). 16.99 (978-0-8050-9365-0(6), 9780805093650, Holt, Henry & Co. Bks. For Young Readers) Holt, Henry & Co.
Trine, Greg. The Grateful Fred. Montijo, Rhode, illus. 3rd rev. ed. 2006. (Melvin Beederman, Superhero Ser.: 3). (ENG.). 144p. (J). (gr. 2-5). pap. 8.99 (978-0-8050-7922-7(X), 9780805079227) Square Fish.
Voigt, Cynthia. Orfe. 2009. (ENG.). 162p. (YA). (gr. 7). pap. 8.99 (978-1-4169-9842-6(X), Simon Pulse) Simon Pulse.
Winters, Ben H. The Secret Life of Ms. Finkleman. 2011. (ENG.). 272p. (J). (gr. 3-7). pap. 5.99 (978-0-06-196543-2(X)) HarperCollins Pubs.
Yolanda And Reese. The Boy Who Loved to Be Like Michael Jackson. Harrell, Maurice, illus. 2012. 32p. 24.95 (978-1-4560-8506-3(9)) America Star Bks.

ROCKEFELLER, JOHN D. (JOHN DAVISON), 1839-1937

John D. Rockefeller: Oil Baron & Philanthropist. rev. exp. ed. 2004. (American Business Leaders Ser.). (Illus.). 128p. (YA). (gr. 6-12). 23.95 (978-1-931798-38-9(9)) Reynolds, Morgan Inc.
Laughlin, Rosemary. John D. Rockefeller: Oil Baron & Philanthropist. 2004. (American Business Leaders Ser.). (Illus.). 128p. (J). (gr. 5-18). 21.95 (978-1-883846-59-6(5)) Reynolds, Morgan Inc.
Parker, Lewis K. John D. Rockefeller & the Oil Industry. (American Tycoons Ser.). 24p. 2009. (gr. 3-3). 42.50 (978-1-61511-392-7(4)) 2003. (Illus.). (J). lib. bdg. 22.60 (978-0-8239-6446-8(9)) Rosen Publishing Group, Inc., The. (PowerKids Pr.).

ROCKET FLIGHT

see Space Flight

ROCKETRY

see also Guided Missiles; Rockets (Aeronautics); Space Vehicles

Asimov, Isaac & Hantula, Richard. Exploring Outer Space. 2005. (Isaac Asimov's 21st Century Library of the Universe). (Illus.). 32p. (gr. 2-6). lib. bdg. 26.00 (978-0-8368-3981-4(1), Gareth Stevens Learning Library) Stevens, Gareth Publishing LLLP.
Dahl, Michael. On the Launch Pad: A Counting Book about Rockets, 1 vol. Alderman, Derrick & Shea, Denise, illus. 2004. (Know Your Numbers Ser.). (ENG.). 24p. (gr. -1-2). per. 8.95 (978-1-4048-1119-5(2)) Picture Window Bks.
Dartford, Mark. Missiles & Rockets. 2003. (Military Hardware in Action Ser.). (ENG., Illus.). 48p. (gr. 5-9). lib. bdg. 25.26 (978-0-8225-4709-9(0)) Lerner Publishing Group.
Dorling Kindersley Publishing Staff. DK Readers L3: Rocket Science: Rocket Science. 2015. (DK Readers Ser.). (ENG., Illus.). 64p. (J). (gr. 2-4). 14.99 (978-1-4654-3580-4(8), DK Children) Dorling Kindersley Publishing, Inc.
Eason, Sarah. How Does a Rocket Work? 2010. (How Does It Work? Ser.). (Illus.). 32p. (J). (gr. 3-6). 26.00 (978-1-4339-3477-3(9)); pap. 10.50 (978-1-4339-3478-0(7)) Stevens, Gareth Publishing LLLP. (Gareth Stevens Learning Library).
Feldman, Heather. Sputnik: The First Satellite. 2003. (Space Firsts Ser.). (Illus.). 24p. (J). lib. bdg. 22.60 (978-0-8239-6244-0(X), PowerKids Pr.) Rosen Publishing Group, Inc., The.
Ferrie, Chris. Rocket Science for Babies. 2017. (Baby University Ser.: 0). (ENG., Illus.). 24p. (J). bds. 9.99 **(978-1-4926-5625-8(9)**, Sourcebooks Jabberwocky) Sourcebooks, Inc.
Gross, Miriam. All about Rockets. 2009. (Blast Off! Ser.). 24p. (gr. 2-3). 42.50 (978-1-61511-617-1(6)); (J). lib. bdg. 22.60 (978-1-4358-2735-6(X)) Rosen Publishing Group, Inc., The. (PowerKids Pr.).
Hirschmann, Kris. Blast Off. 2006. (Illus.). 63p. (J). (978-0-439-55092-5(0)) Scholastic, Inc.
Miller, Ron. Rockets. 2007. (Space Innovations Ser.). (ENG., Illus.). 112p. (gr. 6-8). lib. bdg. 31.93 (978-0-8225-7153-7(6)) Lerner Publishing Group.
Mooney, Carla. Rocketry: Investigate the Science & Technology of Rockets & Ballistics. Denham, Caitlin, illus. 2014. (Build It Yourself Ser.). (ENG.). 128p. (J). (gr. 3-7). 22.95 (978-1-61930-232-7(2)) Open City Bks.
Otfinoski, Steven. Rockets. 2006. (Great Inventions Ser.). (Illus.). 128p. (gr. 8-7). lib. bdg. 29.95 (978-0-7614-2232-7(3), Benchmark Bks.) Marshall Cavendish Corp.
Patchett, Kaye. Robert Goddard: Rocket Pioneer. 2003. (Giants of Science Ser.). (ENG., Illus.). 64p. (J). (gr. 3-7). lib. bdg. 28.35 (978-1-56711-888-9(7), Blackbirch Pr., Inc.) Cengage Gale.
Peak, Doris-Jean. Wernher Von Braun: Alabama's Rocket Scientist. 2009. (Alabama Roots Biography Ser.). (Illus.). 112p. (J). (978-1-59421-044-0(6)) Seacoast Publishing, Inc.
Skurzynski, Gloria. This Is Rocket Science: True Stories of the Risk-Taking Scientists Who Figure Out Ways to Explore Beyond. 2010. (ENG., Illus.). 80p. (J). (gr. 5-18). lib. bdg. 28.90 (978-1-4263-0598-6(2), National Geographic Children's Bks.) National Geographic Society.
Skurzynski, Gloria & National Geographic Kids Staff. This Is Rocket Science: True Stories of the Risk-Taking Scientists Who Figure Out Ways to Explore Beyond. 2010. (ENG., Illus.). 80p. (J). (gr. 5-18). 18.95 (978-1-4263-0597-9(4), National Geographic Children's Bks.) National Geographic Society.
Spangenburg, Ray & Moser, Diane Kit. Wernher Von Braun: Out of the Fire, the Stars. 2nd rev. ed. 2008. (Makers of Modern Science Ser.). 192p. (gr. 6-12). 35.00 (978-0-8160-6179-2(3), Chelsea Hse.) Facts On File, Inc.
Spilsbury, Louise. Robert Goddard & the Rocket, 01 vols., 1. 2016. (Inventions That Changed the World Ser.). (ENG.). 32p. (J). pap. 10.00 (978-1-5081-4639-1(X), PowerKids Pr.) Rosen Publishing Group, Inc., The.
Upgrade kit dsm-3 Flight&rocketry. (J). 2004. (978-1-59242-530-3(5)) 2003. (978-1-59242-413-9(9)) Delta Education, LLC.

ROCKETS (AERONAUTICS)

see also Guided Missiles

Baker, David. Rockets & Launch Vehicles. 2008. (Exploring Space Ser.). (Illus.). 32p. (J). (gr. 4-6). lib. bdg. 26.00 (978-1-59036-771-1(5)) Weigl Pubs., Inc.
Baker, David & Kissock, Heather. Rockets. 2016. (J). **(978-1-4896-5821-0(1)**, AV2 by Weigl) Weigl Pubs., Inc.
Baker, David & Kissock, Heather. Rockets & Launch Vehicles. 2008. (Exploring Space Ser.). (Illus.). 32p. (J). (gr. 4-6). pap. 9.95 (978-1-59036-772-8(3)) Weigl Pubs., Inc.
Dahl, Michael. On the Launch Pad: A Counting Book about Rockets, 1 vol. Alderman, Derrick & Shea, Denise, illus. 2004. (Know Your Numbers Ser.). (ENG.). 24p. (gr. -1-2). per. 8.95 (978-1-4048-1119-5(2)) Picture Window Bks.
Dorling Kindersley Publishing Staff. Spaceships & Rockets. 2016. (DK Readers Ser.). (ENG., Illus.). 48p. (J). (gr. k-2). pap. 3.99 (978-1-4654-4511-7(0), DK Children) Dorling Kindersley Publishing, Inc.
Eason, Sarah. How Does a Rocket Work? 2010. (How Does It Work? Ser.). (Illus.). 32p. (J). (gr. 3-6). 26.00 (978-1-4339-3477-3(9)); pap. 10.50 (978-1-4339-3478-0(7)) Stevens, Gareth Publishing LLLP. (Gareth Stevens Learning Library).
Gendell, Megan. Rocking & Roving: Everything You Wanted to Know about Rockets, Rovers, & Robots. 2008. (Illus.). 31p. (J). (978-0-545-04460-8(X)) Scholastic, Inc.
Graham, Ian. Build the Rocket. 2014. (Build It Ser.). (ENG., Illus.). 32p. (J). (gr. k). 19.95 (978-1-60710-952-5(2), Silver Dolphin Bks.) Readerlink Distribution Services, LLC.
Graham, Ian & Salariya, David. Planes, Rockets — And Other — Flying Machines. Hewetson, N. J., illus. 2014. (Time Shift Speed Ser.). 32p. (gr. 3-6). 31.35 **(978-1-908973-95-5(1))** Book Hse. GBR. Dist: Black Rabbit Bks.
Gross, Miriam. All about Rockets. 2009. (Illus.). 24p. (J). (gr. 2-5). pap. 8.25 (978-1-4358-3133-9(0), PowerKids Pr.) Rosen Publishing Group, Inc., The.
Latham, Donna. Superfast Rockets. 2005. (Ultimate Speed Ser.). (Illus.). 32p. (YA). (gr. 3-6). lib. bdg. 25.27 (978-1-59716-083-4(0)) Bearport Publishing Co., Inc.
Linde, Barbara M. Rocket Scientists, 01 vols., 1. 2016. (Out of the Lab: Extreme Jobs in Science Ser.). (ENG., Illus.). 32p. (J). pap. 10.00 (978-1-4994-1855-2(8), PowerKids Pr.) Rosen Publishing Group, Inc., The.
Miller, Ron. Rockets. 2007. (Space Innovations Ser.). (ENG., Illus.). 112p. (gr. 6-8). lib. bdg. 31.93 (978-0-8225-7153-7(6)) Lerner Publishing Group.
Morey, Allan. Rockets. 2017. (Space Tech Ser.). (ENG., Illus.). 24p. (J). (gr. 3-7). lib. bdg. 25.95 **(978-1-62617-705-5(8)**, Epic Bks.) Bellwether Media.
Murphy, Maggie. High-Tech DIY Projects with Flying Objects. 2014. (Maker Kids Ser.). (Illus.). 32p. (J). (gr. 3-6). pap. 70.50 (978-1-4777-6660-6(X), PowerKids Pr.) Rosen Publishing Group, Inc., The.
My Rocket: KinderWords, 6 Packs. (Kinderstarters Ser.). 8p. (gr. -1-1). 21.00 (978-0-7635-8693-5(5)) Rigby Education.
Otfinoski, Steven. Rockets. 2006. (Great Inventions Ser.). (Illus.). 128p. (gr. 8-7). lib. bdg. 29.95 (978-0-7614-2232-7(3), Benchmark Bks.) Marshall Cavendish Corp.
Raketen und Raumfahrt. (GER.). 40p. (978-3-411-08191-2(0)) Bibliographisches Institut & F. A. Brockhaus AG DEU. Dist: i. b. d., Ltd.
Roby, Cynthia A. Building Aircraft & Spacecraft: Aerospace Engineers, 01 vols., 1. 2016. (Engineers Rule Ser.). (ENG., Illus.). 32p. (J). pap. 11.75 (978-1-5081-4528-8(8), PowerKids Pr.) Rosen Publishing Group, Inc., The.
Rocket Science. 2004. (Formula Fun Ser.). (Illus.). 48p. (J). (978-1-84229-586-1(1)) Top That! Publishing PLC.
Rockets: Level O, 6 vols. (Wonder Worldtm Ser.). 48p. 39.95 (978-0-7802-2958-7(4)) Wright Group/McGraw-Hill.
Skurzynski, Gloria. This Is Rocket Science: True Stories of the Risk-Taking Scientists Who Figure Out Ways to Explore Beyond. 2010. (ENG., Illus.). 80p. (J). (gr. 5-18). lib. bdg. 28.90 (978-1-4263-0598-6(2), National Geographic Children's Bks.) National Geographic Society.
Skurzynski, Gloria & National Geographic Kids Staff. This Is Rocket Science: True Stories of the Risk-Taking Scientists Who Figure Out Ways to Explore Beyond. 2010. (ENG., Illus.). 80p. (J). (gr. 5-18). 18.95 (978-1-4263-0597-9(4), National Geographic Children's Bks.) National Geographic Society.
Zappa, Marcia. Rockets & Satellites, 1 vol. 2011. (Universe Set 2 Ser.). (ENG., Illus.). 32p. (gr. 3-5). 27.07 (978-1-61714-691-6(9), Buddy Bks.) ABDO Publishing Co.

ROCKETS (AERONAUTICS)—FICTION

Achatz, Eric. The Adventures of Ryan Alexander: The Great Space Chase. 2010. 52p. pap. 23.50 (978-1-4269-3763-7(6)) Trafford Publishing.
Albee, Sarah, et al. To the Center of the Earth! 2008. (Backyardigans Ser.). (ENG.). 24p. (J). pap. 3.99 (978-1-4169-7094-1(0), Simon Spotlight/Nickelodeon) Simon Spotlight/Nickelodeon.
Anderson, Derek. Romeo & Lou Blast Off. Anderson, Derek, illus. 2014. (ENG., Illus.). 32p. (J). (gr. -1-3). 16.99 (978-1-4814-1932-1(3), Simon & Schuster Bks. For Young Readers) Simon & Schuster Bks. For Young Readers.
Anderson, Lynne. Rocket Ship Shapes: Set Of 6. 2011. (Early Connections Ser.). (J). pap. 37.00 net. (978-1-4108-1091-5(7)) Benchmark Education Co.
Auerbach, Annie. The Grosse Adventures Vol. 3: Trouble at Twilight Cave, 1 vol. Nicholas, Jamar, illus. 2009. (Tokyopop Ser.). (ENG.). 96p. (gr. 2-6). 25.65 (978-1-59961-562-2(2)) Spotlight.
Bergman, Mara. Oliver Who Would Not Sleep! Maland, Nick, illus. 2007. (J). (978-0-439-92827-4(3), Levine, Arthur A. Bks.) Scholastic, Inc.
Blackburn, Sheila M. Stewie Scraps & the Star Rocket. 2008. 76p. pap. (978-1-903853-87-0(7)) Brilliant Pubns.
Capucilli, Alyssa Satin. Ralph & the Rocket Ship. Cole, Henry, illus. 2016. (Ready-To-Reads Ser.). (ENG.). 24p. (J). (gr. -1-1). pap. 3.99 (978-1-4814-5866-5(3), Simon Spotlight) Simon Spotlight.
Condon, Bill. Race to the Moon, 1 vol. rev. ed. 2013. (Fiction Readers Ser.). (ENG., Illus.). 28p. (J). (gr. 3-3). pap. 8.99 (978-1-4333-5605-6(8)) Shell Educational Publishing.
—Race to the Moon. rev. ed. 2013. (Fiction Readers Ser.). (ENG., Illus.). 28p. (gr. 3-3). pap. 19.96 (978-1-4807-1727-5(4)) Teacher Created Materials, Inc.
Hambrick, Sharon. Tommy's Rocket. Manning, Maurie J., illus. 2003. (Fig Street Kids Ser.). 83p. (J). (gr. 1-2). 7.49 (978-1-59166-186-3(2)) BJU Pr.
Hamening, Gail. How Did Clancey Get His Color?, 1 vol. 2009. 45p. pap. 24.95 (978-1-60836-440-4(2)) America Star Bks.
Hillert, Margaret. Up, up, & Away. Spinks, Scott, illus. 2016. (BeginningtoRead Ser.). (ENG.). 32p. (J). (gr. 1-2). 22.60 (978-1-59953-806-8(7)) Norwood Hse. Pr.
Hooke, R. Schuyler. Thomas & the Jet Engine. 2009. (Step into Reading Ser.). (ENG., Illus.). 32p. (J). (gr. k-3). pap. 3.99 (978-0-375-84289-4(6), Random Hse. Bks. for Young Readers) Random Hse. Children's Bks.
Ishwaran, Wobine. A Journey into Space: Kary to the Moon. 2008. 24p. pap. 11.49 (978-1-4343-6717-4(7)) AuthorHouse.
Korda, Lerryn & Korda, Lerryn. Rocket to the Moon. Korda, Lerryn & Korda, Lerryn, illus. 2010. (Playtime with Little Nye Ser.). (ENG., Illus.). 32p. (J). (— 1). 8.99 (978-0-7636-4652-3(0)) Candlewick Pr.
Lalley, Kristine. Show & Tell. 2006. (Neighborhood Readers Ser.). (ENG.). 12p. (gr. -1-3). pap. 5.90 (978-1-4042-6465-6(5), Rosen Classroom) Rosen Publishing Group, Inc., The.
Lee, Ingrid. George Most Wanted, 1 vol. Denis, Stephane, illus. 2005. (Orca Echoes Ser.). (ENG.). 64p. (J). (gr. 2-3). per. 6.95 (978-1-55143-472-8(5)) Orca Bk. Pubs. USA.
Logan, Bob. Rocket Town. 2011. (ENG., Illus.). 24p. (J). (gr. -1-k). bds. 7.99 (978-1-4022-4186-4(0), Sourcebooks Jabberwocky) Sourcebooks, Inc.
Mai, Lily. Bertie Boom's Trip to the Moon. 2010. (Illus.). 20p. 12.49 (978-1-4520-1379-4(9)) AuthorHouse.
Milgrim, David. Go, Otto, Go! Milgrim, David, illus. 2016. (Adventures of Otto Ser.). (ENG., Illus.). 32p. (J). (gr. -1-k). pap. 3.99 (978-1-4814-6723-0(9), Simon Spotlight) Simon Spotlight.
Morrissey, Dean & Krensky, Stephen. The Crimson Comet. Morrissey, Dean, illus. 2006. (Illus.). 32p. (J). (gr. k-4). 17.89 (978-0-06-008070-9(1)) HarperCollins Pubs.
Oliver, Lin. Revenge of the Itty-Bitty Brothers. Gilpin, Stephen, illus. 2009. (Who Shrunk Daniel Funk? Ser.: 3). (ENG.). 176p. (J). (gr. 3-7). 14.99 (978-1-4169-0961-3(3), Simon & Schuster Bks. For Young Readers) Simon & Schuster Bks. For Young Readers.
Project Blastoff. 2015. (Astrotwins Ser.). (ENG., Illus.). 224p. (J). (gr. 3-7). 17.99 (978-1-4814-1545-3(X), Simon & Schuster/Paula Wiseman Bks.) Simon & Schuster/Paula Wiseman Bks.
Ross, Diana. The Little Red Engine & the Rocket. Wood, Leslie, illus. 2005. (Little Red Engine Ser.: 1). (ENG.). 32p. (J). (gr. k-2). pap. 8.99 (978-0-233-00146-3(8)) Andre Deutsch GBR. Dist: Independent Pubs. Group.
Santillo, LuAnn. Lift-Off. Santillo, LuAnn, ed. 2003. (Half-Pint Kids Readers Ser.). (Illus.). 7p. (J). (gr. -1-1). pap. 1.00 (978-1-59256-043-1(1)) Half-Pint Kids, Inc.
Sawler, Kimberly. Rocket & the Magical Cosmic Candies. Walls, Ty, illus. 2006. 32p. (J). (gr. 4-7). 18.95 (978-1-933285-51-1(6)) Brown Books Publishing Group.
Weston, Greg. The Inventors. 2009. 202p. pap. 13.95 (978-1-4092-6096-7(8)) Lulu Pr., Inc.
Wilde, Oscar. El Famoso Cohete. Zwerger, Lisbeth, illus. (SPA.). 72p. (J). (978-84-392-8693-6(7)) Gaviota Ediciones ESP. Dist: Lectorum Pubns., Inc.
Wilson, Zachary. A Circle in the Sky. Adinolfi, JoAnn, illus. (Rookie Ready to Learn Ser.). (J). 2011. (ENG.). 40p. pap. 5.95 (978-0-531-26746-2(6)) 2011. 40p. (gr. -1-k). lib. bdg. 23.00 (978-0-531-26446-1(7)) 2006. (ENG.). 32p. (gr. k-2). lib. bdg. 19.50 (978-0-531-12570-0(X)) Scholastic Library Publishing. (Children's Pr.).
—Un Circulo en el Cielo. Adinolfi, JoAnn, illus. 2011. (Rookie Ready to Learn Español Ser.). (SPA.). 40p. (J). pap. 5.95 (978-0-531-26791-2(1), Children's Pr.) Scholastic Library Publishing.
Wilson, Zachary & Adinolfi, JoAnn, Un Circulo en el Cielo. Adinolfi, JoAnn, illus. 2011. (Rookie Ready to Learn Español Ser.). (SPA., Illus.). 40p. (J). lib. bdg. 23.00 (978-0-531-26123-1(9), Children's Pr.) Scholastic Library Publishing.

ROCKETS (AERONAUTICS)—MODELS

Shores, Lori. Cómo Hacer un Cohete Efervescente. 2010. (Divertirse con la Ciencia/Hands-On Science Fun Ser.).Tr. of How to Build a Fizzy Rocket. (SPA. ENG & MUL.). 24p. (gr. k-1). lib. bdg. 26.65 (978-1-4296-6105-8(4)) Capstone Press of Coughlan Cos.
—How to Build a Fizzy Rocket, 1 vol. 2010. (Hands-On Science Fun Ser.). (ENG.). 24p. (gr. k-1). 26.65 (978-1-4296-4491-4(5)); pap. 41.70 (978-1-4296-5574-3(7)) Capstone Press of Coughlan Cos. (Pebble Plus).

ROCKS

see also Crystallography; Geology; Mineralogy; Stone

ABDO Publishing Company Staff. Rocks & Minerals. 2014. (Rocks & Minerals Ser.: 8). (ENG.). 48p. (gr. 8-12). lib. bdg. 262.32 (978-1-62403-383-4(0)) ABDO Publishing Co.
Allen, Nancy Kelly. Earth's Rock Cycle. 2009. (Rock It! Ser.). 24p. (ENG.). (J). (gr. 3-6). pap. 8.25 (978-1-4358-3185-8(3)); (gr. 3-4). 42.50 (978-1-60852-480-8(9), PowerKids Pr.); (YA). (gr. 2-5). lib. bdg. 22.60 (978-1-4358-2762-2(7)) Rosen Publishing Group, Inc., The.
—Granite & Other Igneous Rocks. 2009. 24p. (Illus.). (J). (gr. 3-6). pap. 8.25 (978-1-4358-3181-0(0), PowerKids Pr.); (gr. 3-4). 42.50 (978-1-60852-483-9(3), PowerKids Pr.); (J). (gr. 2-5). lib. bdg. 22.60 (978-1-4358-2758-5(9)) Rosen Publishing Group, Inc., The.
—Identifying Rocks. 2009. (Rock It! Ser.). (ENG., Illus.). 24p. (J). (gr. 3-6). pap. 8.25 (978-1-4358-3186-5(1)); 24p. (gr. 3-4). 42.50 (978-1-60852-486-0(8), PowerKids Pr.); (YA). (gr. 2-5). lib. bdg. 22.60 (978-1-4358-2763-9(5)) Rosen Publishing Group, Inc., The.
—Limestone & Other Sedimentary Rocks. 2009. (Rock It! Ser.). 24p. (ENG., Illus.). (J). (gr. 3-6). pap. 8.25 (978-1-4358-3182-7(9), PowerKids Pr.); (gr. 3-4). 42.50 (978-1-60852-489-1(2), PowerKids Pr.); (YA). (gr. 2-5). lib. bdg. 22.60 (978-1-4358-2759-2(7)) Rosen Publishing Group, Inc., The.
—Minerals & Rocks. 2009. (Rock It! Ser.). 24p. (ENG.). (J). (gr. 3-6). pap. 8.25 (978-1-4358-3184-1(5)); (gr. 3-4). 42.50 (978-1-60852-492-1(2), PowerKids Pr.); (YA). (gr. 2-5). lib. bdg. 22.60 (978-1-4358-2761-5(9)) Rosen Publishing Group, Inc., The.
—Slate & Other Metamorphic Rocks. 2009. (Rock It! Ser.). 24p. (ENG., Illus.). (J). (gr. 3-6). pap. 8.25 (978-1-4358-3183-4(7), PowerKids Pr.); (gr. 3-4). 42.50 (978-1-60852-495-2(7), PowerKids Pr.); (YA). (gr. 2-5). lib. bdg. 22.60 (978-1-4358-2760-8(0)) Rosen Publishing Group, Inc., The.
Aloian, Molly. What Are Igneous Rocks? 2010. (ENG.). 32p. (J). pap. (978-0-7787-7233-0(0)) Crabtree Publishing Co.
—What Are Metamorphic Rocks? 2010. (ENG.). 32p. (J). pap. (978-0-7787-7234-7(9)); lib. bdg. (978-0-7787-7229-3(2)) Crabtree Publishing Co.
Anderson, Michael. Investigating Minerals, Rocks, & Fossils. 2011. (Illus.). 88p. (J). lib. bdg. 31.70 (978-1-61530-500-1(9)) Rosen Publishing Group, Inc., The.
Aston, Dianna Hutts. A Rock Is Lively. Long, Sylvia, illus. (ENG.). 40p. (J). (gr. k-3). 2015. 7.99 (978-1-4521-4555-6(5)) 2012. 16.99 (978-1-4521-0645-8(2)) Chronicle Bks. LLC.
—A Rock Is Lively. 2015. (J). lib. bdg. 18.40 (978-0-606-37444-6(2)) Turtleback Bks.
Atwood, Frederick D. Rocks & Minerals - Pb: A Portrait of the Natural World. 2013. (Portrait of the Natural World Ser.). (Illus.). 72p. pap. 9.95 (978-1-59764-332-0(7)) New Line Bks.
Barker, Charles Ferguson. Under Ohio: The Story of Ohio's Rocks & Fossils. Barker, Charles Ferguson, illus. 2007. (Illus.). 56p. (J). (gr. 3-7). 26.95 (978-0-8214-1755-3(X)) Ohio Univ. Pr.
Basher, Simon & Green, Dan. Rocks & Minerals: A Gem of a Book! Basher, Simon, illus. 2009. (Basher Science Ser.). (ENG., Illus.). 128p. (J). (gr. 5-9). pap. 8.99

(978-0-7534-6314-7(8), 9780753463147, Kingfisher) Roaring Brook Pr.

Baxter, Roberta. Sedimentary Rocks. 2016. (Geology Rocks! Ser.). (ENG.). 24p. (J). (gr. 3-6). 28.50 (978-1-5038-0805-8(X), 210640) Child's World, Inc., The.

Benchmark Education Company, LLC Staff, compiled by. Rocks & Minerals: Theme Set. 2006. (J). 215.00 (978-1-4108-7135-0(5)) Benchmark Education Co.

—Rocky Tales & Earth Systems. 2005. spiral bd. 225.00 (978-1-4108-5819-1(7)) Benchmark Education Co.

Blevins, Wiley. Rocks & Minerals, 6 vols., Set. 2004. (Phonics Readers Books 37-72 Ser.). (ENG.). 8p. (gr. k-1). pap. 35.70 (978-0-7368-4083-5(4), Phonics Readers) Capstone Press of Coughlan Cos.

Bowman, Chris. Rocks. 2014. (Earth Science Rocks! Ser.). (ENG., Illus.). 24p. (J). (gr. k-3). lib. bdg. 25.95 (978-1-60014-981-8(2), Blastoff! Readers) Bellwether Media.

Bramwell, Martyn. Rocks & Fossils. Bramwell, Martyn, ed. Jackson, Ian & Suttie, Alan, illus. rev. ed. 2007. (Hobby Guides). 31p. (J). pap. 6.99 (978-0-7945-1526-3(6), Usborne) EDC Publishing.

Brannon, Cecelia H. A Look at Igneous Rocks. 2016. (Rock Cycle Ser.). (ENG.). 32p. (J). (gr. 3-4). pap. 10.52 (978-0-7660-7316-6(5)); (Illus.). 25.27 (978-0-7660-7318-0(1)) Enslow Pubs., Inc.

—A Look at Metamorphic Rocks. 2016. (Rock Cycle Ser.). (ENG.). 32p. (J). (gr. 3-4). pap. 10.52 (978-0-7660-7320-3(3)); (Illus.). 25.27 (978-0-7660-7322-7(X)) Enslow Pubs., Inc.

—A Look at Sedimentary Rocks. 2016. (Rock Cycle Ser.). (ENG.). 32p. (J). (gr. 3-4). pap. 10.52 (978-0-7660-7336-4(X)); (Illus.). 25.27 (978-0-7660-7338-8(6)) Enslow Pubs., Inc.

Brasch, Nicolas. Why Do Volcanoes Erupt? 2010. (Solving Science Mysteries Ser.). (Illus.). 24p. (J). pap. 8.25 (978-1-4488-0401-6(9), PowerKids Pr.); (YA). (gr. 3-6). lib. bdg. 22.60 (978-1-4488-0400-9(0)) Rosen Publishing Group, Inc., The.

—Why Do Volcanoes Erupt? All about Earth Science. 2010. (Illus.). 24p. (J). 49.50 (978-1-4488-0402-3(7), 1307173, PowerKids Pr.) Rosen Publishing Group, Inc., The.

Braun, Eric. Let's Rock! Science Adventures with Rudie the Origami Dinosaur, 1 vol. Christoph, Jamey, illus. 2013. (Origami Science Adventures Ser.). (ENG.). 24p. (gr. 3-4). pap. 6.95 (978-1-4048-8068-9(2)); lib. bdg. 27.32 (978-1-4048-7971-3(4)) Picture Window Bks.

Bredeson, Carmen. Weird but True Rocks. 2011. (Weird but True Science Ser.). (Illus.). 24p. (J). (gr. k-18). pap. 7.95 (978-1-59845-370-6(X), Enslow Elementary); (gr. 5-9). lib. bdg. 22.60 (978-0-7660-3864-6(5)) Enslow Pubs., Inc.

Bredeson, Carmen & Cousins, Lindsey. Can You Find These Rocks? 2012. (All about Nature Ser.). 24p. (J). (gr. -1-1). (Illus.). pap. 7.95 (978-1-4644-0066-7(0), Enslow Elementary); 22.60 (978-0-7660-3979-7(X)) Enslow Pubs., Inc.

Brian, Bethany. How the Rock Cycle Works. 2009. (Science Kaleidoscope Ser.). 32p. (gr. 4-4). 47.90 (978-1-60853-036-6(1), PowerKids Pr.) Rosen Publishing Group, Inc., The.

Brinkman, Patricia. Discover Rock Types. 2006. (J). pap. (978-1-4108-6497-0(9)) Benchmark Education Co.

—Discover the Rock Cycle. 2006. (J). pap. (978-1-4108-6496-3(0)) Benchmark Education Co.

—The Rock Cycle. 2006. (J). pap. (978-1-4108-6493-2(6)) Benchmark Education Co.

—Rock Types. 2006. (J). pap. (978-1-4108-6494-9(4)) Benchmark Education Co.

Bryan, Bethany. How the Rock Cycle Works. 2009. (Real Life Readers Ser.). 32p. (gr. 4-5). pap. 10.00 (978-1-4358-0151-6(2), Rosen Classroom); (J). lib. bdg. 25.25 (978-1-4358-2984-8(0), PowerKids Pr.) Rosen Publishing Group, Inc., The.

Burns, T. D. BOOST Rocks & Minerals Coloring Book. 2013. (BOOST Educational Ser.). (ENG.). 48p. (J). (gr. 3-5). pap. 5.99 (978-0-486-49437-1(3)) Dover Pubns., Inc.

Burton, Margie, et al. Big & Little. 2011. (Early Connections Ser.). (J). (978-1-61672-284-5(3)) Benchmark Education Co.

—Rocks. 2011. (Early Connections Ser.). (J). (978-1-61672-536-5(2)) Benchmark Education Co.

Callery, Sean. Rocks & Minerals. 2010. (Unpredictable Nature Ser.). (Illus.). 48p. (J). (gr. 3-18). lib. bdg. 19.95 (978-1-4222-2005-4(2)) Mason Crest.

Cardenas, Ernesto & Saavedra, Patricia. Rocas. l.t. ed. 2006. (SPA., Illus.). 16p. pap. 4.95 (978-1-933668-18-5(0)) Milo Educational Bks. & Resources.

Cardenas, Ernesto A. Rocks. 2009. pap. 4.95 (978-1-60698-072-9(6)) Milo Educational Bks. & Resources.

Challoner, Jack. Find Out about Rocks & Minerals: With 23 Projects & More Than 350 Pictures. 2013. (ENG., Illus.). 64p. (J). (gr. k-8). 9.99 (978-1-84322-747-2(9), Armadillo) Anness Publishing GBR. Dist: National Bk. Network.

Challoner, Jack & Walshaw, Rodney. Rocks & Minerals: Crystals; Erosion; Geology; Fossils. 2015. (ENG., Illus.). 64p. 12.99 (978-1-86147-465-0(2), Armadillo) Anness Publishing GBR. Dist: National Bk. Network.

Christian, Peggy. If You Find a Rock. Lember, Barbara Hirsch, photos by. 2008. (ENG., Illus.). 32p. (J). (gr. -1-3). pap. 7.99 (978-0-15-206354-2(4)) Houghton Mifflin Harcourt Publishing Co.

Clarke, Phillip & Tudhope, Simon, eds. 100 Rocks & Minerals to Spot. 2009. (Spotter's Cards Ser.). 52p. (J). 9.99 (978-0-7945-2255-1(6), Usborne) EDC Publishing.

Close, Edward. Earth's Treasures: Rocks & Minerals: Rocks & Minerals, 1 vol., 1. 2014. (Discovery Education: Earth & Space Science Ser.). (ENG.). 32p. (gr. 3-6). 26.25 (978-1-4777-6170-0(5), PowerKids Pr.) Rosen Publishing Group, Inc., The.

Colich, Abby. Rock, 1 vol. 2013. (Exploring Materials Ser.). (ENG.). 24p. (gr. -1-1). 22.65 (978-1-4329-8018-4(1)); pap. 6.95 (978-1-4329-8026-9(2)) Heinemann-Raintree. (Acorn).

Conklin, Wendy. The Rock Cycle. 2015. (Science Readers: Content & Literacy Ser.). (ENG., Illus.). 32p. (gr. 4-4). pap. 8.99 (978-1-4807-4688-6(6)) Teacher Created Materials, Inc.

Corriel, Michele. Weird Rocks, 1 vol. Bilyeu, Dan, illus. 2013. (ENG.). 36p. (J). 12.00 (978-0-87842-597-6(7)) Mountain Pr. Publishing Co., Inc.

Cull, Selby. Rocks & Minerals. 2009. (Restless Earth Ser.). (Illus.). 112p. (YA). (gr. 5-9). 35.00 (978-0-7910-9702-1(1)) Facts On File, Inc.

Culp, Jennifer. What Are Sedimentary Rocks?, 01 vols., 1. 2016. (Junior Geologist Ser.). (ENG., Illus.). 32p. (J). pap. 12.90 (978-1-5081-0046-1(2), Britannica Educational Publishing) Rosen Publishing Group, Inc., The.

Dayton, Connor. Crystals. (Rocks & Minerals Ser.). 24p. (gr. 2-3). 2009. 42.50 (978-1-60852-498-3(1), PowerKids Pr.) 2007. (Illus.). (YA). lib. bdg. 22.60 (978-1-4042-3687-5(2)) Rosen Publishing Group, Inc., The.

—Rocks & Minerals, 6 bks., Set. Incl. Crystals. lib. bdg. 22.60 (978-1-4042-3687-5(2)); Fossils. lib. bdg. 22.60 (978-1-4042-3689-9(9)); Gemstones. lib. bdg. 22.60 (978-1-4042-3686-8(4)); Minerals. lib. bdg. 22.60 (978-1-4042-3691-2(0)); Rock Formations. lib. bdg. 22.60 (978-1-4042-3690-5(2)); Volcanic Rocks. lib. bdg. 22.60 (978-1-4042-3688-2(0)); (Illus.). 24p. (YA). (gr. 2-5). 2007. 2007. Set lib. bdg. 127.50 (978-1-4042-3610-3(4), PowerKids Pr.) Rosen Publishing Group, Inc., The.

—Volcanic Rocks. (Rocks & Minerals Ser.). 24p. (gr. 2-3). 2009. 42.50 (978-1-60852-503-4(1), PowerKids Pr.) 2007. (Illus.). (YA). lib. bdg. 22.60 (978-1-4042-3688-2(0)) Rosen Publishing Group, Inc., The.

Dee, Willa. Earth's Rock Cycle, 1 vol., 1. 2014. (Rocks: the Hard Facts Ser.). (ENG.). 24p. (J). (gr. 3-6). 23.60 (978-1-4777-2903-8(8), PowerKids Pr.) Rosen Publishing Group, Inc., The.

—Unearthing Igneous Rocks, 1 vol., 1. 2014. (Rocks: the Hard Facts Ser.). (ENG.). 24p. (J). (gr. 3-6). 23.60 (978-1-4777-2901-4(1), PowerKids Pr.) Rosen Publishing Group, Inc., The.

—Unearthing Metamorphic Rocks, 1 vol., 1. 2014. (Rocks: the Hard Facts Ser.). (ENG.). 24p. (J). (gr. 3-6). 23.60 (978-1-4777-2902-1(X), PowerKids Pr.) Rosen Publishing Group, Inc., The.

—Unearthing Sedimentary Rocks, 1 vol., 1. 2014. (Rocks: the Hard Facts Ser.). (ENG.). 24p. (J). (gr. 3-6). 23.60 (978-1-4777-2900-7(3), PowerKids Pr.) Rosen Publishing Group, Inc., The.

DeWitt, Lockwood. Dig It! Hixson, Bryce, illus. 2003. (J). per. 14.95 (978-1-931801-02-7(9)) Loose In The Lab.

Dickmann, Nancy. The Rock Cycle. 2016. (Earth Figured Out Ser.). (ENG., Illus.). 32p. (J). (gr. 4-4). pap. 10.58 (978-1-5026-0870-3(7)) Cavendish Square Publishing.

Dorling Kindersley Publishing Staff. Pocket Genius: Rocks & Minerals. 2016. (Pocket Genius Ser.). (ENG., Illus.). 160p. (J). (gr. 3-7). pap. 4.99 (978-1-4654-4590-2(0), DK Children) Dorling Kindersley Publishing, Inc.

—The Rock & Gem Book. 2016. (ENG., Illus.). 192p. (J). (gr. 3-7). 22.99 (978-1-4654-5070-8(X), DK Children) Dorling Kindersley Publishing, Inc.

—Rocks & Minerals. 2014. (ENG.). (J). 96p. (gr. 2-4). pap. 12.99 (978-1-4654-1654-4(4)); 56p. (gr. k-4). 10.99 (978-1-4654-1559-2(9)) Dorling Kindersley Publishing, Inc. (DK Children).

Dorling Kindersley Publishing Staff & Dennie, Devin P. My Book of Rocks & Minerals. 2017. (ENG., Illus.). 96p. (J). (gr. 1-4). 12.99 **(978-1-4654-6190-2(6)**, DK Children) Dorling Kindersley Publishing, Inc.

Dunlop, Jenna & Morganelli, Adrianna. Minerals. 2004. (Rocks, Minerals, & Resources Ser.). (ENG., Illus.). 32p. (J). lib. bdg. (978-0-7787-1415-6(2)) Crabtree Publishing Co.

Earth Rocks. (Illus.). (J). (gr. 3-6). 103.50 (978-0-8239-7284-5(4), Reading Power) Rosen Publishing Group, Inc., The.

Earth's Rocky Past. 2015. (Earth's Rocky Past Ser.). (ENG.). 32p. (J). (gr. 4-4). pap., pap., pap. 360.00 (978-1-4994-1286-4(X), PowerKids Pr.) Rosen Publishing Group, Inc., The.

EDC Publishing, creator. Rocks & Fossils Kid Kit. 2009. (Usborne Kid Kits Ser.). (Illus.). (J). (gr. 5). pap. 15.99 (978-1-60130-025-6(5)) EDC Publishing.

Encyclopaedia Britannica, Inc. Staff, compiled by. Britannica Illustrated Science Library: Rocks & Minerals, 16 vols. 2008. (Illus.). (J). 29.95 (978-1-59339-396-0(2)) Encyclopaedia Britannica, Inc.

Estigarribia, Diana. Learing about Rocks, Weathering, & Erosion with Graphic Orgainzers. 2005. (Graphic Organizers in Science Ser.). (Illus.). 24p. (J). (gr. 3-5). lib. bdg. 21.25 (978-1-4042-2806-1(3), PowerKids Pr.) Rosen Publishing Group, Inc., The.

—Learning about Rocks, Weathering, & Erosion with Graphic Organizers. (Graphic Organizers in Science Ser.). 24p. 2009. (gr. 3-4). 42.50 (978-1-61513-044-3(6)) 2006. (ENG., Illus.). (gr. 4-6). pap. 8.25 (978-1-4042-5042-0(5)) Rosen Publishing Group, Inc., The. (PowerKids Pr.).

Farndon, John. Rocks, Gems, Minerals. 2016. (ENG., Illus.). 120p. (J). (gr. 6-10). 24.95 (978-1-77085-740-7(0), 9781770857407) Firefly Bks., Ltd.

—Rocks, Minerals & Gems. 2016. (ENG., Illus.). 120p. (J). (gr. 6-10). pap. 12.95 (978-1-77085-868-8(7), 9781770858688) Firefly Bks., Ltd.

Faulkner, Rebecca. Igneous Rock. 2016. (Geology Rocks! Ser.). (ENG.). 48p. (gr. 6-8). pap. 9.49 (978-1-4109-8526-2(1), Raintree Freestyle) Heinemann-Raintree.

Flood, Nancy Bo. Sand to Stone: And Back Again. Kuyper, Tony, photos by. 2009. (ENG., Illus.). 32p. (J). (gr. -1-k). pap. 9.95 (978-1-55591-657-2(0)) Fulcrum Publishing.

Freeman, Marcia S. Let's Look at Rocks. 2003. (ENG.). 16p. (gr. 1-2). pap. 6.00 (978-1-59515-258-9(X)) Rourke Educational Media.

Gardner, Robert. Smashing Science Projects about Earth's Rocks & Minerals. LaBaff, Tom, illus. 2007. (Rockin' Earth Science Experiments Ser.). 48p. (J). (gr. 3-4). lib. bdg. 25.27 (978-0-7660-2731-2(7), Enslow Elementary) Enslow Pubs., Inc.

Glaser, Rebecca. Rocks. 2012. (ENG., Illus.). 24p. (J). lib. bdg. 25.65 (978-1-62031-028-1(7)) Jump! Inc.

Goldman, Phyllis B., ed. Monkeyshines on Rocks & Minerals. (Illus.). 148p. (J). (gr. -1-7). reprint ed. pap. 26.95 (978-1-888325-14-0(3)) Allosaurus Pubs.

Gosman, Gillian. What Do You Know about Rocks? 2013. (20 Questions: Earth Science Ser.). (J). 24p. (gr. 3-6). pap. 8.25 (978-1-4488-9850-3(1)); 24p. (gr. 3-6). lib. bdg. 22.60 (978-1-4488-9696-7(7)); (978-1-4488-9851-0(X)) Rosen Publishing Group, Inc., The. (PowerKids Pr.).

Graphic Organizers in Science. (Illus.). (J). (gr. 3-5). 119.70 (978-1-4042-2955-6(8)) Rosen Publishing Group, Inc., The.

Green, Dan. Rocks & Minerals. 2013. (Scholastic Discover More Ser.). (ENG.). 112p. (J). (gr. 5-9). 15.99 (978-0-545-50511-6(9), Scholastic Reference) Scholastic, Inc.

Green, Jen. Rocks & Soil. 2008. (Our Earth Ser.). (Illus.). 24p. (YA). (gr. 1-4). lib. bdg. 21.25 (978-1-4042-4271-5(6)) Rosen Publishing Group, Inc., The.

Gregorovna, Anna. Inside Earth: Rocks & Minerals. 2012. (InfoMax Readers Ser.). (ENG., Illus.). 24p. (J). (gr. 1-2). pap. 8.25 (978-1-4488-9043-9(8), Rosen Classroom) Rosen Publishing Group, Inc., The.

Hamilton, John. Landslides, 1 vol. 2006. (Nature's Fury Ser.). (ENG., Illus.). 32p. (gr. 3-8). 27.07 (978-1-59679-331-6(7), Abdo & Daughters) ABDO Publishing Co.

Hand, Carol. Experiments with Rocks & Minerals. 2011. (True Bk Ser.). (ENG., Illus.). 48p. (J). pap. 6.95 (978-0-531-26648-9(6)); lib. bdg. 29.00 (978-0-531-26348-8(7)) Scholastic Library Publishing. (Children's Pr.).

Hansen, Grace. Rocas. 2016. (¡Súper Geología! Ser.). (SPA.). 24p. (J). (gr. 1-6). pap. 7.95 (978-1-4966-0682-2(5)) Capstone Classroom.

—Rocks, 1 vol. 2016. (ENG., Illus.). 24p. (J). (978-1-62970-909-3(3), 1391189) ABDO Publishing Co.

Hantula, Richard. Rocks & Fossils. 2007. (Gareth Stevens Vital Science: Earth Science Ser.). (Illus.). 48p. (gr. 5-12). pap. 14.05 (978-0-8368-7876-9(0), Gareth Stevens Secondary Library) Stevens, Gareth Publishing LLLP.

Harkrader, Lisa. What Is a Rock? 2016. (Spring Forward Ser.). (J). (gr. 2). (978-1-4900-9456-4(3)) Benchmark Education Co.

Harrison, Lorraine. All Kinds of Rocks. 2013. (InfoMax Readers Ser.). (ENG.). 24p. (J). (gr. 2-3). pap. 49.50 (978-1-4777-2408-8(7)); (Illus.). pap. 8.25 (978-1-4777-2407-1(9)) Rosen Publishing Group, Inc., The. (Rosen Classroom).

Hatch Jr., B. J. Butch. Professor Rock Ltd. Chatham, Dennis J., illus. 2003. 32p. (J). 14.95 (978-1-56167-808-2(2)) American Literary Pr.

Hirsch, Rebecca. Rock Cycle, 1 vol. 2014. (Rocks & Minerals Ser.). (ENG.). 48p. (gr. 8-12). lib. bdg. 32.79 (978-1-62403-389-6(X)) ABDO Publishing Co.

—Sedimentary Rocks, 1 vol. 2014. (Rocks & Minerals Ser.). (ENG.). 48p. (gr. 8-12). lib. bdg. 32.79 (978-1-62403-390-2(3)) ABDO Publishing Co.

Hirschmann, Kris. Rocks & Minerals. 2004. (World Discovery Science Readers Ser.). (Illus.). 31p. (J). pap. 4.95 (978-0-439-56630-8(4)) Scholastic, Inc.

Hodge, Judith. Riches from Earth & Las riquezas de la Tierra: 6 English, 6 Spanish Adaptations. 2011. (ENG & SPA.). (J). 97.00 net. (978-1-4108-5716-3(6)) Benchmark Education Co.

Hoffman, Steven M. Rock Study: A Guide to Looking at Rocks. 2011. (Rock It! Ser.). (Illus.). 24p. (J). pap. 8.25 (978-1-4488-2713-8(2)); lib. bdg. 22.60 (978-1-4488-2562-2(8)) Rosen Publishing Group, Inc., The. (PowerKids Pr.).

Hosford, William G. Geo the Geode. Hosford, William G., illus. 2006. (Illus.). 32p. (J). lib. bdg. 19.95 (978-0-9776562-0-2(9), CN0601) WGH Arts LLC.

Howell, Sara. The Rock Cycle. 2017. (J). **(978-1-5383-0028-2(1))** Rosen Publishing Group, Inc., The.

Hutmacher, Kimberly. Fossils & Rocks. 2012. (ENG.). 24p. (gr. 4-5). pap. 8.95 (978-1-61810-236-2(2)) Rourke Educational Media.

Hyde, Natalie. How to Be a Rock Collector. 2012. (Let's Rock! Ser.). (ENG., Illus.). 32p. (J). (gr. 3-6). lib. bdg. (978-0-7787-7212-5(8)) Crabtree Publishing Co.

—What Are Sedimentary Rocks? 2010. (ENG.). 32p. (J). pap. (978-0-7787-7235-4(7)) Crabtree Publishing Co.

—What Is the Rock Cycle? 2010. (ENG.). 32p. (J). pap. (978-0-7787-7236-1(5)); lib. bdg. (978-0-7787-7231-6(4)) Crabtree Publishing Co.

Hyler, Nelson W. The How & Why Wonder Book of Rocks & Minerals. Blackwood, Paul E., ed. Shannon, Kenyon, illus. 2011. 52p. 36.95 (978-1-258-10482-5(2)) Literary Licensing, LLC.

Jennings, Terry. Rocas y Suelos (Rocks & Soils) (SPA.). 32p. (J). 6.95 (978-84-348-1912-2(0)) SM Ediciones ESP. Dist: AIMS International Bks., Inc.

Korb, Rena. Radical Rocks, 1 vol. Reibeling, Brandon, illus. 2007. (Science Rocks Ser.). (ENG.). 32p. (gr. -1-4). 28.50 (978-1-60270-040-6(0), Looking Glass Library- Nonfiction) Magic Wagon.

Lang, Sheri. I Sort Rocks: Putting Data in Order. 2017. (Computer Science for the Real World Ser.). 8p. (gr. 5-6). pap. 6.20 **(978-1-5383-5020-1(3)**, Rosen Classroom) Rosen Publishing Group, Inc., The.

Larson, Kirsten. Rock Cycle. 2016. (Let's Explore Science Ser.). (ENG., Illus.). 48p. (gr. 5-8). 35.64 (978-1-68191-398-8(4)) Rourke Educational Media.

Lawrence, Ellen. Baking & Crushing: A Look at Metamorphic Rock. 2015. (Illus.). 24p. (J). lib. bdg. (978-1-62724-300-1(3)) Bearport Publishing Co., Inc.

—Famous Rocks. 2015. (Illus.). 24p. (J). lib. bdg. (978-1-62724-297-4(X)) Bearport Publishing Co., Inc.

—How Do People Use Rocks? 2014. (Science Slam!: Rock-Ology Ser.). (ENG.). 24p. (J). (gr. -1-3). lib. bdg. 23.93 (978-1-62724-303-2(8)) Bearport Publishing Co., Inc.

—How Do Volcanoes Make Rock? A Look at Igneous Rock. 2015. (Illus.). 24p. (J). lib. bdg. (978-1-62724-298-1(8)) Bearport Publishing Co., Inc.

—How Do Water & Wind Change Rock? A Look at Sedimentary Rock. 2015. (Illus.). 24p. (J). lib. bdg. (978-1-62724-299-8(6)) Bearport Publishing Co., Inc.

—Rocks & Minerals. 2015. (FUN-Damental Experiments Ser.). (ENG.). 24p. (J). (gr. -1-3). lib. bdg. 23.93 (978-1-62724-540-1(5)) Bearport Publishing Co., Inc.

—What Are Rocks Made Of? 2015. (Illus.). 24p. (J). lib. bdg. (978-1-62724-302-5(X)) Bearport Publishing Co., Inc.

—What Is the Rock Cycle? 2015. (Illus.). 24p. (J). lib. bdg. (978-1-62724-304-9(6)) Bearport Publishing Co., Inc.

Let's Rock, 7 vols., Set. Incl. Crystals. Spilsbury, Louise & Spilsbury, Richard. pap. 8.29 (978-1-4329-4692-0(7)); Fossils. Spilsbury, Louise & Spilsbury, Richard. pap. 8.29 (978-1-4329-4690-6(0)); Igneous Rocks. Oxlade, Chris. pap. 8.29 (978-1-4329-4687-6(0)); Metamorphic Rocks. Oxlade, Chris. pap. 8.29 (978-1-4329-4688-3(9)); Minerals. Spilsbury, Louise & Spilsbury, Richard. pap. 8.29 (978-1-4329-4691-3(9)); Sedimentary Rocks. Oxlade, Chris. pap. 8.29 (978-1-4329-4689-0(7)); Soil. Spilsbury, Louise & Spilsbury, Richard. pap. 8.29 (978-1-4329-4693-7(5)); (gr. 3-6). (Let's Rock Ser.). (ENG.). 32p. 2011. Set pap. 55.93 (978-1-4329-4694-4(3)); Set lib. bdg. 199.92 (978-1-4329-4686-9(2)) Heinemann-Raintree. (Heinemann InfoSearch).

Lilly, Melinda. Rocks. (Read & Do Science Ser.). (Illus.). (J). 20.64 (978-1-58952-647-1(3)) Rourke Educational Media.

—Rocks. Thompson, Scott M., photos by. 2005. (Rourke Discovery Library). (Illus.). 24p. (J). (gr. 1-4). lib. bdg. 14.95 (978-1-59515-404-0(3), 1244275) Rourke Educational Media.

Lindeen, Carol K. Lo Básico de las Rocas. Translation Services Staff & Translations.com Staff, trs. from ENG. 2010. (Lo Básico de la Naturaleza/Nature Basics Ser.).Tr. of Rock Basics. (SPA, ENG & MUL.). 24p. (gr. k-1). lib. bdg. 21.99 (978-1-4296-5348-0(5)) Capstone Press of Coughlan Cos.

Lindeen, Mary. Investigating the Rock Cycle. 2015. (ENG., Illus.). 40p. (J). (gr. 3-5). 29.32 (978-1-4677-8058-2(8)) Lerner Publishing Group.

Lockwood, Sophie. Experiment with Rocks. 2010. (Explorer Junior Library: Science Explorer Junior Ser.). (ENG.). 32p. (gr. 3-6). lib. bdg. 28.50 (978-1-60279-836-6(2), 200538) Cherry Lake Publishing.

—Super Cool Science Experiments: Rocks. 2009. (Explorer Library: Science Explorer Ser.). (ENG., Illus.). 32p. (gr. 4-8). lib. bdg. 28.50 (978-1-60279-523-5(1), 200283) Cherry Lake Publishing.

A Look at Earth's Rocks. 2017. (Look at Earth's Rocks Ser.). 32p. (gr. 2-2). pap. 63.00 **(978-1-4824-6283-8(4))**; lib. bdg. 159.60 **(978-1-4824-6281-4(8))** Stevens, Gareth Publishing LLLP.

Lowery, Lawrence F. Spenser & the Rocks: I Wonder Why. 2013. (I Wonder Why Ser.). (ENG., Illus.). 36p. (J). (gr. k-3). pap. 11.95 (978-1-938946-11-0(1)) National Science Teachers Assn.

MacAulay, Kelley. Why Do We Need Rocks & Minerals? 2014. (ENG., Illus.). 24p. (J). (978-0-7787-0492-8(0)); pap. (978-0-7787-0496-6(3)) Crabtree Publishing Co.

Maloof, Torrey. Rocks & Minerals, 1 vol. rev. ed. 2014. (Science Readers: Content & Literacy Ser.). (ENG.). 32p. (gr. 2-2). pap. 8.99 (978-1-4807-4610-7(X)) Teacher Created Materials, Inc.

Mattern, Joanne. Igneous Rocks & the Rock Cycle. (Shaping & Reshaping of Earth's Surface Ser.). 24p. (gr. 4-4). 2009. 42.50 (978-1-60854-214-7(9), PowerKids Pr.) 2006. (Illus.). (YA). lib. bdg. 22.60 (978-1-4042-3196-2(X)) Rosen Publishing Group, Inc., The.

—Metamorphic Rocks & the Rock Cycle. (Shaping & Reshaping of Earth's Surface Ser.). 24p. (gr. 4-4). 2009. 42.50 (978-1-60854-215-4(7), PowerKids Pr.) 2006. (Illus.). (YA). lib. bdg. 22.60 (978-1-4042-3194-8(3)) Rosen Publishing Group, Inc., The.

—Minerals & the Rock Cycle. (Shaping & Reshaping of Earth's Surface Ser.). 24p. (gr. 4-4). 2009. 42.50 (978-1-60854-218-5(1), PowerKids Pr.) 2006. (Illus.). (YA). lib. bdg. 22.60 (978-1-4042-3199-3(4)) Rosen Publishing Group, Inc., The.

—Sedimentary Rocks & the Rock Cycle. (Shaping & Reshaping of Earth's Surface Ser.). 24p. (gr. 4-4). 2009. 42.50 (978-1-60854-224-6(6), PowerKids Pr.) 2006. (Illus.). (YA). lib. bdg. 22.60 (978-1-4042-3195-5(1)) Rosen Publishing Group, Inc., The.

McCarthy, Cecilia Pinto. Metamorphic Rocks. 2016. (Geology Rocks! Ser.). (ENG.). 24p. (J). (gr. 3-6). 28.50 (978-1-5038-0802-7(5), 210638) Child's World, Inc., The.

McConnell, William. Rocks & Fossils. (Reading Room Collection 1 Ser.). 16p. (gr. 2-3). 2009. 37.50 (978-1-60851-950-7(3), PowerKids Pr.) 2006. (Illus.). (J). lib. bdg. 17.25 (978-1-4042-3344-7(X)) Rosen Publishing Group, Inc., The.

Meierhenry, Mark V. & Volk, David. The Mystery of the Round Rocks. Folkerts, Jason, illus. 2007. 44p. (J). (gr. 2-5). pap. 13.95 (978-0-9777955-3-6(5), South Dakota State Historical Society Pr.) South Dakota State Historical Society Pr.

Melon, Zach. Rocky's Rock Collection. 2013. (Rosen Readers Ser.). (ENG.). 24p. (J). (gr. 2-3). pap. 49.50 (978-1-4777-2244-2(0), Rosen Classroom); pap. 8.25 (978-1-4777-2243-5(2)) Rosen Publishing Group, Inc., The.

Meredith, Susan. Las Rocas, los Minerales y el Suelo. 2012. (SPA & ENG.). 48p. (gr. 4-8). pap. 10.95 (978-1-61810-470-0(5)) Rourke Educational Media.

—Rocks, Minerals, & Soil. 2009. (Let's Explore Science Ser.). (Illus.). 48p. (gr. 4-8). (J). lib. bdg. 32.79 (978-1-60694-411-0(8)); (ENG., pap. 10.95 (978-1-60694-529-2(7)) Rourke Educational Media.

Miles, Lisa. Rocks & Minerals. 2003. (Usborne Hotshots Ser.). (ENG., Illus.). 1p. (YA). (gr. 2-18). pap. 2.95 (978-0-7460-2790-5(7)) EDC Publishing.

—Usborne Rocks & Minerals Sticker Book. Khan, Sarah & Armstrong, Carrie, eds. Freeman, Mike & Julings, Emma, photos by. rev. ed. 2006. (Spotter's Guides Sticker Books - New Format Ser.). (Illus.). 16p. (J). (gr. 2-5). pap. 8.99 (978-0-7945-1413-6(8), Usborne) EDC Publishing.

Mills, Nathan & Roza, Greg. Exploring Rocks & Minerals. 2012. (Rosen Readers Ser.). (ENG., Illus.). 24p. (J). (gr. 1-2). pap. 8.25 (978-1-4488-8830-6(1), 1348003); pap. 49.50 (978-1-4488-8831-3(X), 1348003) Rosen Publishing Group, Inc., The. (Rosen Classroom).

Moore, Elizabeth. Looking at Rocks, 1 vol. 2011. (Wonder Readers Early Level Ser.). (ENG.). (gr. -1-1). 32p. pap. 5.99 (978-1-4296-7809-4(7)); 16p. pap. 35.94 (978-1-4296-8123-0(3)) Capstone Press of Coughlan Cos. (Wonder Readers).

Morgan, Ben & Palmer, Douglas. Rock & Fossil Hunter. 2015. (ENG., Illus.). 72p. (J). (gr. 3-7). pap. 9.99 (978-1-4654-3015-1(6), DK Children) Dorling Kindersley Publishing, Inc.

Morgan, Sally. Rocks. 2011. (Earth Cycles Ser.). 32p. (YA). (gr. 3-6). lib. bdg. 28.50 (978-1-59920-525-0(4)) Black Rabbit Bks.

Mortensen, Lori. Salt Rocks! 2016. (Spring Forward Ser.). (J). (gr. 2). (978-1-4900-9436-6(9)) Benchmark Education Co.

Nagle, Frances. What Are Sedimentary Rocks? 2017. (Look at Earth's Rocks Ser.). 32p. (gr. 2-2). 26.60 **(978-1-4824-6240-1(0))** Stevens, Gareth Publishing LLLP.

—What Is the Rock Cycle? 2017. (Look at Earth's Rocks Ser.). 32p. (gr. 2-2). pap. 10.50 **(978-1-4824-6019-3(X))** Stevens, Gareth Publishing LLLP.

National Geographic Kids Staff & Honovich, Nancy. Rocks & Minerals. 2016. (ENG., Illus.). 160p. (J). (gr. 3-7). lib. bdg. 22.90 (978-1-4263-2302-7(6), National Geographic Children's Bks.) National Geographic Society.

—Rocks & Minerals: Find Adventure! - Go Outside! - Have Fun! - Be a Rock Hound! 2016. (ENG., Illus.). 160p. (J). (gr. 3-7). pap. 12.99 (978-1-4263-2301-0(8), National Geographic Children's Bks.) National Geographic Society.

Natural History Museum Collection Staff. Rocks & Minerals Sticker Book. 2013. (ENG.). 14p. (J). (gr. -1-1). pap. 7.99 (978-0-565-09300-6(2)) Natural History Museum Pubns. GBR. Dist: Independent Pubs. Group.

Nelson, Maria. Igneous Rocks. 2013. 24p. (J). (gr. 2-5). 22.60 (978-1-4339-8313-9(3)); pap. 8.15 (978-1-4339-8314-6(1)); pap. 48.90 (978-1-4339-8315-3(X)) Stevens, Gareth Publishing LLLP.

—Metamorphic Rocks. 2013. (That Rocks! Ser.). 24p. (J). (gr. 2-5). pap. 8.15 (978-1-4339-8318-4(4)); pap. 48.90 (978-1-4339-8319-1(2)); lib. bdg. 22.60 (978-1-4339-8317-7(6)) Stevens, Gareth Publishing LLLP.

—The Rock Cycle. 2013. (That Rocks! Ser.). (Illus.). 24p. (J). (gr. 2-5). pap. 8.15 (978-1-4339-8326-9(5)); lib. bdg. 22.60 (978-1-4339-8325-2(7)) Stevens, Gareth Publishing LLLP.

—Sedimentary Rocks. 2013. (That Rocks! Ser.). 24p. (J). (gr. 2-5). pap. 48.90 (978-1-4339-8323-8(0)); (Illus.). pap. 8.15 (978-1-4339-8322-1(2)); (Illus.). lib. bdg. 22.60 (978-1-4339-8321-4(4)) Stevens, Gareth Publishing LLLP.

—Weathering & Erosion. 2013. (That Rocks! Ser.). (Illus.). 24p. (J). (gr. 2-5). pap. 8.15 (978-1-4339-8330-6(3)); lib. bdg. 22.60 (978-1-4339-8329-0(X)) Stevens, Gareth Publishing LLLP.

Nelson, Robin. Rocks. 2005. (First Step Nonfiction Ser.). (J). (Illus.). 23p. (gr. -1-3). lib. bdg. 18.60 (978-0-8225-2599-8(2), Lerner Pubns.); pap. 5.95 (978-0-8225-5375-5(9)) Lerner Publishing Group.

Newson, Lesley & Wadsworth, Pamela. Rhagor Am Greigiau, Pridd a Thywydd. 2005. (WEL., Illus.). 24p. pap. (978-1-85596-238-5(1)) Dref Wen.

Nsrc, prod. Science & Technology for Children BOOKS: Rocks & Minerals. 2007. (J). (978-1-933008-40-0(7), Science and Technology Concepts (STC)) Smithsonian Science Education Ctr. (SSEC).

O'Donoghue, Michael. Rocks & Minerals of the World. 2004. (World Book's Science & Nature Guides Ser.). (Illus.). 80p. (J). (978-0-7166-4217-6(4)) World Bk., Inc.

O'Neal, Claire. A Project Guide to Rocks & Minerals. 2010. (Earth Science Projects for Kids Ser.). (Illus.). 48p. (J). (gr. 4-7). lib. bdg. 29.95 (978-1-58415-866-0(2)) Mitchell Lane Pubs., Inc.

Ostopowich, Melanie. The Rock Cycle. (Focus on Earth Science Ser.). (gr. 3-6). 2015. (ENG.). (J). lib. bdg. 27.13 (978-1-4896-4093-2(2), AV2 by Weigl) 2010. (Illus.). 24p. (J). pap. 11.95 (978-1-60596-968-8(0)) 2010. (Illus.). 24p. (YA). lib. bdg. 25.70 (978-1-60596-967-1(2)) 2006. (Illus.). 24p. (J). lib. bdg. 24.45 (978-1-59036-209-9(8)) Weigl Pubs., Inc.

—Rocks. (Focus on Earth Science Ser.). 2015. (ENG.). (J). (gr. 3-6). lib. bdg. 27.13 (978-1-4896-4089-5(4), AV2 by Weigl) 2010. (Illus.). 24p. (J). (gr. 3-5). pap. 11.95 (978-1-60596-962-6(1)) 2010. (Illus.). 24p. (YA). (gr. 3-6). lib. bdg. 25.70 (978-1-60596-961-9(3)) 2004. (Illus.). 24p. (J). lib. bdg. 24.45 (978-1-59036-210-5(1)) Weigl Pubs., Inc.

Owen, Ruth. Science & Craft Projects with Rocks & Soil. 2013. (Get Crafty Outdoors Ser.). (ENG., Illus.). 32p. (J). (gr. k-3). 26.50 (978-1-4777-0246-8(6)); pap. 11.75 (978-1-4777-0255-0(5)) Rosen Publishing Group, Inc., The. (PowerKids Pr.).

Owings, Lisa. Igneous Rocks, 1 vol. 2014. (Rocks & Minerals Ser.). (ENG.). 48p. (gr. 8-12). lib. bdg. 32.79 (978-1-62403-387-2(3)) ABDO Publishing Co.

Oxlade, Chris. Igneous Rocks, 1 vol. 2011. (Let's Rock Ser.). (ENG.). 32p. (gr. 3-6). 33.32 (978-1-4329-4679-1(X)); pap. 8.29 (978-1-4329-4687-6(0)) Heinemann-Raintree. (Heinemann InfoSearch).

—Metamorphic Rocks, 1 vol. 2011. (Let's Rock Ser.). (ENG.). 32p. (gr. 3-6). 33.32 (978-1-4329-4680-7(3)); pap. 8.29 (978-1-4329-4688-3(9)) Heinemann-Raintree. (Heinemann InfoSearch).

—Rocas Ígneas. 2011. (Las Rocas Ser.). (SPA.). 32p. (gr. 3-5). pap. 8.29 (978-1-4329-5659-2(0), Heinemann InfoSearch) Heinemann-Raintree.

—Rocas Metamórficas. 2011. (Las Rocas Ser.). (SPA.). 32p. (gr. 3-5). pap. 8.29 (978-1-4329-5660-8(4)); lib. bdg. 33.32 (978-1-4329-5652-3(3)) Heinemann-Raintree. (Heinemann InfoSearch).

—Rocas Sedimentarias. 2011. (Las Rocas Ser.). (SPA.). 32p. (gr. 3-5). pap. 8.29 (978-1-4329-5662-2(0)); lib. bdg. 33.32 (978-1-4329-5654-7(X)) Heinemann-Raintree. (Heinemann InfoSearch).

—Rocks. 2016. (Rock On! Ser.). (ENG., Illus.). 32p. (gr. 2-4). lib. bdg. 30.65 (978-1-4109-8135-6(5), Raintree Perspectives) Heinemann-Raintree.

—Rocks & Minerals, 1 vol. (Essential Physical Science Ser.). (ENG., 48p. (gr. 4-6). 2014. Illus.). 33.32 (978-1-4329-8150-1(1)) 2013. pap. 9.95 (978-1-4329-8159-4(5)) Heinemann-Raintree. (Heinemann InfoSearch).

—Sedimentary Rocks, 1 vol. 2011. (Let's Rock Ser.). (ENG.). 32p. (gr. 3-6). 33.32 (978-1-4329-4681-4(1)); pap. 8.29 (978-1-4329-4689-0(7)) Heinemann-Raintree. (Heinemann InfoSearch).

Pellant, Chris & Pellant, Helen. Granite & Other Igneous Rocks. 2007. (Guide to Rocks & Minerals Ser.). (Illus.). 32p. (gr. 3-6). lib. bdg. 26.00 (978-0-8368-7906-3(6), Gareth Stevens Learning Library) Stevens, Gareth Publishing LLLP.

—Marble & Other Metamorphic Rocks. 2007. (Guide to Rocks & Minerals Ser.). (Illus.). 32p. (gr. 3-6). lib. bdg. 26.00 (978-0-8368-7907-0(4), Gareth Stevens Learning Library) Stevens, Gareth Publishing LLLP.

—Rocks. 2008. (Rock Stars Ser.). (Illus.). 24p. (J). (gr. 1-4). lib. bdg. 23.00 (978-0-8368-9225-3(9)) Stevens, Gareth Publishing LLLP.

—Sandstone & Other Sedimentary Rocks. 2007. (Guide to Rocks & Minerals Ser.). (Illus.). 32p. (gr. 3-6). lib. bdg. 26.00 (978-0-8368-7909-4(0), Gareth Stevens Learning Library) Stevens, Gareth Publishing LLLP.

Peters, Elisa. What Are Igneous Rocks?, 01 vols., 1. 2016. (Junior Geologist Ser.). (ENG., Illus.). 32p. (J). pap. 12.90 (978-1-5081-0047-8(0), Britannica Educational Publishing) Rosen Publishing Group, Inc., The.

Petersen, Christine. Rockin' Rocks, 1 vol. 2010. (Rock on!: a Look at Geology Ser.). (ENG.). 32p. (YA). (gr. 3-6). 27.07 (978-1-60453-746-8(9)) ABDO Publishing Co.

Peterson, Judy Monroe. What Are Metamorphic Rocks?, 01 vols., 1. 2016. (Junior Geologist Ser.). (ENG., Illus.). 32p. (J). pap. 12.90 (978-1-5081-0048-5(9), Britannica Educational Publishing) Rosen Publishing Group, Inc., The.

Phelan, Glen. Rocks & Minerals. 2007. (Nonfiction Reading & Writing Workshops Ser.). (ENG., Illus.). 32p. (J). pap. 17.95 (978-0-7922-4571-1(7)) CENGAGE Learning.

Pinet, Michele. Be Your Own Rock & Mineral Expert. Greenbaum, Fay, tr. from FRE. Korkos, Alain, illus. 2003. 40p. (J). (gr. 5-7). 14.95 (978-0-8069-9580-9(7)) Sterling Publishing Co., Inc.

Prokos, Anna. Rocks & Minerals. 2004. (Discovery Channel School Science Ser.). (Illus.). 32p. (gr. 4-8). lib. bdg. 26.00 (978-0-8368-3384-3(8), Gareth Stevens Learning Library) Stevens, Gareth Publishing LLLP.

Rafferty, John P. Rocks. 2011. (Illus.). xvii, 276p. lib. bdg. 51.70 (978-1-61530-492-9(4)) Rosen Publishing Group, Inc., The.

Rajczak Nelson, Kristen. What Are Igneous Rocks? 2017. (Look at Earth's Rocks Ser.). 32p. (gr. 2-2). pap. 63.00 (978-1-4824-6252-4(4)) Stevens, Gareth Publishing LLLP.

—What Are Metamorphic Rocks? 2017. (Look at Earth's Rocks Ser.). 32p. (gr. 2-2). pap. 10.50 (978-1-4824-6248-7(6)) Stevens, Gareth Publishing LLLP.

Rau, Dana Meachen. Rocks & Minerals. 2009. (21st Century Skills Library: Real World Science Ser.). (ENG.). 32p. (gr. 4-8). lib. bdg. 28.50 (978-1-60279-463-4(4), 200233) Cherry Lake Publishing.

Red Hot Rocks!, 6 Packs. (Bookweb Ser.). 32p. (gr. 6-18). 34.00 (978-0-7578-0911-8(1)) Rigby Education.

Reid, Struan & McConnell, William. Rocks & Fossils. 2006. (Rosen Real Readers Big Bookstm Ser.). (ENG.). 16p. (gr. 2-3). 37.95 (978-1-4042-6221-8(0)) Rosen Publishing Group, Inc., The.

Reynolds, Shaye. Volcanoes. 2016. (Spotlight on Earth Science Ser.). 00024p. (J). (gr. 4-6). pap. 10.00 (978-1-4994-2537-6(6), PowerKids Pr.) Rosen Publishing Group, Inc., The.

Reynolds, Toby & Calver, Paul. Rocks, Crystals, & Gems. 2016. (Visual Explorers Ser.). (ENG., Illus.). 32p. (J). (gr. 3-7). pap. 6.99 (978-1-4380-0828-8(7)) Barron's Educational Series, Inc.

Riley, Peter. Rocks & Soil. 2016. (Moving up with Science Ser.). 00032p. (J). (gr. 3-4). pap. 10.00 (978-1-4994-3153-7(8), PowerKids Pr.) Rosen Publishing Group, Inc., The.

Rissman, Rebecca. Rocks & Soil. 2013. (Real Size Science Ser.). (ENG., Illus.). 24p. (gr. -1-1). 22.65 (978-1-4329-7882-2(9)); pap. 6.95 (978-1-4329-7889-1(6)) Heinemann-Raintree. (Acorn).

The Rock Cycle. 2013. (That Rocks! Ser.). 24p. (J). (gr. 2-5). pap. 48.90 (978-1-4339-8327-6(3)) Stevens, Gareth Publishing LLLP.

Rocks & Minerals. 2005. 48p. (J). per. 6.99 (978-1-59441-202-8(2), CD-104110) Carson-Dellosa Publishing, LLC.

Rocks & Minerals. 2009. (Hammond Undercover Ser.). 72p. (J). (gr. 3-7). 15.95 (978-0-8437-1932-1(X)) Hammond World Atlas Corp.

Rosinsky, Natalie M. & Picture Window Books Staff. Las Rocas: Duras, Blandas, Lisas y Ásperas. Robledo, Sol, tr. from ENG. John, Matthew, illus. 2007. (Ciencia Asombrosa Ser.). (SPA.). 24p. (gr. k-4). 26.65 (978-1-4048-3225-1(4)) Picture Window Bks.

Royston, Angela. Rock: Let's Look at a Pebble. 2005. (J). (978-1-4109-1826-0(2)); (ENG.). 24p. pap. (978-1-4109-1833-8(5)) Steck-Vaughn.

Roza, Greg. Exploring Rocks & Minerals. 2012. (Exploring Earth & Space Ser.). (ENG., Illus.). 24p. (J). (gr. 1-3). 22.60 (978-1-4488-8576-3(0), 1348003, PowerKids Pr.) Rosen Publishing Group, Inc., The.

Rupert, Matthews. Visual Factfinder Rocks & Fossils. 2008. 512p. pap. (978-1-84810-080-0(9)) Miles Kelly Publishing, Ltd.

Rupp, Rebecca. Rocks. 2004. (J). (978-1-58017-540-1(6)); pap. (978-1-58017-539-5(2)) Storey Publishing, LLC.

Russell, Carol & Russell, Tally. I Like Rocks! Russell, Fletch, photos by. 2011. (Illus.). 32p. pap. 12.95 (978-1-4634-3271-3(2)) AuthorHouse.

Salas, Laura Purdie. A Rock Can Be . . Dabija, Violeta, illus. 2015. (ENG.). 32p. (J). (gr. k-2). lib. bdg. 17.99 (978-1-4677-2110-3(7), Millbrook Pr.) Lerner Publishing Group.

Salzano, Tammi J. Rocks, Minerals, & Gemstones. Jankowski, Daniel, illus. 2009. 24p. (J). pap. (978-0-545-19868-4(2)) Scholastic, Inc.

Scholastic, Inc. Staff, contrib. by. Rocks & Minerals. 2015. (Scholastic Discover More Reader, Level 2 Ser.). (ENG.). 32p. (J). (gr. 1-3). pap. 3.99 (978-0-545-83947-1(5), Scholastic Reference) Scholastic, Inc.

Scholastic, Inc. Staff, et al. Rocks, Minerals & Gems. 2016. (ENG.). 224p. (J). (gr. 3-7). 19.99 (978-0-545-94719-0(7), Scholastic Nonfiction) Scholastic, Inc.

Schuh, Mari C. Learning about Rocks, 1 vol. 2011. (Science Builders Ser.). (ENG.). 24p. (gr. k-1). pap. 7.29 (978-1-4296-7108-8(4)); pap. 41.70 (978-1-4296-7114-9(9)); lib. bdg. 26.65 (978-1-4296-6072-3(4)) Capstone Press of Coughlan Cos. (Pebble Plus).

The Shaping & Reshaping of Earth's Surface. (Illus.). (J). (gr. k-6). 127.50 (978-1-4042-3296-9(6)) Rosen Publishing Group, Inc., The.

Sian revision rock Origins. 2004. (J). (978-1-59242-063-6(X)) Delta Education, LLC.

Simon, Seymour. Rocks & Minerals. 2017. 48p. (J). (gr. 1-5). pap. 6.99 **(978-0-06-228917-9(9))** HarperCollins Pubs.

Slade, Suzanne. The Rock Cycle. (Cycles in Nature Ser.). 24p. (gr. 3-3). 2009. 42.50 (978-1-61512-116-8(1), PowerKids Pr.) 2007. (Illus.). (YA). lib. bdg. 22.60 (978-1-4042-3493-2(4)) Rosen Publishing Group, Inc., The.

Sohn, Emily & Wright, Pam. Earth Materials: The Mystery Rocks. 2011. (IScience Readers Ser.). 32p. (J). (gr. 3-4). lib. bdg. 22.60 (978-1-59953-418-3(5)) Norwood Hse. Pr.

Spilsbury, Louise. What Is the Rock Cycle?, 1 vol., 1. 2014. (Let's Find Out! Ser.). (ENG., Illus.). 32p. (J). (gr. 3-6). 23.45 (978-1-62275-266-9(X)) Rosen Publishing Group, Inc., The.

Stamper, Judith Bauer. Rocks & Minerals. 2010. (Illus.). 32p. (J). pap. (978-0-545-28544-5(5)) Scholastic, Inc.

Stewart, Melissa. Extreme Rocks & Minerals! 2007. (Smithsonian Q & A Ser.). (ENG., Illus.). 48p. (J). (gr. k-4). pap. 8.99 (978-0-06-089981-3(6), Collins) HarperCollins Pubs.

Storey, Rita. Rocks & Stones. 2007. (How We Use Materials/Watts Ser.). (Illus.). 30p. (J). (gr. 4-7). lib. bdg. 28.50 (978-1-59920-006-4(6)) Black Rabbit Bks.

Sundance/Newbridge LLC Staff. Rocks & Soil. 2007. (Early Science Ser.). (gr. k-3). 18.95 (978-1-4007-6441-9(6)); pap. 6.10 (978-1-4007-6437-2(8)) Sundance/Newbridge Educational Publishing.

Swanson, Jennifer. Metamorphic Rocks, 1 vol. 2014. (Rocks & Minerals Ser.). (ENG.). 48p. (gr. 8-12). lib. bdg. 32.79 (978-1-62403-388-9(1)) ABDO Publishing Co.

Symes, R. F. DK Eyewitness Books: Rocks & Minerals: Rocks & Minerals. 2014. (DK Eyewitness Bks.). (ENG.). 72p. (J). (gr. 3-7). pap. 9.99 (978-1-4654-2056-5(8), DK Children) Dorling Kindersley Publishing, Inc.

Taylor-Butler, Christine. Experiments with Rocks, 1 vol. 2011. (My Science Investigations Ser.). (ENG.). 32p. (gr. 1-3). pap. 8.29 (978-1-4329-5366-9(4)); 27.32 (978-1-4329-5360-7(5)) Heinemann-Raintree. (Heinemann First Library).

That Rocks! 2013. (That Rocks! Ser.). 24p. (J). (gr. 2-5). 135.60 (978-1-4339-8333-7(8)); pap. 48.90 (978-1-4339-9737-2(1)); pap. 293.40 (978-1-4339-9738-9(X)) Stevens, Gareth Publishing LLLP.

Tomecek, Steve. Rocks & Minerals. Poling, Kyle, illus. 2010. (Jump into Science Ser.). (ENG.). 32p. (J). (gr. -1-3). 16.95 (978-1-4263-0538-2(9)); lib. bdg. 25.90 (978-1-4263-0539-9(7)) National Geographic Society. (National Geographic Children's Bks.).

Tomecek, Steve & National Geographic Kids Staff. National Geographic Kids Everything Rocks & Minerals: Dazzling Gems of Photos & Info That Will Rock Your World. 2011. (ENG., Illus.). 64p. (J). (gr. 3-7). pap. 12.95 (978-1-4263-0768-3(3), National Geographic Children's Bks.) National Geographic Society.

Tomecek, Steve the Dirtmeister. Rocks & Minerals: Dazzling Gems of Photos & Info That Will Rock Your World. 2011. (National Geographic Kids Everything Ser.). (ENG., Illus.). 64p. (J). (gr. 3-7). 25.90 (978-1-4263-0801-7(9), National Geographic Children's Bks.) National Geographic Society.

Trueit, Trudi Strain. Rocks, Gems, & Minerals. 2003. (Watts Library). (ENG.). 64p. (gr. 5-7). pap. 8.95 (978-0-531-16241-5(9), Watts, Franklin) Scholastic Library Publishing.

Tuchman, Gail. Rocks & Minerals. 2015. (Scholastic Reader Level 2 Ser.). lib. bdg. 13.55 (978-0-606-37757-7(3)) Turtleback Bks.

Wadsworth, Pamela. Creigiau, Pridd a Thywydd. 2005. (WEL., Illus.). 24p. pap. (978-1-85596-237-8(3)) Dref Wen.

Wadsworth, Pamela & Tate, Sylvia. Golwg Gyntaf Ar Greigiau, Pridd a Thywydd. 2005. (WEL., Illus.). 24p. pap. (978-1-85596-253-8(5)) Dref Wen.

Walker, Kate. Rocks. 2011. (Investigating Earth Ser.). 32p. (gr. 2). 28.50 (978-1-60870-560-3(9)) Marshall Cavendish Corp.

Walker, Sally M. Marveling at Minerals. 2013. (Searchlight Books (tm) — Do You Dig Earth Science? Ser.). (ENG.). 40p. (gr. 3-5). lib. bdg. 27.93 (978-1-4677-0022-1(3), Lerner Pubns.); (Illus.). pap. 8.95 (978-1-4677-0792-3(9)) Lerner Publishing Group.

—Researching Rocks. 2013. (Searchlight Books (tm) — Do You Dig Earth Science? Ser.). (ENG., Illus.). 40p. (gr. 3-5). pap. 8.95 (978-1-4677-0793-0(7)); lib. bdg. 27.93 (978-1-4677-0018-4(5), Lerner Pubns.) Lerner Publishing Group.

—Rocks. (Illus.). 48p. 2007. (J). pap. 8.95 (978-0-8225-6621-2(4)) 2006. (ENG., (gr. 2-5). lib. bdg. 26.60 (978-0-8225-5947-4(1), Lerner Pubns.) Lerner Publishing Group.

Wallace, Nancy Elizabeth. Rocks! Rocks! Rocks!, 0 vols. 2009. (ENG., Illus.). 48p. (J). (gr. -1-3). 17.99 (978-0-7614-5528-8(0), 9780761455288, Amazon Children's Publishing) Amazon Publishing.

Watts, Pam. The Rock Cycle. 2016. (Geology Rocks! Ser.). (ENG.). 24p. (J). (gr. 3-6). 28.50 (978-1-5038-0804-1(1), 210642) Child's World, Inc., The.

Weakland, Mark. Yogi Bear's Guide to Rocks. Beach, Bryan, illus. 2015. (Yogi Bear's Guide to the Great Outdoors Ser.). (ENG.). 32p. (gr. 1-2). lib. bdg. 27.99 (978-1-4914-6548-6(4)) Capstone Press of Coughlan Cos.

Weathering & Erosion. 2013. (That Rocks! Ser.). 24p. (J). (gr. 2-5). pap. 48.90 (978-1-4339-8331-3(1)) Stevens, Gareth Publishing LLLP.

Wermund, Jerry. The World According to Rock. Sansevero, Tony, illus. 2005. 48p. (J). pap. (978-0-9726255-1-7(8)) Rockon Publishing.

What Happens to Rock? 6 Each of 1 Student Book, 6 vols. (Sunshinetm Science Ser.). 24p. (gr. 1-2). 41.95 (978-0-7802-2720-0(4)) Wright Group/McGraw-Hill.

What Happens to Rock? Big Book. (Sunshinetm Science Ser.). 24p. (gr. 1-2). 37.50 (978-0-7802-2794-1(8)) Wright Group/McGraw-Hill.

Williams, Zella. Experiments on Rocks & the Rock Cycle. (Do-It-Yourself Science Ser.). 24p. (gr. 2-3). 2009. 47.90 (978-1-61512-187-8(0), PowerKids Pr.) 2007. (Illus.). (YA). lib. bdg. 25.25 (978-1-4042-3660-8(0)) Rosen Publishing Group, Inc., The.

Woolley, A. Rocks & Minerals. 2004. (Spotter's Guides). (Illus.). 64p. (J). lib. bdg. 13.95 (978-1-58086-309-4(4)) EDC Publishing.

Woolley, Alan. Rocks & Minerals Spotter's Guide: With Internet Links. Freeman, Mike, photos by. rev. ed. 2007. (Spotter's Guides). (Illus.). 64p. (J). pap. 5.99 (978-0-7945-1304-7(2), Usborne) EDC Publishing.

Wooster, Patricia. Show Me Rocks & Minerals. 2013. (My First Picture Encyclopedias Ser.). (ENG., Illus.). 32p. (gr. 1-2). 7.95 (978-1-4765-3346-9(6), Aplus Bks.) Capstone Press of Coughlan Cos.

—Show Me Rocks & Minerals: My First Picture Encyclopedia, 1 vol. 2013. (My First Picture Encyclopedias Ser.). (ENG.). 32p. (gr. 1-2). 27.32 (978-1-4765-0116-1(5)); pap. 8.10 (978-1-4765-3350-6(4)) Capstone Press of Coughlan Cos. (Aplus Bks.).

Yomtov, Nel. Rocks & the People Who Love Them, 1 vol. Foss, Timothy, illus. 2012. (Adventures in Science Ser.). (ENG.). 32p. (gr. 3-4). pap. 8.10 (978-1-4296-7988-6(3)); pap. 47.70 (978-1-4296-8466-8(6)) Capstone Press of Coughlan Cos. (Graphic Library).

York, J. Igneous Rocks. 2016. (Geology Rocks! Ser.). (ENG.). 24p. (J). (gr. 3-6). 28.50 (978-1-5038-0801-0(7), 210637) Child's World, Inc., The.

Zappa, Marcia. Rocks, 1 vol. 2010. (Big Buddy Bks.). (ENG., Illus.). 32p. (J). (gr. 2-5). 28.50 (978-1-61613-494-5(1), 1315160) ABDO Publishing Co.

Zemlicka, Shannon. From Rock to Road. 2004. (Start to Finish Ser.). (J). pap. 4.95 (978-0-8225-2146-4(6)); 18.60 (978-0-8225-1391-9(9), Lerner Pubns.) Lerner Publishing Group.

Zoehfeld, Kathleen Weidner. National Geographic Readers: Rocks & Minerals. 2012. (Readers Ser.). (ENG., Illus.). 32p. (J). (gr. k-3). lib. bdg. 13.90 (978-1-4263-1039-3(0), National Geographic Children's Bks.) National Geographic Society.

—Rocks & Minerals. 2012. (Readers Ser.). (ENG., Illus.). 32p. (J). (gr. k-3). pap. 3.99 (978-1-4263-1038-6(2), National Geographic Children's Bks.) National Geographic Society.

ROCKS—AGE

see Geology, Stratigraphic

ROCKS—FICTION

Agha-Khan, Aliyar. Cyrus & Kaleo Go Rock Hunting. 2012. 32p. pap. 12.99 (978-1-4634-1567-9(2)) AuthorHouse.

Backus, Leatha F. Annie & Timmy's Magic Pebbles. 2008. 32p. per. 24.95 (978-1-4241-9513-8(6)) America Star Bks.

Barker, Charles Ferguson. Under Ohio: The Story of Ohio's Rocks & Fossils. 2016. (ENG.). 56p. pap. 17.95 (978-0-8214-2195-6(6)) Ohio Univ. Pr.

Bowlby, Linda S. The Rock Garden. Helms, Dana, illus. 2008. 29p. (J). (gr. -1-3). pap. 9.95 (978-0-9779993-4-7(3)) Red Earth Publishing.

Bradfield, Roger. Hello, Rock. 2012. (ENG., Illus.). 28p. (J). 9.95 (978-1-930900-64-6(3)) Purple Hse. Pr.

—!Hola, Piedrita!/Hello, Rock. 2012. (SPA., Illus.). 25p. (J). (gr. -1-3). 9.95 (978-1-930900-65-3(1)) Purple Hse. Pr.

Briggs, Molly Anne. Momma's Favorite Rock. 2006. (J). pap. 8.00 (978-0-8059-7070-8(3)) Dorrance Publishing Co., Inc.

Caddy, David. The Reef. 2005. 144p. (Orig.). (J). pap. 13.50 (978-1-920731-29-8(6)) Fremantle Pr. AUS. Dist: Independent Pubs. Group.

Canavan, Charles Patrick. Rocky's Road to Sunshine. 2013. (ENG., Illus.). 30p. (J). pap. 19.95 (978-1-4787-1251-0(1)) Outskirts Pr., Inc.

Carney, Charles. A Day Just for Daddies. 2011. (Illus.). 24p. (J). 15.99 (978-1-60010-439-8(8)) Idea & Design Works, LLC.

Carney, Mary Lou. The Treasure Rock. 2009. 32p. 14.00 (978-0-687-64537-4(9)) Abingdon Pr.

Chorao, Kay. Ed & Kip. Chorao, Kay, illus. (I Like to Read(r) Ser.). (ENG., Illus.). 24p. (J). (gr. -1-3). 2015. 6.99 (978-0-8234-3398-8(6)) 2014. 14.95 (978-0-8234-2903-5(2)) Holiday Hse., Inc.

Ciraolo, Simona, illus. Hug Me. 2014. (ENG.). 32p. (J). (gr. -1-2). 17.95 (978-1-909263-49-9(4)) Flying Eye Bks. GBR. Dist: Consortium Bk. Sales & Distribution.

Cook, Sherry & Johnson, Terri. Ronnie Rock, 26. Kuhn, Jesse, illus. l.t. ed. 2006. (Quirkles — Exploring Phonics through Science Ser.: 18). 32p. (J). 7.99 (978-1-933815-17-6(5), Quirkles, The) Creative 3, LLC.

The Coolest Rock. (Early Intervention Levels Ser.). 31.86 (978-0-7362-0668-6(X)) CENGAGE Learning.

Cornfield, Lynda Ellis. Rocks for Clean Oceans. 2009. 28p. pap. 13.99 (978-1-4389-8417-9(0)) AuthorHouse.

Dey, Joy M. Agate: What Good Is a Moose? Johnson, Nikki, illus. 2007. 32p. (J). (gr. -1-3). 17.95 (978-0-942235-73-9(8)) Lake Superior Port Cities, Inc.

Dreyer, Ellen. The Glow Stone, 1 vol. 2006. (ENG.). 224p. (YA). (gr. 7-18). 15.95 (978-1-56145-370-2(6)) Peachtree Pubs.

Fagan, Cary. Ella May & the Wishing Stone. Cote, Genevieve, illus. 2011. (ENG.). 32p. (J). (gr. -1-1). 17.95 (978-1-77049-225-7(9), Tundra Bks.) Tundra Bks. CAN. Dist: Penguin Random Hse. LLC.

Ferry, Beth. Stick & Stone. Lichtenheld, Tom, illus. 2015. (ENG.). 48p. (J). (gr. -1-3). 16.99 (978-0-544-03256-9(X), HMH Books For Young Readers) Houghton Mifflin Harcourt Publishing Co.

Fitzsimmons, Christy. Krissy & the Indians, 1 vol. Steckler, Megan, illus. 2009. 28p. pap. 24.95 (978-1-61546-206-3(6)) America Star Bks.

Formento, Alison. These Rocks Count! Snow, Sarah, illus. 2014. (These Things Count! Ser.). (ENG.). 32p. (J). (gr. -1-3). 16.99 (978-0-8075-7870-4(3)) Whitman, Albert & Co.

Frazier, Sundee T. Brendan Buckley's Universe & Everything in It. 2008. (ENG.). 208p. (J). (gr. 3-7). 6.99 (978-0-440-42206-8(X), Yearling) Random Hse. Children's Bks.

George, Jean Craighead. A Special Gift for Grammy. Johnson, Steve & Fancher, Lou, illus. 2013. (ENG.). 32p. (J). (gr. -1-3). 17.99 (978-0-06-053176-8(2)) HarperCollins Pubs.

Griffin, Molly Beth. Rhoda's Rock Hunt. Bell, Jennifer A., illus. 2014. (ENG.). 32p. (J). (gr. -1-2). 16.95 (978-0-87351-950-2(7)) Minnesota Historical Society Pr.

Hargis, Alvin. Kingdom of Mystique Series: Book 1. 2007. 25p. pap. 24.95 (978-1-4241-8635-8(8)) PublishAmerica, Inc.

Herndon, Susen A. Janie's World: Under the Rock. 2013. 40p. (gr. 4-6). pap. 16.46 (978-1-4669-7472-2(9)) Trafford Publishing.

Hufford, Lottie. God's Talking Child Rocks. 2012. 28p. pap. 13.95 (978-1-4525-5782-3(9)) Balboa Pr.

King, Steve. The Stone Dragon. 2005. 80p. pap. 16.95 (978-1-4137-9628-5(1)) PublishAmerica, Inc.
Malone, Ladawn. The Master's Garden. 2009. 32p. pap. 14.49 (978-1-4490-3860-1(3)) AuthorHouse.
Martin, Stephen W. Charlotte & the Rock. Cotterill, Samantha, illus. 2017. (ENG.). 32p. (J). (-k). 16.99 (978-1-101-99389-7(8), Dial Bks) Penguin Young Readers Group.
McGuirk, Leslie. If Rocks Could Sing: A Discovered Alphabet. 2011. (ENG., Illus.). 48p. (J). (gr. -1-2). 15.99 (978-1-58246-370-4(0), Tricycle Pr.) Random Hse. Children's Bks.
McRary, Janie. The Rock That Became a Friend. 2011. 24p. pap. 12.74 (978-1-4634-3018-4(3)) AuthorHouse.
Milord, Susan. Pebble: A Story about Belonging. Milord, Susan, illus. 2007. (ENG., Illus.). 32p. (J). (gr. -1-2). 15.99 (978-0-06-085807-0(9)) HarperCollins Pubs.
Murray, Andrew. On a Tall, Tall Cliff. Snow, Alan, illus. (ENG.). 32p. (J). (gr. k-2). 2005. 19.99 (978-0-00-712155-7(5)) 2004. pap. 11.95 (978-0-00-712156-4(3)) HarperCollins Pubs. Ltd. GBR. Dist: Independent Pubs. Group.
Orobosa-Ogbeide, Kathryn. Adam's Magic Pebble. 2012. 20p. pap. 13.77 (978-1-4669-1896-2(9)) Trafford Publishing.
Pair, Regether. The Little Rock Island & a Little Rock Named Sam Who Doesn't Think He Fits In. 2012. 20p. pap. 24.95 (978-1-4626-9807-3(7)) America Star Bks.
Parnell, Paul. Talking Rocks. 2009. 52p. pap. 16.95 (978-1-61546-651-1(7)) America Star Bks.
Perry, Phyllis J. The Secrets of the Rock. Lipking, Ron, illus. 2004. (Fribble Mouse Library Mystery Ser.). 96p. (J). 16.95 (978-1-932146-22-6(9), 1237661) Highsmith Inc.
Weston Woods Staff, creator. Elizabeti's Doll. 2011. 38.75 (978-0-439-84574-8(2)); 18.95 (978-0-439-73629-9(3)) Weston Woods Studios, Inc.
Zito, Ann R. Rock, Stream, Tree. Matheny, Melody, illus. 2010. 52p. pap. 11.00 (978-1-4520-7822-9(X)) AuthorHouse.

ROCKY MOUNTAINS

Aloian, Molly. The Rocky Mountains. 2011. (ENG., Illus.). 48p. (J). pap. (978-0-7787-7570-6(4)); (gr. 4-7). lib. bdg. (978-0-7787-7563-8(1)) Crabtree Publishing Co.
Asnong, Jocey, illus. Rocky Mountain ABCs. 2016. (ENG.). 28p. (— 1). bds. 12.00 (978-1-77160-163-4(9)) Road West Publishing Co.
Bauer, Marion Dane. The Rocky Mountains. Wallace, John, illus. 2006. (Wonders of America Ser.). (ENG.). 32p. (J). (gr. -1-1). pap. 3.99 (978-0-689-86948-8(7), Simon Spotlight) Simon Spotlight.
Brucken, Kelli M. Bristlecone Pines. 2005. (Wonders of the World Ser.). (ENG., Illus.). 48p. (J). (gr. 4-8). lib. bdg. 29.15 (978-0-7377-3061-6(7), Greenhaven Pr., Inc.) Cengage Gale.
Collard, Sneed B., III. Fire Birds. 2015. (Illus.). 48p. (J). (978-0-9844460-7-0(9)) Bucking Horse Bks.
Frisch, Nate. Rocky Mountains National Park: Preserving America. 2016. (Preserving America Ser.). (ENG.). 48p. (J). (gr. 5-9). pap. 12.00 (978-1-62832-182-1(2), Creative Paperbacks) Creative Co., The.
Goyette, Linda. Rocky Mountain Kids, 1 vol. 2008. (ENG., Illus.). 128p. (J). (gr. 3-7). pap. (978-1-897142-32-5(3)) Brindle & Glass Publishing.
Hamilton, John. Rocky Mountain National Park. 2008. (National Parks Set II Ser.). 32p. (gr. 4-9). 27.07 (978-1-60453-094-0(4), Abdo & Daughters) ABDO Publishing Co.
Herrington, Lisa M. Rocky Mountain. 2017. (Rookie National Parks Ser.). (ENG.). 32p. (J). pap. 5.95 **(978-0-531-23905-6(5)**, Children's Pr.) Scholastic Library Publishing.
Hyde, Natalie. Rocky Mountains Research Journal. 2017. (Illus.). 32p. (J). **(978-0-7787-3471-0(4))**; pap. **(978-0-7787-3496-3(X))** Crabtree Publishing Co.
Justesen, Kim Williams. Hey Ranger! Kids Ask Questions about Rocky Mountain National Park. Newhouse, Judy, illus. 2005. (Hey Ranger! Ser.). (ENG.). 48p. (J). (gr. -1-12). pap. 9.95 (978-0-7627-3848-9(0), Falcon Guides) Globe Pequot Pr., The.
Lerner Classroom Staff & Zuehlke, Jeffrey. The Rocky Mountains. 2010. (Lightning Bolt Books (tm) — Famous Places Ser.). (ENG., Illus.). 32p. (gr. k-2). pap. 7.95 (978-0-7613-5585-4(5)) Lerner Publishing Group.
Lonely Planet Publications Staff, et al. Unfolding Journeys Rocky Mountain Explorer, 1 vol. 2016. (Lonely Planet Kids Ser.). (ENG., Illus.). 16p. (J). pap. 17.99 (978-1-78657-107-6(2), 5243) Lonely Planet Pubns.
Loomis, Jennifer A. Wildlife in the Rocky Mountains. Loomis, Jennifer A., photos by. unabr. ed. 2005. (Illus.). 100p. (J). 24.95 (978-0-88045-159-8(9)) Stemmer Hse. Pubs.
Maynard, Charles W. The Rocky Mountains. (Great Mountain Ranges of the World Ser.). 2009. 24p. (gr. 3-3). 42.50 (978-1-61513-171-6(X)) 2004. (J). 21.25 (978-0-8239-6698-1(4)) 2004. (Illus.). 24p. (J). lib. bdg. 22.60 (978-0-8239-6926-5(6)) Rosen Publishing Group, Inc., The. (PowerKids Pr.).
Peluso, Beth A. The Charcoal Forest: How Fire Helps Animals & Plants. Peluso, Beth A., illus. 2007. (Illus.). 56p. (J). (gr. -1-3). pap. 12.00 (978-0-87842-532-7(2)) Mountain Pr. Publishing Co., Inc.
Tarbox, A. D. A Mountain Food Chain: Nature's Bounty. 2nd ed. 2015. (Illus.). 80p. (J). (978-1-60818-540-5(0), Creative Education) Creative Co., The.
Walsh, Steve. Zebulon Montgomery Pike: Explorer & Military Officer. 2011. (ENG & SPA., Illus.). 54p. (J). pap. 8.95 (978-0-86541-123-4(9)) Filter Pr., LLC.
Zeiger, Jennifer. Rocky Mountain National Park. 2017. (True Book — National Parks Ser.). (ENG.). 48p. (J). lib. bdg. 31.00 **(978-0-531-23394-8(4)**, Children's Pr.) Scholastic Library Publishing.
Zuehlke, Jeffrey. The Rocky Mountains. 2010. (Lightning Bolt Books (tm) — Famous Places Ser.). (ENG.). 32p. (gr. k-2). lib. bdg. 26.60 (978-0-7613-4454-4(3), Lerner Pubns.) Lerner Publishing Group.

ROCKY MOUNTAINS—FICTION

Burchfield, Cindy. Gimme, Gimme Moocher Marmots. Burchfield, Cindy, illus. 2007. (Illus.). 48p. per. 18.95 (978-1-59858-457-8(X)) Dog Ear Publishing, LLC.
Burns, Emily. Marked Evidence. 2003. (Rocky Mountain Mysteries Ser.: 3). (J). per. 4.95 (978-0-9723259-2-9(1), RMM3) Covered Wagon Publishing LLC.
Butler, T. Lee. The Ghost on Tanner's Mountain. 2008. 96p. pap. 11.94 (978-1-4357-5963-3(X)) Lulu Pr., Inc.
Cangilla-McAdam, Claudia. Mama's Mysterious Mission. Crum, Anna-Maria, illus. 2007. 32p. (J). (gr. 3-7). 12.95 (978-1-56579-588-4(1)) Fielder, John Publishing.
Carr, Roger Vaughan. The Climb. 2007. 96p. (J). pap. (978-1-4207-0730-4(2)) Sundance/Newbridge Educational Publishing.
Carson, James. The Saddle Boys of the Rockies. 2007. 104p. per. (978-1-4068-4406-1(3)) Echo Library.
—Saddle Boys of the Rockies or Lost on Th. 2007. pap. (978-1-4065-1298-4(2)) Dodo Pr.
Derrick Patricia. Beaser the Bear's Rocky Mountain Christmas. Hoch, Doug, illus. 2007. 32p. (J). (gr. -1-3). 18.95 incl. audio compact disk (978-1-933818-09-2(3)) Animalations.
Derrick, Patricia. Rickity & Snickity at the Balloon Fiesta. Martinez, J-P Loppo, illus. 2007. 32p. (J). (gr. -1-3). 18.95 incl. audio compact disk (978-1-933818-11-5(5)) Animalations.
Duffield, J. W. Bert Wilson in the Rockies. 2006. 26.95 (978-1-4218-2964-7(9)); pap. 11.95 (978-1-4218-3064-3(7)) 1st World Publishing, Inc.
Fabry, Chris & Jenkins, Jerry B. Haunted Waters. 2005. (Red Rock Mysteries Ser.: 1). (ENG., Illus.). 224p. (YA). (gr. -1-7). pap. 6.99 (978-1-4143-0140-2(5), Tyndale Kids) Tyndale Hse. Pubs.
Freitag, Fred. On Hills & Meadows by the River. 2013. 28p. pap. 24.95 (978-1-63000-584-9(3)) America Star Bks.
James, Will. Cowboy in the Making. rev. ed. (Illus.). 104p. (J). (gr. 4-6). pap. 15.00 (978-0-87842-439-9(3), 811) Mountain Pr. Publishing Co., Inc.
Kingston, W. H. G. In the Rocky Mountains. 2007. (Illus.). 228p. per. (978-1-4065-2892-3(7)) Dodo Pr.
Kuhn, Krystyna & Pessah, Jon. The Game. 2012. (ENG.). 320p. (YA). (gr. 7-17). 9.99 (978-1-907411-65-6(8)) Little, Brown Book Group Ltd. GBR. Dist: Hachette Bk. Group.
Marsh, Carole. The Mystery in the Rocky Mountains. 2009. (Real Kids, Real Places Ser.). (Illus.). 145p. (J). lib. bdg. 18.99 (978-0-635-07000-5(6), Marsh, Carole Mysteries) Gallopade International.
Nesbit, Troy. Jinx of Payrock Canyon. 2014. (Wilderness Mystery Ser.). (ENG., Illus.). 282p. (J). (gr. 3-7). pap. 12.95 (978-1-58979-865-6(1)) Taylor Trade Publishing.
Noland, Monica. Slide. 2006. 116p. pap. 19.95 (978-1-4241-4966-7(5)) PublishAmerica, Inc.
Richardson, Steve. Alexander Trout's Amazing Adventure. Lowe, Wesley, illus. 2008. 75p. 16.95 (978-0-9786422-2-8(8)) Impossible Dreams Publishing Co.
Wolfson, Steve. Monster Cheese. Johnson, Bill, illus. 2013. 34p. pap. 10.95 (978-0-9798324-3-7(8)) Argami Productions, LLC.

RODENTS

Antill, Sara. Porcupines. 2010. (Unusual Animals Ser.). (Illus.). 24p. (J). (gr. k-3). (ENG.). pap. 8.15 (978-1-61533-005-8(4)); lib. bdg. 22.60 (978-1-60754-995-6(6)) Windmill Bks.
Borgert-Spaniol, Megan. Capybaras. 2013. (Animal Safari Ser.). (ENG., Illus.). 24p. (J). (gr. k-3). lib. bdg. 25.95 (978-1-60014-908-5(1), Blastoff! Readers) Bellwether Media.
Gagne, Tammy. Backyard Jungle Safari Gray Squirrels: Grey Squirrels. 2015. (ENG., Illus.). 32p. (J). 26.50 (978-1-62469-104-1(8)) Purple Toad Publishing, Inc.
Gaines, Ann. Kids Top 10 Small Mammal Pets. 2015. (American Humane Association Top 10 Pets for Kids Ser.). 48p. (J). (gr. 3-4). 25.27 (978-0-7660-6650-2(9)) Enslow Pubs., Inc.
Ganeri, Anita. Capybara, 1 vol. 2010. (Day in the Life: Rain Forest Animals Ser.). (ENG., Illus.). 24p. (gr. k-2). 23.32 (978-1-4329-4110-9(0)); pap. 6.79 (978-1-4329-4121-5(6)) Heinemann-Raintree. (Heinemann Read & Learn).
Kalman, Bobbie. Baby Rodents. 2013. (ENG., Illus.). 24p. (J). (978-0-7787-1009-7(2)); pap. (978-0-7787-1014-1(9)) Crabtree Publishing Co.
—Guinea Pigs & Other Rodents. 2005. (What Kind of Animal Is It? Ser.). (ENG., Illus.). 32p. (J). (gr. 1-2). lib. bdg. (978-0-7787-2163-5(9)) Crabtree Publishing Co.
—Rodent Rap. 2010. (My World Ser.). (ENG., Illus.). 16p. (J). (gr. k-2). (978-0-7787-9438-7(5)); pap. (978-0-7787-9482-0(2)) Crabtree Publishing Co.
Kalman, Bobbie & Langille, Jacqueline. Les Rongeurs. 2003. (Petit Monde Vivant Ser.). (FRE., Illus.). 32p. (J). pap. 9.95 (978-2-89579-005-1(1)) Bayard Canada Livres CAN. Dist: Crabtree Publishing Co.
Kalman, Bobbie & Miller, Reagan. Les Cochons D'Inde et Autres Rongeurs. 2011. (Petit Monde Vivant (Small Living World) Ser.: No. 76). (FRE., Illus.). 32p. (J). pap. 9.95 (978-2-89579-370-0(0)) Bayard Canada Livres CAN. Dist: Crabtree Publishing Co.
Lunis, Natalie. Capybara: The World's Largest Rodent. 2010. (More SuperSized! Ser.). (Illus.). 24p. (J). (gr. k-3). lib. bdg. 22.61 (978-1-936087-31-0(6)) Bearport Publishing Co., Inc.
Lynette, Rachel. Capybaras. 2013. (Jungle Babies of the Amazon Rain Forest Ser.). 24p. (J). (gr. -1-3). lib. bdg. 21.32 (978-1-61772-753-5(9)) Bearport Publishing Co., Inc.
Markle, Sandra. Los Puercoespines. 2008. (Animales Presas (Animal Prey) Ser.). (SPA.). (J). (gr. 4-7). 25.26 (978-0-7613-3897-0(7)) Lerner Publishing Group.
Mataya, Marybeth. Are You My Rodent?, 1 vol. Williams, Matthew, illus. 2008. (Are You My Pet? Ser.). (ENG.). 32p. (J). (gr. 1-4). 28.50 (978-1-60270-246-2(2)) Magic Wagon.
Morey, Allan. Capybaras. 2017. (Weird & Unusual Animals Ser.). (ENG.). 24p. (gr. 1-4). 20.95 **(978-1-68151-155-9(X))** Amicus Publishing.
Morgan, Sally. Rodents. 2004. (J). lib. bdg. (978-1-59389-177-0(6)) Cherrytree Bks.
Schafer, Susan. Capybaras. 2014. (Giant Animals Ser.). 48p. (J). (gr. 4-6). lib. bdg. 31.36 (978-1-62712-969-5(3)) Cavendish Square Publishing.
Sill, Cathryn. About Rodents: A Guide for Children, 1 vol. Sill, John, illus. 2016. (About... Ser.). (ENG.). 48p. (J). (gr. -1-2). pap. 7.95 (978-1-56145-914-8(3)) Peachtree Pubs.
Sill, Cathryn & Sill, John. About Rodents: A Guide for Children, 1 vol. 2008. (ENG., Illus.). 48p. (J). (gr. k-3). 15.95 (978-1-56145-454-9(0)) Peachtree Pubs.
Stefoff, Rebecca. The Rodent Order. 2008. (Family Trees Ser.). 96p. (gr. 6-18). lib. bdg. 34.21 (978-0-7614-3073-5(3), Benchmark Bks.) Marshall Cavendish Corp.
Thatcher, Henry. Capybaras & Pygmy Mice, 1 vol. 1. 2014. (Big Animals, Small Animals Ser.). (ENG.). 32p. (J). (gr. k-5). 26.25 (978-1-4777-6114-4(4), PowerKids Pr.) Rosen Publishing Group, Inc., The.
Visca, Curt & Visca, Kelley. How to Draw Cartoon Rodents. 2003. (Kid's Guide to Drawing Ser.). (Illus.). 24p. (J). lib. bdg. 25.25 (978-0-8239-6161-0(3), PowerKids Pr.) Rosen Publishing Group, Inc., The.
Visca, Kelly. How to Draw Cartoon Rodents. 2009. (Kid's Guide to Drawing Ser.). 24p. (gr. 3-3). 47.90 (978-1-61511-018-6(6), PowerKids Pr.) Rosen Publishing Group, Inc., The.
World Book, Inc Staff, contrib. by. Hamsters & Other Pet Rodents. 2009. (J). (978-0-7166-1370-1(0)) World Bk., Inc.
Zobel, Derek. Gophers. 2011. (Backyard Wildlife Ser.). (ENG., Illus.). 24p. (J). (gr. k-3). lib. bdg. 25.95 (978-1-60014-597-1(3), Blastoff! Readers) Bellwether Media.

RODENTS—FICTION

Aguayo, Sal. The Tiny Detective. 2008. 48p. pap. 16.95 (978-1-60703-859-7(5)) America Star Bks.
—The Tiny Telepaths: A Continuing Saga, 1 vol. 2010. 62p. pap. 19.95 (978-1-4489-5212-0(3)) America Star Bks.
Bee, William. Stanley the Farmer, 1 vol. Bee, William, illus. 2015. (Stanley Ser.). (ENG., Illus.). 32p. (J). (gr. 1-2). 14.95 (978-1-56145-803-5(1)) Peachtree Pubs.
—Stanley the Mailman, 1 vol. Bee, William, illus. 2016. (Stanley Ser.). (ENG., Illus.). 32p. (J). (gr. -1-2). 14.95 (978-1-56145-867-7(8)) Peachtree Pubs.
—Stanley's Diner, 1 vol. Bee, William, illus. 2015. (Stanley Ser.). (ENG., Illus.). 32p. (J). (gr. -1-2). 14.95 (978-1-56145-802-8(3)) Peachtree Pubs.
—Stanley's Numbers, 1 vol. Bee, William, illus. 2017. (Stanley Ser.). (ENG., Illus.). 20p. (J). (gr. -1 — 1). bds. 6.95 **(978-1-56145-976-6(3))** Peachtree Pubs.
—Stanley's Opposites, 1 vol. Bee, William, illus. 2017. (Stanley Ser.). (ENG., Illus.). 20p. (J). (gr. -1 — 1). bds. 6.95 **(978-1-56145-977-3(1))** Peachtree Pubs.
Bee, William. Stanley's Shapes, 1 vol. Bee, William, illus. 2016. (Stanley Ser.). (ENG., Illus.). 20p. (J). (gr. -1-k). bds. 6.95 (978-1-56145-949-0(6), Freestone) Peachtree Pubs.
Bee, William, illus. Stanley the Mailman. 2016. (J). pap. **(978-1-56145-946-9(1)**, Peachtree Junior) Peachtree Pubs.
Deeks, Graham. Ratrigues & the Invisible Intelligence. 2011. 264p. 27.08 (978-1-4269-7019-1(6)); pap. 17.08 (978-1-4269-7020-7(X)) Trafford Publishing.
Ducharme, P. J. The Adventures of Jungle Foot Rot, 1 vol. 2009. 17p. pap. 24.95 (978-1-60813-918-7(2)) America Star Bks.
Howe, James & Walrod, Amy. Horace & Morris but Mostly Dolores. Walrod, Amy, illus. 2003. (ENG., Illus.). 32p. (J). (gr. -1-3). 7.99 (978-0-689-85675-4(X), Atheneum Bks. for Young Readers) Simon & Schuster Children's Publishing.
Hungry Hedgehog, 6 Packs. (Story Steps Ser.). (gr. k-2). 29.00 (978-0-7635-9583-8(7)) Rigby Education.
Jonell, Lynne. Emmy & the Home for Troubled Girls. Bean, Jonathan, illus. 2010. (Emmy & the Rat Ser.: 2). (ENG.). 384p. (J). (gr. 4-7). pap. 12.99 (978-0-312-60873-6(X), 9780312608736) Square Fish.
—Emmy & the Incredible Shrinking Rat. Bean, Jonathan, illus. 2008. (Emmy & the Rat Ser.: 1). (ENG.). 368p. (J). (gr. 4-7). pap. 8.99 (978-0-312-38460-9(2), 9780312384609) Square Fish.
—Emmy & the Incredible Shrinking Rat. Lt. ed. 2008. 426p. (YA). 23.95 (978-1-4104-0778-8(0)) Thorndike Pr.
—Emmy & the Rats in the Belfry. Bean, Jonathan, illus. 2011. (Emmy & the Rat Ser.: 3). (ENG.). 384p. (J). (gr. 4-7). 17.99 (978-0-8050-9183-0(1), 9780805091830, Holt, Henry & Co. Bks. For Young Readers) Holt, Henry & Co.
Lester, Helen. Hooway for Wodney Wat, 1 vol. Munsinger, Lynn, illus. 2011. (ENG.). 32p. (J). (gr. -1-3). audio compact disk 10.99 (978-0-547-55217-0(3)) Houghton Mifflin Harcourt Publishing Co.
—Wodney Wat's Wobot. Munsinger, Lynn, illus. 2011. (ENG.). 32p. (J). (gr. -1-3). 16.99 (978-0-547-36756-9(2)) Houghton Mifflin Harcourt Publishing Co.
Pevear, Ted F. & Pevear, Linda W. The Date in the Junk Yard. 2012. 28p. 24.95 (978-1-62709-781-9(3)) America Star Bks.
Rylant, Cynthia. The Storm. McDaniels, Preston, illus. 2003. (Lighthouse Family Ser.: 1). (ENG.). 80p. (J). (gr. 1-5). pap. 5.99 (978-0-689-84882-7(X), Simon & Schuster Bks. For Young Readers) Simon & Schuster Bks. For Young Readers.
Stanley the Builder, 1 vol. 2014. (Stanley Ser.). (ENG., Illus.). 32p. (J). (gr. -1-2). 14.95 (978-1-56145-801-1(5)) Peachtree Pubs.
Stanley's Garage, 1 vol. 2014. (Stanley Ser.). (ENG., Illus.). 32p. (J). (gr. -1-2). 14.95 (978-1-56145-804-2(X)) Peachtree Pubs.
Who Painted the Porcupine. (J). 23.50 (978-0-8136-3967-3(0)) Modern Curriculum Pr.
Willems, Mo. Naked Mole Rat Gets Dressed. Willems, Mo, illus. 2009. (ENG., Illus.). 40p. (J). (gr. -1 — 1). 16.99 (978-1-4231-1437-6(X)) Hyperion Pr.
Willems, Mo, et al, narrated by. Naked Mole Rat Gets Dressed. 2011. (J). (gr. -1-2). 29.95 (978-0-545-29678-6(1)) Weston Woods Studios, Inc.

RODEOS

ABDO Publishing Company Staff. Xtreme Rodeo. 2013. (Xtreme Rodeo Ser.: 6). 32p. (gr. 3-9). lib. bdg. 162.42 (978-1-61783-976-4(0), Abdo & Daughters) ABDO Publishing Co.
Ambrosek, Renee. Team Roping. 2009. (World of Rodeo Ser.). 48p. (gr. 6-6). 53.00 (978-1-60854-311-3(0), Rosen Reference) Rosen Publishing Group, Inc., The.
Cohn, Jessica. Rodeo. 2nd ed. 2013. (Incredibly Insane Sports Ser.). (Illus.). 48p. (J). (gr. 4-6). 31.95 (978-1-4339-8838-7(0)); pap. 14.05 (978-1-4339-8839-4(9)) Stevens, Gareth Publishing LLLP. (Gareth Stevens Learning Library).
Flood, Nancy Bo. Cowboy Up! Ride the Navajo Rodeo. Sonnemair, Jan, illus. 2013. (ENG.). 48p. (J). (gr. 3-7). 17.95 (978-1-59078-893-6(1), Wordsong) Boyds Mills Pr.
Hamilton, John. Bareback Riding. 2013. (Xtreme Rodeo Ser.). (Illus.). 32p. (J). (gr. 3-9). lib. bdg. 27.07 (978-1-61783-977-1(9), Abdo & Daughters) ABDO Publishing Co.
—Barrel Racing. 2013. (Xtreme Rodeo Ser.). (Illus.). 32p. (J). (gr. 3-9). lib. bdg. 27.07 (978-1-61783-978-8(7), Abdo & Daughters) ABDO Publishing Co.
—Bull Riding. 2013. (Xtreme Rodeo Ser.). (Illus.). 32p. (J). (gr. 3-9). lib. bdg. 27.07 (978-1-61783-979-5(5), Abdo & Daughters) ABDO Publishing Co.
—Rodeo Clown. 2015. (Illus.). 32p. pap. 27.07 (978-1-62403-758-0(5)) ABDO Publishing Co.
—Roping. 2013. (Xtreme Rodeo Ser.). (Illus.). 32p. (J). (gr. 3-9). lib. bdg. 27.07 (978-1-61783-982-5(5), Abdo & Daughters) ABDO Publishing Co.
—Saddle Bronc Riding. 2013. (Xtreme Rodeo Ser.). (Illus.). 32p. (J). (gr. 3-9). lib. bdg. 27.07 (978-1-61783-980-1(9), Abdo & Daughters) ABDO Publishing Co.
—Steer Wrestling. 2013. (Xtreme Rodeo Ser.). (Illus.). 32p. (J). (gr. 3-9). lib. bdg. 27.07 (978-1-61783-981-8(7), Abdo & Daughters) ABDO Publishing Co.
Hamilton, S. L. Rodeo. 2010. (Xtreme Sports Ser.). 32p. (gr. 3-9). 27.07 (978-1-61613-004-6(0), A&D Xtreme) ABDO Publishing Co.
Johnson, Robin. Rodeo. 2009. (ENG., Illus.). 32p. (J). (gr. 3-6). lib. bdg. (978-0-7787-4977-6(0)); (gr. 4-5). pap. (978-0-7787-4993-6(2)) Crabtree Publishing Co.
Kubke, Jane. Bull Riding. 2009. (World of Rodeo Ser.). 48p. (gr. 6-6). 53.00 (978-1-60854-303-8(X), Rosen Reference) Rosen Publishing Group, Inc., The.
Kupperberg, Paul. Rodeo Clowns. (World of Rodeo Ser.). 48p. 2009. (gr. 6-6). 53.00 (978-1-60854-308-3(0), Rosen Reference) 2006. (Illus.). (YA). (gr. 4-7). lib. bdg. 26.50 (978-1-4042-0546-8(2)) Rosen Publishing Group, Inc., The.
Meinking, Mary & Peschke, Marci. Kylie Jean Rodeo Craft Queen, 1 vol. Mourning, Tuesday, illus. 2014. (Kylie Jean Craft Queen Ser.). (ENG.). 32p. (gr. 2-3). lib. bdg. 26.65 (978-1-4795-2190-6(6)) Picture Window Bks.
Munro, Roxie. Rodeo. 2007. (ENG., Illus.). 60p. (J). (gr. -1-3). 15.95 (978-1-933979-03-8(8), 6b65c83d-7b1c-4bb8-b6ff-b33386e4bcdc) Bright Sky Pr.
Murphy, Stuart J. Rodeo Time. Wenzel, David T., illus. 2006. (MathStart 3 Ser.). (ENG.). 40p. (J). (gr. 2-5). pap. 5.99 (978-0-06-055779-9(6)) HarperCollins Pubs.
Petruccio, Steven James. Rodeo Coloring Book. 2004. (Dover History Coloring Book Ser.). (ENG., Illus.). 32p. (J). (gr. -1-2). pap. 3.99 (978-0-486-43330-1(7)) Dover Pubns., Inc.
Pirk, Wendy & Radford, Duane. Rodeo Roundup, 1 vol. 2017. (ENG., Illus.). 64p. (J). pap. 6.99 **(978-1-896124-63-6(1)**, 9781896124636) Dragon Hill Publishing CAN. Dist: Lone Pine Publishing USA.
Rodeo, 6 bks., Set. (SPA.). (J). (gr. 1-4). lib. bdg. 115.62 (978-1-57103-382-6(3)) Rourke Educational Media.
Stone, Lynn M. The Rodeo. 2008. (All about the Rodeo Ser.). (Illus.). 32p. (YA). (gr. 4-7). lib. bdg. 28.50 (978-1-60472-387-8(4)) Rourke Educational Media.
—Rodeo Bronc Riders. 2008. (All about the Rodeo Ser.). (Illus.). 32p. (YA). (gr. 4-7). lib. bdg. 28.50 (978-1-60472-388-5(2)) Rourke Educational Media.
The World of Rodeo, 6 bks., Set. Incl. Barrel Racing. Broyles, Janell. lib. bdg. 29.25 (978-1-4042-0543-7(8)); Bull Riding. Kubke, Jane & Kubke, Jessica. lib. bdg. 29.25 (978-1-4042-0544-4(6)); Rodeo Clowns. Kupperberg, Paul. lib. bdg. 26.50 (978-1-4042-0546-8(2)); Team Roping. Ambrosek, Renee. lib. bdg. 29.25 (978-1-4042-0548-2(9)); (Illus.). 48p. (YA). (gr. 4-7). 2006. Set lib. bdg. 159.00 (978-1-4042-0836-0(4)) Rosen Publishing Group, Inc., The.

RODEOS—FICTION

Beecher, Elizabeth. Roy Rogers & Cowboy Toby. Crawford, Mel, illus. 2011. 30p. 35.95 (978-1-258-03514-3(6)) Literary Licensing, LLC.
Brett, Jan. Armadillo Rodeo. Brett, Jan, illus. 2004. (ENG., Illus.). 32p. (J). (gr. -1-3). pap. 6.99 (978-0-14-240125-5(0), Puffin Books) Penguin Young Readers Group.
Compton, Dawn. Grand Entry. Kollman, Carrie, illus. 2004. 64p. pap. 12.95 (978-1-932196-45-0(5)) WordWright.biz, Inc.
—Leave 'Em Standing. 2005. (Illus.). pap. 12.95 (978-1-932196-73-3(0)) WordWright.biz, Inc.
Dixon, Franklin W. Showdown at Widow Creek. 2016. (Hardy Boys Adventures Ser.: 11). (ENG., Illus.). 128p. (J). (gr. 3-7). 17.99 (978-1-4814-3878-0(6), Aladdin) Simon & Schuster Children's Publishing.
Dunlap, Sonya K. Responza the Bull Learns the Ropes. 2008. 24p. pap. 17.95 (978-0-9815245-5-9(9)) Accelerator Bks.
Enderle, Dotti. The Fat Stock Stampede at the Houston Livestock Show & Rodeo, 1 vol. Galey, Chuck, illus. 2008. (ENG.). 32p. (J). (gr. 1-3). 16.99 (978-1-58980-443-2(0)) Pelican Publishing Co., Inc.
Gallagher, Diana G. Monica & the Crushworthy Cowboy, 1 vol. 2011. (Monica Ser.). (ENG.). 88p. (gr. 2-3). lib. bdg. 26.65 (978-1-4342-2554-2(2)) Stone Arch Bks.
Garretson, Jerri. Kansas Tall Tales: Tenth Anniversary Anthology. Garretson, Jerri & Dollar, Diane A., illus. 2008. 106p. (J). pap. 19.95 (978-0-9659712-7-0(9)) Ravenstone Pr.
Gowar, Mick. Rodeo Rider, 1 vol. Hall, Francois, illus. 2013. (Start Reading Ser.). (ENG.). 24p. (gr. k-1). pap. 7.95 (978-1-4765-4133-4(7)) Capstone Press of Coughlan Cos.
Halvorson, Marilyn. Bull Rider, 1 vol. 2003. (Orca Soundings Ser.). (ENG.). 128p. (YA). (gr. 8-12). pap. 9.95 (978-1-55143-233-5(1)) Orca Bk. Pubs. USA.
—Monteur de Taureau: (Bull Rider), 1 vol. 2011. (FRE.). 128p. (YA). (gr. 7-12). pap. 9.95 (978-1-55469-859-2(6)) Orca Bk. Pubs. USA.
Krulik, Nancy & dePaola, Tomie. Rootin' Tootin' Cow Dog #8. Braun, Sebastien, illus. 2015. (Magic Bone Ser.: 8). (ENG.). 128p. (J). (gr. 1-3). bds. 4.99 (978-0-448-48097-8(2), Grosset & Dunlap) Penguin Young Readers Group.
Leipold, Judith. Destiny's Wild Ride, a Tall Tale of the Legendary Hub Hubbell. White, David, illus. 2013. 32p. 24.95 (978-1-61493-168-3(2)); pap. 14.95 (978-1-61493-167-6(4)) Peppertree Pr., The.
Lewis, Ashley. Roads to Rodeos. 2008. 32p. pap. 24.95 (978-1-60563-259-9(7)) America Star Bks.
Peck, Robert Newton. Horse Thief. 2003. 277p. (YA). (gr. 7). 13.65 (978-0-7569-1461-5(2)) Perfection Learning Corp.
Peschke, Marci. Rodeo Queen, 1 vol. Mourning, Tuesday, illus. 2011. (Kylie Jean Ser.). (ENG.). 112p. (gr. 2-3). pap. 5.95

PQR

(978-1-4048-6618-8(3)); lib. bdg. 22.65 (978-1-4048-5961-6(6)) Picture Window Bks. (Kylie Jean).

Rodman, Dennis & Warburton, Dustin. Dennis the Wild Bull. 2013. (ENG.). 32p. (J). (gr. -1-5). pap. 16.00 (978-0-615-75249-5(7)) Neighborhood Pubs.

Santillo, LuAnn. The Best Tricks. Santillo, LuAnn, ed. 2003. (Half-Pint Kids Readers Ser.). (Illus.). 7p. (J). (gr. -1-1). pap. 1.00 (978-1-59256-082-0(2)) Half-Pint Kids, Inc.

Sargent, Dave & Sargent, Pat. Rusty: (Red Roan) Be Strong & Brave, 30 vols., Vol. 52. Lenoir, Jane, illus. 2003. (Saddle up Ser.: Vol. 52). 42p. (J). pap. 10.95 (978-1-56763-804-2(X)); lib. bdg. 23.60 (978-1-56763-803-5(1)) Ozark Publishing.

Townsend, Tom. The Ballad of Ol' Hook. 2006. (YA). pap. 9.95 (978-1-932196-91-7(9)) WordWright.biz, Inc.

Williams, Suzanne Morgan. Bull Rider. (ENG.). 256p. (YA). (gr. 7). 2010. pap. 8.99 (978-1-4424-1252-1(6)) 2009. 17.99 (978-1-4169-6130-7(5)) McElderry, Margaret K. Bks. (McElderry, Margaret K. Bks.).

RODRIGUEZ, ALEX, 1975-

Clark, Travis. Alex Rodriguez. 2010. (Role Model Athletes Ser.). (Illus.). 64p. (YA). (gr. 7-12). 22.95 (978-1-4222-0488-7(X)) Mason Crest.

Gaspar, Joe. Alex Rodriguez. 2010. (Reading Power: Baseball's MVPs Ser.). (Illus.). 24p. (J). pap. 8.85 (978-1-4488-1793-1(5), PowerKids Pr.); (gr. 3-6). lib. bdg. 22.60 (978-1-4488-0634-8(8)) Rosen Publishing Group, Inc., The.

Hoffman, Mary Ann. Alex Rodriguez: Baseball Star. (Sports Superstars Ser.). 24p. (gr. 1-1). 2009. 42.50 (978-1-60853-173-8(2), PowerKids Pr.) 2007. (Illus.). (J). lib. bdg. 22.60 (978-1-4042-3533-5(7)) Rosen Publishing Group, Inc., The.

—Alex Rodriguez: Baseball Star/Estrella del Beisbol. 2009. (Amazing Athletes/Atletas increibles Ser.). (SPA.). 24p. (gr. 1-2). 42.50 (978-1-61511-303-3(7), Editorial Buenas Letras) Rosen Publishing Group, Inc., The.

—Alex Rodriguez: Baseball Star/Estrella del Beisbol. Alaman, Eduardo, tr. 2007. (Amazing Athletes/Atletas increibles Ser.). (SPA., Illus.). 24p. (J). (gr. 2-5). lib. bdg. 22.60 (978-1-4042-7598-0(3)) Rosen Publishing Group, Inc., The.

Kappes, Serena. Alex Rodriguez. 2006. (Sports Heroes & Legends Ser.). (Illus.). 106p. (J). (gr. 3-7). lib. bdg. 27.93 (978-0-8225-5963-4(3), Lerner Pubns.) Lerner Publishing Group.

—Alex Rodriguez: Hot Corner, Hot Shot. 2012. (USA TODAY Lifeline Biographies Ser.). (ENG.). 112p. (gr. 6-12). lib. bdg. 34.60 (978-0-7613-8155-6(4)) Lerner Publishing Group.

Kjelle, Marylou Morano. Alex Rodriquez: Professional Baseball Player. 2005. (Robbie Reader Ser.). (Illus.). 32p. (J). (gr. 4-8). lib. bdg. 25.70 (978-1-58415-394-8(6)) Mitchell Lane Pubs., Inc.

Rappoport, Ken. Alex Rodriguez: Champion Baseball Star. 2012. (Sports Star Champions Ser.). (Illus.). 48p. (J). (gr. 5-18). 25.27 (978-0-7660-4026-7(7)) Enslow Pubs., Inc.

—Super Sports Star Alex Rodriguez. 2004. (Super Sports Star Ser.). (Illus.). 48p. (J). lib. bdg. 25.27 (978-0-7660-2138-9(6)) Enslow Pubs., Inc.

Rodríguez Gonzalez, Tania. Alex Rodriguez. 2012. (Superstars of Baseball ENGLISH Ser.). 32p. (J). (gr. 4). 19.95 (978-1-4222-2674-2(3)); (SPA., Illus.). 19.95 (978-1-4222-2621-6(2)) Mason Crest.

Torsiello, David P. Read about Alex Rodriguez. 2011. (I Like Sports Stars! Ser.). (Illus.). 24p. (J). (gr. k-18). pap. 7.95 (978-1-59845-302-7(5), Enslow Elementary); (gr. 1-4). lib. bdg. 22.60 (978-0-7660-3828-8(9)) Enslow Pubs., Inc.

Uschan, Michael V. Alex Rodriguez. 2011. (People in the News Ser.). 128p. (YA). (gr. 7-12). lib. bdg. 33.95 (978-1-4205-0350-0(2)) Cengage Gale.

Weber, Terri Smith. Alex Rodrigues: Improving His Game. 2004. (J). pap. (978-1-932724-19-6(2), Bios for Kids) Panda Publishing, L.L.C.

—Alex Rodriguez: Improving His Game. 2004. (J). lib. bdg. (978-1-932724-18-9(4), Bios for Kids) Panda Publishing, L.L.C.

—Alex Rodriguez: Mejorando Su Juego. 2003. (SPA.). (J). pap. (978-0-9740180-6-5(6)); lib. bdg. (978-0-9740180-5-8(8)) Panda Publishing, L.L.C. (Bios for Kids).

Zuehlke, Jeffrey. Alex Rodriguez. (Amazing Athletes Ser.). 32p. 2005. (Illus.). (J). (gr. 2-5). per. 5.95 (978-0-8225-2311-6(6)) 2005. (Illus.). (J). (gr. 3-7). lib. bdg. 23.93 (978-0-8225-2427-4(9)) 2009. (ENG.). (gr. 2-5). 25.26 (978-0-8225-8871-9(4)) 2009. (ENG.). (gr. 2-5). pap. 7.95 (978-0-8225-8872-6(2), First Avenue Editions) Lerner Publishing Group.

—Alex Rodriguez (Revised Edition) 2009. pap. 40.95 (978-0-7613-4773-6(9)) Lerner Publishing Group.

ROEBLING, WASHINGTON AUGUSTUS, 1837-1926

Ratliff, Thomas. You Wouldn't Want to Work on the Brooklyn Bridge! An Enormous Project That Seemed Impossible. Bergin, Mark, illus. 2009. (You Wouldn't Want to Ser.). (ENG.). 32p. (J). (gr. 3-18). pap. 9.95 (978-0-531-20519-8(3)) Scholastic Library Publishing.

Ratliff, Tom. You Wouldn't Want to Work on the Brooklyn Bridge! An Enormous Project That Seemed Impossible. Bergin, Mark, illus. 2009. (You Wouldn't Want to Ser.). (ENG.). 32p. (J). (gr. 3-12). 29.00 (978-0-531-21328-5(5)) Scholastic Library Publishing.

ROENTGEN RAYS

see X-Rays

ROGERS, BUCK (FICTITIOUS CHARACTER)—FICTION

Lawrence, James. Buck Rogers in the 25th Century - The Gray Morrow Years, 1979-1981, Vol. 1. Herman, Daniel, ed. 2013. (ENG., Illus.). 240p. (YA). 49.99 (978-1-61345-034-5(6), 9781613450345) Hermes Pr.

ROGERS, ROBERT, 1731-1795

Bruchac, Marge. Malian's Song. Maughan, William L., illus. 2006. (Vermont Folklife Center Children's Book Ser.). (ENG.). 32p. (J). (gr. -1-3). 16.95 (978-0-916718-26-8(3)) Vermont Folklife Ctr.

Gauch, Patricia Lee. The Impossible Major Rogers. Parker, Robert Andrew, illus. 2008. (J). (978-1-59078-334-4(4)) Boyds Mills Pr.

Quasha, Jennifer. Robert Rogers: Rogers' Rangers & the French & Indian War. 2005. (Library of American Lives & Times). (Illus.). 112p. (J). (gr. 4-8). lib. bdg. 34.60 (978-0-8239-5731-6(4)) Rosen Publishing Group, Inc., The.

—Robert Rogers: Rogers' Rangers, & the French & Indian War. 2009. (Library of American Lives & Times Ser.). 112p. (gr. 5-5). 69.20 (978-1-60853-503-3(7)) Rosen Publishing Group, Inc., The.

ROGERS RANGERS

Quasha, Jennifer. Robert Rogers: Rogers' Rangers, & the French & Indian War. 2009. (Library of American Lives & Times Ser.). 112p. (gr. 5-5). 69.20 (978-1-60853-503-3(7)) Rosen Publishing Group, Inc., The.

ROLLER SKATING

see also In-Line Skating; Skateboarding

Blomquist, Christopher. Street Luge in the X Games. 2009. (Kid's Guide to the X Games Ser.). 24p. (gr. 3-3). 42.50 (978-1-61511-211-1(1), PowerKids Pr.) Rosen Publishing Group, Inc., The.

Group/McGraw-Hill, Wright. Roma Roller Skater: Level H, 6 vols. (Take Twostm Ser.). 16p. 29.95 (978-0-322-08965-5(4)) Wright Group/McGraw-Hill.

Jackson, Demi. Roller Derby. 2015. (Daredevil Sports Ser.). (ENG.). 32p. (J). (gr. 1-1). 25.25 (978-1-4824-2999-2(3)) Stevens, Gareth Publishing LLLP.

Loh-Hagan, Virginia. Extreme Street Luging. 2016. (Illus.). 32p. (J). (978-1-63470-488-5(6)) Cherry Lake Publishing.

Shafran, Michael. Skate! Your Guide to Inline, Aggressive, Vert, Street, Roller Hockey, Speed Skating, Dance, Fitness Training, & More. 2003. (Extreme Sports Ser.). (ENG., Illus.). 64p. (J). (gr. 4-7). pap. 8.95 (978-0-7922-5107-1(5), National Geographic Children's Bks.) National Geographic Society.

ROLLER SKATING—FICTION

Ashman, Linda. Samantha on a Roll. Davenier, Christine, illus. 2011. (ENG.). 40p. (J). (gr. -1-4). 17.99 (978-0-374-36399-4(4), 9780374363994, Farrar, Straus & Giroux (BYR)) Farrar, Straus & Giroux.

Dougherty, Meghan. Rise of the Undead Redhead. Birnbach, Alece, illus. 2014. (Dorothy's Derby Chronicles Ser.: 1). (ENG.). 256p. (J). (gr. 3-6). pap. 6.99 (978-1-4022-9535-5(9), Sourcebooks Jabberwocky) Sourcebooks, Inc.

—Woe of Jade Doe. Birnbach, Alece, illus. 2015. (Dorothy's Derby Chronicles Ser.: 2). (ENG.). 288p. (J). (gr. 4-7). pap. 6.99 (978-1-4926-0147-0(0), Sourcebooks Jabberwocky) Sourcebooks, Inc.

Eggers, Jeanette S. Grandmas Don't Rollerskate. 2008. 24p. pap. 12.99 (978-1-4389-1434-3(2)) AuthorHouse.

Jamieson, Victoria. Roller Girl. 2015. (ENG., Illus.). 240p. (J). (gr. 4-7). 20.99 (978-0-525-42967-8(0)); pap. 12.99 (978-0-8037-4016-7(6)) Penguin Young Readers Group. (Dial Bks).

—Roller Girl. 2015. (J). lib. bdg. 24.50 (978-0-606-37112-4(5)) Turtleback Bks.

Johnson, Andi. Rollerskate Kate. 2004. (Illus.). 16p. 9.00 (978-1-84161-115-0(8)) Ravette Publishing, Ltd. GBR. Dist: Parkwest Pubns., Inc.

Nash, Andy. Marcus & His Monkey: For Kids Blessed with Popularity. 2010. (J). (978-0-8127-0452-5(5)) Autumn Hse. Publishing Co.

Rue, Ginger. Aleca Zamm Is Ahead of Her Time. Persico, Zoe, illus. 2017. (Aleca Zamm Ser.: 2). (ENG.). 128p. (J). (gr. 2-5). pap. 6.99 **(978-1-4814-7063-6(9)**, Aladdin) Simon & Schuster Children's Publishing.

Scotton, Rob. The Rain Is a Pain. 2012. (Splat the Cat: I Can Read Ser.). (J). lib. bdg. 13.55 (978-0-606-26861-5(8), Turtleback) Turtleback Bks.

ROMAN ANTIQUITIES

see Classical Antiquities; Rome—Antiquities

ROMAN ART

see Art, Roman

ROMAN CATHOLIC CHURCH

see Catholic Church

ROMAN LITERATURE

see Latin Literature

ROMAN MYTHOLOGY

see Mythology, Classical

ROMAN PHILOSOPHY

see Philosophy, Ancient

ROMANIA

Benge, Janet. Richard Wurmbrand: Love Your Enemies. 2017. (J). pap. **(978-1-57658-987-8(0))** YWAM Publishing.

Burgan, Michael. Dracula's Dark World. 2010. (HorrorScapes Ser.). (Illus.). 32p. (J). (gr. 4-7). lib. bdg. 25.27 (978-1-936087-96-9(0)) Bearport Publishing Co., Inc.

Goldberg, Enid & Itzkowitz, Norman. Valad the Impaler: The Real Count Dracula. 2008. (ENG.). 128p. (J). (gr. 6-12). pap. 5.95 (978-0-531-13898-4(4), Watts, Franklin) Scholastic Library Publishing.

Indovino, Shaina Carmel. The European Union: Facts & Figures. 2012. (J). (978-1-4222-2231-7(4)); (978-1-4222-2240-9(3)); pap. (978-1-4222-2271-3(3)) Mason Crest.

—Romania. 2012. (J). (978-1-4222-2256-0(X)); pap. (978-1-4222-2287-4(X)) Mason Crest.

Kaplan, Arie. Dracula: The Life of Vlad the Impaler. 2011. (Illus.). 64p. (J). 77.70 (978-1-4488-2233-1(5), Rosen Reference); pap. 12.95 (978-1-4488-2232-4(7), Rosen Reference); (gr. 5-9). lib. bdg. 31.95 (978-1-4488-1229-5(1)) Rosen Publishing Group, Inc., The.

Kerns, Ann. Romania in Pictures. 2006. (Visual Geography Series, Second Ser.). (ENG., Illus.). 80p. (gr. 5-12). lib. bdg. 31.93 (978-0-8225-2497-7(X)) Lerner Publishing Group.

Knox, Barbara J. Castle Dracula: Romania's Vampire Home. 2005. (Castles, Palaces, & Tombs Ser.). (Illus.). 32p. (J). (gr. 2-5). lib. bdg. 25.27 (978-1-59716-000-1(8)) Bearport Publishing Co., Inc.

Koestler-Grack, Rachel. Elie Wiesel: Witness for Humanity. 2009. (Life Portraits Ser.). (Illus.). 112p. (J). (gr. 7-12). lib. bdg. 36.00 (978-1-4339-0054-9(8), 1293616) Stevens, Gareth Publishing LLLP.

Molnar, Haya Leah. Under a Red Sky: Memoir of a Childhood in Communist Romania. 2010. (ENG., Illus.). 320p. (J). (gr. 7-12). 24.99 (978-0-374-31840-6(9), Farrar, Straus & Giroux (BYR)) Farrar, Straus & Giroux.

Niver, Heather Moore. Was Count Dracula Real? 2017. (J). **(978-0-7660-9196-2(1))** Enslow Pubs., Inc.

Oprea, Tiberiu. Romania. 2003. (Countries of the World Ser.). (Illus.). 96p. (gr. 5-12). lib. bdg. 31.00 (978-0-8368-2367-7(2)) Stevens, Gareth Publishing LLLP.

Pundyk, Grace. Welcome to Romania. 2004. (Welcome to My Country Ser.). (Illus.). 48p. (gr. 2-5). lib. bdg. 27.00 (978-0-8368-2567-1(5)) Stevens, Gareth Publishing LLLP.

Sabatino, Michael. The Legend of Dracula. 2015. (Famous Legends Ser.). (ENG., Illus.). 32p. (J). (gr. 2-3). 25.25 (978-1-4824-2734-9(6)) Stevens, Gareth Publishing LLLP.

Sheehan, Sean & Nevins, Debbie. Romania. 2015. (Cultures of the World (r) Ser.). (ENG., Illus.). 144p. (J). (gr. 5-5). 47.07 (978-1-5026-0336-4(5)) Cavendish Square Publishing.

Weingarten, Ethan. Transylvania. 2014. (Scariest Places on Earth Ser.). 24p. (J). (gr. 2-5). 22.60 (978-1-4824-1161-4(X)) Stevens, Gareth Publishing LLLP.

ROMANIA—FICTION

Bush, Suzanne & Takes, Deb. Time Will Tell. 2004. 279p. (YA). lib. bdg. 15.95 (978-0-9747426-0-1(0)) Imagining Possibilities.

Fantaskey, Beth. Jessica Rules the Dark Side. 2012. (ENG.). 320p. (YA). (gr. 9). 16.99 (978-0-547-39309-4(1)) Houghton Mifflin Harcourt Publishing Co.

—Jessica's Guide to Dating on the Dark Side. 2010. (ENG., Illus.). 384p. (YA). (gr. 9-18). pap. 8.99 (978-0-547-25940-6(9)) Houghton Mifflin Harcourt Publishing Co.

George, Jessica Day. Silver in the Blood. (ENG.). 368p. (YA). 2016. pap. 9.99 (978-1-68119-024-2(9), 9781681190242) 2015. (gr. 7). 17.99 (978-1-61963-431-2(7), 9781619634312) Bloomsbury Publishing USA. (Bloomsbury USA Childrens).

Keeney, Stephen S. Spencer the Adventurer & the Castle of Bran. 2009. (ENG.). 256p. (J). pap. 14.99 (978-1-934135-31-0(3), Zumaya Thresholds) Zumaya Pubns. LLC.

Marsh, Carole. The Mystery at Dracula's Castle: Transylvania, Romania. (Around the World in 80 Mysteries Ser.). 133p. (J). 2009. 18.99 (978-0-635-07039-5(1), Marsh, Carole Mysteries) 2008. (Illus.). (gr. 3-5). 14.95 (978-0-635-06471-4(5)) 2008. (Illus.). (gr. 3-5). per. 5.95 (978-0-635-06469-1(3), Marsh, Carole Mysteries) Gallopade International.

Matthews, John. Henry Hunter & the Beast of Snagov: Henry Hunter Series #1. 2016. (Henry Hunter Ser.). (ENG., Illus.). 240p. (J). (gr. 2-7). 15.99 (978-1-5107-1038-2(8), Sky Pony Pr.) Skyhorse Publishing Co., Inc.

Stoker, Bram. Drácula. Schuler, Susan, tr. Ruiz, Alfonso, illus. 2010. (Classic Fiction Ser.). (ENG & SPA.). 72p. (gr. 2-3). pap. 7.15 (978-1-4342-2277-0(2), Graphic Revolve en Español) Stone Arch Bks.

—Dracula. Gilbert, Anne Yvonne, illus. 2010. (ENG.). 96p. (J). (gr. 7-18). 19.99 (978-0-7636-4793-3(4), Templar) Candlewick Pr.

—Dracula. Kliros, Thea, illus. abr. ed. 2011. (Dover Children's Thrift Classics Ser.). (ENG.). 96p. (J). (gr. 3-8). reprint ed. pap. 4.00 (978-0-486-29567-1(2)) Dover Pubns., Inc.

—Dracula. Schuler, Susan, tr. Ruiz, Alfonso, illus. 2010. (Classic Fiction Ser.). 72p. pap. 0.90 (978-1-4342-2985-4(8), Graphic Revolve) Stone Arch Bks.

Weber, Lori. Strange Beauty, 1 vol. 2006. (Lorimer SideStreets Ser.). (ENG.). 144p. (YA). (gr. 9-12). 16.95 (978-1-55028-944-2(6), 9781550289442); 9.95 (978-1-55028-941-1(1), 9781550289411) Lorimer, James & Co., Ltd., Pubs. CAN. Dist: Casemate Pubs. & Bk. Distributors, LLC.

White, Kiersten. And I Darken. (ENG.). (YA). (gr. 7). 2017. (And I Darken Ser.: 1). 512p. pap. 10.99 **(978-0-553-52234-1(5)**, Ember) 2016. (Illus.). 496p. 18.99 (978-0-553-52231-0(0), Delacorte Pr.) 2016. (Illus.). 496p. lib. bdg. 21.99 (978-0-553-52232-7(9), Delacorte Pr.) Random Hse. Children's Bks.

—Now I Rise. 2017. (And I Darken Ser.: 2). (ENG.). 480p. (YA). (gr. 7). 18.99 **(978-0-553-52235-8(3))**; lib. bdg. 21.99 **(978-0-553-52236-5(1))** Random Hse. Children's Bks. (Delacorte Pr.).

ROMANIES—FICTION

Blackford, Cheryl. Lizzie & the Lost Baby. 2016. (ENG.). 192p. (J). (gr. 5-7). 16.99 (978-0-544-57099-3(5), HMH Books For Young Readers) Houghton Mifflin Harcourt Publishing Co.

Bryant, Jen. The Fortune of Carmen Navarro. 2011. (ENG.). 240p. (YA). (gr. 7). pap. 8.99 (978-0-375-85097-4(X), Ember) Random Hse. Children's Bks.

Clark, Henry. The Book That Proves Time Travel Happens. 2015. (ENG., Illus.). 416p. (J). (gr. 3-7). 17.00 (978-0-316-40617-8(1)) Little Brown & Co.

Cook, Norman. Sam in the Crimea: A Victorian Adventure Based on the Work of Lord Shaftesbury. 2007. (Illus.). 128p. (J). (gr. 4-7). per. 9.00 (978-1-84625-045-3(5)) DayOne Pubns. GBR. Dist: Send The Light Distribution LLC.

Duey, Kathleen. The Sunset Gates. Rayyan, Omar, illus. 2005. 76p. (J). lib. bdg. 15.00 (978-1-59054-918-6(X)) Fitzgerald Bks.

—True Heart. Rayyan, Omar, illus. 2005. 76p. (J). lib. bdg. 15.00 (978-1-59054-920-9(1)) Fitzgerald Bks.

Dunlap, Susanne. The Musician's Daughter. (ENG.). (YA). (gr. 7). 2010. 352p. pap. 8.99 (978-1-59990-452-8(7), 9781599904528) 2009. 336p. 16.99 (978-1-59990-332-3(6), 9781599903323) Bloomsbury Publishing USA. (Bloomsbury USA Childrens).

Flood, C. J. Infinite Sky. 2015. (ENG., Illus.). 256p. (YA). (gr. 7). pap. 10.99 (978-1-4814-0659-8(0)) Simon & Schuster Children's Publishing.

Gardner, Sally. The Red Necklace. 2009. (ENG.). 400p. (YA). (gr. 7-18). 8.99 (978-0-14-241488-0(3), Speak) Penguin Young Readers Group.

—The Red Necklace: A Story of the French Revolution. l.t. ed. 2008. 583p. 23.95 (978-1-4104-1016-0(1)) Thorndike Pr.

—The Silver Blade. 2010. (ENG.). 384p. (YA). (gr. 7-18). 8.99 (978-0-14-241731-7(9), Speak) Penguin Young Readers Group.

Gypsy Kids: The Adventures of Colby Myers & Mark Howard. 2003. 21.95 (978-1-932277-00-5(5)) Crystal Ball Publishing, LLC.

Kent, Trilby. Medina Hill. 2009. (ENG.). 176p. (YA). (gr. 5-9). 19.95 (978-0-88776-888-0(1), Tundra Bks.) Tundra Bks. CAN. Dist: Penguin Random Hse. LLC.

Lindelauf, Benny. Nine Open Arms. 2014. (ENG., Illus.). 264p. (J). (gr. 3). 16.95 (978-1-59270-146-9(9)) Enchanted Lion Bks., LLC.

Molesworth & Molesworth, Mary Louisa S. Us. 2008. 116p. 22.95 (978-1-60664-989-3(2)) Aegypan.

Molesworth, Mary Louisa S. Us: An Old Fashioned Story. 2007. (ENG.). 142p. pap. 18.99 (978-1-4346-0600-6(7)); 156p. pap. 21.99 (978-1-4346-0675-4(9)) Creative Media Partners, LLC.

Resau, Laura. The Lightning Queen. 2015. (ENG.). 336p. (J). (gr. 3-7). 16.99 (978-0-545-80084-6(6), Scholastic Pr.) Scholastic, Inc.

Roderman, Anna Marie. Two Tales of Courage. 2004. 116p. (YA). pap. 7.95 (978-0-87714-318-5(8)) i-5 Publishing LLC.

Rutkoski, Marie. The Cabinet of Wonders. 2013. (Kronos Chronicles Ser.: 1). (ENG.). 288p. (J). (gr. 5-9). pap. 10.99 (978-1-250-01804-5(8), 9781250018045) Square Fish.

—The Celestial Globe. 2013. (Kronos Chronicles Ser.: 2). (ENG.). 320p. (J). (gr. 5-9). pap. 7.99 (978-1-250-02732-0(2), 9781250027320) Square Fish.

—The Jewel of the Kalderash. 2013. (Kronos Chronicles Ser.: 3). (ENG.). 336p. (J). (gr. 5-9). pap. 7.99 (978-1-250-01025-4(X), 9781250010254) Square Fish.

Strangway, Melissa. Finding Hope. 2012. 82p. pap. 11.65 (978-1-61933-676-6(6)) FastPmcil, Inc.

Surace, Joan. The Story of Lucia. Rockford, Nancy, illus. 2006. (YA). pap. 8.00 (978-0-8059-7062-3(2)) Dorrance Publishing Co., Inc.

ROMANOV, HOUSE OF

Fleming, Candace. The Family Romanov: Murder, Rebellion, & the Fall of Imperial Russia. 2014. (ENG., Illus.). 304p. (YA). (gr. 7). 19.99 (978-0-375-86782-8(1)); lib. bdg. 21.99 (978-0-375-96782-5(6)) Random Hse. Children's Bks. (Schwartz & Wade Bks.).

ROME

Here are entered works about the Roman Empire. Works only on the modern city of Rome are entered under Rome (Italy).

Ancient Romans. 2009. (J). (978-0-7166-2131-7(2)) World Bk., Inc.

AZ Books Staff. Ancient Rome. Naumovets, Elena & Svistunova, Natalia, eds. 2012. (Mysteries of History Ser.). (ENG.). 18p. (J). (gr. 1-3). bds. 17.95 (978-1-61889-090-0(5)) AZ Bks. LLC.

Barber, Nicola. Ancient Roman Sports & Pastimes. 2010. (Ancient Communities: Roman Life Ser.). 32p. (J). (ENG.). pap. 10.60 (978-1-61532-315-9(5)); (Illus.). (gr. 3-6). lib. bdg. 26.50 (978-1-61532-306-7(6)) Rosen Publishing Group, Inc., The. (PowerKids Pr.).

Beller, Susan Provost. Roman Legions on the March: Soldiering in the Ancient Roman Army. 2007. (Soldiers on the Battlefront Ser.). (ENG., Illus.). 112p. (gr. 6-8). lib. bdg. 33.26 (978-0-8225-6781-3(4)) Lerner Publishing Group.

Beston, Clare. Make Your Own Roman Arena. 2014. (Make Your Own Ser.). (ENG.). 20p. (J). (gr. k-2). pap. 7.99 (978-1-905710-17-1(8)) B Small Publishing GBR. Dist: Independent Pubs. Group.

Ganeri, Anita. Gladiators & Ancient Rome. 2009. (History Explorers Ser.). (ENG.). 24p. (J). (gr. k-2). pap. 5.95 (978-1-84696-213-4(7), TickTock Books) Octopus Publishing Group GBR. Dist: Independent Pubs. Group.

—How to Live Like a Roman Gladiator. Epelbaum, Mariano, illus. 2015. (How to Live Like... Ser.). (ENG.). 32p. (J). (gr. 3-6). lib. bdg. 26.65 (978-1-4677-6355-4(1)) Lerner Publishing Group.

Gedacht, Daniel C. Home Life in Ancient Rome. 2004. (Primary Sources of Ancient Civilizations Ser.). (ENG., Illus.). 24p. (gr. 4-8). pap. 8.25 (978-0-8239-8945-4(3), PowerKids Pr.) Rosen Publishing Group, Inc., The.

—Land & Resources of Ancient Rome. 2004. (Primary Sources of Ancient Civilizations Ser.). (ENG., Illus.). 24p. (gr. 4-8). pap. 8.25 (978-0-8239-8943-0(7), PowerKids Pr.) Rosen Publishing Group, Inc., The.

—Politics & Government in Ancient Rome. 2004. (Primary Sources of Ancient Civilizations Ser.). (Illus.). 24p. (ENG.). (gr. 4-8). pap. 8.25 (978-0-8239-8948-5(8)); (J). lib. bdg. 22.60 (978-0-8239-6777-3(8)) Rosen Publishing Group, Inc., The. (PowerKids Pr.).

Gifford, Clive. Romans. Scruton, Ben, illus. 2016. (Reading Ladder Ser.). (ENG.). 32p. (J). (gr. 1-4). pap. 6.99 **(978-1-4052-8043-3(3))** Egmont Bks., Ltd. GBR. Dist: Independent Pubs. Group.

Harrison, Paul. Ancient Roman Clothes. 2010. (Ancient Communities: Roman Life Ser.). (ENG.). 32p. (J). pap. 10.60 (978-1-61532-308-1(2), PowerKids Pr.) Rosen Publishing Group, Inc., The.

—Ancient Roman Homes. 2010. (Ancient Communities: Roman Life Ser.). 32p. (J). (ENG.). pap. 10.60 (978-1-61532-313-5(9)); (Illus.). (gr. 3-6). lib. bdg. 26.50 (978-1-61532-305-0(8)) Rosen Publishing Group, Inc., The. (PowerKids Pr.).

Hinds, Kathryn. Religion. 2004. (Life in the Roman Empire Ser.). 80p. (gr. 6). 34.21 (978-0-7614-1657-9(9), Benchmark Bks.) Marshall Cavendish Corp.

Kuntz, Lynn. The Roman Colosseum. 2004. (Great Structures in History Ser.). (ENG., Illus.). 48p. (J). (gr. 4-7). 27.50 (978-0-7377-1561-3(8), Greenhaven Pr., Inc.) Cengage Gale.

Landau, Elaine. Exploring Ancient Rome with Elaine Landau. 2005. (Exploring Ancient Civilizations with Elaine Landau Ser.). (Illus.). 48p. (J). (gr. 3-4). lib. bdg. 25.27 (978-0-7660-2337-6(0), Enslow Elementary) Enslow Pubs., Inc.

Leoni, Cristiana. In Caesar's Rome with Cicero. Cappon, Manuela, illus. 2008. (Come See My City Ser.). 48p. (gr. 4-8). lib. bdg. 28.50 (978-0-7614-4328-5(2), Benchmark Bks.) Marshall Cavendish Corp.

Life in the Roman Empire. 2016. (Life in the Roman Empire Ser.). 80p. (J). lib. bdg. 142.56 (978-1-5026-2398-0(6)) Cavendish Square Publishing.

Markel, Rita J. Your Travel Guide to Ancient Rome. 2003. (Passport to History Ser.). (ENG., Illus.). 96p. (gr. 5-9). lib. bdg. 26.60 (978-0-8225-3071-8(6)) Lerner Publishing Group.

Nardo, Don. Cause & Effect: Ancient Rome. 2017. (ENG.). 80p. (YA). (gr. 5-12). 39.93 **(978-1-68282-160-2(9))** ReferencePoint Pr., Inc.

Riggs, Sandy. Three Ancient Communities: Text Pairs. 2008. (Bridges/Navigators Ser.). (J). (gr. 3). 89.00 *(978-1-4108-8374-2(4))* Benchmark Education Co.

Shakespeare, William. Antony & Cleopatra. Heims, Neil & Bloom, Harold, eds. 2008. (Bloom's Shakespeare Through the Ages Ser.). 290p. (YA). (gr. 9-12). 50.00 *(978-0-7910-9630-7(0))* Facts On File, Inc.

Wood, Alix. Gladiators: Fighting to the Death. Wood, Alix, illus. 2013. (Illus.). 32p. (J). (gr. 4-6). 26.60 *(978-1-4339-9580-4(8))*; pap. 10.50 *(978-1-4339-9581-1(6))*; pap. 63.00 *(978-1-4339-9582-8(4))* Stevens, Gareth Publishing LLLP.

ROME—ANTIQUITIES

Deckker, Zilah. Ancient Rome: Archaeology Unlocks the Secrets of Rome's Past. 2007. (National Geographic Investigates Ser.). (ENG., Illus.). 64p. (J). (gr. 5-18). 27.90 *(978-1-4263-0129-2(4)*, National Geographic Children's Bks.) National Geographic Society.

Dugan, Christine. Rome, 1 vol. 2007. (Primary Source Readers Ser.). (ENG.). 32p. (J). (gr. 5-5). pap. 8.99 *(978-0-7439-0432-2(X))* Shell Educational Publishing.

Hanel, Rachael. Ancient Rome: An Interactive History Adventure. 2010. (You Choose: Historical Eras Ser.). (ENG.). 112p. (gr. 3-4). pap. 41.70 *(978-1-4296-5101-1(6)*, You Choose Bks.) Capstone Press of Coughlan Cos.

James, Simon. Ancient Rome. 2015. (DK Eyewitness Bks.). (ENG., Illus.). 72p. (J). (gr. 3-7). 19.99 *(978-1-4654-3569-9(7)*, DK Children) Dorling Kindersley Publishing, Inc.

—DK Eyewitness Books: Ancient Rome: Ancient Rome. 2015. (DK Eyewitness Bks.). (ENG., Illus.). 72p. (J). (gr. 3-7). pap. 9.99 *(978-1-4654-3568-2(9)*, DK Children) Dorling Kindersley Publishing, Inc.

MacDonald, Fiona. How to Be a Roman Soldier. Hewetson, Nicholas J., illus. 2008. (How to Be Ser.). (ENG.). 32p. (J). (gr. 3-7). pap. 5.95 *(978-1-4263-0169-8(3)*, National Geographic Children's Bks.) National Geographic Society.

Malam, John. The Romans. 2011. (Dig It: History from Objects Ser.). (Illus.). 32p. (YA). (gr. 2-5). lib. bdg. 26.50 *(978-1-4488-3285-9(3))* Rosen Publishing Group, Inc., The.

Nardo, Don. Roman Roads & Aqueducts. 2014. (History's Great Structures). (ENG., Illus.). 80p. (J). lib. bdg. *(978-1-60152-634-2(2))* ReferencePoint Pr., Inc.

ROME—BIOGRAPHY

Abbott, Jacob. Julius Caesar. 2009. 206p. pap. 10.95 *(978-1-59915-141-0(3))* Yesterday's Classics.

—Nero. 2009. 202p. (J). pap. 12.00 *(978-1-59128-057-6(5))* Canon Pr.

Barter, James. Influential Figures of Ancient Rome. 2003. (Lucent Library of Historical Eras Ser.). (ENG.). 33.45 *(978-1-59018-315-1(0)*, Lucent Bks.) Cengage Gale.

Bridges, Shirin Yim. Agrippina: "Atrocious & Ferocious" Malone, Peter, illus. 2011. (Thinking Girl's Treasury of Dastardly Dames Ser.). (ENG.). 32p. (J). (gr. 3-8). 18.95 *(978-0-9834256-1-8(2))* Goosebottom Bks. LLC.

Forsyth, Fiona. Cicero: Defender of the Republic. 2009. (Ancient Leaders Ser.). 112p. (gr. 5-8). 66.50 *(978-1-61511-420-7(3)*, Rosen Reference) Rosen Publishing Group, Inc., The.

Galford, Ellen. Julius Caesar: The Boy Who Conquered an Empire. 2007. (National Geographic World History Biographies Ser.). (ENG., Illus.). 64p. (J). (gr. 3-7). 17.95 *(978-1-4263-0064-6(6))*; lib. bdg. 27.90 *(978-1-4263-0065-3(4))* National Geographic Society. (National Geographic Children's Bks.).

Goldberg, Jan. Julius Caesar. 2004. (ZB Reads Trio Books). (Illus.). 106p. (gr. 5-7). pap. 5.50 *(978-0-7367-1800-4(1))* Zaner-Bloser, Inc.

Haaren, John. Famous Men of Rome. 2008. 120p. pap. 12.95 *(978-1-60459-524-6(8))* Wilder Pubns., Corp.

Haaren, John H. & Poland, A. B. Famous Men of Ancient Rome: Lives of Julius Caesar, Nero, Marcus Aurelius & Others. 2005. (Dover Children's Classics Ser.). (ENG.). 160p. (J). (gr. 3-8). per. 8.95 *(978-0-486-44361-4(2))* Dover Pubns., Inc.

—Famous Men of Rome (Yesterday's Classics) 2006. (Illus.). 260p. (J). per. 11.95 *(978-1-59915-046-8(8))* Yesterday's Classics.

Hunter, Nick. Julius Caesar, 1 vol. Edwards, Mat, illus. 2013. (Hero Journals). (ENG.). 48p. (gr. 4-6). pap. 9.95 *(978-1-4109-5363-6(7)*, NA-r) Heinemann-Raintree.

—Julius Caesar, 1 vol. 2013. (Hero Journals). (ENG., Illus.). 48p. (gr. 4-6). 33.32 *(978-1-4109-5356-8(4)*, NA-r) Heinemann-Raintree.

Mattern, Joanne. Julius Caesar. 2017. (Junior Biography From Ancient Civilization Ser.). (gr. 4-6). 29.95 *(978-1-68020-024-9(0))* Mitchell Lane Pubs., Inc.

Medina, Nico. Who Was Julius Caesar? Foley, Tim, illus. 2014. (Who Was? Ser.). (ENG.). 112p. (J). (gr. 3-7). pap. 5.99 *(978-0-448-48083-1(2)*, Grosset & Dunlap) Penguin Young Readers Group.

Morgan, Julian. Hadrian: Consolidating the Empire. 2003. (Ancient Leaders Ser.). (Illus.). 112p. (YA). (gr. 5-8). lib. bdg. 34.60 *(978-0-8239-3593-2(0)*, Rosen Reference) Rosen Publishing Group, Inc., The.

Nardo, Don. Influential Figures of Ancient Rome. 2004. (Lucent Library of Historical Eras). (Illus.). 128p. (J). 27.45 *(978-1-59018-285-7(5)*, Lucent Bks.) Cengage Gale.

Orr, Tamra. Marcus Brutus. 2006. (J). lib. bdg. *(978-1-58415-511-9(6))* Mitchell Lane Pubs., Inc.

Rinaldo, Denise. Julius Caesar: Dictator for Life. (Wicked History Ser.). (ENG.). 128p. (J). 2010. (gr. 6-12). pap. 5.95 *(978-0-531-22822-7(3)*, Watts, Franklin) 2009. (gr. 5-9). 31.00 *(978-0-531-21276-9(9))* Scholastic Library Publishing.

Santillan, Beatriz & Morgan, Julian. Hadrian: Emperor of Rome. 2017. (Leaders of the Ancient World Ser.). 112p. (J). (gr. 12-11). 37.10 ***(978-1-5081-7484-4(9)***, Rosen Young Adult) Rosen Publishing Group, Inc., The.

Saxena, Shalini. Nero: Ruthless Roman Emperor. 2016. (History's Most Murderous Villains Ser.). (Illus.). 32p. (J). (gr. 5-4). pap. 10.50 *(978-1-4824-4799-6(1))* Stevens, Gareth Publishing LLLP.

Turner, Tracey. Hard As Nails in Ancient Rome. Lenman, Jamie, illus. 2015. (ENG.). 64p. (J). *(978-0-7787-1513-9(2))* Crabtree Publishing Co.

White, John S. The Boys' & Girls' Plutarch. 2004. reprint ed. pap. 28.95 *(978-1-4191-5511-6(3))*; pap. 1.99 *(978-1-4192-5511-3(8))* Kessinger Publishing, LLC.

Williams, Rose. The Young Romans. 2003. (Anthem Classics Ser.). (LAT & ENG., Illus.). 128p. (J). pap. 26.00 *(978-1-84331-047-1(3))* Anthem Pr. GBR. Dist: Bolchazy-Carducci Pubs.

—The Young Romans. 2007. (LAT & ENG.). pap. 23.00 *(978-0-86516-670-7(6))* Bolchazy-Carducci Pubs.

ROME—FICTION

Angel, Ido. Vipo in Rome: A Trevi Fountain Wish Comes True. 2015. (AV2 Animated Storytime Ser.). (ENG.). (J). lib. bdg. 29.99 *(978-1-4896-3920-2(9)*, AV2 by Weigl) Weigl Pubs., Inc.

Barclay, Katerina & Barclay, Aegea. The Hand of Zeus. Barclay, Katerina, illus. 2004. (Illus.). (J). 29.95 *(978-0-9758803-1-9(4)*, 206 234 2572); 24.95 *(978-0-9758803-0-2(6)*, 206.612.9698) Aegean Design.

Bergvinson, M. E. St. George's Mysterious Cross. 2013. 208p. pap. 23.16 *(978-1-300-13979-9(X))* Lulu Pr., Inc.

Downey, Glen. Gladiators. 2007. (Illus.). 48p. (J). lib. bdg. 23.08 *(978-1-4242-1627-7(3))* Fitzgerald Bks.

Fisher, Meaghan. Giuseppe's Famous Pizza Pies. Barrett, Diana, illus. 2013. 24p. 17.99 *(978-1-938768-34-7(5))*; pap. 8.99 *(978-1-938768-20-0(5))* Gypsy Pubns.

Henty, George Alfred. The Young Carthaginian: A Tale of the Times of Hannibal. 2004. pap. 8.95 *(978-1-57646-874-6(7))* Quiet Vision Publishing.

Hobbs, Leigh. Mr Chicken Arriva a Roma. 2017. (Mr Chicken Ser.). (ENG.). 32p. (J). (gr. -1-3). 17.99 ***(978-1-925266-77-1(X))*** Allen & Unwin AUS. Dist: Independent Pubs. Group.

Holm, Kirsten C. Everyday Life in Ancient Rome. 2012. (Jr. Graphic Ancient Civilizations Ser.). (ENG.). 24p. (J). (gr. 3-6). pap. 10.60 *(978-1-4488-6389-1(9))*; lib. bdg. 25.25 *(978-1-4488-6215-3(9))* Rosen Publishing Group, Inc., The. (PowerKids Pr.).

Jensen, Peder Skytte. Anton & Rosita: All Roads Lead to Rome. 2011. (Illus.). 40p. (gr. 1-2). pap. 20.38 *(978-1-4567-8077-7(8))* AuthorHouse.

Lawrence, Caroline. The Assassins of Rome. 2003. (ENG., Illus.). 224p. (gr. 2-4). pap. 10.99 *(978-1-84255-023-6(3)*, Orion Children's Bks.) Hachette Children's Group GBR. Dist: Hachette Bk. Group.

—The Colossus of Rhodes. 2005. (ENG., Illus.). 224p. (gr. 7-9). pap. 10.99 *(978-1-84255-138-7(8)*, Orion Children's Bks.) Hachette Children's Group GBR. Dist: Hachette Bk. Group.

—The Enemies of Jupiter. 2004. (ENG., Illus.). 224p. (gr. 4-6). pap. 10.99 *(978-1-84255-164-6(7)*, Orion Children's Bks.) Hachette Children's Group GBR. Dist: Hachette Bk. Group.

Lee, Kathy. Captive in Rome. 2005. pap. *(978-1-84427-088-0(2))* Scripture Union.

—A Captive in Rome. 2016. (ENG., Illus.). 146p. (J). pap. *(978-0-281-07633-8(2))* SPCK Publishing.

—Rome in Flames. 2016. (ENG., Illus.). 162p. (J). pap. *(978-0-281-07635-2(9))* SPCK Publishing.

Llorente, Pilar Molina. Aura Gris. (SPA.). 192p. (YA). (gr. 5-8). *(978-84-216-0993-4(9)*, BU3870) Bruño, Editorial ESP. Dist: Lectorum Pubns., Inc.

Marciano, John Bemelmans. Madeline & the Cats of Rome. 2008. (Madeline Ser.). (ENG.). 48p. (J). (gr. 1-3). 17.99 *(978-0-670-06297-3(9)*, Viking Books for Young Readers) Penguin Young Readers Group.

Mitchell, Jack. The Ancient Ocean Blues. 2008. (ENG.). 200p. (YA). (gr. 5-8). pap. 9.95 *(978-0-88776-832-3(6)*, Tundra Bks.) Tundra Bks. CAN. Dist: Penguin Random Hse. LLC.

Nielsen, Jennifer A. Mark of the Thief. 2015. (Mark of the Thief Ser.: 1). (ENG.). 352p. (J). (gr. 4-7). pap. 7.99 *(978-0-545-56155-6(8)*, Scholastic Paperbacks) Scholastic, Inc.

—Mark of the Thief. 2015. (Mark of the Thief Ser.: 1). lib. bdg. 18.40 *(978-0-606-38064-5(7))* Turtleback Bks.

Northfield, Gary. Julius Zebra: Rumble with the Romans! Northfield, Gary, illus. 2016. (ENG., Illus.). 288p. (J). (gr. 2-5). 15.99 *(978-0-7636-7853-1(8))* Candlewick Pr.

Orczy, Emmuska. Unto Caesar. 2008. 260p. 29.95 *(978-1-60664-863-6(2))*; pap. 15.95 *(978-1-60664-110-1(7))* Aegypan.

Platt, Richard. Roman Diary: The Journal of Iliona, a Young Slave. Parkins, David, illus. 2014. (ENG.). 128p. (J). (gr. 4-7). pap. 6.99 *(978-0-7636-7053-5(7))* Candlewick Pr.

Riggs, Sandy. Three Ancient Communities: Set Of 6. 2011. (Navigators Ser.). (J). pap. 44.00 net. *(978-1-4108-5093-5(5))* Benchmark Education Co.

Rogers, Terry, illus. Androcles & the Lion: A Roman Legend. 2003. (Dominie Collection of Myths & Legends). (SPA.). 20p. (J). lib. bdg. *(978-0-7685-2419-2(9))* Dominie Pr., Inc.

—Androcles & the Lion: A Roman Legend. 2004. (SPA & ENG.). 20p. (J). (gr. 3-3). pap. 6.47 net. *(978-0-7685-2122-1(X)*, Dominie Elementary) Pearson Schl.

Scieszka, Jon. See You Later, Gladiator. McCauley, Adam, illus. 2004. (Time Warp Trio Ser.: 9). (ENG.). 96p. (J). (gr. 2-4). pap. 5.99 *(978-0-14-240117-0(X)*, Puffin Books) Penguin Young Readers Group.

—See You Later, Gladiator. McCauley, Adam, illus. 2004. (Time Warp Trio Ser.: No. 9). 87p. (J). (gr. 4-7). 12.65 *(978-0-7569-5986-9(1))* Perfection Learning Corp.

Seven, John. The Dragon of Rome, 1 vol. Phillips, Craig, illus. 2013. (Time-Tripping Faradays Ser.). (ENG.). 160p. (gr. 4-5). 9.95 *(978-1-62370-012-6(4))*; lib. bdg. 26.65 *(978-1-4342-6029-1(1))* Stone Arch Bks.

Seven, John & Phillips, Craig. The Dragon of Rome, 1 vol. 2013. (ENG.). 160p. (YA). pap. *(978-1-4342-6439-8(4))* Stone Arch Bks.

Sienkiewicz, Henryk. Quo Vadis: A Narrative of the Time of Nero. (SPA., Illus.). 168p. (YA). 11.95 *(978-84-7281-132-4(8)*, AF1132) Auriga, Ediciones S.A. ESP. Dist: Continental Bk. Co., Inc.

Snedeker, Caroline Dale. A Triumph for Flavius. 2004. (Illus.). 87p. (J). per. 13.95 *(978-0-9667067-1-0(4))* American Home-School Publishing, LLC.

Strauss, Peggy Guthart. Getting the Boot. 2005. (S. A. S. S. Ser.). (ENG., Illus.). 224p. (YA). (gr. 7-6). 7.99 *(978-0-14-240414-0(4)*, Speak) Penguin Young Readers Group.

Woods, Dave & Inns, Chris. Junior Caesar. 2014. (ENG., Illus.). 64p. (J). (gr. k-2). pap. 5.99 *(978-1-4083-1362-6(6))* Hodder & Stoughton GBR. Dist: Hachette Bk. Group.

ROME—HISTORY

Abbott, Jacob. Hannibal. 2009. (J). pap. 12.00 *(978-1-59128-059-0(1))* Canon Pr.

—Julius Caesar. 2009. (J). pap. 12.00 *(978-1-59128-060-6(5))* Canon Pr.

Ancient Rome. 2003. spiral bd. 16.95 *(978-1-56004-154-2(4))*; spiral bd. 19.95 *(978-1-56004-162-7(5))* Social Studies Schl. Service.

Anderson, Michael. Ancient Rome. 2011. (Illus.). 88p. (J). lib. bdg. 31.70 *(978-1-61530-522-3(X))* Rosen Publishing Group, Inc., The.

Anderson, Zachary. The Fall of Rome & the Rise of Constantinople. 2015. (Exploring the Ancient & Medieval Worlds Ser.). (ENG., Illus.). 160p. (J). (gr. 8-8). lib. bdg. 45.64 *(978-1-5026-0574-0(0))* Cavendish Square Publishing.

—The Rise of the Roman Empire. 2015. (Exploring the Ancient & Medieval Worlds Ser.). (ENG., Illus.). 160p. (J). (gr. 8-8). 45.64 *(978-1-5026-0572-6(4))* Cavendish Square Publishing.

Baikie, James. Peeps at Many Lands: Ancient Rome (Yesterday's Classics) 2008. 128p. pap. 8.95 *(978-1-59915-290-5(8))* Yesterday's Classics.

Barnham, Kay. Gory Gladiators, Savage Centurions, & Caesar's Sticky End: A Menacing History of the Unruly Romans! 2015. (Awfully Ancient Ser.). (ENG., Illus.). 32p. (J). (gr. 5-5). pap. 10.50 *(978-1-4824-3113-1(0))* Stevens, Gareth Publishing LLLP.

Baum, Margaux & Morgan, Julian. Constantine. 2016. (Leaders of the Ancient World Ser.). 00112p. (J). (gr. 6-6). 37.10 *(978-1-5081-7252-9(8))* Rosen Publishing Group, Inc., The.

Baynard, Kate Holland & Baynard, Holland Callaway. Holland Goes to Rome: A brief look at the ancient city, its history & its Culture. 2010. 16p. 12.50 *(978-1-4490-4604-0(5))* AuthorHouse.

Bedwin, Christa. Romans. 2016. (Illus.). 32p. (J). *(978-1-5105-1104-0(0))* SmartBook Media, Inc.

Beesly. Stories from the History of Rome. 2008. 136p. pap. 8.95 *(978-1-59915-264-6(9))* Yesterday's Classics.

Benchmark Education Company. Rome Long Ago (Teacher Guide) 2005. *(978-1-4108-4682-2(2))* Benchmark Education Co.

Benduhn, Tea. Ancient Rome. 2007. (Life Long Ago Ser.). (Illus.). 24p. (gr. 1-4). pap. 8.15 *(978-0-8368-7788-5(8))*; lib. bdg. 22.00 *(978-0-8368-7783-0(7))* Stevens, Gareth Publishing LLLP. (Weekly Reader Leveled Readers).

—La Antigua Roma. 2007. (vida en el pasado (Life Long Ago) Ser.). (SPA., Illus.). 24p. (gr. 1-4). pap. 8.15 *(978-0-8368-8039-7(0))*; lib. bdg. 22.00 *(978-0-8368-8034-2(X))* Stevens, Gareth Publishing LLLP. (Weekly Reader Leveled Readers).

Benoit, Peter. Ancient Rome. 2012. (Ancient World Ser.). (ENG., Illus.). 112p. (J). pap. 9.95 *(978-0-531-25983-2(8))* Scholastic Library Publishing.

—The Ancient World: Ancient Rome. 2012. (ENG., Illus.). 112p. (J). lib. bdg. 34.00 *(978-0-531-25183-6(7)*, Children's Pr.) Scholastic Library Publishing.

Bingham, Jane. Ancient Rome. 2006. (Ancient Civilizations Ser.). (Illus.). 48p. (gr. 5-12). lib. bdg. 31.00 *(978-0-8368-6191-4(4)*, Gareth Stevens Secondary Library) Stevens, Gareth Publishing LLLP.

—Classical Myth: A Treasury of Greek & Roman Legends, Art, & History. 2007. (Myth Ser.). (Illus.). 96p. (J). (gr. 4-7). pap. 7.99 *(978-0-7858-2350-6(6))* Book Sales, Inc.

—Classical Myth: A Treasury of Greek & Roman Legends, Art, & History. 2007. (ENG., Illus.). 96p. (C). (gr. 6-18). lib. bdg. 140.00 *(978-0-7656-8104-1(8)*, Y181755) Routledge.

—How People Lived in Ancient Rome. (How People Lived Ser.). (Illus.). 2009. 32p. (gr. 4-8). pap. 10.60 *(978-1-4358-2622-9(1)*, Rosen Classroom) 2008. 30p. (J). lib. bdg. 26.50 *(978-1-4042-4432-0(8))* Rosen Publishing Group, Inc., The.

Bingham, Jane, et al. Encyclopedia of the Roman World. 2004. (History Encyclopedias Ser.). (Illus.). 128p. (J). 19.95 *(978-0-7945-0117-4(6)*, Usborne) EDC Publishing.

Bodden, Valerie. Ancient Civilization: Rome. 2015. (Ancient Civilization Ser.). (ENG.). 48p. (J). (gr. 5-8). pap. 12.00 *(978-0-89812-981-6(8)*, Creative Paperbacks) Creative Co., The.

—Gladiators. 2017. (J). ***(978-1-60818-813-0(2)***, Creative Education) Creative Co., The.

Bodden, Valerie. Rome. 2014. (J). *(978-1-60818-394-4(7)*, Creative Education) Creative Co., The.

Botham, Noel. Did Romans Really Wash Themselves in Wee? 2015. (Dr. Dino's Learnatorium Ser.). (ENG., Illus.). 160p. (J). (gr. 4-7). pap. 8.99 *(978-1-78219-915-1(2))* Blake, John Publishing, Ltd. GBR. Dist: Independent Pubs. Group.

Brannon, Barbara. Discover Ancient Rome. 2005. (J). pap. *(978-1-4108-5164-2(8))* Benchmark Education Co.

Bridges, Shirin Yim. Agrippina: "Atrocious & Ferocious" 2011. 18.95 *(978-0-938425-65-6(X))*; 18.95 *(978-0-938425-61-8(7))* Goosebottom Bks. LLC.

Brocklehurst, R. Roman Army. 2004. (Discovery Program Ser.). 48p. (J). lib. bdg. 16.95 *(978-1-58086-609-5(3)*, Usborne) EDC Publishing.

Burgen, Michael. Empire of Ancient Rome, Revised Edition. 2nd rev. ed. 2009. (Great Empires of the Past Ser.). (Illus.). 160p. (gr. 6-12). 35.00 *(978-1-60413-159-8(4)*, Chelsea Hse.) Facts On File, Inc.

Burrell, Carol M. Scavella. Did Greek Soldiers Really Hide Inside the Trojan Horse? And Other Questions about the Ancient World. 2010. (Is That a Fact? Ser.). (ENG.). 40p. (gr. 4-6). lib. bdg. 26.60 *(978-0-7613-4912-9(X))* Lerner Publishing Group.

Califf, David J. Battle of Actium. 2003. (Great Battles Through the Ages Ser.). (Illus.). 112p. (gr. 6-12). 30.00 *(978-0-7910-7440-4(4)*, Chelsea Hse.) Facts On File, Inc.

Callery, Sean. The Dark History of Ancient Rome. 2010. (Dark Histories Ser.). 64p. (gr. 5). 32.79 *(978-1-60870-084-4(4))* Marshall Cavendish Corp.

Catel, Patrick. What Did the Ancient Romans Do for Me?, 1 vol. 2010. (Linking the Past & Present Ser.). (ENG., Illus.). 32p. (gr. 3-6). 33.32 *(978-1-4329-3743-0(X))*; pap. 8.29 *(978-1-4329-3750-8(2))* Heinemann-Raintree. (Heinemann InfoSearch).

Church, Alfred J. Stories from Livy. 2008. 212p. pap. 9.95 *(978-1-59915-078-9(6))* Yesterday's Classics.

Coddington, Andrew. Martyrdom: Christians in the Roman Empire. 2016. (Public Persecutions Ser.). 128p. (J). 45.64 *(978-1-5026-2327-0(7))* Cavendish Square Publishing.

Cohn, Jessica. The Ancient Romans. 2012. (Crafts from the Past Ser.). (Illus.). 48p. (J). (gr. 4-6). pap. 14.05 *(978-1-4339-7710-7(9))*; lib. bdg. 31.95 *(978-1-4339-7709-1(5))* Stevens, Gareth Publishing LLLP.

Collins. Romans. 2016. (Collins Fascinating Facts Ser.). (ENG., Illus.). 72p. (J). (gr. 1-3). pap. 10.99 *(978-0-00-816923-7(3))* HarperCollins Pubs. Ltd. GBR. Dist: Independent Pubs. Group.

Cont Media Staff. Ancient Rome. 2008. (Illus.). 48p. (YA). 12.99 *(978-1-931703-26-0(4))* Creative Publishing Consultants.

Cooke, Tim. The Ancient Romans. 2015. (At Home With... Ser.). (Illus.). 32p. (gr. 5-9). lib. bdg. 31.35 *(978-1-78121-082-6(9)*, Brown Bear Bks.) Windmill Bks. Ltd. GBR. Dist: Black Rabbit Bks.

Corbishley, Mike. Ancient Rome. 3rd rev. ed. 2007. (Cultural Atlas for Young People Ser.). (Illus.). 96p. (YA). (gr. 5-9). 35.00 *(978-0-8160-6822-7(4))* Facts On File, Inc.

Corrick, James A. The Bloody, Rotten Roman Empire: The Disgusting Details about Life in Ancient Rome, 1 vol. 2011. (Disgusting History Ser.). (ENG.). 32p. (gr. 3-4). pap. 8.10 *(978-1-4296-6353-3(7))*; pap. 47.70 *(978-1-4296-6475-2(4))* Capstone Press of Coughlan Cos. (Fact Finders).

Cottrell, George. Ancient Rome. 2017. (Unlocking Ancient Civilizations Ser.). (J). (gr. 4-5). pap. 63.00 ***(978-1-5345-2034-9(1))***; 32p. pap. 10.50 ***(978-1-5345-2033-2(3))***; 32p. lib. bdg. 27.25 ***(978-1-5345-2035-6(X))*** Greenhaven Publishing LLC. (KidHaven Publishing).

Cricket Books Staff & Cobblestone Publishing, Inc. Staff. If I Were a Kid in Ancient Rome: Children of the Ancient World. Sheldon, Ken, ed. 2007. (If I Were a Kid In... Ser.). (ENG., Illus.). 32p. (J). (gr. 1-5). 17.95 *(978-0-8126-7930-4(X))* Cricket Bks.

Croy, Anita. Myths & Legends of Ancient Rome. 2015. (Illus.). 64p. (J). *(978-0-7166-2635-0(7))* World Bk., Inc.

Daning, Tom. Mitología Romana: Rómulo y Remo. Obregón, José María, illus. 2009. (Historietas Juveniles: Mitologías (Jr. Graphic Mythologies) Ser.). (SPA.). 24p. (J). (gr. 3-6). lib. bdg. 25.25 *(978-1-4358-8570-7(8))* Rosen Publishing Group, Inc., The.

—Roman Mythology: Romulus & Remus. 2009. (Jr. Graphic Mythologies Ser.). (ENG.). 24p. (J). (gr. 2-3). 47.90 *(978-1-61513-870-8(6)*, PowerKids Pr.) Rosen Publishing Group, Inc., The.

Daning, Tom & Obregón, José María. Mitología Romana: Rómulo y Remo. 2009. (Historietas Juveniles: Mitologías (Jr. Graphic Mythologies) Ser.). (SPA., Illus.). 24p. (J). (gr. 3-8). pap. 10.60 *(978-1-4358-3334-0(1))* Rosen Publishing Group, Inc., The.

Dargie, Richard. Ancient Rome. 2004. (Picturing the Past Ser.). (Illus.). 32p. (J). 15.95 *(978-1-59270-023-3(3))* Enchanted Lion Bks., LLC.

—Rich & Poor in Ancient Rome. 2005. (Rich & Poor in Ser.). (Illus.). 32p. (YA). (gr. 4-7). lib. bdg. 27.10 *(978-1-58340-722-6(7))* Black Rabbit Bks.

Daynes, Katie. See Inside Ancient Rome. Hancock, David, illus. 2006. (See Inside Board Bks.). 16p. (J). (gr. 2-5). bds. 12.99 *(978-0-7945-1321-4(2)*, Usborne) EDC Publishing.

de Souza, Philip & Langley, Andrew. History News: the Roman News. 2009. (History News Ser.). (ENG., Illus.). 32p. (J). (gr. 4-7). pap. 7.99 *(978-0-7636-4199-3(5))* Candlewick Pr.

Deckker, Zilah. Ancient Rome: Archaeology Unlocks the Secrets of Rome's Past. 2007. (National Geographic Investigates Ser.). (ENG., Illus.). 64p. (J). (gr. 5-18). 17.95 *(978-1-4263-0128-5(6)*, National Geographic Children's Bks.) National Geographic Society.

Dickins, Rosie. The Story of Rome. Gower, Teri, illus. 2006. (Usborne Young Reading: Series Two Ser.). 60p. (J). (gr. 2). lib. bdg. 13.99 *(978-1-58086-900-3(9)*, Usborne) EDC Publishing.

Dickinson, Rachel. Tools of the Ancient Romans: A Kid's Guide to the History & Science of Life in Ancient Rome. 2006. (Build It Yourself Ser.). (ENG., Illus.). 144p. (J). (gr. 3-7). pap. 15.95 *(978-0-9749344-5-7(3))* Northern Trails Pr.

Dickmann, Nancy. Ancient Rome. 2016. (History Hunters Ser.). (ENG.). 32p. (gr. 3-4). lib. bdg. 27.99 *(978-1-5157-2550-3(2)*, Edge Bks.) Capstone Press of Coughlan Cos.

Dillard, Sheri. Roman Gladiators. 2015. (Ancient Warriors Ser.). (ENG.). 32p. (J). (gr. 2-5). 28.50 *(978-1-63143-758-8(5)*, 208590) Child's World, Inc., The.

DiPrimio, Pete. Ancient Rome. 2009. (How'd They Do That? Ser.). (Illus.). 64p. (J). (gr. 4-8). 33.95 *(978-1-58415-820-2(4))* Mitchell Lane Pubs., Inc.

Doeden, Matt. Tools & Treasures of Ancient Rome. 2014. (Searchlight Books: What Can We Learn from Early Civilizations? Ser.). (ENG., Illus.). 40p. (gr. 3-5). lib. bdg. 27.93 *(978-1-4677-1433-4(X)*, Lerner Pubns.) Lerner Publishing Group.

Dorling Kindersley Publishing Staff. DK Findout! Ancient Rome. 2016. (DK Find Out! Ser.). (ENG., Illus.). 64p. (J). (gr. 1-4). pap. 10.99 *(978-1-4654-5427-0(6)*, DK Children) Dorling Kindersley Publishing, Inc.

—Pocket Genius: Ancient Rome. 2016. (Pocket Genius Ser.). (ENG., Illus.). 160p. (J). (gr. 3-7). pap. 4.99 *(978-1-4654-4525-4(0)*, DK Children) Dorling Kindersley Publishing, Inc.

—Ultimate Sticker Book: Ancient Rome. 2017. (Ultimate Sticker Bks.). (ENG.). 32p. (J). (gr. k-2). pap. 6.99 *(978-1-4654-6202-2(3)*, DK Children) Dorling Kindersley Publishing, Inc.

Dubois, Muriel L. Ancient Rome: A Mighty Empire, 1 vol. 2011. (Great Civilizations Ser.). (ENG.). 32p. (gr. 3-4). lib. bdg. 27.32 *(978-1-4296-6832-3(6)*, Fact Finders) Capstone Press of Coughlan Cos.

Editors of Kingfisher. Remarkable Romans. 2017. (It's All About... Ser.). (ENG.). 32p. pap. 5.99 *(978-0-7534-7282-8(1)*, 9780753472828, Kingfisher) Roaring Brook Pr.

PQR

Edwards, Laurie J. Exploring Ancient Rome. 2018. (ENG.). 32p. (gr. 3-6). ***(978-1-63235-466-2(7)***, 12-Story Library) Pr. Room Editions LLC.

England, Victoria. Top 10 Worst Things about Ancient Rome. Antram, David, illus. 2012. (Top 10 Worst Ser.). (ENG.). 32p. (J). (gr. 3-6). pap. 10.50 *(978-1-4339-6695-8(6))*; lib. bdg. 26.60 *(978-1-4339-6694-1(8))* Stevens, Gareth Publishing LLLP. (Gareth Stevens Learning Library).

Fact Atlas: Ancient Rome. 2009. (FACT ATLAS Ser.). 72p. (J). 14.95 *(978-0-8437-1929-1(X))* Hammond World Atlas Corp.

Fall of Rome/Byzantium DBA. 2003. spiral bd. 16.95 *(978-1-56004-155-9(2))* Social Studies Schl. Service.

Forsyth, Fiona. Augustus: The First Emperor. (Ancient Leaders Ser.). 112p. (gr. 5-8). 2009. 66.50 *(978-1-61511-419-1(X))* 2003. (Illus.). (YA). lib. bdg. 34.60 *(978-0-8239-3588-8(4))* Rosen Publishing Group, Inc., The. (Rosen Reference).

—Cicero: Defender of the Republic. 2009. (Ancient Leaders Ser.). 112p. (gr. 5-8). 66.50 *(978-1-61511-420-7(3)*, Rosen Reference) Rosen Publishing Group, Inc., The.

Frankel, Karen. Projects about Ancient Rome. 2006. (Hands-On History Ser.). (Illus.). 48p. (gr. 3-7). lib. bdg. 21.95 *(978-0-7614-2260-0(9)*, Benchmark Bks.) Marshall Cavendish Corp.

Galford, Ellen. Julius Caesar: The Boy Who Conquered an Empire. 2007. (National Geographic World History Biographies Ser.). (ENG., Illus.). 64p. (J). (gr. 3-7). 17.95 *(978-1-4263-0064-6(6))*; lib. bdg. 27.90 *(978-1-4263-0065-3(4))* National Geographic Society. (National Geographic Children's Bks.).

Gallagher, Belinda. Why Why Why... Did Romans Race to the Circus? 2010. (Why Why Why Ser.). (Illus.). 32p. (J). (gr. 1-3). lib. bdg. 18.95 *(978-1-4222-1577-7(6))* Mason Crest.

Ganeri, Anita. How the Ancient Romans Lived. 2010. (Life in Ancient Times Ser.). (ENG.). 32p. (J). (gr. 3-6). lib. bdg. 26.60 *(978-1-4339-4094-1(9)*, Gareth Stevens Learning Library) Stevens, Gareth Publishing LLLP.

—How to Live Like a Roman Gladiator. Epelbaum, Mariano, illus. 2015. (How to Live Like... Ser.). (ENG.). 32p. (J). (gr. 3-6). pap. 7.99 *(978-1-4677-7211-2(9))* Lerner Publishing Group.

Gedacht, Daniel C. Economy & Industry in Ancient Rome. 2009. (Primary Sources of Ancient Civilizations Ser.). 24p. (gr. 3-3). 42.50 *(978-1-60851-557-8(5)*, PowerKids Pr.) Rosen Publishing Group, Inc., The.

—Land & Resources in Ancient Rome. 2004. (Primary Sources of Ancient Civilizations Ser.). (Illus.). 24p. (J). lib. bdg. 22.60 *(978-0-8239-6775-9(1)*, PowerKids Pr.) Rosen Publishing Group, Inc., The.

—Politics & Government in Ancient Rome. 2009. (Primary Sources of Ancient Civilizations Ser.). 24p. (gr. 3-3). 42.50 *(978-1-60851-563-9(X)*, PowerKids Pr.) Rosen Publishing Group, Inc., The.

—Technology of Ancient Rome. 2009. (Primary Sources of Ancient Civilizations Ser.). 24p. (gr. 3-3). 42.50 *(978-1-60851-564-6(8)*, PowerKids Pr.) Rosen Publishing Group, Inc., The.

Gifford, Clive. Ancient Rome. 2017. (Best & Worst Jobs Ser.). (ENG., Illus.). 32p. (J). (gr. 4-6). 17.99 *(978-0-7502-8738-8(1)*, Wayland) Hachette Children's Group GBR. Dist: Hachette Bk. Group.

Gould, F. J. The Children's Plutarch: Tales of the Romans. Crane, Walter, illus. 2012. 260p. *(978-1-78139-160-0(2))* Benediction Classics.

Grant, Neil. Every Day Life in Ancient Rome. Cappon, Manuela, tr. Cappon, Manuela, illus. 2003. (Uncovering History Ser.). 46p. (J). lib. bdg. 28.50 *(978-1-58340-249-8(7))* Black Rabbit Bks.

Greenberg, Imogen. The Romans. Greenberg, Isabel, illus. 2016. (Discover... Ser.). (ENG.). 32p. (J). (gr. 3-7). 14.99 *(978-1-84780-856-1(5)*, Frances Lincoln Children's Bks.) Quarto Publishing Group UK GBR. Dist: Hachette Bk. Group.

Greenblatt, Miriam. Julius Caesar & the Roman Republic. 2005. (Rulers & Their Times Ser.). (Illus.). 96p. (J). (gr. 3-7). lib. bdg. 29.93 *(978-0-7614-1836-8(9)*, Benchmark Bks.) Marshall Cavendish Corp.

Guerber, H. A. The Story of the Romans (Yesterday's Classics) 2006. (Illus.). 368p. (J). per. 13.95 *(978-1-59915-012-3(3))* Yesterday's Classics.

Guy, John. Roman Life. 2006. (Life of Early Civilization Ser.). (Illus.). 31p. (J). per. *(978-1-59905-056-0(0))* Saddleback Educational Publishing, Inc.

Haaren, John. Famous Men of Rome. 2008. 120p. pap. 12.95 *(978-1-60459-524-6(8))* Wilder Pubns., Corp.

Haaren, John H. & Poland, A. B. Famous Men of Ancient Rome: Lives of Julius Caesar, Nero, Marcus Aurelius & Others. 2005. (Dover Children's Classics Ser.). (ENG.). 160p. (J). (gr. 3-8). per. 8.95 *(978-0-486-44361-4(2))* Dover Pubns., Inc.

Hamen, Susan E. Ancient Rome, 1 vol. 2014. (Ancient Civilizations Ser.). (ENG.). 112p. (J). (gr. 6-12). lib. bdg. 35.64 *(978-1-62403-542-5(6)*, Essential Library) ABDO Publishing Co.

Hanbury-Murphy, Trudy. Solving the Mysteries of Ancient Rome. 2008. (Digging into History Ser.). 32p. (gr. 4-18). lib. bdg. 29.93 *(978-0-7614-3101-5(2)*, Benchmark Bks.) Marshall Cavendish Corp.

Hanel, Rachael. Ancient Rome: An Interactive History Adventure. 2010. (You Choose: Historical Eras Ser.). (ENG.). 112p. (gr. 3-4). pap. 41.70 *(978-1-4296-5101-1(6)*, You Choose Bks.) Capstone Press of Coughlan Cos.

Hanel, Rachel. Gladiators. 2007. (Fearsome Fighters Ser.). (Illus.). 48p. (YA). (gr. 3-6). lib. bdg. 31.35 *(978-1-58341-535-1(1))* Creative Co., The.

Harrison, Paul. Ancient Roman Clothes. 2010. (Ancient Communities: Roman Life Ser.). (Illus.). 32p. (J). (gr. 3-6). lib. bdg. 26.50 *(978-1-61532-304-3(X)*, PowerKids Pr.) Rosen Publishing Group, Inc., The.

Hawes, Alison. What the Romans Did for the World. 2010. (Crabtree Connections Ser.). (ENG.). 24p. (J). (gr. 3-6). *(978-0-7787-9943-6(3))*; pap. *(978-0-7787-9965-8(4))* Crabtree Publishing Co.

Hinds, Kathryn. The City. 2004. (Life in the Roman Empire Ser.). (Illus.). 80p. (gr. 6). 34.21 *(978-0-7614-1655-5(2)*, Benchmark Bks.) Marshall Cavendish Corp.

—Early Germans: Peoples of the North. 2009. (Barbarians! Ser.). 80p. (gr. 6-8). 35.64 *(978-0-7614-4064-2(X))* Marshall Cavendish Corp.

—Goths. 2009. (Barbarians! Ser.). 80p. (gr. 6-8). 35.64 *(978-0-7614-4065-9(8))* Marshall Cavendish Corp.

—Lin In The Roman Empire Series, 4 Bks, Set. 2004. (Life in the Roman Empire Ser.). (gr. 6). 136.84 *(978-0-7614-1653-1(6))* Marshall Cavendish Corp.

—The Patricians. 2004. (Life in the Roman Empire Ser.). (Illus.). 80p. (gr. 6). 34.21 *(978-0-7614-1654-8(4)*, Benchmark Bks.) Marshall Cavendish Corp.

Hirsch, E. D., Jr., ed. Ancient Rome: Level 3. 2003. tchr. ed. 9.95 *(978-0-7690-5057-7(3))* Pearson Learning.

History's Fearless Fighters. 2015. (History's Fearless Fighters Ser.). (ENG.). 48p. (J). (gr. 5-6). 191.70 *(978-1-4824-2562-8(9))* Stevens, Gareth Publishing LLLP.

Hoblin, Paul. Gladiators, 1 vol. 2013. (Great Warriors Ser.). (ENG.). 48p. (J). (gr. 3-6). lib. bdg. 32.79 *(978-1-61783-722-7(9))*; (Illus.). pap. 15.64 *(978-1-61783-772-2(5)*, Core Library) ABDO Publishing Co.

Hunt, Norman Bancroft. Living in Ancient Rome. 2008. (Living in the Ancient World Ser.). (Illus.). 96p. (YA). (gr. 7-12). 35.00 *(978-0-8160-6340-6(0))* Facts On File, Inc.

Hunter, Nick. Julius Caesar, 1 vol. Edwards, Mat, illus. 2013. (Hero Journals). (ENG.). 48p. (gr. 4-6). pap. 9.95 *(978-1-4109-5363-6(7)*, NA-r) Heinemann-Raintree.

—Julius Caesar, 1 vol. 2013. (Hero Journals). (ENG., Illus.). 48p. (gr. 4-6). 33.32 *(978-1-4109-5356-8(4)*, NA-r) Heinemann-Raintree.

Hurdman, Charlotte, et al. Find Out about Ancient Egypt, Rome & Greece: Exploring the Great Classical Civilizations, with 60 Step-By-Step Projects & 1500 Exciting Images. 2013. (ENG., Illus.). 256p. (J). (gr. 3-7). 17.99 *(978-1-84322-804-2(1)*, Armadillo) Anness Publishing GBR. Dist: National Bk. Network.

Hyde, Natalie. Gladiators. 2016. (ENG., Illus.). 48p. (J). pap. *(978-0-7787-2227-4(9))* Crabtree Publishing Co.

Hynson, Colin. Ancient Rome: The Complete Homework Solution. 2010. (Study Buddies Ser.). (ENG.). 32p. (J). (gr. 4-7). pap. 6.95 *(978-1-84898-182-9(1)*, TickTock Books) Octopus Publishing Group GBR. Dist: Independent Pubs. Group.

Innes, Brian. Ancient Roman Myths. 2010. (Myths from Around the World Ser.). 48p. (gr. 6-8). (YA). lib. bdg. 31.00 *(978-1-4339-3527-5(9))*; (Illus.). (J). pap. 14.05 *(978-1-4339-3528-2(7))* Stevens, Gareth Publishing LLLP. (Gareth Stevens Secondary Library).

Jacobs, Denise. Patricians in the Roman Empire. 2016. (Life in the Roman Empire Ser.). 80p. (J). 35.64 *(978-1-5026-2257-0(2))* Cavendish Square Publishing.

James, Simon. Ancient Rome. 2015. (DK Eyewitness Bks.). (ENG., Illus.). 72p. (J). (gr. 3-7). 19.99 *(978-1-4654-3569-9(7)*, DK Children) Dorling Kindersley Publishing, Inc.

Jeffrey, Gary & Petty, Kate. Julius Caesar: The Life of a Roman General. 2005. (Graphic Nonfiction Biographies Ser.). (ENG., Illus.). 48p. (J). (gr. 4-7). lib. bdg. 31.95 *(978-1-4042-0239-9(0)*, 1241097) Rosen Publishing Group, Inc., The.

Jovinelly, Joann. The Crafts & Culture of the Romans. 2009. (Crafts of the Ancient World Ser.). 48p. (gr. 5-8). 58.50 *(978-1-61512-065-9(3)*, Rosen Reference) Rosen Publishing Group, Inc., The.

Kemp, Ellwood W. Streams of History: Ancient Rome (Yesterday's Classics) 2008. 104p. per. 7.95 *(978-1-59915-256-1(8))* Yesterday's Classics.

Kent, Zachary. Julius Caesar: Ruler of the Roman World. 2006. (Rulers of the Ancient World Ser.). (Illus.). 160p. (YA). (gr. 6-9). lib. bdg. 29.27 *(978-0-7660-2563-9(2))* Enslow Pubs., Inc.

Kerrigan, Michael. Romans. 2010. (Ancients in Their Own Words Ser.). 64p. (gr. 5). 32.79 *(978-1-60870-067-7(4))* Marshall Cavendish Corp.

Klar, Jeremy. The Totally Gross History of Ancient Rome, 01 vols., 1. 2016. (Totally Gross History Ser.). (ENG.). 48p. (J). 30.25 *(978-1-4994-3746-1(3))*; pap. 11.75 *(978-1-4994-3744-7(7))* Rosen Publishing Group, Inc., The. (Rosen Central).

Kops, Deborah. Ancient Rome: A MyReportLinks. com Book. 2005. (Civilizations of the Ancient World Ser.). (Illus.). 48p. (J). lib. bdg. 26.60 *(978-0-7660-5255-0(9)*, MyReportLinks.com Bks.) Enslow Pubs., Inc.

Leoni, Cristiana. In Caesar's Rome with Cicero. Cappon, Manuela, illus. 2008. (Come See My City Ser.). 48p. (gr. 4-8). lib. bdg. 28.50 *(978-0-7614-4328-5(2)*, Benchmark Bks.) Marshall Cavendish Corp.

Litten, Kristyna. Rome: a 3D Keepsake Cityscape. Litten, Kristyna, illus. 2013. (Panorama Pops Ser.). (ENG., Illus.). 15p. (J). (gr. k-12). 8.99 *(978-0-7636-6415-2(4))* Candlewick Pr.

Lowery, Zoe & Morgan, Julian. Nero. 2016. (Leaders of the Ancient World Ser.). 00112p. (J). (gr. 6-6). 37.10 *(978-1-5081-7256-7(0))* Rosen Publishing Group, Inc., The.

Macaulay, David. City: A Story of Roman Planning & Construction. 2012. 21.00 *(978-1-61383-577-7(9))* Perfection Learning Corp.

Macdonald, Fiona. Ancient Rome. 2013. (Illus.). 48p. (J). *(978-1-4351-5083-6(X))* Barnes & Noble, Inc.

—Do You Want to Be a Roman Soldier? 2015. (Do You Want to Be... Ser.). (Illus.). 32p. (gr. 3-6). 28.50 *(978-1-909645-38-7(9))* Book Hse. GBR. Dist: Black Rabbit Bks.

MacDonald, Fiona. How to Be a Roman Soldier. Hewetson, Nicholas J., illus. 2005. (How to Be Ser.). (ENG.). 32p. (J). (gr. 3-7). 14.95 *(978-0-7922-3616-0(5)*, National Geographic Children's Bks.) National Geographic Society.

—How to Be a Roman Soldier. Hewetson, Nicholas, illus. 2005. (How to Be Ser.). (ENG.). 32p. (J). (gr. 3-7). 21.90 *(978-0-7922-3631-3(9)*, National Geographic Children's Bks.) National Geographic Society.

—Romans: Dress, Eat, Write & Play Just Like the Romans. 2008. (Hands-on History Ser.). (ENG., Illus.). 32p. (J). (gr. 3-7). pap. *(978-0-7787-4071-1(4))* Crabtree Publishing Co.

Mackley, Daniel. The City in the Roman Empire. 2016. (Life in the Roman Empire Ser.). 80p. (J). 35.64 *(978-1-5026-2259-4(9))* Cavendish Square Publishing.

Malam, John. Ancient Rome Inside Out. 2017. (Ancient Worlds Inside Out Ser.). (ENG.). 32p. (J). ***(978-0-7787-2882-5(X))***; (Illus.). pap. ***(978-0-7787-2896-2(X))*** Crabtree Publishing Co.

—Life in Ancient Rome. 2011. (Big Picture: Homes Ser.). (ENG.). 24p. (gr. 1-2). pap. 41.70 *(978-1-4296-6731-9(1)*, First Facts) Capstone Press of Coughlan Cos.

—You Wouldn't Want to Be a Roman Galdiator! Antram, David, illus. rev. ed. 2012. (You Wouldn't Want to...: Ancient Civilization Ser.). (ENG.). 40p. (J). pap. 9.95 *(978-0-531-28028-7(4))* Scholastic Library Publishing.

Mara, Wil. The Romans. 2011. (Technology of the Ancients Ser.). 64p. (gr. 5). 32.79 *(978-1-60870-768-3(7))* Marshall Cavendish Corp.

Marcovitz, Hal. Ancient Rome. 2011. (Understanding World History Ser.). (ENG., Illus.). 80p. (YA). (gr. 7-12). lib. bdg. 27.95 *(978-1-60152-186-6(3))* ReferencePoint Pr., Inc.

Marks, Anthony & Tingay, Graham. Romans. Jackson, Ian & Wood, Gerald, illus. 2005. (Illustrated World History Ser.). 96p. (J). (gr. 6-12). lib. bdg. 20.95 *(978-1-58086-782-5(0)*, Usborne) EDC Publishing.

—Romans II. 2010. (Illustrated World History Ser.). 96p. (J). pap. 12.99 *(978-0-7945-2754-9(X)*, Usborne) EDC Publishing.

Mason Crest. Rome, Vol. 8. 2016. (Major World Cities Ser.: Vol. 8). (ENG., Illus.). 48p. (J). (gr. 5-8). 20.95 *(978-1-4222-3545-4(9))* Mason Crest.

Mattern, Joanne. Gladiators. 2009. (ENG., Illus.). 32p. (gr. 4-8). pap. 9.95 *(978-1-60694-541-4(6))* Rourke Educational Media.

—Julius Caesar. 2017. (Junior Biography From Ancient Civilization Ser.). (gr. 4-6). 29.95 *(978-1-68020-024-9(0))* Mitchell Lane Pubs., Inc.

Matthews, Rupert. Gladiators. 2015. (History's Fearless Fighters Ser.). (ENG.). 48p. (J). (gr. 5-6). pap. 14.05 *(978-1-4824-3165-0(3))* Stevens, Gareth Publishing LLLP.

Maynard, Charles W. The Technology of Ancient Rome. (Technology of the Ancient World Ser.). 48p. 2009. (gr. 6-6). 61.20 *(978-1-60854-242-0(4)*, Rosen Reference) 2005. (Illus.). (J). (gr. 5-8). lib. bdg. 29.25 *(978-1-4042-0556-7(X))* Rosen Publishing Group, Inc., The.

McCullough, Naomi V. The Technology of Ancient Rome. 2016. (Ancient Innovations Ser.). 64p. (J). lib. bdg. 34.21 *(978-1-5026-2233-4(5))* Cavendish Square Publishing.

Mehta-Jones, Shilpa. Life in Ancient Rome. 2004. (Peoples of the Ancient World Ser.). (ENG., Illus.). 32p. (J). lib. bdg. *(978-0-7787-2034-8(9))* Crabtree Publishing Co.

Mincks, Margaret. What We Get from Roman Mythology. 2015. (21st Century Skills Library: Mythology & Culture Ser.). (ENG., Illus.). 32p. (J). (gr. 3-6). pap. 14.21 *(978-1-63188-931-8(1)*, 205985) Cherry Lake Publishing.

Morgan, Julian. Hadrian: Consolidating the Empire. 2009. (Ancient Leaders Ser.). 112p. (gr. 5-8). 66.50 *(978-1-61511-423-8(8)*, Rosen Reference) Rosen Publishing Group, Inc., The.

—Nero: Destroyer of Rome. 2009. (Ancient Leaders Ser.). 112p. (gr. 5-8). 66.50 *(978-1-61511-426-9(2)*, Rosen Reference) Rosen Publishing Group, Inc., The.

Morris, Neil. Everyday Life in Ancient Rome. 2008. (Uncovering History Ser.). (ENG., Illus.). 48p. (J). (gr. 2-7). 19.95 *(978-88-89272-54-1(6))* McRae Bks. Srl ITA. Dist: Independent Pubs. Group.

Murrell, Deborah Jane & Dennis, Peter. Gladiator. 2012. (Illus.). 32p. (gr. 3-5). pap. 8.95 *(978-1-926853-52-9(0))* Saunders Bk. Co. CAN. Dist: RiverStream Publishing.

Naden, Corinne J. & Blue, Rose. Ancient Romans & the Colosseum. 2003. (J). *(978-1-58417-316-8(5))*; pap. *(978-1-58417-317-5(3))* Lake Street Pubs.

Nardo, Don. Cause & Effect the Fall of Rome: The Fall of Rome. 2015. (ENG., Illus.). 80p. (J). lib. bdg. *(978-1-60152-794-3(2))* ReferencePoint Pr., Inc.

—Daily Life in Ancient Rome. 2015. (Daily Life in Ancient Civilizations Ser.). (ENG., Illus.). 48p. (gr. 3-6). pap. 8.99 *(978-1-4846-0833-3(X)*, Heinemann InfoSearch) Heinemann-Raintree.

—The Roman Empire. 2005. (World History Ser.). (ENG., Illus.). 96p. (YA). (gr. 7-10). lib. bdg. 33.45 *(978-1-59018-657-2(5)*, Lucent Bks.) Cengage Gale.

—Rome. 2011. (Classical Civilization Ser.). 128p. (YA). (gr. 7-12). 28.95 *(978-1-59935-174-2(9))* Reynolds, Morgan Inc.

Osborne, Mary Pope & Boyce, Natalie Pope. Ancient Rome & Pompeii: A Nonfiction Companion to Vacation under the Volcano. Murdocca, Sal, illus. 2006. (Magic Tree House (R) Fact Tracker Ser.: 14). (ENG.). 128p. (J). (gr. 2-5). 6.99 *(978-0-375-83220-8(3)*, Random Hse. Bks. for Young Readers) Random Hse. Children's Bks.

Park, Louise & Love, Timothy. The Roman Gladiators. 2009. (Ancient & Medieval People Ser.). 32p. (gr. 5). 28.50 *(978-0-7614-4443-5(2))* Marshall Cavendish Corp.

Phipps, Liza & Thompson, Avril. Romans. 2016. (History Showtime Ser.). (ENG., Illus.). 32p. (J). (gr. 2-4). pap. 11.99 *(978-1-4451-1488-0(7)*, Franklin Watts) Hachette Children's Group GBR. Dist: Hachette Bk. Group.

Pistone, Nicholas. Art & Culture of Ancient Rome. 2010. (Ancient Art & Cultures Ser.). 40p. (YA). (gr. 5-8). lib. bdg., E-Book 53.00 *(978-1-61532-965-6(X))* Rosen Publishing Group, Inc., The.

Pistone, Nicholas, et al. Art & Culture of Ancient Rome. 2010. (Ancient Art & Cultures Ser.). (Illus.). 40p. (J). pap. 11.75 *(978-1-61532-885-7(8))*; (YA). (gr. 5-8). lib. bdg. 26.50 *(978-1-4358-3591-7(3))* Rosen Publishing Group, Inc., The.

Platt, Richard. Roman Diary: The Journal of Iliona of Mytilini, Who Was Captured & Sold As a Slave in Rome, AD 107. Parkins, David, illus. 2009. (ENG.). 64p. (J). (gr. 3-7). 18.99 *(978-0-7636-3480-3(8))* Candlewick Pr.

Powell, Jillian. The Romans. 2010. (Gruesome Truth about Ser.). (ENG.). 32p. (J). (gr. 4-6). lib. bdg. 22.60 *(978-1-61533-220-5(0))* Windmill Bks.

Price, Sean. Hannibal of Carthage, 1 vol. 2013. (Hero Journals). (ENG., Illus.). 48p. (gr. 4-6). 33.32 *(978-1-4109-5359-9(9))*; pap. 9.95 *(978-1-4109-5366-7(1))* Heinemann-Raintree. (NA-r).

Rajczak, Kristen. 20 Fun Facts about Women in Ancient Greece & Rome. 2015. (Fun Fact File: Women in History Ser.). (ENG., Illus.). 32p. (J). (gr. 2-3). 25.25 *(978-1-4824-2818-6(0))* Stevens, Gareth Publishing LLLP.

Randolph, Joanne, ed. Living & Working in Ancient Rome. 2017. (Back in Time Ser.). 48p. (gr. 5-6). pap. 11.70 ***(978-0-7660-8973-0(8))*** Enslow Pubs., Inc.

Reece, Katherine E. The Romans: Builders of an Empire. 2005. (Ancient Civilizations Ser.). (Illus.). 48p. (J). (gr. 4-8). lib. bdg. *(978-1-59515-507-8(4)*, 1244352) Rourke Educational Media.

Rice, Rob S. Ancient Roman Warfare. 2009. (Ancient Warfare Ser.). (Illus.). 32p. (J). (gr. 5-8). lib. bdg. 26.00 *(978-1-4339-1974-9(5)*, Gareth Stevens Learning Library) Stevens, Gareth Publishing LLLP.

Ridgley, Sara & Mole, Gavin. Sing It & Say - Ancient Rome. (Illus.). 140p. (J). 10.95 incl. audio *(978-1-85909-390-0(6)*, Warner Bros. Pubns.) Alfred Publishing Co., Inc.

Ridley, Sarah. Life in Roman Times. 2015. (Everyday History Ser.). (Illus.). 32p. (J). 31.35 *(978-1-59920-951-7(9))* Black Rabbit Bks.

Riggs, Kate. Gladiators. 2011. (Great Warriors Ser.). 24p. (J). (gr. k-2). 16.95 *(978-1-60818-000-4(X)*, Creative Education) Creative Co., The.

Rinaldo, Denise. Julius Caesar: Dictator for Life. 2010. (Wicked History Ser.). (ENG.). 128p. (J). (gr. 6-12). pap. 5.95 *(978-0-531-22822-7(3)*, Watts, Franklin) Scholastic Library Publishing.

Robinson, Tony. Romans. unabr. ed. 2015. (Weird World of Wonders Ser.). (ENG., Illus.). 160p. (J). (gr. 4-6). pap. 7.99 *(978-0-330-53389-8(4))* Pan Macmillan GBR. Dist: Independent Pubs. Group.

—Romans & Greeks. 2016. (Weird World of Wonders Ser.). (ENG., Illus.). 320p. (J). (gr. 4-6). pap. 12.99 *(978-1-5098-0539-6(7))* Pan Macmillan GBR. Dist: Independent Pubs. Group.

Rogora, Bernardo. Los Romanos. (Coleccion Bravo). (SPA., Illus.). 76p. (YA). (gr. 5-8). *(978-84-7131-907-4(1)*, EDI30259) Editex, Editorial S.A. ESP. Dist: Lectorum Pubns., Inc.

Romans. 2014. (Ladybird Histories Ser.). (ENG., Illus.). 64p. (J). (gr. 2-4). pap. 13.99 ***(978-0-7232-7730-9(3))*** Penguin Bks., Ltd. GBR. Dist: Independent Pubs. Group.

Roxburgh, Ellis. Cleopatra vs. the Roman Empire: Power, Conquest, & Tragedy. 2016. (History's Greatest Rivals Ser.). (ENG., Illus.). 48p. (J). (gr. 6-8). pap. 14.05 *(978-1-4824-4223-6(X))* Stevens, Gareth Publishing LLLP.

Ryall, Michael. Rome Long Ago. 2005. (J). pap. *(978-1-4108-4634-1(2))* Benchmark Education Co.

Samuels, Charlie. Technology in Ancient Rome. 2013. (Technology in the Ancient World Ser.). 48p. (J). (gr. 4-6). pap. 84.30 *(978-1-4339-9638-2(3))*; pap. 14.05 *(978-1-4339-9637-5(5))*; (ENG., Illus.). lib. bdg. 31.95 *(978-1-4339-9636-8(7))* Stevens, Gareth Publishing LLLP.

Santillian, Beatriz & Morgan, Julian. Hadrian: Emperor of Rome. 2017. (Leaders of the Ancient World Ser.). 112p. (J). (gr. 12-11). 37.10 ***(978-1-5081-7484-4(9)***, Rosen Young Adult) Rosen Publishing Group, Inc., The.

Sasek, Miroslav. This Is Rome. 2007. (This Is ... Ser.). (ENG., Illus.). 64p. (J). (gr. 2-12). 17.95 *(978-0-7893-1549-6(1))* Universe Publishing.

Saxena, Shalini. Nero: Ruthless Roman Emperor. 2016. (History's Most Murderous Villains Ser.). (Illus.). 32p. (J). (gr. 5-4). pap. 10.50 *(978-1-4824-4799-6(1))* Stevens, Gareth Publishing LLLP.

Schomp, Virginia. The Ancient Romans. 2008. (Myths of the World Ser.). (Illus.). 96p. (J). (gr. 6-18). lib. bdg. 34.21 *(978-0-7614-3094-0(6)*, Benchmark Bks.) Marshall Cavendish Corp.

Sewell, E. M. The Child's History of Rome. 2005. reprint ed. pap. 26.95 *(978-1-4179-6641-7(6))* Kessinger Publishing, LLC.

Sheehan, Sean & Levy, Patricia. Ancient Rome. 2010. (Exploring the Ancient World Ser.). (Illus.). 64p. (YA). (gr. 6-8). lib. bdg. 34.60 *(978-1-4339-4160-3(0)*, Gareth Stevens Secondary Library) Stevens, Gareth Publishing LLLP.

Shone, Rob. Spartacus: The Life of a Roman Gladiator. 2009. (Graphic Nonfiction Biographies Ser.). (ENG.). 48p. (YA). (gr. 4-5). 58.50 *(978-1-61513-028-3(4)*, Rosen Reference) Rosen Publishing Group, Inc., The.

Shone, Rob & Ganeri, Anita. Spartacus: The Life of a Roman Gladiator. 2005. (Graphic Nonfiction Biographies Ser.). (ENG., Illus.). 48p. (J). (gr. 4-7). lib. bdg. 31.95 *(978-1-4042-0240-5(4)*, 1241099) Rosen Publishing Group, Inc., The.

Shoulders, Debbie & Shoulders, Michael. G Is for Gladiators: An Ancient Rome Alphabet. Juhasz, Victor, illus. 2010. (Sleeping Bear Alphabets Ser.). (ENG.). 40p. (J). (gr. 1-4). 19.99 *(978-1-58536-457-2(6)*, 202180) Sleeping Bear Pr.

Sims, Lesley. The Roman Soldier's Handbook: Everything a Beginner Soldier Needs to Know. McNee, Ian, illus. 2006. (English Heritage Ser.). 80p. (J). (gr. 4-7). 12.99 *(978-0-7945-0837-1(5)*, Usborne) EDC Publishing.

Smith, Miranda & Steele, Philip. Ancient Worlds: A Thrilling Adventure Through the Ancient Worlds. 2016. (Navigators Ser.). (ENG., Illus.). 80p. (J). 15.99 *(978-0-7534-7239-2(2)*, 9780753472392, Kingfisher) Roaring Brook Pr.

Snedden, Robert. Ancient Rome. 2009. (Technology in Times Past Ser.). (Illus.). 46p. (J). (gr. 4-7). pap. *(978-1-897563-63-2(9))* Saunders Bk. Co.

Sonneborn, Liz. The Romans: Life in Ancient Rome. Hiti, Samuel, illus. 2009. (Life in Ancient Civilizations Ser.). (ENG.). 48p. (gr. 3-6). lib. bdg. 29.27 *(978-0-8225-8679-1(7)*, Millbrook Pr.) Lerner Publishing Group.

Spotlight on Ancient Civilizations: Rome. 2013. (Spotlight on Ancient Civilizations: Rome Ser.). 24p. (J). (gr. 3-4). (ENG.). 141.60 *(978-1-4777-1144-6(9))*; (ENG.). pap. 60.00 *(978-1-4777-2689-1(6))*; pap. 297.00 *(978-1-4777-2690-7(X))* Rosen Publishing Group, Inc., The. (PowerKids Pr.).

Steele, Philip. Ancient Rome: Step into the Time of the Roman Empire, with 15 Step-by-Step Projects & over 370 Exciting Pictures. 2013. (ENG., Illus.). 64p. (J). (gr. 3-7). pap. 12.99 *(978-1-84322-692-5(8))* Anness Publishing GBR. Dist: National Bk. Network.

—Hail! Ancient Romans. 2010. (ENG.). 32p. (J). *(978-0-7787-6624-7(1))*; pap. *(978-0-7787-6631-5(4))* Crabtree Publishing Co.

—The Roman Empire. 2007. (Step Into Ser.). (ENG., Illus.). 64p. (J). (gr. 4-7). pap. 10.99 *(978-1-84476-348-1(X))* Anness Publishing GBR. Dist: National Bk. Network.

—The Roman Empire. 2009. (Passport to the Past Ser.). (Illus.). 64p. (J). (gr. 4-7). lib. bdg. 31.95 (978-1-4358-5176-4(5)) Rosen Publishing Group, Inc., The.
Stewart, David. Inside Ancient Rome. James, John et al, illus. 2005. (Inside... Ser.). 48p. (J). (gr. 5). lib. bdg. 19.95 (978-1-59270-045-5(4)) Enchanted Lion Bks., LLC.
Sullivan, Erin Ash. Ancient Rome: Set Of 6. 2011. (Navigators Ser.). (J). pap. 50.00 net. (978-1-4108-5115-4(X)) Benchmark Education Co.
—Ancient Rome: Text Pairs. 2008. (Bridges/Navigators Ser.). (J). (gr. 6). 89.00 (978-1-4108-8429-9(5)) Benchmark Education Co.
Sylvester, Diane. Ancient Rome. Hillam, Corbin, illus. 2006. (Museum Ser.). 64p. (J). (gr. 5-8). pap. 13.99 (978-0-88160-390-3(2), LW445, Learning Works, The) Creative Teaching Pr., Inc.
Tracy, Kathleen. The Life & Times of Constantine. 2005. (Biography from Ancient Civilizations Ser.). (Illus.). 48p. (J). (gr. 4-8). lib. bdg. 29.95 (978-1-58415-343-6(1)) Mitchell Lane Pubs., Inc.
Trajan's Rome Grades 5-9: The Man, the City, the Empire. (J). tchr. ed., spiral bd. 15.00 (978-0-382-44446-3(9)) Cobblestone Publishing Co.
Turner, Tracey. Hard As Nails in Ancient Rome. Lenman, Jamie, illus. 2015. (ENG.). 64p. (J). (978-0-7787-1513-9(2)) Crabtree Publishing Co.
Van Vleet, Carmella. Explore Ancient Rome! 25 Great Projects, Activities, Experiments. Kim, Alex, illus. 2008. (Explore Your World Ser.). (ENG.). 96p. (J). (gr. k-4). pap. 12.95 (978-0-9792268-4-7(8)) Octavio Publishing.
Von Zumbusch, Amelie. Ancient Roman Culture. 2013. (Spotlight on Ancient Civilizations: Rome Ser.). (ENG.). 24p. (J). (gr. 3-4). 23.60 (978-1-4777-0775-3(1), PowerKids Pr.) Rosen Publishing Group, Inc., The.
—Ancient Roman Daily Life. 2013. (Spotlight on Ancient Civilizations: Rome Ser.). (ENG.). 24p. (J). (gr. 3-4). 23.60 (978-1-4777-0778-4(6), PowerKids Pr.) Rosen Publishing Group, Inc., The.
Vonne, Mira. Gross Facts about the Roman Empire. 2017. (Gross History Ser.). (ENG., Illus.). 32p. (gr. 1-2). lib. bdg. 26.65 (978-1-5157-4156-5(7)) Capstone Press of Coughlan Cos.
Waldron, Melanie. Geography Matters in Ancient Rome. 2015. (Geography Matters in Ancient Civilizations Ser.). (ENG., Illus.). 48p. (gr. 3-6). 33.32 (978-1-4846-0964-4(6), Heinemann InfoSearch) Heinemann-Raintree.
Warrick, Karen Clemens. Hannibal: Great General of the Ancient World. 2006. (Rulers of the Ancient World Ser.). (Illus.). 160p. (J). (gr. 6-12). lib. bdg. 27.93 (978-0-7660-2564-6(0)) Enslow Pubs., Inc.
Weatherill, Sue & Weatherill, Stephen. Romans. 2005. (ENG., Illus.). 24p. (J). (gr. 1-4). pap., act. bk. ed. 7.99 (978-1-902915-34-0(8)) B Small Publishing GBR. Dist: Independent Pubs. Group.
West, David. The Ancient Romans. 2016. (Discovering Ancient Civilizations Ser.). 32p. (gr. 3-3). pap. 10.50 (978-1-4824-5059-0(3)) Stevens, Gareth Publishing LLLP.
Whiting, Jim. The Life & Times of Julius Caesar. 2005. (Biography from Ancient Civilizations Ser.). (Illus.). 48p. (J). (gr. -1-7). lib. bdg. 29.95 (978-1-58415-337-5(7)) Mitchell Lane Pubs., Inc.
—The Life & Times of Nero. 2005. (Biography from Ancient Civilizations Ser.). (Illus.). 48p. (J). (gr. 5-8). lib. bdg. 29.95 (978-1-58415-349-8(0)) Mitchell Lane Pubs., Inc.
Willard Crompton, Samuel. Discovering Ancient Rome, 1 vol. 2015. (Exploring Ancient Civilizations Ser.). (ENG.). 48p. (YA). 51.70 (978-1-62275-832-6(3), Britannica Educational Publishing) Rosen Publishing Group, Inc., The.
Williams, Jane A. A Bluestocking Guide - Ancient Rome: Companion Workbook for Richard J. Maybury's Ancient Rome: How it Affects You Today. Daniels, Kathryn, ed. 2004. (Bluestocking Guide Ser.). 47p. (YA). pap. 9.95 (978-0-942617-48-1(7)) Bluestocking Pr.
Williams, Marcia. The Romans: Gods, Emperors, & Dormice. 2013. (ENG.). 40p. (J). (gr. 3-7). 16.99 (978-0-7636-6581-4(9)) Candlewick Pr.
Williams, Rose. The Young Romans. 2003. (Anthem Classics Ser.). (LAT & ENG., Illus.). 128p. (J). pap. 26.00 (978-1-84331-047-1(3)) Anthem Pr. GBR. Dist: Bolchazy-Carducci Pubs.
—The Young Romans. 2007. (LAT & ENG.). pap. 23.00 (978-0-86516-670-7(6)) Bolchazy-Carducci Pubs.
Woolf, Alex. Meet the Ancient Romans. 2014. (Encounters with the Past Ser.). 32p. (J). (gr. 3-6). 26.60 (978-1-4824-0886-7(4)) Stevens, Gareth Publishing LLLP.
Yonge, Charlotte Mary. Aunt Charlotte's Roman History. 2013. 260p. pap. (978-3-95507-998-7(8)) DOGMA. in Europäischer Hochschulverlag GmbH & Co. KG.
Zumbusch, Amelie von. Ancient Roman Culture. 2013. (Spotlight on Ancient Civilizations: Rome Ser.). (ENG., Illus.). 24p. (J). (gr. 3-4). pap. 10.00 (978-1-4777-0883-5(9), PowerKids Pr.) Rosen Publishing Group, Inc., The.
—Ancient Roman Daily Life. 2013. (Spotlight on Ancient Civilizations: Rome Ser.). (ENG., Illus.). 24p. (J). (gr. 3-4). pap. 10.00 (978-1-4777-0889-7(8), PowerKids Pr.) Rosen Publishing Group, Inc., The.
—The Ancient Roman Economy. 2013. (Spotlight on Ancient Civilizations: Rome Ser.). (ENG.). 24p. (J). (gr. 3-4). pap. 10.00 (978-1-4777-0887-3(1)); lib. bdg. 23.60 (978-1-4777-0777-7(8)) Rosen Publishing Group, Inc., The. (PowerKids Pr.).
—Ancient Roman Geography. 2013. (Spotlight on Ancient Civilizations: Rome Ser.). (ENG., Illus.). 24p. (J). (gr. 3-4). pap. 10.00 (978-1-4777-0891-0(X), PowerKids Pr.) Rosen Publishing Group, Inc., The.
—Ancient Roman Technology. 2013. (Spotlight on Ancient Civilizations: Rome Ser.). (ENG., Illus.). 24p. (J). (gr. 3-4). pap. 10.00 (978-1-4777-0893-4(6), PowerKids Pr.) Rosen Publishing Group, Inc., The.
Zumbusch, Amelie Von & Von Zumbusch, Amelie. Ancient Roman Geography. 2013. (Spotlight on Ancient Civilizations: Rome Ser.). (ENG., Illus.). 24p. (J). (gr. 3-4). 23.60 (978-1-4777-0779-1(4), PowerKids Pr.) Rosen Publishing Group, Inc., The.
—Ancient Roman Technology. 2013. (Spotlight on Ancient Civilizations: Rome Ser.). (ENG.). 24p. (J). (gr. 3-4). 23.60 (978-1-4777-0780-7(8), PowerKids Pr.) Rosen Publishing Group, Inc., The.

ROME—HISTORY—FICTION

Banks, Lynne Reid. Tiger, Tiger. 2007. (ENG.). 208p. (YA). (gr. 7-11). mass mkt. 6.99 (978-0-440-42044-6(X), Laurel Leaf) Random Hse. Children's Bks.
Church, Alfred J. The Aeneid for Boys & Girls. 2008. 100p. pap. 9.05 (978-1-60459-519-2(1)) Wilder Pubns., Corp.
Collins, Tim. Diary of Dorkius Maximus. Pinder, Andrew, illus. 2014. (Diary of Dorkius Maximus Ser.: 1). (ENG.). 192p. (J). (gr. 4-6). pap. 8.99 (978-1-78055-027-5(8)) O'Mara, Michael Bks., Ltd. GBR. Dist: Independent Pubs. Group.
—Diary of Dorkius Maximus in Egypt. Pinder, Andrew, illus. 2014. (Diary of Dorkius Maximus Ser.: 2). (ENG.). 192p. (J). (gr. 4-6). pap. 8.99 (978-1-78055-028-2(6)) O'Mara, Michael Bks., Ltd. GBR. Dist: Independent Pubs. Group.
—Diary of Dorkius Maximus in Pompeii. Pinder, Andrew, illus. 2015. (Diary of Dorkius Maximus Ser.: 3). (ENG.). 192p. (J). (gr. 4-6). pap. 10.99 (978-1-78055-268-2(8)) O'Mara, Michael Bks., Ltd. GBR. Dist: Independent Pubs. Group.
Dalton, Annie. Fighting Fit: Mission - Get into the Gladiator Groove! 2009. (Mel Beeby, Agent Angel Ser.: 6). (ENG.). 192p. (J). (gr. 4-7). pap. 7.99 (978-0-00-720476-2(0)) HarperCollins Pubs. Ltd. GBR. Dist: HarperCollins Pubs.
Henty, George Alfred. The Young Carthaginian: A Story of the Times of Hannibal. 2011. 360p. pap. 19.95 (978-1-61179-162-4(6)) Fireship Pr.
—The Young Carthaginian: A Tale of the Times of Hannibal. 2004. reprint ed. pap. 27.95 (978-1-4191-8911-1(5)); pap. 1.99 (978-1-4192-8911-8(X)); pap. 27.95 (978-1-4191-8911-1(5)) Kessinger Publishing, LLC.
Hulme-Cross, Benjamin. The Gladiator's Victory. Rinaldi, Angelo, illus. 2015. (ENG.). 160p. (J). (978-0-7787-1764-5(X)) Crabtree Publishing Co.
Lampard, Frank. Frankie vs. the Rowdy Romans. 2014. (Frankie's Magic Soccer Ball Ser.: 2). (ENG., Illus.). 112p. (J). (gr. 2-5). pap. 4.99 (978-0-545-66614-5(7), Scholastic Paperbacks) Scholastic, Inc.
Lawrence, Caroline. The Assassins of Rome. 2005. (Roman Mysteries Ser.). (Illus.). 161p. (J). (gr. 3-7). 14.65 (978-0-7569-5879-4(2)) Perfection Learning Corp.
—The Beggar of Volubilis. 2008. (ENG., Illus.). 272p. (gr. 4-6). pap. 10.99 (978-1-84255-604-7(5), Orion Children's Bks.) Hachette Children's Group GBR. Dist: Hachette Bk. Group.
—The Charioteer of Delphi. 2007. (ENG., Illus.). 256p. (gr. 4-6). pap. 10.99 (978-1-84255-544-6(8), Orion Children's Bks.) Hachette Children's Group GBR. Dist: Hachette Bk. Group.
—The Dolphins of Laurentum. 2005. (Roman Mysteries Ser.). (Illus.). 161p. (J). (gr. 6-9). 13.65 (978-0-7569-6538-9(1)) Perfection Learning Corp.
—The Legionary from Londinium. 2013. (ENG., Illus.). 192p. (J). (gr. 7-17). 10.99 (978-1-84255-192-9(2), Orion Children's Bks.) Hachette Children's Group GBR. Dist: Hachette Bk. Group.
—The Man from Pomegranate Street, Bk. 17. 2010. (ENG., Illus.). 272p. (YA). (gr. 7-17). 10.99 (978-1-84255-608-5(8), Orion Children's Bks.) Hachette Children's Group GBR. Dist: Hachette Bk. Group.
—The Prophet from Ephesus. 2009. (ENG., Illus.). 224p. (YA). (gr. 7-17). pap. 10.99 (978-1-84255-606-1(1), Orion Children's Bks.) Hachette Children's Group GBR. Dist: Hachette Bk. Group.
—The Scribes from Alexandria. 2008. (ENG., Illus.). 272p. (gr. 4-6). pap. 10.99 (978-1-84255-605-4(3), Orion Children's Bks.) Hachette Children's Group GBR. Dist: Hachette Bk. Group.
—The Sirens of Surrentum. 2006. (ENG., Illus.). 272p. (gr. 7-9). pap. 10.99 (978-1-84255-506-4(5), Orion Children's Bks.) Hachette Children's Group GBR. Dist: Hachette Bk. Group.
—The Sirens of Surrentum. 2007. (Roman Mysteries Ser.: Bk. 11). (ENG., Illus.). 224p. (J). (gr. 6-9). 16.95 (978-1-59643-084-6(2)) Roaring Brook Pr.
—The Slave-Girl from Jerusalem. 2007. (ENG., Illus.). 240p. (gr. 4-6). pap. 10.99 (978-1-84255-572-9(3), Orion Children's Bks.) Hachette Children's Group GBR. Dist: Hachette Bk. Group.
—Trimalchio's Feast: And Other Mini-Mysteries. 2013. (ENG., Illus.). 144p. (J). (gr. 4-6). pap. 10.99 (978-1-84255-593-4(6), Orion Children's Bks.) Hachette Children's Group GBR. Dist: Hachette Bk. Group.
Lee, Kathy. Rome in Flames. 2005. 144p. pap. (978-1-84427-089-7(0)) Scripture Union.
Livingston, Lesley. The Valiant. 2017. (ENG.). 384p. (YA). (gr. 7). 17.99 (978-0-448-49378-7(0), Razorbill) Penguin Young Readers Group.
Mitchell, Jack. The Roman Conspiracy. 2005. (ENG.). 176p. (J). (gr. 5-8). pap. 8.95 (978-0-88776-713-5(3), Tundra Bks.) Tundra Bks. CAN. Dist: Penguin Random Hse. LLC.
Nielsen, Jennifer A. Mark of the Thief. 2015. (Mark of the Thief Ser.: 1). (ENG.). 352p. (J). (gr. 4-7). 17.99 (978-0-545-56154-9(X), Scholastic Pr.) Scholastic, Inc.
—Rise of the Wolf. 2016. (Mark of the Thief Ser.: 2). (ENG.). 352p. (J). (gr. 4-7). pap. 7.99 (978-0-545-56205-8(8)); 17.99 (978-0-545-56204-1(X)) Scholastic, Inc. (Scholastic Pr.).
—Rise of the Wolf. 2016. (Mark of the Thief Ser.: 2). lib. bdg. 18.40 **(978-0-606-39707-0(8))** Turtleback Bks.
Rubalcaba, Jill. The Wadjet Eye. 2006. (ENG.). 160p. (J). (gr. 5-7). pap. 7.99 (978-0-618-68927-9(3)) Houghton Mifflin Harcourt Publishing Co.
Shakespeare, William. Julius Caesar. Mahbab, Mustashrik, illus. 2008. (ENG.). 208p. (YA). (gr. 7-11). pap. 12.95 (978-0-8109-7072-4(4), Amulet Bks.) Abrams, Inc.
—Julius Caesar, 1 vol. Garcia, Eduardo, illus. 2011. (Shakespeare Graphics Ser.). (ENG.). 88p. (gr. 2-3). pap. 7.15 (978-1-4342-3450-6(9)); lib. bdg. 27.99 (978-1-4342-2631-0(X)) Stone Arch Bks. (Shakespeare Graphics).
Shecter, Vicky Alvear. Cleopatra's Moon. 2013. (ENG.). 368p. (J). (gr. 9). pap. 9.99 (978-0-545-22131-3(5), Levine, Arthur A. Bks.) Scholastic, Inc.
Surget, Alain & Yeardley, Glynne. Danger at the Circus! Parme, Fabrice, illus. 2014. 95p. (J). (978-1-4351-5334-9(0)) Barnes & Noble, Inc.
Sutcliff, Rosemary. The Eagle. movie tie-in ed. 2011. (Roman Britain Trilogy Ser.: 1). (ENG.). 240p. (YA). (gr. 5). pap. 9.99 (978-0-312-56434-6(1), 9780312564346) Square Fish.
—The Eagle of the Ninth. 2010. (Roman Britain Trilogy Ser.: 1). (ENG.). 240p. (YA). (gr. 7). pap. 9.99 (978-0-312-64429-1(9), 9780312644291) Square Fish.
Thompson, Kate. Most Wanted. 2010. (ENG.). 144p. (J). (gr. 3-18). 15.99 (978-0-06-173037-5(8), Greenwillow Bks.) HarperCollins Pubs.
Trease, Geoffrey, text. Word to Caesar. 2005. (J). per. 14.95 (978-0-9766386-2-9(2)) Hillside Education.
Wallace, Lew. Ben-Hur. (SPA., Illus.). (YA). 11.95 (978-84-7281-099-0(2), AF1099) Auriga, Ediciones S.A. ESP. Dist: Continental Bk. Co., Inc.
Weatherby, W. J. Chariots of Fire. Morris, Margery, ed. abr. ed. Date not set. (Nelson Readers Ser.: 2). (J). pap. (978-0-17-557036-2(1)) Addison-Wesley Longman, Inc.

ROME—HISTORY—REPUBLIC, 510-30 B.C.

Ancient Rome II, Grades 5-9: Theater, Sculpture & Painting, Religion, Daily Life, the Roman at Home, Latin Prefixes in English. (Teaching with Primary Sources Ser.). (Illus.). (J). tchr. ed., ring bd. 28.95 (978-0-382-40865-6(9)) Cobblestone Publishing Co.
Bailey, Gerry & Foster, Karen. Julius Caesar's Sandals. Noyes, Leighton, illus. 2008. (Stories of Great People Ser.). (ENG.). 40p. (J). (gr. 3-6). pap. (978-0-7787-3717-9(9)); lib. bdg. (978-0-7787-3695-0(4)) Crabtree Publishing Co.
Baum, Margaux & Thorne, James. Julius Caesar. 2016. (Leaders of the Ancient World Ser.). 00112p. (J). (gr. 6-6). 37.10 (978-1-5081-7248-2(X)) Rosen Publishing Group, Inc., The.
Brooks, Philip. Hannibal. rev. ed. 2015. (Wicked History Ser.). (ENG., Illus.). 144p. (J). lib. bdg. 33.00 (978-0-531-22122-8(9), Children's Pr.) Scholastic Library Publishing.
—Hannibal: Rome's Worst Nightmare. 2008. (Wicked History Ser.). (ENG., Illus.). 128p. (J). 31.00 (978-0-531-18553-7(2), Watts, Franklin) Scholastic Library Publishing.
Cox, Phil Roxbee. Who Were the Romans? 2004. (Starting Point History Ser.). (Illus.). 32p. (J). pap. 4.95 (978-0-7945-0247-8(4), Usborne); lib. bdg. 12.95 (978-1-58086-446-6(5)) EDC Publishing.
Crompton, Samuel Willard. Julius Caesar. 2003. (Ancient World Leaders Ser.). (Illus.). 112p. (J). (gr. 6-12). 30.00 (978-0-7910-7220-2(7), Chelsea Hse.) Facts On File, Inc.
Curry, Jane Louise & Livy. Brave Cloelia: Retold from the Account in the History of Early Rome by the Roman Historian Titus Livius. Crosby, Jeff, illus. 2004. (ENG.). 34p. 17.95 (978-0-89236-763-4(6)) Oxford Univ. Pr., Inc.
Firth, Rachel. Julius Caesar. 2007. (Famous Lives Gift Bks). (Illus.). 64p. (J). 8.99 (978-0-7945-1595-9(9), Usborne) EDC Publishing.
Forsyth, Fiona. Cicero: Defender of the Republic. 2003. (Ancient Leaders Ser.). (Illus.). 112p. (YA). (gr. 5-8). lib. bdg. 34.60 (978-0-8239-3590-1(6), Rosen Reference) Rosen Publishing Group, Inc., The.
Goldberg, Jan. Julius Caesar. 2004. (ZB Reads Trio Books). (Illus.). 106p. (gr. 5-7). pap. 5.50 (978-0-7367-1800-4(1)) Zaner-Bloser, Inc.
Jeffrey, Gary. Julius Caesar: The Life of a Roman General. 2009. (Graphic Nonfiction Biographies Ser.). (ENG.). 48p. (YA). (gr. 4-5). 58.50 (978-1-61513-020-7(9), Rosen Reference) Rosen Publishing Group, Inc., The.
Medina, Nico. Who Was Julius Caesar? Foley, Tim, illus. 2014. (Who Was? Ser.). (ENG.). 112p. (J). (gr. 3-7). pap. 5.99 (978-0-448-48083-1(2), Grosset & Dunlap) Penguin Young Readers Group.
Newsome, Joel. Hannibal. 2017. (J). **(978-1-5026-2869-5(4))** Cavendish Square Publishing.
Rinaldo, Denise. Julius Caesar. rev. ed. 2015. (Wicked History Ser.). (ENG., Illus.). 144p. (J). lib. bdg. 33.00 (978-0-531-22123-5(7), Children's Pr.) Scholastic Library Publishing.
Tracy, Kathleen. The Life & Times of Cicero. 2006. (Biography from Ancient Civilizations Ser.). (Illus.). 48p. (J). (gr. 4-8). lib. bdg. 29.95 (978-1-58415-510-2(8)) Mitchell Lane Pubs., Inc.
Zumbusch, Amelie von. Ancient Roman Government. 2013. (Spotlight on Ancient Civilizations: Rome Ser.). (ENG., Illus.). 24p. (J). (gr. 3-4). pap. 10.00 (978-1-4777-0885-9(5), PowerKids Pr.) Rosen Publishing Group, Inc., The.

ROME—HISTORY—EMPIRE, 30 B.C.-476 A.D.

Allan, Tony. Exploring the Life, Myth, & Art of Ancient Rome. 2011. (Civilizations of the World Ser.). (YA). (gr. 7-12). lib. bdg. 42.60 (978-1-4488-4831-7(8)) Rosen Publishing Group, Inc., The.
Baum, Margaux & Forsyth, Fiona. Augustus. 2016. (Leaders of the Ancient World Ser.). 00112p. (J). (gr. 6-6). 37.10 (978-1-5081-7242-0(0)) Rosen Publishing Group, Inc., The.
Bingham, Jane. Romans. 2017. (Explore! Ser.). (ENG., Illus.). 32p. (J). (gr. 4-6). pap. 11.99 (978-0-7502-8887-3(6), Wayland) Hachette Children's Group GBR. Dist: Hachette Bk. Group.
Bridges, Shirin Yim. Agrippina: "Atrocious & Ferocious" Malone, Peter, illus. 2011. (Thinking Girl's Treasury of Dastardly Dames Ser.). (ENG.). 32p. (J). (gr. 3-8). 18.95 (978-0-9834256-1-8(2)) Goosebottom Bks. LLC.
Brocklehurst, R. Roman Army. 2004. (Discovery Program Ser.). (Illus.). 48p. (J). pap. 8.95 (978-0-7945-0591-2(0)) EDC Publishing.
Bruce, Julia. Conquest! Can You Build a Roman City? Dennis, Peter, illus. 2009. (Step into History Ser.). 32p. (J). (gr. 2-5). lib. bdg. 23.94 (978-0-7660-3478-5(X)) Enslow Pubs., Inc.
Cox, Phil Roxbee. Who Were the Romans? 2004. (Starting Point History Ser.). (Illus.). 32p. (J). pap. 4.95 (978-0-7945-0247-8(4), Usborne) EDC Publishing.
Hawes, Alison. A Roman Soldier's Handbook. 2010. (Crabtree Connections Ser.). (ENG.). 24p. (J). (gr. 3-6). (978-0-7787-9952-8(2)); pap. (978-0-7787-9974-0(3)) Crabtree Publishing Co.
Hinds, Kathryn. Everyday Life in the Roman Empire. 2009. 320p. (YA). (gr. 6-18). 42.79 (978-0-7614-4484-8(X)) Marshall Cavendish Corp.
Jacobs, Pat & MacDonald, Fiona. I Wonder Why Romans Wore Togas. 2012. (I Wonder Why Ser.). (ENG., Illus.). 32p. (J). (gr. k-3). 6.99 (978-0-7534-6795-4(X), 9780753467954, Kingfisher) Roaring Brook Pr.
Lane, Allison. The Countryside in the Roman Empire. 2016. (Life in the Roman Empire Ser.). 80p. (J). 35.64 (978-1-5026-2261-7(0)) Cavendish Square Publishing.
MacDonald, Fiona. How to Be a Roman Soldier. Hewetson, Nicholas J., illus. 2008. (How to Be Ser.). (ENG.). 32p. (J). (gr. 3-7). pap. 5.95 (978-1-4263-0169-8(3), National Geographic Children's Bks.) National Geographic Society.
Markel, Rita J. The Fall of the Roman Empire. 2007. (Pivotal Moments in History Ser.). (ENG., Illus.). 160p. (gr. 9-12). lib. bdg. 38.60 (978-0-8225-5919-1(6)) Lerner Publishing Group.
Whiting, Jim. The Life & Times of Augustus Caesar. 2005. (Biography from Ancient Civilizations Ser.). (Illus.). 48p. (J). (gr. -1-7). lib. bdg. 29.95 (978-1-58415-336-8(9)) Mitchell Lane Pubs., Inc.

ROME (ITALY)

Barber, Nicola. Rome. 2004. (Great Cities of the World Ser.). (Illus.). 48p. (gr. 5-12). lib. bdg. 31.00 (978-0-8368-5040-6(8), Gareth Stevens Secondary Library) Stevens, Gareth Publishing LLLP.
DuTemple, Lesley A. The Pantheon. 2003. (Great Building Feats Ser.). (Illus.). 96p. (J). (gr. 5-9). 27.93 (978-0-8225-0376-7(X)) Lerner Publishing Group.
Foster, Brett & Marcovitz, Hal. Rome. 2005. (Bloom's Literary Places Ser.). (Illus.). 150p. (C). (gr. 9-13). 40.00 (978-0-7910-7839-6(6), Chelsea Hse.) Facts On File, Inc.
In the City of Rome: Individual Title Six-Packs. (Literatura 2000 Ser.). (gr. 2-3). 33.00 (978-0-7635-0203-4(0)) Rigby Education.
Laidlaw, Jill A. Roman City Guidebook. 2010. (Crabtree Connections Ser.). (ENG.). 24p. (J). (gr. 3-6). (978-0-7787-9949-8(2)); pap. (978-0-7787-9971-9(9)) Crabtree Publishing Co.
Lamprell, Klay. Roma - Grandes Secretos para Pequenos Viajeros, 1 vol. 2012. (SPA & ENG.). 96p. (J). pap. 14.99 (978-84-08-10915-0(4), 103550) Lonely Planet Pubns.
Nelson, Drew. 20 Fun Facts about the Colosseum, Vol. 1. 2014. (Fun Fact File: World Wonders! Ser.). (ENG.). 32p. (J). (gr. 2-3). 25.25 (978-1-4824-0462-3(1)) Stevens, Gareth Publishing LLLP.
O'Connor, Jim. Where Is the Colosseum? O'brien, John & Groff, David, illus. 2017. (Where Is? Ser.). (ENG.). 112p. (J). (gr. 3-7). 5.99 (978-0-399-54190-2(X), Grosset & Dunlap) Penguin Young Readers Group.
Rose, Simon. Colosseum. 2012. (J). 27.13 (978-1-61913-249-8(4)); pap. 12.95 (978-1-61913-255-9(9)) Weigl Pubs., Inc.
Rudolph, Jessica. Rome. 2017. (Citified! Ser.). (ENG.). 24p. (J). (gr. k-3). 17.95 **(978-1-68402-235-9(5))** Bearport Publishing Co., Inc.
Svagerko, Keith & Svagerko, Sydney. Sydney Travels to Rome: A Guide for Kids - Let's Go to Italy Series! 2013. 128p. pap. 13.95 (978-1-62646-650-0(5)) Booklocker.com, Inc.

ROME (ITALY)—FICTION

Baccalario, Pierdomenico. The Ring of Fire. Janeczko, Leah D., tr. from ITA. 2010. (Century Ser.). (ENG., Illus.). 320p. (J). (gr. 3-7). pap. 7.99 (978-0-375-85795-9(8), Yearling) Random Hse. Children's Bks.
Bargellini, Demetrio & Stilton, Geronimo. The Coliseum Con. Cooper-McGuinness, Nanette, tr. 2009. (Geronimo Stilton Graphic Novels Ser.). (ENG., Illus.). 56p. (J). (gr. 2-6). 9.99 (978-1-59707-172-7(2), 9781597071727) Papercutz.
Bennardo, Charlotte & Zaman, Natalie. Blonde Ops. 2014. (ENG.). 288p. (YA). (gr. 7). 17.99 (978-1-250-03039-9(0), 9781250030399, St. Martin's Griffin) St. Martin's Pr.
Cerulli, Claudia. Ottavia e I Gatti Di Roma - Octavia & the Cats of Rome: A Bilingual Picture Book in Italian & English. Lätti, Leo, illus. 2013. 40p. pap. (978-1-938712-11-1(0)) Roxby Media Ltd.
Crawford, F. Marion. Cecilia, a Story of Modern Rome. 2011. 172p. pap. 12.99 (978-1-61203-071-5(8)) Bottom of the Hill Publishing.
Drake, Jennifer & Feltham, Sarah. Scotty's Postcards from Rome. 2012. (ENG., Illus.). 27p. (J). pap. 10.95 (978-0-578-10548-2(9)) Drake Feltham Publishing.
Gonzalez, Christina Diaz. Moving Target. 2015. (ENG.). 256p. (J). (gr. 3-7). 17.99 (978-0-545-77318-8(0), Scholastic Pr.) Scholastic, Inc.
—Return Fire. (Moving Target Ser.: 2). (ENG.). (J). (gr. 3-7). 2017. 224p. pap. 6.99 **(978-0-545-77323-2(7))** 2016. 352p. 17.99 (978-0-545-77322-5(9)) Scholastic, Inc. (Scholastic Pr.).
Krulik, Nancy. Follow That Furball. 2013. (Magic Bone Ser.: 3). lib. bdg. 16.00 (978-0-606-32127-3(6), Turtleback) Turtleback Bks.
Loccisano, Rina. Baby Dario Is Born. Baker, David, illus. 2012. 36p. pap. 24.95 (978-1-4560-6099-2(6)) America Star Bks.
Marsh, Carole. The Mystery at the Roman Colosseum. 2006. (Around the World in 80 Mysteries Ser.). (Illus.). 132p. (J). (gr. 4-7). 14.95 (978-0-635-06157-7(0)) Gallopade International.
Messner, Kate. Danger in Ancient Rome. McMorris, Kelley, illus. 2015. (Ranger in Time Ser.: 2). (ENG.). 160p. (J). (gr. 2-5). pap. 5.99 (978-0-545-63917-0(4), Scholastic Pr.) Scholastic, Inc.
Morris, Paula. The Eternal City. 2015. (ENG.). 304p. (J). (gr. 7). 17.99 (978-0-545-25133-4(8)) Scholastic, Inc.
Moss, Marissa. Caravaggio: Painter on the Run. Moss, Marissa, illus. 2016. (ENG., Illus.). 360p. (gr. 6). 16.95 (978-1-939547-29-3(6)) Creston Bks.
—Home, Sweet Rome. 2013. (Mira's Diary Ser.: 0). (ENG., Illus.). 192p. (J). (gr. 4-7). 12.99 (978-1-4022-6609-6(X), 9781402266096, Sourcebooks Jabberwocky) Sourcebooks, Inc.
Murdock, Catherine Gilbert. Heaven Is Paved with Oreos. (ENG.). 208p. (J). (gr. 5-7). 2015. pap. 6.99 (978-0-544-43932-0(5), HMH Books For Young Readers) 2013. 16.99 (978-0-547-62538-6(3)) Houghton Mifflin Harcourt Publishing Co.
Shecter, Vicky Alvear. Cleopatra's Moon. 2011. (ENG.). 368p. (J). (gr. 9-7). 18.99 (978-0-545-22130-6(7), Levine, Arthur A. Bks.) Scholastic, Inc.

ROOMING HOUSES

see Hotels, Motels, etc.

ROOSEVELT, ELEANOR, 1884-1962

Auch, Allison. Women Who Dared & Mujeres que se Atrevieron: 6 English, 6 Spanish Adaptations. 2011. (ENG & SPA.). (J). 97.00 net. (978-1-4108-5692-0(5)) Benchmark Education Co.

Brown, Jonatha A. Eleanor Roosevelt. 2005. (Gente que hay que conocer (People We Should Know- Spanish) Ser.). 24p. (gr. 1-4). (ENG & SPA.). pap. 8.15 (978-0-8368-4591-4(9)); (ENG & SPA.). lib. bdg. 22.00 (978-0-8368-4584-6(6)); (Illus.). pap. 8.15 (978-0-8368-4475-7(0)); (Illus.). lib. bdg. 22.00 (978-0-8368-4468-9(8)) Stevens, Gareth Publishing LLLP. (Weekly Reader Leveled Readers).

Cohen, Della. Eleanor Roosevelt: Proud & Tall. 2005. (Illus.). 16p. (J). pap. (978-0-7367-2879-9(1)) Zaner-Bloser, Inc.

Collard, Sneed B., III. Eleanor Roosevelt: Making the World a Better Place. 2008. (American Heroes Ser.). 48p. (gr. 3-18). lib. bdg. 29.93 (978-0-7614-3069-8(5), Benchmark Bks.) Marshall Cavendish Corp.

Conklin, Wendy. Eleanor Roosevelt, 1 vol. 2007. (Primary Source Readers Ser.). (ENG.). 32p. (J). (gr. 4-5). pap. 8.99 (978-0-7439-0667-8(5)) Shell Educational Publishing.

Doak, Robin S. Eleanor Roosevelt, 1 vol. 2012. (American Biographies Ser.). (ENG.). 48p. (gr. 4-6). pap. 9.95 (978-1-4329-6461-0(5), NA-h) Heinemann-Raintree.

Donnelly, Shannon. Eleanor Roosevelt. Wolek, Guy, illus. 2005. (Heroes of America Ser.). 236p. (gr. 3-8). 27.07 (978-1-59679-260-9(4), Abdo & Daughters) ABDO Publishing Co.

Eleanor Roosevelt. 2005. 12p. (gr. k-4). 2.95 (978-0-635-02622-4(8)) Gallopade International.

Feinberg, Barbara Silberdick. Eleanor Roosevelt: Everything She Could Be. 2003. (Gateway Biography Ser.: 4). (Illus.). 48p. lib. bdg. 23.90 (978-0-7613-2623-6(5), Millbrook Pr.) Lerner Publishing Group.

Fleming, Candace. Our Eleanor: A Scrapbook Look at Eleanor Roosevelt's Remarkable Life. 2005. (ENG., Illus.). 192p. (J). (gr. 4-8). 24.99 (978-0-689-86544-2(9), Atheneum Bks. for Young Readers) Simon & Schuster Children's Publishing.

Haldy, Emma E. Eleanor Roosevelt. Bane, Jeff, illus. 2016. (My Early Library: My Itty-Bitty Bio Ser.). (ENG.). 24p. (J). (gr. k-1). 28.50 (978-1-63470-483-0(5), 207663) Cherry Lake Publishing.

Hubbard-Brown, Janet. Eleanor Roosevelt: First Lady. 2009. (Women of Achievement Ser.). 128p. (gr. 6-12). 35.00 (978-1-60413-076-8(8), Chelsea Hse.) Facts On File, Inc.

Kimmelman, Leslie & Juhasz, Victor. Hot Dog! Eleanor Roosevelt Throws a Picnic. 2014. (ENG., Illus.). 40p. (J). (gr. 3-6). 16.99 (978-1-58536-830-3(X), 203013) Sleeping Bear Pr.

Klein, Dvora. Eleanor Roosevelt. 2009. pap. 13.25 (978-1-60559-059-2(2)) Hameray Publishing Group, Inc.

Kramer, Candice. Eleanor Roosevelt & Marian Anderson. 2005. (J). pap. (978-1-4108-4537-5(0)) Benchmark Education Co.

Lassieur, Allison. Eleanor Roosevelt: Activist for Social Change. 2006. (Great Life Stories Ser.). (ENG., Illus.). 112p. (J). (gr. 6-8). lib. bdg. 30.50 (978-0-531-13871-7(2), Watts, Franklin) Scholastic Library Publishing.

Lee, Sally. Eleanor Roosevelt, 1 vol. 2010. (First Ladies Ser.). (ENG.). 24p. (gr. k-1). pap. 7.29 (978-1-4296-5603-0(4)); pap. 41.70 (978-1-4296-5604-7(2)); lib. bdg. 26.65 (978-1-4296-5010-6(9)) Capstone Press of Coughlan Cos. (Pebble Plus).

MacLeod, Elizabeth. Eleanor Roosevelt: An Inspiring Life. 2006. (Snapshots: Images of People & Places in History Ser.). (ENG., Illus.). 32p. (J). (gr. 3-7). 6.95 (978-1-55337-811-2(3)) Kids Can Pr., Ltd. CAN. Dist: Hachette Bk. Group.

Marsico, Katie. Eleanor Roosevelt: First Lady & Human Rights Advocate, 1 vol. 2008. (Essential Lives Set 2 Ser.). (ENG., Illus.). 112p. (J). (gr. 6-12). lib. bdg. 35.64 (978-1-60453-040-7(5)) ABDO Publishing Co.

Massie, Elizabeth. Eleanor Roosevelt. 2016. (Spring Forward Ser.). (J). (gr. 1). (978-1-4900-9385-7(0)) Benchmark Education Co.

Mattern, Joanne. Eleanor Roosevelt, 1 vol. 2008. (First Ladies Set 1 Ser.). (ENG., Illus.). 32p. (YA). (gr. 1-4). 27.07 (978-1-59928-800-0(1)) ABDO Publishing Co.

—Eleanor Roosevelt: More Than a First Lady. (Women Who Shaped History Ser.). 24p. 2009. (gr. 2-3). 42.50 (978-1-60854-817-0(1)) 2003. (Illus.). (J). lib. bdg. 22.60 (978-0-8239-6501-4(5)) Rosen Publishing Group, Inc., The. (PowerKids Pr.).

Merchant, Peter. Eleanor Roosevelt & the Scary Basement. DiVito, Anna, illus. 2006. (Ready-To-read COFA Ser.). (ENG.). 32p. (J). (gr. k-2). pap. 3.99 (978-0-689-87205-1(4), Simon & Schuster/Paula Wiseman Bks.) Simon & Schuster/Paula Wiseman Bks.

Nabli, Dina E. L. Eleanor Roosevelt First Lady of the World. 2006. 44p. (J). lib. bdg. 15.00 (978-1-4242-0847-0(5)) Fitzgerald Bks.

Rappaport, Doreen. Eleanor, Quiet No More. Kelley, Gary, illus. 2009. (ENG.). 48p. (J). (gr. 1-3). 16.99 (978-0-7868-5141-6(4)) Hyperion Pr.

Rinaldo, Denise. Eleanor Roosevelt: With a Discussion of Respect. 2003. (Values in Action Ser.). (J). (978-1-59203-063-7(7)) Learning Challenge, Inc.

Rosenberg, Pam. Eleanor Roosevelt: First Lady, Humanitarian, & World Citizen. 2003. (Our People Ser.). (ENG., Illus.). 32p. (J). (gr. 3-6). 29.93 (978-1-59296-001-9(4), 200634) Child's World, Inc., The.

Sawyer, Kem Knapp. Eleanor Roosevelt. 2006. (DK Biography Ser.). (ENG., Illus.). 128p. (J). (gr. 5-12). pap. 6.99 (978-0-7566-1496-6(1), DK Children) Dorling Kindersley Publishing, Inc.

Shea, John M. Eleanor Roosevelt in Her Own Words. 2016. (Eyewitness to History Ser.). (ENG., Illus.). 32p. (J). (gr. 4-5). pap. 10.50 (978-1-4824-4062-1(8)) Stevens, Gareth Publishing LLLP.

Stille, Darlene R. Eleanor Roosevelt: First Lady & Civil Rights Activist, 1 vol. Sprunger, Reed, illus. 2013. (Beginner Biographies Set 2 Ser.). (ENG.). 32p. (J). (gr. -1-4). 28.50 (978-1-61641-941-7(5)) Magic Wagon.

Thompson, Gare. Who Was Eleanor Roosevelt? Wolf, Elizabeth, tr. Wolf, Elizabeth & Harrison, Nancy, illus. 2004. (Who Was? Ser.). (ENG.). 112p. (J). (gr. 3-7). pap. 5.99 (978-0-448-43509-1(8), Grosset & Dunlap) Penguin Young Readers Group.

—Who Was Eleanor Roosevelt? Wolf, Elizabeth, illus. 2004. (Who Was... ? Ser.). 106p. (gr. 3-7). 15.00 (978-0-7569-2829-2(X)) Perfection Learning Corp.

—Who Was Eleanor Roosevelt? 2004. (Who Was... ? Ser.). (gr. 3-6). lib. bdg. 16.00 (978-0-613-72563-7(8), Turtleback) Turtleback Bks.

Tieck, Sarah. Eleanor Roosevelt, 1 vol. 2010. (First Biographies Set 6 Ser.). (ENG., Illus.). 32p. (J). (gr. 1-4). 27.07 (978-1-60453-986-8(0)) ABDO Publishing Co.

Time for Kids Magazine Staff. Time for Kids: Eleanor Roosevelt: First Lady of the World. 2005. (Time for Kids Ser.). (ENG., Illus.). 48p. (J). (gr. 2-4). per. 3.99 (978-0-06-057613-4(8)) HarperCollins Pubs.

Tor, Regina, et al. Growing Toward Peace. 2011. 90p. 38.95 (978-1-258-02528-1(0)) Literary Licensing, LLC.

Winget, Mary. Eleanor Roosevelt. (Biography Ser.). (Illus.). 2005. 112p. (gr. 6-12). lib. bdg. 27.93 (978-0-8225-4985-7(9)) 2003. 48p. (J). pap. 8.95 (978-0-8225-4801-0(1), Lerner Pubns.) 2003. 48p. (J). (gr. 3-5). lib. bdg. 26.60 (978-0-8225-4675-7(2)) Lerner Publishing Group.

ROOSEVELT, ELEANOR, 1884-1962—FICTION

Coleman, Evelyn. Circle of Fire. 2009. (Mysteries Through Time Ser.). 160p. (YA). (gr. 4-8). 31.95 (978-1-60754-191-2(2)); pap. 15.25 (978-1-60754-192-9(0)) Windmill Bks.

ROOSEVELT, FRANKLIN D. (FRANKLIN DELANO), 1882-1945

Brennan, Linda Crotta. Franklin D. Roosevelt's Presidency. 2016. (Presidential Powerhouses Ser.). (ENG., Illus.). 104p. (J). (gr. 6-12). 35.99 (978-1-4677-7928-9(8)); 53.32 (978-1-4677-8549-5(0)) Lerner Publishing Group. (Lerner Pubns.).

Caplan, Jeremy. Franklin D Roosevelt A Leader in Troubled Times. 2006. 44p. (J). lib. bdg. 15.00 (978-1-4242-0848-7(3)) Fitzgerald Bks.

Cronkite, Walter, frwd. Great American Presidents. (Illus.). (gr. 4-8). pap. (978-0-7910-8048-1(X), Chelsea Hse.) Facts On File, Inc.

Edison, Erin. Franklin D. Roosevelt, 1 vol. (Presidential Biographies Ser.). (ENG.). 24p. (gr. k-1). 2014. pap. 6.29 (978-1-4765-9630-3(1), Pebble Bks.) 2012. (Illus.). lib. bdg. 26.65 (978-1-4296-8736-2(3), Pebble Plus) Capstone Press of Coughlan Cos.

Elish, Dan. Franklin Delano Roosevelt. 2008. (Presidents & Their Times Ser.). 96p. (gr. 6-18). lib. bdg. 34.21 (978-0-7614-2841-1(0), Benchmark Bks.) Marshall Cavendish Corp.

Ford, Carin T. Franklin D. Roosevelt: The 32nd President. 2006. (Heroes of American History Ser.). (Illus.). 32p. (J). (gr. 4-7). lib. bdg. 23.94 (978-0-7660-2603-2(5), Enslow Elementary) Enslow Pubs., Inc.

Fremon, David K. The Great Depression in United States History. 2014. (In United States History Ser.). 96p. (J). (gr. 5-12). 27.94 (978-0-7660-6087-6(X)); (Illus.). pap. 10.95 (978-0-7660-6088-3(8)) Enslow Pubs., Inc.

Frith, Margaret. Who Was Franklin Roosevelt? Harrison, Nancy & O'brien, John, illus. 2010. (Who Was? Ser.). (ENG.). 112p. (J). (gr. 3-7). pap. 5.99 (978-0-448-45346-0(0), Grosset & Dunlap) Penguin Young Readers Group.

Gosman, Gillian. Franklin D. Roosevelt. 2011. (Life Stories Ser.). (Illus.). 24p. (J). pap. 8.25 (978-1-4488-3182-1(2), PowerKids Pr.); (gr. 1-4). lib. bdg. 22.60 (978-1-4488-3179-1(2), PowerKids Pr.); (ENG & SPA., (gr. 1-4). lib. bdg. 22.60 (978-1-4488-3222-4(5)) Rosen Publishing Group, Inc., The.

Gregory, Josh. Franklin D. Roosevelt: The 32nd President. 2015. (First Look at America's Presidents Ser.). (ENG.). 24p. (J). (gr. -1-3). lib. bdg. 23.93 (978-1-62724-555-5(3)) Bearport Publishing Co., Inc.

Gunderson, Megan M. Franklin D. Roosevelt, 1 vol. 2009. (United States Presidents Ser.). (ENG., Illus.). 40p. (YA). (gr. 3-6). 27.07 (978-1-60453-472-6(9)) ABDO Publishing Co.

Hansen, Grace. Franklin D. Roosevelt. 2015. (Biografías de Los Presidentes de Los Estados Unidos Ser.). (SPA., Illus.). 24p. (gr. k-1). pap. 7.95 (978-1-4966-0407-1(5)) Capstone Classroom.

—Franklin Delano Roosevelt, 1 vol. 2014. (United States President Biographies Ser.). (ENG.). 24p. (J). (gr. 4-8). lib. bdg. 28.50 (978-1-62970-088-5(6)) ABDO Publishing Co.

Jurmain, Suzanne Tripp. Nice Work, Franklin! Day, Larry, illus. 2016. (ENG.). 32p. (J). (gr. k-4). 17.99 (978-0-8037-3800-3(5), Dial Bks) Penguin Young Readers Group.

Kent, Deborah. Franklin Delano Roosevelt: Nothing to Fear! 2006. (Defining Moments Ser.). (Illus.). 32p. (YA). (gr. 2-5). lib. bdg. 25.27 (978-1-59716-272-2(8)) Bearport Publishing Co., Inc.

Kesselring, Mari. How to Analyze the Works of Franklin D. Roosevelt, 1 vol. 2013. (Essential Critiques Set 4 Ser.). (ENG.). 112p. (J). (gr. 6-12). lib. bdg. 35.64 (978-1-61783-643-5(5), Essential Library) ABDO Publishing Co.

Klimo, Kate. Dog Diaries #8: Fala. Jessell, Tim, illus. 2016. (Dog Diaries). (ENG.). 160p. (J). (gr. 2-5). lib. bdg. 12.99 (978-0-553-53491-7(2), Random Hse. Bks. for Young Readers) Random Hse. Children's Bks.

—Fala. Jessell, Tim, illus. 2016. (Dog Diaries). (ENG.). 160p. (J). (gr. 2-5). pap. 7.99 (978-0-553-53490-0(4), Random Hse. Bks. for Young Readers) Random Hse. Children's Bks.

Krull, Kathleen. A Boy Named FDR: How Franklin D. Roosevelt Grew up to Change America. Johnson, Steve & Fancher, Lou, illus. (ENG.). 48p. (J). (gr. 1-4). 2016. 7.99 (978-1-101-93251-3(1), Dragonfly Bks.) 2010. 17.99 (978-0-375-85716-4(8), Knopf Bks. for Young Readers) Random Hse. Children's Bks.

Kudlinski, Kathleen. Franklin Delano Roosevelt: Champion of Freedom. Henderson, Meryl, illus. 2003. (Childhood of Famous Americans Ser.). (ENG.). 192p. (J). (gr. 3-7). pap. 6.99 (978-0-689-85745-4(4), Simon & Schuster/Paula Wiseman Bks.) Simon & Schuster/Paula Wiseman Bks.

Lawson, Barbara Spilman. FDR the Primary Sources. 2016. (Spring Forward Ser.). (J). (gr. 2). (978-1-4900-9434-2(2)) Benchmark Education Co.

Levine, Michelle & Waxman, Laura Hamilton. Franklin D. Roosevelt. 2005. (History Maker Bios Ser.). (Illus.). 48p. (J). (gr. 3-5). 26.60 (978-0-8225-1545-6(8)) Lerner Publishing Group.

Mahaney, Ian F. Franklin Delano Roosevelt. 2016. (Premier Presidents Ser.). (ENG.). 24p. (J). (gr. 1-4). 27.07 (978-1-5038-0851-5(3), 210701) Child's World, Inc., The.

Mara, Wil. Franklin D. Roosevelt. 2004. (Rookie Biographies Ser.). (ENG.). (J). 32p. (gr. 1-2). pap. 4.95 (978-0-516-25823-2(0)); (Illus.). 31p. 20.50 (978-0-516-21844-1(1)) Scholastic Library Publishing. (Children's Pr.).

Margaret, Amy. Franklin D. Roosevelt Library & Museum. (Presidential Libraries Ser.). 24p. 2009. (gr. 3-3). 42.50 (978-1-60851-483-0(8)) 2004. (Illus.). (J). lib. bdg. 22.60 (978-0-8239-6268-6(7)) Rosen Publishing Group, Inc., The. (PowerKids Pr.).

Marrin, Albert. FDR & the American Crisis. (ENG.). 336p. (YA). (gr. 7). 2016. pap. 15.99 (978-0-385-75362-3(4), Ember) 2015. (Illus.). 24.99 (978-0-385-75359-3(4), Knopf Bks. for Young Readers) 2015. (Illus.). lib. bdg. 27.99 (978-0-385-75360-9(8), Knopf Bks. for Young Readers) Random Hse. Children's Bks.

McKown, Robin. Roosevelt's Americ. 2011. 94p. 38.95 (978-1-258-10479-5(2)) Literary Licensing, LLC.

Mis, M. S. How to Draw the Life & Times of Franklin Delano Roosevelt. 2009. (Kid's Guide to Drawing the Presidents of the United States of America Ser.). 32p. (gr. 4-4). 50.50 (978-1-61511-136-7(0), PowerKids Pr.) Rosen Publishing Group, Inc., The.

Mis, Melody S. How to Draw the Life & Times of Franklin Delano Roosevelt. 2007. (Kid's Guide to Drawing the Presidents of the United States of America Ser.). (Illus.). 32p. (YA). (gr. 2-5). 26.50 (978-1-4042-3008-8(4)) Rosen Publishing Group, Inc., The.

Nardo, Don. The Presidency of Franklin D. Roosevelt: Confronting the Great Depression & World War II. 2014. (Greatest U. S. Presidents Ser.). (ENG.). 64p. (gr. 5-7). lib. bdg. 33.99 (978-0-7565-4927-5(2)) Compass Point Bks.

Panchyk, Richard. Franklin Delano Roosevelt for Kids: His Life & Times with 21 Activities. 2007. (For Kids Ser.). (ENG., Illus.). 160p. (J). (gr. 4-8). pap. 14.95 (978-1-55652-657-2(1)) Chicago Review Pr., Inc.

Rice, Earle. FDR & the New Deal. 2009. (Monumental Milestones Ser.). 48p. (YA). (gr. 4-7). lib. bdg. 29.95 (978-1-58415-828-8(X)) Mitchell Lane Pubs., Inc.

Rice, Earle, Jr. How Franklin D. Roosevelt Fought World War II. 2017. (Presidents at War Ser.). 128p. (J). (gr. 8-8). lib. bdg. 37.27 **(978-0-7660-8527-5(9))** Enslow Pubs., Inc.

Roberts, Jeremy. Franklin D. Roosevelt. 2003. (Presidential Leaders Ser.). (Illus.). 112p. (J). (gr. 6-12). lib. bdg. 29.27 (978-0-8225-0095-7(7)) Lerner Publishing Group.

Roome, Hugh. Franklin D. Roosevelt. 2017. (Rookie Biographies Ser.). (ENG.). 32p. (J). pap. 5.95 **(978-0-531-23863-9(6)**, Children's Pr.) Scholastic Library Publishing.

—Franklin D. Roosevelt: American Hero. 2017. (Rookie Biographies Ser.). (ENG.). 32p. (J). lib. bdg. 25.00 **(978-0-531-23229-3(8)**, Children's Pr.) Scholastic Library Publishing.

Saddleback Educational Publishing Staff, ed. Franklin Roosevelt, 1 vol. unabr. ed. 2008. (Graphic Biographies Ser.). (ENG., Illus.). 25p. (YA). (gr. 9-12). pap. 7.95 (978-1-59905-222-9(9)) Saddleback Educational Publishing, Inc.

Shea, John M. Franklin D. Roosevelt in His Own Words. 2014. (Eyewitness to History Ser.). (Illus.). 32p. (J). (gr. 4-6). pap. 63.00 (978-1-4824-1202-4(0)) Stevens, Gareth Publishing LLLP.

Sullivan, Anne Marie. Franklin D. Roosevelt. 2004. (Childhood of the Presidents Ser.). (Illus.). 48p. (J). (gr. 4-18). lib. bdg. 17.95 (978-1-59084-279-9(0)) Mason Crest.

Time for Kids Magazine Staff. Franklin D. Roosevelt - A Leader in Troubled Times. 2005. (Time for Kids Ser.). (ENG., Illus.). 48p. (J). (gr. 2-4). per. 3.99 (978-0-06-057615-8(4)) HarperCollins Pubs.

Van Steenwyk, Elizabeth. First Dog Fala, 1 vol. Montgomery, Michael G., illus. 2008. (ENG.). 32p. (J). (gr. k-3). 16.95 (978-1-56145-411-2(7)) Peachtree Pubs.

Vander Hook, Sue. Franklin D. Roosevelt: 32nd U. S. President, 1 vol. 2008. (Essential Lives Set 2 Ser.). (ENG., Illus.). 112p. (J). (gr. 6-12). lib. bdg. 35.64 (978-1-60453-041-4(3)) ABDO Publishing Co.

Waxman, Laura Hamilton. Franklin D. Roosevelt. 2004. (History Maker Bios Ser.). (J). pap. 6.95 (978-0-8225-2539-4(9), Lerner Pubns.) Lerner Publishing Group.

Wood, Douglas. Franklin & Winston: A Christmas That Changed the World. Moser, Barry, illus. 2011. (ENG.). 40p. (J). (gr. 1-4). 16.99 (978-0-7636-3383-7(6)) Candlewick Pr.

ROOSEVELT, FRANKLIN D. (FRANKLIN DELANO), 1882-1945—FICTION

Klimo, Kate. Fala. 2016. (Dog Diaries: 8). lib. bdg. 18.40 (978-0-606-38448-3(0)) Turtleback Bks.

Kravitz, Danny. Tommy Mcknight & the Great Election. 2016. (Presidential Politics Ser.). (ENG.). 96p. (gr. 3-4). lib. bdg. 26.65 (978-1-4965-2585-7(X), Connect) Stone Arch Bks.

Winthrop, Elizabeth. Franklin Delano Roosevelt: Letters from a Mill Town Girl. Winthrop, Elizabeth, illus. unabr. ed. 2003. (Illus.). (J). (gr. 4-7). 25.95 incl. audio (978-1-59112-213-5(9)) Live Oak Media.

ROOSEVELT, THEODORE, 1858-1919

Adler, David A. Colonel Theodore Roosevelt. 2014. (ENG., Illus.). 144p. (J). (gr. 5). 18.95 (978-0-8234-2950-9(4)) Holiday Hse., Inc.

Baker, Brynn. Roosevelt's Rough Riders: Fearless Cavalry of the Spanish-American War. 2015. (Military Heroes Ser.). (ENG., Illus.). 32p. (gr. 3-4). lib. bdg. 27.32 (978-1-4914-4840-3(7)) Capstone Press of Coughlan Cos.

Benchmark Education Co. Theodore Roosevelt & the Progressive Era. 2014. (PRIME Ser.). (J). (gr. 6-8). pap. (978-1-4509-9496-5(2)) Benchmark Education Co.

Benge, Janet & Benge, Geoff. Heroes of History - Theodore Roosevelt: An American Original. 2004. (ENG., Illus.). 208p. (YA). pap. 9.99 (978-1-932096-10-1(8)) Emerald Bks.

Berne, Emma Carlson. The Presidency of Theodore Roosevelt: Leading from the Bully Pulpit, 1 vol. 2014. (Greatest U. S. Presidents Ser.). (ENG.). 64p. (gr. 5-7). lib. bdg. 33.99 (978-0-7565-4925-1(6)) Compass Point Bks.

Britton, Tamara L. Theodore Roosevelt, 1 vol. 2009. (United States Presidents Ser.). (ENG., Illus.). 40p. (YA). (gr. 3-6). 27.07 (978-1-60453-473-3(7)) ABDO Publishing Co.

Burgan, Michael. Who Was Theodore Roosevelt? Harrison, Nancy & Hoare, Jerry, illus. 2014. (Who Was? Ser.). (ENG.). 112p. (J). (gr. 3-7). 5.99 (978-0-448-47945-3(1), Grosset & Dunlap) Penguin Young Readers Group.

—Who Was Theodore Roosevelt? 2014. (Who Was... ? Ser.). lib. bdg. 16.00 (978-0-606-35691-6(6)) Turtleback Bks.

Collins, James. Theodore Roosevelt: With Buffalo Bill & Farley's Raiders. Cox, Brian T., illus. 2006. (Time Traveler's Adventure Ser.). 56p. (J). 13.50 incl. audio compact disk (978-1-932332-60-5(X)) Toy Box Productions.

DeMauro, Lisa & Time for Kids Editors. Theodore Roosevelt: The Adventurous President. 2005. (Time for Kids Ser.). (ENG., Illus.). 48p. (J). (gr. 2-4). 15.99 (978-0-06-057606-6(5)); pap. 3.99 (978-0-06-057604-2(9)) HarperCollins Pubs.

Elish, Dan. Theodore Roosevelt. 2007. (Presidents & Their Times Ser.). (Illus.). 96p. (gr. 6-7). lib. bdg. 34.21 (978-0-7614-2429-1(6), Benchmark Bks.) Marshall Cavendish Corp.

Fitzpatrick, Brad. Theodore Roosevelt. 2011. (Conservation Heroes Ser.). (Illus.). 144p. (YA). (gr. 6-12). 35.00 (978-1-60413-948-8(X), Chelsea Hse.) Facts On File, Inc.

Garraty, John. Teddy Roosevelt: American Rough Rider. 2017. (Young Voyageur Ser.). (ENG., Illus.). 176p. (YA). (gr. 4-8). pap. 12.99 **(978-0-7603-5437-7(5)**, Voyageur Pr.) Quarto Publishing Group USA.

Gayle, Sharon Shavers & Gayle, Sharon. Teddy Roosevelt: The People's President. Dacey, Bob & Bandelin, Debra, trs. Dacey, Bob & Bandelin, Debra, illus. 2004. (Ready-To-read SOFA Ser.). (ENG.). 32p. (J). (gr. 1-3). pap. 3.99 (978-0-689-85825-3(6), Simon Spotlight) Simon Spotlight.

Gregory, Josh. Theodore Roosevelt: The 26th President. 2015. (First Look at America's Presidents Ser.). (ENG.). 24p. (J). (gr. -1-3). lib. bdg. 23.93 (978-1-62724-557-9(X)) Bearport Publishing Co., Inc.

Harness, Cheryl. The Remarkable Rough-Riding Life of Theodore Roosevelt & the Rise of Empire America. 2007. (Cheryl Harness Histories Ser.). (ENG., Illus.). 144p. (J). (gr. 3-7). 16.95 (978-1-4263-0008-0(5)); (gr. 4-7). lib. bdg. 25.90 (978-1-4263-0009-7(3)) National Geographic Society. (National Geographic Children's Bks.).

Hollihan, Kerrie Logan. Theodore Roosevelt for Kids: His Life & Times, 21 Activities. 2010. (For Kids Ser.). (ENG., Illus.). 144p. (J). (gr. 4-18). pap. 16.95 (978-1-55652-955-9(4)) Chicago Review Pr., Inc.

Jackson, Ellen, ed. My Tour of Europe: By Teddy Roosevelt, Age 10. Brighton, Catherine, illus. 2003. 40p. 14.95 (978-0-7613-1998-6(0), Millbrook Pr.) Lerner Publishing Group.

Kay, Helen. The First Teddy Bear. Detwiler, Susan, illus. 2nd enl. ed. 2005. 38p. (J). (gr. -1-3). 18.95 (978-0-88045-154-3(8)); per. 11.95 (978-0-88045-153-6(X)) Stemmer Hse. Pubs.

Keating, Frank. Theodore. Wimmer, Mike, illus. 2006. (Mount Rushmore Presidential Ser.). (ENG.). 32p. (J). (gr. 1-4). 17.99 (978-0-689-86532-9(5), Simon & Schuster/Paula Wiseman Bks.) Simon & Schuster/Paula Wiseman Bks.

Kerley, Barbara. What to Do about Alice? 2011. (J). (gr. 2-5). 18.95 (978-0-545-29821-6(0)); 29.95 (978-0-545-29679-3(X)) Weston Woods Studios, Inc.

—What to Do about Alice? How Alice Roosevelt Broke the Rules, Charmed the World, & Drove Her Father Teddy Crazy! Fotheringham, Edwin, illus. 2008. (ENG.). 48p. (J). (gr. 2-5). 16.99 (978-0-439-92231-9(3), Scholastic Pr.) Scholastic, Inc.

Mara, Wil. Theodore Roosevelt. 2007. (Rookie Biographies Ser.). (Illus.). 32p. (J). (gr. 1-2). pap. 4.95 (978-0-516-27304-4(3), Children's Pr.) Scholastic Library Publishing.

Marcovitz, Hal. Theodore Roosevelt. 2004. (Childhood of the Presidents Ser.). (Illus.). 48p. (J). (gr. 4-18). lib. bdg. 17.95 (978-1-59084-278-2(2)) Mason Crest.

Marsh, Carole. Theodore Roosevelt. 2004. 12p. (gr. k-4). 2.95 (978-0-635-02362-9(8)) Gallopade International.

McGowen, Tom. The Spanish-American War & Teddy Roosevelt in American History. 2003. (In American History Ser.). (Illus.). 128p. (J). lib. bdg. 26.60 (978-0-7660-1987-4(X)) Enslow Pubs., Inc.

McKay, Sindy. We Both Read-President Theodore Roosevelt. Gampert, John, illus. 2006. (We Both Read Ser.). 44p. (J). (gr. 1-5). 7.99 (978-1-891327-67-4(4)) Treasure Bay, Inc.

McPherson, Stephanie Sammartino. Theodore Roosevelt. 2005. (Presidential Leaders Ser.). (Illus.). 112p. (J). 29.27 (978-0-8225-0999-8(7), Lerner Pubns.) Lerner Publishing Group.

National Geographic Learning Staff. The Mountain Man & the President. 2010. (ENG., Illus.). 48p. (C). (gr. 2-8). pap. 18.95 (978-0-8114-8064-2(X)) National Geographic School Publishing, Inc.

Olson, Nathan, et al. Theodore Roosevelt: Bear of a President, 1 vol. Martin, Cynthia et al, illus. 2007. (Graphic Biographies Ser.). (ENG.). 32p. (gr. 3-4). per. 8.10 (978-0-7368-7901-9(3), 1264944, Graphic Library) Capstone Press of Coughlan Cos.

Rappaport, Doreen. To Dare Mighty Things: The Life of Theodore Roosevelt. Payne, C. F., illus. 2013. (ENG.). 48p. (J). (gr. 1-3). 17.99 (978-1-4231-2488-7(X)) Hyperion Pr.

Rice, Dona Herweck. Teedie: The Boy Who Would Be President. 2015. (Building Fluency Through Reader's Theater Ser.). (ENG., Illus.). 24p. (gr. 1-2). pap. 6.99 (978-1-4938-1513-5(X)) Teacher Created Materials, Inc.

Rosenstock, Barb. The Camping Trip That Changed America: Theodore Roosevelt, John Muir, & Our National Parks. Gerstein, Mordecai, illus. 2012. (ENG.). 32p. (J). (gr. 1-3). 17.99 (978-0-8037-3710-5(6), Dial Bks) Penguin Young Readers Group.

Ruffin, Frances E. How to Draw the Life & Times of Theodore Roosevelt. (Kid's Guide to Drawing the Presidents of the United States of America Ser.). 32p. 2009. (gr. 4-4). 50.50 (978-1-61511-160-2(3), PowerKids Pr.) 2007. (Illus.). (YA). (gr. 2-5). 26.50 (978-1-4042-3002-6(5)) Rosen Publishing Group, Inc., The.

Schwartz, Eric. A World Contender. 2006. (How America Became America Ser.). (Illus.). 96p. (YA). lib. bdg. 22.95 *(978-1-59084-911-8(6))* Mason Crest.

Schwartz, Heather E. Theodore Roosevelt's Presidency. 2016. (Presidential Powerhouses Ser.). (ENG., Illus.). 104p. (J). (gr. 6-12). 35.99 *(978-1-4677-7930-2(X))*; 53.32 *(978-1-4677-8601-0(2))* Lerner Publishing Group. (Lerner Pubns.).

Seiple, Samantha. Death on the River of Doubt: Theodore Roosevelt's Amazon Adventure. 2017. (ENG.). 240p. (J). (gr. 7). 17.99 *(978-0-545-70916-3(4),* Scholastic Pr.) Scholastic, Inc.

Shattuck, Randy. Theodore Roosevelt. 2016. lib. bdg. *(978-1-68048-529-5(6))* Rosen Publishing Group, Inc., The.

Swain, Gwenyth. Theodore Roosevelt. 2004. (History Maker Bios Ser.). (J). pap. 8.95 *(978-0-8225-2542-4(9))*; (ENG., Illus.). 48p. (gr. 3-6). 27.93 *(978-0-8225-1548-7(2))* Lerner Publishing Group. (Lerner Pubns.).

Uhl, Xina M. Theodore Roosevelt. 2016. (Premier Presidents Ser.). (ENG.). 24p. (J). (gr. 1-4). 27.07 *(978-1-5038-0876-8(9),* 210726) Child's World, Inc., The.

Wade, Mary Dodson. Amazing President Theodore Roosevelt. (Amazing Americans Ser.). (Illus.). 24p. (J). 2013. (gr. k-3). pap. 7.95 *(978-0-7660-5979-5(0),* Enslow Elementary) 2009. (gr. 1-3). lib. bdg. 22.60 *(978-0-7660-3284-2(1))* Enslow Pubs., Inc.

Wadsworth, Ginger. Camping with the President. Dugan, Karen, illus. 2009. (ENG.). 32p. (J). (gr. 4-18). 16.95 *(978-1-59078-497-6(9),* Calkins Creek) Boyds Mills Pr.

Weston Woods Staff, creator. What to Do about Alice? 2011. 38.75 *(978-0-545-29822-3(9))* Weston Woods Studios, Inc.

ROOSEVELT, THEODORE, 1858-1919—FICTION

Kennedy Center Staff. Teddy Roosevelt & the Treasure of Ursa Major. Hoyt, Ard, illus. 2011. (ENG.). 128p. (J). (gr. 2-5). pap. 5.99 *(978-1-4169-4860-5(0),* Simon & Schuster Bks. For Young Readers) Simon & Schuster Bks. For Young Readers.

Kimmelman, Leslie. Mind Your Manners, Alice Roosevelt!, 1 vol. Gustavson, Adam, illus. 2009. (ENG.). 32p. (J). (gr. -1-3). 16.95 *(978-1-56145-492-1(3))* Peachtree Pubs.

Lalicki, Tom. Shots at Sea: A Houdini & Nate Mystery. 2011. (Houdini & Nate Mysteries Ser.). 224p. (J). pap. 6.99 *(978-0-312-65920-2(2))* Square Fish.

Mills, Claudia. Being Teddy Roosevelt. Alley, R. W., illus. 2012. (ENG.). 112p. (J). (gr. 2-5). pap. 8.99 *(978-0-312-64018-7(8),* 9780312640187) Square Fish.

ROOSEVELT FAMILY

Panchyk, Richard. Franklin Delano Roosevelt for Kids: His Life & Times with 21 Activities. 2007. (For Kids Ser.). (ENG., Illus.). 160p. (J). (gr. 4-8). pap. 14.95 *(978-1-55652-657-2(1))* Chicago Review Pr., Inc.

ROOSEVELT FAMILY—FICTION

Buckley, Anne. The Day Mrs. Roosevelt Came to Town. 2003. 186p. (YA). (gr. 9-18). per. 9.99 *(978-0-88092-458-0(6))* Royal Fireworks Publishing Co.

ROOSTERS

DaSilva, Barbara, ed. Roosters. 2011. (Applewood's Pictorial America Ser.). (ENG., Illus.). 56p. pap. 9.95 *(978-1-60889-011-8(2))* Applewood Bks.

ROOSTERS—FICTION

Angelastro, Yvonne. The Four Lost Chicks. 2013. 28p. pap. 16.99 *(978-1-4808-0292-6(1))* Archway Publishing.

Auch, Mary Jane. Poultrygeist. Jane, Mary & Auch, Herm, illus. 2004. (ENG.). 32p. (J). (gr. k-3). reprint ed. 6.95 *(978-0-8234-1876-3(6))* Holiday Hse., Inc.

Bell, Anthea, ed. & tr. The Bremen Town Musicians. Bell, Anthea, tr. Lai, Hsin-Shih, illus. 2007. 32p. (J). (gr. -1-3). 17.95 *(978-0-88010-583-5(6),* Bell Pond Bks.) SteinerBooks, Inc.

Black, Michael Ian. Cock-a-Doodle-Doo-Bop. Myers, Matthew, illus. 2015. (ENG.). 40p. (J). (gr. -1-3). 17.99 *(978-1-4424-9510-4(3),* Simon & Schuster Bks. For Young Readers) Simon & Schuster Bks. For Young Readers.

Bobo, W. L. Chickendoodle! Where Are You? 2011. 28p. pap. 21.95 *(978-1-4269-5742-0(4))* Trafford Publishing.

Carle, Eric. Rooster Is off to See the World. 2013. (Eric Carle Ready-To-Read Ser.). lib. bdg. 13.55 *(978-0-606-32063-4(6),* Turtleback) Turtleback Bks.

Caruso, Barbara, reader. Elvis the Rooster Almost Goes to Heaven, 4 bks., Set. unabr. ed. 2006. (Readalongs for Beginning Readers Ser.). (Illus.). (J). (gr. -1-3). pap. 29.95 incl. audio *(978-1-59519-684-2(6))*; pap. 31.95 incl. audio compact disk *(978-1-59519-685-9(4))* Live Oak Media.

Cazet, Denys. Elvis the Rooster & the Magic Words. Cazet, Denys, illus. 2004. (I Can Read Bks.). (ENG., Illus.). 48p. (J). (gr. k-3). 15.99 *(978-0-06-000509-2(2))* HarperCollins Pubs.

—Elvis the Rooster & the Magic Words, 4 bks., Set. unabr. ed. 2006. (Readalongs for Beginning Readers Ser.). (J). (gr. -1-3). pap. 31.95 incl. audio compact disk *(978-1-59519-693-4(5))*; (Illus.). pap. 29.95 incl. audio *(978-1-59519-692-7(7))* Live Oak Media.

Chin, Oliver. Year of the Rooster. Calle, Juan, illus. 2016. (Tales from the Chinese Zodiac Ser.: 12). (ENG.). 40p. (J). (gr. -1). 15.95 *(978-1-59702-125-8(3))* Immedium.

Correa, Shan. Gaff, 1 vol. 2010. (ENG.). 224p. (J). (gr. 3-7). 15.95 *(978-1-56145-526-3(1),* Peachtree Junior) Peachtree Pubs.

Cox, Judy. The Secret Chicken Society. Haley, Amanda, illus. (ENG.). 96p. (J). 2013. pap. 5.99 *(978-0-8234-2765-9(X))* 2012. 15.95 *(978-0-8234-2372-9(7))* Holiday Hse., Inc.

Crummel, Susan Stevens & Stevens, Janet. Cook-a-Doodle-Doo! 2005. (ENG., Illus.). 48p. (J). (gr. -1-3). reprint ed. pap. 7.99 *(978-0-15-205658-2(0))* Houghton Mifflin Harcourt Publishing Co.

Davies, Rob. Henhouse High Jinx: Mr. Stevens & Friends. 2013. 176p. 21.99 *(978-1-4669-9492-8(4))*; pap. 11.99 *(978-1-4669-9491-1(6))* Trafford Publishing.

Davis, Peg. After the Storm: A Napoleon & Marigold Adventure. 2009. 40p. pap. 16.50 *(978-1-60860-222-3(2),* Eloquent Bks.) Strategic Book Publishing & Rights Agency (SBPRA).

—Napoleon & Marigold. 2008. 24p. pap. 13.50 *(978-1-60693-114-1(8),* Eloquent Bks.) Strategic Book Publishing & Rights Agency (SBPRA).

De Anda, Diane. Kikiriki / Quiquiriquí. Hernández, Karina, tr. from ENG. Lechón, Daniel, illus. 2004. (ENG & SPA.). 32p. 16.95 *(978-1-55885-382-9(0),* Piñata Books) Arte Publico Pr.

Deedy, Carmen Agra. The Rooster Who Would Not Be Quiet! Yelchin, Eugene, illus. 2017. (ENG.). 48p. (J). (gr. -1-3). 17.99 *(978-0-545-72288-9(8),* Scholastic Pr.) Scholastic, Inc.

Degman, Lori. Cock-A-Doodle-Oops! Zemke, Deborah, illus. 2014. (ENG.). 36p. (J). (gr. -1-4). 16.95 *(978-1-939547-07-1(5))* Creston Bks.

Dempsey, Kristy. Surfer Chick. Cole, Henry, illus. 2012. (ENG.). 32p. (J). (gr. -1-k). 16.95 *(978-1-4197-0188-7(6),* Abrams Bks. for Young Readers) Abrams, Inc.

Doudna, Kelly. El Peinado Del Gallo, 1 vol. Haberstroh, Anne, illus. 2007. (Cuentos de Animales Ser.).Tr. of Rooster Combs. (SPA & ENG.). 24p. (J). (gr. k-3). lib. bdg. 24.21 *(978-1-59928-663-1(7),* SandCastle) ABDO Publishing Co.

—Rooster Combs, 1 vol. Haberstroh, Anne, illus. 2006. (Animal Tales Ser.). 24p. (J). (gr. k-3). (ENG.). lib. bdg. 24.21 *(978-1-59679-965-3(X),* SandCastle); pap. 48.42 *(978-1-59679-966-0(8))* ABDO Publishing Co.

Edwards, Pamela Duncan. The Mixed-up Rooster. Lloyd, Megan, illus. 2006. 32p. (J). (gr. -1-1). 15.99 *(978-0-06-028999-7(6),* Tegen, Katherine Bks) HarperCollins Pubs.

—The Wrong Way Rooster. Date not set. 32p. (J). (gr. -1-1). pap. 5.99 *(978-0-06-443689-2(6))* HarperCollins Pubs.

Eggleton, Jill. Rabbit & Rooster's Ride: 3-in-1 Package. Taylor, Clive, illus. (Sails Literacy Ser.). 24p. (gr. k-18). 57.00 *(978-0-7578-8617-1(5))* Rigby Education.

—Rabbit & Rooster's Ride: 6 Small Books. Taylor, Clive, illus. (Sails Literacy Ser.). 24p. (gr. k-18). 25.00 *(978-0-7578-7727-8(3))* Rigby Education.

—Rabbit & Rooster's Ride: Big Book Only. Taylor, Clive, illus. (Sails Literacy Ser.). 24p. (gr. k-18). 27.00 *(978-0-7578-6200-7(4))* Rigby Education.

Ekholm, Jan. The Little Red Rascal. 2011. 88p. pap. 30.28 *(978-1-4567-9501-6(5))* AuthorHouse.

Finch, Mary & Messing, Debra. The Little Red Hen. Slater, Kate, illus. 2013. (ENG.). 32p. (J). pap. 7.99 *(978-1-78285-041-0(4))*; (gr. -1-2). 16.99 *(978-1-84686-575-6(1))*; (gr. -1-2). 9.99 *(978-1-84686-751-4(7))* Barefoot Bks., Inc.

Frazier, Laurence. Cranky the Rooster. 2011. 24p. pap. 12.79 *(978-1-4567-6258-2(3))* AuthorHouse.

Freddie. The Rooster's Story. 2009. 28p. pap. 13.99 *(978-1-4389-8827-6(3))* AuthorHouse.

Garrett, Cindy Crawford. Life's Lessons with the Silly Animals Out on the Ranch: What Is Wrong with Bob the Rooster? 2013. 24p. pap. 17.99 *(978-1-4817-0574-5(1))* AuthorHouse.

Giacomucci, Carol. A New Home. 2006. 23p. pap. 10.95 *(978-0-7414-3498-2(9))* Infinity Publishing.

Giles, Lisa. The Adventures of Sunny the Bunny: The Easter Egg Hunt. 2010. 20p. 10.49 *(978-1-4520-1842-3(1))* AuthorHouse.

Green, Jonathan, illus. Amadeus, the Leghorn Rooster. 2004. (J). 17.95 *(978-0-87844-174-7(3))* Sandlapper Publishing Co., Inc.

Grimm, Jacob & Grimm, Wilhelm K. Hut in the Forest, 1 vol. Lawson, Polly, tr. from GER. Stietencron, Bettina, illus. 2007. (Grimm's Fairy Tales Ser.). (ENG.). 28p. (J). *(978-0-86315-615-1(0))* Floris Bks.

Helsel, Sandra. Pokey & the Rooster. Snyder, Joe, illus. 2009. 28p. pap. 9.95 *(978-0-9818488-1-5(8))* Ajoyin Publishing, Inc.

Hillenbrand, Will. Cock-a-Doodle Christmas!, 0 vols. 2010. (ENG.). 32p. (J). (gr. -1-2). pap. 6.99 *(978-0-7614-5718-3(6),* 9780761457183, Amazon Children's Publishing) Amazon Publishing.

Jones, Nancy. The Grandpaws. 2005. 57p. pap. 16.95 *(978-1-4137-4778-2(7))* America Star Bks.

Kelly, Thomas E. The Fox & the Young Rooster. Ward, Kelly, illus. 2011. 44p. pap. 24.95 *(978-1-4626-0343-5(2))* America Star Bks.

Kline, Trish & Donev, Mary. Hoops in the Coop: KA Reader 7. 2007. (Illus.). 32p. (J). per. 20.00 *(978-1-934307-00-7(9))* Ghost Hunter Productions.

Krystosek, Richard. Chicken Scratch. 2013. 36p. pap. 24.95 *(978-1-63000-536-8(3))* America Star Bks.

Lambert, Megan Dowd. A Crow of His Own. Costello, David & Costello, David Hyde, illus. 2015. (ENG.). 32p. (J). (gr. -1-1). lib. bdg. 16.95 *(978-1-58089-447-0(X))* Charlesbridge Publishing, Inc.

—A Crow of His Own. Costello, David, illus. 2014. (J). pap. *(978-1-58089-448-7(8))* Charlesbridge Publishing, Inc.

Landstrom, Lena. Four Hens & a Rooster. Sandin, Joan, tr. from SWE. Landstrom, Olof, illus. 2005. 28p. (J). (gr. -1-3). 16.00 *(978-91-29-66336-5(9))* R & S Bks. SWE. Dist: Macmillan.

Lavette, Lavaille. The Adventures of Roopster Roux: That's Not Punny, 1 vol. Nguyen, Duke, ed. Kuon, Vuthy, illus. 2007. (Roupster Roux Ser.: Vol. 5). (ENG.). 32p. (J). (gr. 3-7). 16.95 *(978-1-58980-483-8(X))* Pelican Publishing Co., Inc.

—Adventures of Roopster Roux: You're So Victor Vain, 1 vol. Kuon, Vuthy, illus. 2007. (Roupster Roux Ser.). (ENG.). 32p. (J). (gr. 3-7). 16.95 *(978-1-58980-484-5(8))* Pelican Publishing Co., Inc.

Levy, Janice. Gonzalo Grabs the Good Life. Slavin, Bill, illus. 2009. (ENG.). 34p. (J). (gr. k-4). 17.50 *(978-0-8028-5326-8(5),* Eerdmans Bks For Young Readers) Eerdmans, William B. Publishing Co.

Meadows, Daisy. Crystal the Snow Fairy. Ripper, Georgie, illus. 2006. (Weather Fairies Ser.: 1). (ENG.). 80p. (Orig.). (J). (gr. -1-3). mass mkt. 4.99 *(978-0-439-81387-7(5),* Scholastic Paperbacks) Scholastic, Inc.

Ocker, Christa Holder. A Rooster Named Lorenz. 2003. (J). per. *(978-1-59196-284-7(6))* Instant Pub.

Okereke, Laurence. Barry & Big Joe. 2007. (ENG., Illus.). 20p. (J). *(978-0-9795739-0-3(4))* Dion's Pubn.

Pearson, Tracey Campbell. Bob. Pearson, Tracey Campbell, illus. 2006. (ENG., Illus.). 32p. (J). (gr. -1-1). reprint ed. 8.99 *(978-0-374-40871-8(8),* 9780374408718) Square Fish.

Robert, Brenda. Rooster Went A' Walkin' 2009. 28p. pap. 13.99 *(978-1-4389-3414-3(9))* AuthorHouse.

Rodriguez, Béatrice. Rooster's Revenge. 2011. (Stories Without Words Ser.). (ENG., Illus.). 32p. (J). (gr. -1). 14.95 *(978-1-59270-112-4(4))* Enchanted Lion Bks., LLC.

Roller, Ellen. Trading Places. Shea, Gary, illus. 2008. (J). pap. 11.95 *(978-0-9792645-0-4(2))* Edgewood Publishing, LLC.

Sattler, Jennifer. Chick 'n' Pug. 2013. (ENG., Illus.). 30p. (J). (gr. -1-1). bds. 7.99 *(978-1-61963-078-9(8),* 9781619630789, Bloomsbury USA Childrens) Bloomsbury Publishing USA.

—A Chick 'n' Pug Christmas. 2014. (ENG., Illus.). 32p. (J). (gr. -1-1). 16.99 *(978-1-59990-602-7(3),* 9781599906027, Bloomsbury USA Childrens) Bloomsbury Publishing USA.

—Chick 'n' Pug Meet the Dude. (ENG., Illus.). (J). (gr. -1-1). 2014. 30p. bds. 7.99 *(978-1-61963-402-2(3),* 9781619634022) 2013. 32p. 17.89 *(978-1-59990-760-4(7),* 9781599907604) 2013. 32p. 16.99 *(978-1-59990-600-3(7),* 9781599906003) Bloomsbury Publishing USA. (Bloomsbury USA Childrens).

—Chick 'n' Pug: the Love Pug. 2015. (ENG., Illus.). 32p. (J). (gr. -1-1). 16.99 *(978-1-61963-672-9(7),* 9781619636729, Bloomsbury USA Childrens) Bloomsbury Publishing USA.

Sattler, Jennifer Gordon. Chick 'n' Pug. 2010. (ENG., Illus.). 32p. (J). (gr. -1-1). 14.99 *(978-1-59990-534-1(5),* 9781599905341, Bloomsbury USA Childrens) Bloomsbury Publishing USA.

Sattler, Jennifer Gordon, illus. A Chick 'n' Pug Christmas. 2014. (J). *(978-1-61963-463-3(5))* Bloomsbury Pr.

Scillian, Devin. Brewster the Rooster. White, Lee, illus. rev. ed. 2007. (ENG.). 32p. (J). (gr. 3-7). 16.95 *(978-1-58536-311-7(1))* Sleeping Bear Pr.

Sommer, Carl. Proud Rooster & Little Hen. Budwine, Greg, illus. 2014. (J). pap. *(978-1-57537-964-7(3))* Advance Publishing, Inc.

—Proud Rooster & Little Hen. 2003. (Another Sommer-Time Story Ser.). (Illus.). 48p. (J). (gr. 1-4). 16.95 incl. audio *(978-1-57537-559-5(1))* Advance Publishing, Inc.

—Proud Rooster & Little Hen. Budwine, Greg, illus. 2003. (Another Sommer-Time Story Ser.). (ENG.). 48p. (J). (gr. 1-4). 16.95 incl. audio compact disk *(978-1-57537-510-6(9))* Advance Publishing, Inc.

—Proud Rooster & Little Hen(Gallito Orgulloso y Gallinita) Budwine, Greg, illus. 2009. (Another Sommer-Time Story Bilingual Ser.). (SPA & ENG.). 48p. (J). 16.95 *(978-1-57537-164-1(2))* Advance Publishing, Inc.

Stewart, Grandmother. George the Rooster Goes to the Apple Orchard. 2007. (ENG., Illus.). 28p. (J). lib. bdg. 14.95 *(978-0-9792135-0-2(9))* Rooster Pubns.

Stewart, Wilson N. Cock-a-Doodle-Who? 2007. (ENG., Illus.). 6p. (J). 15.99 *(978-0-7868-0826-7(8))* Hyperion Bks. for Children.

Stoeke, Janet Morgan. The Loopy Coop Hens. 2013. (Penguin Young Readers Level 2 Ser.). lib. bdg. 13.55 *(978-0-606-28751-7(5),* Turtleback) Turtleback Bks.

Sutton, Jennifer. Little Dude's Big Day. 2012. 60p. pap. 18.95 *(978-1-60976-835-5(3),* Strategic Bk. Publishing) Strategic Book Publishing & Rights Agency (SBPRA).

Terry, Will, illus. Little Rooster's Diamond Button. 2013. (ENG.). 32p. (J). (gr. -1-3). pap. 7.99 *(978-0-8075-4645-1(3))* Whitman, Albert & Co.

Toepperwein, Emilie & Toepperwein, Fritz A. Chinto, the Chaparral Cock. (J). (gr. 4-7). 2.95 *(978-0-910722-04-9(8))* Highland Pr.

Tulien, Sean. The Not-So-Evil Wizard. Cunyat, Pol, illus. 2016. (Thud & Blunder Ser.). (ENG.). 56p. (gr. 2-4). pap. 4.95 *(978-1-4965-3225-1(2))*; lib. bdg. 23.99 *(978-1-4965-3221-3(X))* Stone Arch Bks.

Underwood, Barbara. Brewster Rooster. DeWitt, Robin & Dewitt Grush, Patricia, illus. 2006.Tr. of Carla's New Glasses. (ENG.). 32p. (gr. 1-2). pap. 9.95 *(978-1-57874-108-3(4),* Kaeden Bks.) Kaeden Corp.

Villasenor, Victor. The Stranger & the Red Rooster: El Forastero y el Gallo Rojo. Ventura, Gabriela Baeza, tr. Jara, Jose, illus. 2005. (ENG & SPA.). 26p. (J). (gr. -1-2). 16.95 *(978-1-55885-420-8(7),* Piñata Books) Arte Publico Pr.

Vosloo, Isak. Rooster Lost His Crow: Vossie's Children Book Series. 2012. (Illus.). 32p. pap. 21.35 *(978-1-4678-9679-5(9))* AuthorHouse.

—Rooster Verloor Sy Kraai: 'Oom Vossie Vertel ... ' Kinderboekreeks. 2012. 32p. pap. 21.35 *(978-1-4678-9095-3(2))* AuthorHouse.

Ward, Helen, illus. & retold by. The Rooster & the Fox. Ward, Helen, retold by. 2003. 40p. (J). (gr. k-3). 16.95 *(978-0-7613-1846-0(1),* First Avenue Editions) Lerner Publishing Group.

Ward, Helen & Ward, Helen. The Rooster & the Fox. 2003. (Single Titles Ser.: Vol. 3). 40p. (gr. k-4). lib. bdg. 24.90 *(978-0-7613-2920-6(X),* Millbrook Pr.) Lerner Publishing Group.

Welling, Peter J. Michael le Soufflé & the April Fool, 1 vol. Welling, Peter J., illus. 2003. (ENG., Illus.). 32p. (J). (gr. k-3). 16.99 *(978-1-58980-105-9(9))* Pelican Publishing Co., Inc.

Ziskind, Hélio & Duchesne, Christiane. Le Géant de la Forêt: Un Voyage Musical. Pratt, Pierre, illus. 2014. (FRE.). 48p. (J). (gr. k-2). 16.95 *(978-2-923163-36-9(2))* La Montagne Secrete CAN. Dist: Independent Pubs. Group.

ROOTS (BOTANY)

Aloian, Molly. What Are Bulbs & Roots? 2012. (ENG., Illus.). 24p. (J). *(978-0-7787-4220-3(2))*; pap. *(978-0-7787-4225-8(3))* Crabtree Publishing Co.

Bishop, Celeste. ¿Por Qué Las Plantas Tienen Raíces? / Why Do Plants Have Roots?, 01 vols., 1. 2016. (Partes de la Planta / Plant Parts Ser.). (ENG & SPA., Illus.). 24p. (J). 23.60 *(978-1-5081-4742-8(6),* PowerKids Pr.) Rosen Publishing Group, Inc., The.

—Why Do Plants Have Roots?, 01 vols., 1. 2016. (Plant Parts Ser.). (ENG., Illus.). 24p. (J). pap. 8.25 *(978-1-5081-4225-6(4),* PowerKids Pr.) Rosen Publishing Group, Inc., The.

Blackaby, Susan. Plant Plumbing: A Book about Roots & Stems. DeLage, Charlene, illus. 2003. (Growing Things Ser.). (ENG.). 24p. (gr. -1-2). 26.65 *(978-1-4048-0109-7(X))*; per. 8.95 *(978-1-4048-0385-5(8))* Picture Window Bks.

Bodach, Vijaya K. Roots [Scholastic]. 2010. (Plant Parts Ser.). 24p. pap. 0.52 *(978-1-4296-5059-5(1),* Pebble Plus) Capstone Press of Coughlan Cos.

Bodach, Vijaya Khisty. Roots. 2016. (Plant Parts Ser.). (ENG.). 24p. (gr. k-1). pap. 7.29 *(978-1-5157-4245-6(8),* Pebble Plus) Capstone Press of Coughlan Cos.

Coldwell, Lamar. The Roots of a Tree. 2016. (Rosen REAL Readers: STEM & STEAM Collection). 8p. (gr. 1-k). pap. 5.46 *(978-1-5081-2383-5(7),* Rosen Classroom) Rosen Publishing Group, Inc., The.

Farndon, John. Roots. 2006. (World of Plants (Blackbirch) Ser.). (ENG., Illus.). 24p. (J). (gr. 2-6). lib. bdg. 26.65 *(978-1-4103-0421-6(3),* Blackbirch Pr., Inc.) Cengage Gale.

Higgins, Nadia. Experiment with a Plant's Roots. 2015. (Lightning Bolt Books (tm) — Plant Experiments Ser.). (ENG., Illus.). 32p. (gr. k-2). pap. 8.99 *(978-1-4677-6073-7(0))*; lib. bdg. 26.65 *(978-1-4677-5729-4(2))* Lerner Publishing Group. (Lerner Pubns.).

Kudlinski, Kathleen V. What Do Roots Do? Schuppert, David, illus. (ENG.). 32p. (J). (gr. k-3). 2007. pap. 7.95 *(978-1-55971-980-3(X))* 2005. 15.95 *(978-1-55971-896-7(X))* Cooper Square Publishing Llc.

Mitchell, Melanie S. Roots. 2004. (First Step Nonfiction - Parts of Plants Ser.). (ENG., Illus.). 8p. (gr. -1-1). pap. 4.95 *(978-0-8225-3919-3(5),* Lerner Pubns.) Lerner Publishing Group.

Owen, Ruth. What Do Roots, Stems, Leaves, & Flowers Do? 2014. (World of Plants Ser.). 32p. (J). (gr. 2-5). lib. bdg. 26.25 *(978-1-4777-7137-2(9),* PowerKids Pr.) Rosen Publishing Group, Inc., The.

Sterling, Kristin. Exploring Roots. 2011. (First Step Nonfiction / Let's Look at Plants Ser.). pap. 33.92 *(978-0-7613-8616-2(5))*; (Illus.). 23p. lib. bdg. 21.27 *(978-0-7613-5781-0(5))*; (ENG.). 24p. pap. 6.95 *(978-0-7613-7834-1(0))* Lerner Publishing Group.

Throp, Claire. All about Roots. (All about Plants Ser.). (ENG.). 24p. (gr. -1-1). 2016. pap. 5.99 *(978-1-4846-3848-4(4))* 2014. 22.65 *(978-1-4846-0508-0(X))* Heinemann-Raintree. (Acorn).

Waldron, Melanie. Roots, 1 vol. 2014. (Plant Parts Ser.). (ENG., Illus.). 32p. (gr. 2-4). pap. 8.95 *(978-1-4109-6281-2(4))*; lib. bdg. 30.65 *(978-1-4109-5422-0(6))* Heinemann-Raintree. (Raintree Perspectives).

Whitehouse, Patricia. Las Raíces. 2nd ed. 2010. (Las Plantas Ser.). (SPA.). 24p. (gr. k-2). 23.32 *(978-1-4329-4188-8(7))*; pap. 6.79 *(978-1-4329-4193-2(3))* Heinemann-Raintree.

ROPE

Labrecque, Ellen. Rope Sports, 1 vol. 2011. (Extreme Sports Ser.). (ENG., Illus.). 32p. (gr. 1-2). 29.99 *(978-1-4109-4218-0(X),* Read Me!) Heinemann-Raintree.

ROSES

Kate, Maggie, ed. Glitter Roses Stickers. 2004. (Dover Stickers Ser.). (ENG., Illus.). 2p. (J). (gr. -1-5). 1.99 *(978-0-486-43534-3(2))* Dover Pubns., Inc.

Klose, Liz & Peters, Laura. Roses for Ontario, 1 vol. rev. ed. 2003. (ENG., Illus.). 272p. (gr. 4). pap. 21.95 *(978-1-55105-263-2(6),* 1551052636) Lone Pine Publishing USA.

Lindley, Nancy & Peters, Laura. Roses for Michigan, 1 vol., Vol. 1. rev. ed. 2004. (ENG., Illus.). 272p. (gr. 4). pap. 18.95 *(978-1-55105-367-7(5),* 1551053675) Lone Pine Publishing USA.

Peters, Laura & Jalbert, Brad. Roses for British Columbia, 1 vol. rev. ed. 2003. (ENG., Illus.). 272p. (gr. 4). pap. 21.95 *(978-1-55105-261-8(X),* 155105261X) Lone Pine Publishing USA.

Thomson, Ruth. The Life Cycle of a Rose. 2009. (Learning about Life Cycles Ser.). (J). (ENG.). 24p. (gr. k-5). pap. 8.25 *(978-1-4358-2887-2(9),* PowerKids Pr.); (gr. 2-5). lib. bdg. 22.60 *(978-1-4358-2837-7(2))* Rosen Publishing Group, Inc., The.

ROSES—FICTION

Cohn, Diana. Roses for Isabella. Córdova, Amy, illus. 2011. 32p. (J). 17.95 *(978-0-88010-731-0(6))* SteinerBooks, Inc.

Cook, Cathy T. The Adventures of Rose Bush. 2010. 64p. pap. 10.49 *(978-1-4520-3645-8(4))* AuthorHouse.

De La Ramee, Louise. Bimbi. 2004. reprint ed. pap. 19.95 *(978-1-4191-0998-0(7))*; pap. 1.99 *(978-1-4192-0998-7(1))* Kessinger Publishing, LLC.

Erich, Bev. Pink Roses Everywhere. gif. ed. 2004. (Illus.). 64p. (J). 14.95 *(978-0-9743913-0-4(1))* Snojoy Publishing.

Fernandez, David R. Lady Godiva & the Legend of the Black Rose. 2008. (Illus.). 32p. (J). pap. 8.99 *(978-0-9817521-4-3(4))* Mirror Publishing.

Madonna, pseud. Friends for Life! Fulvimari, Jeffrey, illus. 2007. (English Roses Ser.: 1). (ENG.). 96p. (J). (gr. 3-7). 10.99 *(978-0-14-241114-8(0),* Puffin Books) Penguin Young Readers Group.

Madonna, pseud & Fulvimari, Jeffrey. The Runway Rose. 2009. (English Roses Ser.: 9). (ENG., Illus.). 128p. (J). (gr. 3-7). 9.99 *(978-0-14-241126-1(4),* Puffin Books) Penguin Young Readers Group.

McKee, Mabel A. The Heart of the Rose. (Illus.). (J). reprint ed. pap. *(978-0-9658838-1-8(7))* Barnes Printing.

My Roses. 2003. (J). per. *(978-1-57657-898-8(4))* Paradise Pr., Inc.

Quattlebaum, Mary. Jackson Jones & the Curse of the Outlaw Rose. 2008. (ENG.). 112p. (J). (gr. 3-7). 5.99 *(978-0-440-42138-2(1),* Yearling) Random Hse. Children's Bks.

Randolph, Joanne. Rose: A Flower's Story. 2009. (Nature Stories Ser.). (Illus.). 24p. (J). (gr. -1-2). pap. 8.15 *(978-1-60754-102-8(5))*; lib. bdg. 22.60 *(978-1-60754-101-1(7))* Windmill Bks.

Roses for Renee Set B, 6 vols. 32p. (gr. 1-3). 26.50 *(978-0-7802-8055-7(5))* Wright Group/McGraw-Hill.

Sirotzky, Sara. Red Rose & Blue Butterfly. Weber, Andra, illus. 2012. (ENG.). 32p. (J). (gr. -1-3). 17.95 *(978-1-4507-9594-4(3))* Ampersand, Inc.

Slater, Dashka. Dangerously Ever After. Docampo, Valeria, illus. 2012. (ENG.). 40p. (J). (gr. k-3). 16.99 *(978-0-8037-3374-9(7),* Dial Bks) Penguin Young Readers Group.

Valentina, Marina. Lost in the Roses. 2008. (Illus.). 24p. (J). pap. 5.95 *(978-1-60108-024-0(7))* Red Cygnet Pr.

—Lost in the Roses. Valentina, Marina, illus. 2007. (Illus.). 24p. (J). (gr. -1-1). 14.95 *(978-1-60108-014-1(X))* Red Cygnet Pr.

Wood, Douglas. Aunt Mary's Rose. Shed, Greg & Pham, LeUyen, illus. 2010. (ENG.). 32p. (J). (gr. -1-3). 16.99 *(978-0-7636-1090-6(9))* Candlewick Pr.

Yee, Paul. Roses Sing on New Snow: A Delicious Tale. Chan, Harvey, illus. 32p. (J). 16.95 *(978-0-88899-144-7(4))* Groundwood Bks. CAN. Dist: Publishers Group West (PGW).

ROSH HA-SHANAH

Hashanah, Rosh & Kippur, Yom. Rosh Hashanah & Yom Kippur Coloring Book. 2.99 *(978-1-58330-168-5(2))* Feldheim Pubs.

Kropf, Latifa Berry. It's Shofar Time! Cohen, Tod, photos by. (High Holidays Ser.). (ENG., Illus.). 24p. (J). (gr. -1-1). 2011. pap. 8.95 *(978-0-7613-8307-9(7))* 2006. lib. bdg. 12.95 *(978-1-58013-158-2(1))* Lerner Publishing Group. (Kar-Ben Publishing).

Musleah, Rahel & Jarrett, Judy. Apples & Pomegranates: A Family Seder for Rosh Hashanah. 2004. (ENG & HEB., Illus.). 64p. (J). (gr. k-5). pap. 7.95 *(978-1-58013-123-0(9),* Kar-Ben Publishing) Lerner Publishing Group.

ROSH HA-SHANAH—FICTION

Balsley, Tilda & Fischer, Ellen. I'm Sorry, Grover! A Rosh Hashanah Tale. Leigh, Tom, illus. 2013. (High Holidays Ser.). (ENG.). 24p. (J). (gr. -1-k). lib. bdg. 16.95 *(978-0-7613-7560-9(0),* Kar-Ben Publishing) Lerner Publishing Group.

—I'm Sorry, Grover: A Rosh Hashanah Tale. Leigh, Tom, illus. 2013. (High Holidays Ser.). (ENG.). 24p. (J). (gr. -1-k). 6.95 *(978-0-7613-7561-6(9),* Kar-Ben Publishing) Lerner Publishing Group.

Cohen, Deborah Bodin. Engineer Ari & the Rosh Hashanah Ride. 2008. (High Holidays Ser.). (Illus.). 32p. (J). (gr. -1-3). lib. bdg. 17.95 *(978-0-8225-8648-7(7),* Kar-Ben Publishing) Lerner Publishing Group.

Epstein, Sylvia & Migron, Hagit. How the Rosh Hashanah Challah. 2010. 26p. pap. *(978-965-229-479-1(9))* Gefen Publishing Hse., Ltd.

Gerstein, Mordicai. The White Ram: A Story of Abraham & Isaac. Gerstein, Mordicai, illus. 2006. (ENG., Illus.). 32p. (J). (gr. -1-3). 16.95 *(978-0-8234-1897-8(9))* Holiday Hse., Inc.

Jules, Jacqueline. What a Way to Start a New Year! A Rosh Hashanah Story. Stead, Judy, illus. 2013. (High Holidays Ser.). (ENG.). 24p. (J). (gr. -1-2). 7.95 *(978-0-7613-8117-4(1));* lib. bdg. 16.95 *(978-0-7613-8116-7(3))* Lerner Publishing Group. (Kar-Ben Publishing).

Kimmel, Eric A. Even Higher! A Rosh Hashanah Story by I. L. Peretz. Weber, Jill, illus. 2010. (ENG.). 32p. (J). (gr. -1-3). pap. 6.95 *(978-0-8234-2298-2(4))* Holiday Hse., Inc.

Koster, Gloria. Mitzi's Mitzvah. Conger, Holli, illus. 2013. (ENG.). 12p. (J). (gr. -1 — 1). 5.95 *(978-1-4677-0695-7(7),* Kar-Ben Publishing) Lerner Publishing Group.

Marshall, Linda Elovitz. Talia & the Rude Vegetables. Assirelli, Francesca, illus. 2011. (High Holidays Ser.). (ENG.). 24p. (J). (gr. k-3). pap. 6.95 *(978-0-7613-5218-1(X),* Kar-Ben Publishing) Lerner Publishing Group.

Newman, Tracy. Rosh Hashanah Is Coming! Garofoli, Viviana, illus. 2016. (ENG.). 12p. (gr. -1 — 1). 23.99 *(978-1-5124-0945-1(6),* Kar-Ben Publishing) Lerner Publishing Group.

Ofanansky, Allison. What's the Buzz? Honey for a Sweet New Year. Alpern, Eliyahu, illus. Alpern, Eliyahu, photos by. 2011. (High Holidays Ser.). (J). (gr. -1-k). lib. bdg. 15.95 *(978-0-7613-5640-0(1))* Lerner Publishing Group.

Schnur, Susan. Tashlich at Turtle Rock. Schnur-Fishman, Anna & Steele-Morgan, Alexandra, illus. 2010. (High Holidays Ser.). 32p. (J). (gr. k-4). lib. bdg. 17.95 *(978-0-7613-4509-1(4),* Kar-Ben Publishing) Lerner Publishing Group.

Schnur, Susan & Schnur-Fishman, Anna. Tashlich at Turtle Rock. Steele-Morgan, Alex, illus. 2010. (High Holidays Ser.). (ENG.). 32p. (J). (gr. k-3). pap. 7.95 *(978-0-7613-4510-7(8),* Kar-Ben Publishing) Lerner Publishing Group.

Vander Zee, Ruth & Sneider, Marian. Eli Remembers. Farnsworth, Bill, illus. 2007. (ENG.). 32p. (J). (gr. -1-3). 18.00 *(978-0-8028-5309-7(9),* Eerdmans Bks For Young Readers) Eerdmans, William B. Publishing Co.

Wayland, April Halprin. New Year at the Pier: A Rosh Hashanah Story. Jorisch, Stéphane, illus. 2009. 352p. (J). *(978-0-8037-3110-3(8),* Dial) Penguin Publishing Group.

ROSS, BETSY, 1752-1836

Buckley, James, Jr. Who Was Betsy Ross? O'brien, John & Harrison, Nancy, illus. 2014. (Who Was? Ser.). (ENG.). 112p. (J). (gr. 3-7). 5.99 *(978-0-448-48243-9(6),* Grosset & Dunlap) Penguin Young Readers Group.

Buckley, James. Who Was Betsy Ross? 2014. (Who Was...? Ser.). lib. bdg. 16.00 *(978-0-606-36181-1(2))* Turtleback Bks.

Cox, Vicki. Betsy Ross: Flag for a New Nation. 2005. (Leaders of the American Revolution Ser.). (Illus.). 100p. (gr. 5-8). lib. bdg. 30.00 *(978-0-7910-8618-6(6))* Facts On File, Inc.

Devillier, Christy. Betsy Ross, 1 vol. 2004. (First Biographies Set Iv Ser.). (ENG., Illus.). 32p. (gr. k-4). 27.07 *(978-1-59197-516-8(6),* Buddy Bks.) ABDO Publishing Co.

Harkins, Susan Sales & Harkins, William H. Betsy Ross. 2006. (Profiles in American History Ser.). (Illus.). 48p. (J). (gr. 3-7). lib. bdg. 29.95 *(978-1-58415-446-4(2))* Mitchell Lane Pubs., Inc.

Manera, Alexandria. Betsy Ross. 2003. (Women of the Revolution Ser.). (J). pap. *(978-1-58417-085-3(9));* lib. bdg. *(978-1-58417-022-8(0))* Lake Street Pubs.

Mara, Wil. Betsy Ross. 2006. (Rookie Biographies Ser.). (ENG., Illus.). 32p. (J). (gr. 1-2). per. 4.95 *(978-0-516-25369-5(7),* Children's Pr.) Scholastic Library Publishing.

Olson, Kay Melchisedech. Betsy Ross & the American Flag, 1 vol. Cool, Anna Maria et al, illus. 2005. (Graphic History Ser.). (ENG.). 32p. (gr. 3-4). 30.65 *(978-0-7368-4962-3(9),* Graphic Library) Capstone Press of Coughlan Cos.

Palazzo-Craig, Janet. The Making of the American Flag: Betsy Ross & George Washington. 2009. (Great Moments in American History Ser.). 32p. (gr. 3-3). 47.90 *(978-1-61513-155-6(8))* Rosen Publishing Group, Inc., The.

Randolph, Ryan. Betsy Ross: The American Flag, & Life in a Young America. 2009. (Library of American Lives & Times Ser.). 112p. (gr. 5-5). 69.20 *(978-1-60853-473-9(1))* Rosen Publishing Group, Inc., The.

Randolph, Ryan P. Betsy Ross: The American Flag & Life in Young America. 2005. (Library of American Lives & Times). (Illus.). 112p. (J). (gr. 4-8). lib. bdg. 34.60 *(978-0-8239-5730-9(6))* Rosen Publishing Group, Inc., The.

Silate, Jennifer. Betsy Ross. 2004. (Famous People in American History Ser.). (ENG., Illus.). 32p. (gr. 4-8). pap. 10.00 *(978-0-8239-4176-6(0))* Rosen Publishing Group, Inc., The.

—Betsy Ross: Creadora de la bandera Estadounidense. 2004. (Grandes personajes en la historia de los Estados Unidos Ser.). (SPA.). 32p. (gr. 3-6). pap. 10.00 *(978-0-8239-4222-0(8),* Rosen Classroom) Rosen Publishing Group, Inc., The.

—Betsy Ross: Creadora de la bandera estadounidense (Betsy Ross: Creator of the American Flag) 2009. (Grandes personajes en la historia de los Estados Unidos (Famous People in American History) Ser.). (SPA.). 32p. (gr. 2-3). 47.90 *(978-1-61512-791-7(7),* Editorial Buenas Letras) Rosen Publishing Group, Inc., The.

—Betsy Ross: Creator of the American Flag. 2009. (Primary Sources of Famous People in American History Ser.). 32p. (gr. 2-3). 47.90 *(978-1-60851-657-5(1))* Rosen Publishing Group, Inc., The.

—Betsy Ross: Creator of the American Flag / Creadora de la bandera Estadounidense. 2009. (Famous People in American History/Grandes personajes en la historia de los Estados Unidos Ser.). (ENG & SPA.). 32p. (gr. 2-3). 47.90 *(978-1-61512-539-5(6),* Editorial Buenas Letras) Rosen Publishing Group, Inc., The.

Urwin, Kirsten. Betsy Ross & the Creation of the American Flag. 2015. (Spotlight on American History Ser.). (ENG., Illus.). 24p. (J). (gr. 4-6). pap. 10.00 *(978-1-4994-1789-0(6),* PowerKids Pr.) Rosen Publishing Group, Inc., The.

ROSSINI, GIOACCHINO, 1792-1868

Balfe, Roberta Rymer, et al. A Young Person's Introduction to the Arts Featuring the Opera La Cenerentola (Cinderella) by Gioachino [sic] Rossini: Music, Drama, Language, Costumes, Games, Puzzles. 2008. (Illus.). 24p. (J). *(978-0-9785364-0-4(1))* Young Patronesses of the Opera, The.

ROUND TABLE

see Arthur, King

ROUSSEAU, HENRI, 1844-1910

de Duve, Catherine. Hello Rousseau: Get to Know Rousseau through Stories, Games & Draw-It-Yourself Fun. 2007. 132p. pap. 9.95 *(978-1-59960-001-7(3))* Birdcage Pr.

Markel, Michelle & Rousseau, Henri. The Fantastic Jungles of Henri Rousseau. Hall, Amanda, illus. 2012. (ENG.). 34p. (J). 17.00 *(978-0-8028-5364-6(1),* Eerdmans Bks For Young Readers) Eerdmans, William B. Publishing Co.

Stephens, Pam. Dropping in on Rousseau. 2003. (ENG., Illus.). 32p. (J). 15.95 *(978-1-56290-303-9(9))* Crystal Productions.

ROUSSEAU, JEAN-JACQUES, 1712-1778

Brezina, Corona. Jean-Jacques Rousseau & the Social Contract. 2016. (J). lib. bdg. *(978-1-5081-0227-4(9))* Rosen Publishing Group, Inc., The.

ROUTES OF TRADE

see Trade Routes

ROWAN (FICTITIOUS CHARACTER)—FICTION

Rodda, Emily. Rowan & the Ice Creepers. 2003. (Rowan of Rin Ser.). 272p. (J). (gr. 3-18). 15.99 *(978-0-06-029780-0(8))* HarperCollins Pubs.

—Rowan & the Travelers. 2004. (Rowan of Rin Ser.). (ENG.). 192p. (J). (gr. 3-18). pap. 6.99 *(978-0-06-056072-0(X),* Greenwillow Bks.) HarperCollins Pubs.

—Rowan & the Zebak. 2003. (Rowan of Rin Ser.). (ENG., Illus.). 208p. (J). (gr. 2-18). pap. 5.99 *(978-0-06-441024-3(2),* Harper Trophy) HarperCollins Pubs.

—Rowan of Rin. 2004. (Rowan of Rin Ser.). (ENG., Illus.). 176p. (J). (gr. 3-18). pap. 6.99 *(978-0-06-056071-3(1),* Greenwillow Bks.) HarperCollins Pubs.

ROWING

Brown, Daniel James. The Boys in the Boat (Young Readers Adaptation) The True Story of an American Team's Epic Journey to Win Gold at the 1936 Olympics. (ENG., Illus.). (J). (gr. 5). 2016. 256p. 10.99 *(978-0-14-751685-5(4),* Puffin Books) 2015. 240p. 17.99 *(978-0-451-47592-3(5),* Viking Books for Young Readers) Penguin Young Readers Group.

—The Boys in the Boat (Young Readers Adaptation) The True Story of an American Team's Epic Journey to Win Gold at the 1936 Olympics. 2016. lib. bdg. 22.10 *(978-0-606-39312-6(9))* Turtleback Bks.

ROWING—FICTION

Beauvais, Clémentine. Scam on the Cam. Home, Sarah, illus. 2016. (Sesame Seade Mystery Ser.: 3). (ENG.). 192p. (J). 16.95 *(978-0-8234-3630-9(6))* Holiday Hse., Inc.

Tetlow, Karin. Harry Goes Rowing. Guze, Tessa, illus. 2013. 32p. pap. 11.95 *(978-0-615-75585-4(2))* Juping Horse Pr.

ROWLING, J. K., 1965-

Bucholz, Dinah. The Unofficial Harry Potter Cookbook: From Cauldron Cakes to Knickerbocker Glory — More Than 150 Magical Recipes for Muggles & Wizards. 2010. (Unofficial Cookbook Ser.). (ENG.). 256p. 19.95 *(978-1-4405-0325-2(7))* Adams Media Corp.

Gaines, Ann Graham. J. K. Rowling. 2004. (Blue Banner Biography Ser.). (Illus.). 32p. (J). (gr. 3-8). lib. bdg. 25.70 *(978-1-58415-325-2(3))* Mitchell Lane Pubs., Inc.

Hallett, Cynthia J. & Huey, Peggy J., eds. New Casebooks - J. K. Rowling: Harry Potter, 1 vol. 2012. (New Casebooks Ser.). (ENG., Illus.). 224p. (C). 85.00 *(978-0-230-00849-6(6),* 9780230008496); pap. 29.00 *(978-0-230-00850-2(X),* 9780230008502) Palgrave Macmillan.

Harmin, Karen Leigh. J. K. Rowling: Author of Harry Potter — An Unauthorized Biography. 2006. (People to Know Today Ser.). (Illus.). 128p. (J). (gr. 7-12). lib. bdg. 33.27 *(978-0-7660-1850-1(4))* Enslow Pubs., Inc.

Harrington, Jamie. The Unofficial Guide to Crafting the World of Harry Potter: 30 Magical Crafts for Muggles, Witches, & Wizards Alike. 2016. (ENG., Illus.). 192p. pap. 17.99 *(978-1-4405-9504-2(6))* Adams Media Corp.

Herweck Rice, Dona. A Biography of J. K. Rowling. (Grade 8) 2017. (TIME for KIDS(r) Nonfiction Readers Ser.). (ENG., Illus.). (J). (gr. 8-8). pap. 8.99 ***(978-1-4938-3931-5(4))*** Teacher Created Materials, Inc.

Hunsicker, Jennifer. J. K. Rowling: Author of the Harry Potter Series. 2016. (Famous Female Authors Ser.). (ENG., Illus.). 32p. (gr. 3-4). lib. bdg. 27.99 *(978-1-5157-1328-9(8),* Snap Bks.) Capstone Press of Coughlan Cos.

Moore, P.D. About Harry Potter: What Every Kid Should Know... Moore, Rema Harracksingh- & Delande, J., eds. 2003. (Illus.). 170p. (YA). pap. *(978-0-9543596-3-8(1))* Lux-Verbi Bks.

Peterson-Hilleque, Victoria. How to Analyze the Works of J. K. Rowling, 1 vol. 2011. (Essential Critiques Set 2 Ser.). (ENG., Illus.). 112p. (J). (gr. 6-12). lib. bdg. 35.64 *(978-1-61783-093-8(3))* ABDO Publishing Co.

—J. K. Rowling: Extraordinary Author, 1 vol. 2010. (Essential Lives Set 5 Ser.). (ENG.). 112p. (J). (gr. 6-12). lib. bdg. 35.64 *(978-1-61613-517-1(4))* ABDO Publishing Co.

Pezzi, Bryan. J. K. Rowling. (J). 2012. 28.55 *(978-1-61913-057-9(2))* 2012. pap. 13.95 *(978-1-61913-596-3(5))* 2005. (Illus.). 32p. (gr. 5-7). lib. bdg. 26.00 *(978-1-59036-287-7(X))* Weigl Pubs., Inc.

Pollack, Pam & Belviso, Meg. Who Is J. K. Rowling? Marchesi, Stephen & Harrison, Nancy, illus. 2012. (Who Was? Ser.). (ENG.). 112p. (J). (gr. 3-7). pap. 5.99 *(978-0-448-45872-4(1),* Grosset & Dunlap) Penguin Young Readers Group.

Pollack, Pamela & Belviso, Meg. Who Is J. K. Rowling? 2012. (Who Is... ? Ser.). lib. bdg. 16.00 *(978-0-606-26078-7(1),* Turtleback) Turtleback Bks.

Price, Joan. J. K. Rowling. 2004. (Trailblazers of the Modern World Ser.). (Illus.). 48p. (gr. 5-12). lib. bdg. 31.00 *(978-0-8368-5499-2(3),* Gareth Stevens Secondary Library) Stevens, Gareth Publishing LLLP.

—J.K. Rowling. 2004. (Trailblazers of the Modern World Ser.). (Illus.). 48p. (gr. 5-12). pap. 14.05 *(978-0-8368-5268-4(0),* Gareth Stevens Secondary Library) Stevens, Gareth Publishing LLLP.

Pyne, Erin A. A Fandom of Magical Proportions: S: an Unauthorized History of the Harry Potter Phenomenon. 2007. (Illus.). 84p. (J). per. 8.36 *(978-0-9788138-8-8(X))* Nimble Bks. LLC.

Rice, Dona Herweck. Game Changers: A Biography of J. K. Rowling. 2017. (Time for Kids Nonfiction Readers Ser.). lib. bdg. 19.65 ***(978-0-606-40264-4(0))*** Turtleback Bks.

Rosenberg, Moshe. Morality for Muggles: Ethics in the Bible & the World of Harry Potter. 2011. (J). *(978-1-60280-183-7(5))* Ktav Publishing Hse., Inc.

Senker, Cath. J. K. Rowling: Creator of Harry Potter. 2011. (Famous Lives Ser.). (Illus.). 32p. (YA). (gr. 3-6). lib. bdg. 26.50 *(978-1-4488-3288-0(8))* Rosen Publishing Group, Inc., The.

Sexton, Colleen. J. K. Rowling. 2008. pap. 52.95 *(978-1-57505-984-6(3))* Lerner Publishing Group.

Sexton, Colleen A. J. K. Rowling. (Biography Ser.). (Illus.). 112p. (J). 2007. (gr. -1). lib. bdg. 30.60 *(978-0-8225-7949-6(9))* 2007. (gr. -1). per. 7.95 *(978-0-8225-8749-1(1),* First Avenue Editions) 2005. (gr. 4-7). per. 7.95 *(978-0-8225-3389-4(8))* Lerner Publishing Group.

—J.K. Rowling. 2006. (Just the Facts Biographies Ser.). (Illus.). 112p. (J). 27.93 *(978-0-8225-3423-5(1),* Lerner Pubns.) Lerner Publishing Group.

Sexton, Colleen A. & Cosgrove, Martha. J. K. Rowling. 2006. (Just the Facts Biographies Ser.). (Illus.). 112p. (J). pap. 9.95 *(978-0-8225-5995-5(1),* Lerner Pubns.) Lerner Publishing Group.

Shapiro, Marc. J. K. Rowling: The Wizard Behind Harry Potter. 4th ed. 2007. (ENG., Illus.). 288p. pap. 20.99 *(978-0-312-37697-0(9),* 9780312376970, St. Martin's Griffin) St. Martin's Pr.

Sickels, Amy. Mythmaker: The Story of J. K. Rowling. 2nd rev. ed. 2008. (Who Wrote That? Ser.). (Illus.). 136p. (gr. 6-12). lib. bdg. 35.00 *(978-0-7910-9632-1(7),* Chelsea Hse.) Facts On File, Inc.

Tieck, Sarah. J. K. Rowling, 1 vol. 2010. (First Biographies Set 6 Ser.). (ENG.). 32p. (J). (gr. 1-4). 27.07 *(978-1-60453-987-5(9))* ABDO Publishing Co.

Vos MacDonald, Joan. J. K. Rowling: Banned, Challenged, & Censored. 2008. (Authors of Banned Bks). (Illus.). 160p. (YA). (gr. 3-7). lib. bdg. 35.94 *(978-0-7660-2687-2(6))* Enslow Pubs., Inc.

Westerfeld, Scott & Castro, Adam-Troy. Mind-Rain: Your Favorite Authors on Scott Westerfeld's Uglies Series. Westerfeld, Scott, ed. 2009. (ENG., Illus.). 224p. (J). (gr. 7-12). pap. 17.95 *(978-1-933771-34-2(8))* BenBella Bks.

ROYAL CANADIAN MOUNTED POLICE

Bekkering, Annalise. Mounties: Canadian Icons. 2010. (Illus.). 24p. *(978-1-77071-577-6(0));* pap. *(978-1-77071-584-4(3))* Weigl Educational Pubs. Ltd.

Crewe, Sabrina. Canadian Mounties. 2015. (Canadian Symbols Ser.). (ENG., Illus.). 24p. (gr. k-1). lib. bdg. 26.65 *(978-1-4914-7094-7(1),* Pebble Plus) Capstone Press of Coughlan Cos.

Newhouse, Maxwell. The RCMP Musical Ride. 2004. (ENG., Illus.). 24p. (J). (gr. k-12). 15.95 *(978-0-88776-683-1(8),* Tundra Bks.) Tundra Bks. CAN. Dist: Penguin Random Hse. LLC.

ROYAL CANADIAN MOUNTED POLICE—FICTION

Bekkering, Annalise. Les Gendarmes: Les Emblèmes Canadiens. McMann, Julie, tr. from ENG. 2011. (FRE.). 24p. (YA). (gr. 2-4). *(978-1-77071-410-6(3))* Weigl Educational Pubs. Ltd.

Carter, Anne Laurel. Under a Prairie Sky, 1 vol. Daniel, Alan & Daniel, Lea, illus. 2004. (ENG.). 32p. (J). (gr. -1-3). pap. 7.95 *(978-1-55143-282-3(X))* Orca Bk. Pubs. USA.

ROYALTY

see Kings, Queens, Rulers, etc.; Princes; Princesses

RUBBER

Colich, Abby. Rubber, 1 vol. 2013. (Exploring Materials Ser.). (ENG.). 24p. (gr. -1-1). 22.65 *(978-1-4329-8019-1(X));* pap. 6.95 *(978-1-4329-8027-6(0))* Heinemann-Raintree. (Acorn).

Garry-McCord, Kathleen & Sonsky, Kim. Stamp It! Brush-Free Art Prints & Paint Projects. Sonsky, Kim, illus. 2006. (Illus.). 48p. (J). *(978-0-439-81340-2(9))* Scholastic, Inc.

Gleason, Carrie. The Biography of Rubber. 2005. (How Did That Get There?). (ENG., Illus.). 32p. (J). (gr. 4-5). pap. *(978-0-7787-2522-0(7));* lib. bdg. *(978-0-7787-2486-5(7))* Crabtree Publishing Co.

Levete, Sarah. Rubber. 2006. (Material Matters Ser.). (J). *(978-1-59389-273-9(X))* Chrysalis Education.

Lowery, Lawrence F. Rubber vs. Glass: I Wonder Why. Smith, Phil, illus. 2014. (I Wonder Why Ser.). (ENG.). 36p. (J). (gr. k-3). pap. 11.95 *(978-1-938946-50-9(2))* National Science Teachers Assn.

Ridley, Sarah. A Rubber Tire. 2006. (How It's Made Ser.). (Illus.). 32p. (gr. 1-4). lib. bdg. 26.00 *(978-0-8368-6295-9(3),* Gareth Stevens Learning Library) Stevens, Gareth Publishing LLLP.

SchreyerKarmel. BOUNCE! THE WONDERFUL WORLD OF RUBBER UPPER INTERMEDIATE BOOK WITH ONLINE ACCESS. 2014. (ENG., Illus.). 28p. (J). pap. 9.50 *(978-1-107-64154-9(3))* Cambridge Univ. Pr.

Somervill, Barbara A. The Story Behind Rubber, 1 vol. 2011. (True Stories Ser.). (ENG.). 32p. (gr. 3-3). 30.65 *(978-1-4329-5439-0(3),* NA-h) Heinemann-Raintree.

RUBBER TIRES

see Tires, Rubber

RUDOLPH, WILMA, 1940-1994

Anderson, Jennifer Joline. Wilma Rudolph: Track & Field Inspiration, 1 vol. 2011. (Legendary Athletes Ser.). (ENG., Illus.). 112p. (YA). (gr. 7-12). 34.22 *(978-1-61714-759-3(1))* ABDO Publishing Co.

Baer, Peter. Wilma Rudolph: Gold-Medal Winner. 2013. (InfoMax Readers Ser.). (ENG.). 24p. (J). (gr. 2-3). pap. 8.25 *(978-1-4777-2381-4(1));* pap. 49.50 *(978-1-4777-2383-8(8))* Rosen Publishing Group, Inc., The. (Rosen Classroom).

Baer, Peter & Castle, Grace. Olympic Champion: Wilma Rudolph. 2013. (Rosen Readers Ser.). (ENG.). 24p. (J). (gr. 2-3). pap. 8.25 *(978-1-4777-2385-2(4));* pap. 49.50 *(978-1-4777-2386-9(2))* Rosen Publishing Group, Inc., The. (Rosen Classroom).

Beck, Isabel L., et al. Wilma Rudolph. 2003. (Trophies Ser.). (gr. 6-18). 88.70 *(978-0-15-319349-1(2))* Harcourt Schl. Pubs.

Goddu, Krystyna Poray. What's Your Story, Wilma Rudolph? 2016. (Cub Reporter Meets Famous Americans Ser.). (ENG.). 32p. (J). (gr. k-3). 26.65 *(978-1-4677-8782-6(5))* Lerner Publishing Group.

Harper, Jo. Wilma Rudolph: Olympic Runner. Henderson, Meryl, illus. 2004. (Childhood of Famous Americans Ser.). (ENG.). 192p. (J). (gr. 3-7). pap. 6.99 *(978-0-689-85873-4(6),* Simon & Schuster/Paula Wiseman Bks.) Simon & Schuster/Paula Wiseman Bks.

Krull, Kathleen. Wilma Unlimited. Diaz, David, illus. 2015. 44p. pap. 7.00 *(978-1-61003-502-6(X))* Center for the Collaborative Classroom.

Martin, Isabel. Wilma Rudolph, 1 vol. 2014. (Great African-Americans Ser.). (ENG., Illus.). 24p. (gr. k-1). lib. bdg. 21.99 *(978-1-4914-0503-1(1),* Pebble Bks.) Capstone Press of Coughlan Cos.

Morganelli, Adrianna. Wilma Rudolph: Track & Field Champion. 2016. (Remarkable Lives Revealed Ser.). (ENG.). 32p. (J). (gr. 2-5). *(978-0-7787-2689-0(4))* Crabtree Publishing Co.

Schraff, Anne. Wilma Rudolph: The Greatest Woman Sprinter in History. 2004. (African-American Biographies Ser.). (Illus.). 112p. (J). lib. bdg. 26.60 *(978-0-7660-2291-1(9))* Enslow Pubs., Inc.

Sherrow, Victoria. Wilma Rudolph. Johnson, Larry, illus. 2006. (Yo Solo Biografías Ser.). (ENG & SPA.). 48p. (J). (gr. 2-3). lib. bdg. 23.93 *(978-0-8225-6260-3(X),* Ediciones Lerner) Lerner Publishing Group.

—Wilma Rudolph. Translations.com Staff, tr. Johnson, Larry, illus. 2006. (Yo Solo: Biografías (On My Own Biographies) Ser.). (SPA.). 48p. (gr. 2-4). pap. 6.95 *(978-0-8225-6623-6(0),* Ediciones Lerner) Lerner Publishing Group.

Streissguth, Tom. Wilma Rudolph. (Illus.). 2007. 110p. (YA). pap. 9.95 *(978-0-8225-6693-9(1))* 2006. (ENG., 120p. (gr. 5-12). lib. bdg. 30.60 *(978-0-8225-5958-0(7))* Lerner Publishing Group.

Wade, Mary Dodson. Amazing Olympic Athlete Wilma Rudolph. (Amazing Americans Ser.). (Illus.). 24p. (J). 2013. (gr. k-3). pap. 7.95 *(978-0-7660-5978-8(2),* Enslow Elementary) 2009. (gr. 1-3). lib. bdg. 22.60 *(978-0-7660-3282-8(5))* Enslow Pubs., Inc.

Weakland, Mark. When Wilma Rudolph Played Basketball. Duncan, Daniel, illus. 2016. (Leaders Doing Headstands Ser.). (ENG.). 32p. (gr. 2-3). pap. 7.95 *(978-1-5158-0136-8(5));* lib. bdg. 27.99 *(978-1-4795-9684-3(1))* Picture Window Bks.

—When Wilma Rudolph Played Basketball. Duncan, Daniel, illus. 2017. 32p. (J). *(978-1-5158-0140-5(3))* Picture Window Bks.

RUG AND CARPET INDUSTRY

Miller, Raymond H. Jhalak Man Tamang: Slave Labor Whistleblower. 2006. (Young Heroes Ser.). (ENG., Illus.). 48p. (J). (gr. 3-7). lib. bdg. 30.50 *(978-0-7377-3616-8(X),* Kidhaven) Cengage Gale.

RUGBY FOOTBALL

Callery, Sean. The Rugby World Cup 2015. 2017. (Rugby Focus Ser.). (ENG., Illus.). 32p. (J). (gr. 4-6). 17.99 *(978-0-7502-9387-7(X),* Wayland) Hachette Children's Group GBR. Dist: Hachette Bk. Group.

Fullman, Joe. The Official England Rugby Superstars. 2015. (ENG., Illus.). 32p. (J). (gr. 7). pap. 12.99 *(978-1-78312-143-4(2))* Carlton Bks., Ltd. GBR. Dist: Independent Pubs. Group.

Gagne, Tammy. Day by Day with Calvin Johnson. 2014. (Illus.). 32p. (J). (gr. -1-2). 25.70 *(978-1-61228-633-4(X))* Mitchell Lane Pubs., Inc.

Gifford, Clive. Rugby. 2016. (ENG., Illus.). 32p. (J). (gr. 4-6). pap. 11.99 *(978-1-4451-4965-3(6),* Franklin Watts) Hachette Children's Group GBR. Dist: Hachette Bk. Group.

Jones, Emma. Girls Play Rugby. 2016. (Girls Join the Team Ser.). 24p. (J). (gr. 3-3). pap. 8.25 *(978-1-4994-2105-7(2),* PowerKids Pr.) Rosen Publishing Group, Inc., The.

Jones, Simon. Rugby: Complete Skills. 2015. (Know the Game Ser.). (ENG., Illus.). 64p. pap. 12.00 *(978-1-4729-1960-1(2),* 9781472919601) Bloomsbury Publishing USA.

Mason, Paul. Be a Rugby Expert. 2017. (ENG., Illus.). 32p. (J). (gr. 4-6). pap. 12.99 *(978-1-4451-4239-5(2),* Franklin Watts) Hachette Children's Group GBR. Dist: Hachette Bk. Group.

Purslow, Frances. For the Love of Rugby. 2006. (For the Love of Sports Ser.). (Illus.). 24p. (J). (gr. 3-7). lib. bdg. 24.45 *(978-1-59036-380-5(9))*; per. 8.95 *(978-1-59036-381-2(7))* Weigl Pubs., Inc.
—Rugby. 2013. (J). *(978-1-62127-318-9(0))*; pap. *(978-1-62127-323-3(7))* Weigl Pubs., Inc.
Richards, Jon. Laws of the Game. 2017. (Rugby Focus Ser.). (ENG., Illus.). 32p. (J). (gr. 4-6). pap. 11.99 *(978-0-7502-9479-9(5)*, Wayland) Hachette Children's Group GBR. Dist: Hachette Bk. Group.
—Players & Skills. 2017. (Rugby Focus Ser.). (ENG., Illus.). 32p. (J). (gr. 4-6). pap. 11.99 *(978-0-7502-9481-2(7)*, Wayland) Hachette Children's Group GBR. Dist: Hachette Bk. Group.
—Teamwork & Tactics. 2016. (ENG., Illus.). 32p. (J). (gr. 4-6). pap. 11.99 *(978-0-7502-9480-5(9)*, Wayland) Hachette Children's Group GBR. Dist: Hachette Bk. Group.
Superstars of Pro Football, 27 vols., Set. Incl. Antonio Gates. Kimmich, Ian. (Illus.). (gr. 7-12). 2009. lib. bdg. 22.95 *(978-1-4222-0553-2(3))*; Asante Samuel. Mooney, Carla. (Illus.). (gr. 7-12). 2009. lib. bdg. 22.95 *(978-1-4222-0542-6(8))*; Ben Roethlisberger. Heits, Rudolph T. (gr. 5-18). 2010. lib. bdg. 22.95 *(978-1-4222-1664-4(0))*; Brett Favre. Lourdes-Pitt, H. H. (gr. 5-18). 2010. lib. bdg. 22.95 *(978-1-4222-1662-0(4))*; Brian Urlacher. Uschan, Michael V. (Illus.). (gr. 7-12). 2009. lib. bdg. 22.95 *(978-1-4222-0555-6(X))*; Brian Westbrook. Robson, David W. (Illus.). (gr. 7-12). 2009. lib. bdg. 22.95 *(978-1-4222-0547-1(9))*; Chad Johnson. Angst, Frank. (Illus.). (gr. 5-18). 2009. lib. bdg. 22.95 *(978-1-4222-0556-3(8))*; Champ Bailey. Snow, D. C. (Illus.). (gr. 7-12). 2009. lib. bdg. 22.95 *(978-1-4222-0544-0(4))*; DeMarcus Ware. Heits, Rudolph T. (gr. 5-18). 2010. lib. bdg. 22.95 *(978-1-4222-1665-1(9))*; DeSean Jackson. Puliditor, Seth H. (gr. 5-18). 2010. lib. bdg. 22.95 *(978-1-4222-1663-7(2))*; Donovan McNabb. Chatlien, Michael. (Illus.). (gr. 7-12). 2009. lib. bdg. 22.95 *(978-1-4222-0559-4(2))*; Ed Reed. Gitlin, Martin. (Illus.). (gr. 7-12). 2009. lib. bdg. 22.95 *(978-1-4222-0558-7(4))*; Jason Witten. Heits, Rudolph T. (gr. 5-18). 2010. lib. bdg. 22.95 *(978-1-4222-1666-8(7))*; LaDanian Tomlinson. Lace, William W. (Illus.). (gr. 7-12). 2009. lib. bdg. 22.95 *(978-1-4222-0546-4(0))*; Manning Brothers. Marcovitz, Hal. (Illus.). (gr. 7-12). 2009. lib. bdg. 22.95 *(978-1-4222-0543-3(6)*, 1291172); Plaxico Burress. Grayson, Robert. (Illus.). (gr. 7-12). 2009. lib. bdg. 22.95 *(978-1-4222-0552-5(5))*; Randy Moss. Robson, David. (Illus.). (gr. 7-12). 2009. lib. bdg. 22.95 *(978-1-4222-0550-1(9))*; Tony Gonzalez. Hunter, Amy N. (Illus.). (gr. 7-12). 2009. lib. bdg. 22.95 *(978-1-4222-0541-9(X))*; 64p. (YA). 2011. Set lib. bdg. 619.65 *(978-1-4222-1660-6(8))* Mason Crest.
Woods, Mark & Owen, Ruth. Scrum! 2010. (Top Score Maths Ser.). (Illus.). 32p. pap. *(978-0-237-54281-8(1))* Evans Brothers, Ltd.

RUGBY FOOTBALL—FICTION

Beka. We'll Win with Big Class & Huge Style. 2008. (Rugger Boys Ser.: 2). (ENG., Illus.). 48p. pap. 11.95 *(978-1-905460-44-1(9))* CineBook GBR. Dist: National Bk. Network.
Dafydd, Myrddin ap. Brwydr y Brodyr. 2005. (WEL.). 68p. pap. *(978-0-86381-906-3(0))* Gwasg Carreg Gwalch.
Daley, Laurie & Panckridge, Michael. Live Action. 2007. 224p. *(978-0-207-20053-3(X))* HarperCollins Pubs. Australia.
Folau, Israel & Harding, David. Izzy Folau Bindup - Pushed to the Limit & Standing Tall. 2016. (Izzy Folau Ser.). (ENG.). 352p. (YA). (gr. 7-9). pap. 17.99 *(978-0-14-378093-9(X))* Random Hse. Australia AUS. Dist: Independent Pubs. Group.
—Izzy Folau Bindup 1. 2016. (Izzy Folau Ser.). (ENG.). 352p. (YA). (gr. 7-9). pap. 17.99 *(978-0-14-378092-2(1))* Random Hse. Australia AUS. Dist: Independent Pubs. Group.
Harding, David. Pushed to the Limit. Fosdike, David, illus. 2016. (Israel Folau Ser.: 3). (ENG.). 192p. (J). (gr. 4-7). pap. 9.99 *(978-0-85798-665-8(1))* Random Hse. Australia AUS. Dist: Independent Pubs. Group.
—Standing Tall. Fosdike, David, illus. 2016. (Izzy Folau Ser.: 4). (ENG.). 192p. (J). (gr. 4-7). pap. 9.99 *(978-0-85798-667-2(8))* Random Hse. Australia AUS. Dist: Independent Pubs. Group.
James, Mike. Bootsie - & the Team. 2012. 136p. pap. *(978-1-922022-14-1(4))* Vivid Publishing.
—Bootsie - Just One More. 2012. 136p. pap. *(978-1-922022-29-5(2))* Vivid Publishing.
K. Hall. The Adventures of Ranald the Rugby Player: The First Game. 2012. (Illus.). 28p. pap. 21.35 *(978-1-4685-8319-9(0))* AuthorHouse.
Oliver, Sarah. Be the Best. 2008. (Illus.). 104p. pap. 25.50 *(978-0-9559820-0-2(6))* Oliver, Sarah GBR. Dist: Lulu Pr., Inc.
Siggins, Gerard. Rugby Flyer: Haunting History, Thrilling Tries. 2016. (ENG.). 176p. (J). 13.00 *(978-1-84717-819-0(7))* O'Brien Pr., Ltd., The IRL. Dist: Dufour Editions, Inc.
—Rugby Rebel. 2015. (ENG.). 176p. (J). 12.00 *(978-1-84717-677-6(1))* O'Brien Pr., Ltd., The IRL. Dist: Dufour Editions, Inc.
Smith, Andrew. Winger. Bosma, Sam, illus. (ENG.). (YA). (gr. 7). 2014. 464p. pap. 11.99 *(978-1-4424-4493-5(2))* 2013. 448p. 16.99 *(978-1-4424-4492-8(4))* Simon & Schuster Bks. For Young Readers. (Simon & Schuster Bks. For Young Readers).
Spencer, Adam. The Green Zone Kicker. 2012. 34p. pap. 14.99 *(978-1-105-22672-4(7))* Lulu Pr., Inc.

RUINS

see Extinct Cities

RULERS

see Kings, Queens, Rulers, etc.

RUMANIA

see Romania

RUNAWAYS

Bryfonski, Dedria. Street Teens. 2011. (Opposing Viewpoints Ser.). (ENG., Illus.). 224p. (gr. 10-12). 48.80 *(978-0-7377-5761-3(2))*; pap. 33.80 *(978-0-7377-5762-0(0)*, Greenhaven Pr., Inc.) Cengage Gale.
Krohn, Katherine E. Everything You Need to Know about Living on Your Own. 2005. (Need to Know Library). (Illus.). 64p. (YA). (gr. 7-12). lib. bdg. 31.95 *(978-0-8239-3088-3(2)*, NTLIOW) Rosen Publishing Group, Inc., The.

RUNAWAYS—FICTION

Adams, W. Royce. Jay. 2005. viii, 115p. (YA). pap. *(978-1-58832-120-6(7))* Unlimited Publishing LLC.
Alcott, Louisa May. Under the Lilacs. 2005. 28.95 *(978-1-4218-1487-2(0))*; 280p. pap. 13.95 *(978-1-4218-1587-9(7))* 1st World Publishing, Inc. (1st World Library - Literary Society).
—Under the Lilacs. 2012. (ENG., Illus.). 328p. (gr. 3-9). pap. 17.95 *(978-1-4290-9311-8(0))* Applewood Bks.
—Under the Lilacs. 2007. 228p. pap. 20.99 *(978-1-4346-3618-8(6))*; 248p. pap. 22.99 *(978-1-4346-3635-5(6))* Creative Media Partners, LLC.
—Under the Lilacs. 2005. pap. *(978-1-4065-0105-6(0))* Dodo Pr.
—Under the Lilacs. 2013. (Works of Louisa May Alcott). 302p. reprint ed. lthr. 79.00 *(978-0-7812-1637-1(0))* Reprint Services Corp.
—Under the Lilacs. 2011. 226p. 26.95 *(978-1-4638-9588-4(7))* Rodgers, Alan Bks.
—Under the Lilacs. 2007. 316p. (gr. 4-7). 32.95 *(978-1-4344-8357-7(6))*; per. 19.95 *(978-1-4344-8356-0(8))* Wildside Pr., LLC.
Alderson, Sarah. Out of Control. 2015. (ENG., Illus.). 320p. (J). (gr. 9). 17.99 *(978-1-4814-2716-6(4)*, Simon Pulse) Simon Pulse.
Alger, Horatio. Driven from Home: Carl Crawford's Experience. reprint ed. pap. 79.00 *(978-1-4047-3564-4(X))* Classic Textbooks.
—Driven from Home: Carl Crawford's Experience. 2006. pap. *(978-1-4065-0702-7(4))* Dodo Pr.
—Phil the Fiddler. 2006. pap. *(978-1-4068-0667-0(6))* Echo Library.
Allen, Elanna. Itsy Mitsy Runs Away. Allen, Elanna, illus. 2011. (ENG., Illus.). 40p. (J). (gr. -1-2). 16.99 *(978-1-4424-0671-1(2)*, Atheneum Bks. for Young Readers) Simon & Schuster Children's Publishing.
Almond, David. The Boy Who Swam with Piranhas. Jeffers, Oliver, illus. 2015. (ENG.). 256p. (J). (gr. 4-7). pap. 7.99 *(978-0-7636-7680-3(2))* Candlewick Pr.
Anderson, Max Elliot. Reckless Runaway. 2005. 160p. pap. 10.95 *(978-0-9752880-4-7(0))* Baker Trittin Pr.
Arcos, Carrie. Out of Reach. (ENG.). (YA). (gr. 9). 2013. Illus.). 272p. pap. 9.99 *(978-1-4424-4054-8(6))* 2012. 256p. 16.99 *(978-1-4424-4053-1(8))* Simon Pulse. (Simon Pulse).
Armistead, Cal. Being Henry David. (ENG.). 312p. (YA). (gr. 8-12). 2014. pap. 9.99 *(978-0-8075-0616-5(8))* 2013. 16.99 *(978-0-8075-0615-8(X))* Whitman, Albert & Co.
Arnold, David. Mosquitoland. 2015. (ENG.). 352p. (YA). (gr. 7). 17.99 *(978-0-451-47077-5(X)*, Viking Books for Young Readers) Penguin Young Readers Group.
Arnosky, Jim. The Pirates of Crocodile Swamp. 2009. (ENG.). 240p. (J). (gr. 4-7). 15.99 *(978-0-399-25068-2(9)*, G.P. Putnam's Sons Books for Young Readers) Penguin Young Readers Group.
Ayarbe, Heidi. Compromised. (ENG.). (YA). (gr. 8). 2011. 480p. pap. 8.99 *(978-0-06-172851-8(9))* 2010. 464p. 16.99 *(978-0-06-172849-5(7))* HarperCollins Pubs. (HarperTeen).
Babiak, Alexandra Brittany. The Runaway Jacket, 1 vol. 2009. 40p. pap. 24.95 *(978-1-60749-332-7(2))* America Star Bks.
Bailey, Christine. Girl in the Middle. 2013. 236p. pap. 8.99 *(978-0-9890632-0-3(8))* Vinspire Publishing LLC.
Bare, Bart. Girl. 2010. 188p. (YA). pap. 11.95 *(978-0-9825396-4-4(9))* Canterbury Hse. Publishing, Ltd.
Barnaby, Hannah. Wonder Show. (ENG., 288p. (YA). (gr. 7). 2013. Illus.). pap. 8.99 *(978-0-544-10483-9(8))* 2012. 16.99 *(978-0-547-59980-9(3))* Houghton Mifflin Harcourt Publishing Co.
Barnes, Jennifer Lynn. Trial by Fire. 2012. (Raised by Wolves Ser.: Bk. 2). (ENG.). 368p. (J). (gr. 7). pap. 9.99 *(978-1-60684-333-8(8)*, Carolrhoda Lab™) Lerner Publishing Group.
Barnholdt, Lauren. Right of Way. (ENG., Illus.). (YA). (gr. 9). 2014. 336p. pap. 9.99 *(978-1-4424-5128-5(9))* 2013. 320p. 16.99 *(978-1-4424-5127-8(0))* Simon Pulse. (Simon Pulse).
Barratt, Mark. The Wild Man. 2010. (ENG.). 352p. (YA). (gr. 6-18). pap. 9.00 *(978-0-8028-5377-6(3)*, Eerdmans Bks For Young Readers) Eerdmans, William B. Publishing Co.
Bedford, Martyn. Twenty Questions for Gloria. 2016. (ENG.). 288p. (YA). (gr. 9). 16.99 *(978-0-553-53939-4(6)*, Lamb, Wendy Bks.) Random Hse. Children's Bks.
Black, Holly. Valiant: A Modern Faerie Tale. 2005. (ENG.). 320p. (YA). (gr. 8-18). 17.99 *(978-0-689-86822-1(7)*, McElderry, Margaret K. Bks.) McElderry, Margaret K. Bks.
Blair, Jamie. Leap of Faith. 2013. (ENG., Illus.). 240p. (YA). (gr. 9). 16.99 *(978-1-4424-4713-4(3)*, Simon & Schuster Bks. For Young Readers) Simon & Schuster Bks. For Young Readers.
Blair, Jamie M. Leap of Faith. 2014. (ENG.). 240p. (YA). (gr. 9). pap. 11.99 *(978-1-4424-4716-5(8)*, Simon & Schuster Bks. For Young Readers) Simon & Schuster Bks. For Young Readers.
Boie, Kirsten. The Princess Trap. (ENG.). 416p. (J). (gr. 5-9). 2012. pap. 7.99 *(978-0-545-22262-4(1))* 2010. 17.99 *(978-0-545-22261-7(3))* Scholastic, Inc. (Chicken Hse., The).
Boyne, John. Noah Barleywater Runs Away. Jeffers, Oliver, illus. 2011. (ENG.). 240p. (J). (gr. 3-7). 16.99 *(978-0-385-75246-6(6))* Fickling, David Bks. GBR. Dist: Penguin Random Hse. LLC.
—Noah Barleywater Runs Away. Jeffers, Oliver, illus. 2012. (ENG.). 240p. (J). (gr. 3-7). 7.99 *(978-0-385-75264-0(4)*, Yearling) Random Hse. Children's Bks.
—The Terrible Thing That Happened to Barnaby Brocket. Jeffers, Oliver, illus. (ENG.). 288p. (J). (gr. 3-7). 2014. 6.99 *(978-0-307-97765-6(X)*, Yearling) 2013. 16.99 *(978-0-307-97762-5(5)*, Knopf Bks. for Young Readers) Random Hse. Children's Bks.
Brett, Jan. Home for Christmas. Brett, Jan, illus. 2011. (ENG., Illus.). 32p. (J). (gr. -1-k). 17.99 *(978-0-399-25653-0(9)*, G.P. Putnam's Sons Books for Young Readers) Penguin Young Readers Group.
Brewer, Janey. Mist & Moonlight. 2007. 76p. per. 19.95 *(978-1-4241-9525-1(X))* America Star Bks.
Broach, Elise. The Wolf Keepers. Ratterree, Alice, illus. 2016. (ENG.). 352p. (J). 16.99 *(978-0-8050-9899-0(2)*, 9780805098990, Holt, Henry & Co. Bks. For Young Readers) Holt, Henry & Co.
Brown, Margaret Wise. El Conejito Andarin, 1 vol. Marcuse, Aida E., tr. Hurd, Clement, illus. 2006. (SPA.). 48p. (J). (gr. -1-2). pap. 6.99 *(978-0-06-077694-7(3))* HarperCollins Pubs.
—Goodnight Moon Classic Library: Contains Goodnight Moon, the Runaway Bunny, & My World. Hurd, Clement, illus. 2011. (ENG.). 32p. (J). (gr. -1-1). 14.99 *(978-0-06-199823-2(0))* HarperCollins Pubs.
—The Runaway Bunny. Hurd, Clement, illus. 48p. (J). (gr. -1-3). 2017. (ENG.). 17.99 *(978-0-06-077582-7(3))* 2005. lib. bdg. 18.89 *(978-0-06-077583-4(1))* HarperCollins Pubs.
—The Runaway Bunny Padded Board Book. Hurd, Clement, illus. 2017. 36p. (J). (gr. -1 — 1). bds. 9.99 *(978-0-06-245959-6(7)*, HarperFestival) HarperCollins Pubs.
Brown, Margaret Wise & Marcus, Leonard S. The Runaway Bunny: a 75th Anniversary Retrospective. Hurd, Clement, illus. 2017. 64p. (J). (gr. -1-3). 19.99 *(978-0-06-248994-4(1))* HarperCollins Pubs.
Burgess, Melvin. Smack. 2010. (ENG.). 352p. (YA). (gr. 9-13). pap. 13.99 *(978-0-312-60862-0(4)*, 9780312608620) Square Fish.
Buske, Jody. Wilderness Awakening. 2006. 108p. pap. 19.95 *(978-1-4241-2685-9(1))* PublishAmerica, Inc.
Butcher, Kristin & Labatt, Mary. Sam Finds a Monster. Sarrazin, Marisol, illus. 2003. (Kids Can Read Ser.). (ENG.). 32p. (J). (gr. k-1). 3.95 *(978-1-55337-352-0(9))* Kids Can Pr., Ltd. CAN. Dist: Hachette Bk. Group.
Cabot, Meg. Runaway. 2010. (Airhead Ser.: 3). (ENG.). 320p. (J). (gr. 7-18). 16.99 *(978-0-545-04060-0(4))* Scholastic, Inc.
Carter, Alden R. Walkaway. 2008. (ENG.). 192p. (YA). (gr. 7-18). 16.95 *(978-0-8234-2106-0(6))* Holiday Hse., Inc.
Charles, Norma. The Girl in the Backseat. 2008. (ENG., Illus.). 184p. (YA). (gr. 7-18). per. *(978-1-55380-056-9(7))* Ronsdale Pr.
Choyce, Lesley. Crash, 1 vol. 2013. (Orca Soundings Ser.). (ENG.). 136p. (YA). (gr. 8-12). pap. 9.95 *(978-1-4598-0522-4(4))*; lib. bdg. 16.95 *(978-1-4598-0525-5(9))* Orca Bk. Pubs. USA.
Christie, Ed. The Sweet Smell of Rotten Eggs: Volume Two, the Dude Ranch Rangers. 2009. 108p. pap. 10.95 *(978-1-4401-3764-8(1))* iUniverse, Inc.
Christopher, Matt. Dirt Bike Runaway. 2008. (New Matt Christopher Sports Library). 176p. (J). (gr. 4-6). lib. bdg. 26.60 *(978-1-59953-215-8(8))* Norwood Hse. Pr.
Cleary, Beverly. Runaway Ralph. (Mouse & the Motorcycle Ser.). 175p. (J). (gr. 3-5). pap. 4.50 *(978-0-8072-1394-0(2))*; pap. 4.95 *(978-0-8072-1477-0(9))* Random Hse. Audio Publishing Group. (Listening Library).
Cole, Brock. The Goats. 2003. 20.75 *(978-0-8446-7238-0(6))* Smith, Peter Pub., Inc.
—The Goats. Cole, Brock, illus. 2010. (ENG., Illus.). 192p. (YA). (gr. 7-10). pap. 9.99 *(978-0-312-61191-0(9)*, 9780312611910) Square Fish.
Coley, Patrick. The Chronicles of Maxwell & His Runaways. 2012. 134p. 29.99 *(978-1-4797-0759-1(7))*; pap. 19.99 *(978-1-4797-0758-4(9))* Xlibris Corp.
Collier, James Lincoln. Me & Billy, 0 vols. unabr. ed. 2013. (ENG.). 194p. (J). (gr. 5-7). pap. 9.99 *(978-1-4778-1706-3(9)*, 9781477817063, Amazon Children's Publishing) Amazon Publishing.
Collins, David Paul. Shanghaied. 2011. 320p. 29.95 *(978-1-4620-3184-9(6))*; pap. 19.95 *(978-1-4620-3183-2(8))* iUniverse, Inc.
Collins, Pat Lowery. The Fattening Hut. 2005. (ENG.). 192p. (YA). (gr. 7). pap. 12.95 *(978-0-618-55209-2(X))* Houghton Mifflin Harcourt Publishing Co.
Conford, Ellen. To All My Fans, with Love, From Sylvie. 2013. (ENG.). 200p. (gr. 4). pap. 12.95 *(978-1-939601-01-8(0))* Ig Publishing, Inc.
Coville, Bruce. The Mischief Monster. Coville, Katherine, illus. 2008. (Moongobble & Me Ser.: Bk. 4). (ENG.). 80p. (J). (gr. 1-5). pap. 5.99 *(978-1-4169-0808-1(0)*, Aladdin) Simon & Schuster Children's Publishing.
Curtis, Christopher Paul. Bud, Not Buddy. unabr. ed. 2004. 256p. (J). (gr. 4-7). pap. 36.00 incl. audio *(978-0-8072-8210-6(3)*, LYA 140 S{, Listening Library) Random Hse. Audio Publishing Group.
—Bud, Not Buddy. 2004. (ENG., Illus.). 288p. (J). (gr. 3-7). mass mkt. 7.99 *(978-0-553-49410-5(4)*, Laurel Leaf) Random Hse. Children's Bks.
Curtis, Christopher Paul & Jiménez Rioja, Alberto. Me Llamo Bud, No Buddy. 2016. (SPA.). 240p. (J). (gr. 5-12). pap. 12.99 ***(978-1-63245-639-7(7))*** Lectorum Pubns., Inc.
Cushman, Karen. Will Sparrow's Road. (ENG.). 224p. (J). (gr. 5-7). 2014. pap. 6.99 *(978-0-544-33632-2(1)*, HMH Books For Young Readers) 2012. 16.99 *(978-0-547-73962-5(1))* Houghton Mifflin Harcourt Publishing Co.
Darrow, Sharon. Trash. 2006. (ENG.). 160p. (YA). (gr. 7-12). 16.99 *(978-0-7636-2624-2(4))* Candlewick Pr.
de Harven, Emile. Suivez la Piste. (FRE.). (YA). (gr. 9-12). pap., tchr.'s training gde. ed. 6.95 *(978-0-88436-342-2(2)*, 40811) EMC/Paradigm Publishing.
De la Peña, Matt. We Were Here. 2010. (ENG.). 368p. (YA). (gr. 9). pap. 9.99 *(978-0-385-73670-1(3)*, Ember) Random Hse. Children's Bks.
De Palma, Toni. Under the Banyan Tree. 2007. (ENG.). 192p. (YA). (gr. 7-18). 16.95 *(978-0-8234-1965-4(7))* Holiday Hse., Inc.
DeFelice, Cynthia. Wild Life. 2011. (ENG.). 192p. (J). (gr. 3-7). 17.99 *(978-0-374-38001-4(5)*, 9780374380014, Farrar, Straus & Giroux (BYR)) Farrar, Straus & Giroux.
—Wild Life. 2013. (ENG.). 208p. (J). (gr. 3-7). pap. 7.99 *(978-1-250-03407-6(8)*, 9781250034076) Square Fish.
Downes, Patrick. Come Home, Angus. Kulikov, Boris, illus. 2016. (ENG.). 32p. (J). (gr. -1-k). 17.99 *(978-0-545-59768-5(4))* Scholastic, Inc.
Dragonwagon, Crescent & Zindel, Paul. To Take a Dare. 2016. (ENG.). (YA). (gr. 7-12). pap. 9.99 *(978-1-63168-028-1(5))* Graymalkin Media.
Duggan, Matt. The Royal Woods. 2010. (ENG., Illus.). 244p. (J). (gr. 4-7). pap. *(978-1-55470-060-8(4))* Me to We.
Duling, Astrid. The Guinea Pigs Twiggy & Molly. 2012. 134p. pap. *(978-3-8423-1287-6(3))* Books on Demand GmbH.
Easton, Kelly. The Outlandish Adventures of Liberty Aimes. Swearingen, Greg, illus. 2011. (ENG.). 224p. (J). (gr. 3-7). pap. 6.99 *(978-0-375-83772-2(8)*, Yearling) Random Hse. Children's Bks.
Evans, Richard. If Only. 2015. (ENG., Illus.). 288p. (YA). (gr. 9). pap. 11.99 *(978-1-4814-4853-6(6)*, Simon Pulse) Simon Pulse.
Everheart, Chris. Concrete Gallery. 2014. (ENG.). 96p. (J). *(978-1-63235-053-4(X))* Pr. Room Editions LLC.
Fagan, Cary. Danny, Who Fell in a Hole, 1 vol. Pavlovic, Milan, illus. 2013. (ENG.). 96p. (J). 14.95 *(978-1-55498-311-7(8))* Groundwood Bks. CAN. Dist: Publishers Group West (PGW).
—Danny, Who Fell in a Hole. 2013. 84p. pap. *(978-1-4596-6456-2(6))* ReadHowYouWant.com, Ltd.
Fenn, Jennifer. Flight Risk. 2017. (ENG.). 384p. (YA). 17.99 *(978-1-62672-760-1(0)*, 9781626727601) Roaring Brook Pr.
Finn, Alex. Nothing to Lose. 2004. 288p. (J). 16.99 *(978-0-06-051750-2(6)*, HarperTeen) HarperCollins Pubs.
Foard, Sheila Wood. Harvey Girl. 2006. (ENG., Illus.). 176p. (YA). (gr. 7-12). per. 18.95 *(978-0-89672-570-6(7))* Texas Tech Univ. Pr.
Funke, Cornelia. The Thief Lord. 2004.Tr. of Herr der Diebe. 376p. (J). (gr. 5-18). pap. 44.00 incl. audio *(978-0-8072-2278-2(X)*, Listening Library) Random Hse. Audio Publishing Group.
—Thief Lord. Birmingham, Christian, illus. 2010. (ENG.). 376p. (J). (gr. 3-7). 7.99 *(978-0-545-22770-4(4)*, Chicken Hse., The) Scholastic, Inc.
—The Thief Lord. 2003.Tr. of Herr der Diebe. (gr. 3-6). 18.40 *(978-0-613-84572-4(2)*, Turtleback) Turtleback Bks.
Fusco, Kimberly Newton. Beholding Bee. 2015. (ENG.). 336p. (J). (gr. 3-7). 7.99 *(978-0-375-86808-5(9)*, Yearling) Random Hse. Children's Bks.
Gabriel, Thora. Chessie Bligh & the Scroll of Andelthor. 2006. 284p. (J). 27.95 *(978-0-595-83579-9(1))* iUniverse, Inc.
Gemeinhart, Dan. The Honest Truth. 2015. (ENG.). 240p. (J). (gr. 3-7). pap. 6.99 *(978-0-545-66574-2(4))*; 16.99 *(978-0-545-66573-5(6))* Scholastic, Inc. (Scholastic Pr.).
Gonick, Larry. Kokopelli & Company in Attack of the Smart Pies. 2005. (ENG., Illus.). 192p. (J). 15.95 *(978-0-8126-2740-4(7))* Cricket Bks.
Grant, Vicki. No te Vayas, 1 vol. 2011. (Spanish Soundings Ser.). (SPA.). 160p. (J). (gr. 8-12). pap. 9.95 *(978-1-55469-970-4(3))* Orca Bk. Pubs. USA.
Griffin, Paul. Ten Mile River. 2011. (ENG.). 208p. (YA). (gr. 7-18). 7.99 *(978-0-14-241983-0(4)*, Speak) Penguin Young Readers Group.
The Guardians. 2014. (ENG., Illus.). 288p. (J). (gr. 4-8). pap. 7.99 *(978-1-4814-1834-8(3)*, Aladdin) Simon & Schuster Children's Publishing.
Guest, Jacqueline. At Risk, 1 vol. 2004. (Lorimer SideStreets Ser.). (ENG.). 192p. (YA). (gr. 9-12). 9.95 *(978-1-55028-846-9(6)*, 9781550288469); 16.95 *(978-1-55028-847-6(4)*, 9781550288476) Lorimer, James & Co., Ltd., Pubs. CAN. Dist: Casemate Pubs. & Bk. Distributors, LLC.
Hackl, Jo. Smack Dab in the Middle of Maybe. 2017. (J). ***(978-0-399-55738-5(5))*** Random Hse., Inc.
Hardesty, Ann A. Lucy's Trials in the Black Hills. 2009. 104p. pap. 10.99 *(978-1-4490-5368-0(8))* AuthorHouse.
Hardy, Thomas. THE MAYOR OF CASTERBRIDGE LEVEL 5 UPPER-INTERMEDIATE. 2009. (ENG.). 112p. pap. 14.50 *(978-84-8323-560-7(9))* Cambridge Univ. Pr.
—THE MAYOR OF CASTERBRIDGE LEVEL 5 UPPER-INTERMEDIATE BOOK WITH CD-ROM AND AUDIO CDS (2) PACK, 1 vol. 2009. (ENG.). 112p. pap. 16.50 incl. cd-rom, audio compact disk *(978-84-8323-556-0(0))* Cambridge Univ. Pr.
Harmon, Michael. Skate. 2008. (ENG.). 256p. (YA). (gr. 9). per. 6.99 *(978-0-553-49510-2(0)*, Laurel Leaf) Random Hse. Children's Bks.
Harrison, Emma. Escaping Perfect. 2016. (ENG., Illus.). 336p. (YA). (gr. 9). 17.99 *(978-1-4814-4212-1(0)*, Simon Pulse) Simon Pulse.
—Finding What's Real. 2017. (ENG., Illus.). 304p. (YA). (gr. 9). 17.99 *(978-1-4814-4215-2(5)*, Simon Pulse) Simon Pulse.
Herrick, Steven. The Simple Gift. 2004. (ENG.). 192p. (YA). (gr. 9). pap. 9.99 *(978-0-689-86867-2(7)*, Simon Pulse) Simon Pulse.
Hill, Janet Muirhead. Kendall's Storm. Leonhard, Herb, illus. 2011. (J). pap. 12.00 *(978-0-9820893-0-9(9))* Raven Publishing Inc. of Montana.
—Kyleah's Tree. Leonhard, Herb, illus. 2011. (J). pap. 12.00 *(978-0-9827377-9-8(3))* Raven Publishing Inc. of Montana.
Hillert, Margaret. The Little Runaway. Dumm, Brian, illus. 2016. (BeginningtoRead Ser.). (ENG.). 32p. (J). (gr. k-2). 22.60 *(978-1-59953-801-3(6))* Norwood Hse. Pr.
Hoffman, Alice. Indigo. 2003. (ENG.). 96p. (J). (gr. 3-7). pap. 6.99 *(978-0-439-25636-0(4)*, Scholastic Paperbacks) Scholastic, Inc.
Hopkins, Ellen. Smoke. (ENG., Illus.). (YA). (gr. 9). 2015. 576p. pap. 12.99 *(978-1-4169-8329-3(5))* 2013. 560p. 19.99 *(978-1-4169-8328-6(7))* McElderry, Margaret K. Bks. (McElderry, Margaret K. Bks.).
Horse, Harry. Little Rabbit Runaway. Horse, Harry, illus. 2005. (ENG., Illus.). 32p. (J). (gr. k-1). 15.95 *(978-1-56145-343-6(9))* Peachtree Pubs.
Hubler, Marsha. Southern Belle's Special Gift, 1 vol. 2009. (Keystone Stables Ser.). (ENG.). 128p. (J). pap. 7.99 *(978-0-310-71794-2(9))* Zonderkidz.
Hutchinson, Shaun David. The Five Stages of Andrew Brawley. Larsen, Christine, illus. 2015. (ENG.). 304p. (YA). (gr. 7). 17.99 *(978-1-4814-0310-8(9)*, Simon Pulse) Simon Pulse.
Jackson, Louise A. Exiled! From Tragedy to Triumph on the Missouri Frontier. 2007. (Illus.). 235p. (YA). (gr. 7-9). per. 16.95 *(978-1-57168-948-1(6)*, Eakin Pr.) Eakin Pr.
Johnson, Angela. Bird. 2006. 133p. (gr. 3-7). 16.00 *(978-0-7569-6660-7(4))* Perfection Learning Corp.
Johnson, Terry Lynn. Falcon Wild. 2017. (ENG.). 176p. (J). (gr. 5). lib. bdg. 16.99 ***(978-1-58089-788-4(6))*** Charlesbridge Publishing, Inc.
Joyce, Melanie. Goldilocks. 2009. (Fairydust Fairytales Ser.). (ENG.). 5p. (J). (gr. -1-k). bds. 6.95 *(978-1-84696-962-1(X)*, TickTock Books) Octopus Publishing Group GBR. Dist: Independent Pubs. Group.

Juwell & Precious. Runaway. 2006. (Platinum Teen Ser.). 133p. (YA). (gr. 8-12). per. 6.99 (978-0-9729325-6-1(9)) Precioustymes Entertainment, LLC.

Kaufman, Sashi. The Other Way Around. 288p. (YA). (gr. 8-12). 2017. (ENG.). pap. 9.99 **(978-1-5124-8177-8(7)**, Carolrhoda Bks.) 2014. 17.95 (978-1-4677-0262-1(5)) Lerner Publishing Group.

Kehret, Peg. Runaway Twin. 2011. (ENG.). 208p. (J). (gr. 5-18). 6.99 (978-0-14-241849-9(8), Puffin Books) Penguin Young Readers Group.

Kelly, Tom. Finn's Going. 2007. 278p. (YA). (gr. 8-12). 16.99 (978-0-06-121453-0(1), Greenwillow Bks.) HarperCollins Pubs.

Keplinger, Kody. Run. (ENG.). 304p. (gr. 9). 2017. (J). pap. 10.99 **(978-0-545-83114-7(8)**, Scholastic Paperbacks) 2016. (YA). 17.99 (978-0-545-83113-0(X), Scholastic Pr.) Scholastic, Inc.

Kern, Peggy. Little Peach. 2015. (ENG.). 208p. (YA). (gr. 9). 17.99 (978-0-06-226695-8(0)) HarperCollins Pubs.

Keyes, Morgan. Darkbeast. 2012. (ENG.). 288p. (J). (gr. 5-9). 16.99 (978-1-4424-4205-4(0), McElderry, Margaret K. Bks.) McElderry, Margaret K. Bks.

Klise, Kate. Pop Goes the Circus! Klise, M. Sarah, illus. 2015. (Three-Ring Rascals Ser.: 4). (ENG.). 144p. (J). (gr. 2-5). 15.95 (978-1-61620-464-8(8)) Algonquin Bks. of Chapel Hill.

Konnikova, Svetlana. Grapette, the Runaway Who Rolled Away: A Timeless Tale of Love & Family: A Child Discovering the World. Smishliaev, Anatoli, illus. 2007. (Grapette's Adventures Ser.). (ENG.). 32p. (J). (gr. k-2). 15.95 (978-0-9791758-0-0(1)) Aurora Pubs., Inc.

Lawrence, Iain. The Convicts. 2006. 15.10 (978-0-7569-6901-1(8)) Random House Children's Books GBR. Dist: Perfection Learning Corp.

Lawson, Jessica. Waiting for Augusta. 2016. (ENG., Illus.). 336p. (J). (gr. 3-7). 16.99 (978-1-4814-4839-0(0), Simon & Schuster Bks. For Young Readers) Simon & Schuster Bks. For Young Readers.

Layburn, Joe. Runaways. Williams, John, illus. 2014. (ENG.). 144p. (J). (gr. 4-7). pap. 8.95 (978-1-84780-080-0(7), Frances Lincoln) Quarto Publishing Group UK GBR. Dist: Hachette Bk. Group.

Lean, Sarah. A Hundred Horses. (ENG.). (J). (gr. 3-7). 2015. 240p. pap. 6.99 (978-0-06-212230-8(4)) 2014. 224p. 16.99 (978-0-06-212229-2(0)) HarperCollins Pubs. (Tegen, Katherine Bks).

Leavitt, Martine. My Book of Life by Angel. 2012. (ENG.). 256p. (YA). (gr. 9-13). 17.99 (978-0-374-35123-6(6), 9780374351236, Farrar, Straus & Giroux (BYR)) Farrar, Straus & Giroux.

—My Book of Life by Angel. 2014. (ENG.). 272p. (YA). (gr. 9-13). pap. 11.99 (978-1-250-04003-9(5), 9781250040039) Square Fish.

Lee, Stacey. Under a Painted Sky. 2015. (ENG.). 384p. (YA). (gr. 7). 16.99 (978-0-399-16803-1(6), G.P. Putnam's Sons Books for Young Readers) Penguin Young Readers Group.

—Under a Painted Sky. 2016. lib. bdg. 22.10 (978-0-606-38391-2(3)) Turtleback Bks.

Levin, Betty. Shoddy Cove. 2003. 208p. (J). (gr. 5-18). 15.99 (978-0-06-052271-1(2)) HarperCollins Pubs.

Linka, Catherine. A Girl Called Fearless. 2014. (ENG.). 368p. (YA). (gr. 7). 18.99 (978-1-250-03929-3(0); 9781250039293, St. Martin's Griffin) St. Martin's Pr.

London, Alex. Proxy. 2014. (ENG.). 432p. (YA). (gr. 7). pap. 10.99 (978-0-14-751133-1(X), Speak) Penguin Young Readers Group.

Lovejoy, Sharon. Running Out of Night. 2014. (ENG., Illus.). 304p. (J). (gr. 4-7). lib. bdg. 19.99 (978-0-375-99147-9(6), Delacorte Bks. for Young Readers) Random Hse. Children's Bks.

Lowory, Brigid. Guitar Highway Rose. 2003. (ENG.). 208p. (YA). (gr. 7-12). tchr. ed. 16.95 (978-0-8234-1790-2(5)) Holiday Hse., Inc.

Lowry, Brigid. Guitar Highway Rose. 2006. (ENG.). 208p. (YA). (gr. 8-12). reprint ed. pap. 18.99 (978-0-312-34296-8(9), 9780312342968, St. Martin's Griffin) St. Martin's Pr.

Lynch, Chris. Killing Time in Crystal City. 2015. (ENG., Illus.). 240p. (YA). (gr. 7). 17.99 (978-1-4424-4011-1(2), Simon & Schuster Bks. For Young Readers) Simon & Schuster Bks. For Young Readers.

Mackey, Heather. Dreamwood. 2014. (ENG.). 352p. (J). (gr. 5). 16.99 (978-0-399-25067-5(0), G.P. Putnam's Sons Books for Young Readers) Penguin Young Readers Group.

Madden, Kerry. Jessie's Mountain. 2008. (ENG.). 320p. (J). (gr. 3-7). 16.99 (978-0-670-06154-9(9), Viking Books for Young Readers) Penguin Young Readers Group.

Martin, Ann M. & Godwin, Laura. The Runaway Dolls. Selznick, Brian, illus. (Doll People Ser.: Bk. 3). (ENG.). 352p. (J). (gr. 3-7). 2010. pap. 7.99 (978-0-7868-5585-8(1)) 2008. 17.99 (978-0-7868-5584-1(3)) Hyperion Pr.

—The Runaway Dolls. Selznick, Brian, illus. 2010. (Doll People Ser.: 3). (J). lib. bdg. 18.40 (978-0-606-13987-8(7), Turtleback) Turtleback Bks.

Maruno, Jennifer. Totem, 0 vols. 2014. (ENG.). 168p. (YA). pap. 10.99 (978-1-4597-1934-7(4), 9781459719347) Dundurn CAN. Dist: Ingram Publisher Services.

Marvel, Saga, et al. Marvel Saga. 2009. (Astonishing X-Men Ser.). (Illus.). 152p. pap. 14.99 (978-0-7851-3846-4(3)) Marvel Worldwide, Inc.

Mazer, Harry. Snow Bound. 144p. (YA). (gr. 7-18). pap. 4.99 (978-0-8072-1367-4(5), Listening Library) Random Hse. Audio Publishing Group.

McCusker, Paul & Elmer, Robert. Ripple Effect, 1 vol., Bk. 1. 2008. (Time Thriller Trilogy Ser.: Bk. 1). (ENG., Illus.). 224p. (YA). (gr. 8-11). pap. 9.99 (978-0-310-71436-1(2)) Zondervan.

McKissack, Patricia C. Away West. James, Gordon C. & James, Gordon, illus. 2006. (Scraps of Time Ser.). (ENG.). 144p. (J). (gr. 3-7). 5.99 (978-0-14-240688-5(0), Puffin Books) Penguin Young Readers Group.

Michaelis, Antonia. The Secret of the Twelfth Continent. Hosmer-Dillard, Mollie, tr. from GER. Nievelstein, Ralf, illus. 2013. (ENG.). 288p. (J). (gr. 2-7). 14.95 (978-1-62087-539-1(X), 620539, Sky Pony Pr.) Skyhorse Publishing Co., Inc.

Michaels, Rune. Fix Me. 2011. (ENG., Illus.). 160p. (YA). (gr. 9). 16.99 (978-1-4169-5772-0(3), Atheneum Bks. for Young Readers) Simon & Schuster Children's Publishing.

Mimms, Cory Wheeler. Trailing Tennessee. 2013. (ENG.). 240p. (J). pap. 14.99 (978-1-940052-00-7(9)) Craigmore Creations.

Myers, Bill. The Enemy Closes In, 1 vol. 2009. (Elijah Project Ser.). (ENG.). 128p. (J). (gr. 4-7). pap. 6.99 (978-0-310-71194-0(0)) Zonderkidz.

Nelson, Suzanne. Serendipity's Footsteps. 2015. (ENG.). 368p. (YA). (gr. 7). 17.99 (978-0-385-39212-9(5), Knopf Bks. for Young Readers) Random Hse. Children's Bks.

Niner, Holly L. The Day I Ran Away. Ongaro, Isabella, illus. 2017. (ENG.). 32p. (J). (gr. k-2). 17.95 **(978-1-936261-89-5(8))** Flashlight Pr.

O'Neill, Joan. Rainbow's End. 2007. (ENG.). 288p. (J). (gr. 7-17). pap. 10.95 (978-0-340-91149-5(2)) Hachette Children's Group GBR. Dist: Hachette Bk. Group.

Ostow, Micol. Family. (ENG.). 384p. (J). (gr. 9). 2013. pap. 9.99 (978-1-60684-393-2(1)) 2011. 17.99 (978-1-60684-155-6(6)) Lerner Publishing Group. (Carolrhoda Lab™).

Otis, James. Toby Tyler, or Ten Weeks with a Circus. 2007. 100p. (gr. 4-7). per. (978-1-4068-4370-5(9)) Echo Library.

Parry, Rosanne. Second Fiddle. 2012. (ENG.). 240p. (J). (gr. 3-7). 6.99 (978-0-375-86166-6(1), Yearling) Random Hse. Children's Bks.

Patron, Susan. The Higher Power of Lucky. 2008. (JPN., Illus.). 215p. (J). (978-4-7515-2209-7(4)) Asunaro Shobo.

—The Higher Power of Lucky. 2009. 9.00 (978-0-7848-2460-3(6), Everbind) Marco Bk. Co.

—The Higher Power of Lucky. 2008. 17.00 (978-1-60686-088-5(7)) Perfection Learning Corp.

—The Higher Power of Lucky. Phelan, Matt, illus. (ENG.). (J). (gr. 4-6). 2008. 160p. pap. 7.99 (978-1-4169-7557-1(8), Atheneum Bks. for Young Readers) 2006. 144p. 17.99 (978-1-4169-0194-5(9), Atheneum/Richard Jackson Bks.) Simon & Schuster Children's Publishing.

—The Higher Power of Lucky. 2008. lib. bdg. 18.40 (978-0-606-08934-0(9), Turtleback) Turtleback Bks.

Patterson, James & Raymond, Emily. First Love. 2017. (ENG., Illus.). 384p. mass mkt. 7.99 **(978-1-4555-8500-7(9)**, Jimmy Patterson) Little Brown & Co.

—First Love. Illingworth, Sasha, photos by. 2015. (ENG., Illus.). 336p. (YA). (gr. 10-17). pap. 9.99 (978-0-316-20703-4(9), Jimmy Patterson) Little Brown & Co.

—First Love. 2014. (ENG.). 560p. (YA). pap. 16.00 (978-1-4555-8501-4(7), Jimmy Patterson) Little Brown & Co.

—First Love. 2014. (YA). lib. bdg. 28.20 (978-0-606-35894-1(3)) Turtleback Bks.

Paul, Curtis Christopher. Bud, Not Buddy. 2014. (ENG.). 256p. (J). (gr. 12-12). 11.24 (978-1-63245-063-0(1)) Lectorum Pubns., Inc.

Paulsen, Gary. The Beet Fields. 2011. (ENG.). 174p. (YA). (gr. 9). pap. 7.99 (978-0-375-87305-8(8), Delacorte Bks. for Young Readers) Random Hse. Children's Bks.

—Tasting the Thunder. 144p. (YA). (978-0-330-32705-3(4), Pan) Pan Macmillan.

Pearson, Maggie. The Pop Star Pirates. 2015. (Race Further with Reading Ser.). (ENG., Illus.). 48p. (J). (978-0-7787-2089-8(6)) Crabtree Publishing Co.

Peretti, Frank E. Nightmare Academy. 2008. 352p. (YA). mass mkt. 7.99 (978-1-4003-1017-3(2)) Nelson, Thomas Inc.

Philbrick, Rodman. Freak the Mighty. 20th anniv. ed. 2013. (ENG.). 208p. (J). (gr. 3-7). 16.99 (978-0-545-56645-2(2), Blue Sky Pr., The) Scholastic, Inc.

Posesorski, Sherie. Escape Plans. Pearcey, Dawn, illus. 2005. 272p. (J). (gr. 5). 8.95 (978-1-55050-177-3(1)) Coteau Bks. CAN. Dist: Fitzhenry & Whiteside, Ltd.

Poulsen, David A. Last Sam's Cage. rev. ed. 2004. (ENG.). 224p. (YA). pap. 9.95 (978-1-55263-611-4(9)) Keyhole Pr.

—Last Sam's Cage. rev. ed. 2008. (ENG.). 222p. (YA). (gr. 9-18). per. (978-1-55263-953-5(3)) Me to We.

Preble, Joy. Finding Paris. 2015. (ENG.). 272p. (YA). (gr. 9). 17.99 (978-0-06-232130-5(7)) HarperCollins Pubs.

Ramadurai, Suchitra. The Runaway Peppercorn. Rajagopalan, Ashok, illus. 2005. 28p. (J). (978-81-8146-119-3(3)) Tulika Pubs.

Rapp, Adam. Punkzilla. (ENG., Illus.). 256p. (YA). (gr. 9). 2010. pap. 7.99 (978-0-7636-5297-5(0)) 2009. 16.99 (978-0-7636-3031-7(4)) Candlewick Pr.

Ray, Delia. Finding Fortune. 2015. (ENG.). 288p. (J). (gr. 5-7). 16.99 (978-0-374-30065-4(8), 9780374300654, Farrar, Straus & Giroux (BYR)) Farrar, Straus & Giroux.

Rice, Luanne. The Beautiful Lost. 2017. (ENG.). 304p. (J). (gr. 7). 18.99 **(978-1-338-11107-1(8))** Scholastic, Inc.

Richtel, Matt. Runaway Booger. Wildish, Lee, illus. 2017. 32p. (J). (gr. -1-3). 14.99 (978-0-06-234984-2(8)) HarperCollins Pubs.

Ripley, T. P. Lily Lovebug & the Unconquered Planet. 2013. 170p. pap. (978-1-908910-43-1(7)) Crooked Cat Publishing.

Robbins, Trina. The Bark in Space. Page, Tyler, illus. 2013. (Chicagoland Detective Agency Ser.: 5). (ENG.). 64p. (gr. 4-8). (J). lib. bdg. 29.27 (978-0-7613-8166-2(X)); pap. 6.95 (978-1-4677-0725-1(2)) Lerner Publishing Group. (Graphic Universe™).

Robinson, Anitha. Broken Worlds. 2014. (Broken Worlds Ser.). (ENG.). 200p. (YA). (gr. 8-11). pap. 8.95 (978-1-933767-37-6(5)) CBAY Bks.

Rollins, Ellie. Zip. 2013. (ENG.). 336p. (J). (gr. 3-7). pap. 7.99 (978-1-59514-571-0(0), Razorbill) Penguin Young Readers Group.

Rose, Caroline Starr. Jasper & the Riddle of Riley's Mine. 2017. (ENG.). 288p. (J). (gr. 5). 16.99 (978-0-399-16811-6(7), G.P. Putnam's Sons Books for Young Readers) Penguin Young Readers Group.

Ross, Elizabeth. Belle Epoque. 2014. (ENG.). 352p. (YA). (gr. 7). pap. 9.99 (978-0-385-74147-7(2), Ember) Random Hse. Children's Bks.

Rottman, S. L. Shadow of a Doubt, 1 vol. (ENG.). 224p. (YA). (gr. 7-18). 2005. pap. 7.95 (978-1-56145-354-2(4)) 2003. 14.95 (978-1-56145-291-0(2)) Peachtree Pubs.

Runaway Pony (revised) 2017. (Sandy Lane Stables Ser.). (ENG.). (J). pap. 5.99 **(978-0-7945-3622-0(0)**, Usborne) EDC Publishing.

Rush, Jennifer. Altered. 2013. (Altered Ser.: 1). (ENG.). (YA). (gr. 7-17). 352p. pap. 10.00 (978-0-316-19709-0(2)); 336p. 18.00 (978-0-316-19708-3(4)) Little, Brown Bks. for Young Readers.

Ryan, Darlene. Cuts Like a Knife, 1 vol. 2012. (Orca Soundings Ser.). (ENG.). 128p. (YA). (gr. 8-12). 16.95 (978-1-4598-0120-2(2)); pap. 9.95 (978-1-4598-0119-6(9)) Orca Bk. Pubs. USA.

Ryan, Darlene & Fernández, Queta. De Nadie Mas, 1 vol. 2008. (Spanish Soundings Ser.). (SPA.). 112p. (YA). (gr. 8-12). pap. 9.95 (978-1-55143-969-3(7)) Orca Bk. Pubs. USA.

Saldaña, Jr. A Good Long Way. 2010. 128p. (J). (gr. 6-18). pap. 10.95 (978-1-55885-607-3(2), Piñata Books) Arte Publico Pr.

Sanchez, Priscilla. Champ the Boxing Boxer. 2011. 12p. pap. 8.32 (978-1-4634-7423-2(7)) AuthorHouse.

Scaletta, Kurtis. The Tanglewood Terror. (ENG.). 272p. (J). 2012. (gr. 4-7). 7.99 (978-0-375-86542-8(X), Yearling) 2011. (gr. 3-7). 16.99 (978-0-375-86758-3(9), Knopf Bks. for Young Readers) Random Hse. Children's Bks.

Scanlon, Liz Garton. The Great Good Summer. 2015. (ENG., Illus.). 224p. (J). (gr. 3-7). 16.99 (978-1-4814-1147-9(0), Beach Lane Bks.) Beach Lane Bks.

Schwabach, Karen. The Storm Before Atlanta. 2011. (ENG.). 320p. (J). (gr. 3-7). pap. 6.99 (978-0-375-85867-3(9), Yearling) Random Hse. Children's Bks.

Seidon, Bonnie Bale. The Adventures of Trevor & the Tiger. 2012. 104p. 21.79 (978-1-4669-4389-6(0)); pap. 11.79 (978-1-4669-4391-9(2)) Trafford Publishing.

Selznick, Brian. Wonderstruck. Selznick, Brian, illus. 2011. (ENG., Illus.). 640p. (J). (gr. 4-7). 29.99 (978-0-545-02789-2(6), Scholastic Pr.); 300.00 (978-0-545-38985-3(2)) Scholastic, Inc.

Shaw, Tucker. Oh Yeah, Audrey! 2014. (ENG., Illus.). 256p. (YA). (gr. 8-17). 16.95 (978-1-4197-1223-4(3), Amulet Bks.) Abrams, Inc.

Shepherd, Lee Walker. Gingerhaus & the Runaway Gingerboy. 2007. (Illus.). 32p. (J). spiral bd. 19.99 (978-0-9758995-1-9(1)) Indigo, LLC.

Skovron, Jon. Man Made Boy. (ENG.). 384p. (YA). (gr. 7). 2015. pap. 10.99 (978-0-14-242743-9(8), Speak) 2013. 17.99 (978-0-670-78620-6(9), Viking Books for Young Readers) Penguin Young Readers Group.

Snyder, Zilpha Keatley. William S. & the Great Escape. (ENG.). (J). (gr. 3-7). 2010. 240p. pap. 7.99 (978-1-4169-6764-4(8)) 2009. 224p. 16.99 (978-1-4169-6763-7(X)) Simon & Schuster Children's Publishing. (Atheneum Bks. for Young Readers).

Sommer, Carl. Hopeless to Hopeful. Vignolo, Enrique, illus. 2009. (Quest for Success Ser.). (ENG.). 56p. (YA). pap. 4.95 (978-1-57537-278-5(9)); lib. bdg. 12.95 (978-1-57537-253-2(3)) Advance Publishing, Inc.

—Miserable Millie. Vignolo, Enrique, illus. (J). 2014. pap. (978-1-57537-960-9(0)) 2007. (ENG.). 48p. 16.95 incl. audio compact disk (978-1-57537-521-2(4)) 2007. (ENG.). 48p. (gr. -1-3). 9.95 (978-1-57537-022-4(0)) 2007. (ENG.). 48p. (gr. -1-3). lib. bdg. 16.95 (978-1-57537-071-2(9)) Advance Publishing, Inc.

—Miserable Millie(La Pobrecita Mili) Vignolo, Enrique, illus. 2009. (Another Sommer-Time Story Bilingual Ser.). (SPA & ENG.). 48p. (J). lib. bdg. 16.95 (978-1-57537-160-3(X)) Advance Publishing, Inc.

—The Runaway(La Escapada) Vignolo, Enrique, illus. 2009. (Quest for Success Bilingual Ser.). (SPA & ENG.). 104p. (YA). lib. bdg. 14.95 (978-1-57537-234-1(7)) Advance Publishing, Inc.

Stanley, Shalanda. Drowning Is Inevitable. 2015. (ENG.). 288p. (YA). (gr. 9). 17.99 (978-0-553-50828-4(8), Knopf Bks. for Young Readers) Random Hse. Children's Bks.

Stanton, Angie. Royally Lost. 2014. (ENG.). 336p. (YA). (gr. 8). pap. 9.99 (978-0-06-227258-4(6), HarperTeen) HarperCollins Pubs.

Stokes, K. Lynn. Clouded Visions. 2008. 208p. 24.95 (978-0-595-51980-4(6)); pap. 14.95 (978-0-595-53217-9(9)) iUniverse, Inc.

Stretton, Hesba. Cassy. Hymper, W. & Stacey, W. S., illus. 2006. (Golden Inheritance Ser.: Vol. 9). 117p. (J). pap. (978-0-921100-94-2(9)) Inheritance Pubns.

Tate, Eleanora E. The Minstrel's Melody. 2009. (Mysteries Through Time Ser.). 176p. (gr. 4-8). (YA). pap. 15.25 (978-1-60754-180-6(7)); (Illus.). (J). 31.95 (978-1-60754-179-0(3)) Windmill Bks.

Teele, Elinor. The Mechanical Mind of John Coggin. 2016. (Illus.). 352p. (J). (gr. 3-7). 16.99 (978-0-06-234510-3(9), Waldon Pond Pr.) HarperCollins Pubs.

Thomas, Jacquelin. Split Ends. 2010. (ENG.). 272p. pap. 17.99 (978-1-4165-9879-4(0)) Pocket Books.

Thompson, Ricki. City of Cannibals. 2010. (ENG.). 269p. (YA). (gr. 9-12). 18.95 (978-1-59078-623-9(8), Front Street) Boyds Mills Pr.

Thore, Maria Nilsson. Stay-At-Home Sammy & the Runaway Spot. 2017. (ENG.). 36p. (J). (gr. -1-3). 15.95 (978-0-8234-3677-4(2)) Holiday Hse., Inc.

Tocher, Timothy. Chief Sunrise, John McGraw, & Me. 2004. (ENG.). 168p. (J). (gr. 4-8). 16.95 (978-0-8126-2711-4(3)) Cricket Bks.

Tsiang, Sarah Yi-Mei. Breathing Fire, 1 vol. 2014. (Orca Soundings Ser.). (ENG.). 144p. (YA). (gr. 8-12). pap. 9.95 (978-1-4598-0565-1(8)) Orca Bk. Pubs. USA.

Twain, Mark, pseud. The Adventures of Tom Sawyer. Ingpen, Robert R., illus. 2010. (Sterling Illustrated Classics Ser.). (ENG.). 240p. (J). (gr. 5-18). 19.95 (978-1-4027-6762-3(5)) Sterling Publishing Co., Inc.

—Tom Sawyer, 1 vol. Mullarkey, Lisa, illus. 2010. (Calico Illustrated Classics Ser.: No. 1). (ENG.). 112p. (J). (gr. 3-6). 27.07 (978-1-60270-704-7(9)) Magic Wagon.

—Tom Sawyer. 2009. 196p. (gr. 4-7). pap. 12.99 (978-1-934941-63-8(8)) Red & Black Pubs.

Umminger, Alison. American Girls. 2016. (ENG.). 304p. (YA). 17.99 (978-1-250-07500-0(9), 9781250075000) Flatiron Bks.

Ure, Jean. Gone Missing. 2007. (ENG., Illus.). 192p. (J). (gr. 4-7). pap. 8.99 (978-0-00-722459-3(1), HarperCollins Children's Bks.) HarperCollins Pubs. Ltd. GBR. Dist: HarperCollins Pubs.

VanArsdale, Anthony, illus. Journey on a Runaway Train. 2017. (Boxcar Children Great Adventure Ser.: 1). (ENG.). 160p. (J). (gr. 1-5). 12.99 **(978-0-8075-0695-0(8))**; 6.99 **(978-0-8075-0696-7(6))** Whitman, Albert & Co.

Voigt, Cynthia. The Tale of Birle. 2015. (Tales of the Kingdom Ser.: 2). (ENG., Illus.). 416p. (YA). (gr. 7). 19.99 (978-1-4424-8356-9(3), Atheneum Bks. for Young Readers) Simon & Schuster Children's Publishing.

Volponi, Paul. Homestretch. 2009. (ENG.). 160p. (YA). (gr. 7-18). 16.99 (978-1-4169-3987-0(3), Atheneum Bks. for Young Readers) Simon & Schuster Children's Publishing.

Voss, Dawn. Avenging Aja. 2007. 50p. pap. 15.00 (978-0-615-15324-7(0)) Voss, Dawn L.

Wallace, Brandon. The Journey Home. (Wilder Boys Ser.). (ENG.). 208p. (J). 2017. (gr. 4-8). pap. 7.99 **(978-1-4814-3266-5(4))** 2016. (Illus.). (gr. 3-7). 16.99 (978-1-4814-3267-2(2)) Simon & Schuster Children's Publishing. (Aladdin).

Wallace, Brandon. Wilder Boys. 2017. (Wilder Boys Ser.). (ENG.). 256p. (J). (gr. 4-8). pap. 7.99 (978-1-4814-3263-4(X), Simon & Schuster/Paula Wiseman Bks.) Simon & Schuster/Paula Wiseman Bks.

Walters, Gregory. Fouling Out, 1 vol. 2008. (ENG.). 176p. (J). (gr. 5-10). pap. 8.95 (978-1-55143-714-9(7)) Orca Bk. Pubs. USA.

Wang, Jack, et al. Mark Twain's the Adventures of Huckleberry Finn. 2016. (ENG., Illus.). 24p. (J). (gr. -1 — 1). bds. 9.95 (978-1-4521-5249-3(7)) Chronicle Bks. LLC.

—Mark Twain's the Adventures of Tom Sawyer. 2017. (Cozy Classics Ser.). (ENG., Illus.). 24p. (J). bds. 9.95 (978-1-4521-5250-9(0)) Chronicle Bks. LLC.

Ward, Rachel. Numbers. 2010. (Numbers Ser.: 1). (ENG.). 336p. (J). (gr. 7-12). 17.99 (978-0-545-14299-1(7), Chicken Hse., The) Scholastic, Inc.

Warner, Gertrude Chandler. Journey on a Runaway Train. 2017. (Boxcar Children Great Adventure Ser.: 1). (J). lib. bdg. 17.20 **(978-0-606-40315-3(9))** Turtleback Bks.

Weinbrenner, Darlene. Hannah, Mable, & the Moving Van. 2007. 76p. per. 19.95 (978-1-4241-6563-6(6)) America Star Bks.

Whelan, Gloria. Chu Ju's House. 2004. 240p. (J). (gr. 5-18). lib. bdg. 17.89 (978-0-06-050725-1(X)) HarperCollins Pubs.

—Friend on Freedom River. van Frankenhuyzen, Gijsbert, illus. 2004. (Tales of Young Americans Ser.). (ENG.). 32p. (J). 16.95 (978-1-58536-222-6(0)) Sleeping Bear Pr.

Whipple, Natalie. Transparent. 2013. (ENG.). 368p. (YA). (gr. 8). pap. 9.99 (978-0-06-212016-8(6), HarperTeen) HarperCollins Pubs.

Wilson, Jacqueline. Cookie. Sharratt, Nick, illus. 2010. (ENG.). 352p. (J). (gr. 4-7). pap. 11.99 (978-0-312-64290-7(3), 9780312642907) Square Fish.

Wissing, Caroline. Voiceless. 2012. (ENG.). 240p. (gr. 10-12). pap. 14.95 (978-1-897235-98-0(4)) Thistledown Pr., Ltd. CAN. Dist: Univ. of Toronto Pr.

Withers, Pam. Camp Wild, 1 vol. 2006. (Orca Currents Ser.). (ENG.). 112p. (J). (gr. 5-9). 14.95 (978-1-55143-557-2(8)) Orca Bk. Pubs. USA.

—Camp Wild. 2006. (Orca Currents Ser.). 104p. (gr. 5-9). lib. bdg. 19.95 (978-0-7569-6878-6(X)) Perfection Learning Corp.

Woltz, Anna. A Hundred Hours of Night. Watkinson, Laura, tr. from DUT. 2016. (ENG.). 256p. (YA). (gr. 9). 17.99 (978-0-545-84828-2(8), Levine, Arthur A. Bks.) Scholastic, Inc.

Woodson, Jacqueline. Beneath a Meth Moon: An Elegy. (ENG.). (YA). (gr. 7). 2013. 240p. pap. 8.99 (978-0-14-242392-9(0), Speak) 2012. 144p. 16.99 (978-0-399-25250-1(9), Nancy Paulsen Books) Penguin Young Readers Group.

—Beneath a Meth Moon: An Elegy. 2013. lib. bdg. 19.65 (978-0-606-30566-2(1), Turtleback) Turtleback Bks.

Wright, Richard. Rite of Passage. 2014. (Trophy Bk Ser.). (ENG.). 160p. (J). (gr. 8-12). 13.24 (978-1-63245-325-9(8)) Lectorum Pubns., Inc.

Wunder, Wendy. The Museum of Intangible Things. 2015. (ENG.). 256p. (YA). (gr. 7). pap. 9.99 (978-1-59514-576-5(1), Razorbill) Penguin Young Readers Group.

Wynne-Jones, Tim. Blink & Caution. (ENG., Illus.). 352p. (YA). (gr. 9). 2012. pap. 8.99 (978-0-7636-5697-3(6)) 2011. 16.99 (978-0-7636-3983-9(4)) Candlewick Pr.

—The Maestro. l.t. ed. 2013. 304p. pap. (978-1-4596-6503-3(1)) ReadHowYouWant.com, Ltd.

Yee, Lisa. Absolutely Maybe. 2009. (ENG.). 288p. (J). (gr. 7-18). 16.99 (978-0-439-83844-3(4), Levine, Arthur A. Bks.) Scholastic, Inc.

RUNNING

see Track and Field

RURAL ARCHITECTURE

see Architecture, Domestic

RURAL LIFE—FICTION

Chambers, Vickie. In the Silence of the Hills. Taylor, LaVonne, ed. (Illus.). (YA). (gr. 9-12). (978-0-9627735-1-8(4)) Excellence Enterprises.

Fox, Gaines. Go Fly a Kite: A Juvenile Adventure Novel. 2008. 200p. pap. 24.95 (978-1-60703-573-2(1)) America Star Bks.

Sarja, Jennifer. When Watute Wants Some Water. Phan, Henry et al, illus. 2005. 36p. (J). (gr. -1-3). 20.00 (978-0-9773451-0-6(6)) Youth Inkwell Publishing.

Wright, Lloyd. Gramp's Variety of Stories. 2007. 200p. 24.95 (978-0-595-71311-0(4)); per. 14.95 (978-0-595-47731-9(3)) iUniverse, Inc.

RURAL SOCIOLOGY

see Sociology, Rural

RUSSELL, BILL, 1934-

Hayhurst, Chris. Bill Russell. 2009. (Basketball Hall of Famers Ser.). 112p. (gr. 5-8). 63.90 (978-1-61511-530-3(7), Rosen Reference) Rosen Publishing Group, Inc., The.

RUSSELL, CHARLES M. (CHARLES MARION), 1864-1926

Harris, Lois. Charlie Russell: Tale-Telling Cowboy Artist, 1 vol. 2010. (ENG., Illus.). 32p. (J). (gr. k-3). 16.99 (978-1-58980-758-7(8)) Pelican Publishing Co., Inc.

RUSSIA (FEDERATION)

see also Soviet Union, for works discussing the time period before the dissolution of the former Soviet Union; and Former Soviet Republics, for works discussing collecively the independent countries that emerged from the dissolution of the former Soviet Union.

Beliaev, Edward & Buranbaeva, Oksana. Dagestan. 2005. (Cultures of the World Ser.). (Illus.). 144p. (J). (gr. 3-7). lib. bdg. (978-0-7614-2015-6(0)) Marshall Cavendish Corp.

The check digit for ISBN-10 appears in parentheses after the full ISBN-13

Blake, Kevin. Russia. 2017. (Countries We Come From Ser.). (ENG., Illus.). 32p. (J). (gr. -1-3). 19.95 *(978-1-68402-056-0(5))* Bearport Publishing Co., Inc.

Blomquist, Christopher. A Primary Source Guide to Russia. (Countries of the World). 24p. 2009. (gr. 2-3). 42.50 *(978-1-61512-044-4(0))* 2005. (Illus.). (J). (gr. k-5). lib. bdg. 22.60 *(978-1-4042-2756-9(3))* Rosen Publishing Group, Inc., The. (PowerKids Pr.).

Bowden, Rob & Ransome, Galya. Focus on Russia. 2007. (World in Focus Ser.). 64p. (gr. 5-12). pap. 14.05 *(978-0-8368-6756-5(4))*; (Illus.). lib. bdg. 34.00 *(978-0-8368-6749-7(1))* Stevens, Gareth Publishing LLLP. (Gareth Stevens Secondary Library).

Centore, Michael. Russia, Vol. 12. 2015. (Major Nations in a Global World: Tradition, Culture, & Daily Life Ser.). 64p. (J). (gr. 7). 23.95 *(978-1-4222-3349-8(9))* Mason Crest.

Chanek, Sherilin & National Geographic Learning Staff. Europe & Russia: Geography & Environments. 2007. (Reading Expeditions Ser.). (ENG., Illus.). 64p. pap. 25.95 *(978-0-7922-4374-8(9))* CENGAGE Learning.

—Europe & Russia - People & Places. 2007. (Reading Expeditions Ser.). (ENG., Illus.). 64p. (J). pap. 25.95 *(978-0-7922-4375-5(7))* CENGAGE Learning.

Charting Russia's Future, 2 bks. 9th ed. 2005. 88p. (YA). pap. *(978-1-891306-81-5(2))* Choices Program, Watson Institute, Brown Univ.

Dando, William A. Russia. 2nd rev. ed. 2007. (Modern World Nations Ser.). (Illus.). 141p. (YA). (gr. 7-12). lib. bdg. 35.00 *(978-0-7910-9248-4(8))* Facts On File, Inc.

Frederick, Shane. Alexander Ovechkin. 2015. (Hockey Superstars Ser.). (ENG.). 32p. (gr. 3-4). lib. bdg. 27.99 *(978-1-4914-2141-3(X))* Capstone Press of Coughlan Cos.

Ganeri, Anita. Russia. 2017. (Journey Through Ser.). (ENG., Illus.). 32p. (J). (gr. 4-6). 16.99 ***(978-1-4451-5620-0(2)***, Franklin Watts) Hachette Children's Group GBR. Dist: Hachette Bk. Group.

—Russia. Isik, Semur, illus. 2015. (Country Guides, with Benjamin Blog & His Inquisitive Dog Ser.). (ENG.). 32p. (gr. 1-3). 29.99 *(978-1-4109-7997-1(0)*, Read Me!) Heinemann-Raintree.

George, Enzo. Russia's City of the Dead. 2017. (Crypts, Tombs, & Secret Rooms Ser.). 48p. (gr. 4-5). pap. 84.30 ***(978-1-5382-0644-7(7))*** Stevens, Gareth Publishing LLLP.

Glaser, Jason. Maria Sharapova. 2009. (Sports Idols Ser.). 24p. (gr. 2-3). 42.50 *(978-1-60853-142-4(2)*, PowerKids Pr.) Rosen Publishing Group, Inc., The.

Glencoe McGraw-Hill Staff. Exploring Our World: People, Places & Cultures. 2007. (WORLD & ITS PEOPLE EASTERN Ser.). (ENG., Illus.). 108p. (gr. 6-9). pap. 11.32 *(978-0-07-878170-4(1)*, 0078781701) McGraw-Hill Higher Education.

—Exploring Our World - People, Places, & Cultures: Western Hemisphere, Europe, & Russia. 2007. (WORLD & ITS PEOPLE EASTERN Ser.). (ENG., Illus.). 59p. (gr. 6-9). per. 6.48 *(978-0-07-877728-8(3)*, 0078777283) McGraw-Hill Higher Education.

Haugen, David. Russia. Greenhaven Press Editors, ed. 2013. (Opposing Viewpoints Ser.). (ENG.). 224p. (gr. 10-12). pap. 33.80 *(978-0-7377-6970-8(X))*; lib. bdg. 48.80 *(978-0-7377-6969-2(6))* Cengage Gale. (Greenhaven Pr., Inc.).

Hulick, Kathryn. My Teenage Life in Russia. 2017. (Custom & Cultures of the World Ser.: Vol. 12). (ENG., Illus.). (YA). (gr. 7-12). 23.95 ***(978-1-4222-3910-0(1))*** Mason Crest.

Hunt, Jilly. Russia, 1 vol. 2012. (Countries Around the World Ser.). (ENG.). 48p. (gr. 3-6). pap. 9.95 *(978-1-4329-6136-7(5))*; lib. bdg. 33.32 *(978-1-4329-6110-7(1))* Heinemann-Raintree. (NA-h).

Johnson, Robin. The Urals. 2011. (ENG., Illus.). 48p. (J). pap. *(978-0-7787-7571-3(2))*; (gr. 4-7). lib. bdg. *(978-0-7787-7564-5(X))* Crabtree Publishing Co.

Kalman, Bobbie. Spotlight on Russia. 2010. (ENG.). 32p. (J). pap. *(978-0-7787-3486-4(2))* Crabtree Publishing Co.

Markle, Sandra. The Great Leopard Rescue: Saving the Amur Leopards. 2016. (ENG., Illus.). 48p. (J). (gr. 4-6). 30.65 *(978-1-4677-9247-9(0)*, Millbrook Pr.) Lerner Publishing Group.

Márquez, Herón. Russia in Pictures. 2nd ed. 2003. (Visual Geography Series, Second Ser.). (ENG., Illus.). 80p. (gr. 5-12). 31.93 *(978-0-8225-0937-0(7))* Lerner Publishing Group.

Marsh, Carole. Russia: The Great Bear & Its Dramatic History! 2009. (It's Your World Ser.). 48p. (J). (gr. 2-9). pap. 7.99 *(978-0-635-06809-5(5))* Gallopade International.

Marsico, Katie. Russia. 2010. (Explorer Library: Social Studies Explorer Ser.). (ENG.). 48p. (gr. 4-8). lib. bdg. 31.36 *(978-1-60279-831-1(1)*, 200528) Cherry Lake Publishing.

Maynard, Charles W. The Ural Mountains. 2004. (Great Mountain Ranges of the World Ser.). (Illus.). 24p. (J). lib. bdg. 22.60 *(978-0-8239-6699-8(2)*, PowerKids Pr.) Rosen Publishing Group, Inc., The.

McGraw-Hill Education Editors. Exploring Our World: People, Places, & Culture. 2007. (WORLD & ITS PEOPLE EASTERN Ser.). (ENG & SPA., Illus.). 108p. (gr. 6-9). per. 12.04 *(978-0-07-878172-8(8)*, 0078781728) McGraw-Hill Education.

McGraw-Hill-Glencoe Staff & McGraw-Hill Education Staff. Exploring Our World, Western Hemisphere with Europe & Russia, Student Edition. 2nd ed. 2007. (WORLD & ITS PEOPLE EASTERN Ser.). (ENG.). (gr. 6-9). 98.00 *(978-0-07-874580-5(2)*, 0078745802) McGraw-Hill Education.

McGraw-Hill Staff. Exploring Our World, Western Hemisphere with Europe & Russia. 2007. (WORLD & ITS PEOPLE EASTERN Ser.). (ENG.). (gr. 6-9). cd-rom 104.00 *(978-0-07-879088-1(3)*, 0078790883) McGraw-Hill Education.

Mis, Melody S. How to Draw Russia's Sights & Symbols. 2009. (Kid's Guide to Drawing the Countries of the World Ser.). 48p. (gr. 4-4). 53.00 *(978-1-61511-124-4(7)*, PowerKids Pr.) Rosen Publishing Group, Inc., The.

Moon, Walt K. Exploremos Rusia. 2017. (Bumba Books (tm) en Español — Exploremos Países (Let's Explore Countries) Ser.). (SPA.). 24p. (J). (gr. -1-1). lib. bdg. 25.32 ***(978-1-5124-4125-3(2))*** Lerner Publishing Group.

Moon, Walt K. Let's Explore Russia. 2017. (Bumba Books (tm) — Let's Explore Countries Ser.). (ENG.). 24p. (J). (gr. -1-1). 12.99 ***(978-1-5124-3744-7(1)***, Lerner Pubns.); 38.65 ***(978-1-5124-3012-7(9)***, Lerner Pubns.); 38.65 ***(978-1-5124-3743-0(3)***, Lerner Pubns.); (Illus.). 25.32 *(978-1-5124-3009-7(9))* Lerner Publishing Group.

Murdico, Suzanne J. Russia: A Primary Source Cultural Guide. (Primary Sources of World Cultures Ser.). 128p. 2009. (gr. 4-5). 79.90 *(978-1-60851-929-3(5))* 2005. (Illus.). (J). (gr. 5-8). lib. bdg. 37.25 *(978-1-4042-2913-6(2))* Rosen Publishing Group, Inc., The.

Murray, Julie. Russia, 1 vol. 2013. (Explore the Countries Ser.). (ENG.). 40p. (J). (gr. 2-5). lib. bdg. 29.93 *(978-1-61783-817-0(9)*, Big Buddy Bks.) ABDO Publishing Co.

Nichols, Susan. Vladimir Putin. 2017. ***(978-0-7660-9204-4(6))*** Enslow Pubs., Inc.

Nickles, Greg. Russia: The Culture. 3rd rev. ed. 2008. (Lands, Peoples & Cultures Ser.). (ENG., Illus.). 32p. (J). (gr. 3-7). pap. *(978-0-7787-9672-5(8))* Crabtree Publishing Co.

—Russia: The Land. 3rd rev. ed. 2008. (Lands, Peoples & Cultures Ser.). (ENG., Illus.). 32p. (J). (gr. 3-7). pap. *(978-0-7787-9670-1(1))* Crabtree Publishing Co.

—Russia - The Land. 3rd rev. ed. 2008. (Lands, Peoples & Cultures Ser.). (ENG., Illus.). 32p. (J). (gr. 3-7). lib. bdg. *(978-0-7787-9302-1(8))* Crabtree Publishing Co.

—Russia - The People. 3rd rev. ed. 2008. (Lands, Peoples & Cultures Ser.). (ENG., Illus.). 32p. (J). (gr. 3-7). pap. *(978-0-7787-9671-8(X))* Crabtree Publishing Co.

Nickles, Greg & Kalman, Bobbie. Russia - The Culture. 3rd rev. ed. 2008. (Lands, Peoples & Cultures Ser.). (ENG., Illus.). 32p. (J). (gr. 3-7). lib. bdg. *(978-0-7787-9304-5(4))* Crabtree Publishing Co.

Nickles, Greg & Nickels, Greg. Russia: The People. 3rd rev. ed. 2008. (Lands, Peoples & Cultures Ser.). (ENG., Illus.). 32p. (J). (gr. 3-7). lib. bdg. *(978-0-7787-9303-8(6))* Crabtree Publishing Co.

Pelleschi, Andrea. Russia, 1 vol. 2013. (Countries of the World Set 2 Ser.). (ENG.). 144p. (J). (gr. 6-12). lib. bdg. 37.07 *(978-1-61783-635-0(4)*, Essential Library) ABDO Publishing Co.

Powell, Jillian. Descubramos Rusia. 2007. (Descubramos Países del Mundo (Looking at Countries) Ser.). (SPA & ENG., Illus.). 32p. (gr. 1-5). lib. bdg. 26.00 *(978-0-8368-8187-5(7)*, Gareth Stevens Learning Library) Stevens, Gareth Publishing LLLP.

—Descubramos Rusia (Looking at Russia) 2007. (Descubramos países del mundo (Spanish- Looking at Countries) Ser.). (SPA.). 32p. (gr. 1-5). pap. 10.50 *(978-0-8368-8194-3(X)*, Gareth Stevens Learning Library) Stevens, Gareth Publishing LLLP.

—Looking at Russia. 2007. (Looking at Countries Ser.). 32p. (gr. 1-5). pap. 10.50 *(978-0-8368-8180-6(X))*; (Illus.). lib. bdg. 26.00 *(978-0-8368-8173-8(7))* Stevens, Gareth Publishing LLLP. (Gareth Stevens Learning Library).

Ransome, Galya. Russia in Our World. 2010. (Countries in Our World Ser.). 32p. (gr. 4-7). lib. bdg. 31.35 *(978-1-59920-442-0(8))* Black Rabbit Bks.

Rechner, Amy. Russia. 2017. (Country Profiles Ser.). (ENG., Illus.). 32p. (J). (gr. 3-8). lib. bdg. 26.95 ***(978-1-62617-686-7(8)***, Blastoff! Discovery) Bellwether Media.

Reid, Sue & Collins UK Staff. Spotlight on Russia. 2016. (ENG.). 80p. (J). (gr. 5-6). pap. 9.95 *(978-0-00-816404-1(5))* HarperCollins Pubs. Ltd. GBR. Dist: Independent Pubs. Group.

Roland, James. Growing up in Russia. 2017. (ENG.). 80p. (YA). (gr. 5-12). ***(978-1-68282-223-4(0))*** ReferencePoint Pr., Inc.

Rosenberg, Aaron. Vladimir Putin: President of Russia. (Newsmakers Ser.). 112p. 2009. (gr. 9-10). 63.90 *(978-1-60851-136-5(7))* 2007. (Illus.). (YA). (gr. 7-12). lib. bdg. 34.60 *(978-1-4042-1903-8(X))* Rosen Publishing Group, Inc., The.

Rothstein, Evelyn. Clara's Great War. Uhlig, Elizabeth, illus. 2011. 88p. (J). pap. 12.95 *(978-0-9815345-9-6(7))* Marble Hse. Editions.

Rozett, Louise. Ice Queen: Catherine the Great Seizes Power in Russia. 2011. (J). pap. *(978-0-545-32946-0(9))* Scholastic, Inc.

Russell, Henry & National Geographic Kids Staff. Russia. 2008. (Countries of the World Ser.). (ENG., Illus.). 64p. (J). (gr. 5). lib. bdg. 27.90 *(978-1-4263-0259-6(2)*, National Geographic Children's Bks.) National Geographic Society.

Savage, Jeff. Alex Ovechkin. 2011. (Amazing Athletes Set VIII Ser.). pap. 45.32 *(978-0-7613-8601-8(7))*; (ENG.). 32p. (gr. 2-5). pap. 7.95 *(978-0-7613-7818-1(9))* Lerner Publishing Group.

—Maria Sharapova. 2008. pap. 40.95 *(978-0-8225-9489-5(7))* Lerner Publishing Group.

Senker, Cath. Russia. 2016. (Land & the People Ser.). 48p. (gr. 5-5). pap. 14.05 *(978-1-4824-5095-8(X))* Stevens, Gareth Publishing LLLP.

Sexton, Colleen & Bartell, Jim. Russia. 2010. (Exploring Countries Ser.). (ENG., Illus.). 32p. (J). (gr. 3-7). lib. bdg. 26.95 *(978-1-60014-488-2(8)*, Blastoff! Readers) Bellwether Media.

Snyder, Laurel. Swan: The Life & Dance of Anna Pavlova. Morstad, Julie, illus. 2015. (ENG.). 52p. (J). (gr. 1-4). 17.99 *(978-1-4521-1890-1(6))* Chronicle Bks. LLC.

Steele, Philip. Russia. 2015. (Emerging Nations Ser.). (ENG., Illus.). 48p. (J). (gr. 4-9). 37.10 *(978-1-59920-989-0(6))* Black Rabbit Bks.

Streissguth, Thomas. Russia. 2008. (Country Explorers Ser.). (Illus.). 48p. (J). (gr. 2-5). lib. bdg. 27.93 *(978-0-8225-8664-7(9))* Lerner Publishing Group.

Streissguth, Tom. Russia. 2008. pap. 40.95 *(978-0-8225-9307-2(6))* Lerner Publishing Group.

Suib, Stella. Inside Russia's SVR: The Foreign Intelligence Service. 2009. (Inside the World's Most Famous Intelligence Agencies Ser.). 64p. (gr. 5-5). 58.50 *(978-1-61513-572-1(3))* Rosen Publishing Group, Inc., The.

Thornton, Jeremy. Religious Intolerance: Jewish Immigrants Come to America (1881-1914) 2009. (Primary Sources of Immigration & Migration in America Ser.). 24p. (gr. 3-4). 42.50 *(978-1-60851-783-1(7)*, PowerKids Pr.) Rosen Publishing Group, Inc., The.

Torchinsky, Oleg, et al. Russia. 2015. (Cultures of the World (r) Ser.). (ENG., Illus.). 144p. (J). (gr. 5-5). 47.07 *(978-1-5026-0342-5(X))* Cavendish Square Publishing.

Trenton, Russell, ed. The Russian Revolution: The Fall of the Tsars & the Rise of Communism. 2015. (Age of Revolution Ser.). (ENG.). 128p. (YA). (gr. 9-10). 70.50 *(978-1-68048-033-7(2)*, Britannica Educational Publishing) Rosen Publishing Group, Inc., The.

Vincent, Zu. Catherine the Great: Empress of Russia. 2009. (Wicked History Ser.). (ENG.). 128p. (J). (gr. 6-12). pap. 5.95 *(978-0-531-20738-3(2)*, Watts, Franklin) Scholastic Library Publishing.

Woolf, Alex. Meteor: Perspectives on Asteroid Strikes, 1 vol. 2014. (Disaster Dossiers Ser.). (ENG., Illus.). 56p. (gr. 7-8). 34.65 *(978-1-4846-0182-2(3))* Heinemann-Raintree.

Yomtov, Nelson & Rogers, Stillman. Russia. 2012. (ENG.). 144p. (J). lib. bdg. 40.00 *(978-0-531-27545-0(0))* Scholastic Library Publishing.

Zemlicka, Shannon. Colors of Russia. Reeves, Jeni, illus. (Colors of the World Ser.). 24p. (J). 2005. (gr. 3-6). lib. bdg. 19.93 *(978-1-57505-513-8(9))* 2003. (gr. 1-4). pap. 5.95 *(978-1-57505-564-0(3))* Lerner Publishing Group.

RUSSIA (FEDERATION)—COMMUNISM

see Communism—Soviet Union

RUSSIAN AMERICANS

Behnke, Alison. Russians in America. 2005. (In America Ser.). (ENG., Illus.). 80p. (gr. 5-8). lib. bdg. 27.93 *(978-0-8225-3954-4(3)*, Lerner Pubns.) Lerner Publishing Group.

Bryan, Nichol. Russian Americans, 1 vol. 2004. (One Nation Set 2 Ser.). (ENG.). 32p. (gr. k-6). 27.07 *(978-1-59197-533-5(6)*, Checkerboard Library) ABDO Publishing Co.

Marcovitz, Hal. Russian Americans. (Major American Immigration Ser.). (Illus.). 64p. (YA). 2010. (gr. 9-12). 22.95 *(978-1-4222-0617-1(3))* 2009. (gr. 9-12). 22.95 *(978-1-4222-0513-6(4))* 2007. (gr. 7-18). pap. 9.95 *(978-1-4222-0868-7(0))* Mason Crest.

Moreno, Barry. The Russian Americans. 2007. (Major American Immigration Ser.). (YA). pap. 9.95 *(978-1-4222-0684-3(X))* Mason Crest.

Trumbauer, Lisa. Russian Immigrants. 2004. (Immigration to the United States Ser.). (Illus.). 96p. (gr. 4-9). 35.00 *(978-0-8160-5685-9(4))* Facts On File, Inc.

RUSSIAN AMERICANS—FICTION

Barbara, Cohen. Molly's Pilgrim. 97th rev. ed. 2014. (ENG.). 32p. (J). (gr. 1-5). 8.24 *(978-1-63245-244-3(8))* Lectorum Pubns., Inc.

Best, Cari. Three Cheers for Catherine the Great! Potter, Giselle, illus. 2003. (Catherine the Great Ser.). (ENG.). 32p. (J). (gr. -1-3). pap. 8.99 *(978-0-374-47551-2(2)*, 9780374475512) Square Fish.

Blume, Lesley M. M. The Rising Star of Rusty Nail. 2009. (ENG.). 288p. (J). (gr. 3-7). 7.99 *(978-0-440-42111-5(X)*, Yearling) Random Hse. Children's Bks.

Brosgol, Vera. Anya's Ghost. Brosgol, Vera, illus. 2011. (ENG., Illus.). 224p. (YA). (gr. 7-12). 22.99 *(978-1-59643-713-5(8)*, 9781596437135, First Second Bks.) Roaring Brook Pr.

—Anya's Ghost. Brosgol, Vera, illus. 2014. (ENG., Illus.). 240p. (YA). (gr. 7). pap. 10.99 *(978-1-250-04001-5(9)*, 9781250040015) Square Fish.

Cohen, Barbara. Molly's Pilgrim. Duffy, Daniel Mark & Deraney, Michael J., illus. 97th rev. ed. 2005. (ENG.). 32p. (J). (gr. 2-5). pap. 3.99 *(978-0-688-16280-1(0))* HarperCollins Pubs.

—Molly's Pilgrim. (Literature to Go Ser.). pap., tchr. ed. incl. VHS *(978-0-7919-2685-7(0))* Phoenix Films & Video.

Crowder, Melanie. Audacity. 2016. (ENG.). 400p. (YA). (gr. 7). pap. 10.99 *(978-0-14-751249-9(2)*, Speak) Penguin Young Readers Group.

Crowder, Melanie & Mack, Jeff. Audacity. 2015. (ENG.). 400p. (YA). (gr. 7). bds. 17.99 *(978-0-399-16899-4(0)*, Philomel Bks.) Penguin Young Readers Group.

Devlin, Calla. Right Where You Left Me. 2017. (ENG., Illus.). 256p. (YA). (gr. 9). 17.99 ***(978-1-4814-8699-6(3)***, Atheneum Bks. for Young Readers) Simon & Schuster Children's Publishing.

Greenberger, Tehilla. Gifts to Treasure. Toron, Eli, illus. 2007. (Fun to Read Book.). 224p. (J). per. 10.95 *(978-1-929628-32-2(3))* Hachai Publishing.

Hesse, Karen. Brooklyn Bridge. Sheban, Chris, illus. 2011. (ENG.). 256p. (J). (gr. 5-9). pap. 9.99 *(978-0-312-67428-1(7)*, 9780312674281) Square Fish.

Hill, Kirkpatrick. Dancing at the Odinochka. 2010. (ENG.). 272p. (J). (gr. 5-9). pap. 12.99 *(978-1-4424-1352-8(2)*, McElderry, Margaret K. Bks.) McElderry, Margaret K. Bks.

Kiem, Elizabeth. Dancer, Daughter, Traitor, Spy. 2014. (Bolshoi Saga Ser.: 1). (ENG., Illus.). 292p. (YA). (gr. 9). pap. 10.99 *(978-1-61695-422-2(1)*, Soho Teen) Soho Pr., Inc.

Kirov, Erica. The Chalice of Immortality. 2011. (ENG.). 208p. (J). (gr. 4-7). pap. 7.99 *(978-1-4022-1503-2(7)*, Sourcebooks Jabberwocky) Sourcebooks, Inc.

Mann, Jennifer Ann. Sunny Sweet Is So Dead Meat. 2014. (Sunny Sweet Ser.). (ENG., Illus.). 208p. (YA). (gr. 3-6). 15.99 *(978-1-59990-978-3(2)*, 9781599909783, Bloomsbury USA Childrens) Bloomsbury Publishing USA.

—Sunny Sweet Is So Not Sorry. 2013. (Sunny Sweet Ser.). (ENG., Illus.). 208p. (YA). (gr. 3-6). 15.99 *(978-1-59990-977-6(4)*, 9781599909776, Bloomsbury USA Childrens) Bloomsbury Publishing USA.

Weston Woods Staff, creator. Three Cheers for Catherine the Great. 2011. 18.95 *(978-0-439-80506-3(6))* Weston Woods Studios, Inc.

—Three Cheers for Catherine the Great! 2011. 38.75 *(978-0-439-78620-1(7))* Weston Woods Studios, Inc.

RUSSIAN COMMUNISM

see Communism—Soviet Union

RUSSIAN LANGUAGE

Beullens-Maoui, Nathalie, ed. Animals Habitats: Russian, 01 vols., 1. 2016. (Our Wonderful World Ser.). (ENG & SPA.). 8p. (J). pap. 9.35 *(978-1-5081-1245-7(2)*, Rosen Classroom) Rosen Publishing Group, Inc., The.

Carole Marsh. From Russia with Love! Russian for Kids. 2004. (Little Linguist Ser.). 32p. (gr. 2-6). pap. 5.95 *(978-0-635-02433-6(0))* Gallopade International.

Cartwright, Stephen & Amery, Heather. First Thousand Words in Russian. 2004. (First Thousand Words Ser.). (RUS & ENG., Illus.). 64p. (J). (gr. -1-7). lib. bdg. 20.95 *(978-0-88110-574-2(0))* EDC Publishing.

Fedoruk, Dennis, prod. Bilingual Baby - Flashcard Set - Russian. 2013. (RUS.). (J). 7.99 *(978-1-892703-79-8(3))* Small Fry Beginnings.

Kalz, Jill. My First Russian Phrases, 1 vol. TransPerfect Translations Staff, tr. Fabbri, Daniele, illus. 2012. (Speak Another Language! Ser.). (ENG & RUS.). 32p. (gr. 1-3). lib. bdg. 26.65 *(978-1-4048-7515-9(8))* Picture Window Bks.

Kudela, Katy R. My First Book of Russian Words, 1 vol. Translations.com Staff, tr. 2011. (Bilingual Picture Dictionaries Ser.). 32p. (gr. 1-2). (ENG & MUL.). pap. 8.10 *(978-1-4296-6336-6(7))*; (MUL.). pap. 47.70 *(978-1-4296-6463-9(0))* Capstone Press of Coughlan Cos. (Aplus Bks.).

Marsh, Carole. False Paw! French for Kids. Beard, Chad, ed. 2004. (Little Linguist Ser.). (Illus.). 32p. lib. bdg. 29.95 *(978-0-635-02438-1(1))* Gallopade International.

—From Russia with Love! Russian for Kids. Beard, Chad, ed. 2004. (Little Linguist Ser.). (Illus.). 32p. 29.95 *(978-0-635-02441-1(1))* Gallopade International.

Melling, David, illus. First Russian Words. 2009. (First Words Ser.). (RUS & ENG.). 48p. (J). (gr. 3-18). pap. 12.95 *(978-0-19-911151-0(0))* Oxford Univ. Pr., Inc.

Milet Publishing Staff. Animals - My First Bilingual Book. 2011. (My First Bilingual Book Ser.). (ENG., Illus.). 24p. (J). (gr. k — 1). bds. 7.99 *(978-1-84059-618-2(X))* Milet Publishing.

—Bilingual Visual Dictionary. 2011. (Milet Multimedia Ser.). (ENG & RUS., Illus.). 1p. (J). (gr. k-2). cd-rom 19.95 *(978-1-84059-590-1(6))* Milet Publishing.

—Fruit - My First Bilingual Book. 2011. (My First Bilingual Book Ser.). (ENG., Illus.). 24p. (J). (gr. k — 1). bds. 7.99 *(978-1-84059-634-2(1))* Milet Publishing.

—Milet Bilingual Visual Dictionary. 2012. (Milet Bilingual Visual Dictionary Ser.). (ENG & RUS., Illus.). 148p. (J). (gr. k-2). 34.95 *(978-1-84059-694-6(5))* Milet Publishing.

—My Bilingual Book-Hearing (English-Russian) 2014. (My Bilingual Book Ser.). (ENG & RUS., Illus.). 28p. (J). (gr. -1-k). 9.95 *(978-1-84059-782-0(8))* Milet Publishing.

—My Bilingual Book-Sight (English-Russian) 2014. (My Bilingual Book Ser.). (ENG & RUS., Illus.). 28p. (J). (gr. -1-k). 9.95 *(978-1-84059-798-1(4))* Milet Publishing.

—My Bilingual Book-Smell (English-Russian) 2014. (My Bilingual Book Ser.). (ENG & RUS., Illus.). 28p. (J). (gr. -1-k). 9.95 *(978-1-84059-814-8(X))* Milet Publishing.

—My Bilingual Book-Taste (English-Russian) 2014. (My Bilingual Book Ser.). (ENG & RUS., Illus.). 28p. (J). (gr. -1-k). 9.95 *(978-1-84059-830-8(1))* Milet Publishing.

—My Bilingual Book-Touch (English-Russian) 2014. (My Bilingual Book Ser.). (ENG & RUS., Illus.). 28p. (J). (gr. -1-k). 9.95 *(978-1-84059-846-9(8))* Milet Publishing.

—My First Bilingual Book - Colors. 2011. (My First Bilingual Book Ser.). (ENG.). 24p. (J). (gr. k — 1). bds. 7.99 *(978-1-84059-603-8(1))* Milet Publishing.

—My First Bilingual Book - Vegetables. 2011. (My First Bilingual Book Ser.). (ENG., Illus.). 24p. (J). (gr. k — 1). bds. 8.99 *(978-1-84059-666-3(X))* Milet Publishing.

—My First Bilingual Book-Home (English-Russian) 2011. (My First Bilingual Book Ser.). (ENG., Illus.). 24p. (J). (gr. k — 1). bds. 7.99 *(978-1-84059-650-2(3))* Milet Publishing.

—My First Bilingual Book-Jobs (English-Russian) 2012. (My First Bilingual Book Ser.). (ENG & RUS., Illus.). 24p. (J). (gr. k — 1). bds. 7.99 *(978-1-84059-710-3(0))* Milet Publishing.

—My First Bilingual Book-Music (English-Russian) 2012. (My First Bilingual Book Ser.). (ENG & RUS., Illus.). 24p. (J). (gr. k — 1). bds. 7.99 *(978-1-84059-726-4(7))* Milet Publishing.

—My First Bilingual Book-Opposites (English-Russian) 2012. (My First Bilingual Book Ser.). (ENG & RUS., Illus.). 24p. (J). (gr. k — 1). bds. 7.99 *(978-1-84059-742-4(9))* Milet Publishing.

—My First Bilingual Book-Sports (English-Russian) 2012. (My First Bilingual Book Ser.). (ENG & RUS., Illus.). 24p. (J). (gr. k — 1). bds. 7.99 *(978-1-84059-758-5(5))* Milet Publishing.

The Rosetta Stone Language Library: Russian Level 1. 2005. (J). (gr. 1-18). cd-rom 209.00 *(978-1-883972-60-8(4))* Rosetta Stone Ltd.

The Rosetta Stone Language Library: Russian Level 2. 2005. (J). (gr. 1-18). cd-rom 239.00 *(978-1-883972-61-5(2))* Rosetta Stone Ltd.

Tcachenco, Natalya. The Best on the East Mystery & Adventures, Vol. 1. 2006th ed. 2005. Orig. Title: The best on the East. (Illus.). (J). 19.99 *(978-0-9754433-4-7(8)*, Language Transformer Bks.) Velichko, Vera.

Turhan, Sedat. New Bilingual Visual Dictionary (English-Russian) 2nd ed. 2017. (New Bilingual Visual Dictionary Ser.). (ENG & RUS., Illus.). 144p. (J). (gr. k-2). 19.95 ***(978-1-78508-891-9(2))*** Milet Publishing.

York, M. J. Learn Russian Words. Petelinsek, Kathleen, illus. 2014. (Foreign Language Basics Ser.). (ENG.). 24p. (J). (gr. 2-5). 27.07 *(978-1-62687-378-0(X)*, 207125) Child's World, Inc., The.

RUSSIAN LITERATURE

Woodworth, Bradley & Richards, Constance E., eds. St. Petersburg. 2005. (Bloom's Literary Places Ser.). (Illus.). 150p. (C). (gr. 9-13). lib. bdg. 40.00 *(978-0-7910-7837-2(X)*, Chelsea Hse.) Facts On File, Inc.

RUSSIAN SATELLITES

see Communist Countries

RUSSIANS—UNITED STATES

Parker, Lewis K. Russian Colonies in the Americas. (European Colonies in the Americas Ser.). 24p. 2009. (gr. 2-2). 42.50 *(978-1-61512-319-3(9))* 2003. (Illus.). (J). lib. bdg. 22.60 *(978-0-8239-6470-3(1))* Rosen Publishing Group, Inc., The. (PowerKids Pr.).

RUSSO-TURKISH WAR, 1853-1856

see Crimean War, 1853-1856

RUTH (BIBLICAL FIGURE)

Dorn, Owen A. Ruth: A Love Story. 2003. (God's People Ser.). (Illus.). pap. 6.99 *(978-0-8100-1348-3(7))* Northwestern Publishing Hse.

Frank, Penny. La Nueva Familia de Rut.Tr. of Ruth's New Family. (SPA.). (J). 1.99 *(978-1-56063-785-1(4)*, 490315) Editorial Unilit.

MacKenzie, Carine. Bible Heroes Ruth. 2013. (Bible Art Ser.). (ENG.). 16p. (J). act. bk. ed. 1.99 *(978-1-84550-092-4(X)*,

1dddfc7c-5d21-456d-9725-776cca86c003) Christian Focus Pubns. GBR. Dist: Bookmasters Distribution.

—Ruth: The Harvest Girl. McLaren, Duncan, illus. 2012. (Bible Time Ser.). (ENG.). 32p. (J). (gr. -1-2). pap. 3.99 (978-1-84550-173-0(X), 3811ae37-6768-4f8e-99ee-b432698842f5) Christian Focus Pubns. GBR. Dist: Bookmasters Distribution.

MacLean, Ruth. The Happy Harvest: A Puzzle Book about Ruth. rev. ed. 2008. (Puzzle Ser.). (ENG.). 24p. (J). 4.99 (978-1-84550-405-2(4), 940a47e5-80f8-4841-9210-d657fd18414c) Christian Focus Pubns. GBR. Dist: Bookmasters Distribution.

Sanders, Karen Nordberg. Ruth & Naomi. Rooney, Ronnie, illus. 2007. 16p. (J). (gr. k-4). 1.99 (978-0-7586-1283-0(4)) Concordia Publishing Hse.

Schur, Maxine Rose. The Story of Ruth. Connelly, Gwen, illus. 2005. 32p. (J). (gr. 2-4). lib. bdg. 16.95 (978-1-58013-114-8(X)); (ENG.). (gr. 1-3). per. 9.95 (978-1-58013-130-8(1)) Lerner Publishing Group. (Kar-Ben Publishing).

Zondervan, A. Ruth & Naomi, 1 vol. Miles, David, illus. 2015. (I Can Read! / Adventure Bible Ser.). (ENG.). 32p. (J). pap. 3.99 (978-0-310-74650-8(7)) Zonderkidz.

RUTH (BIBLICAL FIGURE)—FICTION

Lundy, Charlotte. Thank You, Ruth & Naomi. Waldrep, Evelyn L., ed. Sagasti, Miriam, illus. 2004. 32p. (J). (gr. k-4). 15.95 (978-0-9741817-0-7(6)) Bay Light Publishing.

Silverberg, Selma Kritzer. Naomi's Song. 2009. (ENG.). 142p. (gr. 7-18). pap. 14.00 (978-0-8276-0886-3(1)) Jewish Pubn. Society.

RUTH, BABE, 1895-1948

Christopher, Matt. Babe Ruth. 2006. (Matt Christopher Legends in Sports Ser.). (Illus.). 91p. (gr. 3-7). 15.00 (978-0-7569-6922-6(0)) Perfection Learning Corp.

Collins, Tracy Brown. Babe Ruth. (Baseball Superstars Ser.). (gr. 6-12). 2009. 128p. pap. 11.95 (978-0-7910-9897-4(4), Checkmark Bks.) 2008. (Illus.). 122p. lib. bdg. 30.00 (978-0-7910-9570-6(3), Chelsea Hse.) Facts On File, Inc.

Holub, Joan. Who Was Babe Ruth? Hammond, Ted & Harrison, Nancy, illus. 2012. (Who Was? Ser.). (ENG.). 112p. (J). (gr. 3-7). pap. 5.99 (978-0-448-45586-0(2), Grosset & Dunlap) Penguin Young Readers Group.

—Who Was Babe Ruth? 2012. (Who Was... ? Ser.). lib. bdg. 16.00 (978-0-606-23650-8(3), Turtleback) Turtleback Bks.

Moss, Marissa. Mighty Jackie: The Strike-Out Queen. Payne, C. F., tr. Payne, C. F., illus. 2004. (ENG.). 32p. (J). (gr. k-3). 18.99 (978-0-689-86329-5(2), Simon & Schuster/Paula Wiseman Bks.) Simon & Schuster/Paula Wiseman Bks.

Murphy, Frank. Babe Ruth Saves Baseball! Walz, Richard, illus. 2005. (Step into Reading Ser.: Vol. 3). (ENG.). 48p. (J). (gr. k-3). pap. 3.99 (978-0-375-83048-8(0), Random Hse. Bks. for Young Readers) Random Hse. Children's Bks.

—Babe Ruth Saves Baseball. Walz, Richard, illus. 2005. (Step into Reading Ser.). 46p. (gr. 1-3). 14.00 (978-0-7569-5161-0(5)) Perfection Learning Corp.

Patrick, Jean L. S. The Baseball Adventure of Jackie Mitchell, Girl Pitcher vs. Babe Ruth. Hammond, Ted & Carbajal, Richard, illus. 2011. (History's Kid Heroes Ser.). 32p. pap. 51.02 (978-0-7613-7635-4(6)); (ENG.). (gr. 3-5). pap. 8.95 (978-0-7613-7072-7(2)) Lerner Publishing Group. (Graphic Universe™).

—The Baseball Adventure of Jackie Mitchell, Girl Pitcher vs. Babe Ruth. Trover, Zachary et al, illus. 2011. (History's Kid Heroes Ser.). (ENG.). 32p. (gr. 3-5). 26.60 (978-0-7613-6180-0(4)) Lerner Publishing Group.

—La Nina Que Poncho A Babe Ruth. Reeves, Jeni, illus. 2007. (Yo Solo - Historia (on My Own - History) Ser.). 48p. (J). (gr. 4-7). per. 6.95 (978-0-8225-7788-1(7)) Lerner Publishing Group.

—La Niña Que Ponchó a Babe Ruth. Translations.com Staff, tr. from ENG. Reeves, Jeni, illus. 2007. (Yo Solo - Historia (on My Own - History) Ser.).Tr. of Girl Who Struck Out Babe Ruth. (SPA.). 48p. (gr. 2-4). lib. bdg. 25.26 (978-0-8225-7785-0(2)) Lerner Publishing Group.

—La Nina Que Poncho a Babe Ruth; the Girl Who Struck Out Babe Ruth. 2008. pap. 40.95 (978-0-8225-9725-4(X)) Lerner Publishing Group.

Saddleback Educational Publishing Staff, ed. Babe Ruth, 1 vol. unabr. ed. 2008. (Graphic Biographies Ser.). (ENG., Illus.). 25p. (YA). (gr. 9-12). pap. 7.95 (978-1-59905-215-1(6)) Saddleback Educational Publishing, Inc.

Shaughnessy, Dan. The Legend of the Curse of the Bambino. Payne, C. F., illus. 2005. (ENG.). 32p. (J). (gr. k-3). 16.95 (978-0-689-87235-8(6), Simon & Schuster/Paula Wiseman Bks.) Simon & Schuster/Paula Wiseman Bks.

Tavares, Matt. Becoming Babe Ruth. Tavares, Matt, illus. 2013. (ENG., Illus.). 40p. (J). (gr. k-3). 16.99 (978-0-7636-5646-1(1)) Candlewick Pr.

Yomtov, Nel. The Bambino: The Story of Babe Ruth's Legendary 1927 Season, 1 vol. Foley, Tim, illus. 2011. (American Graphic Ser.). (ENG.). 32p. (gr. 3-4). pap. 8.10 (978-1-4296-6265-9(4)); pap. 47.70 (978-1-4296-6433-2(9)) Capstone Press of Coughlan Cos. (Graphic Library).

Yomtov, Nelson. The Bambino: The Story of Babe Ruth's Legendary 1927 Season, 1 vol. Foley, Tim, illus. 2010. (American Graphic Ser.). (ENG.). 32p. (gr. 3-4). lib. bdg. 30.65 (978-1-4296-5473-9(2), Graphic Library) Capstone Press of Coughlan Cos.

RUTH, GEORGE HERMAN, 1895-1948

see Ruth, Babe, 1895-1948

RUTHERFORD, ERNEST, 1871-1937

Pasachoff, Naomi E. Ernest Rutherford: Father of Nuclear Science. 2005. (Great Minds of Science Ser.). (Illus.). 128p. (J). lib. bdg. 26.60 (978-0-7660-2441-0(5)) Enslow Pubs., Inc.

S

SABBATH

Abraham, Michelle Shapiro & Koffsky, Ann D. Shavua Tov! A Good Week. 2008. (HEB & ENG.). (J). (978-0-8074-1084-4(5)) URJ Pr.

Bernhard, Durga Yael. Around the World in One Shabbat: Jewish People Celebrate the Sabbath Together. 2011. (ENG., Illus.). 32p. (J). (gr. -1-1). 18.99 (978-1-58023-433-7(X), 9781580234337, Jewish Lights Publishing) LongHill Partners, Inc.

Bird, Rebecca. My Sunday Quiet Book. 2017. (ENG.). (J). pap. 39.99 **(978-1-4621-1936-3(0))** Cedar Fort, Inc./CFI Distribution.

Danis, Naomi. It's Tot Shabbat! Cohen, Tod, photos by. 2011. (Shabbat Ser.). (ENG., Illus.). 24p. (J). (gr. -1-1). lib. bdg. 14.95 (978-0-7613-4515-2(9), Kar-Ben Publishing) Lerner Publishing Group.

Duncan, Aubrey. Understanding God's Sabbath: A Decision to Make. 2004. per. 12.95 (978-0-9749490-0-0(0), 500) Advent Truth Ministries.

Ellingson, Jessica B. The Sacrament Is for Me. Jensen, Chase, illus. 2016. (ENG.). (gr. k-3). 14.99 (978-1-4621-1880-9(1)) Cedar Fort, Inc./CFI Distribution.

Holdaway, Chelsea. The Sabbath Is a Special Day: A Sacrament Meeting Activity Book. 2017. (ENG.). (J). (gr. -1-k). pap. 5.99 **(978-1-4621-2105-2(5))** Cedar Fort, Inc./CFI Distribution.

Kimmel, Eric A. Joseph & the Sabbath Fish. Peluso, Martina, illus. 2011. (Shabbat Ser.). (ENG.). 32p. (J). (gr. k-3). pap. 7.95 (978-0-7613-5909-8(5), Kar-Ben Publishing) Lerner Publishing Group.

Krinsky, Rivkah. Touch of Shabbat: A Touch & Feel Book. Becker, Boruch, illus. 2011. (J). bds. 9.95 (978-0-8266-0019-6(0)) Kehot Pubn. Society.

Lieberman, Naomi. Shabbos, Shabbos I Love You. Rosenfeld, D. L., ed. Zmora, Avram, illus. 2013. (ENG.). 32p. (J). 10.95 (978-1-929628-70-4(6)) Hachai Publishing.

Newman, Tracy. Shabbat Is Coming! Garofoli, Viviana, illus. 2014. (Shabbat Ser.). (ENG.). 12p. (J). (gr. -1 — 1). 5.95 (978-1-4677-1367-2(8), Kar-Ben Publishing) Lerner Publishing Group.

Simon, Norma. Every Friday Night. Weiss, Harvey, illus. (Festival Series of Picture Storybooks). (J). (gr. -1). spiral bd. 4.50 (978-0-8381-0708-9(7)) United Synagogue of America Bk. Service.

Sofer, Barbara. Ilan Ramon: Israel's First Astronaut. 2004. (General Jewish Interest Ser.). (J). pap. 6.95 (978-0-929371-49-8(6)) Lerner Publishing Group.

—Shabbat Shalom: Israel's First Astronaut. 2004. (Illus.). 12p. (J). 16.95 (978-0-930494-91-9(1), Kar-Ben Publishing) Lerner Publishing Group.

SABBATH—FICTION

Abramson, Susan & Dvorkin, Aaron. Who Hogged the Hallah? A Shabbat Shabang. 2008. (Illus.). 80p. (J). pap. 9.95 (978-0-9659546-5-5(X)) Oak Leaf Systems.

Barash, Chris. One Fine Shabbat. Mai-Wyss, Tatjana, illus. 2016. (ENG.). 12p. (gr. -1 — 1). (J). 5.99 (978-1-4677-5871-0(X)); 23.99 (978-1-4677-9614-9(X)) Lerner Publishing Group. (Kar-Ben Publishing).

Ben-Gur, Naomi. The Cricket & the Ant: A Shabbat Story. Kober, Shahar, illus. 2016. (ENG.). 32p. (gr. -1-3). lib. bdg. 17.99 (978-1-4677-8935-6(6), Kar-Ben Publishing) Lerner Publishing Group.

Berman, Seryl. Around the Shabbos Table. Binus, Ari, illus. 2008. 40p. (J). (gr. -1-k). pap. 10.95 (978-1-929628-44-5(7)) Hachai Publishing.

Cohen, Deborah. The Seventh Day. Hall, Melanie, illus. 2005. (ENG.). 24p. (J). (gr. -1-2). 16.95 (978-0-929371-24-5(0)); per. 8.95 (978-1-58013-125-4(5)) Lerner Publishing Group. (Kar-Ben Publishing).

A Dinosaur Goes to Church. 2013. (ENG., Illus.). 32p. (J). 14.99 (978-1-62108-423-5(X)) Covenant Communications, Inc.

Fabiyi, Jan Goldin. Where Shabbat Lives. Ramá, Sue, illus. 2008. (ENG.). 12p. (J). (gr. -1 — 1). pap. 5.95 (978-0-8225-8946-4(X), Kar-Ben Publishing) Lerner Publishing Group.

Fox, Kate & Read, Abigail. Dear Mom: A Journal All about You Written by Me. 2014. (ENG.). 96p. 12.99 (978-1-84601-469-7(7), Spruce) Octopus Publishing Group GBR. Dist: Hachette Bk. Group.

Fox, Tamar. No Baths at Camp. Vasquez, Natalia, illus. 2013. (ENG.). 32p. (J). (gr. -1-3). pap. 7.95 (978-0-7613-8121-1(X)); lib. bdg. 17.95 (978-0-7613-8120-4(1)) Lerner Publishing Group. (Kar-Ben Publishing).

Gehl, Laura. Koala Challah. Mola, Maria, illus. 2017. (ENG.). 24p. (gr. -1-1). pap. 7.99 **(978-1-5124-2088-3(3)**, Kar-Ben Publishing) Lerner Publishing Group.

Gellman, Ellie B. Shai's Shabbat Walk. Conger, Holli, illus. 2014. (ENG.). 12p. (gr. -1). 5.95 (978-1-4677-4949-7(4), Kar-Ben Publishing) Lerner Publishing Group.

Herman, Michael. The Cholent Brigade. Harmer, Sharon, illus. 2017. (ENG.). 24p. (gr. -1-2). 17.99 **(978-1-5124-0844-7(1)**, Kar-Ben Publishing) Lerner Publishing Group.

Herman, Michael. Under the Sabbath Lamp. Massari, Alida, illus. 2017. (ENG.). 32p. (J). (gr. -1-2). 17.99 (978-1-5124-0841-6(7), Kar-Ben Publishing) Lerner Publishing Group.

Kimmel, Eric A. Joseph & the Sabbath Fish. Peluso, Martina, illus. 2011. (Shabbat Ser.). (ENG.). 32p. (J). (gr. k-3). lib. bdg. 17.95 (978-0-7613-5908-1(7), Kar-Ben Publishing) Lerner Publishing Group.

Kimmelman, Leslie. The Shabbat Puppy, 0 vols. Zollars, Jaime, illus. 2012. (Shofar Ser.: 0). (ENG.). 32p. (J). (gr. -1-3). 17.99 (978-0-7614-6145-6(0), 9780761461456, Amazon Children's Publishing) Amazon Publishing.

Koffsky, Ann D., illus. Kayla & Kugel. 2015. (J). (978-1-68115-502-9(8)); (978-0-87441-898-9(4)) Behrman Hse., Inc.

—Shabbat Shalom, Hey! 2015. (J). (ENG.). 24p. (gr. -1-k). lib. bdg. 16.95 (978-1-4677-4917-6(6)); 6.99 (978-1-4677-6208-3(3)) Lerner Publishing Group. (Kar-Ben Publishing).

Levine, Anna. Jodie's Shabbat Surprise. Topaz, Ksenia, illus. 2015. (J). (gr. k-3). (ENG.). 32p. lib. bdg. 17.95 (978-1-4677-3465-3(9)); 6.99 (978-1-4677-6204-5(0)) Lerner Publishing Group. (Kar-Ben Publishing).

Manushkin, Fran. Many Days, One Shabbat, 0 vols. Monescillo, Maria, illus. 2011. (ENG.). 24p. (J). (gr. -1-3). 12.99 (978-0-7614-5965-1(0), 9780761459651, Amazon Children's Publishing) Amazon Publishing.

Marshall, Linda Elovitz. Shh... Shh... Shabbat. Golubeva, Evgenia, illus. 2016. (ENG.). 12p. (gr. -1 — 1). 5.99 (978-1-4677-5873-4(6)); 23.99 (978-1-4677-9615-6(8)) Lerner Publishing Group. (Kar-Ben Publishing).

McClain, Jennie. Monday I Was a Monkey: A "Tale" of Reverence. Eichelberger, Jennifer, illus. 2011. (J). (978-1-60861-243-7(0)) Covenant Communications.

Meltzer, Amy. The Shabbat Princess. Avilés, Martha, illus. 2011. (Shabbat Ser.). (ENG.). 32p. (J). (gr. -1-2). pap. 7.95 (978-0-7613-5106-1(X)); lib. bdg. 17.95 (978-0-7613-5142-9(6)) Lerner Publishing Group. (Kar-Ben Publishing).

Millner, Denene. Early Sunday Morning. Brantley-Newton, Vanessa, illus. 2017. (Denene Millner Bks.). (ENG.). 40p. (J). 17.95 (978-1-57284-211-3(3)) Agate Publishing, Inc.

Newman, Tracy. Shabbat Hiccups. Exelby, Ilana, illus. 2016. (ENG.). 32p. (J). (gr. -1-3). 16.99 (978-0-8075-7312-9(4)) Whitman, Albert & Co.

Rauchwerger, Diane Levin & Levin, Diane. Dinosaur on Shabbat. Wolff, Jason, illus. 2006. (ENG.). 24p. (J). (gr. -1-1). lib. bdg. 15.95 (978-1-58013-159-9(X), Kar-Ben Publishing) Lerner Publishing Group.

Rouss, Sylvia A. The Littlest Candlesticks. Hannon, Holly, illus. 2005. (Littlest Ser.). 32p. (J). 14.95 (978-1-930143-48-7(6)); pap. 9.95 (978-1-930143-49-4(4)) Simcha Media Group. (Devora Publishing).

Shulimson, Sarene. Lights Out Shabbat. Ebbeler, Jeffrey, illus. 2012. (Shabbat Ser.). (ENG.). 32p. (J). (gr. -1-2). lib. bdg. 17.95 (978-0-7613-7564-7(3), Kar-Ben Publishing) Lerner Publishing Group.

Sigal, Maxine Handelman. Shabbat Angels. Rothenberg, Joani, illus. 2003. (gr. k-3). 13.95 (978-0-8074-0865-0(4), 164051) URJ Pr.

Silberman, Shoshana. A Family Haggadah II, Vol. 2. Kahn, Katherine Janus, illus. l.t. ed. 2003. 64p. (J). pap. 6.95 (978-1-58013-014-1(3), Kar-Ben Publishing) Lerner Publishing Group.

Snyder, Laurel. Baxter, the Pig Who Wanted to Be Kosher. Goldin, David, illus. 2010. (ENG.). 32p. (J). (gr. -1-2). 15.99 (978-1-58246-315-5(8), Tricycle Pr.) Random Hse. Children's Bks.

—Baxter, the Pig Who Wanted to Be Kosher. 2010. (J). pap. 2.46 (978-1-58246-373-5(5), Tricycle Pr.) Ten Speed Pr.

Sschweiger-dmiel, Izhak. Hanna's Sabbath Dress. Eitan (tchernov), Ora, illus. 2012. (ENG.). 32p. (J). (gr. -1-3). 16.99 (978-1-4424-7439-0(4), Simon & Schuster Bks. For Young Readers) Simon & Schuster Bks. For Young Readers.

Swartz, Daniel J. Bim & Bom: A Shabbat Tale. Iwai, Melissa, illus. rev. ed. 2011. (Shabbat Ser.). (ENG.). 24p. (J). (gr. -1-1). pap. 8.95 (978-0-7613-6717-8(9), Kar-Ben Publishing) Lerner Publishing Group.

Walker, Yonette. Soul Soup Sunday. 2012. 24p. pap. 15.99 (978-1-4691-8226-1(2)) Xlibris Corp.

Wasserman, Mira. Too Much of a Good Thing. Carolan, Christine, illus. 2003. 32p. (J). (gr. -1-3). pap. 6.95 (978-1-58013-066-0(6)); (ENG.). 15.95 (978-1-58013-082-0(8)) Lerner Publishing Group. (Kar-Ben Publishing).

SABOTAGE

Bascomb, Neal. Sabotage: The Mission to Destroy Hitler's Atomic Bomb. 2016. (ENG., Illus.). 320p. (J). (gr. 7). 17.99 (978-0-545-73243-7(3), Levine, Arthur A. Bks.) Scholastic, Inc.

Hoose, Phillip. The Boys Who Challenged Hitler: Knud Pedersen & the Churchill Club. 2015. (ENG., Illus.). 208p. (YA). (gr. 7-12). 19.99 (978-0-374-30022-7(4), 9780374300227, Farrar, Straus & Giroux (BYR)) Farrar, Straus & Giroux.

SABOTAGE—FICTION

Abdo, Kenny. Give Me Liberty or Give Me Detention!, 1 vol. Doucet, Bob, illus. 2013. (Haven't Got a Clue! Ser.). (ENG.). 80p. (J). (gr. 3-6). lib. bdg. 27.07 (978-1-61641-953-0(9), Calico Chapter Bks) Magic Wagon.

Bailey, Kristin. Rise of the Arcane Fire. 2014. (Secret Order Ser.: 2). (ENG., Illus.). 464p. (YA). (gr. 9). 17.99 (978-1-4424-6802-3(5), Simon Pulse) Simon Pulse.

Baker, Jennifer. The Lying Game. 2014. (ENG., Illus.). 192p. (YA). (gr. 7). pap. 13.99 (978-1-4814-2878-1(0), Simon Pulse) Simon Pulse.

BookSource Staff, compiled by. Sports Sabotage. 2012. (Hardy Boys: Secret Files Ser.: 8). lib. bdg. 16.00 (978-0-606-23673-7(2), Turtleback) Turtleback Bks.

Bossley, Michele Martin. Cracked, 1 vol. 2007. (Orca Currents Ser.). (ENG.). (J). (gr. 5-9). 112p. lib. bdg. 14.95 (978-1-55143-702-6(3)); 128p. per. 9.95 (978-1-55143-700-2(7)) Orca Bk. Pubs. USA.

—Tampered, 1 vol. 2013. (Orca Currents Ser.). (ENG.). 136p. (J). (gr. 5-9). pap. 9.95 (978-1-4598-0356-5(6)); lib. bdg. 16.95 (978-1-4598-0357-2(4)) Orca Bk. Pubs. USA.

Brezenoff, Steve. Bowling Lane Without Any Strikes. 2013. (Field Trip Mysteries Ser.). (ENG.). 88p. (gr. 2-3). pap. 35.70 (978-1-4342-6231-8(6)) Stone Arch Bks.

—The Bowling Lane Without Any Strikes. Calo, Marcos, illus. 2013. (Field Trip Mysteries Ser.). (ENG.). 88p. (gr. 2-3). pap. 6.10 (978-1-4342-6212-7(X)); lib. bdg. 25.32 (978-1-4342-5979-0(X)) Stone Arch Bks.

Brouwer, Sigmund. Scarlet Thunder, 1 vol. 2008. (Orca Sports Ser.). (ENG.). 176p. (YA). (gr. 6-10). pap. 9.95 (978-1-55143-911-2(5)) Orca Bk. Pubs. USA.

Burroughs, Scott, illus. Sports Sabotage. 2012. (Hardy Boys: the Secret Files Ser.: 8). (ENG.). 112p. (J). (gr. 1-4). pap. 5.99 (978-1-4424-2316-9(1), Aladdin) Simon & Schuster Children's Publishing.

Coman, Carolyn. The Memory Bank. Shepperson, Rob, illus. 2010. (J). 263p. pap. (978-0-545-21067-6(4)); (ENG.). 288p. (gr. 3-7). 16.99 (978-0-545-21066-9(6)) Scholastic, Inc. (Levine, Arthur A. Bks.).

Darlison, Aleesah. Willow's Victory Cancelled. Brailsford, Jill, illus. 2017. (Unicorn Riders Ser.). (ENG.). 112p. (gr. 3-5). pap. 5.95 (978-1-4795-6557-3(1)) Picture Window Bks.

Dixon, Franklin W. The Race Is On. Burroughs, Scott, illus. 2015. (Hardy Boys: the Secret Files Ser.: 19). (ENG.). 96p. (J). (gr. 1-4). pap. 5.99 (978-1-4814-2271-0(5), Aladdin) Simon & Schuster Children's Publishing.

—Running on Fumes. 2005. 150p. (J). lib. bdg. 16.92 (978-1-4242-0384-0(8)) Fitzgerald Bks.

Fisch, Sholly. Challenge of the Super Friends, 1 vol. Brizuela, Dario, illus. 2013. (DC Super Friends Ser.). (ENG.). 32p. (gr. 1-2). lib. bdg. 22.60 (978-1-4342-4701-8(5)) Stone Arch Bks.

Harvey, Jacqueline. Alice-Miranda in China. 2017. (Alice-Miranda Ser.: 14). (ENG.). 336p. (J). (gr. 3-7). pap. 9.99 (978-0-85798-520-0(5)) Random Hse. Australia AUS. Dist: Independent Pubs. Group.

Hawking, Lucy & Hawking, Stephen W. George & the Big Bang. Parsons, Garry, illus. 2012. (George's Secret Key Ser.). (ENG.). 336p. (J). (gr. 3-7). 22.99 (978-1-4424-4005-0(8), Simon & Schuster Bks. For Young Readers) Simon & Schuster Bks. For Young Readers.

Hawking, Stephen W. & Hawking, Lucy. George & the Big Bang. Parsons, Garry, illus. 2013. (George's Secret Key Ser.). (ENG.). 304p. (J). (gr. 3-7). pap. 11.99 (978-1-4424-4006-7(6), Simon & Schuster Bks. For Young Readers) Simon & Schuster Bks. For Young Readers.

Keene, Carolyn. The Clue at Black Creek Farm. 2015. 171p. (J). (978-1-4806-8613-7(1), Simon & Schuster/Paula Wiseman Bks.) Simon & Schuster/Paula Wiseman Bks.

—Designed for Disaster. Pamintuan, Macky, illus. 2011. (Nancy Drew & the Clue Crew Ser.: 29). (ENG.). 96p. (J). (gr. 1-4). pap. 5.99 (978-1-4169-9439-8(4), Aladdin) Simon & Schuster Children's Publishing.

—Once upon a Crime. 2nd ed. 2006. (Nancy Drew: Girl Detective Super Mystery Ser.: 2). (ENG.). 192p. (J). (gr. 3-7). pap. 6.99 (978-1-4169-1248-4(7), Aladdin) Simon & Schuster Children's Publishing.

—Sabotage at Willow Woods. 2014. (Nancy Drew Diaries: 5). (ENG., Illus.). 176p. (J). (gr. 3-7). pap. 6.99 (978-1-4424-9392-6(5), Aladdin) Simon & Schuster Children's Publishing.

—Trails of Treachery. 2008. (Nancy Drew: Girl Detective Ser.). 136p. (gr. 3-7). 15.00 (978-0-7569-8295-9(2)) Perfection Learning Corp.

MacGregor, Roy. Peril at the World's Biggest Hockey Tournament. 2008. (ENG.). 160p. (YA). (gr. 3-7). mass mkt. 6.99 (978-0-7710-5607-9(9), Screech Owls) McClelland & Stewart CAN. Dist: Penguin Random Hse. LLC.

Metz, Melinda. The Droid of Doom. McKenzie, Heath, illus. 2016. (S. M. A. R. T. S. Ser.). (ENG.). 128p. (gr. 3-6). pap. 9.95 (978-1-4965-3017-2(9)) Stone Arch Bks.

—S. M. A. R. T. S. & the Droid of Doom. McKenzie, Heath, illus. 2016. (S. M. A. R. T. S. Ser.). (ENG.). 128p. (gr. 3-6). lib. bdg. 22.65 (978-1-4965-3015-8(2)) S.M.A.R.T.S. Learning System.

—S. M. A. R. T. S. & the Mars Mission Mayhem. McKenzie, Heath, illus. 2016. (S. M. A. R. T. S. Ser.). (ENG.). 128p. (gr. 3-6). lib. bdg. 22.65 (978-1-4965-3016-5(0)) S.M.A.R.T.S. Learning System.

Morgan, Alex. Sabotage Season. (Kicks Ser.). (ENG., Illus.). (J). (gr. 3-7). 2014. 192p. pap. 6.99 (978-1-4424-8576-1(0)) 2013. 176p. 15.99 (978-1-4424-8574-7(4)) Simon & Schuster Bks. For Young Readers. (Simon & Schuster Bks. For Young Readers).

Peril at Granite Peak. 2014. (Hardy Boys Adventures Ser.: 5). (ENG., Illus.). 160p. (J). (gr. 3-7). pap. 6.99 (978-1-4424-9395-7(X), Aladdin) Simon & Schuster Children's Publishing.

Probst, Jeff & Tebbetts, Chris. The Sabotage. 2015. (Stranded, Shadow Island Ser.: 2). lib. bdg. 17.20 (978-0-606-36792-9(6)) Turtleback Bks.

Stilton, Thea. Thea Stilton & the Chocolate Sabotage. 2014. (Thea Stilton Ser.: 19). (ENG., Illus.). 176p. (J). (gr. 2-5). pap. 8.99 (978-0-545-64656-7(1), Scholastic Paperbacks) Scholastic, Inc.

Sutherland, Tui T. & Sutherland, Kari H. The Menagerie. 2015. (Menagerie Ser.: 3). (ENG.). 368p. (J). (gr. 3-7). 16.99 (978-0-06-078067-8(3)) HarperCollins Pubs.

Terrell, Brandon. The Undercover Cheerleader. Epelbaum, Mariano, illus. 2017. (Snoops, Inc Ser.). (ENG.). 112p. (gr. 4-6). lib. bdg. 26.65 **(978-1-4965-5061-3(7))** Stone Arch Bks.

Wolff, Tracy. Book 2: Sabotage. 2016. (Mars Bound Ser.). (ENG.). (J). (gr. 2-8). lib. bdg. 28.50 **(978-1-62402-198-5(0))** ABDO Publishing Co.

SABRINA, THE TEENAGE WITCH (FICTITIOUS CHARACTER)—FICTION

Aguirre-Sacasa, Roberto. Chilling Adventures of Sabrina. Hack, Robert, illus. 2016. (Chilling Adventures of Sabrina Ser.). (ENG.). 176p. pap. 17.99 (978-1-62738-987-7(3)) Archie Comic Pubns., Inc.

Gallagher, Mike. Sabrina Animated. Manak, Dave, illus. 2011. (Archie & Friends All-Stars Ser.: 13). (ENG.). 128p. (J). (gr. 4-7). pap. 9.95 (978-1-879794-80-1(2), Archie Comics) Archie Comic Pubns., Inc.

Golliher, Bill. Best of Sabrina the Teenage Witch. G!, Holly, illus. 2011. (Archie & Friends All-Stars Ser.: 15). (ENG.). 128p. (J). (gr. 4-7). pap. 9.95 (978-1-879794-75-7(6), Archie Comics) Archie Comic Pubns., Inc.

SACAGAWEA

Buffalohead, Julie, illus. Sacagawea. 2005. (Libros Ilustrados (Picture Bks.)). (SPA & ENG.). 40p. (J). (gr. 3-6). 16.95 (978-0-8225-3191-3(7), Ediciones Lerner) Lerner Publishing Group.

Buffalohead, Julie & Erdrich, Liselotte. Sacagawea. Buffalohead, Julie, illus. 2003. (ENG., Illus.). 40p. (J). (gr. 3-6). 17.95 (978-0-87614-646-0(9), Carolrhoda Bks.) Lerner Publishing Group.

Collard, Sneed B., III. Sacagawea: Brave Shoshone Girl. 2006. (American Heroes Ser.). (Illus.). 48p. (gr. 3-7). lib. bdg. 29.93 (978-0-7614-2166-5(1), Benchmark Bks.) Marshall Cavendish Corp.

Cooke, Tim. Sacagawea. 2016. (Meet the Greats Ser.). 00048p. (J). pap. 14.05 **(978-1-4824-5960-9(4))** Stevens, Gareth Publishing LLLP.

Cosson, Jody. Sacagawea: Indian Guide, 1 vol. Soud, illus. 2008. (Beginner Biographies Ser.). (ENG.). 32p. (gr. -1-3).

28.50 *(978-1-60270-252-3(7),* Looking Glass Library-Nonfiction) Magic Wagon.
Crosby, Michael T. Sacagawea: Lewis & Clark's Pathfinder. 2007. 144p. (J). (gr. 6-18). 25.95 *(978-1-59556-026-1(2))* OTTN Publishing.
DeFord, Diane. Sacagawea. 2009. pap. 13.25 *(978-1-60559-069-1(X))* Hameray Publishing Group, Inc.
Doremus, Robert, illus. Sacagawea. 2014. (History's All-Stars Ser.). (ENG.). 208p. (J). (gr. 3-7). pap. 6.99 *(978-1-4814-1499-9(2),* Simon & Schuster/Paula Wiseman Bks.) Simon & Schuster/Paula Wiseman Bks.
Dunn, Joeming W. Sacagawea, 1 vol. Espinosa, Rod, illus. 2008. (Bio-Graphics Ser.). (ENG.). 32p. 28.50 *(978-1-60270-176-2(8),* Graphic Planet- Nonfiction) ABDO Publishing Co.
Feinstein, Stephen. Lee Sobre Sacagawea/Read about Sacagawea. 2006. (I Like Biographies! Bilingual Ser.). (ENG & SPA., Illus.). (J). (gr. 1-3). lib. bdg. 22.60 *(978-0-7660-2674-2(4),* Enslow Elementary) Enslow Pubs., Inc.
—Read about Sacagawea. 2004. (I Like Biographies! Ser.). (Illus.). 24p. (J). lib. bdg. 22.60 *(978-0-7660-2297-3(8))* Enslow Pubs., Inc.
Ford, Carin T. Sacagawea: Meet an American Legend. 2003. (Meeting Famous People Ser.). (Illus.). 32p. (J). lib. bdg. 22.60 *(978-0-7660-2004-7(5))* Enslow Pubs., Inc.
Franklin, Virgil. The Story of Sacagawea. 2009. (Reading Room Collection 2 Ser.). 24p. (gr. 3-4). 42.50 *(978-1-60851-997-2(X),* PowerKids Pr.) Rosen Publishing Group, Inc., The.
Frazier, Neta. Path to the Pacific: The Story of Sacagawea. 2017. (Great Leaders & Events Ser.). (ENG.). (J). (gr. 4-8). lib. bdg. 35.99 ***(978-1-942875-44-4(4))*** Quarto Publishing Group USA.
Frazier, Neta Lohnes. Path to the Pacific: The Story of Sacagawea. 2016. (Young Voyageur Ser.). (ENG., Illus.). 208p. (J). (gr. 4-9). pap. 12.99 *(978-0-7603-5227-4(5),* Voyageur Pr.) Quarto Publishing Group USA.
Griffiths, Katie. Sacagawea. 2017. (J). ***(978-1-5026-2747-6(7))*** Cavendish Square Publishing.
Gunderson, Jessica Sarah. Sacagawea: Journey into the West, 1 vol. Martin, Cynthia & Schultz, Barbara, illus. 2006. (Graphic Biographies Ser.). (ENG.). 32p. (gr. 3-4). 30.65 *(978-0-7368-6499-2(7),* Graphic Library) Capstone Press of Coughlan Cos.
—Sacagawea: Journey into the West, 1 vol. Martin, Cynthia & Schulz, Barbara, illus. 2006. (Graphic Biographies Ser.). (ENG.). 32p. (gr. 3-4). per. 8.10 *(978-0-7368-9663-4(5),* Graphic Library) Capstone Press of Coughlan Cos.
Haldy, Emma E. Sacagawea. Bane, Jeff, illus. 2016. (My Early Library: My Itty-Bitty Bio Ser.). (ENG.). 24p. (J). (gr. k-1). 28.50 *(978-1-63470-482-3(7),* 207659) Cherry Lake Publishing.
Jazynka, Kitson. Sacagawea. 2015. (Readers Bios Ser.). (ENG., Illus.). 32p. (J). (gr. 1-4). pap. 3.99 *(978-1-4263-1963-1(0),* National Geographic Children's Bks.) National Geographic Society.
King, Margaret. The Legacy & Legend of Sacagawea. 2017. (Primary Source Readers Ser.). (Illus.). 32p. (J). (gr. 4-5). pap. 8.99 *(978-1-4938-3793-9(1))* Teacher Created Materials, Inc.
Krensky, Stephen. Sacagawea. Magnuson, Diana, illus. 2005. 32p. (J). lib. bdg. 15.00 *(978-1-59054-954-4(6))* Fitzgerald Bks.
Krull, Kathleen. Sacajawea. Collins, Matt, illus. 2015. (Women Who Broke the Rules Ser.). (ENG.). 48p. (J). (gr. 1-4). 16.99 *(978-0-8027-3799-1(4),* 9780802737991, Bloomsbury USA Childrens) Bloomsbury Publishing USA.
Lohof, Arle & Jensen, Joyce. My Story as Told by Sacagawea. Little, Gary, illus. 2006. 32p. (J). (gr. 1-2). 3.95 *(978-0-9711667-3-8(0))* Outlook Publishing, Inc.
Lynette, Rachel. Sacagawea. 2013. (Pioneer Spirit: the Westward Expansion Ser.). 24p. (J). (gr. 3-6). 22.60 *(978-1-4777-0782-1(4));* pap. 49.50 *(978-1-4777-0898-9(7));* (ENG., Illus.). pap. 8.25 *(978-1-4777-0897-2(9))* Rosen Publishing Group, Inc., The. (PowerKids Pr.).
Marcovitz, Hal. Sacagawea: Guide for the Lewis & Clark Expedition. 2007. (Illus.). 63p. (J). pap. 12.00 *(978-1-4223-6712-4(6))* DIANE Publishing Co.
Marsh, Carole. Sacagawea: Native American Heroine: Native American Heroine. 2003. 12p. (gr. k-4). 2.95 *(978-0-635-02143-4(9))* Gallopade International.
McAneney, Caitie. The Life of Sacagawea. 2016. (Native American Biographies Ser.). (Illus.). 32p. (J). (gr. 5-4). 26.25 *(978-1-5081-4819-7(8),* PowerKids Pr.) Rosen Publishing Group, Inc., The.
Nelson, Maria. The Life of Sacagawea. 2012. (Famous Lives Ser.). (ENG., Illus.). 24p. (J). (gr. k-3). lib. bdg. 22.60 *(978-1-4339-6357-5(4));* (gr. 1-4). pap. 8.15 *(978-1-4339-6359-9(0))* Stevens, Gareth Publishing LLLP.
Norwich, Grace. Sacajawea. Vanarsdale, Anthony, illus. 2012. (I Am Ser.). (ENG.). 128p. (J). (gr. 3-7). pap. 5.99 *(978-0-545-40574-4(2),* Scholastic Paperbacks) Scholastic, Inc.
Petrie, Kristin. Sacagawea, 1 vol. 2007. (Explorers Set 2 Ser.). (ENG., Illus.). 32p. (gr. 4-7). 27.07 *(978-1-59679-749-9(5),* Checkerboard Library) ABDO Publishing Co.
Rausch, Monica. Sacagawea. 2007. (Grandes personajes (Spanish- Great Americans) Ser.). 24p. (gr. 1-4). (SPA.). pap. 8.15 *(978-0-8368-7991-9(0));* (Illus.). pap. 8.15 *(978-0-8368-7692-5(X));* (Illus.). lib. bdg. 22.00 *(978-0-8368-7685-7(7))* Stevens, Gareth Publishing LLLP. (Weekly Reader Leveled Readers).
Rausch, Monica L. Sacagawea. 2007. (Grandes personajes (Great Americans) Ser.). (SPA., Illus.). 24p. (gr. 1-4). lib. bdg. 22.00 *(978-0-8368-7984-1(8),* Weekly Reader Leveled Readers) Stevens, Gareth Publishing LLLP.
Sanford, William R. & Green, Carl R. Sacagawea: Courageous American Indian Guide. 2012. (Courageous Heroes of the American West Ser.). (Illus.). 48p. (J). (gr. 5-18). 22.60 *(978-0-7660-4006-9(2))* Enslow Pubs., Inc.
Shepherd, Jodie. Sacagawea. 2015. (Rookie Biographies(tm) Ser.). (ENG., Illus.). 32p. (J). lib. bdg. 25.00 *(978-0-531-21414-5(1),* Children's Pr.) Scholastic Library Publishing.
St. George, Judith. Sacagawea. 2006. pap. 8.75 *(978-0-15-365175-5(X))* Harcourt Schl. Pubs.
Sutcliffe, Jane. Sacagawea. 2009. (History Maker Biographies Ser.). (ENG.). 48p. (gr. 3-6). 27.93 *(978-0-7613-4222-9(2),* Lerner Pubns.) Lerner Publishing Group.
Tieck, Sarah. Sacagawea, 1 vol. 2006. (Buddy Book Ser.). (ENG., Illus.). 32p. (gr. -1-3). 27.07 *(978-1-59679-789-5(4),* Buddy Bks.) ABDO Publishing Co.

SACCO-VANZETTI TRIAL, DEDHAM, MASS., 1921

Hinton, Kerry. The Trial of Sacco & Vanzetti: A Primary Source Account. 2009. (Great Trials of the Twentieth Century Ser.). 64p. (gr. 5-8). 58.50 *(978-1-61513-220-1(1))* Rosen Publishing Group, Inc., The.

SACRED ART

see Christian Art and Symbolism

SACRED MUSIC

see Church Music

SAFETY EDUCATION

see also Accidents—Prevention

Abramovitz, Melissa. Abc's of Health & Safety. Morris, Alexander, illus. 2012. 16p. pap. 9.95 *(978-1-61633-276-1(X))* Guardian Angel Publishing, Inc.
Acosta, Jamey & Reid, Stephanie. Health & Safety, 1 vol. 2010. (Early Childhood Themes Ser.). (ENG., Illus.). 16p. (J). (gr. -1-2). pap. 19.99 *(978-1-4333-1809-2(1));* pap. 6.99 *(978-1-4333-1808-5(3))* Shell Educational Publishing.
Adams, Jeanne. Tyler's Safe Day, Everyday Safety for Children. 2009. 24p. pap. 13.50 *(978-1-60860-465-4(9),* Eloquent Bks.) Strategic Book Publishing & Rights Agency (SBPRA).
Adler, Rebecca. Keep Me Safe at Home & in My Community: A handbook on Safety for Young Children & their Families. 2009. 52p. pap. 20.49 *(978-1-4389-0585-3(8))* AuthorHouse.
Adult Guide to Staying Safe. 2003. (YA). *(978-0-88441-663-0(1))* Girl Scouts of the USA.
Amaso, Marcellus Chigbo. 100 Tips for a School Child's Daily Safety Guide. 2013. 120p. 29.99 *(978-1-4797-7243-8(7));* pap. 19.99 *(978-1-4797-4951-5(6))* Xlibris Corp.
American Academy of Pediatrics (AAP) Staff. Blast! - Babysitter Lessons & Safety Training. 3rd rev. ed. 2016. (ENG.). 72p. pap. 13.95 ***(978-1-284-13580-0(2))*** Jones & Bartlett Learning, LLC.
Bair, Carolyn. Fireman Dave Goes to School. 2012. 16p. pap. 13.99 *(978-1-4685-4194-6(3))* AuthorHouse.
Barr, Linda. The Water Patrol: Saving Surfers' Lives in Big Waves. 2005. (High Five Reading - Blue Ser.). (ENG., Illus.). 48p. (gr. 3-4). per. 9.00 *(978-0-7368-5749-9(4),* High Five Reading (RBL)) Capstone Press of Coughlan Cos.
Bell, Nasherall, creator. Child Safety at Home, School & Play l.t. ed. 2004. (Illus.). 32p. (J). pap. *(978-0-9729753-3-9(0))* Really Big Coloring Bks., Inc.
Bellisario, Gina. Be Aware! My Tips for Personal Safety. Kurilla, Renee, illus. 2014. (Cloverleaf Books — My Healthy Habits Ser.). (ENG.). 24p. (gr. k-2). lib. bdg. 23.93 *(978-1-4677-1351-1(1),* Millbrook Pr.) Lerner Publishing Group.
Benchmark Education Company, LLC Staff, compiled by. Safety. 2006. (J). 91.00 *(978-1-4108-7046-9(4))* Benchmark Education Co.
Berry, Joy. Help Me Be Good about Being Careless. 2009. (Help Me Be Good Ser.). 32p. pap. 7.95 *(978-1-60577-103-8(1))* Berry, Joy Enterprises.
Berry, Joy Wilt. A Book about Being Careless. 2005. (Illus.). (J). *(978-0-7172-8582-2(0))* Scholastic, Inc.
Beylon, Cathy. Safety First Coloring Book. 2006. (Dover Coloring Bks.). (ENG., Illus.). 32p. (J). (gr. -1-2). pap. 3.99 *(978-0-486-45164-0(X))* Dover Pubns., Inc.
Blaine, Victor. Safe in Your Home. 2016. (Safety Smarts Ser.). 00024p. (J). (gr. k-1). pap. 8.25 *(978-1-4994-2787-5(5),* PowerKids Pr.) Rosen Publishing Group, Inc., The.
—Safe on the Playground. 2016. (Safety Smarts Ser.). 00024p. (J). (gr. k-1). pap. 8.25 *(978-1-4994-2785-1(9),* PowerKids Pr.) Rosen Publishing Group, Inc., The.
Boothroyd, Jennifer. Caution in the Kitchen! Germs, Allergies, & Other Health Concerns. 2016. (Lightning Bolt Books — Healthy Eating Ser.). (ENG., Illus.). 32p. (J). (gr. 1-3). 26.65 *(978-1-4677-9473-2(2),* Lerner Pubns.) Lerner Publishing Group.
Boyer, Richard G. Oddo Safety Series, 4 vols., Set. (Illus.). (J). (gr. -1-6). lib. bdg. 44.60 *(978-0-87783-170-9(X))* Oddo Publishing, Inc.
Brady, Janeen J. Safety Kids Vol. 3: Protect Their Minds. 24p. (J). (gr. k-6). pap. 4.95 *(978-0-944803-82-0(2))* Brite Music, Inc.
Campbell, Maureen & Yoerg, Sharon. Bridges to Safety: A Practical Guide for Adults to Help Teens Teach Conflict Resolution & Character Skills to Children. 2004. (Illus.). 118p. per. 24.94 incl. cd-rom *(978-0-9716772-0-3(4))* Six Seconds.
Candy Cane Press, creator. Safe at Play: Outdoor Safety. 2005. (ENG., Illus.). 14p. (J). (gr. -1-k). bds. 12.95 *(978-0-8249-6593-8(0),* Ideal Pubns.) Worthy Publishing.
Casanueva, Idilian. You May Touch Here! Puedes Tocar Aqui! Caceres, Marangelie, illus. 2007. 16p. per. 10.95 *(978-1-59858-327-4(1))* Dog Ear Publishing, LLC.
Caviezel, Giovanni. Fireman's Safety Hints. Mesturini, C., illus. 2012. (Little People Shape Bks.). (ENG.). 10p. (J). (gr. k-2). bds. 8.99 *(978-0-7641-6594-8(1))* Barron's Educational Series, Inc.
—Policeman's Safety Hints. 2013. (ENG.). 12p. (J). (gr. -1-2). bds. 8.99 *(978-0-7641-6721-8(9))* Barron's Educational Series, Inc.
Cicola, Amanda, et al. Health & Safety 1: Gym Class; Shopping for Lunch; Good for You; My Happy Heart; Just Like Me; Staying Safe; Always Brush Your Teeth; A Visit to the Doctor, 8 bks. Simon, Sue A. et al, illus. 2005. (ENG.). 8p. (J). pap. 120.00 *(978-1-893986-26-8(8))* Keep Bks.
Council Guide to Staying Safe. 2003. (YA). *(978-0-88441-664-7(X))* Girl Scouts of the USA.
Croft, Jennifer. Everything You Need to Know about Guns in Your Home. 2005. (Need to Know Library). (Illus.). 64p. (YA). (gr. 7-12). lib. bdg. 31.95 *(978-0-8239-3162-0(5),* NTGUHO) Rosen Publishing Group, Inc., The.
Cumberland, Diana. Listen to Your Body: Empowering Children to Be Safe. 2013. 40p. pap. 15.95 *(978-1-4525-8559-8(8),* Balboa Pr.) Author Solutions, Inc.
Decker, William. Safe at School. 2016. (Safety Smarts Ser.). 00024p. (J). (gr. k-1). pap. 8.25 *(978-1-4994-2764-6(6),* PowerKids Pr.) Rosen Publishing Group, Inc., The.
—Safe in the Car. 2016. (Safety Smarts Ser.). 00024p. (J). (gr. k-1). pap. 8.25 *(978-1-4994-2788-2(3),* PowerKids Pr.) Rosen Publishing Group, Inc., The.
Desalle, Nicole. Safe at Home. 2011. pap. 39.95 *(978-0-7664-3751-7(5))* Abrams & Co. Pubs., Inc.
—Safe at Play. 2011. pap. 39.95 *(978-0-7664-3752-4(3))* Abrams & Co. Pubs., Inc.
—Safe at School. 2011. pap. 39.95 *(978-0-7664-3750-0(7))* Abrams & Co. Pubs., Inc.
Doeden, Matt. Safety Smarts: How to Manage Threats, Protect Yourself, Get Help, & More. 2012. (USA TODAY Teen Wise Guides: Lifestyle Choices Ser.). (ENG., Illus.). 64p. (gr. 8-12). lib. bdg. 31.93 *(978-0-7613-7022-2(6))* Lerner Publishing Group.
Don't Panic. 2003. (Illus.). pap. 5.60 *(978-0-7398-7505-6(1))* Steck-Vaughn.
Don't Stick Sticks up Your Nose! Don't Stuff Stuff in Your Ears! 2013. (Don't Stick Sticks up Your Nose! Don't Stuff Stuff in Your Ears! Ser.). (ENG.). 22p. bds. 5.99 *(978-0-9888861-0-0(3),* 9780988886100) Dontstickdontstuff.
Duncan, David A. Dude, Where's Your Helmet?, 1 vol. 2009. (ENG., Illus.). 48p. (J). pap. *(978-1-897522-59-2(2))* RMB Rocky Mountain Bks.
Etingoff, Kim. Navigating Cyberspace. Stephens, Ronald, ed. 2014. (Safety First Ser.: 11). 48p. (J). (gr. 5-18). 20.95 *(978-1-4222-3049-7(X))* Mason Crest.
Eye on the Sky. 2015. (Eye on the Sky Ser.). (ENG.). 32p. (J). (gr. 3-4). pap., pap., pap. 63.00 *(978-1-4824-3461-3(X))* Stevens, Gareth Publishing LLLP.
Feigh, Alison. I Can Play It Safe. Logan, Laura, illus. 2008. (ENG.). 32p. (J). (gr. -1-3). 14.99 *(978-1-57542-285-5(9))* Free Spirit Publishing, Inc.
First Aid & Home Safety. (YA). (gr. 6-12). pap. 10.95 *(978-0-8224-4366-7(X))* Globe Fearon Educational Publishing.
Ford, Jean. Growth & Development. Forman, Sara, ed. 2013. (Young Adult's Guide to the Science of Health Ser.: 15). 128p. (J). (gr. 7-18). 24.95 *(978-1-4222-2810-4(X))* Mason Crest.
French, Cathy. People Who Keep You Safe. 2011. (Early Connections Ser.). (J). *(978-1-61672-239-5(8))* Benchmark Education Co.
Giles, Sophie & Davies, Kate. The Children's Book of Keeping Safe. 2014. (ENG., Illus.). 320p. (J). pap. 10.00 *(978-1-84135-909-0(2))* Award Pubns. Ltd. GBR. Dist: Parkwest Pubns., Inc.
Gogerly, Liz. Looking after Me. Gordon, Mike, illus. 2008. (ENG.). 32p. (J). (gr. -1-3). *(978-0-7787-4109-1(5))* Crabtree Publishing Co.
—Safety. Gordon, Mike, illus. 2008. (Looking after Me Ser.). (ENG.). 32p. (J). (gr. -1-3). pap. *(978-0-7787-4120-6(6));* lib. bdg. *(978-0-7787-4113-8(3))* Crabtree Publishing Co.
Goldsmith, Mike & Johnson, Jinny. Being Safe. 2009. (Now We Know About... Ser.). (ENG., Illus.). 24p. (J). (gr. k-3). pap. *(978-0-7787-4734-5(4));* lib. bdg. *(978-0-7787-4717-8(4))* Crabtree Publishing Co.
Goodbody, Slim. Avoiding Injuries. McGinnis, Ben, illus. Pinchbeck, Chris, photos by. 2007. (Slim Goodbody Good Health Guides). 32p. (J). (gr. 2-6). lib. bdg. 26.00 *(978-0-8368-7739-7(X),* Gareth Stevens Learning Library) Stevens, Gareth Publishing LLLP.
—Keeping Safe. McGinnis, Ben, illus. Pinchbeck, Chris, photos by. 2007. (Slim Goodbody Good Health Guides). 32p. (gr. 2-6). lib. bdg. 26.00 *(978-0-8368-7743-4(8),* Gareth Stevens Learning Library) Stevens, Gareth Publishing LLLP.
Grossblatt, Ben. Keep Out! Door Alarm: Build Your Own Key-Card Security System! 2004. (Illus.). 24p. (J). *(978-0-439-66835-4(2))* Scholastic, Inc.
Guard, Anara. What If a Stranger Approaches You?, 1 vol. Madden, Colleen M., illus. 2011. (Danger Zone Ser.). (ENG.). 24p. (gr. 1-2). pap. 7.49 *(978-1-4048-7031-4(8));* lib. bdg. 25.99 *(978-1-4048-6683-6(3))* Picture Window Bks.
—What If There Is a Fire?, 1 vol. Pfleegor, Gina, illus. 2011. (Danger Zone Ser.). (ENG.). 24p. (gr. 1-2). lib. bdg. 25.99 *(978-1-4048-6685-0(X))* Picture Window Bks.
—What If You Get Lost?, 1 vol. Jones, Dani, illus. 2011. (Danger Zone Ser.). (ENG.). 24p. (gr. 1-2). lib. bdg. 25.99 *(978-1-4048-6684-3(1))* Picture Window Bks.
—What If You Need to Call 911?, 1 vol. Laughead, Mike, illus. 2011. (Danger Zone Ser.). (ENG.). 24p. (gr. 1-2). lib. bdg. 25.99 *(978-1-4048-6682-9(5))* Picture Window Bks.
Hahn, Donna M. Staying Safe When I Go Out. 2009. 24p. pap. 12.00 *(978-1-4389-6498-0(6))* AuthorHouse.
Head, Honor. Being Safe Out & About. 2017. (Keep Yourself Safe Ser.). (ENG., Illus.). 24p. (J). (gr. k-2). 16.99 *(978-1-4451-4430-6(1),* Franklin Watts) Hachette Children's Group GBR. Dist: Hachette Bk. Group.
Herrington, Lisa M. Internet Safety. 2012. (Rookie Read-About(tm) Safety Ser.). (ENG., Illus.). 32p. (J). lib. bdg. 25.00 *(978-0-531-28971-6(0));* (gr. -1-1). pap. 5.95 *(978-0-531-29273-0(8))* Scholastic Library Publishing.
—Stranger Safety. 2012. (Rookie Read-About(tm) Safety Ser.). (ENG., Illus.). 32p. (J). lib. bdg. 25.00 *(978-0-531-28972-3(9));* pap. 5.95 *(978-0-531-29274-7(6))* Scholastic Library Publishing.
Higgins, Melissa. You're in Charge: Basic Rules Every Babysitter Needs to Know, 1 vol. 2014. (Babysitter's Backpack Ser.). (ENG., Illus.). 32p. (gr. 3-4). lib. bdg. 27.99 *(978-1-4914-0764-6(6),* Snap Bks.) Capstone Press of Coughlan Cos.
Holt, Rinehart and Winston Staff. Decisions for Health Blue, Chptr. 13: Preventing Abuse. 4th ed. 2004. pap. 11.20 *(978-0-03-068047-2(6))* Holt McDougal.
—Decisions for Health Blue, Chptr. 19: Safety. 4th ed. 2004. pap. 11.20 *(978-0-03-068054-0(9))* Holt McDougal.
—Decisions for Health Green Chptr. 15: Health & Safety. 4th ed. 2004. pap. 11.20 *(978-0-03-068037-3(9))* Holt McDougal.
—Decisions for Health Red Chptr. 17: Personal Safety. 4th ed. 2004. pap. 11.20 *(978-0-03-068044-1(1))* Holt McDougal.
Hord, Colleen. My Safe Community. 2011. (ENG., Illus.). 24p. (gr. k-2). pap. 8.95 *(978-1-61741-997-3(4))* Rourke Educational Media.
Hunt, Jilly. Safety. 2010. (Being Healthy, Feeling Great Ser.). (ENG.). 32p. (J). pap. 10.60 *(978-1-61532-383-8(X),* PowerKids Pr.); (YA). (gr. 3-6). lib. bdg. 26.50 *(978-1-61532-382-1(1))* Rosen Publishing Group, Inc., The.
Jackman, Vernon. Bunnies & Butterflies in the Backyard & the Pirates Who Know Where They Live: Stories That Help Children Learn & Remember Their Address & Telephone Number. Theagene, Jeannisse, illus. l.t. ed. 2010. (ENG.). 32p. (J). pap. 6.99 *(978-0-9829371-1-2(3))* New Kid Safety.
Jackson, Joann. Green Light, Red Light, Go! 2008. 20p. per. 24.95 *(978-1-60441-778-4(1))* America Star Bks.
Jakubiak, David J. A Smart Kid's Guide to Avoiding Online Predators. (Illus.). 24p. (J). 2010. pap. 8.25 *(978-1-4358-3354-8(6))* 2009. (gr. 2-6). lib. bdg. 22.60 *(978-1-4042-8117-2(7))* Rosen Publishing Group, Inc., The. (PowerKids Pr.).
—A Smart Kid's Guide to Social Networking Online. 2010. (Illus.). 24p. (J). pap. 8.25 *(978-1-4358-3358-6(9),* 1300427, PowerKids Pr.) Rosen Publishing Group, Inc., The.
James, Cindy. Ten Easy Tips for Staying Safe. 2009. (Reading Room Collection 2 Ser.). 24p. (gr. 3-4). 42.50 *(978-1-60851-991-0(0),* PowerKids Pr.) Rosen Publishing Group, Inc., The.
James, Sara. Safety. 2013. (Junior Martial Arts Ser.: 9). 32p. (J). (gr. 4-18). 19.95 *(978-1-4222-2737-4(5))* Mason Crest.
Jennings, Rosemary. Safe on Your Bike. 2016. (Safety Smarts Ser.). 00024p. (J). (gr. k-1). pap. 8.25 *(978-1-4994-2784-4(0),* PowerKids Pr.) Rosen Publishing Group, Inc., The.
Joyce, Julie. What Should You Do? Safety Tips for Kids. 2004. (J). 3.95 *(978-0-9656808-4-4(3),* KidBk-1) Dynamic Publishing Co., Inc.
Kahn, doc, Robert. Bobby & Mandee's Good Touch/Bad Touch: Children's Safety Book. Hardie, Chris, illus. 2011. (ENG.). 25p. pap. 6.95 *(978-1-935274-54-4(6))* Future Horizons, Inc.
Kallio, Jamie. 12 Tips for Staying Safe. 2017. (Illus.). 32p. (J). *(978-1-62143-509-9(1))* Pr. Room Editions LLC.
Kallio, Jamie & Ringstad, Arnold. 12 Tips for Staying Safe. 2016. (Healthy Living Ser.). (ENG., Illus.). 32p. (J). pap. 9.95 *(978-1-63235-385-6(7))* Pr. Room Editions LLC.
Keevish, Michele C. When a Stranger Says Hello. 2008. 16p. per. 24.95 *(978-1-4241-8669-3(2))* America Star Bks.
Knowlton, MaryLee. Safety at Home. Andersen, Gregg, photos by. 2008. (Staying Safe Ser.). (ENG., Illus.). 32p. (J). (gr. -1-3). lib. bdg. *(978-0-7787-4316-3(0))* Crabtree Publishing Co.
—Safety at School. Andersen, Gregg, photos by. 2008. (Staying Safe Ser.). (ENG., Illus.). 32p. (J). (gr. -1-3). lib. bdg. *(978-0-7787-4317-0(9))* Crabtree Publishing Co.
—Safety at the Playground. Andersen, Gregg, photos by. 2008. (Staying Safe Ser.). (ENG., Illus.). 32p. (J). (gr. -1-3). lib. bdg. *(978-0-7787-4318-7(7))* Crabtree Publishing Co.
Knowlton, MaryLee & Dowdy, Penny. Safety at School. Andersen, Gregg, photos by. 2008. (Staying Safe Ser.). (ENG., Illus.). 32p. (J). (gr. -1-3). pap. *(978-0-7787-4322-4(5))* Crabtree Publishing Co.
—Safety at the Playground. Andersen, Gregg, photos by. 2008. (Staying Safe Ser.). (ENG., Illus.). 32p. (J). (gr. -1-3). pap. *(978-0-7787-4323-1(3))* Crabtree Publishing Co.
Kreiner, Anna. Todo lo que necesitas saber sobre la violencia en la escuela (Everything You Need to Know about Violence in School) 2009. (Todo lo que necesitas (the Need to Know Library) Ser.). (SPA.). 64p. (gr. 6-6). 58.50 *(978-1-60854-411-0(7),* Editorial Buenas Letras) Rosen Publishing Group, Inc., The.
LaBerge, Margaret M. Sara Safety, School Safety Pamphlet. Lucas, Stacey L. et al, illus. 2004. (J). pap. *(978-0-9755561-0-8(X))* Reading Resc.
Lee, Sally. Staying Safe Online. 2012. (Staying Safe Ser.). (ENG.). 24p. (gr. 1-2). pap. 41.70 *(978-1-4296-8389-0(9),* First Facts) Capstone Press of Coughlan Cos.
Leslie, Natalie Johnson & Leslie, H. Steve. Surviving School Violence. 2010. 20p. 15.99 *(978-1-4490-6397-9(7))* AuthorHouse.
Letizia, Kenneth M. Go Ask Ally: Wearing Seat Belts Doesn't Change Lives, Not Wearing Them Does. 2011. 32p. (gr. 1-2). pap. 14.39 *(978-1-4567-6326-8(1))* AuthorHouse.
Lindeen, Mary & Kesselring, Susan. Being Safe at Home. McGeehan, Dan & Moore, David, Jr., illus. 2011. (Be Safe Ser.). (ENG.). 24p. (J). (gr. k-3). lib. bdg. 27.07 *(978-1-60954-299-3(1),* 200079) Child's World, Inc., The.
—Being Safe in Your Neighborhood. McGeehan, Dan & Moore, David, illus. 2011. (Be Safe Ser.). (ENG.). 24p. (J). (gr. k-3). lib. bdg. 27.07 *(978-1-60954-370-9(X),* 200081) Child's World, Inc., The.
Llewelyn, Claire. Stay Safe! 2006. (Qeb Looking after Me Ser.). (Illus.). 24p. (J). lib. bdg. 16.95 *(978-1-59566-195-1(6))* QEB Publishing Inc.
Lombardo, Jennifer & Mooney, Carla. Social Networking: Staying Safe in the Online World. 2017. (Hot Topics Ser.). 120p. (YA). (gr. 7-7). lib. bdg. 39.40 ***(978-1-5345-6021-5(1),*** Lucent Pr.) Greenhaven Publishing LLC.
Lyons, Shelly. Safety in My Neighborhood. 2013. (My Neighborhood Ser.). (ENG.). 24p. (gr. k-1). pap. 41.70 *(978-1-62065-888-8(7));* pap. 7.29 *(978-1-62065-887-1(9));* lib. bdg. 26.65 *(978-1-62065-102-5(5))* Capstone Press of Coughlan Cos. (Pebble Plus).
Mara, Wil. Community Connections: What Should I Do?, 8 vols., Set. Incl. What Should I Do? At the Pool. lib. bdg. 25.64 *(978-1-61080-056-3(7),* 201054); What Should I Do? If a Stranger Comes Near. lib. bdg. 25.64 *(978-1-61080-049-5(4),* 201040); What Should I Do? If I See a Stray Animal. (Illus.). (J). lib. bdg. 25.64 *(978-1-61080-050-1(8),* 1330905); What Should I Do? If There Is a Fire. lib. bdg. 25.64 *(978-1-61080-053-2(2),* 201048); What Should I Do? In the Car. lib. bdg. 25.64 *(978-1-61080-052-5(4),* 201046); What Should I Do? Near a Busy Street. (Illus.). (J). lib. bdg. 25.64 *(978-1-61080-051-8(6),* 1330910); What Should I Do? On My Bike. lib. bdg. 25.64 *(978-1-61080-055-6(9),* 201052); What Should I Do? On the Playground. lib. bdg. 25.64 *(978-1-61080-054-9(0),* 201050); 24p. (gr. 2-5). 2011. Set lib. bdg. 205.12 *(978-1-61080-145-4(8))* Cherry Lake Publishing.
—What Should I Do? If a Stranger Comes Near. 2011. (Community Connections: What Should I Do? Ser.). (ENG.).

S

24p. (gr. 2-5). lib. bdg. 25.64 (978-1-61080-049-5(4), 201040) Cherry Lake Publishing.

—What Should I Do? If I See a Stray Animal. 2011. (Community Connections: What Should I Do? Ser.). (ENG., Illus.). 24p. (J). (gr. 2-5). lib. bdg. 25.64 (978-1-61080-050-1(8), 1330905) Cherry Lake Publishing.

—What Should I Do? Near a Busy Street. 2011. (Community Connections: What Should I Do? Ser.). (ENG., Illus.). 24p. (J). (gr. 2-5). lib. bdg. 25.64 (978-1-61080-051-8(6), 1330910) Cherry Lake Publishing.

Marlowe, Christie. Protecting Your Body: Germs, Super Bugs, Poison & Deadly Diseases. Stephens, Ronald, ed. 2014. (Safety First Ser.: 11). 48p. (J). (gr. 5-18). 20.95 (978-1-4222-3051-0(1)) Mason Crest.

Mattern, Joanne. Staying Safe at Home. 2007. (Safety First Ser.). (Illus.). 24p. (gr. k-3). pap. 8.15 (978-0-8368-7798-4(5)); (ENG & SPA., pap. 8.15 (978-0-8368-8063-2(3)); lib. bdg. 22.00 (978-0-8368-7791-5(8)) Stevens, Gareth Publishing LLLP. (Weekly Reader Leveled Readers).

—Staying Safe at Home (la Seguridad en Casa) 2007. (Safety First / la Seguridad Es lo Primero Ser.). (ENG & SPA., Illus.). 24p. (gr. k-3). lib. bdg. 22.00 (978-0-8368-8056-4(0), Weekly Reader Leveled Readers) Stevens, Gareth Publishing LLLP.

—Staying Safe at School/la Seguridad en la Escuela. 2007. (Safety First / la Seguridad Es lo Primero Ser.). (ENG & SPA., Illus.). 24p. (gr. k-3). lib. bdg. 22.00 (978-0-8368-8057-1(9), Weekly Reader Leveled Readers) Stevens, Gareth Publishing LLLP.

—Staying Safe at School/La Seguridad en La Escuela. 2007. (Safety First / la Seguridad Es lo Primero Ser.). 24p. (gr. k-3). (ENG & SPA.). pap. 8.15 (978-0-8368-8064-9(1)); (Illus.). pap. 8.15 (978-0-8368-7799-1(3)); (Illus.). lib. bdg. 22.00 (978-0-8368-7792-2(6)) Stevens, Gareth Publishing LLLP. (Weekly Reader Leveled Readers).

—Staying Safe in the Car. 2007. (Safety First Ser.). (Illus.). 24p. (gr. k-3). pap. 8.15 (978-0-8368-7800-4(0)); lib. bdg. 22.00 (978-0-8368-7793-9(4)) Stevens, Gareth Publishing LLLP. (Weekly Reader Leveled Readers).

—Staying Safe in the Car (la Seguridad en el Auto) 2007. (Safety First / la Seguridad Es lo Primero Ser.). (ENG & SPA., Illus.). 24p. (gr. k-3). lib. bdg. 22.00 (978-0-8368-8058-8(7), Weekly Reader Leveled Readers) Stevens, Gareth Publishing LLLP.

—Staying Safe in the Car (la seguridad en el Auto) 2007. (Safety First / la Seguridad Es lo Primero Ser.). (ENG & SPA.). 24p. (gr. k-3). pap. 8.15 (978-0-8368-8065-6(X), Weekly Reader Leveled Readers) Stevens, Gareth Publishing LLLP.

—Staying Safe on My Bike. 2007. (Safety First Ser.). (Illus.). 24p. (gr. k-3). pap. 8.15 (978-0-8368-7801-1(9)); lib. bdg. 22.00 (978-0-8368-7794-6(2)) Stevens, Gareth Publishing LLLP. (Weekly Reader Leveled Readers).

—Staying Safe on My Bike/La Seguridad en Mi Bicicleta. 2007. (Safety First / la Seguridad Es lo Primero Ser.). (SPA., Illus.). 24p. (gr. k-3). lib. bdg. 22.00 (978-0-8368-8059-5(5), Weekly Reader Leveled Readers) Stevens, Gareth Publishing LLLP.

—Staying Safe on the School Bus. 2007. (Safety First Ser.). (Illus.). 24p. (gr. k-3). pap. 8.15 (978-0-8368-7802-8(7)); lib. bdg. 22.00 (978-0-8368-7795-3(0)) Stevens, Gareth Publishing LLLP. (Weekly Reader Leveled Readers).

—Staying Safe on the School Bus/La Seguridad en el Autobús Escol Ar. 2007. (Safety First / la Seguridad Es lo Primero Ser.). (SPA., Illus.). 24p. (gr. k-3). lib. bdg. 22.00 (978-0-8368-8060-1(9), Weekly Reader Leveled Readers) Stevens, Gareth Publishing LLLP.

—Staying Safe on the Street. 2007. (Safety First Ser.). (Illus.). 24p. (gr. k-3). pap. 8.15 (978-0-8368-7803-5(5)); lib. bdg. 22.00 (978-0-8368-7796-0(9)) Stevens, Gareth Publishing LLLP. (Weekly Reader Leveled Readers).

—Staying Safe on the Street (la Seguridad en la Calle) 2007. (Safety First / la Seguridad Es lo Primero Ser.). (SPA & ENG., Illus.). 24p. (gr. k-3). lib. bdg. 22.00 (978-0-8368-8061-8(7), Weekly Reader Leveled Readers) Stevens, Gareth Publishing LLLP.

McCurry, Chris & Waddington, Emma. Why Do I Have to Eat My Greens? Big Issues for Little People Around Health & Well-Being. Thomas, Louis, illus. 2016. (Life & Soul Library). (ENG.). 32p. (J). (gr. -1-3). 12.99 (978-1-84780-865-3(4), Frances Lincoln Children's Bks.) Quarto Publishing Group UK GBR. Dist: Hachette Bk. Group.

McKay, Sindy. We Both Read-Being Safe. Photodisc-Getty Staff, Images, photos by. 2003. (We Both Read Ser.). (Illus.). 44p. (J). (gr. 1-2). 7.99 (978-1-891327-51-3(8)); pap. 4.99 (978-1-891327-52-0(6)) Treasure Bay, Inc.

Meachen Rau, Dana. Safety on the Go. 2009. (Bookworms: Safe Kids Ser.). (SPA & ENG.). 32p. (gr. k-2). 15.95 (978-0-7614-4085-7(2)) Marshall Cavendish GBR. Dist: Marshall Cavendish Corp.

Meiners, Cheri J. Be Careful & Stay Safe. Johnson, Meredith, illus. 2006. (Learning to Get Along(r) Ser.). (ENG.). 40p. (J). (gr. -1-3). pap. 10.95 (978-1-57542-211-4(5)) Free Spirit Publishing, Inc.

Miller, Shannon. Don't Talk to Strangers Online. 2013. (Internet DOs & DON'ts Ser.). (Illus.). 24p. (J). (gr. k-2). 22.60 (978-1-4777-0755-5(7)); (ENG., pap. 8.25 (978-1-4777-1564-2(9)); pap. 49.50 (978-1-4777-1565-9(7)) Rosen Publishing Group, Inc., The. (PowerKids Pr.).

Minton, Eric. Smartphone Safety, 1 vol., 1. 2014. (Stay Safe Online Ser.). (ENG.). 32p. (J). (gr. 4-6). 26.25 (978-1-4777-2935-9(6), PowerKids Pr.) Rosen Publishing Group, Inc., The.

Myers, Connie Ellis. Words to Say out Loud: A Safety Book for Children. 2007. (Illus.). 84p. (J). spiral bd. 19.99 (978-0-9799127-0-2(9)) Say Out Loud, LLC.

Nelson, Robin. Staying Safe in Emergencies. 2006. (Pull Ahead Books: Health Ser.). (ENG., Illus.). 32p. (gr. k-3). lib. bdg. 22.60 (978-0-8225-3391-7(X)) Lerner Publishing Group.

Nelson, Sara. Stay Safe! How You Can Keep Out of Harm's Way. 2009. pap. 52.95 (978-0-7613-4688-3(0)) Lerner Publishing Group.

Nelson, Sara Kirsten. Stay Safe! How You Can Keep Out of Harm's Way. Desrocher, Jack, illus. 2008. (Health Zone Ser.). (ENG.). 64p. (gr. 4-7). lib. bdg. 30.60 (978-0-8225-7551-1(5)) Lerner Publishing Group.

Newsom, Tony. High School Student Safety Tips. 2007. (ENG., Illus.). 95p. (YA). pap. 8.99 (978-0-9787143-5-2(0)) Carrington Bks.

—Middle School Student Safety Tips. 2007. (ENG., Illus.). 43p. (YA). pap. 8.99 (978-0-9787143-4-5(2)) Carrington Bks.

—Student Safety Tips: 40 that Every 1st - 2nd Grader Must Know!, 2 vols., Vol. 2. 2nd ed. 2007. (ENG., Illus.). 48p. pap. 6.99 (978-0-9787143-1-4(8)) Carrington Bks.

—Student Safety Tips: 45 that Every 3rd - 5th Grader Must Know!, 2 vols., Spanish Edition. 2nd ed. 2007. (ENG., Illus.). 52p. pap. 6.99 (978-0-9787143-2-1(6)) Carrington Bks.

No Way! A Book about Staying Safe for Girls Ages 4-6. 2003. (YA). (978-0-88441-660-9(7)) Girl Scouts of the USA.

Obert, Lois. Help! Willie's Choking! 2006. (ENG., Illus.). (J). 7.95 (978-1-57166-370-2(3)) Quixote Pr.

Olson, Karen W. Living Safe, Playing Safe. Hamelin, Marie-Micheline, illus. 2005. (Caring for Me Ser.). (ENG.). 20p. (J). pap. 10.95 (978-1-894778-33-6(2)) Theytus Bks., Ltd. CAN. Dist: Univ. of Toronto Pr.

—Living Safe, Playing Safe. George, Leonard, Jr., illus. 2009. (Caring for Me Ser.). (ENG.). 20p. pap. 9.95 (978-1-894778-51-0(0)) Theytus Bks., Ltd. CAN. Dist: Univ. of Toronto Pr.

Oregon Center for Applied Science, creator. Bike Smart. 2006. (J). cd-rom 19.95 (978-1-933898-09-4(7)) Oregon Ctr. for Applied Science, Inc.

—Walk Smart: Children's Pedestrian Safety Program. 2005. (J). cd-rom 19.95 (978-1-933898-10-0(0)) Oregon Ctr. for Applied Science, Inc.

Parker, Helen. Lift Stick & Learn: Emergency. 2006. (Illus.). 12p. (J). (gr. -1-k). (978-1-84610-282-0(0)) Make Believe Ideas.

Pettiford, Rebecca. Crossing Guards. 2015. (J). lib. bdg. 25.65 (978-1-62031-156-1(9), Bullfrog Bks.) Jump! Inc.

Pinnell, Gay Su, et al. Health & Safety 2: Safety First; Don't Be a Couch Potato; Birthday Shots; Just in Case; Time Out; Home Sick; the Eye Doctor; the Big Race, 8 bks., Set. Simon, Sue A. et al, illus. 2005. (ENG.). 8p. (J). pap. 120.00 (978-1-893986-27-5(6)) Keep Bks.

Raatma, Lucia. Staying Safe Around Strangers, 1 vol. 2011. (Staying Safe Ser.). (ENG.). 24p. (gr. 1-2). pap. 7.29 (978-1-4296-7195-8(5)); pap. 41.70 (978-1-4296-7196-5(3)); lib. bdg. 25.32 (978-1-4296-6821-7(0)) Capstone Press of Coughlan Cos. (First Facts).

—Staying Safe on the Playground. 2011. (Staying Safe Ser.). (ENG.). 24p. (gr. 1-2). pap. 41.70 (978-1-4296-7198-9(X), First Facts) Capstone Press of Coughlan Cos.

Raatma, Lucia & Lee, Sally. Staying Safe. (Staying Safe Ser.). (ENG.). 24p. (gr. 1-2). 2012. pap. 250.20 (978-1-4296-8391-3(0)) 2012. pap. 29.16 (978-1-4296-8390-6(2)) 2012. lib. bdg. 151.92 (978-1-4296-8153-7(5)) 2012. lib. bdg. 50.64 (978-1-4296-8152-0(7)) 2011. pap. 21.87 (978-1-4296-7201-6(3)) 2011. pap. 166.80 (978-1-4296-7202-3(1)) 2011. lib. bdg. 101.28 (978-1-4296-6835-4(0)) Capstone Press of Coughlan Cos. (First Facts).

Rau, Dana Meachen. School Safety: Seguridad en la Escuela. 2009. (Bookworms — Bilingual Editions: Safe Kids/Ninos Seguros Ser.). (SPA & ENG.). 32p. (gr. k-2). lib. bdg. 15.95 (978-0-7614-4782-5(2)) Marshall Cavendish Corp.

Rau, Dana Meachen & Meachen Rau, Dana. Safety at Home: Seguridad en la Casa. 2009. (Bookworms: Safe Kids Ser.). (SPA & ENG.). 32p. (gr. k-2). 15.95 (978-0-7614-4089-5(5)) Marshall Cavendish Corp.

—School Safety: Seguridad en la Escuela. 2009. (Bookworms: Safe Kids Ser.). (SPA & ENG.). 32p. (gr. k-2). 15.95 (978-0-7614-4090-1(9)) Marshall Cavendish Corp.

Raymer, Dottie. Staying Home Alone. 2015. (Smart Girl's Guide Ser.). lib. bdg. 24.50 (978-0-606-37237-4(7)) Turtleback Bks.

Richardson, Sarah J. What If? The What Ifs of Childhood Safety, 1 bk. 2004. 120p. (J). per. 9.99 (978-0-9752982-0-6(8)) 4 Childrens Sake Pubns.

Riggs, Sandy. Safe Streets. 2006. (Reader's Clubhouse Level 2 Reader Ser.). (ENG., Illus.). 24p. (J). (gr. 1-4). pap. 3.99 (978-0-7641-3300-8(4)) Barron's Educational Series, Inc.

Rissman, Rebecca. No Running in the House: Safety Tips Every Babysitter Needs to Know, 1 vol. 2014. (Babysitter's Backpack Ser.). (ENG., Illus.). 32p. (gr. 3-4). 27.99 (978-1-4914-0765-3(4), Snap Bks.) Capstone Press of Coughlan Cos.

—Should Henry Wear a Helmet? Staying Safe, 1 vol. 2013. (What Would You Do? Ser.). (ENG., Illus.). 24p. (gr. -1-1). pap. 6.29 (978-1-4329-7247-9(2)); lib. bdg. 22.65 (978-1-4329-7241-7(3)) Heinemann-Raintree. (Acorn).

Rivera, Sheila. Emergencies. 2007. (First Step Nonfiction - Safety Ser.). (ENG.). 8p. (gr. -1-1). pap. 4.95 (978-0-8225-6824-7(1)) Lerner Publishing Group.

—Home Safety. 2007. (First Step Nonfiction - Safety Ser.). (ENG.). 8p. (gr. -1-1). pap. 4.95 (978-0-8225-6823-0(3)) Lerner Publishing Group.

—School Safety. 2007. (First Step Nonfiction - Safety Ser.). (ENG., Illus.). 8p. (J). (gr. -1-1). pap. 4.95 (978-0-8225-6822-3(5)) Lerner Publishing Group.

Robinson, Beth. The Safe Touch Book. Green, Noel, illus. 2013. 20p. (J). mass mkt. 8.99 (978-0-9799092-2-1(8)) Robinson, Beth.

Rothman, Kevin F. Coping with Dangers on the Internet. 2005. (Coping Ser.). (Illus.). 192p. (YA). (gr. 7-12). lib. bdg. 34.60 (978-0-8239-3201-6(X)) Rosen Publishing Group, Inc., The.

Safety Always Matters (SAM), Vol. II. 12p. (J). (gr. k-3). 29.50 (978-1-883994-05-1(5)); 29.50 (978-1-883994-04-4(7)) Safety Always Matters, Inc.

Safety Smarts. 2016. (Safety Smarts Ser.). 00024p. (J). (gr. k-1). 165.20 (978-1-4994-2690-8(9), PowerKids Pr.) Rosen Publishing Group, Inc., The.

Salzmann, Mary Elizabeth. Wear a Helmet! Healthy Safety Habits, 1 vol. 2014. (Healthy Habits Ser.). (ENG.). 24p. (J). (gr. -1-3). 24.21 (978-1-62403-533-3(7)) ABDO Publishing Co.

Schaefer, Adam. Manteneroe Fuera de Peligro, 1 vol. 2010. (Salud y el Estado Fisico Ser.).Tr. of Staying Safe. (SPA.). 32p. (gr. 1-3). 27.32 (978-1-4329-4446-9(0)); pap. 8.29 (978-1-4329-4451-3(7)) Heinemann-Raintree.

Scholastic Library Publishing. Rookie Read: About Safety. 2012. (J). 138.00 (978-0-531-24325-1(7), Children's Pr.) Scholastic Library Publishing.

Schulz, Kathy. Always Be Safe. 2011. (Rookie Ready to Learn — Out & about: in My Community Ser.). (Illus.). 40p. (J). (gr. -1-k). lib. bdg. 25.00 (978-0-531-27175-9(7), Children's Pr.) Scholastic Library Publishing.

—Always Be Safe. Potter, Katherine, illus. 2003. (Rookie Reader Skill Set Ser.). (ENG.). (J). (gr. k-2). pap. 4.95 (978-0-516-26965-8(8), Children's Pr.) Scholastic Library Publishing.

Senker, Cath. Keeping Safe. 2008. (Healthy Choices Ser.). (Illus.). 24p. (J). (gr. 3-7). lib. bdg. 22.60 (978-1-4042-4300-2(3), PowerKids Pr.) Rosen Publishing Group, Inc., The.

Simms, Mattie. The (Q) Kids Help Center. 2006. per. 9.99 (978-0-9772077-0-1(6)) Kanlearn, Inc.

Smith, K. Be Safe on the Bus: Learning the B Sound. 2009. (PowerPhonics Ser.). 24p. (gr. 1-1). 39.90 (978-1-60851-434-2(X), PowerKids Pr.) Rosen Publishing Group, Inc., The.

Spikes, James L. Taffey Pop Kids Presents the Adventures of Lemmon Head & Mudd Duck: What to Do if Someone Tries to Grab YOU!!! Spikes, Leon, Jr., illus. 2007. 32p. (J). 14.95 (978-0-9771438-0-1(5)) Taffey Pop Kids Publishing.

Staley, Erin. Improving Community Health & Safety Through Service Learning, 1 vol. 2015. (ENG.). 80p. (YA). 34.60 (978-1-4777-7955-2(8), Rosen Young Adult) Rosen Publishing Group, Inc., The.

Stephens, Ronald, ed. Road Safety. 2014. (Safety First Ser.: 11). 48p. (J). (gr. 5-18). 20.95 (978-1-4222-3052-7(X)) Mason Crest.

—Stranger Danger. 2014. (Safety First Ser.: 11). 48p. (J). (gr. 5-18). 20.95 (978-1-4222-3054-1(6)) Mason Crest.

Tedesco, Ann & Alimonti, Frederick. Not Everyone Is Nice: Helping Children Learn Caution with Strangers. DePrince, Erik & Volinski, Jessica, illus. 2003. (Let's Talk Ser.). (ENG.). 48p. (J). pap. 9.95 (978-0-88282-233-4(0)) New Horizon Pr. Pubs., Inc.

Thomas, Pat. I Can Be Safe: A First Look at Safety. Harker, Lesley, illus. 2003. (First Look At... Ser.). (ENG.). 32p. (J). pap. 7.99 (978-0-7641-2460-0(9)) Barron's Educational Series, Inc.

Thompson, Gary. What Every Teen Should Know Before Getting Behind the Wheel Alone: A Guide to Increasing Your Child's Safety While Reducing Your Auto Repair Expenses. 2004. 131p. (YA). per. 9.95 (978-0-9749763-1-0(8)) Guiding Horizons.

Tieck, Sarah. Be Safe, 1 vol. 2012. (ENG.). 32p. 27.07 (978-1-61783-231-4(6), Buddy Bks.) ABDO Publishing Co.

Tomsi, Cathy. Take a Stand. 2011. pap. 39.95 (978-0-7664-3753-1(1)) Abrams & Co. Pubs., Inc.

—Tell Someone You Trust. 2011. pap. 39.95 (978-0-7664-3754-8(X)) Abrams & Co. Pubs., Inc.

Traveling Wild. 2014. (Traveling Wild Ser.). 32p. (J). (gr. 3-6). 106.40 (978-1-4824-1180-5(6)) Stevens, Gareth Publishing LLLP.

Unger, Karen. Don't Go There! Staying Safe for Girls Ages 6-8. 2003. (Illus.). 48p. (J). (978-0-88441-661-6(5)) Girl Scouts of the USA.

—I Don't Think So! A Book about Staying Safe for Girls Ages 8-11. 2003. (Illus.). 41p. (J). (978-0-88441-662-3(3)) Girl Scouts of the USA.

Urban Donahue, Jill. Play It Smart: Playground Safety, 1 vol. Mashéris, Bob, illus. 2008. (How to Be Safe! Ser.). (ENG.). 24p. (gr. k-2). 26.65 (978-1-4048-4823-8(1)) Picture Window Bks.

van der Zande, Irene. Kidpower Safety Comics: An Introduction to "People Safety" for Young Children Ages 3 to 10 & Their Adults. Golert, Amanda, illus. 2011. 44p. (J). pap. (978-0-9796191-4-4(9)) van der Zande, Irene.

Van Sant, Barb. Kid Sense! Good Answers to Your Child's Tough Questions about Personal Safety. 2010. 39p. pap. 12.95 (978-0-578-06778-0(1)) Boulder Street Bks. LLC.

Walker, Gloria. Stop & Go Safety. 2008. 24p. (J). pap. 14.95 (978-1-883589-91-2(6)) Clark Publishing, Inc.

Weber, Rebecca. Safety Basics. 2012. (Health & Your Body Ser.). (ENG.). 24p. (gr. k-1). pap. 41.70 (978-1-4296-8346-3(5)); lib. bdg. 26.65 (978-1-4296-7694-6(9)) Capstone Press of Coughlan Cos. (Pebble Plus).

Weekley, Randy J. Strangers, Bullies, Safety & More (Spanish Version) A How to Guide to Child Safety. 2008. (SPA., Illus.). 54p. (J). pap. 16.99 (978-1-59879-632-2(1), Lifevest) Lifevest Publishing, Inc.

Wood, Ira. How to Stay Safe at Home & On-line. 2009. (Reading Room Collection 2 Ser.). 24p. (gr. 3-4). 42.50 (978-1-60851-972-9(4), PowerKids Pr.) Rosen Publishing Group, Inc., The.

21st Century Safety & Privacy. 2013. (21st Century Safety & Privacy Ser.). 64p. (J). (gr. 5-8). 159.75 (978-1-4488-9579-3(0)); pap. 388.50 (978-1-4777-1678-6(5)); pap. 64.75 (978-1-4777-1677-9(7)) Rosen Publishing Group, Inc., The.

SAFETY EDUCATION—FICTION

Anielski, Angela. My Safe Space: I Don't Know You! 2009. 36p. (J). pap. 19.95 (978-1-4327-3774-0(0)) Outskirts Pr., Inc.

Bernstein, Susan H. N. E. Pominonous Epstein Minds His Mind. (E. Pominonous Epstein Ser.). 18p. (J). (gr. -1-3). pap. 8.95 (978-0-9706596-0-6(1)) Bernstein, Susan.

Blacknall, Sharon. The Abc's & 123's of Child Safety. 2012. 46p. pap. 17.45 (978-1-4624-0437-7(5), Inspiring Voices) Author Solutions, Inc.

Blazin' Hot: Coloring/Activity Book (English) 2005. (Illus.). (J). 2.99 (978-0-9770455-0-1(1)) Mighty Kids Media.

Blazin' Hot: Coloring/Activity Book (English) Incl. Stickers. 2007. (J). 2.99 (978-1-933934-51-8(4)) Mighty Kids Media.

Blazin' Hot: Picture Book (English) NL 9x9 with Snipe. 2007. (J). 5.99 (978-1-933934-46-4(8)) Mighty Kids Media.

Cain, Janan. Roonie B. Moonie: Lost & Alone. 2007. (Illus.). 32p. (J). (gr. -1-3). 15.95 (978-0-9740190-8-6(9)) Illumination Arts Publishing Co., Inc.

Camping Caper: Coloring/Activity Book (English) incl. Stickers. 2007. (Illus.). (J). 2.99 (978-1-933934-65-5(4)) Mighty Kids Media.

Camping Caper: Picture Book (English) 8x8. 2007. (Illus.). (J). 5.99 (978-1-933934-64-8(6)) Mighty Kids Media.

Chatton, Julie. Trains: Safe & Sound. 2008. 24p. pap. 13.50 (978-1-60693-307-7(8), Eloquent Bks.) Strategic Book Publishing & Rights Agency (SBPRA).

Chessen, Sherri. Gorp's Secret: An Empowering Tale in Pumpernickel Park. Bronson, Linda, illus. 2008. (ENG.). 36p. (J). 16.95 (978-0-9724249-3-6(8)) Gorp Group Pr., The.

Chriscoe, Sharon. Scary Weather, Scaredy Cat, 1 vol. 2008. (ENG.). 48p. 24.95 (978-1-60474-143-8(0)) America Star Bks.

Christopher, Matt. Into the Danger Zone. Koelsch, Michael, illus. 6th ed. 2004. (ENG.). 64p. (J). (gr. 1-4). pap. 13.99 (978-0-316-76267-0(9), Tingley, Megan Bks.) Little, Brown Bks. for Young Readers.

—Wild Ride. Koelsch, Michael, illus. 7th ed. 2005. (ENG.). 64p. (J). (gr. 1-4). pap. 13.99 (978-0-316-76263-2(6)) Little, Brown Bks. for Young Readers.

Cook, Julia. The Bubble Wrap Queen. Valentine, Allison, illus. 2008. (ENG.). 32p. (J). (gr. -1-3). pap. 9.95 (978-1-931636-83-4(4)) National Ctr. For Youth Issues.

—Scoop. Venting, Elisabeth, illus. 2007. 32p. (J). 15.95 (978-1-934073-07-0(5)) National Ctr. For Youth Issues.

Cool by the Pool: Coloring / Activity Book incl Snipe. 2007. (Illus.). (J). 2.99 (978-0-9770455-8-7(7)) Mighty Kids Media.

Cool by the Pool: Picture Book (English) 8x8. 2007. (J). 5.99 (978-1-933934-37-2(9)) Mighty Kids Media.

Cool by the Pool: Picture Book (English) NL 9x9 with Snipe. 2007. (J). 5.99 (978-1-933934-47-1(6)) Mighty Kids Media.

Crowley, Kerry. The Smart Thing to Do. 2006. 60p. pap. 7.61 (978-1-4116-7126-3(0)) Lulu Pr., Inc.

Danger Alert: Coloring/Activity Book (English) Incl. Stickers. 2007. (J). 2.99 (978-1-933934-54-9(9)) Mighty Kids Media.

Danger Alert: Picture Book (English) 8x8. 2007. (J). 5.99 (978-1-933934-39-6(5)) Mighty Kids Media.

Danger Alert: Picture Book (English) 9x9 with Snipe. 2007. (J). 5.99 (978-1-933934-49-5(2)) Mighty Kids Media.

Denice, Sonia. Chow-E-Chowz: Saved by a Whistle. 2011. 44p. pap. 18.46 (978-1-4567-1020-0(6)) AuthorHouse.

Diggle, David Mark. Douglas: Pays the Price for Not Paying Attention. Preuss, Sarah Louise, illus. 2011. 24p. (J). pap. (978-0-9871658-5-5(2)) Diggle de Doo Productions Pty, Ltd.

Duracell and the National Center for Missing & Exploited Children (NCMEC), creator. The Great Tomato Adventure: A Story about Smart Safety Choices. 2007. 0.00 (978-0-9795307-0-8(9)) Duracell & the National Ctr. for Missing & Exploited Children (NCMEC).

Dyan, Penelope. When Touching Is Bad. Dyan, Penelope, illus. 2013. (Illus.). 34p. pap. 11.95 (978-1-61477-088-6(3)) Bellissima Publishing, LLC.

Educational Adventures, creator. Cool by the Pool: Coloring/Activity Book (Spanish) w/ Snipe. 2007. (Illus.). (J). per. 2.99 (978-1-933934-73-0(5)) Mighty Kids Media.

—Cool by the Pool: Picture Book (Spanish) 9x9. 2007. (Illus.). (J). per. 5.99 (978-1-933934-72-3(7)) Mighty Kids Media.

—Danger Alert: Coloring/Activity Book (Spanish) w/ Snipe. 2006. (Illus.). (J). 2.99 (978-1-933934-06-8(9)) Mighty Kids Media.

—Danger Alert: Picture Book (Spanish) 9x9. 2006. (Illus.). (J). 5.99 (978-1-933934-04-4(2)) Mighty Kids Media.

—Free Wheelin' Coloring/Activity Book (English) w/ Snipe. 2007. (J). 2.99 (978-1-933934-52-5(2)) Mighty Kids Media.

—Free Wheelin' Picture Book (Spanish) w/ Snipe. 2006. (Illus.). (J). 5.99 (978-0-9770455-6-3(0)) Mighty Kids Media.

—Poison Patrol: Coloring/Activity Book (Spanish) w/ Snipe. 2006. (Illus.). (J). 2.99 (978-1-933934-02-0(6)) Mighty Kids Media.

—Poison Patrol: Picture Book (Spanish) 9x9. 2006. (Illus.). (J). 5.99 (978-1-933934-00-6(X)) Mighty Kids Media.

—Street Smarts: Coloring/Activity Book (Spanish) w/ Snipe. 2006. (Illus.). (J). 2.99 (978-1-933934-19-8(0)) Mighty Kids Media.

—Street Smarts: Picture Book (Spanish) 9x9. 2007. (Illus.). (J). per. 5.99 (978-1-933934-77-8(8)) Mighty Kids Media.

Ennis, Nancy. When Mommy & Daddy Say No, They Still Love You. Meadows, Cynthia, illus. 2014. (ENG.). 24p. (J). 14.95 net. (978-1-61254-198-3(4)) Brown Books Publishing Group.

Faulk, Terry. Joe the Roadside Crow. 2010. 20p. 12.99 (978-1-4490-7006-9(X)) AuthorHouse.

Free Wheelin' Picture Book (English) NL 9x9 with Snipe. 2007. (J). 5.99 (978-1-933934-48-8(4)) Mighty Kids Media.

Glickman, Claudia. Skin Sense. 2007. (Illus.). 16p. (J). (978-0-615-16242-3(8)) L.G. Publishing.

Goodnight, Craig. Condor the Police K-9 In: Never Talk to Strangers. 2011. 28p. pap. 12.25 (978-1-4520-7644-7(8)) AuthorHouse.

Gopinath, Karin Ursula. Friends in the Garden. Sutanto, Tommy, illus. 2008. 34p. (J). per. 19.95 (978-0-9800637-0-7(1)) Lotus Art Works Inc.

Hallinan, P. K. Let's Be Safe. (Illus.). (J). 2012. 24p. bds. 7.99 (978-0-8249-1888-0(6)) 2007. (ENG., 32p. (gr. -1-3). 8.99 (978-0-8249-5529-8(3)) Worthy Publishing. (Ideal Pubns.).

Haslett, Katherine A. The Day Amy Met the Prime Minister & Mrs. Blair. 2007. (Illus.). 32p. (J). pap. 8.00 (978-0-8059-7353-2(2)) Dorrance Publishing Co., Inc.

Health New England, creator. Sammie Sportz My Summer of Sports Safety. 2007. (Illus.). 16p. (J). 9.95 (978-0-9777159-3-0(0)) Health New England.

Hill, Maree. Nurse Nerid. 2011. 28p. pap. 28.03 (978-1-4568-5419-5(4)) Xlibris Corp.

Jacobs, Paul DuBois & Swender, Jennifer. Fire Drill. Lee, Huy Voun, illus. 2010. (ENG.). 32p. (J). (gr. -1-2). 17.99 (978-0-8050-8953-0(5), 9780805089530, Holt, Henry & Co. Bks. For Young Readers) Holt, Henry & Co.

Joyce, Irma. Never Talk to Strangers. Buckett, George, illus. 2009. (ENG.). 32p. (J). (gr. -1-2). 9.99 (978-0-375-84964-0(5), Golden Bks.) Random Hse. Children's Bks.

Judith Mader. I Went to Safety Town! 2009. 40p. pap. 16.99 (978-1-4389-0129-9(1)) AuthorHouse.

Lane, Kathleen. The Best Worst Thing. 2016. (ENG.). 208p. (J). (gr. 3-7). 16.99 (978-0-316-25781-7(8)) Little Brown & Co.

Larson, Jason. Me & My Safety. 2009. 28p. pap. 16.99 (978-1-4490-4445-9(X)) AuthorHouse.

Marcotte, David A. Be Wary of Strangers. 2005. (ENG., Illus.). 36p. per. 14.95 (978-1-932672-47-3(8)) Outskirts Pr., Inc.

Matalonis, Anne. The Fox Behind the Chatterbox. McGhee, Chelsea, illus. 2008. 32p. pap. 17.95 (978-1-59858-783-8(8)) Dog Ear Publishing, LLC.

Mayo, Margaret. Emergency! Ayliffe, Alex, illus. 2003. 32p. (J). (gr. -1-1). 14.95 (978-0-87614-922-5(0), Carolrhoda Bks.) Lerner Publishing Group.

Mishica, Clare. Samantha Stays Safe. Dubin, Jill, illus. 2012. 32p. (J). pap. 8.00 (978-1-935014-40-9(4)) Hutchings, John Pubs.

Murphy, Stuart J. Percy Juega con Cuidado. 2011. (I See I Learn Ser.). (SPA & ENG., Illus.). 32p. (J). (-k). 14.95 (978-1-58089-484-5(4)); pap. 6.95 (978-1-58089-485-2(2)) Charlesbridge Publishing, Inc.

Omawumi Kola-Lawal, Constance. We Learn about Road Safety. 2013. 32p. pap. (978-1-909204-29-4(3)) BookPublishingWorld.

Pace, Anne Marie. Never Ever Talk to Strangers. Francis, Guy, illus. 2010. (J). (978-0-545-24229-5(0)) Scholastic, Inc.

Pendziwol, Jean E. Once upon a Dragon: Stranger Safety for Kids (and Dragons) Gourbault, Martine, illus. 2006. (ENG.). 32p. (J). (gr. -1-2). 7.95 (978-1-55337-969-0(1)) Kids Can Pr., Ltd. CAN. Dist: Hachette Bk. Group.

Poison Patrol: Coloring/Activity (English) Incl. Posters, Stickers. 2007. (J). 2.99 (978-1-933934-53-2(0)) Mighty Kids Media.

Poison Patrol: Picture Book 8x8. 2007. (J). 5.99 (978-1-933934-40-2(9)) Mighty Kids Media.

Poison Patrol: Picture Book (English) 9x9 with Snipe. 2007. (J). 5.99 (978-1-933934-50-1(6)) Mighty Kids Media.

Porter, Rhonda. Brody Learns about Strangers, 1 vol. 2009. 29p. pap. 19.95 (978-1-61546-699-3(1)) PublishAmerica, Inc.

Potter, Noel Gyro. Plan B, 1 vol. Cannon, Joseph, illus. 2010. (Adventures of Marshall & Art Set 2 Ser.). (ENG.). 32p. (gr. -1-4). 28.50 (978-1-60270-736-8(7), Looking Glass Library) ABDO Publishing Co.

—Stranger Danger, 1 vol. Cannon, illus. 2010. (Adventures of Marshall & Art Set 2 Ser.). (ENG.). 32p. (gr. -1-4). 28.50 (978-1-60270-738-2(3), Looking Glass Library) ABDO Publishing Co.

Russell, Pamela L. R. Bee Careful! My Big Kid Safety Manual. 2012. 20p. pap. 17.99 (978-1-4685-9831-5(7)) AuthorHouse.

Sargent, Dave & Sargent, David M. Bob White: Use Good Judgement, 20 vols., Vol. 3. Lenoir, Jane, illus. 2003. (Feather Tales Ser.: No. 3). 42p. (J). pap. 10.95 (978-1-56763-724-3(8)) Ozark Publishing.

Sargent, David M. Bob White: Use Good Judgement, 20 vols., Vol. 3. Lenoir, Jane, illus. 2003. (Feather Tales Ser.: No. 3). 42p. (J). lib. bdg. 20.95 (978-1-56763-723-6(X)) Ozark Publishing.

Scoop. 2007. (J). 15.95 (978-1-934073-00-1(8)) National Ctr. For Youth Issues.

Shaw, Natalie. Be Careful, Friend! Craig, Karen, illus. 2010. (Yo Gabba Gabba! Ser.). (ENG.). 26p. (J). (gr. -1 — 1). bds. 5.99 (978-1-4169-9534-0(X), Simon Spotlight) Simon Spotlight.

Slater, Teddy. Emergency, Call 911. Lewis, Anthony, illus. 2010. 16p. (J). (978-0-545-24601-9(6)) Scholastic, Inc.

—Fire Prevention. Lewis, Anthony, illus. 2010. 16p. (J). (978-0-545-24603-3(2)) Scholastic, Inc.

—Home Safe Home. Smith, Jamie, illus. 2010. 16p. (J). (978-0-545-24606-4(7)) Scholastic, Inc.

—Safety in the Bus. Smith, Jamie, illus. 2010. 16p. (J). (978-0-545-24602-6(4)) Scholastic, Inc.

—Stranger Danger. Lewis, Anthony, illus. 2010. 16p. (J). (978-0-545-24605-7(9)) Scholastic, Inc.

—Street Safety. Smith, Jamie, illus. 2010. 16p. (J). (978-0-545-24604-0(0)) Scholastic, Inc.

Street Smarts: Coloring/Activity Book (English) Incl. Stickers. 2006. (Illus.). (J). 2.99 (978-1-933934-18-1(2)) Mighty Kids Media.

Street Smarts: Picture Book 9x9 with Snipe. 2006. (Illus.). (J). 5.99 (978-1-933934-17-4(4)) Mighty Kids Media.

Street Smarts: Picture Book (English) 8x8. 2006. (Illus.). (J). 5.99 (978-1-933934-16-7(6)) Mighty Kids Media.

Thomas, Kate. Mother Duck Knows the Way. Larkins, Mona, illus. 2005. 32p. (J). 8.95 (978-1-58374-122-1(4)) Chicago Spectrum Pr.

Townsend, Peter. Shelly & Muffin's Big Lesson Learned. 2008. 11p. pap. 24.95 (978-1-60672-379-1(0)) America Star Bks.

Tuchman, Lauryn & Silverhardt, Lauryn. A Visit to the Firehouse. Craig, Karen, illus. 2009. (Blue's Clues Ser.). (ENG.). 24p. (J). (gr. -1-2). pap. 3.99 (978-1-4169-7193-1(9), Simon Spotlight/Nickelodeon) Simon Spotlight/Nickelodeon.

Weeks, Kermit. All of Life Is a School. Project Firefly, illus. 2007. 64p. (J). 19.95 (978-0-9790267-0-6(9)) KWIP, Inc.

Willis, Jeanne. Cottonball Colin. Ross, Tony, illus. 2008. 26p. (J). (gr. -1-4). 16.00 (978-0-8028-5331-8(5), Eerdmans Bks For Young Readers) Eerdmans, William B. Publishing Co.

Yolen, Jane. How Do Dinosaurs Stay Safe? Teague, Mark, illus. 2015. (ENG.). 40p. (J). (gr. -1-k). 16.99 (978-0-439-24104-5(9), Blue Sky Pr., The) Scholastic, Inc.

SAFETY MEASURES

see Accidents—Prevention

also subjects with the subdivision Safety Measures, e.g. Aeronautics—Safety Measures

SAHARA

Aloian, Molly. The Sahara Desert. 2012. (ENG.). 32p. (J). (978-0-7787-0714-1(8)); (Illus.). pap. (978-0-7787-0722-6(9)) Crabtree Publishing Co.

Chapman, S. I. mon. In the Desert. 2006. (Illus.). 111p. (J). lib. bdg. 20.00 (978-1-4242-0628-5(6)) Fitzgerald Bks.

Fine, Jil. Sahara: El Desierto Mas Grande del Mundo. 2004. (Maravillas Naturales (Natures Greatest Hits) Ser.). (SPA.). 24p. (J). (gr. 3-6). lib. bdg. 22.60 (978-0-8239-6879-4(0), Editorial Buenas Letras) Rosen Publishing Group, Inc., The.

—Sahara: El desierto más grande del mundo (the Sahara: World's Largest Desert) 2009. (Maravillas naturales (Natures Greatest Hits) Ser.). (SPA.). 24p. (gr. 2-2). 42.50 (978-1-61514-365-8(3), Editorial Buenas Letras) Rosen Publishing Group, Inc., The.

—The Sahara: World's Largest Desert. 2009. (Nature's Greatest Hits Ser.). 24p. (gr. 2-2). 42.50 (978-1-61514-842-4(6), PowerKids Pr.) Rosen Publishing Group, Inc., The.

Franchino, Vicky. Sahara Desert. 2016. (Community Connections: Getting to Know Our Planet Ser.). (ENG.). 24p. (J). (gr. 2-5). 27.07 (978-1-63470-518-9(1), 207803) Cherry Lake Publishing.

Heinrichs, Ann. The Sahara Desert. 2008. (Nature's Wonders Ser.). 96p. (gr. 6-18). lib. bdg. 35.64 (978-0-7614-2855-8(0), Benchmark Bks.) Marshall Cavendish Corp.

Lappi, Megan. The Sahara Desert. 2005. 32p. pap. 9.95 (978-1-59036-274-7(8)) Weigl Pubs., Inc.

—Sahara Desert. 2013. (J). (978-1-62127-477-3(2)); pap. (978-1-62127-483-4(7)) Weigl Pubs., Inc.

—The Sahara Desert: The Largest Desert in the World. 2006. (Natural Wonders Ser.). (Illus.). 32p. (J). (gr. 3-7). 15.60 (978-0-7569-6997-4(2)) Perfection Learning Corp.

—The Sahara Desert: The Largest Desert in the World. 2006. (Natural Wonders Ser.). (Illus.). 32p. (J). (gr. 5-6). lib. bdg. 26.00 (978-1-59036-452-9(X)); per. 9.95 (978-1-59036-458-1(9), 1266427) Weigl Pubs., Inc.

Publishers, Wayland & Newland, Sonya. Trekking the Sahara Desert. 2016. (Travelling Wild Ser.). (ENG., Illus.). 32p. (J). (gr. 4-6). 17.99 (978-0-7502-8584-1(2), Wayland) Hachette Children's Group GBR. Dist: Hachette Bk. Group.

Reynolds, Jan. Sahara, 1 vol. 2007. (Vanishing Cultures Ser.). (ENG., Illus.). 32p. (978-1-60060-146-0(4)); (J). (gr. 4-7). 10.95 (978-1-60060-131-6(6)) Lee & Low Bks., Inc.

Weintraub, Aileen. The Sahara Desert: The Biggest Desert. 2009. (Great Record Breakers in Nature Ser.). 24p. (gr. 3-4). 42.50 (978-1-61513-186-0(8), PowerKids Pr.) Rosen Publishing Group, Inc., The.

Zuravicky, Orli. The Amazon & the Sahara: Using Double Line Graphs & Double Bar Graphs. (PowerMath Ser.). 32p. 2009. (ENG., Illus.). (gr. 4-5). pap. 10.00 (978-0-8239-8868-6(6)) 2009. (gr. 4-5). 47.90 (978-1-60851-401-4(3)) 2004. (Illus.). (J). lib. bdg. 23.95 (978-0-8239-8981-2(X)) Rosen Publishing Group, Inc., The. (PowerKids Pr.).

SAHARA—FICTION

Cunnane, Kelly. Deep in the Sahara. Hadadi, Hoda, illus. 2013. (ENG.). 40p. (J). (gr. -1-3). 17.99 (978-0-375-87034-7(2), Schwartz & Wade Bks.) Random Hse. Children's Bks.

Davies, Stephen. Outlaw. 2011. (ENG.). 304p. (YA). (gr. 7). 16.99 (978-0-547-39017-8(3)) Houghton Mifflin Harcourt Publishing Co.

Smith, Lisa. Makini, the Impala with a Crooked Horn. 2011. 24p. pap. 24.95 (978-1-4626-2608-3(4)) America Star Bks.

Terman, Douglas. By Balloon to the Sahara. 2015. (ENG.). 144p. (J). pap. 6.99 (978-1-937133-48-1(6)) Chooseco LLC.

Turner, Tracey. Lost in the Desert of Dread. 2014. (ENG., Illus.). 128p. (J). (978-0-7787-0725-7(3)) Crabtree Publishing Co.

SAILING

see also Boats and Boating; Navigation; Yachts and Yachting

Bruce, Julia. Sail! Can You Command a Sea Voyage? Dennis, Peter, illus. 2009. (Step into History Ser.). 32p. (J). (gr. 2-5). lib. bdg. 23.94 (978-0-7660-3477-8(1)) Enslow Pubs., Inc.

Davison, Tim & Kibble, Steve. Sailing for Kids. 2nd ed. 2015. (ENG., Illus.). 48p. pap. 18.70 **(978-1-909911-26-0(7))** Fernhurst Bks. GBR. Dist: Casemate Pubs. & Bk. Distributors, LLC.

Gamble, Adam & Jasper, Mark. Good Night Boats. Veno, Joe, illus. 2016. (Good Night Our World Ser.). (ENG.). 20p. (J). (— 1). bds. 9.95 (978-1-60219-500-4(5)) Good Night Bks.

Henderson, Richard. First Sail, 1 vol. Wharton, Jennifer Heyd, illus. 2009. (ENG.). 48p. (J). (gr. -1-3). 15.95 (978-0-87033-442-9(5), 9780870334429, Cornell Maritime Pr./Tidewater Pubs.) Schiffer Publishing, Ltd.

Ives, Burl. Sailing on a Very Fine Day. Myers, Bernice & Myers, Lou, illus. 2011. 32p. pap. 35.95 (978-1-258-04002-4(6)) Literary Licensing, LLC.

Mosenthal, Basil, et al. Getting Afloat: All You Need to Know about Sailing Small Boats. 2003. (ENG., Illus.). 80p. pap. (978-0-7136-5278-9(0), Adlard Coles) Bloomsbury Publishing Plc.

Newland, Sonya. Sailing the Caribbean Islands. 2016. (Travelling Wild Ser.). (ENG., Illus.). 32p. (J). (gr. 4-6). 17.99 (978-0-7502-9865-0(0), Wayland) Hachette Children's Group GBR. Dist: Hachette Bk. Group.

Porter, Suzie. Sailing. 2011. (Get Outdoors Ser.). (Illus.). 32p. (J). (gr. 4-6). lib. bdg. 25.25 (978-1-4488-3297-2(7), PowerKids Pr.) Rosen Publishing Group, Inc., The.

Sisk, Siobhan. Would You Dare Sail Around the World? 2016. (Would You Dare? Ser.). 00032p. (J). pap. 10.50 **(978-1-4824-5826-8(8))**; lib. bdg. 26.60 **(978-1-4824-5828-2(4))** Stevens, Gareth Publishing LLLP.

Teitelbaum, Michael. Sailing. 2012. (Extreme Sports Ser.). (ENG., Illus.). 32p. (J). (gr. 2-5). lib. bdg. 28.50 (978-1-60973-184-7(0), 201130) Child's World, Inc., The.

Veigele, William J. Sea Bag of Memories: Images, Poems, Thoughts, & Crafts of the small Ship Sailors of World War II. 2003. 320p. (YA). (gr. 10-18). 39.95 (978-0-9645867-4-1(6)) Astral Publishing Co.

SAILING—FICTION

Appelt, Kathi. Keeper. Hall, August, illus. (ENG.). (J). (gr. 3-7). 2012. 432p. pap. 8.99 (978-1-4169-5061-5(3)) 2010. 416p. 17.99 (978-1-4169-5060-8(5)) Simon & Schuster Children's Publishing. (Atheneum Bks. for Young Readers).

Arvidson, Douglas. Brothers of the Fire Star. Scarborough, Rob, illus. 2012. 207p. (YA). pap. 15.95 (978-1-890109-91-2(6), Cross Time) Crossquarter Publishing Group.

Ballantyne, R. M. The Crew of the Water Wagtail. 2011. 146p. pap. 12.95 (978-1-60664-550-5(1)) Rodgers, Alan Bks.

—Red Rooney: Or, the Last of the Crew. 2007. (R. M. Ballantyne Collection). (Illus.). 408p. 22.00 (978-1-934554-08-1(1)) Vision Forum, Inc., The.

Ballantyne, Robert Michael. Red Rooney: The Last of the Crew. 2007. (ENG.). 270p. pap. 21.99 (978-1-4346-3693-5(3)); 302p. pap. 24.99 (978-1-4346-3741-3(7)) Creative Media Partners, LLC.

Basham, Tom. Sailing Home. Calvert, Lissa, illus. 2012. 168p. (978-1-77097-370-1(2)) FriesenPress.

Basham, Tom & Calvert, Lissa. Sailing Home. 2012. 168p. pap. (978-1-77097-371-8(0)) FriesenPress.

Beach, John & Lubotsky, Dana, readers. The Wanderer. unabr. ed. 2004. 320p. (J). (gr. 4-7). pap. 36.00 incl. audio (978-0-8072-0864-9(7), LYA 199 SP, Listening Library) Random Hse. Audio Publishing Group.

Bell, Loman. Old Glory. Bell, Loman, illus. 2012. (Illus.). 40p. pap. (978-0-9866065-8-8(8)) Wood Islands Prints.

Benchmark Education Co., LLC. Sail with Me Big Book. 2014. (Shared Reading Foundations Ser.). (J). (gr. -1). (978-1-4509-9447-7(4)) Benchmark Education Co.

Blackstone, Stella. Una Isla Bajo el Sol. Ceccoli, Nicoletta, illus. 2003. (SPA.). 24p. (J). pap. 6.99 (978-1-84148-144-9(0)) Barefoot Bks., Inc.

Blackstone, Stella & Barefoot Books Staff. An Island in the Sun. Ceccoli, Nicoletta, illus. 2005. (ENG.). 24p. (J). pap. 6.99 (978-1-84148-079-4(7)) Barefoot Bks., Inc.

Borgenicht, David & Lurie, Alexander. Deadly Seas: You Decide How to Survive! 2015. (WorstCase Scenario Ultimate Adventure Ser.). (ENG., Illus.). 204p. (gr. 3-8). 47.10 (978-1-59920-981-4(0)) Black Rabbit Bks.

Bradford, Arthur. Benny's Brigade. Hanawalt, Lisa, illus. 2012. (ENG.). 48p. 19.95 (978-1-936365-61-6(8)) McSweeney's Publishing.

Brown, Jeff. The Flat Stanley Collection, Set. Pamintuan, Macky, illus. 2013. (Flat Stanley Ser.). 400p. (J). (gr. 1-5). pap. 14.99 (978-0-06-180247-8(6)) HarperCollins Pubs.

—Stanley, Flat Again! Nash, Scott & Pamintuan, Macky, illus. (Flat Stanley Ser.). (ENG.). 96p. (J). (gr. 2-5). 2009. pap. 4.99 (978-0-06-442173-7(2)) 2003. 15.99 (978-0-06-009551-2(2)) HarperCollins Pubs.

Bukiet, Melvin Jules. Undertown. 2013. (ENG.). 304p. (J). (gr. 3-7). 17.95 (978-1-4197-0589-2(X), Amulet Bks.) Abrams, Inc.

Burgess, Lisa Maria. Juma's Dhow Race. Gugu, Abdul M., illus. 2013. 32p. 19.95 (978-1-939604-09-5(5)); pap. 9.99 (978-1-939604-05-7(2)) Barranca Pr.

Carlos the Sailor Visits Atlantic City. 2005. (J). pap. 12.95 (978-0-9766889-0-7(5)) ComteQ Publishing.

Clements, Andrew. In Harm's Way. Stower, Adam, illus. (Benjamin Pratt & the Keepers of the School Ser.: 4). (ENG.). (J). (gr. 2-5). 2014. 240p. pap. 7.99 (978-1-4169-3910-8(5)) 2013. 224p. 14.99 (978-1-4169-3889-7(3)) Simon & Schuster Children's Publishing. (Atheneum Bks. for Young Readers).

—We the Children. 2011. (Benjamin Pratt & the Keepers of the School Ser.: 1). (ENG.). 176p. (J). (gr. 2-5). pap. 7.99 (978-1-4169-3907-8(5), Atheneum Bks. for Young Readers) Simon & Schuster Children's Publishing.

—The Whites of Their Eyes. Stower, Adam, illus. (Benjamin Pratt & the Keepers of the School Ser.: 3). (ENG.). (J). (gr. 2-5). 2013. 240p. pap. 6.99 (978-1-4169-3909-2(1)) 2012. 224p. 14.99 (978-1-4169-3888-0(5)) Simon & Schuster Children's Publishing. (Atheneum Bks. for Young Readers).

Coates, Paul. Tim & the Iceberg, 1 vol. Haywood, Ian Benfold, illus. 2011. (ENG.). 32p. (J). (gr. k-3). 16.95 (978-1-59572-205-8(X)); pap. 6.95 (978-1-59572-206-5(8)) Star Bright Bks., Inc.

Collingwood, Harry. Under the Chilean Flag. 2009. 184p. 26.95 (978-1-60664-598-7(6)); pap. 13.95 (978-1-60664-330-3(4)) Rodgers, Alan Bks.

Costello, David Hyde. Little Pig Saves the Ship. Costello, David Hyde, illus. 2017. (ENG., Illus.). 32p. (J). (gr. -1-2). 14.99 (978-1-58089-715-0(0)) Charlesbridge Publishing, Inc.

Creech, Sharon. The Wanderer. Diaz, David, illus. 2011. (ENG.). 304p. (J). (gr. 3-7). pap. 6.99 (978-0-06-441032-8(3)) HarperCollins Pubs.

Daynes, Katie, retold by. Sinbad. 2005. (Young Reading Series 1 Ser.). 48p. (J). (gr. 2-18). pap. 5.95 (978-0-7945-0825-8(1), Usborne) EDC Publishing.

DeGorsky, Gregory J. The Christmas Pirate. DeGorsky, Jon, ed. 2007. (ENG., Illus.). 80p. (J). pap. 4.95 (978-0-9678542-3-6(7)) Magnetic Image, Inc.

Dogiakis, Helen. Captain Terry the Pirate Cow's Adventure to Italy. 2011. 32p. pap. 14.99 (978-1-4567-3131-1(9)) AuthorHouse.

Eggleton, Jill. Sailor Sam in Trouble. Storey, Jim, illus. 2004. (Rigby Sails Early Ser.). (ENG.). 16p. (gr. 1-2). pap. 6.95 (978-0-7578-9295-0(7)) Houghton Mifflin Harcourt Publishing Co.

Ering, Timothy Basil. The Unexpected Love Story of Alfred Fiddleduckling. Ering, Timothy Basil, illus. 2017. (ENG., Illus.). 48p. (J). (-k). 15.99 (978-0-7636-6432-9(4)) Candlewick Pr.

Espluga, Maria. I Am a Sailor. 2009. (I Am A... (Alphabet Soup) Ser.). (Illus.). 24p. (J). (gr. k-1). pap. 8.15 (978-1-60754-255-1(2)); lib. bdg. 22.60 (978-1-60754-254-4(4)) Windmill Bks.

—I, Sailor: Yo, Marinero. 2009. (SPA & ENG.). 28p. (J). 13.95 (978-1-931398-53-4(4)) Me+Mi Publishing.

Ezirim, E. C. Jet Black & the Ebony Knights. 2010. 40p. 16.99 (978-1-4520-7567-9(0)) AuthorHouse.

Floerchinger, Lori Liddic. Ocean of Dreams. Floerchinger, Jeremy, illus. 2008. 36p. pap. 24.95 (978-1-60703-003-4(9)) America Star Bks.

Griffin, Paul. Adrift. 2015. (ENG.). 240p. (J). (gr. 7). 17.99 (978-0-545-70939-2(3), Scholastic Pr.) Scholastic, Inc.

Gurney, Stella. Sally Sets Sail. Worsley, Belinda, illus. 2009. (Get Ready (Windmill Books) Ser.). 32p. (J). (gr. k-2). lib. bdg. 22.60 (978-1-60754-261-2(7)) Windmill Bks.

Hopkinson, Deborah. Sailing for Gold. Farnsworth, Bill, illus. 2005. 76p. (J). lib. bdg. 15.00 (978-1-59054-915-5(5)) Fitzgerald Bks.

Johnson, Julia, ed. Arabian Star. Climent, Henry, illus. 2009. (ENG.). 52p. 11.99 (978-1-905299-84-3(2), Stacey International) Stacey Publishing GBR. Dist: Casemate Pubs. & Bk. Distributors, LLC.

Johnston, James D. The Adventures of Lucas & Celi: Lucas Stows Away. 2009. 32p. pap. 12.99 (978-1-4343-6372-5(4)) AuthorHouse.

Kisko, Stephen. Sailing the Puddles. 2013. 36p. pap. 12.95 (978-1-62838-002-6(0)) Page Publishing Inc.

Lumley, Jemima. The Journey Home from Grandpa's. Fatus, Sophie, illus. 2010. (ENG.). 16p. (J). (gr. -1-3). pap. 5.99 (978-1-84686-277-9(9)) Barefoot Bks., Inc.

Lund, Deb. Dinosailors. Fine, Howard, illus. 2008. (ENG.). 36p. (J). (gr. -1-3). pap. 6.99 (978-0-15-206124-1(X)) Houghton Mifflin Harcourt Publishing Co.

Martin, Ann M. & Godwin, Laura. The Doll People Book 4 the Doll People Set Sail. Helquist, Brett, illus. 2016. (Doll People Ser.). (ENG.). 304p. (J). (gr. 3-7). pap. 7.99 (978-1-4231-3998-0(4)) Hyperion Bks. for Children.

McDougal-Littell Publishing Staff. The True Confessions of Charlotte Doyle. 2004. (McDougal Littell Literature Connections Ser.). (ENG., Illus.). 272p. (gr. 7-7). 18.50 (978-0-395-87477-6(7), 2-70837) Great Source Education Group, Inc.

Mercier, Deborah. The Captain's Hat. Mills, Faythe, illus. 2007. 32p. (J). 17.99 (978-0-9799410-0-9(8)) Minnewaska Pr.

Meyer, L. A. Bloody Jack: Being an Account of the Curious Adventures of Mary "Jacky" Faber, Ship's Boy. 2nd ed. 2010. (Bloody Jack Adventures Ser.: 1). (ENG., Illus.). 304p. (YA). (gr. 7-12). reprint ed. pap. 9.99 (978-0-15-205085-6(X)) Houghton Mifflin Harcourt Publishing Co.

Mitchen, Scott. Will of the Pirates. 2008. 180p. 22.95 (978-0-595-70652-5(5)) iUniverse, Inc.

Myers, Byrona. Yo Ho for Strawberry Roam! Jauss, Anne Marie, illus. 2011. 154p. 41.95 (978-1-258-08204-8(7)) Literary Licensing, LLC.

Neale, Jonathan. Lost at Sea. 2004. (ENG.). 112p. (J). (gr. 5-7). reprint ed. pap. 8.95 (978-0-618-43236-3(1)) Houghton Mifflin Harcourt Publishing Co.

Oppenheim, Shulamith. Rescuing Einstein's Compass. Juhasz, George, illus. 2003. (ENG.). 32p. (J). (gr. k-3). 15.95 (978-1-56656-507-3(3), Interlink Bks.) Interlink Publishing Group, Inc.

Optic, Oliver, pseud. Sunny Shores; or, Young America in Italy & Austria a Story of Travel & Adventure by William T Adams. 2006. 428p. per. 26.99 (978-1-4255-4627-4(7)) Michigan Publishing.

Otis, James. Raising the Pearl. 2011. 302p. 48.95 (978-1-258-10248-7(X)) Literary Licensing, LLC.

Parrish, Fayrene. Pancho Saves the Day: Shipmates Learning Adventures Venture. Parrish, Fayrene, illus. 2010. (Illus.). 42p. (J). 15.95 (978-0-9826717-8-8(4)) Parrish, Fayrene.

Parry, Rosanne. The Turn of the Tide. 2016. (ENG., Illus.). 304p. (J). (gr. 3-7). 16.99 (978-0-375-86972-3(7), Random Hse. Bks. for Young Readers) Random Hse. Children's Bks.

Peters, Stephanie True. The First & Final Voyage: The Sinking of the Titanic, 1 vol. Proctor, Jon, illus. 2008. (Historical Fiction Ser.). (ENG.). 56p. (gr. 2-3). pap. 6.25 (978-1-4342-0494-3(4), Graphic Flash) Stone Arch Bks.

Prins, Piet. The Sailing Sleuths. Kramer, Jaap, illus. 2006. 137p. (J). pap. (978-1-894666-46-6(1)) Inheritance Pubns.

—Stefan Derksen's Polar Adventure. 2004. (Illus.). 237p. (J). pap. (978-1-894666-67-1(4)) Inheritance Pubns.

Punter, R. Stories of Pirates. 2004. (Young Reading Ser.: Vol. 1). 48p. (J). (gr. 2-18). pap. 5.99 (978-0-7945-0583-7(X)) EDC Publishing.

Ransome, Arthur. Swallowdale. Ransome, Arthur, illus. 2010. (Swallows & Amazons Ser.). (Illus.). 431p. (YA). pap. 14.95 (978-1-56792-421-3(2)) Godine, David R. Pub.

—Swallowdale. 2014. (ENG., Illus.). 464p. (gr. 4-13). 24.95 (978-1-4683-0956-0(0), 460956) Overlook Pr., The.

—We Didn't Mean to Go to Sea. 2010. (ENG.). 100p. (gr. 2). pap. 22.95 (978-1-906582-05-0(X)) Aurora Metro Pubns. Ltd. GBR. Dist: Consortium Bk. Sales & Distribution.

Root, Phyllis. Lilly & the Pirates. Shepperson, Rob, illus. (ENG.). (J). 2013. 180p. (gr. 3-7). pap. 8.95 (978-1-62091-027-6(6)) 2010. 116p. (gr. 4-6). 16.95 (978-1-59078-583-6(5), Front Street) Boyds Mills Pr.

Schaaf, Ron. Tiger's Quest: Rounding Cape Horn. 2007. (J). (978-0-9787555-0-8(2)) Hickory Tales Publishing.

Smith, Buckley. Moonsailors. Smith, Buckley, illus. 2007. (ENG., Illus.). 40p. (J). (gr. -1-7). 14.95 (978-0-937822-95-1(7)) WoodenBoat Pubns.

Stevenson, Robin. A Thousand Shades of Blue, 1 vol. 2008. (ENG.). 240p. (YA). (gr. 7-12). pap. 12.95 (978-1-55143-921-1(2)) Orca Bk. Pubs. USA.

Treasure Island: A Growing Field Adventure. 2011. (Illus.). 64p. (J). 16.95 (978-0-9770391-4-2(5)) Growing Field Bks.

Wait, Lea. Seaward Born. 2004. (ENG., Illus.). 160p. (J). (gr. 3-7). pap. 8.99 (978-0-689-84860-5(9), McElderry, Margaret K. Bks.) McElderry, Margaret K. Bks.

Winfield, Arthur M. The Rover Boys on the Ocean. 2007. 232p. 26.95 (978-1-4218-4138-0(X)); per. 11.95 (978-1-4218-4236-3(X)) 1st World Publishing, Inc. (1st World Library - Literary Society).

Winkler, Ashley & Winkler, Michael. One Good Quest Deserves Another: A Crown of Amaranth Story. 2009. 292p. 28.95 (978-0-595-71039-3(5)); pap. 18.95 (978-0-595-47365-6(2)) iUniverse, Inc.

Zwingelberg, Wc. The Adventures of Will W. Wilson. 2006. (Illus.). 80p. per. 12.00 (978-1-4251-0579-2(3)) Trafford Publishing.

SAILING—HISTORY

Jackson, Tom. Land & Water Transportation. 2012. (FAYFT: Invention & Technology Ser.). 64p. (gr. 4-10). lib. bdg. 39.95 (978-1-936333-42-4(2)) Brown Bear Bks.

SAILOR MOON (FICTITIOUS CHARACTER)—FICTION

Takeuchi, Naoko. Sailor Moon. (Sailor Moon Ser.: Vol. 5). (ENG., Illus.). 2012. 176p. (gr. 8-12). pap. 10.99 (978-1-61262-001-5(9)) 2011. 176p. pap. 10.99 (978-1-935429-75-3(2)) 2011. 248p. pap. 10.99 (978-1-935429-74-6(4))No. 8. 2012. 200p. (gr. 8-12). pap. 10.99 (978-1-61262-004-6(3))Set, Vols. 1-6. 2012. 1200p. pap. 65.94 (978-1-61262-396-2(4)) Vol. 3. 2012. 176p. (gr. 8-12). pap. 10.99 (978-1-935429-76-0(0)) Vol. 10. 2013. 200p. (gr. 8-12). pap. 10.99 (978-1-61262-006-0(X)) Vol. 11. 2013. 200p. (gr. 8-12). pap. 10.99 (978-1-61262-007-7(8)) Vol. 12. 2013. 200p. (gr. 8-12). pap. 10.99 (978-1-61262-008-4(6)) Kodansha America, Inc.

—Sailor Moon 4. 2012. (Sailor Moon Ser.: Vol. 4). (ENG., Illus.). 176p. (gr. 8-12). pap. 10.99 (978-1-61262-000-8(0)) Kodansha America, Inc.

—Sailor Moon 9. 2013. (Sailor Moon Ser.: Vol. 9). (ENG., Illus.). 264p. (gr. 8-12). pap. 10.99 (978-1-61262-005-3(1)) Kodansha America, Inc.

SAILORS

see also Naval Biography

also names of countries with the subhead Navy, e.g. United States—Navy, etc.

Anderson, Dale. Soldiers & Sailors in the American Revolution. 2005. (World Almanac Library of the American Revolution Ser.). 48p. (gr. 5-12). pap. 14.05 (978-0-8368-5938-6(3)); lib. bdg. 31.00 (978-0-8368-5929-4(4)) Stevens, Gareth Publishing LLLP. (Gareth Stevens Secondary Library).

Brown, Chris. Shiver Me Timbers: A Fun Book of Pirates, Sailors, & Other Sea-Farers. 2006. (ENG., Illus.). 32p. (J). (gr. 4-7). pap. 8.95 *(978-0-7145-3303-2(3))* Consortium Bk. Sales & Distribution.

Duder, Tessa, ed. Down to the Sea Again: True Sea Stories for Young Newzealanders. 2005. 256p. (J). *(978-1-86950-476-2(3))* HarperCollins Pubs. New Zealand NZL. Dist: HarperCollins Pubs. Australia.

Fern, Tracey E. Dare the Wind: The Record-Breaking Voyage of Eleanor Prentiss & the Flying Cloud. McCully, Emily Arnold, illus. 2014. (ENG.). 540p. (J). (gr. k-3). 17.99 *(978-0-374-31699-0(6)*, 9780374316990, Farrar, Straus & Giroux (BYR)) Farrar, Straus & Giroux.

Goldish, Meish. Navy: Civilian to Sailor. 2010. (Becoming a Soldier Ser.). 24p. (YA). (gr. 3-6). lib. bdg. 22.61 *(978-1-936088-14-0(2))* Bearport Publishing Co., Inc.

Gunderson, Jessica. Your Life as a Cabin Boy on a Pirate Ship. Burns, Mike, illus. 2012. (Way It Was Ser.). (ENG.). 32p. (gr. 2-3). pap. 8.95 *(978-1-4048-7249-3(3))*; lib. bdg. 26.65 *(978-1-4048-7159-5(4))* Picture Window Bks.

Janveau, Teri-Lynn & Thompson, Allister. Sailing for Glory: The Story of Captain Angus Walters & the Bluenose. Thompson, Samantha, illus. 2006. (Stories of Canada Ser.: 10). (ENG.). 72p. (J). 18.95 *(978-1-894917-09-4(X)*, Napoleon & Co.) Dundum CAN. Dist: Ingram Publisher Services.

Llanas, Sheila Griffin. Women of the U. S. Navy: Making Waves, 1 vol. 2010. (Women in the U. S. Armed Forces Ser.). (ENG.). 32p. (gr. 3-4). lib. bdg. 27.99 *(978-1-4296-5448-7(1)*, Snap Bks.) Capstone Press of Coughlan Cos.

Loveless, Antony. Nuclear Submariners. 2009. (World's Most Dangerous Jobs Ser.). (ENG., Illus.). 32p. (J). (gr. 3-6). pap. *(978-0-7787-5111-3(2))*; lib. bdg. *(978-0-7787-5097-0(3))* Crabtree Publishing Co.

Micklos, John. How the Revolutionary War Was Won. 2008. (Revolutionary War Library). (Illus.). 48p. (J). (gr. 3-4). lib. bdg. 25.27 *(978-0-7660-3016-9(4)*, Enslow Elementary) Enslow Pubs., Inc.

—Why We Won the American Revolution — Through Primary Sources. 2013. (American Revolution Through Primary Sources Ser.). 48p. (J). (gr. 4-18). 25.27 *(978-0-7660-4134-9(4))* Enslow Pubs., Inc.

—Why We Won the American Revolution—Through Primary Sources. 2013. (American Revolution Through Primary Sources Ser.). 48p. (J). (gr. 4-10). pap. 8.95 *(978-1-4644-0192-3(6))* Enslow Pubs., Inc.

Miller, Adam, et al. Courage under Fire: Tales of Bravery, 1 vol. 2014. (Courage under Fire Ser.). (ENG.). 32p. (gr. 3-4). 111.96 *(978-1-4765-9939-7(4)*, Edge Bks.) Capstone Press of Coughlan Cos.

—Courage under Fire: True Stories of Bravery from the U. S. Army, Navy, Air Force, & Marines, 1 vol. 2014. (Courage under Fire Ser.). (ENG., Illus.). 112p. (gr. 3-4). pap. 9.95 *(978-1-4914-1065-3(5))* Capstone Press of Coughlan Cos.

Miller, Nancy. My Mom Is in the Navy, 01 vols., 1. 2016. (Military Families Ser.). (ENG., Illus.). 24p. (J). pap. 8.25 *(978-1-5081-4438-0(9)*, PowerKids Pr.) Rosen Publishing Group, Inc., The.

Prentzas, G. S. Lost at Sea. 2015. (Illus.). 32p. (J). lib. bdg. *(978-1-62724-290-5(2))* Bearport Publishing Co., Inc.

Raum, Elizabeth. World War II Naval Forces, 1 vol. 2013. (You Choose: World War II Ser.). (ENG., Illus.). 112p. (gr. 3-4). pap. 6.95 *(978-1-62065-720-1(1)*, You Choose Bks.) Capstone Press of Coughlan Cos.

—World War II Naval Forces: An Interactive History Adventure. 2013. (You Choose: World War II Ser.). (ENG.). 112p. (gr. 3-4). pap. 41.70 *(978-1-62065-721-8(X))*; (Illus.). lib. bdg. 31.99 *(978-1-4296-4780-9(9))* Capstone Press of Coughlan Cos. (You Choose Bks.).

Reed, Jennifer. Marineros de la Armada de EE. UU. 2010. (Gente de Las Fuerzas Armadas de EE. UU. /People of the Armed Forces Ser.).Tr. of Sailors of the U. S. Navy. (MUL & SPA.). 24p. (gr. k-1). lib. bdg. 26.65 *(978-1-4296-6117-1(8))* Capstone Press of Coughlan Cos.

—Sailors of the U. S. Navy [Scholastic]. 2010. (People of the U. S. Armed Forces Ser.). (ENG.). 24p. pap. 0.49 *(978-1-4296-5806-5(1)*, Pebble Plus) Capstone Press of Coughlan Cos.

Russo, Kristen J. Surprising Facts about Being a Navy Sailor. 2017. (What You Didn't Know about the U. S. Military Life Ser.). (ENG.). 32p. (gr. 3-4). lib. bdg. 27.99 ***(978-1-5157-7430-3(9)**, Edge Bks.)* Capstone Press of Coughlan Cos.

Sheinkin, Steve. The Port Chicago 50: Disaster, Mutiny, & the Fight for Civil Rights. 2014. (ENG., Illus.). 208p. (J). (gr. 5-9). 19.99 *(978-1-59643-796-8(0)*, 9781596437968) Roaring Brook Pr.

Taylor, Kathleen. Eddie & Bingo: A Friendship Tale. Taylor, Kathleen, illus. 2011. (Illus.). 42p. (J). pap. 21.95 *(978-1-59299-558-5(6))* Inkwater Pr.

SAILORS—FICTION

Ballantyne, R. M. The Crew of the Water Wagtail. 2011. 146p. 24.95 *(978-1-4638-9596-9(8))* Rodgers, Alan Bks.

—The Young Trawler. 2011. 250p. 27.95 *(978-1-4638-9496-2(1))* Rodgers, Alan Bks.

Barchers, Suzanne. The Shipwrecked Sailor: A Tale from Egypt. Hehenberger, Shelly, illus. 2015. (Tales of Honor Ser.). (ENG.). 32p. (gr. 1-3). lib. bdg. 26.60 *(978-1-939656-86-5(9))* Red Chair Pr.

Barron, Liz. Salcombe Seaside Fairies: Kevin the Crabshell Fairy. 2010. (Illus.). 24p. pap. 11.49 *(978-1-4490-6142-5(7))* AuthorHouse.

Becker, Lindsey. The Star Thief. 2017. (ENG., Illus.). 416p. (J). (gr. 3-7). 16.99 *(978-0-316-34856-0(2))* Little, Brown Bks. for Young Readers.

Benchmark Education Co., LLC. Sail with Me Big Book. 2014. (Shared Reading Foundations Ser.). (J). (gr. -1). *(978-1-4509-9447-7(4))* Benchmark Education Co.

Bower, Tamara. The Shipwrecked Sailor: An Egyptian Tale with Hieroglyphs. Bower, Tamara, illus. 2016. (ENG., Illus.). 32p. (J). (gr. 2-5). 16.99 *(978-1-4814-2525-4(0)*, Atheneum Bks. for Young Readers) Simon & Schuster Children's Publishing.

Child, Neil. The Creek. 2012. 82p. pap. 19.95 *(978-1-4626-6027-8(4))* America Star Bks.

Collingwood, Harry. The Rover's Secret. 2011. 274p. 29.95 *(978-1-4638-9505-1(4))* Rodgers, Alan Bks.

Cooper, Mark A. Fledgling: Jason Steed. 2010. (ENG.). 240p. (J). (gr. 3-7). pap. 10.99 *(978-1-4022-3999-1(6)*, Sourcebooks Jabberwocky) Sourcebooks, Inc.

Jenkins, Amanda. Mere Moments A Story of Pearl Harbor, the Day the Towers Fell. 2011. (Readers' & Writers' Genre Workshop Ser.). (J). pap. *(978-1-4509-3019-2(0))* Benchmark Education Co.

Moore, Jordan. Sinbad the Sailor, 1 vol. rev. ed. 2013. (Fiction Readers Ser.). (ENG., Illus.). 32p. (J). (gr. 3-3). pap. 8.99 *(978-1-4333-5647-6(3))* Shell Educational Publishing.

Priestley, Chris. Tales of Terror from the Black Ship. Roberts, David, illus. 2008. (Tales of Terror Ser.: 1). (ENG.). 256p. (YA). (gr. 3-6). 12.99 *(978-1-59990-290-6(7)*, 9781599902906, Bloomsbury USA Childrens) Bloomsbury Publishing USA.

Russell, Krista. Chasing the Nightbird, 1 vol. 2011. (ENG.). 192p. (YA). (gr. 5-9). 15.95 *(978-1-56145-597-3(0)*, Peachtree Junior) Peachtree Pubs.

Sala, George Augustus. Captain Dangerous. 2011. 130p. 24.95 *(978-1-4638-9899-1(1))*; 124p. pap. 10.95 *(978-1-4638-0142-7(4))*; 126p. pap. 10.95 *(978-1-4638-0141-0(6))*; 130p. pap. 10.95 *(978-1-4638-0140-3(8))* Rodgers, Alan Bks.

Schorr, Titus. The Stars & Stripes, 01 vols., 1. 2016. (Rosen REAL Readers: Social Studies Nonfiction / Fiction: Family, Community, & the World Ser.). (ENG.). 12p. (J). pap. 6.33 *(978-1-5081-1958-6(9)*, Rosen Classroom) Rosen Publishing Group, Inc., The.

Stanmore, Tony. Tide of Chance: A Holiday Adventure. 2010. (Illus.). 60p. pap. 10.49 *(978-1-4520-0650-5(4))* AuthorHouse.

Tweed, Susan Larned. A Sailor's Adventure: Sailing Stormy Seas. 2012. 24p. pap. 11.50 *(978-1-61897-522-5(6)*, Strategic Bk. Publishing) Strategic Book Publishing & Rights Agency (SBPRA).

SAILORS' LIFE

see Seafaring Life

SAINT LAWRENCE RIVER

Cooke, Tim. The St. Lawrence River. 2003. (Rivers of North America Ser.). (Illus.). 32p. (gr. 2-6). lib. bdg. 26.00 *(978-0-8368-3762-9(2)*, Gareth Stevens Learning Library) Stevens, Gareth Publishing LLLP.

Lackey, Jennifer. Jacques Cartier: Exploring the St. Lawrence River. 2006. (In the Footsteps of Explorers Ser.). (ENG., Illus.). 32p. (J). (gr. 4-7). pap. *(978-0-7787-2466-7(2))* Crabtree Publishing Co.

Woog, Adam. Jacques Cartier. 2009. (Great Explorers Ser.). (Illus.). 112p. (gr. 6-12). 30.00 *(978-1-60413-430-8(5)*, Chelsea Hse.) Facts On File, Inc.

SAINT LAWRENCE RIVER VALLEY

Peppas, Lynn. The St. Lawrence: River Route to the Great Lakes. 2010. (Rivers Around the World Ser.). (ENG., Illus.). 32p. (J). (gr. 5-8). pap. *(978-0-7787-7470-9(8))*; lib. bdg. *(978-0-7787-7447-1(3))* Crabtree Publishing Co.

SAINT LOUIS (MO.)

Greenspan, Judy. Dropping in on St. Louis. 2017. (Dropping in On Ser.). (ENG.). (J). (gr. 3-5). 32.80 ***(978-1-68342-175-7(2))*** Rourke Educational Media.

Klein, Carol Swartout. Painting for Peace in Ferguson. 2nd ed. 2015. (ENG.). 54p. (J). (gr. 2-3). 25.95 *(978-0-9963901-0-1(3))*; pap. 15.95 *(978-0-9892079-9-7(4))* TreeHse. Publishing Group.

Murray, Julie. Gateway Arch, 1 vol. 2003. (Buddy Book Ser.). (ENG., Illus.). 24p. (gr. k-4). 25.65 *(978-1-57765-671-5(7)*, Buddy Bks.) ABDO Publishing Co.

Publications International Ltd. Staff. Yesterday & Today St. Louis. 2009. 192p. 24.95 *(978-1-4127-1576-8(8))* Publications International, Ltd.

SAINT LOUIS (MO.)—FICTION

Holley, Marietta. Samantha at the St. Louis Exposition. 2007. 188p. pap. 19.99 *(978-1-4264-6038-8(4))* Creative Media Partners, LLC.

Ingalls, Ann. Fairy Floss. Blanco, Migy, illus. 2017. (ENG.). 40p. (J). (gr. -1-3). 17.99 *(978-1-4998-0238-2(2))* Little Bee Books Inc.

Jacobs, Lily. The Littlest Bunny in St. Louis: An Easter Adventure. Dunn, Robert, illus. 2015. (ENG.). 32p. (J). (-3). 9.99 *(978-1-4926-1201-8(4)*, Sourcebooks Jabberwocky) Sourcebooks, Inc.

James, Eric. A Halloween Scare in St. Louis. Le Ray, Marina, illus. 2015. (ENG.). 32p. (J). (-5). 9.99 *(978-1-4926-2401-1(2)*, 9781492624011, Sourcebooks Jabberwocky) Sourcebooks, Inc.

—Santa's Sleigh Is on Its Way to St. Louis: A Christmas Adventure. Dunn, Robert, illus. 2016. (ENG.). 32p. (J). (-2). 12.99 *(978-1-4926-4356-2(4)*, 9781492643562, Sourcebooks Jabberwocky) Sourcebooks, Inc.

Ludwig, Elisa. Pretty Wanted. 2015. (Pretty Crooked Trilogy Ser.: 3). (ENG.). 336p. (YA). (gr. 8). 17.99 *(978-0-06-206612-1(9)*, Tegen, Katherine Bks) HarperCollins Pubs.

MacColl, Michaela & Nichols, Rosemary. Freedom's Price. 2015. (Hidden Histories Ser.). (ENG., Illus.). 288p. (J). (gr. 3-7). 17.95 *(978-1-62091-624-7(X)*, Calkins Creek) Boyds Mills Pr.

Olswanger, Anna. Shlemiel Crooks. Goodman Koz, Paula, illus. 2008. 36p. (J). pap. 11.95 *(978-1-58838-236-8(2)*, Junebug Bks.) NewSouth, Inc.

—Shlemiel Crooks. Koz, Paula Goodman, illus. 2005. 36p. (J). (gr. 2-4). 15.95 *(978-1-58838-165-1(X))* NewSouth, Inc.

Smallman, Steve. Santa Is Coming to St. Louis. Dunn, Robert, illus. 2013. (ENG.). 32p. (J). (-3). 9.99 *(978-1-4022-9000-8(4)*, Sourcebooks Jabberwocky) Sourcebooks, Inc.

ST. LOUIS CARDINALS (BASEBALL TEAM)

Epstein, Brad. St. Louis Cardinals ABC. 2013. (My First Alphabet Books (Michaelson Entertainment) Ser.). (ENG., Illus.). 28p. (J). bds. *(978-1-60730-211-7(X))* Michaelson Entertainment.

Frisch, Aaron. St. Louis Cardinals. 2009. (World Series Champions Ser.). (Illus.). 23p. (J). (gr. 2-3). 24.25 *(978-1-58341-688-4(9)*, Creative Education) Creative Co., The.

Gilbert, Sara. St. Louis Cardinals. 2013. (Illus.). 24p. (J). 25.65 *(978-1-60818-271-8(1)*, Creative Education) Creative Co., The.

—The Story of the St. Louis Cardinals. 2011. (Baseball: the Great American Game Ser.). (Illus.). 48p. (J). (gr. 5-8). lib. bdg. 34.25 *(978-1-60818-053-0(0)*, Creative Education) Creative Co., The.

—World Series Champs: St. Louis Cardinals. 2013. (World Series Champions Ser.). (ENG.). 24p. (J). (gr. 1-3). pap. 7.99 *(978-0-89812-822-2(6)*, Creative Paperbacks) Creative Co., The.

Gitlin, Martin. St. Louis Cardinals, 1 vol. 2011. (Inside MLB Ser.). (ENG., Illus.). 48p. (YA). (gr. 3-6). lib. bdg. 32.79 *(978-1-61714-056-3(2))* ABDO Publishing Co.

Gitlin, Marty. St. Louis Cardinals, 1 vol. 2014. (Inside MLB Ser.). (ENG., Illus.). 48p. (J). (gr. 3-6). lib. bdg. 32.79 *(978-1-62403-482-4(9)*, SportsZone) ABDO Publishing Co.

Kelley, K. C. St. Louis Cardinals. 2014. (Favorite Baseball Teams Ser.). (ENG.). 32p. (J). (gr. 1-4). 28.50 *(978-1-62323-979-4(6)*, 206756) Child's World, Inc., The.

Kennedy, Mike & Stewart, Mark. Meet the Cardinals. 2010. (Smart about Sports Ser.). 24p. (J). (gr. k-3). lib. bdg. 22.60 *(978-1-59953-373-5(1))* Norwood Hse. Pr.

MacRae, Sloan. The St. Louis Cardinals. 2012. (Illus.). 24p. (J). 49.50 *(978-1-4488-5152-2(1))*; pap. 8.25 *(978-1-4488-5151-5(3))*; lib. bdg. 22.60 *(978-1-4488-5009-9(6))* Rosen Publishing Group, Inc., The. (PowerKids Pr.).

Mattern, Joanne. Albert Pujols. 2007. (Robbie Reader Ser.). (Illus.). 32p. (J). (gr. 2-5). lib. bdg. 25.70 *(978-1-58415-596-6(5))* Mitchell Lane Pubs., Inc.

—Albert Pujols: Baseball Superstar, 1 vol. 2011. (Superstar Athletes Ser.). (ENG.). 24p. (gr. 1-2). pap. 7.29 *(978-1-4296-7301-3(X))*; pap. 41.70 *(978-1-4296-7302-0(8))* Capstone Press of Coughlan Cos.

Needham, Tom. Albert Pujols: MVP on & off the Field. 2007. (Sports Stars with Heart Ser.). (Illus.). 128p. (J). (gr. 5-9). lib. bdg. 33.27 *(978-0-7660-2866-1(6))* Enslow Pubs., Inc.

O'Hearn, Michael. The Story of the St. Louis Cardinals. 2007. (Baseball, the Great American Game Ser.). (Illus.). 48p. (YA). (gr. 4-7). lib. bdg. 32.80 *(978-1-58341-551-1(3))* Creative Co., The.

Publications International Ltd. Staff. Yesterday & Today St Louis Cardinals. 2007. 144p. *(978-1-4127-1504-1(0)*, 1412715040, PIL Kids) Publications International, Ltd.

Sandler, Michael. David Eckstein & the St. Louis Cardinals: 2006 World Series. 2008. (World Series Superstars). (Illus.). 24p. (J). (gr. 1-4). lib. bdg. 22.61 *(978-1-59716-636-2(7))* Bearport Publishing Co., Inc.

Stewart, Mark. The St. Louis Cardinals. 2012. (Team Spirit Ser.). 48p. (J). (gr. 3-6). lib. bdg. 29.27 *(978-1-59953-494-7(0))* Norwood Hse. Pr.

Stout, Glenn & Williams, Ike. Against All Odds: Never Give Up. 2012. (Good Sports Ser.). (ENG., Illus.). 144p. (J). (gr. 5-7). pap. 5.99 *(978-0-547-88734-0(5))* Houghton Mifflin Harcourt Publishing Co.

SAINT PATRICK'S DAY

Aloian, Molly. Saint Patrick's Day. 2009. (Celebrations in My World Ser.). (ENG., Illus.). 32p. (J). (gr. k-2). pap. *(978-0-7787-4776-5(X))*; (gr. 1-3). *(978-0-7787-4758-1(1))* Crabtree Publishing Co.

Balian, Lorna. Leprechauns Never Lie, 1 vol. Balian, Lorna, illus. 2004. (ENG., Illus.). 32p. (J). 14.95 *(978-1-932065-37-4(7))* Star Bright Bks., Inc.

Berendes, Mary. St. Patrick's Day Shamrocks. 2015. (Our Holiday Symbols Ser.). (ENG.). 24p. (J). (gr. 1-4). 25.64 *(978-1-63143-746-5(1)*, 208555) Child's World, Inc., The.

Freeman, Dorothy Rhodes. St. Patrick's Day. rev. ed. 2008. (Best Holiday Bks.). (Illus.). 48p. (J). (gr. 3-7). lib. bdg. 25.27 *(978-0-7660-3046-6(6))* Enslow Pubs., Inc.

Gnojewski, Carol. Fun St. Patrick's Day Crafts. 2015. (Kid Fun Holiday Crafts! Ser.). 32p. (J). (gr. 3-4). 23.94 *(978-0-7660-6230-6(9))*; pap. 7.95 *(978-0-7660-6231-3(7)*, Enslow Elementary) Enslow Pubs., Inc.

—St. Patrick's Day Crafts. 2004. (Fun Holiday Crafts Kids Can Do! Ser.). (Illus.). 32p. (J). lib. bdg. 23.94 *(978-0-7660-2256-0(0))* Enslow Pubs., Inc.

Goeller, Dorothy. St. Patrick's Day. 2010. (All about Holidays Ser.). (Illus.). 24p. (J). 22.60 *(978-0-7660-3808-0(4))*; pap. 7.95 *(978-1-59845-177-1(4))* Enslow Pubs., Inc. (Enslow Elementary).

Grack, Rachel. Saint Patrick's Day. 2017. (Celebrating Holidays! Ser.). (ENG.). 24p. (J). (gr. k-3). lib. bdg. 25.95 ***(978-1-62617-623-2(X)**, Blastoff! Readers)* Bellwether Media.

Keogh, Josie. St. Patrick's Day. 2013. (PowerKids Readers: Happy Holidays! Ser.). (ENG., Illus.). 24p. (J). (gr. k-2). pap. 8.25 *(978-1-4488-9714-8(9))*; lib. bdg. 22.60 *(978-1-4488-9628-8(2))* Rosen Publishing Group, Inc., The. (PowerKids Pr.).

—St. Patrick's Day: Día de San Patricio. Alamán, Eduardo, tr. from SPA. 2013. (PowerKids Readers: Happy Holidays! / ¡Felices Fiestas! Ser.). (ENG & SPA., Illus.). 24p. (gr. k-2). lib. bdg. 22.60 *(978-1-4488-9971-5(0)*, PowerKids Pr.) Rosen Publishing Group, Inc., The.

Landau, Elaine. Celebrating St. Patrick's Day. 2012. (Celebrating Holidays Ser.). 48p. (J). (gr. 3-18). 25.27 *(978-0-7660-4035-9(6)*, Enslow Elementary) Enslow Pubs., Inc.

—What Is St. Patrick's Day? 2011. (I Like Holidays! Ser.). (Illus.). 24p. (J). (gr. 1-4). lib. bdg. 22.60 *(978-0-7660-3704-5(5))* Enslow Pubs., Inc.

Lindeen, Mary. St. Patrick's Day. 2015. (BeginningtoRead Ser.). (ENG., Illus.). 32p. (J). (gr. k-2). lib. bdg. 22.60 *(978-1-59953-687-3(0))* Norwood Hse. Pr.

Lynette, Rachel. Let's Throw a St. Patrick's Day Party! 2011. (J). pap. 8.25 *(978-1-4488-2737-4(X))*; lib. bdg. 22.60 *(978-1-4488-2574-5(1))* Rosen Publishing Group, Inc., The. (PowerKids Pr.).

McGee, Randel. Paper Crafts for St. Patrick's Day. 2011. (Paper Craft Fun for Holidays Ser.). (Illus.). 48p. (J). (gr. 2-5). lib. bdg. 25.27 *(978-0-7660-3725-0(8))*; (gr. 3-18). pap. 8.95 *(978-1-59845-337-9(8)*, Enslow Elementary) Enslow Pubs., Inc.

McNeil, Niki, et al. HOCPP 1062 Saint Patrick's Day. 2006. spiral bd. 20.00 *(978-1-60308-062-0(7))* In the Hands of a Child.

Mercer, Abbie. Happy St. Patrick's Day. (Holiday Fun Ser.). 24p. 2009. (gr. 2-3). 42.50 *(978-1-61513-377-2(1)*, PowerKids Pr.) 2007. (Illus.). (J). (gr. -1-3). lib. bdg. 22.60 *(978-1-4042-3811-4(5))* Rosen Publishing Group, Inc., The.

Miller, Heather. Celebrate St. Patrick's Day. 2006. (Celebrate Holidays Ser.). (Illus.). 104p. (J). (gr. 5-6). lib. bdg. 33.27 *(978-0-7660-2581-3(0))* Enslow Pubs., Inc.

Murray, Julie. Saint Patrick's Day, 1 vol. 2011. (Holidays Set 3 Ser.). (ENG., Illus.). 24p. (J). (gr. 1-4). 25.65 *(978-1-61783-042-6(9))* ABDO Publishing Co.

Owen, Ruth. St. Patrick's Day Origami, 1 vol. 2015. (Holiday Origami Ser.). (ENG.). 32p. (J). 27.50 *(978-1-4777-5718-5(X)*, PowerKids Pr.) Rosen Publishing Group, Inc., The.

Ponto, Joanna. St. Patrick's Day. 2016. (Story of Our Holidays Ser.). (ENG., Illus.). 32p. (J). (gr. 3-3). 25.27 *(978-0-7660-7461-3(7))*; pap. 10.52 *(978-0-7660-7473-6(0))* Enslow Pubs., Inc.

Roop, Peter & Roop, Connie. Let's Celebrate St. Patrick's Day. Connelly, Gwen, illus. 2003. 32p. (J). (gr. 3-6). pap. 6.95 *(978-0-7613-1782-1(1))*; (J). (gr. 3-6). pap. 6.95 *(978-0-7613-1782-1(1))*; lib. bdg. 22.90 *(978-0-7613-2505-5(0))* Lerner Publishing Group. (Millbrook Pr.).

Sebra, Richard. It's St. Patrick's Day! 2017. (Bumba Books (tm) — It's a Holiday! Ser.). (ENG.). 24p. (J). (gr. -1-1). 12.99 ***(978-1-5124-3705-8(0)**, Lerner Pubns.)*; 38.65 ***(978-1-5124-3704-1(2)**, Lerner Pubns.)*; (Illus.). 25.32 *(978-1-5124-2561-1(3))*; (Illus.). 38.65 ***(978-1-5124-2740-0(3)**, Lerner Pubns.)* Lerner Publishing Group.

Smith, Mary Lou. Celebrate Saint Patrick's Day. 2015. (Our Holidays Ser.). (ENG., Illus.). 24p. (J). (gr. 1-1). pap. 8.22 *(978-1-5026-0418-7(3))* Cavendish Square Publishing.

Wallace, Nancy K. Fettuccine & Four-Leaf Clovers: A Readers' Theater Script & Guide, 1 vol. Mata, Nina, illus. 2016. (ENG.). 32p. (J). *(978-1-62402-112-1(3))* Magic Wagon.

Williams, Colleen Madonna Flood. My Adventure on St. Patrick's Day. 2007. 44p. (J). 8.99 *(978-1-59092-556-0(4))* Blue Forge Pr.

York, M. J. Celebrating St. Patrick's Day. 2017. (Welcome, Spring! Ser.). (ENG.). 24p. (J). (gr. -1-2). lib. bdg. 27.07 *(978-1-5038-1655-8(9)*, 211505) Child's World, Inc., The.

Zocchi, Judy. On Saint Patrick's Day. Wallis, Rebecca, illus. 2005. (Holiday Happenings Ser.). 32p. (J). pap. 10.95 *(978-1-59646-232-8(9))*; per. 10.95 *(978-1-59646-233-5(7))* Dingles & Co.

—On Saint Patrick's Day/el día de San Patricio. Wallis, Rebecca, illus. 2005. (Holiday Happenings Ser.).Tr. of día de San Patricio. (ENG & SPA.). 32p. (J). pap. 10.95 *(978-1-59646-234-2(5))*; lib. bdg. 21.65 *(978-1-891997-40-2(8))*; per. 10.95 *(978-1-59646-235-9(3))* Dingles & Co.

SAINT PATRICK'S DAY—FICTION

Bouthyette, Valerie, illus. The Leprechaun Trap. 2008. 40p. (J). pap. 10.95 *(978-0-9800835-0-7(8))* Clinch Media.

Callahan, Sean. The Leprechaun Who Lost His Rainbow, 1 vol. Cote, Nancy, illus. 2010. (ENG.). 32p. (J). (gr. 1-3). pap. 6.99 *(978-0-8075-4455-6(8))* Whitman, Albert & Co.

—Shannon & the World's Tallest Leprechaun. Kemly, Kathleen, illus. 2008. (ENG.). 32p. (J). (gr. 2-3). lib. bdg. 15.95 *(978-0-8075-7326-6(4))* Whitman, Albert & Co.

Flor Ada, Alma. Celebra el Dia De3 San Patricio con Samantha y Lola. Lavandeira, Sandra, illus. 2006. (Cuentos para Celebrar / Stories to Celebrate Ser.). (SPA.). 30p. (gr. k-6). per. 11.95 *(978-1-59820-117-8(4)*, Alfaguara) Santillana USA Publishing Co., Inc.

Flor Ada, Alma & Campoy, F. Isabel. Celebrate St. Patrick's Day with Samantha & Lola. Hayes, Joe & Franco, Sharon, trs. 2006. (Stories to Celebrate Ser.). (Illus.). 30p. (gr. k-6). per. 11.95 *(978-1-59820-129-1(8)*, Alfaguara) Santillana USA Publishing Co., Inc.

Gorgas, Paula Blais. Little Lost Leprechaun. (Illus.). (J). 2007. 20p. per. 11.99 *(978-0-9797574-5-7(2))* 2006. 24p. lib. bdg. 24.95 *(978-0-9778651-4-7(2))* Dragonfly Publishing, Inc.

Harimann, Sierra. Puppies on Parade. 2014. (Illus.). 30p. (J). pap. *(978-0-545-59211-6(9))* Scholastic, Inc.

Heling, Kathryn & Hembrook, Deborah. Ten Lucky Leprechauns. Johnson, Jay, illus. 2013. (ENG.). 24p. (J). (gr. -1-k). pap. 3.99 *(978-0-545-43648-9(6)*, Cartwheel Bks.) Scholastic, Inc.

—Ten Lucky Leprechauns. 2013. lib. bdg. 13.55 *(978-0-606-31493-0(8)*, Turtleback) Turtleback Bks.

Hillert, Margaret. It's St. Patrick's Day, Dear Dragon. Schimmell, David, illus. 2008. (BeginningtoRead Ser.). 32p. (J). (gr. k-2). lib. bdg. 22.60 *(978-1-59953-161-8(5))* Norwood Hse. Pr.

—It's St. Patrick's Day, Dear Dragon. del Risco, Eida, tr. Schimmell, David, illus. 2008. (BeginningtoRead Ser.). 32p. (J). (-2). pap. 11.94 *(978-1-60357-086-2(1))* Norwood Hse. Pr.

Holub, Joan. Good Luck! A St. Patrick's Day Story. Terry, Will, illus. 2007. (Ant Hill Ser.). (ENG.). 24p. (J). (gr. -1-k). lib. bdg. 11.89 *(978-1-4169-2560-6(0)*, Aladdin Library) Simon & Schuster Children's Publishing.

—Good Luck! A St. Patrick's Day Story. Terry, Will, illus. 2007. (Ant Hill Ser.). (ENG.). 24p. (J). (gr. -1-k). pap. 3.99 *(978-1-4169-0955-2(9)*, Simon Spotlight) Simon Spotlight.

Lee, Quinlan B. & Bridwell, Norman. Happy St. Patrick's Day, Clifford! Haefele, Steve, illus. 2010. (Clifford the Big Red Dog Ser.). (J). *(978-0-545-23401-6(8))* Scholastic, Inc.

Matheis, Mickie. A Berry Lucky St. Patrick's Day. Thomas, Laura, illus. 2015. (Strawberry Shortcake Ser.). (ENG.). 24p. (J). (gr. -1-k). 4.99 *(978-0-448-48420-4(X)*, Grosset & Dunlap) Penguin Young Readers Group.

McGuirk, Leslie. Lucky Tucker. McGuirk, Leslie, illus. 2008. (ENG., Illus.). 24p. (J). (gr. -1-k). pap. 4.99 *(978-0-7636-3389-9(5))* Candlewick Pr.

—Lucky Tucker. 2008. 14.75 *(978-1-4178-1914-0(6)*, Turtleback) Turtleback Bks.

McNamara, Margaret & Gordon, Mike. The Luck of the Irish. 2007. (Robin Hill School Ser.). (SPA & ENG., Illus.). 32p. (J). (gr. -1-1). pap. 3.99 *(978-1-4169-1539-3(7)*, Simon Spotlight) Simon Spotlight.

Meadows, Daisy. Lindsay the Luck Fairy. 2013. (Rainbow Magic — Special Edition Ser.). lib. bdg. 17.20 *(978-0-606-31512-8(8)*, Turtleback) Turtleback Bks.

Rey, H. A. Happy St. Patrick's Day. 2014. (Curious George Ser.). (ENG., Illus.). 14p. (J). (— 1). bds. 7.99

(978-0-544-08888-7(3)) Houghton Mifflin Harcourt Publishing Co.

Rockwell, Anne F. St. Patrick's Day. Rockwell, Lizzy, illus. 2010. 40p. (J). (gr. -1-3). (ENG.). 14.99 (978-0-06-050197-6(9)); lib. bdg. 15.89 (978-0-06-050198-3(7)) HarperCollins Pubs.

Roy, Ron. March Mischief. Gurney, John Steven, illus. 2010. (Calendar Mysteries Ser.: 3). (ENG.). 80p. (J). (gr. 1-4). 4.99 (978-0-375-85663-1(3), Random Hse. Bks. for Young Readers) Random Hse. Children's Bks.

—March Mischief. 2010. (Calendar Mysteries Ser.: 3). lib. bdg. 14.75 (978-0-606-12460-7(8), Turtleback) Turtleback Bks.

Sanrio. Happy St. Patrick's Day, Hello Kitty. 2015. (Hello Kitty Ser.). (J). lib. bdg. 17.15 (978-0-606-37239-8(3)) Turtleback Bks.

Slater, Teddy. The Luckiest St. Patrick's Day Ever! Long, Ethan, illus. (J). 2008. (ENG.). 32p. (gr. -1-3). pap. 5.99 (978-0-545-03943-7(6), Cartwheel Bks.) 2007. (978-0-439-86648-4(0)) Scholastic, Inc.

Stone Arch Books. St. Patrick's Day & Easter, 1 vol. Nguyen, Dustin, illus. 2014. (Batman: Li'l Gotham Ser.). (ENG.). 32p. (gr. 2-3). 22.60 (978-1-4342-9219-3(3)) Stone Arch Bks.

Sypolt, Carl W. Fibber Lygood at Christmas, Easter, & St. Patrick's Day. 2006. 108p. (J). pap. 10.95 (978-0-7414-2982-7(9)) Infinity Publishing.

Thaler, Mike. St. Patrick's Day from the Black Lagoon. Lee, Jared, illus. 2011. 61p. (J). (978-0-545-27328-2(5)) Scholastic, Inc.

Wallace, Adam. How to Catch a Leprechaun. Elkerton, Andy, illus. 2016. (ENG.). 32p. (J). (-6). 10.99 (978-1-4926-3291-7(0), 9781492632917, Sourcebooks Jabberwocky) Sourcebooks, Inc.

Wing, Natasha. The Night Before St. Patrick's Day. Wummer, Amy, illus. 2009. (Night Before Ser.). (ENG.). 32p. (J). (gr. -1-3). pap. 4.99 (978-0-448-44852-7(1), Grosset & Dunlap) Penguin Young Readers Group.

Wojciechowski, Susan. A Fine St. Patrick's Day. Curry, Tom, illus. 2008. (ENG.). 40p. (J). (gr. -1-2). pap. 7.99 (978-0-385-73640-4(1), Dragonfly Bks.) Random Hse. Children's Bks.

SAINT PETERSBURG (RUSSIA)

Langley, Andrew. St. Petersburg. 2005. (Great Cities of the World Ser.). (Illus.). 48p. (gr. 5-12). lib. bdg. 31.00 (978-0-8368-5054-3(8), Gareth Stevens Secondary Library) Stevens, Gareth Publishing LLLP.

SAINT PETERSBURG (RUSSIA)—HISTORY

Dyan, Penelope. Water & Blood — A Kid's Guide to St Petersburg, Russi. Weigand, John D., photos by. 2011. (Illus.). 34p. pap. 11.95 (978-1-61477-001-5(8)) Bellissima Publishing, LLC.

Woodworth, Bradley & Richards, Constance E., eds. St. Petersburg. 2005. (Bloom's Literary Places Ser.). (Illus.). 150p. (C). (gr. 9-13). lib. bdg. 40.00 (978-0-7910-7837-2(X), Chelsea Hse.) Facts On File, Inc.

SAINT PETERSBURG (RUSSIA)—HISTORY—SIEGE, 1941-1944

Anderson, M. T. Symphony for the City of the Dead: Dmitri Shostakovich & the Siege of Leningrad. 2015. (ENG., Illus.). 464p. (YA). (gr. 9). 25.99 (978-0-7636-6818-1(4)) Candlewick Pr.

SAINT VALENTINE'S DAY

see Valentine's Day

SAINTS

see also Legends

Amadeo, Diana M. Holy Friends: Thirty Saints & Blesseds of the Americas. Curreli, Augusta & Lombardo, Irina, illus. 2005. 134p. (J). (gr. 3-7). 19.95 (978-0-8198-3384-6(3)) Pauline Bks. & Media.

Barnes, Kathleen. I Love to See the Temple Reprint. 2009. 32p. pap. 8.95 (978-1-60641-112-4(8)) Deseret Bk. Co.

—Sacrament Time. 2009. 32p. pap. 9.95 (978-1-60641-113-1(6)) Deseret Bk. Co.

Baum, Margaux & Morgan, Julian. Constantine. 2016. (Leaders of the Ancient World Ser.). 00112p. (J). (gr. 6-6). 37.10 (978-1-5081-7252-9(8)) Rosen Publishing Group, Inc., The.

Benson, Robert Hugh. An Alphabet of Saints. Symington, Lindsay, illus. 2013. (ENG.). 32p. (J). (gr. -1-k). reprint ed. 16.95 (978-1-930873-12-4(3), Neumann Pr.) TAN Bks.

Bernier-Grand, Carmen T. Our Lady of Guadalupe, 0 vols. Engel, Tonya, illus. 2012. (ENG.). 32p. (J). (gr. 3-7). 17.99 (978-0-7614-6135-7(3), 9780761461357, Amazon Children's Publishing) Amazon Publishing.

Betz, Eva K. Saint Brigid & the Cows. Peterson, Russell, illus. 2013. (ENG.). 48p. (J). (gr. k-3). 12.95 (978-1-930873-95-7(6), Neumann Pr.) TAN Bks.

Billington, Rachel. The Life of Saint Francis. (Illus.). 48p. pap. 11.99 (978-0-340-71427-0(1)) Hodder & Stoughton GBR. Dist: Trafalgar Square Publishing.

Boutet de Monvel, Maurice. The Story of Joan of Arc. 2010. (Dover Children's Classics Ser.). (ENG., Illus.). 64p. (J). (gr. 4-7). pap. 14.99 (978-0-486-47026-9(1)) Dover Pubns., Inc.

Brassey, Richard. George & the Dragon & Other Saintly Stories. 2003. (Illus.). 40p. pap. (978-1-84255-082-3(9), Orion Children's Bks.) Hachette Children's Group.

Brassey, Richard, illus. George & the Dragon & Other Saintly Stories. 2003. 40p. (978-1-84255-019-9(5), Orion Children's Bks.) Hachette Children's Group.

Briere, Euphemia. Victor Constantinus, Maximus Augustus: The Life of Saint Constantine, the First Christian Emperor & His Mother, Saint Helena. 2003. (Illus.). (J). 4.00 (978-0-913026-90-8(5), VC) St. Nectarios Pr.

Brown, Don. Across a Dark & Wild Sea. 2004. (Illus.). (J). (gr. k-3). spiral bd. (978-0-616-14616-3(7)) Canadian National Institute for the Blind/Institut National Canadien pour les Aveugles.

Brown, Laura Rhoderica. Saint John Neumann: Missionary to Immigrants. Esquinaldo, Virginia, illus. 2016. (J). pap. (978-0-8198-9066-5(9)) Pauline Bks. & Media.

Buell, Jean. God's Heroes: A Child's Book of Saints. Larkin, Jean, ed. 2006. (Illus.). 32p. (J). (gr. -1-3). pap. 3.95 (978-1-933178-30-1(2)) Pflaum Publishing Group.

Burnett, Allan. Columba & All That. Anderson, Scoular, illus. 2007. (ENG.). 128p. pap. (978-1-84158-571-0(8)) Birlinn, Ltd.

Butterfield, Moira. Religion & Saints. 2016. (Discover the Anglo-Saxons Ser.). (ENG., Illus.). 32p. (J). (gr. 4-6). pap. 11.99 (978-1-4451-3339-3(3), Franklin Watts) Hachette Children's Group GBR. Dist: Hachette Bk. Group.

Canton, William. Childs Book of Saints. 2006. pap. 27.95 (978-1-4286-3503-6(3)) Kessinger Publishing, LLC.

—A Child's Book of Saints. Robinson, T. H., illus. 2013. 268p. pap. 12.75 (978-1-936639-22-9(X)) St. Augustine Academy Pr.

Carr, Simonetta. Augustine of Hippo. Lowe, Wes, illus. 2009. (ENG.). 62p. (J). 18.00 (978-1-60178-073-7(7)) Reformation Heritage Bks.

Cash, Marie Romero. Santos: A Coloring Book of New Mexican Saints. 2008. 80p. (J). pap. 10.95 (978-0-86534-701-4(8)) Sunstone Pr.

Chryssavgis, John & Rouvelas, Marilyn. Saint Anthony the Great. Brent, Isabelle, illus. 2015. (ENG.). 28p. (J). (gr. k-2). 17.95 (978-1-937786-46-5(3), Wisdom Tales) World Wisdom, Inc.

Daniel-Rops, Henri. Golden Legend of Young Saints. 2009. Orig. Title: Légende Dorée de Mes Filleuls. (J). pap. 15.95 (978-1-933184-37-1(X)) Sophia Institute Pr.

DeDomenico, Elizabeth Marie. Saint John Vianney: A Priest for All People. Hatke, Ben, illus. 2008. (Encounter the Saints Ser.). 122p. (J). (gr. 4-7). pap. 7.95 (978-0-8198-7115-2(X)) Pauline Bks. & Media.

Demi. Joan of Arc, 0 vols. 2011. (ENG.). 56p. (J). (gr. 3-7). 19.99 (978-0-7614-5953-8(7), 9780761459538, Amazon Children's Publishing) Amazon Publishing.

—Saint Francis of Assisi. 2012. (ENG., Illus.). 56p. (J). (gr. -1-3). 19.95 (978-1-937786-04-5(8)) World Wisdom, Inc.

Denham, Joyce. Saint Francis of Assisi. Temporin, Elena, illus. 2008. (ENG.). 32p. (J). (gr. k-6). pap. 9.95 (978-1-55725-571-6(7)) Paraclete Pr., Inc.

—Stories of the Saints. Stevens, Judy, illus. 2003. 48p. (J). pap. 11.99 (978-0-7459-4637-5(2), Lion Books) Lion Hudson PLC GBR. Dist: Trafalgar Square Publishing.

—Stories of the Saints. Stevens, Judy, illus. 2007. (ENG.). 48p. (J). (gr. 4-7). pap. 9.95 (978-1-55725-534-1(2)) Paraclete Pr., Inc.

Donaghy, Thomas J. My Golden Book of Saints. 2009. (Illus.). 42p. (J). bds. 9.95 (978-0-89942-363-0(9)) Catholic Bk. Publishing Corp.

Driscoll, Christ. And God Blessed the Irish: The Story of Patrick. Kelley, Patrick, illus. 2007. 59p. (J). (gr. 3-7). 14.95 (978-1-929039-40-1(9)) Ambassador Bks., Inc.

Ernest, Brother. A Story of St. John Bosco. 2013. (ENG., Illus.). 32p. (J). (gr. k-2). 12.95 (978-0-911845-04-4(6), Neumann Pr.) TAN Bks.

Flanagan, Anne. Saints of America Col/Act Bk. 24p. pap. 1.25 (978-0-8198-7086-5(2), 332-382) Pauline Bks. & Media.

Flavin, Pamela. An Alphabet of Saints for Young People. 2009. (Illus.). 64p. pap. (978-1-84748-533-5(2)) Athena Pr.

Flavius, Brother. A Story of St. Catherine of Alexandria. 2013. (ENG., Illus.). 32p. (J). (gr. k-2). 12.95 (978-0-911845-03-7(8), Neumann Pr.) TAN Bks.

Gallery, Philip D. Can You Find Saints? Introducing Your Child to Holy Men & Women. Harlow, Janet L., tr. Harlow, Janet L., illus. 2003. (J). (ENG.). 41p. (gr. 2-4). 16.99 (978-0-86716-487-9(5)); 40p. (978-2-89507-437-3(2)) Franciscan Media.

Giraldo, Maria Loretta. Saints & Their Stories. Moran, Margaret Edward, tr. Bertelle, Nicoletta, illus. 2010.Tr. of I Santi: i miei primi Amici. 168p. (J). (gr. 2-5). 19.95 (978-0-8198-7134-3(6)) Pauline Bks. & Media.

Glavich, Mary Kathleen. Saint Therese of Lisieux: The Way of Love. Esquinaldo, Virginia, tr. Esquinaldo, Virginia, illus. 2003. (Encounter the Saints Ser.). 132p. (J). pap. 5.95 (978-0-8198-7074-2(9), 332-370) Pauline Bks. & Media.

Gray, Tricia. The Wondrous Adventures of St. Francis of Assisi. rev. ed. 2003. (Illus.). 164p. (J). pap. 14.95 (978-0-86716-480-0(8)) Franciscan Media.

Haldy, Emma E. Mother Teresa. Bane, Jeff, illus. 2017. (My Early Library: My Itty-Bitty Bio Ser.). (ENG.). 24p. (J). (gr. k-1). lib. bdg. 28.50 (978-1-63472-154-7(3), 209188) Cherry Lake Publishing.

Heffernan, Anne Eileen. 57 Stories of Saints. Rizzo, Jerry, illus. 3rd ed. 2006. 531p. (J). pap. 16.95 (978-0-8198-2681-7(2)) Pauline Bks. & Media.

Heffernan, Eileen. Fifty-Seven Stories of Saints. Rizzo, Jerry, illus. 2003. (J). 552p. pap. 16.95 (978-0-8198-2674-9(X), 332-094); 549p. (978-0-8198-2675-6(8)) Pauline Bks. & Media.

Hilliam, David. Joan of Arc: Heroine of France. 2004. (Leaders of the Middle Ages Ser.). (Illus.). 112p. (J). lib. bdg. 34.60 (978-1-4042-0164-4(5)) Rosen Publishing Group, Inc., The.

—Thomas Becket: English Saint & Martyr. 2009. (Leaders of the Middle Ages Ser.). 112p. (gr. 5-8). 66.50 (978-1-61513-902-6(8), Rosen Reference) Rosen Publishing Group, Inc., The.

Hodges, Margaret. The Legend of Saint Christopher. Watson, Richard Jesse, illus. 2009. (ENG.). 32p. (J). (gr. k-5). 9.00 (978-0-8028-5360-8(9), Eerdmans Bks For Young Readers) Eerdmans, William B. Publishing Co.

—The Legend of Saint Christopher. Watson, Richard J., illus. 2004. 32p. (J). (gr. 2-6). 18.00 (978-0-8028-5077-5(4)) Eerdmans, William B. Publishing Co.

Hoyt, Megan. Hildegard's Gift. Hill, David, illus. 2014. (ENG.). 32p. (J). pap. 15.99 (978-1-61261-358-1(6)) Paraclete Pr., Inc.

Hubbard, Margaret Ann. Saint Louis & the Last Crusade. Barton, Harry, illus. 2013. (ENG.). 157p. pap. 9.95 (978-1-58617-647-1(1)) Ignatius Pr.

Hunt, Jeanne. Celebrating Saints & Seasons: Hundreds of Activities for Catholic Children. 2010. (ENG.). 192p. pap. 12.99 (978-0-86716-959-1(1)) Franciscan Media.

Hyde, Katherine. Lucia: Saint of Light. 2009. 32p. 18.50 (978-0-9822770-4-1(0)) Ancient Faith Publishing.

Jablonski, Patricia Edward. Saint Andre Bessette: Miracles in Montreal. Kiwak, Barbara, illus. 2010. (J). (gr. 4-7). pap. 7.95 (978-0-8198-7140-4(0)) Pauline Bks. & Media.

Joan of Arc. 2010. (Women of Achievement Ser.). (Illus.). 128p. (gr. 6-12). 35.00 (978-1-60413-710-1(X), Chelsea Hse.) Facts On File, Inc.

Kudlinski, Kathleen. Joan of Arc. 2008. (DK Biography Ser.). (ENG., Illus.). 128p. (J). (gr. 5-12). pap. 6.99 (978-0-7566-3526-8(8), DK Children) Dorling Kindersley Publishing, Inc.

Lace, William W. Joan of Arc & the Hundred Years' War in World History. 2003. (In World History Ser.). (Illus.). 128p. (J). (gr. 5-12). lib. bdg. 27.94 (978-0-7660-1938-6(1)) Enslow Pubs., Inc.

Lang, Leonora Blanche. The Book of Saints & Heroes. Lang, Andrew, ed. Ford, H. J., illus. 2012. 344p. pap. 13.50 (978-1-936639-18-2(1)) St. Augustine Academy Pr.

Llewellyn, Claire. Saints & Angels. 2003. (ENG., Illus.). 64p. (J). (gr. 5-9). tchr. ed. 16.99 (978-0-7534-5588-3(9), 9780753455883, Kingfisher) Roaring Brook Pr.

Lovasik, Lawrence G. Los Angeles. (Illus.). (J). 1.50 (978-0-89942-465-1(1)) Catholic Bk. Publishing Corp.

Lovasik, Lawrence G. & Winkler, J. Book of Saints, Set, No. I-XXI. gif. ed. (Saint Joseph Picture Books Ser.). (Illus.). (J). 17.50 (978-0-89942-314-2(0), 314/GS, Resurrection Pr.) Catholic Bk. Publishing Corp.

Lovasik, Lorenzo G. Primer Libro de los Santos: La Historia de Sus Vidas y Sus Ejemplos. 2007. (Illus.). 96p. 5.95 (978-0-89942-137-7(7)) Catholic Bk. Publishing Corp.

Macdonald, Fiona. You Wouldn't Want to Be Joan of Arc! A Mission You Might Want to Miss. Antram, David, illus. 2010. (You Wouldn't Want to Ser.). (ENG.). 32p. (J). 29.00 (978-0-531-20473-3(1)); (gr. 3-18). pap. 9.95 (978-0-531-22828-9(2)) Scholastic Library Publishing.

Marsh, Emily Beata. Saint John Bosco: Champion for the Young. Alfano, Wayne, illus. 2015. 128p. (J). pap. 8.95 (978-0-8198-9045-0(6)) Pauline Bks. & Media.

Matas, Toni. Saint Francis of Assisi, Messenger of Peace. Picanyol, illus. 2013. 64p. (J). 8.95 (978-0-8198-7297-5(0)) Pauline Bks. & Media.

—St. Ignatius of Loyola, Leading the Way. Picanyol, illus. 2013. (J). 8.95 (978-0-8198-7298-2(9)) Pauline Bks. & Media.

McGrath, Michael O'Neill, illus. Patrons & Protectors: In Times of Need. 2003. (Patrons & Protectors Ser.: Vol. 3). 58p. (J). 18.95 (978-1-56854-410-6(3)) Liturgy Training Pubns.

McGrew, Michael. Saint Brendan & the Voyage Before Columbus. Litz, Mamie Saebz, illus. 2005. 32p. 9.95 (978-0-8091-6705-0(0), 6705-0) Paulist Pr.

McKenzie, Janet P. RACE for Heaven's Catholic Study Guides for Mary Fabyan Windeatt's Saint Biographies Grade 5: Saint Rose of Lima, Saint Martin de Porres, King David & His Songs, & Blessed Marie of New France. 2007. 108p. (J). per. 24.95 (978-1-934185-07-0(8)) Biblio Resource Pubns., Inc.

—RACE for Heaven's Catholic Study Guides for Mary Fabyan Windeatt's Saint Biographies Grade 6: Saint Dominic, the Children of Fatima, Saint John Masias, & Saint Benedict. 2007. 112p. (J). per. 24.95 (978-1-934185-08-7(6)) Biblio Resource Pubns., Inc.

—RACE for Heaven's Catholic Study Guides for Mary Fabyan Windeatt's Saint Biographies Grade 7: The Curé of Ars (St. John Vianney), the Little Flower (St. Therese of the Child Jesus), Saint Hyacinth of Poland, & Saint Louis de Montfort. 2007. 124p. (J). per. 24.95 (978-1-934185-09-4(4)) Biblio Resource Pubns., Inc.

—RACE for Heaven's Catholic Study Guides for Mary Fabyan Windeatt's Saint Biographies Grade 8: Saint Margaret Mary, Saint Francis Solano, Pauline Jaricot, & Saint Paul the Apostle. 2007. 156p. (YA). per. 24.95 (978-1-934185-10-0(8)) Biblio Resource Pubns., Inc.

—RACE for Heaven's Catholic Study Guides for Mary Fabyan Windeatt's Saint Biographies Grades 3 And 4: Saint Thomas Aquinas, the Patron Saint of First Communicants, Saint Catherine of Siena, & the Miraculous Medal. 2007. 108p. (J). per. 24.95 (978-1-934185-06-3(X)) Biblio Resource Pubns., Inc.

—Reading the Saints: Lists of Catholic Books for Children Plus Book Collecting Tips for the Home & School Library. 2007. 228p. (J). per. 24.95 (978-1-934185-00-1(0)) 2nd ed. 2013. (ENG.). 278p. pap. 29.95 (978-1-934185-45-2(0)) Biblio Resource Pubns., Inc.

Mitchell, Patricia. Saints Tell Their Stories. Casco, Maria Cristina Lo, illus. 2009. 62p. (J). (gr. k-5). 12.95 (978-1-59325-161-1(0)) Word Among Us Pr.

Monahan, Joan. St. Therese of Lisieux: Missionary of Love. 2003. (Illus.). 144p. 9.95 (978-0-8091-6710-4(7), 6710-7) Paulist Pr.

Moore, Armando. Clare of Assisi. (Illus.). 31p. 7.95 (978-1-875570-63-8(2)) St Pauls Pubns. AUS. Dist: St Pauls/Alba Hse. Pubs.

Morgan, Julian. Constantine: Ruler of Christian Rome. 2009. (Ancient Leaders Ser.). 112p. (gr. 5-8). 66.50 (978-1-61511-422-1(X), Rosen Reference) Rosen Publishing Group, Inc., The.

Morse, Letitia M. Yellow Roses on Her Feet. 2008. (J). pap. (978-0-9815075-0-7(6)) Bienna Bks.

Mortimer, Sheila. St Patrick & the Shamrock. Catchpole, Diana, illus. 2004. 8p. (J). 10.95 (978-0-7171-3755-8(4)) M.H. Gill & Co. U. C. IRL. Dist: Dufour Editions, Inc.

Muldoon, Kathleen M. Little Book of Saints, 2 bks. Mattozzi, Patricia R., illus. 2005. 24p. (J). Vol. 2. pap. 3.95 (978-0-8198-4511-5(6), 332-187) Vol. I. pap. 3.95 (978-0-8198-4510-8(8), 332-186) Pauline Bks. & Media.

Muldoon, Kathleen M. & Wallace, Susan Helen. My First Book of Saints. Mattozzi, Patricia R. & Kinarney, Tom, illus. 2012. 128p. (J). 12.95 (978-0-8198-4917-5(0)) Pauline Bks. & Media.

Murphy, Sally. Meet Mary MacKillop. Martinez, Sonia, illus. 2013. (Meet... Ser.). (ENG.). 32p. (J). (gr. -1). 18.99 (978-1-74275-721-6(9)) Random Hse. Australia AUS. Dist: Independent Pubs. Group.

Petras, Julie A. Draw & Tell Saints. 2004. (J). pap. 12.95 (978-1-59276-048-0(1)) Our Sunday Visitor, Publishing Div.

Plum, Paul S., et al. Teach Me about Saints. 2003. 24p. (J). per. 4.95 (978-1-931709-84-2(X)) Our Sunday Visitor, Publishing Div.

Pochocki, Ethel. Saints & Heroes. Owens, Mary Beth, illus. 2012. 258p. (YA). pap. 15.95 (978-1-932350-51-7(9)) Bethlehem Bks.

—Saints & Heroes for Kids. rev. exp. ed. 2005. (Illus.). 224p. (J). pap. 14.95 (978-0-86716-554-8(5)) Franciscan Media.

Pollack, Pamela D. & Belviso, Meg. Who Was Joan of Arc? Thomson, Andrew & Harrison, Nancy, illus. 2016. (Who Was? Ser.). (ENG.). 112p. (J). (gr. 3-7). pap. 5.99 (978-0-448-48304-7(1), Grosset & Dunlap) Penguin Young Readers Group.

—Who Was Joan of Arc? 2016. (Who Was... ? Ser.). lib. bdg. 16.00 (978-0-606-38395-0(6)) Turtleback Bks.

Puhalo, Lazar. Lives of Saints for Young People: Twelve Saints. Date not set. (YA). (gr. 7-12). 28p. pap. 4.50 (978-1-879038-34-9(X), 9002); Vol. 1. 28p. pap. 4.50 (978-1-879038-33-2(1), 9001); Vol. 3. 32p. pap. 4.50 (978-1-879038-35-6(8), 9003); Vol. 4. 42p. pap. 4.50 (978-1-879038-36-3(6), 9004); Vol. 5. 32p. pap. 4.50 (978-1-879038-37-0(4), 9005); Vol. 6. 28p. pap. 4.50 (978-1-879038-38-7(2), 9006); Vol. 7. 78p. pap. 6.50 (978-1-879038-39-4(0), 9007); Vol. 8. 32p. pap. (978-1-879038-40-0(4), 9008); Vol. 9. 28p. pap. 4.50 (978-1-879038-41-7(2), 9009); Vol. 10. 28p. pap. (978-1-879038-42-4(0), 9010) Synaxis Pr.

Ross, Nancy Wilson. Joan of Arc. 2003. vii, 182p. pap. 29.00 (978-0-7581-5017-2(2)) Textbook Pubs.

Ross Williamson, Hugh. The Young People's Book of Saints: Sixty-Three Saints of the Western Church from the First to the Twentieth Century. Connelly, Sheila, illus. 2009. (J). 15.95 (978-1-933184-62-3(0)) Sophia Institute Pr.

Saints: Lives & Illuminations. 2007. (Illus.). 39p. (J). (gr. 3-7). per. 10.00 (978-0-8028-5332-5(3), Eerdmans Bks For Young Readers) Eerdmans, William B. Publishing Co.

Sanders, Nancy I. Mary, 1 vol. 2014. (Get to Know Ser.). (ENG.). 112p. (J). pap. 7.99 (978-0-310-74480-1(6)) Zonderkidz.

Sanderson, Ruth. More Saints: Lives & Illuminations. Sanderson, Ruth, illus. 2007. (Illus.). 40p. (J). (gr. 1). 20.00 (978-0-8028-5272-4(6), Eerdmans Bks For Young Readers) Eerdmans, William B. Publishing Co.

—Saints: Lives & Illuminations. Sanderson, Ruth, illus. (Illus.). 2010. (ENG.). 160p. (J). (gr. 3-18). 16.00 (978-0-8028-5365-3(X), Eerdmans Bks For Young Readers) 2004. 40p. 20.00 (978-0-8028-5220-5(3)) Eerdmans, William B. Publishing Co.

Schmidt, Gary D. Martin de Porres: The Rose in the Desert. Diaz, David, illus. 2012. (ENG.). 32p. (J). (gr. 1-4). lib. bdg. 16.99 (978-0-547-61218-8(4)) Houghton Mifflin Harcourt Publishing Co.

Schroedel, Jenny. The Blackbird's Nest: Saint Kevin of Ireland. Montross, Doug, illus. 2004. 32p. (J). 18.00 (978-0-88141-258-1(9)) St. Vladimir's Seminary Pr.

Seco, Nina S. & Pilutik, Anastasia D. Saints Adrian & Natalie. Duckworth, Ruth, illus. Date not set. (Cloud of Witnesses Ser.). (Orig.). (J). (gr. -1-1). pap. (978-0-913026-29-8(8)) St. Nectarios Pr.

Self, David. The Loyola Treasury of Saints: From the Time of Jesus to the Present Day. Hall, Amanda, illus. 2003. (ENG.). 224p. (J). (gr. 2-7). 28.95 (978-0-8294-1785-2(0)) Loyola Pr.

Steedman, Amy. In God's Garden: Stories of the Saints for Children. rev. ed. 2003. (Illus.). 192p. (J). (gr. -1-3). 23.95 (978-1-929291-32-8(9)) Roman Catholic Bks.

Stott, Apryl, illus. Brigid & the Butter: A Legend about Saint Brigid of Ireland. 2017. 25p. (J). pap. (978-0-8198-1233-9(1)) Pauline Bks. & Media.

Streit, Jakob. Brother Francis: The Life of Francis of Assisi. Kuettel, Nina, tr. from GER. 2013. (ENG., Illus.). 56p. (J). pap. 10.00 (978-1-936367-40-5(8)) Waldorf Publications.

Swaim, Colleen. Lleven Su Fuego Al Mundo: Jóvenes Que Alcanzaron la Santidad. 2012. (SPA.). (J). (978-0-7648-2176-9(8)) Liguori Pubns.

—Radiate: More Stories of Daring Teen Saints. 2012. (J). (978-0-7648-2147-9(4)) Liguori Pubns.

Thiel, Kristin. Joan of Arc. 2017. (J). **(978-1-5026-2791-9(4))** Cavendish Square Publishing.

Thompson, Paul B. Joan of Arc: Warrior Saint of France. 2007. (Rulers of the Middle Ages Ser.). (Illus.). 160p. (YA). (gr. 6-12). lib. bdg. 35.94 (978-0-7660-2716-9(3)) Enslow Pubs., Inc.

Trouvé, Marianne Lorraine. Saint Catherine Labouré: And Our Lady of the Miraculous Medal. 2011. (ENG.). (J). pap. 7.95 (978-0-8198-7224-1(5)) Pauline Bks. & Media.

Trouve, Marianne Lorraine. Saint Clare of Assisi: A Light for the World. Peterson, Mary Joseph, illus. 2009. (J). pap. 7.95 (978-0-8198-7122-0(2)) Pauline Bks. & Media.

Vazquez, Ana Maria & Dean, Jennings. Blessed Pier Giorgio Frassati: Journey to the Summit. Stewart, Don, illus. 2004. (Encounter Ser.: 18). 144p. (J). pap. 5.95 (978-0-8198-1165-3(3), 332-028) Pauline Bks. & Media.

Visconti, Guido. Clare & Francis. Landmann, Bimba, illus. 2004. 40p. 20.00 (978-0-8028-5269-4(6)) Eerdmans, William B. Publishing Co.

Wallace, Susan F. S. P. & Wright, Melissa. Saints for Young Readers for Every Day, 2 vols., Vol. 1. Aven, Jamie H., illus. 3rd ed. 2005. (J). pap. 15.95 (978-0-8198-7081-0(1), 332-377) Pauline Bks. & Media.

Wallace, Susan Helen. Little Book of Saints: Volume 4, 4. Kinarney, Tom, illus. 2009. (J). 4.95 (978-0-8198-4527-6(2)) Pauline Bks. & Media.

—Saint Bakhita of Sudan: Forever Free. Alfano, Wayne, illus. 2006. (Encounter the Saints Ser.: 21). 102p. (J). pap. 7.95 (978-0-8198-7094-0(3)) Pauline Bks. & Media.

—Saint Faustina Kowalska: Messenger of Mercy. Waites, Joan, illus. 2007. (Encounter the Saints Ser.: 23). (J). pap. 7.95 (978-0-8198-7101-5(X)) Pauline Bks. & Media.

—Saint Gianna Beretta Molla: The Gift of Life. 2012. (ENG., Illus.). 101p. (J). pap. 7.95 (978-0-8198-7182-4(6)) Pauline Bks. & Media.

—Saint Katharine Drexel: The Total Gift. Kiwak, Barbara, illus. 2003. (Encounter the Saints Ser.: Vol. 15). 144p. (J). pap. 5.95 (978-0-8198-7068-1(4), 332-365) Pauline Bks. & Media.

—Saint Teresa of Avila: Joyful in the Lord. Kiwak, Barbara, illus. 2008. (Encounter the Saints Ser.: No. 24). 106p. (J). (gr. 4-7). pap. 7.95 (978-0-8198-7116-9(8)) Pauline Bks. & Media.

Wilkinson, Philip. Joan of Arc: The Teenager Who Saved Her Nation. (National Geographic World History Biographies Ser.). (ENG., Illus.). 64p. (J). (gr. 3-7). 2009. pap. 7.99 (978-1-4263-0415-6(3)) 2007. 17.95 (978-1-4263-0116-2(2)) 2007. lib. bdg. 27.90 (978-1-4263-0117-9(0)) National Geographic Society. (National Geographic Children's Bks.).

Windeatt, Mary F. Saint Catherine of Siena: The Story of the Girl Who Saw Saints in the Sky. Beccard, Helen L., illus.

2009. (ENG.). 65p. (J). (gr. 3-7). reprint ed. pap. 7.95 *(978-0-89555-421-5(6))* TAN Bks.
—Saint Hyacinth of Poland: The Story of the Apostle of the North. Mary Jean, illus. 2009. (ENG.). 208p. (J). (gr. 1-8). reprint ed. pap. 13.95 *(978-0-89555-422-2(4))* TAN Bks.
—Saint John Masias: Marvelous Dominican Gatekeeper of Lima, Peru. Sister Mary of the Compassion, illus. 2009. Orig. Title: Warrior in White. (ENG.). 156p. (J). (gr. 3-9). pap. 11.95 *(978-0-89555-428-4(3))* TAN Bks.
—Saint Louis de Montfort: The Story of Our Lady's Slave. Grout, Paul A., illus. 2009. Orig. Title: Our Lady's Slave: the Story of St. Louis Mary Grignion de Montfort. (ENG.). 211p. (J). (gr. 2-9). reprint ed. pap. 13.95 *(978-0-89555-414-7(3))* TAN Bks.
—Saint Maria Goretti. Harmon, Gedge, illus. 2009. (ENG.). 32p. (J). (gr. k-2). reprint ed. pap., stu. ed. 4.50 *(978-0-89555-374-4(0))* TAN Bks.
Windeatt, Mary Fabyan & Ignatz, Marie. Vocabulary Quiz Workbook: Based on 6 Great Saints' Lives by Mary Fabyan Windeatt. Lester, Mary Frances, ed. 2004. (ENG.). 200p. (gr. 5-9). pap., wbk. ed. 21.95 *(978-0-89555-743-8(6)*, 1841) TAN Bks.
Windle, Margaret. Assorted Saints & the Virtues. 2006. (Illus.). 64p. (J). 11.99 *(978-0-9798889-1-5(3))* Growing with the Saints, Inc.
Winter, Jonah. The Secret World of Hildegard. Winter, Jeanette, illus. 2007. (J). *(978-0-439-50738-7(3)*, Levine, Arthur A. Bks.) Scholastic, Inc.
Wolny, Philip. Joan of Arc: French Soldier & Saint. 2017. (Women Who Changed History Ser.). 48p. (gr. 10-12). pap. 14.05 ***(978-1-68048-645-2(4)***, Britannica Educational Publishing) Rosen Publishing Group, Inc., The.
Woodfield, Elaine. Stories of the Saints V1, 4 vols. Staggenborg, Kim, illus. 2009. (J). pap. 13.95 *(978-0-9788376-8-6(1))* Catholic Heritage Curricula.
—Stories of the Saints V2, 4 vols. Staggenborg, Kim, illus. 2009. (J). pap. 0.00 *(978-0-9788376-9-3(X))* Catholic Heritage Curricula.
Zarin, Cynthia. Saints among the Animals. Gore, Leonid, illus. 2012. (ENG.). 96p. (J). (gr. 2-7). pap. 6.99 *(978-1-4424-7296-9(0)*, Atheneum Bks. for Young Readers) Simon & Schuster Children's Publishing.

SAINTS—FICTION

Boyce, Frank Cottrell. Millions. 2005. 247p. (gr. 3-7). 19.00 *(978-0-7569-5439-0(8))* Perfection Learning Corp.
Clayden, Julie & Joliffe, Angela. Martha. 2006. (First Word Heroes Ser.). (ENG., Illus.). 14p. bds. 7.99 *(978-1-904637-23-3(X)*, 190463723X) Authentic Media GBR. Dist: EMI CMG Distribution.
Davidson, Alice Joyce. St. Therese: the Little Flower. Swanson, Maggie, illus. 2006. 24p. (J). 7.95 *(978-0-88271-214-7(4))* Regina Pr., Malhame & Co.
Evangelista, Susan. Tommy's New Shell, 2nd in series. Coke, Sherrie, illus. 2005. 24p. (J). bds. 19.95 *(978-0-9769602-0-1(6))* Evangelista, Susan.
Everett-Green, Evelyn. A Heroine of France. 2006. (ENG.). 188p. pap. 19.99 *(978-1-4264-7060-8(6))* 2007. 206p. pap. 22.99 *(978-1-4264-7136-0(X))* Creative Media Partners, LLC.
Farley, Donna. The Ravens of Fame: A Tale of Saint Cuthbert. 2010. 32p. pap. 14.95 *(978-0-9822770-5-8(9))* Ancient Faith Publishing.
Hunger, Bill. When Two Saints Meet. Ripley, Jill, ed. Martin, Alice et al, illus. 100p. (Orig.). (YA). (gr. 6-12). pap. 9.95 *(978-0-9625782-0-5(7))* Two Saints Publishing.
Hurley, Tonya. The Blessed. Watkins, Abbey, illus. 2012. (Blessed Ser.). (ENG.). 416p. (YA). (gr. 9). 17.99 *(978-1-4424-2951-2(8)*, Simon & Schuster Bks. For Young Readers) Simon & Schuster Bks. For Young Readers.
—Passionaries. (Blessed Ser.). (ENG., Illus.). 368p. (YA). (gr. 9). 2015. pap. 12.99 *(978-1-4424-2955-0(0))* 2014. 17.99 *(978-1-4424-2954-3(2))* Simon & Schuster Bks. For Young Readers. (Simon & Schuster Bks. For Young Readers).
—Precious Blood. Watkins, Abbey, illus. 2013. (Blessed Ser.). (ENG.). 432p. (YA). (gr. 9). pap. 9.99 *(978-1-4424-2952-9(6)*, Simon & Schuster Bks. For Young Readers) Simon & Schuster Bks. For Young Readers.
Jackson, Dessi. The Saint & His Bees. Brandenburg, Claire, illus. 2013. 28p. pap. 9.99 *(978-1-62395-487-1(8))* Xist Publishing.
Kuck, Anna. Seven Holy Sleepers: Amazing Saints. 2012. 38p. pap. 15.95 *(978-1-4497-7065-5(7)*, WestBow Pr.) Author Solutions, Inc.
Mora, Pat. The Song of Francis & the Animals. Frampton, David, illus. 2005. 32p. (J). (gr. -1-2). 16.00 *(978-0-8028-5253-3(X))* Eerdmans, William B. Publishing Co.
Nobisso, Josephine. Francis Woke up Early. Hyde, Maureen, illus. 2011. (ENG.). 32p. (J). (gr. k-2). 17.95 *(978-0-940112-20-9(5))*; pap. 9.95 *(978-0-940112-22-3(1))* Gingerbread Hse.
Roberts, Esyllt Nest, et al. Dwynwen. 2005. (WEL., Illus.). 36p. pap. *(978-0-86381-468-6(9))* Gwasg Carreg Gwalch.
Rupp, Dain Christopher. The Greatest Saint Stories A-Z: (Book 1 of 2: A-M) 2008. 32p. per. 24.95 *(978-1-60441-067-9(1))* America Star Bks.
Shanghai Animation Studio Staff & Tang, Sanmu. Three Monks. Ying, Wu, tr. from CHI. 2010. (Favorite Children's Ser.). (ENG., Illus.). 32p. (J). (gr. -1-3). pap. 5.95 *(978-1-60220-973-2(1))* BetterLink Pr., Inc.
Song-i, Yoon. Saint Teresa of Avila, God's Troublemaker. 2014. (ENG., Illus.). 208p. (J). pap. 14.95 *(978-0-8198-9038-2(3))* Pauline Bks. & Media.
Steedman, Amy. Our Island Saints (Yesterday's Classics) 2006. (J). per. 9.95 *(978-1-59915-031-4(X))* Yesterday's Classics.
Strasser, Myrna A. Saint Francis & the Nativity, 1 vol. Bianchi, Fausto, illus. 2010. (ENG.). 40p. (J). (gr. -1-2). 16.99 *(978-0-310-70890-2(7))* Zonderkidz.
Thottam, Meena, adapted by. The Sage's Daughter. 2006. (J). 3.95 *(978-0-9776917-2-2(1)*, Curcumin Bks.) Davlaw Press.
Welborn, Amy. Adventures in Assisi: on the Path with St. Francis: On the Path with St. Francis. Engelhart, Ann Kissane, illus. 2014. (ENG.). 32p. (J). (gr. k-3). 15.99 *(978-1-61636-650-6(8))* Franciscan Media.
Williamson, Denise J. Forbidden Gates. 2008. (J). 8.99 *(978-1-59166-853-4(0))* BJU Pr.
Willoughby, R. Peter Puts His Foot in It! Buckley, Joel, illus. 2004. 64p. pap. *(978-1-85999-765-9(1))* Scripture Union.
Windeatt, Mary F. Saint Teresa of Avila. Harmon, Gedge, illus. 2009. (ENG.). 32p. (J). (gr. k-2). reprint ed. pap., stu. ed. 4.50 *(978-0-89555-372-0(4))* TAN Bks.

SAINTS—LEGENDS

Forest, Jim. Saint Nicholas & the Nine Gold Coins. Andrejev, Vladislav, illus. 2015. (J). *(978-0-88141-511-7(1))* St. Vladimir's Seminary Pr.
Knijpenga, Siegwart. Stories of the Saints: A Collection for Children. 2nd ed. 2012. (ENG., Illus.). 224p. (J). (gr. 4-7). pap. *(978-0-86315-929-9(X))* Floris Bks.
McAllister, Margaret. Stories of the Saints. Massari, Alida, illus. 2015. (ENG.). 48p. (J). (gr. 2-4). 17.99 *(978-0-7459-6445-4(1))* Lion Hudson PLC GBR. Dist: Independent Pubs. Group.
Rock, Lois. Saintly Tales & Legends. Balit, Christina, illus. 2004. 100p. (J). 15.95 *(978-0-8198-7083-4(8)*, 332-379) Pauline Bks. & Media.

SALADS

Beck, Isabel L., et al. Trophies Kindergarten: The Salad. 2003. (Trophies Ser.). (gr. k-6). 13.80 *(978-0-15-329524-9(4))* Harcourt Schl. Pubs.
Dolbear, Emily. How Did That Get to My Table? Salad. 2009. (Community Connections: How Did That Get to My Table? Ser.). (ENG.). 24p. (gr. 2-5). lib. bdg. 25.64 *(978-1-60279-473-3(1)*, 200262) Cherry Lake Publishing.
Head, Honor. Salad. 2010. (J). 24.25 *(978-1-59920-259-4(X))* Black Rabbit Bks.
Kuskowski, Alex. Cool Sides & Salads, 1 vol. 2014. (Cool Home Cooking Ser.). (ENG.). 32p. (gr. 3-6). 28.50 *(978-1-62403-503-6(5))* ABDO Publishing Co.

SALAMANDERS

Borgert-Spaniol, Megan. Salamanders. 2012. (Backyard Wildlife Ser.). (ENG., Illus.). 24p. (J). (gr. k-3). lib. bdg. 25.95 *(978-1-60014-723-4(2)*, Blastoff! Readers) Bellwether Media.
Bredeson, Carmen. Fun Facts about Salamanders! 2007. (I Like Reptiles & Amphibians! Ser.). (Illus.). 24p. (J). (gr. 1-3). lib. bdg. 22.60 *(978-0-7660-2790-9(2)*, Enslow Elementary) Enslow Pubs., Inc.
Carr, Aaron. Salamander. 2014. (J). *(978-1-4896-3106-0(2))* Weigl Pubs., Inc.
Clark, Willow & Rockwood, Leigh. Salamanders Are Gross! 2010. (Creepy Crawlies Ser.). (Illus.). 24p. (J). (ENG.). pap. 8.25 *(978-1-4488-1365-0(4)*, PowerKids Pr.); lib. bdg. 22.60 *(978-1-4488-0702-4(6))* Rosen Publishing Group, Inc., The.
Curtis, Jennifer Keats & Frederick, J. Adam. Salamander Season, 1 vol. Bersani, Shennen, illus. 2015. (ENG.). 32p. (J). (gr. 1-4). 17.95 *(978-1-62855-556-1(4))* Arbordale Publishing.
—Temporada de Salamandras. Bersani, Shennen, illus. 2015. (SPA.). 32p. (J). (gr. 1-4). pap. 9.95 *(978-1-62855-574-5(2))* Arbordale Publishing.
Dibble, Traci. Can You See the Salamander? 2016. (1-3Y Animals Ser.). (ENG., Illus.). 12p. (J). pap. 5.99 ***(978-1-63437-667-9(6))*** American Reading Co.
Goldish, Meish. Slimy Salamanders. 2010. (Amphibiana Ser.). (Illus.). 24p. (YA). (gr. k-3). lib. bdg. 22.61 *(978-1-936087-37-2(5))* Bearport Publishing Co., Inc.
Guillain, Charlotte. Life Story of a Salamander, 1 vol. 2014. (Animal Life Stories Ser.). (ENG., Illus.). 32p. (gr. 1-3). 27.32 *(978-1-4846-0490-8(3)*, Heinemann First Library) Heinemann-Raintree.
Hibbert, Clare. Salamanders. 2009. (Extreme Pets Ser.). (YA). (gr. 4-7). 28.50 *(978-1-59920-235-8(2))* Black Rabbit Bks.
Kolpin, Molly. Salamanders. 2010. (Amphibians Ser.). (ENG.). 24p. (gr. k-1). pap. 41.70 *(978-1-4296-5091-5(5))*; lib. bdg. 26.65 *(978-1-4296-3990-3(3))* Capstone Press of Coughlan Cos. (Pebble Plus).
Kralovansky, Susan. Salamander or Lizard?, 1 vol. 2014. (This or That? Ser.). (ENG.). 24p. (gr. 5-10). lib. bdg. 25.65 *(978-1-62403-289-9(3)*, Super SandCastle) ABDO Publishing Co.
McNab, Chris. Frogs, Toads, & Salamanders. 2006. (Nature's Monsters Ser.). (Illus.). 32p. (gr. 2-6). lib. bdg. 26.00 *(978-0-8368-6172-3(8)*, Gareth Stevens Learning Library) Stevens, Gareth Publishing LLLP.
Murray, Julie. Salamanders, 1 vol. 2005. (Animal Kingdom Set II Ser.). (ENG., Illus.). 24p. (gr. k-4). 25.65 *(978-1-59197-334-8(1)*, Buddy Bks.) ABDO Publishing Co.
Nelson, Robin. Salamanders. 2009. pap. 34.95 *(978-0-7613-4109-3(9))*; (ENG.). 24p. 23.93 *(978-0-7613-4065-2(3)*, Lerner Pubns.) Lerner Publishing Group.
Plattner, Josh. Salamander: Master of Regrowth, 1 vol. 2016. (ENG., Illus.). 24p. (J). *(978-1-62403-740-5(2))* ABDO Publishing Co.
Pope, Kristen. Salamanders. 2015. (Endangered Animals Ser.). (ENG.). 24p. (J). (gr. 1-4). 27.07 *(978-1-63143-971-1(5)*, 208806) Child's World, Inc., The.
Rudolph, Jessica. Mi Piel Tiene Bultos y es Babosa. 2015. (Pistas de Animales Ser.). (SPA.). 24p. (J). (gr. -1-3). lib. bdg. 23.93 *(978-1-62724-584-5(7))* Bearport Publishing Co., Inc.
—My Skin Is Bumpy & Slimy (Fire Salamander) 2014. (Zoo Clues Ser.). 24p. (J). (gr. -1-3). lib. bdg. 23.93 *(978-1-62724-115-1(9))* Bearport Publishing Co., Inc.
Schafer, Susan. Chinese Giant Salamanders. 2014. (Giant Animals Ser.). 48p. (J). (gr. 4-6). lib. bdg. 31.36 *(978-1-62712-960-2(X))* Cavendish Square Publishing.
Silverman, Buffy. Can You Tell a Gecko from a Salamander? 2012. (Animal Look-Alikes Ser.). 32p. (gr. k-2). pap. 45.32 *(978-0-7613-9255-2(6))*; (ENG.). pap. 7.95 *(978-0-7613-8552-3(5))*; (ENG.). lib. bdg. 26.60 *(978-0-7613-6737-6(3)*, Lerner Pubns.) Lerner Publishing Group.
Squire, Ann O. Chinese Giant Salamander: The World's Biggest Amphibian. 2007. (SuperSized! Ser.). (Illus.). 24p. (J). (gr. k-3). lib. bdg. 21.28 *(978-1-59716-386-6(4)*, 1265931) Bearport Publishing Co., Inc.
Stewart, Melissa. Salamander or Lizard? How Do You Know? 2011. (Which Animal Is Which? Ser.). (Illus.). 24p. (J). (gr. k-18). pap. 7.95 *(978-1-59845-238-9(X)*, Enslow Elementary); lib. bdg. 22.60 *(978-0-7660-3679-6(0))* Enslow Pubs., Inc.
Sweeney, Alyse. Mudpuppies. 2010. (Amphibians Ser.). (ENG.). 24p. (gr. k-1). pap. 41.70 *(978-1-4296-5089-2(3)*, Pebble Plus) Capstone Press of Coughlan Cos.
Tomljanovic, Tatiana. Caring for Your Salamander. 2006. (Caring for Your Pet Ser.). (Illus.). 32p. (J). (gr. 3-7). per. 9.95 *(978-1-59036-477-2(5))*; lib. bdg. 26.00 *(978-1-59036-476-5(7))* Weigl Pubs., Inc.
Winnick, Nick. Salamanders. 2009. (Backyard Animals Ser.). (Illus.). 24p. (J). (gr. 3-5). pap. 8.95 *(978-1-60596-085-2(3))*; lib. bdg. 24.45 *(978-1-60596-084-5(5))* Weigl Pubs., Inc.
Woodward, John. Salamanders. 2008. (Nature's Children Ser.). (Illus.). 52p. (J). *(978-0-7172-6261-8(8))* Grolier, Ltd.

SALEM (FICTITIOUS CHARACTER)—FICTION

Hemphill, Stephanie. Wicked Girls: A Novel of the Salem Witch Trials. 2013. (ENG.). 432p. (YA). (gr. 8). pap. 9.99 *(978-0-06-185330-2(5))* HarperCollins Pubs.

SALEM (MASS.)—HISTORY

Angelini, Josephine. Trail of Tears. 2015. (Worldwalker Trilogy Ser.: 2). (SPA & ENG.). 352p. (YA). (gr. 7). 17.99 *(978-1-250-05090-8(1)*, 9781250050908) Feiwel & Friends.
Aronson, Marc. Witch-Hunt: Mysteries of the Salem Witch Trials. 2005. (Illus.). 272p. (YA). (gr. 7-12). 16.65 *(978-0-7569-5659-2(5))* Perfection Learning Corp.
Benoit, Peter. The Salem Witch Trials. 2013. (ENG.). 64p. (J). 30.00 *(978-0-531-28206-9(6))*; pap. 8.95 *(978-0-531-27671-6(6))* Scholastic Library Publishing.
Crewe, Sabrina & Uschan, Michael V. The Salem Witch Trials. 2004. (Events That Shaped America Ser.). (Illus.). 32p. (gr. 3-6). lib. bdg. 26.00 *(978-0-8368-3406-2(2)*, Gareth Stevens Learning Library) Stevens, Gareth Publishing LLLP.
Dellaccio, Tanya & Nardo, Don. The Salem Witch Trials: A Crisis in Puritan New England. 2017. (American History Ser.). 104p. (YA). (gr. 7-7). lib. bdg. 39.40 ***(978-1-5345-6039-0(4)***, Lucent Pr.) Greenhaven Publishing LLC.
Doeden, Matt. The Salem Witch Trials: An Interactive History Adventure, 1 vol. (You Choose: History Ser.). (ENG.). 112p. (gr. 3-4). 2011. pap. 6.95 *(978-1-4296-6272-7(7))* 2011. pap. 41.70 *(978-1-4296-6440-0(1))* 2010. 31.99 *(978-1-4296-5478-4(3))* Capstone Press of Coughlan Cos. (You Choose Bks.).
Dunn, Joeming W. The Salem Witch Trials, 1 vol. Martin, Cynthia, illus. 2008. (Graphic History Ser.). (ENG.). 32p. 28.50 *(978-1-60270-186-1(5)*, Graphic Planet- Nonfiction) ABDO Publishing Co.
Forten, Charlotte. Diary of Charlotte Forten: A Free Black Girl Before the Civil War, 1 vol. 2014. (First-Person Histories Ser.). (ENG.). 32p. (gr. 3-4). lib. bdg. 27.32 *(978-1-4765-4196-9(5)*, Fact Finders) Capstone Press of Coughlan Cos.
Fradin, Judith Bloom & Fradin, Dennis Brindell. The Salem Witch Trials. 2008. (Turning Points in U. S. History Ser.). 48p. (gr. 3-18). lib. bdg. 31.36 *(978-0-7614-3013-1(X)*, Benchmark Bks.) Marshall Cavendish Corp.
Hinds, Maurene J. Witchcraft on Trial: From the Salem Witch Hunts to the Crucible. 2009. (Famous Court Cases That Became Movies Ser.). (Illus.). 104p. (J). (gr. 7-12). lib. bdg. 33.27 *(978-0-7660-3055-8(5))* Enslow Pubs., Inc.
Holub, Joan. What Were the Salem Witch Trials? 2015. (What Was... ? Ser.). lib. bdg. 16.00 *(978-0-606-36761-5(6))* Turtleback Bks.
Holub, Joan & dePaola, Tomie. What Were the Salem Witch Trials? Putra, Dede & McVeigh, Kevin, illus. 2015. (What Was? Ser.). (ENG.). 112p. (J). (gr. 3-7). 5.99 *(978-0-448-47905-7(2)*, Grosset & Dunlap) Penguin Young Readers Group.
Kent, Deborah. Witchcraft Trials: Fear, Betrayal, & Death in Salem. 2009. (America's Living History Ser.). (Illus.). 128p. (J). (gr. 5-9). lib. bdg. 33.27 *(978-0-7660-2906-4(9))* Enslow Pubs., Inc.
Landau, Elaine. The Salem Witchcraft Trials: Would You Join the Madness? 2014. (What Would You Do? Ser.). (Illus.). 48p. (J). (gr. 3-4). lib. bdg. 25.27 *(978-0-7660-4224-7(3)*, Enslow Elementary) Enslow Pubs., Inc.
MacBain, Jenny. The Salem Witch Trials: A Primary Source History of the Witchcraft Trials in Salem, Massachusetts. (Primary Sources in American History Ser.). 64p. (gr. 5-8). 2009. 58.50 *(978-1-60851-503-5(6))* 2003. (Illus.). lib. bdg. 31.95 *(978-0-8239-3683-0(X)*, Rosen Reference) Rosen Publishing Group, Inc., The.
Martin, Michael. The Salem Witch Trials, 1 vol. Bascle, Brian, illus. 2005. (Graphic History Ser.). (ENG.). 32p. (gr. 3-4). per. 8.10 *(978-0-7368-5246-3(8)*, Graphic Library) Capstone Press of Coughlan Cos.
Stern, Steven L. Witchcraft in Salem. 2010. (HorrorScapes Ser.). 32p. (YA). (gr. 4-7). lib. bdg. 25.27 *(978-1-936088-00-3(2))* Bearport Publishing Co., Inc.
Uschan, Michael V. The Salem Witch Trials. 2004. (Landmark Events in American History Ser.). (Illus.). 48p. (gr. 5-12). pap. 14.05 *(978-0-8368-5415-2(2))*; lib. bdg. 31.00 *(978-0-8368-5387-2(3))* Stevens, Gareth Publishing LLLP. (Gareth Stevens Secondary Library).
Wallis, Jeffrey. Trials in Salem. 2005. (Houghton Mifflin Social Studies Leveled Readers). (Illus.). 16p. (J). pap. *(978-0-618-56037-0(8))* Houghton Mifflin Harcourt Publishing Co.

SALES PERSONNEL

see also Advertising; Business; Marketing

Blane, Francisco. At theTag Sale: Lap Book. 2009. (My First Reader's Theater Set B Ser.). (J). 28.00 *(978-1-4108-8535-7(6))* Benchmark Education Co.
Carlson Berne, Emma. Run Your Own Bake Sale. 2014. (Young Entrepreneurs Ser.). 32p. (J). (gr. 4-6). pap. 10.00 *(978-1-4777-3007-2(9)*, PowerKids Pr.) Rosen Publishing Group, Inc., The.
Clark, Betty. Choosing a Career in Real Estate. 2009. (World of Work Ser.). 64p. (gr. 5-5). 58.50 *(978-1-60854-335-9(8))* Rosen Publishing Group, Inc., The.
Ensaff, Najoud, et al. Retail Careers. 2011. (Been There! Ser.). 32p. (gr. 3-6). lib. bdg. 31.35 *(978-1-59920-473-4(8))* Black Rabbit Bks.
Ferguson. Careers in Focus: Retail. 3rd rev. ed. 2007. (Careers in Focus Ser.). (Illus.). 192p. (gr. 6-12). 32.95 *(978-0-8160-6593-6(4)*, Ferguson Publishing Co.) Facts On File, Inc.
Gard, Carolyn. Cool Careers Without College for People Who Love to Sell Things. 2009. (Cool Careers Without College Ser.). 144p. (gr. 6-6). 66.50 *(978-1-61511-979-0(5))* Rosen Publishing Group, Inc., The.
Houghton, Gillian. Goods & Services. 2009. (Invest Kids Ser.). 24p. (ENG., Illus.). (J). (gr. 2-5). pap. 8.25 *(978-1-4358-3210-7(8)*, 1291654); (gr. 2-3). 42.50 *(978-1-61513-617-9(7))*; (Illus.). (J). lib. bdg. 22.60 *(978-1-4358-2775-2(9)*, 1291654) Rosen Publishing Group, Inc., The. (PowerKids Pr.).
Jacobson, Ryan. Get a Job Making Stuff to Sell. Cannell, Jon, illus. 2014. (You're in Business! Ser.). 40p. (J). (gr. 5-9). lib. bdg. 27.93 *(978-1-4677-3837-8(9)*, Lerner Pubns.) Lerner Publishing Group.
Meinking, Mary. Start Your Crafting Business. 2017. (Build Your Business Ser.). (ENG.). 32p. (gr. 3-4). lib. bdg. 27.99 ***(978-1-5157-6690-2(X))*** Capstone Press of Coughlan Cos.
Mozer, Mindy. Careers As a Commissioned Sales Representative. 2013. (Essential Careers Ser.). 80p. (YA). (gr. 7-12). 33.25 *(978-1-4777-1794-3(3))* Rosen Publishing Group, Inc., The.
Scheunemann, Pam. Cool Jobs for Super Sales Kids: Ways to Make Money Selling Stuff, 1 vol. 2011. (Cool Kid Jobs Ser.). (ENG.). 32p. (gr. 3-6). 28.50 *(978-1-61613-197-5(7)*, Checkerboard Library) ABDO Publishing Co.
Sheen, Barbara. Careers in Sales & Marketing. 2015. (ENG., Illus.). 80p. (YA). lib. bdg. *(978-1-60152-812-4(4))* ReferencePoint Pr., Inc.
Sun-Tzu & Gagliardi, Gary. Strategy for Sales Managers: Sun Tzu's the Art of War Plus Book Series. 2005. (Art of War Plus Ser.). (Illus.). 192p. 16.95 *(978-1-929194-33-9(1)*, Art of War Plus Bks.) Clearbridge Publishing.

SALES PERSONNEL—FICTION

Andrews, Jan. The Auction. (Illus.). (J). 13.95 *(978-0-88899-110-2(X))*; pap. 5.95 *(978-0-88899-168-3(1))* Groundwood Bks. CAN. Dist: Publishers Group West (PGW).
McOmber, Rachel B., ed. McOmber Phonics Storybooks: The Lemonade Sale. rev. ed. (Illus.). (J). *(978-0-944991-41-1(6))* Swift Learning Resources.
Merrill, Jean. The Elephant Who Liked to Smash Small Cars. Solbert, Ronni, illus. 2015. (ENG.). 40p. (J). (gr. -1-2). 14.95 *(978-1-59017-872-0(6)*, NYR Children's Collection) New York Review of Bks., Inc., The.

SALES PERSONNEL—VOCATIONAL GUIDANCE

Endsaff, Najoud & Rooney, Anne. Retail Careers. 2010. (In the Workplace Ser.). 48p. (J). 35.65 *(978-1-60753-093-0(7))* Amicus Publishing.

SALESMEN

see Sales Personnel

SALINGER, J. D. (JEROME DAVID), 1919-2010

Kerr, Christine. Bloom's How to Write about J. D. Salinger. 2007. (Bloom's How to Write about Literature Ser.). 280p. (C). (gr. 9-12). 45.00 *(978-0-7910-9483-9(9))*, Chelsea Hse.) Facts On File, Inc.

SALK, JONAS, 1914-1995

Hantula, Richard. Jonas Salk. 2004. (Trailblazers of the Modern World Ser.). (Illus.). 48p. (gr. 5-12). lib. bdg. 31.00 *(978-0-8368-5100-7(5)*, Gareth Stevens Secondary Library) Stevens, Gareth Publishing LLLP.
Llanas, Sheila. Jonas Salk: Medical Innovator & Polio Vaccine Developer, 1 vol. 2013. (Essential Lives Set 8 Ser.). (ENG., Illus.). 112p. (J). (gr. 6-12). lib. bdg. 35.64 *(978-1-61783-896-5(9)*, Essential Library) ABDO Publishing Co.
Marsh, Carole. Jonas Salk. 2004. 12p. (gr. k-4). 2.95 *(978-0-635-02377-3(6))* Gallopade International.
McLeese, Don. Jonas Salk. 2005. (Rourke Discovery Library). (Illus.). 24p. (J). (gr. 2-5). lib. bdg. *(978-1-59515-436-1(1))* Rourke Educational Media.
McPherson, Stephanie Sammartino. Jonas Salk: Conquering Polio. 128p. (J). (gr. 6-18). 20.95 *(978-1-58013-207-7(3)*, Kar-Ben Publishing) Lerner Publishing Group.
Reis, Ronald A. Jonas Salk: Microbiologist. 2005. (Ferguson Career Biographies Ser.). (Illus.). 120p. (gr. 6-12). 25.00 *(978-0-8160-6186-0(6)*, Ferguson Publishing Co.) Facts On File, Inc.
Sherrow, Victoria. Jonas Salk: Beyond the Microscope. 2nd rev. ed. 2008. (Makers of Modern Science Ser.). (Illus.). 146p. (gr. 6-12). 35.00 *(978-0-8160-6180-8(7)*, Chelsea Hse.) Facts On File, Inc.
Tocci, Salvatore. Jonas Salk: Creator of the Polio Vaccine. 2003. (Great Minds of Science Ser.). (Illus.). 128p. (J). (gr. 4-10). lib. bdg. 27.94 *(978-0-7660-2097-9(5))* Enslow Pubs., Inc.

SALMON

Best, B. J. Salmon. 2016. (Migrating Animals Ser.). 24p. (J). pap. 8.22 *(978-1-5026-2102-3(9))*; lib. bdg. 24.21 *(978-1-5026-2104-7(5))* Cavendish Square Publishing.
Catt, Thessaly. Migrating with the Salmon. 2011. (Animal Journeys Ser.). (Illus.). 24p. (YA). (gr. 1-4). lib. bdg. 22.60 *(978-1-4488-2545-5(8))* Rosen Publishing Group, Inc., The.
Cosson, M. J. Salmon: A Journey Home. 2016. (Illus.). 32p. (J). *(978-1-4896-4523-4(3))* Weigl Pubs., Inc.
—Salmon Migration. 2012. (Animal Migrations Ser.). (ENG., Illus.). 32p. (J). (gr. 2-5). lib. bdg. 29.93 *(978-1-60973-625-5(7)*, 201202) Child's World, Inc., The.
Glimmerveen, Ulco. Leaper: The Amazing Life of the Salmon. (Illus.). 32p. (J). pap. *(978-1-86943-042-9(5))* Scholastic New Zealand Ltd.
Harasymiw, Mark. The Bizarre Life Cycle of A Salmon. 2012. (Strange Life Cycles Ser.). (Illus.). 24p. (J). (gr. 2-5). 22.60 *(978-1-4339-7059-7(7))*; pap. 8.15 *(978-1-4339-7060-3(0))* Stevens, Gareth Publishing LLLP. (Gareth Stevens Learning Library).
Kalman, Bobbie & Sjonger, Rebecca. The Life Cycle of a Salmon. 2006. (Life Cycle Ser.). (ENG., Illus.). 32p. (J). (gr. -1-3). pap. *(978-0-7787-0705-9(9))* Crabtree Publishing Co.
—Les Saumons. Briere, Marie-Josee, tr. from ENG. 2008. (Petit Monde Vivant Ser.). (FRE., Illus.). 32p. (J). (gr. 3-7). pap. 9.95 *(978-2-89579-180-5(5))* Bayard Canada Livres CAN. Dist: Crabtree Publishing Co.
Migrating with the Salmon. 2011. (Animal Journeys Ser.). (Illus.). 24p. (J). pap. 8.25 *(978-1-4488-2674-2(8)*, PowerKids Pr.) Rosen Publishing Group, Inc., The.

Miller, Debbie S. & Eiler, John H. A King Salmon Journey. Van Zyle, Jon, illus. 2014. 44p. 15.95 *(978-1-60223-230-3(X))*; 32p. pap. 12.95 *(978-1-60223-231-0(8))* Univ. of Alaska Pr.
Murray, Julie. Salmon, 1 vol. 2007. (Life Cycles Ser.). (ENG.). 24p. (gr. 4-7). 25.65 *(978-1-59928-710-2(2)*, Buddy Bks.) ABDO Publishing Co.
Reed-jones, Carol. Salmon Stream. Maydak, Michael S., illus. 2004. (Sharing Nature with Children Book Ser.). 32p. (J). (gr. 4-7). 16.95 *(978-1-58469-014-6(3))*; (ENG.). pap. 7.95 *(978-1-58469-013-9(5))* Dawn Pubns.
Ritchie, Scot. P'ésk'a & the First Salmon Ceremony, 1 vol. 2015. (ENG., Illus.). 32p. (J). (gr. -1-2). 18.95 *(978-1-55498-718-4(0))* Groundwood Bks. CAN. Dist: Publishers Group West (PGW).
Royston, Angela. El Salmón, 1 vol. 2010. (Ciclo de Vida Ser.). (SPA & ENG.). 32p. (gr. 1-3). pap. 7.99 *(978-1-4329-4386-8(3))* Heinemann-Raintree.
Sexton, Colleen. The Life Cycle of a Salmon. 2010. (Life Cycles Ser.). (ENG., Illus.). 24p. (J). (gr. k-3). lib. bdg. 25.95 *(978-1-60014-311-3(3)*, Blastoff! Readers) Bellwether Media.
Thomson, Ruth. The Life Cycle of a Salmon. 2007. (Learning about Life Cycles Ser.). (Illus.). 24p. (J). (gr. 3-7). lib. bdg. 22.60 *(978-1-4042-3712-4(7)*, PowerKids Pr.) Rosen Publishing Group, Inc., The.
Winkelman, Barbara Gaines. Sockeye's Journey Home: The Story of a Pacific Salmon. Popeo, Joanie, illus. 2005. (Smithsonian Oceanic Collection: Vol. 19). (ENG.). 32p. (J). (gr. -1-2). 15.95 *(978-1-56899-829-9(5)*, B4019) Soundprints.
Winkelman, Barbara Gaines & Thomas, Peter. Sockeye's Journey Home: The Story of a Pacific Salmon. Popeo, Joanie, illus. 2003. (ENG.). 32p. (J). (gr. -1-3). 9.95 *(978-1-56899-834-3(1)*, PB4069) Soundprints.

SALOMON, HAYM, 1740-1785

Amler, Jane Frances. Haym Salomon: Patriot Banker of the American Revolution. (Library of American Lives & Times Ser.). 112p. 2009. (gr. 5-6). 69.20 *(978-1-60853-487-6(1))* 2005. (Illus.). (YA). (gr. 4-8). lib. bdg. 34.60 *(978-0-8239-6629-5(1))* Rosen Publishing Group, Inc., The.

SALOONS

see Restaurants

SALT

Centore, Michael. Salt. 2017. (J). ***(978-1-4222-3742-7(7))*** Mason Crest.
Dunlop, Jenna & Zronik, John. Salt. 2004. (Rocks, Minerals, & Resources Ser.). (ENG., Illus.). 32p. (J). lib. bdg. *(978-0-7787-1411-8(X))* Crabtree Publishing Co.
Furgang, Adam. Salty & Sugary Snacks: The Incredibly Disgusting Story. 2011. (Incredibly Disgusting Food Ser.). (Illus.). 48p. (YA). pap. 11.75 *(978-1-4488-2283-6(1)*, Rosen Reference); (gr. 5-9). lib. bdg. 29.25 *(978-1-4488-1267-7(4))* Rosen Publishing Group, Inc., The.
Kjelle, Marylou Morano. The Properties of Salts. 2009. (Library of Physical Science Ser.). 24p. (gr. 4-4). 42.50 *(978-1-60853-793-8(5)*, PowerKids Pr.) Rosen Publishing Group, Inc., The.
Kuhn, Betsy. The Force Born of Truth: Mohandas Gandhi & the Salt March, India, 1930. 2010. (Civil Rights Struggles around the World Ser.). (ENG., Illus.). 160p. (gr. 9-12). lib. bdg. 38.60 *(978-0-8225-8968-6(0))* Lerner Publishing Group.
Kurlansky, Mark. The Story of Salt. Schindler, S. D., illus. (ENG.). 48p. (J). (gr. -1-3). 2014. 8.99 *(978-0-14-751166-9(6)*, Puffin Books) 2006. 17.99 *(978-0-399-23998-4(7)*, G.P. Putnam's Sons Books for Young Readers) Penguin Young Readers Group.
—The Story of Salt. 2014. lib. bdg. 19.65 *(978-0-606-35715-9(7))* Turtleback Bks.
Lawrence, Ellen. Why Is Seawater Salty? 2016. (Drip, Drip, Drop: Earth's Water Ser.). (ENG., Illus.). 24p. (J). (gr. -1-3). 17.95 *(978-1-943553-22-8(X))* Bearport Publishing Co., Inc.
Masters, Nancy Robinson. Salt. 2008. (21st Century Skills Library: Global Products Ser.). (ENG.). 32p. (gr. 4-8). lib. bdg. 28.50 *(978-1-60279-120-6(1)*, 200108) Cherry Lake Publishing.
Nelson, Robin. From Sea to Salt. 2003. (Start to Finish Ser.). (ENG., Illus.). 24p. (gr. k-3). 19.93 *(978-0-8225-0946-2(6)*, Lerner Pubns.) Lerner Publishing Group.
Owings, Lisa & Nelson, Robin. From Sea to Salt. 2015. (Start to Finish, Second Ser.). (ENG., Illus.). 24p. (J). (gr. k-3). pap. 6.95 *(978-1-4677-6113-0(3))*; lib. bdg. 23.93 *(978-1-4677-6019-5(6))* Lerner Publishing Group. (Lerner Pubns.).
Perritano, John. Salt, Vol. 12. 2015. (North American Natural Resources Ser.). (Illus.). 64p. (J). (gr. 7). 23.95 *(978-1-4222-3388-7(X))* Mason Crest.
Strom, Laura Layton. The Rock We Eat - Salt. 2007. (Shockwave: Economics & Geography Ser.). (ENG., Illus.). 36p. (J). (gr. 3-5). 25.00 *(978-0-531-17799-0(8)*, Children's Pr.) Scholastic Library Publishing.
Woolf, Alex. The Story of Salt. 2016. (Story of Food Ser.). (ENG., Illus.). 32p. (J). (gr. 4-6). 16.99 *(978-0-7502-9658-8(5)*, Wayland) Hachette Children's Group GBR. Dist: Hachette Bk. Group.

SALUTATIONS

see Etiquette; Letter Writing

SALVADOR

see El Salvador

SALVAGE

see also Shipwrecks; Skin Diving

Dybvik, Tina. Trendy Jewelry for the Crafty Fashionista, 1 vol. 2011. (Fashion Craft Studio Ser.). (ENG.). 32p. (gr. 3-4). lib. bdg. 27.99 *(978-1-4296-6549-0(1)*, Snap Bks.) Capstone Press of Coughlan Cos.
Hewitt, Sally. Reduce & Reuse. 2008. (Rise & Shine Ser.). (ENG., Illus.). 32p. (J). (gr. 3-7). pap. *(978-0-7787-4102-2(8))* Crabtree Publishing Co.
Jones, Jen. Cool Crafts with Newspapers, Magazines, & Junk Mail: Green Projects for Resourceful Kids, 1 vol. 2010. (Green Crafts Ser.). (ENG.). 32p. (gr. 3-4). lib. bdg. 27.99 *(978-1-4296-4764-9(7)*, Snap Bks.) Capstone Press of Coughlan Cos.
Jones, Jen & Sirrine, Carol. Re-Craft: Unique Projects That Look Great (And Save the Planet) 2011. (Craft It Yourself Ser.). (ENG.). 112p. (gr. 3-4). pap. 12.95 *(978-1-4296-6637-4(4))* Capstone Young Readers of Coughlan Cos.
Laughlin, Kara L. Beautiful Bags for the Crafty Fashionista, 1 vol. 2011. (Fashion Craft Studio Ser.). (ENG.). 32p. (gr. 3-4). lib. bdg. 27.99 *(978-1-4296-6550-6(5)*, Snap Bks.) Capstone Press of Coughlan Cos.
Nunn, Daniel. Cardboard, 1 vol. 2011. (From Trash to Treasures Ser.). (ENG.). 24p. (gr. k-2). 23.32 *(978-1-4329-5150-4(5)*, Heinemann Read & Learn) Heinemann-Raintree.
—Jars & Pots, 1 vol. 2011. (From Trash to Treasures Ser.). (ENG.). 24p. (gr. k-2). 23.32 *(978-1-4329-5154-2(8)*, Heinemann Read & Learn) Heinemann-Raintree.
Otfinoski, Steven. Recycling & Upcycling: Science, Technology, Engineering. 2016. (Calling All Innovators: a Career for You Ser.). (ENG., Illus.). 64p. (J). lib. bdg. 32.00 *(978-0-531-23002-2(3)*, Children's Pr.) Scholastic Library Publishing.
Sirrine, Carol. Cool Crafts with Old Jeans: Green Projects for Resourceful Kids. 2010. (Green Crafts Ser.). (ENG.). 32p. (gr. 3-4). lib. bdg. 27.99 *(978-1-4296-4006-0(5)*, Snap Bks.) Capstone Press of Coughlan Cos.
Wilcox, Charlotte. Recycling. 2008. pap. 52.95 *(978-0-8225-9329-4(7))* 2007. (ENG., Illus.). 48p. (gr. 4-8). lib. bdg. 27.93 *(978-0-8225-6768-4(7))* Lerner Publishing Group.

SALVAGE—FICTION

Michaels, Craig. Blackbeard's Treasure. 2008. (J). *(978-0-936389-99-8(0))* Tudor Pubs., Inc.

SALVATION ARMY

Marsico, Katie. The Salvation Army. 2014. (Community Connections: How Do They Help? Ser.). (ENG.). 24p. (J). (gr. 2-5). 25.64 *(978-1-63188-029-2(2)*, 205523) Cherry Lake Publishing.

SAMOAN ISLANDS

Burgan, Michael. Puerto Rico y Otras Areas Perifericas. 2004. (World Almanac Ser.).Tr. of Puerto Rico & Other Outlying Areas. (SPA.). 48p. (gr. 4-9). lib. bdg. 31.00 *(978-0-8368-5726-9(7)*, GHS32693, Gareth Stevens Learning Library) Stevens, Gareth Publishing LLLP.

SAMOAN ISLANDS—FICTION

Bessey, Siân Ann. Uprising in Samoa: A Novel. 2004. 178p. (J). *(978-1-59156-890-2(0))* Covenant Communications.
Bundschuh, Rick. Burned, 1 vol. 2014. (Faithgirlz / Soul Surfer Ser.). (ENG.). 128p. (J). pap. 7.99 *(978-0-310-74555-6(1))* Zonderkidz.
Watson, Leilani. Sina & the Eel: A Tale from Samoa. Cooper, Jenny, illus. 2016. 24p. (J). pap. *(978-1-927244-56-2(0))* Flying Start Bks.
—Sina & the Eel (Big Book Edition) A Tale from Samoa. Cooper, Jenny, illus. 2016. 24p. (J). pap. *(978-1-927244-66-1(8))* Flying Start Bks.

SAMSON (BIBLICAL JUDGE)

Barberet, Denise-Renée. Samson. (Money at its Best: Millionaires of the Old Testament Ser.). 112p. (YA). (gr. 7-12). 2009. 24.95 *(978-1-4222-0475-7(8))* 2007. pap. 14.95 *(978-1-4222-0850-2(8))* Mason Crest.

SAMSON (BIBLICAL JUDGE)—FICTION

Samson 4 book Set. 2007. (J). mass mkt. *(978-0-9769722-4-2(7))* Leslie, Beverly J.

SAMURAI

Bodden, Valerie. Samurai. 2017. (J). ***(978-1-60818-815-4(9)***, Creative Education) Creative Co., The.
Dawson, Patricia. Samurai: Warlords of Japan. 2015. (History's Greatest Warriors Ser.). (ENG., Illus.). 48p. (J). (gr. 4-4). 31.36 *(978-1-5026-0125-4(7))* Cavendish Square Publishing.
Doeden, Matt. Life as a Samurai. 2010. (You Choose: Warriors Ser.). (ENG.). 112p. (gr. 3-4). pap. 41.70 *(978-1-4296-5726-6(X)*, You Choose Bks.) Capstone Press of Coughlan Cos.
Farndon, John. How to Live Like a Samurai Warrior. Pinelli, Amerigo, illus. 2016. (How to Live Like... Ser.). (ENG.). 32p. (J). (gr. 3-6). 26.65 *(978-1-5124-0630-6(9))* Lerner Publishing Group.
Green, John. Samurai Stained Glass Coloring Book. 2008. (Dover Stained Glass Coloring Book Ser.). (ENG., Illus.). 32p. (gr. 3-8). 6.99 *(978-0-486-46558-6(6))* Dover Pubns., Inc.
—Samurai Warriors. 2008. (Dover History Coloring Book Ser.). (ENG., Illus.). 32p. (gr. 3-8). 3.95 *(978-0-486-46559-3(4))* Dover Pubns., Inc.
Hanel, Rachel. Samurai. 2007. (Fearsome Fighters Ser.). (Illus.). 48p. (YA). (gr. 3-6). lib. bdg. 31.35 *(978-1-58341-538-2(6))* Creative Co., The.
Hepperman, Christina. Samurai, 1 vol. 2013. (Great Warriors Ser.). (ENG.). 48p. (J). (gr. 3-6). lib. bdg. 32.79 *(978-1-61783-727-2(X))* ABDO Publishing Co.
Heppermann, Christine. Samurai. 2013. (Great Warriors EBook Ser.). (ENG., Illus.). 48p. (J). pap. 15.64 *(978-1-61783-777-7(6)*, Core Library) ABDO Publishing Co.
Hubbard, Ben. Samurai Warriors. 2016. (Conquerors & Combatants Ser.). 224p. (YA). lib. bdg. 55.00 *(978-1-5026-2459-8(1))* Cavendish Square Publishing.
Lee, Adrienne. Samurai, 1 vol. Martin, Cynthia, illus. 2013. (Legendary Warriors Ser.). (ENG.). 32p. (gr. 1-2). 26.65 *(978-1-4765-3113-7(7)*, Blazers) Capstone Press of Coughlan Cos.
Lüsted, Marcia Amidon. Samurai Science: Armor, Weapons, & Battlefield Strategy. 2016. (Warrior Science Ser.). (ENG., Illus.). 32p. (gr. 3-4). 27.99 *(978-1-4914-8124-0(2))* Capstone Press of Coughlan Cos.
Macdonald, Fiona. Do You Want to Be a Samurai Warrior? 2015. (Do You Want to Be... Ser.). (Illus.). 32p. (gr. 3-6). 28.50 *(978-1-909645-39-4(7))* Book Hse. GBR. Dist: Black Rabbit Bks.
MacDonald, Fiona. How to Be a Samurai Warrior. James, John, illus. 2005. (How to Be Ser.). (ENG.). 32p. (J). (gr. 3-7). lib. bdg. 21.90 *(978-0-7922-3633-7(5)*, National Geographic Children's Bks.) National Geographic Society.
Macdonald, Fiona. You Wouldn't Want to Be a Samurai! A Deadly Career You'd Rather Not Pursue. Antram, David, illus. 2009. (You Wouldn't Want to Ser.). (ENG.). 32p. (J). 29.00 *(978-0-531-21325-4(0))*; (gr. 3-18). pap. 9.95 *(978-0-531-20516-7(9))* Scholastic Library Publishing.
MacDonald, Fiona & Donnelly, S. E. How to Be a Samurai Warrior. James, John, illus. 2005. (How to Be Ser.). (ENG.). 32p. (J). (gr. 3-7). 14.95 *(978-0-7922-3618-4(1)*, National Geographic Children's Bks.) National Geographic Society.
Main Idea & Details Spanish Version, Gr. 1-3. 2005. (Spanish Version Ser.). (J). per. *(978-1-58232-147-9(7))* ECS Learning Systems, Inc.
Malam, John. Samurai. 2013. (Illus.). 48p. (J). *(978-1-4351-5097-3(X))* Barnes & Noble, Inc.
—Samurai. 2010. (Remarkable Man & Beast Ser.). (Illus.). 48p. (J). (gr. 3-18). lib. bdg. 19.95 *(978-1-4222-1973-7(9))* Mason Crest.
Matthews, Rupert. Samurai. 2015. (History's Fearless Fighters Ser.). (ENG., Illus.). 48p. (J). (gr. 5-6). pap. 14.05 *(978-1-4824-3177-3(7))* Stevens, Gareth Publishing LLLP.
McLeese, Don. Samurai. 2009. 32p. pap. 7.99 *(978-0-8249-1444-8(9)*, Ideal Pubns.) Worthy Publishing.
Murrell, Deborah Jane & Dennis, Peter. Samurai. 2012. (Illus.). 32p. (gr. 3-5). pap. 8.95 *(978-1-926853-55-0(5))* Saunders Bk. Co. CAN. Dist: RiverStream Publishing.
Ollhoff, Jim. Samurai, 1 vol. 2008. (World of Martial Arts Ser.). (ENG.). 32p. (gr. 4-8). 27.07 *(978-1-59928-983-0(0)*, Abdo & Daughters) ABDO Publishing Co.
Osborne, Mary Pope & Boyce, Natalie Pope. Ninjas & Samurai: A Nonfiction Companion to Magic Tree House #5: Night of the Ninjas. Murdocca, Sal, illus. 2014. (Magic Tree House - Fact Tracker Ser.: 30). (ENG.). 128p. (J). (gr. 2-5). 6.99 *(978-0-385-38632-6(X)*, Random Hse. Bks. for Young Readers) Random Hse. Children's Bks.
—Ninjas & Samurai: A Nonfiction Companion to Magic Tree House #5: Night of the Ninjas. 2014. (Magic Tree House Fact Tracker Ser.: 30). lib. bdg. 16.00 *(978-0-606-36017-3(4))* Turtleback Bks.
Park, Louise & Love, Timothy. The Japanese Samurai. 2009. (Ancient & Medieval People Ser.). 32p. (gr. 5). 28.50 *(978-0-7614-4448-0(3))* Marshall Cavendish Corp.
Riggs, Kate. Great Warriors - Samurai. 2011. (Great Warriors Ser.). (ENG.). 24p. (J). (gr. 1-3). pap. 9.99 *(978-0-89812-574-0(X)*, Creative Paperbacks) Creative Co., The.
—Samurai. 2011. (Great Warriors Ser.). 24p. (J). (gr. k-2). 16.95 *(978-1-60818-003-5(4)*, Creative Education) Creative Co., The.
Sepahban, Lois. Samurai Warriors. 2015. (Ancient Warriors Ser.). (ENG.). 32p. (J). (gr. 2-5). 28.50 *(978-1-63143-759-5(3)*, 208591) Child's World, Inc., The.
Turnbull, Stephen R. The Most Daring Raid of the Samurai. 2011. (Most Daring Raids in History Ser.). (Illus.). 64p. (YA). (gr. 7-12). lib. bdg. 31.95 *(978-1-4488-1872-3(9))* Rosen Publishing Group, Inc., The.

SAMURAI—FICTION

Bradford, Chris. The Ring of Earth. 4th ed. 2010. (Young Samurai Ser.: 4). (ENG., Illus.). 336p. (YA). (gr. 7). pap. 8.99 *(978-0-14-133253-6(0)*, Penguin Global) Penguin Publishing Group.
—The Ring of Fire. 6th ed. 2011. (Young Samurai Ser.: 6). (ENG., Illus.). 352p. (YA). (gr. 7). pap. 10.95 *(978-0-14-133255-0(7))* Penguin Bks., Ltd. GBR. Dist: Independent Pubs. Group.
—The Ring of Sky. 8th ed. 2012. (Young Samurai Ser.: 8). (ENG., Illus.). 384p. (YA). (gr. 7). pap. 10.95 *(978-0-14-133972-6(1))* Penguin Bks., Ltd. GBR. Dist: Independent Pubs. Group.
—The Ring of Water. 5th ed. 2011. (Young Samurai Ser.: 5). (ENG., Illus.). 320p. (YA). (gr. 7). pap. 8.99 *(978-0-14-133254-3(9))* Penguin Bks., Ltd. GBR. Dist: Independent Pubs. Group.
—The Ring of Wind. 7th ed. 2012. (Young Samurai Ser.: 7). (ENG., Illus.). 368p. (YA). (gr. 7). 8.99 *(978-0-14-133971-9(3)*, Penguin Global) Penguin Publishing Group.
—The Way of the Warrior, Bk. 1. 2008. (Young Samurai Ser.: 1). (ENG., Illus.). 352p. (J). (gr. 6-10). pap. 12.99 ***(978-0-14-132430-2(9))*** Penguin Bks., Ltd. GBR. Dist: Independent Pubs. Group.
—Young Samurai the Way of the Dragon. l.t. ed. 2012. (Young Samurai Ser.). (ENG.). 644p. (J). (gr. 9-12). 23.99 *(978-1-4104-4466-0(X))* Thorndike Pr.
—Young Samurai: the Way of the Sword. 2011. 448p. pap. 7.99 *(978-1-4231-2937-0(7))* Hyperion Pr.
—Young Samurai the Way of the Sword. l.t. ed. 2012. (Young Samurai Ser.). (ENG.). 547p. (J). (gr. 6-9). 23.99 *(978-1-4104-4404-2(X))* Thorndike Pr.
Crilley, Mark. Brody's Ghost Volume 6. Crilley, Mark, illus. 2015. (ENG., Illus.). 112p. pap. 7.99 *(978-1-61655-461-3(4))* Dark Horse Comics.
Duey, Kathleen. Samurai, 6 vols. 2006. (Time Soldiers Ser.: Bk. 6). (ENG., Illus.). 96p. (J). (gr. k-2). per. 5.95 *(978-1-929945-63-4(9))* Big Guy Bks., Inc.
—Samurai. Epstein, Eugene, illus. l.t. ed. 2006. (Time Soldiers Ser.: Bk. 6). (ENG.). 48p. (J). (gr. k-2). 15.95 *(978-1-929945-62-7(0))* Big Guy Bks., Inc.
—Samurai. Epstein, Eugene, illus. Gould, Robert, photos by. 2007. (Time Soldiers Ser.). (ENG.). 96p. (gr. k-2). 24.21 *(978-1-59961-229-4(1))* Spotlight.
Falk, Nick. The Curse of the Oni. Flowers, Tony, illus. 2016. (Samurai vs Ninja Ser.: 4). (ENG.). 96p. (J). (gr. 1-3). pap. 7.99 *(978-0-85798-640-5(6))* Random Hse. Australia AUS. Dist: Independent Pubs. Group.
—The Day of the Undead. Flowers, Tony, illus. 2016. (Samurai vs Ninja Ser.: 3). (ENG.). 96p. (J). (gr. 1-3). pap. 7.99 *(978-0-85798-638-2(4))* Random Hse. Australia AUS. Dist: Independent Pubs. Group.
Fanning, Kieran. The Black Lotus: The Samurai Wars. 2016. (ENG.). 304p. (J). (gr. 3-7). 16.99 *(978-0-545-94028-3(1)*, Chicken Hse., The) Scholastic, Inc.
Fussell, Sandy. Owl Ninja. James, Rhian Nest, illus. 2011. (Samurai Kids Ser.: 2). (ENG.). 272p. (J). (gr. 4-7). 15.99 *(978-0-7636-5003-2(X))* Candlewick Pr.
—Samurai Kids #4: Monkey Fist. James, Rhian Nest, illus. 2012. (Samurai Kids Ser.: 4). (ENG.). 272p. (J). (gr. 4-7). pap. 6.99 *(978-0-7636-5827-4(8))* Candlewick Pr.
—Shaolin Tiger. James, Rhian Nest, illus. 2011. (Samurai Kids Ser.: 3). (ENG.). 272p. (J). (gr. 4-7). pap. 6.99 *(978-0-7636-5702-4(6))* Candlewick Pr.
—White Crane. James, Rhian Nest, illus. 2010. (Samurai Kids Ser.: 1). (ENG.). 256p. (J). (gr. 4-7). 15.99 *(978-0-7636-4503-8(6))* Candlewick Pr.
Gerstein, Mordicai, illus. Three Samurai Cats: A Story from Japan. 2004. (ENG.). 32p. (J). (gr. k-3). 6.95 *(978-0-8234-1877-0(4))* Holiday Hse., Inc.
Gibsen, Cole. Katana. 2012. (Katana Novel Ser.: 1). (ENG.). 384p. (YA). pap. 9.95 *(978-0-7387-3040-0(8)*, Flux) North Star Editions.
—Senshi. 2013. (Katana Novel Ser.: 2). (ENG.). 384p. (YA). pap. 9.99 *(978-0-7387-3261-9(3)*, Flux) North Star Editions.
—Shinobi. 2014. (Katana Novel Ser.: 3). (ENG.). 288p. (YA). pap. 9.99 *(978-0-7387-3911-3(1)*, Flux) North Star Editions.
Goto, Scott. Perfect Sword. Goto, Scott, illus. 2010. (ENG., Illus.). 48p. (J). (gr. 1-4). pap. 8.95 *(978-1-57091-698-4(5))* Charlesbridge Publishing, Inc.
Gratz, Alan. Samurai Shortstop. 2008. (ENG.). 288p. (YA). (gr. 7-18). 7.99 *(978-0-14-241099-8(3)*, Speak) Penguin Young Readers Group.
Haibara, Yak & Haibara, Yak. Sengoku Basara: Samurai Legends Volume 2: Samurai Legends Volume 2, 2 vols. 2013. (ENG., Illus.). 424p. (YA). pap. 19.99 *(978-1-926778-59-4(6)*, 9781926778594) UDON Entertainment Corp. CAN. Dist: Diamond Comic Distributors, Inc.
Haugaard, Erik Christian & Haugaard, Erik C. The Revenge of the Forty-Seven Samurai. 2005. (ENG.). 240p. (J). (gr. 5-7). pap. 14.95 *(978-0-618-54896-5(3))* Houghton Mifflin Harcourt Publishing Co.
—The Samurai's Tale. 2005. (ENG.). 256p. (J). (gr. 5-7). pap. 7.99 *(978-0-618-61512-4(1))* Houghton Mifflin Harcourt Publishing Co.
Hoobler, Dorothy & Hoobler, Thomas. The Demon in the Teahouse. 2005. 181p. (J). (gr. 4-7). 13.65 *(978-0-7569-6725-3(2))* Perfection Learning Corp.
—The Ghost in the Tokaido Inn. 2005. (ENG.). 240p. (J). (gr. 3-7). 6.99 *(978-0-14-240541-3(8)*, Puffin Books) Penguin Young Readers Group.
—The Ghost in the Tokaido Inn. 2005. 214p. (J). (gr. 4-7). 14.65 *(978-0-7569-6403-0(2))* Perfection Learning Corp.
—In Darkness, Death. 2005. (Puffin Sleuth Novels Ser.). 195p. (J). (gr. 5-9). 14.65 *(978-0-7569-5457-4(6))* Perfection Learning Corp.
—Seven Paths to Death. 2009. (ENG.). 208p. (YA). (gr. 7-7). 7.99 *(978-0-14-241466-8(2)*, Puffin Books) Penguin Young Readers Group.
—The Sword That Cut the Burning Grass. 2006. 211p. (gr. 5-9). 17.00 *(978-0-7569-6907-3(7))* Perfection Learning Corp.
Hulme-Cross, Benjamin. The Samurai's Assassin. Rinaldi, Angelo, illus. 2015. (ENG.). 160p. (J). *(978-0-7787-1766-9(6))* Crabtree Publishing Co.
Martin, Benjamin. Revenge of the Akuma Clan: (Samurai Awakening Book 2) 2016. (ENG.). 320p. (J). (gr. 7-12). 8.99 *(978-0-8048-4738-4(X))* Tuttle Publishing.
—Samurai Awakening. 2012. (ENG.). 320p. (J). (gr. 7-12). 17.99 *(978-4-8053-1228-5(9))* Tuttle Publishing.
—Samurai Awakening: (Samurai Awakening Book 1) 2016. (ENG.). 320p. (J). (gr. 7-12). 8.99 *(978-0-8048-4737-7(1))* Tuttle Publishing.
Namioka, Lensey. Valley of the Broken Cherry Trees. 2005. (ENG.). 1p. pap. 7.95 *(978-0-8048-3610-4(8))* Tuttle Publishing.
Orlean, Susan & Bradford, Chris. Young Samurai the Way of the Warrior. l.t. ed. 2011. (Young Samurai Ser.). (ENG.). 628p. (J). 23.99 *(978-1-4104-4329-8(9))* Thorndike Pr.
Phillips, Dee. Samurai: The Story of a Warrior. 2015. (Yesterday's Voices Ser.). (YA). lib. bdg. 19.60 *(978-0-606-36675-5(X))* Turtleback Bks.
Preus, Margi. The Bamboo Sword. 2015. (ENG., Illus.). 352p. (YA). (gr. 5-9). 16.95 *(978-1-4197-0807-7(4)*, Amulet Bks.) Abrams, Inc.
Richard, Laurent. The Championship! Gauvin, Edward, tr. Ryser, Nicolas, illus. 2014. (ENG.). 64p. (J). (gr. 2-5). pap. 6.95 *(978-1-4677-4459-1(X))*; (Tao, the Little Samurai Ser.: 4). lib. bdg. 29.27 *(978-1-4677-2097-7(6))* Lerner Publishing Group. (Graphic Universe™).
—Clowns & Dragons! Gauvin, Edward, tr. from FRE. Ryser, Nicolas, illus. 2014. (Tao, the Little Samurai Ser.: 3). (ENG.). 56p. (J). (gr. 2-5). lib. bdg. 29.27 *(978-1-4677-2096-0(8)*, Graphic Universe™) Lerner Publishing Group.
—Ninjas & Knock Outs! Gauvin, Edward, tr. from FRE. Ryser, Nicolas, illus. 2014. (Tao, the Little Samurai Ser.: 2). (ENG.). 64p. (J). (gr. 2-5). lib. bdg. 29.27 *(978-1-4677-3272-7(9)*, Graphic Universe™) Lerner Publishing Group.
—Pranks & Attacks! Gauvin, Edward, tr. from FRE. Ryser, Nicolas, illus. 2014. (Tao, the Little Samurai Ser.: 1). (ENG.). 64p. (J). (gr. 2-5). lib. bdg. 29.27 *(978-1-4677-2095-3(X)*, Graphic Universe™) Lerner Publishing Group.
—Wild Animals! Gauvin, Edward, tr. from FRE. Ryser, Nicolas, illus. 2014. (Tao, the Little Samurai Ser.: 5). (ENG.). 64p. (J). (gr. 2-5). lib. bdg. 29.27 *(978-1-4677-2098-4(4)*, Graphic Universe™) Lerner Publishing Group.
Sakai, Stan. Usagi Yojimbo Vol. 3: Al Filo de la Vida y la Muerte. 2007. (SPA., Illus.). 200p. reprint ed. pap. 15.95 *(978-1-59497-319-2(9))* Public Square Bks.
—Usagi Yojimbo Vol. 4: Estaciones. 2007. (SPA., Illus.). 200p. reprint ed. pap. 15.95 *(978-1-59497-320-8(2))* Public Square Bks.
—Usagi Yojimbo Vol. 5: Segadora. 2007. (SPA., Illus.). 256p. reprint ed. pap. 17.95 *(978-1-59497-321-5(0))* Public Square Bks.
—Usagi Yojimbo Vol. 6: Primeras Andanzas. 2007. (SPA., Illus.). 128p. reprint ed. pap. 12.95 *(978-1-59497-322-2(9))* Public Square Bks.
—Usagi Yojimbo Vol. 7: Samurai (en Español) 2007. (SPA., Illus.). 144p. reprint ed. pap. 14.95 *(978-1-59497-323-9(7))* Public Square Bks.
—The Usagi Yojimbo Saga, Vol. 2, Bk. 2. 2015. (ENG., Illus.). 672p. pap. 24.99 *(978-1-61655-610-5(2))* Dark Horse Comics.
—Usagi Yojimbo Saga Volume 3. Sakai, Stan, illus. 2015. (ENG., Illus.). 616p. pap. 24.99 *(978-1-61655-611-2(0))* Dark Horse Comics.
—Usagi Yojimbo Saga Volume 3 Ltd. Ed. Sakai, Stan, illus. 2015. (ENG., Illus.). 618p. 79.99 *(978-1-61655-673-0(0))* Dark Horse Comics.
Samurai. (Awesome Adventures Ser.). 16p. (J). *(978-2-7643-0167-8(7))* Phidal Publishing, Inc./Editions Phidal, Inc.

S

Sazaklis, John & Foxe, Steve. Drift's Samurai Showdown. 2015. (J). *(978-0-316-30190-9(6))* Little Brown & Co.

Scieszka, Jon. Ay, Samuray!Tr. of Sam Samurai. (SPA.). (J). 7.95 *(978-958-04-6867-7(2))* Norma S.A. COL. Dist: Distribuidora Norma, Inc.

—Sam Samurai. McCauley, Adam, illus. 2004. (Time Warp Trio Ser.: 10). (ENG.). 96p. (J). (gr. 2-4). pap. 5.99 *(978-0-14-240088-3(2),* Puffin Books) Penguin Young Readers Group.

—Sam Samurai. McCauley, Adam, illus. 2006. (Time Warp Trio Ser.: No. 10). 85p. (gr. 4-7). 15.00 *(978-0-7569-6779-6(1))* Perfection Learning Corp.

Snow, Maya. Blade's Edge. 2009. 245p. (J). lib. bdg. 17.89 *(978-0-06-124391-2(4))* HarperCollins Pubs.

—Chasing the Secret. 2010. (Sisters of the Sword Ser.: 2). (ENG.). 272p. (J). (gr. 5). pap. 6.99 *(978-0-06-124392-9(2))* HarperCollins Pubs.

—Sisters of the Sword. 2008. (Sisters of the Sword Ser.). (J). (gr. 5-18). 288p. 16.99 *(978-0-06-124387-5(6))*; 275p. lib. bdg. 17.89 *(978-0-06-124388-2(4))* HarperCollins Pubs.

Stilton, Geronimo. The Way of the Samurai. 2012. (Geronimo Stilton Ser.: No. 49). (ENG.). 128p. (J). (gr. 2-5). pap. 7.99 *(978-0-545-34101-1(9),* Scholastic Paperbacks) Scholastic, Inc.

—The Way of the Samurai. 2012. (Geronimo Stilton Ser.: 49). lib. bdg. 18.40 *(978-0-606-26094-7(3),* Turtleback) Turtleback Bks.

Tsunetomo, Yamamoto & Wilson, William Scott. Hagakure: The Code of the Samurai, 1 vol. Kutsuwada, Chie, illus. 2011. (ENG.). 144p. pap. 14.95 *(978-4-7700-3120-4(3))* Kodansha America, Inc.

SAN (AFRICAN PEOPLE)

Banting, Erinn. Galapagos Islands. 2012. (J). *(978-1-61913-523-9(X))*; pap. *(978-1-61913-436-2(5))* Weigl Pubs., Inc.

Watson, Galadriel. Bushmen of Southern Africa with Code. 2012. (World Cultures Ser.). (ENG., Illus.). 32p. (J). (gr. 4-7). pap. 13.95 *(978-1-61913-529-1(9),* AV2 by Weigl) Weigl Pubs., Inc.

Watson, Galadriel Findlay. Bushmen of Southern Africa. (J). 2012. *(978-1-61913-094-4(7))* 2005. (Illus.). 32p. (gr. 4-8). lib. bdg. 26.00 *(978-1-59036-222-8(5))* Weigl Pubs., Inc.

SAN ANTONIO (TEX.)

Fradin, Dennis Brindell. The Alamo. 2006. (Turning Points in U. S. History Ser.). (Illus.). 46p. (J). (gr. 3-7). lib. bdg. 29.93 *(978-0-7614-2127-6(0),* Benchmark Bks.) Marshall Cavendish Corp.

Keller, Susanna & Levy, Janey. A Primary Source Investigation of the Alamo. 2015. (Uncovering American History Ser.). (ENG., Illus.). 64p. (J). (gr. 5-6). 32.95 *(978-1-4994-3507-8(X),* Rosen Central) Rosen Publishing Group, Inc., The.

McReynolds, Stacy. San Antonio Zoo. 2003. (Great Zoos of the United States Ser.). (Illus.). 24p. (J). lib. bdg. 22.60 *(978-0-8239-6319-5(5),* PowerKids Pr.) Rosen Publishing Group, Inc., The.

Puck. 123 San Antonio: A Cool Counting Book. 2013. (Cool Counting Bks.). (ENG.). 22p. (J). (— 1). bds. 8.95 *(978-1-938093-17-3(8))* Duo Pr. LLC.

San Antonio: the River City: Third Grade Guided Reading Level O. (On Our Way to English Ser.). (gr. 3-18). 34.50 *(978-0-7578-7144-3(5))* Rigby Education.

SAN ANTONIO (TEX.)—FICTION

Casad, Mary Brooke. Bluebonnet at the Alamo, 1 vol. Vincent, Benjamin, illus. 2013. (ENG.). 32p. (J). (gr. k-3). 16.99 *(978-1-4556-1806-4(3))* Pelican Publishing Co., Inc.

Flor Ada, Alma. Quiero Ayudar! Dominguez, Angela, illus. 2010.Tr. of Let Me Help! (ENG & SPA.). 32p. (J). (gr. -1-3). 16.95 *(978-0-89239-232-2(0))* Lee & Low Bks., Inc.

In the City of San Antonio: Lap Book. (Pebble Soup Explorations Ser.). 16p. (gr. -1-18). 21.00 *(978-0-7578-1659-8(2))* Rigby Education.

In the City of San Antonio: Small Book. (Pebble Soup Explorations Ser.). 16p. (gr. -1-18). 5.00 *(978-0-7578-1699-4(1))* Rigby Education.

López, Diana. Ask My Mood Ring How I Feel. 2013. (ENG.). 336p. (J). (gr. 3-7). 17.00 *(978-0-316-20996-0(1))* Little Brown & Co.

Milligan, Bryce. Comanche Captive. 2005. (Illus.). 168p. (YA). (gr. 7). per. *(978-1-57168-849-1(8))* Eakin Pr.

Perelstein, Jennifer. Who Moved the Masterpieces? A Visit to the Mcnay Art Museum. 2010. 30p. pap. 15.99 *(978-1-60844-585-1(2))* Dog Ear Publishing, LLC.

Smallman, Steve. Santa Is Coming to San Antonio. Dunn, Robert, illus. 2015. (ENG.). 32p. (J). (-3). 9.99 *(978-1-4926-2632-9(5),* Sourcebooks Jabberwocky) Sourcebooks, Inc.

Villareal, Ray. Body Slammed! 2012. (YA). pap. 11.95 *(978-1-55885-749-0(4),* Piñata Books) Arte Publico Pr.

SAN ANTONIO (TEX.)—HISTORY

Boehm Jerome, Kate. San Antonio & the State of Texas: Cool Stuff Every Kid Should Know. 2011. (Arcadia Kids Ser.). (ENG., Illus.). 48p. (J). (gr. 3-6). pap. 9.99 *(978-1-4396-0089-4(9))* Arcadia Publishing.

Collard, Sneed B., III. David Crockett: Fearless Frontiersman. 2006. (American Heroes Ser.). (Illus.). 40p. (J). (gr. 3-7). lib. bdg. 28.50 *(978-0-7614-2160-3(2),* Benchmark Bks.) Marshall Cavendish Corp.

Espinosa, Rod. The Battle of the Alamo, 1 vol. Espinosa, Rod, illus. 2007. (Graphic History Ser.). (ENG., Illus.). 32p. (gr. 3-7). 28.50 *(978-1-60270-073-4(7),* Graphic Planet-Nonfiction) ABDO Publishing Co.

Gibson, Karen. San Antonio. 2009. (Class Trip Ser.). (Illus.). 48p. (J). (gr. 2-5). lib. bdg. 29.95 *(978-1-58415-811-0(5))* Mitchell Lane Pubs., Inc.

Koestler-Grack, Rachel A. Daily Life in a Southwestern Settlement: San Antonio. 2003. (J). *(978-1-58417-012-9(3))*; pap. *(978-1-58417-075-4(1))* Lake Street Pubs.

SAN DIEGO CHARGERS (FOOTBALL TEAM)

Burgess, Zack. Meet the San Diego Chargers. 2016. (Big Picture Sports Ser.). (ENG., Illus.). 24p. (J). (gr. k-3). lib. bdg. 22.60 *(978-1-59953-729-0(X))* Norwood Hse. Pr.

Epstein, Brad M. San Diego Chargers 101. 2010. (ENG., Illus.). 24p. (J). bds. *(978-1-60730-126-4(1),* 101 Bk.) Michaelson Entertainment.

Howell, Brian. San Diego Chargers. 2015. (Insider's Guide to Pro Football Ser.). (ENG.). 32p. (J). (gr. k-3). 28.50 *(978-1-63407-002-7(X),* 208837) Child's World, Inc., The.

Kimmich, Ian. Antonio Gates. 2009. (Superstars of Pro Football Ser.). (Illus.). 64p. (YA). (gr. 7-12). lib. bdg. 22.95 *(978-1-4222-0553-2(3))* Mason Crest.

Omoth, Tyler. The Story of the San Diego Chargers. 2009. (NFL Today Ser.). (Illus.). 48p. (YA). (gr. 5-9). 22.95 *(978-1-58341-769-0(9))* Creative Co., The.

Schmalzbauer, Adam. The History of the San Diego Chargers. 2004. (NFL Today Ser.). (Illus.). 32p. (YA). (gr. 5-9). 18.95 *(978-1-58341-312-8(X))* Creative Co., The.

Stewart, Mark. The San Diego Chargers. rev. ed. 2012. (Team Spirit Ser.). (ENG.). 48p. (J). (gr. 3-6). lib. bdg. 29.27 *(978-1-59953-537-1(8))* Norwood Hse. Pr.

Whiting, Jim. NFL Today: San Diego Chargers. 2013. (NFL Today Ser.). (ENG.). 48p. (J). (gr. 4-7). pap. 12.00 *(978-0-89812-871-0(4),* Creative Paperbacks) Creative Co., The.

—The Story of the San Diego Chargers. 2013. (J). 35.65 *(978-1-60818-318-0(1),* Creative Education) Creative Co., The.

Wilson, Bernie. San Diego Chargers, 1 vol. 2010. (Inside the NFL Ser.). (ENG.). 48p. (YA). (gr. 3-6). lib. bdg. 32.79 *(978-1-61714-026-6(0))* ABDO Publishing Co.

Wyner, Zach. San Diego Chargers. (Illus.). 32p. 2015. pap. *(978-1-4896-0883-3(4))* 2014. (ENG.). (J). (gr. 4-7). lib. bdg. 28.55 *(978-1-4896-0882-6(6),* AV2 by Weigl) Weigl Pubs., Inc.

SAN DIEGO PADRES (BASEBALL TEAM)

Goodman, Michael E. The Story of the San Diego Padres. 2011. (J). 35.65 *(978-1-60818-054-7(9),* Creative Education) Creative Co., The.

Hawkes, Brian. The Story of the San Diego Padres. 2007. (Baseball, the Great American Game Ser.). (Illus.). 48p. (YA). (gr. 4-7). lib. bdg. 32.80 *(978-1-58341-552-8(1))* Creative Co., The.

Stewart, Mark. The San Diego Padres. 2012. (Team Spirit Ser.). 48p. (J). (gr. 3-6). lib. bdg. 29.27 *(978-1-59953-495-4(9))* Norwood Hse. Pr.

Wilson, Bernie. San Diego Padres, 1 vol. (Inside MLB Ser.). (ENG., Illus.). 48p. (gr. 3-6). 2011. (YA). lib. bdg. 32.79 *(978-1-61714-057-0(0))* 2014. (J). lib. bdg. 32.79 *(978-1-62403-483-1(7),* SportsZone) ABDO Publishing Co.

SAN FRANCISCO (CALIF.)

Gamble, Adam. Good Night San Francisco. Cohen, Santiago, illus. 2006. (Good Night Our World Ser.). (ENG.). 22p. (J). (gr. k — 1). bds. 9.95 *(978-0-9777979-5-0(3))* Good Night Bks.

Hanson, Anders. Let's Go by Cable Car, 1 vol. Craig, Diane, ed. 2008. (Let's Go Ser.). (ENG., Illus.). 24p. (J). (gr. k-3). lib. bdg. 24.21 *(978-1-59928-896-3(6),* SandCastle) ABDO Publishing Co.

Hollander, Barbara Gottfried. Harvey Milk: The First Openly Gay Elected Official in the United States. 2017. (J). ***(978-1-5383-8093-2(5),*** Rosen Young Adult) Rosen Publishing Group, Inc., The.

Luiso, Lisa. What Daddy Sees in San Francisco. 2007. (Illus.). 30p. (J). lib. bdg. 19.95 *(978-1-933732-37-4(7))* Big Ransom Studio.

—What Mommy Sees in San Francisco. abr. ed. 2007. (J). lib. bdg. 19.95 *(978-1-933732-28-2(8))* Big Ransom Studio.

Mackay, Stephanie, illus. San Francisco Monsters. 2017. (ENG.). 22p. (J). (gr. -1). bds. 9.99 ***(978-2-924734-03-2(7))*** City Monsters Bks. CAN. Dist: Publishers Group West (PGW).

Puck. 123 San Francisco. Somers, Kevin, illus. 2009. (Cool Counting Bks.). (ENG.). 22p. (J). (gr. k — 1). bds. 8.95 *(978-0-9796213-8-3(0))* Duo Pr. LLC.

Sasek, Miroslav. This Is San Francisco. 2003. (This Is ... Ser.). (ENG., Illus.). 64p. (J). (gr. 2-12). 17.95 *(978-0-7893-0962-4(9))* Universe Publishing.

Segal, Robin. ABC in San Francisco. 2008. (All 'Bout Cities Ser.). (ENG.). 32p. (J). (gr. -1-k). *(978-0-9719697-9-7(5))* Murray Hill Bks., LLC.

Skewes, John & Mullin, Michael. Larry Gets Lost in San Francisco. Skewes, John, illus. 2009. (Larry Gets Lost Ser.). (ENG., Illus.). 32p. (J). (gr. -1-2). 17.99 *(978-1-57061-567-2(5),* Little Bigfoot) Sasquatch Bks.

Stanborough, Rebecca. Golden Gate Bridge. 2016. (Engineering Wonders Ser.). (ENG., Illus.). 32p. (gr. 3-4). lib. bdg. 27.32 *(978-1-4914-8196-7(X),* Fact Finders) Capstone Press of Coughlan Cos.

Trounce, Charlotte. San Francisco: A 3D Keepsake Cityscape. Trounce, Charlotte, illus. 2013. (Panorama Pops Ser.). (ENG., Illus.). 30p. (J). (gr. k-4). 8.99 *(978-0-7636-6471-8(5))* Candlewick Pr.

Turner, Barbara. A Day in San Francisco, Vol. 1. l.t. ed. 2003. (Illus.). 32p. (J). per. 14.95 *(978-0-9747019-0-5(4))* Turner, Barbara.

Wearing, Judy, et al. Golden Gate Bridge. 2014. (Illus.). 24p. (J). *(978-1-62127-463-6(2))* Weigl Pubs., Inc.

Weintraub, Aileen. Alcatraz Island Light: The West Coast's First Lighthouse. 2003. (Great Lighthouses of North America Ser.). (Illus.). 24p. (YA). (gr. 3-6). 22.60 *(978-0-8239-6171-9(0))* Rosen Publishing Group, Inc., The.

Wyner, Zach. Golden State Warriors. 2014. (On the Hardwood Ser.). (gr. 3-8). pap. 8.95 *(978-1-61570-913-7(4))* Scobre Pr. Corp.

Zschock, Martha Day. Journey Around San Francisco from A to Z. 2003. (Journeys Ser.). (Illus.). 32p. (J). (gr. 1-6). 17.95 *(978-1-889833-49-1(5),* Commonwealth Editions) Applewood Bks.

SAN FRANCISCO (CALIF.)—BRIDGES

Ashley, Susan. The Golden Gate Bridge. 2004. (Weekly Reader Early Learning Library). (Illus.). 24p. (J). (gr. 1-4). lib. bdg. 22.00 *(978-0-8368-4140-4(9),* 1228634, Weekly Reader Leveled Readers) Stevens, Gareth Publishing LLLP.

Eggers, Dave. This Bridge Will Not Be Gray. Nichols, Tucker, illus. 2015. (ENG.). 104p. (gr. -1). 19.95 *(978-1-940450-47-6(0))* McSweeney's Publishing.

Wearing, Judy. Golden Gate Bridge. 2009. (Structural Wonders Ser.). (Illus.). 32p. (J). (gr. 4-6). lib. bdg. 26.00 *(978-1-60596-136-1(1))* Weigl Pubs., Inc.

Wearing, Judy & Riddolls, Tom. Golden Gate Bridge. 2009. (Structural Wonders Ser.). (Illus.). 32p. (J). (gr. 4-6). 10.95 *(978-1-60596-137-8(X))* Weigl Pubs., Inc.

Zuehlke, Jeffrey. The Golden Gate Bridge. 2009. (Lightning Bolt Books (tm) — Famous Places Ser.). (ENG., Illus.). 32p. (J). (gr. k-2). 26.60 *(978-0-8225-9407-9(2),* 1299390, Lerner Pubns.) Lerner Publishing Group.

SAN FRANCISCO (CALIF.)—EARTHQUAKE AND FIRE, 1906

see San Francisco Earthquake and Fire, Calif., 1906

SAN FRANCISCO (CALIF.)—FICTION

Allen, Skye. The Songbird Thief. 2016. (Oaktown Fey Ser.). (ENG., Illus.). (YA). pap. 14.99 ***(978-1-63477-003-3(X),*** Harmony Ink Pr.) Dreamspinner Pr.

Allison, Jennifer. Gilda Joyce, Psychic Investigator. 2006. (Gilda Joyce Ser.). (ENG.). 336p. (J). (gr. 5-18). reprint ed. 8.99 *(978-0-14-240698-4(8),* Puffin Books) Penguin Young Readers Group.

Argueta, Jorge. Xochitl & the Flowers. Angel, Carl, illus. 2013. (ENG.). 32p. (J). (gr. k). pap. 9.95 *(978-0-89239-224-7(X))* Lee & Low Bks., Inc.

—Xochitl & the Flowers (Xochitl, la Nina de Las Flores) Angel, Carl, illus. 2003.Tr. of Xochitl, la Nina de Las Flores. (ENG & SPA.). 32p. (J). 16.95 *(978-0-89239-181-3(2))* Lee & Low Bks., Inc.

Averbeck, Jim. A Hitch at the Fairmont. Bertozzi, Nick, illus. (ENG.). 416p. (J). (gr. 3-7). 2015. pap. 7.99 *(978-1-4424-9448-0(4))* 2014. 16.99 *(978-1-4424-9447-3(6),* Atheneum Bks. for Young Readers) Simon & Schuster Children's Publishing.

Bennett, Jenn. The Anatomical Shape of a Heart. 2015. (ENG.). 304p. (YA). (gr. 7). 17.99 *(978-1-250-06645-9(X),* 9781250066459) Feiwel & Friends.

Bills, Randall N. Detective Mysteries. 2008. 92p. pap. 6.95 *(978-0-9796392-1-0(2))* Adventure Boys Inc.

Birthday Vicious. 2014. (Ashley Project Ser.: 3). (ENG., Illus.). 304p. (J). (gr. 4-8). pap. 7.99 *(978-1-4424-9038-3(1),* Aladdin) Simon & Schuster Children's Publishing.

Bjorkman, Lauren. Miss Fortune Cookie. 2012. (ENG.). 288p. (YA). (gr. 9-13). 16.99 *(978-0-8050-8951-6(9),* Holt, Henry & Co. Bks. For Young Readers) Holt, Henry & Co.

Bliss, Bryan. No Parking at the End Times. 2015. (ENG.). 272p. (YA). (gr. 9). 17.99 *(978-0-06-227541-7(0),* Greenwillow Bks.) HarperCollins Pubs.

Bloncourt, Nelson & Botero, Fernando. Botero: Paintings & Works on Paper. Polyansky, Nikita, illus. 2013. (ENG.). 252p. 125.00 *(978-0-9881745-1-1(0))* Glitterati, Inc.

Braswell, Liz. The Fallen. movie tie-in ed. 2011. (Nine Lives of Chloe King Ser.: 1). (ENG.). 256p. (YA). (gr. 9). pap. 8.99 *(978-1-4424-4134-7(8),* Simon Pulse) Simon Pulse.

Brenner, Summer. Ivy, Homeless in San Francisco. Bowes, Brian, illus. 2nd ed. 2011. (ENG.). 176p. (J). (gr. 4-7). pap. 15.00 *(978-1-60486-317-8(X))* PM Pr.

Brezenoff, Steve. The Crook Who Crossed the Golden Gate Bridge, 1 vol. Canga, C. B., illus. 2010. (Field Trip Mysteries Ser.). (ENG.). 88p. (gr. 2-3). 25.32 *(978-1-4342-2138-4(5))*; pap. 6.10 *(978-1-4342-2770-6(7))* Stone Arch Bks.

Bross, Lanie. Fates. (ENG.). (YA). (gr. 7). 2015. 354p. pap. 9.99 *(978-0-385-74283-2(5),* Ember) 2014. 336p. 17.99 *(978-0-385-74282-5(7),* Delacorte Pr.) Random Hse. Children's Bks.

Brown, Jeff. Escape to California. 2014. (Flat Stanley's Worldwide Adventures Ser.: 12). (J). lib. bdg. 14.75 *(978-0-606-35951-1(6))* Turtleback Bks.

Bruton, Seth. I'm So Cute, You Can't Be Mad. Hicks, Kaylee, illus. 2012. 24p. pap. 13.97 *(978-1-61204-897-0(8),* Strategic Bk. Publishing) Strategic Book Publishing & Rights Agency (SBPRA).

Bullen, Alexandra. Wish. 2010. (ENG.). 336p. (J). (gr. 9). pap. 9.99 *(978-0-545-13906-9(6))* Scholastic, Inc.

Bunting, Eve. Pop's Bridge. Payne, C. F., illus. 2006. (ENG.). 32p. (J). (gr. -1-3). 17.99 *(978-0-15-204773-3(5))* Houghton Mifflin Harcourt Publishing Co.

Buzbee, Lewis. Bridge of Time. 2013. (ENG.). 320p. (J). (gr. 5-9). pap. 14.99 *(978-1-250-02734-4(9),* 9781250027344) Square Fish.

Carson, John & Carson, Marlene. Ramblin' Rose: The Chinese Fortune Cookie. 2008. 291p. pap. 8.99 *(978-0-9800034-1-3(5))* BBM Bks.

Chambliss Bertman, Jennifer. Book Scavenger. 2015. (Book Scavenger Ser.). (ENG., Illus.). 368p. (J). (gr. 4-9). 16.99 *(978-1-62779-115-1(9),* 9781627791151, Holt, Henry & Co. Bks. For Young Readers) Holt, Henry & Co.

—Book Scavenger. 2016. (Book Scavenger Ser.). (ENG.). 368p. (J). pap. 7.99 *(978-1-250-07980-0(2),* 9781250079800) Square Fish.

—The Unbreakable Code. 2017. (Book Scavenger Ser.). (ENG., Illus.). 368p. (J). 16.99 *(978-1-62779-116-8(7),* 9781627791168, Holt, Henry & Co. Bks. For Young Readers) Holt, Henry & Co.

Childs, Tera Lynn. Sweet Legacy. 2013. (Sweet Venom Ser.: 3). (ENG.). 384p. (YA). (gr. 8). 17.99 *(978-0-06-200185-6(X),* Tegen, Katherine Bks) HarperCollins Pubs.

—Sweet Shadows. (Sweet Venom Ser.: 2). (ENG.). (YA). (gr. 8). 2013. 352p. pap. 9.99 *(978-0-06-200184-9(1))* 2012. 336p. 17.99 *(978-0-06-200183-2(3))* HarperCollins Pubs. (Tegen, Katherine Bks).

—Sweet Venom. (Sweet Venom Ser.: 1). (ENG.). (YA). (gr. 8). 2012. 384p. pap. 9.99 *(978-0-06-200182-5(5))* 2011. 352p. 17.99 *(978-0-06-200181-8(7))* HarperCollins Pubs. (Tegen, Katherine Bks).

Choldenko, Gennifer. Chasing Secrets. 2015. (ENG.). 288p. (J). (gr. 4-7). lib. bdg. 19.99 *(978-0-375-99063-2(1),* Lamb, Wendy Bks.) Random Hse. Children's Bks.

—Chasing Secrets. 2016. lib. bdg. 18.40 *(978-0-606-38879-5(6))* Turtleback Bks.

Chronicle Books Staff. San Francisco, Baby! Jenkins, Ward, illus. 2012. (ENG.). 24p. (J). (gr. -1 — 1). 12.99 *(978-1-4521-0620-5(7))* Chronicle Bks. LLC.

Clark, Brenda. Spiro & Zinger Rescue the Orphans: Spiro the Shooting Star - Book Three, 1 vol. 2010. 70p. pap. 19.95 *(978-1-4489-3992-3(5))* America Star Bks.

Craft, Elizabeth. Flavor of the Day. 2013. (@cafe Ser.: 4). (ENG., Illus.). 192p. (YA). (gr. 7). pap. 13.99 *(978-1-4814-2113-3(1),* Simon Pulse) Simon Pulse.

—I'll Have What He's Having. 2013. (@cafe Ser.: 2). (ENG., Illus.). 208p. (YA). (gr. 7). pap. 14.99 *(978-1-4814-2111-9(5),* Simon Pulse) Simon Pulse.

—Love Bytes. 2013. (@cafe Ser.: 1). (ENG., Illus.). 224p. (YA). (gr. 7). pap. 15.99 *(978-1-4814-2110-2(7),* Simon Pulse) Simon Pulse.

—Make Mine to Go. 2013. (@cafe Ser.: 3). (ENG., Illus.). 192p. (YA). (gr. 7). pap. 13.99 *(978-1-4814-2112-6(3),* Simon Pulse) Simon Pulse.

Crowder, Melanie. Three Pennies. 2017. (ENG., Illus.). 192p. (J). (gr. 3-7). 16.99 ***(978-1-4814-7187-9(2),*** Atheneum Bks. for Young Readers) Simon & Schuster Children's Publishing.

De la Cruz, Melissa. The Ashley Project. 2014. (Ashley Project Ser.: 1). (ENG., Illus.). 288p. (J). (gr. 4-8). pap. 6.99 *(978-1-4424-9033-8(0),* Aladdin) Simon & Schuster Children's Publishing.

—Jealous? 2008. (Ashleys Ser.: Bk. 2). (ENG.). 256p. (J). (gr. 4-8). pap. 9.99 *(978-1-4169-3407-3(3),* Simon & Schuster Bks. For Young Readers) Simon & Schuster Bks. For Young Readers.

—Popularity Takeover. 2015. (Ashley Project Ser.: 4). (ENG., Illus.). 272p. (J). (gr. 4-8). 17.99 *(978-1-4814-0974-2(3),* Aladdin) Simon & Schuster Children's Publishing.

Dixon, Franklin W. Comic con Artist. 21st ed. 2008. (Hardy Boys (All New) Undercover Brothers Ser.: 21). (ADY & ENG., Illus.). 192p. (J). (gr. 3-7). pap. 5.99 *(978-1-4169-5498-9(8),* Aladdin) Simon & Schuster Children's Publishing.

Doctorow, Cory. Homeland. (ENG.). (YA). (gr. 8). 2014. 448p. pap. 12.99 *(978-0-7653-3370-4(8),* 9780765333704) 2013. 400p. 17.99 *(978-0-7653-3369-8(4),* 9780765333698) Doherty, Tom Assocs., LLC. (Tor Teen).

—Homeland. 2014. (YA). lib. bdg. 24.50 *(978-0-606-38513-8(4))* Turtleback Bks.

—Little Brother. (ENG.). (YA). (gr. 8-13). 2010. 432p. pap. 12.99 *(978-0-7653-2311-8(7),* 9780765323118) 2008. 384p. 19.99 *(978-0-7653-1985-2(3),* 9780765319852) Doherty, Tom Assocs., LLC. (Tor Teen).

—Little Brother. 2010. (YA). lib. bdg. 24.50 *(978-0-606-14347-9(5),* Turtleback) Turtleback Bks.

Dreher, Ruth. Ralph the Red Engine. 2010. 36p. pap. 15.49 *(978-1-4520-2169-0(4))* AuthorHouse.

Duey, K. & Bale, K. A. Salvados! Terremoto. 2003. (Survival Ser.).Tr. of Survival! Earthquake. (SPA.). (J). pap. 9.95 *(978-0-9715256-5-8(X))* Planeta Publishing Corp.

Duey, Kathleen & Bale, Karen A. Earthquake: San Francisco 1906. 2014. (Survivors Ser.). (ENG., Illus.). 160p. (J). (gr. 3-7). pap. 6.99 *(978-1-4814-0079-4(7),* Aladdin) Simon & Schuster Children's Publishing.

Ee, Susan. Angelfall, 0 vols. 2012. (Penryn & the End of Days Ser.: 1). (ENG.). 288p. (YA). (gr. 9-12). pap. 7.99 *(978-0-7614-6327-6(5),* 9780761463276, Amazon Children's Publishing) Amazon Publishing.

—Angelfall. 2012. 256p. pap. 12.99 *(978-0-9835970-1-8(4))* Dream, Feral LLC.

—World After, 0 vols. 2013. (Penryn & the End of Days Ser.: 2). (ENG.). 320p. (YA). (gr. 9-12). pap. 7.99 *(978-1-4778-1728-5(X),* 9781477817285, Amazon Children's Publishing) Amazon Publishing.

Emerson, Scott. The Case of the Cat with the Missing Ear: From the Notebooks of Edward R. Smithfield, D. V. M. Mullett, Viv, illus. 2011. (Adventures of Samuel Blackthorne Ser.: 1). (ENG.). 240p. (J). (gr. 3-7). pap. 11.99 *(978-0-689-87615-8(7),* Simon & Schuster Bks. For Young Readers) Simon & Schuster Bks. For Young Readers.

Finley, Leah. The One & Only Mr C. 2009. 82p. pap. 8.95 *(978-1-935118-75-6(7))* Bellissima Publishing, LLC.

Freeman, Don. Fly High, Fly Low. Freeman, Don, illus. (ENG., Illus.). 64p. (J). (gr. -1-k). 2004. reprint ed. 16.99 *(978-0-670-03685-1(4),* Viking Books for Young Readers) 50th anniv. ed. 2007. 7.99 *(978-0-14-240817-9(4),* Puffin Books) Penguin Young Readers Group.

—Fly High, Fly Low. Freeman, Don, illus. 2007. (Illus.). 56p. (gr. -1-3). 18.00 *(978-0-7569-8001-6(1))* Perfection Learning Corp.

French, Mary B. Bear-Ly There with Compass. Coffey, Kevin, illus. 2012. 122p. pap. 6.00 *(978-0-9852821-0-3(X))* Mary B./French.

Gagnon, Michelle. Unearthly Things. 2017. (ENG.). 288p. (YA). (gr. 9). 18.99 *(978-1-61695-696-7(8),* Soho Teen) Soho Pr., Inc.

Garis, Howard R. Dick Hamilton's Airship. 2008. 160p. 25.95 *(978-1-60664-781-3(4))*; pap. 13.95 *(978-1-60664-155-2(7))* Aegypan.

Gloster, Dean. Dessert First. 2016. (ENG.). 304p. (YA). 17.99 *(978-1-4405-9454-0(6),* Simon Pulse) Simon Pulse.

Grant, Michael & Applegate, Katherine. Eve & Adam. 2013. (ENG.). 304p. (YA). (gr. 8-12). pap. 9.99 *(978-1-250-03419-9(1),* 9781250034199) Square Fish.

Gregory, Kristiana & Campbell, Mary Exa Atkins. Earthquake at Dawn. 2003. (Great Episodes Ser.). (ENG., Illus.). 224p. (J). (gr. 5-7). pap. 13.95 *(978-0-15-204681-1(X))* Houghton Mifflin Harcourt Publishing Co.

Honeyman, Kay. The Fire Horse Girl. 2016. (ENG.). 336p. (J). (gr. 7). pap. 9.99 *(978-0-545-40311-5(1),* Levine, Arthur A. Bks.) Scholastic, Inc.

Hopkinson, Deborah. Into the Firestorm: A Novel of San Francisco 1906. 2008. (Yearling Bks.). (ENG.). 208p. (J). (gr. 3-7). per. 6.99 *(978-0-440-42129-0(2),* Yearling) Random Hse. Children's Bks.

Jacobs, Lily. The Littlest Bunny in San Francisco: An Easter Adventure. Dunn, Robert, illus. 2015. (ENG.). 32p. (J). (-3). 9.99 *(978-1-4926-1192-9(1),* Sourcebooks Jabberwocky) Sourcebooks, Inc.

James, Eric. A Halloween Scare in San Francisco. Le Ray, Marina, illus. 2015. (ENG.). 32p. (J). (-5). 9.99 *(978-1-4926-2399-1(7),* 9781492623991, Sourcebooks Jabberwocky) Sourcebooks, Inc.

—Santa's Sleigh Is on Its Way to San Francisco: A Christmas Adventure. Dunn, Robert, illus. 2016. (ENG.). 32p. (J). (-2). 12.99 *(978-1-4926-4354-8(8),* 9781492643548, Sourcebooks Jabberwocky) Sourcebooks, Inc.

Kleinman, Estelle. Al Capone Does My Shirts. Friedland, Joyce & Kessler, Rikki, eds. 2007. (Al Capone on Alcatraz Ser.: Bk. 1). (Illus.). 38p. pap. 16.95 *(978-0-7675-3758-2(0))* Learning Links Inc.

Kleven, Elisa, illus. The Horribly Hungry Gingerbread Boy: A San Francisco Story. 2016. 40p. (J). *(978-1-59714-352-3(9))* Heyday.
Krueger, Jim & Rogers, Bud. The Argon Deception, 1 vol. Padilla, Ariel, illus. 2008. (Z Graphic Novels / Tomo Ser.). (ENG.). 160p. (J). (gr. 4-7). pap. 6.99 *(978-0-310-71303-6(X))* Zondervan.
Laberje, Reji. Max Explores San Francisco. Fenech, Liza, illus. 2014. (Max Explores Ser.). (ENG.). 20p. (J). (— 1). bds. 9.95 *(978-1-62937-005-7(3))* Triumph Bks.
Larson, Kirby. Hattie Ever After. 2014. (ENG.). 256p. (YA). (gr. 7). pap. 8.99 *(978-0-375-85090-5(2),* Ember) Random Hse. Children's Bks.
Laurence, Yep. Dragonwings. 25th rev. ed. 2014. (Golden Mountain Chronicles Ser.). (ENG.). 336p. (J). (gr. 12-12). 11.24 *(978-1-63245-143-9(3))* Lectorum Pubns., Inc.
Lee, Milly. Landed. Choi, Yangsook, illus. 2006. (ENG.). 40p. (J). (gr. 2-6). 17.99 *(978-0-374-34314-9(4),* 9780374343149, Farrar, Straus & Giroux (BYR)) Farrar, Straus & Giroux.
Lee, Milly, et al. Earthquake. Choi, Yangsook, illus. 2003. (Avenues Ser.). (ENG.). 32p. (C). (gr. k-2). pap. 21.95 *(978-0-374-39964-1(6))* National Geographic School Publishing, Inc.
Lee, Stacey. Outrun the Moon. 2016. (ENG.). 400p. (YA). (gr. 7). 17.99 *(978-0-399-17541-1(5),* G.P. Putnam's Sons Books for Young Readers) Penguin Young Readers Group.
Madonia, Kristen-Paige. Fingerprints of You. 2013. (ENG., Illus.). 272p. (YA). (gr. 9). pap. 9.99 *(978-1-4424-2921-5(6),* Simon & Schuster Bks. For Young Readers) Simon & Schuster Bks. For Young Readers.
—Fingerprints of You. Ribera, Terry, illus. 2012. (ENG.). 272p. (YA). (gr. 9). 16.99 *(978-1-4424-2920-8(8),* Simon & Schuster Bks. For Young Readers) Simon & Schuster Bks. For Young Readers.
—Invisible Fault Lines. 2016. (ENG.). 320p. (YA). (gr. 7). 17.99 *(978-1-4814-3071-5(8),* Simon & Schuster Bks. For Young Readers) Simon & Schuster Bks. For Young Readers.
Marsh, Carole. The Ghost of the Golden Gate Bridge. 2009. (Real Kids, Real Places Ser.). (Illus.). 146p. (J). lib. bdg. 18.99 *(978-0-635-07047-0(2),* Marsh, Carole Mysteries) Gallopade International.
Mcallister, Herb West. Doo West to Toadstool. 2011. 44p. pap. 21.99 *(978-1-4628-5530-8(X))* Xlibris Corp.
McDonald, Megan. Julie Story Collection. Hunt, Robert, illus. 2007. 472p. pap. 29.95 *(978-1-59369-450-0(4))* American Girl Publishing, Inc.
McKernan, Victoria. Son of Fortune. 2015. (ENG.). 448p. (YA). (gr. 7). pap. 9.99 *(978-0-375-85786-7(9),* Ember) Random Hse. Children's Bks.
McNeil, Gretchen. Possess. (ENG.). (YA). (gr. 8). 2012. 400p. pap. 9.99 *(978-0-06-206072-3(4))* 2011. 384p. 17.99 *(978-0-06-206071-6(6))* HarperCollins Pubs.
Messner, Kate. Escape from the Great Earthquake. McMorris, Kelley, illus. 2017. (Ranger in Time Ser.: 6). (ENG.). 160p. (J). (gr. 2-5). pap. 5.99 ***(978-0-545-90983-9(X))*** Scholastic, Inc.
Morris, Paris & Florzak, Douglas. My Twins Are Coming Home. 2010. (ENG., Illus.). 24p. (J). pap. 12.95 *(978-0-9760095-5-9(2))* New Year Publishing.
Morris, Paris & Singer, Thom. I'm Having Twins, 1 vol. 2010. (ENG., Illus.). 24p. (J). pap. 12.95 *(978-0-9760095-4-2(4))* New Year Publishing.
Moss, Marissa. Mira's Diary: California Dreaming. Moss, Marissa, illus. 2016. (ENG., Illus.). 190p. (J). (gr. 2-8). 12.99 *(978-1-939547-22-4(9))* Creston Bks.
Murphy, Pat. The Wild Girls. unabr. ed. 2007. (YA). (gr. 6-9). audio compact disk 45.00 *(978-0-7393-5988-4(6))* Random Hse. Audio Publishing Group.
Myers, Jason. The Mission. 2009. (ENG.). 384p. (YA). (gr. 9-18). pap. 9.99 *(978-1-4169-8455-9(0),* Simon Pulse) Simon Pulse.
Novesky, Amy. Me, Frida. Diaz, David, illus. (ENG.). 32p. (J). (gr. k-2). 2015. 9.95 *(978-1-4197-1516-7(X))* 2010. 18.99 *(978-0-8109-8969-6(7))* Abrams, Inc. (Abrams Bks. for Young Readers).
Osborne, Mary Pope. Earthquake in the Early Morning. unabr. ed. 2004. (Magic Tree House Ser.: No. 24). 71p. (J). (gr. k-3). pap. 17.00 incl. audio *(978-0-8072-0933-2(3),* S FTR 256 SP, Listening Library) Random Hse. Audio Publishing Group.
Perkins, Stephanie. Lola & the Boy Next Door. (ENG.). (YA). (gr. 9). 2013. 368p. pap. 10.99 *(978-0-14-242201-4(0),* Speak) 2011. 352p. 16.99 *(978-0-525-42328-7(1),* Dutton Books for Young Readers) Penguin Young Readers Group.
Pollak, Dale. Velocity: From the Front Line to the Bottom Line. 2010. (ENG.). 144p. 29.95 *(978-0-9760095-7-3(9))* New Year Publishing.
Rai, Sarbjit. Elfins in San Francisco. 2009. 24p. pap. 11.49 *(978-1-4389-8014-0(0))* AuthorHouse.
Rankin, Cindy. Under the Ashes. 2016. (ENG.). 240p. (J). (gr. 3-7). 16.99 *(978-0-8075-3635-3(0))* Whitman, Albert & Co.
Reich, Susanna. Penelope Bailey Takes the Stage, 1 vol. 2006. (ENG.). 32p. (J). (gr. 3-7). 16.95 *(978-0-7614-5287-4(7))* Marshall Cavendish Corp.
Reiss, Kathryn. The Silver Guitar: A Julie Mystery. Ansfield, Elizabeth, ed. Giovine, Sergio, illus. 2011. (ENG.). 192p. (YA). (gr. 4-18). pap. 6.95 *(978-1-59369-756-3(2))* American Girl Publishing, Inc.
—The Strange Case of Baby H. 2009. (Mysteries Through Time Ser.). 144 - 176p. (YA). (gr. 4-8). 31.95 *(978-1-60754-423-4(7));* pap. 15.25 *(978-1-60754-424-1(5))* Windmill Bks.
—The Tangled Web: A Julie Mystery. Tibbles, Jean-Paul, illus. 2009. (ENG.). 168p. (J). (gr. 4-18). 10.95 *(978-1-59369-475-3(X));* pap. 6.95 *(978-1-59369-476-0(8))* American Girl Publishing, Inc.
Resnicoff, Stan. The BIG Parade: San Francisco. 2012. (ENG.). (J). pap. *(978-1-4675-1539-9(6))* Independent Pub.
Robbins, Trina. A Match Made in Heaven. Ota, Yuko & Studio, Xian Nu, illus. 2013. (My Boyfriend Is a Monster Ser.: 8). (ENG.). 128p. (YA). (gr. 7-12). pap. 9.95 *(978-1-4677-0732-9(5),* Graphic Universe™) Lerner Publishing Group.
—A Match Made in Heaven. Xian Nu Studio Staff, illus. 2013. (My Boyfriend Is a Monster Ser.: 8). (ENG.). 128p. (YA). (gr. 7-12). lib. bdg. 29.27 *(978-0-7613-6857-1(4),* Graphic Universe™) Lerner Publishing Group.
Robles, Anthony. Lakas & the Manilatown Fish. Angel, Carl, illus. 2015. (ENG & TGL.). 32p. (J). pap. 9.95 *(978-0-89239-211-7(8),* Children's Book Press) Lee & Low Bks., Inc.
Robles, Anthony D. & Children's Book Press Staff. Lakas & the Manilatown Fish (Si Lakas at Ang Isdang Manilatown) de Jesus, Eloisa D. & de Guzman, Magdalena, trs. Angel, Carl, illus. 2003.Tr. of Si Lakas at Ang Isdang Manilatown. (ENG & TAG.). 32p. (J). 16.95 *(978-0-89239-182-0(0))* Lee & Low Bks., Inc.
Roy, Ron. The New Year Dragon Dilemma. Gurney, John Steven, illus. 2011. (to Z Mysteries Ser.). (ENG.). 144p. (J). (gr. 1-4). 5.99 *(978-0-375-86880-1(1),* Random Hse. Bks. for Young Readers) Random Hse. Children's Bks.
Sager, Ryan K. The World's Greatest Chocolate-Covered Pork Chops. 2017. (ENG.). 256p. (J). (gr. 3-7). 16.99 ***(978-1-4847-6761-0(6))*** Hyperion Bks. for Children.
San Francisco Shake-Up, 6 Packs. (Greetings Ser.: Vol. 3). (gr. 3-5). 31.00 *(978-0-7635-2075-5(6))* Rigby Education.
Say, Allen. The Favorite Daughter. 2013. (J). pap. *(978-0-545-17663-7(8),* Levine, Arthur A. Bks.) Scholastic, Inc.
—The Favorite Daughter. Say, Allen, illus. 2013. (ENG., Illus.). 32p. (J). (gr. -1-3). 17.99 *(978-0-545-17662-0(X),* Levine, Arthur A. Bks.) Scholastic, Inc.
Schnell, David. The Night Before Baseball at the Park by the Bay. Pamintuan, Macky, illus. 2013. (ENG.). 32p. 0.00 *(978-0-9891043-0-2(3))* Prospect Palo Alto Publishing.
Schomer-Wendel, Gretchen & Schomer, Adam Anthony. Becka Goes to San Francisco. 2009. (Becka & the Big Bubble Ser.). (Illus.). 32p. (J). (gr. -1-2). 22.60 *(978-1-60754-107-3(6));* pap. 10.55 *(978-1-60754-108-0(4))* Windmill Bks.
Scott, Michael. The Alchemyst. 2009. (ENG., Illus.). 375p. (gr. 6-10). 19.00 *(978-1-60686-514-9(5))* Perfection Learning Corp.
—The Alchemyst. (Secrets of the Immortal Nicholas Flamel Ser.: Bk. 1). (ENG.). 400p. (YA). (gr. 7). 2008. pap. 10.99 *(978-0-385-73600-8(2),* Ember) 2007. (Illus.). 16.99 *(978-0-385-73357-1(7),* Delacorte Bks. for Young Readers) Random Hse. Children's Bks.
—The Warlock. 2011. (Secrets of the Immortal Nicholas Flamel Ser.: 5). (ENG.). 400p. (YA). (gr. 7-18). 18.99 *(978-0-385-73533-9(2),* Delacorte Bks. for Young Readers) Random Hse. Children's Bks.
—The Warlock the Secrets of the Immortal Nicholas Flamel. l.t. ed. 2011. (Secrets of the Immortal Nicholas Flamel Ser.). (ENG.). 486p. 23.99 *(978-1-4104-4157-7(1))* Thorndike Pr.
Senzai, N. H. Saving Kabul Corner. 2014. (Kabul Chronicles Ser.). (ENG., Illus.). 288p. (J). (gr. 3-7). 16.99 *(978-1-4424-8494-8(2),* Simon & Schuster/Paula Wiseman Bks.) Simon & Schuster/Paula Wiseman Bks.
—Shooting Kabul. (Kabul Chronicles Ser.). (ENG.). (J). (gr. 3-7). 2011. 288p. pap. 7.99 *(978-1-4424-0195-2(8))* 2010. 272p. 18.99 *(978-1-4424-0194-5(X))* Simon & Schuster/Paula Wiseman Bks. (Simon & Schuster/Paula Wiseman Bks.).
Shulman, Dee. My Totally Secret Diary - Reality TV Nightmare. 2012. (ENG., Illus.). 144p. (J). (gr. 2-4). pap. 10.99 *(978-1-86230-424-6(6),* Red Fox) Random House Children's Books GBR. Dist: Independent Pubs. Group.
Silvano, Wendi. Love Is All Around San Francisco. Czernichowska, Joanna, illus. 2016. (ENG.). 32p. (J). (-6). 12.99 *(978-1-4926-2959-7(6),* Sourcebooks Jabberwocky) Sourcebooks, Inc.
Simmons, Andrew & Averdonz, N. R. I Was an Eighth-Grade Ninja, 1 vol. Padilla, Ariel, illus. 2007. (Z Graphic Novels / Tomo Ser.). (ENG.). 160p. (J). (gr. 3-7). pap. 6.99 *(978-0-310-71300-5(5))* Zondervan.
Sims, Lori. Starvin' Marvin & Skinny Minnie Shake up San Francisco. 2009. 78p. (YA). pap. 9.95 *(978-1-4327-3651-4(5))* Outskirts Pr., Inc.
Smallman, Steve. Santa Is Coming to San Francisco. Dunn, Robert, illus. 2012. (ENG.). 32p. (J). (-3). 9.99 *(978-1-4022-7548-7(X),* Sourcebooks Jabberwocky) Sourcebooks, Inc.
Spradlin, Michael P. & Smith, Roland. Alcatraz. 2014. (I, Q Ser.). (ENG.). 272p. (J). (gr. 5-7). 16.99 *(978-1-58536-826-6(1),* 203667); pap. 9.99 *(978-1-58536-825-9(3),* 203727) Sleeping Bear Pr.
Stone, Tamara Ireland. Time after Time. 2014. (ENG.). 368p. (YA). (gr. 7-12). pap. 9.99 *(978-1-4231-5981-0(0))* Hyperion Bks. for Children.
Sully, Katherine. Night-Night San Francisco. Poole, Helen, illus. 2017. (ENG.). 20p. (J). (-1). bds. 9.99 *(978-1-4926-4765-2(9),* 9781492647652, Sourcebooks Jabberwocky) Sourcebooks, Inc.
Tarshis, Lauren. I Survived the San Francisco Earthquake 1906. 2012. (I Survived Ser.: 5). (ENG.). 112p. (J). (gr. 2-5). pap. 4.99 *(978-0-545-20699-0(5),* Scholastic Paperbacks) Scholastic, Inc.
—I Survived the San Francisco Earthquake 1906. 2012. (I Survived . Ser.: No. 5). lib. bdg. 14.75 *(978-0-606-23936-3(7),* Turtleback) Turtleback Bks.
The Calaiacovo Family. The Amazing Adventures of Ruby & Rubette: San Francisco. 2010. 32p. pap. 14.49 *(978-1-4490-6948-3(7))* AuthorHouse.
Thomas, Roger B. The Accidental Marriage. 2014. (ENG.). 219p. 19.95 *(978-1-58617-908-3(X))* Ignatius Pr.
Thomson, Celia & Braswell, Liz. The Nine Lives of Chloe King: The Fallen; the Stolen; the Chosen. 2011. (Nine Lives of Chloe King Ser.). (ENG.). 784p. (YA). (gr. 9). pap. 13.99 *(978-1-4424-3570-4(4),* Simon Pulse) Simon Pulse.
Trine, Greg. Dinos Are Forever. Dormer, Frank W., illus. (Adventures of Jo Schmo Ser.: 1). (ENG.). 112p. (J). (gr. 1-4). 2014. pap. 5.99 *(978-0-544-00325-5(X),* HMH Books For Young Readers) 2012. 12.99 *(978-0-547-76341-5(7))* Houghton Mifflin Harcourt Publishing Co.
—Pinkbeard's Revenge. Dormer, Frank W., illus. (Adventures of Jo Schmo Ser.: 4). (ENG.). 128p. (J). (gr. 1-4). 2015. pap. 5.99 *(978-0-544-45601-3(7),* HMH Books For Young Readers) 2013. 12.99 *(978-0-547-80797-3(X))* Houghton Mifflin Harcourt Publishing Co.
—Wyatt Burp Rides Again. Dormer, Frank W., illus. (Adventures of Jo Schmo Ser.: 2). (ENG.). 112p. (J). (gr. 1-4). 2014. pap. 5.99 *(978-0-544-01899-0(0),* HMH Books For Young Readers) 2012. 12.99 *(978-0-547-80795-9(3))* Houghton Mifflin Harcourt Publishing Co.
Walton, Rick. 10 Little Monsters Go to San Fransisco. Smiley, Jess Smart, illus. 2015. (ENG.). 32p. (J). 16.95 *(978-1-942672-99-9(3))* Familius LLC.
Wendel, Gretchen Schomel, et al. Becka Goes to San Francisco. Renthrope, Damon, illus. 2007. (ENG.). 32p. (J). 11.99 *(978-1-933754-12-3(5))* Waterside Publishing.
Wiggin, Kate Douglas. The Girl & the Kingdom. 2011. 60p. 16.95 *(978-1-4638-9982-0(3))* Rodgers, Alan Bks.
—Polly Oliver's Problem. 2007. 108p. per. 9.95 *(978-1-60312-369-3(5))* Aegypan.
Yang, Belle. Hannah Is My Name. Yang, Belle, illus. 2007. (Illus.). (J). (gr. k-4). 14.65 *(978-0-7569-8124-2(7))* Perfection Learning Corp.
—Hannah Is My Name: A Young Immigrant's Story. Yang, Belle, illus. 2007. (ENG., Illus.). 32p. (J). (gr. k-4). pap. 6.99 *(978-0-7636-3521-3(9))* Candlewick Pr.
Yep, Laurence. Child of the Owl. (Golden Mountain Chronicles). (J). pap., stu. ed. *(978-0-13-053125-4(1))* Prentice Hall (Schl. Div.).
—The Earth Dragon Awakes: The San Francisco Earthquake of 1906. (ENG., Illus.). 128p. (J). (gr. 3-7). 2008. pap. 6.99 *(978-0-06-000846-8(6))* 2006. 14.99 *(978-0-06-027524-2(3))* HarperCollins Pubs.
—The Magic Paintbrush. Wang, Suling, illus. 2003. (ENG.). 96p. (J). (gr. 3-7). pap. 6.99 *(978-0-06-440852-3(3))* HarperCollins Pubs.
—The Magic Paintbrush. Wang, Suling, illus. 2003. 89p. (J). (gr. 3-7). 12.65 *(978-0-7569-1444-8(2))* Perfection Learning Corp.
—The Tiger's Apprentice. 2005. (Tiger's Apprentice Ser.: Bk. 1). 184p. (J). lib. bdg. 24.62 *(978-1-4242-0449-6(6))* Fitzgerald Bks.
—The Tiger's Apprentice. 2005. (Tiger's Apprentice (Tandem Library) Ser.). 184p. (gr. 5-9). 17.00 *(978-0-7569-5074-3(0))* Perfection Learning Corp.
—Tiger's Blood. 2005. (Tiger's Apprentice Ser.: Bk. 2). (ENG.). 240p. (J). (gr. 5-18). 15.99 *(978-0-06-001016-4(9))* HarperCollins Pubs.
Zakatchenko, Lilian. Girls from Brazil, 1 vol. 2010. 16p. 24.95 *(978-1-4489-3834-6(1))* PublishAmerica, Inc.
Zarr, Sara. The Lucy Variations. 2014. (ENG.). 336p. (YA). (gr. 7-17). pap. 10.00 *(978-0-316-20500-9(1))* Little, Brown Bks. for Young Readers.
Zschock, Martha Day. Hello, San Francisco! 2012. (Hello! Ser.). (ENG., Illus.). 16p. (J). (gr. -1-k). bds. 9.95 *(978-1-933212-65-4(9),* Commonwealth Editions) Applewood Bks.

SAN FRANCISCO (CALIF.)—HISTORY

Accord Publishing Staff & Andrews McMeel Publishing Staff. San Francisco. 2014. (ENG., Illus.). 12p. (J). bds. 12.99 *(978-1-4494-5583-5(2))* Andrews McMeel Publishing.
Adams, Jennifer. My Little Cities: San Francisco. Pizzoli, Greg, illus. 2017. (ENG.). 22p. (J). (gr. -1 — 1). bds. 9.99 ***(978-1-4521-5391-9(4))*** Chronicle Bks. LLC.
Aretha, David. No Compromise: The Story of Harvey Milk. 2009. (Civil Rights Leaders Ser.). 100p. (YA). (gr. 5-9). lib. bdg. 28.95 *(978-1-59935-129-2(3))* Reynolds, Morgan Inc.
Barter, James. San Francisco in the 1960s. 2003. (Travel Guide To Ser.). (ENG., Illus.). 96p. (J). 30.85 *(978-1-59018-359-5(2),* Lucent Bks.) Cengage Gale.
Canasi, Brittany. Dropping in on San Francisco. 2017. (Dropping in On Ser.). (ENG.). (J). (gr. 3-5). 32.80 ***(978-1-68342-172-6(8))*** Rourke Educational Media.
Carr, Aaron. Golden Gate Bridge. 2014. (Illus.). 24p. (J). *(978-1-4896-2894-7(0))* Weigl Pubs., Inc.
Cooke, Tim. 1906 San Francisco Earthquake. 2005. (Disasters Ser.). (Illus.). 32p. (gr. 2-6). lib. bdg. 26.00 *(978-0-8368-4494-8(7),* Gareth Stevens Learning Library) Stevens, Gareth Publishing LLLP.
Dyan, Penelope. Halfway to the Stars! a Kid's Guide to San Francisco. Weigand, John D., photos by. 2009. (Illus.). 44p. pap. 11.95 *(978-1-935118-88-6(9))* Bellissima Publishing, LLC.
Epstein, Brad M. San Francisco 49ers 101. 2010. (ENG., Illus.). 24p. (J). bds. *(978-1-60730-127-1(X),* 101 Bk.) Michaelson Entertainment.
Evanson, Ashley. San Francisco: A Book of Numbers. Evanson, Ashley, illus. 2015. (Hello, World Ser.). (ENG., Illus.). 14p. (J). (— 1). bds. 6.99 *(978-0-448-48914-8(7),* Grosset & Dunlap) Penguin Young Readers Group.
Freedman, Russell. Angel Island: Gateway to Gold Mountain. 2016. (ENG., Illus.). 96p. (J). (gr. 5-7). pap. 10.99 *(978-0-544-81089-1(9),* HMH Books For Young Readers) Houghton Mifflin Harcourt Publishing Co.
Grinapol, Corinne. Harvey Milk: Pioneering Gay Politician, 1 vol. 2015. (ENG., Illus.). 112p. (J). 35.60 *(978-1-4777-7899-9(3),* Rosen Young Adult) Rosen Publishing Group, Inc., The.
Herold, Vickey. Discover A Gold Rush Community: San Francisco. 2006. (J). pap. *(978-1-4108-6431-4(6))* Benchmark Education Co.
—A Gold Rush Community: San Francisco. 2006. (J). pap. *(978-1-4108-6428-4(6))* Benchmark Education Co.
Hoena, Blake. Building the Golden Gate Bridge: An Interactive Engineering Adventure, 1 vol. 2014. (You Choose: Engineering Marvels Ser.). (ENG., Illus.). 112p. (gr. 3-4). 31.99 *(978-1-4914-0398-3(5),* You Choose Bks.) Capstone Press of Coughlan Cos.
Hollander, Barbara Gottfried. Harvey Milk: The First Openly Gay Elected Official in the United States. 2017. (J). pap. ***(978-1-5383-8092-5(7),*** Rosen Young Adult) Rosen Publishing Group, Inc., The.
Johnson, Rebecca L. & National Geographic Learning Staff. The San Francisco Earthquake. 2007. (Content-Based Chapter Bks.). (ENG., Illus.). 68p. (C). pap. 26.95 *(978-0-7922-5864-3(9))* National Geographic School Publishing, Inc.
Krensky, Stephen. Lizzie Newton & the San Francisco Earthquake. 2010. pap. 56.72 *(978-0-7613-6928-8(7))* Lerner Publishing Group.
Lester, Brian. San Francisco 49ers, 1 vol. 2010. (Inside the NFL Ser.). (ENG.). 48p. (YA). (gr. 3-6). lib. bdg. 32.79 *(978-1-61714-027-3(9))* ABDO Publishing Co.
McDougall, Chros. San Francisco Earthquake & Fire, 1 vol. 2013. (History's Greatest Disasters Ser.). (ENG.). 48p. (J). (gr. 3-6). lib. bdg. 32.79 *(978-1-61783-959-7(0))* ABDO Publishing Co.
McDougall, Chrs. San Francisco Earthquake & Fire Paperback. 2013. (J). pap. 15.64 *(978-1-62403-024-6(6),* Core Library) ABDO Publishing Co.
O'Connell, Jennifer. The Eye of the Whale: A Rescue Story, 1 vol. O'Connell, Jennifer, illus. 2013. (Tilbury House Nature Book Ser.: 0). (ENG., Illus.). 32p. (gr. 1-7). 17.95 *(978-0-88448-335-9(5),* 884335) Tilbury Hse. Pubs.
Publications International Ltd. Staff. Yesterday & Today San Francisco. 2008. 192p. 24.95 *(978-1-4127-1575-1(X))* Publications International, Ltd.
Shea, Tess & Pohlen, Jerome. San Francisco Baby: A Local Baby Book. Lemay, Violet, illus. 2013. (Local Baby Bks.). (ENG.). 22p. (— 1). bds. 8.95 *(978-1-938093-16-6(X))* Duo Pr. LLC.
Skewes, John. Larry Loves San Francisco! Skewes, John, illus. 2014. (Larry Gets Lost Ser.). (ENG., Illus.). 20p. (J). (— 1). bds. 9.99 *(978-1-57061-912-0(3),* Little Bigfoot) Sasquatch Bks.
Tanaka, Shelley. Earthquake! A Day That Changed America. Craig, David, illus. 2006. 48p. (J). (gr. 4-8). reprint ed. 17.00 *(978-1-4223-5635-7(3))* DIANE Publishing Co.
Van Meter, Larry A. Yerba Buena. 2007. (Colonial Settlements in America Ser.). (Illus.). 100p. (YA). (gr. 5-9). lib. bdg. 30.00 *(978-0-7910-9338-2(7))* Facts On File, Inc.
Walsh, Kenneth C. H. You Are There! San Francisco 1906. 2017. (J). pap. 8.97 *(978-1-4938-3617-8(X))* Teacher Created Materials, Inc.
White, Tekla. San Francisco Bay Area Missions. 2007. (Exploring California Missions Ser.). (ENG., Illus.). 64p. (gr. 4-7). lib. bdg. 27.93 *(978-0-8225-0900-4(8),* Lerner Pubns.) Lerner Publishing Group.
Wood, Anita. City Doodles San Francisco, 1 vol. 2013. (ENG., Illus.). 240p. (J). pap., pap. 9.99 *(978-1-4236-3286-3(9))* Gibbs Smith, Publisher.

SAN FRANCISCO EARTHQUAKE AND FIRE, CALIF., 1906

Cooke, Tim. 1906 San Francisco Earthquake. 2005. (Disasters Ser.). (Illus.). 32p. (gr. 2-6). lib. bdg. 26.00 *(978-0-8368-4494-8(7),* Gareth Stevens Learning Library) Stevens, Gareth Publishing LLLP.
Hoobler, Dorothy & Hoobler, Thomas. What Was the San Francisco Earthquake? Hammond, Ted, illus. 2016. (What Was? Ser.). (ENG.). 112p. (J). (gr. 3-7). 5.99 *(978-0-399-54159-9(4));* lib. bdg. 15.99 *(978-0-399-54212-1(4))* Penguin Young Readers Group. (Grosset & Dunlap).
—What Was the San Francisco Earthquake? Hammond, Ted, illus. 2016. (What Was... ? Ser.). (ENG.). 112p. (J). (gr. 3-7). 16.00 *(978-0-606-39329-4(3))* Turtleback Bks.
Krensky, Stephen. Lizzie Newton & the San Francisco Earthquake. 2010. pap. 56.72 *(978-0-7613-6928-8(7))* Lerner Publishing Group.
McDougall, Chros. San Francisco Earthquake & Fire, 1 vol. 2013. (History's Greatest Disasters Ser.). (ENG.). 48p. (J). (gr. 3-6). lib. bdg. 32.79 *(978-1-61783-959-7(0))* ABDO Publishing Co.
McDougall, Chrs. San Francisco Earthquake & Fire Paperback. 2013. (J). pap. 15.64 *(978-1-62403-024-6(6),* Core Library) ABDO Publishing Co.
Slavicek, Louise Chipley. The San Francisco Earthquake & Fire Of 1906. 2008. (Great Historic Disasters Ser.). (Illus.). 128p. (gr. 5-8). 35.00 *(978-0-7910-9650-5(5),* Chelsea Hse.) Facts On File, Inc.
Walsh, Kenneth C. H. You Are There! San Francisco 1906. 2017. (J). pap. 8.97 *(978-1-4938-3617-8(X))* Teacher Created Materials, Inc.
—You Are There! San Francisco 1906. 2017. (Time for Kids Nonfiction Readers Ser.). lib. bdg. 19.65 ***(978-0-606-40271-2(3))*** Turtleback Bks.
Worth, Richard. The San Francisco Earthquake. 2005. (Environmental Disasters Ser.). (Illus.). 112p. (gr. 6-12). 35.00 *(978-0-8160-5756-6(7))* Facts On File, Inc.

SAN FRANCISCO GIANTS (BASEBALL TEAM)

Connery-Boyd, Peg. San Francisco Giants. 2016. (Hawk's Nest Activity Bks.: 0). (ENG.). 64p. (J). (gr. k-3). pap., act. bk. ed. 8.99 *(978-1-4926-3370-9(4))* Sourcebooks, Inc.
Frisch, Aaron. San Francisco Giants. 2009. (World Series Champions Ser.). (Illus.). 23p. (J). (gr. 2-3). 24.25 *(978-1-58341-690-7(0),* Creative Education) Creative Co., The.
Gilbert, Sara. San Francisco Giants. 2013. (Illus.). 24p. (J). 25.65 *(978-1-60818-272-5(X),* Creative Education) Creative Co., The.
—World Series Champs: San Francisco Giants. 2013. (World Series Champions Ser.). (ENG.). 24p. (J). (gr. 1-3). pap. 9.99 *(978-0-89812-823-9(4),* Creative Paperbacks) Creative Co., The.
Gitlin, Martin. San Francisco Giants, 1 vol. 2011. (Inside MLB Ser.). (ENG., Illus.). 48p. (YA). (gr. 3-6). lib. bdg. 32.79 *(978-1-61714-058-7(9))* ABDO Publishing Co.
Gitlin, Marty. San Francisco Giants, 1 vol. 2014. (Inside MLB Ser.). (ENG., Illus.). 48p. (J). (gr. 3-6). lib. bdg. 32.79 *(978-1-62403-484-8(5),* SportsZone) ABDO Publishing Co.
Goodman, Michael E. The Story of the San Francisco Giants. 2011. (J). 35.65 *(978-1-60818-055-4(7),* Creative Education) Creative Co., The.
Monnig, Alex. San Francisco Giants. 2014. (Favorite Baseball Teams Ser.). (ENG.). 32p. (J). (gr. 1-4). 28.50 *(978-1-62323-978-7(8),* 206755) Child's World, Inc., The.
Monning, Alex. San Francisco Giants. 2016. (J). ***(978-1-4896-5947-7(1),*** AV2 by Weigl) Weigl Pubs., Inc.
Richardson, Adele. The Story of the San Francisco Giants. 2007. (Baseball, the Great American Game Ser.). (Illus.). 48p. (YA). (gr. 4-7). lib. bdg. 32.80 *(978-1-58341-499-6(1))* Creative Co., The.
Stewart, Mark. The San Francisco Giants. 2012. (Team Spirit Ser.). 48p. (J). (gr. 3-6). lib. bdg. 29.27 *(978-1-59953-496-1(7))* Norwood Hse. Pr.
Tometich, Annabelle. Superstars of the San Francisco Giants. 2014. (Pro Sports Superstars Ser.). 24p. (J). 27.10 *(978-1-60753-596-6(3))* Amicus Publishing.

SANATORIUMS

see Hospitals

S

SAND

Brannon, Cecelia H. A Look at Sand, Silt, & Mud. 2016. (Rock Cycle Ser.). (ENG.). 32p. (J). (gr. 3-4). pap. 10.52 *(978-0-7660-7332-6(7))*; (Illus.). 25.27 *(978-0-7660-7334-0(3))* Enslow Pubs., Inc.

Gurney, Beth. Sand & Soil. 2004. (Rocks, Minerals, & Resources Ser.). (ENG., Illus.). 32p. (J). pap. *(978-0-7787-1449-1(7))* Crabtree Publishing Co.

Lawrence, Ellen. Is Sand a Rock? 2015. (Illus.). 24p. (J). lib. bdg. *(978-1-62724-301-8(1))* Bearport Publishing Co., Inc.

Prager, Ellen J. Sand. Woodman, Nancy, illus. 2006. (Jump into Science Ser.). (ENG.). 32p. (J). (gr. -1-3). per. 6.95 *(978-0-7922-5583-3(6))*, National Geographic Children's Bks.) National Geographic Society.

Rau, Dana Meachen. Building Sandcastles. 2012. (How-To Library). (ENG.). 32p. (gr. 3-6). 28.50 *(978-1-61080-468-4(6)*, 202078); pap. 14.21 *(978-1-61080-642-8(5)*, 202252) Cherry Lake Publishing.

SAND CREEK MASSACRE, COLO., 1864—FICTION

Reeder, Red. Whispering Wind: A Story of the Massacre at Sand Creek. Wilson, Charles Banks, illus. 2011. 216p. 44.95 *(978-1-258-05996-5(7))* Literary Licensing, LLC.

SAND DUNES

Peggy J. Parks. Sand Dunes. 2004. (Wonders of the World Ser.). (ENG.). (J). 29.15 *(978-0-7377-2057-0(3)*, Kidhaven) Cengage Gale.

Robinson, Fay. Sand Dunes. 2016. (Spring Forward Ser.). (J). (gr. 2). *(978-1-4900-9464-9(4))* Benchmark Education Co.

SAND DUNES—FICTION

Barchers, Suzanne I. To the Dunes with Luce, 1 vol. 2011. (Targeted Phonics Ser.). (ENG., Illus.). 16p. (J). (gr. k-2). pap. 5.99 *(978-1-4333-2918-0(2))* Teacher Created Materials, Inc.

Baumer, Dawn McVay, creator. Dune Daze: Silver Lake. 2004. (Illus.). (J). *(978-0-9754960-0-8(X))* Butters Pr.

SANDBURG, CARL, 1878-1967

Murcia, Rebecca Thatcher. Carl Sandburg. 2007. (Poets & Playwrights Ser.). (Illus.). 112p. (J). (gr. 3-7). lib. bdg. 37.10 *(978-1-58415-430-3(6))* Mitchell Lane Pubs., Inc.

SANDWICHES

Ashley, Susan. I Can Make a Sandwich. 2004. (I Can Do It! Ser.). (Illus.). 24p. (gr. k-3). pap. 8.15 *(978-0-8368-4330-9(4))*; lib. bdg. 21.00 *(978-0-8368-4323-1(1))* Stevens, Gareth Publishing LLLP. (Weekly Reader Leveled Readers).

Blake, Susannah. Sandwiches & Snacks. 2009. (Make & Eat Ser.). (ENG., Illus.). 24p. (J). (gr. 3-5). pap. 9.40 *(978-1-4358-2931-2(X)*, PowerKids Pr.) Rosen Publishing Group, Inc., The.

—Sandwiches & Snacks. Crawford, Andy, photos by. 2009. (Make & Eat Ser.). (Illus.). 24p. (J). (gr. 5). 25.25 *(978-1-4358-2857-5(7)*, PowerKids Pr.) Rosen Publishing Group, Inc., The.

Dale, Jay. My Big Sandwich, 1 vol. Meldrum, Ned, photos by. 2012. (Engage Literacy Red Ser.). (ENG., Illus.). 32p. (gr. k-2). pap. 5.99 *(978-1-4296-8834-5(3)*, Engage Literacy) Capstone Press of Coughlan Cos.

Deering, Alison. Fish & Fowl: Easy & Awesome Sandwiches for Kids. Lentz, Bob, illus. 2017. (Between the Bread Ser.). (ENG.). 48p. (gr. 4-5). lib. bdg. 31.32 ***(978-1-5157-3920-3(1))*** Capstone Press of Coughlan Cos.

—More Meat Please! Delicious Sandwiches for Meat-Eating Kids. Lentz, Bob, illus. 2017. (Between the Bread Ser.). (ENG.). 48p. (gr. 4-5). lib. bdg. 31.32 ***(978-1-5157-3921-0(X))*** Capstone Press of Coughlan Cos.

—Sandwiches! More Than You've Ever Wanted to Know about Making & Eating America's Favorite Food. Lentz, Bob, illus. 2017. (ENG.). 144p. (gr. 4-5). pap. 15.95 ***(978-1-62370-816-0(8))*** Capstone Young Readers of Coughlan Cos.

Fauchald, Nick. On-the-Go Schwarmas: And Other Middle-Eastern Dishes. Rooney, Ronnie, illus. 2009. (Kids Dish Ser.). (ENG.). 32p. (gr. 1-3). lib. bdg. 27.32 *(978-1-4048-5192-4(5))* Picture Window Bks.

LaPenta, Marilyn. Super 'Wiches. 2011. (Yummy Tummy Recipes Ser.). 24p. (J). (gr. 1-4). lib. bdg. 22.61 *(978-1-61772-306-3(1))* Bearport Publishing Co., Inc.

Larson, Jennifer S. Tasty Sandwiches. Cohen, Brie, photos by. 2013. (You're the Chef Ser.). (ENG., Illus.). 32p. (J). (gr. 3-5). lib. bdg. 26.60 *(978-0-7613-6643-0(1)*, Millbrook Pr.) Lerner Publishing Group.

Nolan, Janet. PBandJ Hooray! 2016. (J). *(978-1-4896-3870-0(9))* Weigl Pubs., Inc.

—PB&J Hooray! Your Sandwich's Amazing Journey from Farm to Table. Patton, Julia, illus. 2014. (ENG.). 32p. (J). (gr. -1-3). 16.99 *(978-0-8075-6397-7(8))* Whitman, Albert & Co.

Shaw-Russell, Susan. Build Your Own Burger Sticker Activity Book. 2010. (Dover Little Activity Books Stickers Ser.). (ENG., Illus.). 4p. (J). (gr. k-3). pap. 1.99 *(978-0-486-47592-9(1))* Dover Pubns., Inc.

Tuminelly, Nancy. Cool Sandwich Food Art: Easy Recipes That Make Food Fun to Eat!, 1 vol. 2011. (Cool Food Art Ser.). (ENG., Illus.). 32p. (gr. 3-6). 28.50 *(978-1-61613-366-5(X)*, Checkerboard Library) ABDO Publishing Co.

SANGER, MARGARET, 1883-1966

Archer, Jules. The Feminist Revolution: A Story of the Three Most Inspiring & Empowering Women in American History: Susan B. Anthony, Margaret Sanger, & Betty Friedan. rev. ed. 2015. (Jules Archer History for Young Readers Ser.). (ENG., Illus.). 200p. (J). (gr. 6). 16.99 *(978-1-63220-603-9(X)*, Sky Pony Pr.) Skyhorse Publishing Co., Inc.

Cox, Vicki. Margaret Sanger. 2004. (Women in Medicine Ser.). (Illus.). 112p. (gr. 6-12). 30.00 *(978-0-7910-8030-6(7)*, Chelsea Hse.) Facts On File, Inc.

SANITARY AFFAIRS

see Sanitation

SANITATION

see also Cemeteries; Health; Public Health; Refuse and Refuse Disposal; Water—Purification; Water-Supply; World War, 1939-1945—Medical Care

Forest, Anne. Sanitation Workers, 01 vols., 1. 2016. (Hands-On Jobs Ser.). (ENG., Illus.). 24p. (J). pap. 8.25 *(978-1-5081-4371-0(4)*, PowerKids Pr.) Rosen Publishing Group, Inc., The.

Marsico, Katie. Stinky Sanitation Inventions. 2013. (Awesome Inventions You Use Every Day Ser.). (ENG., Illus.). 32p. (gr. 3-6). lib. bdg. 26.60 *(978-1-4677-1090-9(3)*, Lerner Pubns.) Lerner Publishing Group.

Murray, Julie. School, 1 vol. 2009. (That's Gross! A Look at Science Ser.). (ENG., Illus.). 32p. (J). (gr. 2-5). 28.50 *(978-1-60453-557-0(1))* ABDO Publishing Co.

Robertson, Charmaine. My Uncle Is a Sanitation Worker. 2016. (Rosen REAL Readers: Social Studies Nonfiction / Fiction: Family, Community, & the World Ser.). 12p. (gr. 1-k). pap. 6.33 *(978-1-5081-2311-8(X)*, Rosen Classroom) Rosen Publishing Group, Inc., The.

Silverstein, Alvin, et al. Poop Collectors, Armpit Sniffers, & More: The Yucky Jobs Book. Kelley, Gerald, illus. 2010. (Yucky Science Ser.). 48p. (J). 25.27 *(978-0-7660-3316-0(3))* Enslow Pubs., Inc.

Zamosky, Lisa. Sanitation Workers Then & Now, 1 vol. 2006. (Primary Source Readers Ser.). (ENG.). 32p. (J). (gr. 2-2). pap. 8.99 *(978-0-7439-9382-1(9))* Shell Educational Publishing.

SANTA CLAUS

Bauchman, Della. The Many Faces of Sant. 2009. 24p. pap. 13.99 *(978-1-4490-4988-1(5))* AuthorHouse.

Bonnett, Rosalind, illus. Santa Flap Book. 2012. (Flap Bks). 10p. (J). bds. 7.99 *(978-0-7945-3316-8(7)*, Usborne) EDC Publishing.

Bonnice, Sherry. Christmas & Santa Claus Folklore. 2004. (North American Folklore Ser.). (Illus.). 112p. (J). (gr. 7-18). lib. bdg. 22.95 *(978-1-59084-330-7(4))* Mason Crest.

Color All About: Santa: A Giant Coloring Book about What Santa Does When It's Not Christmas. 2004. (Illus.). (J). *(978-0-9763307-4-5(1))*; (SPA & ENG.). *(978-0-9763307-8-3(4))* Food Marketing Consultants, Inc.

Demi. The Legend of Saint Nicholas. Demi, illus. 2003. (ENG., Illus.). 40p. (J). (gr. k-5). 21.99 *(978-0-689-84681-6(9)*, McElderry, Margaret K. Bks.) McElderry, Margaret K. Bks.

Furman, M. E. A World of Cookies for Santa: Follow Santa's Tasty Trip Around the World. Gal, Susan, illus. 2017. (ENG.). 48p. (J). (gr. -1-3). 16.99 ***(978-0-544-22620-3(8)***, HMH Books For Young Readers) Houghton Mifflin Harcourt Publishing Co.

Heald, Glenn. Santa Talks! The Life Story of Saint Nicholas. 2013. 96p. pap. 11.95 *(978-1-4759-5069-4(1))* iUniverse, Inc.

Hill, David W. & Hill, Anita R. The Case Of: Is Santa Claus Real? 2012. (ENG.). 63p. pap. 24.95 *(978-1-4327-7713-5(0))* Outskirts Pr., Inc.

Hippie Bob. Jesus Believes in Santa Claus: A Christmas Dream... 2009. 40p. pap. 19.99 *(978-1-4389-7936-6(3))* AuthorHouse.

Jeffers, H. Paul. Legends of Santa Claus. 2005. (Biography Ser.). (Illus.). 112p. (J). (gr. 6-12). lib. bdg. 27.93 *(978-0-8225-4983-3(2))* Lerner Publishing Group.

Jones, Bryony. Where's Santa? Whelon, Chuck, illus. 2015. (ENG.). 32p. (J). (gr. k-3). 12.99 *(978-1-4814-0619-2(1)*, Aladdin) Simon & Schuster Children's Publishing.

Jones, Vanessa. Santa's Secret. 2008. (Illus.). 24p. pap. 12.99 *(978-1-4389-3333-7(9))* AuthorHouse.

Kalman, Bobbie. Santa Claus. 2010. (ENG., Illus.). 16p. (J). *(978-0-7787-9505-6(5))*; pap. *(978-0-7787-9530-8(6))* Crabtree Publishing Co.

Keitz, Roderick K., illus. The North Pole Chronicles, 4 bks., Set. Incl. Christmas Eve Tradition. Thompson, R. W., Jr. (gr. -1-3). 1993. 8.95 *(978-0-9636442-1-3(1))*; Shopping Trip. Thompson, R. W., Jr. (gr. -1-3). 1995. 8.95 *(978-0-9636442-2-0(X))*; Star on the Pole. Thompson, R. W. 1996. 8.95 *(978-0-9636442-3-7(8))*; Wow! I Got to Go to the North Pole. Thompson, R. W., Jr. (gr. -1-3). 1994. 8.95 *(978-0-9636442-0-6(3))*; 16p. (J). (Illus.). 29.95 *(978-0-9636442-8-2(9))* North Pole Chronicles.

Keller, Irene. Santa Visits the Thingumajigs. Keller, Dick, illus. 2005. (ENG.). 28p. (J). (gr. -1-k). bds. 7.95 *(978-0-8249-6619-5(8)*, Ideal Pubns.) Worthy Publishing.

Kramer, Mark. Santa Claws: A True Story. 2009. (Illus.). 25p. (J). pap. 15.95 *(978-1-4327-4793-0(2))* Outskirts Pr., Inc.

Kurtz, John. Santa Claus Christmas Paper Dolls. 2013. (Dover Paper Dolls Ser.). (ENG.). 32p. (J). (gr. 1-5). pap. 9.99 *(978-0-486-49424-1(1))* Dover Pubns., Inc.

Laughing Elephant Staff. The Truth about Santa Claus. 2007. (ENG., Illus.). 37p. (J). (gr. -1-3). 19.95 *(978-1-59583-187-3(8)*, 9781595831873, Green Tiger Pr.) Laughing Elephant.

Light, Kayte. Nicholas & the Spirit of Love. 2013. 16p. pap. 7.99 *(978-1-4624-0631-9(9)*, Inspiring Voices) Author Solutions, Inc.

Lomax M.Ed., L. E. A Saint Called Nicholas: The Christmas Legends Series, Vol. I. 2012. 52p. pap. 23.99 *(978-1-4582-0584-1(3)*, Abbott Pr.) Author Solutions, Inc.

Marzollo, Jean. I Spy Santa Claus. Wick, Walter, illus. 2006. (Scholastic Reader Level 1 Ser.). (ENG.). 32p. (J). (gr. -1-3). per. 3.99 *(978-0-439-78414-6(X))* Scholastic, Inc.

Mazurkiewicz, Jessica & Dahlen, Noelle. 3-D Coloring Book—Here Comes Santa Claus! 2011. (Dover 3-D Coloring Book Ser.). (ENG., Illus.). 32p. (J). (gr. 2-6). pap. 5.99 *(978-0-486-48413-6(0))* Dover Pubns., Inc.

Miller, Jocelyn. My Carry-Along Santa Activity Book: Christmas Fun with Stickers. Hughes, Cathy, illus. 2013. (ENG.). 32p. (J). (gr. k-2). pap. 9.99 *(978-0-7459-6419-5(2))* Lion Hudson PLC GBR. Dist: Independent Pubs. Group.

Moritz, Dianne, adapted by. Santa Lives! The Night Before Christmas. 2005. (Charming Petite Ser.). (Illus.). 64p. (J). 4.95 *(978-0-88088-467-9(3))* Peter Pauper Pr. Inc.

Publications International Ltd. Staff, ed. Rudolph the Red-Nosed Reindeer: My First Library. 2010. 10p. (J). bds. 12.98 *(978-1-60553-819-8(1))* Phoenix International Publications, Inc.

—Rudolph the Red-Nosed Reindeer: Book & Cuddly Rudolph. 2010. (J). 5.98 *(978-1-60553-750-4(0))* Phoenix International Publications, Inc.

—Rudolph the Red-Nosed Reindeer (Look & Find) 2010. 24p. (J). 7.98 *(978-1-60553-958-4(9))* Phoenix International Publications, Inc.

Schmidt, Marsha & Schmidt, Matt. The Santa Claus Project: Stories of Discovery about a Man in a Red Suit. 2012. 62p. (J). pap. 11.95 *(978-1-4772-6777-6(8))* AuthorHouse.

Stiegemeyer, Julie. Saint Nicholas: The Real Story of the Christmas Legend. Ellison, Chris, illus. 2003. 32p. (J). 13.49 *(978-0-7586-0376-0(2))* Concordia Publishing Hse.

Taplin, Sam. First Sticker Book Santa. 2011. (First Sticker Bks). 16p. (J). pap. 6.99 *(978-0-7945-3130-0(X)*, Usborne) EDC Publishing.

Tonn, Mary Jane. Jolly Old Santa Claus. 2008. (ENG., Illus.). 30p. (J). (gr. -1-1). pap. 3.95 *(978-0-8249-5513-7(7)*, Ideal Pubns.) Worthy Publishing.

Walsh, William S. The Story of Santa Klaus: Told for Children of All Ages from Six To. 2007. (ENG.). 216p. per. 24.95 *(978-1-4304-4232-5(8))* Kessinger Publishing, LLC.

Wick, Walter. Can You See What I See? - Christmas Read-and-Seek. Wick, Walter, illus. 2008. (Scholastic Reader Level 1 Ser.). (ENG., Illus.). 32p. (J). (gr. -1-3). pap. 3.99 *(978-0-545-07887-0(3))* Scholastic, Inc.

Yzermans, Vincent A. Wonderworker: The True Story of How St. Nicholas Became Santa Claus. 2004. (Illus.). 64p. pap. 12.95 *(978-0-87946-278-9(7)*, 249) ACTA Pubns.

SANTA CLAUS—FICTION

Aboff, Marcie. Santa's Big Red Helper. Haefele, Steve, illus. 2005. (Clifford Ser.). (ENG.). 80p. (J). (gr. k — 1). 2.99 *(978-0-439-79150-2(2))* Scholastic, Inc.

Agee, Jon. Little Santa. (ENG., Illus.). (J). 2015. 34p. (— 1). bds. 7.99 *(978-0-525-42940-1(9))* 2013. 40p. (gr. -1-k). 17.99 *(978-0-8037-3906-2(0))* Penguin Young Readers Group. (Dial Bks).

Allan, Nicholas. Father Christmas Needs a Wee! Allan, Nicholas, illus. 2009. (ENG., Illus.). 32p. (J). (gr. -1-k). pap. 13.99 *(978-1-86230-825-1(X)*, Red Fox) Random House Children's Books GBR. Dist: Independent Pubs. Group.

Anderson, Danny. Santa's Spy. 2012. 28p. pap. 15.99 *(978-1-4771-1007-2(0))* Xlibris Corp.

Anderson, Derek. How the Easter Bunny Saved Christmas. Anderson, Derek, illus. 2006. (ENG., Illus.). 40p. (J). (gr. -1-3). 17.99 *(978-0-689-87634-9(3)*, Simon & Schuster Bks. For Young Readers) Simon & Schuster Bks. For Young Readers.

Andes, Mary Lou. Santa's Prayer. Mattozzi, Patricia, illus. 2007. (J). (gr. -1-k). bds. 11.95 incl. cd-rom *(978-0-8198-7100-8(1))* Pauline Bks. & Media.

Andreae, Giles. I Love You Father Christmas. Dodd, Emma, illus. 2016. (ENG.). 24p. (J). (gr. -1 — 1). bds. 8.99 *(978-1-4083-3808-7(4)*, Orchard Bks.) Hachette Children's Group GBR. Dist: Hachette Bk. Group.

Angel. Santa Claus's Journey to Texusilver. 2009. 28p. pap. 12.49 *(978-1-4490-2432-1(7))* AuthorHouse.

Angel, Bruce. I Believe in Santa Claus. 2006. 121p. pap. 19.95 *(978-1-4241-1486-3(1))* PublishAmerica, Inc.

Anonymous. Rudolph Saves the Day. 2014. (J). lib. bdg. 14.75 *(978-0-606-36126-2(X))* Turtleback Bks.

—Rudolph the Red-Nosed Reindeer: Rudolph Saves the Day. 2014. (Rudolph the Red-Nosed Reindeer Ser.: 2). (ENG., Illus.). 24p. (J). (gr. -1-2). 4.99 *(978-1-250-05049-6(9)*, 9781250050496) Square Fish.

Antoine, Leon. Santa's Destiny: A Legend Reborn, 1 vol. 2010. 48p. pap. 16.95 *(978-1-4512-9281-7(3))* America Star Bks.

Aoki, Hisako. Santa's Favorite Story: Santa Tells the Story of the First Christmas. Gantschev, Ivan, illus. 2007. (ENG.). 28p. (J). (gr. -1-3). 9.99 *(978-1-4169-5029-5(X)*, Simon & Schuster Bks. For Young Readers) Simon & Schuster Bks. For Young Readers.

Apples for Santa. 2007. (Little Elf Set 1 Ser.). (J). 7.33 *(978-1-932570-73-1(X))* Pioneer Valley Bks.

Argenta, Joan. Santa Claus Comes to the Thomas Family. 2011. 16p. (gr. -1). pap. 8.43 *(978-1-4567-7846-0(3))* AuthorHouse.

Arnold, Tedd. Fly Guy's Ninja Christmas. Arnold, Tedd, illus. 2016. (Fly Guy Ser.: 16). (ENG., Illus.). 32p. (J). (gr. -1-3). 6.99 *(978-0-545-66277-2(X))* Scholastic, Inc.

Aronson, Jeff & Aronson, Miriam. Little Mike & Maddie's Christmas Book. Aronson, Jeff & Zephyr, Jay, illus. 2007. 32p. (J). 16.00 *(978-0-9795302-2-7(9)*, CrumbGobbler Pr.) Downtown Wetmore Pr.

Atamer, Bilie. A Christmas Party for Santa. 2013. 36p. pap. 13.95 *(978-1-61244-187-0(4))* Halo Publishing International.

Atamer, Billie. The Magic Sleigh. 2013. 28p. pap. 13.95 *(978-1-61244-213-6(7))* Halo Publishing International.

Attia, Stephan. Other Christmas Stories. 2009. 42p. pap. 19.68 *(978-0-557-11189-3(7))* Lulu Pr., Inc.

Auerbach, Annie. Santa's Sleigh. Pagnoni, Roberta, illus. 2017. (ENG.). 12p. (J). (gr. -1-k). bds. 5.99 ***(978-1-4380-5000-3(3))*** Barron's Educational Series, Inc.

Badalamenti, Andrew. Around the World in One Night. Santa's Secrets Unwrapped! 2008. 28p. 14.50 *(978-0-615-25180-6(3))* Badalamenti, Andrew.

Bailey, Linda. When Santa Was a Baby. Godbout, Geneviève, illus. 2015. (ENG.). 36p. (J). (gr. -1-2). 16.99 *(978-1-77049-556-2(8)*, Tundra Bks.) Tundra Bks. CAN. Dist: Penguin Random Hse. LLC.

Bailey, Tressie. The Little Box Kittens meet Santa Claus. 2009. 37p. pap. 24.10 *(978-0-557-03198-6(2))* Lulu Pr., Inc.

Bak, Jenny. Ten Gifts from Santa Claus: A Counting Book. Harding, Niall, illus. 2011. (ENG.). 22p. (J). (gr. -1-k). 14.99 *(978-1-4052-5127-3(1))* Egmont Bks., Ltd. GBR. Dist: Independent Pubs. Group.

Baker, Tommy. Santa Claus, the Fourth Wise Man. 2012. (ENG.). (J). 26p. pap. 13.95 *(978-1-4327-9630-3(5))*; 25p. pap. 18.95 *(978-1-4327-9774-4(3))* Outskirts Pr., Inc.

Balian, Lorna. Bah! Humbug?, 1 vol. 2006. (ENG., Illus.). 32p. (J). (gr. -1-3). 15.95 *(978-1-59572-036-8(7))* Star Bright Bks., Inc.

Banda, Rey A. The Magical City of Northopolis; a Christmas Story. Patlan, Alyssa A., illus. 2012. 50p. (-18). pap. 16.95 *(978-0-615-69125-1(0))* Northopolis.

Barrett, Judi. Santa from Cincinnati. Hawkes, Kevin, illus. 2012. (ENG.). 48p. (J). (gr. -1-3). 16.99 *(978-1-4424-2993-2(3)*, Atheneum Bks. for Young Readers) Simon & Schuster Children's Publishing.

Bass, William E. A Gift for Sant. Salazar, Vivian Rose, illus. 2012. 36p. pap. 24.95 *(978-1-4626-6731-4(7))* America Star Bks.

—Santa Revisits His Secret Little Helper. Salazar, Vivian, illus. 2012. 26p. 24.95 *(978-1-4626-5396-6(0))* America Star Bks.

Bates, Susan Welch. The Rag Picker's Christmas. 2008. 17p. pap. 24.95 *(978-1-60672-967-0(5))* America Star Bks.

Baugh, Helen. Rudy's Windy Christmas. Mantle, Ben, illus. 2015. (ENG.). 32p. (J). (gr. -1-3). 16.99 *(978-0-8075-7173-6(3))* Whitman, Albert & Co.

Baum, L. Frank. A Kidnapped Santa Claus. 2011. 24p. 12.95 *(978-1-4638-9603-4(4))*; pap. 6.95 *(978-1-4638-0070-3(3))* Rodgers, Alan Bks.

—L Frank Baum's Book of Santa Claus. 2007. 84p. per. 7.99 *(978-1-60459-118-7(8))* Wilder Pubns., Corp.

—The Life & Adventures of Santa Claus. 2007. 112p. 22.95 *(978-1-60312-592-5(2))* Aegypan.

—The Life & Adventures of Santa Claus. 2008. (ENG.). 216p. pap. 24.95 *(978-1-55709-180-2(3))* Applewood Bks.

—The Life & Adventures of Santa Claus. Clark, Mary Cowles, illus. 2011. 200p. *(978-1-84902-560-7(6))* Benediction Classics.

—The Life & Adventures of Santa Claus. Clark, Mary, illus. 2007. 156p. (gr. 4-7). 23.95 *(978-1-60206-778-3(3))*; per. 9.95 *(978-1-60206-777-6(5))* Cosimo, Inc.

—The Life & Adventures of Santa Claus. Clark, Mary Cowles, illus. 2015. (Penguin Christmas Classics Ser.). (ENG.). 176p. (gr. 12). 16.00 *(978-0-14-312853-3(1)*, Penguin Classics) Penguin Publishing Group.

Becker, Curt. The Sad Sant. Fariss, Michelle, illus. 2009. 36p. pap. 14.95 *(978-1-60844-161-7(X))* Dog Ear Publishing, LLC.

Bedford, David. I've Seen Santa! Warnes, Tim, illus. 2006. 32p. (J). (gr. -1-3). 15.95 *(978-1-58925-058-1(3))* Tiger Tales.

Bell, Jonas Fearon, des. Oh! Christmas Tree: A Fun-To-Find Lift-the-Flap Book. 2013. (ENG., Illus.). 20p. (gr. -1). bds. 8.99 *(978-1-77093-498-6(7))* Flowerpot Pr.

Bennett, Richard Grant, et al. Secret Santa. 2015. 17.99 *(978-1-4621-1739-0(2))* Cedar Fort, Inc./CFI Distribution.

Benson, Julian. The Christmas Dog: Lc's Worst Day Ever! 2012. 20p. pap. 24.95 *(978-1-4626-9816-5(6))* America Star Bks.

Benson, Nicky. The Spirit of Christmas: A Giving Tradition. 2014. 32p. 12.99 *(978-1-58925-188-5(1))* Tiger Tales.

Bently, Peter. The Tooth Fairy's Christmas. Parsons, Garry, illus. 2014. (J). *(978-1-4351-5739-2(7))* Barnes & Noble, Inc.

Berenstain, Stan & Berenstain, Jan. The Berenstain Bears Meet Santa Bear (Deluxe Edition) 2016. (First Time Books(R) Ser.). (ENG., Illus.). 32p. (J). (gr. -1-2). pap. 6.99 *(978-0-399-55767-5(9)*, Random Hse. Bks. for Young Readers) Random Hse. Children's Bks.

Berger, Samantha. Santa's Reindeer Games. Manders, John, illus. 2011. (J). *(978-0-545-36866-7(9))* Scholastic, Inc.

Bergeron, Denys. Les Bottes du Pere Noel. 2004. (Arion Pratique Ser.). (FRE., Illus.). 92p. (J). *(978-2-921493-88-8(8)*, Spotlight Poets) Arion.

Biedrzycki, David. Santa Retires. Biedrzycki, David, illus. 2012. (ENG., Illus.). 32p. (J). (gr. -1-3). 16.95 *(978-1-58089-293-3(0))*; pap. 7.95 *(978-1-58089-294-0(9))* Charlesbridge Publishing, Inc.

—Santa's New Jet. Biedrzycki, David & Bonnet, Rosalinde, illus. 2011. (ENG.). 32p. (J). (gr. -1-2). 16.95 *(978-1-58089-291-9(4))*; pap. 7.95 *(978-1-58089-292-6(2))* Charlesbridge Publishing, Inc.

—Santa's New Jet. 2007. (Illus.). (J). pap. *(978-0-545-00238-7(9))* Scholastic, Inc.

Bigalow, Stephen W. Who Is Santa? And How Did He Get to the North Pole? Megenhardt, Bill, illus. 2013. (ENG.). 144p. (J). (gr. 4-7). 19.95 *(978-0-9773757-3-8(0))* Profit Publishing.

Biggs, Brian. Everything Goes: Santa Goes Everywhere! Biggs, Brian, illus. 2013. (ENG., Illus.). 24p. (J). (gr. -1 — 1). bds. 7.99 *(978-0-06-195817-5(4))* HarperCollins Pubs.

Bizzarro, Grace. Christmas on the Internet. Bohart, Lisa, illus. 2013. 20p. pap. 12.95 *(978-1-61493-197-3(6))* Peppertree Pr., The.

Blessing, Victor. Santa Claus Got Sick Because. 2009. 24p. pap. 12.99 *(978-1-4490-1126-0(8))* AuthorHouse.

Bolin, Ken & Bolin, Corrine. Santa SP: Santa Clauses of the South Pole. 2003. (J). pap. 9.00 *(978-0-8059-6190-4(9))* Dorrance Publishing Co., Inc.

Boyd, Ken. Tinsel Tail Mouse. 2009. 48p. pap. 16.25 *(978-1-60860-403-6(9)*, Eloquent Bks.) Strategic Book Publishing & Rights Agency (SBPRA).

Bradbury, Lynne. Santa Claus Has a Busy Night. (Christmas Titles Ser.: No. S808-6). (Illus.). (J). 3.95 *(978-0-7214-5077-3(6)*, Dutton Juvenile) Penguin Publishing Group.

Bratun, Katy. Gingerbread Mouse. Bratun, Katy, illus. 2003. (Illus.). 32p. (J). (gr. -1-2). lib. bdg. 13.89 *(978-0-06-009081-4(2))* HarperCollins Pubs.

Brenner, Tom. And Then Comes Christmas. Christy, Jana, illus. 2014. (ENG.). 32p. (J). (gr. -1-3). 15.99 *(978-0-7636-5342-2(X))* Candlewick Pr.

Brett, Jan. The Animals' Santa. Brett, Jan, illus. 2014. (ENG., Illus.). 32p. (J). (gr. -1-k). 17.99 *(978-0-399-25784-1(5))*, G.P. Putnam's Sons Books for Young Readers) Penguin Young Readers Group.

Bridgman, C. A. Santa's Hawaiian Vacation. (J). 14.95 *(978-0-681-32827-3(4))* Booklines Hawaii, Ltd.

Bridwell, Norman. Clifford's Christmas Treasury. 2005. (Illus.). 96p. (gr. -1-3). pap. 10.99 *(978-0-439-79137-3(5))* Scholastic, Inc.

Briggs, Raymond. The Snowman & the Snowdog. 2015. (Step into Reading Ser.). (ENG., Illus.). 32p. (J). (gr. -1-1). 12.99 *(978-0-385-38735-4(0)*, Random Hse. Bks. for Young Readers) Random Hse. Children's Bks.

Brinkley, Lonnie. I Believe: Lost at the North Pole. 2008. (Illus.). 450p. (J). 29.95 *(978-0-9801215-3-7(1))* Big Bear Publishing U.S.

Brooks, Walter R. Freddy & the North Pole. Wiese, Kurt, illus. 2013. (ENG.). 322p. (gr. 4-13). pap. 10.99 *(978-1-4683-0320-9(1)*, 460320) Overlook Pr., The.

Brown, Jeff. Stanley's Christmas Adventure. Nash, Scott & Pamintuan, Macky, illus. 2010. (Flat Stanley Ser.). (ENG.). 96p. (J). (gr. 2-5). pap. 4.99 *(978-0-06-442175-1(9))* HarperCollins Pubs.

—Stanley's Christmas Adventure. 2010. (Flat Stanley Ser.). (J). (gr. -1-3). lib. bdg. 14.75 *(978-0-613-68466-8(4)*, Turtleback) Turtleback Bks.

Brown, Tricia. Musher's Night Before Christmas, 1 vol. Dubac, Debra, illus. 2011. (Night Before Christmas Ser.). (ENG.). 32p. (J). (gr. k-3). 16.99 *(978-1-58980-843-0(6))* Pelican Publishing Co., Inc.

Browning, Tom & Moore, Clement C. The Night Before Christmas. 2009. (ENG., Illus.). 48p. (J). (gr. k). 14.95 *(978-1-4027-5484-5(1)*, Sterling Innovation) Sterling Publishing Co., Inc.
Buckham, Derek. The Santa Stories. 2008. 81p. pap. 34.50 *(978-1-4092-4803-3(8))* Lulu Pr., Inc.
Burgess, Thornton W. The Christmas Reindeer. Chase, Rhoda, illus. 2013. (Dover Children's Classics Ser.). (ENG.). 160p. (J). (gr. k-3). pap. 5.99 *(978-0-486-49153-0(6))* Dover Pubns., Inc.
Byrne, Barbara. The Magic Bell On. 2003. 13p. 12.66 *(978-1-4116-1078-1(4))* Lulu Pr., Inc.
Califi, Matt. The Gnome Exchange Program: North Pole Rescue. 2017. (ENG.). (J). (gr. 3-7). pap. 17.99 ***(978-1-4621-2012-3(1)***, Sweetwater Bks.) Cedar Fort, Inc./CFI Distribution.
Campbell, H. David. Stanley: The Littlest Elf. 2012. 48p. pap. 21.99 *(978-1-4685-6257-6(6))* AuthorHouse.
Campbell, Suzy. Pennies for Christmas, 1 vol. 2010. 24p. 24.95 *(978-1-4512-0553-4(8))* PublishAmerica, Inc.
Candlewick Press Staff. Peppa Pig & the Lost Christmas List. Candlewick Press Staff, illus. 2014. (Peppa Pig Ser.). (ENG., Illus.). 32p. (J). (-k). 5.99 *(978-0-7636-7456-4(7)*, Candlewick Entertainment) Candlewick Pr.
—Peppa Pig & the Lost Christmas List. 2014. (Peppa Pig Ser.). lib. bdg. 16.00 *(978-0-606-35868-2(4))* Turtleback Bks.
Cannon, Sherrill S. Santa's Birthday Gift. 2009. 24p. pap. 11.50 *(978-1-60860-824-9(7)*, Eloquent Bks.) Strategic Book Publishing & Rights Agency (SBPRA).
Caro, Joe. Santa's Christmas Train. Shih, Lin, illus. 2005. 32p. pap. *(978-0-9628078-2-4(6))* Cowboy Collector Pubns.
—Santa's Christmas Train Coloring Book. Shih, Lin, illus. 2005. 32p. pap. *(978-0-9628078-5-5(0))* Cowboy Collector Pubns.
Carothers, Nina. Red Ed & the True Meaning of Christmas. Nilsen, Richard J., ed. Padovano, Chris, illus. 2013. 32p. pap. 12.97 *(978-1-937376-27-7(3))* All Star Pr.
Caviezel, Giovanni. Santa. Mesturini, Cristina, illus. 2012. (Mini People Shape Bks.). (ENG.). 10p. (J). bds. 4.99 *(978-0-7641-6578-8(X))* Barron's Educational Series, Inc.
—Santa's Toyshop. Rigo, Laura, illus. 2012. (ENG.). 10p. (J). (gr. -1-k). bds. 6.99 *(978-0-7641-6546-7(1))* Barron's Educational Series, Inc.
Chand, Emlyn. Courtney Saves Christmas. Giffin, Noelle, illus. 2012. 60p. 21.95 *(978-1-62253-114-1(0))* Evolved Publishing.
Chandler, Jeffery. The Christmas Santa Overslept. 2008. 13p. pap. 24.95 *(978-1-60703-421-6(2))* America Star Bks.
Child, Jeremy. Santa. Leach, Emma, illus. 2010. (Snow Shakers Ser.). (ENG.). 8p. (J). (gr. -1-k). bds. 4.99 *(978-0-7641-6384-5(1))* Barron's Educational Series, Inc.
Christian, Norma. A Christmas Mouse. 2012. 32p. pap. 13.99 *(978-1-4624-0328-8(X)*, Inspiring Voices) Author Solutions, Inc.
Christmas Book - Santa Claus. 2005. (J). bds. *(978-1-4194-0074-2(6))* Paradise Pr., Inc.
Christ's Santa. 2004. (YA). 19.95 *(978-0-9747815-0-1(9))* Life's Journey of Hope Pubns.
Chronicle Books Staff, et al. Little Reindeer. 2006. (Little Finger Puppet Board Bks.: FING). (ENG., Illus.). 12p. (J). (gr. -1 — 1). bds. 6.99 *(978-0-8118-5457-3(4))* Chronicle Bks. LLC.
Clark, Ruth E. Florida Santa: Is He Real? How Do We Know It? Caterisano, Sarah, illus. 2008. (ENG.). 32p. (J). (gr. -1-3). 16.95 *(978-0-9792963-0-7(7))* Hibiscus Publishing.
Claus, Nancy. Santa's Hat. Ferchaud, Steve, illus. 2006. (J). *(978-0-9746747-6-6(1))* Cypress Bay Publishing.
—Santa's Prize. Ferchaud, Steve, illus. 2006. (J). *(978-0-9746747-5-9(3))* Cypress Bay Publishing.
Claus, Santa. The Santa Legends Present: The Lost Button. 2005. (J). cd-rom 12.00 *(978-1-59971-079-2(X))* Aardvark Global Publishing.
—Santa's World: North Pole Series, Volume 1. 2006. (J). bds. 17.95 *(978-0-9787129-0-7(0))* North Pole Pr.
Coffelt, Soraya Diase. It's Not about You Mr. Santa Claus: A Love Letter about the True Meaning of Christmas. 2014. (Love Letters Book Ser.). (ENG., Illus.). 34p. pap. 8.99 *(978-1-63047-261-0(1))* Morgan James Publishing.
Coffin, Douglas. One Maine Christmas Eve, 1 vol. Coffin, Douglas, illus. 2015. (ENG., Illus.). 32p. (gr. -1-12). 16.95 *(978-0-88448-469-1(6)*, 884469) Tilbury Hse. Pubs.
Coldon, Christine. Emmalynn: Wondrously Magical Christmas Eve. 2012. 56p. pap. 24.99 *(978-1-4685-8735-7(8))* AuthorHouse.
Collict, Joan E. Robot Horse: A Christmas Tale. 2012. 20p. pap. 13.77 *(978-1-4669-6318-4(2))* Trafford Publishing.
Conners, Lauren. The Stuffed Frog in Santa's Sack. 2009. 28p. pap. 12.49 *(978-1-4490-4623-1(1))* AuthorHouse.
Conteh, Gerald. I Still Believe in Santa. 2007. 188p. per. 14.95 *(978-1-60264-014-6(9))* Virtualbookworm.com Publishing, Inc.
Cookies for Santa. 2006. (Little Elf Set 1 Ser.). (J). 7.33 *(978-1-932570-75-5(6))* Pioneer Valley Bks.
Cooper, Margaret. The Christmas Horse. Bohart, Lisa, illus. 2008. 32p. pap. 12.95 *(978-0-9821654-9-2(8))* Peppertree Pr., The.
Cornell-Castle, Violet R. Santa's Elves. 2008. 32p. pap. 18.65 *(978-1-4363-5899-6(X))* Xlibris Corp.
Craig, Barbara J. Santa's Magical Key. 2010. 20p. 10.49 *(978-1-4520-4399-9(X))* AuthorHouse.
Creamer, Joan Klatil. The Magic Sceptre - the Legend of Blue Santa Claus. Creamer, Joan Klatil, illus. 2006. (Illus.). 32p. (J). 16.95 *(978-0-9778476-3-1(2))* Silver Snowflake Publishing.
Crisp, Dan. Santa's Missing Reindeer. Crisp, Dan, illus. 2011. (ENG., Illus.). 12p. (J). (gr. -1-k). 12.99 *(978-0-230-71291-1(6))* Macmillan Pubs., Ltd. GBR. Dist: Independent Pubs. Group.
Crissey, Brian. The Loneliest Christmas Tree. Crissey, Noah, illus. 2004. 32p. (J). bds. 25.00 *(978-1-893183-35-3(1)*, 598) Granite Publishing, LLC.
Crissey, Brian L. The Loneliest Christmas Tree. Crissey, Noah, illus. 2004. (J). *(978-1-930724-13-6(6))*; *(978-1-930724-12-9(8))* Granite Publishing, LLC.
Crofoot, Nancy. Christmas in the Barn, 1 vol. Rawat, Tania, illus. 2009. 37p. pap. 24.95 *(978-1-61582-585-1(1))* America Star Bks.
Cronin, Doreen. Click, Clack, Ho! Ho! Ho! Lewin, Betsy, illus. 2015. (Click, Clack Book Ser.). (ENG.). 40p. (J). (gr. -1-2). 17.99 *(978-1-4424-9673-6(8))* Simon & Schuster Children's Publishing.
Crowley-Ranelli, D. Holiday Island: Santa in a Bathing Suit? 2009. 56p. pap. 9.95 *(978-1-60860-268-1(0)*, Eloquent Bks.) Strategic Book Publishing & Rights Agency (SBPRA).
Crowson, Andrew. Flip Flap Christmas. Crowson, Andrew, illus. 2003. (Illus.). 12p. (J). bds. *(978-1-85602-476-1(8)*, Pavilion Children's Books) Pavilion Bks.
Cummings, David W. How Biddikins & Buddikins Made Santa Claus Work Fast! 2005. (J). pap. 15.00 *(978-0-8059-6814-9(8))* Dorrance Publishing Co., Inc.
Cummings, Priscilla. Santa Claws: The Christmas Crab, 1 vol. Ramsey, Marcy Dunn, illus. 2009. (ENG.). 30p. (J). 10.50 *(978-0-87033-576-1(6)*, 9780870335761, Cornell Maritime Pr./Tidewater Pubs.) Schiffer Publishing, Ltd.
Curran, John. When I First Saw Santa. 2011. 20p. 10.03 *(978-1-4567-2708-6(7))* AuthorHouse.
Cuyler, Margery. That's Good! That's Bad! on Santa's Journey. 2015. (J). lib. bdg. 17.20 *(978-0-606-37582-5(1))* Turtleback Bks.
Daley-Prado, M. The Super Heroes Save Christmas! 2007. 24p. per. 24.95 *(978-1-4241-9123-9(8))* America Star Bks.
Daly, Jerald James. An Early Snow (the Visions Come) 2008. 180p. pap. 24.95 *(978-1-60703-610-4(X))* America Star Bks.
Daly, Kathleen N. Jingle Bells. Miller, J. P., illus. 2015. (Little Golden Book Ser.). (ENG.). 24p. (J). (-k). 4.99 *(978-0-553-51112-3(2)*, Golden Bks.) Random Hse. Children's Bks.
Daniels, Johanna. What About Claus? 2005. (Illus.). 32p. 15.95 *(978-0-9711106-8-7(9))* Mountaintop Pr.
Danowski, Jeffrey K. The Teddy Bear Necklace. 2012. 218p. 29.95 *(978-1-4626-9762-5(3))* America Star Bks.
Davenport, Kathy. Holly's Best Friend. 2010. 36p. 17.49 *(978-1-4520-2065-5(5))* AuthorHouse.
Davies, Margo. Do You Believe in Santa Claus? 2003. (J). 6.00 *(978-0-9708959-7-4(6)*, Accent Pubns.) Ajoyin Publishing, Inc.
Davis, Anne Shirley. No Red Suit for Santa? 2008. 16p. pap. 8.49 *(978-1-4389-2418-2(6))* AuthorHouse.
de Las Casas, Dianne. The House That Santa Built, 1 vol. Stone-Barker, Holly, illus. 2013. (ENG.). 32p. (J). (gr. -1-k). 16.99 *(978-1-4556-1750-0(4))* Pelican Publishing Co., Inc.
DeLand, M. Maitland. Baby Santa's Worldwide Christmas Adventure. Wilson, Phil, illus. 2010. 32p. (J). 14.95 *(978-1-60832-062-2(6))* Greenleaf Book Group.
Delrusso, Diana. Pages, the Book-Maker Elf. Schwab, Jordan, illus. 2008. 68p. pap. 23.49 *(978-1-4343-9844-4(7))* AuthorHouse.
Dempster, Al. Santa's Toy Shop (Disney) RH Disney Staff, illus. 2015. (Little Golden Book Ser.). (ENG.). 24p. (J). (-k). 4.99 *(978-0-7364-3401-0(1)*, Golden/Disney) Random Hse. Children's Bks.
Dempster, Al. Walt Disney's Santa's Toy Shop. 2015. (Illus.). (J). ***(978-0-7364-3402-7(X))*** Mouse Works.
Depken, Kristen L. Rudolph the Red-Nosed Reindeer. Karl, Linda, illus. 2014. (My Readers Ser.). (ENG.). 32p. (J). (gr. k-2). 15.99 *(978-1-250-05044-1(8)*, 9781250050441) Square Fish.
DePrisco, Dorothea. Randall Reindeer's Naughty & Nice Report. Reagan, Susan, illus. 2011. (ENG.). (J). (gr. -1-3). 24.95 *(978-1-61524-365-5(8)*, Intervisual/Piggy Toes) Bendon, Inc.
Dineen, Kaite. What Santa Wants You to Know: A Story of Santa's Love for Jesus, 1 vol. 2010. 34p. pap. 24.95 *(978-1-4489-7071-1(7))* PublishAmerica, Inc.
Disney Book Group Staff. Mickey Saves Santa. Disney Storybook Artists Staff, illus. 2009. (ENG.). 24p. (J). (gr. -1-k). pap. 5.99 *(978-1-4231-1846-6(4))* Disney Pr.
Dodd, Melissa. Santa Sheds, 1 vol. 2009. 17p. pap. 24.95 *(978-1-60749-208-5(3))* America Star Bks.
Dodson, Bert. Helping Santa: My First Christmas Adventure with Grandma. Dodson, Bert, illus. 2011. (ENG., Illus.). 32p. (J). (gr. 1-3). 17.95 *(978-1-59373-093-2(4))* Bunker Hill Publishing, Inc.
Donaldson, Julia. Stick Man. Scheffler, Axel, illus. (ENG.). 32p. (J). (gr. -1-3). 2016. 12.99 *(978-0-545-94789-3(8))* 2009. 16.99 *(978-0-545-15761-2(7))* Scholastic, Inc. (Levine, Arthur A. Bks.).
Donovan, Dan. A Christmas Tail! 2008. 28p. pap. 14.50 *(978-1-4389-1220-2(X))* AuthorHouse.
Donovan, Jane Monroe. Small, Medium & Large. Donovan, Jane Monroe, illus. 2010. (ENG., Illus.). 32p. (J). (gr. 1-4). 15.95 *(978-1-58536-447-3(9)*, 202172) Sleeping Bear Pr.
Dorman, Brandon. Santa's Stowaway. Dorman, Brandon, illus. 2009. (ENG., Illus.). 40p. (J). (gr. -1-3). 16.99 *(978-0-06-135188-4(1)*, Greenwillow Bks.) HarperCollins Pubs.
Dove, Karen. A Gift for Santa. 2012. 50p. 23.99 *(978-1-61996-793-9(6))*; pap. 12.99 *(978-1-61996-792-2(8))* Salem Author Services.
Drake, Rudy. Dushan, 1 vol. 2010. 20p. 24.95 *(978-1-4489-4875-8(4))* PublishAmerica, Inc.
Driscoll, Colleen. Piper the Elf Trains Santa. Dumm, Brian, illus. 2012. (ENG.). 32p. (J). 16.95 *(978-0-938467-56-4(5))* Headline Bks., Inc.
Dubel, Dorothy. The Magical Shoes of Santa's Elves(c). 2011. 24p. pap. 15.99 *(978-1-4568-7883-2(2))* Xlibris Corp.
Dunham, Terri Hoover. The Legend of Papa Noel: A Cajun Christmas Story. Knorr, Laura, illus. 2006. (Legends Ser.). (ENG.). 32p. (J). (gr. -1-3). 17.95 *(978-1-58536-256-1(5))* Sleeping Bear Pr.
Dunrea, Olivier. Merry Christmas, Ollie! (Gossie & Friends Ser.). (ENG., Illus.). (J). (gr. k — 1). 2011. 30p. bds. 6.99 *(978-0-547-37016-3(4))* 2008. 32p. 12.95 *(978-0-618-53242-1(0))* Houghton Mifflin Harcourt Publishing Co.
—Merry Christmas, Ollie (Reader) 2015. (Gossie & Friends Ser.). (ENG., Illus.). 32p. (J). (gr. -1 — 1). pap. 3.99 *(978-0-544-55394-1(2)*, HMH Books For Young Readers) Houghton Mifflin Harcourt Publishing Co.
Dunsany, Taylor. The Little Witch Who Lost Her Broom & Other Stories. 2008. 48p. pap. 8.95 *(978-0-595-52506-5(7))* iUniverse, Inc.
Duval, Kathy. The Three Bears' Christmas. Meisel, Paul, illus. (ENG.). 32p. (J). (gr. -1-3). 2006. 6.95 *(978-0-8234-2039-1(6))* 2005. 16.95 *(978-0-8234-1871-8(5))* Holiday Hse., Inc.
—The Three Bears' Christmas. Meisel, Paul, illus. 2007. (J). *(978-0-545-05421-8(4))* Scholastic, Inc.
Eight Jolly Reindeer. 2014. (ENG., Illus.). 16p. (J). (gr. -1 — 1). bds. 6.99 *(978-0-545-65145-5(X)*, Cartwheel Bks.) Scholastic, Inc.
Eldridge, Les. Santa's Cat. Eldridge, Les & Casey, James, illus. 2003. 24p. (J). *(978-1-877338-03-8(6))* Steele Roberts Aotearoa Ltd.
Elliott, Alan. Willy the Texas Longhorn, 1 vol. Ford, Stephanie, illus. 2013. (ENG.). 32p. (J). (gr. k-3). 16.99 *(978-1-4556-1870-5(5))* Pelican Publishing Co., Inc.
Emmett, Jonathan. The Santa Trap, 1 vol. Bernatene, Poly, illus. 2012. (ENG.). 32p. (J). 15.95 *(978-1-56145-670-3(5))* Peachtree Pubs.
Evert, Lori. The Christmas Wish. Breiehagen, Per, illus. Breiehagen, Per, photos by. 2013. (ENG.). 48p. (J). (gr. -1-2). 17.99 *(978-0-449-81681-3(8)*, Random Hse. Bks. for Young Readers) Random Hse. Children's Bks.
—The Christmas Wish. Breiehagen, Per, illus. Breiehagen, Per, photos by. 2013. (J). *(978-0-449-81942-5(6))* Random Hse., Inc.
Falk, Barbara Bustetter & Hyman, Helen Kandel. Don't Park on the Roof. 2007. 36p. per. 21.32 *(978-1-4257-7096-9(7))* Xlibris Corp.
Fambro, Sonja Grimsley. Santa Spent the Night with Me! 2011. 52p. pap. 25.06 *(978-1-4634-4626-0(8))* AuthorHouse.
—When Santa Goes to Church. 2011. 84p. pap. 32.26 *(978-1-4634-5983-3(1))* AuthorHouse.
Faulconer, Charlotte. The Green Button Wish. 2010. 28p. pap. 12.49 *(978-1-4490-8003-7(0))* AuthorHouse.
Fearne, Peter. My Week with Father Christmas. 2006. 176p. per. *(978-1-84667-021-3(7))* Derwent Pr., The.
Federici, Diane Marie. The Christmas Stocking. 2006. (J). pap. 8.00 *(978-0-8059-6874-3(1))* Dorrance Publishing Co., Inc.
Felden, Georgia. When Jesus Hired Santa. 2006. (J). pap. *(978-0-9790444-8-9(0))* Dynasty Publishing, Inc.
Feldman, Thea. Rudolph the Red-Nosed Reindeer - The Classic Story. Madrid, Erwin, illus. 50th ed. 2014. (Rudolph the Red-Nosed Reindeer Ser.). (ENG.). 40p. (J). (gr. -1-3). 12.99 *(978-1-250-04760-1(9)*, 9781250047601) Square Fish.
Ferguson, Sarah & Duchess of York Staff. Little Red's Christmas Story. Williams, Sam, illus. 2011. (ENG.). 40p. (J). (gr. -1-2). pap. 19.99 *(978-1-4424-3076-1(1)*, Simon & Schuster/Paula Wiseman Bks.) Simon & Schuster/Paula Wiseman Bks.
Figley, Marty Rhodes. Santa's Underwear. Kelley, Marty, illus. 2016. (ENG.). 32p. (J). (gr. k-3). 16.99 *(978-1-58536-954-6(3)*, 204109) Sleeping Bear Pr.
Franklin, Kathleen. Uncle Holly saves Christmas. 2010. (Illus.). 32p. 14.89 *(978-1-4520-9689-6(9))* AuthorHouse.
Frazee, Marla. Santa Claus the World's Number One Toy Expert. 2010. (ENG., Illus.). 32p. (J). (gr. -1-3). pap. 7.99 *(978-0-547-48074-9(1))* Houghton Mifflin Harcourt Publishing Co.
Froeb, Lori. Fisher-Price Little People Christmastime Is Here! 2015. (Fisher Price Lift the Flap Ser.). (ENG., Illus.). 10p. (J). (gr. -1-k). bds. 9.99 *(978-0-7944-3534-9(3))* Reader's Digest Assn., Inc., The.
Fry, Michael & Jackson, Bradley. The Naughty List. Fry, Michael, illus. 2015. (ENG., Illus.). 240p. (J). (gr. 3-7). 12.99 *(978-0-06-235475-4(2))* HarperCollins Pubs.
Fuggle, Debbie. The Two Little Fir Trees. 2012. 28p. pap. 32.70 *(978-1-4691-3253-2(2))* Xlibris Corp.
Garcia, Jeffrey. Santa Claus & the Molokai Mules. 2009. 32p. 17.95 *(978-0-9840942-0-2(2))* Garcia, Jeffrey.
Garis, Howard Roger. Johnnie & Billie Bushytail. 2004. reprint ed. pap. 15.95 *(978-1-4191-2786-1(1))*; pap. 1.99 *(978-1-4192-2786-8(6))* Kessinger Publishing, LLC.
Garland, Michael. Oh, What a Christmas! Garland, Michael, illus. 2011. (ENG., Illus.). 40p. (J). (gr. -1-3). 16.99 *(978-0-545-24210-3(X)*, Scholastic Pr.) Scholastic, Inc.
Garner, Ellen. Santa's Elves & the Tickets. Street, James, illus. 2012. 56p. pap. 12.99 *(978-0-615-55920-9(4))* EG Bks.
Garza, Xavier. Charro Claus & the Tejas Kid. 2008. (SPA & ENG., Illus.). 40p. (J). (gr. k-6). 17.95 *(978-1-933693-24-8(X))* Cinco Puntos Pr.
Gausselin, Richard J. How the Grandmas & Grandpas Saved Christmas. 2012. 24p. pap. 17.99 *(978-1-4772-4771-6(8))* AuthorHouse.
Gerencher, Jane. Santa's Sugar. Patch, Michael, illus. 2012. 51p. 15.50 *(978-0-9852501-3-3(5))* Inkwell Books LLC.
Gerver, Jane E. The Santa Snatcher. Spaziante, Patrick, illus. 2004. 32p. (J). lib. bdg. 15.00 *(978-1-4242-0959-0(5))* Fitzgerald Bks.
Gevry, C. C. A Christmas Kindness. Mabey, Coline, illus. 2012. 24p. pap. 11.99 *(978-0-9852661-4-1(7))* 4RV Publishing, LLC.
Godley, Marie. The Special Christmas Bear. 2007. (Illus.). 52p. per. *(978-1-84748-005-7(5))* Athena Pr.
Gomi, Taro. Presents Through the Window. 2016. (ENG., Illus.). 36p. (J). (gr. -1-k). 15.99 *(978-1-4521-5138-0(5))* Chronicle Bks. LLC.
Goodrich, Carter & Moore, Clement C. A Creature Was Stirring: One Boy's Night Before Christmas. Goodrich, Carter, illus. 2006. (ENG., Illus.). 40p. (J). (gr. -1-3). 17.99 *(978-0-689-86399-8(3)*, Simon & Schuster Bks. For Young Readers) Simon & Schuster Bks. For Young Readers.
Gordon, Peggy T. Santa's Secret. 2009. 24p. pap. 15.99 *(978-1-4415-5330-0(4))* Xlibris Corp.
Goss, Matt. Bear Crimbo. 2010. (ENG., Illus.). 72p. (J). 17.95 *(978-0-9815381-3-6(4))* Hilton Publishing Co.
Graham, Brandon. Perverts of the Unknown. Graham, Brandon, illus. 2003. (ENG., Illus.). 56p. pap. 10.99 *(978-1-56163-374-6(7))* NBM Publishing Co.
Grampa Ralph. Santa's New Boots, 1 vol. 2010. 48p. pap. 16.95 *(978-1-4489-5981-5(0))* America Star Bks.
Grandpa. The Beginning of Meet the Müsh-Mice: (a Visit to the North Pole) 2012. 34p. 29.95 *(978-1-4626-9377-1(6))* America Star Bks.
Green, Rod. Santa Claus: The Magical World of Father Christmas. 2014. (ENG., Illus.). 32p. (J). (gr. 1). 12.95 *(978-1-78312-076-5(2))* Carlton Bks., Ltd. GBR. Dist: Sterling Publishing Co., Inc.
Greenberg, Nicki. The Naughtiest Reindeer Goes South. 2017. (Naughtiest Reindeer Ser.: 3). (ENG.). 32p. (J). (gr. -1-1). 12.99 ***(978-1-76029-311-6(3))*** Allen & Unwin AUS. Dist: Independent Pubs. Group.
Greene, Rhonda Gowler. Santa's Stuck. Cole, Henry, illus. 2006. (ENG.). 32p. (J). (gr. -1-3). pap. 5.99 *(978-0-14-240686-1(4)*, Puffin Books) Penguin Young Readers Group.
Gregory, Larry. A Christmas Surprise. Woolmer, Nancy, illus. 2004. 24p. pap. 24.95 *(978-1-4137-3014-2(0))* PublishAmerica, Inc.
Grimmer, Constance Marie. Santa's Christmas Dogs: A Legend Begins... 2009. 28p. pap. 15.49 *(978-1-4490-5920-0(1))* AuthorHouse.
H M Bricker & Bricker, Howard Michael. The Christmas Santa Had No Beard. Dall, John, illus. 2011.Tr. of Navidad Que Santa Claus No Tovo Barba. (ENG & SPA.). 34p. (J). 15.45 *(978-0-615-42163-6(6))* H M Bricker.
Hagen, Carol L. The Night Henry Ford Met Santa. Faulkner, Matt, illus. 2006. (ENG.). 32p. (J). (gr. k-6). 17.95 *(978-1-58536-132-8(1))* Sleeping Bear Pr.
Haig, Matt. A Boy Called Christmas. Mould, Chris, illus. 2016. (ENG.). 240p. (J). (gr. 3-7). 16.99 *(978-0-399-55265-6(0)*, Knopf Bks. for Young Readers) Random Hse. Children's Bks.
Hale, Bruce. Santa on the Loose! Garbot, Dave, illus. 2012. (ENG.). 32p. (J). (gr. -1-3). 7.99 *(978-0-06-202262-2(8))* HarperCollins Pubs.
Hall, Annalisa. Tak & Lolly: Santa Clause at Church. 2009. 51p. pap. 6.99 *(978-0-557-04923-3(7))* Lulu Pr., Inc.
Hall, Martha Gamble. A Note from Sant. 2008. 16p. pap. 10.99 *(978-1-4389-2308-6(2))* AuthorHouse.
Hammon, Darrel L. Christmas Beneath the Lake: From the Adventures of Bob the Bullfrog. 2012. (ENG.). (J). (-18). 25p. pap. 23.95 *(978-1-4327-7916-0(8))*; 35p. pap. 17.95 *(978-1-4787-1910-6(9))* Outskirts Pr., Inc.
Hansen, Eric. Ian, Ceo, North Pole. 2008. 108p. pap. 9.95 *(978-1-60693-554-5(2)*, Eloquent Bks.) Strategic Book Publishing & Rights Agency (SBPRA).
Hardin, Holly. Aurora of the Northern Lights. 2009. 31p. (J). pap. 18.95 *(978-1-4327-2439-9(8))* Outskirts Pr., Inc.
Harley, Bill. Dear Santa: The Letters of James B. Dobbins. Alley, R. W., illus. 2005. 32p. (J). (ENG.). 15.99 *(978-0-06-623778-7(5))*; lib. bdg. 16.89 *(978-0-06-623779-4(3))* HarperCollins Pubs.
Harper, Stephan J. One Christmas Story. Steuerwald, Joy, illus. 2003. 32p. (J). lib. bdg. 16.95 *(978-0-9741800-0-7(9))* Inspire Press, Inc.
Harris, Danielle. The Second Chance Sant. 2012. 28p. pap. 24.95 *(978-1-4626-6778-9(3))* America Star Bks.
Harrison, Michael. Cop's Night Before Christmas, 1 vol. Miles, David, illus. 2010. (Night Before Christmas Ser.). (ENG.). 32p. (J). (gr. k-3). 16.99 *(978-1-58980-800-3(2))* Pelican Publishing Co., Inc.
Harry, Rebecca. Snow Bunny's Christmas Wish. Harry, Rebecca, illus. 2013. (ENG., Illus.). 32p. (J). (gr. -1-3). 16.99 *(978-0-545-54103-9(4)*, Orchard Bks.) Scholastic, Inc.
Hassett, Ann. The Finest Christmas Tree. Hassett, John, illus. 2010. (ENG.). 32p. (J). (gr. -1-3). pap. 6.99 *(978-0-547-40623-7(1))* Houghton Mifflin Harcourt Publishing Co.
Hatch, Justina. Charlie the Caterpillar, 1 vol. 2010. 44p. pap. 24.95 *(978-1-4489-9256-0(7))* PublishAmerica, Inc.
Hatfield, Kara. The Real Story of Sant. 2011. 30p. pap. 16.95 *(978-1-4626-1022-8(6))* America Star Bks.
Hazlehurst, Pam. Santa's Dilemm. 2012. (Illus.). 24p. pap. 19.82 *(978-1-4772-5079-2(4))* AuthorHouse.
Head, Jean. Andrew's Christmas Dream. 2012. 28p. pap. 5.00 *(978-1-937260-19-4(4))* Sleepytown Pr.
Healey, Richard (Dick). Holly the Christmas Dove. 2005. 36p. (J). 13.28 *(978-1-4116-5496-9(X))* Lulu Pr., Inc.
Heible, Beverly. A Christmas Party on River Row. 2012. 98p. 22.95 *(978-1-62709-018-6(5))*; pap. 17.95 *(978-1-4626-9575-1(2))* America Star Bks.
Heidecker, Samie. Who's Looking at Whom? Christmas, 1 vol. 2010. 38p. 24.95 *(978-1-4489-4855-0(X))* PublishAmerica, Inc.
Heierbacher, Michael. Yo Ho Ho Merry Christmas. 2010. (Illus.). 28p. (J). pap. 15.95 *(978-1-4327-6484-5(5))* Outskirts Pr., Inc.
Helen, Grace. Santa's Way. 2012. 32p. pap. 24.95 *(978-1-4626-7356-8(2))* America Star Bks.
Help for Santa. 2006. (Little Elf Set 1 Ser.). (J). 7.33 *(978-1-932570-76-2(4))* Pioneer Valley Bks.
Henderson, Richard. One Christmas Night. Shackelford, David, illus. 2008. 32p. (J). 15.95 *(978-0-615-17629-1(1))* St. Clair Publishing.
Higgins, Tiffany A. We've Seen Sant. Higgins, Clark L., illus. 2011. 26p. pap. 12.27 *(978-1-61204-267-1(8)*, Eloquent Bks.) Strategic Book Publishing & Rights Agency (SBPRA).
Hill, Kathi Harper. The Christmas Closet & Other Works. 2012. (ENG.). 48p. 16.99 *(978-1-936815-58-6(3))* Yawn's Bks. & More, Inc.
Hineman, Jonathan. Goodbye, Santa. Cruz, Cheryl, illus. 2013. 26p. (J). 16.95 *(978-1-60131-172-6(9))* Big Tent Bks.
Hodgson, Julie. The Magic of Christmas. 2007. 26p. 18.95 *(978-1-84799-350-2(8))* Lulu Pr., Inc.
Hoffer, Rod. The Strange Christmas Dream. 2012. 64p. pap. 24.99 *(978-1-4772-5949-8(X))* AuthorHouse.
Holm, H. R. Forever Santa. 2009. 14p. (J). pap. 2.99 *(978-1-59955-345-0(7))* Cedar Fort, Inc./CFI Distribution.
Holub, Joan. The Knights Before Christmas. Magoon, Scott, illus. 2015. (ENG.). 32p. (J). (gr. k-3). 16.99 *(978-0-8050-9932-4(8)*, 9780805099324, Holt, Henry & Co. Bks. For Young Readers) Holt, Henry & Co.
Hooper, Ruth. Santa's Factory. Charbonnel, Olivier & Mostyn, David, illus. 2004. 6p. (J). (gr. k-4). reprint ed. 16.00 *(978-0-7567-7585-8(X))* DIANE Publishing Co.
Hopkins, Charles. Santa's Frost Covered Sleigh Lay Broken in the Snow. 2007. pap. 17.00 *(978-0-8059-8935-9(8))* Dorrance Publishing Co., Inc.
Houghton Mifflin and Company Publishing Staff & Rey, H. A. The Family Christmas Treasury with CD & Downloadable Audio. 2013. (ENG., Illus.). 288p. (J). (gr. -1-3). 18.99 *(978-0-544-09249-5(X))* Houghton Mifflin Harcourt Publishing Co.
Howe, James. The Fright Before Christmas. Mack, Jeff, illus. (Bunnicula & Friends Ser.: 5). (ENG.). 48p. (J). (gr. 1-3).

S

2007. pap. 3.99 *(978-0-689-86941-9(X))* 2006. 16.99 *(978-0-689-86939-6(8))* Simon Spotlight. (Simon Spotlight).

Humphrey, Eleanor Cairns. Building Santa's Work Shop from Tales of the Crystal Cave. 2012. 268p. pap. 27.95 *(978-1-4626-7820-4(3))* America Star Bks.

Humphreys, Stephen. Harold Saves Christmas: A Harold & Charlie adventure Story. 2011. (Illus.). 28p. pap. 12.49 *(978-1-4520-9994-1(4))* AuthorHouse.

Hunter, Sara Hoagland. The Lighthouse Santa. Miner, Julia, illus. 2011. 36p. (J). (gr. -1-3). 17.95 *(978-1-61168-006-5(9))* Univ. Pr. of New England.

Hurley, Wes. How the Winter Frog Came to Was: Or, How to Get a Nice Surprise on Thanksgiving! Lee, Susan, illus. 2007. 36p. per. 24.95 *(978-1-4241-8395-1(2))* America Star Bks.

Hurst, Joshua. One Day at the North Pole. Johnson, Jared, illus. 2008. 44p. pap. 24.95 *(978-1-60703-327-1(5))* America Star Bks.

Inches, Alison. Santa Claus Is Green! How to Have an Eco-Friendly Christmas. Kirwan, Wednesday, illus. 2009. (Little Green Bks.). (ENG.). 24p. (J). (gr. -1-1). pap. 5.99 *(978-1-4169-7223-5(4),* Little Simon) Little Simon.

Iosue, Marilyn. Santa's Busy Day. 2007. pap. 17.00 *(978-0-8059-8761-4(4))* Dorrance Publishing Co., Inc.

Irvine, Patricia McCune. Haunted Pavilion: And Other Short Stories. 2003. 144p. 21.95 *(978-0-595-75249-2(7))* iUniverse, Inc.

Ismail, Yasmeen. Christmas for Greta & Gracie. Ismail, Yasmeen, illus. 2016. (ENG., Illus.). 32p. (J). (gr. -1-2). 15.99 *(978-0-7636-8943-8(2),* Nosy Crow) Candlewick Pr.

It's Santa. 2003. (J). per. *(978-1-57657-909-1(3))* Paradise Pr., Inc.

J. Katyn. Boo & the Halloween Grin. 2011. 36p. pap. *(978-1-4269-7197-6(4))* Trafford Publishing (UK) Ltd.

Jackson, Kate. Santa's Special Helper: A Spot-the-Difference Christmas Adventure! 2016. (ENG.). 18p. (J). bds. 7.99 *(978-1-4926-4175-9(8),* 9781492641759, Sourcebooks Jabberwocky) Sourcebooks, Inc.

Jacobson, Ryan. The Case of the Florida Freeze, 1 vol. Belkholm, Erica, illus. l.t. ed. 2005. (Santa Claus: Super Spy Ser.). (ENG.). 80p. (J). per. 4.99 *(978-0-9774122-0-4(2),* Getchu Bks.) Lake 7 Creative, LLC.

James, Eric. Santa's Sleigh Is on Its Way to Alabama. Dunn, Robert, illus. 2015. (ENG.). 32p. (J). (-2). 12.99 *(978-1-4926-2763-0(1),* Sourcebooks Jabberwocky) Sourcebooks, Inc.

—Santa's Sleigh Is on Its Way to California. Dunn, Robert, illus. 2015. (ENG.). 32p. (J). (-2). 12.99 *(978-1-4926-2747-0(X),* Sourcebooks Jabberwocky) Sourcebooks, Inc.

—Santa's Sleigh Is on Its Way to Colorado. Dunn, Robert, illus. 2015. (ENG.). 32p. (J). (-2). 12.99 *(978-1-4926-2756-2(9),* Sourcebooks Jabberwocky) Sourcebooks, Inc.

—Santa's Sleigh Is on Its Way to Florida. Dunn, Robert, illus. 2015. (ENG.). 32p. (J). (-2). 12.99 *(978-1-4926-2743-2(7),* Sourcebooks Jabberwocky) Sourcebooks, Inc.

—Santa's Sleigh Is on Its Way to Georgia. Dunn, Robert, illus. 2015. (ENG.). 32p. (J). (-2). 12.99 *(978-1-4926-2744-9(5),* Sourcebooks Jabberwocky) Sourcebooks, Inc.

—Santa's Sleigh Is on Its Way to Illinois. Dunn, Robert, illus. 2015. (ENG.). 32p. (J). (-2). 12.99 *(978-1-4926-2746-3(1),* Sourcebooks Jabberwocky) Sourcebooks, Inc.

—Santa's Sleigh Is on Its Way to Indiana. Dunn, Robert, illus. 2015. (ENG.). 32p. (J). (-2). 12.99 *(978-1-4926-2753-1(4),* Sourcebooks Jabberwocky) Sourcebooks, Inc.

—Santa's Sleigh Is on Its Way to Iowa. Dunn, Robert, illus. 2015. (ENG.). 32p. (J). (-2). 12.99 *(978-1-4926-2749-4(6),* Sourcebooks Jabberwocky) Sourcebooks, Inc.

—Santa's Sleigh Is on Its Way to Kentucky. Dunn, Robert, illus. 2015. (ENG.). 32p. (J). (-2). 12.99 *(978-1-4926-2761-6(5),* Sourcebooks Jabberwocky) Sourcebooks, Inc.

—Santa's Sleigh Is on Its Way to Louisiana. Dunn, Robert, illus. 2015. (ENG.). 32p. (J). (-2). 12.99 *(978-1-4926-2762-3(3),* Sourcebooks Jabberwocky) Sourcebooks, Inc.

—Santa's Sleigh Is on Its Way to Michigan. Dunn, Robert, illus. 2015. (ENG.). 32p. (J). (-2). 12.99 *(978-1-4926-2741-8(0),* Sourcebooks Jabberwocky) Sourcebooks, Inc.

—Santa's Sleigh Is on Its Way to Minnesota. Dunn, Robert, illus. 2015. (ENG.). 32p. (J). (-2). 12.99 *(978-1-4926-2748-7(8),* Sourcebooks Jabberwocky) Sourcebooks, Inc.

—Santa's Sleigh Is on Its Way to Missouri. Dunn, Robert, illus. 2015. (ENG.). 32p. (J). (-2). 12.99 *(978-1-4926-2759-3(3),* Sourcebooks Jabberwocky) Sourcebooks, Inc.

—Santa's Sleigh Is on Its Way to My House. Dunn, Robert, illus. 2015. (ENG.). 32p. (J). (-2). 12.99 *(978-1-4926-2740-1(2),* Sourcebooks Jabberwocky) Sourcebooks, Inc.

—Santa's Sleigh Is on Its Way to New Jersey. Dunn, Robert, illus. 2015. (ENG.). 32p. (J). (-2). 12.99 *(978-1-4926-2758-6(5),* Sourcebooks Jabberwocky) Sourcebooks, Inc.

—Santa's Sleigh Is on Its Way to New York. Dunn, Robert, illus. 2015. (ENG.). 32p. (J). (-2). 12.99 *(978-1-4926-2751-7(8),* Sourcebooks Jabberwocky) Sourcebooks, Inc.

—Santa's Sleigh Is on Its Way to North Carolina. Dunn, Robert, illus. 2015. (ENG.). 32p. (J). (-2). 12.99 *(978-1-4926-2750-0(X),* Sourcebooks Jabberwocky) Sourcebooks, Inc.

—Santa's Sleigh Is on Its Way to Ohio. Dunn, Robert, illus. 2015. (ENG.). 32p. (J). (-2). 12.99 *(978-1-4926-2742-5(9),* Sourcebooks Jabberwocky) Sourcebooks, Inc.

—Santa's Sleigh Is on Its Way to Pennsylvania. Dunn, Robert, illus. 2015. (ENG.). 32p. (J). (-2). 12.99 *(978-1-4926-2745-6(3),* Sourcebooks Jabberwocky) Sourcebooks, Inc.

—Santa's Sleigh Is on Its Way to South Carolina. Dunn, Robert, illus. 2015. (ENG.). 32p. (J). (-2). 12.99 *(978-1-4926-2757-9(7),* Sourcebooks Jabberwocky) Sourcebooks, Inc.

—Santa's Sleigh Is on Its Way to Tennessee. Dunn, Robert, illus. 2015. (ENG.). 32p. (J). (-2). 12.99 *(978-1-4926-2752-4(6),* Sourcebooks Jabberwocky) Sourcebooks, Inc.

—Santa's Sleigh Is on Its Way to Texas. Dunn, Robert, illus. 2015. (ENG.). 32p. (J). (-2). 12.99 *(978-1-4926-2739-5(9),* Sourcebooks Jabberwocky) Sourcebooks, Inc.

—Santa's Sleigh Is on Its Way to Virginia. Dunn, Robert, illus. 2015. (ENG.). 32p. (J). (-2). 12.99 *(978-1-4926-2754-8(2),* Sourcebooks Jabberwocky) Sourcebooks, Inc.

—Santa's Sleigh Is on Its Way to Washington. Dunn, Robert, illus. 2015. (ENG.). 32p. (J). (-2). 12.99 *(978-1-4926-2760-9(7),* Sourcebooks Jabberwocky) Sourcebooks, Inc.

—Santa's Sleigh Is on Its Way to Wisconsin. Dunn, Robert, illus. 2015. (ENG.). 32p. (J). (-2). 12.99 *(978-1-4926-2755-5(0),* Sourcebooks Jabberwocky) Sourcebooks, Inc.

—Santa's Sleigh Is on Its Way to Arkansas: A Christmas Adventure. Dunn, Robert, illus. 2016. (ENG.). 32p. (J). (-2). 12.99 *(978-1-4926-4317-3(3),* 9781492643173, Sourcebooks Jabberwocky) Sourcebooks, Inc.

—Santa's Sleigh Is on Its Way to Boise: A Christmas Adventure. Dunn, Robert, illus. 2016. (ENG.). 32p. (J). (-2). 12.99 *(978-1-4926-4318-0(1),* 9781492643180, Sourcebooks Jabberwocky) Sourcebooks, Inc.

—Santa's Sleigh Is on Its Way to Boston: A Christmas Adventure. Dunn, Robert, illus. 2016. (ENG.). 32p. (J). (-2). 12.99 *(978-1-4926-4319-7(X),* 9781492643197, Sourcebooks Jabberwocky) Sourcebooks, Inc.

—Santa's Sleigh Is on Its Way to Canada: A Christmas Adventure. Dunn, Robert, illus. 2016. (ENG.). 32p. (J). (-2). 12.99 *(978-1-4926-4321-0(1),* 9781492643210, Sourcebooks Jabberwocky) Sourcebooks, Inc.

—Santa's Sleigh Is on Its Way to Charleston: A Christmas Adventure. Dunn, Robert, illus. 2016. (ENG.). 32p. (J). (-2). 12.99 *(978-1-4926-4322-7(X),* 9781492643227, Sourcebooks Jabberwocky) Sourcebooks, Inc.

—Santa's Sleigh Is on Its Way to Cincinnati: A Christmas Adventure. Dunn, Robert, illus. 2016. (ENG.). 32p. (J). (-2). 12.99 *(978-1-4926-4324-1(6),* 9781492643241, Sourcebooks Jabberwocky) Sourcebooks, Inc.

—Santa's Sleigh Is on Its Way to Connecticut: A Christmas Adventure. Dunn, Robert, illus. 2016. (ENG.). 32p. (J). (-2). 12.99 *(978-1-4926-4325-8(4),* 9781492643258, Sourcebooks Jabberwocky) Sourcebooks, Inc.

—Santa's Sleigh Is on Its Way to Delaware: A Christmas Adventure. Dunn, Robert, illus. 2016. (ENG.). 32p. (J). (-2). 12.99 *(978-1-4926-4326-5(2),* 9781492643265, Sourcebooks Jabberwocky) Sourcebooks, Inc.

—Santa's Sleigh Is on Its Way to Edmonton: A Christmas Adventure. Dunn, Robert, illus. 2016. (ENG.). 32p. (J). (-2). 12.99 *(978-1-4926-4327-2(0),* 9781492643272, Sourcebooks Jabberwocky) Sourcebooks, Inc.

—Santa's Sleigh Is on Its Way to Hawaii: A Christmas Adventure. Dunn, Robert, illus. 2016. (ENG.). 32p. (J). (-2). 12.99 *(978-1-4926-4328-9(9),* 9781492643289, Sourcebooks Jabberwocky) Sourcebooks, Inc.

—Santa's Sleigh Is on Its Way to Kansas: A Christmas Adventure. Dunn, Robert, illus. 2016. (ENG.). 32p. (J). (-2). 12.99 *(978-1-4926-4330-2(0),* 9781492643302, Sourcebooks Jabberwocky) Sourcebooks, Inc.

—Santa's Sleigh Is on Its Way to Kansas City: A Christmas Adventure. Dunn, Robert, illus. 2016. (ENG.). 32p. (J). (-2). 12.99 *(978-1-4926-4331-9(9),* 9781492643319, Sourcebooks Jabberwocky) Sourcebooks, Inc.

—Santa's Sleigh Is on Its Way to Las Vegas: A Christmas Adventure. Dunn, Robert, illus. 2016. (ENG.). 32p. (J). (-2). 12.99 *(978-1-4926-4332-6(7),* 9781492643326, Sourcebooks Jabberwocky) Sourcebooks, Inc.

—Santa's Sleigh Is on Its Way to Los Angeles: A Christmas Adventure. Dunn, Robert, illus. 2016. (ENG.). 32p. (J). (-2). 12.99 *(978-1-4926-4333-3(5),* 9781492643333, Sourcebooks Jabberwocky) Sourcebooks, Inc.

—Santa's Sleigh Is on Its Way to Maine: A Christmas Adventure. Dunn, Robert, illus. 2016. (ENG.). 32p. (J). (-2). 12.99 *(978-1-4926-4334-0(3),* 9781492643340, Sourcebooks Jabberwocky) Sourcebooks, Inc.

—Santa's Sleigh Is on Its Way to Maryland: A Christmas Adventure. Dunn, Robert, illus. 2016. (ENG.). 32p. (J). (-2). 12.99 *(978-1-4926-4335-7(1),* 9781492643357, Sourcebooks Jabberwocky) Sourcebooks, Inc.

—Santa's Sleigh Is on Its Way to Massachusetts: A Christmas Adventure. Dunn, Robert, illus. 2016. (ENG.). 32p. (J). (-2). 12.99 *(978-1-4926-4336-4(X),* 9781492643364, Sourcebooks Jabberwocky) Sourcebooks, Inc.

—Santa's Sleigh Is on Its Way to Mississippi: A Christmas Adventure. Dunn, Robert, illus. 2016. (ENG.). 32p. (J). (-2). 12.99 *(978-1-4926-4337-1(8),* 9781492643371, Sourcebooks Jabberwocky) Sourcebooks, Inc.

—Santa's Sleigh Is on Its Way to Montana: A Christmas Adventure. Dunn, Robert, illus. 2016. (ENG.). 32p. (J). (-2). 12.99 *(978-1-4926-4338-8(6),* 9781492643388, Sourcebooks Jabberwocky) Sourcebooks, Inc.

—Santa's Sleigh Is on Its Way to Nevada: A Christmas Adventure. Dunn, Robert, illus. 2016. (ENG.). 32p. (J). (-2). 12.99 *(978-1-4926-4340-1(8),* 9781492643401, Sourcebooks Jabberwocky) Sourcebooks, Inc.

—Santa's Sleigh Is on Its Way to New England: A Christmas Adventure. Dunn, Robert, illus. 2016. (ENG.). 32p. (J). (-2). 12.99 *(978-1-4926-4341-8(6),* 9781492643418, Sourcebooks Jabberwocky) Sourcebooks, Inc.

—Santa's Sleigh Is on Its Way to New Hampshire: A Christmas Adventure. Dunn, Robert, illus. 2016. (ENG.). 32p. (J). (-2). 12.99 *(978-1-4926-4342-5(4),* 9781492643425, Sourcebooks Jabberwocky) Sourcebooks, Inc.

—Santa's Sleigh Is on Its Way to New Mexico: A Christmas Adventure. Dunn, Robert, illus. 2016. (ENG.). 32p. (J). (-2). 12.99 *(978-1-4926-4343-2(2),* 9781492643432, Sourcebooks Jabberwocky) Sourcebooks, Inc.

—Santa's Sleigh Is on Its Way to New York City: A Christmas Adventure. Dunn, Robert, illus. 2016. (ENG.). 32p. (J). (-2). 12.99 *(978-1-4926-4344-9(0),* 9781492643449, Sourcebooks Jabberwocky) Sourcebooks, Inc.

—Santa's Sleigh Is on It's Way to Newfoundland: A Christmas Adventure. Dunn, Robert, illus. 2016. (ENG.). 32p. (J). (-2). 12.99 *(978-1-4926-4505-4(2),* 9781492645054, Sourcebooks Jabberwocky) Sourcebooks, Inc.

—Santa's Sleigh Is on Its Way to North Dakota: A Christmas Adventure. Dunn, Robert, illus. 2016. (ENG.). 32p. (J). (-2). 12.99 *(978-1-4926-4345-6(9),* 9781492643456, Sourcebooks Jabberwocky) Sourcebooks, Inc.

—Santa's Sleigh Is on It's Way to Nova Scotia: A Christmas Adventure. Dunn, Robert, illus. 2016. (ENG.). 32p. (J). (-2). 12.99 *(978-1-4926-4508-5(7),* 9781492645085, Sourcebooks Jabberwocky) Sourcebooks, Inc.

—Santa's Sleigh Is on Its Way to Oklahoma: A Christmas Adventure. Dunn, Robert, illus. 2016. (ENG.). 32p. (J). (-2). 12.99 *(978-1-4926-4346-3(7),* 9781492643463, Sourcebooks Jabberwocky) Sourcebooks, Inc.

—Santa's Sleigh Is on Its Way to Pittsburgh: A Christmas Adventure. Dunn, Robert, illus. 2016. (ENG.). 32p. (J). (-2). 12.99 *(978-1-4926-4351-7(3),* 9781492643517, Sourcebooks Jabberwocky) Sourcebooks, Inc.

—Santa's Sleigh Is on Its Way to Portland: A Christmas Adventure. Dunn, Robert, illus. 2016. (ENG.). 32p. (J). (-2). 12.99 *(978-1-4926-4352-4(1),* 9781492643524, Sourcebooks Jabberwocky) Sourcebooks, Inc.

—Santa's Sleigh Is on Its Way to Rhode Island: A Christmas Adventure. Dunn, Robert, illus. 2016. (ENG.). 32p. (J). (-2). 12.99 *(978-1-4926-4353-1(X),* 9781492643531, Sourcebooks Jabberwocky) Sourcebooks, Inc.

—Santa's Sleigh Is on Its Way to South Dakota: A Christmas Adventure. Dunn, Robert, illus. 2016. (ENG.). 32p. (J). (-2). 12.99 *(978-1-4926-4355-5(6),* 9781492643555, Sourcebooks Jabberwocky) Sourcebooks, Inc.

—Santa's Sleigh Is on Its Way to Tampa Bay: A Christmas Adventure. Dunn, Robert, illus. 2016. (ENG.). 32p. (J). (-2). 12.99 *(978-1-4926-4357-9(2),* 9781492643579, Sourcebooks Jabberwocky) Sourcebooks, Inc.

—Santa's Sleigh Is on Its Way to Tulsa: A Christmas Adventure. Dunn, Robert, illus. 2016. (ENG.). 32p. (J). (-2). 12.99 *(978-1-4926-4359-3(9),* 9781492643593, Sourcebooks Jabberwocky) Sourcebooks, Inc.

—Santa's Sleigh Is on Its Way to Utah: A Christmas Adventure. Dunn, Robert, illus. 2016. (ENG.). 32p. (J). (-2). 12.99 *(978-1-4926-4360-9(2),* 9781492643609, Sourcebooks Jabberwocky) Sourcebooks, Inc.

James G. Normand. Santa's Secret Trick. 2009. (Illus.). 52p. pap. 20.49 *(978-1-4389-5788-3(2))* AuthorHouse.

Jarvis, Cathy. Red Beard Santa's Biker Buddy. 2013. 36p. pap. 15.49 *(978-1-4669-9587-1(4))* Trafford Publishing.

Jatkowska, Ag. Santa Sticker Fun. Jatkowska, Ag, illus. 2016. (ENG., Illus.). 56p. (J). (gr. -1-3). pap. 9.99 ***(978-1-5098-2786-2(2))*** Pan Macmillan GBR. Dist: Independent Pubs. Group.

Jeffers, Susan. The Twelve Days of Christmas. Jeffers, Susan, illus. 2013. (ENG., Illus.). 40p. (J). (gr. -1-3). 17.99 *(978-0-06-206615-2(3))* HarperCollins Pubs.

Jeffers, Susan, illus. The Twelve Days of Christmas. 2013. (J). *(978-0-06-206616-9(1))* Harper & Row Ltd.

Johansen, Tesia. The Christmas Secret. Johnson, Gary & Johansen, Tesia, illus. 2011. 28p. pap. 24.95 *(978-1-4626-3242-8(4))* America Star Bks.

Johnston, Patches. Mark's Mixed-up Months. 2004. 33p. pap. 24.95 *(978-1-4137-2432-5(9))* PublishAmerica, Inc.

Jones, Carl. Rudy the Rangifer & Why Her Nose Turned Orange. 2007. 64p. pap. 14.99 *(978-0-9748266-3-9(4))* Grampa Jones's Publishing Co.

Jones, Christianne C. The Santa Shimmy. Randall, Emma, illus. 2015. (Holiday Jingles Ser.). (ENG.). 20p. (gr. -1 — 1). bds. 5.99 *(978-1-4795-6494-1(X))* Picture Window Bks.

Jones, Ernest, illus. The Great Mix Up. 2005. (ENG.). 42p. (J). 17.99 *(978-0-9772282-0-1(7))* B. T. Brooks.

Jones, Sandy. Anya's Gift: A Tale of Two Christmases, 1 vol. Yourell, Pam, illus. 2009. 48p. pap. 24.95 *(978-1-61546-129-5(9))* America Star Bks.

Jordan, L. W. Santa Heads South: Casey's Christmas Surprise. Lasson, Matt, illus. 2008. 40p. per. 24.95 *(978-1-60441-374-8(3))* America Star Bks.

Joyce, William & Geringer, Laura. Nicholas St. North & the Battle of the Nightmare King. Bk. 1. Joyce, William, illus. 2011. (Guardians Ser.: 1). (ENG., Illus.). 240p. (J). (gr. 2-6). 15.99 *(978-1-4424-3048-8(6),* Atheneum Bks. for Young Readers) Simon & Schuster Children's Publishing.

Karr, Lily. My Santa Claus. Johnson, Jay, illus. 2012. (ENG.). 12p. (J). (gr. -1-k). bds. 4.99 *(978-0-545-43649-6(4))* Scholastic, Inc.

Keane, Michael. The Night Santa Got Lost: How NORAD Saved Christmas. Garland, Michael, illus. (ENG.). 28p. (J). (gr. -1). 2012. 14.95 *(978-1-59698-810-1(X),* Little Patriot Pr.) 2015. 16.99 *(978-1-62157-398-2(2),* Regnery Kids) Regnery Publishing, Inc., An Eagle Publishing Co.

Kelley, True. The Dog Who Saved Santa. Kelley, True, illus. 2008. (ENG., Illus.). 32p. (J). (gr. -1-3). 16.95 *(978-0-8234-2120-6(1))* Holiday Hse., Inc.

Kessler, Leonard. That's Not Santa! (Hello Reader! Ser.). (FRE., Illus.). (J). pap. 5.99 *(978-0-590-24360-5(8))* Scholastic, Inc.

Kibblesmith, Daniel & Quach, A. P. Santa's Husband. 2017. 32p. 16.99 ***(978-0-06-274874-4(2),*** Collins Design) HarperCollins Pubs.

Kilgore, Lee. The Riddle of the Rustled Reindeer: A Christmas Mystery. 2009. 50p. pap. 16.95 *(978-1-61546-863-8(3))* America Star Bks.

Klein, Abby. Secret Santa Surprise! McKinley, John, illus. 2015. 86p. (J). ***(978-0-545-86357-5(0))*** Scholastic, Inc.

Klimo, Kate. Dragon Keepers #6: the Dragon at the North Pole. Shroades, John, illus. (Dragon Keepers Ser.). (ENG.). 176p. (J). (gr. 3-7). 2014. 6.99 *(978-0-375-87117-7(9),* Yearling) 2013. 15.99 *(978-0-375-87066-8(0),* Random Hse. Bks. for Young Readers) Random Hse. Children's Bks.

Kneen, Maggie. The First Christmas: An Angel Came to Nazareth. 2010. (ENG., Illus.). 24p. (J). (gr. -1-1). 9.99 *(978-0-8118-7662-9(4))* Chronicle Bks. LLC.

Knights, Harry B. Luigi & the Lost Wish, 1 vol. Calico World Entertainment Staff, illus. 2003. (Nicholas Stories Ser.: 4). (ENG.). 56p. (J). (gr. k-3). 16.95 *(978-1-58980-162-2(8))* Pelican Publishing Co., Inc.

—The Maiden Voyage of Kris Kringle, 1 vol. Calico World Entertainment Staff, illus. 2003. (Nicholas Stories Ser.: 3). (ENG.). 56p. (J). (gr. k-3). 16.95 *(978-1-58980-161-5(X))* Pelican Publishing Co., Inc.

Koontz, Dean. Robot Santa: The Further Adventures of Santa's Twin. Parks, Phil, illus. 2004. (Santa's Twin Ser.: Bk. 2). 72p. (J). 20.89 *(978-0-06-050944-6(9))* HarperCollins Pubs.

—Santa's Twin. Parks, Phil, illus. 2004. (Santa's Twin Ser.: Bk. 1). (ENG.). 64p. pap. 12.95 *(978-0-06-057223-5(X),* William Morrow Paperbacks) HarperCollins Pubs.

Kremer, Kevin. Santa's Our Substitute Teacher. Ely, Dave, illus. 2006. 150p. (gr. 4-7). per. 5.99 *(978-0-9663335-4-1(3),* 703-001) Snow In Sarasota Publishing.

Kulka, Joe. Christmas Coal Man. Kulka, Joe, illus. 2015. (ENG., Illus.). 32p. (J). (gr. k-3). lib. bdg. 17.99 *(978-1-4677-1607-9(3),* Carolrhoda Bks.) Lerner Publishing Group.

—The Christmas Coal Man. Kulka, Joe, illus. 2015. (ENG., Illus.). 32p. (J). (gr. k-3). 17.99 *(978-1-4677-8808-3(2),* Carolrhoda Bks.) Lerner Publishing Group.

Kurtz, John. Claus Kids Christmas Coloring Book. 2011. (Dover Holiday Coloring Book Ser.). (ENG.). 32p. (J). (gr. k-5). pap. 3.99 *(978-0-486-48292-7(8))* Dover Pubns., Inc.

—Claus Kids Stickers. 2011. (Dover Little Activity Books Stickers Ser.). (ENG.). 4p. (J). (gr. k-3). pap. 1.50 *(978-0-486-48294-1(4))* Dover Pubns., Inc.

La Porte, Mary Ellen. The Almost Christmas Story. 2011. 44p. pap. 18.99 *(978-1-4520-9946-0(4))* AuthorHouse.

Lambert, Lydia. Scrub-A-Dub Reindeer: Bath Mitt & Bath Book Set. Jones, Anna, illus. 2015. (Scrub-A-Dub Bath Mitt & Bath Book Sets Ser.). (ENG.). 8p. (J). (gr. -1 — 1). 9.99 *(978-1-4380-7584-6(7))* Barron's Educational Series, Inc.

—Scrub-A-Dub Santa: Bath Mitt & Bath Book Set. Jones, Anna, illus. 2015. (Scrub-A-Dub Bath Mitt & Bath Book Sets Ser.). (ENG.). 8p. (J). (gr. -1 — 1). 9.99 *(978-1-4380-7585-3(5))* Barron's Educational Series, Inc.

Lansley, Oliver. Holly & Ivan's Christmas Adventure. 2012. (ENG., Illus.). 96p. (J). (gr. k-5). pap. 16.95 *(978-1-84943-136-1(1))* Oberon Bks., Ltd. GBR. Dist: Consortium Bk. Sales & Distribution.

L.A.S., Alex. Magnificent Sir Johnny & Santa Claus. 2011. 36p. pap. 24.95 *(978-1-4626-3401-9(X))* America Star Bks.

Lee, Chris. Becoming a Sant: A Guidebook for Parents & Santa's Helpers. 2008. 48p. pap. 16.95 *(978-1-60563-449-4(2))* America Star Bks.

Lee, Stan. Stan Lee's Superhero Christmas. Jessell, Tim, illus. 2nd ed. 2016. (ENG.). (J). (gr. k-2). 27.95 ***(978-1-59687-526-5(7),*** ipicturebooks) ibooks, Inc.

Lee, Stan. Superhero Christmas. Jessell, Tim, illus. 2004. 32p. (J). (gr. -1-2). 16.89 *(978-0-06-056560-2(8))* HarperCollins Pubs.

Lepage, Michaele. A Year at Santa's Workshop. 2009. 32p. pap. 14.55 *(978-1-4343-7989-4(2))* AuthorHouse.

LePage, Michaele L. & Lovass-Nagy, Nicole. A Year at the North Pole. 2009. 31p. 16.95 *(978-0-557-06430-4(9))* Lulu Pr., Inc.

Letter to Santa. 2003. (Traditional Christmas Stories Ser.). 32p. (J). 4.98 *(978-0-7525-8845-2(1))* Parragon, Inc.

Leuck, Laura. Santa Claws. Grimly, Gris, illus. 2006. (ENG.). 32p. (J). (gr. -1-3). 16.95 *(978-0-8118-4992-0(9))* Chronicle Bks. LLC.

Levine, Whitney Joy. The Tiniest Reindeer. 2008. 24p. pap. 12.99 *(978-1-4389-3102-9(6))* AuthorHouse.

Lewis, Anne Margaret. The Runaway Santa. Zenz, Aaron, illus. 2015. (ENG.). 40p. (J). (gr. -1-k). 15.99 *(978-1-63450-589-5(1),* Sky Pony Pr.) Skyhorse Publishing Co., Inc.

Lewis, J. Patrick. The Snowflake Sisters. Desimini, Lisa, illus. 2012. (ENG.). 32p. (J). (gr. -1-3). pap. 16.99 *(978-1-4424-6719-4(3),* Atheneum Bks. for Young Readers) Simon & Schuster Children's Publishing.

Lewis, Michael G. The Great Pirate Christmas Battle, 1 vol. Jaskiel, Stan, illus. 2014. (ENG.). 32p. (J). (gr. k-3). 16.99 *(978-1-4556-1934-4(5))* Pelican Publishing Co., Inc.

Lincoln, Dallas Ford. The Sawmill Sant. 2011. 36p. pap. 16.95 *(978-1-4626-4335-6(3))* America Star Bks.

Lindstrom, Ken. Grandpa, Is There Really a Santa Claus? 2008. 20p. pap. 10.99 *(978-1-4389-2127-3(6))* AuthorHouse.

Lippman, Peter. Santa's Workshop. (ENG.). (J). bds. 79.60 *(978-0-7611-0489-6(5),* 20489) Workman Publishing Co., Inc.

Little Bee Books Staff. My Santa Book. 2015. (ENG., Illus.). 12p. (J). (gr. -1 — 1). bds. 5.99 *(978-1-4998-0129-3(7))* Little Bee Books Inc.

Little, Paul D. The Christmas Chips. 2009. 44p. pap. 15.50 *(978-1-60860-578-1(7),* Eloquent Bks.) Strategic Book Publishing & Rights Agency (SBPRA).

Litwin, Eric. Pete the Cat Saves Christmas. Dean, James, illus. (Pete the Cat Ser.). 40p. (J). (gr. -1-3). 2014. (ENG.). 17.99 *(978-0-06-211062-6(4))* 2012. lib. bdg. 18.89 *(978-0-06-211063-3(2))* HarperCollins Pubs.

Lizana, Robert V. Two Weeks Before Christmas. 2012. 24p. pap. 17.99 *(978-1-4772-7164-3(3))* AuthorHouse.

Lombardi, Elizabeth L. Jonathan's Journey. 2012. (ENG.). (J). *(978-1-62148-014-3(3))* SteinerBooks, Inc.

Lutz, Nancie Anne. Patsy & Freckles Make Christmas Cookies. Lutz, Nancie Anne, illus. 2005. (Illus.). 25p. (J). *(978-0-9760064-1-1(3))* Dollworks.

MacGuire, Maxine. Maddie & the Naughty Elf: Santa Learns a Lesson, 1 vol. 2010. 36p. 24.95 *(978-1-4489-8250-9(2))* PublishAmerica, Inc.

MacLennan, David. Santa's Stormy Christmas Eve. Parkinson, Cheryl, tr. Parkinson, Cheryl, illus. 2004. 32p. 7.95 *(978-0-9731960-0-9(9))* Full Satchel Pr. CAN. Dist: Wilson & Assocs.

Madaras, Diana. Kitty Humbug's Christmas Tail. Madaras, Diana & Nielsen, Ric, illus. 2009. 24p. 17.99 *(978-1-892344-56-4(4))* Palomino Publishing.

Mader, C. Roger, illus. Stowaway in a Sleigh. 2016. (ENG.). 32p. (J). (gr. -1-3). 17.99 *(978-0-544-48174-9(7),* HMH

Books For Young Readers) Houghton Mifflin Harcourt Publishing Co.

Major, Kevin. The House of Wooden Santas, 1 vol. Pratt, Ned, photos by. gif. ed. 2004. (ENG., Illus.). 96p. (J). 34.95 (978-0-88995-249-2(3)) Red Deer Pr. CAN. Dist: Fitzhenry & Whiteside, Ltd.

A Manatee Christmas. 2007. (Illus.). 32p. (J). lib. bdg. 15.99 (978-0-9771059-7-7(0)) Thomas Expressions, LLC.

Marsh, Carole. The Story of Santa Claus. 2003. 12p. (J). (gr. k-4). pap. 2.95 (978-0-635-02151-9(X)) Gallopade International.

Martini, T. J. Christmas Lost & Found. Kiejna, Magdalenea, illus. 2017. (J). per. 15.99 (978-0-9705018-7-5(0)) Wings, Inc.

Matsuura, Richard & Matsuura, Ruth. Gift from Santa. Chao, Linus, illus. (J). 7.95 (978-1-887916-06-6(7)) Orchid Isle Publishing Co.

McAnulty, Stacy. Dear Santasaurus. Kaminsky, Jef, illus. 2013. (ENG.). 32p. (J). (gr. k-3). 15.95 (978-1-59078-876-9(1)) Boyds Mills Pr.

McArdle, Donald. Santa's Newest Friend. 2007. 25p. (J). 21.50 (978-0-615-14212-8(5)) McArdle, Donald.

McDade Jr, Bert M. Why Santa Claus Comes at Christmas. Swope, Brenda, illus. 2011. 32p. pap. 24.95 (978-1-4560-0921-2(4)) America Star Bks.

McFarlane, Sheryl. Island Santa, 1 vol. Lott, Sheena, illus. 2012. (ENG.). 32p. (J). (gr. k). 19.95 (978-0-9880536-0-1(8)) Queen Alexandra Foundation for Children CAN. Dist: Orca Bk. Pubs. USA.

McGuirk, Leslie. Ho, Ho, Ho, Tucker! McGuirk, Leslie, illus. 2010. (Candlewick Storybook Animations Ser.). (ENG., Illus.). 32p. (J). (-k). 8.99 (978-0-7636-5043-8(9)) Candlewick Pr.

McLean, Michael & McLean, Scott. Fairy Tale Christmas. 2014. (ENG., Illus.). 176p. (J). (gr. 3-9). 15.99 (978-1-60907-930-7(2), Shadow Mountain) Shadow Mountain Publishing.

McMahan, Gregg. Christmas Honey. 2012. (ENG.). pap. 10.00 (978-1-4675-5319-3(0)) Independent Pub.

Metzger, Steve. Waiting for Santa. Edgson, Alison, illus. 2015. (ENG.). 32p. (J). (gr. 2-6). 16.99 (978-1-58925-199-1(7)) Tiger Tales.

Milgrim, David. See Santa Nap. Milgrim, David, illus. 2016. (Adventures of Otto Ser.). (ENG., Illus.). 32p. (J). (gr. -1-k). pap. 3.99 (978-1-4814-6787-2(5), Simon Spotlight) Simon Spotlight.

Mitter, Matt. Fisher-Price Little People: Santa's Helpers. 2016. (ENG.). 12p. (J). (gr. -1-k). bds. 5.99 (978-0-7944-3799-2(0)) Studio Fun International.

Modugno, Maria. Santa Claus & the Three Bears. Dyer, Jane & Dyer, Brooke, illus. 2013. (ENG.). 40p. (J). (gr. -1-3). 17.99 (978-0-06-170023-1(1)) HarperCollins Pubs.

Moore, Brian L. The Story Behind Santa Sacks. Mulligan, Todd, illus. 2004. 32p. (978-0-9732651-0-1(8)) Hills-n-Hollows Publishing.

Moore, Clement C. Grumpy Santa. Spiridellis, Gregg & Spiridellis, Evan, illus. 2003. (ENG.). (J). (978-0-439-53039-2(3), Orchard Bks.) Scholastic, Inc.

—My First Night Before Christmas. Newsom, Tom, illus. 2008. (ENG.). 12p. (J). 9.95 (978-1-58117-808-1(5), Intervisual/Piggy Toes) Bendon, Inc.

—The Night Before Christmas. Newsom, Tom, illus. 2007. (ENG.). 18p. (J). (gr. -1-3). 19.95 (978-1-4037-2947-7(6), Intervisual/Piggy Toes) Bendon, Inc.

—The Night Before Christmas, Set. gif. ed. 2012. (ENG.). 48p. (J). 29.95 (978-1-60433-296-4(4), Applesauce Pr.) Cider Mill Pr. Bk. Pubs., LLC.

Morozumi, Atsuko. The Elves' First Christmas. 2009. (Illus.). 32p. (J). (gr. -1-1). 16.95 (978-1-935021-61-2(3)) Price, Mathew Ltd.

Muncaster, Harriet. The Biggest Smallest Christmas Present. Muncaster, Harriet, illus. 2016. (ENG., Illus.). 32p. (J). (-k). 16.99 (978-0-399-16432-3(4), G.P. Putnam's Sons Books for Young Readers) Penguin Young Readers Group.

Mundt, A. S. The Letter. 2011. 36p. pap. 14.49 (978-1-4634-3936-1(9)) AuthorHouse.

Murail, Marie-aude & Murail, Elvire. Santa's Last Present. Blake, Quentin, illus. 2004. (ENG.). 32p. (J). (gr. 3-7). 12.95 (978-1-56145-319-1(6)) Peachtree Pubs.

Murphy, T. M. Saving Santa's Seals. Taylor, Adam, illus. 2009. (LeapKids Ser.). (ENG.). 170p. (J). (gr. 1-5). pap. 10.95 (978-0-9815148-8-8(X)) Leapfrog Pr.

Nesbø, Jo. Silent (but Deadly) Night. Lowery, Mike, illus. 2017. (J). pap. **(978-1-5344-1000-8(7)**, Simon & Schuster/Paula Wiseman Bks.) Simon & Schuster/Paula Wiseman Bks.

Nguyen, Anthony. Santa with His Reindeer. 2004. pap. 8.00 (978-0-8059-6261-1(1)) Dorrance Publishing Co., Inc.

Nivens, Karen. Benjamin P. Blizzard: Welcome to Christmastown. Grisham, Jason, illus. 2007. 48p. (J). per. (978-0-9798154-1-6(X)) Living Waters Publishing Co.

Norman, Travis D. Christmas Island. Baker, David, illus. 2011. 28p. pap. 24.95 (978-1-4560-9800-1(4)) America Star Bks.

The North Pole Is Sinking! 2005. (J). 9.99 (978-0-9773674-0-5(1)) Blue State Pr.

Nosy Crow Staff. Roly Poly Looks for Santa Claus: A Tiny Tab Book. Ho, Jannie, illus. 2016. (Tiny Tab Ser.). (ENG.). 8p. (J). (— 1). bds. 7.99 (978-0-7636-8938-4(6), Nosy Crow) Candlewick Pr.

Nyaradi, J. A. Catching Santa. 2006. 140p. pap. 11.95 (978-0-7414-3462-3(8)) Infinity Publishing.

O., Lila. Lulabelle's Jewels: The Christmas Wish of Mrs. Claus. 2008. 20p. pap. 12.49 (978-1-4389-3189-0(1)) AuthorHouse.

O, Lila & O., Lila. Lula Belle's Jewels: The Christmas Wish of Mrs. Claus. 2011. 28p. pap. 17.50 (978-1-4634-3326-0(3)) AuthorHouse.

O'Dea, Kendra J. Polar Bear Pond. 2007. (Illus.). 62p. (J). per. 11.95 (978-0-9799162-0-5(8)) Shortbread Hill Bk. Co.

O'Donnell, Kevin & Gon, Zang Sung. Stone Age Santa. Kim, Boo Young et al, illus. 2007. (ENG.). 184p. (J). (gr. 4-7). per. 11.95 (978-1-58818-153-4(7)) Hill Street Pr., LLC.

Pallotta, Jerry. Dinosaur Christmas. McWilliam, Howard, illus. 2013. (ENG.). 32p. (J). (gr. k-2). 12.99 (978-0-545-43360-0(6)) Scholastic, Inc.

—Santa Pups. Terry, Will, illus. 2016. (ENG.). 32p. (J). (gr. -1-k). 6.99 (978-0-545-48479-4(0)) Scholastic, Inc.

—Santa Pups. Terry, Will, illus. 2016. (ENG.). 32p. (J). (gr. -1-k). 17.20 (978-0-606-39130-6(4)) Turtleback Bks.

Partridge, Helen L. Blinky: The Bear Who Wouldn't Hibernate. 2008. 32p. per. 24.95 (978-1-4241-9261-8(7)) America Star Bks.

Pasquali, Elena. Santa's Midnight Sleighride. Vagnozzi, Barbara, illus. 2013. (Finger-Trail Animal Tales Ser.). (ENG.). 10p. (J). (gr. -1-k). bds. 9.99 (978-0-7459-6242-9(4)) Lion Hudson PLC GBR. Dist: Independent Pubs. Group.

Patterson, James. SantaKid. Garland, Michael, illus. 2004. (ENG.). 48p. (J). (gr. -1-1). 17.99 (978-0-316-00061-1(2), Jimmy Patterson) Little Brown & Co.

Peet, Amanda & Troyer, Andrea. Dear Santa, Love, Rachel Rosenstein. Davenier, Christine, illus. 2015. (ENG.). 40p. (J). (gr. -1-2). 20.99 (978-0-553-51062-1(2)); 17.99 (978-0-553-51061-4(4)) Random Hse. Children's Bks. (Doubleday Bks. for Young Readers).

Pelham, David. Here Comes Santa: A Mini Holiday Pop-Up. Pelham, David, illus. 2008. (ENG., Illus.). 18p. (J). 11.99 (978-1-4169-5440-8(6), Little Simon) Little Simon.

Perry, Rex, illus. 'Twas the Night Before Christmas. 2004. 24p. (J). lib. bdg. 8.00 (978-1-4242-0641-4(3)) Fitzgerald Bks.

Pingk, Rubin. Samurai Santa: A Very Ninja Christmas. Pingk, Rubin, illus. 2015. (ENG., Illus.). 40p. (J). (gr. -1-3). 17.99 (978-1-4814-3057-9(2), Simon & Schuster Bks. For Young Readers) Simon & Schuster Bks. For Young Readers.

Pingry, Patricia A. Dear Santa... Rasmussen, Wendy, illus. 2005. (ENG.). 24p. (J). (gr. -1-k). bds. 6.95 (978-0-8249-6618-8(X), Ideal Pubns.) Worthy Publishing.

Plehal, Christopher J. Yes, Virginia: There Is a Santa Claus. Bernardin, James, illus. 2010. (ENG.). 32p. (J). (gr. -1-2). 16.99 (978-0-06-200173-3(6)) HarperCollins Pubs.

Ploog, Michael G. L. Frank Baum's the Life & Adventures of Santa Claus. Ploog, Michael G., illus. 2003. (Illus.). 80p. (YA). (gr. 7-12). reprint ed. 25.00 (978-0-7567-6682-5(6)) DIANE Publishing Co.

Powell Zalewski, Amy. Maybe the Truth about Santa. Mugambi, Christina Nkirote, illus. 2005. 32p. (J). (gr. -1-3). 15.00 (978-0-9773608-1-9(4)) Shiny Red Ball Publishing.

Poydar, Nancy. Brave Santa. 2004. (ENG., Illus.). 32p. (J). (gr. k-3). tchr. ed. 16.95 (978-0-8234-1821-3(9)) Holiday Hse., Inc.

Priddy, Roger. Santa Claus. 2012. (Funny Faces Ser.). (ENG., Illus.). 10p. (J). (gr. -1-1). bds. 8.99 (978-0-312-51558-4(8), 9780312515584, Priddy Bks.) St. Martin's Pr.

Primavera, Elise. Auntie Claus & the Key to Christmas. 2011. (ENG., Illus.). 40p. (J). (gr. -1-3). pap. 7.99 (978-0-547-57679-4(X)) Houghton Mifflin Harcourt Publishing Co.

—Auntie Claus Gift Edition. Primavera, Elise, illus. 2015. (ENG., Illus.). 40p. (J). (gr. -1-3). 17.99 (978-0-544-53872-6(2), HMH Books For Young Readers) Houghton Mifflin Harcourt Publishing Co.

Provencio, Marta. The Christmas Dragon. 2013. 24p. pap. 12.99 (978-1-4808-0379-4(0)) Archway Publishing.

Publications International Ltd. Staff, ed. Rudolph the Red-Nosed Reindeer(r): A Flashlight Adventure Sound Book. 2014. 14p. (J). (978-1-4508-9047-2(4), 1450890474) Publications International, Ltd.

Punter, Russell. Stories of Santa. Webb, Philip, illus. 2006. (Young Reading Series 1 Gift Bks.). 48p. (J). 8.99 (978-0-7945-1476-1(6), Usborne) EDC Publishing.

R., Charlie. The Christmas Mama Santa Delivered the Toys. 2012. 36p. 19.95 (978-1-4626-6824-3(0)) PublishAmerica, Inc.

Rader, Laura. When Santa Lost His Ho! Ho! Ho! Rader, Laura, illus. 2008. (ENG., Illus.). 40p. (J). (gr. -1-3). 14.99 (978-0-06-114139-3(9)) HarperCollins Pubs.

Rae, Jaci. Collista's Search for the True Meaning of Christmas. 2007. (Illus.). 59p. per. 14.95 (978-0-9746229-1-0(5)) North Shore Records, Inc.

Ralph, Grampa. How Santa Knows. 2007. 56p. pap. 16.95 (978-1-4241-2284-4(8)) America Star Bks.

Random House. Santa's Little Helpers (Team Umizoomi) Ostrom, Bob, illus. 2013. (Pictureback(R) Ser.). (ENG.). 16p. (J). (gr. -1-2). 4.99 (978-0-449-81881-7(0), Random Hse. Bks. for Young Readers) Random Hse. Children's Bks.

Rasmussen, Liz, illus. Too Fat to Fly. 2007. 32p. (J). 16.95 (978-0-9793517-0-9(7)) Silver Bells Publishing Hse.

Rawlinson, Julia. Fletcher & the Snowflake Christmas. Beeke, Tiphanie, illus. 2010. (ENG.). 32p. (J). (gr. -1-2). 16.99 (978-0-06-199033-5(7), Greenwillow Bks.) HarperCollins Pubs.

Reagan, Jean. How to Catch Santa. Wildish, Lee, illus. 2015. (ENG.). 32p. (J). (gr. -1-3). 17.99 (978-0-553-49839-4(8)); lib. bdg. 20.99 (978-0-553-49840-0(1)) Random Hse. Children's Bks. (Knopf Bks. for Young Readers).

Reasoner, Charles. Inside Santa's Toy Shop. Reasoner, Charles, illus. 2007. (Story Book Ser.). (Illus.). 12p. (J). (gr. k-3). bds. (978-1-84666-151-8(X), Tide Mill Pr.) Top That! Publishing PLC.

Reasoner, Charles & Wood, Hannah. Peek-A-Boo Reindeer, 1 vol. Reasoner, Charles, illus. 2014. (Charles Reasoner Peek-A-Boo Bks.). (ENG., Illus.). 10p. (gr. -1 — 1). bds. 12.99 (978-1-4795-5179-8(1)) Picture Window Bks.

Rees, Douglas. Jeannette Claus Saves Christmas. Latyk, Olivier, illus. 2010. (ENG.). 40p. (J). (gr. k-3). 16.99 (978-1-4169-2686-3(0), McElderry, Margaret K. Bks.) McElderry, Margaret K. Bks.

Reindeer. 2003. (Shaped Board Books Ser.). 14p. (J). (gr. -1-k). bds. 9.95 (978-0-7525-8850-6(8)) Parragon, Inc.

Reiss, Mike. Santa's Eleven Months Off, 1 vol. Montgomery, Michael G., illus. (ENG.). (J). 2016. 28p. (gr. -1-3). pap. 7.95 (978-1-56145-962-9(3)) 2007. 32p. (gr. k-3). 16.95 (978-1-56145-421-1(4)) Peachtree Pubs.

Reynolds, Carl. The Turkey Mountain Gang's... . Christmas Adventure! 2010. 44p. pap. 18.49 (978-1-4520-6514-4(4)) AuthorHouse.

Rice, James. Santa's Revenge, 1 vol. Rice, James, illus. 2005. (ENG., Illus.). 32p. (J). (gr. k-3). 16.99 (978-1-58980-250-6(0)) Pelican Publishing Co., Inc.

Rigo, L., illus. Little Reindeer. 2014. (Mini People Shape Bks.). (ENG.). 10p. (J). (gr. -1-2). bds. 4.99 (978-0-7641-6736-2(7)) Barron's Educational Series, Inc.

Rissman, Angelica. Julius & the Lost Letter to Santa. 2003. (J). 7.99 (978-1-59384-019-8(5)) Parklane Publishing.

Ritchie, Joseph R. Where's Santa? Halverson, Lydia, illus. 2006. (ENG.). 14p. (J). (gr. -1-k). bds. 7.95 (978-0-8249-6673-7(2), Ideal Pubns.) Worthy Publishing.

(Robert Thompson), Pau Pau. Santa's Secret Helpers, 1 vol. 2009. 55p. pap. 16.95 (978-1-60836-859-4(9)) America Star Bks.

Robertson, Si & Nelson, Ashley Howard. Uncle Si, the Christmas Elf: Work Hard, Nap Hard. Gilpin, Stephen, illus. 2014. (ENG.). 48p. (J). (gr. -1-3). 29.99 (978-1-4814-1821-8(1), Simon & Schuster Bks. For Young Readers) Simon & Schuster Bks. For Young Readers.

Robinson, George. Elmer the Elf & the Magical Jingle Bells, 1 vol. Foster, Janet, illus. 2008. (ENG.). 33p. 24.95 (978-1-60610-606-8(6)) America Star Bks.

Robinson, Michelle. Goodnight Santa: The Perfect Bedtime Book. East, Nick, illus. 2015. (Goodnight Ser.). (ENG.). 32p. (gr. -1 — 1). pap. 7.99 (978-1-4380-0660-4(8)) Barron's Educational Series, Inc.

Rodriguez, Sergio R. Little Santa & Snowboy: The Childhood Adventures of Santa Claus. 2007. (Illus.). 32p. (J). pap. 8.95 (978-0-615-17411-2(6)) Little Santa Bks., Inc.

Rooks, Elizabeth. Where Does Santa Go on Vacation after Christmas? 2012. 24p. pap. 17.99 (978-1-4772-6535-2(X)) AuthorHouse.

—Where Does Santa Work after Christmas? 2012. 24p. pap. 17.99 (978-1-4772-9210-5(1)) AuthorHouse.

Rookstool, Yakiri. A Christmas Star. 2009. 80p. pap. 9.95 (978-1-60693-855-3(X), Eloquent Bks.) Strategic Book Publishing & Rights Agency (SBPRA).

Rose, M. E. Kangaroo Christmas. Keenan, Brona, illus. 2007. (ENG.). 140p. (YA). 10.95 (978-1-896209-89-0(0)) Bayeux Arts, Inc. CAN. Dist: Chicago Distribution Ctr.

Rosier, Joan. Christmas Stilts. 2008. (ENG.). 24p. 12.99 (978-1-4389-3907-0(8)) AuthorHouse.

Ross, Richard. Arctic Airlift. 2005. (Illus.). 36p. (J). 17.00 (978-0-9763119-0-4(9)) Blue Fox Pr.

Roussos, J. C. A Gift for Santa. 2016. (ENG.). (J). pap. 6.99 **(978-1-942840-20-6(9))** Hocus Pocus Publishing, Inc.

Rowland, Teresa. Blusher's First Christmas. 2012. 64p. (-18). pap. 20.95 (978-1-4525-0718-7(X)) Balboa Pr.

Rumbley, Rose-Mary. Dear Santa: Thanks for the Piano. 2004. (Illus.). 46p. (J). pap. 8.95 (978-1-57168-466-0(2)) Eakin Pr.

Russo, Frank M. The Sleigh. Cittadino, Kyle & Cittadino, Kristen, illus. 2012. 24p. 24.95 (978-1-4626-6916-5(6)); pap. 24.95 (978-1-4626-7662-0(6)) America Star Bks.

Russo, Mallory Kate. The Hotel Christmas. 2012. 24p. pap. 24.95 (978-1-4626-8060-3(7)) America Star Bks.

Ryan, Brittney. The Legend of Holly Claus. Long, Laurel, illus. 2004. (Julie Andrews Collection). 544p. (J). (gr. 4-18). 16.99 (978-0-06-058511-2(0)); lib. bdg. 17.89 (978-0-06-058514-3(5)) HarperCollins Pubs. (Julie Andrews Collection).

Sadler, R. D. The Littlest Bell. 2011. 16p. pap. 10.70 (978-1-4567-5364-1(9)) AuthorHouse.

Sammartino, Joseph & Ozimkowski, Edward. The Legend of Kringle. 2009. 48p. pap. 19.95 (978-1-4490-5241-6(X)) AuthorHouse.

Sansone, V. K. The Carpenter & His Wife. 2009. 32p. pap. 14.98 (978-0-557-19204-5(8)) Lulu Pr., Inc.

Santa. 2003. (Shaped Board Books Ser.). 14p. (J). (gr. -1-k). bds. 9.95 (978-0-7525-8851-3(6)) Parragon, Inc.

Santa & the Elves. 2003. (J). per. (978-1-57657-908-4(5)) Paradise Pr., Inc.

Santa Claus & the Kids on the Farm. 2004. (J). per. 15.99 (978-0-9753533-0-1(6)) Golden Eagle Publishing Hse., Inc.

Santa Gets A Haircut. 2005. (J). 5.95 (978-0-9769321-3-0(X)) Steingart, Nathan Publishing.

Santa Gets New Glasses. 2005. (J). 5.95 (978-0-9769321-2-3(1)) Steingart, Nathan Publishing.

Santa Goes to the Dentist. 2005. (J). 5.95 net. (978-0-9769321-5-4(6)) Steingart, Nathan Publishing.

Santa Niclaus. A Letter from Sant: The Original. 2012. 28p. (-18). pap. 16.09 (978-1-4669-6794-6(3)) Trafford Publishing.

Santa Takes A Vacation. 2005. (J). 5.95 (978-0-9769321-4-7(8)) Steingart, Nathan Publishing.

Santa the Chimney Sweep/the Candy Cane That Found a Home: Wee Voices Collection. 2005. (Illus.). 37p. per. 6.95 (978-0-9764444-9-7(6)) E. J. Publishing.

Santa's Birthday. 2005. (J). 5.95 (978-0-9769321-1-6(3)) Steingart, Nathan Publishing.

Santa's Bodyguard. 2005. (J). (978-0-9771639-0-8(3)) Riverview Foundation.

Santa's Busy Christmas Eve. 2003. (J). 4.99 (978-1-59384-011-2(X)) Parklane Publishing.

Santa's Christmas Cookies. 2003. (J). per. (978-1-57657-708-0(2)) Paradise Pr., Inc.

Santa's Elves Alphabet. 2003. (Illus.). (J). per. (978-1-57657-174-3(2)) Paradise Pr., Inc.

Santa's Hat. 2003. (J). per. (978-1-57657-927-5(1)) Paradise Pr., Inc.

Santa's Jolly Belly. 2003. (J). per. (978-1-57657-923-7(9)) Paradise Pr., Inc.

Santa's Little Helpers. 2003. (J). per. (978-1-57657-809-4(7)); per. (978-1-57657-921-3(2)) Paradise Pr., Inc.

Santa's Suit. 2006. (Little Elf Set 1 Ser.). (J). 7.33 (978-1-932570-71-7(3)) Pioneer Valley Bks.

Santa's Thanksgiving. 2005. (J). 5.95 (978-0-9769321-0-9(5)) Steingart, Nathan Publishing.

Santa's Twinkly Christmas Eve. 2008. (Light up Book Ser.). 8p. (978-1-4075-3500-5(5)) Parragon, Inc.

Sargent, Dave & Sargent, Pat. Sweetpea: (Purple Corn Welsh) Be Happy, 30 vols., Vol. 58. Lenoir, Jane, illus. 2003. (Saddle up Ser.: Vol. 58). 42p. (J). pap. 10.95 (978-1-56763-816-5(3)); lib. bdg. 23.60 (978-1-56763-815-8(5)) Ozark Publishing.

Scarry, Richard. Christmas Mice. Scarry, Richard, illus. 2014. (Little Golden Book Ser.). (ENG., Illus.). 24p. (J). (-k). 4.99 (978-0-385-38421-6(1), Golden Bks.) Random Hse. Children's Bks.

—The Night Before the Night Before Christmas! Scarry, Richard, illus. 2014. (ENG., Illus.). 48p. (J). (gr. -1-2). 14.99 (978-0-385-38804-7(7), Golden Bks.) Random Hse. Children's Bks.

Schatzer, Jeffrey L. The Bird in Santa's Beard: How a Christmas Legend Was Forever Changed. 2004. (Illus.). 34p. (J). (978-0-9749554-0-7(X)) Big Belly Bks.

Scholastic, Inc. Staff, contrib. by. Peppa's Christmas Wish. 2013. (Peppa Pig Ser.). (ENG.). 24p. (J). (gr. -1-k). 4.99 (978-0-545-56511-0(1)) Scholastic, Inc.

Schomer-Wendel, Gretchen & Schomer, Adam Anthony. Becka Goes to the North Pole. 2009. (Becka & the Big Bubble Ser.). (Illus.). 32p. (J). (gr. -1-3). pap. 10.55 (978-1-60754-117-2(3)) Windmill Bks.

Schonewill, Lisa. Tell Me Mama, Is Santa Claus Real? 2005. (J). pap. 9.00 (978-0-8059-6373-1(1)) Dorrance Publishing Co., Inc.

Schorr, Titus. Secret Santa, 01 vols., 1. 2016. (Rosen REAL Readers: Social Studies Nonfiction / Fiction: Family, Community, & the World Ser.). (ENG.). 8p. (J). pap. 5.46 (978-1-5081-1893-0(0), Rosen Classroom) Rosen Publishing Group, Inc., The.

Scillian, Devin. Memoirs of an Elf. Bowers, Tim, illus. 2014. (ENG.). 32p. (J). (gr. 1-4). 16.99 (978-1-58536-910-2(1), 203676) Sleeping Bear Pr.

Scott, Christina. All in A Night's Work. 2006. (J). lib. bdg. 19.95 (978-1-933732-19-0(9)) Big Ransom Studio.

—The Chimney. 2006. (J). lib. bdg. 19.95 (978-1-933732-18-3(0)) Big Ransom Studio.

—The North Pole. 2006. (J). lib. bdg. 19.95 (978-1-933732-17-6(2)) Big Ransom Studio.

Scott, Eric. Santa & the Cyberspace Plot. 2013. 114p. pap. 7.99 (978-1-78333-397-4(9)) Acorn Bks.

Scotton, Rob. Russell's Christmas Magic. Scotton, Rob, illus. 2007. (Illus.). 32p. (J). (gr. -1-2). lib. bdg. 17.89 (978-0-06-059855-6(7)) HarperCollins Pubs.

Sedrak, Asham. The Santa Claus Fox. 2011. 28p. pap. 13.59 (978-1-4670-2484-6(8)) AuthorHouse.

Sellaro, Brendan. Space Santa Holiday Hero. 2012. (ENG., Illus.). 32p. (J). 16.95 (978-0-938467-60-1(3)) Headline Bks., Inc.

Sesko, Frank & Sesko, Mary Ann. Santa & Sam's Big Secret. 2007. 48p. per. 14.95 (978-1-4327-0769-9(8)) Outskirts Pr., Inc.

Seus. Wie der Grinch Weihnachen. pap. 14.95 (978-3-492-23722-2(3)) Piper Verlag GmbH DEU. Dist: Distribooks, Inc.

Shannon, David. It's Christmas, David! Shannon, David, illus. 2010. (ENG., Illus.). 32p. (J). (gr. -1-3). 17.99 (978-0-545-14311-0(X), Blue Sky Pr., The) Scholastic, Inc.

Sharkey, Niamh. Santasaurus. Sharkey, Niamh, illus. (ENG., Illus.). 32p. (J). (gr. -1-2). 2008. pap. 3.99 (978-0-7636-3890-0(0)) 2005. 15.99 (978-0-7636-2671-6(6)) Candlewick Pr.

Sharp, Rhonda Winchell. The Nine Most Famous Reindeer of All. Vandewater, Rena, illus. 2004. 40p. (J). pap. 15.99 (978-0-9748047-8-1(9)) Hickory Bark Productions.

Shaw, Stephanie. A Cookie for Santa. Robert, Bruno, illus. 2014. (ENG.). 32p. (J). (gr. 1-4). 15.99 (978-1-58536-883-9(0), 203675) Sleeping Bear Pr.

Shepherd, Anita. The Santa Genie. 2012. 50p. pap. 7.95 (978-0-9882368-0-6(X)) New Eden Publishing.

Silvano, Wendi J. Turkey Claus, 0 vols. Harper, Lee, illus. 2012. (ENG.). 40p. (J). (gr. -1-3). 16.99 (978-0-7614-6239-2(2), 9780761462392, Two Lions) Amazon Publishing.

Simon, Tom. El Traje Azul de Papa Noel.Tr. of Santa's Blue Suit. (SPA.). 24p. (J). (gr. k-2). 16.95 (978-84-488-0867-9(3), BS3557) Beascoa, Ediciones S.A. ESP. Dist: Lectorum Pubns., Inc.

Sims, Tom. Repo Elf. Perri, Anthony F., illus. 2008. (ENG.). 104p. (J). 12.95 (978-0-9787213-4-3(9), Cambridge House Pr.) Sterling & Ross Pubs.

Smale, Denise L. Santa I Moved! 2012. 20p. pap. 24.95 (978-1-4626-9241-5(9)) America Star Bks.

Smallman, Steve. Santa Is Coming to Alabama. Dunn, Robert, illus. 2013. (ENG.). 32p. (J). (-3). 9.99 (978-1-4022-8821-0(2), Sourcebooks Jabberwocky) Sourcebooks, Inc.

—Santa Is Coming to Alaska. Dunn, Robert, illus. 2013. (ENG.). 32p. (J). (-3). 9.99 (978-1-4022-9517-1(0), Sourcebooks Jabberwocky) Sourcebooks, Inc.

—Santa Is Coming to Albuquerque. Dunn, Robert, illus. 2013. (ENG.). 32p. (J). (-3). 9.99 (978-1-4022-9042-8(X), Sourcebooks Jabberwocky) Sourcebooks, Inc.

—Santa Is Coming to Arizona. Dunn, Robert, illus. 2012. (ENG.). 32p. (J). (-3). 9.99 (978-1-4022-7545-6(5), Sourcebooks Jabberwocky) Sourcebooks, Inc.

—Santa Is Coming to Arkansas. Dunn, Robert, illus. 2013. (ENG.). 32p. (J). (-3). 9.99 (978-1-4022-9066-4(7), Sourcebooks Jabberwocky) Sourcebooks, Inc.

—Santa Is Coming to Asheville. Dunn, Robert, illus. 2013. (ENG.). 32p. (J). (-3). 9.99 (978-1-4022-9030-5(6), Sourcebooks Jabberwocky) Sourcebooks, Inc.

—Santa Is Coming to Atlanta. Dunn, Robert, illus. 2015. (ENG.). 32p. (J). (-3). 9.99 (978-1-4926-2640-4(6), Sourcebooks Jabberwocky) Sourcebooks, Inc.

—Santa Is Coming to Austin. Dunn, Robert, illus. 2013. (ENG.). 32p. (J). (-3). 9.99 (978-1-4022-8973-6(1), Sourcebooks Jabberwocky) Sourcebooks, Inc.

—Santa Is Coming to Baltimore. Dunn, Robert, illus. 2015. (ENG.). 32p. (J). (-3). 9.99 (978-1-4926-2652-7(X), Sourcebooks Jabberwocky) Sourcebooks, Inc.

—Santa Is Coming to Bellingham. Dunn, Robert, illus. 2013. (ENG.). 32p. (J). (-3). 9.99 (978-1-4022-9130-2(2), Sourcebooks Jabberwocky) Sourcebooks, Inc.

—Santa Is Coming to Bentonville. Dunn, Robert, illus. 2013. (ENG.). 32p. (J). (-3). 9.99 (978-1-4022-9109-8(4), Sourcebooks Jabberwocky) Sourcebooks, Inc.

—Santa Is Coming to Birmingham. Dunn, Robert, illus. 2013. (ENG.). 32p. (J). (-3). 9.99 (978-1-4022-9106-7(X), Sourcebooks Jabberwocky) Sourcebooks, Inc.

—Santa Is Coming to Boise. Dunn, Robert, illus. 2013. (ENG.). 32p. (J). (-3). 9.99 (978-1-4022-9118-0(3), Sourcebooks Jabberwocky) Sourcebooks, Inc.

—Santa Is Coming to Boston. Dunn, Robert, illus. 2012. (ENG.). 32p. (J). (-3). 9.99 (978-1-4022-7506-7(4), Sourcebooks Jabberwocky) Sourcebooks, Inc.

—Santa Is Coming to Boulder. Dunn, Robert, illus. 2015. (ENG.). 32p. (J). (-3). 9.99 (978-1-4926-2659-6(7), Sourcebooks Jabberwocky) Sourcebooks, Inc.

—Santa Is Coming to Bozeman. Dunn, Robert, illus. 2013. (ENG.). 32p. (J). (-3). 9.99 (978-1-4022-9045-9(4), Sourcebooks Jabberwocky) Sourcebooks, Inc.

—Santa Is Coming to Brooklyn. Dunn, Robert, illus. 2013. (ENG.). 32p. (J). (-3). 9.99 (978-1-4022-9003-9(9), Sourcebooks Jabberwocky) Sourcebooks, Inc.
—Santa Is Coming to Buffalo. Dunn, Robert, illus. 2013. (ENG.). 32p. (J). (-3). 9.99 (978-1-4022-8858-6(1), Sourcebooks Jabberwocky) Sourcebooks, Inc.
—Santa Is Coming to Cajun Country. Dunn, Robert, illus. 2015. (ENG.). 32p. (J). (-3). 9.99 (978-1-4926-2665-7(1), Sourcebooks Jabberwocky) Sourcebooks, Inc.
—Santa Is Coming to Calgary. Dunn, Robert, illus. 2013. (ENG.). 32p. (J). (-3). 11.99 (978-1-4022-8988-0(X), Sourcebooks Jabberwocky) Sourcebooks, Inc.
—Santa Is Coming to California. Dunn, Robert, illus. 2012. (ENG.). 32p. (J). (-3). 9.99 (978-1-4022-7515-9(3), Sourcebooks Jabberwocky) Sourcebooks, Inc.
—Santa Is Coming to Canada. Dunn, Robert, illus. 2013. (ENG.). 32p. (J). (-3). 11.99 (978-1-4022-8839-5(5), Sourcebooks Jabberwocky) Sourcebooks, Inc.
—Santa Is Coming to Cape Cod. Dunn, Robert, illus. 2013. (ENG.). 32p. (J). (-3). 9.99 (978-1-4022-9078-7(0), Sourcebooks Jabberwocky) Sourcebooks, Inc.
—Santa Is Coming to Charleston. Dunn, Robert, illus. 2013. (ENG.). 32p. (J). (-3). 9.99 (978-1-4022-8985-9(5), Sourcebooks Jabberwocky) Sourcebooks, Inc.
—Santa Is Coming to Charlotte. Dunn, Robert, illus. 2014. (ENG.). 32p. (J). (-3). 9.99 (978-1-4926-0697-0(9), Sourcebooks Jabberwocky) Sourcebooks, Inc.
—Santa Is Coming to Chattanooga. Dunn, Robert, illus. 2015. (ENG.). 32p. (J). (-3). 9.99 (978-1-4926-2651-0(1), Sourcebooks Jabberwocky) Sourcebooks, Inc.
—Santa Is Coming to Chicago. Dunn, Robert, illus. 2012. (ENG.). 32p. (J). (-3). 9.99 (978-1-4022-7509-8(9), Sourcebooks Jabberwocky) Sourcebooks, Inc.
—Santa Is Coming to Cincinnati. Dunn, Robert, illus. 2013. (ENG.). 32p. (J). (-3). 9.99 (978-1-4022-8997-2(9), Sourcebooks Jabberwocky) Sourcebooks, Inc.
—Santa Is Coming to Cleveland. Dunn, Robert, illus. 2014. (ENG.). 32p. (J). (-3). 9.99 (978-1-4926-0703-8(7), Sourcebooks Jabberwocky) Sourcebooks, Inc.
—Santa Is Coming to Colorado. Dunn, Robert, illus. 2013. (ENG.). 32p. (J). (-3). 9.99 (978-1-4022-8815-9(8), Sourcebooks Jabberwocky) Sourcebooks, Inc.
—Santa Is Coming to Columbus. Dunn, Robert, illus. 2013. (ENG.). 32p. (J). (-3). 9.99 (978-1-4022-9036-7(5), Sourcebooks Jabberwocky) Sourcebooks, Inc.
—Santa Is Coming to Connecticut. Dunn, Robert, illus. 2014. (ENG.). 32p. (J). (-3). 9.99 (978-1-4926-0670-3(7), Sourcebooks Jabberwocky) Sourcebooks, Inc.
—Santa Is Coming to Dallas. Dunn, Robert, illus. 2014. (ENG.). 32p. (J). (-3). 9.99 (978-1-4926-0700-7(2), Sourcebooks Jabberwocky) Sourcebooks, Inc.
—Santa Is Coming to Delaware. Dunn, Robert, illus. 2013. (ENG.). 32p. (J). (-3). 9.99 (978-1-4022-9508-9(1), Sourcebooks Jabberwocky) Sourcebooks, Inc.
—Santa Is Coming to Denver. Dunn, Robert, illus. 2015. (ENG.). 32p. (J). (-3). 9.99 (978-1-4926-2644-2(9), Sourcebooks Jabberwocky) Sourcebooks, Inc.
—Santa Is Coming to des Moines. Dunn, Robert, illus. 2015. (ENG.). 32p. (J). (-3). 9.99 (978-1-4926-2646-6(5), Sourcebooks Jabberwocky) Sourcebooks, Inc.
—Santa Is Coming to Duluth. Dunn, Robert, illus. 2013. (ENG.). 32p. (J). (-3). 9.99 (978-1-4022-9027-5(6), Sourcebooks Jabberwocky) Sourcebooks, Inc.
—Santa Is Coming to Durango. Dunn, Robert, illus. 2013. (ENG.). 32p. (J). (-3). 9.99 (978-1-4022-9133-3(7), Sourcebooks Jabberwocky) Sourcebooks, Inc.
—Santa Is Coming to Edmonton. Dunn, Robert, illus. 2013. (ENG.). 32p. (J). (-3). 11.99 (978-1-4022-8991-0(X), Sourcebooks Jabberwocky) Sourcebooks, Inc.
—Santa Is Coming to el Paso. Dunn, Robert, illus. 2015. (ENG.). 32p. (J). (-3). 9.99 (978-1-4926-2634-3(1), Sourcebooks Jabberwocky) Sourcebooks, Inc.
—Santa Is Coming to Florida. Dunn, Robert, illus. 2012. (ENG.). 32p. (J). (-3). 9.99 (978-1-4022-7527-2(7), Sourcebooks Jabberwocky) Sourcebooks, Inc.
—Santa Is Coming to Georgia. Dunn, Robert, illus. 2013. (ENG.). 32p. (J). (-3). 9.99 (978-1-4022-8794-7(1), Sourcebooks Jabberwocky) Sourcebooks, Inc.
—Santa Is Coming to Grand Rapids. Dunn, Robert, illus. 2015. (ENG.). 32p. (J). (-3). 9.99 (978-1-4926-2657-2(0), Sourcebooks Jabberwocky) Sourcebooks, Inc.
—Santa Is Coming to Green Bay. Dunn, Robert, illus. 2013. (ENG.). 32p. (J). (-3). 9.99 (978-1-4022-9112-8(4), Sourcebooks Jabberwocky) Sourcebooks, Inc.
—Santa Is Coming to Hawaii. Dunn, Robert, illus. 2013. (ENG.). 32p. (J). (-3). 9.99 (978-1-4022-9009-1(8), Sourcebooks Jabberwocky) Sourcebooks, Inc.
—Santa Is Coming to Hollywood. Dunn, Robert, illus. 2015. (ENG.). 32p. (J). (-3). 9.99 (978-1-4926-2664-0(3), Sourcebooks Jabberwocky) Sourcebooks, Inc.
—Santa Is Coming to Honolulu. Dunn, Robert, illus. 2015. (ENG.). 32p. (J). (-3). 9.99 (978-1-4926-2653-4(8), Sourcebooks Jabberwocky) Sourcebooks, Inc.
—Santa Is Coming to Houston. Dunn, Robert, illus. 2015. (ENG.). 32p. (J). (-3). 9.99 (978-1-4926-2631-2(7), Sourcebooks Jabberwocky) Sourcebooks, Inc.
—Santa Is Coming to Idaho. Dunn, Robert, illus. 2013. (ENG.). 32p. (J). (-3). 9.99 (978-1-4022-9511-9(1), Sourcebooks Jabberwocky) Sourcebooks, Inc.
—Santa Is Coming to Illinois. Dunn, Robert, illus. 2013. (ENG.). 32p. (J). (-3). 9.99 (978-1-4022-9103-6(5), Sourcebooks Jabberwocky) Sourcebooks, Inc.
—Santa Is Coming to Indiana. Dunn, Robert, illus. 2013. (ENG.). 32p. (J). (-3). 9.99 (978-1-4022-8803-6(4), Sourcebooks Jabberwocky) Sourcebooks, Inc.
—Santa Is Coming to Indianapolis. Dunn, Robert, illus. 2015. (ENG.). 32p. (J). (-3). 9.99 (978-1-4926-2636-7(8), Sourcebooks Jabberwocky) Sourcebooks, Inc.
—Santa Is Coming to Iowa. Dunn, Robert, illus. 2013. (ENG.). 32p. (J). (-3). 9.99 (978-1-4022-8818-0(2), Sourcebooks Jabberwocky) Sourcebooks, Inc.
—Santa Is Coming to Jacksonville. Dunn, Robert, illus. 2015. (ENG.). 32p. (J). (-3). 9.99 (978-1-4926-2635-0(X), Sourcebooks Jabberwocky) Sourcebooks, Inc.
—Santa Is Coming to Jefferson City. Dunn, Robert, illus. 2014. (ENG.). 32p. (J). (-3). 9.99 (978-1-4926-0766-3(5), Sourcebooks Jabberwocky) Sourcebooks, Inc.
—Santa Is Coming to Kansas. Dunn, Robert, illus. 2013. (ENG.). 32p. (J). (-3). 9.99 (978-1-4022-9121-0(3), Sourcebooks Jabberwocky) Sourcebooks, Inc.
—Santa Is Coming to Kansas City. Dunn, Robert, illus. 2013. (ENG.). 32p. (J). (-3). 9.99 (978-1-4022-8855-5(7), Sourcebooks Jabberwocky) Sourcebooks, Inc.
—Santa Is Coming to Kentucky. Dunn, Robert, illus. 2013. (ENG.). 32p. (J). (-3). 9.99 (978-1-4022-8824-1(7), Sourcebooks Jabberwocky) Sourcebooks, Inc.
—Santa Is Coming to Las Vegas. Dunn, Robert, illus. 2013. (ENG.). 32p. (J). (-3). 9.99 (978-1-4022-8836-4(0), Sourcebooks Jabberwocky) Sourcebooks, Inc.
—Santa Is Coming to Los Angeles. Dunn, Robert, illus. 2013. (ENG.). 32p. (J). (-3). 9.99 (978-1-4022-8830-2(1), Sourcebooks Jabberwocky) Sourcebooks, Inc.
—Santa Is Coming to Louisiana. Dunn, Robert, illus. 2012. (ENG.). 32p. (J). (-3). 9.99 (978-1-4022-7536-4(6), Sourcebooks Jabberwocky) Sourcebooks, Inc.
—Santa Is Coming to Louisville. Dunn, Robert, illus. 2015. (ENG.). 32p. (J). (-3). 9.99 (978-1-4926-2639-8(2), Sourcebooks Jabberwocky) Sourcebooks, Inc.
—Santa Is Coming to Lubbock. Dunn, Robert, illus. 2013. (ENG.). 32p. (J). (-3). 9.99 (978-1-4022-9136-4(1), Sourcebooks Jabberwocky) Sourcebooks, Inc.
—Santa Is Coming to Madison. Dunn, Robert, illus. 2014. (ENG.). 32p. (J). (-3). 9.99 (978-1-4926-0706-9(1), Sourcebooks Jabberwocky) Sourcebooks, Inc.
—Santa Is Coming to Maine. Dunn, Robert, illus. 2013. (ENG.). 32p. (J). (-3). 9.99 (978-1-4022-9069-5(1), Sourcebooks Jabberwocky) Sourcebooks, Inc.
—Santa Is Coming to Manchester. Dunn, Robert, illus. 2013. (ENG.). 32p. (J). (-3). 9.99 (978-1-4022-9115-9(9), Sourcebooks Jabberwocky) Sourcebooks, Inc.
—Santa Is Coming to Maryland. Dunn, Robert, illus. 2013. (ENG.). 32p. (J). (-3). 9.99 (978-1-4022-8812-8(3), Sourcebooks Jabberwocky) Sourcebooks, Inc.
—Santa Is Coming to Massachusetts. Dunn, Robert, illus. 2014. (ENG.). 32p. (J). (-3). 9.99 (978-1-4926-0673-4(1), Sourcebooks Jabberwocky) Sourcebooks, Inc.
—Santa Is Coming to Memphis. Dunn, Robert, illus. 2015. (ENG.). 32p. (J). (-3). 9.99 (978-1-4926-2643-5(0), Sourcebooks Jabberwocky) Sourcebooks, Inc.
—Santa Is Coming to Miami. Dunn, Robert, illus. 2013. (ENG.). 32p. (J). (-3). 9.99 (978-1-4022-9051-0(9), Sourcebooks Jabberwocky) Sourcebooks, Inc.
—Santa Is Coming to Michigan. Dunn, Robert, illus. 2012. (ENG.). 32p. (J). (-3). 9.99 (978-1-4022-7539-5(0), Sourcebooks Jabberwocky) Sourcebooks, Inc.
—Santa Is Coming to Minnesota. Dunn, Robert, illus. 2012. (ENG.). 32p. (J). (-3). 9.99 (978-1-4022-7530-2(7), Sourcebooks Jabberwocky) Sourcebooks, Inc.
—Santa Is Coming to Mississippi. Dunn, Robert, illus. 2013. (ENG.). 32p. (J). (-3). 9.99 (978-1-4022-9015-2(2), Sourcebooks Jabberwocky) Sourcebooks, Inc.
—Santa Is Coming to Missoula. Dunn, Robert, illus. 2015. (ENG.). 32p. (J). (-3). 9.99 (978-1-4926-2656-5(2), Sourcebooks Jabberwocky) Sourcebooks, Inc.
—Santa Is Coming to Missouri. Dunn, Robert, illus. 2013. (ENG.). 32p. (J). (-3). 9.99 (978-1-4022-8809-8(3), Sourcebooks Jabberwocky) Sourcebooks, Inc.
—Santa Is Coming to Montana. Dunn, Robert, illus. 2013. (ENG.). 32p. (J). (-3). 9.99 (978-1-4022-9018-3(7), Sourcebooks Jabberwocky) Sourcebooks, Inc.
—Santa Is Coming to My House. Dunn, Robert, illus. 2012. (ENG.). 32p. (J). (-3). 9.99 (978-1-4022-7775-7(X), Sourcebooks Jabberwocky) Sourcebooks, Inc.
—Santa Is Coming to Naperville. Dunn, Robert, illus. 2013. (ENG.). 32p. (J). (-3). 9.99 (978-1-4022-9063-3(2), Sourcebooks Jabberwocky) Sourcebooks, Inc.
—Santa Is Coming to Naples. Dunn, Robert, illus. 2013. (ENG.). 32p. (J). (-3). 9.99 (978-1-4022-9048-0(9), Sourcebooks Jabberwocky) Sourcebooks, Inc.
—Santa Is Coming to Nashville. Dunn, Robert, illus. 2014. (ENG.). 32p. (J). (-3). 9.99 (978-1-4926-0718-2(5), Sourcebooks Jabberwocky) Sourcebooks, Inc.
—Santa Is Coming to Nebraska. Dunn, Robert, illus. 2013. (ENG.). 32p. (J). (-3). 9.99 (978-1-4022-9072-5(1), Sourcebooks Jabberwocky) Sourcebooks, Inc.
—Santa Is Coming to Nevada. Dunn, Robert, illus. 2013. (ENG.). 32p. (J). (-3). 9.99 (978-1-4022-9523-2(5), Sourcebooks Jabberwocky) Sourcebooks, Inc.
—Santa Is Coming to New Brunswick. Dunn, Robert, illus. 2014. (ENG.). 32p. (J). (-3). 11.99 (978-1-4926-0712-0(6), Sourcebooks Jabberwocky) Sourcebooks, Inc.
—Santa Is Coming to New England. Dunn, Robert, illus. 2012. (ENG.). 32p. (J). (-3). 9.99 (978-1-4022-7551-7(X), Sourcebooks Jabberwocky) Sourcebooks, Inc.
—Santa Is Coming to New Hampshire. Dunn, Robert, illus. 2014. (ENG.). 32p. (J). (-3). 9.99 (978-1-4926-0676-5(6), Sourcebooks Jabberwocky) Sourcebooks, Inc.
—Santa Is Coming to New Jersey. Dunn, Robert, illus. 2013. (ENG.). 32p. (J). (-3). 9.99 (978-1-4022-8797-8(6), Sourcebooks Jabberwocky) Sourcebooks, Inc.
—Santa Is Coming to New Mexico. Dunn, Robert, illus. 2013. (ENG.). 32p. (J). (-3). 9.99 (978-1-4022-9520-1(0), Sourcebooks Jabberwocky) Sourcebooks, Inc.
—Santa Is Coming to New Orleans. Dunn, Robert, illus. 2014. (ENG.). 32p. (J). (-3). 9.99 (978-1-4926-0694-9(4), Sourcebooks Jabberwocky) Sourcebooks, Inc.
—Santa Is Coming to New York. Dunn, Robert, illus. 2012. (ENG.). 32p. (J). (-3). 9.99 (978-1-4022-7503-6(X), Sourcebooks Jabberwocky) Sourcebooks, Inc.
—Santa Is Coming to New York City. Dunn, Robert, illus. 2015. (ENG.). 32p. (J). (-3). 9.99 (978-1-4926-2662-6(7), Sourcebooks Jabberwocky) Sourcebooks, Inc.
—Santa Is Coming to Newfoundland. Dunn, Robert, illus. 2014. (ENG.). 32p. (J). (-3). 11.99 (978-1-4926-0715-1(0), Sourcebooks Jabberwocky) Sourcebooks, Inc.
—Santa Is Coming to Niagara Falls. Dunn, Robert, illus. 2015. (ENG.). 32p. (J). (-3). 9.99 (978-1-4926-2655-8(4), Sourcebooks Jabberwocky) Sourcebooks, Inc.
—Santa Is Coming to North Carolina. Dunn, Robert, illus. 2014. (ENG.). 32p. (J). (-3). 9.99 (978-1-4926-0682-6(0), Sourcebooks Jabberwocky) Sourcebooks, Inc.
—Santa Is Coming to North Dakota. Dunn, Robert, illus. 2013. (ENG.). 32p. (J). (-3). 9.99 (978-1-4022-9514-0(6), Sourcebooks Jabberwocky) Sourcebooks, Inc.
—Santa Is Coming to Northern Virginia. Dunn, Robert, illus. 2015. (ENG.). 32p. (J). (-3). 9.99 (978-1-4926-2663-3(5), Sourcebooks Jabberwocky) Sourcebooks, Inc.
—Santa Is Coming to Notre Dame. Dunn, Robert, illus. 2013. (ENG.). 32p. (J). (-3). 9.99 (978-1-4022-9024-4(1), Sourcebooks Jabberwocky) Sourcebooks, Inc.
—Santa Is Coming to Nova Scotia. 2014. (ENG.). 32p. (J). (-3). 11.99 (978-1-4926-0709-0(6), Sourcebooks Jabberwocky) Sourcebooks, Inc.
—Santa Is Coming to Ohio. Dunn, Robert, illus. 2012. (ENG.). 32p. (J). (-3). 9.99 (978-1-4022-7554-8(4), Sourcebooks Jabberwocky) Sourcebooks, Inc.
—Santa Is Coming to Oklahoma. Dunn, Robert, illus. 2013. (ENG.). 32p. (J). (-3). 9.99 (978-1-4022-9012-1(8), Sourcebooks Jabberwocky) Sourcebooks, Inc.
—Santa Is Coming to Oklahoma City. Dunn, Robert, illus. 2015. (ENG.). 32p. (J). (-3). 9.99 (978-1-4926-2637-4(6), Sourcebooks Jabberwocky) Sourcebooks, Inc.
—Santa Is Coming to Omaha. Dunn, Robert, illus. 2013. (ENG.). 32p. (J). (-3). 9.99 (978-1-4022-9006-0(3), Sourcebooks Jabberwocky) Sourcebooks, Inc.
—Santa Is Coming to Oregon. Dunn, Robert, illus. 2013. (ENG.). 32p. (J). (-3). 9.99 (978-1-4022-9075-6(6), Sourcebooks Jabberwocky) Sourcebooks, Inc.
—Santa Is Coming to Orlando. Dunn, Robert, illus. 2015. (ENG.). 32p. (J). (-3). 9.99 (978-1-4926-2633-6(3), Sourcebooks Jabberwocky) Sourcebooks, Inc.
—Santa Is Coming to Ottawa. Dunn, Robert, illus. 2013. (ENG.). 32p. (J). (-3). 11.99 (978-1-4022-8994-1(4), Sourcebooks Jabberwocky) Sourcebooks, Inc.
—Santa Is Coming to Philadelphia. Dunn, Robert, illus. 2012. (ENG.). 32p. (J). (-3). 9.99 (978-1-4022-7518-0(8), Sourcebooks Jabberwocky) Sourcebooks, Inc.
—Santa Is Coming to Pittsburgh. Dunn, Robert, illus. 2013. (ENG.). 32p. (J). (-3). 9.99 (978-1-4022-8982-8(0), Sourcebooks Jabberwocky) Sourcebooks, Inc.
—Santa Is Coming to Portland. Dunn, Robert, illus. 2012. (ENG.). 32p. (J). (-3). 9.99 (978-1-4022-7772-6(5), Sourcebooks Jabberwocky) Sourcebooks, Inc.
—Santa Is Coming to Providence. Dunn, Robert, illus. 2015. (ENG.). 32p. (J). (-3). 9.99 (978-1-4926-2660-2(0), Sourcebooks Jabberwocky) Sourcebooks, Inc.
—Santa Is Coming to Raleigh-Durham. Dunn, Robert, illus. 2015. (ENG.). 32p. (J). (-3). 9.99 (978-1-4926-2642-8(2), Sourcebooks Jabberwocky) Sourcebooks, Inc.
—Santa Is Coming to Rapid City. Dunn, Robert, illus. 2015. (ENG.). 32p. (J). (-3). 9.99 (978-1-4926-2658-9(9), Sourcebooks Jabberwocky) Sourcebooks, Inc.
—Santa Is Coming to Rhode Island. Dunn, Robert, illus. 2014. (ENG.). 32p. (J). (-3). 9.99 (978-1-4926-0727-4(4), Sourcebooks Jabberwocky) Sourcebooks, Inc.
—Santa Is Coming to Salt Lake City. Dunn, Robert, illus. 2015. (ENG.). 32p. (J). (-3). 9.99 (978-1-4926-2645-9(7), Sourcebooks Jabberwocky) Sourcebooks, Inc.
—Santa Is Coming to San Antonio. Dunn, Robert, illus. 2015. (ENG.). 32p. (J). (-3). 9.99 (978-1-4926-2632-9(5), Sourcebooks Jabberwocky) Sourcebooks, Inc.
—Santa Is Coming to San Diego. Dunn, Robert, illus. 2014. (ENG.). 32p. (J). (-3). 9.99 (978-1-4926-0688-8(X), Sourcebooks Jabberwocky) Sourcebooks, Inc.
—Santa Is Coming to San Francisco. Dunn, Robert, illus. 2012. (ENG.). 32p. (J). (-3). 9.99 (978-1-4022-7548-7(X), Sourcebooks Jabberwocky) Sourcebooks, Inc.
—Santa Is Coming to San Jose. Dunn, Robert, illus. 2015. (ENG.). 32p. (J). (-3). 9.99 (978-1-4926-2641-1(4), Sourcebooks Jabberwocky) Sourcebooks, Inc.
—Santa Is Coming to Santa Cruz. Dunn, Robert, illus. 2013. (ENG.). 32p. (J). (-3). 9.99 (978-1-4022-9057-2(8), Sourcebooks Jabberwocky) Sourcebooks, Inc.
—Santa Is Coming to Santa Fe. Dunn, Robert, illus. 2013. (ENG.). 32p. (J). (-3). 9.99 (978-1-4022-9124-1(8), Sourcebooks Jabberwocky) Sourcebooks, Inc.
—Santa Is Coming to Savannah. Dunn, Robert, illus. 2013. (ENG.). 32p. (J). (-3). 9.99 (978-1-4022-8979-8(0), Sourcebooks Jabberwocky) Sourcebooks, Inc.
—Santa Is Coming to Seattle. Dunn, Robert, illus. 2015. (ENG.). 32p. (J). (-3). 9.99 (978-1-4926-2649-7(X), Sourcebooks Jabberwocky) Sourcebooks, Inc.
—Santa Is Coming to Sioux Falls. Dunn, Robert, illus. 2015. (ENG.). 32p. (J). (-3). 9.99 (978-1-4926-2650-3(3), Sourcebooks Jabberwocky) Sourcebooks, Inc.
—Santa Is Coming to South Carolina. Dunn, Robert, illus. 2014. (ENG.). 32p. (J). (-3). 9.99 (978-1-4926-0685-7(5), Sourcebooks Jabberwocky) Sourcebooks, Inc.
—Santa Is Coming to South Dakota. Dunn, Robert, illus. 2013. (ENG.). 32p. (J). (-3). 9.99 (978-1-4022-9021-3(7), Sourcebooks Jabberwocky) Sourcebooks, Inc.
—Santa Is Coming to St. Louis. Dunn, Robert, illus. 2013. (ENG.). 32p. (J). (-3). 9.99 (978-1-4022-9000-8(4), Sourcebooks Jabberwocky) Sourcebooks, Inc.
—Santa Is Coming to Tampa Bay & St. Petersburg. Dunn, Robert, illus. 2013. (ENG.). 32p. (J). (-3). 9.99 (978-1-4022-9054-1(3), Sourcebooks Jabberwocky) Sourcebooks, Inc.
—Santa Is Coming to Tennessee. Dunn, Robert, illus. 2013. (ENG.). 32p. (J). (-3). 9.99 (978-1-4022-8806-7(9), Sourcebooks Jabberwocky) Sourcebooks, Inc.
—Santa Is Coming to Texas. Dunn, Robert, illus. 2012. (ENG.). 32p. (J). (-3). 9.99 (978-1-4022-7512-8(9), Sourcebooks Jabberwocky) Sourcebooks, Inc.
—Santa Is Coming to the Beach. Dunn, Robert, illus. 2015. (ENG.). 32p. (J). (-3). 9.99 (978-1-4926-2846-0(8), Sourcebooks Jabberwocky) Sourcebooks, Inc.
—Santa Is Coming to the Carolinas. Dunn, Robert, illus. 2012. (ENG.). 32p. (J). (-3). 9.99 (978-1-4022-7586-9(2), Sourcebooks Jabberwocky) Sourcebooks, Inc.
—Santa Is Coming to the Great Smoky Mountains. Dunn, Robert, illus. 2013. (ENG.). 32p. (J). (-3). 9.99 (978-1-4022-9033-6(0), Sourcebooks Jabberwocky) Sourcebooks, Inc.
—Santa Is Coming to the Jersey Shore. Dunn, Robert, illus. 2014. (ENG.). 32p. (J). (-3). 9.99 (978-1-4926-0691-8(X), Sourcebooks Jabberwocky) Sourcebooks, Inc.
—Santa Is Coming to the Quad Cities. Dunn, Robert, illus. 2013. (ENG.). 32p. (J). (-3). 9.99 (978-1-4022-9060-2(8), Sourcebooks Jabberwocky) Sourcebooks, Inc.
—Santa Is Coming to the Rockies. Dunn, Robert, illus. 2012. (ENG.). 32p. (J). (-3). 9.99 (978-1-4022-7593-7(5), Sourcebooks Jabberwocky) Sourcebooks, Inc.
—Santa Is Coming to the Twin Cities. Dunn, Robert, illus. 2015. (ENG.). 32p. (J). (-3). 9.99 (978-1-4926-2647-3(3), Sourcebooks Jabberwocky) Sourcebooks, Inc.
—Santa Is Coming to the Valley of the Sun. Dunn, Robert, illus. 2015. (ENG.). 32p. (J). (-3). 9.99 (978-1-4926-2666-4(X), Sourcebooks Jabberwocky) Sourcebooks, Inc.
—Santa Is Coming to the Wisconsin Dells. Dunn, Robert, illus. 2015. (ENG.). 32p. (J). (-3). 9.99 (978-1-4926-2661-9(9), Sourcebooks Jabberwocky) Sourcebooks, Inc.
—Santa Is Coming to Toledo. Dunn, Robert, illus. 2015. (ENG.). 32p. (J). (-3). 9.99 (978-1-4926-2654-1(6), Sourcebooks Jabberwocky) Sourcebooks, Inc.
—Santa Is Coming to Toronto. Dunn, Robert, illus. 2012. (ENG.). 32p. (J). (-3). 9.99 (978-1-4022-7521-0(8), Sourcebooks Jabberwocky) Sourcebooks, Inc.
—Santa Is Coming to Tucson. Dunn, Robert, illus. 2013. (ENG.). 32p. (J). (-3). 9.99 (978-1-4022-8976-7(6), Sourcebooks Jabberwocky) Sourcebooks, Inc.
—Santa Is Coming to Tulsa. Dunn, Robert, illus. 2013. (ENG.). 32p. (J). (-3). 9.99 (978-1-4022-9039-8(X), Sourcebooks Jabberwocky) Sourcebooks, Inc.
—Santa Is Coming to Utah. Dunn, Robert, illus. 2013. (ENG.). 32p. (J). (-3). 9.99 (978-1-4022-8827-2(1), Sourcebooks Jabberwocky) Sourcebooks, Inc.
—Santa Is Coming to Vancouver. Dunn, Robert, illus. 2012. (ENG.). 32p. (J). (-3). 9.99 (978-1-4022-7542-5(0), Sourcebooks Jabberwocky) Sourcebooks, Inc.
—Santa Is Coming to Vermont. Dunn, Robert, illus. 2013. (ENG.). 32p. (J). (-3). 9.99 (978-1-4022-9127-2(2), Sourcebooks Jabberwocky) Sourcebooks, Inc.
—Santa Is Coming to Virginia. Dunn, Robert, illus. 2013. (ENG.). 32p. (J). (-3). 9.99 (978-1-4022-8800-5(X), Sourcebooks Jabberwocky) Sourcebooks, Inc.
—Santa Is Coming to Virginia Beach. Dunn, Robert, illus. 2015. (ENG.). 32p. (J). (-3). 9.99 (978-1-4926-2648-0(1), Sourcebooks Jabberwocky) Sourcebooks, Inc.
—Santa Is Coming to Washington. Dunn, Robert, illus. 2012. (ENG.). 32p. (J). (-3). 9.99 (978-1-4022-7524-1(2), Sourcebooks Jabberwocky) Sourcebooks, Inc.
—Santa Is Coming to Washington DC. Dunn, Robert, illus. 2013. (ENG.). 32p. (J). (-3). 9.99 (978-1-4022-8833-3(6), Sourcebooks Jabberwocky) Sourcebooks, Inc.
—Santa Is Coming to West Virginia. Dunn, Robert, illus. 2013. (ENG.). 32p. (J). (-3). 9.99 (978-1-4022-9100-5(0), Sourcebooks Jabberwocky) Sourcebooks, Inc.
—Santa Is Coming to Wichita. Dunn, Robert, illus. 2015. (ENG.). 32p. (J). (-3). 9.99 (978-1-4926-2638-1(4), Sourcebooks Jabberwocky) Sourcebooks, Inc.
—Santa Is Coming to Wisconsin. Dunn, Robert, illus. 2012. (ENG.). 32p. (J). (-3). 9.99 (978-1-4022-7533-3(1), Sourcebooks Jabberwocky) Sourcebooks, Inc.
—Santa Is Coming to Wyoming. Dunn, Robert, illus. 2014. (ENG.). 32p. (J). (-3). 9.99 (978-1-4926-0679-6(0), Sourcebooks Jabberwocky) Sourcebooks, Inc.
Smallman, Steve, et al. My First Santa's Coming to Michigan. Dunn, Robert, illus. 2015. (ENG.). 18p. (J). bds. 9.99 (978-1-4926-2873-6(5), Sourcebooks Jabberwocky) Sourcebooks, Inc.
—My First Santa's Coming to Minnesota. Dunn, Robert, illus. 2015. (ENG.). 18p. (J). bds. 9.99 (978-1-4926-2879-8(4), Sourcebooks Jabberwocky) Sourcebooks, Inc.
—My First Santa's Coming to New Jersey. Dunn, Robert, illus. 2015. (ENG.). 18p. (J). bds. 9.99 (978-1-4926-2882-8(4), Sourcebooks Jabberwocky) Sourcebooks, Inc.
—My First Santa's Coming to Ohio. Dunn, Robert, illus. 2015. (ENG.). 18p. (J). bds. 9.99 (978-1-4926-2876-7(X), Sourcebooks Jabberwocky) Sourcebooks, Inc.
—My First Santa's Coming to Texas. Dunn, Robert, illus. 2015. (ENG.). 18p. (J). bds. 9.99 (978-1-4926-2870-5(0), Sourcebooks Jabberwocky) Sourcebooks, Inc.
—My First Santa's Coming to My House. Dunn, Robert, illus. 2015. (ENG.). 18p. (J). bds. 9.99 (978-1-4926-2885-9(9), Sourcebooks Jabberwocky) Sourcebooks, Inc.
Smith, Joel D. Santa's Secret Deal: Who Else Signed It, & Where You Can Find Proof of the Deal in Your Room Right Now. 2012. 30p. pap. 14.25 (978-1-4575-1456-6(3)) Dog Ear Publishing, LLC.
Smith, John A. A Special Christmas for Oscar. 2004. 31p. pap. 24.95 (978-1-4137-2892-7(8)) PublishAmerica, Inc.
Snow, Alan. How Santa Really Works. Snow, Alan, illus. 2007. (ENG., Illus.). 48p. (J). (gr. -1-3). 7.99 (978-1-4169-5000-4(1), Atheneum Bks. for Young Readers) Simon & Schuster Children's Publishing.
Snyder, Casey. Miss Fit the Dog Saves Christmas. 2013. 20p. pap. 24.95 (978-1-62709-358-3(3)) America Star Bks.
Sobel, Gerrie. Jacob & His Magical Flying Bears. Torres, Dottie, illus. 2009. 32p. pap. 12.95 (978-1-936051-16-8(8)) Peppertree Pr., The.
Solheim, James. Santa's Secrets Revealed: All Your Questions Answered about Santa's Super Sleigh, His Flying Reindeer, & Other Wonders. Gott, Barry, illus. 2004. (Carolrhoda Picture Books Ser.). 40p. (J). (gr. k-3). 15.95 (978-1-57505-600-5(3)) Lerner Publishing Group.
Sonneborn, Scott. The Computer Meltdown. Lozano, Omar, illus. 2015. (North Police Ser.). (ENG.). 32p. (gr. k-2). lib. bdg. 21.32 (978-1-4795-6485-9(0)) Picture Window Bks.
—The Mystery of Santa's Sleigh. Lozano, Omar, illus. 2015. (North Police Ser.). (ENG.). 32p. (gr. k-2). lib. bdg. 21.32 (978-1-4795-6484-2(2)) Picture Window Bks.
Soper, Stuart A. Milky Saves Christmas. 2011. (Illus.). 290p. pap. 16.00 (978-1-60976-193-6(6), Strategic Bk. Publishing) Strategic Book Publishing & Rights Agency (SBPRA).
Soprano, Sophie, illus. Laughing All the Way. 2008. (J). (978-1-59811-642-7(8)) Covenant Communications.
Sorenson, E. Randy. The First Reindeer Couldn't Fly. 2007. (Illus.). 32p. (J). 17.99 (978-0-615-16939-2(2)) Sorenson, E. Randy.
Special Delivery from Santa. 2003. (J). per. (978-1-57657-810-0(0)); per. (978-1-57657-922-0(0)) Paradise Pr., Inc.

Spencer, John Nicholas. Sleigh Ride with Santa. Spencer, Kay Kincannon, illus. 2012. (ENG.). 26p. (J). pap. 14.95 *(978-1-61296-140-8(1))* Black Rose Writing.

Stainton, Sue. Christmas Magic. Melhuish, Eva, illus. 2007. 32p. (J). (gr. -1-1). lib. bdg. 16.89 *(978-0-06-078572-7(1),* Tegen, Katherine Bks) HarperCollins Pubs.

Stanton, Melissa. My Pen Pal, Santa. Bell, Jennifer A., illus. 2013. (ENG.). 32p. (J). (gr. -1-2). 9.99 *(978-0-375-86992-1(1),* Random Hse. Bks. for Young Readers) Random Hse. Children's Bks.

Stayer, Elizabeth. Santa's Magic Stardust. 2009. 40p. pap. 18.49 *(978-1-4490-2884-8(5))* AuthorHouse.

Stepp, Shirley. Santa Lost His Cell Phone. 2012. 24p. 24.95 *(978-1-4626-5479-6(7))* America Star Bks.

Stoddard, Chad L. Why Is Santa Fat? 2012. 20p. pap. 15.00 *(978-1-4520-0788-5(8))* AuthorHouse.

Stoeke, Janet Morgan. Minerva Louise on Christmas Eve. Stoeke, Janet Morgan, illus. 2009. (ENG., Illus.). 32p. (J). (gr. -1-k). pap. 6.99 *(978-0-14-241449-1(2),* Puffin Books) Penguin Young Readers Group.

Sullivan, E. J. How Santa Got His Elves. Eldredge, Ernie, illus. 2006. (J). (gr. -1-3). 9.95 *(978-1-58173-308-2(9))* Sweetwater Pr.

Sykes, Julie. Bless You, Santa! Warnes, Tim, illus. 2004. 32p. (J). tchr. ed. 15.95 *(978-1-58925-041-3(9))* Tiger Tales.

—Shhh! Warnes, Tim, illus. 2006. (Storytime Board Bks.). 18p. (J). (gr. -1-1). bds. 6.95 *(978-1-58925-796-2(0))* Tiger Tales.

Sylvester, Merrill. Ho-Ho Where Did All My Reindeer Go? The Chicken Leg Detective Service. 2011. 72p. pap. 19.95 *(978-1-4626-0794-5(2))* America Star Bks.

Sypolt, Carl W. Fibber Lygood at Christmas, Easter, & St. Patrick's Day. 2006. 108p. (J). pap. 10.95 *(978-0-7414-2982-7(9))* Infinity Publishing.

Tapler, Judy. Santa Horse. Kohler, Michelle, illus. 2008. 36p. pap. 16.99 *(978-1-4389-2290-4(6))* AuthorHouse.

Taylor, Lillian Webb. Santa's Musical Elves. 2009. 28p. pap. 12.25 *(978-1-60860-146-2(3),* Strategic Bk. Publishing) Strategic Book Publishing & Rights Agency (SBPRA).

Teitelbaum, Michael. Garfield & the Santa Spy. Fentz, Mike, illus. 2004. 92p. (J). *(978-0-439-70543-1(6))* Scholastic, Inc.

Thaler, Mike. The Secret Santa from the Black Lagoon. Lee, Jared D., illus. 2014. 64p. (J). *(978-0-545-78519-8(7))* Scholastic, Inc.

The Bee Guru, Gregg McMahan. Christmas Honey. 2012. (Illus.). 20p. pap. 11.60 *(978-1-4669-5471-7(X))* Trafford Publishing.

Thompson, Emily Weisner & Hussey, Mandy. But What If There's No Chimney? Lampe, Kate, illus. 2016. (ENG.). 24p. 12.00 *(978-0-253-02392-6(0))* Indiana Univ. Pr.

Thompson, Lauren. The Christmas Magic. Muth, Jon J., illus. 2009. (ENG.). 40p. (J). (gr. -1-3). 16.99 *(978-0-439-77497-0(7),* Scholastic Pr.) Scholastic, Inc.

Todd, Michelle, illus. Santa's Workshop. 2017. (ENG.). 12p. (J). (gr. -1-1). 12.99 ***(978-1-4380-5007-2(0))*** Barron's Educational Series, Inc.

Tolkien, J. R. R. Letters from Father Christmas. Tolkien, Baillie, ed. 2004. (ENG., Illus.). 128p. pap. 23.99 *(978-0-618-51265-2(9))* Houghton Mifflin Harcourt Publishing Co.

Tolley, Diane Stringam. Kris Kringle's Magic. 2012. 169p. (J). 14.99 *(978-1-4621-1105-3(X))* Cedar Fort, Inc./CFI Distribution.

Tolley, Diane Stringham & Tolley, Diane Stringam. Carving Angels. 2011. 121p. (J). 12.99 *(978-1-59955-944-5(7),* Bonneville Bks.) Cedar Fort, Inc./CFI Distribution.

Tonn, Mary Jane. Jolly Old Santa Claus. 2010. 32p. pap. 7.99 *(978-0-8249-5624-0(9),* Ideal Pubns.) Worthy Publishing.

Trinidad Joe. Santa's Key West Vacation. 2007. (Illus.). 80p. per. 12.95 *(978-0-9799474-0-7(5))* Seastory Pr.

Trivette, Donna K. One Special Christmas. 2012. 44p. pap. 24.95 *(978-1-4626-9363-4(6))* America Star Bks.

Trondheim, Lewis & Robin, Theirry. Happy Halloween, Li'l Santa. Robin, Thierry, illus. 2003. (ENG.). 51p. 14.95 *(978-1-56163-361-6(5))* NBM Publishing Co.

Tullis, Jamie. Rudolph, I Think You Need Glasses! 2012. 24p. pap. 15.99 *(978-1-4797-1624-1(3))* Xlibris Corp.

Tully, Justin. Lost from the Christmas Mansion. 2008. 141p. pap. 16.95 *(978-1-4092-5106-4(3))* Lulu Pr., Inc.

Turner, Christina. Hello Santa! Turner, Christina, illus. 2007. (Illus.). 16p. (J). (gr. -1). bds. 7.95 *(978-0-9790347-0-1(1))* Mackenzie Smiles, LLC.

Turner, Thomas N. Country Music Night Before Christmas, 1 vol. Rice, James, illus. 2003. (Night Before Christmas Ser.). (ENG.). 32p. (J). (gr. k-3). 16.99 *(978-1-58980-148-6(2))* Pelican Publishing Co., Inc.

Twenstrup, Norm. A Surprise for Santa. DHP, Inc. Staff, ed. (Illus.). 32p. (J). (gr. -1-3). pap. *(978-1-885531-12-4(5))* Mess Hall Writers.

Vaitonis, Steven. Edison the Christmas Elf & the Imperfect Perfect Toy. Blue, Melissa, illus. 2014. 32p. (J). (gr. -1-1). pap. 12.95 *(978-1-939930-33-0(2),* Belle Isle Bks.) Brandylane Pubs., Inc.

Van Allsburg, Chris. The Polar Express. 30th anniv. ed. 2015. (ENG., Illus.). 32p. (J). (gr. -1-3). 19.99 *(978-0-544-58014-5(1),* HMH Books For Young Readers) Houghton Mifflin Harcourt Publishing Co.

—The Polar Express: Sam's Edition. annot. ed. 2006. (J). (gr. k-3). 35.00 *(978-0-618-83659-8(4))* Houghton Mifflin Harcourt Trade & Reference Pubs.

—The Polar Express Big Book. 2014. (ENG., Illus.). 32p. (J). (gr. -1-3). 29.99 *(978-0-544-45798-0(6),* HMH Books For Young Readers) Houghton Mifflin Harcourt Publishing Co.

Van King, L. The Dwarf in the Drawer: A Mischievous Parody. Gonzales, Chuck, illus. 2013. (ENG.). 32p. (J). 19.99 *(978-1-250-04143-2(0),* 9781250041432) Square Fish.

Vanek, Karen & Schmidt, Sharon Vanek. Santa Claus Meets the Tooth Fairy. 2012. 44p. pap. 21.99 *(978-1-4772-4535-4(9))* AuthorHouse.

Velde, Henry. The Night I Became... 2007. (J). per. 16.99 *(978-1-933156-18-7(X),* Visikid Bks.) GSVQ Publishing.

Vine, Deryth. Fiskers Meets Santa Claus. 2013. (Illus.). 40p. pap. *(978-0-9927157-0-0(9))* Tanglin Publishing.

Waiting for Santa. 2004. (J). per. *(978-1-57657-385-3(0));* per. *(978-1-57657-451-5(2))* Paradise Pr., Inc.

Walker-Renner, Christa. Santa's Magic. 2009. 20p. pap. 11.00 *(978-1-4389-8206-9(2))* AuthorHouse.

Wallace, Adam. Only YOU Can Save Christmas! A Help-The-Elf Adventure. Bruner, Garth, illus. 2017. (ENG.). 40p. (J). (gr. 1-5). 16.99 ***(978-1-4926-4136-0(7),*** Sourcebooks Jabberwocky) Sourcebooks, Inc.

Wallace, Carol. The Santa Secret. Björkman, Steve, illus. 2007. (Holiday House Readers: Level 2 Ser.). (ENG.). 40p. (J). (gr. -1-3). 15.95 *(978-0-8234-2022-3(1));* pap. 4.95 *(978-0-8234-2126-8(0))* Holiday Hse., Inc.

Wallace, R. Mike. Saunter. 2009. 36p. pap. 10.75 *(978-1-60693-994-9(7),* Strategic Bk. Publishing) Strategic Book Publishing & Rights Agency (SBPRA).

Wallace, William H. Santa's Magic Key. 2010. 20p. (J). 10.49 *(978-1-4490-8924-5(0))* AuthorHouse.

Walters, Eric & Walters, Christina. The True Story of Santa Claus. Gooderham, Andrew, illus. 2005. 38p. (J). 9.95 *(978-1-894601-11-5(4))* Chestnut Publishing Group CAN. Dist: Hushion Hse. Publishing, Ltd.

Wampol, Pam & Woodard, Heather. Oscar's Dreamzz: The Story of Santa's First Elf. 2013. 40p. pap. *(978-1-4602-0414-6(X))* FriesenPress.

Watt, Fiona. Busy Santa Book. 2011. (Pull-Back Bks). 10p. (J). ring bd. 24.99 *(978-0-7945-3178-2(4),* Usborne) EDC Publishing.

—Santa Claus. 2004. (Sparkly Touchy-Feely Board Bks.). 10p. (J). 15.95 *(978-0-7945-0830-2(8),* Usborne) EDC Publishing.

—That's Not My Santa. (Touchy-Feely Board Bks). 10p. (J). 2008. bds. 9.99 *(978-0-7945-2390-9(0))* 2012. bds. 8.99 *(978-0-7945-3310-6(8))* EDC Publishing. (Usborne).

Webster, Clare L., retold by. The Elf, 1 vol. 2009. 27p. pap. 24.95 *(978-1-60836-775-7(4))* America Star Bks.

Weiner-Booth, Patsy. The Day Santa Met Jesus: A Christmas story & Play. 2009. 56p. pap. 10.99 *(978-1-4490-1090-4(3))* AuthorHouse.

Wellings, Chris R. Sparkles Goes Home for the Holidays. Kennell, Julie, illus. 2011. 40p. pap. 24.95 *(978-1-4560-4120-5(7))* America Star Bks.

—Sparkles Meets the Easter Bunny: The Adventures of Sparkles. Hammersley, Karen, illus. 2011. 48p. pap. 24.95 *(978-1-4560-7063-2(0))* America Star Bks.

Wells, Rosemary. Max's Christmas. 2013. (Max & Ruby Ser.). (ENG.). 32p. (J). (gr. -1-k). 8.99 *(978-0-14-750947-5(5),* Puffin Books) Penguin Young Readers Group.

—Max's Christmas. 2013. (Max & Ruby Ser.). lib. bdg. 18.40 *(978-0-606-32139-6(X),* Turtleback) Turtleback Bks.

—McDuff's New Friend with Plush Box Set. 2003. (Illus.). 28p. (J). 14.99 *(978-0-7868-1866-2(2),* Disney Editions) Disney Pr.

Wendel, Gretchen Schomer & Schomer, Adam Anthony. Becka Goes to San Diego. Renthrope, Damon, illus. 2008. (ENG.). 32p. (J). (gr. -1-3). 11.99 *(978-1-933754-51-2(6))* Waterside Publishing.

Wendel, Gretchen Schomer & Schomer, Adam Anthony. Becka Goes to Chicago. Renthrope, Damon, illus. 2008. (ENG.). 36p. (J). (gr. -1-3). 11.99 *(978-1-933754-52-9(4))* Waterside Publishing.

Wenger, Brahm. Dewey's Magical Sleigh. 2005. (ENG.). 32p. (J). (gr. -1-2). 15.95 *(978-0-9745143-5-2(7))* RandallFraser Publishing.

—Dewey's Magical Sleigh, from the Dewey Doo-it Series. 2005. (ENG., Illus.). 32p. (J). (gr. -1-2). 15.95 incl. lp *(978-0-9745143-6-9(5))* RandallFraser Publishing.

Werkema, Mark A. The Flight Before Christmas. 2004. (YA). pap. 13.95 *(978-1-58961-306-5(6))* PageFree Publishing, Inc.

Werner, James R. Dave's Christmas Surprise & a Puppy Named Oxley. 2008. 28p. pap. 14.95 *(978-1-4327-3298-1(6))* Outskirts Pr., Inc.

Weston Woods Staff, creator. Fletcher & the Snowflake Christmas. 2011. 29.95 *(978-0-545-42619-0(7))* Weston Woods Studios, Inc.

Wheeler, Lisa. The Christmas Boot. Pinkney, Jerry, illus. 2016. (ENG.). 32p. (J). (gr. -1-3). 17.99 *(978-0-8037-4134-8(0),* Dial Bks) Penguin Young Readers Group.

White, S.D. Sing along with the Santa Claus That Never Saw a Child. 2008. 20p. pap. 12.89 *(978-1-4389-0305-7(7))* AuthorHouse.

Whitehouse, Anna. The Last Sant. 2012. 118p. pap. *(978-1-78176-289-9(9))* FeedARead.com.

Whybrow, Ian. Miss Wire's Christmas Surprise. Chichester Clark, Emma, illus. 2007. 45p. (J). (gr. -1-3). pap. 3.95 *(978-0-7534-6136-5(6),* Kingfisher) Roaring Brook Pr.

Wilhite, Cindy. Santa He Sees You When. 2009. 28p. 18.65 *(978-0-557-12852-5(8))* Lulu Pr., Inc.

Wilkins, Nalini. Doby's First Christmas. Robb, Jonathan, illus. 2012. 28p. pap. 12.50 *(978-1-62212-777-1(3),* Strategic Bk. Publishing) Strategic Book Publishing & Rights Agency (SBPRA).

Wilkinson, Thomas M. Willie-off-the-Pickleboat. 2009. 71p. pap. 12.99 *(978-0-557-06181-5(4))* Lulu Pr., Inc.

Willey, Margaret. A Clever Beatrice Christmas. Solomon, Heather M., illus. 2006. (ENG.). 40p. (J). (gr. -1-2). 19.99 *(978-0-689-87017-0(5),* Atheneum Bks. for Young Readers) Simon & Schuster Children's Publishing.

Williams, Hap. Henry the Elf. Graves, Michelle, illus. 2012. 28p. pap. 24.95 *(978-1-4626-8999-6(X))* America Star Bks.

Williams, Sam. Santa's Toys. Gill, Tim, illus. 2003. 14p. bds. *(978-1-85602-274-3(9),* Pavilion Children's Books) Pavilion Bks.

Williamson, K. E. Kayla & the Christmas Monkey. 2010. 28p. pap. 15.49 *(978-1-4520-9749-7(6))* AuthorHouse.

Wilson, Matthew. Scrooge & Santa GN. 2011. (Illus.). 100p. pap. 14.95 *(978-1-897548-98-1(2))* Arcana Studio, Inc.

Witt, Janice. Harold Discovers Santa's Secret: A Very Long Dog with a Very Big Heart. Reznicek, Curtis, illus. 2013. 40p. pap. 11.99 *(978-1-63022-442-4(1))* Speedy Publishing LLC.

Wolf, Carol A. Foggy Dog Discovers Christmas. 2012. 40p. pap. 16.46 *(978-1-4669-6253-8(4))* Trafford Publishing.

Wolfe, Greg. Shmelf the Hanukkah Elf. McWilliam, Howard, illus. 2016. (ENG.). 32p. (J). 16.99 *(978-1-61963-521-0(6),* 9781619635210, Bloomsbury USA Childrens) Bloomsbury Publishing USA.

Wolper, Joanna. The Man Who Could Be Santa. 2008. (Illus.). 78p. (J). pap. *(978-0-88092-765-9(8));* lib. bdg. *(978-0-88092-764-2(X))* Royal Fireworks Publishing Co.

Wood, Douglas. What Santa Can't Do. Cushman, Doug, illus. 2008. (ENG.). 32p. (J). (gr. -1-3). 16.99 *(978-1-4169-6747-7(8),* Simon & Schuster Bks. For Young Readers) Simon & Schuster Bks. For Young Readers.

Wood, Francis Eusene. The Christmas Letter. Wood, Christine & Marken, Jon, eds. McDermott, Robert, illus. Wood, Christine, photos by. 2007. pap. 9.95 *(978-0-9746372-6-6(2))* Tip-Of-The-Moon Publishing Co.

Wreggelsworth, Irene. Help, Children! - The Monsters Kidnapped Santa Claus: Bilingual Book in English & Spanish. Piccione, Dana, illus. 2010. (ENG.). 120p. pap. 26.99 *(978-1-4537-1272-6(0))* CreateSpace Independent Publishing Platform.

Young, H. M. (Hal). The huskies & the christmas Fawn. 2007. 56p. pap. 9.95 *(978-1-4357-0070-3(8))* Lulu Pr., Inc.

Zalesny, Michele. The Elves' Surprise. 2008. (ENG., Illus.). 20p. (J). pap. 9.25 *(978-1-935125-06-8(0))* Robertson Publishing.

Zurcher, Corina. Growing up Claus. 2007. 188p. 21.99 *(978-1-60477-046-9(5));* per. 13.99 *(978-1-60266-917-8(1))* Salem Author Services.

SANTA CLAUS—POETRY

Brallier, Christine, illus. The Night Before Christmas. 2013. (ENG.). 32p. (J). 16.99 *(978-0-9789688-2-3(4))* Brownian Bee Pr.

Brown, Tricia. Alaskan Night Before Christmas, 1 vol. Stacy, Alan, illus. 2008. (Night Before Christmas Ser.). (ENG.). 32p. (gr. 1-3). 16.99 *(978-1-58980-554-5(2))* Pelican Publishing Co., Inc.

Gribnau, Joe. Rocky Mountain Night Before Christmas, 1 vol. Alikhan, Salima, illus. 2007. (Night Before Christmas Ser.). (ENG.). 32p. (J). (gr. k-3). 16.99 *(978-1-58980-317-6(5))* Pelican Publishing Co., Inc.

Layne, Steven L. Preacher's Night Before Christmas, 1 vol. Benioff, Carol, illus. 2006. (Night Before Christmas Ser.). (ENG.). 32p. (J). (gr. k-3). 16.99 *(978-1-58980-321-3(3))* Pelican Publishing Co., Inc.

McWilliams, Amanda & Moore, Clement C. Ozark Night Before Christmas, 1 vol. Rice, James, illus. 2004. (Night Before Christmas Ser.). (ENG.). 32p. (J). (gr. k-3). 16.99 *(978-1-58980-056-4(7))* Pelican Publishing Co., Inc.

Medina, Tony. Just Us. 2004. (Illus.). 48p. (J). (gr. 4-18). pap. 6.95 *(978-0-940975-75-0(0),* Sankofa Bks.) Just Us Bks., Inc.

Moore, Clement C. Era la Víspera de Navidad. 2012.Tr. of Twas the Night Before Christmas. (SPA., Illus.). 32p. (J). 16.95 *(978-0-9879023-5-1(0))* Grafton and Scratch Pubs. CAN. Dist: Bookmasters Distribution.

—The Night Before Christmas. Fujikawa, Gyo, illus. 2007. (ENG.). 32p. (J). (gr. -1-2). 9.95 *(978-1-4027-5065-6(X))* Sterling Publishing Co., Inc.

—The Night Before Christmas. 2006. (J). per. 9.95 *(978-1-4276-0967-0(5))* Aardvark Global Publishing.

—The Night Before Christmas. 2012. (ENG.). 32p. 11.50 *(978-1-84135-796-6(0))* Award Pubns. Ltd. GBR. Dist: Parkwest Pubns., Inc.

—The Night Before Christmas. Fisher, Henry, illus. 2013. 26p. (J). *(978-1-4351-4927-4(0))* Barnes & Noble, Inc.

—The Night Before Christmas. Barrett, Angela, illus. 2012. 30p. (J). *(978-1-4351-4416-3(3))* Barnes & Noble, Inc.

—The Night Before Christmas. Adolphe, Joseph, illus. 2013. (J). 19.95 *(978-1-59530-953-2(5))* Hallmark Card, Inc.

—The Night Before Christmas. Kesler, Matt, illus. 2012. 16p. (J). 29.95 *(978-1-59530-407-0(X))* Hallmark Card, Inc.

—The Night Before Christmas. Engelbreit, Mary, illus. 2011. (ENG.). 40p. (J). (gr. -1-3). 9.99 *(978-0-06-208944-1(7))* HarperCollins Pubs.

—The Night Before Christmas. Watson, Richard Jesse, illus. 2008. (ENG.). 40p. (J). (gr. -1-3). pap. 6.99 *(978-0-06-075744-1(2))* HarperCollins Pubs.

—The Night Before Christmas. Whatley, Bruce, illus. 2004. (ENG.). 32p. (J). (gr. -1 — 1). bds. 6.99 *(978-0-06-073917-1(7),* HarperFestival) HarperCollins Pubs.

—The Night Before Christmas. 2014. (ENG., Illus.). 32p. (J). (gr. -1-k). 10.99 *(978-1-4449-0243-3(1))* Hodder & Stoughton GBR. Dist: Hachette Bk. Group.

—The Night Before Christmas. dePaola, Tomie, illus. 2010. (ENG.). 24p. (J). (gr. -1). bds. 8.95 *(978-0-8234-2284-5(4))* Holiday Hse., Inc.

—The Night Before Christmas. 2008. *(978-1-58865-498-4(2))* Kidsbooks, LLC.

—The Night Before Christmas. Caparo, Antonio Javier, illus. 2017. (ENG.). 40p. (J). (gr. -1-2). 17.99 ***(978-1-5344-0085-6(0),*** Little Simon) Little Simon.

—The Night Before Christmas. 2009. (Illus.). 23p. pap. *(978-0-462-09940-8(7))* Marshall Cavendish.

—The Night Before Christmas. Zwerger, Lisbeth, illus. 2014. (Minedition Minibooks Ser.). (ENG.). 32p. (J). (gr. -1-k). 9.99 *(978-988-8240-88-3(9))* Neugebauer, Michael (Publishing) Limited HKG. Dist: Independent Pubs. Group.

—The Night Before Christmas. Rand, Ted, illus. 2014. (ENG.). 32p. (J). 17.95 *(978-0-7358-4106-2(3))* North-South Bks., Inc.

—The Night Before Christmas. Newsom, Tom, illus. 2012. (J). *(978-1-4508-5375-0(7))* Publications International, Ltd.

—The Night Before Christmas. 2015. (Big Golden Board Book Ser.). (ENG., Illus.). 24p. (J). (-k). bds. 10.99 *(978-0-553-52226-6(4),* Golden Bks.) Random Hse. Children's Bks.

—The Night Before Christmas. Malvern, Corinne, illus. (Little Golden Board Book Ser.). (ENG.). (J). 2014. 26p. (-k). bds. 7.99 *(978-0-385-38474-2(2))* 2011. 24p. (gr. -1-k). 4.99 *(978-0-375-86359-2(1))* Random Hse. Children's Bks. (Golden Bks.).

—The Night Before Christmas. Ercolini, David, illus. 2015. (ENG.). 32p. (J). (gr. -1-k). 16.99 *(978-0-545-39112-2(1),* Orchard Bks.) Scholastic, Inc.

—The Night Before Christmas. 2012. 28p. (gr. -1-2). 14.95 *(978-1-61382-397-2(5))* Simon & Brown.

—The Night Before Christmas. Bell, Bill, illus. 2011. (ENG.). 32p. (J). (gr. k-2). 6.95 *(978-1-61608-470-7(7),* 608470, Sky Pony Pr.) Skyhorse Publishing Co., Inc.

—The Night Before Christmas. Eldredge, Larry, illus. 2006. (Night Before Christmas Ser.). 32p. (J). 9.95 *(978-1-58173-306-8(2));* 26p. bds. 9.95 *(978-1-58173-300-6(3))* Sweetwater Pr.

—The Night Before Christmas. Nowakowski, Marcin, illus. 2016. (ENG.). 32p. (J). (gr. -1-1). pap. 9.99 *(978-1-78445-346-6(3))* Top That! Publishing PLC GBR. Dist: Independent Pubs. Group.

—The Night Before Christmas. Rackham, Arthur, illus. 2012. 32p. pap. 5.99 *(978-1-61720-437-1(4))* Wilder Pubns., Corp.

—The Night Before Christmas. Samuel, Janet, illus. 2012. (ENG.). 24p. (J). bds. 6.99 *(978-0-8249-1884-2(3),* Ideal Pubns.) Worthy Publishing.

—The Night Before Christmas. 2010. (Illus.). 32p. (J). 9.99 *(978-0-8249-5627-1(3),* Ideal Pubns.) Worthy Publishing.

—The Night Before Christmas. Mills, Donald, illus. 2008. 30p. (J). (gr. -1-k). pap. 3.95 *(978-0-8249-5514-4(5),* Ideal Pubns.) Worthy Publishing.

—The Night Before Christmas. Price, Margaret Evans, illus. 2009. (Dover Children's Classics Ser.). (ENG.). 16p. (J). (gr. k-5). pap. 6.99 *(978-0-486-47369-7(4))* Dover Pubns., Inc.

—The Night Before Christmas. Puybaret, Eric, illus. 2010. (Book & CD Ser.). (ENG.). 26p. (J). (gr. k-4). 19.95 *(978-1-936140-06-0(3))* Charlesbridge Publishing, Inc.

—The Night Before Christmas. Gurney, John Steven, illus. 2006. (ENG.). (J). (gr. -1-3). 9.99 *(978-0-439-89557-6(X))* Scholastic, Inc.

—The Night Before Christmas. 2013. (ENG., Illus.). 40p. (J). (gr. -1-3). 18.00 *(978-0-316-07018-8(1))* Little, Brown Bks. for Young Readers.

—The Night Before Christmas. Reid, Barbara, illus. 2014. (ENG.). 32p. (J). (gr. -1-3). 16.99 *(978-0-8075-5625-2(4))* Whitman, Albert & Co.

—The Night Before Christmas, Set. Santore, Charles, illus. gif. ed. 2013. (ENG.). 48p. (J). 14.95 *(978-1-60433-437-1(1),* Applesauce Pr.) Cider Mill Pr. Bk. Pubs., LLC.

—The Night Before Christmas. Reid, Barbara, illus. adapted ed. 2016. (ENG.). 36p. pap. 6.95 ***(978-1-945546-47-1(6))*** Frederic Thomas USA, Inc.

—The Night Before Christmas. Tudor, Tasha, illus. 10th anniv. ed. 2009. 32p. pap. 6.99 *(978-0-316-18947-7(2))* Hachette Bk. Group.

—The Night Before Christmas. Engelbreit, Mary, illus. rev. ed. (ENG.). 40p. (J). (gr. -1-3). 2006. 17.99 *(978-0-06-008160-7(0))*Set. 2007. 25.00 *(978-0-06-136495-2(9),* HarperFestival) HarperCollins Pubs.

—The Night Before Christmas. Birmingham, Christian, illus. 10th anniv. ed. 2005. (ENG.). 48p. (J). (gr. -1-3). 9.95 *(978-0-7624-2416-0(8))* Running Pr. Bk. Pubs.

—The Night Before Christmas: A Brick Story. Brack, Amanda, illus. 2015. (ENG.). 32p. (J). (gr. -1). 12.99 *(978-1-63450-179-8(9),* Sky Pony Pr.) Skyhorse Publishing Co., Inc.

—The Night Before Christmas: A Visit from St. Nicholas. 2008. 48p. 18.99 *(978-1-60641-066-0(0))* Deseret Bk. Co.

—The Night Before Christmas: Or, a Visit from St. Nicholas. Santore, Charles, illus. 2011. 41p. (J). *(978-1-60464-033-5(2))* Appleseed Pr. Bk. Pub. LLC.

—The Night Before Christmas: The Classic Heirloom Edition. Santore, Charles, illus. 2016. (ENG.). 48p. (J). 24.95 *(978-1-60433-677-1(3),* Applesauce Pr.) Cider Mill Pr. Bk. Pubs., LLC.

—'Twas the Night Before Christmas. Whelan, Kat, illus. 2010. (ENG.). 24p. (J). (gr. -1-2). 12.95 *(978-1-58925-858-7(4))* Tiger Tales.

—Twas the Night Before Christmas. 2013. (ENG., Illus.). 32p. (J). pap. 7.95 *(978-0-9879023-1-3(8))* Grafton and Scratch Pubs. CAN. Dist: Bookmasters Distribution.

—Twas the Night Before Christmas: A Visit from St. Nicholas. Smith, Jessie Willcox, illus. 2015. vi, 29p. (J). pap. *(978-1-4677-7805-3(2),* First Avenue Editions) Lerner Publishing Group.

—Twas the Night Before Christmas: Santa Claus for the Benefit of Children of the 21st Century. 2012. (ENG., Illus.). 32p. (J). 15.95 *(978-0-9879023-0-6(X),* 9780987902306) Grafton and Scratch Pubs. CAN. Dist: Bookmasters Distribution.

—A Visit from St. Nicholas. Nast, Thomas, illus. 2006. (ENG.). 24p. (gr. -1-1). pap. 24.95 *(978-1-55709-592-3(2))* Applewood Bks.

Moore, Clement C., ed. & illus. The Night Before Christmas. Moore, Clement C., illus. Winget, Susan, illus. 2004. 32p. 18.00 *(978-0-7412-1939-8(5))* Lang Graphics, Ltd.

—The Night Before Christmas. Moore, Clement C., illus. Gorsline, Douglas, illus. 32p. (J). Random Hse. Children's Bks.

—The Night Before Christmas. Moore, Clement C., illus. Porfirio, Guy, illus. 2004. 20p. (J). 9.95 *(978-0-8249-6553-2(1),* Ideal Pubns.) Worthy Publishing.

Moore, Clement C. & Curto Family, The. The Night Before Christmas. Creative Illustrations Studio & Good Times At Home LLC, illus. 2012. (J). pap. 9.99 *(978-0-9840338-5-0(8))* Good Times at Home LLC.

Moore, Clement C. & Linz, Peter. The Night Before Christmas. Gurney, John Steven, illus. 2006. (ENG.). 32p. (J). (gr. -1-3). 18.95 *(978-0-439-89843-0(9))* Scholastic, Inc.

Moore, Clement C., et al. C'était la Veille de Noel. 2012.Tr. of Twas the Night Before Christmas. (FRE.). 32p. (J). 16.95 *(978-0-9879023-6-8(9))* Grafton and Scratch Pubs. CAN. Dist: Bookmasters Distribution.

Santore, Charles, illus. The Night Before Christmas. 2011. (Classic Edition Ser.). (ENG.). 44p. (J). (gr. -1). 19.95 *(978-1-60433-237-7(9),* Applesauce Pr.) Cider Mill Pr. Bk. Pubs., LLC.

Simmons, Lynn Sheffield. Sugar Lump's Night Before Christmas, 1 vol. Ward, Sue Marshall, illus. 2007. (Night Before Christmas Ser.). (ENG.). 48p. (J). (gr. k-5). 12.95 *(978-1-58980-439-5(2))* Pelican Publishing Co., Inc.

Smith, Jessie Willcox & Moore, Clement C. 'Twas the Night Before Christmas. Smith, Jessie Willcox, illus. 2005. (ENG., Illus.). 32p. (J). (gr. -1-3). 6.99 *(978-0-618-61510-0(5));* 14.00 *(978-0-618-61682-4(9))* Houghton Mifflin Harcourt Publishing Co.

Spirin, Gennady, illus. The Night Before Christmas, 0 vols. ltd. ed. 2006. (ENG.). 32p. (J). (gr. -1-3). 16.99 *(978-0-7614-5298-0(2),* 9780761452980, Amazon Children's Publishing) Amazon Publishing.

Wick, Walter. Can You See What I See? Night Before Christmas. Wick, Walter, photos by. 2005. (Can You See What I See? Ser.). (ENG., Illus.). 40p. (J). (gr. -1-3). 13.99 *(978-0-439-76927-3(2),* Cartwheel Bks.) Scholastic, Inc.

Yates, Philip. A Pirate's Night Before Christmas. Serra, Sebastiá, illus. (ENG.). 32p. (J). (gr. -1-1). 2014. pap. 6.95

S

(978-1-4549-1357-3(6)) 2008. 14.95 *(978-1-4027-4257-6(6))* Sterling Publishing Co., Inc.

SANTA FE (N.M.)

Brown, Rachel K. Santa Fe: Daily Life in a Western Trading Center. 2003. (J). pap. *(978-1-58417-074-7(3))*; lib. bdg. *(978-1-58417-011-2(5))* Lake Street Pubs.

Coll, Ivar Da. Maria Juana. (SPA.). (J). bds. *(978-958-04-4908-9(2))* Norma S.A. COL. Dist: Lectorum Pubns., Inc.

McNeese, Tim. Santa Fe. 2007. (Colonial Settlements in America Ser.). (Illus.). 116p. (YA). (gr. 5-9). lib. bdg. 30.00 *(978-0-7910-9332-0(8))* Facts On File, Inc.

Noble, David Grant. Santa Fe: History of an Ancient City. 2008. (ENG.). 144p. 40.00 *(978-1-934691-03-8(8))*; (Illus.). pap. 19.95 *(978-1-934691-04-5(6))* School for Advanced Research Pr./SAR Pr.

SANTA FE NATIONAL HISTORIC TRAIL

Dean, Arlan. The Santa Fe Trail: From Independence, Missouri to Santa Fe, New Mexico. (Famous American Trails Ser.). 24p. 2009. (gr. 3-3). 42.50 *(978-1-61512-492-3(6))* 2003. (Illus.). (J). lib. bdg. 22.60 *(978-0-8239-6481-9(7))* Rosen Publishing Group, Inc., The. (PowerKids Pr.).

Randolph, Ryan P. The Santa Fe Trail. (Library of the Westward Expansion Ser.). 24p. 2009. (gr. 3-4). 42.50 *(978-1-60853-940-6(7))* 2003. (Illus.). (J). lib. bdg. 22.60 *(978-0-8239-6292-1(X))* Rosen Publishing Group, Inc., The. (PowerKids Pr.).

Thompson, Linda. The Santa Fe Trail. 2005. (Expansion of America Ser.). (Illus.). 48p. (gr. 4-8). 20.95 *(978-1-59515-226-8(1))* Rourke Educational Media.

Williams, Jean K. The Perils of the Santa Fe Trail. 2017. (Landmarks in U. S. History Ser.). (ENG.). 32p. (gr. 3-4). lib. bdg. 27.32 ***(978-1-5157-7117-3(2)***, Fact Finders) Capstone Press of Coughlan Cos.

SANTA FE NATIONAL HISTORIC TRAIL—FICTION

Sperry, Armstrong. Wagons Westward: The Old Trail to Santa Fe. Sperry, Armstrong, illus. 2005. (Illus.). 200p. (YA). (gr. 6-11). reprint ed. pap. 15.00 *(978-0-7567-9693-8(8))* DIANE Publishing Co.

SARATOGA CAMPAIGN, 1777

Burgan, Michael. The Untold Story of the Battle of Saratoga: A Turning Point in the Revolutionary War. 2015. (What You Didn't Know about the American Revolution Ser.). (ENG.). 64p. (gr. 4-8). pap. 8.95 *(978-0-7565-4978-7(7))* Compass Point Bks.

Rushworth, Victoria. Battles of the American Revolution: Saratoga: Text Pairs. 2008. (Bridges/Navigators Ser.). (J). (gr. 5). 81.00 *(978-1-4108-8404-6(X))* Benchmark Education Co.

Vierow, Wendy. The Battle of Saratoga. (Atlas of Famous Battles of the American Revolution Ser.). 24p. 2009. (gr. 3-3). 42.50 *(978-1-60853-330-5(1))* 2003. (Illus.). (J). lib. bdg. 22.60 *(978-0-8239-6332-4(2))* Rosen Publishing Group, Inc., The. (PowerKids Pr.).

SARGASSO SEA

Heller, Ruth. A Sea within a Sea: Secrets of the Sargasso. Heller, Ruth, illus. 2006. (Illus.). 29p. (J). (gr. 4-8). reprint ed. 17.00 *(978-1-4223-5731-6(7))* DIANE Publishing Co.

SASKATCHEWAN

Aksomitis, Linda. L Is for Land of Living Skies: A Saskatchewan Alphabet. Bennett, Lorna, illus. 2010. (Discover Canada Province by Province Ser.). (ENG.). 32p. (J). (gr. 1-3). 17.95 *(978-1-58536-490-9(8))*, 202194) Sleeping Bear Pr.

Glaze, Dave. The Last Flight of the Birdman, 1 vol. 2007. (1912: the Mackenzie Davis Files Ser.). (ENG.). 200p. (J). (gr. 4-7). pap. 7.95 *(978-1-55050-373-9(1))* Coteau Bks. CAN. Dist: Orca Bk. Pubs. USA.

Millar, Ruth. Saskatchewan Heroes & Rogues. 2004. (ENG., Illus.). 240p. (gr. 7-18). pap. 17.95 *(978-1-55050-289-3(1))* Coteau Bks. CAN. Dist: Fitzhenry & Whiteside, Ltd.

SASKATCHEWAN—FICTION

Banks, Lynne Reid. Uprooted - a Canadian War Story. 2014. (ENG.). 336p. (J). 8.99 *(978-0-00-758943-2(3)*, HarperCollins Children's Bks.) HarperCollins Pubs. Ltd. GBR. Dist: HarperCollins Pubs.

Croza, Laurel. From There to Here, 1 vol. James, Matt, illus. 2014. (ENG.). 36p. (J). (gr. -1-2). 18.95 *(978-1-55498-365-0(7))* Groundwood Bks. CAN. Dist: Publishers Group West (PGW).

Draper, Penny. Day of the Cyclone, 1 vol. Sapergia, Barbara, ed. 2012. (Disaster Strikes! Ser.: 7). (ENG.). 176p. (J). (gr. 4-7). pap. 8.95 *(978-1-55050-481-1(9))* Coteau Bks. CAN. Dist: Orca Bk. Pubs. USA.

Dueck, Adele. Racing Home, 1 vol. 2011. (ENG.). 200p. (J). (gr. 4-8). pap. 8.95 *(978-1-55050-450-7(9))* Coteau Bks. CAN. Dist: Orca Bk. Pubs. USA.

Fields, Jan. Track the Turtle Lake Monster, 1 vol. Brundage, Scott, illus. 2016. (ENG.). 80p. (J). lib. bdg. *(978-1-62402-155-8(7))* Magic Wagon.

Porter, Pamela. The Crazy Man. 2013. 164p. pap. *(978-1-4596-6446-3(9))* ReadHowYouWant.com, Ltd.

—I'll Be Watching. 2013. 336p. pap. *(978-1-4596-6449-4(3))* ReadHowYouWant.com, Ltd.

Rathborne, St. George. Canoe Mates in Canada; or, Three Boys Afloat on the Saskatchewan. 2007. 100p. per. *(978-1-4068-3746-9(6))* Echo Library.

SASQUATCH

Bougie, Matt. Bigfoot, the Loch Ness Monster, & Unexplained Creatures. 2017. ***(978-1-5026-2847-3(3))*** Cavendish Square Publishing.

Burgan, Michael. The Unsolved Mystery of Bigfoot. 2013. (Unexplained Mysteries Ser.). (ENG.). 24p. (gr. 1-2). pap. 41.70 *(978-1-62065-807-9(0)*, First Facts); (Illus.). pap. 7.95 *(978-1-62065-806-2(2))*; (Illus.). lib. bdg. 25.32 *(978-1-62065-134-6(3))* Capstone Press of Coughlan Cos.

Chambers, Catherine. Bigfoot. Petney, Ryan, illus. 2015. (Autobiographies You Never Thought You'd Read! Ser.). (ENG.). 32p. (gr. 1-3). 29.99 *(978-1-4109-7961-2(X)*, Read Me!) Heinemann-Raintree.

Collins, Terry. Bigfoot & Adaptation, 1 vol. 2011. (Monster Science Ser.). (ENG.). 32p. (gr. 3-4). pap. 8.10 *(978-1-4296-7327-3(3))*; pap. 47.70 *(978-1-4296-7328-0(1))* Capstone Press of Coughlan Cos. (Graphic Library).

—Bigfoot & Adaptation, 1 vol. Mallea, Cristian, illus. 2011. (Monster Science Ser.). (ENG.). 32p. (gr. 3-4). lib. bdg. 30.65 *(978-1-4296-6579-7(3)*, Graphic Library) Capstone Press of Coughlan Cos.

Colson, Mary. Bigfoot & the Yeti, 1 vol. King, Chris, illus. 2013. (Solving Mysteries with Science Ser.). (ENG.). 48p. (gr. 3-6). pap. 9.95 *(978-1-4109-5505-0(2))* Heinemann-Raintree.

—Bigfoot & the Yeti, 1 vol. 2013. (Solving Mysteries with Science Ser.). (ENG., Illus.). 48p. (gr. 3-6). 29.99 *(978-1-4109-5499-2(4))* Heinemann-Raintree.

Cowley, Stewart & Cox, Greg. Searching for Bigfoot. 2011. (J). pap. 12.95 *(978-1-4488-4768-6(0))*; lib. bdg. 31.95 *(978-1-4488-4760-0(5))* Rosen Publishing Group, Inc., The. (Rosen Reference).

Cox, Greg. Bigfoot. 2005. (Unsolved Mysteries: the Secret Files Ser.). (Illus.). 48p. (J). (gr. 4-7). lib. bdg. 29.25 *(978-0-8239-3561-1(2))* Rosen Publishing Group, Inc., The.

—Bigfoot. 2009. (Unsolved Mysteries: the Secret Files Ser.). 48p. (gr. 5-8). 53.00 *(978-1-60854-692-3(6)*, Rosen Reference) Rosen Publishing Group, Inc., The.

DeMolay, Jack. Bigfoot: A North American Legend. (Jr. Graphic Mysteries Ser.). (ENG.). 24p. 2009. (J). (gr. 2-3). 47.90 *(978-1-61513-840-1(4)*, PowerKids Pr.) 2007. (Illus.). (J). (gr. 2-5). lib. bdg. 25.25 *(978-1-4042-3405-5(5))* 2007. (Illus.). (gr. 3-8). pap. 10.60 *(978-1-4042-2158-1(1))* Rosen Publishing Group, Inc., The.

—Bigfoot: La Leyenda del Hombre-Monstruo. Obregón, José María, tr. 2008. (Historietas Juveniles: Misterios (Jr. Graphic Mysteries) Ser.). (SPA., Illus.). 24p. (J). (gr. 2-5). lib. bdg. 25.25 *(978-1-4358-2536-9(5))* Rosen Publishing Group, Inc., The.

—Bigfoot: La Leyenda del hombre-monstruo (A North American Legend) 2009. (Historietas Juveniles: Misterios (Jr. Graphic Mysteries) Ser.). (SPA.). 24p. (gr. 2-3). 47.90 *(978-1-61513-150-2(1))*, Editorial Buenas Letras) Rosen Publishing Group, Inc., The.

Guiley, Rosemary Ellen & Dennett, Preston E. Bigfoot, Yeti, & Other Ape-Men. 2008. (Mysteries, Legends, & Unexplained Phenomena Ser.). (Illus.). 152p. (YA). (gr. 7-12). 29.95 *(978-0-7910-9386-3(7))* Facts On File, Inc.

Halls, Kelly Milner. In Search of Sasquatch. 2011. (ENG., Illus.). 64p. (J). (gr. 5-7). 18.99 *(978-0-547-25761-7(9))* Houghton Mifflin Harcourt Publishing Co.

Hand, Carol. The Existence of Sasquatch & Yeti, 1 vol. 2012. (Unsolved Mysteries (el) Ser.). (ENG.). 112p. (J). (gr. 6-12). lib. bdg. 35.64 *(978-1-61783-304-5(5)*, Essential Library) ABDO Publishing Co.

Hawkins, John. Bigfoot & Other Monsters. 2012. (Mystery Hunters Ser.). (ENG., Illus.). 32p. (J). (gr. 4-6). pap. 10.60 *(978-1-4488-6445-4(3))*; lib. bdg. 25.25 *(978-1-4488-6431-7(3))* Rosen Publishing Group, Inc., The. (PowerKids Pr.).

Joline Anderson, Jennifer. Bigfoot & Yeti, 1 vol. 2014. (Creatures of Legend Ser.). (ENG., Illus.). 48p. (gr. 3-6). lib. bdg. 32.79 *(978-1-62403-150-2(1))* ABDO Publishing Co.

Karst, Ken. Bigfoot. 2014. (J). *(978-1-60818-402-6(1)*, Creative Education) Creative Co., The.

—Enduring Mysteries: Bigfoot. 2015. (Enduring Mysteries Ser.). (ENG.). 48p. (J). (gr. 5-8). pap. 12.00 *(978-1-62832-073-2(7)*, Creative Paperbacks) Creative Co., The.

Kawa, Katie. The Legend of Bigfoot. 2017. (Famous Legends Ser.). 32p. (gr. 2-3). pap. 10.50 ***(978-1-5382-0368-2(5))*** Stevens, Gareth Publishing LLLP.

Krensky, Stephen. Bigfoot. 2006. (Monster Chronicles Ser.). (Illus.). 48p. (J). (gr. 5-8). lib. bdg. 26.60 *(978-0-8225-5925-2(0)*, Lerner Pubns.) Lerner Publishing Group.

Krohn, Katherine. Encountering Bigfoot: Eyewitness Accounts, 1 vol. Byers, Michael, illus. 2014. (Eyewitness to the Unexplained Ser.). (ENG.). 32p. (gr. 3-4). 30.65 *(978-1-4914-0243-6(1)*, Graphic Library) Capstone Press of Coughlan Cos.

Loh-Hagan, Virginia. Bigfoot. Magic, Myth, & Mystery. 2016. (Magic, Myth, & Mystery Ser.). (ENG.). 32p. (J). (gr. 4-8). 29.93 *(978-1-63471-116-6(5)*, 208575, 45th Parallel Press) Cherry Lake Publishing.

McClellan, Ray. Bigfoot. 2014. (Unexplained Mysteries Ser.). (ENG., Illus.). 24p. (J). (gr. 3-7). lib. bdg. 25.95 *(978-1-62617-103-9(3)*, Epic Bks.) Bellwether Media.

Miller, Heather. Bigfoot. 2006. (Monsters Ser.). (ENG., Illus.). 48p. (J). (gr. 4-8). 27.00 *(978-0-7377-3161-3(3)*, Greenhaven Pr., Inc.) Cengage Gale.

Murray, Laura K. Are They Real?: Bigfoot. 2017. (Are They Real? Ser.). (ENG.). 24p. (J). (gr. 1-3). pap. 8.99 ***(978-1-62832-369-6(8)***, Creative Paperbacks) Creative Co., The.

Murray, Laura K. Bigfoot. 2017. 24p. (J). *(978-1-60818-761-4(6)*, Creative Education) Creative Co., The.

Nagle, Frances. Bigfoot. 2016. (Monsters! Ser.). (Illus.). 32p. (J). (gr. 2-1). pap. 10.50 *(978-1-4824-4855-9(6))* Stevens, Gareth Publishing LLLP.

Noll, Elizabeth. Bigfoot. 2017. (Strange ... but True? Ser.). (ENG., Illus.). 32p. (gr. 3-7). 31.35 ***(978-1-68072-020-4(1))*** Black Rabbit Bks.

Olsen, Sylvia & Charko, Kasia. Sebastian Sasquatch, 1 vol. 2013. (ENG., Illus.). 32p. (J). (gr. -1-3). 9.95 *(978-1-55039-197-8(6))* Sono Nis Pr. CAN. Dist: Orca Bk. Pubs. USA.

Rivkin, Jennifer. Searching for Bigfoot. 2014. (Mysterious Monsters Ser.). (Illus.). 32p. (J). (gr. 3-6). lib. bdg. 26.25 *(978-1-4777-7105-1(0)*, PowerKids Pr.) Rosen Publishing Group, Inc., The.

Shea, Therese. Bigfoot. 2006. (Tony Stead Nonfiction Independent Reading Collection). (ENG.). 24p. (gr. 3-6). pap. 8.85 *(978-1-4042-5675-0(X))* Rosen Publishing Group, Inc., The.

—The Bigfoot Trail. 2014. (Scariest Places on Earth Ser.). 24p. (J). (gr. 2-5). pap. 8.15 *(978-1-4824-0928-4(3))* Stevens, Gareth Publishing LLLP.

Shone, Rob. Bigfoot & Other Strange Beasts. 2009. (Graphic Mysteries Ser.). (ENG.). 48p. (YA). (gr. 5-5). 58.50 *(978-1-61512-961-4(8)*, Rosen Reference) Rosen Publishing Group, Inc., The.

—Bigfoot & Other Strange Beasts. Spender, Nick, illus. 2006. (Graphic Mysteries Ser.). (ENG.). 48p. (YA). (gr. k-3). lib. bdg. 31.95 *(978-1-4042-0793-6(7))* Rosen Publishing Group, Inc., The.

—Bigfoot & Other Strange Beasts. Spender, Nik, illus. 2006. (Graphic Mysteries Ser.). (ENG.). 48p. (gr. 5-8). pap. 14.05 *(978-1-4042-0804-9(6))* Rosen Publishing Group, Inc., The.

Teitelbaum, Michael. Bigfoot Caught on Film: And Other Monster Sightings! 2008. (24/7: Science Behind the Scenes Ser.). (ENG., Illus.). 64p. (J). (gr. 9-12). 29.00 *(978-0-531-12078-1(3)*, Watts, Franklin) Scholastic Library Publishing.

—Wild Man of the Woods! Following in the Footsteps of Bigfoot. 2011. (J). pap. *(978-0-545-32934-7(5))* Scholastic, Inc.

Theisen, Paul. Bigfoot. 2010. (Unexplained Ser.). (ENG., Illus.). 24p. (J). (gr. 3-7). lib. bdg. 25.95 *(978-1-60014-498-1(5)*, Torque Bks.) Bellwether Media.

Tieck, Sarah. Bigfoot, 1 vol. 2016. (ENG., Illus.). 32p. (J). *(978-1-62403-764-1(X))* ABDO Publishing Co.

Troupe, Thomas Kingsley. The Legend of Bigfoot, 1 vol. Dumm, Brian Caleb, illus. 2010. (Legend Has It Ser.). (ENG.). 32p. (gr. 2-4). lib. bdg. 27.32 *(978-1-4048-6032-2(0))* Picture Window Bks.

Walker, Kathryn. Mysteries of Giant Humanlike Creatures. 2008. (ENG., Illus.). 32p. (J). (gr. 3-7). pap. *(978-0-7787-4156-5(7))*; lib. bdg. *(978-0-7787-4143-5(5))* Crabtree Publishing Co.

Woog, Adam. Bigfoot. 2006. (Encounters with Ser.). (ENG., Illus.). 48p. (J). (gr. 4-8). lib. bdg. 29.00 *(978-0-7377-3473-7(6)*, Greenhaven Pr., Inc.) Cengage Gale.

Worth, Bonnie. Looking for Bigfoot. Nelson, Jim, illus. 2010. (Step into Reading Ser.). (ENG.). 48p. (J). (gr. 2-4). pap. 3.99 *(978-0-375-86331-8(1)*, Random Hse. Bks. for Young Readers) Random Hse. Children's Bks.

SATAN

see Devil

SATELLITES, ARTIFICIAL

see Artificial Satellites

SATIRE

Johnston, Marianne. Dealing with Insults / Qué hacer con los Insultos. 2009. (Conflict Resolution Library / Biblioteca solución de conflictos Ser.). (ENG & SPA.). 24p. (gr. 2-3). 42.50 *(978-1-60853-415-9(4)*, Editorial Buenas Letras) Rosen Publishing Group, Inc., The.

—Dealing with Insults/Que Hacer con Los Insultos. Velazquez De Leon, Mauricio, tr. from ENG. 2008. (Conflict Resolution Library / Biblioteca Solución de Conflictos Ser.). (SPA., Illus.). 24p. (J). (gr. k-3). lib. bdg. 22.60 *(978-1-4042-7661-1(0))* Rosen Publishing Group, Inc., The.

SATURN (PLANET)

Allyn, Daisy. Saturn: The Ringed Planet. 2010. (Our Solar System Ser.). 24p. (J). (gr. k-3). (ENG.). pap. 8.15 *(978-1-4339-3840-5(5))*; (Illus.). lib. bdg. 22.60 *(978-1-4339-3839-9(1))* Stevens, Gareth Publishing LLLP.

Asimov, Isaac & Hantula, Richard. Saturno: El Planeta de los Anillos. Porras, Carlos & D'Andrea, Patricia, trs. from ENG. 2003. (Isaac Asimov's Biblioteca del Universo del Siglo XXI).Tr. of Saturn: The Ringed Beauty. (SPA., Illus.). 32p. (gr. 2-6). lib. bdg. 26.00 *(978-0-8368-3860-2(2)*, Gareth Stevens Learning Library) Stevens, Gareth Publishing LLLP.

Austen, Mary. Exploring Saturn. 2017. (J). ***(978-1-5345-2254-1(9)***, KidHaven Publishing) Greenhaven Publishing LLC.

Bloom, J. P. Saturn, 1 vol. 2014. (Planets Ser.). (ENG., Illus.). 24p. (J). (gr. 2-4). lib. bdg. 28.50 *(978-1-62970-720-4(1))* ABDO Publishing Co.

Bortolotti, Dan. Exploring Saturn. 2003. (ENG., Illus.). 64p. (J). (gr. 4-8). pap. 9.95 *(978-1-55297-765-1(X)*, 9781552977651) Firefly Bks., Ltd.

Carson, Mary Kay. Far-Out Guide to Saturn. 2010. (Far-Out Guide to the Solar System Ser.). (Illus.). 48p. (J). pap. 8.95 *(978-1-59845-187-0(1)*, Enslow Elementary); (gr. 2-5). 25.27 *(978-0-7660-3178-4(0))* Enslow Pubs., Inc.

Chiger, Arielle & Elkin, Matthew. 20 Fun Facts about Gas Giants. 2014. (Fun Fact File: Space! Ser.). 32p. (J). (gr. 2-5). 25.25 *(978-1-4824-1001-3(X))*; pap. 10.50 *(978-1-4824-1002-0(8))* Stevens, Gareth Publishing LLLP.

Cosson, M. J. Your Mission to Saturn, 1 vol. 2011. (Planets Ser.). (ENG., Illus.). 32p. (J). (gr. k-3). 28.50 *(978-1-61641-682-9(3))* Magic Wagon.

Geiger, Beth. The Inside Story of Saturn. 2006. (J). 7.80 *(978-1-933798-08-0(4))* Sally Ride Science.

Glaser, Chaya. Saturn: Amazing Rings. 2015. (Out of This World Ser.). (ENG.). 24p. (J). (gr. -1-3). lib. bdg. 23.93 *(978-1-62724-566-1(9))* Bearport Publishing Co., Inc.

—Saturno: Anillos Asombrosos. 2015. (Fuera de Este Mundo Ser.). (SPA., Illus.). 24p. (J). (gr. -1-3). lib. bdg. 23.93 *(978-1-62724-596-8(0))* Bearport Publishing Co., Inc.

Goldstein, Margaret J. Saturn. 2003. (Our Universe Ser.). (ENG., Illus.). 32p. (gr. 2-4). lib. bdg. 22.60 *(978-0-8225-4653-5(1))* Lerner Publishing Group.

Heos, Bridget. Do You Really Want to Visit Saturn? Fabbri, Daniele, illus. 2013. (Do You Really Want to Visit... ? Ser.). (ENG.). 24p. (gr. 1-4). 27.10 *(978-1-60753-200-2(X))* Amicus Publishing.

Hicks, Terry Allan. Saturn. 2009. (Space!). 64p. (gr. 5-18). lib. bdg. 32.79 *(978-0-7614-4249-3(9))* Marshall Cavendish Corp.

Hofer, Charles. Saturn. (Library of Planets Ser.). 2009. 48p. (gr. 5-8). 55.90 *(978-1-60853-821-8(4)*, Rosen Reference) 2008. (J). lib. bdg. 29.25 *(978-1-4358-5075-0(0))* 2005. (ENG.). 48p. (YA). lib. bdg. 27.95 *(978-1-4042-0173-6(4))* Rosen Publishing Group, Inc., The.

Howard, Fran. Saturn, 1 vol. 2007. (Planets Ser.). (ENG.). 32p. (gr. 3-7). 27.07 *(978-1-59928-828-4(1)*, Buddy Bks.) ABDO Publishing Co.

Jefferis, David. Mighty Megaplanets: Jupiter & Saturn. 2008. (Exploring Our Solar System Ser.). (ENG., Illus.). 32p. (J). (gr. 3-7). pap. *(978-0-7787-3753-7(5))* Crabtree Publishing Co.

Lawrence, Ellen. Saturn: The Ringed Wonder. 2013. (Zoom into Space Ser.). 24p. (J). (gr. -1-3). lib. bdg. 23.93 *(978-1-909673-14-4(5))* Ruby Tuesday Books Limited GBR. Dist: Bearport Publishing Co., Inc.

Miller, Ron. Saturn. 2003. (Worlds Beyond Ser.). (Illus.). 80p. (gr. 7-18). lib. bdg. 27.93 *(978-0-7613-2360-0(0)*, Twenty-First Century Bks.) Lerner Publishing Group.

Nichols, Amie. Journey to Saturn, 1 vol. 2014. (Spotlight on Space Science Ser.). (ENG.). 32p. (J). (gr. 5-5). pap. 11.75 *(978-1-4994-0376-3(3)*, PowerKids Pr.) Rosen Publishing Group, Inc., The.

Orme, Helen & Orme, David. Let's Explore Saturn. 2007. (Space Launch! Ser.). (Illus.). 24p. (J). (gr. 1-4). pap. 8.15 *(978-0-8368-8131-8(1))*; lib. bdg. 23.00 *(978-0-8368-7946-9(5))* Stevens, Gareth Publishing LLLP. (Gareth Stevens Learning Library).

Owen, Ruth. Saturn. 2013. (Explore Outer Space Ser.). 32p. (J). (gr. 3-6). 25.25 *(978-1-61533-727-9(X))*; pap. 60.00 *(978-1-61533-772-9(5))*; pap. 10.00 *(978-1-61533-771-2(7))* Windmill Bks.

Owens, L. L. Saturn. McGeehan, Dan, illus. 2011. (Space Neighbors Ser.). (ENG.). 32p. (J). (gr. 1-4). lib. bdg. 27.07 *(978-1-60954-387-7(4)*, 200888) Child's World, Inc., The.

Radomski, Kassandra. The Secrets of Saturn. 2015. (Planets Ser.). (ENG., Illus.). 32p. (gr. 2-4). lib. bdg. 31.99 *(978-1-4914-5868-6(2))* Capstone Press of Coughlan Cos.

Ring, Susan. Saturn. (J). 2013. 27.13 *(978-1-62127-268-7(0))* 2013. pap. 12.95 *(978-1-62127-277-9(X))* 2004. pap. 8.95 *(978-1-59036-227-3(6))* 2004. (Illus.). 24p. (gr. 4-7). lib. bdg. 24.45 *(978-1-59036-100-9(8))* Weigl Pubs., Inc.

Ring, Susan & Roumanis, Alexis. Saturn. 2016. (Illus.). 24p. (J). *(978-1-5105-0989-4(5))* SmartBook Media, Inc.

Roumanis, Alexis. Saturn. 2016. (J). ***(978-1-5105-2055-4(4))*** SmartBook Media, Inc.

—Saturn. 2015. (J). *(978-1-4896-3300-2(6))* Weigl Pubs., Inc.

Saturn. 2nd rev. ed. 2008. (New Solar System Ser.). (Illus.). 32p. (YA). (gr. 3-6). 23.00 *(978-1-60413-213-7(2))* Facts On File, Inc.

Slade, Suzanne. A Look at Saturn. (Astronomy Now! Ser.). 24p. (gr. 2-3). 2009. 42.50 *(978-1-61511-473-3(4)*, PowerKids Pr.) 2007. (Illus.). (J). lib. bdg. 22.60 *(978-1-4042-3830-5(1))* Rosen Publishing Group, Inc., The.

Sparrow, Giles. Destination Saturn. 2009. (Destination Solar System Ser.). (Illus.). 32p. (J). 25.25 *(978-1-4358-3447-7(X))*; pap. 10.00 *(978-1-4358-3461-3(5))* Rosen Publishing Group, Inc., The. (PowerKids Pr.).

Squire, Ann O. Planet Saturn. 2014. (True Book(tm), A — Space Ser.). (ENG.). 48p. (J). lib. bdg. 31.00 *(978-0-531-21156-4(8))* Scholastic Library Publishing.

Steinkraus, Kyla. Giant Gas Planets: Jupiter, Saturn, Uranus, & Neptune. 2014. (ENG.). 24p. (gr. k-3). 28.50 *(978-1-62717-728-3(0))* Rourke Educational Media.

Taylor-Butler, Christine. Saturn. (Scholastic News Nonfiction Readers Ser.). (ENG., Illus.). 24p. (J). (gr. 1-2). 2008. pap. 6.95 *(978-0-531-14767-2(3))* 2007. 22.00 *(978-0-531-14752-8(5))* Scholastic Library Publishing.

Waxman, Laura Hamilton. Saturn. 2009. (Early Bird Astronomy Ser.). (ENG.). 48p. (gr. 2-5). lib. bdg. 26.60 *(978-0-7613-4154-3(4))*; (Illus.). pap. 8.95 *(978-0-7613-4985-3(5)*, Lerner Pubns.) Lerner Publishing Group.

Wimmer, Teresa. Saturn. 2007. (My First Look at: Planets Ser.). (Illus.). 24p. (J). (gr. -1-3). lib. bdg. 24.25 *(978-1-58341-522-1(X)*, Creative Education) Creative Co., The.

World Book, contrib. by. Saturn & Uranus. 2nd ed. 2006. (World Book's Solar System & Space Exploration Library). (Illus.). 64p. (J). *(978-0-7166-9519-6(7))* World Bk., Inc.

World Book, Inc. Staff, contrib. by. Saturn & Uranus. 2006. (World Book's Solar System & Space Exploration Library). (Illus.). 63p. (J). *(978-0-7166-9506-6(5))* World Bk., Inc.

World Book, Inc Staff, contrib. by. Saturn & Uranus. 2010. (J). *(978-0-7166-9535-6(9))* World Bk., Inc.

Zobel, Derek. Saturn. 2010. (Exploring Space Ser.). (ENG., Illus.). 24p. (J). (gr. k-3). lib. bdg. 25.95 *(978-1-60014-407-3(1)*, Blastoff! Readers) Bellwether Media.

SAUDI ARABIA

Anderson, Abby. Saudi Arabia. 2009. pap. 52.95 *(978-0-7613-4734-7(8))* Lerner Publishing Group.

Anderson, Laurie Halse. A Ticket to Saudi Arabia. 2009. (Country Explorers Ser.). (ENG.). 48p. (gr. 2-4). 29.27 *(978-1-58013-595-5(1))* Lerner Publishing Group.

Anderson, Laurie Halse & Milivojevic, JoAnn. A Ticket to Saudi Arabia. 2005. (Ticket to Ser.). (Illus.). 48p. (gr. 2-4). 22.60 *(978-1-57505-147-5(8))* Lerner Publishing Group.

Etheredge, Laura. Saudi Arabia & Yemen. 2011. (Middle East: Region in Transition Ser.). (Illus.). 176p. (YA). (gr. 9-12). lib. bdg. 40.00 *(978-1-61530-335-9(9))* Rosen Publishing Group, Inc., The.

Harper, Robert Alexander & Subanthore, Aswin. Saudi Arabia. 2nd rev. ed. 2007. (Modern World Nations Ser.). (Illus.). 120p. (YA). (gr. 7-12). lib. bdg. 35.00 *(978-0-7910-9516-4(9))* Facts On File, Inc.

Ismail, Vehbi. Muhammad: The Last Prophet. 2011. 190p. 42.95 *(978-1-258-03217-3(1))* Literary Licensing, LLC.

Janin, Hunt & Besheer, Margaret. Saudi Arabia. 2014. (Cultures of the World (r) Ser.). 144p. (J). (gr. 5-10). 47.07 *(978-0-7614-4996-6(5))* Cavendish Square Publishing.

Keating, Susan Katz. Saudi Arabia. (Major Muslim Nations Ser.). 112p. (gr. 7-18). 2010. (YA). 25.95 *(978-1-4222-1385-8(4))* Vol. 13. 2015. (Illus.). (J). lib. bdg. 25.95 *(978-1-4222-3450-1(9))* Mason Crest.

Kehnemui Donnelly, Susan. Al-Rihlah Al-Mudhishah: Jawlah Fi Al-Mamlakah Wa-Aramku Al-Saudiyah. 2010. (ARA., Illus.). 31p. (J). *(978-1-882771-21-9(4))* History Factory.

Klepeis, Alicia. Understanding Saudi Arabia Today. 2014. (Illus.). 63p. (J). (gr. 3-6). 33.95 *(978-1-61228-651-8(8))* Mitchell Lane Pubs., Inc.

Kopp, Megan. Saudi Arabia. 2016. (J). ***(978-1-5105-1905-3(X))*** SmartBook Media, Inc.

—Saudi Arabia. 2014. (J). *(978-1-4896-1026-3(X))* Weigl Pubs., Inc.

Marsico, Katie. The Hottest & the Coldest. 2015. (True Book(tm), a — Extreme Places Ser.). (ENG., Illus.). 48p. (J). lib. bdg. 31.00 *(978-0-531-21844-0(9)*, Children's Pr.) Scholastic Library Publishing.

Mockaitis, Thomas R. Osama Bin Laden: A Biography, 1 vol. 2010. (Greenwood Biographies Ser.). (Illus.). 141p. (C). 39.00 *(978-0-313-35374-1(3)*, GR5374, Greenwood) ABC-CLIO, LLC.

Owings, Lisa. Saudi Arabia. 2012. (Exploring Countries Ser.). (ENG., Illus.). 32p. (J). (gr. 3-7). lib. bdg. 26.95 *(978-1-60014-764-7(X),* Blastoff! Readers) Bellwether Media.
Reed, Jennifer Bond. The Saudi Royal Family. 2nd rev. ed. 2007. (Modern World Leaders Ser.). (Illus.). 120p. (YA). (gr. 7-12). lib. bdg. 30.00 *(978-0-7910-9218-7(6))* Facts On File, Inc.
Saudi Arabia - Enchantment of the World. 2014. (ENG., Illus.). 144p. (J). lib. bdg. 40.00 *(978-0-531-20793-2(5))* Scholastic Library Publishing.
Schaffer, David. Saudi Arabia in the News: Past, Present, & Future. 2006. (Middle East Nations in the News Ser.). (Illus.). 128p. (J). (gr. 4-7). lib. bdg. 34.60 *(978-1-59845-026-2(3),* MyReportLinks.com Bks.) Enslow Pubs., Inc.
Senker, Cath. Saudi Arabia. 2008. (Costume Around the World Ser.). (Illus.). 32p. (gr. 4-6). 28.00 *(978-0-7910-9773-1(0),* Chelsea Clubhouse) Facts On File, Inc.
Sullivan, Laura L. Saudi Arabia. 2017. (J). ***(978-1-5026-2488-8(5))*** Cavendish Square Publishing.
Tracy, Kathleen. We Visit Saudi Arabia. 2011. (Your Land & My Land Ser.). (Illus.). 64p. (J). (gr. 4-7). lib. bdg. 33.95 *(978-1-58415-963-6(4))* Mitchell Lane Pubs., Inc.
Wagner, Heather Lehr. Saudi Arabia. 2nd rev. ed. 2008. (Creation of the Modern Middle East Ser.). (Illus.). 112p. (gr. 6-12). 35.00 *(978-1-60413-023-2(7),* Chelsea Hse.) Facts On File, Inc.
Walsh, Kieran. Saudi Arabia. 2003. (Countries in the News Ser.). (Illus.). 24p. (J). 25.64 *(978-1-58952-681-5(3))* Rourke Educational Media.

SAWYER, TOM (FICTITIOUS CHARACTER)—FICTION

Barchers, Suzanne. The Adventures of Tom Sawyer. rev. ed. 2015. (Great Works). (ENG., Illus.). 72p. (gr. 4-8). pap. 9.99 *(978-1-4258-8973-9(5))* Shell Educational Publishing.
Brook, Henry, retold by. Tom Sawyer. 2008. (Usborne Classics Retold Ser.). 160p. (J). pap. 4.99 *(978-0-7945-2063-2(4),* Usborne) EDC Publishing.
Lawson, Jessica & Twain, Mark. The Tom Sawyer Collection: The Adventures of Tom Sawyer; the Adventures of Huckleberry Finn; the Actual & Truthful Adventures of Becky Thatcher. Bruno, Iacopo, illus. 2014. (ENG.). 944p. (J). (gr. 3-7). 50.99 *(978-1-4814-0536-2(5),* Simon & Schuster Bks. For Young Readers) Simon & Schuster Bks. For Young Readers.
Rigby Education Staff. Tom Sawyer: Jumbled Tumble. (gr. k-2). 26.00 *(978-0-7635-2424-1(7))* Rigby Education.
Ross, Linda B., adapted by. Tom Sawyer: Read Aloud Classics Edition Big Book. 2014. (Read Aloud Classics Ser.). (J). (gr. -1-2). 9.99 *(978-1-4788-0707-0(5))* Newmark Learning LLC.
Tom Sawyer: 6 Small Books. (gr. k-2). 23.00 *(978-0-7635-8507-5(6))* Rigby Education.
Twain, Mark, pseud. The Adventures of Tom Sawyer. Ingpen, Robert R., illus. 2010. (Sterling Illustrated Classics Ser.). (ENG.). 240p. (J). (gr. 5-18). 19.95 *(978-1-4027-6762-3(5))* Sterling Publishing Co., Inc.
—The Adventures of Tom Sawyer. McKowen, Scott, illus. 2004. (Sterling Unabridged Classics Ser.). (ENG.). 224p. (J). (gr. 5). 9.95 *(978-1-4027-1460-3(2))* Sterling Publishing Co., Inc.
—The Adventures of Tom Sawyer: A Song for Aunt Polly. Bates, Amy, illus. 2008. (Easy Reader Classics Ser.). (ENG.). 32p. (gr. -1-3). lib. bdg. 24.21 *(978-1-59961-334-5(4))* Spotlight.
—The Adventures of Tom Sawyer - Literary Touchstone Edition. 2005. 216p. (YA). per. 4.99 *(978-1-58049-596-7(6),* PWH5966) Prestwick Hse., Inc.
—The Adventures of Tom Sawyer, Complete. l.t. ed. 2006. 408p. pap. *(978-1-84637-320-6(4))* Echo Library.
—Las Aventuras de Tom Sawyer.Tr. of Adventures of Tom Sawyer. (SPA.). (YA). *(978-84-7525-151-6(X))* Ediciones Generales Anaya SA.
—Las Aventuras de Tom Sawyer. 2003. (Advanced Reading Ser.).Tr. of Adventures of Tom Sawyer. (SPA.). 124p. (J). 11.95 *(978-84-239-9045-0(1))* Espasa Calpe, S.A. ESP. Dist: Planeta Publishing Corp.
—Avventure di Tom Sawyer. pap. 15.95 *(978-88-451-2151-7(8))* Fabbri Editori - RCS Libri ITA. Dist: Distribooks, Inc.
—A Song for Aunt Polly. Bates, Amy, illus. 2004. (Adventures of Tom Sawyer Ser.: Vol. 1). 32p. (J). *(978-0-7607-3963-1(3))* Barnes & Noble, Inc.
—Tom Sawyer. 2005. 264p. 28.95 *(978-1-4218-0768-3(8),* 1st World Library - Literary Society) 1st World Publishing, Inc.
—Tom Sawyer. 2006. (Classic Retelling Ser.). (Illus.). 224p. (YA). (gr. 8-12). *(978-0-618-12053-6(X),* 2-00218) Holt McDougal.
—Tom Sawyer. 2004. reprint ed. pap. 1.99 *(978-1-4192-5166-5(X))* Kessinger Publishing, LLC.
—Tom Sawyer. (Young Collector's Illustrated Classics Ser.). (Illus.). 192p. (J). (gr. 3-7). 9.95 *(978-1-56156-453-8(2))* Kidsbooks, LLC.
—Tom Sawyer, 1 vol. Mullarkey, Lisa, illus. 2010. (Calico Illustrated Classics Ser.: No. 1). (ENG.). 112p. (J). (gr. 3-6). 27.07 *(978-1-60270-704-7(9))* Magic Wagon.
—Tom Sawyer. (Coleccion Clasicos de la Juventud). (SPA., Illus.). 220p. (J). 12.95 *(978-84-7189-029-0(1),* ORT310) Ortells, Alfredo Editorial S.L. ESP. Dist: Continental Bk. Co., Inc.
—Tom Sawyer. 2009. 196p. (gr. 4-7). pap. 12.99 *(978-1-934941-63-8(8))* Red & Black Pubs.
—Tom Sawyer. 2003. (Timeless Classics Ser.). (SPA., Illus.). 95p. (J). (gr. 5-8). pap. 12.95 *(978-84-372-2235-6(4))* Santillana USA Publishing Co., Inc.
—Tom Sawyer. l.t. ed. 2006. (Classics Ser.). (ENG.). 363p. (J). (gr. 4-7). 22.95 *(978-0-7862-8640-9(7))* Thorndike Pr.
—Tom Sawyer, Detective. (SPA., Illus.). 160p. (YA). 11.95 *(978-84-7281-062-4(3),* AF0623) Auriga, Ediciones S.A. ESP. Dist: Continental Bk. Co., Inc.

SAXONS

see Anglo-Saxons

SAYINGS

see Proverbs; Quotations

SCANDINAVIA

Crabtree Staff & Williams, Brian. Understanding Norse Myths. 2012. (ENG., Illus.). 48p. (J). pap. *(978-0-7787-4532-7(5))* Crabtree Publishing Co.
Ganeri, Anita. How to Live Like a Viking Warrior. Epelbaum, Mariano, illus. 2015. (How to Live Like... Ser.). (ENG.). 32p. (J). (gr. 3-6). lib. bdg. 26.65 *(978-1-4677-6354-7(3))* Lerner Publishing Group.
Greenling, Jason. The Technology of the Vikings. 2016. (Ancient Innovations Ser.). 64p. (J). 34.21 *(978-1-5026-2241-9(6))* Cavendish Square Publishing.
Hopkins, Andrea. Viking Families & Farms. 2009. (Viking Library). 24p. (gr. 3-3). 42.50 *(978-1-60854-257-4(2),* PowerKids Pr.) Rosen Publishing Group, Inc., The.
Kuskowski, Alex. Super Simple Scandinavian Art: Fun & Easy Art from Around the World, 1 vol. 2014. (Super Simple Cultural Art Set 2 Ser.). (ENG.). 32p. (gr. 5-10). lib. bdg. 27.07 *(978-1-62403-283-7(4),* Super SandCastle) ABDO Publishing Co.
Park, Louise & Love, Timothy. The Scandinavian Vikings. 2009. (Ancient & Medieval People Ser.). 32p. (gr. 5). 28.50 *(978-0-7614-4445-9(9))* Marshall Cavendish GBR. Dist: Marshall Cavendish Corp.
Wargin, Kathy-jo. D Is for Dala Horse: A Nordic Countries Alphabet. Graef, Renee, illus. 2010. (Discover the World Ser.). (ENG.). 40p. (J). (gr. 1-3). 17.95 *(978-1-58536-510-4(6),* 202203) Sleeping Bear Pr.
—D Is for Dala Horse: A Nordic Countries Alphabet. 2016. (Av2 Fiction Readalong 2017 Ser.). (ENG.). (J). (gr. k-6). 34.28 ***(978-1-4896-5200-3(0),*** AV2 by Weigl) Weigl Pubs., Inc.
Williams, Brian. Understanding Norse Myths. 2012. (ENG.). 48p. (J). *(978-0-7787-4527-3(9))* Crabtree Publishing Co.

SCARECROWS

Wilde, Kim. How to Make a Scarecrow: Band 00/Lilac. 2006. (Collins Big Cat Ser.). (ENG., Illus.). 16p. (J). (gr. -1-k). pap. 5.99 *(978-0-00-718645-7(2))* HarperCollins Pubs. Ltd. GBR. Dist: Independent Pubs. Group.

SCARECROWS—FICTION

Amery, Heather. Scarecrow's Secret. Tyler, Jenny, ed. Cartwright, Stephen, illus. rev. ed. 2004. (Farmyard Tales Readers Ser.). 16p. (J). pap. 5.95 *(978-0-7945-0751-0(4),* Usborne) EDC Publishing.
Awdry, W. Thomas Scares the Crows. 2016. (Thomas & Friends 8X8 Ser.). lib. bdg. 14.75 *(978-0-606-38895-5(8))* Turtleback Bks.
—Thomas Scares the Crows (Thomas & Friends) 2016. (Pictureback(R) Ser.). (ENG.). 24p. (J). (gr. -1-2). 4.99 *(978-1-101-93831-7(5),* Random Hse. Bks. for Young Readers) Random Hse. Children's Bks.
Banks, Rosemary. Moe the Well Dressed Scarecrow. 2013. 20p. pap. 24.95 *(978-1-4626-9683-3(X))* America Star Bks.
Baum, L. Frank. Oz, the Complete Collection, Volume 3: The Patchwork Girl of Oz; Tik-Tok of Oz; the Scarecrow of Oz. 2013. (Oz, the Complete Collection: 3). (ENG.). 720p. (J). (gr. 3-7). 19.99 *(978-1-4424-8892-2(1),* Aladdin) Simon & Schuster Children's Publishing.
—The Patchwork Girl of Oz; Tik-Tok of Oz; the Scarecrow of Oz, Vol. 3. 2013. (Oz, the Complete Collection: 3). (ENG.). 720p. (J). (gr. 3-7). pap. 12.99 *(978-1-4424-8549-5(3),* Aladdin) Simon & Schuster Children's Publishing.
Baum, L. Frank & Thompson, Ruth Plumly. Oz - The Complete Collection Vol. 5: The Magic of Oz; Glinda of Oz; The Royal Book of Oz. 2013. (Oz, the Complete Collection: 5). (ENG.). 576p. (J). (gr. 3-7). 19.99 *(978-1-4424-8894-6(8),* Aladdin) Simon & Schuster Children's Publishing.
—The Royal Book of Oz. 2011. 160p. (gr. -1-7). 24.95 *(978-1-4638-9602-7(6));* pap. 13.95 *(978-1-60664-507-9(2))* Rodgers, Alan Bks.
—The Royal Book of Oz. 2009. 112p. pap. 8.99 *(978-1-60459-763-9(1))* Wilder Pubns., Corp.
Blyton, Enid. Ugly Old Scarecrow: And Other Stories. 2013. (ENG., Illus.). 192p. (J). 9.95 *(978-1-84135-462-0(7))* Award Pubns. Ltd. GBR. Dist: Parkwest Pubns., Inc.
Broad, Michael. Spooky Ballet!, No. 4. Broad, Michael, illus. 2011. (Agent Amelia Ser.: 4). (ENG., Illus.). 144p. (J). (gr. 2-5). pap. 5.95 *(978-0-7613-8064-1(7),* Darby Creek); lib. bdg. 22.60 *(978-0-7613-8059-7(0))* Lerner Publishing Group.
—#4 Spooky Ballet! 2011. (Agent Amelia Ser.). pap. 33.92 *(978-0-7613-8344-4(1),* Darby Creek) Lerner Publishing Group.
Brown, Ken. The Scarecrow's Hat, 1 vol. Brown, Ken, illus. 2011. (ENG., Illus.). 32p. (J). (gr. -1-1). pap. 7.95 *(978-1-56145-570-6(9))* Peachtree Pubs.
Brown, Phillip A. Haywood & Mel: Haywood Wants to Quit, 1 vol. 2010. 24p. pap. 24.95 *(978-1-4489-8371-1(1))* PublishAmerica, Inc.
Chapman, Catherine. The Magical Scarecrows' Garden. 2009. 160p. pap. 35.95 *(978-1-60860-481-4(0),* Strategic Bk. Publishing) Strategic Book Publishing & Rights Agency (SBPRA).
Cunningham, Darrell. The Adventures of Stan: Book One the Awakening. 2011. (Illus.). 80p. (gr. 4-6). pap. 29.00 *(978-1-4567-7918-4(4))* AuthorHouse.
Dillon, Jana. Jeb Scarecrow's Pumpkin Patch, 1 vol. 2016. (ENG., Illus.). 32p. (J). (gr. k-3). pap. 8.99 *(978-1-4556-2181-1(1))* Pelican Publishing Co., Inc.
Dolan, Penny. At the End of the Garden. 2008. (Tadpoles Ser.). (ENG., Illus.). 24p. (J). (gr. -1-3). pap. *(978-0-7787-3881-7(7));* lib. bdg. *(978-0-7787-3850-3(7))* Crabtree Publishing Co.
Donaldson, Julia. The Scarecrows' Wedding. Scheffler, Axel, illus. 2014. (ENG.). 32p. (J). (gr. -1-3). 17.99 *(978-0-545-72606-1(9),* Levine, Arthur A. Bks.) Scholastic, Inc.
Gordon, Judy Ann. Grammie's Magical Garden: Beyond the Gate. 2012. 68p. pap. 28.99 *(978-1-4772-7973-1(3))* AuthorHouse.
Hernandez, Christopher. Scaredycrow. 2013. lib. bdg. 14.75 *(978-0-606-31953-9(0),* Turtleback) Turtleback Bks.
Keene, Carolyn. The Secret of the Scarecrow. Pamintuan, Macky, illus. 2013. (Nancy Drew & the Clue Crew Ser.: 36). (ENG.). 96p. (J). (gr. 1-4). pap. 4.99 *(978-1-4424-5353-1(2),* Aladdin) Simon & Schuster Children's Publishing.
Kidwell, Justina. The Enchanted Garden & the Curse of the Evil Witch: The Kent Boys' Adventures. 2009. 68p. pap. 19.95 *(978-1-60749-163-7(X))* America Star Bks.
Knight, Chris. Skaggy the Scarecrow: A Halloween Story. 2010. (Illus.). 40p. pap. 18.49 *(978-1-4520-2473-8(1))* AuthorHouse.
Leday, Linda. Sammy the Scarecrow. 2009. 36p. pap. 16.99 *(978-1-4389-4826-3(3))* AuthorHouse.
Long, Loren. Otis & the Scarecrow. Long, Loren, illus. 2014. (Otis Ser.). (ENG., Illus.). 40p. (J). (gr. k-3). 17.99 *(978-0-399-16396-8(4),* Philomel Bks.) Penguin Publishing Group.
Lougher, Jenny. Ted & the Combine Harvester. Lewis, Wayne, illus. 2007. 23p. pap. *(978-1-905553-27-3(7))* BookPublishingWorld.
Masessa, Ed. Scarecrow Magic. Myers, Matt, illus. 2015. (ENG.). 32p. (J). (gr. -1-k). 16.99 *(978-0-545-69109-3(5))* Scholastic, Inc.
McFarland, Kim. A Refugee in Oz. 2010. 164p. pap. 11.95 *(978-0-557-48706-6(4))* Lulu Pr., Inc.
Moulton, Mark Kimball. Scarecrow Pete & His Suitcase of Dreams. Crouch, Karen Hillard, illus. 2005. (ENG.). 36p. (J). (gr. -1-3). 14.95 *(978-0-8249-5151-1(4),* Ideal Pubns.) Worthy Publishing.
Newman, Gerry. Nellie, the Scarecrow: A Dorset Fable. 2003. (Illus.). 188p. pap. 12.50 *(978-1-84426-184-0(0))* Upfront Publishing Ltd. GBR. Dist: Printondemand-worldwide.com.
Norton Kreider, Barbara. Mr Squealy Meets Scarecrow. Dimbylow, Jube, illus. 2013. 24p. pap. *(978-1-921883-53-8(7))* Pick-a-Woo Woo Pubs.
Oblich, Kathleen. Jake & the Scarecrow. 2007. 48p. pap. 16.95 *(978-1-4241-3101-3(4))* PublishAmerica, Inc.
Parker, Emma. The Not So Scary Scarecrow. 2010. (Illus.). pap. *(978-1-877547-88-1(3))* First Edition Ltd.
Pullman, Philip. The Scarecrow & His Servant. Bailey, Peter, illus. (ENG.). 240p. (J). (gr. 3-7). 2007. 7.99 *(978-0-440-42130-6(6),* Yearling) 2005. 15.95 *(978-0-375-81531-7(7),* Knopf Bks. for Young Readers) Random Hse. Children's Bks.
Rylant, Cynthia. Scarecrow. Stringer, Lauren, illus. 2014. 32p. pap. 7.00 *(978-1-61003-181-3(4))* Center for the Collaborative Classroom.
Santa Niclaus. Hay Baggins: The Little Scarecrow Boy. 2012. 140p. pap. 39.88 *(978-1-4669-6918-6(0))* Trafford Publishing.
Sillifant, Alec. Farmer Ham. Spoor, Mike, illus. import ed. 2004. 24p. *(978-1-904511-93-9(7))* Meadowside Children's Bks.
Stine, R. L. Scarecrow Walks at Midnight. 2010. (Classic Goosebumps Ser.: 16). (ENG.). 160p. (J). (gr. 3-7). 6.99 *(978-0-545-17801-3(0),* Scholastic Paperbacks) Scholastic, Inc.
Thompson, Ruth Plumly. The Royal Book of Oz. 2004. reprint ed. pap. 1.99 *(978-1-4192-8123-5(2));* pap. 20.95 *(978-1-4191-8123-8(5))* Kessinger Publishing, LLC.
Whitlock, Matt. Punk 'n Patch. Whitlock, Matt, illus. 2005. (Illus.). 32p. (J). (gr. -1-3). 16.95 *(978-0-9769057-0-7(1))* Little Hero.
Yolen, Jane. The Scarecrow's Dance. Ibatoulline, Bagram, illus. 2009. (ENG.). 32p. (J). (gr. -1-3). 16.99 *(978-1-4169-3770-8(6),* Simon & Schuster Bks. For Young Readers) Simon & Schuster Bks. For Young Readers.

SCENARIOS

see Motion Picture Plays; Television Plays

SCENERY

see Views

SCENERY (STAGE)

see Theaters—Stage Setting and Scenery

SCHALLENBERGER, MOSES, 1826-1909

Wadsworth, Ginger. Survival in the Snow. Orback, Craig, illus. 48p. 2011. (J). pap. 6.95 *(978-0-7613-3941-0(8),* First Avenue Editions) 2009. (ENG.). (gr. 2-4). 25.26 *(978-0-8225-7892-5(1))* Lerner Publishing Group.

SCHLIEMANN, HEINRICH, 1822-1890

Kerns, Ann. Troy. 2008. (Unearthing Ancient Worlds Ser.). (ENG.). 80p. (gr. 5-8). lib. bdg. 30.60 *(978-0-8225-7582-5(5))* Lerner Publishing Group.
Schlitz, Laura Amy. The Hero Schliemann: The Dreamer Who Dug up Troy. Byrd, Robert, illus. 2006. (ENG.). 80p. (J). (gr. 4-7). lib. bdg. 17.99 *(978-0-7636-2283-1(4))* Candlewick Pr.

SCHMIDT, KARL PATTERSON, 1890-1957

Knittel, Patty. Red Coats & Scimitars. 2014. (J). pap. *(978-0-8163-5701-7(3))* Pacific Pr. Publishing Assn.
Wright, A. Gilbert. In the Steps of the Great American Herpetologist. Kalmenoff, Matthew, illus. 2014. (ENG.). 128p. (J). (gr. 2-6). pap. 11.95 *(978-1-59077-360-4(8))* Evans, M. & Co., Inc.

SCHOLARSHIP

see Learning and Scholarship

SCHOLARSHIPS

see also Student Loan Funds

Bercik, Mark. America's Complete Sports Scholarship Guide: Giving Back Something to the Game. Wilding, Diane, ed. 2nd rev. ed. 2003. Orig. Title: America's Sports Scholarship Guide. (Illus.). 272p. (YA). (gr. 4-12). per. 19.95 *(978-0-9721199-1-7(4))* America Sports Publishing.
Contagious Community: Living Beyond Yourself: Connect with God, Connect with Others, Connect with Life. 2008. 175p. pap. *(978-1-57494-431-0(2),* Serendipity Hse.) LifeWay Christian Resources.
McCormick, Lisa Wade. Financial Aid Smarts: Getting Money for School. 2012. (Get Smart with Your Money Ser.). (ENG., Illus.). 64p. (J). (gr. 7-12). pap. 12.95 *(978-1-4488-8266-3(4));* lib. bdg. 31.95 *(978-1-4488-8252-6(4))* Rosen Publishing Group, Inc., The.
Prentzas, G. S. Smart Strategies for Paying for College. 2014. (Financial Security & Life Success for Teens Ser.). (Illus.). 80p. (J). (gr. 7-12). 34.25 *(978-1-4777-7614-8(1))* Rosen Publishing Group, Inc., The.
Rugg, Frederick E. Financial Aid in Less Than 3000 Words. 6p. (YA). 9th rev. ed. 2003. pap. 6.95 *(978-1-883062-51-4(9))* 10th rev. ed. 2004. pap. 6.95 *(978-1-883062-57-6(8))* Rugg's Recommendations.

SCHOOL ADMINISTRATION

see School Management And Organization

SCHOOL AND HOME

see Home and School

SCHOOL ATTENDANCE

see also Child Labor; Dropouts; First Day of School

Davidson, Tish. School Conflict. 2004. (Life Balance Ser.). (ENG., Illus.). 80p. (YA). (gr. 5-8). pap. 6.95 *(978-0-531-15571-4(4),* Watts, Franklin) Scholastic Library Publishing.
Go Back to School with Jack & Annie! 2003. *(978-0-375-88495-5(5))* Random Hse. Children's Bks.
Gordon, Sharon. We Listen. 2007. (J). pap. 6.99 *(978-0-7614-3274-6(4))* Marshall Cavendish Corp.
Hoffman, Joan. First Grade Basics. 2003. (ENG.). 64p. (J). (gr. 1). pap., wbk. ed. 3.99 *(978-1-58947-037-8(0))* School Zone Publishing Co.
—Second Grade Basics. 2003. (ENG.). 64p. (J). (gr. k-3). pap., wbk. ed. 3.99 *(978-1-58947-038-5(9))* School Zone Publishing Co.
Machen Pritchard, M. Ann. Phil the Pill & Friends: Making Positive Choices. Machen Pritchard, M. Ann, illus. 2005. (Illus.). 75p. (J). per. 11.99 *(978-0-9772210-0-4(8),* Phil the Pill & Friends) MAMP Creations.
Murphy, Terri, illus. My School. 2010. (My World Ser.). (ENG.). 24p. (J). (gr. -1-1). pap. 8.15 *(978-1-61533-039-3(9));* lib. bdg. 22.60 *(978-1-60754-953-6(0))* Windmill Bks.
School Zone Interactive Staff. First Grade. 2003. (On-Track Software Ser.). (ENG.). (J). (gr. 1-18). cd-rom 24.99 *(978-1-58947-547-2(X))* School Zone Publishing Co.
School Zone Publishing. Third Grade. 2003. (Power Packs Ser.). (ENG., Illus.). (J). 24.99 *(978-1-58947-533-5(X))* School Zone Publishing Co.
—Third Grade: Builds Skills & Confidence for Success in School! 2003. (Software Ser.). (ENG.). (J). (gr. 3-18). 24.99 *(978-1-58947-538-0(0))* School Zone Publishing Co.
School Zone Publishing Company Staff. School Time Fun. (Illus.). (J). 19.99 incl. audio compact disk *(978-0-88743-958-2(6))* School Zone Publishing Co.

SCHOOL ATTENDANCE—FICTION

Adler, David A. Young Cam Jansen & the New Girl Mystery. Natti, Susanna, illus. 2005. (Young Cam Jansen Ser.: 10). (ENG.). 32p. (J). (gr. 1-3). mass mkt. 3.99 *(978-0-14-240353-2(9),* Penguin Young Readers) Penguin Young Readers Group.
Akubue, Chira. Azuka. 2012. (Illus.). 16p. pap. 18.30 *(978-1-4670-0796-2(X))* AuthorHouse.
Apostolina, M. Hazing Meri Sugarman. 2005. (ENG.). 272p. (YA). pap. 8.99 *(978-1-4169-0610-0(X),* Simon Pulse) Simon Pulse.
Arlen, Richard. Girls' Boarding School. 320p. pap. 6.95 *(978-0-7472-4039-6(6))* Headline Publishing Group GBR. Dist: Trafalgar Square Publishing.
Azuma, Kiyohiko. Azumanga Daioh, Vol. 3. 2004. (Illus.). 172p. (YA). pap. 9.99 *(978-1-4139-0030-9(5))* ADV Manga.
Bentley, Dawn. Fuzzy Bear Goes to School. Nagy, Krisztina, illus. 2005. (Fuzzy Bear Ser.). 10p. (J). 10.95 *(978-1-58117-124-2(2),* Intervisual/Piggy Toes) Bendon, Inc.
Blance, Ellen & Cook, Tony. Monster Goes to School. Date not set. (Illus.). 24p. pap. 129.15 *(978-0-582-18596-8(3))* Addison-Wesley Longman, Ltd. GBR. Dist: Trans-Atlantic Pubns., Inc.
Blyton, Enid. The Naughtiest Girl Is a Monitor. (Illus.). 160p. (J). pap. 6.95 *(978-0-09-945490-8(4))* Random Hse. GBR. Dist: Trafalgar Square Publishing.
Brown, Marc. Arthur & the Cootie-Catcher, Vol. 15. unabr. ed. 2004. (Arthur Chapter Bks.: Bk. 15). 60p. (J). (gr. 2-4). pap. 17.00 incl. audio *(978-0-8072-0346-0(7),* Listening Library) Random Hse. Audio Publishing Group.
—Arthur's off to School. 2004. (ENG., Illus.). 24p. (J). (gr. -1-1). pap. 3.99 *(978-0-316-73378-6(4))* Little, Brown Bks. for Young Readers.
Butcher, A. J. Chaos Rising. 2004. (ENG., Illus.). 240p. (J). (gr. 5-8). pap. 18.99 *(978-0-316-73765-4(8))* Little, Brown Bks. for Young Readers.
—Spy High Mission One. 2004. (ENG.). 224p. (J). (gr. 5-8). pap. 17.99 *(978-0-316-73760-9(7))* Little, Brown Bks. for Young Readers.
Capucilli, Alyssa Satin. Biscuit Loves School. Schories, Pat, illus. 2003. (ENG.). 12p. (J). (gr. -1-1). pap. 9.99 *(978-0-06-009454-6(0),* HarperFestival) HarperCollins Pubs.
Clements, Andrew. Frindle. Selznick, Brian, illus. 105p. (J). (gr. 3-5). pap. 4.50 *(978-0-8072-1522-7(8),* Listening Library) Random Hse. Audio Publishing Group.
—Frindle. unabr. ed. 2004. (Middle Grade Cassette Librariestm Ser.). 105p. (J). (gr. 3-7). pap. 29.00 incl. audio *(978-0-8072-7994-6(3),* S YA 961 SP, Listening Library) Random Hse. Audio Publishing Group.
Couric, Katie. The Brand New Kid. 2004. (Illus.). (J). (gr. -1-3). spiral bd. *(978-0-616-07225-7(2));* spiral bd. *(978-0-616-07226-4(0))* Canadian National Institute for the Blind/Institut National Canadien pour les Aveugles.
Dodd, Christina. Back to School Mom, 18 Copies. 2003. mass mkt. 128.88 *(978-0-06-056267-0(6))* HarperCollins Pubs.
Goldston, Juli-Ette Robin. Bowtie Brownlee Goes to School. 2012. 16p. pap. 14.99 *(978-1-4685-9456-0(7))* AuthorHouse.
Goodman, Jill. Mustang, the Little Dog Who Was Afraid to Go to School. 2004. (Illus.). (J). pap. *(978-1-889636-63-4(0))* Youthlight, Inc.
Hall, Kirsten. First Day of School: All about Shapes & Sizes. Luedecke, Bev, illus. 2004. (Beastieville Ser.). (ENG.). 32p. (J). (gr. k-1). pap. 3.95 *(978-0-516-24654-3(2),* Children's Pr.) Scholastic Library Publishing.
Harper, Jessica. Lizzy's Ups & Downs: NOT an Ordinary School Day. Dupont, Lindsay Harper, illus. 2004. 32p. (J). (gr. -1-3). 15.99 *(978-0-06-052063-2(9))* HarperCollins Pubs.
Harrison, Lisi. Revenge of the Wannabes. 2005. (Clique Ser.: 3). (ENG.). 304p. (YA). (gr. 7-17). pap. 9.99 *(978-0-316-70133-4(5),* Poppy) Little, Brown Bks. for Young Readers.
Hurwitz, Johanna. Fourth-Grade Fuss. Hammond, Andy, illus. 2004. 144p. (J). lib. bdg. 16.89 *(978-0-06-052344-2(1));* (ENG.). (gr. 3-7). 16.99 *(978-0-06-052343-5(3))* HarperCollins Pubs.
Kalar, Bonnie. Miss Lane's Class. Spreen, Kathe, illus. Date not set. 12p. (J). (gr. -1-2). pap. *(978-1-891619-38-0(1))* Corona Pr.
Krulik, Nancy. Who's Afraid of Fourth Grade? John and Wendy Staff, illus. 2004. (Katie Kazoo, Switcheroo Ser.: No. 1). (ENG.). 160p. (J). (gr. 2-4). mass mkt. 4.99 *(978-0-448-43555-8(1),* Grosset & Dunlap) Penguin Young Readers Group.

S

Mazer, Anne. Some Things Never Change. 2004. (Amazing Days of Abby Hayes Ser.: Bk. 13). (Illus.). 101p. (J). (gr. 4-7). 12.65 *(978-0-7569-5302-7(2))* Perfection Learning Corp.
Moss, Marissa. Amelia's Bully Survival Guide. Moss, Marissa, illus. 2006. (Amelia Ser.). (ENG., Illus.). 40p. (J). (gr. 2-5). 9.95 *(978-1-4169-0907-1(9)*, Simon & Schuster/Paula Wiseman Bks.) Simon & Schuster/Paula Wiseman Bks.
Nickelodeon Staff. Hooray for School: Going to School With Nick. 2007. 4.99 *(978-1-4169-5401-9(5)*, Simon Spotlight/Nickelodeon) Simon Spotlight/Nickelodeon.
Parish, Herman. Amelia Bedelia Goes Back to School. Sweat, Lynn, illus. 2004. (Amelia Bedelia Ser.). (ENG.). 20p. (J). (gr. -1-3). pap. 6.99 *(978-0-06-051873-8(1)*, Greenwillow Bks.) HarperCollins Pubs.
Park, Barbara. Junie B., First Grader - Boss of Lunch. Brunkus, Denise, illus. 2003. (Junie B., First Grader Ser.: No. 2). 96p. (J). (gr. k-3). lib. bdg. 11.99 *(978-0-375-90294-9(5)*, Golden Bks.) Random Hse. Children's Bks.
Rice, David L. Because Brian Hugged His Mother. 2004. (Sharing Nature with Children Book Ser.). (Illus.). 32p. (YA). (gr. -1-3). 16.95 *(978-1-883220-90-7(4))* Dawn Pubns.
—Because Brian Hugged His Mother, 1 vol. Thompson, K. Dyble, illus. 2004. (Sharing Nature with Children Book Ser.). (ENG.). 32p. (YA). (gr. -1-3). pap. 7.95 *(978-1-883220-89-1(0))* Dawn Pubns.
Sachar, Louis. Sideways Stories from Wayside School. McCauley, Adam, illus. rev. ed. 2004. (Wayside School Ser.). (ENG.). 128p. (J). (gr. 3-7). pap. 6.99 *(978-0-380-73148-0(7))* HarperCollins Pubs.
Shepard, Sara. Pretty Little Liars. 2006. (Pretty Little Liars Ser.: No. 1). (ENG.). 304p. (YA). (gr. 9-12). 16.99 *(978-0-06-088730-8(3)*, HarperTeen) HarperCollins Pubs.
Starting First Grade. (Tami & Moishy Ser.: Vol. 4). (J). bds. 6.95 *(978-1-58330-968-1(3))* Feldheim Pubs.
Stolarz, Laurie Faria. Red Is for Remembrance. 2005. (Stolarz Ser.: 4). (ENG.). 336p. (YA). pap. 11.99 *(978-0-7387-0760-0(0)*, Flux) North Star Editions.
Williams, Suzanne. The Leo School Trio No. 1: Here Comes Hilary. 2003. 112p. (J). (gr. 2-5). pap. 3.99 *(978-0-439-32988-0(4))* Scholastic, Inc.

SCHOOL DROPOUTS
see Dropouts

SCHOOL ENROLLMENT
see School Attendance

SCHOOL INSPECTION
see School Management And Organization

SCHOOL INTEGRATION
see Segregation in Education

SCHOOL JOURNALISM
see College and School Journalism

SCHOOL LIBRARIES
see also Children's Literature; Libraries
Anderson, Dee. Reading Is Funny! Motivating Kids to Read with Riddles. 2008. (Illus.). 216p. 40.00 *(978-0-8389-0957-7(4))* American Library Assn.
Bloom, Paul. Rules in the Library. 2015. (School Rules Ser.). (ENG., Illus.). 24p. (J). (gr. k-k). pap. 8.15 *(978-1-4824-2649-6(8))* Stevens, Gareth Publishing LLLP.
Buzzeo, Toni. R Is for Research. Wong, Nicole, illus. 2008. (J). (gr. 2-4). 17.95 *(978-1-60213-030-2(2)*, Upstart Bks.) Highsmith Inc.
Morris, Ann. That's Our Librarian! Linenthal, Peter, illus. Linenthal, Peter, photos by. 2003. (That's Our School Ser.). (ENG.). 32p. (gr. k-3). lib. bdg. 22.60 *(978-0-7613-2400-3(3)*, Millbrook Pr.) Lerner Publishing Group.
Murray, Julie. Librarians, 1 vol. 2010. (Buddy Bks.). (ENG.). 32p. (J). (gr. 2-5). 27.07 *(978-1-61613-506-5(9))* ABDO Publishing Co.
Sue, Grandma. The Best Book in the Library. Cherry, Gale, illus. 2010. 20p. 12.49 *(978-1-4490-9704-2(9))* AuthorHouse.

SCHOOL LIFE
see Students

SCHOOL MANAGEMENT AND ORGANIZATION
see also Teaching
Benchmark Education Co., LLC. Safe at School Big Book. 2014. (Shared Reading Foundations Ser.). (J). (gr. -1). *(978-1-4509-9432-3(6))* Benchmark Education Co.
Carroll, Jamuna. School Reform. Berlatsky, Noah, ed. 2010. (Opposing Viewpoints Ser.). (ENG.). 186p. (gr. 10-12). 46.45 *(978-0-7377-4781-2(1)*, Greenhaven Pr., Inc.) Cengage Gale.
Coan, Sharon. Rules at School (Foundations) 2015. (TIME for KIDS(r) Nonfiction Readers Ser.). (ENG., Illus.). 12p. (gr. k-k). 4.99 *(978-1-4938-2065-8(6))* Teacher Created Materials, Inc.
—Trabajadores de Mi Escuela (Workers at My School) 2016. (Nonfiction Readers Ser.). (SPA.). 12p. (J). (gr. k-k). pap. 4.99 *(978-1-4938-3026-8(0))* Teacher Created Materials, Inc.
Coll-Seck, Jayden. Ms. Okafor Is Our Principal, 01 vols., 1. 2016. (Rosen REAL Readers: Social Studies Nonfiction / Fiction: Family, Community, & the World Ser.). (ENG.). 12p. (J). pap. 6.33 *(978-1-5081-1779-7(9)*, Rosen Classroom) Rosen Publishing Group, Inc., The.
Federico, Julie. The Bad Guys: A Students/Teachers Guide to School Safety & Violence Prevention. 2013. 32p. pap. 16.95 *(978-1-4497-9949-6(3)*, WestBow Pr.) Author Solutions, Inc.
Garrett, Winston. What Does a Library Media Specialist Do? 2014. (Jobs in My School Ser.). 24p. (J). (gr. k-2). lib. bdg. 23.60 *(978-1-4777-6546-3(8)*, PowerKids Pr.) Rosen Publishing Group, Inc., The.
—What Does a Library Media Specialist Do? (¿Qué Hace el Especialista de Medios de la Biblioteca Escolar?) de la Vega, Eida, ed. 2014. (Oficios en Mi Escuela / Jobs in My School Ser.). (SPA & ENG.). 24p. (J). (gr. k-2). lib. bdg. 23.60 *(978-1-4777-6796-2(7)*, PowerKids Pr.) Rosen Publishing Group, Inc., The.
Heitkamp, Kristina Lyn. Gay-Straight Alliances: Networking with Other Teens & Allies. 2017. (LGBTQ+ Guide to Beating Bullying Ser.). 64p. (J). (gr. 12-11). 34.45 ***(978-1-5081-7427-1(X)***, Rosen Young Adult) Rosen Publishing Group, Inc., The.
Hudson, David L. Rights of Students. 2nd rev. ed. 2010. (Point/Counterpoint Ser.). 112p. (C). (gr. 9). 35.00 *(978-1-60413-692-0(8)*, Chelsea Hse.) Facts On File, Inc.
Kent, Susan. Learning How to Say Safe at School. 2009. (Violence Prevention Library). 24p. (gr. 2-3). 42.50 *(978-1-60854-266-6(1)*, PowerKids Pr.) Rosen Publishing Group, Inc., The.
Kidde, Rita. What Does a Janitor Do? (¿Qué Hace el Conserje?) de la Vega, Eida, ed. 2014. (Oficios en Mi Escuela / Jobs in My School Ser.). (SPA & ENG.). 24p. (J). (gr. k-2). lib. bdg. 23.60 *(978-1-4777-6791-7(6)*, PowerKids Pr.) Rosen Publishing Group, Inc., The.
—What Does the Principal Do? 2014. (Jobs in My School Ser.). 24p. (J). (gr. k-2). lib. bdg. 23.60 *(978-1-4777-6477-0(1)*, PowerKids Pr.) Rosen Publishing Group, Inc., The.
—What Does the Principal Do? (¿Qué Hace el Director?) de la Vega, Eida, ed. 2014. (Oficios en Mi Escuela / Jobs in My School Ser.). (SPA & ENG.). 24p. (J). (gr. k-2). lib. bdg. 23.60 *(978-1-4777-6790-0(8)*, PowerKids Pr.) Rosen Publishing Group, Inc., The.
Kreiner, Anna. Todo lo que necesitas saber sobre la violencia en la escuela (Everything You Need to Know about Violence in School) 2009. (Todo lo que necesitas (the Need to Know Library) Ser.). (SPA.). 64p. (gr. 6-6). 58.50 *(978-1-60854-411-0(7)*, Editorial Buenas Letras) Rosen Publishing Group, Inc., The.
Liebman, Dan & Liebman, Daniel. President. 2009. (I Want to Be Ser.). (ENG., Illus.). 24p. (J). (gr. -1-2). 14.95 *(978-1-55407-562-1(9)*, 9781554075621); pap. 3.99 *(978-1-55407-563-8(7)*, 9781554075638) Firefly Bks., Ltd.
—Presidente. 2009. (Quiero Ser.). (SPA., Illus.). 24p. (J). (gr. -1-2). 14.95 *(978-1-55407-564-5(5)*, 9781554075645); pap. 5.99 *(978-1-55407-565-2(3)*, 9781554075652) Firefly Bks., Ltd.
Marsico, Katie. Working at a School. 2008. (21st Century Junior Library: Careers Ser.). (ENG.). 24p. (gr. 2-5). lib. bdg. 25.64 *(978-1-60279-266-1(6)*, 200171) Cherry Lake Publishing.
Marx, Jeff. How to Win a High School Election: Advice & Ideas Collected from over 1,000 High School Seniors. 2003. 180p. (gr. 7-12). pap. 14.95 *(978-0-9667824-0-0(2))* Marx, Jeff.
McCune, Susan. Mr. Morgan Keeps Our School Clean, 01 vols., 1. 2016. (Rosen REAL Readers: Social Studies Nonfiction / Fiction: Family, Community, & the World Ser.). (ENG.). 12p. (J). pap. 6.33 *(978-1-5081-1755-1(1)*, Rosen Classroom) Rosen Publishing Group, Inc., The.
Mitchell, Melanie. Principals. (Pull Ahead Bks.). (J). 2005. (Illus.). 32p. lib. bdg. 22.60 *(978-0-8225-1694-1(2))* 2004. pap. 6.95 *(978-0-8225-2535-6(6)*, Lerner Pubns.) Lerner Publishing Group.
Murray, Julie. Principals, 1 vol. 2010. (Going to Work Ser.). (ENG.). 32p. (J). (gr. 2-5). 27.07 *(978-1-61613-508-9(5))* ABDO Publishing Co.
Parnell, Declan. Mr. Wilson Is Our Crossing Guard, 01 vols., 1. 2016. (Rosen REAL Readers: Social Studies Nonfiction / Fiction: Family, Community, & the World Ser.). (ENG.). 8p. (J). pap. 5.46 *(978-1-5081-1704-9(7)*, Rosen Classroom) Rosen Publishing Group, Inc., The.
The School Rules. 2015. (School Rules Ser.). (ENG.). 24p. (gr. k-k). pap., pap., pap. 293.40 *(978-1-4824-3496-5(2))* Stevens, Gareth Publishing LLLP.
Schuh, Mari. Community Helpers at School. 2016. (Community Helpers on the Scene Ser.). (ENG., Illus.). 24p. (gr. k-1). lib. bdg. 21.99 *(978-1-5157-2400-1(X)*, Pebble Bks.) Capstone Press of Coughlan Cos.
Shava, Ryder. Mr. Lagaya Is Our Assistant Principal, 01 vols., 1. 2016. (Rosen REAL Readers: Social Studies Nonfiction / Fiction: Family, Community, & the World Ser.). (ENG.). 12p. (J). pap. 6.33 *(978-1-5081-1782-7(9)*, Rosen Classroom) Rosen Publishing Group, Inc., The.
Verderosa, Laura. At My School. 2010. (Sight Word Readers Ser.). (J). 3.49 *(978-1-60719-606-8(9))* Newmark Learning LLC.

SCHOOL MUSIC
see Music—Study and Teaching; School Songbooks

SCHOOL NEWSPAPERS
see College and School Journalism

SCHOOL NURSING
Garrett, Winston. What Does the School Nurse Do? 2014. (Jobs in My School Ser.). 24p. (J). (gr. k-2). lib. bdg. 23.60 *(978-1-4777-6551-7(4)*, PowerKids Pr.) Rosen Publishing Group, Inc., The.
—What Does the School Nurse Do? (¿Qué Hace la Enfermera de la Escuela?) de la Vega, Eida, ed. 2014. (Oficios en Mi Escuela / Jobs in My School Ser.). (SPA & ENG.). 24p. (J). (gr. k-2). lib. bdg. 23.60 *(978-1-4777-6801-3(7)*, PowerKids Pr.) Rosen Publishing Group, Inc., The.
Morris, Ann. That's Our Nurse! Linenthal, Peter, illus. Linenthal, Peter, photos by. 2003. (That's Our School Ser.). (ENG.). 32p. (gr. k-3). lib. bdg. 22.60 *(978-0-7613-2402-7(X)*, Millbrook Pr.) Lerner Publishing Group.
Vogel, Elizabeth. Meet the School Nurse. 2009. (My School Ser.). 24p. (gr. 1-2). 37.50 *(978-1-61514-708-3(X)*, PowerKids Pr.) Rosen Publishing Group, Inc., The.

SCHOOL ORGANIZATION
see School Management And Organization

SCHOOL PLAYGROUNDS
see Playgrounds

SCHOOL PLAYS
see Plays

SCHOOL SONGBOOKS
Barden, Christine H., et al. Music for Little Mozarts — Little Mozarts Go to Church, Bk 1-2: 10 Favorite Hymns, Spirituals & Sunday School Songs. 2008. (Music for Little Mozarts Ser.: Bk 1-2). (ENG.). 24p. (J). pap. 6.00 *(978-0-7390-5689-9(1))* Alfred Publishing Co., Inc.
—Music for Little Mozarts — Little Mozarts Go to Church, Bk 3-4: 10 Favorite Hymns, Spirituals & Sunday School Songs. 2008. (Music for Little Mozarts Ser.: Bk 3-4). (ENG.). 24p. (J). pap. 6.00 *(978-0-7390-5690-5(5))* Alfred Publishing Co., Inc.
Vogt, Janet. Music Brain Teasers. 2006. pap. 19.95 *(978-0-89328-248-6(0))* Lorenz Corp., The.

SCHOOL SPORTS
see also Coaching (Athletics)
Lewis, Jan, illus. Sports Day. 2012. (First Time Ser.). (ENG.). 24p. (J). *(978-1-84643-488-4(2))* Child's Play International Ltd.
Shivers, Joseph P. & Shivers, Paul L. Harriers: The Making of a Championship Cross Country Team. 2006. (ENG.). 180p. (J). (gr. 7-12). per. 9.95 *(978-1-932802-95-5(9)*, Holy Macro! Bks.) Tickling Keys, Inc.

SCHOOL TEACHING
see Teaching

SCHOOL WITHDRAWALS
see Dropouts

SCHOOLS
see also Boarding Schools; Education; Kindergarten; Public Schools; Universities and Colleges
Abramovitz, Melissa. The 100th Day of School, 1 vol. 2012. (Let's Celebrate Ser.). (ENG., Illus.). 24p. (gr. k-1). lib. bdg. 26.65 *(978-1-4296-8645-7(6)*, Pebble Plus) Capstone Press of Coughlan Cos.
Adamson, Heather. School in Many Cultures. 2016. (Life Around the World Ser.). (ENG.). 24p. (gr. k-1). pap. 7.29 *(978-1-5157-4239-5(3)*, Pebble Plus) Capstone Press of Coughlan Cos.
Allen, Kenny. My School. 2009. (Real Life Readers Ser.). 8p. (gr. k-1). pap. 5.15 *(978-1-4042-7969-8(5)*, Rosen Classroom) Rosen Publishing Group, Inc., The.
Ancona, George. Mi Escuela: My School. 2004. (Somos Latino (We Are Latinos) Ser.). 21.00 *(978-0-516-23686-5(5)*, Watts, Franklin) Scholastic Library Publishing.
Anderson, Sheila. School. 2008. (J). pap. 3.95 *(978-0-8225-8838-2(2))*; pap. 22.95 *(978-0-8225-9374-4(2))* Lerner Publishing Group.
Appleby, Alex. Dinosaurs at School. 2013. (Dinosaur School Ser.). 24p. (J). (gr. k-1). pap. 48.90 *(978-1-4339-9043-4(1))*; (Illus.). pap. 8.15 *(978-1-4339-9042-7(3))*; (ENG., Illus.). lib. bdg. 22.60 *(978-1-4339-9041-0(5))* Stevens, Gareth Publishing LLLP.
Aretha, David. The Story of the Little Rock Nine & School Desegregation in Photographs. 2014. (Story of the Civil Rights Movement in Photographs Ser.). 48p. (J). lib. bdg. 25.27 *(978-0-7660-4235-3(9))* Enslow Pubs., Inc.
Barron's Educational Series Staff & Rigo, L., illus. Off to School. 2010. (ENG.). 10p. (J). (gr. -1-1). bds. 7.99 *(978-0-7641-6363-0(9))* Barron's Educational Series, Inc.
Bell, Cece. El Deafo. Lasky, David, illus. 2014. (ENG.). 248p. (J). (gr. 3-7). 21.95 *(978-1-4197-1020-9(6))*; pap. 10.95 *(978-1-4197-1217-3(9))* Abrams, Inc. (Amulet Bks.).
—El Deafo. 2014. (J). lib. bdg. 22.05 *(978-0-606-36148-4(0))* Turtleback Bks.
Bellamy, Adam. This Is My School. 2016. (All about My World Ser.). (Illus.). 24p. (J). pap. 9.35 *(978-0-7660-8083-6(8))* Enslow Pubs., Inc.
Benjamin, Tina. My Day at School. 2015. (Inside My World Ser.). (ENG.). 24p. (J). (gr. k-k). 22.60 *(978-1-4824-1801-9(0))* Stevens, Gareth Publishing LLLP.
Berendes, Mary. School/la Escuela. Petelinsek, Kathleen, illus. 2008. (WordBooks/Libros de Palabras Ser.). (SPA & ENG.). 24p. (J). (gr. k-3). 25.64 *(978-1-59296-994-4(1)*, 201098) Child's World, Inc., The.
Berry, Joy. I Love Preschool. Regan, Dana, illus. 2010. (Teach Me About Ser.). (ENG.). 20p. (J). (gr. k — 1). bds. 5.99 *(978-1-60577-015-4(9))* Berry, Joy Enterprises.
Blane, Francisco. People at School: Lap Book. 2009. (My First Reader's Theater Set B Ser.). (J). 28.00 *(978-1-935441-00-7(0))* Benchmark Education Co.
Bloom, Paul. Rules in the Classroom. 2015. (School Rules Ser.). (ENG., Illus.). 24p. (J). (gr. k-k). pap. 8.15 *(978-1-4824-2641-0(2))* Stevens, Gareth Publishing LLLP.
Boothroyd, Jennifer. From Chalkboards to Computers: How Schools Have Changed. 2011. (Comparing Past & Present Ser.). pap. 7.95 *(978-0-7613-7840-2(5))*; pap. 45.32 *(978-0-7613-8390-1(5))*; (ENG., Illus.). 32p. lib. bdg. 26.60 *(978-0-7613-6744-4(6))* Lerner Publishing Group.
—Schools. 2006. (First Step Nonfiction Ser.). (Illus.). 8p. (J). pap. 3.95 *(978-0-8225-5729-6(0)*, Lerner Pubns.) Lerner Publishing Group.
Borene, Mark R. Welcome to the School. 2009. 20p. pap. 10.49 *(978-1-4389-7752-2(2))* AuthorHouse.
Bozzo, Linda & Library. Schools of the Past, Present, & Future. 2010. (Imagining the Future Ser.). (Illus.). 24p. (J). lib. bdg. 22.60 *(978-0-7660-3434-1(8)*, Enslow Elementary) Enslow Pubs., Inc.
Brezina, Corona. Standing up to Bullying at School. 2017. (LGBTQ+ Guide to Beating Bullying Ser.). 64p. (J). (gr. 12-11). pap. 12.95 ***(978-1-5081-7429-5(6)***, Rosen Young Adult) Rosen Publishing Group, Inc., The.
Bullard, Lisa. Who Works at Hannah's School? Becker, Paula J., illus. 2017. (Cloverleaf Books (tm) — off to School Ser.). (ENG.). 24p. (J). (gr. k-2). 25.32 ***(978-1-5124-3940-3(1)***, Millbrook Pr.) Lerner Publishing Group.
—Who Works at Hannah's School? Becker, Paula, illus. 2017. (Cloverleaf Books (tm) — off to School Ser.). (ENG.). (J). (gr. k-2). pap. 7.99 ***(978-1-5124-5581-6(4)***, Millbrook Pr.) Lerner Publishing Group.
—William's 100th Day of School. Byrne, Mike, illus. 2017. (Cloverleaf Books (tm) — off to School Ser.). (ENG.). 24p. (J). (gr. k-2). 25.32 ***(978-1-5124-3935-9(5))***; pap. 7.99 ***(978-1-5124-5582-3(2))*** Lerner Publishing Group. (Millbrook Pr.).
Butterfield, Moira. Schools Around the World. 2016. (Children Like Us Ser.). (ENG., Illus.). 32p. (J). (gr. 3-3). pap. 10.58 *(978-1-5026-0846-8(4))* Cavendish Square Publishing.
Canetti, Yanitzia. ABCs of School. 2010. (J). 8.99 *(978-1-59835-277-1(6)*, BrickHouse Education) Cambridge BrickHouse, Inc.
—Abecedario Escolar. 2010. (SPA.). 40p. (J). pap. 8.99 *(978-1-59835-275-7(X)*, BrickHouse Education) Cambridge BrickHouse, Inc.
—Colores escolares/School Colors: A World of Color. 2010. (ENG & SPA.). 24p. (J). pap. 6.99 *(978-1-59835-272-6(5)*, BrickHouse Education) Cambridge BrickHouse, Inc.
Capaccio, George. Schools. 2014. (Life in Colonial America Ser.). 80p. (YA). (gr. 6-8). lib. bdg. 35.64 *(978-1-62712-894-0(8))* Cavendish Square Publishing.
Carr, Aaron. The School. 2013. pap. 12.95 *(978-1-62127-353-0(9))*; (Illus.). 24p. (J). *(978-1-62127-348-6(2))* Weigl Pubs., Inc.
Cassel, Katrina L. The Middle School Survival Manual. 2010. 128p. (J). (gr. 6-18). pap. 8.99 *(978-0-7586-1790-3(9))* Concordia Publishing Hse.
Catherman, Jonathan. The Manual to Middle School: The Do This, Not That Survival Guide for Guys. 2017. (ENG.). 224p. pap. 13.99 ***(978-0-8007-2847-2(5))*** Revell.
Chambers, Catherine & Dorling Kindersley Publishing Staff. School Days Around the World, Level 3. 2007. (DK Readers Ser.). (ENG., Illus.). 48p. (J). (gr. 2-4). pap. 3.99 *(978-0-7566-2548-1(3)*, DK Children) Dorling Kindersley Publishing, Inc.
Civardi, Anne. Going to School Sticker Book. 2008. (First Experiences Sticker Bks). (Illus.). 16p. (J). pap. 6.99 *(978-0-7945-2182-0(7)*, Usborne) EDC Publishing.
Clark, Veronica, et al. Class Assemblies 1, 1 vol. 2010. (and C Black Assembly Packs Ser.). (ENG., Illus.). 64p. (J). pap. 32.95 incl. audio compact disk ***(978-1-4081-2456-7(4))*** HarperCollins Pubs. Ltd. GBR. Dist: Independent Pubs. Group.
—Class Assemblies 2, 1 vol. 2010. (and C Black Assembly Packs Ser.). (ENG., Illus.). 64p. (J). pap. 32.95 incl. audio compact disk ***(978-1-4081-2457-4(2))*** HarperCollins Pubs. Ltd. GBR. Dist: Independent Pubs. Group.
—Class Assemblies 3, 1 vol. 2010. (and C Black Assembly Packs Ser.). (ENG., Illus.). 64p. (J). pap. 32.95 incl. audio compact disk ***(978-1-4081-2458-1(0))*** HarperCollins Pubs. Ltd. GBR. Dist: Independent Pubs. Group.
Cohn, Jessica. On the Job at School. Scheuer, Lauren, illus. 2016. (Core Content Social Studies — on the Job Ser.). (ENG.). 32p. (J). (gr. 2-5). lib. bdg. 26.65 *(978-1-63440-106-1(5))* Red Chair Pr.
Collins, Stan. School Signs. 2003. (ENG.). 10p. (J). (gr. -1). spiral bd. 19.95 *(978-1-930820-35-7(6))* Garlic Pr.
Color All About: A Giant Coloring Book about Fun Things to do at School: Back to School. 2004. (Illus.). 36p. (J). *(978-1-59949-005-2(6))* Food Marketing Consultants, Inc.
Cosmic Debris Etc., Inc. Staff, et al. Middle School. 2009. (Worst Case Scenario Ser.). (ENG., Illus.). 128p. (J). (gr. 6-8). pap. 10.99 *(978-0-8118-6864-8(8))* Chronicle Bks. LLC.
Dale, Jay. Ways We Go to School, 1 vol. 2012. (Engage Literacy Green Ser.). (ENG.). 32p. (gr. k-2). pap. 5.99 *(978-1-4296-9020-1(8)*, Engage Literacy) Capstone Press of Coughlan Cos.
David C. Cook Publishing Company Staff, creator. Action! Cool Theater. 2008. (Bible Fun Stuff for Middle School Ser.). (Illus.). 112p. (J). (gr. 6-8). pap. 16.99 *(978-1-4347-6856-8(2))* Cook, David C.
Desalle, Nicole. Safe at School. 2011. pap. 39.95 *(978-0-7664-3750-0(7))* Abrams & Co. Pubs., Inc.
Donahue, Jill L., et al. Chuckle Squad: Jokes about Classrooms, Sports, Food, Teachers, & Other School Subjects, 1 vol. Haugen, Ryan et al, illus. 2010. (Michael Dahl Presents Super Funny Joke Bks.). (ENG.). 80p. (gr. k-3). 25.32 *(978-1-4048-5773-5(7))* Picture Window Bks.
Dorling Kindersley Publishing Staff. A School Like Mine: A Unique Celebration of Schools Around the World. 2016. (ENG., Illus.). 80p. (J). (gr. 3-7). 19.99 *(978-1-4654-5100-2(5)*, DK Children) Dorling Kindersley Publishing, Inc.
Doudna, Kelly. School Around the World, 1 vol. 2004. (Around the World Ser.). (ENG., Illus.). 24p. (J). (gr. k-3). lib. bdg. 24.21 *(978-1-59197-569-4(7)*, SandCastle) ABDO Publishing Co.
Edwards, Rhonda S. A Living Mascot. Owens, Alana, illus. 2013. (ENG.). 38p. (J). pap. 9.99 *(978-0-7443-2013-8(5))* SynergEbks.
Elliott, Tommy. I Don't Want To: Go to School. 2009. 24p. pap. 13.49 *(978-1-4389-5123-2(X))* AuthorHouse.
Emberley, Rebecca. My School/Mi Escuela. 2005. (SPA & ENG., Illus.). 10p. (J). (gr. -1 — 1). bds. 6.99 *(978-0-316-00050-5(7))* Little, Brown Bks. for Young Readers.
Emmer, Rae. Drama Club. 2009. (School Activities Ser.). 24p. (gr. 1-1). 42.50 *(978-1-60852-998-8(3)*, PowerKids Pr.) Rosen Publishing Group, Inc., The.
—Drama Club / Club de Teatro. 2009. (School Activities / Actividades escolares Ser.). (ENG & SPA.). 24p. (gr. 1-2). 42.50 *(978-1-60853-004-5(3)*, Editorial Buenas Letras) Rosen Publishing Group, Inc., The.
Espejo, Roman. Cell Phones in Schools. Greenhaven Press Editors & Gale Editors, eds. 2014. (At Issue Ser.). (ENG.). 128p. (gr. 10-12). pap. 27.80 *(978-0-7377-6156-6(3)*, Greenhaven Pr., Inc.) Cengage Gale.
—Cell Phones in Schools. Greenhaven Press Editors, ed. 2014. (At Issue Ser.). (ENG.). 128p. (gr. 10-12). lib. bdg. 39.40 *(978-0-7377-6155-9(5)*, Greenhaven Pr., Inc.) Cengage Gale.
Falk, Laine. This Is the Way We Go to School. 2009. (Scholastic News Nonfiction Readers Ser.). (ENG.). 24p. (J). (gr. 1-2). pap. 6.95 *(978-0-531-21440-4(0)*, Children's Pr.); lib. bdg. 22.00 *(978-0-531-21341-4(2))* Scholastic Library Publishing.
Fastje, Shanaya B. Mystery School. 2009. 28p. pap. 13.99 *(978-1-4490-0115-5(7))* AuthorHouse.
Fayetteville Elementary, Students & Staf. Memories of Fayetteville Elementary School. 2007. 124p. per. 16.95 *(978-0-9790446-1-8(8))* Pen & Publish Inc.
Feldman, Ruth Tenzer. Don't Whistle in School: The History of America's Public Schools. 2005. (People's History Ser.). (Illus.). 96p. (gr. 6-12). lib. bdg. 26.60 *(978-0-8225-1745-0(0))* Lerner Publishing Group.
Felix, Rebecca. Patterns at School. 2015. (21st Century Basic Skills Library: Patterns All Around Ser.). (ENG., Illus.). 24p. (J). (gr. k-3). pap. 12.79 *(978-1-63188-934-9(6)*, 205997) Cherry Lake Publishing.
Flash Kids Editors, ed. Ready for School: Grade Pre-K-K (Flash Skills) 2010. (Flash Skills Ser.). (ENG.). 64p. (J). pap. 3.95 *(978-1-4114-3466-0(8)*, Spark Publishing Group) Sterling Publishing Co., Inc.
Foran, Jill. La Petite école: Le Début de la Colonie. Karvonen, Tanjah, tr. from ENG. 2011. (FRE., Illus.). 24p. (gr. 3-6). *(978-1-77071-421-2(9))* Weigl Educational Pubs. Ltd.
—The School House: Pioneers of Canada. 2011. 24p. (YA). (gr. 2-4). *(978-1-77071-680-3(7))*; pap. *(978-1-77071-684-1(X))* Weigl Educational Pubs. Ltd.

Fretland VanVoorst, Jenny. Las Formas en la Escuela. 2015.Tr. of Shapes at School. (SPA., Illus.). 24p. (J). lib. bdg. *(978-1-62031-248-3(4),* Bullfrog Bks.) Jump! Inc.
—Shapes at School. 2015. (Illus.). 24p. (J). lib. bdg. *(978-1-62031-203-2(4),* Bullfrog Bks.) Jump! Inc.
Friedman, Hannah. Everything Sucks: Losing My Mind & Finding Myself in a High School Quest for Cool. 2009. (ENG.). 264p. (YA). (gr. 8-12). pap. 12.95 *(978-0-7573-0775-1(2),* HCI Teens) Health Communications, Inc.
Friedman, Lauri S. School Shootings. 2009. (Writing the Critical Essay Ser.). (ENG., Illus.). 128p. (J). 31.80 *(978-0-7377-4564-1(9),* Greenhaven Pr., Inc.) Cengage Gale.
Fronczak, Blaine. Haley Helps at School. 2013. (Core Math Skills: Numbers & Operations in Base 10 Ser.). 24p. (J). (gr. 1-2). 22.60 *(978-1-4777-2225-1(4));* (ENG.). pap. 8.25 *(978-1-4777-2097-4(9))* Rosen Publishing Group, Inc., The. (Rosen Classroom).
—Haley Helps at School: Use Place Value & Properties of Operations to Add. 2013. (Rosen Math Readers Ser.). (ENG.). 24p. (J). (gr. 1-2). pap. 49.50 *(978-1-4777-2098-1(7),* Rosen Classroom) Rosen Publishing Group, Inc., The.
Gaarder-Juntti, Oona. Shapes at School, 1 vol. 2013. (Shapes Everywhere Ser.). (ENG.). 24p. (gr. k-4). lib. bdg. 25.65 *(978-1-61783-412-7(2),* Super SandCastle) ABDO Publishing Co.
—What in the World Is a Green School?, 1 vol. 2010. (Super SandCastle Ser.). (ENG.). 24p. 25.65 *(978-1-61613-190-6(X),* Super SandCastle) ABDO Publishing Co.
Geatches, Hazel, ed. Schools. 2012. (ENG., Illus.). 32p. pap. 10.00 *(978-0-19-464627-7(0))* Oxford Univ. Pr., Inc.
Gimpel, Diane Marczely. The Columbine Shootings, 1 vol. 2012. (Essential Events Set 8 Ser.). (ENG.). 112p. (J). (gr. 6-12). lib. bdg. 35.64 *(978-1-61783-308-3(8))* ABDO Publishing Co.
Gordon, Sharon. We Share. 2007. (J). pap. 6.99 *(978-0-7614-3276-0(0))* Marshall Cavendish Corp.
—We Tell the Truth. 2007. (J). pap. 6.99 *(978-0-7614-3277-7(9))* Marshall Cavendish Corp.
Gosman, Gillian. Simple Machines at School. 2014. (Simple Machines Everywhere Ser.). (Illus.). 24p. (J). (gr. k-3). pap. 49.50 *(978-1-4777-6645-3(6),* PowerKids Pr.) Rosen Publishing Group, Inc., The.
Graves, Karen M. School in Pioneer Times. 2016. (It's Back to School ... Way Back! Ser.). (ENG., Illus.). 32p. (gr. 3-4). lib. bdg. 27.32 *(978-1-5157-2096-6(9),* Fact Finders) Capstone Press of Coughlan Cos.
Graves, Kerry A. School in the Great Depression. 2016. (It's Back to School ... Way Back! Ser.). (ENG., Illus.). 32p. (gr. 3-4). lib. bdg. 27.32 *(978-1-5157-2098-0(5),* Fact Finders) Capstone Press of Coughlan Cos.
Greathouse, Lisa. Count Me In! School Carnival, 1 vol. 2nd rev. ed. 2011. (TIME for KIDS(r) Nonfiction Readers Ser.). (ENG.). 28p. (J). (gr. 2-2). pap. 6.99 *(978-1-4333-3637-9(5))* Teacher Created Materials, Inc.
Gregoire, Maryellen. Escuelas Viejas y Nuevas (Old & New Schools) 2012. (Wonder Readers Spanish Emergent Ser.). (SPA.). 16p. (gr. -1-1). pap. 35.94 *(978-1-62065-574-0(8))* Capstone Press of Coughlan Cos.
—Old & New Schools, 1 vol. 2012. (Wonder Readers Emergent Level Ser.). (ENG.). (gr. -1-1). 32p. pap. 5.99 *(978-1-4296-9191-8(3));* 16p. pap. 35.94 *(978-1-4296-9201-4(4))* Capstone Press of Coughlan Cos. (Wonder Readers).
Gregory, Cam. When Do I Go to School? 2014. (Little Books of Answers: Level B Ser.). (Illus.). 16p. (gr. k-2). pap. 7.95 *(978-1-927136-11-9(3))* Three Crows Media NZL. Dist: RiverStream Publishing.
Greven, Alec. Rules for School. Acedera, Kei, illus. 2010. (ENG.). 48p. (J). (gr. 1-5). 9.99 *(978-0-06-195170-1(6),* Collins) HarperCollins Pubs.
Group/McGraw-Hill, Wright. My School, Your School: Level E, 6 vols. (Take Twostm Ser.). 16p. 29.95 *(978-0-322-08948-8(4))* Wright Group/McGraw-Hill.
Guest, John. Collective Worship Unwrapped: 33 Tried & Tested Story-Based Assemblies for Primary Schools. 2nd ed. 2013. 132p. pap. *(978-1-84101-618-4(7),* Barnabas in Schools) Bible Reading Fellowship.
Hale, Shannon. Real Friends. Pham, LeUyen, illus. 2017. (ENG.). 224p. (J). 21.99 *(978-1-62672-416-7(4),* 9781626724167, First Second Bks.) Roaring Brook Pr.
Hale, Shannon & Pham, LeUyen. Real Friends. 2017. (J). lib. bdg. 24.50 ***(978-0-606-39954-8(2))*** Turtleback Bks.
Hall, Pamela. A Bully-Free Bus, 1 vol. Ostrom, Bob, illus. 2012. (Bully-Free World Ser.). (ENG.). 24p. (J). (gr. -1-4). 27.07 *(978-1-61641-844-1(3))* Magic Wagon.
Hasday, Judy L. Forty-Nine Minutes of Madness: The Columbine High School Shooting. 2012. (Disasters — People in Peril Ser.). (Illus.). 48p. (J). (gr. 5-18). 25.27 *(978-0-7660-4013-7(5))* Enslow Pubs., Inc.
Healy, Nicholas M. If You Were a Period [LTD Commodities]. Gray, Sara, illus. 2010. (Word Fun Ser.). 24p. pap. 3.50 *(978-1-4048-6252-4(8),* Nonfiction Picture Bks.) Picture Window Bks.
Henningfeld, Diane Andrews. Charter Schools. 2007. (At Issue Ser.). (ENG., Illus.). 128p. (gr. 10-12). pap. 27.80 *(978-0-7377-3915-2(0),* Greenhaven Pr., Inc.) Cengage Gale.
Herrington, Lisa M. Back-to-School Safety. 2012. (Rookie Read-About(tm) Safety Ser.). (ENG., Illus.). 32p. (J). lib. bdg. 25.00 *(978-0-531-28967-9(2));* pap. 5.95 *(978-0-531-29269-3(X))* Scholastic Library Publishing.
Herweck Rice, Dona. La Escuela Alrededor Del Mundo. 2017. (TIME for Kids en Español - Level 3 Ser.). (SPA.). 32p. (gr. 3-3). lib. bdg. 31.99 ***(978-1-5157-5166-3(X))*** Time for Kids Inc AUS. Dist: Capstone Pub.
Hinman, Bonnie. The Scoop on School & Work in Colonial America, 1 vol. 2012. (Life in the American Colonies Ser.). (ENG.). 32p. (gr. 3-4). pap. 8.10 *(978-1-4296-7986-2(7),* Fact Finders) Capstone Press of Coughlan Cos.
Hughes, Susan & Owlkids Books Inc. Staff. Off to Class: Incredible & Unusual Schools Around the World. 2011. (ENG., Illus.). 64p. (J). (gr. 3-7). 22.95 *(978-1-926818-85-6(7));* pap. 14.95 *(978-1-926818-86-3(5))* Owlkids Bks. Inc. CAN. Dist: Publishers Group West (PGW).
Hurt, Avery Elizabeth. Working with Your School to Create a Safe Environment. 2017. (LGBTQ+ Guide to Beating Bullying Ser.). 64p. (J). (gr. 12-11). 34.45 ***(978-1-5081-7435-6(0),*** Rosen Young Adult) Rosen Publishing Group, Inc., The.
The Inside Scoop on American Graduate & Professional Schools. 2004. (C). pap. 4.95 net. *(978-1-884169-33-5(3))* International Educational Improvement Ctr. Pr.
Jack's Pack: KinderReaders Individual Title Six-Packs. (Kinderstarters Ser.). 8p. (gr. -1-1). 21.00 *(978-0-7635-8660-7(9))* Rigby Education.
Jobs in My School. 2014. (Jobs in My School Ser.). 24p. (J). (gr. k-2). 141.60 *(978-1-4777-6561-6(1),* PowerKids Pr.) Rosen Publishing Group, Inc., The.
Jones, Jen. How Much Do You Know about Bullying?, 1 vol. 2011. (Friendship Quizzes Ser.). (ENG.). 32p. (gr. 3-4). lib. bdg. 27.99 *(978-1-4296-6540-7(8),* Snap Bks.) Capstone Press of Coughlan Cos.
Jones, Tammy. We Go to School. 2009. (Sight Word Readers Set A Ser.). (J). 3.49 net. *(978-1-60719-146-9(6))* Newmark Learning LLC.
Kalman, Bobbie. At School. 2010. (ENG.). 16p. (J). *(978-0-7787-9497-4(0));* pap. *(978-0-7787-9522-3(5))* Crabtree Publishing Co.
—La Comunidad de Mi Escuela. 2010. (SPA.). 24p. (J). pap. *(978-0-7787-8590-3(4));* lib. bdg. *(978-0-7787-8564-4(5))* Crabtree Publishing Co.
—My School Community. 2010. (My World Ser.). (ENG., Illus.). 24p. (J). (gr. k-2). *(978-0-7787-9442-4(3));* pap. *(978-0-7787-9486-8(5))* Crabtree Publishing Co.
—School Days Then & Now. 2013. (ENG., Illus.). 24p. (J). *(978-0-7787-0127-9(1));* pap. *(978-0-7787-0209-2(X))* Crabtree Publishing Co.
Kalz, Jill. School Adventure. Cerato, Mattia, illus. 2010. (A-MAZE-Ing Adventures Ser.). (ENG.). 32p. (gr. 1-2). lib. bdg. 26.65 *(978-1-4048-6039-1(8))* Picture Window Bks.
Keller, Carolyn & Seaman, Jim. Allegheny College College Prowler off the Record. 2005. (College Prowler off the Record Guides: Vol. 1). 160p. (YA). (gr. 12-18). pap., stu. ed. 14.95 *(978-1-59658-000-8(3))* College Prowler, Inc.
Kimball, Marrae. The Secret Combination to Middle School: Real Advice from Real Kids, Ideas for Success, & Much More! 2013. 200p. (J). pap. 14.95 *(978-0-9849322-1-4(6))* Find Your Way Publishing, Inc.
Knowlton, MaryLee. Safety at School. Andersen, Gregg, photos by. 2008. (Staying Safe Ser.). (ENG., Illus.). 32p. (J). (gr. -1-3). lib. bdg. *(978-0-7787-4317-0(9))* Crabtree Publishing Co.
Koestler-Grack, Rachel A. School in the Civil Rights Movement. 2016. (It's Back to School ... Way Back! Ser.). (ENG., Illus.). 32p. (gr. 3-4). lib. bdg. 27.32 *(978-1-5157-2099-7(3),* Fact Finders) Capstone Press of Coughlan Cos.
Kreiner, Anna. Todo lo que necesitas saber sobre la violencia en la escuela (Everything You Need to Know about Violence in School) 2009. (Todo lo que necesitas (the Need to Know Library) Ser.). (SPA.). 64p. (gr. 6-6). 58.50 *(978-1-60854-411-0(7),* Editorial Buenas Letras) Rosen Publishing Group, Inc., The.
Kreisman, Rachelle. Places We Go: A Kids' Guide to Community Sites. Haggerty, Tim, illus. 2015. (Start Smart: Community Ser.). (ENG.). 32p. (gr. 1-3). 26.65 *(978-1-937529-36-9(3))* Red Chair Pr.
Kuskowski, Alex. Know Your Numbers: School, 1 vol. 2014. (Numbers 1-20 Ser.). (ENG.). 24p. (J). (gr. k-3). lib. bdg. 24.21 *(978-1-62403-267-7(2),* SandCastle) ABDO Publishing Co.
A la Escuela: Individual Title Six-Packs. (Chiquilibros Ser.). (SPA.). (gr. k-1). 23.00 *(978-0-7635-8594-5(7))* Rigby Education.
Laval, Thierry. Look & Find at School. 2017. (Mini Look & Find Ser.). (ENG.). 14p. (J). 9.95 ***(978-0-531-23081-7(3),*** Children's Pr.) Scholastic Library Publishing.
Lawrence, Ellen. Time for School. 2015. (My World Your World Ser.). (ENG.). 24p. (J). (gr. -1-3). lib. bdg. 23.93 *(978-1-910549-04-9(5))* Bearport Publishing Co., Inc.
Layne, Deborah & Layne, Stephen L. T Is for Teachers: A School Alphabet. Ettlinger, Doris, illus. rev. ed. 2005. (ENG.). 40p. (J). (gr. k-6). 14.95 *(978-1-58536-266-0(2))* Sleeping Bear Pr.
Learning Express Editors. Catholic High School Entrance Exams. 5th ed. 2013. (ENG.). 256p. pap. 18.95 *(978-1-57685-933-9(9))* LearningExpress, LLC.
LeBlanc, Terry. Learning to Recycle with Terry the Trashman. 2004. (J). pap. *(978-0-9755913-0-7(4))* LeBlanc, Terry Leonard.
Lee, April. Helping at School. 2012. (InfoMax Readers Ser.). (ENG., Illus.). 16 pp.p. (J). (gr. k-1). pap. 7.00 *(978-1-4488-8896-2(4),* Rosen Classroom) Rosen Publishing Group, Inc., The.
Lee, Sally. School Long Ago & Today, 1 vol. 2014. (Long Ago & Today Ser.). (ENG.). 24p. (gr. 1-2). 25.32 *(978-1-4914-0296-2(2))* Capstone Press of Coughlan Cos.
Lewis, Clare. Schools Around the World, 1 vol. 2014. (Around the World Ser.). (ENG., Illus.). 24p. (gr. -1-1). 22.65 *(978-1-4846-0370-3(2),* Acorn) Heinemann-Raintree.
Listen & Learn Get Ready for School. 2017. (Listen & Learn First Words Ser.). (ENG.). (J). bds. 19.99 ***(978-0-7945-3985-6(8),*** Usborne) EDC Publishing.
Lucas, Eileen. The Little Rock Nine Stand up for Their Rights. Gustavson, Adam, illus. 2011. 48p. pap. 9.95 *(978-0-7613-7118-2(4));* pap. 56.72 *(978-0-7613-7634-7(8));* (ENG.). (gr. 2-4). lib. bdg. 27.93 *(978-0-7613-5874-9(9),* Millbrook Pr.) Lerner Publishing Group.
Lunis, Natalie. Spooky Schools. 2013. (Scary Places Ser.). 32p. (J). (gr. 4-8). lib. bdg. 25.27 *(978-1-61772-750-4(4))* Bearport Publishing Co., Inc.
Manton, Charlotte. The Community of Lincoln. Stanley, Karen & Bornemeier, Pam, eds. Schellpeper, Kathy, photos by. (Illus.). 116p. (J). (gr. 3-6). pap. 10.50 *(978-0-9671920-0-0(5))* Lincoln Public Schls.
Mara, Wil. The Schoolmaster. 2010. (Colonial People Ser.). 48p. (gr. 3-18). 29.93 *(978-0-7614-4801-3(2))* Marshall Cavendish Corp.
Marks, Jennifer L. School Times, 1 vol. 2010. (Spot It Ser.). (ENG.). 32p. lib. bdg. 8.99 *(978-1-4296-5761-7(8),* Pebble Bks.) Capstone Press of Coughlan Cos.
Marsico, Katie. Good Manners at School, 1 vol. Haslam, John, illus. 2009. (Good Manners Matter! Ser.). (ENG.). 32p. (J). (gr. -1-2). 28.50 *(978-1-60270-608-8(5))* Magic Wagon.
Mattern, Joanne. After School. 2006. (My Day at School Ser.). (Illus.). 24p. (gr. k-3). pap. 8.15 *(978-0-8368-6790-9(4));* lib. bdg. 22.00 *(978-0-8368-6783-1(1))* Stevens, Gareth Publishing LLLP. (Weekly Reader Leveled Readers).
—Eating Lunch at School. 2006. (My Day at School Ser.). 24p. (gr. k-3). pap. 8.15 *(978-0-8368-6791-6(2));* (Illus.). lib. bdg. 22.00 *(978-0-8368-6784-8(X))* Stevens, Gareth Publishing LLLP. (Weekly Reader Leveled Readers).
—Getting Ready for School. 2006. (My Day at School Ser.). (Illus.). 24p. (gr. k-3). pap. 8.15 *(978-0-8368-6792-3(0));* lib. bdg. 22.00 *(978-0-8368-6785-5(8))* Stevens, Gareth Publishing LLLP. (Weekly Reader Leveled Readers).
—Going to School. 2006. (My Day at School Ser.). (Illus.). 24p. (gr. k-3). lib. bdg. 22.00 *(978-0-8368-6786-2(6),* Weekly Reader Leveled Readers) Stevens, Gareth Publishing LLLP.
—In the Classroom. 2006. (My Day at School Ser.). (Illus.). 24p. (gr. k-3). pap. 8.15 *(978-0-8368-6794-7(7));* lib. bdg. 22.00 *(978-0-8368-6787-9(4))* Stevens, Gareth Publishing LLLP. (Weekly Reader Leveled Readers).
—In the Classroom (en el salón de Clases) 2006. (My Day at School/ Mi dia en la escuela Ser.). (SPA., Illus.). 24p. (gr. k-3). lib. bdg. 22.00 *(978-0-8368-7361-0(0),* Weekly Reader Leveled Readers) Stevens, Gareth Publishing LLLP.
—Playing at School. 2006. (My Day at School Ser.). (Illus.). 24p. (gr. k-3). pap. 8.15 *(978-0-8368-6795-4(5));* lib. bdg. 22.00 *(978-0-8368-6788-6(2))* Stevens, Gareth Publishing LLLP. (Weekly Reader Leveled Readers).
—Staying Safe at School/la Seguridad en la Escuela. 2007. (Safety First / la Seguridad Es lo Primero Ser.). (ENG & SPA., Illus.). 24p. (gr. k-3). lib. bdg. 22.00 *(978-0-8368-8057-1(9),* Weekly Reader Leveled Readers) Stevens, Gareth Publishing LLLP.
—Staying Safe at School/La Seguridad en La Escuela. 2007. (Safety First / la Seguridad Es lo Primero Ser.). 24p. (gr. k-3). (ENG & SPA.). pap. 8.15 *(978-0-8368-8064-9(1));* (Illus.). pap. 8.15 *(978-0-8368-7799-1(3));* (Illus.). lib. bdg. 22.00 *(978-0-8368-7792-2(6))* Stevens, Gareth Publishing LLLP. (Weekly Reader Leveled Readers).
Mayer, Kirsten. Meet the Ghouls Character Guidebook. 2014. (ENG., Illus.). 96p. (J). (gr. 3-7). 9.99 *(978-0-316-28361-8(4))* Little, Brown Bks. for Young Readers.
Meister, Cari. La Biblioteca Pública. 2016. (Los Primeros Viajes Escolares (First Field Trips)).Tr. of Public Library. (SPA.). 24p. (J). (gr. k-2). lib. bdg. 25.65 *(978-1-62031-327-5(8),* Bullfrog Bks.) Jump! Inc.
—El Museo de Arte. 2016. (Los Primeros Viajes Escolares (First Field Trips)).Tr. of Art Museum. (SPA.). 24p. (J). (gr. k-2). lib. bdg. 25.65 *(978-1-62031-331-2(6),* Bullfrog Bks.) Jump! Inc.
—Public Library. Fretland VanVoorst, Jenny, ed. 2016. (First Field Trips). 24p. (J). (gr. k-2). lib. bdg. 25.65 *(978-1-62031-296-4(4),* Bullfrog Bks.) Jump! Inc.
Meyer, Terry. Navigating a New School. 2012. (Middle School Survival Handbook Ser.). (ENG., Illus.). 64p. (YA). (gr. 5-8). lib. bdg. 31.95 *(978-1-4488-8312-7(1),* Rosen Reference) Rosen Publishing Group, Inc., The.
Meyer, Terry Teague. Navigating a New School. 2012. (Middle School Survival Handbook Ser.). (ENG., Illus.). 64p. (YA). (gr. 5-8). pap. 12.95 *(978-1-4488-8319-6(9),* Rosen Reference) Rosen Publishing Group, Inc., The.
Michele, Tracey. Map the School. 2011. (ENG., Illus.). 16p. (J). pap. 7.95 *(978-1-59920-590-8(4))* Black Rabbit Bks.
—My School, Your School. 2011. (Learn-Abouts Ser.). (ENG., Illus.). 16p. (J). pap. 7.95 *(978-1-59920-605-9(6))* Black Rabbit Bks.
Milet Publishing Staff. My First Bilingual Book - School. 2014. (My First Bilingual Book Ser.). (Illus.). 20p. (J). (— 1). (FRE & ENG.). bds. 7.99 *(978-1-84059-894-0(8));* (ENG & BEN., bds. 7.99 *(978-1-84059-891-9(3));* (POR & ENG., bds. 7.99 *(978-1-84059-899-5(9));* (ENG & VIE., bds. 7.99 *(978-1-84059-905-3(7));* (ENG & TUR., bds. 7.99 *(978-1-84059-903-9(0));* (ENG & PER., bds. 7.99 *(978-1-84059-893-3(X));* (ENG & CHI., bds. 7.99 *(978-1-84059-892-6(1));* (ENG & GER., bds. 7.99 *(978-1-84059-895-7(6))* Milet Publishing.
—My First Bilingual Book - School (English-Korean) 2014. (My First Bilingual Book Ser.). (ENG & KOR., Illus.). 20p. (J). (— 1). bds. 7.99 *(978-1-84059-897-1(2))* Milet Publishing.
—My First Bilingual Book - School (English-Somali) 2014. (My First Bilingual Book Ser.). (ENG & SOM., Illus.). 20p. (J). (— 1). bds. 7.99 *(978-1-84059-901-5(4))* Milet Publishing.
—School. 2014. (My First Bilingual Book Ser.). (ENG & ITA., Illus.). 20p. (J). (— 1). bds. 7.99 *(978-1-84059-896-4(4))* Milet Publishing.
—School - My First Bilingual Book. 2014. (My First Bilingual Book Ser.). (Illus.). 20p. (J). (— 1). (ENG & ARA.). bds. 7.99 *(978-1-84059-890-2(5));* (ENG & RUS., bds. 7.99 *(978-1-84059-900-8(6));* (ENG & URD., bds. 7.99 *(978-1-84059-904-6(9));* (SPA & ENG., bds. 7.99 *(978-1-84059-902-2(2))* Milet Publishing.
—School - My First Bilingual Book (Szkoła) 2014. (My First Bilingual Book Ser.). (ENG, POL & POR., Illus.). 20p. (J). (— 1). bds. 7.99 *(978-1-84059-898-8(0))* Milet Publishing.
Milla Gorilla Goes to School. 2004. pap. 1.50 *(978-0-87162-934-0(8))* Warner Pr., Inc.
Miller, Amanda. We Help Out at School. 2009. (Scholastic News Nonfiction Readers Ser.). (ENG.). 24p. (J). pap. 6.95 *(978-0-531-21449-7(4));* (gr. 1-2). lib. bdg. 22.00 *(978-0-531-21345-2(5))* Scholastic Library Publishing. (Children's Pr.).
Miller, Jake. Who's Who in a School Community. 2005. (Communities at Work Ser.). (ENG., Illus.). 24p. (gr. 2-3). pap. 8.25 *(978-1-4042-5030-7(1),* PowerKids Pr.) Rosen Publishing Group, Inc., The.
—Who's Who in School Community. (Communities at Work Ser.). 24p. (gr. 2-2). 2009. 42.50 *(978-1-61511-902-8(7))* 2005. (Illus.). (J). lib. bdg. 22.60 *(978-1-4042-2788-0(1))* Rosen Publishing Group, Inc., The. (PowerKids Pr.).
Miller, Reagan. 100th Day of School. 2010. (ENG., Illus.). 32p. (J). *(978-0-7787-4763-5(8));* pap. *(978-0-7787-4781-9(6))* Crabtree Publishing Co.
Mills, Nathan & Rose, Craig. We Help at School. 2012. (Rosen Readers Ser.). (ENG., Illus.). 16p. (J). (gr. k-1). pap. 7.00 *(978-1-4488-8661-6(9),* Rosen Classroom) Rosen Publishing Group, Inc., The.
Mills, Nathan & Sotherden, Nora. Our Classroom Rules. 2012. (Rosen Readers Ser.). (ENG., Illus.). 16p. (J). (gr. k-1). pap. 7.00 *(978-1-4488-8692-0(9),* Rosen Classroom) Rosen Publishing Group, Inc., The.
Modoc Press Editors. Directory of Distance Learning Opportunities: K-12, 1 vol. 2003. 432p. (C). (gr. k-12). 96.00 *(978-1-57356-515-8(6),* OXDLK-12, Greenwood) ABC-CLIO, LLC.
Mortensen, Lori. Manners Matter in the Classroom. Hunt, Lisa, illus. (First Graphics: Manners Matter Ser.). (ENG.). 24p. (gr. 1-2). 2011. pap. 35.70 *(978-1-4296-6392-2(8))* 2010. lib. bdg. 23.99 *(978-1-4296-5333-6(7))* Capstone Press of Coughlan Cos.
—Manners Matter on a Field Trip, 1 vol. Hunt, Lisa, illus. 2010. (First Graphics: Manners Matter Ser.). (ENG.). 24p. (gr. 1-2). lib. bdg. 23.99 *(978-1-4296-5331-2(0))* Capstone Press of Coughlan Cos.
Mortenson, Greg. Stones into Schools: Promoting Peace, One School at a Time. 2011. (ENG.). 240p. (J). (gr. 3-18). 16.99 *(978-0-8037-3687-0(8),* Dial) Penguin Publishing Group.
Mortenson, Greg & Roth, Susan L. Listen to the Wind: The Story of Dr. Greg & Three Cups of Tea. Roth, Susan L., illus. 2009. (Rise & Shine Ser.). (ENG., Illus.). 32p. (J). (gr. 1-3). 16.99 *(978-0-8037-3058-8(6),* Dial Bks) Penguin Young Readers Group.
Moss, Marissa. Amelia's School Survival Guide. Moss, Marissa, illus. 2006. (Amelia Ser.). (ENG., Illus.). 64p. (J). (gr. 2-5). 12.99 *(978-1-4169-0915-6(X),* Simon & Schuster/Paula Wiseman Bks.) Simon & Schuster/Paula Wiseman Bks.
Mullins, Matt. How Did They Build That? School. 2009. (Community Connections: How Did They Build That? Ser.). (ENG.). 24p. (gr. 2-5). lib. bdg. 25.64 *(978-1-60279-487-0(1),* 200257) Cherry Lake Publishing.
Murkoff, Heidi. What to Expect at Preschool. Rader, Laura, illus. 2003. (What to Expect Kids Ser.). (ENG.). 24p. (J). (gr. -1-k). pap. 3.99 *(978-0-06-052920-8(2),* HarperFestival) HarperCollins Pubs.
Murphy, Terri, illus. My School. 2010. (My World Ser.). (ENG.). 24p. (J). (gr. -1-1). pap. 8.15 *(978-1-61533-039-3(9));* lib. bdg. 22.60 *(978-1-60754-953-6(0))* Windmill Bks.
Myers, Dean. School. 2006. *(978-0-06-052311-4(5));* lib. bdg. *(978-0-06-052312-1(3))* HarperCollins Canada, Ltd.
Nagle, Jeanne. Reducing Your Carbon Footprint at School. 2009. (Your Carbon Footprint Ser.). 48p. (gr. 5-5). 53.00 *(978-1-60854-911-5(9),* Rosen Reference) Rosen Publishing Group, Inc., The.
Nations, Susan. Things at School. 2006. (Things in My World Ser.). (Illus.). 16p. (gr. -1-2). lib. bdg. 19.00 *(978-0-8368-6808-1(0),* Weekly Reader Leveled Readers) Stevens, Gareth Publishing LLLP.
Nunn, Daniel & Smith, Sian. Manners at School, 1 vol. 2012. (Oh, Behave! Ser.). (ENG.). 24p. (gr. -1-1). lib. bdg. 22.65 *(978-1-4329-6637-9(5),* Acorn) Heinemann-Raintree.
O'Connell, Eleanor. Schools Around the World. 2016. (Adventures in Culture Ser.). 00024p. (J). pap. 8.15 *(978-1-4824-5589-2(7))* Stevens, Gareth Publishing LLLP.
Orr, Tamra. Violence in Our Schools: Halls of Hope, Halls of Fear. 2003. (Single Title: Social Studies Ser.). (ENG., Illus.). 192p. (YA). 30.50 *(978-0-531-12268-6(9),* Watts, Franklin) Scholastic Library Publishing.
Owens, L. L. Go to School, 1 vol. Davidson, Chris, illus. 2010. (Let's Be Social Ser.). (ENG.). 32p. 28.50 *(978-1-60270-799-3(5),* Looking Glass Library- Nonfiction) Magic Wagon.
Owenz, Roger. Mr Owenz Goes to School. 2009. 24p. pap. 12.99 *(978-1-4490-2655-4(9))* AuthorHouse.
Palmer, Erin. Summer School, Yes or No. 2016. (Seeing Both Sides Ser.). (ENG.). 32p. (gr. 3-6). 32.79 *(978-1-68191-385-8(2))* Rourke Educational Media.
Parramón, José María. Borday, Irene, illus. (Coleccion Estoy En...).Tr. of My Street. (SPA.). 32p. (J). (gr. k-3). 6.36 *(978-84-342-1003-5(7))* Parramon Ediciones S.A. ESP. Dist: Lectorum Pubns., Inc.
—Mi Casa. Borday, Irene, illus. (Coleccion Estoy En...).Tr. of My House. (SPA.). 32p. (J). (gr. k-3). 6.36 *(978-84-342-1002-8(9))* Parramon Ediciones S.A. ESP. Dist: Lectorum Pubns., Inc.
—Mi Jardin. Borday, Irene, illus. (Coleccion Estoy En...).Tr. of My Garden. (SPA.). 32p. (J). (gr. k-3). 6.36 *(978-84-342-1005-9(3))* Parramon Ediciones S.A. ESP. Dist: Lectorum Pubns., Inc.
Parramón, José María & Bordoy, Irene. Mi Calle.Tr. of My Street. (SPA., Illus.). (J). (gr. -1-1). 6.95 *(978-958-04-1277-9(4))* Norma S.A. COL. Dist: Distribuidora Norma, Inc.
Peirce, Lincoln. Big Nate - Say Good-Bye to Dork City. 2015. (Big Nate Ser.). (ENG., Illus.). 224p. (J). 9.99 *(978-1-4494-6225-3(1))* Andrews McMeel Publishing.
Pettiford, Rebecca. El Zoológico. 2016. (Los Primeros Viajes Escolares (First Field Trips)).Tr. of Zoo. (SPA.). 24p. (J). (gr. k-2). lib. bdg. 25.65 *(978-1-62031-333-6(2),* Bullfrog Bks.) Jump! Inc.
Phillips, Clifton C. Rabbits Rule at Night School. 2008. 28p. pap. 8.99 *(978-1-935105-02-2(7))* Avid Readers Publishing Group.
Puppet Rescue, creator. Yaker Goes to School. 2007. (Illus.). 10p. (J). 4.95 *(978-0-9799958-2-8(5))* Puppet Rescue.
Raatma, Lucia. Staying Safe on the School Bus, 1 vol. 2011. (Staying Safe Ser.). (ENG.). 24p. (gr. 1-2). lib. bdg. 25.32 *(978-1-4296-6823-1(7),* First Facts) Capstone Press of Coughlan Cos.
Randolph, Ryan P. Frontier Schools & Schoolteachers. 2009. (Library of the Westward Expansion Ser.). 24p. (gr. 3-4). 42.50 *(978-1-60853-935-2(0),* PowerKids Pr.) Rosen Publishing Group, Inc., The.
Rau, Dana Meachen. School Safety: Seguridad en la Escuela. 2009. (Bookworms — Bilingual Editions: Safe Kids/Ninos Seguros Ser.). (SPA & ENG.). 32p. (gr. k-2). lib. bdg. 15.95 *(978-0-7614-4782-5(2))* Marshall Cavendish Corp.
Rau, Dana Meachen & Meachen Rau, Dana. School Safety: Seguridad en la Escuela. 2009. (Bookworms: Safe Kids Ser.). (SPA & ENG.). 32p. (gr. k-2). 15.95 *(978-0-7614-4090-1(9))* Marshall Cavendish Corp.

S

Raymer, Dottie. School Smarts Projects. McGuinness, Tracy & McGuinness, Tracey, illus. 2007. (American Girl Library). (ENG.). 96p. (J). (gr. 3-7). pap. 8.95 (978-1-59369-005-2(3), American Girl) American Girl Publishing, Inc.

Reid, Stephanie. School, 1 vol. 2011. (Early Childhood Themes Ser.). (ENG.). 16p. (J). (gr. -1-2). pap. 19.99 (978-1-4333-2354-6(0)); pap. 6.99 (978-1-4333-2353-9(2)) Teacher Created Materials, Inc.

Remember: The Journey to School Integration-Display. 2004. (ENG.). 1p. (J). tchr. ed. 162.00 (978-0-618-45334-4(2)) Houghton Mifflin Harcourt Publishing Co.

Rhodes, Corey L. Keep Your Head Up! 2010. 24p. 16.99 (978-1-4490-7580-4(0)) AuthorHouse.

Rice, Dona & Petersen, Casey Null. School Around the World, 1 vol. 2nd rev. ed. 2011. (Nonfiction Readers Ser.). (ENG.). 28p. (J). (gr. 3-3). pap. 8.99 (978-1-4333-3654-6(5)) Teacher Created Materials, Inc.

Rice, Dona Herweck. Big Kid School, 1 vol. 2011. (Early Childhood Themes Ser.). (ENG.). 16p. (J). (gr. -1-2). pap. 6.99 (978-1-4333-2355-3(9)); pap. 19.99 (978-1-4333-2356-0(7)) Teacher Created Materials, Inc.

Rice, Dona Herweck & Petersen, Casey Null. School Around the World, 1 vol. 2nd rev. ed. 2013. (Nonfiction Readers Ser.). (ENG., Illus.). 28p. (J). (gr. 3-3). pap. 25.96 (978-1-4807-1069-6(5)) Shell Educational Publishing.

Ridley, Sarah. School. 2017. (Tell Me What You Remember Ser.). (ENG., Illus.). 24p. (J). (gr. k-2). 17.99 (978-1-4451-4009-4(8), Franklin Watts) Hachette Children's Group GBR. Dist: Hachette Bk. Group.

Rissman, Rebecca. Going to a Beach, 1 vol. 2012. (World of Field Trips Ser.). (ENG.). 24p. (gr. -1-1). lib. bdg. 22.65 (978-1-4329-6064-3(4), Acorn) Heinemann-Raintree.

—Going to a Concert, 1 vol. 2012. (World of Field Trips Ser.). (ENG.). 24p. (gr. -1-1). lib. bdg. 22.65 (978-1-4329-6065-0(2), Acorn) Heinemann-Raintree.

—Going to a Farm, 1 vol. 2012. (World of Field Trips Ser.). (ENG.). 24p. (gr. -1-1). pap. 6.29 (978-1-4329-6075-9(X)); lib. bdg. 22.65 (978-1-4329-6066-7(0)) Heinemann-Raintree. (Acorn).

—Going to a Library, 1 vol. 2012. (World of Field Trips Ser.). (ENG.). 24p. (gr. -1-1). lib. bdg. 22.65 (978-1-4329-6071-1(7), Acorn) Heinemann-Raintree.

—Going to a Museum, 1 vol. 2012. (World of Field Trips Ser.). (ENG.). 24p. (gr. -1-1). pap. 6.29 (978-1-4329-6076-6(8)); lib. bdg. 22.65 (978-1-4329-6067-4(9)) Heinemann-Raintree. (Acorn).

—Going to a Park, 1 vol. 2012. (World of Field Trips Ser.). (ENG.). 24p. (gr. -1-1). lib. bdg. 22.65 (978-1-4329-6068-1(7), Acorn) Heinemann-Raintree.

—Going to a Stadium, 1 vol. 2012. (World of Field Trips Ser.). (ENG.). 24p. (gr. -1-1). lib. bdg. 22.65 (978-1-4329-6069-8(5), Acorn) Heinemann-Raintree.

—Going to a Zoo, 1 vol. 2012. (World of Field Trips Ser.). (ENG.). 24p. (gr. -1-1). lib. bdg. 22.65 (978-1-4329-6070-4(9), Acorn) Heinemann-Raintree.

—Going to School: Comparing Past & Present, 1 vol. 2014. (Comparing Past & Present Ser.). (ENG., Illus.). 24p. (gr. -1-1). pap. 6.95 (978-1-4329-9025-1(X)); lib. bdg. 22.65 (978-1-4329-8991-0(X)) Heinemann-Raintree. (Acorn).

Rivera, Sheila. School Safety. 2007. (First Step Nonfiction - Safety Ser.). (ENG., Illus.). 8p. (J). (gr. -1-1). pap. 4.95 (978-0-8225-6822-3(5)) Lerner Publishing Group.

Robertson, David Alexander. Sugar Falls: A Residential School Story. Henderson, Scott B., illus. 2012. (ENG.). 40p. (YA). (gr. 9-12). pap. (978-1-55379-334-2(X), 9781553793342, HighWater Pr.) Portage & Main Pr.

Rookie Preschool, 12 vols., Set. Incl. Ants Go Marching. Childrens Press Staff. 23.00 (978-0-531-24406-7(7), Children's Pr.); Busy Day, Busy Night: Rain Forest. Hendra, Sue. 23.00 (978-0-531-24407-4(5), Children's Pr.); It's Circle Time! Shapes. Perez, Nomar. 23.00 (978-0-531-24401-2(6)); Jack's Room. Woolf, Julia. 23.00 (978-0-531-24400-5(8), Children's Pr.); Leaves Fall All Around. Mack, Steve. 23.00 (978-0-531-24402-9(4)); Piglets Belong to Pigs. Children's Press, contrib. by. 23.00 (978-0-531-24408-1(3), Children's Pr.); Red, Blue, & Yellow Too! Children's Press, contrib. by. lib. bdg. 23.00 (978-0-531-24403-6(2), Children's Pr.); Sing a Song of Seasons. Children's Press, contrib. by. lib. bdg. 23.00 (978-0-531-24409-8(1), Children's Pr.); Three Little Kittens Get Dressed. Scholastic Library Publishing. lib. bdg. 23.00 (978-0-531-24404-3(0), Children's Pr.); What's the Weather? Rockwell, Lizzy & Fowler, Allan. lib. bdg. 23.00 (978-0-531-24410-4(5)); Who Is Sleeping? Sapp, Karen. lib. bdg. 23.00 (978-0-531-24411-1(3), Children's Pr.); 3-2-1 School Is Fun! Haley, Amanda. 23.00 (978-0-531-24405-0(9)); 24p. (J). (gr. -1). 2009. Set lib. bdg. 276.00 (978-0-531-22775-6(8)) Scholastic Library Publishing.

Rosa-Mendoza, Gladys. My School/Mi Escuela. Murphy, Terri, illus. 2007. (English Spanish Foundations Ser.). (ENG & SPA.). (J). (gr. -1-k). bds. 6.95 (978-1-931398-23-7(2)) Me+Mi Publishing.

Rustad, Martha. Michael Makes Friends at School. Becker, Paula, illus. 2017. (Cloverleaf Books (tm) — off to School Ser.). (ENG.). (J). (gr. k-2). pap. 7.99 **(978-1-5124-5577-9(6))**; lib. bdg. 25.32 **(978-1-5124-3937-3(1))** Lerner Publishing Group. (Millbrook Pr.).

Ruurs, Margriet. My School in the Rain Forest: How Children Attend School Around the World. 2009. (ENG., Illus.). 32p. (J). (gr. 2-4). 17.95 (978-1-59078-601-7(7)) Boyds Mills Pr.

—School Days Around the World. Feagan, Alice, illus. 2015. (Around the World Ser.). (ENG.). 40p. (J). (gr. -1-2). 18.95 (978-1-77138-047-8(0)) Kids Can Pr., Ltd. CAN. Dist: Hachette Bk. Group.

Salzmann, Mary Elizabeth. Money for School, 1 vol. 2010. (Your Piggy Bank: A Guide to Spending & Saving for Kids! Ser.). (ENG.). 24p. (J). (gr. k-3). 27.07 (978-1-61641-031-5(0)) Magic Wagon.

Scholastic News Nonfiction Readers: Kids Like Me (Global Awareness), 5 vols., Set. Incl. This Is the Way We Dress. Behrens, Janice. lib. bdg. 22.00 (978-0-531-21338-4(2)); This Is the Way We Eat Our Food. Falk, Laine. lib. bdg. 22.00 (978-0-531-21339-1(0)); This Is the Way We Go to School. Falk, Laine. lib. bdg. 22.00 (978-0-531-21341-4(2)); This Is the Way We Help at Home. Miller, Amanda. lib. bdg. 22.00 (978-0-531-21340-7(4)); This Is the Way We Play. Miller, Amanda. lib. bdg. 22.00 (978-0-531-21342-1(0)); 24p. (J). (gr. 1-2). 2009. Set lib. bdg. 110.00 (978-0-531-21035-2(9), Children's Pr.) Scholastic Library Publishing.

Scholl, Elizabeth. New York City. 2009. (Class Trip Ser.). (Illus.). 48p. (J). (gr. 2-5). lib. bdg. 29.95 (978-1-58415-808-0(5)) Mitchell Lane Pubs., Inc.

School. 2007. (Busy Books Large Ser.). 5p. (978-1-4054-9499-1(9)); (978-1-4054-9495-3(6)) Parragon, Inc.

The School Rules. 2015. (School Rules Ser.). (ENG.). 24p. (gr. k-k). 135.60 (978-1-4824-2541-3(6)); pap., pap., pap. 48.90 (978-1-4824-3497-2(0)) Stevens, Gareth Publishing LLLP.

Scraper, Katherine. Rules at School. 2006. (Early Explorers Ser.). (J). pap. (978-1-4108-6030-9(2)) Benchmark Education Co.

Senge, Peter, et al. Escuelas Que Aprenden: Un Manual de la Quinta Disciplina para Educadores, Padres de Familiar y Todos los Que Se Interesen en la Educacion. Nannetti, Jorge Cardenas, tr. 2006. (Coleccion Vitral Ser.). (SPA., Illus.). 630p. per. (978-958-04-6511-9(8)) Norma S.A. COL. Dist: Distribuidora Norma, Inc.

Sesame Street Staff, creator. Sesame Street: Elmo & Me! Boxed Set. 2011. 40p. (J). bds. 12.99 (978-1-60745-166-2(2)) Flying Frog Pubs.

Sévigny, Éric, illus. Caillou Goes to School. 2016. (Clubhouse Ser.). (ENG.). 24p. (J). (gr. -1-k). pap. 3.99 (978-2-89718-313-4(6)) Caillouet, Gerry.

Sévigny, Éric, illus. Caillou Va À l'École. 2017. (Château de Cartes Ser.). (FRE.). 24p. (J). (gr. -1). 3.99 **(978-2-89718-314-1(4))** Caillouet, Gerry.

Shapiro, Ouisie. Bullying & Me: Schoolyard Stories, 1 vol. Vote, Steven, photos by. 2010. (ENG., Illus.). 32p. (J). (gr. 3-7). 16.99 (978-0-8075-0921-0(3)) Whitman, Albert & Co.

Sharp, Anne Wallace. Separate but Equal: The Desegregation of America's Schools. 2006. (Lucent Library of Black History). (ENG., Illus.). 104p. (J). (gr. 3-7). lib. bdg. 33.45 (978-1-59018-953-5(1), Lucent Bks.) Cengage Gale.

Shava, Ryder. We Come to School to Learn, 01 vols., 1. 2016. (Rosen REAL Readers: Social Studies Nonfiction / Fiction: Family, Community, & the World Ser.). (ENG.). 8p. (J). pap. 5.46 (978-1-5081-1659-2(8), Rosen Classroom) Rosen Publishing Group, Inc., The.

Silva, Sadie. Finding My School: Sticking to It. 2017. (Computer Science for the Real World Ser.). 8p. (gr. 5-6). pap. 6.20 **(978-1-5383-5113-0(7)**, Rosen Classroom) Rosen Publishing Group, Inc., The.

The Smartest One in Class: Individual Title Six-Packs. (gr. -1-2). 27.00 (978-0-7635-9474-9(1)) Rigby Education.

Smith, Julie. The Magic Pencil: Happy Birthday Kuser Elementary School 1909-2009. 2009. 44p. pap. 19.00 (978-1-4389-7246-6(6)) AuthorHouse.

Smith, Paula. Be the Change in Your School. 2014. (ENG., Illus.). 24p. (J). (978-0-7787-0626-7(5)) Crabtree Publishing Co.

—Schools in Different Places. 2015. (Learning about Our Global Community Ser.). (ENG., Illus.). 24p. (J). (978-0-7787-2013-3(6)) Crabtree Publishing Co.

Stern, Leonard & Price, Roger. Escape from Detention Mad Libs. 2013. (Mad Libs Ser.). (ENG.). 48p. (J). (gr. 3-7). 4.99 (978-0-8431-7379-6(3), Mad Libs) Penguin Young Readers Group.

Stewart, Faith. Teens & Rural Education: Opportunities & Challenges. 2009. (Youth in Rural North America Ser.). (Illus.). 96p. (YA). (gr. 3-7). lib. bdg. 22.95 (978-1-4222-0015-5(9)) Mason Crest.

Swanson Sateren, Shelley. School in Colonial America. 2016. (It's Back to School ... Way Back! Ser.). (ENG., Illus.). 32p. (gr. 3-4). lib. bdg. 27.32 (978-1-5157-2097-3(7), Fact Finders) Capstone Press of Coughlan Cos.

Taylor-Butler, Christine. Think Like a Scientist in the Gym. 2011. (Explorer Junior Library: Science Explorer Junior Ser.). (ENG.). 32p. (gr. 4-8). lib. bdg. 28.50 (978-1-61080-163-8(6), 201096) Cherry Lake Publishing.

Telgemeier, Raina. Smile. 2010. 21.00 (978-1-60686-896-6(9)) Perfection Learning Corp.

—Smile. 2010. (ENG.). 224p. (J). (gr. 3-7). 24.99 (978-0-545-13205-3(3)); (Illus.). pap. 10.99 (978-0-545-13206-0(1)) Scholastic, Inc. (Graphix).

—Smile. 2010. lib. bdg. 22.10 (978-0-606-14082-9(4), Turtleback) Turtleback Bks.

Thaler, Mike. The Class Trip from the Black Lagoon, 1 vol. Lee, Jared, illus. 2011. (Black Lagoon Adventures Ser.: No. 1). (ENG.). 64p. (gr. 3-6). 24.21 (978-1-59961-811-1(7)) Spotlight.

Thornborough, Kathy. School. Petelinsek, Kathleen, illus. 2014. (Talking Hands Ser.). (ENG.). 24p. (J). (gr. k-3). 25.64 (978-1-62687-322-3(4), 207162) Child's World, Inc., The.

Tillman, Charles. The Middle School Rules of Charles Tillman. 2015. (Middle School Rules Ser.). (ENG., Illus.). 176p. (J). (gr. 4-8). 14.99 (978-1-4245-5101-9(3)) BroadStreet Publishing.

Top That Publishing Staff, ed. My School Days Yearbook. 2005. (Illus.). 28p. (978-1-84510-657-7(1)) Top That! Publishing PLC.

Vogel, Elizabeth. Meet the Cafeteria Workers. 2009. (My School Ser.). 24p. (gr. 1-2). 37.50 (978-1-61514-705-2(5), PowerKids Pr.) Rosen Publishing Group, Inc., The.

—Meet the Librarian. 2009. (My School Ser.). 24p. (gr. 1-2). 37.50 (978-1-61514-706-9(3), PowerKids Pr.) Rosen Publishing Group, Inc., The.

—My School, 6 bks. Incl. Meet My Teacher. lib. bdg. 18.75 (978-0-8239-6032-3(3)); Meet the Cafeteria Workers. lib. bdg. 18.75 (978-0-8239-6035-4(8)); Meet the Librarian. lib. bdg. 18.75 (978-0-8239-6031-6(5)); Meet the Principal. lib. bdg. 18.75 (978-0-8239-6033-0(1)); Meet the School Nurse. lib. bdg. 18.75 (978-0-8239-6034-7(X)); Meet the School Secretary. lib. bdg. 18.75 (978-0-8239-6036-1(6)); 24p. (J). (gr. 1). 2002. (Illus.). Set lib. bdg. 88.50 (978-0-8239-7114-5(7), PowerKids Pr.) Rosen Publishing Group, Inc., The.

Watt, Fiona. Sticker Dolly Dressing Back to School. 2012. (Sticker Dolly Dressing Ser.). 34p. (J). pap. 8.99 (978-0-7945-3303-8(5), Usborne) EDC Publishing.

Weekly Reader Editorial Staff. Things at School (Las Cosas de la Escuela) 2006. (Things in My World/ Las cosas de mi mundo Ser.). (SPA., Illus.). 16p. (gr. -1-2). pap. 5.30 (978-0-8368-7227-9(4), Weekly Reader Leveled Readers) Stevens, Gareth Publishing LLLP.

—Things at School/Las Cosas de la Escuela. 2006. (Things in My World/ Las cosas de mi mundo Ser.). (SPA., Illus.). 16p. (gr. -1-2). lib. bdg. 19.00 (978-0-8368-7220-0(7), Weekly Reader Leveled Readers) Stevens, Gareth Publishing LLLP.

Weekly Reader Editorial Staff, contrib. by. Things at School. 2006. (Things in My World Ser.). (Illus.). 16p. (gr. -1-2). pap. 5.30 (978-0-8368-6815-9(3), Weekly Reader Leveled Readers) Stevens, Gareth Publishing LLLP.

Whitney, Brooks. How to Master the School Universe: Homework, Teachers, Tests, Bullies, & Other Ways to Survive the Classroom. Kennedy, Kelly, illus. 2004. 80p. (J). pap. (978-0-439-57902-5(3)) Scholastic, Inc.

Wright, Pamela. Rant Room. 2011. 82p. pap. 19.95 (978-1-4560-9428-7(9)) America Star Bks.

SCHOOLS—ADMINISTRATION

see School Management And Organization

SCHOOLS, COMMERCIAL

see Business Education

SCHOOLS—FICTION

see also Universities and Colleges—Fiction

Abbott, Simon, illus. Happy Street - School. 2016. (Happy Street Ser.). (ENG.). 10p. (J). (gr. -1-k). bds. 9.99 (978-1-4052-7522-4(7)) Egmont Bks., Ltd. GBR. Dist: Independent Pubs. Group.

Abbott, Tony. Firegirl. 2007. (ENG.). 160p. (J). (gr. 3-7). pap. 7.99 (978-0-316-01170-9(3)) Little, Brown Bks. for Young Readers.

Abdel-Fattah, Randa. Does My Head Look Big in This? 2007. 360p. (YA). 25.66 (978-1-4287-4610-7(2)); 25.66 (978-1-4287-4610-7(2)) Follett School Solutions. (Follettbound).

—Does My Head Look Big in This? 2008. (ENG.). 368p. (J). (gr. 7). pap. 9.99 (978-0-439-92233-3(X), Scholastic Paperbacks) Scholastic, Inc.

Abdo, Kenny. All for a Game, 1 vol. Doucet, Bob, illus. 2013. (Haven't Got a Clue! Ser.). (ENG.). 80p. (J). (gr. 3-6). lib. bdg. 27.07 (978-1-61641-950-9(4), Calico Chapter Bks) Magic Wagon.

—Comic Relief, 1 vol. Doucet, Bob, illus. 2013. (Haven't Got a Clue! Ser.). (ENG.). 80p. (J). (gr. 3-6). lib. bdg. 27.07 (978-1-61641-951-6(2), Calico Chapter Bks) Magic Wagon.

—Duck, Dive, Rock & Roll, 1 vol. Doucet, Bob, illus. 2013. (Haven't Got a Clue! Ser.). (ENG.). 80p. (J). (gr. 3-6). lib. bdg. 27.07 (978-1-61641-952-3(0), Calico Chapter Bks) Magic Wagon.

—Give Me Liberty or Give Me Detention!, 1 vol. Doucet, Bob, illus. 2013. (Haven't Got a Clue! Ser.). (ENG.). 80p. (J). (gr. 3-6). lib. bdg. 27.07 (978-1-61641-953-0(9), Calico Chapter Bks) Magic Wagon.

—Psych-Out!, 1 vol. Doucet, Bob, illus. 2013. (Haven't Got a Clue! Ser.). (ENG.). 80p. (J). (gr. 3-6). lib. bdg. 27.07 (978-1-61641-954-7(7), Calico Chapter Bks) Magic Wagon.

—Triple Take, 1 vol. Doucet, Bob, illus. 2013. (Haven't Got a Clue! Ser.). (ENG.). 80p. (J). (gr. 3-6). lib. bdg. 27.07 (978-1-61641-955-4(5), Calico Chapter Bks) Magic Wagon.

ABDO Publishing Company Staff. Chet Gecko Mysteries - 10 Titles. 2008. (Chet Gecko Mystery Ser.). (J). 242.10 (978-1-59961-460-1(X)) Spotlight.

—Dragon Slayer's Academy. 2006. (Dragon Slayers' Academy Ser.). 112p. (gr. 1-6). 145.26 (978-1-59961-121-1(X)) Spotlight.

Abdul-Jabbar, Kareem. Streetball Crew Book One Sasquatch in the Paint. 2015. (Streetball Crew Ser.). (ENG.). 288p. (J). (gr. 3-7). pap. 7.99 (978-1-4231-9254-1(0)) Hyperion Bks. for Children.

Abdul-Jabbar, Kareem & Obstfeld, Raymond. Sasquatch in the Paint. 2013. (Streetball Crew Ser.). (ENG.). 272p. (J). (gr. 3-7). 16.99 (978-1-4231-7870-5(X)) Hyperion Pr.

Aber, Linda Williams. Quien Tiene Manchas; Who's Got Spots? 2008. pap. 34.95 (978-1-58013-759-1(8)) Kane Press, Inc.

Abercrombie, Barbara. The Show-and-Tell Lion. Cravath, Lynne Avril & Avril, Lynne, illus. 2006. (ENG.). 32p. (J). (gr. -1-2). 17.99 (978-0-689-86408-7(6), McElderry, Margaret K. Bks.) McElderry, Margaret K. Bks.

The Abominable Snowman Doesn't Roast Marshmallows, 6 bks., Pack. 2005. 96p. (J). pap. 3.99 (978-0-439-86573-9(5)) Scholastic, Inc.

Abraham, Susan Gonzales & Abraham, Denise Gonzales. Cecilia's Year. (Latino Fiction for Young Adults Ser.). (ENG., Illus.). (J). 2007. 210p. (gr. 4-6). pap. 11.95 (978-1-933693-02-6(9)) 2004. 160p. (gr. 7-9). 16.95 (978-0-938317-87-6(3)) Cinco Puntos Pr.

—Surprising Cecilia. 2005. (Latino Fiction for Young Adults Ser.). (ENG., Illus.). 216p. (J). (gr. -1-7). 16.95 (978-0-938317-96-8(2)) Cinco Puntos Pr.

Abrahams, Peter. Reality Check. 2010. (ENG.). 352p. (YA). (gr. 8). pap. 8.99 (978-0-06-122768-4(4), HarperTeen) HarperCollins Pubs.

Abramsen, Ruth M. Akeelah's Spider. 2008. 36p. per. 13.95 (978-1-59800-440-3(9)) Outskirts Pr., Inc.

Abuhamda, Nasser. A Flower in the Rain. 2009. 40p. pap. 14.95 (978-1-59858-879-8(6)) Dog Ear Publishing, LLC.

Adams, Colleen. School Is Cool! 2006. (Neighborhood Readers Ser.). (ENG.). 8p. (gr. -1-3). pap. 5.15 (978-1-4042-5676-7(8), Rosen Classroom) Rosen Publishing Group, Inc., The.

Adams, Diane. Teacher's Little Helper, 1 vol. Hayashi, Nancy, illus. 2012. (ENG.). 32p. (J). 15.95 (978-1-56145-630-7(6)) Peachtree Pubs.

Adams, Keith. The Tales of Henry Tuffin - Henry Goes to School. Hewitt, Geoff, ed. Mawson, Alan, illus. 2013. 20p. pap. (978-1-78222-103-6(4)) Paragon Publishing, Rothersthorpe.

Adams, Sherred Willcox. Five Little Friends. 2006. pap. 15.95 (978-1-4304-4149-6(6)) Kessinger Publishing, LLC.

Adams, W. Royce. The Computer's Nerd. 2011. 154p. (gr. 4-7). 22.99 (978-0-9712206-9-0(7)) Rairarubia Bks.

Adderson, Caroline. Jasper John Dooley: Not in Love. Clanton, Ben, illus. 2015. (Jasper John Dooley Ser.). (ENG.). 132p. (J). (gr. 2-5). pap. 7.95 (978-1-77138-343-1(7)) Kids Can Pr., Ltd. CAN. Dist: Hachette Bk. Group.

—Jasper John Dooley: Star of the Week. Clanton, Ben, illus. 2014. (Jasper John Dooley Ser.). (ENG.). 128p. (J). (gr. 2-5). pap. 7.95 (978-1-77138-119-2(1)) Kids Can Pr., Ltd. CAN. Dist: Hachette Bk. Group.

Adler, David A. Andy & Tamika. Hillenbrand, Will, illus. 2005. (Andy Russell Ser.: 2). (ENG.). 144p. (J). (gr. 1-4). pap. 5.99 (978-0-15-205446-5(4)) Houghton Mifflin Harcourt Publishing Co.

—Andy & Tamika. Hillenbrand, Will, illus. 2005. (Andy Russell Ser.: Bk. 2). 129p. 16.00 (978-0-7569-4898-6(3)) Perfection Learning Corp.

—Bones & the Cupcake Mystery, No. 3. Newman, Barbara Johansen, illus. 2008. (Bones Ser.: 3). (ENG.). 32p. (J). (gr. 1-3). mass mkt. 3.99 (978-0-14-241147-6(7), Penguin Young Readers) Penguin Young Readers Group.

—Bones & the Math Test. 2010. (Bones Penguin Young Readers Ser.: 6). lib. bdg. 13.55 (978-0-606-10585-9(9), Turtleback) Turtleback Bks.

—Bones & the Math Test Mystery. Newman, Barbara Johansen, illus. 2010. (Bones Ser.: 6). (ENG.). 32p. (J). (gr. 1-3). mass mkt. 3.99 (978-0-14-241519-1(7), Penguin Young Readers) Penguin Young Readers Group.

—Cam Jansen - The First Day of School Mystery, 22 vols. Natti, Susanna, illus. 2005. (Cam Jansen Ser.: 22). (ENG.). 64p. (J). (gr. 2-5). 4.99 (978-0-14-240326-6(1), Puffin Books) Penguin Young Readers Group.

—Cam Jansen - The Mystery Writer Mystery. Allen, Joy, illus. 27th ed. 2008. (Cam Jansen Ser.: 27). (ENG.). 64p. (J). (gr. 2-5). 4.99 (978-0-14-241194-0(9), Puffin Books) Penguin Young Readers Group.

—Cam Jansen & the Graduation Day Mystery. 2012. (Cam Jansen Ser.: 31). (ENG.). 64p. (J). (gr. 2-5). pap. 4.99 (978-0-14-242208-3(8), Puffin Books) Penguin Young Readers Group.

—Cam Jansen & the Graduation Day Mystery. 2012. (Cam Jansen Ser.: 31). lib. bdg. 14.75 (978-0-606-26663-5(1), Turtleback) Turtleback Bks.

—Cam Jansen & the Sports Day Mysteries. Allen, Joy, illus. 2009. (Cam Jansen: A Super Special Ser.). 118p. 16.00 (978-1-60686-431-9(9)) Perfection Learning Corp.

—Cam Jansen & the Sports Day Mysteries: A Super Special. 2009. (Cam Jansen Ser.). lib. bdg. 16.00 (978-0-606-00110-6(7), Turtleback) Turtleback Bks.

—Cam Jansen the Sports Day Mysteries: A Super Special. Allen, Joy, illus. 2009. (Cam Jansen Ser.). (ENG.). 128p. (J). (gr. 2-5). 5.99 (978-0-14-241225-1(2), Puffin Books) Penguin Young Readers Group.

—Danny's Doodles: The Dog Biscuit Breakfast. 2015. (Danny's Doodles Ser.: 3). (ENG., Illus.). 144p. (J). (gr. 2-5). pap. 4.99 (978-1-4926-1665-8(6), Sourcebooks Jabberwocky) Sourcebooks, Inc.

—Danny's Doodles: The Donut Dilemma. 2014. (Danny's Doodles Ser.: 2). (ENG., Illus.). 144p. (J). (gr. 2-5). pap. 4.99 (978-1-4022-8728-2(3), 9781402287282, Sourcebooks Jabberwocky) Sourcebooks, Inc.

—Danny's Doodles: The Jelly Bean Experiment. 2013. (Danny's Doodles Ser.: 1). (ENG.). 112p. (J). (gr. 2-5). pap. 5.99 (978-1-4022-8721-3(6), 9781402287213, Sourcebooks Jabberwocky) Sourcebooks, Inc.

—Danny's Doodles: the Squirting Donuts. 2014. (Danny's Doodles Ser.: 2). (ENG.). 144p. (J). (gr. 2-5). 14.99 (978-1-4926-1401-2(7), Sourcebooks Jabberwocky) Sourcebooks, Inc.

—The Day I Lost My Hampster: And Other True School Stories. 2006. 48p. (978-0-439-80289-5(X)) Scholastic, Inc.

—Don't Talk to Me about the War. 2009. (ENG.). 224p. (J). (gr. 3-7). 7.99 (978-0-14-241372-2(0), Puffin Books) Penguin Young Readers Group.

—Not Wanted by the Police. Franson, Leanne, illus. 2005. (Andy Russell Ser.: Bk. 5). (ENG.). 128p. (J). (gr. 1-4). pap. 5.99 (978-0-15-216719-6(6)) Houghton Mifflin Harcourt Publishing Co.

—The School Play Mystery. Natti, Susanna, illus. 2005. (Cam Jansen Ser.: 21). (ENG.). 64p. (J). (gr. 2-5). 4.99 (978-0-14-240355-6(5), Puffin Books) Penguin Young Readers Group.

—School Trouble for Andy Russell. Hillenbrand, Will, illus. 2005. (Andy Russell Ser.: Bk. 3). (ENG.). 128p. (J). (gr. 1-4). pap. 9.95 (978-0-15-205428-1(6)) Houghton Mifflin Harcourt Publishing Co.

—School Trouble for Andy Russell. Hillenbrand, Will, illus. 2007. (Andy Russell Ser.: Bk. 3). 118p. pap. 6.60 (978-1-4189-5227-3(3)) Houghton Mifflin Harcourt Supplemental Pubs.

—School Trouble for Andy Russell. Hillenbrand, Will, illus. 2008. (Andy Russell Ser.: Bk. 3). (J). (gr. 2-5). pap. 28.95 incl. audio compact disk (978-1-4301-0484-1(8)); pap. 24.95 incl. audio (978-1-4301-0483-4(X)) Live Oak Media.

—The Secret Service Mystery. Natti, Susanna, illus. 2008. (Cam Jansen Ser.: 26). (ENG.). 64p. (J). (gr. 2-5). 4.99 (978-0-14-241074-5(8), Puffin Books) Penguin Young Readers Group.

—The Secret Service Mystery. Natti, Susanna, illus. 2008. (Cam Jansen Ser.: Bk. 26). 57p. (J). (gr. 2-5). 11.65 (978-0-7569-8917-0(5)) Perfection Learning Corp.

—The Speedy Car Mystery, 16 vols. Natti, Susanna, illus. 2010. (Young Cam Jansen Ser.: 16). (ENG.). 32p. (J). (gr. 1-3). 14.99 (978-0-670-06143-3(3), Viking Books for Young Readers) Penguin Young Readers Group.

—Young Cam Jansen & the 100th Day of School, 15 vols. Natti, Susanna, illus. 2010. (Young Cam Jansen Ser.: 15). (ENG.). 32p. (J). (gr. 1-3). mass mkt. 3.99 (978-0-14-241685-3(1), Penguin Young Readers) Penguin Young Readers Group.

—Young Cam Jansen & the 100th Day of School Mystery, 15 vols. Natti, Susanna, illus. 2009. (Young Cam Jansen Ser.: 15). (ENG.). 32p. (J). (gr. 1-3). 13.99 (978-0-670-06172-3(7), Viking Books for Young Readers) Penguin Young Readers Group.

—Young Cam Jansen & the New Girl Mystery. Natti, Susanna, illus. 2005. (Young Cam Jansen Ser.: Bk. 10). 32p. (gr. k-2). 14.00 (978-0-7569-5522-9(X)) Perfection Learning Corp.

—Young Cam Jansen & the Speedy Car Mystery, 16 vols. Natti, Susanna, illus. 2011. (Young Cam Jansen Ser.: 16). (ENG.). 32p. (J). (gr. 1-3). mass mkt. 3.99 (978-0-14-241868-0(4), Penguin Young Readers) Penguin Young Readers Group.

—Young Cam Jansen & the Spotted Cat Mystery, No. 12. Natti, Susanna & Natti, S., illus. 2007. (Young Cam Jansen Ser.: 12). (ENG.). 32p. (J). (gr. 1-3). pap. 3.99 *(978-0-14-241012-7(8)*, Penguin Young Readers) Penguin Young Readers Group.
—Young Cam Jansen & the Spotted Cat Mystery. Natti, Susanna, illus. 2007. (Young Cam Jansen (prebound) Ser.). 31p. (gr. -1-3). 14.00 *(978-0-7569-8155-6(7))* Perfection Learning Corp.
—Young Cam Jansen & the Substitute Mystery, No. 11. Natti, Susanna, illus. 2006. (Young Cam Jansen Ser.: 11). (ENG.). 32p. (J). (gr. 1-3). mass mkt. 3.99 *(978-0-14-240660-1(0)*, Penguin Young Readers) Penguin Young Readers Group.
—Young Cam Jansen & the Zoo Note Mystery. Natti, Susanna, illus. 2013. (Puffin Young Readers, L3 Ser.). (ENG.). 31p. (J). (gr. -1-3). pap. 3.99 *(978-0-448-46633-0(3)*, Puffin) Penguin Publishing Group.
—Young Cam Jansen & the Zoo Note Mystery. Natti, Susanna, illus. 2004. (Young Cam Jansen Ser.: 9). (ENG.). 32p. (J). (gr. 1-3). mass mkt. 3.99 *(978-0-14-240204-7(4)*, Penguin Young Readers) Penguin Young Readers Group.
Adoff, Jaime. Names Will Never Hurt Me. 2005. (ENG.). 192p. (YA). (gr. 7-7). 5.99 *(978-0-14-240457-7(8)*, Speak) Penguin Young Readers Group.
Adornetto, Alexandra. Halo. 2010. (Halo Trilogy Ser.: 1). (ENG.). 496p. (YA). (gr. 7-12). 16.99 *(978-0-312-65626-3(2))* Feiwel & Friends.
—Halo. 2011. (Halo Trilogy Ser.: 1). (ENG.). 512p. (YA). (gr. 7-12). pap. 10.99 *(978-0-312-67436-6(8)*, 9780312674366) Square Fish.
—HALO. 2010. (SPA.). 416p. (YA). pap. 22.95 *(978-84-9918-173-8(2))* Roca Editorial ESP. Dist: Spanish Pubs., LLC.
—Heaven. 2013. (Halo Trilogy Ser.: 3). (ENG.). 448p. (YA). (gr. 7-12). pap. 10.99 *(978-1-250-02941-6(4)*, 9781250029416) Square Fish.
Adrian, Emily. Like It Never Happened. 2015. (ENG.). 368p. (J). (gr. 9). 17.99 *(978-0-525-42823-7(2)*, Dial Bks) Penguin Young Readers Group.
Adrian, Susan. Tunnel Vision: A Novel. 2015. (ENG.). 320p. (YA). (gr. 8-12). 18.99 *(978-1-250-04792-2(7)*, 9781250047922, St. Martin's Griffin) St. Martin's Pr.
Aggarwal, Eash. Paradox. 2010. 90p. pap. 8.99 *(978-0-557-45261-3(9))* Lulu Pr., Inc.
Agnew, Kate. Shout, Show & Tell! Monks, Lydia, illus. 2005. (Green Bananas Ser.). (ENG.). 48p. (J). (gr. -1-1). *(978-0-7787-1040-0(8))* Crabtree Publishing Co.
—Shout, Show, & Tell. Monks, Lydia, illus. 2005. (Green Bananas Ser.). (ENG.). 48p. (J). lib. bdg. *(978-0-7787-1024-0(6))* Crabtree Publishing Co.
Agnew, Kate, et al. Gweiddi, Dangos a Dweud. 2005. (WEL., Illus.). 47p. pap. *(978-1-85596-676-5(X))* Dref Wen.
Agro-Melina, Robert Joseph. Joe & the Mysteries of Dream Hall: The Extra Dwarf & the Purloined Parchment. 2012. 152p. pap. 10.99 *(978-1-4575-1239-1(4))* Dog Ear Publishing, LLC.
Aguirre, Ann. Infinite Risk. 2016. (Immortal Game Ser.: 3). (ENG.). 384p. (YA). 17.99 *(978-1-250-02465-7(X)*, 9781250024657) Feiwel & Friends.
—Public Enemies. 2015. (Immortal Game Ser.: 2). (ENG.). 384p. (YA). (gr. 7). 17.99 *(978-1-250-02466-4(8)*, 9781250024664) Feiwel & Friends.
—Public Enemies. 2015. (ENG.). 384p. (YA). *(978-1-250-07420-1(7))* St. Martin's Pr.
—The Queen of Bright & Shiny Things. 2015. (ENG.). 336p. (YA). (gr. 7). 17.99 *(978-1-250-04750-2(1)*, 9781250047502) Feiwel & Friends.
Ahlberg, Allan. Starting School. braille ed. 2004. (J). (gr. k-3). spiral bd. *(978-0-616-01526-1(7))* Canadian National Institute for the Blind/Institut National Canadien pour les Aveugles.
Ahlberg, Allan & Ahlberg, Janet. Starting School. (ENG., Illus.). 32p. (J). pap. 9.95 *(978-0-14-050737-9(X))* Penguin Bks., Ltd. GBR. Dist: Trafalgar Square Publishing.
Aikawa, Yu. Dark Edge, Vol. 6. Aikawa, Yu, illus. 2006. (Dark Edge Ser.). (ENG., Illus.). 200p. (YA). pap. 9.95 *(978-1-59796-026-7(6))* DrMaster Pubns. Inc.
Ain, Beth. Izzy Kline Has Butterflies. 2017. (ENG.). 176p. (J). (gr. 3-7). 16.99 *(978-0-399-55080-5(1)*, Random Hse. Bks. for Young Readers) Random Hse. Children's Bks.
—Starring Jules (As Herself) 2014. (Starring Jules Ser.: 1). (ENG., Illus.). 160p. (J). (gr. 2-5). pap. 5.99 *(978-0-545-44353-1(9)*, Scholastic Paperbacks) Scholastic, Inc.
—Starring Jules (As Herself) 2014. (Starring Jules Ser.: 1). lib. bdg. 16.00 *(978-0-606-35365-6(8))* Turtleback Bks.
—Starring Jules (in Drama-Rama) Higgins, Anne Keenan, illus. 2013. (Starring Jules Ser.: 2). (ENG.). 176p. (J). (gr. 2-5). 14.99 *(978-0-545-44354-8(7)*, Scholastic Pr.) Scholastic, Inc.
—Starring Jules (Third Grade Debut) (Starring Jules Ser.: 4). (ENG.). 176p. (J). (gr. 2-5). 2015. pap. 5.99 *(978-0-545-44359-3(8))* 2014. 14.99 *(978-0-545-44358-6(X))* Scholastic, Inc. (Scholastic Pr.).
Airgood, Ellen. Prairie Evers. (ENG.). 224p. (J). (gr. 3-7). 2014. pap. 7.99 *(978-0-14-242668-5(7)*, Puffin Books) 2012. 15.99 *(978-0-399-25691-2(1)*, Nancy Paulsen Books) Penguin Young Readers Group.
Aker, Don. One on One. 2014. 144p. (J). (gr. 3-7). pap. 8.99 *(978-0-06-231353-9(3))* HarperCollins Pubs.
Al-Emadi, Hesham. The Savior's Threshold: The Chronicles of Dourren. 2010. 192p. pap. 13.95 *(978-1-4502-1846-7(6))* iUniverse, Inc.
—The Savior's Threshold: The Chronicles of Dourren. 2010. 192p. 23.95 *(978-1-4502-1848-1(2))* iUniverse, Inc.
Al Shaikh, Latifa. I'm Still Waiting for that Chocolate. 2007. 52p. (YA). per. 8.95 *(978-0-595-42982-0(3))* iUniverse, Inc.
Albertalli, Becky. Simon vs. the Homo Sapiens Agenda. (YA). (gr. 9). 2016. 336p. pap. 10.99 *(978-0-06-234868-5(X))* 2015. (ENG.). 320p. 17.99 *(978-0-06-234867-8(1))* HarperCollins Pubs.
Alberto, Daisy. Pete for President! Sims, Blanche, illus. 2004. (Social Studies Connects). 32p. (J). (gr. 1-3). pap. 5.95 *(978-1-57565-142-2(4))* Kane Press, Inc.
Alcántara, Ricardo. Huy, Que Miedo! 13th ed. 2003. (SPA., Illus.). 44p. *(978-84-236-2559-8(1)*, ED6263) Edebé ESP. Dist: Lectorum Pubns., Inc.
Alcott, Jessica. Even When You Lie to Me. 2015. (ENG.). 352p. (YA). (gr. 9). 17.99 *(978-0-385-39116-0(1)*, Crown Books For Young Readers) Random Hse. Children's Bks.
Alcott, Louisa May. Hombrecitos.Tr. of Little Men. (SPA., Illus.). 160p. (YA). 11.95 *(978-84-7281-168-3(9)*, AF1168) Auriga, Ediciones S.A. ESP. Dist: Continental Bk. Co., Inc.
—Jo's Boys. l.t. ed. 2007. (ENG.). 288p. pap. 23.99 *(978-1-4346-0451-4(9))* Creative Media Partners, LLC.
—Jo's Boys. abr. ed. 2011. (Dover Children's Thrift Classics Ser.). (ENG., Illus.). 112p. (J). (gr. 3-8). pap. 4.00 *(978-0-486-40789-0(6))* Dover Pubns., Inc.
—Jo's Boys. l.t. ed. 2005. 424p. pap. *(978-1-84637-067-0(1))* Echo Library.
—Jo's Boys. 2013. (Works of Louisa May Alcott). 366p. reprint ed. lthr. 79.00 *(978-0-7812-1642-5(7))* Reprint Services Corp.
—Little Men. Andreasen, Dan, illus. 2009. (Classic Starts(tm) Ser.). (ENG.). 160p. (J). (gr. 2-4). 6.95 *(978-1-4027-5423-4(X))* Sterling Publishing Co., Inc.
—Little Men. rev. ed. 2006. 352p. 31.95 *(978-1-4218-1800-9(0))*; pap. 15.95 *(978-1-4218-1900-6(7))* 1st World Publishing, Inc. (1st World Library - Literary Society).
—Little Men: Life at Plumfield with Jo's Boys. 2013. (Works of Louisa May Alcott). 292p. reprint ed. lthr. 79.00 *(978-0-7812-1629-6(X))* Reprint Services Corp.
Alcott, Louisa May & Barbarese, J. T. Little Men. 2012. (ENG.). 368p. (gr. 12). mass mkt. 5.95 *(978-0-451-53223-7(6)*, Signet) Penguin Publishing Group.
Alegre, Mari. Destiny. 2011. 174p. 29.99 *(978-1-4568-2040-4(0))* Xlibris Corp.
Alegria, Malin. Border Town #2: Quince Clash. 2012. (Border Town Ser.). (ENG.). 192p. (J). (gr. 7). pap. 5.99 *(978-0-545-40241-5(7)*, Scholastic Paperbacks) Scholastic, Inc.
Aleixandre, Marilar & Aleixandre, Marilar. La Branda Sin Futuro. 2003. (SPA.). 156p. *(978-84-348-7193-9(9)*, SM30543) SM Ediciones ESP. Dist: Lectorum Pubns., Inc.
Alender, Katie. As Dead as It Gets. 2013. (Bad Girls Don't Die Ser.). (ENG.). 448p. (J). (gr. 7-17). pap. 9.99 *(978-1-4231-3778-8(7))* Hyperion Pr.
—Bad Girls Don't Die. 2010. (ENG.). 352p. (J). (gr. 7-17). pap. 8.99 *(978-1-4231-0877-1(9))* Hyperion Pr.
—Famous Last Words. 2014. (ENG.). 320p. (J). (gr. 7). 18.99 *(978-0-545-63997-2(2))* Scholastic, Inc.
—From Bad to Cursed. 2012. (ENG.). 448p. (YA). (gr. 7-17). pap. 9.99 *(978-1-4231-3777-1(9))* Hyperion Pr.
Alexander, Alma. Spellspam. 2008. (Worldweavers Ser.: Bk. 2). (YA). (gr. 7-18). (ENG.). 448p. 17.99 *(978-0-06-083958-1(9))*; 437p. lib. bdg. 18.89 *(978-0-06-083959-8(7))* HarperCollins Pubs. (Eos).
Alexander, Carol. The Bean Trees. Friedland, Joyce & Kessler, Rikki, eds. 2007. (Novel-Ties Ser.). (Illus.). 35p. pap. 16.95 *(978-0-7675-3554-0(5))* Learning Links Inc.
—Class Clown. Friedland, Joyce & Kessler, Rikki, eds. 2007. (Novel-Ties Ser.). (Illus.). 24p. pap. 16.95 *(978-0-7675-1014-1(3))* Learning Links Inc.
—The Golden Compass: A Study Guide. Friedland, Joyce & Kessler, Rikki, eds. 2008. (Novel-Ties Ser.). 30p. pap. 16.95 *(978-0-7675-4254-8(1))* Learning Links Inc.
—The Planet of Junior Brown. Friedland, Joyce & Kessler, Rikki, eds. 2007. (Novel-Ties Ser.). (Illus.). 30p. pap. 16.95 *(978-0-7675-3561-8(8))* Learning Links Inc.
Alexander, Claire. Lucy & the Bully, 1 vol. Alexander, Claire, illus. 2008. (ENG., Illus.). 32p. (J). (gr. -1-3). 16.99 *(978-0-8075-4786-1(7))* Whitman, Albert & Co.
Alexander, Claire, illus. Back to Front & Upside Down. 2012. (ENG.). 26p. (J). 16.00 *(978-0-8028-5414-8(1)*, Eerdmans Bks For Young Readers) Eerdmans, William B. Publishing Co.
Alexander, Kwame. He Said, She Said. 2013. 330p. (YA). lib. bdg. *(978-0-06-211897-4(8))* Harper & Row Ltd.
—He Said, She Said. 2013. (ENG.). 336p. (YA). (gr. 9). 17.99 *(978-0-06-211896-7(X)*, Amistad) HarperCollins Pubs.
Alexander, Michael. Until Wishes Are Fulfilled II: Alec's Story. 2007. 204p. per. 15.50 *(978-1-84426-468-1(8))* Upfront Publishing Ltd. GBR. Dist: Printondemand-worldwide.com.
Alfonsi, Alice. Lizzie for President. 2004. 149p. (J). lib. bdg. 16.92 *(978-1-4242-0681-0(2))* Fitzgerald Bks.
Alger, Horatio. Making His Way. 2005. 28.95 *(978-1-4218-1456-8(0))*; 260p. pap. 13.95 *(978-1-4218-1556-5(7))* 1st World Publishing, Inc. (1st World Library - Literary Society).
—Strive & Succeed. 2007. 172p. 24.95 *(978-1-4344-8359-1(2))*; per. 14.95 *(978-1-4344-8358-4(4))* Wildside Pr., LLC.
Aliki. Play's the Thing. Aliki, illus. 2005. (ENG., Illus.). 32p. (J). 16.99 *(978-0-06-074355-0(7))* HarperCollins Pubs.
Allard, Harry. Miss Nelson Is Missing!, 1 vol. Marshall, James, illus. 2007. (Read along Book & CD Ser.). (ENG.). 32p. (J). (gr. -1-3). audio compact disk 10.99 *(978-0-618-85281-9(6))* Houghton Mifflin Harcourt Publishing Co.
Allard, Harry & Marshall, James. Miss Nelson Has a Field Day. 2015. 32p. pap. 7.00 *(978-1-61003-506-4(2))* Center for the Collaborative Classroom.
Allard, Harry G., Jr. Miss Nelson Has a Field Day, 1 vol. Marshall, James, illus. 2012. (ENG.). 32p. (J). (gr. -1-3). audio compact disk 10.99 *(978-0-547-75376-8(4))* Houghton Mifflin Harcourt Publishing Co.
—Miss Nelson Is Back, 1 vol. Marshall, James, illus. 2011. (ENG.). 32p. (J). (gr. -1-3). audio compact disk 10.99 *(978-0-547-57718-0(4))* Houghton Mifflin Harcourt Publishing Co.
Allard, Harry G., Jr. & Marshall, James. The Miss Nelson Collection. 2014. (ENG., Illus.). 112p. (J). (gr. 1-4). 16.99 *(978-0-544-08222-9(2)*, HMH Books For Young Readers) Houghton Mifflin Harcourt Publishing Co.
Allen, C. William. The African Interior Mission. Lee, Xiongpao, illus. 2006. 232p. (J). pap. 20.00 *(978-0-9653308-5-5(0))* Africana Homestead Legacy Pubs., Inc.
Allen, Crystal. The Laura Line. (J). (gr. 3-7). 2016. 352p. pap. 6.99 *(978-0-06-249021-6(4))* 2013. (ENG.). 336p. 16.99 *(978-0-06-199274-2(7))* HarperCollins Pubs.
—Spirit Week Showdown. Kaban, Eda, illus. (Magnificent Mya Tibbs Ser.: 1). (J). (gr. 3-7). 2017. 256p. pap. 6.99 *(978-0-06-234234-8(7))* 2016. 240p. 16.99 *(978-0-06-234233-1(9))* HarperCollins Pubs.
Allen, Elise & Daryle Connors. Gabby Duran & the Unsittables. 2016. (Gabby Duran Ser.: 1). (J). lib. bdg. 18.40 *(978-0-606-39443-7(5))* Turtleback Bks.
Allen, Jonathan. I'm Not Ready! 2011. (Baby Owl Ser.). (ENG., Illus.). 32p. (J). (gr. -1-k). 16.95 *(978-1-907967-05-4(2))* Boxer Bks., Ltd. GBR. Dist: Sterling Publishing Co., Inc.
Allen, M. E. Gotta Get Some Bish Bash Bosh. 2005. (Illus.). 208p. (J). 15.99 *(978-0-06-073198-4(2)*, HarperTeen) HarperCollins Pubs.
Allen, Nancy. Amazing Grace: A Kentucky Girl with Gumption During World War II. 2014. Orig. Title: Amazing Grace: a Kentucky Girl with Gumption During World War II. (ENG., Illus.). 160p. (gr. 4-7). pap. 14.99 *(978-1-62619-405-2(X)*, History Pr., The) Arcadia Publishing.
Allen, Richard L. Cool to Be in School. 2013. 32p. pap. 9.95 *(978-1-60414-674-5(5))* Fideli Publishing, Inc.
Allison, Jennifer. The Ladies of the Lake. 2007. (Gilda Joyce Ser.). (ENG.). 352p. (J). (gr. 5-18). 9.99 *(978-0-14-240907-7(3)*, Puffin Books) Penguin Young Readers Group.
Allison, John. Bad Machinery Vol. 3: The Case of the Simple Soul. 2014. (ENG., Illus.). 136p. (YA). pap. 19.99 *(978-1-62010-193-3(9)*, 9781620101933) Oni Pr., Inc.
Allyson, Libby. Scottie Rides the Bus. 2004. 27p. pap. 24.95 *(978-1-4137-3298-6(4))* PublishAmerica, Inc.
Almond, David. My Name Is Mina. 2012. (ENG.). 304p. (J). (gr. 5). 6.99 *(978-0-375-87327-0(9)*, Yearling) Random Hse. Children's Bks.
The (Almost) Perfect Guide to Imperfect Boys. 2014. (Mix Ser.). (ENG., Illus.). 304p. (J). (gr. 4-8). pap. 7.99 *(978-1-4814-0563-8(2)*, Aladdin) Simon & Schuster Children's Publishing.
Alonso, Fernando. Sopaboba. 8th ed. 2003. (SPA., Illus.). 136p. *(978-84-239-9025-2(7)*, EC1519) Espasa Calpe, S.A. ESP. Dist: Lectorum Pubns., Inc.
Alphin, Elaine Marie. The Perfect Shot. (Carolrhoda YA Ser.). (ENG.). 360p. (YA). (gr. 6-12). 2011. pap. 9.95 *(978-0-7613-8138-9(4)*, Carolrhoda Lab™) 2005. 16.95 *(978-1-57505-862-7(6)*, Carolrhoda Bks.) Lerner Publishing Group.
—Picture Perfect. 2003. (ENG., Illus.). 256p. (YA). (gr. 5-12). 15.95 *(978-0-8225-0535-8(5))* Lerner Publishing Group.
—Simon Says. 2005. (ENG.). 264p. (YA). (gr. 9-12). pap. 14.95 *(978-0-15-204678-1(X))* Houghton Mifflin Harcourt Publishing Co.
Alpine, Rachele. Operation Pucker Up. 2015. (Mix Ser.). (ENG., Illus.). 256p. (J). (gr. 4-8). 17.99 *(978-1-4814-3236-8(2)*, Aladdin) Simon & Schuster Children's Publishing.
Alsaid, Adi. Never Always Sometimes. 2015. (ENG.). 320p. (YA). 17.99 *(978-0-373-21154-8(6)*, Harlequin Teen) Harlequin Enterprises, Ltd. CAN. Dist: HarperCollins Pubs.
Alsenas, Linas. Beyond Clueless. 2015. (ENG.). 256p. (YA). (gr. 7-11). 16.95 *(978-1-4197-1496-2(1)*, Amulet Bks.) Abrams, Inc.
Altebrando, Tara. The Best Night of Your (Pathetic) Life. 2013. (ENG.). 256p. (YA). (gr. 9). pap. 8.99 *(978-0-14-242640-1(7)*, Speak) Penguin Young Readers Group.
Alter, Anna. Francine's Day. Alter, Anna, illus. 2003. (Illus.). 32p. (J). lib. bdg. 16.89 *(978-0-06-623937-8(0))* HarperCollins Pubs.
Alvarado, Beatriz. Juliana: A girl from the Andes. 2008. 44p. pap. 16.95 *(978-1-4327-0253-3(X))* Outskirts Pr., Inc.
Alvarez, Julia. De Como la Tia Lola Aprendio a Ensenar. 2011. (Tia Lola Stories Ser.). (SPA & ENG.). 160p. (J). (gr. 3-7). 7.99 *(978-0-375-85793-5(1)*, Yearling) Random Hse. Children's Bks.
—Finding Miracles. 2006. (ENG.). 288p. (YA). (gr. 7-12). mass mkt. 6.99 *(978-0-553-49406-8(6)*, Laurel Leaf) Random Hse. Children's Bks.
—How Tia Lola Learned to Teach. 2011. (Tia Lola Stories Ser.). (ENG., Illus.). 144p. (J). (gr. 3-7). pap. 7.99 *(978-0-375-85792-8(3)*, Yearling) Random Hse. Children's Bks.
Amato, Mary. Edgar Allan's Official Crime Investigation Notebook. (ENG.). 176p. (J). 2011. pap. 6.99 *(978-0-8234-2386-6(7))* 2010. (gr. 1-5). 16.95 *(978-0-8234-2271-5(2))* Holiday Hse., Inc.
—Guitar Notes. (ENG., Illus.). 304p. (J). (gr. 7). 2014. pap. 8.99 *(978-1-60684-503-5(9))* 2012. 16.99 *(978-1-60684-124-2(6))* Lerner Publishing Group. (Carolrhoda Lab™).
—Invisible Lines. Caparo, Antonio, illus. 2011. (ENG.). 336p. (gr. 5). 7.99 *(978-1-60684-187-7(4)*, Carolrhoda Bks.) Lerner Publishing Group.
—Our Teacher Is a Vampire & Other (Not) True Stories. Long, Ethan, illus. (ENG.). 256p. (J). (gr. 3-7). 2017. pap. 6.99 *(978-0-8234-3769-6(8))* 2016. 16.95 *(978-0-8234-3553-1(9))* Holiday Hse., Inc.
—Please Write in This Book. Brace, Eric, illus. (ENG.). (J). (gr. 4-7). 2008. 97p. pap. 7.99 *(978-0-8234-2138-1(4))* 2006. 112p. 16.95 *(978-0-8234-1932-6(0))* Holiday Hse., Inc.
—Stinky & Successful: The Riot Brothers Never Stop! Long, Ethan, illus. 2007. (ENG.). 160p. (J). (gr. 2-5). 16.95 *(978-0-8234-2100-8(7))* Holiday Hse., Inc.
—The Word Eater. Ryniak, Christopher, illus. 2005. (ENG.). 151p. (J). (gr. 3-7). reprint ed. pap. 7.99 *(978-0-8234-1940-1(1))* Holiday Hse., Inc.
Ambrose, Adrianne. What I Learned from Being a Cheerleader. 2010. 202p. pap. 12.95 *(978-1-935661-94-8(9)*, Bell Bridge Bks.) BelleBks., Inc.
Amnesty International Staff, ed. Free? Stories about Human Rights. 2010. (ENG., Illus.). 224p. (J). (gr. 5-18). pap. 9.99 *(978-0-7636-4926-5(0))* Candlewick Pr.
Amos, Angela. 'Twas the Fight Before Christmas. 2013. 34p. pap. 12.95 *(978-1-4327-8204-7(5))* Outskirts Pr., Inc.
Anastasio, Dina. Everyone Clapped for Jason: Set Of 6. 2010. (Early Connections Ser.). (J). pap. 37.00 net. *(978-1-4108-1362-6(2))* Benchmark Education Co.
Andersen, Alan Lance. Wizard Academies - Rumpots, Crackpots, & Pooka-Mazed Halfwits. 2008. 174p. pap. 19.96 *(978-0-615-18594-1(0))* Wizard Academies, LLC.
Anderson, Annette Latva. Alone into Darkness: Was It Fate or an Error in Judgment? 2013. (ENG.). 46p. (J). pap. 9.95 *(978-1-4787-1208-4(2))* Outskirts Pr., Inc.
Anderson, Jeff. Zack Delacruz: Me & My Big Mouth. (Zack Delacruz Ser.). (ENG., Illus.). 176p. (J). (gr. 5-8). 2016. pap. 6.95 *(978-1-4549-2127-1(7))* 2015. 12.95 *(978-1-4549-1499-0(8))* Sterling Publishing Co., Inc.
—Zack Delacruz 2 (working Title) 2016. (Zack Delacruz Ser.). (ENG., Illus.). 192p. (J). (gr. 5-8). 12.95 *(978-1-4549-2067-0(X))* Sterling Publishing Co., Inc.
Anderson, Jennifer. Honey Creek Royalty. 2013. 246p. pap. 12.99 *(978-1-62237-148-8(8))* Turquoise Morning Pr.
Anderson, Jessica. Case of the Foul Play on a School Day. 2015. (ENG.). 64p. (gr. 3-6). 29.95 *(978-1-63430-386-6(5))* Rourke Educational Media.
—Case of the Sabotaged Spaghetti. 2015. (ENG.). 64p. (gr. 3-6). 29.95 *(978-1-63430-384-2(9))* Rourke Educational Media.
—Secret of the School Suitor. 2015. (ENG.). 64p. (gr. 3-6). 29.95 *(978-1-63430-383-5(0))* Rourke Educational Media.
Anderson, Jessica Lee. Trudy. 2005. (Milkweed Prize for Children's Literature Ser.). (ENG.). 192p. (J). (gr. 3-8). per. 6.95 *(978-1-57131-659-2(0))* Milkweed Editions.
Anderson, Jodi Lynn. Loser/Queen. Lee, Brittney, illus. 2010. (ENG.). 272p. (YA). (gr. 7-18). pap. 9.99 *(978-1-4169-9646-0(X)*, Simon & Schuster Bks. For Young Readers) Simon & Schuster Bks. For Young Readers.
Anderson, John David. Insert Coin to Continue. (ENG.). 336p. (J). (gr. 3-7). 2017. pap. 7.99 ***(978-1-4814-4705-8(X))*** 2016. (Illus.). 16.99 *(978-1-4814-4704-1(1))* Simon & Schuster Children's Publishing. (Aladdin).
—Ms. Bixby's Last Day. (J). (gr. 3-7). 2017. 336p. pap. 6.99 ***(978-0-06-233818-1(8))*** 2016. 320p. 16.99 *(978-0-06-233817-4(X))* HarperCollins Pubs. (Waldon Pond Pr.).
—Posted. 2017. 384p. (J). (gr. 3-7). 16.99 *(978-0-06-233820-4(X)*, Waldon Pond Pr.) HarperCollins Pubs.
—Sidekicked. 2013. (ENG.). 384p. (J). (gr. 3-7). 16.99 *(978-0-06-213314-4(4)*, Waldon Pond Pr.) HarperCollins Pubs.
Anderson, Laurie Halse. Catalyst. 2003. (ENG.). 256p. (YA). (gr. 7-18). pap. 8.99 *(978-0-14-240001-2(7)*, Speak) Penguin Young Readers Group.
—The Hair of Zoe Fleefenbacher Goes to School. Hoyt, Ard, illus. 2009. (ENG.). 32p. (J). (gr. 1-5). 17.99 *(978-0-689-85809-3(4)*, Simon & Schuster Bks. For Young Readers) Simon & Schuster Bks. For Young Readers.
—New Beginnings #13, 13 vols. 2012. (Vet Volunteers Ser.: 13). (ENG.). 192p. (J). (gr. 3-7). 6.99 *(978-0-14-241675-4(4)*, Puffin Books) Penguin Young Readers Group.
—Prom. 2006. (YA). 1.25 *(978-1-4193-5096-2(X))* Recorded Bks., Inc.
—Speak. 2006. 24.50 *(978-0-8446-7292-2(0))* Smith, Peter Pub., Inc.
—Speak. 2011. (ENG.). 224p. (YA). (gr. 7-12). pap. 10.99 *(978-0-312-67439-7(2)*, 9780312674397) Square Fish.
—Teacher's Pet. 2009. (Vet Volunteers Ser.: 7). (ENG.). 160p. (J). (gr. 3-7). 6.99 *(978-0-14-241252-7(X)*, Puffin Books) Penguin Young Readers Group.
—Twisted. 2014. (ENG.). 288p. (YA). (gr. 7-12). 14.24 *(978-1-63245-343-3(6))* Lectorum Pubns., Inc.
—Twisted. 2011. 11.04 *(978-0-7848-3388-9(5)*, Everbind) Marco Bk. Co.
—Twisted. 2008. (ENG.). 288p. (YA). (gr. 7-18). 9.99 *(978-0-14-241184-1(1)*, Speak) Penguin Young Readers Group.
—Twisted. l.t. ed. 2007. (Literacy Bridge Young Adult Ser.). 299p. (YA). (gr. 7-12). 23.95 *(978-0-7862-9885-3(5))* Thorndike Pr.
Anderson, Lynne. Charlie's Championships & Los campeonatos de Charlie: 6 English, 6 Spanish Adaptations. 2011. (ENG & SPA.). (J). 75.00 net. *(978-1-4108-5655-5(0))* Benchmark Education Co.
Anderson, Pamela Dell. My New School: Afro Boy. Lee, Hanlim & WU, Stacie, illus. 2003. 24p. (J). 12.95 *(978-1-932555-01-1(3))* Watch Me Grow Kids.
—My New School: Afro Girl. Lee, Hanlim & WU, Stacie, illus. 2003. 24p. (J). 12.95 *(978-1-932555-00-4(5))* Watch Me Grow Kids.
—My New School: Asian/Latin Boy. Lee, Hanlim & WU, Stacie, illus. 2003. 24p. (J). 12.95 *(978-1-932555-03-5(X))* Watch Me Grow Kids.
—My New School: Latin/Asian Girl. Lee, Hanlim & WU, Stacie, illus. 2003. 24p. (J). 12.95 *(978-1-932555-02-8(1))* Watch Me Grow Kids.
Anderson, Phil. The Thomas Family Values. 2012. 84p. pap. 13.95 *(978-1-4772-2529-5(3))* AuthorHouse.
Anderson, R. J. A Little Taste of Poison. 2016. (ENG., Illus.). 368p. (J). (gr. 4-7). 17.99 *(978-1-4814-3774-5(7)*, Atheneum Bks. for Young Readers) Simon & Schuster Children's Publishing.
Anderson, Salem. Salem Anderson & Her Private Diary. 2011. 24p. pap. 11.32 *(978-1-4490-7115-8(5))* AuthorHouse.
Anderson, Shannon. Coasting Casey: A Tale of Busting Boredom in School. Madden, Colleen, illus. 2016. (ENG.). 48p. (J). (gr. k-4). 15.99 *(978-1-63198-068-6(2))* Free Spirit Publishing, Inc.
Anderson, William. Hallie's Bad Day, 1 vol. 2009. 48p. pap. 16.95 *(978-1-60836-681-1(2))* America Star Bks.
Andracki, Zenon. Dear Ashley: A Middle Grade Novel. 2006. (ENG.). 84p. per. 19.95 *(978-1-4241-6168-3(1))* America Star Bks.
Andreae, Giles. Captain Flinn & the Pirate Dinosaurs. Ayto, Russell, illus. 2005. (Captain Flinn & the Pirate Dinosaurs Ser.). (ENG.). 32p. (J). (gr. -1-1). 17.99 *(978-1-4169-0713-8(0)*, McElderry, Margaret K. Bks.) McElderry, Margaret K. Bks.
Andrews, D. M. The Serpent in the Glass. 2012. 234p. pap. *(978-1-78176-773-3(4))* FeedARead.com.
Andrews, Jesse. Me & Earl & the Dying Girl. (ENG.). 304p. (YA). (gr. 9-17). 2012. 17.95 *(978-1-4197-0176-4(2)*, Amulet Bks.) 2015. 17.95 *(978-1-4197-2027-7(9))* 2015. 17.95 *(978-1-4197-2013-0(9)*, Amulet Bks.) 2015. pap. 9.95 *(978-1-4197-1960-8(2)*, Amulet Bks.) Abrams, Inc.
—Me & Earl & the Dying Girl. 2015. (CHI.). 320p. (YA). (gr. 9-17). pap. *(978-986-344-282-0(8))* Rye Field Publishing, Co.
—Me & Earl & the Dying Girl. 2015. lib. bdg. 20.80 *(978-0-606-37113-1(3))* Turtleback Bks.

S

Andrews, Julie & Hamilton, Emma Walton. A Spooky, Sparkly Halloween. 2016. (Very Fairy Princess Ser.). (J). lib. bdg. 16.00 *(978-0-606-38317-2(4))* Turtleback Bks.
—Valentines from the Heart. 2015. (Very Fairy Princess Ser.). (J). lib. bdg. 16.00 *(978-0-606-37466-8(3))* Turtleback Bks.
—The Very Fairy Princess Follows Her Heart. Davenier, Christine, illus. 2013. (Very Fairy Princess Ser.). (ENG.). 32p. (J). (gr. -1-3). 16.99 *(978-0-316-18559-2(0))* Little Brown & Co.

Andrews, Julie & Walton Hamilton, Emma. The Very Fairy Princess: Attitude of Gratitude. Davenier, Christine, illus. 2016. (ENG.). 32p. (J). (gr. -1-3). 17.99 *(978-0-316-26588-1(8))* Little, Brown Bks. for Young Readers.

Andrews, Julie, et al. The Very Fairy Princess - Graduation Girl! Davenier, Christine, illus. 2014. (Very Fairy Princess Ser.). (ENG.). 32p. (J). (gr. -1-3). 18.99 *(978-0-316-21960-0(6))* Little, Brown Bks. for Young Readers.

Andrews, Randall. The Last Guardian of Magic. 2008. 448p. (YA). per. 23.95 *(978-0-595-47345-8(8))* iUniverse, Inc.

Angelchild, P. Erotic Memoirs Volume 1. 2007. pap. *(978-1-84747-127-7(7))* Chipmunkapublishing.

Angleberger, Tom. Darth Paper Strikes Back. 2011. (Origami Yoda Ser.). (ENG., Illus.). 176p. (J). (gr. 3-7). 13.95 *(978-1-4197-0027-9(8))*, Amulet Bks.); pap. *(978-1-4197-0254-9(8))* Abrams, Inc.
—Darth Paper Strikes Back, 3 vols. 2011. (Origami Yoda Ser.: 2). (J). *(978-1-4618-4266-8(2))*; 1.25 *(978-1-4640-2485-6(5))* Recorded Bks., Inc.
—Darth Paper Strikes Back. (Origami Yoda Files Ser.: 2). (J). 2015. lib. bdg. 18.40 *(978-0-606-39395-9(1))* 2011. lib. bdg. 25.70 *(978-0-606-33075-6(5)*, Turtleback) Turtleback Bks.
—Emperor Pickletine Rides the Bus. 2014. (Origami Yoda Ser.). (ENG., Illus.). 224p. (J). (gr. 3-7). 13.95 *(978-1-4197-0933-3(X)*, Amulet Bks.) Abrams, Inc.
—Princess Labelmaker to the Rescue! (Origami Yoda Ser.). (ENG., Illus.). (gr. 3-7). 2016. 224p. (J). pap. 7.95 *(978-1-4197-2200-4(X))* 2014. 208p. (YA). 13.95 *(978-1-4197-1052-0(4))* Abrams, Inc. (Amulet Bks.).
—Princess Labelmaker to the Rescue! 2014. (Origami Yoda Files Ser.: 5). (J). lib. bdg. 25.70 *(978-0-606-35237-6(6))* Turtleback Bks.
—The Secret of the Fortune Wookiee. 2015. (Origami Yoda Ser.). (ENG., Illus.). 208p. (J). (gr. 3-7). pap. 7.95 *(978-1-4197-1971-4(8)*, Amulet Bks.) Abrams, Inc.
—The Secret of the Fortune Wookiee. Bell, Cece, illus. 2012. (Origami Yoda Ser.: No. 3). (ENG.). 208p. (J). (gr. 3-7). 13.95 *(978-1-4197-0392-8(7)*, Amulet Bks.) Abrams, Inc.
—The Strange Case of Origami Yoda. 2011. (Illus.). 160p. pap. *(978-0-8109-9877-3(7)*, Amulet Bks.) 2010. (ENG., Illus.). 160p. (J). (gr. 3-7). 13.95 *(978-0-8109-8425-7(3)*, Amulet Bks.) 2010. pap. *(978-0-8109-9650-2(2))* Abrams, Inc.
—The Strange Case of Origami Yoda, 2 vols. 2010. (Origami Yoda Ser.: 1). (J). 48.75 *(978-1-4498-4583-4(5))* Recorded Bks., Inc.
—The Surprise Attack of Jabba the Puppett. 2016. (Origami Yoda Ser.). (ENG.). 240p. (YA). (gr. 3-7). pap. 7.95 *(978-1-4197-2030-7(9)*, Amulet Bks.) Abrams, Inc.
—The Surprise Attack of Jabba the Puppett: An Origami Yoda Book. 2013. (Origami Yoda Ser.: No. 4). (ENG., Illus.). 224p. (YA). (gr. 3-7). 13.95 *(978-1-4197-0858-9(9)*, Amulet Bks.) Abrams, Inc.
—The Surprise Attack of Jabba the Puppett: An Origami Yoda Book. 2013. (Origami Yoda Ser.: 4). (J). 50.75 *(978-1-4703-9686-2(6))*; 48.75 *(978-1-4703-9677-0(7))*; 1.25 *(978-1-4703-9695-4(5))*; 48.75 *(978-1-4703-9650-3(5))*; 168.75 *(978-1-4703-9641-1(6))* Recorded Bks., Inc.
—The Surprise Attack of Jabba the Puppett: An Origami Yoda Book. (Origami Yoda Files Ser.: 4). (J). 2016. lib. bdg. 18.40 *(978-0-606-38208-3(9))* 2013. lib. bdg. 25.70 *(978-0-606-33308-5(8)*, Turtleback) Turtleback Bks.

Angleberger, Tom & Dellinger, Paul. Fuzzy. 2016. (ENG.). 272p. (J). (gr. 3-7). 14.95 *(978-1-4197-2122-9(4)*, Amulet Bks.) Abrams, Inc.

Anglin, M. R. Lucas: Guardian of Truth. 2012. 192p. pap. 8.00 *(978-1-60039-195-8(8))* Lamp Post Inc.

Anselmo, Robert Louis. We're All Different & yet Still the Same. l.t. ed. 2006. (Illus.). 22p. (J). 14.99 *(978-1-59879-107-5(9))*; per. 9.99 *(978-1-59879-088-7(9))* Lifevest Publishing, Inc.

Anstee, Ashlyn. No, No, Gnome! Anstee, Ashlyn, illus. 2016. (ENG., Illus.). 40p. (J). (gr. -1-3). 17.99 *(978-1-4814-3091-3(2)*, Simon & Schuster Bks. For Young Readers) Simon & Schuster Bks. For Young Readers.

Applegate, Anne. The Last Academy. 2013. (ENG.). 320p. (J). (gr. 7). 17.99 *(978-0-545-50204-7(7))* Scholastic, Inc.

Applegate, Katherine. Don't Swap Your Sweater for a Dog. Biggs, Brian, illus. 2008. (Roscoe Riley Rules Ser.: 3). (ENG.). 96p. (J). (gr. 1-5). 15.99 *(978-0-06-114886-6(5))*; pap. 4.99 *(978-0-06-114885-9(7))* HarperCollins Pubs.
—Don't Swap Your Sweater for a Dog. 2016. (Roscoe Riley Rules Ser.: 3). (J). lib. bdg. 14.75 *(978-0-606-38736-1(6))* Turtleback Bks.
—Don't Tap-Dance on Your Teacher. Biggs, Brian, illus. 2009. (Roscoe Riley Rules Ser.: 5). (ENG.). 96p. (J). (gr. 1-5). pap. 4.99 *(978-0-06-114889-7(X))* HarperCollins Pubs.
—Don't Tap-Dance on Your Teacher. Biggs, Brian, illus. 2016. (Roscoe Riley Rules Ser.: 5). (ENG.). 112p. (J). (gr. 1-5). 14.75 *(978-0-606-39252-5(1))* Turtleback Bks.
—Don't Tap-Dance on Your Teacher. 2009. (Roscoe Riley Rules Ser.: 5). (J). lib. bdg. 14.75 *(978-0-606-05007-4(8)*, Turtleback) Turtleback Bks.
—Home of the Brave. 2008. (ENG.). 272p. (J). (gr. 5-9). pap. 7.99 *(978-0-312-53563-6(5)*; 9780312535636) Square Fish.
—Never Glue Your Friends to Chairs. Biggs, Brian, illus. 2008. (Roscoe Riley Rules Ser.: 1). (ENG.). 96p. (J). (gr. 1-5). 15.99 *(978-0-06-114882-8(2))*; pap. 4.99 *(978-0-06-114881-1(4))* HarperCollins Pubs.
—Never Race a Runaway Pumpkin. Biggs, Brian, illus. 2009. (Roscoe Riley Rules Ser.: 7). (ENG.). 96p. (J). (gr. 1-5). 15.99 *(978-0-06-178372-2(2))*; pap. 4.99 *(978-0-06-178370-8(6))* HarperCollins Pubs.
—Never Race a Runaway Pumpkin. 2009. (Roscoe Riley Rules Ser.: 7). (J). lib. bdg. 14.75 *(978-0-606-06090-5(1)*, Turtleback) Turtleback Bks.
—Never Swim in Applesauce. 2016. (Roscoe Riley Rules Ser.: 4). (J). lib. bdg. 14.75 *(978-0-606-38737-8(4))* Turtleback Bks.
—Never Swipe a Bully's Bear. Biggs, Brian, illus. 2008. (Roscoe Riley Rules Ser.: 2). (ENG.). 96p. (J). (gr. 1-5). 15.99 *(978-0-06-114884-2(9))*; pap. 4.99 *(978-0-06-114883-5(0))* HarperCollins Pubs.
—Never Walk in Shoes That Talk. Biggs, Brian, illus. 2009. (Roscoe Riley Rules Ser.: 6). (ENG.). 96p. (J). (gr. 1-5). 14.99 *(978-0-06-114892-7(X))*; pap. 4.99 *(978-0-06-114891-0(1))* HarperCollins Pubs.
—Never Walk in Shoes That Talk. 2009. (Roscoe Riley Rules Ser.: 06). lib. bdg. 14.75 *(978-0-606-05019-7(1)*, Turtleback) Turtleback Bks.

Arai, Kiyoko. Beauty Pop, Vol. 1. 2006. (ENG., Illus.). 208p. pap. 8.99 *(978-1-4215-0575-6(4))* Viz Media.

Archer, Jennifer. Through Her Eyes. 2012. (ENG.). 400p. (YA). (gr. 8). pap. 9.99 *(978-0-06-183459-2(9)*, HarperTeen) HarperCollins Pubs.

Arcos, Carrie. Crazy Messy Beautiful. 2017. (ENG.). 320p. (YA). (gr. 7). 17.99 *(978-0-399-17553-4(9)*, Philomel Bks.) Penguin Young Readers Group.

Arena, Felice & Kettle, Phil. Rotten School Day. Vane, Mitch, illus. 2004. (J). pap. *(978-1-59336-364-2(8))* Mondo Publishing.

Arévalo, Josefina. Lo Que Paulito Olvidó. 2006. (SPA.). (J). *(978-1-59835-006-7(4))* Cambridge BrickHouse, Inc.

Argueta, Jorge. Moony Luna. Gómez, Elizabeth, illus. 2013.Tr. of Luna, Lunita Lunera. (ENG & SPA.). 32p. (J). pap. 9.95 *(978-0-89239-306-0(8)*, Children's Book Press) Lee & Low Bks., Inc.

Argueta, Jorge & Alvarez, Cecilia Concepcion. Moony Luna: Luna, Lunita Lunera. Gomez, Elizabeth, illus. 2005. (ENG & SPA.). 32p. (J). 16.95 *(978-0-89239-205-6(3))* Lee & Low Bks., Inc.

Ariye, Shirley. Our Georgia School: A Wildlife Habitat. 2012. 24p. pap. 11.95 *(978-1-60976-608-5(3)*, Strategic Bk. Publishing) Strategic Book Publishing & Rights Agency (SBPRA).

Armstrong, Kelley. The Gathering. (Darkness Rising Ser.: 1). (YA). (gr. 8). 2012. 384p. pap. 9.99 *(978-0-06-179703-3(0))* 2011. 368p. 17.99 *(978-0-06-179702-6(2))* HarperCollins Pubs.
—The Gathering. (Darkness Rising Ser.: Bk. 1). (YA). 1.25 *(978-1-4498-6189-6(X))*; 100.75 *(978-1-4498-6186-5(5))*; 2013. 102.75 *(978-1-4498-6184-1(9))* Recorded Bks., Inc.

Arnold, Audrey. Elkin's Tail. 2012. (Illus.). 52p. pap. 27.45 *(978-1-4772-2180-8(8))* AuthorHouse.

Arnold, Beth. Elijah Makes New Friends. Arnold, Beth, illus. 2012. (Illus.). 30p. pap. 9.99 *(978-0-9860272-3-9(5))* Get Happy Tips, LLC.

Arnold, Louise. Golden & Grey: An Unremarkable Boy & a Rather Remarkable Ghost. 2006. (ENG., Illus.). 272p. (J). (gr. 3-7). reprint ed. pap. 6.99 *(978-0-689-87585-4(1)*, McElderry, Margaret K. Bks.) McElderry, Margaret K. Bks.
—Golden & Grey: The Nightmares That Ghosts Have. 2007. (ENG.). 304p. (J). (gr. 3-7). pap. 5.99 *(978-0-689-87587-8(8)*, McElderry, Margaret K. Bks.) McElderry, Margaret K. Bks.
—Golden & Grey - A Good Day for Haunting. 2009. (ENG.). 336p. (J). (gr. 3-7). pap. 6.99 *(978-1-4169-0864-7(1)*, McElderry, Margaret K. Bks.) McElderry, Margaret K. Bks.

Arnold, Tedd. Super Fly Guy. Arnold, Tedd, illus. 2006. (Fly Guy Ser.: 2). (ENG., Illus.). 32p. (J). (gr. -1-3). 6.99 *(978-0-439-63904-0(2)*, Cartwheel Bks.) Scholastic, Inc.

Arroyo, Madeline. Calie's Gift. Vavak, S. Dean, illus. 2003. 32p. (gr. 2-5). 16.95 *(978-0-9740061-0-9(6)*, 1234106) Stairway Pubns.

Aryal, Aimee. Hello Herbie Husker! Shrestha, Anuj, illus. 2004. 24p. (J). 14.95 *(978-1-932888-43-0(8))* Mascot Bks., Inc.
—Hello, Pistol Pete! Craig, Megan, illus. 2007. 24p. (J). lib. bdg. 14.95 *(978-1-932888-38-6(1))* Mascot Bks., Inc.

Asch, Frank. Battle in a Bottle. Kanzler, John, illus. 2014. (Class Pets Ser.). (ENG.). 96p. (J). (gr. 2-6). pap. 13.99 *(978-1-4814-3625-0(2)*, Simon & Schuster/Paula Wiseman Bks.) Simon & Schuster/Paula Wiseman Bks.
—The Ghost of P. S. 42. Kanzler, John, illus. 2014. (Class Pets Ser.). (ENG.). 96p. (J). (gr. 2-5). pap. 13.99 *(978-1-4814-3624-3(4)*, Simon & Schuster/Paula Wiseman Bks.) Simon & Schuster/Paula Wiseman Bks.
—Survival School. Kanzler, John, illus. 2014. (Class Pets Ser.). (ENG.). 96p. (J). (gr. 2-6). pap. 13.99 *(978-1-4814-3627-4(9)*, Simon & Schuster/Paula Wiseman Bks.) Simon & Schuster/Paula Wiseman Bks.

Ashburn, Boni. The Class. Gee, Kimberly, illus. 2016. (ENG.). 40p. (J). (gr. -1-3). 17.99 *(978-1-4424-2248-3(3)*, Beach Lane Bks.) Beach Lane Bks.

Ashcraft, Carolyn. Hamlet Goes to School. 2004. (Illus.). 108p. (J). per. 5.99 net. *(978-0-9755232-0-9(1))* Word Seed Publishing.

Asher, Diana Harmon. Sidetracked. 2017. (ENG.). 240p. (J). (gr. 3-7). 16.99 ***(978-1-4197-2601-9(3)**, Amulet Bks.)* Abrams, Inc.

Asher, Jay. Thirteen Reasons Why. 2014. (ENG.). 336p. (YA). 15.24 *(978-1-63245-099-9(2))* Lectorum Pubns., Inc.
—Thirteen Reasons Why. 2009. 11.72 *(978-0-7848-3782-5(1)*, Everbind) Marco Bk. Co.
—Thirteen Reasons Why. (ENG.). (YA). (gr. 7). 2017. 336p. pap. 10.99 ***(978-0-451-47829-0(0))*** 2011. 336p. pap. 10.99 *(978-1-59514-188-0(X))* 2007. 320p. 18.99 *(978-1-59514-171-2(5))* 10th anniv. ed. 2016. 352p. 18.99 *(978-1-59514-788-2(8))* Penguin Young Readers Group. (Razorbill).
—Thirteen Reasons Why. 2011. (ENG.). (YA). (gr. 7-12). lib. bdg. 21.60 ***(978-1-60686-991-8(4))*** Perfection Learning Corp.
—Thirteen Reasons Why. 2011. lib. bdg. 22.10 *(978-0-606-15085-9(4)*, Turtleback) Turtleback Bks.

Asher, Jay & Mackler, Carolyn. The Future of Us. 2012. (ENG., Illus.). 384p. (YA). (gr. 7). pap. 10.99 *(978-1-59514-516-1(8)*, Razorbill) Penguin Young Readers Group.
—The Future of Us. 2012. lib. bdg. 20.85 *(978-0-606-26498-3(1)*, Turtleback) Turtleback Bks.

Ashes to Ashes. 2014. (ENG., Illus.). 400p. (YA). (gr. 9). 18.99 *(978-1-4424-4081-4(3)*, Simon & Schuster Bks. For Young Readers) Simon & Schuster Bks. For Young Readers.

Ashton, Brodi. Diplomatic Immunity. 2016. 368p. (YA). (gr. 8). 17.99 *(978-0-06-236856-0(7))* HarperCollins Pubs.

Ashton, Victoria. Juicy Secrets. 2006. (Confessions of a Teen Nanny Ser.). 208p. (J). lib. bdg. 16.89 *(978-0-06-077526-1(2))*; (ENG.). (YA). (gr. 9-12). 15.99 *(978-0-06-073181-6(8))* HarperCollins Pubs. (HarperTeen).
—Rich Girls. 2006. (Confessions of a Teen Nanny Ser.). (ENG.). 224p. (YA). (gr. 9-12). 15.99 *(978-0-06-073179-3(6))* HarperCollins Pubs.

Asquith, Ros. Letters from an Alien Schoolboy. 2013. (ENG., Illus.). 192p. (J). (gr. 1-5). 12.95 *(978-1-62087-536-0(5)*, 620536, Sky Pony Pr.) Skyhorse Publishing Co., Inc.
—Trixie Ace Ghost Buster. 2008. (Trixie Ser.). (ENG., Illus.). 176p. (J). (gr. 3-6). pap. 7.99 *(978-0-00-725909-0(3))* HarperCollins Pubs. Ltd. GBR. Dist: Independent Pubs. Group.
—Trixie Gets the Witch Factor. 2007. (Trixie Ser.). (ENG., Illus.). 176p. (J). (gr. 3-6). pap. 13.95 *(978-0-00-725910-6(7))* HarperCollins Pubs. Ltd. GBR. Dist: Independent Pubs. Group.

Astro, Ian. Moon School. 2006. (Neighborhood Readers Ser.). (ENG.). 16p. (gr. 1-3). pap. 6.50 *(978-1-4042-7196-8(1)*, Rosen Classroom) Rosen Publishing Group, Inc., The.

Atkins, Catherine. Alt Ed. 2004. (ENG.). 208p. (YA). (gr. 7-12). reprint ed. 6.99 *(978-0-14-240235-1(4)*, Speak) Penguin Young Readers Group.

Atkins, Eddie. McCool School: If I ran the School. 2006. 32p. per. 19.95 *(978-1-59858-155-3(4))* Dog Ear Publishing, LLC.

Atkinson, Elizabeth. From Alice to Zen & Everyone in Between. (gr. 4-7). 2013. (ENG.). 248p. (J). pap. 9.95 *(978-1-4677-0861-6(5)*, Carolrhoda Bks.) 2008. 247p. (YA). 16.95 *(978-0-8225-7271-8(0))* Lerner Publishing Group.

Attack of the Tagger. unabr. ed. 2006. (Shredderman Ser.: Bk. 2). (Illus.). (J). (gr. 3-6). audio compact disk 28.95 *(978-1-59519-759-7(1))* Live Oak Media.

Atwood, D. E. If We Shadows. 2016. (ENG., Illus.). (J). 24.99 ***(978-1-63533-033-5(5))*** 2014. 240p. pap. 14.99 *(978-1-62798-820-9(3))* Dreamspinner Pr. (Harmony Ink Pr.).

Atwood, Megan. Molly Meets Trouble (Whose Real Name Is Jenna) Fleming, Lucy, illus. 2016. (Dear Molly, Dear Olive Ser.). (ENG.). 96p. (gr. 1-3). lib. bdg. 21.99 *(978-1-4795-8696-7(X))* Picture Window Bks.

Auch, M. J. One Plus One Equals Blue. 2014. (ENG.). 288p. (J). (gr. 5-9). pap. 8.99 *(978-1-250-03992-7(4)*, 9781250039927) Square Fish.

Auch, Mary Jane. I Was a Third Grade Spy. Auch, Herm, illus. 2004. 86p. (gr. 2-5). 16.00 *(978-0-7569-4138-3(5))* Perfection Learning Corp.
—I Was a Third Grade Spy. Auch, Herm, illus. 2003. (ENG.). 96p. (J). (gr. 3-7). 5.99 *(978-0-440-41871-9(2)*, Yearling) Random Hse. Children's Bks.

Auerbach, Adam. Edda: A Little Valkyrie's First Day of School. Auerbach, Adam, illus. 2014. (ENG., Illus.). 40p. (J). (gr. -1-3). 16.99 *(978-0-8050-9703-0(1)*, 9780805097030, Holt, Henry & Co. Bks. For Young Readers) Holt, Henry & Co.

Auerbach, Annie & Mike, Norton. Grosse Adventures - The Good, the Bad & the Gassy, Vol. 1. 2006. (Illus.). 96p. pap. 4.99 *(978-1-59816-049-9(4))* TOKYOPOP, Inc.

Aunt Connye. Club House: Stories that Teach. 2012. 76p. pap. 28.99 *(978-1-4670-4413-4(X))* AuthorHouse.

Avi. Don't You Know There's a War On? 2nd ed. 2003. 208p. (J). pap. *(978-0-439-53096-5(2)*, HarperCollins) HarperCollins Pubs.
—Don't You Know There's a War On? 2003. 193p. (gr. 3-7). 18.00 *(978-0-7569-1383-0(7))* Perfection Learning Corp.
—Nothing but the Truth. 2010. (ENG.). 208p. (J). (gr. 5-9). 6.99 *(978-0-545-17415-2(5)*, Scholastic Paperbacks) Scholastic, Inc.
—Nothing but the Truth. 2010. lib. bdg. 17.20 *(978-0-606-12300-6(8)*, Turtleback) Turtleback Bks.
—Romeo & Juliet Together (and Alive!) at Last. 2012. (ENG.). 128p. (J). (gr. 5-9). pap. 6.99 *(978-0-545-43097-5(6)*, Scholastic Paperbacks) Scholastic, Inc.
—School of the Dead. 288p. (J). (gr. 3-7). 2017. pap. 6.99 ***(978-0-06-174086-2(1))*** 2016. 16.99 *(978-0-06-174085-5(3))* HarperCollins Pubs.
—School of the Dead. 2017. (ENG.). (J). (gr. 3-7). lib. bdg. 17.20 ***(978-0-606-40053-4(2))*** Turtleback Bks.

Avi. The Secret School. 2003. (ENG., Illus.). 176p. (J). (gr. 2-5). pap. 7.99 *(978-0-15-204699-6(2)*, 53582853) Houghton Mifflin Harcourt Publishing Co.
—The Secret School. 2003. 157p. (J). (gr. 3-7). 13.60 *(978-0-7569-1625-1(9))* Perfection Learning Corp.

Avi & Vail, Rachel. Never Mind! 2005. (Twin Novels Ser.). 200p. (gr. 5-9). 16.00 *(978-0-7569-5667-7(6))* Perfection Learning Corp.

Ayarbe, Heidi. Compulsion. 2011. (ENG.). 304p. (YA). (gr. 9-18). 17.99 *(978-0-06-199386-2(7))* HarperCollins Pubs.
—Wanted. 2012. (ENG.). 400p. (YA). (gr. 9). 17.99 *(978-0-06-199388-6(3))* HarperCollins Pubs.

Ayres, Katherine. Family Tree. 2012. 116p. pap. 7.99 *(978-1-936495-21-4(X))* BookPartners, LLC.
—Macaroni Boy. 2004. (ENG.). 192p. (J). (gr. 3-7). per. 6.99 *(978-0-440-41884-9(4)*, Yearling) Random Hse. Children's Bks.

Ayton, Shalanna. The Adventures of Missy the Moose. 2009. 68p. pap. 26.99 *(978-1-4389-7827-7(8))* AuthorHouse.

Babiak, Alexandra Brittany. The Runaway Jacket, 1 vol. 2009. 40p. pap. 24.95 *(978-1-60749-332-7(2))* America Star Bks.

Babich, Elaine. You Never Called Me Princess. 2012. 210p. pap. 14.00 *(978-1-105-70209-9(X))* Lulu.com GBR. Dist: Lulu Pr., Inc.

Baccellia, Kim. No More Goddesses. 2013. (ENG.). 252p. (YA). (gr. 3-7). pap. 14.99 *(978-1-61271-012-9(3)*, Zumaya Thresholds) Zumaya Pubns. LLC.

Backes, M. Molly. The Princesses of Iowa. (ENG.). 464p. (YA). (gr. 9). 2014. pap. 9.99 *(978-0-7636-7161-7(4))* 2012. (Illus.). 16.99 *(978-0-7636-5312-5(8))* Candlewick Pr.

Bacon, C. G. Mean Mandy. 2009. 103p. pap. 11.00 *(978-0-557-05740-5(X))* Lulu Pr., Inc.

Bacon, Lee. Joshua Dread. 2013. (Joshua Dread Ser.: 1). (ENG.). 272p. (J). (gr. 4-7). 6.99 *(978-0-307-92998-3(1)*, Yearling) Random Hse. Children's Bks.
—Joshua Dread: the Dominion Key. 2015. (Joshua Dread Ser.: 3). (ENG.). 256p. (J). (gr. 4-7). 6.99 *(978-0-385-37126-1(8)*, Yearling) Random Hse. Children's Bks.

Bacskai, Andrew. Fighting the Legend, 1 vol. unabr. ed. 2011. (District 13 Ser.). (ENG.). 48p. (YA). (gr. 9-12). pap. 7.95 *(978-1-61651-278-1(4))* Saddleback Educational Publishing, Inc.

Badeaux, Dewey. Sam & Skully. Ball, Lauren, illus. 2013. 126p. pap. 12.99 *(978-0-9884057-4-5(1))* Alligator Pr.

Bader, Bonnie. 100 Monsters in My School. Hendrix, Bryan, illus. 2003. (All Aboard Math Reader Ser.). 48p. (gr. -1-3). 14.00 *(978-0-7569-1648-0(8))* Perfection Learning Corp.

Badger, Meredith. Fairy School Dropout Undercover. 2011. (Fairy School Ser.: 2). (ENG., Illus.). 160p. (J). (gr. 2-4). pap. 14.99 *(978-0-312-61951-0(0)*, 9780312619510) Square Fish.

Baier, Jeanne M. The Twins Jeffrey & Jeanne. 2012. 28p. pap. 16.00 *(978-1-4669-5194-5(X))* Trafford Publishing.

Bailey, Charles. Slick Glickman, Unlikely Hero. 2008. 164p. 22.95 *(978-0-595-49014-1(X))*; pap. 12.95 *(978-0-595-48014-2(4))* iUniverse, Inc.

Bailey, Christine. Girl in the Middle. 2013. 236p. pap. 8.99 *(978-0-9890632-0-3(8))* Vinspire Publishing LLC.

Bailey, Em. Shift. 2016. (ENG.). 288p. (YA). (gr. 9). pap. 17.99 ***(978-1-76012-698-8(5))*** Hardie Grant Egmont Pty, Ltd. AUS. Dist: Independent Pubs. Group.

Bailey, Linda. Stanley at School. Slavin, Bill, illus. 2015. (ENG.). 32p. (J). (gr. -1-2). 17.95 *(978-1-77138-096-6(9))* Kids Can Pr., Ltd. CAN. Dist: Hachette Bk. Group.

Baker, Chandler. Teen Hyde: High School Horror. 2017. (High School Horror Ser.: 2). (ENG.). 272p. (YA). 17.99 *(978-1-250-05875-1(9)*, 9781250058751) Feiwel & Friends.

Baker, Kim. Pickle: The (Formerly) Anonymous Prank Club of Fountain Point Middle School. Probert, Tim, illus. 2014. (ENG.). 256p. (J). (gr. 3-7). pap. 7.99 *(978-1-250-04427-3(8)*, 9781250044273) Square Fish.

Baker, Kimberly. Pickle: The (Formerly) Anonymous Prank Club of Fountain Point Middle School. Probert, Tim, illus. 2012. (ENG.). 240p. (J). (gr. 3-7). 16.99 *(978-1-59643-765-4(0)*, 9781596437654) Roaring Brook Pr.

Balaban, Bob. Boy or Beast. Rash, Andy, illus. (Creature from the 7th Grade Ser.: 1). (ENG.). (J). (gr. 5). 2013. 272p. pap. 7.99 *(978-0-14-242542-8(7)*, Puffin Books) 2012. 256p. 15.99 *(978-0-670-01271-8(8)*, Viking Books for Young Readers) Penguin Young Readers Group.

Balan, Judy. Tweenache in the Time of Hashtags. 2016. (Nina the Philosopher Ser.: 1). 192p. 6.99 *(978-93-5177-550-8(X))* HarperCollins Pubs.

Baldwin, Kathleen. A School for Unusual Girls. 2015. (Stranje House Ser.: 1). (ENG.). 352p. (YA). (gr. 8-12). 17.99 *(978-0-7653-7600-8(8)*, 9780765376008, Tor Teen) Doherty, Tom Assocs., LLC.

Baldwin, Rich & Jones, Sandie. The Detective Company. Dawn, Baumer, illus. 2004. 183p. (YA). pap. 9.95 *(978-0-9742920-0-7(1)*, 2001) Buttonwood Pr.

Balgassi, Haemi. Tae's Sonata. 2005. (Reader's Workshop Ser.). (ENG.). 164p. (C). pap. 19.95 *(978-0-7362-2801-5(2))* National Geographic School Publishing, Inc.

Ball, Nate. Alien in My Pocket: Radio Active. Pamintuan, Macky, illus. 2014. (Alien in My Pocket Ser.: 3). (ENG.). 144p. (J). (gr. 1-5). 15.99 *(978-0-06-231493-2(9))* HarperCollins Pubs.
—Alien in My Pocket - Blast Off! Pamintuan, Macky, illus. 2014. (Alien in My Pocket Ser.: 1). (ENG.). 160p. (J). (gr. 1-5). pap. 4.99 *(978-0-06-221623-6(6))* HarperCollins Pubs.
—Alien in My Pocket - The Science Unfair. Pamintuan, Macky, illus. 2014. (Alien in My Pocket Ser.: 2). (ENG.). 144p. (J). (gr. 1-5). pap. 4.99 *(978-0-06-221625-0(2))* HarperCollins Pubs.
—Alien in My Pocket: on Impact! Pamintuan, Macky, illus. 2014. (Alien in My Pocket Ser.: 4). (ENG.). 128p. (J). (gr. 1-5). pap. 4.99 *(978-0-06-221629-8(5))* HarperCollins Pubs.
—Radio Active. 2014. (Alien in My Pocket Ser.: 3). (J). lib. bdg. 14.75 *(978-0-606-35349-6(6))* Turtleback Bks.
—The Science Unfair. Pamintuan, Macky, illus. 2014. (Alien in My Pocket Ser.: 2). (ENG.). 144p. (J). (gr. 1-5). 15.99 *(978-0-06-231494-9(7))* HarperCollins Pubs.
—The Science Unfair. 2014. (Alien in My Pocket Ser.: 2). (J). lib. bdg. 14.75 *(978-0-606-35182-9(5))* Turtleback Bks.

Ball, S. N. Daddies Don't Get Snow Days. Howard, Ellie Nothaus, illus. 2013. (ENG.). 28p. (J). pap. 13.95 *(978-1-4787-1188-9(4))* Outskirts Pr., Inc.

Balliett, Blue. The Wright 3. Helquist, Brett, illus. 2008. 318p. (gr. 4-7). 18.00 *(978-0-7569-8942-2(6))* Perfection Learning Corp.
—The Wright 3. Helquist, Brett, illus. 2007. (ENG.). 352p. (J). (gr. 3-7). pap. 7.99 *(978-0-439-69368-4(3)*, Scholastic Paperbacks) Scholastic, Inc.

Baltazar, Art & Aureliani, Franco. Enter - Nightwing! Baltazar, Art & Aureliani, Franco, illus. 2012. (Tiny Titans Ser.). (ENG., Illus.). 32p. (gr. 1-2). lib. bdg. 22.60 *(978-1-4342-4540-3(3))* Stone Arch Bks.
—Penguins in the Batcave!, 1 vol. Baltazar, Art & Aureliani, Franco, illus. 2012. (Tiny Titans Ser.). (ENG., Illus.). 32p. (gr. 1-2). 22.60 *(978-1-4342-4539-7(X))* Stone Arch Bks.
—Report Card Pickup!, 1 vol. Baltazar, Art & Aureliani, Franco, illus. 2013. (Tiny Titans Ser.). (ENG., Illus.). 32p. (gr. 1-2). lib. bdg. 22.60 *(978-1-4342-4699-8(X))* Stone Arch Bks.
—Sidekick City Elementary, 1 vol. Baltazar, Art & Aureliani, Franco, illus. 2012. (Tiny Titans Ser.). (ENG., Illus.). 32p. (gr. 1-2). lib. bdg. 22.60 *(978-1-4342-4528-1(4))* Stone Arch Bks.

Banash, Jennifer. Silent Alarm. 2015. (ENG.). 336p. (YA). (gr. 7). bds. 17.99 *(978-0-399-25789-6(6)*, G.P. Putnam's Sons Books for Young Readers) Penguin Young Readers Group.

Bancks, Tristan. Mac Slater Hunts the Cool. (Mac Slater Hunts the Cool Ser.). (ENG.). 224p. (J). (gr. 3-7). 2011. pap. 6.99 *(978-1-4169-8575-4(1))* 2010. 15.99 *(978-1-4169-8574-7(3))* Simon & Schuster Bks. For Young Readers. (Simon & Schuster Bks. For Young Readers).
—Noob, Amateur Dentist. Gorissen, Dean, illus. 2015. (Legends in Their Own Lunchbox Ser.). (ENG.). 56p. (gr. 2-3). pap. 7.99 *(978-1-4966-0253-4(6)*, Legends in Their Own Lunchbox) Capstone Classroom.
—Noob & the Librarian Supervillain. Gorissen, Dean, illus. 2015. (Legends in Their Own Lunchbox Ser.). (ENG.). 48p. (gr. 1-2). pap. 7.99 *(978-1-4966-0247-3(1)*, Legends in Their Own Lunchbox) Capstone Classroom.
—Noob, Crimebuster. Gorissen, Dean, illus. 2015. (Legends in Their Own Lunchbox Ser.). (ENG.). 48p. (gr. 1-2). pap. 7.99

(978-1-4966-0241-1(2), Legends in Their Own Lunchbox) Capstone Classroom.
Banerjee, Anjali. Looking for Bapu. 2008. (ENG.). 176p. (J). (gr. 3-7). 6.50 (978-0-553-49425-9(2), Yearling) Random Hse. Children's Bks.
Bang, Molly. When Sophie's Feelings Are Really, Really Hurt. 2015. (ENG., Illus.). 40p. (J). (gr. -1-3). 17.99 (978-0-545-78831-1(5), Blue Sky Pr., The) Scholastic, Inc.
Banim, Lisa. In the Doghouse. 2005. 124p. (J). lib. bdg. 16.92 (978-1-4242-0685-8(5)) Fitzgerald Bks.
Banim, Lisa & Minsky, Terri. The Case of the Kate Haters. 2005. (Illus.). 124p. (J). (978-1-4156-3927-6(2)) Disney Pr.
Banks, Jacqueline Turner. A Day for Vincent Chin & Me. 2005. (ENG.). 128p. (J). (gr. 5-7). pap. 11.95 (978-0-618-54879-8(3)) Houghton Mifflin Harcourt Publishing Co.
Banks, Jacqueline Turner & Turner Banks, Jacqueline. Egg-Drop Blues. 2003. (ENG.). 128p. (J). (gr. 5-7). pap. 10.95 (978-0-618-25080-6(8)) Houghton Mifflin Harcourt Publishing Co.
Banks, Kate & Sheldrake, Rupert. Boy's Best Friend. 2015. (ENG.). 224p. (J). (gr. 3-7). 15.99 (978-0-374-38008-3(2), 9780374380083, Farrar, Straus & Giroux (BYR)) Farrar, Straus & Giroux.
Banks, Piper. Geek Abroad, 2 vols. 2008. (Geek High Ser.: 2). (ENG.). 256p. (YA). (gr. 9-18). 9.99 (978-0-451-22393-7(4), Berkley) Penguin Publishing Group.
—Geek High. 2007. (Geek High Ser.: 1). (ENG.). 256p. (YA). (gr. 9-18). 9.99 (978-0-451-22225-1(3), Berkley) Penguin Publishing Group.
—Revenge of the Geek. 2010. (Geek High Ser.: 4). (ENG.). 256p. (gr. 12-18). 9.99 (978-0-451-23134-5(1), Berkley) Penguin Publishing Group.
Banks, Tyra. Modelland. 2011. 569p. (YA). (gr. 7). 17.99 (978-0-375-97259-1(5), Delacorte Pr) Random House Publishing Group.
Banner, Angela. Ant & Bee & the Secret. 2015. (Ant & Bee Ser.). (ENG., Illus.). 84p. (J). (gr. -1-k). 7.99 (978-1-4052-7515-6(4)) Egmont Bks., Ltd. GBR. Dist: Independent Pubs. Group.
Banville, Vincent. Hennessy. 180p. pap. (978-0-7022-2505-5(3)) Univ. of Queensland Pr.
Baratz-Logsted, Lauren. Angel's Choice. 2006. (ENG.). 256p. (YA). (gr. 9-12). pap. 6.99 (978-1-4169-2524-8(4), Simon Pulse) Simon Pulse.
—Crazy Beautiful. 2011. (ENG.). 204p. (YA). (gr. 7). pap. 12.95 (978-0-547-40310-6(0)) Houghton Mifflin Harcourt Publishing Co.
—The Education of Bet. 2011. (ENG.). 192p. (YA). (gr. 7). pap. 11.99 (978-0-547-55024-4(3)) Houghton Mifflin Harcourt Publishing Co.
—Jackie's Jokes. 2009. (Sisters Eight Ser.: 4). (ENG., Illus.). 128p. (J). (gr. 1-4). pap. 5.99 (978-0-547-05328-8(2)) Houghton Mifflin Harcourt Publishing Co.
Barbara, Cohen. Molly's Pilgrim. 97th rev. ed. 2014. (ENG.). 32p. (J). (gr. 1-5). 8.24 (978-1-63245-244-3(8)) Lectorum Pubns., Inc.
Barber, Tiki & Barber, Ronde. Red Zone. (Barber Game Time Bks.). (ENG., 176p. (J). (gr. 3-7). 2013. Illus.). pap. 7.99 (978-1-4169-6861-0(X)) 2010. 15.99 (978-1-4169-6860-3(1)) Simon & Schuster/Paula Wiseman Bks. (Simon & Schuster/Paula Wiseman Bks.).
Barbour, Ralph Henry. The Half-Back. 2005. 27.95 (978-1-4218-1494-0(3)); 220p. pap. 12.95 (978-1-4218-1594-7(X)) 1st World Publishing, Inc. (1st World Library - Literary Society).
—The Half-Back. 2007. 132p. per. (978-1-4068-3665-3(6)) Echo Library.
—The New Boy at Hilltop & Other Stories. 2006. pap. (978-1-4065-0779-9(2)) Dodo Pr.
Barden, Stephanie. Cinderella Smith. Goode, Diane, illus. (Cinderella Smith Ser.: 1). (ENG.). (J). 2012. 176p. (gr. 3-7). pap. 5.99 (978-0-06-196425-1(5)) 2011. 160p. (gr. 3-7). 16.99 (978-0-06-196423-7(9)) Vol. 3. 2013. 144p. (gr. 1-5). 16.99 (978-0-06-200443-7(3)) HarperCollins Pubs.
—The More the Merrier. Goode, Diane, illus. (Cinderella Smith Ser.: 2). (ENG.). (J). (gr. 3-7). 2013. 160p. pap. 5.99 (978-0-06-200442-0(5)) 2012. 144p. 15.99 (978-0-06-200440-6(9)) HarperCollins Pubs.
Bare, Bart. Girl. 2010. 188p. (YA). pap. 11.95 (978-0-9825396-4-4(9)) Canterbury Hse. Publishing, Ltd.
Bargiel, Nina G. & Amsterdam, Shane. Fintastic Friends Forever. 2016. (Illus.). 32p. (J). (978-1-5182-1661-9(7)) Little Brown & Co.
Barham, Paul Richard. The Adventures of Damen the Duck. 2012. 72p. pap. 41.99 (978-1-4691-5476-3(5)) Xlibris Corp.
Barker, Kathryn. In the Skin of a Monster. 2016. (ENG.). 304p. (YA). (gr. 10). pap. 12.99 (978-1-76011-171-7(6)) Allen & Unwin AUS. Dist: Independent Pubs. Group.
Barkley, Callie. Amy Is a Little Bit Chicken. Bishop, Tracy, illus. 2015. (Critter Club Ser.: 13). (ENG.). 128p. (J). (gr. k-4). pap. 5.99 (978-1-4814-5174-1(X), Little Simon) Little Simon.
—Liz Learns a Lesson. Riti, Marsha, illus. 2013. (Critter Club Ser.: 3). (ENG.). 128p. (J). (gr. -1-2). 16.99 (978-1-4424-6770-5(3)); pap. 5.99 (978-1-4424-6768-2(1)) Little Simon. (Little Simon).
—Liz Learns a Lesson. 2013. (Critter Club Ser.: 3). lib. bdg. 16.00 (978-0-606-32032-0(6), Turtleback) Turtleback Bks.
Barkow, Henriette. The Giant Turnip. Johnson, Richard, illus. 2004. 32p. (J). (ENG & POR.). pap. (978-1-85269-744-0(X)); (POL & ENG.). pap. (978-1-85269-743-3(1)) Mantra Lingua.
Barlow, Andrew. Jellytoes Misses the Bus. Barlow, Andrew, illus. 2005. (Jellytoes Ser.). (ENG., Illus.). 32p. (J). per. 8.95 (978-0-9764336-0-6(5)) MJS Publishing Group LLC.
Barnes, Bobbie Jo. The Message. 2012. 24p. pap. 24.95 (978-1-4626-9047-3(5)) America Star Bks.
Barnes, Derrick. Brand New School, Brave New Ruby. Newton, Vanessa Brantley, illus. 2008. (Ruby & the Booker Boys Ser.: 1). (ENG.). 144p. (J). (gr. 2-5). pap. 5.99 (978-0-545-01760-2(2), Scholastic Paperbacks) Scholastic, Inc.
Barnes, Derrick D. Trivia Queen/Supreme. Newton, Vanessa Brantley, illus. 2008. (Ruby & the Booker Boys Ser.: 2). (ENG.). 144p. (J). (gr. 2-5). pap. 5.99 (978-0-545-01761-9(0)) Scholastic, Inc.
—We Could Be Brothers. 2010. (J). (978-0-545-13574-0(5), Scholastic Pr.) Scholastic, Inc.
Barnes, Jennifer Lynn. Every Other Day. 2013. (ENG.). 352p. (J). (gr. 7). pap. 9.99 (978-1-60684-415-1(6), Carolrhoda Lab™) Lerner Publishing Group.
—The Fixer. 2015. (ENG.). 384p. (YA). (gr. 7). 17.99 (978-1-61963-594-4(1), 9781619635944, Bloomsbury USA Childrens) Bloomsbury Publishing USA.
—The Long Game: A Fixer Novel. (ENG.). 368p. (YA). 2017. pap. 9.99 (978-1-61963-599-9(2), 9781619635999) 2016. 17.99 (978-1-61963-596-8(8), 9781619635968) Bloomsbury Publishing USA. (Bloomsbury USA Childrens).
—Perfect Cover. 2008. (The Squad). (ENG.). 288p. (YA). (gr. 7). mass mkt. 7.99 (978-0-385-73454-7(9), Laurel Leaf) Random Hse. Children's Bks.
—Trial by Fire. 2012. (Raised by Wolves Ser.: Bk. 2). (ENG.). 368p. (J). (gr. 7). pap. 9.99 (978-1-60684-333-8(8), Carolrhoda Lab™) Lerner Publishing Group.
Barnes, John. Tales of the Madman Underground. 2011. (ENG.). 544p. (YA). (gr. 9-18). 9.99 (978-0-14-241702-7(5), Speak) Penguin Young Readers Group.
Barnes, Phil. My Teacher's a Robot! 2015. (ENG.). 63p. (J). (gr. 1-2). mass mkt. 8.95 (978-1-78455-935-9(0), e0384285-e807-49f7-959d-e33332f5b2d5) Austin, Stan AUS. Dist: Bookmasters Distribution.
Barnett, Mac. Billy Twitters & His Blue Whale Problem. Rex, Adam, illus. 2009. (ENG.). 48p. (J). (gr. -1-2). 16.99 (978-0-7868-4958-1(4)) Hyperion Pr.
Barnett, Mac & John, Jory. The Terrible Two. Cornell, Kevin, illus. (Terrible Two Ser.). (ENG.). (J). (gr. 3-7). 2016. 224p. 13.95 (978-1-4197-1680-5(8), Amulet Bks.) 2016. pap. 7.95 (978-1-4197-1925-7(4)) 2015. 224p. 13.95 (978-1-4197-1491-7(0), Amulet Bks.) Abrams, Inc.
—The Terrible Two. 2017. (Terrible Two Ser.: 1). lib. bdg. 18.40 (978-0-606-40723-6(5)); lib. bdg. 18.40 (978-0-606-40724-3(3)) Turtleback Bks.
Barnholdt, Lauren. Aces Up. 2010. (ENG.). 288p. (YA). (gr. 7). pap. 9.99 (978-0-385-73874-3(9), Ember) Random Hse. Children's Bks.
—Devon Delaney Should Totally Know Better. 2009. (Mix Ser.). (ENG.). 288p. (J). (gr. 4-8). pap. 6.99 (978-1-4169-8019-3(9), Aladdin) Simon & Schuster Children's Publishing.
—Fake Me a Match. 2012. (Mix Ser.). (ENG.). 304p. (J). (gr. 4-8). pap. 6.99 (978-1-4424-2259-9(9), Aladdin) Simon & Schuster Children's Publishing.
—Fake Me a Match. 2011. (Mix Ser.). (ENG.). 288p. (J). (gr. 4-9). 15.99 (978-1-4424-2258-2(0), Simon & Schuster/Paula Wiseman Bks.) Simon & Schuster/Paula Wiseman Bks.
—Girl Meets Ghost. 2013. (Girl Meets Ghost Ser.: 1). (ENG.). (J). (gr. 4-9). 240p. pap. 7.99 (978-1-4424-2146-2(0)); 224p. 15.99 (978-1-4424-4246-7(8)) Simon & Schuster Children's Publishing. (Aladdin).
—Hailey Twitch Is Not a Snitch. Beaky, Suzanne, illus. 2010. (Hailey Twitch Ser.: 1). (ENG.). 160p. (J). (gr. 2-4). pap. 6.99 (978-1-4022-2444-7(3), Sourcebooks Jabberwocky) Sourcebooks, Inc.
—The Harder the Fall. (Girl Meets Ghost Ser.: 2). (ENG., (J). (gr. 4-9). 2014. Illus.). 256p. pap. 7.99 (978-1-4424-2147-9(9)) 2013. 240p. 16.99 (978-1-4424-4247-4(6)) Simon & Schuster Children's Publishing. (Aladdin).
—Rules for Secret Keeping. 2011. (Mix Ser.). (ENG.). 304p. (J). (gr. 4-8). pap. 7.99 (978-1-4169-8021-6(0), Aladdin) Simon & Schuster Children's Publishing.
—Sometimes It Happens. (ENG.). (YA). (gr. 9). 2012. 336p. pap. 9.99 (978-1-4424-1315-3(8)) 2011. 320p. 16.99 (978-1-4424-1314-6(X)) Simon Pulse. (Simon Pulse).
—The Thing about the Truth. (ENG.). (YA). (gr. 9). 2013. 320p. pap. 9.99 (978-1-4424-3461-5(9)) 2012. 304p. 16.99 (978-1-4424-3460-8(0)) Simon Pulse. (Simon Pulse).
Barns, Crosby H. Who Programmed the Species? The Theory of Scientific Coincidence. 2008. 36p. pap. 16.99 (978-1-4389-0727-7(3)) AuthorHouse.
Baron, Jeff. Sean Rosen Is Not for Sale. (ENG.). 384p. (J). (gr. 3-7). 2015. pap. 6.99 (978-0-06-218751-2(1)) 2014. 16.99 (978-0-06-218750-5(3)) HarperCollins Pubs. (Greenwillow Bks.).
Barreintez, Elsa. I'm Only Eight, by Reynaldo: I Survived Being Eight. 2010. 46p. pap. 14.95 (978-1-4327-5489-1(0)) Outskirts Pr., Inc.
Barrett, Jennifer. Lethal Delivery, Postage Prepaid. (Thumbprint Mysteries Ser.). 32.86 (978-0-8092-0425-0(8)) McGraw-Hill/Contemporary.
Barrows, Annie & Blackall, Sophie. Ivy + Bean & the Ghost That Had to Go, 1 vol. 2011. (Ivy & Bean Ser.). (ENG., Illus.). 136p. (J). (gr. 1-4). 24.21 (978-1-59961-929-3(6)) Spotlight.
—Ivy + Bean What's the Big Idea?, 1 vol. 2011. (Ivy & Bean Ser.). (ENG., Illus.). 132p. (J). (gr. 1-4). 24.21 (978-1-59961-934-7(2)) Spotlight.
Barrows, Annie, et al. Ivy + Bean What's the Big Idea? Blackall, Sophie, illus. 2010. (ENG.). 128p. (J). (gr. 1-5). 14.99 (978-0-8118-6692-7(0)) Chronicle Bks. LLC.
Barry, Cotter. The Adventures of Morgan Morgan the Rhymester. 2010. 16p. 12.99 (978-1-4520-0116-6(2)) AuthorHouse.
Barry, Dave. The Worst Night Ever. 2016. (Class Trip Ser.). (ENG.). 256p. (J). (gr. 3-7). 13.99 (978-1-4847-0850-7(4)) Hyperion Bks. for Children.
Barshaw, Ruth McNally. Best Friends Fur-Ever. Barshaw, Ruth McNally, illus. 2013. (Ellie Mcdoodle Diaries). (ENG., Illus.). 192p. (YA). (gr. 3-6). 12.99 (978-1-61963-175-5(X), 9781619631755, Bloomsbury USA Childrens) Bloomsbury Publishing USA.
—Ellie McDoodle: Best Friends Fur-Ever. Barshaw, Ruth McNally, illus. 2011. (Ellie Mcdoodle Ser.). (ENG., Illus.). 192p. (YA). (gr. 3-6). pap. 7.99 (978-1-59990-657-7(0), 9781599906577, Bloomsbury USA Childrens) Bloomsbury Publishing USA.
—The Ellie McDoodle Diaries: Ellie for President. Barshaw, Ruth McNally, illus. 2014. (Ellie Mcdoodle Ser.). (ENG., Illus.). 176p. (J). (gr. 3-6). 12.99 (978-1-61963-061-1(3), 9781619630611, Bloomsbury USA Childrens) Bloomsbury Publishing USA.
—The Ellie McDoodle Diaries: Most Valuable Player. Barshaw, Ruth McNally, illus. 2013. (Ellie Mcdoodle Diaries). (ENG., Illus.). 192p. (YA). (gr. 3-6). 12.99 (978-1-61963-176-2(8), 9781619631762, Bloomsbury USA Childrens) Bloomsbury Publishing USA.
—New Kid in School. Barshaw, Ruth McNally, illus. 2013. (Ellie Mcdoodle Diaries). (ENG., Illus.). 192p. (YA). (gr. 3-6). 12.99 (978-1-61963-174-8(1), 9781619631748, Bloomsbury USA Childrens) Bloomsbury Publishing USA.
—The Show Must Go On. Barshaw, Ruth McNally, illus. 2013. (Ellie Mcdoodle Diaries). (ENG., Illus.). 176p. (YA). (gr. 3-6). 12.99 (978-1-61963-059-8(1), 9781619630598, Bloomsbury USA Childrens) Bloomsbury Publishing USA.
Bartlett, Roberta. How I Met an Alien. 2011. 74p. pap. 19.95 (978-1-4560-7818-8(6)) America Star Bks.
Bashline, Trent. How Jake & Daisy Stopped Bullying at Dogwood Elementary. 2011. 32p. pap. 12.79 (978-1-4634-2895-2(2)) AuthorHouse.
Baskin, Nora Raleigh. Anything but Typical. (ENG.). 208p. (J). (gr. 5-9). 2010. pap. 8.99 (978-1-4169-9500-5(5)) 2009. (Illus.). 17.99 (978-1-4169-6378-3(2)) Simon & Schuster Bks. For Young Readers. (Simon & Schuster Bks. For Young Readers).
—Runt. (ENG., Illus.). 208p. (J). (gr. 3-7). 2014. pap. 6.99 (978-1-4424-5808-6(9)) 2013. 15.99 (978-1-4424-5807-9(0)) Simon & Schuster Bks. For Young Readers. (Simon & Schuster Bks. For Young Readers).
Bass, Alexis. Love & Other Theories. 2014. (ENG.). 384p. (YA). (gr. 9). 17.99 (978-0-06-227532-5(1), HarperTeen) HarperCollins Pubs.
—What's Broken Between Us. 2015. (ENG.). 304p. (YA). (gr. 9). 17.99 (978-0-06-227535-6(6), HarperTeen) HarperCollins Pubs.
Bass, Karen. Drummer Girl, 1 vol. 2011. (ENG.). 192p. (YA). (gr. 8-12). pap. 14.95 (978-1-55050-462-0(2)) Coteau Bks. CAN. Dist: Orca Bk. Pubs. USA.
Bass, Patrik Henry. The Zero Degree Zombie Zone. Craft, Jerry, illus. 2014. (ENG.). 144p. (J). (gr. 3-7). 16.99 (978-0-545-13210-7(X), Scholastic Pr.) Scholastic, Inc.
Bast, Michael. Death's Academy. 2014. (J). pap. 14.99 (978-1-4621-1380-4(X), Horizon Pubs.) Cedar Fort, Inc./CFI Distribution.
Basye, Dale E. Blimpo Vol. 3: The Third Circle of Heck. Dob, Bob, illus. 2011. (Heck Ser.). (ENG.). 464p. (J). (gr. 3-7). pap. 7.99 (978-0-375-85677-8(3), Yearling) Random Hse. Children's Bks.
—Fibble. Dob, Bob, illus. 2012. (Heck Ser.). (ENG.). 384p. (J). (gr. 4-7). pap. 6.99 (978-0-375-85679-2(X), Yearling) Random Hse. Children's Bks.
—Precocia: the Sixth Circle of Heck. Dob, Bob, illus. 2013. (Heck Ser.). (ENG.). 432p. (J). (gr. 3-7). 6.99 (978-0-375-86807-8(0), Yearling) Random Hse. Children's Bks.
—Rapacia. Dob, Bob, illus. 2010. (Heck Ser.). (ENG.). 384p. (J). (gr. 3-7). pap. 6.99 (978-0-375-84078-4(8), Yearling) Random Hse. Children's Bks.
—Where the Bad Kids Go. Dob, Bob, illus. 2009. (Heck Ser.). (ENG.). 304p. (J). (gr. 3-7). 6.99 (978-0-375-84076-0(1), Yearling) Random Hse. Children's Bks.
—Wise Acres: the Seventh Circle of Heck. Dob, Bob, illus. 2013. (Heck Ser.). (ENG.). 448p. (J). (gr. 4-7). 16.99 (978-0-307-98185-1(1), Random Hse. Bks. for Young Readers) Random Hse. Children's Bks.
Bateman, Anya. I Just Got a Letter from Allyson Pringle. 2008. 256p. (YA). pap. 15.95 (978-1-60641-028-8(8)) Deseret Bk. Co.
—The Makeover of James Orville Wickenbee. 2007. 262p. (J). pap. (978-1-59038-707-8(4)) Deseret Bk. Co.
Bateman, Teresa. The Bully Blockers Club. Urbanovic, Jackie, illus. 2004. (ENG.). 32p. (J). (gr. 1-3). 6.99 (978-0-8075-0919-7(1)) Whitman, Albert & Co.
Bates, Marni. Invisible. 2013. (Smith High Ser.). (ENG.). 288p. (YA). (gr. 9). pap. 9.95 (978-0-7582-6938-6(2), K-Teen) Kensington Publishing Corp.
Bates, Melinda. Nick Pricer: An American Heir. 2012. 88p. 19.95 (978-1-4697-8478-6(5)); pap. 9.95 (978-1-4697-8476-2(9)) iUniverse, Inc.
Bates, Michelle. Horse in Danger. (Sandy Lane Stables Ser.). 2017. (ENG.). 128p. (YA). pap. 5.99 (978-0-7945-3915-3(7)) 2009. (Illus.). 114p. (J). (gr. 5). pap. 4.99 (978-0-7945-2530-9(X)) EDC Publishing. (Usborne).
Bates, Michelle. Midnight Horse. rev. ed. 2011. (Sandy Lane Stables Ser.). 128p. (J). pap. 4.99 (978-0-7945-2529-3(6), Usborne) EDC Publishing.
Bateson, Catherine. Being Bee. (ENG.). 136p. (J). 2008. (gr. 3-7). pap. 7.95 (978-0-8234-2208-1(9)) 2007. (Illus.). (gr. 4-7). 16.95 (978-0-8234-2104-6(X)) Holiday Hse., Inc.
Bauer, A. C. E. & Shakespeare, William. Come Fall. 2011. (ENG.). 240p. (J). (gr. 3-7). pap. 6.99 (978-0-375-85826-0(1), Yearling) Random Hse. Children's Bks.
Bauer, Joan. Peeled. 2009. (ENG.). 256p. (YA). (gr. 7-18). 8.99 (978-0-14-241430-9(1), Speak) Penguin Young Readers Group.
—Stand Tall. 2005. (ENG.). 192p. (YA). (gr. 7-5). pap. 8.99 (978-0-14-240427-0(6), Speak) Penguin Young Readers Group.
Bauer, Michael Gerard. Don't Call Me Ishmael. 2007. 255p. (YA). (gr. 9-12). lib. bdg. 17.89 (978-0-06-134835-8(X), HarperTeen) HarperCollins Pubs.
Baumgartner, John Robert. Like Losing Your Left Hand. 2011. 244p. pap. 24.95 (978-1-4560-4043-7(X)) America Star Bks.
Baxter, Alice L. Adam's Atomic Adventures. 2007. 76p. per. 8.95 (978-0-595-45616-1(2)) iUniverse, Inc.
Beamer, Cheryl & Beamer, Frank. Yea, It's Hokie Game Day! De Angel, Miguel, illus. 2006. 24p. (J). lib. bdg. 17.95 (978-1-932888-44-7(6)) Mascot Bks., Inc.
Beamish, Diane. Gentle Jack. 2006. 25p. (J). 10.25 (978-1-4116-5553-9(2)) Lulu Pr., Inc.
Bean, Raymond. Investing Well (in Supersonic Spaceships!) Vimislik, Matthew, illus. 2015. (Benji Franklin: Kid Zillionaire Ser.). (ENG.). 88p. (gr. 2-3). lib. bdg. 22.65 (978-1-4965-0368-8(6)) Stone Arch Bks.
—Sweet Farts, 0 vols. unabr. ed. 2012. (Sweet Farts Ser.: 1). (ENG.). 138p. (J). (gr. 4-6). pap. 9.95 (978-1-61218-250-6(X), 9781612182506, Amazon Children's Publishing) Amazon Publishing.
Beasley, Kate. Gertie's Leap to Greatness. Tamaki, Jillian, illus. 2016. (ENG.). 256p. (J). 16.99 (978-0-374-30261-0(8), 9780374302610, Farrar, Straus & Giroux (BYR)) Farrar, Straus & Giroux.
Beaty, Andrea. Artist Ted. Lemaître, Pascal, illus. 2012. (ENG.). 32p. (J). (gr. -1-3). 17.99 (978-1-4169-5374-6(4), McElderry, Margaret K. Bks.) McElderry, Margaret K. Bks.
—Firefighter Ted. Lemaître, Pascal, illus. 2009. (ENG.). 32p. (J). (gr. -1-3). 17.99 (978-1-4169-2821-8(9), McElderry, Margaret K. Bks.) McElderry, Margaret K. Bks.
—Iggy Peck, Architect. Roberts, David, illus. 2007. (ENG.). 32p. (J). (gr. k-17). 17.95 (978-0-8109-1106-2(X), Abrams Bks. for Young Readers) Abrams, Inc.
—Iggy Peck, Architect. Roberts, David, illus. 2010. (ENG.). 32p. (J). (gr. k-17). pap. 7.95 (978-0-8109-8928-3(X)) UK Abrams Bks. for Young Readers.
Beaumier, Randy P. Snapshot Billy: I Remember. 2012. 36p. pap. 24.95 (978-1-4626-1787-6(5)) America Star Bks.
Becher, Susan. Silly Friend. 2010. 28p. pap. 12.50 (978-1-4520-0244-6(4)) AuthorHouse.
Beck, Sharon. The Fish in Our Class. 2011. (Randy's Corner Ser.). (Illus.). 32p. (J). (gr. -1-2). lib. bdg. 25.70 (978-1-58415-978-0(2)) Mitchell Lane Pubs., Inc.
Beck, W. H. Malcolm at Midnight. Lies, Brian, illus. (ENG.). 272p. (J). (gr. 2-5). 2015. pap. 7.99 (978-0-544-33666-7(6), HMH Books For Young Readers) 2012. 16.99 (978-0-547-68100-9(3)) Houghton Mifflin Harcourt Publishing Co.
—Malcolm under the Stars. Lies, Brian, illus. (ENG.). 272p. (J). (gr. 2-5). 2016. pap. 7.99 (978-0-544-81312-0(X)) 2015. 16.99 (978-0-544-39267-0(1)) Houghton Mifflin Harcourt Publishing Co. (HMH Books For Young Readers).
Becker, Bonny. The Magical Ms. Plum. Portnoy, Amy, illus. 2011. (ENG.). 112p. (J). (gr. 1-4). 6.99 (978-0-375-84760-8(X), Yearling) Random Hse. Children's Bks.
Becker, Helaine. Dirk Daring, Secret Agent, 1 vol. 2014. (Dirk Daring, Secret Agent Ser.: 1). (ENG., Illus.). 208p. (J). (gr. 3-6). pap. 9.95 (978-1-4598-0683-2(2)) Orca Bk. Pubs. USA.
—Let Sleeping Dogs Lie, 1 vol. 2016. (Dirk Daring, Secret Agent Ser.: 2). (ENG., Illus.). 240p. (J). (gr. 3-6). pap. 9.95 (978-1-4598-1038-9(4)) Orca Bk. Pubs. USA.
Becker, Suzy. Kate the Great Except When She's Not. Becker, Suzy, illus. 2014. (Kate the Great Ser.: 1). (ENG., Illus.). 272p. (J). (gr. 3-7). 12.99 (978-0-385-38742-2(3), Crown Books For Young Readers) Random Hse. Children's Bks.
—Kate the Great, Except When She's Not. Becker, Suzy, illus. 2014. (Kate the Great Ser.). (ENG., Illus.). 272p. (J). (gr. 3-7). lib. bdg. 15.99 (978-0-385-38743-9(1), Crown Books For Young Readers) Random Hse. Children's Bks.
Beckford, Lois. The Interesting Pen Pal. 2010. 44p. pap. 21.99 (978-1-4415-0878-2(3)) Xlibris Corp.
Beckham, David. Charlie Barker & the Secret of the Deep Dark Woods. 2006. 570p. pap. 33.20 (978-1-4120-9264-7(7)) Trafford Publishing.
Beckley, N. K. The Three-Some: Book 2. 2012. 66p. 24.99 (978-1-4771-2938-8(3)) Xlibris Corp.
—The Writer's Corner: Book 3. 2012. 90p. 24.99 (978-1-4797-1241-0(8)); pap. 15.99 (978-1-4797-1240-3(X)) Xlibris Corp.
Beckwith, Kathy. Critical Mass: I Never Thought It Would Be Like This. . 2003. (ENG.). 192p. (J). pap. 9.95 (978-1-930572-25-6(5)) Educational Media Corp.
Bedford, David A. Angela. 2009. 190p. 25.50 (978-1-60860-755-6(0), Eloquent Bks.) Strategic Book Publishing & Rights Agency (SBPRA).
Bee, Clair. Pitcher's Duel: A Chip Hilton Sports Story. 2011. 224p. (gr. 4-7). 44.95 (978-1-258-09630-4(7)) Literary Licensing, LLC.
BEEBE, Diane. School's Out. 2006. (J). (978-1-4276-0238-1(7)) Aardvark Global Publishing.
Beeny, Emily. Hector the Collector. Graegin, Stephanie, illus. 2017. (ENG.). 40p. (J). 17.99 (978-1-62672-296-5(X), 9781626722965) Roaring Brook Pr.
Beil, Michael D. The Mistaken Masterpiece. 2011. (Red Blazer Girls Ser.). (ENG.). 320p. (J). (gr. 3-7). 16.99 (978-0-375-86740-8(6), Knopf Bks. for Young Readers) Random Hse. Children's Bks.
—The Red Blazer Girls. 2010. (Red Blazer Girls Ser.). (ENG.). 320p. (J). (gr. 3-7). 7.99 (978-0-375-84303-7(5), Yearling) Random Hse. Children's Bks.
—The Red Blazer Girls: the Mistaken Masterpiece. 2012. (Red Blazer Girls Ser.). (ENG.). 336p. (J). (gr. 5). 8.99 (978-0-375-86494-0(6), Yearling) Random Hse. Children's Bks.
—The Red Blazer Girls: the Secret Cellar. 2012. (Red Blazer Girls Ser.). (ENG., Illus.). 288p. (J). (gr. 5). 17.99 (978-0-375-86741-5(4), Knopf Bks. for Young Readers) Random Hse. Children's Bks.
—The Red Blazer Girls: the Vanishing Violin. 2011. (Red Blazer Girls Ser.). (ENG.). 336p. (J). (gr. 3-7). 8.99 (978-0-375-85454-5(1), Yearling) Random Hse. Children's Bks.
—The Secret Cellar. 2013. (Red Blazer Girls Ser.). (ENG., Illus.). 288p. (J). (gr. 5). pap. 8.99 (978-0-375-86495-7(4), Yearling) Random Hse. Children's Bks.
Beitler, Stacey Ann. Willy Goes to School. 2011. 28p. pap. 14.50 (978-1-61204-397-5(6), Strategic Bk. Publishing) Strategic Book Publishing & Rights Agency (SBPRA).
Beka. A Funny Thing Happened on the Way to Paris..., No. 4. 2013. (Dance Class Graphic Novels Ser.). (ENG., Illus.). 48p. (J). (gr. 1-7). 10.99 (978-1-59707-384-4(9), 9781597073844) Papercutz.
Belasen, Amy & Osborn, Jacob. Jenny Green's Killer Junior Year. 2008. (ENG.). 304p. (YA). (gr. 9-18). pap. 14.99 (978-1-4169-6792-7(3), Simon Pulse) Simon Pulse.
Bell, Braden. The Kindling. 2012. (YA). (978-1-4621-1027-8(4)) Cedar Fort, Inc./CFI Distribution.
—Luminescence. 2014. pap. 14.99 (978-1-4621-1405-4(9), Horizon Pubs.) Cedar Fort, Inc./CFI Distribution.
—Penumbras. 2013. (Middle School Magic Ser.). (ENG.). 305p. (J). (gr. 3-7). 14.99 (978-1-4621-1220-3(X), Sweetwater Bks.) Cedar Fort, Inc./CFI Distribution.
Bell, Cece. Chuck & Woodchuck. Bell, Cece, illus. 2016. (ENG., Illus.). 32p. (J). (gr. -1-3). 15.99 (978-0-7636-7524-0(5)) Candlewick Pr.
Bell, Eric. Alan Cole Is Not a Coward. 2017. 272p. (J). (gr. 3-7). 16.99 (978-0-06-256702-4(0), Tegen, Katherine Bks) HarperCollins Pubs.

Bell, Rebecca. Capitano Ricco. Bell, Rebecca, illus. 2005. (Illus.). 36p. (J). 9.95 *(978-1-934138-06-9(1))* Bouncing Ball Bks., Inc.

Bell, Shelia. The Life of Payne: Book II Fairley High Series. 2014. (ENG.). (YA). (gr. 7-18). pap. 9.95 *(978-0-9838935-7-8(8)*, Seraphina) Bonita and Hodge Publishing Group.

Bellisario, Gina. An Extra-Ordinary Girl. Von Innerebner, Jessika, illus. 2016. (Ellie Ultra Ser.). (ENG.). 128p. (gr. 2-3). lib. bdg. 25.99 *(978-1-4965-3139-1(6))* Stone Arch Bks.

—Queen of the Spelling Bee. Von Innerebner, Jessika, illus. 2016. (Ellie Ultra Ser.). (ENG.). 128p. (gr. 2-3). lib. bdg. 25.99 *(978-1-4965-3141-4(8))* Stone Arch Bks.

—Team Earth Takeover. von Innerebner, Jessika, illus. 2017. (Ellie Ultra Ser.). (ENG.). 128p. (gr. 2-3). pap. 6.95 *(978-1-4965-3147-6(7))* Stone Arch Bks.

Benchmark Education Co., LLC. At My School Big Book. 2014. (Shared Reading Foundations Ser.). (J). (gr. -1). *(978-1-4509-9427-9(X))* Benchmark Education Co.

Benjamin, Brooks. My Seventh-Grade Life in Tights. 2016. (ENG.). 304p. (J). (gr. 4-7). 16.99 *(978-0-553-51250-2(1)*, Delacorte Bks. for Young Readers) Random Hse. Children's Bks.

Benn, Iris H. Penelope's New Friends: Early Childhood Life Lesson. 2013. 32p. 29.95 *(978-1-4787-1210-7(4))* Outskirts Pr., Inc.

Bennet, Chloe. Season Three. 2017. (Boywatching Ser.). (ENG.). 288p. (J). (gr. 6-10). 10.99 *(978-1-4083-4512-2(9)*, Orchard Bks.) Hachette Children's Group GBR. Dist: Hachette Bk. Group.

Bennett, Anna Elizabeth. Little Witch. Stone, Helen, illus. 60th anniv. ed. 2013. (ENG.). 128p. (J). (gr. k-3). pap. 12.95 *(978-1-61608-964-1(4)*, 608964, Sky Pony Pr.) Skyhorse Publishing Co., Inc.

Bennett, Cindy C. Geek Girl. 2011. 280p. (J). pap. 15.99 *(978-1-59955-925-4(0))* Bonneville B.V. NLD. Dist: Cedar Fort, Inc./CFI Distribution.

Bennett, Olivia. Who What Wear! The Allegra Biscotti Collection. 2011. (ENG., Illus.). 240p. (J). (gr. 5-7). pap. 8.99 *(978-1-4022-4392-9(8)*, Sourcebooks Jabberwocky) Sourcebooks, Inc.

Bennett, Sandra. Gingerbread Aliens. Welsh, Hayley, illus. 2012. (ENG.). 56p. (J). pap. *(978-0-9872356-4-0(8))* Australian Self Publishing Group/ Inspiring Pubs.

Benoit, Charles. Cold Calls. (ENG.). (gr. 7). 2016. 304p. (YA). pap. 8.99 *(978-0-544-54121-4(9)*, HMH Books For Young Readers) 2014. 288p. (J). 17.99 *(978-0-544-23950-0(4))* Houghton Mifflin Harcourt Publishing Co.

Benson, Amber. Among the Ghosts. Grace, Sina, illus. 2011. (ENG.). 256p. (J). (gr. 3-7). pap. 6.99 *(978-1-4169-9426-8(2)*, Aladdin) Simon & Schuster Children's Publishing.

Benson, Cindy. Chloe & Hairy Go to School. 2012. 32p. pap. 12.99 *(978-0-9855202-9-8(9))* Kids At Heart Publishing, LLC.

Benson, Donna. Spotlight on the Cupcakes: The Cupcakes Club #3. 2008. (ENG.). 115p. (J). pap. 7.95 *(978-0-9799159-2-5(9))* Pink Lemonade, LLC.

Bentley, Catherine & Bentley, Dawn. Hoppy Goes to School. Huerta, Catherine, illus. 2006. (Pet Tales Ser.). (ENG.). 32p. (J). 2.95 *(978-1-59249-558-0(3))* Soundprints.

Bentley, Dawn. Hoppy Goes to School. Huerta, Catherine, illus. 2006. (ENG.). 32p. (J). pap. 9.95 *(978-1-59249-559-7(1))*; (gr. -1-3). 4.95 *(978-1-59249-556-6(7))* Soundprints.

Bentley, Sue. Chocolate Wishes #1. Swan, Angela, illus. 2013. (Magic Bunny Ser.: 1). (ENG.). 128p. (J). (gr. 1-3). pap. 5.99 *(978-0-448-46727-6(5)*, Grosset & Dunlap) Penguin Young Readers Group.

—Classroom Chaos, 2 vols. Swan, Angela & Farley, Andrew, illus. 2008. (Magic Kitten Ser.: 2). (ENG.). 128p. (J). (gr. 1-3). pap. 5.99 *(978-0-448-44999-9(4)*, Grosset & Dunlap) Penguin Young Readers Group.

Benton, Jim. Attack of the 50-Ft. Cupid. Benton, Jim, illus. 2004. (Franny K. Stein, Mad Scientist Ser.: 2). (ENG., Illus.). 112p. (J). (gr. 2-5). 16.99 *(978-0-689-86292-2(X)*, Simon & Schuster Bks. For Young Readers) Simon & Schuster Bks. For Young Readers.

—Attack of the 50-Ft. Cupid, 1 vol. Benton, Jim, illus. 2011. (Franny K. Stein, Mad Scientist Ser.). (ENG., Illus.). 112p. (gr. 3-6). 24.21 *(978-1-59961-818-0(4))* Spotlight.

—The Fran with Four Brains, 1 vol. Benton, Jim, illus. 2011. (Franny K. Stein, Mad Scientist Ser.). (ENG., Illus.). 112p. (gr. 3-6). 24.21 *(978-1-59961-822-7(2))* Spotlight.

—The Fran with Four Brains. 2007. (Franny K. Stein, Mad Scientist Ser.: 6). lib. bdg. 16.00 *(978-1-4177-9038-8(5)*, Turtleback) Turtleback Bks.

—The Frandidate, 1 vol. Benton, Jim, illus. 2011. (Franny K. Stein, Mad Scientist Ser.). (ENG., Illus.). 128p. (gr. 3-6). 24.21 *(978-1-59961-823-4(0))* Spotlight.

—Franny K. Stein, Mad Scientist, 7 vols., Set. Benton, Jim, illus. Incl. Attack of the 50-Ft. Cupid. 112p. 24.21 *(978-1-59961-818-0(4))*; Fran That Time Forgot. 112p. 24.21 *(978-1-59961-820-3(6))*; Fran with Four Brains. 112p. 24.21 *(978-1-59961-822-7(2))*; Frandidate. 128p. 24.21 *(978-1-59961-823-4(0))*; Frantastic Voyage. 112p. 24.21 *(978-1-59961-821-0(4))*; Invisible Fran. 112p. 24.21 *(978-1-59961-819-7(2))*; Lunch Walks among Us. 112p. 24.21 *(978-1-59961-817-3(6))*; (gr. 3-6). (Franny K. Stein, Mad Scientist Ser.). (Illus.). 2011. 169.47 *(978-1-59961-816-6(8))* Spotlight.

—The Invisible Fran. Benton, Jim, illus. 2004. (Franny K. Stein, Mad Scientist Ser.: 3). (ENG., Illus.). 112p. (J). (gr. 2-5). 17.99 *(978-0-689-86293-9(8)*, Simon & Schuster Bks. For Young Readers) Simon & Schuster Bks. For Young Readers.

—The Invisible Fran, 1 vol. Benton, Jim, illus. 2011. (Franny K. Stein, Mad Scientist Ser.). (ENG., Illus.). 112p. (gr. 3-6). 24.21 *(978-1-59961-819-7(2))* Spotlight.

—It's Not My Fault I Know Everything. Benton, Jim, illus. 2009. (Dear Dumb Diary Ser.: 8). (ENG., Illus.). 144p. (J). (gr. 3-7). 6.99 *(978-0-439-82597-9(0)*, Scholastic Paperbacks) Scholastic, Inc.

—It's Not My Fault I Know Everything. 2009. (Dear Dumb Diary Ser.: 8). lib. bdg. 17.20 *(978-0-606-00142-7(5)*, Turtleback) Turtleback Bks.

—Let's Pretend This Never Happened. Benton, Jim, illus. 2004. (Dear Dumb Diary Ser.: 1). (Illus.). 95p. (gr. -1-2). 17.20 *(978-1-4176-3050-9(7)*, Turtleback) Turtleback Bks.

—Lunch Walks among Us. Benton, Jim, illus. (Franny K. Stein, Mad Scientist Ser.: 1). (ENG., Illus.). 112p. (J). (gr. 2-5). 2004. mass mkt. 5.99 *(978-0-689-86295-3(4))* 2003. 16.99 *(978-0-689-86291-5(1))* Simon & Schuster Bks. For Young Readers. (Simon & Schuster Bks. For Young Readers).

—Lunch Walks among Us, 1 vol. Benton, Jim, illus. 2011. (Franny K. Stein, Mad Scientist Ser.). (ENG., Illus.). 112p. (gr. 3-6). 24.21 *(978-1-59961-817-3(6))* Spotlight.

—Lunch Walks among Us. Benton, Jim, illus. 2004. (Franny K. Stein, Mad Scientist Ser.: 1). (Illus.). 102p. (gr. 2-5). lib. bdg. 16.00 *(978-1-4176-4054-6(5)*, Turtleback) Turtleback Bks.

—Nobody's Perfect. I'm As Close As It Gets. Benton, Jim, illus. 2013. (Dear Dumb Diary Year Two Ser.: 3). (ENG., Illus.). 144p. (J). (gr. 3-7). pap. 5.99 *(978-0-545-37764-5(1)*, Scholastic Paperbacks) Scholastic, Inc.

—Nobody's Perfect. I'm As Close As It Gets. 2013. (Dear Dumb Diary: Year Two Ser.: 3). lib. bdg. 16.00 *(978-0-606-31535-7(7)*, Turtleback) Turtleback Bks.

—Okay, So Maybe I Do Have Superpowers. Benton, Jim, illus. 2011. (Dear Dumb Diary Ser.: 11). (ENG., Illus.). 160p. (J). (gr. 3-7). pap. 6.99 *(978-0-545-11615-2(5)*, Scholastic Paperbacks) Scholastic, Inc.

—The Problem with Here Is That It's Where I'm From. 2007. (Dear Dumb Diary Ser.: 6). 17.20 *(978-1-4177-8231-4(5)*, Turtleback) Turtleback Bks.

—School. Hasn't This Gone on Long Enough? Benton, Jim, illus. 2012. (Dear Dumb Diary Year Two Ser.: 1). (ENG., Illus.). 160p. (J). (gr. 3-7). pap. 5.99 *(978-0-545-37761-4(7)*, Scholastic Paperbacks) Scholastic, Inc.

—School. Hasn't This Gone on Long Enough? 2012. (Dear Dumb Diary: Year Two Ser.: 1). lib. bdg. 16.00 *(978-0-606-23731-4(3)*, Turtleback) Turtleback Bks.

—The Super-Nice Are Super-Annoying. 2012. (Dear Dumb Diary: Year Two Ser.: 2). lib. bdg. 16.00 *(978-0-606-26188-3(5)*, Turtleback) Turtleback Bks.

—That's What Friends Aren't For. 2010. (Dear Dumb Diary Ser.: 09). lib. bdg. 17.20 *(978-0-606-06876-5(7)*, Turtleback) Turtleback Bks.

—What I Don't Know Might Hurt Me. Benton, Jim, illus. 2013. (Dear Dumb Diary Year Two Ser.: 4). (ENG., Illus.). 144p. (J). (gr. 3-7). pap. 5.99 *(978-0-545-37765-2(X)*, Scholastic Paperbacks) Scholastic, Inc.

—The Worst Things in Life Are Also Free. Benton, Jim, illus. 2010. (Dear Dumb Diary Ser.: 10). (ENG., Illus.). 160p. (J). (gr. 3-7). pap. 6.99 *(978-0-545-11614-5(7)*, Scholastic Paperbacks) Scholastic, Inc.

Benton, Jim & Kelly, Jamie. Never Do Anything, Ever. Benton, Jim, illus. 2005. (Dear Dumb Diary Ser.: 4). (ENG., Illus.). 144p. (J). (gr. 3-7). pap. 6.99 *(978-0-439-62908-9(X)*, Scholastic Paperbacks) Scholastic, Inc.

—Never Underestimate Your Dumbness. Benton, Jim, illus. 2008. (Dear Dumb Diary Ser.: 7). (ENG., Illus.). 160p. (J). (gr. 3-7). 6.99 *(978-0-439-82596-2(2))* Scholastic, Inc.

Bentz, Lindsay. Really Good Friends. 2007. (ENG.). 182p. pap. 12.95 *(978-1-59526-720-7(4)*, Llumina Pr.) Aeon Publishing Inc.

Benway, Robin. Going Rogue. 2015. (Also Known As Ser.). (ENG.). 320p. (YA). (gr. 7). pap. 9.99 *(978-0-8027-3786-1(2)*, 9780802737861, Bloomsbury USA Childrens) Bloomsbury Publishing USA.

Benz, Derek & Lewis, J. S. The Brimstone Key. 2011. (Grey Griffins: the Clockwork Chronicles Ser.: 1). (ENG.). 400p. (J). (gr. 3-7). pap. 22.99 *(978-0-316-04521-6(7))* Little, Brown Bks. for Young Readers.

—The Brimstone Key Bk. 1. 2010. (Grey Griffins: the Clockwork Chronicles Ser.: 1). (ENG., Illus.). 384p. (J). (gr. 3-7). 15.99 *(978-0-316-04522-3(5))* Little, Brown Bks. for Young Readers.

—The Relic Hunters: Even Heroes Have to Go to School. 2012. (Grey Griffins: the Clockwork Chronicles Ser.: 2). (ENG.). 384p. (J). (gr. 3-7). pap. 7.99 *(978-0-316-04520-9(9))* Little, Brown Bks. for Young Readers.

Berenstain, Jan & Berenstain, Mike. The Berenstain Bears Come Clean for School. Berenstain, Jan & Berenstain, Mike, illus. 2011. (Berenstain Bears Ser.). (ENG., Illus.). 32p. (J). (gr. -1-3). pap. 3.99 *(978-0-06-057395-9(3)*, HarperFestival) HarperCollins Pubs.

Berenstain, Mike. The Berenstain Bears Blessed Are the Peacemakers, 1 vol. 2014. (Berenstain Bears/Living Lights Ser.). (ENG.). 24p. (J). pap. 3.99 *(978-0-310-73481-9(9))* Zonderkidz.

—The Berenstain Bears' Show-And-Tell. Berenstain, Mike, illus. 2017. (Berenstain Bears Ser.). (Illus.). 24p. (J). (gr. -1-3). pap. 3.99 *(978-0-06-235031-2(5)*, HarperFestival) HarperCollins Pubs.

Berenstain, Mike, et al. The Berenstain Bears & the Golden Rule, 1 vol. 2008. (Berenstain Bears/Living Lights Ser.). (ENG., Illus.). 32p. (J). (gr. -1-2). pap. 3.99 *(978-0-310-71247-3(5))* Zonderkidz.

Berenstain, Stan, et al. The Berenstain Bears Go Back to School. Berenstain, Mike, illus. (Berenstain Bears Ser.). (ENG.). 32p. (J). (gr. -1-3). 2009. pap. 6.99 *(978-0-06-052675-7(0))* 2005. 15.99 *(978-0-06-052673-3(4))* HarperCollins Pubs. (HarperFestival).

Berenzy, Alix. Sammy: The Classroom Guinea Pig. Berenzy, Alix, illus. 2008. (ENG., Illus.). 32p. (J). (gr. k-3). pap. 8.99 *(978-0-312-37964-3(1)*, 9780312379643) Square Fish.

Berg, Dorlisa H. Fat Freddy Gets Fit. 2012. 158p. pap. 19.99 *(978-1-4797-6309-2(8))* Xlibris Corp.

Bergen, Lara. Drama Queen. 2007. 164p. (J). pap. *(978-0-545-03702-0(6))* Scholastic, Inc.

—Sophie the Awesome. Tallardy, Laura, illus. 2010. 99p. (J). *(978-0-545-24231-8(2))* Scholastic, Inc.

—Stand up & Cheer. 2013. 134p. (J). pap. *(978-0-545-56280-5(5))* Scholastic, Inc.

Berger, Samantha & Brockenbrough, Martha. Back to School with Bigfoot. Pressler, Dave, illus. 2017. (ENG.). 40p. (J). (gr. -1-3). 16.99 *(978-0-545-85973-8(5))* Scholastic, Inc.

Berk, Josh. The Dark Days of Hamburger Halpin. 2011. (ENG.). 258p. (YA). (gr. 7). pap. 8.99 *(978-0-375-84625-0(5)*, Ember) Random Hse. Children's Bks.

Berk, Sheryl & Berk, Carrie. Designer Drama. 2016. (Fashion Academy Ser.: 3). (ENG.). 192p. (J). (gr. 5-8). pap. 7.99 *(978-1-4926-1353-4(3)*, 9781492613534, Sourcebooks Jabberwocky) Sourcebooks, Inc.

—Fashion Academy. 2015. (Fashion Academy Ser.: 1). (ENG.). 160p. (J). (gr. 5-8). pap. 6.99 *(978-1-4926-0162-3(4)*, Sourcebooks Jabberwocky) Sourcebooks, Inc.

—Model Madness. 2017. (Fashion Academy Ser.: 4). (ENG.). 192p. (J). (gr. 5-8). pap. 7.99 *(978-1-4926-4496-5(X)*, 9781492644965, Sourcebooks Jabberwocky) Sourcebooks, Inc.

Berke, Lindsey Jensen. Am I Pretty? 2013. 28p. 22.99 *(978-1-4808-0106-6(2))*; pap. 16.99 *(978-1-4808-0108-0(9))* Archway Publishing.

Berkowitz, Barbara. The Talent Show. 2009. 108p. 21.49 *(978-1-4389-9826-8(0))*; pap. 10.99 *(978-1-4389-9825-1(2))* AuthorHouse.

Berman, Ali. Misdirected: A Novel. 2014. (ENG., Illus.). 290p. (YA). (gr. 7). 18.95 *(978-1-60980-573-9(9)*, Triangle Square) Seven Stories Pr.

Bernard, Norah S. CLIVE & BRIE. 2006. (YA). per. 8.95 *(978-0-615-15932-4(X))* HELORO Publishing Group.

Bernard, Romily & Bolivar, Commander S. T., III. The Boy Who Knew Too Much. 2016. (Munchem Academy Ser.). (ENG.). 320p. (J). (gr. 3-7). 16.99 *(978-1-4847-5358-3(5))* Disney Pr.

Berry, Eileen M. Haiku on Your Shoes. Regan, Dana, illus. 2005. 56p. (J). (gr. -1-3). per. 7.49 *(978-1-59166-374-4(1))* BJU Pr.

Berry, Julie. The Scandalous Sisterhood of Prickwillow Place. 2014. (ENG.). 368p. (J). (gr. 5-9). 15.99 *(978-1-59643-956-6(4)*, 9781596439566) Roaring Brook Pr.

Berry, Julie & Gardner, Sally Faye. The Rat Brain Fiasco. 2010. (Splurch Academy Ser.: 1). (ENG.). 208p. (J). (gr. 3-7). pap. 6.99 *(978-0-448-45359-0(2)*, Grosset & Dunlap) Penguin Young Readers Group.

Bertram, Debbie & Bloom, Susan. The Best Book to Read. Garland, Michael, illus. 2011. (ENG.). 32p. (J). (gr. -1-2). pap. 7.99 *(978-0-375-87300-3(7)*, Dragonfly Bks.) Random Hse. Children's Bks.

Bertrand, Diane Gonzales. The F Factor. 2010. 256p. (YA). (gr. 6-18). pap. 12.95 *(978-1-55885-598-4(X)*, Piñata Books) Arte Publico Pr.

—El Momento de Trino. Sanmiguel, Rosario, tr. from ENG. 2006. (SPA.). 181p. (J). (gr. 3-7). per. 9.95 *(978-1-55885-473-4(8)*, Piñata Books) Arte Publico Pr.

Bertrand, Diane Gonzales, et al. Adelita & the Veggie Cousins / Adelita y las primas Verduritas. Rodriguez, Tina, illus. 2011. (SPA.). (J). 16.95 *(978-1-55885-699-8(4)*, Piñata Books) Arte Publico Pr.

Besser, Kenneth/R. Arnie Carver & the Plague of Demeverde. 2007. (Illus.). x, 338p. (J). *(978-1-934316-02-3(4))* RTMC Organization, LLC.

Bessler, edward. A Smile for Billy. 2008. 175p. pap. 13.95 *(978-1-4357-4439-4(X))* Lulu Pr., Inc.

Best, Cari. My Three Best Friends & Me, Zulay. Brantley-Newton, Vanessa, illus. 2015. (ENG.). 40p. (J). (gr. -1-3). 17.99 *(978-0-374-38819-5(9)*, 9780374388195, Farrar, Straus & Giroux (BYR)) Farrar, Straus & Giroux.

Bethune, Helen. Way Back When, 1 vol. 2013. (Fiction Readers Ser.). (ENG., Illus.). 28p. (J). (gr. 2-2). pap. 6.99 *(978-1-4333-5570-7(1))* Shell Educational Publishing.

Bette, Grandma. The Excellent Adventures of Max & Madison: Bedtime stories for Youngsters. 2012. 116p. pap. 42.95 *(978-1-4525-0432-2(6))* Balboa Pr.

Beverly, Cleary. Dear Mr. Henshaw. 2014. (Cleary Reissue Ser.). (ENG.). 160p. (J). (gr. 7-12). 10.24 *(978-1-63245-195-8(6))* Lectorum Pubns., Inc.

Bianchi, John. Bird at School. 2016. (1-3Y Bird, Bunny & Bear Ser.). (ENG., Illus.). 16p. (J). pap. 5.99 *(978-1-63437-438-5(X))* American Reading Co.

—Snowed in at Pokeweed Public School. (Illus.). 24p. (J). (gr. 1-5). *(978-1-894323-34-5(3))* Pokeweed Pr.

Bienvenido a nuestra escuela y el primer día de escuela de Katy: Teacher's Guide. 2004. (SPA.). instr.'s gde. ed. *(978-1-4108-2370-0(9))* Benchmark Education Co.

Biggs, Brian. Tinyville Town: Time for School! 2017. (ENG., Illus.). 32p. (J). (gr. -1-k). 16.95 **(978-1-4197-2566-1(1)**, Abrams Appleseed) Abrams, Inc.

Bildner, Phil. Busted. 2013. (ENG., Illus.). 256p. (YA). (gr. 9). pap. 16.99 *(978-1-4814-2171-3(9)*, Simon & Schuster Bks. For Young Readers) Simon & Schuster Bks. For Young Readers.

—A Whole New Ballgame. Probert, Tim, illus. 2015. (Rip & Red Ser.: 1). (ENG.). 256p. (J). (gr. 3-7). 16.99 *(978-0-374-30130-9(1)*, 9780374301309, Farrar, Straus & Giroux (BYR)) Farrar, Straus & Giroux.

—A Whole New Ballgame. 2016. (Rip & Red Ser.: 1). (J). lib. bdg. 17.20 *(978-0-606-38553-4(3))* Turtleback Bks.

Biller, Maxim. Poppy's Biggest Wish. 2006. (ENG., Illus.). 32p. (J). (gr. -1-k). 17.99 *(978-0-7475-8236-6(X)*, Bloomsbury Childrens) Bloomsbury Publishing Plc GBR. Dist: Independent Pubs. Group.

Billingsley, ReShonda Tate. Friends 'Til the End. 2009. (Good Girlz Ser.: 6). (ENG., Illus.). 208p. pap. 11.00 *(978-1-4165-5877-4(2)*, Gallery Bks.) Gallery Bks.

Bingham, Mark Jay. Woolie & the Bully. 2013. 52p. 30.95 *(978-1-4582-0843-9(5))*; pap. 23.95 *(978-1-4582-0844-6(3))* Author Solutions, Inc. (Abbott Pr.).

Binns, B. A. Pull. 2010. 310p. (YA). (gr. 9-18). 16.95 *(978-1-934813-43-0(5))* Westside Bks.

Binns, B. A. & McKenzie, C. Lee. The Princess of Las Pulgas. 2010. 334p. (YA). (gr. 8-18). 16.95 *(978-1-934813-44-7(3))* Westside Bks.

Birchall, Katy. The It Girl. 2016. (It Girl Ser.: 1). (ENG., Illus.). 352p. (J). (gr. 4-8). 16.99 *(978-1-4814-6362-1(4)*, Aladdin) Simon & Schuster Children's Publishing.

—Team Awkward. 2017. (It Girl Ser.: 2). (ENG., Illus.). 304p. (YA). (gr. 4-8). 16.99 *(978-1-4814-6365-2(9)*, Simon & Schuster/Paula Wiseman Bks.) Simon & Schuster/Paula Wiseman Bks.

Birdseye, Tom. Attack of the Mutant Underwear. 2006. (ENG., Illus.). 208p. (J). (gr. 3-7). 7.99 *(978-0-14-240734-9(8)*, Puffin Books) Penguin Young Readers Group.

Birney, Betty G. Adventure According to Humphrey. 2009. (Humphrey Ser.: 5). (ENG.). 128p. (J). (gr. 3-7). 15.99 *(978-0-399-24731-6(9)*, G.P. Putnam's Sons Books for Young Readers) Penguin Young Readers Group.

—Friendship According to Humphrey. (Humphrey Ser.: 2). (ENG.). (J). (gr. 3-7). 2006. 176p. 5.99 *(978-0-14-240633-5(3)*, Puffin Books) 2005. 160p. 15.99 *(978-0-399-24264-9(3)*, G.P. Putnam's Sons Books for Young Readers) Penguin Young Readers Group.

—Friendship According to Humphrey. 2007. (Humphrey Ser.). 150p. (gr. 4-7). 16.00 *(978-0-7569-8277-5(4))* Perfection Learning Corp.

—Humphrey's Mixed-Up Magic Trick. Burris, Priscilla, illus. 2016. (Humphrey's Tiny Tales Ser.: 5). (ENG.). 96p. (J). (gr. k-3). 4.99 *(978-0-14-751461-5(4)*, Puffin Books) Penguin Young Readers Group.

—Humphrey's Playful Puppy Problem. Burris, Priscilla, illus. 2014. (Humphrey's Tiny Tales Ser.: 2). (ENG.). 96p. (J). (gr. k-3). pap. 4.99 *(978-0-14-751484-4(3)*, Puffin Books) Penguin Young Readers Group.

—Humphrey's Really Wheely Racing Day. Burris, Priscilla, illus. 2014. (Humphrey's Tiny Tales Ser.: 1). (ENG.). 96p. (J). (gr. k-3). pap. 4.99 *(978-0-14-751485-1(1)*, Puffin Books) Penguin Young Readers Group.

—Humphrey's School Fair Surprise. Burris, Priscilla, illus. 2016. (Humphrey's Tiny Tales Ser.: 4). (ENG.). 112p. (J). (gr. k-3). 14.99 *(978-0-399-17229-8(7)*, G.P. Putnam's Sons Books for Young Readers) Penguin Young Readers Group.

—Humphrey's School Fair Surprise. 2016. (Humphrey's Tiny Tales Ser.: 04). lib. bdg. 14.75 *(978-0-606-38423-0(5))* Turtleback Bks.

—Imagination According to Humphrey. 2015. (Humphrey Ser.: 11). (ENG.). 128p. (J). (gr. 2-4). 15.99 *(978-0-399-25797-1(7)*, G.P. Putnam's Sons Books for Young Readers) Penguin Young Readers Group.

—Mysteries According to Humphrey. 2013. (According to Humphrey Ser.: 8). lib. bdg. 16.00 *(978-0-606-31699-6(X)*, Turtleback) Turtleback Bks.

—The Princess & the Peabodys. 2007. (ENG.). 256p. (J). (gr. 5-9). 15.99 *(978-0-06-084720-3(4))* HarperCollins Pubs.

—School Days According to Humphrey. (Humphrey Ser.: 7). (ENG.). (J). (gr. 3-7). 2012. 176p. pap. 5.99 *(978-0-14-242106-2(5)*, Puffin Books) 2011. 160p. 15.99 *(978-0-399-25413-0(7)*, G.P. Putnam's Sons Books for Young Readers) Penguin Young Readers Group.

—School Days According to Humphrey. 2012. (According to Humphrey Ser.: 7). lib. bdg. 16.00 *(978-0-606-26085-5(4)*, Turtleback) Turtleback Bks.

—Secrets According to Humphrey. 2015. (Humphrey Ser.: 10). (ENG.). 160p. (J). (gr. 3-7). 5.99 *(978-0-14-751431-8(2)*, Puffin Books) Penguin Young Readers Group.

—Surprises According to Humphrey. (Humphrey Ser.: 4). (ENG.). (J). (gr. 3-7). 2009. 160p. 5.99 *(978-0-14-241296-1(1)*, Puffin Books) 2008. 144p. 15.99 *(978-0-399-24730-9(0)*, G.P. Putnam's Sons Books for Young Readers) Penguin Young Readers Group.

—Surprises According to Humphrey. 2009. (According to Humphrey Ser.: 4). lib. bdg. 16.00 *(978-0-606-00906-5(X)*, Turtleback) Turtleback Bks.

—Trouble According to Humphrey. (Humphrey Ser.: 3). (ENG.). (J). (gr. 3-7). 2008. 192p. 5.99 *(978-0-14-241089-9(6)*, Puffin Books) 2007. 176p. 15.99 *(978-0-399-24505-3(7)*, G.P. Putnam's Sons Books for Young Readers) Penguin Young Readers Group.

—Winter According to Humphrey. 2013. (Humphrey Ser.: 9). (ENG.). 176p. (J). (gr. 3-7). pap. 5.99 *(978-0-14-242759-0(4)*, Puffin Books) Penguin Young Readers Group.

—Winter According to Humphrey. 2013. (According to Humphrey Ser.: 9). lib. bdg. 16.00 *(978-0-606-32138-9(1)*, Turtleback) Turtleback Bks.

—The World According to Humphrey. (Humphrey Ser.: 1). (ENG.). (J). (gr. 3-7). 2005. 144p. pap. 5.99 *(978-0-14-240352-5(0)*, Puffin Books) 2004. 160p. 15.99 *(978-0-399-24198-7(1)*, G.P. Putnam's Sons Books for Young Readers) Penguin Young Readers Group.

—The World According to Humphrey. 2005. (According to Humphrey Ser.: 1). lib. bdg. 16.00 *(978-1-4176-7532-6(2)*, Turtleback) Turtleback Bks.

Bjorkman, Lauren. My Invented Life. 2009. (ENG.). 240p. (YA). (gr. 9-13). 27.99 *(978-0-8050-8950-9(0)*, Holt, Henry & Co. Bks. For Young Readers) Holt, Henry & Co.

Blabey, Aaron. Sunday Chutney. Blabey, Aaron, illus. 2009. (ENG., Illus.). 32p. (J). (gr. -1-k). 16.95 *(978-1-59078-597-3(5)*, Front Street) Boyds Mills Pr.

Black, Holly. The Iron Trial. 2014. (Magisterium Ser.: Bk. 1). pap. *(978-0-545-84067-5(8)*, Scholastic Pr.) Scholastic, Inc.

Black, Holly & Clare, Cassandra. The Bronze Key. 2016. (Magisterium Ser.: 3). (ENG., Illus.). 256p. (J). (gr. 3-7). 17.99 *(978-0-545-52231-1(5)*, Scholastic Pr.) Scholastic, Inc.

—The Iron Trial. (ENG.). (J). 2015. (Magisterium Ser.: 1). 304p. (gr. 3-7). pap. 7.99 *(978-0-545-52226-7(9))* 2014. (Magisterium Ser.: 1). (Illus.). 304p. (gr. 3-7). 17.99 *(978-0-545-52225-0(0))* 2014. (Illus.). 320p. *(978-0-85753-250-3(2))* Scholastic, Inc. (Scholastic Pr.).

—The Iron Trial. 2015. (Magisterium Ser.: 1). lib. bdg. 18.40 *(978-0-606-37028-8(5))* Turtleback Bks.

—Magisterium. la Prueba de Hierro. 2015. (SPA & ENG.). 304p. (J). (gr. 8). pap. 13.95 *(978-607-07-2604-0(9))* Editorial Planeta, S. A. ESP. Dist: Two Rivers Distribution.

Black, Yelena. Dance of Shadows. (Dance of Shadows Ser.). (ENG., Illus.). 384p. (YA). (gr. 7). 2014. pap. 9.99 *(978-1-61963-185-4(7)*, 9781619631854) 2013. 17.99 *(978-1-59990-940-0(5)*, 9781599909400) Bloomsbury Publishing USA. (Bloomsbury USA Childrens).

Blackburn, Sheila M. Stewie Scraps & the Super Sleigh. 2008. 72p. pap. *(978-1-903853-89-4(3))* Brilliant Pubns.

Blacker, Terence. Boy2Girl. 2007. (ENG.). 304p. (YA). (gr. 7-10). per. 12.99 *(978-0-312-37146-3(2)*, 9780312371463) Square Fish.

Blackstone, Matt. Sorry You're Lost. 2014. (ENG.). 320p. (J). (gr. 5-9). 15.99 *(978-0-374-38065-6(1)*, 9780374380656, Farrar, Straus & Giroux (BYR)) Farrar, Straus & Giroux.

Blackwell, Paul E. Undercurrent. 2013. 320p. (YA). (gr. 9). 17.99 *(978-0-06-212350-3(5)*, HarperTeen) HarperCollins Pubs.

Blackwood, Sage. Miss Ellicott's School for the Magically Minded. 2017. 368p. (J). (gr. 3-7). 16.99 *(978-0-06-240263-9(3)*, Tegen, Katherine Bks) HarperCollins Pubs.

Blagden, Scott. Dear Life, You Suck: A Novel. 2015. (ENG.). 320p. (YA). (gr. 9). pap. 9.99 *(978-0-544-33621-6(6)*, HMH Books For Young Readers) Houghton Mifflin Harcourt Publishing Co.

Blake, Jillian. Antisocial. 2017. (ENG.). 256p. (YA). (gr. 9). 17.99 *(978-1-101-93896-6(X)*, Delacorte Pr.) Random Hse. Children's Bks.

Blake, Stephanie. No Quiero Ir a la Escuela. 2007. (SPA., Illus.). 40p. (gr. k-2). 17.99 *(978-84-8470-268-9(5))* Corimbo, Editorial S.L. ESP. Dist: Lectorum Pubns., Inc.

Blakemore, Megan Frazer. The Friendship Riddle. (ENG.). 2016. 384p. (J). pap. 7.99 *(978-1-68119-019-8(2)*, 9781681190198) 2015. 368p. (YA). (gr. 3-6). 16.99 *(978-1-61963-630-9(1)*, 9781619636309) Bloomsbury Publishing USA. (Bloomsbury USA Childrens).

Blanc, Katherine & Ebbeler, Jeffrey. Melvin the Mouth. Mottram, Dave, illus. 2017. (ENG.). 32p. (J). (gr. -1-3). lib. bdg. 16.99 *(978-1-58089-714-3(2))* Charlesbridge Publishing, Inc.

Bland, Anita D. Matilda's Apple. 2011. 24p. pap. 15.99 *(978-1-4653-4329-1(6))* Xlibris Corp.

Blanda, Dominick. The Super Duper Kid Fantastic. 2009. 32p. pap. 14.99 *(978-1-4389-4566-8(3))* AuthorHouse.

Blankenship, Paula. We Both Read-Lulu's Lost Shoes. Reinhart, Larry, illus. 2005. (We Both Read Ser.). 44p. (J). (gr. k-1). 7.99 *(978-1-891327-55-1(0))*; pap. 4.99 *(978-1-891327-56-8(9))* Treasure Bay, Inc.

Bledsoe Jr, Reuben Booo. Bullybuster. 2013. (ENG.). 98p. (J). pap. 14.95 *(978-1-4787-1215-2(5))* Outskirts Pr., Inc.

Blejwas, Emily. Once You Know This. 2017. (ENG.). 240p. (J). (gr. 4-7). 16.99 ***(978-1-5247-0097-3(5))***; lib. bdg. 19.99 ***(978-1-5247-0098-0(3))*** Random Hse. Children's Bks. (Delacorte Bks. for Young Readers).

Block, F. L. My Miserable Life. Hemingway, Edward, illus. 2016. (ENG.). 192p. (J). 13.99 *(978-0-8050-9628-6(0)*, 9780805096286, Holt, Henry & Co. Bks. For Young Readers) Holt, Henry & Co.

Block, Francesca Lia. Pink Smog: Becoming Weetzie Bat. 2012. (Weetzie Bat Ser.: 6). (ENG.). 208p. (YA). (gr. 9). 17.99 *(978-0-06-156598-4(9)*, HarperTeen) HarperCollins Pubs.

—The Waters & the Wild. 2009. (ENG.). 128p. (YA). (gr. 9-18). 16.99 *(978-0-06-145244-4(0)*, HarperTeen) HarperCollins Pubs.

Bloom, Ira. Hearts & Other Body Parts. 2017. (ENG.). 352p. (J). (gr. 9). 17.99 *(978-1-338-03073-0(6)*, Scholastic Pr.) Scholastic, Inc.

Bloom, Steve. The Stand-In. 2016. (ENG.). 360p. (YA). (gr. 8-12). 18.99 *(978-1-5124-1023-5(3))*; 38.65 *(978-1-5124-1121-8(3)*, Carolrhoda Lab™) Lerner Publishing Group.

Bloom, Suzanne. The Bus for Us. Bloom, Suzanne, illus. 2013. (ENG., Illus.). 32p. (J). (gr. k-2). pap. 6.95 *(978-1-62091-441-0(7))* Boyds Mills Pr.

Bloomsbury USA. Lift & Look: at School. 2016. (ENG., Illus.). 12p. (J). bds. 8.99 *(978-1-61963-997-3(1)*, 9781619639973, Bloomsbury Activity Bks.) Bloomsbury Publishing USA.

Bloor, Edward. London Calling. 2008. (ENG., Illus.). 304p. (YA). (gr. 7-9). per. 8.99 *(978-0-375-84363-1(9)*, Ember) Random Hse. Children's Bks.

—Story Time. 2005. (ENG., Illus.). 444p. (YA). (gr. 7-12). reprint ed. pap. 8.99 *(978-0-15-205222-5(4))* Houghton Mifflin Harcourt Publishing Co.

Blount, Patty. Send. 2012. (ENG.). 304p. (YA). (gr. 7-12). pap. 8.99 *(978-1-4022-7337-7(1))* Sourcebooks, Inc.

Blume-D'Ausilio, Carole Ed. D. The Bronx Bully. 2011. 28p. pap. 15.99 *(978-1-4628-5235-2(1))* Xlibris Corp.

Blume, Judy. Cool Zone with the Pain & the Great One. Stevenson, James, illus. 2009. (ENG.). 128p. (J). (gr. 3-7). 5.99 *(978-0-440-42093-4(8)*, Yearling) Random Hse. Children's Bks.

—Friend or Fiend? With the Pain & the Great One. Stevenson, James, illus. 2010. (ENG.). 128p. (J). (gr. 3-7). 5.99 *(978-0-440-42095-8(4)*, Yearling) Random Hse. Children's Bks.

—Going, Going, Gone! with the Pain & the Great One. Stevenson, James, illus. 2010. (ENG.). 128p. (J). (gr. 3-7). 5.99 *(978-0-440-42094-1(6)*, Yearling) Random Hse. Children's Bks.

—Just As Long As We're Together. 2010. (ENG.). 288p. (YA). (gr. 7). pap. 8.99 *(978-0-385-73988-7(5)*, Delacorte Bks. for Young Readers) Random Hse. Children's Bks.

—The One in the Middle Is the Green Kangaroo. Ohi, Debbie Ridpath, illus. 2014. (ENG.). 48p. (J). (gr. 1-5). pap. 5.99 *(978-1-4814-1131-8(4)*, Atheneum Bks. for Young Readers) Simon & Schuster Children's Publishing.

Blythe, Carolita. Revenge of a Not-So-Pretty Girl. 2013. (ENG.). 336p. (YA). (gr. 7). 19.99 *(978-0-375-99081-6(X)*, Delacorte Bks. for Young Readers) Random Hse. Children's Bks.

BMI Staff, compiled by. Fear Street Collection - Set, 98 vols. 2009. (YA). 114.81 *(978-1-60884-415-9(3))* BMI Educational Services.

Boatwright-Cook, Jane. The Skeleton Leaf Stories: Behind the Shutters. 2012. 124p. 23.99 *(978-1-4772-1346-9(5))*; pap. 14.95 *(978-1-4772-1347-6(3))* AuthorHouse.

Boelts, Maribeth. Those Shoes. Jones, Noah Z., illus. 2009. (ENG.). 40p. (J). (gr. k-3). pap. 6.99 *(978-0-7636-4284-6(3))* Candlewick Pr.

Bogaerts, Jorge. El Dia Que Hizo Mucho Viento. (SPA.). 112p. (J). *(978-84-207-3535-1(3))* Grupo Anaya, S.A.

Boggess, Eileen. Mia the Meek. 2006. (ENG.). 155p. (gr. 6-9). per. 14.95 *(978-1-890862-47-3(9))* Bancroft Pr.

—MIA the Meek. 2006. (Mia Fullerton Ser.: Bk. 1). 155p. (J). (gr. 6-11). 16.95 *(978-1-890862-46-6(0))* Bancroft Pr.

—Mia the Melodramatic. 2008. (MIA Fullerton Ser.). 168p. (J). (gr. 6-13). 19.95 *(978-1-890862-56-5(8))* Bancroft Pr.

Boggs, Garnett Reed. Totally Katy: Katy Is Always Planning, but Just How Well do Her Plans Work Out? 2011. 108p. (gr. 4-6). pap. 10.95 *(978-1-4634-3233-1(X))* AuthorHouse.

Boie, Kirsten. The Princess Trap. (ENG.). 416p. (J). (gr. 5-9). 2012. pap. 7.99 *(978-0-545-22262-4(1))* 2010. 17.99 *(978-0-545-22261-7(3))* Scholastic, Inc. (Chicken Hse., The).

Bolger, Kevin. Zombiekins. Blecha, Aaron, illus. 2011. (ENG.). 208p. (J). (gr. 3-7). 6.99 *(978-1-59514-367-9(X)*, Razorbill) Penguin Young Readers Group.

—Zombiekins. 2010. (ENG.). 208p. (J). (gr. 4-7). 10.99 *(978-1-59514-177-4(4)*, Razorbill) Penguin Young Readers Group.

—Zombiekins 2. Blecha, Aaron, illus. 2011. (J). 10.99 *(978-1-59514-432-4(3)*, Razorbill) Penguin Publishing Group.

Bond, Felicia. The Halloween Play. Bond, Felicia, illus. 2008. Orig. Title: The Halloween Performance. (ENG., Illus.). 32p. (J). (gr. -1-1). pap. 7.99 *(978-0-06-135796-1(0))* HarperCollins Pubs.

Bond, Gwenda. Double Down. 2016. (Lois Lane Ser.). (ENG.). 384p. (gr. 9-12). 16.95 *(978-1-63079-038-7(9))* Switch Pr.

—Fallout. (Lois Lane Ser.). (ENG.). 304p. (gr. 9-12). 2016. pap. 9.95 *(978-1-63079-006-6(0))* 2015. 16.95 *(978-1-63079-005-9(2))* Switch Pr.

Bond, Roland. Harvey Plumstead & the Dinnertime Dog. 2012. (Illus.). 96p. (gr. 4-18). pap. 13.66 *(978-1-4772-4317-6(8))* AuthorHouse.

BookSource Staff, compiled by. Robot Rumble. 2013. (Hardy Boys: Secret Files Ser.: 11). lib. bdg. 16.00 *(978-0-606-27027-4(2)*, Turtleback) Turtleback Bks.

Booraem, Ellen. Texting the Underworld. 2013. (ENG.). 320p. (J). (gr. 5). 16.99 *(978-0-8037-3704-4(1)*, Dial Bks) Penguin Young Readers Group.

Borden, Louise. The A+ Custodian. Gustavson, Adam, tr. Gustavson, Adam, illus. 2004. (ENG.). 40p. (J). (gr. 2-5). 17.99 *(978-0-689-84995-4(8)*, McElderry, Margaret K. Bks.) McElderry, Margaret K. Bks.

—The John Hancock Club. Gustavson, Adam, illus. 2007. (ENG.). 48p. (J). (gr. 2-5). 17.99 *(978-1-4169-1813-4(2)*, McElderry, Margaret K. Bks.) McElderry, Margaret K. Bks.

—Kindergarten Luck. Godbout, Geneviève, illus. 2015. (ENG.). 32p. (J). (gr. -1-k). 16.99 *(978-1-4521-1394-4(7))* Chronicle Bks. LLC.

—The Last Day of School. Gustavson, Adam, illus. 2006. (ENG.). 40p. (J). (gr. 2-5). 17.99 *(978-0-689-86869-6(3)*, McElderry, Margaret K. Bks.) McElderry, Margaret K. Bks.

—The Lost-and-Found Tooth. Gustavson, Adam, illus. 2008. (ENG.). 40p. (J). (gr. 2-5). 16.99 *(978-1-4169-1814-1(0)*, McElderry, Margaret K. Bks.) McElderry, Margaret K. Bks.

—Off to First Grade. Schindler, S. D. et al, illus. 2008. (ENG.). 40p. (J). (gr. -1-3). 17.99 *(978-0-689-87395-9(6)*, McElderry, Margaret K. Bks.) McElderry, Margaret K. Bks.

Borden, Louise & Gustavson, Adam. The Day Eddie Met the Author. 2004. (ENG., Illus.). 44p. (J). (gr. 2-5). 7.99 *(978-0-689-86720-0(4)*, McElderry, Margaret K. Bks.) McElderry, Margaret K. Bks.

Bossley, Michele Martin. Swiped, 1 vol. 2006. (Orca Currents Ser.). (ENG.). 136p. (J). (gr. 5-9). per. 9.95 *(978-1-55143-646-3(9))* Orca Bk. Pubs. USA.

Bost, Richard. Taekwon Tales. 2012. 120p. pap. 9.99 *(978-0-9848626-1-0(7))* ImBost Inc.

Bottner, Barbara. Miss Brooks Loves Books! (And I Don't) Emberley, Michael, illus. 2010. (ENG.). 32p. (J). (gr. -1-2). 17.99 *(978-0-375-84682-3(4)*, Knopf Bks. for Young Readers) Random Hse. Children's Bks.

—Priscilla Gorilla. Emberley, Michael, illus. 2017. (ENG.). 40p. (J). (gr. -1-2). 17.99 *(978-1-4814-5897-9(3)*, Atheneum/Caitlyn Dlouhy Books) Simon & Schuster Children's Publishing.

Bouchard, John L. A Taste of Soda. 2006. 92p. pap. 16.95 *(978-1-4241-2482-4(4))* PublishAmerica, Inc.

Boudreau, Helene. Real Mermaids Don't Need High Heels. 2013. (ENG.). 240p. (J). (gr. 4-8). pap. 6.99 *(978-1-4022-6458-0(5)*, Sourcebooks Jabberwocky) Sourcebooks, Inc.

Bowe, Julie. Dance Fever. 2017. (Victoria Torres, Unfortunately Average Ser.). (ENG.). 160p. (gr. 4-4). lib. bdg. 26.65 *(978-1-4965-3819-2(6))* Stone Arch Bks.

—Face the Music. 2015. (Victoria Torres, Unfortunately Average Ser.). (ENG.). 160p. (gr. 4-4). pap. 5.95 *(978-1-4965-0538-5(7))* Stone Arch Bks.

—Formula for Friends. 2015. (Victoria Torres, Unfortunately Average Ser.). (ENG.). 160p. (gr. 4-4). pap. 5.95 *(978-1-4965-0539-2(5))* Stone Arch Bks.

—My Best Frenemy. 2011. (Friends for Keeps Ser.). (ENG.). 256p. (J). (gr. 3-7). 6.99 *(978-0-14-241880-2(3)*, Puffin Books) Penguin Young Readers Group.

—My Forever Friends. 2012. (Friends for Keeps Ser.). (ENG.). 240p. (J). (gr. 3-7). pap. 6.99 *(978-0-14-242104-8(9)*, Puffin Books) Penguin Young Readers Group.

—My Last Best Friend. 2008. (Friends for Keeps Ser.). (ENG., Illus.). 160p. (J). (gr. 2-5). pap. 5.99 *(978-0-15-206197-5(5))* Houghton Mifflin Harcourt Publishing Co.

—My New Best Friend. 2010. (Friends for Keeps Ser.). (ENG.). 192p. (J). (gr. 2-5). pap. 6.99 *(978-0-547-32869-0(9))* Houghton Mifflin Harcourt Publishing Co.

—Pompom Problems. 2015. (Victoria Torres, Unfortunately Average Ser.). (ENG.). 160p. (gr. 4-4). lib. bdg. 26.65 *(978-1-4965-0532-3(8))* Stone Arch Bks.

—So Much Drama. 2016. (Victoria Torres, Unfortunately Average Ser.). (ENG., Illus.). 160p. (gr. 4-4). pap. 5.95 *(978-1-4965-3807-9(2))*; lib. bdg. 26.65 *(978-1-4965-3799-7(8))* Stone Arch Bks.

—Vicka for President! 2016. (Victoria Torres, Unfortunately Average Ser.). (ENG., Illus.). 160p. (gr. 4-4). lib. bdg. 26.65 *(978-1-4965-3800-0(5))* Stone Arch Bks.

Bowen, Anne. I Know an Old Teacher. Gammell, Stephen, illus. 2008. (ENG.). 32p. (J). (gr. k-3). 16.95 *(978-0-8225-7984-7(7)*, Carolrhoda Bks.) Lerner Publishing Group.

—Que Hacen los Maestros? (Despues de Que Te Vas de la Escuela) Gott, Barry, illus. 2007. (Ediciones Lerner Single Titles Ser.). (SPA.). 32p. (J). (gr. k-3). 16.95 *(978-0-8225-6264-1(2)*, Ediciones Lerner) Lerner Publishing Group.

—What Do Teachers Do (After You Leave School)? Gott, Barry, illus. 2006. (ENG.). 32p. (J). (gr. k-3). 16.95 *(978-1-57505-922-8(3)*, Carolrhoda Bks.) Lerner Publishing Group.

Bowen, Fred. Throwing Heat, 1 vol. 2010. (ENG.). 128p. (J). (gr. 2-7). pap. 6.95 *(978-1-56145-540-9(7))* Peachtree Pubs.

Bowie, Barbara Kay. Ready for School: An Activity & Story Book for Parents & Children Entering Kindergarten. 2004. (J). 7.95 *(978-0-9713450-1-0(5))* Educational Expertise, LLC.

Bowyer, Clifford B. The Darkness Within: The Imperium Saga: the Adventures of Kyria, 12 vols., Vol. 9. Brigman, June, illus. 2009. (Imperium Saga: 9). (ENG.). (J). 5.99 *(978-0-9787782-4-8(3))* Silver Leaf Bks., LLC.

Boylan, Jennifer Finney. Falcon Quinn & the Black Mirror. Dorman, Brandon, illus. (Falcon Quinn Ser.: 1). (ENG.). (J). (gr. 5-9). 2011. 512p. pap. 7.99 *(978-0-06-172834-1(9))* 2010. 496p. 16.99 *(978-0-06-172832-7(2))* HarperCollins Pubs. (Tegen, Katherine Bks).

—Falcon Quinn & the Crimson Vapor. 2011. (Falcon Quinn Ser.: 2). (ENG.). 384p. (J). (gr. 5-9). 16.99 *(978-0-06-172835-8(7)*, Tegen, Katherine Bks) HarperCollins Pubs.

Bracken, Beth. The Little Bully, 1 vol. Bell, Jennifer A., illus. 2012. (Little Boost Ser.). (ENG.). 32p. (gr. k-3). lib. bdg. 23.99 *(978-1-4048-6795-6(3)*, Little Boost) Picture Window Bks.

—Too Shy for Show-And-Tell, 1 vol. Bell, Jennifer A., illus. 2012. (Little Boost Ser.). (ENG.). 32p. (gr. k-3). 7.95 *(978-1-4048-7418-3(6)*, Little Boost) Picture Window Bks.

—Too Shy for Show-and-Tell. Bell, Jennifer A., illus. 2011. (Little Boost Ser.). (ENG.). 32p. (gr. k-3). lib. bdg. 23.99 *(978-1-4048-6654-6(X)*, Little Boost) Picture Window Bks.

Bradley, Timothy. Hive Mind, Bk. 1. rev. ed. 2013. (Sci Hi Ser.). (ENG., Illus.). 152p. (J). (gr. 3-6). lib. bdg. 26.96 *(978-1-4807-2612-3(5))* Teacher Created Materials, Inc.

Bradley, Timothy J. Infestation. Bradley, Timothy J., illus. 2013. (ENG., Illus.). 192p. (J). (gr. 3-7). pap. 5.99 *(978-0-545-45904-4(4)*, Scholastic Paperbacks) Scholastic, Inc.

—Time Jump, Bk. 3. 2014. (Sci Hi Ser.). (ENG.). 232p. (J). (gr. 3-6). lib. bdg. 26.96 *(978-1-4807-4217-8(1))* Teacher Created Materials, Inc.

Bradman, Tony. Flora the Fairy's Magic Spells. Carlow, Emma, illus. 2nd ed. 2016. (Reading Ladder Ser.). (ENG.). 48p. (J). (gr. k-2). 7.99 *(978-1-4052-8227-7(4))* Egmont Bks., Ltd. GBR. Dist: Independent Pubs. Group.

—Goldilocks & the Just Right Club. Warburton, Sarah, illus. 2014. (After Happily Ever After Ser.). (ENG.). 56p. (gr. 2-3). pap. 5.05 *(978-1-4342-7963-7(4)*, After Happily Ever After) Stone Arch Bks.

Bradshaw, Jennifer. No School Today, My Son. 2009. 24p. pap. 11.49 *(978-1-4490-4174-8(4))* AuthorHouse.

Brady, Bill. A Charm for Jo. Brady, Laurie, illus. l.t. ed. 2005. (Turtle Books). 32p. (J). (gr. 2-5). lib. bdg. 15.95 *(978-0-944727-48-5(4))* Jason & Nordic Pubs.

Brady, Bill & Brady, Laurie. A Charm for Jo. Fargo, Todd, illus. l.t. ed. 2005. (Turtle Bks.). (ENG.). 32p. (J). (gr. 2-5). pap. 9.95 *(978-0-944727-47-8(6))* Jason & Nordic Pubs.

Braem, Viola Brunette. Woodside: A Novel about the Years from 1930 to 1943. A Fictionalized Autobiography & Funny Events in a One-room School. 2005. (YA). per. 14.95 *(978-0-9772315-0-8(X))* EPS Digital.

Brager, Allison. Off-Colored Rainbows. 2005. 64p. pap. 16.95 *(978-1-4241-0267-9(7))* PublishAmerica, Inc.

Braidich, Victoria. Monday with Meg. 2006. (Neighborhood Readers Ser.). (ENG.). 12p. (gr. -1-3). pap. 5.90 *(978-1-4042-6459-5(0)*, Rosen Classroom) Rosen Publishing Group, Inc., The.

Bramwell, Wendie & Normand, Bridgid. Rhymitis. Kim, Julie J., tr. Kim, Julie J., illus. 2003. 32p. (J). pap. *(978-0-9741388-8-6(6))* Committee for Children.

Brandt, Courtney. A Fine Line. 2008. 164p. pap. 12.95 *(978-0-595-52500-3(8))* iUniverse, Inc.

Brannon, Pat. Filthy Farley O'Charlie Mcbarley. 2007. 48p. per. 16.95 *(978-1-4241-8904-5(7))* PublishAmerica, Inc.

Brashares, Ann. The Here & Now. 2014. 242p. (YA). *(978-0-385-39008-8(4)*, Delacorte Pr) Random House Publishing Group.

—The Here & Now. (ENG.). 256p. (YA). (gr. 7). 2015. pap. 10.99 *(978-0-385-73683-1(5)*, Ember) 2014. 18.99 *(978-0-385-73680-0(0)*, Delacorte Pr.) Random Hse. Children's Bks.

Brauner, Barbara & Mattson, James Iver. The Glitter Trap. Halpin, Abigail, illus. 2014. (Oh My Godmother Ser.). (ENG.). 256p. (J). (gr. 3-7). pap. 6.99 *(978-1-4231-6474-6(1))* Hyperion Bks. for Children.

—Oh My Godmother the Magic Mistake. Halpin, Abigail, illus. 2014. (Oh My Godmother Ser.). (ENG.). 272p. (J). (gr. 3-7). pap. 6.99 *(978-1-4231-6479-1(2))* Hyperion Bks. for Children.

Braver, Vanita. Madison & the Two-Wheeler, 1 vol. DiRocco, Carl, illus. 2007. (ENG.). 32p. (J). (gr. -1-3). 14.95 *(978-1-59572-109-9(6))* Star Bright Bks., Inc.

Bray, Libba. A Great & Terrible Beauty. 2005. (Gemma Doyle Trilogy Ser.: Bk. 1). (ENG.). 432p. (YA). (gr. 7). reprint ed. pap. 9.99 *(978-0-385-73231-4(7)*, Ember) Random Hse. Children's Bks.

Brazil, Angela. The Luckiest Girl in the School. 2007. (ENG.). 210p. per. 20.99 *(978-1-4346-2918-0(X))*; 236p. per. 22.99 *(978-1-4346-2942-5(2))* Creative Media Partners, LLC.

Brecon, Connah. Frank! 2014. (ENG., Illus.). 32p. (J). (gr. -1-17). 16.95 *(978-0-7624-5423-5(7)*, Running Pr. Kids) Running Pr. Bk. Pubs.

Breen, Steve. A Perfect Mess. 2016. (ENG., Illus.). 32p. (J). (-k). 16.99 *(978-0-8037-4156-0(1)*, Dial Bks) Penguin Young Readers Group.

Breese, K. Ryer. Future Imperfect. 2011. (ENG.). 320p. (YA). (gr. 8-18). pap. 22.99 *(978-0-312-64151-1(6)*, 9780312641511, St. Martin's Griffin) St. Martin's Pr.

Breisacher, Cathy. Petunia Pepper's Picture Day. Elden, Christian, illus. 2010. 32p. (J). 14.99 *(978-1-59317-397-5(0))* Warner Pr., Inc.

Bremauntz, M. The Adventures of Marcela & Little Joey: Little Joey Loves Bugs. 2010. 32p. 17.25 *(978-1-4269-4417-8(9))* Trafford Publishing.

Brenner, Emily. On the First Day of Grade School. Whatley, Bruce, illus. 2004. 32p. (J). (gr. -1-1). lib. bdg. 16.89 *(978-0-06-051041-1(2))* HarperCollins Pubs.

Brent-Dyer, Elinor M. Bride Leads the Chalet School. 2011. (ENG., Illus.). 287p. (YA). (gr. 8-12). pap. *(978-1-84745-103-3(9))* Girls Gone By.

Breslaw, Anna. Scarlett Epstein Hates It Here. 2016. (ENG.). 288p. (YA). (gr. 7). 17.99 *(978-1-59514-835-3(3)*, Razorbill) Penguin Young Readers Group.

Brewer, Elly. Jerry & the Jannans. 2006. (ENG.). 320p. (J). (gr. 4-7). pap. 11.99 *(978-0-7475-8213-7(0))* Bloomsbury Publishing Plc GBR. Dist: Independent Pubs. Group.

Brewer, Heather. Chronicles of Vladimir Tod, 2 vols. 2009. (Chronicles of Vladimir Tod Ser.: 2). (ENG.). 288p. (YA). (gr. 7-18). 8.99 *(978-0-14-241342-5(9)*, Speak) Penguin Young Readers Group.

—Eighth Grade Bites. Laud, Julia, illus. 2013. (Chronicles of Vladimir Tod Ser.: 1). (ENG.). 144p. (YA). (gr. 7). pap. 12.99 *(978-0-8037-3811-9(0)*, Dial Bks) Penguin Young Readers Group.

—Eighth Grade Bites. 2008. (Chronicles of Vladimir Tod Ser.: 1). (ENG.). 192p. (YA). (gr. 7). 8.99 *(978-0-14-241187-2(6)*, Speak) Penguin Young Readers Group.

—Eleventh Grade Burns, 4 vols. 2010. (Chronicles of Vladimir Tod Ser.: 4). (ENG.). 320p. (YA). (gr. 7-18). 8.99 *(978-0-14-241647-1(9)*, Speak); 4th ed. 16.99 *(978-0-525-42243-3(9)*, Dutton Books for Young Readers) Penguin Young Readers Group.

—High School Bites, 2 bks. in 1, Set. 2012. (Chronicles of Vladimir Tod Ser.). (ENG.). 512p. (YA). (gr. 7). pap. 8.99 *(978-0-14-242460-5(9)*, Puffin Books) Penguin Young Readers Group.

—Tenth Grade Bleeds. Preseault, N., ed. 2010. (Chronicles of Vladimir Tod Ser.: 3). (ENG.). 304p. (YA). (gr. 7-18). pap. 8.99 *(978-0-14-241560-3(X)*, Speak) Penguin Young Readers Group.

—Tenth Grade Bleeds. 2009. (Chronicles of Vladimir Tod Ser.: 3). (ENG., Illus.). 304p. (YA). (gr. 7-18). 16.99 *(978-0-525-42135-1(1)*, Dutton Books for Young Readers) Penguin Young Readers Group.

—Tenth Grade Bleeds. 2010. (Chronicles of Vladimir Tod Ser.: 03). lib. bdg. 19.65 *(978-0-606-10594-1(8)*, Turtleback) Turtleback Bks.

—The Chronicles of Vladimir Tod. 2011. (Chronicles of Vladimir Tod Ser.: 5). (ENG.). 336p. (YA). (gr. 7-18). 8.99 *(978-0-14-241752-2(1)*, Speak) Penguin Young Readers Group.

—Twelfth Grade Kills. 5th ed. 2010. (Chronicles of Vladimir Tod Ser.: 5). (ENG.). 340p. (YA). (gr. 7-18). 16.99 *(978-0-525-42224-2(2)*, Dutton Books for Young Readers) Penguin Young Readers Group.

Brewis, Alan. Boris Returns A Hero! 2008. 72p. pap. 12.50 *(978-1-4357-4377-9(6))* Lulu Pr., Inc.

Brezenoff, Steve. The Absolute Value of -1. 2010. (Carolrhoda YA Ser.). (ENG.). 296p. (YA). (gr. 9-12). lib. bdg. 16.95 *(978-0-7613-5417-8(4)*, Carolrhoda Bks.) Lerner Publishing Group.

—The Absolute Value Of -1. 2011. (Carolrhoda YA Ser.). (ENG.). 296p. (YA). (gr. 9-12). pap. 9.95 *(978-0-7613-8130-3(9)*, Carolrhoda Lab™) Lerner Publishing Group.

—The Burglar Who Bit the Big Apple, 1 vol. Canga, C. B., illus. 2010. (Field Trip Mysteries Ser.). (ENG.). 88p. (gr. 2-3). 25.32 *(978-1-4342-2139-1(3))* Stone Arch Bks.

—Cheaters. 2013. (Ravens Pass Ser.). (ENG.). 96p. (gr. 2-3). pap. 35.70 *(978-1-4342-6291-2(X))* Stone Arch Bks.

—Cheaters, 1 vol. Pinelli, Amerigo, illus. 2013. (Ravens Pass Ser.). (ENG.). 96p. (gr. 2-3). lib. bdg. 25.32 *(978-1-4342-4616-5(7))* Stone Arch Bks.

—The Crook Who Crossed the Golden Gate Bridge, 1 vol. Canga, C. B., illus. 2010. (Field Trip Mysteries Ser.). (ENG.). 88p. (gr. 2-3). 25.32 *(978-1-4342-2138-4(5))*; pap. 6.10 *(978-1-4342-2770-6(7))* Stone Arch Bks.

—The Ghost Who Haunted the Capitol, 1 vol. Canga, C. B., illus. 2010. (Field Trip Mysteries Ser.). (ENG.). 88p. (gr. 2-3). 25.32 *(978-1-4342-2140-7(7))*; pap. 6.10 *(978-1-4342-2772-0(3))* Stone Arch Bks.

—On the Bus, on the Case, 1 vol. Canga, C. B., illus. 2010. (Field Trip Mysteries Ser.). (ENG.). 240p. (gr. 3-6). 12.95 *(978-1-4342-2531-3(3))* Stone Arch Bks.

—The Painting That Wasn't There, 1 vol. Canga, C. B., illus. 2009. (Field Trip Mysteries Ser.). (ENG.). 88p. (gr. 2-3). lib. bdg. 25.32 *(978-1-4342-1608-3(X))* Stone Arch Bks.

—Ravens Pass. 2013. (Ravens Pass Ser.). (ENG.). 96p. (gr. 2-3). 202.56 *(978-1-4342-6053-6(4))* Stone Arch Bks.

—The Ride That Was Really Haunted, 1 vol. Calo, Marcos, illus. 2011. (Field Trip Mysteries Ser.). (ENG.). 88p. (gr. 2-3). pap. 6.10 *(978-1-4342-3427-8(4))*; lib. bdg. 25.32 *(978-1-4342-3224-3(7))* Stone Arch Bks.

—The Teacher Who Forgot Too Much, 1 vol. Canga, C. B., illus. 2009. (Field Trip Mysteries Ser.). (ENG.). 88p. (gr. 2-3). lib. bdg. 25.32 *(978-1-4342-1609-0(8))* Stone Arch Bks.

—The Village That Almost Vanished, 1 vol. Canga, C. B., illus. 2009. (Field Trip Mysteries Ser.). (ENG.). 88p. (gr. 2-3). lib. bdg. 25.32 *(978-1-4342-1611-3(X))* Stone Arch Bks.

—The Zombie Who Visited New Orleans, 1 vol. Canga, C. B., illus. 2010. (Field Trip Mysteries Ser.). (ENG.). 88p. (gr. 2-3). 25.32 *(978-1-4342-2141-4(5))*; pap. 6.10 *(978-1-4342-2773-7(1))* Stone Arch Bks.

—The Zoo with the Empty Cage, 1 vol. Canga, C. B., illus. 2009. (Field Trip Mysteries Ser.). (ENG.). 88p. (gr. 2-3). lib. bdg. 25.32 *(978-1-4342-1610-6(1))* Stone Arch Bks.

Brian, Kate, pseud. Confessions. 2009. (Private Ser.: No. 4). (ENG.). 240p. (YA). pap. 9.99 *(978-1-4169-9949-2(3)*, Simon & Schuster Bks. For Young Readers) Simon & Schuster Bks. For Young Readers.

—Cruel Love. 2011. (Privilege Ser.). (ENG.). 224p. (YA). (gr. 9). pap. 9.99 *(978-1-4424-0788-6(3)*, Simon & Schuster Bks. For Young Readers) Simon & Schuster Bks. For Young Readers.

—Fake Boyfriend. 2009. (ENG.). 288p. (YA). (gr. 9). pap. 8.99 *(978-1-4169-1368-9(8)*, Simon & Schuster Bks. For Young Readers) Simon & Schuster Bks. For Young Readers.

—Invitation Only. 2009. (Private Ser.: No. 2). (ENG.). 272p. (YA). pap. 9.99 *(978-1-4169-9947-8(7)*, Simon & Schuster Bks. For Young Readers) Simon & Schuster Bks. For Young Readers.

—Megan Meade's Guide to the McGowan Boys. 2006. (ENG.). 288p. (YA). (gr. 7-12). pap. 9.99 *(978-1-4169-0031-3(4)*, Simon & Schuster Bks. For Young Readers) Simon & Schuster Bks. For Young Readers.

—Ominous. 2011. (Private Ser.). (ENG.). 224p. (YA). (gr. 9-18). pap. 9.99 *(978-1-4169-8472-6(0)*, Simon & Schuster Bks. For Young Readers) Simon & Schuster Bks. For Young Readers.

Bridges, Eunice. A Day Like Mine. Goodwin, Adrienne Annette, illus. 2011. 32p. pap. 24.95 *(978-1-4560-5766-4(9))* America Star Bks.

S

Bridwell, Norman. Clifford's School Story Box. Bridwell, Norman, illus. 2015. (ENG., Illus.). (J). (gr. -1-k). 10.99 (978-0-545-83737-8(5)) Scholastic, Inc.

Briggs, Meredith. Polka-Dot Parade. 2007. 52p. per. 16.95 (978-1-4241-8366-1(9)) America Star Bks.

Britt, Fanny. Jane, the Fox & Me, 1 vol. Ouriou, Susan & Morelli, Christelle, trs. from FRE. Arsenault, Isabelle, illus. 2013. (ENG.). 104p. (J). (gr. 5). 19.95 (978-1-55498-360-5(6)) Groundwood Bks. CAN. Dist: Publishers Group West (PGW).

Brix, Liz. Josephine Prairie Dog. 2009. 28p. pap. 12.70 (978-1-4389-4448-7(9)) AuthorHouse.

Broach, Elise. Trouble at School for Marvin & James. Murphy, Kelly, illus. 2017. (Masterpiece Adventures Ser.: 3). (ENG.). 112p. (J). 15.99 (978-1-62779-318-6(6), 9781627793186, Holt, Henry & Co. Bks. For Young Readers) Holt, Henry & Co.

Brockway, Stephanie. Mystic Phyles: Beasts. Masiello, Ralph, illus. 2011. (ENG.). 144p. (J). (gr. 4-7). 15.95 (978-1-57091-718-9(3)) Charlesbridge Publishing, Inc.

Brody, Jessica. The Karma Club. 2011. (ENG.). 288p. (YA). (gr. 7-12). pap. 10.99 (978-0-312-67473-1(2), 9780312674731) Square Fish.

—A Week of Mondays. 2016. (ENG.). 464p. (YA). 17.99 (978-0-374-38270-4(0), 9780374382704, Farrar, Straus & Giroux (BYR)) Farrar, Straus & Giroux.

Bromley, Anne C. & Casilla, Robert. The Lunch Thief, 1 vol. 2010. (ENG., Illus.). 32p. (gr. 3-7). 16.95 (978-0-88448-311-3(8), 884311) Tilbury Hse. Pubs.

Bromley, Peter David. Aunty Liz the Lollipop Lady. 2004. 48p. pap. (978-0-7552-1013-8(1)) Authors OnLine, Ltd.

Brooks, Amy. Dorothy Dainty's Gay Times. l.t. ed. 2007. 118p. pap. 19.99 (978-1-4346-4972-0(5)) Creative Media Partners, LLC.

Brooks, Mel & Reiner, Carl. The 2000 Year Old Man Goes to School. Bennett, James, illus. 2006. 32p. (J). (gr. 4-8). reprint ed. 18.00 (978-1-4223-5622-7(1)) DIANE Publishing Co.

—The 2000 Year Old Man Goes to School. Bennett, James, illus. 2005. (ENG.). 40p. (J). (gr. -1-3). 17.99 (978-0-06-076676-4(X)) HarperCollins Pubs.

Brosgol, Vera. Anya's Ghost. Brosgol, Vera, illus. 2011. (ENG., Illus.). 224p. (YA). (gr. 7-12). 22.99 (978-1-59643-713-5(8), 9781596437135, First Second Bks.) Roaring Brook Pr.

—Anya's Ghost. Brosgol, Vera, illus. 2014. (ENG., Illus.). 240p. (YA). (gr. 7). pap. 10.99 (978-1-250-04001-5(9), 9781250040015) Square Fish.

Brothers, Marilee. Moonstone. 2008. 236p. (YA). pap. 14.95 (978-0-9802453-4-9(6), Bell Bridge Bks.) BelleBks., Inc.

Broutin & Stehr. Baldomero Va A la Escuela. (SPA.). 26p. (978-84-95150-47-9(6)) Corimbo, Editorial S.L.

Brouwer, Sigmund. Justine McKeen, Bottle Throttle, 1 vol. Whamond, Dave, illus. 2016. (Orca Echoes Ser.). (ENG.). 80p. (J). (gr. 2-3). pap. 6.95 (978-1-4598-0731-0(6)) Orca Bk. Pubs. USA.

—Justine Mckeen, Pooper Scooper, 1 vol. Whamond, Dave, illus. 2012. (Orca Echoes Ser.). (ENG.). 64p. (J). (gr. 2-3). pap. 6.95 (978-1-55469-931-5(2)) Orca Bk. Pubs. USA.

—Justine McKeen vs. the Queen of Mean, 1 vol. Whamond, Dave, illus. 2014. (Orca Echoes Ser.). (ENG.). 64p. (J). (gr. 2-3). pap. 6.95 (978-1-4598-0397-8(3)) Orca Bk. Pubs. USA.

—Justine McKeen, Walk the Talk, 1 vol. Whamond, Dave, illus. 2012. (Orca Echoes Ser.). (ENG.). 64p. (J). (gr. 2-3). pap. 6.95 (978-1-55469-929-2(0)) Orca Bk. Pubs. USA.

Brown, Devin. Not Exactly Normal. 2006. 234p. (J). (gr. 4). per. 8.00 (978-0-8028-5287-8(4), Eerdmans Bks For Young Readers) Eerdmans, William B. Publishing Co.

Brown, Gavin. Josh Baxter Levels Up. 2016. (ENG., Illus.). 192p. (J). (gr. 3-7). 12.99 (978-0-545-77294-5(X), Scholastic Pr.) Scholastic, Inc.

Brown, Herman. A Cut Too Far. 2015. (ENG.). 96p. (YA). (gr. 6-12). 27.99 (978-1-4677-5709-6(8)) Lerner Publishing Group.

—The Option. 2014. (Red Zone Ser.: 3). (ENG.). 104p. (YA). (gr. 6-12). pap. 7.95 (978-1-4677-4473-7(5), Darby Creek); lib. bdg. 27.93 (978-1-4677-2128-8(X)) Lerner Publishing Group.

Brown, Jeff. Flat Stanley: Show & Tell, Flat Stanley! Pamintuan, Macky, illus. 2014. (I Can Read Level 2 Ser.). (ENG.). 32p. (J). (gr. -1-3). pap. 3.99 (978-0-06-218975-2(1)) HarperCollins Pubs.

—Show & Tell, Flat Stanley! 2014. (Flat Stanley: I Can Read Ser.). (J). lib. bdg. 13.55 (978-0-606-35493-6(X)) Turtleback Bks.

Brown, Jeffrey. Jedi Academy. 2015. (Star Wars: Jedi Academy Ser.). (ENG.). 112p. (J). (gr. 3-7). 9.99 (978-0-545-85278-4(1)) Scholastic, Inc.

Brown, Jennifer. Hate List. 2017. (ENG.). 528p. (YA). (gr. 10-17). pap. 11.99 **(978-0-316-55678-1(5))** Little, Brown Bks. for Young Readers.

—Hate List. 2011. 10.36 (978-0-7848-3563-0(2), Everbind) Marco Bk. Co.

—How Lunchbox Jones Saved Me from Robots, Traitors, & Missy the Cruel. 2015. (ENG.). 240p. (YA). (gr. 3-6). 16.99 (978-1-61963-454-1(6), 9781619634541, Bloomsbury USA Childrens) Bloomsbury Publishing USA.

—Pennybaker School Is Headed for Disaster. Kissi, Marta, illus. 2017. (ENG.). 320p. (J). 16.99 (978-1-68119-174-4(1), 9781681191744, Bloomsbury USA Childrens) Bloomsbury Publishing USA.

Brown, Judy. School Shutdown. Brown, Judy, illus. 2014. (Petbots Ser.: 2). (ENG., Illus.). 192p. (J). (gr. k-3). pap. 9.99 (978-1-84812-411-0(2)) Bonnier Publishing GBR. Dist: Independent Pubs. Group.

Brown Lcsw, Jennifer. Star's Unexpected News. 2011. 32p. pap. 13.49 (978-1-4389-3567-6(6)) AuthorHouse.

Brown, Liz. The Bully. (Illus.). 90p. (978-1-897039-08-3(5)) High Interest Publishing (HIP).

Brown, Marc. Arthur Turns Green. 2014. (ENG.). 32p. (J). (gr. 1-4). 7.00 (978-0-316-12923-7(2)) Little Brown & Co.

—Arthur Turns Green. 2014. (Arthur Adventures Ser.). (J). lib. bdg. 17.20 (978-0-606-34069-4(6), Turtleback) Turtleback Bks.

—Arthur's Classroom Fib. 2007. (Arthur Step into Reading Ser.). lib. bdg. 13.55 (978-1-4177-7281-0(6), Turtleback) Turtleback Bks.

—Arthur's Teacher Trouble. 2004. (Arthur Adventure Ser.). (J). (gr. k-3). spiral bd. (978-0-616-01603-9(4)); spiral bd. (978-0-616-00406-7(0)) Canadian National Institute for the Blind/Institut National Canadien pour les Aveugles.

—Arturo y el Misterioso Sobre. Sarfatti, Esther, tr. from ENG. 2006. (Libro de Capitulos de Arturo Ser.). (Illus.). 58p. (J). (gr. 6-8). per. 4.99 (978-1-930332-93-5(9)) Lectorum Pubns., Inc.

—Buster Makes the Grade. 2005. (Arthur Chapter Bks.: No. 16). (Illus.). 55p. (J). lib. bdg. 15.00 (978-1-59054-737-3(3)) Fitzgerald Bks.

—La Visita del Senor Rataquemada. Sarfatti, Esther, tr. from ENG. 2003.Tr. of Arthur's Teacher Moves In. (SPA.). (J). (gr. k-2). pap. 6.95 (978-1-930332-41-6(6)) Lectorum Pubns., Inc.

Brown, Monica. Drama Queen. 2016. (Lola Levine Ser.: 2). (J). lib. bdg. 16.00 (978-0-606-38329-5(8)) Turtleback Bks.

—Lola Levine, Drama Queen. 2016. (Lola Levine Ser.: 2). (ENG., Illus.). (J). (gr. 1-5). 112p. pap. 5.99 (978-0-316-25842-5(3)); 96p. 15.99 (978-0-316-25843-2(1)) Little, Brown Bks. for Young Readers.

Brown, Peter. My Teacher Is a Monster! (No, I Am Not.) 2014. (ENG., Illus.). 40p. (J). (gr. -1-3). 18.99 (978-0-316-07029-4(7)) Little, Brown Bks. for Young Readers.

Brown, Roberta Simpson. Scared in School. 2005. (ENG.). 141p. (J). (gr. 6-9). pap. 8.95 (978-0-87483-496-3(1)) August Hse. Pubs., Inc.

Brown Sr., David F. Tabby Goes to School: The First in the Tabatha Adventures Series, 1 vol. Brown Jr., David F., illus. 2009. 20p. pap. 24.95 (978-1-60836-181-6(0)) America Star Bks.

Brown, Tiffany M. Gallery Eleven Twenty-Two. Sefcik, Wendy, illus. 2013. 30p. 17.99 (978-0-9854423-0-9(1)); pap. 9.99 (978-0-9854423-1-6(X)) Brewster Moon.

Brownlee, Browne. Bad Breath. 2007. 108p. 19.95 (978-1-4241-5487-6(1)) America Star Bks.

Bruchac, Joseph. Bearwalker. Comport, Sally Wern, illus. 2010. (ENG.). 240p. (J). (gr. 5). pap. 6.99 (978-0-06-112315-3(3)) HarperCollins Pubs.

Bruna, Dick. The School. 2013. (ENG., Illus.). 28p. (J). (gr. -1 — 1). 7.95 (978-1-84976-215-1(5)) Tate Publishing, Ltd. GBR. Dist: Abrams, Inc.

Bruno, Yvonne. Lisa Finds a New Friend. 2011. 24p. 12.79 (978-1-4567-1780-3(4)) AuthorHouse.

Bryan, Sabrina & DeVillers, Julia. Princess of Gossip. 2008. (ENG.). 384p. pap. 23.99 (978-1-4165-7065-3(9), MTV Bks.) MTV Books.

Bryant, Annie. Bad News/Good News. 2008. (Beacon Street Girls Ser.: 2). (ENG., Illus.). 256p. (J). (gr. 4-8). pap. 7.99 (978-1-4169-6425-4(8), Aladdin) Simon & Schuster Children's Publishing.

—Freaked Out. 2009. (Beacon Street Girls Ser.: 7). (ENG.). 272p. (J). (gr. 4-8). pap. 8.99 (978-1-4169-6433-9(9), Aladdin) Simon & Schuster Children's Publishing.

—Just Kidding. 2009. (Beacon Street Girls Ser.: 10). (ENG.). 256p. (J). (gr. 4-8). pap. 7.99 (978-1-4169-6440-7(1), Aladdin) Simon & Schuster Children's Publishing.

—Lake Rescue. 2008. (Beacon Street Girls Ser.: 6). (ENG.). 256p. (J). (gr. 4-8). pap. 7.99 (978-1-4169-6431-5(2), Aladdin) Simon & Schuster Children's Publishing.

—Letters from the Heart. 2008. (Beacon Street Girls Ser.: 3). (ENG., Illus.). 256p. (J). (gr. 4-8). pap. 6.99 (978-1-4169-6426-1(6), Aladdin) Simon & Schuster Children's Publishing.

—Lucky Charm. 2009. (Beacon Street Girls Ser.: 8). (ENG.). 272p. (J). (gr. 4-8). pap. 9.99 (978-1-4169-6434-6(7), Aladdin) Simon & Schuster Children's Publishing.

—Maeve on the Red Carpet. 2009. (Beacon Street Girls Ser.: No. 3). (ENG.). 240p. (J). (gr. 4-8). pap. 6.99 (978-1-4169-6432-2(0), Aladdin) Simon & Schuster Children's Publishing.

—Promises, Promises. 2008. (Beacon Street Girls Ser.: 5). (ENG.). 304p. (J). (gr. 4-8). pap. 8.99 (978-1-4169-6430-8(4), Aladdin) Simon & Schuster Children's Publishing.

—Worst Enemies/Best Friends. 2008. (Beacon Street Girls Ser.: 1). (ENG.). 240p. (J). (gr. 4-8). pap. 8.99 (978-1-4169-6424-7(X), Aladdin) Simon & Schuster Children's Publishing.

Bryant, Jen. Pieces of Georgia. 2007. (ENG., Illus.). 176p. (J). (gr. 5-9). per. 6.99 (978-0-440-42055-2(5), Yearling) Random Hse. Children's Bks.

Bryant, Mary. Sped Spud: He May Be a Tater, but He's No Dud. 2008. 28p. pap. 24.95 (978-1-60563-436-4(0)) America Star Bks.

—Sped Spud: He May Be a Tater, but He's No Dud, 1 vol. 2010. 28p. 24.95 (978-1-4512-1075-0(2)) PublishAmerica, Inc.

Bubble Guppies, Bubble. Bubble Guppies Come Play with Us. 2015. (Lift-The-Flap Ser.: 5). (ENG.). 10p. (J). (gr. -1-k). bds. 11.99 (978-0-7944-3035-1(X), Reader's Digest Children's Bks.) Studio Fun International.

Buchanan, Paul & Buchanan, P. The Last Place I Want to Be, 1 vol. 2009. 176p. (J). pap. 7.99 (978-0-8254-2408-3(9)) Kregel Pubns.

Buchanan, Selena. Sunday Chimes, 1 vol. 2009. 51p. pap. 16.95 (978-1-4489-2208-6(9)) America Star Bks.

Buckeridge, Anthony. Jennings' Diary. 2008. (Jennings Ser.: 5). (ENG.). 192p. (J). (gr. -1-12). pap. 12.95 (978-0-7551-0163-4(4)) House of Stratus, Inc. GBR. Dist: Gardners Bks. Ltd.

—Jennings' Little Hut. 2008. (Jennings Ser.: 3). (ENG.). 210p. (J). (gr. -1-12). pap. 12.95 (978-0-7551-1367-5(5)) House of Stratus, Inc. GBR. Dist: Gardners Bks. Ltd.

Buckley, Michael. The Fairy-Tale Detectives: And the Unusual Suspects. Ferguson, Peter, illus. 2012. 580p. (J). (978-1-4351-4487-3(2), Amulet Bks.) Abrams, Inc.

—M Is for Mama's Boy. Beavers, Ethen, illus. 2010. (Nerds Ser.). (ENG.). 288p. (J). (gr. 3-7). 16.95 (978-0-8109-8986-3(7)); pap. 6.95 (978-0-8109-9674-8(X)) Abrams, Inc. (Amulet Bks.).

—M Is for Mama's Boy, Bk. 2. 2011. (Nerds Ser.). (ENG., Illus.). 304p. (J). (gr. 3-7). pap. 7.95 (978-1-4197-0023-1(5), Amulet Bks.) Abrams, Inc.

—NERDS: National Espionage, Rescue, & Defense Society. 2009. (N. E. R. D. S. Ser.: 1). (J). 1.25 (978-1-4407-4243-9(X)); 190.75 (978-1-4407-4234-7(0)); 88.75 (978-1-4407-4237-8(5)); 73.75 (978-1-4407-4233-0(2)); 86.75 (978-1-4407-4239-2(1)); 71.75 (978-1-4407-4235-4(9)) Recorded Bks., Inc.

—NERDS Bk. 1: National Espionage, Rescue, & Defense Society. 2010. (Nerds Ser.). (ENG., Illus.). 352p. (J). (gr. 3-7). pap. 7.95 (978-0-8109-8985-6(9), Amulet Bks.) Abrams, Inc.

—Nerds Bk. 1: National Espionage, Rescue, & Defense Society. Beavers, Ethen, illus. 2009. (Nerds Ser.). (ENG.). 336p. (J). (gr. 3-7). 16.95 (978-0-8109-4324-7(7), Amulet Bks.) Abrams, Inc.

—NERDS - National Espionage, Rescue, & Defense Society. 2010. (Nerds Ser.: 1). (J). lib. bdg. 18.40 (978-0-606-15084-2(6), Turtleback) Turtleback Bks.

—NERDS 2: M für Muttersöhnchen. 2011. (SPA.). 260p. (J). (gr. 6-8). pap. 10.99 (978-987-612-335-8(1)) V&R Editoras.

—The Unusual Suspects. 2006. (Sisters Grimm Ser.: Bk. 2). 1.00 (978-1-4237-8623-8(8)) Recorded Bks., Inc.

—The Unusual Suspects. 2017. (Sisters Grimm Ser.: 2). (J). lib. bdg. 19.60 **(978-0-606-39686-8(1))** Turtleback Bks.

—The Unusual Suspects. 2007. (Sisters Grimm Ser.: 2). (J). lib. bdg. 18.40 (978-1-4178-0732-1(6), Turtleback) Turtleback Bks.

—A Very Grimm Guide. Ferguson, Peter, illus. 2012. (Sisters Grimm Ser.). (ENG.). 128p. (J). (gr. 3-7). 16.95 (978-1-4197-0201-3(7), Amulet Bks.) Abrams, Inc.

Buckner, Chuck. The Death of Arkie Baker. 2008. 84p. pap. 8.86 (978-1-4357-4105-8(6)) Lulu Pr., Inc.

Budhos, Marina. Ask Me No Questions. 2007. 159p. (gr. 7-12). 20.00 (978-0-7569-8114-3(X)) Perfection Learning Corp.

—Ask Me No Questions. 2007. (ENG.). 192p. (YA). (gr. 7-12). pap. 10.99 (978-1-4169-4920-6(8), Atheneum Bks. for Young Readers) Simon & Schuster Children's Publishing.

Buffington, Cecil. High School Super-Star: The Junior Year. 2008. 244p. pap. 16.95 (978-0-595-51914-9(8)) iUniverse, Inc.

Bui-Quang, Phuong-Mai. Tea Club. 2006. (YA). per. 10.95 (978-1-59971-581-0(3)) Aardvark Global Publishing.

Bulion, Leslie. The Trouble with Rules, 1 vol. (ENG.). 160p. (J). 2011. pap. 6.95 (978-1-56145-576-8(8)) 2008. (gr. 2-6). 14.95 (978-1-56145-440-2(0)) Peachtree Pubs.

Bunker, Lisa. Felix Yz. 2017. (ENG.). 288p. (J). (gr. 5-9). 16.99 (978-0-425-28850-4(1), Viking Books for Young Readers) Penguin Young Readers Group.

Bunting, Eve. My Special Day at Third Street School. Bloom, Suzanne, illus. 2009. (ENG.). 32p. (J). (gr. k-2). pap. 10.95 (978-1-59078-745-8(5)) Boyds Mills Pr.

Burch, Robert. Queenie Peavey. l.t. ed. 2003. (LRS Large Print Cornerstone Ser.). 166p. (J). lib. bdg. 29.95 (978-1-58118-115-9(9)) LRS.

Burchette, Ruby J. The Dog Went to School, 1 vol. 2010. 48p. pap. 16.95 (978-1-4489-4962-5(9)) America Star Bks.

Burchill, Julie. Sugar Rush. 2005. 288p. (J). lib. bdg. 17.89 (978-0-06-077620-6(X), HarperTeen) HarperCollins Pubs.

Burke, Morgan. Get It Started. 2010. (Party Room Ser.: 1). (ENG.). 272p. (J). (gr. 11). pap. 12.99 (978-1-4424-1420-4(0), Simon Pulse) Simon Pulse.

Burkhart, Alma J. If You Could See Her Smile. Burns, Sandra, illus. 2013. 24p. pap. 8.99 (978-1-938768-32-3(9)) Gypsy Pubns.

Burkhart, Jessica. Chasing Blue. 2009. (Canterwood Crest Ser.: 2). (ENG.). 272p. (J). (gr. 4-8). pap. 7.99 (978-1-4169-5841-3(X), Aladdin) Simon & Schuster Children's Publishing.

—Comeback. 2012. (Canterwood Crest Ser.: 15). lib. bdg. 18.40 (978-0-606-26312-2(8), Turtleback) Turtleback Bks.

—Famous. 2013. (Canterwood Crest Ser.: 18). (ENG.). 240p. (J). (gr. 4-7). pap. 7.99 (978-1-4424-3659-6(X), Aladdin) Simon & Schuster Children's Publishing.

—Jealousy. 2013. (Canterwood Crest Ser.: 17). (ENG.). 208p. (J). (gr. 4-7). pap. 7.99 (978-1-4424-3657-2(3), Aladdin) Simon & Schuster Children's Publishing.

—Masquerade. 2012. (Canterwood Crest Ser.: 16). lib. bdg. 18.40 (978-0-606-26887-5(1), Turtleback) Turtleback Bks.

—Popular. 2012. (Canterwood Crest Ser.: 14). lib. bdg. 18.40 (978-0-606-26311-5(X), Turtleback) Turtleback Bks.

—Unfriendly Competition. 2011. (Canterwood Crest Ser.: 12). (ENG.). 192p. (J). (gr. 4-8). pap. 7.99 (978-1-4424-0386-4(1), Aladdin) Simon & Schuster Children's Publishing.

Burkhart, Jessica & Haley, Patricia. Chosen: Super Special. 2011. (Canterwood Crest Ser.). (ENG.). 304p. (J). (gr. 5-8). pap. 7.99 (978-1-4424-1946-9(6), Aladdin) Simon & Schuster Children's Publishing.

Burkhart, Kiersi. Honor Code. 2017. (ENG.). 320p. (YA). **(978-1-5124-2996-1(1)**, Carolrhoda Bks.) Lerner Publishing Group.

Burkholder, Sheila M. Elsie Waits Patiently. 2004. (Illus.). 32p. (gr. -1-5). 2.70 (978-0-7399-2339-9(0), 2778) Rod & Staff Pubs., Inc.

Burks, Megan. Sally the Circle. 2012. 28p. pap. 21.99 (978-1-4771-3343-9(7)) Xlibris Corp.

Burnett, Eric. Gymnastics Jenny Stands on Her Own. 2003. 108p. pap. 9.95 (978-0-595-27919-7(8)) iUniverse, Inc.

Burnett, Frances Hodgson. A Little Princess. 2008. 156p. 25.95 (978-1-60664-768-4(7)); pap. 13.95 (978-1-60664-141-5(7)) Aegypan.

—A Little Princess. 2008. 212p. (gr. 2-4). 24.99 (978-0-554-38458-0(2)); 27.99 (978-0-554-29155-0(X)) Creative Media Partners, LLC.

—A Little Princess. Aldous, Kate, illus. 2005. 62p. (J). (gr. 4-7). 8.95 (978-0-7945-1123-4(6), Usborne) EDC Publishing.

—A Little Princess. 2012. (ENG., Illus.). 280p. (978-1-905716-04-3(4), Collector's Library, The) Pan Macmillan.

—A Little Princess. Gill, Margery, illus. 2008. (Puffin Classics Ser.). (ENG.). 320p. (J). (gr. 5-7). 5.99 (978-0-14-132112-7(1), Puffin Books) Penguin Young Readers Group.

—A Little Princess. 188p. 2009. pap. 13.95 (978-1-4385-0876-4(X)) 2008. pap. 13.45 (978-1-4385-0194-9(3)) Standard Pubns., Inc. (Book Jungle).

—A Little Princess. McKowen, Scott, illus. 2004. (Sterling Unabridged Classics Ser.). (ENG.). 208p. (J). (gr. 5). 9.95 (978-1-4027-1454-2(8)) Sterling Publishing Co., Inc.

—A Little Princess. Engelbreit, Mary, illus. 2007. (Mary Engelbreit's Classic Library). (ENG.). 304p. (J). (gr. 3-7). 9.99 (978-0-06-008137-9(6), HarperFestival) HarperCollins Pubs.

—A Little Princess. 2012. (Children's Classics Ser.). (ENG.). 186p. pap. 19.99 (978-1-909438-52-1(9), Sovereign) Bollinger, Max GBR. Dist: Lightning Source UK, Ltd.

—A Little Princess. Kliros, Thea, illus. abr. ed. 2012. (Dover Children's Thrift Classics Ser.). (ENG.). 96p. (J). (gr. 3-8). pap. 3.00 (978-0-486-29171-0(5)) Dover Pubns., Inc.

—A Little Princess: Being the whole story of Sara Crewe now told for T. 2007. 196p. per. 19.99 (978-1-4346-7028-1(7)); (ENG.). 210p. per. 22.99 (978-1-4346-7029-8(5)) Creative Media Partners, LLC.

—A Little Princess: The Story of Sara Crewe. (J). 16.95 (978-0-8488-1253-9(0)) Amereon Ltd.

—A Little Princess: The Story of Sara Crewe. Warren, Eliza, ed. Marcos, Pablo, illus. 2006. 239p. (YA). reprint ed. 10.00 (978-0-7567-9835-2(3)) DIANE Publishing Co.

—A Little Princess: The Story of Sara Crewe. 2005. 112p. per. 4.95 (978-1-4209-2529-6(6)) Digireads.com Publishing.

—A Little Princess: The Story of Sara Crewe. 2006. pap. (978-1-4065-0559-7(5)) Dodo Pr.

—A Little Princess: The Story of Sara Crewe. l.t. ed. 2005. 376p. pap. (978-1-84637-117-2(1)) Echo Library.

—A Little Princess: The Story of Sara Crewe. 2004. reprint ed. pap. 22.95 (978-1-4191-0213-4(3)); pap. 1.99 (978-1-4192-0213-1(8)) Kessinger Publishing, LLC.

—A Little Princess: The Story of Sara Crewe. 2006. 204p. (YA). 19.95 (978-1-934169-20-9(X)); pap. 7.95 (978-1-934169-21-6(8)) Norilana Bks.

—A Little Princess: The Story of Sara Crewe. 2005. (Twelve-Point Ser.). lib. bdg. 25.00 (978-1-58287-320-6(8)); lib. bdg. 26.00 (978-1-58287-814-0(5)) North Bks.

—A Little Princess: The Story of Sara Crewe. Rust, Graham, illus. (J). pap. 22.95 (978-0-590-24079-6(X)) Scholastic, Inc.

—A Little Princess: The Story of Sara Crewe. l.t. ed. 2003. 342p. pap. 10.95 (978-0-7862-6247-2(8)) Thorndike Pr.

—A Little Princess: With a Discussion of Generosity. Gribbon, Sean & Jael, trs. Gribbon, Sean & Jael, illus. 2003. (Values in Action Illustrated Classics Ser.). (J). (978-1-59203-050-7(5)) Learning Challenge, Inc.

—Sara Crewe. l.t. ed. 2006. 92p. pap. (978-1-84637-263-6(1)) Echo Library.

—Sara Crewe. 2009. 68p. pap. 7.95 (978-1-60664-388-4(6)) Rodgers, Alan Bks.

—Sara Crewe or What Happened at Miss Minc. 2005. pap. 20.95 (978-0-7661-9708-4(5)) Kessinger Publishing, LLC.

Burnham, Molly B. Teddy Mars: Almost a World Record Breaker. Spencer, Trevor, illus. 2016. (Teddy Mars Ser.: 2). 288p. (J). (gr. 3-7). 16.99 (978-0-06-227813-5(4), Tegen, Katherine Bks) HarperCollins Pubs.

Burns, A. M. Hunters. 2016. (ENG., Illus.). (J). 24.99 **(978-1-63533-031-1(9)**, Harmony Ink Pr.) Dreamspinner Pr.

Burns, Catherine Lloyd. The Good, the Bad & the Beagle. 2014. (ENG.). 336p. (J). (gr. 5-7). 16.99 (978-0-374-30039-5(9), 9780374300395, Farrar, Straus & Giroux (BYR)) Farrar, Straus & Giroux.

—The Half-True Lies of Cricket Cohen. 2017. (ENG.). 256p. (J). 16.99 (978-0-374-30041-8(0), 9780374300418, Farrar, Straus & Giroux (BYR)) Farrar, Straus & Giroux.

Burns, Ellen Flanagan. The Tallest Bridge in the World: A Story about Social Anxiety Disorder. Lewis, Anthony, illus. 2017. (J). **(978-1-4338-2760-0(3)**, Magination Pr.) American Psychological Assn.

Burns, T. R. The Bad Apple. (Merits of Mischief Ser.: 1). (ENG.). (J). (gr. 3-7). 2013. 368p. pap. 7.99 (978-1-4424-4030-2(9)) 2012. 352p. 16.99 (978-1-4424-4029-6(5)) Simon & Schuster Children's Publishing. (Aladdin).

—Watch Your Step. 2015. (Merits of Mischief Ser.: 3). (ENG., Illus.). 464p. (J). (gr. 3-7). pap. 7.99 (978-1-4424-4036-4(8), Aladdin) Simon & Schuster Children's Publishing.

—A World of Trouble. (Merits of Mischief Ser.: 2). (ENG., Illus.). (J). (gr. 3-7). 2014. 400p. pap. 7.99 (978-1-4424-4033-3(3)) 2013. 384p. 16.99 (978-1-4424-4032-6(5)) Simon & Schuster Children's Publishing. (Aladdin).

Burroughs, Scott, illus. Robot Rumble. 2013. (Hardy Boys: the Secret Files Ser.: 11). (ENG.). 96p. (J). (gr. 1-4). pap. 5.99 (978-1-4424-5367-8(2), Aladdin) Simon & Schuster Children's Publishing.

Burt, Steve. Even Odder: More Stories to Chill the Heart. Hagerman, Jessica, illus. 2003. 144p. pap. 14.95 (978-0-9741407-0-4(8)) Burt, Steven E.

Burton, Rebecca. Leaving Jetty Road. 2004. 272p. (978-0-207-20015-1(7)) HarperCollins Pubs. Australia.

Bush, Laura & Hager, Jenna Bush. Read All about It! Brunkus, Denise, illus. 2010. (ENG.). 32p. (J). (gr. -1-3). pap. 6.99 (978-0-06-156077-4(4)) HarperCollins Pubs.

Bushnell, Candace. The Carrie Diaries. (Carrie Diaries: 1). (ENG.). (YA). (gr. 9). 2011. 416p. pap. 9.99 (978-0-06-172892-1(6)) 2010. 400p. 18.99 (978-0-06-172891-4(8)) 2012. 416p. pap. 10.99 (978-0-06-223684-5(9)) HarperCollins Pubs.

Bushweller, Ellie. The Tree with A Hundred Hands. 2008. 40p. 18.50 (978-0-615-24478-5(5)) Bushweller, Ellie.

Bustard, Anne. Anywhere but Paradise. 2015. (ENG.). 288p. (gr. 5). 16.99 (978-1-60684-585-1(3)); (J). 16.99 (978-1-5124-0110-3(2)) Lerner Publishing Group. (Carolrhoda Bks.).

Butcher, Kristin. Cheat, 1 vol. 2010. (Orca Currents Ser.). (ENG.). 128p. (J). (gr. 5-9). pap. 9.95 (978-1-55469-274-3(1)) Orca Bk. Pubs. USA.

Butler, Dori. Late Again! 2005. (J). pap. (978-1-4108-4209-1(6)) Benchmark Education Co.

Butler, Dori Hillestad. Alexandra Hopewell, Labor Coach. 2005. 136p. (J). (gr. 3-6). 15.99 (978-0-8075-0242-6(1)) Whitman, Albert & Co.

—The Buddy Files Bk. 4: The Case of the Fire Alarm. Tugeau, Jeremy, illus. 2011. (Buddy Files Ser.: 4). (ENG.). 144p. (J). (gr. 1-5). pap. 5.99 (978-0-8075-0935-7(3)) Whitman, Albert & Co.

—The Case of the Library Monster. Tugeau, Jeremy, illus. 2012. (Buddy Files Ser.: 5). (J). lib. bdg. 16.00 (978-0-606-23839-7(5), Turtleback) Turtleback Bks.

—The Case of the Library Monster. Tugeau, Jeremy & Crisp, Dan, illus. 2012. (Buddy Files Ser.: 5). (ENG.). 128p. (J). (gr. 1-5). pap. 5.99 (978-0-8075-0936-4(1)) Whitman, Albert & Co.

—The Case of the School Ghost. 2013. (Buddy Files Ser.: 6). lib. bdg. 16.00 (978-0-606-31843-3(7), Turtleback) Turtleback Bks.

—The Case of the School Ghost. Tugeau, Jeremy, illus. (Buddy Files Ser.: 6). (ENG.). (J). (gr. 1-5). 2012. 128p. 14.99 (978-0-8075-0915-9(9))Bk. 6. 2013. 144p. pap. 5.99 (978-0-8075-0937-1(X)) Whitman, Albert & Co.

—Sliding into Home, 1 vol. Casale, Paul, illus. 2003. (Peachtree Junior Publication Ser.). (ENG.). 192p. (J). (gr. 3-7). 14.95 (978-1-56145-222-4(X)) Peachtree Pubs.

—The Truth about Truman School, 1 vol. (ENG.). (J). (gr. 3-7). 2009. 192p. pap. 7.99 (978-0-8075-8096-7(1)) 2008. (Illus.). 176p. lib. bdg. 15.99 (978-0-8075-8095-0(3)) Whitman, Albert & Co.

Butler, Shirley. The First-Class Adventure of Flat Freddie. 2008. 60p. pap. 19.95 (978-1-60672-882-6(2)) America Star Bks.

Butterfield, MaryAnn Milton. You Are Too a Bully! 2013. 126p. (gr. 4-6). 28.99 (978-1-4582-0968-9(7)); pap. 11.99 (978-1-4582-0969-6(5)) Author Solutions, Inc. (Abbott Pr.).

Button, Lana. Willow's Whispers, 0 vols. Howells, Tania, illus. 2014. (Willow Ser.). (ENG.). 32p. (J). (gr. -1-2). pap. 7.95 (978-1-55453-744-0(4)) Kids Can Pr., Ltd. CAN. Dist: Hachette Bk. Group.

Buxbaum, Julie. Tell Me Three Things. (ENG.). (YA). (gr. 7). 2017. 352p. pap. 9.99 (**978-0-553-53567-9(6)**, Ember) 2016. 336p. 17.99 (978-0-553-53564-8(1), Delacorte Pr.) 2016. 336p. lib. bdg. 20.99 (978-0-553-53565-5(X), Delacorte Pr.) Random Hse. Children's Bks.

Buxbaum, Julie. What to Say Next. 2017. (ENG.). 304p. (YA). (gr. 7). 18.99 (978-0-553-53568-6(4), Delacorte Pr.) Random Hse. Children's Bks.

Buyea, Rob. Because of Mr. Terupt. (ENG.). (J). (gr. 3-7). 2011. 304p. 7.99 (978-0-375-85824-6(5), Yearling) 2010. 288p. 16.99 (978-0-385-73882-8(X), Delacorte Bks. for Young Readers) Random Hse. Children's Bks.

—Mr. Terupt Falls Again. 2012. (ENG.). 368p. (J). (gr. 4-7). 16.99 (978-0-385-74205-4(3), Delacorte Bks. for Young Readers) Random Hse. Children's Bks.

Buyea, Robert W. Saving Mr. Terupt. 2015. (ENG.). 384p. (J). (gr. 4-7). lib. bdg. 19.99 (978-0-375-99120-2(4), Delacorte Bks. for Young Readers) Random Hse. Children's Bks.

Buzzeo, Toni. Adventure Annie Goes to Kindergarten. Wummer, Amy, illus. 2013. (ENG.). 32p. (J). (gr. -1-k). mass mkt. 7.99 (978-0-14-242695-1(4), Puffin Books) Penguin Young Readers Group.

—Fire up with Reading! Yoshikawa, Sachiko, illus. 2007. (Mrs. Skorupski Story Ser.). 32p. (J). (gr. -1-3). 17.95 (978-1-932146-91-2(1), Upstart Bks.) Highsmith Inc.

—The Great Dewey Hunt. Yoshikawa, Sachiko, illus. 2009. (Mrs. Skorupski Story Ser.). (J). 36p. (gr. -1-3). 17.95 (978-1-60213-041-8(8)); (978-1-60213-029-6(9)) Highsmith Inc. (Upstart Bks.).

—Our Librarian Won't Tell Us Anything! Yoshikawa, Sachiko, illus. 2006. 32p. (J). (gr. -1-k). lib. bdg. 17.95 (978-1-932146-73-8(3), Upstart Bks.) Highsmith Inc.

Bykowski, Christy. Gluten-Free Me Beckman Goes to School. Thompson, Chad, illus. 2013. 24p. pap. 11.95 (978-1-61244-228-0(5)) Halo Publishing International.

Bylsma, Dan & Bylsma, Jay M. Slam Dunks Not Allowed! 2003. (Illus.). 238p. (YA). (978-0-938682-72-1(5)); pap. (978-0-938682-77-6(6)) River Road Pubns., Inc.

Cabot, Meg. Abandon. 2011. (ENG.). 320p. (J). (gr. 9-18). 17.99 (978-0-545-28410-3(4)) Scholastic, Inc.

—All-American Girl. 2008. (All-American Girl Ser.: 1). (ENG.). 416p. (YA). (gr. 8). pap. 8.99 (978-0-06-147989-2(6), HarperTeen) HarperCollins Pubs.

—All-American Girl. 2008. (All-American Girl Ser.: Vol. 1). 398p. (YA). (gr. 7-12). 19.65 (978-1-4178-2386-4(0), Turtleback) Turtleback Bks.

—Avalon High. 2007. (Avalon High Coronation Ser.: Bk. 1). (ENG.). 320p. (YA). (gr. 8-12). pap. 8.99 (978-0-06-075588-1(1), HarperTeen) HarperCollins Pubs.

—Blast from the Past. 2010. (Allie Finkle's Rules for Girls Ser.: 6). (ENG.). 240p. (J). (gr. 3-7). 15.99 (978-0-545-04048-8(5), Scholastic Pr.) Scholastic, Inc.

—Forever Princess, Vol. X. 2009. (Princess Diaries: 10). (ENG.). 416p. (YA). (gr. 8). pap. 9.99 (978-0-06-123294-7(7), HarperTeen) HarperCollins Pubs.

—From the Notebooks of a Middle-School Princess. 2016. (From the Notebooks of a Middle School Princess Ser.: 1). (J). lib. bdg. 18.40 (978-0-606-38554-1(1)) Turtleback Bks.

—Haunted. 2007. (Mediator Ser.: No. 5). 263p. 18.00 (978-0-7569-7831-0(9)) Perfection Learning Corp.

—Homecoming. Coronado, Jinky, illus. 2008. (Avalon High Coronation Ser.: Bk. 2). (ENG.). 192p. (YA). (gr. 8-18). pap. 9.99 (978-0-06-117709-5(1)) HarperCollins Pubs.

—How to Be Popular: When You're a Social Reject Like Me, Steph L. (ENG.). (YA). 2008. 320p. (gr. 8-12). pap. 8.99 (978-0-06-088014-9(7)) 2006. 304p. (gr. 7-12). 16.99 (978-0-06-088012-5(0)) HarperCollins Pubs. (HarperTeen).

—Hunter's Moon. Coronado, Jinky, illus. 2009. (Avalon High Coronation Ser.: Bk. 3). (ENG.). 160p. (YA). (gr. 8-18). pap. 9.99 (978-0-06-117710-1(5)) HarperCollins Pubs.

—Jinx. 2007. (gr. 7-12). 262p. (YA). lib. bdg. 17.89 (978-0-06-083765-5(9)); (ENG.). 272p. (J). 16.99 (978-0-06-083764-8(0)) HarperCollins Pubs. (HarperTeen).

—The Merlin Prophecy. (Avalon High Coronation Ser.: Bk. 1). 304p. (YA). 2006. (ENG.). (gr. 7-12). 16.99 (978-0-06-075586-7(5)) 2005. (gr. 8-12). lib. bdg. 17.89 (978-0-06-075587-4(3), HarperTeen) HarperCollins Pubs.

—Moving Day. 2009. (Allie Finkle's Rules for Girls Ser.: Bk. 1). (ENG.). 256p. (J). (gr. 3-7). 6.99 (978-0-545-04041-9(8), Scholastic Paperbacks) Scholastic, Inc.

—Moving Day. 2009. (Allie Finkle's Rules for Girls Ser.: 1). lib. bdg. 17.20 (978-0-606-06818-5(X), Turtleback) Turtleback Bks.

—The New Girl. 2008. (Allie Finkle's Rules for Girls Ser.: 2). (ENG.). 240p. (J). (gr. 3-7). 15.99 (978-0-545-04049-5(3), Scholastic Pr.) Scholastic, Inc.

—Party Princess. (ENG., (YA). 2006. (Princess Diaries: Vol. 7). Illus.). 304p. (gr. 7-12). 16.99 (978-0-06-072453-5(6)) Vol. VII. 2008. (Princess Diaries: 7). 320p. (gr. 8). pap. 9.99 (978-0-06-154374-6(8), HarperTeen) HarperCollins Pubs.

—Princess in Love. 2004. (Princess Diaries: Vol. 3). 288p. (J). (gr. 7-18). pap. 38.00 incl. audio (978-0-8072-2284-3(4), Listening Library) Random Hse. Audio Publishing Group.

—Princess in Pink. (ENG.). 2008. (Princess Diaries: 5). 288p. (YA). (gr. 8). pap. 9.99 (978-0-06-154363-0(2), HarperTeen) 2004. (Princess Diaries: Vol. 5). (Illus.). 272p. (J). (gr. 7-18). 15.99 (978-0-06-009610-6(1)) HarperCollins Pubs.

—Princess in Pink. 2008. (Princess Diaries: 5). 256p. (YA). (gr. 7-12). 20.85 (978-1-4178-2563-9(4), Turtleback) Turtleback Bks.

—Princess in the Spotlight. 2008. (Princess Diaries). 222p. (gr. 7-12). 19.00 (978-0-7569-8794-7(6)) Perfection Learning Corp.

—Princess in the Spotlight, unabr. ed. 2004. (Princess Diaries: Vol. 2). 272p. (J). (gr. 7-18). pap. 38.00 incl. audio (978-0-8072-1197-7(4), S YA 332 SP, Listening Library) Random Hse. Audio Publishing Group.

—Princess in the Spotlight Vol. 2. 2008. (Princess Diaries: 2). (ENG.). 256p. (YA). (gr. 8-12). pap. 9.99 (978-0-06-147994-6(2), HarperTeen) HarperCollins Pubs.

—Princess in Training. (ENG., 2005. (Princess Diaries: Vol. 6). Illus.). 288p. (J). (gr. 7-18). 16.99 (978-0-06-009613-7(6)) Vol. VI. 2008. (Princess Diaries: 6). 304p. (YA). (gr. 8). pap. 9.99 (978-0-06-154365-4(9), HarperTeen) HarperCollins Pubs.

—Princess Mia. (ENG.). 2008. (Princess Diaries: Vol. 9). 256p. (J). (gr. 7-18). 16.99 (978-0-06-072461-0(7)) Vol. 9. 2009. (Princess Diaries: 9). 304p. (YA). (gr. 8). pap. 9.99 (978-0-06-072463-4(3), HarperTeen) HarperCollins Pubs.

—Princess Mia. 2009. (Princess Diaries: 9). (YA). lib. bdg. 20.85 (978-0-606-02178-4(7), Turtleback) Turtleback Bks.

—Princess on the Brink. 2007. (Princess Diaries: 8). (ENG.). 272p. (YA). (gr. 8). pap. 9.99 (978-0-06-072460-3(9), HarperTeen) HarperCollins Pubs.

—Ready or Not. (All-American Girl Ser.: 2). 2008. (ENG.). 336p. (YA). (gr. 8). pap. 8.99 (978-0-06-147996-0(9), HarperTeen) 2005. (ENG.). 256p. (J). (gr. 7-18). 16.99 (978-0-06-072450-4(1)) 2nd ed. 2005. 256p. (J). (gr. 7-18). lib. bdg. 16.89 (978-0-06-072451-1(X)) HarperCollins Pubs.

—Shadowland & Ninth Key. 2010. (Mediator Ser.). (ENG.). 544p. (YA). (gr. 8). pap. 9.99 (978-0-06-204020-6(0), HarperTeen) HarperCollins Pubs.

—Stage Fright. 2010. (Allie Finkle's Rules for Girls Ser.: 4). (ENG.). 240p. (J). (gr. 3-7). 6.99 (978-0-545-04046-4(9)) Scholastic, Inc.

—Teen Idol. 2005. (ENG., Illus.). 320p. (YA). (gr. 8-18). reprint ed. pap. 9.99 (978-0-06-009618-2(7), HarperTeen) HarperCollins Pubs.

—Teen Idol. 2005. 291p. (YA). 16.65 (978-0-7569-5735-3(4)) Perfection Learning Corp.

—Twilight. 2005. (Mediator Ser.: No. 6). (ENG.). 256p. (J). 15.99 (978-0-06-072467-2(6)) HarperCollins Pubs.

—When Lightning Strikes; Code Name Cassandra. 2010. (Vanished Ser.: Bks. 1 & 2). (ENG., Illus.). 560p. (YA). (gr. 7). pap. 12.99 (978-1-4424-0629-2(1), Simon Pulse) Simon Pulse.

Cabot, Meg & Cabot, Frank. From the Notebooks of a Middle School Princess. 2015. (From the Notebooks of a Middle School Princess Ser.). (ENG., Illus.). 192p. (J). (gr. 3-7). 16.99 (978-1-250-06602-2(6), 9781250066022) Feiwel & Friends.

Cabral, Jeane. All Aboard the Yellow School Bus: Follow the Bus Through the Pages on a Counting Adventure! Top That Publishing Staff, ed. Petrlik, Andrea, illus. 2008. (Story Book Ser.). 20p. (J). (gr. -1). (978-1-84666-543-1(4), Tide Mill Pr.) Top That! Publishing PLC.

Cach, Lisa. Wake unto Me. 2011. (ENG.). 320p. (YA). (gr. 7-18). 8.99 (978-0-14-241436-1(0), Speak) Penguin Young Readers Group.

Cadenhead, MacKenzie. Sleeper. 2017. (ENG.). 272p. (YA). (gr. 6-12). pap. 10.99 (**978-1-4926-3614-4(2)**) Sourcebooks, Inc.

Calame, Don. Beat the Band. 2010. (ENG., Illus.). 400p. (YA). (gr. 9-18). 16.99 (978-0-7636-4633-2(4)) Candlewick Pr.

—Call the Shots. 2013. (ENG.). 464p. (YA). (gr. 9). pap. 7.99 (978-0-7636-6454-1(5)) Candlewick Pr.

Caletti, Deb. The Six Rules of Maybe. (ENG.). (YA). (gr. 7). 2011. 352p. pap. 9.99 (978-1-4169-7971-5(9)) 2010. 336p. 16.99 (978-1-4169-7969-2(7)) Simon Pulse. (Simon Pulse).

Calin, Marisa. Between You & Me. 2012. (ENG.). 256p. (YA). (gr. 7-12). 16.99 (978-1-59990-758-1(5), 9781599907581, Bloomsbury USA Childrens) Bloomsbury Publishing USA.

Callen, Sharon. Ms. Wilde & Oscar, 1 vol. rev. ed. 2013. (Fiction Readers Ser.). (ENG., Illus.). 32p. (J). (gr. 3-3). pap. 8.99 (978-1-4333-5611-7(2)) Shell Educational Publishing.

—Ms. Wilde & Oscar. rev. ed. 2013. (Fiction Readers Ser.). (ENG., Illus.). 32p. (gr. 3-3). pap. 19.96 (978-1-4807-1733-6(9)) Teacher Created Materials, Inc.

Calloway, Cassidy. Confessions of a First Daughter. 2009. (ENG.). 224p. (YA). (gr. 8-18). pap. 9.99 (978-0-06-172439-8(4), HarperTeen) HarperCollins Pubs.

Calmenson, Stephanie. The Frog Principal. Brunkus, Denise, illus. 2006. (ENG.). 32p. (J). pap. 5.99 (978-0-439-81217-7(8), Scholastic Paperbacks) Scholastic, Inc.

—Ollie's School Day. Carter, Abby, illus. 2012. (ENG.). 24p. (J). 15.95 (978-0-8234-2377-4(8)) Holiday Hse., Inc.

Calmenson, Stephanie & Cole, Joanna. Teacher's Pets. Ross, Heather, illus. 2015. (Ready, Set, Dogs! Ser.: 2). (ENG.). 144p. (J). (gr. 1-4). pap. 5.99 (978-1-250-05705-1(1), 9781250057051) Square Fish.

Calonita, Jen. Belles. 2012. (Belles Ser.: 1). (ENG.). 384p. (YA). (gr. 7-17). pap. 8.99 (978-0-316-09112-1(X), Poppy) Little, Brown Bks. for Young Readers.

—Flunked. 2015. (Fairy Tale Reform School Ser.: 1). (ENG.). 256p. (J). (gr. 5-8). 15.99 (978-1-4926-0156-2(X), 9781492601562, Sourcebooks Jabberwocky) Sourcebooks, Inc.

—Secrets of My Hollywood Life. 2007. (Secrets of My Hollywood Life Ser.: 1). (ENG.). 256p. (J). (gr. 7-17). per. 19.99 (978-0-316-15443-7(1), Poppy) Little, Brown Bks. for Young Readers.

—Tricked. 2017. (Fairy Tale Reform School Ser.: 3). (ENG.). 272p. (J). (gr. 5-8). 15.99 (978-1-4926-3795-0(5), 9781492637950, Sourcebooks Jabberwocky) Sourcebooks, Inc.

Caloyeras, Jennifer. Strays: A Novel. 2015. (ENG.). 219p. (J). pap. 17.95 (978-1-61822-037-0(3), Ashland Creek Pr.) Byte Level Research.

Cameron, Anne. Secrets of the Storm Vortex. Jamieson, Victoria, illus. 2015. (Lightning Catcher Ser.: 3). (ENG.). 464p. (J). (gr. 3-7). 16.99 (978-0-06-211283-5(X), Greenwillow Bks.) HarperCollins Pubs.

—The Storm Tower Thief. Jamieson, Victoria, illus. 2014. (Lightning Catcher Ser.: 2). (ENG.). 432p. (J). (gr. 3-7). 16.99 (978-0-06-211279-8(1), Greenwillow Bks.) HarperCollins Pubs.

Cammuso, Frank. The Dodgeball Chronicles. 2008. (Knights of the Lunch Table Ser.: 1). (ENG., Illus.). 144p. (J). (gr. 2-5). pap. 10.99 (978-0-439-90322-6(X), Graphix) Scholastic, Inc.

—The Dragon Players. 2009. (Knights of the Lunch Table Ser.: 2). (ENG.). 128p. (J). (gr. 4-7). pap. 10.99 (978-0-439-90323-3(8), Graphix) Scholastic, Inc.

—The Misadventures of Salem Hyde: Spelling Trouble. 2013. (Misadventures of Salem Hyde Ser.: 1). (J). lib. bdg. 17.15 (978-0-606-33440-2(8), Turtleback) Turtleback Bks.

Campbell, K. G. Dylan the Villain. Campbell, K. G., illus. 2016. (ENG., Illus.). 32p. (J). (gr. -1-1). 17.99 (978-0-451-47642-5(5), Viking Books for Young Readers) Penguin Young Readers Group.

Campbell, K. G., illus. Dylan the Villain. 2016. (J). (978-0-698-40517-2(X)) Penguin Bks., Ltd.

Campbell, L. A. Cartboy & the Time Capsule. (Cartboy Ser.: 1). (ENG.). 208p. (J). (gr. 3-7). 2015. pap. 6.99 (978-0-7653-7844-6(2), 9780765378446) 2013. (Illus.). 12.99 (978-0-7653-3317-9(1), 9780765333179) Doherty, Tom Assocs., LLC. (Starscape).

Campbell, S. E. Tasting Silver. 2013. 178p. pap. 10.99 (978-1-62237-220-1(4)) Turquoise Morning Pr.

Candlewick Press, Candlewick. Peppa Pig & the Busy Day at School. Candlewick Press, Candlewick & Ladybird Books Staff, illus. 2013. (Peppa Pig Ser.). (ENG.). 32p. (J). (-k). 12.99 (978-0-7636-6525-8(8), Candlewick Entertainment) Candlewick Pr.

Cantor, Jillian. The Life of Glass. 2010. (ENG.). 352p. (YA). (gr. 8-18). 16.99 (978-0-06-168651-1(4), HarperTeen) HarperCollins Pubs.

Capucilli, Alyssa Satin. Biscuit's 100th Day of School. Young, Mary O'Keefe & Schories, Pat, illus. 2006. (Biscuit Ser.). (ENG.). 20p. (J). (gr. -1-1). pap. 6.99 (978-0-06-079467-5(4), HarperFestival) HarperCollins Pubs.

—Not This Bear: A First Day of School Story. Hussey, Lorna, illus. 2015. (ENG.). 32p. (J). (gr. -1-1). 16.99 (978-0-8050-9896-9(8), 9780805098969, Holt, Henry & Co. Bks. For Young Readers) Holt, Henry & Co.

Carbone, Elisa. The Pack. 2006. (ENG.). 160p. (YA). (gr. 7-18). per. 6.99 (978-0-14-240535-2(3), Puffin Books) Penguin Young Readers Group.

Cardi, Annie. The Chance You Won't Return. 2014. (ENG.). 352p. (YA). (gr. 7). 16.99 (978-0-7636-6292-9(5)) Candlewick Pr.

Carey, Anna. Rebecca Is Always Right. 2015. (ENG.). 304p. (J). pap. 13.00 (978-1-84717-565-6(1)) O'Brien Pr., Ltd., The IRL. Dist: Dufour Editions, Inc.

Carleson, J. C. The Tyrant's Daughter. 2015. (ENG.). 304p. (YA). (gr. 7). pap. 9.99 (978-0-449-80999-0(4), Ember) Random Hse. Children's Bks.

Carlson, Melody. Beyond Reach. 2007. (Secret Life of Samantha Mcgregor Ser.: No. 2). (ENG.). 256p. (J). (gr. 7-12). per. 14.99 (978-1-59052-693-4(7), Multnomah) Doubleday Religious Publishing Group, The.

—Bright Purple: Color Me Confused. 2006. (Truecolors Ser.: 10). (ENG.). 224p. (YA). (gr. 4-7). per. 14.99 (978-1-57683-950-8(8), Th1nk Bks.) NavPress Publishing Group.

—Dark Blue: Color Me Lonely. 2004. (Truecolors Ser.: 1). (ENG.). 208p. (YA). pap. 14.99 (978-1-57683-529-6(4), Th1nk Bks.) NavPress Publishing Group.

—Homecoming Queen, 1 vol. 2014. (Carter House Girls Ser.). (ENG.). 224p. (YA). pap. 9.99 (978-0-310-74725-3(2)) Zondervan.

—Last Dance, 1 vol. 2014. (Carter House Girls Ser.). (ENG.). 208p. (YA). pap. 9.99 (978-0-310-74900-4(X)) Zondervan.

—My Name Is Chloe. 2005. (Diary of a Teenage Girl: Bk. 5). 288p. (YA). mass mkt. 7.99 (978-1-59052-736-8(4), Multnomah) Doubleday Religious Publishing Group, The.

—Payback. 2008. (Secret Life of Samantha Mcgregor Ser.: No. 4). (ENG.). 240p. (gr. 8-12). pap. 12.99 (978-1-59052-934-8(0), Multnomah) Doubleday Religious Publishing Group, The.

—Playing with Fire. 2007. (Secret Life of Samantha Mcgregor Ser.: No. 3). (ENG.). 256p. (YA). (gr. 7-12). per. 12.99 (978-1-59052-694-1(5), Multnomah Bks.) Crown Publishing Group.

—Stealing Bradford, 1 vol. 2014. (Carter House Girls Ser.). (ENG.). 224p. (YA). pap. 9.99 (978-0-310-74654-6(X)) Zondervan.

Carlson, Nancy. First Grade, Here I Come! 2006. (Illus.). (J). (978-1-4156-8114-5(7), Viking Adult) Penguin Publishing Group.

—Henry & the Bully. 2012. (ENG.). 32p. (J). (gr. -1-1). pap. 6.99 (978-0-14-242120-8(0), Puffin Books) Penguin Young Readers Group.

—Henry's 100 Days of Kindergarten. Carlson, Nancy, illus. 2007. (ENG., Illus.). 32p. (J). (gr. -1-1). pap. 5.99 (978-0-14-240758-5(5), Puffin Books) Penguin Young Readers Group.

—Henry's 100 Days of Kindergarten. 2007. 16.00 (978-1-4177-5983-5(6), Turtleback) Turtleback Bks.

—Henry's Amazing Imagination. 2010. (ENG.). 32p. (J). (gr. -1-1). pap. 6.99 (978-0-14-241605-1(3), Puffin Books) Penguin Young Readers Group.

—Henry's Show & Tell. Carlson, Nancy, illus. 2012. (Nancy Carlson Picture Bks). (Illus.). 32p. (J). (gr. k-2). (ENG.). 9.95 (978-0-7613-8953-8(9)); 56.72 (978-0-7613-9308-5(0)) Lerner Publishing Group. (Carolrhoda Bks.).

—I Don't Like to Read! Carlson, Nancy & Carlson, illus. 2009. (ENG.). 32p. (J). (gr. k-2). pap. 6.99 (978-0-14-241451-4(4), Puffin Books) Penguin Young Readers Group.

—It's Not My Fault! Carlson, Nancy, illus. 2003. (Illus.). 32p. (J). (gr. k-2). 15.95 (978-1-57505-598-5(8)) Lerner Publishing Group.

—No Es Mi Culpa. Translations.com Staff, tr. from ENG. Carlson, Nancy, illus. 2006. (Spanish Picture Bks.). (SPA., Illus.). 32p. (J). (gr. k-2). lib. bdg. 15.95 (978-0-8225-6501-7(3), Ediciones Lerner) Lerner Publishing Group.

—¡Piensa en Grande! 2005. (Libros Ilustrados (Picture Bks.)). (SPA., Illus.). 32p. (J). (gr. k-2). lib. bdg. 15.95 (978-0-8225-3192-0(5), Ediciones Lerner) Lerner Publishing Group.

—Think Big! 2005. (Illus.). 28p. (J). (gr. -1-3). 15.95 (978-1-57505-622-7(4), Carolrhoda Bks.) Lerner Publishing Group.

Carman, Patrick. Pulse. 2013. (Pulse Ser.: 1). (ENG.). 384p. (YA). (gr. 8). 17.99 (978-0-06-208576-4(X), Tegen, Katherine Bks) HarperCollins Pubs.

Carmi, Rebecca. Amazing Magnetism. Speirs, John, illus. 2003. (Magic School Bus Science Chapter Bks.). 76p. (gr. 2-4). 15.00 (978-0-7569-1576-6(7)) Perfection Learning Corp.

Carmichael, Jodi. Spaghetti Is Not a Finger Food (and Other Life Lessons) Sarah, Ackerley, illus. 2013. (ENG.). 152p. (J). (gr. 1-5). pap. 6.95 (978-1-939775-03-0(5)) March 4th, Inc.

Carmona, Adela. The Boy Who Could See. Chapman, Robert E., illus. 2008. 32p. pap. 24.95 (978-1-60672-697-6(8)) PublishAmerica, Inc.

Carolan, Jill. Sadie's Bargain. 2008. 148p. pap. 10.94 (978-0-615-26231-4(7)) Never Quit Productions, Inc.

Caroll, Robin. Samantha Sanderson at the Movies, 1 vol. 2014. (FaithGirlz / Samantha Sanderson Ser.). (ENG.). 272p. (J). pap. 8.99 (978-0-310-74245-6(5)) Zonderkidz.

—Samantha Sanderson on the Scene, 1 vol. 2014. (FaithGirlz / Samantha Sanderson Ser.). (ENG.). 256p. (J). pap. 8.99 (978-0-310-74247-0(1)) Zonderkidz.

Carr, Annie Roe. Nan Sherwood at Pine Camp or the Old Lum. 2007. pap. (978-1-4065-1294-6(X)) Dodo Pr.

—Nan Sherwood at Rose Ranch. 2007. 124p. per. (978-1-4068-4396-5(2)) Echo Library.

—Nan Sherwood at Rose Ranch or the Old Me. 2007. pap. (978-1-4065-1295-3(8)) Dodo Pr.

Carr, Elias & Karre, Andrew. The Combination. 2011. (Night Fall Ser.). (ENG.). 120p. (YA). (gr. 6-12). pap. 7.95 (978-0-7613-7810-5(3)) Lerner Publishing Group.

Carr, Patrick W. The Legend's Granddaughter: Not Quite Super, Book 1. Dabbs, Douglas, illus. 2007. 281p. (J). pap. (978-0-9793168-0-7(4)) NQSBks.

Carrier, Therese & Carrier, Stephen. Josiah's School Fun Day. Hatfield, Tommy, illus. 2007. 29p. (J). 16.95 (978-0-9797648-0-6(7)) Carrier, Therese.

Carriger, Gail. Curtsies & Conspiracies. (Finishing School Ser.: 2). (ENG.). (YA). (gr. 7-17). 2014. 336p. pap. 10.00 (978-0-316-19020-6(9)) 2013. 320p. 18.00 (978-0-316-19011-4(X)) Little, Brown Bks. for Young Readers.

—Etiquette & Espionage. 2013. (Finishing School Ser.: 1). (ENG.). 320p. (YA). (gr. 7-17). 18.99 (978-0-316-19008-4(X)) Little Brown & Co.

—Etiquette & Espionage. 2013. (Finishing School Ser.: 1). (ENG.). 336p. (YA). (gr. 7-17). pap. 10.99 (978-0-316-19010-7(1)) Little, Brown Bks. for Young Readers.

—Waistcoats & Weaponry. 2014. (Finishing School Ser.: 3). (ENG.). 304p. (YA). (gr. 7-17). 18.00 (978-0-316-19027-5(6)) Little Brown & Co.

—Waistcoats & Weaponry. 2015. (Finishing School Ser.: 3). (ENG.). 320p. (YA). (gr. 7-17). pap. 10.00 (978-0-316-19025-1(X)) Little, Brown Bks. for Young Readers.

Carroll, Jonathan. Meet Julius Carmichael: First Day Blues. Koltun, Amy, illus. 2003. 96p. (J). (gr. 3-6). pap. 6.95 (978-0-9724935-0-5(6)) Striking Presence Pubns.

Carson, Jana. We Both Read-The New Tribe. Treatner, Meryl, illus. 2013. 44p. (J). pap. 4.99 (978-1-60115-264-0(7)); 9.95 (978-1-60115-263-3(9)) Treasure Bay, Inc.

Carter, Alden. Love, Football, & Other Contact Sports. 2008. (ENG.). 261p. (YA). pap. 8.95 (978-0-8234-2165-7(1)) Holiday Hse., Inc.

Carter, Alden R. Love, Football, & Other Contact Sports. 2006. (ENG.). 192p. (YA). (gr. 7-12). 17.95 (978-0-8234-1975-3(4)) Holiday Hse., Inc.

—Wart, Son of Toad, 0 vols. unabr. ed. 2013. (ENG.). 224p. (YA). (gr. 8-10). pap. 9.99 (978-1-4778-1698-1(4), 9781477816981, Amazon Children's Publishing) Amazon Publishing.

Carter, Ally. I'd Tell You I Love You, but Then I'd Have to Kill You. 2016. (Gallagher Girls Ser.: 1). (J). lib. bdg. 20.85 (**978-0-606-39572-4(5)**) Turtleback Bks.

—I'd Tell You I Love You, but Then I'd Have to Kill You (10th Anniversary Edition) 2016. (Gallagher Girls Ser.). (ENG.). 304p. (J). (gr. 5-9). pap. 9.99 (978-1-4847-8505-8(3)) Hyperion Bks. for Children.

—Only the Good Spy Young (10th Anniversary Edition) 2016. (Gallagher Girls Ser.). (ENG.). 288p. (J). (gr. 5-9). pap. 9.99 (978-1-4847-8506-5(1)) Hyperion Bks. for Children.

—Out of Sight, Out of Time. 2016. (Gallagher Girls Ser.: 5). (YA). lib. bdg. 20.85 (978-0-606-38299-1(2)) Turtleback Bks.

—Out of Sight, Out of Time (10th Anniversary Edition) 2016. (Gallagher Girls Ser.). (ENG.). 320p. (YA). (gr. 5-9). pap. 9.99 (978-1-4847-8507-2(X)) Hyperion Bks. for Children.

—United We Spy (10th Anniversary Edition) 2016. (Gallagher Girls Ser.). (ENG.). 320p. (YA). (gr. 5-9). pap. 9.99 (978-1-4847-8508-9(8)) Hyperion Bks. for Children.

Carter, David A. School Bugs. Carter, David A., illus. 2009. (David Carter's Bugs Ser.). (ENG., Illus.). 20p. (J). (gr. -1-2). 12.99 (978-1-4169-5056-1(7), Little Simon) Little Simon.

Carvell, Tim. Planet Tad. Holgate, Doug, illus. (Planet Tad Ser.: 1). 256p. (J). (gr. 3-7). 2014. (ENG.). pap. 6.99 (978-0-06-193438-4(0)) 2012. (ENG.). 12.99 (978-0-06-193436-0(4)) 2012. lib. bdg. 14.89 (978-0-06-193437-7(2)) HarperCollins Pubs.

—Return to Planet Tad. 2014. (Planet Tad Ser.: 2). (ENG., Illus.). 240p. (J). (gr. 3-7). 12.99 (978-0-06-226625-5(X)) HarperCollins Pubs.

Casanova, Mary. Chrissa Stands Strong, Bks. 2. England, Tamara, ed. Jones, Richard, illus. 2009. (ENG.). 130p. (YA). (gr. 3-18). pap. 6.95 (978-1-59369-567-5(5), American Girl) American Girl Publishing, Inc.

Casella, Jody. Thin Space. 2013. (ENG.). 256p. (YA). (gr. 7). 16.99 (978-1-58270-435-7(X)); pap. 10.99 (978-1-58270-392-3(2)) Simon Pulse. (Simon Pulse).

Cass, Isabella. Don't Stop Believing, Bk. 4. 2011. (Superstar High Ser.: 3). (ENG.). 496p. (J). (gr. 4-7). pap. 8.99 *(978-0-552-56092-4(8))* Transworld Publishers Ltd. GBR. Dist: Independent Pubs. Group.

Cassidy, Cathy. Indigo Blue. 2006. (ENG.). 240p. (J). (gr. 5-18). 7.99 *(978-0-14-240703-5(8)*, Puffin Books) Penguin Young Readers Group.

Castan, Mike. Fighting for Dontae. 2012. (ENG.). 144p. (YA). 16.95 *(978-0-8234-2348-4(4))* Holiday Hse., Inc.

—The Price of Loyalty. 2011. (ENG., Illus.). 256p. (YA). (gr. 7-18). 17.95 *(978-0-8234-2268-5(2))* Holiday Hse., Inc.

Castellucci, Cecil. Boy Proof. (ENG.). 208p. (YA). (gr. 9-18). 2005. 15.99 *(978-0-7636-2333-3(4))* 2006. reprint ed. per. 8.99 *(978-0-7636-2796-6(8))* Candlewick Pr.

—Boy Proof, 4 vols. 2005. (YA). 62.75 *(978-1-4193-5131-0(1))* Recorded Bks., Inc.

Castle, M. E. Cloneward Bound. 2013. (Clone Chronicles Ser.: No. 2). (ENG.). 272p. (J). (gr. 3-7). pap. 6.99 *(978-1-60684-473-1(3)*, Darby Creek) Lerner Publishing Group.

—Game of Clones. (Clone Chronicles Ser.: No. 3). (ENG.). 256p. (J). (gr. 3-7). 2014. 15.99 *(978-1-60684-234-8(X))*No. 3. 2015. pap. 6.99 *(978-1-60684-538-7(1))* Lerner Publishing Group. (Darby Creek).

—Popular Clone. 2012. (Clone Chronicles: No. 1). (ENG.). 320p. (J). (gr. 3-7). pap. 6.99 *(978-1-60684-414-4(8))*; 15.99 *(978-1-60684-232-4(3))* Lerner Publishing Group. (Darby Creek).

Catalanotto, Peter & Schembri, Pamela. The Veterans Day Visitor. Catalanotto, Peter, illus. 2008. (Second Grade Friends Ser.). (ENG., Illus.). 64p. (J). (gr. 2-5). 16.99 *(978-0-8050-7840-4(1)*, 9780805078404, Holt, Henry & Co. Bks. For Young Readers) Holt, Henry & Co.

Catling, Patrick Skene. The Chocolate Touch. 2014. (ENG.). 128p. (J). (gr. 3-7). 10.24 *(978-1-63245-319-8(3))* Lectorum Pubns., Inc.

—The Chocolate Touch. 2009. 8.32 *(978-1-55744-369-4(6)*, Everbind) Marco Bk. Co.

—The Chocolate Touch. 2006. 16.00 *(978-0-7569-6383-5(4))* Perfection Learning Corp.

—The Chocolate Touch. 87p. (J). (gr. 3-5). pap. 4.99 *(978-0-8072-1454-1(X)*, Listening Library) Random Hse. Audio Publishing Group.

Catling, Patrick Skene & Catling, P. The Chocolate Touch. Apple, Margot, illus. 2006. 126p. (J). (gr. 3-7). 17.20 *(978-1-4177-3437-5(X)*, Turtleback) Turtleback Bks.

Catling, Patrick Skene & Catling, Patrick S. The Chocolate Touch. Apple, Margot, illus. 2006. (ENG.). 128p. (J). (gr. 3-7). pap. 7.99 *(978-0-688-16133-0(2))* HarperCollins Pubs.

Caudill, Rebecca. Did You Carry the Flag Today, Charley. Grossman, Nancy, illus. 2007. 96p. (J). pap. 7.95 *(978-0-8050-8141-1(0)*, Holt, Henry & Co. Bks. For Young Readers) Holt, Henry & Co.

—Schoolhouse in the Woods. Merwin, Decie, illus. l.t. ed. 2004. (Fairchild Family Story Ser.: Bk. 2). 130p. (J). pap. 10.95 *(978-1-883937-80-5(9))* Bethlehem Bks.

—Schoolroom in the Parlor. Merwin, Decie, illus. l.t. ed. 2005. (Fairchild Family Story Ser.). 145p. (J). (gr. 3-7). pap. 11.95 *(978-1-883937-82-9(5))* Bethlehem Bks.

Certain Signals. 2014. (Gift Ser.). (ENG.). 112p. (YA). (gr. 6-12). lib. bdg. 27.93 *(978-1-4677-3511-7(6))* Lerner Publishing Group.

Cervantes, Angela. Allie, First at Last. 2016. (ENG.). 208p. (J). (gr. 3-7). 16.99 *(978-0-545-81223-8(2)*, Scholastic Pr.) Scholastic, Inc.

Cervantes, Gerard. Hilda Bee's Special Home. 2012. 48p. pap. 17.45 *(978-1-4497-3140-3(6)*, WestBow Pr.) Author Solutions, Inc.

Chabert, Jack. The Locker Ate Lucy! Ricks, Sam, illus. 2014. (Eerie Elementary — Branches Ser.: bk.2). (ENG.). 96p. (J). (gr. 1-3). 15.99 *(978-0-545-62396-4(0))*; pap. 4.99 *(978-0-545-62395-7(2))* Scholastic, Inc.

—The Locker Ate Lucy! 2014. (Eerie Elementary — Branches Ser.: bk.2). (ENG.). (J). lib. bdg. 14.75 *(978-0-606-36052-4(2))* Turtleback Bks.

—Recess Is a Jungle! Ricks, Sam, illus. 2016. (Eerie Elementary — Branches Ser.: bk.3). (ENG.). 96p. (J). (gr. 1-3). 15.99 *(978-0-545-87353-6(3))* Scholastic, Inc.

—Sam Battles the Machine! Ricks, Sam, illus. 2017. (Eerie Elementary — Branches Ser.: bk.6). (ENG.). 96p. (J). (gr. 1-3). pap. 4.99 ***(978-0-545-87378-9(9))*** Scholastic, Inc.

—Sam Battles the Machine! 2017. (Eerie Elementary — Branches Ser.: bk.6). (ENG.). (J). lib. bdg. 14.75 ***(978-0-606-40191-3(1))*** Turtleback Bks.

—School Freezes Over! Ricks, Sam, illus. 2016. (Eerie Elementary — Branches Ser.: bk.5). (ENG.). 96p. (J). (gr. 1-3). pap. 4.99 *(978-0-545-87373-4(8))* Scholastic, Inc.

—The School Is Alive! Ricks, Sam, illus. 2014. (Eerie Elementary — Branches Ser.: bk.1). (ENG.). 96p. (J). (gr. 1-3). 15.99 *(978-0-545-62393-3(6))*; pap. 4.99 *(978-0-545-62392-6(8))* Scholastic, Inc.

—The School Is Alive! 2014. (Eerie Elementary — Branches Ser.: bk.1). (ENG.). (J). lib. bdg. 14.75 *(978-0-606-35822-4(6))* Turtleback Bks.

—The Science Fair Is Freaky! Ricks, Sam, illus. 2016. (Eerie Elementary — Branches Ser.: bk.4). (ENG.). 96p. (J). (gr. 1-3). pap. 4.99 *(978-0-545-87368-0(1))* Scholastic, Inc.

—The Science Fair Is Freaky! 2016. (Eerie Elementary — Branches Ser.: bk.4). (ENG.). (J). lib. bdg. 14.75 *(978-0-606-38806-1(0))* Turtleback Bks.

Chachas, George & Wojtak, James. Doolittle's Very, Very Bad Day. De Soto, Ben, illus. 2011. 26p. (J). pap. 9.95 *(978-0-9793144-2-1(9))* Dragonetti.

Chainani, Soman. The Last Ever After. 2015. (School for Good & Evil Ser.: 3). (ENG., Illus.). 672p. (J). (gr. 3-7). 17.99 *(978-0-06-210495-3(0))* HarperCollins Pubs.

—The School for Good & Evil. (School for Good & Evil Ser.). (J). (gr. 3). 2016. 1760p. pap. 23.97 *(978-0-06-245624-3(5))* 2015. (ENG.). 1334p. 53.97 *(978-0-06-243497-5(7))* HarperCollins Pubs.

—The School for Good & Evil. Bruno, Iacopo, illus. (ENG.). (J). (gr. 3-7). 2014. (School for Good & Evil Ser.: 1). 544p. pap. 7.99 *(978-0-06-210490-8(X))* 2013. (School for Good & Evil Trilogy: No. 1). 400p. 17.99 *(978-0-06-210489-2(6))* HarperCollins Pubs.

—The School for Good & Evil. Bruno, Iacopo, illus. 2014. (School for Good & Evil Ser.: 1). 496p. (J). lib. bdg. 17.20 *(978-0-606-36513-0(3))* Turtleback Bks.

—The School for Good & Evil #4: Quests for Glory. 2017. (School for Good & Evil Ser.: 4). 576p. (J). (gr. 3-7). 17.99 ***(978-0-06-265847-0(6))*** HarperCollins Pubs.

Chainani, Soman. A World Without Princes. 2014. (School for Good & Evil Trilogy: No. 2). 448p. (J). pap. *(978-0-06-233135-9(3))* Harper & Row Ltd.

—A World Without Princes. Bruno, Iacopo, illus. 2014. (School for Good & Evil Trilogy: No. 2). (ENG.). 400p. (J). *(978-0-06-234072-6(7))* Harper & Row Ltd.

—A World Without Princes. Bruno, Iacopo, illus. 2015. (School for Good & Evil Ser.: 2). (ENG.). 512p. (J). (gr. 3-7). pap. 7.99 *(978-0-06-210493-9(4))* HarperCollins Pubs.

—A World Without Princes. 2014. (School for Good & Evil Trilogy: No. 2). (ENG., Illus.). 448p. (J). (gr. 3-7). 17.99 *(978-0-06-210492-2(6))* HarperCollins Pubs.

—A World Without Princes. 2015. (School for Good & Evil Ser.: 2). (J). lib. bdg. 17.20 *(978-0-606-36514-7(1))* Turtleback Bks.

Chaltas, Thalia. Because I Am Furniture. 2010. (ENG.). 368p. (YA). (gr. 7-18). 8.99 *(978-0-14-241510-8(3)*, Speak) Penguin Young Readers Group.

Chambers, Veronica. The Go-Between. 2017. (ENG.). 208p. (YA). (gr. 7). 16.99 ***(978-1-101-93095-3(0)***, Delacorte Pr.) Random Hse. Children's Bks.

Champion, Dionne N., et al. The Spirit of the Baobab Tree. Champion, Dionne N. & Champion, Daryl, illus. 2008. 37p. (J). 31.99 *(978-1-4363-7842-0(7))* Xlibris Corp.

Chandler, Elizabeth. Kissed by an Angel: Evercrossed; Everlasting; Everafter. 2014. (Kissed by an Angel Ser.). (ENG., Illus.). 912p. (YA). (gr. 9). pap. 29.99 *(978-1-4424-9494-7(8)*, Simon Pulse) Simon Pulse.

Chang, Hae-Kyung. Oh No, School! Bisaillon, Josée, illus. 2014. 30p. (J). *(978-1-4338-1333-7(5)*, Magination Pr.) American Psychological Assn.

A Change of Lace. 2014. (Sew Zoey Ser.: 9). (ENG., Illus.). 176p. (J). (gr. 3-7). pap. 6.99 *(978-1-4814-1961-1(7)*, Simon Spotlight) Simon Spotlight.

Changing Schools: Individual Title Six-Packs. (gr. -1-2). 27.00 *(978-0-7635-9440-4(7))* Rigby Education.

Chapman, Clay McLeod. The Tribe - Homeroom Headhunters. 2014. (Tribe Novel Ser.). (ENG., Illus.). 320p. (J). (gr. 3-7). pap. 6.99 *(978-1-4231-5453-2(3))* Hyperion Bks. for Children.

Chapman, Jared. Steve, Raised by Wolves. 2015. (ENG., Illus.). 40p. (J). (gr. -1-3). 17.00 *(978-0-316-25390-1(1))* Little Brown & Co.

Chapman, Lara. Accidentally Evil. 2015. (Mix Ser.). (ENG., Illus.). 240p. (J). (gr. 4-8). pap. 7.99 *(978-1-4814-0110-4(6)*, Aladdin) Simon & Schuster Children's Publishing.

—Flawless. 2011. (ENG.). 272p. (YA). (gr. 7-12). 16.99 *(978-1-59990-631-7(7)*, 9781599906317); pap. 9.99 *(978-1-59990-596-9(5)*, 9781599905969) Bloomsbury Publishing USA. (Bloomsbury USA Childrens).

—The XYZs of Being Wicked. 2014. (ENG., Illus.). 272p. (J). (gr. 4-8). pap. 6.99 *(978-1-4814-0107-4(6)*, Aladdin) Simon & Schuster Children's Publishing.

CHaracter Ed & the Magical Lesson of the Bully. 2004. (J). pap. 15.95 *(978-1-59526-181-6(8))* Aeon Publishing Inc.

Charbonneau, Joelle. The Testing. (Testing Ser.: 1). (ENG.). 352p. (YA). (gr. 7). 2015. pap. 9.99 *(978-0-544-33623-0(2)*, HMH Books For Young Readers) 2013. 17.99 *(978-0-547-95910-8(9))* Houghton Mifflin Harcourt Publishing Co.

Charisse, April. Say Hello to Me: A Story about a Little Girl on the Autism Spectrum. 2012. 16p. pap. 15.99 *(978-1-4685-9475-1(3))* AuthorHouse.

Charles L. Wilson. The Search Is On: The Wild Adventures of Lester & Dora. 2009. 200p. 24.99 *(978-1-4269-1813-1(5))*; pap. 14.99 *(978-1-4269-1812-4(7))* Trafford Publishing.

Charlesworth, Liza. Fish School: An Animal Friends Reader. Smith, Ian, illus. 2015. 16p. (J). pap. ***(978-0-545-85963-9(8))*** Scholastic, Inc.

Charlie Bumpers vs. the Squeaking Skull, 1 vol. 2014. (Charlie Bumpers Ser.). (ENG., Illus.). (J). (gr. 2-4). 10p. 16.95 *(978-1-56145-809-7(0))*; 160p. 13.95 *(978-1-56145-808-0(2))* Peachtree Pubs.

Charlton-Trujillo, E. E. Fat Angie. 2013. (ENG.). 272p. (YA). (gr. 9). 16.99 *(978-0-7636-6119-9(8))* Candlewick Pr.

Chast, Roz. Marco Goes to School. Chast, Roz, illus. 2012. (ENG., Illus.). 32p. (J). (gr. -1-3). 16.99 *(978-1-4169-8475-7(5)*, Atheneum Bks. for Young Readers) Simon & Schuster Children's Publishing.

Chastain, Emma. Confessions of a High School Disaster. 2017. (Chloe Snow's Diary Ser.). (ENG., Illus.). 352p. (YA). (gr. 7). 17.99 *(978-1-4814-8875-4(9)*, Simon Pulse) Simon Pulse.

Chbosky, Stephen. The Perks of Being a Wallflower. 2014. (ENG.). 224p. (gr. 7-12). 18.25 *(978-1-63245-042-5(9))* Lectorum Pubns., Inc.

—The Perks of Being a Wallflower. 2012. (ENG.). 224p. 21.00 *(978-1-4516-9620-2(5))*; pap. 14.99 *(978-1-4516-9619-6(1))* MTV Books. (MTV Bks.).

—The Perks of Being a Wallflower. 2009. 13.77 *(978-0-7848-1530-4(5)*, Everbind) Marco Bk. Co.

—The Perks of Being a Wallflower. 2008. (ENG.). 24.30 *(978-1-60686-308-4(8)*, Covercraft) Perfection Learning Corp.

—The Perks of Being a Wallflower. 2007. 1.25 *(978-1-4281-3271-9(6))* Recorded Bks., Inc.

Cheeseboro, Tyrese. Why Did Ronald Break the Rules? Rules at Home & Rules at School! 2010. 28p. 12.49 *(978-1-4490-8871-2(6))* AuthorHouse.

Chen, Bill. The Musical. Sun, Jun, illus. 2013. (J). *(978-0-9845523-1-3(6))* Heryin Publishing Corp.

Cheng, Andrea. Brushing Mom's Hair. Wong, Nicole, illus. 2009. (ENG.). 64p. (J). (gr. 5-8). 17.95 *(978-1-59078-599-7(1)*, Front Street) Boyds Mills Pr.

—The Year of the Baby. Barton, Patrice, illus. 2014. (Anna Wang Novel Ser.: 2). (ENG.). 176p. (J). (gr. 1-4). pap. 5.99 *(978-0-544-22525-1(2)*, HMH Books For Young Readers) Houghton Mifflin Harcourt Publishing Co.

—The Year of the Book. Halpin, Abigail, illus. (Anna Wang Novel Ser.: 1). (ENG.). 160p. (J). (gr. 1-4). 2013. pap. 5.99 *(978-0-544-02263-8(7))* 2012. 16.99 *(978-0-547-68463-5(0))* Houghton Mifflin Harcourt Publishing Co.

Cheva, Cherry. She's So Money. 2009. (ENG.). 304p. (YA). (gr. 8). pap. 8.99 *(978-0-06-128853-1(5)*, HarperTeen) HarperCollins Pubs.

Child, Lauren. Clarice Bean Spells Trouble. Child, Lauren, illus. 2006. (Clarice Bean Ser.). (Illus.). 189p. (J). (gr. 3-6). 13.65 *(978-0-7569-7919-5(6))* Perfection Learning Corp.

—I Am Going to Save a Panda! 2010. (Charlie & Lola Ser.). lib. bdg. 13.55 *(978-0-606-10628-3(6)*, Turtleback) Turtleback Bks.

—I Am Too Absolutely Small for School. Child, Lauren, illus. (Charlie & Lola Ser.). (ENG., Illus.). 32p. (J). (gr. -1-2). 2004. 16.99 *(978-0-7636-2403-3(9))* 2005. reprint ed. per. 8.99 *(978-0-7636-2887-1(5))* Candlewick Pr.

—I Am Too Absolutely Small for School. 2007. (Charlie & Lola (Shang Yi Publishing) Ser.). (CHI., Illus.). (J). *(978-957-762-437-6(5))* Hsin Yi Pubns.

—I Am Too Absolutely Small for School. Child, Lauren, illus. 2005. (ENG., Illus.). (J). (gr. -1-1). lib. bdg. 14.65 *(978-0-7569-6495-5(4))* Perfection Learning Corp.

—I Can't Stop Hiccuping! 2010. (Charlie & Lola Ser.). lib. bdg. 13.55 *(978-0-606-10629-0(4)*, Turtleback) Turtleback Bks.

—Spells Trouble. Child, Lauren, illus. 2006. (Clarice Bean Ser.). (ENG., Illus.). 192p. (J). (gr. 3-7). pap. 6.99 *(978-0-7636-2903-8(0))* Candlewick Pr.

—Utterly Me, Clarice Bean. Child, Lauren, illus. 2005. (Clarice Bean Ser.). (ENG., Illus.). 208p. (J). (gr. 3-7). reprint ed. pap. 5.99 *(978-0-7636-2788-1(7))* Candlewick Pr.

—Utterly Me, Clarice Bean. Child, Lauren, illus. 2006. (Clarice Bean Ser.). (Illus.). 16.00 *(978-0-7569-6567-9(5))* Perfection Learning Corp.

Child, Lauren, et al. Fi'n Hollol, Carys Blodyn. 2005. (WEL., Illus.). 192p. pap. *(978-1-85596-675-8(1))* Dref Wen.

Children's Press, contrib. by. Show-and-Tell Sam & Other School Stories. 2008. (Rookie Reader Treasury Ser.). (ENG., Illus.). 128p. (J). 11.95 *(978-0-531-21726-9(4)*, Children's Pr.) Scholastic Library Publishing.

Childs, Tera Lynn. Fins Are Forever. 2012. (Forgive My Fins Ser.: 2). (ENG.). 288p. (YA). (gr. 8). pap. 8.99 *(978-0-06-191470-6(3)*, Tegen, Katherine Bks) HarperCollins Pubs.

Childs, Tera Lynn & Childs, Tera. Oh. My. Gods. 2009. (ENG.). 288p. (YA). (gr. 7-18). 7.99 *(978-0-14-241420-0(4)*, Speak) Penguin Young Readers Group.

Chima, Cinda Williams. The Wizard Heir. 2008. (Heir Chronicles Ser.). (ENG.). 480p. (J). (gr. 5-9). pap. 9.99 *(978-1-4231-0488-9(9))* Hyperion Pr.

Chisolm, Melinda. Remembering to Breathe. Cross, Jo Ellen, illus. 2009. 31p. pap. 24.95 *(978-1-60703-914-3(1))* America Star Bks.

Chmakova, Svetlana. Awkward. 2015. (J). lib. bdg. 22.10 *(978-0-606-38218-2(6))* Turtleback Bks.

Choi, Yangsook. The Name Jar. Choi, Yangsook, illus. 2003. (ENG., Illus.). 40p. (J). (gr. -1-2). pap. 7.99 *(978-0-440-41799-6(6)*, Dragonfly Bks.) Random Hse. Children's Bks.

Choldenko, Gennifer. If a Tree Falls at Lunch Period. 2009. (ENG., Illus.). 224p. (J). (gr. 5-7). pap. 7.99 *(978-0-15-206644-4(6))* Houghton Mifflin Harcourt Publishing Co.

Choyce, Lesley. Carrie Loses Her Nerve, 1 vol. Thurman, Mark, illus. 2003. (Formac First Novels Ser.: 26). (ENG.). 64p. (J). (gr. 1-5). 4.95 *(978-0-88780-591-2(4)*, 9780887805912); 14.95 *(978-0-88780-592-9(2)*, 9780887805929) Formac Publishing Co., Ltd. CAN. Dist: Casemate Pubs. & Bk. Distributors, LLC.

—Rat, 1 vol. 2012. (Orca Soundings Ser.). (ENG.). 128p. (YA). (gr. 8-12). pap. 9.95 *(978-1-4598-0300-8(0))*; lib. bdg. 16.95 *(978-1-4598-0301-5(9))* Orca Bk. Pubs. USA.

Chriscoe, Sharon. Scary Weather, Scaredy Cat, 1 vol. 2008. (ENG.). 48p. 24.95 *(978-1-60474-143-8(0))* America Star Bks.

Christopher, Lawrence. The Tickle Fingers: Where Is Pinky? Christopher, Lawrence, illus. 2006. (ENG., Illus.). 24p. (J). (gr. -1-18). 9.95 *(978-0-9712278-3-5(7))* MF Unlimited.

Christopher, Matt. Football Double Threat. 2008. (ENG.). 128p. (J). (gr. 3-7). pap. 5.99 *(978-0-316-01632-2(2))* Little, Brown Bks. for Young Readers.

—QB Blitz. 2011. (ENG.). 144p. (J). (gr. 3-7). pap. 5.99 *(978-0-316-17682-8(6))* Little, Brown Bks. for Young Readers.

—Soccer Scoop. 2007. (New Matt Christopher Sports Library). 133p. (J). (gr. 4-6). lib. bdg. 26.60 *(978-1-59953-117-5(8))* Norwood Hse. Pr.

—Stealing Home. 2004. (ENG.). 144p. (J). (gr. 3-7). pap. 5.99 *(978-0-316-60742-1(8))* Little, Brown Bks. for Young Readers.

Chung, Helena. Jennifer, the Special One. 2004. (J). pap. 8.00 *(978-0-8059-6395-3(2))* Dorrance Publishing Co., Inc.

Ciencin, Scott. Attack of the Cling-Ons, 1 vol. Crowther, Jeff, illus. 2011. (Graphic Sparks Ser.). (ENG.). 40p. (gr. 1-3). pap. 5.95 *(978-1-4342-3067-6(8))*; lib. bdg. 23.99 *(978-1-4342-2637-2(9))* Stone Arch Bks. (Graphic Sparks).

Cinema, Bobby. Princess School. 2012. 68p. 18.66 *(978-1-4669-3968-4(0))*; 18p. pap. 8.66 *(978-1-4669-3967-7(2))* Trafford Publishing.

Ciocca, Donna. Harley & Homer. 2004. (YA). per. 9.95 *(978-0-9747361-2-9(0))* Oak Manor Publishing, Inc.

—Harley & Homer for Hire. 2006. (YA). per. 11.95 *(978-0-9747361-9-8(8))* Oak Manor Publishing, Inc.

Ciocca, Gina. Last Year's Mistake. 2015. (ENG., Illus.). 320p. (YA). (gr. 9). 17.99 *(978-1-4814-3223-8(0)*, Simon Pulse) Simon Pulse.

Cirrone, Dorian. Prom Kings & Drama Queens. 2008. 200p. (YA). (gr. 7). lib. bdg. 17.89 *(978-0-06-114373-1(1)*, HarperTeen) HarperCollins Pubs.

Clampitt, Ed & Fortier, Robert. Team Dawg Trevor's Bully Problem. 2007. (J). per. 14.99 *(978-0-9749378-2-3(7))* Team Dawg Productions, Inc.

Clar, David Austin & David Austin Clar Studio Staff, illus. Surprise Party. 2003. (Rainbow Fish & Friends Ser.). (ENG.). 24p. (J). (gr. -1-2). 9.95 *(978-1-59014-114-4(8))* North-South Bks., Inc.

Clark, Brenda. Spiro & Zinger Rescue the Orphans: Spiro the Shooting Star - Book Three, 1 vol. 2010. 70p. pap. 19.95 *(978-1-4489-3992-3(5))* America Star Bks.

Clark, Bridie. Maybe Tonight? 2013. (Snap Decision Ser.: 1). (ENG.). 224p. (YA). (gr. 7). pap. 9.99 *(978-1-59643-816-3(9))* Roaring Brook Pr.

—You Only Live Once. 2014. (Snap Decision Ser.: 2). (ENG.). 224p. (YA). (gr. 7). pap. 9.99 *(978-1-59643-817-0(7)*, 9781596438170) Roaring Brook Pr.

Clark, Catherine. Frozen Rodeo. 2003. (ENG.). 304p. (J). (gr. 8-18). 15.99 *(978-0-06-009070-8(7))* HarperCollins Pubs.

Clark, Clara Gillow. Secrets of Greymoor. 2009. (ENG., Illus.). 176p. (J). (gr. 5). 15.99 *(978-0-7636-3249-6(X))* Candlewick Pr.

Clark, Eleanor. Victoria Grace: Courageous Patriot. 2007. (Eleanor Ser.: Bk. 2). 209p. (J). (gr. 4-7). 14.99 *(978-0-9753036-8-9(6))* HonorNet.

Clark, Jay. The Edumacation of Jay Baker. 2012. (ENG.). 288p. (YA). (gr. 9-12). pap. 9.99 *(978-1-250-01675-1(4))* Square Fish.

Clark, Kristin Elizabeth. Freakboy. 2016. (ENG.). 448p. (YA). (gr. 7-13). 22.10 *(978-0-606-39285-3(8))* Turtleback Bks.

Clark, Sherryl. Kim's Super Science Day. McKenzie, Heath, illus. 2015. (J). pap. *(978-1-4966-0250-3(1))* Capstone Classroom.

Clark, Sherryl;Perry. Ellyse Perry 2: Magic Feet. 2017. (Ellyse Perry Ser.: 2). (ENG.). 160p. (J). (gr. 4-7). 12.99 ***(978-0-14-378126-4(X))*** Random Hse. Australia AUS. Dist: Independent Pubs. Group.

Clark, Todd. The Ice Cream Kid: Brain Freeze! 2014. (ENG.). 176p. (J). 13.99 *(978-1-4494-4424-2(5))* Andrews McMeel Publishing.

Clarke, Cat. The Pants Project. 2017. (ENG.). 272p. (J). (gr. 4-9). 16.99 *(978-1-4926-3809-4(9)*, 9781492638094, Sourcebooks Jabberwocky) Sourcebooks, Inc.

Clarke, David. Snake Bite: A Novel. 2009. 188p. 23.95 *(978-0-595-71833-7(7))*; pap. 13.95 *(978-0-595-48406-5(9))* iUniverse, Inc.

Clarke, Judith. Al Capsella & Watchdogs. 164p. pap. *(978-0-7022-2294-8(1))* Univ. of Queensland Pr.

Clarke, Kevin & Dutton, Demi. Jenny Can't Read: A Story about Dyslexia & Its Effect on Self-Esteem. 2012. 90p. pap. 13.66 *(978-1-4772-1909-6(9))* AuthorHouse.

Cleary, Beverly. Ellen Tebbits. Darling, Louis & Dockray, Tracy, illus. 2008. (ENG.). 192p. (J). (gr. 3-7). 16.99 *(978-0-688-21264-3(6))* HarperCollins Pubs.

—Muggie Maggie. Tiegreen, Alan & Dockray, Tracy, illus. 2015. (Cleary Reissue Ser.). (ENG.). 96p. (J). (gr. 3-7). reprint ed. pap. 6.99 *(978-0-380-71087-4(0))* HarperCollins Pubs.

—Ramona Empieza el Curso, 1 vol. Bustelo, Gabriela, tr. Giegreen, Alan et al, illus. 2006. (Ramona Ser.: 6).Tr. of Ramona Quimby, Age 8. (SPA.). 224p. (J). (gr. 3-7). pap. *(978-0-688-15487-5(5)*, MR7554) HarperCollins Pubs.

—Ramona la Chinche, 1 vol. Darling, Louis et al, illus. 2006. (Ramona Ser.: 2).Tr. of Ramona the Pest. (SPA.). 192p. (J). (gr. 3-7). pap. 5.99 *(978-0-688-14888-1(3)*, MR2295) HarperCollins Pubs.

—Ramona la Chinche. Palacios, Argentina, tr. Darling, Louis, illus. 2006. (Ramona Quimby Spanish Ser.: 2).Tr. of Ramona the Pest. (SPA.). 181p. (J). (gr. 4-7). lib. bdg. 16.00 *(978-0-613-00464-0(7)*, Turtleback) Turtleback Bks.

—Ramona Quimby, Age 8. Rogers, Jacqueline, illus. 2016. (Ramona Ser.: 6). 208p. (J). (gr. 3-7). 12.99 *(978-0-06-246454-5(X))* HarperCollins Pubs.

—Ramona Quimby, Age 8. Tiegreen, Alan & Rogers, Jacqueline, illus. 2016. (Ramona Ser.: 6). (ENG.). 208p. (J). (gr. 3-7). pap. 6.99 *(978-0-380-70956-4(2))* HarperCollins Pubs.

—Ramona Quimby, Age 8. Tiegreen, Alan et al, illus. 2014. (Ramona Ser.: 6). (ENG.). 208p. (J). (gr. 3-7). 16.99 *(978-0-688-00477-4(6))* HarperCollins Pubs.

—Ramona Quimby, Age 8. (Ramona Quimby Ser.). (J). (gr. 3-5). Random House Publishing Group.

—Ramona Quimby, Age 8. (Ramona Quimby Ser.). 190p. (J). (gr. 3-5). pap. 4.99 *(978-0-8072-1436-7(1)*, Listening Library) Random Hse. Audio Publishing Group.

—Ramona Quimby, Age 8 Read-Aloud Edition. Rogers, Jacqueline, illus. 2016. (Ramona Ser.: 6). 208p. (J). (gr. 3-7). 17.99 *(978-0-06-245327-3(0))* HarperCollins Pubs.

—Ramona the Brave. Tiegreen, Alan et al, illus. 2013. (Ramona Ser.: 3). (ENG.). 208p. (J). (gr. 3-7). 16.99 *(978-0-688-22015-0(0))*; pap. 6.99 *(978-0-380-70959-5(7))* HarperCollins Pubs.

—Ramona the Brave. (Ramona Quimby Ser.). 190p. (J). (gr. 3-5). pap. 4.99 *(978-0-8072-1440-4(X)*, Listening Library) Random Hse. Audio Publishing Group.

—Ramona the Pest. Darling, Louis & Rogers, Jacqueline, illus. 2013. (Ramona Ser.: 2). (SPA & ENG.). 240p. (J). (gr. 3-7). pap. 6.99 *(978-0-380-70954-0(6))* HarperCollins Pubs.

—Ramona the Pest. Darling, Louis et al, illus. 2013. (Ramona Ser.: 2). (ENG.). 240p. (J). (gr. 3-7). 16.99 *(978-0-688-21721-1(4))* HarperCollins Pubs.

—Ramona the Pest. (Ramona Quimby Ser.). (J). (gr. 3-5). Random House Publishing Group.

—Ramona the Pest. (Ramona Quimby Ser.). 192p. (J). (gr. 3-5). pap. 4.99 *(978-0-8072-1438-1(8)*, Listening Library) Random Hse. Audio Publishing Group.

—Ramona's World. Tiegreen, Alan et al, illus. 2014. (Ramona Ser.: 8). (ENG.). 240p. (J). (gr. 3-7). 16.99 *(978-0-688-16816-2(7))* HarperCollins Pubs.

—Ramona's World. Tiegreen, Alan & Rogers, Jacqueline, illus. 2013. (Ramona Ser.: 8). (ENG.). 240p. (J). (gr. 3-7). pap. 7.99 *(978-0-380-73272-2(6))* HarperCollins Pubs.

—Ramona's World. unabr. ed. 2004. (Ramona Quimby Ser.). 194p. (J). (gr. 3-7). pap. 29.00 incl. audio *(978-0-8072-8169-7(7)*, Listening Library) Random Hse. Audio Publishing Group.

—Ramona's World. 2013. (Ramona Quimby Ser.: 8). (J). (gr. 3-6). lib. bdg. 17.20 *(978-0-613-35794-4(9)*, Turtleback) Turtleback Bks.

Clement-Moore, Rosemary. Prom Dates from Hell. 2008. (Maggie Quinn: Girl vs Evil Ser.). (ENG.). 320p. (YA). (gr. 9). pap. 8.99 *(978-0-385-73413-4(1)*, Delacorte Bks. for Young Readers) Random Hse. Children's Bks.

Clements, Andrew. About Average. Elliott, Mark, illus. (ENG.). (J). (gr. 3-7). 2014. 144p. pap. 7.99 *(978-1-4169-9725-2(3))* 2012. 128p. 16.99 *(978-1-4169-9724-5(5))* Simon & Schuster Children's Publishing. (Atheneum Bks. for Young Readers).

—Andrew Clements' School Stories. 2013. (ENG., Illus.). 1856p. (J). (gr. 3-7). pap. 79.99 *(978-1-4424-9386-5(0),* Atheneum Bks. for Young Readers) Simon & Schuster Children's Publishing.
—Back to School. 2006. (ENG., Illus.). 512p. (J). (gr. 3-7). pap. 17.99 *(978-1-4169-2681-8(X),* Atheneum Bks. for Young Readers) Simon & Schuster Children's Publishing.
—Bully Buster. 2014. (Jake Drake Ser. Bk. 1 Ser.). (ENG.). 80p. (J). (gr. 2-5). 9.24 *(978-1-63245-290-0(1))* Lectorum Pubns., Inc.
—Bully Buster. Frazee, Marla & Pedersen, Janet, illus. 2008. (Jake Drake Ser.: Bk. 1). 67p. (gr. 2-5). 15.00 *(978-0-7569-9001-5(7))* Perfection Learning Corp.
—Bully Buster. Pedersen, Janet & Frazee, Marla, illus. 2007. (Jake Drake Ser.: Bk. 1). (ENG.). 80p. (J). (gr. 2-5). pap. 5.99 *(978-1-4169-3933-7(4),* Atheneum Bks. for Young Readers) Simon & Schuster Children's Publishing.
—Fear Itself. Stower, Adam, illus. 2011. (Benjamin Pratt & the Keepers of the School Ser.: 2). (ENG.). (J). (gr. 2-5). 240p. pap. 7.99 *(978-1-4169-3908-5(3));* 224p. 16.99 *(978-1-4169-3887-3(7))* Simon & Schuster Children's Publishing. (Atheneum Bks. for Young Readers).
—Frindle. 2014. (ENG.). 112p. (J). 11.24 *(978-1-63245-158-3(1))* Lectorum Pubns., Inc.
—Head of the Class: Frindle - The Landry News - The Janitor's Boy. Selznick, Brian, illus. 2007. (ENG.). 416p. (J). (gr. 3-7). pap. 20.99 *(978-1-4169-4974-9(7),* Atheneum Bks. for Young Readers) Simon & Schuster Children's Publishing.
—In Harm's Way. Stower, Adam, illus. (Benjamin Pratt & the Keepers of the School Ser.: 4). (ENG.). (J). (gr. 2-5). 2014. 240p. pap. 7.99 *(978-1-4169-3910-8(5))* 2013. 224p. 14.99 *(978-1-4169-3889-7(3))* Simon & Schuster Children's Publishing. (Atheneum Bks. for Young Readers).
—The Jacket. 2014. (ENG.). 96p. (J). (gr. 3-7). 10.24 *(978-1-63245-301-3(0))* Lectorum Pubns., Inc.
—The Jacket. Henderson, McDavid, illus. 2003. (ENG.). 96p. (J). (gr. 3-7). pap. 6.99 *(978-0-689-86010-2(2),* Atheneum Bks. for Young Readers) Simon & Schuster Children's Publishing.
—Jake Drake, Class Clown. Pedersen, Janet, illus. 2007. (Jake Drake Ser.: Bk. 4). (ENG.). 96p. (J). (gr. 2-5). pap. 5.99 *(978-1-4169-4912-1(7),* Atheneum Bks. for Young Readers) Simon & Schuster Children's Publishing.
—Jake Drake, Know-It-All. Frazee, Marla & Pedersen, Janet, illus. 2007. (Jake Drake Ser.: Bk. 2). 88p. (gr. 2-5). 15.00 *(978-0-7569-8212-6(X))* Perfection Learning Corp.
—Jake Drake, Know-It-All. Pedersen, Janet & Frazee, Marla, illus. 2007. (Jake Drake Ser.: Bk. 2). (ENG.). 112p. (J). (gr. 2-5). pap. 5.99 *(978-1-4169-3931-3(8),* Atheneum Bks. for Young Readers) Simon & Schuster Children's Publishing.
—Jake Drake, Teacher's Pet. Pedersen, Janet, illus. 2007. (Jake Drake Ser.: 3). (ENG.). 96p. (J). (gr. 2-5). pap. 5.99 *(978-1-4169-3932-0(6),* Atheneum Bks. for Young Readers) Simon & Schuster Children's Publishing.
—Jake Drake, Teacher's Pet. 2007. (Jake Drake Ser.: 3). lib. bdg. 16.00 *(978-1-4177-9035-7(0),* Turtleback) Turtleback Bks.
—The Last Holiday Concert. 2006. (ENG., Illus.). 176p. (J). (gr. 3-7). pap. 7.99 *(978-0-689-84525-3(1),* Atheneum Bks. for Young Readers) Simon & Schuster Children's Publishing.
—The Last Holiday Concert. Selznick, Brian, illus. 2004. (ENG.). 176p. (J). (gr. 3-7). 17.99 *(978-0-689-84516-1(2),* Atheneum Bks. for Young Readers) Simon & Schuster Children's Publishing.
—The Last Holiday Concert. rev. l.t. ed. 2007. (Literacy Bridge Middle Reader Ser.). 165p. (J). (gr. 3-7). 22.95 *(978-0-7862-9374-2(8))* Thorndike Pr.
—The Losers Club. 2017. (ENG.). 240p. (J). (gr. 3-7). 16.99 ***(978-0-399-55755-2(5),*** Random Hse. Bks. for Young Readers) Random Hse. Children's Bks.
—Lost & Found. Elliott, Mark, illus. (ENG.). (J). (gr. 3-7). 2010. 192p. pap. 7.99 *(978-1-4169-0986-6(9))* 2008. 176p. 16.99 *(978-1-4169-0985-9(0))* Simon & Schuster Children's Publishing. (Atheneum Bks. for Young Readers).
—Lunch Money. Selznick, Brian, illus. (ENG.). (J). (gr. 3-7). 2007. 240p. pap. 7.99 *(978-0-689-86685-2(2))* 2005. 224p. 18.99 *(978-0-689-86683-8(6))* Simon & Schuster Children's Publishing. (Atheneum Bks. for Young Readers).
—Lunch Money. 2007. 17.20 *(978-1-4177-8116-4(5),* Turtleback) Turtleback Bks.
—The Map Trap. Andreasen, Dan, illus. 2016. (ENG.). 160p. (J). (gr. 3-7). pap. 7.99 *(978-1-4169-9728-3(8))* Simon & Schuster Children's Publishing.
—The Map Trap. LaMarche, Jim & Andreasen, Dan, illus. 2014. (ENG.). 144p. (J). (gr. 3-7). 17.99 *(978-1-4169-9727-6(X),* Atheneum Bks. for Young Readers) Simon & Schuster Children's Publishing.
—The Map Trap. 2016. lib. bdg. 18.40 *(978-0-606-38977-8(6))* Turtleback Bks.
—No Talking. 2014. (ENG.). 160p. (J). (gr. 3-7). 11.24 *(978-1-63245-298-6(7))* Lectorum Pubns., Inc.
—No Talking. (J). 2008. 78.75 *(978-1-4361-5835-0(4))* 2007. 54.75 *(978-1-4281-5418-6(3))* 2007. 1.25 *(978-1-4281-5415-5(9))* 2007. 209.75 *(978-1-4281-5419-3(1))* 2007. 52.75 *(978-1-4281-5420-9(5))* 2007. (SPA.). 54.75 *(978-1-4281-5422-3(1))* 2007. 51.75 *(978-1-4281-5424-7(8))* Recorded Bks., Inc.
—No Talking. Elliott, Mark, illus. (ENG.). 160p. (J). (gr. 3-7). 2009. pap. 7.99 *(978-1-4169-0984-2(2))* 2007. 18.99 *(978-1-4169-0983-5(4))* Simon & Schuster Children's Publishing. (Atheneum Bks. for Young Readers).
—No Talking. Elliott, Mark, illus. l.t. ed. 2007. (Literacy Bridge Middle Reader Ser.). 155p. (J). (gr. 3-7). 23.95 *(978-1-4104-0294-3(0))* Thorndike Pr.
—No Talking. 2009. (CHI., Illus.). 180p. (J). pap. 14.95 *(978-7-5309-5645-8(0))* Tianjin Education Pr.
—No Talking. 2009. lib. bdg. 18.40 *(978-0-606-14508-4(7),* Turtleback) Turtleback Bks.
—El Periodico Landry. Selznick, Brian, illus. 2004.Tr. of Landry News. (SPA.). (YA). pap. 9.99 *(978-84-241-7886-4(6))* Everest Editora ESP. Dist: Lectorum Pubns., Inc.
—The Report Card. (ENG., Illus.). (J). (gr. 3-7). 2004. 176p. 18.99 *(978-0-689-84515-4(4))* 2006. 192p. reprint ed. pap. 7.99 *(978-0-689-84524-6(3))* Simon & Schuster Children's Publishing. (Atheneum Bks. for Young Readers).
—Room One: A Mystery or Two. Elliott, Mark, illus. 2008. (ENG.). 192p. (J). (gr. 3-7). pap. 7.99 *(978-0-689-86687-6(9),* Atheneum Bks. for Young Readers) Simon & Schuster Children's Publishing.
—Room One: A Mystery or Two. Blair, Chris & Elliott, Mark, illus. 2006. (ENG.). 176p. (J). (gr. 3-7). 17.99 *(978-0-689-86686-9(0),* Atheneum Bks. for Young Readers) Simon & Schuster Children's Publishing.
—Sin Hablar. 2009.Tr. of No Talking. (SPA.). 156p. (gr. 4-6). pap. 10.99 *(978-84-441-4100-8(3))* Everest Editora ESP. Dist: Lectorum Pubns., Inc.
—Troublemaker. Elliott, Mark, illus. (ENG.). (J). (gr. 3-7). 2013. 176p. pap. 7.99 *(978-1-4169-4932-9(1))* 2011. 160p. lib. bdg. 16.99 *(978-1-4169-4930-5(5))* Simon & Schuster Children's Publishing. (Atheneum Bks. for Young Readers).
—We Hold These Truths. Stower, Adam, illus. 2013. (Benjamin Pratt & the Keepers of the School Ser.: 5). (ENG.). 272p. (J). (gr. 2-5). 14.99 *(978-1-4169-3890-3(7),* Atheneum Bks. for Young Readers) Simon & Schuster Children's Publishing.
—We the Children. 2011. (Benjamin Pratt & the Keepers of the School Ser.: 1). (ENG.). 176p. (J). (gr. 2-5). pap. 7.99 *(978-1-4169-3907-8(5),* Atheneum Bks. for Young Readers) Simon & Schuster Children's Publishing.
—We the Children. Stower, Adam, illus. 2010. (Benjamin Pratt & the Keepers of the School Ser.: 1). (ENG.). 160p. (J). (gr. 2-5). 14.99 *(978-1-4169-3886-6(9),* Atheneum Bks. for Young Readers) Simon & Schuster Children's Publishing.
—The Whites of Their Eyes. Stower, Adam, illus. (Benjamin Pratt & the Keepers of the School Ser.: 3). (ENG.). (J). (gr. 2-5). 2013. 240p. pap. 6.99 *(978-1-4169-3909-2(1))* 2012. 224p. 14.99 *(978-1-4169-3888-0(5))* Simon & Schuster Children's Publishing. (Atheneum Bks. for Young Readers).

Clewarth, John. Firestorm Rising. 2012. (Illus.). 200p. pap. *(978-1-4710-3681-1(2))* Lulu.com.

Cline-Ransome, Lesa. Freedom's School. Ransome, James E., illus. 2015. (ENG.). 32p. (J). (gr. 1-3). 17.99 *(978-1-4231-6103-5(3),* Jump at the Sun) Hyperion Bks. for Children.

Cobb, Amy. Band Camp Rules. 2016. (Band Geeks Set 2 Ser.). (ENG., Illus.). (J). (gr. 3-6). lib. bdg. 27.07 ***(978-1-62402-172-5(7))*** ABDO Publishing Co.
—Dude, Where's My Saxophone?, 1 vol. Cattish, Anna, illus. 2015. (ENG.). 112p. (J). *(978-1-62402-073-5(9))* Magic Wagon.
—First Chair, 1 vol. Cattish, Anna, illus. 2015. (ENG.). 112p. (J). *(978-1-62402-074-2(7))* Magic Wagon.
—Notes from a Pro, 1 vol. Cattish, Anna, illus. 2015. (ENG.). 112p. (J). *(978-1-62402-075-9(5))* Magic Wagon.
—Settling the Score. 2016. (Band Geeks Set 2 Ser.). (ENG.). (J). (gr. 3-6). lib. bdg. 27.07 ***(978-1-62402-175-6(1))*** ABDO Publishing Co.
—Shredding with the Geeks, 1 vol. Cattish, Anna, illus. 2015. (ENG.). 112p. (J). *(978-1-62402-076-6(3))* Magic Wagon.
—Snaring the Trumpet, 1 vol. Cattish, Anna, illus. 2015. (ENG.). 112p. (J). *(978-1-62402-077-3(1))* Magic Wagon.
—Swing Vote for Solo, 1 vol. Cattish, Anna, illus. 2015. (ENG.). 112p. (J). *(978-1-62402-078-0(X))* Magic Wagon.

Cobb, Daryl K. Do Pirates Go to School. 2010. pap. 11.99 *(978-0-578-05535-0(X))* 10 To 2 Children's Bks.

Coben, Harlan. Found. 2014. (Mickey Bolitar Novel Ser.: 3). (ENG.). 336p. (YA). (gr. 7). 18.99 *(978-0-399-25652-3(0),* G.P. Putnam's Sons Books for Young Readers) Penguin Young Readers Group.
—Seconds Away. (Mickey Bolitar Novel Ser.: 2). (ENG.). (YA). (gr. 7). 2012. 352p. 18.99 *(978-0-399-25651-6(2),* G.P. Putnam's Sons Books for Young Readers)Bk. 2. 2013. 368p. pap. 9.99 *(978-0-14-242635-7(0),* Speak) Penguin Young Readers Group.
—Seconds Away. l.t. ed. 2012. (Mickey Bolitar Ser.: 2). (ENG.). 396p. 23.99 *(978-1-4104-5348-8(0))* Thorndike Pr.
—Seconds Away. 2013. (Mickey Bolitar Ser.: 2). lib. bdg. 20.85 *(978-0-606-32141-9(1),* Turtleback) Turtleback Bks.
—Shelter. (Mickey Bolitar Novel Ser.: 1). (ENG.). (YA). (gr. 7-18). 2011. 288p. 18.99 *(978-0-399-25650-9(4),* G.P. Putnam's Sons Books for Young Readers)Bk. 1. 2012. 336p. pap. 9.99 *(978-0-14-242203-8(7),* Speak) Penguin Young Readers Group.
—Shelter. l.t. ed. 2011. (Mickey Bolitar Ser.: Bk. 1). (ENG.). 354p. (J). (gr. 9-12). 23.99 *(978-1-4104-4365-6(5))* Thorndike Pr.
—Shelter. 2012. (Mickey Bolitar Ser.: 1). lib. bdg. 20.85 *(978-0-606-26669-7(0),* Turtleback) Turtleback Bks.

Cobot, Meg. All-American Girl. 2004. 416p. (J). (gr. 7-18). pap. 44.00 incl. audio *(978-0-8072-2281-2(X),* Listening Library) Random Hse. Audio Publishing Group.

Cocca-Leffler, Maryann. Jack's Talent. Cocca-Leffler, Maryann, illus. 2007. (ENG., Illus.). 32p. (J). (gr. -1-3). 17.99 *(978-0-374-33681-3(4),* 9780374336813, Farrar, Straus & Giroux (BYR)) Farrar, Straus & Giroux.
—Mr. Tanen's Ties. Cocca-Leffler, Maryann, illus. 2004. (ENG., Illus.). 32p. (J). (gr. k-2). pap. 6.95 *(978-0-8075-5302-2(6))* Whitman, Albert & Co.
—Princess Kim & Too Much Truth. 2012. (J). 34.28 *(978-1-61913-121-7(8))* Weigl Pubs., Inc.
—Princess Kim & Too Much Truth. Cocca-Leffler, Maryann, illus. 2011. (ENG., Illus.). 32p. (J). (gr. 1-3). 16.99 *(978-0-8075-6618-3(7))* Whitman, Albert & Co.
—Theo's Mood: A Book of Feelings. Cocca-Leffler, Maryann, illus. 2013. (ENG., Illus.). 24p. (J). (gr. -1-3). 15.99 *(978-0-8075-7778-3(2))* Whitman, Albert & Co.

Cocca-Leffler, Maryann, illus. Spotlight on Stacey. 2007. (Social Studies Connects). 32p. (J). (gr. -1-3). pap. 5.95 *(978-1-57565-236-8(6))* Kane Press, Inc.

Cochran, Molly. Legacy. (Legacy Ser.). (ENG.). (YA). (gr. 9). 2012. 448p. pap. 9.99 *(978-1-4424-1740-3(4))* 2011. 432p. 17.99 *(978-1-4424-1739-7(0))* Simon & Schuster/Paula Wiseman Bks. (Simon & Schuster/Paula Wiseman Bks.).
—Poison. (Legacy Ser.). (ENG., 368p. (YA). (gr. 9). 2014. Illus.). pap. 9.99 *(978-1-4424-5051-6(7))* 2012. 17.99 *(978-1-4424-5050-9(9))* Simon & Schuster/Paula Wiseman Bks. (Simon & Schuster/Paula Wiseman Bks.).

Cocks, Heather & Morgan, Jessica. Spoiled. 2012. (ENG.). 384p. (YA). (gr. 10-17). pap. 10.00 *(978-0-316-09827-4(2),* Poppy) Little, Brown Bks. for Young Readers.

Codell, Esmé Raji. Sahara Special. 2003. (ENG., Illus.). 208p. (J). (gr. 3-7). pap. 16.49 *(978-0-7868-2627-8(4))* Hyperion Bks. for Children.
—Sahara Special. 2004. (ENG.). 192p. (J). (gr. 3-7). pap. 6.99 *(978-0-7868-1611-8(2))* Hyperion Pr.
—Vive la Paris. 2006. (ENG.). 224p. (gr. 4-7). 15.99 *(978-0-7868-5124-9(4))* Hyperion Pr.

Cody, Matthew. Powerless. 2011. (Supers of Noble's Green Ser.). (ENG.). 288p. (J). (gr. 3-7). 7.99 *(978-0-375-84489-8(9),* Yearling) Random Hse. Children's Bks.

Cody, Paul. Love Is Both Wave & Particle. 2017. (ENG.). 320p. (YA). 17.99 *(978-1-62672-688-8(4),* 9781626726888) Roaring Brook Pr.

Coe, Victoria J. Fenway & Hattie. 2016. (Fenway & Hattie Ser.). (ENG.). 176p. (J). (gr. 3-7). 15.99 *(978-0-399-17274-8(2),* G.P. Putnam's Sons Books for Young Readers) Penguin Young Readers Group.

Cohen, Barbara. Molly's Pilgrim. Duffy, Daniel Mark & Deraney, Michael J., illus. 97th rev. ed. 2005. (ENG.). 32p. (J). (gr. 2-5). pap. 3.99 *(978-0-688-16280-1(0))* HarperCollins Pubs.
—Molly's Pilgrim. (Literature to Go Ser.). pap., tchr. ed. incl. VHS *(978-0-7919-2685-7(0))* Phoenix Films & Video.

Cohen, Joshua C. Leverage. 2012. (ENG.). 432p. (YA). (gr. 9). pap. 8.99 *(978-0-14-242086-7(7),* Speak) Penguin Young Readers Group.

Cohen, Miriam. Bee My Valentine, 1 vol. Himmler, Ronald, illus. 2009. (ENG.). 32p. (J). (gr. k-3). pap. 5.95 *(978-1-59572-086-3(3))* Star Bright Bks., Inc.
—Bee My Valentine!, 1 vol. Himler, Ronald, illus. 2008. (ENG.). 32p. (J). (gr. k-3). 15.95 *(978-1-59572-085-6(5))* Star Bright Bks., Inc.
—First Grade Takes a Test. 2008. (J). (gr. k-2). 27.95 incl. audio *(978-0-8045-6964-4(9));* 29.95 incl. audio compact disk *(978-0-8045-4187-9(6))* Spoken Arts, Inc.
—First Grade Takes a Test, 1 vol. Himler, Ronald, illus. 2006. (ENG.). 32p. (J). (gr. -1-3). 15.95 *(978-1-59572-054-2(5));* (gr. k-3). pap. 5.95 *(978-1-59572-055-9(3))* Star Bright Bks., Inc.
—First Grade Takes a Test (Spanish/English), 1 vol. Himler, Ronald, illus. 2008. (ENG & SPA.). 32p. (J). (gr. k-3). 15.95 *(978-1-59572-150-1(9));* pap. 5.95 *(978-1-59572-151-8(7))* Star Bright Bks., Inc.
—Jim's Dog Muffins, 1 vol. Himler, Ronald, illus. 2008. 32p. (J). (ENG.). 15.95 *(978-1-59572-099-3(5));* (gr. -1-3). pap. 5.95 *(978-1-59572-100-6(2))* Star Bright Bks., Inc.
—Layla's Head Scarf, 1 vol. Himler, Ronald, illus. 2009. (ENG.). 32p. (J). (gr. -1-3). 15.95 *(978-1-59572-177-8(0));* pap. 5.95 *(978-1-59572-178-5(9))* Star Bright Bks., Inc.
—Tough Jim, 1 vol. Himler, Ronald, illus. (ENG.). 32p. (J). (gr. -1-3). 2008. 15.95 *(978-1-59572-071-9(5))* 2007. pap. 5.95 *(978-1-59572-072-6(3))* Star Bright Bks., Inc.

Cohen, Miriam & Himler, Ronald. El examen de primer Grado, 1 vol. Himler, Ronald, illus. 2006.Tr. of First Grade Takes a Test. (SPA., Illus.). 32p. (J). (gr. k-3). 15.95 *(978-1-59572-153-2(3));* pap. 5.95 *(978-1-59572-152-5(5))* Star Bright Bks., Inc.

Cohen, Morris L. & Cohen, Miriam. Best Friends. 2007. (ENG.). 32p. (J). (gr. -1-3). 10.99 *(978-1-4169-6501-5(7),* Simon & Schuster/Paula Wiseman Bks.) Simon & Schuster/Paula Wiseman Bks.

Cohen, Paula Marantz. Beatrice Bunson's Guide to Romeo & Juliet. 2016. (ENG.). 200p. (J). (gr. 4-9). pap. 11.95 *(978-1-58988-105-1(2))* Dry, Paul Bks., Inc.

Cohn, Rachel. Kill All Happies. 2017. (ENG.). 288p. (YA). (gr. 9-17). 17.99 *(978-1-4231-5722-9(2))* Hyperion Pr.
—Shrimp, 7 vols. 2005. (YA). 171.75 *(978-1-4193-5253-9(9))* Recorded Bks., Inc.
—Shrimp. 2006. (ENG.). 352p. (YA). (gr. 7-12). reprint ed. pap. 6.99 *(978-0-689-86613-5(5),* Simon & Schuster Bks. For Young Readers) Simon & Schuster Bks. For Young Readers.

Colasanti, Susane. All I Need. 2014. (ENG.). 240p. (YA). (gr. 7). pap. 9.99 *(978-0-14-242676-0(8),* Speak) Penguin Young Readers Group.
—Keep Holding On. 2013. (ENG., Illus.). 240p. (YA). (gr. 7). pap. 9.99 *(978-0-14-242633-3(4),* Speak) Penguin Young Readers Group.
—So Much Closer. 2012. (ENG.). 272p. (YA). (gr. 7-18). pap. 8.99 *(978-0-14-242114-7(6),* Speak) Penguin Young Readers Group.
—Something Like Fate. 2011. (ENG., Illus.). 304p. (YA). (gr. 7-18). 9.99 *(978-0-14-241882-6(X),* Speak) Penguin Young Readers Group.
—Take Me There. 2009. (ENG.). 320p. (YA). (gr. 7-18). 9.99 *(978-0-14-241435-4(2),* Speak) Penguin Young Readers Group.
—Waiting for You. 2010. (ENG.). 336p. (YA). (gr. 7-18). 9.99 *(978-0-14-241575-7(8),* Speak) Penguin Young Readers Group.
—When It Happens. 2008. (ENG.). 336p. (YA). (gr. 7-18). 9.99 *(978-0-14-241155-1(8),* Speak) Penguin Young Readers Group.

Colbert, Brandy. Pointe. (ENG.). 352p. (YA). (gr. 9). 2015. pap. 9.99 *(978-0-14-751441-7(X),* Speak) 2014. 17.99 *(978-0-399-16034-9(5),* G.P. Putnam's Sons Books for Young Readers) Penguin Young Readers Group.

Cole, Anjennetta. Cory's Classroom Rules. 2012. 28p. pap. 15.99 *(978-1-4685-3652-2(4))* AuthorHouse.

Cole, Barbara. Anna & Natalie, 1 vol. Himler, Ronald, illus. 2007. (ENG.). 32p. (J). 16.95 *(978-1-59572-105-1(3))* Star Bright Bks., Inc.

Cole, Barbara H. Anna & Natalie, 1 vol. Himler, Ronald, illus. 2010. (ENG.). 32p. (J). pap. 6.95 *(978-1-59572-211-9(4))* Star Bright Bks., Inc.

Cole, Diedra. The Adventures of Chris & Abby: First Day of School. 2012. (ENG.). 34p. (J). pap. 14.95 *(978-1-4327-8170-5(7))* Outskirts Pr., Inc.

Cole, Frank. The Adventures of Hashbrown Winters. 2009. (J). pap. 7.99 *(978-1-59955-303-0(1))* Cedar Fort, Inc./CFI Distribution.
—Hashbrown Winters & the Mashimoto Madness. 2010. 128p. (J). pap. 8.99 *(978-1-59955-378-8(3))* Cedar Fort, Inc./CFI Distribution.
—Hashbrown Winters & the Phantom of Pordunce. 2010. 128p. (J). pap. 7.99 *(978-1-59955-398-6(8))* Cedar Fort, Inc./CFI Distribution.

Cole, Frank L. Hashbrown Winters & Whiz-Tastrophe. 2013. pap. 14.99 *(978-1-4621-1056-8(8),* Bonneville Bks.) Cedar Fort, Inc./CFI Distribution.

Cole, Henry. Eddie the Bully. 2016. (ENG.). 40p. (J). (gr. -1-3). 17.99 *(978-1-4998-0181-1(5))* Little Bee Books Inc.

Cole, Kenneth. Friends & Neighbors: We Love to Learn. Ruebartsch, John, photos by. 2005. (Illus.). (J). pap. 9.95 *(978-0-9770816-1-5(3))* SHARP Literacy, Inc.
—Friends & Neighbors: We Love to Learn. Ruebartsch, John, photos by. 2005. (Illus.). (J). 16.95 *(978-0-9770816-0-8(5))* SHARP Literacy, Inc.

Cole, Myke. The Wildsidhe Chronicles Bk. 6: Car Trouble. 2003. (J). pap. 7.99 *(978-1-890096-18-2(0))* Padwolf Publishing, Inc.

Coleman, Evelyn. Freedom Train. 2012. (ENG.). 160p. (J). (gr. 3-7). pap. 7.99 *(978-1-4424-3652-7(2),* McElderry, Margaret K. Bks.) McElderry, Margaret K. Bks.
—Freedom Train. Riley, David, illus. 2008. (ENG.). 160p. (J). (gr. 3-7). 17.99 *(978-0-689-84716-5(5),* McElderry, Margaret K. Bks.) McElderry, Margaret K. Bks.

Coleman, K. Showdown. 2017. (Gridiron Ser.). (ENG.). (YA). (gr. 6-12). 112p. pap. 7.99 ***(978-1-5124-5354-6(4));*** lib. bdg. 26.65 ***(978-1-5124-3978-6(9))*** Lerner Publishing Group. (Darby Creek).
—Signing Day. 2017. (Gridiron Ser.). (ENG.). (YA). (gr. 6-12). 120p. pap. 7.99 ***(978-1-5124-5355-3(2));*** lib. bdg. 26.65 ***(978-1-5124-3983-0(5))*** Lerner Publishing Group. (Darby Creek).

Coleman, K. R. The Late Hit. 2017. (Gridiron Ser.). (ENG.). 128p. (YA). (gr. 6-12). 26.65 ***(978-1-5124-3982-3(7));*** pap. 7.99 ***(978-1-5124-5352-2(8))*** Lerner Publishing Group. (Darby Creek).

Coleman, Rowan. Musical Star. 2011. (ENG., Illus.). 256p. (J). (gr. 6-9). pap. 9.99 *(978-0-00-724434-8(7))* HarperCollins Pubs. Ltd. GBR. Dist: HarperCollins Pubs.

Colfer, Chris. Struck by Lightning: The Carson Phillips Journal. (ENG.). 272p. (YA). (gr. 10-17). 2013. pap. 10.00 *(978-0-316-23293-7(9))* 2012. 17.99 *(978-0-316-23295-1(5))* Little, Brown Bks. for Young Readers.

Colin, Beatrice & Pinto, Sara. My Invisible Sister. Pinto, Sara, illus. 2011. (ENG., Illus.). 128p. (YA). (gr. 3-6). pap. 6.99 *(978-1-59990-678-2(3),* 9781599906782, Bloomsbury USA Childrens) Bloomsbury Publishing USA.

Collard, Sneed B., III. Dog Sense, 1 vol. (ENG.). 192p. (J). (gr. 3-7). 2008. pap. 7.95 *(978-1-56145-460-0(5))* 2005. 14.95 *(978-1-56145-351-1(X))* Peachtree Pubs.

Collicott, Sharleen. Mildred & Sam & Their Babies. Collicott, Sharleen, illus. 2005. (I Can Read Bks.). (Illus.). 48p. (J). (gr. -1-2). 15.99 *(978-0-06-058111-4(5),* Geringer, Laura Book) HarperCollins Pubs.

Collins, Amanda E. Bff!!! or Not??? 2007. 168p. 30.99 *(978-1-4257-3371-1(9))* Xlibris Corp.

Collins, Charles. Hover for a Day. Seltzer, Jerry, illus. 2006. (ENG.). 56p. (J). 19.95 *(978-1-60131-004-0(8),* Castlebridge Bks.) Big Tent Bks.

Collins, Nancy A. Vamps. 2008. (Vamps Ser.: 1). (ENG.). 256p. (YA). (gr. 9-18). pap. 8.99 *(978-0-06-134917-1(8),* HarperTeen) HarperCollins Pubs.

Collins, P. J. Sarah. Sam & Nate. Jin, Katherine, illus. 2005. 60p. (J). lib. bdg. 20.00 *(978-1-4242-1261-3(8))* Fitzgerald Bks.

Collins, Paul. Lucy & the Red Street Boyz. Bocquée, Christian, illus. 2015. (Legends in Their Own Lunchbox Ser.). (ENG.). 56p. (gr. 2-3). pap. 7.99 *(978-1-4966-0260-2(9),* Legends in Their Own Lunchbox) Capstone Classroom.
—Lucy, Kung-Fu Queen. Bocquée, Christian, illus. 2015. (Legends in Their Own Lunchbox Ser.). (ENG.). 48p. (gr. 1-2). pap. 7.99 *(978-1-4966-0242-8(0),* Legends in Their Own Lunchbox) Capstone Classroom.
—Lucy, the Boss. Bocquée, Christian, illus. 2015. (Legends in Their Own Lunchbox Ser.). (ENG.). 56p. (gr. 2-3). pap. 7.99 *(978-1-4966-0254-1(4),* Legends in Their Own Lunchbox) Capstone Classroom.

Collins, Rudy. Vanessa Owens & the Bond of Sisterhood. 2011. 106p. pap. 19.95 *(978-1-4560-7873-7(9))* America Star Bks.

Collins, Tim. Fangs a Lot: Final Notes from a Totally Lame Vampire. Pinder, Andrew, illus. 2014. (ENG.). 320p. (J). (gr. 5-9). 13.99 *(978-1-4814-2134-8(4),* Aladdin) Simon & Schuster Children's Publishing.
—Notes from a Hairy-Not-Scary Werewolf. Pinder, Andrew, illus. 2013. (ENG.). 288p. (J). (gr. 5-9). 12.99 *(978-1-4424-8207-4(9),* Aladdin) Simon & Schuster Children's Publishing.
—Notes from a Totally Lame Vampire: Because the Undead Have Feelings Too! Pinder, Andrew, illus. 2010. (ENG.). 336p. (J). (gr. 5-9). 12.99 *(978-1-4424-1183-8(X),* Aladdin) Simon & Schuster Children's Publishing.
—Prince of Dorkness: More Notes from a Totally Lame Vampire. Pinder, Andrew, illus. 2011. (ENG.). 336p. (J). (gr. 5-9). 12.99 *(978-1-4424-3388-5(4),* Aladdin) Simon & Schuster Children's Publishing.

Compestine, Ying. The Story of Paper: Amazing Chinese Inventions. Xuan, YongSheng, illus. 2016. (ENG & CHI.). 40p. (J). (gr. -1-3). 15.95 *(978-1-59702-123-4(7))* Immedium.

Complete Nothing. 2014. (True Love Ser.: 2). (ENG., Illus.). 336p. (YA). (gr. 7). pap. 9.99 *(978-1-4424-7720-9(2),* Simon & Schuster Bks. For Young Readers) Simon & Schuster Bks. For Young Readers.

Condie, Ally. Being Sixteen. 2010. (YA). *(978-1-60641-233-6(7))* Deseret Bk. Co.
—Freshman for President. 2008. (ENG.). 304p. (YA). (gr. 8-12). pap. 15.99 *(978-1-59038-913-3(1),* Shadow Mountain) Shadow Mountain Publishing.
—Reunion. 2008. 288p. (YA). pap. 15.95 *(978-1-59038-989-8(1))* Deseret Bk. Co.
—Yearbook. 2006. 208p. (YA). pap. 14.95 *(978-1-59038-690-3(6))* Deseret Bk. Co.

Conford, Ellen. Jenny Archer, Author. Palmisciano, Diane & Brooks, Erik, illus. 2006. (ENG.). 64p. (J). (gr. 1-4). per. 12.99 *(978-0-316-01487-8(7))* Little, Brown Bks. for Young Readers.

Conforto, Lisa. The Very Compromising Adventures of Thumby Blackstone, 1 vol. 2010. 34p. 24.95 *(978-1-4512-0270-0(9))* PublishAmerica, Inc.

Conklin, Jennie Maria. Miss Prudence A Story of Two Girls' Lives. 2004. reprint ed. pap. 1.99 *(978-1-4192-3464-4(1))* Kessinger Publishing, LLC.

Connatser, Scott. Excited about Pre-School. 2011. 32p. pap. 12.77 *(978-1-4567-6564-4(7))* AuthorHouse.

S

Connor, Lexi. The Runaway Spell. 2011. (B Magical Ser.: 3). (ENG.). 144p. (J). (gr. 3-7). pap. 5.99 *(978-0-545-26552-2(5)*, Scholastic Paperbacks) Scholastic, Inc.

Constable, Cathryn. The Wolf Princess. (ENG.). 320p. (J). (gr. 5-9). 2014. pap. 6.99 *(978-0-545-52841-2(0))* 2013. 16.99 *(978-0-545-52839-9(9))* Scholastic, Inc. (Chicken Hse., The).

The Contagious Colors of Mumpley Middle School. 2014. (ENG., Illus.). 288p. (J). (gr. 2-5). pap. 8.99 *(978-1-4424-7830-5(6)*, Atheneum Bks. for Young Readers) Simon & Schuster Children's Publishing.

Converse, P. J. Subway Girl. 2011. (ENG.). 224p. (YA). (gr. 9-18). 16.99 *(978-0-06-157514-3(3)*, HarperTeen) HarperCollins Pubs.

Conway, David. Errol & His Extraordinary Nose. Angaramo, Roberta, illus. 2010. (ENG.). 32p. (J). (gr. -1-3). 16.95 *(978-0-8234-2262-3(3))* Holiday Hse., Inc.

Cook, Eileen. The Education of Hailey Kendrick. 2011. (ENG.). 272p. (YA). (gr. 9-18). 16.99 *(978-1-4424-1325-2(5)*, Simon Pulse) Simon Pulse.

—Fourth Grade Fairy. 2011. (Fourth Grade Fairy Ser.: 1). (ENG.). 176p. (J). (gr. 3-7). pap. 7.99 *(978-1-4169-9811-2(X)*, Aladdin) Simon & Schuster Children's Publishing.

—Getting Revenge on Lauren Wood. 2010. (ENG.). (YA). (gr. 9). 288p. pap. 9.99 *(978-1-4424-0976-7(2))*; 272p. 15.99 *(978-1-4169-7433-8(4))* Simon Pulse. (Simon Pulse).

—Gnome Invasion. 2011. (Fourth Grade Fairy Ser.: 3). (ENG.). 160p. (J). (gr. 3-7). pap. 6.99 *(978-1-4169-9813-6(6)*, Aladdin) Simon & Schuster Children's Publishing.

—Wishes for Beginners. 2011. (Fourth Grade Fairy Ser.: 2). (ENG.). 160p. (J). (gr. 3-7). pap. 6.99 *(978-1-4169-9812-9(8)*, Aladdin) Simon & Schuster Children's Publishing.

Cook, Jacqueline. On to Nationals. 2008. 296p. per. 12.95 *(978-1-4327-1681-3(6))* Outskirts Pr., Inc.

Cook, Kristi. Eternal. 2014. (ENG., Illus.). 432p. (YA). (gr. 9). pap. 9.99 *(978-1-4424-8531-0(0)*, Simon Pulse) Simon Pulse.

—Haven. 2011. (ENG.). 416p. (YA). (gr. 9-18). 16.99 *(978-1-4424-0760-2(3)*, Simon Pulse) Simon Pulse.

—Magnolia. 2014. (ENG., Illus.). 336p. (YA). (gr. 9). 17.99 *(978-1-4424-8535-8(3))*; pap. 10.99 *(978-1-4424-8534-1(5))* Simon Pulse. (Simon Pulse).

—Mirage. 2012. (ENG.). 384p. (YA). (gr. 9). 16.99 *(978-1-4424-4299-3(9)*, Simon Pulse) Simon Pulse.

Cooke, Tobias. The Secret of the Lost Soul: A Ben Street Mystery. 2011. 272p. pap. *(978-1-907499-80-7(6))* Pen Pr. Pubs., Ltd.

A Cool School: Individual Title Six-Packs. (gr. -1-2). 27.00 *(978-0-7635-9442-8(3))* Rigby Education.

Cooling, Wendy, ed. Ten of the Best: School Stories with a Difference. 2009. (ENG., Illus.). 192p. (J). pap. 7.99 *(978-0-00-713339-0(1)*, HarperCollins Children's Bks.) HarperCollins Pubs. Ltd. GBR. Dist: HarperCollins Pubs.

Cooner, Donna. Skinny. (ENG.). 272p. (J). (gr. 7). 2014. pap. 9.99 *(978-0-545-42764-7(9))* 2012. 17.99 *(978-0-545-42763-0(0))* Scholastic, Inc.

Cooney, Caroline B. Code Orange. 2007. 200p. (gr. 7-12). 17.00 *(978-0-7569-8210-2(3))* Perfection Learning Corp.

—Code Orange. 2007. (ENG.). 224p. (YA). (gr. 7-12). mass mkt. 6.99 *(978-0-385-73260-4(0)*, Laurel Leaf) Random Hse. Children's Bks.

—Code Orange. 2007. lib. bdg. 17.20 *(978-1-4177-7788-4(5)*, Turtleback) Turtleback Bks.

—The Lost Songs. 2013. (ENG.). 256p. (YA). (gr. 7). pap. 8.99 *(978-0-385-73967-2(2)*, Ember) Random Hse. Children's Bks.

—The Vampire's Promise. 2011. (ENG.). 496p. (J). (gr. 7-7). pap. 9.99 *(978-0-545-28976-4(9))* Scholastic, Inc.

Cooney, Doug. I Know Who Likes You. Bernardin, James, illus. 2005. (ENG.). 224p. (J). (gr. 3-7). pap. 10.99 *(978-1-4169-0261-4(9)*, Simon & Schuster Bks. For Young Readers) Simon & Schuster Bks. For Young Readers.

Coons, Timothy A. School of Chaos, 1 vol. 2010. 74p. pap. 19.95 *(978-1-4512-9345-6(3))* America Star Bks.

Cooper, Abby. Bubbles. 2017. (ENG.). 272p. (J). 16.99 *(978-0-374-30290-0(1)*; 9780374302900, Farrar, Straus & Giroux (BYR)) Farrar, Straus & Giroux.

—Sticks & Stones. 2016. (ENG.). 288p. (J). 16.99 *(978-0-374-30287-0(1)*, 9780374302870, Farrar, Straus & Giroux (BYR)) Farrar, Straus & Giroux.

—Sticks & Stones. 2017. (J). lib. bdg. 18.40 ***(978-0-606-39950-0(X))*** Turtleback Bks.

Cooper, Ilene. Look at Lucy! Merrell, David, illus. 2009. (Lucy Ser.: No. 3). (ENG.). 112p. (J). (gr. 1-4). 4.99 *(978-0-375-85558-0(0)*, Random Hse. Bks. for Young Readers) Random Hse. Children's Bks.

—Lucy's Tricks & Treats. Merrell, David, illus. 2012. (Lucy Ser.). (ENG.). 112p. (J). (gr. 1-4). 4.99 *(978-0-375-86997-6(2)*, Random Hse. Bks. for Young Readers) Random Hse. Children's Bks.

Cooper, Jay. Mutant Rat Attack! 2017. (Spy Next Door Ser.: 1). (ENG.). 144p. (J). (gr. 2-5). 9.99 *(978-0-545-93297-4(1)*, Scholastic Pr.) Scholastic, Inc.

Cooper, Rose. Gossip from the Girls' Room. 2011. (ENG.). 208p. (J). (gr. 3-7). 12.99 *(978-0-385-73947-4(8)*, Delacorte Bks. for Young Readers) Random Hse. Children's Bks.

—I Text Dead People. 2015. (Dead Serious Ser.). (ENG.). 240p. (J). (gr. 3-7). 15.99 *(978-0-375-99138-7(7)*, Delacorte Bks. for Young Readers) Random Hse. Children's Bks.

Copeland, Cynthia L. Dilly for President. 2005. (Illus.). 64p. (J). (gr. -1-k). pap. 6.95 *(978-0-7613-2442-3(9))*, First Avenue Editions) Lerner Publishing Group.

—The 15 Best Things about Being the New Kid. Vargo, Sharon, illus. 2006. (Silly Millies Ser.). 32p. (J). (gr. -1-3). lib. bdg. 21.27 *(978-0-7613-2889-6(0)*, Millbrook Pr.); (gr. 2). per. 5.95 *(978-0-8225-6473-7(4)*, First Avenue Editions) Lerner Publishing Group.

Coppock, Phil & Bower's 2008-2009 4th Grade Class. Rubber Tuesday. 2010. 70p. pap. 12.95 *(978-1-4327-5751-9(2))* Outskirts Pr., Inc.

Corbett Sampson, Natalie. Game Plan. 2013. 362p. pap. *(978-1-927746-09-7(4))* Fierce Ink Pr. Co-Op, Ltd.

Cordone Warner, Debra. A Busy Day for Baby Duck & Little Boy Blue. 2010. 34p. pap. 19.99 *(978-0-557-59587-7(8))* Lulu Pr., Inc.

Coriell, Shelley. Welcome, Caller, This Is Chloe. 2013. (ENG.). 320p. (YA). (gr. 7-17). pap. 7.95 *(978-1-4197-0545-8(8)*, Amulet Bks.) Abrams, Inc.

Cormier, Robert. The Chocolate War. 191p. (YA). (gr. 7-18). pap. 4.99 *(978-0-8072-1428-2(0)*, Listening Library) Random Hse. Audio Publishing Group.

—The Chocolate War. 30th ed. 2004. (Readers Circle Ser.). (ENG.). 272p. (YA). (gr. 7-12). pap. 9.99 *(978-0-375-82987-1(3)*, Ember) Random Hse. Children's Bks.

Corp, Carey & Langdon, Lorie. Doon, 1 vol. 2014. (Doon Novel Ser.). (ENG.). 416p. (YA). pap. 12.99 *(978-0-310-74239-5(0))* Blink.

Corrigan, Eireann. Accomplice. 2010. (ENG.). 304p. (J). (gr. 7-7). 17.99 *(978-0-545-05236-8(X)*, Scholastic Pr.) Scholastic, Inc.

Cosgrove, Stephen. Flynn "Flea" Flicker: Sticking to the Truth. Arroyo, Fian, illus. 2004. (J). *(978-1-58804-353-5(3))* P C I Education.

—Mizz Buggly: Doing Your Best. Arroyo, Fian, illus. 2004. (J). *(978-1-58804-380-1(0))* P C I Education.

Cosimano, Elle & Carey, Janet Lee. Nearly Found. 2015. (Nearly Boswell Mysteries Ser.). (ENG.). 384p. (YA). (gr. 7-12). 17.99 *(978-0-8037-3927-7(3)*, Kathy Dawson Books) Penguin Young Readers Group.

Costain, Meredith. Stella & the Pet Parade. McGowan, Shane, illus. 2015. (Legends in Their Own Lunchbox Ser.). (ENG.). 48p. (gr. 1-2). pap. 7.99 *(978-1-4966-0243-5(9)*, Legends in Their Own Lunchbox) Capstone Classroom.

Cotler, Steve. Cheesie Mack Is Not Exactly Famous. Holgate, Douglas, illus. 2014. (Cheesie Mack Ser.). (ENG.). 256p. (J). (gr. 3-7). 15.99 *(978-0-385-36984-8(0)*, Random Hse. Bks. for Young Readers) Random Hse. Children's Bks.

—Cheesie Mack Is Running Like Crazy! Holgate, Douglas, illus. (Cheesie Mack Ser.). (ENG.). (J). (gr. 3-7). 2014. 256p. pap. 6.99 *(978-0-307-97716-8(1)*, Yearling) 2013. 240p. 15.99 *(978-0-307-97713-7(7)*, Random Hse. Bks. for Young Readers) Random Hse. Children's Bks.

—Cheesie Mack Is Sort of Freaked Out. Holgate, Douglas, illus. 2014. (Cheesie Mack Ser.). (ENG.). 256p. (J). (gr. 3-7). 15.99 *(978-0-385-36988-6(3)*, Random Hse. Bks. for Young Readers) Random Hse. Children's Bks.

Cottle Street: Individual Title Six-Packs. (Action Packs Ser.). 120p. (gr. 3-5). 44.00 *(978-0-7635-8423-8(1))* Rigby Education.

Cotton, Peter B. When Jungle Jim Comes to Visit Fred the Snake. Lemaire, Bonnie, illus. 2013. 48p. 24.95 *(978-0-9883370-4-6(5))* Fig & The Vine, LLC, The.

Couloumbis, Audrey. Not Exactly a Love Story. 2014. (ENG.). 288p. (YA). (gr. 7). pap. 9.99 *(978-0-375-86606-7(X)*, Ember) Random Hse. Children's Bks.

CourseCrafters Staff, des. Interactive Storybooks - Let's Go to School! 2003. (J). spiral bd. 14.95 *(978-1-58605-961-3(0))* LeapFrog Enterprises, Inc.

—Interactive Storybooks - School Time. 2003. (J). spiral bd. 14.95 *(978-1-58605-960-6(2))* LeapFrog Enterprises, Inc.

Courtin, Thierry. T choupi rentre a l Ecole. 13.95 *(978-2-09-202041-8(2))* Nathan, Fernand FRA. Dist: Distribooks, Inc.

Cousins, Dave. Waiting for Gonzo. 2015. (ENG.). 288p. (YA). pap. 9.99 *(978-0-7387-4199-4(X)*, Flux) North Star Editions.

Cousins, Lucy. Maisy Goes to Preschool: A Maisy First Experiences Book. Cousins, Lucy, illus. 2009. (Maisy Ser.). (ENG., Illus.). 32p. (J). (gr. -1-k). 12.99 *(978-0-7636-4254-9(1))* Candlewick Pr.

Coutts, Alexandra. Young Widows Club. 2015. (ENG.). 304p. (YA). (gr. 7). 17.99 *(978-0-374-30126-2(3)*, 9780374301262, Farrar, Straus & Giroux (BYR)) Farrar, Straus & Giroux.

Coven, Wanda. Heidi Heckelbeck & the Big Mix-Up. Burris, Priscilla, illus. 2016. (Heidi Heckelbeck Ser.: 18). (ENG.). 128p. (J). (gr. k-4). pap. 5.99 *(978-1-4814-7169-5(4)*, Little Simon) Little Simon.

—Heidi Heckelbeck & the Cookie Contest. Burris, Priscilla, illus. 2012. (Heidi Heckelbeck Ser.: 3). (ENG.). 128p. (J). (gr. k-2). 16.99 *(978-1-4424-4166-8(6))*; pap. 5.99 *(978-1-4424-4165-1(8))* Little Simon. (Little Simon).

—Heidi Heckelbeck & the Cookie Contest. 2012. (Heidi Heckelbeck Ser.: 3). lib. bdg. 16.00 *(978-0-606-26328-3(4)*, Turtleback) Turtleback Bks.

—Heidi Heckelbeck & the Secret Admirer. Burris, Priscilla, illus. 2012. (Heidi Heckelbeck Ser.: 6). (ENG.). 128p. (J). (gr. k-4). 16.99 *(978-1-4424-4175-0(5))*; pap. 5.99 *(978-1-4424-4174-3(7))* Little Simon. (Little Simon).

—Heidi Heckelbeck & the Secret Admirer. 2012. (Heidi Heckelbeck Ser.: 6). lib. bdg. 16.00 *(978-0-606-26905-6(3)*, Turtleback) Turtleback Bks.

—Heidi Heckelbeck Casts a Spell. Burris, Priscilla, illus. 2012. (Heidi Heckelbeck Ser.: 2). (ENG.). 128p. (J). (gr. k-4). 16.99 *(978-1-4424-4088-3(0))*; pap. 5.99 *(978-1-4424-3567-4(4))* Little Simon. (Little Simon).

—Heidi Heckelbeck Casts a Spell. 2012. (Heidi Heckelbeck Ser.: 2). lib. bdg. 16.00 *(978-0-606-26327-6(6)*, Turtleback) Turtleback Bks.

—Heidi Heckelbeck Gets Glasses. Burris, Priscilla, illus. 2012. (Heidi Heckelbeck Ser.: 5). (ENG.). 128p. (J). (gr. k-2). pap. 5.99 *(978-1-4424-4171-2(2))*; 15.99 *(978-1-4424-4172-9(0))* Little Simon. (Little Simon).

—Heidi Heckelbeck Gets Glasses. 2012. (Heidi Heckelbeck Ser.: 5). lib. bdg. 16.00 *(978-0-606-26888-2(X)*, Turtleback) Turtleback Bks.

—Heidi Heckelbeck Has a Secret. Burris, Priscilla, illus. 2012. (Heidi Heckelbeck Ser.: 1). (ENG.). 128p. (J). (gr. k-4). 16.99 *(978-1-4424-4087-6(2))*; pap. 5.99 *(978-1-4424-3565-0(8))* Little Simon. (Little Simon).

—Heidi Heckelbeck Has a Secret - Heidi Heckelbeck Casts a Spell - Heidi Heckelbeck & the Cookie Contest. Burris, Priscilla, illus. 2014. (Heidi Heckelbeck Ser.). (ENG.). 384p. (J). (gr. k-4). pap. 8.99 *(978-1-4814-2771-5(7)*, Little Simon) Little Simon.

—Heidi Heckelbeck Makes a Wish. 2016. (Heidi Heckelbeck Ser.: 17). lib. bdg. 16.00 *(978-0-606-38962-4(8))* Turtleback Bks.

—Heidi Heckelbeck Makes a Wish: Super Special! Burris, Priscilla, illus. 2016. (Heidi Heckelbeck Ser.: 17). (ENG.). 160p. (J). (gr. k-4). pap. 5.99 *(978-1-4814-6613-4(5)*, Little Simon) Little Simon.

—Heidi Heckelbeck Tries Out for the Team. Burris, Priscilla, illus. 2017. (Heidi Heckelbeck Ser.: 19). (ENG.). 128p. (J). (gr. k-4). pap. 5.99 *(978-1-4814-7172-5(4)*, Little Simon) Little Simon.

Covey, Sean. Sophie & the Perfect Poem. Curtis, Stacy, illus. 2013. (7 Habits of Happy Kids Ser.: 6). (ENG.). 32p. (J). (gr. -1-1). 7.99 *(978-1-4424-7651-6(6)*, Simon & Schuster Bks. For Young Readers) Simon & Schuster Bks. For Young Readers.

Coville, Bruce. The Monster's Ring. Coville, Katherine, illus. 2008. (Magic Shop Book Ser.: 1). (ENG.). 128p. (J). (gr. 5-7). pap. 6.99 *(978-0-15-206442-6(7))* Houghton Mifflin Harcourt Publishing Co.

—My Teacher Fried My Brains. Pierard, John, illus. 2014. (My Teacher Bks.: 2). (ENG.). 176p. (J). (gr. 3-7). 17.99 *(978-1-4814-0431-0(8)*, Aladdin) Simon & Schuster Children's Publishing.

—My Teacher Is an Alien. Wimmer, Mike, illus. 2014. (My Teacher Bks.: 1). (ENG.). 160p. (J). (gr. 3-7). 17.99 *(978-1-4814-0430-3(X)*, Simon & Schuster/Paula Wiseman Bks.) Simon & Schuster/Paula Wiseman Bks.

—The Skull of Truth: A Magic Shop Book. Lippincott, Gary A., illus. 2007. (Magic Shop Book Ser.: 4). (ENG.). 208p. (J). (gr. 5-7). pap. 7.99 *(978-0-15-206084-8(7))* Houghton Mifflin Harcourt Publishing Co.

—There's an Alien in My Classroom! (Illus.). 201p. (J). pap. 8.95 *(978-0-340-73634-0(8))* Hodder & Stoughton GBR. Dist: Trafalgar Square Publishing.

Cowling, Chani. Cookie Baker, Sweet & Sour. 2008. 24p. pap. 24.95 *(978-1-60703-021-8(7))* America Star Bks.

Cox, Amy. Odetta the Octopus Teacher. 2013. 28p. pap. 24.95 *(978-1-63000-491-0(X))* America Star Bks.

Cox, Judy. Carmen Learns English. Dominguez, Angela N., illus. 2010. (ENG.). 32p. (J). (gr. -1-3). 16.95 *(978-0-8234-2174-9(0))* Holiday Hse., Inc.

—Don't Be Silly, Mrs. Millie!, 0 vols. Mathieu, Joe, illus. 2010. (ENG.). 34p. (J). (gr. k-3). pap. 6.99 *(978-0-7614-5727-5(5)*, 9780761457275, Amazon Children's Publishing) Amazon Publishing.

—Happy Birthday, Mrs. Millie!, 0 vols. Mathieu, Joe, illus. 2012. (ENG.). 32p. (J). (gr. k-3). 16.99 *(978-0-7614-6126-5(4)*, 9780761461265, Amazon Children's Publishing) Amazon Publishing.

—Puppy Power. Björkman, Steve, illus. (ENG.). 96p. (J). 2009. (gr. 2-4). pap. 6.95 *(978-0-8234-2210-4(0))* 2008. (gr. -1-3). 15.95 *(978-0-8234-2073-5(6))* Holiday Hse., Inc.

—Ukulele Hayley. Haley, Amanda, illus. (ENG.). 96p. (J). (gr. 2-5). 2014. pap. 5.99 *(978-0-8234-3190-8(8))* 2013. 16.95 *(978-0-8234-2863-2(X))* Holiday Hse., Inc.

Cox, Steven. Justin's Very Own Drum. Saavedra, Anthony, illus. 2009. 24p. pap. 24.95 *(978-1-60749-553-6(8))* America Star Bks.

Coy, John. Crackback. 2007. 201p. (gr. 7-12). 17.00 *(978-0-7569-8274-4(X))* Perfection Learning Corp.

—Love of the Game. 2011. (4 For 4 Ser.: 3). (ENG.). 192p. (J). (gr. 3-7). 16.99 *(978-0-312-37331-3(7)*, 9780312373313) Feiwel & Friends.

—Love of the Game. 2011. (4 For 4 Ser.: 3). (ENG.). 192p. (J). (gr. 3-7). pap. 8.99 *(978-1-250-00637-0(6)*, 9781250006370) Square Fish.

—Take Your Best Shot. 2012. (4 For 4 Ser.: 4). (ENG.). 192p. (J). (gr. 3-7). 16.99 *(978-0-312-37332-0(5)*, 9780312373320) Feiwel & Friends.

—Top of the Order. 2010. (4 For 4 Ser.: 1). (ENG.). 208p. (J). (gr. 3-7). pap. 8.99 *(978-0-312-61111-8(0)*, 9780312611118) Square Fish.

Cozzo, Karole. How to Keep Rolling after a Fall. 2016. (ENG.). 272p. (YA). pap. 9.99 *(978-1-250-07928-2(4)*, 9781250079282) Feiwel & Friends.

—How to Say I Love You Out Loud. 2015. (ENG.). 240p. (YA). (gr. 7). pap. 9.99 *(978-1-250-06359-5(0))* Feiwel & Friends.

Crabtree, Julie. Discovering Pig Magic. 2008. (ENG.). 144p. (J). (gr. 2-8). 16.95 *(978-1-57131-683-7(3))*; pap. 6.95 *(978-1-57131-684-4(1))* Milkweed Editions.

Crane, Caprice. Confessions of a Hater. 2014. (ENG.). 384p. (YA). (gr. 8). pap. 9.99 *(978-1-250-04433-4(2)*, 9781250044334) Square Fish.

Crane, Carol. Handkerchief Quilt. Palmer, Gary, illus. 2010. (ENG.). 32p. (J). (gr. k-3). 15.95 *(978-1-58536-344-5(8))* Sleeping Bear Pr.

Crane, Cheri J. Moment of Truth: A Novel. 2005. 238p. (YA). *(978-1-59156-727-1(0))* Covenant Communications.

Crayton, Tina Anderson. Sniffles: Each Season Brings New Sniffles. 2012. 12p. pap. 15.99 *(978-1-4772-8454-4(0))* AuthorHouse.

Creagh, Kelly. Enshadowed. 2012. (ENG., Illus.). 448p. (YA). (gr. 7). 17.99 *(978-1-4424-0204-1(0)*, Atheneum Bks. for Young Readers) Simon & Schuster Children's Publishing.

—Enshadowed: A Nevermore Book. 2013. (ENG., Illus.). 464p. (YA). (gr. 7). pap. 9.99 *(978-1-4424-0206-5(7))* Simon & Schuster Children's Publishing.

—Nevermore. (ENG., Illus.). (YA). (gr. 9). 2011. 576p. pap. 9.99 *(978-1-4424-0201-0(6))* 2010. 560p. 17.99 *(978-1-4424-0200-3(8))* Simon & Schuster Children's Publishing. (Atheneum Bks. for Young Readers).

—Oblivion. 2015. (ENG.). 448p. (YA). (gr. 7). 18.99 *(978-1-4424-3627-5(1))* Simon & Schuster Children's Publishing.

Creech, Sharon. Absolutely Normal Chaos. 2012. 230p. (J). (gr. 4-7). lib. bdg. 17.20 *(978-0-613-02936-0(4)*, Turtleback) Turtleback Bks.

—Bloomability. 2012. (Illus.). 272p. (J). (gr. 3-7). pap. 6.99 *(978-0-06-440823-3(X))* HarperCollins Pubs.

—Bloomability. unabr. ed. 2004. 273p. (J). (gr. 4-7). pap. 38.00 incl. audio *(978-0-8072-8754-5(7)*, YA257SP, Listening Library) Random Hse. Audio Publishing Group.

—Bloomability. 2012. (J). (gr. 3-6). 17.20 *(978-0-613-22826-8(X)*, Turtleback) Turtleback Bks.

—A Fine, Fine School. 2004. (Illus.). (J). (gr. k-3). spiral bd. *(978-0-616-11107-9(X))* Canadian National Institute for the Blind/Institut National Canadien pour les Aveugles.

—A Fine, Fine School. Bliss, Harry, illus. 2004. (J). (gr. k-3). spiral bd. *(978-0-616-11106-2(1))* Canadian National Institute for the Blind/Institut National Canadien pour les Aveugles.

—A Fine, Fine School. Bliss, Harry, illus. 2003. (ENG.). 32p. (J). (gr. -1-3). pap. 6.99 *(978-0-06-000728-7(1))* HarperCollins Pubs.

—A Fine, Fine School. 2003. (Illus.). 25.95 incl. audio *(978-1-59112-221-0(X))* Live Oak Media.

—A Fine, Fine School. Bliss, Harry, illus. 2003. pap. 37.95 incl. audio *(978-1-59112-222-7(8))*; pap. 39.95 incl. audio compact disk *(978-1-59112-555-6(3))* Live Oak Media.

—A Fine, Fine School. 2003. (Illus.). (J). (gr. -1-2). 28.95 incl. audio compact disk *(978-1-59112-496-2(4))* Live Oak Media.

—A Fine, Fine School. Bliss, Harry, illus. 2004. (J). (gr. -1-3). 14.65 *(978-0-7569-3179-7(7))* Perfection Learning Corp.

—Hate That Cat. (ENG.). (J). (gr. 3-7). 2010. 176p. pap. 6.99 *(978-0-06-143094-7(3))* 2008. 160p. 16.99 *(978-0-06-143092-3(7))* HarperCollins Pubs.

—Replay. (J). (gr. 3-7). 2013. (ENG.). 224p. pap. 6.99 *(978-0-06-054021-0(4))* 2005. 240p. lib. bdg. 16.89 *(978-0-06-054020-3(6)*, Cotler, Joanna Books) HarperCollins Pubs.

Crews, G. S. The Adventures of Mercy Saint. 2011. 258p. pap. 15.00 *(978-0-9795236-5-6(6))* Crews Pubns., LLC.

Crimi-Trent, Ellen & Priddy, Roger. The Field Trip. 2014. (Schoolies Ser.). (ENG.). 28p. (J). (gr. -1-1). 4.99 *(978-0-312-51662-8(2)*, 9780312516628, Priddy Bks.) St. Martin's Pr.

—School Fair. 2014. (Schoolies Ser.). (ENG.). 28p. (J). (gr. -1-1). 4.99 *(978-0-312-51663-5(0)*, 9780312516635, Priddy Bks.) St. Martin's Pr.

—Schoolies - My Fun Activity Box. 2014. (Schoolies Ser.). (ENG.). (J). (gr. -1-1). act. bk. ed. 14.99 *(978-0-312-51725-0(4)*, 9780312517250, Priddy Bks.) St. Martin's Pr.

—Schoolies: Chalk Fun. 2014. (Schoolies Ser.). (ENG.). 16p. (J). (gr. -1-1). bds. 8.99 *(978-0-312-51722-9(X)*, 9780312517229, Priddy Bks.) St. Martin's Pr.

—Super Sticker Book. 2014. (Schoolies Ser.). (ENG.). 130p. (J). (gr. -1-1). pap. 12.99 *(978-0-312-51724-3(6)*, 9780312517243, Priddy Bks.) St. Martin's Pr.

Croall, Marie P. My Boyfriend Is a Monster - Under His Spell. Park, Hyeondo, illus. 2011. (My Boyfriend Is a Monster Ser.: 4). (ENG.). 128p. (YA). (gr. 7-12). pap. 9.95 *(978-0-7613-7076-5(5)*, Graphic Universe™) Lerner Publishing Group.

—School of Evil, 14 vols. Carruthers, Sandy, illus. 2010. (Twisted Journeys (r) Ser.: 13). (ENG.). 112p. (J). (gr. 4-7). lib. bdg. 27.93 *(978-0-8225-9263-1(0))* Lerner Publishing Group.

—Under His Spell, 4 vols., No. 4. Park, Hyeondo, illus. 2011. (My Boyfriend Is a Monster Ser.: 4). (ENG.). 128p. (YA). (gr. 7-12). 29.27 *(978-0-7613-5602-8(9))* Lerner Publishing Group.

Cronn-Mills, Kirstin. Beautiful Music for Ugly Children. 2012. (ENG.). 288p. (YA). pap. 11.99 *(978-0-7387-3251-0(6)*, Flux) North Star Editions.

Cross, P. C. Summer Job: A Virgil & Cy Mystery. 2008. 260p. pap. 16.95 *(978-0-595-50921-8(5))* iUniverse, Inc.

Cross, Vince. A Club: The Blogs of Abi Goodenough. 2006. (ENG.). 160p. (J). (gr. 4-7). per. 8.99 *(978-0-7459-6019-7(7))* Lion Hudson PLC GBR. Dist: Independent Pubs. Group.

Crossan, Sarah. One. 2015. (ENG.). 400p. (YA). (gr. 8). 17.99 *(978-0-06-211875-2(7)*, Greenwillow Bks.) HarperCollins Pubs.

Crosshill, Tom. The Cat King of Havana. 2016. 368p. (YA). (gr. 8). 17.99 *(978-0-06-242283-5(9)*, Tegen, Katherine Bks) HarperCollins Pubs.

Crow, Kristyn. Zombelina: School Days. Idle, Molly, illus. (ENG.). (J). 2017. 40p. 16.99 *(978-1-61963-641-5(7)*, 9781619636415) 2013. 32p. (gr. -1-3). 16.99 *(978-0-8027-2803-6(0)*, 9780802728036) Bloomsbury Publishing USA. (Bloomsbury USA Childrens).

Crow, Marilee. A Pocketful of Manners. Snider, K. C., illus. 2011. 16p. pap. 9.95 *(978-1-61633-176-4(3))* Guardian Angel Publishing, Inc.

Crow, Melinda Melton. Field Trip for School Bus, 1 vol. Thompson, Chad, illus. 2012. (Wonder Wheels Ser.). (ENG.). 32p. (gr. -1-1). pap. 6.25 *(978-1-4342-4237-2(4))*; lib. bdg. 22.65 *(978-1-4342-4019-4(3))* Stone Arch Bks.

—Helpful Tractor, 1 vol. Thompson, Chad, illus. 2011. (Wonder Wheels Ser.). (ENG.). 32p. (gr. -1-1). pap. 6.25 *(978-1-4342-3382-0(0))*; lib. bdg. 22.65 *(978-1-4342-3027-0(9))* Stone Arch Bks.

—Lucky School Bus, 1 vol. Thompson, Chad, illus. 2011. (Wonder Wheels Ser.). (ENG.). 32p. (gr. -1-1). pap. 6.25 *(978-1-4342-3381-3(2))*; lib. bdg. 22.65 *(978-1-4342-3026-3(0))* Stone Arch Bks.

Crowley, Suzanne. The Very Ordered Existence of Merilee Marvelous. 2007. 380p. (J). (gr. 5-9). 16.99 *(978-0-06-123197-1(5)*, Greenwillow Bks.) HarperCollins Pubs.

Crutcher, Chris. Deadline. (ENG.). (YA). (gr. 9). 2009. 336p. pap. 9.99 *(978-0-06-085091-3(4))* 2007. 320p. 17.99 *(978-0-06-085089-0(2))* HarperCollins Pubs. (Greenwillow Bks.).

—Deadline. 2011. 10.36 *(978-0-7848-3487-9(3)*, Everbind) Marco Bk. Co.

—Period 8. 2013. 288p. (YA). (gr. 9). (ENG.). 17.99 *(978-0-06-191480-5(0))*; lib. bdg. 18.89 *(978-0-06-191481-2(9))* HarperCollins Pubs. (Greenwillow Bks.).

—The Sledding Hill. 2006. (ENG.). 256p. (YA). (gr. 8-12). pap. 9.99 *(978-0-06-050245-4(2)*, Greenwillow Bks.) HarperCollins Pubs.

—Staying Fat for Sarah Byrnes. 2003. (ENG.). 304p. (YA). (gr. 8). pap. 9.99 *(978-0-06-009489-8(3)*, Greenwillow Bks.) HarperCollins Pubs.

—Whale Talk. 2009. (ENG.). 304p. (YA). (gr. 8). pap. 9.99 *(978-0-06-177131-6(7)*, Greenwillow Bks.) HarperCollins Pubs.

—Whale Talk. 2004. 224p. (J). (gr. 7-18). pap. 38.00 incl. audio *(978-0-8072-2289-8(5)*, Listening Library) Random Hse. Audio Publishing Group.

Cuate, Melodie A. Journey to la Salle's Settlement. 2010. (Mr. Barrington's Mysterious Trunk Ser.). (ENG., Illus.). 184p. (J). lib. bdg. 18.95 *(978-0-89672-704-5(1))* Texas Tech Univ. Pr.

—Journey to the Alamo. 2006. (Mr. Barrington's Mysterious Trunk Ser.). (Illus.). 144p. (J). (gr. 4-7). 18.95 *(978-0-89672-592-8(8))* Texas Tech Univ. Pr.

Culbertson, Kim. Songs for a Teenage Nomad. 2010. (ENG.). 256p. (YA). (gr. 7-12). pap. 12.99 *(978-1-4022-4301-1(4))* Sourcebooks, Inc.

The Culverdale School Tales. 2005. (J). per. *(978-1-59872-011-2(2))* Instant Pub.
Cummings, Priscilla. Blindsided. (ENG.). (J). (gr. 5-18). 2011. 256p. 7.99 *(978-0-14-241902-1(8),* Puffin Books) 2010. 240p. 16.99 *(978-0-525-42161-0(0),* Dutton Books for Young Readers) Penguin Young Readers Group.
Cummings, Troy. Attack of the Shadow Smashers. 2013. (Notebook of Doom Ser.: 3). (ENG.). 96p. (J). (gr. 1-3). pap. 4.99 *(978-0-545-55297-4(4))* Scholastic, Inc.
—Attack of the Shadow Smashers. 2013. (Notebook of Doom Ser.: 3). lib. bdg. 14.75 *(978-0-606-32369-7(4),* Turtleback) Turtleback Bks.
—Charge of the Lightning Bugs. Cummings, Troy, illus. 2015. (Notebook of Doom Ser.: 8). (ENG., Illus.). 96p. (J). (gr. 1-3). 15.99 *(978-0-545-79554-8(0));* pap. 4.99 *(978-0-545-79555-5(9))* Scholastic, Inc.
—Chomp of the Meat-Eating Vegetables. 2014. (Notebook of Doom Ser.: 4). (ENG.). 96p. (J). (gr. 1-3). 15.99 *(978-0-545-55300-1(8));* (Illus.). pap. 4.99 *(978-0-545-55299-8(0))* Scholastic, Inc.
—Chomp of the Meat-Eating Vegetables. 2014. (Notebook of Doom Ser.: 4). lib. bdg. 14.75 *(978-0-606-35362-5(3))* Turtleback Bks.
—Day of the Night Crawlers. 2013. (Notebook of Doom Ser.: 2). (ENG.). 96p. (J). (gr. 1-3). 15.99 *(978-0-545-49324-6(2));* pap. 4.99 *(978-0-545-49325-3(0));* E-Book *(978-0-545-49327-7(7))* Scholastic, Inc.
—Day of the Night Crawlers. 2013. (Notebook of Doom Ser.: 2). lib. bdg. 14.75 *(978-0-606-32368-0(6),* Turtleback) Turtleback Bks.
—March of the Vanderpants. 2017. (Notebook of Doom — Branches Ser.: 12). lib. bdg. 14.75 ***(978-0-606-40192-0(X))*** Turtleback Bks.
—March of the Vanderpants - A Branches Book. Cummings, Troy, illus. 2017. (Notebook of Doom Ser.: 12). (ENG., Illus.). 96p. (J). (gr. 1-3). pap. 4.99 ***(978-1-338-03452-3(9));*** lib. bdg. 15.99 ***(978-1-338-03453-0(7))*** Scholastic, Inc.
—The Notebook of Doom #6: Pop of the Bumpy Mummy (a Branches Book) - Library Edition. 2014. (Notebook of Doom Ser.: 6). (ENG.). 96p. (J). (gr. 1-3). 15.99 *(978-0-545-69899-3(5))* Scholastic, Inc.
—The Notebook of Doom Collection, Bks. 1-3. Cummings, Troy, illus. 2016. (Notebook of Doom Ser.). (ENG., Illus.). 288p. (J). (gr. 1-3). pap. 9.99 *(978-1-338-10199-7(4))* Scholastic, Inc.
—Pop of the Bumpy Mummy. Cummings, Troy, illus. 2014. (Notebook of Doom Ser.: 6). (ENG., Illus.). 96p. (J). (gr. 1-3). pap. 4.99 *(978-0-545-69898-6(7))* Scholastic, Inc.
—Rise of the Balloon Goons. 2013. (Notebook of Doom Ser.: 1). (ENG., Illus.). 96p. (J). (gr. 1-3). 15.99 *(978-0-545-49322-2(6));* pap. 4.99 *(978-0-545-49323-9(4))* Scholastic, Inc.
—Rumble of the Coaster Ghost. Cummings, Troy, illus. 2016. (Notebook of Doom Ser.: 9). (ENG., Illus.). 96p. (J). (gr. 1-3). pap. 4.99 *(978-0-545-86497-8(6))* Scholastic, Inc.
—Snap of the Super-Goop: A Branches Book. Cummings, Troy, illus. 2016. (Notebook of Doom Ser.: 1). (ENG., Illus.). 96p. (J). (gr. 1-3). 15.99 *(978-0-545-86500-5(X))* Scholastic, Inc.
—Snap of the Super-Goop - A Branches Book. Cummings, Troy, illus. 2016. (Notebook of Doom Ser.: 1). (ENG., Illus.). 96p. (J). (gr. 1-3). pap. 4.99 *(978-0-545-86499-2(2))* Scholastic, Inc.
—Sneeze of the Octo-Schnozz: a Branches Book (the Notebook of Doom #11) 2016. (Notebook of Doom Ser.: 11). (ENG.). 96p. (J). (gr. 1-3). pap. 4.99 *(978-1-338-03448-6(0))* Scholastic, Inc.
—Whack of the P-Rex. 2014. (Notebook of Doom Ser.: 5). (ENG.). 96p. (J). (gr. 1-3). pap. 4.99 *(978-0-545-69895-5(2))* Scholastic, Inc.
Curtin, Ann. Dreamcatcher. 2015. 201p. (YA). *(978-1-61271-246-8(0))* Zumaya Pubns. LLC.
Cusack, Geraldine O'Connell. Wrecker's Cove. 2013. 100p. pap. *(978-1-78407-081-6(5))* FeedARead.com.
Cuyler, Margery. Hooray for Reading Day! Howard, Arthur, illus. 2008. (Jessica Worries Ser.). (ENG.). 32p. (J). (gr. k-3). 17.99 *(978-0-689-86188-8(5),* Simon & Schuster Bks. For Young Readers) Simon & Schuster Bks. For Young Readers.
—I Repeat, Don't Cheat! Howard, Arthur, illus. 2010. (ENG.). 32p. (J). (gr. k-3). 15.99 *(978-1-4169-7167-2(X),* Simon & Schuster Bks. For Young Readers) Simon & Schuster Bks. For Young Readers.
—Kindness Is Cooler, Mrs. Ruler. Yoshikawa, Sachiko, illus. 2007. (ENG.). 48p. (J). (gr. k-5). 17.99 *(978-0-689-87344-7(1),* Simon & Schuster Bks. For Young Readers) Simon & Schuster Bks. For Young Readers.
—100th Day Worries. Howard, Arthur, illus. 2006. (ENG.). 32p. (J). (gr. k-3). reprint ed. 7.99 *(978-1-4169-0789-3(0),* Simon & Schuster Bks. For Young Readers) Simon & Schuster Bks. For Young Readers.
Dad Goes to School. 2003. (Mom & Dad Ser.). (J). 7.33 *(978-1-58453-252-1(1))* Pioneer Valley Bks.
Dadey, Debbie. Dream of the Blue Turtle. Avakyan, Tatevik, illus. 2014. (Mermaid Tales Ser.: 7). (ENG.). 128p. (J). (gr. 1-4). 16.99 *(978-1-4424-8264-7(8),* Aladdin) Simon & Schuster Children's Publishing.
—Great Green Gator Graduation. Lucas, Margeaux, illus. 2006. (Swamp Monster in Third Grade Ser.). 58p. (J). pap. *(978-0-439-79401-5(3))* Scholastic, Inc.
—The Lost Princess. Avakyan, Tatevik, illus. 2013. (Mermaid Tales Ser.: 5). (ENG.). 128p. (J). (gr. 1-4). 15.99 *(978-1-4424-8258-6(3));* pap. 5.99 *(978-1-4424-8257-9(5))* Simon & Schuster Children's Publishing. (Aladdin).
—Mermaid Tales 4-Books-In-1! Trouble at Trident Academy; Battles of the Best Friends; a Whale of a Tale; Danger in the Deep Blue Sea. Avakyan, Tatevik, illus. 2016. (Mermaid Tales Ser.). (ENG.). 416p. (J). (gr. 1-4). 14.99 *(978-1-4814-7592-1(4),* Aladdin) Simon & Schuster Children's Publishing.
—Treasure in Trident City. Avakyan, Tatevik, illus. 2014. (Mermaid Tales Ser.: 8). (ENG.). 128p. (J). (gr. 1-4). pap. 5.99 *(978-1-4424-8266-1(4),* Aladdin) Simon & Schuster Children's Publishing.
—Trouble at Trident Academy. Avakyan, Tatevik, illus. 2012. (Mermaid Tales Ser.: 1). (ENG.). 112p. (J). (gr. 1-4). 15.99 *(978-1-4424-4978-7(0));* pap. 5.99 *(978-1-4424-2980-2(1))* Simon & Schuster Children's Publishing. (Aladdin).
Dadey, Debby & Dadey, Debbie. Danger in the Deep Blue Sea, 1 vol., Bk. 4. 2015. (Mermaid Tales Ser.). (ENG.). 104p. (J). (gr. 2-4). 24.21 *(978-1-61479-325-0(5),* Spotlight) ABDO Publishing Co.
—Treasure in Trident City, 1 vol., Bk. 8. 2015. (Mermaid Tales Ser.). (ENG.). 120p. (J). (gr. 2-4). 24.21 *(978-1-61479-329-8(8),* Spotlight) ABDO Publishing Co.
—Trouble at Trident Academy, 1 vol., Bk. 1. 2015. (Mermaid Tales Ser.). (ENG.). 104p. (J). (gr. 2-4). 24.21 *(978-1-61479-322-9(0),* Spotlight) ABDO Publishing Co.
Daffern, Brian. Prince Albert Bk. 2: The Beast School. 2005. 160p. (YA). per. 10.95 *(978-0-9709104-6-2(0))* Hickory Tales Publishing.
Dahl, Michael. Cold Feet, 1 vol. Ornia-Blanco, Miguel, illus. 2010. (Monster Street Ser.). (ENG.). 32p. (gr. 1-3). lib. bdg. 23.99 *(978-1-4048-6070-4(3),* Monster Street) Picture Window Bks.
—The Marshmallow Mermaid. Crowther, Jeff, illus. 2010. (Graphic Sparks Ser.). (ENG.). 40p. (gr. 1-3). pap. 5.95 *(978-1-4342-2802-4(9),* Graphic Sparks) Stone Arch Bks.
—Sugar Hero. Crowther, Jeff, illus. (Graphic Sparks Ser.). (ENG.). 40p. (gr. 1-3). 2010. pap. 5.95 *(978-1-4342-2801-7(0))* 2009. lib. bdg. 23.99 *(978-1-4342-1587-1(3))* Stone Arch Bks. (Graphic Sparks).
Dahl, Michael & Nickel, Scott. The Green Queen of Mean. Crowther, Jeff, illus. 2010. (Graphic Sparks Ser.). (ENG.). 40p. (gr. 1-3). pap. 5.95 *(978-1-4342-2803-1(7),* Graphic Sparks) Stone Arch Bks.
Dahl, Roald. Matilda.Tr. of Matilda. (FRE.). (J). pap. 19.95 *(978-2-07-051254-6(1))* Gallimard, Editions FRA. Dist: Distribooks, Inc.
—Matilda. Blake, Quentin & Terrazzini, Daniela Jaglenka, illus. 2013.Tr. of Matilda. (ENG.). 240p. (J). (gr. 3-7). 16.99 *(978-0-14-242427-8(7),* Puffin Books) Penguin Young Readers Group.
—Matilda. Blake, Quentin, illus.Tr. of Matilda. (ENG.). (J). (gr. 3-7). 2007. 256p. 7.99 *(978-0-14-241037-0(3))* 2004. 240p. pap. 7.99 *(978-0-14-240253-5(2))* 2013. 256p. pap. 7.99 *(978-0-14-242538-1(9))* Penguin Young Readers Group. (Puffin Books).
—Matilda. 2007.Tr. of Matilda. 18.40 *(978-1-4177-8613-8(2),* Turtleback) Turtleback Bks.
—MATILDA. 46th ed. 2006. (Alfaguara Juvenil Ser.). (SPA., Illus.). 230p. (J). (gr. 5-8). pap. 12.95 *(978-84-204-6454-1(6))* Ediciones Alfaguara ESP. Dist: Santillana USA Publishing Co., Inc.
Dail, Maggie. Getting to First Base - Chris Struggles to Read. 2006. 157p. pap. 13.95 *(978-1-4116-8125-5(8))* Lulu Pr., Inc.
Dairman, Tara. All Four Stars. 2014. (All Four Stars Ser.: Bk. 1). (ENG.). 288p. (J). (gr. 3-7). 16.99 *(978-0-399-16252-7(6),* G.P. Putnam's Sons Books for Young Readers) Penguin Young Readers Group.
—Stars So Sweet. 2016. (All Four Stars Ser.: Bk. 3). (ENG.). 288p. (J). (gr. 3-7). 16.99 *(978-1-101-99648-5(X),* G.P. Putnam's Sons Books for Young Readers) Penguin Young Readers Group.
Dajani, Suad Farsakh. Grandma's Stories: A Collection of Six Children's Stories. 2013. 40p. 25.99 *(978-1-4808-0051-9(1));* pap. 16.99 *(978-1-4808-0049-6(X))* Archway Publishing.
Dakos, Kalli & DesMarteau, Alicia. Our Principal Promised to Kiss a Pig. DiRocco, Carl, illus. (ENG.). 32p. (J). 2017. (gr. -1-3). pap. 7.99 ***(978-0-8075-6635-0(7))*** 2004. (gr. 2-5). 16.99 *(978-0-8075-6629-9(2))* Whitman, Albert & Co.
Dale, Jay. Captain Ross & the Old Sea Ferry, 1 vol. Smith, Graham, illus. 2012. (Engage Literacy Green Ser.). (ENG.). 32p. (gr. k-2). pap. 5.99 *(978-1-4296-9016-4(X),* Engage Literacy) Capstone Press of Coughlan Cos.
D'Alessandro, Alan. Growing Out of Fear. 2005. 62p. pap. 16.95 *(978-1-4137-8547-0(6))* PublishAmerica, Inc.
Daly, Niki. Nicholas & the Wild Ones: How to Beat the Bullies. 2016. (ENG.). 32p. (J). (gr. -1-3). 18.99 *(978-1-84780-853-0(0),* Frances Lincoln Children's Bks.) Quarto Publishing Group UK GBR. Dist: Hachette Bk. Group.
D'Amico, Carmela. Ella Sets the Stage. D'Amico, Steven, illus. 2006. 41p. (J). pap. 16.99 *(978-0-439-83153-6(9),* Levine, Arthur A. Bks.) Scholastic, Inc.
D'Amico, Carmela & D'Amico, Steve. Ella the Elegant Elephant. 2005. (J). (gr. k-3). 29.95 incl. audio compact disk *(978-0-8045-4128-2(0),* SACD4128) Spoken Arts, Inc.
D'Amico, Carmela & D'Amico, Steven. Ella the Elegant Elephant. 2004. (Illus.). (J). (ENG.). 56p. (gr. -1-3). 17.99 *(978-0-439-62792-4(3));* *(978-0-439-62793-1(1))* Scholastic, Inc. (Levine, Arthur A. Bks.).
—Ella the Elegant Elephant. 2005. (J). (gr. k-3). 27.95 incl. audio *(978-0-8045-6933-0(9),* SAC6933) Spoken Arts, Inc.
D'Amico, Christine. Higgledy-Piggledy: Mabel's World. Bell-Myers, Darcy, illus. 2005. (ENG.). 32p. (J). 16.95 *(978-0-9716631-1-4(4))* Avoomba Group Co.
Dammier, Patti. Got Carrots? Rescued Horse: The Winter Vacation. 2012. 142p. 21.95 *(978-1-4759-2842-6(4))* iUniverse, Inc.
Damon, Emma. Busytime. Damon, Emma, illus. 2010. (Pop-Up Flaps Ser.). (ENG., Illus.). 8p. (J). (gr. k-k). bds. 10.99 *(978-0-230-74454-7(0))* Macmillan Pubs., Ltd. GBR. Dist: Independent Pubs. Group.
Dana, Kimberly. Lucy & Cecee's How to Survive (and Thrive) in Middle School. 2012. 278p. (gr. 4-6). 27.95 *(978-1-4620-3967-8(7));* pap. 17.95 *(978-1-4620-3966-1(9))* iUniverse, Inc.
Daneshvari, Gitty. Class Is Not Dismissed! 2011. (School of Fear Ser.: 2). (ENG.). 336p. (J). (gr. 3-7). pap. 8.99 *(978-0-316-03329-9(4))* Little, Brown Bks. for Young Readers.
—The Final Exam. (School of Fear Ser.: 3). (ENG.). (J). (gr. 3-7). 2012. 352p. pap. 8.99 *(978-0-316-18285-0(0))* 2011. 336p. 16.99 *(978-0-316-18287-4(7))* Little, Brown Bks. for Young Readers.
—Ghoulfriends 'Til the End. 2014. (Monster High Ghoulfriends Ser.: 4). (ENG., Illus.). 256p. (J). (gr. 3-7). 13.99 *(978-0-316-22251-8(8))* Little, Brown Bks. for Young Readers.
—The Ghouls Rule Boxed Set, Set. 2013. (ENG., Illus.). 816p. (J). (gr. 3-7). 39.00 *(978-0-316-32361-1(6))* Little, Brown Bks. for Young Readers.
—School of Fear. 2010. (School of Fear Ser.: 1). (ENG., Illus.). 368p. (J). (gr. 3-7). pap. 8.99 *(978-0-316-03327-5(8))* Little, Brown Bks. for Young Readers.
Daniel: Individual Title Six-Packs. (Literatura 2000 Ser.). (gr. 1-2). 28.00 *(978-0-7635-0129-7(8))* Rigby Education.
Danneberg, Julie. The Big Test. Love, Judy, illus. 2011. (Mrs. Hartwells Classroom Adventures Ser.). (ENG.). 32p. (J). (gr. 1-4). 16.95 *(978-1-58089-360-2(0));* pap. 7.95 *(978-1-58089-361-9(9))* Charlesbridge Publishing, Inc.
—Field-Trip Fiasco. Love, Judy, illus. 2015. (Mrs. Hartwells Classroom Adventures Ser.). (ENG.). 32p. (J). (gr. k-3). 16.95 *(978-1-58089-671-9(5))* Charlesbridge Publishing, Inc.
—First Year Letters. Love, Judy, illus. 2014. 32p. pap. 7.00 *(978-1-61003-320-6(5))* Center for the Collaborative Classroom.
—First Year Letters. Love, Judy, illus. 2003. (Mrs. Hartwells Classroom Adventures Ser.). (ENG.). 32p. (J). (gr. 1-4). 16.95 *(978-1-58089-084-7(9));* pap. 6.95 *(978-1-58089-085-4(7))* Charlesbridge Publishing, Inc.
—¡Que Nervios! El Primer Dia de Escuela. Mlawer, Teresa, tr. Love, Judy, illus. 2006. (Mrs. Hartwells Classroom Adventures Ser.). (SPA & ENG.). 32p. (J). (gr. k-3). pap. 7.95 *(978-1-58089-126-4(8))* Charlesbridge Publishing, Inc.
—Last Day Blues. Love, Judy, illus. 2006. (Mrs. Hartwells Classroom Adventures Ser.). (ENG.). 32p. (J). (gr. k-3). 7.95 *(978-1-58089-104-2(7))* Charlesbridge Publishing, Inc.
Danziger, Paula. Amber Brown Goes Fourth. Ross, Tony, illus. 2007. (Amber Brown Ser.: No. 3). 101p. (gr. 2-5). 15.00 *(978-0-7569-8197-6(2))* Perfection Learning Corp.
—Amber Brown Goes Fourth. (Amber Brown Ser.: No. 3). 112p. (J). (gr. 3-6). pap. 3.99 *(978-0-8072-1291-2(1),* Listening Library) Random Hse. Audio Publishing Group.
—Amber Brown Goes Fourth. Ross, Tony, illus. 2007. (Amber Brown Ser.: 3). (ENG.). 128p. (J). (gr. 2-5). 5.99 *(978-0-14-240901-5(4),* Puffin Books) Penguin Young Readers Group.
—Amber Brown Is Not a Crayon. Ross, Tony, illus. 2006. (Amber Brown Ser.: 1). (ENG.). 96p. (J). (gr. 2-5). 5.99 *(978-0-14-240619-9(8),* Puffin Books) Penguin Young Readers Group.
—Amber Brown Is Not a Crayon. (Amber Brown Ser.: No. 1). 80p. (J). (gr. 3-6). pap. 3.50 *(978-0-8072-1289-9(X),* Listening Library) Random Hse. Audio Publishing Group.
—Amber Brown Sees Red. 2011. (Amber Brown Ser.: No. 6). 7.64 *(978-0-7848-3448-0(2),* Everbind) Marco Bk. Co.
—Amber Brown Sees Red. 2009. (Amber Brown Ser.: 6). (ENG.). 144p. (J). (gr. 2-5). 5.99 *(978-0-14-241261-9(9),* Puffin Books) Penguin Young Readers Group.
—Amber Brown Sees Red. (Amber Brown Ser.: No. 6). 116p. (J). (gr. 3-6). pap. 3.99 *(978-0-8072-1294-3(6),* Listening Library) Random Hse. Audio Publishing Group.
—Amber Brown Sees Red. 2009. (Amber Brown Ser.: 6). (gr. 3-6). lib. bdg. 16.00 *(978-0-613-09442-9(5),* Turtleback) Turtleback Bks.
—Amber Brown Wants Extra Credit. Ross, Tony, illus. 2008. (Amber Brown Ser.: 4). (ENG.). 144p. (J). (gr. 2-5). 5.99 *(978-0-14-241049-3(7),* Puffin Books) Penguin Young Readers Group.
—Amber Brown Wants Extra Credit. (Amber Brown Ser.: No. 4). 120p. (J). (gr. 3-6). pap. 3.99 *(978-0-8072-1292-9(X),* Listening Library) Random Hse. Audio Publishing Group.
—The Cat Ate My Gymsuit. 2006. (ENG.). 176p. (J). (gr. 5-18). 8.99 *(978-0-14-240654-0(6),* Puffin Books) Penguin Young Readers Group.
—Forever Amber Brown. 2008. (Amber Brown Ser.: 5). (ENG.). 128p. (J). (gr. 2-5). 5.99 *(978-0-14-241201-5(5),* Puffin Books) Penguin Young Readers Group.
—Get Ready for Second Grade, Amber Brown. Ross, Tony, illus. 2003. (Is for Amber Ser.). (ENG.). 48p. (J). (gr. 1-3). mass mkt. 3.99 *(978-0-14-250081-1(X),* Penguin Young Readers) Penguin Young Readers Group.
—Get Ready for Second Grade, Amber Brown. Ross, Tony, illus. 2004. (A Is for Amber Ser.). 48p. (gr. k-2). 14.00 *(978-0-7569-2177-4(5))* Perfection Learning Corp.
—Get Ready for Second Grade, Amber Brown. 2003. (Young Amber Brown Easy-To-Read Ser.: 3). (gr. k-3). lib. bdg. 13.55 *(978-0-613-67547-5(9),* Turtleback) Turtleback Bks.
—Orange You Glad It's Halloween, Amber Brown?, 4 bks., Set. Ross, Tony, illus. 2007. (Amber Brown Ser.). (J). (gr. 1-3). pap. 29.95 incl. audio *(978-1-4301-0080-5(X))* Live Oak Media.
—Orange You Glad It's Halloween, Amber Brown? Ross, Tony, illus. 2007. (Is for Amber Ser.). (ENG.). 48p. (J). (gr. 1-3). 3.99 *(978-0-14-240809-4(3),* Penguin Young Readers) Penguin Young Readers Group.
—Orange You Glad It's Halloween, Amber Brown? Ross, Tony, illus. 2007. (Amber Brown Ser.). 48p. (J). (gr. k-3). 11.65 *(978-0-7569-8154-9(9))* Perfection Learning Corp.
—The Pistachio Prescription. 2006. (ENG.). 208p. (J). (gr. 5-18). 8.99 *(978-0-14-240682-3(1),* Puffin Books) Penguin Young Readers Group.
—Second Grade Rules, Amber Brown. Ross, Tony, illus. 2005. (Is for Amber Ser.). (ENG.). 48p. (J). (gr. 1-3). mass mkt. 3.99 *(978-0-14-240421-8(7),* Penguin Young Readers) Penguin Young Readers Group.
—Second Grade Rules, Amber Brown. Ross, Tony, illus. 2005. (Amber Brown Ser.). 48p. (gr. k-2). 14.00 *(978-0-7569-5521-2(1))* Perfection Learning Corp.
—¿Seguiremos Siendo Amigos? 97th ed. 2003.Tr. of Amber Brown is Not a Crayon. (SPA., Illus.). 106p. (gr. 3-5). 24.60 *(978-84-204-4857-2(5),* SAN8575) Harcourt Schl. Pubs.
—Segundo Grado Es Increible, Ambar Dorado. Ross, Tony, illus. 2007. (de Ambar / a Is for Amber Easy-To-Read Ser.).Tr. of Second Grade Rules, Amber Brown. (SPA.). 48p. (gr. k-3). pap. 8.95 *(978-1-59820-594-7(3))* Santillana USA Publishing Co., Inc.
Danziger, Paula, et al. Amber Brown Is on the Move. Lewis, Anthony, illus. 2014. (Amber Brown Ser.: 11). (ENG.). 192p. (J). (gr. 2-5). pap. 6.99 *(978-0-14-751223-9(9),* Puffin Books) Penguin Young Readers Group.
Danzinger, Paula. Get Ready for Second Grade, Amber Brown. Ross, Tony, illus. 2003. pap. 31.95 incl. audio compact disk *(978-1-59112-562-4(6))* Live Oak Media.
Dara Cicciarelli. Sam Loses His Sneaker. Hoke, Jason, illus. 2011. 20p. pap. 24.95 *(978-1-4560-9178-1(6))* America Star Bks.
Darling, Angela. Lindsay Likes Nick Crush: Does He Like Her Too? 2013. (Crush Ser.: 3). (ENG., Illus.). 144p. (J). (gr. 3-7). 15.99 *(978-1-4424-8045-2(9),* Simon Spotlight) Simon Spotlight.
—Lindsay's Surprise Crush. 2013. (Crush Ser.: 3). (ENG., Illus.). 144p. (J). (gr. 3-7). pap. 5.99 *(978-1-4424-8042-1(4),* Simon Spotlight) Simon Spotlight.
Daudet, Alphonse. The Siege of Berlin & Other Stories. 2004. reprint ed. pap. 1.99 *(978-1-4192-8248-5(4));* pap. 15.95 *(978-1-4191-8248-8(X))* Kessinger Publishing, LLC.
David Austin Clar Studio Staff, illus. Surprise Party. 2003. (Rainbow Fish & Friends Ser.). (ENG.). 24p. (J). (gr. -1). 3.99 *(978-1-59014-107-6(5))* North-South Bks., Inc.
David, Stuart. My Brilliant Idea (and How It Caused My Downfall) (ENG.). 240p. (YA). (gr. 7). 2017. pap. 9.99 *(978-0-544-93886-1(0))* 2016. 17.99 *(978-0-544-69961-8(0))* Houghton Mifflin Harcourt Publishing Co. (HMH Books For Young Readers).
Davidson, Danica. Escape from the Overworld. 2015. (Unofficial Overworld Adventure Ser.). (ENG.). 112p. (J). (gr. 1-7). pap. 7.99 *(978-1-63450-103-3(9),* Sky Pony Pr.) Skyhorse Publishing Co., Inc.
Davidson, Jenny. The Explosionist. 2008. 464p. (YA). (gr. 7-18). lib. bdg. 18.89 *(978-0-06-123976-2(3),* HarperTeen) HarperCollins Pubs.
Davies, Jacqueline. The Candy Smash. (Lemonade War Ser.). (ENG., Illus.). 240p. (J). (gr. 2-5). 2014. pap. 7.99 *(978-0-544-22500-8(7),* HMH Books For Young Readers) 2013. 15.99 *(978-0-544-02208-9(4))* Houghton Mifflin Harcourt Publishing Co.
—The Lemonade Crime. 2011. (Lemonade War Ser.: 2). (ENG., Illus.). 160p. (J). (gr. 2-5). 15.99 *(978-0-547-27967-1(1))* Houghton Mifflin Harcourt Publishing Co.
—The Lemonade Crime. 2012. (Lemonade War Ser.: 2). lib. bdg. 18.40 *(978-0-606-24518-0(9),* Turtleback) Turtleback Bks.
—Nothing but Trouble. 2016. (Nothing but Trouble Ser.: 1). 320p. (J). (gr. 3-7). 16.99 *(978-0-06-236988-8(1),* Tegen, Katherine Bks) HarperCollins Pubs.
Davies, Kate, illus. Little Squeak School. 2014. (J). *(978-1-4351-5582-4(3))* Barnes & Noble, Inc.
—Welcome to the Mouse House. 2014. (J). *(978-1-4351-5583-1(1))* Barnes & Noble, Inc.
Davies, Matt. Ben Draws Trouble. 2015. (ENG., Illus.). 32p. (J). (gr. -1-2). 17.99 *(978-1-59643-795-1(2),* 9781596437951) Roaring Brook Pr.
Davies, Mike. Lousy Thinking: Hitching a Ride on a Schoolboy's Mind. 2012. 162p. pap. *(978-1-906954-53-6(4))* Live It Publishing.
Davies, Peter. Molly's Magic Pencil: The Blue Genie. 2011. 28p. (gr. 1-2). 14.99 *(978-1-4567-3018-5(5))* AuthorHouse.
Davis, Diane. Something Is Wrong at My House: A Book about Parents' Fighting. Neely, Keith R., illus. 2010.Tr. of Algo anda mal en mi Casa. (SPA & ENG.). 32p. (J). (gr. -1-3). pap. 9.95 *(978-1-884734-65-6(0))* Parenting Pr., Inc.
Davis, Eleanor. Secret Science Alliance. 2010. (J). *(978-1-59990-143-5(9))* Bloomsbury Publishing USA.
—The Secret Science Alliance. Davis, Eleanor, illus. 2009. (ENG., Illus.). 160p. (YA). (gr. 3-6). pap. 16.99 *(978-1-59990-396-5(2),* 9781599903965, Bloomsbury USA Childrens) Bloomsbury Publishing USA.
—The Secret Science Alliance & the Copycat Crook. Davis, Eleanor, illus. 2009. (ENG., Illus.). 160p. (J). (gr. 3-6). 18.99 *(978-1-59990-142-8(0),* 9781599901428, Bloomsbury USA Childrens) Bloomsbury Publishing USA.
Davis, Graeme. Re-Read Harry Potter & the Chamber of Secrets Today! an Unauthorized Guide. 2008. 112p. pap. 15.49 *(978-1-934840-72-6(6))* Nimble Bks. LLC.
Davis, Heather. The Clearing. 2010. (ENG., Illus.). 224p. (YA). (gr. 9). pap. 8.99 *(978-0-547-26367-0(8))* Houghton Mifflin Harcourt Publishing Co.
Davis Jones, Melanie, et al. The School Box: Field Day - 100th Da of School - One Happy Classroom. Molnar, Albert & McKillip Thornburgh, Rebecca, illus. 2004. (Rookie Reader Ser.). (ENG.). 96p. (J). (gr. k-2). pap. 9.95 *(978-0-516-24554-6(6),* Children's Pr.) Scholastic Library Publishing.
Davis, Katie. Kindergarten Rocks! 2008. (ENG., Illus.). 32p. (J). (gr. -1-3). pap. 7.99 *(978-0-15-206468-6(0))* Houghton Mifflin Harcourt Publishing Co.
Davis, Lois. Happy to Be Me. 2013. 20p. pap. 24.95 *(978-1-63000-789-8(7))* America Star Bks.
Davis, Milton J. Amber & the Hidden City. 2013. 220p. pap. 16.95 *(978-0-9800842-7-6(X))* MVmedia.
Davis, Rebecca. Jake Riley: Irreparably Damaged. 2003. 240p. (J). 16.89 *(978-0-06-051838-7(3))* HarperCollins Pubs.
Davis, Rhonda L. Faces of Darkness: The Daredevil Friends. 2008. 284p. pap. 14.95 *(978-1-934925-75-1(6),* Eloquent Bks.) Strategic Book Publishing & Rights Agency (SBPRA).
Davis, Samira And Edwina. Nikko & Sierra's Adventures: I Hate Knuckle Sandwiches. 2011. 24p. pap. 11.32 *(978-1-4634-0408-6(5))* AuthorHouse.
DAVIS, Tamika. If i knew back then what i know Now. 2010. 119p. pap. 15.00 *(978-0-557-37544-8(4))* Lulu Pr., Inc.
Davis, Tanita S. Peas & Carrots. 2016. (ENG.). 288p. (YA). (gr. 7). 17.99 *(978-0-553-51281-6(1));* lib. bdg. 20.99 *(978-0-553-51282-3(X))* Random Hse. Children's Bks. (Knopf Bks. for Young Readers).
Davis, Terry. If Rock & Roll Were a Machine. 2015. (ENG., Illus.). 256p. (YA). (gr. 7). pap. 10.99 *(978-1-4814-5632-6(6),* Simon & Schuster Bks. For Young Readers) Simon & Schuster Bks. For Young Readers.
Dawe, Ted. Into the River. 2016. (ENG.). 304p. (J). (gr. 7). 17.99 *(978-1-943818-19-8(3))* Polis Bks.
Dawson, Jennifer. Silly Sally Sue. 2013. 24p. pap. 24.95 *(978-1-62709-938-7(7))* America Star Bks.
Dawson, Stephanie Mara. The best recess Ever. 2nd ed. 2004. (Illus.). 28p. (J). per. 15.95 *(978-0-9748990-0-8(3))* Bk. Nook Productions.
Day, Susie. Serafina67 - "Urgently Requires Life" 2010. (ENG.). 256p. (J). (gr. 7-12). 8.99 *(978-0-545-07352-3(9),* Scholastic Paperbacks) Scholastic, Inc.
De Baun, Hillary Hall. The Last Stop Before Heaven. Cooper, Floyd, illus. 2012. (ENG.). 236p. (J). pap. 9.00 *(978-0-8028-5398-1(6),* Eerdmans Bks For Young Readers) Eerdmans, William B. Publishing Co.

S

de Brunhoff, Laurent. Babar et ses Amis a L'Ecole. (Babar Ser.). (FRE., Illus.). 48p. (J). (gr. -1-3). 19.95 (978-0-7859-8802-1(5)) French & European Pubns., Inc.

—Babar et ses Amis Font les Courses. (Babar Ser.). (FRE., Illus.). 48p. (J). (gr. -1-3). 19.95 (978-0-7859-8810-6(6)) French & European Pubns., Inc.

De Campi, Alex. Kat & Mouse, Vol. 3. 2017. (ENG., Illus.). 96p. pap. 5.99 (978-1-59816-550-0(X), 9781598165500) TOKYOPOP, Inc.

—Kat & Mouse Vol. 1: Teacher Torture, 1 vol. Manfredi, Federica, illus. 2009. (Tokyopop Ser.). (ENG.). 96p. (gr. 2-6). 25.65 (978-1-59961-564-6(9)) Spotlight.

—Kat & Mouse Vol. 2: Tripped, 1 vol. Manfredi, Federica, illus. 2009. (Tokyopop Ser.). (ENG.). 96p. (gr. 2-6). 25.65 (978-1-59961-565-3(7)) Spotlight.

—Kat & Mouse Vol. 3: The Ice Storm, 1 vol. Manfredi, Federica, illus. 2009. (Tokyopop Ser.). (ENG.). 96p. (gr. 2-6). 25.65 (978-1-59961-566-0(5)) Spotlight.

De Fonté, Desiree. Jazzy: A Story of Love. 2012. 26p. 24.95 (978-1-4626-5106-1(2)) America Star Bks.

De Goldi, Kate. The 10 PM Question. 2010. (ENG., Illus.). 256p. (YA). (gr. 7-18). 15.99 (978-0-7636-4939-5(2)) Candlewick Pr.

de Kinder, Jan. Red. 2015. (ENG., Illus.). 32p. (J). 16.00 (978-0-8028-5446-9(X), Eerdmans Bks For Young Readers) Eerdmans, William B. Publishing Co.

De la Cruz, Melissa. The Ashley Project. 2014. (Ashley Project Ser.: 1). (ENG., Illus.). 288p. (J). (gr. 4-8). pap. 6.99 (978-1-4424-9033-8(0), Aladdin) Simon & Schuster Children's Publishing.

—The Ashleys. 2008. (Ashleys Ser.: Bk. 1). (ENG.). 272p. (J). (gr. 4-8). pap. 9.99 (978-1-4169-3406-6(5), Simon & Schuster Bks. For Young Readers) Simon & Schuster Bks. For Young Readers.

—Jealous? 2008. (Ashleys Ser.: Bk. 2). (ENG.). 256p. (J). (gr. 4-8). pap. 9.99 (978-1-4169-3407-3(3), Simon & Schuster Bks. For Young Readers) Simon & Schuster Bks. For Young Readers.

—Popularity Takeover. 2015. (Ashley Project Ser.: 4). (ENG., Illus.). 272p. (J). (gr. 4-8). 17.99 (978-1-4814-0974-2(3), Aladdin) Simon & Schuster Children's Publishing.

—Social Order. 2014. (Ashley Project Ser.: 2). (ENG., Illus.). 288p. (J). (gr. 4-8). 16.99 (978-1-4814-0667-3(1), Simon & Schuster/Paula Wiseman Bks.) Simon & Schuster/Paula Wiseman Bks.

de Lint, Charles. The Blue Girl. 2006. (ENG.). 384p. (YA). (gr. 7-18). reprint ed. 7.99 (978-0-14-240545-1(0), Firebird) Penguin Young Readers Group.

De Valera, Sinead. The Magic Gifts: Classic Irish Fairytales. (Illus.). 224p. 16.95 (978-0-86327-822-8(1)) Wolfhound Pr. IRL. Dist: Irish Bks. & Media, Inc.

Dean, Carolee. Comfort. 2004. (ENG.). 256p. (YA). (gr. 7-18). pap. 14.95 (978-0-618-43912-6(9)) Houghton Mifflin Harcourt Publishing Co.

—Forget Me Not. (ENG.). (YA). (gr. 9). 2013. 400p. pap. 11.99 (978-1-4424-3255-0(1)) 2012. 384p. 16.99 (978-1-4424-3254-3(3)) Simon Pulse. (Simon Pulse).

Dean, James. Too Cool for School. 2014. (Pete the Cat I Can Read Ser.). (J). lib. bdg. 13.55 (978-0-606-35062-4(4), Turtleback) Turtleback Bks.

Dean, James & Dean, Kimberly. Too Cool for School. Dean, James & Dean, Kimberly, illus. 2014. (My First I Can Read Ser.). (ENG., Illus.). 32p. (J). (gr. -1-3). 16.99 (978-0-06-211076-3(4)); pap. 3.99 (978-0-06-211075-6(6)) HarperCollins Pubs.

Dean, Zoey. Blonde Ambition. 2004. (A-List Ser.: 3). (ENG.). 240p. (YA). (gr. 10-17). pap. 9.99 (978-0-316-73474-5(8), Poppy) Little, Brown Bks. for Young Readers.

DeAngelo, Jeremy. The Out Crowd. 2006. (J). pap. (978-0-88092-613-3(9)); lib. bdg. (978-0-88092-612-6(0)) Royal Fireworks Publishing Co.

Deb, Capone. Dumplings are Delicious Learning & Activity Guide. Stan, Jaskiel, illus. 2007. 20p. (J). 9.95 (978-0-9728666-9-9(8)) As Simple As That Publishing.

Decker-Ahmed, Stasia. The Weirder the Better. 2011. (ENG.). 175p. (J). (gr. 4-6). pap. 8.99 (978-0-930773-97-7(7)) Black Heron Pr.

DeClements, Barthe. Fourth Grade Wizards. 2008. (ENG.). 128p. (J). (gr. 3-7). 5.99 (978-0-14-241348-7(8), Puffin Books) Penguin Young Readers Group.

—Nothing's Fair in Fifth Grade. 2008. (ENG.). 144p. (J). (gr. 3-7). 5.99 (978-0-14-241349-4(6), Puffin Books) Penguin Young Readers Group.

DeClements, Barthe & Declements, Barthe. Sixth Grade Can Really Kill You. 2008. (ENG.). 160p. (J). (gr. 3-7). 5.99 (978-0-14-241380-7(1), Puffin Books) Penguin Young Readers Group.

Dee, Barbara. Just Another Day in My Insanely Real Life. 2007. (Mix Ser.). (ENG.). 256p. (J). (gr. 4-8). pap. 7.99 (978-1-4169-4739-4(6), Aladdin) Simon & Schuster Children's Publishing.

—Solving Zoe. 2010. (Mix Ser.). (ENG.). 256p. (J). (gr. 4-8). pap. 7.99 (978-1-4169-9159-5(X), Aladdin) Simon & Schuster Children's Publishing.

—Star-Crossed. 2017. (ENG., Illus.). 288p. (J). (gr. 4-8). 16.99 (978-1-4814-7848-9(6), Simon & Schuster/Paula Wiseman Bks.) Simon & Schuster/Paula Wiseman Bks.

—This Is Me from Now On. 2010. (Mix Ser.). (ENG.). 272p. (J). (gr. 4-8). pap. 7.99 (978-1-4169-9414-5(9), Aladdin) Simon & Schuster Children's Publishing.

—Trauma Queen. 2011. (Mix Ser.). (ENG.). 272p. (J). (gr. 4-8). pap. 6.99 (978-1-4424-0923-1(1), Aladdin) Simon & Schuster Children's Publishing.

Dee, Carole. The Bully Returns to Margaret. 2012. 36p. pap. 10.95 (978-1-4626-7766-5(5)) America Star Bks.

Deedy, Carmen Agra. The Library Dragon, 1 vol. White, Michael P., illus. 2012. (ENG.). 32p. (J). 19.95 (978-1-56145-639-0(X)) Peachtree Pubs.

—Return of the Library Dragon, 1 vol. White, Michael P., illus. 2012. (ENG.). 32p. (J). 16.95 (978-1-56145-621-5(7)) Peachtree Pubs.

DeFelice, Cynthia. The Ghost & Mrs. Hobbs. 2010. (Ghost Mysteries Ser.: 2). (ENG.). 208p. (J). (gr. 3-7). pap. 8.99 (978-0-312-62909-0(5), 9780312629090) Square Fish.

Degen, Bruce. I Gotta Draw. Degen, Bruce, illus. 2012. (ENG., Illus.). 40p. (J). (gr. k-4). 16.99 (978-0-06-028417-6(X)) HarperCollins Pubs.

deGroat, Diane. Ants in Your Pants, Worms in Your Plants! Gilbert Goes Green. deGroat, Diane, illus. 2011. (Gilbert Ser.). (ENG., Illus.). 32p. (J). (gr. -1-3). 16.99 (978-0-06-176511-7(2)) HarperCollins Pubs.

—April Fool! Watch Out at School! deGroat, Diane, illus. 2009. (Gilbert Ser.). (Illus.). 32p. (J). (gr. -1-3). (ENG.). 17.99 (978-0-06-143042-8(0)); lib. bdg. 18.89 (978-0-06-143043-5(9)) HarperCollins Pubs.

—Brand-New Pencils, Brand-New Books. deGroat, Diane, illus. (ENG., Illus.). 32p. (J). (gr. -1-3). 2007. pap. 6.99 (978-0-06-072616-4(4)) 2005. 15.99 (978-0-06-072613-3(X)) HarperCollins Pubs.

—Brand-New Pencils, Brand-New Books. deGroat, Diane, illus. 2007. (Gilbert & Friends Ser.). (Illus.). (J). (gr. -1-3). 14.65 (978-0-7569-8087-0(9)) Perfection Learning Corp.

—Happy Birthday to You, You Belong in a Zoo. deGroat, Diane, illus. 2007. (Gilbert & Friends Ser.). (ENG., Illus.). 32p. (J). (gr. -1-3). pap. 6.99 (978-0-06-001029-4(0)) HarperCollins Pubs.

—Happy Birthday to You, You Belong in a Zoo. deGroat, Diane, illus. 2007. (Gilbert & Friends Ser.). (Illus.). (gr. -1-3). 17.00 (978-0-7569-8108-2(5)) Perfection Learning Corp.

—Jingle Bells, Homework Smells. deGroat, Diane, illus. 2003. (ENG., Illus.). 32p. (J). (gr. -1-3). pap. 6.99 (978-0-688-17545-0(7)) HarperCollins Pubs.

—Jingle Bells, Homework Smells. deGroat, Diane, illus. 2008. (Illus.). (J). (gr. -1-3). pap. 16.95 incl. audio (978-1-4301-0419-3(8)) Live Oak Media.

—No More Pencils, No More Books, No More Teacher's Dirty Looks! deGroat, Diane, illus. (Gilbert Ser.). (Illus.). 32p. (J). (gr. -1-3). 2009. (ENG.). pap. 6.99 (978-0-06-079116-2(0)) 2006. 15.99 (978-0-06-079114-8(4)) 2006. lib. bdg. 18.89 (978-0-06-079115-5(2)) HarperCollins Pubs.

—Trick or Treat, Smell My Feet. 4 bks., Set. 2008. (J). (gr. -1-2). pap. 37.95 incl. audio (978-1-4301-0426-1(0)); pap. 39.95 incl. audio compact disk (978-1-4301-0428-5(7)) Live Oak Media.

DeGross, Monalisa. Donavan's Double Trouble. Bates, Amy, illus. 192p. (J). (gr. 2-5). 2008. lib. bdg. 16.89 (978-0-06-077294-9(8)) 2007. (ENG.). 16.99 (978-0-06-077293-2(X)) HarperCollins Pubs. (Amistad).

DeJong, Meindert. The Wheel on the School. 82p. (J). pap. 5.95 (978-0-8072-1539-5(2), Listening Library) Random Hse. Audio Publishing Group.

Delgado, Alvin. Spirit of the Gang. 2007. 192p. pap. 12.95 (978-1-4303-1334-2(X)) Lulu Pr., Inc.

Delios, Louis & Sharma, Vicky. Tomorrow Will Be a New Day. 2011. 20p. pap. (978-1-4269-7318-5(7)) Trafford Publishing (UK) Ltd.

Dellasega, Cheryl. Nugrl90, 0 vols. LaPierre, Karina, illus. 2007. (Bloggrls Ser.: 1). (ENG.). 192p. (YA). (gr. 7-11). pap. 9.99 (978-0-7614-5396-3(2), 9780761453963, Amazon Children's Publishing) Amazon Publishing.

DelleCava, Karen. A Closer Look. 2011. 304p. (YA). (gr. 9-18). 16.95 (978-1-934813-49-2(4)) Westside Bks.

Dellicurti, Dana. Joey's First Day at School. 2008. 24p. per. 14.95 (978-1-4327-1408-6(2)) Outskirts Pr., Inc.

Delsol, Wendy. Flock. 2013. (ENG.). 400p. (YA). (gr. 7). pap. 8.99 (978-0-7636-6467-1(7)) Candlewick Pr.

—Frost. (ENG., Illus.). (YA). (gr. 7). 2012. 384p. pap. 8.99 (978-0-7636-6249-3(6)) 2011. 376p. 15.99 (978-0-7636-5386-6(1)) Candlewick Pr.

—Stork. (ENG., Illus.). (YA). (gr. 7). 2011. 368p. pap. 8.99 (978-0-7636-5687-4(9)) 2010. 357p. 15.99 (978-0-7636-4844-2(2)) Candlewick Pr.

Deluca, Laura. Demon. 2013. 298p. pap. 12.95 (978-1-938397-46-2(0), Pagan Writers Pr.) Mroczka Media.

Delval, Marie-Hélène. L 'Ecole des Geants. pap. 18.95 (978-2-227-72802-8(7)) Bayard Editions FRA. Dist: Distribooks, Inc.

Demas, Corinne. Middle Grade Novel. Date not set. 196p. (J). (gr. 3-7). 15.99 (978-0-06-028725-2(X)); 4.99 (978-0-06-440845-5(0)) HarperCollins Pubs.

—Pirates Go to School. Manders, John, illus. 2011. (ENG.). 32p. (J). (gr. -1-3). 16.99 (978-0-545-20629-7(4), Orchard Bks.) Scholastic, Inc.

DeMatteis, J. M. Imaginalis. 2010. (ENG.). 256p. (J). (gr. 3-7). 16.99 (978-0-06-173286-7(9), Tegen, Katherine Bks) HarperCollins Pubs.

Demcak, Andrew. Ghost Songs. 2016. (ENG., Illus.). (J). 24.99 **(978-1-63533-019-9(X))** 2014. 210p. pap. 14.99 (978-1-62798-795-0(9)) Dreamspinner Pr. (Harmony Ink Pr.).

Demetrios, Heather. Bad Romance. 2017. (ENG.). 368p. (YA). 17.99 (978-1-62779-772-6(6), 9781627797726, Holt, Henry & Co. Bks. For Young Readers) Holt, Henry & Co.

Denchfield, Nick. Charlie Chick Goes to School. Parker, Ant, illus. 2015. (Charlie Chick Ser.). (ENG.). 16p. (J). (-k). 12.99 (978-1-4472-7718-7(X)) Pan Macmillan GBR. Dist: Independent Pubs. Group.

Denice, Sonia. Chow-E-Chowz: Saved by a Whistle. 2011. 44p. pap. 18.46 (978-1-4567-1020-0(6)) AuthorHouse.

Denman, K. L. La Cache: (Stuff We All Get), 1 vol. 2012. (FRE.). 128p. (J). (gr. 5-9). pap. 9.95 (978-1-4598-0314-5(0)) Orca Bk. Pubs. USA.

—Mirror Image, 1 vol. 2007. (Orca Currents Ser.). (ENG.). 128p. (J). (gr. 5-9). per. 9.95 (978-1-55143-665-4(5)) Orca Bk. Pubs. USA.

Denou, Violeta. Teo en la Escuela (Teo at School) (SPA.). 32p. (J). 12.95 (978-84-7176-311-2(7)) Timun Mas, Editorial S.A. ESP. Dist: AIMS International Bks., Inc.

Dent, Grace & Dent, Grace. Diva Without a Cause. 2009. (ENG.). 240p. (YA). (gr. 10-17). pap. 18.99 (978-0-316-03482-1(7), Poppy) Little, Brown Bks. for Young Readers.

dePaola, Tomie. Meet the Barkers: Morgan & Moffat Go to School. dePaola, Tomie, illus. 2003. (Barker Twins Ser.). (ENG., Illus.). 32p. (J). (gr. -1-3). 6.99 (978-0-14-250083-5(6), Puffin Books) Penguin Young Readers Group.

—Meet the Barkers: Morgan & Moffat Go to School. 2005. (J). (gr. k-3). pap. 17.95 incl. audio (978-0-8045-6934-7(7), SAC6934) Spoken Arts, Inc.

—Stagestruck. dePaola, Tomie, illus. 2007. (ENG., Illus.). 32p. (J). (gr. -1-3). pap. 6.99 (978-0-14-240899-5(9), Puffin Books) Penguin Young Readers Group.

—Stagestruck. dePaola, Tomie, illus. 2007. (Illus.). (gr. -1-3). 17.00 (978-0-7569-8159-4(X)) Perfection Learning Corp.

—Trouble in the Barkers' Class. dePaola, Tomie, illus. 2006. (Barker Twins Ser.). (ENG., Illus.). 32p. (J). (gr. -1-3). reprint ed. pap. 6.99 (978-0-14-240585-7(X), Puffin Books) Penguin Young Readers Group.

dePaola, Tomie & de, Paola Tomie. Oliver Button Es una Nena. 2003.Tr. of Oliver Button Is a Sissy. (SPA.). 48p. (J). (gr. k-1). 14.99 (978-84-241-8108-6(5)) Everest Editora ESP. Dist: Lectorum Pubns., Inc.

Derby, Kenneth. The Top Ten Ways to Ruin the First Day of 5th Grade. 2004. (ENG.). 176p. (J). (gr. 4-6). tchr. ed. 16.95 (978-0-8234-1851-0(0)) Holiday Hse., Inc.

Derek the Ghost Staff. Monsters on the March. Fischer, Scott M., illus. 2013. (Scary School Ser.: 2). (ENG.). 272p. (J). (gr. 3-7). pap. 6.99 (978-0-06-196097-0(7)) HarperCollins Pubs.

—The Northern Frights. Fischer, Scott M., illus. 2013. (Scary School Ser.: 3). (ENG.). 272p. (J). (gr. 3-7). 16.99 (978-0-06-196098-7(5)) HarperCollins Pubs.

—Scary School. Fischer, Scott M., illus. (Scary School Ser.: 1). (ENG.). (J). (gr. 3-7). 2012. 272p. pap. 6.99 (978-0-06-196094-9(2)) 2011. 256p. 16.99 (978-0-06-196092-5(6)) HarperCollins Pubs.

Deriso, C. H. Elisabeth & the Unwanted Advice. 2016. (Babysitter Chronicles Ser.). (ENG., Illus.). 160p. (gr. 4-7). lib. bdg. 26.65 (978-1-4965-2757-8(7)) Stone Arch Bks.

Deriso, Christine Hurley. Elisabeth & the Unwanted Advice. 2016. (Babysitter Chronicles Ser.). (ENG., Illus.). 160p. (gr. 4-7). pap. 6.95 (978-1-4914-8864-5(6)) Stone Arch Bks.

—Talia Talk. 2009. 184p. (J). pap. (978-0-375-84496-6(1), Delacorte Pr) Random House Publishing Group.

Derting, Kimberly. Body Finder. 2011. (Body Finder Ser.: 1). (ENG.). 352p. (YA). (gr. 9). pap. 9.99 (978-0-06-177983-1(0)) HarperCollins Pubs.

—Desires of the Dead. 2012. (Body Finder Ser.: 2). (ENG.). 384p. (YA). (gr. 9). pap. 8.99 (978-0-06-177986-2(5)) HarperCollins Pubs.

deRubertis, Barbara. Bobby Baboon's Banana Be-Bop. Alley, R. W., illus. 2010. (Animal Antics A to Z Ser.). 32p. (J). lib. bdg. 22.60 (978-1-57565-305-1(2)); (ENG.). (gr. -1-3). pap. 7.95 (978-1-57565-301-3(X)) Kane Press, Inc.

—Una Coleccion para Kate (A Collection for Kate) Fiammenghi, Gioia, illus. 2007. (Math Matters Ser.). (SPA.). 29p. (J). (gr. -1-3). pap. 5.95 (978-1-57565-240-5(4)) Kane Press, Inc.

—Lana Llama's Little Lamb. Alley, R. W., illus. 2011. (Animal Antics A to Z Ser.). 32p. (J). pap. 45.32 (978-0-7613-7658-3(5)); (ENG.). lib. bdg. 22.60 (978-1-57565-333-4(8)); (gr. -1-3). pap. 7.95 (978-1-57565-324-2(9)) Kane Press, Inc.

—Nina Nandu's Nervous Noggin. Alley, R. W., illus. 2011. (Animal Antics A to Z Ser.). 32p. (J). pap. 45.32 (978-0-7613-7660-6(7)); (ENG.). lib. bdg. 22.60 (978-1-57565-335-8(4)); (gr. -1-3). pap. 7.95 (978-1-57565-326-6(5)) Kane Press, Inc.

—Quentin Quokka's Quick Questions. Alley, R. W., illus. 2011. (Animal Antics A to Z Ser.). 32p. (J). pap. 45.32 (978-0-7613-7663-7(1)); lib. bdg. 22.60 (978-1-57565-338-9(9)); (gr. -1-3). pap. 7.95 (978-1-57565-329-7(X)) Kane Press, Inc.

Derubertis, Barbara. Xavier Ox's Xylophone Experiment. Alley, R. W., illus. 2011. (Animal Antics A to Z Set III Ser.). pap. 45.32 (978-0-7613-8433-5(2)) Kane Press, Inc.

deRubertis, Barbara. Xavier Ox's Xylophone Experiment. Alley, R. W., illus. 2011. (Animal Antics A to Z Ser.). 32p. (J). (ENG.). pap. 7.95 (978-1-57565-349-5(4)); lib. bdg. 22.60 (978-1-57565-357-0(5)) Kane Press, Inc.

—Yoko Yak's Yakety Yakking. Alley, R. W., illus. 2011. (Animal Antics A to Z Ser.). pap. 7.95 (978-1-57565-350-1(8)); lib. bdg. 22.60 (978-1-57565-358-7(3)) Kane Press, Inc.

deRubertis, Barbara & DeRubertis, Barbara. Bobby Baboon's Banana Be-Bop. Alley, R. W., illus. 2012. (Animal Antics A to Z Ser.). 32p. (J). (gr. 2 — 1). cd-rom 7.95 (978-1-57565-395-2(8)) Kane Press, Inc.

—Lana Llama's Little Lamb. Alley, R. W., illus. 2012. (Animal Antics A to Z Ser.). 32p. (J). (gr. 2 — 1). cd-rom 7.95 (978-1-57565-405-8(9)) Kane Press, Inc.

—Nina Nandu's Nervous Noggin. Alley, R. W., illus. 2012. (Animal Antics A to Z Ser.). 32p. (J). (gr. 2 — 1). cd-rom 7.95 (978-1-57565-407-2(5)) Kane Press, Inc.

—Quentin Quokka's Quick Questions. Alley, R. W., illus. 2012. (Animal Antics A to Z Ser.). 32p. (J). (gr. 2 — 1). cd-rom 7.95 (978-1-57565-410-2(5)) Kane Press, Inc.

—Xavier Ox's Xylophone Experiment. Alley, R. W., illus. 2012. (Animal Antics A to Z Ser.). 32p. (J). (gr. 2 — 1). cd-rom 7.95 (978-1-57565-417-1(2)) Kane Press, Inc.

—Yoko Yak's Yakety Yakking. Alley, R. W., illus. 2012. (Animal Antics A to Z Ser.). 32p. (J). (gr. 2 — 1). cd-rom 7.95 (978-1-57565-418-8(0)) Kane Press, Inc.

Desir, C. Fault Line. 2013. (ENG.). 240p. (YA). (gr. 10). 16.99 (978-1-4424-6072-0(5), Simon Pulse) Simon Pulse.

Despain, Bree. The Dark Divine. 2010. (ENG.). 384p. (gr. 7). pap. 9.99 (978-1-60684-154-9(8), Carolrhoda Lab™) Lerner Publishing Group.

Dessen, Sarah. Just Listen. 2008. (ENG.). 400p. (YA). (gr. 7-18). 10.99 (978-0-14-241097-4(7), Speak) Penguin Young Readers Group.

—Just Listen. 2007. 20.00 (978-0-7569-8270-6(7)) Perfection Learning Corp.

—Just Listen. 2008. 22.10 (978-1-4178-2016-0(0), Turtleback) Turtleback Bks.

—What Happened to Goodbye. 2013. (ENG.). 432p. (YA). (gr. 7). pap. 9.99 (978-0-14-242383-7(1), Speak) Penguin Young Readers Group.

—What Happened to Goodbye. 2013. lib. bdg. 20.85 (978-0-606-30864-9(4), Turtleback) Turtleback Bks.

Destiny, A. & Helms, Rhonda. Never Too Late. 2015. (Flirt Ser.). (ENG., Illus.). 224p. (YA). (gr. 7). pap. 9.99 (978-1-4814-5188-8(X), Simon Pulse) Simon Pulse.

Deuker, Carl. Gutless. 2017. (ENG.). 336p. (YA). (gr. 7). pap. 9.99 **(978-1-328-74206-3(7)**, HMH Books For Young Readers) Houghton Mifflin Harcourt Publishing Co.

—Gym Candy. 2008. (ENG.). 320p. (YA). (gr. 7). pap. 9.99 (978-0-547-07631-7(2)) Houghton Mifflin Harcourt Publishing Co.

—Gym Candy. 2008. 313p. 19.00 (978-1-60686-376-3(2)) Perfection Learning Corp.

—High Heat. 2005. (ENG.). 352p. (J). (gr. 8-18). pap. 8.99 (978-0-06-057248-8(5), HarperTeen) HarperCollins Pubs.

Deutsch, Stacia. The Friendship Code. Fernandez, Andrea, illus. 2017. (Girls Who Code Ser.: 1). (ENG.). 144p. (J). (gr. 3-7). 12.99 **(978-0-399-54251-0(5)**, Penguin Workshop) Penguin Young Readers Group.

DeVillers, Julia. How My Private Personal Journal Became a Bestseller. 2005. (ENG.). 224p. (J). (gr. 3-7). 6.99 (978-0-14-240332-7(6), Puffin Books) Penguin Young Readers Group.

—New Girl in Town. Pooler, Paige, illus. (Liberty Porter, First Daughter Ser.: 2). (ENG.). (J). (gr. 3-7). 2011. 224p. pap. 6.99 (978-1-4169-9129-8(8)) 2010. 208p. 15.99 (978-1-4169-9128-1(X)) Simon & Schuster/Paula Wiseman Bks. (Simon & Schuster/Paula Wiseman Bks.).

DeVillers, Julia & Roy, Jennifer. Double Feature. 2012. (Mix Ser.). (ENG.). 288p. (J). (gr. 4-8). pap. 7.99 (978-1-4424-3403-5(1), Aladdin) Simon & Schuster Children's Publishing.

—Triple Trouble. 2014. (Mix Ser.). (ENG., Illus.). 240p. (J). (gr. 4-8). pap. 7.99 (978-1-4424-3406-6(6), Aladdin) Simon & Schuster Children's Publishing.

—Triple Trouble. 2013. (ENG.). 240p. (J). (gr. 4-8). 16.99 (978-1-4424-3405-9(8), Simon & Schuster/Paula Wiseman Bks.) Simon & Schuster/Paula Wiseman Bks.

DeVillers, Julia & Roy, Jennifer Rozines. Double Feature. 2012. (ENG.). 272p. (J). (gr. 4-8). 16.99 (978-1-4424-3402-8(3), Aladdin) Simon & Schuster Children's Publishing.

—Take Two. 2010. (Mix Ser.). (ENG.). 304p. (J). (gr. 4-8). pap. 7.99 (978-1-4169-6731-6(1), Aladdin) Simon & Schuster Children's Publishing.

—Take Two. 2010. (ENG.). 240p. (J). (gr. 4-8). 16.99 (978-1-4169-7533-5(0), Simon & Schuster/Paula Wiseman Bks.) Simon & Schuster/Paula Wiseman Bks.

—Times Squared. 2011. (Mix Ser.). (ENG.). (J). (gr. 4-8). 272p. pap. 7.99 (978-1-4169-6732-3(X)); 240p. 16.99 (978-1-4169-7532-8(2)) Simon & Schuster Children's Publishing. (Aladdin).

—Trading Faces. 2008. (ENG.). 304p. (J). (gr. 4-8). 16.99 (978-1-4169-7531-1(4), Simon & Schuster/Paula Wiseman Bks.) Simon & Schuster/Paula Wiseman Bks.

Devore, Laurie. How to Break a Boy. 2017. (ENG.). 352p. (YA). 17.99 (978-1-250-08286-2(2), 9781250082862) Imprint IND. Dist: Macmillan.

Dewdney, Anna. Llama Llama & the Bully Goat. 2013. (Llama Llama Ser.). (ENG., Illus.). 40p. (J). (gr. -1-k). 17.99 (978-0-670-01395-1(1), Viking Books for Young Readers) Penguin Young Readers Group.

—Llama Llama Misses Mama. 2009. (Llama Llama Ser.). (ENG., Illus.). 40p. (J). (gr. -1-k). 17.99 (978-0-670-06198-3(0), Viking Books for Young Readers) Penguin Young Readers Group.

DeWitt, Fowler. The Contagious Colors of Mumpley Middle School. Montalvo, Rodolfo, illus. 2013. (ENG.). 272p. (J). (gr. 2-5). 16.99 (978-1-4424-7829-9(2), Atheneum Bks. for Young Readers) Simon & Schuster Children's Publishing.

DeWoskin, Rachel. Blind. 2014. (ENG.). 416p. (YA). (gr. 7). 17.99 (978-0-670-78522-3(9), Viking Books for Young Readers) Penguin Young Readers Group.

Dewoskin, Rachel. Blind. 2016. (ENG.). 416p. (YA). (gr. 7). pap. 10.99 (978-0-14-242455-1(2), Speak) Penguin Young Readers Group.

Un Día de Escuela de Oso. 2014. (SPA., Illus.). (J). (978-1-78285-087-8(2)) Barefoot Bks., Inc.

Dickson, Darnell G. Small Town, Big Dreams: A Dane Jordan Sports Novel. 2008. pap. 14.99 (978-1-59955-229-3(9)) Cedar Fort, Inc./CFI Distribution.

Diesen, Deborah. Picture Day Perfection. Santat, Dan, illus. 2013. (ENG.). 32p. (J). (gr. k-2). 17.95 (978-1-4197-0844-2(9), Abrams Bks. for Young Readers) Abrams, Inc.

—The Pout-Pout Fish Goes to School. Hanna, Dan, illus. 2014. (Pout-Pout Fish Adventure Ser.). (ENG.). 32p. (J). (gr. -1-k). 16.99 (978-0-374-36095-5(2), 9780374360955, Farrar, Straus & Giroux (BYR)) Farrar, Straus & Giroux.

Digby, Anne. Boy Trouble at Trebizon. 2016. (Trebizon Ser.). (ENG., Illus.). 192p. (J). (gr. 3-5). pap. 10.99 (978-1-4052-8066-2(2)) Egmont Bks., Ltd. GBR. Dist: Independent Pubs. Group.

—Hockey Term at Trebizon. 2017. (Trebizon Ser.: 9). (ENG., Illus.). 224p. (J). (gr. 3-5). pap. 10.99 **(978-1-4052-8071-6(9))** Egmont Bks., Ltd. GBR. Dist: Independent Pubs. Group.

—Second Term at Trebizon. 2016. (Trebizon Ser.). (ENG., Illus.). 192p. (J). (gr. 4-7). pap. 10.99 (978-1-4052-8064-8(6)) Egmont Bks., Ltd. GBR. Dist: Independent Pubs. Group.

—Summer Camp at Trebizon. 2016. (Trebizon Ser.). (ENG., Illus.). 192p. (J). (gr. 3-6). pap. 10.99 **(978-1-4052-8069-3(7))** Egmont Bks., Ltd. GBR. Dist: Independent Pubs. Group.

—Summer Term at Trebizon. 2016. (Trebizon Ser.). (ENG., Illus.). 208p. (J). (gr. 3-5). pap. 10.99 (978-1-4052-8065-5(4)) Egmont Bks., Ltd. GBR. Dist: Independent Pubs. Group.

Digby, Anne. The Tennis Term at Trebizon. 2016. (Trebizon Ser.). (ENG., Illus.). 192p. (J). (gr. 3-6). pap. 10.99 **(978-1-4052-8068-6(9))** Egmont Bks., Ltd. GBR. Dist: Independent Pubs. Group.

DiGerolamo, Tony. The Wildsidhe Chronicles Bk. 5: The Undercover Dragon. 2003. (J). pap. 7.99 (978-1-890096-17-5(2)) Padwolf Publishing, Inc.

Diggins, Matthew. Andrew & the Secret Gallery. Diggins, Matthew, illus. (Illus.). (J). 2008. 32p. pap. 6.95 (978-1-60108-026-4(3)) 2007. 30p. (gr. 1-5). 15.95 (978-1-60108-016-5(6)) Red Cygnet Pr.

Dillard, Sarah. First Day at Zoo School. Dillard, Sarah, illus. 2014. (ENG., Illus.). 40p. (J). (gr. k-2). 14.99 (978-1-58536-890-7(3), 203670) Sleeping Bear Pr.

Dillon, James. Okay Kevin: A Story to Help Children Discover How Everyone Learns Differently. McHale, Kara, illus. 2017. (ENG.). 36p. (J). 17.95 **(978-1-78592-732-4(9)**, 8785) Kingsley, Jessica Pubs. GBR. Dist: Macmillan Distribution Ltd.

Dillon, Jana. Lucky O'Leprechaun in School, 1 vol. Dillon, Jana, illus. 2003. (Lucky o'Leprechaun Ser.). (ENG., Illus.). 32p. (J). (gr. k-3). 16.99 (978-1-58980-035-9(4)) Pelican Publishing Co., Inc.

Dinan, Kurt. Don't Get Caught. 2016. (ENG.). 336p. (YA). (gr. 8-12). pap. 10.99 (978-1-4926-3014-2(4), 9781492630142) Sourcebooks, Inc.

Dinnison, Kris. You & Me & Him. (ENG.). 288p. (YA). (gr. 9). 2016. pap. 8.99 *(978-0-544-67175-1(9))* 2015. 17.99 *(978-0-544-30112-2(9))* Houghton Mifflin Harcourt Publishing Co. (HMH Books For Young Readers).
Dinosaur School: Set 5. 2016. (Dinosaur School Ser.). 24p. (gr. k-k). pap. 48.90 *(978-1-4824-5337-9(1))*; lib. bdg. 135.60 *(978-1-4824-4517-6(4))* Stevens, Gareth Publishing LLLP.
Dion. Chess with Butterflies. 2006. (Illus.). 65p. (J). (gr. 4). pap. 4.95 *(978-1-881929-43-7(4))* Oxton Hse., Pubs.
Dionne, Erin. Models Don't Eat Chocolate Cookies. 2009. (ENG.). 256p. (J). (gr. 3-7). pap. 6.99 *(978-0-8037-3296-4(1)*, Dial Bks) Penguin Young Readers Group.
—Notes from an Accidental Band Geek. 2012. (ENG.). 304p. (J). (gr. 5). pap. 6.99 *(978-0-14-242247-2(9)*, Puffin Books) Penguin Young Readers Group.
—The Total Tragedy of a Girl Named Hamlet. 2011. (ENG.). 304p. (J). (gr. 3-7). 8.99 *(978-0-14-241748-5(3)*, Puffin Books) Penguin Young Readers Group.
Dipucchio, Kelly. Dog Days of School. 2017. (J). lib. bdg. 16.00 ***(978-0-606-39971-5(2))*** Turtleback Bks.
Dipucchio, Kelly. Grace for President. Pham, LeUyen, illus. 2012. (ENG.). 40p. (J). (gr. 1-3). 16.99 *(978-1-4231-3999-7(2))* Hyperion Pr.
Diroma, Joseph. Pinuccio. Jones, Bob, illus. 2009. 24p. pap. 14.99 *(978-1-60844-036-8(2))* Dog Ear Publishing, LLC.
DiSalvo-Ryan, DyAnne. The Sloppy Copy Slipup. 2005. (ENG., Illus.). 128p. (J). (gr. 2-6). 16.95 *(978-0-8234-1947-0(9))* Holiday Hse., Inc.
Disney Book Group. Girl Meets World Friend Power. No New Art Needed, illus. 2016. (Girl Meets World Junior Novel Ser.). (ENG.). 128p. (J). (gr. 3-7). pap. 5.99 *(978-1-4847-6715-3(2))* Disney Pr.
—Star Darlings Good Wish Gone Bad. Disney Storybook Art Team, illus. 2016. (Star Darlings Ser.). (ENG.). 320p. (J). (gr. 3-7). 13.99 *(978-1-4847-5351-4(8))* Disney Pr.
—World of Reading: Elena of Avalor Isabel's School Adventure: Journey to Crystal Caverns: Level 1. Disney Storybook Art Team, illus. 2017. (World of Reading Ser.). (ENG.). 32p. (J). (gr. 1-3). pap. 4.99 *(978-1-4847-4798-8(4))* Disney Pr.
Disney Book Group Staff. Girl Meets World Follow Your Heart. 2015. (Girl Meets World Junior Novel Ser.). (ENG., Illus.). 128p. (J). (gr. 3-7). pap. 5.99 *(978-1-4847-2812-3(2))* Disney Pr.
Disney Book Group Staff & Ryals, Lexi. Jessie Livin' the Life. 2014. (Jessie Junior Novel Ser.). (ENG.). 128p. (J). (gr. 3-7). pap. 5.99 *(978-1-4231-8411-9(4))* Disney Pr.
Disney Press Staff. School's Out. 2010. 128p. pap. 4.99 *(978-1-4231-2677-5(7))* Disney Pr.
Divine, Jill. Wicked Rabbit. 2011. (Illus.). 86p. pap. 12.95 *(978-1-4457-3797-3(3))* Lulu Pr., Inc.
Divine, L. Drama High - Second Chance. 2006. (ENG., Illus.). 234p. (YA). (gr. 9-12). pap. 9.95 *(978-0-7582-1635-9(1)*, K-Teen/Dafina) Kensington Publishing Corp.
—The Fight, 2 vols. 2006. (ENG., Illus.). 208p. (YA). (gr. 9-12). pap. 9.95 *(978-0-7582-1633-5(5)*, K-Teen/Dafina) Kensington Publishing Corp.
—Frenemies. 2008. (Drama High Ser.: Vol. 4). 218p. (gr. 8-12). 19.95 *(978-0-7569-8832-6(2))* Perfection Learning Corp.
—Hustlin' 2009. (ENG., Illus.). 256p. (YA). (gr. 9). pap. 15.00 *(978-0-7582-3105-5(9)*, K-Teen/Dafina) Kensington Publishing Corp.
—Hustlin' 2009. (Drama High Ser.: 7). lib. bdg. 26.95 *(978-0-606-00156-4(5)*, Turtleback) Turtleback Bks.
—Keep It Movin' 2009. (Drama High Ser.: 8). lib. bdg. 20.80 *(978-0-606-00157-1(3)*, Turtleback) Turtleback Bks.
—Lady J. 2008. (Drama High Ser.: Vol. 5). 214p. (gr. 8-12). 19.95 *(978-0-7569-8833-3(0))* Perfection Learning Corp.
Dixon, Amy. Maurice the Unbeastly. Mountford, Karl James, illus. 2017. (ENG.). 32p. (J). (gr. -1). 16.95 ***(978-1-4549-1953-7(1))*** Sterling Publishing Co., Inc.
Dixon, Franklin W. Bound for Danger. 2016. (Hardy Boys Adventures Ser.: 13). (ENG., Illus.). 144p. (J). (gr. 3-7). pap. 6.99 *(978-1-4814-6831-2(6)*, Aladdin) Simon & Schuster Children's Publishing.
—The Great Escape. Burroughs, Scott, illus. 2015. (Hardy Boys: the Secret Files Ser.: 17). (ENG.). 112p. (J). (gr. 1-4). pap. 4.99 *(978-1-4814-2267-3(7)*, Aladdin) Simon & Schuster Children's Publishing.
—The Race Is On. Burroughs, Scott, illus. 2015. (Hardy Boys: the Secret Files Ser.: 19). (ENG.). 96p. (J). (gr. 1-4). pap. 5.99 *(978-1-4814-2271-0(5)*, Aladdin) Simon & Schuster Children's Publishing.
Doerrfeld, Cori. Truth in Sight. Doerrfeld, Cori & Page, Tyler, illus. 2016. (Cici: a Fairy's Tale Ser.: 2). (ENG.). 48p. (J). (gr. 2-5). lib. bdg. 26.65 *(978-1-4677-6153-6(2)*, Graphic Universe™) Lerner Publishing Group.
Doherty, Berlie. Coconut Comes to School. Bates, Ivan, illus. 2004. (ENG.). 32p. (J). (gr. k-2). 18.00 *(978-0-00-710433-8(2)*, HarperCollins Children's Bks.) HarperCollins Pubs. Ltd. GBR. Dist: Independent Pubs. Group.
Donaldson, Julia. A Gold Star for Zog. Scheffler, Axel, illus. 2012. (ENG.). 32p. (J). (gr. -1-3). 17.99 *(978-0-545-41724-2(4)*, Levine, Arthur A. Bks.) Scholastic, Inc.
—The Wrong Kind of Bark. Parsons, Garry, illus. 2005. (Red Bananas Ser.). (ENG.). 48p. (J). lib. bdg. *(978-0-7787-1073-8(4))*; (gr. 1-3). *(978-0-7787-1089-9(0))* Crabtree Publishing Co.
Dong, Haidan. Of Trouble & Trickery. 2004. 58p. pap. 8.95 *(978-0-595-31170-5(9))* iUniverse, Inc.
Donley, Jan. The Side Door. 2010. (ENG.). 288p. (J). (gr. 9). pap. 14.95 *(978-1-935226-12-3(6))* Spinsters Ink Bks.
Donovan, Gail. 100th Day Fun. Clar, David Austin, illus. 2003. (Rainbow Fish & Friends Ser.). 24p. (J). lib. bdg. 9.95 *(978-1-59014-141-0(5))* Night Sky Bks.
Donovan, Rebecca. Barely Breathing, 0 vols. unabr. ed. 2013. (Breathing Ser.: 2). (ENG.). 512p. (YA). (gr. 10-12). pap. 9.99 *(978-1-4778-1717-9(4)*, 9781477817179, Amazon Children's Publishing) Amazon Publishing.
—The Breathing Series: Books 1 And 2, 0 vols. 2013. (Breathing Ser.). (ENG.). 978p. (YA). (gr. 10-12). pap. 12.99 *(978-1-4778-1695-0(X)*, 9781477816950, Skyscape) Amazon Publishing.
—Reason to Breathe, 0 vols. 2013. (Breathing Ser.: 1). (ENG.). 466p. (YA). (gr. 10-12). pap. 9.99 *(978-1-4778-1714-8(X)*, 9781477817148, Amazon Children's Publishing) Amazon Publishing.
Doodler, Todd H. Super Rawr! Doodler, Todd H., illus. 2016. (ENG., Illus.). 40p. (J). (gr. -1-k). 12.99 *(978-0-545-79969-0(4)*, Scholastic Pr.) Scholastic, Inc.
Doolan, Catherine. Drochla Gruaige. Kelly, Maeve, illus. 2004. (Sraith Sos Ser.: 09). (IRI, ENG & GLE.). 64p. (J). pap. 9.95 *(978-0-86278-866-7(8))* O'Brien Pr., Ltd., The IRL. Dist: Dufour Editions, Inc.
Dorfman, Joaquin. The Long Wait for Tomorrow. 2009. (YA). *(978-0-375-84696-0(4))* Random Hse., Inc.
Doti, James. Jimmy Finds His Voice. Mertins, Lisa, illus. 2013. (J). 14.95 *(978-1-935204-47-3(5))* Salem Author Services.
Doty, M. Surviving High School. 2012. (Surviving High School Ser.: 1). (ENG.). 224p. (YA). (gr. 7-17). pap. 10.00 *(978-0-316-22015-6(9)*, Poppy) Little, Brown Bks. for Young Readers.
Double or Nothing. 2014. (It Takes Two Ser.: 3). (ENG., Illus.). 160p. (J). (gr. 3-7). pap. 6.99 *(978-1-4814-1652-8(9)*, Simon Spotlight) Simon Spotlight.
Doudna, Kelly. Goat Cheese, 1 vol. Haberstroh, Anne, illus. 2006. (Animal Tales Ser.). 24p. (J). (gr. k-3). (ENG.). lib. bdg. 24.21 *(978-1-59679-937-0(4)*, SandCastle); pap. 48.42 *(978-1-59679-938-7(2))* ABDO Publishing Co.
Dougherty, Brandi. The Friendship Experiment. 2009. 147p. (J). pap. *(978-0-545-07929-7(2))* Scholastic, Inc.
—The Valentine's Day Disaster. 2008. 204p. (J). pap. *(978-0-545-03168-4(0))* Scholastic, Inc.
Dougherty, Meghan. Rise of the Undead Redhead. Birnbach, Alece, illus. 2014. (Dorothy's Derby Chronicles Ser.: 1). (ENG.). 256p. (J). (gr. 3-6). pap. 6.99 *(978-1-4022-9535-5(9)*, Sourcebooks Jabberwocky) Sourcebooks, Inc.
Douglas, Babette. Kiss a Me Goes to School. Rockwell, Barry, illus. 2006. (Kiss a Me Teacher Creature Stories Ser.). (J). (gr. -1-3). 9.99 *(978-1-890343-09-5(9))* Kiss A Me Productions, Inc.
Dowding, Philippa. The Gargoyle at the Gates. 2012. (Lost Gargoyle Ser.: 3). (ENG.). 192p. (J). pap. 10.99 *(978-1-4597-0394-0(4)*, 9781459703940) Dundurn CAN. Dist: Ingram Publisher Services.
Dowell, Frances O'Roark. Blasts Off! McDaniels, Preston, illus. 2011. (From the Highly Scientific Notebooks of Phineas L. MacGuire Ser.). (ENG.). 224p. (J). (gr. 3-7). pap. 7.99 *(978-1-4424-2204-9(1)*, Atheneum Bks. for Young Readers) Simon & Schuster Children's Publishing.
—Chicken Boy. Krause, George, photos by. 2007. (ENG., Illus.). 224p. (J). (gr. 5-9). pap. 6.99 *(978-1-4169-3482-0(0)*, Atheneum Bks. for Young Readers) Simon & Schuster Children's Publishing.
—Chicken Boy. 2005. (ENG., Illus.). 208p. (J). (gr. 5-9). 17.99 *(978-0-689-85816-1(7)*, Atheneum Bks. for Young Readers) Simon & Schuster Children's Publishing.
—Erupts! McDaniels, Preston, illus. 2006. (From the Highly Scientific Notebooks of Phineas L. MacGuire Ser.). (ENG.). 176p. (J). (gr. 3-7). 16.99 *(978-1-4169-0195-2(7)*, Atheneum Bks. for Young Readers) Simon & Schuster Children's Publishing.
—The Kind of Friends We Used to Be. (Secret Language of Girl Trilogy Ser.). (ENG., Illus.). (J). (gr. 3-7). 2010. 256p. pap. 7.99 *(978-1-4169-9779-5(2))* 2009. 240p. 16.99 *(978-1-4169-5031-8(1))* Simon & Schuster Children's Publishing. (Atheneum Bks. for Young Readers).
—Phineas L. MacGuire ... Gets Cooking! McDaniels, Preston, illus. 2015. (From the Highly Scientific Notebooks of Phineas L. MacGuire Ser.). (ENG.). 224p. (J). (gr. 3-7). pap. 6.99 *(978-1-4814-0100-5(9))* Simon & Schuster Children's Publishing.
—Phineas L. Macguire... Erupts! McDaniels, Preston, illus. 2007. (From the Highly Scientific Notebooks of Phineas L. MacGuire Ser.). (ENG.). 176p. (J). (gr. 3-7). pap. 6.99 *(978-1-4169-4734-9(5)*, Atheneum Bks. for Young Readers) Simon & Schuster Children's Publishing.
—Phineas L. MacGuire... Gets Slimed! McDaniels, Preston, illus. (From the Highly Scientific Notebooks of Phineas L. MacGuire Ser.). (ENG.). (J). (gr. 3-7). 2010. 224p. pap. 6.99 *(978-1-4169-9775-7(X))* 2007. 208p. 16.99 *(978-1-4169-0196-9(5))* Simon & Schuster Children's Publishing. (Atheneum Bks. for Young Readers).
—Phineas L. MacGuire... Gets Slimed! McDaniels, Preston, illus. l.t. ed. 2008. (From the Highly Scientific Notebooks of Phineas L. MacGuire Ser.). 159p. (J). (gr. 3-7). 22.95 *(978-1-4104-0440-4(4))* Thorndike Pr.
—The Secret Language of Girls. 2005. 247p. (gr. 3-7). 17.00 *(978-0-7569-5463-5(0))* Perfection Learning Corp.
—The Secret Language of Girls. (Secret Language of Girl Trilogy Ser.). (ENG., Illus.). 256p. (J). (gr. 3-7). 2005. pap. 7.99 *(978-1-4169-0717-6(3))* 2004. 19.99 *(978-0-689-84421-8(2))* Simon & Schuster Children's Publishing. (Atheneum Bks. for Young Readers).
—The Secret Language of Girls Trilogy: The Secret Language of Girls; the Kind of Friends We Used to Be; the Sound of Your Voice, Only Really Far Away. 2015. (Secret Language of Girl Trilogy Ser.). (ENG., Illus.). 768p. (J). (gr. 5-9). pap. 22.99 *(978-1-4814-3831-5(X)*, Atheneum Bks. for Young Readers) Simon & Schuster Children's Publishing.
—The Sound of Your Voice, Only Really Far Away. 2013. (Secret Language of Girl Trilogy Ser.). (ENG., Illus.). 240p. (J). (gr. 5-9). 16.99 *(978-1-4424-3289-5(6))* Simon & Schuster Children's Publishing.
—Ten Miles Past Normal. (ENG., 224p. (YA). (gr. 7). 2012. Illus.). pap. 9.99 *(978-1-4169-9586-9(2))* 2011. 16.99 *(978-1-4169-9585-2(4))* Simon & Schuster Children's Publishing. (Atheneum Bks. for Young Readers).
Dower, Laura. Gabi & the Great Big Bakeover. Lazuli, Lilly, illus. 160p. 2017. (J). *(978-1-4747-2213-1(X))* 2016. (ENG.). (gr. 4-5). lib. bdg. 26.65 *(978-1-4965-3119-3(1))* Stone Arch Bks.
—Kiki Takes the Cake. Lazuli, Lilly, illus. 2016. (Dessert Diaries). (ENG.). 160p. (gr. 4-5). lib. bdg. 26.65 *(978-1-4965-3120-9(5))* Stone Arch Bks.
—On the Case. 2004. 170p. (J). lib. bdg. 16.92 *(978-1-4242-0648-3(0))* Fitzgerald Bks.
Downer, Denise. Soul Mates. Frampton, Otis, illus. 2013. (Tombstone Twins Ser.). (ENG.). 48p. (gr. 1-3). lib. bdg. 23.99 *(978-1-4342-2248-0(9))* Stone Arch Bks.
—Tombstone Twins: Soul Mates, 1 vol. Frampton, Otis, illus. 2013. (Tombstone Twins Ser.). (ENG.). 48p. (gr. 1-3). pap. 5.95 *(978-1-4342-3873-3(3))* Stone Arch Bks.
—Tombstone Twins Package: Soul Mates. Frampton, Otis, illus. 2013. (ENG.). 41p. (J). (gr. 2-4). pap. 35.70 *(978-1-4342-3955-6(1))* Stone Arch Bks.
Downing, Erin. A Funny Thing about Love: Dancing Queen; Prom Crashers; Drive Me Crazy. 2011. (ENG.). 656p. (YA). (gr. 7). pap. 9.99 *(978-1-4424-0645-2(3)*, Simon Pulse) Simon Pulse.
Downtown Bookworks Inc. Staff & Turgeon, Carolyn. The Next Full Moon. 2012. (ENG.). 192p. (J). (gr. 4-7). pap. 6.99 *(978-1-935703-34-1(X))* Downtown Bookworks.
Doxey, Heidi. The Jane Journals at Pemberley Prep: Liam Darcy, I Loathe You. 2015. 215p. (YA). pap. 14.99 *(978-1-4621-1682-9(5))* Cedar Fort, Inc./CFI Distribution.
DPWW, ed. High School Musical Actors' Biography. 2007. (J). (gr. 2-7). pap. 6.99 *(978-1-4231-0827-6(2))* Disney Pr.
Drake, Paula. How to Make a Snow Day: The Official Rules & Regulations. 2011. 28p. (gr. -1). pap. 15.00 *(978-1-4567-1830-5(4))* AuthorHouse.
Draper, Sharon M. The Battle of Jericho. (Jericho Trilogy Ser.: 1). (ENG., Illus.). (YA). (gr. 7). 2017. 320p. pap. 9.99 ***(978-1-4814-9029-0(X)***, Atheneum/Caitlyn Dlouhy Books) 2003. 304p. 19.99 *(978-0-689-84232-0(5)*, Atheneum Bks. for Young Readers) Simon & Schuster Children's Publishing.
—The Battle of Jericho. 2005. (Jericho Trilogy Ser.). (ENG., Illus.). 352p. (YA). (gr. 7). mass mkt. 7.99 *(978-0-689-84233-7(3)*, Simon Pulse) Simon Pulse.
—Darkness Before Dawn. 2014. (Hazelwood High Trilogy Ser. 3 Ser.). (ENG.). 288p. (YA). (gr. k-k). 11.24 *(978-1-63245-162-0(X))* Lectorum Pubns., Inc.
—Darkness Before Dawn. 2013. (Hazelwood High Trilogy Ser.: 3). (ENG., Illus.). 256p. (YA). (gr. 7). pap. 9.99 *(978-1-4424-8915-8(4)*, Atheneum Bks. for Young Readers) Simon & Schuster Children's Publishing.
—Darkness Before Dawn. 2013. (Hazelwood High Trilogy Ser.: 3). lib. bdg. 20.85 *(978-0-606-32334-5(1)*, Turtleback) Turtleback Bks.
—Double Dutch. 2004. 183p. (gr. 6-9). 17.00 *(978-0-7569-2934-3(2))* Perfection Learning Corp.
—Double Dutch. 2004. (ENG.). 192p. (J). (gr. 5-9). pap. 7.99 *(978-0-689-84231-3(7)*, Atheneum Bks. for Young Readers) Simon & Schuster Children's Publishing.
—Fire from the Rock. 2014. (ENG.). 240p. (YA). (gr. 7-12). 12.24 *(978-1-63245-286-3(3))* Lectorum Pubns., Inc.
—Fire from the Rock. 2008. (ENG.). 240p. (YA). (gr. 7-18). 7.99 *(978-0-14-241199-5(X)*, Speak) Penguin Young Readers Group.
—Just Another Hero. (Jericho Trilogy Ser.: 3). (ENG., (YA). (gr. 7). 2017. Illus.). 304p. pap. 9.99 ***(978-1-4814-9030-6(3)***, Atheneum/Caitlyn Dlouhy Books) 2009. 288p. 19.99 *(978-1-4169-0700-8(9)*, Atheneum Bks. for Young Readers) Simon & Schuster Children's Publishing.
—Just Another Hero. 2010. (Jericho Trilogy Ser.). (ENG., Illus.). 352p. (YA). (gr. 7). mass mkt. 7.99 *(978-1-4169-0701-5(7)*, Simon Pulse) Simon Pulse.
—Just Another Hero. 2010. (Jericho Trilogy Ser.: 3). lib. bdg. 18.40 *(978-0-606-14725-5(X)*, Turtleback) Turtleback Bks.
—Lost in the Tunnel of Time. Watson, Jesse Joshua, illus. 2011. (Clubhouse Mysteries Ser.: 2). (ENG.). 112p. (J). (gr. 3-7). pap. 5.99 *(978-1-4424-2704-4(3)*, Aladdin) Simon & Schuster Children's Publishing.
—Lost in the Tunnel of Time. Watson, Jesse Joshua, illus. 2011. (Clubhouse Mysteries Ser.: 2). (ENG.). 112p. (J). (gr. 3-7). lib. bdg. 15.99 *(978-1-4424-2703-7(5)*, Simon & Schuster/Paula Wiseman Bks.) Simon & Schuster/Paula Wiseman Bks.
—November Blues. 2011. 9.00 *(978-0-7848-3495-4(4)*, Everbind) Marco Bk. Co.
—November Blues. (Jericho Trilogy Ser.: 2). (ENG., Illus.). (YA). (gr. 7). 2017. 336p. pap. 9.99 ***(978-1-4814-9031-3(1)***, Atheneum/Caitlyn Dlouhy Books) 2007. 320p. 19.99 *(978-1-4169-0698-8(3)*, Atheneum Bks. for Young Readers) Simon & Schuster Children's Publishing.
Draper, Sharon M. Tears of a Tiger. 2014. (Hazelwood High Trilogy Ser. 1 Ser.). (ENG.). 192p. (YA). (gr. 12-12). 12.24 *(978-1-63245-075-3(5))* Lectorum Pubns., Inc.
—Tears of a Tiger. 2007. (Hazelwood High Trilogy: Bk. 1). 45p. ring bd. 54.95 *(978-1-60843-737-5(X))* Prestwick Hse., Inc.
—Tears of a Tiger. 2013. (Hazelwood High Trilogy Ser.: 1). (ENG., Illus.). 192p. (J). (gr. 7). pap. 9.99 *(978-1-4424-8913-4(8)*, Atheneum Bks. for Young Readers) Simon & Schuster Children's Publishing.
—Tears of a Tiger. l.t. ed. 2006. (Hazelwood High Trilogy: Bk. 1). 207p. (YA). (gr. 8-12). per. 10.95 *(978-0-7862-8361-3(0))* Thorndike Pr.
—Tears of a Tiger. 2013. (Hazelwood High Trilogy Ser.: 1). lib. bdg. 20.85 *(978-0-606-32332-1(5)*, Turtleback) Turtleback Bks.
Dream Pony (revised) 2017. (Sandy Lane Stables Ser.). (ENG.). (J). pap. 5.99 ***(978-0-7945-3624-4(7)***, Usborne) EDC Publishing.
Dreissigacker Martin, Susan. Princess Stephanie Stories: The Road Trip & the New School. 2009. 32p. pap. 18.79 *(978-1-4389-1836-5(4))* AuthorHouse.
Driscoll, Laura. Lila the Fair. Sims, Blanche, illus. 2005. (Social Studies Connects). 32p. (J). pap. 5.95 *(978-1-57565-148-4(3))* Kane Press, Inc.
Driving Mom Crazy 6 Packs: Individual Title. (gr. -1-2). 27.00 *(978-0-7635-9446-6(6))* Rigby Education.
Drown, Merle. Lighting the World. 2015. (ENG.). 278p. pap. 18.00 *(978-0-9898971-4-3(1))* Whitepoint Pr.
Drummond, Ree. Charlie Goes to School. deGroat, Diane, illus. 2013. (Charlie the Ranch Dog Ser.). (ENG.). 40p. (J). (gr. -1-3). 17.99 *(978-0-06-221920-6(0))* HarperCollins Pubs.
Du Jardin, Rosamond. A Man for Marcy. 2003. (YA). pap. 12.95 *(978-1-930009-76-9(3)*, 800-691-7779) Image Cascade Publishing.
Dubosarsky, Ursula. The Golden Day. 2013. (ENG.). 160p. (YA). (gr. 7). 15.99 *(978-0-7636-6399-5(9))* Candlewick Pr.
Duey, Kathleen. Skin Hunger. 2008. (Resurrection of Magic Ser.: 1). (ENG.). 368p. (YA). (gr. 7-7). pap. 12.99 *(978-0-689-84094-4(2)*, Atheneum Bks. for Young Readers) Simon & Schuster Children's Publishing.
DuJardin, Rosamond. Boy Trouble. 2003. (YA). pap. 12.95 *(978-1-930009-70-7(4)*, 800-691-7779) Image Cascade Publishing.
—One of the Crowd. 2003. (YA). pap. 12.95 *(978-1-930009-73-8(9)*, 800-691-7779) Image Cascade Publishing.
—Senior Prom. 2003. (YA). pap. 12.95 *(978-1-930009-77-6(1)*, 800-691-7779) Image Cascade Publishing.
Duke, Shirley. Unthinkable. 2010. (Night Fall Ser.). (ENG.). 112p. (YA). (gr. 6-12). pap. 7.95 *(978-0-7613-6157-2(X))* Lerner Publishing Group.
Dumble, Carol. R U My Friend? 2011. 20p. pap. 11.99 *(978-1-4567-1825-1(8))* AuthorHouse.
Dumbleton, Mike. Watch Out for Jamie Joel. 2004. (ENG.). 144p. (J). (gr. 9). pap. 16.95 *(978-1-86508-532-6(4))* Allen & Unwin AUS. Dist: Independent Pubs. Group.
Dunbar, Helene. These Gentle Wounds. 2014. (ENG.). 312p. (YA). pap. 11.99 *(978-0-7387-4027-0(6)*, Flux) North Star Editions.
Duncan, Lois. Killing Mr. Griffin. 2010. (ENG.). 272p. (YA). (gr. 7-17). pap. 10.99 *(978-0-316-09900-4(7))* Little, Brown Bks. for Young Readers.
Duncan, Randy. Miranda & Her Pand. 2009. 28p. pap. 12.49 *(978-1-4389-6132-3(4))* AuthorHouse.
Dungy, Tony. You Can Do It! Bates, Amy June, illus. 2008. (ENG.). 32p. (J). (gr. -1-2). 17.99 *(978-1-4169-5461-3(9)*, Little Simon Inspirations) Little Simon Inspirations.
Dunlap, Susanne. The Academie. 2012. (ENG.). 368p. (YA). 16.99 *(978-1-59990-586-0(8)*, 9781599905860, Bloomsbury USA Childrens) Bloomsbury Publishing USA.
Dunlop, Ed. Sherlock Jones: The Assassination Plot. 2004. 116p. (J). 8.99 *(978-1-59166-315-7(6))* BJU Pr.
Dunsany, Taylor. The Little Witch Who Lost Her Broom & Other Stories. 2008. 48p. pap. 8.95 *(978-0-595-52506-5(7))* iUniverse, Inc.
Dupuis, Jenny Kay & Kacer, Kathy. I Am Not a Number, 1 vol. Newland, Gillian, illus. 2016. (ENG.). 32p. (J). (gr. 3-6). 18.95 *(978-1-927583-94-4(2))* Second Story Pr. CAN. Dist: Orca Bk. Pubs. USA.
Durand, Hallie. Catch That Cookie! 2014. *(978-0-8037-3960-4(5)*, Dial) Penguin Publishing Group.
—Catch That Cookie! Small, David, illus. 2014. (ENG.). 32p. (J). (gr. -1-k). 17.99 *(978-0-525-42835-0(6)*, Dial Bks) Penguin Young Readers Group.
—Dessert First. Davenier, Christine, illus. (ENG.). (J). (gr. 2-5). 2010. 176p. pap. 5.99 *(978-1-4169-6386-8(3))* 2009. 160p. 14.99 *(978-1-4169-6385-1(5))* Simon & Schuster Children's Publishing. (Atheneum Bks. for Young Readers).
—Just Desserts. Davenier, Christine, illus. (ENG.). (J). (gr. 2-5). 2011. 224p. pap. 5.99 *(978-1-4169-6388-2(X))* 2010. 208p. 15.99 *(978-1-4169-6387-5(1))* Simon & Schuster Children's Publishing. (Atheneum Bks. for Young Readers).
—No Room for Dessert. Davenier, Christine, illus. (ENG.). 192p. (J). (gr. 2-5). 2012. pap. 6.99 *(978-1-4424-0361-1(6))* 2011. 15.99 *(978-1-4424-0360-4(8))* Simon & Schuster Children's Publishing. (Atheneum Bks. for Young Readers).
Durst, Sarah Beth. Drink, Slay, Love. (ENG., Illus.). 400p. (YA). (gr. 9). 2012. pap. 10.99 *(978-1-4424-2374-9(9))* 2011. 17.99 *(978-1-4424-2373-2(0))* McElderry, Margaret K. Bks. (McElderry, Margaret K. Bks.).
Durst, Sarah Beth. Roar & Sparkles Go to School. Whitehouse, Ben, illus. 2017. (ENG.). 40p. (J). (gr. -1-1). 16.99 ***(978-0-7624-5986-5(7)***, Running Pr.) Running Pr. Bk. Pubs.
Dwyer, Cynthia. Four-Eyed Philip. Schuepbach, Lynnette, illus. 2007. (J). 14.95 *(978-0-9793296-0-9(4))* Grannie Annie Family Story Celebration, The.
E. S. Townsend. The Secrets of Marsh House. 2013. 208p. pap. *(978-1-907011-44-3(7))* Esteemworld Pubns.
Eaddy, Susan. Poppy's Best Paper. Bonnet, Rosalinde, illus. 2015. (ENG.). 40p. (J). (gr. k-3). lib. bdg. 15.95 *(978-1-58089-614-6(6))* Charlesbridge Publishing, Inc.
—Poppy's Best Paper (1 Hardcover/1 CD) Bonnet, Rosalinde, illus. 2016. (ENG.). (J). (gr. 1-4). audio compact disk 29.95 *(978-1-4301-2187-9(4))* Live Oak Media.
Eagle, Rita. Sniffy the Beagle. Rasmussen, Gerry, illus. 2007. (ENG.). 44p. per. 13.95 *(978-1-59800-537-0(5))* Outskirts Pr., Inc.
Eareckson Tada, Joni & Jensen, Steve. The Meanest Teacher. 2005. (Darcy & Friends Ser.). 144p. (gr. 3-6). pap. 5.99 *(978-1-58134-256-7(X)*, Crossway Bibles) Crossway.
Easley, Maryann. Warriors Daughter. 2007. 150p. pap. 24.95 *(978-1-4241-4875-2(8))* PublishAmerica, Inc.
East, Bob. Tommy Cat & the Haunted Well, 1 vol. 2009. 42p. pap. 24.95 *(978-1-60703-754-5(8))* America Star Bks.
Easton, Kelly. To Be Mona. (ENG.). 224p. (YA). (gr. 7). 2009. pap. 7.99 *(978-1-4169-0055-9(1))* 2008. 16.99 *(978-1-4169-0054-2(3))* McElderry, Margaret K. Bks. (McElderry, Margaret K. Bks.).
Eaton, Kelly Toole. Kelina Makes Her Dreams Come True. 2011. 40p. pap. 21.99 *(978-1-4568-8824-4(2))* Xlibris Corp.
Eaves, Victor Caleb. Vee's the Chapters of Expudict: Book One. 2008. 128p. pap. 12.00 *(978-1-4389-3385-6(1))* AuthorHouse.
Echols, Jennifer. Biggest Flirts. 2014. (Superlatives Ser.). (ENG., Illus.). 336p. (YA). (gr. 9). pap. 9.99 *(978-1-4424-7445-1(9)*, Simon Pulse) Simon Pulse.
—Most Likely to Succeed. 2015. (Superlatives Ser.). (ENG., Illus.). 352p. (YA). (gr. 9). 17.99 *(978-1-4424-7452-9(1)*, Simon Pulse) Simon Pulse.
—The One That I Want. 2012. (ENG.). 288p. (YA). (gr. 7). pap. 9.99 *(978-1-4424-5236-7(6)*, Simon Pulse) Simon Pulse.
—Perfect Couple. 2015. (Superlatives Ser.). (ENG., Illus.). 336p. (YA). (gr. 9). pap. 10.99 *(978-1-4424-7448-2(3)*, Simon Pulse) Simon Pulse.
Eckelberg, Aimie. Walk the Walk. 2010. 32p. 15.00 *(978-1-4520-3644-1(6))* AuthorHouse.
Ecker, Rebecca. Miss Emmalou Strain & the Hunt for Hermie. 2008. 32p. pap. 12.95 *(978-1-4327-0182-6(7))* Outskirts Pr., Inc.
Ecton, Anne Massey. Passing Through Camelot. 2006. (J). *(978-0-88092-620-1(1))* Royal Fireworks Publishing Co.
Edelman, Lana. School Friends. 2012. (Penguin Young Readers Level 2 Ser.). lib. bdg. 13.55 *(978-0-606-26023-7(4)*, Turtleback) Turtleback Bks.

S

Edward, Judy. Calvin Can - Be Happy. Edward, Aaron, illus. 2012. 32p. pap. (978-1-4602-0097-1(7)) FriesenPress.
Edwards, Michelle. Pa Lia's First Day. 2005. (Jackson Friends Ser.: 1). (ENG., Illus.). 64p. (J). (gr. -1-3). pap. 5.99 (978-0-15-205748-0(X)) Houghton Mifflin Harcourt Publishing Co.
—Pa Lia's First Day. 2005. (Jackson Friends Bks.). (Illus.). 55p. (gr. 1-4). 15.95 (978-0-7569-5773-5(7)) Perfection Learning Corp.
—Stinky Stern Forever. 2007. (Jackson Friends Bks.). (Illus.). 49p. (gr. 1-4). 15.95 (978-0-7569-8198-3(0)) Perfection Learning Corp.
—Stinky Stern Forever: A Jackson Friends Book. 2007. (Jackson Friends Ser.). (ENG., Illus.). 56p. (J). (gr. 1-4). pap. 6.95 (978-0-15-206101-2(0)) Houghton Mifflin Harcourt Publishing Co.
—Zero Grandparents. 2005. (Jackson Friends Bks.). (Illus.). 59p. (gr. 1-4). 15.95 (978-0-7569-5774-2(5)) Perfection Learning Corp.
Edwards, Nancy. Mom for Mayor. Chesworth, Michael D., illus. 2006. (ENG.). 96p. (J). (gr. 1-5). 16.95 (978-0-8126-2743-5(1)) Cricket Bks.
Edwards, Pamela Duncan. Gigi & Lulu's Gigantic Fight. Cole, Henry, tr. Cole, Henry, illus. 2004. 40p. (J). (gr. -1-2). lib. bdg. 15.89 (978-0-06-050753-4(5)) HarperCollins Pubs.
Edwards, Pat & Edwards, LaVell. Hello, Cosmo! De Angel, Miguel, illus. 2006. 24p. (J). lib. bdg. 17.95 (978-1-932888-45-4(4)) Mascot Bks., Inc.
Edwardson, Debby Dahl. My Name Is Not Easy, 0 vols. 2013. (ENG.). 256p. (YA). (gr. 7-9). pap. 9.99 (978-1-4778-1629-5(1), 9781477816295, Amazon Children's Publishing) Amazon Publishing.
Efaw, Amy. After. 2010. (ENG.). 368p. (YA). (gr. 7-18). 8.99 (978-0-14-241590-0(1), Speak) Penguin Young Readers Group.
Egan, Kate. Kate & Nate Are Running Late! Yaccarino, Dan, illus. 2012. (ENG.). 36p. (J). (gr. k-2). 16.99 (978-1-250-00080-4(7), 9781250000804) Feiwel & Friends.
Eglington, Tara. How to Keep a Boy from Kissing You. 2016. (ENG.). 320p. (YA). 18.99 (978-1-250-04953-7(9), 9781250049537) St. Martin's Pr.
Ehrenberg, Pamela. Ethan, Suspended. 2009. (ENG.). 272p. (J). (gr. 6-9). pap. 8.50 (978-0-8028-5317-2(X)) 2007. 266p. (YA). (gr. 7-18). 16.00 (978-0-8028-5324-0(2), Eerdmans Bks For Young Readers) Eerdmans, William B. Publishing Co.
Ehrlich, Esther. Nest. (ENG.). 336p. (J). (gr. 5). 2016. pap. 7.99 (978-0-385-38610-4(9), Yearling) 2014. 16.99 (978-0-385-38607-4(9), Lamb, Wendy Bks.) Random Hse. Children's Bks.
Ehrlich, Nikki. Twindergarten. Wagner, Zoey Abbott, illus. 2017. 32p. (J). (gr. -1-3). 15.99 (978-0-06-256423-8(4)) HarperCollins Pubs.
Eisenson, Adam. Hope. 2005. (Illus.). 35p. (J). 14.95 (978-0-9766157-0-5(3)) Lone Star Pubns.
Eland, Lindsay. Five Times Revenge. 2016. 384p. (J). (gr. 3-7). 16.99 (978-0-06-239730-0(3), Greenwillow Bks.) HarperCollins Pubs.
Elder, Joshua. Mail Order Ninja, 1 vol., Vol. 1. Owen, Erich, illus. 2009. (Tokyopop Ser.). (ENG.). 96p. (gr. 2-6). 25.65 (978-1-59961-568-4(1)) Spotlight.
—Mail Order Ninja Vol. 2: Timmy Strikes Back, 1 vol. Owen, Erich, illus. 2009. (Tokyopop Ser.). (ENG.). 104p. (gr. 2-6). 25.65 (978-1-59961-569-1(X)) Spotlight.
Eldridge, Courtney. Ghost Time. 2016. (ENG.). 418p. (YA). pap. 9.99 (978-1-4778-1697-4(6), 9781477816974) Amazon Publishing.
Elfgren, Sara B. & Strandberg, Mats. The Circle. 2014. (Engelsfors Trilogy Ser.: 1). (ENG.). 608p. (gr. 9-13). pap. 13.99 (978-1-4683-0819-8(X), 460819) Overlook Pr., The.
Elish, Dan. The School for the Insanely Gifted. 2011. (ENG.). 304p. (J). (gr. 3-7). 15.99 (978-0-06-113873-7(8)) HarperCollins Pubs.
Elkeles, Simone. How to Ruin a Summer Vacation. 2006. (How to Ruin a Summer Vacation Novel Ser.: 1). (ENG.). 240p. (YA). (gr. 8-12). per. 9.95 (978-0-7387-0961-1(1), Flux) North Star Editions.
—How to Ruin My Teenage Life. 2007. (How to Ruin a Summer Vacation Novel Ser.: 2). (ENG.). 288p. (YA). (gr. 7-12). per. 11.99 (978-0-7387-1019-8(9), Flux) North Star Editions.
—Leaving Paradise. 2007. 20.80 (978-1-4177-8393-9(1), Turtleback) Turtleback Bks.
—Rules of Attraction. 2015. (Perfect Chemistry Novel Ser.). (ENG.). 352p. (YA). (gr. 9). pap. 9.99 (978-1-61963-702-3(2), 9781619637023, Bloomsbury USA Childrens) Bloomsbury Publishing USA.
Ella, Peter Leo. Class Party on the Big Yellow School Bus. Ella, Peter Leo, illus. 2013. (Illus.). 28p. pap. (978-9980-86-513-7(X)) University of Papua New Guinea Press.
Ellen, Connie. Marvel Mansion Gang. 2012. 114p. pap. 12.19 (978-1-4269-5968-4(0)) Trafford Publishing.
Elliott, Laura Malone. Hunter's Best Friend at School. Munsinger, Lynn, illus. 2005. (gr. -1-2). 17.00 (978-0-7569-5786-5(9)) Perfection Learning Corp.
—Hunter's Best Friend at School. Munsinger, Lynn, illus. 2005. (ENG.). 32p. (J). (gr. -1-2). reprint ed. pap. 6.99 (978-0-06-075319-1(6), Tegen, Katherine Bks) HarperCollins Pubs.
—Thanksgiving Day Thanks. Munsinger, Lynn, illus. 2013. (ENG.). 32p. (J). (gr. -1-3). 17.99 (978-0-06-000236-7(0)) HarperCollins Pubs.
Elliott, Rebecca. Eva & the New Owl. 2016. (Owl Diaries: 4). (ENG., Illus.). 80p. (J). (gr. k-2). pap. 4.99 (978-0-545-82559-7(8)) Scholastic, Inc.
—Eva Sees a Ghost. 2015. (Owl Diaries: 2). (ENG., Illus.). 80p. (J). (gr. k-2). 15.99 (978-0-545-78784-0(X)); pap. 4.99 (978-0-545-78783-3(1)) Scholastic, Inc.
—Eva's Treetop Festival, Bk. 1. Elliott, Rebecca, illus. 2015. (Owl Diaries: 1). (ENG., Illus.). 80p. (J). (gr. k-2). pap. 4.99 (978-0-545-68362-3(9)) Scholastic, Inc.
—My Stinky New School. Elliott, Rebecca, illus. 2015. (ENG., Illus.). 32p. (J). (gr. -1-1). 16.99 (978-0-7459-6949-7(6)) Lion Hudson PLC GBR. Dist: Independent Pubs. Group.
—A Woodland Wedding. Elliott, Rebecca, illus. 2016. (Owl Diaries: 3). (ENG., Illus.). 80p. (J). (gr. k-2). 15.99 (978-0-545-82558-0(X)) Scholastic, Inc.
Ellis, Ann Dee. This Is What I Did. 2011. 9.68 (978-0-7848-3387-2(7), Everbind) Marco Bk. Co.
Ellis, Kat. Blackfin Sky. 2014. (ENG.). 304p. (YA). (gr. 2-17). pap. 9.95 (978-0-7624-5401-3(6), Running Pr. Kids) Running Pr. Bk. Pubs.
Ellis, Leanne Statland. Tree Huggers. 2010. (J). pap. (978-0-88092-521-1(3)) Royal Fireworks Publishing Co.
Elmendorf, Dana. South of Sunshine. 2017. (ENG.). 256p. (YA). (gr. 8-12). pap. 9.99 **(978-0-8075-7571-0(2))** Whitman, Albert & Co.
Elwell, Sharon. Caught in the Middle: Reflections of a Middle School Teacher. 2007. 112p. per. 10.95 (978-1-4327-0621-0(7)) Outskirts Pr., Inc.
Emerson, Kevin. Breakout. 2015. (ENG.). 304p. (YA). (gr. 7). 17.99 (978-0-385-39112-2(9), Crown Books For Young Readers) Random Hse. Children's Bks.
—Carlos Is Gonna Get It. 2008. (J). pap. (978-0-439-93526-5(1), Levine, Arthur A. Bks.) Scholastic, Inc.
Emery, Anne. Dinny Gordon Senior. 2004. (J). per. 9.95 (978-1-59511-000-8(3)) Image Cascade Publishing.
—Senior Year. Krush, Beth, illus. 2006. (YA). per. 11.95 (978-1-59511-005-3(4)) Image Cascade Publishing.
—Sorority Girl. 2006. (YA). per. 11.95 (978-1-59511-007-7(0)) Image Cascade Publishing.
Emond, Stephen. Bright Lights, Dark Nights. 2015. (ENG., Illus.). 384p. (YA). (gr. 7). 17.99 (978-1-62672-206-4(4)) Roaring Brook Pr.
—Happyface. 2011. (ENG., Illus.). 336p. (YA). (gr. 7-17). pap. 10.99 (978-0-316-04099-0(1)) Little, Brown Bks. for Young Readers.
Emzer, Counselor. The Day Before Summer Vacation. 2004. 31p. pap. 24.95 (978-1-4137-2680-0(1)) PublishAmerica, Inc.
Endacott, C. R. Afflatus. 2008. 232p. pap. 15.95 (978-0-595-52418-1(4)) iUniverse, Inc.
Enderle, Dotti. Tell No One!, 1 vol. McWilliam, Howard, illus. 2010. (Ghost Detectors Ser.: No. 1). (ENG.). 80p. (J). (gr. 2-5). 27.07 (978-1-60270-692-7(1)) Magic Wagon.
Engelbreit, Mary. Queen of Hearts. Engelbreit, Mary, illus. 2008. (Ann Estelle Stories Ser.). (ENG., Illus.). 32p. (J). (gr. -1-3). pap. 6.99 (978-0-06-008183-6(X)) HarperCollins Pubs.
English, Karen. Birthday Blues. Freeman, Laura, illus. 2010. (ENG.). 96p. (J). (gr. 1-4). pap. 5.99 (978-0-547-24893-6(8)) Houghton Mifflin Harcourt Publishing Co.
—Dog Days. Freeman, Laura, illus. 2014. (Carver Chronicles Ser.). (ENG.). 128p. (J). (gr. 1-4). pap. 5.99 (978-0-544-33912-5(6), HMH Books For Young Readers) Houghton Mifflin Harcourt Publishing Co.
—Don't Feed the Geckos! The Carver Chronicles, Book Three. Freeman, Laura, illus. 2016. (Carver Chronicles Ser.). (ENG.). 144p. (J). (gr. 1-4). pap. 5.99 (978-0-544-81083-9(X), HMH Books For Young Readers) Houghton Mifflin Harcourt Publishing Co.
—Francie. 2007. (ENG.). 208p. (J). (gr. 4-8). per. 8.99 (978-0-312-37383-2(X), 9780312373832) Square Fish.
—The Newsy News Newsletter. Freeman, Laura, illus. 2011. (ENG.). 96p. (J). (gr. 1-4). pap. 5.99 (978-0-547-40626-8(6)) Houghton Mifflin Harcourt Publishing Co.
—Nikki & Deja. Freeman, Laura, illus. 2009. (ENG.). 80p. (J). (gr. -1-3). pap. 5.99 (978-0-547-13362-1(6)) Houghton Mifflin Harcourt Publishing Co.
—Nikki & Deja: Substitute Trouble. Freeman, Laura, illus. 2014. (ENG.). 112p. (J). (gr. 1-4). pap. 5.99 (978-0-544-22388-2(8), HMH Books For Young Readers) Houghton Mifflin Harcourt Publishing Co.
—Wedding Drama. Freeman, Laura, illus. 2013. (ENG.). 112p. (J). (gr. 1-4). pap. 5.99 (978-0-544-00324-8(1)) Houghton Mifflin Harcourt Publishing Co.
Enright, Elizabeth. The Four-Story Mistake. Enright, Elizabeth, illus. 3rd ed. 2008. (Melendy Quartet Ser.: 2). (ENG., Illus.). 208p. (J). (gr. 3-7). per. 8.99 (978-0-312-37599-7(9), 9780312375997) Square Fish.
Ensor, Rod. Getting It. 2007. 216p. per. 14.95 (978-0-595-44800-5(3)) iUniverse, Inc.
Epstein, Adam Jay & Jacobson, Andrew. Starbounders. McClellan, David, illus. 2013. (Starbounders Ser.: 1). (ENG.). 320p. (J). (gr. 3-7). 16.99 (978-0-06-212022-9(0)) HarperCollins Pubs.
—Starbounders Vol. 2: Rebellion. 2014. (Starbounders Ser.: 2). (ENG.). 304p. (J). (gr. 3-7). 16.99 (978-0-06-212027-4(1)) HarperCollins Pubs.
Erikson, Harvey. Basketball Fever... Bring It On! 2014. 206p. pap. 11.95 (978-1-62652-583-2(8), Mill City Press, Inc) Salem Author Services.
Erlings, Fridrik. Fish in the Sky. 2012. (ENG., Illus.). 288p. (YA). (gr. 7). 16.99 (978-0-7636-5888-5(X)) Candlewick Pr.
Erskine, Kathryn. Mockingbird. (ENG.). (J). (gr. 5-18). 2011. 256p. 7.99 (978-0-14-241775-1(0), Puffin Books) 2010. 240p. 16.99 (978-0-399-25264-8(9), Philomel Bks.) Penguin Young Readers Group.
—Mockingbird. (J). 2012. 1.25 (978-1-4407-4671-0(0)) 2010. 74.75 (978-1-4407-4665-9(6)) 2010. 72.75 (978-1-4407-4667-3(2)) 2010. (SPA.). 62.75 (978-1-4407-4663-5(X)) 2010. 64.75 (978-1-4407-4661-1(3)) 2010. 210.75 (978-1-4407-4662-8(1)) Recorded Bks., Inc.
—Mockingbird. 2011. lib. bdg. 18.40 (978-0-606-15356-0(X), Turtleback) Turtleback Bks.
—Quaking. 2010. (ENG.). 256p. (YA). (gr. 7-18). 7.99 (978-0-14-241476-7(X), Speak) Penguin Young Readers Group.
Esham, Barbara. Last to Finish: A Story about the Smartest Boy in Math Class. Gordon, Mike, illus. 2008. 32p. (J). (gr. k-18). 16.95 (978-1-60336-456-0(0), Adventures of Everyday Geniuses, The) Mainstream Connections Publishing.
—Stacey Coolidge's Fancy Smancy Cursive Handwriting. Gordon, Mike, illus. 2008. 32p. (J). (gr. k-18). 16.95 (978-1-60336-462-1(5), Adventures of Everyday Geniuses, The) Mainstream Connections Publishing.
Esola, Mike. Diary of a Dinosaur: The Attack of Benny. 2013. (ENG.). 154p. pap. 10.95 (978-1-4787-1363-0(1)) Outskirts Pr., Inc.
Esprit, Keisha. Serena Goes to School. 2013. 24p. pap. 24.95 (978-1-62709-460-3(1)) America Star Bks.
Esquivel, Rosaura. It's Time for School. 2017. (Let's Tell Time Ser.). 24p. (J). (gr. 4-6). 23.60 **(978-1-5081-5725-0(1)**, PowerKids Pr.) Rosen Publishing Group, Inc., The.
Ethington, Rebecca. Through Glass Omni 1: Omnibus Books 1-3. 2013. 324p. (YA). pap. 13.59 (978-0-9884837-6-7(9)) Imdalind Pr.
Eulberg, Elizabeth. Just Another Girl. 2017. (ENG.). 256p. (J). (gr. 7). 17.99 (978-0-545-95628-4(5)) Scholastic, Inc.
—The Lonely Hearts Club. (ENG.). 304p. (J). 2011. (gr. 3-7). pap. 8.99 (978-0-545-14032-4(3)) 2010. (gr. 9-12). 17.99 (978-0-545-14031-7(5)) Scholastic, Inc.
—Take a Bow. 2012. (ENG.). 288p. (J). (gr. 7). 17.99 (978-0-545-33474-7(8)); 280p. (YA). pap. (978-0-545-43982-4(5)) Scholastic, Inc.
—We Can Work It Out. 2015. (ENG.). 320p. (J). (gr. 7). 17.99 (978-0-545-65461-6(0)) Scholastic, Inc.
Eulo, Elena Yates. The Great Receiver. 2008. (ENG.). 192p. (J). (gr. 7-18). 16.95 (978-0-8234-1888-6(X)) Holiday Hse., Inc.
Evans, Ann. Cry Danger. 2012. 114p. pap. (978-1-907670-27-5(0)) Greenstream Publishing.
Evans, Dustin, illus. Costume Craziness, 1 vol. 2013. (Mystical Pencil Ser.). (ENG.). 32p. (J). (gr. 3-6). 28.50 (978-1-61641-926-4(1)) Magic Wagon.
Evans, John D. The Cut. 2003. (ENG.). 262p. (YA). per. 18.95 (978-1-888725-82-7(6), BeachHouse Bks.) Science & Humanities Pr.
Evans, Leslie, illus. You Have to Be Smart If You're Going to Be Tall/Tienes Que Ser Inteligente Si Vas a Ser Alta. 2006. 46p. (J). (gr. -1-3). per. 16.99 (978-1-59879-217-1(2)) Lifevest Publishing, Inc.
Evans, Mari. Trusting Love. 2014. (ENG., Illus.). 200p. (YA). pap. 14.99 (978-1-62798-955-8(2)) Dreamspinner Pr.
Evans, Rhonda Boone. Johnny Lumpkin Wants a Friend. Evans, Chadrick Michael, illus. 2007. 32p. per. 24.95 (978-1-4241-8614-3(5)) America Star Bks.
Evans, Rose-Marie. The Unexpected Adventure at East Haddam High. 2009. 80p. pap. 10.75 (978-1-60860-182-0(X), Strategic Bk. Publishing) Strategic Book Publishing & Rights Agency (SBPRA).
Evans, Sandra. This Is Not a Werewolf Story. 2016. (ENG., Illus.). 352p. (J). (gr. 4-7). 16.99 (978-1-4814-4480-4(8), Atheneum Bks. for Young Readers) Simon & Schuster Children's Publishing.
Everett, Reese. Wolfpack Gang Is Outta Sight! 2015. (ENG.). 48p. (gr. k-3). 27.07 (978-1-63430-375-0(X)) Rourke Educational Media.
Ewell, Katherine. Dear Killer. 2014. (ENG.). 368p. (YA). (gr. 8). 17.99 (978-0-06-225780-2(3)) HarperCollins Pubs.
Fabian, Cynthia. Orchestra in Our Brain: The Story of a Child with Epilepsy. Stevens, Daniel, illus. 2011. 20p. pap. 10.95 (978-1-60976-783-9(7), Eloquent Bks.) Strategic Book Publishing & Rights Agency (SBPRA).
Fabrikant, Amy. When Kayla Was Kyle. Levine, Jennifer, illus. 2013. 32p. pap. 8.95 (978-1-61286-154-8(7)) Avid Readers Publishing Group.
Facey, La-Toya S. Brielle-Elaine Tries to Fit In! 2011. 24p. pap. 14.99 (978-1-4634-2353-7(5)) AuthorHouse.
Fairlie, Emily. The Magician's Bird. Caparo, Antonio Javier, illus. 2014. (Tuckernuck Mysteries Ser.: 2). (ENG.). 288p. (J). (gr. 3-7). pap. 6.99 (978-0-06-211894-3(3), Tegen, Katherine Bks) HarperCollins Pubs.
—The Magician's Bird. 2013. (Tuckernuck Mysteries Ser.: 2). (ENG.). 288p. (J). (gr. 3-7). 16.99 (978-0-06-211893-6(5), Tegen, Katherine Bks) HarperCollins Pubs.
Falconer, Ian. Olivia Saves the Circus. 2004. (Olivia Ser.). (J). (gr. k-2). spiral bd. (978-0-616-11110-9(X)); spiral bd. (978-0-616-11111-6(8)) Canadian National Institute for the Blind/Institut National Canadien pour les Aveugles.
—Olivia Saves the Circus. Falconer, Ian, illus. 2010. (Classic Board Bks.). (ENG., Illus.). 36p. (J). (gr. -1-2). bds. 7.99 (978-1-4424-1287-3(9), Atheneum Bks. for Young Readers) Simon & Schuster Children's Publishing.
Fallin, Rachel. Little Blessings. 2012. 24p. pap. 17.99 (978-1-4685-6209-5(6)) AuthorHouse.
Falwell, Cathryn & National Geographic Learning Staff. David's Drawings. 2010. (Rise & Shine Ser.). (ENG., Illus.). 32p. (C). (gr. -1-2). pap. 14.95 (978-1-58430-261-2(5)) National Geographic School Publishing, Inc.
Falzon, Adrienne. What Is an Angel? Salzberg, Helen, illus. 2012. 32p. 18.99 (978-0-9855562-2-8(6)) Blue Note Pubns.
Fantaskey, Beth. Jekel Loves Hyde. 2011. (ENG.). 288p. (YA). (gr. 9). pap. 8.99 (978-0-547-55027-5(8)) Houghton Mifflin Harcourt Publishing Co.
—Jessica's Guide to Dating on the Dark Side. 2010. (ENG., Illus.). 384p. (YA). (gr. 9-18). pap. 8.99 (978-0-547-25940-6(9)) Houghton Mifflin Harcourt Publishing Co.
Farber, Erica. Richard Scarry's Readers (Level 2): One, Two, AH-CHOO! Scarry, Huck, illus. 2014. (Richard Scarry's Great Big Schoolhouse Ser.). (ENG.). 24p. (J). (gr. k-1). 12.95 (978-1-4549-0380-2(5)) Sterling Publishing Co., Inc.
Faris, Stephanie. 25 Roses. 2015. (Mix Ser.). (ENG., Illus.). 224p. (J). (gr. 4-8). pap. 7.99 (978-1-4814-2420-2(3), Aladdin) Simon & Schuster Children's Publishing.
—30 Days of No Gossip. 2014. (ENG., Illus.). 208p. (J). (gr. 4-8). 17.99 (978-1-4424-8282-1(6), Aladdin) Simon & Schuster Children's Publishing.
Farizan, Sara. Tell Me Again How a Crush Should Feel. 2014. (ENG.). 304p. (YA). (gr. 9-12). 16.95 (978-1-61620-284-2(X), 73284) Algonquin Bks. of Chapel Hill.
Farley, Camille. Emma Just Wants to be Cool!, 1 vol. 2010. 34p. 24.95 (978-1-4489-4529-0(1)) PublishAmerica, Inc.
Farley, Robin. Mia & the Girl with a Twirl. Ivanov, Olga & Ivanov, Aleksey, illus. 2013. (My First I Can Read Ser.). (ENG.). 32p. (J). (gr. -1-3). 16.99 (978-0-06-208689-1(8)); pap. 3.99 (978-0-06-208688-4(X)) HarperCollins Pubs.
—Mia Dances Back to School! Ivanov, Olga & Ivanov, Aleksey, illus. 2013. (Mia Ser.). (ENG.). 24p. (J). (gr. -1-3). pap. 4.99 (978-0-06-210014-6(9), HarperFestival) HarperCollins Pubs.
—Mia Sets the Stage. Ivanov, Olga & Ivanov, Aleksey, illus. 2013. (My First I Can Read Ser.). (ENG.). 32p. (J). (gr. -1-3). pap. 3.99 (978-0-06-208685-3(5)) HarperCollins Pubs.
Farmer, Penelope. Charlotte Sometimes. Connor, Chris, illus. 2007. (ENG.). 208p. (J). (gr. 7-9). 17.95 (978-1-59017-221-6(3), NYR Children's Collection) New York Review of Bks., Inc., The.
Farrar, F. W. Eric, or, Little by Little. 2007. 276p. per. (978-1-4065-1686-9(4)) Dodo Pr.
Farrar, Frederic William. Eric; or, Little by Little. 2006. 372p. per. 26.99 (978-1-4255-3870-5(3)) Michigan Publishing.
Farrar, Josh. A Song for Bijou. 2013. (ENG.). 304p. (YA). (gr. 5-8). 16.99 (978-0-8027-3394-8(8), 9780802733948, Bloomsbury USA Childrens) Bloomsbury Publishing USA.
Farruggia, M. E. Lost Memories. 2013. 352p. pap. 21.99 (978-1-4582-1247-4(5), Abbott Pr.) Author Solutions, Inc.
Faruqi, Reem & Lyon, Lea. Lailah's Lunchbox, 1 vol. 2015. (ENG., Illus.). 32p. (gr. 1-7). 16.95 (978-0-88448-431-8(9), 884431) Tilbury Hse. Pubs.
Fastje, Shanaya B. Mystery School: Monday Sleepover Disaster. 2009. 24p. pap. 12.99 (978-1-4490-0679-2(5)) AuthorHouse.
Fault Line. 2014. (ENG., Illus.). 256p. (YA). (gr. 10). pap. 11.99 (978-1-4424-6073-7(3), Simon Pulse) Simon Pulse.
Favole, Robert. Monday Redux. 2003. 200p. (YA). 15.99 (978-1-930826-11-3(7)) Flywheel Publishing Co.
Fearing, Mark & Rummel, Tim. Earthling! 2012. (ENG., Illus.). 248p. (J). (gr. 3-7). 22.99 (978-0-8118-7106-8(1)) Chronicle Bks. LLC.
—Earthling. 2012. (ENG., Illus.). 248p. (J). (gr. 3-7). pap. 12.99 (978-1-4521-0906-0(0)) Chronicle Bks. LLC.
Feder, Aliza & Sofer, Rochel. We Need to Talk. 2008. 250p. 18.95 (978-1-934440-30-8(2), Devora Publishing) Simcha Media Group.
Fehlbaum, Beth. Big Fat Disaster. (ENG.). (YA). 2015. 286p. pap. 9.99 (978-1-4405-9267-6(5)) 2014. 288p. 17.99 (978-1-4405-7048-3(5)) Simon Pulse. (Simon Pulse).
—Hope in Patience. 2010. 312p. (YA). (gr. 8-18). 16.95 (978-1-934813-41-6(9)) Westside Bks.
Fehler, Gene. Beanball. 2011. (ENG.). 144p. (YA). (gr. 7). pap. 7.99 (978-0-547-55001-5(4)) Houghton Mifflin Harcourt Publishing Co.
Feinstein, John. The Sixth Man. 2016. (Triple Threat Ser.: 2). (ENG.). 304p. (J). (gr. 5). 18.40 (978-0-606-39342-3(0)) Turtleback Bks.
—The Sixth Man (the Triple Threat, 2) 2015. (Triple Threat Ser.). (ENG.). 304p. (YA). (gr. 5). 16.99 (978-0-385-75350-0(0), Knopf Bks. for Young Readers) Random Hse. Children's Bks.
—The Walk On. 2015. (Triple Threat Ser.). (ENG.). 384p. (J). (gr. 5). pap. 7.99 (978-0-385-75349-4(7), Yearling) Random Hse. Children's Bks.
—The Walk On. 2015. (Triple Threat Ser.: 1). lib. bdg. 18.40 (978-0-606-37704-1(2)) Turtleback Bks.
Feldman, Jody. The Seventh Level. (ENG.). (J). (gr. 5). 2011. 320p. pap. 6.99 (978-0-06-195107-7(2)) 2010. 304p. 16.99 (978-0-06-195105-3(6)) HarperCollins Pubs. (Greenwillow Bks.).
Ferguson, Donald. Chums of Scranton High. 2006. 25.95 (978-1-4218-2935-7(5)); pap. 10.95 (978-1-4218-3035-3(3)) 1st World Publishing, Inc.
—The Chums of Scranton High at Ice Hockey. 2007. 124p. per. (978-1-4065-2361-4(5)) Dodo Pr.
—The Chums of Scranton High on the Cinder Path. 2007. 124p. per. (978-1-4065-2363-8(1)) Dodo Pr.
—The Chums of Scranton High, or, Hugh Morgan's Uphill Fight. 2007. 136p. per. (978-1-4065-2362-1(3)) Dodo Pr.
—The Chums of Scranton High Out for the Pennant, or, in the Three Town League. 2007. 124p. per. (978-1-4065-2364-5(X)) Dodo Pr.
Ferguson, Terrence. Stuttering Sammie: I'm Just Like You, I Just Repeat Some Letters or Words When I Talk. 2012. 24p. 24.95 (978-1-4626-6267-8(6)); pap. 24.95 (978-1-4626-8326-0(6)) America Star Bks.
Ferraiolo, Jack D. The Big Splash. 2008. (ENG.). 288p. (YA). (gr. 5-9). 16.95 (978-0-8109-7067-0(8), Amulet Bks.) Abrams, Inc.
Ferreira, Ninha. The Breakthrough: All Star Cheer Articles - Book 1. 2008. (ENG.). 194p. (YA). per. 13.95 (978-0-9815202-0-9(0)) Higgins Publishing.
Ficklin, Sherry D. Losing Logan. 2014. (ENG.). 304p. (J). (gr. 10-12). pap. 9.95 (978-1-940534-41-1(0)) Clean Teen Publishing.
Field, C. D. The Medicine Tree. 2015. (ENG.). 108p. (YA). (gr. 3-4). mass mkt. 11.95 (978-1-78554-535-1(3), 5ff504aa-2872-45d0-b48e-8fde50a9662c) Austin, Stan AUS. Dist: Bookmasters Distribution.
Fielding, Sarah. The Governess, or, the Little Female Academy. 2007. 140p. (gr. 4-7). per. (978-1-4065-2397-3(6)) Dodo Pr.
Fields, Jan. Facing a Frenemy, 1 vol. 2014. (Meri's Mirror Ser.). (ENG., Illus.). 80p. (J). (gr. 2-5). lib. bdg. 27.07 (978-1-62402-008-7(9), Calico Chapter Bks) Magic Wagon.
—Really New School: An Up2U Action Adventure, 1 vol. To, Vivienne, illus. 2013. (Up2U Adventures Ser.). (ENG.). 80p. (J). (gr. 2-5). lib. bdg. 27.07 (978-1-61641-969-1(5), Calico Chapter Bks) Magic Wagon.
—Tattletale Traitor, 1 vol. 2014. (Meri's Mirror Ser.). (ENG., Illus.). 80p. (J). (gr. 2-5). lib. bdg. 27.07 (978-1-62402-010-0(0), Calico Chapter Bks) Magic Wagon.
—Terrible Twin Mania, 1 vol. 2014. (Meri's Mirror Ser.). (ENG.). 80p. (J). (gr. 2-5). lib. bdg. 27.07 (978-1-62402-011-7(9), Calico Chapter Bks) Magic Wagon.
Figley, Marty Rhodes. The Prairie Adventure of Sarah & Annie, Blizzard Survivors. Hammond, Ted & Carbajal, Richard Pimentel, illus. 2011. (History's Kid Heroes Set III Ser.). pap. 51.02 (978-0-7613-8621-6(1)); (ENG.). 32p. (gr. 3-5). pap. 8.95 (978-0-7613-7808-2(1)) Lerner Publishing Group. (Graphic Universe™).
—The Prairie Adventure of Sarah & Annie, Blizzard Survivors. Hammond, Ted & Carbajal, Richard, illus. 2011. (History's Kid Heroes Ser.). (ENG.). 32p. (gr. 3-5). lib. bdg. 26.60 (978-0-7613-7805-1(7)) Lerner Publishing Group.
Finchler, Judy. Testing Miss Malarkey. O'Malley, Kevin, illus. 2003. (Miss Malarkey Ser.). (ENG.). 32p. (J). (gr. k-4). pap. 7.99 (978-0-8027-7624-2(8), 9780802776242, Bloomsbury USA Childrens) Bloomsbury Publishing USA.
—Testing Miss Malarkey. 2004. (J). (gr. 1-5). 17.95 incl. audio (978-0-8045-6897-5(9)) Spoken Arts, Inc.
Finchler, Judy & O'Malley, Kevin. Miss Malarkey Leaves No Reader Behind. O'Malley, Kevin, illus. 2010. (Miss Malarkey Ser.). (ENG., Illus.). 32p. (J). (gr. k-3). pap. 7.99

(978-0-8027-2098-6(6), 9780802720986, Bloomsbury USA Childrens) Bloomsbury Publishing USA.

Fine, Anne. Friday Surprise. Flook, Helen, illus. 2nd ed. 2016. (Reading Ladder Ser.). (ENG.). 48p. (J). (gr. k-2). pap. 7.99 (978-1-4052-8246-8(0)) Egmont Bks., Ltd. GBR. Dist: Independent Pubs. Group.

Finley, Ucal P. A Proper Place for Boogers. Stroud, Brenda D., illus. 2011. 54p. pap. 12.95 (978-0-9834307-0-4(5)) G Publishing LLC.

Finn, Caitlin. Harold the Misfit. 2012. 24p. pap. 14.93 (978-1-4669-5131-0(1)) Trafford Publishing.

Finn, Perdita. Crashing the Party. Dorman, Brandon, illus. 2007. 109p. (J). (978-0-439-74436-2(9)) Scholastic, Inc.

—Going for the Gold. 2007. 118p. (J). (978-0-439-89208-7(2)) Scholastic, Inc.

—Monster High - Haunted. 2015. (ENG., Illus.). 144p. (J). (gr. 3-7). pap. 5.99 (978-0-316-37739-3(2)) Little, Brown Bks. for Young Readers.

—Monster High: Electrified: the Deluxe Junior Novel. 2017. (ENG.). 144p. (J). (gr. 3-7). 9.99 **(978-0-316-54826-7(X))** Little, Brown Bks. for Young Readers.

—Monster High: Electrified: the Junior Novel. 2017. (ENG.). 144p. (J). (gr. 3-7). pap. 6.99 **(978-0-316-54836-6(7))** Little, Brown Bks. for Young Readers.

Finney, Ruth. A Prayer for Momma. 2007. 38p. pap. 8.00 (978-0-8059-7483-6(0)) Dorrance Publishing Co., Inc.

Finneyfrock, Karen. Starbird Murphy & the World Outside. 2014. (ENG.). 384p. (YA). (gr. 7). 17.99 (978-0-670-01276-3(9), Viking Books for Young Readers) Penguin Young Readers Group.

—The Sweet Revenge of Celia Door. 2014. (ENG.). 288p. (YA). (gr. 7). pap. 9.99 (978-0-14-750995-6(5), Speak) Penguin Young Readers Group.

Fiorella, Christina. Timothy's New School Worries. 2008. 24p. pap. 14.49 (978-1-4343-6364-0(3)) AuthorHouse.

Fisch, Sarah & Bridwell, Norman. Backpack Puppy. Durk, Jim, illus. 2005. (J). pap. (978-0-439-73379-3(0)) Scholastic, Inc.

Fischer, Ellen. If an Elephant Went to School. Wood, Laura, illus. 2015. (ENG.). 32p. (J). (-2). 14.95 (978-1-938063-61-9(9), Mighty Media Kids) Mighty Media Pr.

Fischer, JoAnn. Our Teacher Is A Fish! 2008. (ENG.). 34p. pap. 10.00 (978-1-4196-7477-8(3)) CreateSpace Independent Publishing Platform.

Fishbone, Greg. The Penguins of Doom. 2007. (From the Desk of Septina Nash Ser.). (ENG., Illus.). 182p. (J). (gr. 2-7). 13.95 (978-1-933831-03-9(0)) Blooming Tree Pr.

Fisher, Catherine. Darkwater. 2012. (ENG.). 240p. (YA). (gr. 7). 16.99 (978-0-8037-3818-8(8), Dial Bks) Penguin Young Readers Group.

Fisher, Doris & Sneed, Dani. One Odd Day, 1 vol. Lee, Karen, illus. 2006. (Basic Math Numbers Ser.). (ENG.). 32p. (J). (gr. -1-3). 15.95 (978-0-9768823-3-6(7)) Arbordale Publishing.

Fisher, Jane Smith. On the Air!, Vol. 1. 2003. (Illus.). 96p. (gr. 4-8). pap. 11.95 (978-0-9744235-0-0(5)) Wilson Place Comics.

Fisher-Price Little People. Let's Imagine at School. 2015. (Fisher Price Lift the Flap Ser.). (ENG.). 10p. (J). (gr. -1-k). bds. 9.99 (978-0-7944-3467-0(3), Reader's Digest Children's Bks.) Studio Fun International.

Fisk, Katie. Flying with the Angels. 2008. 62p. pap. 19.95 (978-1-60563-608-5(8)) America Star Bks.

FitzGerald, Dawn. Getting in the Game. 2007. (ENG.). 144p. (J). (gr. 4-8). pap. 16.99 (978-0-312-37753-3(3), 9780312377533) Square Fish.

—Soccer Chick Rules. 2007. (ENG.). 160p. (J). (gr. 5-9). per. 9.99 (978-0-312-37662-8(6), 9780312376628) Square Fish.

Fitzgerald, Mary. Jodie Has Jagged Edges. 2012. (ENG.). 21p. (J). pap. 22.95 (978-1-4327-8839-1(6)) Outskirts Pr., Inc.

Fitzhugh, Louise. Harriet the Spy. 298p. (J). (gr. 3-5). pap. 5.95 (978-0-8072-1535-7(X), Listening Library) Random Hse. Audio Publishing Group.

—Harriet the Spy. 50th anniv. ed. 2014. (ENG.). 336p. (J). (gr. 3-7). 17.99 (978-0-385-37610-5(3), Delacorte Bks. for Young Readers) Random Hse. Children's Bks.

Fitzpatrick, Becca. The Complete Hush, Hush Saga: Hush, Hush; Crescendo; Silence; Finale. 2012. (Hush, Hush Saga Ser.: Bks. 1-4). (ENG.). 1744p. (YA). (gr. 9). 74.99 (978-1-4424-7372-0(X), Simon & Schuster Bks. For Young Readers) Simon & Schuster Bks. For Young Readers.

—Hush, Hush. (SPA.). 368p. 2010. (Hush, Hush Saga: Bk. 1). (YA). pap. 20.95 (978-84-666-4417-4(2)) pap. 13.95 (978-84-9872-932-0(7)) Ediciones B ESP. Dist: Spanish Pubs., LLC.

—Hush, Hush, 3 vols. Ruiz, Derek, ed. 2012. (Hush, Hush Saga: Bk. 1). (Illus.). 120p. (YA). 19.95 (978-0-9836131-1-4(7)) Sea Lion Bks.

—Hush, Hush. (Hush, Hush Saga Ser.: Bk. 1). (ENG.). (YA). (gr. 9-18). 2010. 432p. pap. 11.99 (978-1-4169-8942-4(0)) 2009. 400p. 21.99 (978-1-4169-8941-7(2)) Simon & Schuster Bks. For Young Readers. (Simon & Schuster Bks. For Young Readers).

Flake, Sharon G. Pinned. (ENG.). 240p. (J). 2014. (gr. 9). pap. 9.99 (978-0-545-05733-2(7)) 2012. (gr. 8-9). 17.99 (978-0-545-05718-9(3)) Scholastic, Inc. (Scholastic Pr.).

—The Skin I'm In. 2007. (J). lib. bdg. 19.65 (978-1-4178-0860-1(8), Turtleback) Turtleback Bks.

Flanagan, Liz. Eden Summer. 2017. (ENG.). 288p. (J). (gr. 7). 18.99 **(978-1-338-12120-9(0))** Scholastic, Inc.

Fleischman, Paul. The Dunderheads. Roberts, David, illus. 2012. (ENG.). 56p. (J). (gr. 1-4). pap. 6.99 (978-0-7636-5239-5(3)) Candlewick Pr.

Fleming, Candace. The Fabled Fifth Graders of Aesop Elementary School. 2012. (Aesop Elementary School Ser.). (ENG.). 176p. (J). (gr. 2-5). 7.99 (978-0-375-87187-0(X), Yearling) Random Hse. Children's Bks.

—The Fabled Fourth Graders of Aesop Elementary School. 2009. (Aesop Elementary School Ser.). (ENG.). 192p. (J). (gr. 2-5). 6.99 (978-0-440-42229-7(9), Yearling) Random Hse. Children's Bks.

Fletcher, Alison. Lucy & Lila. Lyles, Christopher, illus. 2016. (ENG.). 32p. (J). (gr. -1-3). 16.99 (978-1-4998-0156-9(4)) Little Bee Books Inc.

Fletcher, Brenden. Yearbook. 2016. (Gotham Academy Ser.: 3). lib. bdg. 29.40 (978-0-606-39222-8(X)) Turtleback Bks.

Fletcher, Ralph. Flying Solo. 2008. (ENG.). 144p. (J). (gr. 5-7). pap. 7.99 (978-0-547-07652-2(5)) Houghton Mifflin Harcourt Publishing Co.

—Spider Boy. 2009. (ENG.). 192p. (J). (gr. 5-7). pap. 6.99 (978-0-547-24820-2(2)) Houghton Mifflin Harcourt Publishing Co.

Flinn, Alex. Diva. 2013. (ENG.). 304p. (YA). (gr. 9). pap. 9.99 (978-0-06-212434-0(X)) 2007. (ENG.). 288p. (J). (gr. 9-12). pap. 8.99 (978-0-06-056846-7(1), HarperTeen) 2006. 263p. (YA). (gr. 7-12). 16.99 (978-0-06-056843-6(7), HarperTeen) 2006. 263p. (YA). (gr. 7-12). lib. bdg. 18.89 (978-0-06-056845-0(3), HarperTeen) HarperCollins Pubs.

—Fade to Black. 2006. (ENG.). 208p. (YA). (gr. 9-12). pap. 9.99 (978-0-06-056842-9(9), HarperTeen) HarperCollins Pubs.

—Mirrored. 2015. (Kendra Chronicles Ser.: 3). (ENG.). 384p. (YA). (gr. 8). 17.99 (978-0-06-213451-6(5)) HarperCollins Pubs.

Flood, Pansie Hart. It's Test Day, Tiger Turcotte. Wummer, Amy, tr. Wummer, Amy, illus. 2004. (Young Reader Fiction Ser.). 72p. (J). (gr. 1-4). pap. 6.95 (978-1-57505-670-8(4)); lib. bdg. 19.93 (978-1-57505-056-0(0), Carolrhoda Bks.) Lerner Publishing Group.

—Sometimey Friend. Marshall, Felicia, illus. 2005. 124p. (J). (gr. 3-7). 15.95 (978-1-57505-866-5(9)) Lerner Publishing Group.

—Tiger's Trouble with Donut Head. Wummer, Amy, illus. 2005. 71p. (J). lib. bdg. 19.93 (978-1-57505-814-6(6), Carolrhoda Bks.) Lerner Publishing Group.

Flor Ada, Alma. Celebra el Cinco de Mayo con un Jarabe Tapatio. Gomez, Marcela & Silva, David, illus. 2006. (Cuentos para Celebrar / Stories to Celebrate Ser.). 30p. (gr. k-6). per. 11.95 (978-1-59820-118-5(2)) Ediciones Alfaguara ESP. Dist: Santillana USA Publishing Co., Inc.

—Celebrate Martin Luther King, Jr. Day with Mrs. Park's Class. Weiss, Monica, illus. 2006. (Stories to Celebrate Ser.). 30p. (gr. k-6). per. 11.95 (978-1-59820-125-3(5), Alfaguara) Santillana USA Publishing Co., Inc.

Flor, Ada Alma. My Name Is Maria Isabel. 2014. (ENG.). 64p. (J). (gr. 12-12). 9.24 (978-1-63245-189-7(1)) Lectorum Pubns., Inc.

Flores-Scott, Patrick. Jumped In. 2013. (ENG.). 304p. (YA). (gr. 7). 16.99 (978-0-8050-9514-2(4), 9780805095142, Holt, Henry & Co. Bks. For Young Readers) Holt, Henry & Co.

—Jumped In. 2014. (ENG., Illus.). 304p. (YA). (gr. 7). pap. 10.99 (978-1-250-05398-5(6), 9781250053985) Square Fish.

Florido, Lorraine. Hugo the Punk. Shami, Susan, ed. Ewing, John, illus. 2013. 108p. (YA). pap. 9.98 (978-0-9818449-6-1(0)) Thinkus Pubs.

Flower, Graham Jessie. Grace Harlowe's Junior Year at High School: Or Fast Friends in the Sororities. 2007. (ENG.). 162p. pap. 19.99 (978-1-4346-1306-6(2)); 178p. pap. 21.99 (978-1-4346-1358-5(5)) Creative Media Partners, LLC.

—Grace Harlowe's Senior Year at High School. 2006. 156p. pap. 19.99 (978-1-4264-1912-6(0)) Creative Media Partners, LLC.

—Grace Harlowe's Senior Year at High School. 2004. reprint ed. pap. 21.95 (978-1-4191-2224-8(X)) Kessinger Publishing, LLC.

—Grace Harlowe's Sophomore Year at High School: The Record of the Girl Chums in Work & Athletics. 2007. 154p. pap. 19.99 (978-1-4264-8570-1(0)); (ENG.). 174p. pap. 21.99 (978-1-4264-8627-2(8)) Creative Media Partners, LLC.

Floyd, Kara. Olivia West vs. Middle School: Round One. 2013. 164p. pap. 11.99 (978-1-937165-34-5(5)) Orange Hat Publishing.

Floyd, Lucy. Conejo y Tortuga van a la Escuela. Flor Ada, Alma & Campoy, F. Isabel, trs. from ENG. Denise, Christopher, illus. 2010. (Green Light Readers Level 1 Ser.).Tr. of Rabbit & Turtle Go to School. (SPA & ENG.). 28p. (J). (gr. -1-3). pap. 3.99 (978-0-547-33898-9(8)) Houghton Mifflin Harcourt Publishing Co.

Flying Solo. 2011. 8.32 (978-0-7848-3634-7(5), Everbind) Marco Bk. Co.

Flynn, Pat. Alex Jackson: Dropping In. 2004. (Illus.). 80p. (Orig.). (J). pap. (978-0-7022-3433-0(8)) Univ. of Queensland Pr.

Flynn, Warren. Return Ticket. 2003. (Illus.). 272p. pap. 13.50 (978-1-920731-90-8(3)) Fremantle Pr. AUS. Dist: Independent Pubs. Group.

Fogelin, Adrian. The Big Nothing. (ENG.). 224p. (J). (gr. 3-7). 2006. pap. 7.95 (978-1-56145-388-7(9)) 2004. 15.95 (978-1-56145-326-9(9)) Peachtree Pubs.

—The Real Question, 1 vol. (ENG.). 256p. (YA). 2009. pap. 7.95 (978-1-56145-501-0(6)) 2006. (gr. 7-18). 15.95 (978-1-56145-383-2(8)) Peachtree Pubs.

Fogleman, Laurie. Jimmy, What Are You Eating?! 2011. 64p. (gr. -1). pap. 9.99 (978-1-4634-1206-7(1)) AuthorHouse.

Fontes, Justine. Deadly Drive. 2013. (Surviving Southside Ser.). (ENG.). 104p. (YA). (gr. 6-12). pap. 7.95 (978-1-4677-0704-6(X)); lib. bdg. 27.93 (978-1-4677-0310-9(9)) Lerner Publishing Group.

—Showdown in Crittertown. 2014. (Cheddar's Tales Ser.). (ENG.). 176p. (J). (gr. 2-4). pap. 5.99 (978-1-4380-0360-3(9)) Barron's Educational Series, Inc.

Ford, Carrie Elizabeth. Anonymous. 2012. 150p. 24.95 (978-1-4626-6158-9(0)) America Star Bks.

Foreman, Matthew Sinclair. Disney Descendants - Secrets Revealed. 2016. (ENG.). 20p. (J). (gr. 3-6). 16.99 (978-0-7944-3750-3(8), Reader's Digest Children's Bks.) Studio Fun International.

Forester, Victoria. The Boy Who Knew Everything. 2015. (ENG.). 416p. (J). (gr. 4-7). 16.99 (978-0-312-62600-6(2), 9780312626006) Feiwel & Friends.

—The Girl Who Could Fly. 2008. (ENG.). 336p. (J). (gr. 4-7). 16.95 (978-0-312-37462-4(3), 9780312374624) Feiwel & Friends.

—The Girl Who Could Fly. Barcellona, Christine, ed. 2015. (ENG.). 352p. (J). (gr. 4-7). pap. 7.99 (978-1-250-07246-7(8), 9781250072467) Square Fish.

Forgetful Fred: 6 Small Books. (gr. k-3). 24.00 (978-0-7635-6237-3(8)) Rigby Education.

Formento, Alison. This Tree Counts!, 1 vol. Snow, Sarah, illus. 2010. (These Things Count! Ser.). (ENG.). 32p. (J). (gr. -1-3). 16.99 (978-0-8075-7890-2(8)) Whitman, Albert & Co.

Forney, Lane. The Super Power Teens 2: A Blast from the Past. 2010. 137p. pap. 14.99 (978-0-557-09707-4(X)) Lulu Pr., Inc.

Fox, Laura. Stan the Timid Turtle: Helping Children Cope with Fears about School Violence. DuFalla, Anita, illus. 2014. (ENG.). 48p. (J). (gr. -1-2). 9.95 (978-0-88282-466-6(X)) New Horizon Pr. Pubs., Inc.

Frampton, David. Beastie ABC. Frampton, David, illus. Date not set. (Illus.). 32p. (J). (gr. -1-1). pap. 5.99 (978-0-06-443653-3(5)) HarperCollins Pubs.

France, Richard. Joshua Stories: Book 1 - New School, New Friends. 2011. (Illus.). 104p. (gr. 4-6). pap. 14.09 (978-1-4567-7732-6(7)) AuthorHouse.

Francis, Melissa. Bite Me! 2009. (ENG.). 304p. (YA). (gr. 9-18). pap. 8.99 (978-0-06-143098-5(6), HarperTeen) HarperCollins Pubs.

Franco, Betsy. Double Play: Monkeying Around with Addition. Cushman, Doug, illus. 2011. (ENG.). 32p. (J). (gr. -1-2). 15.99 (978-1-58246-384-1(0), Tricycle Pr.) Random Hse. Children's Bks.

—Metamorphosis: Junior Year. Franco, Tom & Franco, Betsy, illus. 2009. (ENG.). 128p. (YA). (gr. 9-18). 16.99 (978-0-7636-3765-1(3)) Candlewick Pr.

Frank, Lucy. Lucky Stars. 2014. (ENG.). 304p. (J). (gr. 5-9). pap. 14.99 (978-1-4814-2901-6(9), Atheneum Bks. for Young Readers) Simon & Schuster Children's Publishing.

Frank, Steven B. Armstrong & Charlie. 2017. (ENG.). 304p. (J). (gr. 5-7). 16.99 (978-0-544-82608-3(6), HMH Books For Young Readers) Houghton Mifflin Harcourt Publishing Co.

Frankel, Erin. Nobody! A Story about Overcoming Bullying in Schools. Heaphy, Paula, illus. 2015. (ENG.). 48p. (J). (gr. k-4). 15.99 (978-1-57542-495-8(9)) Free Spirit Publishing, Inc.

Franklin, Emily. Last Night at the Circle Cinema. 2015. (ENG.). 200p. (YA). (gr. 8-12). 18.99 (978-1-4677-7489-5(8)) Lerner Publishing Group.

Frasier, Debra. Miss Alaineus: A Vocabulary Disaster. Frasier, Debra, illus. 2007. (ENG., Illus.). 40p. (J). (gr. -1-3). pap. 7.99 (978-0-15-206053-4(7)) Houghton Mifflin Harcourt Publishing Co.

Frazier, Angie. The Mastermind Plot. 2012. (ENG.). 240p. (J). (gr. 3-7). 16.99 (978-0-545-20864-2(5), Scholastic Pr.) Scholastic, Inc.

Frazier, Sundee T. Brendan Buckley's Sixth-Grade Experiment. 2013. (ENG.). 288p. (J). (gr. 4-7). 6.99 (978-0-385-74051-7(4), Yearling) Random Hse. Children's Bks.

Fredericks, Mariah. Crunch Time. 2007. (ENG.). 336p. (YA). (gr. 7-12). pap. 15.99 (978-1-4169-3973-3(3), Atheneum Bks. for Young Readers) Simon & Schuster Children's Publishing.

—The Girl in the Park. 2013. (ENG.). 224p. (YA). (gr. 9). pap. 8.99 (978-0-449-81591-5(9), Ember) Random Hse. Children's Bks.

—Head Games. 2006. (ENG., Illus.). 272p. (YA). (gr. 7). pap. 6.99 (978-1-4169-1335-1(1), Atheneum Bks. for Young Readers) Simon & Schuster Children's Publishing.

Freeman, Martha. Fourth-Grade Weirdo. 2004. (Illus.). 147p. (gr. 4-7). 15.50 (978-0-7569-4117-8(2)) Perfection Learning Corp.

—The Secret Cookie Club. 2015. (Secret Cookie Club Ser.). (ENG., Illus.). 304p. (J). (gr. 3-7). 16.99 (978-1-4814-1046-5(6), Simon & Schuster Bks. For Young Readers) Simon & Schuster Bks. For Young Readers.

Freeman, Shannon. High School High, 1 vol. 2013. (Port City High Ser.). (ENG.). 199p. (YA). (gr. 9-12). pap. 9.95 (978-1-62250-037-6(7)) Saddleback Educational Publishing, Inc.

—High School High. 2013. (Port City High Ser.: 1). (YA). lib. bdg. 20.80 (978-0-606-31773-3(2), Turtleback) Turtleback Bks.

—Taken, 1 vol. 2013. (Port City High Ser.). (ENG.). 199p. (YA). (gr. 9-12). pap. 9.95 (978-1-62250-038-3(5)) Saddleback Educational Publishing, Inc.

—Traumatized. 2014. (Port City High Ser.: 7). (YA). lib. bdg. 20.80 (978-0-606-36619-9(9)) Turtleback Bks.

Frelinghuysen Eighth Grade Storytellers Staff. Flash Before My Eyes. 2008. 52p. pap. 8.95 (978-0-595-52714-4(0)) iUniverse, Inc.

French, Jackie. My Dad the Dragon. King, Stephen Michael, illus. 2004. 128p. (978-0-207-19950-9(7)) HarperCollins Pubs. Australia.

French, Moira. The Swingewood Stories. 2009. 36p. pap. 16.99 (978-1-4490-4777-1(7)) AuthorHouse.

French, Simon. My Cousin's Keeper. 2014. (ENG.). 240p. (J). (gr. 3-7). 16.99 (978-0-7636-6279-0(8)) Candlewick Pr.

French, Vivian. Princess Charlotte & the Enchanted Rose. Gibb, Sarah, illus. 2007. (Tiara Club Ser.: No. 7). 80p. (J). (gr. 1-4). pap. 3.99 (978-0-06-112441-9(9), Tegen, Katherine Bks) HarperCollins Pubs.

—Princess Katie & the Silver Pony. Gibb, Sarah, illus. 2007. (Tiara Club Ser.: No.2). 80p. (J). (gr. 1-4). 15.99 (978-0-06-112432-7(X), Tegen, Katherine Bks) HarperCollins Pubs.

—The Tiara Club at Ruby Mansions No. 5: Princess Lauren & the Diamond Necklace. 2008. (Tiara Club Ser.). (ENG., Illus.). 80p. (J). (gr. 1-4). pap. 3.99 (978-0-06-143488-4(4), Tegen, Katherine Bks) HarperCollins Pubs.

Frey, Hildegard G. The Camp Fire Girls at School or the Woleho Weavers. 2004. reprint ed. pap. 1.99 (978-1-4192-5575-5(4)); pap. 21.95 (978-1-4191-5575-8(X)) Kessinger Publishing, LLC.

Freytag, Lorna. My Humongous Hamster Goes to School. Freytag, Lorna, illus. 2015. (My Humongous Hamster Ser.). (ENG., Illus.). 32p. (J). (gr. -1-3). 16.99 (978-1-62779-140-3(X), 9781627791403, Holt, Henry & Co. Bks. For Young Readers) Holt, Henry & Co.

Fridolfs, Derek. Secret Hero Society- Study Hall of Justice. Nguyen, Dustin, illus. 2016. 176p. (J). pap. **(978-1-76027-653-9(7))** Scholastic, Inc.

Friedland, Joyce, ed. Cool Zone with Pain & the Great One: Novel-Ties Study Guide. 2011. 29p. pap. 16.95 (978-0-7675-4471-9(4)) Learning Links Inc.

Friedman, Becky. Daniel Goes to School. 2014. (Daniel Tiger's Neighborhood 8X8 Ser.). lib. bdg. 13.55 (978-0-606-35756-2(4)) Turtleback Bks.

Friedman, Darlene. Star of the Week: A Story of Love, Adoption, & Brownies with Sprinkles. Roth, Roger, illus. 2009. (ENG.). 32p. (J). (gr. k-3). 17.99 (978-0-06-114136-2(4)) HarperCollins Pubs.

Friedman, Laurie. Back to School, Mallory. Schmitz, Tamara, illus. (Mallory Ser.: 2). (ENG.). 176p. (J). (gr. 2-5). 2005. per. 5.95 (978-1-57505-865-8(0)) 2004. 15.95 (978-1-57505-658-6(5)) Lerner Publishing Group.

—Back-to-School Rules. Murfin, Teresa, illus. 2011. (Carolrhoda Picture Books Ser.). (ENG.). 32p. (J). (gr. k-3). lib. bdg. 16.95 (978-0-7613-6070-4(0)) Lerner Publishing Group.

—A Clases Otra Vez, Mallory. Anaya, Josefina, tr. from ENG. Schmitz, Tamara, illus. 2008. (Mallory en español (Mallory in Spanish) Ser.).Tr. of Back to School, Mallory. (SPA & ENG.). 176p. (J). (gr. 2-5). pap. 5.95 (978-0-7613-3904-5(3)) Lerner Publishing Group.

—High Five, Mallory! Kalis, Jennifer, illus. (Mallory Ser.: Vol. 26). (ENG.). 160p. (J). 2017. (gr. 2-5). pap. 5.95 **(978-1-5124-5867-1(8))** 2016. (gr. 3-3). E-Book 11.99 (978-1-5124-0898-0(0), 9781512408980) Lerner Publishing Group. (Darby Creek).

—High Five, Mallory! Kalis, Jennifer, illus. 2016. (Mallory Ser.: 26). (ENG.). 160p. (gr. 2-5). 15.95 (978-1-4677-5030-1(1)) Lerner Publishing Group.

—Honestly, Mallory! 2009. pap. 34.95 (978-0-7613-4788-0(7)) Lerner Publishing Group.

—Honestly, Mallory! Pollak, Barbara, illus. (Mallory Ser.: 8). (ENG.). 160p. (J). (gr. 2-5). 2008. pap. 5.95 (978-1-58013-840-6(3), First Avenue Editions) 2007. 15.95 (978-0-8225-6193-4(X), Carolrhoda Bks.) Lerner Publishing Group.

—Mallory Goes Green! Kalis, Jennifer, illus. (Mallory Ser.: 13). (ENG.). 160p. (J). (gr. 2-5). 2011. pap. 5.95 (978-0-7613-3949-6(3)) 2010. 15.95 (978-0-8225-8885-6(4), Carolrhoda Bks.) Lerner Publishing Group.

—Mallory in the Spotlight. Kalis, Jennifer, illus. (Mallory Ser.). 2011. pap. 33.92 (978-0-7613-8359-8(X), Darby Creek) 2011. (ENG.). 160p. (J). (gr. 2-5). pap. 5.95 (978-0-7613-3948-9(5), Darby Creek) 2010. (ENG.). 160p. (J). (gr. 2-5). 15.95 (978-0-8225-8884-9(6), Carolrhoda Bks.) Lerner Publishing Group.

—Mallory Makes a Difference. Kalis, Jennifer, illus. 2017. (Mallory Ser.: 28). (ENG.). 152p. (gr. 2-5). 15.95 **(978-1-4677-5032-5(8))** Lerner Publishing Group.

—Mallory's Guide to Boys, Brothers, Dads, & Dogs. Kalis, Jennifer, illus. (Mallory Ser.). 160p. (J). (gr. 2-5). 2012. pap. 33.92 (978-0-7613-9206-4(8), Darby Creek) 2012. (ENG.). pap. 5.95 (978-0-7613-5250-1(3), Darby Creek) 2011. (ENG.). 15.95 (978-0-8225-8886-3(2), Carolrhoda Bks.) Lerner Publishing Group.

—Not What I Expected. Shaloshvili, Natasha, illus. 2015. (Mostly Miserable Life of April Sinclair Ser.: 5). (ENG.). 176p. (J). (gr. 5-9). 17.99 (978-1-4677-8829-8(5), Darby Creek) Lerner Publishing Group.

—Play It Again, Mallory. Kalis, Jennifer, illus. (Mallory Ser.: 20). (ENG.). 160p. (J). (gr. 2-5). 2014. pap. 5.95 (978-1-4677-0936-1(0)) 2013. 15.95 (978-0-7613-6075-9(1)) Lerner Publishing Group. (Darby Creek).

—Red, White, & True Blue Mallory. Kalis, Jennifer, illus. 2009. (Mallory Ser.: 11). (ENG.). 184p. (J). (gr. 2-5). 15.95 (978-0-8225-8882-5(X), Carolrhoda Bks.) Lerner Publishing Group.

—Step Fourth, Mallory! Kalis, Jennifer, illus. (Mallory Ser.: 10). (ENG.). 176p. (J). (gr. 2-5). 2009. pap. 5.95 (978-1-58013-842-0(X), First Avenue Editions) 2008. 15.95 (978-0-8225-8881-8(1), Carolrhoda Bks.) Lerner Publishing Group.

—Too Much Drama. Shaloshvili, Natasha, illus. 2016. (Mostly Miserable Life of April Sinclair Ser.: 6). (ENG.). 184p. (gr. 5-9). 35.99 (978-1-4677-9570-8(4), Darby Creek) Lerner Publishing Group.

Friedman, Laurie B. Not What I Expected. Shaloshvili, Natasha, illus. 2015. (ENG.). 176p. (J). (gr. 5-9). 17.95 (978-1-4677-8588-4(1)) Lerner Publishing Group.

Friend, Natasha. For Keeps. 2011. (ENG.). 272p. (YA). (gr. 7-18). 7.99 (978-0-14-241846-8(3), Speak) Penguin Young Readers Group.

—Where You'll Find Me. 2016. (ENG.). 272p. (YA). 16.99 (978-0-374-30230-6(8), 9780374302306, Farrar, Straus & Giroux (BYR)) Farrar, Straus & Giroux.

—Where You'll Find Me. 2017. (YA). lib. bdg. 20.85 **(978-0-606-39591-5(1))** Turtleback Bks.

Frino, Michael G. Welcome to Waycool School: Where Learning Is Fun & Lessons are Learned by Everyone! 2010. 32p. pap. 17.25 (978-1-4269-4048-4(3)) Trafford Publishing.

Frino Ph. D., Michael G. Waycool School Takes the Bus. 2011. 40p. pap. (978-1-4269-9003-8(0)) Trafford Publishing (UK) Ltd.

Frizzell, Colin. Chill, 1 vol. 2006. (Orca Soundings Ser.). (ENG.). 128p. (YA). (gr. 8-12). per. 9.95 (978-1-55143-507-7(1)) Orca Bk. Pubs. USA.

Froley, Margaux. Escape Theory. 2014. (ENG., Illus.). 288p. (YA). (gr. 9). pap. 9.99 (978-1-61695-342-3(X), Soho Teen) Soho Pr., Inc.

—Hero Complex. 2015. (ENG., Illus.). 216p. (YA). (gr. 9). pap. 10.99 (978-1-61695-573-1(2), Soho Teen) Soho Pr., Inc.

Frost, Helen. Diamond Willow. 2011. (ENG.). 144p. (J). (gr. 5-9). pap. 7.99 (978-0-312-60383-0(5), 9780312603830) Square Fish.

—Room 214: a Year in Poems. 2014. (ENG., Illus.). 128p. (J). (gr. 5-9). pap. 8.99 (978-1-250-04009-1(4), 9781250040091) Square Fish.

Fruchter, Jason, illus. Daniel Plays at School. 2016. (Daniel Tiger's Neighborhood Ser.). (ENG.). 32p. (J). (gr. -1-k). pap. 3.99 (978-1-4814-6102-3(8), Simon Spotlight) Simon Spotlight.

Fry, Michael. The Odd Squad King Karl. Fry, Michael, illus. 2014. (Odd Squad Book Ser.). (ENG., Illus.). 208p. (J). (gr. 3-7). 12.99 (978-1-4231-9958-8(8)) Hyperion Bks. for Children.

—Zero Tolerance. Fry, Michael, illus. 2013. (Odd Squad Book Ser.). (ENG., Illus.). 240p. (J). (gr. 3-7). 12.99 (978-1-4231-7099-0(7)) Hyperion Pr.

Fujieda, Toru, creator. Dragon Girl. (Dragon Girl Ser.: 1). (ENG., Illus.). (J). (gr. 8-17). 2010. 496p. pap. 20.99 (978-0-7595-3166-6(8)) Vol. 2. 2011. 464p. pap. 20.99 (978-0-7595-3167-3(6)) Orbit. (Yen Pr.).

Fuller, Kimberly. H a Carter. 2012. 138p. 28.99 (978-1-105-83103-4(5)) Lulu Pr., Inc.

Fulton-Vengco, Aletha. Felicidad & Her Pen Pal Kamar. 2009. 33p. 13.90 *(978-0-578-02728-9(3))* Vengco, Aletha Fulton.

Funke, Cornelia. Ghost Knight. 2013.Tr. of Geisterritter. (ENG., Illus.). 352p. (J). (gr. 3-7). pap. 7.99 *(978-0-316-05616-8(2))* Little, Brown Bks. for Young Readers.

Funny School Stories: Learning to Read Box Set. 2016. (I Can Read Level 1 Ser.). 192p. (J). (gr. -1-3). pap. 16.99 *(978-0-06-231336-2(3))* HarperCollins Pubs.

Fuqua, Jonathon Scott. The Reappearance of Sam Webber. 2010. (ENG.). 250p. pap. 12.95 *(978-1-890862-60-2(6))* Bancroft Pr.

Fuss, Kevin. The Brothers Geek. 2010. 180p. 24.99 *(978-1-4490-7366-4(2))* AuthorHouse.

Fussell, Sandy. Owl Ninja. James, Rhian Nest, illus. 2011. (Samurai Kids Ser.: 2). (ENG.). 272p. (J). (gr. 4-7). 15.99 *(978-0-7636-5003-2(X))* Candlewick Pr.

—Shaolin Tiger. James, Rhian Nest, illus. 2011. (Samurai Kids Ser.: 3). (ENG.). 272p. (J). (gr. 4-7). pap. 6.99 *(978-0-7636-5702-4(6))* Candlewick Pr.

—White Crane. James, Rhian Nest, illus. 2010. (Samurai Kids Ser.: 1). (ENG.). 256p. (J). (gr. 4-7). 15.99 *(978-0-7636-4503-8(6))* Candlewick Pr.

Galante, Cecilia. The One & Only Willa Bean. Valiant, Kristi, illus. 2012. (Little Wings Ser.: 4). (ENG.). 112p. (J). (gr. 1-4). pap. 4.99 *(978-0-375-86950-1(6))*, Random Hse. Bks. for Young Readers) Random Hse. Children's Bks.

—Willowood. 2011. (ENG.). 288p. (J). (gr. 4-8). pap. 6.99 *(978-1-4169-8303-3(1))*, Aladdin) Simon & Schuster Children's Publishing.

—Willowood. 2010. (ENG.). 272p. (J). (gr. 4-8). 16.99 *(978-1-4169-8022-3(9))*, Simon & Schuster/Paula Wiseman Bks.) Simon & Schuster/Paula Wiseman Bks.

—The World from up Here. (ENG.). 320p. (J). (gr. 3-7). 2017. pap. 6.99 ***(978-0-545-84846-6(6))*** 2016. 16.99 *(978-0-545-84845-9(8))*, Scholastic Pr.) Scholastic, Inc.

Galbraith, Kathryn O. Sparky & Tidbit. Kelley, Gerald, illus. 2015. (Ready-To-Reads Ser.). (ENG.). 40p. (J). (gr. 1-3). pap. 3.99 *(978-1-4814-0424-2(5))*, Simon Spotlight) Simon Spotlight.

Gale, Eric Kahn. The Bully Book. 2013. (ENG.). 256p. (J). (gr. 3-7). pap. 6.99 *(978-0-06-212513-2(3))* HarperCollins Pubs.

Gall, Chris. Substitute Creacher. 2011. (ENG., Illus.). 40p. (J). (gr. -1-3). 16.99 *(978-0-316-08915-9(X))* Little, Brown Bks. for Young Readers.

Gallagher, Diana G. Advice about School: Claudia Cristina Cortez Uncomplicates Your Life. Garvey, Brann, illus. 2010. (Claudia Cristina Cortez Ser.). (ENG.). 80p. (gr. 2-3). pap. 6.10 *(978-1-4342-2252-7(7))*; 26.65 *(978-1-4342-1905-3(4))* Stone Arch Bks. (Claudia Cristina Cortez).

—Beware! The Complicated Life of Claudia Cristina Cortez, 1 vol. Garvey, Brann, illus. 2009. (Claudia Cristina Cortez Ser.). (ENG.). 88p. (gr. 2-3). 26.65 *(978-1-4342-1575-8(X))*, Claudia Cristina Cortez) Stone Arch Bks.

—Dance Trap: The Complicated Life of Claudia Cristina Cortez, 1 vol. Garvey, Brann, illus. 2007. (Claudia Cristina Cortez Ser.). (ENG.). 88p. (gr. 2-3). per. 6.10 *(978-1-59889-879-8(5))*, Claudia Cristina Cortez) Stone Arch Bks.

—Friends Forever? The Complicated Life of Claudia Cristina Cortez, 1 vol. Garvey, Brann, illus. 2008. (Claudia Cristina Cortez Ser.). (ENG.). 88p. (gr. 2-3). pap. 6.10 *(978-1-4342-0868-2(0))*; lib. bdg. 26.65 *(978-1-4342-0772-2(2))* Stone Arch Bks. (Claudia Cristina Cortez).

—Guilty! The Complicated Life of Claudia Cristina Cortez, 1 vol. Garvey, Brann, illus. 2007. (Claudia Cristina Cortez Ser.). (ENG.). 88p. (gr. 2-3). per. 6.10 *(978-1-59889-881-1(7))*, Claudia Cristina Cortez) Stone Arch Bks.

—Haunted Love, 1 vol. (Claudia & Monica: Freshman Girls Ser.). (ENG.). 144p. (gr. 3-6). 2013. 9.95 *(978-1-4342-6286-8(3))* 2012. lib. bdg. 26.65 *(978-1-4342-3277-9(8))* Stone Arch Bks. (Claudia & Monica: Freshman Girls).

—Homecoming, 1 vol. (Claudia & Monica: Freshman Girls Ser.). (ENG.). 144p. (gr. 3-6). 2013. 9.95 *(978-1-4342-4887-9(9))* 2012. lib. bdg. 26.65 *(978-1-4342-3276-2(X))* Stone Arch Bks. (Claudia & Monica: Freshman Girls).

—Mice Capades, 1 vol. Juarez, Adriana & Puglisi, Adriana, illus. 2013. (Pet Friends Forever Ser.). (ENG.). 88p. (gr. 1-3). pap. 5.95 *(978-1-4795-1863-0(8))*; lib. bdg. 25.32 *(978-1-4048-7500-5(X))* Picture Window Bks.

—Monica & the Doomed Dance, 1 vol. 2010. (Monica Ser.). (ENG.). 88p. (gr. 2-3). 26.65 *(978-1-4342-1982-4(8))* Stone Arch Bks.

—Monica & the School Spirit Meltdown, 1 vol. 2010. (Monica Ser.). (ENG.). 88p. (gr. 2-3). 26.65 *(978-1-4342-1983-1(6))* Stone Arch Bks.

—New Firsts, 1 vol. 2012. (Claudia & Monica: Freshman Girls Ser.). (ENG.). 144p. (gr. 3-6). lib. bdg. 26.65 *(978-1-4342-3275-5(1))*, Claudia & Monica: Freshman Girls) Stone Arch Bks.

—Party! The Complicated Life of Claudia Cristina Cortez, 1 vol. Garvey, Brann, illus. 2008. (Claudia Cristina Cortez Ser.). (ENG.). 88p. (gr. 2-3). pap. 6.10 *(978-1-4342-0867-5(2))*; lib. bdg. 26.65 *(978-1-4342-0771-5(4))* Stone Arch Bks. (Claudia Cristina Cortez).

—Tested, 1 vol. 2012. (Claudia & Monica: Freshman Girls Ser.). (ENG.). 144p. (gr. 3-6). lib. bdg. 26.65 *(978-1-4342-3278-6(6))*, Claudia & Monica: Freshman Girls) Stone Arch Bks.

—Vote! The Complicated Life of Claudia Cristina Cortez, 1 vol. Garvey, Brann, illus. 2008. (Claudia Cristina Cortez Ser.). (ENG.). 88p. (gr. 2-3). pap. 6.10 *(978-1-4342-0866-8(4))*; lib. bdg. 26.65 *(978-1-4342-0770-8(6))* Stone Arch Bks. (Claudia Cristina Cortez).

—Whatever! The Complicated Life of Claudia Cristina Cortez, 1 vol. Garvey, Brann, illus. 2007. (Claudia Cristina Cortez Ser.). (ENG.). 88p. (gr. 2-3). pap. 6.10 *(978-1-59889-880-4(9))*; lib. bdg. 26.65 *(978-1-59889-839-2(6))* Stone Arch Bks. (Claudia Cristina Cortez).

Gallagher, Mary Collins. Ginny Morris & Dads New Girlfriend. Martin, Whitney, illus. 2006. (Ginny Morris Ser.). 63p. (J). (gr. 3-7). 14.95 *(978-1-59147-386-2(1))*; per. 9.95 *(978-1-59147-387-9(X))* American Psychological Assn. (Magination Pr.).

—Nine Is Not an Even Number. Martin, Whitney, illus. 2005. 48p. (J). 14.95 *(978-1-59147-157-8(5))*; pap. 9.95 *(978-1-59147-158-5(3))* American Psychological Assn. (Magination Pr.).

Gallagher, Toni. Twist My Charm - The Popularity Spell. 2015. (Twist My Charm Ser.). (ENG.). 272p. (J). (gr. 3-7). 16.99 *(978-0-553-51115-4(7))*, Random Hse. Bks. for Young Readers) Random Hse. Children's Bks.

—Twist My Charm: Love Potion #11. 2016. (Twist My Charm Ser.). (ENG.). 272p. (J). (gr. 3-7). 16.99 *(978-0-553-51119-2(X))*, Random Hse. Bks. for Young Readers) Random Hse. Children's Bks.

Gallo, Tina & S. I. International Staff. Let's Go, Go, Go! 2010. (Playskool Ser.). (ENG.). 32p. (J). 4.99 *(978-1-4424-0181-5(8))*, Simon Scribbles) Simon Scribbles.

Galveston, Louise. In Todd We Trust. 2015. (ENG., Illus.). 256p. (J). (gr. 3-7). 16.99 *(978-1-59514-679-3(2))*, Razorbill) Penguin Young Readers Group.

Gamblin, Rose Tooley & Hernández, Oscar. Bill's Lunch: El Almuerzo de Bill. 2010. (ENG & SPA., Illus.). 32p. (J). *(978-0-8127-0472-3(X))* Review & Herald Publishing Assn.

Gantos, Jack. Jack Adrift: Fourth Grade Without a Clue. 2005. (Jack Henry Ser.: 1). (ENG.). 208p. (J). (gr. 4-8). pap. 8.99 *(978-0-374-43718-3(1))*, 9780374437183) Square Fish.

—Joey Pigza Swallowed the Key. 2009. 8.30 *(978-0-7848-3764-1(3))*; 8.32 *(978-0-7848-1771-1(5))* Marco Bk. Co. (Everbind).

—Joey Pigza Swallowed the Key. unabr. ed. 2004. (Joey Pigza Ser.: Bk. 1). 154p. (J). (gr. 5-9). pap. 29.00 incl. audio *(978-0-8072-8166-6(2))*, YA120SP, Listening Library) Random Hse. Audio Publishing Group.

—Joey Pigza Swallowed the Key. 2007. (Joey Pigza Ser.: 1). (J). 1.25 *(978-1-4193-6006-0(X))* Recorded Bks., Inc.

—Joey Pigza Swallowed the Key. 2014. (Joey Pigza Ser.: 1). (ENG.). 176p. (J). (gr. 5-9). pap. 7.99 *(978-1-250-06168-3(7))*, 9781250061683) Square Fish.

—Joey Pigza Swallowed the Key. 2014. (Joey Pigza Ser.: 1). (J). lib. bdg. 18.40 *(978-0-606-23019-3(X))*, Turtleback) Turtleback Bks.

—The Key That Swallowed Joey Pigza. 2014. (Joey Pigza Ser.: 5). (ENG.). 160p. (J). (gr. 5-9). 16.99 *(978-0-374-30083-8(6))*, 9780374300838, Farrar, Straus & Giroux (BYR)) Farrar, Straus & Giroux.

—Rotten Ralph Helps Out. Rubel, Nicole, illus. unabr. ed. 2006. (Readalongs for Beginning Readers Ser.). (J). (gr. -1-3). 24.95 incl. audio *(978-1-59519-678-1(1))*; 28.95 incl. audio compact disk *(978-1-59519-679-8(X))* Live Oak Media.

—Rotten Ralph Helps Out, 4 bks., Set. unabr. ed. 2006. (Readalongs for Beginning Readers Ser.). (Illus.). (J). (gr. -1-3). pap. 29.95 incl. audio *(978-1-59519-676-7(5))*; pap. 31.95 incl. audio compact disk *(978-1-59519-677-4(3))* Live Oak Media.

—Rotten Ralph Helps Out. Rubel, Nicole, illus. (Rotten Ralph Rotten Readers Ser.: 1). (ENG.). 48p. (J). (gr. 1-3). 2012. 15.99 *(978-0-312-64172-6(9))*, 9780312641726) 2012. pap. 3.99 *(978-0-312-67281-2(0))*, 9780312672812) 2004. pap. 6.99 *(978-0-374-46355-7(7))*, 9780374463557) Square Fish.

—What Would Joey Do? 2004. (Joey Pigza Ser.: Bk. 3). 240p. (J). (gr. 5-9). pap. 36.00 incl. audio *(978-1-4000-9020-4(2))*, Listening Library) Random Hse. Audio Publishing Group.

Ganz-Schmitt, Sue. Planet Kindergarten. Prigmore, Shane, illus. 2016. (ENG.). 36p. (J). (gr. -1-k). 7.99 *(978-1-4521-5644-6(1))* Chronicle Bks. LLC.

—Planet Kindergarten: 100 Days in Orbit. Prigmore, Shane, illus. 2016. (ENG.). 36p. (J). (gr. -1-k). 16.99 *(978-1-4521-3776-6(5))* Chronicle Bks. LLC.

Ganz, Yaffa. The Adventures of Jeremy & Heddy Levi. Katz, Avi, illus. 2005. 204p. (J). 16.95 *(978-1-930143-50-0(8))*, 3508); pap. 12.95 *(978-1-930143-51-7(6))*, 3516) Simcha Media Group. (Devora Publishing).

Ganzer, Diane. Summer School Blues. 2008. 124p. pap. 9.99 *(978-1-935105-19-0(1))* Avid Readers Publishing Group.

Garant, Andre J. The Circus Kids. 2008. 140p. pap. 11.99 *(978-1-4389-2833-3(5))* AuthorHouse.

Garcia, Cristina. Dreams of Significant Girls. 2011. (ENG.). 256p. (YA). (gr. 9-18). 16.99 *(978-1-4169-7920-3(4))*, Simon & Schuster Bks. For Young Readers) Simon & Schuster Bks. For Young Readers.

Garcia, Cristina. Dreams of Significant Girls. 2012. (ENG.). 256p. (J). (gr. 9). pap. 8.99 *(978-1-4169-7930-2(1))*, Simon & Schuster Bks. For Young Readers) Simon & Schuster Bks. For Young Readers.

Garcia, Kami & Stohl, Margaret. Beautiful Creatures. 2009. (Beautiful Creatures Ser.: 1). (ENG.). 576p. (YA). (gr. 7-17). 17.99 *(978-0-316-04267-3(6))* Little Brown & Co.

—Beautiful Creatures. (Beautiful Creatures Ser.: 1). (ENG.). 592p. (YA). (gr. 7-17). 2010. pap. 12.99 *(978-0-316-07703-3(8))* 2012. mass mkt. 7.99 *(978-0-316-23165-7(7))* 2012. pap. 10.99 *(978-0-316-23167-1(3))* Little, Brown Bks. for Young Readers.

—Beautiful Creatures. 2013. (ENG., Illus.). 240p. (gr. 8-17). 20.00 *(978-0-316-18271-3(0))*, Yen Pr.) Orbit.

—Beautiful Creatures. 2010. (Beautiful Creatures Ser.: 1). (YA). lib. bdg. 23.30 *(978-0-606-26699-4(2))*, Turtleback) Turtleback Bks.

Garden, Nancy. Endgame. 2012. (ENG., Illus.). 304p. (YA). (gr. 7-12). pap. 6.99 *(978-0-15-206377-1(3))* Houghton Mifflin Harcourt Publishing Co.

Gardner, (Grandpa). Starting School. 2011. 32p. pap. 24.95 *(978-1-4560-0903-8(6))* America Star Bks.

Gardner, Graham. Inventing Elliot. 2005. (ENG.). 192p. (YA). (gr. 7-7). 5.99 *(978-0-14-240344-0(X))*, Speak) Penguin Young Readers Group.

—Inventing Elliot. 2005. 181p. (YA). 13.65 *(978-0-7569-5704-9(4))* Perfection Learning Corp.

Garfinkle, D. L. Stuck in the 70's. 2007. 182p. (YA). *(978-1-4287-4661-9(7))* Penguin Publishing Group.

Garland, Michael. Miss Smith Reads Again! 2006. (Illus.). (J). *(978-1-4156-8098-8(1))*, Dutton Juvenile) Penguin Publishing Group.

—Miss Smith's Incredible Storybook. Garland, Michael, illus. (ENG., Illus.). 32p. (J). (gr. -1-2). 2005. pap. 6.99 *(978-0-14-240282-5(6))*, Puffin Books) 2003. 16.99 *(978-0-525-47133-2(2))*, Dutton Books for Young Readers) Penguin Young Readers Group.

—Miss Smith's Incredible Storybook. 2007. 29.95 incl. audio compact disk *(978-0-8045-4159-6(0))*; 27.95 incl. audio *(978-0-8045-6945-3(2))* Spoken Arts, Inc.

—Where's My Homework? Garland, Michael, illus. 2014. (ENG., Illus.). 32p. (J). (gr. -1-k). pap. 6.99 *(978-0-545-43655-7(9))*, Cartwheel Bks.) Scholastic, Inc.

Garrett, Nicole. The Cupid Factor. 2007. 203p. pap. 14.50 *(978-1-4357-0276-9(X))* Lulu Pr., Inc.

Garrett, Troy. Kramer's World. 2010. 204p. pap. 12.50 *(978-1-60693-155-4(5))*, Eloquent Bks.) Strategic Book Publishing & Rights Agency (SBPRA).

Garsee, Jeannine. Before, after, & Somebody in Between. 2008. (ENG., Illus.). 368p. (YA). (gr. 9-12). pap. 8.99 *(978-1-59990-292-0(3))*, 9781599902920, Bloomsbury USA Childrens) Bloomsbury Publishing USA.

—The Unquiet. 2012. (ENG.). 400p. (YA). (gr. 9). 16.99 *(978-1-59990-723-9(2))*, 9781599907239, Bloomsbury USA Childrens) Bloomsbury Publishing USA.

Garton, Sam. Otter Goes to School. Garton, Sam, illus. 2016. (Illus.). 32p. (J). (gr. -1-3). 17.99 *(978-0-06-235225-5(3))* HarperCollins Pubs.

—Otter: Hello, Sea Friends! Garton, Sam, illus. 2016. (My First I Can Read Ser.). (Illus.). 32p. (J). (gr. -1-3). pap. 3.99 *(978-0-06-236660-3(2))* HarperCollins Pubs.

Garvey, Amy. Cold Kiss. 2012. (Cold Kiss Ser.: 1). (ENG.). 336p. (YA). (gr. 8). pap. 8.99 *(978-0-06-199623-8(8))*, HarperTeen) HarperCollins Pubs.

Garvin, Jeff. Symptoms of Being Human. 2016. 352p. (YA). (gr. 9). 17.99 *(978-0-06-238286-3(1))* HarperCollins Pubs.

Gary, Meredith. Sometimes You Get What You Want. Brown, Lisa, illus. 2008. (ENG.). 32p. (J). (gr. -1 — 1). 16.99 *(978-0-06-114015-0(5))* HarperCollins Pubs.

Garza, Xavier. Rooster Joe & the Bully / el Gallo Joe y el Abusón. 2016. (ENG & SPA.). 128p. (J). (gr. 5-8). pap. 9.95 *(978-1-55885-835-0(0))*, Piñata Books) Arte Publico Pr.

Gassman, Julie A. Eleanore Won't Share, 1 vol. Mikhail, Jessica, illus. 2010. (Little Boost Ser.). (ENG.). 32p. (gr. k-3). lib. bdg. 23.99 *(978-1-4048-6358-3(3))*, Little Boost) Picture Window Bks.

Gateley, Edwina, illus. & text. God Goes to School. Gateley, Edwina, text. 2009. 32p. (J). pap. 9.95 *(978-0-8091-6748-7(4))* Paulist Pr.

Gates, J. Gabriel & Keel, Charlene. Ghost Crown. 2012. (Tracks Ser.). (ENG.). 456p. (YA). (gr. 6-12). pap. 9.95 *(978-0-7573-1594-7(1))*, HCI Teens) Health Communications, Inc.

Gatou, Shouji. Full Metal Panic - Overload!, Vol. 5. Nagai, Tomohiro, illus. 2006. (Full Metal Panic: Overload! Ser.). 200p. (YA). pap. 9.99 *(978-1-4139-0342-3(8))* ADV Manga.

Gaulkin, Marianne Quigley. Playdance Studio. Baker, David, illus. 2011. 28p. pap. 24.95 *(978-1-4560-2163-4(X))* America Star Bks.

Gay, Delmas Levi. The Ears at the Top of the Stairs. 2008. 56p. per. 15.99 *(978-1-4363-0273-9(0))* Xlibris Corp.

Gaydos, Nora. Now I'm Growing! - First Day of School. Gutierrez, Akemi, illus. 2011. (ENG.). 30p. (J). (gr. -1-17). 8.99 *(978-1-60169-152-1(1))* Innovative Kids.

Gee, T. S. Dress up for When I Grow Up. 2013. 28p. pap. 24.95 *(978-1-62709-078-0(9))* America Star Bks.

Geesey, Kathleen. Black Fog. 2011. 200p. pap. 24.95 *(978-1-4560-7000-7(2))* America Star Bks.

Geithner, Carole. If Only. 2012. (ENG.). 336p. (J). (gr. 5-9). 16.99 *(978-0-545-23499-3(9))*, Scholastic Pr.) Scholastic, Inc.

Gelenius, Deb. My Mom, My Teacher. 2013. 28p. pap. 11.95 *(978-1-61244-135-1(1))* Halo Publishing International.

Gene, Barbara. Lamar Montgomery & the Freaky Faces Club. 2006. (J). per. 14.95 *(978-1-889743-50-9(X))* Robbie Dean Pr.

George, Bobby & George, June. Montessori: Letter Work. Nassner, Alyssa, illus. 2012. (Montessori Ser.). (ENG.). 24p. (J). (gr. -1-k). bds., bds. 9.95 *(978-1-4197-0411-6(7))*, Abrams Appleseed) Abrams, Inc.

—Montessori: Number Work. Nassner, Alyssa, illus. 2012. (Montessori Ser.). (ENG.). 24p. (J). (gr. -1-k). bds., bds. 9.95 *(978-1-4197-0412-3(5))*, Abrams Appleseed) Abrams, Inc.

Georgiana, Vanessa. Lulu: And the Garden of Life. 2013. 104p. (gr. 4-6). pap. 8.99 *(978-1-4582-0936-8(9))*, Abbott Pr.) Author Solutions, Inc.

Gephart, Donna. How to Survive Middle School. 2011. (ENG.). 256p. (J). (gr. 3-7). 6.99 *(978-0-375-85411-8(8))*, Yearling) Random Hse. Children's Bks.

—Lily & Dunkin. 2016. (ENG.). 352p. (J). (gr. 5). 16.99 *(978-0-553-53674-4(5))*, Delacorte Bks. for Young Readers) Random Hse. Children's Bks.

Geraldi, Michele J. Pennies at Piper Park. 2009. 24p. pap. 12.99 *(978-1-4389-2829-6(7))* AuthorHouse.

Geras, Adèle. Pictures of the Night. 2005. (ENG.). 192p. (YA). (gr. 7-12). pap. 11.95 *(978-0-15-205543-1(6))* Houghton Mifflin Harcourt Publishing Co.

—The Tower Room. 2005. (ENG.). 204p. (YA). (gr. 7-12). pap. 12.95 *(978-0-15-205537-0(1))* Houghton Mifflin Harcourt Publishing Co.

Gerber, Carole. Jessica Mcbean, Tap Dance Queen. Barton, Patrice, illus. 2006. 144p. (J). 13.95 *(978-0-9718348-7-3(3))* Blooming Tree Pr.

—Jessica McBean, Tap Dance Queen. Barton, Patrice, illus. 2007. (ENG.). 144p. (J). (gr. 1-5). pap. 6.95 *(978-0-9718348-9-7(X))* Blooming Tree Pr.

Gerber, Linda. Now & Zen. 2006. (S. A. S. S. Ser.). (ENG., Illus.). 224p. (YA). (gr. 7-18). 7.99 *(978-0-14-240657-1(0))*, Speak) Penguin Young Readers Group.

Gerhardt, Jake. Me & Miranda Mullaly. 2016. (ENG.). 256p. (J). (gr. 5). 16.99 *(978-0-451-47540-4(2))*, Viking Books for Young Readers) Penguin Young Readers Group.

—My Future Ex-Girlfriend. 2017. (ENG.). 240p. (J). (gr. 5). 16.99 *(978-0-451-47541-1(0))*, Viking Books for Young Readers) Penguin Young Readers Group.

Gerrity, Arlene. The Tale of Chicken Noodle & Rabbit Stew - Number Two. 2010. 24p. 10.99 *(978-1-4251-6258-0(4))* Trafford Publishing.

Gervay, Susanne. Being Jack. Wilcox, Cathy, illus. 2015. 167p. (J). *(978-1-61067-455-3(3))* Kane Miller.

—I Am Jack. Cathy, Wilcox, illus. 2013. (ENG.). 144p. (J). pap. 5.99 *(978-1-61067-128-6(7))* Kane Miller.

Ghani, Samna. The Tooth Fairy Goes to School. Williams, Nancy E., ed. Cappoen, Jennifer Tipton, illus. 2013. 44p. (J). pap. 10.98 *(978-1-938526-31-2(7))* Laurus Bks.

Gianferrari, Maria. Hello Goodbye Dog. Barton, Patrice, illus. 2017. (ENG.). 40p. (J). 16.99 *(978-1-62672-177-7(7))*, 9781626721777) Roaring Brook Pr.

Gibbs, Stuart. Evil Spy School. 2015. (Spy School Ser.). (ENG., Illus.). 336p. (J). (gr. 3-7). 17.99 *(978-1-4424-9489-3(1))*, Simon & Schuster Bks. For Young Readers) Simon & Schuster Bks. For Young Readers.

—Spy School. (Spy School Ser.). (ENG., (J). (gr. 3-7). 2013. Illus.). 320p. pap. 7.99 *(978-1-4424-2183-7(5))* 2012. 304p. 17.99 *(978-1-4424-2182-0(7))* Simon & Schuster Bks. For Young Readers. (Simon & Schuster Bks. For Young Readers).

—Spy School Secret Service. 2017. (J). pap. ***(978-1-4814-7783-3(8))***, Simon & Schuster Bks. For Young Readers) Simon & Schuster Bks. For Young Readers.

Gibbs, Stuart. Spy Ski School. 2016. (Spy School Ser.). (ENG., Illus.). 368p. (J). (gr. 3-7). 16.99 *(978-1-4814-4562-7(6))*, Simon & Schuster Bks. For Young Readers) Simon & Schuster Bks. For Young Readers.

Gibsen, Cole. Senshi. 2013. (Katana Novel Ser.: 2). (ENG.). 384p. (YA). pap. 9.99 *(978-0-7387-3261-9(3))*, Flux) North Star Editions.

—Shinobi. 2014. (Katana Novel Ser.: 3). (ENG.). 288p. (YA). pap. 9.99 *(978-0-7387-3911-3(1))*, Flux) North Star Editions.

Gibson, Marley. Radiate. 2012. (ENG.). 416p. (YA). (gr. 7). pap. 21.99 *(978-0-547-61728-2(3))* Houghton Mifflin Harcourt Publishing Co.

Gideon, John. The Little Soup Spoon. 2010. 32p. pap. 12.99 *(978-1-4520-3001-2(4))* AuthorHouse.

Gidney, Craig Laurance. Bereft. 2013. (ENG.). 170p. (J). (gr. 7). pap. 9.95 *(978-0-9849146-4-7(1))* Tiny Stachel Pr.

Gier, Kerstin. Dream a Little Dream. Bell, Anthea, tr. from GER. 2015. (Silver Trilogy Ser.: 1). (ENG.). 336p. (YA). (gr. 7). 17.99 *(978-1-62779-027-7(6))*, 9781627790277, Holt, Henry & Co. Bks. For Young Readers) Holt, Henry & Co.

—Just Dreaming. Bell, Anthea, tr. from GER. 2017. (Silver Trilogy Ser.). (ENG.). 368p. (YA). 18.99 *(978-1-62779-080-2(2))*, 9781627790802, Holt, Henry & Co. Bks. For Young Readers) Holt, Henry & Co.

Gifaldi, David. Toby Scudder, King of the School. 2005. (ENG.). 208p. (J). (gr. 5-7). pap. 12.95 *(978-0-618-55158-3(1))* Houghton Mifflin Harcourt Publishing Co.

Giff, Patricia Reilly. Bears Beware. Bright, Alasdair, illus. 2012. (Zigzag Kids Ser.). (ENG.). 80p. (J). (gr. 1-4). pap. 4.99 *(978-0-375-85913-7(6))*, Yearling) Random Hse. Children's Bks.

—The Big Whopper. Bright, Alasdair, illus. 2010. (Zigzag Kids Ser.). (ENG.). 80p. (J). (gr. 1-4). pap. 4.99 *(978-0-553-49469-3(4))*, Yearling) Random Hse. Children's Bks.

—Eleven. 2009. (ENG.). 176p. (J). (gr. 3-7). 7.99 *(978-0-440-23802-7(1))*, Yearling) Random Hse. Children's Bks.

—Flying Feet. Bright, Alasdair, illus. 2011. (Zigzag Kids Ser.). (ENG.). 80p. (J). (gr. 1-4). 4.99 *(978-0-375-85911-3(X))*, Yearling) Random Hse. Children's Bks.

—Jubilee. (ENG.). 160p. (J). (gr. 3-7). 2017. 6.99 ***(978-0-385-74489-8(7))***, Yearling) 2016. 16.99 *(978-0-385-74486-7(2))*, Lamb, Wendy Bks.) Random Hse. Children's Bks.

—The Number One Kid. Bright, Alasdair, illus. 2010. (Zigzag Kids Ser.). (ENG.). 80p. (J). (gr. 1-4). pap. 4.99 *(978-0-553-49468-6(6))*, Yearling) Random Hse. Children's Bks.

—The Secret at the Polk Street School. (J). (gr. 1-2). pap. 3.99 *(978-0-8072-1274-5(1))*, Listening Library) Random Hse. Audio Publishing Group.

—Star Time. Bright, Alasdair, illus. 2011. (Zigzag Kids Ser.). (ENG.). 80p. (J). (gr. 1-4). 4.99 *(978-0-375-85912-0(8))*, Yearling) Random Hse. Children's Bks.

—Super Surprise. Bright, Alasdair, illus. 2012. (Zigzag Kids Ser.). (ENG.). 80p. (J). (gr. 1-4). pap. 4.99 *(978-0-375-85914-4(4))*, Yearling) Random Hse. Children's Bks.

—Zigzag Zoom. Bright, Alasdair, illus. 2013. (Zigzag Kids Ser.). (ENG.). 80p. (J). (gr. 1-4). pap. 4.99 *(978-0-307-97703-8(X))*, Yearling) Random Hse. Children's Bks.

Giles, Gail. Right Behind You. 2008. (ENG.). 320p. (J). (gr. 10-17). pap. 10.99 *(978-0-316-16637-9(5))* Little, Brown Bks. for Young Readers.

—Shattering Glass. 2004. 215p. (J). (gr. 7-18). pap. 37.00 incl. audio *(978-1-4000-9013-6(X))*, Listening Library) Random Hse. Audio Publishing Group.

Giles, Lamar. Endangered. 2015. (ENG.). 288p. (YA). (gr. 9). 17.99 *(978-0-06-229756-3(2))*, HarperTeen) HarperCollins Pubs.

Gill, Jean. On the Other Hand. 2005. (ENG.). 126p. (J). pap. 11.95 *(978-0-86243-771-8(7))* Y Lolfa GBR. Dist: Dufour Editions, Inc.

Gill, Timothy. Flip & Fin: We Rule the School! Numberman, Neil, illus. 2014. (ENG.). 32p. (J). (gr. -1-3). 14.99 *(978-0-06-224300-3(4))*, Greenwillow Bks.) HarperCollins Pubs.

Gilles, Almira Astudillo. Willie Wins, 1 vol. Angel, Carl, illus. 2013. (ENG.). 32p. (J). (gr. -1-3). 16.95 *(978-1-58430-023-6(X))* Lee & Low Bks., Inc.

Gilley, Jane. Thibault Goes Missing - Book Two of the Troglodyte Trilogy. 2008. 16p. pap. *(978-1-906210-73-1(X))* Grosvenor Hse. Publishing Ltd.

Gilman, Charles. Professor Gargoyle. 2012. (Tales from Lovecraft Middle School Ser.: 1). (ENG., Illus.). 160p. (J). (gr. 4-7). 13.99 *(978-1-59474-591-1(9))* Quirk Bks.

—The Slither Sisters. 2013. (Tales from Lovecraft Middle School Ser.: 2). (ENG., Illus.). 160p. (J). (gr. 4-7). 13.99 *(978-1-59474-593-5(5))* Quirk Bks.

—Tales from Lovecraft Middle School #4: Substitute Creature. 2013. (Tales from Lovecraft Middle School Ser.: 4). (ENG., Illus.). 176p. (J). (gr. 4-7). 13.99 *(978-1-59474-640-6(0))* Quirk Bks.

—Teacher's Pest. 2013. (Tales from Lovecraft Middle School Ser.: 3). (ENG., Illus.). 176p. (YA). (gr. 4-7). 13.99 *(978-1-59474-614-7(1))* Quirk Bks.

Gilman, Grace. Dixie. McConnell, Sarah, illus. 2011. (I Can Read Level 1 Ser.). (ENG.). 32p. (J). (gr. -1-3). 16.99 *(978-0-06-171914-1(5))*; pap. 3.99 *(978-0-06-171913-4(7))* HarperCollins Pubs.

—Dixie & the Best Day Ever. Rogers, Jacqueline, illus. 2014. (I Can Read Level 1 Ser.). (ENG.). 32p. (J). (gr. -1-3). pap. 3.99 *(978-0-06-208659-4(6))* HarperCollins Pubs.
—Dixie & the Big Bully. McConnell, Sarah, illus. 2013. (I Can Read Level 1 Ser.). (ENG.). 32p. (J). (gr. -1-3). 16.99 *(978-0-06-208637-2(5))* HarperCollins Pubs.
—Dixie & the Big Bully. 2013. (Dixie: I Can Read Ser.). (J). lib. bdg. 13.55 *(978-0-606-27136-3(8),* Turtleback) Turtleback Bks.
—Dixie & the Class Treat. Rogers, Jacqueline, illus. 2012. (I Can Read Level 1 Ser.). (ENG.). 32p. (J). (gr. -1-3). 16.99 *(978-0-06-208606-8(5));* pap. 3.99 *(978-0-06-208605-1(7))* HarperCollins Pubs.
—Dixie & the School Trip. 2012. (Dixie: I Can Read Ser.). (J). lib. bdg. 13.55 *(978-0-606-26284-2(9),* Turtleback) Turtleback Bks.
—Dixie Loves School Pet Day. McConnell, Sarah, illus. 2011. (I Can Read Level 1 Ser.). (ENG.). 32p. (J). (gr. -1-3). 16.99 *(978-0-06-171912-7(9));* pap. 3.99 *(978-0-06-171911-0(0))* HarperCollins Pubs.
Gilmore, Grace. The New Kid. Brown, Petra, illus. 2016. (Tales from Maple Ridge Ser.: 6). (ENG.). 128p. (J). (gr. k-4). pap. 5.99 *(978-1-4814-4746-1(7),* Little Simon) Little Simon.
Gilson, Jamie. Bug in a Rug. deGroat, Diane, illus. 2003. (ENG.). 80p. (J). pap. 7.95 *(978-0-618-31670-0(1))* Houghton Mifflin Harcourt Publishing Co.
—My Teacher Is an Idiom. Tilley, Debbie, illus. 2015. (ENG.). 144p. (J). (gr. 1-4). 16.99 *(978-0-544-05680-0(9))* Houghton Mifflin Harcourt Publishing Co.
Gingold, Janet. Danger, Long Division. 2006. 188p. per. 14.99 *(978-1-59092-122-7(4))* Blue Forge Pr.
—Finch Goes Wild. 2007. 280p. (YA). pap. 14.99 *(978-1-59092-385-6(5))* Blue Forge Pr.
Giordano, Anthony. Another Boring Summer... Again! 2009. 154p. (YA). pap. 11.25 *(978-1-60695-077-7(0))* Callanish Pr.
Girard, Franck. Toby Goes Bananas. Bloch, Serge, illus. 2017. (ENG.). 96p. (J). (gr. 2-5). 19.99 ***(978-0-545-85284-5(6))***; pap. 9.99 ***(978-0-545-85283-8(8))*** Scholastic, Inc. (Graphix).
Giris, B. J. Kahmal's Big Day! 2012. 40p. pap. 16.50 *(978-1-4669-3548-8(0))* Trafford Publishing.
Glaser, Linda. Hannah's Way. Gustavson, Adam, illus. 2012. (Shabbat Ser.). 32p. (J). (gr. k-3). (ENG.). pap. 7.95 *(978-0-7613-5138-2(8));* lib. bdg. 17.95 *(978-0-7613-5137-5(X))* Lerner Publishing Group. (Kar-Ben Publishing).
Glass, Alberta. My Seeing Eye Glasses. Buehrle, Jacquelyn, illus. 2011. 28p. pap. 24.95 *(978-1-4560-2829-9(4))* PublishAmerica, Inc.
Glassman, Miriam. Call Me Oklahoma! 2013. (ENG.). 128p. (J). (gr. 2-7). 16.95 *(978-0-8234-2742-0(0))* Holiday Hse., Inc.
Glennon, Michelle. My Big Green Teacher: Please Turn off the Lights. Glennon, Michelle, illus. 2008. (ENG., Illus.). 32p. (J). 19.95 *(978-0-9796625-3-9(2))* GDG Publishing.
—My Big Green Teacher: Seven Generations from Now. Glennon, Michelle, illus. 2008. (Illus.). (J). 19.95 *(978-0-9797952-1-3(4))* GDG Publishing.
—My Big Green Teacher: Take a Deep Breath: Saving Our Rainforests. Glennon, Michelle, illus. 2008. (ENG., Illus.). 32p. (J). 19.95 *(978-0-9797952-0-6(6))* GDG Publishing.
—My Big Green Teacher: Recycling: It's Easy Being Green. Glennon, Michelle, illus. 2007. (Illus.). 32p. (J). 19.95 *(978-0-9796625-6-0(7))* GDG Publishing.
Glickman, Susan. Bernadette & the Lunch Bunch, 1 vol. Allard, Melanie, illus. 2009. (Lunch Bunch Ser.). (ENG.). 123p. (J). (gr. 1-4). pap. 6.95 *(978-1-897187-51-7(3))* Second Story Pr. CAN. Dist: Orca Bk. Pubs. USA.
Glines, Abbi. Under the Lights. 2016. (Field Party Ser.: 2). (ENG., Illus.). 336p. (YA). (gr. 9). 17.99 *(978-1-4814-3889-6(1),* Simon Pulse) Simon Pulse.
Gloster, Dean. Dessert First. 2016. (ENG.). 304p. (YA). 17.99 *(978-1-4405-9454-0(6),* Simon Pulse) Simon Pulse.
Go! Fight! Twin! 2014. (It Takes Two Ser.: 4). (ENG., Illus.). 160p. (J). (gr. 3-7). 17.99 *(978-1-4814-1656-6(1));* pap. 6.99 *(978-1-4814-1655-9(3))* Simon Spotlight. (Simon Spotlight).
Goddard, D. L. Agondray: The Guardian of the Clouds. 2012. (Illus.). 100p. pap. 10.67 *(978-1-4678-8516-4(9))* AuthorHouse.
The Goddess Girls: Pandora the Curious; Pheme the Gossip; Persephone the Daring; Cassandra the Lucky. 2014. (Goddess Girls Ser.). (ENG., Illus.). 1040p. (J). (gr. 3-7). pap. 29.99 *(978-1-4814-2730-2(X),* Aladdin) Simon & Schuster Children's Publishing.
Goff, John. The Take Over. Evans, Patricia, ed. 2012. 196p. (J). pap. 18.99 *(978-0-9841934-8-6(0))* Bryson Taylor Publishing.
Going to School: Individual Title Six-Packs. (Chiquilibros Ser.). (gr. k-1). 23.00 *(978-0-7635-0408-3(4))* Rigby Education.
Gold, Maya. Spellbinding. 2013. (ENG.). 272p. (J). (gr. 7). pap. 8.99 *(978-0-545-43380-8(0))* Scholastic, Inc.
Gold, Maya & Fitzhugh, Louise. Harriet the Spy, Double Agent. 2007. (Harriet the Spy Adventures Ser.). (ENG.). 160p. (J). (gr. 3-7). 6.99 *(978-0-440-41691-3(4),* Yearling) Random Hse. Children's Bks.
Gold, Rachel. Just Girls. 2014. (ENG.). 254p. (J). pap. 16.95 *(978-1-59493-419-3(3))* Bella Bks., Inc.
Goldberg, Whoopi. Toeshoe Trouble. Roos, Maryn, illus. 2009. (ENG.). 160p. (J). (gr. 1-17). pap. 4.99 *(978-0-7868-5261-1(5),* Jump at the Sun) Hyperion Bks. for Children.
Goldblatt, Mark. Finding the Worm. 2015. (ENG.). 352p. (J). (gr. 4-7). 16.99 *(978-0-385-39108-5(0),* Random Hse. Bks. for Young Readers) Random Hse. Children's Bks.
—Finding the Worm (Twerp Sequel) 2016. (ENG.). 368p. (J). (gr. 4-7). 7.99 *(978-0-385-39111-5(0),* Yearling) Random Hse. Children's Bks.
—Twerp. 2013. (ENG.). 288p. (J). (gr. 4-7). 16.99 *(978-0-375-97142-6(4),* Random Hse. Bks. for Young Readers) Random Hse. Children's Bks.
Goldfinger, Jennifer P. Hello, My Name Is Tiger. Goldfinger, Jennifer P., illus. 2016. (Illus.). 40p. (J). (gr. -1-3). 17.99 *(978-0-06-239951-9(9))* HarperCollins Pubs.
Golightly, Holly. School Bites: Blood Drinking 101, 2. 2005. (Illus.). 64p. (YA). per. *(978-0-9745367-3-6(3))* BroadSword Comics/ Jim Balent Studios.
Golightly, Holly, creator. School Bites. 2004. 64p. (YA). per. *(978-0-9745367-2-9(5),* SB1A) BroadSword Comics/ Jim Balent Studios.
Gomez, Sally. Too Many Freckles! Mitchell, Hazel, illus. 2008. (ENG.). 32p. pap. *(978-1-934363-32-4(4))* Zoe Life Publishing.
Gonzales Betrand, Diane. The Story Circle / el Circulo de Cuentos. Martin, Wendy, illus. 2016. (ENG, MUL & SPA.). 32p. (J). (gr. k-3). 17.95 *(978-1-55885-826-8(1),* Piñata Books) Arte Publico Pr.
Gonzales, Rave And Linda. Saved: A Short Story. 2012. 60p. pap. 19.95 *(978-1-4626-7625-5(1))* America Star Bks.
González, Rigoberto & Alvarez, Cecilia Concepcion. Antonio's Card/la Tarjeta de Antonio. 2013. (ENG & SPA., Illus.). 32p. (J). 17.95 *(978-0-89239-204-9(5))* Lee & Low Bks., Inc.
Goo, Maurene. I Believe in a Thing Called Love. 2017. (ENG.). 336p. (YA). 17.99 *(978-0-374-30404-1(1),* 9780374304041, Farrar, Straus & Giroux (BYR)) Farrar, Straus & Giroux.
—Since You Asked... 2013. (YA). pap. *(978-0-545-44822-2(0));* (ENG.). 272p. (J). (gr. 7). 17.99 *(978-0-545-44821-5(2))* Scholastic, Inc. (Scholastic Pr.).
Goobie, Beth. Hello, Groin, 1 vol. 2006. (ENG.). 292p. (YA). (gr. 8-12). 17.95 *(978-1-55143-459-9(8))* Orca Bk. Pubs. USA.
Goode, John. Going the Distance. (YA). 2016. (ENG., Illus.). (gr. 8-12). 24.99 ***(978-1-63533-020-5(3),*** Harmony Ink Pr.) 2015. lib. bdg. *(978-1-63216-620-3(8))* Dreamspinner Pr.
—151 Days. 2016. (ENG., Illus.). (J). 32.99 ***(978-1-63477-925-8(8))*** 2014. 350p. pap. 17.99 *(978-1-62798-747-9(9))* Dreamspinner Pr. (Harmony Ink Pr.).
Goode, Laura. Sister Mischief. 2011. (ENG., Illus.). 384p. (YA). (gr. 9-18). 16.99 *(978-0-7636-4640-0(7))* Candlewick Pr.
Goodman, Carol. Blythewood. 2014. (Blythewood Novel Ser.). (ENG.). 512p. (YA). (gr. 7). pap. 9.99 *(978-0-14-242251-9(7),* Speak) Penguin Young Readers Group.
—Ravencliffe. 2015. (Blythewood Novel Ser.). (ENG.). 432p. (YA). (gr. 7). pap. 10.99 *(978-0-14-242252-6(5),* Speak) Penguin Young Readers Group.
Goodman, Gabriel. The Alliance. 2013. (Surviving Southside Ser.). (ENG.). 104p. (YA). (gr. 6-12). pap. 7.95 *(978-1-4677-0708-4(2),* Darby Creek); lib. bdg. 27.93 *(978-1-4677-0595-0(0))* Lerner Publishing Group.
—The Confessional. 2015. (ENG.). 112p. (YA). (gr. 6-12). 27.99 *(978-1-4677-5712-6(8))* Lerner Publishing Group.
Gorbachev, Valeri. Two Little Chicks Go to School. 2011. (ENG., Illus.). 28p. (J). (gr. -1-3). 6.95 *(978-0-7358-4027-0(X))* North-South Bks., Inc.
Gordon, Amy. Return to Gill Park. 2006. (ENG., Illus.). 240p. (J). (gr. 4-7). 16.95 *(978-0-8234-1998-2(3))* Holiday Hse., Inc.
—Twenty Gold Falcons. (ENG.). 240p. (J). (gr. 3-7). 2012. pap. 8.99 *(978-0-8234-2656-0(4))* 2010. 16.95 *(978-0-8234-2252-4(6))* Holiday Hse., Inc.
Gorgas, Paula Blais. Little Lost Leprechaun. 2007. (Illus.). 20p. (J). per. 11.99 *(978-0-9797574-5-7(2))* Dragonfly Publishing, Inc.
Gorman, Carol. A Midsummer Night's Dork. 2004. (ENG.). 224p. (J). 15.99 *(978-0-06-050718-3(7))* HarperCollins Pubs.
Gorrell, Nancy. Corey's Story. 2007. (ENG., Illus.). 96p. (J). (gr. 2-5). per. 6.99 *(978-1-84550-258-4(2),* f3ae651d-4c6d-4b03-9761-9d54cb71a3e3) Christian Focus Pubns. GBR. Dist: Bookmasters Distribution.
Goscinny, René & Bell, Anthea. Nicholas. Sempé, Jean-Jacques, illus. 2011. (ENG.). 136p. (gr. 7-17). pap. 9.95 *(978-0-7148-6115-9(4))* Phaidon Pr., Inc.
Goslee, S. J. Whatever. 2016. (ENG.). 272p. (YA). 17.99 *(978-1-62672-399-3(0),* 9781626723993) Roaring Brook Pr.
Gosselin, Kim. Sportsercise: A School Story about Exercise-Induced Asthma. Ravanelli, Terry, illus. 2nd ed. 2004. (Children's Asthma Ser.). (J). per. 9.95 *(978-1-891383-25-0(6))* JayJo Bks., LLC.
Gosselink, John. The Defense of Thaddeus A. Ledbetter. 2010. (ENG., Illus.). 240p. (J). (gr. 3-7). 14.95 *(978-0-8109-8977-1(8),* Amulet Bks.) Abrams, Inc.
—Free Thaddeus! 2011. (ENG.). 240p. (J). (gr. 3-7). pap. 6.95 *(978-1-4197-0084-2(7),* Amulet Bks.) Abrams, Inc.
Gould, M. & Gould, R. About Gossip: What Would Jesus Do, 1 vol. Hurst, Debbie, illus. 2009. 28p. pap. 24.95 *(978-1-60749-680-9(1))* America Star Bks.
Gownley, Jim. Amelia & the Gym Class System: #2, 1 vol. Gownley, Jim, illus. 2011. (Amelia Rules! Ser.). (ENG., Illus.). 36p. 24.21 *(978-1-59961-788-6(9))* Spotlight.
Gownley, Jimmy. The Dumbest Idea Ever! 2014. (ENG., Illus.). 240p. (J). (gr. 4-7). 24.99 *(978-0-545-45346-2(1),* Graphix) Scholastic, Inc.
—Her Permanent Record. Gownley, Jimmy, illus. 2012. (Amelia Rules! Ser.). (ENG., Illus.). 160p. (J). (gr. 2-7). 19.99 *(978-1-4169-8615-7(4));* pap. 11.99 *(978-1-4169-8614-0(6))* Simon & Schuster Children's Publishing. (Atheneum Bks. for Young Readers).
—Her Permanent Record. 2012. (Amelia Rules! Ser.: 8). lib. bdg. 23.30 *(978-0-606-26885-1(5),* Turtleback) Turtleback Bks.
—True Things: Adults Don't Want Kids to Know. Gownley, Jimmy, illus. 2010. (Amelia Rules! Ser.). (ENG., Illus.). 176p. (J). (gr. 2-7). 19.99 *(978-1-4169-8611-9(1));* pap. 11.99 *(978-1-4169-8609-6(X))* Simon & Schuster Children's Publishing. (Atheneum Bks. for Young Readers).
—The Tweenage Guide to Not Being Unpopular. Gownley, Jimmy, illus. 2010. (Amelia Rules! Ser.). (ENG., Illus.). 192p. (J). (gr. 2-7). pap. 12.99 *(978-1-4169-8608-9(1),* Atheneum Bks. for Young Readers) Simon & Schuster Children's Publishing.
—The Whole World's Crazy. Gownley, Jimmy, illus. 2011. (Amelia Rules! Ser.). (ENG., Illus.). 176p. (J). (gr. 2-7). 21.99 *(978-1-4424-4538-3(6),* Atheneum Bks. for Young Readers) Simon & Schuster Children's Publishing.
Grab, Daphne. Alive & Well in Prague, New York. 2008. (Laura Geringer Bks.). 247p. (YA). (gr. 7-18). lib. bdg. 17.89 *(978-0-06-125671-4(4),* Geringer, Laura Book) HarperCollins Pubs.
—Halftime. 2010. (J). *(978-0-385-73783-8(1));* *(978-0-385-90693-7(5))* Random House Publishing Group. (Delacorte Pr).
Grabenstein, Chris. Riley Mack & the Other Known Troublemakers. 2012. (Riley Mack Ser.: 1). (ENG.). 272p. (J). (gr. 3-7). 16.99 *(978-0-06-202620-0(8))* HarperCollins Pubs.
—Riley Mack Stirs up More Trouble. 2013. (Riley Mack Ser.: 2). (ENG.). 336p. (J). (gr. 3-7). 16.99 *(978-0-06-202622-4(4))* HarperCollins Pubs.
Grace, Amanda. But I Love Him. 2011. (ENG.). 264p. (YA). (gr. 7-18). pap. 9.95 *(978-0-7387-2594-9(3),* Flux) North Star Editions.
—In Too Deep. 2012. (ENG.). 240p. (YA). pap. 9.95 *(978-0-7387-2600-7(1),* Flux) North Star Editions.
Grace, N. B. Battle of the Bands. 2007. (High School Musical Stories from East High Ser.). 142p. (J). (gr. 3-7). 12.65 *(978-0-7569-8337-6(1))* Perfection Learning Corp.
Graff, Lisa. Absolutely Almost. 2014. (ENG.). 304p. (J). (gr. 3-7). 16.99 *(978-0-399-16405-7(7),* Philomel Bks.) Penguin Young Readers Group.
—Double Dog Dare. (ENG.). (J). (gr. 3-7). 2013. 320p. pap. 7.99 *(978-0-14-242412-4(9),* Puffin Books) 2012. 304p. 16.99 *(978-0-399-25516-8(8),* Philomel Bks.) Penguin Young Readers Group.
—The Life & Crimes of Bernetta Wallflower: The Pros & Cons. 2015. (ENG.). 288p. (J). (gr. 3-7). 7.99 *(978-0-14-751675-6(7),* Puffin Books) Penguin Young Readers Group.
—Sophie Simon Solves Them All. Beene, Jason, illus. 2010. (ENG.). 112p. (J). (gr. 3-5). 14.99 *(978-0-374-37125-8(3),* 9780374371258, Farrar, Straus & Giroux (BYR)) Farrar, Straus & Giroux.
—Sophie Simon Solves Them All. Beene, Jason, illus. 2012. (ENG.). 112p. (J). (gr. 3-5). pap. 6.99 *(978-1-250-02898-3(1),* 9781250028983) Square Fish.
—The Thing about Georgie. 2008. (ENG.). 224p. (J). (gr. 3-7). pap. 6.99 *(978-0-06-087591-6(7))* HarperCollins Pubs.
Graham, Rosemary. Thou Shalt Not Dump the Skater Dude: And Other Commandments I Have Broken. 2008. (ENG.). 288p. (YA). (gr. 7-18). 8.99 *(978-0-14-240851-3(4),* Speak) Penguin Young Readers Group.
Grambling, Lois G. Can I Bring My Pterodactyl to School, Ms. Johnson? Love, Judy, illus. 2006. (Prehistoric Pets Ser.). (ENG.). 32p. (J). (gr. k-3). 7.95 *(978-1-58089-141-7(1))* Charlesbridge Publishing, Inc.
Grandits, John. Seven Rules You Absolutely Must Not Break If You Want to Survive the Cafeteria. Austin, Michael Allen, illus. 2017. (ENG.). 32p. (J). (gr. 1-4). 16.99 *(978-0-544-69951-9(3),* Clarion Bks.) Houghton Mifflin Harcourt Trade & Reference Pubs.
Grandma, Sue. Rocky the Rocking Horse. 2010. 24p. 12.99 *(978-1-4520-7333-0(3))* AuthorHouse.
Grant, Myrna. Ivan & the Hidden Bible. 2006. (Flamingo Fiction 9-13s Ser.). (ENG., Illus.). 144p. (J). (gr. 4-7). per. 6.99 *(978-1-84550-133-4(0),* 9394aef3-942b-4824-b0b8-0ae3449d32e0) Christian Focus Pubns. GBR. Dist: Bookmasters Distribution.
Grant, Vicki. B Negative, 1 vol. 2011. (Orca Soundings Ser.). (ENG.). 136p. (YA). (gr. 8-12). pap. 9.95 *(978-1-55469-841-7(3));* lib. bdg. 16.95 *(978-1-55469-842-4(1))* Orca Bk. Pubs. USA.
—Cochonnet (Pigboy), 1 vol. 2011. (FRE.). 112p. (J). (gr. 5-9). pap. 9.95 *(978-1-4598-0006-9(0))* Orca Bk. Pubs. USA.
—Pigboy. 2007. (Orca Currents Ser.). 101p. (gr. 5). 19.95 *(978-0-7569-8067-2(4))* Perfection Learning Corp.
Grau, Sheila. Dr. Critchlore's School for Minions: Polar Distress. Sutphin, Joe, illus. 2017. (Dr. Critchlore's School for Minions Ser.). (ENG.). 288p. (J). (gr. 3-7). 14.95 *(978-1-4197-2294-3(8),* Amulet Bks.) Abrams, Inc.
Grau, Sheila & Sutphin, Joe. Dr. Critchlore's School for Minions: Gorilla Tactics. 2016. (Dr. Critchlore's School for Minions Ser.). (ENG., Illus.). 304p. (J). (gr. 3-7). 14.95 *(978-1-4197-1371-2(X),* Amulet Bks.) Abrams, Inc.
Gray, Bianca. Back to School: Adventures of Alex & Joey. 2013. 20p. pap. 17.99 *(978-1-4817-0425-0(7))* AuthorHouse.
Gray, Claudia. Spellcaster. 2013. (Spellcaster Ser.: 1). (ENG.). 400p. (YA). (gr. 8). 17.99 *(978-0-06-196120-5(5),* HarperTeen) HarperCollins Pubs.
—Steadfast. (Spellcaster Ser.: 2). (ENG.). (YA). (gr. 8). 2015. 368p. pap. 9.99 *(978-0-06-196123-6(X))* 2014. 352p. 17.99 *(978-0-06-196122-9(1))* HarperCollins Pubs. (HarperTeen).
Green, Corey. Managing Stan: Buckley School Books #1. 2007. (ENG.). 162p. (J). 16.95 *(978-1-934437-01-8(8));* pap. 7.99 *(978-1-934437-02-5(6))* Abligio Bks.
Green, D. L. Kaitlyn & the Competition. 2016. (Babysitter Chronicles Ser.). (ENG.). 160p. (gr. 4-7). pap. 6.95 *(978-1-4914-8861-4(1))* Stone Arch Bks.
—Zeke Meeks. Alves, Josh, illus. 2013. (Zeke Meeks Ser.). (ENG.). 128p. (gr. 2-2). 181.20 *(978-1-4048-8052-8(6));* 90.60 *(978-1-4048-8053-5(4))* Picture Window Bks. (Zeke Meeks).
—Zeke Meeks vs His Big Phony Cousin, 1 vol. Alves, Josh, illus. 2014. (Zeke Meeks Ser.). (ENG.). 128p. (gr. 2-2). pap. 5.95 *(978-1-4795-3810-2(8));* 22.65 *(978-1-4795-2167-8(1))* Picture Window Bks. (Zeke Meeks).
—Zeke Meeks vs the Annoying Princess Sing-Along, 1 vol. Alves, Josh, illus. 2014. (Zeke Meeks Ser.). (ENG.). 128p. (gr. 2-2). 22.65 *(978-1-4795-4828-6(6),* Zeke Meeks) Picture Window Bks.
—Zeke Meeks vs the Crummy Class Play, 1 vol. Alves, Josh, illus. 2014. (Zeke Meeks Ser.). (ENG.). 128p. (gr. 2-2). 22.65 *(978-1-4795-4827-9(8),* Zeke Meeks) Picture Window Bks.
—Zeke Meeks vs the Gruesome Girls, 1 vol. Alves, Josh, illus. 2012. (Zeke Meeks Ser.). (ENG.). 128p. (gr. 2-2). pap. 5.95 *(978-1-4048-7221-9(3));* lib. bdg. 22.65 *(978-1-4048-6805-2(4))* Picture Window Bks. (Zeke Meeks).
—Zeke Meeks vs the Horrendous Halloween, 1 vol. Alves, Josh, illus. 2013. (Zeke Meeks Ser.). (ENG.). 128p. (gr. 2-2). lib. bdg. 22.65 *(978-1-4048-7638-5(3),* Zeke Meeks) Picture Window Bks.
—Zeke Meeks vs the Horrifying TV-Turnoff Week, 1 vol. Alves, Josh, illus. 2012. (Zeke Meeks Ser.). (ENG.). 128p. (gr. 2-2). pap. 5.95 *(978-1-4048-7220-2(5));* lib. bdg. 22.65 *(978-1-4048-6804-5(6))* Picture Window Bks. (Zeke Meeks).
—Zeke Meeks vs the Mother's Day Meltdown. Alves, Josh, illus. 2015. (Zeke Meeks Ser.). (ENG.). 128p. (gr. 2-2). 22.65 *(978-1-4795-2168-5(X),* Zeke Meeks) Picture Window Bks.
—Zeke Meeks vs the No-Fun Fund-Raiser, 1 vol. Alves, Josh, illus. 2013. (Zeke Meeks Ser.). (ENG.). 128p. (gr. 2-2). lib. bdg. 22.65 *(978-1-4048-7640-8(5),* Zeke Meeks) Picture Window Bks.
—Zeke Meeks vs the Pain-In-the-Neck Pets, 1 vol. Alves, Josh, illus. 2014. (Zeke Meeks Ser.). (ENG.). 128p. (gr. 2-2). 22.65 *(978-1-4795-2166-1(3),* Zeke Meeks) Picture Window Bks.
—Zeke Meeks vs the Putrid Puppet Pals, 1 vol. Alves, Josh, illus. 2012. (Zeke Meeks Ser.). (ENG.). 128p. (gr. 2-2). pap. 5.95 *(978-1-4048-7223-3(X));* lib. bdg. 22.65 *(978-1-4048-6803-8(8))* Picture Window Bks. (Zeke Meeks).
—Zeke Meeks vs the Stinkin' Science Fair, 1 vol. Alves, Josh, illus. 2012. (Zeke Meeks Ser.). (ENG.). 128p. (gr. 2-2). pap. 5.95 *(978-1-4048-7222-6(1));* lib. bdg. 22.65 *(978-1-4048-6802-1(X))* Picture Window Bks. (Zeke Meeks).
—Zeke Meeks vs the Super Stressful Talent Show, 1 vol. Alves, Josh, illus. 2013. (Zeke Meeks Ser.). (ENG.). 128p. (gr. 2-2). 8.95 *(978-1-4048-8106-8(9));* lib. bdg. 22.65 *(978-1-4048-7639-2(1))* Picture Window Bks. (Zeke Meeks).
Green, Jessica. Diary of a Would-Be Princess: The Journal of Jillian Jones, 5b. 2007. (Illus.). 236p. (J). (gr. 4-7). 15.95 *(978-1-58089-166-0(7))* Charlesbridge Publishing, Inc.
Green, Poppy. A New Friend. Bell, Jennifer A., illus. 2015. (Adventures of Sophie Mouse Ser.: 1). (ENG.). 128p. (J). (gr. k-4). pap. 5.99 *(978-1-4814-2832-3(2),* Little Simon) Little Simon.
Green, S. E. Killer Instinct. 2014. (ENG., Illus.). 272p. (YA). (gr. 9). 17.99 *(978-1-4814-0285-9(4),* Simon Pulse) Simon Pulse.
Green, Tim. Baseball Great. (Baseball Great Ser.: 1). (ENG.). (J). (gr. 3-7). 2010. 272p. pap. 6.99 *(978-0-06-162688-3(0))* 2009. 256p. 16.99 *(978-0-06-162686-9(4))* HarperCollins Pubs.
—Baseball Great. 2010. (Baseball Great Ser.: 1). (J). lib. bdg. 17.20 *(978-0-606-10356-5(2),* Turtleback) Turtleback Bks.
—First Team. 2015. (ENG.). 352p. (J). (gr. 3-7). pap. 6.99 *(978-0-06-220876-7(4))* HarperCollins Pubs.
—First Team. 2014. (ENG.). 336p. (J). (gr. 3-7). 16.99 *(978-0-06-220875-0(6))* HarperCollins Pubs.
—First Team. 2015. (J). lib. bdg. 17.20 *(978-0-606-37616-7(X))* Turtleback Bks.
—New Kid. 2014. (ENG.). 320p. (J). (gr. 3-7). 16.99 *(978-0-06-220872-9(1))* HarperCollins Pubs.
Greene, Stephanie. Princess Posey & the First Grade Ballet. Sisson, Stéphanie Roth, illus. 2014. (Princess Posey, First Grader Ser.: 9). (ENG.). 96p. (J). (gr. k-3). pap. 5.99 *(978-0-14-751292-5(1),* Puffin Books) Penguin Young Readers Group.
—Princess Posey & the First Grade Parade, Bk. 1. Sisson, Stéphanie Roth, illus. 2010. (Princess Posey, First Grader Ser.: 1). (ENG.). 96p. (J). (gr. k-3). 12.99 *(978-0-399-25167-2(7),* G.P. Putnam's Sons Books for Young Readers) Penguin Young Readers Group.
—Princess Posey & the First Grade Parade, Bk. 1. Sisson, Stéphanie Roth, illus. 2011. (Princess Posey, First Grader Ser.: 1). (ENG.). 96p. (J). (gr. k-3). 5.99 *(978-0-14-241827-7(7),* Puffin Books) Penguin Young Readers Group.
—Princess Posey & the Monster Stew, 4 vols. Sisson, Stéphanie Roth, illus. 2012. (Princess Posey, First Grader Ser.: 4). (ENG.). 96p. (J). (gr. k-3). pap. 5.99 *(978-0-14-242105-5(7),* Puffin Books) Penguin Young Readers Group.
—Princess Posey & the New First Grader. Sisson, Stéphanie Roth, illus. 2013. (Princess Posey, First Grader Ser.: 6). (ENG.). 96p. (J). pap. 4.99 *(978-0-14-242763-7(2),* Puffin Books) Penguin Young Readers Group.
—Princess Posey & the Perfect Present, Bk. 2. Sisson, Stéphanie Roth, illus. 2011. (Princess Posey, First Grader Ser.: 2). (ENG.). 96p. (J). (gr. k-3). 5.99 *(978-0-14-241828-4(5),* Puffin Books); 12.99 *(978-0-399-25462-8(5),* G.P. Putnam's Sons Books for Young Readers) Penguin Young Readers Group.
—Princess Posey & the Tiny Treasure. Sisson, Stéphanie Roth, illus. 2013. (Princess Posey, First Grader Ser.: 5). (ENG.). 96p. (J). (gr. k-3). pap. 5.99 *(978-0-14-242415-5(3),* Puffin Books) Penguin Young Readers Group.
—Queen Sophie Hartley. 2011. (ENG.). 144p. (J). (gr. 2-5). pap. 5.99 *(978-0-547-55021-3(9))* Houghton Mifflin Harcourt Publishing Co.
Greensill, Rowina Anne. James Goes to Play School. 2010. (Illus.). 28p. pap. 12.49 *(978-1-4490-7039-7(6))* AuthorHouse.
Greenwald, Lisa. Pink & Green Is the New Black: Pink & Green Book Three. (Pink & Green Ser.). (ENG.). 280p. (J). (gr. 3-7). 2015. pap. 7.95 *(978-1-4197-1679-9(4))* 2014. 16.95 *(978-1-4197-1225-8(X))* Abrams, Inc. (Amulet Bks.).
—Reel Life Starring Us. (ENG.). (YA). (gr. 3-7). 2013. 320p. pap. 7.95 *(978-1-4197-0426-0(5))* 2011. 304p. 16.95 *(978-1-4197-0026-2(X))* Abrams, Inc. (Amulet Bks.).
Greenwald, Lisa. 11 Before 12. 2017. 416p. (J). (gr. 3-7). 16.99 ***(978-0-06-241174-7(8),*** Tegen, Katherine Bks) HarperCollins Pubs.
Greenwald, Tommy. Charlie Joe Jackson's Guide to Extra Credit. Coovert, J. P., illus. 2012. (Charlie Joe Jackson Ser.: 2). (ENG.). 272p. (J). (gr. 4-7). 15.99 *(978-1-59643-692-3(1),* 9781596436923) Roaring Brook Pr.
—Charlie Joe Jackson's Guide to Extra Credit. Coovert, J. P., illus. 2013. (Charlie Joe Jackson Ser.: 2). (ENG.). 288p. (J). (gr. 4-7). pap. 7.99 *(978-1-250-01670-6(3),* 9781250016706) Square Fish.
—Charlie Joe Jackson's Guide to Extra Credit. 2013. (Charlie Joe Jackson's Guide Ser.: 2). (J). lib. bdg. 18.40 *(978-0-606-28461-5(3),* Turtleback) Turtleback Bks.
—Charlie Joe Jackson's Guide to Making Money. Coovert, J. P., illus. 2014. (Charlie Joe Jackson Ser.: 4). (ENG.). 208p. (J). (gr. 4-7). 13.99 *(978-1-59643-840-8(1),* 9781596438408) Roaring Brook Pr.
—Charlie Joe Jackson's Guide to Not Growing Up. Burniac, Lauren, ed. Coovert, J. P., illus. 2016. (Charlie Joe Jackson Ser.: 6). (ENG.). 192p. (J). 13.99 *(978-1-62672-169-2(6),* 9781626721692) Roaring Brook Pr.
—Charlie Joe Jackson's Guide to Not Reading. Coovert, J. P., illus. 2011. (Charlie Joe Jackson Ser.: 1). (ENG.). 224p. (J). (gr. 4-7). 15.99 *(978-1-59643-691-6(3),* 9781596436916) Roaring Brook Pr.

S

—Charlie Joe Jackson's Guide to Not Reading. 2012. (Charlie Joe Jackson's Guide Ser.: 1). (J). lib. bdg. 17.20 *(978-0-606-26127-2(3),* Turtleback) Turtleback Bks.

—Charlie Joe Jackson's Guide to Planet Girl. Coovert, J. P., illus. 2015. (Charlie Joe Jackson Ser.: 5). (ENG.). 208p. (J). (gr. 4-7). 13.99 *(978-1-59643-841-5(X),* 9781596438415) Roaring Brook Pr.

—Jack Strong Takes a Stand. Mendes, Melissa, illus. 2013. (ENG.). 240p. (J). (gr. 4-7). 15.99 *(978-1-59643-836-1(3),* 9781596438361) Roaring Brook Pr.

—Katie Friedman Gives up Texting! And Lives to Tell about It. Coovert, J. P., illus. 2015. (ENG.). 240p. (J). (gr. 4-7). 13.99 *(978-1-59643-837-8(1),* 9781596438378) Roaring Brook Pr.

—Pete Milano's Guide to Being a Movie Star. Roher, Rebecca, illus. 2016. (ENG.). 256p. (J). 13.99 *(978-1-62672-167-8(X),* 9781626721678) Roaring Brook Pr.

—The Real Us. Burniac, Lauren, ed. Coovert, J. P., illus. 2017. (ENG.). 256p. (J). 16.99 *(978-1-62672-171-5(8),* 9781626721715) Roaring Brook Pr.

Greenway, Glen. Ant Cook & the Giant Sangom. 2008. 144p. pap. 12.95 *(978-1-4327-1898-5(3))* Outskirts Pr., Inc.

Gregg, Stacy. The Auditions, 1. 2010. (Pony Club Rivals Ser.: 1). (ENG.). 288p. (J). (gr. 4-7). 7.99 *(978-0-00-733343-1(9),* HarperCollins Children's Bks.) HarperCollins Pubs. Ltd. GBR. Dist: HarperCollins Pubs.

—Riding Star, 3. 2011. (Pony Club Rivals Ser.: 3). (ENG.). 304p. (J). (gr. 4-7). pap. 7.99 *(978-0-00-733345-5(5),* HarperCollins Children's Bks.) HarperCollins Pubs. Ltd. GBR. Dist: HarperCollins Pubs.

Greig, Allison. Stacey's Adventures. 2006. (Illus.). 64p. pap. *(978-1-84401-035-6(X))* Athena Pr.

Gresh, Dannah. Danika's Totally Terrible Toss. 2008. (Secret Keeper Girl Fiction Ser.). (ENG.). 112p. pap. 7.99 *(978-0-8024-8702-5(5))* Moody Pubs.

Gresh, Dannah & Anderson, Chizuruoke. Yuzi's False Alarm. 2008. (Secret Keeper Girl Fiction Ser.). (ENG.). 96p. pap. 7.99 *(978-0-8024-8704-9(1))* Moody Pubs.

Gresh, Dannah & Mylin, Janet. Just Call Me Kate. 2008. (Secret Keeper Girl Fiction Ser.). (ENG.). 112p. pap. 7.99 *(978-0-8024-8703-2(3))* Moody Pubs.

Gresh, Dannah K. & Weibel, Suzy. T Is for AnTONIa. 2008. (Secret Keeper Girl Fiction Ser.). (ENG.). 96p. pap. 7.99 *(978-0-8024-8705-6(X))* Moody Pubs.

Greve, Meg. Kickin' It. 2015. (ENG.). 48p. (gr. k-3). 27.07 *(978-1-63430-370-5(9))* Rourke Educational Media.

Griffin, Adele. Amandine. 2003. (ENG.). 208p. (gr. 5-9). pap. 6.99 *(978-0-7868-1441-1(1))* Disney Pr.

—The Julian Game. 2011. (ENG.). 208p. (YA). (gr. 7-18). 7.99 *(978-0-14-241973-1(7),* Speak) Penguin Young Readers Group.

—The Knaveheart's Curse. 2009. (Vampire Island Ser.). (ENG.). 160p. (J). (gr. 3-7). 6.99 *(978-0-14-241407-1(7),* Puffin Books) Penguin Young Readers Group.

Griffin, N. Smashie Mcperter & the Mystery of Room 11. Hindley, Kate, illus. 2015. (ENG.). 256p. (J). (gr. 2-5). 15.99 *(978-0-7636-6145-8(7))* Candlewick Pr.

Griffin, Paul. When Friendship Followed Me Home. 2016. (ENG.). 256p. (J). (gr. 5-9). 16.99 *(978-0-8037-3816-4(1),* Dial Bks) Penguin Young Readers Group.

Griffis, Molly Levite. The Rachel Resistance. 224p. 8.95 *(978-1-57168-553-7(7))* Eakin Pr.

Griffiths, Andy. Treasure Fever! 2008. (Schooling Around Ser.: No. 1). 198p. (J). pap. *(978-0-545-09222-7(1))* Scholastic, Inc.

Griffo, Michael. Unwelcome. 2011. (ENG.). 352p. (YA). (gr. 9). pap. 9.95 *(978-0-7582-5339-2(7),* K-Teen) Kensington Publishing Corp.

Grigsby, Susan. First Peas to the Table: How Thomas Jefferson Inspired a School Garden. Tadgell, Nicole, illus. 2012. (ENG.). 32p. (J). (gr. 1-3). 16.99 *(978-0-8075-2452-7(2))* Whitman, Albert & Co.

—In the Garden with Dr. Carver. Tadgell, Nicole, illus. 2012. (J). *(978-1-61913-157-6(9))* Weigl Pubs., Inc.

—In the Garden with Dr. Carver. Tadgell, Nicole, illus. 2010. (ENG.). 32p. (J). (gr. 2-3). 16.99 *(978-0-8075-3630-8(X))* Whitman, Albert & Co.

—Wisteria's Show & Tell Spectacular: Older Than the Dinosaurs. Miller, Alexandra, illus. 2012. (J). *(978-1-934860-12-0(3))* Shenanigan Bks.

Grimes, Nikki. Almost Zero: A Dyamonde Daniel Book. Christie, R. Gregory, illus. 2010. (Dyamonde Daniel Book Ser.: 3). (ENG.). 128p. (J). (gr. 2-4). 11.99 *(978-0-399-25177-1(4),* G.P. Putnam's Sons Books for Young Readers) Penguin Young Readers Group.

—Bronx Masquerade. (ENG.). (YA). (gr. 7). 2017. 192p. pap. 8.99 ***(978-0-425-28976-1(1))*** 2003. 176p. 6.99 *(978-0-14-250189-4(1))* Penguin Young Readers Group. (Speak).

—Bronx Masquerade. 2003. (gr. 7-12). lib. bdg. 17.20 *(978-0-613-81701-1(X),* Turtleback) Turtleback Bks.

—Danitra Brown, Class Clown. Lewis, E. B., illus. 2005. 32p. (J). lib. bdg. 17.89 *(978-0-688-17291-6(1));* (ENG.). (gr. 3). 16.99 *(978-0-688-17290-9(3),* Amistad) HarperCollins Pubs.

—Halfway to Perfect: A Dyamonde Daniel Book, 4 vols. Christie, R. Gregory, illus. 2012. (Dyamonde Daniel Book Ser.: 4). (ENG.). 128p. (J). (gr. 2-4). 10.99 *(978-0-399-25178-8(2),* G.P. Putnam's Sons Books for Young Readers) Penguin Young Readers Group.

—Planet Middle School. 2011. (ENG.). 160p. (YA). 15.99 *(978-1-59990-284-5(2),* 9781599902845, Bloomsbury USA Childrens) Bloomsbury Publishing USA.

Grisham, John. The Scandal. 2017. (Theodore Boone Ser.: 6). lib. bdg. 19.65 ***(978-0-606-40086-2(9))*** Turtleback Bks.

Griswell, Kim T. Rufus Goes to School. Gorbachev, Valeri, illus. 2013. (ENG.). 32p. (J). (gr. -1-1). 14.95 *(978-1-4549-0416-8(X))* Sterling Publishing Co., Inc.

Grogan, John. Marley Goes to School. Cowdrey, Richard, illus. (Marley Ser.). 40p. (J). (gr. -1-3). 2012. (ENG.). 9.99 *(978-0-06-211366-5(6))* 2009. (ENG.). 17.99 *(978-0-06-156151-1(7))* 2009. lib. bdg. 18.89 *(978-0-06-156152-8(5))* HarperCollins Pubs.

Grogan, Shannon. From Where I Watch You. (ENG.). 304p. (YA). (gr. 9). 2016. pap. 10.99 *(978-1-61695-689-9(5))* 2015. 18.99 *(978-1-61695-554-0(6))* Soho Pr., Inc. (Soho Teen).

Gross, S. D. Freddie, Fireman Mike. 2007. (Illus.). 24p. (J). (gr. -1-3). per. 12.99 *(978-1-59879-343-7(8))* Lifevest Publishing, Inc.

Grosso, Mike. I Am Drums. 2016. (ENG.). 256p. (J). (gr. 5-7). 16.99 *(978-0-544-70710-8(9))* Houghton Mifflin Harcourt Publishing Co.

Group/McGraw-Hill, Wright. Secrets & Strays, 6 vols. (D-Man Beans Ser.). 47p. (gr. 4-6). 42.50 *(978-0-322-06258-0(6))* Wright Group/McGraw-Hill.

Grover, Lorie Ann. Hold Me Tight. 2007. (ENG.). 352p. (J). (gr. 5-9). pap. 16.95 *(978-1-4169-6753-8(2),* McElderry, Margaret K. Bks.) McElderry, Margaret K. Bks.

Groves. Back to School, Bk. 15. Date not set. (Illus.). 32p. (J). pap. 129.15 *(978-0-582-18058-1(9))* Addison-Wesley Longman, Ltd. GBR. Dist: Trans-Atlantic Pubns., Inc.

Grund, Carol A. Anna Mei, Blessing in Disguise. 2011. 181p. (J). pap. *(978-0-8198-0796-0(6))* Pauline Bks. & Media.

—Anna Mei, Cartoon Girl. 2010. 140p. (J). (gr. 4-7). pap. 8.95 *(978-0-8198-0788-5(5))* Pauline Bks. & Media.

Grunwell, Jeanne Marie. Mind Games. 2006. (ENG., Illus.). 144p. (J). (gr. 5-7). pap. 10.95 *(978-0-618-68947-7(8))* Houghton Mifflin Harcourt Publishing Co.

Guarente, Gabe. Satan's Prep: A Graphic Novel. 2014. (ENG., Illus.). 112p. (J). (gr. 6). 17.95 *(978-1-62873-592-5(9),* Sky Pony Pr.) Skyhorse Publishing Co., Inc.

Guatemala, Anne. The Story of Señor Pico. Frazao, Catia, illus. 2007.Tr. of Historia del Señor Pico. (ENG & SPA.). 32p. (J). pap. 17.00 *(978-0-8059-7818-6(6))* Dorrance Publishing Co., Inc.

Guerin, F. A. The Witch at NO46: Verbrola. 2011. (Illus.). 140p. pap. 14.69 *(978-1-4567-7118-8(3))* AuthorHouse.

Guerra, Stephanie. Betting Blind, 0 vols. 2014. (ENG.). 256p. (gr. 9-12). pap. 9.99 *(978-1-4778-4785-5(5),* 9781477847855, Skyscape) Amazon Publishing.

—Torn, 0 vols. 2012. (ENG.). 272p. (YA). (gr. 10-12). 17.99 *(978-0-7614-6272-9(4),* 9780761462729, Amazon Children's Publishing) Amazon Publishing.

Guest, Elissa Haden. Iris & Walter - The School Play. Davenier, Christine, illus. 2006. (Iris & Walter Ser.). 44p. (gr. 1-4). 15.95 *(978-0-7569-6679-9(5))* Perfection Learning Corp.

—Iris & Walter & the Substitute Teacher. Davenier, Christine, illus. 2006. (Iris & Walter Ser.). 44p. (gr. 1-4). 15.95 *(978-0-7569-7122-9(5))* Perfection Learning Corp.

Guignard, Lars. The Yogi's Curse. 2013. 342p. pap. *(978-0-9877753-9-9(1))* Guignard, Lars.

Gumfounded. 2004. (J). 13.95 *(978-0-9759866-0-8(0))* Garr, Sherry B.

Gunter, Tina. Monday. 2012. 30p. 24.95 *(978-1-4626-5164-1(X))* America Star Bks.

Gurevich, Margaret. All or Nothing. Hagel, Brooke, illus. 2016. (Chloe by Design Ser.). (ENG.). 96p. (gr. 5-8). lib. bdg. 25.32 *(978-1-4965-3263-3(5))* Stone Arch Bks.

—Back to Basics. Hagel, Brooke, illus. 2016. (Chloe by Design Ser.). (ENG.). 96p. (gr. 5-8). lib. bdg. 25.32 *(978-1-4965-3261-9(9))* Stone Arch Bks.

—Chloe by Design: Measuring Up. Hagel, Brooke, illus. 2016. (Chloe by Design Ser.). (ENG.). 384p. (gr. 4-8). 14.95 *(978-1-62370-727-9(7))* Capstone Young Readers of Coughlan Cos.

—The Final Cut. Hagel, Brooke, illus. 2016. (Chloe by Design Ser.). (ENG.). 96p. (gr. 5-8). lib. bdg. 25.32 *(978-1-4965-3264-0(3))* Stone Arch Bks.

—Made to Measure. Hagel, Brooke, illus. 2016. (Chloe by Design Ser.). (ENG.). 96p. (gr. 5-8). lib. bdg. 25.32 *(978-1-4965-3262-6(7))* Stone Arch Bks.

Gutknecht, Allison. A Cast Is the Perfect Accessory: And Other Lessons I've Learned. Lewis, Stevie, illus. 2014. (ENG.). 160p. (J). (gr. 2-5). 16.99 *(978-1-4424-8396-5(2));* pap. 5.99 *(978-1-4424-8395-8(4))* Simon & Schuster Children's Publishing. (Aladdin).

—Don't Wear Polka-Dot Underwear with White Pants: And Other Lessons I've Learned. Lewis, Stevie, illus. 2013. (ENG.). 160p. (J). (gr. 2-5). pap. 6.99 *(978-1-4424-8392-7(X),* Aladdin) Simon & Schuster Children's Publishing.

—Don't Wear Polka-Dot Underwear with White Pants: And Other Lessons I've Learned. Lewis, Stevie, illus. 2013. (ENG.). 160p. (J). (gr. 2-5). 15.99 *(978-1-4424-8393-4(8),* Simon & Schuster/Paula Wiseman Bks.) Simon & Schuster/Paula Wiseman Bks.

—Never Wear Red Lipstick on Picture Day: And Other Lessons I've Learned. Lewis, Stevie, illus. 2014. (ENG.). 176p. (J). (gr. 2-5). 16.99 *(978-1-4814-2959-7(0));* pap. 6.99 *(978-1-4814-2958-0(2))* Simon & Schuster Children's Publishing. (Aladdin).

Gutman, Dan. Back to School, Weird Kids Rule! Paillot, Jim, illus. 2014. (My Weird School Special Ser.). 144p. (J). (gr. 1-5). lib. bdg. 16.89 *(978-0-06-220686-2(9))* HarperCollins Pubs.

—Bunny Double, We're in Trouble! 2014. (My Weird School Ser.). (J). lib. bdg. 16.00 *(978-0-606-35055-6(1),* Turtleback) Turtleback Bks.

—The Christmas Genie. Santat, Dan, illus. 2010. (ENG.). 176p. (J). (gr. 3-7). pap. 6.99 *(978-1-4169-9002-4(X),* Simon & Schuster Bks. For Young Readers) Simon & Schuster Bks. For Young Readers.

—Coach Hyatt Is a Riot! Paillot, Jim, illus. 2008. (My Weird School Daze Ser.: 4). 112p. (J). (gr. 1-5). lib. bdg. 15.89 *(978-0-06-155408-7(1));* 4th ed. (ENG.). pap. 4.99 *(978-0-06-155406-3(5))* HarperCollins Pubs.

—Deck the Halls, We're off the Walls! Paillot, Jim, illus. 2013. (My Weird School Special Ser.). 144p. (J). (gr. 1-5). (ENG.). pap. 5.99 *(978-0-06-220682-4(6));* lib. bdg. 16.89 *(978-0-06-220683-1(4))* HarperCollins Pubs.

—Dr. Brad Has Gone Mad! 2009. (My Weird School Daze Ser.: 7). (J). lib. bdg. 14.75 *(978-0-606-06969-4(0),* Turtleback) Turtleback Bks.

—Dr. Carbles Is Losing His Marbles! Paillot, Jim, illus. 2007. (My Weird School Ser.: 19). 112p. (J). (ENG.). (gr. 1-5). pap. 4.99 *(978-0-06-123477-4(X));* (gr. 2-5). lib. bdg. 15.89 *(978-0-06-123478-1(8))* HarperCollins Pubs.

—Dr. Carbles Is Losing His Marbles! Paillot, Jim, illus. 2007. (My Weird School Ser.: No. 19). 99p. (J). (gr. 2-5). 11.65 *(978-0-7569-8810-4(1))* Perfection Learning Corp.

—Dr. Nicholas Is Ridiculous! Paillot, Jim, illus. 2013. (My Weirder School Ser.: 8). 112p. (J). (gr. 1-5). 15.89 *(978-0-06-204219-4(X));* (ENG.). pap. 4.99 *(978-0-06-204218-7(1))* HarperCollins Pubs.

—Dr. Nicholas Is Ridiculous! 2013. (My Weirder School Ser.: 8). (J). lib. bdg. 14.75 *(978-0-606-31820-4(8),* Turtleback) Turtleback Bks.

—The Homework Machine. 2014. (ENG.). 176p. (J). (gr. 3-7). 11.24 *(978-1-63245-274-0(X))* Lectorum Pubns., Inc.

—The Homework Machine. 2006. (ENG., Illus.). 160p. (J). (gr. 3-7). 17.99 *(978-0-689-87678-3(5),* Simon & Schuster Bks. For Young Readers) Simon & Schuster Bks. For Young Readers.

—It's Halloween, I'm Turning Green! Paillot, Jim, illus. 2013. (My Weird School Special Ser.). 144p. (J). (gr. 1-5). (ENG.). pap. 5.99 *(978-0-06-220679-4(6));* lib. bdg. 16.89 *(978-0-06-220680-0(X))* HarperCollins Pubs.

—Mayor Hubble Is in Trouble! Paillot, Jim, illus. 2012. (My Weirder School Ser.: 6). 112p. (J). (gr. 1-5). (ENG.). pap. 4.99 *(978-0-06-204212-5(2));* lib. bdg. 15.89 *(978-0-06-204213-2(0))* HarperCollins Pubs.

—Mayor Hubble Is in Trouble! 2012. (My Weirder School Ser.: 6). (J). lib. bdg. 14.75 *(978-0-606-26525-6(2),* Turtleback) Turtleback Bks.

—The Million Dollar Putt. 2007. 69p. (J). (gr. 3-7). 13.65 *(978-0-7569-8281-2(2))* Perfection Learning Corp.

—Miss Brown Is Upside Down! Paillot, Jim, illus. 2015. (My Weirdest School Ser.: 3). (ENG.). 112p. (J). (gr. 1-5). pap. 4.99 *(978-0-06-228427-3(4))* HarperCollins Pubs.

—Miss Daisy Is Crazy! Paillot, Jim, illus. 2004. (My Weird School Ser.: 1). (ENG.). 96p. (J). (gr. 1-5). pap. 4.99 *(978-0-06-050700-8(4))* HarperCollins Pubs.

—Miss Daisy Is Still Crazy! Paillot, Jim, illus. 2016. (My Weirdest School Ser.: 5). 112p. (J). (gr. 1-5). lib. bdg. 15.89 *(978-0-06-228433-4(9))* HarperCollins Pubs.

—Miss Holly Is Too Jolly! Paillot, Jim, illus. 2006. (My Weird School Ser.: 14). (ENG.). 112p. (J). (gr. 1-5). pap. 4.99 *(978-0-06-085382-2(4))* HarperCollins Pubs.

—Miss Klute Is a Hoot! Paillot, Jim, illus. 2014. (My Weirder School Ser.: 11). 112p. (J). (gr. 1-5). 15.89 *(978-0-06-219845-7(9));* (ENG.). pap. 4.99 *(978-0-06-219844-0(0))* HarperCollins Pubs.

—Miss Klute Is a Hoot! 2014. (My Weirder School Ser.: 11). (J). lib. bdg. 14.75 *(978-0-606-35503-2(0))* Turtleback Bks.

—Miss Kraft Is Daft! Paillot, Jim, illus. 2012. (My Weirder School Ser.: 7). 112p. (J). (gr. 1-5). (ENG.). pap. 4.99 *(978-0-06-204215-6(7));* lib. bdg. 15.89 *(978-0-06-204216-3(5))* HarperCollins Pubs.

—Miss Kraft Is Daft! Paillot, Jim, illus. 2012. (My Weirder School Ser.: 7). (J). lib. bdg. 14.75 *(978-0-606-27125-7(2),* Turtleback) Turtleback Bks.

—Miss Laney Is Zany! Paillot, Jim, illus. 2010. (My Weird School Daze Ser.: 8). 112p. (J). (gr. 1-5). (ENG.). pap. 4.99 *(978-0-06-155415-5(4));* lib. bdg. 15.89 *(978-0-06-155417-9(0))* HarperCollins Pubs.

—Miss Laney Is Zany! 2010. (My Weird School Daze Ser.: 8). (J). lib. bdg. 14.75 *(978-0-606-10112-7(8),* Turtleback) Turtleback Bks.

—Miss Lazar Is Bizarre! Paillot, Jim, illus. 2005. (My Weird School Ser.: 9). (ENG.). 96p. (J). (gr. 1-5). pap. 4.99 *(978-0-06-082225-5(2))* HarperCollins Pubs.

—Miss Mary Is Scary! Paillot, Jim, illus. 2010. (My Weird School Daze Ser.: 10). 112p. (J). (gr. 1-5). (ENG.). pap. 4.99 *(978-0-06-170397-3(4));* lib. bdg. 15.89 *(978-0-06-170398-0(2))* HarperCollins Pubs.

—Miss Small Is off the Wall! Paillot, Jim, illus. 2005. (My Weird School Ser.: 5). (ENG.). 112p. (J). (gr. 1-5). pap. 4.99 *(978-0-06-074518-9(5))* HarperCollins Pubs.

—Miss Suki Is Kooky! Paillot, Jim, illus. 2007. (My Weird School Ser.: 17). (ENG.). 112p. (J). (gr. 1-5). pap. 4.99 *(978-0-06-123473-6(7))* HarperCollins Pubs.

—Miss Suki Is Kooky! Paillot, Jim, illus. 2007. (My Weird School Ser.: 17). (J). 14.75 *(978-1-4177-7430-2(4),* Turtleback) Turtleback Bks.

—Mr. Burke Is Berserk! Paillot, Jim, illus. 2012. (My Weirder School Ser.: 4). 112p. (J). (gr. 1-5). (ENG.). pap. 4.99 *(978-0-06-196922-5(2));* lib. bdg. 15.89 *(978-0-06-196923-2(0))* HarperCollins Pubs.

—Mr. Burke Is Berserk! 2012. (My Weirder School Ser.: 4). (J). lib. bdg. 14.75 *(978-0-606-23571-6(X),* Turtleback) Turtleback Bks.

—Mr. Cooper Is Super! Paillot, Jim, illus. 2015. (My Weirdest School Ser.: 1). (ENG.). 112p. (J). (gr. 1-5). pap. 4.99 *(978-0-06-228421-1(5))* HarperCollins Pubs.

—Mr. Cooper Is Super! Paillot, Jim, illus. 2015. (My Weirdest School Ser.: 1). (J). lib. bdg. 14.75 *(978-0-606-36482-9(X))* Turtleback Bks.

—Mr. Docker Is off His Rocker! Paillot, Jim, illus. 2006. (My Weird School Ser.: 10). (ENG.). 112p. (J). (gr. 1-5). pap. 4.99 *(978-0-06-082227-9(9))* HarperCollins Pubs.

—Mr. Granite Is from Another Planet!, No. 3. Paillot, Jim, illus. 2008. (My Weird School Daze Ser.: 3). (ENG.). 112p. (J). (gr. 1-5). pap. 4.99 *(978-0-06-134611-8(X))* HarperCollins Pubs.

—Mr. Harrison Is Embarrassin'! Paillot, Jim, illus. 2011. (My Weirder School Ser.: 2). 112p. (J). (gr. 1-5). (ENG.). pap. 4.99 *(978-0-06-196918-8(4));* lib. bdg. 15.89 *(978-0-06-196919-5(2))* HarperCollins Pubs.

—Mr. Hynde Is Out of His Mind! Paillot, Jim, illus. 2005. (My Weird School Ser.: 6). 112p. (J). (ENG.). (gr. 1-5). pap. 4.99 *(978-0-06-074520-2(7));* (gr. 2-5). lib. bdg. 15.89 *(978-0-06-074521-9(5))* HarperCollins Pubs.

—Mr. Jack Is a Maniac! Paillot, Jim, illus. 2014. (My Weirder School Ser.: 10). 112p. (J). (gr. 1-5). (ENG.). pap. 4.99 *(978-0-06-219841-9(6));* lib. bdg. 15.89 *(978-0-06-219842-6(4))* HarperCollins Pubs.

—Mr. Jack Is a Maniac! 2014. (My Weirder School Ser.: 10). (J). lib. bdg. 13.55 *(978-0-606-35066-2(7),* Turtleback) Turtleback Bks.

—Mr. Klutz Is Nuts!, No. 2. Paillot, Jim, illus. 2004. (My Weird School Ser.: 2). (ENG.). 112p. (J). (gr. 1-5). pap. 4.99 *(978-0-06-050702-2(0))* HarperCollins Pubs.

—Mr. Louie Is Screwy! Paillot, Jim, illus. 2007. (My Weird School Ser.: 20). (ENG.). 112p. (J). (gr. 1-5). pap. 4.99 *(978-0-06-123479-8(6))* HarperCollins Pubs.

—Mr. Macky Is Wacky! Paillot, Jim, illus. 2006. (My Weird School Ser.: 15). (ENG.). 112p. (J). (gr. 1-5). pap. 4.99 *(978-0-06-114151-5(8))* HarperCollins Pubs.

—Mr. Macky Is Wacky! Paillot, Jim, illus. 2006. (My Weird School Ser.: 15). (J). lib. bdg. 14.75 *(978-1-4177-7429-6(0),* Turtleback) Turtleback Bks.

—Mr. Nick Is a Lunatic! Paillot, Jim, illus. 2016. (My Weirdest School Ser.: 6). 112p. (J). (gr. 1-5). pap. 4.99 *(978-0-06-228436-5(3))* HarperCollins Pubs.

—Mr. Sunny Is Funny! Paillot, Jim, illus. 2008. (My Weird School Daze Ser.: 2). 112p. (J). (gr. 1-5). (ENG.). pap. 4.99 *(978-0-06-134609-5(8));* No. 2. lib. bdg. 15.89 *(978-0-06-134610-1(1))* HarperCollins Pubs.

—Mr. Tony Is Full of Baloney! Paillot, Jim, illus. 2010. (My Weird School Daze Ser.: 11). 112p. (J). (gr. 1-5). (ENG.). pap. 4.99 *(978-0-06-170399-7(0));* lib. bdg. 15.89 *(978-0-06-170400-0(8))* HarperCollins Pubs.

—Mrs. Cooney Is Loony! Paillot, Jim, illus. 2005. (My Weird School Ser.: 7). (ENG.). 112p. (J). (gr. 1-5). pap. 4.99 *(978-0-06-074522-6(3))* HarperCollins Pubs.

—Mrs. Dole Is Out of Control! Paillot, Jim, illus. 2008. (My Weird School Daze Ser.: 1). (ENG.). 112p. (J). (gr. 1-5). pap. 4.99 *(978-0-06-134607-1(1))* HarperCollins Pubs.

—Mrs. Jafee Is Daffy! Paillot, Jim, illus. 2009. (My Weird School Daze Ser.: 6). (ENG.). 128p. (J). (gr. 1-5). pap. 4.99 *(978-0-06-155411-7(1))* HarperCollins Pubs.

—Mrs. Jafee Is Daffy! 2009. (My Weird School Daze Ser.: 6). (J). lib. bdg. 14.75 *(978-0-606-05035-7(3),* Turtleback) Turtleback Bks.

—Mrs. Kormel Is Not Normal! Paillot, Jim, illus. 2006. (My Weird School Ser.: 11). (ENG.). 96p. (J). (gr. 1-5). pap. 4.99 *(978-0-06-082229-3(5))* HarperCollins Pubs.

—Mrs. Lane Is a Pain! Paillot, Jim, illus. 2014. (My Weirder School Ser.: 12). 112p. (J). (gr. 1-5). (ENG.). pap. 4.99 *(978-0-06-219847-1(5));* lib. bdg. 15.89 *(978-0-06-219848-8(3))* HarperCollins Pubs.

—Mrs. Lane Is a Pain! 2014. (My Weirder School Ser.: 12). (J). lib. bdg. 14.75 *(978-0-606-35964-1(8))* Turtleback Bks.

—Mrs. Lizzy Is Dizzy! Paillot, Jim, illus. 2010. (My Weird School Daze Ser.: 9). 112p. (J). (gr. 1-5). (ENG.). pap. 4.99 *(978-0-06-155416-2(2));* lib. bdg. 15.89 *(978-0-06-155418-6(9))* HarperCollins Pubs.

—Mrs. Lizzy Is Dizzy! 2010. (My Weird School Daze Ser.: 9). (J). lib. bdg. 14.75 *(978-0-606-10113-4(6),* Turtleback) Turtleback Bks.

—Mrs. Master Is a Disaster! 2017. (My Weirdest School Ser.: 8). lib. bdg. 14.75 ***(978-0-606-40078-7(8))*** Turtleback Bks.

—Mrs. Meyer Is on Fire! Paillot, Jim, illus. 2016. 105p. (J). ***(978-1-4806-9926-7(8))*** Harper & Row Ltd.

—Mrs. Meyer Is on Fire! Paillot, Jim, illus. 2016. (My Weirdest School Ser.: 4). 112p. (J). (gr. 1-5). pap. 4.99 *(978-0-06-228430-3(4))* HarperCollins Pubs.

—Mrs. Patty Is Batty! Paillot, Jim, illus. 2006. (My Weird School Ser.: 13). (ENG.). 112p. (J). (gr. 1-5). pap. 4.99 *(978-0-06-085380-8(8))* HarperCollins Pubs.

—Mrs. Roopy Is Loopy! Paillot, Jim, illus. 2004. (My Weird School Ser.: 3). (ENG.). 96p. (J). (gr. 1-5). pap. 4.99 *(978-0-06-050704-6(7))* HarperCollins Pubs.

—Mrs. Yonkers Is Bonkers! Paillot, Jim, illus. 2007. (My Weird School Ser.: 18). (ENG.). 112p. (J). (gr. 1-5). pap. 4.99 *(978-0-06-123475-0(3))* HarperCollins Pubs.

—Mrs. Yonkers Is Bonkers! Paillot, Jim, illus. 2007. (My Weird School Ser.: 18). (J). 14.75 *(978-1-4177-8222-2(6),* Turtleback) Turtleback Bks.

—Ms. Beard Is Weird! 2012. (My Weirder School Ser.: 5). (J). lib. bdg. 14.75 *(978-0-606-26295-8(4),* Turtleback) Turtleback Bks.

—Ms. Coco Is Loco! Paillot, Jim, illus. 2007. (My Weird School Ser.: 16). (ENG.). 112p. (J). (gr. 1-5). pap. 4.99 *(978-0-06-114153-9(4))* HarperCollins Pubs.

—Ms. Coco Is Loco! Paillot, Jim, illus. 2007. (My Weird School Ser.: 16). (J). 14.75 *(978-1-4177-7428-9(2),* Turtleback) Turtleback Bks.

—Ms. Cuddy Is Nutty! Paillot, Jim, illus. 2015. (My Weirdest School Ser.: 2). 112p. (J). (gr. 1-5). (ENG.). pap. 4.99 *(978-0-06-228424-2(X));* lib. bdg. 15.89 *(978-0-06-228425-9(8))* HarperCollins Pubs.

—Ms. Hannah Is Bananas! Paillot, Jim, illus. 2004. (My Weird School Ser.: 4). (ENG.). 96p. (J). (gr. 1-5). pap. 4.99 *(978-0-06-050706-0(3))* HarperCollins Pubs.

—Ms. Joni Is a Phony! Paillot, Jim, illus. 2017. (My Weirdest School Ser.: 7). 112p. (J). (gr. 1-5). pap. 4.99 *(978-0-06-242929-2(9))* HarperCollins Pubs.

—Ms. Krup Cracks Me Up! Paillot, Jim, illus. 2008. (My Weird School Ser.: 21). (ENG.). 112p. (J). (gr. 1-5). pap. 4.99 *(978-0-06-134605-7(5))* HarperCollins Pubs.

—Ms. Lagrange Is Strange! Paillot, Jim, illus. 2005. (My Weird School Ser.: 8). (ENG.). 112p. (J). (gr. 1-5). pap. 4.99 *(978-0-06-082223-1(6))* HarperCollins Pubs.

—Ms. Leakey Is Freaky! Paillot, Jim, illus. 2011. (My Weird School Daze Ser.: 12). 112p. (J). (gr. 1-5). lib. bdg. 15.89 *(978-0-06-170403-1(2))* HarperCollins Pubs.

—Ms. Leakey Is Freaky! No. 12. Paillot, Jim, illus. 2011. (My Weird School Daze Ser.: 12). (ENG.). 112p. (J). (gr. 1-5). pap. 4.99 *(978-0-06-170402-4(4))* HarperCollins Pubs.

—Ms. Sue Has No Clue! Paillot, Jim, illus. 2013. (My Weirder School Ser.: 9). 112p. (J). (gr. 1-5). (ENG.). pap. 4.99 *(978-0-06-219838-9(6));* lib. bdg. 15.89 *(978-0-06-219839-6(4))* HarperCollins Pubs.

—Ms. Sue Has No Clue! 2013. (My Weirder School Ser.: 9). (J). lib. bdg. 14.75 *(978-0-606-32173-0(X),* Turtleback) Turtleback Bks.

—My Weird School, 4 bks. in 1. Pamintuan, Macky & Paillot, Jim, illus. 2016. (My Weird School Ser.). 384p. (J). (gr. 1-5). 14.99 *(978-0-06-249668-3(9))* HarperCollins Pubs.

—My Weird School. 2017. (My Weird School - I Can Read Ser.). lib. bdg. 13.55 ***(978-0-606-40067-1(2))*** Turtleback Bks.

—My Weird School: Talent Show Mix-Up. Paillot, Jim, illus. 2016. (My Weird School - I Can Read Ser.). (ENG.). 32p. (J). (gr. -1-3). 13.55 *(978-0-606-39276-1(9))* Turtleback Bks.

—My Weird School: Class Pet Mess! Paillot, Jim, illus. 2017. (I Can Read Level 2 Ser.). 32p. (J). (gr. -1-3). pap. 3.99 *(978-0-06-236746-4(3))* HarperCollins Pubs.

—The My Weird School Collection, Bks. 1-4. Paillot, Jim, illus. 2010. (My Weird School Ser.). (J). (gr. 1-5). pap. 16.99 *(978-0-06-189489-3(3))* HarperCollins Pubs.

—My Weird School Daze! Paillot, Jim, illus. 2007. (J). *(978-1-4287-4814-9(8))* HarperCollins Pubs.

—My Weird School Goes to the Museum. Paillot, Jim, illus. 2016. 30p. (J). ***(978-1-5182-2157-6(2))*** Harper & Row Ltd.

—My Weird School Goes to the Museum. Paillot, Jim, illus. 2016. (I Can Read Level 2 Ser.). 32p. (J). (gr. -1-3). pap. 3.99 *(978-0-06-236742-6(0))* HarperCollins Pubs.

—My Weirdest School #8: Mrs. Master Is a Disaster! Paillot, Jim, illus. 2017. (My Weirdest School Ser.: 8). 112p. (J). (gr. 1-5). pap. 4.99 (978-0-06-242933-9(7)) HarperCollins Pubs.
—My Weirdest School #9: Miss Tracy Is Spacey! Paillot, Jim, illus. 2017. (My Weirdest School Ser.: 9). 112p. (J). (gr. 1-5). pap. 4.99 **(978-0-06-242936-0(1))** HarperCollins Pubs.
—Officer Spence Makes No Sense! Paillot, Jim, illus. 2009. (My Weird School Daze Ser.: 5). 112p. (J). (gr. 1-5). (ENG.). pap. 4.99 (978-0-06-155409-4(X)); lib. bdg. 15.89 (978-0-06-155410-0(3)) HarperCollins Pubs.
—Oh, Valentine, We've Lost Our Minds! Paillot, Jim, illus. 2014. (My Weird School Special Ser.). (ENG.). 144p. (J). (gr. 1-5). pap. 5.99 (978-0-06-228403-7(7)) HarperCollins Pubs.
—Oh, Valentine, We've Lost Our Minds! 2014. (My Weird School Ser.). (J). lib. bdg. 16.00 (978-0-606-36460-7(9)) Turtleback Bks.
—Rappy Goes to School. Bowers, Tim, illus. 2016. 40p. (J). (gr. -1-3). 17.99 (978-0-06-229181-3(5)) HarperCollins Pubs.
—The Return of the Homework Machine. (ENG.). (J). (gr. 3-7). 2011. 192p. pap. 7.99 (978-1-4169-5459-0(7)) 2009. 176p. 15.99 (978-1-4169-5416-3(3)) Simon & Schuster Bks. For Young Readers. (Simon & Schuster Bks. For Young Readers).
Guzzardi, Mary. The Magical Ice Skates. 2011. 50p. pap. 24.95 (978-1-4560-3246-3(1)) PublishAmerica, Inc.
Haas, Jessie. Saige. Davis, Sarah, illus. 2012. (American Girl Today Ser.: Bk. 1). lib. bdg. 17.15 (978-0-606-31568-5(3), Turtleback) Turtleback Bks.
—Saige Paints the Sky. Davis, Sarah, illus. 2012. (American Girl Today Ser.: Bk. 2). lib. bdg. 17.15 (978-0-606-31569-2(1), Turtleback) Turtleback Bks.
Haberdasher, Violet. Knightley Academy. 2011. (ENG.). 512p. (J). (gr. 3-7). pap. 5.99 (978-1-4169-9144-1(1), Aladdin) Simon & Schuster Children's Publishing.
—The Secret Prince. 2011. (ENG.). 512p. (J). (gr. 3-7). 16.99 (978-1-4169-9145-8(X), Simon & Schuster/Paula Wiseman Bks.) Simon & Schuster/Paula Wiseman Bks.
—The Secret Prince: A Knightley Academy Book. 2012. (ENG.). 512p. (J). (gr. 3-7). pap. 7.99 (978-1-4169-9146-5(8), Simon & Schuster/Paula Wiseman Bks.) Simon & Schuster/Paula Wiseman Bks.
Haddix, Margaret Peterson. Because of Anya. 2005. 114p. 16.00 (978-0-7569-4922-8(X)) Perfection Learning Corp.
—Children of Refuge. 2017. (Children of Exile Ser.: 2). (ENG., Illus.). 272p. (J). (gr. 5). 17.99 **(978-1-4424-5006-6(1)**, Simon & Schuster Bks. For Young Readers) Simon & Schuster Bks. For Young Readers.
—Dexter the Tough. Elliott, Mark, illus. 2008. (ENG.). 144p. (J). (gr. 2-5). pap. 6.99 (978-1-4169-1170-8(7)) 2007. 141p. pap. 7.99 (978-0-5-377020-3(1)) 2007. (ENG.). 144p. (J). (gr. 2-5). 17.99 (978-1-4169-1159-3(6)) Simon & Schuster Bks. For Young Readers. (Simon & Schuster Bks. For Young Readers).
—Full Ride. (ENG.). (YA). (gr. 7). 2014. 368p. pap. 12.99 (978-1-4424-4279-5(4)) 2013. 352p. 16.99 (978-1-4424-4278-8(6)) Simon & Schuster Bks. For Young Readers. (Simon & Schuster Bks. For Young Readers).
Hahn, Mary Downing. Daphne's Book. 2008. (ENG., Illus.). 192p. (J). (gr. 5-7). pap. 7.99 (978-0-547-01641-2(7)) Houghton Mifflin Harcourt Publishing Co.
—Where I Belong. 2014. (ENG.). 240p. (J). (gr. 5-7). 16.99 (978-0-544-23020-0(5)) Houghton Mifflin Harcourt Publishing Co.
Haig, Matt. To Be a Cat. Curtis, Stacy, illus. (ENG.). 304p. (J). (gr. 3-7). 2014. pap. 8.99 (978-1-4424-5406-4(7)) 2013. 16.99 (978-1-4424-5405-7(9)) Simon & Schuster Children's Publishing.
Hainsworth, Emily. Take the Fall. 2016. 368p. (YA). (gr. 9). 17.99 (978-0-06-209422-3(X)) HarperCollins Pubs.
Halahmy, Miriam. Hidden. 2016. (ENG.). 224p. (J). 16.95 (978-0-8234-3694-1(2)) Holiday Hse., Inc.
Hale, Bruce. The Big Nap. unabr. ed. 2004. (Chet Gecko Mystery Ser.: No. 4). 128p. (J). (gr. 3-6). pap. 17.00 incl. audio (978-0-8072-1707-8(7), S FTR 272 SP, Listening Library) Random Hse. Audio Publishing Group.
—The Big Nap. Hale, Bruce, illus. 2008. (Chet Gecko Mystery Ser.: No. 4). (ENG., Illus.). 128p. (gr. 1-5). 24.21 (978-1-59961-461-8(8)) Spotlight.
—Clark the Shark. Francis, Guy, illus. 2013. (Clark the Shark Ser.). (ENG.). 32p. (J). (gr. -1-3). 17.99 (978-0-06-219226-4(4)) HarperCollins Pubs.
—Curse of the Were-Hyena: A Monstertown Mystery. Hale, Bruce, illus. 2016. (Monstertown Mysteries Ser.). (ENG., Illus.). 220p. (J). (gr. 3-7). 14.99 (978-1-4847-1325-9(7)) Disney Pr.
—Dial M for Mongoose: A Chet Gecko Mystery. 2010. (Chet Gecko Ser.: 15). (ENG., Illus.). 128p. (J). (gr. 2-5). pap. 5.99 (978-0-547-48079-4(2)) Houghton Mifflin Harcourt Publishing Co.
—Farewell, My Lunchbag. 2009. (Chet Gecko Ser.: 3). (ENG., Illus.). 128p. (J). (gr. 2-5). pap. 6.99 (978-0-15-202629-5(0)) Houghton Mifflin Harcourt Publishing Co.
—From Russia with Lunch: A Chet Gecko Mystery. 2010. (Chet Gecko Ser.: 14). (ENG., Illus.). 128p. (J). (gr. 2-5). pap. 6.99 (978-0-547-32862-9(6)) Houghton Mifflin Harcourt Publishing Co.
—Give My Regrets to Broadway. 2005. (Chet Gecko Ser.: 9). (ENG., Illus.). 144p. (J). (gr. 2-5). pap. 5.99 (978-0-15-216730-1(7)) Houghton Mifflin Harcourt Publishing Co.
—Give My Regrets to Broadway. 2005. (Chet Gecko Mystery Ser.). (Illus.). 115p. (gr. 3-7). 16.00 (978-0-7569-5247-1(6)) Perfection Learning Corp.
—The Hamster of the Baskervilles. 2003. (Chet Gecko Ser.: 5). (ENG., Illus.). 144p. (J). (gr. 2-5). pap. 6.99 (978-0-15-202509-0(X)) Houghton Mifflin Harcourt Publishing Co.
—Hiss Me Deadly. Hale, Bruce, illus. 2009. (Chet Gecko Ser.: 13). (ENG., Illus.). 128p. (J). (gr. 2-5). pap. 5.99 (978-0-15-206424-2(9)) Houghton Mifflin Harcourt Publishing Co.
—Key Lardo: A Chet Gecko Mystery. Hale, Bruce, illus. 2007. (Chet Gecko Ser.: 12). (ENG., Illus.). 128p. (J). (gr. 2-5). pap. 5.99 (978-0-15-205235-5(6)) Houghton Mifflin Harcourt Publishing Co.
—The Malted Falcon. 2007. (Chet Gecko Mystery Ser.). (Illus.). 107p. (J). (gr. 4-7). pap. 6.60 (978-1-4189-5239-6(7)) Harcourt Trade Pubs.
—The Malted Falcon. 2008. (Chet Gecko Ser.: 7). (ENG., Illus.). 128p. (J). (gr. 2-5). pap. 5.99 (978-0-15-216712-7(9)) Houghton Mifflin Harcourt Publishing Co.
—The Malted Falcon. Hale, Bruce, illus. 2008. (Chet Gecko Mystery Ser.: No. 7). (ENG., Illus.). 128p. (gr. 1-5). 24.21 (978-1-59961-467-0(7)) Spotlight.
—Murder, My Tweet. 2005. (Chet Gecko Mystery Ser.). (Illus.). 117p. (gr. 3-7). 16.00 (978-0-7569-5248-8(4)) Perfection Learning Corp.
—Murder, My Tweet. Hale, Bruce, illus. 2008. (Chet Gecko Mystery Ser.: No. 10). (ENG., Illus.). 136p. (gr. 1-5). 24.21 (978-1-59961-468-7(5)) Spotlight.
—Mutant Mantis Lunch Ladies! 2017. (Monstertown Mysteries Ser.). (ENG.). 208p. (J). (gr. 3-7). 14.99 (978-1-4847-1324-2(9)) Disney Pr.
—The Mystery of Mr. Nice. Hale, Bruce, illus. 2008. (Chet Gecko Mystery Ser.: No. 2). (ENG., Illus.). 112p. (gr. 1-5). 24.21 (978-1-59961-469-4(3)) Spotlight.
—The Possum Always Rings Twice. Hale, Bruce, illus. 2007. (Chet Gecko Ser.: 11). (ENG., Illus.). 128p. (J). (gr. 2-5). pap. 5.99 (978-0-15-205233-1(X)) Houghton Mifflin Harcourt Publishing Co.
—This Gum for Hire. 2003. (Chet Gecko Ser.: 6). (ENG., Illus.). 144p. (J). (gr. 2-5). pap. 5.99 (978-0-15-202497-0(2)) Houghton Mifflin Harcourt Publishing Co.
—This Gum for Hire. 2007. (Chet Gecko Mystery Ser.). (Illus.). 115p. (J). (gr. 4-7). pap. 6.60 (978-1-4189-5216-7(8)) Houghton Mifflin Harcourt Supplemental Pubs.
—This Gum for Hire. Hale, Bruce, illus. 2008. (Chet Gecko Mystery Ser.: No. 6). (ENG., Illus.). 128p. (gr. 1-5). 24.21 (978-1-59961-471-7(5)) Spotlight.
—Trouble Is My Beeswax. 2004. (Chet Gecko Mystery Ser.). (Illus.). 111p. (gr. 3-7). 16.00 (978-0-7569-3488-0(5)) Perfection Learning Corp.
—Trouble Is My Beeswax. Hale, Bruce, illus. 2008. (Chet Gecko Mystery Ser.: No. 8). (ENG., Illus.). 128p. (gr. 1-5). 24.21 (978-1-59961-472-4(3)) Spotlight.
—Trouble Is My Beeswax: A Chet Gecko Mystery. 2004. (Chet Gecko Ser.: 8). (ENG., Illus.). 144p. (J). (gr. 2-5). pap. 6.99 (978-0-15-216724-0(2)) Houghton Mifflin Harcourt Publishing Co.
Hale, Shannon. Ever after High: Once upon a Time: A Story Collection. 2014. (ENG.). 272p. (J). (gr. 3-7). 12.99 (978-0-316-25821-0(0)) Little, Brown Bks. for Young Readers.
—Ever after High: the Storybox of Legends Boxed Set. 2014. (ENG.). 900p. (J). (gr. 3-7). 45.00 (978-0-316-28720-3(2)) Little, Brown Bks. for Young Readers.
—The Forgotten Sisters. 2015. (Princess Academy Ser.: 3). (ENG.). 336p. (YA). (gr. 5-8). 17.99 (978-1-61963-485-5(6), 9781619634855, Bloomsbury USA Childrens) Bloomsbury Publishing USA.
—Palace of Stone. (Princess Academy Ser.: 2). (ENG.). (YA). (gr. 5-8). 2015. 352p. pap. 7.99 (978-1-61963-257-8(8), 9781619632578) 2012. 336p. 17.99 (978-1-59990-873-1(5), 9781599908731) Bloomsbury Publishing USA. (Bloomsbury USA Childrens).
—Palace of Stone. 2015. (Princess Academy Ser.: 2). (YA). lib. bdg. 18.40 (978-0-606-36439-3(0)) Turtleback Bks.
—Princess Academy. (Princess Academy Ser.: 1). (ENG.). (YA). (gr. 5-8). 2005. 320p. 17.99 (978-1-58234-993-0(2), 9781582349930) 2nd ed. 2015. 336p. pap. 7.99 (978-1-61963-613-2(1), 9781619636132) Bloomsbury Publishing USA. (Bloomsbury USA Childrens).
—Princess Academy. 2009. (Princess Academy Ser.: No. 1). 8.86 (978-0-7848-2867-0(9), Everbind) Marco Bk. Co.
—Princess Academy. 2007. (Princess Academy Ser.: No. 1). 314p. (gr. 5-9). 18.00 (978-0-7569-8180-8(8)) Perfection Learning Corp.
—Princess Academy. (Princess Academy Ser.: No. 1). (978-0-439-88811-0(5), Scholastic) Scholastic, Inc.
—Princess Academy. l.t. ed. 2006. (Princess Academy Ser.: No. 1). 339p. (J). (gr. 5-9). 23.95 (978-0-7862-8733-8(0)) Thorndike Pr.
—Princess Academy. 2015. (Princess Academy Ser.: 1). (YA). lib. bdg. 18.40 (978-0-606-36438-6(2)) Turtleback Bks.
—The Storybook of Legends. 2013. (Ever after High Ser.). (ENG., Illus.). 320p. (J). (gr. 3-7). 14.99 (978-0-316-40122-7(6)) Little, Brown Bks. for Young Readers.
—The Storybook of Legends. 2017. (Ever after High Ser.: 1). (J). lib. bdg. 18.40 **(978-0-606-40630-7(1))** Turtleback Bks.
—The Unfairest of Them All. 2014. (Ever after High Ser.). (ENG.). 336p. (J). (gr. 3-7). 14.99 (978-0-316-28201-7(4)) Little, Brown Bks. for Young Readers.
—A Wonderlandiful World. 2014. (Ever after High Ser.: 3). (ENG.). 336p. (J). (gr. 3-7). 14.99 (978-0-316-28209-3(X)) Little, Brown Bks. for Young Readers.
Hall, Kirsten. My New School. Gott, Barry, illus. 2004. (My First Reader Ser.). (ENG.). 32p. (J). (gr. k-1). pap. 3.95 (978-0-516-25505-7(3), Children's Pr.) Scholastic Library Publishing.
Hall, Rosemary. The Kids Knee Garden from the Adventures with Lamb E. Boy Series. 2008. (ENG.). 30p. pap. 9.13 (978-1-4196-8967-3(3)) CreateSpace Independent Publishing Platform.
Halliday, Gemma. Deadly Cool. 2011. (Deadly Cool Ser.: 1). (ENG.). 320p. (YA). (gr. 8). pap. 8.99 (978-0-06-200331-7(3), HarperTeen) HarperCollins Pubs.
—Social Suicide. 2012. (Deadly Cool Ser.: 2). (ENG.). 288p. (YA). (gr. 8). pap. 8.99 (978-0-06-200332-4(1), HarperTeen) HarperCollins Pubs.
Hallinan, P. K. Let's Learn All We Can! (ENG., Illus.). (J). 24p. pap. 6.55 (978-0-8249-5449-9(1)); 2004. 48p. pap. 9.95 (978-0-8249-5491-8(2)) Worthy Publishing. (Ideal Pubns.).
Halpern, Julie. Into the Wild Nerd Yonder. 2011. (ENG.). 272p. (YA). (gr. 8-13). pap. 16.99 (978-0-312-65307-1(7), 9780312653071) Square Fish.
Hambrick, Sharon. Brain Games. 2009. (J). 8.99 (978-1-59166-954-8(5)) BJU Pr.
—Tommy's Rocket. Manning, Maurie J., illus. 2003. (Fig Street Kids Ser.). 83p. (J). (gr. 1-2). 7.49 (978-1-59166-186-3(2)) BJU Pr.
Hamburg, Jennifer. Hazy Bloom & the Tomorrow Power. Mourning, Tuesday & Harnie, Jenn, illus. 2017. (Hazy Bloom Ser.). (ENG.). 176p. (J). 15.99 (978-0-374-30494-2(7), 9780374304942, Farrar, Straus & Giroux (BYR)) Farrar, Straus & Giroux.
Hamilton, Laura, reader. Vera's First Day of School. unabr. ed. 2006. (Picture Book Readalong Ser.). (Illus.). (J). (gr. -1-3). 25.95 incl. audio (978-1-59519-662-0(5)); pap. 39.95 incl. audio compact disk (978-1-59519-661-3(7));Set. pap. 37.95 incl. audio (978-1-59519-660-6(9)) Live Oak Media.
Hamilton, Pamela Greenhalgh. Snow Day. 2011. 34p. (J). pap. 18.95 (978-1-4327-5743-4(1)) Outskirts Pr., Inc.
Hamilton, Rachel. Louie Lets Loose! (Unicorn in New York #1) 2017. (Unicorn in New York Ser.: 1). (ENG.). 128p. (J). (gr. 2-5). pap. 4.99 **(978-1-338-05508-5(9)**, Scholastic Paperbacks) Scholastic, Inc.
—Louie Takes the Stage! (Unicorn in New York #2) 2017. (Unicorn in New York Ser.: 2). (ENG.). 128p. (J). (gr. 2-5). pap. 4.99 **(978-1-338-05512-2(7)**, Scholastic Paperbacks) Scholastic, Inc.
Hamlyn, Jean. Clumsy Daisy Goes to School. 2009. (Illus.). 36p. pap. 16.99 (978-1-4490-3517-4(5)) AuthorHouse.
Han, Jenny. Clara Lee & the Apple Pie Dream. 2014. (ENG.). 160p. (J). (gr. 3-7). pap. 5.99 (978-0-316-07037-9(8)) Little, Brown Bks. for Young Readers.
Han, Jenny & Vivian, Siobhan. Burn for Burn. (ENG., (YA). (gr. 9). 2013. Illus.). 400p. pap. 10.99 (978-1-4424-4076-0(7)) 2012. 368p. 17.99 (978-1-4424-4075-3(9)) Simon & Schuster Bks. For Young Readers. (Simon & Schuster Bks. For Young Readers).
—Fire with Fire. 2013. (ENG., Illus.). 528p. (YA). (gr. 9). 17.99 (978-1-4424-4078-4(3), Simon & Schuster Bks. For Young Readers) Simon & Schuster Bks. For Young Readers.
Hancock, H. Irving. The High School Captain of the Team. 2006. (ENG.). 156p. pap. 19.99 (978-1-4264-6386-0(3)); 172p. pap. 21.99 (978-1-4264-6460-7(6)) Creative Media Partners, LLC.
—The High School Left End, or Dick & Co. Grilling on the Football Gridiron. 2006. (ENG.). 156p. pap. 19.99 (978-1-4264-6385-3(5)); 174p. pap. 21.99 (978-1-4264-6459-1(2)) Creative Media Partners, LLC.
—The High School Pitcher. 2007. 176p. per. (978-1-4065-1990-7(1)) Dodo Pr.
Hand, Cynthia. Boundless. 2013. (Unearthly Ser.: 3). (ENG.). 448p. (YA). (gr. 8). pap. 9.99 (978-0-06-199621-4(1)); 17.99 (978-0-06-199620-7(3)) HarperCollins Pubs. (HarperTeen).
—Hallowed. 2012. (Unearthly Ser.: 2). (ENG.). (YA). (gr. 8). 432p. pap. 9.99 (978-0-06-199619-1(X)); 416p. 17.99 (978-0-06-199618-4(1)) HarperCollins Pubs. (HarperTeen).
—Unearthly. 2011. (Unearthly Ser.: 1). (ENG.). 464p. (YA). (gr. 8). pap. 9.99 (978-0-06-199617-7(3), HarperTeen) HarperCollins Pubs.
Hanks, Larry R. Stickboy, 1 vol. 2010. 28p. 24.95 (978-1-4489-5141-3(0)) PublishAmerica, Inc.
Hanlon, Abby. Dory & the Real True Friend. 2016. (Dory Ser.: 2). lib. bdg. 18.40 (978-0-606-38846-7(X)) Turtleback Bks.
—Ralph Tells a Story. 0 vols. 2012. (ENG.). 40p. (gr. 1-3). 16.99 (978-0-7614-6180-7(9), 9780761461807, Amazon Children's Publishing) Amazon Publishing.
—The Real True Friend. 2015. (Dory Fantasmagory Ser.: 2). (ENG., Illus.). 160p. (J). (gr. 1-3). 14.99 (978-0-525-42866-4(6), Dial Bks) Penguin Young Readers Group.
Hannan, Peter. My Big Mouth: 10 Songs I Wrote That Almost Got Me Killed. Hannan, Peter, illus. 2011. (ENG., Illus.). 240p. (J). (gr. 3-7). 16.99 (978-0-545-16210-4(6), Scholastic Pr.) Scholastic, Inc.
Hannigan, Katherine. Ida B: ... And Her Plans to Maximize Fun, Avoid Disaster, & (Possibly) Save the World. 2004. 256p. (gr. 4-18). lib. bdg. 16.89 (978-0-06-073025-3(0)); (ENG.). (J). 17.99 (978-0-06-073024-6(2), Greenwillow Bks.) HarperCollins Pubs.
—Ida B: And Her Plans to Maximize Fun Avoid Disaster, & (Possibly) Save the World. 2011. (ENG.). 272p. (J). (gr. 5-9). reprint ed. pap. 6.99 (978-0-06-073026-0(9), Greenwillow Bks.) HarperCollins Pubs.
Hansen, Joyce. Yellow Bird & Me. 2005. (ENG.). 160p. (J). (gr. 5-7). pap. 6.95 (978-0-618-61116-4(9)) Houghton Mifflin Harcourt Publishing Co.
—Yellow Bird & Me. 2005. (163rd Street Ser.). 155p. (gr. 5-9). 16.95 (978-0-7569-6228-9(5)) Perfection Learning Corp.
Hanson, Bonnie Compton. Meet the Ponytail Girls. 2004. (Ponytail Girls Ser.). (Illus.). 208p. (J). pap. 7.99 (978-1-58411-029-3(5), Legacy Pr.) Rainbow Pubs. & Legacy Pr.
Hapka, Catherine A. & Vandenberg, Ellen. How Not to Run for Class President. Palen, Debbie, illus. 2016. (Step into Reading Ser.). (ENG.). 48p. (J). (gr. k-3). 3.99 (978-1-101-93362-6(3), Random Hse. Bks. for Young Readers) Random Hse. Children's Bks.
Hapka, Catherine, pseud. Echo's Lucky Charm. Hibbert, Hollie, illus. 2016. (Dolphin School Ser.: 2). (ENG.). 112p. (J). (gr. 2-5). pap. 4.99 (978-0-545-75025-7(3)) Scholastic, Inc.
—Flip's Surprise Talent. 2016. (Dolphin School Ser.: 4). (ENG., Illus.). 112p. (J). (gr. 2-5). pap. 4.99 (978-0-545-75027-1(X), Scholastic Paperbacks) Scholastic, Inc.
—Friends 4 Ever? 2008. (High School Musical Stories from East High Ser.). 124p. (J). (gr. 3-7). 12.65 (978-0-7569-8820-3(9)) Perfection Learning Corp.
—Splash's Secret Friend. 2016. (Dolphin School Ser.: 3). (ENG., Illus.). 112p. (J). (gr. 2-5). pap. 4.99 (978-0-545-75026-4(1), Scholastic Paperbacks) Scholastic, Inc.
Hapka, Cathy, pseud & Titlebaum, Ellen. How Not to Start Third Grade. Palen, Debbie, illus. 2007. (Step into Reading Ser.). (ENG.). 48p. (J). (gr. 2-4). pap. 3.99 (978-0-375-83904-7(6), Random Hse. Bks. for Young Readers) Random Hse. Children's Bks.
Harcourt School Publishers Staff. Going to School, Unit 1. 3rd ed. 2003. (Horizons Ser.). (Illus.). (gr. 1). pap. 166.70 (978-0-15-340220-3(2)) Harcourt Schl. Pubs.
Hardy, LeAnne. Between Two Worlds: A Novel. 2003. 160p. (J). pap. 7.99 (978-0-8254-2793-0(2)) Kregel Pubns.
Hare, Eric B. Curse Proof. 2007. (Illus.). 95p. (J). 10.99 (978-0-8163-2208-4(2)) Pacific Pr. Publishing Assn.
Harewood, Sean C. It's Only the First Day. 2008. 48p. pap. 19.49 (978-1-4343-7367-0(3)) AuthorHouse.
Harimann, Sierra. Diploma Day. 2011. (Illus.). 30p. (J). pap. (978-0-545-28143-0(1)) Scholastic, Inc.
Harkrader, Lisa. The Adventures of Beanboy. 2012. (ENG., Illus.). 240p. (J). (gr. 5-7). 12.99 (978-0-547-55078-7(2)) Houghton Mifflin Harcourt Publishing Co.
—Cool Beans: The Further Adventures of Beanboy. 2014. (ENG., Illus.). 272p. (J). (gr. 5-7). 16.99 (978-0-544-03904-9(1), HMH Books For Young Readers) Houghton Mifflin Harcourt Publishing Co.
—A Fishy Mystery: Venn Diagrams. Pillo, Cary, illus. 2017. (Math Matters (r) Ser.). (ENG.). 32p. (gr. k-3). (J). 5.95 (978-1-57565-866-7(6)); 23.99 **(978-1-57565-869-8(0))** Kane Press, Inc.
—No Place Like Space: Kindness. Warrick, Jessica, illus. 2017. (How to Be an Earthling (r) Ser.: 5). (ENG.). 64p. (J). (gr. 1-3). lib. bdg. 22.65 (978-1-57565-843-8(7)) Kane Press, Inc.
Harley, Bill. Charlie Bumpers vs. His Big Blabby Mouth, 1 vol. Gustavson, Adam, illus. 2017. (Charlie Bumpers Ser.). (ENG.). 186p. (J). (gr. 2-4). 14.95 **(978-1-56145-940-7(2))** Peachtree Pubs.
—Charlie Bumpers vs. the Really Nice Gnome, 1 vol. Gustavson, Adam, illus. (Charlie Bumpers Ser.). (ENG.). 160p. (J). (gr. 2-4). 2015. pap. 6.95 (978-1-56145-831-8(7)) 2014. 13.95 (978-1-56145-740-3(X)) Peachtree Pubs.
—Charlie Bumpers vs. the Squeaking Skull, 1 vol. Gustavson, Adam, illus. 2015. (Charlie Bumpers Ser.). (ENG.). 176p. (J). (gr. 2-4). pap. 6.95 (978-1-56145-888-2(0)) Peachtree Pubs.
—Charlie Bumpers vs. the Teacher of the Year, 1 vol. Gustavson, Adam, illus. (Charlie Bumpers Ser.). (ENG.). 160p. (J). 2014. pap. 6.95 (978-1-56145-824-0(4)) 2013. (gr. 2-4). 14.95 (978-1-56145-732-8(9)) Peachtree Pubs.
—Lost & Found, 1 vol. Gustavson, Adam, illus. 2012. (ENG.). 32p. (J). 16.95 (978-1-56145-628-4(4)) Peachtree Pubs.
—Night of the Spadefoot Toads, 1 vol. 2008. (ENG.). 192p. (J). (gr. 3-7). 15.95 (978-1-56145-459-4(1)) Peachtree Pubs.
Harmer, Wendy. I Lost My Mobile at the Mall. 2011. (ENG.). 272p. (YA). (gr. 7-18). 10.99 (978-1-935279-97-6(1)) Kane Miller.
Harmon, Michael. Brutal. 2011. (ENG.). 240p. (YA). (gr. 9). pap. 8.99 (978-0-440-23995-6(8), Knopf Bks. for Young Readers) Random Hse. Children's Bks.
—Skate. 2008. (ENG.). 256p. (YA). (gr. 9). per. 6.99 (978-0-553-49510-2(0), Laurel Leaf) Random Hse. Children's Bks.
—Stick. 2015. (ENG.). 240p. (YA). (gr. 9). 17.99 (978-0-385-75436-1(1)); lib. bdg. 20.99 (978-0-385-75437-8(X)) Random Hse. Children's Bks. (Knopf Bks. for Young Readers).
Harney, D. G. Meet Mr. Ugly, 1 vol. 2010. 133p. pap. 24.95 (978-1-4489-5191-8(7)) America Star Bks.
Harold, Gwyneth. Bad Girls in School. 2007. (ENG.). 148p. (YA). (gr. 8-12). per. 17.44 (978-0-435-21517-0(5), 21517) Heinemann.
Harper, Charise Mericle. Just Grace. 2008. (Just Grace Ser.: 1). (ENG., Illus.). 144p. (J). (gr. 1-4). pap. 5.99 (978-0-547-01440-1(6)) Houghton Mifflin Harcourt Publishing Co.
—Just Grace & the Snack Attack. 2010. (Just Grace Ser.: 5). (ENG., Illus.). 176p. (J). (gr. 1-4). pap. 5.99 (978-0-547-40629-9(0)) Houghton Mifflin Harcourt Publishing Co.
—Just Grace & the Super Sleepover. 2014. (Just Grace Ser.: 11). (ENG., Illus.). 208p. (J). (gr. 1-4). 15.99 (978-0-544-04584-2(X)) Houghton Mifflin Harcourt Publishing Co.
—Just Grace & the Trouble with Cupcakes. (Just Grace Ser.: 10). (ENG., Illus.). 208p. (J). (gr. 1-4). 2014. pap. 5.99 (978-0-544-33910-1(X), HMH Books For Young Readers) 2013. 15.99 (978-0-547-87744-0(7)) Houghton Mifflin Harcourt Publishing Co.
—Just Grace, Star on Stage. 2014. (Just Grace Ser.: 9). (ENG., Illus.). 208p. (J). (gr. 1-4). pap. 5.99 (978-0-544-22533-6(3), HMH Books For Young Readers) Houghton Mifflin Harcourt Publishing Co.
—Just Grace Walks the Dog. 2009. (Just Grace Ser.: 3). (ENG., Illus.). 176p. (J). (gr. 1-4). pap. 5.99 (978-0-547-23753-4(7)) Houghton Mifflin Harcourt Publishing Co.
—Still Just Grace. (Just Grace Ser.: 2). (ENG., Illus.). 160p. (J). 2009. (gr. 1-4). pap. 5.99 (978-0-618-93482-9(0)) 2007. (gr. 2-5). 15.99 (978-0-618-64643-2(4)) Houghton Mifflin Harcourt Publishing Co.
Harper, Jamie. Miss Mingo & the Fire Drill. Harper, Jamie, illus. 2012. (ENG., Illus.). 40p. (J). (gr. -1-3). pap. 6.99 (978-0-7636-6086-4(8)) Candlewick Pr.
—Miss Mingo & the First Day of School. Harper, Jamie, illus. 2009. (ENG., Illus.). 32p. (J). (gr. -1-3). pap. 6.99 (978-0-7636-4134-4(0)) Candlewick Pr.
—Miss Mingo & the First Day of School. 2006. (Illus.). 26p. (J). (978-1-4156-9174-8(6)) Candlewick Pr.
—Miss Mingo Weathers the Storm. Harper, Jamie, illus. (ENG., Illus.). 40p. (J). (gr. -1-3). 2017. 6.99 **(978-0-7636-9514-9(9))** 2012. 15.99 (978-0-7636-4931-9(7)) Candlewick Pr.
Harper, Jessica. A Place Called Kindergarten. Karas, G. Brian, illus. 2008. (ENG.). 32p. (J). (gr. -1-k). pap. 6.99 (978-0-14-241174-2(4), Puffin Books) Penguin Young Readers Group.
Harper, Meg. No More School. 2006. 184p. per. (978-1-904529-28-6(3), Back to Front) Solidus.
Harrell, Rob. The Troll Who Cried Wolf. 2015. (Life of Zarf Ser.: 2). (ENG., Illus.). 272p. (J). (gr. 3-7). 14.99 (978-0-8037-4104-1(9), Dial Bks) Penguin Young Readers Group.
—The Trouble with Weasels. 2014. (Life of Zarf Ser.: 1). (ENG.). 288p. (J). (gr. 3-7). 14.99 (978-0-8037-4103-4(0), Dial Bks) Penguin Young Readers Group.
Harrington, Dylan, et al. The Harrington Five & the Case of the School Sandals Err Vandals. 2006. 144p. pap. 11.25 (978-1-4116-7863-5(4)) Lulu Pr., Inc.
Harrington, Kim. The Dead & Buried. 2013. (ENG.). 304p. (J). (gr. 7). 17.99 (978-0-545-33302-3(4)) Scholastic, Inc.
—Perception. 2012. (ENG.). 288p. (J). (gr. 9). 16.99 (978-0-545-23053-7(5)) Scholastic, Inc.
Harris, Ashley Rae. The Prank. 2011. (Night Fall Ser.). (ENG.). 120p. (YA). (gr. 6-12). pap. 7.95 (978-0-7613-7814-3(6)); lib. bdg. 27.93 (978-0-7613-7747-4(6)) Lerner Publishing Group.

S

Harris, Lee. Carla & the Great Talent Show. 2009. 80p. pap. 10.00 (978-1-60860-515-6(9), Strategic Bk. Publishing) Strategic Book Publishing & Rights Agency (SBPRA).
Harris, Michael. Teenagers. 2010. 131p. pap. 13.97 (978-0-557-31733-2(9)) Lulu Pr., Inc.
—TEENAGERS II: High School Blowout!!! 2010. 153p. pap. 16.50 (978-0-557-61163-8(6)) Lulu Pr., Inc.
Harris, Patrice. Grandma Asks: Were You Good at School Today? Harrison, Nicholas, illus. 2013. 26p. pap. 10.00 (978-0-9892358-5-3(8)) CLF Publishing.
Harris, Robie H. I Am Not Going to School Today! Ormerod, Jan, illus. 2003. (ENG.). 32p. (J). (gr. -1-3). 17.99 (978-0-689-83913-9(8), McElderry, Margaret K. Bks.) McElderry, Margaret K. Bks.
Harrison, Emma. Sacked: A Rival High Novel. 2008. (YA). (978-1-4114-0525-7(0), Spark Publishing Group) Sterling Publishing Co., Inc.
—That's a Wrap: A Rival High Novel. 2008. (YA). (978-1-4114-0527-1(7), Spark Publishing Group) Sterling Publishing Co., Inc.
—Toe the Line: A Rival High Novel. 2008. (YA). (978-1-4114-0526-4(9), Spark Publishing Group) Sterling Publishing Co., Inc.
Harrison, Lisi. Alphas. 2009. (Alphas Ser.: 1). (ENG.). 272p. (YA). (gr. 7-17). pap. 9.99 (978-0-316-03579-8(3), Poppy) Little, Brown Bks. for Young Readers.
—Back & Deader Than Ever. 2013. (Monster High Ser.: 4). (ENG.). 256p. (YA). (gr. 7-17). pap. 9.99 (978-0-316-18667-4(8), Poppy) Little, Brown Bks. for Young Readers.
—Best Friends for Never. 2004. (Clique Ser.: 2). (ENG.). 208p. (YA). (gr. 7-17). pap. 9.99 (978-0-316-70131-0(9), Poppy) Little, Brown Bks. for Young Readers.
—Bratfest at Tiffany's, No. 9. 2008. (Clique Ser.: 9). (ENG., Illus.). 256p. (YA). (gr. 7-17). per. 9.99 (978-0-316-00680-4(7), Poppy) Little, Brown Bks. for Young Readers.
—Charmed & Dangerous: The Clique Prequel. 2012. (Clique Ser.). (ENG.). 208p. (YA). (gr. 7-17). pap. 8.99 (978-0-316-05536-9(0), Poppy) Little, Brown Bks. for Young Readers.
—Dial L for Loser. 2006. (Clique Ser.: 6). (ENG.). 272p. (J). (gr. 7-17). per. 9.99 (978-0-316-11504-9(5), Poppy) Little, Brown Bks. for Young Readers.
—Dial L for Loser. 2008. (Clique Novels Ser.). 268p. 20.00 (978-1-60686-291-9(X)) Perfection Learning Corp.
—The Ghoul Next Door. (Monster High Ser.: 2). (ENG.). 256p. (YA). (gr. 7-17). 2012. pap. 8.99 (978-0-316-18666-7(X)) 2011. 16.99 (978-0-316-09911-0(2)) Little, Brown Bks. for Young Readers. (Poppy).
—It's Not Easy Being Mean, No. 7. rev. ed. 2007. (Clique Ser.: 7). (ENG.). 224p. (J). (gr. 7-17). per. 9.99 (978-0-316-11505-6(3), Poppy) Little, Brown Bks. for Young Readers.
—It's Not Easy Being Mean. 2008. (Clique Ser.). 193p. 20.00 (978-1-60686-330-5(4)) Perfection Learning Corp.
—Monster High. 2010. (SPA.). 448p. (YA). (gr. 8-12). mass mkt. 19.99 (978-607-11-0641-4(9)) Aguilar, Altea, Taurus, Alfaguara, S.A. de C.V MEX. Dist: Two Rivers Distribution.
—Monster High. (Monster High Ser.: 1). (ENG.). 272p. (YA). (gr. 7-17). 2011. pap. 8.99 (978-0-316-17621-7(4)) 2010. 16.99 (978-0-316-09918-9(X)) Little, Brown Bks. for Young Readers. (Poppy).
—Monster High. 2011. (Monster High Ser.: 1). (YA). lib. bdg. 19.65 (978-0-606-23459-7(4), Turtleback) Turtleback Bks.
—Monster High: the Scary Cute Collection. 2013. (Monster High Ser.). (ENG.). 1056p. (J). (gr. 7-17). pap. 38.00 (978-0-316-24908-9(4), Poppy) Little, Brown Bks. for Young Readers.
—Monster High: Where There's a Wolf, There's a Way. 2011. (Monster High Ser.: 3). (ENG., Illus.). 256p. (YA). (gr. 7-17). 17.99 (978-0-316-09919-6(8), Poppy) Little, Brown Bks. for Young Readers.
—Sealed with a Diss. 2007. (Clique Ser.: 8). (ENG.). 272p. (YA). (gr. 7-17). pap. 9.99 (978-0-316-11506-3(1), Poppy) Little, Brown Bks. for Young Readers.
—Sealed with a Diss. 2008. (Clique Novels Ser.). 248p. 20.00 (978-1-60686-345-9(2)) Perfection Learning Corp.
—A Tale of Two Pretties. 2011. (Clique Ser.: 14). (ENG.). 224p. (YA). (gr. 7-17). pap. 9.99 (978-0-316-08442-0(5), Poppy) Little, Brown Bks. for Young Readers.
—These Boots Are Made for Stalking. 12th ed. 2010. (Clique Ser.: 12). (ENG.). 256p. (YA). (gr. 7-17). pap. 9.99 (978-0-316-00683-5(1), Poppy) Little, Brown Bks. for Young Readers.
—Top of the Feud Chain. 2011. (Alphas Ser.: 4). (ENG.). 240p. (YA). (gr. 7-17). pap. 9.99 (978-0-316-03582-8(3), Poppy) Little, Brown Bks. for Young Readers.
—Where There's a Wolf, There's a Way. 2012. (Monster High Ser.: 3). (ENG., Illus.). 272p. (YA). (gr. 7-17). pap. 9.99 (978-0-316-18668-1(6), Poppy) Little, Brown Bks. for Young Readers.
Harrison, Zac. Crash Landing, 1 vol. 2013. (Hyperspace High Ser.). (ENG.). 288p. (gr. 4-8). 27.32 (978-1-4342-6306-3(1)) Stone Arch Bks.
—Frozen Enemies, 1 vol. 2013. (Hyperspace High Ser.). (ENG.). 288p. (gr. 4-8). 27.32 (978-1-4342-6307-0(X)) Stone Arch Bks.
—Galactic Battle, 1 vol. 2014. (Hyperspace High Ser.). (ENG., Illus.). 288p. (gr. 4-8). 27.32 (978-1-4342-6569-2(2)) Stone Arch Bks.
—Hyperspace High, 1 vol. (Hyperspace High Ser.). (ENG.). 288p. (gr. 4-8). 2014. 54.64 (978-1-4342-8935-3(4)) 2013. 109.28 (978-1-4342-6314-8(2)) 2013. pap. 35.80 (978-1-4342-9039-7(5)) Stone Arch Bks.
—Robot Warriors, 1 vol. 2013. (Hyperspace High Ser.). (ENG.). 288p. (gr. 4-8). pap. 8.95 (978-1-4342-6312-4(6)); 27.32 (978-1-4342-6308-7(8)) Stone Arch Bks.
—Space Plague, 1 vol. 2014. (Hyperspace High Ser.). (ENG., Illus.). 288p. (gr. 4-8). 27.32 (978-1-4342-6568-5(4)) Stone Arch Bks.
—Warlord's Revenge, 1 vol. 2013. (Hyperspace High Ser.). (ENG.). 288p. (gr. 4-8). pap. 8.95 (978-1-4342-6313-1(4)); 27.32 (978-1-4342-6309-4(6)) Stone Arch Bks.
Hart, Alison. Anna's Blizzard, 1 vol. Bachem, Paul, illus. 2017. (ENG.). 160p. (J). (gr. 2-4). pap. 7.95 **(978-1-68263-002-0(1))** Peachtree Pubs.
Hart, Alison. Dive Right In. Studios, Arcana, illus. 2011. (ENG.). 120p. (J). pap. 8.95 (978-1-59369-909-3(3)) American Girl Publishing, Inc.
Hart, Carla. A Kid Named Cancer: A Story about a Bully & How He Got Treated. 2009. 50p. pap. 16.50 (978-1-60693-659-7(X), Eloquent Bks.) Strategic Book Publishing & Rights Agency (SBPRA).
Hart, Caryl & Lord, Leonie. The Wolf Who Wouldn't Go to School. 2015. (ENG.). 32p. (J). (gr. -1-k). pap. 8.99 (978-1-4380-0620-8(9)) Barron's Educational Series, Inc.
Hart, Louise. Rosie's Rule. 2004. 96p. pap. 19.95 (978-1-4137-0546-1(4)) America Star Bks.
Hartinger, Brent. Geography Club. (ENG.). 240p. 2003. (J). 17.99 (978-0-06-001221-2(8)) 2004. (YA). (gr. 9). reprint ed. pap. 9.99 (978-0-06-001223-6(4), HarperTeen) HarperCollins Pubs.
Hartley, Steve. Oliver Fibbs & the Giant Boy-Munching Bugs. Lum, Bernice, illus. unabr. ed. 2015. (Oliver Fibbs Ser.: 2). (ENG.). 192p. (J). (gr. 2-5). pap. 8.99 (978-1-4472-2024-4(2)) Pan Macmillan GBR. Dist: Independent Pubs. Group.
Hartley, Susan. Bienvenido a nuestra Escuela: Fiction-to-Fact Big Book. enl. ed. 2004. (SPA.). (J). pap. 26.00 (978-1-4108-2364-9(4), 23644) Benchmark Education Co.
Harvey, Jacqueline. Alice-Miranda at School. 2012. (ENG.). 272p. (J). (gr. 2-5). 7.99 (978-0-385-73994-8(X), Yearling) Random Hse. Children's Bks.
Harvey, Keith. Tiberius Goes to School. Brown, Kate & Hickman, Paula, illus. 2014. (ENG.). 24p. pap. 8.95 (978-1-84135-919-9(X)) Award Pubns. Ltd. GBR. Dist: Parkwest Pubns., Inc.
—Tiberius Goes to School. Brown, Kait, illus. 2010. (Tiberius Tales Ser.). 24p. (J). (gr. -1-2). pap. 8.15 (978-1-60754-837-9(2)); lib. bdg. 22.60 (978-1-60754-833-1(X)) Windmill Bks.
Harvey, Pam & Panckridge, Michael. In the Deep End. 2007. 224p. (978-0-207-20064-9(5)) HarperCollins Pubs. Australia.
Hasak-Lowy, Todd. 33 Minutes. Barton, Bethany, illus. (ENG.). 224p. (J). (gr. 3-7). 2014. pap. 7.99 (978-1-4424-4501-7(7)) 2013. 16.99 (978-1-4424-4500-0(9)) Simon & Schuster Children's Publishing. (Aladdin).
Hasbro. My Little Pony: Ponyville Reading Adventures. 2015. (Passport to Reading Level 2 Ser.). (ENG., Illus.). 192p. (J). (gr. -1-3). 9.99 (978-0-316-33740-3(4)) Little, Brown Bks. for Young Readers.
Hassan, Michael. Crash & Burn. (ENG.). 544p. (YA). (gr. 9). 2014. pap. 9.99 (978-0-06-211291-0(0)) 2013. 18.99 (978-0-06-211290-3(2)) HarperCollins Pubs.
Haston, Meg. How to Rock Best Friends & Frenemies. 2013. (How to Rock Ser.: 2). (ENG.). 352p. (J). (gr. 3-7). pap. 8.00 (978-0-316-06827-7(6), Poppy) Little, Brown Bks. for Young Readers.
—How to Rock Braces & Glasses. 2011. (How to Rock Ser.: 1). (ENG.). 336p. (J). (gr. 3-7). 16.99 (978-0-316-06825-3(X), Poppy) Little, Brown Bks. for Young Readers.
—How to Rock Braces & Glasses. 2012. (How to Rock Ser.: 1). (ENG.). 352p. (J). (gr. 3-7). pap. 8.00 (978-0-316-06824-6(1), Poppy) Little, Brown Bks. for Young Readers.
Hathaway, Jill. Impostor. 2013. (Slide Ser.: 2). (ENG.). 272p. (YA). (gr. 9). 17.99 (978-0-06-207798-1(8)) HarperCollins Pubs.
—Slide. (Slide Ser.: 1). (ENG.). (YA). (gr. 9). 2013. 272p. pap. 9.99 (978-0-06-207796-7(1)) 2012. 256p. 17.99 (978-0-06-207790-5(2)) HarperCollins Pubs.
Hattie, Jay. The Boy Who Didn't Try. 2011. 16p. pap. 9.00 (978-1-4634-1634-8(2)) AuthorHouse.
Hautman, Pete. The Big Crunch. 2011. (ENG.). 288p. (J). (gr. 7-8). 17.99 (978-0-545-24075-8(1), Scholastic Pr.) Scholastic, Inc.
—Blank Confession. (ENG.). 176p. (YA). (gr. 7). 2011. pap. 10.99 (978-1-4169-1328-3(9)) 2010. 16.99 (978-1-4169-1327-6(0)) Simon & Schuster Bks. For Young Readers. (Simon & Schuster Bks. For Young Readers).
—Invisible. Hautman, Pete, illus. 2006. (ENG., Illus.). 160p. (YA). (gr. 7-12). reprint ed. pap. 9.99 (978-0-689-86903-7(7), Simon & Schuster Bks. For Young Readers) Simon & Schuster Bks. For Young Readers.
—Sweetblood. 2010. (ENG.). 208p. (YA). (gr. 7). pap. 8.99 (978-1-4424-0755-8(7), Simon & Schuster Bks. For Young Readers) Simon & Schuster Bks. For Young Readers.
Hautzig, Deborah. Little Witch Learns to Read. Wickstrom, Sylvie K., illus. 2003. (Step into Reading Ser.). (ENG.). 48p. (J). (gr. k-3). pap. 3.99 (978-0-375-82179-0(1), Random Hse. Bks. for Young Readers) Random Hse. Children's Bks.
Havill, Juanita. Jamaica's Blue Marker. O'Brien, Anne Sibley, illus. 2003. (ENG.). 32p. (J). (gr. -1-3). pap. 7.99 (978-0-618-36917-1(1)) Houghton Mifflin Harcourt Publishing Co.
Hawes, Adrienne Hill. Moving Danielle. 2008. 22p. pap. 24.95 (978-1-4241-4977-3(0)) America Star Bks.
Hawkins, A. D. The Time Princess. 2013. 208p. pap. (978-1-78299-661-3(3)) FeedARead.com.
Hawkins, Rachel. Miss Mayhem. 2015. (Rebel Belle Ser.: 2). (ENG.). 288p. (YA). (gr. 7). 17.99 (978-0-399-25694-3(6), G.P. Putnam's Sons Books for Young Readers) Penguin Young Readers Group.
—Rebel Belle. 2015. (Rebel Belle Ser.: 1). (ENG.). 368p. (YA). (gr. 7). pap. 9.99 (978-0-14-751435-6(5), Speak) Penguin Young Readers Group.
—School Spirits. 2014. (Hex Hall Novel Ser.). (ENG.). 304p. (YA). (gr. 7-12). pap. 9.99 (978-1-4231-4850-0(9)) Hyperion Bks. for Children.
—School Spirits. 2013. (Hex Hall Novel Ser.). (ENG.). 304p. (YA). (gr. 7-12). 17.99 (978-1-4231-4849-4(5)) Hyperion Pr.
Hawkins-Rodgers, Donzella. No Bulley Destroys Chloe's Hairdo. 2003. (Illus.). 32p. (J). (gr. 3-18). pap. 10.95 (978-1-884242-58-8(8)) Multicultural Pubns.
—No Bulley Destroy's Chloe's Hairdo. Hewins, Shirley, illus. 2003. 32p. (J). (gr. 3-18). lib. bdg. 16.95 (978-1-884242-56-4(1)) Multicultural Pubns.
Hawkins, Wendy. Binky Goes to School. 2009. 20p. pap. 13.99 (978-1-4389-6990-9(2)) AuthorHouse.
Haworth-Attard, Barbara. My Life from Air-Bras to Zits. 2009. (ENG.). 288p. (YA). (gr. 7-10). pap. 9.95 (978-0-7387-1483-7(6), Flux) North Star Editions.
Hayes, Angela. The Mop Heads, 1 vol. Polly Jr., Jimmy Wayne, illus. 2009. 14p. pap. 24.95 (978-1-61546-006-9(3)) America Star Bks.
Hayes, Daniel. Flyers. 2013. (ENG.). 208p. (YA). (gr. 7). pap. 10.99 (978-1-4424-8881-6(6), Simon & Schuster Bks. For Young Readers) Simon & Schuster Bks. For Young Readers.
Hayes, Gwen. Dreaming Awake. 2012. (ENG.). 332p. (YA). (gr. 7-18). 9.99 (978-0-451-23554-1(1), Berkley) Penguin Publishing Group.
—Falling Under. 2011. (ENG.). 336p. (YA). (gr. 7-18). 9.99 (978-0-451-23268-7(2), Berkley) Penguin Publishing Group.
Hayes, Sonia. Urban Goddess. 2007. 224p. (YA). per. 9.95 (978-0-9777573-1-2(5)) NUA Multimedia.
Haynes, Marilee. A. K. A. Genius. 2013. (ENG.). 208p. (YA). 9.95 (978-0-8198-0830-1(X)) Pauline Bks. & Media.
—Genius under Construction. 2014. (ENG.). (YA). pap. (978-0-8198-3126-2(3)) Pauline Bks. & Media.
—Pictures of Me. 2016. 149p. (J). pap. (978-0-8198-6019-4(0)) Pauline Bks. & Media.
Hays, Anna Jane. Kindergarten Countdown. Davick, Linda, illus. 2013. (ENG.). 24p. (J). (gr. -1-2). 6.99 (978-0-385-75371-5(3), Dragonfly Bks.) Random Hse. Children's Bks.
Haywood, Carolyn. B Is for Betsy. 2004. (ENG., Illus.). 144p. (J). (gr. 1-4). pap. 5.95 (978-0-15-205099-3(X)) Houghton Mifflin Harcourt Publishing Co.
—Back to School with Betsy. 2004. (ENG., Illus.). 160p. (J). (gr. 1-4). pap. 11.95 (978-0-15-205101-3(5)) Houghton Mifflin Harcourt Publishing Co.
—Betsy & Billy. 2004. (ENG., Illus.). 144p. (J). (gr. 1-4). pap. 6.99 (978-0-15-205100-6(7)) Houghton Mifflin Harcourt Publishing Co.
Hazelton, Tanya & Bonanni, Constance. Ian's Golden Passage. 2009. 168p. pap. 9.99 (978-1-935105-33-6(7)) Avid Readers Publishing Group.
HB Staff. Today Is Monday. 97th ed. 2003. (Signatures Ser.). (gr. 1-18). pap. 16.50 (978-0-15-308169-9(4)) Harcourt Schl. Pubs.
Headley, Justina Chen. The Patch. Vane, Mitch, illus. 2007. (ENG.). 32p. (J). (gr. k-3). pap. 7.95 (978-1-58089-170-7(5)) Charlesbridge Publishing, Inc.
Hearst, Allyson. White Pajamas: A Karate Story. 2011. 68p. pap. 19.95 (978-1-4626-3871-0(6)) America Star Bks.
Heasley, Gwendolyn. Where I Belong. 2011. (Where I Belong Ser.: 1). (ENG.). 304p. (YA). (gr. 8-18). pap. 9.99 (978-0-06-197884-5(1), HarperTeen) HarperCollins Pubs.
Heath, Michael. Garlic Bread for Eugene. 2013. (ENG.). 112p. (J). (gr. 4-6). pap. 7.95 (978-1-9835-0124-1(7)) Turn the Page Publishing.
Heiligman, Deborah. Cool Dog, School Dog, 0 vols. 2013. (ENG.). 32p. (J). (gr. -1-3). pap. 9.99 (978-1-4778-1670-7(4), 9781477816707, Amazon Children's Publishing) Amazon Publishing.
Helgeson, Kat. Say No to the Bro. 2017. (ENG., Illus.). 272p. (YA). (gr. 9). 17.99 **(978-1-4814-7193-0(7)**, Simon & Schuster Bks. For Young Readers) Simon & Schuster Bks. For Young Readers.
Helget, Nicole. The End of the Wild. 2017. (ENG., Illus.). 272p. (J). (gr. 3-7). 16.99 (978-0-316-24511-1(9)) Little, Brown Bks. for Young Readers.
The Hell House Experience. 2008. (ENG.). 70p. 14.99 (978-0-9817520-8-2(X)) Torch Legacy Pubns.
Heller, Alyson. After-School Sports Club Adventures. Björkman, Steve, illus. 2016. (J). **(978-1-4814-7741-3(2))** Simon & Schuster Children's Publishing.
Heller, Alyson. Soccer Day. Björkman, Steve, illus. 2009. (After-School Sports Club Ser.). (ENG.). 32p. (J). (gr. -1-1). pap. 3.99 (978-1-4169-9410-7(6), Simon Spotlight) Simon Spotlight.
Helmetag Murdock, Kita. Future Flash. 2014. (ENG.). 208p. (J). (gr. 2-7). 12.95 (978-1-62873-822-3(7), Sky Pony Pr.) Skyhorse Publishing Co., Inc.
Helms, Rhonda. Promposal. 2015. (ENG., Illus.). 224p. (YA). (gr. 7). pap. 9.99 (978-1-4814-2231-4(6), Simon Pulse) Simon Pulse.
Helmso, Candy Grant. Cakewalk. Taylor, Stephen, illus. 2003. (Books for Young Learners). (ENG.). 16p. (J). pap. 5.75 net. (978-1-57274-250-5(X), 2727, Bks. for Young Learners) Owen, Richard C. Pubs., Inc.
Henderson, Lauren. Kiss Me Kill Me. 2009. (ENG.). 272p. (YA). (gr. 9). pap. 8.99 (978-0-385-73488-2(3), Delacorte Pr.) Random Hse. Children's Bks.
—Kiss of Death. 2012. (ENG.). 318p. (YA). (gr. 9). pap. 9.99 (978-0-385-73780-7(7), Ember) Random Hse. Children's Bks.
Hendrickson, David H. Cracking the Ice. 2011. (YA). 365p. (gr. 9-18). 16.95 (978-1-934813-55-3(9)); 366p. (978-1-934813-56-0(7)) Westside Bks.
Heneghan, James. Hit Squad, 1 vol. 2003. (Orca Soundings Ser.). (ENG.). 128p. (YA). (gr. 8-12). pap. 9.95 (978-1-55143-269-4(2)) Orca Bk. Pubs. USA.
—Hit Squad. 2004. (Orca Soundings Ser.). 106p. 19.95 (978-0-7569-4300-4(0)) Perfection Learning Corp.
Hengel, Katherine. No Easy Race, 1 vol. unabr. ed. 2011. (District 13 Ser.). (ENG.). 47p. (YA). (gr. 9-12). pap. 7.95 (978-1-61651-277-4(6)) Saddleback Educational Publishing, Inc.
—Wings, 1 vol. unabr. ed. 2011. (District 13 Ser.). (ENG.). 48p. (YA). (gr. 9-12). pap. 7.95 (978-1-61651-280-4(6)) Saddleback Educational Publishing, Inc.
Henkes, Kevin. Chrysanthemum. 2004. (Illus.). (J). (gr. k-3). spiral bd. (978-0-616-14575-3(6)) Canadian National Institute for the Blind/Institut National Canadien pour les Aveugles.
—Chrysanthemum. Henkes, Kevin, illus. (ENG., Illus.). 32p. (J). (gr. -1-3). 2008. pap. 7.99 (978-0-688-14732-7(1)) 2007. pap. 24.99 (978-0-06-111974-3(1)) HarperCollins Pubs. (Greenwillow Bks.).
—Chrysanthemum. 2008. (J). (gr. -1-2). lib. bdg. 17.20 (978-0-613-00459-6(0), Turtleback) Turtleback Bks.
—Crisantemo. 2017.Tr. of Chrysanthemum. (SPA.). (J). pap. **(978-1-63245-664-9(8))** Lectorum Pubns., Inc.
—Crisantemo. Mlawer, Teresa, tr. from ENG. 2006.Tr. of Chrysanthemum. (Illus.). 31p. (gr. 4-7). 19.00 (978-0-7569-7316-2(3)) Perfection Learning Corp.
—Lilly Adore l'École! pap. 16.95 (978-2-07-054873-6(2)) Gallimard, Editions FRA. Dist: Distribooks, Inc.
—Lilly's Purple Plastic Purse. Henkes, Kevin, illus. 10th anniv. ed. 2006. (ENG., Illus.). 40p. (J). (gr. -1-4). 17.99 (978-0-688-12897-5(1), Greenwillow Bks.) HarperCollins Pubs.
—Lilly's Purple Plastic Purse. Henkes, Kevin, illus. (Illus.). pap. 16.95 incl. audio (978-0-87499-686-9(4)); pap. incl. audio (978-0-87499-688-3(0)); pap. 18.95 incl. audio compact disk (978-1-59112-347-7(X)); pap. incl. audio compact disk (978-1-59112-557-0(X)) Live Oak Media.
—Lilly's Purple Plastic Purse 20th Anniversary Edition. Henkes, Kevin, illus. 20th ed. 2016. (Illus.). 40p. (J). (gr. -1-3). 17.99 (978-0-06-242419-8(X), Greenwillow Bks.) HarperCollins Pubs.
—Lily y Su Bolso de Plastico Morado. 2017.Tr. of Lilly's Purple Plastic Purse. (SPA.). (J). pap. **(978-1-63245-667-0(2))** Lectorum Pubns., Inc.
—Prudencia Se Preocupa. 2017.Tr. of Wemberly Worried. (SPA.). (J). pap. **(978-1-63245-666-3(4))** Lectorum Pubns., Inc.
—Wemberly Worried. Henkes, Kevin, illus. (Illus.). pap. 16.95 incl. audio (978-0-87499-806-1(9)); pap. 39.95 incl. audio compact disk (978-1-59112-561-7(8)); pap. incl. audio (978-0-87499-808-5(5)); pap. 18.95 incl. audio compact disk (978-1-59112-359-0(3)) Live Oak Media.
—The Year of Billy Miller. Henkes, Kevin, illus. 2013. (Illus.). 240p. (J). (gr. 3-7). (ENG.). 16.99 (978-0-06-226812-9(0)); lib. bdg. 17.89 (978-0-06-226813-6(9)) HarperCollins Pubs. (Greenwillow Bks.).
—The Year of Billy Miller. Henkes, Kevin, illus. 2015. (ENG., Illus.). (J). (gr. 3-7). lib. bdg. 17.60 **(978-1-62765-762-4(2))** Perfection Learning Corp.
—The Year of Billy Miller. 2015. (J). lib. bdg. 17.20 (978-0-606-36977-0(5)) Turtleback Bks.
Hennessy, Claire. Afterwards. 2005. 188p. (YA). pap. (978-1-84223-207-1(X)) Poolbeg Pr.
Hennesy, Carolyn. Pandora Gets Jealous. 2009. (Mythic Misadventures Ser.). (ENG., Illus.). 288p. (YA). (gr. 3-6). pap. 7.99 (978-1-59990-291-3(5), 9781599902913, Bloomsbury USA Childrens) Bloomsbury Publishing USA.
Henry, Isabelle. The Hundred-Penny Rub. 2008. 36p. pap. 16.99 (978-1-4343-4912-5(8)) AuthorHouse.
Henshon, Suzanna E. Spiders on the Ceiling. 2006. (J). (978-0-88092-614-0(7)) Royal Fireworks Publishing Co.
Hensley, Joy N. Rites of Passage. 2014. (ENG.). 416p. (YA). (gr. 8). 17.99 (978-0-06-229519-4(5), HarperTeen) HarperCollins Pubs.
Hensley, Judith Victoria. Terrible Tin. 2008. 136p. pap. 14.95 (978-0-9795103-3-5(3)) Ascended Ideas.
Hepler, Heather. Frosted Kisses. 2015. (ENG.). 272p. (J). (gr. 7). 17.99 (978-0-545-79055-0(7)) Scholastic, Inc.
—Love? Maybe. 2013. (ENG.). 288p. (YA). (gr. 7). pap. 8.99 (978-0-14-242386-8(6), Speak) Penguin Young Readers Group.
Hepler, Linda McGhee. How to Survive Seventh Grade (If You're Lucky) 2008. 146p. pap. 24.95 (978-1-60563-610-8(X)) America Star Bks.
Herbach, Geoff. Fat Boy vs. the Cheerleaders. 2014. (ENG.). 320p. (YA). (gr. 7-12). 16.99 (978-1-4022-9141-8(8), 9781402291418) Sourcebooks, Inc.
—Gabe Johnson Takes Over. 2015. (ENG.). 352p. (YA). (gr. 6-12). pap. 9.99 (978-1-4926-0865-3(3)) Sourcebooks, Inc.
—Stupid Fast. 2011. (Felton Reinstein Trilogy Ser.: 1). (ENG.). 320p. (YA). (gr. 7-12). pap. 10.99 (978-1-4022-5630-1(2), 9781402256301) Sourcebooks, Inc.
Herman, Charlotte. My Chocolate Year: A Novel with 12 Recipes. Pham, LeUyen, illus. 2008. (ENG.). 176p. (J). (gr. 3-7). 15.99 (978-1-4169-3341-0(7), Simon & Schuster Bks. For Young Readers) Simon & Schuster Bks. For Young Readers.
Herman, Gail. Time for School, Little Dinosaur. Fleming, Michael, illus. 2017. (Step into Reading Ser.). (ENG.). 32p. (J). (gr. -1-1). pap. 3.99 **(978-0-399-55645-6(1))**; lib. bdg. 12.99 **(978-0-399-55646-3(X))** Random Hse. Children's Bks. (Random Hse. Bks. for Young Readers).
Hermes, Patricia. The Wild Year Bk. 3: Joshua's Oregon Trail Diary. 2003. (My America Ser.). (ENG., Illus.). 112p. (J). 12.95 (978-0-439-37055-4(8)) Scholastic, Inc.
Hernandez, David. No More Us for You. 2009. (YA). 281p. lib. bdg. 17.89 (978-0-06-117334-9(7)); (ENG.). 288p. (gr. 9-18). 16.99 (978-0-06-117333-2(9)) HarperCollins Pubs. (HarperTeen).
Hershey, Mary. My Big Sister Is So Bossy She Says You Can't Read This Book. 2006. (ENG., Illus.). 176p. (J). (gr. 3-7). per. 6.99 (978-0-553-48797-8(3), Yearling) Random Hse. Children's Bks.
Heyliger, William. Quarterback Hothead. Grubb, W. B., illus. 2011. 262p. 47.95 (978-1-258-09738-7(9)) Literary Licensing, LLC.
Hickey, Joshalyn M. Good Morning Lovey! Chaveevah, Banks Ferguson, illus. 2005. (ENG.). 28p. (J). 12.00 (978-0-9718939-3-1(4)) BaHar Publishing, L.C.
Hicks, Faith Erin. Friends with Boys. Hicks, Faith Erin, illus. 2012. (ENG., Illus.). 224p. (YA). (gr. 7-11). pap. 16.99 (978-1-59643-556-8(9), 9781596435568, First Second Bks.) Roaring Brook Pr.
Hicks, John Bryant. The Day Charlie Lost His Weirdiness. 2nd ed. 2007. (J). per. 5.99 (978-0-9742829-4-7(4)) Quiet Man Publishing.
Higgins, Chris. The Secrets Club: No Match for Dani. 3rd ed. 2016. (Secrets Club Ser.: 3). (ENG.). 176p. (J). (gr. 2-4). pap. 9.99 (978-0-14-133524-7(6)) Penguin Bks., Ltd. GBR. Dist: Independent Pubs. Group.
Higgins, M. G. Bi-Normal, 1 vol. 2013. (Gravel Road Ser.). (ENG.). 191p. (YA). (gr. 9-12). pap. 9.95 (978-1-62250-004-8(0)) Saddleback Educational Publishing, Inc.
—Falling Out of Place, 1 vol. 2013. (Gravel Road Ser.). (ENG.). 191p. (YA). (gr. 9-12). pap. 9.95 (978-1-62250-021-5(0)) Saddleback Educational Publishing, Inc.
—Falling Out of Place. 2013. (Gravel Road Ser.). (YA). lib. bdg. 20.80 (978-0-606-26963-6(0), Turtleback) Turtleback Bks.
—I'm Just Me. 2014. (Gravel Road Ser.). (YA). lib. bdg. 20.80 (978-0-606-35220-8(1)) Turtleback Bks.

Higgins, Nadia. Zombie Field Day: Zombie Zappers Book 2. (Zombie Zappers Ser.). 64p. (J). 2014. (gr. 5-9). pap. 9.95 (978-1-62285-006-8(8)) 2013. (Illus.). 15.95 (978-1-62285-005-1(X)) Enslow Pubs., Inc.

Hileman, Linda L. Dawn's Secret. 2006. (J). per. 9.95 (978-1-59571-117-5(1)) Word Association Pubs.

Hill, Andrew G. The Song of the Seraphim. 2009. 196p. pap. 13.95 (978-1-60860-194-3(3), Strategic Bk. Publishing) Strategic Book Publishing & Rights Agency (SBPRA).

Hill, Eric. Spot Goes to School. Hill, Eric, illus. 2004. (Spot Ser.). (ENG., Illus.). 24p. (J). (gr. -1-k). 6.99 (978-0-14-240167-5(6), Warne) Penguin Young Readers Group.

Hill, Joyce. A Penny in My Pocket. 2007. 220p. 27.95 (978-0-9795818-0-9(X)); pap. 14.95 (978-0-9795818-1-6(8)) Mushgush Pr.

Hill, Kirkpatrick. The Year of Miss Agnes. 2003. (Aladdin Historical Fiction Ser.). 115p. (gr. 3-7). 17.00 (978-0-7569-1407-3(8)) Perfection Learning Corp.

Hillert, Margaret. Come to School, Dear Dragon. Pullan, Jack, illus. 2016. (BeginningtoRead Ser.). (ENG.). 32p. (J). (-2). lib. bdg. 22.60 (978-1-59953-764-1(8)) Norwood Hse. Pr.

—Ven a la Escuela, Querido Dragón. Pullan, Jack, illus. 2017. (BeginningtoRead Ser.).Tr. of Come to School, Dear Dragon. (ENG & SPA.). 32p. (J). (-2). 22.60 **(978-1-59953-827-3(X))** Norwood Hse. Pr.

Hillert, Margaret. Who Goes to School? Woodworth, Viki, illus. 2016. (BeginningtoRead Ser.). (ENG.). 32p. (J). (gr. -1-2). pap. 11.94 (978-1-60357-949-0(4)); (gr. k-2). 22.60 (978-1-59953-808-2(3)) Norwood Hse. Pr.

Hillner, Brenda. The Invisible Girl. 2012. 86p. 19.10 (978-1-4669-5398-7(5)); pap. 9.10 (978-1-4669-5396-3(9)) Trafford Publishing.

Hills, Frederic F. & Hills, Tad. Rocket's 100th Day of School. 2014. (Rocket Ser.). (ENG.). 32p. (J). (gr. 1-4). pap. 3.99 (978-0-385-39097-2(1), Random Hse. Bks. for Young Readers) Random Hse. Children's Bks.

Hilton, Charlotte. Adventure of the Pen Pot Pals. 2009. 36p. pap. 16.99 (978-1-4389-4434-0(9)) AuthorHouse.

Hilton, Nette. Sprite Downberry. 2008. 288p. (978-0-7322-8548-7(8)) HarperCollins Pubs. Australia.

Hilton, Perez. The Boy with Pink Hair. Hill, Jenn, illus. 2011. (ENG.). 32p. (J). (gr. -1-k). 17.99 (978-0-451-23420-9(0), Celebra Young Readers) Penguin Publishing Group.

Himle, Lisa. Hands as Warm as Toast. Langton, Bruce, illus. 2006. 32p. (J). (gr. -1-3). 17.95 (978-1-58726-298-2(3), Mitten Pr.) Ann Arbor Editions LLC.

Hiranandani, Veera. The Whole Story of Half a Girl. 2013. (ENG.). 224p. (J). (gr. 4-7). 6.99 (978-0-375-87167-2(5), Yearling) Random Hse. Children's Bks.

Hirschmann, Kris. A Serious Case of the Sillies. Jennings, C. S., illus. 2013. 32p. (J). pap. (978-0-545-56765-7(3)) Scholastic, Inc.

Hites, Kati. Winnie & Waldorf: Disobedience School. Hites, Kati, illus. 2016. (Illus.). 40p. (J). (gr. -1-3). 17.99 (978-0-06-231162-7(X)) HarperCollins Pubs.

Hobbs, Valerie. Minnie McClary Speaks Her Mind. 2013. (ENG.). 240p. (J). (gr. 4-8). pap. 9.99 (978-1-250-03408-3(6), 9781250034083) Square Fish.

Hoblin, Paul. False Start. 2017. (Gridiron Ser.). (ENG.). 128p. (YA). (gr. 6-12). 26.65 **(978-1-5124-3979-3(7))**; pap. 7.99 **(978-1-5124-5351-5(X))** Lerner Publishing Group. (Darby Creek).

Hodge, Merle. For the Life of Laetitia. 2003. 21.25 (978-0-8446-7246-5(7)) Smith, Peter Pub., Inc.

Hodkin, Michelle. The Unbecoming of Mara Dyer. (Mara Dyer Trilogy Ser.: 1). (ENG., Illus.). (YA). (gr. 9). 2012. 480p. pap. 12.99 (978-1-4424-2177-6(0)) 2011. 464p. 21.99 (978-1-4424-2176-9(2)) Simon & Schuster Bks. For Young Readers. (Simon & Schuster Bks. For Young Readers).

Hoeffner, Karol Ann. Surf Ed. 2010. (ENG.). 288p. (YA). (gr. 9). pap. 13.99 (978-1-4424-1418-1(9), Simon Pulse) Simon Pulse.

Hoena, Blake. Trouble with Cheating. Regan, Dana, illus. 2014. (Jess & Jaylen Ser.). (ENG.). 48p. (J). (gr. 1-4). 27.07 (978-1-63143-442-6(X), 208266) Child's World, Inc., The.

Hoena, Blake A. Raw. Cano, Fernando, illus. 2013. (Tony Hawk: Live2Skate Ser.). (ENG.). 72p. (gr. 3-4). pap. 35.70 (978-1-4342-6268-4(5), Tony Hawk's 900 Revolution) Stone Arch Bks.

—Raw, 1 vol. Cano, Fernando, illus. 2013. (Tony Hawk: Live2Skate Ser.). (ENG.). 72p. (gr. 4-5). pap. 5.95 (978-1-4342-6188-5(3)); lib. bdg. 25.32 (978-1-4342-4086-6(X)) Stone Arch Bks.

—Swamp Sting!, 1 vol. Facio, Sebastian, illus. 2011. (Graphic Sparks Ser.). (ENG.). 40p. (gr. 1-3). pap. 5.95 (978-1-4342-3065-2(1)); lib. bdg. 23.99 (978-1-4342-2960-1(2)) Stone Arch Bks. (Graphic Sparks).

Hoestlandt, Jo. Robin del Bosque. (SPA.). (J). 7.95 (978-958-04-5041-2(2)) Norma S.A. COL. Dist: Distribuidora Norma, Inc.

Hoff, Syd. Danny & the Dinosaur. 2017. (Danny & the Dinosaur — I Can Read Ser.). lib. bdg. 13.55 **(978-0-606-40063-3(X))** Turtleback Bks.

Hoff, Syd. Danny & the Dinosaur: School Days. Hoff, Syd, illus. 2017. (I Can Read Level 1 Ser.). (Illus.). 32p. (J). (gr. -1-3). pap. 3.99 (978-0-06-228161-6(5)) HarperCollins Pubs.

Hoffman, Mary. Bravo, Grace! 2011. (ENG.). 112p. (J). (gr. 3-7). 5.99 (978-0-14-241850-5(1), Puffin Books) Penguin Young Readers Group.

—Encore, Grace! 2011. (ENG.). 112p. (J). (gr. 3-7). 5.99 (978-0-14-241854-3(4), Puffin Books) Penguin Young Readers Group.

—Princess Grace. Van Wright, Cornelius & Hu, Ying-Hwa, illus. 2008. (ENG.). 32p. (J). (gr. -1-3). 18.99 (978-0-8037-3260-5(0), Dial Bks) Penguin Young Readers Group.

Holder, Amy. The Lipstick Laws. 2011. (ENG.). 240p. (YA). (gr. 7-18). pap. 13.99 (978-0-547-36306-6(0)) Houghton Mifflin Harcourt Publishing Co.

Holder, Nancy. Pretty Little Devils. 2009. (ENG.). 272p. (YA). (gr. 7-18). 8.99 (978-1-59514-269-6(X), Razorbill) Penguin Young Readers Group.

Holland, Frances. Ryan's Praying Mantis, 1 vol. 2009. 19p. pap. 24.95 (978-1-60749-432-4(9)) PublishAmerica, Inc.

Holland, L. Tam. The Counterfeit Family Tree of Vee Crawford-Wong. (ENG.). 368p. (YA). (gr. 9). 2014. pap. 9.99 (978-1-4424-1265-1(8)) 2013. 17.99 (978-1-4424-1264-4(X)) Simon & Schuster Children's Publishing.

Holliday, S. L. My Identity Christ-Is: Stay in the Game. 2012. (ENG.). 166p. (J). pap. 12.95 (978-1-4787-1827-7(7)) Outskirts Pr., Inc.

Holm, Jennifer L. Eighth Grade Is Making Me Sick. 2015. (Ginny Davis Year in Stuff Ser.: 2). lib. bdg. 18.40 (978-0-606-37710-2(7)) Turtleback Bks.

—Eighth Grade Is Making Me Sick: Ginny Davis's Year in Stuff. Castaldi, Elicia, illus. 2012. (Ginny Davis's Year in Stuff Ser.). (ENG.). 128p. (J). (gr. 3-7). 15.99 (978-0-375-86851-1(8), Random Hse. Bks. for Young Readers) Random Hse. Children's Bks.

—Middle School Is Worse Than Meatloaf: A Year Told Through Stuff. Castaldi, Elicia, illus. (ENG.). 128p. (J). (gr. 3-7). 2011. pap. 8.99 (978-1-4424-3663-3(8)) 2007. 12.99 (978-0-689-85281-7(9)) Simon & Schuster Children's Publishing. (Atheneum Bks. for Young Readers).

Holm, Jennifer L. Swing It, Sunny. Holm, Matthew, illus. 2017. (Sunny Ser.: 2). (ENG.). 224p. (J). (gr. 3-7). 24.99 **(978-0-545-74170-5(X))**; pap. 12.99 **(978-0-545-74172-9(6))** Scholastic, Inc. (Graphix).

Holm, Jennifer L. & Holm, Matthew. Babymouse for President. Holm, Jennifer L. & Holm, Matthew, illus. 2012. (Babymouse Ser.: 16). (ENG., Illus.). 96p. (J). (gr. 2-5). 12.99 (978-0-375-96780-1(X)); pap. 6.99 (978-0-375-86780-4(5)) Random Hse. Children's Bks. (Random Hse. Bks. for Young Readers).

—Babymouse Tales from the Locker Presents Lights, Camera, Messy Whiskers. 2017. (Babymouse Tales from the Locker Ser.: 1). (ENG., Illus.). 208p. (J). (gr. 3-7). 13.99 (978-0-399-55438-4(6), Random Hse. Bks. for Young Readers) Random Hse. Children's Bks.

—Brave New Pond. Holm, Jennifer L. & Holm, Matthew, illus. 2011. (Squish Ser.: No. 2). (ENG., Illus.). 96p. (J). (gr. 3-7). 12.99 (978-0-375-93784-2(6)); pap. 6.99 (978-0-375-84390-7(6)) Random Hse. Children's Bks. (Random Hse. Bks. for Young Readers).

—Dragonslayer. Holm, Jennifer L. & Holm, Matthew, illus. 2009. (Babymouse Ser.: 11). (ENG., Illus.). 96p. (J). (gr. 2-5). pap. 6.99 (978-0-375-85712-6(5)); lib. bdg. 12.99 (978-0-375-95712-3(X)) Random Hse. Children's Bks. (Random Hse. Bks. for Young Readers).

—Extreme Babymouse. Holm, Jennifer L. & Holm, Matthew, illus. 2013. (Babymouse Ser.: 17). (ENG., Illus.). 96p. (J). (gr. 2-5). pap. 6.99 (978-0-307-93160-3(9)); lib. bdg. 12.99 (978-0-375-97096-2(7)) Random Hse. Children's Bks. (Random Hse. Bks. for Young Readers).

—Extreme Babymouse. 2013. (Babymouse Ser.: 17). lib. bdg. 17.20 (978-0-606-26999-5(1), Turtleback) Turtleback Bks.

—Mad Scientist. Holm, Jennifer L. & Holm, Matthew, illus. 2011. (Babymouse Ser.: No. 14). (ENG., Illus.). 96p. (J). (gr. 2-5). pap. 6.99 (978-0-375-86574-9(8)); lib. bdg. 12.99 (978-0-375-96574-6(2)) Random Hse. Children's Bks. (Random Hse. Bks. for Young Readers).

—The Musical. Holm, Jennifer L. & Holm, Matthew, illus. 2009. (Babymouse Ser.: 10). (ENG., Illus.). 96p. (J). (gr. 2-5). pap. 6.99 (978-0-375-84388-4(4)); lib. bdg. 12.99 (978-0-375-93791-0(9)) Random Hse. Children's Bks. (Random Hse. Bks. for Young Readers).

—Our Hero. 2005. (Babymouse Ser.: 2). (ENG., Illus.). 96p. (J). (gr. 2-5). pap. 6.99 (978-0-375-83230-7(0)); lib. bdg. 12.99 (978-0-375-93230-4(5)) Random Hse. Children's Bks. (Random Hse. Bks. for Young Readers).

—Super Amoeba. Holm, Jennifer L. & Holm, Matthew, illus. 2011. (Squish Ser.: No. 1). (ENG., Illus.). 96p. (J). (gr. 3-7). pap. 6.99 (978-0-375-84389-1(2)); lib. bdg. 12.99 (978-0-375-93783-5(8)) Random Hse. Children's Bks. (Random Hse. Bks. for Young Readers).

Holm, Jennifer L., et al. Comics Squad: Recess! 2014. (Comics Squad Ser.). (ENG., Illus.). 144p. (J). (gr. 2-5). pap. 7.99 (978-0-385-37003-5(2), Random Hse. Bks. for Young Readers) Random Hse. Children's Bks.

Holm, Jennifer L., et al. Comics Squad #3: Detention! 2017. (Comics Squad Ser.: 3). (ENG., Illus.). 160p. (J). (gr. 2-5). lib. bdg. 12.99 **(978-0-553-51268-7(4)**, Random Hse. Bks. for Young Readers) Random Hse. Children's Bks.

Holm, Matthew & Follett, Jonathan. Marvin & the Moths. 2016. (ENG.). 352p. (J). (gr. 3-7). 16.99 (978-0-545-87674-2(5), Scholastic Pr.) Scholastic, Inc.

Holm, Matthew & Holm, Jennifer L. Lunch! 2016. (Comics Squad Ser.: 2). lib. bdg. 18.40 (978-0-606-38446-9(4)) Turtleback Bks.

Holmes, Elizabeth. The Normal Kid. 2012. (Exceptional Reading & Language Arts Titles for Intermediate Grades Ser.). (ENG.). 248p. (J). (gr. 4-9). 17.95 (978-0-7613-8085-6(X), Carolrhoda Bks.) Lerner Publishing Group.

Holmes, Kimberly. Digibots Classroom Adventures. Lawson, Devin, illus. 2004. (J). (978-0-9755725-0-4(4), 1238415) Digibots Corp.

Holmes, Lynda. Spring Cleaning. 2006. 55p. pap. 16.95 (978-1-4241-4324-5(1)) PublishAmerica, Inc.

Holmes, Sara Lewis. Letters from Rapunzel. 2007. 184p. (J). (gr. 3-7). lib. bdg. 16.89 (978-0-06-078074-6(6)) HarperCollins Pubs.

—Operation Yes. 2009. (ENG.). 256p. (J). (gr. 4-7). 16.99 (978-0-545-10795-2(4), Levine, Arthur A. Bks.) Scholastic, Inc.

Holmes, Stephanie. Grady Goes to Puppy School. 2011. 20p. (gr. 1-2). pap. 11.99 (978-1-4634-1000-1(X)) AuthorHouse.

Holmqvist, Carin. African Tales. 2010. 64p. pap. 28.70 (978-0-557-18184-1(4)) Lulu Pr., Inc.

Holt, Kimberly Willis. Navy Brat. Davenier, Christine, illus. 2011. (Piper Reed Ser.: 1). (ENG.). 176p. (J). (gr. 3-6). pap. 6.99 (978-0-312-62548-1(0), 9780312625481) Square Fish.

—Piper Reed, Clubhouse Queen. Davenier, Christine, illus. 2011. (Piper Reed Ser.: 2). (ENG.). 160p. (J). (gr. 3-6). 15.99 (978-0-8050-9431-2(8), 9780805094312, Holt, Henry & Co. Bks. For Young Readers) Holt, Henry & Co.

—Piper Reed, Clubhouse Queen. Davenier, Christine, illus. 2011. (Piper Reed Ser.: 2). (ENG.). 176p. (J). (gr. 3-6). pap. 6.99 (978-0-312-61676-2(7), 9780312616762) Square Fish.

Holt, Theresa. What If I Wet My Pants. 2011. 28p. pap. 15.99 (978-1-4628-5319-9(6)) Xlibris Corp.

Holub, Joan. Apple Countdown. Smith, Jan, illus. 2009. (ENG.). 32p. (J). (gr. -1-3). 16.99 (978-0-8075-0398-0(3)) Whitman, Albert & Co.

—Big Heart! A Valentine's Day Tale. Terry, Will, illus. 2007. (Ant Hill Ser.). (ENG.). 24p. (J). (gr. -1-k). lib. bdg. 13.89 (978-1-4169-2562-0(7), Simon & Schuster/Paula Wiseman Bks.) Simon & Schuster/Paula Wiseman Bks.

—Big Heart! A Valentine's Day Tale. Terry, Will, illus. 2007. (Ant Hill Ser.). (ENG.). 24p. (J). (gr. -1-k). pap. 3.99 (978-1-4169-0957-6(5), Simon Spotlight) Simon Spotlight.

—Groundhog Weather School. Sorra, Kristin, illus. 2009. (ENG.). 32p. (J). (gr. k-3). 16.99 (978-0-399-24659-3(2), G.P. Putnam's Sons Books for Young Readers) Penguin Young Readers Group.

—Groundhog Weather School: Fun Facts about Weather & Groundhogs. Sorra, Kristin, illus. 2013. (ENG.). 32p. (J). (gr. k-3). 6.99 (978-0-14-750945-1(9), Puffin Books) Penguin Young Readers Group.

—Twinkle, Star of the Week. Nicholls, Paul, illus. 2012. (J). (978-1-61913-137-8(4)) Weigl Pubs., Inc.

Holub, Joan & Williams, Suzanne. Aphrodite the Beauty. (Goddess Girls Ser.: 3). (ENG.). 176p. (J). (gr. 3-7). 2013. 17.99 (978-1-4424-5751-5(1)) 2010. pap. 7.99 (978-1-4169-8273-9(6)) Simon & Schuster Children's Publishing. (Aladdin).

—Aphrodite the Diva. 2013. (Goddess Girls Ser.: 6). (ENG., Illus.). 288p. (J). (gr. 3-7). 15.99 (978-1-4424-7478-9(5), Aladdin) Simon & Schuster Children's Publishing.

—Artemis the Brave. (Goddess Girls Ser.: 4). (ENG.). 240p. (J). (gr. 3-7). 2013. 17.99 (978-1-4424-6139-0(X)) 2010. pap. 7.99 (978-1-4169-8274-6(4)) Simon & Schuster Children's Publishing. (Aladdin).

—Artemis the Loyal. 2013. (Goddess Girls Ser.: 7). (ENG., Illus.). 288p. (J). (gr. 3-7). 16.99 (978-1-4424-8594-5(9), Aladdin) Simon & Schuster Children's Publishing.

—Athena the Brain. (Goddess Girls Ser.: 1). (ENG.). 176p. (J). (gr. 3-7). 2012. 16.99 (978-1-4424-5765-2(1)) 2010. pap. 7.99 (978-1-4169-8271-5(X)) Simon & Schuster Children's Publishing. (Aladdin).

—Athena the Wise. (Goddess Girls Ser.: 5). (ENG., 256p. (J). (gr. 3-7). 2013. Illus.). 17.99 (978-1-4424-7477-2(7)) 2011. pap. 7.99 (978-1-4424-2097-7(9)) Simon & Schuster Children's Publishing. (Aladdin).

—Calliope the Muse. 2016. (Goddess Girls Ser.: 20). (ENG., Illus.). 256p. (J). (gr. 3-7). 17.99 (978-1-4814-5005-8(0), Simon & Schuster/Paula Wiseman Bks.) Simon & Schuster/Paula Wiseman Bks.

—Medusa the Mean. (Goddess Girls Ser.: 8). (ENG., 256p. (J). (gr. 3-7). 2013. Illus.). 16.99 (978-1-4424-8595-2(7)) 2012. pap. 7.99 (978-1-4424-3379-3(5)) Simon & Schuster Children's Publishing. (Aladdin).

—Medusa the Mean. 2012. (Goddess Girls Ser.: 8). lib. bdg. 18.40 (978-0-606-26348-1(9), Turtleback) Turtleback Bks.

—Pandora the Curious. 2012. (Goddess Girls Ser.: 9). (ENG.). 256p. (J). (gr. 3-7). 16.99 (978-1-4424-5975-5(1)); pap. 7.99 (978-1-4424-4935-0(7)) Simon & Schuster Children's Publishing. (Aladdin).

—Pandora the Curious. 2012. (Goddess Girls Ser.: 9). lib. bdg. 18.40 (978-0-606-26903-2(7), Turtleback) Turtleback Bks.

—Persephone the Daring. 2013. (Goddess Girls Ser.: 11). lib. bdg. 18.40 (978-0-606-32050-4(4), Turtleback) Turtleback Bks.

—Persephone the Phony. (Goddess Girls Ser.: 2). (ENG.). 160p. (J). (gr. 3-7). 2012. 17.99 (978-1-4424-5752-2(X)) 2010. (Illus.). pap. 7.99 (978-1-4169-8272-2(8)) Simon & Schuster Children's Publishing. (Aladdin).

—Rapunzel Cuts Loose. 2014. (Grimmtastic Girls Ser.: 4). lib. bdg. 16.00 (978-0-606-36064-7(6)) Turtleback Bks.

—Red Riding Hood Gets Lost. 2014. (Grimmtastic Girls Ser.: 2). (ENG.). 192p. (J). (gr. 3-7). pap. 5.99 (978-0-545-51984-7(5)) Scholastic, Inc.

—Sleeping Beauty Dreams Big. 2015. (Grimmtastic Girls Ser.: 5). (ENG.). 192p. (J). (gr. 3-7). pap. 5.99 (978-0-545-78393-4(3), Scholastic Paperbacks) Scholastic, Inc.

—Snow White Lucks Out. 2014. (Grimmtastic Girls Ser.: 3). lib. bdg. 16.00 (978-0-606-35852-1(8)) Turtleback Bks.

—Snowflake Freezes Up. 2016. (Grimmtastic Girls Ser.: 7). (ENG.). 192p. (J). (gr. 3-7). pap. 5.99 (978-0-545-94534-9(8), Scholastic Paperbacks) Scholastic, Inc.

Homework, 6 Packs. (gr. -1-2). 27.00 (978-0-7635-9453-4(9)) Rigby Education.

Honeycutt, Natalie. The Best-Laid Plans of Jonah Twist. 2014. (ENG.). 128p. (J). (gr. 2-5). pap. 13.99 (978-1-4814-3107-1(2), Simon & Schuster Bks. For Young Readers) Simon & Schuster Bks. For Young Readers.

Honeyman, Kay. Interference. 2016. (ENG.). 352p. (YA). (gr. 7). 17.99 (978-0-545-81232-0(1), Levine, Arthur A. Bks.) Scholastic, Inc.

Hood-Caddy, Karen. Howl. 2011. (Wild Place Adventure Ser.: 1). (ENG.). 256p. (J). (gr. 6-8). pap. 9.99 (978-1-926607-25-2(2)) Dundurn CAN. Dist: Ingram Publisher Services.

Hooks, Gwendolyn. The Best Trick: A Pet Club Story, 1 vol. Byrne, Mike, illus. 2010. (Pet Club Ser.). (ENG.). 32p. (gr. 1-2). 22.65 (978-1-4342-2052-3(4)); pap. 6.25 (978-1-4342-2794-2(4)) Stone Arch Bks.

Hoole, Elissa Janine. Sometimes Never, Sometimes Always. 2013. (ENG.). 360p. (YA). pap. 9.99 (978-0-7387-3722-5(4), Flux) North Star Editions.

Hooper, Mary. Down to Earth. Harker, Lesley, illus. 2008. (Two Naughty Angels Ser.). (ENG.). 96p. (J). (gr. 2-4). pap. 11.95 (978-0-7475-9061-3(3)) Bloomsbury Publishing Plc GBR. Dist: Independent Pubs. Group.

—The Ghoul at School. Harker, Lesley, illus. 2008. (Two Naughty Angels Ser.). (ENG.). 96p. (J). (gr. 2-4). pap. 11.95 (978-0-7475-9060-6(5)) Bloomsbury Publishing Plc GBR. Dist: Independent Pubs. Group.

—Round the Rainbow. Harker, Lesley, illus. 2008. (Two Naughty Angels Ser.). (ENG.). 96p. (J). (gr. 2-4). pap. 11.95 (978-0-7475-9062-0(1)) Bloomsbury Publishing Plc GBR. Dist: Independent Pubs. Group.

Hoover, P. J. The Emerald Tablet. 2012. (ENG.). 296p. (J). (gr. 6-9). pap. 8.95 (978-1-933767-19-2(7)) CBAY Bks.

—The Navel of the World. 2013. (ENG.). 304p. (J). (gr. 6-9). pap. 8.95 (978-1-933767-20-8(0)) CBAY Bks.

—Tut. 2016. (J). lib. bdg. 20.85 (978-0-606-38442-1(1)) Turtleback Bks.

—Tut: The Story of My Immortal Life. 2014. (Tut: My Immortal Life Ser.: 1). (ENG.). 320p. (J). (gr. 4-7). 15.99 (978-0-7653-3468-8(2), 9780765334688, Starscape) Doherty, Tom Assocs., LLC.

Hopkins, Audrey. Vinny Drake Is One. Flook, Helen, illus. 2007. (Tiger Ser.). (ENG.). 64p. (J). (gr. 2-4). pap. 9.95 (978-1-84270-437-0(0)) Andersen Pr. GBR. Dist: Independent Pubs. Group.

Hopkins, Cathy. Friend Me: Mates, Dates, & Inflatable Bras; Mates, Dates, & Cosmic Kisses; Mates, Dates, & Designer Divas. 2009. (Mates, Dates Ser.). (ENG.). 528p. (YA). (gr. 7). pap. 8.99 (978-1-4169-7836-7(4), Simon Pulse) Simon Pulse.

—Mates, Dates, & Inflatable Bras. 2011. (Mates, Dates Ser.). (ENG.). 176p. (YA). (gr. 7). pap. 9.99 (978-1-4424-3113-3(X), Simon Pulse) Simon Pulse.

—Teen Queens & Has-Beens. 2010. (Truth or Dare Ser.). (ENG.). 192p. (YA). (gr. 7). pap. 9.99 (978-1-4424-1416-7(2), Simon Pulse) Simon Pulse.

Hopkins, Ellen. Crank. (ENG., (YA). (gr. 9). 2013. Illus.). 576p. pap. 12.99 (978-1-4424-7181-8(6)) 2010. 544p. 21.99 (978-1-4169-9513-5(7)) McElderry, Margaret K. Bks. (McElderry, Margaret K. Bks.).

—Crank. 2013. lib. bdg. 24.50 (978-0-606-35118-8(3)) Turtleback Bks.

—The Crank Trilogy: Crank; Glass; Fallout. 2013. (ENG., Illus.). 1952p. (YA). (gr. 9). pap. 38.99 (978-1-4424-9959-1(1), McElderry, Margaret K. Bks.) McElderry, Margaret K. Bks.

—Rumble. 2016. (ENG., Illus.). 576p. (YA). (gr. 9). pap. 12.99 (978-1-4424-8285-2(0), McElderry, Margaret K. Bks.) McElderry, Margaret K. Bks.

Hopkinson, Deborah. A Letter to My Teacher. Carpenter, Nancy, illus. 2017. (ENG.). 40p. (J). (gr. -1-3). 17.99 (978-0-375-86845-0(3), Schwartz & Wade Bks.) Random Hse. Children's Bks.

Horowitz, Anthony. Point Blanc. 2004. (Alex Rider Ser.: Bk. 2). (SPA.). 264p. pap. 7.95 (978-84-414-1410-5(6)) Editorial Edaf, S.L. ESP. Dist: Spanish Pubs., LLC.

—Point Blank. 2006. (Alex Rider Ser.). (ENG.). 320p. (J). (gr. 5-18). 8.99 (978-0-14-240612-0(0), Puffin Books) Penguin Young Readers Group.

—Return to Groosham Grange: The Unholy Grail. 2010. (ENG.). 224p. (J). (gr. 5-18). 7.99 (978-0-14-241571-9(5), Puffin Books) Penguin Young Readers Group.

Horse, Harry. Little Rabbit Goes to School. Horse, Harry, illus. 2004. (ENG., Illus.). 32p. (J). (gr. k-1). 15.95 (978-1-56145-320-7(X)) Peachtree Pubs.

Hosford, Kate. Infinity & Me. Swiatkowska, Gabi, illus. 2012. (Carolrhoda Picture Bks.). (ENG.). 32p. (J). (gr. k-4). lib. bdg. 16.95 (978-0-7613-6726-0(8)) Lerner Publishing Group.

Houran, Lori Haskins. Alien in the Outfield: Perseverance. Warrick, Jessica, illus. 2017. (How to Be an Earthling (r) Ser.: 6). (ENG.). 64p. (J). (gr. 1-3). lib. bdg. 22.65 (978-1-57565-844-5(5)) Kane Press, Inc.

—Alien in the Outfield: Perseverance. Warrick, Jessica, illus. 2017. (How to Be an Earthling (r) Ser.: 6). (ENG.). 64p. (J). (gr. 1-3). 6.99 (978-1-57565-848-3(8)) Kane Press, Inc.

—Earth's Got Talent! Warrick, Jessica, illus. 2016. (How to Be an Earthling (r) Ser.: 4). (ENG.). 64p. (gr. 1-3). lib. bdg. 22.65 (978-1-57565-827-8(5)) Kane Press, Inc.

—Earth's Got Talent! Courage. Warrick, Jessica, illus. 2016. (How to Be an Earthling (r) Ser.: 4). (ENG.). 64p. (gr. 1-3). 34.65 (978-1-57565-829-2(1)) Kane Press, Inc.

—Greetings, Sharkling! Warrick, Jessica, illus. 2016. (How to Be an Earthling (r) Ser.: 2). (ENG.). 64p. (gr. 1-3). 22.65 (978-1-57565-821-6(6)) Kane Press, Inc.

Houtman, Jacqueline. The Reinvention of Edison Thomas. (ENG.). 192p. (J). (gr. 3-7). 2012. pap. 8.95 (978-1-59078-951-3(2)) 2010. 17.95 (978-1-59078-708-3(0), Front Street) Boyds Mills Pr.

Howard, Denise. Greentown Elementary: The Seafood Nightmare. 2012. (ENG.). pap. (978-1-4675-3556-4(7)) Independent Pub.

Howard, Elizabeth Fitzgerald. Virgie Goes to School with Us Boys. Lewis, E. B., illus. 2005. (gr. k-3). 18.00 (978-0-7569-5088-0(0)) Perfection Learning Corp.

—Virgie Goes to School with Us Boys. Lewis, E. B., illus. 2005. (ENG.). 32p. (J). (gr. k-3). reprint ed. 7.99 (978-0-689-87793-3(5), Aladdin) Simon & Schuster Children's Publishing.

Howard, Kate, illus. On Our Way to First Grade. 2015. 32p. (J). (978-0-545-82340-1(4)) Scholastic, Inc.

Howard, Victoria. The Adventures of Max: The Bolognese Dog. 2012. 72p. pap. 28.99 (978-1-4772-6560-4(0)) AuthorHouse.

Howe, James. Addie on the Inside. (Misfits Ser.). (ENG., Illus.). (J). (gr. 5-9). 2012. 240p. pap. 8.99 (978-1-4169-1385-6(8)) 2011. 224p. 16.99 (978-1-4169-1384-9(X)) Simon & Schuster Children's Publishing. (Atheneum Bks. for Young Readers).

—The Complete Misfits Collection: The Misfits; Totally Joe; Addie on the Inside; Also Known As Elvis. 2015. (Misfits Ser.). (ENG., Illus.). 1072p. (J). (gr. 5-9). pap. 27.99 (978-1-4814-2898-9(5), Atheneum Bks. for Young Readers) Simon & Schuster Children's Publishing.

—The Misfits. 2003. (Misfits Ser.). (ENG.). 304p. (J). (gr. 5-9). mass mkt. 7.99 (978-0-689-83956-6(1), Atheneum Bks. for Young Readers) Simon & Schuster Children's Publishing.

—Totally Joe. (Misfits Ser.). (ENG.). (J). 2007. 224p. (gr. 4-8). pap. 7.99 (978-0-689-83958-0(8)) 2005. (Illus.). 208p. (gr. 5-9). 17.99 (978-0-689-83957-3(X)) Simon & Schuster Children's Publishing. (Atheneum Bks. for Young Readers).

Howe, Katherine. Conversion. (ENG.). 432p. (YA). (gr. 7). 2015. pap. 10.99 (978-0-14-751155-3(0), Speak) 2014. 18.99 (978-0-399-16777-5(3), G.P. Putnam's Sons Books for Young Readers) Penguin Young Readers Group.

Howland, Ashley. The Homework Goblin. 2013. 24p. pap. 13.97 (978-1-62516-301-1(0), Strategic Bk. Publishing) Strategic Book Publishing & Rights Agency (SBPRA).

Hrdlitschka, Shelley. Allegra, 1 vol. 2013. (ENG.). 280p. (YA). (gr. 8-12). pap. 12.95 (978-1-4598-0197-4(0)) Orca Bk. Pubs. USA.

Hubbard, Jenny. And We Stay. 2014. (ENG.). 240p. (YA). (gr. 9). lib. bdg. 19.99 (978-0-375-98955-1(2), Delacorte Pr.) Random Hse. Children's Bks.

—Paper Covers Rock. 2012. (ENG.). 192p. (YA). (gr. 9). pap. 7.99 (978-0-385-74056-2(5), Ember) Random Hse. Children's Bks.

Hubbell, Patricia. Teacher! Sharing, Helping, Caring, 0 vols. Speir, Nancy, illus. 2009. (ENG.). 32p. (J). (gr. -1-3). 16.99 (978-0-7614-5574-5(4), 9780761455745, Amazon Children's Publishing) Amazon Publishing.

Hubert. Adrian & the Tree of Secrets. 2014. (ENG., Illus.). 128p. (gr. 6). pap. 18.95 (978-1-55152-556-3(9)) Arsenal Pulp Pr. CAN. Dist: Consortium Bk. Sales & Distribution.

Hudson, Ella. Hudson Hates School. 2014. (ENG., Illus.). 32p. (J). (gr. k-3). pap. 8.99 (978-1-84780-375-7(X), Frances Lincoln) Quarto Publishing Group UK GBR. Dist: Hachette Bk. Group.

Hudson, Iris. Mac & the Messmaker. Smath, Jerry, illus. 2005. (Social Studies Connects). 32p. (J). (gr. k-2). pap. 5.95 (978-1-57565-158-3(0)) Kane Press, Inc.

Hudson, Wade. The Two Tyrones. Page, Mark, illus. 2004. 32p. (J). lib. bdg. 15.00 (978-1-4242-0239-3(6)) Fitzgerald Bks.

—The Two Tyrones. Page, Mark, illus. 2004. (Just for You Ser.). (ENG.). 32p. (gr. 2-3). pap. 3.99 (978-0-439-56866-1(8), Teaching Resources) Scholastic, Inc.

Hue, Wendy. Tópé Arrives. 2011. (Illus.). 100p. pap. 12.10 (978-1-4567-7640-4(1)) AuthorHouse.

Huelin, Jodi. Alvin & the Big Art Show. 2013. (I Can Read! Level 2 Ser.). (J). lib. bdg. 13.55 (978-0-606-35040-2(3), Turtleback) Turtleback Bks.

—Alvin & the Substitute Teacher. 2013. (I Can Read! Level 2 Ser.). (J). lib. bdg. 13.55 (978-0-606-32462-5(3), Turtleback) Turtleback Bks.

Hueller, Andy. Skipping Stones at the Center of the Earth: A Middle Grade Novel. 2011. (J). pap. 8.99 (978-1-59955-488-4(7), Bonneville Bks.) Cedar Fort, Inc./CFI Distribution.

Hueller, P. W. Wolf High. 2014. (ENG.). 96p. (J). (978-1-63235-055-8(6)) Pr. Room Editions LLC.

Hugelmeyer, Michele. Alex King, Famous Fourth Grader. 2007. 78p. pap. 8.99 (978-1-4303-0821-8(4)) Lulu Pr., Inc.

Hughes, Alison. On a Scale of Idiot to Complete Jerk, 1 vol. 2014. (ENG., Illus.). 144p. (J). (gr. 4-7). pap. 9.95 (978-1-4598-0484-5(8)) Orca Bk. Pubs. USA.

Hughes, Dawn Marie. Deadwood: Haunted Stories. 2006. 94p. pap. 16.95 (978-1-4241-2600-2(2)) PublishAmerica, Inc.

Hughes, Diane. Wilbur Goes to School. 2011. 20p. pap. 11.99 (978-1-4670-3964-2(0)) AuthorHouse.

Hughes, Mark Peter. Lemonade Mouth. movie tie-in ed. 2011. (ENG.). 352p. (YA). (gr. 7-7). pap. 8.99 (978-0-385-74208-5(8), Ember) Random Hse. Children's Bks.

—Lemonade Mouth Puckers Up. 2013. (ENG.). 300p. (YA). (gr. 7). pap. 9.99 (978-0-385-73713-5(0), Ember) Random Hse. Children's Bks.

Hughes, Shirley. Bobbo Goes to School. Hughes, Shirley, illus. 2013. (ENG., Illus.). 32p. (J). (gr. -1-2). 16.99 (978-0-7636-6524-1(X)) Candlewick Pr.

Hughes, Thomas. Tom Brown's School Days by an Old Boy. 2004. reprint ed. pap. 1.99 (978-1-4192-9039-8(8)) Kessinger Publishing, LLC.

—Tom Browns Schooldays. 2006. pap. (978-1-4068-1407-1(5)) Echo Library.

Hulme, Joy N. Climbing the Rainbow. 2004. 224p. (J). 15.99 (978-0-380-81572-2(9)) HarperCollins Pubs.

Hulst, W. G. van de & Hulst, Willem G. van de, illus. The Secret in the Box. 2014. (J). (978-1-928136-17-0(6)) Inheritance Pubns.

Humphrey, Anna. Mission (un)Popular. 2013. (ENG.). 416p. (J). (gr. 5-9). pap. 6.99 (978-1-4231-2321-7(2)) Hyperion Pr.

—Rhymes with Cupid. 2010. (ENG.). 240p. (YA). (gr. 8). pap. 7.99 (978-0-06-193501-5(8), HarperTeen) HarperCollins Pubs.

Huneke, Amanda. A Monster at School, 1 vol. Wolek, Guy, illus. 2013. (Monster on the Loose Ser.). (ENG.). 32p. (J). (gr. -1-4). 28.50 (978-1-61641-931-8(8)) Magic Wagon.

—A Monster on the Bus, 1 vol. Wolek, Guy, illus. 2013. (Monster on the Loose Ser.). (ENG.). 32p. (J). (gr. -1-4). 28.50 (978-1-61641-933-2(4)) Magic Wagon.

Hunt, Lynda Mullaly. COMO PEZ EN EL ÁRBOL: UNA NOVELA SOBRE LA DISLEXIA. 2016. (SPA.). 240p. (J). (gr. 4). pap. 13.95 (978-84-15594-69-7(0), Nube De Tinta) Penguin Random House Grupo Editorial ESP. Dist: Two Rivers Distribution.

—Fish in a Tree. (ENG.). (J). (gr. 5). 2017. 304p. 8.99 (978-0-14-242642-5(3), Puffin Books) 2015. 288p. 16.99 (978-0-399-16259-6(3), Nancy Paulsen Books) Penguin Young Readers Group.

—Fish in a Tree. 2017. lib. bdg. 19.65 **(978-0-606-39991-3(7))** Turtleback Bks.

Huntley, Amy. The Everafter. 2010. (ENG.). 272p. (YA). (gr. 8). pap. 9.99 (978-0-06-177681-6(5)) HarperCollins Pubs.

Hurley, Tonya. Ghostgirl. 2010. (Ghostgirl Ser.: 1). (ENG.). 336p. (YA). (gr. 7-17). pap. 9.99 (978-0-316-03635-1(8)) Little, Brown Bks. for Young Readers.

—Ghostgirl. Frieyro, Alicia, tr. Impey, Allison & Phillips, Craig, illus. 2009. (SPA.). 1200p. (YA). (gr. 8-12). pap. 19.99 (978-607-11-0185-3(9), Alfaguara Juvenil) Santillana USA Publishing Co., Inc.

—Homecoming. 2010. (Ghostgirl Ser.: 2). (ENG.). 304p. (YA). (gr. 7-17). pap. 10.00 (978-0-316-08943-2(5)) Little, Brown Bks. for Young Readers.

—Lovesick. 2011. (Ghostgirl Ser.: 3). (ENG.). 320p. (YA). (gr. 7-17). pap., pap. 9.99 (978-0-316-13316-6(7)) Little, Brown Bks. for Young Readers.

Hurst, Elva. When School Bells Call: Based on a True Story. 2015. (Farm Life Ser.). (ENG.). 80p. (J). pap. 6.99 (978-0-7369-6092-2(9)) Harvest Hse. Pubs.

Hurwitz, Johanna. Amazing Monty. McGrory, Anik, illus. 2013. (Monty Ser.). (ENG.). 112p. (J). (gr. k-4). pap. 5.99 (978-0-7636-6561-6(4)) Candlewick Pr.

—Mighty Monty: More First-Grade Adventures. McGrory, Anik, illus. 2010. (Monty Ser.). (ENG.). 112p. (J). (gr. 1-4). pap. 5.99 (978-0-7636-4786-5(1)) Candlewick Pr.

Hurwitz, Johanna & McCrory, Anik. Mostly Monty. McGrory, Anik, illus. 2008. (Monty Ser.: 1). (ENG.). 96p. (J). (gr. 1-4). pap. 5.99 (978-0-7636-4062-0(X)) Candlewick Pr.

Hurwitz, Kathleen A. Timothy's Tic. Mc Kelvey, Shawn, illus. 2008. 40p. (gr. -1 — 1). 16.99 (978-1-4389-1924-9(7)) AuthorHouse.

Hurwitz, Michele Weber. Calli Be Gold. 2012. (ENG.). 208p. (J). (gr. 3-7). 6.99 (978-0-375-86528-2(4), Yearling) Random Hse. Children's Bks.

Huser, Glen. Skinnybones & the Wrinkle Queen, 1 vol. 2008. (ENG.). 192p. (J). (gr. 6-10). pap. 8.95 (978-0-88899-733-3(7)) Groundwood Bks. CAN. Dist: Publishers Group West (PGW).

Hutchins, Hazel. TJ & the Quiz Kids, 1 vol. 2007. (Orca Young Readers Ser.). (ENG.). 136p. (J). (gr. 3-6). pap. 5.95 (978-1-55143-731-6(7)) Orca Bk. Pubs. USA.

Hutchinson, Shaun David, et al. Violent Ends: A Novel in Seventeen Points of View. (ENG., Illus.). (YA). (gr. 9). 2016. 368p. pap. 10.99 (978-1-4814-3746-2(1)) 2015. 352p. 17.99 (978-1-4814-3745-5(3)) Simon Pulse. (Simon Pulse).

Hyde, Catherine Ryan. Jumpstart the World. 2011. (ENG.). 192p. (YA). (gr. 9). pap. 7.99 (978-0-375-86626-5(4), Ember) Random Hse. Children's Bks.

Hyde, Noreen. The Adventures of Miss Chief: Miss Chief Goes to School. Pushee, Marisa, illus. 2007. 28p. per. 9.95 (978-1-59858-368-7(9)) Dog Ear Publishing, LLC.

Hyman, Fracaswell. Mango Delight. Morrison, Frank, illus. 2017. (ENG.). 224p. (J). (gr. 4-8). 14.95 **(978-1-4549-2332-9(6))** Sterling Publishing Co., Inc.

Hymas, Allison K. Under Locker & Key. 2017. (Max Ser.). (ENG., Illus.). 256p. (J). (gr. 4-8). pap. 7.99 (978-1-4814-6342-3(X), Simon & Schuster/Paula Wiseman Bks.) Simon & Schuster/Paula Wiseman Bks.

Iannantuano, Theresa. Who Took My Lunch? 2012. 24p. pap. 15.99 (978-1-4771-1582-4(X)) Xlibris Corp.

Ide, Laurie S. & Langcaon, Jeff. Super Puffy. 2004. (Illus.). 32p. (J). 12.95 (978-1-56647-686-7(0)) Mutual Publishing LLC.

Ignatow, Amy. The Awesomely Awful Melodies. 2014. (Popularity Papers). (ENG., Illus.). 208p. (J). (gr. 3-7). pap. 8.95 (978-1-4197-1308-8(6), Amulet Bks.) Abrams, Inc.

—The Popularity Papers. 2011. (Popularity Papers). (ENG., Illus.). 208p. (J). (gr. 3-7). pap. 8.95 (978-0-8109-9723-3(1), Amulet Bks.) Abrams, Inc.

—The Popularity Papers: Research for the Social Improvement & General Betterment of Lydia Goldblatt & Julie Graham-Chang. 2010. (Popularity Papers). (ENG., Illus.). 208p. (J). (gr. 3-7). 16.95 (978-0-8109-8421-9(0), Amulet Bks.) Abrams, Inc.

—The Popularity Papers: The Less-Than-Hidden Secrets & Final Revelations of Lydia Goldblatt & Julie Graham-Chang. 2014. (Popularity Papers). (ENG., Illus.). 208p. (J). (gr. 3-7). 15.95 (978-1-4197-1270-8(5), Amulet Bks.) Abrams, Inc.

—Words of (Questionable) Wisdom. 2013. (Popularity Papers). (ENG., Illus.). 208p. (J). (gr. 3-7). pap. 8.95 (978-1-4197-0535-9(0), Amulet Bks.) Abrams, Inc.

Igneri, David S. The Boy & Girl Who Hated History. Wigley, Audrey Watson, illus. 2009. 44p. pap. 24.95 (978-1-61546-828-7(5)) America Star Bks.

Ikegami, Aiko. Friends. Ikegami, Aiko, illus. 2016. (ENG., Illus.). 32p. (J). (gr. -1-3). 16.99 (978-0-8075-2550-0(2)) Whitman, Albert & Co.

Imam, Seema & Imam, Ibrahim. I am Listening. 2007. (I Am Good Ser.). (Illus.). 32p. (J). mass mkt. (978-0-9787849-8-0(7)) Lucent Interpretations, LLC.

Immenschuh, Marilyn Y. Samantha & the Kids of Room 220. 2007. 148p. per. 11.95 (978-0-595-46842-3(X)) iUniverse, Inc.

Imperato, Teresa. Fiona's Fairy Magic. Huang, Benrei, illus. 2005. 14p. (J). 10.95 (978-1-58117-322-2(9), Intervisual/Piggy Toes) Bendon, Inc.

In a World Just Right. 2015. (ENG., Illus.). 432p. (YA). (gr. 7). 18.99 (978-1-4814-1660-3(X)) Simon & Schuster Children's Publishing.

Inagaki, Riichiro. Eyeshield 21, Vol. 8. Murata, Yusuke, illus. 2006. (Eyeshield 21 Ser.: 8). (ENG.). 208p. pap. 9.99 (978-1-4215-0637-1(8)) Viz Media.

—Eyeshield 21, Vol. 9. Murata, Yusuke, illus. 2006. (ENG.). 208p. (gr. 11). pap. 9.99 (978-1-4215-0638-8(6)) Viz Media.

Incomprehensible, Vordak T. & Seegert, Scott. Rule the School. Martin, John, illus. 2011. (Vordak the Incomprehensible Ser.: No. 2). (ENG.). 192p. (J). (gr. 5). 13.99 (978-1-60684-014-6(2), Darby Creek) Lerner Publishing Group.

Ingold, Jeanette. Mountain Solo. 2005. (ENG.). 320p. (YA). (gr. 7-12). pap. 15.95 (978-0-15-205358-1(1)) Houghton Mifflin Harcourt Publishing Co.

Irbinskas, Heather. The Lost Kachina. Albert, Robert & Anthis, Brian, illus. 2004. 32p. (J). 15.95 (978-1-885772-33-6(5)) Kiva Publishing, Inc.

Ireland, Justina. Vengeance Bound. (ENG., (YA). (gr. 9). 2014. Illus.). 336p. pap. 9.99 (978-1-4424-4463-8(0)) 2013. 320p. 17.99 (978-1-4424-4462-1(2)) Simon & Schuster Bks. For Young Readers. (Simon & Schuster Bks. For Young Readers).

Irwin, Ms. Judy. We're Done. 2012. 104p. pap. (978-0-9877088-4-7(8)) Irwin, Judy.

Iserson, David. Firecracker. 2014. (ENG.). 336p. (YA). (gr. 7). pap. 9.99 (978-1-59514-681-6(4), Razorbill) Penguin Young Readers Group.

Ius, Dawn. Anne & Henry. Watcher, Jill, illus. 2015. (ENG.). 304p. (YA). (gr. 9). 18.99 (978-1-4814-3941-1(3), Simon Pulse) Simon Pulse.

Iyengar, Malathi Michelle. Romina's Rangoli. Wanardi, Jennifer, illus. 2007. (Romina's Rangoli Ser.). 32p. (J). (gr. -1-3). 16.95 (978-1-885008-32-9(5), Shen's Bks.) Lee & Low Bks., Inc.

Jablonski, Carla. Thicker Than Water. 2007. (ENG.). 272p. (YA). (gr. 9-12). 8.99 (978-1-59514-123-1(5), Razorbill) Penguin Young Readers Group.

Jackson, Al, Jr. Adventures of Middle School: The Handbook. 2013. (ENG.). 60p. (YA). pap. 12.95 (978-1-4787-0892-6(1)) Outskirts Pr., Inc.

Jackson, Ellen. The Cupcake Thief. 2008. pap. 34.95 (978-1-58013-765-2(2)) Kane Press, Inc.

—The Cupcake Thief. Sims, Blanche, illus. 2007. (Social Studies Connects). 32p. (J). (gr. -1-3). pap. 5.95 (978-1-57565-247-4(1)) Kane Press, Inc.

Jackson, Ladain. Rare Vision. 2013. 100p. pap. 8.99 (978-1-937165-35-2(3)) Orange Hat Publishing.

Jackson, Marcus. Because My Teacher Said I Can. 2011. 24p. pap. 13.86 (978-1-4567-6492-0(6)) AuthorHouse.

Jacobs, Evan. Screaming Quietly, 1 vol. 2013. (Gravel Road Ser.). (ENG.). 212p. (YA). (gr. 9-12). pap. 9.95 (978-1-62250-003-1(2)) Saddleback Educational Publishing, Inc.

—Varsity 170, 1 vol., Bk. 10. 2015. (Gravel Road Ser.). (ENG.). (YA). (gr. 9-12). pap. 9.95 (978-1-62250-889-1(0)) Saddleback Educational Publishing, Inc.

Jacobs, John. I Wanna Be. 2006. (Illus.). 144p. 9.95 (978-0-9774659-6-5(9)) Cameo Pubns., LLC.

Jacobs, John Hornor & Priest, A. Breakthrough. 2014. (Red Zone Ser.: 2). (ENG.). 104p. (YA). (gr. 6-12). lib. bdg. 27.93 (978-1-4677-2131-8(X)) Lerner Publishing Group.

Jacobs, Lana. Ella's School Picture Day. 2015. (Ella the Elephant Ser.). (ENG.). 32p. (J). (gr. 1-2). pap. 3.99 (978-0-448-48922-3(8), Penguin Young Readers) Penguin Young Readers Group.

—Show-And-Tell. 2013. (Penguin Young Readers Level 2 Ser.). lib. bdg. 13.55 (978-0-606-31694-1(9), Turtleback) Turtleback Bks.

Jacobs, Paul DuBois & Swender, Jennifer. Fire Drill. Lee, Huy Voun, illus. 2010. (ENG.). 32p. (J). (gr. -1-2). 17.99 (978-0-8050-8953-0(5), 9780805089530, Holt, Henry & Co. Bks. For Young Readers) Holt, Henry & Co.

Jacobson, Jennifer Richard. Andy Shane & the Queen of Egypt. Carter, Abby, illus. 2009. (Andy Shane Ser.: 3). (ENG.). 64p. (J). (gr. k-3). 4.99 (978-0-7636-4404-8(8)) Candlewick Pr.

—Andy Shane & the Queen of Egypt. 2009. (Andy Shane Ser.: 3). lib. bdg. 14.75 (978-0-606-06592-4(X), Turtleback) Turtleback Bks.

—Andy Shane & the Very Bossy Dolores Starbuckle. Carter, Abby, illus. 2006. (Andy Shane Ser.: 1). (ENG.). 64p. (J). (gr. k-3). 4.99 (978-0-7636-3044-7(6)) Candlewick Pr.

—Andy Shane & the Very Bossy Dolores Starbuckle. Carter, Abby, illus. 2008. (Andy Shane Ser.). (J). (gr. -1-3). 25.95 incl. audio (978-1-4301-0321-9(3)); pap. 16.95 incl. audio (978-1-4301-0320-2(5)) Live Oak Media.

—Andy Shane Is Not in Love. 2009. (Andy Shane Ser.: 4). lib. bdg. 14.75 (978-0-606-06618-1(7), Turtleback) Turtleback Bks.

Jacques, Taryn Elise. What's Wrong with the New Girl? Reilly, Meghan M., illus. 2004. 33p. pap. 24.95 (978-1-4137-1999-4(6)) PublishAmerica, Inc.

Jaden, Denise. Losing Faith. 2010. (ENG.). 400p. (YA). (gr. 9-18). pap. 9.99 (978-1-4169-9609-5(5), Simon Pulse) Simon Pulse.

Jager, Hartmut. The Secret of the Green Paint: Annette Vetter Adventure #2. 2007. (Illus.). 196p. (YA). pap. 9.95 (978-0-944851-28-9(2)) Earth Star Pubns.

Jahn-Clough, Lisa. Me, Penelope. 2009. (ENG.). 208p. (YA). (gr. 9). pap. 12.99 (978-0-547-07632-4(0)) Houghton Mifflin Harcourt Publishing Co.

Jaimet, Kate. Dunces Rock, 1 vol. 2014. (ENG.). 224p. (J). (gr. 4-7). pap. 9.95 (978-1-4598-0585-9(2)) Orca Bk. Pubs. USA.

Jakubowski, Michele. Dodgeball, Drama, & Other Dilemmas. Montalto, Luisa, illus. (Sidney & Sydney Ser.). (ENG.). 128p. (gr. 1-3). 2016. pap. 6.95 (978-1-4795-6755-3(8)) 2013. 8.95 (978-1-4795-2116-6(7)) 2013. lib. bdg. 25.32 (978-1-4048-8061-0(5)) Picture Window Bks.

—Sidney & Sydney. 2013. (Sidney & Sydney Ser.). (ENG.). 128p. (gr. 1-3). 50.64 (978-1-4795-1696-4(1)) Picture Window Bks.

—Third Grade Mix-Up, 1 vol. Montalto, Luisa, illus. 2013. (Sidney & Sydney Ser.). (ENG.). 128p. (gr. 1-3). 8.95 (978-1-4048-8104-4(2)); lib. bdg. 25.32 (978-1-4048-8001-6(1)) Picture Window Bks.

James, Brian. Ahoy, Ghost Ship Ahead! Zivoin, Jennifer, illus. 2007. (Pirate School Ser.: 2). (ENG.). 64p. (J). (gr. 1-3). pap. 3.99 (978-0-448-44625-7(1), Grosset & Dunlap) Penguin Young Readers Group.

—Treasure Trouble. Zivoin, Jennifer, illus. 2008. (Pirate School Ser.: 5). (ENG.). 64p. (J). (gr. 1-3). pap. 3.99 (978-0-448-44782-7(7), Grosset & Dunlap) Penguin Young Readers Group.

—Yo-Ho-Ho! Zivoin, Jennifer, illus. 2008. (Pirate School Ser.: 7). (ENG.). 64p. (J). (gr. 1-3). pap. 3.99 (978-0-448-44887-9(4), Grosset & Dunlap) Penguin Young Readers Group.

—Zombie Blondes. 2009. (ENG.). 256p. (YA). (gr. 7-12). pap. 8.99 (978-0-312-57375-1(8), 9780312573751) Square Fish.

James, Cheryl D. Leah's Treasure Book. 2012. 36p. pap. 16.99 (978-1-4624-0422-3(7), Inspiring Voices) Author Solutions, Inc.

James, Howe. The Misfits. 2014. (Misfits Ser.). (ENG.). 304p. (J). 11.24 (978-1-63245-171-2(9)) Lectorum Pubns., Inc.

James, Mike. Bootsie - & the Team. 2012. 136p. pap. (978-1-922022-14-1(4)) Vivid Publishing.

—Bootsie - Just One More. 2012. 136p. pap. (978-1-922022-29-5(2)) Vivid Publishing.

James, Syrie & James, Ryan M. Forbidden. 2012. (ENG.). 416p. (YA). (gr. 8). pap. 9.99 (978-0-06-202789-4(1), HarperTeen) HarperCollins Pubs.

Jamieson, Victoria. All's Faire in Middle School, 9 vols. 2017. (ENG.). (J). pap. 116.91 **(978-0-525-48668-8(2))**; (Illus.). 248p. (gr. 4-7). 20.99 **(978-0-525-42998-2(0))**; (Illus.). 248p. (gr. 4-7). pap. 12.99 **(978-0-525-42999-9(9))** Penguin Young Readers Group. (Dial Bks).

—All's Faire in Middle School. 2017. lib. bdg. 24.50 **(978-0-606-40484-6(8))** Turtleback Bks.

Jamieson, Victoria. The Great Pet Escape. Jamieson, Victoria, illus. 2016. (Pets on the Loose! Ser.). (ENG., Illus.). 64p. (J). 15.99 (978-1-62779-105-2(1), 9781627791052, Holt, Henry & Co. Bks. For Young Readers) Holt, Henry & Co.

Jamison, Jo Lynn & Elliott, Lela Mae. Siren's Call of the Caves, 1 vol. 2009. 55p. pap. 16.95 (978-1-4489-8627-9(3)) PublishAmerica, Inc.

Janovitz, Marilyn. We Love School (¡Nos Encanta la Escuela!) Janovitz, Marilyn, illus. 2009. (ENG & SPA., Illus.). 32p. (J). (gr. -1-k). 7.95 (978-0-7358-2246-7(8)) North-South Bks., Inc.

Jansen, Karen. The Coming of an Astronaut. 2009. 68p. pap. 9.99 (978-1-60911-076-5(5), Eloquent Bks.) Strategic Book Publishing & Rights Agency (SBPRA).

Jardine, Kathy & Jardine, Ashley. The Durples: Go to School. 2010. 28p. pap. 17.99 (978-1-4490-3405-4(5)) AuthorHouse.

Jarek, Janice. Emma & Her Angels. 2012. 24p. 24.95 (978-1-4626-6255-5(2)) America Star Bks.

Jarman, Benjamin. Tony's Last Touchdown. 2012. (Champion Sports Story Ser.). 104p. (J). (gr. 3-18). pap. 10.95 (978-1-4644-0004-9(0)); 27.94 (978-0-7660-3885-1(8)) Enslow Pubs., Inc.

Jarman, Julia. Harry the Clever Spider at School. Fowkes, Charlie, illus. 2007. (Collins Big Cat Ser.). (ENG.). 128p. (J). (gr. 1-2). pap. 6.99 (978-0-00-718670-9(3)) HarperCollins Pubs. Ltd. GBR. Dist: Independent Pubs. Group.

—The Magic Backpack. Gon, Adriano, illus. 2003. (Flying Foxes Ser.). (ENG.). 48p. (J). lib. bdg. (978-0-7787-1487-3(X)) Crabtree Publishing Co.

Jasper, Rick & Reece, Richard. The Late Bus. 2011. (Night Fall Ser.). (ENG.). 112p. (YA). (gr. 6-12). pap. 7.95 (978-0-7613-7812-9(X)); lib. bdg. 27.93 (978-0-7613-7745-0(X)) Lerner Publishing Group.

Jean Emily Myers, Emily Myers & Jean Emily Myers. Mickey's Mini Farm. Tanner Voyles, illus. 2009. 32p. pap. 21.99 (978-1-4389-5544-5(8)) AuthorHouse.

Jeffs, Dixie. Pokey's Chance. 2013. 24p. pap. 24.95 (978-1-62709-292-0(7)) America Star Bks.

Jellen, Michelle. Spain or Shine. 2005. (S. A. S. S. Ser.). (ENG., Illus.). 224p. (YA). (gr. 7-7). 7.99 (978-0-14-240368-6(7), Speak) Penguin Young Readers Group.

Jempsa, Alice B. Why Does Everything Happen to Me? 2011. 28p. (gr. -1). pap. 13.54 (978-1-4269-5005-6(5)) Trafford Publishing.

Jenkins, A. M. Out of Order. 2003. 256p. (J). lib. bdg. 16.89 (978-0-06-623969-9(9)) HarperCollins Pubs.

—Repossessed. 2008. (ENG.). 240p. (YA). (gr. 8). pap. 9.99 (978-0-06-083570-5(2), HarperTeen) HarperCollins Pubs.

Jenkins, Amanda. Mere Moments A Story of Pearl Harbor, the Day the Towers Fell. 2011. (Readers' & Writers' Genre Workshop Ser.). (J). pap. (978-1-4509-3019-2(0)) Benchmark Education Co.

Jenkins, Jerry B. & Fabry, Chris. Dead End. 2006. (Red Rock Mysteries Ser.: 15). (ENG.). 248p. (YA). (gr. 3-7). per. 6.99 (978-1-4143-0154-9(5), Tyndale Kids) Tyndale Hse. Pubs.

—Instant Menace. 2006. (Red Rock Mysteries Ser.: 9). (ENG.). 256p. (YA). (gr. 3-7). per. 6.99 (978-1-4143-0148-8(0), Tyndale Kids) Tyndale Hse. Pubs.

Jennings, Patrick. Guinea Dog. (Guinea Dog Ser.). (ENG.). 192p. (gr. 3-7). 2011. (J). 6.99 (978-1-60684-153-2(X)) 2010. 15.99 (978-1-60684-053-5(3)) Lerner Publishing Group. (Darby Creek).

—Guinea Dog 2. 2013. (Guinea Dog Ser.). (ENG.). 176p. (J). (gr. 3-7). 15.99 (978-1-60684-452-6(0), Darby Creek) Lerner Publishing Group.

—Lucky Cap. 2011. (ENG.). 224p. (J). (gr. 4-7). 15.99 (978-1-60684-054-2(1), Carolrhoda Bks.) Lerner Publishing Group.

—Odd, Weird & Little. 2014. (ENG.). 160p. (J). (gr. 3-7). 15.99 (978-1-60684-374-1(5), Carolrhoda Bks.) Lerner Publishing Group.

—Wish Riders. 2006. (ENG.). 288p. (gr. 5-9). 15.99 (978-1-4231-0010-2(7)) Hyperion Pr.

Jensen, Melissa. The Fine Art of Truth or Dare. 2012. (ENG.). 400p. (YA). (gr. 7-18). 8.99 (978-0-14-242090-4(5), Speak) Penguin Young Readers Group.

Jensen, Olivia. Thomas & the Bully. 2009. 16p. pap. 8.49 (978-1-4389-1848-8(8)) AuthorHouse.

Jeremiah, Omari. Paper Boy Four: L. O. E. P. S. Worst Nightmare. Rollins, Berni, illus. 2007. 96p. (YA). (gr. 7-12). pap. 12.99 (978-1-929188-15-4(3)) Morton Bks.

—Paperboy 3: The School of Doom. Rollins, Bernie, illus. 2006. 75p. pap. 12.99 (978-1-929188-13-0(7)) Morton Bks.

Jerry, Spinelli. Loser. 2014. (ENG.). 224p. (J). (gr. 7-7). 11.24 (978-1-63245-207-8(3)) Lectorum Pubns., Inc.

—Stargirl. 2014. (ENG.). 208p. (YA). 11.24 (978-1-63245-152-1(2)) Lectorum Pubns., Inc.

Jiménez, Francisco. La Mariposa. Silva, Simon, illus. 2004. 38p. (J). (gr. k-4). reprint ed. pap. 14.00 (978-0-7567-8433-1(6)) DIANE Publishing Co.

Jinks, Catherine. Evil Genius. 2007. 486p. (J). (978-1-4287-3510-1(0)) Harcourt Trade Pubs.

—Evil Genius. 2008. (ENG., Illus.). 496p. (YA). (gr. 7). pap. 9.99 (978-0-15-206185-2(1)) Houghton Mifflin Harcourt Publishing Co.

Jocelyn, Marthe. Mable Riley: A Reliable Record of Humdrum, Peril, & Romance. 2007. 279p. (gr. 4-7). 17.00 (978-0-7569-8183-9(2)) Perfection Learning Corp.

—What We Hide. (ENG.). 288p. (YA). (gr. 9). 2015. pap. 9.99 (978-0-375-85544-3(0), Ember) 2014. 16.99 (978-0-385-73847-7(1), Lamb, Wendy Bks.) Random Hse. Children's Bks.

Johannes, Shelley. Beatrice Zinker, Upside down Thinker. Johannes, Shelley, illus. 2017. (Beatrice Zinker, Upside down Thinker Ser.). (ENG., Illus.). 160p. (J). (gr. 2-5). 14.99 **(978-1-4847-6738-2(1))** Hyperion Bks. for Children.

Johansson, J. R. Insomnia. 2013. (Night Walkers Ser.: 1). (ENG.). 360p. (YA). pap. 9.99 (978-0-7387-3593-1(0), Flux) North Star Editions.

Johns, Eric. Mindreaders. 2007. 184p. pap. 16.95 (978-1-4357-0121-2(6)) Lulu Pr., Inc.

Johnson, Angela. A Certain October. (ENG.). 176p. (YA). (gr. 9). 2013. pap. 9.99 (978-0-689-87065-1(5)) 2012. 16.99 (978-0-689-86505-3(8)) Simon & Schuster Bks. For Young Readers. (Simon & Schuster Bks. For Young Readers).

—Sweet, Hereafter. 2011. (ENG.). 128p. (YA). (gr. 7). pap. 8.99 (978-0-689-87386-7(7), Simon & Schuster Bks. For Young Readers) Simon & Schuster Bks. For Young Readers.

—Sweet, Hereafter, Bk. 3. 2010. 128p. (YA). (gr. 9-18). pap. 16.99 (978-1-4169-9995-9(7)) Simon & Schuster Children's Publishing.

Johnson-Choong, Shelly. The Jewelry Box. 2nd ed. 2004. (YA). reprint ed. pap. 10.95 (978-1-932280-40-1(5), 80405) Granite Publishing & Distribution.

Johnson, Christine. Nocturne. (ENG.). (YA). (gr. 7). 2012. 384p. pap. 9.99 (978-1-4424-0777-0(8)) 2011. 368p. 16.99 (978-1-4424-0776-3(X)) Simon Pulse. (Simon Pulse).

Johnson, Donna. The Story of the Little Red Leaf. Johnson, Emily, illus. l.t. ed. 2006. (ENG.). 22p. (J). 25.00 *(978-0-9778774-0-9(X))* Choice Point Editions.
Johnson, Dwayne. My Angel. 2013. (Illus.). 12p. pap. 18.30 *(978-1-4817-8188-6(X))* AuthorHouse.
Johnson, J. J. This Girl Is Different, 1 vol. 2011. (ENG.). 288p. (YA). (gr. 7-11). 16.95 *(978-1-56145-578-2(4))* Peachtree Pubs.
Johnson, Kristel. Even When We Are Apart. 2008. 20p. pap. 24.95 *(978-1-60610-435-4(7))* America Star Bks.
Johnson, LouAnne. Muchacho. 2011. (ENG.). 208p. (YA). (gr. 7). pap. 9.99 *(978-0-375-85903-8(9),* Ember) Random Hse. Children's Bks.
Johnson, Margaret. Ask Alice, 1 vol. 2011. (ENG.). 64p. pap. 14.25 incl. audio compact disk *(978-84-8323-958-2(2))* Cambridge Univ. Pr.
Johnson, Maureen. Devilish. 2013. (ENG.). 304p. (YA). (gr. 7). pap. 9.99 *(978-0-14-750855-3(X),* Speak) Penguin Young Readers Group.
—The Madness Underneath. 2013. (Shades of London Ser.: 2). (ENG.). 304p. (YA). (gr. 7). pap. 9.99 *(978-0-14-242754-5(3),* Speak) Penguin Young Readers Group.
—The Name of the Star. (Shades of London Ser.: 1). (ENG.). (YA). (gr. 7). 2012. 400p. pap. 10.99 *(978-0-14-242205-2(3),* Speak) 2011. 368p. 16.99 *(978-0-399-25660-8(1),* G.P. Putnam's Sons Books for Young Readers) Penguin Young Readers Group.
—Scarlett Fever. (ENG.). 352p. (J). (gr. 7-7). 2011. pap. 9.99 *(978-0-545-09633-1(2))* 2010. 16.99 *(978-0-439-89928-4(1))* Scholastic, Inc.
Johnson, Patricia. Make Your Own Magic Soil: Life's Lessons on Sustainable Living. 2013. 60p. 24.99 *(978-1-4797-0525-2(X));* pap. 15.99 *(978-1-4797-0524-5(1))* Xlibris Corp.
Johnson, Peter. The Life & Times of Benny Alvarez. 2014. (ENG.). 224p. (J). (gr. 3-7). 16.99 *(978-0-06-221596-3(5))* HarperCollins Pubs.
Johnson, Richard, illus. The Giant Turnip. 2004. 24p. (J). *(978-1-85269-745-7(8)); (978-1-85269-741-9(5)); (978-1-85269-736-5(9)); (978-1-85269-748-8(2)); (978-1-85269-747-1(4))* Mantra Lingua.
Johnson, Sandi. My Teacher Is an Alien. Durant, Sybrina, ed. Sturgen, Bobbi, illus. 2014. (ENG.). 30p. (J). (gr. k-5). pap. 12.99 *(978-1-929063-75-8(X),* 285) Moons & Stars Publishing For Children.
Johnson, Shane L., illus. OLIVIA Trains Her Cat. (Olivia TV Tie-In Ser.). (ENG.). 24p. (J). (gr. -1-1). 2010. 16.99 *(978-1-4424-1383-2(2))* 2009. pap. 3.99 *(978-1-4169-8296-8(5))* Simon Spotlight. (Simon Spotlight).
Johnson, Temeka & Phillips, Quency. Decisions, Decisions, Decisions. 2010. 32p. 19.99 *(978-1-4520-5758-3(3))* AuthorHouse.
Johnson, Varian. The Great Greene Heist. 2014. (ENG.). 240p. (J). (gr. 4-7). 16.99 *(978-0-545-52552-7(7),* Levine, Arthur A. Bks.) Scholastic, Inc.
—To Catch a Cheat. 2016. (ENG.). 256p. (J). (gr. 3-7). 16.99 *(978-0-545-72239-1(X),* Levine, Arthur A. Bks.) Scholastic, Inc.
Johnston, E. K. Exit, Pursued by a Bear. 2016. (ENG.). 256p. (YA). (gr. 9). 17.99 *(978-1-101-99458-0(4),* Dutton Books for Young Readers) Penguin Young Readers Group.
—Prairie Fire. 2015. (J). 18.99 *(978-1-4677-6181-9(8));* (ENG.). 304p. (gr. 6-12). 18.99 *(978-1-4677-3909-2(X))* Lerner Publishing Group.
—The Story of Owen: Dragon Slayer of Trondheim. 2014. 312p. (J). (gr. 6-12). 17.95 *(978-1-4677-1066-4(0),* Carolrhoda Lab™) Lerner Publishing Group.
Johnston, Tony. First Grade, Here I Come! Sweet, Melissa & Walker, David, illus. 2015. (ENG.). 32p. (J). (gr. k-2). 8.99 *(978-0-545-20143-8(8),* Cartwheel Bks.) Scholastic, Inc.
—The Spoon in the Bathroom Wall. 2006. (ENG., Illus.). 144p. (J). (gr. 2-5). pap. 10.95 *(978-0-15-205625-4(4))* Houghton Mifflin Harcourt Publishing Co.
Jonas. JONAS #5: about Face. 5th ed. 2010. 128p. pap. 4.99 *(978-1-4231-1773-5(5))* Disney Pr.
—Three's a Crowd. 6th ed. 2010. 128p. pap. 4.99 *(978-1-4231-2282-1(8))* Disney Pr.
JONAS #8: Prep School Party. 2010. 128p. pap. 4.99 *(978-1-4231-2673-7(4))* Disney Pr.
Jones, Andrea. The Spitting Twins. Kulka, Joe, illus. 2004. 32p. (J). *(978-1-58394-095-2(2),* Frog Ltd.) North Atlantic Bks.
Jones, Birdy. Blossom Plays Possum: (Because She's Shy) McDonnell, Janet, illus. 2017. 32p. (J). 15.95 ***(978-1-4338-2735-8(2),*** Magination Pr.) American Psychological Assn.
Jones, Carrie. Need. 2009. (Need Ser.). (ENG.). 336p. (YA). (gr. 7). pap. 9.99 *(978-1-59990-453-5(5),* 9781599904535, Bloomsbury USA Childrens) Bloomsbury Publishing USA.
Jones, Carrie, et al. After Obsession. 2012. (ENG.). 336p. (YA). (gr. 7-12). pap. 9.99 *(978-1-59990-913-4(8),* 9781599909134, Bloomsbury USA Childrens) Bloomsbury Publishing USA.
Jones, Darynda. Death & the Girl He Loves. 2013. (Darklight Ser.: 3). (ENG.). 272p. (YA). (gr. 8-12). pap. 9.99 *(978-0-312-62522-1(7),* 9780312625221, St. Martin's Griffin) St. Martin's Pr.
Jones, Ena. Clayton Stone, Facing Off. 2016. (ENG.). 224p. (J). 16.95 *(978-0-8234-3648-4(9))* Holiday Hse., Inc.
Jones, Janey Louise. Cloudberry Castle, 1 vol. 2010. (ENG., Illus.). 176p. (J). (gr. 2-5). 11.95 *(978-0-86315-765-3(3))* Floris Bks. GBR. Dist: SteinerBooks, Inc.
Jones, Jasmine, adapted by. Lizzie Loves Ethan. 2003. (Lizzie Mcguire Ser.). (Illus.). 152p. (J). 12.65 *(978-0-7569-2721-9(8))* Perfection Learning Corp.
Jones, Jasmine & Alfonsi, Alice. My Second Way Cool, Set. 2nd gif. novel rev. ed. 2004. (ENG.). 144p. (gr. 3-7). 12.99 *(978-0-7868-4678-8(X))* Disney Pr.
Jones, Jen. Brooke's Quest for Captain, No. 2. 2011. (Team Cheer Ser.). (ENG.). 112p. (gr. 4-4). lib. bdg. 25.32 *(978-1-4342-2995-3(5),* Team Cheer) Stone Arch Bks.
—Brooke's Quest for Captain: # 2, 1 vol. 2012. (Team Cheer Ser.). (ENG.). 112p. (gr. 4-4). pap. 7.19 *(978-1-4342-4250-1(1),* Team Cheer) Stone Arch Bks.
—The Competition for Gaby, No. 4. 2011. (Team Cheer Ser.). (ENG.). 112p. (gr. 4-4). lib. bdg. 25.32 *(978-1-4342-2997-7(1),* Team Cheer) Stone Arch Bks.
—The Competition for Gaby: # 4, 1 vol. 2012. (Team Cheer Ser.). (ENG.). 112p. (gr. 4-4). pap. 7.19 *(978-1-4342-4252-5(8),* Team Cheer) Stone Arch Bks.
—Delaney vs. the Bully. Franco, Paula, illus. 2015. (Sleepover Girls Ser.). (ENG.). 128p. (gr. 3-5). lib. bdg. 22.65 *(978-1-4965-0541-5(7))* Stone Arch Bks.
—Faith & the Camp Snob, No. 1. 2011. (Team Cheer Ser.). (ENG.). 112p. (gr. 4-4). lib. bdg. 25.32 *(978-1-4342-2994-6(7),* Team Cheer) Stone Arch Bks.
—Faith & the Camp Snob: # 1, 1 vol. 2012. (Team Cheer Ser.). (ENG.). 112p. (gr. 4-4). pap. 7.19 *(978-1-4342-4249-5(8),* Team Cheer) Stone Arch Bks.
—Lissa & the Fund-Raising Funk, No. 3. 2011. (Team Cheer Ser.). (ENG.). 112p. (gr. 4-4). lib. bdg. 25.32 *(978-1-4342-2996-0(3),* Team Cheer) Stone Arch Bks.
—Lissa & the Fund-Raising Funk: # 3, 1 vol. 2012. (Team Cheer Ser.). (ENG.). 112p. (gr. 4-4). pap. 7.19 *(978-1-4342-4251-8(X),* Team Cheer) Stone Arch Bks.
—The New Ashley. Franco, Paula, illus. 2014. (Sleepover Girls Ser.). (ENG.). 128p. (gr. 3-5). lib. bdg. 22.65 *(978-1-4342-9758-7(6))* Stone Arch Bks.
—Save Our Squad, Gaby, No. 7. Adams, Liz, illus. 2012. (Team Cheer Ser.). (ENG.). 112p. (gr. 4-4). lib. bdg. 25.32 *(978-1-4342-4035-4(5))* Stone Arch Bks.
—Save Our Squad, Gaby: #7, 1 vol. 2013. (Team Cheer Ser.). (ENG.). 112p. (gr. 4-4). pap. 7.19 *(978-1-4342-4265-5(X),* Team Cheer) Stone Arch Bks.
—Team Cheer. 2013. (Team Cheer Ser.). (ENG.). 112p. (gr. 4-4). pap. 55.60 *(978-1-4342-6326-1(6),* Team Cheer) Stone Arch Bks.
Jones, Lori M. Riley's Heart MacHine. Hammond, Julie, illus. 2012. 16p. pap. 9.95 *(978-1-61633-312-6(X))* Guardian Angel Publishing, Inc.
Jones, Marcia Thornton. A Very Haunted Holiday. 2006. (Ghostville Elementary Ser.: Bk. 15). (Illus.). 67p. (J). pap. *(978-0-439-88361-0(X))* Scholastic, Inc.
Jones, Marcia Thornton & Dadey, Debbie. Dragons Do Eat Homework. Dreidemy, Joëlle, illus. 2007. 64p. (J). *(978-0-545-00234-9(6))* Scholastic, Inc.
—Guys & Ghouls. Francis, Guy, illus. 2006. (Ghostville Elementary Ser.: Bk. 13). 81p. *(978-0-439-79402-2(1))* Scholastic, Inc.
Jones, Melanie Davis. Field Day. Molnar, Albert, illus. 2011. (Rookie Ready to Learn — Out & about: in My Community Ser.). 40p. (J). (gr. -1-k). lib. bdg. 25.00 *(978-0-531-27176-6(5));* (ENG.). pap. 5.95 *(978-0-531-26826-1(8))* Scholastic Library Publishing. (Children's Pr.).
Jones, Nicky. Toby Fletcher's Fly-Away Tree. 2013. 182p. pap. *(978-1-78299-798-6(9))* FeedARead.com.
Jones, Patrick. Always Faithful. 2015. (ENG.). 112p. (YA). (gr. 6-12). lib. bdg. 27.99 *(978-1-4677-8052-0(9));* 7.99 *(978-1-4677-9014-7(1))* Lerner Publishing Group. (Darby Creek).
—At the Center. 2016. (Bounce Ser.). (ENG.). 104p. (YA). (gr. 6-12). 26.65 *(978-1-5124-1122-5(1))* Lerner Publishing Group.
—Barrier. 2014. (Alternative Ser.). (ENG.). 104p. (YA). (gr. 6-12). pap. 7.95 *(978-1-4677-4481-2(6),* Darby Creek); lib. bdg. 27.93 *(978-1-4677-3899-6(9))* Lerner Publishing Group.
—Bridge. 2014. (Alternative Ser.). (ENG.). 96p. (YA). (gr. 6-12). lib. bdg. 27.93 *(978-1-4677-3903-0(0))* Lerner Publishing Group.
—Combat Zone. 2015. (ENG.). 96p. (YA). (gr. 6-12). pap. 7.99 *(978-1-4677-8094-0(4))* Lerner Publishing Group.
—Controlled. 2014. (Alternative Ser.). (ENG.). 112p. (YA). (gr. 6-12). pap. 7.95 *(978-1-4677-4483-6(2),* Darby Creek); lib. bdg. 27.93 *(978-1-4677-3902-3(2))* Lerner Publishing Group.
—Heart or Mind. 2016. (Unbarred Ser.). (ENG., Illus.). 120p. (YA). (gr. 6-12). lib. bdg. 27.99 *(978-1-5124-0003-8(3),* Darby Creek) Lerner Publishing Group.
—Heart or Mind. 2016. (Unbarred Ser.). (ENG., Illus.). 120p. (YA). (gr. 6-12). pap. 7.99 *(978-1-5124-0091-5(2),* Darby Creek) Lerner Publishing Group.
—Heart or Mind. 2016. (Unbarred Ser.). (ENG.). 120p. (YA). (gr. 6-12). 42.65 *(978-1-5124-0092-2(0),* Darby Creek) Lerner Publishing Group.
—Out of the Tunnel. 2014. (Red Zone Ser.: 1). (ENG.). 104p. (YA). (gr. 6-12). pap. 7.95 *(978-1-4677-4471-3(9),* Darby Creek); lib. bdg. 27.93 *(978-1-4677-2126-4(3))* Lerner Publishing Group.
—Outburst. 2014. (Alternative Ser.). (ENG.). 104p. (YA). (gr. 6-12). lib. bdg. 27.93 *(978-1-4677-3901-6(4))* Lerner Publishing Group.
—Outburst. 2014. (Alternative Ser.). (ENG.). 104p. (YA). (gr. 6-12). pap. 7.95 *(978-1-4677-4484-3(0),* Darby Creek) Lerner Publishing Group.
—Pass It Forward. 2016. (Bounce Ser.). (ENG.). 104p. (YA). (gr. 6-12). lib. bdg. 26.65 *(978-1-5124-1125-6(6),* Darby Creek) Lerner Publishing Group.
—Target. 2014. (Alternative Ser.). (ENG.). 128p. (YA). (gr. 6-12). pap. 7.95 *(978-1-4677-4485-0(9),* Darby Creek); lib. bdg. 27.93 *(978-1-4677-3900-9(6))* Lerner Publishing Group.
—To the Point. 2016. (Bounce Ser.). (ENG.). 96p. (YA). (gr. 6-12). lib. bdg. 26.65 *(978-1-5124-1124-9(8),* Darby Creek) Lerner Publishing Group.
Jones, Patrick & Chartier, Brent. At All Costs. 2014. (Red Zone Ser.: 4). 104p. (YA). (gr. 6-12). (ENG.). pap. 7.95 *(978-1-4677-4475-1(1));* lib. bdg. 27.93 *(978-1-4677-2129-5(8))* Lerner Publishing Group. (Darby Creek).
—Collateral Damage. 2015. (ENG.). 128p. (YA). (gr. 6-12). pap. 7.99 *(978-1-4677-8091-9(X))* Lerner Publishing Group.
Jones, Pixy. Teen Dumb Come. 2008. 285p. pap. 17.50 *(978-0-557-00089-0(0))* Lulu Pr., Inc.
Jones, Traci L. Silhouetted by the Blue. 2011. (ENG.). 208p. (J). (gr. 5-9). 16.99 *(978-0-374-36914-9(3),* 9780374369149, Farrar, Straus & Giroux (BYR)) Farrar, Straus & Giroux.
—Standing Against the Wind. 2010. (ENG.). 208p. (YA). (gr. 7-9). pap. 11.99 *(978-0-312-62293-0(7),* 9780312622930) Square Fish.
Joosse, Barbara M. Wally Wants to Hug. Ashdown, Rebecca, illus. 2017. (ENG.). 32p. (J). (gr. -1-3). 16.99 *(978-1-4998-0404-1(0))* Little Bee Books Inc.
Jordan, Jesse. This Is Not the End. 2016. (ENG.). 450p. (gr. 6). pap. 9.99 *(978-1-942546-30-6(0))* Nodin Pr.
Jordan, Rosa. The Goatnappers. 2007. (ENG.). 224p. (J). (gr. 3-7). 14.95 *(978-1-56145-400-6(1))* Peachtree Pubs.
Jordan, Sophie. Firelight. (Firelight Ser.: 1). (ENG.). (YA). (gr. 8). 2011. 352p. pap. 9.99 *(978-0-06-193509-1(3))* 2010. 336p. 16.99 *(978-0-06-193508-4(5))* HarperCollins Pubs.
Jordan, Taylor. Movin' on In. Wummer, Amy, illus. 2005. (Social Studies Connects). 32p. (J). (gr. 1-3). pap. 5.95 *(978-1-57565-159-0(9))* Kane Press, Inc.
Joseph, Bruchac. Eagle Song. 2014. (ENG.). 80p. (J). (gr. 12-12). 9.24 *(978-1-63245-103-3(4))* Lectorum Pubns., Inc.
Joseph, Danielle. Shrinking Violet. 2009. (ENG.). 320p. pap. 19.99 *(978-1-4165-9696-7(8),* MTV Bks.) MTV Books.
Joshi, Bhabika. Mortals: Hayden Roux Chronicles. 2009. 208p. 24.95 *(978-1-4401-5014-2(1));* pap. 14.95 *(978-1-4401-5016-6(8))* iUniverse, Inc.
Joyal, Lisa. Swahili for Beginners, 1 vol. 2008. (ENG., Illus.). 176p. (YA). (gr. 5-9). pap. *(978-1-894549-69-1(4),* Sumach Pr.) Canadian Scholars.
Joyce, Carol. Just Friends. 2011. 228p. (gr. 10-12). 33.95 *(978-1-4497-2972-1(X));* pap. 17.95 *(978-1-4497-2971-4(1))* Author Solutions, Inc. (WestBow Pr.).
Joyce, Sandie May. Aunt Sandie Goes to School - the Comics. 2008. 55p. pap. 22.50 *(978-0-557-02295-3(9))* Lulu Pr., Inc.
Joyce, William. Billy's Booger. Joyce, William, illus. 2015. (ENG., Illus.). 40p. (J). (gr. -1-3). 17.99 *(978-1-4424-7351-5(7))* Simon & Schuster Children's Publishing.
Joyner, Andrew. Boris for the Win. 2013. (Boris Ser.: 3). (ENG.). 80p. (J). (gr. k-2). pap. 4.99 *(978-0-545-48449-7(9))* Scholastic, Inc.
—Boris for the Win. 2013. (Boris Ser.: 3). lib. bdg. 14.75 *(978-0-606-31976-8(X),* Turtleback) Turtleback Bks.
Ju-Yeon, Rhim. President Dad, 7 vols., Vol. 5. Ju-Yeon, Rhim, illus. 5th rev. ed. 2006. (President Dad Ser.). (Illus.). 208p. per. 9.99 *(978-1-59532-238-8(8))* TOKYOPOP, Inc.
Juby, Susan. Getting the Girl: A Guide to Private Investigation, Surveillance, & Cookery. 2010. (ENG.). 352p. (YA). (gr. 8). pap. 8.99 *(978-0-06-076528-6(3),* HarperTeen) HarperCollins Pubs.
Juby, Susan & Wells, Rosemary. The Truth Commission. 2015. (ENG., Illus.). 320p. (YA). (gr. 9). bds. 18.99 *(978-0-451-46877-2(5),* Viking Books for Young Readers) Penguin Young Readers Group.
Judd, Merlynne. Circle of Friendship. 2010. 76p. pap. 24.99 *(978-1-4520-6783-4(X))* AuthorHouse.
Judge, Malcolm. Jonny Jakes Investigates the Hamburgers of Doom. Brown, Alan, illus. 2016. (Middle-Grade Novels Ser.). (ENG.). 240p. (gr. 4-7). lib. bdg. 26.65 *(978-1-4965-2678-6(3))* Stone Arch Bks.
—Jonny Jakes Investigates the Old School Ghoul. Brown, Alan, illus. 2016. (Middle-Grade Novels Ser.). (ENG.). 240p. (gr. 4-7). lib. bdg. 25.99 *(978-1-4965-2829-2(8))* Stone Arch Bks.
Jukes, Mavis. The New Kid. (ENG.). 288p. (J). 2012. (gr. 4-7). 7.99 *(978-0-375-85367-8(7),* Yearling) 2011. (gr. 3-7). 14.99 *(978-0-375-85879-6(2),* Knopf Bks. for Young Readers) Random Hse. Children's Bks.
Jules, Jacqueline. Duck for Turkey Day. Mitter, Kathryn, illus. (ENG.). 32p. (J). 2017. (gr. k-2). pap. 7.99 ***(978-0-8075-1735-2(6))*** 2009. (gr. 1-3). 16.99 *(978-0-8075-1734-5(8))* Whitman, Albert & Co.
Jules, Jacqueline. Freddie Ramos Zooms to the Rescue, Bk. 3. Benitez, Miguel, illus. 2011. (Zapato Power Ser.: Book 3). (ENG.). 96p. (J). (gr. 1-5). 14.99 *(978-0-8075-9482-7(2))* Whitman, Albert & Co.
Julie, Aunt. Paddleduck! Julie, A Little Girl from Texas. 2011. 56p. (gr. 2-4). pap. 8.95 *(978-1-4269-2584-9(0))* Trafford Publishing.
Jung, Mike. Geeks, Girls, & Secret Identities. Maihack, Mike, illus. 2012. (J). (ENG.). 320p. (gr. 3-7). 16.99 *(978-0-545-33548-5(5));* pap. *(978-0-545-33549-2(3))* Scholastic, Inc. (Levine, Arthur A. Bks.).
—Unidentified Suburban Object. (ENG.). 272p. (J). (gr. 3-7). 2017. pap. 6.99 ***(978-0-545-78227-2(9))*** 2016. 16.99 *(978-0-545-78226-5(0),* Levine, Arthur A. Bks.) Scholastic, Inc.
Kade, Stacey. The Ghost & the Goth. 2011. (ENG.). 304p. (J). (gr. 7-17). pap. 8.99 *(978-1-4231-2487-0(1))* Hyperion Pr.
Kahler, A. R. Echoes of Memory. 2017. (Ravenborn Ser.: 2). (ENG., Illus.). 336p. (YA). (gr. 9). 17.99 *(978-1-4814-3260-3(5),* Simon Pulse) Simon Pulse.
—Shades of Darkness. 2016. (Ravenborn Ser.: 1). (ENG., Illus.). 304p. (YA). (gr. 9). 17.99 *(978-1-4814-3257-3(5),* Simon Pulse) Simon Pulse.
Kain, P. G. The Social Experiments of Dorie Dilts: The School for Cool. 2008. (Mix Ser.). (ENG.). 288p. (J). (gr. 4-8). pap. 13.99 *(978-1-4169-3520-9(7),* Simon & Schuster/Paula Wiseman Bks.) Simon & Schuster/Paula Wiseman Bks.
Kalman, Maira. Smartypants: Pete in School. 2005. (J). 27.95 incl. audio *(978-0-8045-6929-3(0),* SAC6929); 29.95 incl. audio compact disk *(978-0-8045-4105-3(1),* SACD4105) Spoken Arts, Inc.
Kalomas, Alice & Kerr, Lenora. Sir Wrinkles Goes to School. Utomo, Gabhor, illus. 2005. (J). 16.95 *(978-0-9766639-1-1(0))* Sir Wrinkles Pr.
Kamateros, Litsa & Morfonios, Nia. Sarah's Socks: My World of Autism. 2010. 24p. pap. 10.95 *(978-1-61633-023-1(6))* Guardian Angel Publishing, Inc.
Kanakia, Rahul. Enter Title Here. 2016. (ENG., Illus.). 352p. (YA). (gr. 9-17). 17.99 *(978-1-4847-2387-6(2))* Hyperion Bks. for Children.
Kaneyoshi, Izumi. Doubt!!, Vol. 4. Kaneyoshi, Izumi, illus. 2005. (Doubt Ser.: 4). (ENG., Illus.). 192p. pap. 9.99 *(978-1-59116-984-0(4))* Viz Media.
Kann, Victoria. Pinkalicious: School Rules! Kann, Victoria, illus. 2010. (I Can Read Level 1 Ser.). (ENG., Illus.). 32p. (J). (gr. -1-3). 16.99 *(978-0-06-192886-4(0))* HarperCollins Pubs.
—School Lunch. Kann, Victoria, illus. 2015. (Pinkalicious Ser.). (ENG., Illus.). 24p. (J). (gr. -1-3). pap. 4.99 *(978-0-06-224590-8(2),* HarperFestival) HarperCollins Pubs.
—School Rules! Kann, Victoria, illus. 2010. (I Can Read Level 1 Ser.). (ENG., Illus.). 32p. (J). (gr. -1-3). pap. 3.99 *(978-0-06-192885-7(2))* HarperCollins Pubs.
Kann, Victoria & Kann, Elizabeth. Purplicious. Kann, Victoria, illus. 2007. (Illus.). 40p. (J). (gr. k-3). (ENG.). 17.99 *(978-0-06-124405-6(8));* lib. bdg. 17.89 *(978-0-06-124406-3(6))* HarperCollins Pubs.
Kantar, Andrew. Game Face. Keleher, Fran, illus. 2013. 160p. pap. 12.95 *(978-1-61160-566-2(0))* Whiskey Creek Restorations.
Kantor, Melissa. The Amanda Project. 2011. 287p. (J). 8.99 *(978-0-06-202706-1(9),* HarperTeen) HarperCollins Pubs.
—Better Than Perfect. 2015. (ENG.). 336p. (YA). (gr. 8). 17.99 *(978-0-06-227923-1(8),* HarperTeen) HarperCollins Pubs.
—If I Have a Wicked Stepmother, Where's My Prince? 2005. 283p. (YA). *(978-1-4156-2763-1(0))* Hyperion Pr.
—Maybe One Day. 2014. (ENG.). 400p. (YA). (gr. 8). 17.99 *(978-0-06-227920-0(3),* HarperTeen) HarperCollins Pubs.
Kaplan, Arie. The New Kid from Planet Glorf, 1 vol. Bradley, Jessica, illus. 2013. (Comics Land Ser.). (ENG.). 32p. (gr. k-2). 7.95 *(978-1-4342-4272-3(2));* lib. bdg. 25.32 *(978-1-4342-4032-3(0))* Stone Arch Bks.
Kaplan, Isabel. Hancock Park. 2010. (ENG.). 272p. (YA). (gr. 9). pap. 8.99 *(978-0-06-137370-1(2),* HarperTeen) HarperCollins Pubs.
Kappler, Kathleen. Whitney's School Morning. 2004. 38p. pap. 24.95 *(978-1-4137-3711-0(0))* PublishAmerica, Inc.
Karalius, Kimberly. Love Charms & Other Catastrophes. 2016. (Grimbaud Ser.). (ENG.). 384p. (YA). pap. 10.99 *(978-1-250-08404-0(0),* 9781250084040) Feiwel & Friends.
Karapetkova, Holly. Las Serpientes en el Tercer Grado. 2012.Tr. of Snakes in Third Grade. (SPA & ENG.). 24p. (gr. 2-3). pap. 8.95 *(978-1-61810-545-5(0))* Rourke Educational Media.
Karas, Phyllis. The Hate Crime. 2004. 190p. (YA). pap. 13.95 *(978-0-595-33138-3(6),* Authors Choice Pr.) iUniverse, Inc.
Kares, P. S. The Prairie Orphans' Journey. 2008. 32p. per. 24.95 *(978-1-4241-8396-8(0))* America Star Bks.
Kargman, Jill & Karasyov, Carrie. Bittersweet Sixteen. 2006. (YA). (gr. 7-12). (ENG.). 240p. 15.99 *(978-0-06-077844-6(X));* 230p. lib. bdg. 16.89 *(978-0-06-077845-3(8))* HarperCollins Pubs.
Karo, Aaron. Me You Us (Previously Published As Galgorithm) 2016. lib. bdg. 22.10 ***(978-0-606-39928-9(3))*** Turtleback Bks.
Karre, Elizabeth. Calling the Shots. 2014. (Gift Ser.). 104p. (gr. 6-12). (J). lib. bdg. 27.93 *(978-1-4677-3514-8(0));* (ENG.). (YA). pap. 7.95 *(978-1-4677-4478-2(6))* Lerner Publishing Group. (Darby Creek).
—Certain Signals. 2014. (Gift Ser.). (ENG.). 112p. (YA). (gr. 6-12). pap. 7.95 *(978-1-4677-4479-9(4),* Darby Creek) Lerner Publishing Group.
—The Fight. 2013. (Surviving Southside Ser.). (ENG.). 128p. (YA). (gr. 6-12). pap. 7.95 *(978-1-4677-0709-1(0));* lib. bdg. 27.93 *(978-1-4677-0596-7(9))* Lerner Publishing Group.
Kashyap, Keshni. Tina's Mouth: An Existential Comic Diary. Araki, Mari, illus. 10th ed. 2012. (ENG.). 256p. 18.95 *(978-0-618-94519-1(9))* Houghton Mifflin Harcourt Publishing Co.
Kasper, Kathy. Mary Jean Learns to Shine. 2008. 51p. pap. 16.95 *(978-1-60441-680-0(7))* America Star Bks.
Katar, Al. Captain Scratch: Island of Sirmanj. 2007. (J). 21.99 *(978-1-934035-31-3(9))* Trent's Prints.
Katcher, Brian. Almost Perfect. 2010. (ENG.). 368p. (YA). (gr. 9). pap. 9.99 *(978-0-385-73665-7(7),* Delacorte Bks. for Young Readers) Random Hse. Children's Bks.
—Playing with Matches. 2009. (ENG.). 304p. (YA). (gr. 9). mass mkt. 8.99 *(978-0-385-73545-2(6),* Laurel Leaf) Random Hse. Children's Bks.
Kate, Lauren. Fallen. (Fallen Ser.: Bk. 1). (ENG.). (YA). (gr. 7). 2010. 480p. pap. 10.99 *(978-0-385-73913-9(3),* Ember) 2009. 464p. 17.99 *(978-0-385-73893-4(5),* Delacorte Pr.) Random Hse. Children's Bks.
—Fallen. 2010. (Fallen Ser.: 1). lib. bdg. 22.10 *(978-0-606-15168-9(0),* Turtleback) Turtleback Bks.
—Oscuros. 2011. (Vintage Espanol Ser.: Bk. 1).Tr. of Fallen. (SPA.). 416p. (YA). (gr. 5). pap. 9.95 *(978-0-307-74500-2(7),* Vintage Espanol) Knopf Doubleday Publishing Group.
—Passion. (Fallen Ser.: Bk. 3). (ENG.). (YA). (gr. 7). 2012. 448p. pap. 10.99 *(978-0-385-73917-7(6),* Ember) 2011. 432p. 17.99 *(978-0-385-73916-0(8),* Delacorte Pr.) Random Hse. Children's Bks.
—Passion. 2012. (Fallen Ser.: 3). lib. bdg. 22.10 *(978-0-606-26410-5(8),* Turtleback) Turtleback Bks.
—Torment. (Fallen Ser.: Bk. 2). (ENG.). (YA). (gr. 7). 2011. 480p. pap. 10.99 *(978-0-385-73915-3(X),* Ember) 2010. 464p. 17.99 *(978-0-385-73914-6(1),* Delacorte Pr.) Random Hse. Children's Bks.
—Torment. 2011. (Fallen Ser.: 2). lib. bdg. 22.10 *(978-0-606-22247-1(2),* Turtleback) Turtleback Bks.
—Tormento. 2011. (Vintage Espanol Ser.: Bk. 2).Tr. of Torment. (SPA.). 416p. (YA). (gr. 7). pap. 9.95 *(978-0-307-74512-5(0),* Vintage Espanol) Knopf Doubleday Publishing Group.
—Unforgiven. (Fallen Ser.). (ENG.). 368p. (YA). (gr. 7). 2016. pap. 10.99 *(978-0-385-74264-1(9),* Ember) 2015. 18.99 *(978-0-385-74263-4(0),* Delacorte Pr.) 2015. lib. bdg. 21.99 *(978-0-375-99068-7(2),* Delacorte Pr.) Random Hse. Children's Bks.
Kats, Jewel. Miss Popular Steals the Show: Girls in Wheelchairs Rule! Stenton, Murray, illus. 2014. 37p. (J). pap. 14.95 *(978-1-61599-236-2(7))* Loving Healing Pr., Inc.
Katschke, Judy. First Grade Feast!/By Judy Katschke; Illustrated by Clare Elsom. Elsom, Clare, illus. 2014. 32p. (J). pap. *(978-0-545-75844-4(0))* Scholastic, Inc.
Katz, Alan. Don't Say That Word! Catrow, David, illus. 2007. (ENG.). 32p. (J). (gr. -1-3). 17.99 *(978-0-689-86971-6(1),* McElderry, Margaret K. Bks.) McElderry, Margaret K. Bks.
—Ricky Vargas: The Funniest Kid in the World. Curtis, Stacy, illus. 2011. (J). pap. *(978-0-545-24583-8(4),* Cartwheel Bks.) Scholastic, Inc.
—That Stinks! A Punny Show-and-Tell. Gilpin, Stephen, illus. 2016. (ENG.). 32p. (J). (gr. -1-3). 17.99 *(978-1-4169-7880-0(1),* Simon & Schuster Bks. For Young Readers) Simon & Schuster Bks. For Young Readers.
Katz, Danny. Little Lunch Four. Vane, Mitch, illus. 2005. (Little Lunch Ser.). 64p. (J). pap. *(978-1-876372-84-2(2),* Black Dog Books) Walker Bks. Australia Pty. Ltd.
Katz, Karen. Rosie Goes to Preschool. 2015. (ENG., Illus.). 40p. (J). (-k). 16.99 *(978-0-385-37917-5(X),* Schwartz & Wade Bks.) Random Hse. Children's Bks.
Katz, Susan B. ABC School's for Me! Munsinger, Lynn, illus. 2015. (ENG.). 32p. (J). (gr. -1-k). 16.99 *(978-0-545-53092-7(X),* Scholastic Pr.) Scholastic, Inc.

S

Kaufman, Sashi. Wired Man & Other Freaks of Nature. 2016. (ENG.). 264p. (YA). (gr. 9-12). 17.99 *(978-1-4677-8563-1(6)*, Carolrhoda Bks.); 35.99 *(978-1-4677-9564-7(X)*, Carolrhoda Lab™) Lerner Publishing Group.

Kaufman, Seufert. Wee Wilhelmina & Her Magic Marbles. 2012. (ENG.). pap. *(978-1-4675-4364-4(0))* Independent Pub.

Kay, Verla. Hornbooks & Inkwells. Schindler, S. D., illus. 2011. (ENG.). 32p. (J). (gr. -1-3). 16.99 *(978-0-399-23870-3(0)*, G.P. Putnam's Sons Books for Young Readers) Penguin Young Readers Group.

Kaye, Marilyn. Jill's Happy Un-Birthday: The after School Club. 2014. (ENG., Illus.). 80p. (J). (gr. 3-7). pap. 13.99 *(978-1-4814-2885-9(3)*, Simon & Schuster/Paula Wiseman Bks.) Simon & Schuster/Paula Wiseman Bks.

Keane, Dave. First Day Frights. Keane, Dave, illus. 2012. (I Can Read Level 2 Ser.). (ENG., Illus.). 32p. (J). (gr. -1-3). pap. 3.99 *(978-0-06-085475-1(8))* HarperCollins Pubs.

—Monster School: First Day Frights. Keane, Dave, illus. 2012. (I Can Read Level 2 Ser.). (ENG., Illus.). 32p. (J). (gr. -1-3). 16.99 *(978-0-06-085476-8(6))* HarperCollins Pubs.

Kear, Nicole C. The Fix-It Friends: Have No Fear! Dockray, Tracy, illus. 2017. (Fix-It Friends Ser.). (ENG.). 144p. (J). 16.99 *(978-1-250-11577-5(9)*, 9781250115775) Imprint IND. Dist: Macmillan.

—The Fix-It Friends: Sticks & Stones. Dockray, Tracy, illus. 2017. (Fix-It Friends Ser.: 2). (ENG.). 144p. (J). pap. 5.99 *(978-1-250-08586-3(1)*, 9781250085863) Imprint IND. Dist: Macmillan.

—The Fix-It Friends: the Show Must Go On. Dockray, Tracy, illus. 2017. (Fix-It Friends Ser.: 3). (ENG.). 160p. (J). pap. 5.99 ***(978-1-250-08668-6(X)***, 9781250086686) Imprint IND. Dist: Macmillan.

—The Fix-It Friends: Wish You Were Here. Dockray, Tracy, illus. 2017. (Fix-It Friends Ser.: 4). (ENG.). 160p. (J). pap. 5.99 ***(978-1-250-08670-9(1)***, 9781250086709) Imprint IND. Dist: Macmillan.

Keating, Jess. How to Outrun a Crocodile When Your Shoes Are Untied. 2014. (My Life Is a Zoo Ser.: 1). (ENG.). 288p. (J). (gr. 4-7). pap. 7.99 *(978-1-4022-9755-7(6)*, 9781402297557, Sourcebooks Jabberwocky) Sourcebooks, Inc.

—How to Outswim a Shark Without a Snorkel. 2015. (My Life Is a Zoo Ser.: 2). (ENG.). 304p. (J). (gr. 4-7). pap. 7.99 *(978-1-4022-9758-8(0)*, 9781402297588, Sourcebooks Jabberwocky) Sourcebooks, Inc.

Keeble, Helen. No Angel. 2013. (ENG.). 384p. (YA). (gr. 8). pap. 9.99 *(978-0-06-208227-5(2)*, HarperTeen) HarperCollins Pubs.

Keeling, Evan. CrumbSnatchers. 2008. 60p. (J). per. 5.95 *(978-0-9796902-4-2(2))* Silent Devil Productions.

Keene, Carolyn. Double Take. Pamintuan, Macky, illus. 2009. (Nancy Drew & the Clue Crew Ser.: 21). (ENG.). 112p. (J). (gr. 1-4). pap. 5.99 *(978-1-4169-7812-1(7)*, Aladdin) Simon & Schuster Children's Publishing.

—Earth Day Escapade. Pamintuan, Macky, illus. 2009. (Nancy Drew & the Clue Crew Ser.: 18). (ENG.). 96p. (J). (gr. 1-4). pap. 5.99 *(978-1-4169-7218-1(8)*, Aladdin) Simon & Schuster Children's Publishing.

Kehoe, Stasia Ward. The Sound of Letting Go. 2014. (ENG.). 400p. (YA). (gr. 7). 17.99 *(978-0-670-01553-5(9)*, Viking Books for Young Readers) Penguin Young Readers Group.

Keil, Melissa. Life in Outer Space, 1 vol. (ENG.). 320p. (YA). (gr. 7-11). 2016. pap. 9.95 ***(978-1-56145-975-9(5))*** 2013. 16.95 *(978-1-56145-742-7(6))* Peachtree Pubs.

Kellerman, Faye & Kellerman, Aliza. Prism. (YA). 2010. (ENG.). 288p. (gr. 8). pap. 8.99 *(978-0-06-168724-2(3))* 2009. 272p. (gr. 7-18). lib. bdg. 17.89 *(978-0-06-168722-8(7)*, HarperTeen) HarperCollins Pubs.

Kelley, Gretchen. Superheroes Don't Eat Veggie Burgers. 2016. (ENG.). 272p. (J). 16.99 *(978-1-62779-089-5(6)*, 9781627790895, Holt, Henry & Co. Bks. For Young Readers) Holt, Henry & Co.

Kelley, Jane. Sol-Ray Man & the Freaky Flood. 2017. (Escapades of Clint Mccool Ser.: 2). lib. bdg. 16.00 ***(978-0-606-40112-8(1))*** Turtleback Bks.

Kelley, Marty. Fame, Fortune, & the Bran Muffins of Doom. Kelley, Marty, illus. 2012. (ENG., Illus.). 144p. (J). 16.95 *(978-0-8234-2606-5(8))* Holiday Hse., Inc.

—Lucky Break. Kelley, Marty, illus. 2017. (Molly Mac Ser.). (ENG., Illus.). 56p. (gr. k-2). lib. bdg. 22.65 *(978-1-5158-0837-4(8))* Picture Window Bks.

—The Messiest Desk. 2009. (J). *(978-1-55933-319-1(7))* Zino Pr. Children's Bks.

Kelley, True. School Lunch. Kelley, True, illus. 2005. (ENG., Illus.). 32p. (J). (gr. -1-3). 16.95 *(978-0-8234-1894-7(4))* Holiday Hse., Inc.

Kelly, Claire. Nellie in the News. Hicks, Faith, illus. 2007. 48p. (J). lib. bdg. 23.08 *(978-1-4242-1631-4(1))* Fitzgerald Bks.

Kelly, David A. The Gold Medal Mess. Brundage, Scott, illus. 2016. (Most Valuable Players Ser.: 1). (ENG.). 128p. (J). (gr. 1-4). 4.99 *(978-0-553-51319-6(2)*, Random Hse. Bks. for Young Readers) Random Hse. Children's Bks.

Kelly, Erin Entrada. Blackbird Fly. Peterschmidt, Betsy, illus. 2015. (ENG.). 304p. (J). (gr. 3-7). 16.99 *(978-0-06-223861-0(2)*, Greenwillow Bks.) HarperCollins Pubs.

Kelly, Jamie & Benton, Jim. Never Underestimate Your Dumbness. 2008. (Dear Dumb Diary Ser.). (Illus.). 150p. (gr. 4-7). 16.00 *(978-0-7569-8814-2(4))* Perfection Learning Corp.

Kelly, Joan L. The Dna Connection: Tannenhauser's Theory. 2013. 198p. pap. 9.99 *(978-1-936453-25-2(8))* Bezalel Bks.

Kelly, Katy. Here's the Thing about Me. Rex, Adam, illus. 2006. (Lucy Rose Ser.). (ENG.). 160p. (J). (gr. 3-7). reprint ed. per. 6.99 *(978-0-440-42026-2(1)*, Yearling) Random Hse. Children's Bks.

Kelly, Keith. Peace Comes to Ajani. Kelly, Keith, illus. 2009. (Illus.). 56p. (J). pap. 9.95 *(978-0-932112-59-0(5))* Carolina Wren Pr.

Kelm, Tracy Martin. Light. 2011. 116p. pap. 11.95 *(978-1-4327-6308-4(3))* Outskirts Pr., Inc.

Kemnitz, Dianna. Another Lesson for Jack. 2012. 42p. 24.95 *(978-1-4626-6897-7(6))* America Star Bks.

Kenah, Katharine. The Best Chef in Second Grade. Carter, Abby, illus. (I Can Read Level 2 Ser.). 48p. (J). 2008. (ENG.). (gr. k-3). pap. 3.99 *(978-0-06-053563-6(6))* 2007. (gr. -1-3). lib. bdg. 16.89 *(978-0-06-053562-9(8))* HarperCollins Pubs.

—The Best Teacher in Second Grade. Carter, Abby, illus. 2007. (I Can Read Level 2 Ser.). (ENG.). 48p. (J). (gr. k-3). pap. 3.99 *(978-0-06-053566-7(0))* HarperCollins Pubs.

—The Best Teacher in Second Grade. Carter, Abby, illus. 2007. (I Can Read Bks.). 48p. (gr. -1-3). 14.00 *(978-0-7569-8105-1(0))* Perfection Learning Corp.

—Scholastic Reader Level 1: the Saturday Triplets #3: Teacher Trouble! Lyon, Tammie, illus. 2013. (Scholastic Reader Level 1 Ser.). (ENG.). 32p. (J). (gr. -1-2). pap. 3.99 *(978-0-545-48145-8(7))* Scholastic, Inc.

Kendall, Grace, ed. I See Reality: Twelve Short Stories about Real Life. 2016. (ENG.). 304p. (YA). 17.99 *(978-0-374-30258-0(8)*, 9780374302580, Farrar, Straus & Giroux (BYR)) Farrar, Straus & Giroux.

Kendall, Jane F. Maestoso Petra. Sanderson, Ruth, illus. 2010. (Horse Diaries: No. 4). (ENG.). 160p. (J). (gr. 3-7). pap. 7.99 *(978-0-375-85842-0(3)*, Random Hse. Bks. for Young Readers) Random Hse. Children's Bks.

Kenley, Holli. Another Way: A Novel. 2015. 155p. (YA). pap. *(978-1-61599-259-1(6))* Loving Healing Pr., Inc.

Kenneally, Miranda. Defending Taylor. 2016. (Hundred Oaks Ser.: Bk. 7). (ENG.). 304p. (YA). (gr. 8-12). pap. 10.99 *(978-1-4926-3008-1(X)*, 9781492630081) Sourcebooks, Inc.

—Stealing Parker. 2012. (Hundred Oaks Ser.: Bk. 2). (ENG.). 256p. (YA). (gr. 7-12). pap. 10.99 *(978-1-4022-7187-8(5))* Sourcebooks, Inc.

Kenney, Rebecca. The Silent. 2009. (YA). 8.99 *(978-1-60682-054-4(0)*, JourneyForth) BJU Pr.

Kent, Renee Holmes. Robyn Flies Home, Vol. 4. 2004. (Adventures in Misty Falls Ser.: Vol. 4). (Illus.). 100p. (gr. 4-7). pap. 4.99 *(978-1-56309-764-5(8)*, N007106) New Hope Pubs.

—Tell the Truth, Cassie, Vol. 6. 2004. (Adventures in Misty Falls Ser.: Vol. 6). (Illus.). 100p. (J). (gr. 4-7). pap. 4.99 *(978-1-56309-452-1(5)*, N007110) New Hope Pubs.

Kenyon, Sherrilyn. Inferno. 2014. (Chronicles of Nick Ser.: 4). (ENG.). 464p. (YA). (gr. 7). pap. 11.99 *(978-1-250-00286-0(9)*, 9781250002860, St. Martin's Griffin) St. Martin's Pr.

—Infinity, Vol. 1. Ahn, JiYoung, illus. 2013. (Dark-Hunters Ser.: 1). (ENG.). 240p. (gr. 11-17). 13.00 *(978-0-316-19053-4(5)*, Yen Pr.) Orbit.

—Infinity. (Chronicles of Nick Ser.: 1). (ENG.). 480p. (YA). (gr. 7-18). 2011. pap. 11.99 *(978-0-312-60304-5(5)*, 9780312603045) 2010. 19.99 *(978-0-312-59907-2(2)*, 9780312599072) St. Martin's Pr. (St. Martin's Griffin).

—Invincible. (Chronicles of Nick Ser.: 2). (ENG.). 432p. (YA). (gr. 7). 2012. pap. 11.99 *(978-0-312-60327-4(4)*, 9780312603274) 2011. 27.99 *(978-0-312-59906-5(4)*, 9780312599065) St. Martin's Pr. (St. Martin's Griffin).

Keplinger, Kody. The DUFF: Designated Ugly Fat Friend. (ENG.). (YA). (gr. 10-17). 2011. 304p. pap. 10.99 *(978-0-316-08424-6(7))* 2015. 320p. pap. 10.00 *(978-0-316-38180-2(2))* Little, Brown Bks. for Young Readers. (Poppy).

—Shut Out. 2012. (ENG.). 288p. (YA). (gr. 10-17). pap. 10.99 *(978-0-316-17555-5(2)*, Poppy) Little, Brown Bks. for Young Readers.

Kerick, Mia. Us Three. 2016. (ENG., Illus.). (J). 24.99 ***(978-1-63477-989-0(4))*** 2014. 180p. pap. 14.99 *(978-1-62798-908-4(0))* Dreamspinner Pr. (Harmony Ink Pr.).

Kerns, Ann. I Date Dead People. Gorman, Mike & Görrissen, Janina, illus. 2012. (My Boyfriend Is a Monster Ser.: 5). (ENG.). 128p. (YA). (gr. 7-12). pap. 9.95 *(978-0-7613-8549-3(5)*, Graphic Universe™) Lerner Publishing Group.

—I Date Dead People. Görrissen, Janina, illus. 2012. (My Boyfriend Is a Monster Ser.: 5). (ENG.). 128p. (YA). (gr. 7-12). lib. bdg. 29.27 *(978-0-7613-6007-0(7))* Lerner Publishing Group.

Kerr, B. Modern Persona: Valhalla High School. 2007. 296p. (YA). per. 18.95 *(978-0-595-44412-0(1))* iUniverse, Inc.

Kerr, Esme. Mischief at Midnight. 2016. (ENG.). 272p. (J). (gr. 3-7). 16.99 *(978-0-545-90403-2(X)*, Chicken Hse., The) Scholastic, Inc.

Kerr, M. E., pseud. If I Love You, Am I Trapped Forever?, 0 vols. 2011. (ENG.). 192p. (J). (gr. 7-9). pap. 9.99 *(978-0-7614-5839-5(5)*, 9780761458395, Amazon Children's Publishing) Amazon Publishing.

Kerz, Anna. The Mealworm Diaries, 1 vol. 2009. (ENG.). 160p. (J). (gr. 4-7). pap. 9.95 *(978-1-55143-982-2(4))* Orca Bk. Pubs. USA.

Kessler, Jackie Morse. Loss. 2012. (Riders of the Apocalypse Ser.: 3). (ENG.). 272p. (YA). (gr. 7). pap. 8.99 *(978-0-547-71215-4(4))* Houghton Mifflin Harcourt Publishing Co.

—Loss. 2012. (Riders of the Apocalypse Ser.: 3). lib. bdg. 19.65 *(978-0-606-24742-9(4)*, Turtleback) Turtleback Bks.

—Rage. 2011. (Riders of the Apocalypse Ser.: 2). (ENG.). 240p. (YA). (gr. 7-18). pap. 9.99 *(978-0-547-44528-1(8))* Houghton Mifflin Harcourt Publishing Co.

Kevin, Henkes. Chrysanthemum. 2014. (ENG.). 32p. (J). (gr. k-3). 11.24 *(978-1-63245-281-8(2))* Lectorum Pubns., Inc.

Kew, Trevor. Trading Goals, 1 vol. 2009. (Lorimer Sports Stories Ser.). (ENG.). 144p. (J). (gr. 4-8). 16.95 *(978-1-55277-425-0(2)*, 9781552774250) Lorimer, James & Co., Ltd., Pubs. CAN. Dist: Casemate Pubs. & Bk. Distributors, LLC.

Khorana, Aditi. Mirror in the Sky. 2016. (ENG.). 352p. (YA). (gr. 7). 17.99 *(978-1-59514-856-8(6)*, Razorbill) Penguin Young Readers Group.

Kids Can Learn Franklin Staff, ed. Ready for School. 2004. 32p. pap. *(978-1-55337-605-7(6))* Kids Can Pr., Ltd.

Kidwell, Leigh-Anne. The Year I Lost My Popularity! 2005. 115p. pap. 19.95 *(978-1-4137-8376-6(7))* PublishAmerica, Inc.

Killeen, James. Top of the Class! Martinez, Heather, illus. 2011. (Little Golden Book Ser.). (ENG.). 24p. (J). (gr. -1-2). 3.99 *(978-0-375-86568-8(3)*, Golden Bks.) Random Hse. Children's Bks.

Kim, Derek Kirk. Vanishing Point. Kim, Derek Kirk, illus. 2012. (Tune Ser.: 1). (ENG., Illus.). 160p. pap. 17.99 *(978-1-59643-516-2(X)*, 9781596435162, First Second Bks.) Roaring Brook Pr.

Kimmel, E. Cody. In the Eye of the Storm. Snow, Scott, illus. 2003. (Adventures of Young Buffalo Bill Ser.). (ENG.). 144p. (J). (gr. 3-7). 15.99 *(978-0-06-029115-0(X))* HarperCollins Pubs.

Kimmel, Elizabeth Cody. In the Eye of the Storm. Snow, Scott, illus. 2003. (Adventures of Young Buffalo Bill Ser.). 144p. (J). (gr. 3-7). lib. bdg. 16.89 *(978-0-06-029116-7(8))* HarperCollins Pubs.

—Leading Ladies. Mingus, Cathi, illus. 2012. (Forever Four Ser.: 2). (ENG.). 224p. (J). (gr. 3-7). pap. 6.99 *(978-0-448-45549-5(8)*, Grosset & Dunlap) Penguin Young Readers Group.

—Lily B. on the Brink of Love. 2005. (ENG.). 192p. (J). 15.99 *(978-0-06-075541-6(5))* HarperCollins Pubs.

—The Reinvention of Moxie Roosevelt. 2011. (ENG.). 256p. (J). (gr. 5-18). 6.99 *(978-0-14-241870-3(6)*, Puffin Books) Penguin Young Readers Group.

—Suddenly Supernatural: Scaredy Kat. 2010. (Suddenly Supernatural Ser.: 2). (ENG.). 272p. (J). (gr. 3-7). pap. 5.99 *(978-0-316-08745-2(9))* Little, Brown Bks. for Young Readers.

—Suddenly Supernatural: School Spirit. 2010. (Suddenly Supernatural Ser.: 1). (ENG.). 336p. (J). (gr. 3-7). pap. 7.99 *(978-0-316-07821-4(2))* Little, Brown Bks. for Young Readers.

Kinard, Kami. The Boy Prediction: Notes & Observations of Tabitha Reddy. 2014. (ENG., Illus.). 272p. (J). (gr. 3-7). 12.99 *(978-0-545-57586-7(9)*, Scholastic Pr.) Scholastic, Inc.

—The Boy Project. 2016. (ENG.). 256p. (J). (gr. 4-7). pap. 6.99 *(978-0-545-34516-3(2)*, Scholastic Paperbacks) Scholastic, Inc.

Kindig, Tess. Luv @ First Site. 2004. 128p. (J). pap. 5.99 *(978-1-4003-0325-0(7))* Nelson, Thomas Inc.

King, A. S. Ask the Passengers. 2013. (ENG.). 336p. (YA). (gr. 10-17). pap. 10.99 *(978-0-316-19467-9(0))* Little, Brown Bks. for Young Readers.

—I Crawl Through It. 2015. (ENG.). 336p. (YA). (gr. 10-17). 18.00 *(978-0-316-33409-9(X))* Little, Brown Bks. for Young Readers.

King, Bart. The Drake Equation. 2016. (ENG.). 320p. (J). (gr. 3-7). 16.99 *(978-1-4847-2552-8(2))* Disney Pr.

—The Drake Equation. 2017. (ENG.). 320p. (J). (gr. 3-7). pap. 7.99 ***(978-1-4847-2554-2(9))*** Hyperion Bks. for Children.

King, J. Eric & Graham, Greg. Byron Carmichael Book One: The Human Corpse Trade. Mizer, Lindsay, ed. Warner, Michael, illus. 2008. (ENG.). 408p. (gr. 8-12). 18.95 *(978-0-615-15770-2(X))* G & K Publishing.

King, Jane. Welcome to Chillsville Elementary. 2013. (Ghoul School Ser.: 1). (ENG.). 80p. (J). (gr. 1-4). pap. 13.99 *(978-1-4814-2162-1(X)*, Simon & Schuster/Paula Wiseman Bks.) Simon & Schuster/Paula Wiseman Bks.

King, Zelda. The Class Surprise. 2006. (Neighborhood Readers Ser.). (ENG.). 16p. (gr. 1-3). pap. 6.50 *(978-1-4042-6994-1(0)*, Rosen Classroom) Rosen Publishing Group, Inc., The.

Kinney, Jeff. Cabin Fever. 2011. (Diary of a Wimpy Kid Ser.). (ENG., Illus.). 224p. (J). (gr. 3-7). 13.95 *(978-1-4197-0223-5(8)*, Amulet Bks.) Abrams, Inc.

—Cabin Fever, 2 vols. 2011. (Diary of a Wimpy Kid Ser.: 6). (J). 44.75 *(978-1-4640-2151-0(1))*; 44.75 *(978-1-4640-2152-7(X))*; 46.75 *(978-1-4640-2148-0(1))*; *(978-1-4640-2149-7(X))*; 1.25 *(978-1-4640-4524-0(0))* Recorded Bks., Inc.

—Cabin Fever. 2011. (Diary of a Wimpy Kid Ser.: 6). (J). lib. bdg. 25.70 *(978-0-606-23667-6(8)*, Turtleback) Turtleback Bks.

—Carnet de Bord de Greg Heffley. Zimmerman, Natalie, tr. 2012. (Journal d'un Degonfle Ser.: Vol. 1). (FRE., Illus.). 223p. (J). (gr. 4-8). pap. *(978-2-02-101196-8(8))* Editions du Seuil.

—El Diario de Greg, un Renacuajo. Morán, Esteban, tr. 2008. (SPA.). 218p. (J). (gr. 3-6). 17.99 *(978-1-933032-52-8(9))* Lectorum Pubns., Inc.

—Diary of a Wimpy Kid. 2014. pap. *(978-1-4197-1499-3(6))* 2013. pap. *(978-1-4197-1176-3(8))* 2009. pap. *(978-0-8109-8888-0(7))* 2007. (Diary of a Wimpy Kid Ser.). (ENG., Illus.). 224p. (J). (gr. 2-8). 13.95 *(978-0-8109-9313-6(9))* 2007. pap. *(978-0-8109-8893-4(3))* 2007. pap. *(978-0-8109-8292-5(7))* 2007. (Diary of a Wimpy Kid Ser.: Bk. 1). 217p. pap. *(978-0-8109-9455-3(0))*Bks. 1-4. 2014. (ENG.). 896p. (J). (gr. 3-7). 56.00 *(978-1-4197-1669-0(7))* Abrams, Inc. (Amulet Bks.).

—Diary of a Wimpy Kid. (Diary of a Wimpy Kid Ser.). (CHI., Illus.). (J). 2009. (gr. 4-8). ***(978-986-84847-4-0(X))*** 2008. (gr. 3-7). ***(978-986-84847-0-2(7))*** DaskoviK, Izdatel'sko-torgovaja korporacija.

—Diary of a Wimpy Kid. 2013. (Diary of a Wimpy Kid Ser.: 16). (CHI.). (J). pap. 13.95 *(978-7-5405-7891-6(2))* Guangdong New Era Publishing Hse. CHN. Dist: Chinasprout, Inc.

—Diary of a Wimpy Kid. 2009. (Diary of a Wimpy Kid Ser.: Bk. 1). 1.00 *(978-1-4074-4434-5(4))* 2008. (Diary of a Wimpy Kid Ser.: 1). (J). 75.75 *(978-1-4361-3290-9(8))* 2008. (Diary of a Wimpy Kid Ser.: 1). (J). 44.75 *(978-1-4281-8196-0(2))* 2008. (Diary of a Wimpy Kid Ser.: 1). (J). 46.75 *(978-1-4281-8194-6(6))* 2008. (Diary of a Wimpy Kid Ser.: 1). (J). 1.25 *(978-1-4281-8191-5(1))* 2008. (Diary of a Wimpy Kid Ser.: 1). (J). 173.75 *(978-1-4281-8195-3(4))* 2008. (Diary of a Wimpy Kid Ser.: 1). (J). 46.75 *(978-1-4281-8198-4(9))* 2008. (Diary of a Wimpy Kid Ser.: 1). (J). 44.75 *(978-1-4281-8200-4(4))* Recorded Bks., Inc.

—Diary of a Wimpy Kid. 2007. (Diary of a Wimpy Kid Ser.: 1). (Illus.). 217p. (J). lib. bdg. 25.70 *(978-0-606-23662-1(7)*, Turtleback) Turtleback Bks.

—Hard Luck. 2013. (Diary of a Wimpy Kid Ser.: Bk. 8). (ENG., Illus.). 224p. (J). (gr. 3-7). 13.95 *(978-1-4197-1132-9(6)*, Amulet Bks.) Abrams, Inc.

—Hard Luck. 2013. (Diary of a Wimpy Kid Ser.: 8). (J). lib. bdg. 25.70 *(978-0-606-32062-7(8)*, Turtleback) Turtleback Bks.

—The Last Straw. 2009. (Diary of a Wimpy Kid Ser.). (Illus.). (J). (gr. 3-7). (ENG.). 224p. 13.95 *(978-0-8109-7068-7(6)*, Amulet Bks.); 218p. pap. *(978-0-8109-7108-0(9))* Abrams, Inc.

—The Last Straw. 2009. (Diary of a Wimpy Kid Ser.: 3). (ENG.). 224p. (J). (gr. 4-6). pap. 17.95 *(978-1-4395-8262-6(9)*, 0008062297, Paw Prints) Baker & Taylor, CATS.

—The Last Straw. 2009. (Diary of a Wimpy Kid Ser.: Bk. 3). (JPN., Illus.). 221p. (J). *(978-4-591-10910-6(0))* Poplar Publishing.

—The Last Straw. 2010. (Diary of a Wimpy Kid Ser.: 3). (J). 1.25 *(978-1-4407-2984-3(0))* 2010. (Diary of a Wimpy Kid Ser.: 3). (J). 46.75 *(978-1-4407-2976-8(X))* 2009. (Diary of a Wimpy Kid Ser.: 3). (J). 75.75 *(978-1-4407-2986-7(7))* 2009. (Diary of a Wimpy Kid Ser.: 3). (J). 44.75 *(978-1-4407-2982-9(4))* 2009. (Diary of a Wimpy Kid Ser.: 3). (J). 44.75 *(978-1-4407-2978-2(6))* 2009. (Diary of a Wimpy Kid Ser.: 3). (J). 45.75 *(978-1-4407-2980-5(8))* 2009. (Diary of a Wimpy Kid Ser.: 3). (J). 173.75 *(978-1-4407-2977-5(8))* 2009. (Diary of a Wimpy Kid Ser.: Bk. 3). 1.00 *(978-1-4416-1788-0(4))* Recorded Bks., Inc.

—The Last Straw. 2009. (Diary of a Wimpy Kid Ser.: 3). (Illus.). 217p. (J). lib. bdg. 25.70 *(978-0-606-23664-5(3)*, Turtleback) Turtleback Bks.

—Rodrick Rules. 2008. (Diary of a Wimpy Kid Ser.). (Illus.). (J). (ENG.). 224p. (gr. 3-7). 13.95 *(978-0-8109-9473-7(9)*, Amulet Bks.); 216p. pap. 4.99 *(978-0-8109-9552-9(2))* Abrams, Inc.

—Rodrick Rules. 2008. (Diary of a Wimpy Kid Ser.: Bk. 2). (JPN., Illus.). 220p. (J). *(978-4-591-10464-4(8))* Poplar Publishing.

—Rodrick Rules, 2 vols. (Diary of a Wimpy Kid Ser.: 2). (J). 2010. 173.75 *(978-1-4361-3864-2(7))* 2010. 75.75 *(978-1-4407-0420-8(1))* 2009. 1.25 *(978-1-4361-3860-4(4))* 2009. 46.75 *(978-1-4361-3863-5(9))* 2009. 44.75 *(978-1-4361-3869-7(8))* 2009. 44.75 *(978-1-4361-3865-9(5))* 2009. (gr. 4-8). 46.75 *(978-1-4361-3867-3(1))* Recorded Bks., Inc.

—Rodrick Rules. 2008. (Diary of a Wimpy Kid Ser.: 2). (J). lib. bdg. 25.70 *(978-0-606-23663-8(5)*, Turtleback) Turtleback Bks.

—The Third Wheel. 2012. (ENG.). (J). (gr. 3-7). pap. 8.49 *(978-1-4197-0729-2(9))* Abrams, Inc.

Kirby, Stan. Captain Awesome & the Easter Egg Bandit. O'Connor, George, illus. 2015. (Captain Awesome Ser.: 13). (ENG.). 128p. (J). (gr. k-4). pap. 5.99 *(978-1-4814-2558-2(7)*, Little Simon) Little Simon.

—Captain Awesome & the Missing Elephants. O'Connor, George, illus. 2014. (Captain Awesome Ser.: 10). (ENG.). 128p. (J). (gr. k-4). 16.99 *(978-1-4424-8995-0(2))*; pap. 5.99 *(978-1-4424-8994-3(4))* Little Simon. (Little Simon).

—Captain Awesome & the New Kid. O'Connor, George, illus. 2012. (Captain Awesome Ser.: 3). (ENG.). 128p. (J). (gr. k-4). 16.99 *(978-1-4424-4200-9(X))*; pap. 5.99 *(978-1-4424-4199-6(2))* Little Simon. (Little Simon).

—Captain Awesome & the New Kid. 2012. (Captain Awesome Ser.: 3). lib. bdg. 16.00 *(978-0-606-26324-5(1)*, Turtleback) Turtleback Bks.

—Captain Awesome & the Ultimate Spelling Bee. O'Connor, George, illus. 2013. (Captain Awesome Ser.: 7). (ENG.). 128p. (J). (gr. k-4). 17.99 *(978-1-4424-5156-8(4))*; pap. 5.99 *(978-1-4424-5158-2(0))* Little Simon. (Little Simon).

—Captain Awesome & the Ultimate Spelling Bee. 2013. (Captain Awesome Ser.: 7). lib. bdg. 16.00 *(978-0-606-27035-9(3)*, Turtleback) Turtleback Bks.

—Captain Awesome Gets Crushed. O'Connor, George, illus. 2013. (Captain Awesome Ser.: 9). (ENG.). 128p. (J). (gr. k-2). pap. 5.99 *(978-1-4424-8212-8(5))*; 16.99 *(978-1-4424-8213-5(3))* Little Simon. (Little Simon).

—Captain Awesome Gets Crushed. 2013. (Captain Awesome Ser.: 9). lib. bdg. 16.00 *(978-0-606-32331-4(7)*, Turtleback) Turtleback Bks.

—Captain Awesome Saves the Winter Wonderland. O'Connor, George, illus. 2012. (Captain Awesome Ser.: 6). (ENG.). 128p. (J). (gr. k-4). 16.99 *(978-1-4424-4335-8(9))*; pap. 5.99 *(978-1-4424-4334-1(0))* Little Simon. (Little Simon).

—Captain Awesome Saves the Winter Wonderland. 2012. (Captain Awesome Ser.: 6). lib. bdg. 16.00 *(978-0-606-26894-3(4)*, Turtleback) Turtleback Bks.

—Captain Awesome to the Rescue! O'Connor, George, illus. 2012. (Captain Awesome Ser.: 1). (ENG.). 128p. (J). (gr. k-2). 16.99 *(978-1-4424-4090-6(2))*; pap. 5.99 *(978-1-4424-3561-2(5))* Little Simon. (Little Simon).

—Captain Awesome to the Rescue! 2012. (Captain Awesome Ser.: 1). lib. bdg. 16.00 *(978-0-606-26322-1(5)*, Turtleback) Turtleback Bks.

—Captain Awesome vs. the Spooky, Scary House. O'Connor, George, illus. 2013. (Captain Awesome Ser.: 8). (ENG.). 128p. (J). (gr. k-2). 16.99 *(978-1-4424-7255-6(3))*; pap. 5.99 *(978-1-4424-7254-9(5))* Little Simon. (Little Simon).

—Captain Awesome vs. the Spooky, Scary House. 2013. (Captain Awesome Ser.: 8). lib. bdg. 16.00 *(978-0-606-32048-1(2)*, Turtleback) Turtleback Bks.

Kirk, David. Truckeroo School. Kirk, David, illus. 2017. (ENG., Illus.). 40p. (J). 17.99 *(978-1-250-01690-4(8)*, 9781250016904) Feiwel & Friends.

Kittle, Katrina. Reasons to Be Happy. 2011. (ENG.). 288p. (J). (gr. 6-8). pap. 10.99 *(978-1-4022-6020-9(2)*, Sourcebooks Jabberwocky) Sourcebooks, Inc.

Kittscher, Kristen. The Wig in the Window. (J). (gr. 3-7). 2016. 384p. pap. 6.99 *(978-0-06-211051-0(9))* 2013. (ENG.). 368p. 16.99 *(978-0-06-211050-3(0))* HarperCollins Pubs.

Klass, David. Home of the Braves. 2004. 355p. (YA). (gr. 7-12). 17.65 *(978-0-7569-2805-6(2))* Perfection Learning Corp.

—Losers Take All. 2015. (ENG.). 320p. (YA). (gr. 7). 17.99 *(978-0-374-30136-1(0)*, 9780374301361, Farrar, Straus & Giroux (BYR)) Farrar, Straus & Giroux.

—Losers Take All. 2016. (YA). lib. bdg. 20.85 *(978-0-606-39480-2(X))* Turtleback Bks.

—You Don't Know Me. 2010. (ENG.). 288p. (YA). (gr. 9-12). pap. 9.99 *(978-0-312-65302-6(6))* Square Fish.

Klass, David & Klass, Perri. Second Impact. 2013. (ENG.). 288p. (YA). (gr. 7). 16.99 *(978-0-374-37996-4(3)*, 9780374379964, Farrar, Straus & Giroux (BYR)) Farrar, Straus & Giroux.

—Second Impact. 2014. (ENG.). 304p. (YA). (gr. 7). pap. 10.99 *(978-1-250-04436-5(7)*, 9781250044365) Square Fish.

Klein, Abby. Don't Sit on My Lunch! Mckinley, John & McKinley, John, illus. 2005. (Ready, Freddy! Ser.: 4). (ENG.). 96p. (J). (gr. -1-3). 5.99 *(978-0-439-55602-6(3)*, Blue Sky Pr., The) Scholastic, Inc.

—The One Hundredth Day of School! McKinley, John, illus. 2008. (Ready, Freddy! Ser.: Bk. 13). 94p. (J). (gr. -1-3). 11.65 *(978-0-7569-8836-4(5))* Perfection Learning Corp.

—Ready, Set, Snow! McKinley, John, illus. 2009. (Ready, Freddy! Ser.: 16). (ENG.). 96p. (J). (gr. -1-3). pap. 5.99 *(978-0-439-89596-5(0))* Scholastic, Inc.

—Second Grade Rules! McKinley, John, illus. 2014. 85p. (J). pap. *(978-0-545-69031-7(5))* Scholastic, Inc.

—Secret Santa Surprise! McKinley, John, illus. 2015. 86p. (J). ***(978-0-545-86357-5(0))*** Scholastic, Inc.

—Thanks for Giving. McKinley, John, illus. 2009. (Ready, Freddy! Reader List: No. 4). 32p. (J). pap. *(978-0-545-14176-5(1))* Scholastic, Inc.

—Thanksgiving Turkey Trouble. McKinley, John, illus. 2008. (Ready, Freddy! Ser.: Bk. 15). 95p. (gr. -1-3). 16.00 *(978-0-7569-8838-8(1))* Perfection Learning Corp.

—Tooth Trouble. 2011. (Ready, Freddy Ser.: Bk. 1). 8.32 *(978-0-7848-3613-2(2),* Everbind) Marco Bk. Co.

Klein, Adria F. Max Goes to School. Gallagher-Cole, Mernie, illus. 2007. (Read-It! Readers: the Life of Max Ser.). (ENG.). 24p. (gr. -1-2). per. 3.95 *(978-1-4048-3059-2(6),* Easy Readers) Picture Window Bks.

—Max Va a la Escuela, 1 vol. Lozano, Clara, tr. Gallagher-Cole, Mernie, illus. 2007. (Read-It! Readers en Español: la Vida de Max Ser.). (SPA.). 24p. (gr. -1-3). per. 3.95 *(978-1-4048-3037-0(5),* Easy Readers) Picture Window Bks.

—Tool School. Rowland, Andrew, illus. 2013. (Tool School Ser.). (ENG.). 32p. (gr. -1-1). 181.20 *(978-1-4342-8842-4(0))* Stone Arch Bks.

Klein, Jen. Shuffle, Repeat. (ENG.). (YA). (gr. 7). 2017. 352p. pap. 9.99 ***(978-0-553-50985-4(3),*** Ember) 2016. 336p. 17.99 *(978-0-553-50982-3(9),* Random Hse. Bks. for Young Readers) Random Hse. Children's Bks.

Kleinman, Estelle. The City of Ember. Friedland, Joyce & Kessler, Rikki, eds. 2007. (Novel-Ties Ser.). (Illus.). 31p. pap. 16.95 *(978-0-7675-3754-4(8))* Learning Links Inc.

—Tears of a Tiger. Friedland, Joyce & Kessler, Rikki, eds. 2008. (Novel-Ties Ser.). (Illus.). 31p. pap. 16.95 *(978-0-7675-4259-3(2))* Learning Links Inc.

Kleinman, Liza & Gideon, Brook. Azalea, Unschooled, 1 vol. 2015. (ENG.). 140p. pap. 16.95 *(978-1-939017-58-1(0),* d2789d05-6972-4d6e-b723-d28acd3a7d7f) Islandport Pr., Inc.

Klimpton, Diana. Amy Wild, Animal Talker - the Musical Mouse. 2013. pap. 4.99 *(978-0-7945-3145-4(8),* Usborne) EDC Publishing.

Kline, Lisa Williams. Write Before Your Eyes. 2010. (ENG.). 192p. (J). (gr. 3-7). 6.99 *(978-0-440-42251-8(5),* Yearling) Random Hse. Children's Bks.

Kline, Suzy. Horrible Harry & the Dead Letters. Remkiewicz, Frank et al, illus. 2009. (Horrible Harry Ser.). (ENG.). 80p. (J). (gr. 2-4). 3.99 *(978-0-14-241457-6(3),* Puffin Books) Penguin Young Readers Group.

—Horrible Harry & the Dragon War. Remkiewicz, Frank, illus. 2003. (Horrible Harry Ser.). (ENG.). 64p. (J). (gr. 2-4). 4.99 *(978-0-14-250166-5(2),* Puffin Books) Penguin Young Readers Group.

—Horrible Harry & the Dragon War. 2003. (Horrible Harry Ser.: 14). lib. bdg. 14.75 *(978-0-613-92539-6(4),* Turtleback) Turtleback Bks.

—Horrible Harry & the Goog. Remkiewicz, Frank & Frank, Remkiewicz, illus. 2006. (Horrible Harry Ser.). (ENG.). 64p. (J). (gr. 2-4). pap. 4.99 *(978-0-14-240728-8(3),* Puffin Books) Penguin Young Readers Group.

—Horrible Harry & the Goog. Remkiewicz, Frank, illus. 2006. (Horrible Harry Ser.). 56p. (gr. 2-5). 14.00 *(978-0-7569-6948-6(4))* Perfection Learning Corp.

—Horrible Harry & the Hallway Bully. Wummer, Amy, illus. (Horrible Harry Ser.: 31). (ENG.). 80p. (J). 2015. (gr. 1-3). 4.99 *(978-0-14-750967-3(X),* Puffin Books) 2014. (gr. 2-4). 14.99 *(978-0-670-01551-1(2),* Viking Books for Young Readers) Penguin Young Readers Group.

—Horrible Harry & the Holidaze. Remkiewicz, Frank, illus. 2004. (Horrible Harry Ser.). (ENG.). 80p. (J). (gr. 2-4). 4.99 *(978-0-14-240205-4(2),* Puffin Books) Penguin Young Readers Group.

—Horrible Harry & the June Box. Wummer, Amy, illus. 2012. (Horrible Harry Ser.). (ENG.). 80p. (J). (gr. 2-4). pap. 4.99 *(978-0-14-242185-7(5),* Puffin Books) Penguin Young Readers Group.

—Horrible Harry & the Locked Closet. Remkiewicz, Frank, illus. 2005. (Horrible Harry Ser.). 68p. (gr. 2-5). 14.00 *(978-0-7569-5825-1(3))* Perfection Learning Corp.

—Horrible Harry & the Missing Diamond. Wummer, Amy, illus. (Horrible Harry Ser.: 30). (ENG.). 80p. (J). (gr. 2-4). 2014. pap. 4.99 *(978-0-14-242228-1(2),* Puffin Books) 2013. 14.99 *(978-0-670-01426-2(5),* Viking Books for Young Readers) Penguin Young Readers Group.

—Horrible Harry & the Mud Gremlins. Remkiewicz, Frank, illus. 2004. (Horrible Harry Ser.). 50p. (gr. 2). 14.00 *(978-0-7569-2815-5(X))* Perfection Learning Corp.

—Horrible Harry & the Scarlet Scissors. Wummer, Amy, illus. (Horrible Harry Ser.). (ENG.). 80p. (J). (gr. 2-4). 2013. pap. 4.99 *(978-0-14-242671-5(7),* Puffin Books) 2012. 14.99 *(978-0-670-01306-7(4),* Viking Books for Young Readers) Penguin Young Readers Group.

—Horrible Harry & the Secret Treasure. Wummer, Amy, illus. (Horrible Harry Ser.). (ENG.). 80p. (J). (gr. 2-4). 2012. 4.99 *(978-0-14-242021-8(2),* Puffin Books) 2011. 14.99 *(978-0-670-01181-0(9),* Viking Books for Young Readers) Penguin Young Readers Group.

—Horrible Harry & the Stolen Cookie. Wummer, Amy, illus. 2013. (Horrible Harry Ser.: 29). (ENG.). 80p. (J). (gr. 2-4). 14.99 *(978-0-670-01425-5(7),* Viking Books for Young Readers) Penguin Young Readers Group.

—Horrible Harry & the Triple Revenge. Remkiewicz, Frank, illus. (Horrible Harry Ser.). (ENG.). 64p. (J). (gr. 2-4). 2008. 4.99 *(978-0-14-241081-3(0),* Puffin Books) 2006. 13.99 *(978-0-670-06077-1(1),* Viking Books for Young Readers) Penguin Young Readers Group.

—Horrible Harry & the Wedding Spies. Wummer, Amy, illus. 2016. (Horrible Harry Ser.: 32). (ENG.). 80p. (J). (gr. 2-5). 4.99 *(978-0-14-750968-0(8),* Puffin Books) Penguin Young Readers Group.

—Horrible Harry & the Wedding Spies. 2016. (Horrible Harry Ser.: 32). lib. bdg. 14.75 *(978-0-606-38389-9(1))* Turtleback Bks.

—Horrible Harry Cracks the Code. Remkiewicz, Frank, illus. 2008. (Horrible Harry Ser.). (ENG.). 80p. (J). (gr. 2-4). 4.99 *(978-0-14-241247-3(3),* Puffin Books) Penguin Young Readers Group.

—Horrible Harry Goes Cuckoo. Wummer, Amy, illus. 2011. (Horrible Harry Ser.). (ENG.). 80p. (J). (gr. 2-4). 4.99 *(978-0-14-241876-5(5),* Puffin Books) Penguin Young Readers Group.

—Horrible Harry Goes to Sea: Puffine Chapters. Remkiewicz, Frank, illus. 2003. (Horrible Harry Ser.). (ENG.). 64p. (J). (gr. 2-4). 4.99 *(978-0-14-250002-6(X),* Puffin Books) Penguin Young Readers Group.

—Horrible Harry Goes to Sea: Puffine Chapters. 2003. (Horrible Harry Ser.: 13). (gr. 3-6). lib. bdg. 14.75 *(978-0-613-61629-4(4),* Turtleback) Turtleback Bks.

—Horrible Harry on the Ropes. Remkiewicz, Frank & Wummer, Amy, illus. 2011. (Horrible Harry Ser.). (ENG.). 80p. (J). (gr. 2-4). 4.99 *(978-0-14-241695-2(9),* Puffin Books) Penguin Young Readers Group.

—Horrible Harry on the Ropes, 24 vols. Wummer, Amy, illus. 2009. (Horrible Harry Ser.: 24). (ENG.). 80p. (J). (gr. 2-4). 14.99 *(978-0-670-01097-4(9),* Viking Books for Young Readers) Penguin Young Readers Group.

—Horrible Harry Takes the Cake. Remkiewicz, Frank, illus. 2007. (Horrible Harry Ser.). (ENG.). 64p. (J). (gr. 2-4). 4.99 *(978-0-14-240939-8(1),* Puffin Books) Penguin Young Readers Group.

—Horrible Harry Takes the Cake. Remkiewicz, Frank, illus. 2007. (Horrible Harry Ser.). 45p. (gr. 2-5). 14.00 *(978-0-7569-8158-7(1))* Perfection Learning Corp.

Kline, Suzy & Remkiewicz, Frank. Horrible Harry Bugs the Three Bears. Remkiewicz, Frank & Remkiewicz, illus. 2009. (Horrible Harry Ser.). (ENG.). 80p. (J). (gr. 2-4). 4.99 *(978-0-14-241295-4(3),* Puffin Books) Penguin Young Readers Group.

Kline, Suzy & Wells, Rosemary. Horrible Harry & the Birthday Girl. Wummer, Amy, illus. 2016. (Horrible Harry Ser.: 34). (ENG.). 80p. (J). (gr. 2-5). bds. 14.99 *(978-0-451-47331-8(0),* Viking Books for Young Readers) Penguin Young Readers Group.

—Horrible Harry & the Top-Secret Hideout. Wummer, Amy, illus. 2015. (Horrible Harry Ser.: 33). (ENG.). 80p. (J). (gr. 1-3). bds. 14.99 *(978-0-451-47329-5(9),* Viking Books for Young Readers) Penguin Young Readers Group.

—Horrible Harry & the Wedding Spies. Wummer, Amy, illus. 2015. (Horrible Harry Ser.: 32). (ENG.). 80p. (J). (gr. 2-5). bds. 14.99 *(978-0-670-01552-8(0),* Viking Books for Young Readers) Penguin Young Readers Group.

Klise, James. Love Drugged. 2010. (ENG.). 312p. (YA). (gr. 7-18). pap. 9.95 *(978-0-7387-2175-0(1),* Flux) North Star Editions.

Klise, Kate. Regarding the Bathrooms: A Privy to the Past. Klise, Kate & Klise, M. Sarah, illus. 2008. (Regarding The ... Ser.: Bk. 4). (ENG.). 160p. (J). (gr. 2-5). pap. 6.99 *(978-0-15-206261-3(0))* Houghton Mifflin Harcourt Publishing Co.

—Regarding the Sink: Where, Oh Where, Did Waters Go? Klise, M. Sarah, illus. 2006. (Regarding The ... Ser.: Bk. 2). (ENG.). 144p. (J). (gr. 2-5). pap. 6.99 *(978-0-15-205544-8(4))* Houghton Mifflin Harcourt Publishing Co.

Klise, Kate & Klise, Kate. Regarding the Bees: A Lesson, in Letters, on Honey, Dating, & Other Sticky Subjects. Klise, M. Sarah, illus. 2009. (Regarding The ... Ser.: Bk. 5). (ENG.). 144p. (J). (gr. 2-5). pap. 6.99 *(978-0-15-206668-0(3))* Houghton Mifflin Harcourt Publishing Co.

Klise, Kate & Klise, M. Sarah. Regarding the Trees: A Splintered Saga Rooted in Secrets. 2007. (Regarding The ... Ser.: Bk. 3). (ENG., Illus.). 160p. (J). (gr. 2-5). pap. 7.99 *(978-0-15-206090-9(1))* Houghton Mifflin Harcourt Publishing Co.

—The Show Must Go On! 2014. (Three-Ring Rascals Ser.: 1). (ENG., Illus.). 160p. (J). (gr. 2-5). pap. 5.95 *(978-1-61620-406-8(0),* 73406) Algonquin Bks. of Chapel Hill.

Knife, Ivan M. Uses the. Black Thursday. 2010. 108p. pap. 15.99 *(978-1-4500-6311-1(X))* Xlibris Corp.

Knight, Chris. Karen Bighead: The Story of a Little Girl with a Big Head. 2011. (Illus.). 24p. 12.12 *(978-1-4520-7730-7(4))* AuthorHouse.

Knight, Karsten. Wildefire. 2011. (ENG.). 400p. (YA). (gr. 9-18). 16.99 *(978-1-4424-2117-2(7),* Simon & Schuster Bks. For Young Readers) Simon & Schuster Bks. For Young Readers.

Knowles, Jo. Read Between the Lines. 2015. (ENG.). 336p. (YA). (gr. 9). 16.99 *(978-0-7636-6387-2(5))* Candlewick Pr.

Knowlton, Laurie. N 2 Deep. 2004. 128p. (J). pap. 5.99 *(978-1-4003-0327-4(3))* Nelson, Thomas Inc.

Knudsen, Michelle. Argus. Wesson, Andrea, illus. 2011. (ENG.). 32p. (J). (gr. -1-3). 15.99 *(978-0-7636-3790-3(4))* Candlewick Pr.

—El Caso de Vivian la Vampira. Wummer, Amy, illus. 2008. (Science Solves It! en Espanol Ser.). (SPA.). 32p. (J). (gr. -1-3). pap. 5.95 *(978-1-57565-277-1(3))* Kane Press, Inc.

—El Caso de Vivian la Vampira (the Case of Vampire Vivian) Wummer, Amy, illus. 2009. (Science Solves It! (r) en Espanol Ser.). (SPA.). (gr. 1-3). pap. 33.92 *(978-0-7613-4800-9(X))* Lerner Publishing Group.

—A Slimy Story. Billin-Frye, Paige, illus. 2004. 32p. (J). lib. bdg. 20.00 *(978-1-4242-1150-0(6))* Fitzgerald Bks.

—A Slimy Story. Billin-Frye, Paige, illus. 2004. (Science Solves It! Ser.). 32p. (J). (gr. -1-3). pap. 5.95 *(978-1-57565-144-6(0))* Kane Press, Inc.

Knudsen, Shannon. Rise Above. 2014. (Red Zone Ser.: 6). (ENG.). 104p. (YA). (gr. 6-12). pap. 7.95 *(978-1-4677-4476-8(X),* Darby Creek) Lerner Publishing Group.

—Testing the Truth. 2015. (ENG.). 104p. (YA). (gr. 6-12). 27.99 *(978-1-4677-5708-9(X))* Lerner Publishing Group.

Knudson, Michelle. The Case of Vampire Vivian. Wummer, Amy, illus. 2003. (Science Solves It! Ser.). 32p. (J). pap. 5.95 *(978-1-57565-127-9(0))* Kane Press, Inc.

Knudson, Mike & Wilkinson, Steve. Bases Loaded. 2011. (Raymond & Graham Ser.). (ENG.). 160p. (J). (gr. 3-7). 6.99 *(978-0-14-241751-5(3),* Puffin Books) Penguin Young Readers Group.

—Dancing Dudes. Curtis, Stacy, illus. 2010. (Raymond & Graham Ser.). (ENG.). 144p. (J). (gr. 3-7). 6.99 *(978-0-14-241508-5(1),* Puffin Books) Penguin Young Readers Group.

—Raymond & Graham Rule the School. Curtis, Stacy, illus. 2009. (Raymond & Graham Ser.). (ENG.). 144p. (J). (gr. 3-7). 6.99 *(978-0-14-241426-2(3),* Puffin Books) Penguin Young Readers Group.

Kobayashi, Jin. School Rumble. (JPN., Illus.). (YA). Vol. 1. pap. *(978-4-06-363244-6(X))* Vol. 2. 162p. pap. *(978-4-06-363290-3(3))* Vol. 3. 158p. pap. *(978-4-06-363321-4(7))* Vol. 4. 154p. pap. *(978-4-06-363346-7(2))* Kodansha, Ltd.

Kocek, Sara. Promise Me Something. 2013. (ENG.). 320p. (YA). (gr. 8-12). 16.99 *(978-0-8075-6641-1(1))* Whitman, Albert & Co.

Koch, Edward R. Relay. 2009. 188p. pap. 12.95 *(978-1-59858-989-4(X))* Dog Ear Publishing, LLC.

Koertge, Ron. Now Playing: Stoner & Spaz II. 2011. (ENG., Illus.). 224p. (YA). (gr. 9-18). 16.99 *(978-0-7636-5081-0(1))* Candlewick Pr.

—Stoner & Spaz. 2011. (ENG., Illus.). 192p. (YA). (gr. 9). pap. 7.99 *(978-0-7636-5757-4(3))* Candlewick Pr.

Koertge, Ronald. Where the Kissing Never Stops. 2005. (ENG.). 256p. (YA). (gr. 9-18). per. 6.99 *(978-0-7636-2696-9(1))* Candlewick Pr.

Kogler, Jennifer. The Otherworldlies. 2008. 400p. (J). lib. bdg. 17.89 *(978-0-06-073960-7(6));* (ENG.). (gr. 5-18). 16.99 *(978-0-06-073959-1(2))* HarperCollins Pubs. (Eos).

Kogler, Jennifer Anne. The Siren's Cry. 2011. (ENG.). 384p. (YA). (gr. 8). 16.99 *(978-0-06-199443-2(X),* HarperTeen) HarperCollins Pubs.

Koja, Kathe. Buddha Boy. 2004. (ENG.). 128p. (YA). (gr. 7-11). reprint ed. 6.99 *(978-0-14-240209-2(5),* Speak) Penguin Young Readers Group.

—Buddha Boy. 2004. 117p. (gr. 3-7). 16.00 *(978-0-7569-3117-9(7))* Perfection Learning Corp.

—Straydog. 2004. (ENG.). 128p. (YA). (gr. 7-18). reprint ed. 7.99 *(978-0-14-240071-5(8),* Speak) Penguin Young Readers Group.

—Talk. 2008. (ENG.). 144p. (YA). (gr. 7-12). per. 16.99 *(978-0-312-37605-5(7),* 9780312376055) Square Fish.

Kolb, Joseph J. Reservation Dreams. 2004. 185p. pap. 24.95 *(978-1-4137-3054-8(X))* America Star Bks.

Kolczynski, Sean. The Night Before Middle School! 2012. 28p. pap. 21.99 *(978-1-4771-4794-8(2))* Xlibris Corp.

Konigsberg, Bill. Honestly Ben. 2017. (ENG.). 336p. (J). (gr. 9). 17.99 *(978-0-545-85826-7(7))* Scholastic, Inc.

—Openly Straight. (ENG.). 336p. (J). (gr. 9). 2015. pap. 9.99 *(978-0-545-79865-5(5))* 2013. 17.99 *(978-0-545-50989-3(0))* Scholastic, Inc. (Levine, Arthur A. Bks.).

Konigsburg, E. L. The View from Saturday. 280p. (YA). (gr. 5-18). pap. 4.95 *(978-0-8072-1511-1(2),* Listening Library) Random Hse. Audio Publishing Group.

Kopley, Richard. The Remarkable David Wordsworth. Fazio, Michael, illus. 2013. 30p. (J). pap. *(978-1-936172-67-2(4))* Elfrig Publishing.

Korelitz, Jean Hanff. Interference Powder, 0 vols. 2006. (ENG.). 146p. (J). (gr. 4-7). pap. 7.99 *(978-0-7614-5275-1(3),* 9780761452751, Amazon Children's Publishing) Amazon Publishing.

—Interference Powder, 1 vol. 2003. (ENG.). 300p. (J). 15.95 *(978-0-7614-5139-6(0))* Marshall Cavendish Corp.

Korman, Gordon. Framed. (J). 2011. (ENG.). 240p. (gr. 3-7). pap. 6.99 *(978-0-545-19763-2(5),* Scholastic Paperbacks) 2010. *(978-0-545-27081-6(2),* Scholastic Pr.) 2010. (Swindle Ser.: 3). (ENG.). 240p. (gr. 4-7). 16.99 *(978-0-545-17849-5(5),* Scholastic Pr.) Scholastic, Inc.

—Jake, Reinvented (repackage) 2017. (ENG.). 192p. (J). (gr. 5-9). pap. 8.99 ***(978-1-4847-9842-3(2))*** Hyperion Bks. for Children.

—No More Dead Dogs. 2017. Orig. Title: Touchdown Stage Left. (J). lib. bdg. 17.20 ***(978-0-606-40570-6(4))*** Turtleback Bks.

—No More Dead Dogs (repackage) 2017. (ENG.). 240p. (J). (gr. 5-9). pap. 6.99 *(978-1-4847-9844-7(9))* Hyperion Bks. for Children.

—Pop. 272p. (YA). (gr. 8). 2011. pap. 9.99 *(978-0-06-174261-3(9))* 2009. 16.99 *(978-0-06-174228-6(7))* HarperCollins Pubs.

—Restart. 2017. (ENG.). 256p. (J). (gr. 3-7). 16.99 ***(978-1-338-05377-7(9),*** Scholastic Pr.) Scholastic, Inc.

—Schooled. 2008. (ENG.). 224p. (J). (gr. 3-7). pap. 6.99 *(978-1-4231-0516-9(8))* Hyperion Bks. for Children.

—Schooled. 2010. 17.00 *(978-1-60686-894-2(2))* Perfection Learning Corp.

—Schooled. (J). 2012. 1.25 *(978-1-4281-7185-5(1))* 2008. 70.75 *(978-1-4361-1568-1(X))* 2008. 69.75 *(978-1-4281-7190-9(8))* 2007. 147.75 *(978-1-4281-7189-3(4))* 2007. 92.75 *(978-1-4281-7192-3(4))* 2007. 90.75 *(978-1-4281-7194-7(0))* 2007. 71.75 *(978-1-4281-7188-6(6))* Recorded Bks., Inc.

—Schooled. 2008. (J). lib. bdg. 17.20 *(978-1-4178-2839-5(0),* Turtleback) Turtleback Bks.

—Slacker. 2016. (ENG.). 240p. (J). (gr. 3-7). 16.99 *(978-0-545-82315-9(3),* Scholastic Pr.) Scholastic, Inc.

—Ungifted. 288p. (J). (gr. 5). 2014. pap. 7.99 *(978-0-06-174267-5(8))* 2012. 16.99 *(978-0-06-174266-8(X))* 2012. lib. bdg. 17.89 *(978-0-06-174268-2(6))* HarperCollins Pubs.

—The 6th Grade Nickname Game (repackage) 2017. (ENG.). 160p. (J). (gr. 3-7). pap. 5.99 *(978-1-4847-9840-9(6))* Hyperion Bks. for Children.

Korman, Susan. Bad Deal. 2011. (Surviving Southside Ser.). (ENG.). 104p. (YA). (gr. 6-12). lib. bdg. 27.93 *(978-0-7613-6152-7(9))* Lerner Publishing Group.

—Overexposed. 2013. (Surviving Southside Ser.). (ENG.). 104p. (YA). (gr. 6-12). lib. bdg. 27.93 *(978-1-4677-0312-3(5))* Lerner Publishing Group.

Korman, Susan J. Bad Deal. (Surviving Southside Ser.). (ENG.). 104p. (YA). (gr. 6-12). 2015. 34.65 *(978-1-4677-6006-5(4),* Lerner Digital) 2011. pap. 7.95 *(978-0-7613-6166-4(9))* Lerner Publishing Group.

—Overexposed. 2013. (Surviving Southside Ser.). (ENG.). 104p. (YA). (gr. 6-12). pap. 7.95 *(978-1-4677-0706-0(6),* Darby Creek) Lerner Publishing Group.

Korngold, Jamie. Sadie & the Big Mountain. Fortenberry, Julie, illus. 2012. (Lag B'Omer & Shavuot Ser.). (ENG.). 32p. (J). (gr. -1-1). pap. 7.95 *(978-0-7613-6494-8(3));* lib. bdg. 17.95 *(978-0-7613-6492-4(7))* Lerner Publishing Group. (Kar-Ben Publishing).

Kosara, Victoria. Graduation Party. Durk, Jim, illus. 2010. (J). pap. *(978-0-545-23400-9(X))* Scholastic, Inc.

Kosgei, William. The Talented & Gifted: African Writers Series. 2013. 106p. pap. 10.95 *(978-1-62516-165-9(4),* Strategic Bk. Publishing) Strategic Book Publishing & Rights Agency (SBPRA).

Koss, Amy Goldman. Poison Ivy. 2008. (ENG.). 192p. (J). (gr. 5-9). pap. 8.99 *(978-0-312-38453-1(X),* 9780312384531) Square Fish.

Kostecki-Shaw, Jenny Sue. My Travelin' Eye. Kostecki-Shaw, Jenny Sue, illus. 2008. (ENG., Illus.). 40p. (J). (gr. -1-2). 18.99 *(978-0-8050-8169-5(0),* 9780805081695, Holt, Henry & Co. Bks. For Young Readers) Holt, Henry & Co.

Koster, Gloria. The Peanut-Free Café. Cocca-Leffler, Maryann, illus. 2012. (ENG.). 32p. (J). (gr. 1-3). pap. 7.99 *(978-0-8075-6387-8(0))* Whitman, Albert & Co.

Kotecki, Nathan. The Suburban Strange. (Suburban Strange Ser.). (ENG.). (YA). (gr. 9). 2013. 384p. pap. 8.99 *(978-0-544-10479-2(X))* 2012. 368p. 16.99 *(978-0-547-72996-1(0))* Houghton Mifflin Harcourt Publishing Co.

Kovanchak, Danielle. It's about Time. 2009. 44p. pap. 16.99 *(978-1-4389-7023-3(4))* AuthorHouse.

Kowitt, H. N. Jinx of the Loser. 2013. (Loser List Ser.: 3). (ENG.). 208p. (J). (gr. 3-7). 9.99 *(978-0-545-50794-3(4),* Scholastic Pr.) Scholastic, Inc.

—Take Me to Your Loser. 2013. (Loser List Ser.: 4). (ENG.). 240p. (J). (gr. 3-7). 9.99 *(978-0-545-50795-0(2),* Scholastic Pr.) Scholastic, Inc.

Kowitt, Holly. The Principal's Bra Is Missing. Kowitt, Holly, illus. 2017. (ENG., Illus.). 224p. (J). 16.99 *(978-1-250-09132-1(2),* 9781250091321) Feiwel & Friends.

Kraft, Erik P. Lenny & Mel. Kraft, Erik P., illus. 2012. (Ready-for-Chapters Ser.). (ENG., Illus.). 64p. (J). (gr. 2-5). pap. 6.99 *(978-0-689-85891-8(4),* Aladdin) Simon & Schuster Children's Publishing.

—Lenny & Mel after-School Confidential. Kraft, Erik P., illus. 2012. (Lenny & Mel Ser.). (ENG., Illus.). 64p. (J). (gr. 2-5). pap. 6.99 *(978-1-4424-6314-1(7),* Simon & Schuster/Paula Wiseman Bks.) Simon & Schuster/Paula Wiseman Bks.

Kramer, Stacy & Thomas, Valerie. Karma Bites. 2010. (ENG.). 348p. (J). (gr. 5-7). pap. 18.99 *(978-0-547-36301-1(X))* Houghton Mifflin Harcourt Publishing Co.

Kraus, Daniel. Rotters. 2012. (ENG.). 464p. (YA). (gr. 9). pap. 10.99 *(978-0-385-73858-3(7),* Ember) Random Hse. Children's Bks.

Kraus, Jeanne. Get Ready for Jetty! My Journal about Adhd & Me. 2012. (J). pap. 9.95 *(978-1-4338-1197-5(9));* (Illus.). 14.95 *(978-1-4338-1196-8(0))* American Psychological Assn. (Magination Pr.).

Kraus, Jeanne R. Annie's Plan: Taking Charge of Schoolwork & Homework. Beyl, Charles, illus. 2006. 48p. (J). (gr. 2-5). 14.95 *(978-1-59147-481-4(7));* pap. 9.95 *(978-1-59147-482-1(5))* American Psychological Assn. (Magination Pr.).

Kreidler, Shannon. The Adventures of Sally the Squirrel: Interactive... Educational & Earn Gold Stars. 2013. 28p. pap. 15.99 *(978-1-4797-7674-0(2))* Xlibris Corp.

Krensky, Stephen. Big Bad Wolves at School. Sneed, Brad, illus. 2007. (ENG.). 32p. (J). (gr. -1-3). 18.99 *(978-0-689-83799-9(2),* Simon & Schuster Bks. For Young Readers) Simon & Schuster Bks. For Young Readers.

Kristina Takes the Stage. 2008. (Illus.). 56p. (J). mass mkt. 10.95 *(978-0-9792361-3-6(4))* Inspire U., LLC.

Kroll, Steven. Patches Lost & Found, 0 vols. Gott, Barry, illus. 2005. (ENG.). 32p. (J). (gr. k-4). pap. 5.95 *(978-0-7614-5217-1(6),* 9780761452171, Amazon Children's Publishing) Amazon Publishing.

Kropp, Alex. Hacker! (Illus.). 93p. *(978-1-897039-09-0(3))* High Interest Publishing (HIP).

Krosoczka, Jarrett J. Lunch Lady & the Author Visit Vendetta. 2009. (Lunch Lady Ser.). (ENG.). 96p. (J). (gr. 3-7). pap. 6.99 *(978-0-375-86094-2(0),* Knopf Bks. for Young Readers) Random Hse. Children's Bks.

—Lunch Lady & the Cyborg Substitute. 2009. (Lunch Lady Ser.). (ENG.). 96p. (J). (gr. 3-7). pap. 6.99 *(978-0-375-84683-0(2));* lib. bdg. 12.99 *(978-0-375-94683-7(7))* Random Hse. Children's Bks. (Knopf Bks. for Young Readers).

—Lunch Lady & the Mutant Mathletes. 2012. (Lunch Lady Ser.). (ENG., Illus.). 96p. (J). (gr. 2-5). pap. 6.99 *(978-0-375-87028-6(8));* lib. bdg. 12.99 *(978-0-375-97028-3(2))* Random Hse. Children's Bks. (Knopf Bks. for Young Readers).

—Lunch Lady & the Mutant Mathletes. 2012. (Lunch Lady Ser.: 7). lib. bdg. 17.20 *(978-0-606-23871-7(9),* Turtleback) Turtleback Bks.

—Lunch Lady & the Picture Day Peril. 2012. (Lunch Lady Ser.). (ENG., Illus.). 96p. (J). (gr. 2-5). pap. 6.99 *(978-0-375-87035-4(0));* lib. bdg. 12.99 *(978-0-375-97035-1(5))* Random Hse. Children's Bks. (Knopf Bks. for Young Readers).

—Lunch Lady & the Picture Day Peril. 2012. (Lunch Lady Ser.: 8). lib. bdg. 17.20 *(978-0-606-26811-0(1),* Turtleback) Turtleback Bks.

—Lunch Lady & the Schoolwide Scuffle. 2014. (Lunch Lady Ser.). (ENG., Illus.). 96p. (J). (gr. 2-5). pap. 6.99 *(978-0-385-75279-4(2));* lib. bdg. 12.99 *(978-0-385-75280-0(6))* Random Hse. Children's Bks. (Knopf Bks. for Young Readers).

—Lunch Lady & the Schoolwide Scuffle. 2014. (Lunch Lady Ser.: 10). lib. bdg. 17.20 *(978-0-606-32235-5(3),* Turtleback) Turtleback Bks.

—Lunch Lady & the Video Game Villain. 2013. (Lunch Lady Ser.). (ENG.). 96p. (J). (gr. 2-5). pap. 6.99 *(978-0-307-98079-3(0));* lib. bdg. 12.99 *(978-0-307-98080-9(4))* Random Hse. Children's Bks. (Knopf Bks. for Young Readers).

S

—Lunch Lady & the Video Game Villain. 2013. (Lunch Lady Ser.: 9). lib. bdg. 17.20 (978-0-606-27003-8(5), Turtleback) Turtleback Bks.

—Max for President. 2008. (ENG.). 40p. (J). (gr. -1-2). pap. 6.99 (978-0-440-41789-7(9), Dragonfly Bks.) Random Hse. Children's Bks.

—A New Class. 2016. (Star Wars: Jedi Academy Ser.: 4). (ENG.). 176p. (J). (gr. 3-7). 12.99 (978-0-545-87573-8(0)) Scholastic, Inc.

Krossing, Karen. Cut the Lights, 1 vol. 2013. (Orca Limelights Ser.). (ENG.). 136p. (J). (gr. 6-9). pap. 9.95 (978-1-4598-0413-5(9)) Orca Bk. Pubs. USA.

—The Yo-Yo Prophet, 1 vol. 2011. (ENG.). 248p. (YA). (gr. 7-12). pap. 12.95 (978-1-55469-827-1(8)) Orca Bk. Pubs. USA.

Krueger, Kathryn L. Road to Grandma's House. 2005. 128p. pap. 13.95 (978-1-59800-366-6(6)) Outskirts Pr., Inc.

Krulik, Nancy. Attack of the Tighty Whities! Blecha, Aaron, illus. 2012. (George Brown, Class Clown Ser.: 7). (ENG.). 128p. (J). (gr. 2-4). pap. 4.99 (978-0-448-45575-4(7), Grosset & Dunlap) Penguin Young Readers Group.

—Attack of the Tighty Whities! 2012. (George Brown, Class Clown Ser.: 7). lib. bdg. 14.75 (978-0-606-23651-5(1), Turtleback) Turtleback Bks.

—Be Nice to Mice!, No. 20. John and Wendy Staff, illus. 2006. (Katie Kazoo, Switcheroo Ser.: 20). (ENG.). 80p. (J). (gr. 2-4). pap. 4.99 (978-0-448-44132-0(2), Grosset & Dunlap) Penguin Young Readers Group.

—Burp or Treat ... Smell My Feet! Super Special. Blecha, Aaron, illus. 2014. (George Brown, Class Clown Ser.: No. 3). (ENG.). 208p. (J). (gr. 2-4). 5.99 (978-0-448-46115-1(3), Grosset & Dunlap) Penguin Young Readers Group.

—Dance Your Pants Off!, No. 9. Blecha, Aaron, illus. 2013. (George Brown, Class Clown Ser.: 9). (ENG.). 128p. (J). (gr. 2-4). pap. 5.99 (978-0-448-45679-9(6), Grosset & Dunlap) Penguin Young Readers Group.

—Dance Your Pants Off! 2013. (George Brown, Class Clown Ser.: 9). lib. bdg. 14.75 (978-0-606-29802-5(9), Turtleback) Turtleback Bks.

—Don't Be Such a Turkey! John and Wendy Staff, illus. 2010. (Katie Kazoo, Switcheroo Ser.). (ENG.). 160p. (J). (gr. 2-4). pap. 4.99 (978-0-448-45448-1(3), Grosset & Dunlap) Penguin Young Readers Group.

—Don't Sneeze! 2017. (Kid from Planet Z Ser.: 2). lib. bdg. 16.00 (978-0-606-40108-1(3)) Turtleback Bks.

—Eww! What's on My Shoe? 2013. (George Brown, Class Clown Ser.: 11). lib. bdg. 14.75 (978-0-606-32126-6(8), Turtleback) Turtleback Bks.

—Flower Power. John and Wendy Staff, illus. 2008. (Katie Kazoo, Switcheroo Ser.: 27). (ENG.). 80p. (J). (gr. 2-4). pap. 4.99 (978-0-448-44674-5(X), Grosset & Dunlap) Penguin Young Readers Group.

—Free the Worms! John and Wendy Staff, illus. 2008. (Katie Kazoo, Switcheroo Ser.: 28). (ENG.). 80p. (J). (gr. 2-4). pap. 3.99 (978-0-448-44675-2(8), Grosset & Dunlap) Penguin Young Readers Group.

—Free the Worms! John & Wendy, illus. 2008. (Katie Kazoo, Switcheroo Ser.). 78p. (J). 11.65 (978-0-7569-8807-4(1)) Perfection Learning Corp.

—Friends for Never, 14 vols. John and Wendy Staff, illus. 2004. (Katie Kazoo, Switcheroo Ser.: 14). (ENG.). 80p. (J). (gr. 2-4). pap. 4.99 (978-0-448-43606-7(X), Grosset & Dunlap) Penguin Young Readers Group.

—Hair Today, Gone Tomorrow!, 34 vols., No. 34. John and Wendy Staff, illus. 2010. (Katie Kazoo, Switcheroo Ser.: 34). (ENG.). 80p. (J). (gr. 2-4). pap. 3.99 (978-0-448-45231-9(6), Grosset & Dunlap) Penguin Young Readers Group.

—How Do You Pee in Space? 2014. (George Brown, Class Clown Ser.: 13). lib. bdg. 14.75 (978-0-606-36163-7(4)) Turtleback Bks.

—How I Survived Middle School: Madame President. 2006. 104p. pap. (978-0-439-90090-4(5)) Scholastic, Inc.

—I Hate Rules! John and Wendy Staff, illus. 2006. (Katie Kazoo, Switcheroo Ser.: 5). (ENG.). 80p. (J). (gr. 2-4). pap. 4.99 (978-0-448-43100-0(9), Grosset & Dunlap) Penguin Young Readers Group.

—I Heard a Rumor. Martini, Angela, illus. 2007. (How I Survived Middle School Ser.: No. 3). 105p. (J). (978-0-439-90091-1(3)) Scholastic, Inc.

—Lice Check, No. 12. Blecha, Aaron, illus. 2014. (George Brown, Class Clown Ser.: 12). (ENG.). 128p. (J). (gr. 2-4). 4.99 (978-0-448-46112-0(9), Grosset & Dunlap) Penguin Young Readers Group.

—Lice Check. 2014. (George Brown, Class Clown Ser.: 12). lib. bdg. 14.75 (978-0-606-34144-8(7), Turtleback) Turtleback Bks.

—Major League Mess-Up. John and Wendy Staff, illus. 2008. (Katie Kazoo, Switcheroo Ser.: 29). (ENG.). 80p. (J). (gr. 2-4). pap. 4.99 (978-0-448-44676-9(6), Grosset & Dunlap) Penguin Young Readers Group.

—No Biz Like Show Biz. John and Wendy Staff, illus. 2007. (Katie Kazoo, Switcheroo Ser.: 24). (ENG.). 80p. (J). (gr. 2-4). pap. 4.99 (978-0-448-44440-6(2), Grosset & Dunlap) Penguin Young Readers Group.

—No Bones about It. John and Wendy Staff, illus. 12th ed. 2004. (Katie Kazoo, Switcheroo Ser.: 12). (ENG.). 80p. (J). (gr. 2-4). pap. 3.99 (978-0-448-43358-5(3), Grosset & Dunlap) Penguin Young Readers Group.

—No Messin' with My Lesson. John and Wendy Staff, illus. 11th ed. 2004. (Katie Kazoo, Switcheroo Ser.: 11). (ENG.). 80p. (J). (gr. 2-4). pap. 4.99 (978-0-448-43357-8(5), Grosset & Dunlap) Penguin Young Readers Group.

—On Your Mark, Get Set, Laugh! John and Wendy Staff, illus. 2004. (Katie Kazoo, Switcheroo Ser.: 13). (ENG.). 80p. (J). (gr. 2-4). pap. 4.99 (978-0-448-43605-0(1), Grosset & Dunlap) Penguin Young Readers Group.

—Red, White, & - Achoo! John and Wendy Staff, illus. 2010. (Katie Kazoo, Switcheroo Ser.: 33). (ENG.). 80p. (J). (gr. 2-4). pap. 3.99 (978-0-448-45230-2(8), Grosset & Dunlap) Penguin Young Readers Group.

—Something's Fishy, No. 26. John and Wendy Staff, illus. 2007. (Katie Kazoo, Switcheroo Ser.: 26). (ENG.). 80p. (J). (gr. 2-4). pap. 4.99 (978-0-448-44442-0(9), Grosset & Dunlap) Penguin Young Readers Group.

—Super Burp!, No. 1. Blecha, Aaron, illus. 2010. (George Brown, Class Clown Ser.: 1). (ENG.). 128p. (J). (gr. 2-4). pap. 5.99 (978-0-448-45367-5(3), Grosset & Dunlap) Penguin Young Readers Group.

—Three Cheers For... Who? John and Wendy Staff, illus. 2011. (Katie Kazoo, Switcheroo Ser.: 35). (ENG.). 80p. (J). (gr. 2-4). pap. 3.99 (978-0-448-45449-8(1), Grosset & Dunlap) Penguin Young Readers Group.

—Tip-Top Tappin' Mom!, 31 vols. John and Wendy Staff, illus. 2009. (Katie Kazoo, Switcheroo Ser.: 31). (ENG.). 80p. (J). (gr. 2-4). pap. 4.99 (978-0-448-45041-4(0), Grosset & Dunlap) Penguin Young Readers Group.

—Trouble Magnet. Blecha, Aaron, illus. 2010. (George Brown, Class Clown Ser.: 2). (ENG.). 128p. (J). (gr. 2-4). pap. 5.99 (978-0-448-45368-2(1), Grosset & Dunlap) Penguin Young Readers Group.

—Vote for Suzanne. John and Wendy Staff, illus. 2008. (Katie Kazoo, Switcheroo Ser.: No. 7). (ENG.). 160p. (J). (gr. 2-4). pap. 4.99 (978-0-448-44678-3(2), Grosset & Dunlap) Penguin Young Readers Group.

—What's Black & White & Stinks All Over? Blecha, Aaron, illus. 2011. (George Brown, Class Clown Ser.: 4). (ENG.). 128p. (J). (gr. 2-4). pap. 5.99 (978-0-448-45370-5(3), Grosset & Dunlap) Penguin Young Readers Group.

—A Whirlwind Vacation. John and Wendy Staff, illus. 2005. (Katie Kazoo, Switcheroo Ser.: No. 2). (ENG.). 160p. (J). (gr. 2-4). mass mkt. 4.99 (978-0-448-43748-4(1), Grosset & Dunlap) Penguin Young Readers Group.

Krulik, Nancy & Burwasser, Amanda Elizabeth. Science No Fair! Project Droid #1. Moran, Mike, illus. 2016. (Project Droid Ser.). (ENG.). 112p. (J). (gr. 1-4). 13.99 (978-1-5107-1018-4(3), Sky Pony Pr.) Skyhorse Publishing Co., Inc.

Krulik, Nancy & dePaola, Tomie. A Royal Pain in the Burp, No. 15A. Blecha, Aaron, illus. 2015. (George Brown, Class Clown Ser.: 15). (ENG.). 128p. (J). (gr. 1-3). bds. 4.99 (978-0-448-48283-5(5), Grosset & Dunlap) Penguin Young Readers Group.

Krulik, Nancy E. Flower Power. John and Wendy Staff, illus. 2008. (Katie Kazoo, Switcheroo Ser.). 78p. (gr. 2-5). 14.00 (978-0-7569-8806-7(3)) Perfection Learning Corp.

Kuenzler, Lou. The Dragon Dance. 2017. (Princess DisGrace Ser.). (ENG., Illus.). 272p. (J). (gr. 3-7). 15.99 (978-0-553-53781-9(4), Random Hse. Bks. for Young Readers) Random Hse. Children's Bks.

Kuhlman, Evan. Brother from a Box. Bruno, Iacopo, illus. (ENG.). 288p. (J). (gr. 4-7). 2013. pap. 6.99 (978-1-4424-2659-7(4)) 2012. 16.99 (978-1-4424-2658-0(6)) Simon & Schuster Children's Publishing. (Atheneum Bks. for Young Readers).

—The Last Invisible Boy. Coovert, J. P., illus. (ENG.). 240p. (J). (gr. 5-9). 2010. pap. 6.99 (978-1-4169-6089-8(9)) 2008. 16.99 (978-1-4169-5797-3(9)) Simon & Schuster Children's Publishing. (Atheneum Bks. for Young Readers).

Kuhn, Douglas Wolcik. The Summer of the Monarch Butterflies. 2012. 28p. pap. 24.95 (978-1-4626-9302-3(4)) America Star Bks.

Kuipers, Alice. Lost for Words. 2010. 224p. (YA). (gr. 8-18). 16.99 (978-0-06-142922-4(8), HarperTeen) HarperCollins Pubs.

Kurkosky, Tina. Bunny Brothers. 2011. 24p. pap. 24.95 (978-1-4626-3608-2(X)) America Star Bks.

Kuroda, Yosuke & Hayashiya, Shizuru. Onegai Teacher, No. 2. 2003. 120p. pap. 9.95 (978-1-58899-179-9(2)) ComicsOne Corp./Dr. Masters.

Kurtagich, Dawn. The Dead House. 2015. (ENG., Illus.). 432p. (J). (gr. 10-17). 18.00 (978-0-316-29868-1(9)) Little, Brown Bks. for Young Readers.

Kurzweil, Allen. Leon & the Spitting Image. Bertholf, Bret, illus. (ENG.). 320p. (J). (gr. 3-18). 2005. pap. 7.99 (978-0-06-053932-0(1), Greenwillow Bks.) 2003. 16.99 (978-0-06-053930-6(5)) HarperCollins Pubs.

Kuskowski, Alex. Line Up, 1 vol. unabr. ed. 2011. (District 13 Ser.). (ENG.). 48p. (YA). (gr. 9-12). pap. 7.95 (978-1-61651-279-8(2)) Saddleback Educational Publishing, Inc.

Kyi, Tanya Lloyd. My Time as Caz Hazard, 1 vol. 2004. (Orca Soundings Ser.). (ENG.). 128p. (YA). (gr. 8-12). pap. 9.95 (978-1-55143-319-6(2), 1234557) Orca Bk. Pubs. USA.

—Truth. 2003. (YA). (gr. 7-18). pap. 7.95 (978-1-55143-235-9(8)) Orca Bk. Pubs. USA.

—Truth. 2004. (Orca Soundings Ser.). 108p. 19.95 (978-0-7569-4346-2(9)) Perfection Learning Corp.

Kyle, Sherry. Love, Lexi: Letters to God. 2016. (ENG.). 224p. (YA). pap. 12.99 (978-1-4964-0963-8(9)) Tyndale Hse. Pubs.

La Clair, Claire. School Crossing Guard. 2012. 24p. pap. 24.95 (978-1-4626-7541-8(7)) PublishAmerica, Inc.

Laban, Elizabeth. The Tragedy Paper. (ENG.). 320p. (YA). (gr. 7). 2014. pap. 9.99 (978-0-307-93048-4(3), Ember) 2013. (Illus.). 17.99 (978-0-375-87040-8(7), Knopf Bks. for Young Readers) Random Hse. Children's Bks.

Labatt, Mary. Sam Gets Lost. Sarrazin, Marisol, tr. Sarrazin, Marisol, illus. 2004. (Kids Can Read Ser.: Vol. 1). (ENG.). 32p. (J). (gr. k-1). 3.95 (978-1-55337-563-0(7)) Kids Can Pr., Ltd. CAN. Dist: Hachette Bk. Group.

—Sam Goes to School. Sarrazin, Marisol, tr. Sarrazin, Marisol, illus. 2004. (Kids Can Read Ser.: Vol. 1). (ENG.). 32p. (J). (gr. k-1). 4.95 (978-1-55337-565-4(3)) Kids Can Pr., Ltd. CAN. Dist: Hachette Bk. Group.

LaBree Stute, Lela. Freedom Pugs! 2010. 38p. pap. 19.99 (978-0-557-42621-8(9)) Lulu Pr., Inc.

Lachtman, Ofelia Dumas. Pepita & the Bully: Pepita y la Peleonera. Baeza Ventura, Gabriela, tr. Pardo DeLange, Alex, illus. 2011. (SPA & ENG.). 32p. (J). (gr. -1-3). 16.95 (978-1-55885-689-9(7), Piñata Books) Arte Publico Pr.

Lackey, Mercedes & Edghill, Rosemary. Conspiracies. 2011. (Shadow Grail Ser.: 2). (ENG.). 352p. (YA). (gr. 8-12). pap. 19.99 (978-0-7653-1762-9(1), 9780765317629, Tor Teen) Doherty, Tom Assocs., LLC.

—Shadow Grail #4: Victories. 2014. (Shadow Grail Ser.: 4). (ENG.). 256p. (YA). (gr. 8-12). pap. 11.99 (978-0-7653-1764-3(8), 9780765317643, Tor Teen) Doherty, Tom Assocs., LLC.

LaCour, Nina. Hold Still. 2010. (ENG.). 272p. (YA). (gr. 7-18). 10.99 (978-0-14-241694-5(0), Speak) Penguin Young Readers Group.

LaFleur, John & Dubin, Shawn. The Misadventures of Dreary & Naughty, 1 vol. 2013. (ENG., Illus.). 64p. (J). 14.99 (978-0-7643-4494-7(3), 9780764344947) Schiffer Publishing, Ltd.

LaFleur, Suzanne. Eight Keys. 2012. (ENG.). 224p. (J). (gr. 4-7). 6.99 (978-0-375-87213-6(2), Yearling) Random Hse. Children's Bks.

—Love, Aubrey. 2011. (ENG.). 272p. (J). (gr. 3-7). pap. 7.99 (978-0-375-85159-9(3), Yearling) Random Hse. Children's Bks.

Lagercrantz, Rose. My Happy Life. Eriksson, Eva, illus. 2013. (ENG.). 136p. (J). (gr. k-3). 16.95 (978-1-877579-35-6(1)) Gecko Pr. NZL. Dist: Lerner Publishing Group.

Lagrou, Patrick. Born among the Dolphins. 2008. (Born among the Dolphins Ser.: 1). (ENG & DUT.). 154p. (J). (gr. 3-18). 19.95 (978-1-60537-022-4(3)) Clavis Publishing.

Laínez, René Colato. I Am Rene, the Boy. Graullera, Fabiolla, illus. 2005.Tr. of Yo Soy Rene, el Nino. (ENG & SPA.). 32p. (J). (gr. -1-2). 16.95 (978-1-55885-378-2(2), Piñata Books) Arte Publico Pr.

—René Has Two Last Names/René Tiene Dos Apellidos. Laínez, René Colato & Graullera Ramírez, Fabiola, illus. 2009. (SPA & ENG.). 32p. (J). (gr. -1-3). 16.95 (978-1-55885-530-4(0)) Arte Publico Pr.

Laird, Elizabeth & Davison, Roz. Jungle School. Sim, David, illus. 2006. (Green Bananas Ser.). (ENG.). 48p. (J). (gr. -1-3). (978-0-7787-1042-4(4)); lib. bdg. (978-0-7787-1026-4(2)) Crabtree Publishing Co.

Lakes, Lofton & Metu, illus. The Dream Team. 2007. 48p. (YA). pap. (978-0-9799320-0-7(9)) Pinkney, Gail.

Lakin, Patricia. Max & Mo Go Apple Picking. Floca, Brian, illus. 2007. (Max & Mo Ser.). (ENG.). 32p. (J). (gr. -1-1). pap. 3.99 (978-1-4169-2535-4(X), Simon Spotlight) Simon Spotlight.

—Max & Mo Make a Snowman. Floca, Brian, illus. 2007. (Max & Mo Ser.). (ENG.). 32p. (J). (gr. -1-1). pap. 3.99 (978-1-4169-2537-8(6), Simon Spotlight) Simon Spotlight.

—Max & Mo's First Day at School. Floca, Brian, illus. 2007. (Max & Mo Ser.). (ENG.). 32p. (J). (gr. -1-1). pap. 3.99 (978-1-4169-2533-0(3), Simon Spotlight) Simon Spotlight.

Laks, Shan. The Tale of Brave Ritchie: Be Aware of Strangers; Beat the Bullies & Exercise Changes Health. 2012. 76p. pap. 42.05 (978-1-4797-2882-4(9)) Xlibris Corp.

LaMarche, Una. You in Five Acts. 2016. (ENG.). 352p. (YA). (gr. 7). 17.99 (978-1-101-99893-9(8), Razorbill) Penguin Young Readers Group.

Lambert, Janet. Hi Neighbor: A Sugar Bradley Story. 2003. (J). pap. 9.95 (978-1-930009-82-0(8), 800-691-7779) Image Cascade Publishing.

—Sweet As Sugar: A Sugar Bradley Story. 2003. (YA). pap. 9.95 (978-1-930009-81-3(X), 800-691-7779) Image Cascade Publishing.

Laminack, Lester L. Jake's 100th Day of School, 1 vol. Love, Judy, illus. (ENG.). 32p. (J). (gr. k-3). 2008. pap. 8.95 (978-1-56145-463-1(X)) 2006. 16.95 (978-1-56145-355-9(2)) Peachtree Pubs.

—Snow Day!, 1 vol. Gustavson, Adam, illus. 2007. (ENG.). 32p. (J). (gr. k-2). 16.95 (978-1-56145-418-1(4)) Peachtree Pubs.

Lancett, Peter. Seeing Red. 2008. (Cutting Edge Ser.). (ENG.). 224p. pap. (978-1-84167-696-8(9)) Ransom Publishing Ltd.

Landon, Kristen. Life in the Pit. 2008. (ENG., Illus.). 248p. (YA). (gr. 5-13). pap. 8.95 (978-1-933831-08-4(1)) Blooming Tree Pr.

Lane, Melaina. Chubs. . Another Day at School. 2011. 20p. 9.14 (978-1-4251-7330-2(6)) Trafford Publishing.

Lang, Diane & Buchanan, Michael. The Fat Boy Chronicles. 2010. (Fat Boy Chronicles Ser.). (ENG.). 224p. (J). (gr. 7-11). pap. 9.95 (978-1-58536-543-2(2), 202220) Sleeping Bear Pr.

Langan, Paul. The Fallen. 2006. (Bluford Ser.: No. 11). 144p. (YA). (gr. 7-18). pap. 4.95 (978-1-59194-066-1(4)) Townsend Pr.

Langcaon, Jeff, illus. My Grandpa's Battleship Missouri Tour. 2007. (J). 14.95 (978-1-56647-831-1(6)) Mutual Publishing LLC.

Lange, Erin Jade. Dead Ends. 2013. (ENG.). 336p. (YA). (gr. 9). 17.99 (978-1-61963-080-2(X), 9781619630802, Bloomsbury USA Childrens); 288p. pap. 17.99 (978-1-61963-081-9(8)) Bloomsbury Publishing USA.

LaPorte, Tom. Hembree Hopefuls: A Hembree Elementary Story. 2003. 164p. (gr. 2-13). pap. 11.95 (978-0-595-27537-3(0), Weekly Reader Teacher's Pr) iUniverse, Inc.

Larbalestier, Justine & Brennan, Sarah Rees. Team Human. (ENG.). 352p. (YA). (gr. 8). 2013. pap. 9.99 (978-0-06-208965-6(X)) 2012. 17.99 (978-0-06-208964-9(1)) HarperCollins Pubs. (HarperTeen).

Larkin, Jim & Rambo, Lee Elliot. Books for Oliver. Brown, Dan, illus. 2006. (J). (978-1-59336-336-9(2)); pap. (978-1-59336-337-6(0)) Mondo Publishing.

Larsen, C. S. The Chronicles of Marvin Archibald Trekker: Boy Magician Book 1 - Penguins of Choice. l.t. ed. 2006. (Illus.). 163p. (YA). per. 5.99 (978-0-9779844-1-1(9)) KnowledgeGain Inc.

Larsen, Elizabeth. Open House at Buster's New School: Season 1, Book 2: Buster Hardings, 1 vol. 2010. 85p. pap. 19.95 (978-1-60749-559-8(7)) America Star Bks.

Larsen, Kirsten & National Geographic Learning Staff. The Ghost Town Mystery. Smath, Jerry, illus. 2010. (Rise & Shine Ser.). (ENG.). 32p. (C). (gr. -1-3). pap. 9.95 (978-1-57565-257-3(9)) National Geographic School Publishing, Inc.

Larson, Kirsten. The Ghost Town Mystery. 2008. pap. 34.95 (978-1-58013-773-7(3)) Kane Press, Inc.

Larson, M. A. Pennyroyal Academy. 2014. (Pennyroyal Academy Ser.: 1). (ENG.). 320p. (J). (gr. 5). 16.99 (978-0-399-16324-1(7), G.P. Putnam's Sons Books for Young Readers) Penguin Young Readers Group.

Lascarso, Laura. Counting Backwards. (ENG., Illus.). 288p. (YA). (gr. 9). 2013. pap. 9.99 (978-1-4424-0691-9(7)) 2012. 16.99 (978-1-4424-0690-2(9), Atheneum Bks. for Young Readers) Simon & Schuster Children's Publishing.

Lathan, Betty Jean. Are You Sure That's My Child? 2011. 48p. pap. 31.99 (978-1-4628-5759-3(0)) Xlibris Corp.

Latimer, Brenda. I See God. 2008. (Illus.). 28p. 12.95 (978-0-9797429-2-7(7)) Halo Publishing International.

Laubach, Melody. Words & Thoughts. 2008. 28p. pap. 17.95 (978-1-4327-2596-9(3)) Outskirts Pr., Inc.

Lauren, Christina. The House. 2015. (ENG., Illus.). 384p. (YA). (gr. 9). 18.99 (978-1-4814-1371-8(6)) Simon & Schuster Children's Publishing.

Laurens, Jennifer. Falling for Romeo. 2007. (YA). per. 12.95 (978-1-933963-94-5(8)) Grove Creek Publishing, LLC.

Laurie Douglas, Inez. No One Heard His Cry. 2008. 185p. pap. 11.95 (978-1-4327-2870-0(9)) Outskirts Pr., Inc.

Lavoie, Jennifer. Andy Squared. 2012. (ENG.). 264p. (J). (gr. 7). pap. 11.95 (978-1-60282-743-1(5)) Bold Strokes Bks.

Lawrence, Lisa. Rodent, 1 vol. 2016. (ENG.). 288p. (YA). (gr. 8-12). pap. 14.95 (978-1-4598-0976-5(9)) Orca Bk. Pubs. USA.

Lawrence, Michael. Ryan's Brain. 2006. (Jiggy Mccue Ser.). (ENG., Illus.). 336p. (J). (gr. 4-6). pap. 8.99 (978-1-84616-227-5(0)) Hodder & Stoughton GBR. Dist: Hachette Bk. Group.

Lawson, Barbara. Three Little Pigs Go to School. 2012. 28p. pap. 24.95 (978-1-4626-8185-3(9)) America Star Bks.

Lay, Kathryn. Crown Me! 2004. (ENG.). 208p. (J). (gr. 4-6). tchr. ed. 17.95 (978-0-8234-1845-9(6)) Holiday Hse., Inc.

—The Substitutes: An Up2U Action Adventure, 1 vol. Calo, Marcos, illus. 2015. (ENG.). 80p. (J). (978-1-62402-095-7(X)) Magic Wagon.

Lazebnik, Claire. Epic Fail. 2011. (ENG.). 304p. (YA). (gr. 8-18). pap. 9.99 (978-0-06-192126-1(2), HarperTeen) HarperCollins Pubs.

Lcg. The Pencil Monster! 2011. 28p. pap. 14.95 (978-0-557-94993-9(9)) Lulu Pr., Inc.

Leader, Jessica. Nice & Mean. 2010. (Mix Ser.). (ENG.). 272p. (J). (gr. 4-8). pap. 6.99 (978-1-4169-9160-1(3), Aladdin) Simon & Schuster Children's Publishing.

LeapFrog Staff. Ozzie & Mack. 2008. (J). pap. 49.99 (978-1-59319-924-1(4)); pap. 39.99 (978-1-59319-976-0(7)) LeapFrog Enterprises, Inc.

Lears, Laurie. Stay Away from Rat Boy! Hansen, Red, illus. 2009. (ENG.). 32p. (J). (gr. 2-3). 16.99 (978-0-8075-6789-0(2)) Whitman, Albert & Co.

Leaver, Trisha. The Secrets We Keep. 2015. (ENG.). 304p. (YA). (gr. 7). 17.99 (978-0-374-30046-3(1), Farrar, Straus & Giroux (BYR)) Farrar, Straus & Giroux.

Leavitt, Lindsey. Going Vintage. 2013. (ENG.). 320p. (YA). (gr. 7-12). 16.99 (978-1-59990-787-1(9), 9781599907871, Bloomsbury USA Childrens) Bloomsbury Publishing USA.

—Sean Griswold's Head. (ENG.). (YA). (gr. 7-12). 2012. 304p. pap. 9.99 (978-1-59990-911-0(1), 9781599909110) 2011. 288p. 16.99 (978-1-59990-498-6(5), 9781599904986) Bloomsbury Publishing USA. (Bloomsbury USA Childrens).

Leavitt, Lindsey & Mellom, Robin. The Pages Between Us. Dening, Abby, illus. 2016. (Pages Between Us Ser.: 1). 288p. (J). (gr. 3-7). 16.99 (978-0-06-237771-5(X)) HarperCollins Pubs.

Leavitt, Martine. Calvin: Just because You See Something Doesn't Mean It's Really There. 2015. (ENG.). 192p. (YA). (gr. 7). 17.99 (978-0-374-38073-1(2), 9780374380731, Farrar, Straus & Giroux (BYR)) Farrar, Straus & Giroux.

Leblanc, Louise. Maddie Stands Tall. Cummins, Sarah, tr. from FRE. Gay, Marie-Louise, illus. 2005. (Formac First Novels Ser.: 54). (ENG.). 64p. (J). (gr. 2-5). 14.95 (978-0-88780-683-4(X), 9780887806834) Formac Publishing Co., Ltd. CAN. Dist: Casemate Pubs. & Bk. Distributors, LLC.

—Maddie Stands Tall, 1 vol. Cummins, Sarah, tr. from FRE. Gay, Marie-Louise, illus. 2005. (Formac First Novels Ser.: 54). (ENG.). 64p. (J). (gr. 2-5). 4.95 (978-0-88780-682-7(1), 9780887806827) Formac Publishing Co., Ltd. CAN. Dist: Casemate Pubs. & Bk. Distributors, LLC.

—Maddie's Big Test. Cummins, Sarah, tr. from FRE. Gay, Marie-Louise, illus. 2006. (Formac First Novels Ser.: 58). (ENG.). 64p. (J). (gr. 2-5). 14.95 (978-0-88780-718-3(6), 9780887807183) Formac Publishing Co., Ltd. CAN. Dist: Casemate Pubs. & Bk. Distributors, LLC.

—Maddie's Big Test, 1 vol. Cummins, Sarah, tr. from FRE. Gay, Marie-Louise, illus. 2006. (Formac First Novels Ser.). (ENG.). 64p. (J). (gr. 2-5). 4.95 (978-0-88780-714-5(3), 9780887807145) Formac Publishing Co., Ltd. CAN. Dist: Casemate Pubs. & Bk. Distributors, LLC.

Lee, Honest & Gilbert, Matthew J. The Disastrous Magical Wishes of Classroom 13. Dreidemy, Joëlle, illus. 2017. (Classroom 13 Ser.: 2). (ENG.). 128p. (J). (gr. 1-5). 15.99 (978-0-316-46454-3(6)); pap. 5.99 (978-0-316-46456-7(2)) Little, Brown Bks. for Young Readers.

—The Disastrous Magical Wishes of Classroom 13. 2017. (Classroom 13 Ser.: 2). (J). lib. bdg. 16.00 (978-0-606-40638-3(7)) Turtleback Bks.

—The Fantastic & Terrible Fame of Classroom 13. 2018. (Classroom 13 Ser.: 3). (J). lib. bdg. 16.00 (978-0-606-40639-0(5)) Turtleback Bks.

—The Unlucky Lottery Winners of Classroom 13. Dreidemy, Joëlle, illus. 2017. (Classroom 13 Ser.: 1). (ENG.). 128p. (J). (gr. 1-5). 15.99 (978-0-316-46465-9(1)); pap. 5.99 (978-0-316-46462-8(7)) Little, Brown Bks. for Young Readers.

Lee, Howard. Jamshid & the Lost Mountain of Light. 2008. (ENG.). 248p. pap. 14.99 (978-1-4196-8958-1(4)) CreateSpace Independent Publishing Platform.

Lee, Jared D., illus. The Dentist from the Black Lagoon, 1 vol. 2014. (ENG.). 32p. (J). 24.21 (978-1-61479-197-3(X)) Spotlight.

Lee, Jenny. Elvis & the Underdogs. Light, Kelly, illus. 2013. (Elvis & the Underdogs Ser.: 1). (ENG.). 304p. (J). (gr. 3-7). 16.99 (978-0-06-223554-1(0)) HarperCollins Pubs.

Lee, Kathy. Space Invaders. 2011. 144p. pap. (978-1-84427-507-6(8)) Scripture Union.

Lee, Penny. Schoolio: Pets, Projects & Pandemonium. 2013. 72p. pap. (978-1-4602-0568-6(5)) FriesenPress.

Lee, Quinlan B. & Bridwell, Norman. Clifford's Best School Day. Haefele, Steve, illus. 2007. (J). (978-0-545-02844-8(2)) Scholastic, Inc.

Lee, Stacey. The Secret of a Heart Note. 2016. 384p. (YA). (gr. 8). 17.99 (978-0-06-242832-5(2), Tegen, Katherine Bks) HarperCollins Pubs.

Lee, Vanessa. The Beauty Queen & the School Nerd. 2007. 78p. (YA). (gr. 4-6). per. 8.95 (978-0-595-45936-0(6)) iUniverse, Inc.

Lee Wardlaw. Seventh-Grade Weirdo. 2010. 160p. pap. 11.95 (978-1-4401-8263-1(9)) iUniverse, Inc.

Lefebvre, Jason. Too Much Glue. Retz, Zac, illus. 2013. (ENG.). 32p. (J). (gr. k-2). 16.95 *(978-1-936261-27-7(8))* Flashlight Pr.

LeFlore, Lyah B. The World Is Mine. Warfield, D. L., illus. 2009. (Come Up Ser.). (ENG.). 304p. (YA). (gr. 9-18). pap. 8.99 *(978-1-4169-7963-0(8),* Simon Pulse) Simon Pulse.

Lehrhaupt, Adam. Chicken in School. Kober, Shahar, illus. 2017. 40p. (J). (gr. -1-3). 17.99 *(978-0-06-236413-5(8))* HarperCollins Pubs.

Lemieux, Jean. Toby & the Mysterious Creature. Cummins, Sarah, tr. from FRE. Casson, Sophie, illus. 2008. (Formac First Novels Ser.). (ENG.). 64p. (J). (gr. 2-5). 14.95 *(978-0-88780-761-9(5),* 9780887807619) Formac Publishing Co., Ltd. CAN. Dist: Casemate Pubs. & Bk. Distributors, LLC.

Lemieux, Jean & Casson, Sophie. Toby & the Mysterious Creature, 1 vol. Cummins, Sarah, tr. from FRE. Casson, Sophie, illus. 2008. (Formac First Novels Ser.). (ENG., Illus.). 64p. (J). (gr. 2-5). 5.95 *(978-0-88780-759-6(3),* 9780887807596) Formac Publishing Co., Ltd. CAN. Dist: Casemate Pubs. & Bk. Distributors, LLC.

Lennon, Maria T. Confessions of a So-Called Middle Child. 2014. (ENG.). 304p. (J). (gr. 3-7). pap. 6.99 *(978-0-06-212691-7(1))* HarperCollins Pubs.

—Watch Out, Hollywood! More Confessions of a So-Called Middle Child. 2014. (ENG.). 224p. (J). (gr. 3-7). 16.99 *(978-0-06-212693-1(8))* HarperCollins Pubs.

Leonard, Elise. Monday Morning Blitz. 2007. (Al's World Ser.: 1). (ENG.). 144p. (J). (gr. 5-9). pap. 8.99 *(978-1-4169-3464-6(2),* Simon & Schuster/Paula Wiseman Bks.) Simon & Schuster/Paula Wiseman Bks.

Leslie, Robyn. Rinny & the Trail of Clues. 2003. Orig. Title: Miss President & the Trail of Clues. (Illus.). 192p. (J). pap. 7.95 *(978-0-9727388-8-0(6))* Sugar Ducky Bks., Inc.

Lester, Helen. Hooway for Wodney Wat, 1 vol. Munsinger, Lynn, illus. 2011. (ENG.). 32p. (J). (gr. -1-3). audio compact disk 10.99 *(978-0-547-55217-0(3))* Houghton Mifflin Harcourt Publishing Co.

—Tackylocks & the Three Bears. Munsinger, Lynn, illus. 2004. (Tacky the Penguin Ser.). (ENG.). 32p. (J). (gr. -1-3). 6.99 *(978-0-618-43953-9(6))* Houghton Mifflin Harcourt Publishing Co.

—Wodney Wat's Wobot. Munsinger, Lynn, illus. 2011. (ENG.). 32p. (J). (gr. -1-3). 16.99 *(978-0-547-36756-9(2))* Houghton Mifflin Harcourt Publishing Co.

Lethcoe, Jason. The Capture of the Crimson Cape. Lethcoe, Jason, illus. 2006. (Amazing Adventures from Zoom's Academy Ser.). (ENG., Illus.). 144p. (J). (gr. 4-7). pap. 12.95 *(978-0-345-48356-0(1),* Ballantine Bks.) Random House Publishing Group.

—Zoom's Academy. 2006. (ENG., Illus.). 304p. (J). (gr. 4-7). pap. 14.95 *(978-0-345-49641-6(8),* Ballantine Bks.) Random House Publishing Group.

Lettera, Janine Hamel. My First Day of School. 2012. 16p. pap. 7.31 *(978-1-4251-1614-9(0))* Trafford Publishing.

Leuck, Laura. My Creature Teacher. Nash, Scott, illus. 2004. (ENG.). 32p. (J). (gr. -1-1). 15.99 *(978-0-06-029694-0(1))* HarperCollins Pubs.

Leveen, Tom. Manicpixiedreamgirl. 2014. (ENG.). 256p. (YA). (gr. 9). pap. 8.99 *(978-0-375-87021-7(0),* Ember) Random Hse. Children's Bks.

—Random. 2014. (ENG., Illus.). 224p. (YA). (gr. 9). 17.99 *(978-1-4424-9956-0(7),* Simon Pulse) Simon Pulse.

—Sick. 2014. (ENG.). 288p. (YA). (gr. 9-17). pap. 8.95 *(978-1-4197-1228-9(4),* Amulet Bks.) Abrams, Inc.

Levine, Gail Carson. The Wish. 2005. (ENG.). 256p. (J). (gr. 3-7). pap. 6.99 *(978-0-06-075911-7(9),* HarperTeen) HarperCollins Pubs.

—The Wish. 2004. 197p. (gr. 3-7). 16.00 *(978-0-7569-4272-4(1))* Perfection Learning Corp.

Levine, Kristin. The Lions of Little Rock. (ENG.). (J). (gr. 5-9). 2013. 320p. pap. 7.99 *(978-0-14-242435-3(8),* Puffin Books) 2012. 304p. 16.99 *(978-0-399-25644-8(X),* G.P. Putnam's Sons Books for Young Readers) Penguin Young Readers Group.

Levithan, David. Another Day. 2015. (ENG.). 336p. (YA). (gr. 7). lib. bdg. 20.99 *(978-0-385-75621-1(6));* 17.99 *(978-0-385-75620-4(8))* Random Hse. Children's Bks. (Knopf Bks. for Young Readers).

—Every You, Every Me. Levithan, David & Farmer, Jonathan, photos by. 2012. (ENG., Illus.). 256p. (YA). (gr. 7). pap. 9.99 *(978-0-375-85451-4(7),* Ember) Random Hse. Children's Bks.

—Every You, Every Me. Farmer, Jonathan, photos by. 2012. (Illus.). lib. bdg. 20.85 *(978-0-606-26816-5(2),* Turtleback) Turtleback Bks.

—The Realm of Possibility. 2006. (ENG.). 224p. (YA). (gr. 7-12). reprint ed. pap. 9.99 *(978-0-375-83657-2(8),* Ember) Random Hse. Children's Bks.

Levithan, David & Ehrenhaft, Daniel. 21 Proms. l.t. ed. 2007. (YA). 22.95 *(978-0-7862-9866-2(9))* Thorndike Pr.

Levy, Elizabeth. A Hare-Raising Tale. Gerstein, Mordicai, illus. unabr. ed. 2006. (First Chapter Bks.). (J). (gr. 2-4). pap. 20.95 incl. audio compact disk *(978-1-59519-705-4(2));* pap. 17.95 incl. audio *(978-1-59519-704-7(4))* Live Oak Media.

Levy, Janice. School Rules for Diva Duck, 1 vol. Madden, Colleen M., illus. 2012. (Diva Duck Ser.). (ENG.). 32p. (J). (gr. -1-4). 28.50 *(978-1-61641-889-2(3))* Magic Wagon.

—Showtime for Flip-Flop, 1 vol. Madden, Colleen M., illus. 2011. (Flip-Flop Adventure Ser.). (ENG.). 32p. (J). (gr. k-3). 28.50 *(978-1-61641-654-6(8))* Magic Wagon.

Levy, Joanne. Crushing It. 2017. (Mix Ser.). (ENG., Illus.). 240p. (J). (gr. 4-8). pap. 7.99 *(978-1-4814-6473-4(6),* Aladdin) Simon & Schuster Children's Publishing.

Lewis, Doreen. The Bubblegum Babes' Guide to Sixth Grade. 2005. (J). per. 9.95 *(978-0-9769193-0-8(3))* Helm Publishing.

Lewis, Fiona. Dreaming in Color. 2011. (ENG.). 304p. (J). (gr. 7). pap. 16.95 *(978-0-9845318-5-1(8))* Tiny Stachel Pr.

Lewis, Jan, illus. School. 2012. (First Time Ser.). (ENG.). 24p. (J). *(978-1-84643-491-4(2))* Child's Play International Ltd.

Lewis, Jill. A Mom in a Million. Gulbis, Stephen, illus. 2005. 32p. (J). *(978-1-84458-368-3(6),* Pavilion Children's Books) Pavilion Bks.

Lewis, Judith. Not Like Any Bird I've Ever Heard. 2011. 24p. pap. 24.95 *(978-1-4626-2730-1(7))* America Star Bks.

Lewis, Kelly. What Do We Do at School? 2016. (Spring Forward Ser.). (J). (gr. k). *(978-1-4900-6021-7(9))* Benchmark Education Co.

Liberto, Lorenzo. Matt the Rat & His Magic Cloud / Raton Mateo y Su Nube Magica: A Day at School / un Dia de Escuela. Gomez, Rocio, ed. Torres, Irving, illus. 2003. (Matt the Rat Ser. / La Serie de Ratón Mateo). (ENG & SPA.). 32p. (J). lib. bdg. 20.00 *(978-0-9743668-0-7(3))* Harvest Sun Pr., LLC.

Lichtman, Wendy. Secrets, Lies, & Algebra. 2008. (Do the Math Ser.: 1). (ENG., Illus.). 208p. (YA). (gr. 8-8). pap. 6.99 *(978-0-06-122957-2(1),* Greenwillow Bks.) HarperCollins Pubs.

—The Writing on the Wall. 2008. (Do the Math Ser.: 2). (ENG.). 224p. (YA). (gr. 8-9). 16.99 *(978-0-06-122958-9(X),* Greenwillow Bks.) HarperCollins Pubs.

Lieb, Josh. I Am a Genius of Unspeakable Evil & I Want to Be Your Class President. 2010. (ENG.). 304p. (J). (gr. 5-7). 8.99 *(978-1-59514-354-9(8),* Razorbill) Penguin Young Readers Group.

Light, Steve. Have You Seen My Lunch Box? Light, Steve, illus. 2017. (ENG., Illus.). 18p. (J). (-k). bds. 6.99 *(978-0-7636-9068-7(6))* Candlewick Pr.

Lim, Rebecca. Exile (Mercy, Book 2) 2016. (Mercy Ser.: 2). (ENG.). 304p. (J). pap. 9.99 *(978-0-00-816904-6(7),* HarperCollins Children's Bks.) HarperCollins Pubs. Ltd. GBR. Dist: HarperCollins Pubs.

—Mercy (Mercy, Book 1) 2016. (Mercy Ser.: 1). (ENG.). 288p. (J). pap. 9.99 *(978-0-00-816903-9(9),* HarperCollins Children's Bks.) HarperCollins Pubs. Ltd. GBR. Dist: HarperCollins Pubs.

Limbaugh, Rush H., III. Rush Revere & the Brave Pilgrims: Time-Travel Adventures with Exceptional Americans. 2013. (ENG., Illus.). 224p. 19.99 *(978-1-4767-5586-1(8),* Threshold Editions) Threshold Editions.

—Rush Revere & the First Patriots: Time-Travel Adventures with Exceptional Americans. 2014. (Rush Revere Ser.: 2). (ENG., Illus.). 256p. 19.99 *(978-1-4767-5588-5(4),* Threshold Editions) Threshold Editions.

Limbaugh, Rush H., III & Limbaugh, Kathryn Adams. Rush Revere & the American Revolution. 2014. (ENG.). 256p. 19.99 *(978-1-4767-8987-3(8),* Threshold Editions) Threshold Editions.

—Rush Revere & the American Revolution. Hiers, Christopher, illus. 2014. 244p. (J). pap. *(978-1-4767-8989-7(4),* Threshold Editions) Threshold Editions.

Lin, Grace. The Year of the Dog. 2007. (Pacy Lin Novel Ser.). (ENG., Illus.). 160p. (J). (gr. 3-7). per. 6.99 *(978-0-316-06002-8(X))* Little, Brown Bks. for Young Readers.

—The Year of the Dog. 2007. (Illus.). 134p. (gr. 3-7). 16.00 *(978-0-7569-8143-3(3))* Perfection Learning Corp.

Lindner, Brooke. Hooray for School! Going to School with Nick Jr. Hall, Susan & Hall, Susan, illus. 2008. (ENG.). 16p. (J). (gr. -1-2). pap. 6.99 *(978-1-4169-5861-1(4),* Simon Spotlight/Nickelodeon) Simon Spotlight/Nickelodeon.

Lindo, Elvira. Manolito Four-Eyes, 0 vols. Emilio, Urberuaga & Urberuaga, Emilio, illus. 2010. (Manolito Four-Eyes Ser.: 1). (ENG.). 155p. (J). (gr. 3-7). pap. 9.99 *(978-0-7614-5729-9(1),* 9780761457299, Amazon Children's Publishing) Amazon Publishing.

—Manolito Gafotas, 0 vols. Urberuaga, Emilio, illus. 2010. (SPA & ENG.). 192p. (J). (gr. 3-7). pap. 9.99 *(978-0-7614-5730-5(5),* 9780761457305, Amazon Children's Publishing) Amazon Publishing.

Lindquist, N. J. The Best of Friends. 2016. (Circle of Friends Ser.: Vol. 1). (ENG., Illus.). (YA). pap. ***(978-1-927692-03-5(2))*** That's Life! Communications.

Lindsay, Elizabeth. Bugs & Butterflies. 2012. (Silverlake Fairy School Ser.). 100p. (J). pap. 4.99 *(978-0-7945-3066-2(4),* Usborne) EDC Publishing.

—Dancing Magic. 2012. (Silverlake Fairy School Ser.). 100p. (J). pap. 4.99 *(978-0-7945-3067-9(2),* Usborne) EDC Publishing.

—Ready to Fly. 2011. (Silverlake Fairy School Ser.). 123p. (J). pap. 7.99 *(978-0-7945-3064-8(8),* Usborne) EDC Publishing.

—Stardust Surprise. 2012. (Silverlake Fairy School Ser.). 100p. (J). pap. 4.99 *(978-0-7945-3065-5(6),* Usborne) EDC Publishing.

—Wands & Charms (Book 2) 2011. (Silverlake Fairy School Ser.). 117p. (J). pap. 4.99 *(978-0-7945-3063-1(X),* Usborne) EDC Publishing.

Lindstrom, Eric. Not If I See You First. 2015. (ENG.). 320p. (YA). (gr. 10-17). 18.00 *(978-0-316-25985-9(3))* Little Brown & Co.

Linke, Glenn Colin. The Gargantuan Boy. 2011. 102p. pap. 30.50 *(978-1-60976-079-3(4),* Eloquent Bks.) Strategic Book Publishing & Rights Agency (SBPRA).

Linn, Laurent. Draw the Line. Linn, Laurent, illus. 2016. (ENG., Illus.). 528p. (YA). (gr. 7). 17.99 *(978-1-4814-5280-9(0),* McElderry, Margaret K. Bks.) McElderry, Margaret K. Bks.

Lipinski, Maureen. Cleopatra Ascending. 2013. (Shadow's Edge Novel Ser.: 2). (ENG.). 240p. (YA). pap. 9.99 *(978-0-7387-3193-3(5),* Flux) North Star Editions.

Lipp, Frederick. Fatima. Lindmark, Margaret, illus. 2006. 32p. (J). pap. *(978-1-59336-302-4(8))* Mondo Publishing.

Lippmann, Wilfried. The Gift of Eye. 2008. 140p. (gr. 7-12). pap. 11.95 *(978-0-595-52251-4(3))* iUniverse, Inc.

Lipsey, Shelia E. House of Cars: Book 1 Fairley High Series. 2013. (ENG.). 158p. (YA). pap. 6.99 *(978-0-9838935-4-7(3),* Seraphina) Bonita and Hodge Publishing Group.

Lipsyte, Robert. Center Field. 2010. (ENG.). 288p. (YA). (gr. 8-18). 17.99 *(978-0-06-055704-1(4),* HarperTeen) HarperCollins Pubs.

—The Twinning Project. (ENG.). (J). (gr. 5-7). 2014. 288p. pap. 6.99 *(978-0-544-22522-0(8),* HMH Books For Young Readers) 2012. 272p. 16.99 *(978-0-547-64571-1(6))* Houghton Mifflin Harcourt Publishing Co.

Little Airplane Productions & Scanlon, Michael, illus. Off to School! 2009. (Wonder Pets! Ser.). (ENG.). 24p. (J). pap. 3.99 *(978-1-4169-7197-9(1),* Simon Spotlight/Nickelodeon) Simon Spotlight/Nickelodeon.

Little, Robert. Fun Day in Mrs. Walker's Class. Galey, Chuck, illus. 2005. 32p. (J). *(978-0-9701863-6-2(3))* Reide Publishing.

Littman, Sarah Darer. Life, After. 2010. (ENG.). 288p. (J). (gr. 7-18). 17.99 *(978-0-545-15144-3(9),* Scholastic Pr.) Scholastic, Inc.

—Want to Go Private? (ENG.). 336p. (J). 2013. (gr. 7). pap. 10.99 *(978-0-545-15147-4(3))* 2011. (gr. 9-9). 17.99 *(978-0-545-15146-7(5),* Scholastic Pr.) Scholastic, Inc.

Litwin, Eric. Rocking in My School Shoes. Dean, James, illus. 2011. (Pete the Cat Ser.). 40p. (J). (gr. -1-3). (ENG.). 17.99 *(978-0-06-191024-1(4));* lib. bdg. 17.89 *(978-0-06-191025-8(2))* HarperCollins Pubs.

Litwin, Eric, ed. Rocking in My School Shoes. 2011. *(978-0-545-50106-4(7))* Scholastic, Inc.

Liu, Carol & Caldarone, Marybeth Sidoti. Arlene on the Scene. 2010. 206p. (J). (gr. 3-5). pap. 7.95 *(978-1-934572-54-2(3))* Emerald Bk. Co.

Livingston, Lesley. Starling. 2075. (ENG.). 368p. (J). (gr. 8). 9.99 *(978-0-06-206308-3(1),* HarperTeen) HarperCollins Pubs.

Llewellyn, Claire. Late for School Yellow Band. Pérez, Moni, illus. 2016. (Cambridge Reading Adventures Ser.). (ENG.). 16p. pap. 6.56 *(978-1-107-57679-7(2))* Cambridge Univ. Pr.

Lloyd-Jones, Emily. The Hearts We Sold. 2017. (ENG.). 400p. (YA). (gr. 10-17). 17.99 ***(978-0-316-31459-6(5))*** Little Brown & Co.

Lo, Catherine. How It Ends. 2016. (ENG.). 304p. (YA). (gr. 9). 17.99 *(978-0-544-54006-4(9),* HMH Books For Young Readers) Houghton Mifflin Harcourt Publishing Co.

Lobo, Chris. Brand New Day: (of School) 2008. 36p. pap. 24.95 *(978-1-60441-973-3(3))* America Star Bks.

Lockard, Lynn. Gone Batty!!! 2009. 40p. pap. 16.99 *(978-1-4389-8516-9(9))* AuthorHouse.

Lockhart, E. The Boy Book: A Study of Habits & Behaviors, Plus Techniques for Taming Them. 2008. (Ruby Oliver Quartet Ser.). (ENG.). 224p. (YA). (gr. 7). pap. 8.99 *(978-0-385-73209-3(0),* Delacorte Pr.) Random Hse. Children's Bks.

—The Boyfriend List: 15 Guys, 11 Shrink Appointments, 4 Ceramic Frogs & Me, Ruby Oliver. 2006. (Ruby Oliver Quartet Ser.). (ENG.). 256p. (YA). (gr. 7-12). reprint ed. pap. 9.99 *(978-0-385-73207-9(4),* Ember) Random Hse. Children's Bks.

—Dramarama. 2007. (ENG.). 320p. (YA). 24.80 *(978-1-4287-4612-1(9))* Hyperion Pr.

—Fly on the Wall: How One Girl Saw Everything. 2007. (ENG., Illus.). 192p. (YA). (gr. 7-12). pap. 8.99 *(978-0-385-73282-6(1),* Delacorte Pr) Random House Publishing Group.

—Real Live Boyfriends: Yes. Boyfriends, Plural. If My Life Weren't Complicated, I Wouldn't Be Ruby Oliver. 2011. (Ruby Oliver Quartet Ser.). (ENG.). 240p. (J). (gr. 7). pap. 8.99 *(978-0-385-73429-5(8),* Ember) Random Hse. Children's Bks.

—The Treasure Map of Boys: Noel, Jackson, Finn, Hutch, Gideon - And Me, Ruby Oliver. 2010. (Ruby Oliver Quartet Ser.). (ENG.). 256p. (J). (gr. 7). pap. 8.99 *(978-0-385-73427-1(1),* Delacorte Pr.) Random Hse. Children's Bks.

Lodding, Linda Ravin. The Busy Life of Ernestine Buckmeister. Beaky, Suzanne, illus. 2011. (ENG.). 32p. (J). (gr. -1-1). 16.95 *(978-0-9799746-9-4(0))* Flashlight Pr.

Loewen, Nancy. The Last Day of Kindergarten, 0 vols. Yoshikawa, Sachiko, illus. 2011. (ENG.). 32p. (J). (gr. -1-1). 16.99 *(978-0-7614-5807-4(7),* 9780761458074, Amazon Children's Publishing) Amazon Publishing.

Logsted, Greg. Alibi Junior High. (ENG.). 256p. (J). (gr. 5-9). 2011. pap. 6.99 *(978-1-4169-4814-8(7))* 2009. (Illus.). 16.99 *(978-1-4169-7959-3(X))* Simon & Schuster/Paula Wiseman Bks. (Simon & Schuster/Paula Wiseman Bks.).

Lois, Lowry. The Birthday Ball. Feiffer, Jules, illus. 2011. (ENG.). 192p. (J). (gr. 5-7). pap. 7.99 *(978-0-547-57710-4(9))* Houghton Mifflin Harcourt Publishing Co.

—Gooney Bird & All Her Charms. Thomas, Middy, illus. 2014. (Gooney Bird Greene Ser.). (ENG.). 160p. (J). (gr. 1-4). 16.99 *(978-0-544-11354-1(3))* Houghton Mifflin Harcourt Publishing Co.

—Gooney Bird & the Room Mother. Thomas, Middy, illus. 2006. (Gooney Bird Ser.: No. 2). (ENG.). 80p. (J). (gr. 3-7). 5.99 *(978-0-440-42133-7(0),* Yearling) Random Hse. Children's Bks.

—Gooney Bird Greene. Middy Chilman, Thomas, illus. 2004. (Gooney Bird Ser.: No. 1). 88p. (gr. 2-5). 16.00 *(978-0-7569-2583-3(5))* Perfection Learning Corp.

—Gooney Bird Is So Absurd. Thomas, Middy, illus. 2013. (Gooney Bird Greene Ser.). (ENG.). 112p. (J). (gr. 1-4). pap. 5.99 *(978-0-547-87559-0(2))* Houghton Mifflin Harcourt Publishing Co.

—Gooney Bird on the Map. Thomas, Middy, illus. (Gooney Bird Greene Ser.). (ENG.). 128p. (J). (gr. 1-4). 2013. pap. 5.99 *(978-0-547-85088-7(3))* 2011. 16.99 *(978-0-547-55622-2(5))* Houghton Mifflin Harcourt Publishing Co.

—Gooney the Fabulous. 2009. (Gooney Bird Ser.: No. 3). (ENG.). 96p. (J). (gr. 3-7). 5.99 *(978-0-440-42253-2(1),* Yearling) Random Hse. Children's Bks.

Lombard, Jenny. Drita, My Homegirl. 2008. (ENG.). 144p. (J). (gr. 3-7). 5.99 *(978-0-14-240905-3(7),* Puffin Books) Penguin Young Readers Group.

—Drita, My Homegirl. 2008. 135p. (J). (gr. 4-6). 13.65 *(978-0-7569-8919-4(1))* Perfection Learning Corp.

Lon Rogers. The Between Season. 2009. 280p. pap. 17.95 *(978-1-4401-8368-3(6))* iUniverse, Inc.

Lonczak, Heather Suzanne. Mookey the Monkey Gets over Being Teased. Ramsey, Marcy Dunn, illus. 2006. 32p. (J). (gr. -1-3). 14.95 *(978-1-59147-479-1(5));* 9.95 *(978-1-59147-480-7(9))* American Psychological Assn. (Magination Pr.).

London, Jonathan. Froggy Goes to School. Remkiewicz, Frank, illus. 2006. (Froggy Ser.). 28p. (gr. -1-1). 16.00 *(978-0-7569-6986-8(7))* Perfection Learning Corp.

Longmeyer, C. M. My Life As a Third Grade Werewolf. Blanding, Dexter, illus. 2014. (ENG.). (J). (gr. 2-3). pap. 7.99 *(978-0-635-11144-9(6))* Gallopade International.

—My Life As a Third Grade Zombie. Blanding, Dexter, illus. 2013. (My Life As a Third Grade... Ser.). (ENG.). (J). (gr. -1-3). pap. 7.99 *(978-0-635-11131-9(4))* Gallopade International.

Longstreet, Barbara, et al. Woodsey School Kids Thanksgiving Feast. 2004. 28p. pap. 24.95 *(978-1-4137-1992-5(9))* PublishAmerica, Inc.

Look, Lenore. Alvin Ho: Allergic to Babies, Burglars, & Other Bumps in the Night. Pham, LeUyen, illus. 2013. (Alvin Ho Ser.). (ENG.). 192p. (J). (gr. 1-4). 15.99 *(978-0-375-87033-0(4),* Schwartz & Wade Bks.) Random Hse. Children's Bks.

—Alvin Ho: Allergic to Birthday Parties, Science Projects, & Other Man-Made Catastrophes. Pham, LeUyen, illus. 2011. (Alvin Ho Ser.). (ENG.). 192p. (J). (gr. 1-4). 6.99 *(978-0-375-87369-0(4),* Yearling) Random Hse. Children's Bks.

—Alvin Ho: Allergic to Girls, School, & Other Scary Things. Pham, LeUyen, illus. 2009. (Alvin Ho Ser.). (ENG.). 192p. (J). (gr. 1-4). 6.99 *(978-0-375-84930-5(0),* Yearling) Random Hse. Children's Bks.

—Alvin Ho: Allergic to Babies, Burglars, & Other Bumps in the Night. Pham, LeUyen, illus. 2014. (Alvin Ho Ser.). (ENG.). 192p. (J). (gr. 1-4). 6.99 *(978-0-385-38600-5(1),* Yearling) Random Hse. Children's Bks.

—Ruby Lu, Brave & True. 2004. (Illus.). 104p. (J). lib. bdg. 15.00 *(978-1-4242-0914-9(5))* Fitzgerald Bks.

—Ruby Lu, Brave & True. Wilsdorf, Anne, illus. 2006. (Ruby Lu Ser.). 105p. (J). (gr. 1-5). 11.65 *(978-0-7569-6553-2(5))* Perfection Learning Corp.

—Ruby Lu, Brave & True. Wilsdorf, Anne, illus. 2006. (ENG.). 112p. (J). (gr. 1-5). pap. 6.99 *(978-1-4169-1389-4(0),* Atheneum Bks. for Young Readers) Simon & Schuster Children's Publishing.

—Ruby Lu, Star of the Show. Choi, Stef, illus. (ENG.). 144p. (J). (gr. 1-5). 2012. pap. 6.99 *(978-1-4169-1776-2(4))* 2011. 15.99 *(978-1-4169-1775-5(6))* Simon & Schuster Children's Publishing. (Atheneum Bks. for Young Readers).

Lopez, Lorraine. Call Me Henri. 2012. (ENG.). 242p. pap. 19.95 *(978-0-8101-2893-4(4))* Curbstone Pr.

Lord, Bette Bao. In the Year of the Boar & Jackie Robinson. Simont, Marc, illus. 2003. (ENG.). 176p. (J). (gr. 3-7). pap. 6.99 *(978-0-06-440175-3(8))* HarperCollins Pubs.

—In the Year of the Boar & Jackie Robinson. 2009. 8.32 *(978-0-7848-0826-9(0),* Everbind) Marco Bk. Co.

—In the Year of the Boar & Jackie Robinson. (J). 2008. 67.75 *(978-1-4281-8016-1(8))* 2004. 46.75 *(978-1-4025-9147-1(0))* Recorded Bks., Inc.

—In the Year of the Boar & Jackie Robinson. 2003. (J). (gr. 3-6). 16.00 *(978-0-8085-7599-3(6),* Turtleback) Turtleback Bks.

Lord, Emery. The Start of Me & You. 2015. (ENG.). 384p. (YA). (gr. 7). 17.99 *(978-1-61963-359-9(0),* 9781619633599, Bloomsbury USA Childrens) Bloomsbury Publishing USA.

Lore, Pittacus. I Am Number Four. (YA). (gr. 9). 2016. (Lorien Legacies: the Lost Files Ser.). 416p. pap. 9.99 *(978-0-06-238771-4(5))* 2011. (Lorien Legacies Ser.: 1). (ENG.). 496p. pap. 9.99 *(978-0-06-196957-7(5))* 2010. (Lorien Legacies Ser.: 1). (ENG.). 448p. 17.99 *(978-0-06-196955-3(9))* 2011. (Lorien Legacies Ser.: 1). (ENG.). 496p. pap. 9.99 *(978-0-06-211655-0(X))* 2011. (Lorien Legacies Ser.: 1). (ENG.). 480p. 17.99 *(978-0-06-202624-8(0))* HarperCollins Pubs.

—I Am Number Four. 2009. (Lorien Legacies Ser.: Bk. 1). 11.04 *(978-0-7848-3715-3(5),* Everbind) Marco Bk. Co.

—I Am Number Four. 2011. (I Am Number Four Ser.: Vol. 1). (ENG.). 440p. (gr. 9-12). 20.00 *(978-1-61383-207-3(9))* Perfection Learning Corp.

—I Am Number Four. 2011. (Lorien Legacies Ser.: 1). (YA). lib. bdg. 20.85 *(978-0-606-23545-7(0),* Turtleback) Turtleback Bks.

—I Am Number Four: The Lost Files: Rebel Allies. 2015. (Lorien Legacies: the Lost Files Ser.). (ENG.). 416p. (YA). (gr. 9). pap. 9.99 *(978-0-06-236404-3(9))* HarperCollins Pubs.

—I Am Number Four: The Lost Files: Secret Histories. 2013. (Lorien Legacies: the Lost Files Ser.). (ENG.). 416p. (YA). (gr. 9). pap. 9.99 *(978-0-06-222367-8(4))* HarperCollins Pubs.

—Secret Histories. 2013. (Lorien Legacies: the Lost Files Ser.). (YA). lib. bdg. 20.85 *(978-0-606-31823-5(2),* Turtleback) Turtleback Bks.

Lorenz, Albert. The Exceptionally, Extraordinarily Ordinary First Day of School. 2010. (ENG., Illus.). 32p. (J). (gr. 1-4). 15.95 *(978-0-8109-8960-3(3),* Abrams Bks. for Young Readers) Abrams, Inc.

Lorenzi, Natalie Dias. Flying the Dragon. (ENG.). 240p. (J). (gr. 4-7). 2014. pap. 8.95 *(978-1-58089-435-7(6))* 2012. 16.95 *(978-1-58089-434-0(8))* Charlesbridge Publishing, Inc.

Lorey, Dean. Monster Law. 2009. 304p. 10.99 *(978-0-06-134048-2(0))* HarperCollins Pubs.

Lorimer, Janet. The Bad Luck Play, 1 vol. unabr. ed. 2010. (Q Reads Ser.). (ENG.). 32p. (YA). (gr. 9-12). pap. 6.95 *(978-1-61651-198-2(2))* Saddleback Educational Publishing, Inc.

—Student Bodies, 1 vol. unabr. ed. 2010. (Q Reads Ser.). (ENG.). 32p. (YA). (gr. 9-12). pap. 6.95 *(978-1-61651-219-4(9))* Saddleback Educational Publishing, Inc.

Lottridge, Celia Barker. Wings to Fly, 1 vol. 3rd ed. 2007. (ENG.). 144p. (J). (gr. 2-7). pap. 8.95 *(978-0-88899-844-6(9))* Groundwood Bks. CAN. Dist: Publishers Group West (PGW).

Loughead, Deb. Sidetracked, 1 vol. 2012. (Orca Sports Ser.). (ENG.). 136p. (YA). (gr. 6-10). pap. 9.95 *(978-1-4598-0250-6(0))* Orca Bk. Pubs. USA.

Louis, Sachar. There's a Boy in the Girls' Bathroom. 2014. (ENG.). 208p. (J). (gr. 7-12). 11.24 *(978-1-63245-256-6(1))* Lectorum Pubns., Inc.

Love, D. Anne. Defying the Diva. 2008. (ENG., Illus.). 272p. (YA). (gr. 7-12). 17.99 *(978-1-4169-3481-3(2),* McElderry, Margaret K. Bks.) McElderry, Margaret K. Bks.

—Picture Perfect. 2010. (ENG.). 304p. (YA). (gr. 7). pap. 8.99 *(978-0-689-87391-1(3),* McElderry, Margaret K. Bks.) McElderry, Margaret K. Bks.

—Semiprecious. (ENG.). 304p. (J). (gr. 5-9). 2009. pap. 6.99 *(978-0-689-87389-8(1))* 2006. (Illus.). 17.99 *(978-0-689-85638-9(5))* McElderry, Margaret K. Bks. (McElderry, Margaret K. Bks.).

Love, Maryann Cusimano. You Are My Wonders. Ichikawa, Satomi & Lewin, Ted, illus. 2012. (ENG.). 32p. (J). (gr. -1-2).

16.99 (978-0-399-25293-8(2), Philomel Bks.) Penguin Young Readers Group.

Lovelady, W. f. The Adventures of Johnny Saturday: Back to the Drawing Board. 2012. 76p. pap. 12.95 (978-1-4685-5286-7(4)) AuthorHouse.

Lovell, Brandy. Crazy Colours. Mitchell, Tina, illus. 2011. 42p. pap. (978-0-9867761-0-6(6)) Bing Long Bks.

Lowe, E. Van. Never Slow Dance with a Zombie. 2009. (ENG.). 256p. (J). (gr. 8-12). pap. 18.99 (978-0-7653-2040-7(1), 9780765320407, Tor Teen) Doherty, Tom Assocs., LLC.

Lowe, Natasha. The Marvelous Magic of Miss Mabel. 2016. (Poppy Pendle Ser.). (ENG., Illus.). 288p. (J). (gr. 3-7). 16.99 (978-1-4814-6533-5(3), Simon & Schuster/Paula Wiseman Bks.) Simon & Schuster/Paula Wiseman Bks.

—The Power of Poppy Pendle. (Poppy Pendle Ser.). (ENG., 272p. (J). (gr. 3-7). 2013. Illus.). pap. 7.99 (978-1-4424-4926-8(8)) 2012. 16.99 (978-1-4424-4679-3(X)) Simon & Schuster/Paula Wiseman Bks. (Simon & Schuster/Paula Wiseman Bks.).

Loye, Scott. Moon Ring. 2011. 160p. (gr. 10-12). 22.95 (978-1-4502-9682-3(3)); pap. 12.95 (978-1-4502-9680-9(7)) iUniverse, Inc.

Lubar, David. The Big Stink. 2010. (Nathan Abercrombie, Accidental Zombie Ser.: 4). (ENG.). 176p. (J). (gr. 3-7). pap. 7.99 (978-0-7653-2510-5(1), 9780765325105, Starscape) Doherty, Tom Assocs., LLC.

—The Bully Bug: A Monsterrific Tale. 2014. (Monsterrific Tales Ser.). (ENG., Illus.). 144p. (J). (gr. 3-7). 24.99 (978-0-7653-3082-6(2), 9780765330826, Starscape) Doherty, Tom Assocs., LLC.

—Dead Guy Spy. 2010. (Nathan Abercrombie, Accidental Zombie Ser.: 2). (ENG.). 176p. (J). (gr. 3-7). pap. 8.99 (978-0-7653-2507-5(1), 9780765325075, Starscape) Doherty, Tom Assocs., LLC.

—The Gloomy Ghost. 2014. (Monsterrific Tales Ser.). (ENG., Illus.). 144p. (J). (gr. 3-7). 15.99 (978-0-7653-3080-2(6), 9780765330802, Starscape) Doherty, Tom Assocs., LLC.

—Hyde & Shriek: A Monsterrific Tale. 2013. (Monsterrific Tales Ser.). (ENG., Illus.). 144p. (J). (gr. 3-7). 14.99 (978-0-7653-3081-9(4), 9780765330819, Starscape) Doherty, Tom Assocs., LLC.

—My Rotten Life. 2009. (Nathan Abercrombie, Accidental Zombie Ser.: 1). (ENG., Illus.). 160p. (J). (gr. 3-7). pap. 8.99 (978-0-7653-1634-9(X), 9780765316349, Starscape) Doherty, Tom Assocs., LLC.

—Sleeping Freshmen Never Lie. 2007. (ENG.). 288p. (YA). (gr. 7-18). 10.99 (978-0-14-240780-6(1), Speak) Penguin Young Readers Group.

—Sophomores & Other Oxymorons. 2015. (ENG.). 432p. (YA). (gr. 7). 17.99 (978-0-525-42970-8(0), Dutton Books for Young Readers) Penguin Young Readers Group.

—Wizards of the Game. 2004. (ENG.). 176p. (J). (gr. 3-7). 6.99 (978-0-14-240215-3(X), Puffin Books) Penguin Young Readers Group.

Lucan, Dawn. My Challenge Memories. 2011. 108p. pap. 8.95 (978-1-4583-4714-5(1)) Lulu Pr., Inc.

Lucas, Sally & Lucas, Margeaux. Dancing Dinos Go to School. 2006. (Step into Reading Ser.: Vol. 1). (ENG., Illus.). 32p. (J). (gr. -1-1). pap. 4.99 (978-0-375-83241-3(6), Random Hse. Bks. for Young Readers) Random Hse. Children's Bks.

Luck, Gail. Bumduggle Davis Beats the Boobrats or the Inauguration of the Motherless Club. 2011. 146p. pap. 12.50 (978-1-61204-727-0(0), Strategic Bk. Publishing) Strategic Book Publishing & Rights Agency (SBPRA).

—Bumduggle Davis Joins the Dots: Or It's All There in Black & White. 2012. 166p. pap. 13.50 (978-1-62212-379-7(4), Strategic Bk. Publishing) Strategic Book Publishing & Rights Agency (SBPRA).

Luddy, Karon. Spelldown: The Big-Time Dreams of a Small-Town Word Whiz. 2008. (Mix Ser.). (ENG.). 224p. (J). (gr. 4-8). pap. 10.99 (978-1-4169-5452-1(X), Simon & Schuster/Paula Wiseman Bks.) Simon & Schuster/Paula Wiseman Bks.

Ludwig, Elisa. Pretty Crooked. 2012. (Pretty Crooked Trilogy Ser.: 1). (ENG.). 368p. (YA). (gr. 8). 17.99 (978-0-06-206606-0(4), Tegen, Katherine Bks) HarperCollins Pubs.

Ludwig, Trudy. Confessions of a Former Bully. Adams, Beth, illus. (ENG.). 48p. (J). 2012. (gr. 3-7). pap. 7.99 (978-0-307-93113-9(7), Dragonfly Bks.) 2010. (gr. 1-4). 15.99 (978-1-58246-309-4(3), Tricycle Pr.) Random Hse. Children's Bks.

—Confessions of a Former Bully. 2012. lib. bdg. 18.40 (978-0-606-26382-5(9), Turtleback) Turtleback Bks.

—The Invisible Boy. Barton, Patrice, illus. 2013. (ENG.). 40p. (J). (gr. 1-4). 16.99 (978-1-58246-450-3(2), Knopf Bks. for Young Readers) Random Hse. Children's Bks.

—Just Kidding. Gustavson, Adam, illus. 2006. (ENG.). 32p. (J). (gr. 1-4). 15.99 (978-1-58246-163-2(5), Tricycle Pr.) Random Hse. Children's Bks.

—Too Perfect. Fields, Lisa, illus. 2009. (ENG.). 32p. (J). (gr. 1-4). 15.99 (978-1-58246-258-5(5), Tricycle Pr.) Random Hse. Children's Bks.

—Trouble Talk. Prevost, Mikela, illus. 2008. (ENG.). 32p. (J). (gr. 1-4). 15.99 (978-1-58246-240-0(2), Tricycle Pr.) Random Hse. Children's Bks.

Luedeke, Lisa. Smashed. (ENG., 336p. (YA). (gr. 9). 2013. Illus.). pap. 10.99 (978-1-4424-2780-8(9)) 2012. 16.99 (978-1-4424-2779-2(5)) McElderry, Margaret K. Bks. (McElderry, Margaret K. Bks.).

Lunsford, Susie. The Magical Wishing Well Forest Series. 2006. pap. 25.32 (978-1-4134-9491-4(9)) Xlibris Corp.

Lupa, Mary R. Stacy Takes the Train to School. Andriyevskaya, Yevgeniya, illus. 2009. 20p. (J). pap. 10.95 (978-1-4327-1609-7(3)) Outskirts Pr., Inc.

Lupica, Mike. Long Shot, 1 vol. 2012. (Comeback Kids Ser.). (ENG.). 192p. (J). (gr. 4-8). lib. bdg. 27.07 (978-1-59961-176-1(7)) Spotlight.

—Qb 1. 2013. (ENG.). 272p. (J). (gr. 5). 17.99 (978-0-399-25228-0(2), Philomel Bks.) Penguin Publishing Group.

—Qb 1. 2014. (ENG.). 288p. (J). (gr. 5). pap. 7.99 (978-0-14-751152-2(6), Puffin Books) Penguin Young Readers Group.

—Safe at Home, 1 vol. 2012. (Comeback Kids Ser.). (ENG.). 192p. (J). (gr. 4-8). lib. bdg. 27.07 (978-1-59961-177-8(5)) Spotlight.

—Travel Team. 2004. (ENG.). 288p. (J). (gr. 3-7). 17.99 (978-0-399-24150-5(7), Philomel Bks.) Penguin Young Readers Group.

—Travel Team. l.t. ed. 2005. (Thorndike Literacy Bridge Ser.). 400p. (J). (gr. 4-7). lib. bdg. 23.95 (978-0-7862-7415-4(8)) Thorndike Pr.

—True Legend. (ENG.). (J). (gr. 5). 2013. 320p. pap. 7.99 (978-0-14-242650-0(4), Puffin Books) 2012. 304p. 17.99 (978-0-399-25227-3(4), Philomel Bks.) Penguin Young Readers Group.

—Two-Minute Drill, 1 vol. 2012. (Comeback Kids Ser.). (ENG.). 192p. (J). (gr. 4-8). lib. bdg. 27.07 (978-1-59961-179-2(1)) Spotlight.

Lutz, Nancie Anne. Patsy Ann Back Again. Lutz, Nancie Anne, illus. 2005. (Illus.). 25p. (J). pap. 14.50 (978-0-9760064-0-4(5)) Dollworks.

Lux, Josephine Kei & Doerflinger, Marion. Daydreaming Daisy Part of the Daydreamer's Club Series. 2009. 40p. pap. 17.50 (978-1-60860-252-0(4), Eloquent Bks.) Strategic Book Publishing & Rights Agency (SBPRA).

Luzzatto, Caroline. Interplanetary Avenger. 2005. (ENG., Illus.). 128p. (J). (gr. 3-7). 16.95 (978-0-8234-1933-3(9)) Holiday Hse., Inc.

Lyga, Barry. The Astonishing Adventures of Fanboy & Goth Girl. 2007. (ENG.). 320p. (YA). (gr. 7-12). pap. 9.99 (978-0-618-91652-8(0)) Houghton Mifflin Harcourt Publishing Co.

—Boy Toy. 2009. (ENG.). 416p. (YA). (gr. 9). pap. 9.99 (978-0-547-07634-8(7)) Houghton Mifflin Harcourt Publishing Co.

—Goth Girl Rising. 2011. (ENG.). 400p. (YA). (gr. 9). pap. 8.99 (978-0-547-40308-3(9)) Houghton Mifflin Harcourt Publishing Co.

—Hero Type. 2009. (ENG.). 312p. (YA). (gr. 7). pap. 8.99 (978-0-547-24877-6(6)) Houghton Mifflin Harcourt Publishing Co.

—Mangaman. Doran, Colleen, illus. 2011. (ENG.). 144p. (YA). (gr. 7). 19.99 (978-0-547-42315-9(2)) Houghton Mifflin Harcourt Publishing Co.

Lyle, Patrice. The Case of the Invisible Witch. 2013. 194p. pap. 9.99 (978-1-61603-034-6(8)) Leap Bks.

Lynch, Chris. Inexcusable. 2005. (ENG., Illus.). 176p. (YA). (gr. 7-18). 19.99 (978-0-689-84789-9(0), Atheneum Bks. for Young Readers) Simon & Schuster Children's Publishing.

—Inexcusable: 10th Anniversary Edition. 10th ed. 2015. (ENG., Illus.). 192p. (YA). (gr. 8). pap. 9.99 (978-1-4814-3202-3(8), Simon & Schuster Bks. For Young Readers) Simon & Schuster Bks. For Young Readers.

—Sins of the Fathers. 2006. 232p. (YA). (gr. 9-12). lib. bdg. 17.89 (978-0-06-074038-2(8), HarperTeen) HarperCollins Pubs.

Lynch, F. Michael. I Will Always Need You. 2008. 24p. pap. 14.50 (978-1-60693-141-7(5), Eloquent Bks.) Strategic Book Publishing & Rights Agency (SBPRA).

Lynch, Janet Nichols. Addicted to Her. 2010. (ENG.). 256p. (YA). (gr. 7-18). pap. 17.95 (978-0-8234-2186-2(4)) Holiday Hse., Inc.

—Messed Up. 2009. (ENG.). 320p. (YA). (gr. 7-18). 17.95 (978-0-8234-2185-5(6)) Holiday Hse., Inc.

—Peace Is a Four-Letter Word. 2005. 158p. (YA). (gr. 8-12). per. 9.95 (978-1-59714-014-0(7), Great Valley Bks.) Heyday.

Lynellen Sullivan & Bryan Castle. Poppers to the Rescue: Book 1 of the Popcorn Series. 2010. 72p. pap. 8.95 (978-1-4401-9764-2(4)) iUniverse, Inc.

Lynn, Erin. Speed Demon. 2008. (ENG.). 192p. (YA). (gr. 9-18). 9.99 (978-0-425-22366-6(3), Berkley) Penguin Publishing Group.

Lyon, George Ella. The Pirate of Kindergarten. Avril, Lynne, illus. 2010. (ENG.). 40p. (J). (gr. -1-3). 17.99 (978-1-4169-5024-0(9), Atheneum/Richard Jackson Bks.) Simon & Schuster Children's Publishing.

Lyons, C. J. Broken. 2014. (ENG.). 320p. (YA). (gr. 7-12). pap. 9.99 (978-1-4022-9230-9(9)) Sourcebooks, Inc.

Lytton, Deborah. Ruby Starr. 2017. (Ruby Starr Ser.: 1). (ENG.). 272p. (J). (gr. 3-7). pap. 7.99 (978-1-4926-4577-1(X), Sourcebooks Jabberwocky) Sourcebooks, Inc.

M. Alvarado. We Are Different, but the Same. 2012. 16p. pap. 15.99 (978-1-4685-4425-1(X)) AuthorHouse.

MacDonald, Alan. Alien Attack! Baines, Nigel, illus. 2015. (ENG.). 192p. (YA). (gr. 2-4). pap. 9.99 (978-1-4088-2524-2(4), 9781408825242, Bloomsbury USA Childrens) Bloomsbury Publishing USA.

—Fangs!, 1 vol. Roberts, David, illus. 2012. (Dirty Bertie Ser.). (ENG.). 112p. (gr. 1-3). pap. 4.95 (978-1-4342-4267-9(6)); 25.32 (978-1-4342-4601-1(9)) Stone Arch Bks.

MacDonald, Maryann. Starring Francie O'Leary. Richards, Virginia Helen, illus. 2010. 64p. (J). (gr. 1-3). pap. 6.95 (978-0-8198-7132-9(X)) Pauline Bks. & Media.

MacDowell, Diane. Adventures of Timkin: The Early Years. 2012. 28p. pap. 19.99 (978-1-4772-7101-8(5)) AuthorHouse.

MacDowell, Maureen. Tomorrow Is the First Day of School. Hergenrother, Max, illus. 2007. 32p. (J). 15.95 (978-0-9791463-0-5(5)) Wading River Bks., LLC.

MacGregor, Roy. The Kindergarten Caper: The Screech Owls Prequel. 2008. (ENG.). 144p. (YA). (gr. 3-7). mass mkt. 6.99 (978-0-7710-5608-6(7), Screech Owls) McClelland & Stewart CAN. Dist: Penguin Random Hse. LLC.

MacHale, D.j. Black Moon Rising. 2017. (J). pap. (978-1-101-93260-5(0)) Random Hse., Inc.

Machon, Daphne E. Charlee's New Glasses. 2013. (Illus.). 16p. pap. 8.50 (978-1-78035-736-2(2), Fastprint Publishing) Upfront Publishing Ltd. GBR. Dist: Printondemand-worldwide.com.

Maciejewski, Mark. I Am Fartacus. 2017. (Max Ser.). (ENG., Illus.). 336p. (J). (gr. 4-8). pap. 7.99 (978-1-4814-6419-2(1), Simon & Schuster/Paula Wiseman Bks.) Simon & Schuster/Paula Wiseman Bks.

Maciel, Amanda. Lucky Girl. 2017. 320p. (YA). (gr. 9). 17.99 (978-0-06-230533-6(6)) HarperCollins Pubs.

—Tease. (ENG.). 336p. (YA). (gr. 9). 2015. pap. 9.99 (978-0-06-230531-2(X)) 2014. 17.99 (978-0-06-230530-5(1)) HarperCollins Pubs.

Mack, Jeff. Clueless Mcgee. Mack, Jeff, illus. 2012. (Clueless Mcgee Ser.: 1). (ENG., Illus.). 240p. (J). (gr. 3-7). 12.99 (978-0-399-25749-0(7), Philomel Bks.) Penguin Young Readers Group.

—Clueless McGee & the Inflatable Pants, Bk. 2. Mack, Jeff, illus. 2013. (Clueless Mcgee Ser.: 2). (ENG., Illus.). 256p. (J). (gr. 3-7). 12.99 (978-0-399-25750-6(0), Philomel Bks.) Penguin Young Readers Group.

—Clueless Mcgee Gets Famous. Mack, Jeff, illus. 2014. (Clueless Mcgee Ser.: 3). (ENG., Illus.). 288p. (J). (gr. 3-7). 12.99 (978-0-399-25751-3(9), Philomel Bks.) Penguin Young Readers Group.

Mack, W. C. Athlete vs. Mathlete. 2013. (Athlete vs. Mathlete Ser.). (ENG.). (YA). (gr. 3-6). 192p. 16.99 (978-1-61963-129-8(6), 9781619631298); 192p. pap. 7.99 (978-1-59990-938-7(3), 9781599909387); 208p. 16.99 (978-1-59990-915-8(4), 9781599909158); (Illus.). 208p. pap. 7.99 (978-1-59990-858-8(1), 9781599908588) Bloomsbury Publishing USA. (Bloomsbury USA Childrens).

Mackall, Dandi Daley. Larger-Than-Life Lara. 2016. (ENG.). 176p. 14.99 (978-1-4964-1429-8(2)) Tyndale Hse. Pubs.

—Natalie: School's First Day of Me, 1 vol. Blakeslee, Lys, illus. 2009. (That's Nat! Ser.). (ENG.). 96p. (J). (gr. 1-4). pap. 4.99 (978-0-310-71568-9(7)) Zonderkidz.

—Natalie & the Downside-Up Birthday, 1 vol. Blakeslee, Lys, illus. 2009. (That's Nat! Ser.). (ENG.). 96p. (J). (gr. 1-4). pap. 4.99 (978-0-310-71569-6(5)) Zonderkidz.

—Natalie Really Very Much Wants to Be a Star, 1 vol. Blakeslee, Lys, illus. 2009. (That's Nat! Ser.). (ENG.). 96p. (J). (gr. 1-4). pap. 4.99 (978-0-310-71567-2(9)) Zonderkidz.

Mackey, Weezie Kerr. Throwing Like a Girl, 0 vols. 2010. (ENG.). 272p. (YA). (gr. 7-9). pap. 9.99 (978-0-7614-5606-3(6), 9780761456063, Amazon Children's Publishing) Amazon Publishing.

Mackintosh, David. The Frank Show. 2012. (ENG., Illus.). 32p. (J). (gr. k-2). 16.95 (978-1-4197-0393-5(5), Abrams Bks. for Young Readers) Abrams, Inc.

—Marshall Armstrong Is New to Our School. 2011. (ENG., Illus.). 32p. (J). (gr. k-2). 17.95 (978-1-4197-0036-1(7), Abrams Bks. for Young Readers) Abrams, Inc.

Mackler, Carolyn. Infinite in Between. 2015. (ENG.). 480p. (YA). (gr. 8). 17.99 (978-0-06-173107-5(2), HarperTeen) HarperCollins Pubs.

—Vegan Virgin Valentine. 2004. (ENG., Illus.). 240p. (YA). (gr. 9-18). 16.99 (978-0-7636-2155-1(2)) Candlewick Pr.

MacLachlan, Patricia. Word after Word after Word. 2010. (ENG.). 128p. (J). (gr. 1-5). 16.99 (978-0-06-027971-4(0), Tegen, Katherine Bks) HarperCollins Pubs.

MacLellan, Erin. Run from the Nun! 2003. (ENG.). 128p. (J). (gr. 4-6). tchr. ed. 16.95 (978-0-8234-1796-4(4)) Holiday Hse., Inc.

Maddox, Jake. Dance Team Dilemma, 1 vol. Wood, Katie, illus. 2013. (Jake Maddox Girl Sports Stories Ser.). (ENG.). 72p. (gr. 2-3). pap. 5.95 (978-1-4342-4201-3(3)); lib. bdg. 25.32 (978-1-4342-4014-9(2)) Stone Arch Bks.

—Dance Team Drama. 2016. (Jake Maddox JV Girls Ser.). (ENG.). 96p. (gr. 3-4). pap. 5.95 (978-1-4965-3678-5(9)); lib. bdg. 25.99 (978-1-4965-3674-7(6)) Stone Arch Bks.

—Heavyweight Takedown. 2015. (Jake Maddox JV Ser.). (ENG.). 96p. (gr. 3-4). lib. bdg. 25.99 (978-1-4342-9638-2(5)) Stone Arch Bks.

—Home-Field Football, 1 vol. Tiffany, Sean, illus. 2012. (Jake Maddox Sports Stories Ser.). (ENG.). 72p. (gr. 2-3). pap. 5.95 (978-1-4342-4206-8(4)); 25.32 (978-1-4342-4008-8(8)) Stone Arch Bks.

—Hoop Hustle. Aburto, Jesus, illus. 2015. (Jake Maddox Sports Stories Ser.). (ENG.). 72p. (gr. 2-3). lib. bdg. 25.32 (978-1-4965-0494-4(1)) Stone Arch Bks.

—Relay Race Breakdown, 1 vol. Garcia, Eduardo, illus. 2012. (Jake Maddox Sports Stories Ser.). (ENG.). 72p. (gr. 2-3). pap. 5.95 (978-1-4342-3903-7(9)); lib. bdg. 25.32 (978-1-4342-3289-2(1)) Stone Arch Bks.

—Second-Chance Soccer, 1 vol. Ray, Mike, illus. 2014. (Jake Maddox JV Ser.). (ENG.). 96p. (gr. 3-4). 25.99 (978-1-4342-9154-7(5)) Stone Arch Bks.

—Slap-Shot Slump. 2015. (Jake Maddox JV Ser.). (ENG.). 96p. (gr. 3-4). lib. bdg. 25.99 (978-1-4342-9635-1(0)) Stone Arch Bks.

—Touchdown Triumph. Aburto, Jesus, illus. 2015. (Jake Maddox Sports Stories Ser.). (ENG.). 72p. (gr. 2-3). lib. bdg. 25.32 (978-1-4965-0492-0(5)) Stone Arch Bks.

—Track & Field Takedown, 1 vol. Garcia, Eduardo, illus. 2012. (Jake Maddox Sports Stories Ser.). (ENG.). 72p. (gr. 2-3). pap. 5.95 (978-1-4342-3901-3(2)); lib. bdg. 25.32 (978-1-4342-3287-8(5)) Stone Arch Bks.

Madge, Amy. The Adventures of Kwun-Gee & Uba Dooba Boy. 2012. 24p. 29.95 (978-1-4626-9270-5(2)) America Star Bks.

Madison, Alan. Velma Gratch & the Way Cool Butterfly. Hawkes, Kevin, illus. 2007. (ENG.). 40p. (J). (gr. -1-3). 17.99 (978-0-375-83597-1(0), Schwartz & Wade Bks.) Random Hse. Children's Bks.

—Velma Gratch & the Way Cool Butterfly. Hawkes, Kevin, illus. 2012. (ENG.). 40p. (J). (gr. -1-3). pap. 7.99 (978-0-307-97804-2(4), Dragonfly Bks.) Random Hse. Children's Bks.

Madonna, pseud. Ready, Set, Vote! 2009. (English Roses Ser.: 10). (ENG., Illus.). 128p. (J). (gr. 3-7). 9.99 (978-0-14-241127-8(2), Puffin Books) Penguin Young Readers Group.

Magaziner, Lauren. Pilfer Academy: A School So Bad It's Criminal. 2016. (ENG.). 272p. (J). (gr. 3-7). 16.99 (978-0-8037-3919-2(2), Dial Bks) Penguin Young Readers Group.

Magnus, Kellie. Little Lion Goes to School. Robinson, Michael, illus. l.t. ed. 2003. 16p. (J). 9.99 (978-0-9744211-0-0(3)) Media Magic New York.

Magoon, Kekla. Camo Girl. 2012. (ENG.). 224p. (J). (gr. 3-9). pap. 7.99 (978-1-4169-7805-3(4), Aladdin) Simon & Schuster Children's Publishing.

—Camo Girl. 2011. (ENG., Illus.). 224p. (J). (gr. 3-9). 16.99 (978-1-4169-7804-6(6), Simon & Schuster/Paula Wiseman Bks.) Simon & Schuster/Paula Wiseman Bks.

—37 Things I Love (in No Particular Order) 2012. (ENG.). 224p. (YA). (gr. 9-13). 16.99 (978-0-8050-9465-7(2), Holt, Henry & Co. Bks. For Young Readers) Holt, Henry & Co.

—37 Things I Love (in No Particular Order) 2013. (ENG.). 240p. (YA). (gr. 9-13). pap. 14.99 (978-1-250-03430-4(2), 9781250034304) Square Fish.

Mahoney, Daniel J. Monstergarten. Kaminsky, Jef, illus. 2013. (ENG.). 40p. (J). (gr. -1-k). 16.99 (978-1-250-01441-2(7), 9781250014412) Feiwel & Friends.

Mahony, Mary. Harry Scores A Hat Trick, Pawns, Pucks, & Scoliosis: The Sequel to Stand Tall, Harry. Pasternack, Susan, ed. Larkin, Catherine, illus. 2003. 130p. (YA). (gr. 5-8). per. 14.95 (978-0-9658879-3-9(6)) Redding Pr.

—School is Not for Me, Jeremy James Conor McGee. Frederick, Sarah, illus. 2009. (J). pap. 7.95 (978-0-9658879-4-6(4)) Redding Pr.

Maihack, Mike. Secret of the Time Tablets (Cleopatra in Space #3) 2016. (Cleopatra in Space Ser.: 3). (ENG.). 192p. (J). (gr. 3-7). pap. 12.99 (978-0-545-83867-2(3), Graphix) Scholastic, Inc.

—The Thief & the Sword. 2015. (Cleopatra in Space Ser.: 2). (ENG., Illus.). 192p. (J). (gr. 3-7). 22.99 (978-0-545-52844-3(5), Graphix) Scholastic, Inc.

Maizel, Rebecca. Infinite Days. 2010. (Vampire Queen Ser.: 1). (ENG.). 336p. (YA). (gr. 7-18). pap. 9.99 (978-0-312-64991-3(6), 9780312649913, St. Martin's Griffin) St. Martin's Pr.

Maldonado, Torrey. Secret Saturdays. 2012. (ENG.). 208p. (YA). (gr. 7-18). 7.99 (978-0-14-241747-8(5), Puffin Books) Penguin Young Readers Group.

—Secret Saturdays. 2012. lib. bdg. 18.40 (978-0-606-23645-4(7), Turtleback) Turtleback Bks.

Malone, Lee Gjertsen. The Last Boy at St. Edith's. 2016. (Max Ser.). (ENG., Illus.). 272p. (J). (gr. 3-7). 16.99 (978-1-4814-4435-4(2), Aladdin) Simon & Schuster Children's Publishing.

—The Last Boy at St. Edith's. 2017. lib. bdg. 18.40 (978-0-606-40157-9(1)) Turtleback Bks.

Maloney, Peter. A Bump on the Head. 2003. (Just Schoolin' Around Ser.). (Illus.). 32p. (J). pap. (978-0-439-39520-5(8)) Scholastic, Inc.

Maloney, Peter & Zekauskas, Felicia. Thanks for Nothing! 2003. (Illus.). 31p. (J). (978-0-439-55360-5(1)) Scholastic, Inc.

Maltby, Robert I. Diquan & the Book Monster, 1 vol. 2009. 39p. pap. 24.95 (978-1-61546-964-2(8)) America Star Bks.

Mammay, Judith. It's Time. Fargo, Todd, illus. l.t. ed. 2007. 32p. (J). pap. 9.95 (978-0-944727-20-1(4)); lib. bdg. 15.95 (978-0-944727-21-8(2)) Jason & Nordic Pubs. (Turtle Bks.).

—Knowing Joseph. (ENG., Illus.). 256p. (J). (gr. 2-7). 2009. pap. 8.95 (978-1-933831-06-0(5)) 2008. 13.95 (978-1-933831-05-3(7)) Blooming Tree Pr.

Man-Kong, Mary & Tillworth, Mary. Princess Charm School (Barbie) Golden Books Staff, illus. 2011. (Little Golden Book Ser.). (ENG.). 24p. (J). (gr. -1-2). 3.99 (978-0-375-87361-4(9), Golden Bks.) Random Hse. Children's Bks.

Manaster, Ilana. Doreen. 2016. (ENG.). 336p. (YA). (gr. 2-17). 16.95 (978-0-7624-5962-9(X), Running Pr. Kids) Running Pr. Bk. Pubs.

Mancusi, Mari. Gamer Girl. 2010. (ENG.). 256p. (YA). (gr. 7-18). 7.99 (978-0-14-241509-2(X), Speak) Penguin Young Readers Group.

Mandel, Lee. Barf for Lunch. 2012. 184p. pap. 8.99 (978-0-9831996-4-9(7)) Creative Dragon Pr.

Mangum, Kay Lynn. When the Bough Breaks. 2007. 352p. (YA). pap. 15.95 (978-1-59038-748-1(1)) Deseret Bk. Co.

Mangum, Lisa. The Hourglass Door. (Hourglass Door Trilogy: Bk. 1). (YA). 2010. 408p. mass mkt. 7.99 (978-1-60641-679-2(0)) 2009. 432p. (gr. 9-18). 18.95 (978-1-60641-093-6(8)) Shadow Mountain Publishing. (Shadow Mountain).

Manley, Curtis. Shawn Loves Sharks. Subisak, Tracy, illus. 2017. (ENG.). 32p. (J). 17.99 (978-1-62672-134-0(3), 9781626721340) Roaring Brook Pr.

Mann, Elizabeth. Little Man: A Novel. 2014. (ENG., Illus.). 208p. (J). (gr. 5-7). 18.95 (978-1-931414-49-4(1), 9781931414494) Mikaya Pr.

Mann, Jennifer Ann. Sunny Sweet Is So Dead Meat. 2014. (Sunny Sweet Ser.). (ENG., Illus.). 208p. (YA). (gr. 3-6). 15.99 (978-1-59990-978-3(2), 9781599909783, Bloomsbury USA Childrens) Bloomsbury Publishing USA.

Mann, Jennifer K. I Will Never Get a Star on Mrs. Benson's Blackboard. Mann, Jennifer K., illus. (ENG., Illus.). 40p. (J). (gr. k-3). 2017. 6.99 (978-0-7636-9299-5(9)) 2015. 16.99 (978-0-7636-6514-2(2)) Candlewick Pr.

Manny goes to Preschool. 2010. 32p. pap. 3.99 (978-1-4231-3403-9(6)) Disney Pr.

Mansbach, Adam & Zweibel, Alan. Benjamin Franklin: Huge Pain in My... 2015. (Benjamin Franklin Ser.). (ENG., Illus.). 208p. (J). (gr. 5-9). 12.99 (978-1-4847-1304-4(4)) Hyperion Bks. for Children.

—Benjamin Franklin: Huge Pain in My... 2017. (Benjamin Franklin Ser.). (ENG.). 224p. (J). (gr. 5-9). pap. 7.99 (978-1-4847-2537-5(9)) Hyperion Bks. for Children.

Mantell, Paul & Christopher, Matt. Mountain Bike Mania. l.t. ed. 2007. (New Matt Christopher Sports Library). 160p. (J). (gr. 4-6). lib. bdg. 26.60 (978-1-59953-108-3(9)) Norwood Hse. Pr.

Manushkin, Fran. The Big Lie, 1 vol. Lyon, Tammie, illus. 2009. (Katie Woo Ser.). (ENG.). 32p. (gr. k-2). 21.32 (978-1-4048-5497-0(5)) Picture Window Bks.

—Elect Me!, 1 vol. Demski, James, Jr., illus. 2008. (Read-It! Readers: Social Studies). (ENG.). 32p. (gr. k-2). 21.32 (978-1-4048-4911-2(4), Easy Readers) Picture Window Bks.

—Katie & the Class Pet, 1 vol. Lyon, Tammie, illus. 2011. (Katie Woo Ser.). (ENG.). 32p. (gr. k-2). pap. 5.95 (978-1-4048-6856-4(9)); lib. bdg. 21.32 (978-1-4048-6520-4(9)) Picture Window Bks.

—Katie & the Fancy Substitute, 1 vol. 2014. (Katie Woo Ser.). (ENG.). 32p. (gr. k-2). 21.32 (978-1-4795-5188-0(0)) Picture Window Bks.

—Katie Finds a Job, 1 vol. Lyon, Tammie, illus. 2011. (Katie Woo Ser.). (ENG.). 32p. (gr. k-2). pap. 5.95 (978-1-4048-6614-0(0)); lib. bdg. 21.32 (978-1-4048-6513-6(6)) Picture Window Bks.

—Katie Woo. Lyon, Tammie, illus. 2013. (Katie Woo Ser.). (ENG.). 32p. (gr. k-2). pap. 130.90 (978-1-4048-8063-4(1)); pap. 23.80 (978-1-4048-8062-7(3)); lib. bdg. 596.96

(978-1-4048-8054-2(2)); lib. bdg. 85.28 (978-1-4048-8055-9(0)) Picture Window Bks.
—Katie Woo Loves School, 1 vol. Lyon, Tammie, illus. 2013. (Katie Woo Ser.). (ENG.). 96p. (gr. k-2). pap. 4.95 (978-1-4795-2027-5(6)) Picture Window Bks.
—Katie Woo Rules the School, 1 vol. Lyon, Tammie, illus. 2011. (Katie Woo Ser.). (ENG.). 96p. (gr. k-2). pap. 4.95 (978-1-4048-7908-9(0)) Picture Window Bks.
—Katie's Lucky Birthday, 1 vol. Lyon, Tammie, illus. 2011. (Katie Woo Ser.). (ENG.). 32p. (gr. k-2). pap. 5.95 (978-1-4048-6612-6(4)); lib. bdg. 21.32 (978-1-4048-6514-3(4)) Picture Window Bks.
—Make-Believe Class, 1 vol. Lyon, Tammie, illus. 2010. (Katie Woo Ser.). (ENG.). 32p. (gr. k-2). lib. bdg. 21.32 (978-1-4048-5732-2(X)) Picture Window Bks.
—Moo, Katie Woo! Lyon, Tammie, illus. 2013. (J). pap. 35.70 (978-1-4048-8093-1(3)); (ENG.). 32p. lib. bdg. 21.32 (978-1-4048-7653-8(7)) Picture Window Bks.
—No More Teasing, 1 vol. Lyon, Tammie, illus. 2009. (Katie Woo Ser.). (ENG.). 32p. (gr. k-2). 21.32 (978-1-4048-5492-5(4)) Picture Window Bks.
—No Valentines for Katie, 1 vol. Lyon, Tammie, illus. 2010. (Katie Woo Ser.). (ENG.). 32p. (gr. k-2). lib. bdg. 21.32 (978-1-4048-5986-9(1)); pap. 5.95 (978-1-4048-6365-1(6)) Picture Window Bks.
—Pedro, First-Grade Hero. Lyon, Tammie, illus. 2016. (Pedro Ser.). (ENG.). 96p. (gr. k-2). pap. 4.95 (978-1-5158-0112-2(8)) Pedro Pubns. GBR. Dist: Capstone Pub.
—Pedro for President. Lyon, Tammie, illus. 2016. (Pedro Ser.). (ENG.). 32p. (gr. k-2). lib. bdg. 21.32 (978-1-5158-0087-3(3)) Pedro Pubns. GBR. Dist: Capstone Pub.
—Who Needs Glasses?, 1 vol. Lyon, Tammie, illus. 2013. (Katie Woo Ser.). (ENG.). 32p. (gr. k-2). pap. 5.95 (978-1-4048-8049-8(6)); lib. bdg. 21.32 (978-1-4048-7655-2(3)) Picture Window Bks.
Manushkin, Fran & Lyon, Tammie. Basta de Burlas, 1 vol. Lyon, Tammie, illus. 2012. (Katie Woo en Español Ser.). (SPA., Illus.). 32p. (gr. k-2). pap. 6.95 (978-1-4048-7677-4(4)); lib. bdg. 21.32 (978-1-4048-7525-8(5)) Picture Window Bks.
—La Gran Mentira, 1 vol. Lyon, Tammie, illus. 2012. (Katie Woo en Español Ser.). (SPA., Illus.). 32p. (gr. k-2). pap. 6.95 (978-1-4048-7678-1(2)); lib. bdg. 21.32 (978-1-4048-7522-7(0)) Picture Window Bks.
Manzak, Bonnie. The Big Red Cat. 2011. 32p. pap. 21.99 (978-1-4568-6607-5(9)) Xlibris Corp.
Marchetta, Melina. Looking for Alibrandi. 2006. (ENG.). 320p. (YA). (gr. 7-12). reprint ed. per. 9.99 (978-0-375-83694-7(2), Knopf Bks. for Young Readers) Random Hse. Children's Bks.
—Saving Francesca. 2006. (ENG.). 258p. (YA). (gr. 7-12). reprint ed. per. 8.99 (978-0-375-82983-3(0), Knopf Bks. for Young Readers) Random Hse. Children's Bks.
Marciniak, Christine. Always Ali. 2015. 258p. (YA). (978-1-61271-279-6(7)) Zumaya Pubns. LLC.
—Honestly, Ali! 2014. (YA). (978-1-61271-249-9(5)) Zumaya Pubns. LLC.
—Reality Ali. 2012. (J). (978-1-61271-075-4(1)); (978-1-61271-076-1(X)); pap. 13.99 (978-1-61271-074-7(3)) Zumaya Pubns. LLC.
Marcionette, Jake. Just Jake. Villa, Victor Rivas, illus. 2014. (Just Jake Ser.: No. 1). (ENG.). 160p. (J). (gr. 3-7). 11.99 (978-0-448-46692-7(9), Grosset & Dunlap) Penguin Young Readers Group.
—Just Jake: Dog Eat Dog. Villa, Victor Rivas, illus. 2015. (Just Jake Ser.: No. 2). (ENG.). 196p. (J). (gr. 3-7). 11.99 (978-0-448-46693-4(7), Grosset & Dunlap) Penguin Young Readers Group.
Marcus, Kimberly. Exposed. 2012. (ENG.). 272p. (YA). (gr. 9). pap. 8.99 (978-0-375-86591-6(8), Ember) Random Hse. Children's Bks.
Margaret I. Pascuzzo. Anton Finds a Treasure. Bicking, Judith, illus. 2008. 16p. pap. 12.00 (978-1-4251-8683-8(1)) Trafford Publishing.
Margolin, Phillip & Rome, Ami Margolin. Vanishing Acts. 2012. (ENG.). 176p. (J). (gr. 3-7). pap. 8.99 (978-0-06-188558-7(4)) HarperCollins Pubs.
Margolis, Leslie. Boys Are Dogs. (Annabelle Unleashed Ser.). (ENG.). (YA). (gr. 3-6). 2009. 224p. pap. 6.99 (978-1-59990-381-1(4), 9781599903811) 2008. (Illus.). 208p. 15.99 (978-1-59990-221-0(4), 9781599902210) Bloomsbury Publishing USA. (Bloomsbury USA Childrens).
—Everybody Bugs Out. (Annabelle Unleashed Ser.). (ENG.). (YA). (gr. 3-12). 2012. 224p. pap. 6.99 (978-1-59990-828-1(X), 9781599908281) 2011. 208p. 15.99 (978-1-59990-526-6(4), 9781599905266) Bloomsbury Publishing USA. (Bloomsbury USA Childrens).
—Girls Acting Catty. (Annabelle Unleashed Ser.). (ENG.). (YA). (gr. 3-6). 2010. 208p. pap. 6.99 (978-1-59990-520-4(5), 9781599905204) 2009. 192p. 15.99 (978-1-59990-237-1(0), 9781599902371) Bloomsbury Publishing USA. (Bloomsbury USA Childrens).
—Girl's Best Friend. (Maggie Brooklyn Mystery Ser.). (ENG.). (YA). (gr. 3-12). 2011. 288p. pap. 7.99 (978-1-59990-690-4(2), 9781599906904) 2010. 272p. 14.99 (978-1-59990-525-9(6), 9781599905259) Bloomsbury Publishing USA. (Bloomsbury USA Childrens).
—One Tough Chick. (Annabelle Unleashed Ser.). (ENG.). (YA). (gr. 3-6). 2014. 192p. pap. 6.99 (978-1-61963-161-8(X), 9781619631618) 2013. 176p. 15.99 (978-1-59990-961-5(8), 9781599909615) Bloomsbury Publishing USA. (Bloomsbury USA Childrens).
—The Secrets at the Chocolate Mansion. 2013. (Maggie Brooklyn Mystery Ser.). (ENG.). 256p. (YA). (gr. 3-6). 16.99 (978-1-61963-036-9(2), 9781619630369, Bloomsbury USA Childrens) Bloomsbury Publishing USA.
—Secrets at the Chocolate Mansion. 2014. (Maggie Brooklyn Mystery Ser.). (ENG.). 272p. (YA). (gr. 3-6). pap. 7.99 (978-1-61963-493-0(7), 9781619634930, Bloomsbury USA Childrens) Bloomsbury Publishing USA.
—Vanishing Acts. (Maggie Brooklyn Mystery Ser.). (ENG.). (YA). (gr. 3-6). 2013. 256p. pap. 6.99 (978-1-59990-981-3(2), 9781599909813) 2012. 240p. 15.99 (978-1-59990-536-5(1), 9781599905365) Bloomsbury Publishing USA. (Bloomsbury USA Childrens).
Marin, Victoria. Aiden's Waltz. 2012. 24p. pap. 15.99 (978-1-4691-6271-3(7)) Xlibris Corp.
Marino, Peter. Dough Boy. 2005. (ENG.). 176p. (YA). (gr. 7-12). 17.95 (978-0-8234-1873-2(1)) Holiday Hse., Inc.
Marioile, Mathieu. Changing Moon. MiniKim et al, illus. 2010. (Nola's Worlds Ser.: 1). (ENG.). 136p. (J). (gr. 6-9). 30.60 (978-0-7613-6502-0(8)) Lerner Publishing Group.
—Changing Moon. Jeffrey, Erica Olson, tr. from FRE. MiniKim et al, illus. 2010. (Nola's Worlds Ser.: 1). (ENG.). 136p. (J). (gr. 6-9). pap. 9.95 (978-0-7613-6538-9(9), Graphic Universe™) Lerner Publishing Group.
—Changing Moon. rev. ed. 2010. pap. 56.72 (978-0-7613-6953-0(8)) Lerner Publishing Group.
Mariz, Rae. The Unidentified. (ENG.). 304p. (YA). (gr. 8). 2012. pap. 8.99 (978-0-06-180209-6(3)) 2010. 16.99 (978-0-06-180208-9(5)) HarperCollins Pubs.
Markey, Kevin. Wall Ball. 2011. (Super Sluggers Ser.). (ENG.). 208p. (J). (gr. 3-7). pap. 5.99 (978-0-06-115223-8(4)) HarperCollins Pubs.
Marlow, Herb. The Classroom Vandal. 2003. (J). 19.95 (978-1-893595-36-1(6)) Four Seasons Bks., Inc.
Marmon, Jim. Alexander Barnaby Meadowlark. 2007. 132p. per. 19.95 (978-1-4241-7662-5(X)) America Star Bks.
Marois, Andre. The Sandwich Thief. Doyon, Patrick, illus. 2016. (ENG.). 160p. (J). (gr. 1-4). 14.99 (978-1-4521-4659-1(4)) Chronicle Bks. LLC.
Marr Osb, Andrew. From Beyond to Here: Merendael's Gift & Other Stories. 2012. 320p. (gr. 4-6). 29.95 (978-1-4759-3460-1(2)); pap. 19.95 (978-1-4759-3458-8(0)) iUniverse, Inc.
Marsh, Carole. Adventure to the Eight Wonders of the World. 2007. (Field Trips (Gallopade International) Ser.). (Illus.). 118p. (J). (gr. 2-9). per. 5.99 (978-0-635-06335-9(2)) Gallopade International.
—Adventure to the Planet Mars! 2007. (Field Trips (Gallopade International) Ser.). (Illus.). 114p. (J). (gr. 4-9). per. 5.99 (978-0-635-06336-6(0)) Gallopade International.
Marsh, Robert. Monster & Me, 1 vol. Percival, Tom, illus. 2009. (Monster & Me Ser.). (ENG.). 40p. (gr. 1-3). lib. bdg. 23.99 (978-1-4342-1589-5(X), Graphic Sparks) Stone Arch Bks.
—Monster in the Outfield, 1 vol. Percival, Tom, illus. 2009. (Monster & Me Ser.). (ENG.). 40p. (gr. 1-3). lib. bdg. 23.99 (978-1-4342-1590-1(3), Graphic Sparks) Stone Arch Bks.
—Monster Moneymaker, 1 vol. Percival, Tom, illus. 2010. (Monster & Me Ser.). (ENG.). 40p. (gr. 1-3). lib. bdg. 23.99 (978-1-4342-1891-9(0), Graphic Sparks) Stone Arch Bks.
Marshall, Jane Garrett. The Christmas Tree That Cried. Tomasek, Dean, illus. 2013. 106p. pap. 24.99 (978-0-9896247-0-1(6)) WRB Pub.
Marshall, Rita. I Still Hate to Read! Delessert, Etienne, illus. 2008. (ENG.). 32p. (J). (gr. 1-3). 19.95 (978-1-56846-174-8(7), Creative Editions) Creative Co., The.
Marshall, Stacey A. Captain Courage & the Fear-Squishing Shoes. Morse, Michelle, illus. 2012. 16p. pap. 9.95 (978-1-61633-319-5(7)) Guardian Angel Publishing, Inc.
Marston, Carrie. Catch Me If You Can. 2012. 82p. (gr. 10-12). pap. 9.95 (978-1-4497-6706-8(0), WestBow Pr.) Author Solutions, Inc.
Martín Anguita, Carmen & Carmen, Martín Anguita. Marta y Su Dragón (Martha & Her Dragon) Cortazar, Alicia Canas, illus. 2008. (SPA.). 32p. (J). 10.99 (978-84-241-5444-8(4)) Everest Editora ESP. Dist: Lectorum Pubns., Inc.
—El Primer Día de Colegio de David. Cortazar, Alicia Canas, illus. 2008. (SPA.). 32p. (J). 10.99 (978-84-241-5790-6(7)) Everest Editora ESP. Dist: Lectorum Pubns., Inc.
Martin, Ann M. Belle Teal. 2004. (Illus.). 214p. (gr. 4-7). 17.00 (978-0-7569-2929-9(6)) Perfection Learning Corp.
—Family Tree Book Three: Best Kept Secret. 2014. (ENG.). 224p. (J). (gr. 3-7). 16.99 (978-0-545-35944-3(9), Scholastic Pr.) Scholastic, Inc.
—Here Today. 2005. 308p. (gr. 5-9). 18.00 (978-0-7569-5104-7(6)) Perfection Learning Corp.
—Here Today. 2005. (ENG.). 336p. (J). (gr. 3-7). pap. 7.99 (978-0-439-57945-2(7), Scholastic Paperbacks) Scholastic, Inc.
Martin, Bill, Jr. & Sampson, Michael. Kitty Cat, Kitty Cat, Are You Going to School?, 0 vols. Bryant, Laura J., illus. 2013. (ENG.). 24p. (J). (gr. -1-2). 16.99 (978-1-4778-1722-3(0), 9781477817223, Amazon Children's Publishing) Amazon Publishing.
Martin, C. K. Kelly. The Lighter Side of Life & Death. 2010. (YA). pap. (978-0-375-84590-1(9)) Random Hse. Children's Bks.
Martin Ed.D., Pamela. Include Me. 2013. 48p. pap. (978-1-4602-2643-8(7)) FriesenPress.
Martin, Sheila. Muddy Water. 2005. pap. 16.95 (978-1-4137-8551-7(4)) PublishAmerica, Inc.
Martinez, Angel. The Story of Natalie: Natalie gets prepare for a day of School. 2011. 28p. pap. 13.95 (978-1-4633-0761-5(6)) Palibrio.
Martinez, Claudia Guadalupe. The Smell of Old Lady Perfume. 2008. (ENG., Illus.). 248p. (J). (gr. 4-9). 15.95 (978-1-933693-18-7(5)) Cinco Puntos Pr.
Martinez, Claudia Guadalupe. Smell of Old Lady Perfume. 2011. (ENG., Illus.). 256p. (J). (gr. 4-10). pap. 7.95 (978-1-933693-88-0(6)) Cinco Puntos Pr.
Martinez, Jessica. The Space Between Us. (ENG., (YA). (gr. 9). 2013. Illus.). 416p. pap. 9.99 (978-1-4424-2056-4(1)) 2012. 400p. 16.99 (978-1-4424-2055-7(3)) Simon Pulse. (Simon Pulse).
Marty, Joyce D. I Was in School When...,Dane's Great Day. 2004. (J). 17.00 (978-0-9753992-0-0(9)) Martin Publishing.
Mary-Todd, Jonathan. Lock-In. 2011. (Night Fall Ser.). (ENG.). 112p. (YA). (gr. 6-12). pap. 7.95 (978-0-7613-7815-0(4)); lib. bdg. 27.93 (978-0-7613-7743-6(3)) Lerner Publishing Group.
Marzullo, Re. Sped. 2013. 214p. pap. 9.99 (978-0-9889618-0-7(6)) Sauvignon Pr.
Masciola, Carol. The Yearbook. 2015. (ENG.). 224p. (YA). 17.99 (978-1-4405-8897-6(X), Simon Pulse) Simon Pulse.
Mason, Charlene. William's First Day of Preschool. 2012. 24p. pap. 24.95 (978-1-4626-7471-8(2)) America Star Bks.
Mason, Jane B. Without Annette. 2016. (ENG.). 336p. (YA). (gr. 7). 18.99 (978-0-545-81995-4(4), Scholastic Pr.) Scholastic, Inc.
Mason, Jane B. & Hines-Stephens, Sarah. Let Sleeping Dogs Spy. Phillips, Craig, illus. 2012. 91p. (J). pap. (978-0-545-37470-5(7)) Scholastic, Inc.
Mason, Richard. The Red Scarf: A Country Boy's Christmas Story. 2011. (ENG.). 155p. (J). (gr. 3-7). pap. 11.95 (978-0-87483-954-8(8)) August Hse. Pubs., Inc.
Mass, Wendy. Heaven Looks a Lot Like the Mall. 2008. (ENG.). 256p. (J). (gr. 7-17). pap. 10.00 (978-0-316-05850-6(5)) Little, Brown Bks. for Young Readers.
—Leap Day. 2006. (ENG.). 208p. (YA). (gr. 7-17). per. 10.99 (978-0-316-05828-5(9)) Little, Brown Bks. for Young Readers.
—A Mango-Shaped Space. 2005. (ENG.). 240p. (YA). (gr. 3-7). per. 8.99 (978-0-316-05825-4(4)) Little, Brown Bks. for Young Readers.
Massaro, Michael. Tonny Towne & the Amazing Brain. 2011. (ENG.). 248p. pap. 9.55 (978-1-4565-2044-1(X)) CreateSpace Independent Publishing Platform.
Massey, Carol. Not a Friend. 2005. 79p. pap. 9.95 (978-0-7414-2319-1(7)) Infinity Publishing.
Masterson, Josephine. Henry's Hamster Goes to School. 2015. (Rosen REAL Readers: STEM & STEAM Collection). (ENG.). 8p. pap. 5.46 (978-1-4994-9595-9(1), Rosen Classroom) Rosen Publishing Group, Inc., The.
Mata, Julie. Kate Walden Directs: Bride of Slug Man. 2015. (ENG., Illus.). 288p. (J). (gr. 3-7). 16.99 (978-1-4231-9460-6(8)) Disney Pr.
—Kate Walden Directs: Bride of Slug Man. 2016. (Kate Walden Directs Ser.). (ENG.). 288p. (J). (gr. 3-7). pap. 6.99 (978-1-4847-4746-9(1)) Hyperion Bks. for Children.
—Night of the Zombie Chickens. 2014. (Kate Walden Ser.). (ENG., Illus.). 288p. (J). (gr. 3-7). 16.99 (978-1-4231-9459-0(4)) Hyperion Bks. for Children.
Matharu, Taran. The Novice. 2015. (Summoner Trilogy: Bk. 1). (ENG.). 384p. (YA). (gr. 7). 18.99 (978-1-250-06712-8(X), 9781250067128) Feiwel & Friends.
—The Novice. Barcellona, Christine, ed. 2016. (Summoner Trilogy Ser.: Bk. 1). (ENG.). 384p. (YA). pap. 10.99 (978-1-250-08005-9(3), 9781250080059) Square Fish.
—The Novice. 2016. (Summoner Trilogy: Bk. 1). (ENG.). (YA). (gr. 7-12). lib. bdg. 22.10 **(978-0-606-39884-8(8))** Turtleback Bks.
Matheis, Mickie. Save the School Bus! (PAW Patrol) Petrossi, Fabrizio, illus. 2017. (Little Golden Book Ser.). (ENG.). 24p. (J). (-k). 4.99 **(978-1-5247-1665-3(0)**, Golden Bks.) Random Hse. Children's Bks.
Mathieu, Jennifer. Moxie. 2017. (YA). pap. **(978-1-250-10426-7(2))** Roaring Brook Pr.
Matlin, Marlee & Cooney, Doug. Nobody's Perfect. 2006. (ENG., Illus.). 240p. (J). (gr. 3-7). 15.95 (978-0-689-86986-0(X), Simon & Schuster Bks. For Young Readers) Simon & Schuster Bks. For Young Readers.
Matranga, Cindy. It Never Rains in Sunny California. 2010. 32p. pap. 12.99 (978-1-4389-4816-4(6)) AuthorHouse.
Mattel. Monster High: Great Scarrier Reef 8x8. 2016. (ENG., Illus.). 24p. (J). (gr. -1-3). pap. 3.99 (978-0-316-30127-5(2)) Little, Brown Bks. for Young Readers.
—Monster High: Great Scarrier Reef Reader. 2016. (Passport to Reading Level 3 Ser.). (ENG., Illus.). 32p. (J). (gr. -1-3). pap. 3.99 (978-0-316-30130-5(2)) Little, Brown Bks. for Young Readers.
—Monster High: Great Scarrier Reef: the Deluxe Junior Novel. 2016. (ENG.). 144p. (J). (gr. 3-7). 9.99 (978-0-316-27046-5(6)) Little, Brown Bks. for Young Readers.
Matthews, Ian. Albert the Big Eyed Squirrel. 2011. 25p. (J). pap. 15.95 (978-1-4327-5904-9(3)) Outskirts Pr., Inc.
Matthews, Owen. How to Win at High School. 2015. (ENG.). 496p. (YA). (gr. 9). 17.99 (978-0-06-233686-6(X), HarperTeen) HarperCollins Pubs.
Maurer, Shari. Change of Heart. 2010. 290p. (YA). 16.95 (978-1-934813-36-2(2)) Westside Bks.
May, Eleanor. Albert Starts School. Melmon, Deborah, illus. 2015. (Mouse Math (r) Ser.). (ENG.). 32p. (J). (gr. -1-1). 22.60 (978-1-57565-741-7(4)) Kane Press, Inc.
—The Bay School Blogger. 2008. pap. 34.95 (978-1-58013-772-0(5)) Kane Press, Inc.
—Mac & Cheese, Pleeeeeze! 2008. pap. 34.95 (978-1-58013-780-5(6)) Kane Press, Inc.
—Mac & Cheese, Pleeeeze! Palmisciano, Diane, illus. 2008. (Math Matters Ser.). (ENG.). 32p. (J). (gr. -1-3). pap. 5.95 (978-1-57565-260-3(9)) Kane Press, Inc.
May, J. E. Louis' School Days. 2007. 252p. 97.99 (978-1-4280-7719-5(7)); per. 90.99 (978-1-4280-7714-0(6)) IndyPublish.com.
May, Kyla. Coco: My Delicious Life. 2013. (Lotus Lane Ser.: 2). (ENG., Illus.). 96p. (J). (gr. 1-3). 15.99 (978-0-545-49615-5(2)); pap. 4.99 (978-0-545-44514-6(0)) Scholastic, Inc.
—Coco: My Delicious Life. 2013. (Lotus Lane Ser.: 2). lib. bdg. 14.75 (978-0-606-31978-2(6), Turtleback) Turtleback Bks.
—Kiki: My Stylish Life. 2013. (Lotus Lane Ser.: 1). (ENG.). 96p. (J). (gr. 1-3). pap. 4.99 (978-0-545-44512-2(4)) Scholastic, Inc.
—Kiki: My Stylish Life. 2013. (Lotus Lane Ser.: 1). lib. bdg. 14.75 (978-0-606-31977-5(8), Turtleback) Turtleback Bks.
—Kiki Bk. 1: My Stylish Life. 2013. (Lotus Lane Ser.: 1). (ENG.). 96p. (J). (gr. 1-3). lib. bdg. 15.99 (978-0-545-49613-1(6)) Scholastic, Inc.
—Mika: My New Life. 2013. (Lotus Lane Ser.: 4). (ENG.). 96p. (J). (gr. 1-3). pap. 4.99 (978-0-545-44519-1(1)) Scholastic, Inc.
—Mika: My New Life. 2013. (Lotus Lane Ser.: 4). lib. bdg. 14.75 (978-0-606-32365-9(1), Turtleback) Turtleback Bks.
Mayer, Kirsten. Attack of the Evil Minions! Miller, Ed, illus. 2013. (ENG.). 32p. (J). (gr. -1-3). 12.99 (978-0-316-23444-3(3)) Little, Brown Bks. for Young Readers.
—Monster High: Ghoul Spirit: A Monster High Doodle Book. GONZALES, Chuck, illus. 2013. (ENG.). 128p. (J). (gr. 1-17). 12.99 (978-0-316-24655-2(7)) Little, Brown Bks. for Young Readers.
Mayer, Mercer. Little Critter: Going to the Sea Park. Mayer, Mercer, illus. 2017. (My First I Can Read Ser.). (Illus.). 40p. (J). (gr. -1-3). 9.99 **(978-0-06-257281-3(4))** HarperCollins Pubs.
—Little Critter: Just Pick Us, Please! Mayer, Mercer, illus. 2017. (My First I Can Read Ser.). (Illus.). 32p. (J). (gr. -1-3). pap. 3.99 **(978-0-06-243142-4(0))** HarperCollins Pubs.
Mayhall, Robin. He Loves Me, He Loves Me Not. Cella, Kristen & Tiede, Dirk, illus. 2013. (My Boyfriend Is a Monster Ser.: 7). (ENG.). 128p. (YA). (gr. 7-12). lib. bdg. 29.27 (978-0-7613-6005-6(0), Graphic Universe™) Lerner Publishing Group.
—He Loves Me, He Loves Me Not. Cella, Kristen et al, illus. 2013. (My Boyfriend Is a Monster Ser.: 7). (ENG.). 128p. (YA). (gr. 7-12). pap. 9.95 (978-0-7613-8548-6(7), Graphic Universe™) Lerner Publishing Group.
Maynard, Joyce. The Cloud Chamber. 2006. (ENG.). 288p. (YA). (gr. 7-7). pap. 13.99 (978-1-4169-2699-3(2), Simon Pulse) Simon Pulse.
Mazer, Anne. Good Things Come in Small Packages. 2003. (Amazing Days of Abby Hayes Ser.: Bk. 12). (Illus.). 101p. (J). (gr. 4-7). 12.65 (978-0-7569-3935-9(6)) Perfection Learning Corp.
—It's Music to My Ears. 2005. (Amazing Days of Abby Hayes Ser.). (Illus.). 110p. (J). (gr. 3-7). 12.65 (978-0-7569-5910-4(1)) Perfection Learning Corp.
—Now You See It, Now You Don't. 2005. (Amazing Days of Abby Hayes Ser.: Bk. 15). (Illus.). 126p. (J). (gr. 4-7). 12.65 (978-0-7569-5932-6(2)) Perfection Learning Corp.
—Some Things Never Change. 2004. (Amazing Days of Abby Hayes Ser.: Bk. 13). (Illus.). 101p. (J). (gr. 4-7). 12.65 (978-0-7569-5302-7(2)) Perfection Learning Corp.
—That's the Way the Cookie Crumbles. 2005. (Amazing Days of Abby Hayes Ser.: Bk. 16). (Illus.). 119p. (J). (gr. 3-7). 12.65 (978-0-7569-6480-1(6)) Perfection Learning Corp.
Mazer, Norma Fox. Crazy Fish. 2007. (ENG., Illus.). 160p. (J). (gr. 2-5). pap. 11.95 (978-0-15-206373-3(0)) Houghton Mifflin Harcourt Publishing Co.
—Ten Ways to Make My Sister Disappear. 2007. (ENG.). 128p. (J). (gr. 4-7). 16.99 (978-0-439-83983-9(1), Levine, Arthur A. Bks.) Scholastic, Inc.
—Ten Ways to Make My Sister Disappear. l.t. ed. 2008. (Thorndike Literacy Bridge Ser.). 207p. (J). (gr. 4-7). 22.95 (978-1-4104-0510-4(9)) Thorndike Pr.
McAnulty, Stacy. Goldie Blox Rules the School! 2017. (Goldie Blox Ser.). lib. bdg. 17.20 **(978-0-606-40256-9(X))** Turtleback Bks.
McBride, Kristina. The Tension of Opposites. 2011. (ENG.). 288p. (J). (gr. 9). pap. 8.99 (978-1-60684-213-3(7), Carolrhoda Lab™) Lerner Publishing Group.
McBride, Susan. Very Bad Things. 2014. (ENG.). 240p. (YA). (gr. 7). lib. bdg. 20.99 (978-0-385-90704-0(4), Delacorte Pr.) Random Hse. Children's Bks.
McBrier, Page. Beatrice's Goat. Lohstoeter, Lori, illus. 2004. (ENG.). 40p. (J). (gr. -1-3). reprint ed. 7.99 (978-0-689-86990-7(8), Aladdin) Simon & Schuster Children's Publishing.
McCafferty, Megan. Jessica Darling's It List 2: The (Totally Not) Guaranteed Guide to Friends, Foes & Faux Friends. 2015. (Jessica Darling's It List Ser.: 2). (ENG.). 208p. (J). (gr. 3-7). pap. 8.00 (978-0-316-24503-6(8), Poppy) Little, Brown Bks. for Young Readers.
—The (Totally Not) Guaranteed Guide to Popularity, Prettiness & Perfection. 2014. (Jessica Darling's It List Ser.: 1). (ENG.). 240p. (J). (gr. 3-7). pap. 8.99 (978-0-316-24498-5(8), Poppy) Little, Brown Bks. for Young Readers.
—The (Totally Not) Guaranteed Guide to Stressing, Obsessing & Second-Guessing. 2015. (Jessica Darling's It List Ser.: 3). (ENG.). 224p. (J). (gr. 3-7). 17.00 (978-0-316-33324-5(7)) Little Brown & Co.
McCarthy, Jenna & Evans, Carolyn. Maggie Malone Makes a Splash. 2015. (Maggie Malone Ser.: 3). (ENG.). 192p. (J). (gr. 4-7). pap. 8.99 (978-1-4022-9312-2(7), Sourcebooks Jabberwocky) Sourcebooks, Inc.
McCarthy, Jenna, et al. Maggie Malone & the Mostly Magical Boots. 2014. (Maggie Malone Ser.: 1). (ENG.). 224p. (J). (gr. 3-6). pap. 6.99 (978-1-4022-9306-1(2), 9781402293061, Sourcebooks Jabberwocky) Sourcebooks, Inc.
McCarty, Peter. Henry in Love. McCarty, Peter, illus. 2009. (ENG., Illus.). 48p. (J). (gr. -1-1). 16.99 (978-0-06-114288-8(3)) HarperCollins Pubs.
McClintock, Norah. My Side, 1 vol. 2013. (Orca Soundings Ser.). (ENG.). 128p. (YA). (gr. 8-12). pap. 9.95 (978-1-4598-0511-8(9)); lib. bdg. 16.95 (978-1-4598-0517-0(8)) Orca Bk. Pubs. USA.
McCombie, Karen. My Big (Strange) Happy Family. Monks, Lydia, illus. 2009. (J). pap. (978-0-385-73597-1(9), Yearling) Random Hse. Children's Bks.
McConnell, Edith J. Their Times. 2004. 44p. (J). per. 11.66 (978-1-4116-1370-6(8)) Lulu Pr., Inc.
McConville, Alexandra. The Adventures of Sass-O-Frask: A Tale of Kindness. 2012. 32p. pap. 19.99 (978-1-4772-6006-7(4)) AuthorHouse.
McCormick, Wilfred. The Three-Two Pitch: A Bronc Burnett Story. 2011. 192p. 42.95 (978-1-258-10008-7(8)) Literary Licensing, LLC.
McCourt, Lisa. It's Time for School. Moore, Cyd, illus. 2017. (Stinky Face Ser.). (ENG.). 32p. (J). (— 1). bds. 6.99 **(978-1-338-13582-4(1)**, Cartwheel Bks.) Scholastic, Inc.
McCranie, Stephen. Mal & Chad - The Biggest, Bestest Time Ever! McCranie, Stephen, illus. 2011. (Mal & Chad Ser.: 1). (ENG., Illus.). 224p. (J). (gr. 3-7). 9.99 (978-0-399-25221-1(5), Philomel Bks.) Penguin Young Readers Group.
Mccroary, Greg. Mia. 2008. (ENG., Illus.). 1p. (J). 6.95 (978-1-74110-636-7(2)) New Holland Pubs. Pty. Ltd. AUS. Dist: Tuttle Publishing.
McCullough, Dicy. Tired of School. 2011. 28p. pap. 15.99 (978-1-4628-9229-7(9)) Xlibris Corp.
McCullough, Kelly. School for Sidekicks. 2015. (ENG.). 336p. (J). (gr. 4-9). 16.99 (978-1-250-03926-2(6), 9781250039262) Feiwel & Friends.
McCully, Emily Arnold. My Heart Glow: Alice Cogswell, Thomas Gallaudet, & the Birth of American Sign Language. McCully, Emily Arnold, illus. 2008. (ENG., Illus.). 40p. (gr. 1-4). 15.99 (978-1-4231-0028-7(X)) Hyperion Pr.
—School. McCully, Emily Arnold, illus. 2005. (Illus.). 32p. (J). lib. bdg. 16.89 (978-0-06-623857-9(9)) HarperCollins Pubs.
McCune, Susan. Mr. Morgan Saves the Day, 01 vols., 1. 2016. (Rosen REAL Readers: Social Studies Nonfiction / Fiction: Family, Community, & the World Ser.). (ENG.). 12p. (J). pap. 6.33 (978-1-5081-1940-1(6), Rosen Classroom) Rosen Publishing Group, Inc., The.

S

McDaniel, Lurlene. Hit & Run. 2013. (ENG.). 192p. (YA). (gr. 7). pap. 8.99 (978-0-385-74381-5(5), Ember) Random Hse. Children's Bks.
—Letting Go of Lisa. 2007. (ENG.). 192p. (YA). (gr. 7-12). mass mkt. 6.99 (978-0-440-23868-3(4), Laurel Leaf) Random Hse. Children's Bks.
—Prey. 2010. (ENG.). 208p. (YA). (gr. 7). mass mkt. 7.99 (978-0-440-24015-0(8), Laurel Leaf) Random Hse. Children's Bks.
—Red Heart Tattoo. 2013. (ENG.). 224p. (YA). (gr. 7). pap. 8.99 (978-0-440-24019-8(0), Ember) Random Hse. Children's Bks.
McDaniels, Preston, illus. Phineas L. MacGuire ... Gets Cooking! 2014. (From the Highly Scientific Notebooks of Phineas L. MacGuire Ser.). (ENG.). 208p. (J). (gr. 3-7). 16.99 (978-1-4814-0099-2(1), Atheneum Bks. for Young Readers) Simon & Schuster Children's Publishing.
McDonald, Abby. The Anti-Prom. (ENG., Illus.). 288p. (YA). (gr. 9). 2012. pap. 7.99 (978-0-7636-5847-2(2)) 2011. 16.99 (978-0-7636-4956-2(2)) Candlewick Pr.
—Sophomore Switch. 2010. (ENG., Illus.). 304p. (YA). (gr. 9). pap. 8.99 (978-0-7636-4774-2(8)) Candlewick Pr.
McDonald, Megan. Around the World in 8 1/2 Days. 2007. (Judy Moody Ser.: 7). (SPA.). (J). 1.25 (978-1-4281-3376-1(3)) Recorded Bks., Inc.
—Around the World in 8 1/2 Days. Reynolds, Peter H., illus. 2010. (Judy Moody Ser.: 7). (ENG.). 176p. (J). (gr. 1-4). 15.99 (978-0-7636-4864-0(7)) Candlewick Pr.
—Around the World in 8 1/2 Days. 2010. (Judy Moody Ser.: 7). lib. bdg. 16.00 (978-0-606-12349-5(0), Turtleback) Turtleback Bks.
—Around the World in 8 1/2 Days, Bk. 7. Reynolds, Peter H., illus. 2010. (Judy Moody Ser.: 7). (ENG.). 176p. (J). (gr. 1-4). pap. 5.99 (978-0-7636-4863-3(9)) Candlewick Pr.
—Beetle Mcgrady Eats Bugs! Manning, Jane K., illus. 2005. (ENG.). 32p. (J). (gr. k-5). 17.99 (978-0-06-001354-7(0), Greenwillow Bks.) HarperCollins Pubs.
—The Doctor Is In! Reynolds, Peter H., illus. 2010. (Judy Moody Ser.: 5). (ENG.). 176p. (J). (gr. 1-4). 15.99 (978-0-7636-4862-6(0)); pap. 5.99 (978-0-7636-4861-9(2)) Candlewick Pr.
—The Doctor Is In! 2010. (Judy Moody Ser.: 5). lib. bdg. 16.00 (978-0-606-12343-3(1), Turtleback) Turtleback Bks.
—The Holly Joliday. Reynolds, Peter H., illus. 2008. (Judy Moody Ser.: No. 1). (ENG.). 96p. (J). (gr. k-3). pap. 7.99 (978-0-7636-4113-9(8)) Candlewick Pr.
—The Incredible Shrinking Kid. Reynolds, Peter H., illus. 2013. (Stink Ser.: 1). (ENG.). (J). (gr. 1-4). 112p. 12.99 (978-0-7636-6388-9(3)); 128p. pap. 4.99 (978-0-7636-6426-8(X)) Candlewick Pr.
—It's Picture Day Today! Tillotson, Katherine, illus. 2009. (ENG.). 36p. (J). (gr. -1-3). 16.99 (978-1-4169-2434-0(5), Atheneum/Richard Jackson Bks.) Simon & Schuster Children's Publishing.
—Judy Moody. 2010. (Judy Moody Ser.: 1). lib. bdg. 16.00 (978-0-606-12330-3(X), Turtleback) Turtleback Bks.
—Judy Moody & Stink in the School's Out Collection. Reynolds, Peter H., illus. 2015. (Judy Moody Ser.). (ENG.). (J). (gr. 1-4). pap. 19.97 (978-0-7636-8018-3(4)) Candlewick Pr.
—Judy Moody & the Bad Luck Charm. 2013. (Judy Moody Ser.: 11). lib. bdg. 16.00 (978-0-606-32099-3(7), Turtleback) Turtleback Bks.
—Judy Moody Predicts the Future. Reynolds, Peter H., illus. 2010. (Judy Moody Ser.: 4). (ENG.). 160p. (J). (gr. 1-4). 15.99 (978-0-7636-4858-9(2)); pap. 5.99 (978-0-7636-4857-2(4)) Candlewick Pr.
—Judy Moody Predicts the Future. 2010. (Judy Moody Ser.: 4). lib. bdg. 16.00 (978-0-606-12341-9(5), Turtleback) Turtleback Bks.
—Judy Moody Saves the World! Reynolds, Peter H., illus. 2004. (Judy Moody Ser.: Bk. 3). 144p. (J). (gr. 1-5). 13.65 (978-0-7569-2588-8(6)) Perfection Learning Corp.
—Judy Moody Saves the World! Reynolds, Peter H., illus. 2010. (Judy Moody Ser.: 3). (ENG.). 160p. (J). (gr. 1-4). 15.99 (978-0-7636-4860-2(4)) Candlewick Pr.
—Judy Moody Saves the World! 2010. (Judy Moody Ser.: 3). lib. bdg. 16.00 (978-0-606-12340-2(7), Turtleback) Turtleback Bks.
—Judy Moody Saves the World!, Bk. 3. Reynolds, Peter H., illus. 2010. (Judy Moody Ser.: 3). (ENG.). 160p. (J). (gr. 1-4). pap. 5.99 (978-0-7636-4859-6(0)) Candlewick Pr.
—Solar System Superhero. Reynolds, Peter H., illus. 2013. (Stink Ser.: 5). (ENG.). (J). (gr. 1-4). 144p. pap. 4.99 (978-0-7636-6425-1(1));Bk. 5. 128p. 12.99 (978-0-7636-6392-6(1)) Candlewick Pr.
—Solar System Superhero, 1 vol. Reynolds, Peter H., illus. 2012. (Stink Ser.: No. 2). (ENG.). 144p. (J). (gr. 2-5). 24.21 (978-1-59961-197-6(X)) Spotlight.
—Solar System Superhero. 2013. (Stink Ser.: 5). lib. bdg. 14.75 (978-0-606-31591-3(8), Turtleback) Turtleback Bks.
—Stink. 2013. (Stink Ser.: 1). lib. bdg. 14.75 (978-0-606-31587-6(X), Turtleback) Turtleback Bks.
—Stink: The Incredible Shrinking Kid. Reynolds, Peter H., illus. 2010. (Stink Ser.: No. 1). 112p. (J). (gr. k-4). 24.21 (978-1-59961-686-5(6)) Spotlight.
—Stink - The Super-Incredible Collection, Bks. 1-3. Reynolds, Peter H., illus. 2013. (Stink Ser.). (ENG.). 352p. (J). (gr. k-3). pap. 14.97 (978-0-7636-6831-0(1)) Candlewick Pr.
—Stink & the Attack of the Slime Mold. Reynolds, Peter H., illus. 2016. (Stink Ser.: 10). (ENG.). 144p. (J). (gr. 1-4). 12.99 (978-0-7636-5554-9(6)) Candlewick Pr.
—Stink & the Attack of the Slime Mold. Reynolds, Peter H., illus. 2017. (Stink Ser.: 10). (ENG.). (J). (gr. 1-4). lib. bdg. 14.75 **(978-0-606-39836-7(8))** Turtleback Bks.
—Stink & the Incredible Super-Galactic Jawbreaker. Reynolds, Peter H., illus. 2013. (Stink Ser.: 2). (ENG.). (J). (gr. 1-4). 144p. pap. 4.99 (978-0-7636-6420-6(0));Bk. 2. 128p. 12.99 (978-0-7636-6389-6(1)) Candlewick Pr.
—Stink & the Incredible Super-Galactic Jawbreaker. Reynolds, Peter H., illus. 2010. (Stink Ser.: No. 2). 128p. (J). (gr. k-4). 24.21 (978-1-59961-684-1(X)) Spotlight.
—Stink & the Incredible Super-Galactic Jawbreaker. 2013. (Stink Ser.: 2). lib. bdg. 14.75 (978-0-606-31588-3(8), Turtleback) Turtleback Bks.
—Stink & the Ultimate Thumb-Wrestling Smackdown. Reynolds, Peter H., illus. 2013. (Stink Ser.: 6). (ENG.). 144p. (J). (gr. 1-4). pap. 4.99 (978-0-7636-6423-7(5));Bk. 6. 12.99 (978-0-7636-6393-3(X)) Candlewick Pr.
—Stink & the Ultimate Thumb-Wrestling Smackdown, 1 vol. Reynolds, Peter H., illus. 2012. (Stink Ser.: No. 2). (ENG.). 144p. (J). (gr. 2-5). 24.21 (978-1-59961-194-5(5)) Spotlight.
—Stink, el Increíble Niño Menguante. 2008. (SPA.). 272p. (J). (gr. 3-5). pap. 7.95 (978-1-60396-193-6(3)) Ediciones Alfaguara ESP. Dist: Two Rivers Distribution.
—Stink y el increíble Rompemuelas Supergaláctico. 2008. (SPA.). 207p. (J). (gr. 3-5). pap. 7.95 (978-1-60396-194-3(1)) Ediciones Alfaguara ESP. Dist: Two Rivers Distribution.
—Was in a Mood. Reynolds, Peter H., illus. 2010. (Judy Moody Ser.: 1). (ENG.). 176p. (J). (gr. 1-4). pap. 5.99 (978-0-7636-4849-7(3)) Candlewick Pr.
—Was in a Mood. Reynolds, Peter H., illus. 2010. (Judy Moody Ser.: 1). (ENG.). 160p. (J). (gr. 1-4). 15.99 (978-0-7636-4850-3(7)) Candlewick Pr.
McElligott, Matthew & Tuxbury, Larry David. Benjamin Franklinstein Lives! McElligott, Matthew, illus. 2010. (Benjamin Franklinstein Ser.: 1). (ENG., Illus.). 128p. (J). (gr. 3-7). 12.99 (978-0-399-25229-7(0), G.P. Putnam's Sons Books for Young Readers) Penguin Young Readers Group.
Mcgee, Ken. Forever. 2013. 224p. pap. 15.49 (978-1-62509-504-6(X)) Salem Author Services.
Mcghee, Alison. Countdown to Kindergarten. Bliss, Harry, illus. 2006. (ENG.). 32p. (J). (gr. -1-3). reprint ed. pap. 6.99 (978-0-15-205586-8(X)) Houghton Mifflin Harcourt Publishing Co.
—Countdown to Kindergarten. Bliss, Harry, illus. pap. 39.95 incl. audio (978-1-59112-929-5(X)); pap. incl. audio compact disk (978-1-59112-469-6(7)); 2004. (J). 28.95 incl. audio compact disk (978-1-59112-928-8(1)) Live Oak Media.
—Julia Gillian (and the Dream of the Dog) Kozjan, Drazen, illus. (Julia Gillian Ser.). (ENG.). 336p. (J). (gr. 3-7). 2011. pap. 6.99 (978-0-545-03353-4(5)) 2010. 16.99 (978-0-545-03351-0(9)) Scholastic, Inc. (Scholastic Pr.).
—Mrs. Watson Wants Your Teeth. Bliss, Harry, illus. 2007. 32p. (J). reprint ed. 16.00 (978-1-4223-6777-3(0)) DIANE Publishing Co.
—Mrs. Watson Wants Your Teeth. Bliss, Harry, illus. 2008. (ENG.). 36p. (J). (gr. -1-3). pap. 6.00 (978-0-15-206348-1(X)) Houghton Mifflin Harcourt Publishing Co.
—Mrs. Watson Wants Your Teeth. Bliss, Harry, illus. unabr. ed. 2007. (Picture Book Readalong Ser.). (J). (gr. -1-2). 28.95 incl. audio compact disk (978-1-59519-902-7(0)) Live Oak Media.
McGhee, Katie Mariah. The Case of the Missing Chimpanzee from Classroom C2. McGhee, Katie Mariah & Herrera, Aaron Jeremiah, illus. 2012. 28p. 24.95 (978-1-4560-0039-4(X)) America Star Bks.
McGinnis, Bsn. Call My Mom!! 2013. 24p. pap. 14.99 (978-1-4669-5595-0(3)) Trafford Publishing.
McGinty, Alice B. Eliza's Kindergarten Pet, 0 vols. Speir, Nancy, illus. 2010. (ENG.). 32p. (J). (gr. k-3). 15.99 (978-0-7614-5702-2(X), 9780761457022, Amazon Children's Publishing) Amazon Publishing.
—Eliza's Kindergarten Surprise, 0 vols. Speir, Nancy, illus. 2013. (ENG.). 34p. (J). (gr. k-3). pap. 9.99 (978-1-4778-1683-7(6), 9781477816837, Amazon Children's Publishing) Amazon Publishing.
McGovern, DeeDee. Zachary, the Adventure Boy!, 1 vol. 2009. 88p. pap. 19.95 (978-1-4489-8249-3(9)) America Star Bks.
McGowan, Angel. Stomp Out the Bullying! 2011. (ENG.). 28p. (J). pap. 14.95 (978-1-4327-7994-8(X)) Outskirts Pr., Inc.
McGowan, Anthony. The Knife That Killed Me. 2011. (ENG.). 224p. (YA). (gr. 9). pap. 8.99 (978-0-375-85516-0(5), Ember) Random Hse. Children's Bks.
McGowan, Joby. Bossy Bianc. 2011. 20p. pap. 24.95 (978-1-4626-2908-4(3)) America Star Bks.
McGroary, Mary Beth. My Teacher Hates Me. 2012. 24p. 24.95 (978-1-4626-6012-4(6)) America Star Bks.
McGuigan, Mary Ann. Morning in a Different Place. 2009. (ENG.). 195p. (YA). (gr. 7-18). 17.95 (978-1-59078-551-5(7), Front Street) Boyds Mills Pr.
McInnes, Nicole. Brianna on the Brink. 2013. (ENG.). 176p. (YA). (gr. 10). 16.95 (978-0-8234-2741-3(2)) Holiday Hse., Inc.
McKay, Hilary. Cold Enough for Snow. Melling, David, tr. Melling, David, illus. 2003. (Pudding Bag School Ser.: Bk. 2). 144p. (J). pap. (978-0-340-87750-0(2), Hodder Children's Books) Hachette Children's Group.
—Lulu & the Duck in the Park. Lamont, Priscilla, illus. (Lulu Ser.: Book 1). (ENG.). (J). (gr. 1-5). 2012. 104p. 13.99 (978-0-8075-4808-0(1))Bk. 1. 2014. 112p. 4.99 (978-0-8075-4809-7(X)) Whitman, Albert & Co.
McKay, Kirsty. The Assassin Game. 2016. (ENG.). 336p. (YA). (gr. 6-12). pap. 10.99 (978-1-4926-3275-7(9), 9781492632757) Sourcebooks, Inc.
McKay, Sindy. We Both Read-My Day (Picture Book) Johnson, Meredith, illus. 2007. (We Both Read Ser.). 44p. (J). (gr. -1-2). lib. bdg. 14.95 (978-1-60115-005-9(9)) Treasure Bay, Inc.
McKee, Rosie. Tara Takes a Vote: Gathering Data. 2017. (Computer Science for the Real World Ser.). 8p. (gr. 5-6). pap. 6.20 **(978-1-5383-5000-3(9)**, Rosen Classroom) Rosen Publishing Group, Inc., The.
McKenna, K. J. Take Three Girls. 2005. 96p. pap. 10.00 (978-1-4116-6290-2(3)) Lulu Pr., Inc.
McKenney, M. W. Roosevelt Junior High. 2008. 73p. pap. 19.95 (978-1-60672-157-5(7)) America Star Bks.
McKenzie, C. Lee. The Princess of Las Pulgas. 2010. (ENG.). (YA). (978-1-934813-46-1(X)) Westside Bks.
McKenzie, Sophie. In a Split Second. 2015. (ENG., Illus.). 368p. (YA). (gr. 7). 17.99 (978-1-4814-1394-7(5)) Simon & Schuster Children's Publishing.
McKinlay, Meg. Duck for a Day. Rudge, Leila, illus. 2012. (ENG.). 96p. (J). (gr. 2-4). 12.99 (978-0-7636-5784-0(0)) Candlewick Pr.
McKinley, Mary. Beau, Lee, the Bomb & Me. 2014. (Rusty Winters Ser.: 1). (ENG.). 256p. (YA). (gr. 13). pap. 9.95 (978-1-61773-255-3(9), K-Teen) Kensington Publishing Corp.
—Rusty Summer. 2015. (Rusty Winters Ser.: 2). (ENG.). 352p. (YA). (gr. 9). pap. 9.95 (978-1-61773-257-7(5)) Kensington Publishing Corp.
McKinty, Adrian. Deviant. 2011. (ENG.). 368p. (YA). (gr. 9-17). 16.95 (978-0-8109-8420-2(2), Amulet Bks.) Abrams, Inc.
McKissack, Fredrick, Jr. Shooting Star. 2010. (ENG.). 288p. (YA). (gr. 7). pap. 9.99 (978-1-4169-9774-0(1), Atheneum Bks. for Young Readers) Simon & Schuster Children's Publishing.
McKissack, Fredrick L. Shooting Star. 2009. (ENG., Illus.). 288p. (YA). (gr. 7-18). 16.99 (978-1-4169-4745-5(0), Atheneum Bks. for Young Readers) Simon & Schuster Children's Publishing.
McKissack, Robert L. Try Your Best. Cepeda, Joe, illus. 2004. (Green Light Readers Level 2 Ser.). (ENG.). 24p. (J). (gr. -1-3). pap. 3.95 (978-0-15-205090-0(6)) Houghton Mifflin Harcourt Publishing Co.
—Try Your Best. Cepeda, Joe, illus. 2005. (Green Light Readers Level 2 Ser.). (gr. k-2). 13.95 (978-0-7569-5630-1(7)) Perfection Learning Corp.
McKnight, Marty. Jim Nasium. 2015. (Jim Nasium Ser.). (ENG.). 88p. (gr. 2-3). 101.28 (978-1-4965-2010-4(6)) Stone Arch Bks.
—Jim Nasium Is a Basket Case. Jones, Chris B., illus. 2015. (Jim Nasium Ser.). (ENG.). 88p. (gr. 2-3). pap. 5.95 (978-1-4965-0526-2(3)) Stone Arch Bks.
—Jim Nasium Is a Hockey Hazard. Jones, Chris B., illus. 2015. (Jim Nasium Ser.). (ENG.). 88p. (gr. 2-3). pap. 5.95 (978-1-4965-0524-8(7)) Stone Arch Bks.
—Jim Nasium Is a Soccer Goofball. Jones, Chris B., illus. 2015. (Jim Nasium Ser.). (ENG.). 88p. (gr. 2-3). pap. 5.95 (978-1-4965-0525-5(5)) Stone Arch Bks.
—Jim Nasium Is a Strikeout King. Jones, Chris, illus. 2016. (Jim Nasium Ser.). (ENG.). 88p. (gr. 2-3). lib. bdg. 25.32 (978-1-4965-3025-7(X)) Stone Arch Bks.
—Jim Nasium Is a Tennis Mismatch. Jones, Chris, illus. 2016. (Jim Nasium Ser.). (ENG.). 88p. (gr. 2-3). lib. bdg. 25.32 (978-1-4965-3026-4(8)) Stone Arch Bks.
McLaughlin, Emma & Kraus, Nicola. The Real Real. 2009. (ENG.). 336p. (YA). (gr. 9). pap. 9.99 (978-0-06-172042-0(9)) HarperCollins Pubs.
McLellan, Gretchen Brandenburg. Mrs. Mcbee Leaves Room 3, 1 vol. Zong, Grace, illus. 2017. (ENG.). 32p. (J). (gr. -1-2). 16.95 (978-1-56145-944-5(5)) Peachtree Pubs.
McMahen, Chris. Klutzhood, 1 vol. 2007. (ENG.). 168p. (J). (gr. 4-7). per. 7.95 (978-1-55143-710-1(4)) Orca Bk. Pubs. USA.
—Tabloidology, 1 vol. 2009. (ENG.). 176p. (J). (gr. 4-7). pap. 9.95 (978-1-55469-009-1(9)) Orca Bk. Pubs. USA.
McMahon, P. J. Case of the Psychic Hamster. Manders, John, illus. 2005. 153p. (J). lib. bdg. 15.38 (978-1-4242-0404-5(6)) Fitzgerald Bks.
McMahon, Susan. Wee Mary from Derry. 2008. 12p. pap. 24.95 (978-1-60610-876-5(X)) America Star Bks.
McManis, Margaret. Olé! Cinco de Mayo!, 1 vol. Harrington, David, illus. 2013. (ENG.). 32p. (J). (gr. k-3). 16.99 (978-1-4556-1754-8(7)) Pelican Publishing Co., Inc.
McMann, Lisa. Bang. (Visions Ser.: 2). (ENG., (YA). (gr. 9). 2014. Illus.). 272p. pap. 9.99 (978-1-4424-6628-9(6)) 2013. 256p. 16.99 (978-1-4424-6625-8(1)) Simon Pulse. (Simon Pulse).
—Fade. (Wake Ser.: Bk. 2). (ENG., (YA). (gr. 9-18). 2010. Illus.). 272p. pap. 10.99 (978-1-4169-7448-2(2)) 2009. 256p. 17.99 (978-1-4169-5358-6(2)) Simon Pulse. (Simon Pulse).
—Wake. 2008. (Wake Ser.: Bk. 1). (ENG.). 224p. (YA). (gr. 9). pap. 11.99 (978-1-4169-7447-5(4)); 17.99 (978-1-4169-5357-9(4)) Simon Pulse. (Simon Pulse).
McManus, Karen M. One of Us Is Lying. 2017. (ENG.). 368p. (YA). (gr. 9). 17.99 **(978-1-5247-1468-0(2))**; lib. bdg. 20.99 **(978-1-5247-1469-7(0))** Random Hse. Children's Bks. (Delacorte Pr.).
McMillan, Bruce. Mouse Views. 2014. 32p. pap. 7.00 (978-1-61003-308-4(6)) Center for the Collaborative Classroom.
McMillan, Melody DeFields. Addison Addley & the Things That Aren't There, 1 vol. 2008. (Orca Young Readers Ser.). (ENG.). 96p. (J). (gr. 3-6). pap. 7.95 (978-1-55143-949-5(2)) Orca Bk. Pubs. USA.
McMullan, Kate. Beware! It's Friday the 13th, 1 vol. Basso, Bill, illus. 2006. (Dragon Slayers' Academy Ser.: No. 13). (ENG.). 112p. (gr. 1-7). 24.21 (978-1-59961-122-8(8)) Spotlight.
—Class Trip to the Cave of Doom, 3 vols. Basso, Bill, illus. 2003. (Dragon Slayers' Academy Ser.: 3). (ENG.). 112p. (J). (gr. 2-5). pap. 5.99 (978-0-448-43110-9(6), Grosset & Dunlap) Penguin Young Readers Group.
—Class Trip to the Cave of Doom, 1 vol. Basso, Bill, illus. 2006. (Dragon Slayers' Academy Ser.: No. 3). (ENG.). 112p. (gr. 1-7). 24.21 (978-1-59961-123-5(6)) Spotlight.
—Countdown to the Year 1000. Basso, Bill, illus. 2003. (Dragon Slayers' Academy Ser.: 8). (ENG.). 112p. (J). (gr. 2-5). pap. 5.99 (978-0-448-43508-4(X), Grosset & Dunlap) Penguin Young Readers Group.
—Countdown to the Year 1000, 1 vol. Basso, Bill, illus. 2007. (Dragon Slayers' Academy Ser.: No. 8). (ENG.). 107p. (gr. 2-5). 24.21 (978-1-59961-376-5(X)) Spotlight.
—A Fine Start Bk. 3: Meg's Prairie Diary. 2003. (My America Ser.). (ENG.). 112p. (J). 12.95 (978-0-439-37061-5(2)) Scholastic, Inc.
—Five Days till Summer. Alley, R. W., illus. 2014. (Pearl & Wagner Ser.: 5). (ENG.). 48p. (J). (gr. 1-3). pap. 3.99 (978-0-448-48137-1(5), Penguin Young Readers) Penguin Young Readers Group.
—Fluffy's Happy Halloween. Smith, Mavis, illus. 2004. (Fluffy, the Classroom Guinea Pig Ser.). 40p. (J). lib. bdg. 15.00 (978-1-59054-464-8(1)) Fitzgerald Bks.
—Four Eyes. Alley, R. W., illus. 2013. (Pearl & Wagner Ser.: 4). (ENG.). 48p. (J). (gr. 1-3). pap. 3.99 (978-0-448-47781-7(5), Penguin Young Readers) Penguin Young Readers Group.
—The Ghost of Sir Herbert Dungeonstone, 1 vol. Basso, Bill, illus. 2006. (Dragon Slayers' Academy Ser.: No. 12). (ENG.). 112p. (gr. 1-7). 24.21 (978-1-59961-124-2(4)) Spotlight.
—Help! It's Parent's Day at DSA. Basso, Bill, illus. 2004. (Dragon Slayers' Academy Ser.: 10). (ENG.). 112p. (J). (gr. 2-5). pap. 4.99 (978-0-448-43220-5(X), Grosset & Dunlap) Penguin Young Readers Group.
—Help! It's Parent's Day at DSA, 1 vol. Basso, Bill, illus. 2006. (Dragon Slayers' Academy Ser.: No. 10). (ENG.). 112p. (gr. 1-7). 24.21 (978-1-59961-125-9(2)) Spotlight.
—The New Kid at School. Basso, Bill & Gilpin, Stephen, illus. 2003. (Dragon Slayers' Academy Ser.: 1). (ENG.). 112p. (J). (gr. 2-5). mass mkt. 5.99 (978-0-448-43108-6(4), Grosset & Dunlap) Penguin Young Readers Group.
—The New Kid at School, 1 vol. Basso, Bill, illus. 2006. (Dragon Slayers' Academy Ser.: No. 1). (ENG.). 112p. (gr. 1-7). 24.21 (978-1-59961-126-6(0)) Spotlight.
—One Funny Day. Alley, R. W., illus. 2012. (Pearl & Wagner Ser.: 1). (ENG.). 48p. (J). (gr. 1-3). pap. 3.99 (978-0-448-45866-3(7), Penguin Young Readers) Penguin Young Readers Group.
—Pearl & Wagner: Five Days till Summer. 2014. (Penguin Young Readers Level 3 Ser.). lib. bdg. 13.55 (978-0-606-35727-2(0)) Turtleback Bks.
—Pig Latin - Not Just for Pigs! Basso, Bill, illus. 2005. (Dragon Slayers' Academy Ser.: 14). (ENG.). 112p. (J). (gr. 2-5). pap. 5.99 (978-0-448-43820-7(8), Grosset & Dunlap) Penguin Young Readers Group.
—Revenge of the Dragon Lady. 2005. (Dragon Slayers Academy Ser.: No. 2). (J). 28.75 (978-1-4193-1910-5(8)) Recorded Bks., Inc.
—School! Adventures at the Harvey N. Trouble Elementary School. Booth, George, illus. 2012. (ENG.). 176p. (J). (gr. 1-4). pap. 8.99 (978-0-312-55595-5(4), 9780312555955) Square Fish.
—School's Out... Forever! Basso, Bill & Gilpin, Stephen, illus. 2012. (Dragon Slayers' Academy Ser.: 20). (ENG.). 112p. (J). (gr. 2-5). pap. 4.99 (978-0-448-44571-7(9), Grosset & Dunlap) Penguin Young Readers Group.
—Two Good Friends. Alley, R. W., illus. 2011. (Pearl & Wagner Ser.: 2). (ENG.). 48p. (J). (gr. 1-3). pap. 3.99 (978-0-448-45690-4(7), Penguin Young Readers) Penguin Young Readers Group.
—Wheel of Misfortune. Basso, Bill, illus. 2003. (Dragon Slayers' Academy Ser.: 7). (ENG.). 112p. (J). (gr. 2-5). pap. 5.99 (978-0-448-43507-7(1), Grosset & Dunlap) Penguin Young Readers Group.
—Wheel of Misfortune, 1 vol. Basso, Bill, illus. 2007. (Dragon Slayers' Academy Ser.: No. 7). (ENG.). 109p. (gr. 2-5). 24.21 (978-1-59961-381-9(6)) Spotlight.
—97 Ways to Train a Dragon. Basso, Bill, illus. 2003. (Dragon Slayers' Academy Ser.: 9). (ENG.). 112p. (J). (gr. 2-5). pap. 5.99 (978-0-448-43177-2(7), Grosset & Dunlap) Penguin Young Readers Group.
McMullen, Beth. Mrs. Smith's Spy School for Girls. 2017. (J). pap. **(978-1-4814-9021-4(4)**, Simon & Schuster/Paula Wiseman Bks.) Simon & Schuster/Paula Wiseman Bks.
McMullen, Judy. Stephanie & the Excellent E's. 2012. (ENG.). pap. (978-1-4675-4211-1(3)) Independent Pub.
McNamara, Margaret. Butterfly Garden. Gordon, Mike, illus. 2012. (Robin Hill School Ser.). (ENG.). 32p. (J). (gr. -1-1). 15.99 (978-1-4424-3643-5(3)); pap. 3.99 (978-1-4424-3642-8(5)) Simon Spotlight. (Simon Spotlight).
—Butterfly Garden. 2012. (Robin Hill School Ready-To-Read Ser.). lib. bdg. 13.55 (978-0-606-23694-2(5), Turtleback) Turtleback Bks.
—Class Mom. Gordon, Mike, illus. 2009. (Robin Hill School Ser.). (ENG.). 32p. (J). (gr. -1-1). pap. 3.99 (978-1-4169-5537-5(2), Simon Spotlight) Simon Spotlight.
—Class Picture Day. Gordon, Mike, illus. 2011. (Robin Hill School Ser.). (ENG.). 32p. (J). (gr. -1-1). 15.99 (978-1-4424-3611-4(5)); pap. 3.99 (978-1-4169-9173-1(5)) Simon Spotlight. (Simon Spotlight).
—The Counting Race. Gordon, Mike, illus. 2003. (Robin Hill School Ser.). (ENG.). 32p. (J). (gr. -1-1). pap. 3.99 (978-0-689-85539-9(7), Simon Spotlight) Simon Spotlight.
—Dad Goes to School. Gordon, Mike, illus. 2007. (Robin Hill School Ser.). (ENG.). 32p. (J). (gr. -1-1). pap. 3.99 (978-1-4169-1541-6(9), Simon Spotlight) Simon Spotlight.
—Earth Day. Gordon, Mike, illus. 2009. (Robin Hill School Ser.). (ENG.). 32p. (J). (gr. -1-1). pap. 3.99 (978-1-4169-5535-1(6), Simon Spotlight) Simon Spotlight.
—Election Day. Gordon, Mike, illus. 2008. (Robin Hill School Ser.). (J). (gr. -1-1). pap. 16.95 (978-1-4301-0598-5(4)) Live Oak Media.
—Fall Leaf Project. Gordon, Mike, illus. 2006. (Robin Hill School Ser.). (ENG.). 32p. (J). (gr. -1-1). pap. 3.99 (978-1-4169-1537-9(0), Simon Spotlight) Simon Spotlight.
—The First Day of School. Gordon, Mike, illus. 2008. (Robin Hill School Ser.). (J). (gr. -1-3). pap. 16.95 (978-1-4301-0604-3(2)) Live Oak Media.
—The First Day of School. Gordon, Mike, illus. 2005. (Robin Hill School Ser.). (ENG.). 32p. (J). (gr. -1-1). pap. 3.99 (978-0-689-86914-3(2), Simon Spotlight) Simon Spotlight.
—First-Grade Bunny. Gordon, Mike, illus. 2005. (Robin Hill School Ser.). (ENG.). 32p. (J). (gr. -1-1). pap. 3.99 (978-0-689-86427-8(2), Simon Spotlight) Simon Spotlight.
—The Garden Project. Gordon, Mike, illus. 2010. (Robin Hill School Ser.). (ENG.). 32p. (J). (gr. -1-1). pap. 3.99 (978-1-4169-9171-7(9), Simon Spotlight) Simon Spotlight.
—Groundhog Day. Gordon, Mike, illus. 2005. (Robin Hill School Ser.). 32p. (J). (gr. -1-3). 11.65 (978-0-7569-7146-5(2)) Perfection Learning Corp.
—Groundhog Day. Gordon, Mike, illus. 2006. (Robin Hill School Ser.). (ENG.). 32p. (J). (gr. -1-1). pap. 3.99 (978-1-4169-0507-3(3), Simon Spotlight) Simon Spotlight.
—Happy Graduation! Gordon, Mike, illus. 2008. (Robin Hill School Ser.). (J). (gr. -1-1). pap. 16.95 (978-1-4301-0610-4(7)) Live Oak Media.
—Happy Graduation! Gordon, Mike, illus. 2006. (Robin Hill School Ser.). (ENG.). 32p. (J). (gr. -1-1). pap. 3.99 (978-1-4169-0509-7(X), Simon Spotlight) Simon Spotlight.
—Happy Thanksgiving. Gordon, Mike, illus. 2005. (Robin Hill School Ser.). (ENG.). 32p. (J). (gr. -1-1). pap. 3.99 (978-1-4169-0505-9(7), Simon Spotlight) Simon Spotlight.
—How Many Seeds in a Pumpkin? Karas, G. Brian, illus. 2007. (Mr. Tiffin's Classroom Ser.). (ENG.). 40p. (J). (gr. -1-2). 17.99 (978-0-375-84014-2(1), Schwartz & Wade Bks.) Random Hse. Children's Bks.
—Martin Luther King Jr. Day. Gordon, Mike, illus. 2007. (Robin Hill School Ser.). (ENG.). 32p. (J). (gr. -1-1). pap. 3.99 (978-1-4169-3494-3(4), Simon Spotlight) Simon Spotlight.
—One Hundred Days (Plus One) Gordon, Mike, illus. 2008. (Robin Hill School Ser.). (J). (gr. -1-3). pap. 16.95 (978-1-4301-0616-6(6)) Live Oak Media.
—One Hundred Days (Plus One) Gordon, Mike, illus. 2003. (Ready-to-Read Robin Hill School Ser.). 32p. (J). (gr. -1-3). 11.65 (978-0-7569-1805-7(7)) Perfection Learning Corp.
—One Hundred Days (Plus One) Gordon, Mike, illus. 2003. (Robin Hill School Ser.). (ENG.). 32p. (J). (gr. -1-1). pap. 3.99 (978-0-689-85535-1(4), Simon Spotlight) Simon Spotlight.

—Picking Apples. Gordon, Mike, illus. 2009. (Robin Hill School Ser.). (ENG.). 32p. (J). (gr. -1-1). pap. 3.99 *(978-1-4169-5539-9(9)*, Simon Spotlight) Simon Spotlight.

—The Playground Problem. Gordon, Mike, illus. 2004. (Robin Hill School Ser.). (ENG.). 32p. (J). (gr. -1-1). pap. 3.99 *(978-0-689-85876-5(0)*, Simon Spotlight) Simon Spotlight.

—A Poem in Your Pocket. Karas, G. Brian, illus. 2015. (Mr. Tiffin's Classroom Ser.). (ENG.). 40p. (J). (gr. -1-3). 16.99 *(978-0-307-97947-6(4)*, Schwartz & Wade Bks.) Random Hse. Children's Bks.

—Presidents' Day. Gordon, Mike, illus. 2010. (Robin Hill School Ser.). (ENG.). 32p. (J). (gr. -1-1). pap. 3.99 *(978-1-4169-9170-0(0)*, Simon Spotlight) Simon Spotlight.

—The Pumpkin Patch. Gordon, Mike, illus. 2005. (Ready-to-Read Ser.). 32p. (J). lib. bdg. 15.00 *(978-1-59054-932-2(5))* Fitzgerald Bks.

—Secret Santa. Gordon, Mike, illus. 2012. (Robin Hill School Ser.). (ENG.). 32p. (J). (gr. -1-1). 15.99 *(978-1-4424-3649-7(2))*; pap. 3.99 *(978-1-4424-3648-0(4))* Simon Spotlight. (Simon Spotlight).

—Too Many Valentines. Gordon, Mike, illus. 2003. (Robin Hill School Ser.). (ENG.). 32p. (J). (gr. -1-1). pap. 3.99 *(978-0-689-85537-5(0)*, Simon Spotlight) Simon Spotlight.

—A Tooth Story. Gordon, Mike, illus. 2004. (Robin Hill School Ser.). (ENG.). 32p. (J). (gr. -1-1). pap. 3.99 *(978-0-689-86423-0(X)*, Simon Spotlight) Simon Spotlight.

—Wash Your Hands! Gordon, Mike, illus. 2010. (Robin Hill School Ser.). (ENG.). 32p. (J). (gr. -1-1). pap. 3.99 *(978-1-4169-9172-4(7)*, Simon Spotlight) Simon Spotlight.

McNamara, Margaret & Gordon, Mike. The Luck of the Irish. 2007. (Robin Hill School Ser.). (SPA & ENG., Illus.). 32p. (J). (gr. -1-1). pap. 3.99 *(978-1-4169-1539-3(7)*, Simon Spotlight) Simon Spotlight.

McNeal, Laura & McNeal, Tom. Crooked. 2007. (ENG.). 368p. (YA). (gr. 7-11). pap. 9.99 *(978-0-375-84191-0(1)*, Ember) Random Hse. Children's Bks.

McNish, Cliff. Angel. (Exceptional Reading & Language Arts Titles for Intermediate Grades Ser.). (YA). 2012. (ENG.). 312p. (gr. 7-12). pap. 9.95 *(978-0-7613-8501-1(0)*, Carolrhoda Lab™) 2008. 311p. (gr. 8-12). 16.95 *(978-0-8225-8900-6(1))* Lerner Publishing Group.

McOmber, Rachel B., ed. McOmber Phonics Storybooks: The Wizz Kid. rev. ed. (Illus.). (J). *(978-0-944991-23-7(8))* Swift Learning Resources.

McPhail, J. A. Dawn of Day. Battis, Gwen, illus. 2012. 200p. 17.99 *(978-0-9851196-2-1(4))* Rowe Publishing and Design.

McPhee, Peter. New Blood, 1 vol. 2007. (Lorimer SideStreets Ser.). (ENG.). 168p. (YA). (gr. 9-12). 9.95 *(978-1-55028-996-1(9)*, 9781550289961) Lorimer, James & Co., Ltd., Pubs. CAN. Dist: Casemate Pubs. & Bk. Distributors, LLC.

McQuestion, Karen. Life on Hold, 0 vols. unabr. ed. 2011. (ENG.). 196p. (gr. 4-6). pap. 9.95 *(978-1-935597-27-8(2)*, 9781935597278, Skyscape) Amazon Publishing.

McTrustry, Chris. Cleopatra's Report, 1 vol. rev. ed. 2013. (Fiction Readers Ser.). (ENG., Illus.). 32p. (J). (gr. 3-3). pap. 8.99 *(978-1-4333-5639-1(2))* Shell Educational Publishing.

McVoy, Terra Elan. After the Kiss. (ENG.). (YA). (gr. 9). 2011. 416p. pap. 10.99 *(978-1-4424-0216-4(4))* 2010. 400p. 16.99 *(978-1-4424-0211-9(3))* Simon Pulse. (Simon Pulse).

Mcwherter, Barbara. Little Pumpkin & Sally: It's O. K. to Be Different. 2008. 26p. pap. 24.95 *(978-1-60563-199-8(X))* America Star Bks.

Meacham, Margaret. A Fairy's Guide to Understanding Humans. 2007. (ENG.). 160p. (J). (gr. 5-18). 16.95 *(978-0-8234-2078-0(7))* Holiday Hse., Inc.

—A Mid-Semester Night's Dream. 2004. (ENG.). 144p. (J). (gr. 4-6). tchr. ed. 16.95 *(978-0-8234-1815-2(4))* Holiday Hse., Inc.

Mead, Richelle. Blood Promise. 2010. (Vampire Academy Ser.: 4). (ENG.). 528p. (YA). (gr. 7-18). 9.99 *(978-1-59514-310-5(6)*, Razorbill) Penguin Young Readers Group.

—Blood Promise. 2010. (Vampire Academy Ser.: 4). lib. bdg. 20.85 *(978-0-606-14565-7(6)*, Turtleback) Turtleback Bks.

—Frostbite. 2008. (Vampire Academy Ser.: Bk. 2). (ENG.). 335p. (YA). (gr. 7-18). pap. 10.99 *(978-1-59514-175-0(8)*, Razorbill) Penguin Publishing Group.

—Frostbite. Vieceli, Emma, illus. 2012. (Vampire Academy Ser.: 2). (ENG.). 144p. (YA). (gr. 7-18). pap. 12.99 *(978-1-59514-430-0(7)*, Razorbill) Penguin Young Readers Group.

—Frostbite. 2012. (Vampire Academy (Graphic Novels) Ser.: 2). lib. bdg. 24.50 *(978-0-606-23631-7(7)*, Turtleback) Turtleback Bks.

—Shadow Kiss. 2013. (Vampire Academy (Graphic Novels) Ser.: 3). lib. bdg. 24.50 *(978-0-606-34129-5(3)*, Turtleback) Turtleback Bks.

—Spirit Bound. 2011. (Vampire Academy Ser.: 5). (ENG.). 512p. (YA). (gr. 7-18). 9.99 *(978-1-59514-366-2(1)*, Razorbill) Penguin Young Readers Group.

—Vampire Academy. 2007. (Vampire Academy Ser.: Bk. 1). (ENG.). 336p. (J). (gr. 7-18). pap. 10.99 *(978-1-59514-174-3(X)*, Razorbill) Penguin Publishing Group.

—Vampire Academy. 2010. (SPA.). 256p. (gr. 8-12). pap. 16.99 *(978-607-11-0456-4(4)*, Alfaguara) Santillana USA Publishing Co., Inc.

—Vampire Academy. Vieceli, Emma, illus. 2011. (Vampire Academy Ser.: 1). (ENG.). 144p. (J). (gr. 7-18). pap. 12.99 *(978-1-59514-429-4(3)*, Razorbill) Penguin Young Readers Group.

—Vampire Academy 10th Anniversary Edition. 2016. (ENG.). 512p. (YA). (gr. 7). pap. 11.99 *(978-0-448-49429-6(9)*, Razorbill) Penguin Young Readers Group.

—Vampire Academy Box Set 1-3, 3 vols. 2013. (Vampire Academy Ser.). (ENG.). 1152p. (YA). (gr. 7). pap., pap., pap. 30.97 *(978-1-59514-775-2(6)*, Razorbill) Penguin Young Readers Group.

—Vampire Academy Box Set 1-6, 6 vols. 2013. (Vampire Academy Ser.). (ENG.). 2784p. (YA). (gr. 7). pap., pap., pap. 60.94 *(978-1-59514-758-5(6)*, Razorbill) Penguin Young Readers Group.

—Vampire Academy Box Set 4-6, 3 vols. 2013. (Vampire Academy Ser.). (ENG.). 1648p. (YA). (gr. 7). pap., pap., pap. 29.97 *(978-1-59514-787-5(X)*, Razorbill) Penguin Young Readers Group.

Meade, L. T. The Rebel of the School. 2007. (ENG.). 272p. pap. 21.99 *(978-1-4346-4869-3(9))*; 302p. pap. 24.99 *(978-1-4346-4870-9(2))* Creative Media Partners, LLC.

—Red Rose & Tiger Lily or in a Wider Wo. 2004. reprint ed. pap. 28.95 *(978-0-7661-8345-2(9))* Kessinger Publishing, LLC.

Meadowbrook Press. Meadowbrook Kids Three Book Back to School Set. 2005. 250p. pap. 26.85 *(978-0-689-05307-8(X))* Meadowbrook Pr.

Meadows, Daisy. Carly the School Fairy. 2015. (Rainbow Magic Special Edition Ser.). (Illus.). (J). (ENG.). 176p. (gr. 2-5). pap. 6.99 *(978-0-545-70827-2(3)*, Scholastic Paperbacks); 155p. ***(978-1-4806-8807-0(X))*** Scholastic, Inc.

—Kathryn the Gym Fairy. 2016. (Rainbow Magic — the School Day Fairies Ser.: 4). lib. bdg. 14.75 *(978-0-606-38792-7(7))* Turtleback Bks.

Meaney, Flynn. The Boy Recession. 2012. (ENG.). 256p. (YA). (gr. 10-17). 17.99 *(978-0-316-10213-1(X)*, Poppy) Little, Brown Bks. for Young Readers.

Mechling, Lauren & Moser, Laura. All Q, No A: More Tales of a 10th-Grade Social Climber. 2006. (ENG.). 288p. (YA). (gr. 7-12). pap. 15.95 *(978-0-618-66378-1(9))* Houghton Mifflin Harcourt Publishing Co.

Mechling, Lauren, et al. The Rise & Fall of a 10th Grade Social Climber. 2005. (ENG.). 304p. (YA). (gr. 7). pap. 16.99 *(978-0-618-55519-2(6))* Houghton Mifflin Harcourt Publishing Co.

Meddaugh, Susan. The Show Must Go On. 2012. (Martha Speaks Ser.). (ENG., Illus.). 96p. (J). (gr. 1-4). 14.99 *(978-0-547-69145-9(9))*; pap. 5.99 *(978-0-547-69147-3(5))* Houghton Mifflin Harcourt Publishing Co.

Medina, Juana. Juana & Lucas. Medina, Juana, illus. 2016. (ENG., Illus.). 96p. (J). (gr. k-3). 14.99 *(978-0-7636-7208-9(4))* Candlewick Pr.

Medina, Kathleen. Born into Greyworld. 2008. 220p. 29.99 *(978-1-4363-2619-3(2))*; pap. 19.99 *(978-1-4363-2618-6(4))* Xlibris Corp.

Medina, Meg. Yaqui Delgado Wants to Kick Your Ass. (ENG., 272p. (YA). (gr. 9). 2014. Illus.). pap. 7.99 *(978-0-7636-7164-8(9))* 2013. 16.99 *(978-0-7636-5859-5(6))* Candlewick Pr.

Meek, Carol. Believer Boy's Power. 2007. 32p. (J). pap. 9.00 *(978-0-8059-7249-8(8))* Dorrance Publishing Co., Inc.

Meens, Estelle, illus. Boss No More. 2014. (J). *(978-1-4338-1641-3(5)*, Magination Pr.) American Psychological Assn.

Meister, Cari. Buzz Beaker & the Race to School, 1 vol. McGuire, Bill, illus. 2011. (Buzz Beaker Bks.). (ENG.). 32p. (gr. 2-3). pap. 6.25 *(978-1-4342-3057-7(0))*; lib. bdg. 22.65 *(978-1-4342-2528-3(3))* Stone Arch Bks.

—Tiny Goes Back to School. Davis, Rich, illus. 2014. (Tiny Ser.). (ENG.). 32p. (J). (gr. k-1). pap. 3.99 *(978-0-448-48134-0(0)*, Penguin Young Readers) Penguin Young Readers Group.

_Meli, Ayani & D., Jessie. God Says I've Changed Your Dna: Walk As Children of the Light. Mallette, Dania, illus. 2013. 24p. pap. 12.00 *(978-0-9846315-7-5(7))* JWD Publishing.

Melissa, De La Cruz, et al. 21 Proms. Levithan, David & Ehrenhaft, Daniel, eds. 2015. (ENG.). 304p. (J). (gr. 7). pap. 9.99 *(978-0-545-79867-9(1)*, PUSH) Scholastic, Inc.

Mellom, Robin. The Classroom Trick Out My School! Gilpin, Stephen, illus. 2014. (Classroom Novel Ser.). (ENG.). 288p. (J). (gr. 3-7). 12.99 *(978-1-4231-5065-7(1))* Hyperion Bks. for Children.

—Ditched: A Love Story. 2013. (ENG.). 288p. (YA). (gr. 7-17). pap. 8.99 *(978-1-4231-4351-2(5))* Disney Pr.

Meminger, Neesha. Shine, Coconut Moon. 2010. (ENG.). 256p. (YA). (gr. 9). pap. 10.99 *(978-1-4424-0305-5(5)*, McElderry, Margaret K. Bks.) McElderry, Margaret K. Bks.

Menard, Lucille. The Top of the Bottom: Inky to the Rescue, Volume 1. 2013. 38p. pap. 12.50 *(978-0-9887969-6-6(1))* Four Menards, The.

Menard, Michele Rose. The Ghoul in Our School. Menard, Adrienne, illus. 2013. 36p. pap. 11.95 *(978-0-9887969-9-7(6))* Four Menards, The.

Menchin, Scott. Harry Goes to Dog School. Menchin, Scott, illus. 2012. (ENG., Illus.). 32p. (J). (gr. -1-3). 16.99 *(978-0-06-195801-4(8))* HarperCollins Pubs.

mendelsohn, martha. Bromley Girls. 2015. (ENG.). 192p. (YA). pap. 14.95 *(978-0-89672-922-3(2))* Texas Tech Univ. Pr.

Mendle, Jane. My Ultimate Sister Disaster: A Novel. 2010. (ENG.). 208p. (YA). (gr. 7-18). pap. 18.99 *(978-0-312-36904-0(2)*, 9780312369040, St. Martin's Griffin) St. Martin's Pr.

Mercer, Sienna. Fangtastic! 2007. (My Sister the Vampire Ser.: 2). (ENG.). 208p. (J). (gr. 3-7). per. 6.99 *(978-0-06-087115-4(6))* HarperCollins Pubs.

Merkel, Ruth Vitrano. Ann: 1833-1897. 2006. (Hannah's Girls Ser.). (Illus.). 112p. (J). (gr. 4-7). per. 9.99 *(978-0-8280-1951-4(7))* Review & Herald Publishing Assn.

—Grace: 1890-1973, 6. 2006. (Hannah's Girls Ser.). (Illus.). 128p. (J). (gr. 4-7). per. 9.99 *(978-0-8280-1953-8(3))* Review & Herald Publishing Assn.

—Marilla 1851-1916, 6 bks. 2006. (Hannah's Girls Ser.). (Illus.). 144p. (J). (gr. 4-7). per. 9.99 *(978-0-8280-1952-1(5))* Review & Herald Publishing Assn.

—Ruthie: Born 1931. 2007. (Hannah's Girls Ser.). (Illus.). 144p. (J). (gr. 4-7). per. 9.99 *(978-0-8280-1954-5(1))* Review & Herald Publishing Assn.

Merschel, Michael. Revenge of the Star Survivors. 2017. (ENG.). 320p. (J). (gr. 5-8). 17.95 *(978-0-8234-3667-5(5))* Holiday Hse., Inc.

Messer, Celeste M. The Broken Wing: The Adventures of Andi O'Malley. Hoeffner, Deb, illus. 2004. (Adventures of Andi O'Malley Ser.). 82-92p. (J). (gr. 4-7). 4.95 *(978-0-9702171-1-0(0))* AshleyAlan Enterprises.

Messner, Kate. All the Answers. (ENG.). 2016. 272p. (J). pap. 7.99 *(978-1-68119-020-4(6)*, 9781681190204) 2015. 256p. (YA). (gr. 3-6). 16.99 *(978-1-61963-374-2(4)*, 9781619633742) Bloomsbury Publishing USA. (Bloomsbury USA Childrens).

—The Brilliant Fall of Gianna Z. (ENG.). 224p. 2017. (J). pap. 8.99 ***(978-1-68119-547-6(X)***, 9781681195476) 2010. (YA). (gr. 3-6). pap. 8.99 *(978-0-8027-2173-0(7)*, 9780802721730) Bloomsbury Publishing USA. (Bloomsbury USA Childrens).

—The Brilliant Fall of Gianna Z. 2017. (J). lib. bdg. 19.65 ***(978-0-606-40595-9(X))*** Turtleback Bks.

—Marty McGuire. Floca, Brian, illus. 2011. (ENG.). 144p. (J). (gr. 2-5). pap. 5.99 *(978-0-545-14246-5(6)*, Scholastic Pr.) Scholastic, Inc.

—Marty McGuire Digs Worms! Floca, Brian, illus. 2012. (ENG.). 176p. (J). (gr. -1-3). pap. 5.99 *(978-0-545-14247-2(4)*, Scholastic Pr.) Scholastic, Inc.

—Sea Monster & the Bossy Fish. Rash, Andy, illus. 2013. (ENG.). 40p. (J). (gr. -1-k). 16.99 *(978-1-4521-1253-4(3))* Chronicle Bks. LLC.

—Sea Monster's First Day. Rash, Andy, illus. 2011. (ENG.). 36p. (J). (gr. -1-3). 16.99 *(978-0-8118-7564-6(4))* Chronicle Bks. LLC.

—The Seventh Wish. 2016. (ENG.). 240p. (J). 16.99 *(978-1-61963-376-6(0)*, 9781619633766, Bloomsbury USA Childrens) Bloomsbury Publishing USA.

Metz, Melinda. Bri's Big Crush. 2016. (Babysitter Chronicles Ser.). (ENG.). 160p. (gr. 4-7). lib. bdg. 26.65 *(978-1-4965-2756-1(9)*, 1400591) Stone Arch Bks.

—The Droid of Doom. McKenzie, Heath, illus. 2016. (S. M. A. R. T. S. Ser.). (ENG.). 128p. (gr. 3-6). pap. 9.95 *(978-1-4965-3017-2(9))* Stone Arch Bks.

—The Mars Mission Mayhem. McKenzie, Heath, illus. 2016. (S. M. A. R. T. S. Ser.). (ENG.). 128p. (gr. 3-6). pap. 9.95 *(978-1-4965-3018-9(7))* Stone Arch Bks.

—S. M. A. R. T. S. & the 3-D Danger. McKenzie, Heath, illus. 2015. (S. M. A. R. T. S. Ser.). (ENG.). 128p. (gr. 3-6). 22.65 *(978-1-4965-0465-4(8))* S.M.A.R.T.S. Learning System.

—S. M. A. R. T. S. & the Droid of Doom. McKenzie, Heath, illus. 2016. (S. M. A. R. T. S. Ser.). (ENG.). 128p. (gr. 3-6). lib. bdg. 22.65 *(978-1-4965-3015-8(2))* S.M.A.R.T.S. Learning System.

—S. M. A. R. T. S. & the Mars Mission Mayhem. McKenzie, Heath, illus. 2016. (S. M. A. R. T. S. Ser.). (ENG.). 128p. (gr. 3-6). lib. bdg. 22.65 *(978-1-4965-3016-5(0))* S.M.A.R.T.S. Learning System.

—S. M. A. R. T. S. & the Missing UFO. McKenzie, Heath, illus. 2015. (S. M. A. R. T. S. Ser.). (ENG.). 128p. (gr. 3-6). lib. bdg. 22.65 *(978-1-4965-0466-1(6))* S.M.A.R.T.S. Learning System.

—S. M. A. R. T. S. & the Poison Plates. McKenzie, Heath, illus. 2015. (S. M. A. R. T. S. Ser.). (ENG.). 128p. (gr. 3-6). 22.65 *(978-1-4965-0464-7(X))* S.M.A.R.T.S. Learning System.

Metzger, Joanna. The Space Program. Elizalde, Marcelo, illus. 2006. 142p. (J). *(978-1-59336-695-7(7))* Mondo Publishing.

Metzger, Lois. A Trick of the Light. (ENG.). 208p. (YA). (gr. 9). 2014. pap. 9.99 *(978-0-06-213309-0(8))* 2013. 17.99 *(978-0-06-213308-3(X))* HarperCollins Pubs.

Metzger, Steve. Five Spooky Ghosts Playing Tricks at School. Harrald-Pilz, Marilee, illus. 2005. (J). *(978-0-439-80381-6(0))* Scholastic, Inc.

Meunier, Sylvain. Ma Premiere de Classe. Eudes-Pascal, Elisabeth, tr. 2003. (Roman Jeunesse Ser.). (FRE., Illus.). 96p. (J). (gr. 4-7). pap. *(978-2-89021-634-1(9))* Diffusion du livre Mirabel (DLM).

Meyer, Stephenie. Amanecer. Pallarés, José Miguel & Sánchez, María Jesús, trs. 2008.Tr. of Breaking Dawn. (SPA.). 832p. (gr. 8-12). pap. 19.99 *(978-607-11-0033-7(X)*, Alfaguara Juvenil) Santillana USA Publishing Co., Inc.

—Crepusculo. 2015.Tr. of Twilight. (ENG & SPA.). 736p. (gr. 7). pap. 14.99 *(978-607-11-0163-1(8)*, Punto de Lectura) Santillana USA Publishing Co., Inc.

—Eclipse. 2009. (Twilight Saga Ser.: 3). (ENG.). 640p. (YA). (gr. 7-17). pap. 15.99 *(978-0-316-02765-6(0))* Little Brown & Co.

—Eclipse. 2007. (Twilight Saga Ser.: 3). (ENG.). 640p. (YA). (gr. 7-17). 19.99 *(978-0-316-16020-9(2))* Little, Brown Bks. for Young Readers.

—Eclipse. 2008. 576p. *(978-1-904233-91-6(0)*, Atom Books) Little, Brown Book Group Ltd.

—Eclipse. 2011. (Twilight Saga: Bk. 3). 13.08 *(978-0-7848-3531-9(4)*, Everbind) Marco Bk. Co.

—Eclipse. 2010. (Twilight Saga: Bk. 3). 629p. (YA). (gr. 9-12). 22.10 *(978-1-60686-303-9(7))* Perfection Learning Corp.

—Eclipse. Pallarés, José Miguel & Sánchez, María Jesús, trs. 2007. (SPA.). 870p. (YA). (gr. 8-12). pap. 15.99 *(978-1-60396-022-9(8)*, Punto de Lectura) Santillana USA Publishing Co., Inc.

—Eclipse. 2007. (Twilight Saga Spanish Ser.: 3). (SPA.). 637p. (gr. 7-12). lib. bdg. 28.15 *(978-1-4177-9862-9(9)*, Turtleback) Turtleback Bks.

—Luna Nueva. Pallares, Jose Miguel, tr. from ENG. 2009.Tr. of New Moon. (SPA.). 280p. (YA). (gr. 8-12). pap. 11.99 *(978-1-60396-698-6(6)*, Punto de Lectura) Santillana USA Publishing Co., Inc.

—Luna Nueva. Pallarés, José Miguel & Sánchez, María Jesús, trs. from ENG. 2007.Tr. of New Moon. (SPA.). 696p. (YA). (gr. 8-12). per. 15.99 *(978-970-58-0023-8(5)*, Alfaguara) Santillana USA Publishing Co., Inc.

—New Moon. (Twilight Saga Ser.: 2). (ENG.). 608p. (gr. 7-17). 2008. (YA). pap. 15.99 *(978-0-316-02496-9(1))* 2006. (J). 19.99 *(978-0-316-16019-3(9)*, Tingley, Megan Bks.) Little, Brown Bks. for Young Readers.

—New Moon. 2011. (Twilight Saga: Bk. 2). 11.72 *(978-0-7848-3535-7(7)*, Everbind) Marco Bk. Co.

—New Moon. 2008. (Twilight Saga: Bk. 2). 563p. (gr. 9-12). 21.00 *(978-1-60686-336-7(3))* Perfection Learning Corp.

—Twilight. 2008. (Twilight Saga: Bk. 1). (CHI.). 375p. (YA). pap. *(978-7-5448-0333-5(3))* Jieli Publishing Hse.

—Twilight. (Twilight Saga Ser.: 1). (ENG.). 544p. (YA). (gr. 7-17). 2005. 19.99 *(978-0-316-16017-9(2))* 2006. reprint ed. pap. 15.99 *(978-0-316-01584-4(9))* Little, Brown Bks. for Young Readers. (Tingley, Megan Bks.).

—Twilight. 2008. 480p. pap. *(978-1-905654-34-5(0)*, Atom Books) Little, Brown Book Group Ltd.

—Twilight. 2009. (Twilight Saga: Bk. 1). 11.72 *(978-0-7848-1934-0(3)*, Everbind) Marco Bk. Co.

—Twilight. (Twilight Saga Ser.: 1). (ENG.). 2012. 224p. (gr. 7-17). pap. 14.99 *(978-0-316-20488-0(9))* 2011. (Illus.). 240p. (gr. 7-17). 19.99 *(978-0-316-13319-7(1))* 2010. (Illus.). 224p. 19.99 *(978-0-7595-2943-4(4))* Orbit. (Yen Pr.).

—Twilight. Kim, Young, illus. collector's ed. 2012. (Twilight Saga Ser.: 0). (ENG.). 464p. (gr. 7-17). 24.99 *(978-0-316-21717-0(4)*, Yen Pr.) Orbit.

—Twilight. (Twilight Saga: Bk. 1). 2010. 498p. (YA). (gr. 9-12). 20.10 *(978-1-60686-352-7(5))* 2006. 21.00 *(978-0-7569-6825-0(9))* Perfection Learning Corp.

—Twilight. (Twilight Ser.: 1). (YA). 2007. 1.25 *(978-1-4193-9974-9(8))* 2006. 87.75 *(978-1-4193-9975-6(6))* Recorded Bks., Inc.

—Twilight. 2006. (Twilight Saga Ser.: 1). (Illus.). 498p. (YA). (gr. 9-12). lib. bdg. 28.15 *(978-1-4177-5591-2(1)*, Turtleback) Turtleback Bks.

Meyerhoff, Jenny. The Barftastic Life of Louie Burger. Week, Jason, illus. 2013. (Barftastic Life of Louie Burger Ser.: 1). (ENG.). 240p. (J). (gr. 3-6). 13.99 *(978-0-374-30518-5(8)*, 9780374305185, Farrar, Straus & Giroux (BYR)) Farrar, Straus & Giroux.

—Class B. U. R. P. Week, Jason, illus. 2014. (Barftastic Life of Louie Burger Ser.: 2). (ENG.). 288p. (J). (gr. 3-6). 13.99 *(978-0-374-30521-5(8)*, 9780374305215, Farrar, Straus & Giroux (BYR)) Farrar, Straus & Giroux.

—Green Thumbs-Up! Chatelain, Éva, illus. 2015. (Friendship Garden Ser.: 1). (ENG.). 176p. (J). (gr. 2-5). pap. 5.99 *(978-1-4814-3904-6(9)*, Aladdin) Simon & Schuster Children's Publishing.

Michael-Angelo Goes to School. 2012. (Illus.). 34p. pap. 9.99 *(978-1-937107-10-9(8))* Morning Joy Media.

Michaelis, Antonia. The Storyteller. 2012. (ENG.). 416p. (YA). (gr. 9-17). 19.95 *(978-1-4197-0047-7(2)*, Amulet Bks.) Abrams, Inc.

Michelle, Sara. The Beginning: Book 5, 1 vol. unabr. ed. 2012. (My New Normal Ser.: 5). (ENG.). 97p. (YA). (gr. 9-12). pap. 8.95 *(978-1-61651-785-4(9))* Saddleback Educational Publishing, Inc.

Michener, Tara. Summer Camp Survival. 2010. 76p. pap. 10.99 *(978-1-4520-6297-6(8))* AuthorHouse.

Mickelson, Marcia. The Huaca. 2013. (J). pap. 16.99 *(978-1-4621-1190-9(4)*, Horizon Pubs.) Cedar Fort, Inc./CFI Distribution.

Mikaelsen, Ben. Ghost of Spirit Bear. (Spirit Bear Ser.: 2). (ENG.). (J). (gr. 5). 2010. 176p. pap. 6.99 *(978-0-06-009009-8(X))* 2008. 160p. 16.99 *(978-0-06-009007-4(3))* HarperCollins Pubs.

Milanes, Janelle. The Victoria in My Head. 2017. (ENG., Illus.). 400p. (YA). (gr. 7). 17.99 ***(978-1-4814-8089-5(8)***, Simon Pulse) Simon Pulse.

Miles, Chris. Spurt. 2017. (ENG., Illus.). 272p. (J). (gr. 6-9). 16.99 *(978-1-4814-7972-1(5)*, Simon & Schuster Bks. For Young Readers) Simon & Schuster Bks. For Young Readers.

Miles, Elizabeth. Envy. (Fury Ser.: 2). (ENG.). (YA). (gr. 9). 2013. Illus.). 416p. pap. 9.99 *(978-1-4424-2222-3(X))* 2012. 400p. 17.99 *(978-1-4424-2221-6(1))* Simon Pulse. (Simon Pulse).

—Eternity. 2013. (Fury Ser.: 3). (ENG., Illus.). 336p. (YA). (gr. 9). 17.99 *(978-1-4424-2227-8(0))*; pap. 9.99 *(978-1-4424-2228-5(9))* Simon Pulse. (Simon Pulse).

—Fury, 11 vols. 2012. (YA). 110.75 *(978-1-4640-3957-7(7))*; 271.75 *(978-1-4640-3955-3(0))*; 126.75 *(978-1-4640-3958-4(5))*; 112.75 *(978-1-4640-3954-6(2))* Recorded Bks., Inc.

—Fury. (Fury Ser.). (ENG.). (YA). (gr. 9). 2012. 400p. pap. 9.99 *(978-1-4424-2225-4(4))* 2011. 384p. 17.99 *(978-1-4424-2224-7(6))* Simon Pulse. (Simon Pulse).

Miller, Amanda E. Pete the Pencil. 2008. 20p. pap. 24.95 *(978-1-60610-814-7(X))* America Star Bks.

Miller, Andrew. Arthur Dudley Dunstan. 2009. 47p. pap. 12.03 *(978-0-557-07115-9(1))* Lulu Pr., Inc.

Miller, Ashley Edward & Stentz, Zack. Colin Fischer. 2012. (Colin Fischer Ser.: 1). (ENG.). 256p. (YA). (gr. 7). 17.99 *(978-1-59514-578-9(8)*, Razorbill) Penguin Young Readers Group.

Miller, Kristine Elizabeth. Albert's Lunch Box. 2008. 24p. pap. 24.95 *(978-1-60672-096-7(1))* America Star Bks.

Miller, Lauren. Free to Fall. 2014. (ENG.). 480p. (YA). (gr. 8). 17.99 *(978-0-06-219980-5(3)*, HarperTeen) HarperCollins Pubs.

Miller, Lee. Ete: (Extraterrestrial Elements) 2006. 80p. pap. 16.95 *(978-1-4241-3498-4(6))* PublishAmerica, Inc.

Miller, Pat Zietlow. Sophie's Squash Go to School. Wilsdorf, Anne, illus. 2016. (ENG.). 40p. (J). (gr. -1-2). 17.99 *(978-0-553-50944-1(6)*, Schwartz & Wade Bks.) Random Hse. Children's Bks.

Millman, M. C. Always Something Else: The whimsical adventures of Elisheva Raskin. 2005. (Illus.). 160p. (J). 14.95 *(978-1-932443-23-3(1)*, ASEH) Judaica Pr., Inc., The.

—Always Something Else 2. 2006. (Illus.). 160p. (J). 14.95 *(978-1-932443-43-1(6)*, ASE2H) Judaica Pr., Inc., The.

Mills, Arthur. The Crawl Space. Mills, Arthur & Tichelaar, Tyler, eds. 2012. (ENG., Illus.). 254p. (J). pap. 9.99 *(978-0-9860166-0-8(8))* Branching Plot Bks.

Mills, Claudia. Annika Riz, Math Whiz. Shepperson, Rob, illus. 2014. (Franklin School Friends Ser.: 2). (ENG.). 128p. (J). (gr. 2-5). 15.99 *(978-0-374-30335-8(5)*, 9780374303358, Farrar, Straus & Giroux (BYR)) Farrar, Straus & Giroux.

—Basketball Disasters. Francis, Guy, illus. 2013. (Mason Dixon Ser.). (ENG.). 176p. (J). (gr. 2-5). pap. 6.99 *(978-0-375-87276-1(0)*, Yearling) Random Hse. Children's Bks.

—Being Teddy Roosevelt. Alley, R. W., illus. 2007. (ENG.). 96p. (J). (gr. 2-5). 16.99 *(978-0-374-30657-1(5)*, 9780374306571, Farrar, Straus & Giroux (BYR)) Farrar, Straus & Giroux.

—Being Teddy Roosevelt. Alley, R. W., illus. 2012. (ENG.). 112p. (J). (gr. 2-5). pap. 8.99 *(978-0-312-64018-7(8)*, 9780312640187) Square Fish.

—Cody Harmon, King of Pets. Shepperson, Rob, illus. 2016. (Franklin School Friends Ser.: 5). (ENG.). 144p. (J). 15.99 *(978-0-374-30223-8(5)*, 9780374302238, Farrar, Straus & Giroux (BYR)) Farrar, Straus & Giroux.

—How Oliver Olson Changed the World. Maione, Heather Harms, illus. 2009. (ENG.). 112p. (J). (gr. 2-5). 15.95 *(978-0-374-33487-1(0)*, 9780374334871, Farrar, Straus & Giroux (BYR)) Farrar, Straus & Giroux.

—How Oliver Olson Changed the World. Maione, Heather, illus. 2011. (ENG.). 128p. (J). (gr. 2-5). pap. 6.99 *(978-0-312-67282-9(9)*, 9780312672829) Square Fish.

—Izzy Barr, Running Star. Shepperson, Rob, illus. 2015. (Franklin School Friends Ser.: 3). (ENG.). 144p. (J). (gr. 2-5). 15.99 *(978-0-374-33578-6(8)*, 9780374335786, Farrar, Straus & Giroux (BYR)) Farrar, Straus & Giroux.

—Kelsey Green, Reading Queen, 1 vol. Shepperson, Rob, illus. 2013. (Franklin School Friends Ser.: 1). (ENG.). 128p.

S

(J). (gr. 2-5). 15.99 (978-0-374-37485-3(6), 9780374374853, Farrar, Straus & Giroux (BYR)) Farrar, Straus & Giroux.
—Kelsey Green, Reading Queen. Shepperson, Rob, illus. 2014. (Franklin School Friends Ser.: 1). (ENG.). 144p. (J). (gr. 2-5). pap. 5.99 (978-1-250-03405-2(1), 9781250034052) Square Fish.
—The Nora Notebooks, Book 2: the Trouble with Babies. Kath, Katie, illus. 2016. (Nora Notebooks Ser.). (ENG.). 192p. (J). (gr. 2-5). 12.99 (978-0-385-39165-8(X), Knopf Bks. for Young Readers) Random Hse. Children's Bks.
—The Trouble with Ants. Kath, Katie, illus. (Nora Notebooks Ser.: 1). (ENG.). 176p. (J). (gr. 2-5). 2016. 6.99 (978-0-385-39163-4(3), Yearling) 2015. lib. bdg. 17.99 (978-0-385-39162-7(5), Knopf Bks. for Young Readers) Random Hse. Children's Bks.
—The Trouble with Friends. Kath, Katie, illus. 2017. (Nora Notebooks Ser.). (ENG.). 192p. (J). (gr. 2-5). 12.99 (978-0-385-39169-6(2), Knopf Bks. for Young Readers) Random Hse. Children's Bks.
—Zero Tolerance. 2013. (ENG.). 240p. (J). (gr. 3-7). 16.99 (978-0-374-33312-6(2), 9780374333126, Farrar, Straus & Giroux (BYR)) Farrar, Straus & Giroux.
—Zero Tolerance. 2014. (ENG.). 256p. (J). (gr. 3-7). pap. 6.99 (978-1-250-04422-8(7), 9781250044228) Square Fish.
—7 X 9 = Trouble! Karas, G. Brian, illus. 2004. 103p. (J). (gr. 2-5). 13.60 (978-0-7569-3397-5(8)) Perfection Learning Corp.
Mills, David. Sam's First Day. Finlay, Lizzie, illus. 2004. 24p. (J). (978-1-85269-702-0(4)); (978-1-85269-637-5(0)); (978-1-85269-636-8(2)); (978-1-85269-635-1(4)); (PER & ENG.). (978-1-85269-634-4(6)); (978-1-85269-631-3(1)); (978-1-85269-630-6(3)); (TUR & ENG.). (978-1-85269-644-3(3)); (978-1-85269-646-7(X)); (978-1-85269-645-0(1)); (978-1-85269-643-6(5)); (978-1-85269-642-9(7)); (978-1-85269-640-5(0)); (978-1-85269-639-9(7)) Mantra Lingua.
Mills, David & Finlay, Lizzie. Sam's First Day. 2004. (Illus.). 24p. (J). (978-1-85269-641-2(9)) Mantra Lingua.
Mills, Emma. First & Then. 2015. (ENG.). 272p. (YA). (gr. 9-12). 17.99 (978-1-62779-235-6(X), 9781627792356, Holt, Henry & Co. Bks. For Young Readers) Holt, Henry & Co.
—This Adventure Ends. 2016. (ENG.). 320p. (YA). 17.99 (978-1-62779-935-5(4), 9781627799355, Holt, Henry & Co. Bks. For Young Readers) Holt, Henry & Co.
Mills, Lauren A. Minna's Patchwork Coat. 2015. (ENG., Illus.). 288p. (J). (gr. 3-7). 17.00 (978-0-316-40621-5(X)) Little Brown & Co.
Mills, Nathan & Holtz, Mary Elizabeth. Sabrina's School. 2012. (Rosen Readers Ser.). (ENG., Illus.). 16p. (J). (gr. k-1). pap. 7.00 (978-1-4488-8719-4(4), Rosen Classroom) Rosen Publishing Group, Inc., The.
Mills, Wendy. Positively Beautiful. (ENG.). 368p. (YA). 2016. pap. 9.99 (978-1-68119-025-9(7), 9781681190259) 2015. (gr. 9). 17.99 (978-1-61963-341-4(8), 9781619633414) Bloomsbury Publishing USA. (Bloomsbury USA Childrens).
Mills, Wynette. Nana's Backyard Alphabet. 2012. 36p. pap. 15.99 (978-1-4771-4061-1(1)) Xlibris Corp.
Millsap, Ella. A Portrait of a Church in Stone: The Keeper of the Honeybees. 2013. 62p. (J). pap. 12.00 (978-0-9891960-3-1(8)) Professional Publishing Hse. LLC.
Minsky, Terri. All over It! 2005. (Illus.). 138p. (J). (978-1-4156-0271-3(9)) Disney Pr.
Misra, Michelle. Birthday Surprise. Chaffey, Samantha, illus. 2016. (Angel Wings Ser.: 2). (ENG.). 128p. (J). (gr. 1-4). pap. 5.99 (978-1-4814-5800-9(0), Aladdin) Simon & Schuster Children's Publishing.
—Secrets & Sapphires. Chaffey, Samantha, illus. 2016. (Angel Wings Ser.: 3). (ENG.). 128p. (J). (gr. 1-4). pap. 5.99 (978-1-4814-5803-0(5), Aladdin) Simon & Schuster Children's Publishing.
—Secrets & Sapphires. Chaffey, Samantha, illus. 2016. (Angel Wings Ser.: 3). (ENG.). 128p. (J). (gr. 1-4). 16.99 (978-1-4814-5804-7(3), Simon & Schuster/Paula Wiseman Bks.) Simon & Schuster/Paula Wiseman Bks.
Miss Gomez's Third Grade Class Staff. Wacky Stories from Wisdom Academy for Young Scientists. 2013. (ENG.). 63p. (YA). pap. 16.95 (978-1-4787-1103-2(5)) Outskirts Pr., Inc.
Mistretta, T. P. C. Jay Francis. The Parkour Code. 2010. 114p. pap. 13.95 (978-0-557-38476-1(1)) Lulu Pr., Inc.
Mitchard, Jacquelyn. All We Know of Heaven. 2008. (ENG.). 320p. (YA). (gr. 8-18). 16.99 (978-0-06-134578-4(4), HarperTeen) HarperCollins Pubs.
Mitchell, Devon L. The Candy Dragon: Torchy's Adventures of Starting School. 2009. 40p. pap. 16.99 (978-1-4389-4626-9(0)) AuthorHouse.
Mitchell, Ed. You Never Can Tell What's Least Expected Most. 2009. 232p. pap. 18.95 (978-1-4092-5434-8(8)) Lulu Pr., Inc.
Mitchell, Julie & Chambers, Mal. Bertha. 2008. (Rigby Focus Forward: Level G Ser.). (Illus.). 24p. (J). (gr. 4-7). pap. (978-1-4190-3703-0(X), Rigby) Pearson Education Australia.
Mitchell, Julie & Konye, Paul. The Bully. 2008. (Rigby Focus Forward: Level K Ser.). (Illus.). 24p. (J). (gr. 4-7). pap. (978-1-4190-3784-9(6), Rigby) Pearson Education Australia.
Mittal, Anjali. The Convent Rules. 2009. (Illus.). 80p. pap. 10.49 (978-1-4389-8575-6(4)) AuthorHouse.
Mlynowski, Sarah. Don't Even Think about It. 2014. (ENG.). 336p. (YA). (gr. 7). 17.99 (978-0-385-73738-8(6), Delacorte Pr.) Random Hse. Children's Bks.
—Frogs & French Kisses. 2007. (Magic in Manhattan Ser.: No. 2). (ENG.). 304p. (YA). (gr. 7). pap. 8.99 (978-0-385-73185-0(X), Delacorte Pr.) Random Hse. Children's Bks.
—Gimme a Call. 2011. (ENG.). 320p. (YA). (gr. 7). pap. 9.99 (978-0-385-73589-6(8), Ember) Random Hse. Children's Bks.
—Parties & Potions. 2010. (Magic in Manhattan Ser.: No. 4). (ENG., Illus.). 368p. (YA). (gr. 7). pap. 10.99 (978-0-385-73646-6(0), Ember) Random Hse. Children's Bks.
Mlynowski, Sarah, et al. Sticks & Stones. (ENG.). 208p. (J). (gr. 3-7). 2017. (Upside-Down Magic Ser.: 2). pap. 5.99 (**978-0-545-80050-1(1)**) 2016. (Upside-down Magic Ser.: No. 2). 14.99 (978-0-545-80049-5(8), Scholastic Pr.) Scholastic, Inc.
Mlynowski, Sarah, et al. Upside-Down Magic. (J). 2016. (Upside-Down Magic Ser.: 1). (ENG.). 208p. (gr. 3-7). pap. 5.99 (978-0-545-80046-4(3)) 2015. (Upside-down Magic Ser.: No. 1). (ENG.). 208p. (gr. 3-7). 14.99 (978-0-545-80045-7(5), Scholastic Pr.) 2015. 196p. pap. (978-0-545-90822-1(1), Scholastic Pr.) Scholastic, Inc.
Mobin-Uddin, Asma. My Name Is Bilal. Kiwak, Barbara, illus. 2005. (ENG.). 32p. (J). (gr. 1-7). 16.95 (978-1-59078-175-3(9)) Boyds Mills Pr.
Moffitt, Debra. Best Kept Secret. 2011. (Pink Locker Society Novels Ser.: 2). (ENG.). 128p. (J). (gr. 3-7). pap. 16.99 (978-0-312-64503-8(1), 9780312645038, St. Martin's Griffin) St. Martin's Pr.
—Girls in Charge. 2011. (Pink Locker Society Novels Ser.: 4). (ENG.). 208p. (J). (gr. 3-7). pap. 18.99 (978-0-312-64506-9(6), 9780312645069, St. Martin's Griffin) St. Martin's Pr.
Mohr, L. C. Krumbuckets. Musheno, Erica, illus. 2007. (ENG.). 144p. (J). (gr. 2-7). 13.95 (978-0-9769417-6-7(7)) Blooming Tree Pr.
Mohsenian, Javad. 9/11 Children. 2006. (ENG.). 128p. per. 10.95 (978-0-7414-3218-6(8)) Infinity Publishing.
Moiser, Liam. Moore Field School & the Mystery. 2013. 118p. pap. 10.95 (978-1-62516-767-3(3), Strategic Bk. Publishing) Strategic Book Publishing & Rights Agency (SBPRA).
Moisher, Phil. Long Before I Knew Better. 2011. 70p. pap. 19.95 (978-1-4560-4007-9(3)) America Star Bks.
Molinari, Laurice E. Pillars of Fire, 1 vol. 2016. (Ether Novel Ser.). (ENG.). 368p. (J). pap. 8.99 (978-0-310-73562-5(9)) Zonderkidz.
Molinari, Laurice Elehwany. The Ether: Vero Rising, 1 vol. 2014. (Ether Novel Ser.). (ENG.). 368p. (J). pap. 8.99 (978-0-310-73561-8(0)) Zonderkidz.
—Pillars of Fire, 1 vol. 2015. (Ether Novel Ser.). (ENG.). 368p. (J). 16.99 (978-0-310-73556-4(4)) Zonderkidz.
Mongredien, Sue. Oliver Moon's Fangtastic Sleepover. 2011. (Oliver Moon Ser.). 92p. (J). pap. 4.99 (978-0-7945-3094-5(X), Usborne) EDC Publishing.
Monir, Alexandra. The Girl in the Picture. 2016. (ENG.). 272p. (YA). (gr. 7). 17.99 (978-0-385-74390-7(4), Delacorte Pr.) Random Hse. Children's Bks.
A Monkey Ate My Homework. 2007. 32p. pap. 4.50 (978-0-8341-2287-1(1), 083-412-2871) Beacon Hill Pr. of Kansas City.
Monks, Lydia. Mungo Monkey Goes to School. 2014. (ENG., Illus.). 14p. (J). (gr. -1-k). 13.99 (978-1-4052-6909-4(X)) Egmont Bks., Ltd. GBR. Dist: Independent Pubs. Group.
Monninger, Joseph. Game Change. 2017. (ENG.). 240p. (YA). (gr. 9). 17.99 (**978-0-544-53122-2(1)**, HMH Books For Young Readers) Houghton Mifflin Harcourt Publishing Co.
Monroe, Chris. Monkey with a Tool Belt & the School Mystery. Monroe, Chris, illus. 2017. (ENG., Illus.). 32p. (gr. -1-2). 17.99 (**978-1-5124-3010-3(2)**, Carolrhoda Bks.) Lerner Publishing Group.
Monroe, Mary. Milagro en la Escuela Monty. 2010. (SPA.). 188p. pap. 13.95 (978-1-61764-099-5(9)) AuthorHouse.
Monroe, Mary A. Tagger: Graffiti Was His Life - & Soul. 2011. 176p. 29.99 (978-1-4567-5028-2(3)); pap. 19.99 (978-1-4567-5029-9(1)) AuthorHouse.
Monstrata, Nessi. Monster High Diaries: Cleo & the Creeperific Mummy Makeover. 2016. (Monster High Diaries: 5). (ENG.). 160p. (J). (gr. 3-7). 9.99 (978-0-316-26636-9(1)) Little, Brown Bks. for Young Readers.
—Monster High Diaries: Frankie Stein & the New Ghoul in School. 2015. (Monster High Diaries: 2). (ENG., Illus.). 160p. (J). (gr. 3-7). 9.99 (978-0-316-30094-0(2)) Little, Brown Bks. for Young Readers.
Mont, Eve Marie. A Phantom Enchantment. 2014. (Unbound Ser.). (ENG.). 288p. (YA). (gr. 13). pap. 9.95 (978-0-7582-6950-8(1), K-Teen) Kensington Publishing Corp.
Montes, Marisa. A Crazy Mixed-Up Spanglish Day. Cepeda, Joe, illus. 2004. (Get Ready for Gabi Ser.). 120p. (gr. 2-5). 14.00 (978-0-7569-3403-3(6)) Perfection Learning Corp.
—A Crazy Mixed-Up Spanglish Day. Cepeda, Joe, illus. 2003. (Get Ready for Gabi Ser.). 128p. (J). 12.95 (978-0-439-51710-2(9), Scholastic Paperbacks) Scholastic, Inc.
Montgomery, Arch. Jake. 2004. 218p. (YA). (gr. 8-12). 19.95 (978-1-890862-31-2(2)) Bancroft Pr.
Montgomery, L. M. Anne of Avonlea. 2011. 214p. (gr. 4-7). pap. 15.95 (978-1-4638-0054-3(1)) Rodgers, Alan Bks.
—Emily Climbs: Emily of New Moon Series. 2014. (Emily Ser.: 2). (ENG.). 368p. (YA). (gr. 5-12). pap. 8.99 (978-1-4022-8915-6(4)) Sourcebooks, Inc.
Montgomery, Lewis B. The Case of the Crooked Campaign. Wummer, Amy, illus. 2012. (Milo & Jazz Mysteries (r) Ser.: 9). (ENG.). 112p. (J). (gr. 2-5). pap. 6.95 (978-1-57565-436-2(9)); lib. bdg. 22.60 (978-1-57565-435-5(0)) Kane Press, Inc.
—The Case of the Diamonds in the Desk. Wummer, Amy, illus. 2012. (Milo & Jazz Mysteries Ser.). 96p. (J). (gr. 2-5). pap. 39.62 (978-0-7613-9207-1(6)); (ENG.). pap. 6.95 (978-1-57565-391-4(5)); lib. bdg. 22.60 (978-1-57565-392-1(3)) Kane Press, Inc.
—The Case of the Haunted Haunted House, Vol. 3. Wummer, Amy, illus. 2009. (Milo & Jazz Mysteries Ser.). 96p. (J). (gr. k-3). 22.60 (978-1-57565-297-9(8)); (ENG.). (gr. 3-7). pap. 6.95 (978-1-57565-295-5(1)) Kane Press, Inc.
—The Case of the Haunted Haunted House. Wummer, Amy, illus. 2012. (Milo & Jazz Mysteries Ser.: Vol. 3). (ENG.). (J). (gr. 2-4). pap. 20.95 incl. audio compact disk (978-1-4301-1206-8(9)) Live Oak Media.
—The Case of the Locked Box. Wummer, Amy, illus. 2013. (ENG.). (J). (gr. 2-4). (Milo & Jazz Mysteries (r) Ser.: 11). 112p. pap. 6.95 (978-1-57565-626-7(4)); (Milo & Jazz Mysteries Ser.: Vol. 11). 106p. lib. bdg. 22.60 (978-1-57565-625-0(6)) Kane Press, Inc.
Moore, Julianne. Best Friends Forever. Pham, LeUyen, illus. 2017. (Step into Reading Ser.). (ENG.). 32p. (J). (gr. -1-1). 15.99 (978-0-375-97369-7(9), Random Hse. Bks. for Young Readers) Random Hse. Children's Bks.
—Freckleface Strawberry & the Really Big Voice. Pham, LeUyen, illus. 2016. (ENG.). 40p. (J). (gr. -1-2). 19.99 (978-0-375-97370-3(2), Doubleday Bks. for Young Readers) Random Hse. Children's Bks.
—Freckleface Strawberry: Backpacks! Pham, LeUyen, illus. 2015. (Step into Reading Ser.). (ENG.). 32p. (J). (gr. -1-1). lib. bdg. 15.99 (978-0-375-97367-3(2), Random Hse. Bks. for Young Readers) Random Hse. Children's Bks.
Moore, Meredith. I Am Her Revenge. 2015. (ENG.). 336p. (YA). (gr. 7). 17.99 (978-1-59514-782-0(9), Razorbill) Penguin Young Readers Group.
Moore, Stephanie. Better Than Picture Perfect. 2014. (Sharp Sisters Ser.: 2). (ENG.). 160p. (YA). (gr. 6-12). pap. 7.95 (978-1-4677-4486-7(7), Darby Creek) Lerner Publishing Group.
—Make Something of It. 2014. (Sharp Sisters Ser.: 1). (ENG.). 152p. (YA). (gr. 6-12). pap. 7.95 (978-1-4677-4488-1(3), Darby Creek) Lerner Publishing Group.
Moore, Stephanie Perry. Back That Thing. 2015. (Illus.). 103p. (YA). 9.99 (978-1-4677-7892-3(3)) Lerner Publishing Group.
—Better Than Picture Perfect. 2014. (Sharp Sisters Ser.: 2). (ENG.). 160p. (YA). (gr. 6-12). lib. bdg. 27.93 (978-1-4677-3725-8(9)) Lerner Publishing Group.
—Enjoying True Peace, 1 vol. 2010. (Yasmin Peace Ser.: 5). (ENG.). 176p. pap. 6.99 (978-0-8024-8606-6(1), Lift Every Voice) Moody Pubs.
—Forever Hot/Truly Fine. 2013. (Grovehill Giants Ser.). (YA). lib. bdg. 26.90 (978-0-606-31877-8(1), Turtleback) Turtleback Bks.
—Give It Up. 2015. (YA). 9.99 (978-1-4677-7886-2(9)); (Swoop List Ser.: 1). (ENG., Illus.). 128p. (gr. 6-12). lib. bdg. 27.99 (978-1-4677-5804-8(3)) Lerner Publishing Group.
—Make Something of It. 2014. (Sharp Sisters Ser.: 1). (ENG.). 152p. (YA). (gr. 6-12). lib. bdg. 27.93 (978-1-4677-3722-7(4)) Lerner Publishing Group.
—On Your Knees. 2015. (Swoop List Ser.: 2). (ENG., Illus.). 128p. (YA). (gr. 6-12). lib. bdg. 27.99 (978-1-4677-5805-5(1)) Lerner Publishing Group.
—Sit on Top. 2015. (Swoop List Ser.: 4). (ENG., Illus.). 112p. (YA). (gr. 6-12). pap. 9.99 (978-1-4677-6052-2(8)) Lerner Publishing Group.
—Yell Out/Do You. 2012. (Lockwood Lions Ser.). (YA). lib. bdg. 26.90 (978-0-606-26493-8(0), Turtleback) Turtleback Bks.
Moore, Stephanie Perry & Moody Publishing Staff. Believing in Hope. 2009. (Yasmin Peace Ser.: 2). (ENG.). 176p. (gr. 7-10). pap. 7.99 (978-0-8024-8603-5(7), Lift Every Voice) Moody Pubs.
Moore, Stephanie Perry & Moore, Derrick. Forever Hot/Truly Fine, 1 vol. 2013. (Grovehill Giants Ser.: Bk. 1). (ENG.). 318p. (YA). (gr. 9-12). pap. 14.95 (978-1-62250-683-5(9)) Saddleback Educational Publishing, Inc.
—Golden Heart - Deep Soul, 1 vol. 2013. (Grovehill Giants Ser.: Bk. 2). (ENG.). 320p. (YA). (gr. 9-12). pap. 14.95 (978-1-62250-684-2(7)) Saddleback Educational Publishing, Inc.
—Golden Heart/Deep Soul. 2013. (Grovehill Giants Ser.). (YA). lib. bdg. 26.90 (978-0-606-31878-5(X), Turtleback) Turtleback Bks.
Mora, Pat. The Rainbow Tulip. Sayles, Elizabeth, illus. 2003. (ENG.). 32p. (J). (gr. k-3). 6.99 (978-0-14-250009-5(7), Puffin Books) Penguin Young Readers Group.
—Rainbow Tulip. 2014. 17.00 (978-1-63419-680-2(5)) Perfection Learning Corp.
Mora, Pat & Martinez, Libby. I Pledge Allegiance. Barton, Patrice, illus. 2014. (ENG.). 40p. (J). (gr. -1-2). 16.99 (978-0-307-93181-8(1), Knopf Bks. for Young Readers) Random Hse. Children's Bks.
Moracho, Cristina. Althea & Oliver. 2014. (ENG.). 384p. (YA). (gr. 9). 17.99 (978-0-670-78539-1(3), Viking Books for Young Readers) Penguin Young Readers Group.
Morait, Tracey. Goalden Girl. 2007. 160p. pap. 13.95 (978-1-84799-758-6(9)) Lulu Pr., Inc.
Moreillon, Judi. Ready & Waiting for You. Stock, Catherine, illus. 2013. (ENG.). 32p. (J). 17.00 (978-0-8028-5355-4(2), Eerdmans Bks For Young Readers) Eerdmans, William B. Publishing Co.
Morgan, Alex. Hat Trick. 2015. (Kicks Ser.). (ENG., Illus.). 128p. (J). (gr. 3-7). 16.99 (978-1-4814-5096-6(4), Simon & Schuster Bks. For Young Readers) Simon & Schuster Bks. For Young Readers.
—Saving the Team. 2014. (Kicks Ser.). (ENG., Illus.). 192p. (J). (gr. 3-7). pap. 6.99 (978-1-4424-8571-6(X), Simon & Schuster Bks. For Young Readers) Simon & Schuster Bks. For Young Readers.
—Saving the Team. Franco, Paula, illus. 2013. (Kicks Ser.). (ENG.). 176p. (J). (gr. 3-7). 17.99 (978-1-4424-8570-9(1), Simon & Schuster Bks. For Young Readers) Simon & Schuster Bks. For Young Readers.
Morgan, Amanda K. Secrets, Lies, & Scandals. (ENG.). (YA). (gr. 9). 2017. 368p. pap. 10.99 (978-1-4814-4955-7(9)) 2016. (Illus.). 352p. 17.99 (978-1-4814-4954-0(0)) Simon Pulse. (Simon Pulse).
Morgan, Amanda K. Such a Good Girl. 2017. (ENG., Illus.). 288p. (YA). (gr. 9). 17.99 (**978-1-4814-4957-1(5)**, Simon Pulse) Simon Pulse.
Morgan, Melissa J. Freaky Tuesday, 17 vols. 2007. (Camp Confidential Ser.: 17). (ENG.). 160p. (J). (gr. 3-7). pap. 4.99 (978-0-448-44651-6(0), Grosset & Dunlap) Penguin Young Readers Group.
Morgan, Michaela. Mouse with No Name. Mikhail, Jess, illus. 2004. (ENG.). 24p. (J). lib. bdg. 23.65 (978-1-59646-682-1(0)) Dingles & Co.
Morgan, Nicolette, illus. All about Me: Briana's Neighborhood. 2007. 24p. (J). 15.99 (978-0-9793904-0-1(0)) It's Me Briana, LLC.
Morgan, Ruth. Batter Splatter! Mikhail, Jess, illus. 2005. (ENG.). 24p. (J). lib. bdg. 23.65 (978-1-59646-704-0(5)) Dingles & Co.
Morgan, Winter. Hidden in the Chest. 2017. (Unofficial Minecrafters Academy Ser.: 5). lib. bdg. 18.40 (**978-0-606-40310-8(8)**) Turtleback Bks.
Morgan, Winter. Skeleton Battle: The Unofficial Minecrafters Academy Series, Book Two. 2016. (Unofficial Minecrafters Academy Ser.). (ENG.). 112p. (J). (gr. 1-7). pap. 7.99 (978-1-5107-0595-1(3), Sky Pony Pr.) Skyhorse Publishing Co., Inc.
Moriarty, Jaclyn. The Ghosts of Ashbury High. (ENG.). 496p. (J). (gr. 7). 2012. pap. 10.99 (978-0-545-06973-1(4)) 2010. 18.99 (978-0-545-06972-4(6)) Scholastic, Inc. (Levine, Arthur A. Bks.).
—The Murder of Bindy MacKenzie. 2008. (ENG.). 496p. (J). (gr. 7-12). pap. 9.99 (978-0-439-74052-4(5), Levine, Arthur A. Bks.) Scholastic, Inc.
Morimoto, Diana. Max, He Likes it that Way, 1 vol. 2010. 24p. pap. 24.95 (978-1-4489-6851-0(8)) PublishAmerica, Inc.
Morin, James F. Rothshield Chasing Shadows. 2006. pap. 14.95 (978-1-59330-422-5(6)) Aventine Pr.
Moritzky, Kayla. The Great I Don't Know. 2009. 28p. pap. 15.49 (978-1-4389-8651-7(3)) AuthorHouse.
Moritzky, Sager. The Super Bad Slime Ball from Outer Space. 2011. 28p. pap. 14.99 (978-1-4389-8652-4(1)) AuthorHouse.
Morpurgo, Michael. Snakes & Ladders. Wilson, Anne, illus. 2006. (Yellow Bananas Ser.). (ENG.). 48p. (J). (gr. -1-3). lib. bdg. (978-0-7787-0952-7(3)) Crabtree Publishing Co.
Morris, Chad. Cragbridge Hall, Book 2: The Avatar Battle. 2014. (Cragbridge Hall Ser.: 2). (ENG., Illus.). 360p. (J). (gr. 3-9). 17.99 (978-1-60907-809-6(8), Shadow Mountain) Shadow Mountain Publishing.
—Cragbridge Hall, Book 3: The Impossible Race. 2015. (Cragbridge Hall Ser.: 3). (ENG., Illus.). 432p. (J). (gr. 3-9). 18.99 (978-1-60907-979-6(5), Shadow Mountain) Shadow Mountain Publishing.
Morris, Kimberly. Take Me to Your Weeder. Warrick, Jessica, illus. 2016. (How to Be an Earthling (r) Ser.: 3). (ENG.). 64p. (gr. 1-3). lib. bdg. 22.65 (978-1-57565-824-7(0)) Kane Press, Inc.
—Take Me to Your Weeder: Responsibility. Warrick, Jessica, illus. 2016. (How to Be an Earthling (r) Ser.: 3). (ENG.). 64p. (gr. 1-3). 34.65 (978-1-57565-826-1(7)) Kane Press, Inc.
Morris, Taylor. The BFF Breakup. 2011. (Mix Ser.). (ENG.). 288p. (J). (gr. 4-8). pap. 6.99 (978-1-4424-0758-9(1), Aladdin) Simon & Schuster Children's Publishing.
Morrison, Julia. Wishes. Fabian, Gabriella, illus. 2013. 42p. pap. 10.00 (978-1-883651-65-7(4)) Winters Publishing.
Morrissey, Lynda I. Monsters in My Class. 2013. 32p. pap. (978-1-4602-2017-7(X)) FriesenPress.
Morse, Scott. Magic Pickle. Morse, Scott, illus. 2008. (Magic Pickle Ser.). (ENG., Illus.). 112p. (J). (gr. 2-5). pap. 9.99 (978-0-439-87995-8(7), Graphix) Scholastic, Inc.
Mortensen, Lori. First Day, No Way!, 1 vol. Simard, Remy, illus. (My First Graphic Novel Ser.). (ENG.). 32p. (gr. k-2). 2011. pap. 6.25 (978-1-4342-3102-4(X)) 2010. 24.65 (978-1-4342-2015-8(X)) Stone Arch Bks. (My First Graphic Novel).
—The Lost Lunch, 1 vol. Simard, Remy, illus. (My First Graphic Novel Ser.). (ENG.). 32p. (gr. k-2). 2011. pap. 6.25 (978-1-4342-3103-1(8)) 2010. 24.65 (978-1-4342-2014-1(1)) Stone Arch Bks. (My First Graphic Novel).
Mortenson, Greg & Husain, Farzana. Listen to the Children: The Story of Dr. Greg & Stones into Schools. Roth, Susan L., illus. 2011. (ENG.). 32p. (J). (gr. 1-3). 17.99 (978-0-8037-3593-4(6), Dial) Penguin Publishing Group.
Morton, Carlene. The Library Pages. Docampo, Valeria, illus. 2010. 32p. (J). (gr. k-4). 17.95 (978-1-60213-045-6(0), Upstart Bks.) Highsmith Inc.
Moser, Lisa. The Monster in the Backpack. Jones, Noah Z., illus. 2013. (Candlewick Sparks Ser.). (ENG.). 40p. (J). (gr. k-4). pap. 3.99 (978-0-7636-6643-9(2)) Candlewick Pr.
Mosher, Jennifer. Who Caught the Yawn? & Where Did the Sneeze Go? Sharp, Todd, illus. 2013. 38p. pap. (978-0-9874832-3-2(4)) MoshPit Publishing.
Mosley, Walter. When the Thrill Is Gone, 3 vols. 2012. (Leonid McGill Mystery Ser.: Bk. 3). (ENG.). 384p. (gr. 12). 16.00 (978-0-451-23565-7(7), Berkley) Penguin Publishing Group.
Moss, Marissa. The All-New Amelia. Moss, Marissa, illus. (ENG., Illus.). (J). 2013. 5.99 (978-1-4169-1289-7(4)) 2007. 40p. (gr. 2-5). 12.99 (978-1-4169-0908-8(7)) Simon & Schuster/Paula Wiseman Bks. (Simon & Schuster/Paula Wiseman Bks.).
—Amelia Writes Again. Moss, Marissa, illus. (Amelia Ser.). (ENG., Illus.). (J). (gr. 2-5). 2012. 32p. pap. 6.99 (978-1-4169-1285-9(1)) 2006. 40p. 12.99 (978-1-4169-0904-0(4)) Simon & Schuster/Paula Wiseman Bks. (Simon & Schuster/Paula Wiseman Bks.).
—Amelia's 5th-Grade Notebook. Moss, Marissa, illus. 2006. (Amelia Ser.). (ENG., Illus.). 40p. (J). (gr. 2-5). 12.99 (978-1-4169-0912-5(5), Simon & Schuster/Paula Wiseman Bks.) Simon & Schuster/Paula Wiseman Bks.
—Amelia's 6th-Grade Notebook. Moss, Marissa, illus. 2005. (Amelia Ser.). (ENG., Illus.). 80p. (J). (gr. 4-7). 12.99 (978-0-689-87040-8(X), Simon & Schuster/Paula Wiseman Bks.) Simon & Schuster/Paula Wiseman Bks.
—Amelia's Back-to-School Survival Guide: Vote 4 Amelia - Amelia's Guide to Babysitting. Moss, Marissa, illus. 2012. (Amelia Ser.). (ENG., Illus.). 160p. (J). (gr. 5-8). 12.99 (978-1-4424-4349-5(9), Simon & Schuster/Paula Wiseman Bks.) Simon & Schuster/Paula Wiseman Bks.
—Amelia's BFF. Moss, Marissa, illus. 2011. (Amelia Ser.). (ENG., Illus.). 64p. (J). (gr. 5-8). 9.99 (978-1-4424-0376-5(4), Simon & Schuster/Paula Wiseman Bks.) Simon & Schuster/Paula Wiseman Bks.
—Amelia's Boy Survival Guide. Moss, Marissa, illus. 2012. (Amelia Ser.). (ENG., Illus.). 80p. (J). (gr. 4-8). 9.99 (978-1-4424-4084-5(8), Simon & Schuster/Paula Wiseman Bks.) Simon & Schuster/Paula Wiseman Bks.
—Amelia's Middle-School Graduation Yearbook. 2015. (ENG., Illus.). 80p. (J). (gr. 4-8). 12.95 (978-1-939547-09-5(1)) Creston Bks.
—Amelia's Middle School Survival Guide: Amelia's Most Unforgettable Embarrassing Moments, Amelia's Guide to Gossip. Moss, Marissa, illus. 2009. (Amelia Ser.). (ENG., Illus.). 160p. (J). (gr. 5-8). 14.99 (978-1-4169-7987-6(5), Simon & Schuster/Paula Wiseman Bks.) Simon & Schuster/Paula Wiseman Bks.
—Blood Diaries: Tales of a 6th-Grade Vampire. Moss, Marissa, illus. 2014. (ENG., Illus.). 136p. (J). (gr. 2-7). 13.00 (978-1-939547-05-7(9)) Creston Bks.
—The Fake Friend! Moss, Marissa, illus. 2012. (Daphne's Diary of Daily Disasters Ser.). (ENG., Illus.). 96p. (J). (gr. 2-5). 9.99 (978-1-4424-4014-2(7)); pap. 5.99 (978-1-4424-4015-9(5)) Simon & Schuster/Paula Wiseman Bks. (Simon & Schuster/Paula Wiseman Bks.).
—The Name Game! Moss, Marissa, illus. 2011. (Daphne's Diary of Daily Disasters Ser.). (ENG., Illus.). 80p. (J). (gr. 2-5). pap. 5.99 (978-1-4424-1738-0(2)); lib. bdg. 9.99 (978-1-4424-2676-4(4)) Simon & Schuster/Paula Wiseman Bks. (Simon & Schuster/Paula Wiseman Bks.).
—The Vampire Dare! Moss, Marissa, illus. 2011. (Daphne's Diary of Daily Disasters Ser.). (ENG., Illus.). 80p. (J). (gr. 2-5). pap. 5.99 (978-1-4424-1737-3(4)); lib. bdg. 9.99 (978-1-4424-2677-1(2)) Simon & Schuster/Paula Wiseman Bks. (Simon & Schuster/Paula Wiseman Bks.).

—Vote 4 Amelia. Moss, Marissa, illus. 2007. (Amelia Ser.). (ENG., Illus.). 80p. (J). (gr. 4-7). 9.99 *(978-1-4169-2789-1(1),* Simon & Schuster/Paula Wiseman Bks.) Simon & Schuster/Paula Wiseman Bks.
Moss, Peggy. Say Something, 1 vol. Lyon, Lea, illus. 2004. (ENG.). 32p. (gr. 2-7). 16.95 *(978-0-88448-261-1(8),* 884261) Tilbury Hse. Pubs.
Moss, Peggy & Lyon, Lea. Say Something, 1 vol. 2008. (ENG., Illus.). 32p. (J). (gr. 1-7). pap. 7.95 *(978-0-88448-310-6(X))* Tilbury Hse. Pubs.
—Say Something: 10TH Anniversary Edition. 2013. (ENG., Illus.). 32p. (gr. 2-7). pap. 7.95 *(978-0-88448-360-1(6),* 884360) Tilbury Hse. Pubs.
Moss, Peggy & Weber, Penny. One of Us, 1 vol. 2010. (ENG., Illus.). 32p. (gr. 1-7). 16.95 *(978-0-88448-322-9(3),* 884322) Tilbury Hse. Pubs.
Mostoller, Marcia. Emma's Dilemm. 2011. 42p. pap. 16.95 *(978-1-4560-9859-9(4))* America Star Bks.
Mounts, Samia. Frunk the Skunk. Matricardi, Luca, illus. 2008. (ENG.). 150p. (J). (gr. 4-6). pap. 9.95 *(978-0-9798841-0-8(1))* 4N Publishing LLC.
Moverley, Richard. The Reluctant Rajput. Dean, David, illus. 2005. (Yellow Go Bananas Ser.). (ENG.). 48p. (J). (gr. 3-4). lib. bdg. *(978-0-7787-2723-1(8))* Crabtree Publishing Co.
Mukherjee, Sonya. Gemini. 2016. (ENG., Illus.). 336p. (YA). (gr. 9). 17.99 *(978-1-4814-5677-7(6),* Simon & Schuster Bks. For Young Readers) Simon & Schuster Bks. For Young Readers.
Muldoon Zappa, Shana & Zappa, Ahmet. Leona's Unlucky Mission. Disney Storybook Art Team, illus. 2016. (Star Darlings Ser.: 3). (ENG.). 176p. (J). (gr. 3-7). pap. 6.99 *(978-1-4231-7768-5(1))* Disney Pr.
Mulford, Carolyn. The Feedsack Dress. 2007. (YA). per. 7.95 *(978-0-9713497-4-2(6))* Cave Hollow Pr.
Mullarkey, Lisa. The Artsy Fartsy Auction: Book 8, 1 vol. Harris, Phyllis, illus. 2012. (Katharine the Almost Great Ser.). (ENG.). 80p. (J). (gr. 1-4). 27.07 *(978-1-61641-829-8(X))* Magic Wagon.
—Battle of the Bunks, 1 vol. Franco, Paula, illus. 2016. (ENG.). 112p. (J). lib. bdg. *(978-1-62402-162-6(X))* Magic Wagon.
—Bent Out of Shape, 1 vol. Harris, Phyllis, illus. 2009. (Katharine the Almost Great Ser.: No. 1). (ENG.). 80p. (J). (gr. 1-4). 27.07 *(978-1-60270-582-1(8))* Magic Wagon.
—The Biggest Star by Far, 1 vol. Harris, Phyllis, illus. 2009. (Katharine the Almost Great Ser.: No. 1). (ENG.). 80p. (J). (gr. 1-4). 27.07 *(978-1-60270-581-4(X))* Magic Wagon.
—Can't Keep Trackula of Jackula, 1 vol. Harris, Phyllis, illus. 2009. (Katharine the Almost Great Ser.: No. 1). (ENG.). 80p. (J). (gr. 1-4). 27.07 *(978-1-60270-584-5(4))* Magic Wagon.
—The Ding Dong Ditch-A-Roo: Book 9, 1 vol. Harris, Phyllis, illus. 2012. (Katharine the Almost Great Ser.). (ENG.). 80p. (J). (gr. 1-4). 27.07 *(978-1-61641-830-4(3))* Magic Wagon.
—A Feast of Fun, 1 vol. Franco, Paula, illus. 2016. (ENG.). 112p. (J). lib. bdg. *(978-1-62402-163-3(8))* Magic Wagon.
—A Filming Fiasco, 1 vol. Franco, Paula, illus. 2016. (ENG.). 112p. (J). lib. bdg. *(978-1-62402-164-0(6))* Magic Wagon.
—Hair's Looking at You: Book 12, 1 vol. Harris, Phyllis, illus. 2012. (Katharine the Almost Great Ser.). (ENG.). 80p. (J). (gr. 1-4). 27.07 *(978-1-61641-833-5(8))* Magic Wagon.
—Hopes in Hiding, 1 vol. Franco, Paula, illus. 2016. (ENG.). 112p. (J). lib. bdg. *(978-1-62402-165-7(4))* Magic Wagon.
—Major Mama Drama, 1 vol. Harris, Phyllis, illus. 2009. (Katharine the Almost Great Ser.: No. 1). (ENG.). 80p. (J). (gr. 1-4). 27.07 *(978-1-60270-580-7(1))* Magic Wagon.
—The Purr-Fect-O Present: Book 10, 1 vol. Harris, Phyllis, illus. 2012. (Katharine the Almost Great Ser.). (ENG.). 80p. (J). (gr. 1-4). 27.07 *(978-1-61641-831-1(1))* Magic Wagon.
—The Red, White, & Blue Crew, 1 vol. Harris, Phyllis, illus. 2009. (Katharine the Almost Great Ser.: No. 1). (ENG.). 80p. (J). (gr. 1-4). 27.07 *(978-1-60270-583-8(6))* Magic Wagon.
—TJ Zaps a Nightmare: Stopping Blackmail Bullying #5, 1 vol. LaCoste, Gary, illus. 2012. (TJ Trapper, Bully Zapper Ser.). (ENG.). 80p. (J). (gr. 2-5). lib. bdg. 27.07 *(978-1-61641-909-7(1),* Calico Chapter Bks) Magic Wagon.
—TJ Zaps the Freeze Out: Stopping the Silent Treatment #3, 1 vol. LaCoste, Gary, illus. 2012. (TJ Trapper, Bully Zapper Ser.). (ENG.). 80p. (J). (gr. 2-5). lib. bdg. 27.07 *(978-1-61641-907-3(5),* Calico Chapter Bks) Magic Wagon.
—TJ Zaps the New Kid: Stopping a Social Bully #1, 1 vol. LaCoste, Gary, illus. 2012. (TJ Trapper, Bully Zapper Ser.). (ENG.). 80p. (J). (gr. 2-5). lib. bdg. 27.07 *(978-1-61641-905-9(9),* Calico Chapter Bks) Magic Wagon.
—TJ Zaps the Rumor Mill: Stopping Gossip #4, 1 vol. LaCoste, Gary, illus. 2012. (TJ Trapper, Bully Zapper Ser.). (ENG.). 80p. (J). (gr. 2-5). lib. bdg. 27.07 *(978-1-61641-908-0(3),* Calico Chapter Bks) Magic Wagon.
—TJ Zaps the Smackdown: Stopping a Physical Bully #6, 1 vol. LaCoste, Gary, illus. 2012. (TJ Trapper, Bully Zapper Ser.). (ENG.). 80p. (J). (gr. 2-5). lib. bdg. 27.07 *(978-1-61641-910-3(5),* Calico Chapter Bks) Magic Wagon.
—Uses Her Common Cents, 1 vol. Harris, Phyllis, illus. 2009. (Katharine the Almost Great Ser.: No. 1). (ENG.). 80p. (J). (gr. 1-4). 27.07 *(978-1-60270-579-1(8))* Magic Wagon.
—The Write Stuff: Book 7, 1 vol. Harris, Phyllis, illus. 2012. (Katharine the Almost Great Ser.). (ENG.). 80p. (J). (gr. 1-4). 27.07 *(978-1-61641-828-1(1))* Magic Wagon.
Mullican, Judy. Jonah Starts School. Cress, Michelle H., illus. l.t. ed. 2003. (HRL Little Book Ser.). 8p. (J). (gr. -1-1). pap. 10.95 *(978-1-57332-269-0(5));* pap. 10.95 *(978-1-57332-268-3(7))* Carson-Dellosa Publishing, LLC. (HighReach Learning, Incorporated).
Mulligan, Andy. Ribblestrop. (Ribblestrop Ser.). (ENG., Illus.). (J). (gr. 3-7). 2016. 400p. pap. 7.99 *(978-1-4424-9905-8(2))* 2014. 384p. 16.99 *(978-1-4424-9904-1(4))* Beach Lane Bks. (Beach Lane Bks.).
—Ribblestrop Forever! 2016. (Ribblestrop Ser.). (ENG., Illus.). 320p. (J). (gr. 3-7). 16.99 *(978-1-4424-9910-2(9),* Beach Lane Bks.) Beach Lane Bks.
Mullins, Julie. School Play Stars. Maddock, Monika, illus. 2005. (Girlz Rock! Ser.). (J). pap. *(978-1-59336-706-0(6))* Mondo Publishing.
Muluka, B. Kandu & the Lake. 2004. (Illus.). 44p. pap. *(978-9966-25-165-7(0))* Heinemann Kenya, Limited (East African Educational Publishers Ltd E.A.E.P.) KEN. Dist: Michigan State Univ. Pr.
Muncaster, Harriet. Isadora Moon Goes to School. 2017. (Isadora Moon Ser.: 1). (ENG.). 128p. (J). (gr. 1-4). 14.99 *(978-0-399-55821-4(7),* Random Hse. Bks. for Young Readers) Random Hse. Children's Bks.
Munday, Evan. Loyalist to a Fault: The Dead Kid Detective Agency #3. 2015. (Dead Kid Detective Agency Ser.: 3). (ENG., Illus.). 320p. (J). (gr. 2-7). pap. 11.95 *(978-1-77041-074-9(0))* Purple Bear Bks., Inc.
Munsch, Robert. Get Out of Bed! 2004. (Illus.). (J). (gr. k-3). spiral bd. *(978-0-616-04557-2(3));* spiral bd. *(978-0-616-03049-3(5))* Canadian National Institute for the Blind/Institut National Canadien pour les Aveugles.
—Kiss Me, I'm Perfect! Martchenko, Michael, illus. 2008. (J). (gr. -1-3). 11.65 *(978-0-7569-9007-7(6))* Perfection Learning Corp.
—El Traje de Nieve de Tomás. Aguirre, Rigo, tr. from ENG. Martchenko, Michael, illus. 2004. (Munsch for Kids Ser.). (SPA.). 24p. (J). (gr. -1-2). pap. 7.95 *(978-1-55037-854-2(6),* 9781550378542) Annick Pr., Ltd. CAN. Dist: Publishers Group West (PGW).
Murail, Marie-aude. Sin Azúcar, Gracias. 2003. (la Orilla Del Viento Ser.). (SPA.). 101p. (J). pap. 8.50 *(978-968-16-6725-2(5))* Fondo de Cultura Economica USA.
Murdoch, Patricia. Exposure, 1 vol. 2006. (Orca Soundings Ser.). (ENG.). 128p. (YA). (gr. 8-12). per. 9.95 *(978-1-55143-493-3(8))* Orca Bk. Pubs. USA.
—Revelación, 1 vol. 2008. (Spanish Soundings Ser.). (SPA.). 112p. (YA). (gr. 8-12). pap. 9.95 *(978-1-55469-053-4(6))* Orca Bk. Pubs. USA.
Murdock, Catherine Gilbert. Front & Center. 2009. (ENG.). 272p. (YA). (gr. 7-18). 16.00 *(978-0-618-95982-2(3))* Houghton Mifflin Harcourt Publishing Co.
Mureddu, R. The Laundromat. 2011. 96p. pap. 19.95 *(978-1-4560-8389-2(9))* America Star Bks.
Murozumi, Hikaru & Inokuma, Shinobu. The School of Water Business. (Illus.). (YA). 206p. pap. *(978-4-09-153102-5(4));* Vol. 4. 2005. (JPN., 205p. mass mkt. *(978-4-09-153104-9(0));* Vol. 5. (JPN., 205p. mass mkt. *(978-4-09-153105-6(9))* Shogakukan.
Murphy, Brendán. Ready for School, Murphy? [8x8 with Stickers]. Murphy, Brendán, illus. 2017. (ENG., Illus.). 40p. (J). (gr. -1-k). pap. 5.99 ***(978-1-368-00299-8(4))*** Hyperion Bks. for Children.
Murphy, Eileen. 3 Big Steps. Montgomery, Violet, illus. 2008. 25p. pap. 24.95 *(978-1-60563-310-7(0))* America Star Bks.
Murphy, Jill. A Bad Spell for the Worst Witch. Murphy, Jill, illus. 2014. (Worst Witch Ser.). (ENG., Illus.). 128p. (J). (gr. 3-7). pap. 5.99 *(978-0-7636-7252-2(1))* Candlewick Pr.
—The Worst Witch Saves the Day. Murphy, Jill, illus. 2014. (Worst Witch Ser.). (ENG., Illus.). 160p. (J). (gr. 3-7). pap. 5.99 *(978-0-7636-7255-3(6))* Candlewick Pr.
—The Worst Witch to the Rescue. Murphy, Jill, illus. 2014. (Worst Witch Ser.). (ENG., Illus.). 176p. (J). (gr. 3-7). 14.99 *(978-0-7636-6999-7(7))* Candlewick Pr.
Murphy, Jim. Revenge of the Green Banana. 2017. (ENG.). 224p. (J). (gr. 5-7). 16.99 *(978-0-544-78677-6(7),* Clarion Bks.) Houghton Mifflin Harcourt Trade & Reference Pubs.
Murphy, Pat. The Wild Girls. unabr. ed. 2007. (YA). (gr. 6-9). audio compact disk 45.00 *(978-0-7393-5988-4(6))* Random Hse. Audio Publishing Group.
Murphy, Sally. Pearl Verses the World. Potter, Heather, illus. 2011. (ENG.). 80p. (J). (gr. 3-7). 14.99 *(978-0-7636-4821-3(3))* Candlewick Pr.
Murphy, Stuart J. Freda Is Found. 2011. (I See I Learn Ser.). (ENG., Illus.). 32p. (J). (-k). 14.95 *(978-1-58089-462-3(3));* pap. 6.95 *(978-1-58089-463-0(1))* Charlesbridge Publishing, Inc.
—Freda Stops a Bully. Jones, Tim, illus. 2012. (I See I Learn Ser.). (ENG.). 32p. (J). (-k). 14.95 *(978-1-58089-466-1(6));* pap. 6.95 *(978-1-58089-467-8(4))* Charlesbridge Publishing, Inc.
—Great Choice, Camille! 2013. (I See I Learn Ser.). (ENG., Illus.). 32p. (J). (-k). pap. 6.95 *(978-1-58089-477-7(1));* lib. bdg. 14.95 *(978-1-58089-476-0(3))* Charlesbridge Publishing, Inc.
Murray, Alison. Hickory Dickory Dog. Murray, Alison, illus. 2014. (ENG., Illus.). 32p. (J). (-k). 16.99 *(978-0-7636-6826-6(5))* Candlewick Pr.
Murray, C. J. Shayna Gladstone: In Search of the Scientist. 2011. 148p. 22.95 *(978-1-4502-8992-4(4));* pap. 12.95 *(978-1-4502-8990-0(8))* iUniverse, Inc.
Murray, Fisher C & Murray, Colleen O. One & Only Bernadette P. McMull. 2009. (ENG.). 32p. pap. 10.95 *(978-1-933916-52-1(4),* Ferne Pr.) Nelson Publishing & Marketing.
Murray, Jaye. Bottled Up. 2004. (ENG.). 224p. (YA). (gr. 7-12). reprint ed. 6.99 *(978-0-14-240240-5(0),* Speak) Penguin Young Readers Group.
Murray, Laura. The Gingerbread Man Loose in the School. Lowery, Mike, illus. 2011. (ENG.). 32p. (J). (gr. k-3). 16.99 *(978-0-399-25052-1(2),* G.P. Putnam's Sons Books for Young Readers) Penguin Young Readers Group.
Murray, Laura & McPike, Elizabeth. The Gingerbread Man Loose at Christmas. Lowery, Mike, illus. 2015. (ENG.). 32p. (J). (gr. k-k). 16.99 *(978-0-399-16866-6(4),* G.P. Putnam's Sons Books for Young Readers) Penguin Young Readers Group.
Murray, Stuart A. P. Todd Goes for the Goal. 2012. (Champion Sports Story Ser.). 104p. (J). (gr. 3-18). pap. 10.95 *(978-1-4644-0000-1(8));* lib. bdg. 27.94 *(978-0-7660-3887-5(4))* Enslow Pubs., Inc.
Murtagh, Ciaran. Megastar. Wesson, Tim, illus. 2016. (Fincredible Diary of Fin Spencer Ser.: 2). (ENG.). 224p. (J). (gr. 4-7). pap. 7.99 *(978-1-84812-447-9(3))* Bonnier Publishing GBR. Dist: Independent Pubs. Group.
Musolf, Nell. Jessica James. 2003. (J). per. *(978-0-9740833-0-8(5))* Port Town Publishing.
My Awesome School Planner. 2008. (Best Friends Club Ser.). 160p. *(978-1-4075-3175-5(1))* Parragon, Inc.
My First Day at School. 2005. (J). 16.95 *(978-0-9769004-0-5(8))* Sinanan, Cindy.
My Teacher Glows in the Dark. 2014. (My Teacher Bks.: 3). (ENG., Illus.). 192p. (J). (gr. 3-7). 17.99 *(978-1-4814-0432-7(6),* Simon & Schuster/Paula Wiseman Bks.) Simon & Schuster/Paula Wiseman Bks.
Myers, Edward. Duck & Cover. 2004. 200p. (J). per. 11.95 *(978-0-9674477-8-0(X))* Montemayor Pr.
—Ice. 2005. 222p. (J). per. 12.95 net. *(978-0-9674477-9-7(8))* Montemayor Pr.
Myers, Lily. This Impossible Light. 2017. (ENG.). 352p. (YA). (gr. 7). 17.99 *(978-0-399-17372-1(2),* Philomel Bks.) Penguin Young Readers Group.
Myers, Suzanne. I'm from Nowhere. 2017. (ENG.). 304p. (YA). (gr. 9). pap. 10.99 *(978-1-61695-706-3(9),* Soho Teen) Soho Pr., Inc.
Myers, Walter Dean. The Beast. 2005. 17.00 *(978-0-7569-5107-8(0))* Perfection Learning Corp.
—The Cruisers. (ENG.). 144p. (J). (gr. 5-9). 2015. (News Crew Ser.). pap. 6.99 *(978-0-545-82874-1(0))* 2011. (Cruisers Ser.: 1). pap. 5.99 *(978-0-439-91633-2(X))* 2010. (Cruisers Ser.: 1). 15.99 *(978-0-439-91626-4(7))* Scholastic, Inc. (Scholastic Pr.).
—Game. (ENG.). (YA). (gr. 8). 2009. 240p. pap. 9.99 *(978-0-06-058296-8(0))* 2008. 224p. 17.99 *(978-0-06-058294-4(4))* HarperCollins Pubs. (HarperTeen).
—Game. 2011. 10.36 *(978-0-7848-3476-3(8),* Everbind) Marco Bk. Co.
—Oh, Snap! 2013. (Cruisers Ser.: Bk. 4). (ENG.). 128p. (J). (gr. 5-9). 17.99 *(978-0-439-91629-5(1),* Scholastic Pr.) Scholastic, Inc.
—Shooter. (ENG.). 2004. 224p. (J). 15.99 *(978-0-06-029519-6(8),* HarperTeen) 2005. 256p. (YA). (gr. 9-17). reprint ed. pap. 9.99 *(978-0-06-447290-6(6),* Amistad) HarperCollins Pubs.
—Slam! 2008. (ENG.). 288p. (J). (gr. 7). pap. 8.99 *(978-0-545-05574-1(1),* Scholastic Paperbacks) Scholastic, Inc.
—Slam! 2008. (Point Signature Ser.). 266p. (gr. 7-12). lib. bdg. 19.65 *(978-0-613-12111-8(2),* Turtleback) Turtleback Bks.
—A Star Is Born. (J). 2015. (News Crew Ser.). (ENG.). 176p. (gr. 5-9). pap. 6.99 *(978-0-545-82876-5(7),* Scholastic Pr.) 2012. (Cruisers Ser.: Bk. 3). *(978-0-439-91631-8(3))* 2012. (Cruisers Ser.: Bk. 3). (ENG.). 176p. (gr. 5-9). 17.99 *(978-0-439-91628-8(3))* Scholastic, Inc.
Myracle, Lauren. Awesome Blossom. 2013. (Flower Power Ser.). (ENG.). 272p. (J). (gr. 4-8). 17.95 *(978-1-4197-0405-5(2),* Amulet Bks.) Abrams, Inc.
—Awesome Blossom: A Flower Power Book. 2013. (Flower Power Ser.). (ENG.). 272p. (J). (gr. 3-7). pap. 7.95 *(978-1-4197-0791-9(4),* Amulet Bks.) Abrams, Inc.
—Bliss. 2008. (ENG.). 464p. (YA). (gr. 9-17). 16.95 *(978-0-8109-7071-7(6),* Amulet Bks.) Abrams, Inc.
—Eleven. 2005. (Winnie Years Ser.). (ENG.). 224p. (J). (gr. 3-7). reprint ed. pap. 7.99 *(978-0-14-240346-4(6),* Puffin Books) Penguin Young Readers Group.
—The Fashion Disaster That Changed My Life. 2008. (ENG.). 160p. (J). (gr. 5-18). 6.99 *(978-0-14-240717-2(8),* Puffin Books) Penguin Young Readers Group.
—Friends of a Feather. Henry, Jed, illus. 2015. (Life of Ty Ser.: 3). (ENG.). 144p. (J). (gr. 1-4). 5.99 *(978-0-14-242320-2(3),* Puffin Books); 12.99 *(978-0-525-42288-4(9),* Dutton Books for Young Readers) Penguin Young Readers Group.
—The Life of Ty - Non-Random Acts of Kindness. Henry, Jed, illus. 2015. (Life of Ty Ser.: 2). (ENG.). 128p. (J). (gr. 1-4). 5.99 *(978-0-14-242319-6(X),* Puffin Books) Penguin Young Readers Group.
—Luv Ya Bunches, Bk. 1. 2009. (Flower Power Ser.). (ENG., Illus.). 352p. (J). (gr. 3-7). 16.95 *(978-0-8109-4211-0(9),* Amulet Bks.) Abrams, Inc.
—Luv Ya Bunches: A Flower Power Book. 2010. (Flower Power Ser.). (ENG.). 352p. (J). (gr. 3-7). pap. 8.95 *(978-0-8109-8982-5(4),* Amulet Bks.) Abrams, Inc.
—Oopsy Daisy. 2012. (Flower Power Ser.). (ENG.). 368p. (J). (gr. 3-7). pap. 8.95 *(978-1-4197-0418-5(4),* Amulet Bks.) Abrams, Inc.
—Penguin Problems. Henry, Jed, illus. 2013. (Life of Ty Ser.: 1). (ENG.). 128p. (J). (gr. 1-4). 12.99 *(978-0-525-42264-8(1),* Dutton Books for Young Readers) Penguin Young Readers Group.
—Penguin Problems. 2014. (Life of Ty Ser.: 1). lib. bdg. 16.00 *(978-0-606-34213-1(3),* Turtleback) Turtleback Bks.
—Rhymes with Witches. (ENG.). (YA). (gr. 8-17). 2006. 272p. pap. 7.95 *(978-0-8109-9215-3(9))* 2005. 224p. 16.95 *(978-0-8109-5859-3(7),* Amulet Bks.) Abrams, Inc.
—Ten. (Winnie Years Ser.). (ENG.). (J). (gr. 3-7). 2012. 240p. pap. 7.99 *(978-0-14-242134-5(0),* Puffin Books) 2011. 272p. 16.99 *(978-0-525-42356-0(7),* Dutton Books for Young Readers) Penguin Young Readers Group.
—Thirteen. 2009. (Winnie Years Ser.). (ENG.). 272p. (J). (gr. 3-7). 7.99 *(978-0-14-241370-8(4),* Puffin Books) Penguin Young Readers Group.
—Violet in Bloom. 2010. (Flower Power Ser.). (ENG., Illus.). 384p. (J). (gr. 3-7). 16.95 *(978-0-8109-8983-2(2),* Amulet Bks.) Abrams, Inc.
Nagda, Ann Whitehead. Kevin Keeps Up. 2012. (ENG.). 96p. (J). 15.95 *(978-0-8234-2657-7(2))* Holiday Hse., Inc.
—The Perfect Cat-Sitter. Roth, Stephanie, illus. 2007. (ENG.). 96p. (J). (gr. 4-7). 15.95 *(978-0-8234-2112-1(0))* Holiday Hse., Inc.
—Tarantula Power! 2007. (ENG., Illus.). 96p. (J). (gr. 2-5). 15.95 *(978-0-8234-1991-3(5))* Holiday Hse., Inc.
—The Valentine Cat. Roth, Stephanie, illus. 2008. (ENG.). 32p. (J). (gr. 2-5). 16.95 *(978-0-8234-2123-7(6))* Holiday Hse., Inc.
Nakakuma, Chie. Whazzup, Wolly Ayaka? 2007. 128p. per. 10.95 *(978-0-595-44646-9(9))* iUniverse, Inc.
Nana, Auntie. I Can't Go to School Today. 2012. pap. 12.95 *(978-0-7414-8105-4(7))* Infinity Publishing.
—I Can't Go to School Today with CD. 2012. pap. 16.95 *(978-0-7414-7756-9(4))* Infinity Publishing.
Napoli, Linda. Sailing Away on a Windy Day. 2012. 24p. pap. 17.32 *(978-1-4797-2962-3(0))* Xlibris Corp.
Nash, Andy. Melinda & Her Mule: For Kids Blessed with a Strong Will. 2008. (J). *(978-0-8127-0453-2(3))* Autumn Hse. Publishing Co.
Na'Shae. The Magic Chronicles: Ice. 2008. 80p. pap. 9.99 *(978-0-9814650-6-7(4))* G Publishing LLC.
Nathoo, Aalaynah. The World above Us!!! 2012. 16p. pap. 15.99 *(978-1-4772-3222-4(2))* AuthorHouse.
Nayeri, Daniel and Dina. Another Faust. 2010. (ENG., Illus.). 400p. (YA). (gr. 9). pap. 8.99 *(978-0-7636-4834-3(5))* Candlewick Pr.
—Another Jekyll, Another Hyde. 2012. (ENG., Illus.). 400p. (YA). (gr. 9). 17.99 *(978-0-7636-5261-6(X))* Candlewick Pr.
Naylor, Phyllis Reynolds. Alice in April. 2011. (Alice Ser.: 5). (ENG.). 192p. (J). (gr. 5-9). pap. 6.99 *(978-1-4424-2757-0(4),* Atheneum Bks. for Young Readers) Simon & Schuster Children's Publishing.
—Alice in Blunderland. 2005. 200p. (J). (gr. 2-7). 13.65 *(978-0-7569-5075-0(9))* Perfection Learning Corp.
—Alice in Blunderland. 2012. (Alice Ser.). (ENG., Illus.). 240p. (J). (gr. 2-7). pap. 5.99 *(978-1-4424-4643-4(9),* Atheneum Bks. for Young Readers) Simon & Schuster Children's Publishing.
—Alice in Charge. (Alice Ser.: 22). (ENG., (YA). (gr. 9). 2011. Illus.). 304p. pap. 8.99 *(978-1-4169-7555-7(1))* 2010. 336p. 16.99 *(978-1-4169-7552-6(7))* Simon & Schuster Children's Publishing. (Atheneum Bks. for Young Readers).
—Alice in Lace. 2009. (Alice McKinley Ser.: No. 8). (ENG.). 160p. (J). pap. 7.99 *(978-1-4169-7543-4(8),* Simon & Schuster/Paula Wiseman Bks.) Simon & Schuster/Paula Wiseman Bks.
—Alice on Her Way. 2006. (Alice McKinley Ser.: No. 17). 322p. (gr. 9-12). 17.00 *(978-0-7569-6909-7(3))* Perfection Learning Corp.
—Alice on Her Way. 2006. (Alice Ser.: No. 17). (ENG.). 352p. (YA). (gr. 9-12). mass mkt. 6.99 *(978-0-689-87091-0(4),* Simon Pulse) Simon Pulse.
—Alice on the Outside. 2012. (Alice Ser.: 11). (ENG., Illus.). 208p. (J). (gr. 5-9). pap. 6.99 *(978-1-4424-3495-0(3),* Atheneum Bks. for Young Readers) Simon & Schuster Children's Publishing.
—All but Alice. 2011. (Alice Ser.: 4). (ENG.). 192p. (J). (gr. 5-9). pap. 6.99 *(978-1-4424-2756-3(6),* Atheneum Bks. for Young Readers) Simon & Schuster Children's Publishing.
—Almost Alice. 2008. (Alice Ser.: 20). (ENG.). 288p. (YA). (gr. 9-18). 16.99 *(978-0-689-87096-5(5),* Atheneum Bks. for Young Readers) Simon & Schuster Children's Publishing.
—Almost Alice. 2009. (Alice Ser.: 20). (ENG.). 288p. (YA). (gr. 9). mass mkt. 6.99 *(978-0-689-87097-2(3),* Simon Pulse) Simon Pulse.
—Dangerously Alice. 2007. (Alice Ser.: 19). (ENG.). 304p. (YA). (gr. 9-12). 15.99 *(978-0-689-87094-1(9),* Atheneum Bks. for Young Readers) Simon & Schuster Children's Publishing.
—Dangerously Alice. 2008. (Alice Ser.: No. 19). (ENG.). 320p. (YA). mass mkt. 6.99 *(978-0-689-87095-8(7),* Simon Pulse) Simon Pulse.
—Eating Enchiladas, 0 vols. Ramsey, Marcy, illus. 2011. (Simply Sarah Ser.: 0). (ENG.). 80p. (J). (gr. 1-4). pap. 9.99 *(978-0-7614-5885-2(9),* 9780761458852, Amazon Children's Publishing) Amazon Publishing.
—I Like Him, He Likes Her: Alice Alone; Simply Alice; Patiently Alice. 2010. (Alice Ser.). (ENG.). 640p. (YA). (gr. 7). pap. 12.99 *(978-1-4424-0978-1(9),* Atheneum Bks. for Young Readers) Simon & Schuster Children's Publishing.
—Including Alice. 2005. (Alice McKinley Ser.: No. 16). 277p. (J). (gr. 4-7). 13.65 *(978-0-7569-5460-4(6))* Perfection Learning Corp.
—Incredibly Alice. (Alice Ser.: 23). (ENG., (YA). (gr. 9). 2012. Illus.). 304p. pap. 8.99 *(978-1-4169-7556-4(X))* 2011. 288p. 16.99 *(978-1-4169-7553-3(5))* Simon & Schuster Children's Publishing. (Atheneum Bks. for Young Readers).
—Lovingly Alice. 2004. (Alice Bks.). 166p. (J). (gr. 4-6). 13.65 *(978-0-7569-6604-1(3))* Perfection Learning Corp.
—Lovingly Alice. 2006. (Alice Ser.). (ENG., Illus.). 176p. (J). (gr. 4-7). pap. 5.99 *(978-0-689-84400-3(X),* Atheneum Bks. for Young Readers) Simon & Schuster Children's Publishing.
—Outrageously Alice. 2011. (Alice Ser.: 9). (ENG., Illus.). 176p. (J). (gr. 5-9). pap. 6.99 *(978-1-4424-2853-9(8),* Atheneum Bks. for Young Readers) Simon & Schuster Children's Publishing.
—Please Don't Be True: Dangerously Alice; Almost Alice; Intensely Alice. 2011. (Alice Ser.). (ENG., Illus.). 768p. (YA). (gr. 9). pap. 12.99 *(978-1-4424-1721-2(8),* Atheneum Bks. for Young Readers) Simon & Schuster Children's Publishing.
—Reluctantly Alice. 2011. (Alice Ser.: 3). (ENG.). 240p. (J). (gr. 5-9). pap. 6.99 *(978-1-4424-2361-9(7),* Atheneum Bks. for Young Readers) Simon & Schuster Children's Publishing.
—Reluctantly Alice. 2008. (Alice McKinley Ser.: No. 3). (ENG.). 208p. (J). pap. 5.99 *(978-1-4169-5876-5(2),* Simon & Schuster/Paula Wiseman Bks.) Simon & Schuster/Paula Wiseman Bks.
—Simply Alice. 2003. (Alice Ser.: 14). (ENG., Illus.). 240p. (YA). (gr. 7). mass mkt. 5.99 *(978-0-689-85965-6(1),* Simon Pulse) Simon Pulse.
—Starting with Alice. 2004. (Alice Bks.). 181p. (J). (gr. 4-7). 12.65 *(978-0-7569-2940-4(7))* Perfection Learning Corp.
—Starting with Alice. 2012. (Alice Ser.). (ENG., Illus.). 224p. (J). (gr. 2-7). pap. 6.99 *(978-1-4424-4642-7(0),* Atheneum Bks. for Young Readers) Simon & Schuster Children's Publishing.
—You & Me & the Space in Between: Alice in Charge; Incredibly Alice; Alice on Board. 2013. (Alice Ser.). (ENG., Illus.). 880p. (YA). (gr. 9). pap. 10.99 *(978-1-4424-8664-5(3),* Atheneum Bks. for Young Readers) Simon & Schuster Children's Publishing.
Neal-Bailey, Ashley L. I Don't Want To. 2007. 20p. per. 24.95 *(978-1-4241-8928-1(4))* America Star Bks.
Neel, Julien. Down in the Dumps. Neel, Julien, illus. 2012. (Lou! Ser.: 3). (ENG., Illus.). 48p. (J). (gr. 6-9). pap. 8.95 *(978-0-8225-9165-8(0),* Graphic Universe™) Lerner Publishing Group.
Neel, Julien & Burrell, Carol klio. Down in the Dumps. Neel, Julien, illus. 2012. (Lou! Ser.: 3). (ENG., Illus.). 48p. (J). (gr. 6-9). lib. bdg. 27.93 *(978-0-7613-8779-4(X),* Graphic Universe™) Lerner Publishing Group.
Neely, Wilma F. Aaron & Abbey Go to School: Trevor Tutors His Friends. 2009. 28p. pap. 12.49 *(978-1-4389-5420-2(4))* AuthorHouse.
Neenan, Colin. Idiot! A Love Story with Drama, Betrayal & E-mail. 2004. (Illus.). 152p. (YA). (gr. 7-13). per. 8.95 *(978-0-9746481-1-8(6))* Brown Barn Bks.
—Thick. 2006. 126p. (YA). (gr. 7-16). per. 6.95 *(978-0-9746481-9-4(1))* Brown Barn Bks.
Nees, Susan. Class Pets. 2013. (Missy's Super Duper Royal Deluxe Ser.: 2). (ENG., Illus.). 80p. (J). (gr. k-2). pap. 4.99 *(978-0-545-43852-0(7))* Scholastic, Inc.
—Class Pets. 2013. (Missy's Super Duper Royal Deluxe Ser.: 2). lib. bdg. 14.75 *(978-0-606-31980-5(8),* Turtleback) Turtleback Bks.
—Picture Day. 2013. (Missy's Super Duper Royal Deluxe Ser.: 1). (ENG., Illus.). 80p. (J). (gr. k-2). 15.99

S

(978-0-545-49609-4(8)); pap. 4.99 (978-0-545-43851-3(9)) Scholastic, Inc.
—Picture Day. 2013. (Missy's Super Duper Royal Deluxe Ser.: 1). lib. bdg. 14.75 (978-0-606-31979-9(4), Turtleback) Turtleback Bks.
—School Play. 2013. (Missy's Super Duper Royal Deluxe Ser.: 3). (ENG., Illus.). 80p. (J). (gr. k-2). pap. 4.99 (978-0-545-43853-7(5)) Scholastic, Inc.
Neff, Henry H. The Fiend & the Forge. 2011. (Tapestry Ser.). (ENG., Illus.). 560p. (J). (gr. 3-7). 7.99 (978-0-375-83899-6(6), Yearling) Random Hse. Children's Bks.
—The Hound of Rowan. 2008. (Tapestry Ser.: 1). (ENG., Illus.). 448p. (J). (gr. 3-7). 7.99 (978-0-375-83895-8(3), Yearling) Random Hse. Children's Bks.
—The Maelstrom: Book Four of the Tapestry. Neff, Henry H., illus. 2013. (Tapestry Ser.). (ENG., Illus.). 480p. (J). (gr. 3-7). 7.99 (978-0-375-87148-1(9), Yearling) Random Hse. Children's Bks.
—The Second Siege. 2010. (Tapestry Ser.). (ENG., Illus.). 512p. (J). (gr. 3-7). 7.99 (978-0-375-83897-2(X), Yearling) Random Hse. Children's Bks.
Neil Wallace, Sandra. Muckers. 2013. (ENG.). 288p. (YA). (gr. 7). 16.99 (978-0-375-86754-5(6), Knopf Bks. for Young Readers) Random Hse. Children's Bks.
Neill, Chloe. Charmfall. 2012. (Dark Elite Ser.: 3). (ENG.). 288p. (YA). (gr. 9). 9.99 (978-0-451-23080-5(9), Berkley) Penguin Publishing Group.
Nelid, Piper. At the School Store, 01 vols., 1. 2016. (Rosen REAL Readers: STEM & STEAM Collection). (ENG.). 8p. (J). pap. 5.46 (978-1-5081-1511-3(7), Rosen Classroom) Rosen Publishing Group, Inc., The.
Nelson, Blake. Boy. 2017. (ENG., Illus.). 368p. (YA). (gr. 9). 18.99 **(978-1-4814-8813-6(9)**, Simon Pulse) Simon Pulse.
—Destroy All Cars. 2011. (ENG.). 224p. (J). (gr. 9-10). pap. 9.99 (978-0-545-10475-3(0), Scholastic Paperbacks) Scholastic, Inc.
—The New Rules of High School. 2004. (ENG.). 240p. (YA). (gr. 7-18). reprint ed. 7.99 (978-0-14-240242-9(7), Speak) Penguin Young Readers Group.
—Paranoid Park. 2008. (ENG.). 192p. (YA). (gr. 7-18). 6.99 (978-0-14-241156-8(6), Puffin Books) Penguin Young Readers Group.
Nelson, James Gary. Dientecito y la Placa Peligros. Burnstead, Debbie, illus. 2011. 16p. pap. 9.95 (978-1-61633-132-0(1)) Guardian Angel Publishing, Inc.
Nelson, Jim. Crosstown Crush. 2005. 82p. Vol. 1, Bk. 1. (YA). pap. 9.00 (978-1-4116-5266-8(5)) Vol. 1,Bk. 2. pap. 9.00 (978-1-4116-6654-2(2)) Lulu Pr., Inc.
Nelson, R. A. Breathe My Name. 2008. (ENG.). 320p. (YA). (gr. 7-18). 9.99 (978-1-59514-186-6(3), Razorbill) Penguin Young Readers Group.
—Teach Me. 2007. (ENG.). 272p. (YA). (gr. 9-12). 8.99 (978-1-59514-085-2(9), Razorbill) Penguin Young Readers Group.
Nelson, Shareese. The Me Inside. 2009. 20p. 10.99 (978-1-4389-4937-6(5)) AuthorHouse.
Nelson, Sheila K. The Backpack Bears' Adventure: Friendship. 2009. 24p. pap. 16.50 (978-1-4490-0554-2(3)) AuthorHouse.
Nelson, Suzanne. You're Bacon Me Crazy. 2014. 248p. (J). pap. (978-0-545-65268-1(5)) Scholastic, Inc.
Neri, G. Chess Rumble. Watson, Jesse Joshua, illus. 2007. (ENG.). 64p. (J). (gr. 3-7). 18.95 (978-1-58430-279-7(8)) Lee & Low Bks., Inc.
Nero, Molly. Smarty Pig & the Test Taking Terror. Turchan, Monique, illus. 2012. 28p. pap. 12.95 (978-1-61244-055-2(X)) Halo Publishing International.
Ness, Berthetta. Originals: Short Stories for Children. 2007. (YA). pap. (978-1-57579-351-1(2)) Pine Hill Pr.
Ness, Patrick. A Monster Calls: Inspired by an Idea from Siobhan Dowd. (ENG.). 240p. (YA). (gr. 7). 2016. pap. 9.99 (978-0-7636-9215-5(8)) 2015. pap. 12.00 (978-0-7636-8081-7(8)) Candlewick Pr.
—A Monster Calls: Inspired by an Idea from Siobhan Dowd. Kay, Jim, illus. (ENG.). 224p. (YA). (gr. 7). 2013. pap. 12.00 (978-0-7636-6065-9(5)) 2011. 16.99 (978-0-7636-5559-4(7)) Candlewick Pr.
—A Monster Calls: Inspired by an Idea from Siobhan Dowd. 2011. (Playaway Children Ser.). (YA). (gr. 7-12). 54.99 (978-1-4558-4499-9(3)) Findaway World, LLC.
—A Monster Calls: Inspired by an Idea from Siobhan Dowd. 2013. lib. bdg. 23.30 (978-0-606-31603-3(5), Turtleback) Turtleback Bks.
—The Rest of Us Just Live Here. (YA). 2016. 336p. (gr. 9). pap. 9.99 (978-0-06-240317-9(6), HarperTeen) 2015. (ENG.). 336p. (gr. 9-12). 17.99 (978-0-06-240316-2(8), HarperTeen) 2015. 352p. (978-1-4063-3116-5(3)) 2015. 317p. (978-0-06-241563-9(8)) HarperCollins Pubs.
Neubecker, Robert. Fall Is for School. Neubecker, Robert, illus. 2017. (ENG., Illus.). 32p. (J). (gr. -1-k). 17.99 **(978-1-4847-3254-0(5))** Disney Pr.
New York Hall of Science Staff. Charlie & Kiwi: An Evolutionary Adventure. Reynolds, Peter H. & Fable Vision Studios Staff, illus. 2011. (ENG.). 48p. (J). (gr. -1-3). 16.99 (978-1-4424-2112-7(6), Atheneum Bks. for Young Readers) Simon & Schuster Children's Publishing.
Newman, Yvette. Missy's Day with Butterflies. 2007. 84p. pap. 11.96 (978-1-4357-0172-4(0)) Lulu Pr., Inc.
Nez, John. One Smart Cookie. Nez, John, illus. 2006. (ENG., Illus.). 32p. (J). (gr. k-3). lib. bdg. 16.99 (978-0-8075-6099-0(5)) Whitman, Albert & Co.
Nichols, C. D. Kids Courageous. 2010. 66p. pap. 9.99 (978-1-60911-809-9(X), Eloquent Bks.) Strategic Book Publishing & Rights Agency (SBPRA).
Nichols, Lee. Deception. 2010. (Haunting Emma Ser.). (ENG.). 336p. (YA). (gr. 9-12). 16.99 (978-1-59990-308-8(3), 9781599903088); pap. 9.99 (978-1-59990-421-4(7), 9781599904214) Bloomsbury Publishing USA. (Bloomsbury USA Childrens).
Nichols, Travis. Matthew Meets the Man. 2012. (ENG., Illus.). 176p. (YA). (gr. 6-9). 24.99 (978-1-59643-545-2(3), 9781596435452) Roaring Brook Pr.
Nickel, Scott. Attack of the Mutant Lunch Lady. Smith, Andy J., illus. 2008. (Graphic Sparks Ser.). (ENG.). 40p. (gr. 1-3). per. 5.95 (978-1-4342-0501-8(0), Graphic Sparks) Stone Arch Bks.
—Invasion of the Gym Class Zombies. Luxich, Matt, illus. 2008. (Graphic Sparks Ser.). (ENG.). 40p. (gr. 1-3). pap. 5.95 (978-1-4342-0503-2(7)); lib. bdg. 23.99 (978-1-4342-0453-0(7)) Stone Arch Bks. (Graphic Sparks).
—Secret of the Summer School Zombies, 1 vol. Luxich, Matt, illus. 2008. (School Zombies Ser.). (ENG.). 40p. (gr. 1-3). 23.99 (978-1-4342-0760-9(9)); pap. 5.95 (978-1-4342-0856-9(7)) Stone Arch Bks. (Graphic Sparks).
Nickel, Scott & Dahl, Michael. The Evil Echo, 1 vol. Crowther, Jeff, illus. 2010. (Princess Candy Ser.). (ENG.). 40p. (gr. 1-3). 23.99 (978-1-4342-1977-0(1)); pap. 5.95 (978-1-4342-2804-8(5)) Stone Arch Bks. (Graphic Sparks).
Nickelodeon Staff & LeapFrog Staff/Nickelodeon. Dora the Explorer: Dora Goes to School. 2008. (J). 13.99 (978-1-59319-985-2(6)) LeapFrog Enterprises, Inc.
The Night Before Kindergarten. 2014. (Night Before Ser.). (ENG.). 32p. (J). (gr. 7-12). 8.24 (978-1-63245-263-4(4)) Lectorum Pubns., Inc.
Night, P. J. The Show Must Go On! 2011. (You're Invited to a Creepover Ser.: 4). (ENG.). 160p. (J). (gr. 3-7). pap. 6.99 (978-1-4424-2905-5(4), Simon Spotlight) Simon Spotlight.
—Show Must Go On!, 1 vol. 2013. (You're Invited to a Creepover Ser.). (ENG.). 160p. (J). (gr. 3-6). lib. bdg. 24.21 (978-1-61479-063-1(9), Essential Library) ABDO Publishing Co.
—The Show Must Go On! 2011. (Creepover Ser.: 4). lib. bdg. 16.00 (978-0-606-23748-2(8), Turtleback) Turtleback Bks.
—Truth or Dare ..., 1 vol. 2013. (You're Invited to a Creepover Ser.). (ENG.). 160p. (J). (gr. 3-6). lib. bdg. 24.21 (978-1-61479-065-5(5), Essential Library) ABDO Publishing Co.
—Truth or Dare... 2011. (You're Invited to a Creepover Ser.: 1). (ENG., Illus.). 160p. (J). (gr. 3-7). pap. 6.99 (978-1-4424-2096-0(0), Simon Spotlight) Simon Spotlight.
Nigro, D. M. The Wolfman, the Shrink & the Eighth-Grade Election. 2006. 116p. (J). pap. 13.50 (978-1-931201-66-7(8)) Twilight Times Bks.
Nijkamp, Marieke. This Is Where It Ends. 2016. (ENG.). 288p. (YA). (gr. 8-12). 17.99 (978-1-4926-2246-8(X), 9781492622468) Sourcebooks, Inc.
—This Is Where It Ends. 2016. lib. bdg. 22.10 (978-0-606-39479-6(6)) 2017. lib. bdg. 22.10 **(978-0-606-39992-0(5))** Turtleback Bks.
Nikki, Grimes. Bronx Masquerade. 2014. (ENG.). 176p. (YA). 11.24 (978-1-63245-077-7(1)) Lectorum Pubns., Inc.
Nimble, Jacque. Prank Wars. 2011. (School Gyrls Ser.). (ENG.). 144p. (J). (gr. 3-7). pap. 5.99 (978-1-4424-0880-7(4), Simon & Schuster/Paula Wiseman Bks.) Simon & Schuster/Paula Wiseman Bks.
Nimmo, Jenny. Midnight for Charlie Bone. 2003. (Children of the Red King Ser.: Bk. 1). (J). (gr. 2-6). per. 4.99 (978-0-439-48839-6(7)) Scholastic, Inc.
Nishimori, Hiroyuki. Cheeky Angel, Vol. 13. Nishimori, Hiroyuki, illus. 2006. (Cheeky Angel Ser.). (ENG., Illus.). 208p. pap. 9.99 (978-1-4215-0447-6(2)) Viz Media.
Nixon, Kareh. The Little Women in My House. 2012. 24p. pap. 14.93 (978-1-4669-6302-3(6)) Trafford Publishing.
No Place to Fall. 2014. (ENG.). 368p. (YA). (gr. 9). 17.99 (978-0-06-227099-3(0)) HarperCollins Pubs.
Nobisso, Josephine. En Ingles, por Supuesto. Ziborova, Dasha, illus. 2003. Orig. Title: In English, of Course. (SPA & ENG.). 32p. (J). (gr. k-2). 16.95 (978-0-940112-14-8(0)) Gingerbread Hse.
—En ingles, por Supuesto. Ziborova, Dasha, illus. 2003. Orig. Title: In English, of Course. (SPA & ENG.). 32p. (J). (gr. k-2). pap. 8.95 (978-0-940112-16-2(7)) Gingerbread Hse.
—In English, of Course. Ziborova, Dasha, illus. 2003.Tr. of En Ingles, Por Supuesto. 32p. (J). (gr. -1). (SPA & ENG.). 16.95 (978-0-940112-07-0(8)); (ENG.). pap. 8.95 (978-0-940112-08-7(6)) Gingerbread Hse.
Noble, Trinka Hakes. Jimmy's Boa & the Bungee Jump Slam Dunk. Kellogg, Steven, illus. 2005. 28p. (gr. -1-3). 16.00 (978-0-7569-5765-0(6)) Perfection Learning Corp.
—Lizzie & the Last Day of School. McLeod, Kris Aro, illus. 2015. (ENG.). 32p. (J). (gr. k-2). 15.99 (978-1-58536-895-2(4), 203811) Sleeping Bear Pr.
—The Orange Shoes. Ettinger, Doris, illus. rev. ed. 2007. (ENG.). 40p. (J). (gr. k-6). 16.95 (978-1-58536-277-6(8)) Sleeping Bear Pr.
Noe, Katherine Schlick. Something to Hold. 2011. (ENG., Illus.). 256p. (J). (gr. 5-7). 17.99 (978-0-547-55813-4(9)) Houghton Mifflin Harcourt Publishing Co.
Noël, Alyson. Art Geeks & Prom Queens. 2011. (ENG.). 240p. (YA). (gr. 7-12). pap. 9.99 (978-0-312-61922-0(7), 9780312619220, St. Martin's Griffin) St. Martin's Pr.
—Five Days of Famous. 2016. (ENG.). 304p. (J). (gr. 5). 16.99 (978-0-553-53796-3(2), Delacorte Bks. for Young Readers) Random Hse. Children's Bks.
—Shadowland. 2010. (Immortals Ser.: 3). (ENG.). 368p. (YA). (gr. 7-12). pap. 9.99 (978-0-312-65005-6(1), 9780312650056, St. Martin's Griffin) St. Martin's Pr.
Nolan, Lea. Illusion. 2015. (ENG., Illus.). 370p. (YA). (gr. 7). pap. 19.99 (978-1-943892-53-2(9)) Entangled Publishing, LLC.
Nolen, Gale. Johnny, My Favorite Mouse. Cain, Doreyl Ammons, illus. 2007. 32p. (J). per. 18.95 (978-0-9753023-7-8(X)) Ammons Communications, Ltd.
Nordling, Lee. Belinda the Unbeatable. Roberts, Scott, illus. 2017. (Game for Adventure Ser.). (ENG.). 32p. (J). (gr. k-3). pap. 6.99 **(978-1-5124-5413-0(3))**; lib. bdg. 25.32 **(978-1-5124-1331-1(3))** Lerner Publishing Group. (Graphic Universe™).
Norris, Elizabeth. Unraveling. (Unraveling Ser.: 1). (ENG.). (YA). (gr. 8). 2013. 480p. pap. 9.99 (978-0-06-210374-1(1)) 2012. 464p. 17.99 (978-0-06-210373-4(3)) HarperCollins Pubs.
Norris, Shana. Something to Blog About. 2008. (ENG.). 256p. (J). (gr. 2-7). 16.95 (978-0-8109-9474-4(7), Amulet Bks.) Abrams, Inc.
—Troy High. 2009. (ENG.). 272p. (YA). (gr. 7-11). 16.95 (978-0-8109-4647-7(5), Amulet Bks.) Abrams, Inc.
Northrop, Michael. Gentlemen. 2009. (ENG.). 256p. (J). (gr. 9-18). 17.99 (978-0-545-09749-9(5), Scholastic Pr.) Scholastic, Inc.
—Plunked. 2014. (ENG.). 256p. (J). (gr. 3-7). pap. 7.99 (978-0-545-29715-8(X), Scholastic Paperbacks) Scholastic, Inc.
—Trapped. (ENG.). 240p. (J). 2012. (gr. 7). pap. 9.99 (978-0-545-21013-3(5)) 2011. (gr. 9-10). 17.99 (978-0-545-21012-6(7)) Scholastic, Inc. (Scholastic Pr.).
Norton, Tamra. Molly Mormon? Myth or Me? 2011. (Illus.). 170p. (YA). pap. 11.99 (978-1-55517-606-8(2), Bonneville Bks.) Cedar Fort, Inc./CFI Distribution.
—Shayla Witherwood: A Half-Faerie Tale. 2012. pap. 16.99 (978-1-59955-963-6(3)) Cedar Fort, Inc./CFI Distribution.
Nöstlinger, Christine. Nuevas Historias de Franz en la Escuela. (Torre de Papel Ser.). (SPA.). (J). (gr. 2). 7.95 (978-958-04-1013-3(5)) Norma S.A. COL. Dist: Distribuidora Norma, Inc.
Nosy Crow Staff. Violet Rose & the Little School. Ho, Jannie, illus. 2016. (ENG.). 52p. (J). (gr. -1-3). 8.99 (978-0-7636-9002-1(3), Nosy Crow) Candlewick Pr.
Nothing Ever Happens 6 Packs. Individual Title. (gr. -1-2). 27.00 (978-0-7635-9467-1(9)) Rigby Education.
Novel Units, Inc. Staff, creator. Surviving the Applewhites Student Packet. 2004. (J). (gr. 7-8). stu. ed. 12.99 (978-1-58130-868-6(X)) Novel Units, Inc.
—Surviving the Applewhites Teacher Guide. 2004. (J). (gr. 7-8). tchr. ed. 11.99 (978-1-58130-867-9(1)) Novel Units, Inc.
Novik, Naomi. Will Supervillains Be on the Final? Liberty Vocational. Li, Yishan, illus. 2011. (ENG.). 192p. pap. 10.99 (978-0-345-51656-5(7), Del Rey) Random House Publishing Group.
Nowinski, Hanna. Meg & Linus. 2017. (ENG.). 336p. (YA). 17.99 (978-1-250-09860-3(2), 9781250098603) Feiwel & Friends.
Nowlin, Laura. This Song Is (Not) for You. 2016. (ENG.). 240p. (YA). (gr. 8-12). pap. 9.99 (978-1-4926-0290-3(6), 9781492602903) Sourcebooks, Inc.
Ntihemuka, Patty Froese. Hyacinth Doesn't Go to Jail: And, Hyacinth Doesn't Miss Christmas. 2009. (J). pap. 10.99 (978-0-8163-2372-2(0)) Pacific Pr. Publishing Assn.
—Hyacinth Doesn't Grow Up: And Hyacinth Doesn't Drown. 2010. (J). pap. 10.99 (978-0-8163-2386-9(0)) Pacific Pr. Publishing Assn.
Numeroff, Laura Joffe. If You Take a Mouse to School. 2004. (Illus.). (J). (gr. k-3). spiral bd. (978-0-616-14593-7(4)); spiral bd. (978-0-616-14594-4(2)) Canadian National Institute for the Blind/Institut National Canadien pour les Aveugles.
—Si Llevas un Ratón a la Escuela, 1 vol. Bond, Felicia, illus. 2003. (If You Give... Ser.).Tr. of If You Take a Mouse to School. (SPA.). 32p. (J). (gr. -1-3). 16.99 (978-0-06-052340-4(9)) HarperCollins Pubs.
—Time for School, Mouse! Bond, Felicia, illus. 2008. (If You Give... Ser.). (ENG.). 24p. (J). (gr. -1 — 1). bds. 6.99 (978-0-06-143307-8(1), HarperFestival) HarperCollins Pubs.
—Time for School, Mouse! Lap Edition. Bond, Felicia, illus. 2016. (If You Give... Ser.). 24p. (J). (gr. -1-3). bds. 12.99 (978-0-06-242741-0(5)) HarperCollins Pubs.
Nydam, Anne. The Bad Advice of Grandma Hasenfuss. 2010. 112p. pap. 14.00 (978-0-557-26037-9(X)) Lulu Pr., Inc.
Oakes, Colleen. Blood of Wonderland. 2017. (Queen of Hearts Ser.: 2). (YA). (gr. 8). 352p. pap. 9.99 **(978-0-06-240977-5(8))**; 336p. 17.99 (978-0-06-240976-8(X)) HarperCollins Pubs. (HarperTeen).
Oakes, Cory Putman. Dinosaur Boy. 2015. (Dinosaur Boy Ser.: 1). (ENG.). 224p. (J). (gr. 3-7). 12.99 (978-1-4926-0537-9(9), 9781492605379, Sourcebooks Jabberwocky) Sourcebooks, Inc.
—Dinosaur Boy Saves Mars. 2016. (Dinosaur Boy Ser.: 2). (ENG.). 224p. (J). (gr. 3-7). 18.40 (978-0-606-39306-5(4)) Turtleback Bks.
Oates, Joyce Carol. Sexy. 2005. 272p. (J). (gr. 7-18). 16.99 (978-0-06-054149-1(0), HarperTeen) HarperCollins Pubs.
—Two or Three Things I Forgot to Tell You. (ENG.). (YA). (gr. 9). 2013. 304p. pap. 9.99 (978-0-06-211048-0(9)) 2012. 288p. 17.99 (978-0-06-211047-3(0)) HarperCollins Pubs. (HarperTeen).
Oberne, Sharon. Kelsey. 2006. 88p. (YA). pap. 13.95 (978-1-58909-340-9(2)) Bookstand Publishing.
Obioha, Natalie O. Emotions. 2010. 120p. pap. 19.99 (978-1-4500-2791-5(1)) Xlibris Corp.
O'Brien, Caragh M. The Vault of Dreamers. 2014. (ENG., Illus.). 432p. (YA). (gr. 7-12). 17.99 (978-1-59643-938-2(6), 9781596439382) Roaring Brook Pr.
Obstacles in Our Way: Individual Title Six-Packs. (gr. k-1). 23.00 (978-0-7635-9067-3(3)) Rigby Education.
Ocean, Davy. Deep-Sea Disaster. Blecha, Aaron, illus. 2014. (Shark School Ser.: 1). (ENG.). 128p. (J). (gr. 1-4). 17.99 (978-1-4814-0679-6(5), Aladdin) Simon & Schuster Children's Publishing.
—Deep-Sea Treasury: Deep-Sea Disaster; Lights! Camera! Hammerhead!; Squid-Napped; the Boy Who Cried Shark. Blecha, Aaron, illus. 2015. (Shark School Ser.). (ENG.). 528p. (J). (gr. 1-4). 14.99 (978-1-4814-5115-4(4), Aladdin) Simon & Schuster Children's Publishing.
—Splash Dance. Blecha, Aaron, illus. 2015. (Shark School Ser.: 6). (ENG.). 128p. (J). (gr. 1-4). pap. 5.99 (978-1-4814-0694-9(9), Aladdin) Simon & Schuster Children's Publishing.
Oceanak, Karla. Dumbstruck. Spanjer, Kendra, illus. 2011. (Aldo Zelnick Comic Novel Ser.: 4). (ENG.). 160p. (J). (gr. 3-7). 12.95 (978-1-934649-16-9(3)) Bailiwick Pr.
Ockler, Sarah. #scandal. 2014. (ENG., Illus.). 416p. (YA). (gr. 9). 17.99 (978-1-4814-0124-1(6), Simon Pulse) Simon Pulse.
O'Connell, Jenny. The Book of Luke. 2007. (ENG.). 304p. pap. 11.00 (978-1-4165-2040-5(6), MTV Bks.) MTV Books.
O'Connell, Rebecca. Penina Levine Is a Hard-boiled Egg. Lue Sue, Majella, illus. 2009. (ENG.). 192p. (J). (gr. 3-7). pap. 18.99 (978-0-312-55026-4(X), 9780312550264) Square Fish.
O'connell, Tyne. A Royal Match. 2011. (Calypso Chronicles Ser.). (ENG.). 512p. (YA). pap. 9.99 (978-1-59990-751-2(8), 9781599907512, Bloomsbury USA Childrens) Bloomsbury Publishing USA.
O'Connor, Barbara. Fame & Glory in Freedom, Georgia. 2008. (ENG.). 112p. (J). (gr. 3-7). pap. 8.99 (978-0-374-40018-7(0), 9780374400187) Square Fish.
O'connor, Jane. Best Reading Buddies. 2016. (Fancy Nancy - I Can Read! Ser.). (J). lib. bdg. 13.55 (978-0-606-39273-0(4)) Turtleback Bks.
O'Connor, Jane. The Dazzling Book Report. Glasser, Robin Preiss & Enik, Ted, illus. 2009. (I Can Read Level 1 Ser.). (ENG.). 32p. (J). (gr. -1-3). pap. 3.99 (978-0-06-170368-3(0)) HarperCollins Pubs.
—Every Day Is Earth Day. Ivanov, Aleksey et al, illus. 2010. (I Can Read Level 1 Ser.). (ENG.). 32p. (J). (gr. -1-3). 16.99 (978-0-06-187327-0(6)) HarperCollins Pubs.
—Every Day Is Earth Day. Ivanov, Aleksey et al, illus. 2010. (I Can Read Level 1 Ser.). (ENG.). 32p. (J). (gr. -1-3). pap. 3.99 (978-0-06-187326-3(8)) HarperCollins Pubs.
—Fancy Day in Room 1-A. Glasser, Robin Preiss, illus. 2012. (I Can Read Level 1 Ser.). (ENG.). 32p. (J). (gr. -1-3). 16.99 (978-0-06-208305-0(8)); pap. 3.99 (978-0-06-208304-3(X)) HarperCollins Pubs.
—Fancy Day in Room 1-A. 2012. (Fancy Nancy - I Can Read! Ser.). (J). lib. bdg. 13.55 (978-0-606-26259-0(8), Turtleback) Turtleback Bks.
—Fancy Nancy: My Family History. Glasser, Robin Preiss et al, illus. 2010. (I Can Read Level 1 Ser.). (ENG.). 32p. (J). (gr. -1-3). 16.99 (978-0-06-188270-8(4)) HarperCollins Pubs.
—Fancy Nancy: Nancy Clancy, Super Sleuth. 2013. (Nancy Clancy Ser.: 1). (J). lib. bdg. 14.75 (978-0-606-31795-5(3), Turtleback) Turtleback Bks.
—Fancy Nancy: Pajama Day. Drainville, Beth et al, illus. 2009. (I Can Read Level 1 Ser.). (ENG.). 32p. (J). (gr. -1-3). 16.99 (978-0-06-170371-3(0)) HarperCollins Pubs.
—Fancy Nancy: The Dazzling Book Report. Glasser, Robin Preiss & Enik, Ted, illus. 2009. (I Can Read Level 1 Ser.). (ENG.). 32p. (J). (gr. -1-3). 16.99 (978-0-06-170369-0(9)) HarperCollins Pubs.
—Fancy Nancy: The Dazzling Book Report. Glasser, Robin Preiss & Enik, Ted, illus. 2009. (Fancy Nancy Ser.). 32p. lib. bdg. 14.00 (978-1-60686-531-6(5)) Perfection Learning Corp.
—Fancy Nancy: The Show Must Go On. Glasser, Robin Preiss & Enik, Ted, illus. 2009. (I Can Read Level 1 Ser.). (ENG.). 32p. (J). (gr. -1-3). 16.99 (978-0-06-170373-7(7)) HarperCollins Pubs.
—Fancy Nancy & the Boy from Paris. Enik, Ted & Glasser, Robin Preiss, illus. 2008. (I Can Read Level 1 Ser.). (ENG.). 32p. (J). (gr. -1-3). 16.99 (978-0-06-123610-5(1)); pap. 3.99 (978-0-06-123609-9(8)) HarperCollins Pubs.
—Fancy Nancy & the Too-Loose Tooth. Glasser, Robin Preiss & Enik, Ted, illus. 2012. (I Can Read Level 1 Ser.). (ENG.). 32p. (J). (gr. -1-3). 16.99 (978-0-06-208301-2(5)); pap. 3.99 (978-0-06-208302-9(3)) HarperCollins Pubs.
—Fancy Nancy & the Too-Loose Tooth. 2012. (Fancy Nancy - I Can Read! Ser.). (J). lib. bdg. 13.55 (978-0-606-23551-8(5), Turtleback) Turtleback Bks.
—Fancy Nancy Collector's Quintet. Glasser, Robin Preiss, illus. 2009. (I Can Read Level 1 Ser.). (J). (gr. k-3). pap. 16.99 (978-0-06-171905-9(6)) HarperCollins Pubs.
—Fancy Nancy: Nancy Clancy Seeks a Fortune. Glasser, Robin Preiss & Bracken, Carolyn, illus. 2016. (Nancy Clancy Ser.: 7). 144p. (J). (gr. 1-5). 9.99 (978-0-06-226969-0(0)) HarperCollins Pubs.
—Fancy Nancy: Nancy Clancy, Soccer Mania. Glasser, Robin Preiss, illus. (Nancy Clancy Ser.: 6). (J). (gr. 1-5). 2016. 144p. pap. 4.99 (978-0-06-226966-9(6)) 2015. (ENG.). 128p. 9.99 (978-0-06-226967-6(4)) HarperCollins Pubs.
—Fancy Nancy Sees Stars. Glasser, Robin Preiss & Enik, Ted, illus. 2008. (I Can Read Level 1 Ser.). (ENG.). 32p. (J). (gr. -1-3). 16.99 (978-0-06-123612-9(8)); pap. 3.99 (978-0-06-123611-2(X)) HarperCollins Pubs.
—Fancy Nancy: Time for Puppy School. Glasser, Robin Preiss, illus. 2017. (I Can Read Level 1 Ser.). 32p. (J). (gr. -1-3). pap. 3.99 (978-0-06-237786-9(8)) HarperCollins Pubs.
—Lulu Goes to Witch School. Sinclair, Bella, illus. 2013. (I Can Read Level 2 Ser.). (ENG.). 48p. (J). (gr. -1-3). 16.99 (978-0-06-223351-6(3)); pap. 3.99 (978-0-06-223350-9(5)) HarperCollins Pubs.
—My Family History. Glasser, Robin Preiss et al, illus. 2010. (I Can Read Level 1 Ser.). (ENG.). 32p. (J). (gr. -1-3). pap. 3.99 (978-0-06-188271-5(2)) HarperCollins Pubs.
—My Family History. 2010. (Fancy Nancy - I Can Read! Ser.). (J). lib. bdg. 13.55 (978-0-606-14988-4(0), Turtleback) Turtleback Bks.
—Nancy Clancy - Super Sleuth. Glasser, Robin Preiss, illus. 2013. (Nancy Clancy Ser.: 1). (ENG.). 144p. (J). (gr. 1-5). pap. 5.99 (978-0-06-208419-4(4)) HarperCollins Pubs.
—Nancy Clancy, Secret Admirer. Glasser, Robin Preiss, illus. 2013. (Nancy Clancy Ser.: 2). (ENG.). 144p. (J). (gr. 1-5). pap. 4.99 (978-0-06-208420-0(8)) HarperCollins Pubs.
—Nancy Clancy, Secret Admirer. 2013. (Nancy Clancy Ser.: 2). (J). lib. bdg. 14.75 (978-0-606-35045-7(4), Turtleback) Turtleback Bks.
O'connor, Jane. Nancy Clancy, Soccer Mania. Glasser, Robin Preiss, illus. 2016. (Nancy Clancy Ser.: 6). (ENG.). 144p. (J). (gr. 1-5). 14.75 (978-0-606-39270-9(X)) Turtleback Bks.
O'Connor, Jane. Nancy Clancy, Star of Stage & Screen. 2016. (Nancy Clancy Ser.: 5). (J). lib. bdg. 14.75 (978-0-606-38153-6(8)) Turtleback Bks.
—Nancy Clancy, Super Sleuth, 3 vols. Glasser, Robin Preiss, illus. 2012. (Nancy Clancy Ser.: 1). (ENG.). 128p. (J). (gr. 1-5). 9.99 (978-0-06-208293-0(0)) HarperCollins Pubs.
—Nancy Clancy's Tres Charming, 3 vols., Set. Glasser, Robin Preiss, illus. 2013. (Fancy Nancy Ser.). (ENG.). 384p. (J). (gr. 1-5). 24.99 (978-0-06-227793-0(6)) HarperCollins Pubs.
—Pajama Day. Drainville, Beth et al, illus. 2009. (I Can Read Level 1 Ser.). (ENG.). 32p. (J). (gr. -1-3). pap. 3.99 (978-0-06-170370-6(2)) HarperCollins Pubs.
—Poet Extraordinaire! Glasser, Robin Preiss, illus. 2010. (Fancy Nancy Ser.). (ENG.). 32p. (J). (gr. -1-2). 12.99 (978-0-06-189643-9(8)) HarperCollins Pubs.
—Secret Admirer, 3 vols. Glasser, Robin Preiss, illus. 2013. (Fancy Nancy Ser.: Bk. 2). (ENG.). 128p. (J). (gr. 1-5). 9.99 (978-0-06-208295-4(7)) HarperCollins Pubs.
—The Show Must Go On. Enik, Ted & Glasser, Robin Preiss, illus. 2009. (I Can Read Level 1 Ser.). (ENG.). 32p. (J). (gr. -1-3). pap. 3.99 (978-0-06-170372-0(9)) HarperCollins Pubs.
—Splendid Speller. Glasser, Robin Preiss, illus. 2011. (I Can Read Level 1 Ser.). (ENG.). 32p. (J). (gr. -1-3). 16.99 (978-0-06-200176-4(0)); pap. 3.99 (978-0-06-200175-7(2)) HarperCollins Pubs.
—Super Sleuth. Glasser, Robin Preiss, illus. 2015. (Fancy Nancy Ser.). (ENG.). 256p. (J). (gr. 1-5). 12.99 (978-0-06-240364-3(8)) HarperCollins Pubs.

O'connor, Jane. Time for Puppy School. 2017. (Fancy Nancy - I Can Read! Ser.). lib. bdg. 13.55 **(978-0-606-40059-6(1))** Turtleback Bks.

O'Connor, Jane. The 100th Day of School. Glasser, Robin Preiss & Enik, Ted, illus. 2009. (I Can Read Level 1 Ser.). (ENG.). 32p. (J). (gr. -1-3). 16.99 (978-0-06-170375-1(3)); pap. 3.99 (978-0-06-170374-4(5)) HarperCollins Pubs.

O'Connor, Jane & Preiss-Glasser, Robin. It's Backward Day! Enik, Ted, illus. 2016. 32p. (J). (978-1-4806-9929-8(2)) Harper & Row Ltd.

O'Dell, Kathleen. Agnes Parker... Girl in Progress. 2004. (ENG.). 176p. (J). (gr. 2-5). reprint ed. 6.99 (978-0-14-240228-3(1), Puffin Books) Penguin Young Readers Group.

—Agnes Parker... Keeping Cool in Middle School. 2008. (ENG.). 160p. (J). (gr. 3-7). 6.99 (978-0-14-241181-0(7), Puffin Books) Penguin Young Readers Group.

O'Doherty, David. Danger Is Totally Everywhere: School of Danger. 2017. (Danger Is Everywhere Ser.: 3). (ENG., Illus.). 240p. (J). (gr. 3-7). 13.99 **(978-0-316-50202-3(2))** Little, Brown Bks. for Young Readers.

Oelschlager, Vanita. Knees: The Mixed up World of a Boy with Dyslexia. Rossi, Joe, illus. 2012. (ENG.). 128p. (J). (gr. k-5). pap. 9.95 (978-0-9826366-9-5(5)) VanitaBooks.

Ofanansky, Allison. What's the Buzz? Honey for a Sweet New Year. Alpern, Eliyahu, photos by. 2014. (ENG., Illus.). 32p. (J). (gr. -1-5). 8.95 (978-1-4677-5706-5(3), Kar-Ben Publishing) Lerner Publishing Group.

—What's the Buzz? Honey for a Sweet New Year. Alpern, Eliyahu, illus. Alpern, Eliyahu, photos by. 2011. (High Holidays Ser.). (J). (gr. -1-k). lib. bdg. 15.95 (978-0-7613-5640-0(1)) Lerner Publishing Group.

Off to School: Individual Title Six-Packs. (Story Steps Ser.). (gr. k-2). 29.00 (978-0-7635-9577-7(2)) Rigby Education.

Oh, Jiwon. Mr. Monkey's Classroom. Oh, Jiwon, illus. 2005. (Illus.). 32p. (J). (gr. -1-2). lib. bdg. 15.89 (978-0-06-055722-5(2)) HarperCollins Pubs.

O'Hara, Mo. Jurassic Carp. Jagucki, Marek, illus. 2017. (My Big Fat Zombie Goldfish Ser.: 6). (ENG.). 224p. (J). pap. 6.99 **(978-1-250-10260-7(X)**, 9781250102607) Square Fish.

Ohlin, Nancy. Consent. 2015. (ENG., Illus.). 288p. (YA). (gr. 9). 17.99 (978-1-4424-6490-2(9), Simon Pulse) Simon Pulse.

—Thorn Abbey. 2013. (ENG.). 304p. (YA). (gr. 9). 16.99 (978-1-4424-6486-5(0), Simon Pulse) Simon Pulse.

O'Keefe, Susan Heyboer. My Life & Death by Alexandra Canarsie, 1 vol. 2006. (ENG.). 217p. (YA). (gr. 7-18). pap. 7.95 (978-1-56145-387-0(0)) Peachtree Pubs.

Okugas, Juanaiga. The tales of Mew the Cat. 2011. 92p. pap. 35.30 (978-1-4567-3480-0(6)) AuthorHouse.

Oliver, Carmen. Bears Make the Best Reading Buddies. Claude, Jean, illus. 2016. (Fiction Picture Bks.). (ENG.). 32p. (gr. -1-1). lib. bdg. 21.27 (978-1-4795-9181-7(5), Fiction Picture Bks.) Picture Window Bks.

Oliver, Ilanit. Olivia & the Best Teacher Ever. 2012. (Olivia 8x8 Ser.). lib. bdg. 13.55 (978-0-606-26367-2(5), Turtleback) Turtleback Bks.

Oliver, Lauren. Before I Fall. (ENG.). (YA). (gr. 9). 2016. 544p. pap. 10.99 (978-0-06-172681-1(8)) 2010. 480p. 17.99 (978-0-06-172680-4(X)) HarperCollins Pubs.

—Before I Fall. 2010. 368p. pap. (978-0-340-98090-3(7), Hodder Paperbacks) Hodder & Stoughton.

—Before I Fall. 2016. (YA). lib. bdg. 22.10 (978-0-606-23576-1(0), Turtleback) Turtleback Bks.

Oliver, Lin. Almost Identical. 2012. (Almost Identical Ser.: 1). (ENG.). 224p. (J). (gr. 3-7). pap. 7.99 (978-0-448-45191-6(3), Grosset & Dunlap) Penguin Young Readers Group.

—Twice as Nice. 2014. (Almost Identical Ser.: 4). (ENG.). 224p. (J). (gr. 3-7). 6.99 (978-0-448-46447-3(0), Grosset & Dunlap) Penguin Young Readers Group.

—Two-Faced, No. 2. 2012. (Almost Identical Ser.: 2). (ENG.). 224p. (J). (gr. 3-7). pap. 7.99 (978-0-448-45192-3(1), Grosset & Dunlap) Penguin Young Readers Group.

Olker, Constance. The Punctuation Pals Meet at School. 2005. (Illus.). 40p. (J). per. 18.95 (978-1-933449-07-4(1)) Nightengale Pr.

—The Punctuation Pals Meet at School. Guzman, Minerva, illus. 2004. (Punctuation Pals Ser.). 24p. (J). (gr. 1-18). 19.95 (978-0-9743348-6-8(3)) Nightengale Pr.

—The Punctuation Pals Meet at School. l.t. ed. 2005. (Illus.). 18p. (J). per. 16.95 (978-0-9761289-4-6(2)) Nightengale Pr.

Olsen EdS, Marci. Lessons to Live by: Character Building Books for School-Age Children. 2008. 52p. pap. 24.95 (978-1-60474-501-6(0)) America Star Bks.

Olson, Norah. Twisted Fate. 2015. (ENG.). 272p. (YA). (gr. 8). 17.99 (978-0-06-227204-1(7)) HarperCollins Pubs.

Olswanger, Anna. Greenhorn. Nerlove, Miriam, illus. 2012. (ENG.). (J). E-Book 9.99 (978-1-60306-159-9(2)); 48p. 17.95 (978-1-58838-235-1(4)) NewSouth, Inc. (NewSouth Bks.).

Onwusilikam, Ify Chinedum. The Drama Queen. 2009. 56p. pap. 10.00 (978-1-60860-126-4(9), Strategic Bk. Publishing) Strategic Book Publishing & Rights Agency (SBPRA).

Opio, Leoncio. The Adventures of Mr. Nimbus & the School House Bullies. 2012. 98p. pap. 19.95 (978-1-4626-9442-6(X)) America Star Bks.

Oram, Hiawyn. Filbert, the Good Little Fiend. Liao, Jimmy, illus. 2013. (ENG.). 32p. (J). (gr. -1-2). 15.99 (978-0-7636-5870-0(7)) Candlewick Pr.

Oramas, Jennifer. Peter's Purpose. Huseman, Ryan, illus. 2012. 34p. 24.95 (978-1-4626-6585-3(3)) America Star Bks.

O'Reilly, Sean. The Missing Mummy, 1 vol. 2011. (Mighty Mighty Monsters Ser.). (ENG.). 48p. (gr. 2-3). lib. bdg. 23.99 (978-1-4342-3218-2(2)) Stone Arch Bks.

—New Monster in School, 1 vol. Arcana Studio, Arcana, illus. 2010. (Mighty Mighty Monsters Ser.). (ENG.). 48p. (gr. 2-3). lib. bdg. 23.99 (978-1-4342-2151-3(2)) Stone Arch Bks.

—Science Fair Nightmare, 1 vol. (Mighty Mighty Monsters Ser.). (ENG., 48p. (gr. 2-3). 2013. Illus.). pap. 6.10 (978-1-4342-4226-6(9)) 2012. lib. bdg. 23.99 (978-1-4342-3891-7(1)) Stone Arch Bks.

Orme, David & Orme, Helen. Up for It? 2008. (Backstreet Ser.). (ENG., Illus.). 36p. pap. (978-1-84167-769-9(8)) Ransom Publishing Ltd.

Orme, Helen. Moving. 2008. (Siti's Sisters Ser.). (ENG., Illus.). 36p. pap. (978-1-84167-689-0(6)) Ransom Publishing Ltd.

—Rats! 2008. (Backstreet Ser.). (ENG., Illus.). 36p. pap. (978-1-84167-772-9(8)) Ransom Publishing Ltd.

—Taken for a Ride. Brett, Cathy, illus. 2007. (Siti's Sisters Ser.). (ENG.). 36p. (J). per. (978-1-84167-596-1(2)) Ransom Publishing Ltd.

—Trouble with Teachers. Brett, Cathy, illus. 2007. (Siti's Sisters Ser.). (ENG.). 36p. (J). per. (978-1-84167-599-2(7)) Ransom Publishing Ltd.

—Who's Who? 2008. (Siti's Sisters Ser.). (ENG., Illus.). 36p. pap. (978-1-84167-687-6(X)) Ransom Publishing Ltd.

—Won't Talk, Can't Talk. 2008. (Backstreet Ser.). (Illus.). 36p. pap. (978-1-84167-777-4(9)) Ransom Publishing Ltd.

Ormerod, Jan. Molly & Her Dad. Thompson, Carol, illus. 2008. 32p. (978-1-921272-55-4(4)) Little Hare Bks. AUS. Dist: HarperCollins Pubs. Australia.

Ormerod, Nicola. Roxy May, Help My Boyfriend Is a Fairy. 2012. 224p. pap. (978-1-909402-03-4(6)) Vamptasy Publishing.

Orr, Wendy. Wanted! - A Guinea Pig Called Henry. Castelao, Patricia, illus. 2012. (Rainbow Street Shelter Ser.: 3). (ENG.). 128p. (J). (gr. 2-5). 15.99 (978-0-8050-8933-2(0), 9780805089332, Holt, Henry & Co. Bks. For Young Readers) Holt, Henry & Co.

Osa, Nancy. Cuba 15. 2011. 10.54 (978-0-7848-3376-6(1), Everbind) Marco Bk. Co.

Oseman, Alice. Solitaire. 2015. (ENG.). 368p. (YA). (gr. 8). 17.99 (978-0-06-233568-5(5), HarperTeen) HarperCollins Pubs.

O'Shaughnessy McKenna, Colleen. Third Grade Wedding Bells? Roth, Stephanie, illus. 2006. (Third Grade Ser.). (ENG.). 160p. (J). (gr. 2-5). 15.95 (978-0-8234-1943-2(6)) Holiday Hse., Inc.

Oshima, Towa. High School Girls, Vol. 5. 2005. (High School Girls Ser.). (ENG., Illus.). 200p. (YA). pap. 9.95 (978-1-59796-058-8(6)) DrMaster Pubns. Inc.

—High School Girls Volume 1-6 Set. 2007. (ENG., Illus.). 200p. pap. 44.95 (978-1-59796-072-4(1)) DrMaster Pubns. Inc.

Osterlund, Anne. Academy 7. 2009. (ENG.). 272p. (YA). (gr. 7-18). pap. 8.99 (978-0-14-241437-8(9), Speak) Penguin Young Readers Group.

Ostler, Heather. The Siren's Secret. 2013. 16.99 (978-1-4621-1223-4(4), Horizon Pubs.) Cedar Fort, Inc./CFI Distribution.

Ostow, Micol. GoldenGirl. 2009. (Bradford Ser.). (ENG.). 224p. (YA). (gr. 9-18). pap. 9.99 (978-1-4169-6118-5(6), Simon Pulse) Simon Pulse.

Ostrovski, Emil. Away We Go. 2016. 272p. (YA). (gr. 9). 17.99 (978-0-06-223855-9(8), Greenwillow Bks.) HarperCollins Pubs.

Owens, L. L. The New Girl. Tolson, Scott, illus. 2004. 27p. (978-1-57021-029-7(2)) Comprehensive Health Education Foundation.

Oxenbury, Helen. Primer Dia de Escuela (First Day of School) 4th ed. (SPA., Illus.). 24p. (J). 7.50 (978-84-261-2002-1(4)) Juventud, Editorial ESP. Dist: AIMS International Bks., Inc.

P. Cotton & Clyde & the Chameleons. 2011. 28p. (gr. -1 — 1). pap. 13.99 (978-1-4520-9675-9(9)) AuthorHouse.

Pace, Anne Marie. A Teacher for Bear. Wohnoutka, Mike, illus. 2011. (J). (978-0-545-37776-8(5)) Scholastic, Inc.

Pace, Marisa. Gina Goes to School: Over & over Again. 2017. (Computer Science for the Real World Ser.). 8p. (gr. 5-6). pap. 6.20 **(978-1-5383-5086-7(6)**, Rosen Classroom) Rosen Publishing Group, Inc., The.

Padian, Maria. Brett McCarthy: Work in Progress. 2009. (ENG.). 288p. (YA). (gr. 7). pap. 8.99 (978-0-440-24055-6(7), Knopf Bks. for Young Readers) Random Hse. Children's Bks.

Padula, Stacy A. Montgomery Lake High #2-When Darkness Tries to Hide. 2011. 146p. pap. 11.50 (978-1-60976-857-7(4), Eloquent Bks.) Strategic Book Publishing & Rights Agency (SBPRA).

Page, Winter. Breaking Free. 2016. (ENG., Illus.). (J). 24.99 **(978-1-63477-943-2(6))** 2014. 180p. pap. 14.99 (978-1-62798-914-5(5)) Dreamspinner Pr. (Harmony Ink Pr.).

Palacio, R. J. Auggie & Me: Three Wonder Stories. 2015. (ENG.). 320p. (J). (gr. 3-7). 16.99 (978-1-101-93485-2(9), Knopf Bks. for Young Readers) Random Hse. Children's Bks.

—Wonder. 2015. (JPN.). 420p. (J). (978-4-593-53495-1(X)) Holp Shuppan, Publishing.

—Wonder. 2015. (SPA.). 160p. (J). (gr. 3-7). pap. 9.95 (978-607-31-3242-8(5)) Penguin Random House Grupo Editorial, S.A. de C.V. MEX. Dist: Two Rivers Distribution.

—Wonder. (ENG.). (J). (gr. 3-7). 2015. 176p. 12.99 (978-0-553-49907-0(6)) 2012. 320p. 16.99 (978-0-375-86902-0(6)) 2012. 320p. lib. bdg. 19.99 (978-0-375-96902-7(0)) Random Hse. Children's Bks. (Knopf Bks. for Young Readers).

—Wonder. l.t. ed. 2013. (ENG.). 482p. 23.99 (978-1-4104-5741-7(9)) Thorndike Pr.

—Wonder. 2012. lib. bdg. 29.40 (978-0-606-36646-5(6)) Turtleback Bks.

Palatini, Margie. The Zoey Zone. Palatini, Margie, illus. 2010. (ENG., Illus.). 192p. (J). (gr. 3-6). pap. 6.99 (978-0-06-113900-0(9), Tegen, Katherine Bks) HarperCollins Pubs.

Pallotta, Jerry. How Will I Get to School This Year? Biedrzycki, David, illus. 2011. (J). (978-0-545-26659-8(9)) Scholastic, Inc.

—What I Saw in the Teachers' Lounge. McWilliam, Howard, illus. 2012. (J). (978-0-545-38472-8(9)) Scholastic, Inc.

Palmer, Iva-Marie. Gabby Garcia's Ultimate Playbook. 2017. (Gabby Garcia's Ultimate Playbook Ser.: 1). 304p. (J). (gr. 3-7). 12.99 (978-0-06-239180-3(1), Tegen, Katherine Bks) HarperCollins Pubs.

Palmer, Robin. Geek Charming. 2009. (ENG.). 368p. (YA). (gr. 7-18). 7.99 (978-0-14-241122-3(1), Speak) Penguin Young Readers Group.

—Sealed with a Kiss, 2 vols., No. 2. 2010. (Yours Truly, Lucy B. Parker Ser.: 2). (ENG.). 224p. (J). (gr. 5-18). 6.99 (978-0-14-241501-6(4), Puffin Books) Penguin Young Readers Group.

Pam, Miss. Never Never Be a Bully. Stutz, Chris, illus. 2011. 24p. pap. 24.95 (978-1-4626-4325-7(6)) America Star Bks.

Papell, David. Harlem Awakenings. 2007. 48p. pap. 12.95 (978-0-615-17531-7(7)) Papell, David.

—Harlem Awakenings Color Edition. 2007. 50p. pap. 26.95 (978-0-615-17931-5(2)) Papell, David.

Pardoe, David. Jasper Tippett's Amazing Journey to Page 42. 2006. (Illus.). 132p. pap. (978-1-84401-785-0(0)) Athena Pr.

Parente, Peter. Boomer to the Rescue. Ivanov, Aleksey, illus. l.t. ed. 2005. 28p. 15.95 (978-0-9745052-3-7(4), Peeper & Friends) Tree Of Life Publishing.

Parish, Herman. Amelia Bedelia Chapter Book #5. Avril, Lynne, illus. 2014. (Amelia Bedelia Ser.). (ENG.). 160p. (J). (gr. 1-5). 9.99 (978-0-06-233399-5(2), Greenwillow Bks.) HarperCollins Pubs.

—Amelia Bedelia Chapter Book #9: Amelia Bedelia on the Job. Avril, Lynne, illus. 2016. (Amelia Bedelia Ser.). 160p. (J). (gr. 1-5). pap. 4.99 (978-0-06-233412-1(3), Greenwillow Bks.) HarperCollins Pubs.

—Amelia Bedelia, Cub Reporter. Sweat, Lynn, illus. 2012. (I Can Read Level 2 Ser.). (ENG.). 64p. (J). (gr. -1-3). 16.99 (978-0-06-209510-7(2)); pap. 3.99 (978-0-06-209509-1(9)) HarperCollins Pubs. (Greenwillow Bks.).

—Amelia Bedelia Hits the Trail. Avril, Lynne, illus. 2013. (I Can Read Level 1 Ser.). (ENG.). 32p. (J). (gr. -1-3). 16.99 (978-0-06-209527-5(7), Greenwillow Bks.) HarperCollins Pubs.

—Amelia Bedelia Joins the Club. Avril, Lynne, illus. 2014. (I Can Read Level 1 Ser.). (ENG.). 32p. (J). (gr. -1-3). 16.99 (978-0-06-222131-5(0)); pap. 3.99 (978-0-06-222130-8(2)) HarperCollins Pubs. (Greenwillow Bks.).

—Amelia Bedelia, Rocket Scientist? Sweat, Lynn, illus. (I Can Read Level 2 Ser.). 64p. (J). 2007. (ENG.). (gr. k-3). pap. 3.99 (978-0-06-051889-9(8), Greenwillow Bks.) 2005. (gr. 1-18). 15.99 (978-0-06-051887-5(1)) 2005. (gr. k-4). lib. bdg. 17.89 (978-0-06-051888-2(X), Greenwillow Bks.) HarperCollins Pubs.

—Amelia Bedelia, Rocket Scientist? Sweat, Lynn, illus. 2007. (I Can Read Ser.). 64p. 14.00 (978-0-7569-8058-0(5)) Perfection Learning Corp.

—Amelia Bedelia, Rocket Scientist? Sweat, Lynn, illus. 2007. (Amelia Bedelia: I Can Read! Ser.: 19). (J). lib. bdg. 13.55 (978-1-4177-8068-6(1), Turtleback) Turtleback Bks.

—Amelia Bedelia Shapes Up! Avril, Lynne, illus. 2014. (Amelia Bedelia Ser.). (ENG.). 160p. (J). (gr. 1-5). pap. 4.99 (978-0-06-233396-4(8), Greenwillow Bks.) HarperCollins Pubs.

—Amelia Bedelia Talks Turkey. Sweat, Lynn, illus. (I Can Read Level 2 Ser.). (ENG.). 64p. (J). (gr. k-3). 2009. pap. 3.99 (978-0-06-084354-0(3)) 2008. 16.99 (978-0-06-084352-6(7)) HarperCollins Pubs. (Greenwillow Bks.).

—Amelia Bedelia Talks Turkey. Parish, Herman & Sweat, Lynn, illus. 2008. (Amelia Bedelia Ser.). 64p. (J). (gr. k-4). lib. bdg. 17.89 (978-0-06-084353-3(5), Greenwillow Bks.) HarperCollins Pubs.

—Amelia Bedelia Talks Turkey. 2009. (Amelia Bedelia: I Can Read! Ser.). (J). lib. bdg. 13.55 (978-0-606-06937-3(2), Turtleback) Turtleback Bks.

—Amelia Bedelia's Backpack Bundle. Sweat, Lynn, illus. 2012. 192p. (J). (978-1-4351-4392-0(2), Greenwillow Bks.) HarperCollins Pubs.

—Amelia Bedelia's First Day of School. Avril, Lynne, illus. (Amelia Bedelia Ser.). (ENG.). 32p. (J). (gr. -1-3). 2015. pap. 6.99 (978-0-06-154457-6(4)) 2011. 9.99 (978-0-06-203274-4(7)) 2009. 16.99 (978-0-06-154455-2(8)) HarperCollins Pubs. (Greenwillow Bks.).

—Amelia Bedelia's First Field Trip. 2013. (Amelia Bedelia Picture Bks.). (J). lib. bdg. 17.20 (978-0-606-31818-1(6), Turtleback) Turtleback Bks.

—Amelia Bedelia's First Valentine. Avril, Lynne, illus. (Amelia Bedelia Ser.). (ENG.). 32p. (J). (gr. -1-3). 2014. pap. 6.99 (978-0-06-154460-6(4)) 2011. 9.99 (978-0-06-203275-1(5)) 2009. 16.99 (978-0-06-154458-3(2)) HarperCollins Pubs. (Greenwillow Bks.).

—Amelia Bedelia's First Valentine. 2014. (Amelia Bedelia Picture Bks.). (J). lib. bdg. 17.20 (978-0-606-35971-9(0)) Turtleback Bks.

—Amelia Bedelia's First Vote. Avril, Lynne, illus. 2012. (Amelia Bedelia Ser.). 32p. (J). (gr. -1-3). (ENG.). 16.99 (978-0-06-209405-6(X)); lib. bdg. 17.89 (978-0-06-209406-3(8)) HarperCollins Pubs. (Greenwillow Bks.).

Parish, Peggy. Teach Us, Amelia Bedelia. Sweat, Lynn, illus. 2005. (Amelia Bedelia Ser.). 58p. (gr. -1-3). 14.00 (978-0-7569-4804-7(5)) Perfection Learning Corp.

Parisi, Mark. Do Not Open! Parisi, Mark, illus. 2017. (Marty Pants Ser.: 1). (Illus.). 256p. (J). (gr. 3-7). 12.99 (978-0-06-242776-2(8)) HarperCollins Pubs.

Park, Barbara. Aloha-Ha-Ha! Brunkus, Denise, illus. (Junie B. Jones Ser.: 26). (ENG.). 128p. (J). (gr. 1-4). 2007. per. 4.99 (978-0-375-83404-2(4)) 2006. lib. bdg. 13.95 (978-0-375-93403-2(0)) Random Hse. Children's Bks. (Random Hse. Bks. for Young Readers).

—Boss of Lunch. Brunkus, Denise, illus. 2003. (Junie B. Jones Ser.: No. 2). (ENG.). 96p. (J). (gr. 1-4). 4.99 (978-0-375-80294-2(0), Random Hse. Bks. for Young Readers) Random Hse. Children's Bks.

—Boss of Lunch. 2003. (Junie B. Jones Ser.: 19). (gr. k-3). lib. bdg. 14.75 (978-0-613-63168-6(4), Turtleback) Turtleback Bks.

—Cheater Pants. Brunkus, Denise, tr. Brunkus, Denise, illus. 2004. (Junie B. Jones Ser.: No. 4). (ENG.). 96p. (J). (gr. 1-4). 4.99 (978-0-375-82302-2(6), Random Hse. Bks. for Young Readers) Random Hse. Children's Bks.

—Cheater Pants. Brunkus, Denise, illus. 2003. (Junie B. Jones Ser.: No. 4). (ENG.). 96p. (J). (gr. 1-4). lib. bdg. 13.99 (978-0-375-92301-2(2), Random Hse. Bks. for Young Readers) Random Hse. Children's Bks.

—Dumb Bunny. Brunkus, Denise, illus. 2007. (Junie B. Jones Ser.: No. 11). (ENG.). 128p. (J). (gr. 1-4). lib. bdg. 14.99 (978-0-375-93809-2(5), Random Hse. Bks. for Young Readers) Random Hse. Children's Bks.

—Jingle Bells, Batman Smells! Brunkus, Denise, illus. 2009. (Junie B. Jones Ser.: No. 8). (ENG.). 128p. (J). (gr. 1-4). 4.99 (978-0-375-82809-6(5), Random Hse. Bks. for Young Readers) Random Hse. Children's Bks.

—Junie B., First Grader - Aloha-Ha-Ha! Brunkus, Denise, illus. 2007. (Junie B. Jones Ser.). 119p. (gr. 1-4). 15.00 (978-0-7569-8085-6(2)) Perfection Learning Corp.

—Junie B. First Grader - Aloha-Ha-Ha! 2007. (Junie B. Jones Ser.: 26). lib. bdg. 14.75 (978-1-4177-8157-7(2), Turtleback) Turtleback Bks.

—Junie B. Jones & Her Big Fat Mouth. unabr. ed. 2004. (Junie B. Jones Ser.: No. 3). 69p. (J). (gr. k-3). pap. 17.00 incl. audio (978-0-8072-0780-2(2), LFTR 239 SP, Listening Library) Random Hse. Audio Publishing Group.

—Junie B. Jones & Some Sneaky Peeky Spying. unabr. ed. 2004. (Junie B. Jones Ser.: No. 4). 66p. (J). (gr. k-3). pap. 17.00 incl. audio (978-0-8072-0781-9(0), LFTR 240 SP, Listening Library) Random Hse. Audio Publishing Group.

—Junie B. Jones y Su Gran Bocota. Brunkus, Denise, illus. 2005. (Junie B. Jones Ser.).Tr. of Junie B. Jones & Her Big Fat Mouth. (SPA.). 80p. (J). (gr. 2-5). pap. 4.99 (978-0-439-42516-2(6), Scholastic en Espanol) Scholastic, Inc.

—Junie B. Jones's Third Boxed Set Ever!, 4 vols., Bks. 9-12. Brunkus, Denise, illus. 2003. (Junie B. Jones Ser.). (ENG.). (J). (gr. 1-4). 19.96 (978-0-375-82552-1(5), Random Hse. Bks. for Young Readers) Random Hse. Children's Bks.

—Junie B.'s Essential Survival Guide to School. Brunkus, Denise, illus. 2013. (Junie B. Jones Ser.). (ENG.). 144p. (J). (gr. 1-4). 12.99 (978-0-449-81783-4(0), Random Hse. Bks. for Young Readers) Random Hse. Children's Bks.

—One-Man Band. Brunkus, Denise, tr. Brunkus, Denise, illus. 2004. (Junie B. Jones Ser.: No. 5). (ENG.). 96p. (J). (gr. 1-4). 4.99 (978-0-375-82536-1(3), Random Hse. Bks. for Young Readers) Random Hse. Children's Bks.

—Shipwrecked, No. 23. Brunkus, Denise, illus. 2005. (Junie B. Jones Ser.: No. 6). (ENG.). 96p. (J). (gr. 1-4). mass mkt. 4.99 (978-0-375-82805-8(2), Random Hse. Bks. for Young Readers) Random Hse. Children's Bks.

—Skinnybones. 2016. (ENG.). 160p. (J). (gr. 3-7). 12.99 (978-0-394-94988-8(9), Yearling) Random Hse. Children's Bks.

—Toothless Wonder. Brunkus, Denise, illus. 2003. (Junie B. Jones Ser.: Bk. 3). 80p. (gr. 1-4). 15.00 (978-0-7569-1621-3(6)) Perfection Learning Corp.

—Turkeys We Have Loved & Eaten, No. 28. Brunkus, Denise, illus. 2012. (Junie B. Jones Ser.: 28). (ENG.). 144p. (J). (gr. 1-4). lib. bdg. 14.99 (978-0-375-97063-4(0), Random Hse. Bks. for Young Readers) Random Hse. Children's Bks.

—Turkeys We Have Loved & Eaten (and Other Thankful Stuff), No. 28. Brunkus, Denise, illus. 2012. (Junie B. Jones Ser.). (ENG.). 144p. (J). (gr. 1-4). 11.99 (978-0-375-87063-7(6), Random Hse. Bks. for Young Readers) Random Hse. Children's Bks.

Parker Ma Csac, Nacole A. A Day in the Life of Ruby. 2011. 28p. pap. 16.25 (978-1-4634-1152-7(9)) AuthorHouse.

Parker, S. M. The Girl Who Fell. (ENG., Illus.). (YA). (gr. 11). 2017. 384p. pap. 10.99 (978-1-4814-3724-0(0)) 2016. 368p. 17.99 (978-1-4814-3725-7(9)) Simon Pulse. (Simon Pulse).

Parkhurst, Johanna. Here's to You, Zeb Pike [Library Edition]. 2014. 180p. pap. 14.99 (978-1-62798-526-0(3), Harmony Ink Pr.) Dreamspinner Pr.

Parkkola, Seita. The School of Possibilities. Silver, Annira & Gass, Marja, trs. from FIN. Ikonen, Jani, illus. 2010. (ENG.). 368p. (J). (gr. 4-7). 12.99 (978-1-4022-1835-4(4), Sourcebooks Jabberwocky) Sourcebooks, Inc.

Parks, Marquin. Wrinkles Wallace: Knights of Night School. 2012. 174p. pap. 12.00 (978-0-9832330-5-3(5)) Meridia Pubs. LLC.

Parnell, Declan. Mom Comes to School, 01 vols., 1. 2016. (Rosen REAL Readers: STEM & STEAM Collection). (ENG.). 12p. (J). pap. 6.33 (978-1-5081-1611-0(3), Rosen Classroom) Rosen Publishing Group, Inc., The.

—School Rules!, 01 vols., 1. 2016. (Rosen REAL Readers: Social Studies Nonfiction / Fiction: Family, Community, & the World Ser.). (ENG.). 8p. (J). pap. 5.46 (978-1-5081-1848-0(5), Rosen Classroom) Rosen Publishing Group, Inc., The.

Parnell, Robyn. The Mighty Quinn. DeYoe, Katie & DeYoe, Aaron, illus. 2013. (ENG.). 272p. (gr. 2-7). pap. 10.95 (978-1-938063-10-7(4), Mighty Media Junior Readers) Mighty Media Pr.

Parr, Todd. Otto Goes to School. 2013. (Passport to Reading Level 1 Ser.). (J). lib. bdg. 14.75 (978-0-606-31740-5(6), Turtleback) Turtleback Bks.

—Teachers Rock! 2016. (ENG., Illus.). 32p. (J). (gr. -1-1). 16.99 (978-0-316-26512-6(8)) Little, Brown Bks. for Young Readers.

Parsley, Elise. If You Ever Want to Bring an Alligator to School, Don't! Parsley, Elise, illus. 2015. (ENG., Illus.). 40p. (J). (gr. -1-1). 17.00 (978-0-316-37657-0(4)) Little Brown & Co.

Pascal, Francine. The Ruling Class. 2010. (ENG.). 208p. (YA). (gr. 9). pap. 10.99 (978-1-4424-1423-5(5), Simon Pulse) Simon Pulse.

—Terror de la Escuela. Orig. Title: The Bully. (SPA.). 120p. (J). 6.95 (978-84-272-3789-6(8)) Molino, Editorial ESP. Dist: AIMS International Bks., Inc.

Passen, Lisa. The Attack of the 50-Foot Teacher. 2005. (Illus.). 28p. (J). (gr. k-4). reprint ed. 16.00 (978-0-7567-9665-5(2)) DIANE Publishing Co.

Pastis, Stephan. Now Look What You've Done. 2016. (Timmy Failure Ser.: 2). lib. bdg. 18.40 (978-0-606-37947-2(9)) Turtleback Bks.

—Timmy Failure: the Book You're Not Supposed to Have. Pastis, Stephan, illus. 2016. (Timmy Failure Ser.). (ENG., Illus.). 304p. (J). (gr. 3-7). 14.99 (978-0-7636-9004-5(X)) Candlewick Pr.

Paterson, Katherine. Marvin One Too Many. Clark Brown, Jane, illus. 2003. 28.95 incl. audio compact disk (978-1-59112-635-5(5)); 28.95 incl. audio compact disk (978-1-59112-635-5(5)); 25.95 incl. audio (978-1-59112-254-8(6)); pap. 31.95 incl. audio compact disk (978-1-59112-636-2(3)) Live Oak Media.

Patrick, Cat. Forgotten. 2012. (ENG.). 320p. (J). (gr. 7-17). pap. 8.99 (978-0-316-09460-3(9)) Little, Brown Bks. for Young Readers.

—Revived. 2013. (ENG.). 368p. (YA). (gr. 7-17). pap. 10.99 (978-0-316-09463-4(3)) Little, Brown Bks. for Young Readers.

Patterson, C. Marie. Little Dinky's Love for Basketball. 2009. 24p. pap. 15.99 (978-1-4415-1255-0(1)) Xlibris Corp.

Patterson, Eric. Nature Boy Nature Strikes Back. Wright, Chris, illus. 2008. 108p. pap. 6.95 (978-1-935105-15-2(9)) Avid Readers Publishing Group.

Patterson, James. Middle School: Escape to Australia. Griffo, Daniel, illus. 2017. (Middle School Ser.: 9). (ENG.). 288p. (J).

(gr. 3-7). 13.99 *(978-0-316-27262-9(0),* Jimmy Patterson) Little Brown & Co.

—Public School Superhero. 2015. (ENG., Illus.). 304p. (J). (gr. 3-7). 13.99 *(978-0-316-32214-0(8),* Jimmy Patterson) Little Brown & Co.

—School's Out - Forever. 2008. (Maximum Ride Ser.: Bk. 2). 418p. (gr. 4-7). 18.00 *(978-0-7569-8349-9(5))* Perfection Learning Corp.

—School's Out - Forever. 2007. (Maximum Ride Ser.: 2). (YA). lib. bdg. 20.85 *(978-1-4177-7493-7(2),* Turtleback) Turtleback Bks.

—The Worst Years of My Life. 2014. lthr. 79.00 *(978-1-62715-524-3(4))* Leatherbound Bestsellers.

—The Worst Years of My Life. 2012. 18.00 *(978-1-61383-331-5(8))* Perfection Learning Corp.

Patterson, James & Bergen, Julia. Ultimate Showdown. 2014. (Middle School Ser.: 5). (ENG., Illus.). 256p. (J). (gr. 3-7). 13.99 *(978-0-316-32211-9(3),* Jimmy Patterson) Little Brown & Co.

Patterson, James & Grabenstein, Chris. House of Robots. Neufeld, Juliana, illus. (House of Robots Ser.: 1). (ENG.). (J). (gr. 3-7). 2015. 336p. pap. 7.99 *(978-0-316-34679-5(9))* 2014. 352p. 13.99 *(978-0-316-40591-1(4))* Little Brown & Co. (Jimmy Patterson).

—House of Robots. 2015. (J). lib. bdg. 18.40 *(978-0-606-37527-6(9))* Turtleback Bks.

—I Even Funnier: A Middle School Story. Park, Laura, illus. 2013. (I Funny Ser.: 2). (ENG.). 368p. (J). (gr. 3-7). 13.99 *(978-0-316-20697-6(0),* Jimmy Patterson) Little Brown & Co.

—I Funny TV: A Middle School Story. Park, Laura, illus. 2015. (I Funny Ser.: 4). (ENG.). 336p. (J). (gr. 3-7). 13.99 *(978-0-316-30109-1(4),* Jimmy Patterson) Little Brown & Co.

—Jacky Ha-Ha. Kerascoët, illus. 2016. (ENG.). 384p. (J). (gr. 3-7). 13.99 *(978-0-316-26249-1(8),* Jimmy Patterson) Little Brown & Co.

—Jacky Ha-Ha. 2017. (Jacky Ha-Ha Ser.). (J). lib. bdg. 18.40 ***(978-0-606-40732-8(4))*** Turtleback Bks.

—Pottymouth & Stoopid. Gilpin, Stephen, illus. 2017. (ENG.). 336p. (J). (gr. 3-7). 13.99 *(978-0-316-34963-5(1))* Little Brown & Co.

—Robots Go Wild. Neufeld, Juliana, illus. 2015. (House of Robots Ser.: 2). (ENG.). 336p. (J). (gr. 3-7). 13.99 *(978-0-316-28479-0(3),* Jimmy Patterson) Little Brown & Co.

Patterson, James & Papademetriou, Lisa. Big Fat Liar. Swaab, Neil, illus. 2014. (Middle School Ser.: Bk. 3). (ENG.). 304p. (J). (gr. 3-7). 13.99 *(978-0-316-32203-4(2),* Jimmy Patterson) Little Brown & Co.

—Homeroom Diaries. Keino, illus. 2014. (ENG.). 272p. (YA). (gr. 7-17). 18.00 *(978-0-316-20762-1(4),* Jimmy Patterson) Little Brown & Co.

Patterson, James & Tebbetts, Chris. How I Survived Bullies, Broccoli, & Snake Hill. Park, Laura, illus. 2013. (Middle School Ser.: 4). (ENG.). 336p. (J). (gr. 3-7). 14.00 *(978-0-316-23175-6(4),* Jimmy Patterson) Little Brown & Co.

—Just My Rotten Luck. Park, Laura, illus. 2015. (Middle School Ser.: 7). (ENG.). 320p. (J). (gr. 3-7). 13.99 *(978-0-316-28477-6(7),* Jimmy Patterson) Little Brown & Co.

—Middle School: Dog's Best Friend. Tejido, Jomike, illus. 2016. (Middle School: Book 8 Ser.: 8). (ENG.). 256p. (J). (gr. 3-7). 13.99 *(978-0-316-34954-3(2),* Jimmy Patterson) Little Brown & Co.

—Public School Superhero. Thomas, Cory, illus. 2016. (ENG.). 304p. (J). (gr. 3-7). pap. 7.99 *(978-0-316-26598-0(5),* Jimmy Patterson) Little Brown & Co.

—The Worst Years of My Life. Park, Laura, illus. (Middle School Ser.: Bk. 1). (ENG.). (J). (gr. 3-7). 2014. 320p. 13.99 *(978-0-316-32202-7(4),* Jimmy Patterson) 2013. pap. 0.01 *(978-0-316-25251-5(4))* 2012. 336p. pap. 8.00 *(978-0-316-10169-1(9),* Jimmy Patterson) Little Brown & Co.

—The Worst Years of My Life. Park, Laura, illus. 2012. (Middle School Ser.: 1). (J). lib. bdg. 18.45 *(978-0-606-26164-7(8),* Turtleback) Turtleback Bks.

Patterson, James & Tebbetts, Christopher. From Hero to Zero. Park, Laura, illus. 2017. (J). pap. ***(978-0-316-35756-2(1))*** Little Brown & Co.

Patterson, James, et al. Public School Superhero. 2015. *(978-0-316-34231-5(9))* Little, Brown Bks. for Young Readers.

Patterson, Rebecca. The Gordon Star. Rees, Mary, illus. 2006. (ENG.). 32p. (J). (gr. k-2). 17.95 *(978-0-86264-893-0(9))* Andersen Pr. GBR. Dist: Independent Pubs. Group.

Patti, Caroline. The World Spins Madly On. 2008. 144p. 21.95 *(978-0-595-71087-4(5));* pap. 11.95 *(978-0-595-47439-4(X))* iUniverse, Inc.

Pattou, Edith. Mrs. Spitzer's Garden. Tusa, Tricia, illus. gif. ed. 2007. (ENG.). 32p. (J). (gr. -1-3). 12.99 *(978-0-15-205802-9(8))* Houghton Mifflin Harcourt Publishing Co.

Paul, Marcy Beller. Underneath Everything. Davis, Bill, illus. 2015. (ENG.). 304p. (YA). (gr. 9). 17.99 *(978-0-06-232721-5(6))* HarperCollins Pubs.

Paul, Volponi. Black & White. 2014. (ENG.). 208p. (YA). 11.24 *(978-1-63245-196-5(4))* Lectorum Pubns., Inc.

Pauley, Kimberly. Cat Girl's Day Off, 1 vol. 2012. (ENG.). 336p. (YA). 17.95 *(978-1-60060-883-4(3),* Tu Bks.) Lee & Low Bks., Inc.

Paulsen, Gary. Liar, Liar. 2012. (ENG.). 128p. (J). (gr. 3-7). 6.99 *(978-0-375-86611-1(6),* Yearling) Random Hse. Children's Bks.

—Molly Mcginty Has a Really Good Day. 2006. (Illus.). 105p. (J). (gr. 3-7). 13.15 *(978-0-7569-6621-8(3))* Perfection Learning Corp.

—Mudshark. 2010. (ENG.). 96p. (J). (gr. 3-7). 6.99 *(978-0-553-49464-8(3),* Yearling) Random Hse. Children's Bks.

—Six Kids & a Stuffed Cat. 2016. (ENG., Illus.). 144p. (J). (gr. 3-7). 16.99 *(978-1-4814-5223-6(1),* Simon & Schuster Bks. For Young Readers) Simon & Schuster Bks. For Young Readers.

—Vote. 2013. (ENG.). 144p. (J). (gr. 4-7). 12.99 *(978-0-385-74228-3(2),* Lamb, Wendy Bks.) Random Hse. Children's Bks.

—Vote: The Theory, Practice, & Destructive Properties of Politics. 2014. (ENG.). 144p. (J). (gr. 4-7). pap. 6.99 *(978-0-385-74229-0(0),* Yearling) Random Hse. Children's Bks.

Payne, C. C. Lula Bell on Geekdom, Freakdom, & the Challenges of Bad Hair, 0 vols. 2012. (ENG.). 276p. (J). (gr. 3-7). 16.99 *(978-0-7614-6225-5(2),* 9780761462255, Amazon Children's Publishing) Amazon Publishing.

Payne, Gregory. Chase to the Brazen Head. 2010. (ENG.). 228p. (YA). (gr. 4-7). pap. 11.95 *(978-988-18094-6-9(0))* Haven Bks.

Payne, Jody. Miss Spellin' Helen. Payne, Rachel & Song, Danielle, illus. 2012. 148p. pap. 6.99 *(978-0-9846667-0-0(5))* Absalon Pr.

Payne, K. E. Another 365 Days. 2013. (ENG.). 264p. (J). (gr. 7). pap. 11.95 *(978-1-60282-775-2(3))* Bold Strokes Bks.

—365 Days. 2011. (ENG.). 280p. (J). (gr. 7). pap. 13.95 *(978-1-60282-540-6(8))* Bold Strokes Bks.

Payton, Belle. Even the Score. 2015. (It Takes Two Ser.: 5). (ENG., Illus.). 160p. (J). (gr. 3-7). pap. 6.99 *(978-1-4814-1951-2(X),* Simon Spotlight) Simon Spotlight.

—May the Best Twin Win. 2015. (It Takes Two Ser.: 7). (ENG., Illus.). 160p. (J). (gr. 3-7). pap. 6.99 *(978-1-4814-3134-7(X),* Simon Spotlight) Simon Spotlight.

—Twice the Talent. 2016. (It Takes Two Ser.: 11). (ENG., Illus.). 160p. (J). (gr. 3-7). pap. 6.99 *(978-1-4814-5263-2(0),* Simon Spotlight) Simon Spotlight.

—Two Cool for School. 2014. (It Takes Two Ser.: 2). (ENG., Illus.). 160p. (J). (gr. 3-7). 16.99 *(978-1-4814-0645-1(0),* Simon Spotlight) Simon Spotlight.

—Two Steps Back. 2015. (It Takes Two Ser.: 6). (ENG., Illus.). 160p. (J). (gr. 3-7). 17.99 *(978-1-4814-2519-3(6),* Simon Spotlight) Simon Spotlight.

PeachMoon Publishing. The Adventures of Lucky the Lizard Las aventuras del lagarto Lucky. 2008. (ENG & SPA., Illus.). 100p. (J). pap. 19.95 *(978-0-9795831-4-8(4))* PeachMoon Publishing.

—Lucky Goes to School. 2007. (J). pap. 9.95 *(978-0-9795831-1-7(X))* PeachMoon Publishing.

Pearce, Jackson. As You Wish. (ENG.). 304p. (YA). (gr. 8). 2010. pap. 8.99 *(978-0-06-166154-9(6))* 2009. 16.99 *(978-0-06-166152-5(X))* HarperCollins Pubs. (HarperTeen).

—The Doublecross: (And Other Skills I Learned As a Superspy) (ENG.). 304p. 2016. (J). pap. 7.99 *(978-1-61963-939-3(4),* 9781619639393) 2015. (YA). (gr. 3-6). 16.99 *(978-1-61963-414-5(7),* 9781619634145) Bloomsbury Publishing USA. (Bloomsbury USA Childrens).

Pearce, Richard & Story, Ken. Dorkman. 2006. (YA). mass mkt. 8.50 *(978-0-9753367-8-6(9))* Onstage Publishing, LLC.

Pearsall, Shelley. All of the Above. Steptoe, Javaka, illus. 2008. (ENG.). 256p. (J). (gr. 3-7). per. 8.00 *(978-0-316-11526-1(6))* Little, Brown Bks. for Young Readers.

—All Shook Up. 2009. (ENG.). 272p. (J). (gr. 3-7). 6.99 *(978-0-440-42139-9(X),* Yearling) Random Hse. Children's Bks.

Pearson, Joanna. The Rites & Wrongs of Janice Wills. 2011. (YA). pap. *(978-0-545-19774-8(0));* (ENG.). 224p. (J). (gr. 9-7). 16.99 *(978-0-545-19773-1(2))* Scholastic, Inc. (Levine, Arthur A. Bks.).

Peck, Richard. The Best Man, 5 vols. (ENG.). (J). 2017. 44.95 ***(978-0-525-48687-9(9),*** Puffin Books) 2017. 256p. (gr. 4-7). 8.99 ***(978-0-14-751579-7(3),*** Puffin Books) 2016. 240p. (gr. 4-7). 16.99 *(978-0-8037-3839-3(0),* Dial Bks) Penguin Young Readers Group.

Peers, Bobbie. William Wenton & the Impossible Puzzle. 2017. (William Wenton Ser.: 1). (ENG., Illus.). 272p. (J). (gr. 3-7). 16.99 ***(978-1-4814-7825-0(7),*** Aladdin) Simon & Schuster Children's Publishing.

Peets, Risa. It's OK to Be Different: An Amazing School Day. 2013. (ENG., Illus.). 76p. (J). pap. 7.99 *(978-1-937008-17-8(7))* Heart to Heart Publishing, Inc.

Peirce, Lincoln. Big Nate. 2012. (ENG.). 224p. pap. 12.99 *(978-1-4494-1144-2(4))* Andrews McMeel Publishing.

—Big Nate: Mr. Popularity. Peirce, Lincoln, illus. 2014. (Big Nate Ser.). (ENG., Illus.). 224p. (J). (gr. 3-7). pap. 9.99 *(978-0-06-208700-3(2))* HarperCollins Pubs.

—Big Nate: Revenge of the Cream Puffs. 2016. (Big Nate Ser.: 15). (ENG.). 184p. (J). (gr. 3-7). pap. 9.99 *(978-1-4494-6228-4(6))* Andrews McMeel Publishing.

—Big Nate: The Crowd Goes Wild! Peirce, Lincoln, illus. 2014. (Big Nate Ser.). (ENG., Illus.). 224p. (J). 9.99 *(978-1-4494-3634-6(X))* Andrews McMeel Publishing.

—Big Nate: Thunka, Thunka, Thunka. 2016. (Big Nate Ser.: Vol. 14). (ENG., Illus.). (J). (gr. 3-6). 29.99 ***(978-1-4494-7581-9(7))*** Andrews McMeel Publishing.

—Big Nate — Genius Mode. 2013. (Big Nate Graphic Novels Ser.). (J). lib. bdg. 20.85 *(978-0-606-31802-0(X),* Turtleback) Turtleback Bks.

—Big Nate — Here Goes Nothing. 2012. (Big Nate Graphic Novels Ser.: 6). (J). lib. bdg. 20.85 *(978-0-606-26526-3(0),* Turtleback) Turtleback Bks.

—Big Nate — In a Class by Himself. Peirce, Lincoln, illus. 2015. (Big Nate Ser.: 1). (ENG., Illus.). 224p. (J). (gr. 3-7). pap. 6.99 *(978-0-06-228359-7(6))* HarperCollins Pubs.

—Big Nate — In a Class by Himself. 2010. pap. *(978-0-06-199287-2(9))* HarperCollins Pubs.

—Big Nate — In a Class by Himself. 2015. (Big Nate Ser.: 1). (J). lib. bdg. 17.20 *(978-0-606-36505-5(2))* Turtleback Bks.

—Big Nate — Mr. Popularity. 2014. (Big Nate Graphic Novels Ser.: 4). (J). lib. bdg. 20.85 *(978-0-606-35482-0(4))* Turtleback Bks.

—Big Nate — Welcome to My World. 2015. (Big Nate Ser.: 13). (ENG., Illus.). 176p. (J). pap. 9.99 *(978-1-4494-6226-0(X))* Andrews McMeel Publishing.

—Big Nate - The Crowd Goes Wild! 2014. (Big Nate Graphic Novels Ser.). lib. bdg. 20.85 *(978-0-606-36143-9(X))* Turtleback Bks.

—Big Nate & Friends. 2011. (Illus.). 224p. (J). (Big Nate Ser.: 3). (ENG.). pap. 9.99 *(978-1-4494-2043-7(5));* *(978-0-545-46801-5(9)); (978-1-60744-837-2(8))* Andrews McMeel Publishing.

—Big Nate Blasts Off. Peirce, Lincoln, illus. 2016. (Big Nate Ser.: 8). (ENG., Illus.). 224p. (J). (gr. 3-7). 13.99 *(978-0-06-211111-6(6))* HarperCollins Pubs.

—Big Nate Doodlepalooza. Peirce, Lincoln, illus. (Illus.). 224p. (J). (gr. 3-7). 2016. (Big Nate Activity Book Ser.: 3). pap. 6.99 *(978-0-06-234952-1(X))* 2013. (Big Nate Ser.). (ENG., 10.99 *(978-0-06-211114-2(0))* HarperCollins Pubs.

—Big Nate Goes for Broke. Peirce, Lincoln, illus. (Big Nate Ser.: 4). (Illus.). 224p. (J). (gr. 3-7). 2016. pap. 6.99 *(978-0-06-236753-2(6))* 2012. (ENG., 12.99 *(978-0-06-199661-0(0))* 2012. lib. bdg. 14.89 *(978-0-06-199662-7(9))* HarperCollins Pubs.

—Big Nate Goes for Broke. 2016. (Big Nate Ser.: 4). 224p. (J). lib. bdg. 17.20 *(978-0-606-38137-6(6))* Turtleback Bks.

—Big Nate Lives It Up. Peirce, Lincoln, illus. 2015. (Big Nate Ser.: 7). (Illus.). 224p. (J). (gr. 3-7). lib. bdg. 13.89 *(978-0-06-211109-8(4))* HarperCollins Pubs.

—Big Nate Makes the Grade. 2012. (Big Nate Graphic Novels Ser.). (Illus.). 224p. lib. bdg. 20.85 *(978-0-606-26308-5(X),* Turtleback) Turtleback Bks.

—Big Nate on a Roll. Peirce, Lincoln, illus. 2011. (Big Nate Ser.: 3). (Illus.). 224p. (J). (gr. 3-7). (ENG.). 12.99 *(978-0-06-194438-3(6));* lib. bdg. 14.89 *(978-0-06-194439-0(4))* HarperCollins Pubs.

—Big Nate Out Loud. 2011. (Big Nate Ser.: 2). (ENG., Illus.). 224p. (J). pap. 9.99 *(978-1-4494-0718-6(8))* Andrews McMeel Publishing.

—Big Nate Strikes Again. Peirce, Lincoln, illus. 2010. (Big Nate Ser.: 2). (Illus.). 224p. (J). (gr. 3-7). (ENG.). 12.99 *(978-0-06-194436-9(X));* lib. bdg. 14.89 *(978-0-06-194437-6(8))* HarperCollins Pubs.

—Big Nate: Thunka, Thunka, Thunka. 2016. (ENG., Illus.). 176p. (J). (gr. 3-6). pap. 9.99 *(978-1-4494-6227-7(8))* Andrews McMeel Publishing.

—Big Nate's Greatest Hits. 2015. (ENG., Illus.). 376p. (J). pap. 12.99 *(978-1-4494-6489-9(0))* Andrews McMeel Publishing.

—Great Minds Think Alike. 2014. (Big Nate Ser.: 8). (ENG.). 224p. (J). 9.99 *(978-1-4494-3635-3(8))* Andrews McMeel Publishing.

—In a Class by Himself. Peirce, Lincoln, illus. (Big Nate Ser.: 1). (Illus.). (J). (gr. 3-7). 2010. (ENG.). 224p. 12.99 *(978-0-06-194434-5(3))* 2010. 224p. lib. bdg. 14.89 *(978-0-06-194435-2(1))* 2012. (ENG., 240p. 12.99 *(978-0-06-220773-9(3))* HarperCollins Pubs.

—Nate el Grande Ataca de Nuevo. 2015.Tr. of Big Nate Strikes Again. (SPA.). 216p. (J). (gr. 3-5). 17.99 *(978-1-933032-79-5(0))* Lectorum Pubns., Inc.

—Thunka, Thunka, Thunka. 2016. (Big Nate Graphic Novels Ser.). lib. bdg. 20.85 *(978-0-606-38234-2(8))* Turtleback Bks.

—Welcome to My World. 2015. (Big Nate Graphic Novels Ser.). lib. bdg. 20.85 *(978-0-606-37391-3(8))* Turtleback Bks.

—What Could Possibly Go Wrong? Peirce, Lincoln, illus. 2012. (Big Nate Comix Ser.: 1). (ENG., Illus.). 224p. (J). (gr. 3-7). pap. 9.99 *(978-0-06-208694-5(4))* HarperCollins Pubs.

Peirce, Lincoln, illus. Big Nate Flips Out. 2013. 216p. (J). *(978-0-06-224637-0(2))* Harper & Row Ltd.

Peirce, Lincoln, et al. Big Nate Makes the Grade. Peirce, Lincoln, illus. 2012. (Big Nate Ser.: 4). (ENG., Illus.). 224p. (J). 9.99 *(978-1-4494-2566-1(6))* Andrews McMeel Publishing.

Pemberton, Teresa. Trissy's New Shoes. 2013. 32p. pap. 13.95 *(978-1-4497-9337-1(1),* WestBow Pr.) Author Solutions, Inc.

Pendergrass, Daphne. Daniel Plays at School. 2016. (Daniel Tiger's Neighborhood Ready-To-Read Ser.). lib. bdg. 13.55 *(978-0-606-38991-4(1))* Turtleback Bks.

Penn, Audrey. A. D. D. Not B. A. D. Wyrick, Monica, illus. 2003. (New Child & Family Press Titles Ser.). 32p. pap. 9.95 *(978-0-87868-849-4(8),* 8498, Child & Family Pr.) Child Welfare League of America, Inc.

—A. D. D. Not B. A. D. Wyrick, Monica Dunsky, illus. 2006. (ENG.). 32p. (J). (gr. -1-3). 7.99 *(978-0-9749303-7-4(7))* Tanglewood Pr.

—Un Beso en Mi Mano. Harper, Ruth E. & Leak, Nancy M., illus. 2006. (Kissing Hand Ser.). (SPA & ENG.). 32p. (J). (gr. -1-3). 16.95 *(978-1-933718-01-9(3))* Tanglewood Pr.

—The Kissing Hand. Gibson, Barbara Leonard, illus. 2014. (Kissing Hand Ser.). (ENG.). 14p. (J). (-k). bds. 7.99 *(978-1-933718-77-4(3))* Tanglewood Pr.

—The Kissing Hand. Harper, Ruth E. & Leak, Nancy M., illus. 2007. (Kissing Hand Ser.). (ENG.). 32p. (J). (gr. -1-3). 28.95 *(978-1-933718-07-1(2));* 12.95 *(978-1-933718-10-1(2))* Tanglewood Pr.

Penn, Audrey, et al, illus. The Kissing Hand. 2010. 23.05 *(978-0-7569-9299-6(0))* Natl Bk. Network.

Penn, Audrey & Gibson, Barbara L. Chester Raccoon & the Big Bad Bully. 2008. (Kissing Hand Ser.). (ENG., Illus.). 32p. (J). (gr. -1-3). 16.95 *(978-1-933718-15-6(3))* Tanglewood Pr.

Penn, Linda M. Clayton's Birding Adventure: A Young Boy Learns the Secret Ways of Birds. 2013. 46p. pap. 10.95 *(978-0-9852488-5-7(8))* Racing to Joy Pr. LLC.

Pennels, Geraldine. The School Shenanigans of Amy & Nontand. 2009. 152p. pap. 33.50 *(978-1-60860-496-8(9),* Strategic Bk. Publishing) Strategic Book Publishing & Rights Agency (SBPRA).

Penner, Evelyn. The Kid Who Ate Dog Food. Chullabrahm, T. M., illus. 2008. 32p. (J). 15.99 *(978-0-9796500-0-0(3))* Peppernut Publishing.

Pennypacker, Sara. Clementine. Frazee, Marla, illus. (ENG.). (J). 2008. 160p. (gr. 2-5). pap. 5.99 *(978-0-7868-3883-7(3))* 2006. 144p. (gr. 1-3). 14.99 *(978-0-7868-3882-0(5))* Hyperion Pr.

—Clementine, Friend of the Week. Frazee, Marla, illus. (Clementine Book Ser.). (ENG.). 176p. (J). 2011. (gr. 1-3). pap. 5.99 *(978-1-4231-1560-1(0))* 2010. (gr. 2-5). 14.99 *(978-1-4231-1355-3(1))* Hyperion Pr.

—Clementine's Letter. Frazee, Marla, illus. (Clementine Book Ser.). (ENG.). 160p. (J). (gr. 1-3). 2009. pap. 5.99 *(978-0-7868-3885-1(X))* 2008. 16.99 *(978-0-7868-3884-4(1))* Hyperion Pr.

—The Talented Clementine. Frazee, Marla, illus. (Clementine Book Ser.). (ENG.). (J). 2008. 160p. (gr. 1-3). pap. 5.99 *(978-0-7868-3871-4(X))* 2007. 144p. (gr. 2-5). 14.99 *(978-0-7868-3870-7(1))* Hyperion Pr.

—Waylon! One Awesome Thing. Frazee, Marla, illus. 2016. (Waylon Ser.). (ENG.). 204p. (J). (gr. 1-3). 15.99 *(978-1-4847-0152-2(6))* Disney Pr.

Peretti, Frank E. Hangman's Curse. 2008. 352p. (YA). mass mkt. 7.99 *(978-1-4003-1016-6(4))* Nelson, Thomas Inc.

—Nightmare Academy. 2008. 352p. (YA). mass mkt. 7.99 *(978-1-4003-1017-3(2))* Nelson, Thomas Inc.

Pérez, Ashley Hope. Out of Darkness. 2015. (ENG., Illus.). 408p. (YA). (gr. 8-12). 18.99 *(978-1-4677-4202-3(3),* Carolrhoda Lab™) Lerner Publishing Group.

Pérez, Celia C. The First Rule of Punk. 2017. (ENG., Illus.). 336p. (J). (gr. 4-7). 16.99 ***(978-0-425-29040-8(9),*** Viking Books for Young Readers) Penguin Young Readers Group.

Perez, Marlene. The Comeback. 2009. (ENG.). 208p. (J). (gr. 7). pap. 8.99 *(978-0-545-08807-7(0))* Scholastic, Inc.

—Dead Is a Battlefield. 2012. (Dead Is Ser.: 6). (ENG.). 240p. (YA). (gr. 7). pap. 7.99 *(978-0-547-60734-4(2))* Houghton Mifflin Harcourt Publishing Co.

—Dead Is a Battlefield. 2012. (Dead Is Ser.: 6). lib. bdg. 18.40 *(978-0-606-24759-7(9),* Turtleback) Turtleback Bks.

—Dead Is a Killer Tune. 2012. (Dead Is Ser.: 7). lib. bdg. 18.40 *(978-0-606-26623-9(2),* Turtleback) Turtleback Bks.

—Dead Is a State of Mind. 2009. (Dead Is Ser.: 2). (ENG., Illus.). 192p. (YA). (gr. 7-18). pap. 7.99 *(978-0-15-206210-1(6))* Houghton Mifflin Harcourt Publishing Co.

—Dead Is Just a Dream. (Dead Is Ser.: 8). (ENG.). 176p. (YA). (gr. 7). 2014. pap. 7.99 *(978-0-544-33634-6(8),* HMH Books For Young Readers) 2013. 16.99 *(978-0-544-10262-0(2))* Houghton Mifflin Harcourt Publishing Co.

—Dead Is Just a Dream. 2014. (Dead Is Ser.: 8). lib. bdg. 18.40 *(978-0-606-35990-0(7))* Turtleback Bks.

—Dead Is Just a Rumor. 2010. (Dead Is Ser.: 4). (ENG., Illus.). 224p. (YA). (gr. 7-18). pap. 7.99 *(978-0-547-34592-5(5))* Houghton Mifflin Harcourt Publishing Co.

—Dead Is Not an Option. 2011. (Dead Is Ser.: 5). (ENG.). 256p. (YA). (gr. 7-18). pap. 7.99 *(978-0-547-34593-2(3))* Houghton Mifflin Harcourt Publishing Co.

—Dead Is the New Black. 2008. (Dead Is Ser.: 1). (ENG., Illus.). 208p. (YA). (gr. 7-18). pap. 8.99 *(978-0-15-206408-2(7))* Houghton Mifflin Harcourt Publishing Co.

Perez-Martinez, Irella. Suyensita & Her Adventures. 2011. 48p. pap. 21.99 *(978-1-4568-5767-7(3))* Xlibris Corp.

Perl, Erica S. The Capybara Conspiracy: A Novel in Three Acts. 2016. (ENG.). 192p. (J). (gr. 5). 16.99 *(978-0-399-55171-0(9),* Knopf Bks. for Young Readers) Random Hse. Children's Bks.

—Dotty. Denos, Julia, illus. 2010. (ENG.). 32p. (J). (gr. -1-3). 16.95 *(978-0-8109-8962-7(X),* Abrams Bks. for Young Readers) Abrams, Inc.

—Ferocious Fluffity: A Mighty Bite-Y Class Pet. Cole, Henry, illus. 2016. (ENG.). 32p. (J). (gr. k-2). 16.95 *(978-1-4197-2182-3(8),* Abrams Bks. for Young Readers) Abrams, Inc.

Perritano, John. The Egyptian Prophecy, 1 vol. Laughead, Mike, illus. 2014. (Kid Squad Saves the World Ser.). (ENG.). 112p. (J). (gr. 8-12). 27.07 *(978-1-62402-039-1(9))* Magic Wagon.

Perry, Chrissie. Private List for Camp Success. 2017. (Penelope Perfect Ser.: 2). lib. bdg. 16.00 ***(978-0-606-40211-8(X))*** Turtleback Bks.

Perry, Ellyse;Clark. Double Time. 2017. (Ellyse Perry Ser.: 4). (ENG.). 160p. (J). (gr. 4-7). 12.99 *(978-0-14-378130-1(8))* Random Hse. Australia AUS. Dist: Independent Pubs. Group.

Perry, Ellyse;Clark. Ellyse Perry 1: Pocket Rocket. 2017. (Ellyse Perry Ser.: 1). (ENG.). 160p. (J). (gr. 4-7). 12.99 ***(978-0-14-378124-0(3))*** Random Hse. Australia AUS. Dist: Independent Pubs. Group.

Perry, Fred. Gold Digger - Platinum, Vol. 2. 2011. (ENG.). 132p. (YA). pap., pap. 14.99 *(978-0-9831823-4-4(5),* 9780983182344) Antarctic Pr., Inc.

Perry, Jolene. Has to Be Love. 2015. (ENG.). 272p. (YA). (gr. 8-12). 16.99 *(978-0-8075-6557-5(1))* Whitman, Albert & Co.

—Stronger Than You Know. 2014. (ENG.). 256p. (YA). (gr. 8-12). 16.99 *(978-0-8075-3155-6(3))* Whitman, Albert & Co.

Perry, Laurie. Kaycee's New School, 1 vol. 2009. 48p. pap. 16.95 *(978-1-61582-638-4(6))* America Star Bks.

Perry, M. LaVora. Taneesha Never Disparaging. Cooper, Floyd, illus. 2008. (ENG.). 216p. (J). (gr. 2-7). pap. 8.95 *(978-0-86171-550-3(0))* Wisdom Pubns.

Peschke, Marci. Daisy & the Spring Dance, 1 vol., Bk. 6. Pilz, M. H., illus. 2011. (Growing up Daisy Ser.). (ENG.). 80p. (gr. 3-8). 27.07 *(978-1-61641-119-0(8),* Calico Chapter Bks) Magic Wagon.

—Daisy for President, 1 vol., Bk. 2. Pilz, M. H., illus. 2011. (Growing up Daisy Ser.). (ENG.). 80p. (gr. 3-8). 27.07 *(978-1-61641-115-2(5),* Calico Chapter Bks) Magic Wagon.

—Daisy Has the Holiday Blues, 1 vol., Bk. 5. Pilz, MH, illus. 2011. (Growing up Daisy Ser.). (ENG.). 80p. (gr. 3-8). 27.07 *(978-1-61641-118-3(X),* Calico Chapter Bks) Magic Wagon.

—Daisy's Fall Festival, 1 vol., Bk. 4. Pilz, M. H., illus. 2011. (Growing up Daisy Ser.). (ENG.). 80p. (gr. 3-8). 27.07 *(978-1-61641-117-6(1),* Calico Chapter Bks) Magic Wagon.

—Daisy's Field Trip Adventure, 1 vol., Bk. 3. Pilz, M. H., illus. 2011. (Growing up Daisy Ser.). (ENG.). 80p. (gr. 3-8). 27.07 *(978-1-61641-116-9(3),* Calico Chapter Bks) Magic Wagon.

—Daisy's Summer Essay, 1 vol., Bk. 1. Pilz, M. H., illus. 2011. (Growing up Daisy Ser.). (ENG.). 80p. (gr. 3-8). 27.07 *(978-1-61641-114-5(7),* Calico Chapter Bks) Magic Wagon.

—Drama Queen, 1 vol. Mourning, Tuesday, illus. 2011. (Kylie Jean Ser.). (ENG.). 112p. (gr. 2-3). lib. bdg. 22.65 *(978-1-4048-6757-4(0),* Kylie Jean) Picture Window Bks.

—Drama Queen, 1 vol. Mourning, Tuesday, illus. 2011. (Kylie Jean Ser.). (ENG.). 112p. (gr. 2-3). pap. 5.95 *(978-1-4048-6616-4(7),* Kylie Jean) Picture Window Bks.

—Green Queen, 1 vol. Mourning, Tuesday, illus. 2014. (Kylie Jean Ser.). (ENG.). 112p. (gr. 2-3). 22.65 *(978-1-4795-2351-1(8),* Kylie Jean) Picture Window Bks.

—Pirate Queen, 1 vol. Mourning, Tuesday, illus. 2013. (Kylie Jean Ser.). (ENG.). 112p. (gr. 2-3). 8.95 *(978-1-4048-8103-7(4));* lib. bdg. 22.65 *(978-1-4048-7581-4(6))* Picture Window Bks. (Kylie Jean).

—Spelling Queen, 1 vol. Mourning, Tuesday, illus. 2012. (Kylie Jean Ser.). (ENG.). 112p. (gr. 2-3). pap. 5.95 *(978-1-4048-7212-7(4));* lib. bdg. 22.65 *(978-1-4048-6801-4(1))* Picture Window Bks. (Kylie Jean).

—Valentine Queen, 1 vol. Mourning, Tuesday, illus. 2014. (Kylie Jean Ser.). (ENG.). 112p. (gr. 2-3). 22.65 *(978-1-4795-2352-8(6),* Kylie Jean) Picture Window Bks.

Peters, Julie Anne. Keeping You a Secret. 2005. (ENG., Illus.). 272p. (YA). (gr. 10-17). pap. 10.00 *(978-0-316-00985-0(7),* Tingley, Megan Bks.) Little, Brown Bks. for Young Readers.

Peterson, Donna. The Misadventures of Phillip Isaac Penn. 2011. 96p. pap. 7.99 *(978-1-59955-893-6(9))* Cedar Fort, Inc./CFI Distribution.

Peterson, Lois. Disconnect, 1 vol. 2012. (Orca Currents Ser.). (ENG.). 136p. (J). (gr. 5-9). pap. 9.95

(978-1-4598-0143-1(1)); lib. bdg. 16.95 (978-1-4598-0144-8(X)) Orca Bk. Pubs. USA.
Peterson, Shelley. Sundancer. Drake, Marybeth, illus. rev. ed. 2007. (ENG.). 264p. (YA). (gr. 7-12). pap. 7.95 (978-1-55263-842-2(1)) Leaf Storm Pr.
Peterson, Tina L. Oscar & the Amazing Gravity Repellent. Bonet, Xavier, illus. 2015. (Middle-Grade Novels Ser.). (ENG.). 224p. (gr. 4-7). lib. bdg. 26.65 (978-1-4965-0000-7(8)) Stone Arch Bks.
Petert. Joetakecarer. 2012. 12p. (-18). pap. 10.67 (978-1-4669-6739-7(0)) Trafford Publishing.
Petrillo, Genevieve & Lyon, Lea. Keep Your Ear on the Ball, 1 vol. Lyon, Lea, illus. 2007. (ENG., Illus.). 32p. (J). (gr. -1-3). 16.95 (978-0-88448-296-3(0)) Tilbury Hse. Pubs.
Petroff, Shani. Careful What You Wish For. McKenney, J. David, illus. 2010. (Bedeviled Ser.: 3). (ENG.). 240p. (J). (gr. 3-7). pap. 6.99 (978-0-448-45113-8(1), Grosset & Dunlap) Penguin Young Readers Group.
—Daddy's Little Angel, No. 1. McKenney, J. David, illus. 2009. (Bedeviled Ser.: 1). (ENG.). 240p. (J). (gr. 5-7). pap. 7.99 (978-0-448-45111-4(5), Grosset & Dunlap) Penguin Young Readers Group.
—The Good, the Bad, & the Ugly Dress. McKenney, J. David, illus. 2010. (Bedeviled Ser.: 2). (ENG.). 240p. (J). (gr. 5-7). pap. 6.99 (978-0-448-45112-1(3), Grosset & Dunlap) Penguin Young Readers Group.
—Romeo & What's Her Name. 2017. (ENG.). 224p. (YA). pap. 9.99 (978-1-250-11114-2(5), 9781250111142) Feiwel & Friends.
Pett, Mark & Rubinstein, Gary. The Girl Who Never Made Mistakes. Pett, Mark, illus. 2011. (ENG., Illus.). 32p. (J). (gr. k-3). 16.99 (978-1-4022-5544-1(6), Sourcebooks Jabberwocky) Sourcebooks, Inc.
Peyo. Off to School! Peyo, illus. 2011. (Smurfs Classic Ser.). (ENG., Illus.). 32p. (J). (gr. k-2). pap. 3.99 (978-1-4424-2138-7(X)); lib. bdg. 15.99 (978-1-4424-3062-4(1)) Simon Spotlight. (Simon Spotlight).
Phelps, Elizabeth Stuart & Robert Williams Wood. Gypsy's Cousin Joy. l.t. ed. 2007. (ENG.). 160p. pap. 21.99 (978-1-4264-9775-9(X)) Creative Media Partners, LLC.
Philbin, Joanna. The Daughters Break the Rules. 2011. (Daughters Ser.: 2). (ENG.). 304p. (J). (gr. 7-17). pap., pap. 10.00 (978-0-316-04905-4(0), Poppy) Little, Brown Bks. for Young Readers.
—The Daughters Take the Stage. 2011. (Daughters Ser.: 3). (ENG.). 304p. (J). (gr. 7-17). pap. 8.99 (978-0-316-04908-5(5), Poppy) Little, Brown Bks. for Young Readers.
Phillipps, J. C. Wink: The Ninja Who Wanted to Be Noticed. 2009. (ENG.). 40p. (J). (gr. -1-k). 15.99 (978-0-670-01092-9(8), Viking Books for Young Readers) Penguin Young Readers Group.
Phillips, Barry. Cave Express. 2010. 84p. pap. 12.61 (978-0-557-25038-7(2)) Lulu Pr., Inc.
Phillips, Dee. The Ghostly Secret of Lakeside School. 2016. (Cold Whispers II Ser.). (ENG.). 32p. (J). (gr. 2-6). 19.95 (978-1-944102-33-3(7)) Bearport Publishing Co., Inc.
Phillips, Lyda. Mr Touchdown. 2008. 184p. 23.95 (978-1-4401-0976-8(1)); pap. 13.95 (978-1-60528-029-5(1)) iUniverse, Inc. (iUniverse Star).
Phillips-Poovey, Lisa. Lucy Wants to Go to School. 2013. 32p. pap. 10.95 (978-1-936912-71-1(6)) Parsons Porch Bks.
Phillips, Ruby Ann. Dream Birthday, 1 vol. Isik, Semur, illus. 2014. (Krystal Ball Ser.). (ENG.). 112p. (gr. 2-3). 25.32 (978-1-4795-2178-4(7)) Picture Window Bks.
—Fortune Cookie Fiasco. Isik, Semur, illus. 2015. (Krystal Ball Ser.). (ENG.). 112p. (gr. 2-3). lib. bdg. 25.32 (978-1-4795-5874-2(5)) Picture Window Bks.
—The Great & Powerful, 1 vol. Isik, Semur, illus. 2014. (Krystal Ball Ser.). (ENG.). 112p. (gr. 2-3). 25.32 (978-1-4795-2179-1(5)) Picture Window Bks.
Philpot, Chelsey. Even in Paradise. 2014. (ENG.). 368p. (YA). (gr. 8). 17.99 (978-0-06-229369-5(9)) HarperCollins Pubs.
Picano, Jaime Gianna. The Mood Ring Adventure. 2008. 128p. pap. 11.95 (978-0-595-47958-0(8)) iUniverse, Inc.
Pichon, Liz. Everything's Amazing (Sort Of) Pichon, Liz, illus. 2015. (Tom Gates Ser.: 3). (ENG., Illus.). 416p. (J). (gr. 3-7). 12.99 (978-0-7636-7473-1(7)) Candlewick Pr.
—Excellent Excuses (and Other Good Stuff) 2016. (Brilliant World of Tom Gates Ser.: 2). lib. bdg. 18.40 (978-0-606-37941-0(X)) Turtleback Bks.
—Tom Gates: Excellent Excuses (And Other Good Stuff) Pichon, Liz, illus. 2015. (Tom Gates Ser.: 2). (ENG., Illus.). 352p. (J). (gr. 3-7). 12.99 (978-0-7636-7474-8(5)) Candlewick Pr.
—TOM GATES: FESTIVAL DE GENIALIDADES (MÁS O MENOS) 2013. (SPA.). 410p. (J). pap. 21.99 (978-84-216-8814-4(6)) Lectorum Pubns., Inc.
Picoult, Jodi & van Leer, Samantha. Between the Lines. (ENG., Illus.). 368p. (YA). (gr. 7). 2013. pap. 12.99 (978-1-4516-3581-2(8)) 2012. 19.99 (978-1-4516-3575-1(3)) Atria/Emily Bestler Bks. (Atria/Emily Bestler Bks.).
Pierce, Seth J. The Day the School Blew Up. 2009. (J). pap. 12.99 (978-0-8163-2329-6(1)) Pacific Pr. Publishing Assn.
Pike, Aprilynne. Hechizos. 2012.Tr. of Spells. (UND & SPA.). 352p. (YA). pap. 18.95 (978-84-96886-27-8(1)) Ediciones Urano S. A. ESP. Dist: Spanish Pubs., LLC.
—Illusions. 2012. (Wings Ser.: 3). (ENG.). 400p. (YA). (gr. 8). pap. 8.99 (978-0-06-166811-1(7), HarperTeen) HarperCollins Pubs.
—Life after Theft. 2013. (Life after Theft Ser.). (ENG.). 352p. (YA). (gr. 8). 17.99 (978-0-06-199900-0(8), HarperTeen) HarperCollins Pubs.
—Sleep No More. 2014. (ENG.). 352p. (YA). (gr. 8). 17.99 (978-0-06-199903-1(2), HarperTeen) HarperCollins Pubs.
—Spells. (Wings Ser.: 2). (ENG.). (YA). (gr. 8). 2011. 384p. pap. 9.99 (978-0-06-166808-1(0)) 2010. 368p. 16.99 (978-0-06-166806-7(0)) HarperCollins Pubs. (HarperTeen).
—Spells, 7 vols. 2010. (YA). 78.75 (978-1-4407-8375-3(6)) Recorded Bks., Inc.
Pike, Tabitha R. Dragon Tears: The Legacy. 2011. 232p. pap. 24.95 (978-1-4560-6664-2(1)) America Star Bks.
Pilger, Seamus. Fart Squad. Gilpin, Stephen, illus. 2015. (Fart Squad Ser.: 1). (ENG.). 112p. (J). (gr. 1-5). pap. 4.99 (978-0-06-229045-8(2), HarperFestival) HarperCollins Pubs.
—Unidentified Farting Objects. Gilpin, Stephen, illus. 2016. (Fart Squad Ser.: 3). 112p. (J). (gr. 1-5). pap. 4.99 (978-0-06-229049-6(5)) HarperCollins Pubs.
Pilkey, Dav. Big, Bad Battle of the Bionic Booger Boy: The Night of the Nasty Nostril Nuggets. 2003. (Captain Underpants Ser.: 6). (gr. 3-6). lib. bdg. 16.00 (978-0-613-68836-9(8), Turtleback) Turtleback Bks.
—El Capitan Calzoncillos y la Furia de la Supermujer Macroelastica. 2003. (Captain Underpants Ser.: 5). (SPA & ENG., Illus.). 176p. (J). (gr. 2-5). pap. 5.99 (978-0-439-53820-6(3), Scholastic en Espanol) Scholastic, Inc.
—El Capitan Calzoncillos y la Ridicula Historia de los Seres del Inodoro Morado. 2008. (Captain Underpants Ser.). (SPA., Illus.). 176p. (J). (gr. 2-5). pap. 5.99 (978-0-545-02583-6(4), Scholastic en Espanol) Scholastic, Inc.
—Captain Underpants & the Attack of the Talking Toilets. Pilkey, Dav, illus. 2014. (Captain Underpants Ser.: Bk. 2). (ENG., Illus.). 160p. (J). (gr. 2-5). 9.99 (978-0-545-59932-0(6)) Scholastic, Inc.
—Captain Underpants & the Attack of the Talking Toilets. 2004. (Captain Underpants Ser.: No. 2). (J). lib. bdg. 19.95 (978-0-439-68436-1(6), Scholastic, Inc.) Scholastic, Inc.
—Captain Underpants & the Big, Bad Battle of the Bionic Booger Boy Part 1: The Night of the Nasty Nostril Nuggets. (Captain Underpants Ser.: Bk. 6). (J). 2004. lib. bdg. 19.95 (978-0-439-68438-5(2), Scholastic, Inc.) 2003. (ENG., Illus.). 176p. (gr. 2-5). 18.99 (978-0-439-37609-9(2)) Scholastic, Inc.
—Captain Underpants & the Big, Bad Battle of the Bionic Booger Boy Part 1: The Night of the Nasty Nostril Nuggets. Pilkey, Dav, illus. 2003. (Captain Underpants Ser.: 6). (ENG., Illus.). 176p. (J). (gr. 2-5). pap. 5.99 (978-0-439-37610-5(6)) Scholastic, Inc.
—Captain Underpants & the Big, Bad Battle of the Bionic Booger Boy Part 2: The Revenge of the Ridiculous Robo-Boogers. 2004. (Captain Underpants Ser.: Bk. 7). (J). lib. bdg. 19.95 (978-0-439-68437-8(4), Scholastic, Inc.) Scholastic, Inc.
—Captain Underpants & the Big, Bad Battle of the Bionic Booger Boy Part 2: The Revenge of the Ridiculous Robo-Boogers. Pilkey, Dav, illus. 2003. (Captain Underpants Ser.: 7). (ENG., Illus.). 176p. (J). (gr. 2-5). 18.99 (978-0-439-37611-2(4)); pap. 5.99 (978-0-439-37612-9(2)) Scholastic, Inc.
—Captain Underpants & the Big, Bad Battle of the Bionic Booger Boy Part 2: The Revenge of the Ridiculous Robo-Boogers. 2003. (Captain Underpants Ser.: 7). lib. bdg. 16.00 (978-0-613-68837-6(6), Turtleback) Turtleback Bks.
—Captain Underpants & the Invasion of the Incredibly Naughty Cafeteria Ladies from Outer Space: (and the Subsequent Assault of the Equally Evil Lunchroom Zombie Nerds) 2004. (Captain Underpants Ser.: No. 3). (J). lib. bdg. 19.95 (978-0-439-68439-2(0), Scholastic, Inc.) Scholastic, Inc.
—Captain Underpants & the Invasion of the Incredibly Naughty Cafeteria Ladies from Outer Space: Color Edition. 2014. (Captain Underpants Ser.: 3). (ENG., Illus.). 160p. (J). (gr. 2-5). 9.99 (978-0-545-69470-4(1)) Scholastic, Inc.
—Captain Underpants & the Perilous Plot of Professor Poopypants. 2004. (Captain Underpants Ser.: No. 4). (J). lib. bdg. 19.95 (978-0-439-68440-8(4), Scholastic, Inc.) Scholastic, Inc.
—Captain Underpants & the Sensational Saga of Sir Stinks-a-Lot. Pilkey, Dav, illus. 2015. (Captain Underpants Ser.: 12). (ENG., Illus.). 208p. (J). (gr. 2). 9.99 (978-0-545-50492-8(9)) Scholastic, Inc.
—Captain Underpants & the Sensational Saga of Sir Stinks-a-Lot. Pilkey, Dav, illus. 2015. (Captain Underpants Ser.: 12). (ENG., Illus.). 208p. (J). (gr. 2). lib. bdg. 20.85 (978-0-606-37924-3(X)) Turtleback Bks.
—Captain Underpants & the Wrath of the Wicked Wedgie Woman. 2004. (Captain Underpants Ser.: No. 5). (J). lib. bdg. 19.95 (978-0-439-68441-5(2), Scholastic, Inc.) Scholastic, Inc.
Pilkons, Alyssa. Confessions of a Teenage Lima Bean. 2009. 232p. pap. 14.98 (978-1-4303-1132-4(0)) Lulu Pr., Inc.
Pin, Isabel. Bumblebee Blues. James, J. Alison, tr. from GER. 2003. (Illus.). 32p. (J). (gr. k-3). 15.95 (978-0-7358-1813-2(4)); lib. bdg. 16.50 (978-0-7358-1814-9(2)) North-South Bks., Inc. (Michael Neugebauer Bks.).
Pincus, Gregory K. The Homework Strike. 2017. (ENG.). 272p. (J). (gr. 3-7). 16.99 (978-0-439-91301-0(2)) Scholastic, Inc.
—The 14 Fibs of Gregory K. 2013. (J). pap. (978-0-439-91300-3(4)); (ENG.). 240p. (gr. 3-7). 17.99 (978-0-439-91299-0(7)) Scholastic, Inc. (Levine, Arthur A. Bks.).
Pinder, Eric. I'd Rather Be Riding My Bike. Cardinal, John, illus. l.t. ed. 2013. 42p. (gr. k-1). pap. 10.95 (978-1-62253-401-2(8)) Evolved Publishing.
Pink, Randi. Wearing White. 2016. (ENG.). 288p. (YA). 17.99 (978-1-250-07021-0(X), 9781250070210) Feiwel & Friends.
Pinkwater, Daniel M. The Education of Robert Nifkin. 2005. (ENG.). 192p. (YA). (gr. 7). pap. 12.95 (978-0-618-55208-5(1)) Houghton Mifflin Harcourt Publishing Co.
—Yo-Yo Man. Davis, Jack E., illus. 2007. (ENG.). 32p. (J). (gr. -1-3). 16.99 (978-0-06-055502-3(5)) HarperCollins Pubs.
Pinto, Amy B. Sophie's Perfume. 2012. 100p. 19.95 (978-1-4759-2715-3(0)) iUniverse, Inc.
Piper, Deb. From A— to Zulinski. 2008. (J). pap. (978-0-88092-713-0(5)); lib. bdg. (978-0-88092-712-3(7)) Royal Fireworks Publishing Co.
Pippenger, Jack G. The Young Rebel. 2007. 292p. 27.95 (978-0-595-86314-3(0)); per. 17.95 (978-0-595-41077-4(4)) iUniverse, Inc.
Pitcher, Chelsea. The S-Word. 2013. (ENG.). 320p. pap. 19.99 (978-1-4516-9516-8(0), Gallery Bks.) Gallery Bks.
Pitcock, Tiffany. Just Friends. 2017. (ENG.). 320p. (YA). pap. 10.99 (978-1-250-08405-7(9), 9781250084057) Feiwel & Friends.
Pittar, Gill. Milly, Molly & Henry (book W/dolls) 2006. 28p. pap. (978-1-86972-103-9(9)) Milly Molly Bks.
—Milly, Molly & Jimmy's Seeds (book W/dolls) 2006. 28p. pap. (978-1-86972-091-9(1)) Milly Molly Bks.
—Milly, Molly & the Stowaways (book W/dolls) 2006. 28p. pap. (978-1-86972-106-0(3)) Milly Molly Bks.
Piven, Hanoch. My Best Friend Is as Sharp as a Pencil: And Other Funny Classroom Portraits. 2010. (ENG., Illus.). 40p. (J). (gr. -1-3). 17.99 (978-0-375-85338-8(3), Schwartz & Wade Bks.) Random Hse. Children's Bks.
Pixley, Marcella. Freak. 2013. (ENG.). 160p. (YA). (gr. 7-10). pap. 10.99 (978-1-250-02742-9(X), 9781250027429) Square Fish.
Plourde, Lynn. Book Fair Day. Wickstrom, Thor, illus. 2006. (J). (978-1-4156-8095-7(7), Dutton Juvenile) Penguin Publishing Group.
—Maxi's Secrets: (or What You Can Learn from a Dog) (ENG.). 272p. (J). (gr. 5). 2017. 8.99 **(978-0-399-54568-9(9)**, Puffin Books) 2016. 16.99 (978-0-399-54567-2(0), Nancy Paulsen Books) Penguin Young Readers Group.
Plourde, Lynn. You're Wearing That to School?! Cornelison, Sue, illus. 2013. (ENG.). 32p. (J). (gr. -1-3). 16.99 (978-1-4231-5510-2(6)) Disney Pr.
Plum-Ucci, Carol. The Body of Christopher Creed. 2008. (ENG., Illus.). 272p. (YA). (gr. 7). pap. 7.99 (978-0-15-206386-3(2)) Houghton Mifflin Harcourt Publishing Co.
Poblocki, Dan. The Nightmarys. 2011. (ENG.). 336p. (J). (gr. 3-7). pap. 7.99 (978-0-375-84257-3(8), Yearling) Random Hse. Children's Bks.
Poindexter, Stephanie. Octavious & His Busy Tentacles. 2010. 21p. 13.50 (978-0-557-30136-2(X)) Lulu Pr., Inc.
Pointon, Janet. A Matter of Choice. 2008. 82p. pap. 11.51 (978-1-4092-3108-0(9)) Lulu Pr., Inc.
Polacco, Patricia. The Art of Miss Chew. Polacco, Patricia, illus. 2012. (ENG., Illus.). 40p. (J). (gr. k-3). 17.99 (978-0-399-25703-2(9), G.P. Putnam's Sons Books for Young Readers) Penguin Young Readers Group.
—Bully. Polacco, Patricia, illus. 2012. (ENG., Illus.). 48p. (J). (gr. 2-5). 17.99 (978-0-399-25704-9(7), G.P. Putnam's Sons Books for Young Readers) Penguin Young Readers Group.
—The Junkyard Wonders. Polacco, Patricia, illus. 2010. (ENG., Illus.). 48p. (J). (gr. 1-4). 17.99 (978-0-399-25078-1(6), Philomel Bks.) Penguin Young Readers Group.
—The Lemonade Club. Polacco, Patricia, illus. 2007. (ENG., Illus.). 48p. (J). (gr. 1-4). 17.99 (978-0-399-24540-4(5), Philomel Bks.) Penguin Young Readers Group.
—Mr. Wayne's Masterpiece. Polacco, Patricia, illus. 2014. (ENG., Illus.). 40p. (J). (gr. k-3). 17.99 (978-0-399-16095-0(7), G.P. Putnam's Sons Books for Young Readers) Penguin Young Readers Group.
Polak, Monique. The Leggings Revolt, 1 vol. 2016. (Orca Currents Ser.). (ENG.). 144p. (J). (gr. 5-9). pap. 9.95 (978-1-4598-1189-8(5)) Orca Bk. Pubs. USA.
—Leggings Revolt. 2016. (Orca Currents Ser.). lib. bdg. 20.80 (978-0-606-38696-8(3)) Turtleback Bks.
Polonsky, Ami. Gracefully Grayson. 2016. (ENG., Illus.). 250p. (J). (gr. 5-9). pap. 8.99 (978-1-4847-2365-4(1)) Hyperion Bks. for Children.
—Gracefully Grayson. 2014. (ENG.). 256p. (J). (gr. 5-9). 16.99 (978-1-4231-8527-7(7)) Hyperion Pr.
Polsky, Sara. This Is How I Find Her. (ENG.). 272p. (YA). (gr. 8-12). 2015. pap. 9.99 (978-0-8075-7880-3(0)) 2013. 16.99 (978-0-8075-7877-3(0)) Whitman, Albert & Co.
Pons, Lele & De la Cruz, Melissa. Surviving High School: Do It for the Vine: A Novel. 2017. (ENG.). 272p. (gr. 8). pap. 11.99 (978-1-5011-2054-1(9), Gallery Bks.) Gallery Bks.
Ponti, James. Vanished! 2017. (Framed! Ser.: 2). (ENG., Illus.). 384p. (J). (gr. 3-7). 16.99 **(978-1-4814-3633-5(3)**, Aladdin) Simon & Schuster Children's Publishing.
Popescu, Petru. Birth of the Pack. rev. ed. 2007. (ENG.). 352p. (YA). (gr. 8-12). pap. 20.99 (978-0-7653-1641-7(2), 9780765316417, Tor Teen) Doherty, Tom Assocs., LLC.
Port City High Sample Set: High School High/Taken/Deported/the Public Eye. 2013. (ENG.). (YA). (gr. 8-12). pap. 39.80 (978-1-62250-697-2(9)) Saddleback Educational Publishing, Inc.
Porter, Rhonda. Brody Meets a Bully. 2008. 16p. pap. 24.95 (978-1-60610-311-1(3)) America Star Bks.
Portes, Andrea. Anatomy of a Misfit. 2014. (ENG.). 336p. (YA). (gr. 9). 17.99 (978-0-06-231364-5(9), HarperTeen) HarperCollins Pubs.
Portis, Antoinette. Kindergarten Diary. Portis, Antoinette, illus. 2010. (Illus.). 32p. (J). (gr. -1-3). (ENG.). 12.99 (978-0-06-145691-6(8)); lib. bdg. 14.89 (978-0-06-145692-3(6)) HarperCollins Pubs.
Portman, Frank. King Dork. 2007. 344p. 19.00 (978-0-7569-7950-8(1)) Perfection Learning Corp.
—King Dork. 2008. (ENG.). 368p. (YA). (gr. 9-12). pap. 9.99 (978-0-385-73450-9(6), Delacorte Bks. for Young Readers) Random Hse. Children's Bks.
Poskitt, Kjartan. Agatha Parrot & the Odd Street School Ghost. Hargis, Wes, illus. (ENG.). 160p. (J). (gr. 2-5). 2017. pap. 6.99 (978-0-544-93530-3(6), HMH Books For Young Readers) 2016. 16.99 (978-0-544-50672-5(3)) Houghton Mifflin Harcourt Publishing Co.
Poskitt, Kjartan & Hargis, Wes. Agatha Parrot & the Thirteenth Chicken. 2017. (Agatha Parrot Ser.). (ENG., Illus.). 160p. (J). (gr. 2-5). 16.99 (978-0-544-50909-2(9)) Houghton Mifflin Harcourt Publishing Co.
Posner, Richard. Goodnight Cinderella. 2014. (ENG.). 248p. (J). (gr. 8-11). pap. 15.95 (978-1-59077-314-7(4)) Evans, M. & Co., Inc.
Posner-Sanchez, Andrea. A Royal Pet Problem. RH Disney Staff, illus. 2015. (Little Golden Book Ser.). (ENG.). 24p. (J). (-k). 4.99 (978-0-7364-3308-2(2), Golden/Disney) Random Hse. Children's Bks.
Potter, Dave. Storm Clouds over Mountain View Middle School. 2009. 60p. pap. 9.99 (978-1-60860-665-8(1), Strategic Bk. Publishing) Strategic Book Publishing & Rights Agency (SBPRA).
Potter, Ellen. Going Places. Leng, Qin, illus. 2017. 108p. (J). (978-1-101-93961-1(3)) Knopf, Alfred A. Inc.
—Olivia Kidney & the Secret Beneath the City. 2009. (ENG.). 336p. (J). (gr. 3-7). 9.99 (978-0-14-241263-3(5), Puffin Books) Penguin Young Readers Group.
—Piper Green & the Fairy Tree. Leng, Qin, illus. 2015. (Piper Green & the Fairy Tree Ser.). (ENG.). 112p. (J). (gr. 2-4). pap. 5.99 (978-0-553-49926-1(2), Yearling) Random Hse. Children's Bks.
—Piper Green & the Fairy Tree: Going Places. Leng, Qin, illus. 2017. (Piper Green & the Fairy Tree Ser.). (ENG.). (J). (gr. 2-4). 20.95 **(978-1-4301-2680-5(9))** Live Oak Media.
—Piper Green & the Fairy Tree: Going Places. Leng, Qin, illus. 2017. (Piper Green & the Fairy Tree Ser.). (ENG.). 128p. (J). (gr. 2-4). lib. bdg. 17.99 (978-1-101-93962-8(1), Knopf Bks. for Young Readers) Random Hse. Children's Bks.
—Piper Green & the Fairy Tree: Too Much Good Luck. Leng, Qin, illus. 2015. (Piper Green & the Fairy Tree Ser.). (ENG.). 128p. (J). (gr. 2-4). 14.99 (978-0-553-49927-8(0), Knopf Bks. for Young Readers) Random Hse. Children's Bks.
Powell, Jillian. Sam's Sunflower. Boccardo, Johanna, illus. 2008. (Tadpoles Ser.). (ENG.). 24p. (J). (gr. -1-3). pap. (978-0-7787-3895-4(7)); lib. bdg. (978-0-7787-3864-0(7)) Crabtree Publishing Co.
Powell Zalewski, Amy. Summer School in the City. 2006. (Illus.). 32p. (J). (gr. 1-8). 15.00 (978-0-9773608-2-6(2)) Shiny Red Ball Publishing.
Power, Timothy. The Boy Who Howled. 2012. (ENG.). 272p. (YA). (gr. 3-12). pap. 7.99 (978-1-59990-852-6(2), 9781599908526, Bloomsbury USA Childrens) Bloomsbury Publishing USA.
Poydar, Nancy. The Bad-News Report Card. Poydar, Nancy, illus. 2006. (ENG., Illus.). 32p. (J). (gr. -1-3). 16.95 (978-0-8234-1992-0(4)) Holiday Hse., Inc.
—The Biggest Test in the Universe. Poydar, Nancy, illus. 2005. (ENG., Illus.). 32p. (J). (gr. -1-3). 16.95 (978-0-8234-1944-9(4)) Holiday Hse., Inc.
—Bunny Business. 2003. (ENG., Illus.). 32p. (J). (gr. k-3). tchr. ed. 16.95 (978-0-8234-1771-1(9)) Holiday Hse., Inc.
—Fish School. 2009. (ENG., Illus.). 32p. (J). (gr. -1-3). 16.95 (978-0-8234-2140-4(6)) Holiday Hse., Inc.
—The Perfectly Horrible Halloween. Poydar, Nancy, illus. 2005. (ENG., Illus.). 32p. (J). (gr. k-3). pap. 6.95 (978-0-8234-1769-8(7)) Holiday Hse., Inc.
—Zip, Zip... Homework. Poydar, Nancy, illus. 2008. (ENG., Illus.). 32p. (J). (gr. -1-3). 16.95 (978-0-8234-2090-2(6)) Holiday Hse., Inc.
Prasad, Sheela. Apocrit. 2012. 348p. 30.00 (978-0-615-66700-3(7)) Silent Hse. Pr.
Pratts, Christine. Tabby Wise for School Secretary. 2005. 61p. pap. 8.99 (978-1-4116-4935-4(4)) Lulu Pr., Inc.
Preble, Laura. The Queen Geek Social Club. 2006. (ENG.). 336p. (YA). (gr. 7-18). 15.00 (978-0-425-21164-9(9), Berkley) Penguin Publishing Group.
Preller, James. Bystander. 2011. (ENG.). 256p. (YA). (gr. 5-9). pap. 8.99 (978-0-312-54796-7(X), 9780312547967) Square Fish.
—Jigsaw Jones: The Case of the Glow in the Dark Ghost. 2017. (Jigsaw Jones Mysteries Ser.). (ENG., Illus.). 96p. (J). pap. 4.99 (978-1-250-11020-6(3), 9781250110206) Feiwel & Friends.
—Jigsaw Jones: The Case of the Smelly Sneaker. 2017. (Jigsaw Jones Mysteries Ser.). (ENG.). 96p. (J). pap. 4.99 (978-1-250-11080-0(7), 9781250110800) Feiwel & Friends.
—Jigsaw Jones: the Case from Outer Space. 2017. (Jigsaw Jones Mysteries Ser.). (ENG., Illus.). 96p. (J). pap. 4.99 (978-1-250-11017-6(3), 9781250110176) Feiwel & Friends.
—Jigsaw Jones: the Case of the Bicycle Bandit. 2017. (Jigsaw Jones Mysteries Ser.). (ENG., Illus.). 96p. (J). pap. 4.99 (978-1-250-11084-8(X), 9781250110848) Feiwel & Friends.
—Jigsaw Jones: the Case of the Mummy Mystery. 2017. (Jigsaw Jones Mysteries Ser.). (ENG., Illus.). 96p. (J). pap. 4.99 (978-1-250-11082-4(3), 9781250110824) Feiwel & Friends.
—A Pirate's Guide to First Grade. Ruth, Greg, illus. 2013. (ENG.). 48p. (J). (gr. -1-1). 7.99 (978-1-250-02721-4(7), 9781250027214) Square Fish.
—A Pirate's Guide to First Grade. 2013. (J). lib. bdg. 18.40 (978-0-606-31896-9(8), Turtleback) Turtleback Bks.
—A Pirate's Guide to Recess. Ruth, Greg, illus. 2013. (ENG.). 36p. (J). (gr. -1-1). 16.99 (978-1-250-00515-1(9), 9781250005151) Feiwel & Friends.
Prendergast, Gabrielle. Audacious, 1 vol. 2015. (ENG.). 336p. (YA). (gr. 8-12). pap. 12.95 (978-1-4598-0264-3(0)) Orca Bk. Pubs. USA.
Press, J. Abra-Ca-Doodle! 2013. (Doodles of Sam Dibble Ser.: 4). lib. bdg. 14.75 (978-0-606-32125-9(X), Turtleback) Turtleback Bks.
—The Doodles of Sam Dibble. Kline, Michael, illus. 2013. (Doodles of Sam Dibble Ser.: 1). (ENG.). 128p. (J). (gr. 1-3). pap. 4.99 (978-0-448-46107-6(2)); No. 4. 4.99 (978-0-448-46110-6(2)) Penguin Young Readers Group. (Grosset & Dunlap).
—The Doodles of Sam Dibble. 2013. (Doodles of Sam Dibble Ser.: 1). lib. bdg. 14.75 (978-0-606-29777-6(4), Turtleback) Turtleback Bks.
—Double Trouble #2. Kline, Michael, illus. 2013. (Doodles of Sam Dibble Ser.: 2). (ENG.). 128p. (J). (gr. 1-3). pap. 4.99 (978-0-448-46108-3(0), Grosset & Dunlap) Penguin Young Readers Group.
Preston, Mary Lou. Do You Know What Wildcats Do at School in P. E. Class? Wildcat's First Day in Class. 2006. (J). pap. 8.00 (978-0-8059-7013-5(4)) Dorrance Publishing Co., Inc.
Prévert, Jacques. En Sortant de l'Ecole. (FRE.). (J). pap. (978-2-07-050633-0(9)) Gallimard, Editions FRA. Dist: Distribooks, Inc.
Price, Allison W. A. The Dragons & the Words of Knowledge. 2009. 112p. pap. 14.98 (978-0-557-05766-5(3)) Lulu Pr., Inc.
Priddy, Roger & Crimi-Trent, Ellen. Making Friends. 2013. (Schoolies Ser.). (ENG., Illus.). 28p. (J). (gr. -1-1). 4.99 (978-0-312-51610-9(X), 9780312516109, Priddy Bks.) St. Martin's Pr.
—My School Day. 2013. (Schoolies Ser.). (ENG., Illus.). 32p. (J). (gr. -1-1). 14.99 (978-0-312-51607-9(X), 9780312516079, Priddy Bks.) St. Martin's Pr.
—School House. 2013. (Schoolies Ser.). (ENG., Illus.). 14p. (J). (gr. -1-1). 14.99 (978-0-312-51613-0(4), 9780312516130, Priddy Bks.) St. Martin's Pr.
Priest, A. L. Breakthrough. 2014. (Red Zone Ser.: 2). (ENG.). 104p. (YA). (gr. 6-12). pap. 7.95 (978-1-4677-4472-0(7), Darby Creek) Lerner Publishing Group.
Primavera, Elise. Louise the Big Cheese & the Back-To-School Smarty-Pants. Goode, Diane, illus. 2011. (ENG.). 40p. (J). (gr. k-3). 16.99 (978-1-4424-0600-1(3), Simon & Schuster/Paula Wiseman Bks.) Simon & Schuster/Paula Wiseman Bks.

S

Prime, Derek. Sarah & Paul Go Back to School Bk. 1: Discover about God & the Bible. 2006. (Sarah & Paul Ser.). (ENG., Illus.). 128p. (J). (gr. 2-5). per. 6.99 *(978-1-84550-157-0(8)*, df1071c4-5480-4c1a-9480-a93d741bf494) Christian Focus Pubns. GBR. Dist: Bookmasters Distribution.

Prinz, Yvonne. Still There, Clare. 2005. (ENG.). 4p. (J). pap., tchr. ed. *(978-1-55192-821-0(3))* Raincoast Bk. Distribution CAN. Dist: Publishers Group West (PGW).

Prisant, Guillermo Murray. Que Miedo! rev. ed. 2006. (Castillo del Terror Ser.). (SPA & ENG.). 112p. (J). (gr. 6-9). pap. 6.95 *(978-970-20-0338-0(5))* Castillo, Ediciones, S. A. de C. V. MEX. Dist: Macmillan.

Prochovnic, Dawn Babb. The Best Day in Room A: Sign Language for School Activities, 1 vol. Bauer, Stephanie, illus. 2009. (Story Time with Signs & Rhymes Ser.). (ENG.). 32p. (gr. -1-3). 28.50 *(978-1-60270-667-5(0)*, Looking Glass Library) ABDO Publishing Co.

Prom Crashers. 2014. (Romantic Comedies Ser.). (ENG., Illus.). 256p. (YA). (gr. 9). pap. 12.99 *(978-1-4814-2747-0(4)*, Simon Pulse) Simon Pulse.

Prom Etiquette Scrapbook. 2011. 128p. 8.99 *(978-1-4231-4566-0(6))* Disney Pr.

Prom: He Said/She Said. 2011. 256p. (J). 12.99 *(978-1-4231-4565-3(8))* Disney Pr.

Prose, Francine. After. 2003. 336p. (J). (gr. 5-18). lib. bdg. 17.89 *(978-0-06-008082-2(5)*, Cotler, Joanna Books) 2004. (ENG.). 352p. (YA). (gr. 8). reprint ed. pap. 9.99 *(978-0-06-008083-9(3)*, HarperTeen) HarperCollins Pubs.

—Bullyville. 2007. 260p. (YA). (gr. 7-12). 16.99 *(978-0-06-057497-0(6))*; lib. bdg. 17.89 *(978-0-06-057498-7(4))* HarperCollins Pubs. (HarperTeen).

—Bullyville. 2011. 10.36 *(978-0-7848-3625-5(6)*, Everbind) Marco Bk. Co.

—Touch. 2010. (ENG.). 272p. (YA). (gr. 9). pap. 8.99 *(978-0-06-137519-4(5)*, HarperTeen) HarperCollins Pubs.

Publications International Ltd. Staff. Little Lift & Listen Sound Dora Go to School. 2007. 12p. (J). 10.98 *(978-1-4127-8575-4(8)*, PIL Kids) Publications International, Ltd.

Publications International Ltd. Staff, ed. Finding Nemo - Let's Go to School. 2011. 12p. (J). bds. *(978-1-4508-0510-0(8))* Publications International, Ltd.

—Record-A-Memory School Years. 2011. 16p. (J). 25.98 *(978-1-4508-1341-9(0))* Publications International, Ltd.

Pugh, Tracey D. A Show & Tell Lesson. McCracken, Jaime, photos by. l.t. ed. 2006. (Illus.). 32p. (J). 12.95 *(978-1-59879-105-1(2))* Lifevest Publishing, Inc.

Pugin-Rodas, M. C. The Eight Ball Club: Ocean of Fire. 2007. (ENG., Illus.). 144p. pap. 15.95 *(978-0-9793761-2-2(2))* ESOL Publishing.

Pugliano-Martin, Carol. My Little Red Lunchbox Book. Ottinger, Jon, illus. 2004. (Sparkle Shape Bks.). 10p. (J). (gr. -1-18). bds. 6.99 *(978-1-57151-716-6(2))* Playhouse Publishing.

Pulver, Robin. The Case of the Incapacitated Capitals. Reed, Lynn Rowe, illus. 2012. (ENG.). 32p. (J). (gr. -1-3). 16.95 *(978-0-8234-2402-3(2))* Holiday Hse., Inc.

—The Case of the Incapacitated Capitals. Reed, Lynn Rowe, illus. 2013. (ENG.). 32p. (J). (gr. -1-3). pap. 7.99 *(978-0-8234-2914-1(8))* Holiday Hse., Inc.

—Happy Endings: A Story about Suffixes. Reed, Lynn Rowe, illus. 2013. (ENG.). (J). (gr. 1-3). pap. 44.95 *(978-1-4301-1435-2(5))* Live Oak Media.

—Happy Endings: A Story about Suffixes. 2013. 18.95 *(978-1-4301-1433-8(9))* Live Oak Media.

—Me First! Prefixes Lead the Way. Reed, Lynn Rowe, illus. 2016. (ENG.). 32p. (J). 16.95 *(978-0-8234-3644-6(6))* Holiday Hse., Inc.

—Never Say Boo! Lucke, Deb, illus. 2009. (ENG.). 32p. (J). (gr. -1-3). 16.95 *(978-0-8234-2110-7(4))* Holiday Hse., Inc.

—Nouns & Verbs Have a Field Day. Reed, Lynn Rowe, illus. 2007. (ENG.). 32p. (J). (gr. -1-3). 7.99 *(978-0-8234-2097-1(3))* Holiday Hse., Inc.

—Nouns & Verbs Have a Field Day. Reed, Lynn Rowe, illus. 2013. pap. 18.95 incl. audio compact disk *(978-1-4301-1115-3(1))* Live Oak Media.

—Persuading Miss Doover. Sisson, Stéphanie Roth, illus. 2015. (J). *(978-0-8234-3426-8(5))* Holiday Hse., Inc.

—Punctuation Takes a Vacation. Reed, Lynn Rowe, illus. 2004. (ENG.). 32p. (J). (gr. k-3). reprint ed. pap. 7.99 *(978-0-8234-1820-6(0))* Holiday Hse., Inc.

—Punctuation Takes a Vacation. Reed, Lynn Rowe, illus. 2009. (J). (gr. 1-3). 29.95 incl. audio compact disk *(978-1-4301-0708-8(1))* Live Oak Media.

—Silent Letters Loud & Clear. Reed, Lynn Rowe, illus. (ENG.). 32p. (J). (gr. 1-3). 2010. pap. 7.99 *(978-0-8234-2309-5(3))* 2008. 16.95 *(978-0-8234-2127-5(9))* Holiday Hse., Inc.

—Thank You, Miss Doover. Sisson, Stéphanie Roth, illus. 2010. (ENG.). 32p. (J). (gr. k-3). 17.95 *(978-0-8234-2046-9(9))* Holiday Hse., Inc.

Pulver, Robin & Reed, Lynn Rowe. Happy Endings: A Story about Suffixes. 2012. (ENG., Illus.). 32p. (J). pap. 7.95 *(978-0-8234-2434-4(0))* Holiday Hse., Inc.

Pung, Alice. Lucy & Linh. 2016. (ENG.). 352p. (YA). (gr. 7). 17.99 *(978-0-399-55048-5(8)*, Knopf Bks. for Young Readers) Random Hse. Children's Bks.

—Marly's Business. 2016. (Our Australian Girl Ser.: 2). (ENG.). 144p. (J). (gr. 3-7). 7.99 *(978-0-14-330850-8(5))* Penguin Books Australia AUS. Dist: Independent Pubs. Group.

Pung, Alice & Masciullo, Lucia. Marly Walks on the Moon. 2016. (Our Australian Girl Ser.: 4). (ENG.). 144p. (J). (gr. 3-7). 12.99 *(978-0-14-330852-2(1))* Penguin Books Australia AUS. Dist: Independent Pubs. Group.

Purves, William C. Fairmont Forever. 2011. 180p. pap. 13.95 *(978-1-4502-3878-6(5))* iUniverse, Inc.

Puttock, Simon. Mouse's First Night at Moonlight School. Pye, Ali, illus. 2015. (ENG.). 32p. (J). (gr. -1-2). 16.99 *(978-0-7636-7607-0(1)*, Nosy Crow) Candlewick Pr.

Quackenbush, Robert. First Grade Jitters. Nascimbene, Yan, illus. 2010. (ENG.). 32p. (J). (gr. k-2). 16.99 *(978-0-06-077632-9(3))* HarperCollins Pubs.

Qualls, Shirley. Marigold Duck Comes to Our School. 2009. 28p. pap. 12.49 *(978-1-4389-8386-8(7))* AuthorHouse.

Queen Rania of Jordan Al Abdullah Staff, et al. The Sandwich Swap. Tusa, Tricia, illus. 2010. (ENG.). 32p. (J). (gr. -1-2). 16.99 *(978-1-4231-2484-9(7))* Hyperion Pr.

Quick, Matthew. Boy21. 2013. (ENG.). 272p. (YA). (gr. 7-17). pap. 10.99 *(978-0-316-12796-7(5))* Little, Brown Bks. for Young Readers.

—Sorta Like a Rock Star. 2011. (ENG.). 384p. (YA). (gr. 7-17). pap., pap. 10.99 *(978-0-316-04353-3(2))* Little, Brown Bks. for Young Readers.

Quintanilla, Billie. Never Again a Homeless Christmas! 2012. 28p. pap. 24.95 *(978-1-4626-5197-9(6))* America Star Bks.

Quintero, Isabel. Gabi, a Girl in Pieces. 2014. (ENG.). 208p. (J). pap. 11.95 *(978-1-935955-95-5(0))*; (YA). 17.95 *(978-1-935955-94-8(2))* Cinco Puntos Pr.

Quintero, Sofia. Efrain's Secret. 2011. (ENG.). 276p. (YA). (gr. 9). pap. 8.99 *(978-0-440-24062-4(X)*, Ember) Random Hse. Children's Bks.

Quitzel, Ivey. Out of Control. 2009. 132p. pap. 11.00 *(978-0-557-08762-4(7))* Lulu Pr., Inc.

R. N., Lavanya. The Bookworm. Suleman, Shilo Shiv, illus. 2013. (ENG.). 32p. (J). (gr. k). pap. 9.95 *(978-81-8190-180-4(0))* Karadi Tales Co. Pvt, Ltd. IND. Dist: Consortium Bk. Sales & Distribution.

Rach, W. Dennis. The Goofy Principal at Silly School. 2007. (J). per. *(978-0-9792579-0-2(5))* Rach, W. Dennis.

Rad, Charles J. The Boy they called a Snowball. 2007. 140p. pap. 20.95 *(978-1-84753-461-3(9))* Lulu Pr., Inc.

Rae, Angela. All of Us. 2009. 81p. pap. 12.99 *(978-0-557-05491-6(5))* Lulu Pr., Inc.

—The Choices Witch Make Us. 2008. 113p. pap. 15.95 *(978-1-4357-4287-1(7))* Lulu Pr., Inc.

Rae, Kristin. What You Always Wanted: An If Only Novel. 2016. (If Only... Ser.). (ENG.). 320p. (YA). pap. 9.99 *(978-1-61963-345-2(0)*, 9781619633452, Bloomsbury USA Childrens) Bloomsbury Publishing USA.

Raiku, Makoto, contrib. by. Zatchbell!, Vol. 3. 2005. 200p. 9.99 *(978-1-4215-0208-3(9))* Viz Media.

Raines, Jennifer. Alex & Andrew Swap Places. 2008. 32p. per. 24.95 *(978-1-4241-8938-0(1))* America Star Bks.

Rainey. School Is Cool. Huggens, Karin, illus. 2004. (J). *(978-0-9666199-9-7(4))* DreamDog Pr.

Rameaka, Thomas. Bee Haven. 2006. (ENG.). 188p. per. 24.95 *(978-1-4241-5646-7(7))* America Star Bks.

Ramesh, Serita. Jason & the Ingenious Number Trick: A Story about Patterns. 2010. 28p. pap. 15.49 *(978-1-4490-4740-5(8))* AuthorHouse.

Ramirez, Terry. Growing up with Olivi: The Beguiling Blue-Haired Beauty of Boysenberry Lane. 2009. 96p. pap. 9.95 *(978-0-595-47668-8(6))* iUniverse, Inc.

Ramona Quimby, Age 8. 2005. (J). *(978-1-59564-976-8(X))* Steps To Literacy, LLC.

Ramos, Juan Antonio. El Principe de Blancanieves. (Torre de Papel Ser.). (SPA.). (J). (gr. 4-18). 8.95 *(978-958-04-3943-1(5))* Norma S.A. COL. Dist: Distribuidora Norma, Inc.

Ramos, Pilar. UN LARGO DIA. (SPA.). 32p. (J). 10.00 *(978-84-342-2518-3(2))* Parramon Ediciones S.A. ESP. Dist: Distribuidora Norma, Inc.

Randall, Thomas. The Waking: A Winter of Ghosts. 2011. (YA). pap. 9.99 *(978-1-59990-252-4(4)*, Bloomsbury USA Childrens) Bloomsbury Publishing USA.

—The Waking: Dreams of the Dead. 2nd ed. 2010. (ENG., Illus.). 304p. (YA). (gr. 7-18). pap. 8.99 *(978-1-59990-585-3(X)*, 9781599905853, Bloomsbury USA Childrens) Bloomsbury Publishing USA.

Randall, Thomas & Golden, Christopher. Spirits of the Noh. 2011. (ENG.). 272p. (YA). (gr. 7-18). pap. 9.99 *(978-1-59990-251-7(6)*, 9781599902517, Bloomsbury USA Childrens) Bloomsbury Publishing USA.

Randle, Kristen D. The Only Alien on the Planet. 2009. (ENG.). 240p. (YA). (gr. 7-12). pap. 11.99 *(978-1-4022-2669-4(1)*, 9781402226694, Sourcebooks Jabberwocky) Sourcebooks, Inc.

—Slumming. 2003. (Illus.). 240p. (J). lib. bdg. 16.89 *(978-0-06-001023-2(1)*, HarperTeen) HarperCollins Pubs.

Random House. Farm Alarm! (Team Umizoomi) Fruchter, Jason, illus. 2014. (Step into Reading Ser.). (ENG.). 24p. (J). (gr. -1-1). pap. 3.99 *(978-0-385-38508-4(0)*, Random Hse. Bks. for Young Readers) Random Hse. Children's Bks.

Random House & McAnulty, Stacy. Goldie Blox Rules the School! Random House, illus. 2017. (Stepping Stone Book(TM) Ser.). (ENG., Illus.). 128p. (J). (gr. 1-4). 6.99 *(978-0-399-55634-0(6)*, Random Hse. Bks. for Young Readers) Random Hse. Children's Bks.

Random House Staff. Time for School! (Bubble Guppies) Random House Staff, illus. 2013. (Pictureback(R) Ser.). (ENG., Illus.). 16p. (J). (gr. -1-2). pap. 4.99 *(978-0-449-81447-5(5)*, Random Hse. Bks. for Young Readers) Random Hse. Children's Bks.

Rankin, Laura. Ruthie & the (Not So) Teeny Tiny Lie. Rankin, Laura, illus. 2007. (ENG., Illus.). 32p. (J). (gr. -1-3). 17.99 *(978-1-59990-010-0(6)*, 9781599900100, Bloomsbury USA Childrens) Bloomsbury Publishing USA.

Ransom, Candice. Amanda Panda Quits Kindergarten. Grove, Christine, illus. 2017. (ENG.). 32p. (J). (gr. -1-2). 17.99 *(978-0-399-55455-1(6)*, Doubleday Bks. for Young Readers) Random Hse. Children's Bks.

Ransom, Jeanie Franz. Don't Squeal Unless It's a Big Deal: A Tale of Tattletales. Urbanovic, Jackie, illus. 2005. (J). 32p. 14.95 *(978-1-59147-239-1(3))*; 28p. (gr. -1-3). pap. 9.95 *(978-1-59147-240-7(7))* American Psychological Assn. (Magination Pr.).

—There's a Cat in Our Class! A Tale about Getting Along. Langdo, Bryan, illus. 2016. 32p. (J). *(978-1-4338-2262-9(8)*, Magination Pr.) American Psychological Assn.

Rapson, Helen. Reggie Did It!, 1 vol. 2009. 49p. pap. 16.95 *(978-1-60813-161-7(0))* America Star Bks.

Rasheed, Leila. Socks, Shocks & Secrets. 2013. (Fantastic Diary of Bathsheba Claric de Trop Ser.). 293p. (J). pap. 5.99 *(978-0-7945-3029-7(X)*, Usborne) EDC Publishing.

Rateau, Loy. David's Prayers: A Boy's Perseverance of Conquering the Enemy. 2005. 17.00 *(978-0-8059-9834-4(9))* Dorrance Publishing Co., Inc.

Rather, Sherri. Upside down Danny, 1 vol. Rather, Sherri, illus. 2009. (Illus.). 27p. pap. 24.95 *(978-1-61582-924-8(5))* America Star Bks.

Rathmann, Peggy. Ruby the Copycat. 2006. (ENG., Illus.). 32p. (J). (gr. -1-3). per. 6.99 *(978-0-439-47228-9(8)*, Teaching Resources) Scholastic, Inc.

Ray, Delia. Ghost Girl: A Blue Ridge Mountain Story. 2016. (ENG.). 272p. (J). (gr. 5-7). pap. 6.99 *(978-0-544-70633-0(1)*, HMH Books For Young Readers) Houghton Mifflin Harcourt Publishing Co.

—Here Lies Linc. (ENG.). 320p. (J). (gr. 3-7). 2012. 7.99 *(978-0-375-86538-1(1)*, Yearling) 2011. 16.99 *(978-0-375-86757-6(0)*, Knopf Bks. for Young Readers) Random Hse. Children's Bks.

Ray, Gracie. Falling Slowly. 2012. 270p. *(978-1-105-59084-9(4))* Lulu.com.

Reagan, Jean. How to Amaze a Teacher. Wildish, Lee, illus. 2017. (ENG.). 32p. (J). (gr. -1-3). 17.99 *(978-0-553-53825-0(X)*, Knopf Bks. for Young Readers) Random Hse. Children's Bks.

Real Bout High School, Vol. 6. 2005. (YA). pap. 9.99 *(978-1-59182-523-4(7))* TOKYOPOP, Inc.

RealBuzz Studios Staff. Hits & Misses. 2007. 128p. (YA). No. 1. pap. 4.97 *(978-1-59789-569-9(5))*No. 3. pap. 4.97 *(978-1-59789-571-2(7))*No. 4. pap. 4.97 *(978-1-59789-572-9(5))* Barbour Publishing, Inc. (Barbour Bks.).

Reasoner, Charles. A Day at School. 2009. (Inside Outside Board Bks.). (Illus.). (J). bds. 10.99 *(978-1-934650-56-1(0))* Just For Kids Pr., LLC.

Reavis, Vicky 'A' Blevins. The Night Before Christmas. 2013. 72p. pap. 17.95 *(978-1-4241-2838-9(2))* America Star Bks.

Reber, Deborah & Goode, Caroline. Love, Love, Love: Language of Love; Cupidity. 2010. (ENG.). 480p. (YA). (gr. 7-18). mass mkt. 9.99 *(978-1-4424-0313-0(6)*, Simon Pulse) Simon Pulse.

Recess. 2004. (At School Ser.). (J). 7.33 *(978-1-58453-268-2(8))* Pioneer Valley Bks.

Rech, Lindsay Faith. It Started with a Dare. 2010. (ENG.). 312p. (YA). (gr. 7-18). pap. 17.99 *(978-0-547-23558-5(5))* Houghton Mifflin Harcourt Publishing Co.

Recorvits, Helen. My Name Is Yoon. Swiatkowska, Gabi, illus. 2003. (ENG.). 32p. (J). (gr. -1-3). 17.99 *(978-0-374-35114-4(7)*, 9780374351144, Farrar, Straus & Giroux (BYR)) Farrar, Straus & Giroux.

—My Name Is Yoon. Swiatkowska, Gabi, illus. 2014. (ENG.). 32p. (J). (gr. -1-3). 6.99 *(978-1-250-05711-2(6)*, 9781250057112) Square Fish.

Recorvits, Helen & Recorvits, H. Yoon & the Jade Bracelet. Swiatkowska, Gabi, illus. 2008. (ENG.). 32p. (J). (gr. -1-3). 18.99 *(978-0-374-38689-4(7)*, 9780374386894, Farrar, Straus & Giroux (BYR)) Farrar, Straus & Giroux.

Red & Green Choices by Green Irene: Niki's Next Grade. 2003. (J). per. 14.50 *(978-0-9742280-1-3(X))* Green Irene.

Redgate, Riley. Noteworthy. 2017. (ENG.). 400p. (YA). (gr. 8-17). 17.95 *(978-1-4197-2373-5(1)*, Amulet Bks.) Abrams, Inc.

—Seven Ways We Lie. (ENG.). 2017. 368p. (YA). pap. 9.95 *(978-1-4197-2348-3(0))* 2016. 352p. (J). (gr. 8-17). 17.95 *(978-1-4197-1944-8(0))* Abrams, Inc. (Amulet Bks.).

Reece, Colleen L. Wilderness Warriors. 2012. 114p. 18.95 *(978-1-61633-309-6(X))*; pap. 8.95 *(978-1-61633-310-2(3))* Guardian Angel Publishing, Inc.

Reed, Amy Lynn. The Nowhere Girls. 2017. (YA). pap. ***(978-1-4814-8174-8(6)***, Simon Pulse) Simon Pulse.

Reedy, Trent. Divided We Fall. 2014. (Divided We Fall Ser.: 1). (ENG.). 384p. (J). (gr. 9). pap. 9.99 *(978-0-545-54368-2(1))*; 17.99 *(978-0-545-54367-5(3))* Scholastic, Inc. (Levine, Arthur A. Bks.).

Rees, Douglas. Uncle Pirate. Auth, Tony, illus. (ENG.). 112p. (J). (gr. 2-5). 2009. pap. 6.99 *(978-1-4169-4763-9(9))* 2008. 15.99 *(978-1-4169-4762-2(0))* McElderry, Margaret K. Bks. (McElderry, Margaret K. Bks.).

—Uncle Pirate to the Rescue. Auth, Tony, illus. 2010. (ENG.). 112p. (J). (gr. 2-5). pap. 6.99 *(978-1-4169-7505-2(5)*, McElderry, Margaret K. Bks.) McElderry, Margaret K. Bks.

—Vampire High. 2010. (ENG.). 240p. (YA). (gr. 7-18). pap. 9.99 *(978-0-385-73920-7(6)*, Delacorte Bks. for Young Readers) Random Hse. Children's Bks.

Reeves, Pamela. United We Stand, a Story about Two Bullies. LaGrange, Tiffany, illus. 2009. 24p. pap. 12.95 *(978-1-936051-36-6(2))* Peppertree Pr., The.

Regan, Peter. Riverside: Spring Fever. 2007. (ENG.). 112p. (J). pap. 10.95 *(978-1-901737-56-1(X))* Anvil Bks., Ltd. IRL. Dist: Dufour Editions, Inc.

Reid, David. The Shade Girls Were Right. 2012. (ENG.). 23p. (J). pap. 14.95 *(978-1-4327-8179-8(0))* Outskirts Pr., Inc.

Reid, Isabelle. Serafina Moon. 2009. 48p. pap. *(978-1-84923-771-0(9))* YouWriteOn.

Reilly, Carmel & Young, Karen. Buzz & Zip Get Lost. 2008. (Rigby Focus Forward: Level G Ser.). (Illus.). 24p. (J). (gr. 4-7). pap. *(978-1-4190-3704-7(8)*, Rigby) Pearson Education Australia.

Reindeer Flight School. 2003. (J). per. *(978-1-57657-920-6(4))*; per. *(978-1-57657-808-7(9))* Paradise Pr., Inc.

Reinhardt, Dana. A Brief Chapter in My Impossible Life. 2007. (ENG.). 256p. (YA). (gr. 9-12). pap. 8.99 *(978-0-375-84691-5(3)*, Ember) Random Hse. Children's Bks.

—We Are the Goldens. 2015. (ENG.). 208p. (YA). (gr. 9). pap. 9.99 *(978-0-385-74258-0(4)*, Ember) Random Hse. Children's Bks.

Reisman, Michael. Simon Bloom, the Gravity Keeper. 2009. (ENG.). 320p. (J). (gr. 3-7). 8.99 *(978-0-14-241368-5(2)*, Puffin Books) Penguin Young Readers Group.

Reisz, Kristopher. Unleashed. 2010. (ENG.). 352p. (YA). (gr. 9). pap. 9.99 *(978-1-4424-0637-7(2)*, Simon Pulse) Simon Pulse.

Reiter, Douglas. Back to School in Cedar Heights. 2006. 79p. pap. 19.95 *(978-1-4137-9058-0(5))* America Star Bks.

Rempel, Leah. Hey, Hmong Girl, Whassup? The Journal of Choua Vang. 2004. (Illus.). v, 138p. (YA). pap. *(978-0-9723721-5-2(6))* Hamline Univ. Pr.

Remza, Freddie. Ride the Wave. 2011. 272p. pap. 16.95 *(978-1-4327-6642-9(2))* Outskirts Pr., Inc.

Renee Daeumler Thompson. I Made a Bad Choice. 2009. 16p. pap. 8.49 *(978-1-4389-7561-0(9))* AuthorHouse.

Rennert, Laura Joy. Emma, the Extra Ordinary Princess. Florian, Melanie, illus. 2009. (J). *(978-0-525-42152-8(1)*, Dutton Juvenile) Penguin Publishing Group.

Rennison, Louise. A Midsummer Tights Dream. 2013. (Misadventures of Tallulah Casey Ser.: 2). (ENG.). 272p. (YA). (gr. 8). pap. 9.99 *(978-0-06-179938-9(6)*, HarperTeen) HarperCollins Pubs.

Rentala, Sita Kanaka Valli. Ocean Flows: In Prose: Zcumby's Judo (on Global Warming) 2010. 44p. (J). pap. 19.99 *(978-1-4490-8780-7(9))* AuthorHouse.

Rentas, Donna. Leticia Goes to School. 2008. 16p. pap. 24.95 *(978-1-4241-8966-3(7))* America Star Bks.

Restle, Hope Madeline. Brianna in Pink. 2007. 156p. per. 11.95 *(978-0-595-47401-1(2))* iUniverse, Inc.

Revenge of the Bully. 2014. (How to Beat the Bully Ser.). (ENG., Illus.). 288p. (J). (gr. 3-7). 17.99 *(978-1-4424-5677-8(9)*, Simon & Schuster/Paula Wiseman Bks.) Simon & Schuster/Paula Wiseman Bks.

Rex, Adam. Fat Vampire: A Never Coming of Age Story. 2011. (ENG.). 336p. (YA). (gr. 9). pap. 8.99 *(978-0-06-192092-9(4))* HarperCollins Pubs.

—School's First Day of School. Robinson, Christian, illus. 2016. (ENG.). 40p. (J). (gr. -1-3). 17.99 *(978-1-59643-964-1(5)*, 9781596439641) Roaring Brook Pr.

Rex, Michael. The Egg of Misery. Rex, Michael, illus. 2012. (Fangbone! Third Grade Barbarian Ser.). (ENG., Illus.). 128p. (J). (gr. 2-4). E-Book *(978-1-101-55043-4(0)*, G.P. Putnam's Sons Books for Young Readers) Penguin Young Readers Group.

—The Egg of Misery: Fangbone, Third Grade Barbarian. Rex, Michael, illus. 2012. (Fangbone! Third Grade Barbarian Ser.: 2). (ENG., Illus.). 128p. (J). (gr. 2-4). 7.99 *(978-0-399-25522-9(2)*, G.P. Putnam's Sons Books for Young Readers) Penguin Young Readers Group.

—Fangbone! Third-Grade Barbarian. 2012. (Illus.). 120p. (J). *(978-0-545-44042-4(4)*, Putnam Juvenile) Penguin Publishing Group.

Rey, H. A. Time for School. 2011. (Curious George Ser.). (ENG., Illus.). 16p. (J). (gr. -1-3). 5.99 *(978-0-547-42230-5(X))* Houghton Mifflin Harcourt Publishing Co.

Rey, H. A., et al. Curious George & the Firefighters. 2007. (Curious George Ser.). (ENG., Illus.). 24p. (J). (gr. -1-3). bds. 11.99 *(978-0-618-89194-8(3))* Houghton Mifflin Harcourt Publishing Co.

Rey, Margret & Rey, H. A. Curious George's First Day of School. Hines, Anna Grossnickle, illus. 2005. (Curious George Ser.). (ENG.). 24p. (J). (gr. -1-3). 13.99 *(978-0-618-60563-7(0))*; pap. 4.99 *(978-0-618-60564-4(9))* Houghton Mifflin Harcourt Publishing Co.

—Curious George's First Day of School. Vipah Interactive Staff, illus. 2005. (Read along Book & CD Ser.). (ENG.). 24p. (J). (gr. -1-3). audio compact disk 10.99 *(978-0-618-60565-1(7))* Houghton Mifflin Harcourt Publishing Co.

Reynolds, Aaron. Tiger Moth: Adventures of an Insect Ninja, 1 vol. Lervold, Erik, illus. 2011. (Tiger Moth Ser.). (ENG.). 128p. (gr. 2-5). pap. 7.95 *(978-1-4342-3032-4(5)*, Graphic Sparks) Stone Arch Bks.

Reynolds, Aaron & Rash, Andy. Superhero School. Rash, Andy, illus. 2009. (ENG., Illus.). 32p. (J). (gr. k-2). 17.99 *(978-1-59990-166-4(8)*, 9781599901664, Bloomsbury USA Childrens) Bloomsbury Publishing USA.

Reynolds, Paul A. Sydney & Simon: To the Moon & Beyond! Reynolds, Peter H., illus. 2017. (ENG.). 48p. (J). (gr. 1-4). lib. bdg. 12.99 *(978-1-58089-679-5(0))* Charlesbridge Publishing, Inc.

Reynolds, Peter H. The Dot. Reynolds, Peter H., illus. 2003. (Creatrilogy Ser.). (ENG., Illus.). 32p. (J). (gr. k-12). 15.00 *(978-0-7636-1961-9(2)*, 53509533) Candlewick Pr.

Reynolds, Wendy. Moby for Justice. 2006. 17.00 *(978-0-8059-8861-1(0))* Dorrance Publishing Co., Inc.

Rhae, Sympne. My Name Is Johnson? l.t. ed. 2006. (Illus.). 53p. (J). per. 13.75 *(978-0-9770043-9-3(2))* New Global Publishing.

Rhodes, Jewell Parker. Towers Falling. 2016. (ENG., Illus.). 240p. (J). (gr. 3-7). 16.99 *(978-0-316-26222-4(6))* Little, Brown Bks. for Young Readers.

Rhuday-Perkovich, Olugbemisola. 8th Grade Super Zero. 2011. (ENG.). 336p. (J). (gr. 4-7). pap. 7.99 *(978-0-545-09725-3(8)*, Levine, Arthur A. Bks.) Scholastic, Inc.

Rhude, Steven. Natalie's Glasses, 1 vol. 2011. (ENG.). 80p. (J). (gr. k-2). pap. 19.95 *(978-1-926916-16-3(6))* MacIntyre & Purcell Publishing CAN. Dist: Independent Pubs. Group.

Ribar, Lindsay. The Art of Wishing. (ENG.). (YA). (gr. 7). 2014. 336p. pap. 9.99 *(978-0-14-242529-9(X)*, Speak) 2013. 320p. 17.99 *(978-0-8037-3827-0(7)*, Dial Bks) Penguin Young Readers Group.

—The Fourth Wish. 2014. (Art of Wishing Ser.). (ENG.). 368p. (YA). (gr. 7). 17.99 *(978-0-8037-3828-7(5)*, Kathy Dawson Books) Penguin Young Readers Group.

Rice, Morgan. Before Dawn (Vampire, Fallen-Book 1) 2016. (ENG., Illus.). 118p. (J). pap. 6.99 *(978-1-63291-611-2(8))* Morgan Rice Bks.

Richard, Laurent. Clowns & Dragons! Gauvin, Edward, tr. from FRE. Ryser, Nicolas, illus. 2014. (Tao, the Little Samurai Ser.: 3). (ENG.). 56p. (J). (gr. 2-5). lib. bdg. 29.27 *(978-1-4677-2096-0(8)*, Graphic Universe™) Lerner Publishing Group.

—Ninjas & Knock Outs! Gauvin, Edward, tr. from FRE. Ryser, Nicolas, illus. 2014. (Tao, the Little Samurai Ser.: 2). (ENG.). 64p. (J). (gr. 2-5). lib. bdg. 29.27 *(978-1-4677-3272-7(9)*, Graphic Universe™) Lerner Publishing Group.

Richards, Anthony Lee. The Golden Bird, 1 vol. 2009. 56p. pap. 16.95 *(978-1-60703-712-5(2))* America Star Bks.

Richards, Justin. Licence to Fish, Vol. 3. 2011. (Agent Alfie Ser.). (ENG., Illus.). 176p. (J). (gr. 2-4). 6.99 *(978-0-00-727359-1(2))* HarperCollins Pubs. Ltd. GBR. Dist: Independent Pubs. Group.

—Sorted! 2009. (Agent Alfie Ser.: 2). (ENG., Illus.). 176p. (J). (gr. 2-4). pap. 6.99 *(978-0-00-727358-4(4)*, HarperCollins Children's Bks.) HarperCollins Pubs. Ltd. GBR. Dist: HarperCollins Pubs.

—Thunder Raker, 1. 2008. (Agent Alfie Ser.: 1). (ENG., Illus.). 144p. (J). (gr. 2-4). pap. 6.99 *(978-0-00-727357-7(6)*, HarperCollins Children's Bks.) HarperCollins Pubs. Ltd. GBR. Dist: HarperCollins Pubs.

Richards, Natalie D. Gone Too Far. 2015. (ENG.). 320p. (YA). (gr. 7-12). pap. 9.99 *(978-1-4022-8554-7(X)*, 9781402285547) Sourcebooks, Inc.

—Six Months Later. 2013. (ENG.). 336p. (YA). (gr. 6-12). pap. 10.99 *(978-1-4022-8551-6(5),* 9781402285516) Sourcebooks, Inc.

Richardson, S. Lee. The Backyard Series Volume Two: The Baby Bear Scare Story. 2012. 28p. pap. 24.95 *(978-1-4626-9615-4(5))* America Star Bks.

Richardson, Sharde. Watched. 2011. (ENG.). 290p. (YA). pap. 12.99 *(978-0-9831498-0-4(1))* Jolt.

Richler, Mordecai. First Spy Case. Eyolfson, Norman, illus. 2003. (Jacob Two-Two Ser.). (ENG.). 144p. (J). (gr. 3-7). pap. 6.95 *(978-0-88776-694-7(3))* Tundra Bks. CAN. Dist: Random Hse., Inc.

—Jacob Two-Two's First Spy Case. Petricic, Dusan, illus. 2009. (Jacob Two-Two Ser.). (ENG.). 168p. (J). (gr. 4-7). 10.95 *(978-0-88776-927-6(6))* Tundra Bks. CAN. Dist: Random Hse., Inc.

Richmond, Peter. Always a Catch. 2014. (ENG.). 288p. (YA). (gr. 7). 17.99 *(978-0-399-25055-2(7),* Philomel Bks.) Penguin Young Readers Group.

Richter, Jutta. The Cat: Or, How I Lost Eternity. Brailovsky, Anna, tr. from GER. Berner, Rotraut Susanne, illus. 2007. (ENG.). 80p. (J). (gr. 1-6). 14.00 *(978-1-57131-676-9(0))* Milkweed Editions.

Ridell, Chris. Ottoline va al colegio/ Ottolina Goes To School. 2008. (SPA.). 172p. (J). 13.95 *(978-84-263-6833-1(6))* Vives, Luis Editorial (Edelvives) ESP. Dist: Baker & Taylor Bks.

Rifkin, Sherri & Bennett, Olivia. The Allegra Biscotti Collection. 2010. (ENG., Illus.). 256p. (J). (gr. 6-8). pap. 11.99 *(978-1-4022-4391-2(X),* Sourcebooks Jabberwocky) Sourcebooks, Inc.

Rigby Education Staff. When I Go to School. (Illus.). (J). 20.00 *(978-0-7635-6441-4(9),* 764419C99) Rigby Education.

Rigby, Jill. I Put It Right There! I Swear! The story of one boy's master plan to overcome executive functioning Difficulties! 2011. 28p. pap. 12.77 *(978-1-4634-3710-7(2))* AuthorHouse.

Riggs, Shannon. Not in Room 204: Breaking the Silence of Abuse. Zollars, Jaime, illus. 2017. (ENG.). 32p. (J). (-3). pap. 7.99 ***(978-0-8075-5766-2(8))*** Whitman, Albert & Co.

Riker, Richard K. School Days Daze. Lt. ed. 2005. (Illus.). 168p. (J). 15.95 *(978-0-9760416-0-3(X))* Safe Harbor Pubns.

Rim, Sujean. Birdie's First Day of School. 2015. (ENG., Illus.). 40p. (J). (gr. -1-3). 17.00 *(978-0-316-40745-8(3))* Little Brown & Co.

Rinaldi, Ann. The Education of Mary: A Little Miss of Color, 1832. 2005. 176p. (J). pap. *(978-0-7868-1377-3(6))* Hyperion Pr.

Ripken, Cal, Jr. & Cowherd, Kevin. Super Slugger. 2013. (ENG.). 200p. (YA). (gr. 3-7). pap. 6.99 *(978-1-4231-4004-7(4))* Hyperion Pr.

Rippin, Sally. The Copycat Kid. Fukuoka, Aki, illus. 2015. 42p. (J). *(978-1-61067-449-2(9))* Kane Miller.

—The Little Lie. Fukuoka, Aki, illus. 2014. 43p. (J). *(978-1-61067-291-7(7))* Kane Miller.

Rise Above. 2014. (Red Zone Ser.: 6). (ENG.). 104p. (YA). (gr. 6-12). lib. bdg. 27.93 *(978-1-4677-2127-1(1))* Lerner Publishing Group.

Rissi, Anica Mrose. Anna, Banana, & the Friendship Split. Park, Meg, illus. 2015. (Anna, Banana Ser.: 1). (ENG.). 128p. (J). (gr. 1-5). 16.99 *(978-1-4814-1605-4(7),* Simon & Schuster Bks. For Young Readers) Simon & Schuster Bks. For Young Readers.

—The Teacher's Pet. OHora, Zachariah, illus. 2017. (ENG.). 40p. (J). (gr. -1-k). 17.99 *(978-1-4847-4364-5(4))* Disney Pr.

Ritter, Joshua & Ellis-Ritter, Karen. Be It Every Day! 2012. 40p. pap. 20.99 *(978-1-4634-5231-5(4))* AuthorHouse.

Rivers, Phoebe. Mischief Night. 2012. (Saranormal Ser.: 3). (ENG.). 160p. (J). (gr. 3-7). 15.99 *(978-1-4424-5380-7(X));* pap. 5.99 *(978-1-4424-5221-3(8))* Simon Spotlight. (Simon Spotlight).

Roat, Sharon Huss. Between the Notes. 2015. (ENG.). 400p. (YA). (gr. 9). 17.99 *(978-0-06-229172-1(6),* HarperTeen) HarperCollins Pubs.

Roat, Sharon Huss. How to Disappear. 2017. 384p. (YA). (gr. 8). 17.99 ***(978-0-06-229175-2(0),*** HarperTeen) HarperCollins Pubs.

Robb, Diane Burton. The Alphabet War: A Story about Dyslexia. Piazza, Gail, illus. 2004. (ENG.). 32p. (J). (gr. 2-3). 16.99 *(978-0-8075-0302-7(9))* Whitman, Albert & Co.

Robberecht, Thierry. Superhero School. Goossens, Philippe, illus. 2012. (ENG.). 30p. (J). (gr. -1-k). 16.95 *(978-1-60537-140-5(8))* Cobblestone Publishing Co.

Robbins, Jacqui. The New Girl... & Me. Phelan, Matt, illus. 2006. (ENG.). 32p. (J). (gr. -1-2). 17.99 *(978-0-689-86468-1(X),* Atheneum/Richard Jackson Bks.) Simon & Schuster Children's Publishing.

—Two of a Kind. Phelan, Matt, illus. 2009. (ENG.). 32p. (J). (gr. -1-2). 17.99 *(978-1-4169-2437-1(X),* Atheneum Bks. for Young Readers) Simon & Schuster Children's Publishing.

Robbins, Trina. The Big Flush. Page, Tyler, illus. 2012. (Chicagoland Detective Agency Ser.: 4). (ENG.). 64p. (gr. 4-8). pap. 6.95 *(978-0-8225-9161-0(8));* lib. bdg. 29.27 *(978-0-7613-8165-5(1))* Lerner Publishing Group. (Graphic Universe™).

—The Drained Brains Caper. Page, Tyler, illus. 2010. (Chicagoland Detective Agency Ser.: 1). (ENG.). 64p. (gr. 4-8). pap. 6.95 *(978-0-7613-5635-6(5),* Graphic Universe™); lib. bdg. 29.27 *(978-0-7613-4601-2(5))* Lerner Publishing Group.

—A Match Made in Heaven. Ota, Yuko & Studio, Xian Nu, illus. 2013. (My Boyfriend Is a Monster Ser.: 8). (ENG.). 128p. (YA). (gr. 7-12). pap. 9.95 *(978-1-4677-0732-9(5),* Graphic Universe™) Lerner Publishing Group.

—A Match Made in Heaven. Xian Nu Studio Staff, illus. 2013. (My Boyfriend Is a Monster Ser.: 8). (ENG.). 128p. (YA). (gr. 7-12). lib. bdg. 29.27 *(978-0-7613-6857-1(4),* Graphic Universe™) Lerner Publishing Group.

Robert, Cormier. The Chocolate War. 2014. (ENG.). 272p. (J). 12.24 *(978-1-63245-138-5(7))* Lectorum Pubns., Inc.

Roberts, Barbara. The Adventures of Phoebe Flower: Stories of a Girl with ADHD. 2010. (ENG.). 176p. (J). (gr. 2-6). pap. 14.95 *(978-0-9714609-6-6(5))* Advantage Bks., LLC.

Roberts, D. W. Pep Squad Mysteries Book 2:the Haunting of Townsand Hall. 2009. 77p. pap. 8.95 *(978-0-557-05289-9(0))* Lulu Pr., Inc.

Roberts, Justin. The Smallest Girl in the Smallest Grade. Robinson, Christian, illus. 2014. (ENG.). 32p. (J). (gr. -1-k). 16.99 *(978-0-399-25743-8(8),* G.P. Putnam's Sons Books for Young Readers) Penguin Young Readers Group.

Roberts, LaDawna. The Haunted Birthday Party. 2007. 48p. per. 16.95 *(978-1-4241-8723-2(0))* America Star Bks.

Roberts, Lisa Brown. Playing the Player. 2015. (ENG., Illus.). 316p. (J). pap. 17.99 *(978-1-943892-56-3(3))* Entangled Publishing, LLC.

Robertson, Elysia Hill. Tool of Life My Pink School Books. Robertson, Elysia Hill, illus. 2005. (Illus.). 112p. (J). per. 12.95 *(978-0-9764444-3-5(7),* EJWV-004) E. J. Publishing.

Robertson, J. Jean. Everyone Goes to School. 2015. (ENG.). 24p. (gr. k-3). 28.50 *(978-1-63430-359-0(8))* Rourke Educational Media.

—Vote for Me! Mones, Marc, illus. 2012. (ENG.). 24p. (gr. 1-2). pap. 8.95 *(978-1-61810-316-1(4))* Rourke Educational Media.

Robertson, Jean. Grandpa Comes to First Grade. Dufalla, Anita, illus. 2011. (ENG.). 24p. (gr. k-1). pap. 8.95 *(978-1-61236-004-1(1))* Rourke Educational Media.

Robertson, Kathy & Hooker, Jennifer. Jasmine & Chad Make New Friends. 2012. 28p. pap. 15.99 *(978-1-4797-1656-2(1))* Xlibris Corp.

Robico. My Little Monster 3. 2014. (My Little Monster Ser.). (ENG., Illus.). 176p. (YA). (gr. 9). pap. 10.99 *(978-1-61262-599-7(1))* Kodansha America, Inc.

—My Little Monster 4. 2014. (My Little Monster Ser.). (ENG., Illus.). 176p. (YA). pap. 10.99 *(978-1-61262-600-0(9))* Kodansha America, Inc.

Robins, E. The Easy Way. 2004. (Carter High Chronicles (High-Interest Readers) Ser.). (Illus.). 48p. (J). per. 4.95 *(978-1-56254-683-0(X),* SP683X) Saddleback Educational Publishing, Inc.

—Too Late. 2004. (Carter High Chronicles (High-Interest Readers) Ser.). (Illus.). 48p. (J). per. 3.95 *(978-1-56254-693-9(7),* SP6937) Saddleback Educational Publishing, Inc.

Robins, Eleanor. Be Fair, 1 vol. unabr. ed. 2011. (Carter High Senior Year Ser.). (ENG.). 49p. (YA). (gr. 9-12). pap. 7.95 *(978-1-61651-323-8(3))* Saddleback Educational Publishing, Inc.

—Boy of Their Dreams, 1 vol. unabr. ed. 2011. (Carter High Chronicles Ser.). (ENG.). 51p. (YA). (gr. 9-12). pap. 7.95 *(978-1-61651-305-4(5))* Saddleback Educational Publishing, Inc.

—Drama Club Mystery, 1 vol. unabr. ed. 2011. (Carter High Mysteries Ser.). (ENG.). 47p. (YA). (gr. 9-12). 7.95 *(978-1-61651-562-1(7))* Saddleback Educational Publishing, Inc.

—Easy Pass, 1 vol. unabr. ed. 2011. (Choices Ser.). (ENG.). 51p. (YA). (gr. 9-12). 7.95 *(978-1-61651-596-6(1))* Saddleback Educational Publishing, Inc.

—The Easy Way, 1 vol. unabr. ed. 2011. (Carter High Chronicles Ser.). (ENG.). 51p. (YA). (gr. 9-12). pap. 7.95 *(978-1-61651-307-8(1))* Saddleback Educational Publishing, Inc.

—The Fastest Runner, 1 vol. unabr. ed. 2011. (Carter High Chronicles Ser.). (ENG.). 52p. (YA). (gr. 9-12). pap. 7.95 *(978-1-61651-308-5(X))* Saddleback Educational Publishing, Inc.

—The Field Trip Mystery, 1 vol. unabr. ed. 2011. (Carter High Mysteries Ser.). (ENG.). 48p. (YA). (gr. 9-12). 7.95 *(978-1-61651-563-8(5))* Saddleback Educational Publishing, Inc.

—It Does Matter, 1 vol. unabr. ed. 2011. (Carter High Senior Year Ser.). (ENG.). 49p. (YA). (gr. 9-12). pap. 7.95 *(978-1-61651-324-5(1))* Saddleback Educational Publishing, Inc.

—It Is Not a Date, 1 vol. unabr. ed. 2011. (Carter High Chronicles Ser.). (ENG.). 51p. (YA). (gr. 9-12). pap. 7.95 *(978-1-61651-309-2(8))* Saddleback Educational Publishing, Inc.

—Just Be Yourself, 1 vol. unabr. ed. 2011. (Carter High Senior Year Ser.). (ENG.). 50p. (YA). (gr. 9-12). pap. 7.95 *(978-1-61651-325-2(X))* Saddleback Educational Publishing, Inc.

—The Last Time, 1 vol. unabr. ed. 2011. (Carter High Senior Year Ser.). (ENG.). 49p. (YA). (gr. 9-12). pap. 7.95 *(978-1-61651-326-9(8))* Saddleback Educational Publishing, Inc.

—Lucky Falcon Mystery, 1 vol. unabr. ed. 2011. (Carter High Mysteries Ser.). (ENG.). 47p. (YA). (gr. 9-12). 7.95 *(978-1-61651-565-2(1))* Saddleback Educational Publishing, Inc.

—No Exceptions, 1 vol. unabr. ed. 2011. (Choices Ser.). (ENG.). 52p. (YA). (gr. 9-12). 7.95 *(978-1-61651-597-3(X))* Saddleback Educational Publishing, Inc.

—One Date Too Many. (Carter High Chronicles (High-Interest Readers) Ser.). 2004. (Illus.). 48p. (J). per. 3.95 *(978-1-56254-689-2(9),* SP6899) 2011. (ENG.). 50p. (YA). (gr. 9-12). pap. 7.95 *(978-1-61651-310-8(1))* Saddleback Educational Publishing, Inc.

—One More Chance, 1 vol. unabr. ed. 2011. (Carter High Senior Year Ser.). (ENG.). 51p. (YA). (gr. 9-12). pap. 7.95 *(978-1-61651-327-6(6))* Saddleback Educational Publishing, Inc.

—The Right Kind of Win. 2004. (Carter High Chronicles (High-Interest Readers) Ser.). (Illus.). 48p. (J). per. 3.95 *(978-1-56254-691-5(0),* SP6910) Saddleback Educational Publishing, Inc.

—The Secret Admirer Mystery, 1 vol. unabr. ed. 2011. (Carter High Mysteries Ser.). (ENG.). 48p. (YA). (gr. 9-12). 7.95 *(978-1-61651-567-6(8))* Saddleback Educational Publishing, Inc.

—Someone to Count, 1 vol. unabr. ed. 2011. (Carter High Senior Year Ser.). (ENG.). 50p. (YA). (gr. 9-12). pap. 7.95 *(978-1-61651-328-3(4))* Saddleback Educational Publishing, Inc.

—Time to Move On, 1 vol. unabr. ed. 2011. (Carter High Senior Year Ser.). (ENG.). 50p. (YA). (gr. 9-12). pap. 7.95 *(978-1-61651-329-0(2))* Saddleback Educational Publishing, Inc.

—Too Late, 1 vol. unabr. ed. 2011. (Carter High Chronicles Ser.). (ENG.). 52p. (YA). (gr. 9-12). pap. 7.95 *(978-1-61651-312-2(8))* Saddleback Educational Publishing, Inc.

—Trust Me, 1 vol. unabr. ed. 2011. (Choices Ser.). (ENG.). 52p. (YA). (gr. 9-12). 7.95 *(978-1-61651-599-7(6))* Saddleback Educational Publishing, Inc.

—The Worst Year Ever, 1 vol. unabr. ed. 2011. (Carter High Senior Year Ser.). (ENG.). 50p. (YA). (gr. 9-12). pap. 7.95 *(978-1-61651-330-6(6))* Saddleback Educational Publishing, Inc.

Robinson, A. M. Vampire Crush. 2010. (ENG.). 416p. (YA). (gr. 8-18). pap. 8.99 *(978-0-06-198971-1(1),* HarperTeen) HarperCollins Pubs.

Robinson, Barbara. The Best Halloween Ever. 2006. (Illus.). 117p. (J). (gr. 3-7). 13.65 *(978-0-7569-6985-1(9))* Perfection Learning Corp.

—The Best School Year Ever. 2005. (Trophy Bk.). (ENG.). 176p. (J). (gr. 3-18). pap. 5.99 *(978-0-06-440492-1(7))* HarperCollins Pubs.

Robinson, Craig & Mansbach, Adam. Jake the Fake Keeps It Real. Knight, Keith, illus. 2017. (Jake the Fake Ser.: 1). (ENG.). 144p. (J). (gr. 3-7). 13.99 *(978-0-553-52351-5(1),* Crown Books For Young Readers) Random Hse. Children's Bks.

Robley Blake, Colleen. I Can't Wait till I'm Five. 2006. (J). 9.95 *(978-0-9767342-0-8(6))* Imaajinn This.

Robshaw, Brandon. Big Wish. 2016. (ENG.). 240p. (J). (gr. 3-7). 16.99 *(978-0-545-90410-0(2),* Chicken Hse., The) Scholastic, Inc.

Rocha, Ruth. Lines, Squiggles, Letters, Words. Matoso, Madalena, illus. 2016. (ENG.). 40p. (J). (gr. -1-k). 16.95 *(978-1-59270-208-4(2))* Enchanted Lion Bks., LLC.

Roche, Denis. The Best Class Picture Ever! 2003. (Illus.). (J). pap. *(978-0-439-57819-6(1),* Scholastic Pr.) Scholastic, Inc.

Rockwell, Anne F. Father's Day. Rockwell, Lizzy, illus. 2005. 40p. (J). (gr. -1-1). lib. bdg. 15.89 *(978-0-06-051378-8(0))* HarperCollins Pubs.

—First Day of School. 2006. *(978-0-06-050192-1(8))* HarperCollins Canada, Ltd.

—First Day of School. Rockwell, Lizzy, illus. (ENG.). 40p. (J). (gr. -1-3). 2013. pap. 6.99 *(978-0-06-050193-8(6))* 2011. 16.99 *(978-0-06-050191-4(X))* HarperCollins Pubs.

—Presidents' Day. Rockwell, Lizzy, illus. 2009. (ENG.). 40p. (J). (gr. -1-1). pap. 6.99 *(978-0-06-050196-9(0))* HarperCollins Pubs.

—Presidents' Day. Rockwell, Lizzy, illus. 2007. (ENG.). 40p. (J). (gr. -1-1). 16.99 *(978-0-06-050194-5(4))* HarperCollins Pubs.

—St. Patrick's Day. Rockwell, Lizzy, illus. 2010. 40p. (J). (gr. -1-3). (ENG.). 14.99 *(978-0-06-050197-6(9));* lib. bdg. 15.89 *(978-0-06-050198-3(7))* HarperCollins Pubs.

—Welcome to Kindergarten. Rockwell, Anne F., illus. 2004. (ENG., Illus.). 32p. (J). (gr. -1-1). pap. 7.99 *(978-0-8027-7664-8(7),* 9780802776648, Bloomsbury USA Childrens) Bloomsbury Publishing USA.

Rockwell, Anne F. & Rockwell. 100 School Days. Rockwell, Lizzy, illus. 2004. (ENG.). 40p. (J). (gr. -1-3). pap. 6.99 *(978-0-06-443727-1(2))* HarperCollins Pubs.

Roddie, Shen. Baby Goes Too. Stojic, Manya, illus. 2003. 32p. (YA). *(978-1-85602-460-0(1),* Pavilion Children's Books) Pavilion Bks.

Rodkey, Geoff. The Tapper Twins Go to War (with Each Other) 2015. (Tapper Twins Ser.: 1). (ENG., Illus.). 240p. (J). (gr. 3-7). 13.99 *(978-0-316-29779-0(8))* Little Brown & Co.

—The Tapper Twins Go to War (with Each Other) 2016. (Tapper Twins Ser.: 1). (ENG., Illus.). 240p. (J). (gr. 3-7). pap. 5.99 *(978-0-316-31597-5(4))* Little, Brown Bks. for Young Readers.

—The Tapper Twins Run for President. 2016. (Tapper Twins Ser.: 3). (ENG., Illus.). 304p. (J). (gr. 3-7). 13.99 *(978-0-316-29785-1(2))* Little, Brown Bks. for Young Readers.

—The Tapper Twins Tear up New York. 2015. (Tapper Twins Ser.: 2). (ENG., Illus.). 288p. (J). (gr. 3-7). 13.99 *(978-0-316-29783-7(6))* Little Brown & Co.

—The Tapper Twins Tear up New York. 2016. (Tapper Twins Ser.: 2). (ENG., Illus.). 288p. (J). (gr. 3-7). pap. 5.99 *(978-0-316-31601-9(6))* Little, Brown Bks. for Young Readers.

Rodman, Mary Ann. First Grade Stinks!, 1 vol. Spiegel, Beth, illus. 2006. (ENG.). 32p. (J). (gr. k-3). 15.95 *(978-1-56145-377-1(3))* Peachtree Pubs.

—Yankee Girl. 2008. (ENG.). 240p. (J). (gr. 4-6). pap. 9.99 *(978-0-312-53576-6(7),* 9780312535766) Square Fish.

Rodman, Sean. Infiltration, 1 vol. 2011. (Orca Soundings Ser.). (ENG.). (gr. 8-12). 128p. (J). 16.95 *(978-1-55469-986-5(X));* 144p. (YA). pap. 9.95 *(978-1-55469-985-8(1))* Orca Bk. Pubs. USA.

Rodriguez, Cindy L. When Reason Breaks. 2015. (ENG.). 304p. (YA). (gr. 7-12). 17.99 *(978-1-61963-412-1(0),* 9781619634121, Bloomsbury USA Childrens) Bloomsbury Publishing USA.

Rodriguez Ferrer, Janel. The Arts-Angels Track 1: Drawn to You. 2012. 252p. pap. 8.99 *(978-1-936214-91-4(1))* Wyatt-MacKenzie Publishing.

Roecker, Lisa & Roecker, Laura. The Liar Society. 2011. (Liar Society Ser.: 1). (ENG.). 368p. (YA). (gr. 7-12). pap. 9.99 *(978-1-4022-5633-2(7))* Sourcebooks, Inc.

Roesti, Delores. Mareena Maree Mulligan & the Flying Wheelchair: Book 2: The Busybodies. 2008. 102p. pap. 10.95 *(978-0-7414-4477-6(1))* Infinity Publishing.

Rogers, Kelly. Buyer Beware, 1 vol. Peterschmidt, Betsy, illus. 2016. (ENG.). 48p. (J). lib. bdg. 28.50 *(978-1-62402-167-1(0))* Magic Wagon.

—The Key, 1 vol. Peterschmidt, Betsy, illus. 2016. (ENG.). 48p. (J). lib. bdg. *(978-1-62402-169-5(7))* Magic Wagon.

—Study Group. Peterschmidt, Betsy, illus. 2016. (ENG.). 48p. (J). lib. bdg. *(978-1-62402-170-1(0))* Magic Wagon.

Rogers, Lon. The Between Season. 2009. 280p. 27.95 *(978-1-4401-8370-6(8))* iUniverse, Inc.

Rogers, Suzanne. Pawsitive Tails. 2012. 40p. *(978-1-77097-298-8(6))* FriesenPress.

Rogers Yaeger, Nancy. Constantine Goes to School. Grace, Bill, illus. 2006. 60p. (J). (gr. 2-5). *(978-1-4050-5714-1(9))* Macmillan Caribbean.

Roland, Timothy. Monkey Me & the Golden Monkey. Roland, Timothy, illus. 2014. (Monkey Me Ser.: 1). (ENG., Illus.). 96p. (J). (gr. 1-3). pap. 4.99 *(978-0-545-55976-8(6))* Scholastic, Inc.

—Monkey Me & the Golden Monkey. 2014. (Monkey Me Ser.: 1). lib. bdg. 14.75 *(978-0-606-35354-0(2))* Turtleback Bks.

—Monkey Me & the Pet Show. 2014. (Monkey Me Ser.: 2). (ENG.). 96p. (J). (gr. 1-3). 15.99 *(978-0-545-55981-2(2))* Scholastic, Inc.

—Monkey Me & the Pet Show. 2014. (Monkey Me Ser.: 2). lib. bdg. 14.75 *(978-0-606-35359-5(3))* Turtleback Bks.

—Monkey Me & the School Ghost. 2014. (Illus.). 90p. (J). *(978-1-4844-3840-4(X))* Scholastic, Inc.

—Monkey Me & the School Ghost. 2014. (Monkey Me Ser.: 4). lib. bdg. 14.75 *(978-0-606-36053-1(0))* Turtleback Bks.

—Our Crazy Class Election. 2007. (Illus.). 90p. (J). *(978-0-545-00401-5(2))* Scholastic, Inc.

—The Pet Show. 2014. (Monkey Me Ser.: 2). (ENG.). 96p. (J). (gr. 1-3). pap. 4.99 *(978-0-545-55980-5(4))* Scholastic, Inc.

Roller, Pat Kellogg. Pink Hat's Adventure with Kites. Salazar, Riana, illus. Roller, John, photos by. 2009. 36p. pap. 10.95 *(978-1-59858-957-3(1))* Dog Ear Publishing, LLC.

Rollins, Danielle. Breaking. 2017. (ENG.). 304p. (YA). 17.99 *(978-1-61963-740-5(5),* 9781619637405, Bloomsbury USA Childrens) Bloomsbury Publishing USA.

Roman, Dave. Astronaut Academy: Re-Entry. Roman, Dave, illus. 2013. (Astronaut Academy Ser.: 2). (ENG., Illus.). 192p. (J). (gr. 5-9). pap. 9.99 *(978-1-59643-621-3(2),* 9781596436213, First Second Bks.) Roaring Brook Pr.

—Zero Gravity. Roman, Dave, illus. 2011. (Astronaut Academy Ser.: 1). (ENG., Illus.). 192p. (J). (gr. 5-9). 17.99 *(978-1-59643-756-2(1),* 9781596437562); pap. 9.99 *(978-1-59643-620-6(4),* 9781596436206) Roaring Brook Pr. (First Second Bks.).

Romanek, Trudee. Raising the Stakes, 1 vol. 2015. (Orca Limelights Ser.). (ENG.). 160p. (J). (gr. 6-9). pap. 9.95 *(978-1-4598-0779-2(0))* Orca Bk. Pubs. USA.

Romano, Juliana. First There Was Forever. 2016. (ENG.). 416p. (YA). (gr. 9). pap. 10.99 *(978-0-14-751391-5(X),* Speak) Penguin Young Readers Group.

Rone, Trenton. Once upon a Hamster 2003. (YA). spiral bd. 14.95 *(978-0-9744437-3-7(5))* Imagination Workshop, The.

Roos, Stephen. The Gypsies Never Came. Liepke, Peter, photos by. 2010. (ENG., Illus.). 128p. (J). (gr. 3-7). pap. 7.99 *(978-1-4424-2940-6(2),* Simon & Schuster Bks. For Young Readers) Simon & Schuster Bks. For Young Readers.

—Recycling George. 2010. (ENG.). 144p. (J). (gr. 3-7). pap. 8.99 *(978-1-4424-2941-3(0),* Simon & Schuster Bks. For Young Readers) Simon & Schuster Bks. For Young Readers.

Roper, Robert, illus. Dora Goes to School. 2004. (Dora the Explorer Ser.: Vol. 8). (ENG.). 24p. (J). pap. 3.99 *(978-0-689-86494-0(9),* Simon Spotlight/Nickelodeon) Simon Spotlight/Nickelodeon.

Rosario, Joann. Secret Swan King. 2004. 27p. (J). pap. 10.00 *(978-0-9758746-0-8(8),* 1246169) J.G.R. Enterprises.

Rose, Jasmine. The Last Caterpillar Princess. 2011. 16p. pap. 8.64 *(978-1-4634-1953-0(8))* AuthorHouse.

Rose, Sandra. My Mom Has Wheels. Talbott, Sherri, illus. 2009. 28p. pap. 24.95 *(978-1-60836-889-1(0))* America Star Bks.

Rose, Sue. Jinxed! 2006. (Unfabulous! Ser.). (Illus.). 118p. (J). *(978-1-4156-5170-4(1))* Scholastic, Inc.

Rosen, Michael J. A School for Pompey Walker. 2012. (ENG.). (J). pap. *(978-1-4675-1412-5(8))* Independent Pub.

Rosenberg, Madelyn & Crockett, Mary. Dream Boy. 2014. (ENG.). 336p. (YA). (gr. 7-12). pap. 9.99 *(978-1-4022-9583-6(9),* 9781402295836) Sourcebooks, Inc.

Roske, Melissa. Kat Greene Comes Clean. 2017. (ENG.). 224p. (J). (gr. 4-7). lib. bdg. 16.99 *(978-1-58089-776-1(2))* Charlesbridge Publishing, Inc.

Ross, Chudney. Lone Bean. 2012. (ENG.). 208p. (J). (gr. 3-7). 16.99 *(978-0-06-166011-5(6),* Amistad) HarperCollins Pubs.

Ross, Jay. Bungalow 29. Klimko, Andrew, illus. 2015. 92p. pap. 5.99 *(978-0-9771994-0-2(1))* Visor Bks.

Roth, Carol. Five Little Ducklings Go to School. Julian, Sean, illus. 2015. (ENG.). 32p. (J). (gr. -1-2). 17.95 *(978-0-7358-4132-1(2))* North-South Bks., Inc.

Rothberg, Abraham. Pinocchio's Sister: A Feminist Fable. 2005. 159p. pap. 11.95 *(978-1-4116-4347-5(X))* Lulu Pr., Inc.

Rothstein, Evelyn. Evelyn & the Two Evas. Uhlig, Elizabeth, illus. 2013. 63p. (YA). pap. 12.95 *(978-0-9834030-5-0(8))* Marble Hse. Editions.

—My Great Grandpa Dave. 2007. (J). per. 12.95 *(978-0-9786745-1-9(0))* Marble Hse. Editions.

Rottman, S. L. Shadow of a Doubt, 1 vol. 2005. (ENG.). 224p. (YA). (gr. 7-18). pap. 7.95 *(978-1-56145-354-2(4))* Peachtree Pubs.

Rountree, Wendy. Lost Soul. 2003. 87p. (J). pap. 19.95 *(978-1-59129-975-2(6))* America Star Bks.

Rouseau, Jasmine. Bizzy Bee Goes to School. 2012. 32p. pap. 19.99 *(978-1-4685-4884-6(0))* AuthorHouse.

Rouss, Sylvia A. No Rules for Michael. Simon, Susan, illus. 2004. (ENG.). 24p. (J). (gr. -1-1). pap. 6.95 *(978-1-58013-044-8(5),* Kar-Ben Publishing) Lerner Publishing Group.

—Sammy Spider's First Day of School. Kahn, Katherine, illus. 2009. (Kar-Ben Favorites Ser.). (ENG.). 32p. (J). (gr. -1-2). 16.95 *(978-0-8225-8583-1(9),* Kar-Ben Publishing) Lerner Publishing Group.

—Sammy Spider's First Day of School. Kahn, Katherine Janus, illus. 2009. (Kar-Ben Favorites Ser.). (ENG.). 32p. (J). (gr. -1-2). pap. 7.95 *(978-0-8225-8584-8(7),* Kar-Ben Publishing) Lerner Publishing Group.

Rouss, Sylvia A. & Rouss, Shannan. A Watermelon in the Sukkah. Iosa, Ann, illus. 2013. 24p. 17.95 *(978-1-4677-1642-0(1));* (ENG.). (J). (gr. -1-2). 16.95 *(978-0-7613-8118-1(X),* Kar-Ben Publishing); (ENG.). (J). (gr. -1-2). 7.95 *(978-0-7613-8119-8(8),* Kar-Ben Publishing) Lerner Publishing Group.

Rovetch, L. Bob. Hot Dog & Bob: And the Dangerously Dizzy Attack of the Hypno Hamsters. Whamond, Dave, illus. 2007. (Hot Dog & Bob Ser.: HOTD). (ENG.). 96p. (J). (gr. 1-5). per. 4.95 *(978-0-8118-5602-7(X))* Chronicle Bks. LLC.

Rowling, J. K. Harrius Potter et Camera Secretorum. Needham, Peter, tr. from ENG. 2007. (Harry Potter Ser.).Tr. of Harry Potter & the Chamber of Secrets. (LAT & ENG., Illus.). 288p. (YA). (gr. 5). 23.95 *(978-1-59990-067-4(X),* 9781599900674, Bloomsbury USA Childrens) Bloomsbury Publishing USA.

S

—Harrius Potter et Philosophi Lapis. Needham, Peter, tr. from ENG. 2003. (Harry Potter Ser.).Tr. of Harry Potter & the Philosopher's Stone. (LAT & ENG., Illus.). 256p. (YA). (gr. 7). 29.99 (978-1-58234-825-4(1), 9781582348254, Bloomsbury USA Childrens) Bloomsbury Publishing USA.

—Harry Potter à l'École des Sorciers. Menard, Jean-François, tr. from ENG. 2007. (Harry Potter Ser.: Year 1).Tr. of Harry Potter & the Sorcerer's Stone. 311p. (J). per. 14.95 (978-2-07-061236-9(8)) Gallimard, Editions FRA. Dist: Distribooks, Inc.

—Harry Potter & the Chamber of Secrets. 2009. 9.64 (978-0-7848-1444-4(9), Everbind) Marco Bk. Co.

—Harry Potter & the Chamber of Secrets. unabr. ed. 2004. (Harry Potter Ser.: Year 2). 352p. (J). (gr. 3-18). pap. 46.00 incl. audio (978-0-8072-8207-6(3), S YA 137 SP, Listening Library) Random Hse. Audio Publishing Group.

—Harry Potter & the Chamber of Secrets. (Harry Potter Ser.: 2). (J). 2006. 1.25 (978-1-4193-8079-2(6)) 2003. 78.75 (978-1-4025-6698-1(0)) Recorded Bks., Inc.

—Harry Potter & the Chamber of Secrets. (Harry Potter Ser.: Year 2). (RUS., Illus.). 28.95 (978-5-8451-0947-7(7)) Rosmen-Izdat RUS. Dist: Distribooks, Inc.

—Harry Potter & the Chamber of Secrets. Kay, Jim, illus. 2016. (Harry Potter Ser.: 2). (ENG.). 272p. (J). (gr. 3). 39.99 (978-0-545-79132-8(4)); 275.00 (978-1-338-11986-2(9)) Scholastic, Inc. (Levine, Arthur A. Bks.).

—Harry Potter & the Chamber of Secrets. l.t. ed. 2003. (Harry Potter Ser.: Year 2). (ENG.). 466p. pap. 13.95 (978-1-59413-001-4(9)) Thorndike Pr.

—Harry Potter & the Chamber of Secrets. 2013. (Harry Potter (Kazu Kibuishi Illustrations) Ser.: 2). lib. bdg. 24.50 (978-0-606-32346-8(5), Turtleback) Turtleback Bks.

—Harry Potter & the Deathly Hallows. (Illus.). 2008. 832p. pap. (978-0-7475-9586-1(0)) 2007. (ENG., 608p. (978-0-7475-9106-1(7)) Bloomsbury Publishing Plc.

—Harry Potter & the Deathly Hallows. braille ed. 2007. (Harry Potter Ser.: Year 7). (J). (gr. 4-7). 34.99 (978-0-939173-57-0(3)) National Braille Pr.

—Harry Potter & the Deathly Hallows. 2010. 25.00 (978-1-60686-882-9(9)) Perfection Learning Corp.

—Harry Potter & the Deathly Hallows, 17 vols. 2007. (Harry Potter Ser.: 7). (YA). 131.75 (978-1-4281-6652-3(1)); 129.79 (978-1-4281-6654-7(8)) Recorded Bks., Inc.

—Harry Potter & the Deathly Hallows. GrandPré, Mary, illus. (Harry Potter Ser.: 7). (ENG.). (J). 2009. 784p. (gr. 4-7). pap. 14.99 (978-0-545-13970-0(8), Levine, Arthur A. Bks.) 2007. 784p. (gr. 5-9). 34.99 (978-0-545-01022-1(5)) 2007. 816p. (gr. 4-7). 65.00 (978-0-545-02937-7(6), Levine, Arthur A. Bks.) Scholastic, Inc.

—Harry Potter & the Deathly Hallows. l.t. ed. 2009. (ENG.). 970p. pap. 14.95 (978-1-59413-355-8(7), Large Print Pr.) 2007. (Harry Potter Ser.: Year 7). (Illus.). 969p. (J). (gr. 4-7). 34.95 (978-0-7862-9665-1(8)) Thorndike Pr.

—Harry Potter & the Deathly Hallows. (Harry Potter (Kazu Kibuishi Illustrations) Ser.: 7). 2013. lib. bdg. 29.40 (978-0-606-32351-2(1)) 2009. lib. bdg. 26.95 (978-0-606-00420-6(3)) Turtleback Bks. (Turtleback).

—Harry Potter & the Deathly Hallows. Bar-hillel, Gili, tr. from ENG. 2007. (Harry Potter Ser.: Year 7). (HEB., Illus.). 568p. (J). (gr. 4-7). pap. (978-965-482-635-8(6)) Yediot Aharonot Bks., Miscal.

—Harry Potter & the Goblet of Fire. 2009. 10.24 (978-0-7848-1587-8(9), Everbind) Marco Bk. Co.

—Harry Potter & the Goblet of Fire. (Harry Potter Ser.: 4). (J). 2006. 1.25 (978-1-4193-8531-5(3)) 2003. 101.75 (978-1-4025-6702-5(2)) Recorded Bks., Inc.

—Harry Potter & the Goblet of Fire. GrandPré, Mary, illus. l.t. ed. 2003. (Harry Potter Ser.: Vol. 4). (ENG.). 936p. pap. 11.66 (978-1-59413-003-8(5)) Thorndike Pr.

—Harry Potter & the Goblet of Fire. 2013. (Harry Potter (Kazu Kibuishi Illustrations) Ser.: 4). lib. bdg. 26.95 (978-0-606-32348-2(1), Turtleback) Turtleback Bks.

—Harry Potter & the Half-Blood Prince. 2005. (ENG.). cd-rom (978-0-7475-8258-8(0)) Bloomsbury Publishing Plc.

—Harry Potter & the Half-Blood Prince, 9 vols. braille ed. 2005. (Harry Potter Ser.: Year 6). (J). (gr. 4-8). 29.99 (978-0-939173-39-6(5), HALF) National Braille Pr.

—Harry Potter & the Half-Blood Prince. GrandPré, Mary, illus. 2006. (Harry Potter Ser.: Year 6). 652p. (gr. 4-8). 23.00 (978-0-7569-6765-9(1)) Perfection Learning Corp.

—Harry Potter & the Half-Blood Prince. (Harry Potter Ser.: 6). (J). 2007. 1.25 (978-1-4193-5430-4(2)) 2006. 110.75 (978-1-4193-5436-6(1)) 2006. 193.75 (978-1-4193-5432-8(9)) 2005. 113.75 (978-1-4193-5434-2(5)) Recorded Bks., Inc.

—Harry Potter & the Half-Blood Prince. GrandPré, Mary, illus. (Harry Potter Ser.: 6). (ENG.). 672p. (J). (gr. 4-8). 2005. 29.99 (978-0-439-78454-2(9)) 2006. reprint ed. per. 12.99 (978-0-439-78596-9(0)) Scholastic, Inc. (Levine, Arthur A. Bks.).

—Harry Potter & the Half-Blood Prince. (Illus.). (J). (gr. 4-7). 2007. (ENG.). 832p. per. 14.95 (978-1-59413-221-6(6)) 2005. (Harry Potter Ser.: Year 6). 831p. 29.95 (978-0-7862-7745-2(9)) Thorndike Pr. (Large Print Pr.).

—Harry Potter & the Half-Blood Prince. 2013. (Harry Potter (Kazu Kibuishi Illustrations) Ser.: 6). lib. bdg. 26.95 (978-0-606-32350-5(3), Turtleback) Turtleback Bks.

—Harry Potter & the Half Blood Prince - Chinese Language. 2005. (Harry Potter Ser.: Year 6). (CHI.). 496p. (YA). (gr. 4-8). pap. 28.95 (978-7-02-005323-0(8), HAP06) People's Literature Publishing Hse. CHN. Dist: Chinasprout, Inc.

—Harry Potter & the Order of the Phoenix. (ENG.). 768p. (J). (gr. 6-10). pap. (978-0-7475-6107-1(9)) Bloomsbury Publishing Plc.

—Harry Potter & the Order of the Phoenix. 2008. (978-977-14-2697-4(4)) Nahdat Misr Bkshop for Printing and Pubs.

—Harry Potter & the Order of the Phoenix, 13 vols. braille ed. 2003. (Harry Potter Ser.: Year 5). (YA). 29.99 (978-0-939173-38-9(7)) National Braille Pr.

—Harry Potter & the Order of the Phoenix. 2003. (Harry Potter Ser.: Year 5). (CHI.). 575p. (YA). pap. 26.95 (978-7-02-004327-9(5), HAP05) People's Literature Publishing Hse. CHN. Dist: Chinasprout, Inc.

—Harry Potter & the Order of the Phoenix. 2004. (Harry Potter Ser.). 870p. (gr. 4-6). 16.49 (978-0-7569-4163-5(6)) Perfection Learning Corp.

—Harry Potter & the Order of the Phoenix. 2003. (ENG.). 768p. (978-1-55192-570-7(2)) Raincoast Bk. Distribution.

—Harry Potter & the Order of the Phoenix. GrandPré, Mary, illus. (Harry Potter Ser.: 5). (ENG.). (J). (gr. 3-7). 2004. 896p. mass mkt. 12.99 (978-0-439-35807-1(8), Scholastic Paperbacks) 2003. 870p. 29.99 (978-0-439-35806-4(X)) Scholastic, Inc.

—Harry Potter & the Order of the Phoenix. l.t. ed. 2003. (Harry Potter Ser.: Year 5). 1093p. 29.95 (978-0-7862-5778-2(4), Large Print Pr.) Thorndike Pr.

—Harry Potter & the Order of the Phoenix. GrandPré, Mary, illus. l.t. ed. 2003. (Thorndike Young Adult Ser.). (ENG.). 1232p. (J). (gr. 4-7). per. 14.95 (978-1-59413-112-7(0), Large Print Pr.) Thorndike Pr.

—Harry Potter & the Order of the Phoenix. (Harry Potter (Kazu Kibuishi Illustrations) Ser.: 5). 2013. lib. bdg. 26.95 (978-0-606-32349-9(X)) 2004. lib. bdg. 24.50 (978-0-613-99916-8(9)) Turtleback Bks. (Turtleback).

—Harry Potter & the Philosopher's Stone. 2014. (ENG., Illus.). 352p. (978-1-4088-5589-8(5)) Bloomsbury Publishing Plc.

—Harry Potter & the Prisoner of Azkaban. 2009. 9.64 (978-0-7848-1542-7(9), Everbind) Marco Bk. Co.

—Harry Potter & the Prisoner of Azkaban. 2005. (Harry Potter Ser.: Year 3). (CHI.). 260p. (YA). pap. 16.95 (978-7-02-003345-4(8), HAP03) People's Literature Publishing Hse. CHN. Dist: Chinasprout, Inc.

—Harry Potter & the Prisoner of Azkaban, 10 vols. 2003. (Harry Potter Ser.: 3). (J). 84.75 (978-1-4025-6700-1(6)) Recorded Bks., Inc.

—Harry Potter & the Prisoner of Azkaban. l.t. ed. 2003. (Harry Potter Ser.: Year 3). (ENG.). 592p. pap. 13.95 (978-1-59413-002-1(7), Large Print Pr.) Thorndike Pr.

—Harry Potter & the Prisoner of Azkaban. 2013. (Harry Potter (Kazu Kibuishi Illustrations) Ser.: 3). lib. bdg. 24.50 (978-0-606-32347-5(3), Turtleback) Turtleback Bks.

—Harry Potter & the Sorcerer's Stone. 2014. (ENG.). lthr. 79.00 (978-1-62715-772-8(7)) Leatherbound Bestsellers.

—Harry Potter & the Sorcerer's Stone. 2009. 8.44 (978-0-7848-2438-2(X)); 10.84 (978-0-7848-1357-7(4)) Marco Bk. Co. (Everbind).

—Harry Potter & the Sorcerer's Stone. 2003. (Harry Potter Ser.: Year 1). (CHI.). 191p. (YA). pap. 14.95 (978-7-02-003343-0(1), HAP01) People's Literature Publishing Hse. CHN. Dist: Chinasprout, Inc.

—Harry Potter & the Sorcerer's Stone. (Harry Potter Ser.: 1). (J). 2004. 1.25 (978-1-4025-6757-5(X)) 2003. 80.75 (978-1-4025-6696-7(4)) Recorded Bks., Inc.

—Harry Potter & the Sorcerer's Stone. Kay, Jim, illus. 2015. (Harry Potter Ser.: 1). (ENG.). 256p. (J). (gr. 3). 39.99 (978-0-545-79035-2(2), Levine, Arthur A. Bks.) Scholastic, Inc.

—Harry Potter & the Sorcerer's Stone, Bk. 1. 2013. (Harry Potter Ser.: 1). (ENG., Illus.). 336p. (J). (gr. 4). pap. 12.99 (978-0-545-58288-9(1)) Scholastic, Inc.

—Harry Potter & the Sorcerer's Stone. 2013. (Harry Potter (Kazu Kibuishi Illustrations) Ser.: 1). lib. bdg. 24.50 (978-0-606-32345-1(7), Turtleback) Turtleback Bks.

—Harry Potter e a Camara Secreta. (Harry Potter Ser.: Year 2).Tr. of Harry Potter & the Chamber of Secrets. (POR.). pap. 28.95 (978-85-325-1166-9(X)) Rocco, Editora, Ltda BRA. Dist: Distribooks, Inc.

—Harry Potter e a Pedra Filosofal. (Harry Potter Ser.: Year 1).Tr. of Harry Potter & the Philospher's Stone. (POR.). pap. 28.95 (978-85-325-1101-0(5)) Rocco, Editora, Ltda BRA. Dist: Distribooks, Inc.

—Harry Potter e a Prisioneiro de Azkaban. (Harry Potter Ser.: Year 3).Tr. of Harry Potter & the Prisioner of Azkaban. (POR.). pap. 29.95 (978-85-325-1206-2(2)) Rocco, Editora, Ltda BRA. Dist: Distribooks, Inc.

—Harry Potter e il Prigioniero di Azkaban. (Harry Potter Ser.: Year 3).Tr. of Harry Potter & the Prisoner of Azkaban. (ITA.). pap. 32.95 (978-88-7782-852-1(8)) Salani ITA. Dist: Distribooks, Inc.

—Harry Potter e o Cálice de Fogo. (Harry Potter Ser.: Year 4).Tr. of Harry Potter & the Goblet of Fire. (POR.). pap. 38.95 (978-85-325-1252-9(6)) Rocco, Editora, Ltda BRA. Dist: Distribooks, Inc.

—Harry Potter y el Prisionero de Azkaban. 2004. (Harry Potter Ser.: Year 3).Tr. of Harry Potter & the Prisioner of Azkaban. (SPA., Illus.). 360p. (gr. 3-18). 17.95 (978-84-7888-519-0(6), SAL1889) Emece Editores ESP. Dist: Lectorum Pubns., Inc.

—Harry Potter y el Prisionero de Azkaban. 2015. (Harry Potter Spanish Ser.: 3).Tr. of Harry Potter & the Prisoner of Azkaban. (SPA.). (gr. 3-6). lib. bdg. 28.10 (978-0-613-35958-0(5), Turtleback) Turtleback Bks.

—Harry Potter y la Camara Secreta. 2004. (Harry Potter Ser.: Year 2).Tr. of Harry Potter & the Chamber of Secrets. (SPA., Illus.). 288p. (YA). (gr. 3-18). 15.95 (978-84-7888-495-7(5), SAL4595) Emece Editores ESP. Dist: Lectorum Pubns., Inc.

—Harry Potter y la Piedra Filosofal. 2004. (Harry Potter Ser.: Year 1).Tr. of Harry Potter & the Sorcerer's Stone. (SPA., Illus.). 256p. (YA). (gr. 7-18). 15.95 (978-84-7888-445-2(9), SAL2819) Emece Editores ESP. Dist: Lectorum Pubns., Inc.

Rowling, J. K. & Scholastic, Inc. Staff. Harry Potter. 2007. (Harry Potter Ser.: Years 1-7). (ENG.). (J). (gr. 3-7). 205.93 (978-0-545-04425-7(1), Levine, Arthur A. Bks.) Scholastic, Inc.

Roy, James. Chaz at the Fish Market. Gorissen, Dean, illus. 2015. (J). pap. (978-1-4966-0251-0(X)) Capstone Classroom.

Roy, Keri Anne & Holt, K. A. Brains for Lunch: A Zombie Novel in Haiku?! Wilson, Gahan, illus. 2010. (ENG.). 96p. (J). (gr. 4-9). 22.99 (978-1-59643-629-9(8), 9781596436299) Roaring Brook Pr.

Roy, Ron. The School Skeleton. Gurney, John Steven, illus. 2003. (to Z Mysteries Ser.: 19). (ENG.). 96p. (J). (gr. 1-4). pap. 4.99 (978-0-375-81368-9(3), Random Hse. Bks. for Young Readers) Random Hse. Children's Bks.

—The School Skeleton. Gurney, John Steven, illus. 2003. (to Z Mysteries Ser.: 19). (gr. k-3). lib. bdg. 14.75 (978-0-613-62405-3(X), Turtleback) Turtleback Bks.

Rubens, Michael. Sons of The 613. 2012. (ENG.). 320p. (YA). (gr. 7). 16.99 (978-0-547-61216-4(8)) Houghton Mifflin Harcourt Publishing Co.

Rubino-Bradway, Caitlen. Ordinary Magic. 2012. (ENG.). 288p. (YA). (gr. 3-12). 16.99 (978-1-59990-725-3(9), 9781599907253, Bloomsbury USA Childrens) Bloomsbury Publishing USA.

Ruby, Laura. Bad Apple. (ENG.). (YA). (gr. 8). 2011. 272p. pap. 8.99 (978-0-06-124333-2(7)) 2009. 256p. 16.99 (978-0-06-124330-1(2)) HarperCollins Pubs. (HarperTeen).

—Good Girls. 2008. (ENG.). 304p. (YA). (gr. 9-12). pap. 8.99 (978-0-06-088225-9(5)) 2006. 288p. (J). lib. bdg. 17.89 (978-0-06-088224-2(7)) 2006. (ENG.). 288p. (YA). (gr. 9-12). 16.99 (978-0-06-088223-5(9)) HarperCollins Pubs. (HarperTeen).

Rud, Jeff. Centerville. 2016. (Orca Sports Ser.). lib. bdg. 20.80 (978-0-606-38688-3(2)) Turtleback Bks.

Rudetsky, Seth. My Awesome - Awful Popularity Plan. 2013. (ENG.). 224p. (YA). (gr. 7). pap. 8.99 (978-0-375-89997-3(9), Ember) Random Hse. Children's Bks.

Rudolph, Shaina & Royer, Danielle. All My Stripes: A Story for Children with Autism. Zivoin, Jennifer, illus. 2014. (J). pap. (978-1-4338-1917-9(1), Magination Pr.) American Psychological Assn.

Rue, Ginger. Aleca Zamm Is a Wonder. Persico, Zoe, illus. 2017. (Aleca Zamm Ser.: 1). (ENG.). 160p. (J). (gr. 2-5). 16.99 **(978-1-4814-7061-2(2)**, Aladdin) Simon & Schuster Children's Publishing.

Rue, Ginger. Rock 'n' Roll Rebel. 2016. (Tig Ripley Ser.). (ENG.). 349p. (J). (gr. 4-7). 16.99 (978-1-58536-945-4(4), 204106) Sleeping Bear Pr.

Rue, Nancy. So Not Okay, 1 vol. 2014. (Mean Girl Makeover Ser.). (ENG.). 304p. (J). pap. 9.99 (978-1-4003-2370-8(3)) Nelson, Thomas Inc.

—You Can't Sit with Us - Mean Girl Makeover, 1 vol. 2014. (Mean Girl Makeover Ser.). (ENG.). 224p. (J). pap. 9.99 (978-1-4003-2371-5(1)) Nelson, Thomas Inc.

Rue, Nancy N. Sophie Steps Up, 1 vol. 2009. (Faithgirlz! Ser.: No. 4). (ENG.). 128p. (J). pap. 6.99 (978-0-310-71841-3(4)) Zonderkidz.

—Sophie's Drama, 1 vol. 2009. (Faithgirlz! Ser.: No. 11). (ENG.). 178p. (J). pap. 6.99 (978-0-310-71844-4(9)) Zonderkidz.

—Sophie's Friendship Fiasco. 2009. (Faithgirlz! Ser.: No. 7). (ENG.). 128p. (J). pap. 6.99 (978-0-310-71842-0(2)) Zonderkidz.

—Totally Unfair, 1 vol. 2005. ('Nama Beach High Ser.). (ENG.). 160p. (YA). pap. 6.99 (978-0-310-25183-5(4)) Zondervan.

Rumble. 2014. (ENG., Illus.). 560p. (YA). (gr. 9). 19.99 (978-1-4424-8284-5(2), McElderry, Margaret K. Bks.) McElderry, Margaret K. Bks.

Rumford, James. Rain School. 2010. (ENG., Illus.). 32p. (J). (gr. -1-3). 17.99 (978-0-547-24307-8(3)) Houghton Mifflin Harcourt Publishing Co.

Rummel, Verna. My School, 1 vol. 2010. 16p. 24.95 (978-1-4489-6214-3(5)) PublishAmerica, Inc.

Rundell, Katherine. Cartwheeling in Thunderstorms. Castrillón, Melissa, illus. 2014. (ENG.). 256p. (J). (gr. 3-7). 17.99 (978-1-4424-9061-1(6), Simon & Schuster Bks. For Young Readers) Simon & Schuster Bks. For Young Readers.

—Cartwheeling in Thunderstorms. 2016. lib. bdg. 18.40 (978-0-606-38273-1(9)) Turtleback Bks.

Rupert Goes to School: Level M, 6 vols. 128p. (gr. 2-3). 49.95 (978-0-7699-1028-4(9)) Shortland Pubns. (U. S. A.) Inc.

Rupp, Rebecca. Octavia Boone's Big Questions about Life, the Universe & Everything. 2010. (ENG., Illus.). 192p. (J). (gr. 4-7). 15.99 (978-0-7636-4491-8(9)) Candlewick Pr.

—Sarah Simpson's Rules for Living. 2008. (ENG., Illus.). 96p. (J). (gr. 3-7). 14.99 (978-0-7636-3220-5(1)) Candlewick Pr.

Rusackas, Francesca. I Love You All Day Long. Burris, Priscilla, illus. 2004. (ENG.). 32p. (J). (gr. -1-k). reprint ed. pap. 6.99 (978-0-06-050278-2(9)) HarperCollins Pubs.

Russell Brown, Eleanor. A C Robat Goes to Circus School. 2009. 32p. pap. 14.49 (978-1-4389-3939-1(6)) AuthorHouse.

Russell, David O. & Auseon, Andrew. Alienated. 2010. (ENG.). 352p. (J). (gr. 3-7). pap. 5.99 (978-1-4169-8299-9(X), Aladdin) Simon & Schuster Children's Publishing.

Russell, Rachel Renée. Dork Diaries Set, Set. Russell, Rachel Renée, illus. 2011. (Dork Diaries: Nos. 1-3). (ENG., Illus.). 928p. (J). (gr. 4-8). 41.99 (978-1-4424-2662-7(4), Aladdin) Simon & Schuster Children's Publishing.

—How to Dork Your Diary. Russell, Rachel Renée, illus. 2011. (Dork Diaries: No. 3.5). (ENG., Illus.). 288p. (J). (gr. 4-8). 13.99 (978-1-4424-2233-9(5), Aladdin) Simon & Schuster Children's Publishing.

—Locker Hero. Russell, Rachel Renée, illus. 2016. (Misadventures of Max Crumbly Ser.: 1). (ENG., Illus.). 320p. (J). (gr. 4-8). 13.99 (978-1-4814-6001-9(3), Aladdin) Simon & Schuster Children's Publishing.

—Middle School Mayhem. Russell, Rachel Renée, illus. 2017. (Misadventures of Max Crumbly Ser.: 2). (ENG., Illus.). 240p. (J). (gr. 4-8). 13.99 **(978-1-4814-6003-3(X)**, Aladdin) Simon & Schuster Children's Publishing.

—Tales from a Not-So-Dorky Drama Queen, 3 vols. unabr. ed. 2015. (Dork Diaries: 8). (ENG.). 320p. (gr. 4-8). audio compact disk 14.99 (978-1-4423-7023-4(8)) Simon & Schuster Audio.

—Tales from a Not-So-Dorky Drama Queen. Russell, Rachel Renée, illus. 2015. (Dork Diaries: Bk. 9). (ENG., Illus.). 352p. (J). (gr. 4-8). 13.99 (978-1-4424-8769-7(0), Aladdin Paperbacks) Simon & Schuster Children's Publishing.

—Tales from a Not-So-Fabulous Life. Russell, Rachel Renée, illus. 2009. (Dork Diaries: 1). (ENG., Illus.). 304p. (J). (gr. 4-8). 13.99 (978-1-4169-8006-3(7), Aladdin) Simon & Schuster Children's Publishing.

—Tales from a Not-So-Fabulous Life. 2009. (Dork Diaries: 1). lib. bdg. 25.75 (978-0-606-32419-9(4), Turtleback) Turtleback Bks.

—Tales from a Not-So-Friendly Frenemy. Russell, Rachel Renée, illus. 2016. (Dork Diaries: 11). (ENG., Illus.). 288p. (J). (gr. 4-8). 13.99 (978-1-4814-7920-2(2), Aladdin) Simon & Schuster Children's Publishing.

—Tales from a Not-So-Graceful Ice Princess. Russell, Rachel Renée, illus. 2012. (Dork Diaries: 4). (ENG., Illus.). 368p. (J). (gr. 4-8). 13.99 (978-1-4424-1192-0(9), Aladdin) Simon & Schuster Children's Publishing.

—Tales from a Not-So-Happily Ever After. 2014. (Dork Diaries: 8). lib. bdg. 25.75 (978-0-606-36241-2(X)) Turtleback Bks.

—Tales from a Not-So-Happy Heartbreaker. Russell, Rachel Renée, illus. 2013. (Dork Diaries: 6). (ENG., Illus.). 352p. (J). (gr. 4-8). 13.99 (978-1-4424-4963-3(2), Aladdin) Simon & Schuster Children's Publishing.

—Tales from a Not-So-Happy Heartbreaker. 2013. (Dork Diaries: 6). lib. bdg. 25.75 (978-0-606-32424-3(0), Turtleback) Turtleback Bks.

—Tales from a Not-So-Perfect Pet Sitter. Russell, Rachel Renée, illus. 2015. (Dork Diaries: 10). (ENG., Illus.). 320p. (J). (gr. 4-8). 13.99 (978-1-4814-5704-0(7), Aladdin) Simon & Schuster Children's Publishing.

—Tales from a Not-So-Perfect Pet Sitter. Russell, Rachel Renée, illus. 2015. (Dork Diaries: 10). (ENG., Illus.). 320p. (J). (gr. 4-8). lib. bdg. 25.75 (978-0-606-37923-6(1)) Turtleback Bks.

—Tales from a Not-So-Popular Party Girl. Russell, Rachel Renée, illus. 2010. (Dork Diaries: 2). (ENG., Illus.). 288p. (J). (gr. 4-8). 13.99 (978-1-4169-8008-7(3), Aladdin) Simon & Schuster Children's Publishing.

—Tales from a Not-So-Popular Party Girl. 2010. (Dork Diaries: 2). lib. bdg. 25.75 (978-0-606-32420-5(8), Turtleback) Turtleback Bks.

—Tales from a Not-So-Smart Miss Know-It-All. Russell, Rachel Renée, illus. 2012. (Dork Diaries: 5). (ENG., Illus.). 368p. (J). (gr. 4-8). 13.99 (978-1-4424-4961-9(6), Aladdin) Simon & Schuster Children's Publishing.

—Tales from a Not-So-Talented Pop Star. Russell, Rachel Renée, illus. 2011. (Dork Diaries: 3). (ENG., Illus.). 336p. (J). (gr. 4-8). 13.99 (978-1-4424-1190-6(2), Aladdin) Simon & Schuster Children's Publishing.

Russell, Rachel Renée, et al. Tales from a Not-So-Popular Party Girl. 2010. (ENG.). pap. (978-1-4424-4042-5(2), Aladdin Paperbacks) Simon & Schuster Children's Publishing.

Russell, Randy. Dead Rules. 2011. (ENG.). 384p. (YA). (gr. 8-18). 16.99 (978-0-06-198670-3(4), HarperTeen) HarperCollins Pubs.

Rutkoski, Marie. The Shadow Society. 2013. (ENG.). 448p. (YA). (gr. 7-12). pap. 9.99 (978-1-250-03424-3(8)) Square Fish.

Rutland, Mirium. Miss Pistachios Big Day. 2007. (Illus.). 48p. pap. (978-1-58690-063-2(3)) Mould, Paul Publishing.

Ruzima, Keza. Girl Power: The Adventures of a Teenage Circle. 2009. 112p. pap. 23.75 (978-1-60860-647-4(3), Eloquent Bks.) Strategic Book Publishing & Rights Agency (SBPRA).

Ryan, Amy Kathleen. Vibes. 2010. (ENG.). 264p. (YA). (gr. 9). pap. 14.95 (978-0-547-24889-9(X)) Houghton Mifflin Harcourt Publishing Co.

Ryan, Carol. A Bridge Through Time, 1 vol. 2010. 276p. pap. 27.95 (978-1-4489-4254-1(3)) PublishAmerica, Inc.

Ryan, Darlene. Responsible, 1 vol. 2007. (Orca Soundings Ser.). (ENG.). (YA). (gr. 8-12). 128p. pap. 9.95 (978-1-55143-685-2(X)); 112p. lib. bdg. 14.95 (978-1-55143-687-6(6)) Orca Bk. Pubs. USA.

Ryan, Hugh. The Hunt. 2012. 90p. (J). (978-0-545-46306-5(8)) Scholastic, Inc.

Ryan, Margaret. Magic Mistakes! Murfin, Teresa, illus. 2010. (Airy Fairy Ser.). (ENG.). 80p. (gr. 2-4). lib. bdg. 24.21 (978-1-59961-499-1(5)) Spotlight.

Ryan, Pam Muñoz. Tony Baloney: Pen Pal. Fotheringham, Ed, illus. 2014. 39p. (J). pap. (978-0-545-69227-4(X), Scholastic Pr.) Scholastic, Inc.

Ryan, Sara. Empress of the World. 2003. (ENG.). 304p. (YA). (gr. 9-18). 8.99 (978-0-14-250059-0(3), Speak) Penguin Young Readers Group.

Ryan, Tom. Big Time, 1 vol. 2014. (Orca Limelights Ser.). (ENG.). 144p. (J). (gr. 6-9). pap. 9.95 (978-1-4598-0461-6(9)) Orca Bk. Pubs. USA.

Rylander, Chris. Codename Zero. 2014. (Codename Conspiracy Ser.: 1). (ENG.). 368p. (J). (gr. 3-7). 16.99 (978-0-06-212008-3(5), Waldon Pond Pr.) HarperCollins Pubs.

—Countdown Zero. 2015. (Codename Conspiracy Ser.: 2). (ENG.). 368p. (J). (gr. 3-7). 16.99 (978-0-06-212011-3(5), Waldon Pond Pr.) HarperCollins Pubs.

—The Fourth Stall. (Fourth Stall Ser.: 1). (ENG.). (J). (gr. 3-7). 2011. 320p. 16.99 (978-0-06-199496-8(0))Pt. II. 2012. 288p. 16.99 (978-0-06-199630-6(0))Pt. 3. 2014. 320p. pap. 6.99 (978-0-06-212006-9(9))Pt. III. 2013. 304p. 16.99 (978-0-06-212005-2(0)) HarperCollins Pubs. (Waldon Pond Pr.).

Rylant, Cynthia. Mr. Putter & Tabby Ring the Bell. Howard, Arthur, illus. (Mr. Putter & Tabby Ser.). (ENG.). 44p. (J). (gr. 1-4). 2012. pap. 5.99 (978-0-547-85075-7(1)) 2011. 14.99 (978-0-15-205071-9(X)) Houghton Mifflin Harcourt Publishing Co.

—Mr. Putter & Tabby Ring the Bell. Howard, Arthur, illus. 2012. (Mr. Putter & Tabby Ser.). lib. bdg. 16.00 (978-0-606-26614-7(3), Turtleback) Turtleback Bks.

Saab, Julie. Little Lola. Gothard, David, illus. 2014. (ENG.). 32p. (J). (gr. -1-3). 16.99 (978-0-06-227457-1(0), Greenwillow Bks.) HarperCollins Pubs.

Sachar, Louis. Fuzzy Mud. 2015. (KOR.). 228p. (J). (gr. 5). pap. (978-89-364-5671-9(7)) Chang-jag and Bipyeong Co.

—Fuzzy Mud. 2015. (CHI.). 240p. (J). pap. (978-986-211-551-0(3)) Hsaio Lu Publishing Co., Ltd.

—Fuzzy Mud. (ENG.). (J). (gr. 5). 2017. 208p. 7.99 (978-0-385-37022-6(9), Yearling) 2015. (Illus.). 192p. 16.99 (978-0-385-74378-5(5), Delacorte Bks. for Young Readers) 2015. (Illus.). 192p. lib. bdg. 19.99 (978-0-375-99129-5(8), Delacorte Bks. for Young Readers) Random Hse. Children's Bks.

—Fuzzy Mud. 2017. lib. bdg. 18.40 **(978-0-606-39871-8(6))** Turtleback Bks.

—Gets a Little Stranger. 150p. (J). (gr. 3-5). pap. 4.99 (978-0-8072-1543-2(0)); 2004. pap. 29.00 incl. audio (978-0-8072-8141-3(7), S YA 116 SP) Random Hse. Audio Publishing Group. (Listening Library).

—Gets a Little Stranger. 2003. (Wayside School Ser.). (J). (gr. 3-6). lib. bdg. 16.00 (978-0-613-86690-3(8), Turtleback) Turtleback Bks.

—Marvin Redpost #2: Why Pick on Me? Record, Adam, illus. 2015. (Marvin Redpost Ser.: 2). (ENG.). 96p. (J). (gr. 1-4). lib. bdg. 12.99 (978-0-553-53541-9(2), Random Hse. Bks. for Young Readers) Random Hse. Children's Bks.

—Marvin Redpost #3: Is He a Girl? Record, Adam, illus. 2015. (Marvin Redpost Ser.: 3). (ENG.). 96p. (J). (gr. 1-4). lib. bdg.

12.99 *(978-0-553-53542-6(0)*, Random Hse. Bks. for Young Readers) Random Hse. Children's Bks.
—Marvin Redpost #5: Class President. Record, Adam, illus. 2015. (Marvin Redpost Ser.: 5). (ENG.). 96p. (J). (gr. 1-4). lib. bdg. 12.99 *(978-0-553-53543-3(9)*, Random Hse. Bks. for Young Readers) Random Hse. Children's Bks.
—Marvin Redpost #6: a Flying Birthday Cake? Record, Adam, illus. 2015. (Marvin Redpost Ser.: 6). (ENG.). 96p. (J). (gr. 1-4). lib. bdg. 12.99 *(978-0-553-53544-0(7)*, Random Hse. Bks. for Young Readers) Random Hse. Children's Bks.
—Sideways Stories from Wayside School. McCauley, Adam, illus. (Wayside School Ser.). (ENG.). 128p. (J). (gr. 3-7). 2003. pap. 6.99 *(978-0-380-69871-4(4))* 2004. pap. 6.99 *(978-0-380-73148-0(7))* HarperCollins Pubs.
—Sideways Stories from Wayside School. 124p. (J). (gr. 3-5). pap. 4.99 *(978-0-8072-1458-9(2)*, Listening Library) Random Hse. Audio Publishing Group.
—Sideways Stories from Wayside School. 2003. (Wayside School Ser.). (J). (gr. 3-6). lib. bdg. 17.20 *(978-0-613-87805-0(1)*, Turtleback) Turtleback Bks.
—Someday Angeline. Samuels, Barbara, illus. 2005. (Avon Camelot Bks.). (ENG.). 192p. (J). (gr. 3-7). pap. 5.99 *(978-0-380-83444-0(8))* HarperCollins Pubs.
—The Wayside School Collection, 3 vols., Set. McCauley, Adam, illus. 2004. (Wayside School Ser.). 496p. (J). (gr. 3-7). pap. 17.97 *(978-0-380-79171-2(4))* HarperCollins Pubs.
—Wayside School Gets a Little Stranger. Schick, Joel & McCauley, Adam, illus. 2003. (Wayside School Ser.). (ENG.). 176p. (J). (gr. 3-7). pap. 5.99 *(978-0-380-72381-2(6))* HarperCollins Pubs.
—Wayside School Gets a Little Stranger. McCauley, Adam, illus. rev. ed. 2004. (Wayside School Ser.). (ENG.). 160p. (J). (gr. 3-7). pap. 6.99 *(978-0-380-73149-7(5))* HarperCollins Pubs.
—Wayside School Is Falling Down. McCauley, Adam, illus. (Wayside School Ser.). (ENG.). (J). (gr. 3-7). 2003. 192p. pap. 6.99 *(978-0-380-75484-7(3))* 2004. 160p. pap. 6.99 *(978-0-380-73150-3(9))* HarperCollins Pubs.
—Wayside School Is Falling Down. 179p. (J). (gr. 3-5). pap. 4.99 *(978-0-8072-1461-9(2)*, Listening Library) Random Hse. Audio Publishing Group.
—Wayside School Is Falling Down. 2003. (Wayside School Ser.). (J). (gr. 3-6). lib. bdg. 17.20 *(978-0-613-89269-8(0)*, Turtleback) Turtleback Bks.
Sachs, Marilyn. The Bears' House. 2008. 80p. (gr. 4-7). pap. 8.95 *(978-0-595-53553-8(4))* iUniverse, Inc.
—The Fat Girl. 2nd ed. 2007. (ENG.). 240p. (YA). (gr. 8-12). per. 8.95 *(978-0-7387-1000-6(8)*, Flux) North Star Editions.
Sackier, Shelley. Dear OPL. 2015. (ENG.). 240p. (J). (gr. 5-8). pap. 7.99 *(978-1-4926-0859-2(9)*, 9781492608592) Sourcebooks, Inc.
Sadd, Kenn. Crazy Cracked Pots. 2009. 144p. pap. 24.95 *(978-1-61546-673-3(8))* America Star Bks.
Saddleback Educational Publishing Staff, ed. Be Fair. 2011. (Carter High Senior Year Ser.). (ENG.). 16p. (YA). (gr. 9-12). cd-rom 7.95 *(978-1-61651-333-7(0))* Saddleback Educational Publishing, Inc.
—Boy of Their Dreams. 2011. (Carter High Chronicles Ser.). (ENG.). 16p. (YA). (gr. 9-12). tchr. ed. 7.95 incl. cd-rom *(978-1-61651-315-3(2))* Saddleback Educational Publishing, Inc.
—Don't Blame Me. 2011. (Carter High Chronicles Ser.). (ENG.). 16p. (YA). (gr. 9-12). tchr. ed. 7.95 incl. cd-rom *(978-1-61651-317-7(9))* Saddleback Educational Publishing, Inc.
—The Easy Way. 2011. (Carter High Chronicles Ser.). (ENG.). 16p. (YA). (gr. 9-12). tchr. ed. 7.95 incl. cd-rom *(978-1-61651-316-0(0))* Saddleback Educational Publishing, Inc.
—The Fastest Runner. 2011. (Carter High Chronicles Ser.). (ENG.). 16p. (YA). (gr. 9-12). cd-rom 7.95 *(978-1-61651-318-4(7))* Saddleback Educational Publishing, Inc.
—It Is Not a Date. 2011. (Carter High Chronicles Ser.). (ENG.). 16p. (YA). (gr. 9-12). cd-rom 7.95 *(978-1-61651-319-1(5))* Saddleback Educational Publishing, Inc.
—One Date Too Many. 2011. (Carter High Chronicles Ser.). (ENG.). 16p. (YA). (gr. 9-12). tchr. ed. 7.95 incl. cd-rom *(978-1-61651-320-7(9))* Saddleback Educational Publishing, Inc.
—Right Kind of Win. 2011. (Carter High Chronicles Ser.). (ENG.). 16p. (YA). (gr. 9-12). cd-rom 7.95 *(978-1-61651-321-4(7))* Saddleback Educational Publishing, Inc.
—Too Late. 2011. (Carter High Chronicles Ser.). (ENG.). 16p. (YA). (gr. 9-12). cd-rom 7.95 *(978-1-61651-322-1(5))* Saddleback Educational Publishing, Inc.
Saddlewick, A. B. Monstrous Maud: Freaky Sleepover. Horne, Sarah, illus. 2013. (Monstrous Maud Ser.: 3). (ENG.). 128p. (J). (gr. k-2). pap. 6.99 *(978-1-78055-074-9(X))* O'Mara, Michael Bks., Ltd. GBR. Dist: Independent Pubs. Group.
—Monstrous Maud: School Scare. Horne, Sarah, illus. 2013. (Monstrous Maud Ser.: 4). (ENG.). 128p. (J). (gr. k-2). pap. 6.99 *(978-1-78055-075-6(8))* O'Mara, Michael Bks., Ltd. GBR. Dist: Independent Pubs. Group.
Saft, Lauren. Those Girls. 2016. (ENG.). 336p. (YA). (gr. 10-17). pap. 9.99 *(978-0-316-26016-9(9)*, Poppy) Little, Brown Bks. for Young Readers.
Sage, Angie. Gargoyle Hall: An Araminta Spookie Adventure. 2015. (Araminta Spookie Adventure Ser.: 1). (ENG., Illus.). 224p. (YA). (gr. 3-6). 16.99 *(978-1-61963-626-2(3)*, 9781619636262, Bloomsbury USA Childrens) Bloomsbury Publishing USA.
Said, Taunya D. Smart Alec- Alex: The 5th Grade Schedule Change. 2009. 53p. (YA). pap. 10.95 *(978-1-4327-4187-7(X))* Outskirts Pr., Inc.
Salane, Jeffrey. Justice. (ENG.). 288p. (J). (gr. 3-7). 2016. (Lawless Ser.: 2). pap. 6.99 *(978-0-545-45032-4(2))* 2015. 16.99 *(978-0-545-45031-7(4))* Scholastic, Inc. (Scholastic Pr.).
—Lawless. (J). 2013. 277p. *(978-0-545-54882-3(9))*Bk. 1. 2015. (ENG.). 288p. (gr. 3-7). pap. 6.99 *(978-0-545-45030-0(6))* Scholastic, Inc. (Scholastic Pr.).
—Lawless: Book 1. 2013. (Lawless Ser.). (ENG.). 288p. (J). (gr. 5-9). 16.99 *(978-0-545-45029-4(2)*, Scholastic Pr.) Scholastic, Inc.
—Mayhem. 2016. (Lawless Ser.: 3). (ENG.). 304p. (J). (gr. 3-7). 17.99 *(978-0-545-45033-1(0)*, Scholastic Pr.) Scholastic, Inc.
Saldaña, Jr. A Good Long Way. 2010. 128p. (J). (gr. 6-18). pap. 10.95 *(978-1-55885-607-3(2)*, Piñata Books) Arte Publico Pr.
Saldana, Rene. Case of Pen Gone Missing/El Caso de la Pluma Perdida. Villarroel, Carolina, tr. from ENG. Mora, Giovanni, illus. 2009. (SPA & ENG.). 80p. (J). (gr. 3-7). pap. 9.95 *(978-1-55885-555-7(6)*, Piñata Books) Arte Publico Pr.
Saldana, Rene, Jr. A Mystery Bigger Than Big / un Misterio Mas Grande Que Grandisimo: A Mickey Rangel Mystery / Colección Mickey Rangel, Detective Privado. 2016. (Mickey Rangel Mystery / Coleccion Mickey Rangel, Detective P Ser.). (MUL, ENG & SPA., Illus.). 64p. (J). (gr. 3-6). pap. 9.95 *(978-1-55885-824-4(5)*, Piñata Books) Arte Publico Pr.
Saldin, Erin. The Girls of No Return. 2012. (YA). pap. *(978-0-545-31027-7(X))*; (ENG.). 352p. (J). (gr. 9-9). 17.99 *(978-0-545-31026-0(1))* Scholastic, Inc. (Levine, Arthur A. Bks.).
Saldivar, Jose A. The Adventures of Oskar: Oskar's New School. Nilsson, Janet Busbey, ed. Jasnoch, Dorothy, illus. 2013. (ENG.). 32p. pap. 13.99 *(978-1-937752-07-1(0))* Owl About Bks. Pub., Inc.
Sales, Leila. Mostly Good Girls. (ENG.). 368p. (YA). (gr. 9). 2011. pap. 9.99 *(978-1-4424-0680-3(1))* 2010. 17.99 *(978-1-4424-0679-7(8))* Simon Pulse. (Simon Pulse).
—This Song Will Save Your Life. 2013. (ENG.). 288p. (YA). (gr. 7). 18.99 *(978-0-374-35138-0(4)*, 9780374351380, Farrar, Straus & Giroux (BYR)) Farrar, Straus & Giroux.
—Tonight the Streets Are Ours. 2015. (ENG.). 352p. (YA). (gr. 7). 17.99 *(978-0-374-37665-9(4)*, 9780374376659, Farrar, Straus & Giroux (BYR)) Farrar, Straus & Giroux.
Salisbury, Graham. Calvin Coconut: Rocket Ride. Rogers, Jacqueline, illus. 2013. (Calvin Coconut Ser.). (ENG.). 160p. (J). (gr. 2-5). pap. 6.99 *(978-0-375-86508-4(X)*, Yearling) Random Hse. Children's Bks.
—Calvin Coconut: Dog Heaven. Rogers, Jacqueline, illus. 2011. (Calvin Coconut Ser.). (ENG.). 160p. (J). (gr. 3-7). 6.99 *(978-0-375-84602-1(6)*, Yearling) Random Hse. Children's Bks.
—Calvin Coconut: Zoo Breath. Rogers, Jacqueline, illus. 2011. (Calvin Coconut Ser.). (ENG.). 160p. (J). (gr. 3-7). 6.99 *(978-0-375-84603-8(4)*, Yearling) Random Hse. Children's Bks.
—Kung Fooey. Rogers, Jacqueline, illus. 2012. (Calvin Coconut Ser.). (ENG.). 144p. (J). (gr. 2-5). 6.99 *(978-0-375-86506-0(3)*, Yearling) Random Hse. Children's Bks.
—Trouble Magnet. Rogers, Jacqueline, illus. 2010. (Calvin Coconut Ser.). (ENG.). 160p. (J). (gr. 3-7). pap. 6.99 *(978-0-375-84600-7(X)*, Yearling) Random Hse. Children's Bks.
Salom, Susie. Kyle Finds Her Way. 2016. (ENG.). 256p. (J). (gr. 4-7). 16.99 *(978-0-545-85266-1(8)*, Levine, Arthur A. Bks.) Scholastic, Inc.
Salter, Helen. Does Snogging Count as Exercise? 2011. (ENG.). 256p. (YA). (gr. 7). pap. 12.99 *(978-1-4424-3111-9(3)*, Simon Pulse) Simon Pulse.
Saltzberg, Barney. Crazy Hair Day. Saltzberg, Barney, illus. 2008. (ENG., Illus.). 32p. (J). (gr. k-3). pap. 6.99 *(978-0-7636-2464-4(0))* Candlewick Pr.
—Crazy Hair Day. Saltzberg, Barney, illus. 2011. (Illus.). (J). (gr. k-3). 29.95 *(978-0-545-13450-7(1))* Weston Woods Studios, Inc.
—Crazy Hair Day, 5 bks., Set. 2011. (J). (gr. k-3). 38.75 *(978-0-545-15157-3(0))* Weston Woods Studios, Inc.
—Crazy Hair Day Big Book. Saltzberg, Barney, illus. 2008. (ENG., Illus.). 32p. (J). (gr. k-3). pap. 24.99 *(978-0-7636-3969-3(9))* Candlewick Pr.
—Star of the Week. Saltzberg, Barney, illus. 2010. (ENG., Illus.). 32p. (J). (gr. k-3). pap. 6.99 *(978-0-7636-3076-8(4))* Candlewick Pr.
Salzmann, Mary Elizabeth. Presidential Seal, 1 vol. 2007. (Critter Chronicles Ser.). (ENG., Illus.). 24p. (J). (gr. k-3). lib. bdg. 24.21 *(978-1-59928-464-4(2)*, SandCastle) ABDO Publishing Co.
Sampson, Jeff. Vesper. 2011. (Deviants Ser.: 1). (ENG.). 304p. (YA). (gr. 8-18). 16.99 *(978-0-06-199276-6(3))* HarperCollins Pubs.
—Vesper: A Deviants Novel. 2011. (Deviants Ser.: 1). (ENG.). 320p. (YA). (gr. 8). pap. 8.99 *(978-0-06-199277-3(1))* HarperCollins Pubs.
Sanchez, Alex. Getting It. Mehta, Sangeeta, ed. 2007. (ENG., Illus.). 240p. (YA). (gr. 7-12). pap. 8.99 *(978-1-4169-0898-2(6)*, Simon & Schuster Bks. For Young Readers) Simon & Schuster Bks. For Young Readers.
—The God Box. Del Rosario, Michael, ed. 2009. (ENG., Illus.). 272p. (YA). (gr. 7). pap. 10.99 *(978-1-4169-0900-2(1)*, Simon & Schuster Bks. For Young Readers) Simon & Schuster Bks. For Young Readers.
—Rainbow Boys. 2003. (ENG., Illus.). 262p. (YA). (gr. 7). pap. 9.99 *(978-0-689-85770-6(5)*, Simon & Schuster Bks. For Young Readers) Simon & Schuster Bks. For Young Readers.
—So Hard to Say. Weiss, Jennifer, ed. 2006. (ENG., Illus.). 232p. (YA). (gr. 7-12). reprint ed. pap. 11.99 *(978-1-4169-1189-0(8)*, Simon & Schuster Bks. For Young Readers) Simon & Schuster Bks. For Young Readers.
Sanchez, Jenny Torres. Death, Dickinson, & the Demented Life of Frenchie Garcia. 2013. (ENG.). 272p. (YA). (gr. 2-17). pap. 10.95 *(978-0-7624-4680-3(3)*, Running Pr. Kids) Running Pr. Bk. Pubs.
Sanchez, Lorrie Christel & Blank, Carol. Virgil: The Bully from Cyberspace. Margolis, Al, illus. 2013. 54p. (J). 20.99 *(978-0-9891338-0-7(X))* Utterly Global.
—Virgil: The Bully from Cyberspace Teacher Edition. Margolis, Al, illus. 2013. 88p. 99.00 *(978-0-9891338-1-4(8))* Utterly Global.
Sanchez, Pete. A Friend for Petro. 2008. 73p. pap. 19.95 *(978-1-60474-902-1(4))* America Star Bks.
Sand-Eveland, Cyndi. Dear Toni. 2008. (ENG., Illus.). 136p. (J). (gr. 3-7). 14.95 *(978-0-88776-876-7(8)*, Tundra Bks.) Tundra Bks. CAN. Dist: Penguin Random Hse. LLC.
Sandberg, Winter. Private Display of Affection. 2016. (ENG., Illus.). (YA). (gr. 8-12). 24.99 ***(978-1-63533-065-6(3)**,* Harmony Ink Pr.) Dreamspinner Pr.
Sandberg, Winter. Private Display of Affection [Library Edition]. 2014. 210p. pap. 14.99 *(978-1-62798-537-6(9)*, Harmony Ink Pr.) Dreamspinner Pr.
Sandell, Lisa Ann. A Map of the Known World. (ENG.). 288p. (J). (gr. 7-7). 2011. pap. 8.99 *(978-0-545-06971-7(8))* 2009. 16.99 *(978-0-545-06970-0(X))* Scholastic, Inc. (Scholastic Pr.).
Sanders, Rob. Ruby Rose: Off to School She Goes! Ohi, Debbie Ridpath, illus. 2016. 32p. (J). (gr. -1-3). 15.99 *(978-0-06-223569-5(9))* HarperCollins Pubs.
Sanders, Stephanie S. Villain School: Good Curses Evil. 2011. (ENG.). 240p. (YA). (gr. 3-12). pap. 6.99 *(978-1-59990-848-9(4)*, 9781599908489, Bloomsbury USA Childrens) Bloomsbury Publishing USA.
—Villain School: Hero in Disguise. 2012. (ENG.). 240p. (YA). (gr. 5-8). 15.99 *(978-1-59990-907-3(3)*, 9781599909073, Bloomsbury USA Childrens) Bloomsbury Publishing USA.
Sandoval, Alex. Zack Goes to School. 2009. 20p. pap. 10.50 *(978-1-4389-5537-7(5))* AuthorHouse.
Sanrio. Hello Kitty: What Will You Be a to Z? 2013. (ENG., Illus.). 32p. (J). (gr. k-2). 12.95 *(978-1-4197-0911-1(9)*, Abrams Bks. for Young Readers) Abrams, Inc.
—Let's Go to School. 2014. (ENG.). 32p. (J). (-2). 9.99 *(978-1-4022-9660-4(6)*, Sourcebooks Jabberwocky) Sourcebooks, Inc.
Sansone, V. K. Katie Bear: Fun Days at School. WillowRaven, Aidana, illus. 2007. 84p. pap. 16.95 *(978-0-9798154-7-8(9))* Living Waters Publishing Co.
—Katie Bear & Friends (Book One) 2009. 36p. pap. 16.97 *(978-0-557-09358-8(9))* Lulu Pr., Inc.
—A Strange Day at the Zoo. 2009. 32p. pap. 14.98 *(978-0-557-06519-6(4))* Lulu Pr., Inc.
Santomero, Angela C., adapted by. You Are Special, Daniel Tiger! 2014. (Daniel Tiger's Neighborhood Ser.). (ENG., Illus.). 26p. (J). (gr. -1-2). 12.99 *(978-1-4814-1915-4(3)*, Simon Spotlight) Simon Spotlight.
Santopolo, Jill. The Nina, the Pinta, & the Vanishing Treasure. 2009. (Alec Flint Mystery Ser.: 1). (ENG.). 192p. (J). (gr. 2-5). pap. 6.99 *(978-0-439-90353-0(X)*, Scholastic Paperbacks) Scholastic, Inc.
Santoro, Scott. Which Way to Witch School? Santoro, Scott, illus. (ENG., Illus.). (J). (gr. -1-2). 2012. pap. 5.99 *(978-0-06-078183-5(1))* 2010. 16.99 *(978-0-06-078181-1(5))* HarperCollins Pubs.
Sappenfield, Heather. The View from Who I Was. 2015. (ENG.). 336p. (YA). pap. 11.99 *(978-0-7387-4174-1(4)*, Flux) North Star Editions.
Sarfatti, Esther, tr. from ENG. Berto Da la Talla. 2006. (Libro de Capitulos de Arturo Ser.). (Illus.). 55p. (J). (gr. 6-8). per. 4.99 *(978-1-930332-94-2(7))* Lectorum Pubns., Inc.
Sargent, Dave. Sammy Goes to School #8, 10 vols. 2007. (Little Stinker Ser.: 8). (J). lib. bdg. 23.60 *(978-1-59381-294-2(9))* Ozark Publishing.
—Sammy Goes to School #8 (PB), 10 vols. 2007. (Little Stinker Ser.: 8). (J). pap. 10.95 *(978-1-59381-295-9(7))* Ozark Publishing.
Sargent, Dave & Sargent, Pat. Zeb: (Zebra Dun) Be Prepared, 30 vols., Vol. 60. Lenoir, Jane, illus. 2003. (Saddle up Ser.: Vol. 60). 42p. (J). pap. 10.95 *(978-1-56763-718-2(3))*; lib. bdg. 23.60 *(978-1-56763-717-5(5))* Ozark Publishing.
Sarn, Amélie & Trouillot, Virgile. Looking for Trouble. 2009. (Groove High Ser.). (Illus.). 112p. (YA). (gr. 5-8). 31.95 *(978-1-60754-206-3(4)*, 1293914); pap. 15.25 *(978-1-60754-207-0(2)*, 1293914) Windmill Bks.
—Love Is in the Air. Ducrest, Olivier, illus. 2009. (Groove High Ser.). 112p. (YA). (gr. 5-8). 31.95 *(978-1-60754-212-4(9)*, 1293915); pap. 15.25 *(978-1-60754-213-1(7)*, 1293915) Windmill Bks.
Sarratt, Carla. Freshman Focus Carter G Woodson High Sc. 2006. 292p. pap. 14.95 *(978-1-4327-0109-3(6))* Outskirts Pr., Inc.
Sarratt, Carla R. Just Be. 2008. 312p. pap. 14.95 *(978-1-4327-2212-8(3))* Outskirts Pr., Inc.
Sateren, Shelley Swanson. The Lunchroom Fight. Sullivan, Mary, illus. 2013. (Max & Zoe Ser.). (ENG.). 32p. (gr. k-2). lib. bdg. 21.32 *(978-1-4048-7199-1(3)*, Max & Zoe) Picture Window Bks.
—Max & Zoe. Sullivan, Mary, illus. (Max & Zoe Ser.). (ENG.). 32p. (gr. k-2). 2014. pap. 19.80 *(978-1-4795-5043-2(4))* 2013. 255.84 *(978-1-4795-1695-7(3))* 2013. 85.28 *(978-1-4795-1694-0(5))* 2013. pap. 19.80 *(978-1-4048-8064-1(X))* Picture Window Bks. (Max & Zoe).
—Max & Zoe at Recess, 1 vol. Sullivan, Mary, illus. 2012. (Max & Zoe Ser.). (ENG.). 32p. (gr. k-2). lib. bdg. 21.32 *(978-1-4048-7200-4(0)*, Max & Zoe) Picture Window Bks.
—Max & Zoe at School, 1 vol. Sullivan, Mary, illus. (Max & Zoe Ser.). (ENG.). 32p. (gr. k-2). 2013. pap. 5.19 *(978-1-4048-8059-7(3))* 2011. lib. bdg. 21.32 *(978-1-4048-6211-1(0))* Picture Window Bks. (Max & Zoe).
—Max & Zoe at the Library, 1 vol. Sullivan, Mary, illus. 2011. (Max & Zoe Ser.). (ENG.). 32p. (gr. k-2). lib. bdg. 21.32 *(978-1-4048-6210-4(2)*, Max & Zoe) Picture Window Bks.
—Max & Zoe: the Lunchroom Fight, 1 vol. Sullivan, Mary, illus. 2013. (Max & Zoe Ser.). (ENG.). 32p. (gr. k-2). pap. 5.19 *(978-1-4795-2328-3(3)*, Max & Zoe) Picture Window Bks.
—Max & Zoe: Too Many Tricks, 1 vol. Sullivan, Mary, illus. 2013. (Max & Zoe Ser.). (ENG.). 32p. (gr. k-2). pap. 5.19 *(978-1-4795-2327-6(5)*, Max & Zoe) Picture Window Bks.
—The School Concert. Sullivan, Mary, illus. 2012. (Max & Zoe Ser.). (ENG.). 32p. (gr. k-2). lib. bdg. 21.32 *(978-1-4048-7198-4(5)*, Max & Zoe) Picture Window Bks.
—The Science Fair. Sullivan, Mary, illus. 2013. (Max & Zoe Ser.). (ENG.). 32p. (gr. k-2). lib. bdg. 21.32 *(978-1-4048-7202-8(7)*, Max & Zoe) Picture Window Bks.
—Too Many Tricks. Sullivan, Mary, illus. 2013. (Max & Zoe Ser.). (ENG.). 32p. (gr. k-2). lib. bdg. 21.32 *(978-1-4048-7197-7(7)*, Max & Zoe) Picture Window Bks.
—The Very Best Art Project. Sullivan, Mary, illus. 2013. (Max & Zoe Ser.). (ENG.). 32p. (gr. k-2). lib. bdg. 21.32 *(978-1-4048-7201-1(9)*, Max & Zoe) Picture Window Bks.
Sathre, Vivian. J. B. Wigglebottom & the Parade of Pets: True Ringside Tales, BBQ, & down-Home Recipes. O'Neill, Catharine, illus. 2013. (ENG.). 96p. (J). (gr. 2-5). pap. 13.99 *(978-1-4814-2159-1(X)*, Atheneum Bks. for Young Readers) Simon & Schuster Children's Publishing.
Sauer, Tammi. Ginny Louise & the School Field Day. Munsinger, Lynn, illus. 2016. (ENG.). 32p. (J). (gr. -1-k). 16.99 *(978-1-4847-3044-7(5))* Disney Pr.
—Ginny Louise & the School Showdown. Munsinger, Lynn, illus. 2015. (ENG.). 32p. (J). (gr. -1-k). 16.99 *(978-1-4231-6853-9(4))* Disney Pr.
—Mostly Monsterly. Magoon, Scott, illus. 2010. (ENG.). 40p. (J). (gr. -1-3). 17.99 *(978-1-4169-6110-9(0)*, Simon & Schuster/Paula Wiseman Bks.) Simon & Schuster/Paula Wiseman Bks.
Saunders, Brianna. The Magic Marble. 2013. 32p. pap. 24.95 *(978-1-63004-598-2(5))* America Star Bks.
Saunders, Kate. Beswitched. 2012. (ENG.). 272p. (J). (gr. 4-7). 7.99 *(978-0-375-87329-4(5)*, Yearling) Random Hse. Children's Bks.
Sawyer, Kim Vogel. Katy's New World, 1 vol. 2010. (Katy Lambright Ser.: No. 1). (ENG.). 208p. (YA). (gr. 8-11). pap. 9.99 *(978-0-310-71924-3(0))* Zondervan.
Say, Allen. The Favorite Daughter. 2013. (J). pap. *(978-0-545-17663-7(8)*, Levine, Arthur A. Bks.) Scholastic, Inc.
—The Favorite Daughter. Say, Allen, illus. 2013. (ENG., Illus.). 32p. (J). (gr. -1-3). 17.99 *(978-0-545-17662-0(X)*, Levine, Arthur A. Bks.) Scholastic, Inc.
Sazaklis, John. The Dangers of Dog Walking. Robinson, Lee, illus. 2016. (Billy Burger, Model Citizen Ser.). (ENG.). 96p. (gr. 2-3). lib. bdg. 22.65 *(978-1-4965-2587-1(6))* Stone Arch Bks.
—The Ferret Fiasco. Robinson, Lee, illus. 2016. (Billy Burger, Model Citizen Ser.). (ENG.). 96p. (gr. 2-3). lib. bdg. 22.65 *(978-1-4965-2589-5(2))* Stone Arch Bks.
—Jumping for Junk Food. Robinson, Lee, illus. 2016. (Billy Burger, Model Citizen Ser.). (ENG.). 96p. (gr. 2-3). lib. bdg. 22.65 *(978-1-4965-2586-4(8))* Stone Arch Bks.
—Recess Is Ruined. Robinson, Lee, illus. 2016. (Billy Burger, Model Citizen Ser.). (ENG.). 96p. (gr. 2-3). lib. bdg. 22.65 *(978-1-4965-2588-8(4))* Stone Arch Bks.
S.C.A.M. 170p. (J). pap. *(978-1-4114-0441-0(6)*, SparkNotes) Barnes & Noble, Inc.
Scarry, Richard. My School Backpack. 2012. (ENG., Illus.). 56p. (J). (gr. -1-k). bds. 9.99 *(978-1-4380-7295-1(3))* Barron's Educational Series, Inc.
—Richard Scarry's Great Big Schoolhouse. 2008. (ENG., Illus.). 72p. (J). (gr. -1-2). 14.95 *(978-1-4027-5820-1(0))* Sterling Publishing Co., Inc.
Schachner, Judy. Class Action. 2017. (Skippyjon Jones Ser.). lib. bdg. 19.65 ***(978-0-606-40104-3(0))*** Turtleback Bks.
—Skippyjon Jones, Class Action. (Skippyjon Jones Ser.). (ENG.). (J). 2017. (-k). pap. 8.99 ***(978-0-425-28892-4(7)**,* Puffin Books) 2011. 32p. (gr. -1-k). 17.99 *(978-0-525-42228-0(5)*, Dutton Books for Young Readers) Penguin Young Readers Group.
Schaefer, Lola M. Mittens at School. Hartung, Susan Kathleen, illus. 2012. (My First I Can Read Ser.). (ENG.). 32p. (J). (gr. -1-3). 16.99 *(978-0-06-170224-2(2))*; pap. 3.99 *(978-0-06-170223-5(4))* HarperCollins Pubs.
—Mittens at School. 2012. (My First I Can Read Ser.). (J). lib. bdg. 13.55 *(978-0-606-26292-7(X)*, Turtleback) Turtleback Bks.
Schanen, Adriana Brad. Partners in Slime. Santoso, Charles, illus. (Quinny & Hopper Ser.). (ENG.). 272p. (J). (gr. 3-7). 2017. pap. 6.99 ***(978-1-4847-7822-7(7))*** 2016. 15.99 *(978-1-4847-7506-6(6))* Hyperion Bks. for Children.
Schanen, Adriana Brad. Quinny & Hopper. Swearingen, Greg, illus. 2014. (ENG.). 240p. (J). (gr. 3-7). 15.99 *(978-1-4231-7829-3(7))* Hyperion Bks. for Children.
Schantz, Sarah Elizabeth. Fig. 2016. (ENG.). 352p. (YA). (gr. 9). pap. 10.99 *(978-1-4814-2359-5(2)*, McElderry, Margaret K. Bks.) McElderry, Margaret K. Bks.
Schechter, Lynn R. My Big Fat Secret: How Jenna Takes Control of Her Emotions & Eating. Chin, Jason, illus. 2009. 48p. (J). (gr. 3-7). 14.95 *(978-1-4338-0540-0(5))*; pap. 9.95 *(978-1-4338-0541-7(3))* American Psychological Assn. (Magination Pr.).
Scheerger, Sarah Lynn. Are You Still There. 2015. (ENG.). 288p. (YA). (gr. 8-12). 16.99 *(978-0-8075-4557-7(0))* Whitman, Albert & Co.
Scheier, Leah. Your Voice Is All I Hear. 2015. (ENG.). 336p. (YA). (gr. 8-12). pap. 9.99 *(978-1-4926-1441-8(6))* Sourcebooks, Inc.
Scheppmann, Andrew. Disney Descendants - Good or Evil? A Mash-Up Challenge. 2016. (ENG.). 96p. (J). (gr. 1-4). 9.99 *(978-0-7944-3772-5(9))* Studio Fun International.
Schindler, Holly. A Blue So Dark. 2010. (ENG.). 288p. (YA). (gr. 9-18). pap. 11.99 *(978-0-7387-1926-9(9)*, Flux) North Star Editions.
—Feral. 2014. (ENG.). 432p. (YA). (gr. 8). 17.99 *(978-0-06-222020-2(9)*, HarperTeen) HarperCollins Pubs.
Schizas, Lea. Bubba & Giganto: Odds Against Us. 2008. 68p. (J). pap. *(978-0-9797513-6-3(5))* 4RV Publishing, LLC.
Schleuning, Todd & Schleuning, Cheryl. The Misphits: Story of Snake. Vene, Alessandro, illus. 2013. (ENG.). (J). (gr. -1-3). 15.95 *(978-1-62086-302-2(2))* Mascot Bks., Inc.
Schmatz, Pat. Bluefish. (ENG.). 240p. (YA). (gr. 7). 2013. pap. 6.99 *(978-0-7636-6341-4(7))* 2011. (Illus.). 15.99 *(978-0-7636-5334-7(9))* Candlewick Pr.
—Mousetraps. Hauser, Bill, illus. 2008. (ENG.). 192p. (YA). (gr. 7-12). 17.95 *(978-0-8225-8657-9(6)*, Carolrhoda Bks.) Lerner Publishing Group.
Schmid, Paul. Hugs from Pearl. Schmid, Paul, illus. 2011. (ENG., Illus.). 40p. (J). (gr. -1-2). 14.99 *(978-0-06-180434-2(7))* HarperCollins Pubs.
—Oliver & His Alligator. Schmid, Paul, illus. 2013. (ENG., Illus.). 40p. (J). (gr. -1-k). 15.99 *(978-1-4231-7437-0(2))* Disney Pr.
Schmidt, Gary D. Okay for Now. (ENG.). 368p. (J). (gr. 5-7). 2013. pap. 7.99 *(978-0-544-02280-5(7))* 2011. (Illus.). 16.99 *(978-0-547-15260-8(4))* Houghton Mifflin Harcourt Publishing Co.
—Okay for Now. 2011. (Playaway Children Ser.). (J). (gr. 5-9). 54.99 *(978-1-61707-313-7(X))* Random Hse., Inc.
—Okay for Now. 2013. lib. bdg. 18.40 *(978-0-606-31670-5(1)*, Turtleback) Turtleback Bks.
—The Wednesday Wars. (ENG.). 272p. (J). (gr. 5-7). 2009. pap. 7.99 *(978-0-547-23760-2(X))* 2007. 16.99 *(978-0-618-72483-3(4))* Houghton Mifflin Harcourt Publishing Co.

S

—The Wednesday Wars. 2008. *(978-0-545-10562-0(5))* Scholastic, Inc.
—The Wednesday Wars. 2009. lib. bdg. 18.40 *(978-0-606-10573-6(5),* Turtleback) Turtleback Bks.
Schmidt, René. Leaving Fletchville, 1 vol. 2008. (ENG.). 168p. (J). (gr. 3-7). pap. 9.95 *(978-1-55143-945-7(X))* Orca Bk. Pubs. USA.
Schmidt, Tiffany. Bright Before Sunrise. 2015. (ENG.). 304p. (YA). (gr. 7). pap. 9.99 *(978-0-8027-3502-7(9),* 9780802735027, Bloomsbury USA Childrens) Bloomsbury Publishing USA.
Schmitt, Gary. R. O. Dents in the School. 2009. 73p. pap. 19.95 *(978-1-60813-737-4(6))* America Star Bks.
Schmitt, H. D. Pee Wee Pickle Goes to Kinder-Garden. Spears, Sheri, illus. 2008. 20p. pap. 24.95 *(978-1-60672-731-7(1))* America Star Bks.
Schnee-Bosch, Penny. Mommy Always Comes Back. Bosch, David, illus. 2013. 40p. pap. 13.95 *(978-0-9727993-6-2(2))* Athanata Arts, Ltd.
Schnee, Silke. Prince Noah & the School Pirates. Sistig, Heike, illus. 2016. (Prince Noah Book Ser.). (ENG.). 32p. (J). 16.00 *(978-0-87486-765-7(7))* Plough Publishing Hse.
Schneider, Robyn. The Beginning of Everything. (ENG.). 352p. (YA). (gr. 8). 2014. pap. 9.99 *(978-0-06-221714-1(3),* Tegen, Katherine Bks) 2013. 17.99 *(978-0-06-221713-4(5))* HarperCollins Pubs.
Schnell, Selynn. The Backpack Jungle. 2011. 48p. pap. 16.95 *(978-1-4560-3332-3(8))* America Star Bks.
Schoenberg, Jane. Stuey Lewis Against All Odds: Stories from the Third Grade, 1 vol. Evans, Cambria, illus. 2012. (Stuey Lewis Ser.: 2). (ENG.). 144p. (J). (gr. 1-4). 15.99 *(978-0-374-39901-6(8),* 9780374399016, Farrar, Straus & Giroux (BYR)) Farrar, Straus & Giroux.
—Stuey Lewis Against All Odds: Stories from the Third Grade. Evans, Cambria, illus. 2013. (Stuey Lewis Ser.: 2). (ENG.). 160p. (J). (gr. 1-4). pap. 8.99 *(978-1-250-03404-5(3),* 9781250034045) Square Fish.
Scholastic. The Pokémon School Challenge. 2017. (Pokémon Ser.: 1). (ENG.). 96p. (J). (gr. 2-5). pap. 4.99 ***(978-1-338-14861-9(3))*** Scholastic, Inc.
Scholz, Susie. I'm Not Going to School Today. 2008. 32p. pap. 12.50 *(978-1-60693-109-7(1),* Eloquent Bks.) Strategic Book Publishing & Rights Agency (SBPRA).
School Days. collector's gif. ed. 2003. (J). bds., act. bk. ed. *(978-0-9744302-0-1(X))* School Days.
School Days, Cool Days! Level J, 6 vols. 128p. (gr. 2-3). 41.95 *(978-0-7699-0989-9(2))* Shortland Pubns. (U. S. A.) Inc.
The School Play: Individual Title Six-Packs. (gr. -1-2). 27.00 *(978-0-7635-9473-2(3))* Rigby Education.
School Time. 2003. (J). per. *(978-1-57657-892-6(5))* Paradise Pr., Inc.
Schories, Pat, illus. Biscuit's Graduation Day. 2005. (J). *(978-1-4155-9660-9(3),* HarperFestival) HarperCollins Pubs.
Schorr, Bill & Smith, Ralph. Tucker Grizzwell's Worst Week Ever. 2017. (ENG.). 248p. (J). pap. 9.99 *(978-1-4494-6910-8(8))* Andrews McMeel Publishing.
Schotter, Roni. Doo-Wop Pop. Collier, Bryan, illus. 2008. 40p. (J). (gr. -1-3). lib. bdg. 17.89 *(978-0-06-057974-6(9),* Amistad) HarperCollins Pubs.
Schraff, Anne. The Accuser, 1 vol. unabr. ed. 2010. (Q Reads Ser.). (ENG.). 32p. (YA). (gr. 9-12). pap. 6.95 *(978-1-61651-188-3(5))* Saddleback Educational Publishing, Inc.
—A Boy Called Twister, 1 vol. unabr. ed. 2010. (Urban Underground Ser.). (ENG.). 180p. (YA). (gr. 9-12). pap. 9.95 *(978-1-61651-002-2(1))* Saddleback Educational Publishing, Inc.
—A Boy Called Twister. 2010. (Urban Underground — Harriet Tubman High School Ser.). (YA). lib. bdg. 20.80 *(978-0-606-14271-7(1),* Turtleback) Turtleback Bks.
—The Fairest, 1 vol. unabr. ed. 2011. (Urban Underground Ser.). (ENG.). 179p. (YA). (gr. 9-12). pap. 9.95 *(978-1-61651-007-7(2))* Saddleback Educational Publishing, Inc.
—Going for Gold. 2008. 124p. lib. bdg. 13.95 *(978-0-7569-8403-8(3))* Perfection Learning Corp.
—The Haunting of Hawthorne. 2008. (Passages Ser.). 125p. (YA). (gr. 7-9). lib. bdg. 13.95 *(978-0-7569-8379-6(7))* Perfection Learning Corp.
—If You Really Loved Me, 1 vol. unabr. ed. 2010. (Urban Underground Ser.). (ENG.). 181p. (YA). (gr. 9-12). pap. 9.95 *(978-1-61651-003-9(X))* Saddleback Educational Publishing, Inc.
—Like a Broken Doll, 1 vol. unabr. ed. 2011. (Urban Underground Ser.). (ENG.). 182p. (YA). (gr. 9-12). pap. 9.95 *(978-1-61651-005-3(6))* Saddleback Educational Publishing, Inc.
—Lost & Found. Langan, Paul, ed. 2007. (Bluford High Ser.). 133p. (gr. 8-12). 16.00 *(978-0-7569-8076-4(3))* Perfection Learning Corp.
—Lost & Found. 2007. (Bluford High — Scholastic Ser.: 1). lib. bdg. 16.00 *(978-1-4177-7141-7(0),* Turtleback) Turtleback Bks.
—A Matter of Trust. 2007. (Bluford High — Scholastic Ser.: 2). lib. bdg. 16.00 *(978-1-4177-7142-4(9),* Turtleback) Turtleback Bks.
—No Fear, 1 vol. unabr. ed. 2011. (Urban Underground Ser.). (ENG.). 198p. (YA). (gr. 9-12). pap. 9.95 *(978-1-61651-268-2(7))* Saddleback Educational Publishing, Inc.
—One of Us, 1 vol. unabr. ed. 2010. (Urban Underground Ser.). (ENG.). 180p. (YA). (gr. 9-12). pap. 9.95 *(978-1-61651-004-6(8))* Saddleback Educational Publishing, Inc.
—Outrunning the Darkness, 1 vol. unabr. ed. 2010. (Urban Underground Ser.). (ENG.). 191p. (YA). (gr. 9-12). pap. 9.95 *(978-1-61651-000-8(5))* Saddleback Educational Publishing, Inc.
—The Power of the Rose. 2008. (Passages Ser.). 94p. (YA). (gr. 7-12). pap. 8.50 *(978-0-7891-7541-0(X));* (J). lib. bdg. 13.95 *(978-0-7569-8381-9(9))* Perfection Learning Corp.
—The Price of Friendship. 2008. (Passages Ser.). 138p. (J). (gr. 4-6). lib. bdg. 13.95 *(978-0-7569-8373-4(8))* Perfection Learning Corp.
—The Quality of Mercy. 2011. (Urban Underground — Harriet Tubman High School Ser.). (YA). lib. bdg. 20.80 *(978-0-606-14800-9(0),* Turtleback) Turtleback Bks.
—Secrets in the Shadows. Langan, Paul, ed. 2007. (Bluford High Ser.). 126p. (gr. 8-12). 16.00 *(978-0-7569-8078-8(X))* Perfection Learning Corp.
—Secrets in the Shadows. 2007. (Bluford High — Scholastic Ser.: 3). lib. bdg. 16.00 *(978-1-4177-7149-3(6),* Turtleback) Turtleback Bks.
—Shadows of Guilt, 1 vol. unabr. ed. 2010. (Urban Underground Ser.). (ENG.). 179p. (YA). (gr. 9-12). pap. 9.95 *(978-1-61651-001-5(3))* Saddleback Educational Publishing, Inc.
—Someone to Love Me. 2007. (Bluford High — Scholastic Ser.: 4). lib. bdg. 16.00 *(978-1-4177-7151-6(8),* Turtleback) Turtleback Bks.
—Sounds of Terror, 1 vol. unabr. ed. 2010. (Q Reads Ser.). (ENG.). 32p. (YA). (gr. 9-12). pap. 6.95 *(978-1-61651-206-4(7))* Saddleback Educational Publishing, Inc.
—The Stranger, 1 vol. unabr. ed. 2011. (Urban Underground Ser.). (ENG.). 200p. (YA). (gr. 9-12). pap. 9.95 *(978-1-61651-266-8(0))* Saddleback Educational Publishing, Inc.
—To Be Somebody. 2008. (Passages Ser.). 120p. (J). (gr. 4-6). lib. bdg. 13.95 *(978-0-7569-8390-1(8))* Perfection Learning Corp.
—Vengeance, 1 vol. unabr. ed. 2012. (Urban Underground Ser.). (ENG.). 204p. (YA). (gr. 9-12). pap. 9.95 *(978-1-61651-961-2(4))* Saddleback Educational Publishing, Inc.
—Waters Edge, 1 vol. unabr. ed. 2011. (Urban Underground Ser.). (ENG.). 197p. (YA). (gr. 9-12). pap. 9.95 *(978-1-61651-589-8(9))* Saddleback Educational Publishing, Inc.
—Wildflower, 1 vol. unabr. ed. 2011. (Urban Underground Ser.). (ENG.). 183p. (YA). (gr. 9-12). pap. 9.95 *(978-1-61651-009-1(9))* Saddleback Educational Publishing, Inc.
—Winners & Losers, 1 vol. unabr. ed. 2012. (Urban Underground Ser.). (ENG.). 204p. (YA). (gr. 9-12). pap. 9.95 *(978-1-61651-962-9(2))* Saddleback Educational Publishing, Inc.
Schraff, Anne E. The Outcasts. 2012. (Urban Underground — Harriet Tubman High School Ser.: 21). (YA). lib. bdg. 20.80 *(978-0-606-23794-9(1),* Turtleback) Turtleback Bks.
—The Rescuers. 2012. (Urban Underground — Harriet Tubman High School Ser.: 25). (YA). lib. bdg. 20.80 *(978-0-606-23798-7(4),* Turtleback) Turtleback Bks.
—Second Chances. 2013. (Urban Underground — Harriet Tubman High School Ser.). (YA). lib. bdg. 20.80 *(978-0-606-31584-5(5),* Turtleback) Turtleback Bks.
—Someone to Love Me. 2007. (Bluford High Ser.). 162p. (gr. 8-12). 16.00 *(978-0-7569-8079-5(8))* Perfection Learning Corp.
—Vengeance. 2012. (Urban Underground — Cesar Chavez High School Ser.: 29). (YA). lib. bdg. 20.80 *(978-0-606-26599-7(6),* Turtleback) Turtleback Bks.
—Winners & Losers. 2012. (Urban Underground — Cesar Chavez High School Ser.: 30). (YA). lib. bdg. 20.80 *(978-0-606-26600-0(3),* Turtleback) Turtleback Bks.
Schreiber, Ellen. Cryptic Cravings. 2012. (Vampire Kisses Ser.: 8). (ENG.). 240p. (YA). (gr. 8). pap. 9.99 *(978-0-06-168947-5(5),* Tegen, Katherine Bks) HarperCollins Pubs.
—Full Moon Kisses. 2013. (Full Moon Ser.: 3). (ENG.). 224p. (YA). (gr. 8). pap. 9.99 *(978-0-06-198654-3(2),* Tegen, Katherine Bks) HarperCollins Pubs.
—Love Bites. 2011. (Vampire Kisses Ser.: 7). (ENG.). 208p. (YA). (gr. 8). pap. 8.99 *(978-0-06-168944-4(0),* Tegen, Katherine Bks) HarperCollins Pubs.
—Magic of the Moonlight. (Full Moon Ser.: 2). (ENG.). (YA). (gr. 8). 2012. 256p. pap. 9.99 *(973-0-06-198656-7(9))* 2011. 240p. 17.99 *(978-0-06-198657-4(7))* HarperCollins Pubs. (Tegen, Katherine Bks).
—Once in a Full Moon. 2011. (Full Moon Ser.: 1). (ENG.). 320p. (YA). (gr. 8). pap. 8.99 *(978-0-06-198652-9(6),* Tegen, Katherine Bks) HarperCollins Pubs.
—Royal Blood No. 6. 2009. (Vampire Kisses Ser.: 6). (ENG.). 208p. (YA). (gr. 8-18). 17.99 *(978-0-06-128887-6(X),* Tegen, Katherine Bks) HarperCollins Pubs.
—Vampire Kisses Boxed Set: Vampire Kisses; Kissing Coffins; Vampireville. 2008. (Vampire Kisses Ser.: Nos. 1-3). (J). pap. 15.99 *(978-0-06-169160-7(7),* HarperTeen) HarperCollins Pubs.
Schreiber, Joe. Con Academy. 2016. (ENG.). 240p. (YA). (gr. 9). pap. 9.99 *(978-0-544-81355-7(3),* HMH Books For Young Readers) Houghton Mifflin Harcourt Publishing Co.
—Lenny Cyrus, School Virus. Smith, Matt, illus. 2014. (ENG.). 288p. (J). (gr. 5-7). pap. 6.99 *(978-0-544-33628-5(3),* HMH Books For Young Readers) Houghton Mifflin Harcourt Publishing Co.
Schreiber, Sam. Raise Your Voice. 2004. (Illus.). 187p. (J). pap. *(978-0-439-73083-9(X))* Scholastic, Inc.
Schroeder, Lisa. Falling for You. 2013. (ENG., (YA). (gr. 9). Illus.). 384p. pap. 9.99 *(978-1-4424-4400-3(2));* 368p. 16.99 *(978-1-4424-4399-0(5))* Simon Pulse. (Simon Pulse).
Schumacher, Julie. Black Box. 2010. (ENG.). 176p. (YA). (gr. 7-18). pap. 7.99 *(978-0-440-24064-8(6),* Delacorte Bks. for Young Readers) Random Hse. Children's Bks.
Schusterman, Michelle. Friends, Fugues, & Fortune Cookies. Kote, Genevieve, illus. 2014. (I Heart Band Ser.: 2). (ENG.). 208p. (J). (gr. 3-7). 6.99 *(978-0-448-45684-3(2),* Grosset & Dunlap) Penguin Young Readers Group.
—I Heart Band #1. Kote, Genevieve, illus. 2014. (I Heart Band Ser.: 1). (ENG.). 208p. (J). (gr. 3-7). 6.99 *(978-0-448-45683-6(4),* Grosset & Dunlap) Penguin Young Readers Group.
Schusterman, Michelle & Kote, Geneviève. Sleepovers, Solos, & Sheet Music. 2014. (I Heart Band Ser.: 3). (ENG.). 208p. (J). (gr. 3-7). 6.99 *(978-0-448-45685-0(0),* Grosset & Dunlap) Penguin Young Readers Group.
Schwab, Victoria. Second Chances. 2014. (Everyday Angel Ser.: 2). (ENG.). 208p. (J). (gr. 3-7). pap. 6.99 *(978-0-545-52847-4(X),* Scholastic Paperbacks) Scholastic, Inc.
Schwartz, Amy. The Boys Team. Schwartz, Amy, illus. 2014. (ENG., Illus.). 40p. (J). (gr. -1-1). 19.99 *(978-1-4814-2534-6(X),* Atheneum Bks. for Young Readers) Simon & Schuster Children's Publishing.
Schwartz, Amy & Marcus, Leonard S. Oscar: The Big Adventure of a Little Sock Monkey. Schwartz, Amy, illus. 2006. (Illus.). 32p. (J). (gr. -1-2). 16.99 *(978-0-06-072622-5(9),* Tegen, Katherine Bks) HarperCollins Pubs.
Schweizer, Chris. The Creeps: Book 1: Night of the Frankenfrogs. 2015. (ENG., Illus.). 128p. (J). (gr. 3-7). 17.95 *(978-1-4197-1379-8(5),* Amulet Bks.) Abrams, Inc.
Scieszka, Jon. Baloney (Henry P.) Smith, Lane, illus. 2005. (gr. -1-3). 17.00 *(978-0-7569-5494-9(0))* Perfection Learning Corp.
—Math Curse. 2004. (Illus.). (J). (gr. k-4). spiral bd. *(978-0-616-01778-4(2))* Canadian National Institute for the Blind/Institut National Canadien pour les Aveugles.
—Science Verse. Smith, Lane, illus. 2004. (ENG.). 40p. (J). (gr. 2-5). 17.99 *(978-0-670-91057-1(0),* Viking Books for Young Readers) Penguin Young Readers Group.
—Spaceheadz. Prigmore, Shane, illus. (Spaceheadz Ser.: 3). (ENG.). (J). (gr. 2-5). 2012. 224p. pap. 7.99 *(978-1-4169-7956-2(5))* 2011. 224p. 15.99 *(978-1-4169-7955-5(7))* 2010. 176p. 14.99 *(978-1-4169-7951-7(4))*Set. 2013. 864p. pap. 23.99 *(978-1-4424-9858-7(7))* Simon & Schuster Bks. For Young Readers. (Simon & Schuster Bks. For Young Readers).
—SPHDZ 4 Life! Prigmore, Shane, illus. 2013. (Spaceheadz Ser.: 4). (ENG.). 192p. (J). (gr. 2-5). pap. 5.99 *(978-1-4169-7958-6(1))*;Bk. 4. 16.99 *(978-1-4169-7957-9(3))* Simon & Schuster Bks. For Young Readers. (Simon & Schuster Bks. For Young Readers).
—SPHDZ Book #1! Prigmore, Shane, illus. 2011. (Spaceheadz Ser.: 1). (ENG.). 192p. (J). (gr. 2-5). pap. 7.99 *(978-1-4424-1986-5(5),* Simon & Schuster Bks. For Young Readers) Simon & Schuster Bks. For Young Readers.
—SPHDZ Book #2! Prigmore, Shane, illus. (Spaceheadz Ser.: 2). (ENG.). (J). (gr. 2-5). 2011. 256p. pap. 7.99 *(978-1-4169-7954-8(9))* 2010. 240p. 14.99 *(978-1-4169-7953-1(0))* Simon & Schuster Bks. For Young Readers. (Simon & Schuster Bks. For Young Readers).
—2095. Smith, Lane, illus. 2005. (Time Warp Trio Ser.: No. 5). 72p. (gr. 4-7). 15.00 *(978-0-7569-5989-0(6))* Perfection Learning Corp.
Scott B, Bryon. The School by Blue Lake. 2010. 60p. pap. 27.99 *(978-1-4520-1658-0(5))* AuthorHouse.
Scott, Elizabeth. Love You Hate You Miss You. (ENG.). (YA). (gr. 8). 2010. 304p. pap. 8.99 *(978-0-06-112285-9(8))* 2009. 288p. 16.99 *(978-0-06-112283-5(1))* HarperCollins Pubs. (HarperTeen).
—Miracle. (ENG., Illus.). (YA). (gr. 9). 2013. 240p. pap. 9.99 *(978-1-4424-1707-6(2))* 2012. 220p. 16.99 *(978-1-4424-1706-9(4))* Simon Pulse. (Simon Pulse).
—Perfect You. 2008. (ENG.). 304p. (YA). (gr. 9-12). pap. 9.99 *(978-1-4169-5355-5(8),* Simon Pulse) Simon Pulse.
Scott, Kieran. Geek Magnet. 2009. (ENG.). 320p. (YA). (gr. 7-18). 8.99 *(978-0-14-241417-0(4),* Speak) Penguin Young Readers Group.
—I Was a Non-Blonde Cheerleader. 2007. (ENG.). 272p. (YA). (gr. 7-18). 8.99 *(978-0-14-240910-7(3),* Speak) Penguin Young Readers Group.
—Only Everything. 2014. (True Love Ser.: 1). (ENG., Illus.). 352p. (YA). (gr. 7). pap. 9.99 *(978-1-4424-7716-2(4),* Simon & Schuster Bks. For Young Readers) Simon & Schuster Bks. For Young Readers.
—She's So Dead to Us. (He's So/She's So Trilogy Ser.). (ENG.). (YA). (gr. 7). 2011. 304p. pap. 9.99 *(978-1-4169-9952-2(3))* 2010. 288p. 16.99 *(978-1-4169-9951-5(5))* Simon & Schuster Bks. For Young Readers. (Simon & Schuster Bks. For Young Readers).
—Something True. 2015. (True Love Ser.: 3). (ENG., Illus.). 288p. (YA). (gr. 7). pap. 9.99 *(978-1-4424-7723-0(7))* Simon & Schuster Children's Publishing.
—This Is So Not Happening. (He's So/She's So Trilogy Ser.). (ENG., 320p. (YA). (gr. 7). 2013. Illus.). pap. 9.99 *(978-1-4169-9956-0(6))* 2012. 16.99 *(978-1-4169-9955-3(8))* Simon & Schuster Bks. For Young Readers. (Simon & Schuster Bks. For Young Readers).
Scott, Kieran & Scott, Kiernan. Brunettes Strike Back. 2007. (ENG.). 272p. (YA). (gr. 7-18). 8.99 *(978-0-14-240778-3(X),* Speak) Penguin Young Readers Group.
Scott, Ladena Mae. Bossy Rossy. 2013. 36p. pap. 18.41 *(978-1-4669-8965-8(3))* Trafford Publishing.
Scott, Mary Ann. New Girl, 1 vol. 2003. (ENG.). 208p. (YA). *(978-1-55041-725-8(8))* Fitzhenry & Whiteside, Ltd.
Scott, Michele. Dark Harmony: A Vivienne Taylor Horse Lover's Mystery, 0 vols. 2014. (Fairmont Riding Academy Ser.: 2). (ENG.). 384p. (YA). (gr. 7-12). pap. 9.99 *(978-1-4778-4726-8(X),* 9781477847268, Amazon Children's Publishing) Amazon Publishing.
—Perfect Harmony: A Vivienne Taylor Horse Lover's Mystery, 0 vols. 2014. (Fairmont Riding Academy Ser.). (ENG.). 274p. (YA). (gr. 7-9). pap. 9.99 *(978-1-4778-4779-4(0),* 9781477847794, Skyscape) Amazon Publishing.
—Silent Harmony, 0 vols. unabr. ed. 2013. (Fairmont Riding Academy Ser.: 1). (ENG.). 256p. (YA). (gr. 7-12). pap. 9.99 *(978-1-4778-1713-1(1),* 9781477817131, Amazon Children's Publishing) Amazon Publishing.
Scotton, Rob. Back to School, Splat! Scotton, Rob, illus. 2011. (Splat the Cat Ser.). (ENG., Illus.). 24p. (J). (gr. -1-3). pap. 3.99 *(978-0-06-197851-7(5),* HarperFestival) HarperCollins Pubs.
—Love, Splat. Scotton, Rob, illus. (Splat the Cat Ser.). (ENG., Illus.). 40p. (J). (gr. -1-2). 2011. 9.99 *(978-0-06-207776-9(7))* 2008. 16.99 *(978-0-06-083157-8(X))* HarperCollins Pubs.
—The Name of the Game. Scotton, Rob, illus. 2012. (I Can Read Level 1 Ser.). (ENG., Illus.). 32p. (J). (gr. -1-3). 16.99 *(978-0-06-209015-7(1))* HarperCollins Pubs.
—On with the Snow. 2013. (Splat the Cat 8X8 Ser.). (J). lib. bdg. 13.55 *(978-0-606-27152-3(X),* Turtleback) Turtleback Bks.
—Sings Flat. Scotton, Rob, illus. 2011. (I Can Read Level 1 Ser.). (ENG., Illus.). 32p. (J). (gr. -1-3). 16.99 *(978-0-06-197854-8(9))* HarperCollins Pubs.
—Splat & the Cool School Trip. Scotton, Rob, illus. 2013. (Splat the Cat Ser.). (ENG., Illus.). 40p. (J). (gr. -1-3). 17.99 *(978-0-06-213386-1(1))* HarperCollins Pubs.
—Splat the Cat. Scotton, Rob, illus. 2008. (Splat the Cat Ser.). (Illus.). 40p. (J). (gr. -1-3). (ENG.). 17.99 *(978-0-06-083154-7(5));* lib. bdg. 17.89 *(978-0-06-083155-4(3))* HarperCollins Pubs.
—Splat the Cat. 2011. (J). (gr. -1-2). 29.95 *(978-0-545-23794-9(7))* Weston Woods Studios, Inc.
—Splat the Cat: Big Reading Collection. Scotton, Rob, illus. 2012. (I Can Read Level 1 Ser.). (ENG., Illus.). 100p. (J). (gr. k-3). pap. 16.99 *(978-0-06-209029-4(1))* HarperCollins Pubs.
—Splat the Cat Sings Flat. Scotton, Rob, illus. 2011. (I Can Read Level 1 Ser.). (ENG., Illus.). 32p. (J). (gr. -1-3). pap. 3.99 *(978-0-06-197853-1(1))* HarperCollins Pubs.
—Up in the Air at the Fair. 2014. (Splat the Cat: I Can Read Ser.). (J). lib. bdg. 13.55 *(978-0-606-35059-4(4),* Turtleback) Turtleback Bks.
Scotton, Rob & Driscoll, Laura. I Scream for Ice Cream. 2015. (Splat the Cat: I Can Read Ser.). (J). lib. bdg. 13.55 *(978-0-606-36948-0(1))* Turtleback Bks.
Scroggs, Kirk. Snoop Troop - Sloppy Joe Stink-O-Rama. 2015. (Snoop Troop Ser.: 3). (ENG., Illus.). 192p. (J). (gr. 3-7). 13.99 *(978-0-316-24278-3(0))* Little, Brown Bks. for Young Readers.
Scruggs, Sheldon. Tyler: The Strongest Boy on the Block. 2012. 140p. pap. 12.95 *(978-1-4575-1355-8(2))* Dog Ear Publishing, LLC.
Seals, Hollie. When You Can't Find the Words. 2007. 144p. per. 11.95 *(978-0-595-45023-7(7))* iUniverse, Inc.
Searl, Duncan. Ellen Tebbits. Friedland, Joyce & Kessler, Rikki, eds. 2007. (Novel-Ties Ser.). (Illus.). 26p. pap. 16.95 *(978-0-7675-3531-1(6))* Learning Links Inc.
Searl, Duncan, et al. Keep the Lights Burning, Abbie. Friedland, Joyce & Kessler, Rikki, eds. 2007. (Novel-Ties Ser.). (Illus.). 25p. pap. 16.95 *(978-0-7675-1456-9(4))* Learning Links Inc.
Second and Fourth Grade Franklin Elementary. The Cat Has Class! 2007. (Illus.). 32p. (J). (gr. k-10). 16.95 *(978-0-929915-71-5(2))* Headline Bks., Inc.
Sedell, Kirsten J. Remembering Sarah: A Child's Story. 2007. (J). *(978-0-9800838-0-4(X))* Sedell, Kirsten.
Sedoti, Chelsea. The Hundred Lies of Lizzie Lovett. 2017. (ENG.). 400p. (YA). (gr. 8-12). 17.99 *(978-1-4926-3608-3(8),* 9781492636083) Sourcebooks, Inc.
Seeberger, Beverley, illus. Razzle Dazzler. 2007. (J). per. 15.00 *(978-0-9713589-8-0(2))* Ubaviel's Gifts.
Seegert, Scott & Martin, John. Sci-Fi Junior High. 2017. (Sci-Fi Junior High Ser.: 1). (ENG., Illus.). 320p. (J). (gr. 3-7). 13.99 *(978-0-316-31516-6(8),* Jimmy Patterson) Little Brown & Co.
Segal, Douglas. I Can Go to School: An I-Can-Do-It Book. Widdowson, Kay, illus. 2007. (ENG.). 10p. (J). (gr. -1-k). bds. 10.95 *(978-1-58117-594-3(9),* Intervisual/Piggy Toes) Bendon, Inc.
Segal, Zoe. Confessions of a Tenth-Grade Social Climber. 2005. 290p. (YA). *(978-0-618-44981-1(7))* Houghton Mifflin Harcourt Publishing Co.
Selfors, Suzanne. Ever after High. 2015. (School Story Ser.). (ENG.). 652p. (J). (gr. 3-7). 42.00 *(978-0-316-30101-5(9))* Little, Brown Bks. for Young Readers.
—Ever after High: General Villainy: A Destiny Do-Over Diary. 2015. (ENG., Illus.). 160p. (J). (gr. 3-7). 9.99 *(978-0-316-40126-5(9))* Little, Brown Bks. for Young Readers.
—Kiss & Spell. 2015. (Ever after High Ser.: Bk. 2). (ENG., Illus.). 224p. (J). (gr. 3-7). 13.99 *(978-0-316-40131-9(5))* Little, Brown Bks. for Young Readers.
—Next Top Villain. 2015. (School Story Ser.). (ENG., Illus.). 224p. (J). (gr. 3-7). 13.99 *(978-0-316-40128-9(5))* Little Brown & Co.
—A Semi-Charming Kind of Life. 2015. (Ever after High Ser.: Bk. 3). 213p. (J). *(978-0-316-40135-7(8))* Little Brown & Co.
Sellers, Sandra. Gran's Story II: A Shy Maiden Finds Her Voice in the Tune of an Old Fiddle. 2010. 28p. pap. 16.99 *(978-1-4269-2776-8(2))* Trafford Publishing.
—Gran's Story IV: Gathering Wild Violets. 2011. 24p. (gr. -1). pap. 15.99 *(978-1-4269-5707-9(6))* Trafford Publishing.
Selzer, Adam. I Kissed a Zombie, & I Liked It. 2010. (ENG.). 192p. (YA). (gr. 7-18). pap. 7.99 *(978-0-385-73503-2(0),* Delacorte Bks. for Young Readers) Random Hse. Children's Bks.
Sempe & Goscinny. Los Recreos del Pequeno Nicolas. 2003. (SPA., Illus.). 116p. (J). (gr. 3-5). pap. 9.95 *(978-84-204-4814-5(1))* Santillana USA Publishing Co., Inc.
Serafin, Jordan. Bella: The Crooked Hat Witch. Rubino, Alisa A., illus. 2004. (J). *(978-0-932991-57-7(2))* Place In The Woods, The.
Serle, Rebecca. When You Were Mine. (ENG., (YA). (gr. 9). 2013. Illus.). 368p. pap. 9.99 *(978-1-4424-3314-4(0))* 2012. 352p. 16.99 *(978-1-4424-3313-7(2))* Simon Pulse. (Simon Pulse).
Serwacki, Kevin & Pallace, Chris. Joey & Johnny - The Ninjas - Get Mooned. Serwacki, Kevin & Pallace, Chris, illus. 2015. (Joey & Johnny, the Ninjas Ser.: 1). (ENG., Illus.). 320p. (J). (gr. 3-7). 12.99 *(978-0-06-229933-8(6))* HarperCollins Pubs.
Seuling, Barbara. Robert & the Great Escape. Brewer, Paul, illus. 2003. (Robert Bks.). (ENG.). 120p. (J). 15.95 *(978-0-8126-2700-8(8))* Cricket Bks.
—Robert & the Happy Endings. Brewer, Paul, illus. 2007. (Robert Bks.). (ENG.). 160p. (J). (gr. 1-4). 16.95 *(978-0-8126-2748-0(2))* Cricket Bks.
—Robert & the Lemming Problem. Brewer, Paul, illus. 2003. (Robert Bks.). (ENG.). 120p. (J). 15.95 *(978-0-8126-2686-5(9))* Cricket Bks.
—Robert & the Practical Jokes. Brewer, Paul, illus. 2006. (Robert Bks.). (ENG.). 150p. (J). (gr. k-4). 16.95 *(978-0-8126-2741-1(5))* Cricket Bks.
—Robert Finds a Way. Brewer, Paul, illus. 2005. (Robert Bks.). (ENG.). 150p. (J). 15.95 *(978-0-8126-2734-3(2))* Cricket Bks.
—Robert Takes a Stand. Brewer, Paul, illus. 2004. (Robert Bks.). (ENG.). 120p. (J). 15.95 *(978-0-8126-2712-1(1))* Cricket Bks.
S.E.W. The Year at Widows' Creek: The Beginning. 2009. 44p. pap. 17.49 *(978-1-4389-5546-9(4))* AuthorHouse.
Sewell, Kristin. A Collection of Seven Children's Stories. 2012. 80p. pap. 28.99 *(978-1-4685-3770-3(9))* AuthorHouse.
Sewer, Anecia. Why Transfer Day, Anyway? Samuel, Karen, illus. 2007. 16p. (J). 15.99 *(978-0-9752986-0-2(7))* Research Institute Pr., The.

Seyforth, Edward L. A Horribly Frightening Deception, 1 vol. 2009. 75p. pap. 19.95 *(978-1-61546-260-5(0))* America Star Bks.

Shade, Jeff. An Unusual Education. 2010. (J). pap. *(978-0-88092-317-0(2))* Royal Fireworks Publishing Co.

Sham And Geri Mahabir. Freddie Learns Responsibility. 2009. 24p. pap. 13.99 *(978-1-4389-5573-5(1))* AuthorHouse.

Shang, Wendy Wan-Long. The Great Wall of Lucy Wu. 2013. (ENG.). 320p. (J). (gr. 3-7). pap. 7.99 *(978-0-545-16216-6(5),* Scholastic Paperbacks) Scholastic, Inc.

Shank, Marilyn Sue. Child of the Mountains. 2013. (ENG.). 272p. (J). (gr. 4-7). 6.99 *(978-0-375-87331-7(7),* Yearling) Random Hse. Children's Bks.

Shann, Taylor. Strange Day. 2003. (J). 13.00 *(978-0-9679552-4-7(6))* Mushroom Cloud Pr. of Orlando.

Sharkey, Niamh. I'm a Happy Hugglewug: Laugh & Play the Hugglewug Way. Sharkey, Niamh, illus. 2008. (ENG., Illus.). 34p. (J). (gr. k-k). bds. 6.99 *(978-0-7636-3981-5(8))* Candlewick Pr.

Sharmat, Marjorie Weinman & Sharmat, Mitchell. The Princess of the Fillmore Street School. Brunkus, Denise, illus. 2005. (Olivia Sharp: Agent for Secrets Ser.). (ENG.). 80p. (J). (gr. 3-7). 5.99 *(978-0-440-42060-6(1),* Yearling) Random Hse. Children's Bks.

Sharp, N. L. Effie's Image. 2008. (ENG., Illus.). 29p. pap. 8.95 *(978-0-9759829-2-1(3))* Prairieland Pr.

Shaw, LaVerne. Mesa Magic. 2006. 184p. per. 19.95 *(978-1-59879-238-6(5))* Lifevest Publishing, Inc.

Shaw, Susan. One of the Survivors. (ENG.). 208p. (J). (gr. 5-9). 2011. pap. 6.99 *(978-1-4169-6389-9(8))* 2009. 15.99 *(978-1-4169-6129-1(1))* McElderry, Margaret K. Bks. (McElderry, Margaret K. Bks.).

—Safe. 2007. (ENG.). 176p. (YA). (gr. 9-18). pap. 14.00 *(978-0-525-47829-4(9),* Dutton Books for Young Readers) Penguin Young Readers Group.

Shaw, Tucker. Anxious Hearts. (ENG.). 272p. (YA). (gr. 7-17). 2011. pap. 6.95 *(978-0-8109-9711-0(8))* 2010. 16.95 *(978-0-8109-8718-0(X))* Abrams, Inc. (Amulet Bks.).

—The Girls. 2010. (ENG.). 224p. (YA). (gr. 7-11). pap. 7.95 *(978-0-8109-8991-7(3),* Amulet Bks.) Abrams, Inc.

Shaw, Tucker & Luce, Clare Boothe. The Girls. 2009. (ENG.). 208p. (YA). (gr. 7-11). 17.95 *(978-0-8109-8348-9(6),* Amulet Bks.) Abrams, Inc.

Shea, Bob. Dinosaur vs. School. Shea, Bob, illus. (Dinosaur vs. Book Ser.). (ENG., Illus.). (J). (gr. -1-k). 2016. 32p. bds. 7.99 *(978-1-4231-6094-6(0))* 2014. 40p. 16.99 *(978-1-4231-6087-8(8))* Hyperion Bks. for Children.

Shea, John & Harmon, Michael B. A Kid from Southie. 2011. 240p. (YA). (gr. 9-18). 16.95 *(978-1-934813-53-9(2))* Westside Bks.

Shefelman, Janice Jordan. Anna Maria's Gift. Papp, Robert, illus. 2011. (Stepping Stone Book Ser.). (ENG.). 112p. (J). (gr. 2-5). pap. 4.99 *(978-0-375-85882-6(2),* Random Hse. Bks. for Young Readers) Random Hse. Children's Bks.

Sheinmel, Courtney. The Kindness Club. 2016. (Kindness Club Ser.). (ENG.). 224p. (J). 15.99 *(978-1-68119-091-4(5),* 9781681190914, Bloomsbury USA Childrens) Bloomsbury Publishing USA.

—Scaredy Cat. Bell, Jennifer A., illus. 2016. (Stella Batts Ser.). (ENG.). 160p. (J). (gr. 1-3). 9.99 *(978-1-58536-919-5(5),* 204026) Sleeping Bear Pr.

—Sincerely: Sincerely, Sophie; Sincerely, Katie. 2010. (ENG.). 400p. (J). (gr. 3-7). 15.99 *(978-1-4169-4010-4(3),* Simon & Schuster Bks. For Young Readers) Simon & Schuster Bks. For Young Readers.

—Sincerely: Sincerely, Sophie, Sincerely, Katie. 2011. (ENG.). 416p. (J). (gr. 3-7). pap. 7.99 *(978-1-4169-4022-7(7),* Simon & Schuster Bks. For Young Readers) Simon & Schuster Bks. For Young Readers.

—Stella Batts: None of Your Beeswax. Bell, Jennifer A., illus. 2014. (Stella Batts Ser.). (ENG.). 160p. (J). (gr. 1-3). 9.99 *(978-1-58536-853-2(9),* 203677) Sleeping Bear Pr.

—Superstar. Bell, Jennifer A., illus. 2015. (Stella Batts Ser.). (ENG.). 184p. (J). (gr. 1-3). pap. 5.99 *(978-1-58536-856-3(3),* 203956) Sleeping Bear Pr.

Sheinmel, Courtney & Bell, Jennifer A. Stella Batts: Needs a New Name. 2012. (Stella Batts Ser.). (ENG., Illus.). 160p. (J). (gr. 1-3). pap. 5.99 *(978-1-58536-183-0(6),* 202266); lib. bdg. 9.99 *(978-1-58536-185-4(2),* 202267) Sleeping Bear Pr.

Sheldon, Dyan. The Crazy Things Girls Do for Love. (ENG.). 352p. (YA). (gr. 7). 2013. pap. 8.99 *(978-0-7636-6468-8(5))* 2011. (Illus.). 16.99 *(978-0-7636-5018-6(8))* Candlewick Pr.

—Planet Janet. (ENG., 240p. (YA). (gr. 9-18). 2004. Illus.). pap. 6.99 *(978-0-7636-2556-6(6))* 2003. 14.99 *(978-0-7636-2048-6(3))* Candlewick Pr.

Sheldon, Kaylene Kauwila. A Day with Makana. 2007.Tr. of I Kekahi la me Makana. (ENG & HAW.). (J). lib. bdg. *(978-0-9773495-2-4(7))* Na Kamalei Koolauloa Early Education Program.

Shelton, Crystal G. Theodore's Rings. 2013. 24p. pap. 24.95 *(978-1-62709-378-1(8))* America Star Bks.

Shen, Prudence. Nothing Can Possibly Go Wrong. Hicks, Faith Erin, illus. 2013. (ENG.). 288p. (YA). (gr. 7). pap. 17.99 *(978-1-59643-659-6(X),* 9781596436596, First Second Bks.) Roaring Brook Pr.

Shepard, Sara. Burned. 2013. (Pretty Little Liars Ser.: 12). (ENG.). 352p. (YA). (gr. 9). pap. 9.99 *(978-0-06-208193-3(4))* HarperCollins Pubs.

—Burned. 2013. (Pretty Little Liars Ser.: 12). (YA). lib. bdg. 20.85 *(978-0-606-32177-8(2),* Turtleback) Turtleback Bks.

—Crushed. 2014. (Pretty Little Liars Ser.: 13). (YA). lib. bdg. 20.85 *(978-0-606-35497-4(2))* Turtleback Bks.

—Deadly. (Pretty Little Liars Ser.: 14). (ENG.). (YA). (gr. 9). 2014. 336p. pap. 10.99 *(978-0-06-219975-1(7))* 2013. 320p. 17.99 *(978-0-06-219974-4(9),* HarperTeen) HarperCollins Pubs.

—Deadly. 2014. (Pretty Little Liars Ser.: 14). (YA). lib. bdg. 20.85 *(978-0-606-35972-6(9))* Turtleback Bks.

—Flawless. (Pretty Little Liars Ser.: 2). (ENG.). (YA). (gr. 9-12). 2008. 352p. pap. 10.99 *(978-0-06-088735-3(4))* 2007. 352p. 16.99 *(978-0-06-088733-9(8))* 2010. 368p. pap. 8.99 *(978-0-06-205987-1(4))* HarperCollins Pubs. (HarperTeen).

—Flawless. 2008. (Pretty Little Liars Ser.: 2). (YA). lib. bdg. 20.85 *(978-0-606-12267-2(2),* Turtleback) Turtleback Bks.

—The Good Girls. 2015. (Perfectionists Ser.: 2). (ENG.). 368p. (YA). (gr. 9). 17.99 *(978-0-06-207452-2(0),* HarperTeen) HarperCollins Pubs.

—Heartless. 2010. (Pretty Little Liars Ser.: 7). (ENG.). (YA). (gr. 9-18). 304p. pap. 10.99 *(978-0-06-156616-5(0));* 288p. 16.99 *(978-0-06-156614-1(4))* HarperCollins Pubs. (HarperTeen).

—Perfect. (Pretty Little Liars Ser.: No. 3). (ENG.). (YA). (gr. 9-12). 2007. 320p. 16.99 *(978-0-06-088736-0(2))*No. 3. 2008. 336p. pap. 9.99 *(978-0-06-088738-4(9))* HarperCollins Pubs. (HarperTeen).

—The Perfectionists. 2014. (Perfectionists Ser.: 1). (ENG.). 336p. (YA). (gr. 9). 17.99 *(978-0-06-207469-0(5))* HarperCollins Pubs.

—Pretty Little Liars. (Pretty Little Liars Ser.: 1). (YA). (gr. 9-12). 2007. (ENG.). 304p. pap. 9.99 *(978-0-06-088732-2(X))* 2010. (ENG.). 304p. pap. 9.99 *(978-0-06-200954-8(0))*Set, Bks. 1-4. 2009. pap. 29.99 *(978-0-06-180131-0(3))* HarperCollins Pubs. (HarperTeen).

—Pretty Little Liars Bind-Up #2: Perfect & Unbelievable. 2014. (Pretty Little Liars Ser.). (ENG.). 672p. (YA). (gr. 9). pap. 10.99 *(978-0-06-232293-7(1),* HarperTeen) HarperCollins Pubs.

—Pretty Little Secrets. (Pretty Little Liars Companion Novel Ser.). (ENG.). (YA). (gr. 9). 2013. 480p. pap. 9.99 *(978-0-06-212592-7(3))* 2012. 464p. 17.99 *(978-0-06-212591-0(5))* HarperCollins Pubs. (HarperTeen).

—Ruthless. (Pretty Little Liars Ser.: 10). (ENG.). (YA). (gr. 9). 2012. 368p. pap. 10.99 *(978-0-06-208187-2(X))* 2011. 352p. 17.99 *(978-0-06-208186-5(1))* HarperCollins Pubs. (HarperTeen).

—Ruthless. 2012. (Pretty Little Liars Ser.: 10). (YA). lib. bdg. 20.85 *(978-0-606-26873-8(1),* Turtleback) Turtleback Bks.

—Stunning. 2013. (Pretty Little Liars Ser.: 11). (ENG.). 336p. (YA). (gr. 9). pap. 10.99 *(978-0-06-208190-2(X),* HarperTeen) HarperCollins Pubs.

—Stunning. 2013. (Pretty Little Liars Ser.: 11). (YA). lib. bdg. 20.85 *(978-0-606-31813-6(5),* Turtleback) Turtleback Bks.

—Toxic. 2014. (Pretty Little Liars Ser.: 15). (ENG.). 352p. (J). (gr. 9). 17.99 *(978-0-06-228701-4(X),* HarperTeen) HarperCollins Pubs.

—Twisted. (Pretty Little Liars Ser.: 9). (ENG.). (YA). (gr. 9). 2012. 336p. pap. 10.99 *(978-0-06-208102-5(0))* 2011. 320p. 16.99 *(978-0-06-208101-8(2))* HarperCollins Pubs. (HarperTeen).

—Twisted. 2012. (Pretty Little Liars Ser.: 9). (YA). lib. bdg. 20.85 *(978-0-606-26288-0(1),* Turtleback) Turtleback Bks.

—Unbelievable. 2008. (Pretty Little Liars Ser.: No. 4). (ENG.). 352p. (J). (gr. 9-18). 16.99 *(978-0-06-088739-1(7),* HarperTeen) HarperCollins Pubs.

—Wanted. (Pretty Little Liars Ser.: 8). (ENG.). (YA). (gr. 9). 2011. 288p. pap. 9.99 *(978-0-06-156619-6(5))* 2010. 272p. 16.99 *(978-0-06-156617-2(9))* HarperCollins Pubs. (HarperTeen).

—Wicked. (Pretty Little Liars Ser.: 5). (ENG.). (YA). (gr. 9). 2009. 336p. pap. 9.99 *(978-0-06-156610-3(1))* 5th ed. 2008. 320p. 17.99 *(978-0-06-156607-3(1))* HarperCollins Pubs. (HarperTeen).

Shepherd, Jodie. Sesame Street Elmo Goes to School. Moroney, Christopher, illus. 2012. (Lift-The-Flap Ser.: 1). (ENG.). 10p. (J). (gr. -1-k). bds. 10.99 *(978-0-7944-2585-2(2),* Reader's Digest Children's Bks.) Studio Fun International.

Sherrard, Valerie. Speechless. 2007. (ENG.). 176p. (YA). (gr. 6). pap. 12.99 *(978-1-55002-701-3(8),* Boardwalk Bks.) Dundurn CAN. Dist: Ingram Publisher Services.

Shields, Gillian. Eternal. (Immortal Ser.: 3). (ENG.). (YA). (gr. 8). 2012. 384p. pap. 9.99 *(978-0-06-200040-8(3))* 2011. 368p. 16.99 *(978-0-06-200039-2(X))* HarperCollins Pubs. (Tegen, Katherine Bks).

Shortt, Yvonne. A New York City Public School Goes Green. 2009. 44p. pap. 19.95 *(978-0-557-07182-1(8))* Lulu Pr., Inc.

Shreeve, Elizabeth. Oliver at the Window. McDonald, Candice Hartsough, illus. 2009. (ENG.). 32p. (J). (gr. -1-1). 16.95 *(978-1-59078-548-5(7),* Front Street) Boyds Mills Pr.

Shreve, Steve. Stan & the Toilet Monster, 0 vols. 2011. (ENG.). 164p. (J). (gr. 2-6). 12.99 *(978-0-7614-5977-4(4),* 9780761459774, Amazon Children's Publishing) Amazon Publishing.

Shreve, Susan Richards. Kiss Me Tomorrow. 2006. 220p. (J). *(978-1-4156-5592-4(8),* Levine, Arthur A. Bks.) Scholastic, Inc.

Shubert's Choice. 2004. (YA). 9.00 *(978-1-889609-26-3(9))* Loving Guidance, Inc.

Shull, Megan. The Swap. 400p. (J). (gr. 5-9). 2016. pap. 7.99 *(978-0-06-231170-2(0))* 2014. (ENG.). 16.99 *(978-0-06-231169-6(7))* HarperCollins Pubs. (Tegen, Katherine Bks).

Shulman, Polly. Enthusiasm. 2007. (ENG.). 224p. (YA). (gr. 7-18). pap. 8.99 *(978-0-14-240935-0(9),* Speak) Penguin Young Readers Group.

Shultz, Charles M. & Katschke, Judy. It's Time for School, Charlie Brown, 1 vol. Lo Blanco, Nick, illus. 2011. (Peanuts Ready-To-Reads Ser.). (ENG.). 32p. (gr. -1-2). lib. bdg. 24.21 *(978-1-59961-802-9(8))* Spotlight.

Shusterman, Neal. Antsy Does Time. 2010. (ENG.). 256p. (J). (gr. 5-18). pap. 6.99 *(978-0-14-241487-3(5),* Puffin Books) Penguin Young Readers Group.

—Dread Locks. 2006. (Dark Fusion Ser.: 1). (ENG.). 176p. (YA). (gr. 7-18). 7.99 *(978-0-14-240599-4(X),* Speak) Penguin Young Readers Group.

—The Shadow Club Rising. 2003. (ENG.). 208p. (YA). (gr. 7-7). 6.99 *(978-0-14-250089-7(5),* Speak) Penguin Young Readers Group.

Siddoway, Richard M. The Cottage Park Puzzle. 2015. 200p. (YA). pap. 14.99 *(978-1-4621-1562-4(4))* Cedar Fort, Inc./CFI Distribution.

Sidney, Margaret. Five Little Peppers at School. 2011. 208p. 26.95 *(978-1-4638-9924-0(6))* Rodgers, Alan Bks.

Sierra, Judy. We Love Our School! A Read-Together Rebus Story. Davick, Linda, illus. 2011. (ENG.). 24p. (J). (gr. -1-2). 7.99 *(978-0-375-86728-6(7),* Knopf Bks. for Young Readers) Random Hse. Children's Bks.

Siggins, Gerard. Rugby Warrior: Back in School. Back in Sport. Back in Time. 2014. (ENG., Illus.). 176p. (J). pap. 14.00 *(978-1-84717-591-5(0))* O'Brien Pr., Ltd., The IRL. Dist: Dufour Editions, Inc.

Sigmon-Heck, Christina. The Birthday Wish. 2012. 24p. pap. 24.95 *(978-1-4626-6207-4(2))* America Star Bks.

Silberberg, Alan. The Awesome, Almost 100% True Adventures of Matt & Craz. Silberberg, Alan, illus. (ENG., Illus.). 336p. (J). (gr. 4-8). 2014. pap. 7.99 *(978-1-4169-9433-6(5))* 2013. 16.99 *(978-1-4169-9432-9(7))* Simon & Schuster Children's Publishing. (Aladdin).

Silva, Kenny. The Card. 2007. 84p. per. 19.95 *(978-1-60441-320-5(4))* America Star Bks.

Silver, Shana & Shane, Rachel. Alice in Wonderland High. 2015. (ENG.). 300p. (YA). 17.99 *(978-1-4405-8466-4(4),* Simon Pulse) Simon Pulse.

Silverman, Erica. Favorite Stories from Cowgirl Kate & Cocoa: School Days. Lewin, Betsy, illus. 2014. (Green Light Readers Level 2 Ser.). (ENG.). 32p. (J). (gr. 1-4). 12.99 *(978-0-544-23017-0(5),* HMH Books For Young Readers) Houghton Mifflin Harcourt Publishing Co.

—School Days. Lewin, Betsy, illus. 2008. (Cowgirl Kate & Cocoa Ser.). (ENG.). 48p. (J). (gr. 1-4). pap. 5.95 *(978-0-15-206130-2(4))* Houghton Mifflin Harcourt Publishing Co.

Simeton, Julia. Mom, Why Can't I Catch Up? 2009. 20p. pap. 12.95 *(978-1-4389-7620-4(8))* AuthorHouse.

Simmons, Andrew & Averdonz, N. R. I Was an Eighth-Grade Ninja, 1 vol. Padilla, Ariel, illus. 2007. (Z Graphic Novels / Tomo Ser.). (ENG.). 160p. (J). (gr. 3-7). pap. 6.99 *(978-0-310-71300-5(5))* Zondervan.

Simmons, Cari & Alexander, Heather. Bending over Backwards. 2015. (Picture Perfect Ser.: 1). (ENG.). 224p. (J). (gr. 3-7). pap. 6.99 *(978-0-06-231022-4(4))* HarperCollins Pubs.

Simmons, Cari & Douglas, Lola. You First. 2015. (Picture Perfect Ser.: 2). (ENG.). 256p. (J). (gr. 3-7). pap. 6.99 *(978-0-06-231058-3(5))* HarperCollins Pubs.

Simmons, Cari & Zulkey, Claire. Best Frenemies. 2015. (Picture Perfect Ser.: 3). (ENG., Illus.). 224p. (J). (gr. 3-7). pap. 6.99 *(978-0-06-231845-9(4))* HarperCollins Pubs.

Simmons, Ted. Diablo Creek. 2007. (ENG.). 168p. (YA). pap. *(978-0-9776958-7-4(5))* CyPress Pubns.

Simon, Charnan. Dance Team. 2013. (Surviving Southside Ser.). (ENG.). 104p. (YA). (gr. 6-12). pap. 7.95 *(978-1-4677-0707-7(4),* Darby Creek); lib. bdg. 27.93 *(978-1-4677-0313-0(3))* Lerner Publishing Group.

—Plan B. 2011. (Surviving Southside Ser.). (ENG.). 104p. (YA). (gr. 6-12). pap. 7.95 *(978-0-7613-6163-3(4));* lib. bdg. 27.93 *(978-0-7613-6149-7(9))* Lerner Publishing Group.

—Shattered Star. (Surviving Southside Ser.). (ENG.). 104p. (YA). (gr. 6-12). 2015. 34.65 *(978-1-4677-6011-9(0),* Lerner Digital) 2011. pap. 7.95 *(978-0-7613-6168-8(5))* 2011. lib. bdg. 27.93 *(978-0-7613-6154-1(5))* Lerner Publishing Group.

Simon, Coco. Alexis Cool As a Cupcake. 2013. (Cupcake Diaries: 8). (ENG., Illus.). 160p. (J). (gr. 3-7). 16.99 *(978-1-4424-8569-3(8),* Simon Spotlight) Simon Spotlight.

—Alexis Cool as a Cupcake. 2012. (Cupcake Diaries: 8). lib. bdg. 16.00 *(978-0-606-26334-4(9),* Turtleback) Turtleback Bks.

—Alexis Gets Frosted. (Cupcake Diaries: 12). (ENG., Illus.). 160p. (J). (gr. 3-7). 2014. 17.99 *(978-1-4424-9612-5(6))* 2013. pap. 6.99 *(978-1-4424-6867-2(X))* Simon Spotlight. (Simon Spotlight).

—Alexis Gets Frosted. 2013. (Cupcake Diaries: 12). lib. bdg. 17.20 *(978-0-606-27026-7(4),* Turtleback) Turtleback Bks.

—Alexis the Icing on the Cupcake. 2014. (Cupcake Diaries: 20). (ENG., Illus.). 160p. (J). (gr. 3-7). pap. 6.99 *(978-1-4814-0468-6(7),* Simon Spotlight) Simon Spotlight.

—The Cupcake Diaries Collection: Katie & the Cupcake Cure; Mia in the Mix; Emma on Thin Icing; Alexis & the Perfect Recipe. 2012. (Cupcake Diaries). (ENG.). 640p. (J). (gr. 3-7). pap. 23.99 *(978-1-4424-8445-0(4),* Simon Spotlight) Simon Spotlight.

—Emma: Sugar & Spice & Everything Nice. 2013. (Cupcake Diaries: 15). lib. bdg. 16.00 *(978-0-606-32052-8(0),* Turtleback) Turtleback Bks.

—Emma, Smile & Say "Cupcake!" 2014. (Cupcake Diaries: 11). (ENG., Illus.). 160p. (J). (gr. 3-7). 17.99 *(978-1-4424-9611-8(8),* Simon Spotlight) Simon Spotlight.

—Katie & the Cupcake Cure. (Cupcake Diaries: 1). (ENG., 160p. (J). (gr. 3-7). 2013. Illus.). 15.99 *(978-1-4424-7490-1(4))* 2011. pap. 6.99 *(978-1-4424-2275-9(0))* Simon Spotlight. (Simon Spotlight).

—Katie & the Cupcake Cure; Mia in the Mix; Emma on Thin Icing, 3 in 1 bks. 2015. (Cupcake Diaries). (ENG., Illus.). 480p. (J). (gr. 3-7). pap. 8.99 *(978-1-4814-5756-9(X),* Simon Spotlight) Simon Spotlight.

—Katie & the Cupcake War. 2014. (Cupcake Diaries: 9). (ENG., Illus.). 160p. (J). (gr. 3-7). 17.99 *(978-1-4424-9609-5(6),* Simon Spotlight) Simon Spotlight.

—Katie, Batter Up! 2013. (Cupcake Diaries: 5). (ENG., Illus.). 160p. (J). (gr. 3-7). 17.99 *(978-1-4424-8564-8(7),* Simon Spotlight) Simon Spotlight.

—Katie Sprinkles & Surprises. 2013. (Cupcake Diaries: 17). (ENG., Illus.). 160p. (J). (gr. 3-7). 17.99 *(978-1-4424-8591-4(4));* pap. 6.99 *(978-1-4424-8590-7(6))* Simon Spotlight. (Simon Spotlight).

—Katie Sprinkles & Surprises. 2013. (Cupcake Diaries: 17). lib. bdg. 17.20 *(978-0-606-32327-7(9),* Turtleback) Turtleback Bks.

—Katie's New Recipe. (Cupcake Diaries: 13). (ENG., Illus.). 160p. (J). (gr. 3-7). 2014. 16.99 *(978-1-4814-0379-5(6))* 2013. pap. 5.99 *(978-1-4424-7168-9(9))* Simon Spotlight. (Simon Spotlight).

—Katie's New Recipe. 2013. (Cupcake Diaries: 13). lib. bdg. 16.00 *(978-0-606-27034-2(5),* Turtleback) Turtleback Bks.

—Mia: A Matter of Taste. 2013. (Cupcake Diaries: 14). lib. bdg. 16.00 *(978-0-606-32042-9(3),* Turtleback) Turtleback Bks.

—Mia: Fashion Plates & Cupcakes. 2014. (Cupcake Diaries: 18). lib. bdg. 16.00 *(978-0-606-35436-3(0))* Turtleback Bks.

—Mia a Matter of Taste. 2013. (Cupcake Diaries: 14). (ENG., Illus.). 160p. (J). (gr. 3-7). 15.99 *(978-1-4424-7480-2(7));* pap. 6.99 *(978-1-4424-7435-2(1))* Simon Spotlight. (Simon Spotlight).

—Mia Fashion Plates & Cupcakes. 2014. (Cupcake Diaries: 18). (ENG., Illus.). 160p. (J). (gr. 3-7). pap. 5.99 *(978-1-4424-9790-0(4),* Simon Spotlight) Simon Spotlight.

—Mia in the Mix. (Cupcake Diaries: 2). (ENG., 160p. (J). (gr. 3-7). 2013. Illus.). 15.99 *(978-1-4424-7491-8(2))* 2011. pap. 6.99 *(978-1-4424-2277-3(7))* Simon Spotlight. (Simon Spotlight).

—Mia the Way the Cupcake Crumbles. 2015. (Cupcake Diaries: 26). (ENG., Illus.). 160p. (J). (gr. 3-7). pap. 6.99 *(978-1-4814-4167-4(1),* Simon Spotlight) Simon Spotlight.

—Mia's Baker's Dozen. (Cupcake Diaries: 6). (ENG., 160p. (J). (gr. 3-7). 2013. Illus.). 17.99 *(978-1-4424-8566-2(3))* 2012. pap. 6.99 *(978-1-4424-4613-7(7))* Simon Spotlight. (Simon Spotlight).

—Mia's Baker's Dozen. 2012. (Cupcake Diaries: 6). lib. bdg. 17.20 *(978-0-606-26570-6(8),* Turtleback) Turtleback Bks.

—Mia's Boiling Point. 2014. (Cupcake Diaries: 10). (ENG., Illus.). 160p. (J). (gr. 3-7). 17.99 *(978-1-4424-9610-1(X),* Simon Spotlight) Simon Spotlight.

—Mia's Boiling Point. 2012. (Cupcake Diaries: 10). lib. bdg. 16.00 *(978-0-606-26895-0(2),* Turtleback) Turtleback Bks.

Simon, Coco & West, Tracey. MIA, the Way the Cupcake Crumbles. 2015. 127p. (J). *(978-1-4806-9834-5(2),* Simon Spotlight) Simon Spotlight.

Simon, Jenne. Lalaloopsy: School Day! Hill, Prescott, illus. 2012. (Lalaloopsy Ser.). (ENG.). 32p. (J). (gr. -1-3). pap. 3.99 *(978-0-545-40321-4(9))* Scholastic, Inc.

Simon, Kitty. Preschool Here I Come! 2011. 20p. 11.99 *(978-1-4567-5779-3(2))* AuthorHouse.

Simon, Norma. All Families Are Special. Flavin, Teresa, illus. 2013. (AV2 Fiction Readalong Ser.: Vol. 59). (ENG.). 32p. (J). (gr. k-3). 34.28 *(978-1-62127-867-2(0),* AV2 by Weigl) Weigl Pubs., Inc.

—All Families Are Special. Flavin, Teresa, illus. 2003. (ENG.). 32p. (J). (gr. k-3). 16.99 *(978-0-8075-2175-5(2))* Whitman, Albert & Co.

Simone, Kriss. Fairy Forest. 2007. 86p. pap. 7.78 *(978-1-84799-156-0(4))* Lulu Pr., Inc.

Simone, Ni-Ni. No Boyz Allowed. 2012. lib. bdg. 20.80 *(978-0-606-26377-1(2),* Turtleback) Turtleback Bks.

Simpson, N. J. Not So Random. 2011. 200p. pap. 13.67 *(978-0-557-83059-6(1))* Lulu Pr., Inc.

Simpson, Rodney. Frannie Fern Goes to Kindergarten. 2011. 52p. pap. 20.26 *(978-1-4490-5455-7(2))* AuthorHouse.

Sinclair, Gardine. Keira at Stageschool. 2013. 186p. (J). pap. *(978-1-78299-387-2(8))* FeedARead.com.

—Stageschool by the Sea. 2013. 176p. (J). pap. *(978-1-78299-389-6(4))* FeedARead.com.

Singleton, Linda Joy. Dead Girl Walking. 2008. (Dead Girl Ser.: 1). (ENG.). 312p. (YA). (gr. 8-18). pap. 9.95 *(978-0-7387-1405-9(4),* Flux) North Star Editions.

—Don't Die, Dragonfly. Karre, Andrew, ed. 2004. (Seer Ser.: 1). (ENG.). 288p. (YA). pap. 9.95 *(978-0-7387-0526-2(8))* Llewellyn Pubns.

—Witch Ball. 2006. (Seer Ser.: 3). (ENG.). 216p. (YA). (gr. 3-7). pap. 9.95 *(978-0-7387-0821-8(6),* Flux) North Star Editions.

Sirod, G. p. & Sirod, G. P. Scabs. 2010. 190p. pap. *(978-1-84923-457-3(4))* YouWriteOn.

Sirowy, Alexandra. First We Were IV. 2017. (ENG., Illus.). 448p. (YA). (gr. 7). 18.99 ***(978-1-4814-7842-7(7),*** Simon & Schuster Bks. For Young Readers) Simon & Schuster Bks. For Young Readers.

Sise, Katie. The Boyfriend App. 2013. (ENG.). 320p. (YA). (gr. 8). 17.99 *(978-0-06-219526-5(3))* HarperCollins Pubs.

—The Pretty App. 2015. (ENG.). 352p. (YA). (gr. 8). 17.99 *(978-0-06-219529-6(8))* HarperCollins Pubs.

Sitomer, Alan Lawrence. Hip-Hop High School. 2006. 368p. (J). *(978-0-7868-3831-8(0),* Jump at the Sun) Hyperion Bks. for Children.

Skarmeas, Nancy. My First Day of School. 2nd ed. 2010. (Illus.). 32p. (J). (gr. -1-1). 8.99 *(978-0-8249-5622-6(2),* Ideal Pubns.) Worthy Publishing.

Skármeta, Antonio. The Composition, 1 vol. Ruano, Alfonso, illus. 2003. (ENG.). 32p. (J). (gr. 3-18). pap. 7.95 *(978-0-88899-550-6(4))* Groundwood Bks. CAN. Dist: Publishers Group West (PGW).

Skead, Robert & Simmel, Mike. Mighty Mike Bounces Back: A Boy's Life with Epilepsy. 2011. 64p. (J). 14.95 *(978-1-4338-1043-5(3));* pap. 9.95 *(978-1-4338-1042-8(5))* American Psychological Assn. (Magination Pr.).

Skeers, Linda & National Geographic Learning Staff. The Impossible Patriotism Project. Hoyt, Ard, illus. 2010. (Rise & Shine Ser.). (ENG.). 32p. (C). (gr. -1-1). pap. 11.95 *(978-0-14-241391-3(7))* National Geographic School Publishing, Inc.

Skipper, Angelic. Launching Out into the Deep. 2006. 14p. 9.81 *(978-1-4116-7345-8(X))* Lulu Pr., Inc.

Skogen, Jennifer. Distant Deep #5. 2015. (Haunting of Grey Hills Ser.). (ENG.). 200-216p. (YA). (gr. 9-12). lib. bdg. 27.13 *(978-1-68076-033-0(5),* Epic Pr.) ABDO Publishing Co.

—Forests of the Night #2. 2015. (Haunting of Grey Hills Ser.). (ENG.). 200-216p. (YA). (gr. 9-12). lib. bdg. 27.13 *(978-1-68076-030-9(0),* Epic Pr.) ABDO Publishing Co.

—Sinews of Thy Heart #4. 2015. (Haunting of Grey Hills Ser.). (ENG.). 200-216p. (J). (gr. 9-12). lib. bdg. 27.13 *(978-1-68076-032-3(7),* 1391657, Epic Pr.) ABDO Publishing Co.

Skovron, Jon. Misfit. 2011. (ENG.). 384p. (YA). (gr. 9-17). 16.95 *(978-1-4197-0021-7(9),* Amulet Bks.) Abrams, Inc.

Skye, obert. Batneezer. Skye, obert, illus. 2016. (Creature from My Closet Ser.: 6). (ENG., Illus.). 208p. (J). 13.99 *(978-1-62779-163-2(9),* 9781627791632, Holt, Henry & Co. Bks. For Young Readers) Holt, Henry & Co.

—Pinocula. Skye, obert, illus. 2013. (Creature from My Closet Ser.: 3). (ENG., Illus.). 256p. (J). (gr. 4-7). 12.99 *(978-0-8050-9689-7(2),* 9780805096897, Holt, Henry & Co. Bks. For Young Readers) Holt, Henry & Co.

—Potterwookiee. Skye, obert, illus. 2012. (Creature from My Closet Ser.: 2). (ENG., Illus.). 256p. (J). (gr. 4-7). 13.99 *(978-0-8050-9451-0(2),* 9780805094510, Holt, Henry & Co. Bks. For Young Readers) Holt, Henry & Co.

—Witherwood Reform School. Thompson, Keith, illus. 2015. (Witherwood Reform School Ser.: 1). (ENG.). 240p. (J). (gr. 4-7). 16.99 *(978-0-8050-9879-2(8),* 9780805098792, Holt, Henry & Co. Bks. For Young Readers) Holt, Henry & Co.

—Wonkenstein. Skye, obert, illus. 2011. (Creature from My Closet Ser.: 1). (ENG., Illus.). 240p. (J). (gr. 4-7). 12.99 *(978-0-8050-9268-4(4),* 9780805092684, Holt, Henry & Co. Bks. For Young Readers) Holt, Henry & Co.

—Wonkenstein. Skye, obert, illus. 2015. (Creature from My Closet Ser.: 1). (ENG., Illus.). 256p. (J). (gr. 4-7). pap. 6.99 *(978-1-250-01022-3(5),* 9781250010223) Square Fish.

S

Slate, Joseph. Miss Bindergarten & the Best Friends. Wolff, Ashley, illus. 2014. (Penguin Young Readers, Level 2 Ser.). (ENG.). 32p. (J). (gr. 1-2). pap. 3.99 *(978-0-448-48132-6(4)*, Penguin Young Readers) Penguin Young Readers Group.

—Miss Bindergarten Celebrates the Last Day of Kindergarten. Wolff, Ashley, illus. 2008. (ENG.). 40p. (J). (gr. -1-k). pap. 7.99 *(978-0-14-241060-8(8)*, Puffin Books) Penguin Young Readers Group.

—Miss Bindergarten Has a Wild Day in Kindergarten. Wolff, Ashley, illus. 2006. (ENG.). 40p. (J). (gr. -1-k). reprint ed. pap. 6.99 *(978-0-14-240709-7(7)*, Puffin Books) Penguin Young Readers Group.

—Miss Bindergarten Takes a Field Trip with Kindergarten. Wolff, Ashley, illus. 2004. (ENG.). 40p. (J). (gr. -1-k). pap. 6.99 *(978-0-14-240139-2(0)*, Puffin Books) Penguin Young Readers Group.

Slate, Joseph & Bader, Bonnie. Miss Bindergarten & the Very Wet Day. Wolff, Ashley, illus. 2015. (Penguin Young Readers, Level 2 Ser.). (ENG.). 32p. (J). (gr. 1-2). 3.99 *(978-0-448-48700-7(4)*, Penguin Young Readers) Penguin Young Readers Group.

Slater, David Michael. Comin' Through, 1 vol. Rooney, Ronnie, illus. 2007. (Missy Swiss & More Ser.). (ENG.). 32p. (gr. -1-4). 28.50 *(978-1-60270-008-6(7)*, Looking Glass Library) ABDO Publishing Co.

—Milo & the Monster, 1 vol. Ebbeler, Jeff, illus. 2009. (David Michael Slater Set 2 Ser.). (ENG.). 32p. (gr. -1-4). 28.50 *(978-1-60270-656-9(5)*, Looking Glass Library) ABDO Publishing Co.

Sloan, Holly Goldberg. Counting by 7s. 2015. (CHI.). 392p. (J). pap. *(978-986-6104-68-8(0))* DaskoviK, Izdatel'sko-torgovaja korporacija.

—Counting by 7s. 2013. (ENG.). 384p. (YA). (gr. 5). 17.99 *(978-0-8037-3855-3(2)*, Dial Bks) Penguin Publishing Group.

—Counting by 7s. 2014. (ENG.). 400p. (J). (gr. 5). 8.99 *(978-0-14-242286-1(X)*, Puffin Books) Penguin Young Readers Group.

—Counting by 7s. 2014. (ENG.). (J). (gr. 5). lib. bdg. 19.60 ***(978-1-62765-616-0(2))*** Perfection Learning Corp.

—Counting by 7s. 2014. (gr. 5-8). lib. bdg. 19.65 *(978-0-606-36583-3(4))* Turtleback Bks.

Slocombe, Megan. A Trip to Italy. 2013. 34p. pap. *(978-3-7103-0389-0(3))* united p.c. Verlag.

Smadja, Brigitte. Tarte aux Escargots. pap. 17.95 *(978-2-211-03633-7(3))* Archimede Editions FRA. Dist: Distribooks, Inc.

Small, Wylie J. The Great Prune Caper. 2009. 94p. pap. 9.98 *(978-1-84728-350-4(0))* Lulu Pr., Inc.

Smiley, Jane. Pie in the Sky. 2013. (Horses of Oak Valley Ranch Ser.). (ENG.). 272p. (J). (gr. 5). 6.99 *(978-0-375-87131-3(4)*, Yearling) Random Hse. Children's Bks.

Smith, Alexander Gordon. Hellraisers. 2015. (Devil's Engine Ser.: 1). (ENG.). 352p. (YA). (gr. 7). 17.99 *(978-0-374-30169-9(7)*, 9780374301699, Farrar, Straus & Giroux (BYR)) Farrar, Straus & Giroux.

Smith, Andrew. Stand-off. Bosma, Sam, illus. 2016. (ENG.). 432p. (YA). (gr. 7). pap. 10.99 *(978-1-4814-1830-0(0)*, Simon & Schuster Bks. For Young Readers) Simon & Schuster Bks. For Young Readers.

—Winger. Bosma, Sam, illus. (ENG.). (YA). (gr. 7). 2014. 464p. pap. 11.99 *(978-1-4424-4493-5(2))* 2013. 448p. 16.99 *(978-1-4424-4492-8(4))* Simon & Schuster Bks. For Young Readers. (Simon & Schuster Bks. For Young Readers).

Smith, Carrie. Mary's Lamb Goes to School: Lap Book Edition. Corbalán, Begoña, illus. 2016. (My First Reader's Theater Tales Ser.). (J). (gr. k). *(978-1-5021-5506-1(0))* Benchmark Education Co.

—Mary's Lamb Goes to School: Small Book Edition. Corbalán, Begoña, illus. 2016. (My First Reader's Theater Tales Ser.). (J). (gr. k). *(978-1-5021-5511-5(7))* Benchmark Education Co.

Smith, Cynthia Leitich. Diabolical. 2012. (Tantalize Ser.). (ENG., Illus.). 368p. (YA). (gr. 9). 17.99 *(978-0-7636-5118-3(4))* Candlewick Pr.

Smith, E. K. Alien Dude! & the Attack of Wormzilla!! Grosshauser, Peter, illus. 2014. (Alien Dude! Ser.). (ENG.). 64p. (J). (gr. 2-4). pap. 4.99 *(978-0-9883792-0-6(1))* Zip Line Publishing.

—Alien Dude! Mr. Evil Potato Man & the Food Fight. Grosshauser, Peter, illus. 2014. (Alien Dude! Ser.). (ENG.). 64p. (J). (gr. 2-4). pap. 4.99 *(978-0-9883792-1-3(X))* Zip Line Publishing.

Smith, Evelyn. The First Fifth Form. Wiles, Frank, illus. 2013. 176p. pap. *(978-1-909423-05-3(X))* Bks. to Treasure.

—The Small Sixth Form. Wiles, Frank, illus. 2013. 200p. pap. *(978-1-909423-08-4(4))* Bks. to Treasure.

Smith, Heather. Baygirl, 1 vol. 2013. (ENG.). 288p. (YA). (gr. 8-12). pap. 12.95 *(978-1-4598-0274-2(8))* Orca Bk. Pubs. USA.

Smith, James. The Wonderer of Time. 2006. 52p. pap. 16.95 *(978-1-4241-3316-1(5))* PublishAmerica, Inc.

Smith, Jane. It's the First Day of Preschool, Chloe Zoe! Smith, Jane, illus. 2016. (Chloe Zoe Ser.). (ENG., Illus.). 32p. (J). (gr. -1-3). 12.99 *(978-0-8075-2456-5(5))* Whitman, Albert & Co.

Smith, Julie. Hearts for the Homeless. 2012. 28p. pap. 19.99 *(978-1-4685-5602-5(9))* AuthorHouse.

Smith, Kourtney. The Adventures of Stanley the Staple. 2013. 28p. pap. 24.95 *(978-1-63004-276-9(5))* America Star Bks.

Smith, L. J. Dark Visions: The Strange Power - The Possessed - The Passion. 2009. (Dark Visions Ser.: Bks 1-3). (ENG.). 752p. (YA). (gr. 7). pap. 9.99 *(978-1-4169-8956-1(0)*, Simon Pulse) Simon Pulse.

Smith-Ready, Jeri. This Side of Salvation. 2014. (ENG., Illus.). 384p. (YA). (gr. 9). 17.99 *(978-1-4424-3948-1(3)*, Simon Pulse) Simon Pulse.

Smith, Stuart. My School's a Zoo! Catrow, David, illus. 2004. 40p. (J). (gr. k-3). lib. bdg. 16.89 *(978-0-06-028511-1(7))* HarperCollins Pubs.

Smith, Yeardley. I, Lorelei. 2009. 352p. (J). (gr. 3-7). lib. bdg. 17.89 *(978-0-06-149345-4(7)*, Geringer, Laura Book) HarperCollins Pubs.

Snadowsky, Daria. Anatomy of a Boyfriend. 2008. (ENG.). 272p. (YA). (gr. 9). pap. 8.99 *(978-0-440-23944-4(3)*, Ember) Random Hse. Children's Bks.

Snicket, Lemony, pseud. Cauchemar a la Scierie. pap. 24.95 *(978-2-09-282357-6(4))* Nathan, Fernand FRA. Dist: Distribooks, Inc.

Snodgrass, Lady Cecily. The Really Rotten Princess & the Cupcake Catastrophe. Lester, Mike, illus. 2013. (Really Rotten Princess Ser.). (ENG.). 32p. (J). (gr. k-2). 16.99 *(978-1-4424-8974-5(X))*; pap. 3.99 *(978-1-4424-8973-8(1))* Simon Spotlight. (Simon Spotlight).

Snyder, Susan E. Shivers & Shakes. 2006. (Illus.). 31p. (J). (gr. k-2). 9.95 *(978-0-9767163-5-8(6))* Kotzig Publishing, Inc.

Snyder, Zilpha Keatley. The Unseen. 2005. 199p. 16.00 *(978-0-7569-5670-7(6))* Perfection Learning Corp.

Soderberg, Erin. Puppy Pirates Super Special #2: Best in Class. 2017. (Puppy Pirates Ser.: 2). (ENG.). 128p. (J). (gr. 1-4). lib. bdg. 12.99 ***(978-1-5247-1329-4(5))***; (Illus.). 5.99 ***(978-1-5247-1328-7(7))*** Random Hse. Children's Bks. (Random Hse. Bks. for Young Readers).

Soderberg, Erin. The Quirks in Circus Quirkus. 2014. (Quirks Ser.). (ENG., Illus.). (YA). (gr. 3-6). 256p. pap. 7.99 *(978-1-61963-663-7(8)*, 9781619636637); 240p. 13.99 *(978-1-59990-790-1(9)*, 9781599907901) Bloomsbury Publishing USA. (Bloomsbury USA Childrens).

Solomon, Michelle & Pereira, Lavinia. Too Big! Faust, Laurie A., illus. 2009. 24p. pap. 10.96 *(978-1-4251-8949-5(0))* Trafford Publishing.

Sones, Sonya. What My Girlfriend Doesn't Know. 2011. 9.68 *(978-0-7848-3389-6(3)*, Everbind) Marco Bk. Co.

—What My Girlfriend Doesn't Know. 2013. (ENG., Illus.). 320p. (YA). (gr. 7). pap. 9.99 *(978-1-4424-9384-1(4)*, Simon & Schuster Bks. For Young Readers) Simon & Schuster Bks. For Young Readers.

Sonneborn, Scott. Pete Bogg: King of the Frogs. Aburtov, illus. 2013. (Pete Bogg Ser.). (ENG.). 48p. (gr. 1-3). pap. 5.95 *(978-1-4342-3872-6(5))*; lib. bdg. 23.99 *(978-1-4342-3284-7(0))* Stone Arch Bks.

Sonnenblick, Jordan. After Ever After. (ENG.). 272p. (J). 2014. pap. 9.99 *(978-0-545-72287-2(X))* 2010. (gr. 7-12). 17.99 *(978-0-439-83706-4(5)*, Scholastic Pr.) Scholastic, Inc.

—Curveball: The Year I Lost My Grip. 304p. 2014. (ENG.). (J). (gr. 7). pap. 9.99 *(978-0-545-32070-2(4)*, Scholastic Paperbacks) 2012. pap. 17.99 *(978-0-545-39311-9(6))* Scholastic, Inc.

—Dodger for President. 2010. (Dodger & Me Ser.: 2). (ENG.). 192p. (J). (gr. 3-7). pap. 8.99 *(978-0-312-61112-5(9)*, 9780312611125) Square Fish.

—Drums, Girls, & Dangerous Pie. 2005. (ENG.). 288p. (J). (gr. 7-12). 18.99 *(978-0-439-75519-1(0)*, Scholastic Pr.) Scholastic, Inc.

—Falling over Sideways. (ENG.). 272p. (J). (gr. 7). 2017. pap. 9.99 ***(978-0-545-86325-4(2))*** 2016. 17.99 *(978-0-545-86324-7(4)*, Scholastic Pr.) Scholastic, Inc.

—The Secret Sheriff of Sixth Grade. 2017. (ENG.). 208p. (J). (gr. 4-7). 16.99 ***(978-0-545-86320-9(1)***, Scholastic Pr.) Scholastic, Inc.

Sonnenblick, Jordan. Zen & the Art of Faking It. (ENG.). 272p. (J). (gr. 7-12). 2010. 9.99 *(978-0-439-83709-5(X)*, Scholastic Paperbacks) 2007. 16.99 *(978-0-439-83707-1(3)*, Scholastic Pr.) Scholastic, Inc.

Sookraj, Esther. Good with Words Bueno con las Palabras. 2010. 24p. pap. 15.99 *(978-1-4500-4169-0(8))* Xlibris Corp.

Soto, Gary. Accidental Love. 2008. (ENG., Illus.). 192p. (YA). (gr. 7). pap. 9.99 *(978-0-15-206113-5(4))* Houghton Mifflin Harcourt Publishing Co.

Souliere, Lisa. Toasters Are Easy, School Not So Much. Rockwell, Joanna, illus. 2012. 20p. pap. 10.95 *(978-1-60976-654-2(7)*, Strategic Bk. Publishing) Strategic Book Publishing & Rights Agency (SBPRA).

The Sound of Your Voice, Only Really Far Away. 2014. (Secret Language of Girl Trilogy Ser.). (ENG., Illus.). 256p. (J). (gr. 5-9). pap. 7.99 *(978-1-4424-3290-1(X)*, Atheneum Bks. for Young Readers) Simon & Schuster Children's Publishing.

Sovern, Megan Jean. The Meaning of Maggie. 2015. (ENG.). 232p. (J). (gr. 3-7). pap. 6.99 *(978-1-4521-2876-4(6))* Chronicle Bks. LLC.

Sowunmi, Lakeysha. Apple Leaves. 2009. 48p. pap. 17.49 *(978-1-4490-2055-2(0))* AuthorHouse.

Spalding, Amy. The New Guy (and Other Senior Year Distractions) 2016. (ENG.). 320p. (YA). (gr. 7-17). 17.99 *(978-0-316-38278-6(7)*, Poppy) Little, Brown Bks. for Young Readers.

Spanabel, H. A. Skyler & the Skunks. 2009. 48p. pap. *(978-1-84923-954-7(1))* YouWriteOn.

Sparks, Kerry. Frost Bites. 2009. 92p. pap. 11.49 *(978-1-4389-5414-1(X))* AuthorHouse.

Sparks, Megan. Falling Hard, 1 vol. 2013. (Roller Girls Ser.). (ENG.). 256p. (gr. 8-10). 12.95 *(978-1-62370-023-2(X))* Capstone Young Readers of Coughlan Cos.

—Hell's Belles, 1 vol. 2013. (Roller Girls Ser.). (ENG.). 256p. (gr. 8-10). 12.95 *(978-1-62370-024-9(8))* Capstone Young Readers of Coughlan Cos.

—Hell's Belles/By Megan Sparks. 2013. 255p. (YA). *(978-1-62370-022-5(1))* Capstone Young Readers of Coughlan Cos.

Spencer, James. Sally Small & the Judith-Situation. 2011. 86p. pap. *(978-1-908147-61-5(X))* YouWriteOn.

Spiegelman, Nadja. Zig & Wikki in Something Ate My Homework. Loeffler, Trade, illus. 2013. (ENG.). 40p. (J). (gr. -1-3). pap. 6.99 *(978-1-935179-38-2(1))* TOON Books / RAW Junior, LLC.

Spiegelman, Nadja & Loeffler, Trade. Zig & Wikki in Something Ate My Homework. 2013. (Toon Books Level 3 Ser.). lib. bdg. 14.75 *(978-0-606-32252-2(3)*, Turtleback) Turtleback Bks.

Spindler, Rebecca Williams & Spindler, Madelyn. Life According to Liz. 2012. 204p. pap. 12.95 *(978-0-9848050-5-1(2)*, Little Creek Bks.) Jan-Carol Publishing, INC.

Spinelli, Eileen. Miss Fox's Class Earns a Field Trip. Kennedy, Anne, illus. 2012. (J). *(978-1-61913-122-4(6))* Weigl Pubs., Inc.

—Miss Fox's Class Earns a Field Trip, 1 vol. Kennedy, Anne, illus. 2010. (Miss Fox's Class Ser.). (ENG.). 32p. (J). (gr. 1-3). 16.99 *(978-0-8075-5169-1(4))* Whitman, Albert & Co.

—Miss Fox's Class Gets It Wrong. Kennedy, Anne, illus. 2012. (Miss Fox's Class Ser.). (ENG.). 32p. (J). (gr. -1-3). 16.99 *(978-0-8075-5165-3(1))* Whitman, Albert & Co.

—Miss Fox's Class Goes Green. Kennedy, Anne, illus. 2012. (J). 34.28 *(978-1-61913-123-1(4))* Weigl Pubs., Inc.

—Miss Fox's Class Goes Green. Kennedy, Anne, illus. 2011. (Miss Fox's Class Ser.). (ENG.). 32p. (J). (gr. 1-3). 6.99 *(978-0-8075-5167-7(8))* Whitman, Albert & Co.

—Miss Fox's Class Shapes Up. Kennedy, Anne, illus. 2011. (ENG.). 32p. (J). (gr. 1-3). 16.99 *(978-0-8075-5171-4(6))* Whitman, Albert & Co.

—Peace Week in Miss Fox's Class. Kennedy, Anne, illus. 2012. (J). *(978-1-61913-155-2(2))* Weigl Pubs., Inc.

Spinelli, Jerry. Fourth Grade Rats. 2012. (ENG.). 160p. (J). (gr. 2-5). pap. 5.99 *(978-0-545-46478-9(1)*, Levine, Arthur A. Bks.) Scholastic, Inc.

—Fourth Grade Rats. 2012. lib. bdg. 16.00 *(978-0-606-26731-1(X)*, Turtleback) Turtleback Bks.

—Loser. 2003. (ENG.). 224p. (J). (gr. 3-7). pap. 6.99 *(978-0-06-054074-6(5))* HarperCollins Pubs.

—Loser. 2003. (J). (gr. 3-6). lib. bdg. 17.20 *(978-0-613-66899-6(5)*, Turtleback) Turtleback Bks.

—Smiles to Go. 2009. (ENG.). 272p. (J). (gr. 5). pap. 6.99 *(978-0-06-447197-8(7))* HarperCollins Pubs.

—Stargirl. 2003. (EMC Masterpiece Series Access Editions). xiv, 199p. (YA). 12.99 *(978-0-8219-2504-1(0)*, 35378) EMC/Paradigm Publishing.

—Stargirl. unabr. ed. 2004. 192p. (J). (gr. 7-18). pap. 40.00 incl. audio *(978-0-8072-0855-7(8)*, LYA 323 SP, Listening Library) Random Hse. Audio Publishing Group.

—Stargirl. 2004. (ENG.). 208p. (YA). (gr. 7). mass mkt. 7.99 *(978-0-440-41677-7(9)*, Laurel Leaf) Random Hse. Children's Bks.

—There's a Girl in My Hammerlock. 2008. 199p. (gr. 4-8). 16.00 *(978-0-7569-8465-6(3))* Perfection Learning Corp.

—Third Grade Angels. Bell, Jennifer, illus. 2014. (ENG.). 160p. (J). (gr. 2-5). pap. 5.99 *(978-0-545-38773-6(6)*, Levine, Arthur A. Bks.) Scholastic, Inc.

Spirn, Michele Sobel. I Am the Turkey. Allen, Joy, illus. 2007. (I Can Read Bks.). 48p. (gr. -1-3). 14.00 *(978-0-7569-8055-9(0))* Perfection Learning Corp.

Spirn, Michele Sobel & Spirn, Michele S. I Am the Turkey. Allen, Joy, illus. (I Can Read Level 2 Ser.). 48p. (J). (gr. k-3). 2006. (ENG.). pap. 3.99 *(978-0-06-053232-1(7))* 2004. 15.99 *(978-0-06-053230-7(0))* HarperCollins Pubs.

Spradlin, Michael P. Live & Let Shop. 2005. (Spy Goddess Ser.: Bk. 1). (ENG., Illus.). 224p. (gr. 7-18). 15.99 *(978-0-06-059407-7(1))* HarperCollins Pubs.

Spratt, R. A. Friday Barnes, No Rules. Gosier, Phil, illus. 2017. (Friday Barnes Mysteries Ser.). (ENG.). 272p. (J). 13.99 *(978-1-62672-639-0(6)*, 9781626726390) Roaring Brook Pr.

—Under Suspicion. Gosier, Phil, illus. 2016. (Friday Barnes Mysteries Ser.). (ENG.). 288p. (J). 13.99 *(978-1-62672-299-6(4)*, 9781626722996) Roaring Brook Pr.

Spring, Melanie. Practice Makes Perfect. 2014. (Varsity Novel Ser.: 3). (ENG.). 192p. (YA). (gr. 7-17). pap. 10.00 *(978-0-316-22733-9(1)*, Poppy) Little, Brown Bks. for Young Readers.

—Turn It Up. 2014. (Varsity Novel Ser.: 2). (ENG.). 208p. (YA). (gr. 7-17). pap. 10.00 *(978-0-316-22724-7(2))* Little Brown & Co.

Springer, Kristina. Cici Reno Knows It All. 2016. (Yoga Girls Ser.). (ENG.). 192p. (J). (gr. 5-8). 14.95 *(978-1-4549-1751-9(2))* Sterling Publishing Co., Inc.

Springer, Nancy. Possessing Jessie. 2010. (ENG.). 128p. (YA). (gr. 7-18). pap. 16.95 *(978-0-8234-2259-3(3))* Holiday Hse., Inc.

Springfield, Pepper. Perfecto Pet Show. Caldwell, Kristy, illus. 2017. (Bobs & Tweets Ser.: 2). (ENG.). 80p. (J). (gr. -1-3). 9.99 ***(978-0-545-87073-3(9))*** Scholastic, Inc.

Springstubb, Tricia. Cody & the Mysteries of the Universe. Wheeler, Eliza, illus. 2016. (ENG.). 144p. (J). (gr. 2-5). 14.99 *(978-0-7636-5858-8(8))* Candlewick Pr.

—Cody & the Rules of Life. Wheeler, Eliza, illus. 2017. (ENG.). 176p. (J). (gr. 2-5). 14.99 *(978-0-7636-7920-0(8))* Candlewick Pr.

Sproule, Acquanetta M. Scamp. 2010. 40p. pap. 18.00 *(978-0-557-37187-7(2))* Lulu Pr., Inc.

Spurling, Wesley. Books for Jacob. 2009. 24p. pap. 14.79 *(978-1-4389-2231-7(0))* AuthorHouse.

—Gerry the Giraffe. 2009. 36p. pap. 16.99 *(978-1-4389-4223-0(0))* AuthorHouse.

Spurr, Judy. Trapped. 2007. 84p. per. 8.95 *(978-0-595-43915-7(2))* iUniverse, Inc.

Spyri, Johanna. How Wiseli Was Provided For. 2006. 108p. per. 9.95 *(978-1-59818-473-0(3))* Aegypan.

—Rico & Stineli. 2006. 148p. (gr. 4-7). per. 11.95 *(978-1-59818-873-8(9))* Aegypan.

St. Claire, Roxanne. They All Fall Down. (ENG.). 352p. (YA). (gr. 7). 2016. pap. 9.99 *(978-0-385-74272-6(X)*, Ember) 2014. 17.99 *(978-0-385-74271-9(1)*, Delacorte Pr.) Random Hse. Children's Bks.

St. Crow, Lili. Betrayals. 2009. (Strange Angels Ser.: 2). (ENG., Illus.). 304p. (YA). (gr. 7-18). 9.99 *(978-1-59514-252-8(5)*, Razorbill) Penguin Young Readers Group.

—Betrayals, 10 vols. 2010. (Strange Angels Ser.: 2). (YA). 95.75 *(978-1-4407-7156-9(1))* Recorded Bks., Inc.

—Betrayals. 2009. (Strange Angels Ser.: 2). lib. bdg. 20.85 *(978-0-606-09020-9(7)*, Turtleback) Turtleback Bks.

St. James, James. Freak Show. 2008. (ENG.). 304p. (YA). (gr. 9-18). 8.99 *(978-0-14-241231-2(7)*, Puffin Books) Penguin Young Readers Group.

Stadelmann, Amy Marie. The Super-Smelly Moldy Blob. Stadelmann, Amy Marie, illus. 2016. (Olive & Beatrix Ser.: 2). (ENG., Illus.). 80p. (J). (gr. k-2). 15.99 *(978-0-545-81485-0(5))* Scholastic, Inc.

Stahl, Mary Louise. Louie. 2003. 122p. (YA). 20.95 *(978-0-595-74889-1(9))*; pap. 10.95 *(978-0-595-28750-5(6))* iUniverse, Inc.

Stahler, David, Jr. Spinning Out. 2011. (ENG.). 288p. (YA). (gr. 7-17). 16.99 *(978-0-8118-7780-0(9))* Chronicle Bks. LLC.

Stalling-Patton, Deborah. Shypoodle: Getting to Know You. 2009. 40p. pap. 17.99 *(978-1-4389-3899-8(3))* AuthorHouse.

Stamper, Judith Bauer. Rocky Road Trip. Gangloff, Hope, illus. 2004. (Magic School Bus Science Chapter Bks.). 89p. (gr. 2-5). lib. bdg. 15.00 *(978-0-7569-3093-6(6))* Perfection Learning Corp.

Stampler, Ann Redisch. Afterparty. 2013. (ENG., Illus.). 416p. (YA). (gr. 9). 17.99 *(978-1-4424-2324-4(2)*, Simon Pulse) Simon Pulse.

—Where It Began. 2013. (ENG.). 384p. (YA). (gr. 9). pap. 9.99 *(978-1-4424-2322-0(6)*, Simon Pulse) Simon Pulse.

Standiford, Natalie. Breaking up Is Really, Really Hard to Do. 2005. (ENG.). 224p. (YA). (gr. 7-17). pap. 18.99 *(978-0-316-11041-9(8))* Little, Brown Bks. for Young Readers.

—The Dating Game, No. 1. 2005. (ENG.). 224p. (YA). (gr. 7-17). pap. 18.99 *(978-0-316-11040-2(X))* Little, Brown Bks. for Young Readers.

—Ex-Rating. 4th rev. ed. 2006. (ENG.). 224p. (YA). (gr. 7-17). per. 17.99 *(978-0-316-15876-3(3))* Little, Brown Bks. for Young Readers.

—The Only Girl in School. 2016. (ENG.). 224p. (J). (gr. 3-7). 16.99 *(978-0-545-82996-0(8)*, Scholastic Pr.) Scholastic, Inc.

—Speed Dating. 5th ed. 2006. (ENG.). 224p. (J). (gr. 8-12). per. 18.99 *(978-0-316-11530-8(4))* Little, Brown Bks. for Young Readers.

—Switched at Birthday. 2014. (ENG.). 240p. (J). (gr. 3-7). 16.99 *(978-0-545-34650-4(9)*, Scholastic Pr.) Scholastic, Inc.

Standish, Burt L. Frank Merriwell in Camp. Rudman, Jack, ed. 2003. (Frank Merriwell Ser.). (YA). (gr. 9-18). 29.95 *(978-0-8373-9324-7(8))*; pap. 9.95 *(978-0-8373-9024-6(9)*, FM-024) Merriwell, Frank Inc.

—Frank Merriwell's Chums. 2007. (ENG.). 228p. pap. 20.99 *(978-1-4346-3282-1(2))*; 264p. pap. 23.99 *(978-1-4346-3283-8(0))* Creative Media Partners, LLC.

Stanek, Robert, pseud. The Bugville Critters Go to School. 2007. (ENG.). 28p. (J). per. 9.99 *(978-1-57545-145-9(X))* RP Media.

—The Bugville Critters Have a Sleepover. 2008. (ENG.). 28p. (J). per. 9.99 *(978-1-57545-146-6(8))* RP Media.

—The Bugville Critters Make New Friends: Buster Bee's School Days #2. 2008. (ENG., Illus.). 60p. (J). per. 18.95 *(978-1-57545-168-8(9))* RP Media.

—The Bugville Critters So Many Lessons to Learn. 2009. (Illus.). 68p. (J). pap. 18.95 *(978-1-57545-237-1(5)*, Reagent Pr. Bks. for Young Readers) RP Media.

—Go to School. 2008. (ENG., Illus.). 28p. (J). pap. 5.29 *(978-1-57545-188-6(3))* RP Media.

—Have Trouble at School. 2009. (Illus.). 24p. pap. 9.99 *(978-1-57545-212-8(X))*; 52p. (J). pap. 14.95 *(978-1-57545-204-3(9))* RP Media. (Reagent Pr. Bks. for Young Readers).

—Robert Stanek's Bugville Critters Storybook Treasury. 2008. (ENG., Illus.). 132p. (J). per. 24.95 *(978-1-57545-171-8(9))* RP Media.

—Robert Stanek's Bugville Critters Storybook Treasury Volume 2 (the Bugville Critters Storybook Collection, Volume 2), 4 vols., Vol. 2. 2008. (ENG., Illus.). 124p. (J). per. 24.95 *(978-1-57545-173-2(5))* RP Media.

—Stay after School. 2009. (Bugville Critters Ser.: No. 10). (ENG., Illus.). 52p. (J). 14.95 *(978-1-57545-206-7(5)*, Reagent Pr. Bks. for Young Readers) RP Media.

—Visit City Hall. 2009. (Bugville Critters Ser.: No. 12). (ENG., Illus.). 52p. (J). 14.95 *(978-1-57545-208-1(1)*, Reagent Pr. Bks. for Young Readers) RP Media.

Staniszewski, Anna. The Dirt Diary. 2014. (Dirt Diary Ser.: 1). (ENG.). 256p. (J). (gr. 5-9). pap. 6.99 *(978-1-4022-8636-0(8)*, 9781402286360, Sourcebooks Jabberwocky) Sourcebooks, Inc.

Stapleton, Rhonda. Flirting with Disaster. 2010. (ENG.). 256p. (YA). (gr. 7-18). pap. 9.99 *(978-1-4169-7465-9(2)*, Simon Pulse) Simon Pulse.

Stark, Henry. Heart Lessons. 2008. (ENG.). 502p. pap. 19.99 *(978-1-4196-4881-6(0))* CreateSpace Independent Publishing Platform.

Starkey, Scott. How to Beat the Bully Without Really Trying. (How to Beat the Bully Ser.). (ENG.). 272p. (J). (gr. 3-7). 2013. pap. 7.99 *(978-1-4424-8473-3(X))* 2012. 15.99 *(978-1-4424-1685-7(8))* Simon & Schuster/Paula Wiseman Bks. (Simon & Schuster/Paula Wiseman Bks.).

Staunton, Ted. Morgan & the Money. Slavin, Bill, illus. 2008. (First Novel Ser.). (ENG.). 64p. (J). (gr. 1-5). *(978-0-88780-776-3(3))* Formac Publishing Co., Ltd.

—Morgan & the Money, 1 vol. Shannon, Ben, illus. 2008. (Formac First Novels Ser.). (ENG.). 64p. (gr. 1-5). 4.95 *(978-0-88780-774-9(7)*, 9780887807749) Formac Publishing Co., Ltd. CAN. Dist: Casemate Pubs. & Bk. Distributors, LLC.

—Pucker up, Morgan, 1 vol. Slavin, Bill, illus. 2008. (Formac First Novels Ser.). (ENG.). 64p. (J). (gr. 2-3). 5.95 *(978-0-88780-744-2(5)*, 9780887807442); 14.95 *(978-0-88780-746-6(1)*, 9780887807466) Formac Publishing Co., Ltd. CAN. Dist: Casemate Pubs. & Bk. Distributors, LLC.

Stavans, Ilan. Golemito. Villegas, Teresa, illus. 2013. (ENG.). 32p. (J). 16.95 *(978-1-58838-292-4(3)*, NewSouth Bks.) NewSouth, Inc.

Stead, Rebecca. Goodbye Stranger. (ENG.). (J). (gr. 5). 2017. 320p. 7.99 *(978-0-307-98086-1(3)*, Yearling) 2015. 304p. 16.99 *(978-0-385-74317-4(3)*, Lamb, Wendy Bks.) 2015. 304p. lib. bdg. 19.99 *(978-0-375-99098-4(4)*, Lamb, Wendy Bks.) Random Hse. Children's Bks.

—Liar & Spy. (ENG.). (J). (gr. 3-7). 2013. 208p. 7.99 *(978-0-375-85087-5(2)*, Yearling) 2012. 192p. 15.99 *(978-0-385-73743-2(2)*, Lamb, Wendy Bks.) Random Hse. Children's Bks.

Steinberg, D. J. Kindergarten, Here I Come! Chambers, Mark, illus. 2012. (ENG.). 32p. (J). (gr. -1-k). pap. 3.99 *(978-0-448-45624-9(9)*, Grosset & Dunlap) Penguin Young Readers Group.

Steiner, Hartley. This Is Gabriel - Making Sense of School: A Book about Sensory Processing Disorder. 2nd rev. ed. 2012. (ENG., Illus.). 32p. pap. 9.95 *(978-1-935567-34-9(9))* Sensory Resources.

Steinkellner, Teddy. Trash Can Days: A Middle School Saga. 2013. (Trash Can Days Ser.). (ENG.). 352p. (J). (gr. 5-9). 16.99 *(978-1-4231-6632-0(9))* Disney Pr.

Steinkellner, Teddy. Two Roads from Here. 2017. (ENG., Illus.). 448p. (YA). (gr. 9). 17.99 ***(978-1-4814-3061-6(0)***, Simon & Schuster Bks. For Young Readers) Simon & Schuster Bks. For Young Readers.

Steinkraus, Kyla. Gumshoe Gang Cracks the Case. 2015. (ENG.). 64p. (gr. 3-6). 29.95 *(978-1-63430-381-1(4))* Rourke Educational Media.

—Table Wars! Dufalla, Anita, illus. 2012. (ENG.). 24p. (gr. 2-3). pap. 8.95 *(978-1-61810-330-7(X))* Rourke Educational Media.

Step up 2: the Streets. 2008. 160p. pap. 4.99 *(978-1-4231-1319-5(5))* Disney Pr.

Stephenson, Lynda. Dancing with Elvis. (YA). (gr. 7). 2006. (ENG.). 331p. per. 8.00 *(978-0-8028-5300-4(5))* 2005. 323p. 17.00 *(978-0-8028-5293-9(9))* Eerdmans, William B. Publishing Co. (Eerdmans Bks For Young Readers).

Stern, A. J. Check, Please!, 3 vols. Marts, Doreen Mulryan, illus. 2010. (Frankly, Frannie Ser.: 3). (ENG.). 128p. (J). (gr. 1-3). pap. 5.99 *(978-0-448-45352-1(5),* Grosset & Dunlap) Penguin Young Readers Group.

—Fashion Frenzy. Marts, Doreen Mulryan, illus. 2011. (Frankly, Frannie Ser.: 6). (ENG.). 128p. (J). (gr. 1-3). pap. 5.99 *(978-0-448-45544-0(7),* Grosset & Dunlap) Penguin Young Readers Group.

—Frankly, Frannie, 1 vol. Marts, Doreen Mulryan, illus. 2010. (Frankly, Frannie Ser.: 1). (ENG.). 128p. (J). (gr. 1-3). pap. 5.99 *(978-0-448-45348-4(7),* Grosset & Dunlap) Penguin Young Readers Group.

—Frankly, Frannie: Books 1-3. Marts, Doreen Mulryan, illus. 2014. (Frankly, Frannie Ser.). (ENG.). 384p. (J). (gr. 1-3). 8.99 *(978-0-448-48461-7(7),* Grosset & Dunlap) Penguin Young Readers Group.

—Miss Fortune, 7 vols. Marts, Doreen Mulryan, illus. 2012. (Frankly, Frannie Ser.: 7). (ENG.). 128p. (J). (gr. 1-3). pap. 5.99 *(978-0-448-45748-2(2),* Grosset & Dunlap) Penguin Young Readers Group.

—Principal for the Day. Marts, Doreen Mulryan, illus. 2011. (Frankly, Frannie Ser.: 5). (ENG.). 128p. (J). (gr. 1-3). pap. 5.99 *(978-0-448-45542-6(0),* Grosset & Dunlap) Penguin Young Readers Group.

Stern, Ricki & Worcester, Heidi P. Adventure: Lonely Leader. Bates, Amy, illus. 2003. (Beryl E. Bean Ser.: No. 3). 64p. (J). lib. bdg. 16.89 *(978-0-06-028774-0(8))* HarperCollins Pubs.

Sternberg, Julie. Everything's Changed. Wright, Johanna, illus. 2017. (Top-Secret Diary of Celie Valentine Ser.). (ENG.). 160p. (J). (gr. 2-6). 16.95 *(978-1-62979-672-7(7))* Boyds Mills Pr.

—Like Carrot Juice on a Cupcake. Cordell, Matthew, illus. 2014. (Eleanor Ser.). (ENG.). 192p. (J). (gr. 1-4). 15.95 *(978-1-4197-1033-9(8),* Amulet Bks.) Abrams, Inc.

Stevens, Eric. Finn Reeder, Flu Fighter: How I Survived a Worldwide Pandemic, the School Bully, & the Craziest Game of Dodge Ball Ever. Fraser, Kay, illus. 2009. (Finn Reeder Ser.). (ENG.). 80p. (gr. 2-3). lib. bdg. 26.65 *(978-1-4342-2450-7(3))* Capstone Digital.

—Flu Fighter: How I Survived a Worldwide Pandemic, the School Bully, & the Craziest Game of Dodge Ball Ever. Fraser, Kay, illus. 2010. (Finn Reeder Ser.). (ENG.). 80p. (gr. 3-4). 9.99 *(978-1-4342-2562-7(3))* Capstone Digital.

Stevens, Janet & Crummel, Susan Stevens. The Little Red Pen. Stevens, Janet, illus. 2011. (ENG., Illus.). 56p. (J). (gr. 1-4). 17.99 *(978-0-15-206432-7(X))* Houghton Mifflin Harcourt Publishing Co.

Stevens, Robin. Murder Is Bad Manners. 2015. (Wells & Wong Mystery Ser.). (ENG., Illus.). 320p. (J). (gr. 5). 17.99 *(978-1-4814-2212-3(X),* Simon & Schuster Bks. For Young Readers) Simon & Schuster Bks. For Young Readers.

Stevenson, Peggy. Meet the Spencers & the Smart Knots. 2009. 48p. pap. 16.95 *(978-1-60813-517-2(9))* America Star Bks.

Stevenson, Robin. Attitude, 1 vol. 2013. (Orca Limelights Ser.). (ENG.). 144p. (J). (gr. 6-9). pap. 9.95 *(978-1-4598-0382-4(5))* Orca Bk. Pubs. USA.

—Impossible Things, 1 vol. 2008. (ENG.). 192p. (J). (gr. 4-8). pap. 8.95 *(978-1-55143-736-1(8))* Orca Bk. Pubs. USA.

—Out of Order, 1 vol. 2007. (ENG.). 232p. (YA). (gr. 7-12). per. 9.95 *(978-1-55143-693-7(0))* Orca Bk. Pubs. USA.

Stevenson, Sarah Jamila. The Latte Rebellion. 2011. (ENG., Illus.). 336p. (YA). (gr. 9-18). pap. 9.95 *(978-0-7387-2278-8(2),* Flux) North Star Editions.

Stewart, Dianne C. Quimbaya. 2008. (ENG.). 200p. (gr. 1-18). pap. 8.95 *(978-0-9667359-8-7(6),* BeanPole Bks.) Harren Communications, LLC.

Stewart, Kenneth. The Kickball Kid. 2012. 24p. pap. 24.95 *(978-1-4626-7683-5(9))* America Star Bks.

Stewart, Kiera. Fetching. 2012. (ENG.). 304p. (YA). (gr. 5-9). pap. 7.99 *(978-1-4231-4245-4(4))* Hyperion Pr.

Stewart, Mark R. Malcolm's Cubby House. Swope, Brenda, illus. 2011. 28p. pap. 24.95 *(978-1-4560-0958-8(3))* America Star Bks.

Stewart, Trenton Lee. The Mysterious Benedict Society. Tingley, Megan, ed. Sudyka, Diana, illus. 2010. (Mysterious Benedict Society Ser.: 3). (ENG.). 400p. (J). (gr. 3-7). pap. 8.99 *(978-0-316-04550-6(0))* Little, Brown Bks. for Young Readers.

—The Mysterious Benedict Society. Ellis, Carson, illus. (Mysterious Benedict Society Ser.: 1). (ENG.). (J). (gr. 3-7). 2008. 512p. pap. 9.99 *(978-0-316-00395-7(6))* 2007. 496p. 19.00 *(978-0-316-05777-6(0),* Tingley, Megan Bks.) 2015. 512p. 12.99 *(978-0-316-26501-0(2))* Little, Brown Bks. for Young Readers.

—The Mysterious Benedict Society. unabr. ed. 2007. (Mysterious Benedict Society Ser.: Bk. 1). (ENG.). (J). (gr. 3-7). 25.50 *(978-0-307-28440-2(9),* Listening Library (Audio)) Penguin Random House Audio Publishing Group.

—The Mysterious Benedict Society. 2009. 17.45 *(978-1-60686-527-9(7))* Perfection Learning Corp.

—The Mysterious Benedict Society. 2010. (Mysterious Benedict Society Ser.: 3). (J). lib. bdg. 19.65 *(978-0-606-15117-7(6),* Turtleback) Turtleback Bks.

—The Mysterious Benedict Society. Ellis, Carson, illus. 2008. (Mysterious Benedict Society Ser.: 1). 485p. (J). (gr. 3-7). lib. bdg. 19.65 *(978-1-4178-1817-4(4),* Turtleback) Turtleback Bks.

—The Mysterious Benedict Society: 10th Anniversary Edition. Ellis, Carson, illus. 2017. (ENG.). 528p. (J). (gr. 3-7). 18.99 *(978-0-316-46491-8(0))* Little, Brown Bks. for Young Readers.

—The Mysterious Benedict Society & the Prisoner's Dilemma. Sudyka, Diana, illus. 2009. (Mysterious Benedict Society Ser.: 3). (ENG.). 400p. (J). (gr. 3-7). 18.99 *(978-0-316-04552-0(7))* Little, Brown Bks. for Young Readers.

Stier, Catherine. Bugs in My Hair?! Lyon, Tammie, illus. 2012. (J). 34.28 *(978-1-61913-111-8(0))* Weigl Pubs., Inc.

—Bugs in My Hair?!, 1 vol. Lyon, Tammie, illus. 2010. (ENG.). 32p. (J). (gr. 1-3). pap. 6.99 *(978-0-8075-0909-8(4))* Whitman, Albert & Co.

—What's Bugging Nurse Penny? A Story about Lice. Beaky, Suzanne, illus. 2013. (ENG.). 32p. (J). (gr. -1-3). 16.99 *(978-0-8075-8803-1(2))* Whitman, Albert & Co.

Stiles, Norman. On My Very First School Day I Met... Mayer, Bill, illus. 2005. 32p. (J). (gr. -1). 9.95 *(978-0-689-03924-9(7),* Milk & Cookies) ibooks, Inc.

Stillman, Josh. The Chinese Finger Trap. 2012. 116p. pap. 11.50 *(978-1-59330-803-2(5))* Aventine Pr.

Stilton, Geronimo. A Fabumouse School Adventure. 2009. (Geronimo Stilton Ser.: 38). (ENG.). 128p. (J). (gr. 2-5). pap. 7.99 *(978-0-545-02138-8(3),* Scholastic Paperbacks) Scholastic, Inc.

—A Fabumouse School Adventure. 2009. (Geronimo Stilton Ser.: 38). lib. bdg. 18.40 *(978-0-606-00229-5(4),* Turtleback) Turtleback Bks.

—Thea Stilton & the Dragon's Code. 2009. (Geronimo Stilton Special Edition Ser.: No. 1). (Illus.). 158p. 18.00 *(978-1-60686-420-3(3))* Perfection Learning Corp.

—Thea Stilton & the Dragon's Code. 2009. (Thea Stilton Ser.: 1). lib. bdg. 19.65 *(978-0-606-00231-8(6),* Turtleback) Turtleback Bks.

Stilton, Geronimo & Stilton, Thea. Thea Stilton & the Ghost of the Shipwreck. 2010. (Thea Stilton Ser.: 3). lib. bdg. 19.65 *(978-0-606-06843-7(0),* Turtleback) Turtleback Bks.

Stilton, Thea. A Mouseford Musical. 2015. (Illus.). 128p. (J). pap. *(978-0-545-78905-9(2))* Scholastic, Inc.

Stine, R. L. Battle of the Dum Diddys. Park, Trip, illus. 2007. (Rotten School Ser.: 12). (ENG.). 128p. (J). (gr. 3-7). 12.99 *(978-0-06-078833-9(X))* HarperCollins Pubs.

—Battle of the Dum Diddys, 1 vol. Park, Trip, illus. 2011. (Rotten School Ser.: No. 12). (ENG.). 128p. (gr. 2-5). 24.21 *(978-1-59961-836-4(2))* Spotlight.

—The Big Blueberry Barf-Off! Park, Trip, illus. 2005. (Rotten School Ser.: No. 1). 128p. (J). (ENG.). 6.99 *(978-0-06-078586-4(1));* lib. bdg. 14.89 *(978-0-06-078587-1(X))* HarperCollins Pubs.

—The Big Blueberry Barf-Off!, 1 vol. Park, Trip, illus. 2011. (Rotten School Ser.: No. 1). (ENG.). 128p. (gr. 2-5). 24.21 *(978-1-59961-825-8(7))* Spotlight.

—Creature Teacher: The Final Exam. 2014. (Goosebumps Most Wanted Ser.: 6). (ENG.). 160p. (J). (gr. 3-7). pap. 6.99 *(978-0-545-62773-3(7),* Scholastic Paperbacks) Scholastic, Inc.

—Dudes, the School Is Haunted!, 1 vol. Park, Trip, illus. 2011. (Rotten School Ser.: No. 7). (ENG.). 128p. (gr. 2-5). 24.21 *(978-1-59961-831-9(1))* Spotlight.

—The Good, the Bad & the Very Slimy, 1 vol. Park, Trip, illus. 2011. (Rotten School Ser.: No. 3). (ENG.). 128p. (gr. 2-5). 24.21 *(978-1-59961-827-2(3))* Spotlight.

—Got Cake? Park, Trip, illus. 2007. (Rotten School Ser.: 13). (ENG.). 128p. (J). (gr. 3-7). 12.99 *(978-0-06-123269-5(6))* HarperCollins Pubs.

—The Great Smelling Bee, 1 vol. Park, Trip, illus. 2011. (Rotten School Ser.: No. 2). (ENG.). 128p. (gr. 2-5). 24.21 *(978-1-59961-826-5(5))* Spotlight.

—The Heinie Prize, 1 vol. Park, Trip, illus. 2011. (Rotten School Ser.: No. 6). (ENG.). 128p. (gr. 2-5). 24.21 *(978-1-59961-830-2(3))* Spotlight.

—How I Met My Monster. 2013. (Goosebumps: Most Wanted Ser.: 3). (ENG.). 160p. (J). (gr. 3-7). pap. 6.99 *(978-0-545-41800-3(3),* Scholastic Paperbacks) Scholastic, Inc.

—How I Met My Monster. 2013. (Goosebumps Most Wanted Ser.: 3). lib. bdg. 17.20 *(978-0-606-31534-0(9),* Turtleback) Turtleback Bks.

—Lose, Team, Lose!, 1 vol. Park, Trip, illus. 2011. (Rotten School Ser.: No. 4). (ENG.). 128p. (gr. 2-5). 24.21 *(978-1-59961-828-9(1))* Spotlight.

—The New Girl. 2006. (Fear Street Ser.: Bk. 1). (ENG., Illus.). 176p. (YA). (gr. 7-12). mass mkt. 7.99 *(978-1-4169-1810-3(8),* Simon Pulse) Simon Pulse.

—Night of the Creepy Things. Park, Trip, illus. (Rotten School Ser.: Bk. 14). 4.99 *(978-0-06-123274-9(2))* HarperCollins Pubs.

—Party Poopers. Park, Trip, illus. (Rotten School Ser.: Bk. 9). 4.99 *(978-0-06-078826-1(7))* HarperCollins Pubs.

—Party Poopers, 1 vol. Park, Trip, illus. 2011. (Rotten School Ser.: No. 9). (ENG.). 128p. (gr. 2-5). 24.21 *(978-1-59961-833-3(8))* Spotlight.

—Punk'd & Skunked, 1 vol. Park, Trip, illus. 2011. (Rotten School Ser.: No. 11). (ENG.). 128p. (gr. 2-5). 24.21 *(978-1-59961-835-7(4))* Spotlight.

—Punk'd & Skunked. Park, Trip, illus. 2007. (Rotten School Ser.: 11). (ENG.). 128p. (J). (gr. 3-7). 6.99 *(978-0-06-078830-8(5))* HarperCollins Pubs.

—Rotten School, 12 vols. Set. Park, Trip, illus. Incl. Battle of the Dum Diddys. 24.21 *(978-1-59961-836-4(2));* Big Blueberry Barf-Off! 24.21 *(978-1-59961-825-8(7));* Dudes, the School Is Haunted! 24.21 *(978-1-59961-831-9(1));* Good, the Bad & the Very Slimy. 24.21 *(978-1-59961-827-2(3));* Great Smelling Bee. 24.21 *(978-1-59961-826-5(5));* Heinie Prize. 24.21 *(978-1-59961-830-2(3));* Lose, Team, Lose! 24.21 *(978-1-59961-828-9(1));* Party Poopers. 24.21 *(978-1-59961-833-3(8));* Punk'd & Skunked. 24.21 *(978-1-59961-835-7(4));* Rottenest Angel. 24.21 *(978-1-59961-834-0(6));* Shake, Rattle, & Hurl! 24.21 *(978-1-59961-829-6(X));* Teacher from Heck. 24.21 *(978-1-59961-832-6(X));* (gr. 2-5). (Rotten School Ser.). (Illus.). 128p. 2011. 290.52 *(978-1-59961-824-1(9))* Spotlight.

—Rotten School #12: Battle of the Dum Diddys. Park, Trip, illus. 4.99 *(978-0-06-078835-3(6))* HarperCollins Pubs.

—Rotten School #15: Calling All Birdbrains. Park, Trip, illus. 4.99 *(978-0-06-123277-0(7))* HarperCollins Pubs.

—Rotten School #16: Dumb Clucks. Park, Trip, illus. 4.99 *(978-0-06-123280-0(7))* HarperCollins Pubs.

—The Rottenest Angel, 1 vol. Park, Trip, illus. 2011. (Rotten School Ser.: No. 10). (ENG.). 128p. (gr. 2-5). 24.21 *(978-1-59961-834-0(6))* Spotlight.

—The Rottenest Angel. Park, Trip, illus. 2006. (Rotten School Ser.: 10). (ENG.). 128p. (J). (gr. 3-7). 6.99 *(978-0-06-078827-8(5))* HarperCollins Pubs.

—Shake, Rattle, & Hurl! Park, Trip, illus. 2006. (Rotten School Ser.: No. 5). (ENG.). 128p. (J). (gr. 3-7). 6.99 *(978-0-06-078811-7(9))* HarperCollins Pubs.

—Shake, Rattle, & Hurl!, 1 vol. Park, Trip, illus. 2011. (Rotten School Ser.: No. 5). (ENG.). 128p. (gr. 2-5). 24.21 *(978-1-59961-829-6(X))* Spotlight.

—The Teacher from Heck, 1 vol. Park, Trip, illus. 2011. (Rotten School Ser.: No. 8). (ENG.). 128p. (gr. 2-5). 24.21 *(978-1-59961-832-6(X))* Spotlight.

—Why I Quit Zombie School. 2011. (Goosebumps Hall of Horrors Ser.: 4). (ENG.). 160p. (J). (gr. 3-7). pap. 6.99 *(978-0-545-28932-0(7),* Scholastic Paperbacks) Scholastic, Inc.

Stolarz, Laurie Faria. White Is for Magic. Karre, Andrew, ed. 2004. (Stolarz Ser.: 2). (ENG.). 312p. (YA). pap. 11.99 *(978-0-7387-0443-2(1),* Flux) North Star Editions.

Stone, Kate. Moose Goes to School. 2012. (ENG.). 16p. (J). bds. 10.99 *(978-1-4494-1788-8(4))* Andrews McMeel Publishing.

Stone, Phoebe. The Boy on Cinnamon Street. 2012. 234p. (J). *(978-0-545-43368-6(1),* Levine, Arthur A. Bks.) Scholastic, Inc.

—Deep down Popular. 2010. (ENG.). 288p. (J). (gr. 4-7). 6.99 *(978-0-439-80244-4(X),* Levine, Arthur A. Bks.) Scholastic, Inc.

Stone, Sonja. Desert Dark. 2016. (ENG.). 336p. (YA). (gr. 7). 17.95 *(978-0-8234-3562-3(8))* Holiday Hse., Inc.

Stone, Tamara Ireland. Every Last Word. (ENG.). (YA). (gr. 7-12). 2017. 384p. pap. 9.99 *(978-1-4847-2364-7(3))* 2015. 368p. 17.99 *(978-1-4847-0527-8(0))* Hyperion Bks. for Children.

—Every Last Word. 2017. (ENG.). (YA). (gr. 7-12). lib. bdg. 20.85 ***(978-0-606-39885-5(6))*** Turtleback Bks.

Stone, Tamara Ireland. Time after Time. 2014. (ENG.). 368p. (YA). (gr. 7-12). pap. 9.99 *(978-1-4231-5981-0(0))* Hyperion Bks. for Children.

Stone, Tanya Lee. A Bad Boy Can Be Good for a Girl. 2007. (ENG.). 240p. (YA). (gr. 7-11). per. 8.99 *(978-0-553-49509-6(7),* Lamb, Wendy Bks.) Random Hse. Children's Bks.

Storrie, Paul D. Made for Each Other, 2 vols. Cowgur, Eldon, illus. 2011. (My Boyfriend Is a Monster Ser.: 2). (ENG.). 128p. (YA). (gr. 7-12). 29.27 *(978-0-7613-5601-1(0))* Lerner Publishing Group.

—#02 Made for Each Other. Cowgur, Eldon, illus. 2011. (My Boyfriend Is a Monster Ser.). 128p. (YA). pap. 56.72 *(978-0-7613-7604-0(6),* Graphic Universe™) Lerner Publishing Group.

Stoudemire, Amar'e. Home Court. Jessell, Tim, illus. 2012. (STAT: Standing Tall & Talented Ser.: 1). (ENG.). 144p. (J). (gr. 3-7). pap. 5.99 *(978-0-545-38759-0(0),* Scholastic Pr.) Scholastic, Inc.

—Home Court. 2012. (STAT: Standing Tall & Talented Ser.: 1). lib. bdg. 16.00 *(978-0-606-26169-2(9),* Turtleback) Turtleback Bks.

Stout, Katie M. Hello, I Love You. 2015. (ENG.). 304p. (YA). pap. *(978-1-250-08195-7(5),* St. Martin's Griffin) St. Martin's Pr.

—Hello, I Love You: A Novel. 2015. (ENG.). 304p. (YA). (gr. 7-12). 18.99 *(978-1-250-05259-9(9),* 9781250052599, St. Martin's Griffin) St. Martin's Pr.

Stout, Shawn K. Don't Chicken Out. Ying, Victoria, illus. 2013. (Not-So-Ordinary Girl Ser.: 3). (ENG.). 176p. (J). (gr. 1-5). pap. 5.99 *(978-1-4169-7111-5(4),* Aladdin) Simon & Schuster Children's Publishing.

—Don't Chicken Out. Ying, Victoria, illus. 2013. (Not-So-Ordinary Girl Ser.: 3). (ENG.). 176p. (J). (gr. 1-5). 15.99 *(978-1-4169-7929-6(8),* Simon & Schuster/Paula Wiseman Bks.) Simon & Schuster/Paula Wiseman Bks.

—Miss Matched. Martini, Angela, illus. 2013. (Not-So-Ordinary Girl Ser.: 2). (ENG.). 176p. (J). (gr. 1-5). pap. 5.99 *(978-1-4424-7404-8(1),* Aladdin) Simon & Schuster Children's Publishing.

—Miss Matched. Martini, Angela, illus. 2013. (Not-So-Ordinary Girl Ser.: 2). (ENG.). 160p. (J). (gr. 1-5). 15.99 *(978-1-4424-7405-5(X),* Simon & Schuster/Paula Wiseman Bks.) Simon & Schuster/Paula Wiseman Bks.

—Penelope Crumb Is Mad at the Moon. 2015. (Penelope Crumb Ser.: 4). (ENG., Illus.). 208p. (J). (gr. 2-4). pap. 6.99 *(978-0-14-242638-8(5),* Puffin Books) Penguin Young Readers Group.

Strand, Jeff. Elrod McBugle on the Loose. 2006. (ENG.). 136p. (YA). per. 9.25 *(978-0-7599-4325-4(7))* Hard Shell Word Factory.

Strange, Jason. Basement of the Undead, 1 vol. Parks, Phil, illus. 2011. (Jason Strange Ser.). (ENG.). 72p. (gr. 2-3). pap. 6.25 *(978-1-4342-3433-9(9));* lib. bdg. 25.32 *(978-1-4342-3234-2(4))* Stone Arch Bks.

—Faceless Friend, 1 vol. Parks, Phil, illus. 2011. (Jason Strange Ser.). (ENG.). 72p. (gr. 2-3). pap. 6.25 *(978-1-4342-3431-5(2));* lib. bdg. 25.32 *(978-1-4342-3232-8(8))* Stone Arch Bks.

Strasnick, Lauren. Nothing Like You. 2010. (ENG.). 240p. (YA). (gr. 9). pap. 8.99 *(978-1-4169-8265-4(5),* Simon Pulse) Simon Pulse.

—Then You Were Gone. 2013. (ENG.). 272p. (YA). (gr. 9). 16.99 *(978-1-4424-2715-0(9),* Simon Pulse) Simon Pulse.

Strasser, Todd. Con-Fidence. 2006. (ENG.). 164p. (J). (gr. 4-7). pap. 6.95 *(978-0-8234-2061-2(2))* Holiday Hse., Inc.

—Give a Boy a Gun. 2012. (ENG.). 224p. (YA). (gr. 7). pap. 10.99 *(978-1-4424-3356-4(6),* Simon & Schuster Bks. For Young Readers) Simon & Schuster Bks. For Young Readers.

—The Wave. 2013. (ENG.). 144p. (YA). (gr. 7). pap. 9.99 *(978-0-307-97912-4(1),* Ember) Random Hse. Children's Bks.

—Wish You Were Dead. (ENG.). 240p. (gr. 9). 2010. (J). pap. 8.99 *(978-1-60684-138-9(6))* 2009. 16.99 *(978-1-60684-007-8(X))* Lerner Publishing Group. (Carolrhoda Lab™).

Stratemeyer, Edward. The Mystery at Putnam Hall: Or the School Chums' Strange Discovery. 2007. (ENG.). 186p. pap. 19.99 *(978-1-4346-1186-4(8));* 204p. pap. 22.99 *(978-1-4346-1257-1(0))* Creative Media Partners, LLC.

—The Rover Boys in the Air: From College Campus to the Clouds. 2007. 188p. pap. 19.99 *(978-1-4346-3802-1(2))* Creative Media Partners, LLC.

Street, Sharon & National Geographic Learning Staff. My Friend & I. 2007. (Windows on Literacy Ser.). (ENG., Illus.). 12p. (J). pap. 10.95 *(978-0-7922-8949-4(8))* CENGAGE Learning.

Strickland, Sharon. Even Though: A Story about Being Different, 1 vol. 2009. 15p. pap. 24.95 *(978-1-60813-821-0(6))* PublishAmerica, Inc.

Strickler, Ashley. Once upon A Time. 2007. 212p. pap. 12.95 *(978-1-4327-0207-6(6))* Outskirts Pr., Inc.

Stringam, Jean. How Not to Cry in Public. 2013. 390p. pap. 16.99 *(978-0-9855540-1-9(0))* Dollison Road Bks.

Strohmeyer, Sarah. Smart Girls Get What They Want. 2013. (ENG.). 368p. (YA). (gr. 8). pap. 9.99 *(978-0-06-195341-5(5))* HarperCollins Pubs.

Stromberg, Ronica. Living It up to Live It Down. 2009. (J). lib. bdg. *(978-0-88092-752-9(6))* Royal Fireworks Publishing Co.

Stroud, Scott. Grumpy Mr. Grady. Hunt, Jim, illus. 2007. 24p. (J). 8.95 *(978-1-60131-008-8(0),* Castlebridge Bks.) Big Tent Bks.

Struyk-Bonn, Chris. Nice Girls Endure. 2016. (ENG.). 256p. (gr. 9-12). 16.95 *(978-1-63079-047-9(8))* Switch Pr.

Stryker, Robin. Goldie, the Homeless Calico Cat. Rubino, Alisa A., illus. 2005. (J). pap. *(978-0-932991-35-5(1))* Place In The Woods, The.

Sturges, Philemon. I Love School! Halpern, Shari, illus. 2014. 32p. pap. 7.00 *(978-1-61003-329-9(9))* Center for the Collaborative Classroom.

—I Love School! Halpern, Shari, illus. 32p. (J). (gr. -1-1). 2004. lib. bdg. 14.89 *(978-0-06-009285-6(8))* 2006. (ENG.). reprint ed. pap. 6.99 *(978-0-06-009286-3(6))* HarperCollins Pubs.

Sturman, Jennifer. And Then Everything Unraveled. 2010. (ENG.). 256p. (J). (gr. 7). 8.99 *(978-0-545-08723-0(6))* Scholastic, Inc.

—And Then I Found Out the Truth. 2010. (ENG.). 272p. (J). (gr. 7-18). 16.99 *(978-0-545-08724-7(4))* Scholastic, Inc.

Stuve-Bodeen, Stephanie. Babu's Song. Boyd, Aaron, illus. 2003. (ENG.). 32p. (J). 16.95 *(978-1-58430-058-8(2))* Lee & Low Bks., Inc.

—La Escuela de Elizabeti. Sarfatti, Esther, tr. from ENG. Hale, Christy, illus. 2007. (SPA.). 32p. (J). (gr. -1-2). pap. 9.95 *(978-1-60060-235-1(5))* Lee & Low Bks., Inc.

Style Guide Staff & Fruchter, Jason, illus. Daniel Goes to School. 2014. (Daniel Tiger's Neighborhood Ser.). (ENG.). 24p. (J). (gr. -1-7). pap. 3.99 *(978-1-4814-0318-4(4),* Simon Spotlight) Simon Spotlight.

Style Guide, Style, illus. School Is Awesome! 2014. (Yo Gabba Gabba! Ser.). (ENG.). 24p. (J). (gr. -1-1). pap. 3.99 *(978-1-4814-0930-8(1),* Simon Spotlight) Simon Spotlight.

Suen, Anastasia. Don't Forget! A Responsibility Story, 1 vol. Ebbeler, Jeff, illus. 2008. (Main Street School - Kids with Character Ser.). (ENG.). 32p. (gr. -1-4). 28.50 *(978-1-60270-269-1(1),* Looking Glass Library) ABDO Publishing Co.

—Girls Can, Too! A Tolerence Story, 1 vol. Ebbeler, Jeff, illus. 2008. (Main Street School - Kids with Character Ser.). (ENG.). 32p. (gr. -1-4). 28.50 *(978-1-60270-271-4(3),* Looking Glass Library) ABDO Publishing Co.

—A Great Idea? An Up2U Character Education Adventure, 1 vol. Dippold, Jane, illus. 2015. (ENG.). 80p. (J). *(978-1-62402-093-3(3))* Magic Wagon.

—Helping Sophia, 1 vol. Ebbeler, Jeffrey, illus. 2007. (Main Street School - Kids with Character Ser.). (ENG.). 32p. (gr. -1-4). 28.50 *(978-1-60270-030-7(3),* Looking Glass Library) ABDO Publishing Co.

—New Girl: An Up2U Character Education Adventure, 1 vol. Dippold, Jane, illus. 2013. (Up2U Adventures Ser.). (ENG.). 80p. (J). (gr. 2-5). lib. bdg. 27.07 *(978-1-61641-968-4(7),* Calico Chapter Bks) Magic Wagon.

—Raising the Flag, 1 vol. Ebbeler, Jeffrey, illus. 2007. (Main Street School - Kids with Character Ser.). (ENG.). 32p. (gr. -1-4). 28.50 *(978-1-60270-031-4(1),* Looking Glass Library) ABDO Publishing Co.

—Scissors, Paper & Sharing, 1 vol. Ebbeler, Jeffrey, illus. 2007. (Main Street School - Kids with Character Ser.). (ENG.). 32p. (gr. -1-4). 28.50 *(978-1-60270-032-1(X),* Looking Glass Library) ABDO Publishing Co.

—Show Some Respect, 1 vol. Ebbeler, Jeffrey, illus. 2007. (Main Street School - Kids with Character Ser.). (ENG.). 32p. (gr. -1-4). 28.50 *(978-1-60270-033-8(8),* Looking Glass Library) ABDO Publishing Co.

—Times Tables Cheat, 1 vol. Ebbeler, Jeffrey, illus. 2007. (Main Street School - Kids with Character Ser.). (ENG.). 32p. (gr. -1-4). 28.50 *(978-1-60270-034-5(6),* Looking Glass Library) ABDO Publishing Co.

—Vote for Isaiah! A Citizenship Story, 1 vol. Ebbeler, Jeff, illus. 2008. (Main Street School - Kids with Character Ser.). (ENG.). 32p. (gr. -1-4). 28.50 *(978-1-60270-274-5(8),* Looking Glass Library) ABDO Publishing Co.

Sullivan, Dana. Ozzie & the Art Contest. Sullivan, Dana, illus. 2013. (ENG., Illus.). 15.99 *(978-1-58536-820-4(2))* Sleeping Bear Pr.

Sullivan, Deirdre. Ming Goes to School. Löfdahl, Maja, illus. 2016. (ENG.). 32p. (J). (gr. -1-k). 16.99 *(978-1-5107-0050-5(1),* Sky Pony Pr.) Skyhorse Publishing Co., Inc.

Sullivan, Derek E. Biggie. 2015. (ENG.). 272p. (YA). (gr. 8-12). 16.99 *(978-0-8075-0727-8(X))* Whitman, Albert & Co.

Sullivan, Jenny. Magic Apostrophe. 2003. (ENG.). 216p. pap. 19.95 *(978-1-85902-116-3(6))* Beekman Bks., Inc.

Sullivan, Maureen. Cabbages & Queens. Ferrando, Carol, illus. 2010. 57p. (J). pap. *(978-0-9820381-3-0(5))* MoJo InkWorks.

Sullivan, Michael. Escapade Johnson & the Witches of Belknap County. Kolitsky, Joy, illus. 2008. (Escapade Johnson Ser.). (ENG.). 99p. (J). (gr. 2-4). pap. 3.95 *(978-1-929945-90-0(6))* Big Guy Bks., Inc.

Summers, Courtney. Cracked up to Be. 2008. (ENG.). 224p. (YA). (gr. 9-18). pap. 12.99 *(978-0-312-38369-5(X),* 9780312383695, St. Martin's Griffin) St. Martin's Pr.

—Some Girls Are. 2010. (ENG.). 256p. (YA). (gr. 9-18). pap. 11.99 *(978-0-312-57380-5(4),* 9780312573805, St. Martin's Griffin) St. Martin's Pr.

S

—This Is Not a Test. 2012. (ENG.). 336p. (YA). (gr. 8). pap. 10.99 (978-0-312-65674-4(2), 9780312656744, St. Martin's Griffin) St. Martin's Pr.
—What Goes Around: Two Books in One: Cracked up to Be & Some Girls Are. 2013. (ENG.). 480p. (YA). (gr. 9-12). pap. 9.99 (978-1-250-03844-9(8), 9781250038449, St. Martin's Griffin) St. Martin's Pr.
Summy, Barrie. The Disappearance of Emily H. 2015. (ENG.). 256p. (J). (gr. 5). 16.99 (978-0-385-73943-6(5), Delacorte Bks. for Young Readers) Random Hse. Children's Bks.
Sundquist, Josh. Love & First Sight. 2017. (ENG.). 288p. (YA). (gr. 7-17). 17.99 (978-0-316-30535-8(9)) Little Brown & Co.
Supplee, Suzanne. Artichoke's Heart. 2009. (ENG.). 288p. (YA). (gr. 7-18). 8.99 (978-0-14-241427-9(1), Speak) Penguin Young Readers Group.
—When Irish Guys Are Smiling. 2008. (S. A. S. S. Ser.). (ENG.). 224p. (YA). (gr. 7-18). 6.99 (978-0-14-241016-5(0), Speak) Penguin Young Readers Group.
Susanne, Gervay & Gervay, Susanne. Being Jack. Wilcox, Cathy, illus. 2016. (ENG.). 192p. (J). pap. 5.99 (978-1-61067-379-2(4)) Kane Miller.
Sutcliffe, Kathy. When Romeo Kissed Mercutio. 2012. (ENG.). 240p. pap. (978-1-922120-28-1(6), IP Digital) Interactive Pubns. Pty, Ltd.
Sutherland, Suzanne. Something Wiki. 2015. (ENG.). 160p. (J). pap. 12.99 (978-1-4597-2821-9(1)) Dundurn CAN. Dist: Ingram Publisher Services.
Sutherland, Tui T. Moon Rising. 2016. (Wings of Fire Ser.: 6). (ENG.). 336p. (J). (gr. 3-7). pap. 6.99 (978-0-545-68536-8(2)) Scholastic, Inc.
—This Must Be Love. 256p. (J). 2005. pap. 7.99 (978-0-06-056477-3(6), Harper Trophy) 2004. (gr. 7-18). lib. bdg. 16.89 (978-0-06-056476-6(8)) HarperCollins Pubs.
Suzy, Kline. Horrible Harry in Room 2B. 2014. (Horrible Harry Ser. No. 1 Ser.). (ENG.). 64p. (J). (gr. 3-7). 8.24 (978-1-63245-257-3(X)) Lectorum Pubns., Inc.
Swaab, Neil. Class Election. 2016. (Secrets to Ruling School Ser.: 2). (ENG., Illus.). 240p. (YA). (gr. 5-9). 13.95 (978-1-4197-2126-7(7), Amulet Bks.) Abrams, Inc.
—Without Even Trying, Bk. 1. 2015. (Secrets to Ruling School Ser.). (ENG., Illus.). 240p. (J). (gr. 5-9). 13.95 (978-1-4197-1221-0(7), Amulet Bks.) Abrams, Inc.
Swain, Cynthia. Sorting at the Nature Center. 2006. (Early Explorers Ser.). (J). pap. (978-1-4108-6039-2(6)) Benchmark Education Co.
Swallow, Pamela. It Only Looks Easy. 2009. (ENG.). 192p. (J). (gr. 3-7). pap. 9.99 (978-0-312-56114-7(8), 9780312561147) Square Fish.
Swan, Bill. Mud Happens, 1 vol. 2005. (Lorimer Sports Stories Ser.: 82). (ENG.). 112p. (J). (gr. 4-8). 16.95 (978-1-55028-899-5(7), 9781550288995); 8.95 (978-1-55028-898-8(9), 9781550288988) Lorimer, James & Co., Ltd., Pubs. CAN. Dist: Casemate Pubs. & Bk. Distributors, LLC.
Swanson, Matthew. The Real McCoys. Behr, Robbi, illus. 2017. (J). pap. **(978-1-250-09853-5(X))** ETT Imprint.
Sweeney, Joyce. Players, 1 vol. 2005. (ENG.). 32p. (YA). (gr. 7-12). reprint ed. pap. 6.95 (978-0-7614-5236-2(2)) Marshall Cavendish Corp.
—Waiting for June, 0 vols. 2006. (ENG.). 158p. (YA). (gr. 10-12). pap. 7.99 (978-0-7614-5329-1(6), 9780761453291, Amazon Children's Publishing) Amazon Publishing.
Sydor, Colleen & Constantin, Pascale. Camilla Chameleon. Constantin, Pascale, illus. 2007. (ENG., Illus.). 32p. (J). (gr. -1-3). pap. 6.95 (978-1-55453-164-6(0)) Kids Can Pr., Ltd. CAN. Dist: Hachette Bk. Group.
Szish, Jill Henry. TJ & the Good Luck Cricket. Perry, Jennifer A., illus. 2007. 32p. per. 24.95 (978-1-4241-8502-3(5)) America Star Bks.
Tackett, Wendy. The Snow Wish. 2011. 100p. (gr. 4-6). 19.95 (978-1-4620-2608-1(7)); pap. 9.95 (978-1-4620-2606-7(0)) iUniverse, Inc.
Taekema, Sylvia. Ripple Effect, 1 vol. 2015. (ENG.). 144p. (J). (gr. 4-7). pap. 9.95 (978-1-4598-0872-0(X)) Orca Bk. Pubs. USA.
Talbot, Rose. The Adventures of Peanut, the Sugar Glider. 2007. 80p. per. 15.99 (978-1-4257-9629-7(X)) Xlibris Corp.
Talley, Robin. Lies We Tell Ourselves. 2016. (ENG.). 416p. pap. 9.99 (978-0-373-21204-0(6), Harlequin Teen) Harlequin Enterprises, Ltd. CAN. Dist: HarperCollins Pubs.
Tan, Valerie Genevivie. Hello! I'm Sha Sha: Join Sha Sha in Her New School. 2009. (Illus.). 50p. (J). pap. 14.95 (978-1-4327-4195-2(0)) Outskirts Pr., Inc.
Tanen, Sloane. Appetite for Detention. Hagen, Stefan, illus. Hagen, Stefan, photos by. 2008. (ENG.). 80p. (YA). (gr. 7-18). 14.99 (978-1-59990-075-9(0), 9781599900759, Bloomsbury USA Childrens) Bloomsbury Publishing USA.
Tanigawa, Nagaru. The Boredom of Haruhi Suzumiya. 2010. (Haruhi Suzumiya Ser.: 3). (ENG., Illus.). 224p. (YA). (gr. 10-17). 24.00 (978-0-316-03886-7(5)); pap. 18.00 (978-0-316-03887-4(3)) Little, Brown Bks. for Young Readers.
—The Disappearance of Haruhi Suzumiya. 2010. (Haruhi Suzumiya Ser.: 4). (ENG., Illus.). 192p. (YA). (gr. 10-17). pap. 18.00 (978-0-316-03889-8(X)) Little, Brown Bks. for Young Readers.
—The Dissociation of Haruhi Suzumiya. 2013. (Haruhi Suzumiya Ser.: 9). (ENG., Illus.). 192p. (YA). (gr. 10-17). pap. 8.99 (978-0-316-03894-2(6)) Little, Brown Bks. for Young Readers.
—The Sigh of Haruhi Suzumiya. 2009. (Haruhi Suzumiya Ser.: Bk. 1). (Illus.). 208p. (YA). (gr. 10-18). 14.99 (978-0-316-03881-2(4)) Hachette Bk. Group.
—The Surprise of Haruhi Suzumiya. 2013. (Haruhi Suzumiya Ser.: 10). (ENG., Illus.). 368p. (YA). (gr. 10-17). 24.00 (978-0-316-03898-0(9)); pap. 10.99 (978-0-316-03897-3(0)) Little, Brown Bks. for Young Readers.
Tanigawa, Nagaru, et al. The Melancholy of Suzumiya Haruhi-Chan. 2012. (Melancholy of Suzumiya Haruhi-Chan Ser.: 6). (ENG., Illus.). 160p. (gr. 11-17). pap. 11.99 (978-0-316-22914-2(8), Yen Pr.) Orbit.
Tarkington, Booth. Ramsey Milholland. 2009. 108p. 22.95 (978-1-60664-679-3(6)); 104p. pap. 9.95 (978-1-60664-308-2(8)) Rodgers, Alan Bks.
Tarshis, Lauren. Emma-Jean Lazarus Fell in Love. 2010. (ENG.). 176p. (J). (gr. 5-18). 6.99 (978-0-14-241568-9(5), Puffin Books) Penguin Young Readers Group.
—Emma-Jean Lazarus Fell Out of a Tree. 2008. (ENG., Illus.). 224p. (J). (gr. 5-18). 7.99 (978-0-14-241150-6(7), Puffin Books) Penguin Young Readers Group.
Taschek, Karen. The Risen Horse. 2010. (ENG.). 248p. (YA). (gr. 7-18). pap. 15.95 (978-0-8263-4837-1(8)) Univ. of New Mexico Pr.
Tashjian, Janet. Einstein the Class Hamster. Tashjian, Jake, illus. 2013. (Einstein the Class Hamster Ser.: 1). (ENG.). 160p. (J). (gr. 2-5). 12.99 (978-0-8050-9610-1(8), 9780805096101, Holt, Henry & Co. Bks. For Young Readers) Holt, Henry & Co.
—Einstein the Class Hamster & the Very Real Game Show. Tashjian, Jake, illus. 2014. (Einstein the Class Hamster Ser.: 2). (ENG.). 176p. (J). (gr. 2-5). 12.99 (978-1-62779-026-0(8), 9781627790260, Holt, Henry & Co. Bks. For Young Readers) Holt, Henry & Co.
—Einstein the Class Hamster Saves the Library. Tashjian, Jake, illus. 2015. (Einstein the Class Hamster Ser.: 3). (ENG.). 192p. (J). (gr. 2-5). 13.99 (978-1-62779-061-1(6), 9781627790611, Holt, Henry & Co. Bks. For Young Readers) Holt, Henry & Co.
—My Life As a Cartoonist. Tashjian, Jake, illus. 2013. (My Life Ser.: 3). (ENG.). 272p. (J). (gr. 4-7). 13.99 (978-0-8050-9609-5(4), 9780805096095, Holt, Henry & Co. Bks. For Young Readers) Holt, Henry & Co.
—My Life As a Gamer. Tashjian, Jake, illus. 2015. (My Life Ser.: 5). (ENG.). 272p. (J). (gr. 4-7). 13.99 (978-0-8050-9851-8(8), 9780805098518, Holt, Henry & Co. Bks. For Young Readers) Holt, Henry & Co.
—My Life As a Joke. Tashjian, Jake, illus. 2014. (My Life Ser.: 4). (ENG.). 272p. (J). (gr. 4-7). 13.99 (978-0-8050-9850-1(X), 9780805098501, Holt, Henry & Co. Bks. For Young Readers) Holt, Henry & Co.
—My Life as a Stuntboy. Tashjian, Jake, illus. 2011. (My Life Ser.: 2). (ENG.). 272p. (J). (gr. 4-7). 15.99 (978-0-8050-8904-2(7), 9780805089042, Holt, Henry & Co. Bks. For Young Readers) Holt, Henry & Co.
—My Life as a Stuntboy. Tashjian, Jake, illus. 2015. (My Life Ser.: 2). (ENG.). 288p. (J). (gr. 4-7). pap. 7.99 (978-1-250-01038-4(1), 9781250010384) Square Fish.
Tatulli, Mark. Desmond Pucket & the Cloverfield Junior High Carnival of Horrors. 2016. (Desmond Pucket Ser.: 3). (ENG., Illus.). 240p. (J). 13.99 (978-1-4494-6628-2(1)) Andrews McMeel Publishing.
—Desmond Pucket & the Mountain Full of Monsters. 2014. (Desmond Pucket Ser.: 2). (ENG.). 240p. (J). 13.99 (978-1-4494-3549-3(1)) Andrews McMeel Publishing.
—Desmond Pucket & the Mountain Full of Monsters. 2015. (Desmond Pucket Ser.: 2). lib. bdg. 20.85 (978-0-606-38232-8(1)) Turtleback Bks.
—Desmond Pucket Makes Monster Magic. 2015. (Desmond Pucket Ser.: 1). lib. bdg. 20.85 (978-0-606-38231-1(3)) Turtleback Bks.
Tayleur, Karen. Promises! Vote for David Mortimore Baxter. Garvey, Brann, illus. 2007. (David Mortimore Baxter Ser.). (ENG.). 96p. (gr. 2-3). per. 6.05 (978-1-59889-208-6(8), David Mortimore Baxter) Stone Arch Bks.
Taylor, Chet. Last, but Not Least. 2007. (Illus.). 20p. (J). per. 11.99 (978-0-9797574-8-8(7)) Dragonfly Publishing, Inc.
Taylor, Chloe. Knot Too Shabby! Zhang, Nancy, illus. 2014. (Sew Zoey Ser.: 7). (ENG.). 176p. (J). (gr. 3-7). pap. 5.99 (978-1-4814-1398-5(8), Simon Spotlight) Simon Spotlight.
—Lights, Camera, Fashion! Zhang, Nancy, illus. 2013. (Sew Zoey Ser.: 3). (ENG.). 176p. (J). (gr. 3-7). 15.99 (978-1-4424-8980-6(4)); pap. 5.99 (978-1-4424-8979-0(0)) Simon Spotlight. (Simon Spotlight).
—Stitches & Stones. Zhang, Nancy, illus. 2013. (Sew Zoey Ser.: 4). (ENG.). 176p. (J). (gr. 3-7). 16.99 (978-1-4424-9803-7(X));Bk. 4. pap. 5.99 (978-1-4424-9802-0(1)) Simon Spotlight. (Simon Spotlight).
Taylor, Chloë. A Tangled Thread. Zhang, Nancy, illus. 2014. (Sew Zoey Ser.: 6). (ENG.). 176p. (J). (gr. 3-7). 16.99 (978-1-4814-0444-0(X), Simon Spotlight) Simon Spotlight.
Taylor, Chloe. A Tangled Thread. Zhang, Nancy, illus. 2014. (Sew Zoey Ser.: 6). (ENG.). 176p. (J). (gr. 3-7). pap. 5.99 (978-1-4814-0443-3(1), Simon Spotlight) Simon Spotlight.
Taylor, G. P. The First Escape. 2008. (Dopple Ganger Chronicles Ser.: 1). (ENG., Illus.). 288p. (J). (gr. 3-7). 19.99 (978-1-4143-1947-6(9), SaltRiver) Tyndale Hse. Pubs.
—The Secret of Indigo Moon. 2009. (Dopple Ganger Chronicles Ser.: 2). (ENG., Illus.). 304p. (J). (gr. 3-7). 19.99 (978-1-4143-1948-3(7), SaltRiver) Tyndale Hse. Pubs.
Taylor, Kara. Deadly Little Sins. 2014. (Prep School Confidential Novel Ser.: 3). (ENG.). 288p. (YA). (gr. 7). pap. 19.99 (978-1-250-03363-5(2), 9781250033635, St. Martin's Griffin) St. Martin's Pr.
Taylor, Laini. Daughter of Smoke & Bone. 2011. (ENG.). 432p. (YA). (gr. 10-17). 20.00 (978-0-316-13402-6(3)) Little Brown & Co.
—Daughter of Smoke & Bone. 2012. (ENG.). (YA). (gr. 10-17). 448p. pap. 12.99 (978-0-316-13399-9(X)); 624p. pap. 28.99 (978-0-316-22435-2(9)) Little, Brown Bks. for Young Readers.
—Daughter of Smoke & Bone. 2012. (Daughter of Smoke & Bone Ser.: 1). (YA). lib. bdg. 24.50 (978-0-606-26704-5(2), Turtleback) Turtleback Bks.
—Days of Blood & Starlight. 2012. (ENG., (YA). (gr. 10-17). Illus.). 528p. 18.99 (978-0-316-13397-5(3)); 688p. 39.99 (978-0-316-22433-8(2)) Little, Brown Bks. for Young Readers.
Taylor, Mari Jo. Not One of the Robot Children. 2005. 11.00 (978-0-8059-9791-0(1)) Dorrance Publishing Co., Inc.
Taylor Sr., Anthony. I Pray. 2012. 20p. pap. 24.95 (978-1-4626-8113-6(1)) America Star Bks.
Teague, Monica. Diary of a Teenager in Junior High. 2011. 32p. pap. 16.95 (978-1-4560-8552-0(2)) America Star Bks.
Tebbetts, Chris & Patterson, James. Middle School, the Worst Years of My Life. Park, Laura, illus. 2016. (Middle School Ser.: 1). (ENG.). 320p. (J). (gr. 3-7). pap. 7.99 (978-0-316-27691-7(X), Jimmy Patterson) Little Brown & Co.
Telgemeier, Raina. Drama. 2012. lib. bdg. 22.10 (978-0-606-26738-0(7), Turtleback) Turtleback Bks.
Teller, Janne. Nothing. Aitken, Martin, tr. (ENG., 240p. (YA). (gr. 7). 2012. Illus.). pap. 10.99 (978-1-4424-4116-3(X)) 2010. 16.99 (978-1-4169-8579-2(4)) Simon & Schuster Children's Publishing. (Atheneum Bks. for Young Readers).
Terheyden, Jerry, reader. Crow Boy. 2004. (Illus.). (J). (gr. -1-2). 28.95 incl. audio compact disk (978-1-59112-802-1(1)) Live Oak Media.
Terrell, Brandon. The Cursed Stage. Epelbaum, Mariano, illus. 2017. (Snoops, Inc Ser.). (ENG.). 112p. (gr. 4-6). lib. bdg. 26.65 (978-1-4965-4346-2(7)) Stone Arch Bks.
—Dive for the Goal Line. 2014. (ENG.). 80p. (J). (978-1-63235-046-6(7)) Pr. Room Editions LLC.
—High Drama. 2015. (ENG.). 112p. (YA). (gr. 6-12). 27.99 (978-1-4677-5710-2(1)) Lerner Publishing Group.
—Take Away. 2014. (Red Zone Ser.: 5). (ENG.). 104p. (YA). (gr. 6-12). lib. bdg. 27.93 (978-1-4677-2130-1(1)) Lerner Publishing Group.
Terrian, Michael W. Chalie's Brand New Coat. 2011. 24p. pap. 12.50 (978-1-4670-3858-4(X)) AuthorHouse.
Terry, Teri. Fractured. 2014. (Slated Ser.: 2). (ENG.). 352p. (YA). (gr. 7). pap. 9.99 (978-0-14-242504-6(4), Speak) Penguin Young Readers Group.
—Shattered. (Slated Ser.: 3). (ENG.). (YA). (gr. 7). 2015. 336p. pap. 9.99 (978-0-14-242507-7(9), Speak) 2014. 320p. 17.99 (978-0-399-16174-2(0), Nancy Paulsen Books) Penguin Young Readers Group.
—Slated. 2013. (Slated Ser.: 1). (ENG.). 368p. (YA). (gr. 7). pap. 9.99 (978-0-14-242503-9(6), Speak) Penguin Young Readers Group.
Testa, Maggie. OLIVIA Loves Halloween. Osterhold, Jared, illus. 2014. (Olivia TV Tie-In Ser.). (ENG.). 24p. (J). (gr. -1-1). pap. 3.99 (978-1-4814-0462-4(8), Simon Spotlight) Simon Spotlight.
Tewkesbury, Alexa. Paul's Potty Pages. 2008. (ENG., Illus.). 128p. (J). (978-1-85345-456-1(7)) Crusade for World Revival.
Thaler, Mike. The Art Teacher from the Black Lagoon, 1 vol. Lee, Jared, illus. 2012. (Black Lagoon Set 2 Ser.: No. 2). (ENG.). 32p. (J). (gr. 1-4). lib. bdg. 24.21 (978-1-59961-952-1(0)) Spotlight.
—The Author Visit from the Black Lagoon. Lee, Jared D., illus. 2010. 61p. (J). **(978-0-545-27327-5(7))** Scholastic, Inc.
—The Author Visit from the Black Lagoon, 1 vol. Lee, Jared, illus. 2012. (Black Lagoon Adventures Ser.: No. 2). (ENG.). 64p. (J). (gr. 2-5). 24.21 (978-1-59961-960-6(1)) Spotlight.
—Back-to-School Fright from the Black Lagoon, 1 vol. Lee, Jared, illus. 2012. (Black Lagoon Adventures Ser.: No. 2). (ENG.). 64p. (J). (gr. 2-5). 24.21 (978-1-59961-961-3(X)) Spotlight.
—The Big Game from the Black Lagoon. Lee, Jared D., illus. 2013. 63p. (J). pap. (978-0-545-61639-3(5)) Scholastic, Inc.
—Black Lagoon, 6 vols., Set. Lee, Jared, illus. Incl. Gym Teacher from the Black Lagoon. lib. bdg. 24.21 (978-1-59961-794-7(3)); Librarian from the Black Lagoon. lib. bdg. 24.21 (978-1-59961-795-4(1)); Music Teacher from the Black Lagoon. lib. bdg. 24.21 (978-1-59961-796-1(X)); Principal from the Black Lagoon. lib. bdg. 24.21 (978-1-59961-797-8(8)); School Nurse from the Black Lagoon. lib. bdg. 24.21 (978-1-59961-798-5(6)); Teacher from the Black Lagoon. lib. bdg. 24.21 (978-1-59961-799-2(4)); (gr. -1-2). (Black Lagoon Set 1 Ser.: 6). (ENG., Illus.). 32p. 2011. Set lib. bdg. 145.26 (978-1-59961-793-0(5)) Spotlight.
—The Book Fair from the Black Lagoon. Lee, Jared, illus. 2006. pap. (978-0-439-88348-1(2)) Scholastic, Inc.
—The Bully from the Black Lagoon. Lee, Jared, illus. 2008. (From the Black Lagoon Ser.). (gr. -1-3). 14.00 (978-0-7569-8834-0(9)) Perfection Learning Corp.
—The Bully from the Black Lagoon. Lee, Jared, illus. (J). 2008. (ENG.). 32p. (gr. -1-3). pap. 3.99 (978-0-545-06521-4(6), Cartwheel Bks.) 2004. (978-0-439-68072-1(7)) Scholastic, Inc.
—The Bully from the Black Lagoon, 1 vol. Lee, Jared, illus. 2012. (Black Lagoon Set 2 Ser.: No. 2). (ENG.). 32p. (J). (gr. 1-4). lib. bdg. 24.21 (978-1-59961-953-8(9)) Spotlight.
—The Christmas Party from the Black Lagoon. Lee, Jared, illus. 2006. 64p. (J). pap. (978-0-439-87160-0(3)) Scholastic, Inc.
—The Class Election from the Black Lagoon, 1 vol. Lee, Jared, illus. 2011. (Black Lagoon Adventures Ser.: No. 1). (ENG.). 64p. (gr. 3-6). 24.21 (978-1-59961-810-4(9)) Spotlight.
—The Class Picture Day from the Black Lagoon. Lee, Jared D., illus. 2012. 64p. (J). pap. (978-0-545-47666-9(6)) Scholastic, Inc.
—The Computer Teacher from the Black Lagoon. Lee, Jared, illus. 2007. (J). (978-0-439-87133-4(6)) Scholastic, Inc.
—The Computer Teacher from the Black Lagoon, 1 vol. Lee, Jared, illus. 2012. (Black Lagoon Set 2 Ser.: No. 2). (ENG.). 32p. (J). (gr. 1-4). lib. bdg. 24.21 (978-1-59961-955-2(5)) Spotlight.
—The Custodian from the Black Lagoon, 1 vol. 2014. (From the Black Lagoon Ser.). (ENG., Illus.). 32p. (J). (gr. 1-4). lib. bdg. 24.21 (978-1-61479-196-6(1)) Spotlight.
—Earth Day from the Black Lagoon. Lee, Jared D., illus. 2013. 64p. (J). (978-0-545-47669-0(0)) Scholastic, Inc.
—The Field Day from the Black Lagoon. Lee, Jared, illus. 2008. (From the Black Lagoon Ser.). 64p. (gr. 2-5). 14.00 (978-0-7569-8801-2(2)) Perfection Learning Corp.
—The Field Day from the Black Lagoon. Lee, Jared, illus. 2008. (Black Lagoon Adventures Ser.: 6). (ENG.). 64p. (J). (gr. 2-5). pap. 4.99 (978-0-439-68076-9(X)) Scholastic, Inc.
—The Field Day from the Black Lagoon, 1 vol. Lee, Jared, illus. 2011. (Black Lagoon Adventures Ser.: No. 1). (ENG.). 64p. (gr. 3-6). 24.21 (978-1-59961-812-8(5)) Spotlight.
—The Gym Teacher from the Black Lagoon, 1 vol. Lee, Jared, illus. 2011. (Black Lagoon Set 1 Ser.: No. 1). (ENG.). 32p. (gr. -1-2). lib. bdg. 24.21 (978-1-59961-794-7(3)) Spotlight.
—The Gym Teacher from the Black Lagoon. Lee, Jared, illus. (J). (gr. -1-3). 2009. pap. 18.95 incl. audio compact disk (978-0-545-19706-9(6)) 2008. (ENG.). 32p. pap. 3.99 (978-0-545-06931-1(9)) Weston Woods Studios, Inc.
—Hubie Cool: Vampire Hunter. Lee, Jared D., illus. 2015. 64p. (J). pap. **(978-0-545-85075-9(4))** Scholastic, Inc.
—The Librarian from the Black Lagoon, 1 vol. Lee, Jared, illus. 2011. (Black Lagoon Set 1 Ser.: No. 1). (ENG.). 32p. (gr. -1-2). lib. bdg. 24.21 (978-1-59961-795-4(1)) Spotlight.
—The Little League Team from the Black Lagoon, 1 vol. Lee, Jared, illus. 2011. (Black Lagoon Adventures Ser.: No. 1). (ENG.). 64p. (gr. 3-6). 24.21 (978-1-59961-813-5(3)) Spotlight.
—Meatloaf Monster from the School Cafeteria. Lee, Jared D., illus. 2012. (J). pap. (978-0-545-48570-8(3)) Scholastic, Inc.
—The Music Teacher from the Black Lagoon, 1 vol. Lee, Jared, illus. 2011. (Black Lagoon Set 1 Ser.: No. 1). (ENG.). 32p. (gr. -1-2). lib. bdg. 24.21 (978-1-59961-796-1(X)) Spotlight.
—The New Kid from the Black Lagoon. 2004. (Black Lagoon Ser.). (Illus.). 32p. (978-0-439-55719-1(4)) Scholastic, Inc.
—The New Kid from the Black Lagoon, 1 vol. Lee, Jared, illus. 2012. (Black Lagoon Set 2 Ser.: No. 2). (ENG.). 32p. (J). (gr. 1-4). lib. bdg. 24.21 (978-1-59961-956-9(3)) Spotlight.
—The Principal from the Black Lagoon. Lee, Jared, illus. 2009. (From the Black Lagoon Ser.). 14.00 (978-1-60686-507-1(2)) Perfection Learning Corp.
—The Principal from the Black Lagoon. Lee, Jared, illus. 2008. (Black Lagoon Adventures Ser.). (ENG.). 32p. (J). (gr. -1-3). pap. 3.99 (978-0-545-06932-8(7), Cartwheel Bks.) Scholastic, Inc.
—The Principal from the Black Lagoon, 1 vol. Lee, Jared, illus. 2011. (Black Lagoon Set 1 Ser.: No. 1). (ENG.). 32p. (gr. -1-2). lib. bdg. 24.21 (978-1-59961-797-8(8)) Spotlight.
—The Reading Challenge from the Black Lagoon. Lee, Jared D., illus. 2015. 64p. (J). pap. (978-0-545-78521-1(9)) Scholastic, Inc.
—The School Carnival from the Black Lagoon. Lee, Jared, illus. 2005. 64p. (J). pap. (978-0-439-80075-4(7)) Scholastic, Inc.
—The School Carnival from the Black Lagoon, 1 vol. Lee, Jared, illus. 2012. (Black Lagoon Adventures Ser.: No. 2). (ENG.). 64p. (J). (gr. 2-5). 24.21 (978-1-59961-962-0(8)) Spotlight.
—The School Nurse from the Black Lagoon, 1 vol. Lee, Jared, illus. 2011. (Black Lagoon Set 1 Ser.: No. 1). (ENG.). 32p. (gr. -1-2). lib. bdg. 24.21 (978-1-59961-798-5(6)) Spotlight.
—School Play from the Black Lagoon, 1 vol. 2014. (Black Lagoon Adventures Set 3 Ser.). (ENG.). 64p. (J). (gr. 3-6). lib. bdg. 24.21 (978-1-61479-205-5(4)) Spotlight.
—The School Secretary from the Black Lagoon. Lee, Jared, illus. 2006. (J). (978-0-439-80077-8(3)) Scholastic, Inc.
—The Science Fair from the Black Lagoon, 1 vol. Lee, Jared, illus. 2011. (Black Lagoon Adventures Ser.: No. 1). (ENG.). 64p. (gr. 3-6). 24.21 (978-1-59961-814-2(1)) Spotlight.
—The Secret Santa from the Black Lagoon. Lee, Jared D., illus. 2014. 64p. (J). (978-0-545-78519-8(7)) Scholastic, Inc.
—The Talent Show from the Black Lagoon, 1 vol. Lee, Jared, illus. 2011. (Black Lagoon Adventures Ser.: No. 1). (ENG.). 64p. (gr. 3-6). 24.21 (978-1-59961-815-9(X)) Spotlight.
—The Teacher from the Black Lagoon. Lee, Jared, illus. 2008. (From the Black Lagoon Ser.). (gr. -1-3). 14.00 (978-0-7569-8779-4(2)) Perfection Learning Corp.
—The Teacher from the Black Lagoon. Lee, Jared D., illus. 2008. (Black Lagoon Adventures Ser.). (ENG.). 32p. (J). (gr. -1-3). pap. 3.99 (978-0-545-06522-1(4), Cartwheel Bks.) Scholastic, Inc.
—The Teacher from the Black Lagoon, 1 vol. Lee, Jared, illus. 2011. (Black Lagoon Set 1 Ser.: No. 1). (ENG.). 32p. (gr. -1-2). lib. bdg. 24.21 (978-1-59961-799-2(4)) Spotlight.
—The Teacher from the Black Lagoon. Lee, Jared, illus. 2004. (J). (gr. k-3). 18.95 (978-1-55592-495-9(6)) Weston Woods Studios, Inc.
—Vacation Bible Snooze, 1 vol. Lee, Jared, illus. 2010. (Tales from the Back Pew Ser.). (ENG.). 32p. (J). (gr. 1-4). pap. 3.99 (978-0-310-71596-2(2)) Zonderkidz.
—The Vice Principal from the Black Lagoon. Lee, Jared, illus. 2007. (J). pap. (978-0-439-87132-7(8)) Scholastic, Inc.
—The 100th Day of School from the Black Lagoon. Lee, Jared, illus. 2012. 64p. (J). pap. (978-0-545-37325-8(5)) Scholastic, Inc.
Thaler, Mike, text. The Substitute Teacher from the Black Lagoon, 1 vol. 2014. (ENG., Illus.). 32p. (J). 24.21 (978-1-61479-199-7(6)) Spotlight.
Thame, Val. Witches in Deed. l.t. ed. 2007. 100p. per. (978-1-905665-25-9(3)) Pollinger In Print.
Tharp, Tim. Knights of the Hill Country. 2008. 233p. 17.00 (978-1-60686-365-7(7)) Perfection Learning Corp.
—Knights of the Hill Country. 2013. (ENG.). 240p. (YA). (gr. 7). pap. 8.99 (978-0-449-81287-7(1), Ember) Random Hse. Children's Bks.
—Mojo. 2014. (ENG.). 288p. (YA). (gr. 7). pap. 8.99 (978-0-375-86402-5(4), Ember) Random Hse. Children's Bks.
—The Spectacular Now. (ENG.). 304p. (YA). (gr. 9). 2010. pap. 8.99 (978-0-375-86502-2(0), Knopf Bks. for Young Readers) 2013. pap. 9.99 (978-0-385-75430-9(2), Ember) Random Hse. Children's Bks.
The Book Company, ed. School. (Sparkle Bks.). (ENG.). (J). bds. 4.99 (978-1-74047-331-6(0)) Book Co. Publishing Pty, Ltd., The AUS. Dist: Penton Overseas, Inc.
The Equality Of Genders Project. Billy Conquers the Bully. 2009. 16p. pap. 8.49 (978-1-4389-5376-2(3)) AuthorHouse.
Thiel, Annie. Danny Is Moving. Edwards, William M., illus. 2006. (Playdate Kids Ser.). 32p. (J). (gr. -1-3). 14.95 (978-1-933721-02-6(2)) Playdate Kids Publishing.
Thielbar, Melinda. The Ancient Formula: A Mystery with Fractions. Pantoja, Tintin, illus. 2011. (Manga Math Mysteries Ser.: 5). (ENG.). 46p. (gr. 3-5). pap. 6.95 (978-0-7613-8134-1(1), Graphic Universe™) Lerner Publishing Group.
—The Ancient Formula No. 5: A Mystery with Fractions. Pantoja, Tintin, illus. 2010. (Manga Math Mysteries Ser.: 5). (ENG.). 48p. (gr. 3-5). 29.27 (978-0-7613-4907-5(3)) Lerner Publishing Group.
—The Fishy Fountain. Lin, Yali, illus. 2010. (Manga Math Mysteries Ser.: 6). (ENG.). 48p. (gr. 3-5). 29.27 (978-0-7613-4908-2(1)) Lerner Publishing Group.
—The Fishy Fountain: A Mystery with Multiplication & Division. Lin, Yali, illus. 2011. (Manga Math Mysteries Ser.: 6). (ENG.). 48p. (gr. 3-5). pap. 6.95 (978-0-7613-8135-8(X), Graphic Universe™) Lerner Publishing Group.
—The Hundred-Dollar Robber. Pantoja, Tintin, illus. 2010. (Manga Math Mysteries Ser.: 2). (ENG.). 48p. (gr. 3-5). pap. 6.95 (978-0-7613-5243-3(0), Graphic Universe™) Lerner Publishing Group.
—The Hundred-Dollar Robber. 2nd rev. ed. 2010. pap. 39.62 (978-0-7613-6943-1(0)) Lerner Publishing Group.
—The Hundred-Dollar Robber: A Mystery with Money. Pantoja, Maria Kristina, illus. 2009. (Manga Math Mysteries Ser.: 2).

(ENG.). 48p. (gr. 3-5). 29.27 (978-0-7613-3854-3(3)) Lerner Publishing Group.
—The Kung Fu Puzzle. 4th rev. ed. 2010. pap. 39.62 (978-0-7613-6945-5(7)) Lerner Publishing Group.
—The Kung Fu Puzzle: A Mystery with Time & Temperature. Helmer, Der-Shing, illus. 2010. (Manga Math Mysteries Ser.: 4). (ENG.). 46p. (gr. 3-5). pap. 6.95 (978-0-7613-5246-4(5), Graphic Universe™) Lerner Publishing Group.
—The Kung Fu Puzzle: A Mystery with Time & Temperature. Ota, Yuko & Helmer, Der-Shing, illus. 2009. (Manga Math Mysteries Ser.: No. 4). 48p. (J). (gr. 2-5). 29.27 (978-0-7613-3856-7(X)) Lerner Publishing Group.
—The Lost Key. Pantoja, Tintin, illus. 2010. (Manga Math Mysteries Ser.: 1). (ENG.). 45p. (gr. 3-5). pap. 6.95 (978-0-7613-5244-0(9), Graphic Universe™) Lerner Publishing Group.
—The Lost Key. rev. ed. 2010. pap. 39.62 (978-0-7613-6942-4(2)) Lerner Publishing Group.
—#5 the Ancient Formula: A Mystery with Fractions. Pantoja, Tintin, illus. 2011. (Manga Math Mysteries Set II Ser.). pap. 39.62 (978-0-7613-8362-8(X), Graphic Universe™) Lerner Publishing Group.
—#6 the Fishy Fountain: A Mystery with Multiplication & Division. Lin, Yali, illus. 2011. (Manga Math Mysteries Set II Ser.). pap. 39.62 (978-0-7613-8363-5(8), Graphic Universe™) Lerner Publishing Group.
Thomas, G. D. Keep Your Head Down. 2012. 160p. pap. 11.00 (978-1-78035-281-7(6), Fastprint Publishing) Upfront Publishing Ltd. GBR. Dist: Printondemand-worldwide.com.
Thomas, Jatavius. Weird Things Happening at Southside Middle School: And Other Stories. 2010. 52p. pap. 8.95 (978-1-4502-4049-9(6)) iUniverse, Inc.
Thomas, Lex. The Burnouts. (Quarantine Ser.: 3). (ENG.). 400p. (gr. 9-12). 2016. pap. 9.99 (978-1-5124-0419-7(5), Carolrhoda Bks.) 2014. (J). 17.99 (978-1-60684-338-3(9), Carolrhoda Lab™) Lerner Publishing Group.
—The Loners. (Quarantine Ser.: No. 1). (ENG.). 416p. (gr. 9). 2013. (J). pap. 9.99 (978-1-60684-438-0(5)) 2012. 17.99 (978-1-60684-329-1(X)) Lerner Publishing Group. (Carolrhoda Lab™).
Thomas, Peggy. Snow Dance, 1 vol. Facklam, Paul, illus. 2008. (ENG.). 32p. (J). (gr. 1-3). 16.99 (978-1-58980-478-4(3)) Pelican Publishing Co., Inc.
Thomas, Rob. Rats Saw God. 2009. 9.00 (978-0-7848-2881-6(4), Everbind) Marco Bk. Co.
—Rats Saw God. 2010. (ENG.). 202p. 17.10 (978-0-7569-8366-6(5)) Perfection Learning Corp.
—Rats Saw God. 2013. (ENG.). 224p. (YA). (gr. 7). 16.99 (978-1-4424-5976-2(X)); (Illus.). pap. 10.99 (978-1-4424-5738-6(4)) Simon & Schuster Bks. For Young Readers. (Simon & Schuster Bks. For Young Readers).
Thomas, Terri. J Mac Is the Freestyle King! Sefcik, Wendy, illus. 2010. 38p. pap. 20.00 (978-1-60844-453-3(8)) Dog Ear Publishing, LLC.
Thompson, Anne. Arrow Sparrow. 2009. (Illus.). 32p. pap. (978-1-84549-369-1(9), Swirl) arima publishing.
Thompson, Brian. Reject High. 2013. 270p. pap. 11.95 (978-0-9891056-0-6(1)) Great Nation Publishing.
Thompson, C. Michael. Twinsational. 2009. 120p. (YA). pap. 14.95 (978-1-4327-3033-8(9)) Outskirts Pr., Inc.
Thompson, Colin. The Floods #2: School Plot. Scrambly, Crab, illus. 2008. (Floods Ser.). (J). (ENG.). 224p. 15.99 (978-0-06-113861-4(4)); 256p. lib. bdg. 16.89 (978-0-06-113855-3(X)) HarperCollins Pubs.
Thompson, Dorothy. Dewey Does Adding & Subtractions Bk. 2: Activity Sports Book. 2004. (Dewey Does Ser.). (Illus.). 44p. (J). (gr. -1-3). pap., act. bk. ed. 4.95 (978-0-9711474-2-3(6)) A B C-123 Publishing.
Thompson, Holly. Falling into the Dragon's Mouth. Huynh, Matt, illus. 2016. (ENG.). 352p. (J). 17.99 (978-1-62779-134-2(5), 9781627791342, Holt, Henry & Co. Bks. For Young Readers) Holt, Henry & Co.
—Orchards. 2012. (ENG.). 336p. (YA). (gr. 7). pap. 9.99 (978-0-385-73978-8(8), Ember) Random Hse. Children's Bks.
Thompson, Kelly. Lasting. 2005. 120p. pap. 19.95 (978-1-4137-9653-7(2)) PublishAmerica, Inc.
Thompson, Lauren. Mouse Loves School. Erdogan, Buket, illus. 2011. (Mouse Ser.). (ENG.). 24p. (J). (gr. -1-k). pap. 3.99 (978-1-4424-2898-0(8)); lib. bdg. 16.99 (978-1-4424-2899-7(6)) Simon Spotlight. (Simon Spotlight).
—Mouse's First Day of School. Erdogan, Buket, illus. 2010. (Mouse Ser.). (ENG.). 34p. (J). (gr. -1 — 1). bds. 7.99 (978-1-4169-9476-3(9), Little Simon) Little Simon.
Thompson, Lauren & Jackson, Livia. Mouse's First Day of School. Erdogan, Buket, illus. 2003. (Mouse Ser.). (ENG.). 32p. (J). (gr. -1-3). 15.99 (978-0-689-84727-1(0), Simon & Schuster Bks. For Young Readers) Simon & Schuster Bks. For Young Readers.
Thompson, Shannon Raines. Mad about Miller. Stone, Kathrine Thompson, ed. Shehan, Terece, illus. 2006. 24p. (YA). 12.95 (978-1-59971-853-8(7)) Aardvark Global Publishing.
—Nuts about Neal. Stone, Kathrine Thompson, ed. Shehan, Terece, illus. 2006. 24p. (YA). 12.95 (978-1-59971-852-1(9)) Aardvark Global Publishing.
Thompson, Tate. Senioritis. 2nd ed. 2003. (YA). per. 13.50 (978-0-943864-47-1(X)) Davenport, May Pubs.
Thompson, Tolya L. Catchin' Cooties Consuelo. Harrold, Brian, illus. 2004. (Smarties Ser.: 3). (SPA.). (J). 16.00 (978-0-9708296-3-4(9)) Savor Publishing Hse., Inc.
Thompson, Vivian L. Neat! Said Jeremy. 2003. 33p. (J). pap. 8.95 (978-0-7414-1579-0(8)) Infinity Publishing.
Thomson, Melissa. Keena Ford & the Field Trip Mix-Up. 2010. (Keena Ford Ser.). (ENG.). 112p. (J). (gr. 1-3). 5.99 (978-0-14-241572-6(3), Puffin Books) Penguin Young Readers Group.
—Keena Ford & the Secret Journal Mix-Up. Morrison, Frank, illus. 2011. (Keena Ford Ser.). (ENG.). 128p. (J). (gr. 1-3). 5.99 (978-0-14-241937-3(0), Puffin Books) Penguin Young Readers Group.
Thor, Annika. The Lily Pond. Schenck, Linda, tr. 2012. (ENG.). 224p. (J). (gr. 4-7). 7.99 (978-0-385-74040-1(9), Yearling) Random Hse. Children's Bks.
Thor, Annika & Schenck, Linda. Deep Sea. 2015. (ENG.). 240p. (YA). (gr. 9). 20.99 (978-0-375-99132-5(8), Delacorte Pr.) Random Hse. Children's Bks.
Thorne, Bella. Autumn Falls. 2014. (ENG.). 224p. (YA). (gr. 7). lib. bdg. 21.99 (978-0-375-99161-5(1), Delacorte Pr.) Random Hse. Children's Bks.
—Autumn's Kiss. 2015. (ENG.). 240p. (YA). (gr. 7). 18.99 (978-0-385-74435-5(8), Delacorte Pr.) Random Hse. Children's Bks.
Thorne, Bella. Autumn's Wish. (ENG.). 320p. (YA). (gr. 7). 2017. pap. 9.99 (**978-0-385-74438-6(2)**, Ember) 2016. 18.99 (978-0-385-74437-9(4), Delacorte Pr.) Random Hse. Children's Bks.
Thorne, Jenn Marie. The Inside of Out. 2016. (ENG.). 400p. (YA). (gr. 7). 17.99 (978-0-8037-4058-7(1), Dial Bks) Penguin Young Readers Group.
Thorpe, Kiki. Before the Bell. RH Disney Staff & Christy, Jana, illus. 2015. (Never Girls Ser.: 9). (ENG.). 128p. (J). (gr. 1-4). lib. bdg. 12.99 (978-0-7364-8167-0(2), RH/Disney) Random Hse. Children's Bks.
Thrash, Maggie. We Know It Was You. 2016. (Strange Ser.). (ENG., Illus.). 352p. (YA). (gr. 9). 17.99 (978-1-4814-6200-6(8), Simon Pulse) Simon Pulse.
Thydell, Johanna & Martens, Helle. There's a Pig in My Class! Ramel, Charlotte, illus. 2014. (ENG.). 32p. (J). (gr. -1-3). 16.95 (978-0-8234-3168-7(1)) Holiday Hse., Inc.
Tidd, Louise Vitellaro. Lo Haré Después. Translations.com Staff, tr. from ENG. Handelman, Dorothy, photos by. 2007. (Lecturas para niños de verdad - Nivel 2 (Real Kids Readers - Level 2) Ser.).Tr. of I'll Do It Later. (SPA., Illus.). 32p. (gr. k-3). per. 5.95 (978-0-8225-7805-5(0)) Lerner Publishing Group.
—Ya Te Enteraste? Handelman, Dorothy, photos by. 2007. (Lecturas para niños de verdad - Nivel 2 (Real Kids Readers - Level 2) Ser.).Tr. of Did You Hear About Jake? (SPA., Illus.). 32p. (J). (gr. -1-3). per. 5.95 (978-0-8225-7802-4(6), Ediciones Lerner) Lerner Publishing Group.
Tidwell, Deborah Swayne. Magic Eraser: And the Substitute Teacher. 2008. 24p. pap. 12.99 (978-1-4343-8107-1(2)) AuthorHouse.
Tilley. Damaged. 2011. (ENG.). 260p. (gr. 9-13). pap. 11.95 (978-988-18967-0-4(3)) Haven Bks.
Time, Nicholas O. Going, Going, Gone. 2016. (In Due Time Ser.: 1). (ENG., Illus.). 160p. (J). (gr. 3-7). pap. 6.99 (978-1-4814-6729-2(8), Simon Spotlight) Simon Spotlight.
—Going, Going, Gone. 2016. (In Due Time Ser.: 1). lib. bdg. 17.20 (978-0-606-38985-3(7)) Turtleback Bks.
Tinti, Natalie. Magic in Us. the Power of Imagination: The Power of Imagination, bks. 1, vol. 2. T, N., illus. ed. 2013. (Sewing a Friendship Ser.). (ENG.). 116p. (J). pap. 12.95 (978-0-9842625-3-3(9)) Tintinatie Publishing Hse.
Titherington, Karen M. Gavin Goes to Kindergarten! Prepare Your Child for the First Day of School. 2011. (Illus.). 80p. (J). 19.99 (978-0-9795741-6-0(1)) Bloated Toe Publishing.
Toader, Alex. Max's Journal: The Adventures of Shark Boy & Lava Girl. Rodriguez, Robert, illus. 2005. 128p. (J). (978-1-933104-03-4(1)) Troublemaker Publishing, LP.
Tobias, Anne B. Harry's Problem First Loose Tooth. Tobias, Tom, illus. 2008. 16p. pap. 9.95 (978-0-9818683-9-4(8)) Peppertree Pr., The.
Tobin, Jim. The Very Inappropriate Word. Coverly, Dave, illus. 2013. (ENG.). 36p. (J). (gr. k-3). 16.99 (978-0-8050-9474-9(1), 9780805094749, Holt, Henry & Co. Bks. For Young Readers) Holt, Henry & Co.
Todd, Strasser. Give a Boy a Gun. 2014. (ENG.). 208p. (YA). 11.24 (978-1-63245-176-7(X)) Lectorum Pubns., Inc.
Toews, Rita. The Bully: A Discussion & Activity Story. Ljungberg, Jon, illus. 2011. 40p. (J). pap. 11.95 (978-1-59850-102-5(X)) Youthlight, Inc.
Toffler-Corrie, Laura. My Totally Awkward Supernatural Crush. 2013. (ENG.). 352p. (J). (gr. 7). 17.99 (978-1-59643-733-3(2)) Roaring Brook Pr.
Toki, Sela Tuita. Pati Loves to Walk Barefoot to School. 2009. 44p. pap. 24.95 (978-1-60749-433-1(7)) America Star Bks.
Tokio, Marnelle. Room 207. Hendry, Linda, illus. 2006. (ENG.). 120p. (J). (gr. 4-7). pap. 8.95 (978-0-88776-695-4(1), Tundra Bks.) Tundra Bks. CAN. Dist: Penguin Random Hse. LLC.
Tolan, Stephanie S. Surviving the Applewhites. 2012. (Applewhites Ser.: 1). (ENG.). 240p. (J). (gr. 5-18). pap. 6.99 (978-0-06-441044-1(7)) HarperCollins Pubs.
—Surviving the Applewhites. l.t. ed. 2005. pap. 10.95 (978-0-7862-7259-4(7), Large Print Pr.) Thorndike Pr.
Toliver, K. S. Pam Brown Is Picture Perfect!! 2008. 28p. pap. 12.95 (978-1-4327-2058-2(9)) Outskirts Pr., Inc.
Toliver, Wendy. The Secret Life of a Teenage Siren. 2012. (Romantic Comedies Ser.). (ENG.). 304p. (YA). (gr. 7). pap. 14.99 (978-1-4424-7494-9(7), Simon Pulse) Simon Pulse.
Toriyama, Akira. Dragon Ball Z. Toriyama, Akira, illus. 2006. (Dragon Ball Z Ser.: 25). (ENG., Illus.). 208p. pap. 9.99 (978-1-4215-0404-9(9)) Viz Media.
—Dragon Ball Z, Vol. 22. Toriyama, Akira, illus. 2005. (ENG., Illus.). 192p. pap. 9.99 (978-1-4215-0051-5(5)) Viz Media.
—Dragon Ball Z, Vol. 24. Toriyama, Akira, illus. 2006. (ENG., Illus.). 208p. pap. 9.99 (978-1-4215-0273-1(9)) Viz Media.
Torres, Jose A. Joey Kanga Roo: First Day of School. 2009. 36p. pap. 15.99 (978-1-4389-3964-3(7)) AuthorHouse.
Tosten, S. Kennedy. Troy's Amazing Universe Bk. 1: M for Mall. 2003. (Illus.). 116p. (YA). (gr. 2-18). pap. 13.95 (978-1-59113-318-6(1)) Booklocker.com, Inc.
Toten, Teresa. The Unlikely Hero of Room 13B. 2015. (ENG.). 304p. (YA). (gr. 7). 17.99 (978-0-553-50786-7(9), Delacorte Pr.) Random Hse. Children's Bks.
Townley, Roderick. Sky. 2010. (ENG.). 272p. (YA). (gr. 7). pap. 12.99 (978-1-4423-3973-6(X), Atheneum Bks. for Young Readers) Simon & Schuster Children's Publishing.
Tracy, Judith. The Wildsidhe Chronicles Bk. 3: Dark Proposal. 2003. (J). pap. 7.99 (978-1-890096-15-1(6)) Padwolf Publishing, Inc.
Tracy, Kathleen. The Hamster in Our Class. 2011. (Randy's Corner Ser.). (Illus.). 32p. (J). (gr. -1-2). lib. bdg. 25.70 (978-1-58415-980-3(4)) Mitchell Lane Pubs., Inc.
—The Turtle in Our Class. 2011. (Randy's Corner Ser.). (Illus.). (J). (gr. -1-2). lib. bdg. 25.70 (978-1-58415-979-7(0)) Mitchell Lane Pubs., Inc.
Tracy, Kristen. Bessica Lefter Bites Back. 2013. (ENG.). 272p. (J). (gr. 5). 6.99 (978-0-375-87295-2(7), Yearling) Random Hse. Children's Bks.
—Camille McPhee Fell under the Bus. 2010. (ENG.). 304p. (J). (gr. 3-7). 7.99 (978-0-375-84546-8(1), Yearling) Random Hse. Children's Bks.
—Project (un)Popular Book #1. (Project (un)Popular Ser.). (ENG.). 336p. (J). (gr. 5). 2017. 7.99 (**978-0-553-51051-5(7)**, Yearling) 2016. 16.99 (978-0-553-51048-5(7), Delacorte Bks. for Young Readers) Random Hse. Children's Bks.
—Project (un)Popular Book #2: Totally Crushed. 2017. (Project (un)Popular Ser.: 2). (ENG.). 224p. (J). (gr. 5). 16.99 (**978-0-553-51052-2(5)**, Delacorte Bks. for Young Readers) Random Hse. Children's Bks.
—The Reinvention of Bessica Lefter. 2012. (ENG.). 320p. (J). (gr. 5). 7.99 (978-0-375-84547-5(X), Yearling) Random Hse. Children's Bks.
—Too Cool for This School. 2015. (ENG.). 288p. (J). (gr. 5). 6.99 (978-0-375-87296-9(5), Yearling) Random Hse. Children's Bks.
Tracy, Kristen. Totally Crushed. 2017. 211p. (J). (**978-0-553-51053-9(3)**, Delacorte Pr) Random House Publishing Group.
Trailblazers! Individual Title Six-Packs. (Action Packs Ser.). 104p. (gr. 3-5). 44.00 (978-0-7635-2992-5(3)) Rigby Education.
Trapped by a Teacher: Individual Title Six-Packs. (Action Packs Ser.). 128p. (gr. 3-5). 44.00 (978-0-7635-3309-0(2)) Rigby Education.
Traylor, Javier. A Day at School with Sally Sue. 2012. 40p. pap. 24.95 (978-1-4137-8929-4(3)) America Star Bks.
Traylor, Marci. What Will I Be? 2008. 40p. pap. 19.50 (978-1-4389-0247-0(6)) AuthorHouse.
Tregay, Sarah. Fan Art. DeJesus, Melissa, illus. 2014. (ENG.). 368p. (YA). (gr. 8). 17.99 (978-0-06-224315-7(2), Tegen, Katherine Bks) HarperCollins Pubs.
Trevino, David. A Colorful Carnival of Kids in the Kingdom of Marbles: Mission #1 the Cemetery Ghost. 2011. 126p. pap. 19.95 (978-1-4626-1087-7(0)) America Star Bks.
Trice, Linda. Kenya's Song. Johnson, Pamela, illus. 2013. (ENG.). 32p. (J). (gr. -1-3). pap. 7.95 (978-1-57091-847-6(3)); lib. bdg. 17.95 (978-1-57091-846-9(5)) Charlesbridge Publishing, Inc.
Trine, Greg. Dinos Are Forever. Dormer, Frank W., illus. (Adventures of Jo Schmo Ser.: 1). (ENG.). 112p. (J). (gr. 1-4). 2014. pap. 5.99 (978-0-544-00325-5(X), HMH Books For Young Readers) 2012. 12.99 (978-0-547-76341-5(7)) Houghton Mifflin Harcourt Publishing Co.
Trionfo, Nikki. Shatter. 2017. (YA). pap. 18.99 (**978-1-4621-2013-0(X)**, Horizon Pubs.) Cedar Fort, Inc./CFI Distribution.
Trivas, Tracy. The Wish Stealers. 2011. (ENG.). 288p. (J). (gr. 3-7). pap. 7.99 (978-1-4169-8726-0(6), Aladdin) Simon & Schuster Children's Publishing.
Tromly, Stephanie. Trouble Is a Friend of Mine. 2015. (ENG.). 336p. (YA). (gr. 7-12). 17.99 (978-0-525-42840-4(2), Kathy Dawson Books) Penguin Young Readers Group.
Tromly, Stephanie. Trouble Makes a Comeback. (ENG.). (YA). (gr. 7). 2017. 320p. pap. 10.99 (**978-0-14-751544-5(0)**, Speak) 2016. 304p. 17.99 (978-0-525-42841-1(0), Kathy Dawson Books) Penguin Young Readers Group.
Trouble in the Barkers' Class. 2005. (J). 29.95 incl. audio compact disk (978-0-8045-4134-3(5)); 27.95 incl. audio (978-0-8045-6935-4(5)) Spoken Arts, Inc.
Trueit, Trudi. No Girls Allowed (Dogs Okay) Paillot, Jim, illus. 2010. (Secrets of a Lab Rat Ser.). (ENG.). 144p. (J). (gr. 3-7). pap. 5.99 (978-1-4169-6111-6(9), Aladdin) Simon & Schuster Children's Publishing.
—No Girls Allowed (Dogs Okay) Paillot, Jim, illus. 2009. (Secrets of a Lab Rat Ser.). (ENG.). 128p. (J). (gr. 3-7). 14.99 (978-1-4169-7592-2(6), Simon & Schuster/Paula Wiseman Bks.) Simon & Schuster/Paula Wiseman Bks.
—Scab for Treasurer? Paillot, Jim, illus. 2011. (Secrets of a Lab Rat Ser.). (ENG.). 160p. (J). (gr. 3-7). pap. 5.99 (978-1-4169-6113-0(5), Aladdin) Simon & Schuster Children's Publishing.
—Scab for Treasurer? Paillot, Jim, illus. 2011. (Secrets of a Lab Rat Ser.). (ENG.). 160p. (J). (gr. 3-7). 15.99 (978-1-4169-7594-6(2), Simon & Schuster/Paula Wiseman Bks.) Simon & Schuster/Paula Wiseman Bks.
—The Sister Solution. Valencia, Adrian, illus. 2015. (Mix Ser.). (ENG.). 240p. (J). (gr. 4-8). pap. 7.99 (978-1-4814-3239-9(7), Aladdin) Simon & Schuster Children's Publishing.
—Stealing Popular. 2012. (Mix Ser.). (ENG.). 240p. (J). (gr. 4-8). pap. 6.99 (978-1-4424-4154-5(2), Aladdin) Simon & Schuster Children's Publishing.
Trufant, Robert & Mullins, Tinnesha. Angel Fingers Series: Na'dyd Goes to School. 2004. (Angel Fingers Ser.). (Illus.). 19p. (J). (gr. -1-2). 14.95 (978-0-9760160-0-7(1)) Mullins Pubns. & Apparel, LLC.
Trumbo, Stephen. Friends of the Forest. 2008. 39p. pap. 24.95 (978-1-60563-781-5(5)) America Star Bks.
Tsang, Evonne. I Love Him to Pieces. Görrissen, Janina, illus. 2011. (My Boyfriend Is a Monster Ser.: 1). (ENG.). 128p. (YA). (gr. 7-12). 29.27 (978-0-7613-6004-9(2)) Lerner Publishing Group.
—#01 I Love Him to Pieces. Görrissen, Janina, illus. 2011. (My Boyfriend Is a Monster Ser.). 128p. (YA). pap. 56.72 (978-0-7613-7602-6(X), Graphic Universe™) Lerner Publishing Group.
Tuck, Pamela M. As Fast As Words Could Fly, 1 vol. Velasquez, Eric, illus. 2013. (ENG.). 40p. (J). 18.95 (978-1-60060-348-3(3)) Lee & Low Bks., Inc.
Tucker, Jasmin. Robot School. 2010. 28p. 12.49 (978-1-4520-5011-9(2)) AuthorHouse.
Tullson, Diane. Lockdown, 1 vol. 2008. (Orca Soundings Ser.). (ENG.). 128p. (YA). (gr. 8-12). pap. 9.95 (978-1-55143-916-7(6)) Orca Bk. Pubs. USA.
Tuma, Refe & Tuma, Susan. What the Dinosaurs Did at School. 2017. (What the Dinosaurs Did Ser.: 2). (ENG., Illus.). 40p. (J). (gr. -1-3). 17.99 (**978-0-316-55289-9(5)**) Little, Brown Bks. for Young Readers.
Turnbull, Ann. Deep Water. 3rd ed. 2013. 102p. pap. (978-1-78132-160-7(4)) SilverWood Bks.
Turnbull-Kennedy, Tiffany. No School for Evil Eraser! 2011. (Illus.). 48p. pap. 16.59 (978-1-4634-3965-1(2)) AuthorHouse.
Turpin, Nick. Molly Is New. Raga, Silvia, illus. 2010. 32p. pap. (978-1-84089-650-3(7)) Zero to Ten, Ltd.
Two Peas in a Pod: 7. 2013. 68p. pap. 12.95 (978-1-4772-7082-0(5)) AuthorHouse.
Uegaki, Chieri. Suki's Kimono. Jorisch, Stéphane, illus. 2005. (ENG.). 32p. (J). (gr. -1-3). pap. 8.95 (978-1-55337-752-8(4)) Kids Can Pr., Ltd. CAN. Dist: Hachette Bk. Group.
Ugezene, Esther I. KiKi, the School Truant. 2005. per. 10.00 (978-0-9767678-1-7(3)) Professional Publishing Hse. LLC.
Ulrich, Maureen. Breakaway, 1 vol. 2012. (ENG.). 272p. (YA). (gr. 9-12). pap. 12.95 (978-1-55050-512-2(2)) Coteau Bks. CAN. Dist: Orca Bk. Pubs. USA.
Umezu, Kazuo. The Drifting Classroom. Roman, Annette, ed. Umezu, Kazuo, illus. 2007. (Drifting Classroom Ser.: 9). (ENG., Illus.). 192p. pap. 9.99 (978-1-4215-0961-7(X)) Viz Media.
Underwood, Deborah. A Balloon for Isabel. Rankin, Laura, illus. 2010. (ENG.). 32p. (J). (gr. -1-2). 16.99 (978-0-06-177987-9(3), Greenwillow Bks.) HarperCollins Pubs.
Underwood, Deborah. Here Comes Teacher Cat. Rueda, Claudia, illus. 2017. (ENG.). 88p. (J). (-k). 16.99 (**978-0-399-53905-3(0)**, Dial Bks) Penguin Young Readers Group.
Unsworth, Anne. Danny Is Dyslexic. 2011. 68p. (gr. 4-6). pap. 12.10 (978-1-4567-8417-1(X)) AuthorHouse.
Urban, Linda. A Crooked Kind of Perfect. (ENG., Illus.). 224p. (J). (gr. 5-7). 2009. pap. 7.99 (978-0-15-206608-6(X)) 2007. 16.00 (978-0-15-206007-7(3)) Houghton Mifflin Harcourt Publishing Co.
Urdahl, Catherine. Polka-Dot Fixes Kindergarten. Kemble, Mai S., illus. 2011. (ENG.). 32p. (J). (gr. -1-3). 16.95 (978-1-57091-737-0(X)); pap. 7.95 (978-1-57091-738-7(8)) Charlesbridge Publishing, Inc.
Ure, Jean. Dazzling Danny. Donnelly, Karen, illus. 2011. (ENG.). 96p. (J). pap. 5.99 (978-0-00-713370-3(7)) HarperCollins Pubs. Ltd. GBR. Dist: HarperCollins Pubs.
—Hunky Dory. 2011. (ENG., Illus.). 192p. (J). pap. 7.99 (978-0-00-722460-9(5), HarperCollins Children's Bks.) HarperCollins Pubs. Ltd. GBR. Dist: HarperCollins Pubs.
Urey, Gary. Super Schnoz & the Gates of Smell. Long, Ethan, illus. (Super Schnoz Ser.: 1). (ENG.). 160p. (J). (gr. 3-7). 2015. pap. 6.99 (978-0-8075-7560-4(7)) 2013. 14.99 (978-0-8075-7555-0(0)) Whitman, Albert & Co.
Ursu, Anne. Breadcrumbs. McGuire, Erin, illus. 2013. (ENG.). 336p. (J). (gr. 3-7). pap. 6.99 (978-0-06-201506-8(0), Waldon Pond Pr.) HarperCollins Pubs.
—Breadcrumbs. McGuire, Erin, illus. 2012. 320p. 55.00 (978-0-449-01400-4(2)) Random Hse., Inc.
—Breadcrumbs. 2013. (J). lib. bdg. 17.20 (978-0-606-27130-1(9), Turtleback) Turtleback Bks.
Usher, Carolyn. Chip Takes Off. 2013. (ENG.). 167p. (YA). pap. 8.95 (978-1-4787-1637-2(1)) Outskirts Pr., Inc.
Uttley, Tracy. Molly Mcsholly Conquers Kindergarten. 2004. 32p. (J). bds. 15.95 (978-1-59298-077-2(5)) Beaver's Pond Pr., Inc.
Uvezian, Verne. The Day Benny Stuck His Neck Out. 2011. 12p. (gr. 1-2). 9.95 (978-1-4567-3119-9(X)) AuthorHouse.
Vail, Rachel. Flabbersmashed about You. Heo, Yumi, illus. 2012. (ENG.). 32p. (J). (gr. -1-3). 16.99 (978-0-312-61345-7(8), 9780312613457) Feiwel & Friends.
—If We Kiss. 2005. (If We Kiss Ser.: Bk. 1). (ENG.). 272p. (J). 15.99 (978-0-06-056914-3(X)) HarperCollins Pubs.
—If You Only Knew. 2014. (Friendship Ring Ser.: 1). (ENG.). 176p. (J). (gr. 5). pap. 7.99 (978-0-14-751118-8(6), Puffin Books) Penguin Young Readers Group.
—Kiss Me Again. 2012. (If We Kiss Ser.: 2). (ENG.). 256p. (YA). (gr. 8). 17.99 (978-0-06-194717-9(2), HarperTeen) HarperCollins Pubs.
—Not That I Care. 2014. (Friendship Ring Ser.: 3). (ENG.). 176p. (J). (gr. 5). pap. 7.99 (978-0-14-751120-1(8), Puffin Books) Penguin Young Readers Group.
—Please, Please, Please. 2014. (Friendship Ring Ser.: 2). (ENG.). 176p. (J). (gr. 5). pap. 7.99 (978-0-14-751119-5(4), Puffin Books) Penguin Young Readers Group.
—Unfriended. (ENG.). (J). (gr. 5). 2015. 304p. 8.99 (978-0-14-751154-6(2), Puffin Books) 2014. 288p. 16.99 (978-0-670-01307-4(2), Viking Books for Young Readers) Penguin Young Readers Group.
—Well, That Was Awkward. 2017. (ENG.). 320p. (J). (gr. 5). 16.99 (978-0-670-01308-1(0), Viking Books for Young Readers) Penguin Young Readers Group.
—What Are Friends For? 2014. (Friendship Ring Ser.: 4). (ENG.). 176p. (J). (gr. 5). pap. 7.99 (978-0-14-751121-8(6), Puffin Books) Penguin Young Readers Group.
—You, Maybe: The Profound Asymmetry of Love in High School. (YA). 2007. (ENG.). 224p. (gr. 8-12). pap. 7.99 (978-0-06-056919-8(0)) 2006. (ENG.). 208p. (gr. 7-12). 15.99 (978-0-06-056917-4(4)) 2006. 199p. (gr. 7-12). lib. bdg. 16.89 (978-0-06-056918-1(2)) HarperCollins Pubs.
Vail, Rachel & Avi. Never Mind! 2005. (ENG.). 208p. (J). (gr. 5-18). reprint ed. pap. 6.99 (978-0-06-054316-7(7)) HarperCollins Pubs.
Vaizey, George de Horne. Etheldreda the Ready. Horrell, Charles, illus. 2007. 200p. per. (978-1-4065-4688-0(7)) Dodo Pr.
—Tom & Some Other Girls. Tarrant, Percy, illus. 2007. 208p. per. (978-1-4065-4698-9(4)) Dodo Pr.
Valdes, Leslie. Dora Goes to School. Roper, Robert, illus. 2005. (Dora the Explorer Ser.: 8). 22p. (J). lib. bdg. 15.00 (978-1-59054-791-5(8)) Fitzgerald Bks.
Valentine, Sally. The Ghost of the Charlotte Lighthouse. 2006. (J). (978-1-59531-013-2(4)) North Country Bks., Inc.
Valentino, Amanda & Bell, Cathleen Davitt. Unraveled, Bk. 4. 2012. (Amanda Project Ser.: 4). (ENG.). 352p. (YA). (gr. 8). pap. 8.99 (978-0-06-174219-4(8), HarperTeen) HarperCollins Pubs.
van Diepen, Allison. Light of Day. 2015. (ENG.). 320p. (YA). (gr. 9). 17.99 (978-0-06-230347-9(3)) HarperCollins Pubs.
—Snitch. 2013. (ENG., Illus.). 320p. (YA). (gr. 9). pap. 11.99 (978-1-4424-8165-7(X), Simon Pulse) Simon Pulse.
Van Dolzer, Krista. Don't Vote for Me. 2016. (ENG.). 240p. (J). (gr. 5-8). pap. 7.99 (978-1-4926-3184-2(1), 9781492631842, Sourcebooks Jabberwocky) Sourcebooks, Inc.
—Don't Vote for Me. 2015. (ENG.). 240p. (J). (gr. 5-8). 15.99 (978-1-4926-0941-4(2), 9781492609414, Sourcebooks Jabberwocky) Sourcebooks, Inc.
Van Draanen, Wendelin. Attack of the Tagger. Biggs, Brian, illus. unabr. ed. 2006. (Shredderman Ser.: Bk. 2). (J). (gr. 3-6). audio 24.95 (978-1-59519-758-0(3)) Live Oak Media.

S

—Attack of the Tagger. Biggs, Brian, illus. 2006. (Shredderman Ser.: Bk. 2). (ENG.). 176p. (J). (gr. 1-4). 6.99 *(978-0-440-41913-6(1)*, Yearling) Random Hse. Children's Bks.

—Confessions of a Serial Kisser. 2009. (ENG.). 304p. (YA). (gr. 7-18). pap. 9.99 *(978-0-375-84249-8(7)*, Ember) Random Hse. Children's Bks.

—Enemy Spy. Biggs, Brian, illus. 2006. (Shredderman Ser.: Bk. 4). (ENG.). 192p. (J). (gr. 1-4). 6.99 *(978-0-440-41915-0(8)*, Yearling) Random Hse. Children's Bks.

—Meet the Gecko. Biggs, Brian, illus. 2006. (Shredderman Ser.: Bk. 3). (ENG.). 176p. (J). (gr. 1-4). 5.99 *(978-0-440-41914-3(X)*, Yearling) Random Hse. Children's Bks.

—The Running Dream. 2011. (ENG.). 352p. (YA). (gr. 7-18). 16.99 *(978-0-375-86667-8(1)*, Knopf Bks. for Young Readers) Random Hse. Children's Bks.

—Sammy Keyes & the Dead Giveaway. 2008. (Sammy Keyes Ser.: Bk. 10). (J). 64.99 *(978-1-60640-639-7(6))* Findaway World, LLC.

—Sammy Keyes & the Dead Giveaway. unabr. ed. 2006. (Sammy Keyes Ser.: Bk. 10). (J). (gr. 5-7). pap. 54.95 incl. audio compact disk *(978-1-59519-771-9(0))*; pap. 36.95 incl. audio *(978-1-59519-770-2(2))* Live Oak Media.

—Sammy Keyes & the Dead Giveaway. 2007. (Sammy Keyes Ser.: Bk. 10). (ENG., Illus.). 304p. (J). (gr. 5-7). per. 7.99 *(978-0-440-41911-2(5)*, Yearling) Random Hse. Children's Bks.

—Sammy Keyes & the Night of Skulls. 2012. (Sammy Keyes Ser.: 14). (ENG.). 336p. (J). (gr. 5-7). 8.99 *(978-0-375-85457-6(6)*, Yearling) Random Hse. Children's Bks.

—Sammy Keyes & the Wedding Crasher. 2011. (Sammy Keyes Ser.: Bk. 13). (ENG.). 320p. (J). (gr. 5). 7.99 *(978-0-375-85456-9(8)*, Yearling) Random Hse. Children's Bks.

—Secret Identity. Biggs, Brian, illus. 2006. (Shredderman Ser.: Bk. 1).Tr. of Al Haqiqa Wara ¿Al Fatak¿. (ENG.). 144p. (J). (gr. 1-4). reprint ed. 6.99 *(978-0-440-41912-9(3)*, Yearling) Random Hse. Children's Bks.

—Shredderman: Secret Identity. Biggs, Brian, illus. unabr. ed. 2006. (Shredderman Ser.: Bk. 1).Tr. of Shredderman - Al Haqiqa Wara ¿Al Fatak¿. (J). (gr. 2-4). audio 24.95 *(978-1-59519-762-7(1))* Live Oak Media.

—Shredderman: Secret Identity. unabr. ed. 2006. (Shredderman Ser.: Bk. 1).Tr. of Shredderman - Al Haqiqa Wara ¿Al Fatak¿. (Illus.). (J). (gr. 2-4). pap. 28.95 incl. audio compact disk *(978-1-59519-763-4(X))* Live Oak Media.

Van Kersen, Elizabeth. Who's Riley. 2005. (Illus.). 50p. (J). per. 8.99 *(978-1-932338-90-4(X))* Lifevest Publishing, Inc.

Van Leeuwen, Jean. Amanda Pig, First Grader. Schweninger, Ann, illus. 2007. (Oliver & Amanda Ser.). 40p. (J). *(978-1-4287-4781-4(8)*, Dial) Penguin Publishing Group.

—Amanda Pig, First Grader. Schweninger, Ann, illus. 2009. (Oliver & Amanda Ser.). (ENG.). 48p. (J). (gr. 1-3). mass mkt. 3.99 *(978-0-14-241276-3(7)*, Penguin Young Readers) Penguin Young Readers Group.

Van Slyke, Rebecca. Dad School. Burris, Priscilla, illus. 2016. (ENG.). 32p. (J). (gr. -1-2). 19.99 *(978-0-385-38896-2(9)*, Doubleday Bks. for Young Readers) Random Hse. Children's Bks.

—Mom School. Burris, Priscilla, illus. 2015. (ENG.). 32p. (J). (gr. -1-2). 16.99 *(978-0-385-38892-4(6)*, Doubleday Bks. for Young Readers) Random Hse. Children's Bks.

Van Stockum, Hilda. A Day on Skates: The Story of a Dutch Picnic. Van Stockum, Hilda, illus. 2007. (Illus.). 40p. (J). (gr. 1). 19.95 *(978-1-932350-18-0(7))* Bethlehem Bks.

Van Tol, Alex. Food Freak. 2017. (Orca Currents Ser.). lib. bdg. 20.80 ***(978-0-606-40452-5(X))*** Turtleback Bks.

Vance, Talia. Silver. 2012. (Bandia Novel Ser.: 1). (ENG.). 384p. (YA). pap. 9.99 *(978-0-7387-3303-6(2)*, Flux) North Star Editions.

Vande Velde, Vivian. 8 Class Pets + 1 Squirrel ÷ 1 Dog = Chaos. Björkman, Steve, illus. (ENG.). 80p. (J). 2012. pap. 6.99 *(978-0-8234-2594-5(0))* 2011. 15.95 *(978-0-8234-2364-4(6))* Holiday Hse., Inc.

Vandever, Daniel W. Fall in Line, Holden. Frank, LaFrenda, ed. Vandever, Daniel W., illus. 2017. (Illus.). 32p. (J). ***(978-1-893354-50-0(4))*** Salina Bookshelf Inc.

Vaughan, M. M. The Ability. Bruno, Iacopo, illus. (Ability Ser.). (ENG.). (YA). (gr. 3-7). 2014. 352p. pap. 6.99 *(978-1-4424-5201-5(3))* 2013. 336p. 15.99 *(978-1-4424-5200-8(5))* McElderry, Margaret K. Bks. (McElderry, Margaret K. Bks.).

—Mindscape. Bruno, Iacopo, illus. 2015. (Ability Ser.). (ENG.). 336p. (YA). (gr. 3-7). pap. 7.99 *(978-1-4424-5205-3(6)*, McElderry, Margaret K. Bks.) McElderry, Margaret K. Bks.

Vaughan, M. M. & Caletti, Deb. The Last Forever. Bruno, Iacopo, illus. 2016. (ENG.). 352p. (YA). (gr. 7-7). pap. 10.99 *(978-1-4424-5002-8(9)*, Simon & Schuster Bks. For Young Readers) Simon & Schuster Bks. For Young Readers.

Vaughn, Lauren Roedy. OCD, the Dude, & Me. 2013. (ENG.). 240p. (YA). (gr. 9). 16.99 *(978-0-8037-3843-0(9)*, Dial Bks) Penguin Young Readers Group.

Vaupel, Robin. My Contract with Henry. 2003. (ENG.). 192p. (J). (gr. 4-6). tchr. ed. 16.95 *(978-0-8234-1701-8(8))* Holiday Hse., Inc.

Vega, Danielle. The Merciless. 2014. (Merciless Ser.: 1). (ENG.). 288p. (YA). (gr. 9). 17.99 *(978-1-59514-722-6(5)*, Razorbill) Penguin Young Readers Group.

Vega, Denise. Click Here: (To Find Out How I Survived Seventh Grade) 2006. (ENG., Illus.). 224p. (J). (gr. 5-17). reprint ed. per. 7.99 *(978-0-316-98559-8(7))* Little, Brown Bks. for Young Readers.

—Rock On: A Story of Guitars, Gigs, Girls, & a Brother (Not Necessarily in That Order) 2012. (ENG., Illus.). 304p. (YA). (gr. 7-17). 17.99 *(978-0-316-13310-4(8))* Little, Brown Bks. for Young Readers.

—Rock On: A Story of Guitars, Gigs, Girls, & a Brother (not Necessarily in That Order) 2013. (ENG., Illus.). 304p. (YA). (gr. 7-17). pap. 8.99 *(978-0-316-13309-8(4))* Little, Brown Bks. for Young Readers.

Velasquez, Gloria. Tyrone's Betrayal. 2006. (Roosevelt High School Series Bks.). 135p. (J). (gr. 3-7). per. 9.95 *(978-1-55885-465-9(7)*, Piñata Books) Arte Publico Pr.

Venditti, Robert. Attack of the Alien Horde. Higgins, Dusty, illus. 2015. (Miles Taylor & the Golden Cape Ser.: 1). (ENG.). 304p. (J). (gr. 4-7). 16.99 *(978-1-4814-0542-3(X))* Simon & Schuster, Inc.

—Rise of the Robot Army. Higgins, Dusty, illus. 2016. (Miles Taylor & the Golden Cape Ser.: 2). (ENG.). 304p. (J). (gr. 4-7). 16.99 *(978-1-4814-0557-7(8)*, Simon & Schuster Bks. For Young Readers) Simon & Schuster Bks. For Young Readers.

Ventura, Marne. Anxious Adam Braves the Test. Trinidad, Leo, illus. 2016. (Worry Warriors Ser.). (ENG.). 96p. (gr. 2-4). pap. 5.95 *(978-1-4965-3650-1(9))*; lib. bdg. 25.99 *(978-1-4965-3611-2(8))* Stone Arch Bks.

—Jittery Jake Conquers Stage Fright. Trinidad, Leo, illus. 2016. (Worry Warriors Ser.). (ENG.). 96p. (gr. 2-4). lib. bdg. 25.99 *(978-1-4965-3612-9(6))* Stone Arch Bks.

—Nervous Nellie Fights First-Day Frenzy. Trinidad, Leo, illus. 2016. (Worry Warriors Ser.). (ENG.). 96p. (gr. 2-4). lib. bdg. 25.99 *(978-1-4965-3613-6(4))* Stone Arch Bks.

Verday, Jessica. The Haunted. (ENG.). (YA). (gr. 9). 2011. 496p. pap. 11.99 *(978-1-4169-7896-1(8))* 2010. 480p. 17.99 *(978-1-4169-7895-4(X))* Simon Pulse. (Simon Pulse).

—The Hidden. (ENG.). 400p. (YA). (gr. 9). 2012. pap. 12.99 *(978-1-4169-7898-5(4))* 2011. 17.99 *(978-1-4169-7897-8(6))* Simon Pulse. (Simon Pulse).

—The Hollow. (ENG.). (YA). (gr. 7). 2010. 528p. pap. 11.99 *(978-1-4169-7894-7(1))*No. 1. 2009. 544p. 17.99 *(978-1-4169-7893-0(3))* Simon Pulse. (Simon Pulse).

Verdi, Jessica. My Life after Now. 2013. (ENG.). 304p. (YA). (gr. 7-12). pap. 9.99 *(978-1-4022-7785-6(7)*, 9781402277856) Sourcebooks, Inc.

Vergo, Franny. Jonathan Ray & His Superhero Pack: Respect. 2012. 42p. pap. 16.50 *(978-1-4685-7602-3(X))* AuthorHouse.

Vernick, Audrey. First Grade Dropout. Cordell, Matthew, illus. 2015. (ENG.). 32p. (J). (gr. -1-3). 16.99 *(978-0-544-12985-6(7)*, Clarion Bks.) Houghton Mifflin Harcourt Trade & Reference Pubs.

—Is Your Buffalo Ready for Kindergarten? Jennewein, Daniel, illus. 2010. (ENG.). 32p. (J). (gr. -1-3). 16.99 *(978-0-06-176275-8(X))* HarperCollins Pubs.

—Second Grade Holdout. Cordell, Matthew, illus. 2017. (ENG.). 32p. (J). (gr. -1-3). 16.99 *(978-0-544-87681-1(4)*, Clarion Bks.) Houghton Mifflin Harcourt Trade & Reference Pubs.

Vernon, Ursula. Curse of the Were-Wiener. 3rd ed. (Dragonbreath Ser.: 3). (ENG.). 208p. (J). (gr. 3-7). 2014. pap. 6.99 *(978-0-14-751321-2(9)*, Puffin Books) 2010. 12.99 *(978-0-8037-3469-2(7)*, Dial Bks) Penguin Young Readers Group.

—Curse of the Were-Wiener. 2014. (Dragonbreath Ser.: 3). lib. bdg. 17.20 *(978-0-606-35710-4(6))* Turtleback Bks.

—Dragonbreath. Vernon, Ursula, illus. (Dragonbreath Ser.: 1). (ENG., Illus.). 160p. (J). (gr. 3-7). 2012. pap. 6.99 *(978-0-14-242095-9(6)*, Puffin Books) 2009. 12.99 *(978-0-8037-3363-3(1)*, Dial Bks) Penguin Young Readers Group.

—Dragonbreath. 2012. (Dragonbreath Ser.: 1). lib. bdg. 17.20 *(978-0-606-26665-9(8)*, Turtleback) Turtleback Bks.

Vic Visits Ground Zero. 2004. (J). *(978-0-9761102-0-0(2))* Adams, Evelyn.

Vicente, Alidis. The Shameless Shenanigans of Mister Malo / Las Terribles Travesuras de Mister Malo: The Mister Malo Series / Serie Mister Malo. 2017. (ENG & SPA.). 115p. (J). (gr. 4-8). pap. 9.95 ***(978-1-55885-853-4(9)***, Piñata Books) Arte Publico Pr.

Viehl, Lynn. Dead of Night. 2012. (Youngbloods Ser.: 2). (ENG.). 312p. (YA). pap. 9.95 *(978-0-7387-2646-5(X)*, Flux) North Star Editions.

Viguie, Debbie & Holder, Nancy. Unleashed. 2012. (Wolf Spring Chronicles Ser.). (ENG.). 400p. (YA). (gr. 7). pap. 9.99 *(978-0-385-74099-9(9)*, Ember) Random Hse. Children's Bks.

Villareal, Ray. Alamo Wars. 2008. 187p. (J). (gr. 6-18). pap. 10.95 *(978-1-55885-513-7(0)*, Piñata Books) Arte Publico Pr.

—Body Slammed! 2012. (YA). pap. 11.95 *(978-1-55885-749-0(4)*, Piñata Books) Arte Publico Pr.

Villoro, Juan. El Profesor Ziper y la Fabulosa Guitarra Electrica. El Fisgsn, illus. 2005. (Infantil Ser.). (SPA.). 96p. (J). (gr. 5-8). pap. 9.95 *(978-968-19-0206-3(8))* Santillana USA Publishing Co., Inc.

Viorst, Judith. Alexander, Who's Trying His Best to Be the Best Boy Ever. 2014. (ENG., Illus.). 40p. (J). (gr. -1-3). 17.99 *(978-1-4814-2353-3(3)*, Atheneum Bks. for Young Readers) Simon & Schuster Children's Publishing.

—And Two Boys Booed. Blackall, Sophie, illus. 2014. (ENG.). 32p. (J). (gr. -1-3). 16.99 *(978-0-374-30302-0(9)*, 9780374303020, Farrar, Straus & Giroux (BYR)) Farrar, Straus & Giroux.

A Visit to the Schoolhouse. 2003. (J). per. *(978-1-57657-903-9(4))* Paradise Pr., Inc.

Vivat, Booki. Frazzled: Everyday Disasters & Impending Doom. Vivat, Booki, illus. 2016. (Illus.). 240p. (J). (gr. 3-7). 12.99 *(978-0-06-239879-6(2))* HarperCollins Pubs.

Vivian, Siobhan. The List. (ENG.). 336p. (J). (gr. 9). 2014. pap. 9.99 *(978-0-545-16918-9(6)*, Scholastic Paperbacks) 2012. 17.99 *(978-0-545-16917-2(8)*, PUSH) Scholastic, Inc.

—Not That Kind of Girl. 2010. (ENG.). 336p. (J). (gr. 9-9). 17.99 *(978-0-545-16915-8(1)*, PUSH) Scholastic, Inc.

—Same Difference. 2014. (ENG.). 304p. (J). pap. 9.99 *(978-0-545-75802-4(5))* Scholastic, Inc.

Vizzini, Ned. Be More Chill. 2011. 9.68 *(978-0-7848-3414-5(8)*, Everbind) Marco Bk. Co.

Vizzini, Ned. Be More Chill. 2005. (ENG.). 304p. (J). (gr. 5-9). per. 8.99 *(978-0-7868-0996-7(5))* Disney Publishing Worldwide.

Voake, Steve. Daisy Dawson & the Secret Pond. Meserve, Jessica, illus. 2010. (Daisy Dawson Ser.: 2). (ENG.). 96p. (J). (gr. 1-4). pap. 5.99 *(978-0-7636-4730-8(6))* Candlewick Pr.

Vogiel, Eva. Facing the Music. 2003. 284p. 19.95 *(978-1-880582-94-7(5))* Judaica Pr., Inc., The.

Voigt, Cynthia & Marcus, Barry David. Bad Girls in Love. 2004. (ENG., Illus.). 240p. (J). (gr. 4-8). pap. 11.99 *(978-0-689-86620-3(8)*, Atheneum Bks. for Young Readers) Simon & Schuster Children's Publishing.

Volponi, Paul. Crossing Lines. 2011. (ENG.). 256p. (YA). (gr. 7). E-Book *(978-1-101-52904-1(0))*; 16.99 *(978-0-670-01214-5(9))* Penguin Young Readers Group. (Viking Books for Young Readers).

—The Hand You're Dealt. 2010. (ENG.). 192p. (YA). (gr. 7). pap. 11.99 *(978-1-4169-3990-0(3)*, Atheneum Bks. for Young Readers) Simon & Schuster Children's Publishing.

—Top Prospect. 2016. (ENG.). 280p. (gr. 4-9). (J). 17.99 *(978-1-4677-9433-6(3))*; 35.99 *(978-1-5124-0887-4(5))* Lerner Publishing Group. (Carolrhoda Bks.).

Vosailagi, Jo, illus. Pentapus. 2006. 120p. per. 12.56 *(978-1-4120-9272-2(8))* Trafford Publishing.

Votruba, Erik C. The Cowboy Mile. 2009. 231p. pap. 14.99 *(978-0-557-09002-0(4))* Lulu Pr., Inc.

Vrabel, Beth. A Blind Guide to Normal. 2016. (ENG.). 272p. (J). (gr. 2-7). 16.99 *(978-1-5107-0228-8(8)*, Sky Pony Pr.) Skyhorse Publishing Co., Inc.

—Pack of Dorks. (Pack of Dorks Ser.). (ENG.). 240p. (J). (gr. 2-7). 2015. pap. 7.99 *(978-1-5107-0179-3(6))* 2014. 15.95 *(978-1-62914-623-2(4))* Skyhorse Publishing Co., Inc. (Sky Pony Pr.).

Vrettos, Adrienne Maria. Best Friends for Never. 2016. (ENG.). 240p. (J). (gr. 3-7). 16.99 *(978-0-545-56149-5(3)*, Scholastic Pr.) Scholastic, Inc.

—The Exile of Gigi Lane. (ENG.). (YA). (gr. 7). 2011. 368p. pap. 8.99 *(978-1-4424-2121-9(5))* 2010. 352p. 16.99 *(978-1-4169-2433-3(7))* McElderry, Margaret K. Bks. (McElderry, Margaret K. Bks.).

—Sight. 2008. (ENG.). 272p. (YA). (gr. 7). pap. 8.99 *(978-1-4169-0658-2(4)*, McElderry, Margaret K. Bks.) McElderry, Margaret K. Bks.

Vulliamy, Clara. Bear with Sticky Paws Goes to School. Vulliamy, Clara, illus. 2010. (ENG., Illus.). 32p. pap. 7.95 *(978-1-58925-424-4(4))* Tiger Tales.

Wagman, Diana. Extraordinary October. 2016. (ENG.). 264p. (YA). (gr. 6). 18.95 *(978-1-63246-036-3(X))* Ig Publishing, Inc.

Wagstaff, Janiel. Stella Writes an Opinion. 2015. (ENG.). (J). (gr. -1-3). pap. 7.95 *(978-1-63133-022-3(5))* Staff Development for Educators.

Walde, Christine. The Candy Darlings. 2006. (ENG.). 310p. (YA). (gr. 9-12). per. 18.95 *(978-0-618-58969-2(4))* Houghton Mifflin Harcourt Publishing Co.

Walden, Mark. Dreadnought. (H. I. V. E. Ser.: 4). (ENG.). (J). (gr. 3-7). 2012. 320p. pap. 8.99 *(978-1-4424-1368-9(9))* 2011. 304p. 16.99 *(978-1-4424-2186-8(X))* Simon & Schuster Bks. For Young Readers. (Simon & Schuster Bks. For Young Readers).

—Escape Velocity. (H. I. V. E. Ser.: 3). (ENG.). (J). (gr. 3-7). 2012. 368p. pap. 8.99 *(978-1-4424-1367-2(0))* 2011. 352p. 16.99 *(978-1-4424-2185-1(1))* Simon & Schuster Bks. For Young Readers. (Simon & Schuster Bks. For Young Readers).

—H. I. V. E. Higher Institute of Villainous Education. 2007. (H. I. V. E. Ser.: 1). (ENG., Illus.). 320p. (J). (gr. 3-7). 17.99 *(978-1-4169-3571-1(1)*, Simon & Schuster Bks. For Young Readers) Simon & Schuster Bks. For Young Readers.

—The Higher Institute of Villainous Education. 2008. (H. I. V. E. Ser.: 1). (ENG.). 320p. (J). (gr. 3-7). pap. 8.99 *(978-1-4169-3572-8(X)*, Simon & Schuster Bks. For Young Readers) Simon & Schuster Bks. For Young Readers.

—The Overlord Protocol. (H. I. V. E. Ser.: 2). (ENG.). 384p. (J). (gr. 3-7). 2009. pap. 7.99 *(978-1-4169-3574-2(6))* 2008. 18.99 *(978-1-4169-3573-5(8))* Simon & Schuster Bks. For Young Readers. (Simon & Schuster Bks. For Young Readers).

—Rogue. (H. I. V. E. Ser.: 5). (ENG.). (J). (gr. 3-7). 2012. 320p. pap. 8.99 *(978-1-4424-1369-6(7))* 2011. 304p. 16.99 *(978-1-4424-2187-5(8))* Simon & Schuster Bks. For Young Readers. (Simon & Schuster Bks. For Young Readers).

Wales, Sid. Freddie & Mee. Bryant, Kerry, illus. 2013. 28p. pap. *(978-1-78222-097-8(6))* Paragon Publishing, Rothersthorpe.

Walker, Brian F. Black Boy White School. 2012. (ENG.). 256p. (YA). (gr. 9). 17.99 *(978-0-06-191483-6(5)*, HarperTeen) HarperCollins Pubs.

Walker, Kate. I Hate Books! Cox, David, illus. 2007. (ENG.). 88p. (J). (gr. 1-4). 16.95 *(978-0-8126-2745-9(8))* Cricket Bks.

Walker, Kristin. A Match Made in High School. 2010. (ENG.). 288p. (YA). (gr. 7-18). 9.99 *(978-1-59514-257-3(6)*, Razorbill) Penguin Young Readers Group.

Walker, Landry Q. Super Hero School: #3, 1 vol. Jones, Eric, illus. 2013. (Supergirl: Cosmic Adventures in the 8th Grade Ser.). (ENG.). 32p. (gr. 2-3). 22.60 *(978-1-4342-4719-3(8))* Stone Arch Bks.

—Supergirl: Cosmic Adventures in the 8th Grade. Jones, Eric, illus. 2013. (Supergirl: Cosmic Adventures in the 8th Grade Ser.). (ENG.). 32p. (gr. 2-3). lib. bdg. 45.20 *(978-1-4342-8831-8(5))*; lib. bdg. 135.60 *(978-1-4342-8830-1(7))*; lib. bdg. 45.20 *(978-1-4342-4367-6(2))* Stone Arch Bks.

Walker, Landry Q. & Mason, Joey. Evil in a Skirt! #5, 1 vol. Jones, Eric, illus. 2013. (Supergirl: Cosmic Adventures in the 8th Grade Ser.). (ENG.). 32p. (gr. 2-3). 22.60 *(978-1-4342-6045-1(3))* Stone Arch Bks.

Walker, Nan. The Bay School Blogger. Wummer, Amy, illus. 2008. (Social Studies Connects Ser.). 32p. (J). (gr. -1-3). pap. 5.95 *(978-1-57565-258-0(7))* Kane Press, Inc.

—Spork Out of Orbit. Warrick, Jessica, illus. 2016. (How to Be an Earthling (r) Ser.: 1). (ENG.). 64p. (gr. 1-3). 22.65 *(978-1-57565-818-6(6))* Kane Press, Inc.

—Spork Out of Orbit: Spork Respect. Warrick, Jessica, illus. 2016. (How to Be an Earthling (r) Ser.: 1). (ENG.). 64p. (gr. 1-3). 34.65 *(978-1-57565-820-9(8))* Kane Press, Inc.

Walker-Renner, Christa. Santa's Magic. 2009. 20p. pap. 11.00 *(978-1-4389-8206-9(2))* AuthorHouse.

Wall, Laura. Goose Goes to School. Wall, Laura, illus. 2015. (ENG., Illus.). 48p. (J). (gr. -1-3). 12.99 *(978-0-06-232437-5(3))* HarperCollins Pubs.

Wallace, Barbara Brooks. The Perils of Peppermints. 2005. (ENG., Illus.). 272p. (J). (gr. 3-7). pap. 12.99 *(978-0-689-85045-5(X)*, Simon & Schuster/Paula Wiseman Bks.) Simon & Schuster/Paula Wiseman Bks.

Wallace, Jason. Out of Shadows. 2011. (ENG., Illus.). 272p. (J). (gr. 10-18). 17.95 *(978-0-8234-2342-2(5))* Holiday Hse., Inc.

Wallace, Kim. Erik & Isabelle Senior Year at Foresthill High. 2008. (Foresthill High Ser.). 220p. (YA). (gr. 8-12). per. 12.00 *(978-0-9755848-3-5(9))* Foglight Pr.

Wallace, Nancy Elizabeth. The Kindness Quilt, 0 vols. 2006. (ENG., Illus.). 48p. (J). (gr. -1-k). 16.99 *(978-0-7614-5313-0(X)*, 9780761453130, Amazon Children's Publishing) Amazon Publishing.

—Recycle Every Day!, 0 vols. Wallace, Nancy Elizabeth, illus. 2006. (ENG., Illus.). 41p. (J). (gr. -1-3). pap. 9.99 *(978-0-7614-5290-4(7)*, 9780761452904, Amazon Children's Publishing) Amazon Publishing.

Wallace, Nancy K. Movie Mishaps, 1 vol. Chronister, Amanda, illus. 2013. (Abby & the Book Bunch Ser.). (ENG.). 80p. (J). (gr. 2-5). 27.07 *(978-1-61641-914-1(8))* Magic Wagon.

—Out to Lunch, 1 vol. Chronister, Amanda, illus. 2013. (Abby & the Book Bunch Ser.). (ENG.). 80p. (J). (gr. 2-5). 27.07 *(978-1-61641-916-5(4))* Magic Wagon.

—Presumed Missing, 1 vol. Chronister, Amanda, illus. 2013. (Abby & the Book Bunch Ser.). (ENG.). 80p. (J). (gr. 2-5). 27.07 *(978-1-61641-917-2(2))* Magic Wagon.

Wallace, Rich. Pressure Point, 1 vol. Heitz, Tim, illus. 2016. (Game Face Ser.). (ENG.). 112p. (J). (gr. 3-7). 27.07 *(978-1-62402-135-0(2))* Magic Wagon.

—Shots on Goal. 2005. (ENG.). 160p. (YA). (gr. 7-11). per. 5.99 *(978-0-679-88671-6(0)*, Laurel Leaf) Random Hse. Children's Bks.

—Southpaw. 2006. 105p. (J). lib. bdg. 15.38 *(978-1-4242-2166-0(8))* Fitzgerald Bks.

—Southpaw. 6th ed. 2007. (Winning Season Ser.). (ENG.). 128p. (J). (gr. 3-7). 5.99 *(978-0-14-240785-1(2)*, Puffin Books) Penguin Young Readers Group.

—War & Watermelon. 2012. (ENG.). 192p. (J). (gr. 5-18). pap. 6.99 *(978-0-14-242138-3(3)*, Puffin Books) Penguin Young Readers Group.

—Wicked Cruel. 2015. (ENG.). 208p. (J). (gr. 5). pap. 6.99 *(978-0-375-86514-5(4)*, Yearling) Random Hse. Children's Bks.

Wallach, Tommy. We All Looked Up. 2015. (ENG., Illus.). 384p. (YA). (gr. 9). 17.99 *(978-1-4814-1877-5(7)*, Simon & Schuster Bks. For Young Readers) Simon & Schuster Bks. For Young Readers.

Walsh, Jean. Gaffer Samson's Luck. 2003. (J). (gr. 3-18). 20.25 *(978-0-8446-7252-6(1))* Smith, Peter Pub., Inc.

Walters, Eric. Au Pas, Camarade, 1 vol. 2011. (FRE., Illus.). 144p. (J). (gr. 5-9). pap. 9.95 *(978-1-4598-0003-8(6))* Orca Bk. Pubs. USA.

—Ed Spécial, 1 vol. 2011. (FRE.). 144p. (J). (gr. 5-9). pap. 9.95 *(978-1-55469-857-8(X))* Orca Bk. Pubs. USA.

—In a Flash, 1 vol. 2008. (Orca Currents Ser.). (ENG.). 112p. (J). (gr. 5-9). pap. 9.95 *(978-1-55469-034-3(X))* Orca Bk. Pubs. USA.

—Laggan Lard Butts, 1 vol. 2006. (Orca Currents Ser.). (ENG.). (J). (gr. 5-9). per. 9.95 *(978-1-55143-518-3(7))* Orca Bk. Pubs. USA.

—Special Edward, 1 vol. 2009. (Orca Currents Ser.). (ENG.). (J). (gr. 5-9). 112p. 16.95 *(978-1-55469-096-1(X))*; 136p. pap. 9.95 *(978-1-55469-092-3(7))* Orca Bk. Pubs. USA.

Waltman, Kevin. Next. 2013. (D-Bow High School Hoops Ser.). (ENG.). 216p. (J). 16.95 *(978-1-935955-64-1(0))*; pap. 11.95 *(978-1-935955-65-8(9))* Cinco Puntos Pr.

—Quicks. 2016. (D-Bow High School Hoops Ser.). (ENG.). 216p. (J). (gr. 6). 16.95 *(978-1-941026-61-8(3))* Cinco Puntos Pr.

—Slump. 2014. (D-Bow High School Hoops Ser.). (ENG.). 216p. (J). 16.95 *(978-1-941026-00-7(1))* Cinco Puntos Pr.

Walton, Evangeline. The Misadventures of Rufus & Misha: Two Dogs Who Are Smart Enough to Go to School. 2013. 24p. pap. 14.93 *(978-1-4669-9970-1(5))* Trafford Publishing.

Walton, K. M. Cracked. 2012. (ENG.). (YA). (gr. 9). 336p. pap. 11.99 *(978-1-4424-2917-8(8))*; 320p. 16.99 *(978-1-4424-2916-1(X))* Simon Pulse. (Simon Pulse).

—Empty. 2013. (ENG., (YA). (gr. 9). Illus.). 272p. pap. 10.99 *(978-1-4424-5358-6(3))*; 256p. 16.99 *(978-1-4424-5359-3(1))* Simon Pulse. (Simon Pulse).

Walton, Rick. Mr. President Goes to School, 1 vol. Sneed, Brad, illus. (ENG.). 32p. (J). (gr. -1-3). 2015. pap. 7.95 *(978-1-56145-892-9(9))* 2010. 15.95 *(978-1-56145-538-6(5))* Peachtree Pubs.

Walvoord, Linda & Walvoord. Rosetta, Rosetta, Sit by Me!, 0 vols. Velasquez, Eric, illus. 2004. (ENG.). 80p. (J). (gr. 3-6). 14.95 *(978-0-7614-5171-6(4)*, 9780761451716, Amazon Children's Publishing) Amazon Publishing.

Wamsley, Jody. What Am I Gonna Do? Turchan, Monique, illus. 2013. 24p. pap. 11.95 *(978-1-61244-070-5(3))* Halo Publishing International.

Wang, Corrie. The Takedown. 2017. (ENG.). 384p. (YA). (gr. 9-17). 17.99 *(978-1-4847-5742-0(4))* Disney Publishing Worldwide.

Ward, Dan. Meet the Boomer Sisters. 2006. 131p. pap. 13.95 *(978-1-4116-6927-7(4))* Lulu Pr., Inc.

Warden, Andrew J. Grecko the Gecko Starts School. 2010. 24p. 17.93 *(978-1-4269-0375-5(8))* Trafford Publishing.

Wardlaw, Lee. 101 Ways to Bug Your Friends & Enemies. 2011. (ENG.). 288p. (J). (gr. 5-18). 6.99 *(978-0-14-241949-6(4)*, Puffin Books) Penguin Young Readers Group.

—101 Ways to Bug Your Teacher. 2005. (ENG.). 256p. (J). (gr. 3-7). pap. 6.99 *(978-0-14-240331-0(8)*, Puffin Books) Penguin Young Readers Group.

Warner, Gertrude Chandler, creator. Hidden in the Haunted School. 2016. (Boxcar Children Mysteries Ser.: 144). (ENG.). 128p. (J). (gr. 1-5). 15.99 *(978-0-8075-0718-6(0))* Whitman, Albert & Co.

Warner, Sally. The Dragon Slayer! Biggs, Brian, illus. 2013. (EllRay Jakes Ser.: 4). (ENG.). 144p. (J). (gr. 1-3). 14.99 *(978-0-670-78497-4(4)*, Viking Books for Young Readers) Penguin Young Readers Group.

—EllRay Jakes Is a Rock Star, 2 vols. Harper, Jamie, illus. 2012. (EllRay Jakes Ser.: 2). (ENG.). 128p. (J). (gr. 1-3). 5.99 *(978-0-14-241989-2(3)*, Puffin Books) Penguin Young Readers Group.

—Ellray Jakes Is a Rock Star! 2012. (EllRay Jakes Ser.: 2). lib. bdg. 16.00 *(978-0-606-23633-1(3)*, Turtleback) Turtleback Bks.

—EllRay Jakes Is Magic. Biggs, Brian, illus. 2014. (EllRay Jakes Ser.: 6). (ENG.). (J). (gr. 1-3). 160p. 14.99 *(978-0-670-78500-1(8)*, Viking Books for Young Readers); 176p. pap. 5.99 *(978-0-14-242360-8(2)*, Puffin Books) Penguin Young Readers Group.

—Ellray Jakes Is Magic. 2014. (EllRay Jakes Ser.: 6). lib. bdg. 16.00 *(978-0-606-34215-5(X)*, Turtleback) Turtleback Bks.
—EllRay Jakes Is Not a Chicken, 1 vol. Harper, Jamie, illus. 2012. (EllRay Jakes Ser.: 1). (ENG.). 128p. (J). (gr. 1-3). 5.99 *(978-0-14-241988-5(5)*, Puffin Books) Penguin Young Readers Group.
—EllRay Jakes Is Not a Chicken! 2012. (EllRay Jakes Ser.: 1). lib. bdg. 16.00 *(978-0-606-23632-4(5)*, Turtleback) Turtleback Bks.
—Ellray Jakes Rocks the Holidays! 2014. (EllRay Jakes Ser.: 7). lib. bdg. 16.00 *(978-0-606-36188-0(X))* Turtleback Bks.
—EllRay Jakes Stands Tall. Biggs, Brian, illus. 2016. (EllRay Jakes Ser.). (ENG.). (J). (gr. 1-3). 176p. 5.99 *(978-0-14-751253-6(0)*, Puffin Books); 160p. 14.99 *(978-0-451-46913-7(5)*, Viking Books for Young Readers) Penguin Young Readers Group.
—EllRay Jakes the Dragon Slayer. 2013. (EllRay Jakes Ser.: 4). lib. bdg. 16.00 *(978-0-606-32136-5(5)*, Turtleback) Turtleback Bks.
—Ellray Jakes the Dragon Slayer, No. 4. Biggs, Brian, illus. 2013. (EllRay Jakes Ser.: 4). (ENG.). 144p. (J). (gr. 1-3). pap. 5.99 *(978-0-14-242358-5(0)*, Puffin Books) Penguin Young Readers Group.
—EllRay Jakes the Recess King! Biggs, Brian, illus. 2015. (EllRay Jakes Ser.: 8). (ENG.). 176p. (J). (gr. 1-3). 5.99 *(978-0-14-751252-9(2)*, Puffin Books); 14.99 *(978-0-451-46911-3(9)*, Viking Books for Young Readers) Penguin Young Readers Group.
—EllRay Jakes Walks the Plank! 2013. (EllRay Jakes Ser.: 3). lib. bdg. 16.00 *(978-0-606-30188-6(7)*, Turtleback) Turtleback Bks.
—Excellent Emma. Harper, Jamie, illus. 2010. (Emma Ser.). (ENG.). 144p. (J). (gr. 3-7). 6.99 *(978-0-14-241569-6(3)*, Puffin Books) Penguin Young Readers Group.
—Rocks the Holidays! Biggs, Brian, illus. 2014. (EllRay Jakes Ser.: 7). (ENG.). 160p. (J). (gr. 1-3). 14.99 *(978-0-451-46909-0(7)*, Viking Books for Young Readers) Penguin Young Readers Group.
—Super Emma. Harper, Jamie, illus. 2008. (Emma Ser.). (ENG.). 112p. (J). (gr. 3-7). 5.99 *(978-0-14-241088-2(8)*, Puffin Books) Penguin Young Readers Group.
—Walks the Plank! Harper, Jamie, illus. (EllRay Jakes Ser.: 3). (ENG.). 128p. (J). (gr. 1-3). 2013. pap. 5.99 *(978-0-14-242409-4(9)*, Puffin Books) 2012. 14.99 *(978-0-670-06306-2(1)*, Viking Books for Young Readers) Penguin Young Readers Group.
Warner, Sally & Harper, Jamie. Excellent Emma. Harper, Jamie, illus. 2009. (Emma Ser.). (ENG., Illus.). 144p. (J). (gr. 3-7). 14.99 *(978-0-670-06310-9(X)*, Viking Books for Young Readers) Penguin Young Readers Group.
Washington, Kathleen. The School Bully. 2006. 9.00 *(978-0-8059-8201-5(9))* Dorrance Publishing Co., Inc.
Wasserman, Robin. Life, Starring Me! 2009. (Candy Apple Ser.). 182p. (J). *(978-0-545-19777-9(5))* Scholastic, Inc.
—Lust. 2005. (Seven Deadly Sins Ser.: 1). (ENG.). 256p. (YA). (gr. 9-12). pap. 9.99 *(978-0-689-87782-7(X)*, Simon Pulse) Simon Pulse.
—Pride. 2006. (Seven Deadly Sins Ser.: 3). (ENG.). 256p. (YA). (gr. 9-12). pap. 8.99 *(978-0-689-87784-1(6)*, Simon Pulse) Simon Pulse.
—Pride - Wrath Vol. 2. 2013. (Seven Deadly Sins Ser.: 2). (ENG., Illus.). 592p. (YA). (gr. 9). pap. 9.99 *(978-1-4424-7506-9(4)*, Simon Pulse) Simon Pulse.
—Seven Deadly Sins Vol. 3: Sloth; Gluttony; Greed. 2013. (ENG., Illus.). 880p. (YA). (gr. 9). pap. 10.99 *(978-1-4424-7508-3(0)*, Simon Pulse) Simon Pulse.
—Sloth. 2006. (Seven Deadly Sins Ser.: 5). (ENG.). 256p. (YA). (gr. 9). pap. 9.99 *(978-1-4169-0718-3(1)*, Simon Pulse) Simon Pulse.
—Wrath. 2006. (Seven Deadly Sins Ser.: 4). (ENG., Illus.). 256p. (YA). (gr. 9-12). pap. 9.99 *(978-0-689-87785-8(4)*, Simon Pulse) Simon Pulse.
Wassner, Gary. The Mystery of the Jubilee Emerald. 2006. (J). pap. *(978-1-59336-712-1(0))* Mondo Publishing.
Watase, Yuu. Absolute Boyfriend, Vol. 3, 6 vols. 2007. (ENG., Illus.). 200p. pap. 9.99 *(978-1-4215-1003-3(0))* Viz Media.
Waters, Cassie. Dive In! 2012. (Pool Girls Ser.: 1). (ENG.). 160p. (J). (gr. 3-7). 15.99 *(978-1-4424-5375-3(3))*; pap. 5.99 *(978-1-4424-4144-6(5))* Simon Spotlight. (Simon Spotlight).
Waters, Daniel. Break My Heart 1,000 Times. 2013. (ENG., Illus.). 352p. (YA). (gr. 7-17). pap. 9.99 *(978-1-4231-2228-9(3))* Hyperion Pr.
Watkins, Steve. Down Sand Mountain. (ENG., Illus.). 336p. (YA). (gr. 7). 2011. pap. 7.99 *(978-0-7636-4835-0(3))* 2008. 16.99 *(978-0-7636-3839-9(0))* Candlewick Pr.
Watson, Cristy. Living Rough, 1 vol. 2011. (Orca Currents Ser.). (ENG.). 128p. (J). (gr. 5-9). 9.95 *(978-1-55469-434-1(5))*; lib. bdg. 16.95 *(978-1-55469-888-2(X))* Orca Bk. Pubs. USA.
Watson, Paul. The Robot. 2011. (ENG.). 272p. (YA). (gr. 7). E-Book *(978-1-101-54326-9(4)*, Razorbill) Penguin Young Readers Group.
Watson, Renée. Piecing Me Together. 2017. (ENG.). 272p. (YA). 17.99 *(978-1-68119-105-8(9)*, 9781681191058, Bloomsbury USA Childrens) Bloomsbury Publishing USA.
Watson, Stephanie. The Club. 2010. (Night Fall Ser.). (ENG.). 112p. (YA). (gr. 6-12). pap. 7.95 *(978-0-7613-6162-6(6))* Lerner Publishing Group.
Watson, Stephanie Elaine. Elvis & Olive: Super Detectives. 2010. (ENG.). 288p. (J). (gr. 3-7). 15.99 *(978-0-545-15148-1(1)*, Scholastic Pr.) Scholastic, Inc.
Watts, Jeri. Kizzy Ann Stamps. (ENG., Illus.). 192p. (J). (gr. 4-7). 2013. pap. 5.99 *(978-0-7636-6976-8(8))* 2012. 15.99 *(978-0-7636-5895-3(2))* Candlewick Pr.
Watts, Leander. Beautiful City of the Dead. 2007. (ENG.). 256p. (YA). (gr. 7-12). pap. 14.99 *(978-0-618-59499-3(X))* Houghton Mifflin Harcourt Publishing Co.
Waudby, Jeannie. One of Us. 2015. (ENG.). 320p. (YA). (gr. 7). 16.95 *(978-0-7624-5799-1(6)*, Running Pr. Kids) Running Pr. Bk. Pubs.
Waxman, Rachel. The Crickhowell School for the Muses. 2013. (ENG.). 228p. (YA). pap. 14.95 *(978-1-56474-541-5(4)*, Fithian Pr) Daniel & Daniel, Pubs., Inc.
We Hold These Truths. 2014. (Benjamin Pratt & the Keepers of the School Ser.: 5). (ENG., Illus.). 288p. (J). (gr. 2-5). pap. 7.99 *(978-1-4169-3911-5(3)*, Atheneum Bks. for Young Readers) Simon & Schuster Children's Publishing.
Weatherly, L. A. Them. 2013. (ENG.). 80p. (YA). (gr. 6-12). pap. 6.95 *(978-1-78112-185-6(0))*; lib. bdg. 22.60 *(978-1-78112-184-9(2))* Lerner Publishing Group.
Weaver, Will. Clay. 2004. 232p. (YA). (gr. 8-12). 14.65 *(978-0-7569-4594-7(1))* Perfection Learning Corp.
Webb, Dave. Barkley Rules. 2011. 148p. pap. 9.99 *(978-1-4575-0607-9(6))* Dog Ear Publishing, LLC.
Webb, Derek & Webb, Arthur. Is. 2011. (ENG., Illus.). 182p. (J). (gr. 7). pap. 11.95 *(978-1-906998-11-0(6))* Parthian Bks. GBR. Dist: Independent Pubs. Group.
Webb, Mack H., Jr. Danny & the Detention Demons. Espinola, Nicole & Nealon, Eve, illus. l.t. ed. 2007. 52p. (J). per. 15.95 *(978-0-9779576-2-0(4))* Pilinut Pr., Inc.
Weber, Penny, illus. On My Way to School. 2009. (J). pap. 13.95 *(978-0-9842146-0-0(7))* Concinnity Initiatives.
Webster, Frank V. The Boys of Bellwood School. 2004. reprint ed. pap. 20.95 *(978-1-4191-5509-3(1))*; pap. 1.99 *(978-1-4192-5509-0(6))* Kessinger Publishing, LLC.
Weeks, Sarah. Cheese: A Combo of Oggie Cooder & Oggie Cooder, Party Animal. 2016. (ENG.). 352p. (J). (gr. 2-5). pap. 8.99 *(978-0-545-93957-7(7))* Scholastic, Inc.
—Oggie Cooder. 2009. (Oggie Cooder Ser.: Vol. 1). (ENG.). 176p. (J). (gr. 2-5). 5.99 *(978-0-439-92794-9(3)*, Scholastic Paperbacks) Scholastic, Inc.
—Oggie Cooder - Party Animal! 2011. (Oggie Cooder Ser.). (ENG.). 176p. (J). (gr. 2-5). pap. 6.99 *(978-0-439-92796-3(X)*, Scholastic Paperbacks) Scholastic, Inc.
Weeks, Sarah & Varadarajan, Gita. Save Me a Seat. 2016. (ENG.). 240p. (J). (gr. 3-7). 16.99 *(978-0-545-84660-8(9)*, Scholastic Pr.) Scholastic, Inc.
Weil, Zoe. Claude & Medea: The Hellburn Dogs. 2007. (ENG., Illus.). 103p. (J). (gr. 2-7). per. 12.00 *(978-1-59056-105-8(8))* Lantern Bks.
Weingarten, Lynn. The Secret Sisterhood of Heartbreakers. (ENG.). (YA). (gr. 8). 2013. 368p. pap. 9.99 *(978-0-06-192619-8(1))* 2011. 352p. 17.99 *(978-0-06-192618-1(3))* HarperCollins Pubs. (HarperTeen).
Weissman, Elissa Brent. Standing for Socks. Sonkin, Jessica, illus. (ENG.). 224p. (J). (gr. 3-7). 2010. pap. 6.99 *(978-1-4169-9777-1(6))* 2009. 15.99 *(978-1-4169-4801-8(5))* Simon & Schuster Children's Publishing. (Atheneum Bks. for Young Readers).
Welch, Ginger. The Dream Reader. 2012. 76p. 19.95 *(978-1-4626-7276-9(0))*; pap. 19.95 *(978-1-4626-8291-1(X))* America Star Bks.
Welch, Willy. Grumbly Bunnies. Lyon, Tammie Speer, illus. 2004. 32p. (J). 15.95 *(978-1-58089-086-1(5))* Charlesbridge Publishing, Inc.
Wellings, Chris R. How Sparkles Came About: The Adventures of Sparkles. Nunnally, Carson, illus. 2011. 32p. pap. 24.95 *(978-1-4560-4119-9(3))* America Star Bks.
Wells, Carolyn. Patty at Home. 2011. 182p. 26.95 *(978-1-4638-9971-4(8))* Rodgers, Alan Bks.
Wells, Robison. Variant. (Variant Ser.: 1). (ENG.). (YA). (gr. 8). 2012. 400p. pap. 9.99 *(978-0-06-202609-5(7))* 2011. 384p. 17.99 *(978-0-06-202608-8(9))* HarperCollins Pubs. (HarperTeen).
Wells, Rosemary. Eduardo: El Primer Dia de Colegio. 2003. Orig. Title: Edward's First Day at School. (SPA., Illus.). 22p. (J). (gr. -1-k). 12.95 *(978-1-56014-620-9(6))* Santillana USA Publishing Co., Inc.
—Emily's First 100 Days of School. Wells, Rosemary, illus. 2005. (ENG., Illus.). 64p. (J). (gr. -1-1). pap. 9.99 *(978-0-7868-1354-4(7))* Hyperion Pr.
—Emily's First 100 Days of School. 2006. (Illus.). (J). (gr. -1-4). 18.95 *(978-0-439-84903-6(9)*, WPCD654) Weston Woods Studios, Inc.
—Hands Off, Harry! Wells, Rosemary, illus. 2011. (ENG., Illus.). 40p. (J). (gr. -1-1). 14.99 *(978-0-06-192112-4(2)*, Tegen, Katherine Bks) HarperCollins Pubs.
—Otto Runs for President. Wells, Rosemary, illus. 2011. (Illus.). (J). (gr. -1-4). 29.95 *(978-0-545-10690-0(7))* Weston Woods Studios, Inc.
—Yoko. Wells, Rosemary, illus. 2009. (ENG., Illus.). 32p. (J). (gr. -1-1). pap. 6.99 *(978-1-4231-1983-8(5))* Hyperion Pr.
Wells, Rosemary & Rosemary, Wells. Yoko. Varela, Sandra Lopez, tr. Wells, Rosemary, illus. 2003. (SPA., Illus.). 34p. (J). (gr. k-2). pap. 8.50 *(978-84-241-8034-8(8))* Everest Editora ESP. Dist: Lectorum Pubns., Inc.
Wells, Tina. Mackenzie Blue. 2013. (Mackenzie Blue Ser.: 1). (ENG.). 224p. (J). (gr. 3-7). pap. 6.99 *(978-0-06-158310-0(3))* HarperCollins Pubs.
—Mackenzie Blue. Segawa, Michael, illus. 2009. (Mackenzie Blue Ser.: 1). (ENG.). 224p. (J). (gr. 3-7). 12.99 *(978-0-06-158308-7(1))* HarperCollins Pubs.
—Mackenzie Blue Vol. 5: Double Trouble. Segawa, Michael, illus. 2014. (Mackenzie Blue Ser.: 5). (ENG.). 224p. (J). (gr. 3-7). pap. 6.99 *(978-0-06-224412-3(4))* HarperCollins Pubs.
—Mixed Messages. (Mackenzie Blue Ser.: 4). (ENG.). (J). (gr. 3-7). 2013. 224p. pap. 6.99 *(978-0-06-158319-3(7))* 2010. 208p. 12.99 *(978-0-06-158317-9(0))* HarperCollins Pubs.
—The Secret Crush. 2013. (Mackenzie Blue Ser.: 2). (ENG.). 240p. (J). (gr. 3-7). pap. 6.99 *(978-0-06-158313-1(8))* HarperCollins Pubs.
—The Secret Crush. Segawa, Michael, illus. 2009. (Mackenzie Blue Ser.: 2). (ENG.). 240p. (J). (gr. 3-7). 10.99 *(978-0-06-158311-7(1))* HarperCollins Pubs.
Wells, Tom. Strange Seasons: Summer. 2008. 212p. 24.95 *(978-0-595-50888-4(X))*; pap. 14.95 *(978-0-595-52016-9(2))* iUniverse, Inc.
Welton, Jude. Adam's Alternative Sports Day: An Asperger Story. 2004. (ENG., Illus.). 112p. (J). pap. 20.95 *(978-1-84310-300-4(1)*, 5356) Kingsley, Jessica Pubs. GBR. Dist: Macmillan Distribution Ltd.
Wenberg, Michael. Stringz. 2010. 216p. (YA). (gr. 6-10). 16.95 *(978-1-934813-33-1(8))* Westside Bks.
Wenger, Brahm. Dewey Doo-It at the Jingle Jangle Jamboree: A Musical Storybook Inspired by Arnold Schwarzenegger to Benefit Inner-City Games. 2006. (ENG.). 32p. (J). (gr. -1-3). 18.95 *(978-0-9745143-4-5(9))* RandallFraser Publishing.
Wertheim, L. Jon & Moskowitz, Tobias J. The Rookie Bookie. (ENG., Illus.). 272p. (J). (gr. 3-7). 2015. pap. 7.00 *(978-0-316-24979-9(3))* 2014. 17.00 *(978-0-316-24981-2(5))* Little, Brown Bks. for Young Readers.
West, Kasie. P. S. I Like You. 2016. (ENG.). 336p. (YA). (gr. 7). 17.99 *(978-0-545-85097-1(5))* Scholastic, Inc.
—Pivot Point. 2013. (Pivot Point Ser.: Bk. 1). (ENG.). 352p. (YA). (gr. 8). 17.99 *(978-0-06-211737-3(8)*, HarperTeen) HarperCollins Pubs.
—Split Second. 2015. (Pivot Point Ser.: Bk. 2). (ENG.). 384p. (YA). (gr. 8). pap. 9.99 *(978-0-06-211739-7(4)*, HarperTeen) HarperCollins Pubs.
Westem, Colleen. Why Elephants Don't Ride School Buses. 2011. 16p. (gr. 1-2). pap. 10.67 *(978-1-4269-6865-5(5))* Trafford Publishing.
Westlund, Emmaline. Fatim. 2012. 42p. pap. 16.95 *(978-1-4626-9660-4(0))* America Star Bks.
Weston Woods Staff, creator. Crazy Hair Day. 2011. 18.95 *(978-0-545-15156-6(2))* Weston Woods Studios, Inc.
—Emily's First 100 Days of School. 2011. 38.75 *(978-0-439-84892-3(X))* Weston Woods Studios, Inc.
—The Gym Teacher from the Black Lagoon. 2011. 38.75 *(978-0-545-19711-3(2))* Weston Woods Studios, Inc.
—How Do Dinosaurs Go to School? 2011. 38.75 *(978-0-545-19712-0(0))* Weston Woods Studios, Inc.
—Miss Nelson Is Missing. 2011. 18.95 *(978-0-439-72847-8(9))*; 29.95 *(978-0-439-73499-8(1))*; 38.75 *(978-0-439-72853-9(3))* Weston Woods Studios, Inc.
—Otto Runs for President. 2011. 18.95 *(978-0-545-31400-8(3))*; 38.75 *(978-0-545-31401-5(1))* Weston Woods Studios, Inc.
—Ready, Freddy! #1: Tooth Trouble. 2011. 20.95 *(978-0-545-05008-1(1))* Weston Woods Studios, Inc.
—Ready, Freddy! #3: Homework Hassles. 2011. 20.95 *(978-0-545-05007-4(3))* Weston Woods Studios, Inc.
—Ready, Freddy! #4: Don't Sit on My Lunch! 2011. 20.95 *(978-0-545-05006-7(5))* Weston Woods Studios, Inc.
—Will I Have a Friend? 2011. 38.75 *(978-0-439-72970-3(X))* Weston Woods Studios, Inc.
Weyn, Suzanne. The Bar Code Tattoo. 2012. (ENG.). 256p. (J). (gr. 7). pap. 9.99 *(978-0-545-47054-4(4)*, Scholastic Paperbacks) Scholastic, Inc.
—Beaten. (Surviving Southside Ser.). (ENG.). 104p. (YA). (gr. 6-12). 2015. 34.65 *(978-1-4677-6007-2(2)*, Lerner Digital) 2011. pap. 7.95 *(978-0-7613-6164-0(2))* 2011. lib. bdg. 27.93 *(978-0-7613-6150-3(2))* Lerner Publishing Group.
—Full Impact. 2013. (Surviving Southside Ser.). (ENG.). 104p. (YA). (gr. 6-12). pap. 7.95 *(978-1-4677-0705-3(8))*; lib. bdg. 27.93 *(978-1-4677-0311-6(7))* Lerner Publishing Group.
—Recruited. 2011. (Surviving Southside Ser.). (ENG.). 104p. (YA). (gr. 6-12). pap. 7.95 *(978-0-7613-6167-1(7))*; lib. bdg. 27.93 *(978-0-7613-6153-4(7))* Lerner Publishing Group.
Whamond, Dave. Oddrey. 2012. 32p. *(978-1-926973-52-4(6))* Owlkids Bks. Inc.
Whamond, Dave & Owlkids Books Inc. Staff. Oddrey & the New Kid. 2013. (Oddrey Ser.: 2). (ENG., Illus.). 32p. (J). (gr. -1-3). 16.95 *(978-1-926973-90-6(9)*, Owlkids) Owlkids Bks. Inc. CAN. Dist: Publishers Group West (PGW).
Wheeler, Lisa. New Pig in Town. Ansley, Frank, illus. 2003. (Fitch & Chip Ser.: 1). (ENG.). 48p. (J). (gr. 1-3). 16.99 *(978-0-689-84950-3(8)*, Atheneum/Richard Jackson Bks.) Simon & Schuster Children's Publishing.
—When Pigs Fly. Ansley, Frank, illus. 2005. 48p. (J). lib. bdg. 15.00 *(978-1-59054-996-4(1))* Fitzgerald Bks.
—When Pigs Fly. Ansley, Frank, illus. 2005. (Fitch & Chip Ser.). 48p. (gr. 1-3). 14.00 *(978-0-7569-5472-7(X))* Perfection Learning Corp.
—When Pigs Fly. Ansley, Frank, illus. 2003. (Fitch & Chip Ser.: 2). (ENG.). 48p. (J). (gr. 1-3). 16.99 *(978-0-689-84951-0(6)*, Atheneum/Richard Jackson Bks.) Simon & Schuster Children's Publishing.
Whipple, Natalie. Transparent. 2013. (ENG.). 368p. (YA). (gr. 8). pap. 9.99 *(978-0-06-212016-8(6)*, HarperTeen) HarperCollins Pubs.
Whitaker, Alecia. The Queen of Kentucky. 2013. (ENG.). 384p. (YA). (gr. 7-17). pap. 8.99 *(978-0-316-12494-2(X)*, Poppy) Little, Brown Bks. for Young Readers.
Whitaker, Nathan. Snap Decision, 1 vol. 2015. (Game Face Ser.). (ENG.). 272p. (J). pap. 8.99 *(978-0-310-73703-2(6))* Zonderkidz.
White, Amy Brecount. Forget-Her-Nots. 2010. (ENG.). 384p. (YA). (gr. 8-18). 16.99 *(978-0-06-167298-9(X)*, Greenwillow Bks.) HarperCollins Pubs.
White, Andrea. Window Boy. 2008. (ENG.). 256p. (J). (gr. 4-7). 17.95 *(978-1-933979-14-4(3)*, 9781933979144) Bright Sky Pr.
—Windows on the World. 2011. 238p. (J). 18.95 *(978-1-60898-105-2(3))*; pap. 9.95 *(978-1-60898-106-9(1))* namelos llc.
White, Dorine. The Emerald Ring (Cleopatra's Legacy) 2013. 183p. (YA). pap. 13.99 *(978-1-4621-1133-6(5)*, Horizon Pubs.) Cedar Fort, Inc./CFI Distribution.
White, Kiersten. Illusions of Fate. 2014. (ENG.). 288p. (YA). (gr. 8). 17.99 *(978-0-06-213589-6(9)*, HarperTeen) HarperCollins Pubs.
White, Michelle A. Anthony with an A. 2011. 16p. pap. 9.50 *(978-1-4634-1641-6(5))* AuthorHouse.
White, Russ. Cat Got Your Tongue? A Book of Idioms. Cornelison, Reuel, illus. l.t. ed. 2004. 44p. (J). per. *(978-0-9742885-0-5(0)*, 00) White, Russ.
White, Toni. Ridge Street Prom. 2008. 182p. pap. 12.96 *(978-1-4357-1966-8(2))* Lulu Pr., Inc.
Whitesides, Tyler. Curse of the Broomstaff. 2013. (Janitors Ser.: 3). (ENG., Illus.). 384p. (J). (gr. 5). 18.99 *(978-1-60907-605-4(2)*, Shadow Mountain) Shadow Mountain Publishing.
—Heroes of the Dustbin. 2015. (Janitors Ser.: Bk. 5). (Illus.). vii, 408p. (J). 18.99 *(978-1-62972-065-4(8)*, Shadow Mountain) Deseret Bk. Co.
—Janitors. 2011. (Janitors Ser.: Bk. 1). pap. 34.99 *(978-1-60908-075-4(0))*; (J). 17.99 *(978-1-60908-056-3(4))* Deseret Bk. Co.
—Janitors. 2012. (Janitors Ser.: 1). (ENG., Illus.). 320p. (J). (gr. 5). pap. 7.99 *(978-1-60907-065-6(8)*, Shadow Mountain) Shadow Mountain Publishing.
—Secrets of New Forest Academy. 2013. (Janitors Ser.: 2). (ENG., Illus.). 368p. (J). (gr. 5). pap. 8.99 *(978-1-60907-546-0(3)*, Shadow Mountain) Shadow Mountain Publishing.
—Strike of the Sweepers. 2014. (Janitors Ser.: 4). (ENG., Illus.). 400p. (J). (gr. 5). 18.99 *(978-1-60907-907-9(8)*, Shadow Mountain) Shadow Mountain Publishing.
Whitmore, Hugh. The Three Madelines. Wilson, Raylene Jenee & Gibbons, Deanna, illus. 2012. 124p. pap. 15.95 *(978-0-9848314-4-9(4))* Sincerity Publishing.
Whittemore, Jo. Brooke's Not-So-Perfect Plan. 2016. (Confidentially Yours Ser.: 1). (Illus.). 320p. (J). (gr. 3-7). pap. 6.99 *(978-0-06-235893-6(6))* HarperCollins Pubs.
—Confidentially Yours #3: Heather's Crush Catastrophe. 2016. (Confidentially Yours Ser.: 3). 288p. (J). (gr. 3-7). 6.99 ***(978-0-06-235897-4(9))*** HarperCollins Pubs.
—D Is for Drama. 2012. (Mix Ser.). (ENG.). 272p. (J). (gr. 4-8). pap. 6.99 *(978-1-4424-4152-1(6)*, Aladdin) Simon & Schuster Children's Publishing.
—Front Page Face-Off. 2010. (ENG.). 240p. (J). (gr. 4-8). pap. 5.99 *(978-1-4169-9169-4(7)*, Aladdin) Simon & Schuster Children's Publishing.
—Odd Girl In. 2011. (Mix Ser.). (ENG.). 240p. (J). (gr. 4-8). pap. 6.99 *(978-1-4424-1284-2(4)*, Aladdin) Simon & Schuster Children's Publishing.
Whitten, A. J. The Cellar. 2011. (ENG.). 288p. (YA). (gr. 7-18). pap. 16.99 *(978-0-547-23253-9(5))* Houghton Mifflin Harcourt Publishing Co.
—The Well. 2009. (ENG., Illus.). 336p. (YA). (gr. 7-18). pap. 18.95 *(978-0-547-23229-4(2))* Houghton Mifflin Harcourt Publishing Co.
Who Will Look Out for Danny? Individual Title Six-Packs. (Action Packs Ser.). 120p. (gr. 3-5). 44.00 *(978-0-7635-8420-7(7))* Rigby Education.
Whybrow, Ian. Harry & the Dinosaurs Go to School. Reynolds, Adrian, illus. 2015. (ENG.). 32p. (J). (gr. -1-2). 7.99 *(978-0-553-53400-9(9)*, Dragonfly Bks.) Random Hse. Children's Bks.
—Little Wolf's Book of Badness. Ross, Tony, illus. 2005. (Middle Grade Fiction Ser.). 132p. (gr. 3-6). 14.95 *(978-1-57505-410-0(8))* Lerner Publishing Group.
—Little Wolf's Haunted Hall for Small Horrors. Ross, Tony, illus. (Middle Grade Fiction Ser.). (J). 2005. 132p. (gr. 3-6). 14.95 *(978-1-57505-412-4(4))* 2004. 125p. (gr. 4-7). per. 6.95 *(978-1-57505-794-1(8))* Lerner Publishing Group.
Whytock, Cherry. My Cup Runneth Over: The Life of Angelica Cookson Potts. Whytock, Cherry, illus. 2012. (ENG., Illus.). 192p. (YA). (gr. 7). pap. 9.99 *(978-1-4424-6055-3(5)*, Simon Pulse) Simon Pulse.
Wicke, Ed. Bullies. 2nd rev. ed. 2003. 212p. (J). per. 9.99 *(978-0-9677652-2-8(6)*, BlacknBlue Pr. UK) Blacknblue Pr.
Wientge, Kristi. Karma Khullar's Mustache. 2017. (ENG., Illus.). 272p. (J). (gr. 3-7). 16.99 ***(978-1-4814-7770-3(6)***, Simon & Schuster Bks. For Young Readers) Simon & Schuster Bks. For Young Readers.
—Karma Khullar's Mustache. 2017. (J). pap. ***(978-1-4814-7771-0(4)***, Simon & Schuster Bks. For Young Readers) Simon & Schuster Bks. For Young Readers.
Wiggins, Rosie. Adventures at a Ray of Hope Preschool. 2007. 32p. per. 12.95 *(978-1-4327-1657-8(3))* Outskirts Pr., Inc.
Wiggins, Thalia. Greg & the Cheat Sheets, 1 vol. Tate, Don, illus. 2012. (Making Choices: the Mcnair Cousins Ser.). (ENG.). 64p. 27.07 *(978-1-61641-630-0(0)*, Calico Chapter Bks) Magic Wagon.
—James Cheats!, 1 vol. Tate, Don, illus. 2012. (Making Choices: the Mcnair Cousins Ser.). (ENG.). 64p. 27.07 *(978-1-61641-633-1(5)*, Calico Chapter Bks) Magic Wagon.
Wight, Eric. Frankie Pickle & the Mathematical Menace. Wight, Eric, illus. 2011. (Frankie Pickle Ser.). (ENG., Illus.). 96p. (J). (gr. 2-5). 9.99 *(978-1-4169-8972-1(2)*, Simon & Schuster Bks. For Young Readers) Simon & Schuster Bks. For Young Readers.
Wilcut-Bledsoe, Robin. The Imagination of Hollie Mason. 2008. 88p. pap. 19.95 *(978-1-60703-804-7(8))* America Star Bks.
Wilde, Jerry. Peace in the Halls: Stories & Activities to Manage Anger & Prevent School Violence. 2003. 112p. (YA). (gr. 4-12). pap. 9.95 *(978-0-9657610-4-8(5))* LGR Publishing, Inc.
Wiley, Gordon. Journey Finds Family. 2009. 68p. pap. 10.49 *(978-1-4389-5265-9(1))* AuthorHouse.
Wilhelm, Doug. The Revealers. 2011. (ENG.). 240p. (YA). (gr. 5-9). pap. 7.99 *(978-0-312-56374-5(4)*, 9780312563745) Square Fish.
Wilhelm, Hans. I Love School! Wilhelm, Hans, illus. 2010. (Scholastic Reader Level 1 Ser.). (ENG., Illus.). 32p. (J). (gr. -1-k). pap. 3.99 *(978-0-545-13474-3(9)*, Cartwheel Bks.) Scholastic, Inc.
Wilkinson, Brenda. Ludell. 2014. (ENG., Illus.). 228p. (J). (-9). pap. 12.95 *(978-1-939601-16-2(9))* Ig Publishing, Inc.
Wilkinson, Lili. Pink. (ENG.). 320p. (YA). (gr. 8). 2012. pap. 9.99 *(978-0-06-192654-9(X))* 2011. 16.99 *(978-0-06-192653-2(1))* HarperCollins Pubs. (HarperTeen).
Willard, Elizabeth Kimmel. Mary Ingalls on Her Own. 2007. (Little House Sequel Ser.). (ENG.). 192p. (J). (gr. 3-7). 16.99 *(978-0-06-000905-2(5))* HarperCollins Pubs.
Willems, Mo. Knuffle Bunny Too: A Case of Mistaken Identity. Willems, Mo, illus. rev. ed. 2007. (Knuffle Bunny Ser.). (ENG., Illus.). 48p. (J). (gr. -1-k). 17.99 *(978-1-4231-0299-1(1))* Hyperion Pr.
Willems, Mo & Willems, Trixie, narrated by. Knuffle Bunny Too: A Case of Mistaken Identity. 2011. (J). (gr. -1-2). 29.95 *(978-0-545-13456-9(0))* Weston Woods Studios, Inc.
Williams Aber, Linda. Quien Tiene Manchas? Fiammenghi, Gioia, illus. 2007. (Math Matters Ser.). (SPA.). 32p. (J). (gr. -1-3). pap. 5.95 *(978-1-57565-251-1(X))* Kane Press, Inc.
Williams, Bonnie. Meet Teddy Rex! Gordon, John, illus. 2012. (Dino School Ser.). (ENG.). 24p. (J). (gr. -1-1). 15.99 *(978-1-4424-4996-1(9))*; pap. 3.99 *(978-1-4424-4995-4(0))* Simon Spotlight. (Simon Spotlight).
—Say Cheese, Teddy Rex! Gordon, John, illus. 2016. (Dino School Ser.). (J). (ENG.). 24p. (gr. -1-1). pap. 3.99 *(978-1-4814-6609-7(7))*; ***(978-1-5182-1896-5(2))*** Simon Spotlight. (Simon Spotlight).
Williams, C. E. Cj's World: My First Day of Second Grade. 2012. 28p. pap. 24.95 *(978-1-4626-6249-4(8))* America Star Bks.
Williams, Felisha. I'm No Bully, Am I? 2012. 24p. (-18). pap. 15.99 *(978-1-4797-0973-1(5))* Xlibris Corp.
—The Milk Chocolate Kid. 2012. 24p. (-18). pap. 15.99 *(978-1-4797-0971-7(9))* Xlibris Corp.
Williams, Heather. Nellie Oleson Meets Laura Ingalls. 2007. (Little House Ser.). 234p. (J). (gr. 3-7). lib. bdg. 16.89 *(978-0-06-124249-6(7))* HarperCollins Pubs.

S

Williams, Katie. Absent. 2013. (ENG.). 180p. (YA). (gr. 7-12). 16.99 *(978-0-8118-7150-1(9))* Chronicle Bks. LLC.

Williams, Katie & Chronicle Books Staff. The Space Between Trees. 2010. (ENG.). 280p. (YA). (gr. 9-17). 17.99 *(978-0-8118-7175-4(4))* Chronicle Bks. LLC.

Williams, Lori. Being Me. 2003. (Summit Books Ser.). 268p. (J). (gr. 3-6). lib. bdg. 13.95 *(978-0-7569-1372-4(1))*; pap. 6.95 *(978-0-7891-6024-9(2))* Perfection Learning Corp.

Williams, Maiya. Kaboom Academy. 2016. (ENG.). 240p. (J). (gr. 5). 6.99 *(978-0-449-81615-8(X)*, Yearling) Random Hse. Children's Bks.

Williams, Rozanne Lanczak. The Author with the Fancy Purple Pen. Richard, Ilene, illus. (Learn to Write Ser.). 16p. (J). 2007. (gr. -1-3). pap. 8.99 *(978-1-59198-346-0(0))* 2006. (gr. k-2). pap. 2.99 *(978-1-59198-299-9(5)*, 6189) Creative Teaching Pr., Inc.

—Emily Santos, Star of the Week. Burris, Priscilla, illus. 2006. (Learn to Write Ser.). 16p. (J). (gr. k-2). pap. 2.99 *(978-1-59198-298-2(7)*, 6194) Creative Teaching Pr., Inc.

—Emily Santos, Star of the Week. Maio, Barbara, ed. Burris, Priscilla, illus. 2006. (J). per. 8.99 *(978-1-59198-358-3(4))* Creative Teaching Pr., Inc.

—Room 9 Writes a Report. Lucas, Margeaux, illus. 2006. (Learn to Write Ser.). 16p. (J). (gr. k-2). pap. 3.49 *(978-1-59198-297-5(9)*, 6193) Creative Teaching Pr., Inc.

—Room 9 Writes a Report. Maio, Barbara, ed. Lucas, Margeaux, illus. 2006. (J). per. 8.99 *(978-1-59198-357-6(6))* Creative Teaching Pr., Inc.

—Tess Builds a Snowman. Harris, Jenny B., illus. 2006. (Learn to Write Ser.). 8p. (J). (gr. k-2). pap. 3.49 *(978-1-59198-286-9(3)*, 6180) Creative Teaching Pr., Inc.

—Tess Builds a Snowman. Maio, Barbara & Faulkner, Stacey, eds. Harris, Jenny B., illus. 2006. (J). per. 6.99 *(978-1-59198-337-8(1))* Creative Teaching Pr., Inc.

—When You Go Walking. Briles, Patty, illus. 2006. (Learn to Write Ser.). 16p. (J). (gr. k-2). pap. 3.49 *(978-1-59198-292-0(8)*, 6188) Creative Teaching Pr., Inc.

Williams, Sam. School Bus Bunny Bus. Trotter, Stuart, illus. 2006. (ENG.). 10p. (J). (gr. -1-1). 12.95 *(978-1-905417-17-9(9))* Boxer Bks., Ltd. GBR. Dist: Sterling Publishing Co., Inc.

Williams, Shanica. Amy Goes Shopping for School. 2012. 16p. pap. 15.99 *(978-1-4772-1360-5(0))* AuthorHouse.

Williams, Shannon. School Rules! Nelson, Anndria, illus. 2010. 36p. pap. 16.99 *(978-1-4520-3924-4(0))* AuthorHouse.

Williams, Stanley R. Not Me. 2008. 47p. pap. 24.95 *(978-1-4241-9577-0(2))* America Star Bks.

Williams, Suzanne. Master of Minds? Carter, Abby, illus. 2004. 58p. (J). lib. bdg. 15.00 *(978-1-4242-0911-8(0))* Fitzgerald Bks.

—Master of Minds? Carter, Abby, illus. 2004. (Marvelous Mind of Matthew Mcghee Age 8 Ser.). 58p. (J). 11.65 *(978-0-7569-5530-4(0))* Perfection Learning Corp.

Williams, T. E. Fluffy!! 2011. 24p. 16.25 *(978-1-4520-3743-1(4))* AuthorHouse.

Williamson, Greg. Why Do I Have to Wear Glasses? Popko, Wendy, illus. 2005. (J). 12.99 *(978-0-9666076-5-9(1))* Peerless Publishing, L.L.C.

—Why Do I Have to Wear Glasses? Popkp, Wendy, illus. 2005. (J). pap. 7.99 *(978-0-9666076-3-5(5))* Peerless Publishing, L.L.C.

Williamson, Lisa. The Art of Being Normal. 2016. (ENG.). 352p. (YA). 17.99 *(978-0-374-30237-5(5)*, 9780374302375, Farrar, Straus & Giroux (BYR)) Farrar, Straus & Giroux.

Willink, Jocko. Way of the Warrior Kid: From Wimpy to Warrior the Navy SEAL Way. Bozak, Jon, illus. 2017. (Way of the Warrior Kid Ser.: 1). (ENG.). 192p. (J). 13.99 ***(978-1-250-15107-0(4)***, 9781250151070) Feiwel & Friends.

Willis, Jeanne. Be Gentle, Python! Birchall, Mark, illus. 2005. (Picture Bks.). 28p. (J). (gr. k-2). 7.95 *(978-1-57505-508-4(2))* Lerner Publishing Group.

—Lucinda Belinda Melinda Mccool. Ross, Tony, illus. 2016. (ENG.). 32p. (J). (-k). 16.99 *(978-1-78344-202-7(6))* Andersen Pr. GBR. Dist: Independent Pubs. Group.

—No Biting, Puma! Birchall, Mark, illus. 2005. (Picture Bks.). 28p. (J). (gr. k-2). 7.25 *(978-1-57505-509-1(0))* Lerner Publishing Group.

Willis, Meredith Sue. Meli's Way. 2015. 178p. (YA). *(978-1-932727-15-9(9))* Montemayor Pr.

Willis, S. J. The Wishwasher. 2011. 128p. (gr. 4-6). pap. 13.32 *(978-1-4567-8751-6(9))* AuthorHouse.

Willner-Pardo, Gina. The Hard Kind of Promise. 2011. (ENG.). 204p. (J). (gr. 5-7). pap. 12.99 *(978-0-547-55017-6(0))* Houghton Mifflin Harcourt Publishing Co.

Willoughby, Holly & Willoughby, Kelly. Best Friends Forever. 2017. (School for Stars Ser.). (ENG.). 192p. (J). (gr. 4-6). 7.99 *(978-1-4440-1461-7(7)*, Orion Children's Bks.) Hachette Children's Group GBR. Dist: Hachette Bk. Group.

—The Princess Rescue. 2017. (School for Stars Ser.). (ENG.). 208p. (J). (gr. 4-6). pap. 7.99 *(978-1-4440-1459-4(5)*, Orion Children's Bks.) Hachette Children's Group GBR. Dist: Hachette Bk. Group.

Willsea, Hedley. The Heath of the Graves. 2009. 371p. pap. 31.50 *(978-1-4092-2226-2(8))* Lulu Pr., Inc.

Willson, Sarah. Cookie Crisis! Ross, Sharon & Bergman, Shannon, illus. 2005. 32p. (J). lib. bdg. 15.00 *(978-1-59054-981-0(3))* Fitzgerald Bks.

Wilson, Bob, illus. Football Fred, Vol. 4. 2003. (ENG.). 80p. (J). pap. *(978-0-330-37091-2(X)*, Pan) Pan Macmillan.

Wilson, Bryan M. Benjamin's Report Card Blues. 2011. 28p. pap. 12.95 *(978-1-4567-3530-2(6))* AuthorHouse.

Wilson, Debra. 65 Mustang: A Novel. 2011. 300p. pap. *(978-1-934922-47-7(1))* IBJ Custom Publishing.

Wilson, Jacqueline. Candyfloss. Sharratt, Nick, illus. 2008. (ENG.). 352p. (J). (gr. 4-7). pap. 9.99 *(978-0-312-38418-0(1)*, 9780312384180) Square Fish.

—Cookie. Sharratt, Nick, illus. 2010. (ENG.). 352p. (J). (gr. 4-7). pap. 11.99 *(978-0-312-64290-7(3)*, 9780312642907) Square Fish.

Wilson, Martin. We Now Return to Regular Life. 2017. (ENG.). 384p. (YA). (gr. 9). 17.99 ***(978-0-7352-2782-8(9)***, Dial Bks) Penguin Young Readers Group.

Wilson, Martin. What They Always Tell Us. 2010. (ENG.). 304p. (YA). (gr. 9). pap. 8.99 *(978-0-385-73508-7(1)*, Delacorte Bks. for Young Readers) Random Hse. Children's Bks.

Wilson-Max, Ken & Quarto Generic Staff. Lenny Goes to Nursery School. Wilson-Max, Ken, illus. 2014. (ENG., Illus.). 32p. (J). (gr. -1-k). 15.99 *(978-1-84780-317-7(2)*, Frances Lincoln) Quarto Publishing Group UK GBR. Dist: Hachette Bk. Group.

Wilson, N. D. Ninja Boy Goes to School. 2014. (ENG., Illus.). 32p. (J). (gr. -1-3). 16.99 *(978-0-375-86584-8(5)*, Random Hse. Bks. for Young Readers) Random Hse. Children's Bks.

Wilson, Troy. Perfect Man, 1 vol. Griffiths, Dean, illus. 2005. (ENG.). 32p. (J). (gr. -1-3). per. 9.95 *(978-1-55143-435-3(0))* Orca Bk. Pubs. USA.

Winerip, Michael. Adam Canfield: The Last Reporter. 2009. (Adam Canfield of the Slash Ser.: 3). (ENG., Illus.). 384p. (J). (gr. 3-7). 16.99 *(978-0-7636-2342-5(3))* Candlewick Pr.

—Adam Canfield of the Slash. (Adam Canfield of the Slash Ser.: 1). (ENG., Illus.). 336p. (J). (gr. 3-7). 2007. per. 7.99 *(978-0-7636-2794-2(1))* 2005. 15.99 *(978-0-7636-2340-1(7))* Candlewick Pr.

—Adam Canfield the Last Reporter. 2010. (Adam Canfield of the Slash Ser.: 3). (ENG., Illus.). 384p. (J). (gr. 3-7). 7.99 *(978-0-7636-4838-1(8))* Candlewick Pr.

—Adam Canfield Watch Your Back! 2009. (Adam Canfield of the Slash Ser.: 2). (ENG., Illus.). 352p. (J). (gr. 3-7). 7.99 *(978-0-7636-4412-3(9))* Candlewick Pr.

Winfield, Arthur M. The Rover Boys at School. 2007. 236p. 27.95 *(978-1-4218-4132-8(0))*; per. 12.95 *(978-1-4218-4230-1(0))* 1st World Publishing, Inc. (1st World Library - Literary Society).

—The Rover Boys at School. 2004. reprint ed. pap. 1.99 *(978-1-4192-8115-0(1))* Kessinger Publishing, LLC.

Winfrey, Kerry. Love & Other Alien Experiences. 2017. (ENG.). 272p. (YA). pap. 10.99 *(978-1-250-11952-0(9)*, 9781250119520) Feiwel & Friends.

Wing, Natasha. The Night Before Class Picture Day. 2016. (Night Before Ser.). lib. bdg. 14.75 *(978-0-606-38834-4(6))* Turtleback Bks.

—The Night Before First Grade. Zemke, Deborah, illus. (Night Before Ser.). (ENG.). 32p. (J). (gr. k-1). 2014. 12.99 *(978-0-448-48256-9(8))* 2005. pap. 4.99 *(978-0-448-43747-7(3))* Penguin Young Readers Group. (Grosset & Dunlap).

—The Night Before Preschool. Wummer, Amy, illus. 2011. (Night Before Ser.). (ENG.). 32p. (J). (gr. -1-k). pap. 4.99 *(978-0-448-45451-1(3)*, Grosset & Dunlap) Penguin Young Readers Group.

—The Night Before the 100th Day of School. Pierce, Mindy, illus. 2005. (Night Before Ser.). (ENG.). 32p. (J). (gr. -1-3). pap. 4.99 *(978-0-448-43923-5(9)*, Grosset & Dunlap) Penguin Young Readers Group.

Winget, Susan. Tucker's Four-Carrot School Day. Winget, Susan, illus. 2005. (ENG., Illus.). 40p. (J). (gr. -1-k). 12.99 *(978-0-06-054642-7(5))* HarperCollins Pubs.

Winkler, Henry & Oliver, Lin. Bookmarks Are People Too! Garrett, Scott, illus. 2014. (Here's Hank Ser.: 1). (ENG.). 128p. (J). (gr. 1-3). 14.99 *(978-0-448-48239-2(8))*; No. 1. 5.99 *(978-0-448-47997-2(4))* Penguin Young Readers Group. (Grosset & Dunlap).

—Bookmarks Are People Too! 2014. (Here's Hank Ser.: 1). lib. bdg. 16.00 *(978-0-606-34142-4(0)*, Turtleback) Turtleback Bks.

—A Brand-New Me! Watson, Jesse Joshua & Heitz, Tim, illus. 2010. (Hank Zipzer Ser.: 17). (ENG.). 160p. (J). (gr. 3-7). pap. 5.99 *(978-0-448-45210-4(3)*, Grosset & Dunlap) Penguin Young Readers Group.

—The Curtain Went Up, My Pants Fell Down. Watson, Jesse Joshua, illus. 2007. (Hank Zipzer Ser.: 11). (ENG.). 160p. (J). (gr. 3-7). pap. 5.99 *(978-0-448-44267-9(1)*, Grosset & Dunlap) Penguin Young Readers Group.

—Help! Somebody Get Me Out of Fourth Grade! Watson, Jesse Joshua & Heitz, Tim, illus. 2004. (Hank Zipzer Ser.: 7). (ENG.). 160p. (J). (gr. 3-7). mass mkt. 5.99 *(978-0-448-43619-7(1)*, Grosset & Dunlap) Penguin Young Readers Group.

—Holy Enchilada! Heyer, Carol et al, illus. 2004. (Hank Zipzer Ser.: 6). (ENG.). 160p. (J). (gr. 3-7). pap. 5.99 *(978-0-448-43353-0(2)*, Grosset & Dunlap) Penguin Young Readers Group.

—I Got a D in Salami. Watson, Jesse Joshua et al, illus. 2004. (Hank Zipzer Ser.: 6). (ENG.). 176p. (J). (gr. 3-7). mass mkt. 5.99 *(978-0-448-43163-5(7)*, Grosset & Dunlap) Penguin Young Readers Group.

—I Got a D in Salami. 2004. (Hank Zipzer Ser.: No. 2). 128p. (J). (gr. 2-6). pap. 29.00 incl. audio *(978-1-4000-9007-5(5)*, Listening Library) Random Hse. Audio Publishing Group.

—Life of Me: Enter at Your Own Risk. Watson, Jesse Joshua, illus. 2008. (Hank Zipzer Ser.: 14). (ENG.). 256p. (J). (gr. 3-7). pap. 6.99 *(978-0-448-44376-8(7)*, Grosset & Dunlap) Penguin Young Readers Group.

—The Life of Me (Enter at Your Own Risk) 2008. (Hank Zipzer Ser.: No. 14). (Illus.). 186p. (gr. 3-7). 16.00 *(978-0-7569-8819-7(5))* Perfection Learning Corp.

—Niagara Falls, or Does It? Watson, Jesse Joshua et al, illus. 2004. (Hank Zipzer Ser.: 1). (ENG.). 144p. (J). (gr. 3-7). pap. 5.99 *(978-0-448-43162-8(9)*, Grosset & Dunlap) Penguin Young Readers Group.

—Niagara Falls, or Does It? 2004. (Hank Zipzer Ser.: No. 1). 128p. (J). (gr. 2-6). pap. 29.00 incl. audio *(978-1-4000-9006-8(7)*, Listening Library) Random Hse. Audio Publishing Group.

—Summer School! What Genius Thought That Up? 2006. (Hank Zipzer Ser.: No. 8). (Illus.). 157p. (J). (gr. 3-9). lib. bdg. 24.21 *(978-1-59961-107-5(4))* Spotlight.

—A Tale of Two Tails. Watson, Jesse Joshua, illus. 2008. (Hank Zipzer Ser.: 15). (ENG.). 160p. (J). (gr. 3-7). pap. 5.99 *(978-0-448-44378-2(3)*, Grosset & Dunlap) Penguin Young Readers Group.

—Zero to Hero. 2012. (Ghost Buddy Ser.: 1). (ENG.). 176p. (J). (gr. 3-7). pap. 5.99 *(978-0-545-29882-7(2)*, Scholastic Paperbacks) Scholastic, Inc.

—The Zippity Zinger, 4 vols. Heitz, Tim, illus. 2004. (Hank Zipzer Ser.: 4). (ENG.). 160p. (J). (gr. 3-7). mass mkt. 5.99 *(978-0-448-43193-2(9)*, Grosset & Dunlap) Penguin Young Readers Group.

—The Zippity Zinger. 2004. (Hank Zipzer Ser.: No. 4). 160p. (J). (gr. 2-6). pap. 29.00 incl. audio *(978-1-4000-9009-9(1)*, Listening Library) Random Hse. Audio Publishing Group.

—The Zippity Zinger. 2006. (Hank Zipzer Ser.: No. 4). 154p. (J). (gr. 3-9). lib. bdg. 24.21 *(978-1-59961-103-7(1))* Spotlight.

Winn, Sheridan. The Sprite Sisters: Magic at Drysdale's School (Vol 7) Winn, Christopher, illus. 2013. 256p. pap. *(978-0-9574231-2-1(8))* Winn, Sheridan.

Winner, Ramona Moreno. It's Okay to Be Different! (Esta Bien Ser Diferente!) Velasquez, Nicole, illus. Date not set. (ENG & SPA.). 40p. (J). (gr. k-3). 9.95 *(978-0-9651174-0-1(5))* BrainStorm 3000.

Winston, Sherri. President of the Whole Fifth Grade. 2012. (President Ser.: 1). (ENG.). 288p. (J). (gr. 3-7). pap. 8.00 *(978-0-316-11433-2(2))* Little, Brown Bks. for Young Readers.

—President of the Whole Sixth Grade. 2015. (ENG.). 320p. (J). (gr. 3-7). 17.00 *(978-0-316-37723-2(6))* Little Brown & Co.

Winter, Ariel S. One of a Kind. Hitch, David, illus. 2012. (ENG.). 32p. (J). (gr. -1-2). 15.99 *(978-1-4424-2016-8(2)*, Aladdin) Simon & Schuster Children's Publishing.

Winters, Ben H. The Mystery of the Missing Everything. (ENG.). 272p. (J). (gr. 3-7). 2012. pap. 6.99 *(978-0-06-196546-3(4))* 2011. 16.99 *(978-0-06-196544-9(8))* HarperCollins Pubs.

—The Secret Life of Ms. Finkleman. (ENG.). (J). (gr. 3-7). 2011. 272p. pap. 5.99 *(978-0-06-196543-2(X))* 2010. 256p. 16.99 *(978-0-06-196541-8(3))* HarperCollins Pubs.

Winters, Kay. My Teacher for President. Brunkus, Denise, illus. 2008. (ENG.). 32p. (J). (gr. k-3). pap. 6.99 *(978-0-14-241170-4(1)*, Puffin Books) Penguin Young Readers Group.

—My Teacher for President. Brunkus, Denise, illus. 2008. (gr. -1-k). 17.00 *(978-0-7569-8925-5(6))* Perfection Learning Corp.

—The Teeny Tiny Ghost & the Monster, Vol. 3. Munsinger, Lynn, illus. 2004. (ENG.). 32p. (J). (gr. -1-3). 14.99 *(978-0-06-028884-6(1))* HarperCollins Pubs.

—This School Year Will Be the Best! Andriani, Renee, illus. 2010. (ENG.). 32p. (J). (gr. 1-3). 16.99 *(978-0-525-42275-4(7)*, Dutton Books for Young Readers) Penguin Young Readers Group.

—This School Year Will Be the Best! Andriani, Renee, illus. 2013. (ENG.). 32p. (J). (gr. 1-3). mass mkt. 6.99 *(978-0-14-242696-8(2)*, Puffin Books) Penguin Young Readers Group.

Wise, Anna. The Vala of Trinity: Book One Norse Series, 1 vol. 2009. 195p. pap. 24.95 *(978-1-61582-763-3(3))* America Star Bks.

Wise, Rachel. Cast Your Ballot! 2013. (Dear Know-It-All Ser.: 9). (ENG., Illus.). 160p. (J). (gr. 3-7). 15.99 *(978-1-4424-8793-2(3))*; pap. 5.99 *(978-1-4424-8792-5(5))* Simon Spotlight. (Simon Spotlight).

—Everyone's a Critic. 2013. (Dear Know-It-All Ser.: 5). (ENG.). 160p. (J). (gr. 3-7). 15.99 *(978-1-4424-6821-4(1))*; pap. 5.99 *(978-1-4424-6820-7(3))* Simon Spotlight. (Simon Spotlight).

—Late Edition. 2014. (Dear Know-It-All Ser.: 11). (ENG., Illus.). 160p. (J). (gr. 3-7). pap. 5.99 *(978-1-4424-9724-5(6)*, Simon Spotlight) Simon Spotlight.

—A Level Playing Field. 2012. (Dear Know-It-All Ser.: 3). (ENG.). 160p. (J). (gr. 3-7). 15.99 *(978-1-4424-5384-5(2))*; pap. 5.99 *(978-1-4424-5326-5(5))* Simon Spotlight. (Simon Spotlight).

—Old Story, New Twist. 2012. (Dear Know-It-All Ser.: 4). (ENG.). 160p. (J). (gr. 3-7). 15.99 *(978-1-4424-5385-2(0))*; pap. 5.99 *(978-1-4424-5328-9(1))* Simon Spotlight. (Simon Spotlight).

—Read All about It! 2012. (Dear Know-It-All Ser.: 1). (ENG.). 176p. (J). (gr. 3-7). 15.99 *(978-1-4424-5382-1(6))*; pap. 5.99 *(978-1-4424-4402-7(9))* Simon Spotlight. (Simon Spotlight).

—Set the Record Straight! 2012. (Dear Know-It-All Ser.: 2). (ENG.). 160p. (J). (gr. 3-7). 15.99 *(978-1-4424-5383-8(4))*; pap. 5.99 *(978-1-4424-4445-4(2))* Simon Spotlight. (Simon Spotlight).

Wiseman, Rosalind. Boys, Girls & Other Hazardous Materials. 2011. (ENG.). 304p. (YA). (gr. 7-18). 8.99 *(978-0-14-241819-2(6)*, Speak) Penguin Young Readers Group.

Wishinsky, Frieda. Jennifer Jones Won't Leave Me Alone. Layton, Neal, illus. 2005. (Carolrhoda Picture Bks.). 32p. (J). (gr. -1-3). per. 6.95 *(978-1-57505-921-1(5))*; (gr. k-2). 15.95 *(978-0-87614-921-8(2))* Lerner Publishing Group.

—Queen of the Toilet Bowl, 1 vol. 2005. (Orca Currents Ser.). (ENG., Illus.). 112p. (J). (gr. 5-9). per. 9.95 *(978-1-55143-364-6(8))* Orca Bk. Pubs. USA.

Witschen, Kay. Johnny Coalboy. Luckemeyer, Norma, illus. 2003. (J). per. 5.95 *(978-0-9741352-0-5(8))* Dwitt Publishing.

Wittlinger, Ellen. Sandpiper. 2007. (ENG.). 288p. (YA). (gr. 7-12). pap. 6.99 *(978-1-4169-3651-0(3)*, Simon & Schuster Bks. For Young Readers) Simon & Schuster Bks. For Young Readers.

Wizner, Jake. Spanking Shakespeare. Ewing, Richard, illus. 2008. (ENG.). 304p. (YA). (gr. 9). pap. 8.99 *(978-0-375-85594-8(7)*, Ember) Random Hse. Children's Bks.

—Spanking Shakespeare. 2007. (YA). *(978-0-375-84086-9(9))* Random Hse. Children's Bks.

Wodehouse, P. G. Mike at Wrykyn. 2013. 189p. reprint ed. lthr. 69.00 *(978-0-7426-3265-3(2))* Classic Bks.

Wojciechowski, Susan. Beany & the Magic Crystal. Natti, Susanna, illus. 2005. (Beany Adventures Ser.). 87p. (J). lib. bdg. 13.65 *(978-0-7569-5836-7(9))* Perfection Learning Corp.

—Beany (Not Beanhead) Natti, Susanna, illus. 2005. (Beany Adventures Ser.). 68p. (J). lib. bdg. 12.65 *(978-0-7569-5835-0(0))* Perfection Learning Corp.

Wojtowicz, Jen. The Boy Who Grew Flowers. Adams, Steve, illus. 2012. (ENG.). 32p. (J). (gr. k-5). 8.99 *(978-1-84686-749-1(5))* Barefoot Bks., Inc.

Wojtowicz, Jen & Wojzowitz, Jen. The Boy Who Grew Flowers. Adams, Steve, illus. 2005. (ENG.). 32p. (J). (gr. -1-3). 16.99 *(978-1-84148-686-4(8))* Barefoot Bks., Inc.

Wolek, Guy, illus. OLIVIA & the School Carnival. 2010. (Olivia TV Tie-In Ser.). (ENG.). 24p. (J). (gr. -1-2). pap. 3.99 *(978-1-4424-0870-8(7)*, Simon Spotlight) Simon Spotlight.

Wolf, Aline D. Our Peaceful Classroom. 2017. (ENG.). (Orig.). (J). 19.95 ***(978-0-939195-54-1(2))*** Parent Child Pr., Inc.

Wolf, Joan M. Someone Named Eva. 2009. (ENG., Illus.). 208p. (J). (gr. 5-7). pap. 7.99 *(978-0-547-23766-4(9))* Houghton Mifflin Harcourt Publishing Co.

Wolf, Sara. Forget Me Always. 2016. (Lovely Vicious Ser.: 2). (ENG.). 250p. (YA). pap. 9.99 *(978-1-63375-317-4(4)*, 9781633753174) Entangled Publishing, LLC.

Wolff, Virginia Euwer. This Full House. (ENG.). 496p. (YA). (gr. 9). 2011. pap. 9.99 *(978-0-06-158306-3(5))* 2009. (Make Lemonade Trilogy: No. 3). 17.99 *(978-0-06-158304-9(9))* HarperCollins Pubs. (HarperTeen).

Wolfgang, Jane. Art Today. 2013. (ENG., Illus.). 32p. (J). 14.95 *(978-1-56290-706-8(9))* Crystal Productions.

Wolitzer, Meg. Belzhar. (ENG.). 272p. (YA). (gr. 9). 2015. 10.99 *(978-0-14-242629-6(6)*, Speak) 2014. 17.99 *(978-0-525-42305-8(2)*, Dutton Books for Young Readers) Penguin Young Readers Group.

Wonder, 2 vols., Set. 2014. (ENG.). 432p. (J). (gr. 3-7). 31.98 *(978-0-553-49906-3(8)*, Knopf Bks. for Young Readers) Random Hse. Children's Bks.

Wonderley, Stanley. A Boy & His Horse. 2012. 19.95 *(978-0-7414-7806-1(4))*; pap. 11.95 *(978-0-7414-7805-4(6))* Infinity Publishing.

Wong, Janet S. & Wong, Janet G. Minn & Jake. Cote, Genevieve, illus. 2008. (ENG.). 160p. (J). (gr. 2-5). pap. 9.99 *(978-0-374-40021-7(0)*, 9780374400217, Farrar, Straus & Giroux (BYR)) Farrar, Straus & Giroux.

Wong, Joyce Lee. Seeing Emily. 2005. (ENG., Illus.). 288p. (J). (gr. 7-11). 16.95 *(978-0-8109-5757-2(4)*, Abrams Bks. for Young Readers) Abrams, Inc.

Wood, Fiona. Six Impossible Things. 2015. (ENG.). 304p. (YA). (gr. 7-17). 18.00 *(978-0-316-24216-5(0))* Little Brown & Co.

—Six Impossible Things. 2016. (ENG.). 304p. (YA). (gr. 7-17). pap. 9.99 *(978-0-316-29941-1(3)*, Poppy) Little, Brown Bks. for Young Readers.

—Wildlife. 2016. (ENG.). 416p. (YA). (gr. 10-17). pap. 9.99 *(978-0-316-24208-0(X)*, Poppy) Little, Brown Bks. for Young Readers.

Wood, Kristen. Find Masked Rider. 2008. 19.95 *(978-1-935159-06-3(2))* My Campus Adventure, Inc.

Woodard, Amy. The Day the Teacher Rode a Horse to School. 2008. 24p. pap. 24.95 *(978-1-60441-736-4(6))* America Star Bks.

Woodberry, Gareth. Gakeva Gluntok's New School. 2005. 65p. pap. 16.95 *(978-1-4137-9894-4(2))* PublishAmerica, Inc.

Wooding, Chris. Silver. 2014. (ENG.). 320p. (J). (gr. 7). 17.99 *(978-0-545-60392-8(7)*, Scholastic Pr.) Scholastic, Inc.

Woodlan Jr. Sr. High Students. Devon Makes a Promise. 2008. 36p. pap. 14.00 *(978-0-9817264-2-7(9))* Pen & Publish Inc.

Woodrow, Allan. Class Dismissed. (ENG.). 272p. (J). (gr. 3-7). 2017. pap. 6.99 ***(978-0-545-80072-3(2)***, Scholastic Paperbacks) 2015. 16.99 *(978-0-545-80071-6(4)*, Scholastic Pr.) Scholastic, Inc.

—Unschooled. 2017. (ENG.). 288p. (J). (gr. 3-7). 16.99 ***(978-1-338-11688-5(6)***, Scholastic Pr.) Scholastic, Inc.

Woods, Brenda. Emako Blue. 2005. (ENG.). 128p. (YA). (gr. 7-18). 6.99 *(978-0-14-240418-8(7)*, Speak) Penguin Young Readers Group.

—Emako Blue. 2005. 124p. (gr. 7). 16.00 *(978-0-7569-5495-6(9))* Perfection Learning Corp.

Woods, Elizabeth. Choker. (ENG.). 240p. (YA). (gr. 9). 2012. pap. 9.99 *(978-1-4424-1234-7(8))* 2011. (Illus.). 16.99 *(978-1-4424-1233-0(X))* Simon & Schuster Bks. For Young Readers. (Simon & Schuster Bks. For Young Readers).

Woodson, Jacqueline. Each Kindness. Lewis, E. B., illus. 2012. (ENG.). 32p. (J). (gr. k-3). 17.99 *(978-0-399-24652-4(5)*, Nancy Paulsen Books) Penguin Young Readers Group.

—Feathers. (ENG.). (J). (gr. 5-18). 2010. 160p. 8.99 *(978-0-14-241550-4(2)*, Speak) 2007. 128p. 16.99 *(978-0-399-23989-2(8)*, G.P. Putnam's Sons Books for Young Readers) Penguin Young Readers Group.

—If You Come Softly & Behind You. 2010. (ENG.). 352p. (YA). (gr. 7-18). 8.99 *(978-0-14-241918-2(4)*, Puffin Books) Penguin Young Readers Group.

Wortche, Allison. Rosie Sprout's Time to Shine. Barton, Patrice, illus. 2011. (ENG.). 40p. (J). (gr. -1-2). 17.99 *(978-0-375-86721-7(X)*, Knopf Bks. for Young Readers) Random Hse. Children's Bks.

Wray, Patricia. Sasha, the Dreamer, 1 vol. 2009. 192p. pap. 24.95 *(978-1-60672-885-7(7))* PublishAmerica, Inc.

Wright, Betty Ren. The Blizzard. Himler, Ronald, illus. 2003. (ENG.). 32p. (J). (gr. k-3). 17.95 *(978-0-8234-1656-1(9))* Holiday Hse., Inc.

Wright, Bil. Putting Makeup on the Fat Boy. (ENG., 240p. (YA). (gr. 7). 2012. Illus.). pap. 9.99 *(978-1-4169-4004-3(9))* 2011. 16.99 *(978-1-4169-3996-2(2))* Simon & Schuster Bks. For Young Readers. (Simon & Schuster Bks. For Young Readers).

Wright, Gail R. The Adventures of Alfred in the Greatest Fruit of All: Conflicts & Resolutions. 2011. 112p. (gr. 1-2). 28.95 *(978-1-4497-1586-1(9))*; pap. 11.95 *(978-1-4497-1585-4(0))* Author Solutions, Inc. (WestBow Pr.).

Wright, Lanikka. The Fab Four 2: Eva's Obsession. 2012. (ENG.). 244p. pap. 13.95 *(978-1-4327-9846-8(4))* Outskirts Pr., Inc.

Wright, Lloyd. Gramp's Variety of Stories. 2007. 200p. 24.95 *(978-0-595-71311-0(4))*; per. 14.95 *(978-0-595-47731-9(3))* iUniverse, Inc.

Wright, Pauline. Why Did My Dad Go to War? 2008. 48p. pap. 19.49 *(978-1-4343-4677-3(3))* AuthorHouse.

Wyatt, Cherokee. The Adventures of Margaret Mouse: School Days. Redmon, Angela M., illus. l.t. ed. 2004. 32p. (J). 6.95 *(978-0-9761326-0-8(5))* www.margaretmouse.com publishing co.

Wyatt, Leslie J. Poor Is Just a Starting Place. 2005. (ENG.). 192p. (J). (gr. 6-17). 16.95 *(978-0-8234-1884-8(7))* Holiday Hse., Inc.

Wymer, Tracy Edward. Soar. (ENG., Illus.). 288p. (J). (gr. 3-7). 2017. pap. 7.99 ***(978-1-4814-4712-6(2))*** 2016. 17.99 *(978-1-4814-4711-9(4))* Simon & Schuster Children's Publishing. (Aladdin).

Wynne-Jones, Tim. Rex Zero & the End of the Word. 2013. (ENG.). 208p. (J). (gr. 3-7). pap. 8.99 *(978-0-312-64460-4(4)*, 9780312644604) Square Fish.

—Rex Zero, King of Nothing. 2013. (ENG.). 240p. (J). (gr. 3-7). pap. 6.99 *(978-0-312-67478-6(3),* 9780312674786) Square Fish.

Yaccarino, Dan. Class Pet Squad: Journey to the Center of Town. 2016. (ENG., Illus.). 144p. (J). 13.99 *(978-1-250-02462-6(5),* 9781250024626) Feiwel & Friends.

Yagmin, Daniel, Jr., illus. Norton B. Nice. 2009. (J). *(978-1-60108-018-9(2))* Red Cygnet Pr.

Yang, Gene Luen. American Born Chinese. 2011. 10.04 *(978-0-7848-3435-0(0),* Everbind) Marco Bk. Co.

—American Born Chinese. 2011. 20.00 *(978-1-60686-920-8(5))* 2007. 29.00 *(978-0-7569-7745-0(2))* Perfection Learning Corp.

—American Born Chinese. Yang, Gene Luen & Pien, Lark, illus. 2007. (ENG.). 240p. (YA). (gr. 7-18). 23.99 *(978-1-59643-373-1(6),* 9781596433731, First Second Bks.) Roaring Brook Pr.

—American Born Chinese. Yang, Gene Luen, illus. rev. ed. 2006. (ENG., Illus.). 240p. (YA). (gr. 7-12). pap. 18.99 *(978-1-59643-152-2(0),* 9781596431522, First Second Bks.) Roaring Brook Pr.

—American Born Chinese. Yang, Gene Luen, illus. 2008. (ENG., Illus.). 240p. (YA). (gr. 7-12). pap. 10.99 *(978-0-312-38448-7(3),* 9780312384487) Square Fish.

—American Born Chinese. 2008. (YA). lib. bdg. 22.10 *(978-0-606-14484-1(6),* Turtleback) Turtleback Bks.

—Secret Coders. Holmes, Mike, illus. 2015. (Secret Coders Ser.: 1). (ENG.). 96p. (J). (gr. 3-7). 17.99 *(978-1-62672-276-7(5),* 9781626722767); pap. 9.99 *(978-1-62672-075-6(4),* 9781626720756) Roaring Brook Pr. (First Second Bks.).

—Secrets & Sequences. Holmes, Mike, illus. 2017. (Secret Coders Ser.: 3). (ENG.). 112p. (J). pap. 10.99 *(978-1-62672-077-0(0),* 9781626720770, First Second Bks.) Roaring Brook Pr.

—Secrets & Sequences. 2017. (Secret Coders Ser.: 3). (J). lib. bdg. 22.10 ***(978-0-606-40345-0(0))*** Turtleback Bks.

Yangsook, Choi. The Name Jar. 2014. (ENG.). 40p. (J). (gr. k-2). 11.24 *(978-1-63245-313-6(4))* Lectorum Pubns., Inc.

Yankovic, Al, pseud. My New Teacher & Me! Hargis, Wes, illus. 2013. (ENG.). 40p. (J). (gr. -1-3). 17.99 *(978-0-06-219203-5(5))* HarperCollins Pubs.

—When I Grow Up. Hargis, Wes, illus. 2011. (ENG.). 32p. (J). (gr. -1-3). 17.99 *(978-0-06-192691-4(4))* HarperCollins Pubs.

Yarnell, Duane. The Winning Basket. 2005. pap. 26.95 *(978-1-4191-5930-5(5))* Kessinger Publishing, LLC.

Yashima, Taro. Crow Boy. Yashima, Taro, illus. 2004. (Illus.). 34p. (J). (gr. k-3). reprint ed. pap. 14.00 *(978-0-7567-7102-7(1))* DIANE Publishing Co.

—Crow Boy. Yashima, Taro, illus. (Illus.). pap. 35.95 incl. audio compact disk *(978-1-59112-803-8(X))* Live Oak Media.

Yates, Alma J. Sammy's Song: A Novel. 2005. 272p. (J). *(978-1-59156-945-9(1))* Covenant Communications.

Yatscoff, Edward R. Archie's Gold. 2013. 200p. pap. *(978-0-9869678-7-0(4))* Yatscoff, Edward R.

Yee, Lisa. Bobby the Brave (Sometimes) Santat, Dan, illus. 2012. (ENG.). 160p. (J). (gr. 2-5). pap. 5.99 *(978-0-545-05595-6(4),* Levine, Arthur A. Bks.) Scholastic, Inc.

—Bobby vs. Girls (Accidentally) Santat, Dan, illus. 2010. (ENG.). 176p. (J). (gr. 2-5). pap. 5.99 *(978-0-545-05593-2(8),* Levine, Arthur A. Bks.) Scholastic, Inc.

—The Kidney Hypothetical: or How to Ruin Your Life in Seven Days:Or How to Ruin Your Life in Seven Days. 2015. (ENG.). 272p. (J). (gr. 7). 17.99 *(978-0-545-23094-0(2))* Scholastic, Inc.

—The Kidney Hypothetical, or, How to Ruin Your Life in Seven Days. 2016. (ENG.). 272p. (J). (gr. 7). pap. 9.99 *(978-0-545-23095-7(0))* Scholastic, Inc.

—Stanford Wong Flunks Big-Time. 2007. (Apple Signature Edition Ser.). (ENG., Illus.). 320p. (J). (gr. 3-7). per. 6.99 *(978-0-439-62248-6(4),* Levine, Arthur A. Bks.) Scholastic, Inc.

—Supergirl at Super Hero High. Random House Staff, illus. 2016. (ENG.). 240p. (J). (gr. 3-7). 13.99 *(978-1-101-94062-4(X),* Random Hse. Bks. for Young Readers) Random Hse. Children's Bks.

—Warp Speed. (ENG.). 320p. (J). 2013. (gr. 3-7). pap. 6.99 *(978-0-545-15400-0(6))* 2011. (gr. 4-7). 16.99 *(978-0-545-12276-4(7))* Scholastic, Inc. (Levine, Arthur A. Bks.).

Yeh, Kat. The Way to Bea. 2017. (ENG.). 352p. (J). (gr. 3-7). 16.99 ***(978-0-316-23667-6(5))*** Little, Brown Bks. for Young Readers.

Yeh, Shao-Min. What Do You See? 2011. 28p. pap. 15.99 *(978-1-4628-5030-3(8))* Xlibris Corp.

Yep, Laurence & Ryder, Joanne. A Dragon's Guide to Making Your Human Smarter. GrandPré, Mary, illus. 2016. (Dragon's Guide Ser.). (ENG.). 304p. (J). (gr. 3-7). 16.99 *(978-0-385-39232-7(X),* Crown Books For Young Readers) Random Hse. Children's Bks.

Yochum, Nikki. Shy Cheyenne & the Substitute Teacher. 2010. 36p. pap. 13.95 *(978-1-60911-140-3(0),* Eloquent Bks.) Strategic Book Publishing & Rights Agency (SBPRA).

Yolen, Jane. How Do Dinosaurs Go to School? Teague, Mark, illus. 2007. (How Do Dinosaurs... Ser.). (ENG.). 40p. (J). (gr. -1-k). 16.99 *(978-0-439-02081-7(6))* Scholastic, Inc.

—How Do Dinosaurs Go to School? Teague, Mark, illus. 2011. (J). (gr. -1-3). 18.95 *(978-0-545-19707-6(4));* 29.95 *(978-0-545-19700-7(7))* Weston Woods Studios, Inc.

—A Plague of Unicorns. 2015. (J). pap. *(978-0-310-74610-2(8))* Zondervan.

Yoo, David. The Detention Club. (ENG.). 304p. (J). (gr. 5). 2012. pap. 6.99 *(978-0-06-178380-7(3))* 2011. 16.99 *(978-0-06-178378-4(1))* HarperCollins Pubs.

Yoon, Salina. Bear's Big Day. 2017. (ENG., Illus.). 32p. (J). bds. 7.99 *(978-1-68119-436-3(8),* 9781681194363, Bloomsbury USA Childrens) Bloomsbury Publishing USA.

Young, Janet Ruth. The Babysitter Murders. 2011. (ENG., Illus.). 336p. (YA). (gr. 9-18). 16.99 *(978-1-4169-5944-1(0),* Atheneum Bks. for Young Readers) Simon & Schuster Children's Publishing.

Young, Jessica. Art-Rageous. Secheret, Jessica, illus. 2015. (Finley Flowers Ser.). (ENG.). 128p. (gr. 2-3). 8.95 *(978-1-4795-5960-2(1),* Finley Flowers) Picture Window Bks.

—Fin-Tastic Fashion. Secheret, Jessica, illus. 2017. (Finley Flowers Ser.). (ENG.). 128p. (gr. 2-3). lib. bdg. 25.32 ***(978-1-4795-9804-5(6),*** Finley Flowers) Picture Window Bks.

—Finley Flowers Collection. Secheret, Jessica, illus. 2016. (Finley Flowers Ser.). (ENG.). 256p. (gr. 2-3). 9.99 *(978-1-4795-9850-2(X),* Finley Flowers) Picture Window Bks.

—New & Improved. Secheret, Jessica, illus. 2015. (Finley Flowers Ser.). (ENG.). 128p. (gr. 2-3). 8.95 *(978-1-4795-5959-6(8),* Finley Flowers) Picture Window Bks.

—Original Recipe. Secheret, Jessica, illus. 2015. (Finley Flowers Ser.). (ENG.). 128p. (gr. 2-3). 8.95 *(978-1-4795-5878-0(8),* Finley Flowers) Picture Window Bks.

—Room to Bloom. Secheret, Jessica, illus. 2017. (Finley Flowers Ser.). (ENG.). 128p. (gr. 2-3). lib. bdg. 25.32 ***(978-1-4795-9806-9(2),*** Finley Flowers) Picture Window Bks.

—Super Spooktacular. Secheret, Jessica, illus. 2017. (Finley Flowers Ser.). (ENG.). 128p. (gr. 2-3). lib. bdg. 25.32 ***(978-1-4795-9807-6(0),*** Finley Flowers) Picture Window Bks.

Young, Judy. Promise. 2016. (ENG.). 368p. (J). (gr. 4-6). pap. 8.99 *(978-1-58536-915-7(2),* 204079) Sleeping Bear Pr.

Young, Karen Romano. Stuck in the Middle (of Middle School) A Novel in Doodles. 2013. (ENG., Illus.). 112p. (J). (gr. 3-7). 12.99 *(978-0-312-55596-2(2),* 9780312555962) Feiwel & Friends.

—Stuck in the Middle (of Middle School) A Novel in Doodles. 2014. (ENG., Illus.). 128p. (J). (gr. 3-7). pap. 6.99 *(978-1-250-03997-2(5),* 9781250039972) Square Fish.

Young, Paige. The Homework Dilemma. 2011. 26p. pap. 16.95 *(978-1-4626-2366-2(2))* America Star Bks.

Yovanoff, Brenna. Places No One Knows. 2016. (ENG.). 384p. (YA). (gr. 9). 17.99 *(978-0-553-52263-1(9),* Delacorte Pr.) Random Hse. Children's Bks.

Yoyo. Ready for School. 2005. 40p. bds. *(978-90-5843-890-4(2))* YoYo Bks.

Yum, Hyewon. Mom, It's My First Day of Kindergarten!, 1 vol. Yum, Hyewon, illus. 2012. (ENG., Illus.). 36p. (J). (gr. -1-2). 16.99 *(978-0-374-35004-8(3),* 9780374350048, Farrar, Straus & Giroux (BYR)) Farrar, Straus & Giroux.

Yunisa. Schoolaholic Princess 1: the Miracle Boys. 2008. 242p. pap. 15.88 *(978-1-4357-6026-4(3))* Lulu Pr., Inc.

—Schoolaholic Princess 2: Romansa Singapura. 2008. 232p. pap. 14.88 *(978-1-4357-6044-8(1))* Lulu Pr., Inc.

—Schoolaholic Princess 3: Simfoni Cinta. 2008. 220p. pap. 14.88 *(978-1-4357-6045-5(X))* Lulu Pr., Inc.

Yusuf, Hanna S. & Day, Cansarra. Katie Mcchoir. 2010. 80p. pap. 10.49 *(978-1-4490-7378-7(6))* AuthorHouse.

Zadoff, Allen. Boy Nobody. 2013. (Unknown Assassin Ser.: 1). (ENG.). 352p. (YA). (gr. 10-17). 18.00 *(978-0-316-19968-1(0))* Little Brown & Co.

—Food, Girls, & Other Things I Can't Have. 2011. (ENG., Illus.). 320p. (gr. 8). pap. 9.99 *(978-0-7613-6384-4-151-8(3),* Carolrhoda Lab™) Lerner Publishing Group.

Zamorsky, Tania & Burnett, Frances Hodgson. A Little Princess. Corvino, Lucy, illus. 2005. (Classic Starts(tm) Ser.). (ENG.). 160p. (J). (gr. 2-4). 6.95 *(978-1-4027-1275-3(8))* Sterling Publishing Co., Inc.

Zann, Tara. Wild Child: Forest's First Day of School. Ermos, George & Widdowson, Dan, illus. 2017. (Wild Child Ser.: 2). (ENG.). 144p. (J). pap. 5.99 *(978-1-250-10387-1(8),* 9781250103871) Imprint IND. Dist: Macmillan.

Zappa, Ahmet & Zappa, Shane Muldoon. Sage & the Journey to the Wish World. Bonatakis, Shannon & Disney Storybook Art Team, illus. 2015. (Star Darlings Ser.: 1). (ENG.). 176p. (J). (gr. 3-7). pap. 6.99 *(978-1-4231-6643-6(4))* Disney Pr.

Zappa, Shana Muldoon. Star Darlings Bind up #1: Sage/Libby/Leona. Disney Storybook Art Team, illus. 2016. (Star Darlings Ser.). (ENG.). 480p. (J). (gr. 3-7). pap. 12.99 *(978-1-4847-8295-8(X))* Disney Pr.

—Star Darlings Bind up #2: Vega/Scarlet/Cassie. Disney Storybook Art Team, illus. 2016. (Star Darlings Ser.). (ENG.). 464p. (J). (gr. 3-7). pap. 12.99 *(978-1-4847-8296-5(8))* Disney Pr.

—Star Darlings Bind up #3: Piper/Astra/Tessa. Disney Storybook Art Team, illus. 2016. (Star Darlings Ser.). (ENG.). 464p. (J). (gr. 3-7). pap. 12.99 *(978-1-4847-8297-2(6))* Disney Pr.

—Star Darlings Collection Vol. 4: Adora Finds a Friend; Clover's Parent Fix-Up; Gemma & the Worst Wish Ever. Disney Storybook Art Team, illus. 2016. (Star Darlings Ser.). (ENG.). 464p. (J). (gr. 3-7). pap. 12.99 *(978-1-4847-8293-4(3))* Disney Pr.

Zappa, Shana Muldoon & Zappa, Ahmet. Cassie Comes Through. Disney Storybook Art Team, illus. 2016. (Star Darlings Ser.: 6). (ENG.). 176p. (J). (gr. 3-7). pap. 6.99 *(978-1-4847-1425-6(3))* Disney Pr.

—Piper's Perfect Dream. Disney Storybook Art Team, illus. 2016. (Star Darlings Ser.: 7). (ENG.). 176p. (J). (gr. 3-7). pap. 6.99 *(978-1-4847-1426-3(1))* Disney Pr.

Zappia, Francesca. Eliza & Her Monsters. 2017. 400p. (YA). (gr. 9). 17.99 *(978-0-06-229013-7(4),* Greenwillow Bks.) HarperCollins Pubs.

Zarins, Kim. Sometimes We Tell the Truth. 2016. ***(978-1-4814-7554-9(1))*** Simon & Schuster, Inc.

—Sometimes We Tell the Truth. 2016. (ENG., Illus.). 448p. (YA). (gr. 9). 17.99 *(978-1-4814-6499-4(X),* Simon Pulse) Simon Pulse.

Zarr, Sara. Sweethearts. 2009. (ENG.). 224p. (YA). (gr. 7-17). pap. 10.99 *(978-0-316-01456-4(7))* Little, Brown Bks. for Young Readers.

Zatch Bell 1: The Lightning Boy From Another World. 2005. 24.98 *(978-1-4215-0215-1(1))* Viz Media.

Zeitlin, Meredith. Freshman Year & Other Unnatural Disasters. 2013. (ENG.). 288p. (YA). (gr. 7). pap. 8.99 *(978-0-14-242421-6(8),* Speak) Penguin Young Readers Group.

Zemach, Kaethe. Ms. McCaw Learns to Draw. (J). 2008. (ENG., Illus.). 32p. (gr. -1-3). 16.99 *(978-0-439-82914-4(3))* 2006. *(978-0-439-82915-1(1))* Scholastic, Inc. (Levine, Arthur A. Bks.).

Zepeda, Frank. A Wad of Gum. 2012. 40p. pap. 19.99 *(978-1-105-73944-6(9))* Lulu Pr., Inc.

Zepf, Máire. Don't Go to School! Krüse, Tarsila, illus. 2017. (ENG.). 40p. (J). (gr. -1). 14.95 ***(978-1-4549-2359-6(8))*** Sterling Publishing Co., Inc.

Zevin, Gabrielle. Memoirs of a Teenage Amnesiac. 2011. 9.46 *(978-0-7848-3492-3(X),* Everbind) Marco Bk. Co.

—Memoirs of a Teenage Amnesiac. 2009. (ENG.). 304p. (YA). (gr. 9-13). pap. 10.99 *(978-0-312-56128-4(8),* 9780312561284) Square Fish.

Zia, Farhana. The Garden of My Imaan, 1 vol. (ENG.). (J). (gr. 3-6). 2016. 232p. pap. 7.95 *(978-1-56145-921-6(6))* 2013. 192p. 15.95 *(978-1-56145-698-7(5))* Peachtree Pubs.

Zidrou. Ducoboo: In the Corner! Godi, illus. 2007. (Ducoboo Ser.: 2). (ENG.). 48p. (J). (gr. 4-7). pap. 9.99 *(978-1-905460-26-7(0))* CineBook GBR. Dist: National Bk. Network.

—Ducoboo: The Class Struggle. Spear, Luke, tr. from FRE. Godi & Grobet, Veronique, illus. 2010. (Ducoboo Ser.: 4). (ENG.). 46p. (J). (gr. 3-17). pap. 11.95 *(978-1-84918-031-3(8))* CineBook GBR. Dist: National Bk. Network.

—Ducoboo No. 3: Your Answers or Your Life! Godi, illus. 2008. (Ducoboo Ser.: 3). (ENG.). 48p. pap. 11.95 *(978-1-905460-28-1(7))* CineBook GBR. Dist: National Bk. Network.

Ziegesar, Cecily von. Adored. 2009. (It Girl Ser.: 8). (ENG.). 240p. (YA). (gr. 10-17). pap. 9.99 *(978-0-316-02509-6(7),* Tingley, Megan Bks.) Little, Brown Bks. for Young Readers.

—I Like It Like That. 2004. (Gossip Girl Ser.: 5). (ENG.). 224p. (YA). (gr. 10-17). pap. 10.99 *(978-0-316-73518-6(3),* Poppy) Little, Brown Bks. for Young Readers.

—Nobody Does It Better. 7th ed. 2005. (Gossip Girl Ser.: 7). (ENG.). 256p. (YA). (gr. 10-17). pap. 10.99 *(978-0-316-73512-4(4),* Poppy) Little, Brown Bks. for Young Readers.

—Only in Your Dreams. 2006. (Gossip Girl Ser.: 9). (ENG.). 256p. (YA). (gr. 10-17). per. 10.99 *(978-0-316-01182-2(7),* Poppy) Little, Brown Bks. for Young Readers.

—Would I Lie to You. 2006. (Gossip Girl Ser.: 10). (ENG.). 224p. (YA). (gr. 10-17). per. 10.99 *(978-0-316-01183-9(5),* Poppy) Little, Brown Bks. for Young Readers.

—You're the One That I Want. 2004. (Gossip Girl Ser.: 6). (ENG.). 256p. (YA). (gr. 10-17). pap. 11.99 *(978-0-316-73516-2(7),* Poppy) Little, Brown Bks. for Young Readers.

Ziegesar, Cecily von, creator. Don't You Forget about Me. 2007. (Gossip Girl Ser.: 11). (ENG.). 304p. (YA). (gr. 10-17). per. 10.99 *(978-0-316-01184-6(3),* Poppy) Little, Brown Bks. for Young Readers.

Ziegler, Jennifer. How Not to Be Popular. 2010. (ENG.). 348p. (YA). (gr. 7). mass mkt. 8.99 *(978-0-440-24024-2(7),* Delacorte Bks. for Young Readers) Random Hse. Children's Bks.

—Sass & Serendipity. 2012. (ENG.). 384p. (YA). (gr. 7). pap. 9.99 *(978-0-375-85964-9(0),* Ember) Random Hse. Children's Bks.

Zielinski, Valerie & Skaletski, Roslyn. The Adventures of Bella. 2011. 48p. pap. 14.00 *(978-1-4634-2018-5(8))* AuthorHouse.

Zimelman, Nathan. How the Second Grade Got $8,205. 50 to Visit the Statue of Liberty. Slavin, Bill, illus. 2017. (ENG.). 32p. (J). (gr. -1-3). pap. 7.99 ***(978-0-8075-3435-9(8))*** Whitman, Albert & Co.

Zoellick, Todd. Daniel Harrington Fairbanks the Third & the Dog That Wouldn't Bark. 2009. 52p. pap. 20.49 *(978-1-4490-1047-8(4))* AuthorHouse.

Zumo. An Awesome Run: Selected Works, 1978-2008. 2008. 284p. 31.99 *(978-1-4389-2394-9(5))* AuthorHouse.

Zurchin, Cynthia, et al. The Whale Done School: Transforming a School's Culture by Catching Students Doing Things Right. 2012. 124p. pap. 14.95 *(978-1-4685-9536-9(9))* AuthorHouse.

50 Cent Staff. Playground. Akana, Lizzi, illus. 2012. (ENG.). 320p. (YA). (gr. 7). pap. 9.99 *(978-1-59514-478-2(1),* Razorbill) Penguin Young Readers Group.

SCHOOLS—MANAGEMENT AND ORGANIZATION

see School Management And Organization

SCHOOLS, MILITARY

see Military Education

SCHUBERT, FRANZ, 1797-1828

Summerer, Eric Michael. Franz Peter Schubert. (Primary Source Library of Famous Composers Ser.). 32p. 2009. (gr. 4-4). 42.50 *(978-1-60854-107-2(X))* 2006. (Illus.). (J). (gr. -1-3). lib. bdg. 23.95 *(978-1-4042-2768-2(7))* Rosen Publishing Group, Inc., The. (PowerKids Pr.).

Wheeler, Opal & Deucher, Sybil. Franz Schubert & his Merry Friends. Greenwalt, Mary, illus. 2008. 128p. (J). pap. 13.95 *(978-1-933573-13-7(9))* Zeezok Publishing, LLC.

SCHULZ, CHARLES M. (CHARLES MONROE), 1922-2000

Marvis, Barbara J. Charles Schulz. 2004. (Robbie Reader Ser.). (Illus.). 32p. (J). (gr. 1-4). lib. bdg. 25.70 *(978-1-58415-289-7(3))* Mitchell Lane Pubs., Inc.

Perkins, Chloe. The Great American Story of Charlie Brown, Snoopy, & the Peanuts Gang! Burroughs, Scott, illus. 2017. (History of Fun Stuff Ser.). (ENG.). 48p. (J). (gr. 1-3). pap. 3.99 ***(978-1-4814-9553-0(4),*** Simon Spotlight) Simon Spotlight.

Schuman, Michael. Charles Schulz. 2017. ***(978-0-7660-9209-9(7))*** Enslow Pubs., Inc.

SCHUMANN, CLARA, 1819-1896

Shichtman, Sandra H. & Indenbaum, Dorothy. The Joy of Creation: The Story of Clara Schumann. 2011. (Classical Composers Ser.). (Illus.). 159p. lib. bdg. 28.95 *(978-1-59935-123-0(4))* Reynolds, Morgan Inc.

SCIENCE

see also Astronomy; Bacteriology; Biology; Botany; Chemistry; Crystallography; Ethnology; Forensic Sciences; Fossils; Geology; Mathematics; Meteorology; Metrology; Mineralogy; Natural History; Physics; Physiology; Space Sciences; Zoology

also headings beginning with the word Scientific

ABDO Publishing. Cutting-Edge Science & Technology. 2016. (Cutting-Edge Science & Technology Ser.: 8). (ENG.). 112p. (J). (gr. 6-12). lib. bdg. 285.12 *(978-1-62403-911-9(1),* Essential Library) ABDO Publishing Co.

Abdo Publishing. Science in the Real World, 1 vol. 2013. (Science in the Real World Ser.: 8). 48p. (J). (gr. 3-6). lib. bdg. 262.32 *(978-1-61783-737-1(7))* ABDO Publishing Co.

ABDO Publishing. STEM in the Real World. 2016. (STEM in the Real World Ser.: 6). (ENG.). 48p. (J). (gr. 3-6). lib. bdg. 196.74 *(978-1-68078-037-6(9))* ABDO Publishing Co.

ABDO Publishing Company. Beginning to End Set 1. 2006. (Beginning to End Set 1 Ser.). 205.20 *(978-1-59679-833-5(5),* Buddy Bks.) ABDO Publishing Co.

—More Super Simple Science. 2013. (More Super Simple Science Ser.: 6). 32p. (J). (gr. k-4). lib. bdg. 162.42 *(978-1-61783-848-4(9),* Super SandCastle) ABDO Publishing Co.

ABDO Publishing Company Staff. Science of Life. 2014. (Science of Life Ser.: 6). (ENG.). 48p. (gr. 3-6). lib. bdg. 196.74 *(978-1-62403-156-4(0))* ABDO Publishing Co.

ABDO Publishing Company Staff & Doudna, Kelly. Science Made Simple. 2007. (Science Made Simple Ser.: 24). (ENG.). 24p. (J). (gr. k-3). lib. bdg. 581.04 *(978-1-59928-578-8(9),* SandCastle) ABDO Publishing Co.

Abel, Simone, illus. First Look - Science, 9 vols. Incl. And Everyone Shouted, Pull! A First Look at Forces & Motion. Llewellyn, Claire. 26.65 *(978-1-4048-0656-6(3));* Hen Can't Help It: A First Look at the Life Cycle of a Chicken. Godwin, Sam. 26.65 *(978-1-4048-0653-5(9));* Trouble with Tadpoles: A First Look at the Life Cycle of a Frog. Godwin, Sam. 26.65 *(978-1-4048-0654-2(7));* (gr. -1-2). (First Look: Science Ser.). (ENG., Illus.). 32p. 2004. 133.25 o.p. *(978-1-4048-0661-0(X))* Picture Window Bks.

Accelerated Curriculum for Science Grade 11 Exit Taks Student Edition. 2005. (Region IV ESC Resources for Science Ser.). spiral bd. *(978-1-932797-27-5(0))* Region IV Education Service Ctr.

ACT Science Reasoning Victory Student Textbook. 2nd ed. 2005. per. *(978-1-58894-034-6(9))* Cambridge Educational Services, Inc.

Action Science. 2010. (Action Science Ser.). (ENG.). 32p. (gr. 3-4). pap. 190.80 *(978-1-4296-5134-9(2),* Fact Finders) Capstone Press of Coughlan Cos.

Action Science [Capstone Sole Source]. 2010. (Action Science Ser.). 32p. lib. bdg. 103.96 *(978-1-4296-5836-2(3),* Fact Finders) Capstone Press of Coughlan Cos.

¿Adonde Van los Residuos? (Coleccion Primeros Pasos en la Ciencia). (SPA., Illus.). (J). (gr. 1-3). pap. *(978-950-724-216-8(3),* LMA8222) Lumen ARG. Dist: Lectorum Pubns., Inc.

A.H.Hashmi. Children's Science Encyclopedia. 2009. 518p. pap. *(978-81-223-1061-0(3))* Mahal, Pustak Pubs., Booksellers & Order Suppliers.

Aire. (Coleccion Jugando Con la Ciencia). (SPA., Illus.). 39p. (J). pap. 9.95 *(978-950-11-0681-7(0),* SGM341) Sigmar ARG. Dist: Continental Bk. Co., Inc.

Akass, Susan. My First Science Book: Explore the Wonders of Science with This Fun-Filled Guide: Kitchen Chemistry, Fantasticphysics, Backyard Biology. 2015. (ENG., Illus.). 112p. (J). (gr. 7-11). pap. 14.95 *(978-1-78249-254-2(2),* CICO Books) Ryland Peters & Small GBR. Dist: WIPRO.

Alaina, Maria. Wonder Readers Next Steps: Science. 2013. (Wonder Readers Next Steps: Science Ser.). (ENG.). 20p. (gr. -1-1). lib. bdg. 67.95 *(978-1-4765-3754-2(2));* lib. bdg. 135.90 *(978-1-4765-3753-5(4))* Capstone Press of Coughlan Cos. (Wonder Readers).

Amazing Science, 12 bks. Incl. Dirt: The Scoop on Soil. Rosinsky, Natalie M. Boyd, Sheree, illus. 2002. 26.65 *(978-1-4048-0012-0(3));* Electricity: Bulbs, Batteries, & Sparks. Stille, Darlene R. Boyd, Sheree, illus. 2004. 26.65 *(978-1-4048-0245-2(2));* Energy: Heat, Light, & Fuel. Stille, Darlene R. Boyd, Sheree, illus. 2004. 26.65 *(978-1-4048-0249-0(5));* Motion: Push & Pull, Fast & Slow. Stille, Darlene R. Boyd, Sheree, tr. Boyd, Sheree, illus. 2004. 26.65 *(978-1-4048-0250-6(9));* Rocks: Hard, Soft, Smooth, & Rough. Rosinsky, Natalie M. John, Matthew, illus. 2002. 26.65 *(978-1-4048-0015-1(8));* Sound: Loud, Soft, High, & Low. Rosinsky, Natalie M. John, Matthew, illus. 2002. 26.65 *(978-1-4048-0016-8(6));* (gr. k-4). (Amazing Science Ser.). (ENG.). 24p. 2004. 319.80 o.p. *(978-1-4048-0244-5(4))* Picture Window Bks.

Amazing World of Science & Math. 2016. (Amazing World of Science & Math Ser.). 48p. (gr. 5-5). pap. 56.20 *(978-1-4824-5335-5(5));* lib. bdg. 127.80 *(978-1-4824-4970-9(6))* Stevens, Gareth Publishing LLLP.

Anderson, James. The Science of Magic (Grade 6) 2016. (TIME for KIDS(r) Nonfiction Readers Ser.). (Illus.). 64p. (J). (gr. 6-6). pap. 10.99 *(978-1-4938-3606-2(4))* Teacher Created Materials, Inc.

Anderson, James D. The Science of Magic. 2016. (Time for Kids Nonfiction Readers Ser.). (ENG.). (J). (gr. 5-8). lib. bdg. 22.10 ***(978-0-606-39542-7(3))*** Turtleback Bks.

Anderson, Kelli. This Book Is a Planetarium: And Other Extraordinary Pop-Up Contraptions. 2017. (ENG., Illus.). 5p. 40.00 *(978-1-4521-3621-9(1))* Chronicle Bks. LLC.

Animal Eaters of the Pond: 6 Each of 1 Student Book, 6 vols. (Sunshinetm Science Ser.). 24p. (gr. 1-2). 41.95 *(978-0-7802-2696-8(8))* Wright Group/McGraw-Hill.

Animal Eaters of the Pond: Big Book. (Sunshinetm Science Ser.). 24p. (gr. 1-2). 37.50 *(978-0-7802-2782-8(4))* Wright Group/McGraw-Hill.

Animal Fibers: 6 Each of 1 Student Book, 6 vols. (Sunshinetm Science Ser.). 24p. (gr. 1-2). 41.95 *(978-0-7802-1434-7(X))* Wright Group/McGraw-Hill.

Animal Fibers: Big Book. (Sunshinetm Science Ser.). 24p. (gr. 1-2). 37.50 *(978-0-7802-1435-4(8))* Wright Group/McGraw-Hill.

Animales Nocturnos de la Selva. (Colección Ventana Transparente). (SPA., Illus.). (J). (gr. 3-5). *(978-950-11-1280-1(2),* SG5231) Sigmar ARG. Dist: Lectorum Pubns., Inc.

Animals & Their Teeth, 6 vols. (Sunshinetm Science Ser.). 24p. (gr. 1-2). 41.95 *(978-0-7802-1443-9(9))* Wright Group/McGraw-Hill.

Animals & Their Teeth: Big Book. (Sunshinetm Science Ser.). 24p. (gr. 1-2). 37.50 *(978-0-7802-1444-6(7))* Wright Group/McGraw-Hill.

Applied Science, Set. 2010. (Extreme! Ser.). (ENG.). 32p. (gr. 3-4). pap. 429.30 *(978-1-4296-5136-3(9),* Fact Finders) Capstone Press of Coughlan Cos.

Applin, D. G., et al. AQA Modular Science for GCSE. 2003. (ENG., Illus.). 336p. pap. *(978-0-7487-7286-5(3))* Nelson Thornes Ltd.

Arnold, Brian. Quick Revision KS3 Science. 2007. (Illus.). 46p. pap. 9.95 *(978-0-340-94308-3(4),* Hodder Education) Hodder Education Group GBR. Dist: Trans-Atlantic Pubns., Inc.

Arnold, Nick. Esa Fascinante Arqueologia. 2003. (Coleccion Esa Gran Cultura).Tr. of Awesome Archaeology. (SPA., Illus.). 160p. (YA). (gr. 5-8). 7.96 (978-84-272-2139-0(8)) Molino, Editorial ESP. Dist: Lectorum Pubns., Inc.

Arnold, Nick & De Saulles, Tony. Ese Voluminoso Cerebro. De Saulles, Tony, tr. 2003. (Coleccion Esa Horrible Cienca). (SPA., Illus.). 158p. (YA). (978-84-272-2065-2(0), ML31376) Molino, Editorial ESP. Dist: Lectorum Pubns., Inc.

Arnold, Nick, et al. Esas Funestas Fuerzas. De Saulles, Tony, tr. 2003. (Coleccion Esa Horrible Cienca). (SPA., Illus.). 160p. (YA). (978-84-272-2054-6(5), ML8313) Molino, Editorial ESP. Dist: Lectorum Pubns., Inc.

Art & Architecture. 2010. (Experimenting with Everyday Science Ser.). (Illus.). 176p. (J). (gr. 6-12). 35.00 (978-1-60413-168-0(3), Chelsea Hse.) Facts On File, Inc.

Asimov, Isaac & Hantula, Richard. Science Fiction: Vision of Tomorrow? 2005. (Isaac Asimov's 21st Century Library of the Universe). (Illus.). 32p. (gr. 2-6). lib. bdg. 26.00 (978-0-8368-3952-4(8), Gareth Stevens Learning Library) Stevens, Gareth Publishing LLLP.

at Science, Editors. The League of Scientists: Ghost in the Water. Al-Greene, Bob, illus. 2014. (League of Scientists Ser.). (ENG.). 192p. (J). (gr. 5-9). pap. 12.95 (978-0-9700106-2-9(1)) Platypus Media, L.L.C.

Atlas de la Prehistoria. (Coleccion Atlas del Saber). (SPA., Illus.). (YA). (gr. 4-18). 20.95 (978-950-11-0889-7(9), SGM74) Sigmar ARG. Dist: Continental Bk. Co., Inc.

Atlas de la Tierra. (Coleccion Atlas del Saber). (SPA., Illus.). (YA). (gr. 4-18). 20.95 (978-950-11-0916-0(X), SGM16) Sigmar ARG. Dist: Continental Bk. Co., Inc.

Atlas de los Pueblos. (Coleccion Atlas del Saber). (SPA., Illus.). (YA). (gr. 4-18). 20.95 (978-950-11-0917-7(8), SGM73) Sigmar ARG. Dist: Continental Bk. Co., Inc.

Atlas del Espacio. (Coleccion Atlas del Saber). (SPA., Illus.). (YA). (gr. 4-18). 20.95 (978-950-11-0887-3(2), SGM72) Sigmar ARG. Dist: Continental Bk. Co., Inc.

Baeuerle, Patrick A. & Landa, Norbert. Microexplorers - Physical Science Series, 4 bks. (Illus.). (J). (gr. k-6). lib. bdg. 75.80 (978-1-56674-946-6(8)) Forest Hse. Publishing Co., Inc.

Bailey, Jacqui. Science Works, 4 bks. Lilly, Matthew, illus. Incl. Monster Bones: The Story of a Dinosaur Fossil. (ENG., Illus.). 32p. (gr. 3-6). 2004. 27.99 (978-1-4048-0565-1(6)); (Science Works). (ENG.). Illus.). 32p. 2004. 111.96 o.p. (978-1-4048-0571-2(0)) Picture Window Bks.

Baker, Lawrence W. Space Exploration - Primary Sources, 4.0. 2004. (Space Exploration Reference Library). (ENG.). 800p. 372.00 (978-0-7876-9208-7(5), Greenhaven Pr., Inc.) Cengage Gale.

Baldwin, Comingore. Access to Science for Infants & Toddlers. 2012. 21p. (J). pap. 19.99 (978-1-4691-9785-2(5)) Xlibris Corp.

Balice, Mary Lee, ed. Information Science. 2016. (Study of Science Ser.). 96p. (gr. 8-8). 72.50 (978-1-68048-231-7(9), Britannica Educational Publishing) Rosen Publishing Group, Inc., The.

Bardley, Kimberly Brubaker. POP! a Book about Bubbles. Miller, Margaret, photos by. 2015. (Illus.). 40p. pap. 6.00 (978-1-61003-614-6(X)) Center for the Collaborative Classroom.

Baredes, Carla & Lotersztain, Ileana. Preguntas que Ponen los Pelos de Punta: Sobre el Aqua y el Fuego. Basile, Javier, illus. 2004. (SPA.). pap. (978-987-98042-1-6(X)) Iamique, Ediciones.

—Preguntas que Ponen los Pelos de Punta: Sobre la Tierra y el Sol. Basile, Javier, illus. 2004. (SPA.). pap. (978-987-98042-0-9(1)) Iamique, Ediciones.

Barnes, John, et al. Science, Maths & Technology. 2003. (ENG., Illus.). 184p. pap. (978-0-7487-7121-9(2)) Nelson Thornes Ltd.

Barnham, Kay. Could I Sit on a Cloud? And Other Questions about Science, 1 vol. 2013. (Questions You Never Thought You'd Ask Ser.). (ENG.). 32p. (gr. 1-3). 29.99 (978-1-4109-5199-1(5)); pap. 8.95 (978-1-4109-5205-9(3)) Heinemann-Raintree. (Read Me!).

Barr, George. Sports Science for Young People. 2011. (Dover Children's Science Bks.). (ENG., Illus.). 176p. (J). (gr. 3-8). pap. 11.95 (978-0-486-26527-8(7), 26527-7) Dover Pubns., Inc.

Basher, Simon & Budzik, Mary. Basher Basics: Creative Writing. Basher, Simon, illus. 2013. (Basher Basics Ser.). (ENG., Illus.). 64p. (J). (gr. 3-7). pap. 7.99 (978-0-7534-7055-8(1), 9780753470558, Kingfisher) Roaring Brook Pr.

Basic Science Mysteries: Activities, Quizzes & Tests. 2003. Vol. 1. spiral bd. (978-1-928629-92-4(X)) Vol. 2. spiral bd. (978-1-928629-93-1(8)) Paradigm Accelerated Curriculum.

Basic Science Mysteries: Text. 2003. Vol. 1. spiral bd. (978-1-928629-90-0(3)) Vol. 2. spiral bd. (978-1-928629-91-7(1)) Paradigm Accelerated Curriculum.

Basic Science Mysteries Full Kit (with TRK) 2005. (Illus.). 796p. (YA). 75.00 (978-1-59476-096-9(9)) Paradigm Accelerated Curriculum.

Bauer, David. Everything Is Matter!, 6 vols., Set. 2003. (Yellow Umbrella Early Level Ser.). (ENG.). 16p. (gr. k-1). pap. 35.70 (978-0-7368-3019-5(7), Yellow Umbrella Bks.) Capstone Press of Coughlan Cos.

Baxter, Fiona, et al. Cambridge Primary Science Stage 4 Learner's Book. 2014. (Cambridge Primary Science Ser.). (ENG., Illus.). 104p. pap. 19.94 (978-1-107-67450-9(6)) Cambridge Univ. Pr.

Be a Plant Scientist: Level L, 6 vols. (Take-Twostm Ser.). 16p. 36.95 (978-0-322-03403-7(5)) Wright Group/McGraw-Hill.

Beacon Science. 2004. per. (978-1-932948-04-2(X)) Student Pr. Initiative.

Beck, Esther. Cool Biological Clues: What Hair, Bones, & Bugs Tell Us, 1 vol. 2009. (Cool CSI Ser.). (ENG., Illus.). 32p. (YA). (gr. 3-6). 28.50 (978-1-60453-483-2(4)) ABDO Publishing Co.

—Cool Crime Scene Basics: Securing the Scene, 1 vol. 2009. (Cool CSI Ser.). (ENG., Illus.). 32p. (YA). (gr. 3-6). 28.50 (978-1-60453-484-9(2)) ABDO Publishing Co.

—Cool Forensic Tools: Technology at Work, 1 vol. 2009. (Cool CSI Ser.). (ENG., Illus.). 32p. (YA). (gr. 3-6). 28.50 (978-1-60453-486-3(9)) ABDO Publishing Co.

—Cool Physical Evidence: What's Left Behind, 1 vol. 2009. (Cool CSI Ser.). (ENG., Illus.). 32p. (YA). (gr. 3-6). 28.50 (978-1-60453-487-0(7)) ABDO Publishing Co.

—Cool Written Records: The Proof Is in the Paper, 1 vol. 2009. (Cool CSI Ser.). (ENG., Illus.). 32p. (YA). (gr. 3-6). 28.50 (978-1-60453-488-7(5)) ABDO Publishing Co.

Becker, Helaine. Magic up Your Sleeve: Amazing Illusions, Tricks, & Science Facts You'll Never Believe. Dávila, Claudia, illus. 2010. (ENG.). 64p. (J). (gr. 3-6). pap. 10.95 (978-1-897349-76-2(9), Maple Tree Pr.) Owlkids Bks. Inc. CAN. Dist: Publishers Group West (PGW).

—Science on the Loose: Amazing Activities & Science Facts You'll Never Believe. Dávila, Claudia & Owlkids Books Inc. Staff, illus. 2008. (ENG.). 64p. (J). (gr. 3-6). pap. 10.95 (978-1-897349-19-9(X), Maple Tree Pr.) Owlkids Bks. Inc. CAN. Dist: Publishers Group West (PGW).

Benchmark Education Company, LLC Staff, compiled by. Bloom & Grow & Simple Systems. 2005. spiral bd. 225.00 (978-1-4108-5804-7(9)) Benchmark Education Co.

—Early Science Theme Set. 2006. (J). 1475.00 (978-1-4108-7064-3(2)) Benchmark Education Co.

—Early/Fluent Science Theme Set. 2006. (J). 810.00 (978-1-4108-7084-1(7)) Benchmark Education Co.

—English Explorers Science Set. 2007. (English Explorers Ser.). (J). spiral bd. 4595.00 (978-1-4108-9740-4(0)) Benchmark Education Co.

—My First Reader's Theater Lap Books. 2009. (My First Reader's Theater Ser.). (J). (gr. k-1). 575.00 (978-1-4108-8455-8(4)) Benchmark Education Co.

—Science & Technology. 2006. spiral bd. 115.00 (978-1-4108-6923-4(7)) 2006. spiral bd. 105.00 (978-1-4108-6935-7(0)) 2005. spiral bd. 42.00 (978-1-4108-3880-3(3)) 2005. spiral bd. 235.00 (978-1-4108-4520-7(6)) 2005. spiral bd. 255.00 (978-1-4108-5444-5(2)) 2005. spiral bd. 145.00 (978-1-4108-5445-2(0)) 2005. spiral bd. 170.00 (978-1-4108-5855-9(3)) 2005. spiral bd. 130.00 (978-1-4108-5856-6(1)) 2005. spiral bd. 110.00 (978-1-4108-3866-7(8)) 2005. spiral bd. 125.00 (978-1-4108-3842-1(0)) 2005. spiral bd. 60.00 (978-1-4108-3843-8(9)) 2005. spiral bd. 55.00 (978-1-4108-3855-1(2)) 2005. spiral bd. 115.00 (978-1-4108-3854-4(4)) Benchmark Education Co.

—Science As Inquiry. 2005. spiral bd. 80.00 (978-1-4108-3918-3(4)); spiral bd. 85.00 (978-1-4108-5848-1(0)); spiral bd. 55.00 (978-1-4108-3919-0(2)) Benchmark Education Co.

—Science as Inquiry. 2005. spiral bd. 145.00 (978-1-4108-5435-3(3)); spiral bd. 85.00 (978-1-4108-4516-0(8)) Benchmark Education Co.

—Science Classroom Library. 2005. spiral bd. 390.00 (978-1-4108-6019-4(1)) Benchmark Education Co.

—Science in Personal & Social Perspectives. 2006. spiral bd. 185.00 (978-1-4108-6948-7(2)) 2006. spiral bd. 295.00 (978-1-4108-6944-9(X)) 2006. spiral bd. 205.00 (978-1-4108-6929-6(6)) 2005. spiral bd. 185.00 (978-1-4108-5854-2(5)) 2005. spiral bd. 245.00 (978-1-4108-5853-5(7)) 2005. spiral bd. 335.00 (978-1-4108-5443-8(4)) 2005. spiral bd. 375.00 (978-1-4108-5442-1(6)) 2005. spiral bd. 300.00 (978-1-4108-4519-1(2)) 2005. spiral bd. 35.00 (978-1-4108-3877-3(3)) 2005. spiral bd. 75.00 (978-1-4108-3863-6(3)) 2005. spiral bd. 80.00 (978-1-4108-3857-5(9)) 2005. spiral bd. 140.00 (978-1-4108-3856-8(0)) 2005. spiral bd. 225.00 (978-1-4108-3862-9(5)) Benchmark Education Co.

—Science in Personal Social Perspectives. 2005. spiral bd. 125.00 (978-1-4108-3846-9(3)); spiral bd. 90.00 (978-1-4108-3847-6(1)) Benchmark Education Co.

—Science Standards Set. 2006. pap. 215.00 (978-1-4108-6953-1(9)) 2006. pap. 350.00 (978-1-4108-6952-4(0)) 2006. spiral bd. 1195.00 (978-1-4108-6951-7(2)) 2006. spiral bd. 785.00 (978-1-4108-6937-1(7)) 2006. spiral bd. 2065.00 (978-1-4108-6950-0(4)) 2006. spiral bd. 195.00 (978-1-4108-6941-8(5)) 2006. spiral bd. 1075.00 (978-1-4108-6940-1(7)) 2005. spiral bd. 6110.00 (978-1-4108-5446-9(9)) Benchmark Education Co.

—Science Strands Set. 2005. spiral bd. 695.00 (978-1-4108-5562-6(7)); spiral bd. 2580.00 (978-1-4108-5459-9(0)) Benchmark Education Co.

—Science, Technology & Society. 2005. spiral bd. 185.00 (978-1-4108-3753-0(X)) Benchmark Education Co.

—Science, Technology, & Society. 2005. spiral bd. 70.00 (978-1-4108-3954-1(0)); spiral bd. 80.00 (978-1-4108-3961-9(3)); spiral bd. 80.00 (978-1-4108-3962-6(1)); spiral bd. 145.00 (978-1-4108-4499-6(4)); spiral bd. 110.00 (978-1-4108-5425-4(6)); spiral bd. 115.00 (978-1-4108-5841-2(3)); spiral bd. 74.00 (978-1-4108-5842-9(1)) Benchmark Education Co.

—Science Text Set. 2005. spiral bd. 175.00 (978-1-4108-3839-1(0)); spiral bd. 315.00 (978-1-4108-3824-7(2)); spiral bd. 1025.00 (978-1-4108-3822-3(6)); spiral bd. 4475.00 (978-1-4108-3820-9(X)); spiral bd. 715.00 (978-1-4108-3818-6(8)); spiral bd. 200.00 (978-1-4108-3840-7(4)) Benchmark Education Co.

—Science Texts Set. 2005. (Navigators Ser.). (J). spiral bd. 875.00 (978-1-4108-5309-7(8)) Benchmark Education Co.

—Science Theme: Science in Personal & Social Perspectives. 2005. spiral bd. 115.00 (978-1-4108-5313-4(6)) Benchmark Education Co.

—Science Themes. 2006. spiral bd. 2460.00 (978-1-4108-7022-3(7)); spiral bd. 1295.00 (978-1-4108-7037-7(5)) Benchmark Education Co.

—Science Themes: Levels N-P Grade 3. 2006. (J). 1050.00 (978-1-4108-7109-1(6)) Benchmark Education Co.

—Science Themes: Levels Q-R Grade 4. 2006. (J). 1025.00 (978-1-4108-7123-7(1)) Benchmark Education Co.

—Science Themes: Levels S-U Grade 5. 2006. (J). 1080.00 (978-1-4108-7138-1(X)) Benchmark Education Co.

—Science Themes: Levels V-X Grade 6. 2006. (J). 765.00 (978-1-4108-7150-3(9)) Benchmark Education Co.

—Spanish Science Standard Set. 2005. spiral bd. 3455.00 (978-1-4108-5857-3(X)) Benchmark Education Co.

Bennett, Andrea T. & Kessler, James H. Sunlight, Skyscrapers, & Soda-Pop: The Wherever-You-Look Science Book. Sarecky, Melody, illus. 2003. (J). 12.95 (978-0-8412-3870-1(7)) American Chemical Society.

Berenstain, Stan, et al. The Berenstain Bears' Big Book of Science & Nature. 2013. (Dover Children's Science Bks.). (ENG.). 192p. (J). (gr. k-3). pap. 14.99 (978-0-486-49834-8(4)) Dover Pubns., Inc.

Bergethon, Peter R. Marty's Miraculous Monday Reader. Date not set. (Illus.). (J). (gr. k-3). pap. (978-1-58447-011-3(9)) Symmetry Learning Systems.

—Measuring My World: Student Science Journal. Date not set. (Illus.). (J). pap. (978-1-58447-006-9(2)) Symmetry Learning Systems.

—Understanding My World: Student Science Journal. Date not set. (Illus.). (J). pap. (978-1-58447-008-3(9)) Symmetry Learning Systems.

Bernardy, Catherine J., et al. Let's Investigate, 12 Vol., Set. (Illus.). 384p. (J). 167.40 (978-0-88682-667-3(5)) Creative Co., The.

Big Book Collection. 2003. (Scott Foresman Science Ser.). (gr. 1-18). 138.60 (978-0-328-00684-7(X)); (gr. 3-18). 138.60 (978-0-328-00686-1(6)) Addison-Wesley Educational Pubs., Inc.

Billings, Henry, et al. The Outer Edge - Cool Science. 2005. (Jt: Non-Fiction Reading Ser.). (ENG., Illus.). 120p. (gr. 6-12). per. 25.56 (978-0-07-869053-2(6), 0078690536) SRA/McGraw-Hill.

Bingham, Jane & Hile, Lori. Solving Mysteries with Science. 2013. (Solving Mysteries with Science Ser.). (ENG.). 48p. (gr. 5-5). pap. 35.96 (978-1-4109-4995-0(8)) Heinemann-Raintree.

Biskup, Agnieszka, et al. Ciencia Gráfica. Strictly Spanish, LLC., tr. Erwin, Steve, illus. 2012. (Ciencia Gráfica Ser.). (SPA.). 32p. (gr. 3-4). lib. bdg. 122.60 (978-1-4296-9241-0(3)) Capstone Press of Coughlan Cos.

—Graphic Science & Engineering in Action. Baez, Marcelo, illus. 2013. (Graphic Science & Engineering in Action Ser.). (ENG.). 32p. (gr. 3-4). lib. bdg. 122.60 (978-1-4296-9938-9(8), Graphic Library) Capstone Press of Coughlan Cos.

—LOL Physical Science. Lum, Bernice, illus. 2012. (LOL Physical Science Ser.). (ENG.). 32p. (gr. 3-4). 54.64 (978-1-4296-9153-6(0), Fact Finders) Capstone Press of Coughlan Cos.

BJU Staff. Science Activity Manual St Gr6. 2004. pap. 15.00 (978-1-59166-008-8(4)) BJU Pr.

—Science Student Notebook Grd 1. 2004. pap. 7.50 (978-1-57924-927-4(2)) BJU Pr.

—Science Student Notebook Grd 3. 2004. pap. 7.50 (978-1-57924-929-8(9)) BJU Pr.

—Science Student Text Grd 1. 2004. 23.50 (978-1-57924-908-3(6)) BJU Pr.

—Science Student Text Grd 3. 2004. 23.50 (978-1-57924-914-4(0)) BJU Pr.

—Science Student Text Grd 6. 2004. pap. 17.00 (978-1-59166-006-4(8)) BJU Pr.

Blane, Francisco. Up & Down: Lap Book. 2009. (My First Reader's Theater Set B Ser.). (J). 28.00 (978-1-60634-989-2(9)) Benchmark Education Co.

Blastoff! - Group 2, 5 bks., Set. 142.50 (978-0-7614-1400-1(2), Benchmark Bks.) Marshall Cavendish Corp.

Block, Cheryl. The Rainbow Web. 2005. (Illus.). 32p. (J). 19.95 (978-0-9761625-0-6(4)) Block Publishing.

Board, Jon & Cross, Alan. Cambridge Primary Science Stage 1 Learner's Book. 2014. (Cambridge Primary Science Ser.). (ENG., Illus.). 68p. pap. 17.44 (978-1-107-61138-2(5)) Cambridge Univ. Pr.

—Cambridge Primary Science Stage 2 Learner's Book. 2014. (Cambridge Primary Science Ser.). (ENG., Illus.). 78p. pap. 17.44 (978-1-107-61139-9(3)) Cambridge Univ. Pr.

—Cambridge Primary Science Stage 3 Learner's Book. 2014. (Cambridge Primary Science Ser.). (ENG., Illus.). 80p. pap. 17.44 (978-1-107-61141-2(5)) Cambridge Univ. Pr.

Bodach, Vijaya Khisty. Sink or Float? 2008. (Discovering & Exploring Science Ser.). (Illus.). 16p. (J). (gr. -1-3). lib. bdg. 12.95 (978-0-7569-8414-4(9)) Perfection Learning Corp.

—What Is Missing? 2008. (Discovering & Exploring Science Ser.). (Illus.). 16p. (J). (gr. -1-3). lib. bdg. 12.95 (978-0-7569-8253-9(7)) Perfection Learning Corp.

Body Numbers, 6 pack. (Discovery World Ser.). 16p. (gr. 1-2). 28.00 (978-0-7635-8467-2(3)) Rigby Education.

Body Parts: KinderFacts Individual Title Six-Packs. (Kinderstarters Ser.). 8p. (gr. -1-1). 21.00 (978-0-7635-8741-3(9)) Rigby Education.

Body Talk: Individual Title Six-Packs. (Story Steps Ser.). (gr. k-2). 32.00 (978-0-7635-9815-0(1)) Rigby Education.

Bolte, Mari. Super Science Projects: You Can Make & Share. 2015. (Sleepover Girls Crafts Ser.). (ENG., Illus.). 64p. (gr. 3-4). pap. 9.95 (978-1-62370-422-3(7)) Capstone Press of Coughlan Cos.

Bones Sets: 1 Each of 3 Big Books. (Sunshinetm Science Ser.). (gr. 1-2). 93.95 (978-0-7802-0530-7(8)) Wright Group/McGraw-Hill.

Bones Sets: 1 Each of 3 Student Books. (Sunshinetm Science Ser.). (gr. 1-2). 17.95 (978-0-7802-0271-9(6)) Wright Group/McGraw-Hill.

Books Are Fun Exclusive Let's Start Science 5 Set. 2005. (J). lib. bdg. (978-1-59566-165-4(4)) QEB Publishing Inc.

Boring, Mel & Dendy, Leslie. Guinea Pig Scientists: Bold Self-Experimenters in Science & Medicine. Mordan, C. B. & Mordan, C., illus. rev. ed. 2005. (ENG.). 224p. (J). (gr. 5-12). 19.99 (978-0-8050-7316-4(7), 9780805073164, Holt, Henry & Co. Bks. For Young Readers) Holt, Henry & Co.

Bow, James. Impossible Science. 2012. (ENG.). 32p. (J). (978-0-7787-8009-0(0)); pap. (978-0-7787-8014-4(7)) Crabtree Publishing Co.

Bradley, Timothy. The Science of Monsters (Grade 6) 2016. (TIME for KIDS(r) Nonfiction Readers Ser.). (Illus.). 64p. (J). (gr. 6-6). 10.99 (978-1-4938-3607-9(2)) Teacher Created Materials, Inc.

Branigan, Carrie. First Steps in Science: Big Story Book. 2003. (ENG., Illus.). 24p. (J). 75.00 (978-0-7487-6865-3(3)) Nelson Thornes Ltd. GBR. Dist: Trans-Atlantic Pubns., Inc.

—Image Bank. 2003. (ENG., Illus.). 96p. (J). 150.00 (978-0-7487-6866-0(1)) Nelson Thornes Ltd. GBR. Dist: Trans-Atlantic Pubns., Inc.

Brasch, Nicolas. Theme Parks, Playgrounds, & Toys. 2010. (Science Behind Ser.). (Illus.). 32p. (J). lib. bdg. 28.50 (978-1-59920-562-5(9)) Black Rabbit Bks.

Brecher, Erwin. Are There Rainbows on the Moon? Over 200 Bizarre, Weird & Wonderful Puzzles with Science. 2013. (ENG., Illus.). 288p. 20.95 (978-1-78097-107-0(9)) Carlton Bks., Ltd. GBR. Dist: Independent Pubs. Group.

Brewer, Ebenezer Cobham. A Guide to the Scientific Knowledge of Things Familiar by Rev Dr Brewer Carefully Revised, & Adapted for Use in Families & Schools of the U. 2006. 504p. per. 29.99 (978-1-4255-5648-8(5)) Michigan Publishing.

Britannica, Learning Library. Science & Nature. 2003. (Illus.). 64p. 14.95 (978-1-59339-033-4(5)) Encyclopaedia Britannica, Inc.

Brocker, Susan & Furgang, Kathy. Pioneers in Medicine: Set Of 6. 2011. (Navigators Ser.). (J). pap. 48.00 net. (978-1-4108-0422-8(4)) Benchmark Education Co.

Bronson, Cary. I am Not a Flying Elephant Fish! A Children's Science Book on the Butterfly. Gomer, William, illus. l.t. ed. 2004. 32p. (J). lib. bdg. 14.95 (978-0-9746094-0-9(4)) Connect With Your Kid Bks.

Brown Bag Science Set Gr. 1-2. 2004. (J). (978-1-57022-470-6(6)) ECS Learning Systems, Inc.

Brown Bag Science Set Gr. 3-4. 2004. (J). (978-1-57022-471-3(4)) ECS Learning Systems, Inc.

Brown, Jordan. Unmasking the Science of Superpowers! Burroughs, Scott, illus. 2016. (Science of Fun Stuff Ser.). (ENG.). 48p. (J). (gr. 1-3). pap. 3.99 (978-1-4814-6778-0(6), Simon Spotlight) Simon Spotlight.

Buckley, Arabella. The Fairy-Land of Science. 2007. 204p. 19.99 (978-1-59986-737-3(0)); per. 9.99 (978-1-59986-823-3(7)) Filiquarian Publishing, LLC.

—The Fairy-Land of Science (Yesterday's Classics) 2006. (Illus.). 244p. (J). per. 10.95 (978-1-59915-024-6(7)) Yesterday's Classics.

Buckley, Arabella Burton. The Fairy Land of Science. 2004. reprint ed. pap. 20.95 (978-1-4191-6179-7(2)) Kessinger Publishing, LLC.

Bulging Brains. (YA). (gr. 5-8). pap. (978-0-439-14976-1(2)) Scholastic GBR. Dist: Lectorum Pubns., Inc.

Burncrot, Curt & Dunlap, Shiree. Testing Targets: For Science of the Physical Creation. Zyp, Nicole & Robinson, Heldi, eds. 2004. 19p. (YA). (gr. 9-12). pap. 5.00 (978-1-888786-44-6(2)) Basic Skills Assessment & Educational Services.

Burgan, Michael, et al. Captured Science History. 2017. (Captured Science History Ser.). (ENG.). 64p. (gr. 5-7). 138.60 **(978-0-7565-5660-0(0)**, CPB Grades 4-8) Compass Point Bks.

Calhoun, Yael, ed. Science News Flash Set, 4-Volumes. 2007. (Science News Flash Ser.). (gr. 6-12). 127.80 (978-0-7910-9660-4(2), Chelsea Hse.) Facts On File, Inc.

Cambridge Studios. Interactive World Issues, Set. 2nd ed. 2003. (C). (gr. 6-12). cd-rom 55.31 (978-0-07-255648-3(X), 9780072556483) Glencoe/McGraw-Hill.

Canavan, Thomas. Why Do Ice Cubes Float? Questions & Answers about the Science of Everyday Materials. 2013. (Science F. A. Q. Ser.). (Illus.). 32p. (gr. 3-6). 31.35 (978-1-78212-396-5(2)) Arcturus Publishing GBR. Dist: Black Rabbit Bks.

Canetti, Yanitzia. Rhyming Tongue Twisters Science: Science. 2010. 32p. (J). pap. 6.99 (978-1-59835-265-8(2), BrickHouse Education) Cambridge BrickHouse, Inc.

—Trabalenguas Científicos. 2010. 32p. (J). pap. 6.99 (978-1-59835-264-1(4), BrickHouse Education) Cambridge BrickHouse, Inc.

Capstone Press. Nasty (But Useful!) Science. 2010. (Nasty (but Useful!) Science Ser.). (ENG.). 32p. lib. bdg. 103.96 (978-1-4296-5921-5(1), Fact Finders) Capstone Press of Coughlan Cos.

Carangelo, Audrey & Hess, Debra. Radiation, Rats, & Mutant Monsters! 2007. (Read on! Special Edition: Level RA Ser.). (Illus.). 23p. (J). (gr. 4-7). pap. 18.51 (978-1-4190-3506-7(1)) Steck-Vaughn.

Carlton Books UK. Science Museum. 2013. (ENG.). 24p. (J). (gr. k-2). pap., act. bk. ed. 8.99 (978-1-78097-347-0(0)) Carlton Bks., Ltd. GBR. Dist: Independent Pubs. Group.

Cave, Holly. Really, Really Big Questions about Science. Aspinall, Marc, illus. 2014. (Really Really Big Questions Ser.). (ENG.). 64p. (J). (gr. 4-7). 16.99 (978-0-7534-7181-4(7), 9780753471814, Kingfisher) Roaring Brook Pr.

Cells & Things. 2004. (Illus.). lib. bdg. 7.95 (978-0-8225-4371-8(0)) Lerner Publishing Group.

Challoner, Jack. Start-Up Science, 8 bks., Set. Incl. Big & Small. lib. bdg. 24.26 (978-0-8172-4319-7(4)); Fast & Slow. lib. bdg. 24.26 (978-0-8172-4320-3(8)); Floating & Sinking. lib. bdg. 16.98 (978-0-8172-4317-3(8)); Hot & Cold. lib. bdg. 24.76 (978-0-8172-4323-4(2)); Light & Dark. lib. bdg. 24.76 (978-0-8172-4321-0(6)); Loud & Quiet. lib. bdg. 24.26 (978-0-8172-4318-0(6)); Push & Pull. lib. bdg. 24.26 (978-0-8172-4316-6(X)); Wet & Dry. lib. bdg. 24.26 (978-0-8172-4322-7(4)); 32p. (J). (gr. 1-4). 1996. (Illus.). Set lib. bdg. 135.84 (978-0-8172-4324-1(0)) Heinemann-Raintree.

Chang, Maria L. & Zile, Susan Van. Science: Graphic Organizers & Mini-Lessons. 2006. (Best Practices in Action Ser.). (ENG., Illus.). 48p. pap. 10.99 (978-0-439-54896-0(9), Teaching Resources) Scholastic, Inc.

Chasse, Betsy & Captured Light Distribution, creators. The Little Book of Bleeps. 2004. (Illus.). 14.95 (978-0-9761074-0-8(6)) Captured Light Distribution, LLC.

Chelsea Clubhouse Science Exploration. (Illus.). (J). 418.50 (978-0-7910-7274-5(6), Chelsea Hse.) Facts On File, Inc.

Chesebro, Doreen & Badasch, Shirley. Student Activity Guide for Health Science Fundamentals. 2nd ed. 2015. (ENG.). 516p. (C). pap. 38.60 (978-0-13-425212-4(8)) Pearson Education.

Children's Big Book of Questions & Answers. 2011. (Illus.). 224p. (J). (978-1-4351-3677-9(2)) Barnes & Noble, Inc.

Christopher, Garrett. Look at These Animals: A Content Area Reader-science. 2005. (Sadlier Phonics Reading Program). (Illus.). 16p. (gr. k-2). 25.20 (978-0-8215-7812-4(X)) Sadlier, William H. Inc.

Ciencias. (Enciclopedias Everest Internacional Ser.). (SPA., Illus.). (YA). (gr. 5-8). 41.95 *(978-84-241-9405-5(5)*, EV7495) Everest Editora ESP. Dist: Lectorum Pubns., Inc.

Ciencias Naturales. (Coleccion Ciencas Naturales Ser.). (SPA., Illus.). (J). Bk. 1. (gr. 1). pap. 8.95 *(978-968-416-500-7(5)*, FN5005)Bk. 2. (gr. 2). pap. 10.95 *(978-968-416-489-5(0)*, FN4890)Bk. 3. (gr. 3). pap. 10.95 *(978-968-416-490-1(4)*, FN4904)Bk. 4. (gr. 4). pap. 10.95 *(978-968-416-491-8(2)*, FN4912)Bk. 5. (gr. 5). pap. 11.95 *(978-968-416-492-5(0)*, FN4920)Bk. 6. (gr. 6). pap. 12.95 *(978-968-416-493-2(9)*, FN4939) Fernandez USA Publishing.

Cientificos! (SPA.). (J). Vol. 7. wbk. ed. 15.00 *(978-958-04-6435-8(9))* Vol. 8. wbk. ed. 15.00 *(978-958-04-6436-5(7))* Vol. 9. wbk. ed. 15.00 *(978-958-04-6437-2(5))* Norma S.A. COL. Dist: Distribuidora Norma, Inc.

Cientificos! Ciencia Integrada 1. (SPA.). (J). 30.00 *(978-958-04-5245-4(8))* Norma S.A. COL. Dist: Distribuidora Norma, Inc.

Cientificos! Ciencia Integrada 2. (SPA.). (J). 30.00 *(978-958-04-5246-1(6))* Norma S.A. COL. Dist: Distribuidora Norma, Inc.

Cientificos! Ciencia Integrada 3. (SPA.). (J). 30.00 *(978-958-04-5247-8(4))* Norma S.A. COL. Dist: Distribuidora Norma, Inc.

Cientificos! Ciencia Integrada 4. 35.00 *(978-958-04-5248-5(2))* Norma S.A. COL. Dist: Distribuidora Norma, Inc.

Cientificos! Ciencia Integrada 5. (SPA.). (J). 40.00 *(978-958-04-5249-2(0))* Norma S.A. COL. Dist: Distribuidora Norma, Inc.

Cientificos! Ciencia Integrada 6. (SPA.). (J). 45.00 *(978-958-04-5250-8(4))* Norma S.A. COL. Dist: Distribuidora Norma, Inc.

Cipriano, Jeri S. Let's Look at Rocks, 6 vols., Set. 2003. (Yellow Umbrella Early Level Ser.). (ENG.). 16p. (gr. k-1). pap. 35.70 *(978-0-7368-3015-7(4)*, Yellow Umbrella Bks.) Capstone Press of Coughlan Cos.

Clarke, Phillip. Mysteries & Marvels of Science - Internet Linked. rev. ed. 2008. (Mysteries & Marvels of Science Ser.). 96p. (J). pap. 16.99 *(978-0-7945-1985-8(7)*, Usborne) EDC Publishing.

Clarke, Phillip, et al. The Usborne Internet-Linked Mysteries & Marvels of Science. Furnival, Keith, illus. 2005. 96p. (J). *(978-0-439-81568-0(1))* Scholastic, Inc.

Claybourne, Anna. Whiz Kid Science, 1 vol. Scott, Kimberly & Dean, Venetia, illus. 2014. (Whiz Kid Science Ser.). (ENG.). 32p. (gr. 2-4). 179.94 *(978-1-4109-6751-0(4)*, Read Me!) Heinemann-Raintree.

Cleary, Brian P. Mrs. Riley Bought Five Itchy Aardvarks & Other Painless Tricks for Memorizing Science Facts. Sandy, J. P., illus. 2008. (Adventures in Memory Ser.). (ENG.). 48p. (gr. 4-6). 26.60 *(978-0-8225-7819-2(0))* Lerner Publishing Group.

Cleveland, Don. How Do We Know How the Brain Works. 2005. (Great Scientific Questions & the Scientists Who Answered Them Ser.). (Illus.). 112p. (J). (gr. 7-12). lib. bdg. 34.60 *(978-1-4042-0078-4(9))* Rosen Publishing Group, Inc., The.

Clouds, Rain, & Fog: Big Book. (Sunshinetm Science Ser.). 24p. (gr. 1-2). 37.50 *(978-0-7802-1374-6(2))* Wright Group/McGraw-Hill.

Cloyd, J. B. Rocks We Use: A Content Area Reader. 2005. (Emergent/Early (Prek-2) Science Package Ser.). 12p. (gr. k-2). 25.20 *(978-0-8215-7813-1(8))* Sadlier, William H. Inc.

Cobb, Vicki. What's the Big Idea? Amazing Science Questions for the Curious Kid. 2010. (ENG., Illus.). 208p. (J). (gr. 3-6). pap. 19.95 *(978-1-61608-013-6(2)*, 1310418) Skyhorse Publishing Co., Inc.

—What's the BIG Idea? Amazing Science Questions for the Curious Kid. 2013. (ENG., Illus.). 208p. (J). (gr. 2-5). pap. 12.95 *(978-1-62087-685-5(X)*, 620685, Sky Pony Pr.) Skyhorse Publishing Co., Inc.

—Where's the Science Here? Classroom Library. 2008. pap. 34.95 *(978-0-8225-8979-2(6))* Lerner Publishing Group.

—Where's the Science Here? Complete Library. 2008. pap. 210.95 *(978-0-8225-9379-9(3))* Lerner Publishing Group.

Collard, Sneed B., III. Science Adventures, 4 bks., Set. Incl. In the Deep Sea. 44p. (YA). (gr. 3-6). lib. bdg. 29.93 *(978-0-7614-1952-5(7))*; In the Rain Forest Canopy. 44p. (J). (gr. 3-7). lib. bdg. 29.93 *(978-0-7614-1954-9(3)*, Benchmark Bks.); In the Wild. 48p. (gr. 4-7). lib. bdg. 29.93 *(978-0-7614-1955-6(1)*, Benchmark Bks.); On the Coral Reefs. 43p. (YA). (gr. 3-6). lib. bdg. 29.93 *(978-0-7614-1953-2(5))*; (Illus.). 2005. 119.71 *(978-0-7614-1951-8(9)*, Benchmark Bks.) Marshall Cavendish Corp.

Collins. Collins Fascinating Facts - Science. rev. ed. 2016. (Collins Fascinating Facts Ser.). (ENG., Illus.). 72p. (J). (gr. 1-3). pap. 10.99 *(978-0-00-816918-3(7))* HarperCollins Pubs. Ltd. GBR. Dist: Independent Pubs. Group.

Collins Publishers Staff & Collins KS3 Staff. KS3 Science. 2014. (ENG., Illus.). 144p. (YA). (gr. 6-9). pap. 12.95 *(978-0-00-756282-4(9))* HarperCollins Pubs. Ltd. GBR. Dist: Independent Pubs. Group.

Collins, Terry, et al. Monster Science. Mallea, Cristian & Gervasio, illus. 2013. (Monster Science Ser.). (ENG.). 32p. (gr. 3-4). lib. bdg. 275.85 *(978-1-4765-0427-8(X))*; lib. bdg. 61.30 *(978-1-4765-0426-1(1))* Capstone Press of Coughlan Cos. (Graphic Library).

Collins UK Publishing Staff & Collins KS3 Staff. KS3 Science. 2014. (ENG.). 216p. (YA). (gr. 6-9). pap. 17.95 *(978-0-00-756283-1(7))* HarperCollins Pubs. Ltd. GBR. Dist: Independent Pubs. Group.

—KS3 Science, Year 7. 2014. (ENG.). 80p. (J). (gr. 6-7). pap., wbk. ed. 8.95 *(978-0-00-756273-2(X))* HarperCollins Pubs. Ltd. GBR. Dist: Independent Pubs. Group.

—KS3 Science, Year 8. 2014. (ENG.). 80p. (YA). (gr. 7-8). pap., wbk. ed. 8.95 *(978-0-00-756274-9(8))* HarperCollins Pubs. Ltd. GBR. Dist: Independent Pubs. Group.

—KS3 Science, Year 9. 2014. (ENG.). 80p. (YA). (gr. 8-9). pap., wbk. ed. 8.95 *(978-0-00-756275-6(6))* HarperCollins Pubs. Ltd. GBR. Dist: Independent Pubs. Group.

Collins UK Publishing Staff & Letts KS2 Staff. Maths, English & Science Test Practice Papers. 2016. (Letts KS2 Success Ser.). (ENG.). 280p. (gr. 3-6). pap. 20.95 *(978-1-84419-836-8(7))* HarperCollins Pubs. Ltd. GBR. Dist: Independent Pubs. Group.

Collison, Paul, et al. Nelson Modular Science, Bk. 1. 2nd rev. ed. 2005. (ENG., Illus.). 296p. (YA). pap. 36.50 *(978-0-7487-6856-1(4))* Nelson Thornes Ltd. GBR. Dist: Trans-Atlantic Pubns., Inc.

Contemporary Issues in Science, 8 vols., Set. 2nd rev. ed. 2012. (Contemporary Issues in Science Ser.). (C). (gr. 9). 280.00 *(978-0-8160-8303-9(7))* Facts On File, Inc.

Cook, Sherry & Johnson, Terri. Andy Acid, 26 vols. Kuhn, Jesse, illus. I.t. ed. 2006. (Quirkles — Exploring Phonics through Science Ser.: 1). 32p. (J). 7.99 *(978-1-933815-00-8(0)*, Quirkles, The) Creative 3, LLC.

—Botanist Bert, 26 vols. Kuhn, Jesse, illus. I.t. ed. 2006. (Quirkles — Exploring Phonics through Science Ser.: 2). 32p. (J). 7.99 *(978-1-933815-01-5(9)*, Quirkles, The) Creative 3, LLC.

—Colorful Caroline, 26 vols. Kuhn, Jesse, illus. I.t. ed. 2006. (Quirkles — Exploring Phonics through Science Ser.: 3). 32p. (J). 7.99 *(978-1-933815-02-2(7)*, Quirkles, The) Creative 3, LLC.

—Density Dan, 26 vols. Kuhn, Jesse, illus. I.t. ed. 2006. (Quirkles — Exploring Phonics through Science Ser.: 4). 32p. (J). 7.99 *(978-1-933815-03-9(5)*, Quirkles, The) Creative 3, LLC.

—Friction Fred, 26 vols. Kuhn, Jesse, illus. I.t. ed. 2006. (Quirkles — Exploring Phonics through Science Ser.: 6). 32p. (J). 7.99 *(978-1-933815-05-3(1)*, Quirkles, The) Creative 3, LLC.

Cooke, Andy, et al. Spectrum 8. 2003. (Spectrum Key Stage 3 Science Ser.). (ENG., Illus.). 168p. pap. 12.95 *(978-0-521-75007-3(5))* Cambridge Univ. Pr.

—Spectrum Year 9. 2003. (Spectrum Key Stage 3 Science Ser.). (ENG., Illus.). 184p. pap. 13.50 *(978-0-521-75010-3(5))* Cambridge Univ. Pr.

Core Concepts. 2013. (Core Concepts Ser.). 96p. (YA). (gr. 7-12). 346.00 *(978-1-4777-0568-1(6))* Rosen Publishing Group, Inc., The.

Core Concepts: Set 2. 2013. (Core Concepts Ser.). 96p. (YA). (gr. 7-12). 346.00 *(978-1-4777-2727-0(2))* Rosen Publishing Group, Inc., The.

Core Concepts: Sets 1 - 3. 2014. (Core Concepts Ser.). 96p. (YA). (gr. 7-12). 1068.00 *(978-1-4777-8100-5(5))* Rosen Publishing Group, Inc., The.

Corliss, William R. Scientific Anomalies & other Provocative Phenomena. 2003. (Illus.). 300p. (Orig.). (YA). (gr. 9-12). pap. 17.95 *(978-0-915554-45-4(3))* Sourcebook Project, The.

Cornsweet, Tom. Why Is Everything! Doing Science. 2009. 260p. 29.95 *(978-0-595-51834-0(6))*; pap. 19.95 *(978-0-595-52871-4(6))* iUniverse, Inc.

Corrigan, Patricia. Bringing Science to Life: A Guide from the St. Louis Science Center. 2007. 128p. (J). pap. 16.00 *(978-1-933370-16-3(5))* Reedy Pr.

Cover Your Bases. 2004. (YA). ring bd. *(978-0-9747576-0-5(8))* Event-Based Science Institute, Inc.

Crews, G. Ellen G Goes Fishing. marion, designs & proctor, brian, illus. 2007. 28p. pap. 4.99 *(978-0-9795236-0-1(5))* Crews Pubns., LLC.

Cuaderno Cientificos! 4, Vol. 4. (SPA.). (J). wbk. ed. 15.00 *(978-958-04-5346-8(2))* Norma S.A. COL. Dist: Distribuidora Norma, Inc.

Cuaderno Cientificos! 5, Vol. 5. (SPA.). (J). wbk. ed. 15.00 *(978-958-04-5347-5(0))* Norma S.A. COL. Dist: Distribuidora Norma, Inc.

Cuaderno Cientificos! 6, Vol. 6. (SPA.). (J). wbk. ed. 15.00 *(978-958-04-5348-2(9))* Norma S.A. COL. Dist: Distribuidora Norma, Inc.

Cullen, Dave. Big Book of Science. Leeks, David, illus. 2004. 48p. (J). 7.99 *(978-1-85854-532-5(3))* Brimax Books Ltd. GBR. Dist: Byeway Bks.

Culp, Jennifer. Ancient Chinese Technology. 2016. (Spotlight on the Rise & Fall of Ancient Civilizations Ser.). 48p. (J). (gr. 6-6). pap. 11.75 *(978-1-4777-8897-4(2))* Rosen Publishing Group, Inc., The.

Cutting-Edge STEM Careers. 2014. (Cutting-Edge STEM Careers Ser.). 128p. (J). pap. 75.40 *(978-1-4777-8106-7(4)*, Rosen Classroom) Rosen Publishing Group, Inc., The.

Cutting Machines, 6 vols. (Sunshinetm Science Ser.). 24p. (gr. 1-2). 31.50 *(978-0-7802-0302-0(X))*; 36.95 *(978-0-7802-0553-6(7))* Wright Group/McGraw-Hill.

Dalgleish, Sharon. It's a Mystery. 2003. (Real Deal Ser.). (Illus.). 32p. (J). pap. *(978-0-7608-6692-4(9))* Sundance/Newbridge Educational Publishing.

Davidson, Avelyn. Dollars & Sense: Economics & Science. 2007. (Shockwave: Economics & Geography Ser.). (ENG., Illus.). 36p. (J). (gr. 3-5). 25.00 *(978-0-531-17750-1(5)*, Children's Pr.) Scholastic Library Publishing.

Davidson, Gary, des. Mesozoic & Cenozoic, 2 vols. 2004. (Time Line Companion Bks.). (Illus.). (J). per. 8.50 *(978-0-9745560-1-7(7))* Azoka Co., The.

—Paleozoic Era, 2 vols. 2004. (Time Line Companion Bks.). (Illus.). 65p. (J). per. *(978-0-9745560-0-0(9))* Azoka Co., The.

Davies, Kate. What's Science All About? 2010. (Science Stories Ser.). 283p. (YA). (gr. 3-18). pap. 15.99 *(978-0-7945-2120-2(7)*, Usborne) EDC Publishing.

Day Two PSAE Student Textbook. 3rd ed. 2005. per. *(978-1-58894-035-3(7))* Cambridge Educational Services, Inc.

Days We Celebrate, 6 vols. (Book2WebTM Ser.). (gr. 4-8). 36.50 *(978-0-322-02846-3(9))* Wright Group/McGraw-Hill.

De Long, Ron, et al. Dream-Makers Science: Art & Science. De Long, Ron et al, eds. 2007. (Illus.). 104p. spiral bd. 9.99 *(978-0-86696-328-2(6))* Binney & Smith, Inc.

De Waard, Nancy & De Waard, E. John. Science Challenge Level 2: 190 Fun & Creative Brainteasers for Kids, Level 2. 2005. (Challenge Ser.). (Illus.). 192p. (J). per. 9.95 *(978-1-59647-068-2(2)*, EAS002) Good Year Bks.

deMarin, Layne. Wonder Readers: Science. (Wonder Readers: Science Ser.). (ENG.). 20p. (gr. k-1). 2012. lib. bdg. 67.95 *(978-1-4296-9620-3(6))* 2012. lib. bdg. 158.55 *(978-1-4296-9621-0(4))* 2011. lib. bdg. 90.60 *(978-1-4296-8638-9(3))* Capstone Press of Coughlan Cos. (Wonder Readers).

Diagram Group Staff. Science Visual Resources Set. 2006. (Science Visual Resources Ser.). 208p. (gr. 6-12). 396.00 *(978-0-8160-6161-7(0))* Facts On File, Inc.

Different Kinds of Bread: 6 Each of 1 Student Book, 6 vols. (Sunshinetm Science Ser.). 24p. (gr. 1-2). 41.95 *(978-0-7802-2726-2(3))* Wright Group/McGraw-Hill.

Different Kinds of Bread: Big Book. (Sunshinetm Science Ser.). 24p. (gr. 1-2). 37.50 *(978-0-7802-2797-2(2))* Wright Group/McGraw-Hill.

Discover Series: Science, Nature, Wildlife, 11 bks. (Illus.). (J). (gr. 3-6). lib. bdg. 175.45 *(978-1-56674-935-0(2))* Forest Hse. Publishing Co., Inc.

Discovery!, 13 vols., Set. Incl. Circulating Life: Blood Transfusion from Ancient Superstition to Modern Medicine. Winner, Cherie. (Illus.). 112p. 2007. lib. bdg. 31.93 *(978-0-8225-6606-9(0))*; Death: Corpses, Cadavers, & Other Grave Matters. Murray, Elizabeth A. 112p. 2010. lib. bdg. 31.93 *(978-0-7613-3851-2(9))*; Dinosaur Eggs Discovered! Unscrambling the Clues. Dingus, Lowell. (Illus.). 112p. 2007. lib. bdg. 31.93 *(978-0-8225-6791-2(1))*; Investigating Climate Change: Scientists' Search for Answers in a Warming World. Johnson, Rebecca L. (Illus.). 112p. 2008. lib. bdg. 31.93 *(978-0-8225-6792-9(X))*; Invisible Invaders: Dangerous Infectious Diseases. Goldsmith, Connie. (Illus.). 112p. 2006. 31.93 *(978-0-8225-3416-7(9))*; Killer Rocks from Outer Space: Asteroids, Comets, & Meteorites. Koppes, Steven N. (Illus.). 112p. 2003. lib. bdg. 31.93 *(978-0-8225-2861-6(4))*; Little People & a Lost World: An Anthropological Mystery. Goldenberg, Linda. (Illus.). 112p. 2006. lib. bdg. 31.93 *(978-0-8225-5983-2(8))*; Mass Extinction: Examining the Current Crisis. Andryszewski, Tricia. (Illus.). 112p. 2008. lib. bdg. 31.93 *(978-0-8225-7523-8(X))*; Mutants, Clones, & Killer Corn: Unlocking the Secrets of Biotechnology. Seiple, Todd & Seiple, Samantha. (Illus.). 112p. 2005. lib. bdg. 31.93 *(978-0-8225-4860-7(7))*; Neandertals: A Prehistoric Puzzle. La Pierre, Yvette. (Illus.). 112p. 2008. lib. bdg. 31.93 *(978-0-8225-7524-5(8))*; Outbreak: Disease Detectives at Work. 2nd rev. ed. Friedlander, Mark P. 128p. 2009. 31.93 *(978-0-8225-9039-2(5))*; Parasites: Latching on to a Free Lunch. Fleisher, Paul. (Illus.). 112p. (J). 2006. lib. bdg. 31.93 *(978-0-8225-3415-0(0))*; Superbugs Strike Back: When Antibiotics Fail. Goldsmith, Connie. (Illus.). 112p. 2007. lib. bdg. 31.93 *(978-0-8225-6607-6(9))*; (gr. 6-12). 2010. Set lib. bdg. 415.09 *(978-0-8225-8203-8(1)*, Twenty-First Century Bks.) Lerner Publishing Group.

Dise, Molly. Fun at the Zoo! 2011. (Science Ser.). (ENG.). 16p. (gr. -1-1). 25.95 *(978-1-4296-8672-3(3)*, Wonder Readers) Capstone Press of Coughlan Cos.

DiSiena, Laura Lyn & Eliot, Hannah. Rainbows Never End: And Other Fun Facts. Oswald, Pete, illus. 2014. (Did You Know? Ser.). (ENG.). 32p. (J). (gr. -1-3). 17.99 *(978-1-4814-0277-4(3))*; pap. 5.99 *(978-1-4814-0275-0(7))* Little Simon. (Little Simon).

A Divertirse Con la Ciencia. 2010. (Divertirse con la Ciencia/Hands-On Science Fun Ser.).Tr. of Hands-On Science Fun. (MUL.). 24p. (gr. k-1). 106.60 *(978-1-4296-6109-6(7))* Capstone Press of Coughlan Cos.

Dobson. Holt Science Spectacular: Physical Science. 6th ed. 2006. stu. ed. 79.33 *(978-0-03-039093-7(1))* Harcourt Schl. Pubs.

Dorling Kindersley Publishing Staff. All about Everything. 2014. (ENG., Illus.). 304p. (J). (gr. 4-7). pap. 12.99 *(978-1-4654-1746-6(X)*, DK Children) Dorling Kindersley Publishing, Inc.

—Pocket Genius: Science. 2016. (Pocket Genius Ser.). (ENG., Illus.). 160p. (J). (gr. 3-7). pap. 4.99 *(978-1-4654-4591-9(9)*, DK Children) Dorling Kindersley Publishing, Inc.

—Science. (ENG.). (J). 2013. 60p. (gr. -1-1). pap. 6.99 *(978-1-4654-1727-5(3))* 2011. (Illus.). 72p. (gr. 3-7). 16.99 *(978-0-7566-7161-7(2))* Dorling Kindersley Publishing, Inc. (DK Children).

—Science: Facts at Your Fingertips. 2013. (Pocket Genius Ser.). (ENG., Illus.). 160p. (J). (gr. 3-7). 7.99 *(978-1-4654-0883-9(5)*, DK Children) Dorling Kindersley Publishing, Inc.

—Science, 2nd Edition. 2nd ed. 2016. (ENG., Illus.). 512p. 50.00 *(978-1-4654-5420-1(9)*, DK) Dorling Kindersley Publishing, Inc.

—Science, Grade 1. 2013. (ENG.). 60p. (J). (gr. k-4). pap. 6.99 *(978-1-4654-1728-2(1)*, DK Children) Dorling Kindersley Publishing, Inc.

—Science, Grade 2. 2013. (ENG.). 60p. (J). (gr. 1-3). pap. 6.99 *(978-1-4654-1729-9(X)*, DK Children) Dorling Kindersley Publishing, Inc.

—Science Grade 3. 2013. (ENG.). 60p. (J). (gr. 2-4). pap. 6.99 *(978-1-4654-1730-5(3)*, DK Children) Dorling Kindersley Publishing, Inc.

—Science, Grade Pre-K: Learn & Experience. 2013. (ENG.). 60p. (J). (gr. -1-k). pap. 6.99 *(978-1-4654-1726-8(5)*, DK Children) Dorling Kindersley Publishing, Inc.

Dorling Kindersley Publishing Staff & Winston, Robert. Utterly Amazing Science. 2014. (ENG., Illus.). 32p. (J). (gr. 3-7). 19.99 *(978-1-4654-1421-2(5)*, DK Children) Dorling Kindersley Publishing, Inc.

Dotlich, Rebecca Kai. What Is Science? Yoshikawa, Sachiko, illus. rev. ed. 2006. (ENG.). 32p. (J). (gr. -1-2). 18.99 *(978-0-8050-7394-2(9)*, 9780805073942, Holt, Henry & Co. Bks. For Young Readers) Holt, Henry & Co.

Doudna, Kelly. It's My Mission to Make a Definition!, 1 vol. 2007. (Science Made Simple Ser.). (ENG., Illus.). 24p. (J). (gr. k-3). lib. bdg. 24.21 *(978-1-59928-600-6(9)*, SandCastle) ABDO Publishing Co.

—Super Simple Science, 6 vols., Set. Incl. Super Simple Things to Do with Balloons: Fun & Easy Science for Kids. lib. bdg. 25.65 *(978-1-61714-672-5(2))*; Super Simple Things to Do with Bubbles: Fun & Easy Science for Kids. 25.65 *(978-1-61714-673-2(0))*; Super Simple Things to Do with Plants: Fun & Easy Science for Kids. lib. bdg. 25.65 *(978-1-61714-674-9(9))*; Super Simple Things to Do with Pressure: Fun & Easy Science for Kids. lib. bdg. 25.65 *(978-1-61714-675-6(7))*; Super Simple Things to Do with Temperature: Fun & Easy Science for Kids. lib. bdg. 25.65 *(978-1-61714-676-3(5))*; Super Simple Things to Do with Water: Fun & Easy Science for Kids. lib. bdg. 25.65 *(978-1-61714-677-0(3))*; (J). (gr. k-3). (Super Simple Science Ser.). (Illus.). 24p. 2011. 153.90 *(978-1-61714-671-8(4)*, Super SandCastle) ABDO Publishing Co.

Doyle, James. A Young Scientist's Guide to Faulty Freaks of Nature, 1 vol. Brozyna, Andrew, illus. 2013. (ENG.). 160p. (J). (gr. 5-6). 14.99 *(978-1-4236-2455-4(6))* Gibbs Smith, Publisher.

—A Young Scientist's Guide to Faulty Freaks of Nature: Including 20 Experiments for the Sink, Bathtub & Backyard (Large Print 16pt) 2013. 200p. pap. *(978-1-4596-5848-6(5))* ReadHowYouWant.com, Ltd.

Driver, Stephanie Schwartz & Garcia, Rachel. I Wish I Knew That Science: Cool Stuff You Need to Know. 2012. (J). *(978-1-60652-387-2(2))* Reader's Digest Assn., Inc., The.

Duke, Shirley. Animal Science. 2012. (ENG., Illus.). 48p. (gr. 4-6). pap. 10.95 *(978-1-61810-257-7(5))* Rourke Educational Media.

—Enterprise Stem. 2011. (ENG., Illus.). 48p. (gr. 4-6). pap. 10.95 *(978-1-61741-983-6(4))* Rourke Educational Media.

Dunn, Justine. Hey! There's Science in My Literature! Grades 1-2. Radtke, Becky, illus. 2007. (Rigby Best Teachers Press Ser.). 96p. per. 13.99 *(978-1-4190-2848-9(0))* Houghton Mifflin Harcourt Supplemental Pubs.

Dunn, Karen Lewit. What's the Solution? 2008. (Discovering & Exploring Science Ser.). (Illus.). 16p. (J). (gr. -1-3). lib. bdg. 12.95 *(978-0-7569-8433-5(5))* Perfection Learning Corp.

Dunne, Abbie. Life Science. 2016. (Life Science Ser.). (ENG.). 24p. (gr. k-1). pap. 41.70 *(978-1-5157-1384-5(9)*, Pebble Plus) Capstone Press of Coughlan Cos.

—Physical Science. 2016. (Physical Science Ser.). (ENG.). 24p. (gr. k-1). pap. 41.70 *(978-1-5157-1386-9(5)*, Pebble Plus) Capstone Press of Coughlan Cos.

DynaNotes Grade 8 Science TAKS Review Guide. 2006. (YA). pap. *(978-1-933854-28-1(6))* DynaStudy, Inc.

DynaNotes Grade 8 Science TAKS Review Guide Transparency Set. 2006. (YA). trans. *(978-1-933854-32-8(4))* DynaStudy, Inc.

DynaNotes Laboratory Review Guide. 2007. (J). pap. *(978-1-933854-61-8(8))* DynaStudy, Inc.

DynaNotes Laboratory Review Guide Transparency Set. 2007. (J). trans. *(978-1-933854-69-4(3))* DynaStudy, Inc.

DynaNotes Mass Transparency Set. 2007. (J). trans. *(978-1-933854-53-3(7))* DynaStudy, Inc.

Early Fluency Set 2: 1 Each of 8 Big Books. (Sunshinetm Science Ser.). (gr. 1-2). 296.50 *(978-0-7802-1764-5(0))* Wright Group/McGraw-Hill.

Early Fluency Set 2: 1 Each of 8 Big Books, 1 Each of 8 Student Books, 1 Teacher Guide, & 1 Duplicate Masters Book. (Sunshinetm Science Ser.). (gr. 1-2). 391.50 *(978-0-7802-1763-8(2))* Wright Group/McGraw-Hill.

Early Fluency Set 2: 1 Each of 8 Student Books. (Sunshinetm Science Ser.). (gr. 1-2). 55.95 *(978-0-7802-1765-2(9))* Wright Group/McGraw-Hill.

Early Fluency Set 3. (Sunshinetm Science Ser.). (gr. 1-2). 296.50 *(978-0-7802-1767-6(5))* Wright Group/McGraw-Hill.

Early Fluency Set 3: 1 Each of Student Books. (Sunshinetm Science Ser.). (gr. 1-2). 55.95 *(978-0-7802-1768-3(3))* Wright Group/McGraw-Hill.

Early Fluency Set 4: 1 Each of 8 Big Books. (Sunshinetm Science Ser.). (gr. 1-2). 296.50 *(978-0-7802-2800-9(6))* Wright Group/McGraw-Hill.

Early Fluency Set 4: 1 Each of 8 Student Books. (Sunshinetm Science Ser.). (gr. 1-2). 55.96 *(978-0-7802-2801-6(4))* Wright Group/McGraw-Hill.

Early Fluency Set 5: 1 Each of 8 Big Books. (Sunshinetm Science Ser.). (gr. 1-2). 296.50 *(978-0-7802-2803-0(0))* Wright Group/McGraw-Hill.

Early Fluency Set 5: 1 Each of 8 Student Books. (Sunshinetm Science Ser.). (gr. 1-2). 55.95 *(978-0-7802-2804-7(9))* Wright Group/McGraw-Hill.

Early Fluency Set 6: 1 Each of 8 Big Books. (Sunshinetm Science Ser.). (gr. 1-2). 296.50 *(978-0-7802-2806-1(5))* Wright Group/McGraw-Hill.

Early Fluency Set 6: 1 Each of 8 Big Books, 1 Each of 8 Student Books, 1 Teacher Guide, & 1 Duplicate Master Book. (Sunshinetm Science Ser.). (gr. 1-2). 391.50 *(978-0-7802-2805-4(7))* Wright Group/McGraw-Hill.

Early Fluency Set 6: 1 Each of 8 Student Books. (Sunshinetm Science Ser.). (gr. 1-2). 55.95 *(978-0-7802-2807-8(3))* Wright Group/McGraw-Hill.

Earth & Space Classroom Library. (gr. k-2). lib. bdg. 54.95 *(978-0-7368-3284-7(X))* Red Brick Learning.

Education.com. All Sorts of Science: A Workbook Full of Science Fun Facts. 2015. (ENG.). 128p. (J). (gr. 5-5). pap. 7.99 *(978-0-486-80273-2(6))* Dover Pubns., Inc.

—Creatures & Counting: A Workbook of Counting, Sorting, & Discovery. 2015. (ENG.). 128p. (J). (gr. -1-k). pap. 7.99 *(978-0-486-80274-9(4))* Dover Pubns., Inc.

—Earth & Sky: A Workbook of Science Facts & Math Practice. 2015. (ENG.). 112p. (J). (gr. 3-3). pap. 7.99 *(978-0-486-80269-5(8))* Dover Pubns., Inc.

Edwards, Mark, et al. Connecting Science. 2008. (Illus.). 228p. (gr. 12-13). pap., stu. ed. 39.50 *(978-0-340-94598-8(2))* Hodder Education Group GBR. Dist: Trans-Atlantic Pubns., Inc.

Ehlke, Paul. Clouds: Science Information in American Sign Language: A Paws Science Adventure. 2003. (J). cd-rom 29.95 *(978-0-9752933-2-4(X))* Institute for Disabilities Research & Training, Inc.

Eikum, John. The 4th Dimension & Beyond: Imagining Worlds with 0, 1, 2, 3, 4 Dimensions & More. 2007. 120p. (J). per. 16.95 *(978-1-59298-172-4(0))* Beaver's Pond Pr., Inc.

Elementary Science 2000: Big Book Collection. 2003. (gr. k-18). 138.60 *(978-0-328-00683-0(1))* Addison-Wesley Educational Pubs., Inc.

Elliott, Cathy. Can You Guess What It Is? 2008. (Discovering & Exploring Science Ser.). (Illus.). 16p. (J). (gr. -1-3). lib. bdg. 12.95 *(978-0-7569-8418-2(1))* Perfection Learning Corp.

Emergent Set: 1 Each of 8 Student Books. (Sunshinetm Science Ser.). (gr. 1-2). 48.95 *(978-0-7802-0568-0(5))* Wright Group/McGraw-Hill.

Emergent Set: 1 Each of Student Books, Vol. 2. (Sunshinetm Science Ser.). (gr. 1-2). 48.95 *(978-0-7802-0570-3(7))* Wright Group/McGraw-Hill.

Enciclopedia Ilustrada de Ciencia Naturaleza (Understanding Science & Nature), 16 bks. Incl. Comportamiento de los Animales (Animal Behavior) 17.95 *(978-0-7835-3358-2(6))*; Cuerpo Humano (Human Body) 17.95 *(978-0-7835-3350-6(0))*; Era de la Computadora. 17.95 *(978-0-7835-3375-9(6))*; Espacio y Planetas. 17.95 *(978-0-7835-3370-4(5))*; Estructura de la Materia (Structure of Matter) 17.95 *(978-0-7835-3383-4(7))*; Evolucion de la

S

Vida. 17.95 *(978-0-7835-3354-4(3))*; Fuerzas Fisicas (Physical Forces) 17.95 *(978-0-7835-3395-7(0))*; Geografia. 17.95 *(978-0-7835-3387-2(X))*; Insectos y Aranas. 17.95 *(978-0-7835-3398-8(5))*; Maquinas e Inventos (Machines & Inventions) 17.95 *(978-0-7835-3400-8(0))*; Mundo Submarino (Underwater World) 17.95 *(978-0-7835-3397-1(7))*; Planeta Tierra (Planet Earth) 17.95 *(978-0-7835-3396-4(9))*; Plantas (Plant Life) 17.95 *(978-0-7835-3399-5(3))*; Tiempo y Clima (Weather & Climate) 17.95 *(978-0-7835-3366-7(7))*; Transporte y la Navegacion (Transportation) 17.95 *(978-0-7835-3379-7(9))*; 152p. (YA). (gr. 6-18). 1996. (Illus.). Set lib. bdg. 319.20 *(978-0-7835-3391-9(8))* Time-Life, Inc.

Encyclopaedia Britannica Publishers, Inc. Staff. Britannica Illustrated Science Library, 16 vols., Set. 2008. (Illus.). 1664p. (YA). (gr. 5-8). 425.00 *(978-1-59339-382-3(2))* Encyclopaedia Britannica, Inc.

Endres, Hollie J. What Computers Do, 6 vols., Set. 2003. (Yellow Umbrella Early Level Ser.). (ENG.). 16p. (gr. k-1). pap. 35.70 *(978-0-7368-3018-8(9)*, Yellow Umbrella Bks.) Capstone Press of Coughlan Cos.

Enz, Tammy & Biskup, Agnieszka. Superman Science. 2016. (Superman Science Ser.). (ENG.). 32p. (gr. 3-4). 109.28 *(978-1-5157-0932-9(9)*, DC Super Heroes) Stone Arch Bks.

Enz, Tammy, et al. Graphic Science & Engineering in Action. Baez, Marcelo, illus. 2013. (Graphic Science & Engineering in Action Ser.). (ENG.). 32p. (gr. 3-4). pap. 190.80 *(978-1-62065-708-9(2))*; pap. 31.80 *(978-1-62065-707-2(4))* Capstone Press of Coughlan Cos. (Graphic Library).

Equipo Staff. 1000 Preguntas y Respuestas. (SPA., Illus.). 96p. (J). (gr. 3-5). *(978-84-305-8671-4(7)*, SU2565) Susaeta Ediciones, S.A. ESP. Dist: Lectorum Pubns., Inc.

Esbaum, Jill & National Geographic Kids Staff. Little Kids First Big Book of How. 2016. (National Geographic Little Kids First Big Bks.). (ENG., Illus.). 128p. (J). (gr. -1-3). 14.99 *(978-1-4263-2329-4(8)*, National Geographic Children's Bks.) National Geographic Society.

Essential Words Science(Intermediate) Intermediate/Middle School. 2005. (Illus.). 37p. (J). 8.95 *(978-0-9764217-2-6(0))* New Leaf Educ., Inc.

Evan-Moor. English / Spanish Science Activities, Grades 1-3. 2005. (ENG & SPA.). 304p. (gr. 1-3). pap. 26.99 *(978-1-55799-860-6(4)*, EMC 5306) Evan-Moor Educational Pubs.

—Hands-on Science-20 Themes: Grades 1-3. 2005. (ENG.). 208p. (J). (gr. 1-3). pap. 21.99 *(978-1-55799-935-1(X)*, EMC 5000) Evan-Moor Educational Pubs.

—Science Centers, Grades 1-2. 2007. (Take It to Your Seat Ser.). (ENG., Illus.). 192p. (J). (gr. 1-2). pap. 21.99 *(978-1-55799-961-0(9)*, EMC 5002) Evan-Moor Educational Pubs.

—Science Centers, Grades 3-4. 2007. (Take It to Your Seat Ser.). (ENG., Illus.). 192p. (J). (gr. 3-4). pap. 21.99 *(978-1-55799-962-7(7)*, EMC 5003) Evan-Moor Educational Pubs.

—Science Centers Grades PreK-K. 2007. (Take It to Your Seat Ser.). (ENG., Illus.). 192p. (J). (gr. -1). pap. 21.99 *(978-1-59673-090-8(0)*, EMC 5004) Evan-Moor Educational Pubs.

—Spanish / English Read & nderstand Science Grades 4-6. 2007. (Spanish/English Read & Understand Ser.). (ENG., Illus.). 304p. (J). (gr. 4-6). pap. 29.99 *(978-1-59673-077-9(3)*, EMC 5312) Evan-Moor Educational Pubs.

Evans, David & Williams, Claudette. Make It Change. (Let's Explore Science Ser.). (Illus.). (J). 12.95 *(978-0-590-74511-6(5))* Scholastic, Inc.

Explore-a-Science Series. (J). (gr. k-6). 300.00 *(978-0-669-19316-9(X))* Houghton Mifflin Harcourt School Pubs.

Fabre, Jean Henri. The Secret of Everyday Things. Bicknell, Florence Constable, tr. 2008. 404p. pap. 14.95 *(978-1-59915-252-3(5))* Yesterday's Classics.

Facts on File, Inc. Staff, ed. Science in Focus, 6 Vols., Set. 2006. (Science in Focus Ser.). 48p. (gr. 4-6). 135.00 *(978-0-7910-9444-0(8)*, Chelsea Clubhouse) Facts On File, Inc.

Fantastic Science Journeys. 2015. (Fantastic Science Journeys Ser.). (ENG.). 32p. (J). (gr. 2-3). 151.50 *(978-1-4824-1637-4(9))* Stevens, Gareth Publishing LLLP.

Farndon, John. Questions & Answers Science & Nature. 2012. (Illus.). 224p. (J). *(978-1-4351-4352-4(3))* Barnes & Noble, Inc.

—Stuff You Need Know! 2015. (ENG., Illus.). 80p. (J). (gr. 4-7). pap. 12.95 *(978-1-77085-494-9(0)*, 9781770854949) Firefly Bks., Ltd.

—Stuff You Need to Know! 2015. (ENG., Illus.). 80p. (J). (gr. 4-7). 19.95 *(978-1-77085-656-1(0)*, 9781770856561) Firefly Bks., Ltd.

Farndon, John & Graham, Ian. Discovering Science. 2010. (Science Library). 40p. (J). (gr. 3-18). lib. bdg. 19.95 *(978-1-4222-1548-7(2))* Mason Crest.

Faucets & Water Sets: 1 Each of 3 Student Books. (Sunshinetm Science Ser.). (gr. 1-2). 20.95 *(978-0-7802-2815-3(4))* Wright Group/McGraw-Hill.

Ferrie, Chris. ABC's of Science. 2017. (Baby University Ser.: 0). (ENG.). 26p. (J). bds. 9.99 ***(978-1-4926-5631-9(3)***, Sourcebooks Jabberwocky) Sourcebooks, Inc.

Film Ideas Staff, creator. The Little Scientist: Here I Am! Camouflage. 2013. 89.00 *(978-1-60572-707-3(5))* Film Ideas, Inc.

Fischer, Stephen David & Caroll, Joseph. Science Detective Beginning: Higher-Order Thinking Reading Writing in Science. 2012. (Science Detective Ser.). 112p. (gr. 3-4). pap. 19.99 *(978-0-89455-834-4(X))* Critical Thinking Co., The.

Flash Kids Editors, Flash Kids, ed. Summer Study, Grade 1. 2016. (Summer Study Ser.). (ENG., Illus.). 160p. (J). (gr. 1-1). pap. 9.95 *(978-1-4114-7857-2(6)*, Spark Publishing Group) Sterling Publishing Co., Inc.

Fleming, Christine. Art As Science. 2007. (Shockwave: Science in Practice Ser.). 36p. (J). lib. bdg. 6.95 *(978-0-531-15461-8(0)*, Children's Pr.) Scholastic Library Publishing.

Flip Chart. 2003. (Scott Foresman Science Ser.). (gr. 3-18). suppl. ed. 262.50 *(978-0-673-59353-5(3))* Addison-Wesley Educational Pubs., Inc.

Floating & Sinking, 6 vols. (Sunshinetm Science Ser.). 24p. (gr. 1-2). 31.50 *(978-0-7802-0296-2(1))*; 36.95 *(978-0-7802-0547-5(2))* Wright Group/McGraw-Hill.

Flynn, Riley. Finding Information & Making Arguments. 2016. (Science & Engineering Practices Ser.). (ENG., Illus.). 24p. (gr. k-1). lib. bdg. 26.65 *(978-1-5157-0948-0(5)*, Pebble Plus) Capstone Press of Coughlan Cos.

—Science & Engineering Practices. 2016. (Science & Engineering Practices Ser.). (ENG.). 24p. (gr. k-1). pap. 27.80 *(978-1-5157-1388-3(1)*, Pebble Plus) Capstone Press of Coughlan Cos.

—Using Facts & Investigating. 2016. (Science & Engineering Practices Ser.). (ENG., Illus.). 24p. (gr. k-1). lib. bdg. 26.65 *(978-1-5157-0949-7(3)*, Pebble Plus) Capstone Press of Coughlan Cos.

—Using Models & Math in Science. 2016. (Science & Engineering Practices Ser.). (ENG., Illus.). 24p. (gr. k-1). lib. bdg. 26.65 *(978-1-5157-0950-3(7)*, Pebble Plus) Capstone Press of Coughlan Cos.

Focus on Science Practice Test Book. 2005. (Focus on Science Ser.). 32p. pap. 30.60 *(978-1-4042-5212-7(6)*, Rosen Classroom) Rosen Publishing Group, Inc., The.

Focus on Science Transparencies. 2005. (Focus on Science Ser.). 44.00 *(978-1-4042-5213-4(4)*, Rosen Classroom) Rosen Publishing Group, Inc., The.

Forte, Imogene. Ready to Learn Beginning Science. 2003. (Illus.). 64p. per. 7.95 *(978-0-86530-598-4(6))* Incentive Pubns., Inc.

—Ready to Learn Following Directions. 2003. (Illus.). 64p. per. 7.95 *(978-0-86530-596-0(X))* Incentive Pubns., Inc.

—Science Fun. 2004. (Fun Things to Make & Do Ser.). (Illus.). (J). per. 9.95 *(978-0-86530-606-6(0))* Incentive Pubns., Inc.

Forte, Imogene & Schurr, Sandra. Standards-Based Science Graphic Organizers & Rubrics. 2004. 128p. (J). per. 13.95 *(978-0-86530-628-8(1))* Incentive Pubns., Inc.

Foster, Patience. Pocket Scientist. 2004. (ENG.). 1p. (J). 8.95 *(978-0-7945-0209-6(1))* EDC Publishing.

Foster, Ruth. Nonfiction Reading Comprehension - Science. 2006. (ENG.). 144p. pap. 16.99 *(978-1-4206-8026-3(9))* Teacher Created Resources, Inc.

—Nonfiction Reading Comprehension - Science, Grade 3. 2006. (ENG.). 144p. pap. 16.99 *(978-1-4206-8021-8(8))* Teacher Created Resources, Inc.

Freaky True Science. 2015. (Freaky True Science Ser.). (ENG.). 32p. (J). (gr. 4-5). 159.60 *(978-1-4824-2554-3(8))*; pap., pap., pap. 63.00 *(978-1-4824-3470-5(9))*; pap., pap., pap. 378.00 *(978-1-4824-3469-9(5))* Stevens, Gareth Publishing LLLP.

Freaky True Science: Set 2. 2016. (Freaky True Science Ser.). 32p. (gr. 5-4). pap. 63.00 *(978-1-4824-5396-6(7))*; lib. bdg. 159.60 *(978-1-4824-4608-1(1))* Stevens, Gareth Publishing LLLP.

Frith, Alex. See Inside Science. 2007. 16p. (J). bds. 12.99 *(978-0-7945-1549-2(5)*, Usborne) EDC Publishing.

—100 Things to Know about Science. 2015. (Illustrated Dictionaries Ser.). (ENG.). 128p. (J). (gr. k-5). pap. 12.99 *(978-0-7945-3502-5(X)*, Usborne) EDC Publishing.

From Flowers to Fruit: 6 Each of 1 Student Book, 6 vols. (Sunshinetm Science Ser.). 24p. (gr. 1-2). 41.95 *(978-0-7802-2686-9(0))* Wright Group/McGraw-Hill.

From Flowers to Fruit: Big Book. (Sunshinetm Science Ser.). 24p. (gr. 1-2). 37.50 *(978-0-7802-2777-4(8))* Wright Group/McGraw-Hill.

Fry, Jenny & Award, Anna. The Ultimate Book of Questions & Answers. 2012. (ENG., Illus.). 48p. (J). 24.95 *(978-1-899762-93-4(0))* Award Pubns. Ltd. GBR. Dist: Parkwest Pubns., Inc.

Fuerst, Jeffrey B. Look at it Go! Lap Book. 2009. (My First Reader's Theater Set B Ser.). (J). 28.00 *(978-1-935441-02-1(7))* Benchmark Education Co.

Furgang, Kathy. A Challenging Game of True or False. 2015. (Fact or Fib? Ser.). (ENG., Illus.). 208p. (J). (gr. 3). pap. 7.95 *(978-1-4549-1588-1(9))* Sterling Publishing Co., Inc.

—Fact or Fib? A Challenging Game of True or False. 2014. (Fact or Fib? Ser.: 1). (ENG., Illus.). 208p. (J). (gr. 3). pap. 7.95 *(978-1-4549-0982-8(X))* Sterling Publishing Co., Inc.

—Fact or Fib? 2: A Challenging Game of True or False. 2014. (Fact or Fib? Ser.: 1). (ENG., Illus.). 208p. (J). (gr. 3). pap. 7.95 *(978-1-4549-0983-5(8))* Sterling Publishing Co., Inc.

—Fact or Fib? 4: A Challenging Game of True or False. 2015. (Fact or Fib? Ser.). (ENG., Illus.). 208p. (J). (gr. 3). pap. 7.95 *(978-1-4549-1589-8(7))* Sterling Publishing Co., Inc.

—Working with Electricity & Magnetism: Set Of 6. 2011. (Navigators Ser.). (J). pap. 48.00 net. *(978-1-4108-0438-9(0))* Benchmark Education Co.

Ganeri, Anita. Fearsome Forces of Nature, 1 vol. 2012. (Extreme Nature Ser.). (ENG.). 32p. (gr. 1-3). pap. 8.29 *(978-1-4109-4701-7(7))*; lib. bdg. 29.99 *(978-1-4109-4696-6(7))* Heinemann-Raintree. (Read Me!).

Gardner, Jane. Black Achievement in Science: Environmental Science, Vol. 10. Pouson, Mel, ed. 2016. (Black Achievement in Science Ser.: Vol. 10). (ENG., Illus.). 64p. (J). (gr. 7-12). 23.95 *(978-1-4222-3559-1(9))* Mason Crest.

Georgia Striving Readers Science K-5. 2012. (CAP-Marketing Ser.). (ENG.). (gr. k-5). pap. 1782.84 *(978-1-62065-957-1(3))* Capstone Press of Coughlan Cos.

Getting Cold! Getting Hot!, 6 vols. (Sunshinetm Science Ser.). 24p. (gr. 1-2). 37.50 *(978-0-7802-1405-7(6))*; 41.95 *(978-0-7802-1404-0(8))* Wright Group/McGraw-Hill.

Getting Rid of Waste Water: 6 Each of 1 Student Book, 6 vols. (Sunshinetm Science Ser.). 24p. (gr. 1-2). 41.95 *(978-0-7802-2692-0(5))* Wright Group/McGraw-Hill.

Getting Rid of Waste Water: Big Book. (Sunshinetm Science Ser.). 24p. (gr. 1-2). 37.50 *(978-0-7802-2780-4(8))* Wright Group/McGraw-Hill.

Getting the Water We Need: 6 Each of 1 Student Book, 6 vols. (Sunshinetm Science Ser.). 24p. (gr. 1-2). 41.95 *(978-0-7802-2690-6(9))* Wright Group/McGraw-Hill.

Getting the Water We Need: Big Book. (Sunshinetm Science Ser.). 24p. (gr. 1-2). 37.50 *(978-0-7802-2779-8(4))* Wright Group/McGraw-Hill.

Gillespie, Lisa Jane. Science 100. Lozano, Luciano & Du, Yukai, illus. 2017. (ENG.). 64p. (J). (gr. 2-5). 22.99 *(978-1-84780-843-1(3)*, Wide Eyed Editions) Quarto Publishing Group UK GBR. Dist: Hachette Bk. Group.

Gilpin, Rebecca & Pratt, Leonie. Big Book of Science Things to Make & Do. Thompson, Josephine, illus. 2008. (Big Book of Science Things to Make & Do Ser.). 95p. (J). (gr. 1). pap. 14.99 *(978-0-7945-1923-0(7)*, Usborne) EDC Publishing.

Glencoe McGraw-Hill Staff. Motion, Forces, & Energy. 2nd ed. 2004. (Glen Sci: Motion, Forces, Ener Ser.). (ENG., Illus.). 248p. (gr. 6-8). stu. ed. 32.40 *(978-0-07-861770-6(7)*, 0078617707) McGraw-Hill Higher Education.

—The Nature of Matter. 2nd ed. 2004. (Glen Sci: the Nature of Matter Ser.). (ENG., Illus.). 192p. (gr. 6-8). stu. ed. 32.40 *(978-0-07-861765-2(0)*, 0078617650) McGraw-Hill Higher Education.

Glencoe McGraw-Hill Staff, creator. Glencoe Science: Level Blue - Reinforcement. 2004. (Integrated Science Ser.). (ENG., Illus.). 85p. (gr. 8-8). pap., stu. ed., pupil's gde. ed. 7.88 *(978-0-07-867169-2(8)*, 0078671698) McGraw-Hill Education.

—Glencoe Science: Level Green. 2004. (Integrated Science Ser.). (ENG., Illus.). 91p. (gr. 7-7). pap., stu. ed., pupil's gde. ed. 7.88 *(978-0-07-867188-3(4)*, 0078671884) McGraw-Hill Education.

—Glencoe Science Level Blue, Level Blue. 2003. (Illus.). 818p. (J). lib. bdg., stu. ed. 74.64 *(978-0-07-828242-3(X))* Glencoe/McGraw-Hill.

Goldsmith, Mike. Everything You Need to Know about Science. 2013. (Everything You Need to Know Ser.). (ENG., Illus.). 160p. (J). (gr. k-4). pap. 12.99 *(978-0-7534-6945-3(6)*, 9780753469453, Kingfisher) Roaring Brook Pr.

Gottlieb. Matter, Motion & Machines. 2004. (Wonders of Science Ser.). (ENG.). (gr. 7-12). 176p. pap., tchr. ed. 27.70 *(978-0-7398-9185-8(5))*; (Illus.). 144p. pap. 24.55 *(978-0-7398-9179-7(0))* Houghton Mifflin Harcourt Publishing Co.

Gow, Mary. Robert Boyle: Pioneer of Experimental Chemistry. 2005. (Great Minds of Science Ser.). (Illus.). 128p. (J). lib. bdg. 27.94 *(978-0-7660-2501-1(2))* Enslow Pubs., Inc.

Graf, Mike & Snedden, Robert. Science Missions, 6 vols., Set. Incl. Mapping Earth from Space. (ENG.). 56p. (gr. 3-3). 2011. pap. 9.95 *(978-1-4109-4001-8(2)*, Raintree Freestyle Express); (Science Missions Ser.). (ENG.). 56p. 2011. Set pap. 29.85 o.p. *(978-1-4109-4002-5(0)*, Raintree Freestyle Express) Heinemann-Raintree.

Graham, Amy. Astonishing Ancient World Scientists: Eight Great Brains. 2009. (Great Scientists & Famous Inventors Ser.). (Illus.). 128p. (J). (gr. 5-9). lib. bdg. 34.60 *(978-1-59845-079-8(4))* Enslow Pubs., Inc.

Grant, R. G. Superstars of Science. Basher, Simon, illus. 2015. (ENG.). 96p. (J). (gr. 3-7). pap. 7.99 *(978-0-545-82627-3(6)*, Scholastic Paperbacks) Scholastic, Inc.

—Superstars of Science: The Brave, the Bold, & the Brainy. 2015. lib. bdg. 18.40 *(978-0-606-37753-9(0))* Turtleback Bks.

Graphic Science. (Graphic Science Ser.). (ENG.). 32p. (gr. 3-4). 2016. lib. bdg. 459.75 *(978-1-5157-4022-3(6))* 2010. pap. 15.90 *(978-1-4296-4996-4(8))* 2010. lib. bdg. 61.30 *(978-1-4296-4450-1(8))* Capstone Press of Coughlan Cos. (Graphic Library).

Graphic Science Collection. 2010. (Graphic Science Ser.). (ENG.). 32p. (gr. 3-4). pap. 174.90 *(978-1-4296-5148-6(2)*, Graphic Library) Capstone Press of Coughlan Cos.

Great Minds of Science, 19 bks., Set. (Illus.). (J). (gr. 4-10). lib. bdg. 398.05 *(978-0-89490-566-7(X))* Enslow Pubs., Inc.

Green, Jen, et al. Show Me Science, 1 vol. 2014. (Show Me Science Ser.). (ENG.). 32p. (gr. 3-5). lib. bdg. 183.90 *(978-1-4329-8753-4(4)*, Raintree Perspectives) Heinemann-Raintree.

Greenling, Jason. The Technology of Ancient China. 2016. (Ancient Innovations Ser.). 64p. (J). 34.21 *(978-1-5026-2235-8(1))* Cavendish Square Publishing.

Greenwood, Rosie. I Wonder Why Volcanoes Blow Their Tops: And Other Questions about Natural Disasters. 2013. (I Wonder Why Ser.). (ENG., Illus.). 32p. (J). (gr. k-3). 6.99 *(978-0-7534-6935-4(9)*, 9780753469354, Kingfisher) Roaring Brook Pr.

Groessen und Masse. (Duden-Schuelerhilfen Ser.). (GER.). 96p. (J). (gr. 4-5). *(978-3-411-02610-4(3))* Bibliographisches Institut & F. A. Brockhaus AG DEU. Dist: International Bk. Import Service, Inc.

Group/McGraw-Hill, Wright. Cold Facts about Ice Ages, 6 vols. (Book2WebTM Ser.). (gr. 4-8). 36.50 *(978-0-322-04434-0(0))* Wright Group/McGraw-Hill.

—Dreams of Flight, 6 vols. (Book2WebTM Ser.). (gr. 4-8). 36.50 *(978-0-322-04433-3(2))* Wright Group/McGraw-Hill.

—Earth & Physical Science: Color & Light, 6 vols. (Book2WebTM Ser.). (gr. 4-8). 36.50 *(978-0-322-04429-6(4))* Wright Group/McGraw-Hill.

—Earth & Physical Science: Exploring Electricity, 6 vols. (Book2WebTM Ser.). (gr. 4-8). 36.50 *(978-0-322-04428-9(6))* Wright Group/McGraw-Hill.

—Famous Shipwrecks, 6 vols. (Book2WebTM Ser.). (gr. 4-8). 36.50 *(978-0-322-04458-6(8))* Wright Group/McGraw-Hill.

—Inventors Create Tomorrow, 6 vols. (Book2WebTM Ser.). (gr. 4-8). 36.50 *(978-0-322-04469-2(3))* Wright Group/McGraw-Hill.

—Mountain Majesty, 6 vols. (Book2WebTM Ser.). (gr. 4-8). 36.50 *(978-0-322-04440-1(5))* Wright Group/McGraw-Hill.

—People on the Path Toward Human Rights, 6 vols. (Book2WebTM Ser.). (gr. 4-8). 36.50 *(978-0-322-04466-1(9))* Wright Group/McGraw-Hill.

—Wonder World Complete Sets: Science Set - 1 Each of 97 Titles. (Wonder Worldtm Ser.). (gr. k-6). 501.95 *(978-0-322-06714-1(6))* Wright Group/McGraw-Hill.

—Wonder World Early & Upper Emergent Sets: Science Set - 1 Each of 49 Titles. (Wonder Worldtm Ser.). (gr. k-6). 229.50 *(978-0-322-06721-9(9))* Wright Group/McGraw-Hill.

—Wonder World Early Fluency & Fluency: Science Set - 1 Each of 48 Titles. (Wonder Worldtm Ser.). (gr. k-6). 299.50 *(978-0-322-06717-2(0))* Wright Group/McGraw-Hill.

Groves, Marcia, et al. Science & Technology in the Middle Ages. 2004. (Medieval World Ser.). (ENG., Illus.). 32p. (J). pap. *(978-0-7787-1386-9(5))* Crabtree Publishing Co.

Guest, John. Amazing True Facts. 2012. (Illus.). 224p. *(978-1-4351-4353-1(1))* Barnes & Noble, Inc.

Gutman, Dan. My Weird School Fast Facts: Space, Humans, & Farts. Paillot, Jim, illus. 2017. (My Weird School Fast Facts Ser.). 192p. (J). (gr. 1-5). pap. 5.99 *(978-0-06-230626-5(X))* HarperCollins Pubs.

Hagler, Gina. The Technology of Ancient India. 2016. (Spotlight on the Rise & Fall of Ancient Civilizations Ser.). 48p. (YA). (gr. 6-6). pap. 11.75 *(978-1-4777-8942-1(1))* Rosen Publishing Group, Inc., The.

Hall, Derek. Life Sciences. 2009. (FAYFT: Great Scientists Ser.). 64p. (gr. 4-10). 39.95 *(978-1-933834-45-0(5))* Brown Bear Bks.

Hall, Kirsten. Glow-In-The-Dark Zombie Science. Myers, Lawrence E., illus. 2009. 32p. (J). pap. *(978-0-545-22626-4(0))* Scholastic, Inc.

Halls, Kelly Milner & Holland, Simon. Lie Detector. Cosgrove, Lee, illus. 2015. (Lie Detector Ser.). (ENG.). 32p. (gr. k-3). 109.28 *(978-1-4795-8525-0(4))* Picture Window Bks.

Hands: Level B, 6 vols. 8p. 24.95 *(978-0-7802-8915-4(3))* Wright Group/McGraw-Hill.

Hands-On Science. 2016. (Hands-On Science Ser.). 48p. (J). lib. bdg. 167.58 *(978-0-7660-8392-9(6))* Enslow Pubs., Inc.

Hands-On Science Fun. 2010. (Hands-On Science Fun Ser.). (ENG.). 24p. (gr. k-1). pap. 27.80 *(978-1-4296-6217-8(4)*, Pebble Plus) Capstone Press of Coughlan Cos.

Hansen, Amy S. & Olien, Rebecca. First Graphics: Science Mysteries. Scott, Korey & McDee, Katie, illus. 2011. (First Graphics: Science Mysteries Ser.). (ENG.). 24p. (gr. 1-2). lib. bdg. 47.98 *(978-1-4296-6099-0(6))* Capstone Press of Coughlan Cos.

—First Graphics: Science Mysteries: A Science Mystery. Scott, Korey & McDee, Katie, illus. 2011. (First Graphics: Science Mysteries Ser.). (ENG.). 24p. (gr. 1-2). pap. 25.16 *(978-1-4296-7181-1(5))*; pap. 142.80 *(978-1-4296-7182-8(3))* Capstone Press of Coughlan Cos.

Hansen, Grace. Science Facts to Surprise You!, 1 vol. 2014. (Seeing Is Believing Ser.). (ENG.). 24p. (J). lib. bdg. 28.50 *(978-1-62970-734-1(1))* ABDO Publishing Co.

Hansen, Merrily P. A Close-Up Look at Plants: A Content Area Reader-Science. 2005. (Sadlier Phonics Reading Program). (Illus.). 16p. (gr. k-2). 25.20 *(978-0-8215-7811-7(1))* Sadlier, William H. Inc.

Harbo, Christopher L. Monster Science. Aón, Carlos, illus. 2013. (Monster Science Ser.). (ENG.). 32p. (gr. 3-4). pap. 15.90 *(978-1-4765-3673-6(2)*, Graphic Library) Capstone Press of Coughlan Cos.

—Monster Science. An, Carlos, illus. 2013. (Monster Science Ser.). (ENG.). 32p. (gr. 3-4). pap. 79.50 *(978-1-4765-3674-3(0)*, Graphic Library) Capstone Press of Coughlan Cos.

Harcourt School Publishers, creator. Energy Transfer & Weather: Lessons 2-3. 2006. (ENG.). pap. 27.00 *(978-0-15-354814-7(2))* Harcourt Schl. Pubs.

—Matter Matters! 2006. (ENG.). pap. 27.00 *(978-0-15-354738-6(3))* Harcourt Schl. Pubs.

Harcourt School Publishers Staff. Harcourt Science: Physical Science Instant Reader CD-ROM Teacher's Guide. 2nd ed. 2003. (Harcourt Science Ser.). (gr. k-18). tchr. ed. 8.00 incl. cd-rom *(978-0-15-324957-0(9))* Harcourt Schl. Pubs.

Harris, Nancy & Rissman, Rebecca. Be the Best at Science, 1 vol. 2012. (Top Tips Ser.). (ENG.). 32p. (gr. 1-3). 29.99 *(978-1-4109-4766-6(1)*, Read Me!) Heinemann-Raintree.

Harris, Tim. Life Science. 2015. (Science Q & A Ser.). (ENG.). 32p. (J). (gr. 5-5). pap. 10.58 *(978-1-5026-0621-1(6))* Cavendish Square Publishing.

Hassard, Jack. Science As Inquiry. 2004. (Illus.). 280p. pap. 19.95 *(978-0-673-57731-3(7))* Good Year Bks.

Hauck, Max M. Science versus Crime. 2008. (Essentials of Forensic Science Ser.). (Illus.). 201p. (gr. 6-12). 35.00 *(978-0-8160-5508-1(4))* Facts On File, Inc.

Hawkins, Jay. Really Horrible Science Facts. 2013. (Really Horrible Facts Ser.). 32p. (J). (gr. k-3). 25.25 *(978-1-61533-745-3(8))*; pap. 60.00 *(978-1-61533-808-5(X))*; pap. 10.00 *(978-1-61533-807-8(1))* Windmill Bks.

Heer, Margreet de. Science: A Discovery in Comics. 2013. (Discovery in Comics Ser.). (ENG., Illus.). 194p. 19.99 *(978-1-56163-750-8(5))* NBM Publishing Co.

Hello From 2030: The Science of the Future & You. 2014. (ENG., Illus.). 224p. (J). (gr. 3-7). 15.99 *(978-1-58270-474-6(0))* Aladdin/Beyond Words.

Hensley, Wendie & Licata, Annette. Science. 2007. (Painless Junior Ser.). (ENG., Illus.). 216p. (gr. 4-7). per. 8.99 *(978-0-7641-3719-8(0))* Barron's Educational Series, Inc.

Hestermann, Josh & Hestermann, Bethanie. Marine Science for Kids: Exploring & Protecting Our Watery World, Includes Cool Careers & 21 Activities. 2017. (For Kids Ser.). (ENG.). 144p. (J). (gr. 4). pap. 18.99 ***(978-1-61373-536-7(7))*** Chicago Review Pr., Inc.

Hewitt, Sally. Listen Up!, 5 vols. 2005. (QEB Let's Start! Science Ser.). (Illus.). 24p. (J). (gr. 1-4). lib. bdg. 15.95 *(978-1-59566-086-2(0))* QEB Publishing Inc.

—Look Here!, 5 vols. 2005. (QEB Let's Start! Science Ser.). (Illus.). 24p. (J). (gr. 1-4). lib. bdg. 15.95 *(978-1-59566-087-9(9))* QEB Publishing Inc.

—Smell That!, 5 vols. 2005. (QEB Let's Start! Science Ser.). (Illus.). 24p. (J). (gr. 1-4). lib. bdg. 15.95 *(978-1-59566-088-6(7))* QEB Publishing Inc.

—Tastes Good!, 5 vols. 2005. (QEB Let's Start! Science Ser.). (Illus.). 24p. (J). (gr. 1-4). lib. bdg. 15.95 *(978-1-59566-089-3(5))* QEB Publishing Inc.

—Touch That!, 5 vols. 2005. (QEB Let's Start! Science Ser.). (Illus.). 24p. (J). (gr. 1-4). lib. bdg. 15.95 *(978-1-59566-090-9(9))* QEB Publishing Inc.

Hicks, Kelli. Analyze This: Testing Ingredients. 2012. (ENG., Illus.). 24p. (gr. 4-5). pap. 8.95 *(978-1-61810-243-0(5))* Rourke Educational Media.

—I Can Prove It! Investigating Science. 2012. (ENG.). 24p. (gr. 4-5). pap. 8.95 *(978-1-61810-244-7(3))* Rourke Educational Media.

Hile, Lori, et al. Solving Mysteries with Science. 2013. (Solving Mysteries with Science Ser.). (ENG.). 48p. (gr. 3-6). pap. 71.92 *(978-1-4109-5509-8(5))*; pap. 35.96 *(978-1-4109-5508-1(7))*; lib. bdg. 119.96 *(978-1-4109-5502-9(8))*; lib. bdg. 149.95 *(978-1-4109-5503-6(6))* Heinemann-Raintree.

Hilltree, Angela. ABC Coloring Book: Creation Science & Geology. 2004. (Illus.). 26p. (J). 6.50 *(978-1-931941-10-5(6))* Media Angels, Inc.

Hirschmann, Kris & Herndon, Ryan. Test Your Smarts! Science. 2009. (Illus.). 80p. (J). pap. *(978-0-545-12041-8(1))* Scholastic, Inc.

Hixson, Bryce. Newton Take 3. Hixson, Bryce, illus. 2003. (Illus.). (J). per. 14.95 *(978-0-9660965-3-8(3))* Loose In The Lab.

—What's Up? Hixson, Bryce, illus. 2003. (Illus.). (J). per. 14.95 *(978-1-931801-05-8(3))* Loose In The Lab.

Hoena, Blake A. If Books. 2012. (If Bks.). (ENG.). 32p. (gr. 1-2). pap. 190.80 *(978-1-4296-9254-0(5))*; pap. 24.30 *(978-1-4296-9253-3(7))*; lib. bdg. 54.64 *(978-1-4296-9113-0(1))* Capstone Press of Coughlan Cos. (Aplus Bks.).

Holden, Arianne. It's Fun to Learn about Science: A Busy Picture Book Full of Fabulous Facts & Things to Do! 2016. (ENG., Illus.). 32p. (J). (gr. -1-12). 9.99 *(978-1-86147-742-2(2)*, Armadillo) Anness Publishing GBR. Dist: National Bk. Network.

Holden, Edward S. The Sciences. 2009. (Illus.). 254p. pap. 11.95 *(978-1-59915-338-4(6))* Yesterday's Classics.

Holland, Simon. What Came Before the Big Bang? 2017. (ENG., Illus.). 128p. (J). (gr. 4). pap. 12.95 ***(978-1-78312-155-7(6))*** Carlton Bks., Ltd. GBR. Dist: Sterling Publishing Co., Inc.

Holmes. Gateway Science. 5th ed. (J). Level 3. 349.98 *(978-0-07-030003-3(8))*Level K. 23.61 *(978-0-07-029942-9(0))* Macmillan/McGraw-Hill Schl. Div.

Holt, Rinehart and Winston Staff. Environmental Science Chptr. 8: Population & Communities. 4th ed. Date not set. pap. 11.20 *(978-0-03-068067-0(0))* Holt McDougal.

—Environmental Science Chptr. 9: The Human Population. 4th ed. Date not set. pap. 11.20 *(978-0-03-068068-7(9))* Holt McDougal.

—Harcourt Science & Technology: Strategies & Practice Answer Key. 4th ed. 2004. (Illus.). pap. 6.00 *(978-0-03-019863-2(1))* Holt McDougal.

—Holt Science & Technology. 4th annot. ed. 2004. tchr. ed. 128.80 *(978-0-03-073174-7(7))* Holt McDougal.

—Holt Science & Technology: Chapter Resources. 5th ed. 2005. pap. 87.36 *(978-0-03-030632-7(9))* Holt McDougal.

—Holt Science & Technology: Directed Reading Answer Key. 4th ed. 2004. (Illus.). pap. 11.20 *(978-0-03-037018-2(3))* Holt McDougal.

—Holt Science & Technology: Directed Reading Worksheets. 4th ed. 2004. pap. 15.00 *(978-0-03-036993-3(2))*; pap. 15.00 *(978-0-03-036994-0(0))*; pap. 15.00 *(978-0-03-036992-6(4))* Holt McDougal.

—Holt Science & Technology: Enhanced Online Edition - Short Course. 5th ed. 2004. (J). (gr. k). 18.60 *(978-0-03-030493-4(8))*; (gr. 1). 18.60 *(978-0-03-030496-5(2))*; (gr. 2). 18.60 *(978-0-03-030501-6(2))* Holt McDougal.

—Holt Science & Technology: Physical Science. 5th ed. 2004. (Holt Science & Technology Ser.). (Illus.). pap., stu. ed. 17.13 *(978-0-03-030161-2(0))* Holt McDougal.

—Holt Science & Technology: Physical Science: Reading & Comprehension Guide. 5th ed. 2004. (Holt Science & Technology Ser.). pap. 17.13 *(978-0-03-036063-3(3))* Holt McDougal.

—Holt Science & Technology: Physical Science: Special Needs Workbook. 5th ed. 2004. (Holt Science & Technology Ser.). pap., wbk. ed. 17.13 *(978-0-03-036056-5(0))* Holt McDougal.

—Holt Science & Technology: Program Introduction Booklet. 5th ed. 2004. (Illus.). 4.33 *(978-0-03-030162-9(9))* Holt McDougal.

—Life Science: Directed Reading & Vocabulary Workbook. 5th ed. 2004. (Holt Science & Technology Ser.). (SPA., Illus.). pap., wbk. ed. 17.13 *(978-0-03-036057-2(9))* Holt McDougal.

—Life Science: Study Guide. 5th ed. 2004. (Holt Science & Technology Ser.). (SPA., Illus.). pap., stu. ed. 17.13 *(978-0-03-030151-3(3))* Holt McDougal.

—Life Science 2005. 5th ed. 2004. (Holt Ciencias y Technologia Ser.). (SPA & ENG., Illus.). 912p. (gr. 6-6). stu. ed. 110.60 *(978-0-03-021179-9(4))* Houghton Mifflin Harcourt Publishing Co.

—Physical Science: Chapter Resources. 5th ed. 2004. (Holt Science & Technology Ser.). (Illus.). pap. 290.13 *(978-0-03-030126-1(2))* Holt McDougal.

—Physical Science: Directed Reading & Vocabulary Workbook. 5th ed. 2004. (Holt Science & Technology Ser.). (SPA., Illus.). pap., wbk. ed. 17.13 *(978-0-03-036059-6(5))* Holt McDougal.

—Physical Science 2005. 5th ed. 2004. (Holt Ciencias y Technologia Ser.). (SPA & ENG., Illus.). 848p. (gr. 8-8). stu. ed. 110.60 *(978-0-03-021272-7(3))* Houghton Mifflin Harcourt Publishing Co.

—Science Skills Workshop. 2nd ed. 2009. (Holt Biology Ser.). (ENG.). 192p. (gr. 6-12). pap. 34.25 *(978-0-03-064424-5(0))* Houghton Mifflin Harcourt Publishing Co.

Hopper, Whitney. Time to Go to the Science Museum! Work with Time. 2014. (Math Masters: Measurement & Data Ser.). 24p. (J). (gr. 2-3). 23.60 *(978-1-4777-6406-0(2))*; (ENG.). pap. 8.25 *(978-1-4777-4819-0(9))* Rosen Publishing Group, Inc., The. (Rosen Classroom).

Hosley, Maria. Dinosaurs, 1 vol. 2007. (First Drawings Ser.). (ENG., Illus.). 24p. 25.65 *(978-1-59679-802-1(5)*, Buddy Bks.) ABDO Publishing Co.

How Are They Built?, 6 bks., Set. (J). (gr. 4-8). lib. bdg. 179.57 *(978-1-58952-133-9(1))* Rourke Educational Media.

How Bread Is Made: 6 Each of 1 Student Book, 6 vols. (Sunshinetm Science Ser.). 24p. (gr. 1-2). 41.95 *(978-0-7802-2724-8(7))* Wright Group/McGraw-Hill.

How Bread Is Made: Big Book. (Sunshinetm Science Ser.). 24p. (gr. 1-2). 37.50 *(978-0-7802-2796-5(4))* Wright Group/McGraw-Hill.

How Can We See in the Dark?, 6 vols. (Sunshinetm Science Ser.). 24p. (gr. 1-2). 36.95 *(978-0-7802-0556-7(1))*; 31.50 *(978-0-7802-0305-1(4))* Wright Group/McGraw-Hill.

Hubble Science Cards. 2003. (Illus.). 44p. 7.99 *(978-0-9741147-0-5(7))* Phlare, Inc.

Hudson, Terry, et al. Oxford International Primary Science, Bk. 6. 2014. (ENG., Illus.). 152p. pap., wbk. ed. 27.00 *(978-0-19-839482-2(9))* Oxford Univ. Pr., Inc.

—Oxford International Primary Science Bk. 2: Primary 4-11 Oxford International Primary Science. 2014. (ENG., Illus.). 112p. pap., wbk. ed. 18.00 *(978-0-19-839478-5(0))* Oxford Univ. Pr., Inc.

—Oxford International Primary Science 4. 2014. (ENG., Illus.). 144p. pap., stu. ed. 23.00 *(978-0-19-839480-8(2))* Oxford Univ. Pr., Inc.

—Oxford International Primary Science, Stage 1. 2014. (ENG., Illus.). 112p. pap., wbk. ed. 18.00 *(978-0-19-839477-8(2))* Oxford Univ. Pr., Inc.

—Oxford International Primary Science, Stage 3. 2014. (ENG., Illus.). 144p. pap., stu. ed. 23.00 *(978-0-19-839479-2(9))* Oxford Univ. Pr., Inc.

—Oxford International Primary Science, Stage 5. 2014. (ENG., Illus.). 152p. pap., wbk. ed. 27.00 *(978-0-19-839481-5(0))* Oxford Univ. Pr., Inc.

Huffman, Julie. 101 Ways to Gross Out Your Friends. Paillot, Jim, illus. 2017. (101 Ser.). (ENG.). 144p. (J). (gr. 3-5). 33.32 *(978-1-942875-16-1(9))* Quarto Publishing Group USA.

Hughes, Colin & Wade, Winnie. How to Be a Wizard at Science Investigations. (J). (gr. 3-6). pap. *(978-1-876367-30-5(X))* Wizard Bks.

—How to Be Brilliant at Living Things. 2004. (Illus.). 48p. pap. 30.00 *(978-1-897675-66-3(6))* Brilliant Pubns. GBR. Dist: Parkwest Pubns., Inc.

Hunter, Dru. How Do We Apply Science? Think Like a Scientist. 2016. (Think Like a Scientist Ser.). (ENG.). 48p. (J). (gr. 5-9). pap. 12.00 *(978-1-62832-197-5(0)*, Creative Paperbacks) Creative Co., The.

Hurd. Physical Science. 3rd ed. (J). 59.47 *(978-0-13-982158-5(9))* Prentice Hall (Schl. Div.).

Ignotofsky, Rachel. I Love Science: A Journal for Self-Discovery & Big Ideas. 2017. (ENG., Illus.). 192p. 14.99 *(978-1-60774-980-6(7)*, Ten Speed Pr.) Potter/TenSpeed/Harmony.

Innes, Brian. Forensic Science. 2004. (Crime & Detection Ser.). (Illus.). 96p. (YA). (gr. 7-18). lib. bdg. 22.95 *(978-1-59084-373-4(8))* Mason Crest.

Instructional Resources. 2003. (Scott Foresman Science Ser.). (gr. 6-18). suppl. ed. 47.95 *(978-0-673-59337-5(1))* Addison-Wesley Educational Pubs., Inc.

Integrated Science for the Caribbean, Bk. 1. 2015. (ENG.). 224p. (J). pap., stu. ed. 24.95 *(978-0-00-811595-1(8))* HarperCollins Pubs. Ltd. GBR. Dist: Independent Pubs. Group.

Interactive Transparency Package. 2003. (gr. k-18). suppl. ed. 109.15 *(978-0-673-59454-9(8))*; (gr. 1-18). suppl. ed. 109.15 *(978-0-673-59455-6(6))*; (gr. 2-18). suppl. ed. 109.15 *(978-0-673-59456-3(4))*; (gr. 3-18). suppl. ed. 109.15 *(978-0-673-59457-0(2))*; (gr. 4-18). suppl. ed. 109.15 *(978-0-673-59458-7(0))*; (gr. 5-18). suppl. ed. 109.15 *(978-0-673-59459-4(9))*; (gr. 6-18). suppl. ed. 109.15 *(978-0-673-59460-0(2))* Addison-Wesley Educational Pubs., Inc.

Iopeners: Big Book Collection, 20 vols. 2005. (J). (gr. k-18). 525.95 *(978-0-7652-4972-2(3))*; (gr. 1-18). 587.50 *(978-0-7652-4976-0(6))* Modern Curriculum Pr.

Iopeners: Classroom Library. 2005. (J). (gr. k-18). 440.50 *(978-0-7652-4969-2(3))*; (gr. 1-18). 518.50 *(978-0-7652-4973-9(1))*; (gr. 2-18). 518.50 *(978-0-7652-4977-7(4))*; (gr. 3-18). 616.50 *(978-0-7652-4980-7(4))*; (gr. 4-18). 616.50 *(978-0-7652-4983-8(9))*; (gr. 5-18). 694.50 *(978-0-7652-4986-9(3))*; (gr. 6-18). 694.50 *(978-0-7652-4989-0(8))* Modern Curriculum Pr.

Iopeners: Science Library, 10 vols. 2005. (J). (gr. k-18). 220.95 *(978-0-7652-4970-8(7))* Modern Curriculum Pr.

Is it Floating?, 6 vols. (Sunshinetm Science Ser.). 24p. (gr. 1-2). 36.95 *(978-0-7802-0546-8(4))*; 31.50 *(978-0-7802-0295-5(3))* Wright Group/McGraw-Hill.

Issues, Evidence & You Complete Materials Package. 2003. (Illus.). (YA). tchr. ed., ring bd. *(978-1-887725-71-2(7))* Lab-Aids, Inc.

Issues, Evidence & You Complete Materials Package: Includes Teacher's Guide & Student Books. 2003. (Illus.). (YA). *(978-1-887725-72-9(5))* Lab-Aids, Inc.

Issues, Evidence & You Complete Materials Package for Chicago Public Schools. 2003. (Illus.). (YA). ring bd. *(978-1-887725-84-2(9))* Lab-Aids, Inc.

Ivanoff, George. How to Make a Fake Death Ray into a Real Laser. 2007. 96p. (J). *(978-1-4207-0735-9(3))* Sundance/Newbridge Educational Publishing.

Jacobs, Daniel. For Your Information. Date not set. (Early Science Big Bks.). (Illus.). 16p. (J). (gr. -1-2). pap. 16.95 *(978-1-58273-123-0(3))* Sundance/Newbridge Educational Publishing.

James, Frank A. J. L., ed. Christmas at the Royal Institution: An Anthology of Lectures by M Faraday, J Tyndall, R S Ball, S P Thompson, E R Lankester, W H Bragg, W L Bragg, R L Gregory, & I Stewart. 2008. (Illus.). 366p. *(978-981-277-108-7(5))* World Scientific Publishing Co. Pte Ltd.

James, Frank A. L., ed. Christmas at the Royal Institution: An Anthology of Lectures by M Faraday, J Tyndall, R S Ball, S P Thompson, E R Lankester, W H Bragg, W L Bragg, R L Gregory, & I Stewart. 2008. (Illus.). 366p. pap. *(978-981-277-109-4(3))* World Scientific Publishing Co. Pte Ltd.

Jason Science Adventure: Aquatic Field Study. 2004. (J). *(978-0-9763809-0-0(0))* JASON Project, The.

Jo, Eun-sook. Ah I'm Full. Cowley, Joy, ed. Kwon, Yeong-mook, illus. 2015. (Science Storybooks Ser.). (ENG.). 32p. (J). (gr. k-3). 26.65 *(978-1-925233-59-9(6))* Lerner Publishing Group.

Johnson, Rebecca L. Machines - Simple & Compound. 2007. (Language, Literacy, & Vocabulary - Reading Expeditions Ser.). (ENG., Illus.). 36p. (J). pap. 18.95 *(978-0-7922-5439-3(2))* CENGAGE Learning.

Johnson, Rose. Discoveries in Life Science That Changed the World, 1 vol. 2015. (ENG.). 48p. (YA). 30.25 *(978-1-4777-8607-9(4)*, Rosen Reference) Rosen Publishing Group, Inc., The.

Jones, Mary, et al. Cambridge Checkpoint Science Coursebook 7. 2012. (ENG., Illus.). 191p. pap. 33.69 *(978-1-107-61333-1(7))* Cambridge Univ. Pr.

—Cambridge Checkpoint Science Coursebook 9. 2013. (ENG., Illus.). 188p. pap. 33.69 *(978-1-107-62606-5(4))* Cambridge Univ. Pr.

—Cambridge Checkpoint Science Workbook 7. 2012. (ENG., Illus.). 96p. pap. 15.94 *(978-1-107-62285-2(9))* Cambridge Univ. Pr.

—Cambridge Checkpoint Science Workbook 9. 2013. (ENG., Illus.). 120p. pap. 15.94 *(978-1-107-69574-0(0))* Cambridge Univ. Pr.

—Combined & Co-Ordinated Sciences. 2017. (Cambridge International IGCSE Ser.). (ENG.). 680p. pap. 49.94 incl. cd-rom *(978-1-316-63101-0(X))* Cambridge Univ. Pr.

Kalman, Bobbie. El Ciclo de Vida de la Abeja. 2005. (Serie Ciclos de Vida Ser.). (SPA., Illus.). 32p. (J). lib. bdg. *(978-0-7787-8666-5(8))*; (gr. 1-4). pap. *(978-0-7787-8712-9(5))* Crabtree Publishing Co.

Kalman, Bobbie & Langille, Jacqueline. ¿Qué Es el Ciclo de Vida? 2005. (Ciencia de los Seres Vivos Ser.). (SPA., Illus.). 32p. (J). (gr. 2-4). pap. *(978-0-7787-8800-3(8))* Crabtree Publishing Co.

Karapetian, Marjam. Bilingual Content Dictionary: English to Spanish. 2004. (SPA & ENG.). 13.95 *(978-0-9764829-4-9(0))*; 15.95 *(978-0-9764829-5-6(9))* WizdomInc.

Kassnoff, David. What Degree Do I Need to Pursue a Career in Information Technology & Information Systems?, 1 vol. 2015. (ENG., Illus.). 80p. (J). 34.60 *(978-1-4777-7865-4(9)*, Rosen Young Adult) Rosen Publishing Group, Inc., The.

Kenney, Karen Latchana. Science in Action. 2016. (Science in Action Ser.: 6). (ENG.). 32p. (J). (gr. 3-6). lib. bdg. 162.42 *(978-1-62403-959-1(6)*, Checkerboard Library) ABDO Publishing Co.

Kinser, Kathy. Doomed to Disappear? Endangered Species: Set Of 6. 2011. (Navigators Ser.). (J). pap. 48.00 net. *(978-1-4108-0418-1(6))* Benchmark Education Co.

Kirkland, Kyle. Frontiers of Science, 8 vols., Set. 2010. (Frontiers of Science Ser.). (C). (gr. 9). 316.00 *(978-0-8160-8302-2(9))* Facts On File, Inc.

Koellhoffer, Tara. Science News for Kids, 6-Volume Set. 2006. (Science News for Kids Ser.). 144p. (gr. 4-6). 180.00 *(978-0-7910-9292-7(5)*, Chelsea Clubhouse) Facts On File, Inc.

Kops, Deborah. Were Early Computers Really the Size of a School Bus? And Other Questions about Inventions. 2011. (Is That a Fact? Ser.). (ENG.). 40p. (gr. 4-6). 26.60 *(978-0-7613-6098-8(0))* Lerner Publishing Group.

Kramer, Alan. Under the Sea with Jacques Cousteau. 2004. (Reader's Theater Ser.). (J). pap. *(978-1-4108-0801-1(7))* Benchmark Education Co.

—The Wright Brothers at Kitty Hawk. 2004. (Reader's Theater Ser.). (J). pap. *(978-1-4108-0794-6(0))* Benchmark Education Co.

Kroll, Jennifer. The Science of Superpowers (Grade 6) 2016. (TIME for KIDS(r) Nonfiction Readers Ser.). (Illus.). 64p. (J). (gr. 6-6). 10.99 *(978-1-4938-3608-6(0))* Teacher Created Materials, Inc.

Kroutil Artists, creator. The Elements: A Fun, Easy to Learn, Introduction to the Elements in Character! 2004. (YA). per. 24.95 *(978-1-932689-00-6(1))* EDGEucation Publishing.

Lacey, Minna. Look Inside Science. 2011. (Look Inside Board Bks). 13p. (J). ring bd. 15.99 *(978-0-7945-2946-8(1)*, Usborne) EDC Publishing.

LaCompte, Angie. I Am a Scientist. 2011. (Science Ser.). (ENG.). 16p. (gr. -1-1). 25.95 *(978-1-4296-8535-1(2)*, Wonder Readers) Capstone Press of Coughlan Cos.

Ladybird I'm Ready... for Science! 2016. (ENG., Illus.). 48p. (J). (gr. k-2). 11.99 *(978-0-241-23835-6(8))* Penguin Bks., Ltd. GBR. Dist: Independent Pubs. Group.

Language Arts Explorer, 26 vols., Set. Incl. Save the Planet: Compost It. Barker, David. 32p. 2010. lib. bdg. 28.50 *(978-1-60279-656-0(4)*, 200349); Save the Planet: Growing Your Own Garden. Hirsch, Rebecca. 32p. 2010. lib. bdg. 28.50 *(978-1-60279-657-7(2)*, 200350); Save the Planet: Helping Endangered Animals. Hirsch, Rebecca. 32p. 2010. lib. bdg. 28.50 *(978-1-60279-658-4(0)*, 200351); Save the Planet: Keeping Water Clean. Farrell, Courtney. 32p. 2010. lib. bdg. 28.50 *(978-1-60279-659-1(9)*, 200352); Save the Planet: Local Farms & Sustainable Foods. Vogel, Julia. 32p. 2010. lib. bdg. 28.50 *(978-1-60279-660-7(2)*, 200353); Save the Planet: Protecting Our Natural Resources. Hirsch, Rebecca. 32p. 2010. lib. bdg. 28.50 *(978-1-60279-661-4(0)*, 200354); Save the Planet: Reduce, Reuse, & Recycle. Minden, Cecilia. 32p. 2010. lib. bdg. 28.50 *(978-1-60279-662-1(9)*, 200355); Save the Planet: Using Alternative Energies. Farrell, Courtney. 32p. 2010. lib. bdg. 28.50 *(978-1-60279-663-8(7)*, 200356); Set. Language Arts Explorer: History Digs. Cherry Lake Publishing Staff. (J). 2011. lib. bdg. 285.00 *(978-1-61080-243-7(8))*; Set. Language Arts Explorer: Science Lab. Cherry Lake Publishing Staff. (J). 2011. lib. bdg. 228.00 *(978-1-61080-245-1(4))*; (gr. 4-8). 2011. Set lib. bdg. 741.00 *(978-1-61080-239-0(X))* Cherry Lake Publishing.

Lassieur, Allison & Lusted, Marcia Amidon. Warrior Science. 2016. (Warrior Science Ser.). (ENG.). 32p. (gr. 3-4). 111.96 *(978-1-4914-8147-9(1)*, Edge Bks.) Capstone Press of Coughlan Cos.

Leavitt, Amie Jane, et al. The Science Behind Natural Phenomena. 2016. (Science Behind Natural Phenomena Ser.). (ENG.). 32p. (gr. 3-4). 111.96 *(978-1-5157-0809-4(8)*, Edge Bks.) Capstone Press of Coughlan Cos.

Leber, Nancy. What Plants & Animals Need, 6 vols., Set. 2003. (Phonics Readers 1-36 Ser.). (ENG.). 8p. (gr. k-1). pap. 29.70 *(978-0-7368-3215-1(7)*, Phonics Readers) Capstone Press of Coughlan Cos.

Lemonick, Michael D. Science Alive, No. 1. 2005. 48p. (J). *(978-0-7868-2106-8(X))* Hyperion Bks. for Children.

—Science Alive, No. 2. 2005. (J). *(978-0-7868-0134-3(4))* Hyperion Pr.

Lerner, K. Lee, et al. U-X-L Doomed: The Science Behind Disasters. 2015. (J). *(978-1-4103-1777-3(3))* Cengage Gale.

LernerClassroom Editors, ed. Cool Science Set III: Classroom Library. 2008. pap. 34.95 *(978-0-8225-9175-7(8))* Lerner Publishing Group.

—Cool Science Set III: Complete Library. 2008. pap. 210.95 *(978-0-8225-9281-5(9))* Lerner Publishing Group.

Let's Explore Science, 33 vols., Set. Incl. MP3 Players. Sturm, Jeanne. 2008. lib. bdg. 31.36 *(978-1-60472-332-8(7))*; Rocks, Minerals, & Soil. Meredith, Susan. 2009. lib. bdg. 32.79 *(978-1-60694-411-0(8))*; (Illus.). 48p. (J). (gr. 4-8). 2011. lib. bdg. o.p. *(978-1-61590-875-2(7))* Rourke Educational Media.

Let's Find Out! 2014. (Let's Find Out! Ser.). 32p. (J). (gr. 3-6). 562.80 *(978-1-62275-539-4(1))*; pap. 309.60 *(978-1-62275-771-8(8))* Rosen Publishing Group, Inc., The.

Let's Find Out! Complete Set. 2016. (Let's Find Out! Ser.). 32p. (gr. 3-2). 1858.20 *(978-1-5081-0232-8(5)*, Britannica Educational Publishing) Rosen Publishing Group, Inc., The.

Let's Find Out! Physical Science. 2014. (Let's Find Out! Ser.). 32p. (J). (gr. 3-6). 281.40 *(978-1-62275-756-5(4))*; 140.70 *(978-1-62275-517-2(0))* Rosen Publishing Group, Inc., The.

Leveled Reader Collection. 2003. (Scott Foresman Science Ser.). (gr. k-18). 198.00 *(978-0-673-65126-6(6))*; (gr. 1-18). 198.00 *(978-0-673-65127-3(4))*; (gr. 2-18). 198.00 *(978-0-673-65128-0(2))*; (gr. 3-18). 231.00 *(978-0-673-65129-7(0))*; (gr. 4-18). 231.00 *(978-0-673-65130-3(4))*; (gr. 5-18). 231.00 *(978-0-673-65131-0(2))*; (gr. 6-18). 231.00 *(978-0-673-65132-7(0))* Addison-Wesley Educational Pubs., Inc.

Levete, Sarah. Science Fact or Fiction? You Decide! 2010. (ENG.). 32p. (J). pap. *(978-0-7787-9916-0(6))*; (Illus.). *(978-0-7787-9895-8(X)*, 1325460) Crabtree Publishing Co.

Levy, Joel. The Universe Explained, 1 vol., 1. 2014. (Guide for Curious Minds Ser.). (ENG.). 136p. (YA). (gr. 7-12). 38.25 *(978-1-4777-2958-8(5))* Rosen Publishing Group, Inc., The.

Life Science, Set. 2010. (Extreme! Ser.). (ENG.). 32p. (gr. 3-4). pap. 429.30 *(978-1-4296-5138-7(5)*, Fact Finders) Capstone Press of Coughlan Cos.

Lift-The-Flap Questions & Answers about Science IR. 2017. (Lift-The-Flap Questions & Answers Ser.). (ENG.). (J). bds. 14.99 ***(978-0-7945-3940-5(8)***, Usborne) EDC Publishing.

Literature Library. 2003. (Literature Library). (gr. k-18). 105.85 *(978-0-673-59585-0(4))*; (gr. 1-18). 105.85 *(978-0-673-59586-7(2))*; (gr. 2-18). 105.85 *(978-0-673-59587-4(0))*; (gr. 3-18). 105.85 *(978-0-673-59588-1(9))*; (gr. 4-18). 35.30 *(978-0-673-59589-8(7))*; (gr. 5-18). 35.30 *(978-0-673-59590-4(0))*; (gr. 6-18). 35.30 *(978-0-673-59591-1(9))* Addison-Wesley Educational Pubs., Inc.

S

Littlefield, Cindy A. Awesome Ocean Science. 2006. (Williamson Kids Can! Ser.). (ENG., Illus.). 120p. (J). (gr. 4-7). pap. 12.95 *(978-0-8249-6796-3(8)*, Ideal Pubns.) Worthy Publishing.

Living on the Edge Series, 5 bks., Set. 128.21 *(978-0-7614-1436-0(3)*, Benchmark Bks.) Marshall Cavendish Corp.

Llewellyn, Claire. Caliente y Frio. (Coleccion de Lado a Lado Ser.). (SPA., Illus.). (J). (gr. k-3). 11.16 *(978-970-656-279-1(6)*, CM30003) Publicaciones Citem, S.A. de C.V. MEX. Dist: Lectorum Pubns., Inc.

—Dia y Noche. (Coleccion de Lado a Lado Ser.). (SPA., Illus.). 11.16 *(978-970-656-281-4(8)*, CM30004) Publicaciones Citem, S.A. de C.V. MEX. Dist: Lectorum Pubns., Inc.

—Diminuto y Enorme. (Coleccion de Lado a Lado Ser.). (SPA., Illus.). 11.16 *(978-970-656-280-7(X)*, CM30005) Publicaciones Citem, S.A. de C.V. MEX. Dist: Lectorum Pubns., Inc.

—Tierra y Mar. (Coleccion de Lado a Lado Ser.). (SPA., Illus.). (J). (gr. k-3). 11.16 *(978-970-656-282-1(6)*, CM30006) Publicaciones Citem, S.A. de C.V. MEX. Dist: Lectorum Pubns., Inc.

Lo Bosco, Maryellen. Famous Immigrant Scientists. 2017. (J). ***(978-0-7660-9244-0(5))*** Enslow Pubs., Inc.

Londt, Claire, et al. English Matters for Zambia Basic Education Grade 3 Pupil's Book. 2nd ed. 2007. pap., stu. ed. 5.75 *(978-0-521-68755-3(1))* Cambridge Univ. Pr.

A Look into Space: Individual Title Six-Packs. (Discovery World Ser.). 12p. (gr. k-1). 28.00 *(978-0-7635-8452-8(5))* Rigby Education.

Ludeke, Kenneth L. & Ludeke, Amalia H. A Day with Anion, an Ion Science. 2013. 28p. (J). pap. 24.95 *(978-1-63000-636-5(X))* America Star Bks.

Lunis, Natalie. Backyard Scientist. Date not set. (Thinking Like a Scientist Ser.). (Illus.). 20p. (J). pap. 16.95 *(978-1-58273-107-0(1))* Sundance/Newbridge Educational Publishing.

Lunis, Natalie & White, Nancy. Being a Scientist. Date not set. (Thinking Like a Scientist Ser.). (Illus.). 20p. (J). pap. 16.95 *(978-1-58273-085-1(7))* Sundance/Newbridge Educational Publishing.

—Exploring Everyday Wonders. Date not set. (Thinking Like a Scientist Ser.). (Illus.). 20p. (J). pap. 16.95 *(978-1-58273-368-5(6))* Sundance/Newbridge Educational Publishing.

—Popcorn Science. Date not set. (Thinking Like a Scientist Ser.). (Illus.). 20p. (J). pap. 16.95 *(978-1-58273-370-8(8))* Sundance/Newbridge Educational Publishing.

—A World of Change. Date not set. (Thinking Like a Scientist Ser.). (Illus.). 20p. (J). pap. 16.95 *(978-1-58273-077-6(6))* Sundance/Newbridge Educational Publishing.

Luz. (Coleccion Jugando Con la Ciencia). (SPA., Illus.). 39p. (J). pap. 9.95 *(978-950-11-0683-1(7)*, SGM35X) Sigmar ARG. Dist: Continental Bk. Co., Inc.

MacGregor, Fiona, et al. Collins Primary Science - Student's Book Stage 3. 2015. (Collins International Primary Science Ser.). (ENG.). 96p. (J). (gr. 2). pap. 12.95 *(978-0-00-758616-5(7))* HarperCollins Pubs. Ltd. GBR. Dist: Independent Pubs. Group.

Maclaine, James. Lift-The-Flap General Knowledge IR. 2015. (Lift-The-Flap Board Bks.). (ENG.). 16p. (J). (gr. k-5). 14.99 *(978-0-7945-3418-9(X)*, Usborne) EDC Publishing.

Mara, Wil. The Mesopotamians. 2011. (Technology of the Ancients Ser.). 64p. (gr. 5). 32.79 *(978-1-60870-767-6(9))* Marshall Cavendish Corp.

—The Romans. 2011. (Technology of the Ancients Ser.). 64p. (gr. 5). 32.79 *(978-1-60870-768-3(7))* Marshall Cavendish Corp.

Marine Science. 2009. (Twentieth-Century Science Ser.). (Illus.). 320p. (J). (gr. 6-12). 49.50 *(978-0-8160-5534-0(3))* Facts On File, Inc.

Mason, Adrienne. Motion, Magnets & More. Dávila, Claudia, illus. 2011. (ENG.). 128p. (J). (gr. -1-2). 18.95 *(978-1-55453-707-5(X))* Kids Can Pr., Ltd. CAN. Dist: Hachette Bk. Group.

Mast, Steven. God's Wonderful World: Science 5. 2004. (God's World Science Ser.). (Illus.). 272p. (gr. 5-18). 15.10 *(978-0-7399-0614-9(3)*, 14501) Rod & Staff Pubs., Inc.

—God's Wonderful World: Science 5 Tests. 2004. (God's World Science Ser.). 31p. (gr. 5-18). 1.95 *(978-0-7399-0615-6(1)*, 14511) Rod & Staff Pubs., Inc.

Math Attack: Exploring Life Science with Math. 2016. (Math Attack: Exploring Life Science with Math Ser.). 00032p. (J). (gr. 3-4). 157.50 (978-1-4994-3195-7(3), PowerKids Pr.) Rosen Publishing Group, Inc., The.

Mattern, Joanne. Can Lightning Strike the Same Place Twice? And Other Questions about Earth, Weather, & the Environment. 2010. (Is That a Fact? Ser.). 40p. (YA). (gr. 3-6). lib. bdg. 26.60 (978-0-8225-9081-1(6)) Lerner Publishing Group.

Mayes, Susan. Starting Point Science: What Makes It Rain? / What Makes a Flower Grow? / Where Does Electricity Come from? / What's under the Ground? Amery, Heather, ed. rev. ed. 2007. (Starting Point Science Ser.). (Illus.). 98p. (J). (gr. 4-7). 13.99 (978-0-7945-1626-0(2), Usborne) EDC Publishing.

McDougal-Littell Publishing Staff. Integrated Course. l.t. ed. 2004. (McDougal Littell Middle School Science Ser.). (ENG.). 128p. (gr. 7-7). 86.05 (978-0-618-42301-9(X), 2-01159) Great Source Education Group, Inc.

—Integrated Course 3. l.t. ed. 2004. (McDougal Littell Middle School Science Ser.). (ENG.). 128p. (gr. 8-8). 86.05 (978-0-618-42303-3(6), 2-01161) Great Source Education Group, Inc.

—Modules: Physical Science - Diversity of Living Things. 2004. (McDougal Littell Science Ser.). (ENG.). 64p. (gr. 6-8). pap., lab manual ed. 15.30 (978-0-618-43724-5(X), 2-01217) Great Source Education Group, Inc.

—Modules: Physical Science; Ecology Unit. 2004. (McDougal Littell Science Ser.). (ENG.). 40p. (gr. 6-8). pap., lab manual ed. 15.30 (978-0-618-43728-3(2), 2-01221) Great Source Education Group, Inc.

—Modules: Physical Science; Life over Time. 2004. (McDougal Littell Science Ser.). (ENG.). 40p. (gr. 6-8). pap., lab manual ed. 15.30 (978-0-618-43731-3(2), 2-01224) Great Source Education Group, Inc.

—Modules: Physical Science; Visual Glossary. 2004. (McDougal Littell Science Ser.). (ENG.). 48p. (gr. 6-8). pap. 28.65 (978-0-618-41587-8(4), 2-01136) Great Source Education Group, Inc.

—Physical Science. 2004. (McDougal Littell Middle School Science Ser.). (ENG.). 112p. (gr. 6-8). 84.85 (978-0-618-30369-4(3), 2-01004) Great Source Education Group, Inc.

—Science: Integrated Course 1. l.t. ed. 2004. (McDougal Littell Middle School Science Ser.). (ENG.). 128p. (gr. 6-6). 86.05 (978-0-618-42299-9(4), 2-01157) Great Source Education Group, Inc.

McFall, Sally, ed. Pro/Con 2, 6 vols. 2003. (Illus.). 1392p. (YA). 339.00 (978-0-7172-5753-9(3)) Scholastic Library Publishing.

—Pro/Con 3, 12 vols. 2004. (Illus.). (YA). 339.00 (978-0-7172-5927-4(7), Grolier) Scholastic Library Publishing.

McGill, Jordan. Life Science Fair Projects. 2011. (J). (978-1-61690-330-5(9)); (gr. 3-5). pap. 12.95 (978-1-61690-658-0(8), AV2 by Weigl); (Illus.). 24p. (gr. 3-6). 27.13 (978-1-61690-654-2(5)) Weigl Pubs., Inc.

McGraw-Hill-Glencoe Staff. The Air Around You. 2nd ed. 2004. (Glen Sci: the Air above Us Ser.). (ENG., Illus.). 192p. (gr. 6-8). lib. bdg., stu. ed. 31.44 (978-0-07-861758-4(8), 0078617588) McGraw-Hill Higher Education.

—Glencoe Science. 2004. (Integrated Science Ser.). (ENG., Illus.). 75p. (gr. 6-6). pap., stu. ed., pupil's gde. ed. 7.88 (978-0-07-867216-3(3), 0078672163) McGraw-Hill Education.

McGraw-Hill Staff. Life Science Animations. 2nd ed. 2004. (gr. 6-12). cd-rom (978-0-07-248438-0(1)) Glencoe/McGraw-Hill.

McGraw-Hill Staff, creator. Science. 2004. (Integrated Science Ser.). (ENG., Illus.). 346p. (gr. 6-6). stu. ed., per. 21.32 (978-0-07-867214-9(7), 0078672147) McGraw-Hill Education.

Meissner, David. Habitat Rescue: Set Of 6. 2010. (Navigators Ser.). (J). pap. 44.00 net. (978-1-4108-0411-2(9)) Benchmark Education Co.

Merrell, Patrick. iFlush Swimming in Science. 2013. (ENG., Illus.). 96p. (J). (gr. 1-6). 12.95 (978-1-60710-783-5(X), Portable Pr.) Readerlink Distribution Services, LLC.

Michels, Dia & Levy, Nathan. 101 Things Everyone Should Know about Science TEST BOOKLET. 2007. (101 Things Everyone Should Know Ser.). (ENG., Illus.). 16p. (YA). 2.95 (978-0-9678020-4-6(0)) Science, Naturally!

Michels, Michael, et al. Cooperative Learning & Science High School Activities. 2005. per. (978-1-879097-74-2(5)) Kagan Publishing.

Miles Kelly Staff. Science: Family Flip Quiz. 2003. (Family Flip Quiz Ser.). (Illus.). 152p. (J). spiral bd. 12.95 (978-1-84236-073-6(6)) Miles Kelly Publishing, Ltd. GBR. Dist: Independent Pubs. Group.

Mills, Nathan & Ludlow, Susan. From Ice to Steam. 2012. (Rosen Readers Ser.). (ENG., Illus.). 24p. (J). (gr. 1-2). pap. 8.25 (978-1-4488-8812-2(3), Rosen Classroom) Rosen Publishing Group, Inc., The.

Mills, Nathan & Worthy, Shanya. Ana's Community Helpers. 2012. (Rosen Readers Ser.). (ENG., Illus.). 16p. (J). (gr. k-1). pap. 7.00 (978-1-4488-8698-2(8), Rosen Classroom) Rosen Publishing Group, Inc., The.

Mitchell, Ainslie. Collecting Seashells. Walker, Anna, illus. 2005. (Science (Harcourt) Ser.). 14p. pap. 6.00 (978-0-15-349999-9(0)) Harcourt Schl. Pubs.

Mitchell Lane Publishers Inc. Staff. A Robbie Reader-Science Biography, 5 vols., Set. 2005. (Robbie Reader Ser.). (Illus.). 32p. (gr. 1-4). lib. bdg. 128.50 (978-1-58415-351-1(2)) Mitchell Lane Pubs., Inc.

Mitchem, James. The Big Book of Things to Make. 2013. (ENG.). 128p. (J). (gr. 2-5). 16.99 (978-1-4654-0255-4(1), DK Children) Dorling Kindersley Publishing, Inc.

MoCasins: Level A. 8p. 20.95 (978-0-322-00624-9(4)) Wright Group/McGraw-Hill.

Modern Staff. Apple Tree. 2003. 38.95 (978-0-8136-4107-2(1)) Modern Curriculum Pr.

Modules: Physical Science; English Learners Package. 2005. (gr. 6-12). (978-0-618-41579-3(3), 2-01131) Holt McDougal.

Modules: Physical Science; How Stuff Works Express Magazine. 2005. (gr. 6-12). (978-0-618-41615-8(3), 2-01137) Holt McDougal.

Modules: Physical Science; Lab Generator. 2005. (gr. 6-12). cd-rom (978-0-618-42033-9(9), 2-01147) Holt McDougal.

Modules: Physical Science; Process & Lab Skills PE. 2005. (Module: Physical Science Ser.). (gr. 6-18). (978-0-618-41364-5(2), 2-01113); (gr. 7-18). (978-0-618-41365-2(0), 2-01114); (gr. 8-18). (978-0-618-41366-9(9), 2-01115) Holt McDougal.

Modules: Physical Science; Science Toolkit. 2005. (gr. 6-12). (978-0-618-41583-0(1), 2-01134) Holt McDougal.

Modules: Physical Science; Standardized Test Practice PE. 2005. (gr. 6-12). cd-rom (978-0-618-41372-0(3), 2-01121); (gr. 7-18). (978-0-618-41371-3(5), 2-01120) Holt McDougal.

Moehlenpah, Arlo. Creation Versus Evolution: Scientific & Religious Considerations. 2003. 36p. (YA). (978-0-9667054-6-1(7)) Doing Good Ministries.

Monroe, Elliot. Interdependence of Species. 2016. (Spotlight on Ecology & Life Science Ser.). 00024p. (J). (gr. 4-6). pap. 10.00 (978-1-4994-2595-6(3), PowerKids Pr.) Rosen Publishing Group, Inc., The.

Monster Science. 2011. (Monster Science Ser.). (ENG.). 32p. (gr. 3-4). pap. 286.20 (978-1-4296-7338-9(9)); pap. 47.70 (978-1-4296-7337-2(0)); lib. bdg. 153.25 (978-1-4296-6583-4(1)) Capstone Press of Coughlan Cos. (Graphic Library).

Morris, Paul & Deo, Patricia. Sciences. 2016. (ENG.). 160p. pap. 21.75 (978-1-4718-8037-7(0)) Hodder Education Group GBR. Dist: Ingram Publisher Services.

Morrison, Karen. International Science Coursebook 3. 2009. (Illus.). 152p. pap. 39.50 (978-0-340-96602-0(5)) Hodder Education Group GBR. Dist: Trans-Atlantic Pubns., Inc.

Morrison, Karen, et al. Collins International Primary Science. 2015. (Collins International Primary Science Ser.). (ENG.). 96p. (gr. 3). pap., stu. ed. 12.95 (978-0-00-758620-2(5)) HarperCollins Pubs. Ltd. GBR. Dist: Independent Pubs. Group.

—Collins Primary Science - Student's Book Stage 6. 2015. (Collins International Primary Science Ser.). (ENG.). 96p. (J). (gr. 5). pap. 12.95 (978-0-00-758627-1(2)) HarperCollins Pubs. Ltd. GBR. Dist: Independent Pubs. Group.

Morter, Peter. Atlas Visual de los Descubrimientos. (SPA., Illus.). 412p. (YA). (gr. 5-8). (978-84-216-1814-1(8), BU4892) Bruño, Editorial ESP. Dist: Lectorum Pubns., Inc.

Mother Goose Cares about Math & Science: Professional Development Manual. 2004. (978-0-9753985-2-4(0)) Mother Goose Programs.

Mother Goose Programs, prod. What's the BIG Idea? Shapes & Spaces Librarian Manual. 2008. 70p. pap. (978-0-9753985-9-3(8)) Mother Goose Programs.

El Motin del Amistad: Libros Aventuras (Adventure Books) 2003. (MacMillan/McGraw-Hill. Estudios Sociales Ser.). (ENG & SPA.). (gr. 5-18). (978-0-02-150125-0(4)) Macmillan/McGraw-Hill Schl. Div.

Movimiento. (Coleccion Jugando Con la Ciencia). (SPA., Illus.). 39p. (J). pap. 9.95 (978-950-11-0684-8(5), SGM325) Sigmar ARG. Dist: Continental Bk. Co., Inc.

Moving up with Science. 2016. (Moving up with Science Ser.). 00032p. (J). (gr. 3-4). 157.50 (978-1-4994-3192-6(9), PowerKids Pr.) Rosen Publishing Group, Inc., The.

Mullins, Lisa & Smith, Elizabeth. Science in the Renaissance. 2009. (Renaissance World Ser.). (ENG., Illus.). 32p. (J). (gr. 5-8). pap. (978-0-7787-4614-0(3)) Crabtree Publishing Co.

El Mundo de la Ciencia. (Coleccion Lo Sabias?). (SPA., Illus.). 44p. (J). 12.95 (978-950-11-0940-5(2), SGM9402) Sigmar ARG. Dist: Continental Bk. Co., Inc.

Murphy, Glenn. Disgusting Science: A Revolting Look at What Makes Things Gross. unabr. ed. 2014. (ENG., Illus.). 160p. (J). (gr. 2-4). pap. 7.99 (978-1-4472-5299-3(3)) Pan Macmillan GBR. Dist: Independent Pubs. Group.

—Supergeek Vol. 1: Dinosaurs, Brains & Supertrains. 2014. (Supergeek! Ser.). (ENG., Illus.). 208p. (J). (gr. 4-7). pap. 7.99 (978-1-4472-2716-8(6)) Pan Macmillan GBR. Dist: Independent Pubs. Group.

—Supergeek Vol. 1: Robots, Space & Furry Animals. 2014. (Supergeek! Ser.). (ENG., Illus.). 208p. (J). (gr. 4-7). pap. 7.99 (978-1-4472-2732-8(8)) Pan Macmillan GBR. Dist: Independent Pubs. Group.

—Why Is Snot Green? And Other Extremely Important Questions (And Answers) Phillips, Mike, illus. 2009. (ENG.). 240p. (J). (gr. 3-7). pap. 13.99 (978-1-59643-500-1(3), 9781596435001) Square Fish.

Murphy, Lisa. Even More Fizzle Bubble Pop & Wow! Simple Science for Young Children. rev. ed. 2003. Orig. Title: Fizzle Bubble Pop & Wow! (ENG., Illus.). 120p. pap. 19.95 (978-0-9706634-2-9(0)) Redleaf Pr.

Museums: Collections to Share, 6 vols. (Book2WebTM Ser.). (gr. 4-8). 36.50 (978-0-322-02986-6(4)) Wright Group/McGraw-Hill.

My Big Book of Science. 2004. (Illus.). 48p. (J). pap. 5.99 (978-1-85854-843-2(8)) Brimax Books Ltd. GBR. Dist: Byeway Bks.

My Body Does Strange Stuff! 2013. (My Body Does Strange Stuff! Ser.). 24p. (J). (gr. 1-3). 135.60 (978-1-4339-9673-3(1)); pap. 293.40 (978-1-4339-9764-8(9)); pap. 48.90 (978-1-4339-9763-1(0)) Stevens, Gareth Publishing LLLP.

My Feet: Big Book: Level C. 8p. 20.95 (978-0-322-00364-4(4)) Wright Group/McGraw-Hill.

My World of Science: Set 1. (Illus.). (J). (gr. 1-2). 96.00 (978-1-4042-3379-9(2)) Rosen Publishing Group, Inc., The.

My World of Science: Set 2. (Illus.). (J). (gr. 1-2). 96.00 (978-1-4042-3289-1(3)) Rosen Publishing Group, Inc., The.

My World of Science Set 1. (ENG & SPA., Illus.). (J). (gr. 4-8). 96.00 (978-1-4042-7568-3(1), Editorial Buenas Letras) Rosen Publishing Group, Inc., The.

Nasty (but Useful!) Science. 2010. (Nasty (but Useful!) Science Ser.). (ENG.). 32p. (gr. 3-4). pap. 31.80 (978-1-4296-6348-9(0)); lib. bdg. 81.96 (978-1-4296-4540-9(7)) Capstone Press of Coughlan Cos. (Fact Finders).

National Geographic Kids Staff. Science Encyclopedia: Atom Smashing, Food Chemistry, Animals, Space, & More! 2016. (ENG., Illus.). 304p. (J). (gr. 3-7). 24.99 (978-1-4263-2542-7(8), National Geographic Children's Bks.) National Geographic Society.

National Science Resources Center, creator. Science & Technology for Children Books: Animal Studies. 2004. (J). (978-1-933008-00-4(8)) Smithsonian Science Education Ctr. (SSEC).

Natural Science Mysteries Full Kit. 2005. (Illus.). 856p. (YA). 75.00 (978-1-59476-097-6(7)) Paradigm Accelerated Curriculum.

Nature's Fury: Lightning!, Killer Quake! & Hurricane!, 3 cass.; set. gif. ed. 2004. (NOVA Ser.). (gr. 7-18). 49.95 incl. VHS (978-1-884738-68-5(0), WG027) WGBH Boston Video.

NCPTA Staff, et al. SATs Practice in Science Age 11. (Illus.). 32p. pap. 6.99 (978-0-340-71046-3(2), Coronet) Hodder & Stoughton GBR. Dist: Trafalgar Square Publishing.

Nelson, Robin. Float & Sink. 2004. (Illus.). 22p. 5.95 (978-0-8225-5296-3(5)); 24p. (J). lib. bdg. 18.60 (978-0-8225-5135-5(7)) Lerner Publishing Group.

—Magnets. 2005. (Forces & Motion Ser.). (Illus.). 22p. (J). pap. 5.95 (978-0-8225-5298-7(1), Lerner Pubns.) Lerner Publishing Group.

—Push & Pull. 2005. (Forces & Motion Ser.). (Illus.). 22p. (J). pap. 5.95 (978-0-8225-5299-4(X)) Lerner Publishing Group.

—Se Congela y Se Derrite. Castañer, Mercedes & Fitzpatrick, Julia, trs. 2003. (Mi Primer Paso Al Mundo Real - el Agua (First Step Nonfiction - Water) Ser.). (SPA., Illus.). 24p. (gr. k-2). lib. bdg. 23.93 (978-0-8225-4865-2(8)) Lerner Publishing Group.

Nichols, Susan. Al-Karaji: Tenth Century Mathematician & Engineer. 2016. (Physicians, Scientists, & Mathematicians of the Islamic World Ser.). 112p. (J). (gr. 6-6). 37.10 (978-1-5081-7143-0(2)) Rosen Publishing Group, Inc., The.

Nsrc. Science & Technology for Children Books: Microworlds. 2004. (Illus.). 64p. (J). (978-1-933008-04-2(0)) Smithsonian Science Education Ctr. (SSEC).

Nuevo Investiguemos 1: Ciencias Naturales y de la Salud. (SPA.). (J). (gr. 1). (978-958-02-1575-2(8)) Editorial Voluntad S.A. COL. Dist: Distribuidora Norma, Inc.

Nuevo Investiguemos 2: Ciencias Naturales y de la Salud. (SPA.). (J). (gr. 2). (978-958-02-1576-9(6)) Editorial Voluntad S.A. COL. Dist: Distribuidora Norma, Inc.

Nuevo Investiguemos 3: Ciencias Naturales y de la Salud. (SPA.). (J). (gr. 3). (978-958-02-1577-6(4)) Editorial Voluntad S.A. COL. Dist: Distribuidora Norma, Inc.

Nuevo Investiguemos 4: Ciencias Naturales y de la Salud. (SPA.). (J). (gr. 4). (978-958-02-1578-3(2)) Editorial Voluntad S.A. COL. Dist: Distribuidora Norma, Inc.

Nuevo Investiguemos 5: Ciencias Naturales y de la Salud. (SPA.). (J). (gr. 5). (978-958-02-1579-0(0)) Editorial Voluntad S.A. COL. Dist: Distribuidora Norma, Inc.

Nuevo Investiguemos 6: Ciencias Naturales y de la Salud. (SPA.). (978-958-02-1534-9(0)) Editorial Voluntad S.A. COL. Dist: Distribuidora Norma, Inc.

Nuevo Investiguemos 8: Ciencias Naturales y de la Salud. (SPA.). (YA). (gr. 8). (978-958-02-1536-3(7)) Editorial Voluntad S.A. COL. Dist: Distribuidora Norma, Inc.

Ohio 8th Gr Science. 2007. 52p. pap. 8.95 (978-0-9769459-5-6(9)) Hollandays Publishing Corp.

Okido Staff. What's Inside? See-Through Pages & Magic Surprises! 2013. (ENG., Illus.). 96p. (J). (gr. -1-3). 19.95 (978-0-500-65019-6(5), 565019) Thames & Hudson.

Oliver, Clare. Tell Me Who Lives in Space? And More about Space. 2004. (Illus.). 32p. (J). pap. (978-1-84458-057-6(1), Pavilion Children's Books) Pavilion Bks.

O'Meara, Stephen James. Are You Afraid Yet? The Science Behind Scary Stuff. Kaposy, Jeremy, illus. 2009. (ENG.). 80p. (J). (gr. 4-7). 17.95 (978-1-55453-294-0(9)); pap. 9.95 (978-1-55453-295-7(7)) Kids Can Pr., Ltd. CAN. Dist: Hachette Bk. Group.

One Each of 8 Big Books. (Sunshinetm Science Ser.). (gr. 1-2). 250.50 (978-0-7802-0567-3(7)) Wright Group/McGraw-Hill.

Operation: Top Secret. 2005. (J). per. (978-1-932855-33-3(5)) becker&mayer! books.

Orme, David. Extreme Science. 2008. (Trailblazers Ser.). (ENG., Illus.). 36p. pap. (978-1-84167-648-7(9)) Ransom Publishing Ltd.

—Extreme Science. 2009. (Fact to Fiction Ser.). (Illus.). 36p. (J). lib. bdg. 16.95 (978-0-7569-9279-8(6)) Perfection Learning Corp.

Orme, Helen. What Things Are Made Of. 2010. (Science Everywhere! Ser.). 24p. 24.25 (978-1-84898-298-7(4)) Black Rabbit Bks.

Osborne, Mary Pope & Boyce, Natalie Pope. Magic Tree House Incredible Fact Book. Murdocca, Sal, illus. 2016. (Magic Tree House Ser.). (ENG.). 144p. (J). (gr. 2-5). 16.99 (978-0-399-55117-8(4), Random Hse. Bks. for Young Readers) Random Hse. Children's Bks.

Out of the Lab: Extreme Jobs in Science. 2013. (Out of the Lab: Extreme Jobs in Science Ser.). 32p. (J). (gr. 3-6). 151.50 (978-1-4777-1540-6(1)); pap. 60.00 (978-1-4777-2734-8(5)); pap. 360.00 (978-1-4777-2735-5(3)) Rosen Publishing Group, Inc., The. (PowerKids Pr.).

Oxford, ed. Graphic Library - Science Complete Program. 2013. (Graphic Science Ser.). (ENG.). 32p. (gr. 3-4). pap. 1535.55 (978-1-4765-3740-5(2), Graphic Library) Capstone Press of Coughlan Cos.

Oxlade, Chris. Why Why Why... Do Magnets Push & Pull? 2010. (Why Why Why Ser.). 32p. (J). (gr. 1-3). lib. bdg. 18.95 (978-1-4222-1583-8(0)) Mason Crest.

Oxlade, Chris, et al. Science: Practical Projects, 8 vols. 2012. (ENG., Illus.). 64p. (J). (gr. 3-7). pap. 20.00 (978-1-84322-796-0(7)) Anness Publishing GBR. Dist: National Bk. Network.

Padilla, Michael J., et al. Adventures in Life, Earth, & Physical Science, 3 vols. 2003. (ENG.). 866p. (YA). (gr. 6-8). stu. ed. 433.00 (978-0-13-115416-2(8)) Prentice Hall Pr.

—Discoveries in Life, Earth, & Physical Science, 3 vols. 2003. (ENG.). 858p. (YA). (gr. 6-8). 429.00 (978-0-13-115415-5(X), Prentice Hall) Pearson Schl.

—Investigations in Life, Earth, & Physical Science, 3 vols. 2003. (ENG.). 890p. (YA). (gr. 6-8). 445.00 (978-0-13-115414-8(1), Prentice Hall) Pearson Schl.

Paizee, Daphne, et al. Collins International Primary Science. 2015. (Collins International Primary Science Ser.). (ENG.). 96p. (gr. 4). pap., stu. ed. 12.95 (978-0-00-758623-3(X)) HarperCollins Pubs. Ltd. GBR. Dist: Independent Pubs. Group.

Paris, John Ayrton. Philosophy in Sport Made Science in Earnest: Being an Attempt to Illustrate the First Principles of Natural Philosophy by the Aid of the Popular Toys & Sports. Cruikshank, George, illus. 2013. (Cambridge Library Collection - Education Ser.). (ENG.). Volume 1. 340p. pap. 40.99 (978-1-108-05739-4(X))Volume 2. 328p. pap. 40.99 (978-1-108-05740-0(3))Volume 3. 220p. pap. 30.99 (978-1-108-05741-7(1)) Cambridge Univ. Pr.

Parker, Steve. Complete Guides Our World. 2012. (ENG.). 144p. (J). (978-1-4351-4406-4(6)) Barnes & Noble, Inc.

—Science. 2014. (100 Facts You Should Know Ser.). 48p. (J). (gr. 4-6). pap. 84.95 (978-1-4824-1189-8(X)) Stevens, Gareth Publishing LLLP.

Pauli, Gunter. La Bruja del Desierto. 2007. (Zeri Fables Ser.).Tr. of Desert Witch. (ENG & SPA., Illus.). 32p. (J). (gr. k-3). pap. 9.95 (978-958-692-844-1(6)) Fondo Editorial Grania, Fundacion Hogares Juveniles Campesinos COL. Dist: Chelsea Green Publishing.

—Can Apples Fly? 2007. (Zeri Fables Ser.). (ENG & SPA., Illus.). 32p. (J). (gr. k-3). pap. 9.95 (978-958-692-854-0(3)) Fondo Editorial Grania, Fundacion Hogares Juveniles Campesinos COL. Dist: Chelsea Green Publishing.

—Cold Feet (Pies Frios) 2007. (Zeri Fables Ser.). (ENG & SPA., Illus.). 32p. (J). (gr. k-3). pap. 9.95 (978-958-692-861-8(6)) Fondo Editorial Grania, Fundacion Hogares Juveniles Campesinos COL. Dist: Chelsea Green Publishing.

—El Oso y el Zorro. 2007. (Zeri Fables Ser.). (ENG & SPA., Illus.). 32p. (J). (gr. k-3). pap. 9.95 (978-958-692-840-3(3)) Fondo Editorial Grania, Fundacion Hogares Juveniles Campesinos COL. Dist: Chelsea Green Publishing.

—Red Rice (Arroces Rojos) 2007. (Zeri Fables Ser.). (ENG & SPA., Illus.). 32p. (J). (gr. k-3). pap. 9.95 (978-958-692-831-1(4)) Fondo Editorial Grania, Fundacion Hogares Juveniles Campesinos COL. Dist: Chelsea Green Publishing.

—Tree Candy. 2007. (Zeri Fables Ser.). (ENG & SPA., Illus.). 32p. (J). (gr. k-3). pap. 9.95 (978-958-692-836-6(5)) Fondo Editorial Grania, Fundacion Hogares Juveniles Campesinos COL. Dist: Chelsea Green Publishing.

Pemberton, Rose. Inheritance & Variation of Traits. 2016. (Spotlight on Ecology & Life Science Ser.). 00024p. (J). (gr. 4-6). pap. 10.00 (978-1-4994-2569-7(4), PowerKids Pr.) Rosen Publishing Group, Inc., The.

Perricone, Mike. The Big Bang. 2009. (Science Foundations Ser.). (Illus.). 128p. (YA). (gr. 7-12). lib. bdg. 35.00 (978-1-60413-015-7(6)) Facts On File, Inc.

Petersen, Christine. Plants Need Sunlight. 2008. (21st Century Junior Library: Plants Ser.). (ENG.). 24p. (gr. 2-5). lib. bdg. 27.07 (978-1-60279-273-9(9), 200178) Cherry Lake Publishing.

Peterson, R. E. (Robert Evans). Peterson's Familiar Science; 2006. 600p. per. 32.99 (978-1-4255-6416-2(X)) Michigan Publishing.

Petheram, Louise, et al. Ascent! 2003. (ENG.). Bk. 2. 200p. pap. (978-0-7487-6795-3(9))Bk. 3. 240p. pap. (978-0-7487-6796-0(7)) Nelson Thornes Ltd.

PH Inc. Staff. Parade of Life: Animals. 2nd ed. (J). pap., act. bk. ed. (978-0-13-225616-2(9)) Prentice Hall (Schl. Div.).

—PH Science Ecology Earth. (J). pap., act. bk. ed. (978-0-13-225582-0(0)) Prentice Hall (Schl. Div.).

—PH Science Evolution. 2nd ed. (J). pap., act. bk. ed. (978-0-13-225541-7(3)) Prentice Hall (Schl. Div.).

Physical, Module B. 2003. (Scott Foresman Science Ser.). (gr. 3-18). suppl. ed. 15.50 (978-0-328-03436-9(3)); (gr. 4-18). suppl. ed. 15.50 (978-0-328-03440-6(1)); (gr. 5-18). suppl. ed. 16.00 (978-0-328-03444-4(4)); (gr. 6-18). suppl. ed. 16.00 (978-0-328-03448-2(7)) Addison-Wesley Educational Pubs., Inc.

Physical Science, Set. 2010. (Extreme! Ser.). (ENG.). 32p. (gr. 3-4). pap. 286.20 (978-1-4296-5139-4(3), Fact Finders) Capstone Press of Coughlan Cos.

Physical Science. 2013. (Physical Science Ser.). 48p. (J). (gr. 4-6). 191.70 (978-1-4339-9681-8(2)); pap. 505.80 (978-1-4339-9810-2(6)) Stevens, Gareth Publishing LLLP.

Physical Science, 4 vols., Set. Incl. All about Temperature. Auch, Alison. lib. bdg. 26.65 (978-1-4296-6608-4(0)); All Kinds of Motion. Waters, Jennifer. lib. bdg. 26.65 (978-1-4296-6607-7(2)); (gr. k-1). (Physical Science Ser.). (ENG.). 24p. 2010. 79.95 o.p. (978-1-4296-4430-3(3), Pebble Plus) Capstone Press of Coughlan Cos.

Physical Science: Physical Science Unit Resource Materials. 2005. (gr. 6-12). (978-0-618-41242-6(5), 2-01097) Holt McDougal.

Plant Eaters of the Pond: 6 Each of 1 Student Book, 6 vols. (Sunshinetm Science Ser.). 24p. (gr. 1-2). 41.95 (978-0-7802-2698-2(4)) Wright Group/McGraw-Hill.

Plant Eaters of the Pond: Big Book. (Sunshinetm Science Ser.). 24p. (gr. 1-2). 37.50 (978-0-7802-2783-5(2)) Wright Group/McGraw-Hill.

Platt, Richard & Biesty, Stephen. Stephen Biesty's Incredible Cross-Sections Book. (Illus.). (J). pap. 24.95 (978-0-590-73870-5(4)) Scholastic, Inc.

Plummer, Todd. Superhero Science: Kapow! Comic Book Crime Fighters Put Physics to the Test. 2009. (Current Science Ser.). (ENG.). 48p. (J). (gr. 4-6). pap. 8.95 (978-1-4339-2247-3(9), Gareth Stevens Learning Library) Stevens, Gareth Publishing LLLP.

Plummer, Todd, et al. Superhero Science: Kapow! Comic Book Crime Fighters Put Physics to the Test. 2009. (Current Science Ser.). (ENG.). 48p. (YA). (gr. 4-7). lib. bdg. 31.00 (978-1-4339-2243-5(6)) Stevens, Gareth Publishing LLLP.

Pocket Scientist: The Blue Book. 2004. (Illus.). 290p. (J). 8.99 (978-0-7945-0148-8(6), Usborne) EDC Publishing.

The Pond: 6 Each of 1 Student Book, 6 vols. (Sunshinetm Science Ser.). 24p. (gr. 1-2). 41.95 (978-0-7802-2694-4(1)) Wright Group/McGraw-Hill.

The Pond: Big Book. (Sunshinetm Science Ser.). 24p. (gr. 1-2). 37.50 (978-0-7802-2781-1(6)) Wright Group/McGraw-Hill.

Pond Life Sets: 1 Each of 3 Big Books. (Sunshinetm Science Ser.). (gr. 1-2). 111.50 (978-0-7802-2820-7(0)) Wright Group/McGraw-Hill.

Pond Life Sets: 1 Each of 3 Student Books. (Sunshinetm Science Ser.). (gr. 1-2). 20.95 (978-0-7802-2821-4(9)) Wright Group/McGraw-Hill.

Prentice-Hall Staff. Building Block. (J). pap., act. bk. ed. (978-0-13-402140-9(1)) Prentice Hall (Schl. Div.).

—Learning System Integrated Science, Bk. 1. (J). pap., act. bk. ed. 21.97 (978-0-13-402199-7(1)) Prentice Hall (Schl. Div.).

—Things Fall Apart. 2nd ed. (J). stu. ed. (978-0-13-716846-0(2)) Prentice Hall (Schl. Div.).

Pressberg, Dava. Producers, Consumers, & Decomposers. 2016. (Spotlight on Ecology & Life Science Ser.). 00024p. (J). (gr. 4-6). 26.25 *(978-1-4994-2594-9(5),* PowerKids Pr.) Rosen Publishing Group, Inc., The.

Primary Sources of Revolutionary Scientific Discoveries & Theories, 8 bk. set. 2005. (YA). (gr. 5-8). lib. bdg. 234.00 *(978-1-4042-0373-0(7))* Rosen Publishing Group, Inc., The.

Prism the Rainbow Pony. 2004. (Region IV ESC Resources for Science Ser.). per. *(978-1-932797-90-9(4))* Region IV Education Service Ctr.

Profiles in Science, bks. 14, vol. 14. Incl. Curious Bones: Mary Anning & the Birth of Paleontology. Goodhue, Thomas W. (Illus.). 112p. (YA). (gr. 6-12). 2004. lib. bdg. 23.95 *(978-1-883846-93-0(5),* First Biographies); Double Stars: The Story of Caroline Herschel. Venkatraman, Padma. (Illus.). 176p. (gr. 6-12). 2007. lib. bdg. 27.95 *(978-1-59935-042-4(4));* Fire, Water, & Air: The Story of Antoine Lavoisier. Baxter, Roberta. (J). 2009. 28.95 *(978-1-59935-087-5(4));* Galileo Galilei & the Science of Motion. Boerst, William J. (Illus.). 144p. (YA). (gr. 6-12). 2004. lib. bdg. 26.95 *(978-1-931798-00-6(1));* Great Explainer: The Story of Richard Feynman. LeVine, Harry, III. 144p. (YA). (gr. 7-10). 2009. 28.95 *(978-1-59935-113-1(7));* Ibn Al-Haytham: First Scientist. Steffens, Bradley. (Illus.). 128p. (J). (gr. 4-7). 2007. lib. bdg. 27.95 *(978-1-59935-024-0(6));* Johannes Kepler: Discovering the Laws of Celestial Motion. Boerst, William J. (Illus.). 144p. (YA). (gr. 6-12). 2004. lib. bdg. 26.95 *(978-1-883846-98-5(6),* First Biographies); Lise Meitner: Discoverer of Nuclear Fission. Barron, Rachel Stiffler. (Illus.). 112p. (YA). (gr. 6-12). 2004. lib. bdg. 23.95 *(978-1-883846-52-7(8),* First Biographies); Louis Pasteur & the Founding of Microbiology. Ackerman, Jane. (Illus.). 144p. (YA). (gr. 6-12). 2004. 26.95 *(978-1-931798-13-6(3));* New Elements: The Story of Marie Curie. (Illus.). 144p. (J). (gr. 4-7). 2006. lib. bdg. 27.95 *(978-1-59935-023-3(8));* Nicholas Copernicus & the Founding of Modern Astronomy. Boerst, William J. (Illus.). 144p. (YA). (gr. 6-12). 2004. lib. bdg. 26.95 *(978-1-883846-99-2(4),* First Biographies); Nikola Tesla & the Taming of Electricity. Aldrich, Lisa J. (Illus.). 160p. (J). (gr. 3-7). 2005. lib. bdg. 26.95 *(978-1-931798-46-4(X));* Rosalind Franklin & the Structure of Life. Polcovar, Jane. (Illus.). 144p. (J). (gr. 3-7). 2006. lib. bdg. 27.95 *(978-1-59935-022-6(X));* Scheduling the Heavens: The Story of Edmond Halley. Fox, Mary Virginia. (Illus.). 128p. (gr. 6-12). 2007. lib. bdg. 27.95 *(978-1-59935-021-9(1));* Skeptical Chemist: The Story of Robert Boyle. Baxter, Roberta. (Illus.). 128p. (gr. 6-12). 2006. lib. bdg. 27.95 *(978-1-59935-025-7(4));* Tycho Brahe: Mapping the Heavens. Boerst, William J. (Illus.). 144p. (YA). (gr. 6-12). 2004. 26.95 *(978-1-883846-97-8(8),* First Biographies); 2007. Set lib. bdg. 405.30 *(978-1-59935-033-2(5))* Reynolds, Morgan Inc.

Publishers, Chelsea House, creator. Scientific American Set, 8-Volumes. 2007. (Scientific American Ser.). (gr. 5-8). 240.00 *(978-0-7910-9811-0(7),* Chelsea Hse.) Facts On File, Inc.

QEB Start Reading & Writing National Book Stores Edition: What's in the Sky? 2006. (J). per. *(978-1-59566-266-8(9))* QEB Publishing Inc.

Raintree. Itlp 2004 Grade 4 Science Stat. 2004. pap. *(978-1-4109-1570-2(0));* pap. *(978-1-4109-1619-8(7))* Harcourt Schl. Pubs.

—Itlp 2004 Grades 2-4 Science S. 2004. pap. *(978-1-4109-1571-9(9));* pap. *(978-1-4109-1567-2(0));* pap. *(978-1-4109-1569-6(7))* Harcourt Schl. Pubs.

Reader dsm-3 sink or float Ea. 2004. (J). *(978-1-59242-525-9(9))* Delta Education, LLC.

Reading First Through Science Grade 1. 2005. (ENG.). 10.95 *(978-0-9766802-8-4(9))* Educational Tools, Inc.

Reading First Through Science Grade 2. 2008. 10.95 *(978-0-9766802-7-7(0))* Educational Tools, Inc.

Reading First Through Science Grade 4. 2005. (ENG., Illus.). *(978-0-9766802-6-0(2))* Educational Tools, Inc.

The Reading Room Collection: Science. (J). (gr. 2-3). 79.50 *(978-1-4042-3384-3(9))* Rosen Publishing Group, Inc., The.

Regan, Michael. Bad Days in Science & Invention. 2017. (Whoops! a History of Bad Days Ser.). (ENG., Illus.). 48p. (gr. 5-8). lib. bdg. 33.32 *(978-1-4109-8563-7(6))* Heinemann-Raintree.

Rhodes, Immacula A. Shoe Box Learning Centers - Science: 30 Instant Centers with Reproducible Templates & Activities That Help Kids Learn Important Science Skills & Concepts-Independently! 2012. (ENG.). 80p. (gr. k-2). pap. 12.99 *(978-0-439-61652-2(2),* Teaching Resources) Scholastic, Inc.

Rhodes, Immacula A. & Julio, Susan. Science: 10 Ready-to-Go Games That Help Children Learn Key Science Concepts & Vocabulary — Independently. 2009. (File-Folder Games in Color Ser.). (ENG.). 144p. pap. 19.99 *(978-0-439-51764-5(8),* Teaching Resources) Scholastic, Inc.

Rice, Dona. All in the Family, 1 vol. rev. ed. 2014. (Science Readers: Content & Literacy Ser.). (ENG., Illus.). 24p. (J). (gr. 1-1). 22.96 *(978-1-4938-1150-2(9))* Teacher Created Materials, Inc.

—Science Detectives, 1 vol. rev. ed. 2014. (Science Readers: Content & Literacy Ser.). (ENG., Illus.). 24p. (gr. 1-1). pap. 8.99 *(978-1-4807-4574-2(X))* Teacher Created Materials, Inc.

Rice, William B. The World of Rocks & Minerals, 1 vol. 2007. (Science Readers Ser.). (ENG., Illus.). 32p. (J). (gr. 4-4). pap. 8.99 *(978-0-7439-0553-4(9))* Shell Educational Publishing.

Richards, Jon & Flaherty, Michael. Science Factory, 6 vols., Set. 2008. (J). (gr. 4-6). lib. bdg. 151.50 *(978-1-4042-4251-7(1))* Rosen Publishing Group, Inc., The.

Ring, Susan. Design It! Build It! Date not set. (Early Science Big Bks.). (Illus.). 16p. (J). (gr. -1-2). pap. 16.95 *(978-1-58273-121-6(7))* Sundance/Newbridge Educational Publishing.

—The Ocean, 6 vols., Set. 2003. (Yellow Umbrella Early Level Ser.). (ENG.). 16p. (gr. k-1). pap. 35.70 *(978-0-7368-2997-7(0),* Yellow Umbrella Bks.) Capstone Press of Coughlan Cos.

—Show Us Your Wings, 6 vols., Set. 2003. (Yellow Umbrella Early Level Ser.). (ENG.). 16p. (gr. k-1). pap. 35.70 *(978-0-7368-2999-1(7),* Yellow Umbrella Bks.) Capstone Press of Coughlan Cos.

Ringstad, Arnold. Weird-But-True Facts about Science. Petelinsek, Kathleen, illus. 2013. (Weird-But-True Facts Ser.). (ENG.). 32p. (J). (gr. 2-5). 28.50 *(978-1-61473-417-8(8),* 205121) Child's World, Inc., The.

Ripley, Catherine. Why? The Best Ever Question & Answer Book about Nature, Science & the World Around You. Ritchie, Scot & Owlkids Books Inc. Staff, illus. 2nd ed. 2010. (ENG.). 192p. (J). (gr. -1-4). 21.95 *(978-1-926818-00-9(8),* Owlkids) Owlkids Bks. Inc. CAN. Dist: Publishers Group West (PGW).

Rissman, Rebecca. Real Size Science. 2013. (Real Size Science Ser.). (ENG.). 24p. (gr. -1-1). pap. 35.94 *(978-1-4329-7890-7(X));* lib. bdg. 135.90 *(978-1-4329-7883-9(7))* Heinemann-Raintree. (Acorn).

Roberts, Don & Roberts, Susan. Things That Scratch: The Story of Abrasives. (Illus.). 60p. (YA). (gr. 8-18). pap. 14.95 *(978-1-57555-170-8(5));* pap. 24.95 *(978-1-57555-169-2(1))* Cedar Bay Pr., L.L.C.

Rohrig, Brian. Pure Slime: 50 Incredible Ways to Make Slime Using Household Substances. 2004. (Illus.). 232p. (YA). per. 12.95 *(978-0-9718480-5-4(X))* FizzBang Science.

Roman, Nora. Using a Ruler. 2017. (Super Science Tools Ser.). 24p. (gr. 1-2). pap. 8.15 ***(978-1-4824-6401-6(2))*** Stevens, Gareth Publishing LLLP.

Romer, Ruth. Welcome to Waterworld. 2004. (Reader's Theater Ser.). (J). pap. *(978-1-4108-0796-0(7))* Benchmark Education Co.

Romer, Ruth & Kramer, Candice. Farflings from Farflung. 2004. (Reader's Theater Ser.). (J). pap. *(978-1-4108-0797-7(5))* Benchmark Education Co.

Rookie Read-About(r) Science. 2013. (Rookie Read-About(r) Science Ser.). (J). 92.00 *(978-0-531-21404-6(4),* Children's Pr.) Scholastic Library Publishing.

Rookie Read-About(r) Science: How Things Work (Set Of 7) 2015. (Rookie Read-About(r) Science: How Things Work Ser.). (J). lib. bdg. 161.00 *(978-0-531-22376-5(0),* Children's Pr.) Scholastic Library Publishing.

Rookie Read-About(r) Science — It's a Good Thing..., 7, Set. 2014. (Rookie Read-About(r) Science — It's a Good Thing... Ser.). (J). *(978-0-531-24359-6(1))* Scholastic Library Publishing.

Rookie Read-About Science: Life Science, 6 bks., Set. Incl. Tiny Life in a Puddle. Early, Bobbi. lib. bdg. 20.50 *(978-0-516-25272-8(0));* Tiny Life in the Air. Taylor-Butler, Christine. lib. bdg. 20.50 *(978-0-516-25273-5(9));* Tiny Life in Your Home. Trumbauer, Lisa. lib. bdg. 20.50 *(978-0-516-25274-2(7));* Tiny Life on Plants. Lindstrom, Karin. lib. bdg. 20.50 *(978-0-516-25297-1(6));* Tiny Life on the Ground. Wade, Mary Dodson. 20.50 *(978-0-516-25298-8(4));* Tiny Life on Your Body. Taylor-Butler, Christine. lib. bdg. 20.50 *(978-0-516-25299-5(2));* (Illus.). 32p. (J). (gr. 1-2). 2005. 2005. 117.00 o.p. *(978-0-516-25395-4(6),* Children's Pr.) Scholastic Library Publishing.

Rookie Read-About(r) Science: What's the Difference? (Set Of 6) 2015. (Rookie Read-About(r) Science: What's the Difference? Ser.). (J). lib. bdg. 138.00 *(978-0-531-22420-5(1),* Children's Pr.) Scholastic Library Publishing.

Roselli, Stephanie. The Budding Scientist. 2012. (Budding Ser.). (ENG., Illus.). 72p. pap. 9.95 *(978-0-87659-385-1(6),* Gryphon House Inc) Gryphon Hse., Inc.

Rosen Publishing Staff. Scientific Breakthroughs, 1 vol. 2015. (Scientific Breakthroughs Ser.). (ENG.). 48p. (YA). 151.25 *(978-1-4777-8613-0(9),* Rosen Central) Rosen Publishing Group, Inc., The.

Rossouw, Andre J. & Bitline S. A. 1010. Natural Sciences Matters Grade 8 Learner's Book Afrikaans Translation. 2006. 160p. pap. 14.00 *(978-0-521-67894-0(3))* Cambridge Univ. Pr.

Russell, Anthony. Nelson International Science. 2014. (ENG.). Bk. 1. 104p. (gr. 1-1). pap., stu. ed. 13.00 *(978-1-4085-1720-8(5))*Bk. 2. 80p. (gr. 2-2). pap., stu. ed. 13.00 *(978-1-4085-1721-5(3))*Bk. 3. (Illus.). 88p. (gr. 3-3). pap., stu. ed. 13.00 *(978-1-4085-1722-2(1))*Bk. 4. (Illus.). 96p. (gr. 4-4). pap., stu. ed. 13.00 *(978-1-4085-1723-9(X))*Bk. 5. (Illus.). 96p. (gr. 5-5). pap., stu. ed. 13.00 *(978-1-4085-1724-6(8))*Bk. 6. (Illus.). 136p. (gr. 6-6). pap., stu. ed. 13.00 *(978-1-4085-1725-3(6))* Oxford Univ. Pr., Inc.

—Nelson International Science Workbook 1. 2014. (ENG., Illus.). 96p. (gr. 1-1). spiral bd. 3.00 *(978-1-4085-1726-0(4))* Oxford Univ. Pr., Inc.

—Nelson International Science Workbook 2. 2014. (ENG.). 64p. (gr. 2-2). spiral bd. 3.00 *(978-1-4085-1740-6(X))* Oxford Univ. Pr., Inc.

—Nelson International Science Workbook 3. 2014. (ENG.). 72p. (gr. 3-3). spiral bd. 3.00 *(978-1-4085-1728-4(0))* Oxford Univ. Pr., Inc.

—Nelson International Science Workbook 4. 2014. (ENG., Illus.). 80p. (gr. 4-4). spiral bd. 3.00 *(978-1-4085-1729-1(9))* Oxford Univ. Pr., Inc.

—Nelson International Science Workbook 5. 2014. (ENG., Illus.). 64p. (gr. 5-5). spiral bd. 3.00 *(978-1-4085-1730-7(2))* Oxford Univ. Pr., Inc.

—Nelson International Science Workbook 6. 2014. (ENG.). 96p. (gr. 6-6). spiral bd. 3.00 *(978-1-4085-1731-4(0))* Oxford Univ. Pr., Inc.

Ryles, Briony & Hall, Derek. Medieval Period & the Renaissance. 2010. (CC: Technology Through the Ages Ser.). 112p. (gr. 6-12). 42.80 *(978-1-933834-84-9(6))* Brown Bear Bks.

—Prehistory & the Classical Period. 2010. (CC: Technology Through the Ages Ser.). 112p. (gr. 6-12). 42.80 *(978-1-933834-83-2(8))* Brown Bear Bks.

—The Scientific Revolution. 2010. (Curriculum Connections: Technology Through the Ages Ser.). 112p. 39.95 *(978-1-933834-85-6(4))* Brown Bear Bks.

Saddleback Educational Publishing Staff, creator. Machines & Inventions. 2009. (Factoscope Ser.). (Illus.). 64p. (J). lib. bdg. 19.95 *(978-1-59905-482-7(5))* Saddleback Educational Publishing, Inc.

Saddleback Educational Publishing Staff, ed. Life Science, 1 vol. 2013. (Science Ser.). (ENG.). 112p. (gr. 9-12). pap. 44.95 *(978-1-62250-035-2(0))* Saddleback Educational Publishing, Inc.

—Physical Science, 1 vol. 2013. (Science Ser.). (ENG.). 108p. (gr. 9-12). pap. 44.95 *(978-1-62250-036-9(9))* Saddleback Educational Publishing, Inc.

Saffer, Barbara. ABC Science Riddles. Johnson, Jennifer, illus. 2004. (ABC Riddles Ser.). 32p. (J). (gr. -1-3). 13.95 *(978-0-939217-55-7(4))* Peel Productions, Inc.

Sandler, Michael & Hess, Debra. Checkered Flag! 2007. (Read on! Special Edition: Level AA Ser.). (Illus.). 23p. (J). (gr. 4-7). pap. 4.84 *(978-1-4190-3516-6(9))* Steck-Vaughn.

Sarver, Amy. Science at the Grocery. 2007. (Reading Expeditions Ser.). (ENG., Illus.). 24p. (J). pap. 14.95 *(978-0-7922-4567-4(9))* CENGAGE Learning.

Sarver, Amy & National Geographic Learning Staff. Science at the Mall. 2007. (Reading Expeditions Ser.). (ENG., Illus.). 24p. (J). pap. 14.95 *(978-0-7922-4569-8(5))* CENGAGE Learning.

Schaefer, Lola M. & Endres, Hollie J. Push & Pull, 6 vols., Set. 2003. (Yellow Umbrella Early Level Ser.). (ENG.). 16p. (gr. k-1). pap. 35.70 *(978-0-7368-2998-4(9),* Yellow Umbrella Bks.) Capstone Press of Coughlan Cos.

Scheppler, Bill. Al-Biruni: Master Astronomer & Muslim Scholar of the Eleventh Century. 2009. (Great Muslim Philosophers & Scientists of the Middle Ages Ser.). 112p. (gr. 6-6). 66.50 *(978-1-61513-177-8(9),* Rosen Reference) Rosen Publishing Group, Inc., The.

Scholastic, Inc. Staff. Brain Play 1st-3rd. 2008. (J). 29.99 *(978-0-545-05207-8(6))* Scholastic, Inc.

—Brain Play Preschool-1st. 2008. (J). 29.99 *(978-0-439-81350-1(6))* Scholastic, Inc.

Scholastic Library Publishing. A True Book-Physical Science. 2011. (Spot It Ser.). (ENG.). 32p. (gr. 1-2). lib. bdg. 27.32 *(978-0-531-25935-1(8),* Children's Pr.) Scholastic Library Publishing.

School Zone Staff. Big Science: Hours of Fun! 2006. (ENG.). 320p. (J). (gr. 2-3). pap. 9.99 *(978-1-58947-317-1(5))* School Zone Publishing Co.

Schuette, Sarah L. Science Fun: A Spot-It Challenge, 1 vol. 2011. (Spot It Ser.). (ENG.). 32p. (gr. 1-2). lib. bdg. 27.32 *(978-1-4296-5986-4(6),* Aplus Bks.) Capstone Press of Coughlan Cos.

Schuh, Mari & Alpert, Barbara. Science Builders. 2011. (Science Builders Ser.). (ENG.). 24p. (gr. k-1). pap. 250.20 *(978-1-4296-7118-7(1));* lib. bdg. 133.25 *(978-1-4296-6074-7(0));* pap. 36.45 *(978-1-4296-7117-0(3))* Capstone Press of Coughlan Cos. (Pebble Plus).

Schwartz, David & Schwartz, David M. Q Is for Quark: A Science Alphabet Book. Doner, Kim, illus. 2009. (ENG.). 64p. (J). (gr. 3-7). pap. 9.99 *(978-1-58246-303-2(4),* Tricycle Pr.) Random Hse. Children's Bks.

Schwartz, Linda. Primary Science Quiz Whiz, Vol. 429. VanBlaricum, Pam, ed. Mason, Mark, illus. 2004. 128p. (J). (gr. 1-3). pap. 14.99 *(978-0-88160-372-9(4),* LW-429) Creative Teaching Pr., Inc.

—Social Studies & Science Quiz Whiz 3-5, Vol. 432. VanBlaricum, Pam, ed. Armstrong, Beverly, illus. 2004. 128p. (J). (gr. 3-5). pap. 10.99 *(978-0-88160-375-0(9),* LW-432) Creative Teaching Pr., Inc.

Sci-Hi - Scientists, 6 vols., Set. Incl. Scientists Behind Earth's Processes. Solway, Andrew. pap. 9.95 *(978-1-4109-4051-3(9));* Scientists Behind Energy. Solway, Andrew. pap. 9.95 *(978-1-4109-4052-0(7));* Scientists Behind Living Things. Snedden, Robert. pap. 9.95 *(978-1-4109-4054-4(3));* Scientists Behind Medical Advances. Hartman, Eve & Meshbesher, Wendy. pap. 9.95 *(978-1-4109-4055-1(1));* Scientists Behind Space. Hartman, Eve & Meshbesher, Wendy. pap. 9.95 *(978-1-4109-4056-8(X));* Scientists Behind the Environment. Snedden, Robert. pap. 9.95 *(978-1-4109-4053-7(5));* (gr. 4-4). (Sci-Hi: Scientists Ser.). (ENG.). 48p. 2011. Set pap. 53.94 *(978-1-4109-4057-5(8));* Set lib. bdg. 133.28 *(978-1-4109-4050-6(0))* Heinemann-Raintree. (Sci-Hi).

Science, Set. 2004. (gr. 6). tchr. ed., stu. ed. 47.95 *(978-1-58095-765-6(X),* SCI0615); (Illus.). (gr. 5). tchr. ed., stu. ed. 47.95 *(978-1-58095-762-5(5),* SCI0515) Alpha Omega Pubns., Inc. (Lifepac).

Science. 2011. (New Discovering Careers for Your Future Ser.). (Illus.). 128p. (gr. 4-9). 24.95 *(978-0-8160-8053-3(4),* Ferguson Publishing Co.) Facts On File, Inc.

Science: Chemistry, 11 vols., Set. 2004. (Illus.). (gr. 11). tchr. ed., stu. ed. 47.95 *(978-1-58095-780-9(3),* SCI1115, Lifepac) Alpha Omega Pubns., Inc.

Science: Physics, 11 vols., Set. 2004. (Illus.). (gr. 12). tchr. ed., stu. ed. 47.95 *(978-1-58095-783-0(8),* SCI1215, Lifepac) Alpha Omega Pubns., Inc.

Science: Student Testing Kit. 2004. (Illus.). (J). (gr. 1-8). stu. ed. 5.00 *(978-0-7403-0045-5(8),* SD001); (YA). (gr. 7-12). pap., stu. ed. 5.00 *(978-0-7403-0046-2(6),* SD002) Alpha Omega Pubns., Inc.

Science & Technology for Children Books, MicroWorlds Set, 8 vols. 2004. (Illus.). 64p. (J). *(978-1-933008-16-5(4))* Smithsonian Science Education Ctr. (SSEC).

Science & Technology for Children Books, Physical Sciences & Technology Library Set, 6 vols. 2004. (Illus.). 64p. (J). *(978-1-933008-26-4(1))* Smithsonian Science Education Ctr. (SSEC).

Science & Technology for Children Books, Science Library Set, 12 vols. 2004. (Illus.). 64p. (J). *(978-1-933008-24-0(5))* Smithsonian Science Education Ctr. (SSEC).

Science & You. (Illus.). (J). 502.60 *(978-0-7910-7275-2(4),* Chelsea Hse.) Facts On File, Inc.

Science Explorer, 24 vols., Set. Incl. Super Cool Science Experiments: Bugs. Gray, Susan H. lib. bdg. 28.50 *(978-1-60279-521-1(5),* 200281); Super Cool Science Experiments: Cells. Mullins, Matt. lib. bdg. 28.50 *(978-1-60279-517-4(7),* 200287); Super Cool Science Experiments: Circulation. Orr, Tamra. (Illus.). lib. bdg. 28.50 *(978-1-60279-520-4(7),* 200304); Super Cool Science Experiments: Compounds & Mixtures. Simon, Charnan. (Illus.). lib. bdg. 28.50 *(978-1-60279-536-5(3),* 200288); Super Cool Science Experiments: Digestion. Orr, Tamra B. (Illus.). lib. bdg. 28.50 *(978-1-60279-518-1(5),* 200303); Super Cool Science Experiments: Ecosystems. Mullins, Matt. lib. bdg. 28.50 *(978-1-60279-516-7(9),* 200300); Super Cool Science Experiments: Electricity. Lockwood, Sophie. (Illus.). lib. bdg. 28.50 *(978-1-60279-533-4(9),* 200289); Super Cool Science Experiments: Erosion. Kazunas, Ariel & Simon, Charnan. (Illus.). lib. bdg. 28.50 *(978-1-60279-525-9(8),* 200284); Super Cool Science Experiments: Heat. Lockwood, Sophie. (Illus.). lib. bdg. 28.50 *(978-1-60279-534-1(7),* 200290); Super Cool Science Experiments: Levers & Pulleys. Rau, Dana Meachen. (Illus.). lib. bdg. 28.50 *(978-1-60279-537-2(1),* 200282); Super Cool Science Experiments: Light. Rau, Dana Meachen. (Illus.). lib. bdg. 28.50 *(978-1-60279-531-0(2),* 200285); Super Cool Science Experiments: Magnets. Taylor-Butler, Christine. (Illus.). lib. bdg. 28.50 *(978-1-60279-530-3(4),* 200296); Super Cool Science Experiments: Minerals. Lockwood, Sophie. (Illus.). lib. bdg. 28.50 *(978-1-60279-524-2(X),* 200291); Super Cool Science Experiments: Planet Earth. Mullins, Matt & Plummer, Todd. (Illus.). lib. bdg. 28.50 *(978-1-60279-515-0(0),* 200302); Super Cool Science Experiments: Plants. Gray, Susan H. (Illus.). lib. bdg. 28.50 *(978-1-60279-522-8(3),* 200286); Super Cool Science Experiments: Respiration. Orr, Tamra B. (Illus.). lib. bdg. 28.50 *(978-1-60279-519-8(3),* 200292); Super Cool Science Experiments: Rocks. Lockwood, Sophie. (Illus.). lib. bdg. 28.50 *(978-1-60279-523-5(1),* 200283); Super Cool Science Experiments: Seeds. Gray, Susan H. lib. bdg. 28.50 *(978-1-60279-514-3(2),* 200293); Super Cool Science Experiments: Soil. Franchino, Vicky. (Illus.). lib. bdg. 28.50 *(978-1-60279-526-6(6),* 200297); Super Cool Science Experiments: Solar Energy. Taylor-Butler, Christine. (Illus.). lib. bdg. 28.50 *(978-1-60279-527-3(4),* 200295); Super Cool Science Experiments: Sound. Taylor-Butler, Christine. (Illus.). lib. bdg. 28.50 *(978-1-60279-532-7(0),* 200301); Super Cool Science Experiments: States of Matter. Mullins, Matt & Plummer, Todd. (Illus.). lib. bdg. 28.50 *(978-1-60279-535-8(5),* 200299); Super Cool Science Experiments: Water. Simon, Charnan & Kazunas, Ariel. (Illus.). lib. bdg. 28.50 *(978-1-60279-529-7(0),* 200298); Super Cool Science Experiments: Weather. Orr, Tamra B. (Illus.). lib. bdg. 28.50 *(978-1-60279-528-0(2),* 200294); (gr. 4-8). 32p. 2009. Set lib. bdg. 478.80 *(978-1-60279-588-4(6),* 200243) Cherry Lake Publishing.

Science Fun. 2005. (Little Celebrations Thematic Packages Ser.). (J). (gr. k-3). 133.50 *(978-0-673-75382-3(4))* Celebration Pr.

Science Links. 2005. (Science Links Ser.). (Illus.). 32p. (gr. 4-6). 345.00 *(978-0-7910-7415-2(3),* Chelsea Hse.) Facts On File, Inc.

Science Made Simple, 6 vols., Set. Incl. Atomic & Molecular Structure. Chaffee, Joel. lib. bdg. 31.95 *(978-1-4488-1230-1(5),* Rosen Reference); Cell Biology. Stimola, Aubrey. lib. bdg. 31.95 *(978-1-4488-1234-9(8));* Chemical Reactions. Wolny, Philip. lib. bdg. 31.95 *(978-1-4488-1235-6(6),* Rosen Reference); Electric & Magnetic Phenomena. Galiano, Dean. lib. bdg. 31.95 *(978-1-4488-1231-8(3),* Rosen Reference); Gases & Their Properties. Meyer, Susan. lib. bdg. 31.95 *(978-1-4488-1233-2(X),* Rosen Reference); Motion & Forces. Orr, Tamra. lib. bdg. 31.95 *(978-1-4488-1232-5(1));* (YA). (gr. 5-8). 2011. (Science Made Simple Ser.). (Illus.). 64p. 2011. Set lib. bdg. 175.50 *(978-1-4488-1393-3(X),* Rosen Reference) Rosen Publishing Group, Inc., The.

Science Missions, 6 vols., Set. Incl. Mapping Earth from Space. Graf, Mike & Snedden, Robert. 34.65 *(978-1-4109-3994-4(4));* Mission to Mars. Hartman, Eve & Meshbesher, Wendy. 34.65 *(978-1-4109-3989-0(8));* (gr. 3-3). (Science Missions Ser.). (ENG.). 56p. 2011. 69.30 *(978-1-4109-3995-1(2),* Raintree Freestyle Express) Heinemann-Raintree.

Science on Patrol. 2016. (Science on Patrol Ser.). 00048p. (J). lib. bdg. 191.70 ***(978-1-4824-5860-2(8))*** Stevens, Gareth Publishing LLLP.

Science Program, Early Level. 2003. (Yellow Umbrella Early Level Ser.). (ENG.). 16p. (gr. k-1). pap. 428.40 *(978-0-7368-3068-3(5),* Yellow Umbrella Bks.) Capstone Press of Coughlan Cos.

Science Q & A. 2015. (Science Q & A Ser.). (ENG.). 32p. (J). (gr. 5-5). 171.00 *(978-1-5026-0380-7(2));* pap., pap., pap. 63.48 *(978-1-5026-0697-6(6))* Cavendish Square Publishing.

Science Reading Stories. (J). (gr. 2). *(978-0-8374-0622-0(6),* 656); (gr. 3). *(978-0-8374-0623-7(4),* 657); (gr. 4). *(978-0-8374-0624-4(2),* 658); (gr. 5). *(978-0-8374-0625-1(0),* 659) Weekly Reader Corp.

Science Rocks! Set 2 CD+Book. 2010. (Science Rocks! Set 2 CD+Book Ser.). (Illus.). 32p. lib. bdg. 324.84 incl. cd-rom *(978-1-60270-990-4(4))* ABDO Publishing Co.

Science Rocks! Set 2 Site CD+Book. 2010. (Science Rocks! Set 2 Site CD+Book Ser.). (Illus.). 32p. lib. bdg. 504.84 incl. cd-rom *(978-1-61641-007-0(8))* ABDO Publishing Co.

Science Set, 8 vols. (Content Collections). (gr. k-2). 276.08 *(978-0-7362-2269-3(3))* CENGAGE Learning.

Science Spanish Content Area Standard Set. 2005. spiral bd. 2500.00 *(978-1-4108-4530-6(3))* Benchmark Education Co.

Science Stories, 4 bks. (J). (gr. 2-4). lib. bdg. 59.80 *(978-1-56674-934-3(4))* Forest Hse. Publishing Co., Inc.

Science stories foss spanish models & designs ea Cr05. 2005. (J). *(978-1-59242-592-1(5))* Delta Education, LLC.

Scientific American: Cutting-Edge Science, 6 bks., Set. Incl. Extreme Engineering. Rosen Publishing Group, creator. (Illus.). 120p. 2007. lib. bdg. 34.60 *(978-1-4042-0986-2(7));* Fighting Infectious Diseases. Rosen Editors. (Illus.). 101p. 2006. lib. bdg. 34.60 *(978-1-4042-0988-6(3));* Future of the Web. Rosen Publishing Group, creator. (Illus.). 118p. 2007. lib. bdg. 34.60 *(978-1-4042-0989-3(1));* Nanotech Revolution. Rosen Publishing Group, creator. (Illus.). 136p. 2007. lib. bdg. 34.60 *(978-1-4042-0990-9(5),* 1267059); Tackling Cancer. Rosen Editors. 101p. 2006. lib. bdg. 34.60 *(978-1-4042-0987-9(5));* 21st-Century Robotics. Rosen Publishing Group, creator. (Illus.). 101p. 2007. lib. bdg. 34.60 *(978-1-4042-0985-5(9));* (YA). (gr. 9-12). 2007. Set lib. bdg. 191.70 *(978-1-4042-0939-8(5))* Rosen Publishing Group, Inc., The.

Scientific American Staff. 21st Century Robotics. 2009. (Scientific American Cutting-Edge Science Ser.). 101p. (gr. 9-9). 63.90 *(978-1-60853-072-4(8))* Rosen Publishing Group, Inc., The.

Scott, Foresman and Company Staff. Discover Science. (J). (gr. 1). pap. 12.34 *(978-0-673-42490-7(1));* (gr. 2). pap. 12.90 *(978-0-673-42491-4(X));* (gr. 3). pap. 14.59 *(978-0-673-42492-1(8));* (gr. 4). pap. 16.06 *(978-0-673-42493-8(6));* (gr. 5). pap. 17.00 *(978-0-673-42494-5(4));* (gr. 6). pap. 17.62 *(978-0-673-42495-2(2))* Addison Wesley Schl. (Scott Foresman).

S

Scotti, Alberto Douglas. Cocina y Ciencia. 2012. 44p. (J). (gr. 3-5). pap. 23.99 (978-958-30-3715-3(X)) Juventud, Editorial ESP. Dist: Lectorum Pubns., Inc.

Seeds Grow, 6 vols. (Sunshinetm Science Ser.). 24p. (gr. 1-2). 31.50 (978-0-7802-0290-0(2)); 36.95 (978-0-7802-0541-3(3)) Wright Group/McGraw-Hill.

Shannon, Terry Miller. Forces That Shape Earth. 2016. (Spring Forward Ser.). (J). (gr. 2). (978-1-4900-9438-0(5)) Benchmark Education Co.

Sharkawy, Azza. Share It! 2014. (ENG., Illus.). 24p. (J). (978-0-7787-0781-3(4)) Crabtree Publishing Co.

Sheldon, Ken. Sing-Along & Learn - Science: 12 Lively Learning Songs & Instant Activities That Teach Key Science Concepts. 2010. (ENG., Illus.). 32p. (gr. k-2). 13.99 (978-0-545-09438-2(0), Teaching Resources) Scholastic, Inc.

Shevick, Ed. Great Scientists in Action. Wheeler, Ron, illus. 2004. (Science Action Labs Ser.). 64p. (J). pap. 9.95 (978-1-57310-436-4(1), 1238118) Teaching & Learning Co.

Shoup, Kate. The Technology of Ancient Greece. 2016. (Ancient Innovations Ser.). 64p. (J). 34.21 (978-1-5026-2231-0(9)) Cavendish Square Publishing.

Show What You Know on the OGT, Science Student Self Study Workbook. 2007. (YA). per. 18.95 (978-1-59230-274-1(2)) Englefield & Assocs., Inc.

Showers, Paul. Where Does the Garbage Go? 2015. (Let's Read & Find Out Science Stage 2 Ser.). (J). (gr. k-3). lib. bdg. 17.20 (978-0-613-01320-8(4), Turtleback) Turtleback Bks.

Sian Revision Work: Plane & Simple. 2004. (Science in A Nutshell Ser.). (J). (978-1-59242-089-6(3)) Delta Education, LLC.

Silva Lee, Alfonso. Mi Isla y Yo: La Naturaleza de Cuba. Hayskar, Bonnie J., ed. Lago, Alexis, illus. 2010. (SPA.). 32p. (J). pap. 9.95 (978-1-929165-22-3(6)) PANGAEA.

Singh, Simon. The Code Book. 2016. (ENG.). 272p. (YA). (gr. 7). pap. 9.99 (978-0-385-73062-4(4), Ember) Random Hse. Children's Bks.

Sitarski, Anita. Cold Light: Creatures, Discoveries, & Inventions That Glow. 2007. (ENG., Illus.). 48p. (J). (gr. 4-6). 16.95 (978-1-59078-468-6(5)) Boyds Mills Pr.

Smibert, Angie. Dramatic Discoveries. 2018. (ENG.). 32p. (gr. 3-6). 31.35 **(978-1-63235-419-8(5)**, 12-Story Library) Pr. Room Editions LLC.

Smith, Carrie. We See with Our Eyes: Lap Book. 2009. (My First Reader's Theater Set B Ser.). (J). 28.00 (978-1-60634-992-2(9)) Benchmark Education Co.

Smith, Jodene. Cut & Paste - Science. 2003. (ENG.). 96p. pap. 12.99 (978-0-7439-3706-1(6)) Teacher Created Resources, Inc.

Snedden, Robert. The Medieval World. 2009. (Technology in Times Past Ser.). (Illus.). 46p. (J). (gr. 4-7). pap. (978-1-897563-65-6(5)) Saunders Bk. Co.

Sobey, Ed. Rocket-Powered Science: Invent to Learn! Create, Build & Test Rocket Designs. 2006. (Illus.). 106p. (J). (gr. 4-7). per. 14.95 (978-1-59647-055-2(0)) Good Year Bks.

Solving Science Mysteries, 14 vols., Set. Incl. Why Do Airplanes Fly? Moore, Rob. lib. bdg. 22.60 (978-1-61531-890-2(9)); Why Do Balls Bounce? Moore, Rob. lib. bdg. 22.60 (978-1-61531-889-6(5)); Why Do Diamonds Sparkle? All about Earth's Resources. Bethune, Helen. lib. bdg. 22.60 (978-1-61531-894-0(1)); Why Do Glaciers Grind? Bethune, Helen. lib. bdg. 22.60 (978-1-4488-0391-0(8)); Why Do Monkeys Chatter? Bethune, Helen. lib. bdg. 22.60 (978-1-4488-0394-1(2)); Why Do Shadows Lengthen? Brasch, Nicolas. lib. bdg. 22.60 (978-1-61531-891-9(7)); Why Do Spiders Live in Webs? Brasch, Nicolas. lib. bdg. 22.60 (978-1-4488-0397-2(7)); Why Do Stars Twinkle? McMahon, Michael. lib. bdg. 22.60 (978-1-61531-895-7(X)); Why Does Electricity Flow? Moore, Rob. lib. bdg. 22.60 (978-1-61531-893-3(3)); Why Does Water Evaporate? Moore, Rob. lib. bdg. 22.60 (978-1-61531-892-6(5)); Why Is It So Loud? Brasch, Nicolas. lib. bdg. 22.60 (978-1-61531-888-9(7)); (YA). (gr. 3-6). (Illus.). 24p. 2010. Set lib. bdg. 297.50 (978-1-61531-924-4(7), PowerKids Pr.) Rosen Publishing Group, Inc., The.

Solway, Andrew & Saunders, Nigel. Exploring Physical Science. 2007. (J). 159.00 (978-1-4042-1105-6(5), Rosen Reference) Rosen Publishing Group, Inc., The.

Sonido. (Coleccion Jugando Con la Ciencia). (SPA., Illus.). 39p. (J). pap. 9.95 (978-950-11-0831-6(7), SGM317) Sigmar ARG. Dist: Continental Bk. Co., Inc.

Spilsbury, Louise, et al. Essential Physical Science, 1 vol. 2014. (Essential Physical Science Ser.). (ENG.). 48p. (gr. 4-6). lib. bdg. 266.56 (978-1-4846-0689-6(2), Heinemann InfoSearch) Heinemann-Raintree.

Spilsbury, Louise, et al. Great Scientific Theories. 2017. (Great Scientific Theories Ser.). (ENG.). 32p. (gr. 4-6). 122.60 **(978-1-4109-8748-8(5)**, Raintree Perspectives) Heinemann-Raintree.

Spilsbury, Richard & Spilsbury, Louise. Look Inside. 2013. (Look Inside Ser.). (ENG.). 32p. (gr. 1-3). pap. 47.94 (978-1-4329-7206-6(5)); lib. bdg. 163.92 (978-1-4329-7199-1(9)) Heinemann-Raintree. (Heinemann First Library).

Spilsbury, Richard, et al. Anatomy of an Investigation. 2013. (Anatomy of an Investigation Ser.). (ENG.). 56p. (gr. 7-8). pap. 47.45 (978-1-4329-7611-8(7)); lib. bdg. 103.95 (978-1-4329-7605-7(2)) Heinemann-Raintree.

Stanbury, Jean. How to Dazzle at Being a Scientist. 2004. (Illus.). 48p. pap. 30.00 (978-1-897675-52-6(6)) Brilliant Pubns. GBR. Dist: Parkwest Pubns., Inc.

Staton, Hilarie N. & McCarthy, Tara. Science & Stories Grade K-3: Integrating Science & Literature. 2005. (Illus.). 129p. (gr. k-3). per. 15.95 (978-1-59647-082-8(8)) Good Year Bks.

Steck-Vaughn Staff. Creepy Creatures. 2003. pap. 4.10 (978-0-7398-7629-9(5)) Steck-Vaughn.

—Focus on Science. 2004. (Focus on Science Ser.). (ENG.). 96p. (gr. 1-1). pap. 21.20 (978-0-7398-9144-5(8)); (Illus.). 128p. (gr. 4-4). pap. 24.00 (978-0-7398-9147-6(2));Level C. 64p. (gr. 3-3). pap., tchr. ed. 21.95 (978-0-7398-9152-0(9));Level C. (Illus.). 128p. (gr. 3-3). pap., stu. ed. 24.00 (978-0-7398-9146-9(4));Level D. 64p. (gr. 4-4). pap., tchr. ed. 21.95 (978-0-7398-9153-7(7));Level A. 64p. (gr. 1-1). pap., tchr. ed. 21.95 (978-0-7398-9150-6(2));Level B. 64p. (gr. 2-2). pap., tchr. ed. 21.95 (978-0-7398-9151-3(0));Level B. (Illus.). 96p. (gr. 2-2). pap. 21.20 (978-0-7398-9145-2(6));Level E. (Illus.). 144p. (gr. 5-5). pap. 25.15 (978-0-7398-9148-3(0));Level F. 64p. (gr. 6-6). pap., tchr. ed. 21.95 (978-0-7398-9155-1(3));Level F. (Illus.). 144p. (gr. 6-6). pap. 25.15 (978-0-7398-9149-0(9)) Houghton Mifflin Harcourt Publishing Co.

—Focus on Science 2004, Level E. 2004. (Focus on Science Ser.). (ENG.). 64p. (gr. 5-5). pap., tchr. ed. 21.95 (978-0-7398-9154-4(5)) Houghton Mifflin Harcourt Publishing Co.

—Science: Earth & Space Life, Physical. 2003. (Science Ser.). (ENG.). 176p. (gr. 3-3). pap. 16.99 (978-0-7398-7935-1(9)) Houghton Mifflin Harcourt Publishing Co.

—Science: Life, Physical, Earth & Spac. 2003. (Science Ser.). (ENG.). 176p. (gr. 1-1). pap. 16.99 (978-0-7398-7933-7(2)); (gr. 4-4). pap. 16.99 (978-0-7398-7936-8(7)) Houghton Mifflin Harcourt Publishing Co.

—Science: Life, Physical, Earth & Space. 2003. (Science Ser.). (ENG.). 176p. (gr. 2-2). pap. 16.99 (978-0-7398-7934-4(0)); (gr. 5-5). pap. 16.99 (978-0-7398-7937-5(5)) Houghton Mifflin Harcourt Publishing Co.

—Science Level H-J: Hello, Hello! 2003. (Illus.). pap. (978-0-7398-7635-0(X)) Steck-Vaughn.

—Science - Earth & Space Life - Physical. 2003. (Science Ser.). (ENG.). 176p. (gr. 6-6). pap. 16.99 (978-0-7398-7938-2(3)) Houghton Mifflin Harcourt Publishing Co.

—What Goes up Must Come Down. 2003. pap. 4.10 (978-0-7398-7632-9(5)) Steck-Vaughn.

The STEM Guide to the Universe. 2016. (STEM Guide to the Universe Ser.). 192p. (gr. 9-9). 276.60 (978-1-5081-7165-2(3), Rosen Young Adult) Rosen Publishing Group, Inc., The.

STEM in the Real World. 2015. (STEM in the Real World Ser.). (ENG.). 24p. (gr. 2-3). pap., pap., pap. 297.00 (978-1-4994-1315-1(7), PowerKids Pr.) Rosen Publishing Group, Inc., The.

Sterling Children's, Sterling. Curious Jane. 2017. (ENG., Illus.). 128p. (J). (gr. 1-6). pap. 16.95 (978-1-4549-2235-3(4)) Sterling Publishing Co., Inc.

Steve, Parker. What about Science & Technology. 2008. 40p. pap. (978-1-84810-074-9(4)) Miles Kelly Publishing, Ltd.

Stille, Darlene R. The Case of the Soda Explosion & Other True Science Mysteries for You to Solve, 1 vol. 2012. (Seriously True Mysteries Ser.). (ENG.). 32p. (gr. 3-4). lib. bdg. 27.32 (978-1-4296-7623-6(X), Fact Finders) Capstone Press of Coughlan Cos.

The Story of Science - Group 3, 4 bks., Set. 119.71 (978-0-7614-1424-7(X), Benchmark Bks.) Marshall Cavendish Corp.

Stosch, Dawn. Science Math. 2008. (Math Alive! Ser.). 32p. (gr. 4-18). lib. bdg. 28.50 (978-0-7614-3213-5(2), Benchmark Bks.) Marshall Cavendish Corp.

Stuart, Colin. Why Space Matters to Me. 2015. (ENG., Illus.). 48p. (gr. 3-6). 12.99 (978-1-5124-0201-8(X), Millbrook Pr.) Lerner Publishing Group.

Sundance/Newbridge LLC Staff. Animal Life Cycles. 2004. (Reading PowerWorks Ser.). (gr. 1-3). pap. 6.10 (978-0-7608-9234-3(2)) Sundance/Newbridge Educational Publishing.

Sunshine Science Early Fluency Sets 1-3: 1 Each of 24 Big Books from Sets 1-3. (Sunshine Ser.). (gr. 1-2). 845.95 (978-0-7802-1370-8(X)) Wright Group/McGraw-Hill.

Sunshine Science Early Fluency Sets 1-3: 1 Each of 24 Student Books from Sets 1-3. (gr. 1-2). 167.95 (978-0-7802-1371-5(8)) Wright Group/McGraw-Hill.

Sunshine Science Early Fluency Sets 4-6: 1 Each of 24 Big Books from Sets 4-6. (gr. 1-2). 845.95 (978-0-7802-2924-2(X)) Wright Group/McGraw-Hill.

Sunshine Science Early Fluency Sets 4-6: 1 Each of 24 Student Books from Sets 4-6. (gr. 1-2). 167.95 (978-0-7802-3189-4(9)) Wright Group/McGraw-Hill.

Sunshine Science Emergent Sets: 1 Each of 24 Big Books from Sets 1-3. (gr. 1-2). 750.50 (978-0-7802-2751-4(4)) Wright Group/McGraw-Hill.

Sunshine Science Emergent Sets: 1 Each of 24 Student Books from Sets 1-3. (gr. 1-2). 146.50 (978-0-7802-1944-1(9)) Wright Group/McGraw-Hill.

Superheroes of Science. 2015. (Superheroes of Science Ser.). (ENG.). 48p. (J). (gr. 6-6). 191.70 (978-1-4824-2561-1(0)) Stevens, Gareth Publishing LLLP.

Suzuki, David T. & Hehner, Barbara. Descubre el Cuerpo Humano. 2004. (Juego de la Ciencia Ser.). (SPA., Illus.). 96p. 14.99 (978-84-9754-033-9(6), 87813) Ediciones Oniro S.A. ESP. Dist: Lectorum Pubns., Inc.

Swain, Cynthia. What Do You Think? 2003. (BuildUp Ser.). (J). pap. 22.00 (978-1-4108-0758-8(4)) Benchmark Education Co.

Swanson, Jennifer, et al. LOL Physical Science. Lum, Bernice, illus. 2012. (LOL Physical Science Ser.). (ENG.). 32p. (gr. 3-4). pap. 190.80 (978-1-4296-9305-9(3)); pap. 31.80 (978-1-4296-9304-2(5)) Capstone Press of Coughlan Cos. (Fact Finders).

Syverson, Carolyn. Places to Go! 2011. (Science Ser.). (ENG.). 16p. (gr. -1-1). 25.95 (978-1-4296-8667-9(7), Wonder Readers) Capstone Press of Coughlan Cos.

TAKS Science Preparation Elementary - Student Edition. 2003. (Region IV ESC Resources for Science Ser.). stu. ed., per., wbk. ed. (978-1-932524-62-8(2)) Region IV Education Service Ctr.

TAKS Science Preparation Elementary - Student Edition - Spanish. 2004. (SPA.). stu. ed., per., wbk. ed. (978-1-932524-87-1(8)) Region IV Education Service Ctr.

TAKS Science Preparation Grade 11 Exit. 2004. (Region IV ESC Resources for Science Ser.). stu. ed., per., wbk. ed. (978-1-932524-64-2(9)) Region IV Education Service Ctr.

Taylor, Kim. Action. (Illus.). 32p. (YA). (gr. 3-18). lib. bdg. 27.10 (978-1-931983-72-3(0)) Chrysalis Education.

—Cold. (Illus.). 32p. (YA). (gr. 3-18). lib. bdg. 27.10 (978-1-931983-73-0(9)) Chrysalis Education.

—Pattern. (Illus.). 32p. (YA). (gr. 3-18). lib. bdg. 27.10 (978-1-931983-76-1(3)) Chrysalis Education.

—Structure. (Illus.). 32p. (YA). (gr. 3-18). lib. bdg. 27.10 (978-1-931983-78-5(X)) Chrysalis Education.

Teacher Created Materials Staff, ed. Physical Science: Add-on Pack. 2007. (Science Readers Ser.). 89.99 (978-1-4333-0068-4(0)) Teacher Created Materials, Inc.

—Physical Science: Themed Classroom Reader Set. 2007. (Themed Reader Sets Ser.). pap. 249.99 (978-1-4333-0154-4(7)) Teacher Created Materials, Inc.

Teeth, 6 vols. (Sunshinetm Science Ser.). 24p. (gr. 1-2). 37.50 (978-0-7802-1402-6(1)); 41.95 (978-0-7802-1401-9(3)) Wright Group/McGraw-Hill.

Teeth Sets: 1 Each of 3 Student Books. (Sunshinetm Science Ser.). (gr. 1-2). 20.95 (978-0-7802-1751-5(9)) Wright Group/McGraw-Hill.

Thimmesh, Catherine. The Sky's the Limit: Stories of Discovery by Women & Girls. Sweet, Melissa, illus. 2005. 73p. (J). (gr. 4-8). reprint ed. 16.00 (978-0-7567-9631-0(8)) DIANE Publishing Co.

Thompson, Gene. Kitchen Science. Date not set. (Thinking Like a Scientist Ser.). (Illus.). 20p. (J). pap. 16.95 (978-1-58273-097-4(0)) Sundance/Newbridge Educational Publishing.

Thomson, Ruth. The Science & Inventions Creativity Book: Games, Models to Make, High-Tech Craft Paper, Stickers, & Stencils. 2013. (Creativity Bks.). (ENG., Illus.). 80p. (J). (gr. 1-6). pap. 12.99 (978-1-4380-0251-4(3)) Barron's Educational Series, Inc.

Tilden, Thomasine E. Lewis & Lewis-Tilden, Thomasine E. Mind Readers: Science Examines ESP. 2008. (24/7: Science Behind the Scenes Ser.). (ENG., Illus.). 64p. (J). (gr. 9-12). pap. 7.95 (978-0-531-17532-3(4), Watts, Franklin) Scholastic Library Publishing.

TIME for Kids Science Guide. (J). (978-0-06-079271-8(X)) HarperCollins Pubs.

Top That Publishing Staff, ed. Electric Science. 2004. (Top That! Labs Ser.). (Illus.). 24p. (J). (978-1-84510-152-7(9)) Top That! Publishing PLC.

—Lets Go Bubbletastic. 2005. (Illus.). 48p. (978-1-84510-548-8(6)) Top That! Publishing PLC.

—Mirror Science. 2004. (Top That! Labs Ser.). (Illus.). 24p. (J). (978-1-84510-155-8(3)) Top That! Publishing PLC.

Trefil, James. (WCS)Sciences. 4th ed. 2004. pap., stu. ed. 71.95 (978-0-471-72701-9(6)) Wiley, John & Sons, Inc.

—(WCS)Sciences: With eGrade Set. 4th ed. 2004. pap., stu. ed. 71.95 (978-0-471-72702-6(4)) Wiley, John & Sons, Inc.

Trefil, James, et al. Life Science 2005. l.t. ed. 2004. (McDougal Littell Middle School Science Ser.). (ENG., Illus.). 128p. (gr. 6-8). 84.85 (978-0-618-30367-0(7), 2-01002) Great Source Education Group, Inc.

Troupe, Thomas Kingsley. The Garbage Gang's Super Science Questions, 4 vols. Toye, Derek, illus. (Garbage Gang's Super Science Questions Ser.). (ENG.). 24p. (gr. k-2). 2015. 106.60 (978-1-4795-8023-1(6)) 2014. 106.60 (978-1-4795-5562-8(2)) Picture Window Bks.

A True Book(tm) — Extreme Science (Set Of 5) 2014. (True Book — Extreme Science Ser.). (J). lib. bdg. 145.00 (978-0-531-24355-8(9)) Scholastic Library Publishing.

Trumbauer, Lisa. Eating Well, 6 vols., Set. 2003. (Yellow Umbrella Early Level Ser.). (ENG.). 16p. (gr. k-1). pap. 35.70 (978-0-7368-3014-0(6), Yellow Umbrella Bks.) Capstone Press of Coughlan Cos.

—Trees Are Terrific!, 6 vols., Set. 2003. (Yellow Umbrella Early Level Ser.). (ENG.). 16p. (gr. k-1). pap. 35.70 (978-0-7368-3000-3(6), Yellow Umbrella Bks.) Capstone Press of Coughlan Cos.

U X L, ed. UXL Man-Made Disasters, 3 vols. 2015. (ENG.). (J). 286.00 (978-1-4103-1774-2(9), UXL) Cengage Gale.

Uncharted, Unexplored, & Unexplained: Scienctific Advancements of the 19th Century, 16 Bks, Set. 2004. (Illus.). (gr. 4-8). lib. bdg. 319.20 (978-1-58415-322-1(9)) Mitchell Lane Pubs., Inc.

Uncharted, Unexplored, & Unexplained: Scientific Advancements of the 19th Century, 26 vols., Set. Incl. Alexander Graham Bell & the Story of the Telephone. Bankston, John. (gr. 4-8). 2004. lib. bdg. 29.95 (978-1-58415-243-9(5)); Antoine Lavoisier: Father of Modern Chemistry. Kjelle, Marylou. (gr. 4-8). 2004. lib. bdg. 29.95 (978-1-58415-309-2(1)); Auguste & Louis Lumiere: And the Rise of Motion Pictures. Whiting, Jim. (gr. 3-8). 2005. lib. bdg. 29.95 (978-1-58415-365-8(2)); Charles Babbage & the Story of the First Computer. Sherman, Josepha. (gr. 4-8). 2005. lib. bdg. 29.95 (978-1-58415-372-6(5)); Charles Darwin & the Origin of the Species. Whiting, Jim. (gr. 3-8). 2005. lib. bdg. 29.95 (978-1-58415-364-1(4)); Dmitri Mendeleyev & the Periodic Table. Zannos, Susan. (gr. 4-8). 2004. lib. bdg. 29.95 (978-1-58415-267-5(2)); Florence Nightingale & the Advancement of Nursing. Hinman, Bonnie. (gr. 4-8). 2004. lib. bdg. 29.95 (978-1-58415-257-6(5)); Friedrich Miescher & the Story of Nucleic Acid. Tracy, Kathleen. (gr. 4-8). 2005. lib. bdg. 29.95 (978-1-58415-369-6(5)); George Eastman & Photographic Film. Mattern, Joanne. (gr. 4-8). 2004. lib. bdg. 29.95 (978-1-58415-258-3(3)); Gregor Mendel & the Discovery of the Gene. Bankston, John. (gr. 4-8). 2004. lib. bdg. 29.95 (978-1-58415-266-8(4)); Guglielmo Marconi & Radio Waves. Zannos, Susan. (gr. 4-8). 2004. lib. bdg. 29.95 (978-1-58415-265-1(6)); Henry Bessemer: Making Steel from Iron. Tracy, Kathleen. (gr. 4-8). 2005. lib. bdg. 29.95 (978-1-58415-366-5(0)); Henry Cavendish & the Discovery of Hydrogen. Sherman, Josepha. (gr. 4-8). 2005. lib. bdg. 29.95 (978-1-58415-368-9(7)); J. J. Thomson & the Discovery of Electrons. Sherman, Josepha. (gr. 4-8). 2005. lib. bdg. 29.95 (978-1-58415-370-2(9)); James Watt & the Steam Engine. Whiting, Jim. (gr. 4-8). 2005. lib. bdg. 29.95 (978-1-58415-371-9(7)); John Dalton & the Atomic Theory. Kjelle, Marylou. (gr. 4-8). 2004. lib. bdg. 29.95 (978-1-58415-308-5(3)); Joseph Lister & the Story of Antiseptics. Bankston, John. (gr. 4-8). 2004. lib. bdg. 29.95 (978-1-58415-262-0(1)); Joseph Priestly & the Discovery of Oxygen. Conley, Kate A. (gr. 4-8). 2005. lib. bdg. 29.95 (978-1-58415-367-2(9)); Karl Benz & the Single Cylinder Engine. Bankston, John. (gr. 4-8). 2004. lib. bdg. 29.95 (978-1-58415-244-6(3)); Louis Daguerre & the Story of the Daguerreotype. Bankston, John. (gr. 4-8). 2004. lib. bdg. 29.95 (978-1-58415-247-7(8)); Louis Pasteur: Fighter Against Contagious Disease. Kjelle, Marylou Morano. (gr. 4-8). 2005. lib. bdg. 29.95 (978-1-58415-363-4(6), 1244912); Michael Faraday & the Discovery of Electromagnetism. Zannos, Susan. (gr. 4-8). 2004. lib. bdg. 29.95 (978-1-58415-307-8(5)); Pierre & Marie Curie & the Discovery of Radium. Tracy, Kathleen. (gr. 4-8). 2004. lib. bdg. 29.95 (978-1-58415-310-8(5)); Robert Koch & the Study of Anthrax. Tracy, Kathleen. (gr. 4-8). 2004. lib. bdg. 29.95 (978-1-58415-261-3(3)); Samuel Morse & the Telegraph. Zannos, Susan. (gr. 4-8). 2004. lib. bdg. 29.95 (978-1-58415-269-9(9)); Thomas Edison: Great Inventor. Thatcher Murcia, Rebecca. (gr. 4-8). 2004. lib. bdg. 29.95 (978-1-58415-306-1(7)); (Illus.). 48p. (J). 2005. Set lib. bdg. 778.70 (978-1-58415-410-5(1)) Mitchell Lane Pubs., Inc.

Unlocking the Secrets of Science: Profiling 20th Century Achievers in Science, Medicine, & Technology, 30 vols., set. (Illus.). 56p. (J). (gr. 5-6). 718.00 (978-1-58415-163-0(3)) Mitchell Publishing, Inc.

Up in the Air: 6 Each of 1 Anthology, 6 vols. (Wildcats Ser.). 32p. (gr. 2-8). (978-0-322-00596-9(5)) Wright Group/McGraw-Hill.

VanVoorst, Jennifer. Make It Move!, 6 vols., Set. 2003. (Yellow Umbrella Early Level Ser.). (ENG.). 16p. (gr. k-1). pap. 35.70 (978-0-7368-3016-4(2), Yellow Umbrella Bks.) Capstone Press of Coughlan Cos.

—Who Builds?, 6 vols., Set. 2003. (Yellow Umbrella Early Level Ser.). (ENG.). 16p. (gr. k-1). pap. 35.70 (978-0-7368-3001-0(4), Yellow Umbrella Bks.) Capstone Press of Coughlan Cos.

Vecchione, Glen. Science Facts. Harris, Joel & Harris, Sharon, illus. 2007. (ENG.). 352p. (J). (gr. 3-7). pap. 6.95 (978-1-4027-4981-0(3)) Sterling Publishing Co., Inc.

A Visual Exploration of Science: Set 1. 2017. (Visual Exploration of Science Ser.). 96p. (gr. 12-13). 148.40 **(978-1-4994-6657-7(9)**, Rosen Young Adult) Rosen Publishing Group, Inc., The.

Voege, Debra & Science Applications, inc Staff. Science in the Real World Set, 10-Volumes. 2009. (Science in the Real World Ser.). (gr. 4-6). 280.00 (978-1-60413-829-0(7), Chelsea Clubhouse) Facts On File, Inc.

Walch Publishing Staff. Assessment Strategies for Science. 2004. 54p. 24.99 (978-0-8251-5174-3(0)); 80p. (J). pap. 24.99 (978-0-8251-5175-0(9)) Walch Education.

Walch Publishing Staff, creator. Math & Science. 2007. (Daily Warm-Ups Ser.). 204p. (gr. 5-6). tchr. ed., spiral bd. 24.99 (978-0-8251-6447-7(8)) Walch Education.

Waldron, Melanie, et al. Essential Life Science, 1 vol. 2014. (Essential Life Science Ser.). (ENG.). 48p. (gr. 4-6). lib. bdg. 266.56 (978-1-4846-0688-9(4), Heinemann InfoSearch) Heinemann-Raintree.

Walker, Colin, et al. Los Seres Vivos. (Coleccion Conceptos de Ciencia en Big Books). (SPA., Illus.). (J). (gr. k-3). 12.00 net. (978-0-8136-6704-1(6), MD7209) Modern Curriculum Pr.

—La Superficie de la Tierra. (Coleccion Conceptos de Ciencia en Big Books). (SPA., Illus.). (J). (gr. k-3). 12.00 (978-0-8136-6754-6(2), MD7212) Modern Curriculum Pr.

Walker, Kathryn. Mysteries of the Cosmic Joker. 2009. (Unsolved! Ser.). (ENG., Illus.). 32p. (J). (gr. 3-5). pap. (978-0-7787-4161-9(3)); (gr. 4-6). (978-0-7787-4148-0(6)) Crabtree Publishing Co.

Walking, Walking: Big Book: Level D. 8p. 20.95 (978-0-322-00626-3(0)) Wright Group/McGraw-Hill.

Wall Chart. 2003. (Scott Foresman Science Ser.). (gr. 3-18). suppl. ed. 81.90 (978-0-673-65118-1(5)) Addison-Wesley Educational Pubs., Inc.

Warm up to Science for Grade 5. 2005. spiral bd. (978-1-933049-16-8(2)) Region IV Education Service Ctr.

Warming up! Cooling Off! 6 Each of 1 Student Book, 6 vols. (Sunshinetm Science Ser.). 24p. (gr. 1-2). 41.95 (978-0-7802-1407-1(2)) Wright Group/McGraw-Hill.

Warming up! Cooling Off! Big Book. (Sunshinetm Science Ser.). 24p. (gr. 1-2). 37.50 (978-0-7802-1408-8(0)) Wright Group/McGraw-Hill.

Weakland, Mark. Clang! Wile E. Coyote Experiments with Magnetism. Billiau, Loic, illus. 2017. (Wile E. Coyote, Physical Science Genius Ser.). (ENG.). 32p. (gr. 3-5). lib. bdg. 30.65 (978-1-5157-3731-5(4)) Capstone Press of Coughlan Cos.

—Comienza la Ciencia. 2012. (Comienza la Ciencia/Science Starts Ser.).Tr. of Science Starts. (MUL.). 32p. (gr. 1-2). lib. bdg. 81.96 (978-1-4296-8261-9(2), A+ Bilingue/Bilingual) Capstone Press of Coughlan Cos.

—Science Starts. (Science Starts Ser.). (ENG.). 32p. (gr. 1-2). 2011. pap. 190.80 (978-1-4296-6179-9(8)) 2010. pap. 31.80 (978-1-4296-6180-5(1)) Capstone Press of Coughlan Cos. (Aplus Bks.).

—Science Starts, 4 vols., Set. Incl. Bubbles Float, Bubbles Pop. Salas, Laura Purdie. lib. bdg. 27.32 (978-1-4296-5250-6(0)); Gears Go, Wheels Roll. lib. bdg. 27.32 (978-1-4296-5253-7(5)); (gr. 1-2). (Science Starts Ser.). (ENG.). 32p. 2010. Set lib. bdg. 54.64 (978-1-4296-5254-4(3), Aplus Bks.) Capstone Press of Coughlan Cos.

Weakland, Mark & Slade, Suzanne. Wile E. Coyote, Physical Science Genius, 1 vol. Cornia, Christian & Ricci, Andrés Martínez, illus. 2014. (Wile E. Coyote, Physical Science Genius Ser.). (ENG.). 32p. (gr. 3-4). lib. bdg. 122.60 (978-1-4765-6199-8(0)) Capstone Press of Coughlan Cos.

Weird & Wacky Science, 6 bks., Set. (Illus.). (YA). (gr. 4-10). lib. bdg. 113.70 (978-0-89490-662-6(3)) Enslow Pubs., Inc.

Weird Careers in Science. 2005. (Weird Careers in Science Ser.). (Illus.). 64p. (gr. 5-8). 175.00 (978-0-7910-9088-6(4), Chelsea Hse.) Facts On File, Inc.

Weird Science. (Eyes on Adventure Ser.). 32p. (J). (gr. 1). pap. (978-1-882210-82-4(4)) Action Publishing, Inc.

Wells, Robert E. What's Older Than a Giant Tortoise? Wells, Robert E., illus. 2004. (Wells of Knowledge Science Ser.). (ENG., Illus.). 32p. (J). (gr. -1-3). 7.99 (978-0-8075-8832-1(6)) Whitman, Albert & Co.

Wells, Robert E. & Wells, Robert. Como Se Mide el Tiempo? 2003. (SPA.). 176p. (J). (gr. 2-3). 15.99 (978-84-261-3287-1(1)) Juventud, Editorial ESP. Dist: Lectorum Pubns., Inc.

Welsh, Anne Marie & Fenly, Leigh. Wow! Wonders of Water. Garcia, Helena, illus. 2009. 112p. (J). pap. (978-0-88441-732-3(8)) Girl Scouts of the USA.

Westrup, Hugh & Barchers, Suzanne. Let's Explore Physical Science Grades 4-5, 10 bks., Set. 2015. (Science Readers: Content & Literacy Ser.). (ENG., Illus.). 32p. (gr. 4-5). 89.90 (978-1-4938-1429-9(X)) Shell Educational Publishing.

What About..., 10 vols., Set. Incl. Dinosaurs. Matthews, Rupert. lib. bdg. 19.95 (978-1-4222-1558-6(X)); History. Williams, Brian. lib. bdg. 19.95 (978-1-4222-1559-3(8)); How We Live. Williams, Brian. lib. bdg. 19.95 (978-1-4222-1560-9(1));

Human Body. Parker, Steve. lib. bdg. 19.95 (978-1-4222-1561-6(X)); Natural World. Williams, Brian. lib. bdg. 19.95 (978-1-4222-1562-3(8)); People & Places. Williams, Brian. lib. bdg. 19.95 (978-1-4222-1563-0(6)); Planet Earth. Williams, Brian. lib. bdg. 19.95 (978-1-4222-1564-7(4)); Science & Technology. Parker, Steve. lib. bdg. 19.95 (978-1-4222-1565-4(2)); Universe. Williams, Brian. lib. bdg. 19.95 (978-1-4222-1566-1(0)); World Wonders. Williams, Brian. lib. bdg. 19.95 (978-1-4222-1567-8(9)); (J). (gr. 6-8). 2010. (Question & Answer Book Ser.). (Illus.). 40p. 2009. Set lib. bdg. 199.50 (978-1-4222-1557-9(1)) Mason Crest.

What Goes into Bread? 6 Each of 1 Student Book, 6 vols. (Sunshinetm Science Ser.). 24p. (gr. 1-2). 41.95 (978-0-7802-2728-6(X)) Wright Group/McGraw-Hill.

What Goes into Bread? Big Book. (Sunshinetm Science Ser.). 24p. (gr. 1-2). 37.50 (978-0-7802-2798-9(0)) Wright Group/McGraw-Hill.

What Is Rock? 6 Each of 1 Student Book, 6 vols. (Sunshinetm Science Ser.). 24p. (gr. 1-2). 41.95 (978-0-7802-2718-7(2)) Wright Group/McGraw-Hill.

What Is Rock? Big Book. (Sunshinetm Science Ser.). 24p. (gr. 1-2). 37.50 (978-0-7802-2793-4(X)) Wright Group/McGraw-Hill.

What Is Soil? 6 Each of 1 Student Book, 6 vols. (Sunshinetm Science Ser.). 24p. (gr. 1-2). 41.95 (978-0-7802-2722-4(0)) Wright Group/McGraw-Hill.

What Is Soil? Big Book. (Sunshinetm Science Ser.). 24p. (gr. 1-2). 37.50 (978-0-7802-2795-8(6)) Wright Group/McGraw-Hill.

What Is this Skeleton?, 6 vols. (Sunshinetm Science Ser.). 24p. (gr. 1-2). 36.95 (978-0-7802-0550-5(2)); 31.50 (978-0-7802-0298-6(8)) Wright Group/McGraw-Hill.

What Makes Light?, 6 vols. (Sunshinetm Science Ser.). 24p. (gr. 1-2). 36.95 (978-0-7802-0555-0(3)); 31.50 (978-0-7802-0304-4(6)) Wright Group/McGraw-Hill.

What will Float?, 6 vols. (Sunshinetm Science Ser.). 24p. (gr. 1-2). 31.50 (978-0-7802-0297-9(X)) Wright Group/McGraw-Hill.

Wheeler-Toppen, Jodi. Science Experiments That Explode & Implode: Fun Projects for Curious Kids, 1 vol. 2010. (Kitchen Science Ser.). (ENG.). 32p. (gr. 3-4). lib. bdg. 27.99 (978-1-4296-5427-2(9), Edge Bks.) Capstone Press of Coughlan Cos.

White, Nancy. Push, Pull, Play the Game: A Content Area Reader-science. 2005. (Sadlier Phonics Reading Program). (Illus.). 20p. (gr. k-2). 25.20 (978-0-8215-7815-5(4)) Sadlier, William H. Inc.

William H. Sadlier Staff. Float or Sink? 2005. (Emergent/Early (Prek-2) Science Package Ser.). 12p. (gr. -1-2). 25.20 (978-0-8215-7840-7(5)) Sadlier, William H. Inc.

—Splish, Splash! 2005. (Emergent/Early (Prek-2) Science Package Ser.). 12p. (gr. -1-1). 25.20 (978-0-8215-7838-4(3)) Sadlier, William H. Inc.

—What Is the Weather Today? 2005. (Emergent/Early (Prek-2) Science Package Ser.). 12p. (gr. k-2). 25.20 (978-0-8215-7839-1(1)) Sadlier, William H. Inc.

Wolf, Cathrine, ed. Inside Space Jam. Date not set. 64p. (Orig.). (J). (gr. 4-8). pap. 3.95 (978-1-886749-19-1(1)) Sports Illustrated For Kids.

Wollard, Kathy. How Come? Every Kid's Science Questions Explained. Solomon, Debra, illus. 2014. (ENG.). 416p. (J). pap. 16.95 (978-0-7611-7978-8(X), 17978) Workman Publishing Co., Inc.

Wollard, Kathy & Solomon, Debra. El Libro de Los Porqués 2: Las Preguntas Más Difíciles y Las Respuestas Más Fáciles Sobre Las Personas, Los Animales y Las Cosas. Solomon, Debra, tr. 2004. (SPA., Illus.). 208p. 28.99 (978-84-9754-047-6(6), 87432) Ediciones Oniro S.A. ESP. Dist: Lectorum Pubns., Inc.

Wonderful Ears: 6 Each of 1 Student Book, 6 vols. (Sunshinetm Science Ser.). 24p. (gr. 1-2). 41.95 (978-0-7802-1416-3(1)) Wright Group/McGraw-Hill.

Wonderful Ears: Big Book. (Sunshinetm Science Ser.). 24p. (gr. 1-2). 37.50 (978-0-7802-1417-0(X)) Wright Group/McGraw-Hill.

Wonderful Eyes, 6 vols. (Sunshinetm Science Ser.). 24p. (gr. 1-2). 37.50 (978-0-7802-1414-9(5)); 42.95 (978-0-7802-1413-2(7)) Wright Group/McGraw-Hill.

Wonders of the World. (Eyes on Adventure Ser.). 32p. (J). (gr. 1). pap. (978-1-882210-65-7(4)) Action Publishing, Inc.

World Almanac Puzzler Deck for Kids: Science (BoMC) World Almanac Deck: Science, 9-11. 2007. 9.95 (978-0-8118-6242-4(9)) Chronicle Bks. LLC.

World Book, Inc. Staff. World Book's Young Scientist, 10 vols., Vol. 10. 2004. (Illus.). 1,280p. (gr. 3-8). pap., tchr. ed. 249.00 (978-0-7166-2750-0(7), 60031) World Bk., Inc.

World Book, Inc Staff, contrib. by. Earth & Space. 2008. (J). (978-0-7166-3016-6(8)); (978-0-7166-3017-3(6)) World Bk., Inc.

—Science & Technology. 2008. (J). (978-0-7166-3018-0(4)) World Bk., Inc.

World Book, Inc. Staff, contrib. by. World Book's Science & Nature Guides, 12 vols. 2004. (World Book's Science & Nature Guides Ser.). (Illus.). 80p. (gr. 5-9). 319.00 (978-0-7166-4208-4(5), SKU 30119) World Bk., Inc.

World of Science. Date not set. (Children's Reference Ser.). (Illus.). 256p. (J). (978-1-4054-1635-1(1)); 224p. 17.99 (978-1-4054-9924-8(9)) Parragon, Inc.

Yes Magazine Editors. Hoaxed! Fakes & Mistakes in the World of Science. Woo, Howie, illus. 2009. (ENG.). 48p. (J). (gr. 3-7). 16.95 (978-1-55453-206-3(X)) Kids Can Pr., Ltd. CAN. Dist: Hachette Bk. Group.

—Hoaxed! Fakes & Mistakes in the World of Science. Yes Magazine Editors, ed. Woo, Howie, illus. 2009. (ENG.). 48p. (J). (gr. 3-7). pap. 8.95 (978-1-55453-207-0(8)) Kids Can Pr., Ltd. CAN. Dist: Hachette Bk. Group.

You & Your Teeth. (Sunshinetm Science Ser.). 24p. (gr. 1-2). 37.50 (978-0-7802-1441-5(2));Set. 41.95 (978-0-7802-1440-8(4)) Wright Group/McGraw-Hill.

You Wouldn't Want to Live Without... (Set Of 6) 2014. (You Wouldn't Want to Live Without... Ser.). (J). lib. bdg. 174.00 (978-0-531-24362-6(1), Watts, Franklin) Scholastic Library Publishing.

Young Explorers in Science. (J). 105.00 (978-0-8136-4363-2(5)) Modern Curriculum Pr.

Young, Karen Romano. Crime Scene Science: 20 A+ Projects & Experiments - Want to Rock Your Science Fair & Score an A? Goldin, David, illus. 2009. (Science Fair Winners Ser.). (ENG.). 80p. (J). (gr. 5-9). pap. 12.95 (978-1-4263-0521-4(4), National Geographic Children's Bks.) National Geographic Society.

—Crime Scene Science: 20 Projects & Experiments about Clues, Crimes, Criminals, & Other Mysterious Things. Goldin, David, illus. 2009. (Science Fair Winners Ser.). (ENG.). 80p. (J). (gr. 5-9). 24.90 (978-1-4263-0522-1(2), National Geographic Children's Bks.) National Geographic Society.

Zev, Marc, et al. 101 Things Everyone Should Know about Math. 2010. (101 Things You Should Know about Ser.). (ENG., Illus.). 128p. (J). (gr. 5-9). pap. 12.95 (978-0-9678020-3-9(2)) Science, Naturally!

100 Things You Should Know About, 15 vols., Set. (Illus.). 48p. (gr. 3-18). lib. bdg. (978-1-59084-444-1(0)) Mason Crest.

1000 Things You Should Know About, 13 vols., Set. (Illus.). 64p. (gr. 3-18). lib. bdg. (978-1-59084-460-1(2)) Mason Crest.

SCIENCE—DATA PROCESSING

Allen-Conn, B. J. & Rose, Kim. Powerful Ideas in the Classroom Using Squeak to Enhance Math & Science Learning. 2003. (Illus.). 86p. per. (978-0-9743131-0-8(6)) Viewpoints Research Institute, Inc.

Group/McGraw-Hill, Wright. Caretakers of the Earth, 6 vols. (Book2WebTM Ser.). (gr. 4-8). 36.50 incl. 5.25 hd (978-0-322-04470-8(7)) Wright Group/McGraw-Hill.

SCIENCE—DICTIONARIES

American Heritage Dictionary Editors, ed. The American Heritage Student Science Dictionary, Second Edition. 2nd ed. 2014. (ENG., Illus.). 384p. (gr. 7). 19.95 (978-0-547-85731-2(4)) Houghton Mifflin Harcourt Publishing Co.

American Heritage Dictionary Staff, ed. The American Heritage Children's Science Dictionary. 2013. (ENG., Illus.). 288p. (J). (gr. 4-6). 18.95 (978-0-547-85752-7(7)) Houghton Mifflin Harcourt Publishing Co.

Avignon, Marie-Claude. Mi Primer Larousse de las Ciencias: De la Vida y de la Tierra. Larousse Staff, ed. 2006. (Mi Primer Larousse Ser.). (SPA., Illus.). 160p. (gr. -1-3). 19.95 (978-970-22-1231-7(6)) Larousse, Ediciones, S. A. de C. V. MEX. Dist: Houghton Mifflin Harcourt Publishing Co.

Brooks, F. First Encyclopedia of Science II. rev. ed. 2011. (First Encyclopedias Ser.). 64p. (J). pap. 9.99 (978-0-7945-3043-3(5), Usborne) EDC Publishing.

, Chambers, Chambers. School Science Dictionary. 2003. (Illus.). 400p. (978-0-550-10070-2(9), Chambers) Hodder & Stoughton.

Craig, A. & Rosney, C. Science Encyclopedia. 2004. (Encyclopedias Ser.). (Illus.). 128p. (J). 7.95 (978-0-7945-0007-8(2)) EDC Publishing.

Delta science dictionary gr3-4 single Title. 2003. 64p. (J). (gr. 3-4). (978-1-59242-297-5(7)) Delta Education, LLC.

Delta science dictionary gr5-6 single Title. 2003. 80p. (J). (gr. 5-6). (978-1-59242-299-9(3)) Delta Education, LLC.

Dictionary of Science Words: Individual Title Six-Packs. (Discovery World Ser.). 24p. (gr. 1-2). 33.00 (978-0-7635-8482-5(7)) Rigby Education.

Dorling Kindersley Publishing Staff. Encyclopedia of Science. 2006. (ENG., Illus.). 448p. (J). (gr. 5-12). pap. 21.99 (978-0-7566-2220-6(4), DK Children) Dorling Kindersley Publishing, Inc.

—First Science Encyclopedia. (ENG.). (J). 2017. 136p. (gr. 2-5). 16.99 **(978-1-4654-4344-1(4))** 2008. (Illus.). 128p. (gr. k-3). 16.99 (978-0-7566-4296-9(5)) Dorling Kindersley Publishing, Inc. (DK Children).

Dorling Kindersley Publishing Staff. Science. 2014. (Visual Encyclopedia Ser.). (ENG., Illus.). 304p. (J). (gr. 2-5). 29.99 (978-1-4654-2046-6(0), DK Children) Dorling Kindersley Publishing, Inc.

Encyclopaedia Britannica, Inc. Staff. Britannica Illustrated Science Library Series (18 Title Series), 18 vols. 2010. 599.00 (978-1-61535-423-8(9)) Encyclopaedia Britannica, Inc.

Firth, Rachel. First Encyclopedia of Science. 2004. (First Encyclopedias Ser.). (ENG., Illus.). 64p. (J). (gr. 3-18). pap. 9.99 (978-0-7945-0273-7(3), Usborne) EDC Publishing.

—The Usborne Little Encyclopedia of Science: Internet-Linked. Hancock, David, illus. 2006. 64p. (J). 6.99 (978-0-7945-1095-4(7), Usborne) EDC Publishing.

Hackney Blackwell, Amy & Manar, Elizabeth P. UXL Encyclopedia of Science. 2015. (Illus.). 10p. (YA). (978-1-4144-3085-0(X)) Cengage Gale.

Holt, Rinehart and Winston Staff. Earth Science. 5th ed. 2003. (Holt Science & Technology Ser.). (ENG., Illus.). 880p. (gr. 7-7). 103.35 (978-0-03-066478-6(0)) Houghton Mifflin Harcourt Publishing Co.

—Holt Science & Technology: Online Edition Upgrade. 2nd ed. 2003. Level A. 2.60 (978-0-03-037236-0(4))Level K. 2.60 (978-0-03-037248-3(8)) Holt McDougal.

—Life Science. 5th ed. 2003. (Holt Science & Technology Ser.). (ENG., Illus.). 912p. (gr. 6-6). 103.35 (978-0-03-066476-2(4)) Houghton Mifflin Harcourt Publishing Co.

—Physical Science. 5th ed. 2003. (Holt Science & Technology Ser.). (ENG., Illus.). 848p. (gr. 8-8). 103.35 (978-0-03-066481-6(0)) Houghton Mifflin Harcourt Publishing Co.

Jugendhandbuch Naturwissen: Bausteine des Lebens, 6 vols., Vol. 1. (GER.). 144p. (J). pap. 750.00 (978-3-499-16203-9(2), M-7486) French & European Pubns., Inc.

Junior Science, 10 vols., Set. 2009. (gr. 4-9). 230.00 (978-1-60413-554-1(9), Chelsea Hse.) Facts On File, Inc.

Khan, Sarah. First Illustrated Science Dictionary. Robson, Kirsteen, ed. Whatmore, Candice, illus. 2013. (ENG.). 104p. (J). (gr. -1-3). 9.99 (978-0-7945-3383-0(3), Usborne) EDC Publishing.

Oxlade, Chris. Illustrated Dictionary of Science. 2004. (Illustrated Dictionaries Ser.). (Illus.). 382p. (J). lib. bdg. 37.95 (978-1-58086-363-6(9)) EDC Publishing.

Rigby Education Staff. Discovery World Red Dictionary. (Discovery World Ser.). (Illus.). 12p. (gr. 1-2). 31.00 (978-0-7635-2707-5(6)) Rigby Education.

Rogers, Kirsteen. Illustrated Elementary Science Dictionary IR. 2012. (Illustrated Dictionaries Ser.). 136p. (J). pap. 12.99 (978-0-7945-3255-0(1), Usborne) EDC Publishing.

Simon, Seymour. Science Dictionary. 2012. (Dover Children's Science Bks.). (ENG., Illus.). 272p. (J). (gr. 3-8). pap. 19.99 (978-0-486-48865-3(9)) Dover Pubns., Inc.

Stockley, Corinne, et al. The Usborne Illustrated Dictionary of Science. Rogers, Kirsteen, ed. Chen, Kuo Kang & Smith, Guy, illus. rev. ed. 2007. (Illustrated Dictionaries Ser.). 382p. (J). (gr. 4-7). pap. 29.99 (978-0-7945-1847-9(8), Usborne) EDC Publishing.

—The Usborne Illustrated Dictionary of Science: A Complete Reference Guide to Physics, Chemistry & Biology. Rogers, Kirsteen, ed. Smith, G. & Chen, Kuo Kang, trs. 2004. (Illustrated Dictionaries Ser.). (ENG., Illus.). 1p. (J). pap. 29.95 (978-0-7945-0064-1(1), Usborne) EDC Publishing.

Tatchell, Judy. Science Encyclopedia. 2004. (Library of Science Ser.). (Illus.). (J). (gr. 4-18). (ENG.). 1p. 39.95 (978-0-7460-3833-8(X)); 448p. lib. bdg. 47.95 (978-1-58086-337-7(X)) EDC Publishing.

U X L, ed. UXL Encyclopedia of Science, 10 vols. 3rd ed. 2015. (ENG., Illus.). 10p. 819.00 (978-1-4144-3075-1(2), UXL) Cengage Gale.

Westphal, Laurie E. Science Dictionary for Kids: The Essential Guide to Science Terms, Concepts, & Strategies. 2009. (ENG.). 144p. (J). (gr. 4-9). pap. 13.95 (978-1-59363-379-0(3), 9781593633790) Prufrock Pr.

Wilkes, Angela. Science Encyclopedia. Bhachu, Verindr, illus. 2009. (Library of Science Ser Ser.). 448p. (J). 39.99 (978-0-7945-2527-9(X), Usborne) EDC Publishing.

SCIENCE—EXPERIMENTS

see also Science Projects

see also particular branches of science with the subdivision Experiments, e.g. Chemistry—Experiments, etc.

Adamick, Mike. Dad's Book of Awesome Science Experiments: 30 Inventive Experiments to Excite the Whole Family! 2014. (ENG., Illus.). 192p. pap. 18.99 (978-1-4405-7077-3(9)) Adams Media Corp.

AIMS Education Foundation. Ray's Reflections. 2007. (ENG.). 200p. (gr. 4-8). pap., wbk. ed. 21.95 (978-1-881431-84-8(3), 1316) AIMS Education Foundation.

Alexander, Alison, et al. Science Interact 7. 2008. (Illus.). 108p. 36.50 (978-0-340-94897-2(3)) Hodder Education Group GBR. Dist: Trans-Atlantic Pubns., Inc.

Amery, Heather, et al. The Usborne Book of KnowHow. King, Colin, illus. 2008. (Usborne Book Of... Ser.). 127p. (J). (gr. 4-7). 19.99 (978-0-7945-2040-3(5), Usborne) EDC Publishing.

Andrews, Georgina & Knighton, Kate. Usborne 100 Science Experiments: Internet-Linked. Chisholm, Jane, ed. Baggott, Stella, illus. Allman, Howard, photos by. 2006. 96p. (J). (gr. 4-7). 15.99 (978-0-7945-1076-3(0)) EDC Publishing.

—100 Science Experiments. 2006. (Illus.). 96p. (J). (gr. 5). lib. bdg. 23.99 (978-1-58086-879-2(7), Usborne) EDC Publishing.

Ardley, Neil & Dorling Kindersley Publishing Staff. 101 Great Science Experiments. rev. ed. 2014. (ENG., Illus.). 120p. (J). (gr. 3-7). pap. 9.99 (978-1-4654-2826-4(7), DK Children) Dorling Kindersley Publishing, Inc.

Arner, Elizabeth. Weather Detectives. 2004. (Illus.). (J). (gr. 4-6). 40.00 (978-1-57336-404-1(5), I2065) Interaction Pubs., Inc.

Arnold, Nick. DIY Science. 2016. (ENG., Illus.). 120p. (J). (gr. 2). 12.95 (978-1-4549-2224-7(9)) Sterling Publishing Co., Inc.

Austin, John. Labcraft Wizards: Magical Projects & Experiments. 2016. (ENG., Illus.). 256p. (J). (gr. 4). pap. 16.99 (978-1-61373-621-0(5)) Chicago Review Pr., Inc.

Baker, Amber. The Ice Cube Experiment. 2009. (Real Life Readers Ser.). 12p. (gr. 1-2). pap. 5.90 (978-1-4042-7901-8(6), Rosen Classroom) Rosen Publishing Group, Inc., The.

Banqueri, Eduardo & Barres, Joseph M. Everyday Science: 66 Experiments That Explain the Small & Big Things All Around Us. 2016. (ENG., Illus.). 144p. (J). (gr. 3-7). pap. 14.99 (978-1-4380-0862-2(7)) Barron's Educational Series, Inc.

Barr, George. Fascinating Science Experiments for Young People. 2012. (Dover Children's Science Bks.). (ENG., Illus.). 160p. (J). (gr. 3-8). reprint ed. pap. 6.95 (978-0-486-27670-0(8), 27670-8) Dover Pubns., Inc.

Bearce, Stephanie. Explosive Experiments. 2017. (Twisted True Tales from Science Ser.: 0). (ENG., Illus.). 125p. (J). (gr. 4-7). pap. 8.95 (978-1-61821-576-5(0)) Prufrock Pr.

Beck, Esther. Cool Odor Decoders: Fun Science Projects about Smells, 1 vol. 2008. (Cool Science Ser.). (ENG.). 32p. (YA). (gr. 2-5). 28.50 (978-1-59928-909-0(1)) ABDO Publishing Co.

—Cool Sensory Suspense: Fun Science Projects about the Senses, 1 vol. 2008. (Cool Science Ser.). (ENG.). 32p. (YA). (gr. 2-5). 28.50 (978-1-59928-910-6(5)) ABDO Publishing Co.

—Cool Spy Supplies: Fun Top Secret Science Projects, 1 vol. 2008. (Cool Science Ser.). (ENG.). 32p. (YA). (gr. 2-5). 28.50 (978-1-59928-911-3(3)) ABDO Publishing Co.

Becker, Helaine. Science on the Loose: Amazing Activities & Science Facts You'll Never Believe. Dávila, Claudia & Owlkids Books Inc. Staff, illus. 2008. (ENG.). 64p. (J). (gr. 3-6). pap. 10.95 (978-1-897349-19-9(X), Maple Tree Pr.) Owlkids Bks. Inc. CAN. Dist: Publishers Group West (PGW).

Bell-Rehwoldt, Sheri. Science Experiments That Surprise & Delight: Fun Projects for Curious Kids. 2011. (Kitchen Science Ser.). (ENG.). 32p. (gr. 3-4). pap. 47.70 (978-1-4296-6421-9(5), Edge Bks.) Capstone Press of Coughlan Cos.

Bennett, Andrea T. & Kessler, James H. Apples, Bubbles, & Crystals: Your Science ABCs. Sarecky, Melody, illus. 2004. (J). (978-0-8412-3944-9(4)) American Chemical Society.

Bingham, Jane. El Libro de los Experimentos Científicos. (SPA., Illus.). (YA). (gr. 5-8). pap. (978-950-724-263-2(5), LMA8241) Lumen ARG. Dist: Lectorum Pubns., Inc.

Biskup, Agnieszka & Enz, Tammy. Max Axiom Science & Engineering Activities. Baez, Marcelo, illus. 2015. (Max Axiom Science & Engineering Activities Ser.). (ENG.). 32p. (gr. 3-4). pap. 31.80 (978-1-4914-2536-7(9), Graphic Library) Capstone Press of Coughlan Cos.

—Super Cool Science & Engineering Activities. 2015. (ENG., Illus.). 128p. (gr. 3-4). pap. 14.95 (978-1-62370-232-8(1)) Capstone Young Readers of Coughlan Cos.

Blevins, Wiley. You Can Use a Magnifying Glass. 2004. (Rookie Read-About Science Ser.). (ENG., Illus.). 32p. (J). (gr. 1-2). pap. 4.95 (978-0-516-27328-0(0), Children's Pr.) Scholastic Library Publishing.

Brandolini, Anita J. Fizz, Bubble & Flash! Element Explorations & Atom Adventures for Hands-On Science Fun! 2004. (Kids Can Bks.). (ENG., Illus.). 128p. (J). pap. 14.25 (978-1-885593-83-2(X), Ideal Pubns.) Worthy Publishing.

Braun, Eric. Mad Margaret Experiments with the Scientific Method, 1 vol. Boyden, Robin, illus. 2012. (In the Science Lab Ser.). (ENG.). 24p. (gr. 2-3). pap. 9.95 (978-1-4048-7710-8(X)); lib. bdg. 26.65 (978-1-4048-7373-5(2)) Picture Window Bks.

Brown, Jordan D. Crazy Concoctions: A Mad Scientist's Guide to Messy Mixtures. Owsley, Anthony, illus. 2012. (ENG.). 80p. (J). (gr. 3-7). 14.95 (978-1-936140-51-0(9)) Charlesbridge Publishing, Inc.

—Science Stunts: Fun Feats of Physics. Owsley, Anthony, illus. 2016. (ENG.). 80p. (J). (gr. 3-7). 16.95 (978-1-62354-064-7(X)) Charlesbridge Publishing, Inc.

Brunelle, Lynn. Big Science for Little People: 52 Activities to Help You & Your Child Discover the Wonders of Science. 2016. (ENG., Illus.). 144p. (gr. -1-3). pap. 14.95 (978-1-61180-350-1(0), Roost Books) Shambhala Pubns., Inc.

—Pop Bottle Science. Meisel, Paul, illus. 2004. (ENG.). 128p. (gr. 2-6). pap. 17.95 (978-0-7611-2980-6(4), 12980) Workman Publishing Co., Inc.

Brynie, Faith Hickman. Six-Minute Nature Experiments. Whittingham, Kim, illus. 2006. 80p. (J). (gr. 4-8). reprint ed. pap. 11.00 (978-1-4223-5105-5(X)) DIANE Publishing Co.

Butterfield, M. & Edom, H. Science with Air. rev. ed. 2008. (Science Activities Ser.). 24p. (J). pap. 5.99 (978-0-7945-2331-2(5), Usborne) EDC Publishing.

Canavan, Thomas. Awesome Experiments with Living Things. Linley, Adam, illus. 2017. (Mind-Blowing Science Experiments Ser.). 32p. (gr. 4-5). pap. 63.00 **(978-1-5382-0728-4(1))** Stevens, Gareth Publishing LLLP.

—Fantastic Experiments with Forces. Linley, Adam, illus. 2017. (Mind-Blowing Science Experiments Ser.). 32p. (gr. 4-5). pap. 63.00 **(978-1-5382-0731-4(1))** Stevens, Gareth Publishing LLLP.

Candlewick Press, Candlewick. Ruff Ruffman's 44 Favorite Science Activities. WGBH, illus. 2015. (Fetch! with Ruff Ruffman Ser.). (ENG.). 132p. (J). (gr. 3-7). pap. 12.99 (978-0-7636-7432-8(X), Candlewick Entertainment) Candlewick Pr.

Cardenas, Ernesto A. The Science Lab. 2009. pap. 4.95 (978-1-60698-094-1(7)) Milo Educational Bks. & Resources.

Carlson Berne, Emma. Answer! Analyze Your Data. 2014. (Scientific Method in Action Ser.). (Illus.). 24p. (J). (gr. 3-6). 23.60 (978-1-4777-2930-4(5)); pap. 8.25 (978-1-4777-3017-1(6)); pap. 49.50 (978-1-4777-3088-1(5)) Rosen Publishing Group, Inc., The. (PowerKids Pr.).

—Share! Present Your Findings. 2014. (Scientific Method in Action Ser.). (Illus.). 24p. (J). (gr. 3-6). pap. 49.50 (978-1-4777-3089-8(3), PowerKids Pr.) Rosen Publishing Group, Inc., The.

Churchill, E. Richard, et al. 365 More Simple Science Experiments with Everyday Materials. Zweifel, Frances, illus. 2014. (ENG.). 320p. (J). (gr. -1-17). pap. 12.95 (978-1-57912-967-5(6), 81967, Black Dog & Leventhal Pubs. Inc.) Hachette Bks.

—365 Simple Science Experiments with Everyday Materials. Zweifel, Frances, illus. 2013. (ENG.). 306p. (J). (gr. -1-17). pap. 12.99 (978-1-57912-927-9(7), 81927, Black Dog & Leventhal Pubs. Inc.) Hachette Bks.

Ciencia con Todo: Experimentos Simples con las Cosas Que Nos Rodean. (Coleccion Pura Ciencia).Tr. of Everyday Science. (SPA.). (YA). (gr. 5-8). pap. 9.56 (978-950-24-0746-3(6)) Albatros ARG. Dist: Lectorum Pubns., Inc.

Ciencia en Segundos: Experimentos Que Puedes Hacer en 10 Minutos o Menos.Tr. of Science in Seconds. (SPA.). (YA). (gr. 5-8). pap. 9.56 (978-950-24-0748-7(2)) Albatros ARG. Dist: Lectorum Pubns., Inc.

Ciencia Magica: Experimentos Extranos y Asombrosos. (SPA.). (YA). (gr. 5-8). pap. (978-950-24-0747-0(4)) Albatros ARG. Dist: Lectorum Pubns., Inc.

Citro, Asia. The Curious Kid's Science Book: 100+ Creative Hands-On Activities for Ages 4-8. Citro, Asia, photos by. 2015. (ENG., Illus.). 224p. (gr. -1-3). pap. 21.95 (978-1-943147-00-7(0)) Innovation Pr., The.

Claybourne, Anna. Make It Change!, 1 vol. Scott, Kimberly & Dean, Venetia, illus. 2014. (Whiz Kid Science Ser.). (ENG.). 32p. (gr. 2-4). 29.99 (978-1-4109-6746-6(8), Read Me!) Heinemann-Raintree.

—Make It Grow!, 1 vol. Scott, Kimberly & Dean, Venetia, illus. 2014. (Whiz Kid Science Ser.). (ENG.). 32p. (gr. 2-4). 29.99 (978-1-4109-6748-0(4), Read Me!) Heinemann-Raintree.

—Make It Splash!, 1 vol. Scott, Kimberly & Dean, Venetia, illus. 2014. (Whiz Kid Science Ser.). (ENG.). 32p. (gr. 2-4). 29.99 (978-1-4109-6749-7(2), Read Me!) Heinemann-Raintree.

—The Science of a Glass of Water: The Science of States of Matter. 2009. (Science of... Ser.). (Illus.). 32p. (YA). (gr. 3-6). lib. bdg. 26.00 (978-1-4339-0041-9(6)) Stevens, Gareth Publishing LLLP.

Cleland, Jo. I Can Make Colors. 2006. (Science about Me Ser.). (Illus.). 8p. (J). (gr. 3-7). pap. 5.95 (978-1-59515-925-0(8)) Rourke Educational Media.

Cobb, Allan B. Super Science Projects about Animals in Their Habitats. 2005. (Psyched for Science Ser.). (Illus.). 48p. (YA). (gr. 5-8). lib. bdg. 29.25 (978-0-8239-3175-0(7), SCADHO) Rosen Publishing Group, Inc., The.

—Super Science Projects about Oceans. 2005. (Psyched for Science Ser.). (Illus.). 48p. (YA). (gr. 5-8). lib. bdg. 29.25 (978-0-8239-3174-3(9), SCOCEA) Rosen Publishing Group, Inc., The.

—Super Science Projects about Sound. 2005. (Psyched for Science Ser.). (Illus.). 48p. (YA). (gr. 5-8). lib. bdg. 29.25 (978-0-8239-3176-7(5), SCSOUN) Rosen Publishing Group, Inc., The.

Cobb, Vicki. I Face the Wind. Gorton, Julia, illus. 2003. (Science Play Ser.). (ENG.). 40p. (J). (gr. -1-3). 16.99 *(978-0-688-17840-6(5))* HarperCollins Pubs.

—Science Experiments You Can Eat. Carpenter, Tad, illus. 2016. 256p. (J). (gr. 3-7). pap. 9.99 *(978-0-06-237729-6(9))* HarperCollins Pubs.

—Science Surprises: More Than 100 Amazing Experiments. 2015. (ENG., Illus.). 192p. (J). (gr. 3-7). pap. 14.99 *(978-1-63220-316-8(2),* Sky Pony Pr.) Skyhorse Publishing Co., Inc.

—See for Yourself! More Than 100 Amazing Experiments for Science Fairs & School Projects. Klug, Dave, illus. 2nd ed. 2010. (ENG.). 192p. (J). (gr. 1-3). pap. 14.95 *(978-1-61608-083-9(3),* 608083) Skyhorse Publishing Co., Inc.

Cobb, Vicki & Darling, Kathy. We Dare You! Hundreds of Fun Science Bets, Challenges, & Experiments You Can Do at Home. rev. ed. 2015. (ENG., Illus.). 336p. (J). (gr. 2-7). pap. 12.95 *(978-1-62914-631-7(5),* Sky Pony Pr.) Skyhorse Publishing Co., Inc.

—We Dare You! Hundreds of Fun Science Experiments, Tricks, & Games You Can Try at Home. 2009. (ENG., Illus.). 336p. (J). (gr. 2-7). pap. 14.95 *(978-1-60239-775-0(9),* 239775) Skyhorse Publishing Co., Inc.

Conklin, Wendy. Surviving the Wild Backyard. 2015. (Building Fluency Through Reader's Theater Ser.). (ENG., Illus.). 32p. (gr. 4-4). pap. 7.99 *(978-1-4938-1290-5(4))* Teacher Created Materials, Inc.

Connolly, Sean. The Book of Potentially Catastrophic Science: 50 Experiments for Daring Young Scientists. 2010. (Irresponsible Science Ser.). (ENG., Illus.). 306p. (J). (gr. 3-9). 14.95 *(978-0-7611-5687-1(9),* 15687) Workman Publishing Co., Inc.

—The Book of Totally Irresponsible Science: 64 Daring Experiments for Young Scientists. 2008. (Irresponsible Science Ser.). (ENG., Illus.). 205p. (J). (gr. 3-9). 12.95 *(978-0-7611-5020-6(X),* 15020) Workman Publishing Co., Inc.

—The Totally Irresponsible Science Kit: 18 Daring Experiments for Young Scientists. 2015. (Irresponsible Science Ser.). (ENG., Illus.). 72p. (J). pap. 22.95 *(978-0-7611-8178-1(4))* Workman Publishing Co., Inc.

Cook, Trevor. Science Lab Set. 2009. (Illus.). (J). (gr. 4-7). 151.50 *(978-1-4358-2826-1(7),* PowerKids Pr.) Rosen Publishing Group, Inc., The.

Cook, Trevor & Henry, Sally. Awesome Experiments: Electricity & Magnetism, Forces, Plants & Living Things, Heat, Materials, Light & Sound. 2012. (ENG., Illus.). 128p. (J). pap. 9.95 *(978-1-84837-604-5(9))* Arcturus Publishing GBR. Dist: Bookmasters Distribution.

Cool Science, 1 vol., Set. Incl. Cool Distance Assistants: Fun Science Projects to Propel Things. Hopwood, James. 28.50 *(978-1-59928-906-9(7));* Cool Dry Ice Devices: Fun Science Projects with Dry Ice. Hopwood, James. 28.50 *(978-1-59928-907-6(5));* Cool Gravity Activities: Fun Science Projects about Balance. Hopwood, James. 28.50 *(978-1-59928-908-3(3));* Cool Odor Decoders: Fun Science Projects about Smells. Beck, Esther. 28.50 *(978-1-59928-909-0(1));* Cool Sensory Suspense: Fun Science Projects about the Senses. Beck, Esther. 28.50 *(978-1-59928-910-6(5));* Cool Spy Supplies: Fun Top Secret Science Projects. Beck, Esther. 28.50 *(978-1-59928-911-3(3));* (YA). (gr. 2-5). (Cool Science Ser.: 6). (ENG.). 32p. 2008. 171.00 *(978-1-59928-905-2(9),* Checkerboard Library) ABDO Publishing Co.

Crabtree Publishing Co. Staff & Burns, Kylie. What's Going On? Collecting & Recording Your Data. 2009. (Step into Science Ser.). (ENG., Illus.). 32p. (J). (gr. 3-6). pap. *(978-0-7787-5170-0(8));* lib. bdg. *(978-0-7787-5155-7(4))* Crabtree Publishing Co.

—What's the Problem? How to Start Your Scientific Investigation. 2009. (Step into Science Ser.). (ENG., Illus.). 32p. (J). (gr. 3-6). pap. *(978-0-7787-5173-1(2));* lib. bdg. *(978-0-7787-5158-8(9))* Crabtree Publishing Co.

Crabtree Publishing Co. Staff & Challen, Paul. What Just Happened? Reading Results & Making Inferences. 2009. (Step into Science Ser.). (ENG., Illus.). 32p. (J). (gr. 3-6). pap. *(978-0-7787-5171-7(6));* lib. bdg. *(978-0-7787-5156-4(2))* Crabtree Publishing Co.

—What's Going to Happen? Making Your Hypothesis. 2009. (Step into Science Ser.). (ENG., Illus.). 32p. (J). (gr. 3-6). pap. *(978-0-7787-5172-4(4));* lib. bdg. *(978-0-7787-5157-1(0))* Crabtree Publishing Co.

Crabtree Publishing Co. Staff & Hyde, Natalie. What's the Plan? Designing Your Experiment. 2009. (Step into Science Ser.). (ENG., Illus.). 32p. (J). (gr. 3-6). pap. *(978-0-7787-5169-4(4));* lib. bdg. *(978-0-7787-5154-0(6))* Crabtree Publishing Co.

Crabtree Publishing Co. Staff & Johnson, Robin. What Do We Know Now? Drawing Conclusions & Answering the Question. 2009. (Step into Science Ser.). (ENG., Illus.). 32p. (J). (gr. 3-6). pap. *(978-0-7787-5168-7(6));* lib. bdg. *(978-0-7787-5153-3(8))* Crabtree Publishing Co.

Crane, Cody. Phineas & Ferb Big Book of Science Experiments. 2013. (Illus.). 136p. (J). pap. *(978-0-545-48195-3(3))* Scholastic, Inc.

Creative Team of Weldon Owen. 101 Things to Do Before You Grow Up: Fun Activities for You to Check off Your List. 2015. (101 Things Ser.). (ENG.). 144p. (J). (gr. 3-7). spiral bd. 12.95 *(978-1-63322-003-4(6))* Quarto Publishing Group USA.

Crupi, Jaclyn. Super Fun Science with Cool & Challenging Experiments: Learn * Question * Answer. 2017. (ENG.). 48p. (J). (gr. 1-5). 9.99 ***(978-1-4380-5010-2(0))*** Barron's Educational Series, Inc.

Daronco, Mickey & Priesti, Lori. Measuring Tools. 2011. (Early Connections Ser.). (J). *(978-1-61672-641-6(5))* Benchmark Education Co.

David C. Cook Publishing Company Staff, creator. Fun Science That Teaches God's Word for Tweeners. 2008. (BFS Ser.). (Illus.). 120p. (gr. 4-6). per. 19.99 *(978-0-7814-4558-0(2))* Cook, David C.

Davids, Stacy B. Strange but True Science, 1 vol. 2010. (Strange but True Ser.). (ENG.). 32p. (gr. 1-2). lib. bdg. 26.65 *(978-1-4296-4552-2(0),* Blazers) Capstone Press of Coughlan Cos.

Discovery Channel (Firm) Staff, contrib. by. Mythbusters. 2013. (Illus.). 48p. (J). *(978-1-935442-24-0(4),* Beckon Bks.) Southwestern Publishing Group, Inc.

Dorling Kindersley Publishing Staff. It Can't Be True!, No. 2. 2016. (ENG., Illus.). 192p. (J). (gr. 3-7). 19.99 *(978-1-4654-5407-2(1),* DK Children) Dorling Kindersley Publishing, Inc.

Dorling Kindersley Publishing Staff. Look I'm a Scientist. 2017. (ENG., Illus.). 48p. (J). ***(978-0-241-23107-4(8))*** Dorling Kindersley Publishing, Inc.

Dorling Kindersley Publishing Staff & Challoner, Jack. Maker Lab: 28 Super Cool Projects. 2016. (ENG., Illus.). 160p. (J). (gr. 3-7). 19.99 *(978-1-4654-5135-4(8),* DK Children) Dorling Kindersley Publishing, Inc.

Doudna, Kelly. I'll Use a Hand Lens with My Friends!, 1 vol. 2007. (Science Made Simple Ser.). (ENG., Illus.). 24p. (J). (gr. k-3). lib. bdg. 24.21 *(978-1-59928-586-3(X),* SandCastle) ABDO Publishing Co.

—I'm on a Roll with Variable Control!, 1 vol. 2007. (Science Made Simple Ser.). (ENG., Illus.). 24p. (J). (gr. k-3). lib. bdg. 24.21 *(978-1-59928-590-0(8),* SandCastle) ABDO Publishing Co.

—It's a Date, Let's Investigate!, 1 vol. 2007. (Science Made Simple Ser.). (ENG., Illus.). 24p. (J). (gr. k-3). lib. bdg. 24.21 *(978-1-59928-596-2(7),* SandCastle) ABDO Publishing Co.

—It's an Event When We Experiment!, 1 vol. 2007. (Science Made Simple Ser.). (ENG., Illus.). 24p. (J). (gr. k-3). lib. bdg. 24.21 *(978-1-59928-598-6(3),* SandCastle) ABDO Publishing Co.

—The Kid's Book of Simple Everyday Science. 2013. (ENG., Illus.). 112p. (J). (gr. k-4). pap. 13.95 *(978-1-938063-34-3(1),* Mighty Media Kids) Mighty Media Pr.

—Super Simple Things to Do with Balloons: Fun & Easy Science for Kids, 1 vol. 2011. (Super Simple Science Ser.). (ENG., Illus.). 24p. (J). (gr. k-3). lib. bdg. 25.65 *(978-1-61714-672-5(2))* ABDO Publishing Co.

—Super Simple Things to Do with Bubbles: Fun & Easy Science for Kids, 1 vol. 2011. (Super Simple Science Ser.). (ENG., Illus.). 24p. (J). (gr. k-3). 25.65 *(978-1-61714-673-2(0))* ABDO Publishing Co.

—Super Simple Things to Do with Plants: Fun & Easy Science for Kids, 1 vol. 2011. (Super Simple Science Ser.). (ENG., Illus.). 24p. (J). (gr. k-3). lib. bdg. 25.65 *(978-1-61714-674-9(9))* ABDO Publishing Co.

—Super Simple Things to Do with Pressure: Fun & Easy Science for Kids, 1 vol. 2011. (Super Simple Science Ser.). (ENG., Illus.). 24p. (J). (gr. k-3). lib. bdg. 25.65 *(978-1-61714-675-6(7))* ABDO Publishing Co.

—Super Simple Things to Do with Temperature: Fun & Easy Science for Kids, 1 vol. 2011. (Super Simple Science Ser.). (ENG., Illus.). 24p. (J). (gr. k-3). lib. bdg. 25.65 *(978-1-61714-676-3(5))* ABDO Publishing Co.

—Super Simple Things to Do with Water: Fun & Easy Science for Kids, 1 vol. 2011. (Super Simple Science Ser.). (ENG., Illus.). 24p. (J). (gr. k-3). lib. bdg. 25.65 *(978-1-61714-677-0(3))* ABDO Publishing Co.

Doyle, James. A Young Scientist's Guide to Defying Disasters with Skill & Daring: Includes 20 Experiments for the Sink, Bathtub & Backyard, 1 vol. Brozyna, Andrew, illus. 2012. (ENG.). 160p. (J). (gr. 5-6). 14.99 *(978-1-4236-2440-0(8))* Gibbs Smith, Publisher.

Dyer, Janice. Get into Wow-Factor Science. 2017. (Illus.). 32p. (J). ***(978-0-7787-3643-1(1))*** Crabtree Publishing Co.

Ebner, Aviva. Junior Science Experiments on Filetrade; Set, 4-Volumes. 2007. (Experiments Ser.). (gr. 4-9). 740.00 *(978-0-8160-7309-2(0))* Facts On File, Inc.

Ecociencia: Experimentos Ecologicos para Chicos.Tr. of Projects for a Healthy Planet. (SPA.). (YA). (gr. 5-8). pap. 9.56 *(978-950-24-0745-6(8))* Albatros ARG. Dist: Lectorum Pubns., Inc.

Editors of TIME For Kids Magazine. Time for Kids Big Book of Science Experiments: A Step-by-Step Guide. 2011. (ENG., Illus.). 192p. (J). (gr. 3-17). 19.95 *(978-1-60320-893-2(3))* Time Inc. Bks.

Edom, H. Science Activities, Vol. 1. 2010. (Science Activities Ser.). 72p. (J). 13.99 *(978-0-7945-2752-5(3),* Usborne) EDC Publishing.

Edom, Helen. Science with Plants. Abel, Simone, illus. rev. ed. 2007. (Science Activities Ser.). 24p. (J). (gr. 3-7). pap. 5.99 *(978-0-7945-1485-3(5),* Usborne) EDC Publishing.

Enz, Tammy & Biskup, Agnieszka. Max Axiom Science & Engineering Activities. Baez, Marcelo, illus. 2015. (Max Axiom Science & Engineering Activities Ser.). (ENG.). 32p. (gr. 3-4). lib. bdg. 122.60 *(978-1-4914-2535-0(0),* Graphic Library) Capstone Press of Coughlan Cos.

Enz, Tammy & Wheeler-Toppen, Jodi Lyn. Recycled Science. 2016. (Recycled Science Ser.). (ENG.). 32p. (gr. 3-4). lib. bdg. 111.96 *(978-1-5157-0876-6(4),* Edge Bks.) Capstone Press of Coughlan Cos.

Evan-Moor Staff. How to Do Science Experiments with Children: Grades 2-4. 2005. 304p. (J). (gr. 2-4). pap. 29.99 *(978-1-55799-936-8(8),* EMC 5001) Evan-Moor Educational Pubs.

Experiment Central: Understanding Scientific Principles Through Projects, 6 vols. 2nd ed. 2010. (ENG.). (J). 522.00 *(978-1-4144-7613-1(2),* UXL) Cengage Gale.

Experiments for Future STEM Professionals: Set 1. 2016. (Experiments for Future STEM Professionals Ser.). 128p. (gr. 6-6). lib. bdg. 149.08 *(978-0-7660-7502-3(8))* Enslow Pubs., Inc.

Experiments for Future STEM Professionals: Set 2. 2016. (Experiments for Future STEM Professionals Ser.). 128p. (J). lib. bdg. 149.08 *(978-0-7660-8391-2(8))* Enslow Pubs., Inc.

Experiments for Future STEM Professionals: Sets 1 - 2. 2016. (Experiments for Future STEM Professionals Ser.). 128p. (J). lib. bdg. 298.16 *(978-0-7660-8471-1(X))* Enslow Pubs., Inc.

Exploratorium Staff. Exploralab. 2013. (ENG.). 128p. (J). 24.95 *(978-1-61628-491-6(9))* Weldon Owen, Inc.

Factastic Challenge, Grades 1-2. 2005. (J). spiral bd. 15.95 *(978-1-932855-17-3(3))* becker&mayer! books.

Factastic Challenge, Grades 3-4. 2005. (J). spiral bd. 15.95 *(978-1-932855-18-0(1))* becker&mayer! books.

Factastic Challenge, Grades 5-6. 2005. (J). spiral bd. 15.95 *(978-1-932855-19-7(X))* becker&mayer! books.

Falk, John H., et al. Bubble Monster: And Other Science Fun. 2003. (Illus.). 176p. (J). (gr. -1-3). pap. 17.95 *(978-1-55652-301-4(7))* Chicago Review Pr., Inc.

Farndon, John. Experimenting with Science, 2 bks., Set. Incl. Experimenting with Chemistry. 104p. lib. bdg. 24.95 *(978-0-7614-3928-8(5));* Experimenting with Physics. 112p. (YA). lib. bdg. 35.64 *(978-0-7614-3929-5(3));* (gr. 4-18). 2008. Set lib. bdg. 71.29 *(978-0-7614-3967-7(6),* Benchmark Bks.) Marshall Cavendish Corp.

Felix, Rebecca. Mini Science Fun. 2017. (Mini Makers Ser.). (ENG.). 32p. (J). (gr. 2-5). 12.99 ***(978-1-5124-3840-6(5),*** Lerner Pubns.); 39.99 ***(978-1-5124-3839-0(1),*** Lerner Pubns.); 39.99 ***(978-1-5124-2812-4(4),*** Lerner Pubns.); (Illus.). 26.65 *(978-1-5124-2634-2(2))* Lerner Publishing Group.

First Science Experiments. 2016. (First Science Experiments Ser.). 32p. (gr. 3-2). 114.00 *(978-1-4994-8098-6(9),* Windmill Bks.) Rosen Publishing Group, Inc., The.

Fredericks, Anthony D. Simple Nature Experiments with Everyday Materials. Zweifel, Frances, illus. 2004. 128p. (J). (gr. 4-8). reprint ed. pap. 6.00 *(978-0-7567-7727-2(5))* DIANE Publishing Co.

Frederickson, A. Experimentos Sencillos con la Naturaleza. 2004. (Juego de la Ciencia Ser.). (SPA., Illus.). 128p. *(978-84-95456-48-9(6),* 87801) Ediciones Oniro S.A.

Freedman, Claire. Monstersaurus. Cort, Ben, illus. 2013. (J). *(978-1-4351-4952-6(1))* Barnes & Noble, Inc.

Gadd, Ken. Applied Science. 2003. (ENG., Illus.). 352p. (YA). pap. 47.50 *(978-0-7487-7044-1(5))* Nelson Thornes Ltd. GBR. Dist: Trans-Atlantic Pubns., Inc.

Gardner, Martin. Martin Gardner's Science Magic: Tricks & Puzzles. 2011. (Dover Magic Bks.). (ENG., Illus.). 96p. (gr. 4). pap. 4.99 *(978-0-486-47657-5(X))* Dover Pubns., Inc.

Gardner, Robert. Bicycle Science Projects: Physics on Wheels. 2004. (Science Fair Success Ser.). (Illus.). 112p. (J). lib. bdg. 27.94 *(978-0-7660-1630-9(7))* Enslow Pubs., Inc.

—Energy Experiments Using Ice Cubes, Springs, Magnets, & More: One Hour or Less Science Experiments. 2012. (Last-Minute Science Projects Ser.). (Illus.). 48p. (J). (gr. 5-18). 25.27 *(978-0-7660-3959-9(5))* Enslow Pubs., Inc.

—Experiments with Electricity & Magnetism. 2017. (Science Whiz Experiments Ser.). 128p. (gr. 5-5). 37.27 ***(978-0-7660-8678-4(X))*** Enslow Pubs., Inc.

—Far-Out Science Projects with Height & Depth: How High Is up? How Low Is Down? 2003. (Sensational Science Experiments Ser.). (Illus.). 48p. (J). (gr. 1-4). lib. bdg. 25.27 *(978-0-7660-2016-0(9))* Enslow Pubs., Inc.

—Forces & Motion Science Fair Projects, Revised & Expanded Using the Scientific Method. LaBaff, Tom & LaBaff, Stephanie, illus. 2010. (Physics Science Projects Using the Scientific Method Ser.). 160p. (J). (gr. 5-18). 35.94 *(978-0-7660-3415-0(1))* Enslow Pubs., Inc.

—Forces & Motion Science Fair Projects Using Water Balloons, Pulleys, & Other Stuff. 2004. (Physics! Best Science Projects Ser.). (Illus.). 128p. (J). lib. bdg. 27.94 *(978-0-7660-2129-7(7))* Enslow Pubs., Inc.

—How Big Is Big? Science Projects with Volume. 2015. (Hot Science Experiments Ser.). 48p. (J). (gr. 3-4). 25.27 *(978-0-7660-6620-5(7))* Enslow Pubs., Inc.

—It's about Time! Science Projects: How Long Does It Take? 2003. (Sensational Science Experiments Ser.). (Illus.). 48p. (J). (gr. 1-4). lib. bdg. 25.27 *(978-0-7660-2012-2(6))* Enslow Pubs., Inc.

—Light, Sound, & Waves Science Fair Projects: Using Sunglasses, Guitars, CDs, & Other Stuff. 2004. (Physics! Best Science Projects Ser.). (Illus.). 128p. (J). lib. bdg. 27.94 *(978-0-7660-2126-6(2))* Enslow Pubs., Inc.

—Melting, Freezing, & Boiling Science Projects with Matter. 2006. (Fantastic Physical Science Experiments Ser.). (Illus.). 48p. (J). (gr. 4-7). lib. bdg. 25.27 *(978-0-7660-2589-9(6),* Enslow Elementary) Enslow Pubs., Inc.

—Planet Earth Science Fair Projects Using the Moon, Stars, Beach Balls, Frisbees, & Other Far-Out Stuff. 2005. (Earth Science! Best Science Projects Ser.). (Illus.). 128p. (J). lib. bdg. 27.94 *(978-0-7660-2362-8(1),* 1238538) Enslow Pubs., Inc.

—Really Hot Science Projects with Temperature: How Hot Is It? How Cold Is It? 2003. (Sensational Science Experiments Ser.). (Illus.). 48p. (J). lib. bdg. 25.27 *(978-0-7660-2015-3(0))* Enslow Pubs., Inc.

—Science Fair Projects about the Properties of Matter Using Marbles, Water, Balloons, & More. Tom, LaBaff, illus. 2004. (Physics! Best Science Projects Ser.). 128p. (J). lib. bdg. 27.94 *(978-0-7660-2128-0(9))* Enslow Pubs., Inc.

—Sizzling Science Projects with Heat & Energy. LaBaff, Tom, illus. 2006. (Fantastic Physical Science Experiments Ser.). 48p. (J). (gr. 3-4). lib. bdg. 25.27 *(978-0-7660-2586-8(1),* Enslow Elementary) Enslow Pubs., Inc.

—Solids, Liquids, & Gases Experiments Using Water, Air, Marbles, & More: One Hour or Less Science Experiments. 2012. (Last-Minute Science Projects Ser.). (Illus.). 48p. (J). (gr. 5-18). 25.27 *(978-0-7660-3962-9(5))* Enslow Pubs., Inc.

—Split-Second Science Projects with Speed: How Fast Does It Go? 2003. (Sensational Science Experiments Ser.). (Illus.). 48p. (J). (gr. 1-4). lib. bdg. 25.27 *(978-0-7660-2017-7(7))* Enslow Pubs., Inc.

—Super-Sized Science Projects with Volume: How Much Space Does It Take Up? 2003. (Sensational Science Experiments Ser.). (Illus.). 48p. (J). lib. bdg. 25.27 *(978-0-7660-2014-6(2))* Enslow Pubs., Inc.

Gardner, Robert & Conklin, Joshua. Experiments for Future Chemists. 2016. (Experiments for Future STEM Professionals Ser.). 128p. (J). (gr. 6-6). lib. bdg. 37.27 *(978-0-7660-7856-7(6))* Enslow Pubs., Inc.

—Experiments for Future Doctors. 2016. (Experiments for Future STEM Professionals Ser.). 128p. (J). (gr. 6-6). 37.27 *(978-0-7660-7854-3(X))* Enslow Pubs., Inc.

—A Kid's Book of Experiments about Light. 2016. (Surprising Science Experiments Ser.). (ENG., Illus.). 48p. (J). (gr. 4-4). 27.93 *(978-0-7660-7205-3(3))* Enslow Pubs., Inc.

—A Kid's Book of Experiments about Sound. 2016. (Surprising Science Experiments Ser.). (ENG., Illus.). 48p. (J). (gr. 4-4). 27.93 *(978-0-7660-7209-1(6))* Enslow Pubs., Inc.

—A Kid's Book of Experiments with Stars. 2016. (Surprising Science Experiments Ser.). (ENG., Illus.). 48p. (J). (gr. 4-4). lib. bdg. 27.93 *(978-0-7660-7270-1(3))* Enslow Pubs., Inc.

Gardner, Robert & Shortelle, Dennis. Slam Dunk! Science Projects with Basketball. 2009. (Score! Sports Science Projects Ser.). (Illus.). 104p. (J). (gr. 5-9). lib. bdg. 33.27 *(978-0-7660-3366-5(X))* Enslow Pubs., Inc.

Garrett, Ginger. Scientists Ask Questions. 2005. (Rookie Read-About Science Ser.). (ENG., Illus.). 32p. (J). (gr. 1-2). pap. 4.95 *(978-0-516-24662-8(3),* Children's Pr.) Scholastic Library Publishing.

Getting Creative with Fab Lab. 2016. (Getting Creative with Fab Lab Ser.). 00064p. (J). (gr. 6-6). 206.70 *(978-1-5081-7366-3(4),* Rosen Central) Rosen Publishing Group, Inc., The.

Gingold, Janet. My Adventure as a Scientist: Advanced My Adventure. 2009. (ENG.). 44p. (J). pap. 8.99 *(978-1-59092-408-2(8))* Blue Forge Pr.

Goodstein, Madeline P. Plastics & Polymers Science Fair Projects Using Hair Gel, Soda Bottles, & Slimy Stuff. 2004. (Chemistry! Best Science Projects Ser.). (Illus.). 128p. (J). lib. bdg. 27.94 *(978-0-7660-2123-5(8))* Enslow Pubs., Inc.

—Water Science Fair Projects Using Ice Cubes, Super Soakers, & Other Wet Stuff. 2004. (Chemistry! Best Science Projects Ser.). (Illus.). 128p. (J). lib. bdg. 27.94 *(978-0-7660-2124-2(6))* Enslow Pubs., Inc.

—Wheels! Science Projects with Bicycles, Skateboards, & Skates. 2009. (Score! Sports Science Projects Ser.). (Illus.). 104p. (J). (gr. 5-9). lib. bdg. 33.27 *(978-0-7660-3107-4(1))* Enslow Pubs., Inc.

Gould, Alan. Hot Water & Warm Homes from Sunlight. Gould, Alan et al, illus. Sneider, Cary I., photos by. rev. ed. 2005. (Great Explorations in Math & Science Ser.). 80p. 13.50 *(978-1-931542-04-3(X),* GEMS) Univ. of California, Berkeley, Lawrence Hall of Science.

Graham, Ian. The Science of a Bicycle: The Science of Forces. 2009. (Science of... Ser.). 32p. (YA). (gr. 3-6). lib. bdg. 26.00 *(978-1-4339-0040-2(8))* Stevens, Gareth Publishing LLLP.

Gray, Susan H. Super Cool Science Experiments: Seeds. 2009. (Explorer Library: Science Explorer Ser.). (ENG.). 32p. (gr. 4-8). lib. bdg. 28.50 *(978-1-60279-514-3(2),* 200293) Cherry Lake Publishing.

Green, Joey. The Electric Pickle: 50 Experiments from the Periodic Table, from Aluminum to Zinc. 2017. (ENG.). 272p. pap. 19.99 ***(978-1-61373-959-4(1))*** Chicago Review Pr., Inc.

Greve, Meg. Science Projects. 2014. (ENG.). 24p. (gr. 3-5). 28.50 *(978-1-62717-690-3(X))* Rourke Educational Media.

Haggis-On-Whey, Doris & Haggis-On-Whey, Benny. Cold Fusion. 2009. (How Ser.). (ENG., Illus.). 64p. (gr. 3). 20.00 *(978-1-934781-21-0(5))* McSweeney's Publishing.

Hands-On Science Fun. (Hands-On Science Fun Ser.). (ENG.). 24p. (gr. k-1). 2011. pap. 333.60 *(978-1-4296-6388-5(X))* 2010. pap. 55.60 *(978-1-4296-6218-5(2))* 2010. lib. bdg. 79.95 *(978-1-4296-5295-7(0))* 2010. lib. bdg. 186.55 *(978-1-4296-5296-4(9))* 2010. lib. bdg. 106.60 *(978-1-4296-4495-2(8))* Capstone Press of Coughlan Cos. (Pebble Plus).

Hands-On Science Fun Collection. 2010. (Hands-On Science Fun Ser.). (ENG.). 24p. (gr. k-1). pap. 27.80 *(978-1-4296-5582-8(8),* Pebble Plus) Capstone Press of Coughlan Cos.

Haslam, Andrew. Earth. 2004. (Make It Work! Science Ser.). (Illus.). 48p. (J). (gr. 3-6). 12.95 *(978-1-58728-376-5(X),* Two-Can Publishing) T&N Children's Publishing.

Haslam, Andrew, et al. Building. (Make It Work! Ser.). (Illus.). 48p. (J). pap. 15.95 *(978-0-590-24332-2(2))* Scholastic, Inc.

Hauser, Jill Frankel. Science Play. Kline, Michael, illus. 2008. (ENG.). 144p. (J). (gr. 4-7). pap. 12.99 *(978-0-8249-6798-7(4),* Ideal Pubns.) Worthy Publishing.

—Science Play: Beginning Discoveries for 2 to 6 Year Olds. Kline, Michael, illus. 2007. (Williamson Little Hands Book Ser.). (ENG.). 144p. (J). (gr. 4-7). 16.99 *(978-0-8249-6799-4(2),* Ideal Pubns.) Worthy Publishing.

—Super Science Concoctions. Kline, Michael, illus. 2008. (ENG.). 160p. (J). (gr. 1-7). 16.99 *(978-0-8249-6802-1(6),* Ideal Pubns.) Worthy Publishing.

Hawbacker, Emily. Energy Lab for Kids: 40 Exciting Experiments to Explore, Create, Harness, & Unleash Energy. 2017. (Lab Ser.). (ENG., Illus.). 144p. (J). (gr. 5-9). pap. 22.99 *(978-1-63159-250-8(5),* Quarry Bks.) Quarto Publishing Group USA.

Hawkins, Jay. Material World: The Science of Matter. 2013. (Big Bang Science Experiments Ser.). (ENG., Illus.). 32p. (gr. 3-6). 26.50 *(978-1-4777-0323-6(3));* pap. 11.75 *(978-1-4777-0367-0(5))* Windmill Bks.

Haysom, John. Science Fair Warm-Up: Learning the Practice of Scientists. 2013. (ENG., Illus.). (J). 55p. pap. *(978-1-936959-20-4(8));* 60p. pap. *(978-1-936959-21-1(6));* 75p. pap. ***(978-1-936959-22-8(4))*** National Science Teachers Assn.

Hedde, Rebecca. Science with Magnets. rev. ed. 2008. (Science Activities Ser.). 24p. (J). pap. 5.99 *(978-0-7945-1406-8(5),* Usborne) EDC Publishing.

Heddle, Rebecca. Science in the Kitchen. Edom, Helen, ed. Davies, Kate, illus. rev. ed. 2007. (Usborne Science Activities Ser.). 24p. (J). (gr. 3-7). pap. 5.99 *(978-0-7945-1405-1(7),* Usborne) EDC Publishing.

Heinecke, Liz Lee. Kitchen Science Lab for Kids: 52 Family Friendly Experiments from the Pantry. 2014. (Lab Ser.). (ENG., Illus.). 144p. (J). (gr. 2-5). pap. 24.99 *(978-1-59253-925-3(4),* 1592539254, Quarry Books) Quarto Publishing Group USA.

Henry, Sally & Cook, Trevor. The Brilliant Book of Experiments. 2013. (ENG., Illus.). 128p. (J). pap. 9.95 *(978-1-84858-394-8(X))* Arcturus Publishing GBR. Dist: Bookmasters Distribution.

—Cool Stuff to Do: Jam-Packed with Brilliant Things to Make & Do! 2012. (ENG.). 128p. (J). pap. 9.95 *(978-1-84858-084-8(3))* Arcturus Publishing GBR. Dist: Bookmasters Distribution.

Heuer, Steve. Spectacular Experiments & Mad Science Kids Love: Science That Dazzles @ Home, School or on the Go! 2010. 204p. pap. 19.99 *(978-1-4490-7041-0(8))* AuthorHouse.

Hewitt, Sally. Plants. (Illus.). 32p. (YA). (gr. 2-18). lib. bdg. 27.10 *(978-1-932333-30-5(4))* Chrysalis Education.

Higgins, Nadia. Experiment with a Plant's Living Environment. 2015. (Lightning Bolt Books (tm) — Plant Experiments Ser.).

(ENG., Illus.). 32p. (gr. k-2). lib. bdg. 26.65 *(978-1-4677-5731-7(4),* Lerner Pubns.) Lerner Publishing Group.

—Experiment with a Plant's Roots. 2015. (Lightning Bolt Books (tm) — Plant Experiments Ser.). (ENG., Illus.). 32p. (gr. k-2). lib. bdg. 26.65 *(978-1-4677-5729-4(2),* Lerner Pubns.) Lerner Publishing Group.

—Experiment with Photosynthesis. 2015. (Lightning Bolt Books (tm) — Plant Experiments Ser.). (ENG., Illus.). 32p. (gr. k-2). 26.65 *(978-1-4677-5732-4(2),* Lerner Pubns.) Lerner Publishing Group.

—Experiment with What a Plant Needs to Grow. 2015. (Lightning Bolt Books (tm) — Plant Experiments Ser.). (ENG., Illus.). 32p. (gr. k-2). lib. bdg. 26.65 *(978-1-4677-5730-0(6),* Lerner Pubns.) Lerner Publishing Group.

Hindman, Susan. Think Like a Scientist in the Classroom. 2011. (Explorer Junior Library: Science Explorer Junior Ser.). (ENG.). 32p. (gr. 4-8). lib. bdg. 28.50 *(978-1-61080-170-6(9),* 201110) Cherry Lake Publishing.

Hoffman, Jane. Backyard Scientist A Science Wonderland for the Very Young: Simple, fun-to-do Science Experiments Ages 2 To 7. 2005. (Illus.). 56p. (J). pap. 8.95 *(978-0-9618663-8-9(1))* Backyard Scientist, Inc.

Holt, Rinehart and Winston Staff. Holt Science & Technology: Inquiry Labs. 5th ed. 2004. (Illus.). pap. 14.60 *(978-0-03-035184-6(7))* Holt McDougal.

—Holt Science & Technology: Labs You Can Eat. 5th ed. 2004. (Illus.). pap. 14.60 *(978-0-03-035183-9(9))* Holt McDougal.

Holzweiss, Kristina & Barth, Amy. I Can Make Exciting Electronics. 2017. (Rookie Star — MakerSpace Projects Ser.). (ENG.). 32p. (J). pap. 5.95 ***(978-0-531-23880-6(6))***; lib. bdg. 25.00 ***(978-0-531-23411-2(8))*** Scholastic Library Publishing. (Children's Pr.).

—I Can Make Marvelous Movers. 2017. (Rookie Star — MakerSpace Projects Ser.). (ENG.). 32p. (J). lib. bdg. 25.00 ***(978-0-531-23413-6(4),*** Children's Pr.) Scholastic Library Publishing.

Homer, Holly, et al. The 101 Coolest Simple Science Experiments. 2016. (ENG., Illus.). 192p. pap. 19.99 *(978-1-62414-133-1(1),* 9781624141331) Page Street Publishing Co.

Hopwood, James. Cool Distance Assistants: Fun Science Projects to Propel Things, 1 vol. 2008. (Cool Science Ser.). (ENG.). 32p. (YA). (gr. 2-5). 28.50 *(978-1-59928-906-9(7))* ABDO Publishing Co.

—Cool Dry Ice Devices: Fun Science Projects with Dry Ice, 1 vol. 2008. (Cool Science Ser.). (ENG.). 32p. (YA). (gr. 2-5). 28.50 *(978-1-59928-907-6(5))* ABDO Publishing Co.

Inventions in Land Vehicles. 2005. (Illus.). 28p. (J). pap. 19.99 incl. audio *(978-0-9724983-0-2(3))* Jazwares Distribution, Inc.

Ives, Rob. Fun Experiments with Matter: Invisible Ink, Giant Bubbles, & More. Sassin, Eva, illus. 2017. (Amazing Science Experiments Ser.). (ENG.). (J). (gr. 3-6). lib. bdg. 26.65 ***(978-1-5124-3216-9(4))*** Lerner Publishing Group.

Janice VanCleave's Wild, Wacky, & Weird Science Experiments: Set 1. 2016. (Janice VanCleave's Wild, Wacky, & Weird Science Experiments Ser.). 64p. (gr. 5-5). 172.25 *(978-1-4777-8960-5(X))*; pap. 64.75 *(978-1-4994-3841-3(9))* Rosen Publishing Group, Inc., The. (Rosen Central).

Janice VanCleave's Wild, Wacky, & Weird Science Experiments: Set 2. 2016. (Janice VanCleave's Wild, Wacky, & Weird Science Experiments Ser.). 00064p. (J). (gr. 5-5). pap. 64.75 *(978-1-4994-6560-0(2),* Rosen Young Adult) Rosen Publishing Group, Inc., The.

Janice VanCleave's Wild, Wacky, & Weird Science Experiments: Set 3. 2017. (Janice VanCleave's Wild, Wacky, & Weird Science Experiments Ser.). 64p. (gr. 10-10). 172.25 ***(978-1-4994-6662-1(5))***; pap. 64.75 ***(978-1-4994-6701-7(X))*** Rosen Publishing Group, Inc., The. (Rosen Central).

Jones, Lorraine. Super Science Projects about Weather & Natural Forces. 2005. (Psyched for Science Ser.). (Illus.). 48p. (YA). (gr. 5-8). lib. bdg. 29.25 *(978-0-8239-3105-7(6),* SCWENA) Rosen Publishing Group, Inc., The.

Der Jugend Brockhaus: Natur und Technik. (GER., Illus.). 640p. (YA). (gr. 5-11). *(978-3-7653-1851-1(5))* Brockhaus, F. A., GmbH DEU. Dist: International Bk. Import Service, Inc.

Kauffman, Dorothy. Science Lab. 2005. (Oxford Picture Dictionary for the Content Areas Ser.). (ENG., Illus.). 24p. pap. 7.56 *(978-0-19-430955-4(X))* Oxford Univ. Pr., Inc.

Kellett, Sarah, et al, eds. Hands-On Science: 50 Kids' Activities from CSIRO. 2017. (ENG.). 128p. (gr. 3-8). pap. 16.50 *(978-1-4863-0614-5(4))* CSIRO Publishing AUS. Dist: Stylus Publishing, LLC.

Kessler, Colleen. A Project Guide to the Solar System. 2010. (Earth Science Projects for Kids Ser.). (Illus.). 48p. (J). (gr. 4-7). lib. bdg. 29.95 *(978-1-58415-867-7(0))* Mitchell Lane Pubs., Inc.

Kitchen Science. 2011. (Kitchen Science Ser.). (ENG.). 32p. (gr. 3-4). pap. 190.80 *(978-1-4296-6422-6(3),* Edge Bks.) Capstone Press of Coughlan Cos.

Kitchen Science, 4 vols., Set. Incl. Science Experiments That Explode & Implode: Fun Projects for Curious Kids. Wheeler-Toppen, Jodi. lib. bdg. 27.99 *(978-1-4296-5427-2(9))*; Science Experiments That Fizz & Bubble: Fun Projects for Curious Kids. Wheeler-Toppen, Jodi. lib. bdg. 27.99 *(978-1-4296-5425-8(2))*; Science Experiments That Fly & Move: Fun Projects for Curious Kids. Lew, Kristi. lib. bdg. 27.99 *(978-1-4296-5426-5(0))*; (gr. 3-4). (Kitchen Science Ser.). (ENG.). 32p. 2010. Set lib. bdg. 83.97 *(978-1-4296-5429-6(5),* Edge Bks.) Capstone Press of Coughlan Cos.

Kneidel, Sally. Creepy Crawlies & the Scientific Method: More Than 100 Hands-On Science Experiments for Children. 2nd ed. 2015. (ENG., Illus.). 240p. (J). (gr. 4-9). pap. 24.95 *(978-1-938486-32-6(3))* Fulcrum Publishing.

Knighton, Kate. 50 Science Things to Make & Do. (50 Things to Make & Do Ser.). (J). 2009. 104p. spiral bd. 9.99 *(978-0-7945-2379-4(X))* 2007. (Illus.). 50p. (gr. 4-7). 9.99 *(978-0-7945-1698-7(X))* EDC Publishing. (Usborne).

Korman, Gordon. Criminal Destiny. 2017. (Masterminds Ser.: 2). (J). lib. bdg. 18.40 ***(978-0-606-39612-7(8))*** Turtleback Bks.

Kraul, Walter. Earth, Water, Fire & Air: Playful Explorations in the Four Elements, 1 vol. Maclean, Donald, tr. from GER. 3rd rev. ed. 2010. Orig. Title: Spielen mit Wasser und Luft & Spielen mit Feuer und Erde. (ENG., Illus.). 104p. (J). (gr. 1-7). pap. 25.00 *(978-0-86315-768-4(8))* Floris Bks. GBR. Dist: SteinerBooks, Inc.

Krautwurst, Terry, et al. Science Smart: Cool Projects for Exploring the Marvels of the Planet Earth. 2004. (ENG., Illus.). 400p. (J). pap. 12.98 *(978-1-4027-1436-8(X))* Sterling Publishing Co., Inc.

Kurzweil, Allen & Kurzweil, Max. Potato Chip Science: 29 Incredible Experiments. 2010. (ENG., Illus.). 96p. (J). (gr. 2-6). 22.95 *(978-0-7611-4825-8(6),* 14825) Workman Publishing Co., Inc.

Ladd, Karol. The Glad Scientist Explores the Human Body. 2004. (Glad Scientist Ser.). pap., act. bk. ed. 6.99 *(978-0-8054-0829-4(0))* B&H Publishing Group.

LaFosse, Michael. Making Origami Science Experiments Step by Step. 2004. (Kid's Guide to Origami Ser.). (Illus.). 24p. (J). lib. bdg. 25.25 *(978-0-8239-6705-6(0),* PowerKids Pr.) Rosen Publishing Group, Inc., The.

LaFosse, Michael G. Making Origami Science Experiments Step by Step. 2009. (Kid's Guide to Origami Ser.). 24p. (gr. 3-4). 47.90 *(978-1-61511-195-4(6),* PowerKids Pr.) Rosen Publishing Group, Inc., The.

Language Arts Explorer: Science Lab, 8 vols., Set. Incl. Science Lab: Gases. Duke, Shirley. lib. bdg. 28.50 *(978-1-61080-203-1(9),* 201182); Science Lab: Motion & Forces. Hirsch, Rebecca. 28.50 *(978-1-61080-205-5(5),* 201186); Science Lab: Properties of Matter. Hirsch, Rebecca. lib. bdg. 28.50 *(978-1-61080-206-2(3),* 201188); Science Lab: Soil. Barker, David M. lib. bdg. 28.50 *(978-1-61080-207-9(1),* 201190); Science Lab: Technological Design. Sirota, Lyn A. lib. bdg. 28.50 *(978-1-61080-208-6(X),* 201192); Science Lab: The Life Cycles of Plants. Hirsch, Rebecca. lib. bdg. 28.50 *(978-1-61080-204-8(7),* 201184); Science Lab: The Transfer of Energy. Zuchora-Walske, Christine. lib. bdg. 28.50 *(978-1-61080-209-3(8),* 201194); Science Lab: Weather Patterns. Hand, Carol. lib. bdg. 28.50 *(978-1-61080-210-9(1),* 201196); 32p. (gr. 4-8). 2011. Set lib. bdg. 228.00 *(978-1-61080-245-1(4))* Cherry Lake Publishing.

Larson, Kirsten. Science Fair Success! 2014. (ENG.). 48p. (gr. 4-6). 35.64 *(978-1-62717-747-4(7))* Rourke Educational Media.

Latta, Sara L. All about Earth: Exploring the Planet with Science Projects. 2015. (Discover Earth Science Ser.). (ENG., Illus.). 32p. (gr. 3-4). lib. bdg. 27.32 *(978-1-4914-4814-4(8))* Capstone Press of Coughlan Cos.

Leavitt, Loralee. Candy Experiments. 2013. (Candy Experiments Ser.: 1). (ENG., Illus.). 160p. (J). pap. 14.99 *(978-1-4494-1836-6(8))* Andrews McMeel Publishing.

—Candy Experiments 2. 2014. (Candy Experiments Ser.: 2). (ENG.). 160p. (J). pap. 14.99 *(978-1-4494-6103-4(4))* Andrews McMeel Publishing.

Lemke, Donald B., et al. Lecciones Sobre la Seguridad en el Trabajo Científico. Smith, Tod G., illus. 2013. (Ciencia Gráfica Ser.). (SPA.). 32p. (gr. 3-4). lib. bdg. 30.65 *(978-1-62065-183-4(1))* Capstone Press of Coughlan Cos.

—Lessons in Science Safety with Max Axiom, Super Scientist, 1 vol. Anderson, Bill & Smith, Tod G., illus. 2007. (Graphic Science Ser.). (ENG.). 32p. (gr. 3-4). 30.65 *(978-0-7368-6834-1(8),* Graphic Library) Capstone Press of Coughlan Cos.

—Lessons in Science Safety with Max Axiom, Super Scientist, 1 vol. Smith, Tod G., illus. 2007. (Graphic Science Ser.). (ENG.). 32p. (gr. 3-4). pap. 8.10 *(978-0-7368-7887-6(4),* Graphic Library) Capstone Press of Coughlan Cos.

Leonard, Sue, ed. Kitchen Science: With over 50 Fantastic Experiments. 2004. (Illus.). 48p. (J). (gr. k-8). reprint ed. 13.00 *(978-0-7567-7285-7(0))* DIANE Publishing Co.

Let's Go! Elementary Science. 2004. spiral bd. 30.00 *(978-1-929075-36-6(3))* Vernier Software & Technology.

Let's Investigate, 6 bks. (J). (gr. 2-6). lib. bdg. 86.70 *(978-1-56674-929-9(8))* Forest Hse. Publishing Co., Inc.

Levine, Shar. Bathtub Science. 2003. (Illus.). 80p. pap. 10.95 *(978-0-8069-7243-5(2))* Sterling Publishing Co., Inc.

Levine, Shar & Johnstone, Leslie. Scary Science: 25 Creepy Experiments. Spires, Ashley, illus. 2011. (ENG.). 64p. (J). (gr. 3-7). pap. 6.99 *(978-0-545-32406-9(8),* Scholastic Paperbacks) Scholastic, Inc.

Lew, Kristi. Science Experiments That Fly & Move: Fun Projects for Curious Kids. (Kitchen Science Ser.). (ENG.). 32p. (gr. 3-4). 2011. pap. 47.70 *(978-1-4296-6420-2(7))* 2010. lib. bdg. 27.99 *(978-1-4296-5426-5(0))* Capstone Press of Coughlan Cos. (Edge Bks.).

Lindsey, Jason. Beyond the Science Lab. MacLure, Ashley, illus. 2012. 82p. pap. 16.95 *(978-0-9854248-4-8(2))* Pinwheel Bks.

Littlefield, Cindy A. Awesome Ocean Science: Investigating the Secrets of the Underwater World. 2004. (Kids Can Bks.). (Illus.). 120p. (J). (gr. 3-5). pap. 12.95 *(978-1-885593-71-9(6),* Ideal Pubns.) Worthy Publishing.

Lockwood, Cate. Science Lab Tools. 2013. (InfoMax Readers Ser.). (ENG.). 24p. (J). (gr. 2-3). pap. 49.50 *(978-1-4777-2304-3(8))*; (Illus.). pap. 8.25 *(978-1-4777-2303-6(X))* Rosen Publishing Group, Inc., The. (Rosen Classroom).

Madgwick, Wendy. Animals & Plants: 10 Easy-to-Follow Experiments for Learning Fun - Find Out about Nature & How Things Live! 2014. (ENG., Illus.). 270p. (J). (gr. -1-12). 8.99 *(978-1-86147-349-3(4),* Armadillo) Anness Publishing GBR. Dist: National Bk. Network.

—First Science Library: Super Materials. 2014. (Illus.). 32p. *(978-1-86147-354-7(0),* Armadillo) Anness Publishing.

Make & Learn. 2014. (Make & Learn Ser.). 32p. (J). (gr. 3-6). 165.00 *(978-1-4777-7095-5(X),* PowerKids Pr.) Rosen Publishing Group, Inc., The.

Make It Work Science, 14 vol. set. 2005. (gr. 4-8). 169.00 *(978-0-7166-4737-9(0))* World Bk., Inc.

Maker Kids. 2014. (Maker Kids Ser.). 32p. (J). (gr. 3-6). 165.00 *(978-1-4777-6662-0(6))*; pap. 70.50 *(978-1-4777-7232-4(4))* Rosen Publishing Group, Inc., The. (PowerKids Pr.).

Maloof, Torrey. What's the Matter with Mr. Fuego? 2015. (Building Fluency Through Reader's Theater Ser.). (ENG., Illus.). 32p. (gr. 5-5). pap. 7.99 *(978-1-4938-1294-3(7))* Teacher Created Materials, Inc.

Mandell, Muriel. Super Science Experiments. Garbot, Dave, illus. 2005. (No-Sweat Science(r) Ser.). (ENG.). 128p. (J). (gr. 3-7). per. 5.95 *(978-1-4027-2149-6(8))* Sterling Publishing Co., Inc.

Margles, Samantha. Star Wars: Science Fair Book. 2013. lib. bdg. 20.85 *(978-0-606-32399-4(6),* Turtleback) Turtleback Bks.

Marine Science Experiments. 2010. (Facts on File Science Experiments Ser.). (Illus.). 176p. (gr. 6-12). 40.00 *(978-0-8160-8168-4(9))* Facts On File, Inc.

Marks, Jennifer L. How to Make a Bouncing Egg, 1 vol. 2011. (Hands-On Science Fun Ser.). (ENG., Illus.). 24p. (gr. k-1). pap. 7.29 *(978-1-4296-6214-7(X),* Pebble Plus) Capstone Press of Coughlan Cos.

Martineau, Susan. Shadows in the Bedroom. Noyes, Leighton, illus. 2011. (Everyday Science Experiments Ser.). (ENG.). 24p. (J). (gr. 3-6). pap. 10.60 *(978-1-61533-410-0(6))*; lib. bdg. 25.25 *(978-1-61533-372-1(X))* Windmill Bks.

Masoff, Joy. Oh, Ick! 117 Science Experiments Guaranteed to Gross Out! 2016. lib. bdg. 26.90 *(978-0-606-38003-4(5))* Turtleback Bks.

McCallum, Ann. Eat Your Science Homework: Recipes for Inquiring Minds. Hernandez, Leeza, illus. 2014. (Eat Your Homework Ser.). (ENG.). 48p. (J). (gr. 2-5). 16.95 *(978-1-57091-298-6(X))* Charlesbridge Publishing, Inc.

McGill, Jordan. Life Science Fair Projects. 2011. (J). *(978-1-61690-330-5(9))*; (gr. 3-5). pap. 12.95 *(978-1-61690-658-0(8),* AV2 by Weigl); (Illus.). 24p. (gr. 3-6). 27.13 *(978-1-61690-654-2(5))* Weigl Pubs., Inc.

McGowan, Chris. Abacus. 2010. (Illus.). 312p. (J). (gr. 5-9). *(978-0-9810831-1-7(0))*; pap. *(978-0-9810831-0-0(2))* Euphausia Pr.

Meiani, Antonella. Air. 2003. (Experimenting with Science Ser.). (Illus.). 40p. (J). (gr. 4-8). lib. bdg. 23.93 *(978-0-8225-0082-7(5))* Lerner Publishing Group.

—Magnetism. 2003. (Experimenting with Science Ser.). (Illus.). 40p. (J). (gr. 4-8). lib. bdg. 23.93 *(978-0-8225-0085-8(X))* Lerner Publishing Group.

Mercer, Bobby. Junk Drawer Chemistry: 50 Awesome Experiments That Don't Cost a Thing. 2015. (Junk Drawer Science Ser.). (ENG., Illus.). 224p. (J). (gr. 4). pap. 14.95 *(978-1-61373-179-6(5))* Chicago Review Pr., Inc.

—Junk Drawer Engineering: 25 Construction Challenges That Don't Cost a Thing. 2017. (Junk Drawer Science Ser.). (ENG.). 224p. (J). (gr. 4). pap. 14.99 *(978-1-61373-716-3(5))* Chicago Review Pr., Inc.

Metz, Lorijo. Using Clocks & Stopwatches. 2013. (Science Tools Ser.). (ENG., Illus.). 24p. (J). (gr. 3-6). 22.60 *(978-1-4488-9689-9(4))*; pap. 8.25 *(978-1-4488-9836-7(6))* Rosen Publishing Group, Inc., The. (PowerKids Pr.).

—Using Scales & Balances. 2013. (Science Tools Ser.). (ENG., Illus.). 24p. (J). (gr. 3-6). 22.60 *(978-1-4488-9686-8(X))*; pap. 8.25 *(978-1-4488-9830-5(7))* Rosen Publishing Group, Inc., The. (PowerKids Pr.).

Mind-Blowing Science Experiments. 2017. (Mind-Blowing Science Experiments Ser.). 32p. (gr. 4-5). pap. 63.00 ***(978-1-5382-0836-6(9))***; lib. bdg. 159.60 ***(978-1-5382-0827-4(X))*** Stevens, Gareth Publishing LLLP.

Mullins, Matt. Think Like a Scientist in the Kitchen. 2011. (Explorer Junior Library: Science Explorer Junior Ser.). (ENG.). 32p. (gr. 4-8). lib. bdg. 28.50 *(978-1-61080-165-2(2),* 201100) Cherry Lake Publishing.

Muntz, Kendra & Kenis, Daniel. Dr. Mollie Cule Reboots the Robot: Awesome Science Activities You Can Do at Home. Carrington, Matt, illus. 2014. 160p. (J). *(978-0-7166-0633-8(X))* World Bk., Inc.

Murphy, Brian. Movement. 2004. (Experiment with Ser.). (SPA., Illus.). 32p. (J). (gr. 2-5). 9.95 *(978-1-58728-248-5(8),* Two-Can Publishing) T&N Children's Publishing.

Murphy, Pat & Klutz Labs Scientists Staff. Lego Chain Reactions. 2015. (ENG.). 64p. (J). (gr. 3). 21.99 *(978-0-545-70330-7(1))* Klutz.

Nagy, Frances. Science with Water. 2007. (Usborne Science Activities Ser.). (Illus.). 24p. (J). (gr. 1). lib. bdg. 13.99 *(978-1-58086-976-8(9))*; pap. 5.99 *(978-0-7945-1484-6(7))* EDC Publishing. (Usborne).

Nasty (But Useful!) Science. 2011. (Nasty (but Useful!) Science Ser.). (ENG.). 32p. (gr. 3-4). pap. 190.80 *(978-1-4296-6474-5(6),* Fact Finders) Capstone Press of Coughlan Cos.

National Geographic Kids Staff, et al. Edible Science: Experiments You Can Eat. 2015. (ENG., Illus.). 80p. (J). (gr. 3-7). pap. 12.99 *(978-1-4263-2111-5(2),* National Geographic Children's Bks.) National Geographic Society.

Navarro, Paula & Jimenez, Angels. Magical Experiments with Light & Color. Cuxart, Bernadette, illus. 2014. (Magic Science Ser.). (ENG.). 36p. (J). (gr. 1-6). pap. 7.99 *(978-1-4380-0426-6(5))* Barron's Educational Series, Inc.

Naylor, Brenda & Naylor, Stuart. The Snowman's Coat & Other Science Questions, 4 vols. Mitchell, Ged, illus. 32p. (J). pap. *(978-0-340-75755-0(8))* Hodder & Stoughton.

Nelson, M. Rae & Krapp, Kristine M. Experiment Central: Understanding Scientific Principles Through Projects. 2nd ed. 2010. (J). *(978-1-4144-7619-3(1))*; *(978-1-4144-7618-6(3))*; *(978-1-4144-7617-9(5))*; *(978-1-4144-7615-5(9))*; *(978-1-4144-7614-8(0))*; *(978-1-4144-7616-2(7))* Cengage Gale. (UXL).

O'Neal, Claire. A Project Guide to Rocks & Minerals. 2010. (Earth Science Projects for Kids Ser.). (Illus.). 48p. (J). (gr. 4-7). lib. bdg. 29.95 *(978-1-58415-866-0(2))* Mitchell Lane Pubs., Inc.

Oxlade, Chris. Earth: Find Out about the Planet, Earthquakes, Volcanoes & Weather with 50 Great Experiments & Projects. 2009. (ENG., Illus.). 64p. (J). (gr. 4-7). pap. 7.99 *(978-1-84476-712-0(4))* Anness Publishing GBR. Dist: National Bk. Network.

—Excellent Science Experiments, 1 vol. 2015. (Excellent Science Experiments Ser.). (ENG.). 32p. (J). 47.00 *(978-1-4994-0345-9(3),* PowerKids Pr.) Rosen Publishing Group, Inc., The.

—Experiments with Air & Water, 1 vol. 2015. (ENG., Illus.). 32p. (J). lib. bdg. 27.50 *(978-1-4777-5793-2(7),* PowerKids Pr.) Rosen Publishing Group, Inc., The.

—Experiments with Electricity & Magnets, 1 vol. 2015. (ENG., Illus.). 32p. (J). pap. 11.75 *(978-1-4777-5962-2(X),* PowerKids Pr.) Rosen Publishing Group, Inc., The.

—Experiments with Matter & Materials, 1 vol. 2015. (ENG.). 32p. (J). lib. bdg. 27.50 *(978-1-4777-5969-1(7),* PowerKids Pr.) Rosen Publishing Group, Inc., The.

—Experiments with Sound & Light, 1 vol. 2015. (ENG., Illus.). 32p. (J). lib. bdg. 27.50 *(978-1-4777-5965-3(4),* PowerKids Pr.) Rosen Publishing Group, Inc., The.

—Simple Experiments with Inclined Planes. 2013. (Science Experiments with Simple Machines Ser.). 32p. (J). (gr. k-3). 26.50 *(978-1-61533-752-1(0))*; pap. 11.75 *(978-1-61533-821-4(7))*; pap. 70.50 *(978-1-61533-822-1(5))* Windmill Bks.

—Simple Experiments with Levers. 2013. (Science Experiments with Simple Machines Ser.). 32p. (J). (gr. k-3). 26.50 *(978-1-61533-756-9(3))*; pap. 11.75 *(978-1-61533-829-0(2))*; pap. 70.50 *(978-1-61533-830-6(6))* Windmill Bks.

—Simple Experiments with Pulleys. 2013. (Science Experiments with Simple Machines Ser.). 32p. (J). (gr. k-3). 26.50 *(978-1-61533-751-4(2))*; pap. 70.50 *(978-1-61533-820-7(9))*; pap. 11.75 *(978-1-61533-819-1(5))* Windmill Bks.

—Simple Experiments with Screws. 2013. (Science Experiments with Simple Machines Ser.). 32p. (J). (gr. k-3). 26.50 *(978-1-61533-753-8(9))*; pap. 70.50 *(978-1-61533-824-5(1))*; pap. 11.75 *(978-1-61533-823-8(3))* Windmill Bks.

—Simple Experiments with Wedges. 2013. (Science Experiments with Simple Machines Ser.). 32p. (J). (gr. k-3). 26.50 *(978-1-61533-755-2(5))*; pap. 11.75 *(978-1-61533-827-6(6))*; pap. 70.50 *(978-1-61533-828-3(4))* Windmill Bks.

—Simple Experiments with Wheels & Axles. 2013. (Science Experiments with Simple Machines Ser.). 32p. (J). (gr. k-3). 26.50 *(978-1-61533-754-5(7))*; pap. 70.50 *(978-1-61533-826-9(8))*; pap. 11.75 *(978-1-61533-825-2(X))* Windmill Bks.

—Super Science Air & Water Experiments: 10 Amazing Experiments with Step by Step Photographs - For. 2016. (ENG., Illus.). (J). pap. ***(978-1-78209-419-7(9))*** Miles Kelly Publishing, Ltd.

—150 Amazing Science Experiments: Fascinating Projects Using Everyday Materials, Demonstrated. 2014. (ENG., Illus.). 256p. pap. 13.99 *(978-1-86147-472-8(5),* Armadillo) Anness Publishing GBR. Dist: National Bk. Network.

—150 Amazing Science Experiments: Fascinating Projects Using Everyday Materials, Demonstrated Step by Step in 1300 Photographs! 2013. (ENG., Illus.). 256p. (J). (gr. 3-7). pap. 17.99 *(978-1-84322-988-9(9),* Armadillo) Anness Publishing GBR. Dist: National Bk. Network.

Oxlade, Chris & Stockley, Corinne. The World of the Microscope. Chen, Kuo Kang et al, illus. 2008. (Usborne Science & Experiments Ser.). 48p. (J). (gr. 5-11). pap. 8.99 *(978-0-7945-1524-9(X),* Usborne) EDC Publishing.

Oxlade, Chris, et al. The Science & History Project Book: 300 Step-By-Step Fun Science Experiments & History Craft Projects for Home Learning & School Study. 2013. (ENG., Illus.). 512p. (J). (gr. 2-7). pap. 17.99 *(978-1-84322-745-8(2),* Armadillo) Anness Publishing GBR. Dist: National Bk. Network.

Parker, Steve & Parker, Jane. Show Me How: I Can Do Science. 2016. (ENG., Illus.). 48p. (J). (gr. -1 — 1). 7.99 *(978-1-86147-404-9(0),* Armadillo) Anness Publishing GBR. Dist: National Bk. Network.

Parker, Steve & Prinja, Raman. Science Club. 2012. (Illus.). 120p. (J). *(978-1-4351-4413-2(9))* Barnes & Noble, Inc.

Parratore, Phil. 101 Hands-On Science Experiments. 2008. (ENG.). 136p. (J). (gr. 4-7). pap. 19.95 *(978-1-59363-317-2(3))* Prufrock Pr.

Pascoe, Elaine. Bugs. Kuhn, Dwight, illus. Kuhn, Dwight, photos by. 2003. 48p. (J). 23.70 *(978-1-56711-458-4(X),* Blackbirch Pr., Inc.) Cengage Gale.

—Flowers. 2003. (Illus.). 48p. (J). 24.95 *(978-1-56711-432-4(6),* Blackbirch Pr., Inc.) Cengage Gale.

Pederson, Bridget & Doudna, Kelly. Don't Be Hasty with Science Safety!, 1 vol. 2007. (Science Made Simple Ser.). (ENG., Illus.). 24p. (J). (gr. k-3). lib. bdg. 24.21 *(978-1-59928-580-1(0),* SandCastle) ABDO Publishing Co.

Perelman, Yakov. Amazing Experiments for Young Physicians. Willams, Brian, tr. 2013. 114p. pap. *(978-2-917260-29-6(7))* Prodinnova.

Pero, Denis. My Little Handbook of Experiments: Sciences, Water & Light, Ecology. 2012. (ENG., Illus.). 144p. (J). (gr. 2). 12.95 *(978-2-7338-2147-3(4))* Auzou, Philippe Editions FRA. Dist: Consortium Bk. Sales & Distribution.

Peterson, Carol. Jump into Science: Themed Science Fairs, 1 vol. Peterson, Carol, illus. 2007. (Illus.). 152p. (C). (gr. 3-7). per. 35.00 *(978-1-59158-413-1(2),* TIP4132, Libraries Unlimited) ABC-CLIO, LLC.

Physical Science with Vernier. 2007. spiral bd. 45.00 *(978-1-929075-47-8(2))* Vernier Software & Technology.

Piazza, Carmelo & Buckley, James. Crazy for Science with Carmelo the Science Fellow. Geran, Chad, illus. 2015. (ENG.). 98p. (J). (gr. 1-4). 19.95 *(978-1-57687-682-4(9),* powerHouse Bks.) powerHouse Cultural Entertainment, Inc.

Pilger, Mary Anne. Science Experiments Index for Young People. 4th rev. ed. 2005. 212p. (C). 65.00 *(978-1-59158-237-3(7),* LU2377, Libraries Unlimited) ABC-CLIO, LLC.

Polinsky, Paige V. Super Simple Experiments with Elements: Fun & Innovative Science Projects. 2016. (ENG., Illus.). 32p. (J). 27.07 *(978-1-68078-168-7(5))* ABDO Publishing Co.

—Super Simple Experiments with Forces: Fun & Innovative Science Projects. 2016. (ENG., Illus.). 32p. (J). *(978-1-68078-169-4(3))* ABDO Publishing Co.

—Super Simple Experiments with Heat & Cold: Fun & Innovative Science Projects. 2016. (ENG., Illus.). 32p. (J). *(978-1-68078-170-0(7))* ABDO Publishing Co.

—Super Simple Experiments with Light & Color: Fun & Innovative Science Projects. 2016. (ENG., Illus.). 32p. (J). *(978-1-68078-171-7(5))* ABDO Publishing Co.

—Super Simple Experiments with Mass: Fun & Innovative Science Projects. 2016. (ENG.). 32p. (J). *(978-1-68078-172-4(3))* ABDO Publishing Co.

Popular Mechanics, ed. The Boy Scientist: 160 Extraordinary Experiments & Adventures. 2012. 242p. pap. 14.99 *(978-1-60796-498-8(8))* Melrovich, Igal.

S

Press, H. J. Science Experiments. 2007. (ENG., Illus.). 352p. (J). (gr. 3-7). pap. 6.95 (978-1-4027-4990-2(2)) Sterling Publishing Co., Inc.

Prize-Winning Science Fair Projects. 2015. (Prize-Winning Science Fair Projects Ser.). (ENG.). 128p. (J). (gr. 7-7). 223.62 (978-0-7660-6700-4(9)) Enslow Pubs., Inc.

Ragsdale, Tyraine D. Science of Grand Hank Lab Book of Experiments. 2005. pap. 24.95 (978-0-9767236-0-8(3)) Grand Hank Productions, Inc.

Rainis, Kenneth G. Forgery: Crime-Solving Science Experiments. 2006. (Forensic Science Projects Ser.). (Illus.). 128p. (J). (gr. 4-7). lib. bdg. 33.27 (978-0-7660-1961-4(6)) Enslow Pubs., Inc.

—Microscope Science Projects & Experiments: Magnifying the Hidden World. 2003. (Science Fair Success Ser.). (Illus.). 128p. (J). lib. bdg. 26.60 (978-0-7660-2090-0(8)) Enslow Pubs., Inc.

Rau, Dana Meachen. Think Like a Scientist on the Playground. 2011. (Explorer Junior Library: Science Explorer Junior Ser.). (ENG.). 32p. (gr. 4-8). lib. bdg. 28.50 (978-1-61080-169-0(5), 201108) Cherry Lake Publishing.

Resler, T. J. How Things Work. 2016. (ENG., Illus.). 208p. (J). (gr. 2-5). 19.99 (978-1-4263-2555-7(X), National Geographic Children's Bks.) National Geographic Society.

Revolutionary Discoveries of Scientific Pioneers. 2013. (Revolutionary Discoveries of Scientific Pioneers Ser.). 80p. (YA). (gr. 7-12). 266.00 (978-1-4777-1818-6(4)) Rosen Publishing Group, Inc., The.

Rice, Dona. Science Detectives, 1 vol. rev. ed. 2014. (Science Readers: Content & Literacy Ser.). (ENG., Illus.). 24p. (gr. 1-1). pap. 8.99 (978-1-4807-4574-2(X)) Teacher Created Materials, Inc.

Richards, Jon. Air & Flight. 2009. (Science Factory Ser.). 32p. (gr. 4-5). 50.50 (978-1-60853-018-2(3), PowerKids Pr.) Rosen Publishing Group, Inc., The.

Rogers, Kirsteen, et al. The Usborne Science Encyclopedia: Internet-Linked. Bhachu, Verinder, illus. 2009. (Usborne Internet-Linked Encyclopedia Ser.). 448p. (J). (gr. 4-7). 19.99 (978-0-7945-2629-0(2), Usborne) EDC Publishing.

Rohrig, Brian. 39 Dazzling Experiments with Dry Ice. 2003. (Illus.). 104p. (YA). per. (978-0-9718480-3-0(3)) FizzBang Science.

—39 Dazzling Experiments with the Mega-Magnet. 2003. (Illus.). 136p. (YA). per. (978-0-9718480-4-7(1)) FizzBang Science.

Rosen Publishing Staff. Excellent Science Experiments, 1 vol. 2015. (Excellent Science Experiments Ser.). (ENG.). 32p. (J). 110.00 (978-1-4777-5723-9(6), PowerKids Pr.) Rosen Publishing Group, Inc., The.

Ross, Michael Elsohn. Kitchen Lab. Seeley, Tim, illus. 2003. (You Are the Scientist Ser.). 48p. (J). (gr. 3-6). lib. bdg. 23.93 (978-0-87614-625-5(6)) Lerner Publishing Group.

—What's the Matter in Mr. Whiskers' Room? Meisel, Paul, illus. 2007. (ENG.). 48p. (J). (gr. 1-4). pap. 7.99 (978-0-7636-3566-4(9)) Candlewick Pr.

—What's the Matter in Mr. Whiskers' Room? 2007. 18.40 (978-1-4177-9071-5(7), Turtleback) Turtleback Bks.

Roth, Jennifer A. Backyard Laboratory. 2007. (Experiment with Science Ser.). (ENG., Illus.). 32p. (J). (gr. 3-6). 27.00 (978-0-531-18542-1(7), Children's Pr.) Scholastic Library Publishing.

Rowe, Brooke. Floating a Paper Clip. Bane, Jeff, illus. 2016. (My Early Library: My Science Fun Ser.). (ENG.). 24p. (J). (gr. k-1). 28.50 (978-1-63471-032-9(0), 208208) Cherry Lake Publishing.

—Shining a Penny. Bane, Jeff, illus. 2016. (My Early Library: My Science Fun Ser.). (ENG.). 24p. (J). (gr. k-1). 28.50 (978-1-63471-030-5(4), 208200) Cherry Lake Publishing.

Royston, Angela. Experiments with a Lemon. 2016. (One-Stop Science Ser.). 32p. (gr. 2-5). 31.35 (978-1-62588-140-3(1), Smart Apple Media) Black Rabbit Bks.

—Experiments with a Ruler. 2016. (One-Stop Science Ser.). 32p. (gr. 2-5). 31.35 (978-1-62588-143-4(6), Smart Apple Media) Black Rabbit Bks.

Roza, Greg. Heads or Tails? Exploring Probability Through Games. 2009. (PowerMath Ser.). (ENG., Illus.). 24p. (gr. 3-4). pap. 8.25 (978-0-8239-8894-5(5), PowerKids Pr.) Rosen Publishing Group, Inc., The.

—Heads or Tails: Exploring Probability Through Games. 2004. (Math Big Bookstm Ser.). (ENG.). 24p. (gr. 3-4). 43.95 (978-0-8239-7644-7(0)) Rosen Publishing Group, Inc., The.

—Where We Play Sports: Measuring the Perimeters of Polygons. 2009. (PowerMath Ser.). (ENG., Illus.). 24p. (gr. 3-4). pap. 8.25 (978-0-8239-8895-2(3), PowerKids Pr.) Rosen Publishing Group, Inc., The.

Rybolt, Thomas R. Soda Pop Science Fair Projects. 2015. (Prize-Winning Science Fair Projects Ser.). (ENG., Illus.). 128p. (J). (gr. 7-7). lib. bdg. 37.27 (978-0-7660-7024-0(7), 1392224) Enslow Pubs., Inc.

—Soda Pop Science Projects: Experiments with Carbonated Soft Drinks. 2004. (Science Fair Success Ser.). (Illus.). 104p. (J). lib. bdg. 27.94 (978-0-7660-2089-4(4)) Enslow Pubs., Inc.

Rybolt, Thomas R. & Mebane, Robert C. Science Experiments for Young People, 5 bks., Set. (Illus.). (YA). (gr. 4-9). lib. bdg. 99.75 (978-0-89490-448-6(5)) Enslow Pubs., Inc.

Sanders, Moira. Gastro Blast: Make Tasty Treats & Learn Great Science: Comics, Quizzes & Questions Answered! Get Ready to Make Science Delicious! 2016. (ENG., Illus.). 128p. (J). (gr. 1-7). pap. 24.95 (978-1-4595-0462-2(3), 9781459504622) Formac Publishing Co., Ltd. CAN. Dist: Casemate Pubs. & Bk. Distributors, LLC.

Scholastic Library Publishing. A True Book-Experiments. 2011. (True Book-Experiments Ser.). (J). 174.00 (978-0-531-20912-7(1), Children's Pr.) Scholastic Library Publishing.

Science Experiments. 2004. (gr. 4). pap. 14.95 (978-0-7403-0221-3(3), SV0401); (gr. 6). pap. 14.95 (978-1-58095-902-5(4), SV0601); (gr. 7). pap. 14.95 (978-1-58095-903-2(2), SV0701); (gr. 8). pap. 14.95 (978-1-58095-904-9(0), SV0801) Alpha Omega Pubns., Inc. (Lifepac).

Science Experiments - Group 3, 6 bks., Set. 153.86 (978-0-7614-1465-0(7), Benchmark Bks.) Marshall Cavendish Corp.

Science Experiments Kid Kit. 2004. (Illus.). 64p. (J). 18.95 (978-1-58086-419-0(8)) EDC Publishing.

Science Experiments with Simple Machines. 2013. (Science Experiments with Simple Machines Ser.). 32p. (J). (gr. k-3). pap. 70.50 (978-1-61533-878-8(0)) Windmill Bks.

Science Explorer Junior, 20 vols., Set. Incl. Experiment with Bugs. Gray, Susan H. 32p. (gr. 3-6). 2010. lib. bdg. 28.50 (978-1-60279-842-7(7), 200550); Experiment with Heat. Lockwood, Sophie. 32p. (gr. 3-6). 2010. lib. bdg. 28.50 (978-1-60279-843-4(5), 200552); Experiment with Liquids. Mullins, Matt. 32p. (gr. 3-6). 2010. lib. bdg. 28.50 (978-1-60279-846-5(X), 200558); Experiment with Magnets. Taylor-Butler, Christine. 32p. (gr. 3-6). 2010. lib. bdg. 28.50 (978-1-60279-844-1(3), 200554); Experiment with Plants. Gray, Susan H. 32p. (gr. 3-6). 2010. lib. bdg. 28.50 (978-1-60279-839-7(7), 200544); Experiment with Rocks. Lockwood, Sophie. 32p. (gr. 3-6). 2010. lib. bdg. 28.50 (978-1-60279-836-6(2), 200538); Experiment with Seeds. Gray, Susan H. 32p. (gr. 3-6). 2010. lib. bdg. 28.50 (978-1-60279-835-9(4), 200536); Experiment with Soil. Franchino, Vicky. 32p. (gr. 3-6). 2010. lib. bdg. 28.50 (978-1-60279-837-3(0), 200540); Experiment with Solar Energy. Taylor-Butler, Christine. 32p. (gr. 3-6). 2010. lib. bdg. 28.50 (978-1-60279-840-3(0), 200546); Experiment with Solids. Gregory, Josh. 32p. (gr. 3-6). 2010. lib. bdg. 28.50 (978-1-60279-845-8(1), 200556); Experiment with Water. Simon, Charnan & Kazunis, Ariel. 32p. (gr. 3-6). 2010. lib. bdg. 28.50 (978-1-60279-838-0(9), 200542); Experiment with Weather. Orr, Tamra. 32p. (gr. 3-6). 2010. lib. bdg. 28.50 (978-1-60279-841-0(9), 200548); Set. Science Explorer Junior: Think Like a Scientist. Cherry Lake Publishing Staff. (J). (gr. 4-8). 2011. lib. bdg. 228.00 (978-1-61080-249-9(7)); 2011. Set lib. bdg. 570.00 (978-1-61080-247-5(0)) Cherry Lake Publishing.

Science Explorer Junior: Think Like a Scientist, 8 vols., Set. Incl. Think Like a Scientist at the Beach. Rau, Dana Meachen. lib. bdg. 28.50 (978-1-61080-168-3(7), 201106); Think Like a Scientist in the Backyard. Mullins, Matt. lib. bdg. 28.50 (978-1-61080-167-6(9), 201104); Think Like a Scientist in the Car. Mullins, Matt. lib. bdg. 28.50 (978-1-61080-164-5(4), 201098); Think Like a Scientist in the Classroom. Hindman, Susan. lib. bdg. 28.50 (978-1-61080-170-6(9), 201110); Think Like a Scientist in the Garden. Mullins, Matt. lib. bdg. 28.50 (978-1-61080-166-9(0), 201102); Think Like a Scientist in the Gym. Taylor-Butler, Christine. lib. bdg. 28.50 (978-1-61080-163-8(6), 201096); Think Like a Scientist in the Kitchen. Mullins, Matt. lib. bdg. 28.50 (978-1-61080-165-2(2), 201100); Think Like a Scientist on the Playground. Rau, Dana Meachen. lib. bdg. 28.50 (978-1-61080-169-0(5), 201108); 32p. (gr. 4-8). (Science Explorer Junior Ser.). 2011. Set lib. bdg. 228.00 (978-1-61080-249-9(7)) Cherry Lake Publishing.

The Science Library, 10 vols., Set. Incl. Animal Life. Parker, Steve. lib. bdg. 19.95 (978-1-4222-1547-0(4)); Discovering Science. Farndon, John & Graham, Ian. lib. bdg. 19.95 (978-1-4222-1548-7(2)); Great Scientists. Farndon, John. lib. bdg. 19.95 (978-1-4222-1549-4(0)); How Things Work. Farndon, John. lib. bdg. 19.95 (978-1-4222-1550-0(4)); Human Body. Parker, Steve. lib. bdg. 19.95 (978-1-4222-1551-7(2)); Inventions. Taylor, Barbara. lib. bdg. 19.95 (978-1-4222-1552-4(0)); Planet Earth. Farndon, John. lib. bdg. 19.95 (978-1-4222-1553-1(9)); Plants. Riley, Peter. lib. bdg. 19.95 (978-1-4222-1554-8(7)); Space. Farndon, John. lib. bdg. 19.95 (978-1-4222-1555-5(5)); Wild Animals. Parker, Steve. lib. bdg. 19.95 (978-1-4222-1556-2(3)); 40p. (J). (gr. 3-18). 2010. Set lib. bdg. 199.50 (978-1-4222-1546-3(6)) Mason Crest.

Science Stories Foss Spanish Ideas & Inventions EA CR05. 2005. (J). (978-1-59242-588-4(7)) Delta Education, LLC.

Science Whiz Experiments. 2017. (Science Whiz Experiments Ser.). 128p. (gr. 5-5). lib. bdg. 223.62 **(978-0-7660-8597-8(X))** Enslow Pubs., Inc.

Science with Magnets Kid Kit. 2004. (Kid Kits Ser.). (Illus.). 24p. (J). 14.95 (978-1-58086-420-6(1)) EDC Publishing.

The Scientific Method in Action. 2014. (Scientific Method in Action Ser.). 24p. (J). (gr. 3-6). 141.60 (978-1-4777-6386-5(4)); pap. 49.50 (978-1-4777-7250-8(2)) Rosen Publishing Group, Inc., The. (PowerKids Pr.).

Sévigny, Eric, illus. The Jungle Explorer. 2010. (Clubhouse Ser.). (ENG.). 24p. (J). (gr. -1-1). pap. 3.95 (978-2-89450-724-7(0)) Caillouet, Gerry.

Shores, Erika L. How to Make Bubbles, 1 vol. (Hands-On Science Fun Ser.). (ENG., 24p. (gr. k-1). 2011. Illus.). pap. 7.29 (978-1-4296-6215-4(8)) 2011. pap. 41.70 (978-1-4296-6387-8(1)) 2010. lib. bdg. 26.65 (978-1-4296-5293-3(4)) Capstone Press of Coughlan Cos. (Pebble Plus).

Shores, Lori. Cómo Hacer un Globo con Olor Misterioso. Translations.com Staff, tr. from ENG. 2010. (Divertirse con la Ciencia/Hands-On Science Fun Ser.).Tr. of How to Make a Mystery Smell Balloon. (MUL, SPA & ENG.). 24p. (gr. k-1). lib. bdg. 26.65 (978-1-4296-6108-9(9)) Capstone Press of Coughlan Cos.

—Hands-On Science Fun. 2010. (Hands-On Science Fun Ser.). (ENG.). 24p. (gr. k-1). pap. 27.80 (978-1-4296-5583-5(6)); pap. 166.80 (978-1-4296-5581-1(X)) Capstone Press of Coughlan Cos. (Pebble Plus).

—How to Build a Fizzy Rocket. 2010. (Hands-On Science Fun Ser.). (ENG.). 24p. (gr. k-1). pap. 41.70 (978-1-4296-5574-3(7), Pebble Plus) Capstone Press of Coughlan Cos.

—How to Build a Tornado in a Bottle. 2010. (Hands-On Science Fun Ser.). (ENG.). 24p. (gr. k-1). pap. 41.70 (978-1-4296-5578-1(X), Pebble Plus) Capstone Press of Coughlan Cos.

—How to Build Flipsticks, 1 vol. 2011. (Hands-On Science Fun Ser.). (ENG., 24p. (gr. k-1). Illus.). pap. 7.29 (978-1-4296-6213-0(1)); pap. 41.70 (978-1-4296-6385-4(5)) Capstone Press of Coughlan Cos. (Pebble Plus).

—How to Make a Liquid Rainbow, 1 vol. 2011. (Hands-On Science Fun Ser.). (ENG., 24p. (gr. k-1). Illus.). pap. 7.29 (978-1-4296-6216-1(6)); pap. 41.70 (978-1-4296-6386-1(3)) Capstone Press of Coughlan Cos. (Pebble Plus).

—How to Make a Mystery Smell Balloon, 1 vol. 2010. (Hands-On Science Fun Ser.). (ENG., 24p. (gr. k-1). Illus.). pap. 7.29 (978-1-4296-5579-8(8)); pap. 41.70 (978-1-4296-5580-4(1)); lib. bdg. 26.65 (978-1-4296-4494-5(X)) Capstone Press of Coughlan Cos. (Pebble Plus).

Shores, Lori & Capstone Press Staff. Hands-On Science Fun, 1 vol. 2010. (Hands-on Science Fun Ser.). (ENG.). 32p. lib. bdg. 95.96 (978-1-4296-5941-3(6), Pebble Plus) Capstone Press of Coughlan Cos.

Sian Phys&Chml Changes. 2004. (Science in A Nutshell Ser.). (J). (978-1-59242-055-1(9)) Delta Education, LLC.

Simon, Seymour & Fauteux, Nicole. Let's Try It Out in the Air. Cushman, Doug, illus. 2003. (Let's Try It Out Ser.). 28p. (J). (gr. -1-3). lib. bdg. 14.65 (978-0-7569-1477-6(9)) Perfection Learning Corp.

—Let's Try It Out in the Water: Hands-on Early-Learning Science Activities. Cushman, Doug, illus. 2003. (Let's Try It Out Ser.). (J). (gr. -1-3). 14.65 (978-0-7569-1478-3(7)) Perfection Learning Corp.

SMARTLAB Creative Team. Indoor Outdoor Science Lab. 2010. 12p. mass mkt. 39.99 (978-1-60380-051-8(4)) becker&mayer! books.

Smith, A. Big Book of Science Experiments. rev. ed. 2011. (Science Experiments Ser.). 96p. (J). pap. 14.99 (978-0-7945-3039-6(7), Usborne) EDC Publishing.

Smith, Chris & Ansell, Dave. Spectacular Science: Exciting Experiments to Try at Home. 2010. (ENG., Illus.). 144p. (gr. 6-18). (978-1-84773-703-8(X)) New Holland Pubs., Ltd.

Smith, Paula. Plan & Investigate It! 2015. (ENG., Illus.). 24p. (J). pap. (978-0-7787-1546-7(9)) Crabtree Publishing Co.

—Prove It! 2015. (ENG., Illus.). 24p. (J). pap. (978-0-7787-1547-4(7)) Crabtree Publishing Co.

Sohn, Emily & Barnett III, Charles. A Crash Course in Forces & Motion with Max Axiom, Super Scientist. Erwin, Steve, illus. 2016. (Graphic Science Ser.). (ENG.). 32p. (gr. 3-4). pap. 8.10 (978-1-5157-4638-6(0), Graphic Library) Capstone Press of Coughlan Cos.

Sohn, Emily & Fellows, Frederick. Variables & Experiments: Getting Across the River. 2011. (IScience Readers Ser.). 48p. (J). (gr. 5-6). lib. bdg. 23.94 (978-1-59953-431-2(2)) Norwood Hse. Pr.

Sohn, Emily & Rompella, Natalie. Fun Science. 2015. (Fun Science Ser.). (ENG.). 24p. (gr. 1-2). 101.28 (978-1-4914-6910-1(2), First Facts) Capstone Press of Coughlan Cos.

Solway, Andrew. The Science of a Loaf of Bread: The Science of Changing Properties. 2009. (Science of... Ser.). (Illus.). 32p. (YA). (gr. 3-6). lib. bdg. 26.00 (978-1-4339-0043-3(2)) Stevens, Gareth Publishing LLLP.

Somervill, Barbara A. What Did You Find Out? Reporting Conclusions. 2006. (Scientific Processes Ser.). (Illus.). 24p. (J). (gr. 3-7). lib. bdg. 21.25 (978-1-4042-3486-4(1), PowerKids Pr.) Rosen Publishing Group, Inc., The.

—What Did You Find Out? Reporting Conclusions. (Think Like a Scientist Ser.). 24p. 2009. (gr. 2-3). 42.50 (978-1-60854-359-5(5), PowerKids Pr.) 2007. (gr. 3-5). pap. 8.25 (978-1-4358-2684-7(1), Rosen Classroom) Rosen Publishing Group, Inc., The.

—What Do You Want to Prove? Planning Investigations. 2006. (Think Like a Scientist Ser.). (Illus.). 24p. (YA). (gr. 2-5). lib. bdg. 22.60 (978-1-4042-3483-3(7)) Rosen Publishing Group, Inc., The.

—What Do You Want to Prove? Planning Investigations. (Think Like a Scientist Ser.). 24p. 2009. (gr. 2-3). 42.50 (978-1-60854-360-1(9), PowerKids Pr.) 2007. (gr. 3-5). pap. 8.25 (978-1-4358-2685-4(X), Rosen Classroom) Rosen Publishing Group, Inc., The.

Spilsbury, Richard & Spilsbury, Louise. What Are Forces & Motion? Exploring Science with Hands-on Activities. 2008. (In Touch with Basic Science Ser.). (Illus.). 32p. (J). (gr. 3-4). lib. bdg. 23.94 (978-0-7660-3095-4(4), Enslow Elementary) Enslow Pubs., Inc.

—What Are Solids, Liquids, & Gases? Exploring Science with Hands-on Activities. 2008. (In Touch with Basic Science Ser.). (Illus.). 32p. (J). (gr. 3-4). lib. bdg. 23.94 (978-0-7660-3094-7(6), Enslow Elementary) Enslow Pubs., Inc.

—What Is Sound? Exploring Science with Hands-on Activities. 2008. (In Touch with Basic Science Ser.). (Illus.). 32p. (J). (gr. 3-4). lib. bdg. 23.94 (978-0-7660-3098-5(9), Enslow Elementary) Enslow Pubs., Inc.

Squire, Ann O. Extreme Experiments. 2014. (True Book(tm), a — Extreme Science Ser.). (ENG.). 48p. (J). lib. bdg. 31.00 (978-0-531-20742-0(0)) Scholastic Library Publishing.

Stillinger, Doug, ed. Battery Science: Make Widgets That Work & Gadgets That Go. 2003. (ENG., Illus.). 56p. (J). (gr. 3-7). 21.95 (978-1-59174-251-7(X), 53643124) Klutz.

Strickling, Jacob. Make Science Fun. 2017. (ENG., Illus.). 192p. (J). 14.99 **(978-1-74257-907-8(8))** New Holland Pubs. Pty, Ltd. AUS. Dist: Midpoint Trade Bks., Inc.

Sturm, Jeanne. Comprension de los Modelos. 2012. (SPA & ENG.). 48p. (gr. 4-8). pap. 10.95 (978-1-61810-472-4(1)) Rourke Educational Media.

—Understanding Models. 2009. (ENG., Illus.). 48p. (gr. 4-8). pap. 10.95 (978-1-60694-528-5(9)) Rourke Educational Media.

Super Science Tools. 2017. (Super Science Tools Ser.). 24p. (gr. 1-2). pap. 48.90 **(978-1-5382-0228-9(X))**; lib. bdg. 135.60 **(978-1-5382-0227-2(1))** Stevens, Gareth Publishing LLLP.

Swanson, Jennifer. Busting Boredom with Experiments. 2017. (Boredom Busters Ser.). (ENG., Illus.). 32p. (gr. 3-4). lib. bdg. 27.99 (978-1-5157-4702-4(6), Edge Bks.) Capstone Press of Coughlan Cos.

Taylor, Barbara. I Wonder Why Soap Makes Bubbles: And Other Questions about Science. 2013. (I Wonder Why Ser.). (ENG., Illus.). 32p. (J). (gr. k-3). 6.99 (978-0-7534-6936-1(7), 9780753469361, Kingfisher) Roaring Brook Pr.

Taylor-Butler, Christine. Bathroom Science. 2016. (ENG., Illus.). 144p. (J). (gr. 2). spiral bd. 14.99 (978-1-62686-587-7(6), Portable Pr.) Readerlink Distribution Services, LLC.

—Experiments with Liquids, 1 vol. 2011. (My Science Investigations Ser.). (ENG.). 32p. (gr. 1-3). 27.32 (978-1-4329-5361-4(3), Heinemann First Library) Heinemann-Raintree.

—Experiments with Magnets & Metals, 1 vol. 2011. (My Science Investigations Ser.). (ENG.). 32p. (gr. 1-3). pap. 8.29 (978-1-4329-5365-2(6), Heinemann First Library) Heinemann-Raintree.

—Experiments with Plants, 1 vol. 2011. (My Science Investigations Ser.). (ENG.). 32p. (gr. 1-3). pap. 8.29 (978-1-4329-5368-3(0)); 27.32 (978-1-4329-5362-1(1)) Heinemann-Raintree. (Heinemann First Library).

—Experiments with Rocks, 1 vol. 2011. (My Science Investigations Ser.). (ENG.). 32p. (gr. 1-3). pap. 8.29 (978-1-4329-5366-9(4)); 27.32 (978-1-4329-5360-7(5)) Heinemann-Raintree. (Heinemann First Library).

—Experiments with Soil, 1 vol. 2011. (My Science Investigations Ser.). (ENG.). 32p. (gr. 1-3). pap. 8.29 (978-1-4329-5369-0(9), Heinemann First Library) Heinemann-Raintree.

—My Science Investigations, 5 vols. 2011. (My Science Investigations Ser.). (ENG.). 32p. (gr. 1-3). pap. 33.16 (978-1-4329-5370-6(2), Heinemann First Library) Heinemann-Raintree.

Thomas, Isabel. Read & Experiment. 2015. (Read & Experiment Ser.). (ENG.). 32p. (gr. 2-4). lib. bdg. 122.60 (978-1-4109-6840-1(5), Raintree Perspectives) Heinemann-Raintree.

Thomas, Lyn. 100% Pure Fake: Gross Out Your Friends & Family with 25 Great Special Effects! 2012. (ENG., Illus.). 48p. (J). (gr. 3-7). 8.95 (978-1-55453-931-4(5)) Kids Can Pr., Ltd. CAN. Dist: Hachette Bk. Group.

Tocci, Salvatore. Experiments with Colors. 2003. (True Bks.). (ENG., Illus.). 48p. (J). 25.00 (978-0-516-22785-6(8), Children's Pr.) Scholastic Library Publishing.

Top That Publishing Staff, ed. Safe & Simple Science Tricks. 2004. (Fun Kits Ser.). (Illus.). 48p. (J). (978-1-904748-75-5(9)) Top That! Publishing PLC.

Unwin, M. Science Activities. 2009. (Science Activities Ser.). 74p. (J). Vol. 2. 13.99 (978-0-7945-2421-0(4)) Vol. 3. 13.99 (978-0-7945-2422-7(2)) EDC Publishing. (Usborne).

VanCleave, Janice. A+ Projects in Physics: Winning Experiments for Science Fairs & Extra Credit. 2003. (VanCleave a+ Science Projects Ser.: 4). (ENG., Illus.). 240p. (gr. 7-12). pap. 16.00 (978-0-471-33098-1(1), Wiley) Wiley, John & Sons, Inc.

—A+ Science Fair Projects. 2003. (ENG., Illus.). 164p. (gr. 7-12). pap. 14.95 (978-0-471-33102-5(3), Jossey-Bass) Wiley, John & Sons, Inc.

—Engineering for Every Kid: Easy Activities That Make Learning Science Fun. 2007. (Science for Every Kid Ser.: 119). (ENG., Illus.). 220p. (gr. 3-7). pap. 14.95 (978-0-471-47182-0(8), Wiley) Wiley, John & Sons, Inc.

—Janice VanCleave's Big Book of Play & Find Out Science Projects. 2007. (ENG., Illus.). 224p. (gr. 3-7). per. 19.95 (978-0-7879-8928-6(2), Jossey-Bass) Wiley, John & Sons, Inc.

—Janice VanCleave's Great Science Project Ideas from Real Kids. 2006. (ENG., Illus.). 144p. (gr. 3-7). pap. 16.00 (978-0-471-47204-9(2), Wiley) Wiley, John & Sons, Inc.

—More of Janice VanCleave's Wild, Wacky, & Weird Earth Science Experiments. 2016. (Janice VanCleave's Wild, Wacky, & Weird Science Experiments Ser.). 00064p. (J). (gr. 5-5). pap. 12.95 (978-1-4994-6549-5(1), Rosen Young Adult) Rosen Publishing Group, Inc., The.

—Super Science Challenges: Hands-On Inquiry Projects for Schools, Science Fairs, or Just Plain Fun! 2007. (ENG., Illus.). 160p. (gr. 3-7). pap. 14.95 (978-0-471-47183-7(6), Wiley) Wiley, John & Sons, Inc.

Vanstone, Emma & Oyler, Amy. Pop, Sizzle, Boom! 101 Science Experiments for the Mad Scientist in Every Kid. Brack, Amanda, illus. 2017. (ENG.). 256p. (J). pap. 14.99 (978-1-250-09282-3(5), 9781250092823) St. Martin's Pr.

Vecchione, Glen. Experimentos Sencillos con la Luz y el Sonido. Elena, Horacio, tr. Elena, Horacio, illus. 2004. (Juego de la Ciencia Ser.). (SPA.). 124p. 10.99 (978-84-9754-043-8(3), 87814) Ediciones Oniro S.A. ESP. Dist: Lectorum Pubns., Inc.

Wakefield, Chris. Dad Did It! 2013. (ENG., Illus.). 32p. pap. 3.25 (978-1-85741-116-4(1)) Southgate Pubs. GBR. Dist: Parkwest Pubns., Inc.

Walker, Pam & Wood, Elaine. Science Experiments on File, 5 vols., Set. 2008. (Experiments Ser.). (gr. 6-12). 925.00 (978-0-8160-7829-5(7)) Facts On File, Inc.

Warner, Penny. Project Book: Ideas, Tips & Techniques for School Projects. Wagner, Amy, ed. Moore, Lishia, illus. Moore, Lishia & Wagner, Amy, photos by. 2007. 80p. pap. 9.98 (978-1-887436-05-2(7)) Woodland Scenics.

Weakland, Mark. Zoom! Wile E. Coyote Experiments with Speed & Velocity. Sordo, Paco, illus. 2017. (Wile E. Coyote, Physical Science Genius Ser.). (ENG.). 32p. (gr. 3-5). lib. bdg. 30.65 (978-1-5157-3734-6(9)) Capstone Press of Coughlan Cos.

West, Krista. Hands-on Projects about Changes in the Earth. 2009. (Great Earth Science Projects Ser.). 24p. (gr. 3-3). 42.50 (978-1-61513-110-5(8), PowerKids Pr.) Rosen Publishing Group, Inc., The.

—Hands-on Projects about Oceans. 2009. (Great Earth Science Projects Ser.). 24p. (gr. 3-3). 42.50 (978-1-61513-112-9(4), PowerKids Pr.) Rosen Publishing Group, Inc., The.

Wheeler-Toppen, Jodi. Science Experiments That Explode & Implode: Fun Projects for Curious Kids. 2011. (Kitchen Science Ser.). (ENG.). 32p. (gr. 3-4). pap. 47.70 (978-1-4296-6418-9(5), Edge Bks.) Capstone Press of Coughlan Cos.

—Science Experiments That Fizz & Bubble: Fun Projects for Curious Kids. (Kitchen Science Ser.). (ENG.). 32p. (gr. 3-4). 2011. pap. 47.70 (978-1-4296-6419-6(3)) 2010. lib. bdg. 27.99 (978-1-4296-5425-8(2)) Capstone Press of Coughlan Cos. (Edge Bks.).

Wheeler-Toppen, Jodi, et al. Girls Science Club. 2012. (Girls Science Club Ser.). (ENG.). 32p. (gr. 3-4). pap. 190.80 (978-1-4296-8522-1(0)); pap. 31.80 (978-1-4296-8521-4(2)); lib. bdg. 83.97 (978-1-4296-8218-3(3)) Capstone Press of Coughlan Cos. (Snap Bks.).

Whitley, Peggy J. & Goodwin, Susan Williams. 99 Jumpstarts for Kids' Science Research, 1 vol. 2005. (Illus.). 264p. (C). per. 37.00 (978-1-59158-261-8(X), LU261X, Libraries Unlimited) ABC-CLIO, LLC.

Wiese, Jim & Shems, Ed. Weird Science: 40 Strange-Acting, Bizarre-Looking, & Barely Believable Activities for Kids. Shems, Ed, illus. 2004. (ENG., Illus.). 132p. (J). (gr. 3-7). pap. 14.95 (978-0-471-46229-3(2), Wiley) Wiley, John & Sons, Inc.

Williams, Jennifer. Oobleck, Slime & Dancing Spaghetti: Twenty Terrific at Home Science Experiments Inspired by Favorite Children's Books. 2009. (ENG., Illus.). 192p. pap. 14.95 *(978-1-933979-34-2(8),* 09eef5a8-0fe3-4734-a09c-0ab0a1faa3bb) Bright Sky Pr.

Williams, Zella. Do-It-Yourself Science, 6 bks., Set. Incl. Experiments about Planet Earth. (J). lib. bdg. 25.25 *(978-1-4042-3662-2(7))*; Experiments about the Natural World. (J). lib. bdg. 25.25 *(978-1-4042-3661-5(9))*; Experiments on Rocks & the Rock Cycle. (YA). lib. bdg. 25.25 *(978-1-4042-3660-8(0))*; Experiments on the Weather. (J). lib. bdg. 25.25 *(978-1-4042-3663-9(5))*; Experiments with Physical Science. (J). lib. bdg. 25.25 *(978-1-4042-3659-2(7))*; Experiments with Solids, Liquids, & Gases. (J). lib. bdg. 25.25 *(978-1-4042-3658-5(9))*; (Illus.). 24p. (gr. 2-5). 2007. 2007. Set lib. bdg. 143.70 *(978-1-4042-3605-9(8),* PowerKids Pr.) Rosen Publishing Group, Inc., The.

—Experiments with Solids, Liquids, & Gases. 2007. (Do-It-Yourself Science Ser.). (Illus.). 24p. (J). 42.30 *(978-1-4042-4013-1(6),* PowerKids Pr.) Rosen Publishing Group, Inc., The.

Winston, Robert. Science Rocks! 2011. (ENG., Illus.). 144p. (J). (gr. 3-7). 19.99 *(978-0-7566-7198-3(1),* DK Children) Dorling Kindersley Publishing, Inc.

Yomtov, Nel. How to Write a Lab Report. Petelinsek, Kathleen, illus. 2013. (Explorer Junior Library: How to Write Ser.). (ENG.). 24p. (J). (gr. 1-4). 25.64 *(978-1-62431-185-7(7),* 203064); pap. 12.79 *(978-1-62431-317-2(5),* 203066) Cherry Lake Publishing.

SCIENCE—EXPERIMENTS—FICTION

Anderson, M. T. The Pox Party. 2006. (Astonishing Life of Octavian Nothing, Traitor to the Nation Ser.: Vol. 1). (ENG., Illus.). 368p. (YA). (gr. 9-12). 17.99 *(978-0-7636-2402-6(0))* Candlewick Pr.

Andros, Camille. Charlotte the Scientist Is Squished. Farley, Brianne, illus. 2017. (ENG.). 40p. (J). (gr. -1-3). 16.99 *(978-0-544-78583-0(5))* Houghton Mifflin Harcourt Publishing Co.

Beaty, Andrea. Ada Twist, Scientist. Roberts, David, illus. 2016. (ENG.). 32p. (J). (gr. k-2). 17.95 *(978-1-4197-2137-3(2),* Abrams Bks. for Young Readers) Abrams, Inc.

Benton, Jim. Attack of the 50-Ft. Cupid. Benton, Jim, illus. 2004. (Franny K. Stein, Mad Scientist Ser.: 2). (ENG., Illus.). 112p. (J). (gr. 2-5). 16.99 *(978-0-689-86292-2(X),* Simon & Schuster Bks. For Young Readers) Simon & Schuster Bks. For Young Readers.

—Attack of the 50-Ft. Cupid, 1 vol. Benton, Jim, illus. 2011. (Franny K. Stein, Mad Scientist Ser.). (ENG., Illus.). 112p. (gr. 3-6). 24.21 *(978-1-59961-818-0(4))* Spotlight.

—Crate of Danger. Benton, Jim, illus. 2005. (Franny K. Stein, Mad Scientist Ser.). (ENG., Illus.). 448p. (J). (gr. 2-5). pap. 23.99 *(978-1-4169-1402-0(1),* Simon & Schuster Bks. For Young Readers) Simon & Schuster Bks. For Young Readers.

—The Fran That Time Forgot, 1 vol. Benton, Jim, illus. 2011. (Franny K. Stein, Mad Scientist Ser.). (ENG., Illus.). 112p. (gr. 3-6). 24.21 *(978-1-59961-820-3(6))* Spotlight.

—The Fran with Four Brains, 1 vol. Benton, Jim, illus. 2011. (Franny K. Stein, Mad Scientist Ser.). (ENG., Illus.). 112p. (gr. 3-6). 24.21 *(978-1-59961-822-7(2))* Spotlight.

—The Fran with Four Brains. 2007. (Franny K. Stein, Mad Scientist Ser.: 6). lib. bdg. 16.00 *(978-1-4177-9038-8(5),* Turtleback) Turtleback Bks.

—The Frandidate. Benton, Jim, illus. 2009. (Franny K. Stein, Mad Scientist Ser.: 7). (ENG., Illus.). 112p. (J). (gr. 2-5). pap. 5.99 *(978-1-4169-0234-8(1),* Simon & Schuster Bks. For Young Readers) Simon & Schuster Bks. For Young Readers.

—The Frandidate, 1 vol. Benton, Jim, illus. 2011. (Franny K. Stein, Mad Scientist Ser.). (ENG., Illus.). 128p. (gr. 3-6). 24.21 *(978-1-59961-823-4(0))* Spotlight.

—Franny K. Stein, Mad Scientist, 7 vols., Set. Benton, Jim, illus. Incl. Attack of the 50-Ft. Cupid. 112p. 24.21 *(978-1-59961-818-0(4))*; Fran That Time Forgot. 112p. 24.21 *(978-1-59961-820-3(6))*; Fran with Four Brains. 112p. 24.21 *(978-1-59961-822-7(2))*; Frandidate. 128p. 24.21 *(978-1-59961-823-4(0))*; Frantastic Voyage. 112p. 24.21 *(978-1-59961-821-0(4))*; Invisible Fran. 112p. 24.21 *(978-1-59961-819-7(2))*; Lunch Walks among Us. 112p. 24.21 *(978-1-59961-817-3(6))*; (gr. 3-6). (Franny K. Stein, Mad Scientist Ser.). (Illus.). 2011. 169.47 *(978-1-59961-816-6(8))* Spotlight.

—Lunch Walks among Us. Benton, Jim, illus. (Franny K. Stein, Mad Scientist Ser.: 1). (ENG., Illus.). 112p. (J). (gr. 2-5). 2004. mass mkt. 5.99 *(978-0-689-86295-3(4))* 2003. 16.99 *(978-0-689-86291-5(1))* Simon & Schuster Bks. For Young Readers. (Simon & Schuster Bks. For Young Readers).

—Lunch Walks among Us, 1 vol. Benton, Jim, illus. 2011. (Franny K. Stein, Mad Scientist Ser.). (ENG., Illus.). 112p. (gr. 3-6). 24.21 *(978-1-59961-817-3(6))* Spotlight.

Bloch, Robert. The Crowded Earth. 2009. 112p. 22.95 *(978-1-60664-648-9(6))*; pap. 9.95 *(978-1-60664-273-3(1))* Rodgers, Alan Bks.

Bodeen, S. A. The Gardener. 2011. (ENG.). 256p. (YA). (gr. 7-12). pap. 9.99 *(978-0-312-65942-4(3),* 9780312659424) Square Fish.

Clements, Andrew. Jake Drake, Know-It-All. Frazee, Marla & Pedersen, Janet, illus. 2007. (Jake Drake Ser.: Bk. 2). 88p. (gr. 2-5). 15.00 *(978-0-7569-8212-6(X))* Perfection Learning Corp.

—Jake Drake, Know-It-All. Pedersen, Janet & Frazee, Marla, illus. 2007. (Jake Drake Ser.: Bk. 2). (ENG.). 112p. (J). (gr. 2-5). pap. 5.99 *(978-1-4169-3931-3(8),* Atheneum Bks. for Young Readers) Simon & Schuster Children's Publishing.

Cooper, Jay. Mutant Rat Attack! 2017. (Spy Next Door Ser.: 1). (ENG.). 144p. (J). (gr. 2-5). 9.99 *(978-0-545-93297-4(1),* Scholastic Pr.) Scholastic, Inc.

Coven, Wanda. Heidi Heckelbeck & the Secret Admirer. 2012. (Heidi Heckelbeck Ser.: 6). lib. bdg. 16.00 *(978-0-606-26905-6(3),* Turtleback) Turtleback Bks.

Dahl, Michael. Maze Monster. Catling, Andy, illus. 2016. (Igor's Lab of Fear Ser.). (ENG.). 40p. (gr. 1-3). lib. bdg. 23.99 *(978-1-4965-3528-3(6))* Stone Arch Bks.

Dashner, James. The Maze Runner & the Scorch Trials, Bks. 1 & 2. collector's ed. 2015. (Maze Runner Ser.). (ENG.). 816p. (YA). (gr. 7). pap. 19.99 *(978-0-553-53824-3(1),* Delacorte Pr.) Random Hse. Children's Bks.

De Marco, Clare. The Mad Scientist Next Door. 2014. (ENG., Illus.). 32p. (J). *(978-0-7787-1305-0(9))* Crabtree Publishing Co.

Dowell, Frances O'Roark. Blasts Off! McDaniels, Preston, illus. 2011. (From the Highly Scientific Notebooks of Phineas L. MacGuire Ser.). (ENG.). 224p. (J). (gr. 3-7). pap. 7.99 *(978-1-4424-2204-9(1),* Atheneum Bks. for Young Readers) Simon & Schuster Children's Publishing.

—Erupts! McDaniels, Preston, illus. 2006. (From the Highly Scientific Notebooks of Phineas L. MacGuire Ser.). (ENG.). 176p. (J). (gr. 3-7). 16.99 *(978-1-4169-0195-2(7),* Atheneum Bks. for Young Readers) Simon & Schuster Children's Publishing.

—Phineas L. MacGuire ... Gets Cooking! McDaniels, Preston, illus. 2015. (From the Highly Scientific Notebooks of Phineas L. MacGuire Ser.). (ENG.). 224p. (J). (gr. 3-7). pap. 6.99 *(978-1-4814-0100-5(9))* Simon & Schuster Children's Publishing.

—Phineas L. Macguire... Erupts! McDaniels, Preston, illus. 2007. (From the Highly Scientific Notebooks of Phineas L. MacGuire Ser.). (ENG.). 176p. (J). (gr. 3-7). pap. 6.99 *(978-1-4169-4734-9(5),* Atheneum Bks. for Young Readers) Simon & Schuster Children's Publishing.

—Phineas L. MacGuire... Gets Slimed! McDaniels, Preston, illus. (From the Highly Scientific Notebooks of Phineas L. MacGuire Ser.). (ENG.). (J). (gr. 3-7). 2010. 224p. pap. 6.99 *(978-1-4169-9775-7(X))* 2007. 208p. 16.99 *(978-1-4169-0196-9(5))* Simon & Schuster Children's Publishing. (Atheneum Bks. for Young Readers).

Galardi Mlis, Judith A. Judi Galardi's Thrae Back Atcha! 2011. 128p. (gr. -1). pap. 16.49 *(978-1-4567-2388-0(X))* AuthorHouse.

Glickman, Susan. Bernadette in the Doghouse, 1 vol. 2011. (Lunch Bunch Ser.). (ENG., Illus.). 122p. (J). (gr. 2-4). pap. 8.95 *(978-1-897187-92-0(0))* Second Story Pr. CAN. Dist: Orca Bk. Pubs. USA.

Grunwell, Jeanne Marie. Mind Games. 2006. (ENG., Illus.). 144p. (J). (gr. 5-7). pap. 10.95 *(978-0-618-68947-7(8))* Houghton Mifflin Harcourt Publishing Co.

Hawking, Lucy & Hawking, Stephen W. George & the Big Bang. Parsons, Garry, illus. 2012. (George's Secret Key Ser.). (ENG.). 336p. (J). (gr. 3-7). 22.99 *(978-1-4424-4005-0(8),* Simon & Schuster Bks. For Young Readers) Simon & Schuster Bks. For Young Readers.

Hawking, Stephen W. & Hawking, Lucy. George & the Big Bang. Parsons, Garry, illus. 2013. (George's Secret Key Ser.). (ENG.). 304p. (J). (gr. 3-7). pap. 11.99 *(978-1-4424-4006-7(6),* Simon & Schuster Bks. For Young Readers) Simon & Schuster Bks. For Young Readers.

Haynes, Natalie. The Great Escape. 2014. (ENG.). 288p. (J). pap. 8.99 *(978-1-4711-2184-5(4),* Simon & Schuster Children's) Simon & Schuster, Ltd. GBR. Dist: Simon & Schuster, Inc.

Howe, James. It Came from Beneath the Bed! 2004. (Tales from the House of Bunnicula Ser.). 112p. (J). (gr. 3-6). pap. 17.00 incl. audio *(978-1-4000-8632-0(9),* Listening Library) Random Hse. Audio Publishing Group.

Hughes, Alison. On a Scale of Idiot to Complete Jerk, 1 vol. 2014. (ENG., Illus.). 144p. (J). (gr. 4-7). pap. 9.95 *(978-1-4598-0484-5(8))* Orca Bk. Pubs. USA.

Hughey, Sue C. Herby's Secret Formula. Hughey, Sue C., illus. 2013. (Illus.). 232p. pap. 11.95 *(978-0-9840358-1-6(8))* Associated Arts Pub.

Jonell, Lynne. The Secret of Zoom. 2009. (ENG.). 304p. (J). (gr. 4-7). 16.99 *(978-0-8050-8856-4(3),* 9780805088564, Holt, Henry & Co. Bks. For Young Readers) Holt, Henry & Co.

Khoury, Jessica. Origin. 2013. (ENG., Illus.). 432p. (YA). (gr. 7). pap. 9.99 *(978-1-59514-596-3(6),* Razorbill) Penguin Young Readers Group.

—Vitro. 2015. (ENG.). 384p. (YA). (gr. 7). pap. 9.99 *(978-1-59514-606-9(7),* Razorbill) Penguin Young Readers Group.

King, Trey. Wrecking Valentine's Day! Wang, Sean, illus. 2015. 24p. (J). ***(978-1-4806-9662-4(5))*** Scholastic, Inc.

Knudsen, Michelle. Argus. Wesson, Andrea, illus. 2011. (ENG.). 32p. (J). (gr. -1-3). 15.99 *(978-0-7636-3790-3(4))* Candlewick Pr.

Kravetz, Nathan. A Monkey's Tale. 2012. 64p. (gr. 4-6). pap. 8.95 *(978-1-4759-5825-6(0))* iUniverse, Inc.

LernerClassroom Editors, ed. Science Solves It! en Espanol: Classroom Set. 2008. pap. 22.95 *(978-1-58013-766-9(0))* Kane Press, Inc.

—Science Solves It! en Espanol: Complete Set. 2008. pap. 138.95 *(978-1-58013-767-6(9))* Kane Press, Inc.

Lynellen Sullivan & Bryan Castle. Poppers to the Rescue: Book 1 of the Popcorn Series. 2010. 72p. pap. 8.95 *(978-1-4401-9764-2(4))* iUniverse, Inc.

Margles, Samantha. Star Wars: Science Fair Book. Scholastic, Inc. Staff, illus. 2013. (Star Wars Ser.). (ENG.). 128p. (J). (gr. 5-9). pap. 9.99 *(978-0-545-52099-7(1))* Scholastic, Inc.

McAlpine, Gordon. The Tell-Tale Start. Zuppardi, Sam, illus. 2013. (Misadventures of Edgar & Allan Poe Ser.: 1). (ENG.). 192p. (J). (gr. 3-7). 15.99 *(978-0-670-78491-2(5),* Viking Books for Young Readers) Penguin Young Readers Group.

McDaniels, Preston, illus. Phineas L. MacGuire ... Gets Cooking! 2014. (From the Highly Scientific Notebooks of Phineas L. MacGuire Ser.). (ENG.). 208p. (J). (gr. 3-7). 16.99 *(978-1-4814-0099-2(1),* Atheneum Bks. for Young Readers) Simon & Schuster Children's Publishing.

Meister, Cari. Buzz Beaker & the Growing Goo, 1 vol. McGuire, Bill, illus. 2011. (Buzz Beaker Bks.). (ENG.). 32p. (gr. 2-3). pap. 6.25 *(978-1-4342-3056-0(2))*; lib. bdg. 22.65 *(978-1-4342-2527-6(5))* Stone Arch Bks.

Mills, Claudia. The Trouble with Ants. Kath, Katie, illus. 2016. (Nora Notebooks Ser.: 1). (ENG.). 176p. (J). (gr. 2-5). 6.99 *(978-0-385-39163-4(3),* Yearling) Random Hse. Children's Bks.

Mull, David Kenneth. His Date for the Dance was His Science Project. 2012. 80p. pap. 9.99 *(978-0-89824-371-0(8))* Royal Fireworks Publishing Co.

O'Hara, Mo. Any Fin Is Possible. Jagucki, Marek, illus. 2016. (My Big Fat Zombie Goldfish Ser.: 4). (ENG.). 224p. (J). (gr. 3-5). 12.99 *(978-1-250-06353-3(1),* 9781250063533) Feiwel & Friends.

Parish, Herman. Amelia Bedelia, Rocket Scientist? Sweat, Lynn, illus. (I Can Read Level 2 Ser.). 64p. (J). 2007. (ENG.). (gr. k-3). pap. 3.99 *(978-0-06-051889-9(8),* Greenwillow Bks.) 2005. (gr. 1-18). 15.99 *(978-0-06-051887-5(1))* 2005. (gr. k-4). lib. bdg. 17.89 *(978-0-06-051888-2(X),* Greenwillow Bks.) HarperCollins Pubs.

Patterson, James. Maximum Ride. 2010. (ENG.). 1392p. (YA). (gr. 5-17). pap., pap. 29.99 *(978-0-316-12825-4(2),* Jimmy Patterson) Little Brown & Co.

Pflugfelder, Bob & Hockensmith, Steve. Nick & Tesla's Secret Agent Gadget Battle. 2014. (Nick & Tesla Ser.: 3). (ENG., Illus.). 256p. (J). (gr. 4-7). 12.95 *(978-1-59474-676-5(1))* Quirk Bks.

—Nick & Tesla's Special Effects Spectacular: A Mystery with Animatronics, Alien Makeup, Camera Gear, & Other Movie Magic You Can Make Yourself! 2015. (Nick & Tesla Ser.: 5). (ENG.). 256p. (J). (gr. 4-7). 12.95 *(978-1-59474-760-1(1))* Quirk Bks.

Press, J. Robots Don't Clean Toilets. Kline, Michael, illus. 2013. (Doodles of Sam Dibble Ser.: 3). (ENG.). 128p. (J). (gr. 1-3). pap. 4.99 *(978-0-448-46109-0(9),* Grosset & Dunlap) Penguin Young Readers Group.

Robbins, Trina. A Midterm Night's Scheme. Page, Tyler, illus. 2014. (Chicagoland Detective Agency Ser.: 6). (ENG.). 64p. (gr. 4-8). lib. bdg. 29.27 *(978-0-7613-8167-9(8),* Graphic Universe™) Lerner Publishing Group.

Roland, Timothy. A Silly Science Experiment. 2007. (Illus.). 91p. (J). *(978-0-545-00400-8(4))* Scholastic, Inc.

Seuling, Barbara. Robert & the Happy Endings. Brewer, Paul, illus. 2007. (Robert Bks.). (ENG.). 160p. (J). (gr. 1-4). 16.95 *(978-0-8126-2748-0(2))* Cricket Bks.

Shelley, Mary. Frankenstein. 2014. (Differentiated Timeless Classics Ser.). (ENG.). 80p. (YA). (gr. 9-12). 12.95 *(978-1-62250-717-7(7))* Saddleback Educational Publishing, Inc.

Tobin, Paul. The Genius Factor: How to Capture an Invisible Cat. Lafontaine, Thierry, illus. 2017. (ENG.). 288p. (J). pap. 7.99 *(978-1-68119-278-9(0),* 9781681192789, Bloomsbury USA Childrens) Bloomsbury Publishing USA.

Wells, H. G. The Invisible Man. Calero, Dennis, illus. 2010. (Classic Fiction Ser.). 72p. pap. 0.60 *(978-1-4342-3208-3(5),* Graphic Revolve) Stone Arch Bks.

Yasuda, Anita. The Slime Attack, 1 vol. Harpster, Steve, illus. 2013. (Dino Detectives Ser.). (ENG.). 32p. (gr. 1-2). pap. 5.95 *(978-1-4342-4833-6(X))*; lib. bdg. 22.65 *(978-1-4342-4153-5(X))* Stone Arch Bks.

SCIENCE—FICTION

see Science Fiction

SCIENCE—HISTORY

ABDO. History of Science, 1 vol. 2014. (History of Science Ser.: 8). (ENG.). 112p. (J). (gr. 6-12). lib. bdg. 285.12 *(978-1-62403-557-9(4),* Essential Library) ABDO Publishing Co.

Anniss, Matt. James Watson & Francis Crick. 2014. (Dynamic Duos of Science Ser.). 48p. (YA). (gr. 5-8). pap. 84.30 *(978-1-4824-1282-6(9))* Stevens, Gareth Publishing LLLP.

—Science vs. Disease. 2013. (Science Fights Back Ser.). (Illus.). 48p. (gr. 4-6). 31.95 *(978-1-4339-8687-1(6))*; pap. 14.05 *(978-1-4339-8688-8(4))* Stevens, Gareth Publishing LLLP. (Gareth Stevens Learning Library).

Atkinson, Mary. The Earth Is Flat! 2007. (Shockwave: Science in Practice Ser.). (ENG., Illus.). 36p. (J). (gr. 3-5). 25.00 *(978-0-531-17580-4(4),* Children's Pr.) Scholastic Library Publishing.

Balchin, Jon. Science: 100 Scientists Who Changed the World. 2003. (Illus.). 224p. 18.95 *(978-1-59270-017-2(9))* Enchanted Lion Bks., LLC.

Benchmark Education Company, LLC Staff, compiled by. HIST & Nature of Science. 2006. spiral bd. 145.00 *(978-1-4108-6949-4(0))* 2005. spiral bd. 135.00 *(978-1-4108-4515-3(X))* 2005. spiral bd. 185.00 *(978-1-4108-5436-0(1))* 2005. spiral bd. 185.00 *(978-1-4108-5437-7(X))* 2005. spiral bd. 85.00 *(978-1-4108-5849-8(9))* 2005. spiral bd. 165.00 *(978-1-4108-5850-4(2))* 2005. spiral bd. 180.00 *(978-1-4108-3848-3(X))* 2005. spiral bd. 60.00 *(978-1-4108-3849-0(8))* 2005. spiral bd. 145.00 *(978-1-4108-3865-0(X))* 2005. spiral bd. 42.00 *(978-1-4108-3878-0(1))* 2005. spiral bd. 42.00 *(978-1-4108-3879-7(X))* Benchmark Education Co.

—Scientific Achievements: Theme Set. 2006. (J). 131.00 *(978-1-4108-7130-5(4))* Benchmark Education Co.

Biesty, Stephen & Platt, Richard. Stephen Biesty's Incredible Explosions: Exploded Views of Astonishing Things. (Illus.). 32p. (J). pap. 22.99 *(978-0-590-24893-8(6))* Scholastic, Inc.

Bryson, Bill. A Really Short History of Nearly Everything. 2009. (ENG., Illus.). 176p. (J). (gr. 3-7). 19.99 *(978-0-385-73810-1(2),* Delacorte Bks. for Young Readers) Random Hse. Children's Bks.

Challoner, Jack. Exploring the Mysteries of Genius & Invention. 2016. (STEM Guide to the Universe Ser.). (ENG.). 96p. (J). (gr. 9-9). lib. bdg. 46.10 *(978-1-4994-6410-8(X))* Rosen Publishing Group, Inc., The.

Claybourne, Anna. Story of Science Kid Kit. 2010. (Kid Kits Ser.). 96p. (J). pap. 17.99 *(978-1-60130-197-0(9),* Usborne) EDC Publishing.

Craig, Diane. Science History Is No Mystery!, 1 vol. 2007. (Science Made Simple Ser.). (ENG., Illus.). 24p. (J). (gr. k-3). lib. bdg. 24.21 *(978-1-59928-616-7(5),* SandCastle) ABDO Publishing Co.

Farndon, John. Science & Technology: The Greatest Innovations in Human History. 2016. (ENG., Illus.). 64p. 12.99 *(978-1-86147-780-4(5),* Armadillo) Anness Publishing GBR. Dist: National Bk. Network.

—The Story of Science & Technology. 2010. (Journey Through History Ser.). (ENG.). 64p. (YA). lib. bdg. 31.95 *(978-1-4488-0621-8(6),* Rosen Reference) Rosen Publishing Group, Inc., The.

Farndon, John & Woolf, Alex. Great Scientists. 2012. (Great People in History Ser.). (ENG.). 128p. (YA). (gr. 8-12). 34.60 *(978-1-4777-0405-9(1))* Rosen Publishing Group, Inc., The.

Faulkner, Nicholas. A Visual History of Science & Technology. 2016. (Visual History of the World Ser.). 00096p. (YA). (gr. 8-8). 37.10 *(978-1-4994-6596-9(3))* Rosen Publishing Group, Inc., The.

Faulkner, Nicholas, ed. 101 Women of STEM. 2016. (People You Should Know Ser.). 184p. (J). (gr. 8-8). lib. bdg. 36.25 *(978-1-68048-511-0(3))* Rosen Publishing Group, Inc., The.

Gow, Mary. Robert Hooke: Creative Genius, Scientist, Inventor. 2006. (Great Minds of Science Ser.). (Illus.). 128p. (J). (gr. 6-10). lib. bdg. 31.93 *(978-0-7660-2547-9(0))* Enslow Pubs., Inc.

Green, Dan. Rebel Science. Lyttleton, David, illus. 2016. (ENG.). 80p. (J). (gr. 3). 14.95 *(978-1-4549-1945-2(0),* 1402430) Sterling Publishing Co., Inc.

Hall, Derek. Chemistry, Earth, & Space Sciences. 2010. (Facts at Your Fingertips Ser.). (YA). (gr. 7-12). 35.65 *(978-1-933834-47-4(1))* Brown Bear Books.

—Physical Sciences. 2009. (FAYFT: Great Scientists Ser.). 64p. (gr. 4-10). 39.95 *(978-1-933834-46-7(3))* Brown Bear Bks.

Herold, Vickey. Discover Science During the Renaissance. 2006. (J). pap. *(978-1-4108-6467-3(7))* Benchmark Education Co.

—Science During the Renaissance. 2006. (J). pap. *(978-1-4108-6464-2(2))* Benchmark Education Co.

Hunter, Dru. What Is Out There? 2015. (Illus.). 48p. (J). *(978-1-60818-594-8(X),* Creative Education) Creative Co., The.

—What Is Out There? Think Like a Scientist. 2016. (Think Like a Scientist Ser.). (ENG.). 48p. (J). (gr. 5-9). pap. 12.00 *(978-1-62832-199-9(7),* Creative Paperbacks) Creative Co., The.

Killcoyne, Hope Lourie, ed. Science: Its History & Development. 2014. (Study of Science Ser.). 160p. (YA). (gr. 7-12). 35.25 *(978-1-62275-421-2(2))* Rosen Publishing Group, Inc., The.

Kortemeier, Todd. Unsung Heroes of Science. 2017. (Unsung Heroes Ser.). (ENG.). 32p. (J). (gr. 3-6). 21.95 *(978-1-63235-309-2(1))* Pr. Room Editions LLC.

—12 Unsung Heroes of Technology. 2017. (Unsung Heroes Ser.). (ENG., Illus.). 32p. (J). (gr. 3-6). 21.95 *(978-1-63235-311-5(3))* Pr. Room Editions LLC.

Krull, Kathleen. Lives of the Scientists: Experiments, Explosions (and What the Neighbors Thought) Hewitt, Kathryn, illus. 2016. (Lives Of ... Ser.). (ENG.). 96p. (J). (gr. 5-7). 8.99 *(978-0-544-81087-7(2),* HMH Books For Young Readers) Houghton Mifflin Harcourt Publishing Co.

Kudlinski, Kathleen V. Boy, Were We Wrong about Dinosaurs! Schindler, S. D., illus. 2005. (ENG.). 32p. (J). (gr. 1-3). 16.99 *(978-0-525-46978-0(8),* Dutton Books for Young Readers) Penguin Young Readers Group.

Kuhtz, Russell. Physical Science. 2016. (Study of Science Ser.). 00104p. (YA). (gr. 8-8). lib. bdg. 36.25 *(978-1-5081-0425-4(5))* Rosen Publishing Group, Inc., The.

Lachner, Elizabeth, ed. Top 101 Scientists. 2016. (People You Should Know Ser.). 184p. (J). (gr. 8-8). lib. bdg. 36.25 *(978-1-68048-510-3(5))* Rosen Publishing Group, Inc., The.

Life in the American Colonies. 2011. (Life in the American Colonies Ser.). (ENG.). 32p. (gr. 3-4). pap. 31.80 *(978-1-4296-7221-4(8),* Fact Finders) Capstone Press of Coughlan Cos.

Machajewski, Sarah. Freaky Science Discoveries. 2015. (Freaky True Science Ser.). (ENG., Illus.). 32p. (J). (gr. 4-5). pap. 10.50 *(978-1-4824-2952-7(7))* Stevens, Gareth Publishing LLLP.

Merlin, Hope, ed. The History of Science, 1 vol., 1. 2014. (Scientific Inquiry Ser.). (ENG.). 112p. (YA). (gr. 9-12). 32.90 *(978-1-62275-116-7(7))* Rosen Publishing Group, Inc., The.

Meyer, Susan. Isaac Newton. 2017. (Leaders of the Scientific Revolution Ser.). 112p. (J). (gr. 12-13). 37.10 ***(978-1-5081-7470-7(9)***, Rosen Young Adult) Rosen Publishing Group, Inc., The.

Oachs, Emily Rose. The 12 Most Influential Scientific Discoveries of All Time. 2018. (ENG.). 32p. (gr. 3-6). 31.35 ***(978-1-63235-413-6(6)***, 12-Story Library) Pr. Room Editions LLC.

Parker, Steve & Malam, John. A Brief Illustrated History of Science. 2017. (Brief Illustrated History Ser.). (ENG.). 32p. (gr. 3-5). lib. bdg. 27.32 *(978-1-5157-2520-6(0),* Fact Finders) Capstone Press of Coughlan Cos.

Perritano, John. Science & Technology, Vol. 9. van Dijk, Ruud, ed. 2016. (Making of the Modern World: 1945 to the Present Ser.). (Illus.). 64p. (J). (gr. 7). 23.95 *(978-1-4222-3641-3(2))* Mason Crest.

Platt, Richard. Stephen Biesty's Incredible Explosions: Exploded Views of Astonishing Things. Biesty, Stephen, illus. 2004. 32p. (J). (gr. 2-8). reprint ed. 20.00 *(978-0-7567-7680-0(5))* DIANE Publishing Co.

Raum, Elizabeth. The Cold, Hard Facts about Science & Medicine in Colonial America, 1 vol. 2011. (Life in the American Colonies Ser.). (ENG.). 32p. (gr. 3-4). pap. 8.10 *(978-1-4296-7215-3(3))*; pap. 47.70 *(978-1-4296-7216-0(1))* Capstone Press of Coughlan Cos. (Fact Finders).

Raum, Elizabeth, et al. Life in the American Colonies. 2011. (Life in the American Colonies Ser.). (ENG.). 32p. (gr. 3-4). pap. 190.80 *(978-1-4296-7222-1(6))*; lib. bdg. 54.64 *(978-1-4296-6493-6(2))* Capstone Press of Coughlan Cos. (Fact Finders).

Samuels, Charlie. Ancient Science: Prehistory-A.D. 500. 2010. (Science Highlights: A Gareth Stevens Timeline Ser.). (ENG.). 48p. (J). (gr. 6-8). pap. 14.05 *(978-1-4339-4137-5(6))*; lib. bdg. 31.95 *(978-1-4339-4136-8(8))* Stevens, Gareth Publishing LLLP. (Gareth Stevens Secondary Library).

—Medieval Science (500-1500) 2010. (Science Highlights: A Gareth Stevens Timeline Ser.). (ENG.). 48p. (J). (gr. 6-8). pap. 14.05 *(978-1-4339-4140-5(6))*; lib. bdg. 31.95 *(978-1-4339-4139-9(2))* Stevens, Gareth Publishing LLLP. (Gareth Stevens Secondary Library).

—Revolutions in Science: 1550-1700. 2010. (Science Highlights: A Gareth Stevens Timeline Ser.). (ENG.). 48p. (J). (gr. 6-8). pap. 14.05 *(978-1-4339-4143-6(0))*; lib. bdg. 31.95 *(978-1-4339-4142-9(2))* Stevens, Gareth Publishing LLLP. (Gareth Stevens Secondary Library).

Scientific Revolution: PowerPoints in World History. 2005. cd-rom 49.95 net. *(978-1-56004-215-0(X))* Social Studies Schl. Service.

Scientific Revolution DBA. 2003. spiral bd. 16.95 *(978-1-56004-168-9(4))* Social Studies Schl. Service.

Spangenburg, Ray & Moser, Diane. The Birth of Science: Ancient Times to 1699. 2nd rev. ed. 2004. (Facts on File

Science Library). (Illus.). 256p. (gr. 6-12). 40.00 *(978-0-8160-4851-9(7))* Facts On File, Inc.

—Science Frontiers, 1946-2001. 2nd rev. ed. 2004. (Facts on File Science Library). (Illus.). 272p. (gr. 6-12). 40.00 *(978-0-8160-4855-7(X))* Facts On File, Inc.

Zuchora-Walske, Christine. Let's Make Some Gold! Science's Biggest Mistakes about Geology & Ecology. 2014. (Science Gets It Wrong Ser.). (Illus.). 32p. (gr. 4-6). pap. 7.95 *(978-1-4677-4549-9(9))*; (ENG., lib. bdg. 26.60 *(978-1-4677-3662-6(7)*, Lerner Pubns.) Lerner Publishing Group.

—Your Head Shape Reveals Your Personality! Science's Biggest Mistakes about the Human Body. 2014. (Science Gets It Wrong Ser.). (Illus.). 32p. (gr. 4-6). pap. 7.95 *(978-1-4677-4551-2(0))*; (ENG., (J). lib. bdg. 26.60 *(978-1-4677-3661-9(9)*, Lerner Pubns.) Lerner Publishing Group.

SCIENCE—METHODOLOGY

see also Logic

Ardizzone, Leonisa. Science — Not Just for Scientists! Easy Explorations for Young Children. 2015. (ENG., Illus.). 96p. pap. 12.95 *(978-0-87659-484-1(4)*, Gryphon House Inc) Gryphon Hse., Inc.

Biskup, Agnieszka. The Amazing Work of Scientists with Max Axiom, Super Scientist, 1 vol. Baez, Marcelo, illus. 2013. (Graphic Science & Engineering in Action Ser.). (ENG.). 32p. (gr. 3-4). pap. 8.10 *(978-1-62065-701-0(5))*; lib. bdg. 30.65 *(978-1-4296-9936-5(1))* Capstone Press of Coughlan Cos. (Graphic Library).

Braun, Eric. Mad Margaret Experiments with the Scientific Method, 1 vol. Boyden, Robin, illus. 2012. (In the Science Lab Ser.). (ENG.). 24p. (gr. 2-3). pap. 9.95 *(978-1-4048-7710-8(X))*; lib. bdg. 26.65 *(978-1-4048-7373-5(2))* Picture Window Bks.

Carlson Berne, Emma. Answer! Analyze Your Data. 2014. (Scientific Method in Action Ser.). (Illus.). 24p. (J). (gr. 3-6). 23.60 *(978-1-4777-2930-4(5))*; pap. 49.50 *(978-1-4777-3088-1(5))*; pap. 8.25 *(978-1-4777-3017-1(6))* Rosen Publishing Group, Inc., The. (PowerKids Pr.)

—Guess! Research & Form a Hypothesis. 2014. (Scientific Method in Action Ser.). (Illus.). 24p. (J). (gr. 3-6). 23.60 *(978-1-4777-2926-7(7)*, PowerKids Pr.) Rosen Publishing Group, Inc., The.

—Look! Make Observations & Ask Questions. 2014. (Scientific Method in Action Ser.). (Illus.). 24p. (J). (gr. 3-6). 23.60 *(978-1-4777-2924-3(0)*, PowerKids Pr.) Rosen Publishing Group, Inc., The.

—Predict! Plan an Experiment. 2014. (Scientific Method in Action Ser.). (Illus.). 24p. (J). (gr. 3-6). pap. 49.50 *(978-1-4777-3086-7(9)*, PowerKids Pr.) Rosen Publishing Group, Inc., The.

—Share! Present Your Findings. 2014. (Scientific Method in Action Ser.). (Illus.). 24p. (J). (gr. 3-6). pap. 49.50 *(978-1-4777-3089-8(3)*, PowerKids Pr.) Rosen Publishing Group, Inc., The.

—Test! Collect & Document Data. 2014. (Scientific Method in Action Ser.). (Illus.). 24p. (J). (gr. 3-6). pap. 8.25 *(978-1-4777-3016-4(8)*, PowerKids Pr.) Rosen Publishing Group, Inc., The.

Carmichael, L. E. Scientific Method in Real World, 1 vol. 2013. (Science in the Real World Ser.). (ENG.). 48p. (J). (gr. 3-6). lib. bdg. 32.79 *(978-1-61783-743-2(1))* ABDO Publishing Co.

—Scientific Method in the Real World. 2013. (Science in the Real World EBook Ser.). (ENG.). 48p. (J). pap. 15.64 *(978-1-61783-793-7(8)*, Core Library) ABDO Publishing Co.

Chappell, Rachel. Solving Science Questions: A Book about the Scientific Process. 2007. (Big Ideas for Young Scientists Ser.). (Illus.). 24p. (J). (gr. 2-5). lib. bdg. *(978-1-60044-542-2(X))* Rourke Educational Media.

deMarin, Layne. Look & Learn. 2011. (Wonder Readers Fluent Level Ser.). (ENG.). 16p. (gr. -1-2). pap. 35.94 *(978-1-4296-8120-9(9)*, Wonder Readers) Capstone Press of Coughlan Cos.

—What Scientists Do. 2011. (Wonder Readers Fluent Level Ser.). (ENG.). (gr. -1-2). 16p. pap. 35.94 *(978-1-4296-8205-3(1))*; 32p. pap. 5.99 *(978-1-4296-7945-9(X))* Capstone Press of Coughlan Cos. (Wonder Readers).

Dempski, Seth. Natalie's Nature Walk: Represent & Interpret Data. 2014. (Math Masters: Measurement & Data Ser.). 24p. (J). (gr. 2-3). 23.60 *(978-1-4777-6440-4(2))*; (ENG.). pap. 8.25 *(978-1-4777-4828-2(8))* Rosen Publishing Group, Inc., The. (Rosen Classroom).

Doudna, Kelly. I'll Use Information for My Explanation!, 1 vol. 2007. (Science Made Simple Ser.). (ENG., Illus.). 24p. (J). (gr. k-3). lib. bdg. 24.21 *(978-1-59928-588-7(6)*, SandCastle) ABDO Publishing Co.

—It's a Date, Let's Investigate!, 1 vol. 2007. (Science Made Simple Ser.). (ENG., Illus.). 24p. (J). (gr. k-3). lib. bdg. 24.21 *(978-1-59928-596-2(7)*, SandCastle) ABDO Publishing Co.

—It's Not Too Late, Let's Communicate!, 1 vol. 2007. (Science Made Simple Ser.). (ENG., Illus.). 24p. (J). (gr. k-3). lib. bdg. 24.21 *(978-1-59928-606-8(8)*, SandCastle) ABDO Publishing Co.

—We Are Wise, Let's Hypothesize!, 1 vol. 2007. (Science Made Simple Ser.). (ENG., Illus.). 24p. (J). (gr. k-3). lib. bdg. 24.21 *(978-1-59928-622-8(X)*, SandCastle) ABDO Publishing Co.

Duke, Shirley. Hypothesis, Theory, Law. 2014. (ENG.). 48p. (gr. 4-6). 35.64 *(978-1-62717-746-7(9))* Rourke Educational Media.

Flatt, Lizann. Collecting Data. 2016. (Get Graphing! Building Data Literacy Skills Ser.). (ENG., Illus.). 24p. (J). (gr. k-3). *(978-0-7787-2633-3(9))* Crabtree Publishing Co.

Flynn, Riley. Using Facts & Investigating. 2016. (Science & Engineering Practices Ser.). (ENG., Illus.). 24p. (gr. k-1). pap. 6.95 *(978-1-5157-0981-7(7)*, Pebble Plus) Capstone Press of Coughlan Cos.

Fries-Gaither, Jessica. Notable Notebooks: Scientists & Their Writings. 2017. (ENG., Illus.). 32p. (J). (gr. 2-4). 18.95 *(978-1-68140-379-3(X))*; pap. 12.95 *(978-1-68140-307-6(2))* National Science Teachers Assn.

Harbo, Christopher L. Frankenstein's Monster & Scientific Methods. An, Carlos, illus. 2013. (Monster Science Ser.). (ENG.). 32p. (gr. 3-4). pap. 47.70 *(978-1-62065-817-8(8)*, Graphic Library) Capstone Press of Coughlan Cos.

—Frankenstein's Monster & Scientific Methods, 1 vol. Aón, Carlos, illus. 2013. (Monster Science Ser.). (ENG.). 32p. (gr. 3-4). lib. bdg. 30.65 *(978-1-4296-9931-0(0)*, Graphic Library) Capstone Press of Coughlan Cos.

Hindman, Susan. Think Like a Scientist in the Classroom. 2011. (Explorer Junior Library: Science Explorer Junior Ser.). (ENG.). 32p. (gr. 4-8). lib. bdg. 28.50 *(978-1-61080-170-6(9)*, 201110) Cherry Lake Publishing.

Hoena, Blake A. If an Egg Hatches... & Other Animal Predictions, 1 vol. 2012. (If Bks.). (ENG., Illus.). 32p. (gr. 1-2). lib. bdg. 27.32 *(978-1-4296-8718-8(5))* Capstone Press of Coughlan Cos.

—If You Have a Magnet... & Other Science Predictions. 2012. (If Bks.). (ENG.). 32p. (gr. 1-2). pap. 47.70 *(978-1-4296-9250-2(2)*, Aplus Bks.) Capstone Press of Coughlan Cos.

Horvath, Joan. What Scientists Actually Do. 2008. (Illus.). 208p. (YA). pap. 16.95 *(978-1-933277-08-0(4))* Stargazer Publishing Co.

Hunter, Dru. How Do We Apply Science? 2015. (Illus.). 48p. (J). *(978-1-60818-592-4(3)*, Creative Education) Creative Co., The.

—How Does It Work? 2015. (Illus.). 48p. (J). *(978-1-60818-593-1(1)*, Creative Education) Creative Co., The.

—How Does It Work? Think Like a Scientist. 2016. (Think Like a Scientist Ser.). (ENG.). 48p. (J). (gr. 5-9). pap. 12.00 *(978-1-62832-198-2(9)*, Creative Paperbacks) Creative Co., The.

—What Is Out There? 2015. (Illus.). 48p. (J). *(978-1-60818-594-8(X)*, Creative Education) Creative Co., The.

—What Is Out There? Think Like a Scientist. 2016. (Think Like a Scientist Ser.). (ENG.). 48p. (J). (gr. 5-9). pap. 12.00 *(978-1-62832-199-9(7)*, Creative Paperbacks) Creative Co., The.

—What Is the Reason? 2015. (Illus.). 48p. (J). *(978-1-60818-595-5(8)*, Creative Education) Creative Co., The.

—What Is the Reason? Think Like a Scientist. 2016. (Think Like a Scientist Ser.). (ENG.). 48p. (J). (gr. 5-9). pap. 12.00 *(978-1-62832-200-2(4)*, Creative Paperbacks) Creative Co., The.

—Where Do We Look for Life? 2015. (Illus.). 48p. (J). *(978-1-60818-596-2(6)*, Creative Education) Creative Co., The.

—Where Do We Look for Life? Think Like a Scientist. 2016. (Think Like a Scientist Ser.). (ENG.). 48p. (J). (gr. 5-9). pap. 12.00 *(978-1-62832-201-9(2)*, Creative Paperbacks) Creative Co., The.

Jerome, Kate Boehm & National Geographic Learning Staff. Thinking It Through. 2007. (Reading Expeditions Ser.). (ENG., Illus.). 24p. (J). pap. 14.95 *(978-0-7922-4593-3(8))* CENGAGE Learning.

Kuskowski, Alex. Science Experiments with Gravity & Motion, 1 vol. 2013. (More Super Simple Science Ser.). (ENG.). 32p. (gr. k-4). lib. bdg. 27.07 *(978-1-61783-850-7(0)*, Super SandCastle) ABDO Publishing Co.

—Science Experiments with Light, 1 vol. 2013. (More Super Simple Science Ser.). (ENG.). 32p. (gr. k-4). lib. bdg. 27.07 *(978-1-61783-851-4(9)*, Super SandCastle) ABDO Publishing Co.

—Science Experiments with Liquid, 1 vol. 2013. (More Super Simple Science Ser.). (ENG.). 32p. (gr. k-4). lib. bdg. 27.07 *(978-1-61783-852-1(7)*, Super SandCastle) ABDO Publishing Co.

—Science Experiments with Magnets, 1 vol. 2013. (More Super Simple Science Ser.). (ENG.). 32p. (gr. k-4). lib. bdg. 27.07 *(978-1-61783-853-8(5)*, Super SandCastle) ABDO Publishing Co.

—Science Experiments with Sight & Sound, 1 vol. 2013. (More Super Simple Science Ser.). (ENG.). 32p. (gr. k-4). lib. bdg. 27.07 *(978-1-61783-854-5(3)*, Super SandCastle) ABDO Publishing Co.

Larson, Kirsten. Using the Scientific Method. 2014. (ENG.). 48p. (gr. 4-6). 35.64 *(978-1-62717-748-1(5))* Rourke Educational Media.

Lemke, Donald B. Investigating the Scientific Method with Max Axiom, Super Scientist, 1 vol. Smith, Tod G. & Milgram, Al, illus. 2008. (Graphic Science Ser.). (ENG.). 32p. (gr. 3-4). per. 8.10 *(978-1-4296-1760-4(8)*, Graphic Library) Capstone Press of Coughlan Cos.

Magner, Laura. The Scientific Method in Fairy Tale Forest. 2007. pap. 14.95 *(978-1-931334-94-5(3))* Pieces of Learning.

Maloof, Torrey. Analyze It!, 1 vol. rev. ed. 2014. (Science Readers: Content & Literacy Ser.). (ENG.). 32p. (gr. 2-2). pap. 8.99 *(978-1-4807-4613-8(4))* Teacher Created Materials, Inc.

McGill, Jordan. Earth Science Fair Projects. 2011. (gr. 3-5). pap. 12.95 *(978-1-61690-655-9(3)*, AV2 by Weigl); (Illus.). 24p. (J). 27.13 *(978-1-61690-651-1(0))* Weigl Pubs., Inc.

—Life Science Fair Projects. 2011. (J). *(978-1-61690-330-5(9))*; (gr. 3-5). pap. 12.95 *(978-1-61690-658-0(8)*, AV2 by Weigl); (Illus.). 24p. (gr. 3-6). 27.13 *(978-1-61690-654-2(5))* Weigl Pubs., Inc.

—Space Science Fair Projects. 2011. (J). (gr. 3-5). pap. 12.95 *(978-1-61690-657-3(X)*, AV2 by Weigl); (Illus.). 24p. 27.13 *(978-1-61690-653-5(7))* Weigl Pubs., Inc.

—Water Science Fair Projects. 2011. (J). *(978-1-61690-332-9(5))*; (gr. 3-5). pap. 12.95 *(978-1-61690-656-6(1)*, AV2 by Weigl); (Illus.). 24p. (gr. 3-6). 27.13 *(978-1-61690-652-8(9))* Weigl Pubs., Inc.

Montgomery, Anne. I Spy, 1 vol. (Science Readers: Content & Literacy Ser.). (ENG., Illus.). 24p. (gr. k-k). 2015. (J). 22.96 *(978-1-4938-1135-9(5))* 2014. pap. 8.99 *(978-1-4807-4525-4(1))* Teacher Created Materials, Inc.

—Tell Me about It, 1 vol. (Science Readers: Content & Literacy Ser.). (ENG., Illus.). 24p. (gr. k-k). 2015. (J). 22.96 *(978-1-4938-1136-6(3))* 2014. pap. 8.99 *(978-1-4807-4526-1(X))* Teacher Created Materials, Inc.

Mullins, Matt. Think Like a Scientist in the Car. 2011. (Explorer Junior Library: Science Explorer Junior Ser.). (ENG.). 32p. (gr. 4-8). lib. bdg. 28.50 *(978-1-61080-164-5(4)*, 201098) Cherry Lake Publishing.

—Think Like a Scientist in the Garden. 2011. (Explorer Junior Library: Science Explorer Junior Ser.). (ENG.). 32p. (gr. 4-8). lib. bdg. 28.50 *(978-1-61080-166-9(0)*, 201102) Cherry Lake Publishing.

—Think Like a Scientist in the Kitchen. 2011. (Explorer Junior Library: Science Explorer Junior Ser.). (ENG.). 32p. (gr. 4-8). lib. bdg. 28.50 *(978-1-61080-165-2(2)*, 201100) Cherry Lake Publishing.

Pederson, Bridget. Its Not Strange, I Know about Change!, 1 vol. 2007. (Science Made Simple Ser.). (ENG., Illus.). 24p. (J). (gr. k-3). lib. bdg. 24.21 *(978-1-59928-604-4(1)*, SandCastle) ABDO Publishing Co.

Porchetta, Renato L. Universal Methodology: UNIVERSAL SCIENTIFIC PROGRAMMING CONTROL-HUMAN INTELLIGENCE AMPLIFICATION MANAGEMENT-SCIENCE of the COMPOSITION of the SIGNIFICANCE,SEMANTICS-SCIENCE of MANAGEMENT-the Mosaic Thinking, 2 vols, Vol.1. 2nd ed. 2007. (ENG., Illus.). 490p. lib. bdg. 100.00 *(978-0-9769931-0-4(4))* Ce Code Efficiency, Inc.

Rainis, Kenneth G. Cell & Microbe Science Fair Projects. rev. exp. ed. 2010. (Biology Science Projects Using the Scientific Method Ser.). (Illus.). 160p. (J). (gr. 5-18). 35.94 *(978-0-7660-3420-4(8))* Enslow Pubs., Inc.

Rau, Dana Meachen. Think Like a Scientist on the Playground. 2011. (Explorer Junior Library: Science Explorer Junior Ser.). (ENG.). 32p. (gr. 4-8). lib. bdg. 28.50 *(978-1-61080-169-0(5)*, 201108) Cherry Lake Publishing.

Rene, Ellen. Science Detectives. 2008. (Illus.). (J). (gr. 3-7). 127.50 *(978-1-4358-2553-6(5)*, PowerKids Pr.) Rosen Publishing Group, Inc., The.

Rice, Dona. Predict It!, 1 vol. 2015. (Science Readers: Content & Literacy Ser.). (ENG., Illus.). 32p. (gr. 3-3). pap. 8.99 *(978-1-4807-4652-7(5))* Teacher Created Materials, Inc.

—Sort It!, 1 vol. rev. ed. 2014. (Science Readers: Content & Literacy Ser.). (ENG., Illus.). 24p. (gr. k-k). pap. 8.99 *(978-1-4807-4535-3(9))* Teacher Created Materials, Inc.

Rice, Dona Herweck. What a Scientist Sees. 2015. (Science Readers: Content & Literacy Ser.). (ENG.). 32p. (gr. 4-4). pap. 8.99 *(978-1-4807-4691-6(6))* Teacher Created Materials, Inc.

—What the Evidence Shows. 2015. (Science Readers: Content & Literacy Ser.). (Illus.). 32p. (gr. 5-5). pap. 8.99 *(978-1-4807-4730-2(0))* Teacher Created Materials, Inc.

Riley, Peter D. Light. 2011. (Real Scientist Investigates Ser.). (Illus.). 32p. (J). (gr. 3-5). lib. bdg. 28.50 *(978-1-59771-281-1(7))* Sea-To-Sea Pubns.

—Materials. 2011. (Real Scientist Investigates Ser.). (Illus.). 32p. (J). (gr. 3-5). lib. bdg. 28.50 *(978-1-59771-282-8(5))* Sea-To-Sea Pubns.

—Space. 2011. (Real Scientist Investigates Ser.). (Illus.). 32p. (J). (gr. 3-5). lib. bdg. 28.50 *(978-1-59771-284-2(1))* Sea-To-Sea Pubns.

Rourke, Brigid. Tools of Science. 2013. (Rosen Readers Ser.). (ENG.). 24p. (J). (gr. 2-3). pap. 8.25 *(978-1-4777-2325-8(0))*; pap. 49.50 *(978-1-4777-2326-5(9))* Rosen Publishing Group, Inc., The. (Rosen Classroom).

Rybolt, Thomas R. & Mebane, Robert C. Environmental Science Fair Projects, Revised & Expanded Using the Scientific Method. LaBaff, Tom & LaBaff, Stephanie, illus. 2010. (Earth Science Projects Using the Scientific Method Ser.). 160p. (J). (gr. 5-18). 35.94 *(978-0-7660-3426-6(7))* Enslow Pubs., Inc.

Smith, Paula. Measure It! 2015. (ENG., Illus.). 24p. (J). pap. *(978-0-7787-1544-3(2))* Crabtree Publishing Co.

—Model It! 2015. (ENG., Illus.). 24p. (J). pap. *(978-0-7787-1545-0(0))* Crabtree Publishing Co.

—Plan & Investigate It! 2015. (ENG., Illus.). 24p. (J). pap. *(978-0-7787-1546-7(9))* Crabtree Publishing Co.

—Prove It! 2015. (ENG., Illus.). 24p. (J). pap. *(978-0-7787-1547-4(7))* Crabtree Publishing Co.

Somervill, Barbara A. Does This Make Sense? Constructing Explanations. 2006. (Scientific Processes Ser.). (Illus.). 24p. (YA). (gr. 2-5). lib. bdg. 21.25 *(978-1-4042-3485-7(3))* Rosen Publishing Group, Inc., The.

—Does This Make Sense? Constructing Explanations. (Think Like a Scientist Ser.). 24p. 2009. (gr. 2-3). 42.50 *(978-1-60854-356-4(0)*, PowerKids Pr.) 2007. (gr. 3-5). pap. 8.25 *(978-1-4358-2681-6(7)*, Rosen Classroom) Rosen Publishing Group, Inc., The.

—Sorting It Out: Evaluating Data. 24p. 2009. (Think Like a Scientist Ser.). (gr. 2-3). 42.50 *(978-1-60854-357-1(9)*, PowerKids Pr.) 2007. (gr. 3-5). pap. 8.25 *(978-1-4358-2682-3(5)*, Rosen Classroom) 2006. (Think Like a Scientist Ser.: Vol. 3). (Illus.). (YA). (gr. 2-5). lib. bdg. 22.60 *(978-1-4042-3487-1(X))* Rosen Publishing Group, Inc., The.

—What Are the Facts? Collecting Information. 2006. (Think Like a Scientist Ser.). (Illus.). 24p. (YA). (gr. 2-5). lib. bdg. 22.60 *(978-1-4042-3484-0(5))* Rosen Publishing Group, Inc., The.

—What Are the Facts? Collecting Information. (Think Like a Scientist Ser.). 24p. 2009. (gr. 2-3). 42.50 *(978-1-60854-358-8(7)*, PowerKids Pr.) 2007. (gr. 3-5). pap. 8.25 *(978-1-4358-2683-0(3)*, Rosen Classroom) Rosen Publishing Group, Inc., The.

—What Did You Find Out? Reporting Conclusions. 2006. (Scientific Processes Ser.). (Illus.). 24p. (J). (gr. 3-7). lib. bdg. 21.25 *(978-1-4042-3486-4(1)*, PowerKids Pr.) Rosen Publishing Group, Inc., The.

—What Did You Find Out? Reporting Conclusions. (Think Like a Scientist Ser.). 24p. 2009. (gr. 2-3). 42.50 *(978-1-60854-359-5(5)*, PowerKids Pr.) 2007. (gr. 3-5). pap. 8.25 *(978-1-4358-2684-7(1)*, Rosen Classroom) Rosen Publishing Group, Inc., The.

—What Do You Want to Prove? Planning Investigations. 2006. (Think Like a Scientist Ser.). (Illus.). 24p. (YA). (gr. 2-5). lib. bdg. 22.60 *(978-1-4042-3483-3(7))* Rosen Publishing Group, Inc., The.

—What Do You Want to Prove? Planning Investigations. (Think Like a Scientist Ser.). 24p. 2009. (gr. 2-3). 42.50 *(978-1-60854-360-1(9)*, PowerKids Pr.) 2007. (gr. 3-5). pap. 8.25 *(978-1-4358-2685-4(X)*, Rosen Classroom) Rosen Publishing Group, Inc., The.

—What's the Big Idea? Forming Hypotheses. 2006. (Scientific Processes Ser.). (Illus.). 24p. (J). (gr. 3-7). lib. bdg. 21.25 *(978-1-4042-3482-6(9)*, PowerKids Pr.) Rosen Publishing Group, Inc., The.

—What's the Big Idea? Forming Hypotheses. (Think Like a Scientist Ser.). 24p. 2009. (gr. 2-3). 42.50 *(978-1-60854-361-8(7)*, PowerKids Pr.) 2007. (gr. 3-5). pap. 8.25 *(978-1-4358-2686-1(8)*, Rosen Classroom) Rosen Publishing Group, Inc., The.

Stefoff, Rebecca. Astrology & Astronomy. 2014. 48p. pap. 29.93 *(978-1-62712-506-2(X))* Cavendish Square Publishing.

—Astrology or Astronomy: Is Your Fate in the Stars? 2013. (J). *(978-0-7614-8144-7(3))* Marshall Cavendish.

—Earth or Sun: Which One Is in the Center? 2013. (J). *(978-0-7614-8147-8(8))* Marshall Cavendish.

Swanson, Diane. Nibbling on Einstein's Brain: The Good, the Bad & the Bogus in Science. Blake, Francis, illus. 2nd rev. ed. 2009. (ENG.). 160p. (J). (gr. 1-12). 24.95 *(978-1-55451-187-7(9)*, 9781554511877); pap. 12.95 *(978-1-55451-186-0(0)*, 9781554511860) Annick Pr., Ltd. CAN. Dist: Publishers Group West (PGW).

Yes Magazine Editors. Science Detectives: How Scientists Solved Six Real-Life Mysteries. Cowles, Rose, illus. 2006. (ENG.). 48p. (J). (gr. 3-7). pap. 8.95 *(978-1-55337-995-9(0))* Kids Can Pr., Ltd. CAN. Dist: Hachette Bk. Group.

Yoder, Eric & Yoder, Natalie. ¡Más Misterios Cortos Que Resuelves con Ciencias! Bercovich, Nadia & Bachelet, Esteban, trs. from ENG. 2016. (One Minute Mysteries Ser.). (ENG & SPA., Illus.). 224p. (J). (gr. 4-8). pap. 12.95 *(978-1-938492-15-0(3))* Science, Naturally!

SCIENCE—PHILOSOPHY

Beck, Esther. Ill Help My Chums Learn about Systems!, 1 vol. 2007. (Science Made Simple Ser.). (ENG., Illus.). 24p. (J). (gr. k-3). lib. bdg. 24.21 *(978-1-59928-584-9(3)*, SandCastle) ABDO Publishing Co.

Gow, Mary. The Great Thinker: Aristotle & the Foundations of Science. 2010. (Great Minds of Ancient Science & Math Ser.). 128p. (J). (gr. 4-7). 33.27 *(978-0-7660-3121-0(7))* Enslow Pubs., Inc.

Harding, Sandra & Figueroa, Robert, eds. Science & Other Cultures. 2003. (ENG.). 304p. (gr. 13-18). 48.95 *(978-0-415-93992-8(5)*, 0415939925) Routledge.

SCIENCE—POETRY

Agard, John. Hello H2O. Kitamura, Satoshi, illus. 2013. (ENG.). 96p. (J). (gr. 2-4). pap. 10.99 *(978-1-4449-1772-7(2))* Hodder & Stoughton GBR. Dist: Hachette Bk. Group.

Shields, Carol Diggory. Science, Fresh Squeezed! Thompson, Richard, illus. 2003. (ENG.). 64p. (J). (gr. -1-7). 14.95 *(978-1-59354-005-0(1)*, Handprint Bks.) Chronicle Bks. LLC.

Vergo, Franny. Sciencepalooza: A Collection of Science Poetry for Primary & Intermediate Students. 2012. 118p. pap. 14.95 *(978-1-4772-1598-2(0))* AuthorHouse.

SCIENCE—RESEARCH

Cherfas, Jeremy. El Genoma Humano. Yanez, Cecilia, tr. 2003. (Essential Science Ser.). (SPA.). 72p. (J). pap. 6.95 *(978-970-690-599-4(5))* Planeta Mexicana Editorial S. A. de C. V. MEX. Dist: Lectorum Pubns., Inc.

Garlick, Mark A. El Universo en Expansion. Barois, Valerian Stoopen, tr. 2003. (Ciencia para Todos Ser.). (SPA.). 72p. (J). pap. 6.95 *(978-970-690-600-7(2))* Planeta Mexicana Editorial S. A. de C. V. MEX. Dist: Lectorum Pubns., Inc.

Tudge, Colin. Alimentos para el Futuro. Barois, Lorena Stoopen, tr. 2003. (Essential Science Ser.). (SPA.). 72p. (J). pap. 6.95 *(978-970-690-603-8(7))* Planeta Mexicana Editorial S. A. de C. V. MEX. Dist: Lectorum Pubns., Inc.

SCIENCE—SOCIAL ASPECTS

see Science and Civilization

SCIENCE—STUDY AND TEACHING

see also Nature Study

Ardizzone, Leonisa. Science — Not Just for Scientists! Easy Explorations for Young Children. 2015. (ENG., Illus.). 96p. pap. 12.95 *(978-0-87659-484-1(4)*, Gryphon House Inc) Gryphon Hse., Inc.

Baxter, Fiona, et al. Cambridge Primary Science Stage 5 Learner's Book. 2014. (Cambridge Primary Science Ser.). (ENG., Illus.). 110p. pap. 19.94 *(978-1-107-66304-6(0))* Cambridge Univ. Pr.

Bendick, Jeanne. Archimedes & the Door of Science: Immortals of Science. 2011. 154p. (gr. 5-8). 41.95 *(978-1-258-01488-9(2))* Literary Licensing, LLC.

Brown, Sam Ed. Bubbles, Rainbows & Worms: Science Experiments for Preschool Children. rev. ed. 2004. (ENG., Illus.). 96p. pap. 14.95 *(978-0-87659-241-0(8)*, 10243, Gryphon House Inc) Gryphon Hse., Inc.

Building Blocks of Science: Human Bodyworks Teacher's Guide (Firsthand Learning) 2007. ring bd. *(978-0-89278-337-3(0))* Carolina Biological Supply Co.

Building Blocks of Science: Light Teacher's Guide. 2007. (Illus.). ring bd. *(978-0-89278-339-7(7))* Carolina Biological Supply Co.

Clausen-Grace, Nicki. What Can You Make? 2006. (Science about Me Ser.). (Illus.). 8p. (J). (gr. 3-7). pap. 5.95 *(978-1-59515-932-8(0))* Rourke Educational Media.

Cleland, Jo. I Can Make Colors. 2006. (Science about Me Ser.). (Illus.). 8p. (J). (gr. 3-7). pap. 5.95 *(978-1-59515-925-0(8))* Rourke Educational Media.

Cotugno, Megan. Measure It!, 1 vol., Set. Incl. Distance, Area, & Volume. Somervill, Barbara A. pap. 8.29 *(978-1-4329-3769-0(3))*; Mass & Weight. Somervill, Barbara A. pap. 8.29 *(978-1-4329-3771-3(5))*; Speed & Acceleration. Somervill, Barbara A. pap. 8.29 *(978-1-4329-3770-6(7))*; Temperature. Rand, Casey. pap. 8.29 *(978-1-4329-3773-7(1))*; Time. Rand, Casey. pap. 8.29 *(978-1-4329-3772-0(3))*; (Illus.). (gr. 3-6). (Measure It! Ser.). (ENG.). 32p. 2010. Set pap. 39.95 *(978-1-4329-3774-4(X)*, Heinemann InfoSearch) Heinemann-Raintree.

Enz, Tammy. Cool Plastic Bottle & Milk Jug Science. 2016. (Recycled Science Ser.). (ENG., Illus.). 32p. (gr. 3-4). lib. bdg. 27.99 *(978-1-5157-0862-9(4))* Capstone Press of Coughlan Cos.

Enz, Tammy & Wheeler-Toppen, Jodi. Whizzy Science with Recyclables: Bring Out Your Science Genius with Soda Bottles, Potato Chip Bags & More Unexpected Stuff. 2016. (Recycled Science Ser.). (ENG.). 112p. (gr. 3-4). pap. 9.95 *(978-1-62370-697-5(1))* Capstone Press of Coughlan Cos.

Good, Keith. Hands-on Science Projects: Classroom Library. 2008. pap. 6.95 *(978-0-8225-9426-0(9))* Lerner Publishing Group.

Harcourt School Publishers Staff. Harcourt Ciencias: CA & National Big Book. 2003. (Harcourt Ciencias Ser.). (SPA., Illus.). 221.70 (978-0-15-321531-5(3)) Harcourt Schl. Pubs.

—Harcourt Ciencias, Grade 1: Grade Level Set: Texas/National Edition. 2003. (Harcourt Ciencias Ser.). (SPA.). (gr. 1-18). tchr. ed. 145.10 (978-0-15-315172-9(2)) Harcourt Schl. Pubs.

—Harcourt Ciencias, Grade 2: Grade Level Set: Texas/National Edition. 2003. (Harcourt Ciencias Ser.). (SPA.). (gr. 2-18). tchr. ed. 145.10 (978-0-15-315173-6(0)) Harcourt Schl. Pubs.

—Harcourt Ciencias, Grade 3 Unit A&B: Life Science. 2003. (Harcourt Ciencias Ser.). (SPA.). (gr. 3-18). tchr. ed. 67.40 (978-0-15-314808-8(X)) Harcourt Schl. Pubs.

—Harcourt Ciencias, Grade 3 Unit E&F: Physical Science. 2003. (Harcourt Ciencias Ser.). (SPA.). (gr. 3-18). tchr. ed. 67.40 (978-0-15-314810-1(1)) Harcourt Schl. Pubs.

—Harcourt Ciencias, Grade 4 Unit A&B: Life Science. 2003. (Harcourt Ciencias Ser.). (SPA.). (gr. 4-18). tchr. ed. 67.40 (978-0-15-314811-8(X)) Harcourt Schl. Pubs.

—Harcourt Ciencias, Grade 4 Unit E&F: Physical Science. 2003. (Harcourt Ciencias Ser.). (SPA.). (gr. 4-18). tchr. ed. 67.40 (978-0-15-314813-2(6)) Harcourt Schl. Pubs.

—Harcourt Ciencias, Grade 5 Unit A&B: Life Science. 2003. (Harcourt Ciencias Ser.). (SPA.). (gr. 5-18). tchr. ed. 70.00 (978-0-15-314814-9(4)) Harcourt Schl. Pubs.

—Harcourt Ciencias, Grade 5 Unit E&F: Physical Science. 2003. (Harcourt Ciencias Ser.). (SPA.). (gr. 5-18). tchr. ed. 70.00 (978-0-15-315037-1(8)) Harcourt Schl. Pubs.

—Harcourt School Publishers Science California: Lab Manual Student Edition Science 08 Grade 4. 2005. pap. 9.00 (978-0-15-352271-0(2)) Harcourt Schl. Pubs.

—Harcourt Science. 2nd ed. 2003. (Harcourt Science Ser.). (Illus.). (gr. 3-18). wbk. ed. 8.70 (978-0-15-323713-3(9)) Harcourt Schl. Pubs.

Holt, Rinehart and Winston Staff. Holt Science & Technology: Science Skills Worksheets. 5th ed. 2004. (Illus.). pap., wbk. ed. 11.60 (978-0-03-035197-6(9)) Holt McDougal.

James, Rosemary. What Do Scientists Do? Solve Problems Involving Measurement & Estimation, 1 vol. 2015. (InfoMax Common Core Math Readers Ser.). (ENG.). 24p. (J). pap. 8.25 (978-1-4777-4603-5(X), Rosen Classroom) Rosen Publishing Group, Inc., The.

Kellett, Sarah, et al, eds. Hands-On Science: 50 Kids' Activities from CSIRO. 2017. (ENG.). 128p. (gr. 3-8). pap. 16.50 (978-1-4863-0614-5(4)) CSIRO Publishing AUS. Dist: Stylus Publishing, LLC.

Kriesberg, Daniel A. Think Green, Take Action: Books & Activities for Kids, 1 vol. 2010. (Illus.). 136p. (C). pap. 30.00 (978-1-59884-378-1(8), A2703P, Libraries Unlimited) ABC-CLIO, LLC.

Latta, Sara L. Positive Reaction! A Crash Course in Science, 1 vol. 2014. (Crash Course Ser.). (ENG.). 64p. (gr. 4-5). lib. bdg. 34.65 (978-1-4914-0772-1(7)) Capstone Press of Coughlan Cos.

Machajewski, Sarah. Discovering STEM at the Restaurant. 2015. (STEM in the Real World Ser.). (ENG., Illus.). 24p. (J). (gr. 2-3). pap. 8.25 (978-1-4994-0924-6(9), PowerKids Pr.) Rosen Publishing Group, Inc., The.

Madanes, Sharon & Workman Publishing Company Staff. Everything You Need to Ace Science in One Big Fat Notebook: A Middle School Study Guide. 2016. (Big Fat Notebooks Ser.). (ENG., Illus.). 528p. (J). (gr. 6-8). pap. 14.95 (978-0-7611-6095-3(7)) Workman Publishing Co., Inc.

Marine Science Experiments. 2010. (Facts on File Science Experiments Ser.). (Illus.). 176p. (gr. 6-12). 40.00 (978-0-8160-8168-4(9)) Facts On File, Inc.

Marks, Jennifer L. How to Make a Bouncing Egg. (Hands-On Science Fun Ser.). (ENG.). 24p. (gr. k-1). 2011. pap. 41.70 (978-1-4296-6384-7(7)) 2010. lib. bdg. 26.65 (978-1-4296-5291-9(8)) Capstone Press of Coughlan Cos. (Pebble Plus).

Maurer, Daniel D. Do You Really Want to Burn Your Toast? A Book about Heat. Alberini, Teresa, illus. 2016. (Adventures in Science Ser.). (ENG.). 24p. (J). (gr. k-3). 20.95 (978-1-60753-961-2(6)) Amicus Publishing.

—Do You Really Want to Skate on Thin Ice? A Book about States of Matter. Alberini, Teresa, illus. 2016. (Adventures in Science Ser.). (ENG.). 24p. (J). (gr. k-3). 20.95 (978-1-60753-958-2(6)) Amicus Publishing.

Miles Kelly Staff. Science. 2003. (Info Bank Ser.). (Illus.). 96p. (J). 7.95 (978-1-84236-152-8(X)) Miles Kelly Publishing, Ltd. GBR. Dist: Independent Pubs. Group.

—Science & Maths. 2003. (Flip Quiz Ser.). (Illus.). 38p. (J). (gr. 10-11). spiral bd. 5.95 (978-1-84236-032-3(9)); (gr. 11-12). spiral bd. 5.95 (978-1-84236-033-0(7)); (gr. 7-9). spiral bd. 5.95 (978-1-84236-030-9(2)); (gr. 9-10). spiral bd. 5.95 (978-1-84236-031-6(0)) Miles Kelly Publishing, Ltd. GBR. Dist: Independent Pubs. Group.

Nagelhout, Ryan. Discovering STEM at the Baseball Game. 2015. (STEM in the Real World Ser.). (ENG., Illus.). 24p. (J). (gr. 2-3). pap. 8.25 (978-1-4994-0916-1(8), PowerKids Pr.) Rosen Publishing Group, Inc., The.

Pobst, Sandy. Scientific Discovery in the Renaissance: Text Pairs. 2008. (Bridges/Navigators Ser.). (J). (gr. 6). 89.00 (978-1-4108-8448-0(1)) Benchmark Education Co.

Roby, Cynthia. Discovering STEM at the Airport. 2015. (STEM in the Real World Ser.). (ENG., Illus.). 24p. (J). (gr. 2-3). pap. 8.25 (978-1-4994-0907-9(9), PowerKids Pr.) Rosen Publishing Group, Inc., The.

—Discovering STEM at the Amusement Park. 2015. (STEM in the Real World Ser.). (ENG., Illus.). 24p. (J). (gr. 2-3). pap. 8.25 (978-1-4994-0910-9(9), PowerKids Pr.) Rosen Publishing Group, Inc., The.

Rourke, Brigid. Tools of Science. 2013. (Rosen Readers Ser.). (ENG.). 24p. (J). (gr. 2-3). pap. 49.50 (978-1-4777-2326-5(9)); pap. 8.25 (978-1-4777-2325-8(0)) Rosen Publishing Group, Inc., The. (Rosen Classroom).

Rowe, Brooke. Building a Lava Lamp. Bane, Jeff, illus. 2016. (My Early Library: My Science Fun Ser.). (ENG.). 24p. (J). (gr. k-1). 28.50 (978-1-63471-026-8(6), 208184) Cherry Lake Publishing.

—Building a Volcano. Bane, Jeff, illus. 2016. (My Early Library: My Science Fun Ser.). (ENG.). 24p. (J). (gr. k-1). 28.50 (978-1-63471-025-1(8), 208180) Cherry Lake Publishing.

—Creating Rain. Bane, Jeff, illus. 2016. (My Early Library: My Science Fun Ser.). (ENG.). 24p. (J). (gr. k-1). 28.50 (978-1-63471-027-5(4), 208188) Cherry Lake Publishing.

Shea, Therese. Discovering STEM at the Zoo. 2015. (STEM in the Real World Ser.). (ENG., Illus.). 24p. (J). (gr. 2-3). pap. 8.25 (978-1-4994-0928-4(1), PowerKids Pr.) Rosen Publishing Group, Inc., The.

Shores, Erika L. How to Make Bubbles. (Hands-On Science Fun Ser.). (ENG.). 24p. (gr. k-1). 2011. pap. 41.70 (978-1-4296-6387-8(1)) 2010. lib. bdg. 26.65 (978-1-4296-5293-3(4)) Capstone Press of Coughlan Cos. (Pebble Plus).

Shores, Lori. How to Build Flipsticks. 2011. (Hands-On Science Fun Ser.). (ENG.). 24p. (gr. k-1). pap. 41.70 (978-1-4296-6385-4(5), Pebble Plus) Capstone Press of Coughlan Cos.

—How to Make a Liquid Rainbow. (Hands-On Science Fun Ser.). (ENG.). 24p. (gr. k-1). 2011. pap. 41.70 (978-1-4296-6386-1(3)) 2010. lib. bdg. 26.65 (978-1-4296-5294-0(2)) Capstone Press of Coughlan Cos. (Pebble Plus).

Skillicorn, Phillipa, et al. Primary Science. 2014. (Collins International Primary Science Ser.). (ENG.). 80p. (J). (gr. -1-k). pap. 6.95 (978-0-00-755148-4(7)) HarperCollins Pubs. Ltd. GBR. Dist: Independent Pubs. Group.

Spilsbury, Richard. I'M Good at Science... What Job Can I Get? 2012. (What's a Good Job for Me? Ser.). (ENG., Illus.). 32p. (J). (gr. 5-6). (978-1-4488-6632-8(4), PowerKids Pr.) Rosen Publishing Group, Inc., The.

Spilsbury, Richard & Spilsbury, Louise. What Are Forces & Motion? Exploring Science with Hands-on Activities. 2008. (In Touch with Basic Science Ser.). (Illus.). 32p. (J). (gr. 3-4). lib. bdg. 23.94 (978-0-7660-3095-4(4), Enslow Elementary) Enslow Pubs., Inc.

—What Are Solids, Liquids, & Gases? Exploring Science with Hands-on Activities. 2008. (In Touch with Basic Science Ser.). (Illus.). 32p. (J). (gr. 3-4). lib. bdg. 23.94 (978-0-7660-3094-7(6), Enslow Elementary) Enslow Pubs., Inc.

—What Is Sound? Exploring Science with Hands-on Activities. 2008. (In Touch with Basic Science Ser.). (Illus.). 32p. (J). (gr. 3-4). lib. bdg. 23.94 (978-0-7660-3098-5(9), Enslow Elementary) Enslow Pubs., Inc.

Staley, Erin. 10 Great Makerspace Projects Using Science. 2017. (Using Makerspaces for School Projects Ser.). 64p. (J). (gr. 11-11). 34.45 **(978-1-4994-3848-2(6)**, Rosen Central) Rosen Publishing Group, Inc., The.

The Study of Science. 2014. (Study of Science Ser.). 160p. (YA). (gr. 7-12). 493.50 (978-1-62275-758-9(0)); 246.75 (978-1-62275-424-3(7)) Rosen Publishing Group, Inc., The.

The Study of Science: Set 2, 1 vol., 1. 2016. (Study of Science Ser.). (ENG.). 96p. (YA). (gr. 8-8). 145.00 (978-1-68048-222-5(X), Britannica Educational Publishing) Rosen Publishing Group, Inc., The.

The Study of Science: Set 3. 2016. (Study of Science Ser.). 00104p. (YA). (gr. 8-8). 217.50 (978-1-5081-0294-6(5), Britannica Educational Publishing) Rosen Publishing Group, Inc., The.

Sundance/Newbridge LLC Staff. Where Plants Live. 2004. (Reading PowerWorks Ser.). (gr. 1-3). 37.50 (978-0-7608-7799-9(8)); pap. 6.10 (978-0-7608-7800-2(5)) Sundance/Newbridge Educational Publishing.

Suzuki, David T. & Helmer, Barbara. Descubre las Plantas. 2004. (Juego de la Ciencia Ser.). (SPA., Illus.). 96p. 14.99 (978-84-9754-062-9(X), 87817) Ediciones Oniro S.A. ESP. Dist: Lectorum Pubns., Inc.

Twist, Clint. Light & Sound. 2010. (Science Everywhere! Ser.). 24p. 24.25 (978-1-84898-297-0(6)) Black Rabbit Bks.

Van Doren, Elizabeth. Get Ready for Kindergarten: Math & Science. 2010. (ENG., Illus.). 240p. (J). (gr. -1-2). 17.95 (978-1-57912-830-2(0), 81830, Black Dog & Leventhal Pubs. Inc.) Hachette Bks.

VanCleave, Janice. Janice VanCleave's Big Book of Play & Find Out Science Projects. 2007. (ENG., Illus.). 224p. (gr. 3-7). per. 19.95 (978-0-7879-8928-6(2), Jossey-Bass) Wiley, John & Sons, Inc.

Weikart, Cindy. The Ohio Graduation Test: Science Study Guide. 2004. 288p. pap., stu. ed. 16.95 (978-1-882203-30-7(5)) Orange Frazer Pr.

Wheeler-Toppen, Jodi. Amazing Cardboard Tube Science. 2016. (Recycled Science Ser.). (ENG., Illus.). 32p. (gr. 3-4). lib. bdg. 27.99 (978-1-5157-0860-5(8)) Capstone Press of Coughlan Cos.

Wiese, Jim. Ancient Science: 40 Time-Traveling, World-Exploring, History-Making Activities for Kids. Shems, Ed, illus. 2003. (ENG.). 128p. (J). (gr. 3-7). pap. 16.00 (978-0-471-21595-0(3), Wiley) Wiley, John & Sons, Inc.

Yoder, Eric & Yoder, Natalie. ¡Más Misterios Cortos Que Resuelves con Ciencias! Bercovich, Nadia & Bachelet, Esteban, trs. from ENG. 2016. (One Minute Mysteries Ser.). (ENG & SPA., Illus.). 224p. (J). (gr. 4-8). pap. 12.95 (978-1-938492-15-0(3)) Science, Naturally!

Young, Karen Romano. Experiments to Do on Your Family. Goldin, David, illus. 2010. (Science Fair Winners Ser.). (ENG.). 80p. (J). (gr. 5-9). 24.90 (978-1-4263-0692-1(X)); pap. 12.95 (978-1-4263-0691-4(1)) National Geographic Society. (National Geographic Children's Bks.).

—Junkyard Science. Goldin, David, illus. 2010. (Science Fair Winners Ser.). (ENG.). 80p. (J). (gr. 5-9). 24.90 (978-1-4263-0690-7(3)); pap. 12.95 (978-1-4263-0689-1(X)) National Geographic Society. (National Geographic Children's Bks.).

SCIENCE—VOCATIONAL GUIDANCE

Brinkerhoff, Shirley. Research Scientist. Riggs, Ernestine G. & Gholar, Cheryl, eds. 2013. (Careers with Character Ser.: 18). 96p. (J). (gr. 7-18). 22.95 (978-1-4222-2765-7(0)) Mason Crest.

Burnett, Betty. Cool Careers Without College for Math & Science Wizards. 2009. (Cool Careers Without College Ser.). 144p. (gr. 6-6). 66.50 (978-1-61511-959-2(0)) Rosen Publishing Group, Inc., The.

Byers, Ann. Jobs As Green Builders & Planners. 2010. (Green Careers Ser.). 80p. (YA). (gr. 7-12). E-Book 61.20 (978-1-4488-0131-2(1)) Rosen Publishing Group, Inc., The.

Cherry Lake Publishing Staff, compiled by. Cool Science Centers. 2009. 32p. lib. bdg. 319.20 (978-1-60279-109-1(0), 200010) Cherry Lake Publishing.

Cool Science Careers. 2011. 32p. lib. bdg. 359.10 (978-1-61080-036-5(2), 200940) Cherry Lake Publishing.

Duke, Shirley. STEM Jobs in Music. 2014. (ENG., Illus.). 48p. (gr. 4-8). 35.64 (978-1-62717-699-6(3)) Rourke Educational Media.

—STEM Jobs with Animals. 2014. (ENG., Illus.). 48p. (gr. 4-8). 35.64 (978-1-62717-698-9(5)) Rourke Educational Media.

Etingoff, Kim. Women Who Built Our Scientific Foundations. Lee-Karlon, Ann, ed. 2013. (Major Women in Science Ser.: 10). 64p. (J). (gr. 7-18). 22.95 (978-1-4222-2933-0(5)) Mason Crest.

Extraordinary Jobs in Health & Science. 2006. (Extraordinary Jobs Ser.). 176p. (gr. 6-12). 40.00 (978-0-8160-5858-7(X), Ferguson Publishing Co.) Facts On File, Inc.

Extreme Science Careers. 2015. (Extreme Science Careers Ser.). (ENG.). 128p. (J). (gr. 7-7). 223.62 (978-0-7660-6696-0(7)) Enslow Pubs., Inc.

French, Lloyd C. On the Job with an Explorer. 2003. (Adventures in Science Professions Ser.). (J). pap. (978-1-58417-123-2(5)); lib. bdg. (978-1-58417-060-0(3)) Lake Street Pubs.

Guillain, Charlotte. Science, 1 vol. 2012. (Jobs If You Like... Ser.). (ENG.). 32p. (gr. 1-3). pap. 8.29 (978-1-4329-6822-9(X), Heinemann First Library) Heinemann-Raintree.

Harmon, Daniel E. Jobs in Environmental Cleanup & Emergency Hazmat Response. 2010. (Green Careers Ser.). 80p. (YA). (gr. 7-12). E-Book 61.20 (978-1-4488-0132-9(X)) Rosen Publishing Group, Inc., The.

Hoyt, Beth Caldwell & Ritter, Erica. The Ultimate Girls' Guide to Science: From Backyard Experiments to Winning the Nobel Prize. Palen, Debbie, illus. 2004. 128p. (J). (gr. 4-12). pap. (978-1-58270-092-2(3)) Beyond Words Publishing, Inc.

Hynson, Colin. Dream Jobs in Science. 2017. (Illus.). 32p. (J). **(978-0-7787-2965-5(6))** Crabtree Publishing Co.

Idzikowski, Lisa. Working in Science. 2018. (ENG.). 32p. (gr. 3-6). **(978-1-63235-448-8(9)**, 12-Story Library) Pr. Room Editions LLC.

Jackson, Donna M. Extreme Scientists: Exploring Nature's Mysteries from Perilous Places. 2014. (Scientists in the Field Ser.). (ENG., Illus.). 80p. (J). (gr. 5-7). pap. 9.99 (978-0-544-25003-1(6), HMH Books For Young Readers) Houghton Mifflin Harcourt Publishing Co.

—Extreme Scientists: Exploring Nature's Mysteries from Perilous Places. 2014. (Scientists in the Field Ser.). lib. bdg. 20.85 (978-0-606-35330-4(5)) Turtleback Bks.

Katirgis, Jane. STEM Jobs in Food & Nutrition. 2014. (ENG., Illus.). 48p. (gr. 4-8). 35.64 (978-1-62717-703-0(5)) Rourke Educational Media.

—STEM Jobs with Cars. 2014. (ENG.). 48p. (gr. 4-8). 35.64 (978-1-62717-702-3(7)) Rourke Educational Media.

Klein, Rebecca T. Careers for Tech Girls in Science. 2015. (Tech Girls Ser.). (ENG., Illus.). 80p. (J). (gr. 7-8). 34.25 (978-1-4994-6103-9(8), Rosen Young Adult) Rosen Publishing Group, Inc., The.

Liebman, Daniel. I Want to Be a Scientist. 2016. (I Want to Be Ser.). (ENG., Illus.). 24p. (J). (gr. -1-2). pap. 3.99 (978-1-77085-789-6(3), 9781770857896) Firefly Bks., Ltd.

Liebman, Daniel & Mlawer, Teresa. Quiero Ser Científico. 2016. (Quiero Ser.). (SPA., Illus.). 24p. (J). (gr. -1-2). pap. 6.99 (978-1-77085-865-7(2), 9781770858657) Firefly Bks., Ltd.

Louv, Barbara. Choose a Career in Science. 2006. (Illus.). 112p. (gr. 3-7). per. 12.95 (978-1-59858-130-0(9)) Dog Ear Publishing, LLC.

Lundgren, Julie K. STEM Jobs with the Environment. 2014. (ENG., Illus.). 48p. (gr. 4-8). 35.64 (978-1-62717-697-2(7)) Rourke Educational Media.

Mahaney, Ian F. Energy in Action, 6 bks., Set. Incl. Electricity. (YA). (gr. 4-7). lib. bdg. 22.60 (978-1-4042-3478-9(0)); Heat. (YA). (gr. 4-7). lib. bdg. 22.60 (978-1-4042-3477-2(2)); Light. (YA). (gr. 4-7). lib. bdg. 22.60 (978-1-4042-3476-5(4)); Sound Waves. (J). (gr. 3-7). lib. bdg. 21.25 (978-1-4042-3480-2(2), PowerKids Pr.); (Illus.). 24p. 2007. 2007. Set lib. bdg. 127.50 (978-1-4042-3504-5(3)) Rosen Publishing Group, Inc., The.

McGuinness, Daniel. Cool Careers Without College for People Who Are Really Good at Science & Math. 2013. (New Cool Careers Without College Ser.). (Illus.). 144p. (J). (gr. 7-12). 35.95 (978-1-4777-1823-0(0)) Rosen Publishing Group, Inc., The.

Mooney, Carla. STEM Jobs in Fashion & Beauty. 2014. (ENG., Illus.). 48p. (gr. 4-8). 35.64 (978-1-62717-700-9(0)) Rourke Educational Media.

—STEM Jobs in Movies. 2014. (ENG.). 48p. (gr. 4-8). 35.64 (978-1-62717-701-6(9)) Rourke Educational Media.

Objects in the Sky, 6 bks., Set. Incl. Exploring Comets. Way, Jennifer. lib. bdg. 22.60 (978-1-4042-3469-7(1), PowerKids Pr.); Exploring Earth. Olien, Rebecca. lib. bdg. 22.60 (978-1-4042-3465-9(9)); Exploring Meteors. Olien, Rebecca. lib. bdg. 22.60 (978-1-4042-3468-0(3), PowerKids Pr.); Exploring the Moon. Olien, Rebecca. lib. bdg. 22.60 (978-1-4042-3466-6(7), PowerKids Pr.); Exploring the Planets in Our Solar System. Olien, Rebecca. lib. bdg. 22.60 (978-1-4042-3467-3(5), PowerKids Pr.); Exploring the Sun. Olien, Rebecca. lib. bdg. 22.60 (978-1-4042-3464-2(0), PowerKids Pr.); (Illus.). 24p. (J). (gr. 3-7). 2007. 2007. Set lib. bdg. 127.50 (978-1-4042-3502-1(7), PowerKids Pr.) Rosen Publishing Group, Inc., The.

Porterfield, Deborah. Great Careers with a High School Diploma: Health Care, Medicine, & Science. 2008. (Great Careers with a High School Diploma Ser.). 115p. (C). (gr. 9). 32.95 (978-0-8160-7047-3(4), Ferguson Publishing Co.) Facts On File, Inc.

Raymos, Rick. STEM Jobs in Sports. 2014. (ENG.). 48p. (gr. 4-8). 35.64 (978-1-62717-696-5(9)) Rourke Educational Media.

Reeves, Diane Lindsey. Career Ideas for Kids Who Like Science. Bond, Nancy, illus. 2nd rev. ed. 2007. (Career Ideas for Kids Ser.). 208p. (gr. 4-9). 32.95 (978-0-8160-6549-3(7), Checkmark Bks.) Facts On File, Inc.

—Find Your Future in Science. 2016. (Bright Futures Press: Find Your Future in STEAM Ser.). (ENG., Illus.). 32p. (J). (gr. 4-6). 29.93 (978-1-63471-898-1(4), 208913) Cherry Lake Publishing.

—Stem. 2017. (Bright Futures Press: World of Work Ser.). (ENG., Illus.). 32p. (J). (gr. 4-7). lib. bdg. 29.93 (978-1-63472-628-3(6), 209546) Cherry Lake Publishing.

Ring, Susan. Scientists at Work. 2005. (Yellow Umbrella Fluent Level Ser.). (ENG., Illus.). 16p. (gr. k-1). pap. 35.70 (978-0-7368-5303-3(0), Yellow Umbrella Bks.) Capstone Press of Coughlan Cos.

Sawyer, Sarah. Careers in DNA Analysis. 2008. (Careers in Forensics Ser.). (Illus.). 64p. (J). (gr. 3-7). lib. bdg. 31.95 (978-1-4042-1343-2(0)) Rosen Publishing Group, Inc., The.

Science. 2010. (What Can I Do Now? Ser.). 240p. (gr. 6-12). 32.95 (978-0-8160-8082-3(8)); (Illus.). 168p. (C). (gr. 9-18). 32.95 (978-0-8160-8153-0(0)) Facts On File, Inc. (Ferguson Publishing Co.).

Snyder, Gail. Careers If You Like Science. 2016. (ENG.). 80p. (J). (gr. 5-12). lib. bdg. (978-1-68282-006-3(8)) ReferencePoint Pr., Inc.

Squire, Ann O. Extreme Science Careers. 2014. (True Book(tm), a — Extreme Science Ser.). (ENG.). 48p. (J). lib. bdg. 31.00 (978-0-531-20744-4(7)) Scholastic Library Publishing.

Suen, Anastasia. Top STEM Careers in Science. 2014. (Cutting-Edge STEM Careers Ser.). (Illus.). 128p. (J). (gr. 9-12). 35.60 (978-1-4777-7664-3(8)) Rosen Publishing Group, Inc., The.

Wendinger, Jennifer. Unusual & Awesome Jobs Using Science: Hollywood Animal Trainer, Cave Diver, & More. 2015. (You Get Paid for THAT? Ser.). (ENG.). 32p. (gr. 3-4). 27.99 (978-1-4914-2031-7(6)) Capstone Press of Coughlan Cos.

SCIENCE—YEARBOOKS

Science Year 2006. 2005. (gr. 5-12). 38.50 (978-0-7166-0559-1(7)) World Bk., Inc.

SCIENCE AND CIVILIZATION

Kidd, J. S. & Kidd, Renee A. Science & Society Set. 2nd rev. ed. 2006. (Science & Society Ser.). 176p. (gr. 6-12). 140.00 (978-0-8160-5603-3(X)) Facts On File, Inc.

Kovacs, Vic. Get into Citizen Science. 2017. 32p. (J). **(978-0-7787-3636-3(9))** Crabtree Publishing Co.

Senker, Cath. Ideas That Changed the World. 2017. (10 Ser.). (ENG., Illus.). 32p. (J). (gr. 4-6). pap. 12.99 **(978-0-7502-9141-5(9)**, Wayland) Hachette Children's Group GBR. Dist: Hachette Bk. Group.

Turney, Jon. Technology - Ethical Debates about the Application of Science. 2008. (Dilemmas in Modern Science Ser.). (ENG., Illus.). 48p. (J). 23.99 (978-0-237-53370-0(7)) Evans Brothers, Ltd. GBR. Dist: Independent Pubs. Group.

SCIENCE AND RELIGION

see Religion and Science

SCIENCE AND SPACE

see Space Sciences

SCIENCE FICTION

see also Time Travel

Abdo Publishing. Star Wars Digests Set 2, 1 vol. 2013. (Star Wars Digests Set 2 Ser.: 4). (ENG.). 80p. (J). (gr. 4-8). lib. bdg. 108.28 (978-1-61479-055-6(8), Essential Library) ABDO Publishing Co.

ABDO Publishing Company Staff. Kid Squad Saves the World, 1 vol. 2014. (Kid Squad Saves the World Ser.: 6). (ENG.). 112p. (J). (gr. 8-12). lib. bdg. 162.42 (978-1-62402-036-0(4), Calico Chapter Bks) Magic Wagon.

—Tom Swift, Young Inventor - 4 Titles. 2007. (Tom Swift, Young Inventor Ser.). (ENG.). 165p. 108.28 (978-1-59961-349-9(2)) Spotlight.

Abnett, Dan. This Ghost Is Toast! Williams, Anthony, illus. 2007. (Real Ghostbusters Ser.). (ENG.). 96p. per. 8.95 (978-1-84576-143-1(X), Titan Bks.) Titan Bks. Ltd. GBR. Dist: Penguin Random Hse. LLC.

Abnett, Dan & Lanning, Andy. Marvel's Guardians of the Galaxy Prelude. Alves, Wellington et al, illus. 2014. (ENG.). 168p. (J). (gr. 4-17). pap. 14.99 (978-0-7851-5410-5(8)) Marvel Worldwide, Inc.

The Abominable Snowman, 6 Vols., Pack. (Bookweb Ser.). 32p. (gr. 3-18). 34.00 (978-0-7635-3935-1(X)) Rigby Education.

Abuhamda, Nasser. A Flower in the Rain. 2009. 40p. pap. 14.95 (978-1-59858-879-8(6)) Dog Ear Publishing, LLC.

Acampora, Michael V. Escape from the Orange Lanterns, 1 vol. Schoening, Dan, illus. 2011. (Green Lantern Ser.). (ENG.). 56p. (gr. 2-3). pap. 4.95 (978-1-4342-3408-7(8), DC Super Heroes) Stone Arch Bks.

—Red Lanterns' Revenge, 1 vol. Schoening, Dan, illus. 2011. (Green Lantern Ser.). (ENG.). 56p. (gr. 2-3). pap. 4.95 (978-1-4342-3409-4(6), DC Super Heroes) Stone Arch Bks.

Acampora, Michael Vincent. Escape from the Orange Lanterns, 1 vol. Schoening, Dan, illus. 2011. (Green Lantern Ser.). (ENG.). 56p. (gr. 2-3). lib. bdg. 26.65 (978-1-4342-2622-8(0), DC Super Heroes) Stone Arch Bks.

—Red Lanterns' Revenge, 1 vol. Schoening, Dan, illus. 2011. (Green Lantern Ser.). (ENG.). 56p. (gr. 2-3). lib. bdg. 26.65 (978-1-4342-2623-5(9), DC Super Heroes) Stone Arch Bks.

Acevedo, Kristy. Contribute. 2017. (Holo Ser.). (ENG.). 300p. (YA). (gr. 7-12). pap. 14.99 (978-1-63163-098-9(9), Jolly Fish Pr.) North Star Editions.

Adams, Jennifer. Frankenstein: An Anatomy Primer, 1 vol. Oliver, Alison, illus. 2014. (ENG.). 22p. (J). (gr. k-1). bds. 9.99 (978-1-4236-3741-7(0)) Gibbs Smith, Publisher.

Adams, John Joseph, ed. Under the Moons of Mars: New Adventures on Barsoom. 2013. (ENG., Illus.). 368p. (YA). (gr. 7). pap. 9.99 (978-1-4424-2030-4(8), Simon & Schuster Bks. For Young Readers) Simon & Schuster Bks. For Young Readers.

—Under the Moons of Mars: New Adventures on Barsoom. Various Artists, illus. 2012. (ENG.). 368p. (YA). (gr. 7). 16.99 (978-1-4424-2029-8(4), Simon & Schuster Bks. For Young Readers) Simon & Schuster Bks. For Young Readers.

Adams, Matthew R. Kord & Harley. O'Reilly, Sean Patrick, ed. 2011. (Illus.). 50p. (YA). pap. 19.95 (978-0-9809204-7-5(7)) Arcana Studio, Inc.

Adams, W. Royce. The Computer's Nerd. 2011. 154p. (gr. 4-7). 22.99 (978-0-9712206-9-0(7)) Rairarubia Bks.

Adina Bates, Shelley. A Lady of Spirit: A Steampunk Adventure Novel. 2014. (ENG.). pap. 13.99 (978-1-939087-15-7(5), Moonshell Bks., Inc.) Shelley Adina.

Adlington, L. J. The Diary of Pelly D. 2008. 304p. (YA). (gr. 9). per. 9.99 (978-0-06-076617-7(4), Greenwillow Bks.) HarperCollins Pubs.

Adrian, Susan. Tunnel Vision: A Novel. 2015. (ENG.). 320p. (YA). (gr. 8-12). 18.99 *(978-1-250-04792-2(7)*, 9781250047922, St. Martin's Griffin) St. Martin's Pr.

Adventures Beyond the Solar System: Planetron & Me. 2005. (J). audio, cd-rom 24.95 *(978-0-9771381-5-9(1))* Williams, Geoffrey T.

Adventures in the Solar System: Planetron & Me. 2005. (J). audio, cd-rom 24.95 *(978-0-9771381-4-2(3))* Williams, Geoffrey T.

Agnew, Kate. Space Saver. Castle, Frances, illus. 2016. (Reading Ladder Ser.). (ENG.). 48p. (J). (gr. k-2). 7.99 *(978-1-4052-8213-0(4))* Egmont Bks., Ltd. GBR. Dist: Independent Pubs. Group.

Aguirre, Ann. Enclave. 2011. (Razorland Trilogy Ser.: 1). (ENG.). 272p. (YA). (gr. 7-18). 18.99 *(978-0-312-65008-7(6)*, 9780312650087) Feiwel & Friends.

—Enclave. 2012. (Razorland Trilogy Ser.: 1). (ENG.). 288p. (YA). (gr. 7). pap. 9.99 *(978-0-312-55137-7(1)*, 9780312551377) Square Fish.

—Horde. 2013. (Razorland Trilogy Ser.: 3). (ENG.). 432p. (YA). (gr. 7). 17.99 *(978-1-250-02463-3(3)*, 9781250024633) Feiwel & Friends.

—Horde. 2014. (Razorland Trilogy Ser.: 3). (ENG.). 464p. (YA). (gr. 7). pap. 10.99 *(978-1-250-05077-9(4)*, 9781250050779) Square Fish.

—Outpost. 2013. (Razorland Trilogy Ser.: 2). (ENG.). 352p. (YA). (gr. 7). pap. 10.99 *(978-1-250-03418-2(3)*, 9781250034182) Square Fish.

—Vanguard. 2017. (Razorland Trilogy Ser.). (ENG.). 368p. (J). 17.99 *(978-1-250-08982-3(4)*, 9781250089823) Feiwel & Friends.

Ahern, Cecelia. Perfect. 2017. (Flawed Ser.). (ENG.). 352p. (YA). 18.99 *(978-1-250-07412-6(6)*, 9781250074126) Feiwel & Friends.

Akins, Karen. Loop. 2014. (ENG.). 336p. (YA). (gr. 7-12). 18.99 *(978-1-250-03098-6(6)*, 9781250030986, St. Martin's Griffin) St. Martin's Pr.

—Twist. 2015. (ENG.). 336p. (YA). (gr. 7-12). 18.99 *(978-1-250-03100-6(1)*, 9781250031006, St. Martin's Griffin) St. Martin's Pr.

Akinyemi, Rowena. Under the Moon, Level 1. Oxford University Press Staff & Bassett, Jennifer, eds. 3rd ed. 2008. (ENG., Illus.). 64p. 9.38 *(978-0-19-478922-6(5))* Oxford Univ. Pr., Inc.

Albee, Sarah. Trevor el Ingenioso; Clever Trevor. 2008. pap. 34.95 *(978-0-7613-3868-0(3))* Kane Press, Inc.

Albee, Sarah, et al. To the Center of the Earth! 2008. (Backyardigans Ser.). (ENG.). 24p. (J). pap. 3.99 *(978-1-4169-7094-1(0)*, Simon Spotlight/Nickelodeon) Simon Spotlight/Nickelodeon.

Albin, Gennifer. Altered. 2013. (Crewel World Ser.: 2). (ENG.). 400p. (YA). (gr. 7). 17.99 *(978-0-374-31642-6(2)*, 9780374316426, Farrar, Straus & Giroux (BYR)) Farrar, Straus & Giroux.

—Altered. 2014. (Crewel World Ser.: 2). (ENG.). 416p. (YA). (gr. 7). pap. 10.99 *(978-1-250-05073-1(1)*, 9781250050731) Square Fish.

—Crewel - Chapters 1-5. 2012. (Crewel World Ser.: 1). (ENG.). 368p. (YA). (gr. 7). 17.99 *(978-0-374-31641-9(4)*, 9780374316419, Farrar, Straus & Giroux (BYR)) Farrar, Straus & Giroux.

—Crewel, Chapters 1-5. 2013. (Crewel World Ser.: 1). (ENG.). 400p. (YA). (gr. 7). pap. 9.99 *(978-1-250-03423-6(X)*, 9781250034236) Square Fish.

—Unraveled. 2014. (Crewel World Ser.: 3). (ENG.). 304p. (YA). (gr. 7). 17.99 *(978-0-374-31643-3(0)*, 9780374316433, Farrar, Straus & Giroux (BYR)) Farrar, Straus & Giroux.

Alexander, Claudia. Windows to Adventure: Windows to the Morning Star. 2012. 68p. pap. 15.99 *(978-1-937781-66-8(6))* Blue Pheonix Bks.

Alexander, Lloyd, et al. Firebirds: An Anthology of Original Fantasy & Science Fiction. Sharyn, November, ed. Vess, Charles, illus. 2005. (ENG.). 432p. (YA). (gr. 7-11). 9.99 *(978-0-14-240320-4(2)*, Firebird) Penguin Young Readers Group.

Alexander, William. Ambassador. 2015. (ENG.). 256p. (J). (gr. 3-7). pap. 7.99 *(978-1-4424-9765-8(3)*, McElderry, Margaret K. Bks.) McElderry, Margaret K. Bks.

—Ambassador. 2015. lib. bdg. 18.40 *(978-0-606-37848-2(0))* Turtleback Bks.

—Nomad. 2015. (ENG., Illus.). 272p. (J). (gr. 3-7). 16.99 *(978-1-4424-9767-2(X)*, McElderry, Margaret K. Bks.) McElderry, Margaret K. Bks.

The Alien Next Door. 2005. (J). audio, cd-rom 24.95 *(978-0-9771381-8-0(6))* Williams, Geoffrey T.

Alixe, Pascal & Klein, Nic, illus. The Iron Nail - Captain America, Vol. 4. 2014. (ENG.). 144p. (J). (gr. 4-17). 24.99 *(978-0-7851-8953-4(X))* Marvel Worldwide, Inc.

Allen, Elise & Conners, Daryle. Gabby Duran & the Unsittables. 2016. (Gabby Duran Ser.). (ENG., Illus.). 240p. (J). (gr. 3-7). pap. 7.99 *(978-1-4847-2542-9(5))* Hyperion Bks. for Children.

Alpert, Mark. The Siege. 2016. (Six Ser.: 2). (ENG.). 288p. (J). (gr. 6-12). 17.99 *(978-1-4926-3170-5(1)*, 9781492631705) Sourcebooks, Inc.

—The Silence. 2017. (Six Ser.: 3). (ENG.). 384p. (J). (gr. 6-12). 17.99 *(978-1-4926-4896-3(5))* Sourcebooks, Inc.

—The Six. 2015. (Six Ser.: 1). (ENG.). 368p. (J). (gr. 6-12). 16.99 *(978-1-4926-1529-3(3)*, 9781492615293) Sourcebooks, Inc.

Ambassador. 2014. (ENG., Illus.). 240p. (J). (gr. 3-7). 16.99 *(978-1-4424-9764-1(5)*, McElderry, Margaret K. Bks.) McElderry, Margaret K. Bks.

Ameet Studio, Ameet. R2-D2 to the Rescue! 2016. (Lego Star Wars Ser.). (ENG.). 64p. (J). (gr. 2-5). pap. 4.99 *(978-0-545-94070-2(2))* Scholastic, Inc.

Ameet Studio Staff. Galactic Freedom Fighters Comics & Activities. 2015. (LEGO Star Wars Ser.). (ENG.). 96p. (J). (gr. 2-5). pap., act. bk. ed. 8.99 *(978-0-545-84237-2(9))* Scholastic, Inc.

—These Aren't the Droids You're Looking For: A Search & Find Book. Ameet Studio Staff, illus. 2014. (LEGO Star Wars Ser.). (ENG., Illus.). 32p. (J). (gr. -1-3). pap. 6.99 *(978-0-545-60804-6(X))* Scholastic, Inc.

Ames, Mildred. Anna to the Infinite Power. 2003. (J). pap. 2.75 *(978-0-590-42707-4(5))* Scholastic, Inc.

Ammann, Michael. Exos. 2003. 108p. (YA). pap. 9.95 *(978-0-595-27121-4(9)*, Writers Club Pr.) iUniverse, Inc.

Anastasiu, Heather. Glitch. 2012. (Glitch Novel Ser.: 1). (ENG.). 336p. (YA). (gr. 7-12). pap. 12.99 *(978-1-250-00299-0(0)*, 9781250002990, St. Martin's Griffin) St. Martin's Pr.

—Override. 2013. (Glitch Novel Ser.: 2). (ENG.). 320p. (YA). (gr. 7-12). pap. 9.99 *(978-1-250-00300-3(8)*, 9781250003003, St. Martin's Griffin) St. Martin's Pr.

—Shutdown. 2013. (Glitch Novel Ser.: 3). (ENG.). 320p. (YA). (gr. 7-12). pap. 9.99 *(978-1-250-00301-0(6)*, 9781250003010, St. Martin's Griffin) St. Martin's Pr.

Anderson, Brian. The Adventures of Commander Zack Proton & the Red Giant. Holgate, Douglas, illus. 2006. (Adventures of Commander Zack Proton Ser.: 1). (ENG.). 128p. (J). (gr. 2-5). pap. 5.99 *(978-1-4169-1364-1(5)*, Simon & Schuster/Paula Wiseman Bks.) Simon & Schuster/Paula Wiseman Bks.

—The Adventures of Commander Zack Proton & the Warlords of Nibblecheese. Holgate, Douglas, illus. 2006. (Adventures of Commander Zack Proton Ser.: 2). (ENG.). 112p. (J). (gr. 2-5). pap. 5.99 *(978-1-4169-1365-8(3)*, Aladdin) Simon & Schuster Children's Publishing.

Anderson, D. M. Killer Cows. 2010. 274p. (YA). pap. 13.99 *(978-1-59080-686-9(7)*, Quake) Echelon Press Publishing.

Anderson, E. V. The Many Lives of Lilith Lane, 0 vols. unabr. ed. 2012. (ENG.). 162p. (YA). (gr. 7-9). pap. 9.99 *(978-1-61109-792-4(4)*, 9781611097924, Amazon Children's Publishing) Amazon Publishing.

Anderson, M. T. The Chamber in the Sky. 2012. (Norumbegan Quartet Ser.: 4). (ENG.). 288p. (J). (gr. 3-7). 17.99 *(978-0-545-33493-8(4)*, Scholastic Pr.) Scholastic, Inc.

—The Empire of Gut & Bone. 2011. (Norumbegan Quartet Ser.: 3). (ENG.). 336p. (J). (gr. 3-7). 17.99 *(978-0-545-13884-0(1)*, Scholastic Pr.) Scholastic, Inc.

—Feed. braille ed. 2003. (J). (gr. 2). spiral bd. *(978-0-616-15869-2(6))* Canadian National Institute for the Blind/Institut National Canadien pour les Aveugles.

—Feed. 2012. (ENG., Illus.). 320p. (YA). (gr. 9). pap. 8.99 *(978-0-7636-6262-2(3))* Candlewick Pr.

—Feed. 2004. 299p. (YA). (gr. 9-12). 15.65 *(978-0-7569-6578-5(0))* Perfection Learning Corp.

—Feed. 2004. 320p. (J). (gr. 7-18). pap. 38.00 incl. audio *(978-1-4000-9022-8(9)*, Listening Library) Random Hse. Audio Publishing Group.

—Feed. 2012. lib. bdg. 19.65 *(978-0-606-26941-4(X)*, Turtleback) Turtleback Bks.

—The Kingdom on the Waves. 2009. (Astonishing Life of Octavian Nothing, Traitor to the Nation Ser.: Vol. 2). (ENG., Illus.). 592p. (YA). (gr. 9). pap. 12.99 *(978-0-7636-4626-4(1))* Candlewick Pr.

—Whales on Stilts! Cyrus, Kurt, illus. 2010. (Pals in Peril Tale Ser.). (ENG.). (J). (gr. 5-9). 208p. 17.99 *(978-1-4424-0695-7(X))*; 224p. pap. 7.99 *(978-1-4424-0701-5(8))* Beach Lane Bks. (Beach Lane Bks.).

—Whales on Stilts! Cyrus, Kurt, illus. 2006. (M. T. Anderson's Thrilling Tales Ser.). 188p. (gr. 5-9). 15.95 *(978-0-7569-7213-4(2))* Perfection Learning Corp.

Anderson, Matt & Hutchins, Eric. White Picket Fences: Double Feature One-shot. 2008. (Illus.). 52p. (YA). pap. 6.95 *(978-0-9801314-9-9(9))* Ape Entertainment.

Anderson, R. J. Quicksilver. 2013. (ENG.). 328p. (YA). (gr. 7-12). 17.95 *(978-0-7613-8799-2(4)*, Carolrhoda Lab™) Lerner Publishing Group.

—Ultraviolet. (ENG.). 312p. (YA). (gr. 7-12). 2013. pap. 9.95 *(978-1-4677-0914-9(X))* 2011. 17.95 *(978-0-7613-7408-4(6))* Lerner Publishing Group. (Carolrhoda Lab™).

Anderson, Suzette. Cybertreks: Wildest West. 2004. 196p. pap. 13.95 *(978-0-595-30840-8(6))* iUniverse, Inc.

Andre Norton. 2010. (Who Wrote That? Ser.). (Illus.). 128p. (gr. 6-12). 35.00 *(978-1-60413-682-1(0)*, Chelsea Hse.) Facts On File, Inc.

Andrews, Jefferri & Andrews, Jonathan. The Macos Adventure. 2013. (ENG.). 212p. (YA). pap. 23.99 *(978-0-9848980-9-1(3)*, BTWEYL) Bks. That Will Enhance Your Life.

Andrews, Jerome. The Initiation. 2006. 40p. pap. 8.50 *(978-1-4116-9167-4(9))* Lulu Pr., Inc.

Angelini, Josephine. Trial by Fire. 2014. (Worldwalker Trilogy: Bk. 1). 384p. (YA). (gr. 7-12). 17.99 *(978-1-250-05088-5(X)*, 9781250050885) Feiwel & Friends.

Angleberger, Tom. Rocket & Groot: Stranded on Planet Stripmall! Angleberger, Tom, illus. 2016. (Marvel Middle Grade Novel Ser.). (ENG., Illus.). 224p. (J). (gr. 3-7). 13.99 *(978-1-4847-1452-2(0)*, Marvel Pr.) Disney Publishing Worldwide.

—Rocket & Groot: Stranded on Planet Strip Mall! Angleberger, Tom, illus. 2017. (Marvel Middle Grade Novel Ser.). (ENG., Illus.). 224p. (J). (gr. 3-7). pap. 7.99 ***(978-1-368-01392-5(9)***, Marvel Pr.) Disney Publishing Worldwide.

Angleberger, Tom. Star Wars - Return of the Jedi: Beware the Power of the Dark Side! McCaig, Iain, illus. 2015. (ENG.). 432p. (J). (gr. 3-7). 17.99 *(978-1-4847-0913-9(6)*, Disney Lucasfilm Press) Disney Publishing Worldwide.

The Annoying Crush. 2014. (Galaxy Zack Ser.: 9). (ENG., Illus.). 128p. (J). (gr. k-4). 16.99 *(978-1-4424-9364-3(X))*; pap. 5.99 *(978-1-4424-9363-6(1))* Little Simon. (Little Simon).

Ant, Exupery. Journee avec le Petit Prince. pap. 10.95 *(978-2-07-054268-0(8))* Gallimard, Editions FRA. Dist: Distribooks, Inc.

Anthony, David & David, Charles. Knightscares #3: (Knightscares): Early Winter's Orb. 2005. (Illus.). 208p. (J). pap. 5.99 *(978-0-9728461-2-7(3))* Sigil Publishing.

Antonios, Joseph. Portal:Earth. 2010. 126p. pap. 12.99 *(978-0-557-40539-8(4))* Lulu Pr., Inc.

Antram, David. How to Draw Science Fiction. 2012. (Illus.). 32p. (J). 70.50 *(978-1-4488-4528-6(9))*; pap. 11.75 *(978-1-4488-4527-9(0))* Rosen Publishing Group, Inc., The. (PowerKids Pr.).

Applegate, K. A., pseud. Aftermath. 2003. (Remnants Ser.: No. 12). 163p. (J). (gr. 4-8). 12.65 *(978-0-7569-5318-8(9))* Perfection Learning Corp.

—Animorphs #7: the Stranger. 2012. (Animorphs Ser.: 7). (ENG.). 176p. (J). (gr. 3-7). pap. 6.99 *(978-0-545-42414-1(3)*, Scholastic Paperbacks) Scholastic, Inc.

—The Capture. 2012. (Animorphs Ser.: 6). (ENG.). 176p. (J). (gr. 3-7). pap. 6.99 *(978-0-545-29158-3(5)*, Scholastic Paperbacks) Scholastic, Inc.

—The Invasion. 2nd ed. 2011. (Animorphs Ser.: 1). (ENG.). 192p. (J). (gr. 3-7). pap. 6.99 *(978-0-545-29151-4(8)*, Scholastic Paperbacks) Scholastic, Inc.

—Survival. 2003. (Remnants Ser.: No. 13). 165p. (J). (gr. 4-8). 12.65 *(978-0-7569-5301-0(4))* Perfection Learning Corp.

—The Visitor. 2nd ed. 2011. (Animorphs Ser.: 2). (ENG.). 192p. (J). (gr. 3-7). pap. 6.99 *(978-0-545-29152-1(6)*, Scholastic Paperbacks) Scholastic, Inc.

Applegate, Katherine. The Capture. 2012. (Animorphs Ser.: 6). lib. bdg. 17.20 *(978-0-606-26194-4(X)*, Turtleback) Turtleback Bks.

—The Stranger. 2012. (Animorphs Ser.: 7). lib. bdg. 17.20 *(978-0-606-26195-1(8)*, Turtleback) Turtleback Bks.

Appleton, Victor. The Adventures of Tom Swift. 2007. 456p. per. 19.95 *(978-1-4344-9982-0(0))* Wildside Pr., LLC.

—Into the Abyss. 2007. (Tom Swift, Young Inventor Ser.). (ENG.). 160p. (gr. 3-7). 27.07 *(978-1-59961-350-5(6))* Spotlight.

—Tom Swift & His Photo Telephone. 2007. 100p. per. *(978-1-4068-1621-1(3))* Echo Library.

—Tom Swift & the Electronic Hydrolung. 2007. (ENG.). 120p. pap. 18.99 *(978-1-4346-3059-5(5))*; 132p. pap. 19.99 *(978-1-4346-3073-5(0))* Creative Media Partners, LLC.

Araujo, André, illus. Avengers A. I. , 12,000 A. D. 2014. (ENG.). 136p. (YA). (gr. 8-17). pap. 16.99 *(978-0-7851-8492-8(9))* Marvel Worldwide, Inc.

Ariga, Hitoshi. Mega Man Gigamix, 2 vols., Vol. 3. 2011. (ENG., Illus.). 224p. (J). pap. 13.95 *(978-1-926778-31-0(6)*, 9781926778310) UDON Entertainment Corp. CAN. Dist: Diamond Comic Distributors, Inc.

Armentrout, Jennifer L. Lux - Beginnings. 2014. (Lux Novel Ser.: Bks. 1-2). (ENG.). 800p. (YA). (gr. 7-12). pap. 12.99 *(978-1-62266-448-1(5)*, 9781622664481); 19.99 *(978-1-62266-481-8(7)*, 9781622664818); pap. 12.99 *(978-1-62266-449-8(3)*, 9781622664498) Entangled Publishing, LLC.

—Obsidian. 2012. (Lux Novel Ser.: 1). (ENG.). 400p. (YA). pap. 9.99 *(978-1-62061-007-7(8)*, 9781620610077) Entangled Publishing, LLC.

—Onyx. 2012. (Lux Novel Ser.: 2). (ENG.). 416p. (YA). pap. 9.99 *(978-1-62061-011-4(6)*, 9781620610114) Entangled Publishing, LLC.

—Opal. 2012. (Lux Novel Ser.: 3). (ENG.). 452p. (YA). (gr. 9). pap. 9.99 *(978-1-62061-009-1(4)*, 9781620610091) Entangled Publishing, LLC.

—Opposition. (ENG.). 2016. (Lux Novel Ser.). 300p. pap. 9.99 *(978-1-63375-694-6(7)*, 9781633756946) 2013. (Lux Ser.: Bk. 5). (J). pap. 9.99 *(978-1-62266-026-1(9)*, Entangled Teen) 2014. (Lux Novel Ser.: 5). 500p. (YA). 19.99 *(978-1-62266-733-8(6)*, 9781622667338) 2014. (Lux Novel Ser.: 5). 500p. (YA). (gr. 7-12). pap. 11.99 *(978-1-62266-264-7(4)*, 9781622662647) Entangled Publishing, LLC.

—Origin. 2013. (ENG.). (Lux Ser.: Bk. 4). (J). pap. 9.99 *(978-1-62061-280-4(1))*; (Lux Novel Ser.: 4). 400p. (YA). (gr. 7-12). pap. 9.99 *(978-1-62266-075-9(7)*, 9781622660759) Entangled Publishing, LLC.

Armstrong, Jennifer. The Kiln. 2004. (Fire-Us Ser.: No. 3). (ENG.). 256p. (J). (gr. 7-18). pap. 5.99 *(978-0-06-447271-5(X))* HarperCollins Pubs.

Armstrong, Jennifer & Butcher, Nancy. The Kiln. 2003. (Fire-Us Ser.: Bk. 3). (ENG.). 208p. (J). (gr. 7-18). 15.99 *(978-0-06-008050-1(7))* HarperCollins Pubs.

Arnett, Mindee. Avalon. 2014. (Avalon Ser.: 1). (ENG.). 432p. (YA). (gr. 8). 17.99 *(978-0-06-223559-6(1))* HarperCollins Pubs.

—Polaris. 2015. (Avalon Ser.: 2). (ENG.). 432p. (YA). (gr. 8). 17.99 *(978-0-06-223562-6(1))* HarperCollins Pubs.

Arnold, Michelle Lee. Mathew Sunburst & the Keepers of the Sky. 2003. 141p. (J). pap. 13.95 *(978-0-7414-1575-2(5))* Infinity Publishing.

Arnold, Shari. Mystique. 2012. (YA). *(978-1-4521-0363-1(1))* Chronicle Bks. LLC.

Arntson, Steven. The Trap. 2017. (ENG.). 256p. (J). (gr. 5-7). pap. 7.99 *(978-0-544-81311-3(1)*, HMH Books For Young Readers) Houghton Mifflin Harcourt Publishing Co.

Artifact Group, The & Shepherd, Jodie. Robot Rampage! 2009. (Backyardigans Ser.). (ENG.). 24p. (J). (gr. -1-1). pap. 3.99 *(978-1-4169-9013-0(5)*, Simon Spotlight/Nickelodeon) Simon Spotlight/Nickelodeon.

Artus, William. The King on the Moon. 2008. 32p. pap. 20.95 *(978-1-4092-3044-1(9))* Lulu Pr., Inc.

Asch, Frank. Time Twister: Journal 3 of a Cardboard Genius. Asch, Frank, illus. 2008. (Journals of a Cardboard Genius Ser.). (ENG., Illus.). 144p. (J). (gr. 2-5). pap. 5.95 *(978-1-55453-231-5(0))* Kids Can Pr., Ltd. CAN. Dist: Hachette Bk. Group.

Ashes, Dustin. Space-Boot Johnny Recharged. 2010. (J). pap. 10.95 *(978-0-7414-5900-8(0))* Infinity Publishing.

Ashman, M. P. The Water Tower. 2017. (ENG.). 177p. (YA). pap. 13.95 ***(978-1-78693-440-6(X)***, e461551a-9f96-4c79-a55f-c4a93b9cedb3) Austin, Stan AUS. Dist: Bookmasters Distribution.

Asimov, Isaac & Asimov, Janet. Norby's Other Secret. 2010. (Dover Children's Classics Ser.). (ENG.). 144p. (J). (gr. 3-12). pap. 6.99 *(978-0-486-47244-7(2))* Dover Pubns., Inc.

Asimov, Isaac & Hantula, Richard. Science Fiction: Vision of Tomorrow? 2005. (Isaac Asimov's 21st Century Library of the Universe). (Illus.). 32p. (gr. 2-6). lib. bdg. 26.00 *(978-0-8368-3952-4(8)*, Gareth Stevens Learning Library) Stevens, Gareth Publishing LLLP.

Asimov, Janet & Asimov, Isaac. Norby the Mixed-Up Robot. 2010. (Dover Children's Classics Ser.). (ENG.). 96p. (J). (gr. 3-12). pap. 5.99 *(978-0-486-47243-0(4))* Dover Pubns., Inc.

The Ask & the Answer: With Bonus Short Story. 2014. (Chaos Walking Ser.). (ENG., Illus.). (YA). (gr. 9). pap. 10.99 *(978-0-7636-7617-9(9))* Candlewick Pr.

Aslan, Austin. The Islands at the End of the World. 2015. (ENG., Illus.). 384p. (YA). (gr. 7). pap. 9.99 *(978-0-385-74403-4(X)*, Ember) Random Hse. Children's Bks.

Asrar, Mahmud & Bennett, Joe, illus. Indestructible Hulk - Humanity Bomb, Vol. 4. 2014. (ENG.). 144p. (J). (gr. 4-17). 24.99 *(978-0-7851-5480-8(9))* Marvel Worldwide, Inc.

Astro, Ian. Moon School. 2006. (Neighborhood Readers Ser.). (ENG.). 16p. (gr. 1-3). pap. 6.50 *(978-1-4042-7196-8(1)*, Rosen Classroom) Rosen Publishing Group, Inc., The.

Atticus, C. J. Stranded in Space: The Stellar Life of Jpeg the Robot Dog. Domschke, Angelika, illus. 2013. 119p. (J). pap. 6.95 *(978-0-9887780-2-3(5))* Atticus, C. J.

Auerbach, Annie & Mike, Norton. Grosse Adventures - The Good, the Bad & the Gassy, Vol. 1. 2006. (Illus.). 96p. pap. 4.99 *(978-1-59816-049-9(4))* TOKYOPOP, Inc.

Avery, Ben & Rogers, Bud. Berlin Breakout, 1 vol. Gaudiamo, Adi Darda, illus. 2008. (Z Graphic Novels / TimeFlyz Ser.). (ENG.). 160p. (J). (gr. 4-7). pap. 6.99 *(978-0-310-71363-0(3))* Zondervan.

Avery, Ben G. Pyramid Peril, 1 vol. Gaudiamo, Adi Darda, illus. 2007. (Z Graphic Novels / TimeFlyz Ser.). (ENG.). 160p. (J). (gr. 3-7). pap. 6.99 *(978-0-310-71361-6(7))* Zondervan.

Avi. Poppy's Return. Floca, Brian, illus. (Poppy Stories Ser.). (J). 2006. (ENG.). 256p. (gr. 3-7). pap. 6.99 *(978-0-06-000014-1(7))* 2005. 240p. lib. bdg. 16.89 *(978-0-06-000013-4(9))* HarperCollins Pubs.

AWRP Meet Superkids. (J). pap., stu. ed. *(978-0-201-21600-4(0))* Addison-Wesley Longman, Inc.

Bach, Ari. Ragnarok. 2016. (ENG., Illus.). (YA). (gr. 9-12). 32.99 ***(978-1-63533-067-0(X)***, Harmony Ink Pr.) Dreamspinner Pr.

Bach, Ari. Valhalla. 2nd ed. 2016. (ENG., Illus.). (YA). (gr. 9-12). 29.99 ***(978-1-63477-990-6(8))*** 2014. 330p. pap. 17.99 *(978-1-62798-718-9(5))* Dreamspinner Pr. (Harmony Ink Pr.).

Bach, Tamara. Girl from Mars. Tanaka, Shelley, tr. from GER. 2008. (ENG.). 160p. (J). (gr. 8). 16.95 *(978-0-88899-724-1(8))* Groundwood Bks. CAN. Dist: Publishers Group West (PGW).

Bachorz, Pam. Candor. 2010. (ENG.). 272p. (gr. 7). pap. 8.99 *(978-1-60684-135-8(1))* Lerner Publishing Group.

—Drought. 2011. (ENG.). 400p. (gr. 7-18). 17.99 *(978-1-60684-016-0(9))* Lerner Publishing Group.

Bacigalupi, Paolo. The Drowned Cities. 2013. (ENG.). 464p. (J). (gr. 10-17). pap. 10.99 *(978-0-316-05622-9(7))* 2012. 448p. (YA). 17.99 *(978-0-316-20037-0(9))* Little, Brown Bks. for Young Readers.

—The Drowned Cities. 2012. 352p. *(978-1-59606-606-2(0))* Subterranean Pr.

—The Drowned Cities. 2013. (J). lib. bdg. 22.10 *(978-0-606-31749-8(X)*, Turtleback) Turtleback Bks.

—Ship Breaker. 2011. (ENG.). 352p. (YA). (gr. 10-17). pap. 10.99 *(978-0-316-05619-9(7))* Little, Brown Bks. for Young Readers.

Baggott, Julianna. Burn. 2014. (Pure Trilogy Ser.: 3). (ENG.). 432p. 26.00 *(978-1-4555-0299-8(5))* Grand Central Publishing.

—Burn. 2014. 420p. (YA). *(978-1-4555-7677-7(8)*, Faithwords) Hachette Nashville.

—Fuse. 2013. (ENG.). 416p. pap. 14.99 *(978-1-4555-2169-2(8))* Grand Central Publishing.

Baikie, Jim, et al. Star Trek: the Classic UK Comics Volume 1: The Classic UK Comics Volume 1. 2016. (Star Trek Ser.). (ENG., Illus.). 244p. 49.99 *(978-1-63140-512-9(8)*, 9781631405129) Idea & Design Works, LLC.

Bailey, Kristin. Legacy of the Clockwork Key. (Secret Order Ser.: 1). (ENG., (YA). (gr. 9). 2014. Illus.). 432p. pap. 9.99 *(978-1-4424-4027-2(9))* 2013. 416p. 17.99 *(978-1-4424-4026-5(0))* Simon Pulse. (Simon Pulse).

—Rise of the Arcane Fire. 2014. (Secret Order Ser.: 2). (ENG., Illus.). 464p. (YA). (gr. 9). 17.99 *(978-1-4424-6802-3(5)*, Simon Pulse) Simon Pulse.

—Shadow of the War Machine. 2015. (Secret Order Ser.: 3). (ENG., Illus.). 448p. (YA). (gr. 9). 17.99 *(978-1-4424-6805-4(X)*, Simon Pulse) Simon Pulse.

Bailey, Mary. Vhan Zeely & the Time Prevaricators. 2009. 192p. 25.50 *(978-1-60693-477-7(5)*, Eloquent Bks.) Strategic Book Publishing & Rights Agency (SBPRA).

Bailey-Peiffer, Stefanie & Bailey-Yarbrough, Caroline. Modie & the Power of the BellKeys. 2004. pap. 8.95 *(978-0-9762502-0-3(9))* Hudson Bks.

Baity, Cameron & Zelkowicz, Benny. The Second Book of Ore Waybound. 2016. (Books of Ore Ser.). (ENG.). 368p. (J). (gr. 5-9). 16.99 *(978-1-4231-6239-1(0))* Hyperion Bks. for Children.

Baker, Chandler. This Is Not the End. 2017. (ENG.). 384p. (YA). (gr. 9-17). 17.99 ***(978-1-4847-5024-7(1))*** Hyperion Bks. for Children.

Balchin, Lance. Mechanica. 2016. (ENG., Illus.). 40p. (J). (gr. 3-7). 17.99 *(978-1-4998-0343-3(5))* Little Bee Books Inc.

Balian, Lorna. Un Fiasco de Bruja, 1 vol. 2003.Tr. of Humbug Witch. (SPA., Illus.). 32p. (J). (gr. -1). pap. 4.95 *(978-1-59572-011-5(1))* Star Bright Bks., Inc.

Ball, Nate. Alien in My Pocket: Radio Active. Pamintuan, Macky, illus. 2014. (Alien in My Pocket Ser.: 3). (ENG.). 144p. (J). (gr. 1-5). pap. 4.99 *(978-0-06-221627-4(9))* HarperCollins Pubs.

—Blast Off! 2014. (Alien in My Pocket Ser.: 1). (J). lib. bdg. 14.75 *(978-0-606-35181-2(7))* Turtleback Bks.

—Forces of Nature. 2015. (Alien in My Pocket Ser.: 6). (J). lib. bdg. 14.75 *(978-0-606-37611-2(9))* Turtleback Bks.

—On Impact! 2014. (Alien in My Pocket Ser.: 4). (J). lib. bdg. 14.75 *(978-0-606-35952-8(4))* Turtleback Bks.

—Space Invaders. 2016. (Alien in My Pocket Ser.: 8). (J). lib. bdg. 14.75 *(978-0-606-38752-1(8))* Turtleback Bks.

Baltazar, Armand. Diego & the Rangers of the Vastlantic. Baltazar, Armand, illus. 2017. (Timeless Ser.: 1). (Illus.). 624p. (J). (gr. 3-7). 19.99 *(978-0-06-240236-3(6)*, Tegen, Katherine Bks) HarperCollins Pubs.

Banim, Lisa. Case of the Missing She-Geek. 2004. 125p. (J). lib. bdg. 16.92 *(978-1-4242-0683-4(9))* Fitzgerald Bks.

Banks, Alex. Jump Boys: Sos. 2013. 200p. pap. *(978-0-9918599-6-2(0))* Novel Ninjutsu.

Banks, Kate & Sheldrake, Rupert. Boy's Best Friend. 2015. (ENG.). 224p. (J). (gr. 3-7). 15.99 *(978-0-374-38008-3(2)*, 9780374380083, Farrar, Straus & Giroux (BYR)) Farrar, Straus & Giroux.

Bankston, John. Ray Bradbury. 2011. (Who Wrote That? Ser.). (Illus.). 140p. (gr. 6-12). 35.00 *(978-1-60413-778-1(9)*, Chelsea Hse.) Facts On File, Inc.

Bao, Karen. Dove Arising. 2016. (Dove Chronicles Ser.: No. 1). (ENG.). 352p. (YA). (gr. 7). pap. 10.99 (978-0-14-751243-7(3), Speak) Penguin Young Readers Group.

Barba, Rick & Gratz, Alan. The Assassination Game. 2012. (ENG.). 320p. (YA). (gr. 7). pap. 7.99 (978-1-4424-2058-8(8), Simon Spotlight) Simon Spotlight.

Barbara Stathi. Sacrifice. 2009. 312p. pap. 18.95 (978-1-4401-7699-9(X)) iUniverse, Inc.

Barbini, F. T. Tijaran Tales: White Child. 2011. 214p. pap. (978-0-7552-1349-8(1)) Authors OnLine, Ltd.

Bardugo, Leigh. Wonder Woman: Warbringer. 2017. (DC Icons Ser.). (ENG.). 384p. (YA). (gr. 7). 18.99 (978-0-399-54973-1(0), Random Hse. Bks. for Young Readers) Random Hse. Children's Bks.

Barlow, Dave. The Seekers. 2004. 48p. 3.95 (978-0-9725230-4-2(9)) Wandering Sage Pubns., LLC.

Barlow, Jeremy. Star Wars Adventures: Boba Fett & the Ship of Fear, 1 vol. 2013. (Star Wars Digests Set 2 Ser.). (ENG.). 80p. (J). (gr. 4-8). lib. bdg. 27.07 (978-1-61479-056-3(6), Essential Library) ABDO Publishing Co.

Barlow, Steve & Skidmore, Steve. Stone Me! Ross, Tony, illus. 2005. (Mad Myths Ser.). 122p. (J). pap. 5.95 (978-1-903015-43-8(X)) Barn Owl Bks, London GBR. Dist: Independent Pubs. Group.

Barnacott, Anthony Royce. Permanoids of Chilon. 2009. 260p. 27.99 (978-1-4389-3824-0(1)) AuthorHouse.

Barnes, Jennifer Lynn. Nobody. 2014. (ENG.). 400p. (J). (gr. 7). pap. 9.99 (978-1-60684-508-0(X), Carolrhoda Lab™) Lerner Publishing Group.

Barnes, John. Losers in Space. 2012. (ENG.). 448p. (YA). (gr. 9-18). 18.99 (978-0-670-06156-3(5), Viking Books for Young Readers) Penguin Young Readers Group.

Barns, Crosby H. Who Programmed the Species? The Theory of Scientific Coincidence. 2008. 36p. pap. 16.99 (978-1-4389-0727-7(3)) AuthorHouse.

Baron, Mike. Nexus Omnibus Volume 3. Warner, Chris, ed. 2013. (ENG., Illus.). 424p. pap. 24.99 (978-1-61655-036-3(8)) Dark Horse Comics.

Baron, Mike & Horse, Dark. Nexus Omnibus Volume 4. Wright, Brendan, ed. 2013. (ENG., Illus.). 416p. 24.99 (978-1-61655-037-0(6)) Dark Horse Comics.

Barr, Lester. Robots Land at Manchester Airport. 2012. (Illus.). 80p. pap. 13.66 (978-1-4772-2248-5(0)) AuthorHouse.

Barrera, J. Mario. Nine Moons. 2005. (ENG & SPA., Illus.). (YA). cd-rom 21.99 (978-0-9752725-2-7(7)) Orion-Cosmos.

Barry, William J. Forever Awakening. 2014. 242p. pap. 18.50 (978-1-61213-113-9(1)) Writer's Coffee Shop, The.

Barth, Kathleen E. The Amazing Adventures of Quigley D Pigley & His Friends: How to Become an Astronaut. 2009. 16p. pap. 8.49 (978-1-4389-8606-7(8)) AuthorHouse.

Bartol, Amy A. Darken the Stars, 0 vols. 2015. (Kricket Ser.: 3). (ENG.). 302p. (YA). pap. 14.95 (978-1-5039-4742-9(4), 9781503947429, 47North) Amazon Publishing.

Bartow, Philip. T & the Jello Castle-Book 2: Bio Bots. 2013. 264p. (J). pap. 13.30 (978-0-9835176-3-4(0)) Institute For Outdoor Awareness, Inc.

The Bash Street Kids Annual 2004. annuals 2003. (Illus.). 96p. (978-0-85116-815-9(9)) Thomson, D.C. & Co., Ltd. GBR. Dist: APG Sales & Distribution Services.

Basic, Zdenko & Sumberac, Manuel, illus. Steampunk: H. G. Wells. 2013. (ENG.). 408p. (YA). (gr. 7-17). 18.95 (978-0-7624-4444-1(4), Running Pr. Kids) Running Pr. Bk. Pubs.

Baum, L. Frank, et al. A Children's Treasury. 2007. 792p. per. 24.95 (978-1-60459-011-1(4)) Wilder Pubns., Corp.

Baxendale, Trevor & BBC. Choose the Future - Terror Moon. 2016. (ENG.). 208p. (J). pap. 9.99 (978-1-4059-2651-5(1), 9781405926515) Penguin Bks., Ltd. GBR. Dist: Diamond Comic Distributors, Inc.

BBC Books Staff. Doctor Who - 12 Doctors 12 Stories. 2014. (ENG.). 528p. (YA). pap. 16.99 (978-0-14-135535-1(2)) Penguin Bks., Ltd. GBR. Dist: Diamond Bk. Distributors.

BBC Children's Books. Twelve Doctors of Christmas. 2016. (ENG., Illus.). 272p. (YA). 14.99 (978-1-4059-2895-3(6), 9781405928953) Penguin Bks., Ltd. GBR. Dist: Diamond Comic Distributors, Inc.

Beach, John, reader. Moo Cow Kaboom! unabr. ed. 2005. (Picture Book Readalong Ser.). (J). (gr. -1-2). 28.95 incl. audio compact disk (978-1-59519-502-9(5)) Live Oak Media.

Beacham, Travis, et al. Tales from Year Zero. 2013. (Pacific Rim Ser.). (ENG., Illus.). 128p. (gr. 8-17). 24.99 (978-0-7851-5394-8(2)) Legendary Comics.

Beagle, Peter S. & Link, Kelly. Superheroes. Horton, Rich, ed. 2013. (ENG.). 384p. pap. 15.95 (978-1-60701-380-8(0), 9781607013808) Prime.

Beauregard, Lynda. Summer Camp Science Mysteries. Helmer, Der-Shing, illus. 2012. (Summer Camp Science Mysteries Ser.). (ENG.). 48p. (gr. 3-6). pap. 52.82 (978-0-7613-9272-9(6));Pack, Set. pap. 316.92 (978-0-7613-9273-6(4)) Lerner Publishing Group. (Graphic Universe™).

Beck, A. E. Master-E: Travel into Mystical Dragon Dimensions: Collision of Fantasy, Science Fiction & Physics. 2010. 212p. pap. 49.49 (978-1-4490-3612-6(0)) AuthorHouse.

Becker, Savan. Starry Night (2nd Edition) 2008. 60p. pap. 25.95 (978-0-615-23554-7(9)) Becker, Savan C.

Beechen, Adam. Justice League Unlimited. 2013. (Justice League Unlimited Ser.). (ENG.). 32p. (gr. 2-3). 90.40 (978-1-4342-3936-5(5)) Stone Arch Bks.

Beechen, Adam & Wong, Walden. Monitor Duty, 1 vol. Barberi, Carlo, illus. 2013. (Justice League Unlimited Ser.). (ENG.). 32p. (gr. 2-3). 22.60 (978-1-4342-6041-3(0)) Stone Arch Bks.

Beecroft, Simon. Ackbar's Underwater Army. 2012. (Star Wars: the Clone Wars DK Readers Ser.). lib. bdg. 13.55 (978-0-606-26457-0(4), Turtleback) Turtleback Bks.

—Chewbacca & the Wookiee Warriors. 2012. (Star Wars: the Clone Wars DK Readers Ser.). lib. bdg. 13.55 (978-0-606-26456-3(6), Turtleback) Turtleback Bks.

—Death Star Battles, Level 3. 2010. (DK Readers Ser.). (ENG.). 48p. (J). (gr. 2-4). 3.99 (978-0-7566-6314-8(8), DK Children) Dorling Kindersley Publishing, Inc.

—Epic Battles, Level 4. 2008. (DK Readers Ser.). (ENG., Illus.). 48p. (J). (gr. 3-7). pap. 3.99 (978-0-7566-3603-6(5), DK Children) Dorling Kindersley Publishing, Inc.

—Jedi Adventures. 2009. (Star Wars: the Clone Wars DK Readers Ser.). lib. bdg. 13.55 (978-0-606-06254-1(8), Turtleback) Turtleback Bks.

—R2-D2 & Friends. 2008. (Star Wars DK Readers Level 2 Ser.). (Illus.). 32p. lib. bdg. 13.55 (978-1-4364-5044-7(6), Turtleback) Turtleback Bks.

—Star Wars: Death Star Battles. 2016. (Star Wars DK Readers Level 3 Ser.). (ENG., Illus.). 48p. (J). (gr. 2-4). lib. bdg. 13.55 (978-0-606-39358-4(7)) Turtleback Bks.

Beecroft, Simon & Dorling Kindersley Publishing Staff. Ready, Set, Podrace! Level 1. 2007. (DK Readers Ser.). (ENG., Illus.). 32p. (J). (gr. k-4). pap. 3.99 (978-0-7566-3274-8(9), DK Children) Dorling Kindersley Publishing, Inc.

Beecroft, Simon & Windham, Ryder. Beware the Dark Side. 2007. (DK Readers Ser.). (ENG., Illus.). 48p. (J). (gr. 3-7). pap. 3.99 (978-0-7566-3114-7(9), DK Children) Dorling Kindersley Publishing, Inc.

—I Want to Be a Jedi, Level 3. 2007. (DK Readers Ser.). (ENG., Illus.). 48p. (J). (gr. 2-4). pap. 3.99 (978-0-7566-3112-3(2), DK Children) Dorling Kindersley Publishing, Inc.

Behling, Steve. Iron Man: Invasion of the Space Phantoms. 2016. (Mighty Marvel Chapter Bks.). (J). lib. bdg. 16.00 (978-0-606-38305-9(0)) Turtleback Bks.

Bell, David. Pink Alert! 2007. (Dawn Gray Ser.). (ENG.). 260p. pap. (978-1-84167-581-7(4)) Ransom Publishing Ltd.

Bell, Janet. Eyes of the Soul. 2003. pap. 24.95 (978-1-4137-0425-9(5)) America Star Bks.

Bell, Sophie. Lilac Attack! 2014. (Ultra Violets Ser.: 3). (ENG., Illus.). 304p. (J). (gr. 3-7). 12.99 (978-1-59514-648-9(2), Razorbill) Penguin Young Readers Group.

Belleza, Rhoda. Empress of a Thousand Skies. 2017. (ENG.). 336p. (YA). (gr. 7). 17.99 (978-1-101-99910-3(1), Razorbill) Penguin Young Readers Group.

Bellin, Joshua David. Survival Colony 9: Forget the Past Fight to Stay Alive. 2015. (ENG., Illus.). 336p. (YA). (gr. 9). pap. 10.99 (978-1-4814-0355-9(9), McElderry, Margaret K. Bks.) McElderry, Margaret K. Bks.

Bendis, Brian Michael. Takio. Oeming, Michael Avon, illus. 2011. (ENG.). 96p. (J). (gr. -1-17). 9.95 (978-0-7851-5326-9(8)) Marvel Worldwide, Inc.

Benintendi, Steve. Underfire. 2003. (Powermark Comics Ser.). (Illus.). 32p. (J). pap. 2.95 (978-0-9705669-2-8(1)) PowerMark Productions.

Benjamin, Harper. Mix & Match - Star Wars. 2015. (Mix & Match Ser.). (ENG.). 12p. (J). (gr. k-1). 14.99 (978-0-7944-3533-2(5), Reader's Digest Children's Bks.) Studio Fun International.

Bennett, Jeffrey. Max Goes to Mars: A Science Adventure with Max the Dog. Okamoto, Alan, illus. 2015. (Science Adventures with Max the Dog Ser.). (ENG.). 32p. (J). (gr. 2-4). 15.00 (978-1-937548-44-5(9)) Big Kid Science.

—Max Goes to the Moon: A Science Adventure with Max the Dog. Okamoto, Alan, illus. 2nd ed. 2012. (Science Adventures with Max the Dog Ser.). (ENG.). 32p. (J). (gr. 2-4). 15.00 (978-1-937548-20-9(1)) Big Kid Science.

—Max Goes to the Space Station: A Science Adventure with Max the Dog. Carroll, Michael, illus. 2013. (Science Adventures with Max the Dog Ser.). (ENG.). 32p. (J). (gr. 2-4). 15.00 (978-1-937548-28-5(7)) Big Kid Science.

Benton, Jim. The Fran That Time Forgot. Benton, Jim, illus. 4th ed. 2005. (Franny K. Stein, Mad Scientist Ser.: 4). (ENG., Illus.). 112p. (J). (gr. 2-5). mass mkt. 5.99 (978-0-689-86298-4(9)); 16.99 (978-0-689-86294-6(6)) Simon & Schuster Bks. For Young Readers. (Simon & Schuster Bks. For Young Readers).

—The Invisible Fran. Benton, Jim, illus. 2005. (Franny K. Stein, Mad Scientist Ser.: 3). (ENG., Illus.). 112p. (J). (gr. 2-5). pap. 6.99 (978-0-689-86297-7(0), Simon & Schuster Bks. For Young Readers) Simon & Schuster Bks. For Young Readers.

—The Invisible Fran, 1 vol. Benton, Jim, illus. 2011. (Franny K. Stein, Mad Scientist Ser.). (ENG., Illus.). 112p. (gr. 3-6). 24.21 (978-1-59961-819-7(2)) Spotlight.

—Let's Do a Thing! 2017. (Victor Shmud, Total Expert Ser.: 1). (ENG.). 128p. (J). (gr. 2-5). pap. 5.99 **(978-0-545-93229-5(7))**; lib. bdg. 16.99 **(978-0-545-93233-2(5))** Scholastic, Inc. (Scholastic Paperbacks).

Benton, Jim. Lunch Walks among Us. Benton, Jim, illus. 2004. (Franny K. Stein, Mad Scientist Ser.: 1). (Illus.). 102p. (gr. 2-5). lib. bdg. 16.00 (978-1-4176-4054-6(5), Turtleback) Turtleback Bks.

Besser, Kenneth/R. Arnie Carver & the Plague of Demeverde. 2007. (Illus.). x, 338p. (J). (978-1-934316-02-3(4)) RTMC Organization, LLC.

Bethell, Zillah. A Whisper of Horses. 2017. (ENG.). 352p. (J). 16.99 (978-1-250-09394-3(5), 9781250093943) Feiwel & Friends.

Bethune, Helen. A Bright New Day, 1 vol. rev. ed. 2013. (Fiction Readers Ser.). (ENG., Illus.). 32p. (J). (gr. 3-3). pap. 8.99 (978-1-4333-5640-7(6)) Shell Educational Publishing.

Bichoman Vuelve de la Tumba. (Fantasmas de Fear Street Coleccion). (SPA.). (YA). (gr. 5-8). pap. 7.95 (978-950-04-1718-1(9), EM9292) Emecé Editores S.A. ARG. Dist: Planeta Publishing Corp., Lectorum Pubns., Inc.

Bick, Ilsa J. Ashes. (Ashes Trilogy Ser.: Bk. 1). (ENG.). 480p. (gr. 9). 2012. (J). pap. 9.99 (978-1-60684-385-7(0)) 2011. 17.99 (978-1-60684-175-4(0)) Lerner Publishing Group. (Carolrhoda Lab™).

—The Dickens Mirror. 2015. (Dark Passages Ser.: 2). (ENG.). 576p. (YA). (gr. 9-12). 18.99 (978-1-5124-0177-6(3), Carolrhoda Lab™) Lerner Publishing Group.

—Monsters. (ENG.). 688p. (J). (gr. 9). 2014. pap. 9.99 (978-1-60684-544-8(6)) 2013. (Ashes Trilogy Ser.: Bk. 3). 18.99 (978-1-60684-177-8(7)) Lerner Publishing Group. (Carolrhoda Lab™).

—Shadows. (Ashes Trilogy Ser.: Bk. 2). (ENG.). 528p. (gr. 9). 2013. (J). pap. 9.99 (978-1-60684-445-8(8)) 2012. 17.99 (978-1-60684-176-1(9)) Lerner Publishing Group. (Carolrhoda Lab™).

—White Space, Bk. 1. 2014. (Dark Passages Ser.: Bk. 1). (ENG.). 560p. (J). (gr. 9). 18.99 (978-1-60684-419-9(9)) Lerner Publishing Group.

Bick, Ilsa J. & Ilsa, Bick. The Dickens Mirror. 2017. (Dark Passages Ser.: 2). (ENG.). 576p. (YA). (gr. 9-12). 9.99 (978-1-5124-4144-4(9), Carolrhoda Bks.) Lerner Publishing Group.

Biggs, Stephen. The Time Barrel. 2009. 152p. pap. (978-1-84923-434-4(5)) YouWriteOn.

Bill Henry Edge. Blip & the Seat of Arthur. 2009. 500p. pap. 24.99 (978-1-4389-5971-9(0)) AuthorHouse.

Bily, Ro. My Red Island in the Sky. 2012. 530p. 34.95 (978-1-4626-6645-4(0)); pap. 34.95 (978-1-4626-6971-4(9)) America Star Bks.

Birch, Kate Jarvik. Tarnished. 2015. (ENG.). 304p. (YA). (gr. 7-12). 16.99 (978-1-63375-127-9(9), 9781633751279) Entangled Publishing, LLC.

Biskup, Agnieszka & Sohn, Emily. Ciencia Gráfica. Martin, Cynthia & Dominquez, Richard, illus. 2013. (Ciencia Gráfica Ser.). (SPA.). 32p. (gr. 3-4). lib. bdg. 122.60 (978-1-62065-185-8(8)) Capstone Press of Coughlan Cos.

—Ciencia Gráfica. Martin, Cynthia & Dominguez, Richard, illus. 2013. (Ciencia Gráfica Ser.). (SPA.). 32p. (gr. 3-4). lib. bdg. 245.20 (978-1-62065-186-5(6)) Capstone Press of Coughlan Cos.

Black, Deirdre. River Run. 2012. (After the Dust Settled Ser.). (ENG.). 120p. (YA). (gr. 6-12). pap. 7.95 (978-0-8225-7274-9(5), Darby Creek); lib. bdg. 27.93 (978-0-7613-8326-0(3)) Lerner Publishing Group.

Black, Holly. Black Heart. (Curse Workers Ser.: 3). (ENG.). (YA). (gr. 9). 2013. 320p. pap. 11.99 (978-1-4424-0347-5(0)) 2012. 304p. 17.99 (978-1-4424-0346-8(2)) McElderry, Margaret K. Bks. (McElderry, Margaret K. Bks.).

—Red Glove. (Curse Workers Ser.: 2). (ENG.). (YA). (gr. 9). 2012. 352p. pap. 12.99 (978-1-4424-0340-6(3)) 2011. 336p. 17.99 (978-1-4424-0339-0(X)) McElderry, Margaret K. Bks. (McElderry, Margaret K. Bks.).

—White Cat. (Curse Workers Ser.: 1). (ENG.). (YA). (gr. 9). 2011. 336p. pap. 8.99 (978-1-4169-6397-4(9)) 2010. 320p. 17.99 (978-1-4169-6396-7(0)) McElderry, Margaret K. Bks. (McElderry, Margaret K. Bks.).

Black, Jenna. Replica. 2013. (Replica Ser.: 1). (ENG.). 368p. (YA). (gr. 8-12). pap. 19.99 (978-0-7653-3371-1(6), 9780765333711, Tor Teen) Doherty, Tom Assocs., LLC.

—Resistance. 2014. (Replica Ser.: 2). (ENG.). 368p. (YA). (gr. 8-12). pap. 9.99 (978-0-7653-3372-8(4), 9780765333728, Tor Teen) Doherty, Tom Assocs., LLC.

—Revolution. 2014. (Replica Ser.: 3). (ENG.). 400p. (YA). (gr. 8-12). pap. 10.99 (978-0-7653-3373-5(2), 9780765333735, Tor Teen) Doherty, Tom Assocs., LLC.

Black, Natalie & Black, Melissa. Double Sided: A Teen Novel. 2010. 124p. 23.50 (978-1-4520-7415-3(1)); pap. 12.99 (978-1-4520-7416-0(X)) AuthorHouse.

Black, Peter Jay. Blackout. 2015. (Urban Outlaws Ser.: 2). (ENG.). 304p. (YA). (gr. 5-8). 16.99 (978-1-61963-592-0(5), 9781619635920, Bloomsbury USA Childrens) Bloomsbury Publishing USA.

—Lockdown. 2016. (Urban Outlaws Ser.: 3). (ENG.). 272p. (J). 16.99 (978-1-61963-834-1(7), 9781619638341, Bloomsbury USA Childrens) Bloomsbury Publishing USA.

—Urban Outlaws. 2014. (Urban Outlaws Ser.: Bk. 1). (ENG., Illus.). 288p. (J). (gr. 5-8). 16.99 (978-1-61963-400-8(7), 9781619634008, Bloomsbury USA Childrens) Bloomsbury Publishing USA.

Blackburn, Sheila M. Stewie Scraps & the Space Racer. 2008. 68p. pap. (978-1-903853-84-9(2)) Brilliant Pubns.

Blackman, Haden. Darth Vader & the Lost Command: Vol 1, 1 vol. 2012. (Star Wars: Darth Vader & the Lost Command Ser.). (ENG., Illus.). 24p. (J). 24.21 (978-1-59961-980-4(6), Graphic Novels) Spotlight.

—Darth Vader & the Lost Command: Vol 2, 1 vol. Leonardi, Rick, illus. 2012. (Star Wars: Darth Vader & the Lost Command Ser.). (ENG.). 24p. (J). 24.21 (978-1-59961-981-1(4), Graphic Novels) Spotlight.

—Darth Vader & the Lost Command: Vol 3, 1 vol. Leonardi, Rick, illus. 2012. (Star Wars: Darth Vader & the Lost Command Ser.). (ENG.). 24p. (J). 24.21 (978-1-59961-982-8(2), Graphic Novels) Spotlight.

—Darth Vader & the Lost Command: Vol 4, 1 vol. Leonardi, Rick, illus. 2012. (Star Wars: Darth Vader & the Lost Command Ser.). (ENG.). 24p. (J). 24.21 (978-1-59961-983-5(0), Graphic Novels) Spotlight.

—Darth Vader & the Lost Command: Vol 5, 1 vol. Leonardi, Rick, illus. 2012. (Star Wars: Darth Vader & the Lost Command Ser.). (ENG.). 24p. (J). 24.21 (978-1-59961-984-2(9), Graphic Novels) Spotlight.

Blackout! Individual Title Six-Packs. (Bookweb Ser.). 32p. (gr. 4-18). 34.00 (978-0-7635-3728-9(4)) Rigby Education.

Blackwell, Paul. Undercurrent. 2014. 320p. (YA). (gr. 9). pap. 9.99 (978-0-06-212352-7(1), HarperTeen) HarperCollins Pubs.

Blade, Adam. Beast Quest 1001 Sticker Book. 2016. (Beast Quest Ser.). (ENG.). 88p. (J). (gr. 2-4). pap. 9.99 (978-1-4083-3773-8(8), Orchard Bks.) Hachette Children's Group GBR. Dist: Hachette Bk. Group.

Blake, Max & Chase, Max. Deadly Mission. 2012. (ENG., Illus.). 128p. (J). pap. (978-1-4088-1579-3(6)) Bloomsbury Pr.

—The Enemy's Lair. 2013. (Star Fighters Ser.). (ENG., Illus.). 144p. (YA). (gr. 2-4). pap. 8.99 (978-1-4088-1580-9(X), 9781408815809, Bloomsbury USA Childrens) Bloomsbury Publishing USA.

Blakemore, Megan Frazer. The Daybreak Bond. 2017. (ENG.). 336p. (J). 16.99 **(978-1-68119-479-0(1)**, 9781681194790, Bloomsbury USA Childrens) Bloomsbury Publishing USA.

Blakemore, Megan Frazer. The Firefly Code. (ENG.). (J). 2017. 368p. pap. 7.99 **(978-1-68119-527-8(5)**, 9781681195278) 2016. 352p. 16.99 (978-1-61963-636-1(0), 9781619636361) Bloomsbury Publishing USA. (Bloomsbury USA Childrens).

—The Firefly Code. 2017. (J). lib. bdg. 18.40 **(978-0-606-40543-0(7))** Turtleback Bks.

Blanchard, Anne & Cerisier, Emmanuel. Arab Science & Invention in the Golden Age. Brent, R. M., tr. from FRE. 2009. (ENG., Illus.). 80p. (J). (gr. 3). 19.95 (978-1-59270-080-6(2)) Enchanted Lion Bks., LLC.

Bland, Ralph. Long Long Time. Barlow, Dave, illus. 2014. 251p. 13.50 (978-1-933300-00-9(0)) Wandering Sage Pubns., LLC.

Bloch, Robert. The Crowded Earth. 2009. 112p. pap. 9.95 (978-1-60664-273-3(1)) Rodgers, Alan Bks.

Block, Francesca Lia. The Island of Excess Love. 2014. (ENG.). 224p. (YA). (gr. 9). 16.99 (978-0-8050-9631-6(0), 9780805096316, Holt, Henry & Co. Bks. For Young Readers) Holt, Henry & Co.

—Love in the Time of Global Warming. 2013. (ENG.). 240p. (YA). (gr. 9-13). 16.99 (978-0-8050-9627-9(2), 9780805096279, Holt, Henry & Co. Bks. For Young Readers) Holt, Henry & Co.

Bobillo, Juan & Dragotta, Nick, illus. FF, Vol. 3. 2013. (ENG.). 128p. (J). (gr. 4-17). pap. 16.99 (978-0-7851-6313-8(1)) Marvel Worldwide, Inc.

Bodeen, S. A. The Gardener. 2011. (ENG.). 256p. (YA). (gr. 7-12). pap. 9.99 (978-0-312-65942-4(3), 9780312659424) Square Fish.

Bodger, Holly. 5 to 1. 2015. (ENG.). 256p. (YA). (gr. 7). 17.99 (978-0-385-39153-5(6), Knopf Bks. for Young Readers) Random Hse. Children's Bks.

Bohls, Steven. Jed & the Junkyard Wars. 2016. (Jed & the Junkyard War Ser.). (ENG.). 304p. (J). (gr. 3-7). 16.99 (978-1-4847-2923-6(4)) Disney Pr.

Bon, Kimberly. Mitchie's Amazing Adventures: Good Bye to Pluto. 2012. 48p. pap. 21.99 (978-1-4685-5133-4(7)) AuthorHouse.

Boné, Thomas H., illus. The Teacher Who Would Not Retire Discovers a New Planet. 2009. (J). 17.95 (978-0-9792918-3-8(6)) Blue Marlin Pubns.

Bortz, Fred. Envisioning Outer Space: Where Science & Fiction Meet. 2015. (J). lib. bdg. (978-1-4677-3740-1(2)) Twenty First Century Bks.

Bow, Erin. The Swan Riders. 2016. (Prisoners of Peace Ser.). (ENG., Illus.). 384p. (YA). (gr. 9). 17.99 (978-1-4814-4274-9(0), McElderry, Margaret K. Bks.) McElderry, Margaret K. Bks.

Bowkett, Steve. Catch Minitales: Short Science Fiction Stories with a Sting! 2003. (ENG.). 152p. (978-1-85539-175-8(9), Network Continuum Education) Bloomsbury Publishing Plc.

Bowman, Erin. Forged. (Taken Ser.: 3). 384p. (YA). (gr. 8). 2016. pap. 9.99 (978-0-06-211733-5(5)) 2015. (ENG.). 17.99 (978-0-06-211732-8(7)) HarperCollins Pubs. (HarperTeen).

Boyd, Charles O'Halloran. Mountains of the North. 2009. 172p. pap. 13.95 (978-1-4401-4228-4(9)) iUniverse, Inc.

Bracken, Alexandra. The Darkest Minds. (Darkest Minds Novel Ser.). (ENG.). 2013. 528p. (YA). (gr. 9-17). pap. 9.99 (978-1-4231-5932-2(2)) 2012. 496p. (J). (gr. 5-9). 17.99 (978-1-4231-5737-3(0)) Hyperion Pr.

—The Darkest Minds. 2013. (Darkest Minds Ser.: 1). (YA). lib. bdg. 20.85 (978-0-606-36533-8(8)) Turtleback Bks.

—In the Afterlight. (Darkest Minds Novel Ser.). (ENG.). (YA). 2015. 592p. (gr. 9-17). pap. 9.99 (978-1-4231-5934-6(9)) 2014. 544p. (gr. 7-12). 18.99 (978-1-4231-5752-6(4)) Hyperion Bks. for Children.

—In the Afterlight. 2015. (Darkest Minds Ser.: 3). (YA). lib. bdg. 20.85 (978-0-606-37505-4(8)) Turtleback Bks.

—Never Fade. 2014. (Darkest Minds Novel Ser.). (ENG.). 544p. (YA). (gr. 7-12). pap. 9.99 (978-1-4231-5933-9(0)) Hyperion Bks. for Children.

—Never Fade. 2013. (Darkest Minds Novel Ser.: Bk. 2). (ENG.). 512p. (J). (gr. 5-9). 17.99 (978-1-4231-5751-9(6)) Hyperion Pr.

—Never Fade. 2014. (Darkest Minds Ser.: 2). (YA). lib. bdg. 20.85 (978-0-606-36534-5(6)) Turtleback Bks.

Brackett, Leigh & Coppel, Jr., Alfred. Planet Stories - Summer 1949. 2008. 128p. (YA). pap. 14.95 (978-1-59798-181-1(8)) Adventure Hse.

Bradley, Marion Zimmer. The Planet Savers. 2011. 100p. 22.95 (978-1-4638-9621-8(2)) Rodgers, Alan Bks.

Bradley, Timothy. Hive Mind, Bk. 1. rev. ed. 2013. (Sci Hi Ser.). (ENG., Illus.). 152p. (J). (gr. 3-6). lib. bdg. 26.96 (978-1-4807-2612-3(5)) Teacher Created Materials, Inc.

Bradman, Tony. Alien. 2012. (Stoke Books Titles Ser.). 64p. (J). (gr. 5-8). pap. 7.95 (978-1-78112-026-2(9)); pap. 45.32 (978-0-7613-9214-9(9)); lib. bdg. 22.60 (978-1-78112-025-5(0)) Stoke Bks.

Brallier, Max. Galactic Hot Dogs 1: Cosmoe's Wiener Getaway. Maguire, Rachel & Kelley, Nichole, illus. 2016. (Galactic Hot Dogs Ser.: 1). (ENG.). 304p. (J). (gr. 3-7). 13.99 (978-1-4814-8098-7(7), Aladdin) Simon & Schuster Children's Publishing.

—Galactic Hot Dogs 2: The Wiener Strikes Back. Maguire, Rachel & Kelley, Nichole, illus. 2016. (Galactic Hot Dogs Ser.: 2). (ENG.). 288p. (J). (gr. 3-7). 13.99 (978-1-4814-2496-7(3), Aladdin) Simon & Schuster Children's Publishing.

Bramlett, Timothy A. Sharkey Explores the Unknown. 2007. pap. 14.95 (978-0-9796444-0-5(2)) Azuria Bks.

Branley, Franklyn M. The Moon Seems to Change. 2015. (Let's Read & Find Out Science Stage 2 Ser.). (J). lib. bdg. 17.20 (978-0-606-37639-6(9)) Turtleback Bks.

Brashares, Ann. The Here & Now. 2015. lib. bdg. 22.10 (978-0-606-37649-5(6)) Turtleback Bks.

Braswell, Liz. The Fallen. movie tie-in ed. 2011. (Nine Lives of Chloe King Ser.: 1). (ENG.). 256p. (YA). (gr. 9). pap. 8.99 (978-1-4424-4134-7(8), Simon Pulse) Simon Pulse.

Bray, Adam. Lego Star Wars: Into Battle! 2015. (DK Adventures Ser.). lib. bdg. 16.00 (978-0-606-36923-7(6)) Turtleback Bks.

Brege, K. B. Champ... A Wave of Terror! Five Ways to Finish. 2006. (Mick Morris Myth Solver Ser.: No. 3). (J). mass mkt. 6.99 (978-0-9774119-2-4(3)) Team B Creative LLC.

Brennan, Herbie. The Secret Prophecy. 2012. (ENG.). 368p. (J). (gr. 3-7). 16.99 (978-0-06-207180-4(7)) HarperCollins Pubs.

Brett, Jan. Hedgie Blasts Off! Brett, Jan, illus. 2006. (ENG., Illus.). 32p. (J). (gr. -1-3). 17.99 (978-0-399-24621-0(5), G.P. Putnam's Sons Books for Young Readers) Penguin Young Readers Group.

Brickwood, L. M. Children of the Moon. 2007. 216p. pap. 14.95 (978-1-920153-03-8(9)) Zulu Planet Pubs. ZAF. Dist: APG Sales & Distribution Services.

Briggs, Elizabeth. Future Shock. 2016. (YA). (Future Shock Ser.: 1). (ENG.). 288p. (gr. 8-12). pap. 9.99 (978-0-8075-2680-4(0)); (978-0-8075-2683-5(5)); (Future Shock Ser.: 1). (ENG.). 272p. (gr. 8-12). 16.99 (978-0-8075-2682-8(7)) Whitman, Albert & Co.

Briggs, Elizabeth. Future Threat. 2017. (Future Shock Ser.: 2). (ENG.). 272p. (YA). (gr. 8-12). 16.99 (978-0-8075-2684-2(3)); pap. 9.99 **(978-0-8075-2686-6(X))** Whitman, Albert & Co.

S

Bright, J. E. Cyborg Superman. Levins, Tim, illus. 2013. (Man of Steel Ser.). (ENG.). 88p. (gr. 2-3). pap. 5.95 (978-1-4342-4219-8(6)) Stone Arch Bks.

—Cyborg Superman, 1 vol. Levins, Tim & DC Comics Staff, illus. 2013. (Man of Steel Ser.). (ENG.). 88p. (gr. 2-3). 26.65 (978-1-4342-4089-7(4)) Stone Arch Bks.

Brindley, John. The City of Screams. 2009. (Exceptional Reading & Language Arts Titles for Intermediate Grades Ser.). (ENG.). 408p. (YA). (gr. 7-12). 18.95 (978-0-7613-3908-3(6)) Lerner Publishing Group.

—The Rule of Claw. Benfold Haywood, Ian P., illus. 2009. (Exceptional Reading & Language Arts Titles for Intermediate Grades Ser.). (ENG.). 408p. (YA). (gr. 7-12). 18.95 (978-1-58013-608-2(7)) Lerner Publishing Group.

Brinley, Bertrand R. The Mad Scientists' Club. Geer, Charles, illus. 50th ed. 2011. (J). 18.95 (978-1-930900-53-0(8)) Purple Hse. Pr.

Britten, Adam. The Man Who Stole a Planet. Hamer, Arthur, illus. 2013. (Captain Valiant Ser.). (ENG.). 160p. (J). (gr. k-3). pap. 9.99 (978-1-84812-347-2(7)) Bonnier Publishing GBR. Dist: Independent Pubs. Group.

Brockington, Drew. CatStronauts: Mission Moon. 2017. (CatStronauts Ser.: 1). (J). lib. bdg. 18.40 **(978-0-606-39900-5(3))** Turtleback Bks.

Brody, Jennifer. Return of the Continuums. 2016. (Continuum Trilogy Ser.: 2). (ENG.). 432p. (YA). 36.95 (978-1-68162-259-0(9)); pap. 14.95 (978-1-68162-258-3(0)) Turner Publishing Co.

—The United Continuums: The Continuum Trilogy, Book 3. 2017. (Continuum Trilogy Ser.: 3). (ENG.). 464p. (YA). pap. 15.99 (978-1-68162-262-0(9)); 36.99 **(978-1-68162-263-7(7))** Turner Publishing Co.

—The 13th Continuum. 2016. (Continuum Trilogy Ser.: 1). (ENG.). 416p. (YA). pap. 14.95 (978-1-68162-254-5(8)) Turner Publishing Co.

Brody, Jessica. Unchanged. 2015. (Unremembered Trilogy Ser.: 3). (ENG.). 432p. (YA). (gr. 7). 17.99 (978-0-374-37989-6(0), 9780374379896, Farrar, Straus & Giroux (BYR)) Farrar, Straus & Giroux.

—Unremembered. 2013. (Unremembered Trilogy Ser.: 1). (ENG.). 320p. (YA). (gr. 7). 17.99 (978-0-374-37991-9(2), 9780374379919, Farrar, Straus & Giroux (BYR)) Farrar, Straus & Giroux.

—Unremembered. 2014. (Unremembered Trilogy Ser.: 1). (ENG.). 352p. (YA). (gr. 7). pap. 9.99 (978-1-250-04002-2(7), 9781250040022) Square Fish.

Brouwer, Sigmund. Ambush. 2009. (Robot Wars Ser.: 3). (ENG.). 304p. (YA). pap. 7.99 (978-1-4143-2311-4(5), Tyndale Kids) Tyndale Hse. Pubs.

—Counterattack. 2009. (Robot Wars Ser.: 4). (ENG.). 304p. (YA). pap. 6.99 (978-1-4143-2312-1(3), Tyndale Kids) Tyndale Hse. Pubs.

—Final Battle. 2009. (Robot Wars Ser.: 5). (ENG.). 320p. (YA). pap. 7.99 (978-1-4143-2313-8(1), Tyndale Kids) Tyndale Hse. Pubs.

Brown, Bruce, et al. Brit - Awol, 3 vols., Vol. 2. Kirkman, Robert, ed. 2008. (ENG., Illus.). 160p. (YA). pap. 14.99 (978-1-58240-864-4(5), 9781582408644) Image Comics.

Brown, Jeff Allan. Floom Shroom the Battling Mushroom. 2009. 100p. pap. 28.99 (978-1-60693-485-2(6), Strategic Bk. Publishing) Strategic Book Publishing & Rights Agency (SBPRA).

Brown, Jeffrey. Jedi Academy. 2015. (Star Wars: Jedi Academy Ser.). (ENG.). 112p. (J). (gr. 3-7). 9.99 (978-0-545-85278-4(1)) Scholastic, Inc.

—Jedi Academy. Brown, Jeffrey, illus. 2013. (Star Wars Jedi Academy Ser.: Bk. 1). (Illus.). 160p. (J). (ENG.). (gr. 3-7). 12.99 (978-0-545-50517-8(8)); pap. (978-0-545-60999-9(2)) Scholastic, Inc.

—The Phantom Bully. 2015. (Star Wars: Jedi Academy Ser.: 3). (ENG., Illus.). 176p. (J). (gr. 3-7). 12.99 (978-0-545-62126-7(7)) Scholastic, Inc.

—Return of the Padawan. Brown, Jeffrey, illus. 2014. (Star Wars Jedi Academy Ser.: Bk. 2). (ENG., Illus.). 176p. (J). (gr. 3-7). 12.99 (978-0-545-62125-0(9)) Scholastic, Inc.

—Sulk. 2009. (Sulk Ser.: 3). (ENG., Illus.). 64p. pap. 6.00 (978-1-60309-055-1(X), 9781603090551) Top Shelf Productions.

Brown, Jennifer. How Lunchbox Jones Saved Me from Robots, Traitors, & Missy the Cruel. 2017. (ENG.). 256p. (J). pap. 7.99 (978-1-68119-441-7(4), 9781681194417, Bloomsbury USA Childrens) Bloomsbury Publishing USA.

—Life on Mars. 2015. (ENG.). 256p. (YA). (gr. 3-6). pap. 7.99 (978-1-61963-671-2(9), 9781619636712, Bloomsbury USA Childrens) Bloomsbury Publishing USA.

Brown, Michele. New Tales from Alice's Wonderland: The Queen of Hearts & the Wibbly Wobbly Jelly. Martyr, Paula, illus. 24p. (J). pap. 7.95 (978-0-233-99536-6(6)) Andre Deutsch GBR. Dist: Trans-Atlantic Pubns., Inc.

Brown, Zachary. The Darkside War. 2015. (Icarus Corps Ser.: 1). (ENG., Illus.). 240p. pap. 14.99 (978-1-4814-3035-7(1), SAGA Press) Simon & Schuster Bks. For Young Readers.

Bruce, Karl. Annie Apple & the Teleportation Phantoms from Outer Space. 2006. (YA). pap. 16.00 (978-0-8059-7156-9(4)) Dorrance Publishing Co., Inc.

Bruchac, Joseph. Arrow of Lightning. 2017. (Killer of Enemies Ser.). (ENG.). 400p. (YA). 19.95 **(978-1-62014-330-8(5)**, Tu Bks.) Lee & Low Bks., Inc.

—Killer of Enemies, 1 vol. 2013. (Killer of Enemies Ser.). (ENG.). 400p. (YA). 19.95 (978-1-62014-143-4(4), Tu Bks.) Lee & Low Bks., Inc.

—Trail of the Dead, 1 vol. 2015. (Killer of Enemies Ser.). (ENG.). 400p. (YA). 19.95 (978-1-62014-261-5(9)) Lee & Low Bks., Inc.

Brunswick, Glen. Non-Humans Volume 1: Runaway American Dream TP: Runaway American Dream TP. 2013. (Illus.). 120p. (YA). pap. 14.99 (978-1-60706-666-8(1)) Image Comics.

Bryers, Paul. Kobal. 2009. 1.00 (978-1-4074-4320-1(8)) Recorded Bks., Inc.

Bryson, Karen Mueller. The Incredibly Awesome Adventures of Puggie Liddel, the Graphic Novel. Tisdel, L. L, illus. 2013. 108p. pap. (978-1-927384-09-1(5)) Zeta Comics.

BubbleGirl, Season. A Doggy Diary. 2006. 93p. (J). per. (978-0-9775120-0-3(2)) Carpe Diem Publishing.

Buckell, Tobias S. & Monti, Joe, eds. Diverse Energies. 2012. (ENG., Illus.). 368p. (YA). pap. 10.95 (978-1-62014-011-6(X)) Lee & Low Bks., Inc.

Buckeridge, Anthony. According to Jennings. 2008. (Jennings Ser.: 6). (ENG.). 190p. (J). (gr. 4-7). pap. 12.95 (978-0-7551-0165-8(0)) House of Stratus, Inc. GBR. Dist: Gardners Bks. Ltd.

Buffagni, Matteo, illus. Avengers Assemble. 2014. (ENG.). 112p. (YA). (gr. 8-17). pap. 16.99 (978-0-7851-6798-3(6)) Marvel Worldwide, Inc.

Buller, Laura. DK Readers L1: Star Wars: What Is a Wookiee? Star Wars: What Is a Wookiee? 2015. (DK Readers Ser.). (ENG., Illus.). 48p. (J). (gr. k-4). 14.99 (978-1-4654-3385-5(6), DK Children) Dorling Kindersley Publishing, Inc.

—Star Wars: Star Pilot. 2015. (Star Wars DK Readers Level 3 Ser.). lib. bdg. 13.55 (978-0-606-37408-8(6)) Turtleback Bks.

—What Is a Wookiee? 2015. (DK Readers Ser.). (ENG., Illus.). 48p. (Orig.). (J). (gr. k-4). pap. 3.99 (978-1-4654-3386-2(4), DK Children) Dorling Kindersley Publishing, Inc.

Bunker, Lisa. Felix Yz. 2017. (ENG.). 288p. (J). (gr. 5-9). 16.99 (978-0-425-28850-4(1), Viking Books for Young Readers) Penguin Young Readers Group.

Bunn, Cullen. Doom Maidens. 2013. (ENG., Illus.). 144p. (YA). (gr. 8-17). pap. 15.99 (978-0-7851-6848-5(6)) Marvel Worldwide, Inc.

Burnam, Michael H. The Last Stop. 2016. (ENG.). 288p. (YA). (gr. 8-17). pap. 12.95 (978-1-78535-117-4(6), Lodestone Bks.) Hunt, John Publishing Ltd. GBR. Dist: National Bk. Network.

Burns, Dal. The Adventures of Phoo. 2006. 148p. pap. 24.95 (978-1-4241-1773-4(9)) PublishAmerica, Inc.

Burroughs, Edgar Rice. The Land That Time Forgot: Graphic Novel. Jones, K. L., illus. 2011. (Campfire Graphic Novels Ser.). (ENG.). 72p. (YA). (gr. 5-12). pap. 9.99 (978-93-80028-38-5(5), Campfire) Steerforth Pr.

—Mars Trilogy: A Princess of Mars - The Gods of Mars - The Warlord of Mars. Fischer, Scott M. et al, illus. 2012. (ENG.). 704p. (YA). (gr. 7). pap. 14.99 (978-1-4424-2387-9(0), Simon & Schuster Bks. For Young Readers) Simon & Schuster Bks. For Young Readers.

Buscema, John & Byrne, John, illus. Avengers: The Legacy of Thanos. 2014. (ENG.). 256p. (J). (gr. 4-17). pap. 34.99 (978-0-7851-8891-9(6)) Marvel Worldwide, Inc.

Butcher, Andrew. The Time of the Reapers, Bk. 1. 2007. (ENG.). 400p. (gr. 7). pap. 12.95 (978-1-904233-94-7(5)) Little, Brown Book Group Ltd. GBR. Dist: Hachette Bk. Group.

Butler, Susan. The Hermit Thrush Sings. unabr. ed. 2003. (YA). 76.75 (978-0-7887-3798-5(8), 41042X4) Recorded Bks., Inc.

Byng, Georgia. Molly Moon Detiene el Mundo. 2004. (SPA.). 358p. (gr. 5-8). 18.99 (978-84-348-9610-9(9)) SM Ediciones ESP. Dist: Lectorum Pubns., Inc.

—Molly Moon, Micky Minus, & the Mind Machine. (Molly Moon Ser.: 4). (ENG.). (J). (gr. 3-7). 2008. 416p. pap. 7.99 (978-0-06-075038-1(3)) 2007. 384p. 16.99 (978-0-06-075036-7(7)) HarperCollins Pubs.

—Molly Moon Stops the World. (J). 2004. (Illus.). 384p. 16.99 (978-0-06-051410-5(8)) 2005. (Molly Moon Ser.: 2). (ENG.). 416p. (gr. 3-7). reprint ed. pap. 7.99 (978-0-06-051415-0(9)) HarperCollins Pubs.

—Molly Moon Viaja a Traes del Tiempo. Crispin, Maria Dolores, tr. 2005. (SPA.). 350p. (978-84-675-0570-2(2)) SM Ediciones.

—Molly Moon's Hypnotic Time Travel Adventure. (ENG.). 400p. (J). 2006. (Molly Moon Ser.: 3). (gr. 3-7). pap. 7.99 (978-0-06-075034-3(0)) 2005. (Illus.). 16.99 (978-0-06-075032-9(4)) HarperCollins Pubs.

—Molly Moon's Hypnotic Time-Travel Adventure. 2005. (Illus.). 400p. (J). lib. bdg. 18.89 (978-0-06-075033-6(2)) HarperCollins Pubs.

Cabot, Meg. Haunted. 2004. (Mediator Ser.: 5). (ENG.). 288p. (YA). (gr. 8-18). pap. 8.99 (978-0-06-075164-7(9), HarperTeen) HarperCollins Pubs.

—Hunter's Moon. Coronado, Jinky, illus. 2009. (Avalon High Coronation Ser.: Bk. 3). (ENG.). 160p. (YA). (gr. 8-18). pap. 9.99 (978-0-06-117710-1(5)) HarperCollins Pubs.

Cadenhead, MacKenzie. Sleeper. 2017. (ENG.). 272p. (YA). (gr. 6-12). pap. 10.99 **(978-1-4926-3614-4(2))** Sourcebooks, Inc.

Calabrese, Linda Lee. It Is What It Is: In a Kid's Mind. 2012. 28p. pap. 24.95 (978-1-4626-5643-1(9)) America Star Bks.

Calandrelli, Emily. ADA Lace, on the Case: An ADA Lace Adventure. Kurilla, Renée, illus. 2017. (Ada Lace Adventure Ser.: 1). (ENG.). 128p. (J). (gr. 1-5). pap. 6.99 **(978-1-4814-8598-2(9)**, Simon & Schuster Bks. For Young Readers) Simon & Schuster Bks. For Young Readers.

—Ada Lace Sees Red. Kurilla, Renée, illus. 2017. (Ada Lace Adventure Ser.: 2). (ENG.). 144p. (J). (gr. 1-5). 16.99 **(978-1-4814-8602-6(0))**; pap. 6.99 **(978-1-4814-8601-9(2))** Simon & Schuster Bks. For Young Readers. (Simon & Schuster Bks. For Young Readers).

Calero, Dennis. You're Not the Captain of Me! 2011. (ENG.). 272p. (J). (gr. 4-7). pap. 9.95 (978-1-59687-375-9(2)) IBks., Inc.

Calhoun, Bonnie S. Lightning: A Novel. 2015. (Stone Braide Chronicles Ser.: 2). (ENG.). 416p. (YA). pap. 13.00 (978-0-8007-2377-4(5)) Revell.

—Thunder: A Novel. 2014. 425p. (YA). pap. (978-0-8007-2416-0(X)) Revell.

Calleja, Seve. El Planeta del Tesoro. 2003. (Disney Collection). (SPA.). 96p. (J). 6.95 (978-84-670-0305-5(7)) Espasa Calpe, S.A. ESP. Dist: Planeta Publishing Corp.

Cameron, Erica. Island of Exiles. 2017. (Ryogan Chronicles Ser.). (ENG.). 400p. (YA). pap. 9.99 (978-1-63375-592-5(4), 9781633755925) Entangled Publishing, LLC.

Cameron, Sharon. The Forgetting. (ENG.). 416p. (gr. 7-7). 2017. (J). pap. 9.99 **(978-1-338-16071-0(0))** 2016. (YA). 18.99 (978-0-545-94521-9(6)) Scholastic, Inc. (Scholastic Pr.).

Campbell, Hazel D. Ramgoat Dashalong: Magical Tales from Jamaica. 2004. (ENG., Illus.). 74p. pap. 5.99 (978-976-610-269-2(4)) Penguin Publishing Group.

Capetta, Amy Rose. Entangled. (ENG.). (YA). (gr. 9). 2014. 352p. pap. 9.99 (978-0-544-33624-7(0), HMH Books For Young Readers) 2013. 336p. 17.99 (978-0-544-08744-6(5)) Houghton Mifflin Harcourt Publishing Co.

—Unmade. (ENG.). 384p. (YA). (gr. 9). 2016. pap. 9.99 (978-0-544-54258-7(4)) 2015. 17.99 (978-0-544-08737-8(2)) Houghton Mifflin Harcourt Publishing Co. (HMH Books For Young Readers).

Caramagna, Joe. Marvel Universe Avengers Assemble Volume 2. 2014. (ENG., Illus.). 88p. (J). (gr. -1-17). pap. 9.99 (978-0-7851-8880-3(0)) Marvel Worldwide, Inc.

—Marvel Universe Guardians of the Galaxy: Cosmic Team-Up. Buscema, Sal, illus. 2014. (ENG.). 96p. (J). (gr. -1-17). pap. 9.99 (978-0-7851-9031-8(7)) Marvel Worldwide, Inc.

Caramagna, Joe, text. Amazing Spider-Man, Vol. 4. 2012. (ENG., Illus.). 96p. (J). (gr. -1-17). pap. 6.99 (978-0-7851-6613-9(0)) Marvel Worldwide, Inc.

—Hulk & the Agents of S. M. A. S. H. 2014. (ENG., Illus.). 96p. (J). (gr. -1-17). pap. 9.99 (978-0-7851-8925-1(4)) Marvel Worldwide, Inc.

Carbone, Courtney. Star Wars: the Phantom Menace (Star Wars) Martinez, Heather, illus. 2015. (Little Golden Book Ser.). (ENG.). 24p. (J). (-k). 4.99 (978-0-7364-3542-0(5), Golden Bks.) Random Hse. Children's Bks.

Carbone, Courtney & Marston, William Moulton. Wonder Woman to the Rescue! Doescher, Erik, illus. 2016. 24p. (J). **(978-1-4806-9760-7(5))** Random Hse., Inc.

Card, Orson Scott. First Meetings: In the Ender Universe. rev. ed. 2004. (Other Tales from the Ender Universe Ser.). (ENG.). 224p. (YA). (gr. 8-12). mass mkt. 6.99 (978-0-7653-4798-5(9), 9780765347985, Tor Teen) Doherty, Tom Assocs., LLC.

—Pathfinder. (ENG.). 672p. (YA). (gr. 7). 2011. pap. 12.99 (978-1-4169-9179-3(4)) 2010. 19.99 (978-1-4169-9176-2(X)) Simon Pulse. (Simon Pulse).

—Pathfinder. l.t. ed. 2011. (Pathfinder Ser.). (ENG.). 802p. 23.99 (978-1-4104-3681-8(0)) Thorndike Pr.

—Ruins. (ENG.). 544p. (YA). (gr. 7). 2013. pap. 12.99 (978-1-4169-9180-9(8)) 2012. 18.99 (978-1-4169-9177-9(8)) Simon Pulse. (Simon Pulse).

—Stonefather. Kidd, Tom, illus. 2008. 112p. 35.00 (978-1-59606-194-1(4)) Subterranean Pr.

—Visitors. 2015. (ENG., Illus.). 608p. (YA). (gr. 7). pap. 12.99 (978-1-4169-9181-6(6), Simon Pulse) Simon Pulse.

Carey, Anna. Eve. (Eve Ser.: 1). (ENG.). (YA). (gr. 8). 2012. 352p. pap. 9.99 (978-0-06-204851-6(1)) 2011. 336p. 17.99 (978-0-06-204850-9(3)) HarperCollins Pubs.

—Eve. 2012. (SPA.). 224p. (YA). pap. 20.95 (978-84-9918-434-0(0)) Roca Editorial ESP. Dist: Spanish Pubs., LLC.

—Once. 2013. (Eve Ser.: 2). (ENG.). 384p. (YA). (gr. 8). pap. 9.99 (978-0-06-204855-4(4)) HarperCollins Pubs.

—Rise. 2013. (Eve Ser.: 3). (ENG.). (YA). (gr. 8). 336p. pap. 9.99 (978-0-06-204858-5(9)); 320p. 17.99 (978-0-06-204857-8(0)) HarperCollins Pubs.

—Rise: An Eve Novel. 2013. (Illus.). 320p. (YA). pap. 9.99 (978-0-06-226273-8(4)) HarperCollins Pubs.

Carlson, Dale. The Human Apes. Carlson, Al & Nicklaus, Carol, illus. 2nd ed. 2005. (ENG.). 155p. (gr. 8-12). reprint ed. pap. 14.95 (978-1-884158-31-5(5)) Team Kreskin Productions, LLC.

Carlson, Dale Bick. The Mountain of Truth. Nicklaus, Carol, illus. 2nd ed. 2005. (ENG.). 169p. (gr. 8-12). reprint ed. pap. 14.95 (978-1-884158-30-8(7)) Team Kreskin Productions, LLC.

Carman, Patrick. The Dark Planet. 2010. (Atherton Ser.: 3). (ENG., Illus.). 368p. (J). (gr. 3-7). pap. 9.99 (978-0-316-16675-1(8)) Little, Brown Bks. for Young Readers.

—The Dark Planet. 2010. (Atherton Ser.: 3). (J). lib. bdg. 20.85 (978-0-606-14737-8(3), Turtleback) Turtleback Bks.

—Pulse. 2013. (Pulse Ser.: 1). (ENG.). 384p. (YA). (gr. 8). 17.99 (978-0-06-208576-4(X), Tegen, Katherine Bks) HarperCollins Pubs.

—Quake. 2015. (Pulse Ser.: 3). (ENG.). 288p. (YA). (gr. 8). 17.99 (978-0-06-208590-0(5)) HarperCollins Pubs.

—Quake: A Pulse Novel. 2016. (Pulse Ser.: 3). 288p. (YA). (gr. 8). pap. 9.99 (978-0-06-208597-9(2), Tegen, Katherine Bks) HarperCollins Pubs.

—Rivers of Fire. 2009. (Atherton Ser.: 2). (ENG., Illus.). 336p. (J). (gr. 3-7). pap. 9.99 (978-0-316-16673-7(1)) Little Brown & Co.

—Tremor. (Pulse Ser.: 2). (ENG.). (YA). (gr. 8). 2015. 384p. pap. 9.99 (978-0-06-208581-8(6)) 2014. 368p. 17.99 (978-0-06-208580-1(8)) HarperCollins Pubs. (Tegen, Katherine Bks).

—Voyagers: Omega Rising (Book 3) 2016. (Voyager Ser.). (ENG., Illus.). 208p. (J). (gr. 3-7). 12.99 (978-0-385-38664-7(8), Random Hse. Bks. for Young Readers) Random Hse. Children's Bks.

Carmody, Isobelle. The Farseekers. 2003. (Obernewtyn Chronicles: Bk. 2). (Illus.). 316p. (J). 13.65 (978-0-7569-4608-1(5)) Perfection Learning Corp.

Carr, Elias & Karre, Andrew. Fight the Wind. 2012. (After the Dust Settled Ser.). (ENG.). 104p. (YA). (gr. 6-12). pap. 7.95 (978-0-8225-9034-7(4), Darby Creek); lib. bdg. 27.93 (978-0-7613-8331-4(X)) Lerner Publishing Group.

Carriger, Gail. Curtsies & Conspiracies. (Finishing School Ser.: 2). (ENG.). (YA). (gr. 7-17). 2014. 336p. pap. 10.00 (978-0-316-19020-6(9)) 2013. 320p. 18.00 (978-0-316-19011-4(X)) Little, Brown Bks. for Young Readers.

—Etiquette & Espionage. 2013. (Finishing School Ser.: 1). (ENG.). 320p. (YA). (gr. 7-17). 18.99 (978-0-316-19008-4(X)) Little Brown & Co.

—Etiquette & Espionage. 2013. (Finishing School Ser.: 1). (ENG.). 336p. (YA). (gr. 7-17). pap. 10.99 (978-0-316-19010-7(1)) Little, Brown Bks. for Young Readers.

—Manners & Mutiny. 2015. (Finishing School Ser.: 4). (ENG., Illus.). 336p. (YA). (gr. 7-17). 18.00 (978-0-316-19028-2(4)) Little, Brown Bks. for Young Readers.

—Waistcoats & Weaponry. 2014. (Finishing School Ser.: 3). (ENG.). 304p. (YA). (gr. 7-17). 18.00 (978-0-316-19027-5(6)) Little Brown & Co.

—Waistcoats & Weaponry. 2015. (Finishing School Ser.: 3). (ENG.). 320p. (YA). (gr. 7-17). pap. 10.00 (978-0-316-19025-1(X)) Little, Brown Bks. for Young Readers.

Carroll, Michael. The Awakening, No. 1. 2008. (Quantum Prophecy Ser.: 1). (ENG.). 288p. (J). (gr. 5-6). 8.99 (978-0-14-241179-7(5), Puffin Books) Penguin Young Readers Group.

—Stronger: A Super Human Clash. 3rd ed. 2013. (Super Human Ser.: 3). (ENG.). 400p. (YA). (gr. 7). pap. 9.99 (978-0-14-242634-0(2), Speak) Penguin Young Readers Group.

Carter, Liane. The Chronicles of Joy. 2008. 244p. pap. (978-1-84923-001-8(3)) YouWriteOn.

Carter, Mike. Access to the Universe. 2005. (Illus.). 160p. (Orig.). pap. (978-0-7344-0696-5(7), Lothian Children's Bks.) Hachette Australia.

Carter, Rachel. Find Me Where the Water Ends. 2014. (ENG.). 352p. (YA). (gr. 9). 17.99 (978-0-06-208111-7(X), HarperTeen) HarperCollins Pubs.

—So Close to You. (ENG.). (YA). (gr. 9). 2013. 336p. pap. 9.99 (978-0-06-208106-3(3)) 2012. 320p. 17.99 (978-0-06-208105-6(5)) HarperCollins Pubs. (HarperTeen).

—This Strange & Familiar Place. 2013. (ENG.). 272p. (YA). (gr. 9). 17.99 (978-0-06-208108-7(X), HarperTeen) HarperCollins Pubs.

Carter-Stephenson, C. J. The Crystal Ship. 2010. (Illus.). 120p. pap. 12.95 (978-1-4457-1369-4(1)) Lulu Pr., Inc.

Caselli, Stefano, illus. Avengers World Vol. 1: A. I. M. Empire. 2014. (ENG.). 120p. (J). (gr. 4-17). pap. 16.99 (978-0-7851-8981-7(5)) Marvel Worldwide, Inc.

Casey, Joe. Godland Finale. 2013. (Illus.). 72p. (YA). pap. 6.99 (978-1-60706-819-8(2)) Image Comics.

Casey, Joe & Reed, Brian. The Amazing Spider-Man: The One & Only. Weeks, Lee et al, illus. 2014. (ENG.). 168p. (J). (gr. 4-17). pap. 16.99 (978-0-7851-9010-3(4)) Marvel Worldwide, Inc.

Castellan, Andrea. Mickey Mouse & the Orbiting Nightmare. 2011. (ENG., Illus.). 128p. (J). pap. (978-1-60886-630-4(0)) Boom! Studios.

Castellucci, Cecil. Shade the Changing Girl Vol. 1: Earth Girl Made Easy. Zarcone, Marley, illus. 2017. (Young Animal Ser.). (ENG.). 144p. pap. 16.99 **(978-1-4012-7099-5(9))** DC Comics.

Castellucci, Cecil. Tin Star. 2014. (Tin Star Ser.: 1). (ENG.). 240p. (YA). (gr. 7). 16.99 (978-1-59643-775-3(8), 9781596437753) Roaring Brook Pr.

Caterer, Claire M. The Key & the Flame. (ENG.). (J). (gr. 3-7). 2015. 496p. pap. 7.99 (978-1-4424-5742-3(2)) 2013. 480p. 17.99 (978-1-4424-5741-6(4)) McElderry, Margaret K. Bks. (McElderry, Margaret K. Bks.).

Cave, Patrick. The Selected. 2010. (ENG.). 416p. (YA). (gr. 9-18). 17.99 (978-1-4169-1573-7(7), Atheneum Bks. for Young Readers) Simon & Schuster Children's Publishing.

—Sharp North. 2009. (ENG.). 528p. (YA). (gr. 9). pap. 8.99 (978-1-4169-1223-1(1), Atheneum Bks. for Young Readers) Simon & Schuster Children's Publishing.

Caveney, Philip. Space Blasters. 2013. (ENG.). 256p. (J). (gr. 4-6). pap. 10.99 (978-1-84939-572-4(1)) Andersen Pr. GBR. Dist: Independent Pubs. Group.

Center for Learning Network Staff. Slaughterhouse-Five: Curriculum Unit. 2005. (Novel Ser.). 76p. (YA). tchr. ed., spiral bd. 19.95 (978-1-56077-789-2(3)) Center for Learning, The.

Cerasi, Chris. Star Wars Adventures: Chewbacca & the Slavers of the Shadowlands, 1 vol. 2013. (Star Wars Digests Set 2 Ser.). (ENG.). 80p. (J). (gr. 4-8). lib. bdg. 27.07 (978-1-61479-057-0(4), Essential Library) ABDO Publishing Co.

Chabot, Jason. Below. 2016. (Broken Sky Chronicles Ser.: 1). (ENG.). 308p. (J). 29.95 (978-1-68162-602-4(0)); (YA). pap. 16.95 (978-1-68162-601-7(2)) Turner Publishing Co.

—Beyond: Broken Sky Chronicles, Book 3. 2017. (Broken Sky Chronicles Ser.: 3). (ENG.). 432p. (J). 35.99 **(978-1-68162-608-6(X))**; (YA). pap. 19.99 (978-1-68162-607-9(1)) Turner Publishing Co.

Chang, Ifay, as told by. Outopians. 2007. (Illus.). 27p. (YA). pap. (978-0-9771594-1-3(8)) TLC Information Services.

Chapman, Elsie. Dualed. 2013. (ENG.). 304p. (YA). (gr. 7). 16.99 (978-0-307-93154-2(4), Random Hse. Bks. for Young Readers) Random Hse. Children's Bks.

Charbonneau, Joelle. Graduation Day. 2014. (Testing Trilogy: Bk. 3). (ENG.). 304p. (J). (gr. 7-12). 17.99 (978-0-547-95921-4(4), HMH Books For Young Readers) Houghton Mifflin Harcourt Publishing Co.

—Independent Study. (ENG.). (YA). (gr. 7). 2015. (Testing Ser.: 2). 336p. pap. 9.99 (978-0-544-43945-0(7), HMH Books For Young Readers) 2014. (Testing Trilogy: Bk. 2). 320p. 17.99 (978-0-547-95920-7(6)) Houghton Mifflin Harcourt Publishing Co.

—Independent Study. 2015. (Testing Ser.: 2). lib. bdg. 20.85 (978-0-606-36832-2(9)) Turtleback Bks.

—The Testing. (Testing Ser.: 1). (ENG.). 352p. (YA). (gr. 7). 2015. pap. 9.99 (978-0-544-33623-0(2), HMH Books For Young Readers) 2013. 17.99 (978-0-547-95910-8(9)) Houghton Mifflin Harcourt Publishing Co.

CHARLES, A. M. A. N. & 1st World Publishing. Dad & Me Go to School. 2006. 24p. per. 9.95 (978-1-4218-9924-4(8)) 1st World Publishing, Inc.

Chartrand, Kenneth. A Martian's Dream of Christmas. 2006. 48p. pap. 16.95 (978-1-4241-4123-4(0)) PublishAmerica, Inc.

Chase, Jeffrey Scott. Andy the Alien. 2006. (J). pap. 16.00 (978-0-8059-7081-4(9)) Dorrance Publishing Co., Inc.

—Andy the Alien Visits the Outer Planets. 2007. (J). pap. 17.00 (978-0-8059-7488-1(1)) Dorrance Publishing Co., Inc.

Chase, Max. Alien Attack. 2012. (Star Fighters Ser.). (ENG., Illus.). 128p. (YA). pap. 5.99 (978-1-59990-850-2(6), 9781599908502, Bloomsbury USA Childrens) Bloomsbury Publishing USA.

—Lethal Combat. 2014. (Star Fighters Ser.). (ENG., Illus.). 128p. (YA). (gr. 2-4). pap. 8.99 (978-1-4088-1582-3(6), 9781408815823, Bloomsbury USA Childrens) Bloomsbury Publishing USA.

—Space Wars! 2014. (Star Fighters Ser.). (ENG., Illus.). 128p. (YA). (gr. 2-4). pap. 8.99 (978-1-4088-1583-0(4), 9781408815830, Bloomsbury USA Childrens) Bloomsbury Publishing USA.

Chatterton, Martin. The Brain Full of Holes, 1 vol. 2010. (ENG.). 256p. (J). (gr. 5-9). 16.95 (978-1-56145-527-0(X)) Peachtree Pubs.

Cherobin. Zoomy Boomy, the Moon, & the Earth: All in its Season, & Seasons Change. 2010. 24p. pap. 14.99 *(978-1-4490-2658-5(3))* AuthorHouse.

Cheung, Jim, et al, illus. Young Avengers. 2010. (ENG.). 352p. (YA). (gr. 8-17). pap. 34.99 *(978-0-7851-4907-1(4))* Marvel Worldwide, Inc.

Cheverton, Mark. Overworld in Flames. 2016. (Gameknight999 Ser.: Bk. 2). (ENG.). 256p. (J). (gr. 3). pap. 9.99 *(978-1-5107-0681-1(X)*, Sky Pony Pr.) Skyhorse Publishing Co., Inc.

Chiaramonti, Gregory. Probie: the Space Probe, Mission One: the Ocean of Europa. 2007. 32p. (J). 16.72 *(978-0-615-13848-0(9))* Chiaramonti, Gregory.

Childress, Jamie. Galactic Treasure Hunt: Lost City of Atlantis. Braun, Chris, illus. 2015. (ENG.). 100p. (J). pap. 4.99 *(978-1-931882-62-0(2))* Adventures Unlimited Pr.

—Galactic Treasure Hunt: Lost City of the Moon. Braun, Chris, illus. 2015. (ENG.). 100p. (J). (gr. -1-7). per. 4.99 *(978-1-931882-45-3(2))* Adventures Unlimited Pr.

—Galactic Treasure Hunt #4: Lost in Time. Braun, Chris, illus. 2008. (Galactic Treasure Hunt Ser.). (ENG.). 176p. (J). pap. 5.99 *(978-1-931882-89-7(4))* Adventures Unlimited Pr.

—Lost Universe. Braun, Chris, illus. 2015. (ENG.). 100p. (J). (gr. 4-7). per. 4.99 *(978-1-931882-74-3(6))* Adventures Unlimited Pr.

Chilton, Claire. Shattered. 2012. 268p. pap. *(978-1-908822-10-9(4))* Ragz Bks.

Choyce, Lesley. Deconstructing Dylan. 2006. (ENG.). 180p. (J). (gr. 7). pap. 12.99 *(978-1-55002-603-0(8)*, Boardwalk Bks.) Dundurn CAN. Dist: Ingram Publisher Services.

Christopher, John. Beyond the Burning Lands. 2015. (Sword of the Spirits Ser.: 2). (ENG., Illus.). 272p. (J). (gr. 5-9). pap. 7.99 *(978-1-4814-1994-9(3)*, Aladdin) Simon & Schuster Children's Publishing.

—The City of Gold & Lead. 2003. (Tripods Ser.). 209p. (YA). (gr. 7). 13.65 *(978-0-7569-5877-0(6))* Perfection Learning Corp.

—The City of Gold & Lead. 2014. (Tripods Ser.: 2). (ENG., Illus.). 304p. (J). (gr. 4-8). 17.99 *(978-1-4814-1476-0(3))*; pap. 7.99 *(978-1-4814-1475-3(5))* Simon & Schuster Children's Publishing. (Aladdin).

—The Pool of Fire. 2014. (Tripods Ser.: 3). (ENG., Illus.). 272p. (J). (gr. 4-8). pap. 7.99 *(978-1-4814-1479-1(8)*, Aladdin) Simon & Schuster Children's Publishing.

—The Tripods Collection: The White Mountains - The City of Gold & Lead - The Pool of Fire - When the Tripods Came. 2014. (Tripods Ser.). (ENG., Illus.). 1088p. (J). (gr. 4-8). pap. 31.99 *(978-1-4814-1505-7(0)*, Aladdin) Simon & Schuster Children's Publishing.

—When the Tripods Came. 2014. (Tripods Ser.). (ENG., Illus.). 240p. (J). (gr. 4-8). pap. 7.99 *(978-1-4814-1481-4(X)*, Aladdin) Simon & Schuster Children's Publishing.

—The White Mountains. 2014. (Tripods Ser.: 1). (ENG., Illus.). 272p. (J). (gr. 4-8). pap. 7.99 *(978-1-4814-1477-7(1)*, Aladdin) Simon & Schuster Children's Publishing.

—The White Mountains. 2014. (Tripods Ser.: 1). (ENG., Illus.). 272p. (J). (gr. 4-8). 17.99 *(978-1-4814-1478-4(X)*, Simon & Schuster/Paula Wiseman Bks.) Simon & Schuster/Paula Wiseman Bks.

—Wild Jack. 2015. (ENG., Illus.). 224p. (J). (gr. 5-9). pap. 7.99 *(978-1-4814-2006-8(2)*, Aladdin) Simon & Schuster Children's Publishing.

Chuks-Samuel, Mary. Captain Rainbow & the Agents: Value My Vote. 2012. (Illus.). 24p. pap. 19.82 *(978-1-4772-1787-0(8))* AuthorHouse.

Ciencin, Scott. Attack of the Cling-Ons, 1 vol. Crowther, Jeff, illus. 2011. (Graphic Sparks Ser.). (ENG.). 40p. (gr. 1-3). pap. 5.95 *(978-1-4342-3067-6(8))*; lib. bdg. 23.99 *(978-1-4342-2637-2(9))* Stone Arch Bks. (Graphic Sparks).

Clare, Cassandra. Lord of Shadows. 2017. (Dark Artifices Ser.: 2). (ENG., Illus.). 720p. (YA). (gr. 9). 24.99 *(978-1-4424-6840-5(8)*, McElderry, Margaret K. Bks.) McElderry, Margaret K. Bks.

Clark, Georgia. Parched. Gams, Allen, illus. 2014. (ENG.). 256p. (YA). (gr. 7). 17.95 *(978-0-8234-2949-3(0))* Holiday Hse., Inc.

Clark, Henry. The Book That Proves Time Travel Happens. 2016. (ENG., Illus.). 432p. (J). (gr. 3-7). pap. 6.99 *(978-0-316-40616-1(3))* Little, Brown Bks. for Young Readers.

Clark, Kent & Snider, Brandon T. Peter Powers & the League of Lying Lizards! Bardin, Dave, illus. 2017. (Peter Powers Ser.: 4). (ENG.). 128p. (J). (gr. 1-5). pap. 5.99 ***(978-0-316-54636-2(4))*** Little, Brown Bks. for Young Readers.

Clark, Kent & Snider, Brandon T. Peter Powers & the Rowdy Robot Raiders. Bardin, Dave, illus. 2017. (Peter Powers Ser.: 2). (ENG.). 128p. (J). (gr. 1-5). pap. 5.99 *(978-0-316-35938-2(6))* Little, Brown Bks. for Young Readers.

Clark, Wook Jin. Megagogo, Vol. 1. 2014. (ENG., Illus.). 176p. (YA). pap. 19.99 *(978-1-62010-117-9(3)*, 9781620101179) Oni Pr., Inc.

Clayton, Emma. The Roar. (ENG.). (J). (gr. 2-7). 2012. 512p. pap. 10.99 *(978-0-439-92785-7(4))* 2009. 496p. 17.99 *(978-0-439-92593-8(2))* Scholastic, Inc. (Chicken Hse., The).

—The Whisper. 2012. 309p. *(978-0-545-43365-5(7)*, Chicken Hse., The) Scholastic, Inc.

CLE, Troy. The Marvelous Effect. 2008. (Marvelous World Ser.: 1). (ENG.). 384p. (J). (gr. 5-9). pap. 8.99 *(978-1-4169-4215-3(7)*, Simon & Schuster Bks. For Young Readers) Simon & Schuster Bks. For Young Readers.

Cle, Troy. Olivion's Favorites. 2009. (Marvelous World Ser.: 2). (ENG.). 352p. (J). (gr. 5-9). 14.99 *(978-1-4169-4216-0(5)*, Simon & Schuster Bks. For Young Readers) Simon & Schuster Bks. For Young Readers.

Clement, Emily Gillespie. Bea & the Smart Kids. 2012. 188p. pap. *(978-1-105-50303-0(8))* Lulu.com.

Clements, Andrew. Things Not Seen. 2004. (ENG.). 256p. (J). (gr. 5-18). reprint ed. pap. 6.99 *(978-0-14-240076-0(9)*, Speak) Penguin Young Readers Group.

—Things Not Seen. 2004. 251p. (gr. 5-9). 17.00 *(978-0-7569-2599-4(1))* Perfection Learning Corp.

—Things Not Seen. 2004. 256p. (J). (gr. 4-7). pap. 38.00 incl. audio *(978-1-4000-9014-3(8)*, Listening Library) Random Hse. Audio Publishing Group.

Clenott, Peter. Devolution. 2013. 280p. pap. *(978-1-927792-14-8(2))* Imajin Bks.

Cohen, Rich. Alex & the Amazing Time Machine. Murphy, Kelly, illus. 2013. (ENG.). 176p. (J). (gr. 3-7). pap. 6.99 *(978-1-250-02729-0(2)*, 9781250027290) Square Fish.

Cohn, Rachel. Beta. 2013. (Beta Novel Ser.). (ENG., Illus.). 336p. (YA). (gr. 9-17). pap. 9.99 *(978-1-4231-5734-2(6))* Hyperion Pr.

—Emergent. 2014. (Beta Novel Ser.). (ENG.). 288p. (YA). (gr. 9-17). 17.99 *(978-1-4231-5720-5(6))* Hyperion Bks. for Children.

Colan, Gene & Heck, Don, illus. The Invincible Iron Man. 2014. (ENG.). 264p. (J). (gr. -1-17). pap. 24.99 *(978-0-7851-8843-8(6))* Marvel Worldwide, Inc.

Colby, J. Z. Trilogy One. Colby, J. Z. et al, illus. 2010. (Nebador Ser.: Books One, Two, and Three). (ENG.). 641p. (YA). pupil's gde. ed. 49.95 *(978-1-936253-17-3(8))* Nebador Archives.

Colby, J. Z. & Persons, Katelynn. Flight Training, Kibi & the Search for Happiness. Colby, J. Z. & Powers, Mireille Xioulan, illus. 2011. (Nebador Ser.: Book Four). 178p. (YA). pap. 10.95 *(978-1-936253-27-2(5))* Nebador Archives.

Cole, Bob. Power Reading: Chapter/Sci-Fi/Dr. Little. Sirrell, Terri, illus. 2004. 25p. (J). (gr. 3-4). vinyl bd. 39.95 *(978-1-883186-63-0(3)*, PPSF1) National Reading Styles Institute, Inc.

—Power Reading: Chapter/Sci-Fi/Dr. Little 2. Ford, David, illus. 2005. 25p. (J). (gr. 3-4). vinyl bd. 39.95 *(978-1-883186-76-0(5)*, PPSF4) National Reading Styles Institute, Inc.

—Power Reading: Chapter/Sci-Fi/Superhero. Ford, David, illus. 2004. 25p. (J). (gr. 3-4). vinyl bd. 39.95 *(978-1-883186-62-3(5)*, PPSF2) National Reading Styles Institute, Inc.

—Power Reading: Chapter/Sci-Fi/Time Warp. Ford, David, illus. 2004. 25p. (J). (gr. 4-18). vinyl bd. 39.95 *(978-1-883186-60-9(9)*, PPSF3) National Reading Styles Institute, Inc.

—Power Reading: Chapter/Sci-Fi/Time Warp 2. Ford, David, illus. 2005. 52p. (J). (gr. 4-18). vinyl bd. 39.95 *(978-1-883186-75-3(7)*, PPSF5) National Reading Styles Institute, Inc.

Cole, Dylan. The Other Worldly Adventures of Tyler Washburn: the New Kid. 2012. (ENG., Illus.). 48p. (J). (gr. -1). 19.95 *(978-1-933492-77-3(5))* Design Studio Pr.

Cole, Frank. The World's Greatest Adventure Machine. 2017. (J). ***(978-0-399-55284-7(2))*** Penguin Publishing Group.

Cole, Frank L. The World's Greatest Adventure Machine. 2017. (ENG.). 320p. (J). (gr. 4-7). 16.99 ***(978-0-399-55282-3(0)**, Delacorte Bks. for Young Readers)* Random Hse. Children's Bks.

Cole, Joanna, et al. The Giant Germ. Degen, Bruce et al, illus. 2010. (Rise & Shine Ser.: 6). (ENG.). 80p. (C). (gr. 2-5). pap. 8.95 *(978-0-439-20420-0(8))* National Geographic School Publishing, Inc.

Cole, Steve. Z. Rex. (ENG.). 256p. (J). (gr. 5-18). 2010. 8.99 *(978-0-14-241712-6(2)*, Puffin Books) 2009. 16.99 *(978-0-399-25253-2(3)*, Philomel Bks.) Penguin Young Readers Group.

Cole, T. M. A Slip in Time: The Book of Eventide. Cole, Raymond A., illus. 2006. (YA). per. 10.75 *(978-0-9777677-0-0(1))* Silver Cloak Pubns.

Colfer, Eoin. The Forever Man. (Warp Ser.). (ENG.). (YA). (gr. 7-12). 2016. 368p. pap. 9.99 *(978-1-4847-2616-7(2))* 2015. 352p. 17.99 *(978-1-4847-2603-7(0))* Hyperion Bks. for Children.

—The Hangman's Revolution. 2014. (W. A. R. P. Ser.: Bk. 2). (ENG.). 384p. (YA). (gr. 7-12). 17.99 *(978-1-4231-6163-9(7))* Disney Pr.

—The Supernaturalist. 2012. (Supernaturalist Ser.). (ENG.). 272p. (J). (gr. 5-9). pap. 7.99 *(978-1-4231-4679-7(4))* Hyperion Pr.

Colfer, Eoin, et al. 12 Doctors 12 Stories. 2014. (ENG., Illus.). 528p. (YA). pap. 16.99 *(978-0-14-135988-5(9)*, 9780141359885) Penguin Bks., Ltd. GBR. Dist: Diamond Comic Distributors, Inc.

Colin, Beatrice & Pinto, Sara. My Invisible Sister. Pinto, Sara, illus. 2011. (ENG., Illus.). 128p. (YA). (gr. 3-6). pap. 6.99 *(978-1-59990-678-2(3)*, 9781599906782, Bloomsbury USA Childrens) Bloomsbury Publishing USA.

Collingwood, Harry. The Log of the 'Flying Fish' 2011. 236p. 26.95 *(978-1-4638-9645-4(X))* Rodgers, Alan Bks.

—The Strange Adventures of Eric Blackburn. 2008. 164p. 25.95 *(978-1-60664-711-0(3))* Rodgers, Alan Bks.

Collins, Suzanne. Catching Fire. 2009. (Hunger Games Trilogy: Bk. 2). (YA). 74.99 *(978-1-61574-572-2(6))* Findaway World, LLC.

—Catching Fire. 2009. 12.04 *(978-0-7848-3842-6(9)*, Everbind) Marco Bk. Co.

—Catching Fire. 2011. 480p. pap. *(978-1-4071-3209-9(1))* Scholastic.

—Catching Fire. (Hunger Games Ser.: 2). (ENG.). (gr. 7). 2014. 448p. (YA). pap. 12.99 *(978-0-545-79188-5(X)*, Tangerine Pr.) 2013. 400p. (YA). pap. 12.99 *(978-0-545-58617-7(8)*, Scholastic Pr.) 2010. (Illus.). 400p. (J). lib. bdg. 22.99 *(978-0-545-31059-8(8)*, Scholastic Pr.) 2009. 400p. (J). 18.99 *(978-0-439-02349-8(1)*, Scholastic Pr.) 2013. 400p. (J). pap. 12.99 *(978-0-545-60368-3(4)*, Scholastic Paperbacks) Scholastic, Inc.

—Catching Fire. l.t. ed. (Hunger Games Trilogy: 2). (ENG.). (YA). 2012. 498p. (gr. 7-12). pap. 14.99 *(978-1-59413-585-9(1)*, Large Print Pr.) 2009. 500p. 23.95 *(978-1-4104-2044-2(2))* Thorndike Pr.

—Catching Fire. 2013. (Hunger Games Trilogy Ser.: 2). lib. bdg. 24.50 *(978-0-606-32025-2(3)*, Turtleback) Turtleback Bks.

—Catching Fire. 2011. (Hunger Games Trilogy: Bk. 2). (CHI.). 344p. (YA). (gr. 7-12). pap. *(978-7-5063-5566-7(3))* Writers' Publishing Hse.

—Gregor & the Prophecy of Bane. 2005. (Underland Chronicles Ser.: 2). (ENG.). 320p. (J). (gr. 3-7). pap. 7.99 *(978-0-439-65076-2(3))* Scholastic, Inc.

—The Hunger Games. 2009. (Hunger Games Trilogy: Bk. 1). 10.85 *(978-0-7848-3801-3(1)*, Everbind) Marco Bk. Co.

—The Hunger Games. 2010. (Hunger Games Trilogy: Bk. 1). (ENG.). 374p. (gr. 7-12). 21.00 *(978-1-60686-581-1(1))* Perfection Learning Corp.

—The Hunger Games. Fournier, Guillaume, tr. 2011. (Hunger Games Trilogy: Bk. 1). (FRE.). 398p. (YA). (gr. 7-12). pap. *(978-2-266-18269-0(2))* Presses Pocket.

—The Hunger Games. 2011. (Hunger Games Trilogy: 1). (YA). 69.75 *(978-1-4561-3196-8(6))* Recorded Bks., Inc.

—The Hunger Games. 2010. (Hunger Games Ser.: 1). (ENG.). 384p. (J). (gr. 7-18). pap. 10.99 *(978-0-439-02352-8(1)*, Scholastic Pr.) Scholastic, Inc.

—The Hunger Games. O'Brien, Tim, illus. 2009. 448p. pap. *(978-1-4071-0908-4(1)*, Scholastic) Scholastic, Inc.

—The Hunger Games. (Hunger Games Ser.: 1). (ENG.). (gr. 7). 2008. 384p. (J). 18.99 *(978-0-439-02348-1(3)*, Scholastic Pr.) 2012. 384p. (J). pap. 12.99 *(978-0-545-42511-7(5))*Set. 2014. (YA). pap. 38.97 *(978-0-545-79191-5(X)*, Scholastic Pr.) Scholastic, Inc.

—The Hunger Games. l.t. ed. (Hunger Games Trilogy: Bk. 1). (ENG.). (YA). 2012. 484p. (gr. 7-12). pap. 14.99 *(978-1-59413-587-3(8)*, Large Print Pr.) 2009. 486p. 23.95 *(978-1-4104-1986-6(X))* Thorndike Pr.

—The Hunger Games. 2010. (Hunger Games Trilogy Ser.: 1). lib. bdg. 22.10 *(978-1-4178-3173-9(1)*, Turtleback) Turtleback Bks.

—The Hunger Games. 2010. (Hunger Games Trilogy: Bk. 1). (CHI.). 324p. (YA). (gr. 7-12). pap. *(978-7-5063-5153-9(6))* Writers' Publishing Hse.

—The Hunger Games: Foil Edition. 2014. (Hunger Games Ser.: 1). (ENG.). 448p. (YA). (gr. 7). pap. 12.99 *(978-0-545-79187-8(1)*, Scholastic Pr.) Scholastic, Inc.

—The Hunger Games Trilogy Set: The Hunger Games; Catching Fire; Mockingjay. 2010. (Hunger Games Ser.: 1). (ENG.). (J). (gr. 7-18). 53.97 *(978-0-545-26535-5(5)*, Scholastic Pr.) Scholastic, Inc.

—The Hunger Games Trilogy Collection. 2014. (Hunger Games Ser.). (ENG.). (J). (gr. 9). pap. 36.97 *(978-0-545-67031-9(4)*, Scholastic Pr.) Scholastic, Inc.

—Los Juegos del Hambre. 2009. (Hunger Games Trilogy: Bk. 1).Tr. of Hunger Games. (SPA.). pap. 19.99 *(978-84-9867-539-9(1))* RBA Libros, S.A. ESP. Dist: Lectorum Pubns., Inc.

—Los Juegos del Hambre. 2012. (Hunger Games Trilogy Spanish Ser.: 1).Tr. of Hunger Games. (SPA.). lib. bdg. 33.05 *(978-0-606-26447-1(7)*, Turtleback) Turtleback Bks.

—LOS JUEGOS DEL HAMBRE. 2012. (Hunger Games Trilogy: Bk. 1). (SPA.). 400p. (J). pap. 19.99 *(978-84-272-0212-2(1))* Molino, Editorial ESP. Dist: Lectorum Pubns., Inc.

—Mockingjay. 2011. (Hunger Games Trilogy: Bk. 3). (CHI.). 435p. (YA). (gr. 7-12). pap. *(978-986-213-216-6(7))* Locus Publishing Co.

—Mockingjay. (Hunger Games Trilogy: 3). (YA). 2011. 77.75 *(978-1-4561-3203-3(2))* 2010. 75.75 *(978-1-4561-3205-7(9))* 2010. 1.25 *(978-1-4640-2636-2(X))* Recorded Bks., Inc.

—Mockingjay. 2011. (Hunger Games Ser.: Vol. 3). (ENG.). 448p. (YA). (gr. 8-12). pap. *(978-1-4071-3210-5(5))* Scholastic Canada, Ltd.

—Mockingjay. 2014. (Hunger Games Ser.: 3). (ENG.). 448p. (YA). (gr. 7). pap. 12.99 *(978-0-545-79190-8(1)*, Scholastic Pr.) 2014. (Hunger Games Ser.: 3). (ENG.). 400p. (YA). (gr. 7). pap. 12.99 *(978-0-545-78829-8(3)*, Scholastic Paperbacks) 2014. (Hunger Games Ser.: 3). (ENG.). 400p. (J). (gr. 7). pap. 12.99 *(978-0-545-66326-7(1)*, Scholastic Pr.) 2010. (Hunger Games Ser.: 3). (ENG.). 400p. (J). (gr. 7-7). lib. bdg. 22.99 *(978-0-545-31060-4(1)*, Scholastic Pr.) 2010. (Hunger Games Ser.: 3). (ENG.). 400p. (J). (gr. 7-18). 18.99 *(978-0-439-02351-1(3)*, Scholastic Pr.) 2010. pap. *(978-0-439-02354-2(8)*, Scholastic Pr.) Scholastic, Inc.

—Mockingjay. l.t. ed. (Hunger Games Trilogy: Bk. 3). (ENG.). (YA). 2012. 502p. (gr. 7-12). pap. 14.99 *(978-1-59413-586-6(X)*, Large Print Pr.) 2010. 503p. 23.99 *(978-1-4104-2841-7(9))* Thorndike Pr.

—Mockingjay. 2014. (Hunger Games Trilogy Ser.: 3). lib. bdg. 24.50 *(978-0-606-36328-0(9))*; lib. bdg. 24.50 *(978-0-606-35133-1(7))* Turtleback Bks.

—Sinsajo. 2010. (Hunger Games Trilogy: Bk. 3).Tr. of Mockingjay. (SPA.). 424p. (J). (gr. 8-12). pap. 19.99 *(978-84-272-0038-8(2))* Molino, Editorial ESP. Dist: Lectorum Pubns., Inc.

—SINSAJO. 2012. (Hunger Games Trilogy: Bk. 3). (SPA.). 424p. (J). pap. 19.99 *(978-84-272-0214-6(8))* Molino, Editorial ESP. Dist: Lectorum Pubns., Inc.

—Sinsajo. 2012. (Hunger Games Trilogy Spanish Ser.: 3).Tr. of Mockingjay. (SPA.). lib. bdg. 33.05 *(978-0-606-26449-5(3)*, Turtleback) Turtleback Bks.

Collins, Terry, et al. Nickolas Flux History Chronicles, 1 vol. Simmons, Mark, illus. 2014. (Nickolas Flux History Chronicles Ser.). (ENG.). 32p. (gr. 3-4). 122.60 *(978-1-4914-0255-9(5)*, Graphic Library) Capstone Press of Coughlan Cos.

Collins, Tim. Sneezy Alien Attack. Dreidemy, Joëlle & Bigwood, John, illus. 2014. (Cosmic Colin Ser.: 2). (ENG.). 128p. (J). (gr. 4-6). pap. 7.99 *(978-1-78055-242-2(4))* O'Mara, Michael Bks., Ltd. GBR. Dist: Independent Pubs. Group.

Collins, Tim & Bigwood, John. Hairy Hamster Horror. 2017. (Cosmic Colin Ser.: 3). (ENG., Illus.). 128p. (J). (gr. 4-6). 8.99 ***(978-1-78055-480-8(X))*** O'Mara, Michael Bks., Ltd. GBR. Dist: Independent Pubs. Group.

—Tricky Time Bomb. 2017. (Cosmic Colin Ser.: 4). (ENG., Illus.). 128p. (J). (gr. 4-6). pap. 8.99 ***(978-1-78055-481-5(8))*** O'Mara, Michael Bks., Ltd. GBR. Dist: Independent Pubs. Group.

Condie, Ally. Juntos. 2011.Tr. of Matched. (SPA.). lib. bdg. 22.05 *(978-0-606-26417-4(5)*, Turtleback) Turtleback Bks.

Condon, Bill. Planet Puzzle, 1 vol. 2013. (Fiction Readers Ser.). (ENG., Illus.). 28p. (J). (gr. 2-2). pap. 6.99 *(978-1-4333-5562-2(0))* Shell Educational Publishing.

Connely, Chris L. & Vaughan, Mark. An Alien from Earth. 2003. 175p. per. 9.95 *(978-0-9745544-0-2(5))* Lewis Lynn Bks.

Conner, Jimmie L. The Adventures of Captain Computerman & His Sidekick Mouseman: The Saving of the Toy Websites. 2005. 77p. pap. 19.95 *(978-1-4137-7457-3(1))* America Star Bks.

The Contagious Colors of Mumpley Middle School. 2014. (ENG., Illus.). 288p. (J). (gr. 2-5). pap. 8.99 *(978-1-4424-7830-5(6)*, Atheneum Bks. for Young Readers) Simon & Schuster Children's Publishing.

Cook, Donna. The Silly Solar System. 2009. pap. 15.00 *(978-1-61623-557-4(8))* Independent Pub.

Cook, Eileen. Remember. 2015. (ENG., Illus.). 320p. (YA). (gr. 9). 17.99 *(978-1-4814-1696-2(0)*, Simon Pulse) Simon Pulse.

Cook, Julia. Hygiene... You Stink! DuFalla, Anita, illus. 2014. (ENG.). 32p. (J). pap. 10.95 *(978-1-934490-62-4(8))* Boys Town Pr.

Cook, Sherry & Johnson, Terri. Gilbert Gas, 26 vols. Kuhn, Jesse, illus. l.t. ed. 2006. (Quirkles — Exploring Phonics through Science Ser.: 7). 32p. (J). 7.99 *(978-1-933815-06-0(X)*, Quirkles, The) Creative 3, LLC.

—Inquisitive Inman, 26 vols. Kuhn, Jesse, illus. l.t. ed. 2006. (Quirkles — Exploring Phonics through Science Ser.: 9). 32p. (J). 7.99 *(978-1-933815-08-4(6)*, Quirkles, The) Creative 3, LLC.

—Kitchen Chemistry Kal, 26 vols. Kuhn, Jesse, illus. l.t. ed. 2006. (Quirkles — Exploring Phonics through Science Ser.: 11). 32p. (J). 7.99 *(978-1-933815-10-7(8)*, Quirkles, The) Creative 3, LLC.

—Mary Motion, 26 vols. Kuhn, Jesse, illus. l.t. ed. 2006. (Quirkles — Exploring Phonics through Science Ser.: 13). 32p. (J). 7.99 *(978-1-933815-12-1(4)*, Quirkles, The) Creative 3, LLC.

—Ollie Oxygen, 26 vols. Kuhn, Jesse, illus. l.t. ed. 2006. (Quirkles — Exploring Phonics through Science Ser.: 15). 32p. (J). 7.99 *(978-1-933815-14-5(0)*, Quirkles, The) Creative 3, LLC.

—Pressure Pete, 26 vols. Kuhn, Jesse, illus. l.t. ed. 2006. (Quirkles — Exploring Phonics through Science Ser.: 16). 32p. (J). 7.99 *(978-1-933815-15-2(9)*, Quirkles, The) Creative 3, LLC.

—Quincy Quake, 26. Kuhn, Jesse, illus. l.t. ed. 2006. (Quirkles — Exploring Phonics through Science Ser.: 17). 32p. (J). 7.99 *(978-1-933815-16-9(7)*, Quirkles, The) Creative 3, LLC.

—Zany Science Zeke, 26. Kuhn, Jesse, illus. l.t. ed. 2006. (Quirkles — Exploring Phonics through Science Ser.: 26). 32p. (J). 7.99 *(978-1-933815-25-1(6)*, Quirkles, The) Creative 3, LLC.

Cooper, Susan. Green Boy. 2013. (ENG., Illus.). 208p. (J). (gr. 3-7). 17.99 *(978-1-4424-8081-0(5)*, McElderry, Margaret K. Bks.) McElderry, Margaret K. Bks.

Cooper, Susan & National Geographic Learning Staff. Green Boy. 2013. (ENG., Illus.). 208p. (J). (gr. 3-7). pap. 7.99 *(978-1-4424-8082-7(3)*, McElderry, Margaret K. Bks.) McElderry, Margaret K. Bks.

Cooper, T. & Glock-Cooper, Allison. Drew. 2014. (Changers Ser.). (ENG., Illus.). 288p. (gr. 6). pap. 11.95 *(978-1-61775-195-0(2)*, Black Sheep) Akashic Bks.

Cornell, Paul & Venditti, Robert. Demon Knights - The Gathering Storm, Vol. 3. 2014. (ENG., Illus.). 256p. pap. 19.99 *(978-1-4012-4269-5(3))* DC Comics.

Cory, Adrian A. On the Eighth Tin. 2014. (ENG.). 194p. (YA). (gr. 8-17). pap. 11.95 *(978-1-78279-368-7(2)*, Lodestone Bks.) Hunt, John Publishing Ltd. GBR. Dist: National Bk. Network.

Cotes, Gilles. OGM et Chant de Mais. Begin, Jean-Guy, illus. 2004. (FRE.). 112p. (J). *(978-2-89599-002-4(6))* Editions de la Paix CAN. Dist: World of Reading, Ltd.

Courage, Nick. The Loudness: A Novel. 2015. (ENG.). 336p. (J). (gr. 3-7). 15.99 *(978-1-63220-414-1(2)*, Sky Pony Pr.) Skyhorse Publishing Co., Inc.

Cousineau, Craig S. Skippy & Oaf: The Battle Against Oxygen Radicals. 2007. (ENG., Illus.). 48p. (J). (gr. 2-4). per. *(978-1-933255-27-9(7))* DNA Pr.

Cousins, Lucy. Maisy Grows a Garden. 2013. (Maisy Ser.). (ENG., Illus.). 16p. (J). (-k). 14.99 *(978-0-7636-6242-4(9))* Candlewick Pr.

—Maisy's Moon Landing: A Maisy First Science Book. Cousins, Lucy, illus. 2017. (Maisy Ser.). (ENG., Illus.). 16p. (J). (-k). 15.99 *(978-0-7636-9040-3(6))* Candlewick Pr.

Coville, Bruce. Aliens Ate My Homework. Coville, Katherine, illus. 2008. (Rod Allbright & the Galactic Patrol Ser.). 179p. (gr. 3-7). 17.00 *(978-0-7569-8466-3(1))* Perfection Learning Corp.

—Aliens Ate My Homework. 179p. (J). (gr. 4-6). pap. 3.99 *(978-0-8072-1503-6(1)*, Listening Library) Random Hse. Audio Publishing Group.

—Aliens Ate My Homework: Rod Allbright & the Galactic Patrol. Coville, Katherine, illus. 2007. (Rod Allbright & the Galactic Patrol Ser.). (ENG.). 192p. (J). (gr. 3-7). pap. 7.99 *(978-1-4169-3883-5(4)*, Aladdin) Simon & Schuster Children's Publishing.

—Aliens Stole My Body. Coville, Katherine, illus. 2008. (Rod Allbright & the Galactic Patrol Ser.). (ENG.). 240p. (J). (gr. 3-7). pap. 7.99 *(978-1-4169-5359-3(0)*, Simon & Schuster/Paula Wiseman Bks.) Simon & Schuster/Paula Wiseman Bks.

—I Left My Sneakers in Dimension X. Coville, Katherine, illus. 2007. (Rod Allbright & the Galactic Patrol Ser.). (ENG.). 192p. (J). (gr. 3-7). pap. 7.99 *(978-1-4169-3882-8(6)*, Simon & Schuster/Paula Wiseman Bks.) Simon & Schuster/Paula Wiseman Bks.

—I Lost My Grandfather's Brain. unabr. ed. 2004. (I Was a Sixth Grade Alien Ser.: Vol. 3). 160p. (J). (gr. 3-6). pap. 29.00 incl. audio *(978-0-8072-8385-1(1)*, YA180SP, Listening Library) Random Hse. Audio Publishing Group.

—I Was a Sixth Grade Alien. (I Was a Sixth Grade Alien Ser.: Vol. 1). 170p. (J). (gr. 4-6). pap. 3.99 *(978-0-8072-8202-1(2))*; 2004. (gr. 3-6). pap. 29.00 incl. audio *(978-0-8072-8201-4(4)*, S YA 138 SP) Random Hse. Audio Publishing Group. (Listening Library).

—The Monsters of Morley Manor. 2003. (Madcap Adventures Ser.). 223p. (gr. 3-7). 17.00 *(978-0-7569-1627-5(5))* Perfection Learning Corp.

—The Monsters of Morley Manor: A Madcap Adventure. 2003. (ENG.). 240p. (J). (gr. 2-5). pap. 7.99 *(978-0-15-204705-4(0))* Houghton Mifflin Harcourt Publishing Co.

—My Teacher Flunked the Planet. Pierard, John, illus. 2005. (My Teacher Bks.: 4). (ENG.). 176p. (J). (gr. 3-7). pap. 6.99 *(978-1-4169-0331-4(3)*, Aladdin) Simon & Schuster Children's Publishing.

—My Teacher Fried My Brains. Pierard, John, illus. 2014. (My Teacher Bks.: 2). (ENG.). 176p. (J). (gr. 3-7). 17.99 *(978-1-4814-0431-0(8)*, Aladdin) Simon & Schuster Children's Publishing.

—My Teacher Is an Alien. unabr. ed. 2004. (My Teacher Is an Alien Ser.: Bk. 1). 123p. (J). (gr. 3-6). pap. 29.00 incl. audio

S

(978-0-8072-8029-4(1), S YA 971 SP, Listening Library) Random Hse. Audio Publishing Group.
—My Teacher Is an Alien. Wimmer, Mike, illus. 2005. (My Teacher Bks.: 1). (ENG.). 160p. (J). (gr. 3-7). pap. 6.99 (978-1-4169-0334-5(8), Aladdin) Simon & Schuster Children's Publishing.
—My Teacher Is an Alien. Wimmer, Mike, illus. 2014. (My Teacher Bks.: 1). (ENG.). 160p. (J). (gr. 3-7). 17.99 (978-1-4814-0430-3(X), Simon & Schuster/Paula Wiseman Bks.) Simon & Schuster/Paula Wiseman Bks.
—The Search for Snout. Coville, Katherine, illus. 2007. (Rod Allbright & the Galactic Patrol Ser.). (ENG.). 224p. (J). (gr. 3-7). pap. 7.99 (978-1-4169-4980-0(1), Simon & Schuster/Paula Wiseman Bks.) Simon & Schuster/Paula Wiseman Bks.
Cowey, James. William Snottengrout - Quapta's Revenge. 2006. 104p. per. (978-1-84667-023-7(3)) Derwent Pr., The.
Cox, Greg. Riese: Kingdom Falling. 2013. (ENG., Illus.). 288p. (YA). (gr. 7). pap. 9.99 (978-1-4424-2970-3(4), Simon & Schuster Bks. For Young Readers) Simon & Schuster Bks. For Young Readers.
Coyle, Katie. Vivian Apple Needs a Miracle. 2017. (ENG.). 304p. (YA). (gr. 7). pap. 9.99 (978-0-544-81318-2(9), HMH Books For Young Readers) Houghton Mifflin Harcourt Publishing Co.
Craig, Joe. Jimmy Coates: Killer. 2007. 261p. (J). (gr. 5-9). 15.99 (978-0-06-077266-6(2)) HarperCollins Pubs.
Crashland. 2014. (Twinmaker Ser.: 2). (ENG.). 480p. (YA). (gr. 8). 17.99 (978-0-06-220324-3(X)) HarperCollins Pubs.
Cremer, Andrea. The Inventor's Secret. (Inventor's Secret Ser.). (ENG.). (YA). (gr. 7). 2015. 416p. pap. 10.99 (978-0-14-751436-7(X), Speak) 2014. 336p. 18.99 (978-0-399-15962-6(2), Philomel Bks.) Penguin Young Readers Group.
—The Turncoat's Gambit. 2016. (Inventor's Secret Ser.: 3). (ENG.). 336p. (YA). (gr. 7). 18.99 (978-0-399-16425-5(1), Philomel Bks.) Penguin Young Readers Group.
Crew, Gary. The Viewer. Tan, Shaun, illus. 2003. (ENG.). 32p. (J). (gr. 1-6). 16.95 (978-1-894965-02-6(7)) Simply Read Bks. CAN. Dist: Ingram Publisher Services.
Crewe, Megan. The Lives We Lost. 2014. (Fallen World Trilogy Ser.). (ENG.). 304p. (YA). (gr. 7-12). pap. 9.99 (978-1-4231-4632-2(8)) Hyperion Bks. for Children.
—A Sky Unbroken, 0 vols. 2015. (Earth & Sky Trilogy Ser.: 3). (ENG., Illus.). 347p. (J). (gr. 7-12). pap. 9.99 (978-1-5039-4657-6(6), 9781503946576, Skyscape) Amazon Publishing.
—The Worlds We Make. 2014. (Fallen World Trilogy Ser.). (ENG.). 288p. (J). (gr. 5-9). 16.99 (978-1-4231-4618-6(2)) Hyperion Bks. for Children.
Crews, G. S. Ellen G Goes to the Haunted Planetarium. Designs, Marion, photos by. 2009. (Illus.). 50p. pap. 20.00 (978-0-9795236-4-9(8)) Crews Pubns., LLC.
Crilley, Mark. Akiko Flights of Fancy. exp. ed. 2007. (Illus.). 264p. pap. 24.95 (978-1-57989-088-9(1)) Sirius Entertainment, Inc.
—The Battle for Boach's Keep Vol. 7. 2004. (Illus.). 144p. pap. 14.95 (978-1-57989-064-3(4)) Sirius Entertainment, Inc.
Crilley, Paul. The Osiris Curse: A Tweed & Nightingale Adventure. 2013. (ENG.). 287p. (J). (gr. 7). 17.99 (978-1-61614-857-7(8)) Prometheus Bks., Pubs.
Crockett, S. D. After the Snow. 2012. (After the Snow Ser.: 1). (ENG.). 304p. (YA). (gr. 7-12). 16.99 (978-0-312-64169-6(9)) Feiwel & Friends.
—After the Snow. 2013. (After the Snow Ser.: 1). (ENG.). 320p. (YA). (gr. 7-12). pap. 9.99 (978-1-250-01676-8(2)) Square Fish.
Crofoot, Betty & Arledge, Roo. Battle for the Multiverse - My Genie & Me Series Book 3. 2013. 92p. pap. 8.95 (978-1-60862-489-8(7)) E-BookTime LLC.
Cross, Julie. Tempest. 2012. (Tempest Trilogy Ser.: 1). (ENG.). (YA). (gr. 9-12). 368p. pap. 9.99 (978-1-250-01120-6(5), 9781250011206); 352p. 17.99 (978-0-312-56889-4(4), 9780312568894) St. Martin's Pr. (St. Martin's Griffin).
—Timestorm: A Tempest Novel. 2014. (Tempest Trilogy Ser.: 3). (ENG.). 368p. (YA). (gr. 9-12). 18.99 (978-0-312-56891-7(6), 9780312568917, St. Martin's Griffin) St. Martin's Pr.
—Vortex. 2013. (Tempest Trilogy Ser.: 2). (ENG.). 368p. (YA). (gr. 9-12). 18.99 (978-0-312-56890-0(8), 9780312568900, St. Martin's Griffin) St. Martin's Pr.
—Vortex: A Tempest Novel. 2013. (Tempest Trilogy Ser.: 2). (ENG.). 384p. (YA). (gr. 9-12). pap. 9.99 (978-1-250-04478-5(2), 9781250044785, St. Martin's Griffin) St. Martin's Pr.
Crossan, Sarah. Breathe. 2013. (Breathe Ser.: 1). (ENG.). 400p. (YA). (gr. 9). pap. 9.99 (978-0-06-211870-7(6), Greenwillow Bks.) HarperCollins Pubs.
Crow, E. J. The Eye Pocket. 2006. (Fantastic Society of Peculiar Adventures Ser.). (ENG., Illus.). 48p. (J). (gr. 2-4). per. (978-1-933255-17-0(X)) DNA Pr.
Cummings, Lindsay. The Murder Complex. 2014. (Murder Complex Ser.: 1). (ENG.). 416p. (YA). (gr. 9). 17.99 (978-0-06-222000-4(4), Greenwillow Bks.) HarperCollins Pubs.
Cunningham, Mary. The Magic Medallion. 2006. (Cynthia's Attic Ser.). 158p. (J). (gr. 4-7). per. 9.99 (978-1-59080-460-5(0)) Echelon Press Publishing.
A Cup of Tea, A Piece of Pie. 2004. (J). 14.95 (978-0-9747363-4-1(1)) Kelly, Kimberly.
Curley, Marianne. The Dark. 2005. (Guardians of Time Ser.). (ENG.). 352p. (YA). (gr. 7-12). per. 8.95 (978-1-58234-664-9(X), 9781582346649, Bloomsbury USA Childrens) Bloomsbury Publishing USA.
Curtis, Simon. Boy Robot. 2016. (ENG., Illus.). 432p. (YA). (gr. 9). 17.99 (978-1-4814-5929-7(5), Simon Pulse) Simon Pulse.
Cushman, Doug. Space Cat. Cushman, Doug, illus. 2006. (I Can Read Bks.). (Illus.). 32p. (gr. -1-3). 14.00 (978-0-7569-6977-6(8)) Perfection Learning Corp.
Cusick, John M. Girl Parts. (ENG., Illus.). 240p. (YA). (gr. 9). 2012. pap. 7.99 (978-0-7636-5644-7(5)) 2010. 16.99 (978-0-7636-4930-2(9)) Candlewick Pr.
Czerneda, Julie E. This Gulf of Time & Stars: Reunification #1. 2015. (Reunification Ser.: 1). (ENG.). 464p. (gr. 12). 25.95 (978-0-7564-0869-5(5), DAW) DAW.

Dael, Do Van. Earth Child. 2012. (Illus.). 24p. pap. 19.82 (978-1-4772-1402-2(X)) AuthorHouse.
Dahl, Michael. A Buried Starship. Levins, Tim & Vecchio, Luciano, illus. 2017. (Superman Tales of the Fortress of Solitude Ser.). (ENG.). 40p. (gr. 1-3). lib. bdg. 24.65 (978-1-4965-4395-0(5), DC Super Heroes) Stone Arch Bks.
—The Museum Monsters. Schoening, Dan, illus. (Superman Ser.). (ENG.). 56p. (gr. 2-3). 2013. pap. 4.95 (978-1-4342-1372-3(2)) 2009. lib. bdg. 26.65 (978-1-4342-1157-6(6)) Stone Arch Bks. (DC Super Heroes).
Dahl, Michael & Nickel, Scott. The Dozer Strikes! Jennings, C. S., illus. 2010. (Incredible Rockhead Ser.). (ENG.). 40p. (gr. 1-3). lib. bdg. 23.99 (978-1-4342-1894-0(5), Graphic Sparks) Stone Arch Bks.
Dahl, Michael, et al. Five Riddles for Robin, 1 vol. Schigiel, Gregg, illus. 2013. (Batman Ser.). (ENG.). 56p. (gr. 2-3). pap. 4.95 (978-1-4342-1366-2(8), DC Super Heroes) Stone Arch Bks.
—The Last Son of Krypton. 2009. (Superman Ser.). (ENG., Illus.). 56p. (gr. 2-3). lib. bdg. 26.65 (978-1-4342-1155-2(X), DC Super Heroes) Stone Arch Bks.
—Last Son of Krypton. 2013. (Superman Ser.). (ENG., Illus.). 56p. (gr. 2-3). pap. 4.95 (978-1-4342-1370-9(6), DC Super Heroes) Stone Arch Bks.
Dahl, Roald. Charlie & the Great Glass Elevator. Blake, Quentin, illus. 2007. (ENG.). 192p. (J). (gr. 3-7). 7.99 (978-0-14-241032-5(2), Puffin Books) Penguin Young Readers Group.
—Charlie & the Great Glass Elevator. Blake, Quentin, illus. 2005. (Puffin Modern Classics Ser.). (ENG.). 176p. (J). (gr. 3-7). pap. 7.99 (978-0-14-240412-6(8), Puffin Books) Penguin Young Readers Group.
—Charlie & the Great Glass Elevator. 2007. 18.40 (978-1-4177-8610-7(8), Turtleback) Turtleback Bks.
Dale, Jeremy. Battle at Three Rivers, Vol. 3. 2014. (ENG., Illus.). 96p. (YA). pap. 8.99 (978-1-939352-55-2(X), 9781939352552) Action Lab Entertainment.
—Into the Woods. 2014. (ENG., Illus.). 96p. (J). pap. 8.99 (978-1-939352-50-7(9), 9781939352507) Action Lab Entertainment.
—Strange Creatures, Vol. 2. 2014. (ENG., Illus.). 96p. (J). pap. 8.99 (978-1-939352-52-1(5), 9781939352521) Action Lab Entertainment.
Daley, Michael J. Rat Trap. 2008. (ENG.). 272p. (J). (gr. 3-7). 16.95 (978-0-8234-2093-3(0)) Holiday Hse., Inc.
—Space Station Rat. 2008. (ENG., Illus.). 181p. (J). (gr. 4-7). 6.95 (978-0-8234-2151-0(1)) Holiday Hse., Inc.
Dalrymple, Farel. The Wrenchies. Dalrymple, Farel, illus. 2014. (ENG., Illus.). 304p. (YA). (gr. 9). pap. 19.99 (978-1-59643-421-9(X), 9781596434219, First Second Bks.) Roaring Brook Pr.
Dalton, Ryan. The Black Tempest. 2017. (Time Shift Trilogy Ser.). (ENG.). 448p. (YA). (gr. 7-12). pap. 14.99 (978-1-63163-106-1(3), Jolly Fish Pr.) North Star Editions.
Daly, Joseph M. Strange Town Volume One: The Woods Behind Trevor Malone's House. 2007. 265p. (YA). pap. 9.99 net. (978-0-9779921-0-2(1)) Wolfs Corner Publishing.
Danziger, Paula. This Place Has No Atmosphere. 2006. (ENG.). 240p. (J). (gr. 5-18). 8.99 (978-0-14-240680-9(5), Puffin Books) Penguin Young Readers Group.
Dare, Danni. Jake Jett: Adventures in Space. 2010. 32p. pap. 12.99 (978-1-4520-4981-6(5)) AuthorHouse.
Dashner, James. The Blade of Shattered Hope. 2010. (13th Reality Ser.: Bk. 3). 432p. (J). 18.99 (978-1-60641-239-8(6), Shadow Mountain) Shadow Mountain Publishing.
—The Blade of Shattered Hope. Dorman, Brandon, illus. 2011. (13th Reality Ser.: 3). (ENG.). 528p. (J). (gr. 3-7). pap. 8.99 (978-1-4424-0871-5(5), Aladdin) Simon & Schuster Children's Publishing.
—The Death Cure. (Maze Runner Ser.: Bk. 3). (ENG.). 352p. (YA). (gr. 7). 2013. pap. 9.99 (978-0-385-73878-1(1)) 2011. 18.99 (978-0-385-73877-4(3)) Random Hse. Children's Bks. (Delacorte Pr.).
—The Death Cure. 2013. (Maze Runner Ser.: 3). lib. bdg. 20.85 (978-0-606-27005-2(1), Turtleback) Turtleback Bks.
—The Eye of Minds. 2013. 310p. (YA). (978-0-385-38370-7(3), Delacorte Pr) Random House Publishing Group.
—The Eye of Minds. (Mortality Doctrine Ser.). (ENG.). (YA). (gr. 7). 2014. 342p. pap. 9.99 (978-0-385-74140-8(5), Ember) 2013. 320p. 18.99 (978-0-385-74139-2(1), Delacorte Pr.) Random Hse. Children's Bks.
—The Fever Code. 2016. (Maze Runner Ser.). (ENG.). 384p. (YA). (gr. 7). 18.99 (978-0-553-51309-7(5)); lib. bdg. 21.99 (978-0-553-51310-3(9)) Random Hse. Children's Bks. (Delacorte Pr.).
—The Game of Lives. 2015. (Mortality Doctrine Ser.). (ENG.). 352p. (YA). (gr. 7). lib. bdg. 21.99 (978-0-375-99003-8(8)); 18.99 (978-0-385-74143-9(X)) Random Hse. Children's Bks. (Delacorte Pr.).
—The Game of Lives (the Mortality Doctrine, Book Three) 2017. (Mortality Doctrine Ser.: 3). (ENG.). 384p. (YA). (gr. 7). pap. 9.99 (**978-0-385-74144-6(8)**, Ember) Random Hse. Children's Bks.
—A Gift of Ice. 2004. (Jimmy Fincher Saga: Bk. 2). 208p. pap. 14.99 (978-1-55517-753-9(0), 1232041) Cedar Fort, Inc./CFI Distribution.
—The Hunt for Dark Infinity. Beus, Bryan, illus. 2009. (13th Reality Ser.: Bk. 2). 446p. (J). 18.95 (978-1-60641-034-9(2), Shadow Mountain) Shadow Mountain Publishing.
—The Hunt for Dark Infinity. Beus, Bryan, illus. 2010. (13th Reality Ser.: 2). (ENG.). 544p. (J). (gr. 3-7). pap. 8.99 (978-1-4169-9153-0(0), Aladdin) Simon & Schuster Children's Publishing.
—The Journal of Curious Letters. Beus, Bryan, illus. 2008. (13th Reality Ser.: Bk. 1). 434p. (J). (gr. 4-7). 17.95 (978-1-59038-831-0(3), Shadow Mountain) Shadow Mountain Publishing.
—The Journal of Curious Letters. Beus, Bryan, illus. 2009. (13th Reality Ser.: 1). (ENG.). 528p. (J). (gr. 3-7). pap. 8.99 (978-1-4169-9152-6(2), Aladdin) Simon & Schuster Children's Publishing.
—The Kill Order. 2014. (Maze Runner Ser.: 0). lib. bdg. 20.85 (978-0-606-35572-8(3)) Turtleback Bks.
—The Maze Runner, 4 vols. (ENG.). (YA). (gr. 7). 2015. 75.96 (978-1-101-93213-1(9), Delacorte Pr.) 2010. (Maze Runner Ser.: 1). 416p. pap. 9.99 (978-0-385-73795-1(5), Delacorte Pr.) 2009. (Maze Runner Ser.: Bk. 1). 384p. 18.99 (978-0-385-73794-4(7), Delacorte Pr.) 2014. (Maze Runner Ser.: 1). 400p. pap. 10.99 (978-0-385-38520-6(X), Delacorte Pr.)Bk. 1. 2014. (Maze Runner Ser.). 400p. 17.99 (978-0-553-51153-6(X), Delacorte Bks. for Young Readers) Random Hse. Children's Bks.
—The Maze Runner. 2010. (Maze Runner Ser.: 1). lib. bdg. 20.85 (978-0-606-15077-4(3), Turtleback) Turtleback Bks.
—The Maze Runner: Virus Letal. 2013. 362p. (YA). pap. 15.99 (978-987-612-565-9(6)) V&R Editoras.
—The Maze Runner & the Scorch Trials, Bks. 1 & 2. collector's ed. 2015. (Maze Runner Ser.). (ENG.). 816p. (YA). (gr. 7). pap. 19.99 (978-0-553-53824-3(1), Delacorte Pr.) Random Hse. Children's Bks.
—The Maze Runner Series, 5 vols. 2016. (ENG.). (YA). (gr. 7). 94.95 (978-1-5247-1434-5(8), Delacorte Pr.) Random Hse. Children's Bks.
—The Maze Runner; The Scorch Trials; The Death Cure; The Kill Order, 4 vols. 2014. (ENG.). (YA). (gr. 7). pap., pap., pap. 39.96 (978-0-385-38889-4(6), Delacorte Pr.) Random Hse. Children's Bks.
—The Maze Runner Trilogy, 3 vols. 2013. (Maze Runner Ser.). (ENG.). (YA). pap., pap., pap. 29.97 (978-0-385-37379-1(1), Ember) Random Hse. Children's Bks.
—A Mutiny in Time. 2012. (Infinity Ring Ser.: Bk. 1). (ENG.). 192p. (J). (gr. 3-7). 12.99 (978-0-545-38696-8(9)); 16.99 (978-0-545-48321-6(2)) Scholastic, Inc.
—A Mutiny in Time. 2015. (Infinity Ring Ser.: 1). lib. bdg. 17.20 (978-0-606-37765-2(4)) Turtleback Bks.
—The Rule of Thoughts. (Mortality Doctrine Ser.). (ENG.). (YA). (gr. 7). 2014. 336p. 18.99 (978-0-385-74141-5(3), Delacorte Pr.)Bk. 2. 2016. 352p. pap. 9.99 (978-0-385-74142-2(1), Ember) Random Hse. Children's Bks.
—The Scorch Trials. (Maze Runner Ser.: 2). (ENG.). (YA). (gr. 7). 2011. 400p. pap. 9.99 (978-0-385-73876-7(5)) 2010. 384p. 18.99 (978-0-385-73875-0(7)) 2015. (Illus.). 384p. 18.99 (978-0-553-53822-9(5)) 2015. 384p. pap. 10.99 (978-0-553-53841-0(1)) Random Hse. Children's Bks. (Delacorte Pr.).
—The Scorch Trials. 2011. (Maze Runner Ser.: 2). lib. bdg. 20.85 (978-0-606-23430-6(6), Turtleback) Turtleback Bks.
—The Void of Mist & Thunder. Dorman, Brandon, illus. 2013. (13th Reality Ser.: 4). (ENG.). 496p. (J). (gr. 3-7). pap. 8.99 (978-1-4424-0873-9(1), Aladdin) Simon & Schuster Children's Publishing.
—The 13th Reality: The Blade of Shattered Hope; the Void of Mist & Thunder. Dorman, Brandon, illus. 2015. (13th Reality Ser.). (ENG.). 976p. (YA). (gr. 7-7). pap. 12.99 (978-1-4814-5702-6(0), Simon & Schuster/Paula Wiseman Bks.) Simon & Schuster/Paula Wiseman Bks.
—The 13th Reality: The Journal of Curious Letters; the Hunt for Dark Infinity. Beus, Bryan, illus. 2015. (13th Reality Ser.). (ENG.). 1024p. (YA). (gr. 7-7). pap. 12.99 (978-1-4814-5315-8(7), Simon & Schuster/Paula Wiseman Bks.) Simon & Schuster/Paula Wiseman Bks.
Davenport, Roger. Wanderer. (ENG.). 2016. 268p. (J). (gr. 6). pap. 8.99 (978-1-5107-0389-6(6)) 2013. 288p. (YA). (gr. 8-12). 16.95 (978-1-62087-541-4(1), 620541) Skyhorse Publishing Co., Inc. (Sky Pony Pr.).
Davey, Owen. Laika: Astronaut Dog. Davey, Owen, illus. 2013. (ENG., Illus.). 32p. (J). (gr. k-3). 15.99 (978-0-7636-6822-8(2), Templar) Candlewick Pr.
David, Charles. Skull in the Birdcage (Knightscares #2, an Epic Fantasy Adventure Series) Knightscares #2. 2003. (Knightscares Ser.: Vol. 2). 208p. (J). per. 5.99 (978-0-9728461-1-0(5), 1222855) Sigil Publishing.
David, Peter. X-Factor - Hell on Earth War, Vol. 20. 2013. (ENG., Illus.). 160p. (YA). (gr. 8-17). pap. 15.99 (978-0-7851-6700-6(5)) Marvel Worldwide, Inc.
David, Peter, et al. The Return of the Worthy. 2007. (Star Trek (Titan Books) Ser.). (ENG., Illus.). 160p. per. 14.95 (978-1-84576-319-0(X), Titan Bks.) Titan Bks. Ltd. GBR. Dist: Penguin Random Hse. LLC.
Davidson, Ellen. When the Third Moon Wanes. 2004. 123p. pap. 19.95 (978-1-4137-2233-8(4)) America Star Bks.
Davidson, Lg. Supernova's Unique Family. 2012. 36p. pap. 20.99 (978-1-4772-6322-8(5)) AuthorHouse.
Davidson, MaryJanice & Alongi, Anthony. The Silver Moon Elm, 3 vols. 2008. (Jennifer Scales Ser.: 3). (ENG.). 288p. (gr. 12-18). 7.99 (978-0-441-01601-3(4), Ace Bks.) Penguin Publishing Group.
Davila, Andrew. Prophecies of the Ancient. 2003. 110p. (YA). pap. 9.95 (978-0-595-26851-1(X)) iUniverse, Inc.
Davis, Adam. Avengers: Age of Ultron: Hulk to the Rescue. 2015. (Passport to Reading Level 2 Ser.). (J). lib. bdg. 13.55 (978-0-606-37215-2(6)) Turtleback Bks.
—Guardians of the Galaxy. 2014. (ENG., Illus.). 24p. (J). (gr. -1-3). pap. 3.99 (978-0-316-29319-8(9)) Little, Brown Bks. for Young Readers.
—Guardians of the Galaxy: Rocket & Groot Fight Back. 2014. (ENG., Illus.). 24p. (J). (gr. -1-3). pap. 4.99 (978-0-316-29323-5(7)) Little, Brown Bks. for Young Readers.
Davis, Alan, et al. The Road to Onslaught. Cruz, Roger et al, illus. 2014. (ENG.). 440p. (J). (gr. 4-17). pap. 39.99 (978-0-7851-8830-8(4)) Marvel Worldwide, Inc.
Davis, Pat. Estelle & the Escape from Mars: A Children's Novel By. 2009. 136p. pap. 10.99 (978-1-4389-5432-5(8)) AuthorHouse.
Davison, Max. Home Collection, Vol. 1. Hebb, Matt & Dalton, Alex, illus. 2016. (ENG.). 112p. (J). (gr. 3-7). pap. 12.99 (978-1-78276-698-8(7)) Titan Bks. Ltd. GBR. Dist: Penguin Random Hse. LLC.
Davroe, A. L. Nexis. 2015. (Tricksters Novel Ser.: 1). (ENG.). 304p. (YA). pap. 9.99 (978-1-63375-017-3(5), 9781633750173) Entangled Publishing, LLC.
Dawson, Delilah S. Hit. 2015. (ENG., Illus.). 336p. (YA). (gr. 9). 17.99 (978-1-4814-2339-7(8), Simon Pulse) Simon Pulse.
—Strike. 2016. (ENG., Illus.). 480p. (YA). (gr. 9). 17.99 (978-1-4814-2342-7(8), Simon Pulse) Simon Pulse.
DC Super Friends. 2013. (DC Super Friends Ser.). (ENG.). 32p. (gr. 1-2). 180.80 (978-1-4342-4856-5(9)) Stone Arch Bks.
de Campi, Alex. Agent Boo, Vol. 1. 2017. (ENG., Illus.). 96p. pap. 4.99 (978-1-59816-802-0(9), 9781598168020) TOKYOPOP, Inc.

De la Cruz, Melissa & Johnston, Michael. Frozen. 2014. (Heart of Dread Ser.: 1). (ENG.). 352p. (YA). (gr. 7). pap. 10.99 (978-0-14-751224-6(7), Speak) Penguin Young Readers Group.
—Golden. 2016. (Heart of Dread Ser.: 3). (ENG.). 272p. (YA). (gr. 7). 17.99 (978-0-399-25756-8(X), G.P. Putnam's Sons Books for Young Readers) Penguin Young Readers Group.
—Stolen Bk. 2: Heart of Dread. 2014. (Heart of Dread Ser.: 2). (ENG.). 304p. (YA). (gr. 7). 17.99 (978-0-399-25755-1(1), G.P. Putnam's Sons Books for Young Readers) Penguin Young Readers Group.
De Saint-Exupéry, Antoine. A Day with the Little Prince. 2003. (Illus.). (J). bds. (978-0-15-204727-6(1), Red Wagon Bks.) Harcourt Children's Bks. CAN. Dist: Harcourt Trade Pubs.
Deconnick, Kelly Sue. Bitch Planet, Volume 2: President Bitch, Vol. 2. 2017. lib. bdg. 26.95 (978-0-606-38898-6(2)) Turtleback Bks.
Deenan, Brendan. Night, Night, Groot. Atkinson, Cale, illus. 2017. (ENG.). 32p. (J). (gr. -1-k). 12.99 (978-1-4847-3282-3(0), Marvel Pr.) Disney Publishing Worldwide.
del Rio, Tania & Staehle, Will. Warren the 13th & the Whispering Woods. 2017. (Warren The 13th Ser.: 2). (ENG., Illus.). 240p. (J). (gr. 5). 16.95 (978-1-59474-929-2(9)) Quirk Bks.
DeLano, Ellie. Traveler. 2017. (ENG., Illus.). 352p. (YA). pap. 10.99 (978-1-250-10040-5(2), 9781250100405) Feiwel & Friends.
DeLonge, Tom & Herbach, Geoff. Strange Times. 2016. (ENG.). 288p. (YA). 17.99 (978-1-943272-21-1(2)) To The Stars...
Denmark, Evangeline. Curio, 1 vol. 2016. (ENG.). 432p. (YA). 17.99 (978-0-310-72966-2(1)) Blink.
Denning, Troy. Tempest. 2006. (Star Wars: Legacy of the Force - Legends Ser.: 3). (ENG.). 400p. mass mkt. 7.99 (978-0-345-47752-1(9), Del Rey) Random House Publishing Group.
Denton, Terry. The Eye of Ulam. 2003. (Storymaze Ser.: Vol. 2). (ENG., Illus.). 132p. (J). (gr. 3-6). pap. 11.99 (978-1-86508-358-2(5)) Allen & Unwin AUS. Dist: Independent Pubs. Group.
—The Ultimate Wave. Denton, Terry, illus. 2003. (Storymaze Ser.: Vol. 1). (ENG., Illus.). 144p. (J). (gr. 3-7). pap. 11.99 (978-1-86508-378-0(X)) Allen & Unwin AUS. Dist: Independent Pubs. Group.
d'Errico, Camilla & Sanders, Scott. Camilla d'Errico's Burn. d'Errico, Camilla, illus. 2009. (ENG., Illus.). 160p. (YA). (gr. 7-18). pap. 9.99 (978-1-4169-7873-2(9), Simon Pulse) Simon Pulse.
Derting, Kimberly. The Countdown. 2016. (Taking Ser.: 3). 384p. (YA). (gr. 9). 17.99 (978-0-06-229366-4(4), HarperTeen) HarperCollins Pubs.
—The Taking. 2014. (Taking Ser.: 1). (ENG.). 368p. (YA). (gr. 9). 17.99 (978-0-06-229360-2(5), HarperTeen) HarperCollins Pubs.
DeStefano, Lauren. Burning Kingdoms. 2015. (Internment Chronicles Ser.: 2). (ENG., Illus.). 320p. (YA). (gr. 7). 19.99 (978-1-4424-8064-3(5), Simon & Schuster Bks. For Young Readers) Simon & Schuster Bks. For Young Readers.
—Fever, 7 vols. 2012. (Chemical Garden Trilogy: Bk. 2). (YA). 102.75 (978-1-4640-1914-2(2)) Recorded Bks., Inc.
—Fever. (Chemical Garden Trilogy Ser.: 2). (ENG.). (YA). (gr. 9). 2013. Illus.). 368p. pap. 9.99 (978-1-4424-0908-8(8)) 2012. 352p. 17.99 (978-1-4424-0907-1(X)) Simon & Schuster Bks. For Young Readers. (Simon & Schuster Bks. For Young Readers).
—Fiebre. (Chemical Garden Trilogy: Bk. 2).Tr. of Fever. (SPA.). 352p. pap. (978-84-96886-28-5(X)) Ediciones Urano S. A.
—The Girl with the Ghost Machine. 2017. (ENG.). 224p. (J). 16.99 (978-1-68119-444-8(9), 9781681194448, Bloomsbury USA Childrens) Bloomsbury Publishing USA.
—Perfect Ruin. White, Teagan, illus. 2013. (Internment Chronicles Ser.: 1). (ENG.). 368p. (YA). (gr. 7). 18.99 (978-1-4424-8061-2(0), Simon & Schuster Bks. For Young Readers) Simon & Schuster Bks. For Young Readers.
—Perfect Ruin. White, Teagan, illus. 2013. (Internment Chronicles Ser.: 1). (ENG.). 368p. (YA). (gr. 7). pap. 10.99 (978-1-4814-1538-5(7)) Simon & Schuster Children's Publishing.
—Sever. 2013. (Chemical Garden Trilogy Ser.: 3). (ENG.). 400p. (YA). (gr. 9). pap. 9.99 (978-1-4424-0910-1(X)) Simon & Schuster.
—Sever. 2013. (Chemical Garden Trilogy Ser.: 3). (ENG.). 384p. (YA). (gr. 9). 17.99 (978-1-4424-0909-5(6), Simon & Schuster Bks. For Young Readers) Simon & Schuster Bks. For Young Readers.
—Wither. (Chemical Garden Ser.: 1). (YA). 1.25 (978-1-4561-2064-1(6)); 256.75 (978-1-4561-2059-7(X)); 90.75 (978-1-4561-2060-3(3)); 2011. 120.75 (978-1-4561-2063-4(8)); 2011. 122.75 (978-1-4561-2061-0(1)) Recorded Bks., Inc.
—Wither. 2011. (Chemical Garden Trilogy Ser.: 1). (ENG.). (YA). (gr. 9). 384p. pap. 10.99 (978-1-4424-0906-4(1)); 368p. 19.99 (978-1-4424-0905-7(3)) Simon & Schuster Bks. For Young Readers. (Simon & Schuster Bks. For Young Readers).
Diamand, Emily. Raiders' Ransom. 2009. (Raiders' Ransom Ser.: 1). (ENG.). 368p. (J). (gr. 3-7). 17.99 (978-0-545-14297-7(0)) Scholastic, Inc.
Diamond, Laura. Endure. 2013. 268p. pap. 11.99 (978-1-940223-45-2(8)) Etopia Pr.
Diaz, Stephanie. Evolution. 2015. (Extraction Ser.: 3). (ENG.). 320p. (YA). (gr. 7). 21.99 (978-1-250-04126-5(0), 9781250041265, St. Martin's Griffin) St. Martin's Pr.
—Extraction. 2014. (Extraction Ser.: 1). (ENG.). 416p. (YA). (gr. 7-12). 18.99 (978-1-250-04117-3(1), 9781250041173, St. Martin's Griffin) St. Martin's Pr.
—Rebellion. 2015. (Extraction Ser.: 2). (ENG.). 336p. (YA). (gr. 7). 19.99 (978-1-250-04125-8(2), 9781250041258, St. Martin's Griffin) St. Martin's Pr.
Dick, Philip K. The Gun. 2011. 26p. pap. 6.95 (978-1-60664-563-5(3)) Rodgers, Alan Bks.
Dietrich, Cale. The Love Interest. 2017. (ENG.). 384p. (YA). 17.99 (978-1-250-10713-8(X), 9781250107138) Feiwel & Friends.
Diggs, Dylan. Palladium: Second Contact. 2006. (J). mass mkt. 3.80 (978-1-886366-13-8(6), 5,000) Sights Productions.

—Palladium: Trust No One. 2006. (J). mass mkt. 3.80 *(978-1-886366-14-5(4))* Sights Productions.

DiGuardo, Maggie & Leventis, Kelly. Celly. 2012. (J). 14.95 *(978-1-937406-17-2(2))* Mascot Bks., Inc.

Dinn, Philip & Jones, Andy. Peg Bearskin. Cohen, Elly, illus. 2003. (ENG.). 32p. (J). pap. *(978-0-9688712-7-0(5))* Running the Goat.

Disney Book Group. Miles from Tomorrowland Journey to the Frozen Planet. Disney Storybook Art Team, illus. 2015. (ENG.). 80p. (J). (gr. -1-k). pap. 4.99 *(978-1-4847-1550-5(0))* Disney Pr.

—Miles from Tomorrowland Spaceship Invader. Disney Storybook Art Team, illus. 2016. (ENG.). 24p. (J). (gr. -1-k). pap. 4.99 *(978-1-4847-1911-4(5))* Disney Pr.

—Rebel Rising. 2017. (ENG.). 416p. (YA). (gr. 7-12). 17.99 *(978-1-4847-8083-1(3),* Disney Lucasfilm Press) Disney Publishing Worldwide.

—Star Wars: The Original Trilogy Stories. 2015. (Storybook Collection). (ENG.). 304p. (J). (gr. -1-k). 16.99 *(978-1-4847-0471-4(1),* Disney Lucasfilm Press) Disney Publishing Worldwide.

—Star Wars Bounty Hunt: Lift-The-Flap Book. 2017. (ENG.). 18p. (J). (gr. 1-3). 12.99 ***(978-1-368-00305-6(2),*** Disney Lucasfilm Press) Disney Publishing Worldwide.

—Star Wars the Force Awakens. 2016. (Read-Along Storybook & CD Ser.). (ENG.). 32p. (J). (gr. 1-3). pap. 6.99 *(978-1-4847-3149-9(2))* Disney Pr.

—Trapped in the Death Star! 2016. (Star Wars: World of Reading Ser.). (J). lib. bdg. 14.75 ***(978-0-606-39174-0(6))*** Turtleback Bks.

—World of Reading Star Wars: Death Star Battle. 2016. (ENG.). 32p. (J). (gr. 1-3). pap. 3.99 *(978-1-4847-3148-2(4),* Disney Lucasfilm Press) Disney Publishing Worldwide.

—World of Reading Star Wars Chaos at the Castle. 2016. (ENG.). 32p. (J). (gr. 1-3). pap. 3.99 *(978-1-4847-7410-6(8),* Disney Lucasfilm Press) Disney Publishing Worldwide.

—World of Reading Star Wars the Fight in the Forest (Level 2) 2017. (World of Reading Ser.). (ENG.). 32p. (J). (gr. 1-3). pap. 4.99 *(978-1-4847-0511-7(4),* Disney Lucasfilm Press) Disney Publishing Worldwide.

—World of Reading Star Wars Trapped in the Death Star! (Level 1) 2016. (World of Reading Ser.). (ENG.). 32p. (J). (gr. 1-3). pap. 4.99 *(978-1-4847-0510-0(6),* Disney Lucasfilm Press) Disney Publishing Worldwide.

Disney Book Group & Fry, Jason. Star Wars Rogue One Rebel Dossier. 2016. (ENG.). 64p. (J). (gr. 3-7). 12.99 *(978-1-4847-8079-4(5),* Disney Lucasfilm Press) Disney Publishing Worldwide.

Disney Book Group & Glass, Calliope. Star Wars Obi-1,2,3. Cook, Katie, illus. 2017. (ENG.). 48p. (J). (gr. -1-k). 12.99 *(978-1-4847-6812-9(4),* Disney Lucasfilm Press) Disney Publishing Worldwide.

Disney Book Group & LucasFilm Press Staff. Finn & Rey Escape! Rood, Brian, illus. 2015. (ENG.). 24p. (J). (gr. 1-3). pap. 4.99 *(978-1-4847-0479-0(7))* Disney Pr.

Disney Book Group & Rucka, Greg. Guardians of the Whills. 2017. (ENG.). 240p. (J). (gr. 5-9). 12.99 *(978-1-4847-8081-7(7),* Disney Lucasfilm Press) Disney Publishing Worldwide.

Disney Book Group, et al. Death Star Battle. 2016. (Star Wars: World of Reading Ser.). (J). lib. bdg. 13.55 *(978-0-606-37540-5(6))* Turtleback Bks.

—Han & Chewie Return! Rood, Brian, illus. 2015. (ENG.). 24p. (J). (gr. 1-3). pap. 3.99 *(978-1-4847-0478-3(9))* Disney Pr.

—Star vs. the Forces of Evil Star & Marco's Guide to Mastering Every Dimension. Plourde, Cindy & Taylor, Devin, illus. 2017. (Guide to Life Ser.). (ENG.). 192p. (J). (gr. 3-7). 12.99 *(978-1-4847-7419-9(1))* Disney Pr.

—World of Reading Star Wars. Rood, Brian, illus. 2015. (World of Reading Ser.). (ENG.). 32p. (J). (gr. 1-3). pap. 3.99 *(978-1-4847-0480-6(0))* Disney Pr.

Disney Book Group Staff. Star Wars: Ewoks Join the Fight, Level 1. 2015. (ENG.). 32p. (J). (gr. 1-3). pap. 3.99 *(978-1-4847-0548-3(3),* Disney Lucasfilm Press) Disney Publishing Worldwide.

—Star Wars: the Empire Strikes Back Read-Along Storybook & CD. 2015. (Read-Along Storybook & CD Ser.). (ENG., Illus.). 32p. (J). (gr. 1-3). pap. 6.99 *(978-1-4847-0686-2(2),* Disney Lucasfilm Press) Disney Publishing Worldwide.

—World of Reading Avengers Boxed Set: Level 1 - Purchase Includes Marvel EBook! Disney Book Group Staff, illus. 2015. (World of Reading Ser.: 2). (ENG., Illus.). 192p. (J). (gr. 1-3). pap. 12.99 *(978-1-4847-0438-7(X),* Marvel Pr.) Disney Publishing Worldwide.

—World of Reading Star Wars Rescue from Jabba's Palace: Level 2. 2015. (World of Reading Ser.). (ENG., Illus.). 32p. (J). (gr. 1-3). pap. 3.99 *(978-1-4847-0501-8(7),* Disney Lucasfilm Press) Disney Publishing Worldwide.

Disney Book Group Staff & DiTerlizzi, Tony. The Adventures of Luke Skywalker, Jedi Knight. McQuarrie, Ralph, illus. 2014. (ENG.). 64p. (J). (gr. 1-3). 19.99 *(978-1-4847-0668-8(4))* Disney Pr.

Disney Book Group Staff & Heddle, Jennifer. Ezra & the Pilot, Level 2. 2014. (World of Reading Ser.). (ENG., Illus.). 32p. (J). (gr. 1-3). pap. 3.99 *(978-1-4847-0486-8(X))* Disney Pr.

—World of Reading Star Wars Rebels. 2015. (World of Reading Ser.). (ENG.). 32p. (J). (gr. 1-3). pap. 3.99 *(978-1-4847-0491-2(6),* Disney Lucasfilm Press) Disney Publishing Worldwide.

Disney Book Group Staff & Kogge, Michael. The Rebellion Begins. 2014. (ENG., Illus.). 176p. (J). (gr. 3-7). pap. 6.99 *(978-1-4847-1475-1(X))* Disney Pr.

—Rise of the Rebels. 2014. (ENG., Illus.). 128p. (J). (gr. 3-7). pap. 5.99 *(978-1-4847-0270-3(0))* Disney Pr.

Disney Book Group Staff & Michaels, Kay. Star Wars Rebels. 2014. (Star Wars: World of Reading Ser.). (J). lib. bdg. 13.55 *(978-0-606-35282-6(1))* Turtleback Bks.

Disney Book Group Staff & Miller, Bryan Q. Disney Comics Tomorrowland. Jones, Kelley, illus. 2014. (Disney Original Graphic Novel Ser.: 1). (ENG.). 176p. (J). (gr. 3-7). pap. 12.99 *(978-1-4231-6229-2(3))* Disney Pr.

Disney Book Group Staff & Peterson, Scott. Meet the Marvel Super Heroes: Includes a Poster of Your Favorite Super Heroes! 2013. (ENG., Illus.). 144p. (J). (gr. 1-3). 12.99 *(978-1-4231-6142-4(4))* Marvel Worldwide, Inc.

Disney Book Group Staff & Rusu, Meredith. Star Wars Rebels: the Inquisitor's Trap. 2014. (ENG.). 24p. (J). (gr. 1-3). pap. 4.99 *(978-1-4847-0468-4(1))* Disney Pr.

Disney Book Group Staff & Rusu, Meredith L. Star Wars - Rebels. 2014. (Read-Along Storybook & CD Ser.). (ENG.). 32p. (J). (gr. 1-3). pap. 6.99 *(978-1-4847-0504-9(1))* Disney Pr.

Disney Book Group Staff & Schaefer, Elizabeth A. Chopper Saves the Day. 2014. (ENG.). 24p. (J). (gr. 1-3). pap. 4.99 *(978-1-4847-0273-4(5))* Disney Pr.

Disney Book Group Staff & Siglain, Michael. Escape from Darth Vader, Level 1. Disney Book Group Staff & Roux, Stephane, illus. 2014. (ENG.). 32p. (J). (gr. 1-3). pap. 3.99 *(978-1-4847-0500-1(9))* Disney Pr.

Disney Book Group Staff & Thornton, Randy. Star Wars: a New Hope Read-Along Storybook & CD. Rood, Brian, illus. 2015. (Read-Along Storybook & CD Ser.). (ENG.). 32p. (J). (gr. 1-3). pap. 6.99 *(978-1-4847-0667-1(6),* Disney Lucasfilm Press) Disney Publishing Worldwide.

Disney Book Group Staff & Windham, Ryder. Ezra's Gamble. 2014. (ENG.). 160p. (J). (gr. 3-7). pap. 6.99 *(978-1-4847-0272-7(7))* Disney Pr.

Disney Book Group Staff, et al. Star Wars Rebels Always Bet on Chopper: Level 1. 2015. (World of Reading Ser.). (ENG., Illus.). 32p. (J). (gr. 1-3). pap. 3.99 *(978-1-4847-0560-5(2),* Disney Lucasfilm Press) Disney Publishing Worldwide.

—Star Wars the Force Awakens: Before the Awakening. Noto, Phil, illus. 2015. (ENG.). 224p. (J). (gr. 3-7). 12.99 *(978-1-4847-2822-2(X))* Disney Pr.

—Zeb to the Rescue, Level 1. 2014. (World of Reading Ser.). (ENG., Illus.). 32p. (J). (gr. 1-3). pap. 3.99 *(978-1-4847-0271-0(9))* Disney Pr.

Disney Press. Avengers: Battle with Ultron. 2015. (Marvel World of Reading Level 2 Ser.). (J). lib. bdg. 13.55 *(978-0-606-36904-6(X))* Turtleback Bks.

Disney Press, et al. Star Wars Rebels: Kanan's Jedi Training. 2015. (Star Wars: World of Reading Ser.). (J). lib. bdg. 13.55 *(978-0-606-36911-4(2))* Turtleback Bks.

Disney Press Editors. Avengers: The New Team. 2015. (Marvel World of Reading Level 1 Ser.). (J). lib. bdg. 13.55 *(978-0-606-36903-9(1))* Turtleback Bks.

—Star Wars Rebels: Always Bet on Chopper. 2015. (Star Wars: World of Reading Ser.). (Illus.). 32p. (J). lib. bdg. 13.55 *(978-0-606-36910-7(4))* Turtleback Bks.

—Star Wars Rebels: Hera's Phantom Flight. 2015. (Star Wars: World of Reading Ser.). (J). lib. bdg. 13.55 *(978-0-606-36909-1(0))* Turtleback Bks.

—Use the Force! 2015. (Star Wars: World of Reading Ser.). (J). lib. bdg. 13.55 *(978-0-606-35923-8(0))* Turtleback Bks.

Disney Press Staff & Heddle, Jennifer. Sabine's Art Attack. 2015. (Star Wars: World of Reading Ser.). (J). lib. bdg. 13.55 *(978-0-606-35928-3(1))* Turtleback Bks.

Disney Press Staff & Rusu, Meredith. The Inquisitor's Trap. 2014. (Star Wars Rebels 8x8 Ser.). (J). lib. bdg. 14.75 *(978-0-606-35926-9(5))* Turtleback Bks.

DiTerlizzi, Tony. The Battle for WondLa. DiTerlizzi, Tony, illus. 2014. (Search for WondLa Ser.: 3). (ENG., Illus.). 496p. (J). (gr. 5). 17.99 *(978-1-4169-8314-9(7),* Simon & Schuster Bks. For Young Readers) Simon & Schuster Bks. For Young Readers.

—A Hero for WondLa, 13 vols. 2012. (Search for Wondra Ser.: 2). (J). 110.75 *(978-1-4640-3934-8(8))* Recorded Bks., Inc.

—A Hero for WondLa. DiTerlizzi, Tony, illus. (Search for WondLa Ser.: 2). (ENG., Illus.). (J). (gr. 5). 2013. 480p. pap. 8.99 *(978-1-4169-8313-2(9))* 2012. 464p. 17.99 *(978-1-4169-8312-5(0))* Simon & Schuster Bks. For Young Readers. (Simon & Schuster Bks. For Young Readers).

—Jimmy Zangwow's Out-of-This-World Moon-Pie Adventure. DiTerlizzi, Tony, illus. 2003. (ENG., Illus.). 40p. (J). (gr. k-3). 7.99 *(978-0-689-85563-4(X),* Simon & Schuster Bks. For Young Readers) Simon & Schuster Bks. For Young Readers.

—The Search for WondLa. DiTerlizzi, Tony, illus. (Search for WondLa Ser.: 1). (ENG., Illus.). (J). (gr. 5). 2012. 512p. pap. 12.99 *(978-1-4169-8311-8(2))* 2010. 496p. 17.99 *(978-1-4169-8310-1(4))* Simon & Schuster Bks. For Young Readers. (Simon & Schuster Bks. For Young Readers).

DiTerlizzi, Tony, et al. El Arbol Metálico. Abreu, Carlos, tr. 2007. (Escritura desatada Ser.). (SPA., Illus.). 116p. (J). (gr. 4-7). 13.95 *(978-84-666-1658-4(6))* Ediciones B ESP. Dist: Spanish Pubs., LLC.

Dixon, Chuck. Perdition's Gate, Vol. 6. Eaglesham, Dale et al, illus. 2004. (Sigil Ser.: Vol. 6). 160p. (YA). pap. 15.95 *(978-1-59314-048-9(7))* CrossGeneration Comics, Inc.

—Resurrection, Vol. 5. Cariello, Sergio et al, illus. 2004. (Crux Ser.: Vol. 5). 160p. (YA). pap. 15.95 *(978-1-59314-053-3(3))* CrossGeneration Comics, Inc.

Dixon, John. Phoenix Island. 2014. (ENG.). 320p. pap. 11.99 *(978-1-4767-3865-9(3),* Gallery Bks.) Gallery Bks.

Dobson, Carol Anne. Freedom. 2013. 130p. pap. *(978-0-9558324-3-7(8))* Appledrane Bks.

Dockter, Debra. Deadly Design. 2015. (ENG.). 368p. (YA). (gr. 7). 17.99 *(978-0-399-17105-5(3),* G.P. Putnam's Sons Books for Young Readers) Penguin Young Readers Group.

Doctorow, Cory. For the Win. 2010. (ENG.). 480p. (YA). (gr. 8-13). 17.99 *(978-0-7653-2216-6(1),* 9780765322166, Tor Teen) Doherty, Tom Assocs., LLC.

—Pirate Cinema. 2013. (ENG.). 384p. (YA). (gr. 7). pap. 9.99 *(978-0-7653-2909-7(3),* 9780765329097, Tor Teen) Doherty, Tom Assocs., LLC.

Doeden, Matt. Can You Survive an Artificial Intelligence Uprising? An Interactive Doomsday Adventure. Fisher-Johnson, Paul, illus. 2016. (You Choose: Doomsday Ser.). (ENG.). 112p. (gr. 3-4). lib. bdg. 31.99 *(978-1-4914-8107-3(2),* You Choose Bks.) Capstone Press of Coughlan Cos.

—Can You Survive an Asteroid Strike? An Interactive Doomsday Adventure. Davidson, Paul, illus. 2016. (You Choose: Doomsday Ser.). (ENG.). 112p. (gr. 3-4). lib. bdg. 31.99 *(978-1-4914-8109-7(9),* You Choose Bks.) Capstone Press of Coughlan Cos.

Doeden, Matt, et al. You Choose: Doomsday. 2016. (You Choose: Doomsday Ser.). (ENG.). 112p. (gr. 3-4). 255.92 *(978-1-4914-8148-6(X),* You Choose Bks.) Capstone Press of Coughlan Cos.

Donbavand, Tommy. Cyber Shock. Gibbons, Alan, ed. 2014. (Read On Ser.). (ENG., Illus.). 640p. (YA). (gr. 7). 9.99 *(978-0-00-746473-9(8))* HarperCollins Pubs. Ltd. GBR. Dist: Independent Pubs. Group.

Doors, Mason. The I T I P. 2012. 36p. pap. 20.99 *(978-1-4772-2046-7(1))* AuthorHouse.

Doran, Colleen. A Distant Soil: the Gathering TP: The Gathering TP. 2013. (Illus.). 240p. (YA). pap. 16.99 *(978-1-60706-689-7(0))* Image Comics.

Dorling Kindersley Publishing Staff. Attack of the Clones. 2013. (LEGO Star Wars DK Reader Ser.). lib. bdg. 13.55 *(978-0-606-32111-2(X),* Turtleback) Turtleback Bks.

—DK Adventures: Star Wars: Jedi Battles: Star Wars: Jedi Battles. 2013. (DK Adventures Ser.). (ENG.). 128p. (J). (gr. 3-7). 16.99 *(978-1-4654-1813-5(X),* DK Children) Dorling Kindersley Publishing, Inc.

—DK Adventures: Star Wars: Sith Wars: Star Wars: Sith Wars. 2013. (DK Adventures Ser.). (ENG., Illus.). 128p. (J). (gr. 3-7). 16.99 *(978-1-4654-1814-2(8),* DK Children) Dorling Kindersley Publishing, Inc.

—Don't Wake the Zillo Beast! 2011. (DK Readers Ser.). (ENG.). 32p. (J). (gr. -1-1). 3.99 *(978-0-7566-8279-8(7),* DK Children) Dorling Kindersley Publishing, Inc.

—Even Droids Need Friends! 2013. (Star Wars DK Readers Pre-Level Ser.). lib. bdg. 13.55 *(978-0-606-31478-7(4),* Turtleback) Turtleback Bks.

—Jedi Battles. 2013. (DK Adventures Ser.). (ENG., Illus.). 128p. (J). (gr. 3-7). pap. 5.99 *(978-1-4654-1724-4(9),* DK Children) Dorling Kindersley Publishing, Inc.

—The Lego(r) Batman. 2016. (ENG.). 64p. (J). (gr. 2-5). 12.99 *(978-1-4654-5633-5(3),* DK Children) Dorling Kindersley Publishing, Inc.

—Masters of the Force. 2012. (Star Wars: the Clone Wars DK Readers Ser.). lib. bdg. 13.55 *(978-0-606-31473-2(3),* Turtleback) Turtleback Bks.

—Meet the Rebels. 2014. (DK Readers Ser.). (ENG.). 32p. (J). (gr. 1-3). 14.99 *(978-1-4654-2268-2(4));* pap. 3.99 *(978-1-4654-2269-9(2))* Dorling Kindersley Publishing, Inc. (DK Children).

—Rogue One. 2016. (Star Wars DK Readers Level 4 Ser.). lib. bdg. 13.55 *(978-0-606-39359-1(5))* Turtleback Bks.

—Secrets of the Rebels. 2015. (Ultimate Sticker Collections). (ENG.). 96p. (J). (gr. 1-4). pap. 12.99 *(978-1-4654-3593-4(X),* DK Children) Dorling Kindersley Publishing, Inc.

—Sith Wars. 2013. (DK Adventures Ser.). (ENG., Illus.). 128p. (J). (gr. 3-7). pap. 5.99 *(978-1-4654-1725-1(7),* DK Children) Dorling Kindersley Publishing, Inc.

—The Clone Wars Character Encyclopedia. 2010. (ENG., Illus.). 208p. (J). (gr. 3-7). 16.99 *(978-0-7566-6308-7(3),* DK Children) Dorling Kindersley Publishing, Inc.

—Who Saved the Galaxy? 2012. (DK Readers Ser.). (ENG., Illus.). 32p. (J). (gr. k-4). pap. 3.99 *(978-0-7566-9808-9(1),* DK Children) Dorling Kindersley Publishing, Inc.

Dorling Kindersley Publishing Staff & Beecroft, Simon. Ackbar's Underwater Army, Level 3. 2012. (DK Readers Ser.). (ENG.). 48p. (J). (gr. 2-4). 3.99 *(978-0-7566-9247-6(4),* DK Children) Dorling Kindersley Publishing, Inc.

—Anakin in Action! 2008. (DK Readers Ser.). (ENG.). 32p. (J). (gr. 1-3). pap. 3.99 *(978-0-7566-4031-6(8),* DK Children) Dorling Kindersley Publishing, Inc.

—Even Droids Need Friends. 2013. (DK Readers Ser.). (ENG.). 32p. (J). (gr. -1-1). pap. 3.99 *(978-1-4654-0182-3(2),* DK Children) Dorling Kindersley Publishing, Inc.

—Even Droids Need Friends! 2013. (DK Readers Ser.). (ENG.). 32p. (J). (gr. -1-1). 14.99 *(978-1-4654-0183-0(0),* DK Children) Dorling Kindersley Publishing, Inc.

—Watch Out for Jabba the Hutt!, Level 1. 2008. (DK Readers Ser.). (ENG.). 32p. (J). (gr. k-2). pap. 3.99 *(978-0-7566-4083-5(0),* DK Children) Dorling Kindersley Publishing, Inc.

Dorling Kindersley Publishing Staff & Fentiman, David. Fight the Empire! 2015. (DK Readers Ser.). (ENG.). 64p. (J). (gr. 2-4). pap. 3.99 *(978-1-4654-1989-7(6),* DK Children) Dorling Kindersley Publishing, Inc.

—Fight the Empire. 2015. (DK Readers Ser.). (ENG.). 64p. (J). (gr. 2-4). 14.99 *(978-1-4654-1988-0(8),* DK Children) Dorling Kindersley Publishing, Inc.

Dorling Kindersley Publishing Staff & Fry, Jason. Rogue One - Secret Mission. 2016. (DK Readers Ser.). (ENG.). 96p. (J). (gr. 3-7). pap. 3.99 *(978-1-4654-5264-1(8),* DK Children) Dorling Kindersley Publishing, Inc.

Dorling Kindersley Publishing Staff & Hibbert, Clare. Boba Fett Jedi Hunter, Level 2. 2011. (DK Readers Ser.). (ENG.). 32p. (J). (gr. 1-3). 3.99 *(978-0-7566-8281-1(9),* DK Children) Dorling Kindersley Publishing, Inc.

—Clone Troopers in Action. 2010. (DK Readers Ser.). (ENG.). 32p. (J). (gr. 1-3). 3.99 *(978-0-7566-6691-0(0),* DK Children) Dorling Kindersley Publishing, Inc.

—Tatooine Adventures, Level 1. 2011. (DK Readers Ser.). (ENG.). 48p. (J). (gr. k-4). 3.99 *(978-0-7566-7128-0(0),* DK Children) Dorling Kindersley Publishing, Inc.

Dorling Kindersley Publishing Staff & Hidalgo, Pablo. Rogue One - The Ultimate Visual Guide. 2016. (ENG., Illus.). 200p. (J). (gr. 4-7). 30.00 *(978-1-4654-5263-4(X),* DK Children) Dorling Kindersley Publishing, Inc.

Dorling Kindersley Publishing Staff & Kent, Lindsay. The Adventures of Han Solo, Level 2. 2011. (DK Readers Ser.). (ENG.). 32p. (J). (gr. -1-1). 3.99 *(978-0-7566-8252-1(5),* DK Children) Dorling Kindersley Publishing, Inc.

Dorling Kindersley Publishing Staff & Khatreja, Himani. DK Readers L2: LEGO Star Wars: Free the Galaxy. 2015. (DK Readers Ser.). (ENG.). 48p. (J). (gr. k-4). pap. 3.99 *(978-1-4654-3793-8(2),* DK Children) Dorling Kindersley Publishing, Inc.

Dorling Kindersley Publishing Staff & Last, Shari. The Adventures of C-3PO. 2014. (DK Readers Ser.). (ENG.). 32p. (J). (gr. 1-3). 14.99 *(978-1-4654-1683-4(8),* DK Children) Dorling Kindersley Publishing, Inc.

Dorling Kindersley Publishing Staff & Nesworthy, Lauren. Rebels: Darth Vader, Jedi Hunter! 2016. (DK Readers Ser.). (ENG., Illus.). 48p. (J). (gr. 1-3). pap. 3.99 *(978-1-4654-5212-2(5),* DK Children) Dorling Kindersley Publishing, Inc.

Dorling Kindersley Publishing Staff & Newsworthy, Lauren. Rebel Power! 2015. (Star Wars DK Readers Level 2 Ser.). lib. bdg. 13.55 *(978-0-606-36925-1(2))* Turtleback Bks.

Dorling Kindersley Publishing Staff & Scott, Heather. Stand Aside - Bounty Hunters! 2009. (DK Readers Ser.). (ENG.). 32p. (J). (gr. 1-3). 3.99 *(978-0-7566-5775-8(X),* DK Children) Dorling Kindersley Publishing, Inc.

Dorling Kindersley Publishing Staff & Stock, Lisa. DK Readers L2: Star Wars: Rey to the Rescue! 2017. (DK Readers Ser.). (ENG.). 48p. (J). (gr. k-2). pap. 3.99 *(978-1-4654-5580-2(9),* DK Children) Dorling Kindersley Publishing, Inc.

Dorling Kindersley Publishing Staff & Wallace, Daniel. Battle for the Galaxy. 2011. (ENG., Illus.). 96p. (J). (gr. 2-5). 12.99 *(978-0-7566-7315-4(1),* DK Children) Dorling Kindersley Publishing, Inc.

Dorling Kindersley Publishing Staff, et al. The Clone Wars - Pirates... & Worse! 2009. (DK Readers Ser.). (ENG., Illus.). 32p. (J). (gr. k-2). 3.99 *(978-0-7566-5773-4(3),* DK Children) Dorling Kindersley Publishing, Inc.

—Darth Maul Sith Apprentice. 2012. (DK Readers Ser.). (ENG.). 48p. (J). (gr. 3-7). 3.99 *(978-0-7566-8866-0(3),* DK Children) Dorling Kindersley Publishing, Inc.

—Planets in Peril. 2010. (DK Readers Ser.). (ENG.). 48p. (J). (gr. 3-7). pap. 3.99 *(978-0-7566-6690-3(2),* DK Children) Dorling Kindersley Publishing, Inc.

—Star Wars Character Encyclopedia, Updated & Expanded. 2016. (ENG., Illus.). 224p. (J). (gr. 2-5). 16.99 *(978-1-4654-4885-9(3),* DK Children) Dorling Kindersley Publishing, Inc.

dos Santos, Steven. The Culling. 2013. (Torch Keeper Ser.: 1). (ENG.). 432p. (YA). pap. 9.99 *(978-0-7387-3537-5(X),* Flux) North Star Editions.

—The Sowing. 2014. (Torch Keeper Ser.: 2). (ENG.). 408p. (YA). pap. 9.99 *(978-0-7387-3540-5(X),* Flux) North Star Editions.

Douglas, Helen. After Eden. 2013. (ENG.). 288p. (YA). (gr. 7). 17.99 *(978-1-61963-130-4(X),* 9781619631304, Bloomsbury USA Childrens) Bloomsbury Publishing USA.

—Chasing Stars. 2016. (ENG.). 352p. (YA). 17.99 *(978-1-61963-410-7(4),* 9781619634107, Bloomsbury USA Childrens) Bloomsbury Publishing USA.

Dowell, Frances O'Roark. Phineas L. Macguire... Blasts Off! McDaniels, Preston, illus. 2008. (From the Highly Scientific Notebooks of Phineas L. MacGuire Ser.). (ENG.). 208p. (J). (gr. 3-7). 16.99 *(978-1-4169-2689-4(5),* Atheneum Bks. for Young Readers) Simon & Schuster Children's Publishing.

—Phineas L. MacGuire... Gets Slimed! McDaniels, Preston, illus. l.t. ed. 2008. (From the Highly Scientific Notebooks of Phineas L. MacGuire Ser.). 159p. (J). (gr. 3-7). 22.95 *(978-1-4104-0440-4(4))* Thorndike Pr.

Dower, Laura. The Beast with 1000 Eyes. Schlafman, Dave, illus. 2009. (Monster Squad Ser.: 3). (ENG.). 144p. (J). (gr. 3-7). pap. 5.99 *(978-0-448-44914-2(5),* Grosset & Dunlap) Penguin Young Readers Group.

—Kiki Takes the Cake. Lazuli, Lilly, illus. 2016. (Dessert Diaries). (ENG.). 160p. (gr. 4-5). lib. bdg. 26.65 *(978-1-4965-3120-9(5))* Stone Arch Bks.

The Dragon Compass: Individual Title Six-Packs. (Bookweb Ser.). 32p. (gr. 6-18). 34.00 *(978-0-7578-0898-2(0))* Rigby Education.

Drake, Raelyn. Realm of Mystics. 2017. (Level Up Ser.). (ENG.). (YA). (gr. 6-12). 120p. pap. 7.99 ***(978-1-5124-5359-1(5));*** lib. bdg. 26.65 ***(978-1-5124-3989-2(4))*** Lerner Publishing Group. (Darby Creek).

Driza, Debra. Mila 2.0. 2013. (Mila 2. 0 Ser.: 1). (ENG.). 480p. (YA). (gr. 8). 17.99 *(978-0-06-209036-2(4),* Tegen, Katherine Bks) HarperCollins Pubs.

—Mila 2.0: Redemption. 2016. (Mila 2. 0 Ser.: 3). (ENG.). 416p. (YA). (gr. 8). 17.99 *(978-0-06-209042-3(9),* Tegen, Katherine Bks) HarperCollins Pubs.

Duane, Diane. High Wizardry, 7 vols. (Young Wizards Ser.: 3). (J). 2006. 90.75 *(978-1-4025-9917-0(X))* 2004. 93.75 *(978-1-4025-8355-1(9))* Recorded Bks., Inc.

—Wizard's Holiday. 2005. (Young Wizards Ser.: 7). (ENG.). 448p. (J). (gr. 5-7). pap. 8.99 *(978-0-15-205207-2(0))* Houghton Mifflin Harcourt Publishing Co.

Ducie, Joe. Crystal Force. 2016. (ENG.). 288p. (YA). (gr. 7). pap. 9.99 *(978-1-4714-0455-9(2))* Bonnier Publishing GBR. Dist: Independent Pubs. Group.

Duckro, Rebecca S. Adventures of Charlie KeeperTechnobrat. 2006. 156p. per. 12.95 *(978-0-595-40498-8(7))* iUniverse, Inc.

Duddle, Jonny. King of Space. Duddle, Jonny, illus. 2013. (ENG., Illus.). 44p. (J). (gr. -1-2). 15.99 *(978-0-7636-6435-0(9),* Templar) Candlewick Pr.

Duey, Kathleen. Time Soldiers, Set. Epstein, Eugene, illus. Gould, Robert, photos by. gif. ed. 2003. (Time Soldiers Ser.). (ENG.). 144p. (J). (gr. k-2). 32.95 *(978-1-929945-23-8(X))* Big Guy Bks., Inc.

Duey, Kathleen & Gould, Robert. Rex. Windler-Cheren, Victoria, tr. Epstein, Eugene, illus. Gould, Robert, photos by. 2003. (Time Soldiers Ser.: Bk. 1). (SPA & ENG.). 48p. (J). (gr. k-4). pap. 8.95 *(978-1-929945-35-1(3))* Big Guy Bks., Inc.

Duffett-Smith, James. Stella & Steve Travel Through Space! Straker, Bethany, illus. 2014. (ENG.). 32p. (J). (gr. -1-k). 14.95 *(978-1-62873-815-5(4),* Sky Pony Pr.) Skyhorse Publishing Co., Inc.

Duggan, Gerry. Nova, Vol. 3. Baldeon, David, illus. 2014. (ENG.). 152p. (J). (gr. 4-17). pap. 16.99 *(978-0-7851-8957-2(2))* Marvel Worldwide, Inc.

Duncan, Alexandra. Blight. 2017. 400p. (YA). (gr. 8). 17.99 *(978-0-06-239699-0(4),* Greenwillow Bks.) HarperCollins Pubs.

—Salvage. (Salvage Ser.: 1). (ENG.). (YA). (gr. 8). 2015. 544p. pap. 9.99 *(978-0-06-222015-8(2))* 2014. 528p. 17.99 *(978-0-06-222014-1(4))* HarperCollins Pubs. (Greenwillow Bks.).

—Sound. 2015. (Salvage Ser.: 2). (ENG.). 496p. (YA). (gr. 8). 17.99 *(978-0-06-222017-2(9),* Greenwillow Bks.) HarperCollins Pubs.

Duncan Gurley, Ann. Esbe's Halo. 2009. 108p. (J). pap. 15.95 *(978-1-4327-3453-4(9))* Outskirts Pr., Inc.

Dunkle, Clare B. The Walls Have Eyes. 2009. (ENG.). 240p. (YA). (gr. 7). 16.99 *(978-1-4169-5379-1(5),* Atheneum Bks. for Young Readers) Simon & Schuster Children's Publishing.

Dunn, Joeming. The Eyes: A Graphic Novel Tour, 1 vol. Espinosa, Rod, illus. 2009. (Graphic Body Ser.). (ENG.). 32p. (J). (gr. 3-6). 28.50 *(978-1-60270-684-2(0))* ABDO Publishing Co.

S

—The Kidneys: A Graphic Novel Tour, 1 vol. Espinosa, Rod, illus. 2009. (Graphic Body Ser.). (ENG.). 32p. (J). (gr. 3-6). 28.50 (978-1-60270-686-6(7)) ABDO Publishing Co.
—The Liver: A Graphic Novel Tour, 1 vol. Espinosa, Rod, illus. 2009. (Graphic Body Ser.). (ENG.). 32p. (J). (gr. 3-6). 28.50 (978-1-60270-687-3(5)) ABDO Publishing Co.
—The Lungs: A Graphic Novel Tour, 1 vol. Espinosa, Rod, illus. 2009. (Graphic Body Ser.). (ENG.). 32p. (J). (gr. 3-6). 28.50 (978-1-60270-688-0(3)) ABDO Publishing Co.
Dunn, Joeming & Espinosa, Rod. The Brain: A Graphic Novel Tour, 1 vol. Espinosa, Rod, illus. 2009. (Graphic Body Ser.). (ENG., Illus.). 32p. (J). (gr. 3-6). 28.50 (978-1-60270-683-5(2)) ABDO Publishing Co.
—The Heart: A Graphic Novel Tour, 1 vol. Espinosa, Rod, illus. 2009. (Graphic Body Ser.). (ENG., Illus.). 32p. (J). (gr. 3-6). 28.50 (978-1-60270-685-9(9)) ABDO Publishing Co.
Dunn, Mark. The Age Altertron, Bk. 1. 2009. (ENG.). 175p. (gr. 4). (978-1-59692-345-4(8)) MacAdam/Cage Publishing, Inc.
Dunn, Pintip. Forget Tomorrow. 2015. (Forget Tomorrow Ser.: 1). (ENG.). 400p. (YA). 16.99 (978-1-63375-238-2(0), 9781633752382) Entangled Publishing, LLC.
DuPrau, Jeanne. The City of Ember Deluxe Edition: The First Book of Ember. 2013. (City of Ember Ser.). (ENG., Illus.). 320p. (J). (gr. 3-7). pap. 8.99 (978-0-385-37135-3(7), Random Hse. Bks. for Young Readers) Random Hse. Children's Bks.
—Voyagers: Escape the Vortex (Book 5) 2016. (Voyager Ser.). (ENG.). 208p. (J). (gr. 3-7). 12.99 (978-0-385-38670-8(2), Random Hse. Bks. for Young Readers) Random Hse. Children's Bks.
Durango, Julia. The Leveller. 2015. (ENG.). 256p. (YA). (gr. 8). 17.99 (978-0-06-231400-0(9), HarperTeen) HarperCollins Pubs.
A Dusk of Demons. 2014. (ENG., Illus.). 288p. (J). (gr. 4-8). pap. 7.99 (978-1-4814-2018-1(6), Aladdin) Simon & Schuster Children's Publishing.
Dutcher, David. Feeble Brainiac & the Lysis Virus. 2005. (ENG., Illus.). 248p. (YA). (gr. 7). per. (978-1-933255-14-9(5)) DNA Pr.
Duyvis, Corinne. On the Edge of Gone. 2016. (ENG.). 464p. (J). (gr. 8-17). 17.95 (978-1-4197-1903-5(3), Amulet Bks.) Abrams, Inc.
—Otherbound. 2014. (ENG.). 400p. (YA). (gr. 9-17). 17.95 (978-1-4197-0928-9(3), Amulet Bks.) Abrams, Inc.
Dyan, Penelope. A Thousand Stars. Dyan, Penelope, illus. 2012. (Illus.). 34p. pap. 11.95 (978-1-61477-049-7(2)) Bellissima Publishing, LLC.
Earls, J S. The Realm Unseen. 2010. 266p. (J). pap. 9.00 (978-1-60039-155-2(9)) Lamp Post Inc.
—The Realm Unseen: Hard Cover. 2010. 266p. 16.00 (978-1-60039-156-9(7)) Lamp Post Inc.
Earth 8 X 8 #2. 2009. 24p. pap. 3.99 (978-1-4231-2203-6(8)) Disney Pr.
Eason, Alethea. Hungry. 2007. 197p. (J). (gr. 5-18). lib. bdg. 16.89 (978-0-06-082555-3(3), Eos) HarperCollins Pubs.
Eastman, Brock D. & Eastman, Brock. Taken. 2011. (Illus.). 315p. (J). pap. (978-1-59638-245-9(7)) P & R Publishing.
Easton, Tom. Seven Second Delay. 2015. (ENG.). 240p. (J). (gr. 7-12). 16.95 (978-0-8234-3209-7(2)) Holiday Hse., Inc.
Eddleman, Peggy. Escape One Danger - Jump into Another.... 2013. (Sky Jumpers Ser.: 1). (ENG.). 288p. (J). (gr. 3-7). lib. bdg. 19.99 (978-0-307-98128-8(2), Random Hse. Bks. for Young Readers) Random Hse. Children's Bks.
—Sky Jumpers. 2013. (Sky Jumpers Ser.). (ENG.). 288p. (J). (gr. 3-7). 16.99 (978-0-307-98127-1(4), Random Hse. Bks. for Young Readers) Random Hse. Children's Bks.
—Sky Jumpers: Book 1. 2014. (Sky Jumpers Ser.). (ENG.). 304p. (J). (gr. 3-7). 7.99 (978-0-307-98130-1(4), Yearling) Random Hse. Children's Bks.
Edmondson, Nathan. The Activity Volume 3. 2015. (ENG., Illus.). 160p. (YA). pap. 16.99 (978-1-60706-759-7(5), 9781607067597) Image Comics.
—Black Widow - The Finely Woven Thread, Vol. 1. 2014. (ENG., Illus.). 144p. (YA). (gr. 8-17). pap. 17.99 (978-0-7851-8819-3(3)) Marvel Worldwide, Inc.
Edwards, Janet. Earth Flight. 2015. (ENG.). 365p. (YA). (gr. 7). 17.99 (978-1-63388-092-4(3), Pyr Bks.) Prometheus Bks., Pubs.
—Earth Girl. 2013. (ENG.). 350p. (YA). (gr. 7). 17.99 (978-1-61614-765-5(2), Pyr Bks.) Prometheus Bks., Pubs.
—Earth Star. 2014. (ENG.). 287p. (YA). (gr. 7). 17.99 (978-1-61614-897-3(7), Pyr Bks.) Prometheus Bks., Pubs.
Edwards, Neil & Pierfederici, Mirco, illus. Dark Avengers: Masters of Evil. 2013. (ENG.). 160p. (YA). (gr. 8-17). pap. 14.99 (978-0-7851-6847-8(8)) Marvel Worldwide, Inc.
Edwards, R. Katie King's Journal. 2004. 376p. (YA). 31.95 (978-0-595-66890-8(9)) iUniverse, Inc.
Egan, Kate. The Divergent Official Illustrated Movie Companion. 2014. (ENG., Illus.). 160p. (YA). (gr. 9). pap. 17.99 (978-0-06-231562-5(5), Tegen, Katherine Bks) HarperCollins Pubs.
—Evil Comes in Pairs. Merkel, Joe F., illus. 2009. (Spider-Man Ser.). 64p. (J). (gr. 2-5). pap. 4.99 (978-0-06-162625-8(2), HarperFestival) HarperCollins Pubs.
—The Hunger Games - Catching Fire. 2013. (ENG., Illus.). 160p. (J). (gr. 7-12). pap. 18.99 (978-0-545-59933-7(4)) Scholastic, Inc.
Elish, Dan. The Attack of the Frozen Woodchucks. Call, Greg, illus. 2008. (ENG.). 256p. (J). (gr. 3-7). 16.99 (978-0-06-113870-6(3), Geringer, Laura Book) HarperCollins Pubs.
Ellcock, Stephen. Stickyscapes Space. Cole, Tom Clohosy & Froese, Tom, illus. 2016. (ENG.). 24p. (J). (gr. 1-5). pap. 14.95 (978-1-78067-843-6(6)) King, Laurence Publishing GBR. Dist: Hachette Bk. Group.
ELLIS, B. J. Mrs. Morgan's Adventures with Aliens. 2008. 249p. 29.50 (978-0-557-00095-1(5)) Lulu Pr., Inc.
Ellis, Sarah. Odd Man Out, 1 vol. 2008. (ENG.). 168p. (J). (gr. 3-7). pap. 8.95 (978-0-88899-703-6(5)) Groundwood Bks. CAN. Dist: Publishers Group West (PGW).
Ellis, Warren. Doom 2099: The Complete Collection by Warren Ellis. Klein, David et al, illus. 2013. (ENG.). 424p. (J). (gr. 4-17). pap. 39.99 (978-0-7851-6754-9(4), Marvel Pr.) Disney Publishing Worldwide.
Elmer, Robert. Beyond Corista, 1 vol. 2009. (Shadowside Trilogy Ser.). (ENG.). 320p. (YA). (gr. 8-11). pap. 9.99 (978-0-310-71423-1(0)) Zondervan.
—Trion Rising, 1 vol. 2008. (Shadowside Trilogy Ser.). (ENG.). 352p. (YA). (gr. 8-11). pap. 9.99 (978-0-310-71421-7(4)) Zondervan.
Else, Barbara. The Queen & the Nobody Boy. Broad, Sam, illus. 2013. (Tales of Fontania Ser.). (ENG.). 328p. (J). (gr. 4-7). (978-1-877579-49-3(1)) Gecko Pr.
Elwood, Tessa. Inherit the Stars. 2015. (ENG.). 304p. (YA). (gr. 2-17). pap. 9.95 (978-0-7624-5840-0(2), Running Pr. Kids) Running Pr. Bk. Pubs.
Elys Dayton, Arwen. Disruptor. 2017. (Seeker Ser.). (ENG.). 384p. (YA). (gr. 9). 18.99 (978-0-385-74411-9(0), Delacorte Pr.) Random Hse. Children's Bks.
—Seeker. 2015. (Seeker Ser.). (ENG.). 480p. (YA). (gr. 9). pap. 9.99 (978-0-385-74408-9(0), Ember) Random Hse. Children's Bks.
—Seeker. 2015. lib. bdg. 20.85 (978-0-606-38458-2(8)) Turtleback Bks.
—Traveler. 2016. (Seeker Ser.). (ENG.). 400p. (YA). (gr. 9). lib. bdg. 21.99 (978-0-375-99149-3(2), Delacorte Pr.) Random Hse. Children's Bks.
Emerson, Kevin. The Dark Shore. (Atlanteans Ser.: 2). (ENG.). (YA). (gr. 8). 2014. 496p. pap. 9.99 (978-0-06-206283-3(2), Tegen, Katherine Bks) 2013. 480p. 17.99 (978-0-06-206282-6(4)) HarperCollins Pubs.
—The Far Dawn. 2014. (Atlanteans Ser.: 3). (ENG.). 368p. (YA). (gr. 8). pap. 9.99 (978-0-06-206286-4(7), Tegen, Katherine Bks) HarperCollins Pubs.
—The Fellowship for Alien Detection. 2013. (ENG.). 432p. (J). (gr. 3-7). 16.99 (978-0-06-207185-9(8), Waldon Pond Pr.) HarperCollins Pubs.
—Last Day on Mars. 2017. (Chronicle of the Dark Star Ser.: 1). 336p. (J). (gr. 3-7). 16.99 (978-0-06-230671-5(5), Waldon Pond Pr.) HarperCollins Pubs.
—The Lost Code. (Atlanteans Ser.: 1). (ENG.). (YA). (gr. 8). 2013. 464p. pap. 9.99 (978-0-06-206280-2(8)) 2012. 448p. 17.99 (978-0-06-206279-6(4)) HarperCollins Pubs. (Tegen, Katherine Bks).
Emmet, Laura. Julie Trent & the Lightning. 2003. 148p. pap. 11.95 (978-0-595-27380-5(7), Writers Club Pr.) iUniverse, Inc.
—Julie Trent & the Tempest. 2003. 136p. pap. 11.95 (978-0-595-27418-5(8), Writers Club Pr.) iUniverse, Inc.
Ende, Michael. La Historia Interminable. Tr. of Unendliche Geschichte. (SPA.). 432p. (YA). (gr. 5-8). 13.95 (978-84-204-2522-1(2), LEC5222) Ediciones Alfaguara ESP. Dist: Lectorum Pubns., Inc.
—La Historia Interminable. Quadflieg, Roswitha & Sáenz, Miguel, trs. Quadflieg, Roswitha, illus. Tr. of Unendliche Geschichte. (SPA.). 424p. (J). 9.95 (978-84-204-3226-7(1)) Ediciones Alfaguara ESP. Dist: Santillana USA Publishing Co., Inc.
—La Historia Interminable. Quadflieg, Roswitha, tr. 57th ed. 2014. Tr. of Unendliche Geschichte. (SPA., Illus.). 419p. 17.95 (978-84-204-6439-8(2)) Ediciones Alfaguara ESP. Dist: Santillana USA Publishing Co., Inc.
—La Historia Interminable. 2003. Tr. of Unendliche Geschichte. (SPA., Illus.). 420p. (J). (gr. 5-8). pap. 12.95 (978-968-19-0254-4(8)) Santillana USA Publishing Co., Inc.
Enderle, Dotti. Book 18: Spaced Out! 2014. (Ghost Detectors Set 3 Ser.). 80p. (J). (gr. 2-5). lib. bdg. 27.07 (978-1-62402-006-3(2), Calico Chapter Bks) Magic Wagon.
—Spaced Out!, 1 vol. McWilliam, Howard, illus. 2016. (ENG.). 80p. (J). (978-1-62402-101-5(8)) Magic Wagon.
Engdahl, Sylvia. Enchantress from the Stars. 2003. (ENG.). 304p. (YA). (gr. 7-18). pap. 8.99 (978-0-14-250037-8(2), Firebird) Penguin Young Readers Group.
—The Far Side of Evil. 2005. (ENG.). 336p. (YA). (gr. 7-7). 22.00 (978-0-14-240293-1(1), Firebird) Penguin Young Readers Group.
Engel, Amy. The Book of Ivy. 2014. (Entangled Teen Ser.). (ENG.). 304p. (YA). (gr. 7-12). pap. 9.99 (978-1-62266-465-8(5), 9781622664658) Entangled Publishing, LLC.
—The Book of Ivy. 2014. (YA). lib. bdg. 20.85 (978-0-606-38239-7(9)) Turtleback Bks.
—The Book of Ivy. 2016. (CHI.). 272p. (YA). (gr. 7-12). pap. (978-986-133-566-7(8)) Yuan Shen Pr. Co., Ltd.
—The Revolution of Ivy. 2015. (ENG.). 400p. (YA). pap. 9.99 (978-1-63375-115-6(5), 9781633751156) Entangled Publishing, LLC.
Engineering is Elementary Team. Kwame's Sound: An Acoustical Engineering Story. 2005. (J). lib. bdg. 15.99 (978-0-9774084-2-9(6)) Engineering is Elementary.
—Michelle's MVP Award: A Chemical Engineering Story. 2005. (J). lib. bdg. 15.99 (978-0-9774084-7-4(7)) Engineering is Elementary.
—A Reminder for Emily: An Electrical Engineering Story. 2006. (J). lib. bdg. 15.99 (978-0-9774084-3-6(4)) Engineering is Elementary.
Englehart, Steve. Jurassic Park: Aftershocks!: Vol. 5, 1 vol. 2013. (Jurassic Park Ser.). (ENG.). 32p. (J). (gr. 4-8). lib. bdg. 24.21 (978-1-61479-187-4(2)) Spotlight.
Epner, Paul. There's a Dachshund in My Bed! Reed, Bill, illus. 2004. 56p. (J). 16.95 (978-0-9743335-8-8(1)) Imaginative Publishing, Ltd.
Epstein, Adam Jay & Jacobson, Andrew. Starbounders. McClellan, David, illus. 2013. (Starbounders Ser.: 1). (ENG.). 320p. (J). (gr. 3-7). 16.99 (978-0-06-212022-9(0)) HarperCollins Pubs.
—Starbounders Vol. 2: Rebellion. 2014. (Starbounders Ser.: 2). (ENG.). 304p. (J). (gr. 3-7). 16.99 (978-0-06-212027-4(1)) HarperCollins Pubs.
Espinosa, Frank. Journey to the Hidden Sea, Vol. 1. 2006. (ENG., Illus.). 304p. (YA). pap. 19.99 (978-1-58240-585-8(9), 9781582405858) Image Comics.
Etienne, Sara Wilson. Lotus & Thorn. 2016. (ENG., Illus.). 464p. (YA). (gr. 9). 17.99 (978-0-399-25669-1(5), G.P. Putnam's Sons Books for Young Readers) Penguin Young Readers Group.
Evans, Joseph. The Trinity Awakening. 2013. 466p. pap. (978-0-9572912-1-8(3)) Evans, Joseph.
Evans, Maz. Who Let the Gods Out? 2017. (ENG.). 320p. (J). (gr. 3-7). 16.99 (978-1-338-06556-5(4), Chicken Hse., The) Scholastic, Inc.
Evans, Richard. Battle of the Ampere. (Michael Vey Ser.: 3). (ENG., Illus.). 320p. (YA). (gr. 7). 2014. pap. 11.99 (978-1-4424-7512-0(9)) 2013. 17.99 (978-1-4424-7511-3(0)) Simon Pulse/Mercury Ink. (Simon Pulse/Mercury Ink).
—An Electrifying Michael Vey Set. 2013. (Michael Vey Ser.). (ENG., Illus.). 1008p. (YA). (gr. 7). 53.99 (978-1-4424-9550-0(2), Simon Pulse/Mercury Ink) Simon Pulse/Mercury Ink.
—Michael Vey 5. 2015. (Michael Vey Ser.: 5). (ENG., Illus.). 288p. (YA). (gr. 7). 18.99 (978-1-4814-4410-1(7), Simon Pulse/Mercury Ink) Simon Pulse/Mercury Ink.
—The Prisoner of Cell 25. (Michael Vey Ser.: 1). (ENG., Illus.). (YA). (gr. 7). 2012. 352p. pap. 11.99 (978-1-4424-6812-2(2)) 2011. 336p. 19.99 (978-1-4516-5650-3(5)) Simon Pulse/Mercury Ink. (Simon Pulse/Mercury Ink).
—Rise of the Elgen. (Michael Vey Ser.: 2). (ENG., Illus.). 352p. (YA). (gr. 7). 2013. pap. 11.99 (978-1-4424-7510-6(2)) 2012. 17.99 (978-1-4424-5414-9(8)) Simon Pulse/Mercury Ink. (Simon Pulse/Mercury Ink).
Everett, Mikaela. The Unquiet. 2015. (ENG.). 464p. (YA). (gr. 9). 17.99 (978-0-06-238127-9(X), Greenwillow Bks.) HarperCollins Pubs.
Faerber, Jay, et al. Universal Heroes. 2006. (Illus.). 136p. (YA). pap. 13.99 (978-0-7851-1857-2(8)) Marvel Worldwide, Inc.
Faircloth, Carson. Games. 2011. 260p. 26.95 (978-1-4620-1029-5(6)); pap. 16.95 (978-1-4620-1027-1(X)) iUniverse, Inc.
Falk, Nick & Flowers, Tony. Tyrannosaurus in the Veggie Patch: Saurus Street 1 (Large Print 16pt) 2013. 102p. pap. (978-1-4596-5771-7(3)) ReadHowYouWant.com, Ltd.
Falkner, Brian. The Assault (Recon Team Angel #1) 2013. (Recon Team Angel Ser.: 1). (ENG.). 304p. (YA). (gr. 7). pap. 9.99 (978-0-375-87190-0(X), Ember) Random Hse. Children's Bks.
—Battlesaurus: Rampage at Waterloo. 2016. (Battlesaurus Ser.: 2). (ENG.). 352p. (YA). 17.99 (978-0-374-30077-7(1), 9780374300777, Farrar, Straus & Giroux (BYR)) Farrar, Straus & Giroux.
—Brain Jack. 2011. (ENG.). 368p. (YA). (gr. 7). pap. 9.99 (978-0-375-84367-9(1), Ember) Random Hse. Children's Bks.
—Ice War (Recon Team Angel #3) 2014. (Recon Team Angel Ser.). (ENG.). 320p. (YA). (gr. 7). 17.99 (978-0-449-81303-4(7), Random Hse. Bks. for Young Readers) Random Hse. Children's Bks.
—Task Force. 2013. (Recon Team Angel Ser.). (ENG., Illus.). 288p. (YA). (gr. 7). 17.99 (978-0-449-81299-0(5), Random Hse. Bks. for Young Readers) Random Hse. Children's Bks.
—Task Force (Recon Team Angel #2) 2014. (Recon Team Angel Ser.). (ENG.). 416p. (YA). (gr. 7). pap. 9.99 (978-0-449-81302-7(9), Ember) Random Hse. Children's Bks.
—The Tomorrow Code. 2009. (ENG.). 368p. (YA). (gr. 7). pap. 9.99 (978-0-375-84365-5(5), Ember) Random Hse. Children's Bks.
Falksen, G. D. The Transatlantic Conspiracy. Iwata, Nat, illus. (ENG.). 240p. (YA). 2017. (gr. 9). pap. 10.99 (978-1-61695-814-5(6)) 2016. (gr. 7). 18.99 (978-1-61695-417-8(5)) Soho Pr., Inc. (Soho Teen).
Falls, Kat. Dark Life. (Dark Life Ser.: 1). (ENG.). 304p. (J). (gr. 3-7). 2011. pap. 7.99 (978-0-545-17815-0(0)) 2010. 16.99 (978-0-545-17814-3(2)) Scholastic, Inc. (Scholastic Pr.).
—Inhuman. 2015. (ENG.). 384p. (J). (gr. 7). pap. 9.99 (978-0-545-37101-8(5), Scholastic Pr.) Scholastic, Inc.
—Rip Tide. 2011. (J). (Dark Life Ser.: 2). (ENG.). 320p. (gr. 3-7). 16.99 (978-0-545-17843-3(6)); 314p. pap. (978-0-545-43175-0(1)) Scholastic, Inc. (Scholastic Pr.).
Farley, C. J. Game World. 2014. (ENG., Illus.). 288p. (J). (gr. 4). pap. 15.95 (978-1-61775-197-4(9), Black Sheep) Akashic Bks.
Farmer, Nancy. The Ear, the Eye & the Arm. 2012. (ENG.). 336p. (J). (gr. 3-7). pap. 7.99 (978-0-545-35661-9(X), Scholastic Paperbacks) Scholastic, Inc.
—The Ear, the Eye, & the Arm. 2012. lib. bdg. 18.40 (978-0-606-23944-8(8), Turtleback) Turtleback Bks.
—The House of the Scorpion. 2004. (ENG., Illus.). 400p. (YA). (gr. 7). reprint ed. pap. 11.99 (978-0-689-85223-7(1), Atheneum Bks. for Young Readers) Simon & Schuster Children's Publishing.
—The House of the Scorpion. 2004. 380p. (gr. 6). lib. bdg. 22.10 (978-1-4176-1900-9(7), Turtleback) Turtleback Bks.
—The Lord of Opium. 2013. (ENG., Illus.). 432p. (YA). (gr. 7). 17.99 (978-1-4424-8254-8(0)) Simon & Schuster Children's Publishing.
Farmer, Penelope. Charlotte Sometimes. Connor, Chris, illus. 2007. (ENG.). 208p. (J). (gr. 7-9). 17.95 (978-1-59017-221-6(3), NYR Children's Collection) New York Review of Bks., Inc., The.
Fearing, Mark & Rummel, Tim. Earthling! 2012. (ENG., Illus.). 248p. (J). (gr. 3-7). 22.99 (978-0-8118-7106-8(1)) Chronicle Bks. LLC.
—Earthling. 2012. (ENG., Illus.). 248p. (J). (gr. 3-7). pap. 12.99 (978-1-4521-0906-0(0)) Chronicle Bks. LLC.
Feasey, Steve. Mutant Rising. 2016. (ENG.). 352p. (YA). (gr. 7). pap. 12.99 (978-1-4088-5572-0(0), 9781408855720, Bloomsbury USA Childrens) Bloomsbury Publishing USA.
Feldstein, Al. Weird Science, Vol. 2. 2007. (ENG., Illus.). 212p. (YA). 49.95 (978-1-888472-69-1(3), 9781888472691, William M. Gaines Agent, INC.) Diamond Bk. Distributors.
Fentiman, David. The Adventures of BB-8. 2016. (Star Wars DK Readers Level 2 Ser.). lib. bdg. 13.55 (978-0-606-38709-5(9)) Turtleback Bks.
—DK Readers L2: Star Wars: the Adventures of BB-8. 2016. (DK Readers Ser.). (ENG., Illus.). 48p. (J). (gr. k-2). pap. 3.99 (978-1-4654-5102-6(1), DK Children) Dorling Kindersley Publishing, Inc.
—DK Readers L3: Star Wars: Finn's Mission. 2016. (DK Readers Ser.). (ENG., Illus.). 64p. (J). (gr. 2-4). pap. 3.99 (978-1-4654-5101-9(3), DK Children) Dorling Kindersley Publishing, Inc.
—Finn's Mission. 2016. (Star Wars DK Readers Level 3 Ser.). lib. bdg. 13.55 (978-0-606-38710-1(2)) Turtleback Bks.
—The Force Awakens. 2015. (DK Readers Ser.). (ENG., Illus.). 48p. (J). (gr. k-2). pap. 3.99 (978-1-4654-3814-0(9), DK Children) Dorling Kindersley Publishing, Inc.
—The Force Awakens: New Adventures. 2015. (DK Readers Ser.). (ENG., Illus.). 48p. (J). (gr. k-2). 14.99 (978-1-4654-3813-3(0), DK Children) Dorling Kindersley Publishing, Inc.
Fentiman, David. New Adventures. 2015. (Illus.). 47p. (J). (978-1-4806-9626-6(9)) Dorling Kindersley Publishing, Inc.
Fentiman, David & Dowsett, Elizabeth. The Amazing Book of Star Wars. 2016. (ENG., Illus.). 48p. (J). (gr. 1-4). 14.99 (978-1-4654-5460-7(8), DK Children) Dorling Kindersley Publishing, Inc.
Ferguson, Alane. The Angel of Death. 2008. (Forensic Mystery Ser.). 258p. 17.00 (978-0-7569-8929-3(9)) Perfection Learning Corp.
Fickling, Phillip. Fillmore & Geary Take Off! Shulman, Mark, illus. 2003. 40p. (J). lib. bdg. (978-1-58717-258-6(5), SeaStar Bks.) Chronicle Bks. LLC.
Fields, Bryan W. Lunchbox & the Aliens. Atteberry, Kevan, illus. 2009. (Froonga Ser.). (ENG.). 208p. (J). (gr. 4-7). pap. 11.99 (978-0-312-56115-4(6), 9780312561154) Square Fish.
Filbach Brothers. Star Wars: Clone Wars Adventures, 1 vol. 2013. (Star Wars Digests Set 2 Ser.). (ENG.). 80p. (J). (gr. 4-8). lib. bdg. 27.07 (978-1-61479-058-7(2)); lib. bdg. 27.07 (978-1-61479-059-4(0)) ABDO Publishing Co. (Essential Library).
Finley, Leah. The One & Only Mr C. 2009. 82p. pap. 8.95 (978-1-935118-75-6(7)) Bellissima Publishing, LLC.
Fisch, Sholly. DC Super Friends. 2013. (DC Super Friends Ser.). (ENG.). 32p. (gr. 1-2). 90.40 (978-1-4342-4855-8(0)) Stone Arch Bks.
Fisch, Sholly, et al. Go! - Party, Party!, Vol. 1. 2015. (ENG., Illus.). 128p. (J). (gr. 2-5). pap. 12.99 (978-1-4012-5242-7(7)) DC Comics.
Fisher, Catherine. Relic Master Part 1. 2013. (Relic Master Ser.). (ENG.). 752p. (YA). (gr. 7). pap. 9.99 (978-0-14-242687-6(3), Firebird) Penguin Young Readers Group.
—Relic Master Part 2. 2013. (Relic Master Ser.). (ENG.). 880p. (YA). (gr. 7). pap. 9.99 (978-0-14-242686-9(5), Firebird) Penguin Young Readers Group.
—The Slanted Worlds. 2015. (Obsidian Mirror Ser.: 2). (ENG.). 384p. (YA). (gr. 7). pap. 9.99 (978-0-14-242678-4(4), Speak) Penguin Young Readers Group.
FitzGerald, Helen. Deviant. 2014. (ENG.). (YA). (gr. 9). pap. 9.99 (978-1-61695-419-2(1), Soho Teen) Soho Pr., Inc.
Fleury, Mike Stevenson. Natural Disaster 2222. 2003. (ENG.). 112p. 19.95 (978-0-595-65436-9(3)); 108p. (YA). pap. 9.95 (978-0-595-25921-2(9)) iUniverse, Inc. (Writers Club Pr.).
Flintham, Thomas. Super Rabbit Boy Powers Up! 2017. (Press Start! — Branches Ser.: 2). lib. bdg. 14.75 (978-0-606-40188-3(1)) Turtleback Bks.
Floreen, Tim. Tattoo Atlas. 2016. (ENG., Illus.). 384p. (YA). (gr. 9). 17.99 (978-1-4814-3280-1(X), Simon Pulse) Simon Pulse.
—Willful Machines. 2016. (ENG., Illus.). 384p. (YA). (gr. 9). pap. 10.99 (978-1-4814-3278-8(8), Simon Pulse) Simon Pulse.
Flynn, Ian. Mega Man 3: Return of Dr. Wily. Bates, Ben, illus. 2012. (Mega Man Ser.: 3). (ENG.). 112p. (gr. 4-7). pap. 11.99 (978-1-936975-11-2(4), Archie Comics) Archie Comic Pubns., Inc.
—Mega Man 4: Spiritus Ex Machina. 2012. (Mega Man Ser.: 4). (ENG.). 112p. (gr. 4-7). pap. 11.99 (978-1-936975-27-3(0), Archie Comics) Archie Comic Pubns., Inc.
Fontana, Shea. Summer Olympus. 2017. (DC Super Hero Girls Ser.: 3). lib. bdg. 20.85 (978-0-606-40123-4(7)) Turtleback Bks.
Fontes, Justine & Fontes, Ron. Casebook: UFOs and/or Alien Encounter. 2009. (Top Secret Graphica Mysteries Ser.). (Illus.). 48p. (YA). (gr. 2-6). 29.25 (978-1-60754-603-0(5)); pap. 11.75 (978-1-60754-604-7(3)) Windmill Bks.
Ford, Sharon Lea. The Pages of Lost Time. 2010. 212p. 24.95 (978-1-60911-127-4(3), Eloquent Bks.) Strategic Book Publishing & Rights Agency (SBPRA).
Forde, Patricia. The List. 2017. (ENG.). 368p. (J). (gr. 5-8). 16.99 (978-1-4926-4796-6(9), 9781492647966, Sourcebooks Jabberwocky) Sourcebooks, Inc.
Forte, Lauren. Ghost Moon (Disney Junior: Miles from Tomorrowland) RH Disney, illus. 2017. (Little Golden Book Ser.). (ENG.). 24p. (J). (-k). 4.99 (978-0-7364-3717-2(7), Golden/Disney) Random Hse. Children's Bks.
Forte, Lauren. Space Race (Disney Junior: Miles from Tomorrowland) RH Disney, illus. 2017. (Little Golden Book Ser.). (ENG.). 24p. (J). (-k). 4.99 (978-0-7364-3569-7(7), Golden/Disney) Random Hse. Children's Bks.
Fosgitt, Jay P. Little Green Men. 2010. (ENG., Illus.). 100p. (YA). pap. 9.95 (978-1-936340-01-9(1), 9781936340019) Ape Entertainment.
Fox, Jennifer. Meet Optimus Prime. 2015. (Passport to Reading Level 1 Ser.). (ENG., Illus.). 32p. (J). (gr. -1-3). pap. 3.99 (978-0-316-40558-4(2)) Little, Brown Bks. for Young Readers.
—Meet Optimus Prime. 2015. (Transformers Passport to Reading Ser.). (J). lib. bdg. 13.55 (978-0-606-35938-2(9)) Turtleback Bks.
Foxe, Steve. Decepticon Island! 2017. (Transformers Passport to Reading Ser.). (J). lib. bdg. 14.75 (978-0-606-39908-1(9)) Turtleback Bks.
—Hot Pursuit! (DC Super Friends) Random House, illus. 2017. (Pictureback(R) Ser.). (ENG.). 24p. (J). (gr. -1-2). pap. 5.99 (978-1-5247-1715-5(0), Random Hse. Bks. for Young Readers) Random Hse. Children's Bks.
Frankel, Jordana. The Isle. 2016. 384p. (YA). (gr. 8). 17.99 (978-0-06-209537-4(4), Tegen, Katherine Bks) HarperCollins Pubs.
—The Ward. (YA). (gr. 8). 2016. 496p. pap. 9.99 (978-0-06-209535-0(8)) 2013. (ENG.). 480p. 17.99 (978-0-06-209534-3(X)) HarperCollins Pubs. (Tegen, Katherine Bks).
Franks, Melissa. Warped! An Adventure Through Time Bk. 1: A What-a-saur? 2008. 96p. pap. 19.95 (978-1-60703-636-4(3)) America Star Bks.
Fraser, Jess, illus. The Legend of the Cosmic Cowboy. 2007. (J). cd-rom 12.99 (978-0-9795190-7-9(1)) Color & Learn.
Frederick, Milner. Douglas Brain. 2008. 208p. per. (978-1-84549-290-8(0)) arima publishing.
Fredley, Nichole. The Sirius, 1 vol. 2010. 534p. pap. 34.95 (978-1-61582-910-1(5)) America Star Bks.
Freer, Dave. Cuttlefish. 2012. (ENG.). 299p. (YA). (gr. 7). 16.95 (978-1-61614-625-2(7)) Prometheus Bks., Pubs.

Freestone, Annie. The Little Mars Rovers. 2008. 36p. pap. 13.95 *(978-1-59858-459-2(6))* Dog Ear Publishing, LLC.
Freitas, Donna. The Body Market. 2017. (Unplugged Ser.: 2). 432p. (YA). (gr. 8). pap. 9.99 ***(978-0-06-211864-6(1))***; 17.99 *(978-0-06-211863-9(3))* HarperCollins Pubs. (HarperTeen).
Frewin Jones, Allan. Thunderbolt. (Hunter & Moon Mystery Ser.: Vol. 5). (Illus.). 171p. (J). pap. 8.99 *(978-0-340-70963-4(4))* Hodder & Stoughton GBR. Dist: Trafalgar Square Publishing.
Frey, James. Endgame - The Fugitive Archives. 2017. (Endgame: the Fugitive Archives Ser.). 352p. (YA). (gr. 9). pap. 9.99 *(978-0-06-233278-3(3))* HarperCollins Pubs.
Frey, James & Johnson-Shelton, Nils. The Calling. (Endgame Ser.: 1). (ENG.). (gr. 9). 2015. 496p. (YA). pap. 10.99 *(978-0-06-233259-2(7))* 2014. 464p. (J). 19.99 *(978-0-06-233258-5(9),* HarperTeen) HarperCollins Pubs.
—The Complete Training Diaries. 2015. (Endgame: the Training Diaries: Nos. 1-3). (ENG.). 416p. (YA). (gr. 9). pap. 9.99 *(978-0-06-233276-9(7))* HarperCollins Pubs.
—Endgame: Rules of the Game. 2017. (Endgame Ser.: 3). 368p. (YA). (gr. 9). pap. 10.99 *(978-0-06-233265-3(1))* HarperCollins Pubs.
—Rules of the Game. 2016. (Endgame Ser.: 3). 352p. (YA). (gr. 9). 19.99 *(978-0-06-233264-6(3))* HarperCollins Pubs.
—Sky Key. 2015. (Endgame Ser.: 2). 512p. (YA). (gr. 9). (ENG.). 19.99 *(978-0-06-233261-5(9))*; pap. 12.00 *(978-0-06-241424-3(0))* HarperCollins Pubs.
Frid, Colt & Frid, Randy. Demons at the Door. 2009. *(978-0-9811847-1-5(5))* Frid Enterprises, Inc.
Friedman, Michael Jan, et al. Convergence. Erwin, Steve et al, illus. 2008. (ENG.). 176p. pap. 14.95 *(978-1-84576-320-6(3),* Titan Bks.) Titan Bks. Ltd. GBR. Dist: Penguin Random Hse. LLC.
Friedman, Stanley. Quantum Outlaws. 2010. 210p. pap. 11.95 *(978-1-935630-09-8(1))* Bellissima Publishing, LLC.
—Quantum Prisoner. 2012. 212p. pap. 11.95 *(978-1-61477-029-9(8))* Bellissima Publishing, LLC.
Fritz, Julie. My Mother Is an Astronaut. 2008. 16p. pap. 10.50 *(978-1-4343-7551-3(X))* AuthorHouse.
Frommer, Abbey C. A New Fight: (Sequel to the Nix), 1 vol. 2010. 116p. pap. 19.95 *(978-1-4489-7959-2(5))* America Star Bks.
Fry, Jason. Darth Maul: Shadow Conspiracy. 2013. lib. bdg. 16.00 *(978-0-606-26775-5(1),* Turtleback) Turtleback Bks.
—Edge of the Galaxy. Balmet, Jean-Paul, illus. 2014. (ENG.). 176p. (J). (gr. 3-7). pap. 6.99 *(978-1-4847-0485-1(1))* Disney Pr.
—Edge of the Galaxy. 2014. 172p. (J). lib. bdg. 17.20 *(978-0-606-36536-9(2))* Turtleback Bks.
—The Jupiter Pirates: Hunt for the Hydra. 2013. (Jupiter Pirates Ser.: 1). (ENG.). 256p. (J). (gr. 3-7). 16.99 *(978-0-06-223020-1(4))* HarperCollins Pubs.
—The Jupiter Pirates: Hunt for the Hydra. 2014. (Jupiter Pirates Ser.: 1). (ENG.). 272p. (J). (gr. 3-7). pap. 6.99 *(978-0-06-223021-8(2))* HarperCollins Pubs.
—Rey's Story. 2016. (Star Wars the Force Awakens Chapter Bks.). (J). lib. bdg. 16.00 *(978-0-606-38302-8(6))* Turtleback Bks.
—Rey's Survival Guide. Barthelmes, Andrew, illus. 2015. (Replica Journal Ser.: 1). (ENG.). 96p. (J). (gr. 1-4). 9.99 *(978-0-7944-3569-1(6))* Studio Fun International.
—Star Wars: Aliens of the Galaxy. 2016. (ENG.). 42p. (J). (gr. k-3). 12.99 *(978-0-7944-3731-2(1),* Reader's Digest Children's Bks.) Studio Fun International.
—Star Wars Rebels: Edge of the Galaxy. 2014. 172p. (J). ***(978-1-4242-6295-3(X),*** Disney Lucasfilm Press) Disney Publishing Worldwide.
Fry, Jason. Star Wars the Force Awakens Chapter Book. 2016. (ENG.). 128p. (J). (gr. 1-3). pap. 5.99 *(978-1-4847-7409-0(4),* Disney Lucasfilm Press) Disney Publishing Worldwide.
Fry, Jason & Harper, Benjamin. Star Wars: Aliens & Ships of the Galaxy. 2016. (ENG.). 96p. (J). (gr. 1-5). 9.99 *(978-0-7944-3588-2(2),* Reader's Digest Children's Bks.) Studio Fun International.
Fry, Jason & Kogge, Michael. Star Wars. 2016. (ENG.). 96p. (J). (gr. 1-3). 9.99 *(978-0-7944-3718-3(4),* Reader's Digest Children's Bks.) Studio Fun International.
Fry, Jason & Weisman, Greg. Servants of the Empire. 2015. 171p. (J). ***(978-1-4242-6297-7(6),*** Disney Lucasfilm Press) Disney Publishing Worldwide.
Fry, Jason, et al. Star Wars Set: The Force Awakens. 2016. (ENG.). 288p. (J). (gr. 1-4). pap. 29.99 *(978-0-7944-3814-2(8),* Reader's Digest Children's Bks.) Studio Fun International.
Fukuda, Andrew. The Prey. 2013. (Hunt Trilogy Ser.: 2). (ENG.). 336p. (YA). (gr. 7-12). pap. 10.99 *(978-1-250-00530-4(2),* 9781250005304); 18.99 *(978-1-250-00511-3(6),* 9781250005113) St. Martin's Pr. (St. Martin's Griffin).
—The Trap. 2013. (Hunt Trilogy Ser.: 3). (ENG.). 320p. (YA). (gr. 7). 18.99 *(978-1-250-00512-0(4),* 9781250005120, St. Martin's Griffin) St. Martin's Pr.
Furman, Simon. Revenge of the Fallen, 1 vol. Davis-Hunt, Jon, illus. 2010. (Transformers: Revenge of the Fallen Movie Adaptation Ser.). (ENG.). 24p. (J). (gr. 3-6). Vol. 1. 24.21 *(978-1-59961-726-8(9))* Vol. 2. 24.21 *(978-1-59961-727-5(7))* Spotlight.
—Revenge of the Fallen, 1 vol., Vol. 3. Milne, Alex, illus. 2010. (Transformers: Revenge of the Fallen Movie Adaptation Ser.). (ENG.). 24p. (J). (gr. 3-6). 24.21 *(978-1-59961-728-2(5))* Spotlight.
—Revenge of the Fallen, 1 vol., Vol. 4. Davis-Hunt, Jon, illus. 2010. (Transformers: Revenge of the Fallen Movie Adaptation Ser.). (ENG.). 24p. (J). (gr. 3-6). 24.21 *(978-1-59961-729-9(3))* Spotlight.
G-Force Gadget Guide. 2009. 48p. pap. 5.99 *(978-1-4231-1805-3(7))* Disney Pr.
Gabel, Claudia & Klam, Cheryl. Elusion. 2014. (Elusion Ser.: 1). (ENG.). 400p. (YA). (gr. 9). 17.99 *(978-0-06-212241-4(X),* Tegen, Katherine Bks) HarperCollins Pubs.
—Etherworld. (Elusion Ser.: 2). 352p. (YA). (gr. 9). 2016. pap. 9.99 *(978-0-06-212245-2(2))* 2015. (ENG.). 17.99 *(978-0-06-212244-5(4))* HarperCollins Pubs. (Tegen, Katherine Bks).
Gage, Brian. The Saddest Little Robot. Otoshi, Kathryn, tr. Otoshi, Kathryn, illus. 2004. (ENG.). 90p. (J). 16.95 *(978-1-932360-05-9(0))* Cricket Bks.
Gagnon, Michelle. Strangelets. 2014. (ENG., Illus.). 280p. (YA). (gr. 9). pap. 9.99 *(978-1-61695-420-8(5),* Soho Teen) Soho Pr., Inc.
Gaiman, NEil & Reaves, Michael. Interworld. (InterWorld Trilogy Ser.: 1). (ENG.). (YA). (gr. 8). 2013. 304p. pap. 9.99 *(978-0-06-212530-9(3),* HarperTeen) 2008. 256p. pap. 9.99 *(978-0-06-123898-7(8))* HarperCollins Pubs.
—Interworld. 2008. (Illus.). 181p. (J). (gr. 5-9). 60.00 *(978-1-59606-173-6(1))* Subterranean Pr.
Gaiman, NEil, et al. Eternity's Wheel. (InterWorld Trilogy Ser.: 3). 288p. (YA). (gr. 8). 2016. pap. 9.99 *(978-0-06-206800-2(8))* 2015. (ENG.). 17.99 *(978-0-06-206799-9(0))* HarperCollins Pubs. (HarperTeen).
—The Silver Dream. (InterWorld Trilogy Ser.: 2). (ENG.). (YA). (gr. 8). 2015. 272p. pap. 9.99 *(978-0-06-206797-5(4))* 2013. 256p. 18.99 *(978-0-06-206796-8(6))* HarperCollins Pubs. (HarperTeen).
Gaither, Stefanie. Into the Abyss. 2016. (ENG., Illus.). 352p. (YA). (gr. 7). 18.99 *(978-1-4814-4995-3(8),* Simon & Schuster Bks. For Young Readers) Simon & Schuster Bks. For Young Readers.
The Galactic Adventures of Team Energy: Episode I: Dr. Slouch & the Candy Factory. 2007. (J). 16.95 *(978-0-9778776-1-4(2))* LGE Performance Systems, Inc.
The Galaxy Zack Collection: A Stellar Four-Book Boxed Set: Hello, Nebulon!; Journey to Juno; the Prehistoric Planet; Monsters in Space! 2014. (Galaxy Zack Ser.). (ENG., Illus.). 512p. (J). (gr. k-4). pap. 23.99 *(978-1-4814-0665-9(5),* Little Simon) Little Simon.
Gallagher, Michael. X-Men, Magneto's Master Plan. Severin, Marie, illus. 24p. (YA). (gr. k-18). 12.95 *(978-0-9627001-6-3(9))* Futech Educational Products, Inc.
—X-Men, Scourge of the Savage Land. Severin, Marie, illus. 24p. (YA). (gr. k-18). 12.95 *(978-0-9627001-7-0(7))* Futech Educational Products, Inc.
Gamble, Paul. The Monster's Daughter. 2017. (Ministry of SUITs Ser.: 2). (ENG.). 384p. (J). 16.99 *(978-1-250-07683-0(8),* 9781250076830) Feiwel & Friends.
Gamow, George. Mr Tompkins Learns the Facts of Life. 2011. (ENG., Illus.). 116p. pap. 27.99 *(978-1-107-40207-2(7))* Cambridge Univ. Pr.
Gant, Gene. Lessons on Destroying the World. 2016. (ENG., Illus.). (J). 24.99 ***(978-1-63533-040-3(8))*** 2014. 200p. pap. 14.99 *(978-1-62798-792-9(4))* Dreamspinner Pr. (Harmony Ink Pr.).
Gardiner, John Reynolds. ALTO SECRETO. (SPA.). 96p. (YA). (gr. 5-8). *(978-84-279-3396-5(7),* NG3489) Noguer y Caralt Editores, S. A. ESP. Dist: Lectorum Pubns., Inc.
Garing, Ken. Planetoid Volume 1 TP. 2013. (ENG., Illus.). 164p. (YA). pap. 15.99 *(978-1-60706-813-6(3),* 9781607068136) Image Comics.
Garner, Em. Contaminated. (ENG.). 336p. (J). (gr. 7). 2014. pap. 9.99 *(978-1-60684-542-4(X))* 2013. 17.99 *(978-1-60684-354-3(0))* Lerner Publishing Group. (Carolrhoda Lab™).
—Contaminated 2 - Mercy Mode. 2014. (ENG.). 341p. (J). (gr. 7). 17.99 *(978-1-60684-356-7(7),* Carolrhoda Lab™) Lerner Publishing Group.
Garvie, Maureen. Amy by Any Other Name. 2009. (ENG.). 256p. (YA). (gr. 7-18). pap. *(978-1-55470-142-1(2))* Me to We.
Gass, Kenneth. Trilobites! 2005. 110p. per. 18.99 net. *(978-0-9634906-8-1(0),* SQP) Specialized Quality Pubns.
Gathering Place Publishers. Stones' Quest in Search of Its Master. 2010. (ENG., Illus.). 472p. (J). 21.95 *(978-0-9754622-5-6(3))* Gathering Place Pubs., Inc.
—Stones' Quest in Search of Its Master: In Search of Its Master 2005. (Stones' Quest Ser.: 1). (ENG., Illus.). 489p. (J). pap. 19.95 *(978-0-9754622-0-1(2))* Gathering Place Pubs., Inc.
Gecko, Gabriel, et al, illus. Iron Man/War Machine: Hands of the Mandarin. 2013. (ENG.). 280p. (J). (gr. 4-17). pap. 24.99 *(978-0-7851-8428-7(7))* Marvel Worldwide, Inc.
Gehrt, Linda. My Trip, My Spaceship. 2004. 26p. pap. 24.95 *(978-1-4137-3392-1(1))* PublishAmerica, Inc.
Geiger, Beth & Fuerst, Jeffrey B. Return to Earth. Wolk-Stanley, Jessica, illus. 2004. (Reader's Theater Ser.). (J). pap. *(978-1-4108-2306-9(7),* A23067) Benchmark Education Co.
Gellineau, Lloyd. The Alien in the Flashlight. 2012. 24p. (-18). pap. 15.99 *(978-1-4797-2339-3(8))* Xlibris Corp.
Geneviève Douyon Flambert. Grace: The Mystical Caribbean Mission. 2009. 152p. pap. 12.95 *(978-0-595-51639-1(4))* iUniverse, Inc.
Geronimo Stilton Staff. Rescue Rebellion. 2015. (Geronimo Stilton Spacemice Ser.: 5). (ENG.). 128p. (J). (gr. 2-5). pap. 6.99 *(978-0-545-83538-1(0),* Scholastic Paperbacks) Scholastic, Inc.
Gerwitz, Felice & Gerwitz, Christina. Dinosaur Quest at Diamond Peak, 3, Vol. 2. 2nd rev. ed. 2007. (Truth Seeker's Mystery Ser.). 208p. (YA). per. 8.99 *(978-1-931941-11-2(4))* Media Angels, Inc.
—The Missing Link: Found, 3, Vol. 1. 2nd rev. ed. 2004. (Truth Seeker's Mystery Ser.). 208p. (YA). per. 8.99 *(978-1-931941-08-2(4))* Media Angels, Inc.
Getson, Denise. Dry Souls. 2011. (ENG.). 200p. (YA). (gr. 8-3). pap. 7.95 *(978-1-933767-12-3(X))* CBAY Bks.
Giants of Anglesey. 2011. 176p. (gr. 4-6). pap. 13.95 *(978-1-4620-3359-1(8))* iUniverse, Inc.
Giarrusso, Chris. G-Man Coming Home. 2013. (ENG., Illus.). 128p. (J). pap. 9.99 *(978-1-60706-571-5(1),* 9781607065715) Image Comics.
Gibbs, Stuart. Space Case. 2015. (Moon Base Alpha Ser.). (ENG., Illus.). 368p. (J). (gr. 3-7). pap. 7.99 *(978-1-4424-9487-9(5),* Simon & Schuster Bks. For Young Readers) Simon & Schuster Bks. For Young Readers.
—Space Case. 2015. (Moon Base Alpha Ser.: 1). lib. bdg. 18.40 *(978-0-606-37883-3(9))* Turtleback Bks.
—Spaced Out. (Moon Base Alpha Ser.). (ENG.). (J). (gr. 3-7). 2017. 368p. pap. 7.99 *(978-1-4814-2337-3(1))* 2016. (Illus.). 352p. 17.99 *(978-1-4814-2336-6(3))* Simon & Schuster Bks. For Young Readers. (Simon & Schuster Bks. For Young Readers).
—Spaced Out. 2017. (Moon Base Alpha Ser.: 2). lib. bdg. 18.40 ***(978-0-606-39762-9(0))*** Turtleback Bks.
Gibson, James E. & Gibson, Sylvia Scott. Treetoe the Space Monster, 1 vol. Gibson, Gregory V., illus. 2010. 28p. 24.95 *(978-1-4489-4896-3(7))* PublishAmerica, Inc.
Gidwitz, Adam. Star Wars - the Empire Strikes Back: So You Want to be a Jedi? McCaig, Iain, illus. 2015. (ENG.). 336p. (J). (gr. 3-7). 17.99 *(978-1-4847-0914-6(4),* 1392359, Disney Lucasfilm Press) Disney Publishing Worldwide.
Gill, David Macinnis. Black Hole Sun. (Black Hole Sun Ser.: 1). (ENG.). (YA). (gr. 9). 2012. 368p. pap. 8.99 *(978-0-06-167306-1(4))* 2010. 352p. 16.99 *(978-0-06-167304-7(8))* HarperCollins Pubs. (Greenwillow Bks.).
—Invisible Sun. (Black Hole Sun Ser.: 2). (ENG.). (YA). (gr. 9). 2013. 400p. pap. 9.99 *(978-0-06-207333-4(8))* 2012. 384p. 16.99 *(978-0-06-207332-7(X))* HarperCollins Pubs. (Greenwillow Bks.).
—Shadow on the Sun. 2013. (Black Hole Sun Ser.: 3). (ENG.). 432p. (YA). (gr. 9). 17.99 *(978-0-06-207335-8(4),* Greenwillow Bks.) HarperCollins Pubs.
Gill, Margaret. The Brain Changers. 2004. 160p. (YA). pap. 12.95 *(978-0-595-31161-3(X))* iUniverse, Inc.
Gill, Michael. Mitsuki. 2008. 32p. pap. 19.99 *(978-1-4363-0938-7(7))* Xlibris Corp.
Gingeleski, Randolph J. The War of Lord Capani. 2008. 58p. pap. 16.95 *(978-1-60563-758-7(0))* America Star Bks.
Gioseffi, Anthony P. Mainframe. 2007. 144p. per. 11.95 *(978-0-595-44953-8(0))* iUniverse, Inc.
Girard, Geoffrey. Project Cain. 2013. (ENG., Illus.). 368p. (YA). (gr. 9). 17.99 *(978-1-4424-7696-7(6),* Simon & Schuster Bks. For Young Readers) Simon & Schuster Bks. For Young Readers.
Glanville, K. L. 2108: Eyes Open. 2012. (ENG.). 280p. (YA). pap. 12.99 *(978-1-61222-210-3(2))* Luminations Media Group, Inc.
Glass, Calliope. Star Wars at-At Attack! 2015. (Star Wars: World of Reading Ser.). (J). lib. bdg. 13.55 *(978-0-606-37538-2(4))* Turtleback Bks.
—World of Reading Star Wars at-At Attack! (Level 1) 2015. (World of Reading Ser.). (ENG.). 32p. (J). (gr. 1-3). pap. 3.99 *(978-1-4847-0549-0(1),* Disney Lucasfilm Press) Disney Publishing Worldwide.
Glass, Calliope & Kennedy, Caitlin. Star Wars ABC-3PO. Cook, Katie, illus. 2016. (ENG.). 48p. (J). (gr. -1-k). 12.99 *(978-1-4847-4142-9(0),* Disney Lucasfilm Press) Disney Publishing Worldwide.
Glur, D. L' Empire Contre Attaque.Tr. of Empire Strikes Back. (FRE.). (J). pap. 11.95 *(978-2-265-06729-5(6))* Fleuve Noir FRA. Dist: Distribooks, Inc.
Golden Books. I Am a Droid (Star Wars) Kennett, Chris, illus. 2016. (Little Golden Book Ser.). (ENG.). 24p. (J). (-k). 4.99 *(978-0-7364-3489-8(5),* Golden Bks.) Random Hse. Children's Bks.
—I Am a Hero (Star Wars) Golden Books, illus. 2017. (Little Golden Book Ser.). (ENG., Illus.). 24p. (J). (-k). 4.99 ***(978-0-7364-3587-1(5),*** Golden Bks.) Random Hse. Children's Bks.
—I Am a Jedi (Star Wars) Cohee, Ron, illus. 2016. (Little Golden Book Ser.). (ENG.). 24p. (J). (-k). 4.99 *(978-0-7364-3487-4(9),* Golden Bks.) Random Hse. Children's Bks.
—I Am a Sith (Star Wars) Kennett, Chris, illus. 2016. (Little Golden Book Ser.). (ENG.). 24p. (J). (-k). 4.99 *(978-0-7364-3607-6(3),* Golden Bks.) Random Hse. Children's Bks.
—I Am a Stormtrooper (Star Wars) Golden Books & Kennett, Chris, illus. 2017. (Little Golden Book Ser.). (ENG.). 24p. (J). (-k). 4.99 *(978-0-7364-3576-5(X),* Golden Bks.) Random Hse. Children's Bks.
—Star Wars: Attack of the Clones (Star Wars) Beavers, Ethen, illus. 2015. (Little Golden Book Ser.). (ENG.). 24p. (J). (-k). 4.99 *(978-0-7364-3546-8(8),* Golden Bks.) Random Hse. Children's Bks.
—Star Wars Little Golden Book Collection (Star Wars) Golden Books, illus. 2016. (Little Golden Book Treasury Ser.). (ENG., Illus.). 176p. (J). (-k). 12.99 *(978-0-7364-3609-0(X),* Golden Bks.) Random Hse. Children's Bks.
Golden Books, illus. Nine Marvel Super Hero Tales. 2017. (Little Golden Book Treasury Ser.). (ENG.). 224p. (J). (-k). 12.99 *(978-1-5247-1783-4(5),* Golden Bks.) Random Hse. Children's Bks.
—Star Wars: I AM A... Little Golden Book Library (Star Wars), 5 vols. 2016. (ENG.). 120p. (J). (-k). 24.95 *(978-0-7364-3638-0(3),* Golden Bks.) Random Hse. Children's Bks.
—The Star Wars Little Golden Book Library (Star Wars), 6 vols. 2015. (ENG.). 144p. (J). (-k). 29.94 *(978-0-7364-3470-6(4),* Golden Bks.) Random Hse. Children's Bks.
Golden Books & Berrios, Frank. Mutants Rule! (Teenage Mutant Ninja Turtles) Golden Books, illus. 2013. (Color & Paint Plus Stickers Ser.). (ENG., Illus.). 128p. (J). (gr. -1-2). pap. 9.99 *(978-0-449-81952-4(3),* Golden Bks.) Random Hse. Children's Bks.
Golden Books Staff. I Am a Pilot (Star Wars) Batson, Alan, illus. 2016. (Little Golden Book Ser.). (ENG.). 24p. (J). (-k). 4.99 *(978-0-7364-3621-2(9),* Golden Bks.) Random Hse. Children's Bks.
—Star Wars: the Force Awakens (Star Wars) Golden Books Staff & Meurer, Caleb, illus. 2016. (Little Golden Book Ser.). (ENG.). 24p. (J). (-k). 4.99 *(978-0-7364-3491-1(7),* Golden Bks.) Random Hse. Children's Bks.
Goldman, Stanley M. The Doorway to Forever: September 2nd, 1666, the First Day of Forever. 2008. (ENG.). 186p. (J). (gr. 7). pap. 9.95 *(978-1-933255-46-0(3))* DNA Pr.
Gompertz, Haley. Pluto's Planet Problems. 2012. 30p. pap. 10.99 *(978-1-60820-712-1(9))* MLR Pr., LLC.
Goobie, Beth. Fixed, 1 vol. 2005. (ENG.). 294p. (YA). (gr. 8-12). 16.95 *(978-1-55143-374-5(5))* Orca Bk. Pubs. USA.
Goodman, Alison. Singing the Dogstar Blues. 2008. 240p. (YA). *(978-0-7322-8863-1(0))* HarperCollins Pubs. Australia.
Goodman, Allegra. The Other Side of the Island. 2009. (ENG.). 288p. (YA). (gr. 7-18). pap. 8.99 *(978-1-59514-196-5(0),* Razorbill) Penguin Young Readers Group.
Goodman, Gabriel. Plague Riders. 2012. (After the Dust Settled Ser.). (ENG.). 112p. (YA). (gr. 6-12). pap. 7.95 *(978-0-8225-9033-0(6),* Darby Creek); lib. bdg. 27.93 *(978-0-7613-8330-7(1))* Lerner Publishing Group.
Gordon, Roderick. Closer, 12 vols. (Tunnels Ser.: 4). (J). 121.75 *(978-1-4498-2159-3(6))*; 1.25 *(978-1-4498-2165-4(0))*; 296.75 *(978-1-4498-2158-6(8))*; 2011. 132.75 *(978-1-4498-2163-0(4))*; 2011. 134.75 *(978-1-4498-2161-6(8))* Recorded Bks., Inc.
—Spiral, 9 vols. 2012. (Tunnels Ser.: 5). (J). 134.75 *(978-1-4618-4517-1(3))*; 121.75 *(978-1-4618-4516-4(5))*; 296.75 *(978-1-4618-4515-7(7))*; 132.75 *(978-1-4618-4519-5(X))* Recorded Bks., Inc.
Gould, Robert & Duey, Kathleen. Time Soldiers - Rex. Epstein, Eugene, illus. Gould, Robert, photos by. 2005. (Time Soldiers Ser.: Bk. 1). (ENG.). 96p. (J). (gr. k-2). per. 5.95 *(978-1-929945-53-5(1))*; per. 5.95 *(978-1-929945-54-2(X))* Big Guy Bks., Inc.
Graceffa, Joey. Children of Eden: A Novel. (ENG.). 288p. (gr. 7-12). 2017. pap. 12.99 ***(978-1-5011-4990-0(3))*** 2016. 18.99 *(978-1-5011-4655-8(6))* Simon & Schuster. (Atria Bks.).
Graham, Brandon & Roy, Simon. Prophet Volume 2: Brothers TP: Brothers TP. 2013. (ENG., Illus.). 172p. (YA). pap. 14.99 *(978-1-60706-749-8(8),* 9781607067498) Image Comics.
Graham, Brandon, et al. Prophet Volume 3: Empire TP: Empire TP. 2014. (ENG., Illus.). 128p. (YA). pap. 14.99 *(978-1-60706-858-7(3),* 9781607068587) Image Comics.
Grange, Emma. The Empire Strikes Back. 2014. (LEGO Star Wars DK Reader Ser.). lib. bdg. 13.55 *(978-0-606-35734-0(3))* Turtleback Bks.
—A New Hope. 2014. (LEGO Star Wars DK Reader Ser.). lib. bdg. 13.55 *(978-0-606-35733-3(5))* Turtleback Bks.
Grant, Michael. BZRK. (ENG.). 400p. (gr. 9). 2013. (J). pap. 9.99 *(978-1-60684-418-2(0))* 2012. 17.99 *(978-1-60684-312-3(5))* Lerner Publishing Group. (Carolrhoda Lab™).
—BZRK Apocalypse. 2014. (ENG.). 400p. (J). (gr. 9). 18.99 *(978-1-60684-408-3(3),* Carolrhoda Lab™) Lerner Publishing Group.
—BZRK Reloaded. (ENG.). 432p. (J). (gr. 9). 2014. pap. 9.99 *(978-1-60684-504-2(7))* 2013. 18.99 *(978-1-60684-394-9(X))* Lerner Publishing Group. (Carolrhoda Lab™).
Grant, Michael. Monster. 2017. (Gone Ser.: 7). 432p. (YA). (gr. 9). 18.99 ***(978-0-06-246784-3(0),*** Tegen, Katherine Bks) HarperCollins Pubs.
Grant, Michael & Applegate, Katherine. Eve & Adam. 2012. (ENG.). 304p. (YA). (gr. 8-12). 17.99 *(978-0-312-58351-4(6),* 9780312583514) Feiwel & Friends.
Gratz, Alan. The Dragon Lantern: A League of Seven Novel. 2015. (League of Seven Ser.: 2). (ENG., Illus.). 336p. (J). (gr. 5-9). 17.99 *(978-0-7653-3823-5(8),* 9780765338235, Starscape) Doherty, Tom Assocs., LLC.
—The League of Seven. Helquist, Brett, illus. 2015. (League of Seven Ser.: 1). (ENG.). 352p. (J). (gr. 5-9). pap. 9.99 *(978-0-7653-3825-9(4),* 9780765338259, Starscape) Doherty, Tom Assocs., LLC.
Grau, Sheila. The Boy with Seventeen Senses. 2016. (ENG.). 256p. (J). (gr. 3-7). 16.95 *(978-1-4197-2119-9(4),* Amulet Bks.) Abrams, Inc.
Gray, Claudia. Defy the Stars. 2017. (Defy the Stars Ser.: 1). (ENG.). 512p. (YA). (gr. 10-17). 17.99 *(978-0-316-39403-1(3))* Little, Brown Bks. for Young Readers.
—Ten Thousand Skies above You. (Firebird Ser.: 2). (YA). (gr. 9). 2016. 448p. pap. 9.99 *(978-0-06-227900-2(9),* HarperTeen) 2015. (ENG.). 432p. 17.99 *(978-0-06-227899-9(1))* HarperCollins Pubs.
Greenburg, Dan. Dude, Where's My Spaceship? Pamintuan, Macky, illus. 2006. (Weird Planet Ser.: No. 1). (ENG.). 96p. (J). (gr. 1-4). 3.99 *(978-0-375-83344-1(7),* Random Hse. Bks. for Young Readers) Random Hse. Children's Bks.
Greene, Janice. Escape from Earth (Science Fiction), 1 vol. 2017. (Pageturners Ser.). (ENG.). 76p. (YA). (gr. 9-12). 8.95 ***(978-1-68021-394-2(6))*** Saddleback Educational Publishing, Inc.
—Under Siege (Science Fiction), 1 vol. 2017. (Pageturners Ser.). (ENG.). 80p. (YA). (gr. 9-12). 8.95 ***(978-1-68021-397-3(0))*** Saddleback Educational Publishing, Inc.
Gregory, David. Visions of Reality. 2007. 236p. per. 15.95 *(978-0-595-44969-9(7))* iUniverse, Inc.
Griffith, Andrew, illus. Transformers: Movie Prequel: Foundation: Vol 1: Dark of the Moon, 1 vol. 2012. (Transformers: Dark of the Moon Movie Prequel Ser.). (ENG.). 24p. (J). 24.21 *(978-1-59961-971-2(7),* Graphic Novels) Spotlight.
—Transformers: Movie Prequel: Foundation: Vol 2, 1 vol. 2012. (Transformers: Dark of the Moon Movie Prequel Ser.). (ENG.). 24p. (J). 24.21 *(978-1-59961-972-9(5),* Graphic Novels) Spotlight.
—Transformers: Movie Prequel: Foundation: Vol 3, 1 vol. 2012. (Transformers: Dark of the Moon Movie Prequel Ser.). (ENG.). 24p. (J). 24.21 *(978-1-59961-973-6(3),* Graphic Novels) Spotlight.
—Transformers: Movie Prequel: Foundation: Vol 4, 1 vol. 2012. (Transformers: Dark of the Moon Movie Prequel Ser.). (ENG.). 24p. (J). 24.21 *(978-1-59961-974-3(1),* Graphic Novels) Spotlight.
Griffiths, Mark. The Impossible Boy. 2014. (ENG., Illus.). 272p. (J). pap. 8.99 *(978-0-85707-539-0(X),* Simon & Schuster Children's) Simon & Schuster, Ltd. GBR. Dist: Simon & Schuster, Inc.
—Technoslime Terror! Chatterton, Martin, illus. 2013. (ENG.). 288p. (J). pap. 6.99 *(978-0-85707-537-6(3),* Simon & Schuster Children's) Simon & Schuster, Ltd. GBR. Dist: Simon & Schuster, Inc.
Grine, Chris. Time Shifters. 2017. (ENG.). 272p. (J). (gr. 3-7). 24.99 ***(978-0-545-92659-1(9))***; pap. 12.99 ***(978-0-545-92657-7(2))*** Scholastic, Inc. (Graphix).
Grisham, Jonathan. The Death of the Universe. 2005. (YA). per. *(978-1-933594-16-3(0))* FBC Pubns. & Printing.
The Guardians. 2014. (ENG., Illus.). 288p. (J). (gr. 4-8). pap. 7.99 *(978-1-4814-1834-8(3),* Aladdin) Simon & Schuster Children's Publishing.
Guffrey, Lindsey. A Psalm for the Solar System. 2013. 24p. pap. 9.00 *(978-0-9896518-0-6(0))* Yorkshire Publishing Group.
Guibert, Emmanuel & Sfar, Joann. Sardine in Outer Space, Vol. 2. Watson, Sasha, tr. from FRE. Sfar, Joann & Pezzali,

S

Walter, illus. 2nd rev. ed. 2006. (Sardine in Outer Space Ser.: 2). (ENG.). 128p. (J). (gr. 1-5). pap. 17.99 *(978-1-59643-127-0(X)*, 9781596431270, First Second Bks.) Roaring Brook Pr.

—Sardine in Outer Space, Vol. 3. Brizzi, Elisabeth & Siegel, Alexis, trs. from FRE. Sfar, Joann & Pezzali, Walter, illus. 3rd rev. ed. 2007. (Sardine in Outer Space Ser.: 3). (ENG.). 112p. (J). (gr. 1-5). pap. 17.99 *(978-1-59643-128-7(8)*, 9781596431287, First Second Bks.) Roaring Brook Pr.

Guillet, Jean-Pierre. La Puce Cosmique et le Rayon Bleuge. Guillet, Francois, illus. 2004. (Des 9 Ans. Ser.). (FRE.). 120p. (J). *(978-2-922565-98-0(X))* Editions de la Paix CAN. Dist: World of Reading, Ltd.

Gutman, Dan. Dr. Brad Has Gone Mad! Paillot, Jim, illus. 2009. (My Weird School Daze Ser.: 7). 112p. (J). (gr. 1-5). lib. bdg. 15.89 *(978-0-06-155414-8(6))* HarperCollins Pubs.

—Mr. Docker Is off His Rocker! Paillot, Jim, illus. 2006. (My Weird School Ser.: 10). (ENG.). 112p. (J). (gr. 1-5). pap. 4.99 *(978-0-06-082227-9(9))* HarperCollins Pubs.

—Mr. Granite Is from Another Planet!, No. 3. Paillot, Jim, illus. 2008. (My Weird School Daze Ser.: 3). (ENG.). 112p. (J). (gr. 1-5). pap. 4.99 *(978-0-06-134611-8(X))* HarperCollins Pubs.

—Mr. Harrison Is Embarrassin'! Paillot, Jim, illus. 2011. (My Weirder School Ser.: 2). 112p. (J). (gr. 1-5). lib. bdg. 15.89 *(978-0-06-196919-5(2))* HarperCollins Pubs.

Haarsma, P. J. Awakening on Orbis 4. 2010. (Softwire Ser.: 4). (ENG., Illus.). 368p. (YA). (gr. 7-18). 16.99 *(978-0-7636-2712-6(7))* Candlewick Pr.

—Betrayal on Orbis. 2008. (Softwire Ser.: 2). (ENG., Illus.). 272p. (YA). (gr. 7-12). 16.99 *(978-0-7636-2710-2(0))* Candlewick Pr.

—The Softwire: Betrayal on Orbis 2. 2009. (Softwire Ser.: 2). (ENG., Illus.). 320p. (YA). (gr. 7). 7.99 *(978-0-7636-4269-3(X))* Candlewick Pr.

—The Softwire: Wormhole Pirates on Orbis 3. 2010. (Softwire Ser.: 3). (ENG., Illus.). 400p. (YA). (gr. 7). 8.99 *(978-0-7636-4777-3(2))* Candlewick Pr.

—Wormhole Pirates on Orbis, Vol. 3. 2009. (Softwire Ser.: 3). (ENG., Illus.). 384p. (YA). (gr. 7). 16.99 *(978-0-7636-2711-9(9))* Candlewick Pr.

Haddix, Margaret Peterson. The Always War. (ENG.). (YA). (gr. 7). 2012. 224p. pap. 8.99 *(978-1-4169-9527-2(7))* 2011. 208p. 16.99 *(978-1-4169-9526-5(9))* Simon & Schuster Bks. For Young Readers. (Simon & Schuster Bks. For Young Readers).

—Among the Barons. 2004. (Shadow Children Ser.). 182p. (gr. 3-7). 17.00 *(978-0-7569-3923-6(2))* Perfection Learning Corp.

—Among the Barons. (Shadow Children Ser.: 4). (ENG.). (J). (gr. 3-7). 2003. 192p. 17.99 *(978-0-689-83906-1(5))* 2004. 208p. reprint ed. pap. 7.99 *(978-0-689-83910-8(3))* Simon & Schuster Bks. For Young Readers. (Simon & Schuster Bks. For Young Readers).

—Among the Brave. 2004. (Shadow Children Ser.: Bk. 5). 132p. (J). lib. bdg. 20.00 *(978-1-4242-0392-5(9))* Fitzgerald Bks.

—Among the Brave. (Shadow Children Ser.: 5). (ENG., Illus.). (J). (gr. 3-7). 2005. 256p. pap. 7.99 *(978-0-689-85795-9(0))* 2004. 240p. 17.99 *(978-0-689-85794-2(2))* Simon & Schuster Bks. For Young Readers. (Simon & Schuster Bks. For Young Readers).

—Among the Enemy. 2006. (Shadow Children Ser.: Bk. 6). (Illus.). 214p. (gr. 3-7). 17.00 *(978-0-7569-6792-5(9))* Perfection Learning Corp.

—Among the Enemy. (Shadow Children Ser.: 6). (ENG., (J). (gr. 3-7). 2006. Illus.). 240p. pap. 7.99 *(978-0-689-85797-3(7))* 2005. 224p. 17.99 *(978-0-689-85796-6(9))* Simon & Schuster Bks. For Young Readers. (Simon & Schuster Bks. For Young Readers).

—Among the Free. 2007. (Shadow Children Ser.: Bk. 7). 194p. (gr. 3-7). 17.00 *(978-0-7569-7953-9(6))* Perfection Learning Corp.

—Among the Free. (Shadow Children Ser.: Bk. 7). (ENG., Illus.). 208p. (J). (gr. 3-7). 2007. pap. 7.99 *(978-0-689-85799-7(3))* 2006. 18.99 *(978-0-689-85798-0(5))* Simon & Schuster Bks. For Young Readers. (Simon & Schuster Bks. For Young Readers).

—Among the Free. 2007. (Shadow Children Ser.: 7). lib. bdg. 18.40 *(978-1-4178-1424-4(1)*, Turtleback) Turtleback Bks.

—Among the Hidden. 2014. (Shadow Children Ser. 1 Ser.). (ENG.). 160p. (J). 11.24 *(978-1-63245-178-1(6))* Lectorum Pubns., Inc.

—Caught. (Missing Ser.: 5). (ENG., (J). (gr. 3-7). 2013. Illus.). 368p. pap. 7.99 *(978-1-4169-8983-7(8))* 2012. 352p. 16.99 *(978-1-4169-8982-0(X))* Simon & Schuster Bks. For Young Readers. (Simon & Schuster Bks. For Young Readers).

—Caught. 2013. (Missing Ser.: 5). lib. bdg. 18.40 *(978-0-606-27045-8(0)*, Turtleback) Turtleback Bks.

—Children of Exile. 2016. (Children of Exile Ser.: 1). (ENG., Illus.). 304p. (J). (gr. 5). 17.99 *(978-1-4424-5003-5(7)*, Simon & Schuster Bks. For Young Readers) Simon & Schuster Bks. For Young Readers.

—Found. (Missing Ser.: 1). (ENG.). (J). (gr. 3-7). 2009. 336p. pap. 7.99 *(978-1-4169-5421-7(X))* 2008. 320p. 17.99 *(978-1-4169-5417-0(1))* Simon & Schuster Bks. For Young Readers. (Simon & Schuster Bks. For Young Readers).

—Game Changer. 2012. (ENG.). 256p. (YA). (gr. 7). 16.99 *(978-0-689-87380-5(8)*, Simon & Schuster Bks. For Young Readers) Simon & Schuster Bks. For Young Readers.

—In over Their Heads. 2017. (Under Their Skin Ser.: 2). (ENG., Illus.). 320p. (J). (gr. 3-7). 16.99 *(978-1-4814-1761-7(4)*, Simon & Schuster Bks. For Young Readers) Simon & Schuster Bks. For Young Readers.

—Redeemed. 2015. (Missing Ser.: 8). (ENG.). 416p. (J). (gr. 3-7). 17.99 *(978-1-4424-9756-6(4)*, Simon & Schuster Bks. For Young Readers) Simon & Schuster Bks. For Young Readers.

—Redeemed. 2016. (Missing Ser.: 8). lib. bdg. 18.40 *(978-0-606-39234-1(3))* Turtleback Bks.

—Revealed. 2015. (Missing Ser.: 7). lib. bdg. 19.65 *(978-0-606-37847-5(2))* Turtleback Bks.

—Risked. 2013. (Missing Ser.: Bk. 6). (ENG., Illus.). 320p. (J). (gr. 3-7). 16.99 *(978-1-4169-8984-4(6)*, Simon & Schuster Bks. For Young Readers) Simon & Schuster Bks. For Young Readers.

—Risked. 2014. (Missing Ser.: 6). lib. bdg. 19.65 *(978-0-606-36096-8(4))* Turtleback Bks.

—Sabotaged. (Missing Ser.: 3). (ENG.). (J). (gr. 3-7). 2011. 400p. pap. 8.99 *(978-1-4169-5425-5(2))* 2010. 384p. 17.99 *(978-1-4169-5424-8(4))* Simon & Schuster Bks. For Young Readers. (Simon & Schuster Bks. For Young Readers).

—Sent. (Missing Ser.: 2). (YA). 2011. 82.75 *(978-1-4407-2678-1(7))* 2009. 1.25 *(978-1-4407-2679-8(5))* 2009. 218.75 *(978-1-4407-2670-5(1))* 2009. 98.75 *(978-1-4407-2675-0(2))* Recorded Bks., Inc.

—Sent. (Missing Ser.: 2). (ENG.). (J). (gr. 3-7). 2010. 336p. pap. 7.99 *(978-1-4169-5423-1(6))* 2009. 320p. 16.99 *(978-1-4169-5422-4(8))* Simon & Schuster Bks. For Young Readers. (Simon & Schuster Bks. For Young Readers).

—Sent. abr. ed. 2009. *(978-1-4424-0767-1(0))* Simon & Schuster Children's Publishing.

—Sent. l.t. ed. 2010. (Missing Ser.: Bk. 2). (ENG.). 346p. 23.99 *(978-1-4104-3245-2(9))* Thorndike Pr.

—Sent. 2010. (Missing Ser.: 2). lib. bdg. 18.40 *(978-0-606-14699-9(7)*, Turtleback) Turtleback Bks.

—Torn. (Missing Ser.: 4). (ENG.). (J). (gr. 3-7). 2012. 368p. pap. 8.99 *(978-1-4169-8981-3(1))* 2011. 352p. 17.99 *(978-1-4169-8980-6(3))* Simon & Schuster Bks. For Young Readers. (Simon & Schuster Bks. For Young Readers).

—Torn. l.t. ed. 2011. (Missing Ser.: Bk. 4). (ENG.). 368p. 23.99 *(978-1-4104-4078-5(8))* Thorndike Pr.

—Torn. 2012. (Missing Ser.: 4). lib. bdg. 18.40 *(978-0-606-26333-7(0)*, Turtleback) Turtleback Bks.

—Turnabout. 2012. (ENG.). 224p. (YA). (gr. 7). pap. 8.99 *(978-1-4424-4603-8(X)*, Simon & Schuster Bks. For Young Readers) Simon & Schuster Bks. For Young Readers.

—Turnabout. 2007. (ENG.). 240p. (YA). (gr. 7-12). mass mkt. 7.99 *(978-1-4169-3653-4(X)*, Simon Pulse) Simon Pulse.

—Under Their Skin. 2016. (Under Their Skin Ser.: 1). (ENG.). 320p. (J). (gr. 3-7). 16.99 *(978-1-4814-1758-7(4)*, Simon & Schuster Bks. For Young Readers) Simon & Schuster Bks. For Young Readers.

—Under Their Skin. 2017. (Under Their Skins Ser.: 1). lib. bdg. 18.40 ***(978-0-606-39756-8(6))*** Turtleback Bks.

Haddon, Mark. Boom! 2011. (ENG.). 208p. (J). (gr. 3-7). 7.99 *(978-0-385-75224-4(5)*, Yearling) Random Hse. Children's Bks.

Hadland, W. Into the Night. 2010. 312p. (gr. 4-6). pap. 19.13 *(978-1-4251-4187-5(0))* Trafford Publishing.

Hagen, Bethany. Landry Park. 2015. (ENG.). 400p. (YA). (gr. 7). pap. 9.99 *(978-0-14-242548-0(6)*, Speak) Penguin Young Readers Group.

Hager, Mandy. Into the Wilderness. 2014. (Blood of the Lamb Ser.). (ENG.). 335p. (YA). (gr. 9). 17.99 *(978-1-61614-863-8(2))* Prometheus Bks., Pubs.

—Resurrection. 2014. (Blood of the Lamb Ser.). (ENG.). 361p. (YA). (gr. 9). 17.99 *(978-1-61614-909-3(4))* Prometheus Bks., Pubs.

Hager, Robert. Saurcana: Terror from the Sea. 2004. (J). *(978-0-9727676-1-3(4))*; pap. *(978-0-9727676-0-6(6))* Hager, Robert.

Haladay, Max. Max Gets Mad. 2006. (Neighborhood Readers Ser.). (ENG.). 8p. (gr. 1-3). pap. 5.15 *(978-1-4042-6811-1(1)*, Rosen Classroom) Rosen Publishing Group, Inc., The.

Hale, Bruce. The Adventures of Space Gecko. (Illus.). (J). 8.95 *(978-0-9621280-2-8(3))* Words & Pictures Publishing, Inc.

Hale, Nathan. One Trick Pony. 2017. (ENG., Illus.). 128p. (J). (gr. 3-7). 14.95 *(978-1-4197-2128-1(3)*, Amulet Bks.) Abrams, Inc.

Hale, Shannon. Dangerous. 2014. (ENG.). 416p. (YA). (gr. 7). 17.99 *(978-1-59990-168-8(4)*, 9781599901688, Bloomsbury USA Childrens) Bloomsbury Publishing USA.

Hale, Shannon & Hale, Dean. The Unbeatable Squirrel Girl: Squirrel Meets World. Mangiatordi, Vitale, illus. 2017. ([Not Part of a Series]; a Squirrel Girl Novel Ser.: 1). (ENG.). 336p. (J). (gr. 3-7). 13.99 *(978-1-4847-8154-8(6)*, Marvel Pr.) Disney Publishing Worldwide.

Halevy, Hanita H. Dragonlions & the Spacemen. Heler, Shraga, illus. 2012. (ENG.). 140p. (J). pap. 13.00 *(978-965-550-085-1(3))* Contento De Semrik ISR. Dist: Bookmasters Distribution.

Hall, Susan, illus. Robot Repairman to the Rescue! 2009. (Backyardigans Ser.). (ENG.). 24p. (J). (gr. -1-2). pap. 3.99 *(978-1-4169-9012-3(7)*, Simon Spotlight/Nickelodeon) Simon Spotlight/Nickelodeon.

Hall, Teri. Away. 2011. (ENG.). 240p. (YA). (gr. 7-18). 16.99 *(978-0-8037-3502-6(2)*, Dial Bks) Penguin Young Readers Group.

—The Line. (ENG.). (J). (gr. 5-18). 2011. 239p. 6.99 *(978-0-14-241776-8(9)*, Puffin Books) 2010. 224p. 16.99 *(978-0-8037-3466-1(2)*, Dial Bks) Penguin Young Readers Group.

Hama, Larry, text. Captain America: The Death of Captain America Prose Novel. 2014. (ENG., Illus.). 344p. (J). (gr. 4-17). 24.99 *(978-0-7851-8996-1(3))* Marvel Worldwide, Inc.

Hambrick, Sharon. Tommy's Rocket. Manning, Maurie J., illus. 2003. (Fig Street Kids Ser.). 83p. (J). (gr. 1-2). 7.49 *(978-1-59166-186-3(2))* BJU Pr.

Hamel, Mike. Dragon's Lair, 5. 2007. (Matterhorn the Brave Ser.: 5). (ENG.). 192p. (J). (gr. 5-11). per. 9.99 *(978-0-89957-837-8(3))* AMG Pubs.

—Jewel Heist, 4. 2007. (Matterhorn the Brave Ser.: 4). (ENG.). 192p. (gr. 8-7). per. 9.99 *(978-0-89957-836-1(5))* AMG Pubs.

—Pyramid Scheme. 2007. (Matterhorn the Brave Ser.: 3). (ENG.). 176p. (J). (gr. 5-7). per. 9.99 *(978-0-89957-835-4(7))* AMG Pubs.

—Rylan the Renegade, 6. 2007. (Matterhorn the Brave Ser.: 6). (ENG.). 192p. (J). (gr. 8-7). per. 9.99 *(978-0-89957-838-5(1))* AMG Pubs.

—The Sword & the Flute. 2007. (Matterhorn the Brave Ser.: 1). (ENG.). 176p. (J). (gr. 5-12). per. 9.99 *(978-0-89957-833-0(0))* AMG Pubs.

—Talis Hunters, Vol. 2. 2007. (Matterhorn the Brave Ser.: 2). (ENG.). 176p. (J). (gr. 5-12). per. 9.99 *(978-0-89957-834-7(9))* AMG Pubs.

Hamilton, Kersten. The Ire of Iron Claw. Hamilton, James, illus. (Gadgets & Gears Ser.: 2). (ENG.). (J). (gr. 2-5). 2016. 192p. pap. 6.99 *(978-0-544-66854-6(5)*, HMH Books For Young Readers) 2015. 176p. 16.99 *(978-0-544-22502-2(3))* Houghton Mifflin Harcourt Publishing Co.

—The Tick-Tock Man. Hamilton, James, illus. 2016. (Gadgets & Gears Ser.: 3). (ENG.). 144p. (J). (gr. 2-5). 16.99 *(978-0-544-43300-7(9))* Houghton Mifflin Harcourt Publishing Co.

Hand, Elizabeth. A New Threat. 2004. (Star Wars Ser.: Vol. 5). 139p. (J). lib. bdg. 20.00 *(978-1-4242-0781-7(9))* Fitzgerald Bks.

Hansen, Lynne. Reckless Revolution. 2007. (YA). *(978-1-4114-9672-9(8)*, Spark Publishing Group) Sterling Publishing Co., Inc.

—Shades of Blue & Gray. 2007. (YA). pap. *(978-1-4114-9674-3(4)*, Spark Publishing Group) Sterling Publishing Co., Inc.

—A Time for Witches. 2007. (YA). *(978-1-4114-9671-2(X)*, Spark Publishing Group) Sterling Publishing Co., Inc.

Hapka, Catherine, pseud. Plants vs. Zombies. 2014. (I Can Read! Level 2 Ser.). (J). lib. bdg. 13.55 *(978-0-606-35477-6(8))* Turtleback Bks.

Hardinge, Frances. A Face Like Glass. 2017. (ENG.). 496p. (YA). (gr. 7-17). 19.95 *(978-1-4197-2484-8(3)*, Amulet Bks.) Abrams, Inc.

Hardy, Melissa. The Geomancer's Compass. 2012. (ENG.). 272p. (YA). (gr. 7). 17.95 *(978-1-77049-292-9(5)*, Tundra Bks.) Tundra Bks. CAN. Dist: Penguin Random Hse. LLC.

Harper, Benjamin. Star Wars Movie Theater Storybook & Lightsaber Projector. 2015. (Movie Theater Ser.: 1). (ENG.). 40p. (J). (gr. k-2). 24.99 *(978-0-7944-3494-6(0))* Studio Fun International.

—Star Wars: the Chewbacca Story. 2016. (ENG.). 32p. (J). (gr. k-3). 17.99 *(978-0-7944-3741-1(9)*, Reader's Digest Children's Bks.) Studio Fun International.

—Star Wars: the Force Awakens: Movie Theater Storybook & BB-8 Projector. 2016. (ENG.). 40p. (J). (gr. 1-3). 24.99 *(978-0-7944-3789-3(3))* Studio Fun International.

—Star Wars: the Power of the Dark Side. 2015. (ENG.). 32p. (J). (gr. 1-4). 17.99 *(978-0-7944-3532-5(7))* Reader's Digest Assn., Inc., The.

HarperCollins Publishers Ltd. Staff, et al. James Cameron's Avatar. movie tie-in ed. 2009. (James Cameron's Avatar Ser.). (ENG., Illus.). 48p. (J). (gr. -1-2). pap. 7.99 *(978-0-06-180124-2(0)*, HarperFestival) HarperCollins Pubs.

Harris, M. G. Ghost Mine. 2017. (Gemini Force I Ser.). (ENG.). 256p. (J). (gr. 7-11). 9.99 *(978-1-4440-1408-2(0)*, Orion Children's Bks.) Hachette Children's Group GBR. Dist: Hachette Bk. Group.

—White Storm. 2016. (Gemini Force I Ser.). (ENG.). 256p. (J). (gr. 7-11). 9.99 *(978-1-4440-1410-5(2)*, Orion Children's Bks.) Hachette Children's Group GBR. Dist: Hachette Bk. Group.

Harris, N. W. The Last Orphans. 2014. (Last Orphans Ser.). (ENG.). 274p. (J). (gr. 7-9). pap. 11.95 *(978-1-940534-89-5(5))* Clean Teen Publishing.

Harrison, Harry. Toy Shop. 2011. 18p. pap. 6.95 *(978-1-60664-572-7(2))* Rodgers, Alan Bks.

Harrison, S. Infinity Rises, 0 vols. 2016. (Infinity Trilogy Ser.: 2). (ENG.). 261p. (YA). (gr. 9-13). pap. 9.99 *(978-1-5039-5225-6(8)*, 9781503952256, Skyscape) Amazon Publishing.

Harrison, Zac. Crash Landing, 1 vol. 2013. (Hyperspace High Ser.). (ENG.). 288p. (gr. 4-8). pap. 8.95 *(978-1-4342-6310-0(X))*; 27.32 *(978-1-4342-6306-3(1))* Stone Arch Bks.

—Frozen Enemies, 1 vol. 2013. (Hyperspace High Ser.). (ENG.). 288p. (gr. 4-8). pap. 8.95 *(978-1-4342-6311-7(8))*; 27.32 *(978-1-4342-6307-0(X))* Stone Arch Bks.

—Galactic Battle, 1 vol. 2014. (Hyperspace High Ser.). (ENG., Illus.). 288p. (gr. 4-8). 27.32 *(978-1-4342-6569-2(2))* Stone Arch Bks.

—Hyperspace High, 1 vol. 2014. (Hyperspace High Ser.). (ENG.). 288p. (gr. 4-8). 54.64 *(978-1-4342-8935-3(4))* Stone Arch Bks.

Harstad, Johan. 172 Hours on the Moon. 2013. (ENG.). 384p. (J). (gr. 8-17). pap. 10.99 *(978-0-316-18289-8(3))* Little, Brown Bks. for Young Readers.

Harstad, Johan & Chace, Tara. 172 Hours on the Moon. 2012. (ENG.). 368p. (gr. 7-17). 17.99 *(978-0-316-18288-1(5))* Little Brown & Co.

Hartley Bellows, Carol. Icey. 2009. 32p. pap. 14.99 *(978-1-4389-4475-3(6))* AuthorHouse.

Hasany, Syed M. Where Is My Stethoscope? 2012. 24p. pap. 14.93 *(978-1-4669-6888-2(5))* Trafford Publishing.

Hasbro. Transformers Rescuebots: Robots to the Rescue! 2016. (ENG.). 12p. (J). (gr. -1-1). bds. 10.99 *(978-0-7944-3685-8(4))* Studio Fun International.

Hasbro Inc. Staff & King, Trey. Transformers Rescue Bots: Training Academy: Firefighters! 2016. (Passport to Reading Level 2 Ser.). (ENG., Illus.). 32p. (J). (gr. -1-1). pap. 3.99 *(978-0-316-38982-2(X))* Little, Brown Bks. for Young Readers.

Hastings, Avery. Feuds. 2014. (Feuds Ser.: 1). (ENG.). 272p. (YA). (gr. 7). 18.99 *(978-1-250-05771-6(X)*, 9781250057716, St. Martin's Griffin) St. Martin's Pr.

Hatke, Ben. Legends of Zita the Spacegirl. Hatke, Ben, illus. 2012. (Zita the Spacegirl Ser.: 2). (ENG., Illus.). 224p. (J). (gr. 3-7). 19.99 *(978-1-59643-806-4(1)*, 9781596438064); pap. 12.99 *(978-1-59643-447-9(3)*, 9781596434479) Roaring Brook Pr. (First Second Bks.).

—Legends of Zita the Spacegirl. 2012. (Zita the Spacegirl Ser.: 2). (J). lib. bdg. 24.50 *(978-0-606-26708-3(5)*, Turtleback) Turtleback Bks.

—Zita the Spacegirl. Hatke, Ben, illus. 2011. (Zita the Spacegirl Ser.: 1). (ENG., Illus.). 192p. (J). (gr. 3-7). 19.99 *(978-1-59643-695-4(6)*, 9781596436954); pap. 12.99 *(978-1-59643-446-2(5)*, 9781596434462) Roaring Brook Pr. (First Second Bks.).

—Zita the Spacegirl. 2011. (Zita the Spacegirl Ser.: 1). (J). lib. bdg. 24.50 *(978-0-606-21623-4(5)*, Turtleback) Turtleback Bks.

Hautman, Pete. The Cydonian Pyramid. (Klaatu Diskos Ser.). (ENG.). 368p. (YA). (gr. 7). 2014. pap. 8.99 *(978-0-7636-6933-1(4))* 2013. 16.99 *(978-0-7636-5404-7(3))* Candlewick Pr.

—The Flinkwater Factor: A Novel in Five Thrilling Episodes. 2015. (Flinkwater Chronicles Ser.: 1). (ENG.). 256p. (J). (gr. 4-8). 16.99 *(978-1-4814-3251-1(6)*, Simon & Schuster Bks. For Young Readers) Simon & Schuster Bks. For Young Readers.

—The Forgetting Machine. 2016. (Flinkwater Chronicles Ser.: 2). (ENG., Illus.). 224p. (J). (gr. 4-8). 16.99 *(978-1-4814-6438-3(8)*, Simon & Schuster Bks. For Young Readers) Simon & Schuster Bks. For Young Readers.

—Hole in the Sky. 2007. (ENG.). 224p. (YA). (gr. 7). pap. 11.95 *(978-1-4169-6822-1(9)*, Simon Pulse) Simon Pulse.

—Mr. Was. 2012. (ENG.). 240p. (YA). (gr. 7). pap. 8.99 *(978-1-4424-3337-3(X)*, Simon & Schuster Bks. For Young Readers) Simon & Schuster Bks. For Young Readers.

—Rash. 2007. (ENG., Illus.). 272p. (YA). (gr. 7-12). pap. 10.99 *(978-0-689-86904-4(5)*, Simon & Schuster Bks. For Young Readers) Simon & Schuster Bks. For Young Readers.

Hawking, Stephen & Hawking, Lucy. George & the Unbreakable Code. Parsons, Garry, illus. 2016. (George's Secret Key Ser.). (ENG.). 352p. (J). (gr. 3-7). 18.99 *(978-1-4814-6627-1(5)*, Simon & Schuster Bks. For Young Readers) Simon & Schuster Bks. For Young Readers.

Hawking, Stephen W. & Hawking, Lucy. George's Cosmic Treasure Hunt. Parsons, Garry, illus. 2009. (George's Secret Key Ser.). (ENG.). 320p. (J). (gr. 3-7). 19.99 *(978-1-4169-8671-3(5)*, Simon & Schuster Bks. For Young Readers) Simon & Schuster Bks. For Young Readers.

—George's Secret Key to the Universe. Parsons, Garry, illus. (George's Secret Key Ser.). (ENG.). (J). (gr. 3-7). 2009. 336p. pap. 12.99 *(978-1-4169-8584-6(0))* 2007. 304p. 22.99 *(978-1-4169-5462-0(7))* Simon & Schuster Bks. For Young Readers. (Simon & Schuster Bks. For Young Readers).

Hawkins, Matt. Think Tank, Vol. 1. 2012. (ENG., Illus.). 120p. (YA). pap. 14.99 *(978-1-60706-660-6(2)*, 9781607066606) Image Comics.

—Think Tank, Vol. 2. 2013. (ENG., Illus.). 160p. (YA). pap. 14.99 *(978-1-60706-745-0(5)*, 9781607067450) Image Comics.

Hawthorne, Mike, illus. Machine Teen: History 101001. 2012. (ENG.). 120p. (J). (gr. 4-17). pap. 14.99 *(978-0-7851-6486-9(3))* Marvel Worldwide, Inc.

Hayes, Vicki C. Sky Watchers. 2014. (Red Rhino Ser.). (J). lib. bdg. 18.40 *(978-0-606-36197-2(9))* Turtleback Bks.

Healey, Karen. When We Wake. 2014. (ENG.). 320p. (YA). (gr. 7-17). pap. 10.99 *(978-0-316-20077-6(8))* Little, Brown Bks. for Young Readers.

—While We Run. 2014. (ENG.). 336p. (YA). (gr. 10-17). 18.00 *(978-0-316-23382-8(X))* Little, Brown Bks. for Young Readers.

Hearn, Julie & Yankus, Marc. Sign of the Raven. 2005. (ENG., Illus.). 336p. (YA). 16.95 *(978-0-689-85734-8(9)*, Atheneum Bks. for Young Readers) Simon & Schuster Children's Publishing.

Heck, Don, et al, illus. Invaders Classic Vol. 1: The Complete Collection. 2014. (ENG.). 512p. (J). (gr. 4-17). pap. 39.99 *(978-0-7851-9057-8(0))* Marvel Worldwide, Inc.

Hein, Connie L. Toliver in Time; for a Journey West: History in a Nutshell. Theobald, Denise, illus. l.t. ed. 2005. 28p. (J). lib. bdg. 17.95 *(978-0-9740855-6-2(1))*; per. 9.95 *(978-0-9740855-7-9(X))* Still Water Publishing.

Hello Mars! 2005. (J). audio, cd-rom 24.95 *(978-0-9771381-6-6(X))* Williams, Geoffrey T.

Heltzel, Anne. Circle Nine. 2011. (ENG.). 272p. (YA). (gr. 9). 16.99 *(978-0-7636-5333-0(0))* Candlewick Pr.

Helvig, Kristi. Burn Out. 2014. (ENG.). 272p. (J). (gr. 9). 17.99 *(978-1-60684-479-3(2)*, Carolrhoda Lab™) Lerner Publishing Group.

—Strange Skies, Bk. 2. 2015. (ENG.). 272p. (gr. 9). 17.99 *(978-1-60684-481-6(4)*, Carolrhoda Lab™) Lerner Publishing Group.

Hemsworth, Jade. Project Mc2: Smart Is the New Cool. 2016. (Illus.). 144p. (J). ***(978-1-250-12632-0(0))*** ETT Imprint.

Henighan, Tom. Mercury Man. 2004. (ENG.). 200p. (YA). (gr. 6). pap. 9.99 *(978-1-55002-508-8(2))* Dundurn CAN. Dist: Ingram Publisher Services.

Henriques, Ben. Max & the Memory Machine. 2010. (J). 12.95 *(978-0-615-38727-7(6))* EB Benjamin, LLC.

Hester, Phil. T. H. U. N. D. E. R. Agents Volume 1. 2014. (T. H. U. N. D. E. R. Agents Ser.). (ENG., Illus.). 104p. pap. 17.99 *(978-1-61377-861-6(9)*, 9781613778616) Idea & Design Works, LLC.

Hickman, Jonathan. Avengers - Rogue Planet, Vol. 5. 2014. (ENG., Illus.). 136p. (YA). (gr. 8-17). 24.99 *(978-0-7851-5477-8(9))* Marvel Worldwide, Inc.

Hicks, Faith Erin. The Adventures of Superhero Girl (Expanded Edition) 2017. (ENG., Illus.). 128p. (gr. 5-9). 16.99 ***(978-1-5067-0336-7(4))*** Dark Horse Comics.

Hidalgo, Pablo. The Phantom Menace. 2012. (Star Wars Ser.). (ENG.). 64p. (J). (gr. -1-3). 9.99 *(978-0-545-38986-0(0))* Scholastic, Inc.

—Star Wars Lightsaber Thumb Wrestling Force Wars. 2016. (ENG., Illus.). 16p. (J). (gr. 1-5). 12.99 *(978-1-4521-5352-0(3))* Chronicle Bks. LLC.

—Star Wars Rebels: Head to Head. 2014. lib. bdg. 19.65 *(978-0-606-36071-5(9))* Turtleback Bks.

—Star Wars Rebels: Head to Head. 2014. (ENG.). 64p. (J). (gr. 3-7). pap. 8.99 *(978-0-545-74642-7(6))* Scholastic, Inc.

Hill, C. J. Echo in Time. (YA). 2014. 387p. *(978-0-06-212395-4(5))* 2013. (Erasing Time Ser.: 2). (ENG.). 400p. (gr. 8). pap. 9.99 *(978-0-06-212396-1(3)*, Tegen, Katherine Bks) HarperCollins Pubs.

—Erasing Time. 2012. (Erasing Time Ser.: 1). (ENG.). 368p. (YA). (gr. 8). 17.99 *(978-0-06-212392-3(0)*, Tegen, Katherine Bks) HarperCollins Pubs.

Hill, Nick. Carlton Casey: Alien Incident. 2007. 100p. per. 9.95 *(978-1-59800-310-9(0))* Outskirts Pr., Inc.

Hilton, Marilyn. Full Cicada Moon. 2017. lib. bdg. 19.65 ***(978-0-606-39789-6(2))*** Turtleback Bks.

Hinkler Books Staff, reader. Barney's Outer Space Adventure. 2004. (J). 9.99 incl. audio compact disk *(978-1-86515-996-6(4))* Hinkler Bks. Pty, Ltd. AUS. Dist: Penton Overseas, Inc.

Hirsch, Jeff. Black River Falls. 2017. (ENG.). 336p. (YA). (gr. 7). pap. 9.99 *(978-0-544-93885-4(2)*, HMH Books For Young Readers) Houghton Mifflin Harcourt Publishing Co.

—The Eleventh Plague. (ENG.). 288p. (J). (gr. 7). 2012. pap. 9.99 *(978-0-545-29015-9(5))* 2011. 17.99 *(978-0-545-29014-2(7))* Scholastic, Inc. (Scholastic Pr.).

—Magisterium. 2012. (ENG.). 320p. (J). (gr. 7). 17.99 *(978-0-545-29018-0(X)*, Scholastic Pr.) Scholastic, Inc.

Hobbs, Constance. Dreamers. 2008. 436p. 50.50 *(978-0-9556783-6-3(6))* Hobbs, Constance GBR. Dist: Lulu Pr., Inc.

Hobbs, Will. Go Big or Go Home. 2009. (ENG.). 208p. (J). (gr. 5). pap. 6.99 *(978-0-06-074143-3(0))* HarperCollins Pubs.

Hockney, Deborah. Jocasta's Gift. 2012. (ENG.). 248p. pap. *(978-1-78088-050-1(2))* Troubador Publishing Ltd.
Hoena, Blake A. Ack's New Pet, 1 vol. Harpster, Steve, illus. 2014. (Eek & Ack Early Chapter Bks.). (ENG.). 32p. (gr. k-2). lib. bdg. 22.65 *(978-1-4342-6406-0(8))* Stone Arch Bks.
—Beyond the Black Hole. Harpster, Steve, illus. 2008. (Graphic Sparks Ser.). (ENG.). 40p. (gr. 1-3). pap. 5.95 *(978-1-4342-0855-2(9),* Graphic Sparks) Stone Arch Bks.
—The Big Mistake, 1 vol. Harpster, Steve, illus. 2014. (Eek & Ack Early Chapter Bks.). (ENG.). 32p. (gr. k-2). lib. bdg. 22.65 *(978-1-4342-6408-4(4))* Stone Arch Bks.
—The Black Hole Report, 1 vol. Harpster, Steve, illus. 2014. (Eek & Ack Early Chapter Bks.). (ENG.). 32p. (gr. k-2). lib. bdg. 22.65 *(978-1-4342-6409-1(2))* Stone Arch Bks.
—Eek & Ack Early Chapter Books, 1 vol. 2014. (Eek & Ack Early Chapter Bks.). (ENG.). 32p. (gr. k-2). 90.60 *(978-1-4342-8457-0(3))* Stone Arch Bks.
—Eek Discovers Earth, 1 vol. Harpster, Steve, illus. 2014. (Eek & Ack Early Chapter Bks.). (ENG.). 32p. (gr. k-2). lib. bdg. 22.65 *(978-1-4342-6407-7(6))* Stone Arch Bks.
—Under the Red Sun, 1 vol. Schoening, Dan, illus. (Superman Ser.). (ENG.). 56p. (gr. 2-3). 2013. pap. 4.95 *(978-1-4342-1375-4(7))* 2009. lib. bdg. 26.65 *(978-1-4342-1159-0(2))* Stone Arch Bks. (DC Super Heroes).
Hoena, Blake A., et al. Poison Ivy's Deadly Garden, 1 vol. (Batman Ser.). (ENG., Illus.). 56p. (gr. 2-3). 2013. pap. 4.95 *(978-1-4342-1368-6(4))* 2009. lib. bdg. 26.65 *(978-1-4342-1152-1(5))* Stone Arch Bks. (DC Super Heroes).
Hoffman, Mary. Trace in Space. (Illus.). 118p. (J). pap. 8.99 *(978-0-340-62669-6(0))* Hodder & Stoughton GBR. Dist: Trafalgar Square Publishing.
Hoffmann, Lou. Key of Behliseth. 2nd ed. 2016. (ENG., Illus.). (J). 27.99 ***(978-1-63533-037-3(8),*** Harmony Ink Pr.) Dreamspinner Pr.
Hofmeyr, David. Stone Rider. 2015. (ENG., Illus.). 336p. (YA). (gr. 7). 18.99 *(978-0-385-74473-7(0),* Delacorte Pr.) Random Hse. Children's Bks.
Holder, Nancy & Viguie, Debbie. Wicked: Witch & Curse. 2009. *(978-1-4351-2000-6(0))* Barnes & Noble, Inc.
Holder, Nancy & Viguié, Debbie. Wicked: Witch & Curse. 2008. (Wicked Ser.). (ENG.). 672p. (YA). (gr. 9). pap. 9.99 *(978-1-4169-7119-1(X),* Simon Pulse) Simon Pulse.
Holliday, Susan. The Time Street Gang & the Rag & Bone Boy. l.t. ed. 2007. 132p. pap. *(978-1-905665-64-8(4))* Pollinger In Print.
Holt, Christopher. Dark Waters. 2013. (Last Dogs Ser.: 2). (J). lib. bdg. 18.40 *(978-0-606-35308-3(9))* Turtleback Bks.
—Journey's End. 2014. (Last Dogs Ser.: 4). (J). lib. bdg. 18.40 *(978-0-606-35944-3(3))* Turtleback Bks.
—The Last Dogs: Dark Waters. Douglas, Allen, illus. 2013. (Last Dogs Ser.: 2). (ENG.). 352p. (J). (gr. 3-7). pap. 7.99 *(978-0-316-20009-7(3))* Little, Brown Bks. for Young Readers.
—The Last Dogs: Journey's End. Douglas, Allen, illus. 2014. (Last Dogs Ser.: 4). (ENG.). 320p. (J). (gr. 3-7). 17.00 *(978-0-316-20007-3(7))* Little, Brown Bks. for Young Readers.
—The Last Dogs: the Long Road. Douglas, Allen, illus. 2014. (Last Dogs Ser.: 3). (ENG.). 352p. (J). (gr. 3-7). pap. 7.99 *(978-0-316-20016-5(6))* Little, Brown Bks. for Young Readers.
—The Long Road. 2014. (Last Dogs Ser.: 3). (J). lib. bdg. 18.40 *(978-0-606-35309-0(7))* Turtleback Bks.
Holt, K. A. Mike Stellar: Nerves of Steel. 2010. (ENG.). 272p. (J). (gr. 3-7). 7.99 *(978-0-375-84557-4(7),* Yearling) Random Hse. Children's Bks.
—Red Moon Rising. 2016. (ENG., Illus.). 336p. (J). (gr. 5-9). 16.99 *(978-1-4814-3626-7(0),* McElderry, Margaret K. Bks.) McElderry, Margaret K. Bks.
Holyoke, Polly. The Neptune Challenge. (ENG.). 352p. (J). 2016. (gr. 5-9). pap. 7.99 *(978-1-4847-1571-0(3))* 2015. (gr. 3-7). 16.99 *(978-1-4847-1345-7(1))* Hyperion Bks. for Children.
Hopper, Ada. March of the Mini Beasts. Ricks, Sam, illus. 2016. (DATA Set Ser.: bk.1). (ENG.). 128p. (J). (gr. k-4). pap. 5.99 *(978-1-4814-5728-6(4),* Little Simon) Little Simon.
Horne, Jay. Published Youth Volume Two. 2010. 61p. pap. 10.99 *(978-0-557-30674-9(4))* Lulu Pr., Inc.
Hosler, Jay. Last of the Sandwalkers. 2015. (ENG., Illus.). 320p. (YA). (gr. 5). pap. 17.99 *(978-1-62672-024-4(X),* 9781626720244, First Second Bks.) Roaring Brook Pr.
Houran, Lori Haskins. Alien in the Outfield: Perseverance. Warrick, Jessica, illus. 2017. (How to Be an Earthling (r) Ser.: 6). (ENG.). 64p. (gr. 1-3). 34.65 ***(978-1-57565-852-0(6))*** Kane Press, Inc.
House, David James. The Key to Space. 2006. (ENM.). 364p. (YA). 24.95 *(978-0-9777086-0-4(8))* House, David.
Houtman, Jacqueline. The Reinvention of Edison Thomas. 2012. (ENG.). 192p. (J). (gr. 3-7). pap. 8.95 *(978-1-59078-951-3(2))* Boyds Mills Pr.
How to Be a Time Lord. 2015. (ENG., Illus.). 176p. (YA). 16.99 *(978-0-7232-9436-8(4),* 9780723294368) Penguin Bks., Ltd. GBR. Dist: Diamond Comic Distributors, Inc.
Howard, Chris. Rootless. 2012. (ENG.). 336p. (J). (gr. 9). 17.99 *(978-0-545-38789-7(2))* Scholastic, Inc.
Howard, Kate, adapted by. Fright Knight! 2016. 71p. (J). ***(978-1-4844-8023-6(6))*** Scholastic, Inc.
Howard, Roger. Safety First. 2008. 328p. pap. 12.95 *(978-1-4327-0449-0(4))* Outskirts Pr., Inc.
Howe, James. Screaming Mummies of the Pharaoh's Tomb II. Helquist, Brett, illus. 2004. (Tales from the House of Bunnicula Ser.: 4). (ENG.). 112p. (J). (gr. 2-5). pap. 6.99 *(978-0-689-83954-2(5),* Atheneum Bks. for Young Readers) Simon & Schuster Children's Publishing.
Howe, Tina Field. Alysa of the Fields: Book One in the Tellings of Xunar-kun. 2006. (Illus.). 320p. (YA). 30.95 *(978-0-9768585-2-2(5))* Howe, Tina Field.
Howson, Imogen. Linked. 2013. (ENG., Illus.). 368p. (YA). (gr. 7). 16.99 *(978-1-4424-4656-4(0),* Simon & Schuster Bks. For Young Readers) Simon & Schuster Bks. For Young Readers.
—Unravel. 2014. (ENG., Illus.). 480p. (YA). (gr. 7). 17.99 *(978-1-4424-4658-8(7),* Simon & Schuster Bks. For Young Readers) Simon & Schuster Bks. For Young Readers.
Howson, Imogen & Smith, Ali. Linked. 2014. (ENG., Illus.). 384p. (YA). (gr. 7). pap. 9.99 *(978-1-4424-4660-1(9),* Simon & Schuster Bks. For Young Readers) Simon & Schuster Bks. For Young Readers.
Hoyle, K. B. Criminal. 2016. (ENG., Illus.). (YA). 31.99 ***(978-1-61213-395-9(9))***; (Breeder Cycle Ser.: Vol. 2). pap. 21.50 ***(978-1-61213-388-1(6))*** Writer's Coffee Shop, The.
Hrdlitschka, Shelley. Sun Signs, 1 vol. 2005. (ENG.). 208p. (YA). (gr. 8-12). pap. 14.95 *(978-1-55143-338-7(9))* Orca Bk. Pubs. USA.
Hubbell, Mary A. The Miracle of Annie's Ring. 2010. 138p. pap. 11.50 *(978-1-60911-530-2(9),* Eloquent Bks.) Strategic Book Publishing & Rights Agency (SBPRA).
Huber, Morgan. Nanite. 2013. 140p. pap. 19.95 *(978-1-63004-633-0(7))* America Star Bks.
Hubert, Jerry. They Were Not Gods: A Space-Age Fairytale. 2003. 170p. (YA). 23.95 *(978-0-595-66091-9(6));* pap. 13.95 *(978-0-595-29970-6(9))* iUniverse, Inc.
Hueller, Andy. Skipping Stones at the Center of the Earth: A Middle Grade Novel. 2011. (J). pap. 8.99 *(978-1-59955-488-4(7),* Bonneville Bks.) Cedar Fort, Inc./CFI Distribution.
Huggins-Cooper, Lynn. Alien Invaders (Invasores Extraterrestres) de La Vega, Eida, tr. Leick, Bonnie, illus. 2005. (SPA & ENG.). 32p. (J). (gr. 4-7). 7.95 *(978-0-9741992-7-6(3),* 626999, Raven Tree Pr.,Csi) Continental Sales, Inc.
—Alien Invaders/Invasores Extraterrestres. de la Vega, Eida, tr. from ENG. Leick, Bonnie, illus. 2005.Tr. of Invasores Extraterrestres. (SPA & ENG.). 32p. (J). (gr. 4-7). 16.95 *(978-0-9724973-9-8(0),* 626999, Raven Tree Pr.,Csi) Continental Sales, Inc.
Hughes, Devon. Escape from Lion's Head. 2017. (Unnaturals Ser.: 2). 384p. (J). (gr. 3-7). 16.99 *(978-0-06-225757-4(9),* Tegen, Katherine Bks) HarperCollins Pubs.
—Unnaturals: The Battle Begins. Richardson, Owen, illus. 2015. (Unnaturals Ser.: 1). (ENG.). 352p. (J). (gr. 3-7). 16.99 *(978-0-06-225754-3(4))* HarperCollins Pubs.
Hughes, Mark Peter. A Crack in the Sky. 2011. (Greenhouse Chronicles Ser.). (ENG.). 416p. (J). (gr. 3-7). 9.99 *(978-0-385-73709-8(2),* Yearling) Random Hse. Children's Bks.
Hughes, Monica. The Game. 2010. (ENG.). 208p. (YA). (gr. 7). pap. 9.99 *(978-1-4424-0939-2(8),* Simon Pulse) Simon Pulse.
—The Golden Aquarians. 2009. (ENG.). 192p. (YA). (gr. 7-7). pap. 9.99 *(978-1-4424-0223-2(7),* Simon & Schuster Bks. For Young Readers) Simon & Schuster Bks. For Young Readers.
—The Keeper of the Isis Light. 2008. Orig. Title: Summerspell. (ENG.). 240p. (J). (gr. 3-7). pap. 11.99 *(978-1-4169-8963-9(3),* Atheneum Bks. for Young Readers) Simon & Schuster Children's Publishing.
—Space Trap. (J). pap. 7.95 *(978-0-88899-202-4(5))* Groundwood Bks. CAN. Dist: Publishers Group West (PGW).
Hunt for Jade Dragon. 2014. (Michael Vey Ser.: No. 4). (ENG., Illus.). 336p. (YA). (gr. 7). 19.99 *(978-1-4814-2438-7(6),* Simon Pulse/Mercury Ink) Simon Pulse/Mercury Ink.
Hunter, Erin. A Dangerous Path. Stevenson, Dave, illus. 2005. (Warriors: the Prophecies Begin Ser.: 5). (ENG.). 336p. (J). (gr. 3-7). pap. 6.99 *(978-0-06-052565-1(7))* HarperCollins Pubs.
Hurst, Melissa E. The Edge of Forever. 2015. (ENG.). 272p. (J). (gr. 6). pap. 14.99 *(978-1-63220-424-0(X),* Sky Pony Pr.) Skyhorse Publishing Co., Inc.
Hussey, Don. Chesapeake Station: It Began with Serenity. 2013. 152p. pap. 12.99 *(978-0-9893324-2-2(X))* Westchester Publishing.
Hutton, Laurie S. & Marsham, Liz. Wonder Woman Classic - A Hero for All. Hood, Josh et al, illus. 2017. 24p. (J). (gr. -1-3). pap. 3.99 *(978-0-06-236081-6(7),* HarperFestival) HarperCollins Pubs.
Iacobucci, Vincent. The Little Book All about Fluguls. 2006. (Illus.). (J). *(978-0-9779390-0-8(6))* Flugul Pubng.
Ilnitzki, Megan. Guardians of the Galaxy Read-Along Storybook & CD. 2017. (Read-Along Storybook & CD Ser.). (ENG.). 32p. (J). (gr. 1-3). pap. 6.99 *(978-1-4847-8153-1(8),* Marvel Pr.) Disney Publishing Worldwide.
Immonen, Stuart, illus. Magnetic North. 2006. (ENG.). 128p. (YA). (gr. 8-17). pap. 12.99 *(978-0-7851-1906-7(X))* Marvel Worldwide, Inc.
Irvine, Alex & Wyatt, Chris. Phase Two: Marvel's Guardians of the Galaxy. 2015. (Marvel Cinematic Universe Ser.). (ENG.). 192p. (J). (gr. 3-7). 10.99 *(978-0-316-25675-9(7))* Little, Brown Bks. for Young Readers.
Irvine, Alexander C. & Preiss, Byron. Have Robot, Will Travel. 2013. 222p. pap. 19.95 *(978-1-59687-959-1(9))* ibooks, Inc.
Isbell, Tom. The Capture. 2016. (Prey Trilogy Ser.: 2). 448p. (YA). (gr. 8). 17.99 *(978-0-06-221605-2(8),* HarperTeen) HarperCollins Pubs.
—The Prey. 2015. (Prey Trilogy Ser.: 1). (ENG.). 416p. (YA). (gr. 8). 17.99 *(978-0-06-221601-4(5),* HarperTeen) HarperCollins Pubs.
Ishwaran, Wobine. A Journey into Space: Kary to the Moon. 2008. 24p. pap. 11.49 *(978-1-4343-6717-4(7))* AuthorHouse.
Ivanoff, George. Gamers' Quest. 2009. (Gamers Ser.: Bk. 1). (ENG.). 208p. (YA). pap. *(978-1-876462-86-4(8),* Ford Street Publishing) Hybrid Pubs.
—How to Make a Fake Death Ray into a Real Laser. 2007. 96p. (J). *(978-1-4207-0735-9(3))* Sundance/Newbridge Educational Publishing.
Izubuchi, Yutaka & Ohnogi, Hiroshi. Rahxephon, Vol. 3. 2006. (RahXephon (Mo Masterbook) Ser.). (ENG., Illus.). 200p. (YA). pap. 7.95 *(978-1-59796-002-1(0))* DrMaster Pubns. Inc.
Jablonski, Carla. The Travelers, Bk. 1. 2009. (Pendragon: Before the War Ser.: 1). (ENG.). 256p. (J). (gr. 5-9). pap. 7.99 *(978-1-4169-6522-0(X),* Aladdin) Simon & Schuster Children's Publishing.
Jackson-Beavers, Rose, et al. A Hole in My Heart. 2004. (ENG.). (YA). per. 10.95 *(978-0-9753634-0-9(9))* Prioritybooks Pubns.
Jackson, Paul B. Luke & Mcnashty's Treasure. 2006. 96p. pap. 16.95 *(978-1-4241-2909-6(5))* PublishAmerica, Inc.
Jacobs, Evan. Emoji of Doom, 1 vol. 2017. (White Lightning Ser.). (ENG.). 91p. (J). (gr. 6-8). pap. 8.95 ***(978-1-68021-354-6(7))*** Saddleback Educational Publishing, Inc.
Jacques, Brian. Redwall. Blevins, Bret, illus. 2007. (Redwall Ser.). (ENG.). 148p. (J). (gr. 5-18). 12.99 *(978-0-399-24481-0(6),* Philomel Bks.) Penguin Young Readers Group.
Jaffe, Charlotte & Doherty, Barbara. The Space Race. 2003. (Illus.). (J). (gr. 2-3). 60.00 *(978-1-57336-395-2(2),* I5077) Interaction Pubs., Inc.
Jakobs, D. Meet Blades the Copter-Bot. 2014. (Transformers Passport to Reading Ser.). (J). lib. bdg. 14.75 *(978-0-606-35295-6(3))* Turtleback Bks.
James, Dalton. The Heroes of Googley Woogley. 2009. 22p. (J). pap. 10.95 *(978-1-4327-2782-6(6))* Outskirts Pr., Inc.
James, Nick. The Pearl Wars. 2011. (Skyship Academy Ser.: 1). (ENG.). 384p. (YA). (gr. 7-18). pap. 9.95 *(978-0-7387-2341-9(X),* Flux) North Star Editions.
—Skyship Academy: Crimson Rising. 2012. (Skyship Academy Ser.: 2). (ENG.). 360p. (YA). pap. 9.99 *(978-0-7387-2342-6(8),* Flux) North Star Editions.
—Skyship Academy: Strikeforce. 2013. (Skyship Academy Ser.: 3). (ENG.). 360p. (YA). pap. 9.99 *(978-0-7387-3637-2(6),* Flux) North Star Editions.
Janicke, Gregory. The Dark Mystery of the Shadow Beasts. 2004. (Illus.). 168p. *(978-983-58-0993-4(3))* Times Edition.
Jansen, Patty. The Far Horizon. 2012. 176p. pap. *(978-0-9872009-4-5(1))* Capricornica Pubns.
Jay, Annabelle. Starsong. 2017. (Sun Dragon Ser.: Vol. 3). (ENG., Illus.). (YA). pap. 14.99 ***(978-1-63533-246-9(X),*** Harmony Ink Pr.) Dreamspinner Pr.
Jayasuriya, Michael. The Time MacHine. 2011. 66p. pap. 15.99 *(978-1-4653-3741-2(5))* Xlibris Corp.
Jazwierska, Jennifer & Popiel, Candice Bataille. Discovery of Glow. 2008. (Glowmundo Ser.). (J). (gr. 2-6). pap. 12.95 *(978-0-9814930-0-8(9))* Elora Media, LLC.
Jinks, Catherine. Evil Genius. 2007. 486p. (J). *(978-1-4287-3510-1(0))* Harcourt Trade Pubs.
—Evil Genius. 2008. (ENG., Illus.). 496p. (YA). (gr. 7). pap. 9.99 *(978-0-15-206185-2(1))* Houghton Mifflin Harcourt Publishing Co.
—Genius Squad. 2009. (ENG., Illus.). 448p. (J). (gr. 7). pap. 8.99 *(978-0-15-206650-5(0))* Houghton Mifflin Harcourt Publishing Co.
—The Genius Wars. 2011. (ENG.). 384p. (YA). (gr. 7). pap. 8.99 *(978-0-547-57727-2(3))* Houghton Mifflin Harcourt Publishing Co.
—Living Hell. 2011. (ENG.). 264p. (YA). (gr. 7). pap. 14.99 *(978-0-547-54998-9(9))* Houghton Mifflin Harcourt Publishing Co.
Johansen, K. V. The Black Box. 2010. (Illus.). 212p. (J). pap. 13.00 *(978-0-9864974-0-7(1))* Sybertooth, Inc. CAN. Dist: Lightning Source, Inc.
Johnson, Bob. The Lost Mine of the Mechanical Spider. Johnson, Bob, illus. 2006. (Squatland Chronicles Ser.). (Illus.). 53p. (J). (gr. -1-3). per. 11.00 *(978-1-60002-185-5(9),* 3977) Mountain Valley Publishing, LLC.
Johnson, Cornelius. Escape from Ketan, 1 vol. 2010. 80p. pap. 19.95 *(978-1-4489-5463-6(0))* America Star Bks.
Johnson, Elana. Abandon: A Possession Novel. 2013. (ENG.). 464p. (YA). (gr. 9). 17.99 *(978-1-4424-8482-5(9));* (Illus.). pap. 9.99 *(978-1-4424-8481-8(0))* Simon Pulse. (Simon Pulse).
—Possession. 2012. (ENG.). 432p. (YA). (gr. 9). pap. 9.99 *(978-1-4424-2126-4(6),* Simon Pulse) Simon Pulse.
—Surrender. 2012. (ENG.). 480p. (YA). (gr. 9). 17.99 *(978-1-4424-4568-0(8),* Simon Pulse) Simon Pulse.
—Surrender: A Possession Novel. 2013. (ENG.). 496p. (YA). (gr. 9). pap. 9.99 *(978-1-4424-4569-7(6),* Simon Pulse) Simon Pulse.
Johnson, Mike. Galileo Seven Part 1, 1 vol. 2013. (Star Trek Ser.). (ENG.). 24p. (J). (gr. 6-12). lib. bdg. 24.21 *(978-1-61479-159-1(7))* Spotlight.
—Galileo Seven Part 2, 1 vol. 2013. (Star Trek Ser.). (ENG.). 24p. (J). (gr. 6-12). lib. bdg. 24.21 *(978-1-61479-160-7(0))* Spotlight.
Johnson, Mike & Parrott, Ryan. Star Trek: Starfleet Academy. Charm, Derek, illus. 2016. (Star Trek Ser.). (ENG.). 120p. (J). pap. 19.99 *(978-1-63140-663-8(9),* 9781631406638) Idea & Design Works, LLC.
Johnson, Mike & Scott, Mairghread. Transformers Prime: Rage of the Dinobots: Rage of the Dinobots. Padilla, Agustin, illus. 2013. (Transformers Ser.). (ENG.). 104p. pap. 17.99 *(978-1-61377-606-3(3),* 9781613776063) Idea & Design Works, LLC.
Johnson, Sandi. Chip Dude from Outer Space. Johnson, Britt, ed. Sturgen, Bobbi, illus. l.t. ed. 2014. (ENG.). 28p. (J). (gr. k-5). pap. 12.99 *(978-1-929063-81-9(4),* 254) Moons & Stars Publishing For Children.
Johnston, E. K. Ahsoka. 2016. (ENG.). 400p. (YA). (gr. 7-17). 17.99 *(978-1-4847-0566-7(1),* Disney Lucasfilm Press) Disney Publishing Worldwide.
Jolley, Alana L. If You Give a Padre a Peppertree. 2008. 24p. pap. 15.99 *(978-1-4257-9308-1(8))* Xlibris Corp.
Jolley, Dan. Alien Adventure on Planet J. Wendt, Matt, illus. 2008. (Twisted Journeys (r) Ser.: 8). (ENG.). 112p. (J). (gr. 4-7). 27.93 *(978-0-8225-6998-5(1),* Graphic Universe™) Lerner Publishing Group.
—Attack of the Mutant Meteors. Witt, David, illus. 2010. (Twisted Journeys (r) Ser.: 14). (ENG.). 112p. (J). (gr. 4-7). pap. 7.95 *(978-0-8225-9255-6(X),* Graphic Universe™); lib. bdg. 27.93 *(978-0-8225-9249-5(5))* Lerner Publishing Group.
—Shipwrecked on Mad Island, No. 11. Huddleston, Courtney, illus. 2009. (Twisted Journeys (r) Ser.: 11). (ENG.). 112p. (J). (gr. 4-7). 27.93 *(978-0-8225-7911-3(1),* Graphic Universe™) Lerner Publishing Group.
Jones, Allan Frewin. Starship. (Hunter & Moon Mystery Ser.: Vol. 5). 169p. (J). pap. 8.99 *(978-0-340-70964-1(2))* Hodder & Stoughton GBR. Dist: Trafalgar Square Publishing.
Jones, Carrie. Flying. 2016. (Flying Ser.: 1). (ENG.). 256p. (YA). 17.99 *(978-0-7653-3657-6(X),* 9780765336576, Tor Teen) Doherty, Tom Assocs., LLC.
Jones, Chris. Cameron Jack & the Ghosts of World War 2. 2010. 120p. pap. 12.49 *(978-1-4520-2839-2(7))* AuthorHouse.
Jones, Diana Wynne. A Tale of Time City. 2012. (ENG.). 384p. (YA). (gr. 7-18). 9.99 *(978-0-14-242015-7(8),* Firebird) Penguin Young Readers Group.
Jordan, Robert. The Hunt Begins. Keegan, Charles, illus. 2005. (Great Hunt Ser.: Bk. 1). 397p. (gr. 5-9). 16.00 *(978-0-7569-5065-1(1))* Perfection Learning Corp.
Jordan, Sophie. Uninvited. (Uninvited Ser.: 1). (ENG.). (YA). (gr. 8). 2015. 400p. pap. 9.99 *(978-0-06-223364-6(5))* 2014. 384p. 17.99 *(978-0-06-223365-3(3))* HarperCollins Pubs. (HarperTeen).
—Unleashed. (Uninvited Ser.: 2). (YA). (gr. 8). 2016. 384p. pap. 9.99 *(978-0-06-223367-7(X))* 2015. (ENG.). 368p. 17.99 *(978-0-06-223371-4(8))* HarperCollins Pubs. (HarperTeen).
Josephs, Rudy & Barba, Rick. The Gemini Agent. 2011. (ENG.). 224p. (YA). (gr. 7). 14.99 *(978-1-4424-1961-2(X));* pap. 7.99 *(978-1-4424-1342-9(5))* Simon Spotlight. (Simon Spotlight).
Joy, Judith Bourassa. A Doorway Through Space: Winner of Mayhaven Award for Children's Fiction. 2008. (ENG.). 224p. (YA). 14.95 *(978-1-932278-17-0(6))* Mayhaven Publishing, Inc.
Jung, Mike. Geeks, Girls, & Secret Identities. Maihack, Mike, illus. 2012. (J). (ENG.). 320p. (gr. 3-7). 16.99 *(978-0-545-33548-5(5));* pap. *(978-0-545-33549-2(3))* Scholastic, Inc. (Levine, Arthur A. Bks.).
The Jupiter Pirates - Curse of the Iris. 2014. (Jupiter Pirates Ser.: 2). (ENG.). 352p. (J). (gr. 3-7). 16.99 *(978-0-06-223023-2(9))* HarperCollins Pubs.
Jury, Walter & Fine, Sarah. Burn. 2015. (ENG.). 352p. (YA). (gr. 7). bds. 17.99 *(978-0-399-16068-4(X),* G.P. Putnam's Sons Books for Young Readers) Penguin Young Readers Group.
—Scan. 2015. (ENG.). 352p. (YA). (gr. 7). pap. 9.99 *(978-0-14-242398-1(X),* Speak) Penguin Young Readers Group.
Kabaya, Kosuke. Android Angels. 2014. (ENG., Illus.). 158p. (YA). pap. 14.95 *(978-1-939012-10-4(4),* 9781939012104) Gen Manga Entertainment, Inc.
Kacvinsky, Katie. Awaken. 2012. (ENG.). 320p. (YA). (gr. 7). pap. 9.99 *(978-0-547-72198-9(6))* Houghton Mifflin Harcourt Publishing Co.
—Awaken. 2012. lib. bdg. 20.85 *(978-0-606-24781-8(5),* Turtleback) Turtleback Bks.
—Middle Ground. 2013. (ENG.). 336p. (YA). (gr. 7). pap. 9.99 *(978-0-544-10480-8(3))* Houghton Mifflin Harcourt Publishing Co.
Kaczynski, Heather. Dare Mighty Things. 2017. 384p. (YA). (gr. 8). 17.99 ***(978-0-06-247986-0(5),*** HarperTeen) HarperCollins Pubs.
Kade, J. V. Bot Wars. 2015. (Bot Wars Ser.). (ENG.). 384p. (J). (gr. 5). 8.99 *(978-0-14-242526-8(5),* Puffin Books) Penguin Young Readers Group.
—The Meta-Rise. 2nd ed. 2014. (Bot Wars Ser.). (ENG., Illus.). 304p. (J). (gr. 5). 17.99 *(978-0-8037-3861-4(7),* Dial Bks) Penguin Young Readers Group.
Kade, Stacey. Project Paper Doll the Rules. 2014. (Project Paper Doll Ser.). (ENG., Illus.). 426p. (YA). (gr. 7-12). pap. 9.99 *(978-1-4231-5379-5(0))* Hyperion Bks. for Children.
—Project Paper Doll the Trials. 2016. (Project Paper Doll Ser.). (ENG.). 336p. (YA). (gr. 7-12). pap. 9.99 *(978-1-4231-9474-3(8))* Hyperion Bks. for Children.
—The Trials. 2015. (Project Paper Doll Ser.). (ENG., Illus.). 336p. (YA). (gr. 7-12). 17.99 *(978-1-4231-8463-8(7))* Hyperion Bks. for Children.
Kahaney, Amelia. The Invisible: A Brokenhearted Novel. 2015. (Brokenhearted Ser.: 2). (ENG.). 304p. (YA). (gr. 8). pap. 9.99 *(978-0-06-223193-2(6),* HarperTeen) HarperCollins Pubs.
Kahn, J. Le Retour du Jedi, Vol. II.Tr. of Return of the Jedi. (FRE.). (J). pap. 11.95 *(978-2-265-06728-8(8))* Fleuve Noir FRA. Dist: Distribooks, Inc.
Kamachi, Kazuma. A Certain Magical Index, Vol. 1. Haimura, Kiyotaka, illus. 2014. (Certain Magical Index Ser.: 1). (ENG.). 224p. (YA). (gr. 8-17). 14.00 *(978-0-316-33912-4(1),* Yen Pr.) Orbit.
Kamat Tarkar, Poorwa Yeshwant. The Cornelius Sign: & the Season Queen Business, 1 vol. 2009. 234p. pap. 24.95 *(978-1-61582-408-3(1))* America Star Bks.
Kang, Lydia. Catalyst. 2016. (Control Duology Ser.). (ENG.). 416p. (YA). (gr. 7). pap. 10.99 *(978-0-14-751604-6(8),* Speak) Penguin Young Readers Group.
Kang, Lydia & Carey, Janet Lee. Catalyst. 2015. (Control Duology Ser.). (ENG.). 400p. (YA). (gr. 7). 17.99 *(978-0-8037-4093-8(X),* Kathy Dawson Books) Penguin Young Readers Group.
Kaplan, Arie. Face Off. White, Dave, illus. 2016. (Lego Star Wars Ser.). (ENG.). 64p. (J). (gr. 2-5). pap. 8.99 *(978-0-545-92541-9(X))* Scholastic, Inc.
Karl, Jean E. The Turning Place: Stories of a Future Past. 2016. (ENG.). 224p. (YA). (gr. 5-8). pap. 7.99 *(978-0-486-80459-0(3))* Dover Pubns., Inc.
Katcher, Brian. The Improbable Theory of Ana & Zak. (YA). (gr. 8). 2016. 352p. pap. 9.99 *(978-0-06-227278-2(0))* 2015. (ENG.). 336p. 17.99 *(978-0-06-227277-5(2))* HarperCollins Pubs. (Tegen, Katherine Bks).
Kaufman, Amie. Illuminae. 2017. lib. bdg. 24.50 ***(978-0-606-39847-3(3))*** Turtleback Bks.
Kaufman, Amie & Kristoff, Jay. Gemina. Lu, Marie, illus. 2016. (Illuminae Files Ser.). (ENG.). 672p. (YA). (gr. 9). 19.99 *(978-0-553-49915-5(7));* lib. bdg. 22.99 *(978-0-553-49916-2(5))* Random Hse. Children's Bks. (Knopf Bks. for Young Readers).
—Illuminae. 2015. (Illuminae Files Ser.). (ENG., Illus.). 608p. (YA). (gr. 9). lib. bdg. 21.99 *(978-0-553-49912-4(2));* 18.99 *(978-0-553-49911-7(4))* Random Hse. Children's Bks. (Knopf Bks. for Young Readers).
Kaufman, Amie & Spooner, Meagan. Their Fractured Light. 2015. (Starbound Ser.). (ENG., Illus.). 430p. (YA). (gr. 7-17). 17.99 *(978-1-4231-7104-1(7))* Hyperion Bks. for Children.
—Their Fractured Light. 2016. (Starbound Ser.). (ENG.). 432p. (YA). (gr. 7-12). pap. 9.99 *(978-1-4847-4783-4(6))* Hyperion Pr.
—These Broken Stars. 2014. (These Broken Stars Ser.). (ENG., Illus.). 410p. (YA). (gr. 7-12). pap. 9.99 *(978-1-4231-7121-8(7))* Hyperion Bks. for Children.

S

—These Broken Stars. 2013. (Starbound Ser.). (ENG., Illus.). 382p. (YA). (gr. 7-12). 17.99 (978-1-4231-7102-7(0)) Hyperion Pr.

—This Shattered World. (Starbound Ser.). (ENG., (YA). (gr. 7-12). 2015. Illus.). 410p. pap. 9.99 (978-1-4231-7122-5(5)) 2014. 400p. 17.99 (978-1-4231-7103-4(9)) Hyperion Bks. for Children.

Kawahara, Reki. Alicization Beginning. 2016. (Sword Art Online Ser.: 9). (ENG., Illus.). 272p. (YA). (gr. 8-17). pap. 14.00 (978-0-316-39042-2(9), Yen Pr.) Orbit.

—Alicization Running. 2017. (Sword Art Online Ser.: 10). (ENG., Illus.). 240p. (YA). (gr. 8-17). pap. 14.00 (978-0-316-39043-9(7), Yen Pr.) Orbit.

—Red Storm Princess, Vol. 2. 2014. (Accel World Ser.: 2). (ENG.). 256p. (YA). (gr. 8-17). pap. 13.00 (978-0-316-29636-6(8), Yen Pr.) Orbit.

Kawahara, Reki. Sword Art Online 11: Alicization Turning. 2017. (Sword Art Online Ser.: 11). (ENG., Illus.). 208p. (YA). (gr. 8-17). pap. 14.00 **(978-0-316-39044-6(5)**, Yen Pr.) Orbit.

Kawahara, Reki & Paul, Stephen. Sword Art Online. Abec, illus. 2014. (YA). **(978-0-316-39049-1(6)**, Yen Pr.) Orbit.

Kawahara, Yumiko. Dolls. Kawahara, Yumiko, illus. (Dolls Ser.: 1). (ENG., Illus.). 1. 2004. 200p. pap. 9.99 (978-1-59116-508-8(3)) Vol. 2. 2005. 216p. pap. 9.99 (978-1-59116-670-2(5)) Viz Media.

Keatinge, Joe. Hell Yeah! Volume 1: Last Days on Earth TP: Last Days on Earth TP. 2012. (ENG., Illus.). 128p. (YA). pap. 9.99 (978-1-60706-607-1(6), 9781607066071) Image Comics.

Keats, Israel. Alien Invasion. 2017. (Level Up Ser.). (ENG.). (J). (gr. 6-12). 120p. pap. 7.99 **(978-1-5124-5356-0(0))**; lib. bdg. 26.65 **(978-1-5124-3984-7(3))** Lerner Publishing Group. (Darby Creek).

—Labyrinth. 2017. (Level Up Ser.). (ENG.). 128p. (YA). (gr. 6-12). 26.65 **(978-1-5124-3987-8(8))**; pap. 7.99 **(978-1-5124-5357-7(9))** Lerner Publishing Group. (Darby Creek).

—The Zephyr Conspiracy. 2017. (Level Up Ser.). (ENG.). (YA). (gr. 6-12). 120p. pap. 7.99 **(978-1-5124-5361-4(7))**; lib. bdg. 26.65 **(978-1-5124-3985-4(1))** Lerner Publishing Group. (Darby Creek).

Keene, Carolyn. Green-Eyed Monster: Book One in the Eco Mystery Trilogy. 2009. (Nancy Drew (All New) Girl Detective Ser.: 39). (ENG.). 176p. (J). (gr. 3-7). pap. 5.99 (978-1-4169-7844-2(5), Aladdin) Simon & Schuster Children's Publishing.

Keeper of the Colony. 2006. (Keeper Ser.). 246p. (J). (gr. 3-9). per. 10.95 (978-1-929976-35-5(6)) Top Pubns., Ltd.

Kellerman, Faye & Kellerman, Aliza. Prism. (YA). 2010. (ENG.). 288p. (gr. 8). pap. 8.99 (978-0-06-168724-2(3)) 2009. 272p. (gr. 7-18). lib. bdg. 17.89 (978-0-06-168722-8(7), HarperTeen) HarperCollins Pubs.

Kelly, Mark. Project Rescue. 2017. (Astrotwins Ser.: 2). lib. bdg. 18.40 **(978-0-606-39745-2(0))** Turtleback Bks.

Kenah, Katharine. The Best Teacher in Second Grade. Carter, Abby, illus. 2007. (I Can Read Bks.). 48p. (gr. -1-3). 14.00 (978-0-7569-8105-1(0)) Perfection Learning Corp.

Kendall, Gillian Murray. The Garden of Darkness. 2014. (ENG.). 336p. (YA). (gr. 6-12). pap. 9.99 (978-1-78108-248-5(0), Ravenstone) Rebellion GBR. Dist: Simon & Schuster, Inc.

Kennedy, Katie. Learning to Swear in America. 2016. (ENG.). 352p. (YA). 17.99 (978-1-61963-909-6(2), 9781619639096, Bloomsbury USA Childrens) Bloomsbury Publishing USA.

—What Goes Up. 2017. (ENG.). 336p. (YA). 17.99 (978-1-61963-912-6(2), 9781619639126, Bloomsbury USA Childrens) Bloomsbury Publishing USA.

Kernaghan, Eileen. The Alchemist's Daughter. 2006. (ENG., Illus.). 144p. pap. 15.95 (978-1-894345-79-8(7)) Thistledown Pr., Ltd. CAN. Dist: Univ. of Toronto Pr.

Kerner, Charlotte. Blueprint. Crawford, Elizabeth D., tr. from GER. 2003. (Young Adult Fiction Ser.). 192p. (YA). (gr. 9-12). 16.95 (978-0-8225-0080-3(9), Carolrhoda Bks.) Lerner Publishing Group.

Kesel, Barbara. Radiant, Vol. 2. Perez, George et al, illus. 2004. (Solus Ser.: Vol. 2). 160p. (YA). pap. 15.95 (978-1-59314-057-1(6)) CrossGeneration Comics, Inc.

Kessler, Liz. Philippa Fisher's Fairy Godsister. 2008. (Philippa Fisher Ser.: 1). (ENG., Illus.). 256p. (J). (gr. 3-7). 15.99 (978-0-7636-4070-5(0)) Candlewick Pr.

Khanlu, Nancy Yousefian. A Trip into Space. 2012. 16p. pap. 7.95 (978-1-4525-0399-8(0)) Get Published.

Khorana, Aditi. Mirror in the Sky. 2016. (ENG.). 352p. (YA). (gr. 7). 17.99 (978-1-59514-856-8(6), Razorbill) Penguin Young Readers Group.

Khoury, Jessica. Kalahari. 2015. (ENG.). 368p. (YA). (gr. 7). 17.99 (978-1-59514-765-3(9), Razorbill) Penguin Young Readers Group.

—Vitro. 2015. (ENG.). 384p. (YA). (gr. 7). pap. 9.99 (978-1-59514-606-9(7), Razorbill) Penguin Young Readers Group.

Kibbie, George Anthon. Bilwok: Dawn of the Trolls. 2015. 183p. (YA). pap. 13.99 (978-1-4621-1663-8(9)) Cedar Fort, Inc./CFI Distribution.

Kiesling, Ralph W. The Exploration, 1 vol. 2009. 253p. pap. 27.95 (978-1-61546-668-9(1)) America Star Bks.

Kim, Derek Kirk. Vanishing Point. Kim, Derek Kirk, illus. 2012. (Tune Ser.: 1). (ENG., Illus.). 160p. pap. 17.99 (978-1-59643-516-2(X), 9781596435162, First Second Bks.) Roaring Brook Pr.

Kim, Susan & Klavan, Laurence. Guardians. 2015. (Wasteland Ser.: 3). (ENG.). 432p. (YA). (gr. 9). 17.99 (978-0-06-211857-8(9), HarperTeen) HarperCollins Pubs.

—Wanderers: A Wasteland Novel. 2015. (Wasteland Ser.: 2). (ENG.). 384p. (YA). (gr. 9). pap. 9.99 (978-0-06-211855-4(2), HarperTeen) HarperCollins Pubs.

—Wasteland. 2013. (Wasteland Ser.: 1). (ENG.). 336p. (YA). (gr. 9). 17.99 (978-0-06-211851-6(X), HarperTeen) HarperCollins Pubs.

Kincaid, S. J. Catalyst. 2014. (Insignia Ser.: 3). (ENG.). 432p. (YA). (gr. 8). 17.99 (978-0-06-209305-9(3), Tegen, Katherine Bks) HarperCollins Pubs.

—The Diabolic. (Diabolic Ser.). (ENG.). (YA). (gr. 9). 2017. 432p. pap. 10.99 **(978-1-4814-7268-5(2))** 2016. (Illus.). 416p. 17.99 (978-1-4814-7267-8(4)) Simon & Schuster Bks. For Young Readers. (Simon & Schuster Bks. For Young Readers).

—Insignia. (Insignia Ser.: 1). (ENG.). (YA). (gr. 8). 2013. 480p. pap. 9.99 (978-0-06-209300-4(2)) 2012. 464p. 17.99 (978-0-06-209299-1(5)) HarperCollins Pubs. (Tegen, Katherine Bks).

—Vortex. (Insignia Ser.: 2). (ENG.). (YA). (gr. 8). 2014. 416p. pap. 9.99 (978-0-06-209303-5(7)) 2013. 400p. 17.99 (978-0-06-209302-8(9)) HarperCollins Pubs. (Tegen, Katherine Bks).

Kinch, Michael. The Blending Time. 2010. (Blending Time Ser.: 1). (ENG.). 264p. (YA). (gr. 9-18). pap. 9.95 (978-0-7387-2067-8(4), Flux) North Star Editions.

—The Fires of New Sun. 2012. (Blending Time Ser.: 2). (ENG.). 288p. (YA). pap. 9.95 (978-0-7387-3076-9(9), Flux) North Star Editions.

—The Rebels of New SUN. 2013. (Blending Time Ser.: 3). (ENG.). 288p. (YA). pap. 9.99 (978-0-7387-3151-3(X), Flux) North Star Editions.

King, Bart. The Drake Equation. 2016. (ENG.). 320p. (J). (gr. 3-7). 16.99 (978-1-4847-2552-8(2)) Disney Pr.

King-cargile, Gillian. Toy & the Test Drive. Krull, Kevin, illus. 2017. (Stuffed Bunny Science Adventure Ser.). (ENG.). 36p. (J). (gr. k-3). 18.99 **(978-0-87580-760-7(7))** Northern Illinois Univ. Pr.

King-Cargile, Gillian. The Toy & the Twister. Krull, Kevin, illus. 2015. (Stuffed Bunny Science Adventure Ser.). (ENG.). 36p. (J). (gr. k-3). 18.99 (978-0-87580-496-5(9)) Northern Illinois Univ. Pr.

King, Carrie. The Life in the Wood with Joni-Pip. 2007. (Illus.). 463p. (978-0-9555246-8-4(7)) Bothy Bks., Corwall, A Div. of Grace & Patrick Pubs., Ltd.

King, J. R. Arianna Kelt & the Renegades of Time: Deluxe Edition, Wizards of Skyhall Book 2. 2008. (ENG.). 252p. (YA). per. 15.95 (978-1-57545-120-6(4)) RP Media.

—Arianna Kelt & the Wizards of Skyhall. 2008. (ENG.). 200p. (J). 18.95 (978-1-57545-164-0(6), Reagent Pr. Echo) RP Media.

King, Kristin. Project: Noah's Ark. 2005. 201p. pap. 24.95 (978-1-4137-6521-2(1)) America Star Bks.

King, Sharon. Oops Was Bullied? Hey, Why Did You Hurt Me That Way? LaRoe, Misty Bailey, illus. 2013. (ENG.). 32p. (J). pap. 16.95 (978-1-4787-1364-7(X)) Outskirts Pr., Inc.

King-smith, Dick. The Water Horse. Parkins, David, illus. 2007. (ENG.). 128p. (J). (gr. 1-4). 5.99 (978-0-375-84231-3(4), Yearling) Random Hse. Children's Bks.

King, Trey. Transformers Rescue Bots: Training Academy: Construction! 2016. (Passport to Reading Level 2 Ser.). (ENG., Illus.). 32p. (J). (gr. -1-1). pap. 3.99 (978-0-316-38973-0(0)) Little, Brown Bks. for Young Readers.

King, Wesley. The Incredible Space Raiders from Space! 2015. (ENG., Illus.). 304p. (J). (gr. 3-7). 16.99 (978-1-4814-2319-9(3), Simon & Schuster Bks. For Young Readers) Simon & Schuster Bks. For Young Readers.

—The Incredible Space Raiders from Space! 2016. lib. bdg. 18.40 (978-0-606-38276-2(3)) Turtleback Bks.

—The Vindico. 2013. (ENG.). 320p. (YA). (gr. 7). pap. 8.99 (978-0-14-242656-2(3), Speak) Penguin Young Readers Group.

Kinney, Scott. Kozmik. O'Reilly, Sean Patrick, ed. 2013. (Illus.). 78p. (J). pap. 14.95 (978-1-927424-51-3(8)) Arcana Studio, Inc.

Kipling, Joe. Blinded by the Light. 2013. 268p. pap. (978-1-909776-00-5(9)) Cillian Pr. Ltd.

Kirby, Matthew J. The Arctic Code. 2016. (Dark Gravity Sequence Ser.: 1). 352p. (J). (gr. 3-7). pap. 6.99 (978-0-06-222488-0(3)) HarperCollins Pubs.

—The Rogue World. 2017. (Dark Gravity Sequence Ser.: 3). 400p. (J). (gr. 3-7). 16.99 (978-0-06-222493-4(X)) HarperCollins Pubs.

—Spell Robbers. 2014. (Quantum League Ser.: No. 1). (ENG.). 272p. (J). (gr. 3-7). 16.99 (978-0-545-50226-9(8), Scholastic Pr.) Scholastic, Inc.

Kirkman, Robert. Super Dinosaur. (ENG., Illus.). Vol. 1. 2011. 128p. (J). pap. 9.99 (978-1-60706-420-6(0), 9781607064206) Vol. 2. 2012. 112p. pap. 12.99 (978-1-60706-568-5(1), 9781607065685) Vol. 3. 2013. 112p. pap. 12.99 (978-1-60706-667-5(X), 9781607066675) Image Comics.

—Super Dinosaur, Vol. 4. 2015. (ENG., Illus.). 128p. (YA). pap. 12.99 (978-1-60706-843-3(5), 9781607068433) Image Comics.

Kirsch, R. A. The Big One: (A Bicycle Tale), 1 vol. 2009. 191p. pap. 24.95 (978-1-60703-341-7(0)) PublishAmerica, Inc.

Kizer, Amber. A Matter of Days. 2016. (ENG.). 288p. (YA). (gr. 7). pap. 9.99 (978-0-385-73974-0(5), Ember) Random Hse. Children's Bks.

Klass, David. Firestorm. 2008. (Caretaker Trilogy Ser.: 1). (ENG.). 320p. (YA). (gr. 9-13). pap. 11.99 (978-0-312-38018-2(6), 9780312380182) Square Fish.

—Firestorm. rev. l.t. ed. 2007. (Caretaker Trilogy: Bk. 1). 435p. (YA). (gr. 9). 23.95 (978-0-7862-9364-3(0)) Thorndike Pr.

—Timelock. 2009. (Caretaker Trilogy Ser.: 3). (ENG.). 256p. (YA). (gr. 9-12). 17.99 (978-0-374-32309-7(7), 9780374323097, Farrar, Straus & Giroux (BYR)) Farrar, Straus & Giroux.

—Timelock. 2010. (Caretaker Trilogy Ser.: 3). (ENG.). 272p. (YA). (gr. 9-12). pap. 8.99 (978-0-312-60863-7(2), 9780312608637) Square Fish.

—Whirlwind. 2009. (Caretaker Trilogy Ser.: 2). (ENG.). 320p. (YA). (gr. 9-12). pap. 18.99 (978-0-312-38429-6(7), 9780312384296) Square Fish.

Klein Bernstein, Sandy. The Door in the Sky. 2012. 268p. pap. 12.95 (978-1-4575-1111-0(8)) Dog Ear Publishing, LLC.

Klein, Joel & Klein, Abby. The Night I Saved the Universe: From the Files of the Galactic Police Department. 2009. 126p. (J). (978-0-545-12933-6(8)) Scholastic, Inc.

Klement, Jon. Rush & the Grey Fox: Ready to Rumble. 2007. 96p. per. (978-1-897217-66-5(8)) Coscom Entertainment.

Kloepfer, John. Galaxy's Most Wanted. Edwards, Nick, illus. 2014. (Galaxy's Most Wanted Ser.: 1). (ENG.). 224p. (J). (gr. 3-7). 12.99 (978-0-06-223101-7(4)) HarperCollins Pubs.

—Galaxy's Most Wanted #2: into the Dorkness. Edwards, Nick, illus. 2016. (Galaxy's Most Wanted Ser.: 2). 272p. (J). (gr. 3-7). pap. 6.99 (978-0-06-223109-3(X)) HarperCollins Pubs.

—Galaxy's Most Wanted #3: Starship Bloopers. Edwards, Nick, illus. 2016. (Galaxy's Most Wanted Ser.: 3). 240p. (J). (gr. 3-7). 12.99 (978-0-06-223106-2(5)) HarperCollins Pubs.

The Knife of Never Letting Go: With Bonus Short Story. 2014. (Chaos Walking Ser.). (ENG., Illus.). 512p. (YA). (gr. 9). pap. 10.99 (978-0-7636-7618-6(7)) Candlewick Pr.

Knutsson, Catherine. Shadows Cast by Stars. (ENG., Illus.). 464p. (YA). (gr. 7). 2013. pap. 11.99 (978-1-4424-0192-1(3)) 2012. 17.99 (978-1-4424-0191-4(5)) Simon & Schuster Children's Publishing. (Atheneum Bks. for Young Readers).

Kochalka, James. The Glorkian Warrior & the Mustache of Destiny. 2016. (Glorkian Warrior Ser.: 3). (ENG., Illus.). 128p. (J). pap. 14.99 (978-1-62672-022-0(3), 9781626720220, First Second Bks.) Roaring Brook Pr.

—The Glorkian Warrior Delivers a Pizza. Kochalka, James, illus. 2014. (Glorkian Warrior Ser.: 1). (ENG., Illus.). 112p. (J). (gr. k-4). pap. 12.99 (978-1-59643-917-7(3), 9781596439177, First Second Bks.) Roaring Brook Pr.

Kogge, Michael. The Force Awakens. deluxe ed. 2016. (ENG.). 192p. (J). (gr. 3-7). 10.99 (978-1-4847-7584-4(8), Disney Lucasfilm Press) Disney Publishing Worldwide.

—Rise of the Rebels. 2014. (Star Wars Rebels Chapter Bks.). (J). lib. bdg. 16.00 (978-0-606-35281-9(3)) Turtleback Bks.

—Star Wars: The Force Awakens Junior Novel. 2016. (J). lib. bdg. 17.20 (978-0-606-38303-5(4)) Turtleback Bks.

—Star Wars Rebels: Battle to the End. 2015. (Star Wars Saga Chapter Book Ser.). (ENG.). 144p. (J). (gr. 1-3). pap. 5.99 (978-1-4847-0487-5(8), Disney Lucasfilm Press) Disney Publishing Worldwide.

Kogge, Michael, adapted by. The Rebellion Begins. 2014. (Illus.). 168p. (J). **(978-1-4242-6294-6(1)**, Disney Lucasfilm Press) Disney Publishing Worldwide.

Kogge, Michael & Disney Book Group Staff. The Force Awakens. 2016. (ENG.). 192p. (J). (gr. 3-7). pap. 6.99 (978-1-4847-0488-2(6), Disney Lucasfilm Press) Disney Publishing Worldwide.

Kopple, Deborah. A Spear of Golden Grass: Short Stories by Norwalk High School Honors English Students. 2010. 216p. (J). pap. 15.95 (978-1-4502-1896-2(2)) iUniverse, Inc.

Korman, Gordon. Masterminds. (Masterminds Ser.: 2). (J). (gr. 3-7). 2017. 336p. 7.99 (978-0-06-230003-4(2)) 2016. 352p. pap. 7.99 (978-0-06-229999-4(9)) 2015. 336p. 16.99 (978-0-06-229996-3(4)) HarperCollins Pubs.

—Masterminds. 2016. (Masterminds Ser.: 1). (J). lib. bdg. 18.40 (978-0-606-38138-3(4)) Turtleback Bks.

Korte, Steve. Wonder Woman - I Am an Amazon Warrior. Ferguson, Lee, illus. 2017. (I Can Read Level 2 Ser.). 32p. (J). (gr. -1-3). pap. 3.99 **(978-0-06-268184-3(2))** HarperCollins Pubs.

—Wonder Woman Movie Deluxe Junior Novel. 2017. 144p. (J). (gr. 1-5). 9.99 **(978-0-06-268190-4(7)**, HarperFestival) HarperCollins Pubs.

—Wonder Woman Movie ICR #2. Ferguson, Lee & Roberts, Jeremy, illus. 2017. (I Can Read Level 2 Ser.). 32p. (J). (gr. -1-3). pap. 3.99 **(978-0-06-268186-7(9))** HarperCollins Pubs.

—Wonder Woman Movie Junior Novel. 2017. 144p. (J). (gr. 1-5). pap. 6.99 **(978-0-06-268188-1(5)**, HarperFestival) HarperCollins Pubs.

Kositsky, Lynne. The Plagues of Kondar. 2014. (Trials of Kondar Ser.). (ENG.). 184p. (YA). pap. 12.99 (978-1-4597-0934-8(9)) Dundurn CAN. Dist: Ingram Publisher Services.

Kostick, Conor. Saga. 2009. (ENG.). 384p. (YA). (gr. 7-18). pap. 9.99 (978-0-14-241422-4(0), Firebird) Penguin Young Readers Group.

Kozlowsky, M. P. Frost. 2016. (ENG.). 352p. (J). (gr. 9). 17.99 (978-0-545-83191-8(1), Scholastic Pr.) Scholastic, Inc.

Kraatz, Jeramey. The Moon Platoon. 2017. (Space Runners Ser.: 1). 352p. (J). (gr. 3-7). 16.99 (978-0-06-244597-1(9)) HarperCollins Pubs.

Kristoff, Amie Kaufman/Jay. ILLUMINAE. EXPEDIENTE_01 (ILLUMINAE 1) 2016. (SPA.). 592p. (J). (gr. 6). pap. 17.95 (978-84-204-8355-9(9), Alfaguara Juvenil) Santillana USA Publishing Co., Inc.

Kriyananda, Swami. The Time Tunnel: A Tale for All Ages & for the Child in You. 2013. (ENG., Illus.). 180p. (J). (gr. 3-7). 14.95 (978-1-56589-270-5(4)) Crystal Clarity Pubs.

Krokos, Dan. The Black Stars. 2015. (ENG., Illus.). 304p. (J). (gr. 3-8). pap. 21.99 (978-0-7653-7668-8(7), 9780765376688, Starscape) Doherty, Tom Assocs., LLC.

—False Future. 2014. (False Memory Novel Ser.). (ENG., Illus.). 320p. (YA). (gr. 9-17). 17.99 (978-1-4231-4987-3(4)) Hyperion Bks. for Children.

—False Sight. 2014. (False Memory Novel Ser.). (ENG., Illus.). 352p. (YA). (gr. 7-12). pap. 8.99 (978-1-4231-4986-6(6)) Hyperion Bks. for Children.

—The Planet Thieves. (ENG., Illus.). 256p. (J). (gr. 3-7). 2014. pap. 9.99 (978-0-7653-7538-4(9), 9780765375384) 2013. 15.99 (978-0-7653-3428-2(3), 9780765334282) Doherty, Tom Assocs., LLC. (Starscape).

Krosoczka, Jarrett J. A New Class. 2016. (Star Wars: Jedi Academy Ser.: 4). (ENG.). 176p. (J). (gr. 3-7). 12.99 (978-0-545-87573-8(0)) Scholastic, Inc.

Kruger, Mark H. Overpowered. 2013. (ENG., Illus.). 432p. (YA). (gr. 7). 17.99 (978-1-4424-3128-7(8), Simon & Schuster Bks. For Young Readers) Simon & Schuster Bks. For Young Readers.

—Overtaken. 2016. (ENG.). 416p. (YA). (gr. 7). pap. 11.99 (978-1-4424-3132-4(6)) Simon & Schuster Children's Publishing.

Krulik, Nancy. Gotcha! Gotcha Back! John and Wendy Staff, illus. 2006. (Katie Kazoo, Switcheroo Ser.: 19). (ENG.). 80p. (J). (gr. 2-4). pap. 4.99 (978-0-448-43768-2(6), Grosset & Dunlap) Penguin Young Readers Group.

—On Thin Ice. John and Wendy Staff, illus. 2007. (Katie Kazoo, Switcheroo Ser.: No. 6). (ENG.). 160p. (J). (gr. 2-4). pap. 5.99 (978-0-448-44447-5(X), Grosset & Dunlap) Penguin Young Readers Group.

Krumwiede, Lana. Archon. 2013. (Psi Chronicles Ser.). (ENG., Illus.). 320p. (J). (gr. 5). 16.99 (978-0-7636-6402-2(2)) Candlewick Pr.

—True Son. 2015. (Psi Chronicles Ser.). (ENG.). 288p. (J). (gr. 5). 15.99 (978-0-7636-7262-1(9)) Candlewick Pr.

Kuhlmann, Torben. Armstrong: The Adventurous Journey of a Mouse to the Moon. 2016. (ENG., Illus.). 128p. (J). 19.95 (978-0-7358-4262-5(0)) North-South Bks., Inc.

Kuper, Tonya. Anomaly. 2014. (Schrodinger's Consortium Ser.: 1). (ENG.). 400p. (YA). (gr. 7-12). pap. 9.99 (978-1-62266-405-4(1), 9781622664054) Entangled Publishing, LLC.

—Enigma. 2017. (Schrodinger's Consortium Ser.: 2). (ENG.). 304p. (YA). pap. 9.99 (978-1-63375-005-0(1), 9781633750050) Entangled Publishing, LLC.

Kuykendall, Roger. All Day September. 2011. 28p. 12.95 (978-1-4638-9782-6(0)); pap. 6.95 (978-1-4638-0109-0(2)) Rodgers, Alan Bks.

Kwaymullina, Ambelin. The Interrogation of Ashala Wolf. (ENG.). 384p. (YA). (gr. 7). 2016. pap. 8.99 (978-0-7636-8020-6(6)) 2014. 17.99 (978-0-7636-6988-1(1)) Candlewick Pr.

Labaff, Stephanie. Draw Aliens & Space Objects in 4 Easy Steps: Then Write a Story. LaBaff, Tom, illus. 2012. (Drawing in 4 Easy Steps Ser.). 48p. (J). (gr. 3-18). pap. 8.95 (978-1-4644-0014-8(8), Enslow Elementary) Enslow Pubs., Inc.

LaFleur, James & Massie, Gordon. Order Of 5ive: The Complete First Season. Dalglish, Rich, ed. 2012. (ENG.). 308p. (YA). pap. 8.99 (978-1-935702-09-2(2)) Middleton Publishing.

Lambert, Eugene. Into the No-Zone. 2017. (Sign of One Trilogy Ser.: 2). (ENG.). 368p. (YA). (gr. 7). pap. 11.99 **(978-1-4052-7736-5(X))** Egmont Bks., Ltd. GBR. Dist: Independent Pubs. Group.

—The Sign of One. 2017. (Sign of One Trilogy Ser.: 1). (ENG.). 400p. (YA). (gr. 7). pap. 11.99 **(978-1-4052-7735-8(1))** Egmont Bks., Ltd. GBR. Dist: Independent Pubs. Group.

Lancaster, J. A. Joe Parker's Prophecy of Zargala. 2010. 392p. pap. 21.18 (978-0-557-26685-2(8)) Lulu Pr., Inc.

Lancaster, Mike A. Dotwav. 2016. (ENG.). 448p. (J). (gr. 6). 17.99 (978-1-5107-0404-6(3), Sky Pony Pr.) Skyhorse Publishing Co., Inc.

—The Future We Left Behind. 2012. (ENG.). 384p. (J). (gr. 7). 16.99 (978-1-60684-410-6(5), Carolrhoda Lab™) Lerner Publishing Group.

—Human. 4. 2012. (ENG.). 240p. (J). (gr. 7). pap. 8.99 (978-1-60684-309-3(5), Carolrhoda Lab™) Lerner Publishing Group.

Land, Greg, illus. Crossover. 2006. (ENG.). 144p. (YA). (gr. 8-17). pap. 12.99 (978-0-7851-1802-2(0)) Marvel Worldwide, Inc.

Landers, Ace. Anakin: Space Pilot. White, David A., illus. 2011. (Lego Star Wars Ser.). (ENG.). 16p. (J). (gr. -1-3). 12.99 (978-0-545-30440-5(7)) Scholastic, Inc.

—Anakin to the Rescue. 2012. (LEGO Star Wars 8X8 Ser.). lib. bdg. 13.55 (978-0-606-26774-8(3), Turtleback) Turtleback Bks.

—Darth Maul's Mission. White, David A., illus. 2011. (Lego Star Wars Ser.). (ENG.). 24p. (J). (gr. -1-3). pap. 3.99 (978-0-545-30441-2(5)) Scholastic, Inc.

—The Empire Strikes Out. 2013. (Lego Star Wars Ser.). (ENG., Illus.). 48p. (J). (gr. 2-5). pap. 4.99 (978-0-545-55224-0(9)) Math Solutions.

—Lego Star Wars: The Yoda Chronicles Trilogy. 2014. (LEGO Star Wars Chapter Bks.). lib. bdg. 18.40 (978-0-606-35414-1(X)) Turtleback Bks.

—A New Hope: Episode 4. 2015. (LEGO Star Wars 8X8 Ser.). lib. bdg. 13.55 (978-0-606-38104-8(X)) Turtleback Bks.

—The Padawan Menace. 2012. (Lego Star Wars Ser.). (ENG.). 32p. (J). (gr. 2-5). pap. 3.99 (978-0-545-40450-1(9), Scholastic Paperbacks) Scholastic, Inc.

—R2-D2 & C-3P0's Guide to the Galaxy. 2016. (Lego Star Wars Ser.). (ENG.). 128p. (J). (gr. 2-5). 12.99 (978-0-545-94894-4(0)) Scholastic, Inc.

—Revenge of the Sith. White, David A., illus. 2015. (Lego Star Wars Ser.). (ENG.). 24p. (J). (gr. -1-3). pap. 3.99 (978-0-545-78524-2(3)) Scholastic, Inc.

—Tales of the Rebellion. Ameet Studio Staff, illus. 2016. (Lego Star Wars Ser.: 3). (ENG.). 64p. (J). (gr. 2-5). pap. 4.99 (978-0-545-87326-0(6)) Scholastic, Inc.

—Yoda's Secret Missions. 2014. (LEGO Star Wars Chapter Bks.: 1). lib. bdg. 14.75 (978-0-606-36070-8(0)) Turtleback Bks.

Landers, Ace & Doodle Pictures Studio Staff. Save the Galaxy! Hyland, Greg, illus. 2011. (Lego Star Wars Ser.). (ENG.). 7p. (J). (gr. -1-3). bds. 9.99 (978-0-545-30101-5(7)) Scholastic, Inc.

Landers, Melissa. Alienated. (Alienated Ser.: 1). (ENG., Illus.). (YA). (gr. 7-12). 2015. 368p. pap. 9.99 (978-1-4231-8525-3(0)) 2014. 348p. 16.99 (978-1-4231-7028-0(8)) Hyperion Bks. for Children.

—Invaded. (Alienated Ser.). (ENG., (YA). (gr. 7-12). 2016. Illus.). 380p. pap. 9.99 (978-1-4231-8526-0(9)) 2015. 368p. 17.99 (978-1-4231-6949-9(2)) Hyperion Bks. for Children.

—Starfall. 2017. (Starflight Ser.). (ENG.). 368p. (YA). (gr. 9-17). 17.99 (978-1-4847-5025-4(X)) Hyperion Bks. for Children.

—Starflight. 2017. (ENG.). 384p. (YA). (gr. 9-17). pap. 9.99 (978-1-4847-4786-5(0)) Hyperion Bks. for Children.

—Starflight. 2016. (ENG., Illus.). 364p. (YA). (gr. 7-12). 17.99 (978-1-4847-2324-1(4)) Hyperion Pr.

Landon, Kristen. The Limit. (ENG.). 304p. (J). (gr. 3-7). 2011. pap. 7.99 (978-1-4424-0272-0(5)) 2010. (Illus.). 16.99 (978-1-4424-0271-3(7)) Simon & Schuster Children's Publishing. (Aladdin).

Lange, Sue. The Perpetual Motion Club. 2013. 208p. pap. 14.95 (978-0-9887488-6-6(X)) Perpetual Motion Machine Publishing.

Lasky, Kathryn. The First Collier. 2006. (Guardians of Ga'hoole Ser.: 9). (ENG.). 208p. (J). (gr. 3-7). 6.99 (978-0-439-79568-5(0), Scholastic Paperbacks) Scholastic, Inc.

—The Rescue. 2004. (Guardians of Ga'Hoole Ser.: 3). (gr. 3-6). lib. bdg. 17.20 (978-0-613-72136-3(5), Turtleback) Turtleback Bks.

Lassiter, Rhiannon. Shadows. 2011. (Hex Ser.: 2). (ENG.). 272p. (YA). (gr. 7). pap. 12.99 (978-1-4424-3103-4(2), Simon Pulse) Simon Pulse.

Lathrop, Brandy. Jalen Goes to Mars. 2008. 22p. pap. 24.95 (978-1-4241-9010-2(X)) America Star Bks.

Lavoie, Jennifer. The First Twenty. 2015. (ENG.). 264p. (J). (gr. 7). pap. 11.95 (978-1-62639-414-8(8)) Bold Strokes Bks.

Lavoie, Rejean. Des Legumes Pour Frank Einstein. Begin, Jean-Guy, illus. 2004. (Des 9 Ans. Ser.: Vol. 44). (FRE.).

The check digit for ISBN-10 appears in parentheses after the full ISBN-13

120p. (J). 8.95 *(978-2-89599-006-2(9))* Editions de la Paix CAN. Dist: World of Reading, Ltd.
Lawrence, David, et al. El Niño Escarabajo. 2004. (SPA.). 32p. *(978-84-7720-794-8(1))* Ediciones Obelisco.
Lawrence, James. Buck Rogers in the 25th Century - The Gray Morrow Years, 1979-1981, Vol. 1. Herman, Daniel, ed. 2013. (ENG., Illus.). 240p. (YA). 49.99 *(978-1-61345-034-5(6),* 9781613450345) Hermes Pr.
Lawrence, Kelsey. Rune. 2006. (Illus.). 92p. pap. 13.50 *(978-1-84426-399-8(1))* Upfront Publishing Ltd. GBR. Dist: Printondemand-worldwide.com.
Lawrence, Michael. Small Eternities. (Withern Rise Ser.). 336p. 2006. (Illus.). (J). (gr. 7). pap. 7.99 *(978-0-06-072482-5(X),* HarperTeen) 2005. (YA). 16.89 *(978-0-06-072481-8(1))* 2005. (ENG.). (J). (gr. 8). 15.99 *(978-0-06-072480-1(3),* Greenwillow Bks.) HarperCollins Pubs.
—The Underwood See. 2007. (Withern Rise Ser.). 372p. (YA). (gr. 9-18). 16.99 *(978-0-06-072483-2(8))* HarperCollins Pubs.
Lawrence, Theo. Mystic City. (Mystic City Trilogy Ser.). (ENG.). 416p. (YA). (gr. 7). 2014. pap. 9.99 *(978-0-385-74161-3(8),* Ember) 2012. 17.99 *(978-0-385-74160-6(X),* Delacorte Pr.) Random Hse. Children's Bks.
—Toxic Heart: a Mystic City Novel. 2015. (Mystic City Trilogy Ser.). (ENG.). 368p. (YA). (gr. 7). pap. 9.99 *(978-0-385-74163-7(4),* Ember) Random Hse. Children's Bks.
Laybourne, Emmy. Sweet. 2015. (ENG.). 288p. (YA). (gr. 8). 17.99 *(978-1-250-05519-4(9))* Feiwel & Friends.
Layne, Steven L. Mergers, 1 vol. (ENG., Illus.). 208p. (YA). (gr. 6-10). 2007. per. 8.95 *(978-1-58980-538-5(0))* 2006. 15.99 *(978-1-58980-183-7(0))* Pelican Publishing Co., Inc.
—Paradise Lost, 1 vol. (ENG.). 312p. (YA). (gr. 7-12). 2013. pap. 8.95 *(978-1-4556-1775-3(X))* 2011. 15.99 *(978-1-58980-590-3(9))* Pelican Publishing Co., Inc.
—This Side of Paradise, 1 vol. 2005. (ENG.). 224p. (YA). (gr. 6-10). pap. 8.95 *(978-1-58980-254-4(3))* Pelican Publishing Co., Inc.
Le Guin, Ursula K. A Wizard of Earthsea. 2012. (Earthsea Cycle Ser.: 1). (ENG.). (YA). (gr. 7). 240p. 17.99 *(978-0-547-85139-6(1));* 264p. pap. 8.99 *(978-0-547-72202-3(8));* 320p. mass mkt. 8.99 *(978-0-547-77374-2(9))* Houghton Mifflin Harcourt Publishing Co.
Le Guin, Ursula K., et al. Diverse Energies, 1 vol. Buckell, Tobias & Monti, Joe, eds. 2012. (ENG.). 368p. (YA). 19.95 *(978-1-60060-887-2(6),* Tu Bks.) Lee & Low Bks., Inc.
Lee, Fonda. Exo. 2017. (ENG.). 384p. (J). (gr. 7). 17.99 *(978-0-545-93343-8(9),* Scholastic Pr.) Scholastic, Inc.
—Zeroboxer. 2015. (ENG.). 360p. (YA). pap. 11.99 *(978-0-7387-4338-7(0),* Flux) North Star Editions.
Lee, Ingrid. George Most Wanted, 1 vol. Denis, Stephane, illus. 2005. (Orca Echoes Ser.). (ENG.). 64p. (J). (gr. 2-3). per. 6.95 *(978-1-55143-472-8(5))* Orca Bk. Pubs. USA.
Lee, Mackenzi. This Monstrous Thing. (YA). (gr. 8). 2017. 400p. pap. 9.99 *(978-0-06-238278-8(0),* Tegen, Katherine Bks) 2015. (ENG.). 384p. 17.99 *(978-0-06-238277-1(2))* HarperCollins Pubs.
Lee, Pat. DrawbotZ. 2014. (Illus.). 72p. (YA). pap. 12.99 *(978-0-9836131-8-3(4))* Sea Lion Bks.
Lee, Quinlan B. Phonics. 2016. (LEGO DC Super Heroes Ser.). (ENG.). (J). (gr. -1-k). pap. 12.99 *(978-0-545-86802-0(5))* Scholastic, Inc.
—Star Wars: Phonics Boxed Set. 2012. (Star Wars Ser.). (ENG.). (J). (gr. k-2). pap. 12.99 *(978-0-545-47952-3(5))* Scholastic, Inc.
Lee, Stan. The Fantastic Four. 2013. (ENG., Illus.). 832p. (J). (gr. -1-17). 99.99 *(978-0-7851-8567-3(4))* Marvel Worldwide, Inc.
—The Fantastic Four Omnibus, Vol. 1. 2013. (ENG., Illus.). 848p. (J). (gr. -1-17). 99.99 *(978-0-7851-8566-6(6))* Marvel Worldwide, Inc.
Lee, Stan & Moore, Stuart. Power Lines. Cullins, Paris, illus. 2016. (Zodiac Ser.). (ENG.). 64p. (J). 12.99 *(978-1-62991-445-9(2),* 9781629914459) Papercutz.
Leflore, Henry. The Aftermath: The Curse of the Blue Flamed Meteor. 2009. 112p. pap. 10.99 *(978-1-4389-9588-5(1))* AuthorHouse.
Leiber, Fritz. The Creature from Cleveland Depths. 2009. 76p. pap. 7.95 *(978-1-60664-286-3(3))* Rodgers, Alan Bks.
Leicht, Martin & Neal, Isla. Mothership. (Ever-Expanding Universe Ser.: 1). (ENG., Illus.). (YA). (gr. 9). 2013. 336p. pap. 9.99 *(978-1-4424-2961-1(5))* 2012. 320p. 16.99 *(978-1-4424-2960-4(7))* Simon & Schuster Bks. For Young Readers. (Simon & Schuster Bks. For Young Readers).
—A Stranger Thing. 2013. (Ever-Expanding Universe Ser.: 2). (ENG., Illus.). 288p. (YA). (gr. 9). 17.99 *(978-1-4424-2963-5(1),* Simon & Schuster Bks. For Young Readers) Simon & Schuster Bks. For Young Readers.
—The World Forgot. 2015. 279p. (YA). pap. *(978-1-4424-2967-3(4),* Simon & Schuster Bks. For Young Readers) Simon & Schuster Bks. For Young Readers.
Leloup, Roger. The Curious Trio. 2012. (Yoko Tsuno Ser.: 7). (ENG., Illus.). 48p. (J). (gr. 3-12). pap. 11.95 *(978-1-84918-127-3(6))* CineBook GBR. Dist: National Bk. Network.
—The Devil's Organ. 2013. (Yoko Tsuno Ser.: 8). (ENG., Illus.). 48p. (J). (gr. 3-12). pap. 11.95 *(978-1-84918-164-8(0))* CineBook GBR. Dist: National Bk. Network.
—The Dragon of Hong Kong - Yoko Tsuno, Vol. 5. 2010. (Yoko Tsuno Ser.: 5). (ENG., Illus.). 46p. (J). (gr. 3-17). pap. 11.95 *(978-1-84918-041-2(5))* CineBook GBR. Dist: National Bk. Network.
—On the Edge of Life. 2007. (Yoko Tsuno Ser.: 1). (ENG., Illus.). 48p. (J). (gr. 4-7). pap. 11.95 *(978-1-905460-32-8(5))* CineBook GBR. Dist: National Bk. Network.
—The Prey & the Ghost. 2009. (Yoko Tsuno Ser.: 3). (ENG., Illus.). 48p. pap. 11.95 *(978-1-905460-56-4(2))* CineBook GBR. Dist: National Bk. Network.
—The Time Spiral. 2008. (Yoko Tsuno Ser.: 2). (ENG., Illus.). 48p. pap. 11.95 *(978-1-905460-43-4(0))* CineBook GBR. Dist: National Bk. Network.
Lemieux, Jean. Toby Shoots for Infinity. Casson, Sophie, illus. 2005. 61p. (J). lib. bdg. 12.00 *(978-1-4242-1201-9(4))* Fitzgerald Bks.
Lemke, Donald. Pranking News. 2016. (Justice League Classic: I Can Read! Ser.). (J). lib. bdg. 13.55 *(978-0-606-38772-9(2))* Turtleback Bks.
Lemke, Donald B. The Amazing Mini-Mutts, 1 vol. Baltazar, Art, illus. 2012. (DC Super-Pets Ser.). (ENG.). 56p. (gr. 2-2). pap. 4.95 *(978-1-4048-7218-9(3));* lib. bdg. 23.99 *(978-1-4048-6488-7(1))* Picture Window Bks. (DC Super-Pets).
Lemke, Donald B., et al. Fun House of Evil, 1 vol. 2013. (Batman Ser.). (ENG., Illus.). 56p. (gr. 2-3). pap. 4.95 *(978-1-4342-1367-9(6),* DC Super Heroes) Stone Arch Bks.
L'Engle, Madeleine. Una Arruga en el Tiempo. 2003. (SPA., Illus.). 206p. (J). (gr. 5-8). pap. 12.95 *(978-84-204-4074-3(4),* KZ744) Santillana USA Publishing Co., Inc.
—A Swiftly Tilting Planet. 228p. (YA). (gr. 5-18). pap. 5.50 *(978-0-8072-1495-4(7),* Listening Library) Random Hse. Audio Publishing Group.
—A Swiftly Tilting Planet. 2007. (Wrinkle in Time Quintet Ser.: 4). (ENG.). 320p. (J). (gr. 5-9). per. 7.99 *(978-0-312-36856-2(9),* 9780312368562) Square Fish.
—A Wind in the Door. 211p. (YA). (gr. 5-18). pap. 5.50 *(978-0-8072-1466-4(3),* Listening Library) Random Hse. Audio Publishing Group.
—A Wind in the Door. 2007. (Wrinkle in Time Quintet Ser.: 2). (ENG.). 256p. (J). (gr. 5-9). per. 6.99 *(978-0-312-36854-8(2),* 9780312368548) Square Fish.
—A Wrinkle in Time. 50th anniv. ed. 2012. (Wrinkle in Time Quintet Ser.: 1). (ENG., Illus.). 280p. (J). (gr. 4-8). 26.99 *(978-0-374-38616-0(1),* 9780374386160, Farrar, Straus & Giroux (BYR)) Farrar, Straus & Giroux.
—A Wrinkle in Time, 2 vols., Set. 20.00 *(978-0-89064-014-2(9))* National Assn. for Visually Handicapped.
—A Wrinkle in Time. 211p. (YA). (gr. 5-18). pap. 5.99 *(978-0-8072-1460-2(4),* Listening Library) Random Hse. Audio Publishing Group.
—A Wrinkle in Time. 2007. (Wrinkle in Time Quintet Ser.: 1). (ENG.). (J). (gr. 5-8). 224p. per. 6.99 *(978-0-312-36755-8(4),* 9780312367558); 256p. per. 6.99 *(978-0-312-36754-1(6),* 9780312367541) Square Fish.
—A Wrinkle in Time. l.t. ed. 2005. 273p. pap. 10.95 *(978-0-7862-7335-5(6),* Large Print Pr.) Thorndike Pr.
—A Wrinkle in Time. (Madeleine L'Engle's Time Quintet Ser.). (J). 2007. 245p. 17.20 *(978-1-4177-8460-8(1))* 50th anniv. ed. 2012. lib. bdg. 20.85 *(978-0-606-23785-7(2))* Turtleback Bks. (Turtleback).
—The Wrinkle in Time Quintet. 2012. (Wrinkle in Time Quintet Ser.). (ENG., Illus.). 1280p. (J). (gr. 4-8). 100.00 *(978-0-374-37596-6(8),* 9780374375966, Farrar, Straus & Giroux (BYR)) Farrar, Straus & Giroux.
—A Wrinkle in Time Trilogy. 2012. (Wrinkle in Time Quintet Ser.). (ENG.). 800p. (J). (gr. 6-9). pap. 20.99 *(978-1-250-00343-0(1),* 9781250003430) Square Fish.
—The Young Unicorns. 2008. (Austin Family Ser.: 3). (ENG.). 304p. (J). (gr. 7-12). pap. 11.99 *(978-0-312-37933-9(1),* 9780312379339) Square Fish.
Leo. The Group, 3 vols., Vol. 2. 2009. (Aldebaran Ser.: 2). (ENG., Illus.). 96p. pap. 19.95 *(978-1-905460-70-0(8))* CineBook GBR. Dist: National Bk. Network.
Leo & LEO, Inc Staff. Aldebaran Vol. 1, 3 vols., Vol. 1. LEO, Inc Staff, illus. 2008. (Aldebaran Ser.: 1). (ENG., Illus.). 104p. pap. 19.95 *(978-1-905460-57-1(0))* CineBook GBR. Dist: National Bk. Network.
Leonard, Krystian. Shining Scars. Kelly, Lucas, illus. 2013. (ENG.). 31p. (J). 16.95 *(978-0-938467-72-4(7))* Headline Bks., Inc.
Lepp, Royden. Secrets of the Cell, Vol. 2. Lepp, Royden, illus. 2017. (Rust Ser.: 2). (ENG., Illus.). 144p. (J). (gr. 5). pap. 14.99 *(978-1-60886-895-7(8),* Archaia Entertainment) Boom! Studios.
—Visitor in the Field, Vol. 1. Lepp, Royden, illus. 2016. (Rust Ser.: 1). (ENG., Illus.). 176p. (J). (gr. 5). pap. 14.99 *(978-1-60886-894-0(X),* Archaia Entertainment) Boom! Studios.
Lestelle, Wende. Science Mouse. 2004. pap. *(978-1-930493-65-0(7))* Athena Pr.
Lester, Cas. Harvey Drew & the Bin Men from Outer Space. 2016. (Harvey Drew Ser.: 1). (ENG., Illus.). 208p. (J). (gr. k-3). pap. 9.99 *(978-1-4714-0223-4(1))* Bonnier Publishing GBR. Dist: Independent Pubs. Group.
—Harvey Drew & the Junk Skunks. 2016. (Harvey Drew Ser.: 3). (ENG., Illus.). 256p. (J). (gr. k-3). pap. 9.99 *(978-1-4714-0334-7(3))* Bonnier Publishing GBR. Dist: Independent Pubs. Group.
Lethcoe, Jason. Song, 3 vols. Altmann, Scott, illus. 2009. (Mysterious Mr. Spines Ser.: 3). (ENG.). 208p. (J). (gr. 5-18). pap. 7.99 *(978-0-448-44655-4(3),* Grosset & Dunlap) Penguin Young Readers Group.
Levigne, Michelle. Commonwealth Universe: Modern Era. 2013. 146p. pap. *(978-1-922066-33-6(8));* 110p. pap. *(978-1-922066-35-0(4));* 110p. pap. *(978-1-922066-31-2(1));* 134p. pap. *(978-1-922066-32-9(X))* Writers Exchange E-Publishing.
Levy, Janey. Edwin Visits Earth. 2006. (Neighborhood Readers Ser.). (ENG.). 16p. (gr. 1-3). pap. 6.50 *(978-1-4042-7160-9(0),* Rosen Classroom) Rosen Publishing Group, Inc., The.
Lewis, Bryan. The Tiny World You Can't See. 2011. 24p. pap. 14.50 *(978-1-4670-2837-0(1))* AuthorHouse.
Lewis, R. C. Spinning Starlight. 2015. (ENG., Illus.). 336p. (YA). (gr. 7-12). 17.99 *(978-1-4231-8515-4(3))* Hyperion Bks. for Children.
—Stitching Snow. (ENG., Illus.). (YA). (gr. 9-17). 2015. 352p. pap. 9.99 *(978-1-4231-9468-2(3))* 2014. 332p. 17.99 *(978-1-4231-8507-9(2))* Hyperion Bks. for Children.
Liddell Nolen, Laura. The Ark. 2015. (Ark Trilogy Ser.: 1). (ENG.). 284p. 19.99 *(978-0-00-812069-6(2),* Harper Voyager) HarperCollins Pubs.
Link, Kelly. Pretty Monsters. 2010. (ENG., Illus.). 416p. (YA). (gr. 7-18). 9.99 *(978-0-14-241672-3(X),* Speak) Penguin Young Readers Group.
Linka, Catherine. A Girl Called Fearless. 2014. (ENG.). 368p. (YA). (gr. 7). 18.99 *(978-1-250-03929-3(0),* 9781250039293, St. Martin's Griffin) St. Martin's Pr.
Liparulo, Robert. Whirlwind, 1 vol. 2010. (Dreamhouse Kings Ser.: 5). (ENG.). 320p. pap. 9.99 *(978-1-59554-892-4(0))* Nelson, Thomas Inc.
Lippert-Martin, Kristen. Incognita. 2016. (Tabula Rasa Saga Ser.: 2). (ENG.). 340p. (YA). (gr. 7-12). 17.99 *(978-1-5124-0577-4(9),* Carolrhoda Bks.) Lerner Publishing Group.
—Tabula Rasa. (ENG.). 337p. (YA). (gr. 7-12). 2016. (Tabula Rasa Saga Ser.: 1). pap. 9.99 *(978-1-5124-2629-8(6))* 2014. 17.99 *(978-1-60684-518-9(7))* Lerner Publishing Group. (Carolrhoda Lab™).
Lipsyte, Robert. The Twin Powers. 2014. (ENG.). 256p. (J). (gr. 5-7). 16.99 *(978-0-547-97335-7(7))* Houghton Mifflin Harcourt Publishing Co.
—The Twinning Project. 2014. (ENG.). 288p. (J). (gr. 5-7). pap. 6.99 *(978-0-544-22522-0(8),* HMH Books For Young Readers) Houghton Mifflin Harcourt Publishing Co.
Liss, David. Randoms. 2016. (Randoms Ser.: 1). (ENG., Illus.). 512p. (J). (gr. 5). pap. 8.99 *(978-1-4814-1780-8(0),* Simon & Schuster Bks. For Young Readers) Simon & Schuster Bks. For Young Readers.
—Rebels. 2016. (Randoms Ser.: 2). (ENG., Illus.). 400p. (J). (gr. 5). 18.99 *(978-1-4814-1782-2(7),* Simon & Schuster Bks. For Young Readers) Simon & Schuster Bks. For Young Readers.
Liss, David. Renegades. 2017. (Randoms Ser.: 3). (ENG., Illus.). 352p. (J). (gr. 5). 18.99 ***(978-1-4814-1785-3(1),*** Simon & Schuster Bks. For Young Readers) Simon & Schuster Bks. For Young Readers.
Liu, Liana. The Memory Key. 2015. (ENG.). 368p. (YA). (gr. 8). 17.99 *(978-0-06-230664-7(2),* HarperTeen) HarperCollins Pubs.
Llongueras, Joan & Masnou, Merce. Kadingir: El Cetro de Zink. 2007. (SPA.). 365p. (J). 18.95 *(978-84-96544-64-2(8))* Roca Editorial ESP. Dist: Spanish Pubs., LLC.
Lloyd-Jones, Emily. Deceptive: An Illusive Novel. 2015. (Illusive Ser.: 2). (ENG.). 432p. (YA). (gr. 7-17). 18.00 *(978-0-316-25464-9(9))* Little Brown & Co.
—Illusive. 2014. (Illusive Ser.: 1). (ENG.). 416p. (YA). (gr. 7-17). 18.00 *(978-0-316-25456-4(8))* Little, Brown Bks. for Young Readers.
Lloyd, Saci. The Carbon Diaries 2015. 2008. (ENG., Illus.). 384p. (YA). pap. *(978-0-340-97015-7(4),* Hodder Children's Books) Hachette Children's Group.
—The Carbon Diaries 2015. 2009. (ENG.). 384p. (YA). (gr. 9-18). 17.95 *(978-0-8234-2190-9(2))* Holiday Hse., Inc.
—The Carbon Diaries 2017. (ENG.). (YA). (gr. 6). 2011. 384p. pap. 8.95 *(978-0-8234-2390-3(5))* 2010. 352p. 17.95 *(978-0-8234-2260-9(7))* Holiday Hse., Inc.
—Momentum. 2012. (ENG.). 224p. (J). 16.95 *(978-0-8234-2414-6(6))* Holiday Hse., Inc.
Lo, Malinda. Adaptation. 2013. (ENG.). 416p. (YA). (gr. 10-17). pap. 10.00 *(978-0-316-19798-4(X))* Little, Brown Bks. for Young Readers.
—Inheritance. 2014. (ENG.). 480p. (YA). (gr. 10-17). pap. 25.99 *(978-0-316-19799-1(8))* Little, Brown Bks. for Young Readers.
Locke, Terry. Spencer Hurley & the Aliens: Book One: the Abduction. Hucks, Robin, ed. 2008. (Spencer Hurley & the Aliens Ser.: 1). (ENG., Illus.). 256p. (J). 12.95 *(978-0-9786940-0-5(7),* SHAB1V1E1CB) Dream Workshop Publishing Co., LLC, The.
Locke, Thomas, pseud. Recruits. 2017. (Recruits Ser.: 1). (ENG.). 384p. (YA). pap. 12.99 *(978-0-8007-2789-5(4));* 25.99 ***(978-0-8007-2865-6(3))*** Revell.
Loesch, Joe. The Tuskegee Airmen: Raiders of the Skies with Buffalo Biff & Farley's Raiders. Hutchinson, Cheryl, ed. 2004. (Backyard Adventure Ser.). (Illus.). 56p. (J). bds. 16.95 incl. audio compact disk *(978-1-932332-27-8(8))* Toy Box Productions.
Lofficier, Randy & Lofficier, Jean-Marc. Robonocchio. Pijuán Aragón, Miren, tr. Martiniere, Stephan, illus. 2004. (SPA.). 128p. (YA). per. 14.95 *(978-1-932983-25-8(2),* Black Coat Pr.) HollywoodComics.com, LLC.
Lois, Lowry. Gathering Blue. (Giver Quartet Ser.: 2). (ENG.). 256p. (YA). (gr. 7). 2013. pap. 9.99 *(978-0-547-90414-6(2))* 2012. 17.99 *(978-0-547-99568-7(7))* Houghton Mifflin Harcourt Publishing Co.
—Gathering Blue. 2013. (Giver Quartet Ser.: 2). lib. bdg. 20.85 *(978-0-606-31673-6(6),* Turtleback) Turtleback Bks.
—The Giver. 2007. (KOR.). 310p. (YA). pap. *(978-89-491-2074-4(7))* Biryongso Publishing Co.
—The Giver. (Giver Quartet Ser.: 1). (ENG.). (YA). (gr. 7). 2014. 240p. pap. 8.99 *(978-0-544-33626-1(7),* HMH Books For Young Readers) 2012. 17.99 *(978-0-547-99566-3(0))* 2014. 256p. 17.99 *(978-0-544-43078-5(6),* HMH Books For Young Readers) Houghton Mifflin Harcourt Publishing Co.
—The Giver. Ibatoulline, Bagram, illus. gif. ed. 2011. (Giver Quartet Ser.: 1). (ENG.). 208p. (YA). (gr. 7). 19.99 *(978-0-547-42477-4(9))* Houghton Mifflin Harcourt Publishing Co.
—The Giver. movie tie-in ed. 2014. (Giver Quartet Ser.: 1). (ENG.). 256p. (J). (gr. 7). pap. 9.99 *(978-0-544-34068-8(X),* HMH Books For Young Readers) Houghton Mifflin Harcourt Publishing Co.
—The Giver. 2014. (ENG.). 192p. (YA). (gr. 3-7). 11.24 *(978-1-63245-036-4(4))* Lectorum Pubns., Inc.
—The Giver. 2009. 9.14 *(978-0-7848-0666-1(7));* 10.52 *(978-0-7848-2389-7(8))* Marco Bk. Co. (Everbind).
—The Giver. 180p. (gr. 5-18). (YA). pap. 5.99 *(978-0-8072-8314-1(2));* 2004. (J). pap. 38.00 incl. audio *(978-0-8072-8313-4(4),* YA159SP) Random Hse. Audio Publishing Group. (Listening Library).
—The Giver, 4 vols. (J). 2009. 55.75 *(978-1-4281-5700-2(X))* 2007. 58.75 *(978-1-4281-5698-2(4))* Recorded Bks., Inc.
—The Giver. l.t. ed. 2004. 226p. (ENG.). pap. 10.95 *(978-0-7862-7153-5(1),* Large Print Pr.); 23.95 *(978-0-7862-7154-2(X))* Thorndike Pr.
—The Giver. 2014. (Giver Quartet Ser.: 1). lib. bdg. 19.65 *(978-0-606-35978-8(8))* Turtleback Bks.
—The Giver Quartet. 2014. (J). *(978-0-544-34063-3(9))* Harcourt.
—The Giver Quartet. 2014. (Giver Quartet Ser.). (ENG.). 784p. (YA). (gr. 7). 29.99 *(978-0-544-34097-8(3),* HMH Books For Young Readers) Houghton Mifflin Harcourt Publishing Co.
—The Giver Quartet Boxed Set. 2014. (Giver Quartet Ser.). (ENG.). 864p. (YA). (gr. 7). 39.99 *(978-0-544-34062-6(0),* HMH Books For Young Readers) Houghton Mifflin Harcourt Publishing Co.
—Messenger. 2012. (Giver Quartet Ser.: 3). (ENG.). 192p. (YA). (gr. 7). 17.99 *(978-0-547-99567-0(9))* Houghton Mifflin Harcourt Publishing Co.
—Messenger. (ENG.). (J). 2009. 176p. (gr. 3-7). mass mkt. 7.99 *(978-0-385-73716-6(5),* Bantam Bks. for Young Readers) 2006. 192p. (gr. 4-7). pap. 9.99 *(978-0-385-73253-6(8),* Ember) 2006. 176p. (gr. 3-7). mass mkt. 7.99 *(978-0-440-23912-3(5),* Laurel Leaf) Random Hse. Children's Bks.
—Passeur. pap. 22.95 *(978-2-211-02166-1(2))* Archimede Editions FRA. Dist: Distribooks, Inc.
—Son. (ENG.). 400p. (YA). (gr. 7). 2014. pap. 9.99 *(978-0-544-33625-4(9),* HMH Books For Young Readers) 2012. (Giver Quartet Ser.: 4). 17.99 *(978-0-547-88720-3(5))* Houghton Mifflin Harcourt Publishing Co.
—Son. l.t. ed. 2013. (Giver Quartet Ser.). (ENG.). 422p. 23.99 *(978-1-4104-5448-5(7))* Thorndike Pr.
—Son. 2014. (Giver Quartet Ser.: 4). lib. bdg. 20.85 *(978-0-606-35979-5(6))* Turtleback Bks.
London, Alex. Guardian. 2014. (ENG.). 352p. (YA). (gr. 7). 17.99 *(978-0-399-16576-4(2),* Philomel Bks.) Penguin Young Readers Group.
—Proxy. 2013. (ENG.). 384p. (YA). (gr. 7). 17.99 *(978-0-399-25776-6(4),* Philomel Bks.) Penguin Young Readers Group.
Long, Christopher E. Hero Worship. 2014. (ENG.). 240p. (YA). pap. 9.99 *(978-0-7387-3909-0(X),* Flux) North Star Editions.
Long, David. Diary of a Time Traveler: Travel the Globe & Meet History's Most Interesting Characters. Stevenson, Nicholas, illus. 2015. (ENG.). 64p. (J). (gr. 2-5). 22.99 *(978-1-84780-704-5(6),* Wide Eyed Editions) Quarto Publishing Group UK GBR. Dist: Hachette Bk. Group.
Long, Ethan. Clara & Clem in Outer Space. 2013. (Penguin Young Readers, Level 1 Ser.). (ENG.). 32p. (J). (gr. k-1). 14.99 *(978-0-448-46722-1(4));* pap. 3.99 *(978-0-448-46721-4(6))* Penguin Young Readers Group. (Penguin Young Readers).
The Lord of Opium. 2014. (ENG., Illus.). 448p. (YA). (gr. 7). pap. 12.99 *(978-1-4424-8255-5(9),* Atheneum Bks. for Young Readers) Simon & Schuster Children's Publishing.
Lord, Pia. The Day the Sun Went Out. 2012. 30p. 24.95 *(978-1-4626-6797-0(X))* America Star Bks.
Lore, Pittacus. The Fate of Ten. 2015. 399p. (YA). *(978-0-06-242452-5(1)); (978-0-06-242751-9(2))* Harper & Row Ltd.
—The Fate of Ten. (Lorien Legacies Ser.: 6). (YA). (gr. 9). 2016. 432p. pap. 10.99 *(978-0-06-219476-3(3))* 2015. (ENG.). 416p. 18.99 *(978-0-06-219475-6(5))* HarperCollins Pubs.
—The Fate of Ten. 2016. (Lorien Legacies Ser.: 6). (YA). lib. bdg. 20.85 *(978-0-606-38760-6(9))* Turtleback Bks.
—Generation One. (Lorien Legacies Reborn Ser.: 1). 416p. (YA). (gr. 9). 2018. pap. 9.99 ***(978-0-06-249370-5(1))*** 2017. 18.99 ***(978-0-06-249374-3(4))*** HarperCollins Pubs.
—I Am Number Four. (YA). (gr. 9). 2016. (Lorien Legacies: the Lost Files Ser.). 416p. pap. 9.99 *(978-0-06-238771-4(5))* 2011. (Lorien Legacies Ser.: 1). (ENG.). 496p. pap. 9.99 *(978-0-06-196957-7(5))* 2010. (Lorien Legacies Ser.: 1). (ENG.). 448p. 17.99 *(978-0-06-196955-3(9))* 2011. (Lorien Legacies Ser.: 1). (ENG.). 496p. pap. 9.99 *(978-0-06-211655-0(X))* 2011. (Lorien Legacies Ser.: 1). (ENG.). 480p. 17.99 *(978-0-06-202624-8(0))* HarperCollins Pubs.
—I Am Number Four. 2009. (Lorien Legacies Ser.: Bk. 1). 11.04 *(978-0-7848-3715-3(5),* Everbind) Marco Bk. Co.
—I Am Number Four. 2011. (I Am Number Four Ser.: Vol. 1). (ENG.). 440p. (gr. 9-12). 20.00 *(978-1-61383-207-3(9))* Perfection Learning Corp.
—I Am Number Four. 2011. (Lorien Legacies Ser.: 1). (YA). lib. bdg. 20.85 *(978-0-606-23545-7(0),* Turtleback) Turtleback Bks.
—I Am Number Four: The Lost Files: Rebel Allies. 2015. (Lorien Legacies: the Lost Files Ser.). (ENG.). 416p. (YA). (gr. 9). pap. 9.99 *(978-0-06-236404-3(9))* HarperCollins Pubs.
—I Am Number Four: The Lost Files: Secret Histories. 2013. (Lorien Legacies: the Lost Files Ser.). (ENG.). 416p. (YA). (gr. 9). pap. 9.99 *(978-0-06-222367-8(4))* HarperCollins Pubs.
—The Legacies. 2012. (Lorien Legacies: the Lost Files Ser.). (YA). lib. bdg. 20.85 *(978-0-606-26874-5(X),* Turtleback) Turtleback Bks.
—The Power of Six. (Lorien Legacies Ser.: 2). (ENG.). (YA). (gr. 9). 2012. 448p. pap. 9.99 *(978-0-06-197457-1(9))* 2011. 416p. 17.99 *(978-0-06-197455-7(2))* HarperCollins Pubs.
—The Power of Six. 2012. (Lorien Legacies Ser.: 2). (YA). lib. bdg. 20.85 *(978-0-606-26289-7(X),* Turtleback) Turtleback Bks.
—The Revenge of Seven. 2014. 371p. (J). *(978-0-06-236719-8(6))* Harper & Row Ltd.
—The Revenge of Seven. (Lorien Legacies Ser.: Bk. 5). (ENG.). 416p. 2015. (YA). (gr. 9). pap. 9.99 *(978-0-06-219473-2(9))* 2014. (J). 17.99 *(978-0-06-219472-5(0))* HarperCollins Pubs.
—The Revenge of Seven. 2015. (Lorien Legacies Ser.: 5). 415p. lib. bdg. 20.85 *(978-0-606-36981-7(3))* Turtleback Bks.
—The Rise of Nine. (Lorien Legacies Ser.: 3). (ENG.). 416p. (YA). (gr. 9). 2013. pap. 9.99 *(978-0-06-197460-1(9))* 2012. 17.99 *(978-0-06-197458-8(7))* HarperCollins Pubs.
—The Rise of Nine. 2013. (Lorien Legacies Ser.: 3). (YA). lib. bdg. 20.85 *(978-0-606-31830-3(5),* Turtleback) Turtleback Bks.
—Secret Histories. 2013. (Lorien Legacies: the Lost Files Ser.). (YA). lib. bdg. 20.85 *(978-0-606-31823-5(2),* Turtleback) Turtleback Bks.
Lore, Pittacus. United As One. 2017. (Lorien Legacies Ser.: 7). (ENG.). (YA). (gr. 9). lib. bdg. 20.85 ***(978-0-606-40055-8(9))*** Turtleback Bks.
Lorimer, Janet. Bugged (Science Fiction), 1 vol. 2017. (Pageturners Ser.). (ENG.). 80p. (YA). (gr. 9-12). 8.95 ***(978-1-68021-393-5(8))*** Saddleback Educational Publishing, Inc.
—Flashback (Science Fiction), 1 vol. 2017. (Pageturners Ser.). (ENG.). 80p. (YA). (gr. 9-12). 8.95 ***(978-1-68021-395-9(4))*** Saddleback Educational Publishing, Inc.
—Murray's Nightmare (Science Fiction), 1 vol. 2017. (Pageturners Ser.). (ENG.). 76p. (YA). (gr. 9-12). 8.95

S

(978-1-68021-396-6(2)) Saddleback Educational Publishing, Inc.

The Lotus Caves. 2014. (ENG., Illus.). 288p. (J). (gr. 4-8). pap. 7.99 *(978-1-4814-1837-9(8)*, Aladdin) Simon & Schuster Children's Publishing.

The Lotus Caves. 2014. (ENG., Illus.). 288p. (J). (gr. 4-8). 17.99 *(978-1-4814-1838-6(6)*, Simon & Schuster/Paula Wiseman Bks.) Simon & Schuster/Paula Wiseman Bks.

Loux, Matthew. The Time Museum. 2017. (Time Museum Ser.: 1). (ENG., Illus.). 256p. (J). pap. 14.99 *(978-1-59643-849-1(5)*, 9781596438491, First Second Bks.) Roaring Brook Pr.

—The Time Museum. 2017. (J). lib. bdg. 26.95 ***(978-0-606-40348-1(5))*** Turtleback Bks.

Lovhaug, Lewis J. Angel Armor: The Cassandra Conflict. 2004. 188p. (YA). pap. 13.95 *(978-0-595-30869-9(4))* iUniverse, Inc.

Lu, Marie. Champion. 2013. (Legend Trilogy: 3). (ENG.). 384p. (YA). (gr. 7). 18.99 *(978-0-399-25677-6(6)*, G.P. Putnam's Sons Books for Young Readers) Penguin Publishing Group.

—Champion. 2014. (Legend Ser.: 3). (ENG.). 416p. (YA). (gr. 7). pap. 9.99 *(978-0-14-751228-4(X)*, Speak) Penguin Young Readers Group.

—Legend. aut. ltd. collector's ed. 2013. (Legend Trilogy: Bk. 1). (Illus.). 306p. (YA). mass mkt. 100.00 net. *(978-1-934267-38-7(4))* Gauntlet, Inc.

—Legend. 2011. (Legend Trilogy: Bk. 1). (ENG.). (YA). (gr. 8-12). 54.99 *(978-1-61657-044-6(X)*, Penguin AudioBooks) Penguin Publishing Group.

—Legend. Kaaris, illus. 2015. (Legend Ser.). (ENG.). 160p. (YA). (gr. 7). pap. 14.99 *(978-0-399-17189-5(4)*, G.P. Putnam's Sons Books for Young Readers) Penguin Young Readers Group.

—Legend. (Legend Ser.: 1). (ENG.). (YA). (gr. 7). 2013. 352p. pap. 9.99 *(978-0-14-242207-6(X)*, Speak) 2011. 320p. 17.99 *(978-0-399-25675-2(X)*, G.P. Putnam's Sons Books for Young Readers) Penguin Young Readers Group.

—Legend. l.t. ed. 2012. (Legend Trilogy: Bk. 1). (ENG.). 394p. (J). (gr. 7-12). 23.99 *(978-1-4104-4606-0(9))* Thorndike Pr.

—Legend. (Legend Graphic Novels Ser.: 1). 2015. lib. bdg. 26.95 *(978-0-606-38424-7(3))* 2013. lib. bdg. 20.85 *(978-0-606-31701-6(5)*, Turtleback) Turtleback Bks.

—Legend Trilogy Boxed Set, 5 vols. 2013. (Legend Trilogy: Bk. 1). (ENG.). 1088p. (YA). (gr. 7). 54.97 *(978-0-399-16667-9(X)*, G.P. Putnam's Sons Books for Young Readers) Penguin Young Readers Group.

—Prodigy. 2013. (Legend Trilogy: Bk. 2). (ENG.). 384p. (YA). (gr. 7). 18.99 *(978-0-399-25676-9(8)*, G.P. Putnam's Sons Books for Young Readers) Penguin Publishing Group.

—Prodigy. 2014. (Legend Ser.: 2). (ENG., Illus.). 416p. (YA). (gr. 7). pap. 10.99 *(978-0-14-242755-2(1)*, Speak) Penguin Young Readers Group.

—Prodigy. l.t. ed. 2013. (Legend Trilogy: Bk. 2). (ENG.). 486p. 23.99 *(978-1-4104-5512-3(2))* Thorndike Pr.

—Prodigy. 2014. (Legend Ser.: 2). lib. bdg. 20.85 *(978-0-606-35716-6(5))* Turtleback Bks.

—Prodigy: The Graphic Novel. 2016. (Legend Trilogy: Bk. 2). (ENG.). 160p. (YA). (gr. 7). pap. 14.99 *(978-0-399-17190-1(8)*, G.P. Putnam's Sons Books for Young Readers) Penguin Young Readers Group.

Lu, Marie. Warcross, 9 vols. 2017. (ENG.). (YA). 170.91 ***(978-0-525-48674-9(7))***; 368p. (gr. 7). 18.99 ***(978-0-399-54796-6(7))*** Penguin Young Readers Group. (G.P. Putnam's Sons Books for Young Readers).

Lubar, David. Hyde & Shriek: A Monsterrific Tale. 2013. (Monsterrific Tales Ser.). (ENG., Illus.). 144p. (J). (gr. 3-7). 14.99 *(978-0-7653-3081-9(4)*, 9780765330819, Starscape) Doherty, Tom Assocs., LLC.

—My Rotten Life. 2009. (Nathan Abercrombie, Accidental Zombie Ser.: 1). (ENG., Illus.). 160p. (J). (gr. 3-7). pap. 8.99 *(978-0-7653-1634-9(X)*, 9780765316349, Starscape) Doherty, Tom Assocs., LLC.

Lucas Book Group Staff & Walker, Landry Q. Alien Book. Scarlet, Tyler, illus. 2016. (ENG.). 352p. (J). (gr. 3-7). 12.99 *(978-1-4847-4141-2(2)*, Disney Lucasfilm Press) Disney Publishing Worldwide.

Lucas Film Book Group. Luke Skywalker. 2016. (Star Wars: Force Awakens 8X8 Ser.). (J). lib. bdg. 14.75 ***(978-0-606-39175-7(4))*** Turtleback Bks.

—Star Wars Poe Dameron 8x8. 2017. (ENG.). 24p. (J). (gr. 1-3). pap. 4.99 *(978-1-4847-0506-3(8)*, Disney Lucasfilm Press) Disney Publishing Worldwide.

—Star Wars: Revenge of the Sith Read-Along Storybook & CD. 2017. (Read-Along Storybook & CD Ser.). (ENG.). 32p. (J). (gr. 1-3). pap. 6.99 *(978-1-4847-8181-4(3)*, Disney Lucasfilm Press) Disney Publishing Worldwide.

—Star Wars Star Wars: Attack of the Clones Read-Along Storybook & CD. 2017. (Read-Along Storybook & CD Ser.). (ENG.). 32p. (J). (gr. 1-3). pap. 6.99 *(978-1-4847-8180-7(5)*, Disney Lucasfilm Press) Disney Publishing Worldwide.

—Trouble on Tatooine. 2017. (Star Wars: World of Reading Ser.). (J). lib. bdg. 14.75 ***(978-0-606-39963-0(1))*** Turtleback Bks.

—World of Reading Star Wars Boxed Set: Level 2. 2017. (ENG.). 192p. (J). (gr. 1-3). pap. 12.99 ***(978-1-368-00587-6(X)***, Disney Lucasfilm Press) Disney Publishing Worldwide.

Lucas Film Book Group. World of Reading Star Wars Trouble on Tatooine (Level 2) 2017. (World of Reading Ser.). (ENG.). 32p. (J). (gr. 1-3). pap. 4.99 *(978-1-4847-9934-5(8)*, Disney Lucasfilm Press) Disney Publishing Worldwide.

Lucas Film Book Group & Ferrari, Alessandro. Star Wars: Prequel Trilogy Graphic Novel. 2017. (ENG., Illus.). 208p. (J). (gr. 3-7). 19.99 *(978-1-368-00274-5(9)*, Disney Lucasfilm Press) Disney Publishing Worldwide.

Lucas Film Book Group & Forbeck, Matt. Star Wars Rogue One Junior Novel. 2017. (ENG.). 192p. (J). (gr. 3-7). 10.99 *(978-1-4847-0509-4(2)*, Disney Lucasfilm Press) Disney Publishing Worldwide.

Lucas Film Book Group & Fry, Jason. Luke & the Lost Jedi Temple. 2016. (ENG.). 24p. (J). (gr. 1-3). pap. 4.99 *(978-1-4847-0505-6(X)*, Disney Lucasfilm Press) Disney Publishing Worldwide.

Lucas Film Book Group & Simonson, Louise. A New Hope: The Rise of a Hero. Simonson, Walter, illus. 2017. (ENG.). 48p. (J). (gr. 1-3). 10.99 *(978-1-4847-9933-8(X)*, Disney Lucasfilm Press) Disney Publishing Worldwide.

Lucas Film Book Group, et al. Join the Resistance, Bk. 1. Wu, Annie, illus. 2017. (Join the Resistance Ser.). (ENG.). 224p. (J). (gr. 5-7). 12.99 *(978-1-4847-0484-4(3)*, Disney Lucasfilm Press) Disney Publishing Worldwide.

Lucas Film Book Group Editors. Poe Dameron. 2017. (Star Wars: Force Awakens 8X8 Ser.). (J). lib. bdg. 14.75 *(978-0-606-39506-9(7))* Turtleback Bks.

Lucas Film Book Group Staff & Holland, Jesse J. Star Wars Finn's Story. Rood, Brian, illus. 2016. (ENG.). 128p. (J). (gr. 1-3). pap. 5.99 *(978-1-4847-9022-9(7)*, Disney Lucasfilm Press) Disney Publishing Worldwide.

Lucas, George. La Guerre des Etoiles, Tome 1.Tr. of Star Wars. (FRE.). (J). pap. 11.95 *(978-2-265-06730-1(X))* Fleuve Noir FRA. Dist: Distribooks, Inc.

Lucas, Luke. Falls the Shadow. 2014. (ENG., Illus.). 352p. (YA). (gr. 7). 18.99 *(978-1-4424-9753-5(X)*, Simon & Schuster Bks. For Young Readers) Simon & Schuster Bks. For Young Readers.

Lucasfilm Book Group. The Heist. 2017. (Star Wars Adventures in Wild Space Ser.: 3). (J). lib. bdg. 16.00 ***(978-0-606-39961-6(5))*** Turtleback Bks.

LucasFilm Book Group. Star Wars: Oversize Graphic Novel. Kawaii Studio Staff & Pastrovicchio, Alessandro, illus. 2016. (ENG.). 208p. (J). (gr. 3-7). 19.99 *(978-1-4847-3784-2(9)*, Disney Lucasfilm Press) Disney Publishing Worldwide.

—Star Wars Adventures in Wild Space the Heist: Book 3. 2017. (Adventures in Wild Space Ser.). (ENG.). 144p. (J). (gr. 1-3). pap. 5.99 *(978-1-368-00314-8(1)*, Disney Lucasfilm Press) Disney Publishing Worldwide.

—Star Wars Galactic Maps: An Illustrated Atlas of the Star Wars Universe. 2016. (ENG.). 80p. (J). (gr. 3-7). 24.99 *(978-1-368-00306-3(0)*, Disney Lucasfilm Press) Disney Publishing Worldwide.

—World of Reading Star Wars Finn & Poe Team Up! 2016. (ENG., Illus.). 32p. (J). (gr. 1-3). pap. 3.99 *(978-1-4847-4143-6(9)*, Disney Lucasfilm Press) Disney Publishing Worldwide.

LucasFilm Book Group & Huddleston, Tom. The Nest. 2017. (Adventures in Wild Space Ser.). (ENG.). 144p. (J). (gr. 1-3). pap. 5.99 *(978-1-368-00316-2(8)*, Disney Lucasfilm Press) Disney Publishing Worldwide.

LucasFilm Book Group & Scott, Cavan. The Snare. 2017. (Adventures in Wild Space Ser.). (ENG.). 144p. (J). (gr. 1-3). pap. 5.99 *(978-1-368-00275-2(7)*, Disney Lucasfilm Press) Disney Publishing Worldwide.

LucasFilm Book Group Staff. World of Reading: Star Wars Listen along: Star Wars: 3 World of Reading Level 2 Readers with CD! 2016. (World of Reading Ser.). (ENG.). 96p. (J). (gr. -1-k). pap. 7.99 *(978-1-4847-9024-3(3)*, Disney Lucasfilm Press) Disney Publishing Worldwide.

Lucasfilm Press. Han & the Rebel Rescue. 2017. (J). lib. bdg. 14.75 ***(978-0-606-39966-1(6))*** Turtleback Bks.

LucasFilm Press. Star Wars: 5-Minute Star Wars Stories. 2015. (ENG.). 176p. (J). (gr. 1-3). 12.99 *(978-1-4847-2820-8(3)*, Disney Lucasfilm Press) Disney Publishing Worldwide.

—Star Wars Han & the Rebel Rescue. 2017. (ENG.). 24p. (J). (gr. 1-3). pap. 4.99 *(978-1-368-00352-0(4)*, Disney Lucasfilm Press) Disney Publishing Worldwide.

Lucasfilm Press & Gray, Claudia. Star Wars - Lost Stars. Noto, Phil, illus. 2015. (ENG.). 560p. (YA). (gr. 7-12). 17.99 *(978-1-4847-2498-9(4)*, Disney Lucasfilm Press) Disney Publishing Worldwide.

LucasFilm Press Staff. The Force Awakens. Rood, Brian, illus. 2015. (World of Reading Ser.). (ENG.). 32p. (J). (gr. 1-3). pap. 3.99 *(978-1-4847-0481-3(9))* Disney Pr.

—Star Wars: Before the Awakening. Noto, Phil, illus. 2015. E-Book *(978-1-4847-3550-3(1))* Disney Publishing Worldwide.

LucasFilm Press Staff & Fry, Jason. The Weapon of a Jedi: A Luke Skywalker Adventure. Noto, Phil, illus. 2015. (ENG.). 192p. (J). (gr. 5-9). 12.99 *(978-1-4847-2496-5(8)*, Disney Lucasfilm Press) Disney Publishing Worldwide.

LucasFilm Press Staff & Rucka, Greg. Smuggler's Run: A Han Solo Adventure. Noto, Phil, illus. 2015. (ENG.). 192p. (J). (gr. 5-9). 12.99 *(978-1-4847-2495-8(X)*, Disney Lucasfilm Press) Disney Publishing Worldwide.

Lunetta, Demitria. In the After. 2013. (In the After Ser.: 1). (ENG.). 464p. (YA). (gr. 8). 17.99 *(978-0-06-210545-5(0)*, HarperTeen) HarperCollins Pubs.

—In the End. 2014. (In the After Ser.: 2). (ENG.). 448p. (YA). (gr. 8). 17.99 *(978-0-06-210548-6(5)*, HarperTeen) HarperCollins Pubs.

Lunn, John. The Aquanauts. 2005. (ENG.). 228p. (J). (gr. 5-9). per. 8.95 *(978-0-88776-727-2(3)*, Tundra Bks.) Tundra Bks. CAN. Dist: Penguin Random Hse. LLC.

Lyen, Taylor Samuel. Pembroke: The Adventures of Arthur Bacterium & Patty Virus. 2012. 180p. (-18). pap. 13.95 *(978-1-4759-5855-3(2))* iUniverse, Inc.

Lyga, Barry. Archvillain. 2010. (Archvillain Ser.: 1). (ENG.). 192p. (J). (gr. 3-7). 16.99 *(978-0-545-19649-9(3)*, Scholastic Pr.) Scholastic, Inc.

Lyga, Barry & DeFranco, Robert. After the Red Rain. 2015. (ENG.). 400p. (YA). (gr. 10-17). 18.00 *(978-0-316-40603-1(1))* Little Brown & Co.

Lynch, Chris. Cyberia. 2008. (Cyberia Ser.: 1). (ENG.). 160p. (J). (gr. 3-7). 16.99 *(978-0-545-02793-9(4)*, Scholastic Pr.) Scholastic, Inc.

—Monkey See, Monkey Don't. 2011. (Cyberia Ser.: 2). (ENG.). 144p. (J). (gr. 3-7). pap. 5.99 *(978-0-545-02797-7(7)*, Scholastic Paperbacks) Scholastic, Inc.

Lyons, Suzanne. Pete Discovers Gravity: Set Of 6. 2011. (Early Connections Ser.). (J). pap. 39.00 net. *(978-1-4108-1559-0(5))* Benchmark Education Co.

Ma, Jyoti & Devi, Chandra. Sparkling Together: Starbright & His Earthling Friends. 2004. (ENG., Illus.). 96p. (J). pap. 19.95 *(978-0-932040-54-1(3)*, 9780932040541) Integral Yoga Pubns.

Maberry, Jonathan. Mars One. 2017. (ENG., Illus.). 448p. (YA). (gr. 7). 17.99 *(978-1-4814-6161-0(3)*, Simon & Schuster Bks. For Young Readers) Simon & Schuster Bks. For Young Readers.

—The Orphan Army. 2015. (Nightsiders Ser.: 1). (ENG., Illus.). 400p. (J). (gr. 3-7). 16.99 *(978-1-4814-1575-0(1)*, Simon & Schuster Bks. For Young Readers) Simon & Schuster Bks. For Young Readers.

—The Orphan Army. 2016. (Nightsiders Ser.: 1). lib. bdg. 18.40 *(978-0-606-38959-4(8))* Turtleback Bks.

—Vault of Shadows. (Nightsiders Ser.: 2). (ENG.). 464p. (J). (gr. 3-7). 2017. pap. 8.99 *(978-1-4814-1579-8(4))* 2016. (Illus.). 16.99 *(978-1-4814-1578-1(6))* Simon & Schuster Bks. For Young Readers. (Simon & Schuster Bks. For Young Readers).

Macaw, Grant. Vigil's End. 2005. (ENG.). 310p. (YA). (gr. 7). per. *(978-1-933255-13-2(7))* DNA Pr.

MacDonald, Tom. Secret of the Tree: Marcus Speer's Ecosentinel. Stieber, Joel, illus. 2009. 300p. 28.95 *(978-0-595-51985-9(7))* iUniverse, Inc.

MacHado, Ana Maria. Un Deseo Loco. (Torre de Papel Ser.). (SPA.). (YA). (gr. 6-18). 8.95 *(978-958-04-4529-6(X)*, NR30565) Norma S.A. COL. Dist: Distribuidora Norma, Inc., Lectorum Pubns., Inc.

MacHale, D. J. The Reality Bug. 2003. (Pendragon Ser.: 4). (ENG., Illus.). 384p. (J). (gr. 5-9). pap. 9.99 *(978-0-7434-3734-9(9)*, Aladdin) Simon & Schuster Children's Publishing.

—Storm. 2014. (SYLO Chronicles Ser.: 2). (ENG.). (J). (gr. 3-7). 512p. pap. 9.99 *(978-1-59514-668-7(7))*; 2nd ed. 496p. 17.99 *(978-1-59514-667-0(9))* Penguin Young Readers Group. (Razorbill).

Machale, D.j. & Loftin, Nikki. Strike: The SYLO Chronicles #3. 2015. (SYLO Chronicles Ser.: 3). (ENG.). 448p. (J). (gr. 3-7). 9.99 *(978-1-59514-670-0(9)*, Razorbill) Penguin Young Readers Group.

Mack, Karen. The Magical Adventures of Sun Beams. 2009. 42p. 31.99 *(978-1-4415-3636-5(1))* Xlibris Corp.

Mackie, Howard & Kavanagh, Terry. Gambit Classic - Volume 2. Janson, Klaus, illus. 2013. (ENG.). 208p. (J). (gr. 4-17). pap. 29.99 *(978-0-7851-6790-7(0))* Marvel Worldwide, Inc.

Mackie, Howard, et al. X-Men - Age of Apocalypse Omnibus Companion. Dodson, Terry et al, illus. 2014. (ENG.). 992p. (J). (gr. 4-17). 99.99 *(978-0-7851-8514-7(3))* Marvel Worldwide, Inc.

Maes, Nicholas. Locksmith. 2008. (Felix Taylor Adventure Ser.: 1). (ENG.). 240p. (J). (gr. 5-8). pap. 11.99 *(978-1-55002-791-4(3)*, Sandcastle Bks.) Dundurn CAN. Dist: Ingram Publisher Services.

Mafi, Tahereh. Ignite Me. 2014. (Shatter Me Ser.: 3). (ENG.). (gr. 9). 416p. (YA). pap. 9.99 *(978-0-06-208558-0(1))*; 352p. (J). 17.99 *(978-0-06-208557-3(3))* HarperCollins Pubs.

—Shatter Me. (Shatter Me Ser.: 1). (ENG.). (YA). (gr. 9). 2012. 464p. pap. 9.99 *(978-0-06-208550-4(6))* 2011. 352p. 17.99 *(978-0-06-208548-1(4))* HarperCollins Pubs.

—Shatter Me. 2012. (Shatter Me Ser.: 1). (YA). lib. bdg. 20.85 *(978-0-606-26868-4(5)*, Turtleback) Turtleback Bks.

—Unite Me: Fracture Me & Destroy Me. 2014. (Shatter Me Ser.). (ENG.). 224p. (YA). (gr. 9). pap. 9.99 *(978-0-06-232796-3(8))* HarperCollins Pubs.

—Unravel Me. 2013. (Shatter Me Ser.: 2). (ENG.). (YA). (gr. 9). 496p. pap. 9.99 *(978-0-06-208554-2(9))*; 480p. 17.99 *(978-0-06-208553-5(0))* HarperCollins Pubs.

—Unravel Me. 2013. (Shatter Me Ser.: 2). (YA). lib. bdg. 20.85 *(978-0-606-35049-5(7)*, Turtleback) Turtleback Bks.

Magno, Carlos, illus. Transformers: Movie Prequel: Rising Storm: Vol 1, 1 vol. 2012. (Transformers: Dark of the Moon Movie Prequel Ser.). (ENG.). 24p. (J). 24.21 *(978-1-59961-975-0(X)*, Graphic Novels) Spotlight.

—Transformers: Movie Prequel: Rising Storm: Vol 2, 1 vol. 2012. (Transformers: Dark of the Moon Movie Prequel Ser.). (ENG.). 24p. (J). 24.21 *(978-1-59961-976-7(8)*, Graphic Novels) Spotlight.

—Transformers: Movie Prequel: Rising Storm: Vol 3, 1 vol. 2012. (Transformers: Dark of the Moon Movie Prequel Ser.). (ENG.). 24p. (J). 24.21 *(978-1-59961-977-4(6)*, Graphic Novels) Spotlight.

—Transformers: Movie Prequel: Rising Storm: Vol 4, 1 vol. 2012. (Transformers: Dark of the Moon Movie Prequel Ser.). (ENG.). 24p. (J). 24.21 *(978-1-59961-978-1(4)*, Graphic Novels) Spotlight.

Magoon, Kekla. Infinity Riders. 2016. (Voyager Ser.). (ENG.). 208p. (J). (gr. 3-7). 12.99 *(978-0-385-38667-8(2)*, Random Hse. Bks. for Young Readers) Random Hse. Children's Bks.

Magro, Mark. Surfacing. 2015. (ENG.). 280p. (YA). (gr. 7). pap. 15.99 *(978-1-63163-054-5(7)*, Jolly Fish Pr.) North Star Editions.

Maguire, K. C. Inside the Palisade. 2015. (ENG.). 173p. (YA). (gr. 8-17). pap. 11.95 *(978-1-78279-715-9(7)*, Lodestone Bks.) Hunt, John Publishing Ltd. GBR. Dist: National Bk. Network.

Mai, Lily. Bertie Boom's Trip to the Moon. 2010. (Illus.). 20p. 12.49 *(978-1-4520-1379-4(9))* AuthorHouse.

Maihack, Mike. Secret of the Time Tablets. 2016. (Cleopatra in Space Ser.: 3). lib. bdg. 24.50 *(978-0-606-38812-2(5))* Turtleback Bks.

Mairghread, Scott. Transformers: Distant Stars: Distant Stars. Howell, Corin & Pitre-Durocher, Sara, illus. 2016. (Transformers Ser.). (ENG.). 120p. pap. 19.99 *(978-1-63140-600-3(0)*, 9781631406003) Idea & Design Works, LLC.

Mak, D P. Invisible Pill. 2005. 44p. pap. *(978-1-84401-210-7(7))* Athena Pr.

Maker, Don. Miranda's Magic. 2013. 152p. pap. 6.63 *(978-0-9859707-4-1(X))* Metacognition Pr.

Malley, Gemma. The Declaration. 2008. (Declaration Ser.). (ENG., Illus.). 320p. (YA). (gr. 7). 10.99 *(978-1-59990-295-1(8)*, 9781599902951, Bloomsbury USA Childrens) Bloomsbury Publishing USA.

—The Declaration, 7 vols. (YA). 2008. 119.75 *(978-1-4281-7284-5(X))* 2007. 245.75 *(978-1-4281-7279-1(3))* 2007. 91.75 *(978-1-4281-7278-4(5))* 2007. 89.75 *(978-1-4281-7280-7(7))* 2007. 121.75 *(978-1-4281-7282-1(3))* 2007. 1.25 *(978-1-4281-7275-3(0))* Recorded Bks., Inc.

—The Legacy. 2011. (Declaration Ser.). (ENG.). 272p. (YA). (gr. 7-18). 17.99 *(978-1-59990-567-9(1)*, 9781599905679, Bloomsbury USA Childrens) Bloomsbury Publishing USA.

Manchee, William. Tarizon the Liberator: Tarizon Trilogy Vol 1. 2008. 340p. (YA). (gr. 7-18). lib. bdg. 24.00 *(978-1-929976-48-5(8)*, TOP) Top Pubns., Ltd.

Mandanna, Sangu. The Lost Girl. 2012. (ENG.). 432p. (YA). (gr. 8). 17.99 *(978-0-06-208231-2(0))* HarperCollins Pubs.

Manning, Matthew K. Batman Character Encyclopedia. 2016. (ENG., Illus.). 208p. (J). (gr. k-4). 16.99 *(978-1-4654-4498-1(X)*, DK Children) Dorling Kindersley Publishing, Inc.

Mansfield, Keith. Battle for Earth. 2011. (Johnny Mackintosh Ser.). (ENG.). 336p. (J). (gr. 4-6). 8.99 *(978-1-84916-329-3(4))* Quercus GBR. Dist: Hachette Bk. Group.

—Johnny Mackintosh & the Spirit of London. 2010. (Johnny Mackintosh,Johnny Mackintosh Trilogy Ser.: 1). (ENG.). 352p. (J). (gr. 4-6). pap. 8.99 *(978-1-84724-774-2(1))* Quercus GBR. Dist: Hachette Bk. Group.

—Star Blaze. 2010. (Johnny Mackintosh,Johnny Mackintosh Trilogy Ser.: 2). (ENG.). 276p. (J). (gr. 4-6). pap. 8.99 *(978-1-84916-126-8(7))* Quercus GBR. Dist: Hachette Bk. Group.

Marazano, Richard. Civilisation, 2 vols. Ponzio, Jean-Michel, illus. 2010. (Chimpanzee Complex Ser.: 3). (ENG.). 55p. pap. 13.95 *(978-1-84918-043-6(1))* CineBook GBR. Dist: National Bk. Network.

—The Sons of Ares, 2 vols. Ponzio, Jean-Michel, illus. 2009. (Chimpanzee Complex Ser.: 1). (ENG.). 56p. pap. 13.95 *(978-1-84918-002-3(4))* CineBook GBR. Dist: National Bk. Network.

Marie, Anna. Hexon. 2012. (ENG.). 66p. pap. 9.95 *(978-1-4327-9112-4(5))* Outskirts Pr., Inc.

Mario. Arriving to Planet Noah. 2011. 68p. 24.99 *(978-1-4628-5905-4(4))*; pap. 15.99 *(978-1-4628-5904-7(6))* Xlibris Corp.

Mariz, Rae. The Unidentified. (ENG.). 304p. (YA). (gr. 8). 2012. pap. 8.99 *(978-0-06-180209-6(3))* 2010. 16.99 *(978-0-06-180208-9(5))* HarperCollins Pubs.

Marlowe, Paul. Sporeville. 2007. (Wellborn Conspiracy Ser.: Bk. 1). 250p. (YA). (gr. 8-12). pap. 10.95 *(978-0-9739505-4-0(4))* Sybertooth, Inc. CAN. Dist: Lightning Source, Inc.

Marman, Richard. Mcalister's Spark. Marman, Richard, illus. 2013. (Illus.). 364p. pap. *(978-1-909302-21-1(X))* Abela Publishing.

Marr, Melissa, et al. Shards & Ashes. 2013. (ENG.). 384p. (YA). (gr. 8). 17.99 *(978-0-06-209846-7(2))*; pap. 9.99 *(978-0-06-209845-0(4))* HarperCollins Pubs.

Marsh, Carole. The Earthshaking Earthquake Mystery. 2007. (Masters of Disasters Ser.). (Illus.). 118p. (J). (gr. 2-9). 14.95 *(978-0-635-06395-3(6))* Gallopade International.

—The Ferocious Forest Fire Mystery. 2008. (Masters of Disasters Ser.). (Illus.). 118p. (J). (gr. 3-5). 14.95 *(978-0-635-06468-4(5))*; per. 5.99 *(978-0-635-06465-3(0))* Gallopade International.

—The Treacherous Tornado Mystery. 2007. (Masters of Disasters Ser.). (Illus.). 118p. (J). (gr. 2-9). 14.95 *(978-0-635-06394-6(8))* Gallopade International.

Marshall, G. Skies of Dawn. 2007. 160p. per. 12.95 *(978-0-595-42946-2(7))* iUniverse, Inc.

Martin, Caroline Jane. The Flow. 2013. (ENG.). 276p. pap. *(978-0-9928101-0-8(8))* Lovell Pr.

Martin-Duttmann, Robin. Zoo on the Moon. 2013. 24p. pap. 12.97 *(978-1-62212-735-1(8)*, Strategic Bk. Publishing) Strategic Book Publishing & Rights Agency (SBPRA).

Martin, Gary & Pennebaker, H. I. Professor Tyme's Timeless Tales: Revenge of the Sargasso Sea Ogre. 2006. (ENG.). 160p. per. 24.95 *(978-1-4241-5701-3(3))* America Star Bks.

Martin, Jenny. Marked. 2016. (ENG.). 368p. (YA). (gr. 7). 17.99 *(978-0-525-42871-8(2)*, Dial Bks) Penguin Young Readers Group.

—Tracked. 2015. (ENG.). 400p. (YA). (gr. 7). 17.99 *(978-0-8037-4012-9(3)*, Dial Bks) Penguin Young Readers Group.

Martin, Laura. The Ark Plan. Deschamps, Eric, illus. (Edge of Extinction Ser.: 1). (J). (gr. 3-7). 2017. 384p. pap. 6.99 *(978-0-06-241623-0(5))* 2016. 368p. 16.99 *(978-0-06-241622-3(7))* HarperCollins Pubs.

Martin, R. Safe Zone. 2017. (Level Up Ser.). (ENG.). (YA). (gr. 6-12). 112p. pap. 7.99 ***(978-1-5124-5360-7(9))***; lib. bdg. 26.65 ***(978-1-5124-3986-1(X))*** Lerner Publishing Group. (Darby Creek).

Martin, T. Michael. The End Games. 2013. (ENG.). 384p. (YA). (gr. 9). 17.99 *(978-0-06-220180-5(8))* HarperCollins Pubs.

Marvel. Avengers: Age of Ultron: Avengers Save the Day. 2015. (Marvel 8x8s Ser.). (J). lib. bdg. 14.75 *(978-0-606-37214-5(8))* Turtleback Bks.

—Avengers: Age of Ultron: Battle at Avengers Tower. 2015. (Marvel 8x8s Ser.). (J). lib. bdg. 13.55 *(978-0-606-37213-8(X))* Turtleback Bks.

—Marvel Avengers Assemble: Built for Action. 2015. (ENG.). 24p. (J). (gr. 1-4). pap. 10.99 *(978-0-7944-3392-5(8)*, Reader's Digest Children's Bks.) Studio Fun International.

—Marvel's Guardians of the Galaxy, Vol. 2. 2017. (ENG., Illus.). 12p. (J). (gr. -1-1). pap. 6.99 *(978-0-316-27170-7(5))* Little, Brown Bks. for Young Readers.

—Marvel's the Avengers Storybook Collection. 2015. (ENG., Illus.). 192p. (J). (gr. -1-3). 11.99 *(978-0-316-25631-5(5))* Little, Brown Bks. for Young Readers.

Marvel & Busse, R. R. Guardians Save the Day Vol. 2. 2017. (Passport to Reading Level 2 Ser.). (ENG., Illus.). 32p. (J). (gr. -1-3). pap. 4.99 *(978-0-316-27169-1(1))* Little, Brown Bks. for Young Readers.

—Meet the Team! 2017. (Passport to Reading Level 2 Ser.). (ENG., Illus.). 32p. (J). (gr. -1-3). pap. 4.99 *(978-0-316-27167-7(5))* Little, Brown Bks. for Young Readers.

—Revenge of the Ravagers. 2017. (ENG., Illus.). 24p. (J). (gr. -1-3). pap. 4.99 *(978-0-316-27161-5(6))* Little, Brown Bks. for Young Readers.

Marvel & Cho, Charles. The Return of Rocket & Groot. 2017. (ENG., Illus.). 24p. (J). (gr. -1-3). pap. 4.99 *(978-0-316-27162-2(4))* Little, Brown Bks. for Young Readers.

Marvel & Marvel Book Group. This Is the Invincible Iron Man. 2012. (Marvel World of Reading Level 1 Ser.). (J). lib. bdg. 13.55 *(978-0-606-23789-5(5)*, Turtleback) Turtleback Bks.

Marvel & McCann, Jim. Guardians of the Galaxy, Vol. 2. 2017. (ENG.). 176p. (J). (gr. 3-7). 9.99 *(978-0-316-27163-9(2))* Little, Brown Bks. for Young Readers.

Marvel Book Group. Avengers - Battle with Ultron, Level 2. 2015. (World of Reading Ser.). (ENG.). 32p. (J). (gr. 1-3). pap. 3.99 *(978-1-4847-1448-5(2)*, Marvel Pr.) Disney Publishing Worldwide.

Marvel Book Group. World of Reading Listen Along. 2017. (World of Reading Ser.). (ENG.). 96p. (J). (gr. -1-k). pap. 7.99 ***(978-1-4847-9948-2(8)***, Marvel Pr.) Disney Publishing Worldwide.

Marvel Book Group, et al. Doctor Strange: Mystery of the Dark Magic. Pham, Khoi & Sotomayor, Chris, illus. 2016. (Mighty Marvel Chapter Book Ser.). (ENG.). 128p. (J). (gr. 3-7). pap. 5.99 *(978-1-4847-3127-7(1)*, Marvel Pr.) Disney Publishing Worldwide.

Marvel Books Staff & Wyatt, Chris. Guardians of the Galaxy. 2014. (ENG.). 144p. (J). (gr. 3-7). pap. 6.99 *(978-0-316-29324-2(5))* Little, Brown Bks. for Young Readers.

Marvel Comics, text. Annihilation Omnibus. 2014. (ENG., Illus.). 880p. (YA). (gr. 8-17). 125.00 *(978-0-7851-8889-6(4))* Marvel Worldwide, Inc.

—Marvel's Agents of S. H. I. E. L. D. 2014. (ENG., Illus.). 240p. (J). (gr. -1-17). 49.99 *(978-0-7851-8998-5(X))* Marvel Worldwide, Inc.

Marvel Comics Staff & Kirby, Jack, texts. Devil Dinosaur. 2014. (ENG., Illus.). 184p. (J). (gr. 4-17). pap. 24.99 *(978-0-7851-9037-0(6))* Marvel Worldwide, Inc.

Marvel Editors. Marvel's Guardians of the Galaxy, Vol. 2. 2017. (Passport to Reading Level 2 Ser.). (J). lib. bdg. 14.75 ***(978-0-606-39906-7(2))***; lib. bdg. 14.75 ***(978-0-606-39905-0(4))*** Turtleback Bks.

Mary-Todd, Jonathan. Pig City. 2012. (After the Dust Settled Ser.). (ENG.). 112p. (YA). (gr. 6-12). pap. 7.95 *(978-0-8225-8746-0(7)*, Darby Creek); lib. bdg. 27.93 *(978-0-7613-8328-4(X))* Lerner Publishing Group.

—Shot Down. 2012. (After the Dust Settled Ser.). (ENG.). 104p. (YA). (gr. 6-12). pap. 7.95 *(978-0-7613-9399-3(4)*, Darby Creek); lib. bdg. 27.93 *(978-0-7613-8329-1(8))* Lerner Publishing Group.

—Snakebite. 2012. (After the Dust Settled Ser.). (ENG.). 120p. (YA). (gr. 6-12). pap. 7.95 *(978-0-8225-8745-3(9)*, Darby Creek); lib. bdg. 27.93 *(978-0-7613-8327-7(1))* Lerner Publishing Group.

Marz, Ron, et al. Progeny Volume 1 TP. 2013. (ENG., Illus.). 144p. (YA). pap. 16.99 *(978-1-60706-748-1(X)*, 9781607067481) Image Comics.

Mashima, Hiro. Rave. 2006. (Rave Ser.). (SPA., Illus.). reprint ed. Vol. 1. 185p. pap. 10.95 *(978-1-59497-175-4(7))* Vol. 3. 184p. pap. 10.95 *(978-1-59497-177-8(3))* Vol. 4. 188p. per. 10.95 *(978-1-59497-178-5(1))* Vol. 5. 192p. pap. 10.95 *(978-1-59497-179-2(X))* Vol. 6. 200p. pap. 10.95 *(978-1-59497-180-8(3))* Public Square Bks.

—Rave: Volume 2, Vol. 2. 2006. (Rave Ser.). (SPA., Illus.). 180p. reprint ed. pap. 10.95 *(978-1-59497-176-1(5))* Public Square Bks.

—Rave: Volume 7, Vol. 7. 2006. (Rave Ser.). (SPA., Illus.). 189p. reprint ed. pap. 10.95 *(978-1-59497-199-0(4))* Public Square Bks.

—Rave: Volume 9, Vol. 9. 2006. (Rave Ser.). (SPA., Illus.). 189p. reprint ed. pap. 10.95 *(978-1-59497-201-0(X))* Public Square Bks.

—Rave, Volume 8, Vol. 8. 2006. (Rave Ser.). (SPA., Illus.). 171p. reprint ed. pap. 10.95 *(978-1-59497-200-3(1))* Public Square Bks.

Mass, Wendy. Pi in the Sky. 2014. (ENG.). 272p. (J). (gr. 3-7). pap. 8.99 *(978-0-316-08917-3(6))* Little, Brown Bks. for Young Readers.

—Voyagers: the Seventh Element (Book 6) 2016. (Voyager Ser.). (ENG.). 208p. (J). (gr. 3-7). 12.99 *(978-0-385-38673-9(7)*, Random Hse. Bks. for Young Readers) Random Hse. Children's Bks.

Mass, Wendy & Brawer, Michael. Archie's Alien Disguise. 2015. (Space Taxi Ser.: 3). (J). lib. bdg. 16.00 *(978-0-606-37517-7(1))* Turtleback Bks.

—B. U. R. P. Strikes Back. 2017. (Space Taxi Ser.: 5). (ENG., Illus.). 144p. (J). (gr. 1-5). pap. 5.99 *(978-0-316-30840-3(4))* Little, Brown Bks. for Young Readers.

—B. U. R. P. Strikes Back. 2017. (Space Taxi Ser.: 5). (J). lib. bdg. 16.00 ***(978-0-606-40226-2(8))*** Turtleback Bks.

Mass, Wendy & Brawer, Michael. The Galactic B. U. R. P. 2016. (Space Taxi Ser.: 4). (ENG., Illus.). 128p. (J). (gr. 1-5). 14.99 *(978-0-316-24331-5(0))*; pap. 5.99 *(978-0-316-24330-8(2))* Little, Brown Bks. for Young Readers.

—The Galactic B. U. R. P. 2016. (Space Taxi Ser.: 4). (J). lib. bdg. 16.00 *(978-0-606-37518-4(X))* Turtleback Bks.

Mass, Wendy & Michael Brawer. Aliens on Earth. 2017. (Space Taxi Ser.: 6). (J). lib. bdg. 16.00 ***(978-0-606-40227-9(6))*** Turtleback Bks.

Mathews, Temple. The New Kid. 2010. (New Kid Ser.). (ENG.). 288p. (J). (gr. 6-11). pap. 9.99 *(978-1-935618-27-0(X))* BenBella Bks.

—The Sword of Armageddon. 2010. ix, 291p. *(978-1-935618-17-1(2))* BenBella Bks.

Matson, Lynne. Nil. 2014. (Nil Ser.: 1). (ENG.). 384p. (YA). (gr. 9-13). 18.99 *(978-0-8050-9771-9(6)*, 9780805097719, Holt, Henry & Co. Bks. For Young Readers) Holt, Henry & Co.

—Nil Unlocked. 2015. (Nil Ser.: 2). (ENG.). 432p. (YA). (gr. 9). 17.99 *(978-1-62779-293-6(7)*, 9781627792936, Holt, Henry & Co. Bks. For Young Readers) Holt, Henry & Co.

Mattern, Joanne. Batter Up! 2005. (J). pap. *(978-1-4108-4193-3(6))* Benchmark Education Co.

Mayer, Kirsten. Meet Team Prime. 2012. (Transformers Passport to Reading Ser.). (J). lib. bdg. 13.55 *(978-0-606-26148-7(6)*, Turtleback) Turtleback Bks.

Maynard, Case. The Surrendered. 2016. (ENG.). 266p. (YA). (gr. 9). pap. 9.95 *(978-0-9970104-7-3(9))* Blaze Publishing, LLC.

Mayne, William. Earthfasts. 2008. (J). (gr. 4-7). 25.25 *(978-0-8446-6430-9(8))* Smith, Peter Pub., Inc.

McBee, Travis. A Little Holiday Thrill. 2008. 66p. pap. 10.99 *(978-0-557-03276-1(8))* Lulu Pr., Inc.

McBride, Earvin, Jr. The Blockheads from Planet Ecto. 2nd unabr. ed. 2003. (Earvin MacBride's Amazing Sci-Fi & Adventure Heroes Ser.). (Illus.). 41p. (YA). (gr. 7-12). pap. 4.95 *(978-1-892511-10-2(X)*, Disposition Sketch Bks.) MacBride, E. J. Pubn., Inc.

McCarthy, Cori. Breaking Sky. 2015. (ENG.). 416p. (YA). (gr. 7-12). 16.99 *(978-1-4926-0141-8(1)*, 9781492601418) Sourcebooks, Inc.

McClellan, Rachel. Escape to Eden. 2016. (ENG.). 295p. (YA). pap. 17.99 *(978-1-4621-1777-2(5)*, Sweetwater Bks.) Cedar Fort, Inc./CFI Distribution.

McClymer, Kelly. Must Love Black. 2008. (ENG.). 192p. (YA). (gr. 7-18). pap. 8.99 *(978-1-4169-4903-9(8)*, Simon Pulse) Simon Pulse.

McCullough, Kelly. School for Sidekicks. 2015. (ENG.). 336p. (J). (gr. 4-9). 16.99 *(978-1-250-03926-2(6)*, 9781250039262) Feiwel & Friends.

McCune, Joshua. Talker 25. 2014. (Talker 25 Ser.: 1). (ENG.). 432p. (YA). (gr. 9). 17.99 *(978-0-06-212191-2(X)*, Greenwillow Bks.) HarperCollins Pubs.

McCusker, Paul & Elmer, Robert. Ripple Effect, 1 vol., Bk. 1. 2008. (Time Thriller Trilogy Ser.: Bk. 1). (ENG., Illus.). 224p. (YA). (gr. 8-11). pap. 9.99 *(978-0-310-71436-1(2))* Zondervan.

McDaniel, Scott, et al, illus. Daredevil & Elektra: Fall from Grace. 2014. (ENG.). 464p. (J). (gr. 4-17). pap. 44.99 *(978-0-7851-8516-1(X))* Marvel Worldwide, Inc.

McDonald, Megan. Solar System Superhero. Reynolds, Peter H., illus. 2013. (Stink Ser.: 5). (ENG.). 144p. (J). (gr. 1-4). pap. 4.99 *(978-0-7636-6425-1(1))* Candlewick Pr.

—Solar System Superhero. 2013. (Stink Ser.: 5). lib. bdg. 14.75 *(978-0-606-31591-3(8)*, Turtleback) Turtleback Bks.

—Stink: the Absolutely Astronomical Collection: Books 4-6. Reynolds, Peter H., illus. 2013. (Stink Ser.). (ENG.). 256p. (J). (gr. k-3). pap. 14.97 *(978-0-7636-6830-3(3))* Candlewick Pr.

McDougal, Anna. Sam's Solar Panels: If... Then. 2017. (Computer Science for the Real World Ser.). 16p. (gr. 7-8). pap. 7.95 ***(978-1-5383-5224-3(9)***, Rosen Classroom) Rosen Publishing Group, Inc., The.

McDougall, Sophia. Mars Evacuees. 2015. 416p. (J). (gr. 3-7). 16.99 *(978-0-06-229399-2(0))* HarperCollins Pubs.

McElligott, Matthew. Mad Scientist Academy: the Space Disaster. 2017. (Mad Scientist Academy Ser.: 3). (ENG.). 40p. (J). (gr. k-3). lib. bdg. 20.99 ***(978-0-553-52383-6(X))***; (Illus.). 17.99 ***(978-0-553-52382-9(1))*** Random Hse. Children's Bks. (Crown Books For Young Readers).

McFarland, Kim. A Refugee in Oz. 2010. 164p. pap. 11.95 *(978-0-557-48706-6(4))* Lulu Pr., Inc.

McGee, Katharine. The Dazzling Heights. 2017. (Thousandth Floor Ser.: 2). 432p. (YA). (gr. 8). 18.99 ***(978-0-06-241862-3(9))*** HarperCollins Pubs.

—The Thousandth Floor. (Thousandth Floor Ser.: 1). (YA). (gr. 8). 2017. 496p. pap. 9.99 ***(978-0-06-241860-9(2))*** 2016. (ENG.). 448p. 18.99 *(978-0-06-241859-3(9))* HarperCollins Pubs.

McGee, Krista. Revolutionary, 1 vol. 2014. (Anomaly Ser.: 3). (ENG.). 320p. (YA). pap. 9.99 *(978-1-4016-8876-9(4))* Nelson, Thomas Inc.

McGinty, Sean. The End of FUN. 2016. (ENG.). 416p. (YA). (gr. 9-17). 17.99 *(978-1-4847-2211-4(6))* Hyperion Bks. for Children.

—The End of Fun. 2017. (ENG.). 416p. (YA). (gr. 9-17). pap. 9.99 *(978-1-4847-2214-5(0))* Hyperion Bks. for Children.

McGowan, Maureen. Compliance, 0 vols. 2014. (Dust Chronicles Ser.: 2). (ENG.). 386p. (YA). (gr. 7-12). pap. 9.99 *(978-1-4778-1696-7(8)*, 9781477816967, Skyscape) Amazon Publishing.

—Deviants, 0 vols. 2014. (Dust Chronicles Ser.: 1). (ENG.). 322p. (YA). (gr. 9-12). pap. 9.99 *(978-1-4778-1032-3(3)*, 9781477810323, Skyscape) Amazon Publishing.

—Glory, 0 vols. 2014. (Dust Chronicles Ser.: 3). (ENG.). 326p. (YA). (gr. 9-12). pap. 9.99 *(978-1-4778-4797-8(9)*, 9781477847978, Amazon Children's Publishing) Amazon Publishing.

McGrath, Robin. Livyers World. 2007. (ENG.). 150p. (J). (gr. 4-7). per. *(978-1-897174-15-9(2))* Creative Bk. Publishing.

McIntyre, Will. Burning Midnight. 2016. (ENG.). 320p. (YA). (gr. 7). 17.99 *(978-0-553-53410-8(6)*, Delacorte Pr.) Random Hse. Children's Bks.

McKinty, Adrian. The Lighthouse Keepers. 2008. (ENG.). 400p. (YA). (gr. 7-11). 17.95 *(978-0-8109-7070-0(8)*, Amulet Bks.) Abrams, Inc.

—The Lighthouse War. 2007. (ENG.). 414p. (J). (gr. 7-17). 16.95 *(978-0-8109-9354-9(6))* Abrams, Inc.

McKissack, Fredrick L., et al. Cyborg. 2011. (Clone Codes Ser.: 2). (ENG.). 144p. (J). (gr. 3-7). 16.99 *(978-0-439-92985-1(7)*, Scholastic Pr.) Scholastic, Inc.

McKissack, Patricia C., et al. The Visitors. 2012. (Clone Codes Ser.). (ENG.). 160p. (J). (gr. 3-7). 16.99 *(978-0-439-92987-5(3)*, Scholastic Pr.) Scholastic, Inc.

McLaughlin, Lauren. Scored. 2012. (ENG.). 240p. (YA). (gr. 9). pap. 8.99 *(978-0-375-86791-0(0)*, Ember) Random Hse. Children's Bks.

McLeod, Bob, illus. The New Mutants, Vol. 1. 2006. (ENG.). 240p. (J). (gr. 4-17). pap. 24.99 *(978-0-7851-2194-7(3))* Marvel Worldwide, Inc.

McMann, Lisa. Going Wild. (Going Wild Ser.: 1). (J). (gr. 3-7). 2017. 400p. pap. 6.99 ***(978-0-06-233715-3(7))*** 2016. 384p. 16.99 *(978-0-06-233714-6(9))* HarperCollins Pubs.

—Predator vs. Prey. 2017. (Going Wild Ser.: 2). 400p. (J). (gr. 3-7). 16.99 ***(978-0-06-233717-7(3))*** HarperCollins Pubs.

McMullen, Sean. Before the Storm. 2009. 262p. (Orig.). pap. 13.95 *(978-1-879462-50-2(8)*, Ford Street Publishing) Hybrid Pubs. AUS. Dist: International Publishers Marketing.

McNaughton, Janet. The Raintree Rebellion. 2007. (ENG.). 252p. (J). mass mkt. 6.99 *(978-0-00-225529-5(4)*, Harper Trophy) HarperCollins Pubs.

McNichol, John. The Tripods Attack! 2008. (Young Chesterton Chronicles Ser.). 367p. (YA). (gr. 8-12). pap. 17.95 *(978-1-933184-26-5(4))* Sophia Institute Pr.

McNiven, Steve, illus. The Sentry, Vol. 2. 2006. (ENG.). 152p. (J). (gr. 4-17). pap. 14.99 *(978-0-7851-1672-1(9))* Marvel Worldwide, Inc.

McOmber, Rachel B., ed. McOmber Phonics Storybooks: Tale of the Green Glob. rev. ed. (Illus.). (J). *(978-0-944991-65-7(3))* Swift Learning Resources.

McPartlin, Moira. The Ways of the Doomed. 2016. (Sun Song Trilogy Ser.: 1). (ENG.). 256p. (YA). (gr. 7). pap. 11.99 *(978-1-908643-88-9(9))* Saraband (Scotland) Ltd. GBR. Dist: Independent Pubs. Group.

McQuerry, Maureen Doyle. The Peculiars. 2012. (ENG.). 368p. (YA). (gr. 7-17). 17.95 *(978-1-4197-0178-8(9)*, Amulet Bks.) Abrams, Inc.

McTrustry, Chris. Cleopatra's Report, 1 vol. rev. ed. 2013. (Fiction Readers Ser.). (ENG., Illus.). 32p. (J). (gr. 3-3). pap. 8.99 *(978-1-4333-5639-1(2))* Shell Educational Publishing.

Meachen Rau, Dana. Mi Lugar Preferido: My Special Space. Kim, Julie J., illus. 2005. (Rookie Reader Español Ser.). 32p. (gr. k-2). 19.50 *(978-0-516-25250-6(X)*, Children's Pr.) Scholastic Library Publishing.

Meadows, Daisy. Marissa the Science Fairy. 2016. (Rainbow Magic — the School Day Fairies Ser.: 1). lib. bdg. 14.75 *(978-0-606-38789-7(7))* Turtleback Bks.

Mears, Richard Chase. Saint Nick & the Space Nicks. Westerfield, William Stephen, illus. l.t. ed. 2004. 32p. (J). 16.95 *(978-0-9754056-0-4(8))* Tuxedo Blue, LLC.

Meddaugh, Susan. Space Dogs. 2012. (Martha Speaks Ser.). (ENG., Illus.). 96p. (J). (gr. 1-4). 14.99 *(978-0-547-68119-1(4))*; pap. 5.99 *(978-0-547-68118-4(6))* Houghton Mifflin Harcourt Publishing Co.

Medina, Kathleen. Born into Greyworld. 2008. 220p. 29.99 *(978-1-4363-2619-3(2))*; pap. 19.99 *(978-1-4363-2618-6(4))* Xlibris Corp.

Medina, Paco & Barberi, Carlo, illus. Nova - Rookie Season, No. 2. 2014. (ENG.). 136p. (J). (gr. 4-17). pap. 16.99 *(978-0-7851-6839-3(7))* Marvel Worldwide, Inc.

Meehan, William. Amulets of Acacia. 2003. 184p. pap. 13.95 *(978-0-595-27163-4(4))* iUniverse, Inc.

Melbourne, Lois. The STEM Club Goes Exploring. 2016. (ENG.). 48p. 15.95 *(978-1-62634-303-0(9))* Greenleaf Book Group.

Melville, Alessandra. Scavengers. 2017. (ENG.). 222p. (J). pap. 13.95 ***(978-1-78693-464-2(7)***, ca3a3b12-3706-4993-b48f-1f7018b57df9) Austin, Stan AUS. Dist: Bookmasters Distribution.

Menge, Dawn & Rhoades, Heath. Queen Vernita Meets Sir HeathyBean the Astronomer. 2010. 33p. (J). pap. 19.95 *(978-1-4327-3120-5(3))* Outskirts Pr., Inc.

Messner, Kate. Wake up Missing. 2014. (ENG.). 288p. (YA). (gr. 5-8). pap. 7.99 *(978-0-8027-3748-9(X)*, 9780802737489, Bloomsbury USA Childrens) Bloomsbury Publishing USA.

Metzen, Chris, et al. Transformers: IDW Collection Phase Two Volume 2: IDW Collection Phase Two Volume 2. Ramondelli, Livio, illus. 2015. (Transformers Ser.: 2). (ENG.). 332p. 49.99 *(978-1-63140-364-4(8)*, 9781631403644) Idea & Design Works, LLC.

Metzger, Joanna. The Space Program. Elizalde, Marcelo, illus. 2006. 142p. (J). *(978-1-59336-695-7(7))* Mondo Publishing.

Meyer, Marissa. Cinder. 2012. (Lunar Chronicles Ser.: 1). (ENG.). 400p. (YA). (gr. 7-12). 19.99 *(978-0-312-64189-4(3)*, 9780312641894) Feiwel & Friends.

—Cinder. 2013. (Lunar Chronicles Ser.: 1). (ENG.). 448p. (YA). (gr. 7-12). pap. 9.99 *(978-1-250-00720-9(8)*, 9781250007209) Square Fish.

—Cinder. l.t. ed. 2012. (Lunar Chronicles: Bk. 1). (ENG.). 496p. (J). (gr. 7-12). 23.99 *(978-1-4104-4607-7(7))* Thorndike Pr.

—Cinder. 2013. (Lunar Chronicles Ser.: 1). (YA). lib. bdg. 20.85 *(978-0-606-28633-6(0)*, Turtleback) Turtleback Bks.

—Cinder. 2015. (Cinder Ser.: 1). (SPA.). 416p. (YA). (gr. 9-12). pap. 20.99 *(978-987-612-927-5(9))* V&R Editoras.

—Cress. 2014. (YA). (Lunar Chronicles: Bk. 3). (ENG.). 560p. (gr. 7-12). 19.99 *(978-0-312-64297-6(0)*, 9780312642976); 552p. *(978-1-250-05632-0(2))* Feiwel & Friends.

—Fairest: Levana's Story. 2016. (Lunar Chronicles Ser.: 0). (YA). lib. bdg. 20.85 *(978-0-606-38438-4(3))* Turtleback Bks.

—Fairest: The Lunar Chronicles: Levana's Story. 2015. (YA). 222p. *(978-1-250-06959-7(9))*; (ENG.). 272p. (gr. 7-12). 17.99 *(978-1-250-06055-6(9)*, 9781250060556) Feiwel & Friends.

—Fairest: The Lunar Chronicles: Levana's Story. Barcellona, Christine, ed. 2016. (Lunar Chronicles Ser.). (ENG.). 288p. (YA). pap. 10.99 *(978-1-250-07355-6(3)*, 9781250073556) Square Fish.

—Scarlet. 2013. (Lunar Chronicles: Bk. 2). (ENG.). 464p. (YA). (gr. 7). 19.99 *(978-0-312-64296-9(2)*, 9780312642969) Feiwel & Friends.

—Scarlet. 2014. (Lunar Chronicles Ser.: 2). (ENG.). 512p. (YA). (gr. 7-12). pap. 9.99 *(978-1-250-00721-6(6)*, 9781250007216) Square Fish.

—Scarlet. l.t. ed. 2013. (Lunar Chronicles: Bk. 2). (ENG.). 572p. 23.99 *(978-1-4104-5623-6(4))* Thorndike Pr.

—Scarlet. 2014. (Lunar Chronicles Ser.: 2). (YA). lib. bdg. 20.85 *(978-0-606-35097-6(7)*, Turtleback) Turtleback Bks.

—Scarlet. 2016. (SPA.). 430p. (YA). (gr. 9-12). pap. 20.99 *(978-987-612-990-9(2))* V&R Editoras.

—Stars Above: A Lunar Chronicles Collection. 2016. (Lunar Chronicles Ser.). (ENG.). 400p. (YA). (gr. 7-12). 17.99 *(978-1-250-09184-0(5)*, 9781250091840) Feiwel & Friends.

—Winter. 2015. (Lunar Chronicles Ser.: 4). (ENG.). 832p. (YA). (gr. 7-12). 22.99 *(978-0-312-64298-3(9)*, 9780312642983) Feiwel & Friends.

—Wires & Nerve. Holgate, Douglas, illus. 2017. (Wires & Nerve Ser.). (ENG.). 240p. (YA). 21.99 *(978-1-250-07826-1(1)*, 9781250078261) Feiwel & Friends.

Michael Vey, the Electric Collection: Michael Vey; Michael Vey 2; Michael Vey 3. 2014. (Michael Vey Ser.). (ENG., Illus.). 1024p. (YA). (gr. 7). pap. 35.99 *(978-1-4814-1411-1(9)*, Simon Pulse/Mercury Ink) Simon Pulse/Mercury Ink.

Michelinie, David, et al. Freemind - The Origin. 2003. (Freemind Ser.). (Illus.). 112p. 14.95 *(978-0-9744225-0-3(9))* Future Comics.

Mikumo, Gakuto. Strike the Blood. Manyako, illus. 2017. (Strike the Blood Ser.: 6). (ENG.). 224p. (YA). (gr. 8-17). pap. 14.00 *(978-0-316-34558-3(X)*, Yen Pr.) Orbit.

Milam, Mary Kay. The Zooming Star Babies. Date not set. (J). pap. *(978-1-890622-65-7(6))* Leathers Publishing.

Miles, Brenda & Sweet, Susan D. Cinderstella: A Tale of Planets Not Princes. Docampo, Valeria, illus. 2016. (J). *(978-1-4338-2270-4(9)*, Magination Pr.) American Psychological Assn.

Milky, D. J. Karma Club, 4 vols., Vol. 1. 2017. (ENG., Illus.). 184p. (YA). (gr. 7-18). pap. 9.99 *(978-1-59182-263-9(7)*, 9781591822639, Tokyopop Kids) TOKYOPOP, Inc.

Miller, Bryan Q. The Guardian, Vol. 1. 2013. (ENG., Illus.). 144p. pap. 14.99 *(978-1-4012-3824-7(6))* DC Comics.

Miller, John Jackson, et al. Star Wars - Knights of the Old Republic, 9 vols., Vol. 1. 2007. (Illus.). 152p. *(978-1-84576-371-8(8))* Titan Bks. Ltd.

Miller, Larry W., Jr. Droptroopers: Gauntlet of Fear. 2007. 208p. per. 14.95 *(978-0-595-47591-9(4))* iUniverse, Inc.

Miller, Lauren. Free to Fall. 2014. (ENG.). 480p. (YA). (gr. 8). 17.99 *(978-0-06-219980-5(3)*, HarperTeen) HarperCollins Pubs.

—Parallel. 2013. (ENG.). 432p. (YA). (gr. 8). 17.99 *(978-0-06-219977-5(3)*, HarperTeen) HarperCollins Pubs.

Miller, Michael & Strickland, AdriAnne. Shadow Run. 2017. (ENG.). 400p. (YA). (gr. 7). 17.99 *(978-0-399-55253-3(7)*, Delacorte Pr.) Random Hse. Children's Bks.

Miller, Sam J. The Art of Starving. 2017. 384p. (YA). (gr. 8). 17.99 ***(978-0-06-245671-7(7)***, HarperTeen) HarperCollins Pubs.

Miller, Wray. Cerulean Blue. 2003. 506p. (YA). per. 18.95 *(978-0-9723948-1-9(8))* MillerWrite, Inc.

Millet, Jason, et al, illus. Beyond Escape! 2007. (Choose Your Own Adventure Ser.: No. 15). 118p. (J). (gr. 4-7). per. 6.99 *(978-1-933390-15-4(8)*, CHCL15) Chooseco LLC.

Millet, Lydia. The Shimmers in the Night. 2012. (Dissenters Ser.). (ENG.). 256p. (J). (gr. 3-7). 16.95 *(978-1-931520-78-2(X)*, Big Mouth Hse.) Small Beer Pr.

Mills, Claudia. The Trouble with Ants. Kath, Katie, illus. 2015. (Nora Notebooks Ser.: 1). (ENG.). 176p. (J). (gr. 2-5). lib. bdg. 17.99 *(978-0-385-39162-7(5)*, Knopf Bks. for Young Readers) Random Hse. Children's Bks.

—The Trouble with Friends. Kath, Katie, illus. 2017. (Nora Notebooks Ser.). (ENG.). 192p. (J). (gr. 2-5). 12.99 *(978-0-385-39169-6(2)*, Knopf Bks. for Young Readers) Random Hse. Children's Bks.

Mindler, Jason. Giralon. 2003. 122p. (YA). 20.95 *(978-0-595-74854-9(6))*; pap. 10.95 *(978-0-595-28581-5(3))* iUniverse, Inc. (Writers Club Pr.).

Minnie & Minnie. The Science Playground: Fun with Science Concepts & Nature. 2009. 48p. pap. 24.99 *(978-1-4389-3466-2(1))* AuthorHouse.

Miranda, Megan. Soulprint. 2015. (ENG.). 368p. (YA). (gr. 7). 17.99 *(978-0-8027-3774-8(9)*, 9780802737748, Bloomsbury USA Childrens) Bloomsbury Publishing USA.

Mitchell, J. Barton. Midnight City. 2013. (Conquered Earth Ser.: 1). (ENG.). 400p. (YA). (gr. 7-12). pap. 9.99 *(978-1-250-03628-5(3)*, 9781250036285, St. Martin's Griffin) St. Martin's Pr.

—Valley of Fires. 2014. (Conquered Earth Ser.: 3). (ENG.). 416p. (YA). (gr. 7-12). 36.99 *(978-1-250-00948-7(0)*, 9781250009487, Dunne, Thomas Bks.) St. Martin's Pr.

Miyazaki, Yuu. Awakening of Silver Beauty, Vol. 2. 2016. (Asterisk War Ser.: 2). (ENG., Illus.). 176p. (YA). (gr. 8-17). pap. 14.00 *(978-0-316-39858-9(6)*, Yen Pr.) Orbit.

Miyazaki, Yuu & okiura. Encounter with a Fiery Princess. 2016. (Asterisk War Ser.: 1). (ENG., Illus.). 192p. (YA). (gr. 8-17). pap. 14.00 *(978-0-316-31527-2(3)*, Yen Pr.) Orbit.

Mlynowski, Sarah. Bras & Broomsticks. 2006. (Magic in Manhattan Ser.: No. 1). (ENG.). 320p. (YA). (gr. 7-12). reprint ed. pap. 8.99 *(978-0-385-73184-3(1)*, Delacorte Pr.) Random Hse. Children's Bks.

Moesta, Rebecca & Anderson, Kevin J. Space Station Crisis. 2011. (Star Challengers Ser.). 184p. (J). (gr. 4-7). 11.99 *(978-1-934857-66-3(1)*, Catalyst Game Labs) InMediaRes Productions.

Moesta, Rebecca, et al. Star Challengers Trilogy. 2013. (J). pap. 18.99 *(978-1-61475-124-3(2)*, WordFire Pr.) WordFire Pr.

Mohr, L. C. Krumbuckets. Musheno, Erica, illus. 2007. (ENG.). 144p. (J). (gr. 2-7). 13.95 *(978-0-9769417-6-7(7))* Blooming Tree Pr.

Monda, Joseph, creator. The Unnaturals. 2007. (Illus.). 32p. (YA). 3.50 *(978-0-615-15138-0(8))* Wild Mind Creations.

Monsters of Men. 2014. (Chaos Walking Ser.). (ENG., Illus.). (YA). (gr. 9). pap. 10.99 *(978-0-7636-7619-3(5))* Candlewick Pr.

Montgomery, Anson. Moon Quest. Semionov, Vladimir, illus. 2008. (Choose Your Own Adventure Ser.: No. 26). 144p. (J). (gr. 2-7). pap. 6.99 *(978-1-933390-26-0(3))* Chooseco LLC.

Montgomery, R. A. Beyond Escape. 2005. (Choose Your Own Adventure Ser.). (Illus.). 118p. (gr. 4-8). pap. 5.50 *(978-0-7608-9703-4(4))* Sundance/Newbridge Educational Publishing.

—The Brilliant Dr. Wogan. 2005. (Choose Your Own Adventure Ser.). (Illus.). 112p. (gr. 4-8). pap. 5.50 *(978-0-7608-9705-8(0))* Sundance/Newbridge Educational Publishing.

—Escape. 2005. (Illus.). 127p. (J). pap. *(978-0-7608-9696-9(8))* Sundance/Newbridge Educational Publishing.

—Prisoner of the Ant People. 2007. 144p. (J). pap. *(978-1-86504-932-8(8))* Chooseco LLC.

—Prisoner of the Ant People. Millet, Jason, illus. 2006. (Choose Your Own Adventure Ser.: No. 10). 144p. (J). (gr. 4-8). per. 6.99 *(978-1-933390-10-9(7)*, CHCL10) Chooseco LLC.

—Prisoner of the Ant People. 2005. (Illus.). 115p. (J). pap. *(978-0-7608-9698-3(4))* Sundance/Newbridge Educational Publishing.

—Project UFO. Semionov, Vladimir & Cannella, Marco, illus. 2008. 144p. (J). (gr. 4-7). pap. 6.99 *(978-1-933390-27-7(1))* Chooseco LLC.

—Punishment: Earth. 2010. 144p. pap. 6.99 *(978-1-933390-36-9(0))* Chooseco LLC.

—Space & Beyond. Yaweera, Sasiprapa & Donploypetch, Jintanan, illus. 2006. (Choose Your Own Adventure Ser.: No. 3). 144p. (J). (gr. 4-8). pap. 6.99 *(978-1-933390-03-1(4)*, CHCL03) Chooseco LLC.

—War with the Evil Power Master. 2005. (Illus.). 123p. (J). pap. *(978-0-7608-9700-3(X))* Sundance/Newbridge Educational Publishing.

—War with the Evil Power Master. Millet, Jason, illus. 2006. (Choose Your Own Adventure Ser.: No. 12). 144p. (J). (gr. 4-8). per. 6.99 *(978-1-933390-12-3(3)*, CHCL12) Chooseco LLC.

Montijo, Rhode. Chews Your Destiny. 2017. (Gum Girl Ser.: 1). (J). lib. bdg. 16.00 ***(978-0-606-39969-2(0))*** Turtleback Bks.

Moore, Stuart. The Age of Bronze. Cullins, Paris & Henrique, Paulo, illus. 2017. (Zodiac Ser.: 3). (ENG.). 64p. (J). 12.99 *(978-1-62991-485-5(1)*, 9781629914855) Papercutz.

Mooring, John L. Cricket's Chronicles: The Third Grade Science Fair. 2010. 24p. pap. 12.99 *(978-1-4490-3278-4(8))* AuthorHouse.

Mordenga, Michael P. Spirit Box. 2007. 280p. per. 17.95 (978-0-595-43785-6(0)) iUniverse, Inc.
Moreau, Chris. The Professor's Telescope. Marek, Jane, illus. 2006. (YA). 10.95 (978-0-9785399-0-0(7)); cd-rom 7.95 (978-0-9785399-2-4(3)) Windows of Discovery.
Moreira, Carol. Membrane. 2013. 282p. pap. (978-1-927746-04-2(3)) Fierce Ink Pr. Co-Op, Ltd.
Morgan, Kass. Day 21. (100 Ser.: 2). (ENG.). 320p. (YA). (gr. 10-17). 2015. pap. 12.99 (978-0-316-23457-3(5)) 2014. 18.00 (978-0-316-23455-9(9)) Little, Brown Bks. for Young Readers.
—Homecoming. 2015. (100 Ser.: 3). (ENG.). 352p. (J). (gr. 10-17). pap. 12.99 (978-0-316-38196-3(9)) Little, Brown Bks. for Young Readers.
Moriarty, Chris. The Inquisitor's Apprentice. Geyer, Mark Edward, illus. 2013. (ENG.). 352p. (J). (gr. 5-7). pap. 7.99 (978-0-547-85084-9(0)) Houghton Mifflin Harcourt Publishing Co.
Morrison, Michele. The Comet's Tale. 2007. 136p. pap. 16.95 (978-1-84753-634-1(4)) Lulu Pr., Inc.
Morse, Scott. Magic Pickle. Morse, Scott, illus. 2008. (Magic Pickle Ser.). (ENG., Illus.). 112p. (J). (gr. 2-5). pap. 9.99 (978-0-439-87995-8(7), Graphix) Scholastic, Inc.
Mosier, Scott & Son, Eugene, illus. Marvel Universe Ultimate Spider-Man Volume 6. 2014. (ENG.). 88p. (J). (gr. -1-17). pap. 9.99 (978-0-7851-8815-5(0)) Marvel Worldwide, Inc.
Moss, Marissa. Alien Eraser Reveals the Secret of Evolution. Moss, Marissa, illus. 2009. (ENG., Illus.). 56p. (J). (gr. 3-7). pap. 6.99 (978-0-7636-4419-2(6)); (Max Disaster Ser.: Bk. 3). 15.99 (978-0-7636-3579-4(0)) Candlewick Pr.
—Alien Eraser to the Rescue. Moss, Marissa, illus. 2009. (Max Disaster Ser.: No. 1). (ENG., Illus.). 56p. (J). (gr. 3-7). pap. 6.99 (978-0-7636-4407-9(2)) Candlewick Pr.
Mould, Paul, ed. The Magnificent Six. 2007. (Illus.). 52p. pap. (978-1-58690-048-9(X)) Mould, Paul Publishing.
Mowry, Chris. Revenge of the Fallen: Alliance, 1 vol. Milne, Alex, illus. 2010. (Transformers: Revenge of the Fallen Movie Prequel Ser.). (ENG.). 24p. (J). (gr. 3-6). Vol. 1. 24.21 (978-1-59961-717-6(X)) Vol. 2. 24.21 (978-1-59961-718-3(8)) Vol. 3. 24.21 (978-1-59961-719-0(6)) Vol. 4. 24.21 (978-1-59961-720-6(X)) Spotlight.
—Revenge of the Fallen: Defiance, 1 vol., Vol. 1. Khanna, Dan, illus. 2010. (Transformers: Revenge of the Fallen Movie Prequel Ser.). (ENG.). 24p. (J). (gr. 3-6). 24.21 (978-1-59961-721-3(8)) Spotlight.
—Revenge of the Fallen: Defiance, 1 vol., Vol. 2. Khanna, Dan & Griffith, Andrew, illus. 2010. (Transformers: Revenge of the Fallen Movie Prequel Ser.). (ENG.). 24p. (J). (gr. 3-6). 24.21 (978-1-59961-722-0(6)) Spotlight.
—Revenge of the Fallen: Defiance, 1 vol., Vol. 4. Duendes del Sur, illus. 2010. (Transformers: Revenge of the Fallen Movie Prequel Ser.). (ENG.). 24p. (J). (gr. 3-6). 24.21 (978-1-59961-724-4(2)) Spotlight.
Moyer, Jenny. Flashfall. 2016. (Flashfall Ser.). (ENG.). 352p. (YA). 17.99 (978-1-62779-481-7(6), 9781627794817, Holt, Henry & Co. Bks. For Young Readers) Holt, Henry & Co.
Mueller, Richard. Zoonauts: The Secret of Animalville. Gosline, Sheldon, ed. Dal Chele, Egido Victor, illus. 2003. 210p. (J). 14.95 (978-0-9719496-6-9(2)) Shangri-La Pubns.
Muller, Jean Powers. Rudolph's Sniffalator. 2011. 20p. pap. 13.77 (978-1-4269-7065-8(X)) Trafford Publishing.
Mullin, Mike. Ashen Winter. (Ashfall Trilogy Ser.). (ENG.). (J). 2013. 580p. (gr. 6). pap. 10.99 (978-1-933718-98-9(6)) 2012. 594p. (gr. 8). 17.95 (978-1-933718-75-0(7)) Tanglewood Pr.
—Ashfall. (Ashfall Trilogy Ser.). (ENG.). 476p. (J). 2012. (gr. 8). pap. 10.95 (978-1-933718-74-3(9)) 2011. (gr. 6). 17.95 (978-1-933718-55-2(2)) Tanglewood Pr.
—Sunrise. 2014. (Ashfall Trilogy Ser.). (ENG.). 466p. (J). (gr. 8). 17.99 (978-1-939100-01-6(1)) Tanglewood Pr.
Munzel, Alexander. Allí Donde Florece el Cardo Sagrado/Where the Holy Thistle Blooms. 2003. (SPA., Illus.). 196p. (J). per. (978-0-9672566-2-7(3)) Technical Software, Inc.
Murguia, Bethanie Deeney. I Feel Five! Murguia, Bethanie Deeney, illus. 2014. (ENG., Illus.). 32p. (J). (gr. -1-3). 14.99 (978-0-7636-6291-2(7)) Candlewick Pr.
Murray, Kirsty. Vulture's Wake. 2010. (ENG.). 256p. (YA). (gr. 7-18). pap. 17.95 (978-0-8234-2282-1(8)) Holiday Hse., Inc.
Murray, Leinster. Space Tug. 2007. 152p. pap. 19.99 (978-1-4264-9420-8(3)); 172p. pap. 21.99 (978-1-4264-9801-5(2)) Creative Media Partners, LLC.
Muth, Jon J. & Buscema, John, illus. Galactus the Devourer. 2014. (ENG.). 184p. (J). (gr. 4-17). pap. 24.99 (978-0-7851-8562-8(3)) Marvel Worldwide, Inc.
My Teacher Glows in the Dark. 2014. (My Teacher Bks.: 3). (ENG., Illus.). 192p. (J). (gr. 3-7). 17.99 (978-1-4814-0432-7(6), Simon & Schuster/Paula Wiseman Bks.) Simon & Schuster/Paula Wiseman Bks.
Myers, Walter Dean. On a Clear Day. 2014. (ENG.). 256p. (YA). (gr. 7). 17.99 (978-0-385-38753-8(9), Crown Books For Young Readers) Random Hse. Children's Bks.
Myklusch, Matt. The Accidental Hero. 2011. (Jack Blank Adventure Ser.: 1). (ENG., Illus.). 496p. (J). (gr. 3-7). pap. 7.99 (978-1-4169-9562-3(5), Aladdin) Simon & Schuster Children's Publishing.
—Jack Blank & the Imagine Nation. 2010. (Jack Blank Adventure Ser.: Bk. 1). (ENG., Illus.). 480p. (J). (gr. 3-7). 16.99 (978-1-4169-9561-6(7), Aladdin) Simon & Schuster Children's Publishing.
Naderi, Babak. The Adventures of Captain Zero. 2009. 16p. pap. 9.00 (978-1-4251-8693-7(9)) Trafford Publishing.
—King of the Universe. 2013. 12p. pap. 14.95 (978-1-4669-8136-2(9)) Trafford Publishing.
Nagatsuki, Tappei. Starting Life in Another World, Vol. 2. 2016. (Re:ZERO -Starting Life in Another World- Ser.: 2). (ENG., Illus.). 256p. (gr. 8-17). pap. 14.00 (978-0-316-39837-4(3), Yen Pr.) Orbit.
Nagatsuki, Tappei, et al. Re: Zero Starting Life in Another World. 2017. (Re:ZERO -Starting Life in Another World- Ser.: 4). (ENG., Illus.). 240p. (YA). (gr. 8-17). pap. 14.00 (978-0-316-39842-8(X), Yen Pr.) Orbit.
Nancy, Farmer. The House of the Scorpion. 2014. (ENG.). 400p. (YA). (gr. 3-6). 14.24 (978-1-63245-268-9(5)) Lectorum Pubns., Inc.
Napton, Robert Place. Son of Merlin Volume 1 TP. 2013. (ENG., Illus.). 160p. (YA). pap. 19.99 (978-1-60706-795-5(1), 9781607067955) Image Comics.
Nayeri, Daniel. Straw House, Wood House, Brick House, Blow: Four Novellas by Daniel Nayeri. Weinberg, James, illus. 2011. (ENG.). 432p. (YA). (gr. 9). 19.99 (978-0-7636-5526-6(0)) Candlewick Pr.
Neary, Paul, illus. S. H. I. E. L. D. Nick Fury vs. S. H. I. E. L. D. 2013. (ENG.). 304p. (J). (gr. 4-17). pap. 29.99 (978-0-7851-8500-0(3)) Marvel Worldwide, Inc.
Neilson, G. E. F. Cosmic Aviators - Book 1 - Flight Edition. 2013. 288p. pap. (978-0-9576132-5-6(3)) Buzzword Pr.
—Cosmic Aviators - Nathaniel's 1st Adventure. 2013. 248p. (978-0-9576132-4-9(5)); 332p. pap. (978-0-9576132-0-1(2)) Buzzword Pr.
Nelson, O. T. The Girl Who Owned a City. 2012. (Exceptional Reading & Language Arts Titles for Intermediate Grades Ser.). (ENG.). 208p. (YA). (gr. 5-12). pap. 9.95 (978-0-7613-5086-6(1)) Lerner Publishing Group.
—The Girl Who Owned a City: Graphic Novel. Delk, Chrissy, illus. 2012. (Single Titles Ser.). (ENG.). 128p. (YA). (gr. 5-12). lib. bdg. 29.27 (978-0-7613-4903-7(0), Graphic Universe™) Lerner Publishing Group.
Nelson, Peter. Herbert's Wormhole: AeroStar & the 3 1/2-Point Plan of Vengeance. Rao, Rohitash, illus. 2013. (Herbert's Wormhole Ser.: 3). (ENG.). 352p. (J). (gr. 3-7). 12.99 (978-0-06-201220-3(7)) HarperCollins Pubs.
Nesbit, E. The Seven Dragons & Other Stories. 2006. 140p. 24.95 (978-1-59818-171-5(8)) Aegypan.
Ness, Patrick. Monsters of Men. Bk. 3. 2010. (Chaos Walking Ser.: 3). (ENG., Illus.). 608p. (YA). (gr. 9-18). 18.99 (978-0-7636-4751-3(9)) Candlewick Pr.
Ness, Patrick & Benedict, A. K. Class: the Stone House. 2017. (Class Ser.: 1). 272p. (YA). (gr. 8). 17.99 **(978-0-06-266617-8(7)**, HarperTeen) HarperCollins Pubs.
Nesworthy, Lauren. Darth Vader, Rebel Hunter! 2016. (Illus.). 48p. (J). **(978-1-5182-1849-1(0))** Dorling Kindersley Publishing, Inc.
Nettrour, Nelani. Nunkey's Adventures, Bk. 1. Nettrour, Autumn, illus. 2003. 70p. (J). pap. 11.95 (978-1-929381-17-3(4), Third Millennium Publishing) Sci Fi-Arizona, Inc.
Nevins, Paul. Dante's War. 2003. 168p. (YA). pap. 12.95 (978-0-595-26743-9(2), Writers Club Pr.) iUniverse, Inc.
Newsome, Eric. The Adventures of Eric: Starry Beginnings. 2009. 51p. pap. 14.95 (978-1-4327-4075-7(X)) Outskirts Pr., Inc.
Nguyen, Taohuu. Mighty Mite 3: Good Mites, Bad Mites. Nguyen, Taohuu, illus. 2007. (Illus.). (J). 14.95 (978-0-9790302-3-9(4)) Amazing Factory, The.
Nichols, Amy K. Now That You're Here. (Duplexity Ser.). (ENG.). (YA). (gr. 7). 2016. 608p. pap. 12.99 (978-0-385-75396-8(9), Ember) 2014. 304p. 16.99 (978-0-385-75389-0(6), Knopf Bks. for Young Readers) Random Hse. Children's Bks.
—While You Were Gone (Duplexity, Part II) 2015. (Duplexity Ser.). (ENG.). 304p. (YA). (gr. 7). 17.99 (978-0-385-75392-0(6), Knopf Bks. for Young Readers) Random Hse. Children's Bks.
Nicholson, William. Viento en Llamas: Siervos del Maestro. Manero Jiménez, Laura, tr. 2005. (Escritura desatada Ser.). (SPA.). 384p. (J). 17.95 (978-84-666-1178-7(9)) Ediciones B ESP. Dist: Independent Pubs. Group.
Nicieza, Mariano. Phazer: A Man Lost in Alternative Universes. Olivetti, Ariel, illus. 2008. 48p. (YA). per. 14.95 (978-0-9740212-7-0(X)) Cedar Grove Bks.
Nikovics, Anne. The Adventures of Katie Ladybug. 2005. 132p. 21.95 (978-1-4184-4002-2(7)) AuthorHouse.
Nimoy, Leonard. Leonard Nimoy's Primortals Vol 1, No. 1: Origins. Chambers, James et al, eds. Eaton, Scot & Barreiro, Mike, illus. 36p. (Orig.). (YA). pap. 2.25 (978-0-9645175-1-6(5)) Big Entertainment, Inc.
Nix, Garth. A Confusion of Princes. 2012. 352p. (YA). (gr. 8). (ENG.). 17.99 (978-0-06-009694-6(2)); lib. bdg. 18.89 (978-0-06-009695-3(0)) HarperCollins Pubs.
—Shade's Children. 2012. (ENG.). 368p. (YA). (gr. 8). pap. 9.99 (978-0-06-207598-7(5)) HarperCollins Pubs.
Nono, Auntie. Solar System Song. Shirasu, Nori, illus. 2004. (J). bds. 1.25 (978-0-9754098-0-0(8)) Accordian Bks.
Norman, Matthew. Domestic Violets. 2011. (P. S. Ser.). (ENG.). 352p. pap. 14.99 (978-0-06-206511-7(4), Harper Perennial) HarperCollins Pubs.
Norris, Elizabeth. Unbreakable. (Unraveling Ser.: 2). (ENG.). 496p. (YA). (gr. 9). 2014. pap. 9.99 (978-0-06-210377-2(6)) 2013. 17.99 (978-0-06-210376-5(8)) HarperCollins Pubs.
—Unraveling. 2013. (Unraveling Ser.: 1). (ENG.). 480p. (YA). (gr. 8). pap. 9.99 (978-0-06-210374-1(1)) HarperCollins Pubs.
North, Phoebe. Starbreak. 2014. (Starglass Sequence Ser.). (ENG., Illus.). 432p. (YA). (gr. 7). 17.99 (978-1-4424-5956-4(5), Simon & Schuster Bks. For Young Readers) Simon & Schuster Bks. For Young Readers.
—Starglass. (Starglass Sequence Ser.). (ENG., Illus.). (YA). (gr. 7). 2014. 464p. pap. 9.99 (978-1-4424-5954-0(9)) 2013. 448p. 17.99 (978-1-4424-5953-3(0)) Simon & Schuster Bks. For Young Readers. (Simon & Schuster Bks. For Young Readers).
Norton, Andre. Key Out of Time. 2007. 140p. per. 11.95 (978-1-60312-081-4(5)) Aegypan.
—The Time Traders. 2007. 236p. per. 12.95 (978-1-4218-2734-6(4)); 27.95 (978-1-4218-2634-9(8)) 1st World Publishing, Inc. (1st World Library - Literary Society).
—The Time Traders. 2007. 172p. pap. 19.99 (978-1-4264-9591-5(9)); (ENG.). 194p. pap. 21.99 (978-1-4264-9972-2(8)) Creative Media Partners, LLC.
—The Time Traders. 2006. pap. (978-1-4068-3561-8(7)) Echo Library.
Norton, Mike & Hopeless, Dennis. The Answer!, Vol.1. Thorpe, Patrick, ed. 2013. (ENG., Illus.). 120p. pap. 12.99 (978-1-61655-197-1(6)) Dark Horse Comics.
Nunez, Kent Hamilton. Mish: The Desert. 2007. 152p. per. 11.95 (978-0-595-47808-8(5)) iUniverse, Inc.
Nybo, B. J. Elmo Jackson Great Yellow Ball. 2005. (978-0-9742322-0-1(3)) New Art & Vision, LLC.
Nye, Bill & Mone, Gregory. Jack & the Geniuses: At the Bottom of the World. Iluzada, Nicholas, illus. 2017. (ENG.). 256p. (J). (gr. 3-7). 13.95 (978-1-4197-2303-2(0), Amulet Bks.) Abrams, Inc.
Nylund, Eric. The Resisters. 2011. (Resisters Ser.). (ENG.). 224p. (J). (gr. 3-7). 16.99 (978-0-375-86856-6(9), Random Hse. Bks. for Young Readers) Random Hse. Children's Bks.
—The Resisters #1: the Resisters. 2012. (Resisters Ser.). (ENG.). 240p. (J). (gr. 5-9). 7.99 (978-0-375-87224-2(8), Yearling) Random Hse. Children's Bks.
—The Resisters #2: Sterling Squadron. 2012. (Resisters Ser.: 2). (ENG.). 320p. (J). (gr. 5-9). 7.99 (978-0-375-87225-9(6), Yearling) Random Hse. Children's Bks.
—The Resisters #3: Titan Base. 2013. (Resisters Ser.: 3). (ENG.). 288p. (J). (gr. 5-9). 7.99 (978-0-307-97854-7(0), Yearling) Random Hse. Children's Bks.
—The Resisters #4: Operation Inferno. 2013. (Resisters Ser.). (ENG.). 288p. (J). (gr. 5-9). 6.99 (978-0-307-97855-4(9), Yearling) Random Hse. Children's Bks.
Nylund, Eric S. The Sterling Squadron. 2012. (Resisters Ser.: 2). (ENG.). 320p. (J). (gr. 5-9). 16.99 (978-0-375-86857-3(7), Random Hse. Bks. for Young Readers) Random Hse. Children's Bks.
Oberne, Sharon. Kelsey. 2006. 88p. (YA). pap. 13.95 (978-1-58909-340-9(2)) Bookstand Publishing.
Obie, Christopher R. Dumisai & the Enchanted Journey. 2003. (J). pap. (978-0-9718530-0-3(2)) Ancestral Light Publishing.
O'Brien, Caragh M. Birthmarked. 2010. (Birthmarked Trilogy Ser.: 1). (ENG., Illus.). 368p. (YA). (gr. 7-18). 18.99 (978-1-59643-569-8(0), 9781596435698) Roaring Brook Pr.
—Birthmarked. 2011. (Birthmarked Trilogy Ser.: 1). (ENG.). 384p. (YA). (gr. 7). pap. 10.99 (978-0-312-67472-4(4), 9780312674724) Square Fish.
—Prized. 2011. (Birthmarked Trilogy Ser.: 2). (ENG., Illus.). 368p. (YA). (gr. 7). 16.99 (978-1-59643-570-4(4), 9781596435704) Roaring Brook Pr.
—Prized. 2012. (Birthmarked Trilogy Ser.: 2). (ENG.). 400p. (YA). (gr. 7). pap. 12.99 (978-1-250-01031-5(4), 9781250010315) Square Fish.
—Promised. 2012. (Birthmarked Trilogy Ser.: 3). (ENG.). 304p. (YA). (gr. 7). 17.99 (978-1-59643-571-1(2), 9781596435711) Roaring Brook Pr.
—Promised. 2013. (Birthmarked Trilogy Ser.: 3). (ENG.). 336p. (YA). (gr. 7-12). pap. 9.99 (978-1-250-03428-1(0), 9781250034281) Square Fish.
—The Rule of Mirrors. 2016. (Vault of Dreamers Trilogy Ser.: 2). (ENG., Illus.). 432p. (YA). (gr. 7). 17.99 (978-1-59643-940-5(8), 9781596439405) Roaring Brook Pr.
—The Vault of Dreamers. 2014. (ENG., Illus.). 432p. (YA). (gr. 7-12). 17.99 (978-1-59643-938-2(6), 9781596439382) Roaring Brook Pr.
O'Brien, Johnny. Day of Deliverance. Hardcastle, Nick, illus. 2010. (Jack Christie Adventure Ser.: 2). (ENG.). 192p. (J). (gr. 4-7). 15.99 (978-0-7636-5075-9(7), Templar) Candlewick Pr.
—Day of the Assassins. Hardcastle, Nick, illus. 2010. (Jack Christie Adventure Ser.: 1). (ENG.). 224p. (J). (gr. 4-7). pap. 6.99 (978-0-7636-4995-1(3), Templar) Candlewick Pr.
—Day of the Assassins: A Jack Christie Novel. Hardcastle, Nick, illus. 2009. (Jack Christie Adventure Ser.: 1). (ENG.). 224p. (J). (gr. 4-7). 15.99 (978-0-7636-4595-3(8), Templar) Candlewick Pr.
O'Callaghan, G. Tektite. 2007. 144p. per. (978-1-84693-025-6(1)) Best Global Publishing Ltd.
O'Connor, Grandma. Rodney the Robot: Why Rodney Rebels. 2008. 52p. pap. 8.95 (978-0-595-51055-9(8)) iUniverse, Inc.
O'Connor, Jane. Fancy Nancy Sees Stars. Glasser, Robin Preiss & Enik, Ted, illus. 2008. (I Can Read Level 1 Ser.). (ENG.). 32p. (J). (gr. -1-3). 16.99 (978-0-06-123612-9(8)); pap. 3.99 (978-0-06-123611-2(X)) HarperCollins Pubs.
Odgers, Sally. Journey to the Center of the Earth, 1 vol. 2013. (Fiction Readers Ser.). (ENG., Illus.). 24p. (J). (gr. 2-2). pap. 6.99 (978-1-4333-5527-1(2)) Shell Educational Publishing.
Offill, Jenny. 11 Experiments That Failed. Carpenter, Nancy, illus. 2011. (ENG.). 40p. (J). (gr. -1-3). 17.99 (978-0-375-84762-2(6), Schwartz & Wade Bks.) Random Hse. Children's Bks.
O'Hely, Eileen. Penny in Space. Phelan, Nicky, illus. 2009. (ENG.). 225p. (J). pap. 14.95 (978-1-85635-571-1(3)) Mercier Pr., Ltd., The IRL. Dist: Dufour Editions, Inc.
Ohnogi, Hiroshi. Rahxephon, Vol. 4. 2006. (RahXephon (Dr Masterbook) Ser.). (ENG., Illus.). 200p. (YA). pap. 7.95 (978-1-59796-003-8(9)) DrMaster Pubns. Inc.
—Rahxephon, Vol. 5. 2006. (RahXephon (Dr Masterbook) Ser.). (ENG., Illus.). 200p. (YA). pap. 7.95 (978-1-59796-004-5(7)) DrMaster Pubns. Inc.
Oliver, Chad. Far from This Earth & Other Stories. Olson, Priscilla, ed. Dennis, Jane, illus. 2003. (NESFA's Choice Ser.: 25). 480p. 24.00 (978-1-886778-48-1(5), NESFA Pr.) New England Science Fiction Assn., Inc.
—A Star Above It & Other Stories. Olson, Priscilla, ed. Dennis, Jane, illus. 2003. (NESFA's Choice Ser.: 24). 480p. 24.00 (978-1-886778-45-0(0), NESFA Pr.) New England Science Fiction Assn., Inc.
Oliver, Lauren. Delirium. (Delirium Trilogy Ser.: 1). (ENG.). 480p. (YA). (gr. 9-18). 2016. pap. 9.99 (978-0-06-172683-5(4)) 2011. 17.99 (978-0-06-211243-9(0)) HarperCollins Pubs.
—Delirium. 2016. (Delirium Ser.: 1). (YA). lib. bdg. 20.85 (978-0-606-23575-4(2), Turtleback) Turtleback Bks.
—Delirium Stories: Hana, Annabel, Raven & Alex. (Delirium Story Ser.). 224p. (YA). (gr. 9). 2016. pap. 9.99 (978-0-06-248432-1(X)) 2013. (ENG.). pap. 9.99 (978-0-06-226778-8(7)) HarperCollins Pubs.
—Delirium Stories: Hana, Annabel, Raven & Alex. (Delirium Ser.). (YA). 2016. lib. bdg. 20.85 (978-0-606-38920-4(2)) 2013. lib. bdg. 20.85 (978-0-606-31834-1(8), Turtleback) Turtleback Bks.
—Pandemonium. (YA). 2016. (Delirium Trilogy Ser.: 2). (ENG.). 400p. (gr. 9). pap. 9.99 (978-0-06-197807-4(8)) 2012. (Delirium Trilogy Ser.: 2). (ENG.). 384p. (gr. 9-18). 17.99 (978-0-06-197806-7(X)) 2012. (Delirium Trilogy: Bk. 2). 375p. (978-0-06-213008-2(0)) HarperCollins Pubs.
—Pandemonium. 2016. (Delirium Ser.: 2). (YA). lib. bdg. 20.85 (978-0-606-27141-7(4), Turtleback) Turtleback Bks.
—Replica. (Replica Ser.: 1). (YA). (gr. 9). 2017. 560p. pap. 12.99 **(978-0-06-239417-0(7))** 2016. 544p. 19.99 (978-0-06-239416-3(9)) HarperCollins Pubs.
—RÉPLICA. 2017. (SPA.). (YA). (gr. 8-12). pap. 21.95 **(978-84-666-6144-7(1))** Ediciones B ESP. Dist: Spanish Pubs., LLC.
—Requiem. 2013. (Delirium Trilogy: Bk. 3). (ENG.). 400p. (J). (gr. 9). 18.99 (978-0-06-201453-5(6)) HarperCollins Pubs.
Oliver, Lauren. Ringer. 2017. (Replica Ser.: 2). 528p. (YA). (gr. 9). 19.99 **(978-0-06-239419-4(3))** HarperCollins Pubs.
Oliver, Lin & Baker, Theo. Sound Bender. 2011. (ENG.). 272p. (J). (gr. 5-9). 16.99 (978-0-545-19692-5(2), Scholastic Pr.) Scholastic, Inc.
The Ologies Collection. 2006. (J). 79.96 (978-0-7636-3509-1(X)) Candlewick Pr.
Olsen, Nora. Swans & Klons. 2013. (ENG.). 192p. (gr. 7). pap. 11.95 (978-1-60282-874-2(1)) Bold Strokes Bks.
Olson, Kayla. The Sandcastle Empire. 2017. 464p. (YA). (gr. 9). 17.99 (978-0-06-248487-1(7), HarperTeen) HarperCollins Pubs.
O'Malley, Kevin. Captain Raptor & the Moon Mystery. O'Brien, Patrick, illus. 2005. (Captain Raptor Ser.). (ENG.). 32p. (J). (gr. k-5). 17.99 (978-0-8027-8935-8(8), 9780802789358, Bloomsbury USA Childrens) Bloomsbury Publishing USA.
O'Malley, Kevin & O'Brien, Patrick. Captain Raptor & the Space Pirates. O'Brien, Patrick, illus. 2007. (Captain Raptor Ser.). (ENG., Illus.). 32p. (J). (gr. k-3). 16.95 (978-0-8027-9571-7(4), 9780802795717) Walker & Co.
O'Reilly, Elaine & Pearson Education Staff. Another World, Pack. 2007.Tr. of En Annan Varld. (ENG.). pap. 17.32 incl. cd-rom (978-1-4058-5206-7(2)) Pearson Education.
O'Reilly, Sean. Science Fair Nightmare, 1 vol. (Mighty Mighty Monsters Ser.). (ENG., 48p. (gr. 2-3). 2013. Illus.). pap. 6.10 (978-1-4342-4226-6(9)) 2012. lib. bdg. 23.99 (978-1-4342-3891-7(1)) Stone Arch Bks.
Ormand, Kate & Louise, Kate. Dark Days. 2014. (ENG.). 256p. (J). (gr. 6). 16.95 (978-1-62873-594-9(5), Sky Pony Pr.) Skyhorse Publishing Co., Inc.
Orme, David. Galactic Shopping Mall. 2008. (Starchasers Ser.). (ENG., Illus.). 48p. pap. (978-1-84167-764-4(7)) Ransom Publishing Ltd.
—Jungle Planet. 2008. (Starchasers Ser.). (ENG., Illus.). 48p. pap. (978-1-84167-768-2(X)) Ransom Publishing Ltd.
—Lost Explorers. 2008. (Starchasers Ser.). (ENG., Illus.). 48p. pap. (978-1-84167-763-7(9)) Ransom Publishing Ltd.
—Planet of the Vampires. 2008. (Starchasers Ser.). (ENG., Illus.). 48p. pap. (978-1-84167-765-1(5)) Ransom Publishing Ltd.
—Space Explorers. 2004. (Shades Ser.). 64p. (J). pap. (978-0-237-52646-7(8)) Evans Brothers, Ltd.
—Ultimate Secret. 2008. (Starchasers Ser.). (ENG., Illus.). 48p. pap. (978-1-84167-766-8(3)) Ransom Publishing Ltd.
Orme, David & Orme, David. Science Fiction. 2008. (Trailblazers Ser.). (ENG., Illus.). 36p. pap. (978-1-84167-693-7(4)) Ransom Publishing Ltd.
O'Rourke, Erica. Dissonance. 2014. (Dissonance Ser.). (ENG., Illus.). 496p. (YA). (gr. 7). 17.99 (978-1-4424-6024-9(5), Simon & Schuster Bks. For Young Readers) Simon & Schuster Bks. For Young Readers.
—Resonance. 2015. (Dissonance Ser.). (ENG., Illus.). 448p. (YA). (gr. 7). 18.99 (978-1-4424-6027-0(X), Simon & Schuster Bks. For Young Readers) Simon & Schuster Bks. For Young Readers.
O'Ryan, Ray. The Annoying Crush. 2014. (Galaxy Zack Ser.: 9). lib. bdg. 16.00 (978-0-606-36093-7(X)) Turtleback Bks.
—Drake Makes a Splash! Jack, Colin, illus. 2014. (Galaxy Zack Ser.: 8). (ENG.). 128p. (J). (gr. k-2). pap. 5.99 (978-1-4424-9360-5(7), Little Simon) Little Simon.
—A Galactic Easter! Jack, Colin, illus. 2014. (Galaxy Zack Ser.: 7). (ENG.). 128p. (J). (gr. k-4). pap. 5.99 (978-1-4424-9357-5(7), Little Simon) Little Simon.
—A Galactic Easter! 2014. (Galaxy Zack Ser.: 7). lib. bdg. 16.00 (978-0-606-35428-8(X)) Turtleback Bks.
—Galaxy Zack: Hello, Nebulon!; Journey to Juno; the Prehistoric Planet. Jack, Colin, illus. 2015. (Galaxy Zack Ser.). (ENG.). 384p. (J). (gr. k-4). pap. 8.99 (978-1-4814-5641-8(5), Little Simon) Little Simon.
—A Green Christmas! Jack, Colin, illus. 2013. (Galaxy Zack Ser.: 6). (ENG.). 128p. (J). (gr. k-2). 16.99 (978-1-4424-8225-8(7)); pap. 4.99 (978-1-4424-8224-1(9)) Little Simon. (Little Simon).
—A Green Christmas! 2013. (Galaxy Zack Ser.: 6). lib. bdg. 14.75 (978-0-606-35185-0(X)) Turtleback Bks.
—A Haunted Halloween. Kraft, Jason, illus. 2015. (Galaxy Zack Ser.: 11). (ENG.). 128p. (J). (gr. k-4). 16.99 (978-1-4814-3491-1(8), Little Simon) Little Simon.
—Hello, Nebulon! Jack, Colin, illus. 2013. (Galaxy Zack Ser.: 1). (ENG.). 128p. (J). (gr. k-2). 16.99 (978-1-4424-5387-6(7)); pap. 5.99 (978-1-4424-5386-9(9)) Little Simon. (Little Simon).
—Hello, Nebulon! 2013. (Galaxy Zack Ser.: 1). lib. bdg. 16.00 (978-0-606-32442-7(9), Turtleback) Turtleback Bks.
—Journey to Juno. Jack, Colin, illus. 2013. (Galaxy Zack Ser.: 2). (ENG.). 128p. (J). (gr. k-4). 17.99 (978-1-4424-5391-3(5)); pap. 5.99 (978-1-4424-5390-6(7)) Little Simon. (Little Simon).
—Journey to Juno. 2013. (Galaxy Zack Ser.: 2). lib. bdg. 16.00 (978-0-606-32443-4(7), Turtleback) Turtleback Bks.
—Monsters in Space! Jack, Colin, illus. 2013. (Galaxy Zack Ser.: 4). (ENG.). 128p. (J). (gr. k-2). 16.99 (978-1-4424-6721-7(5)); pap. 5.99 (978-1-4424-6718-7(5)) Little Simon. (Little Simon).
—Monsters in Space! 2013. (Galaxy Zack Ser.: 4). lib. bdg. 16.00 (978-0-606-32460-1(7), Turtleback) Turtleback Bks.
—Operation Twin Trouble. Kraft, Jason, illus. 2015. (Galaxy Zack Ser.: 12). (ENG.). 128p. (J). (gr. k-4). pap. 5.99 (978-1-4814-4399-9(2), Little Simon) Little Simon.
—The Prehistoric Planet. Jack, Colin, illus. 2013. (Galaxy Zack Ser.: 3). (ENG.). 128p. (J). (gr. k-4). 16.99 (978-1-4424-6716-3(9)); pap. 5.99 (978-1-4424-6715-6(0)) Little Simon. (Little Simon).
—The Prehistoric Planet. 2013. (Galaxy Zack Ser.: 3). lib. bdg. 16.00 (978-0-606-32461-8(5), Turtleback) Turtleback Bks.
—Ready, Set, Blast Off! Kraft, Jason, illus. 2017. (Galaxy Zack Ser.: 15). (ENG.). 128p. (J). (gr. k-4). pap. 5.99 (978-1-4814-8595-1(4), Little Simon) Little Simon.
—Return to Earth! Kraft, Jason, illus. 2015. (Galaxy Zack Ser.: 10). (ENG.). 128p. (J). (gr. k-4). pap. 5.99 (978-1-4814-2181-2(6), Little Simon) Little Simon.

—Science Fair Disaster! Kraft, Jason, illus. 2016. (Galaxy Zack Ser.: 13). (ENG.). 128p. (J). (gr. k-4). pap. 5.99 *(978-1-4814-5876-4(0),* Little Simon) Little Simon.

—Space Camp. Kraft, Jason, illus. 2016. (Galaxy Zack Ser.: 14). (ENG.). 128p. (J). (gr. k-4). pap. 5.99 *(978-1-4814-6300-3(4),* Little Simon) Little Simon.

—Three's a Crowd! Jack, Colin, illus. 2013. (Galaxy Zack Ser.: 5). (ENG.). 128p. (J). (gr. k-4). 16.99 *(978-1-4424-8222-7(2));* pap. 5.99 *(978-1-4424-8221-0(4))* Little Simon. (Little Simon).

—Three's a Crowd! 2013. (Galaxy Zack Ser.: 5). lib. bdg. 16.00 *(978-0-606-35187-4(6))* Turtleback Bks.

O'Ryan, Ray & Jack, Colin. Hello, Nebulon!, 1 vol. 2015. (ENG.). 128p. *(978-1-61479-367-0(0))* ABDO Publishing Co.

Osborne, Mary Pope. Medianoche en la Luna. 2004. (Casa del Arbol Ser.: 8).Tr. of Midnight on the Moon. (SPA.). (J). pap. 5.99 *(978-1-930332-69-0(6))* Lectorum Pubns., Inc.

—Night of the New Magicians. Murdocca, Sal, illus. 2007. (Magic Tree House Merlin Mission Ser.: 7). (ENG.). 144p. (J). (gr. 2-5). 5.99 *(978-0-375-83036-5(7),* Random Hse. Bks. for Young Readers) Random Hse. Children's Bks.

—Night of the New Magicians. 2007. (Magic Tree House Merlin Missions Ser.: 7). lib. bdg. 16.00 *(978-1-4177-9108-8(X),* Turtleback) Turtleback Bks.

Osterlund, Anne. Academy 7. 2009. (ENG.). 272p. (YA). (gr. 7-18). pap. 8.99 *(978-0-14-241437-8(9),* Speak) Penguin Young Readers Group.

Ottaviani, Jim. T-Minus: The Race to the Moon. Cannon, Kevin & Cannon, Zander, illus. 2009. (ENG.). 128p. (J). (gr. 3-7). 21.99 *(978-1-4169-8682-9(0),* Simon & Schuster/Paula Wiseman Bks.) Simon & Schuster/Paula Wiseman Bks.

Outram, Richard. The Adventures of Exokid: Growing Financial Wings. 2013. 40p. pap. 13.95 *(978-1-4575-2130-0(X))* Dog Ear Publishing, LLC.

Overpowered. 2014. (ENG., Illus.). 432p. (YA). (gr. 7). pap. 11.99 *(978-1-4424-3129-4(6),* Simon & Schuster Bks. For Young Readers) Simon & Schuster Bks. For Young Readers.

Oxford University Press Staff & Bassett, Jennifer, eds. Omega Files - Short Stories. 3rd ed. 2008. (ENG., Illus.). 64p. 10.00 *(978-0-19-478913-4(6))* Oxford Univ. Pr., Inc.

Pacheco, Carlos & Klein, Nic, illus. Captain America, Vol. 3. 2014. (ENG.). 136p. (J). (gr. 4-17). 24.99 *(978-0-7851-8951-0(3))* Marvel Worldwide, Inc.

Packard, Edward. Through the Black Hole. Willis, Drew, illus. 2012. (U-Ventures Ser.). (ENG.). 160p. (J). (gr. 3-7). pap. 5.99 *(978-1-4424-3426-4(0),* Simon & Schuster Bks. For Young Readers) Simon & Schuster Bks. For Young Readers.

Page, Cecelia Frances. Adventures on Ancient Continents. 2007. 172p. per. 13.95 *(978-0-595-46358-9(4))* iUniverse, Inc.

Pak, Greg, et al. X-Men - X-Termination. Buffagni, Matteo et al, illus. 2013. (ENG.). 184p. (YA). (gr. 8-17). pap. 24.99 *(978-0-7851-8443-0(0))* Marvel Worldwide, Inc.

Palacios, Tomas. Guardians of the Galaxy. Disney Book Group Staff, illus. 2014. (Beginnings Ser.). (ENG.). 48p. (J). (gr. 1-3). 12.99 *(978-1-4847-0054-9(6),* Marvel Pr.) Disney Publishing Worldwide.

Pallock, Ruth. The Planet Mazol: Book 2 of World Adventures of Jayden. 2011. 82p. pap. 19.95 *(978-1-4560-9004-3(6))* America Star Bks.

Palmer, Kristine. Eigenoids Episode 2: Momentum Sphere Coaster. 2013. 134p. pap. 19.95 *(978-1-63000-928-1(8))* America Star Bks.

Paquette, Ammi-Joan. Paradox. 2014. (ENG.). 240p. (YA). (gr. 7). pap. 9.99 *(978-0-375-87163-4(2),* Ember) Random Hse. Children's Bks.

Park, Louise. New Girl. May, Kyla & Matthews, Melanie, illus. 2015. (Star Girl Ser.). (ENG.). 80p. (gr. 1-4). lib. bdg. 22.65 *(978-1-4795-8275-4(1))* Picture Window Bks.

—Odd One Out. May, Kyla & Matthews, Melanie, illus. 2015. (Star Girl Ser.). (ENG.). 80p. (gr. 1-4). lib. bdg. 22.65 *(978-1-4795-8276-1(X))* Picture Window Bks.

—Three's a Crowd. May, Kyla & Matthews, Melanie, illus. 2015. (Star Girl Ser.). (ENG.). 80p. (gr. 1-4). lib. bdg. 22.65 *(978-1-4795-8278-5(6))* Picture Window Bks.

—Winning Moves. May, Kyla & Matthews, Melanie, illus. 2015. (Star Girl Ser.). (ENG.). 80p. (gr. 1-4). lib. bdg. 22.65 *(978-1-4795-8277-8(8))* Picture Window Bks.

Parker, Derek. Children of Zone. 2015. (ENG., Illus.). 142p. pap. *(978-1-925138-91-7(7))* Connor Court Publishing Pty Ltd.

Parker, Jake. Rescue on Tankium, No. 3. 2011. (Missile Mouse Ser.: 2). (ENG.). 160p. (J). (gr. 3-7). pap. 10.99 *(978-0-545-11717-3(8),* Graphix) Scholastic, Inc.

—Rescue on Tankium3. 2011. (Missile Mouse Ser.: 2). (ENG.). 160p. (J). (gr. 3-7). 21.99 *(978-0-545-11716-6(X),* Graphix) Scholastic, Inc.

Parker, Neal. Lobsterman & the U. F. O. 2014. (ENG., Illus.). 66p. (J). (gr. 3-17). pap. 9.95 *(978-1-60893-350-1(4))* Down East Bks.

Parker, Steve. Robots in Fiction & Films. 2010. (Robot World Ser.). 32p. (J). 28.50 *(978-1-60753-073-2(2))* Amicus Publishing.

Parker, Steve & Pipe, Jim. Robots in Fiction & Films. 2011. (On the Edge Ser.). 32p. (YA). (gr. 3-6). lib. bdg. 28.50 *(978-1-59920-515-1(7))* Black Rabbit Bks.

Parnell, Declan. Brett Meets the Bee Lady, 01 vols., 1. 2016. (Rosen REAL Readers: STEM & STEAM Collection). (ENG.). 12p. (J). pap. 6.33 *(978-1-5081-1518-2(4),* Rosen Classroom) Rosen Publishing Group, Inc., The.

Parry, Jo. Blast Off! 2009. (Wow! Bks.). (Illus.). (J). bds. 12.99 *(978-1-934650-26-4(9))* Just For Kids Pr., LLC.

Parton, Paula. Room 17 - Where History Comes Alive - Missions. Parton, Paula, illus. 2010. (Illus.). 126p. pap. 8.95 *(978-1-935630-19-7(9))* Bellissima Publishing, LLC.

Pascoe, Matt. Chaos Island: A Daisy Albright Adventure. 2010. 72p. pap. 9.99 *(978-1-60911-208-0(3),* Eloquent Bks.) Strategic Book Publishing & Rights Agency (SBPRA).

Pass, Emma. Acid. 2014. (ENG.). 384p. (YA). (gr. 9). 17.99 *(978-0-385-74387-7(4),* Delacorte Pr.) Random Hse. Children's Bks.

Patchett, Mary E. Flight to the Misty Planet. 2011. 236p. 46.95 *(978-1-258-07100-4(2))* Literary Licensing, LLC.

Pati, Geeta. Finny's Voyage Through the Universe: The. 2005. (ENG.). 64p. per. 10.95 *(978-1-59526-019-2(6))* Aeon Publishing Inc.

Patterson, Eric. Carl Nose the Truth. Wright, Christopher, illus. 2007. 104p. (J). pap. 6.95 *(978-0-9797106-6-7(9))* Avid Readers Publishing Group.

Patterson, James. Angel. 2011. (Maximum Ride Ser.). (YA). 54.99 *(978-1-60941-970-7(7))* Findaway World, LLC.

—Angel. (Maximum Ride Ser.: 7). (ENG.). (gr. 5-17). 2012. 352p. pap. 10.00 *(978-0-316-03832-4(6))* 2011. 384p. pap. 22.99 *(978-0-316-12201-6(7))* Little Brown & Co. (Jimmy Patterson).

—Angel. 2012. (Maximum Ride Ser.: 7). lib. bdg. 20.85 *(978-0-606-23452-8(7),* Turtleback) Turtleback Bks.

—Armageddon. 2012. (Daniel X Ser.: 5). (ENG.). 304p. (J). (gr. 3-7). 16.99 *(978-0-316-10179-0(6),* Jimmy Patterson) Little Brown & Co.

—Crazy House. 2017. (Crazy House Ser.: 1). (ENG.). 368p. (YA). (gr. 9-17). 17.99 ***(978-0-316-43131-6(1),*** Jimmy Patterson) Little Brown & Co.

—The Dangerous Days of Daniel X. 2014. lthr. 79.00 *(978-1-62715-506-9(6))* Leatherbound Bestsellers.

—The Dangerous Days of Daniel X. (Daniel X Ser.: 1). (ENG.). 2010. 272p. (J). (gr. 3-7). pap. 8.00 *(978-0-316-11970-2(9),* Jimmy Patterson) 2008. 304p. pap. 20.99 *(978-0-316-03025-0(2))* Little Brown & Co.

—The Dangerous Days of Daniel X. 2010. (Daniel X Ser.: 1). (J). lib. bdg. 18.45 *(978-0-606-14720-0(9),* Turtleback) Turtleback Bks.

—Demons & Druids. 2011. (Daniel X Ser.: 3). (ENG.). 304p. (J). (gr. 3-7). pap., pap. 8.00 *(978-0-316-03830-0(X),* Jimmy Patterson) Little Brown & Co.

—Fang. (ENG.). 2014. (Best of Maximum Ride Ser.: 3). 352p. mass mkt. 8.00 *(978-1-4555-3070-0(0))* 2011. (Maximum Ride Ser.: 6). 368p. (YA). (gr. 5-17). pap. 10.00 *(978-0-316-03831-7(8))* 2010. (Maximum Ride Ser.: 6). 416p. (gr. 5-17). pap. 23.99 *(978-0-316-07106-2(4))* Little Brown & Co. (Jimmy Patterson).

—The Final Warning. 2008. (Maximum Ride Ser.: 4). (ENG.). 304p. (YA). (gr. 5-17). pap. 10.00 *(978-0-316-00287-5(9),* Jimmy Patterson) Little Brown & Co.

—The Final Warning. l.t. ed. 2009. (Maximum Ride Ser.: No. 4). 420p. (YA). 23.95 *(978-1-4104-1626-1(7))* Thorndike Pr.

—Max. 2009. (Maximum Ride Ser.: 5). (ENG.). (YA). (gr. 5-17). 352p. pap. 9.99 *(978-0-316-00290-5(9),* Jimmy Patterson); 416p. 23.99 *(978-0-316-03759-4(1))* Little Brown & Co.

—Maximum Ride. 2015. (Maximum Ride: the Manga Ser.: 9). lib. bdg. 24.50 *(978-0-606-38045-4(0))* Turtleback Bks.

—Maximum Ride Forever. 2015. (Maximum Ride Ser.: 9). (ENG.). 400p. (YA). (gr. 7-17). 19.00 *(978-0-316-20750-8(0),* Jimmy Patterson) Little Brown & Co.

—Nevermore: The Final Maximum Ride Adventure. 2012. (Maximum Ride Ser.: 8). (ENG.). 384p. (YA). (gr. 5-17). 17.99 *(978-0-316-10184-4(2),* Jimmy Patterson) Little Brown & Co.

—Saving the World: And Other Extreme Sports. 3rd rev. ed. 2008. (Maximum Ride Ser.: 3). (ENG.). 432p. (YA). (gr. 5-17). pap. 10.00 *(978-0-316-15427-7(X),* Jimmy Patterson) Little Brown & Co.

—Saving the World & Other Extreme Sports. 2008. (Maximum Ride Ser.: Bk. 5). 429p. (gr. 4-7). 18.00 *(978-0-7569-8353-6(3))* Perfection Learning Corp.

—Saving the World & Other Extreme Sports. l.t. ed. 2007. (Maximum Ride Ser.: No. 3). 489p. (J). (gr. 3-7). 23.95 *(978-0-7862-9887-7(1))* Thorndike Pr.

—School's Out - Forever. 2008. (Maximum Ride Ser.: Bk. 2). 418p. (gr. 4-7). 18.00 *(978-0-7569-8349-9(5))* Perfection Learning Corp.

—School's Out - Forever. 2007. (Maximum Ride Ser.: 2). (YA). lib. bdg. 20.85 *(978-1-4177-7493-7(2),* Turtleback) Turtleback Bks.

—Watch the Skies. 2014. lthr. 79.00 *(978-1-62715-571-7(6))* Leatherbound Bestsellers.

—Watch the Skies. l.t. ed. 2009. (Daniel X Ser.: 2). (ENG.). 352p. pap. 21.99 *(978-0-316-04363-2(X))* Little Brown & Co.

—Watch the Skies. 2010. (Daniel X Ser.: 2). (J). lib. bdg. 18.45 *(978-0-606-10550-7(6),* Turtleback) Turtleback Bks.

Patterson, James & Grabenstein, Chris. Armageddon. 2013. (Daniel X Ser.: 5). (ENG.). 320p. (J). (gr. 3-7). pap. 8.00 *(978-0-316-10177-6(X),* Jimmy Patterson) Little Brown & Co.

—Armageddon. 2013. (Daniel X Ser.: 5). (J). lib. bdg. 18.45 *(978-0-606-31747-4(3),* Turtleback) Turtleback Bks.

—Daniel X: Lights Out. 2015. (Daniel X Ser.: 6). (ENG.). 272p. (J). (gr. 3-7). 17.00 *(978-0-316-20745-4(4),* Jimmy Patterson) Little Brown & Co.

Patterson, James & Ledwidge, Michael. The Dangerous Days of Daniel X. 2009. (Daniel X Ser.: 1). (ENG.). 288p. mass mkt. 7.99 *(978-0-446-50913-8(2),* Jimmy Patterson) Little Brown & Co.

Patterson, James & Rust, Ned. Daniel X. Kye, SeungHui, illus. 2011. (Daniel X: the Manga Ser.: 2). (ENG.). 208p. (gr. 7-17). pap. 12.99 *(978-0-316-07765-1(8),* Yen Pr.) Orbit.

—Watch the Skies. 2010. (Daniel X Ser.: 2). (ENG.). 288p. (J). (gr. 3-7). pap. 8.00 *(978-0-316-11969-6(5),* Jimmy Patterson) Little Brown & Co.

Patterson, James & Sadler, Adam. Demons & Druids. l.t. ed. 2010. (Daniel X Ser.: 3). (ENG.). 320p. 29.99 *(978-0-316-08731-5(9),* Jimmy Patterson) Little Brown & Co.

Patterson, Michael. Blam! O'Reilly, Sean Patrick, ed. 2011. (Illus.). 80p. (YA). pap. 14.95 *(978-1-926914-04-6(X))* Arcana Studio, Inc.

Paulsen, Gary. The Time Hackers. 2006. (ENG.). 96p. (J). (gr. 3-7). 5.99 *(978-0-553-48788-6(4),* Yearling) Random Hse. Children's Bks.

Paye, Won-Ldy & Lippert, Margaret H. Head, Body, Legs: A Story from Liberia. Paschkis, Julie, illus. 2006. (gr. -1-3). lib. bdg. 18.00 *(978-0-7569-6925-7(5))* Perfection Learning Corp.

Pearson, Edwin. Will's Galactic Adventure. 2013. (ENG.). 104p. pap. *(978-1-78306-154-9(5))* Troubador Publishing Ltd.

Pearson, Maggie. Alien Draw. 214p. (J). pap. *(978-0-340-68077-3(6))* Hodder & Stoughton.

Pearson, Mary E. The Adoration of Jenna Fox. 2008. (Jenna Fox Chronicles Ser.: 1). (ENG.). 272p. (YA). (gr. 7-12). 24.99 *(978-0-8050-7668-4(9),* Holt, Henry & Co. Bks. For Young Readers) Holt, Henry & Co.

—The Adoration of Jenna Fox. 2011. 9.46 *(978-0-7848-3478-7(4),* Everbind) Marco Bk. Co.

—The Adoration of Jenna Fox. 2009. (Jenna Fox Chronicles Ser.: 1). (ENG.). 288p. (YA). (gr. 7-12). pap. 10.99 *(978-0-312-59441-1(0),* 9780312594411) Square Fish.

—The Fox Inheritance. 2011. (Jenna Fox Chronicles Ser.: 2). (ENG.). 304p. (YA). (gr. 7-12). 16.99 *(978-0-8050-8829-8(6),* Holt, Henry & Co. Bks. For Young Readers) Holt, Henry & Co.

—The Fox Inheritance. 2013. (Jenna Fox Chronicles Ser.: 2). (ENG.). 320p. (YA). (gr. 7-12). pap. 11.99 *(978-1-250-01032-2(2),* 9781250010322) Square Fish.

Pease, D. Robert. Noah Zarc: Cataclysm. 2nd l.t. ed. 2013. 2. (ENG.). 234p. (gr. 3-8). pap. 11.95 *(978-1-62253-406-7(9))* Evolved Publishing.

—Noah Zarc: Declaration. l.t. ed. 2013. 3. (ENG.). 226p. (gr. 3-8). pap. 11.95 *(978-1-62253-408-1(5))* Evolved Publishing.

—Noah Zarc: Mammoth Trouble. 2nd l.t. ed. 2013. 1. (ENG.). 214p. (gr. 3-8). pap. 11.95 *(978-1-62253-404-3(2))* Evolved Publishing.

—Noah Zarc: Omnibus. l.t. ed. 2013. 4. (ENG.). 630p. (gr. 3-8). 36.95 *(978-1-62253-410-4(7))* Evolved Publishing.

Peevyhouse, Parker. Where Futures End. 2016. (ENG.). 304p. (YA). (gr. 7). 17.99 *(978-0-8037-4160-7(X),* Kathy Dawson Books) Penguin Young Readers Group.

Peredo, Roberto. Acoyani: El Nino y el Poeta. Sanchez, Andres & Arte Y Diseno, Tane, illus. 2nd rev. ed. 2006. (Castillo de la Lectura Naranja Ser.). (SPA & ENG.). 166p. (J). (gr. 4-7). pap. 7.95 *(978-970-20-0146-1(3))* Castillo, Ediciones, S. A. de C. V. MEX. Dist: Macmillan.

Pero, Denis. My First Atlas: Discovery of the World. 2012. (ENG., Illus.). 80p. (J). (gr. 1). 18.95 *(978-2-7338-2148-0(2))* Auzou, Philippe Editions FRA. Dist: Consortium Bk. Sales & Distribution.

Perritano, John. The Science of Movies, 1 vol. 2017. (Red Rhino Nonfiction Ser.). (ENG.). 60p. (J). (gr. 3-8). pap. 8.95 ***(978-1-68021-050-7(5))*** Saddleback Educational Publishing, Inc.

Perritano, Johnrau Dana M. The Science of Movies. 2017. (Red Rhino Nonfiction Ser.). (J). lib. bdg. 19.60 ***(978-0-606-39892-3(9))*** Turtleback Bks.

Perry, Fred & Dlin, Doug. Gold Digger Tech Manual. 2011. (ENG.). 352p. (YA). pap., pap. 19.99 *(978-0-9844879-7-4(2),* 9780984487974) Antarctic Pr., Inc.

Perry, Michael. The Scavengers. 2014. (ENG.). 336p. (J). (gr. 3-7). 16.99 *(978-0-06-202616-3(X))* HarperCollins Pubs.

Peterfreund, Diana. Across a Star-Swept Sea. (Stars Ser.: 2). (ENG.). 464p. (YA). (gr. 8). 2014. pap. 9.99 *(978-0-06-200617-2(7))* 2013. 17.99 *(978-0-06-200616-5(9))* HarperCollins Pubs.

—For Darkness Shows the Stars. (Stars Ser.: 1). (ENG.). (YA). (gr. 8). 2013. 448p. pap. 9.99 *(978-0-06-200615-8(0))* 2012. 416p. 17.99 *(978-0-06-200614-1(2))* HarperCollins Pubs.

—Omega City. 2015. (Omega City Ser.: 1). (ENG.). 336p. (J). (gr. 3-7). 16.99 *(978-0-06-231085-9(2))* HarperCollins Pubs.

Peterson, Megan Cooley. Scooby-Doo! a Science of Electricity Mystery: The Mutant Crocodile. Cornia, Christian, illus. 2017. (Scooby-Doo Solves It with S. T. E. M. Ser.). (ENG.). 32p. (gr. 3-4). lib. bdg. 27.99 *(978-1-5157-3698-1(9))* Capstone Press of Coughlan Cos.

—Scooby-Doo! a Science of Light Mystery: The Angry Alien. Brizuela, Dario, illus. 2017. (Scooby-Doo Solves It with S. T. E. M. Ser.). (ENG.). 32p. (gr. 3-4). lib. bdg. 27.99 *(978-1-5157-3700-1(4))* Capstone Press of Coughlan Cos.

—Scooby-Doo! a Science of Magnetism Mystery: The Magnetic Monster. Cornia, Christian, illus. 2017. (Scooby-Doo Solves It with S. T. E. M. Ser.). (ENG.). 32p. (gr. 3-4). lib. bdg. 27.99 *(978-1-5157-3699-8(7))* Capstone Press of Coughlan Cos.

Peterson, Scott. The Joker Virus, 1 vol. Cavallaro, Mike, illus. 2012. (Dark Knight Ser.). (ENG.). 88p. (gr. 2-3). lib. bdg. 26.65 *(978-1-4342-4096-5(7))* Stone Arch Bks.

—The Ultimate Returns. 4th ed. 2009. (Spectrobes Ser.: No. 3). (ENG.). 144p. (J). (gr. 3-7). pap. 4.99 *(978-1-4231-0811-5(6))* Disney Pr.

Petri, Michelle. The Fvantom: Omegapocalypse. 2007. 212p. per. 14.95 *(978-0-595-45723-6(1))* iUniverse, Inc.

Peyton, Veronica. Silo & the Rebel Raiders. 2016. (ENG.). 304p. (J). (gr. 3-7). 16.99 *(978-0-399-55241-0(3),* Delacorte Bks. for Young Readers) Random Hse. Children's Bks.

Pfeffer, Susan Beth. The Dead & the Gone. 2010. (Last Survivors Ser.: 2). 321p. lib. bdg. 19.65 *(978-0-606-14464-3(1),* Turtleback) Turtleback Bks.

—Life As We Knew It. 2008. (Life As We Knew It Ser.: 1). (ENG., Illus.). 352p. (YA). (gr. 7-18). pap. 9.99 *(978-0-15-206154-8(1))* Houghton Mifflin Harcourt Publishing Co.

—Life As We Knew It. Howard, Arthur, illus. 2006. (Life As We Knew It Ser.: 1). (ENG.). 352p. (YA). (gr. 7-12). 17.99 *(978-0-15-205826-5(5))* Houghton Mifflin Harcourt Publishing Co.

—Life As We Knew It. 2008. (Last Survivors Ser.: 1). 347p. (gr. 7-12). lib. bdg. 19.65 *(978-1-4178-1541-8(8),* Turtleback) Turtleback Bks.

—The Life As We Knew It Collection. 2015. (Life As We Knew It Ser.). (ENG.). 1252p. (YA). (gr. 7). 29.99 *(978-0-544-54263-1(0),* HMH Books For Young Readers) Houghton Mifflin Harcourt Publishing Co.

—The Shade of the Moon. (Life As We Knew It Ser.: 4). (ENG.). 304p. (YA). (gr. 7). 2014. pap. 8.99 *(978-0-544-33615-5(1),* HMH Books For Young Readers) 2013. 17.99 *(978-0-547-81337-0(6))* Houghton Mifflin Harcourt Publishing Co.

—This World We Live In, Bk. 3. 2011. (Life As We Knew It Ser.: 3). (ENG.). 256p. (YA). (gr. 7). pap. 8.99 *(978-0-547-55028-2(6))* Houghton Mifflin Harcourt Publishing Co.

Pflugfelder, Bob & Hockensmith, Steve. Nick & Tesla's High-Voltage Danger Lab: A Mystery with Electromagnets, Burglar Alarms, & Other Gadgets You Can Build Yourself. 2013. (Nick & Tesla Ser.: 1). (ENG., Illus.). 240p. (J). (gr. 4-7). 12.95 *(978-1-59474-648-2(6))* Quirk Bks.

Phelan, James. The Last Thirteen Book Six: 8. 2014. (ENG., Illus.). 192p. (J). pap. *(978-1-4431-3352-4(3))* Kane Miller.

Philbrick, Rodman. The Last Book in the Universe. unabr. ed. 2004. 224p. (J). (gr. 5-9). pap. 36.00 incl. audio *(978-0-8072-8844-3(6),* LYA 272 SP, Listening Library) Random Hse. Audio Publishing Group.

Phillips, Terrie. The Ski Trip. 2006. (Illus.). 38p. (J). lib. bdg. 12.95 *(978-0-9789449-0-2(9))* Tbooks Publishing Co.

Phineas and Ferb. Phineas & Ferb Batter Up! 2010. pap. 5.99 *(978-1-4231-2408-5(1))* Disney Pr.

Pierce, Meredith Ann. Waters Luminous & Deep. 2005. (ENG.). 320p. (YA). (gr. 7-7). 9.99 *(978-0-14-240356-3(3),* Firebird) Penguin Young Readers Group.

Pierce, Tamora. Alanna: The First Adventure. unabr. ed. 2004. (Song of the Lioness Ser.: Bk. 1). 216p. (J). (gr. 6-18). pap. 36.00 incl. audio *(978-0-8072-8772-9(5),* YA263SP, Listening Library) Random Hse. Audio Publishing Group.

Pike, Aprilynne. Glitter. 2016. (ENG., Illus.). 384p. (YA). (gr. 9). 17.99 *(978-1-101-93370-1(4),* Random Hse. Bks. for Young Readers) Random Hse. Children's Bks.

Pillsbury, Samuel H. The Invasion of Planet Wampetter. Angorn, Matthew, illus. 2003. (Planet Wampetter Adventure Ser.). 133p. (J). (gr. 3-8). 15.00 *(978-0-9622036-6-4(1));* pap. 8.95 *(978-1-930085-05-3(2))* Perspective Publishing, Inc.

Pinkwater, Daniel M. Adventures of a Cat-Whiskered Girl. 2011. (ENG., Illus.). 288p. (J). (gr. 5-7). pap. 16.95 *(978-0-547-55002-2(2))* Houghton Mifflin Harcourt Publishing Co.

Pinkwater, Daniel M. Lizard Music. Pinkwater, Daniel M., illus. 2017. (ENG., Illus.). 160p. (J). (gr. 4-7). pap. 9.99 ***(978-1-68137-184-9(7),*** NYRB Kids) New York Review of Bks., Inc., The.

—Lizard Music. 2011. (ENG., Illus.). 160p. (J). (gr. 4-7). 15.95 *(978-1-59017-387-9(2),* NYR Children's Collection) New York Review of Bks., Inc., The.

Piper, Henry Beam. Little Fuzzy. 2007. (ENG.). 172p. per. 19.99 *(978-1-4346-2928-9(7));* 188p. per. 21.99 *(978-1-4346-2952-4(X))* Creative Media Partners, LLC.

Pittman, Eddie. Red's Planet. 2016. (Red's Planet Ser.: 1). (J). lib. bdg. 20.80 *(978-0-606-38203-8(8))* Turtleback Bks.

Platt, Richard & Dorling Kindersley Publishing Staff. Galactic Mission. 2014. (DK Adventures Ser.). (ENG.). 128p. (J). (gr. 3-7). pap. 5.99 *(978-1-4654-1977-4(2),* DK Children) Dorling Kindersley Publishing, Inc.

Plummer, Todd. Superhero Science: Kapow! Comic Book Crime Fighters Put Physics to the Test. 2009. (Current Science Ser.). (ENG.). 48p. (J). (gr. 4-6). pap. 8.95 *(978-1-4339-2247-3(9),* Gareth Stevens Learning Library) Stevens, Gareth Publishing LLLP.

Plummer, Todd, et al. Superhero Science: Kapow! Comic Book Crime Fighters Put Physics to the Test. 2009. (Current Science Ser.). (ENG.). 48p. (YA). (gr. 4-7). lib. bdg. 31.00 *(978-1-4339-2243-5(6))* Stevens, Gareth Publishing LLLP.

Pon, Cindy. Want. 2017. (ENG., Illus.). 336p. (YA). (gr. 9). 18.99 ***(978-1-4814-8922-5(4),*** Simon Pulse) Simon Pulse.

Pope, P. R. Queens of Antares: Volume 1 of the Bloodline Trilogy: Bloodline Returned: Bloodline Returned. 2012. (ENG., Illus.). 224p. pap. *(978-1-908168-01-6(3),* Elsewhen Pr.) Alnpete Ltd.

Popescu, Petru. Footprints in Time. 2008. 256p. (J). (gr. 5). lib. bdg. 17.89 *(978-0-06-088400-0(2),* Geringer, Laura Book) HarperCollins Pubs.

Powell, Huw. The Lost Sword: A Spacejackers Novel. 2016. (Spacejackers Ser.: 2). (ENG.). 320p. (J). 16.99 *(978-1-61963-836-5(3),* 9781619638365, Bloomsbury USA Childrens) Bloomsbury Publishing USA.

—Spacejackers. 2015. (Spacejackers Ser.). (ENG.). 336p. (YA). (gr. 3-6). 16.99 *(978-1-61963-515-9(1),* 9781619635159, Bloomsbury USA Childrens) Bloomsbury Publishing USA.

Powell, William Campbell. Expiration Day. 2014. (ENG.). 336p. (YA). (gr. 8-12). 17.99 *(978-0-7653-3828-0(9),* Tor Teen) Doherty, Tom Assocs., LLC.

Pratchett, Terry. The Bromeliad Trilogy: Truckers, Diggers, & Wings. 2003. 512p. (J). (gr. 5-18). 18.89 *(978-0-06-054855-1(X));* 19.99 *(978-0-06-009493-5(1))* HarperCollins Pubs.

Prendergast, G. S. Zero Repeat Forever. 2017. (Nahx Invasions Ser.: 1). (ENG., Illus.). 496p. (YA). (gr. 9). 17.99 ***(978-1-4814-8184-7(3),*** Simon & Schuster Bks. For Young Readers) Simon & Schuster Bks. For Young Readers.

Prendergast, Gabrielle. Zero Repeat Forever. 2017. (YA). pap. ***(978-1-4814-8185-4(1),*** Simon & Schuster Bks. For Young Readers) Simon & Schuster Bks. For Young Readers.

Press, J. Robots Don't Clean Toilets. Kline, Michael, illus. 2013. (Doodles of Sam Dibble Ser.: 3). (ENG.). 128p. (J). (gr. 1-3). pap. 4.99 *(978-0-448-46109-0(9),* Grosset & Dunlap) Penguin Young Readers Group.

Preston, L. M. Explorer X: Beta. 2012. (ENG.). 264p. (YA). pap. 11.99 *(978-0-9841989-5-5(4))* Phenomenal One Pr.

—The Pack. 2010. (ENG.). 316p. (J). pap. 14.99 *(978-0-9841989-7-9(0))* Phenomenal One Pr.

—The Pack - Retribution: Retribution. 2012. (ENG.). 250p. (YA). (gr. 8-12). pap. 11.99 *(978-0-9850251-0-6(7))* Phenomenal One Pr.

Price, Kevin, ed. The Mystery of Love: A Born Storyteller Collection of Mystery Adventure & Science Fiction Stories. 2013. (Illus.). 308p. pap. *(978-0-9872559-6-9(7),* Crotchet Quaver) Logorythm.

Price, Lissa. Enders. 2014. (ENG.). 288p. (YA). (gr. 7). lib. bdg. 20.99 *(978-0-375-99061-8(5),* Delacorte Pr.) Random Hse. Children's Bks.

—Starters. (ENG.). (YA). (gr. 7). 2013. 384p. pap. 9.99 *(978-0-385-74248-1(7),* Ember) 2012. 352p. 17.99 *(978-0-385-74237-5(1),* Delacorte Pr.) Random Hse. Children's Bks.

Price, Michael & Howard, Kate. Droid Tales. 2015. (Lego Star Wars Ser.). (ENG.). 96p. (J). (gr. 2-5). pap. 7.99 *(978-0-545-87328-4(2))* Scholastic, Inc.

Price, Susan. A Sterkarm Kiss. 2004. (ENG.). 288p. (J). (gr. 7-18). 16.99 *(978-0-06-072197-8(9))* HarperCollins Pubs.

Prior, Natalie Jane & Dawson, Kathy. Lily Quench & the Magician's Pyramid, Vol. 5. 2004. (ENG., Illus.). 176p. (Orig.). (J). (gr. 3-7). 6.99 *(978-0-14-240163-7(3),* Puffin Books) Penguin Young Readers Group.

Project Cain. 2014. (ENG., Illus.). 384p. (YA). (gr. 9). pap. 11.99 *(978-1-4424-7698-1(2),* Simon & Schuster Bks. For Young Readers) Simon & Schuster Bks. For Young Readers.

Protobunker Studio Staff & Wells, H. G. La Guerra de los Mundos. Ruiz, Alfonso, illus. 2010. (Classic Fiction Ser.).

S

(SPA.). 72p. (gr. 2-3). 27.99 *(978-1-4342-2322-7(1)*, Graphic Revolve en Español) Stone Arch Bks.
Pryor, Bonnie. Mr. Munday & the Space Creatures. 2013. (ENG., Illus.). 32p. (J). (gr. -1-3). 16.99 *(978-1-4424-8877-9(8)*, Atheneum Bks. for Young Readers) Simon & Schuster Children's Publishing.
Psycho Backho: Arc of Fury - the Cataclysm. 2005. (YA). per. *(978-1-59620-003-6(0))* Science of Knowledge Pr.
Publications International Ltd. Staff. Wall E Large Sound BK. 2008. 24p. (J). 17.98 *(978-1-4127-8991-2(5)*, PIL Kids) Publications International, Ltd.
Publications International Ltd. Staff, ed. Star Wars: Revenge of the Sith: Play-a-Sound. 2005. (Illus.). 24p. (J). 16.98 *(978-1-4127-3487-5(8)*, 7262800) Publications International, Ltd.
Pugh, Ian. Wolfstorm: The First Danny Piper Adventure. 2010. 388p. 32.95 *(978-1-4269-0239-0(5))* Trafford Publishing.
Pullman, Philip. The Adventures of John Blake: Mystery of the Ghost Ship. Fordham, Fred, illus. 2017. (ENG.). 160p. (J). (gr. 3-7). 19.99 ***(978-1-338-14912-8(1)***, Graphix) Scholastic, Inc.
—The Adventures of John Blake: Mystery of the Ghost Ship. Fordham, Fred, illus. 2017. lib. bdg. 33.05 ***(978-0-606-40195-1(4))*** Turtleback Bks.
Pullman, Philip. La Daga. Gallart, Dolors, tr. 7th ed. 2005. (Escritura desatada Ser.).Tr. of Subtle Knife. (SPA., Illus.). 283p. (YA). (gr. 7-11). 13.95 *(978-84-406-8409-7(6))* Ediciones B ESP. Dist: Independent Pubs. Group.
Purves, Jeff, et al, illus. Hulk Visionaries, Vol. 3. 2006. (ENG.). 192p. (J). (gr. 4-17). pap. 19.99 *(978-0-7851-2095-7(5))* Marvel Worldwide, Inc.
Quesada, Joe & Tieri, Frank. Iron Man by Joe Quesada. Martinez, Alitha et al, illus. 2013. (ENG.). 232p. (J). (gr. 4-17). pap. 24.99 *(978-0-7851-6736-5(6))* Marvel Worldwide, Inc.
Quijano, Jonathan. Make Your Own Sci-Fi Flick, 1 vol. 2012. (Make Your Movie Ser.). (ENG., Illus.). 48p. (gr. 3-4). lib. bdg. 31.99 *(978-1-4296-7531-4(4))* Capstone Press of Coughlan Cos.
Quintana, Adrienne. Eruption. 2015. 282p. (YA). pap. 16.99 *(978-1-4621-1536-5(5))* Cedar Fort, Inc./CFI Distribution.
Rafter, Dan. Gearz. 2010. (ENG., Illus.). 96p. (YA). pap. 17.99 *(978-1-61623-929-9(8))* Bluewater Productions, Inc.
Railes, H. J. Darok 10. 2005. 230p. (J). pap. 9.95 *(978-1-929976-31-7(3))* Top Pubns., Ltd.
—Keeper of the Realm, Vol. 2. 2003. (Illus.). 248p. (J). pap. 9.95 *(978-1-929976-21-8(6))* Top Pubns., Ltd.
Random House. DC Super Hero Girls Activity Journal (DC Super Hero Girls) Random House, illus. 2017. (Official Guide Ser.). (ENG., Illus.). 160p. (J). (gr. 2-4). 13.99 *(978-1-5247-1845-9(9)*, Random Hse. Bks. for Young Readers) Random Hse. Children's Bks.
Random House Disney Staff. Big Hero 6. Random House Disney Staff, illus. 2014. (Little Golden Book Ser.). (ENG., Illus.). 24p. (J). (-k). 4.99 *(978-0-7364-3168-2(3)*, Golden Bks.) Random Hse. Children's Bks.
—Big Hero 6 Big Golden Book (Disney Big Hero 6) Random House Disney Staff, illus. 2014. (Big Golden Book Ser.). (ENG., Illus.). 48p. (J). (gr. k-4). 9.99 *(978-0-7364-3186-6(1)*, Golden Bks.) Random Hse. Children's Bks.
Random House Disney Staff & Fontana, Shea. Super Hero High Yearbook! (DC Super Hero Girls) Random House Disney Staff, illus. 2016. (ENG., Illus.). 96p. (J). (gr. 3-7). pap. 9.99 *(978-1-5247-0106-2(8)*, Random Hse. Bks. for Young Readers) Random Hse. Children's Bks.
Random House Staff. Ooze Control. Navarra, Nino, illus. 2013. (Pictureback(R) Ser.). (ENG.). 16p. (J). (gr. -1-2). pap. 4.99 *(978-0-307-98229-2(7)*, Random Hse. Bks. for Young Readers) Random Hse. Children's Bks.
Raney, Tom, et al, illus. The Infinity War. 2006. (ENG.). 400p. (J). (gr. 4-17). pap. 29.99 *(978-0-7851-2105-3(6))* Marvel Worldwide, Inc.
Rauch, Earl Mac. Buckaroo Banzai TP Vol 02 No Matter Where You Go. 2014. (ENG., Illus.). 158p. (YA). pap. 16.95 *(978-1-936814-72-5(2)*, 9781936814725) Moonstone.
Rauch, Mac & Richter, W. D. BUCKAROO BANZAI: TPB Vol. 1: Return of the Screw: TPB Vol. 1: Return of the Screw. 2014. (ENG., Illus.). 120p. (YA). pap. 15.95 *(978-1-936814-71-8(4)*, 9781936814718) Moonstone.
Rawson, Christopher. Gnomes & Goblins. Cartwright, Stephen, illus. 2004. (Young Reading Series One Ser.). 48p. (J). (gr. 2-18). pap. 5.95 *(978-0-7945-0407-6(8)*, Usborne) EDC Publishing.
Rechlin, Ted & Paper Dolls. Robot Battle Paper Action Figures. 2012. (Dover Paper Dolls Ser.). (ENG.). 32p. (J). (gr. 3-5). pap. 9.99 *(978-0-486-48781-6(4))* Dover Pubns., Inc.
Reese, Jenn. Above World. (ENG.). 368p. (J). (gr. 5). 2013. pap. 7.99 *(978-0-7636-6259-2(3))* 2012. (Illus.). 16.99 *(978-0-7636-5417-7(5))* Candlewick Pr.
—Horizon. 2015. (Above World Ser.). (ENG.). 400p. (J). (gr. 5). pap. 7.99 *(978-0-7636-7667-4(5))* Candlewick Pr.
—Mirage. (Above World Ser.). (ENG.). 368p. (J). (gr. 5). 2014. pap. 7.99 *(978-0-7636-6929-4(6))* 2013. 16.99 *(978-0-7636-5418-4(3))* Candlewick Pr.
Reeve, Philip. Black Light Express. 2017. (ENG.). 352p. (gr. 9-12). 17.95 ***(978-1-63079-096-7(6))*** Switch Pr.
—Cakes in Space. McIntyre, Sarah, illus. 2015. (Not-So-Impossible Tale Ser.). (ENG.). 224p. (J). (gr. 2-5). 12.99 *(978-0-385-38792-7(X)*, Random Hse. Bks. for Young Readers) Random Hse. Children's Bks.
—A Darkling Plain. 2017. (Mortal Engines Ser.: 4). (ENG.). 544p. (J). (gr. 7). pap. 9.99 ***(978-1-338-20115-4(8)***, Scholastic Pr.) Scholastic, Inc.
—Fever Crumb. 2011. (Fever Crumb Ser.). (ENG.). 336p. (J). (gr. 7-7). pap. 9.99 *(978-0-545-22215-0(X)*, Scholastic Pr.) Scholastic, Inc.
—Fever Crumb: a Web of Air. 2013. (Fever Crumb Ser.). (ENG.). 304p. (J). (gr. 7-7). pap. 9.99 *(978-0-545-22217-4(6)*, Scholastic Pr.) Scholastic, Inc.
—Infernal Devices. 2017. (Mortal Engines Ser.: 3). (ENG.). 352p. (J). (gr. 7). pap. 9.99 ***(978-1-338-20114-7(X)***, Scholastic Pr.) Scholastic, Inc.
—Infernal Devices. 2012. (Predator Cities Ser.: 3). lib. bdg. 19.65 *(978-0-606-23951-6(0)*, Turtleback) Turtleback Bks.
—Mortal Engines. 2017. (Mortal Engines Ser.: 1). (ENG.). 320p. (J). (gr. 7). pap. 9.99 ***(978-1-338-20112-3(3)***, Scholastic Pr.) Scholastic, Inc.
—Predator's Gold. 2017. (Mortal Engines Ser.: 2). (ENG.). 336p. (J). (gr. 7). pap. 9.99 ***(978-1-338-20113-0(1)***, Scholastic Pr.) Scholastic, Inc.
—Railhead. 2016. (ENG.). 352p. (gr. 9-12). 16.95 *(978-1-63079-048-6(6))* Switch Pr.
—Scrivener's Moon. 2012. (ENG.). 352p. (J). (gr. 7). 17.99 *(978-0-545-22218-1(4)*, Scholastic Pr.) Scholastic, Inc.
—Starcross: A Stirring Adventure of Spies, Time Travel & Curious Hats. Wyatt, David, illus. 2007. (ENG.). 384p. (YA). (gr. 5-18). 16.95 *(978-1-59990-121-3(8)*, 9781599901213, Bloomsbury USA Childrens) Bloomsbury Publishing USA.
—A Web of Air. 2011. (Fever Crumb Ser.). (ENG.). 304p. (J). (gr. 7-7). 17.99 *(978-0-545-22216-7(8))* Scholastic, Inc.
Reichs, Brendan. Nemesis. 2017. (Project Nemesis Ser.). (ENG.). 464p. (YA). (gr. 7). 17.99 *(978-0-399-54493-4(3)*, G.P. Putnam's Sons Books for Young Readers) Penguin Young Readers Group.
Reichs, Kathy. Code. 2013. (Virals Ser.: 3). (ENG.). 432p. (J). (gr. 5). pap. 8.99 *(978-1-59514-572-7(9)*, Puffin Books) Penguin Young Readers Group.
—Virals. 2014. lthr. 79.00 *(978-1-62715-582-3(1))* Leatherbound Bestsellers.
—Virals. (Virals Ser.: 1). (ENG.). (J). (gr. 5-18). 2011. 480p. 10.99 *(978-1-59514-426-3(9)*, Puffin Books) 2010. 464p. 17.99 *(978-1-59514-342-6(4)*, Razorbill) Penguin Young Readers Group.
—Virals. 2011. 20.00 *(978-1-61383-226-4(5))* Perfection Learning Corp.
Reichs, Kathy & Reichs, Brendan. Code. 2013. (Virals Ser.: 3). lib. bdg. 19.65 *(978-0-606-32140-2(3)*, Turtleback) Turtleback Bks.
—Terminal. 2015. (Virals Ser.: 5). (ENG.). 432p. (J). (gr. 5). 17.99 *(978-1-59514-528-4(1)*, G.P. Putnam's Sons Books for Young Readers) Penguin Young Readers Group.
—Trace Evidence. 2016. (Virals Ser.). lib. bdg. 20.85 *(978-0-606-38400-1(6))* Turtleback Bks.
—Virals. 2011. (Virals Ser.: 1). lib. bdg. 20.85 *(978-0-606-23069-8(6)*, Turtleback) Turtleback Bks.
—Virals Short Stories Omnibus. 2016. (Virals Ser.). (ENG.). 304p. (J). (gr. 5). 9.99 *(978-0-14-751920-7(9)*, Puffin Books) Penguin Young Readers Group.
Reid, Kate. Operation Timewarp. 2003. 195p. pap. *(978-1-84255-203-2(1)*, Orion Children's Bks.) Hachette Children's Group.
Reilly, Carmel & Young, Karen. Buzz Takes Over. 2008. (Rigby Focus Forward: Level I Ser.). (Illus.). 24p. (J). (gr. 4-7). pap. *(978-1-4190-3743-6(9)*, Rigby) Pearson Education Australia.
Reinhart, Matthew & Lucasfilm. A Galactic Pop-Up Adventure. ltd. ed. 2012. (Star Wars Ser.). (ENG.). 10p. (J). (gr. 2-5). 300.00 *(978-0-545-44246-6(X)*, Orchard Bks.) Scholastic, Inc.
Reinhart, Matthew & Lucasfilm Ltd. Staff. A Galactic Pop-Up Adventure. 2012. (Star Wars Ser.). (ENG.). 5p. (J). (gr. 2-5). 36.99 *(978-0-545-17616-3(6)*, Orchard Bks.) Scholastic, Inc.
Reintgen, Scott. Nyxia. 2017. (Nyxia Triad Ser.). (ENG.). 384p. (YA). (gr. 7). 17.99 ***(978-0-399-55679-1(6))***; lib. bdg. 20.99 ***(978-0-399-55680-7(X))*** Random Hse. Children's Bks. (Crown Books For Young Readers).
Reisman, Michael. Simon Bloom, the Gravity Keeper. 2009. (ENG.). 320p. (J). (gr. 3-7). 8.99 *(978-0-14-241368-5(2)*, Puffin Books) Penguin Young Readers Group.
Reiss, Kathryn. Paint by Magic. 2003. (ENG.). 288p. (J). (gr. 5-7). pap. 17.95 *(978-0-15-204925-6(8))* Houghton Mifflin Harcourt Publishing Co.
Remender, Rick. Castaway in Dimension Z, Bk. 2. 2014. (ENG., Illus.). 136p. (J). (gr. 4-17). pap. 19.99 *(978-0-7851-6656-6(4))* Marvel Worldwide, Inc.
—Uncanny Avengers - Avenge the Earth, Vol. 4. 2014. (ENG., Illus.). 136p. (J). (gr. 4-17). 24.99 *(978-0-7851-5423-5(X))* Marvel Worldwide, Inc.
Renick, Sam X. The Adventures of Sammy the Saver In: Will Sammy Ride the World's First Space Coaster?, Vol. 2. Alvarado, Juan, illus. 2003. 32p. (J). pap. 8.95 *(978-0-9713664-1-1(1))* It's A Habit! Co., The.
Revealed. 2014. (Missing Ser.: 7). (ENG., Illus.). 448p. (J). (gr. 3-7). 18.99 *(978-1-4169-8986-8(2)*, Simon & Schuster Bks. For Young Readers) Simon & Schuster Bks. For Young Readers.
Revis, Beth. Across the Universe. 2012. (Across the Universe Trilogy: Bk. 1). (ENG.). (YA). (gr. 7-12). 54.99 *(978-1-61587-857-4(2)*, Penguin AudioBooks) Penguin Publishing Group.
—Across the Universe. 2011. (Across the Universe Ser.: Bk. 1). (ENG.). (YA). (gr. 9-18). 448p. 9.99 *(978-1-59514-467-6(6))*; 416p. 17.99 *(978-1-59514-397-6(1))* Penguin Young Readers Group. (Razorbill).
—Across the Universe. 2011. (Across the Universe Trilogy: 1). lib. bdg. 20.85 *(978-0-606-23139-8(0)*, Turtleback) Turtleback Bks.
—A Million Suns. 2012. (Across the Universe Ser.: 2). (ENG., Illus.). 416p. (YA). (gr. 9). pap. 9.99 *(978-1-59514-537-6(0)*, Razorbill) Penguin Young Readers Group.
—A Million Suns. 2012. (Across the Universe Trilogy: 2). lib. bdg. 20.85 *(978-0-606-26632-1(1)*, Turtleback) Turtleback Bks.
—Shades of Earth. 2013. (Across the Universe Ser.: 3). (ENG.). 448p. (YA). (gr. 9). pap. 9.99 *(978-1-59514-615-1(6)*, Razorbill) Penguin Young Readers Group.
—Shades of Earth. 2013. (Across the Universe Trilogy: 3). lib. bdg. 20.85 *(978-0-606-32117-4(9)*, Turtleback) Turtleback Bks.
Rex, Adam. Smek for President! Rex, Adam, illus. (Smek Smeries Ser.). (ENG., Illus.). 272p. (J). (gr. 3-7). 2016. pap. 7.99 *(978-1-4847-0969-6(1))* 2015. 16.99 *(978-1-4847-0951-1(9))* Hyperion Bks. for Children.
—The True Meaning of Smekday. Rex, Adam, illus. 2015. (ENG., Illus.). 432p. (J). (gr. 3-7). pap. 7.99 *(978-1-4847-2946-5(3))* Hyperion Bks. for Children.
—The True Meaning of Smekday. Rex, Adam, illus. 2009. (Smek Smeries Ser.). (ENG., Illus.). 432p. (J). (gr. 3-7). pap. 7.99 *(978-0-7868-4901-7(0))* Hyperion Pr.
—The True Meaning of Smekday. 2009. (Illus.). 423p. 18.00 *(978-1-60686-525-5(0))* Perfection Learning Corp.
Rex, Michael. The Egg of Misery: Fangbone, Third Grade Barbarian. Rex, Michael, illus. 2012. (Fangbone! Third Grade Barbarian Ser.: 2). (ENG., Illus.). 128p. (J). (gr. 2-4). 7.99 *(978-0-399-25522-9(2)*, G.P. Putnam's Sons Books for Young Readers) Penguin Young Readers Group.
—Fangbone! Third-Grade Barbarian. 2012. (Illus.). 120p. (J). *(978-0-545-44042-4(4)*, Putnam Juvenile) Penguin Publishing Group.
Rey, H. A. Curious George Discovers the Seasons (science Storybook) 2016. (Curious George Ser.). (ENG., Illus.). 32p. (J). (gr. -1-3). 14.99 *(978-0-544-78586-1(X)*, HMH Books For Young Readers) Houghton Mifflin Harcourt Publishing Co.
Reynolds, David West, et al. The Complete Visual Dictionary. Ivanov, Alex, photos by. 2006. (ENG., Illus.). 272p. (J). (gr. 5-12). 40.00 *(978-0-7566-2238-1(7)*, DK Children) Dorling Kindersley Publishing, Inc.
Reynolds, Jason. Miles Morales. Nelson, Kadir, illus. 2017. (Marvel YA Novel Ser.). (ENG.). 272p. (YA). (gr. 7-12). 17.99 ***(978-1-4847-8748-9(X)***, Marvel Pr.) Disney Publishing Worldwide.
RH Disney Staff. The Big Battle. RH Disney Staff, illus. 2014. (Step into Reading Ser.). (ENG., Illus.). 32p. (J). (gr. k-3). 4.99 *(978-0-7364-3245-0(0)*, RH/Disney) Random Hse. Children's Bks.
—Love at First Beep. 2008. (Step into Reading Ser.). (ENG., Illus.). 32p. (J). (gr. k-3). pap. 3.99 *(978-0-7364-2514-8(4)*, RH/Disney) Random Hse. Children's Bks.
RH Disney Staff & Scollon, Bill. Fight to the Finish! RH Disney Staff & Disney Storybook Art Team, illus. 2014. (Step into Reading Ser.). (ENG.). 48p. (J). (gr. k-3). 3.99 *(978-0-7364-3189-7(6)*, RH/Disney) Random Hse. Children's Bks.
Rich, Jamie S. The World Is Flat. 2013. (ENG., Illus.). 168p. (YA). pap. 14.99 *(978-1-60706-791-7(9)*, 9781607067917) Image Comics.
Richard Richtmyer. A Bit of Magic: A Novel. 2009. 116p. pap. 10.95 *(978-1-4401-5565-9(8))* iUniverse, Inc.
Richards, C. J. Battle of the Bots. Fujita, Goro, illus. 2015. (Robots Rule Ser.: 3). (ENG.). 240p. (J). (gr. 2-5). 13.99 *(978-0-544-33932-3(0)*, HMH Books For Young Readers) Houghton Mifflin Harcourt Publishing Co.
—Battle of the Bots. 2017. (Robots Rule Ser.: 3). (ENG.). (J). (gr. 2-5). lib. bdg. 17.20 ***(978-0-606-39811-4(2))*** Turtleback Bks.
Richards, C. J. Lots of Bots. Fujita, Goro, illus. 2015. (Robots Rule Ser.: 2). (ENG.). 224p. (J). (gr. 2-5). 13.99 *(978-0-544-33934-7(7)*, HMH Books For Young Readers) Houghton Mifflin Harcourt Publishing Co.
Richards, Justin. Rewind Assassin. 2007. (Time Runners Ser.: 2). (ENG.). 208p. (J). (gr. 4-7). pap. 8.99 *(978-1-4169-2643-6(7))* Simon & Schuster, Ltd. GBR. Dist: Simon & Schuster, Inc.
Richardson, D. L. Feedback. 2013. 254p. pap. 11.99 *(978-1-939194-83-1(0))* Etopia Pr.
Richardson, Fay Lapka. Dark Is a Color. 2004. 264p. (J). pap. 12.95 *(978-0-9744989-6-6(3))* Fox Song Bks.
Richardson, Mike. Dark Horse Heroes, Vol. 1. Dark Horse Comics Staff & Warner, Christopher S., eds. Hughes, Adam, illus. 2008. (ENG.). 488p. pap. 24.95 *(978-1-59307-734-1(3))* Dark Horse Comics.
Riggs, Carol. The Body Institute. 2015. (ENG.). 368p. (J). pap. 9.99 *(978-1-63375-125-5(2)*, 9781633751255) Entangled Publishing, LLC.
Riggs, Carol. The Lying Planet. 2016. (ENG., Illus.). (YA). (gr. 7). pap. 17.99 ***(978-1-68281-304-1(5))*** Entangled Publishing, LLC.
Riggs, Ransom. Miss Peregrine's Journal for Peculiar Children. 2016. (Miss Peregrine's Peculiar Children Ser.). (ENG.). 192p. (YA). (gr. 9). 14.99 *(978-1-59474-940-7(X))* Quirk Bks.
Riis, Jon. Something for Nothing: A Diploma for Your Life Experience. 2010. 192p. (YA). pap. 17.00 *(978-1-934376-21-8(3))* Balona Bks.
Ripley, T. P. Lily Lovebug & the Unconquered Planet. 2013. 170p. pap. *(978-1-908910-43-1(7))* Crooked Cat Publishing.
Ritchie, Brendan. Beyond Carousel. 2017. (Carousel Ser.). (ENG.). 368p. (YA). (gr. 7). 19.99 ***(978-1-925164-03-9(9))*** Fremantle Pr. AUS. Dist: Independent Pubs. Group.
Robbins, Trina. The Bark in Space. Page, Tyler, illus. 2013. (Chicagoland Detective Agency Ser.: 5). (ENG.). 64p. (gr. 4-8). (J). lib. bdg. 29.27 *(978-0-7613-8166-2(X))*; pap. 6.95 *(978-1-4677-0725-1(2))* Lerner Publishing Group. (Graphic Universe™).
—The Drained Brains Caper. Page, Tyler, illus. 2010. (Chicagoland Detective Agency Ser.: 1). (ENG.). 64p. (gr. 4-8). pap. 6.95 *(978-0-7613-5635-6(5)*, Graphic Universe™); lib. bdg. 29.27 *(978-0-7613-4601-2(5))* Lerner Publishing Group.
—Night of the Living Dogs. Page, Tyler, illus. 2012. (Chicagoland Detective Agency Ser.). 64p. (J). (gr. 4-8). pap. 39.62 *(978-0-7613-9313-9(7)*, Graphic Universe™); (ENG.). lib. bdg. 29.27 *(978-0-7613-4616-6(3))* Lerner Publishing Group.
Roberts, Jeyn. Dark Inside. (ENG.). (YA). (gr. 9). 2012. 352p. pap. 10.99 *(978-1-4424-2352-7(8))* 2011. 336p. 17.99 *(978-1-4424-2351-0(X))* Simon & Schuster Bks. For Young Readers. (Simon & Schuster Bks. For Young Readers).
—Rage Within. (ENG., Illus.). 368p. (YA). (gr. 9). 2013. Illus.). pap. 9.99 *(978-1-4424-2355-8(2))* 2012. 17.99 *(978-1-4424-2354-1(4))* Simon & Schuster Bks. For Young Readers. (Simon & Schuster Bks. For Young Readers).
Roberts, Willo Davis. Girl with the Silver Eyes. 2011. (ENG.). 192p. (J). (gr. 3-7). pap. 7.99 *(978-1-4424-2170-7(3)*, Aladdin) Simon & Schuster Children's Publishing.
Robinson, Anitha. Broken Worlds. 2014. (Broken Worlds Ser.). (ENG.). 200p. (YA). (gr. 8-11). pap. 8.95 *(978-1-933767-37-6(5))* CBAY Bks.
Robinson, Kelley. Naming: Book One of the Magic of Io Series. Curtiss, Melody, illus. 2013. 138p. pap. 8.95 *(978-0-9745865-1-9(X)*, SarahRose Children's Bks.) SarahRose Publishing.
Robinson, Michelle. Goodnight Spaceman: The Perfect Bedtime Book! East, Nick, illus. 2017. (Goodnight Ser.). (ENG.). 32p. (J). (gr. -1 — 1). pap. 7.99 ***(978-1-4380-1086-1(9))*** Barron's Educational Series, Inc.
Robinson, R. M. Death by Paradox. 2014. (Illus.). 320p. (YA). 29.95 *(978-1-939434-14-2(9))* Firefall Editions.
Robson, Jenny. Savannah 2116 Ad. 2005. 144p. pap. *(978-0-624-04230-3(8))* Tafelberg Pubs., Ltd.
Roche, Nick, et al. Transformers: IDW Collection Phase Two Volume 3: IDW Collection Phase Two Volume 3. Milne, Alex & Salgado, Jimbo, illus. 2016. (Transformers Ser.: 3). (ENG.). 332p. 49.99 *(978-1-63140-540-2(3)*, 9781631405402) Idea & Design Works, LLC.
Rockwell, Carey. On the Trail of Space Pirates. Ley, Willy, ed. 2007. 140p. per. 11.95 *(978-1-60312-283-2(4))* Aegypan.
—On the Trail of Space Pirates. 2007. 140p. 24.95 *(978-1-60312-781-3(X))* Aegypan.
—The Revolt on Venus: The TOM CORBETT Space Cadet Adventure. 2007. (ENG.). 180p. pap. 19.99 *(978-1-4264-9548-9(X))*; 202p. pap. 22.99 *(978-1-4264-9929-6(9))* Creative Media Partners, LLC.
—Sabotage in Space. 2007. (ENG.). 162p. pap. 19.99 *(978-1-4264-9345-4(2))* Creative Media Partners, LLC.
—Sabotage in Space. 2007. 108p. per. *(978-1-4068-3959-3(0))* Echo Library.
Rockwell, Carey & Ley, Willy. The Space Pioneers: A Tom Corbett Space Cadet Adventure. Glanzman, Louis, illus. 2011. 220p. 44.95 *(978-1-258-10097-1(5))* Literary Licensing, LLC.
Rockwood, Roy. Lost on the Moon. 2008. 132p. pap. 10.95 *(978-1-60664-236-8(7))* Rodgers, Alan Bks.
—Through Space to Mars. 2008. 128p. (gr. 4-7). 23.95 *(978-1-60664-801-8(2))*; pap. 11.95 *(978-1-60664-173-6(5))* Aegypan.
Rodda, Emily. Isle of the Dead. 2004. (Dragons of Deltora Ser.: No. 3). 195p. (J). lib. bdg. 16.92 *(978-1-4242-0273-7(6))* Fitzgerald Bks.
—Shadowgate. 2004. (Dragons of Deltora Ser.: No. 2). 195p. (J). lib. bdg. 16.92 *(978-1-4242-0274-4(4))* Fitzgerald Bks.
Roe, David & Reader's Digest Editors. Mix & Match. Milne, Alex & Ruffolo, Rob, illus. 2007. (ENG.). 12p. (J). (gr. -1-1). bds. 14.99 *(978-0-7944-1286-9(6))* Reader's Digest Assn., Inc., The.
Rogers, Anne. The magic rainbow large Print. 2008. 332p. pap. 30.95 *(978-1-4092-3059-5(7))* Lulu Pr., Inc.
—The magic rainbow very large Print. 2008. 502p. pap. 39.50 *(978-1-4092-3065-6(1))* Lulu Pr., Inc.
Roland, Timothy. Monkey Me & the School Ghost. 2014. (Monkey Me Ser.: 4). (ENG.). 96p. (J). (gr. 1-3). pap. 4.99 *(978-0-545-55989-8(8))* Scholastic, Inc.
—Monkey Me & the School Ghost. Roland, Timothy, illus. 2014. (Monkey Me Ser.: 4). (ENG., Illus.). 96p. (J). (gr. 1-3). 15.99 *(978-0-545-55990-4(1))* Scholastic, Inc.
Rollins, James. Jake Ransom & the Howling Sphinx. 2012. (Jake Ransom Ser.: 2). (ENG.). 384p. (J). (gr. 5). pap. 7.99 *(978-0-06-147384-5(7))* HarperCollins Pubs.
Roman, Dave. Astronaut Academy: Re-Entry. Roman, Dave, illus. 2013. (Astronaut Academy Ser.: 2). (ENG., Illus.). 192p. (J). (gr. 5-9). pap. 9.99 *(978-1-59643-621-3(2)*, 9781596436213, First Second Bks.) Roaring Brook Pr.
—Zero Gravity. Roman, Dave, illus. 2011. (Astronaut Academy Ser.: 1). (ENG., Illus.). 192p. (J). (gr. 5-9). 17.99 *(978-1-59643-756-2(1)*, 9781596437562, First Second Bks.) Roaring Brook Pr.
Romita, John & Ditko, Steve, illus. X-Men - The Hidden Year, Vol. 2. 2012. (ENG.). 304p. (J). (gr. 4-17). pap. 34.99 *(978-0-7851-6055-7(8))* Marvel Worldwide, Inc.
Rooper, Leah. Jane Unwrapped. 2015. (ENG., Illus.). 290p. (J). pap. 16.99 *(978-1-943892-66-2(0))* Entangled Publishing, LLC.
Rose, Imogen. Initiation: Japanese Language Edition. Galeano, Tomomi, tr. 2013. 482p. pap. 16.99 *(978-1-940015-04-0(9))* Imogen Rose.
Rose, Kathryn. Camelot Burning. 2014. (Metal & Lace Novel Ser.: 1). (ENG.). 384p. (YA). pap. 9.99 *(978-0-7387-3967-0(7)*, Flux) North Star Editions.
Rose, Sue. Jinxed! 2006. (Unfabulous! Ser.). (Illus.). 118p. (J). *(978-1-4156-5170-4(1))* Scholastic, Inc.
Rosenberg, Michael. The Story of Bendalot Part: The Return Home. 2009. (Illus.). 36p. pap. 15.49 *(978-1-4389-8294-6(1))* AuthorHouse.
Rosenblum, Gregg. City 1. 2015. (Revolution 19 Ser.: 3). (ENG.). 288p. (YA). (gr. 8). 17.99 *(978-0-06-212601-6(6)*, HarperTeen) HarperCollins Pubs.
—Fugitive X. 2014. (Revolution 19 Ser.: 2). (ENG.). 272p. (YA). (gr. 8). 17.99 *(978-0-06-212597-2(4)*, HarperTeen) HarperCollins Pubs.
—Revolution 19. (Revolution 19 Ser.: 1). (ENG.). (YA). (gr. 8). 2014. 288p. pap. 9.99 *(978-0-06-212596-5(6))* 2013. 272p. 17.99 *(978-0-06-212595-8(8))* HarperCollins Pubs. (HarperTeen).
Rosenow, Ty. The Historical Adventures of Thomas Balfour. 2012. 186p. pap. 17.95 *(978-1-105-94011-8(X))* Lulu Pr., Inc.
Rosinski & Van Hamme, Jean. Child of the Stars. Rosinski, Adolf, illus. 2007. (Thorgal Ser.: 1). (ENG.). 96p. per. 19.95 *(978-1-905460-23-6(6))* CineBook GBR. Dist: National Bk. Network.
Ross, Joel. The Fog Diver. 2015. (Fog Diver Ser.: 1). (ENG.). 336p. (J). (gr. 3-7). 16.99 *(978-0-06-235293-4(8))* HarperCollins Pubs.
—The Fog Diver. 2016. (J). lib. bdg. 17.20 *(978-0-606-38745-3(5))* Turtleback Bks.
—The Lost Compass. 2016. (Fog Diver Ser.: 2). 352p. (J). (gr. 3-7). 16.99 *(978-0-06-235297-2(0))* HarperCollins Pubs.
Rossi, Veronica. Into the Still Blue. 2014. 392p. (YA). *(978-0-06-229518-7(7))* Harper & Row Ltd.
—Into the Still Blue. 2014. (Under the Never Sky Trilogy: Bk. 3). (ENG.). 400p. (J). (gr. 9). 17.99 *(978-0-06-207209-2(9))* HarperCollins Pubs.
—Under the Never Sky. 2012. (Under the Never Sky Trilogy Ser.: 1). (ENG.). (YA). (gr. 9). 400p. pap. 9.99 *(978-0-06-207204-7(8))*; 384p. 17.99 *(978-0-06-207203-0(X))* HarperCollins Pubs.
Rossing, Nina. Supermassive. 2016. (ENG., Illus.). (J). 27.99 ***(978-1-63533-076-2(9)***, Harmony Ink Pr.) Dreamspinner Pr.
Roth, Veronica. Allegiant. (Divergent Ser.: 3). (YA). (gr. 9). 2016. 592p. pap. 12.99 *(978-0-06-242009-1(7))* 2016. 592p. pap. 12.99 *(978-0-06-202407-7(8))* 2013. (ENG.). 544p. 19.99 *(978-0-06-202406-0(X))* 2016. 592p. 19.99 *(978-0-06-242008-4(9))* HarperCollins Pubs. (Tegen, Katherine Bks).
—Allegiant. Lt. ed. 2016. (Divergent Ser.: 3). (ENG.). 580p. pap. 12.99 *(978-1-59413-960-4(1)*, Large Print Pr.) Thorndike Pr.
—Allegiant. 2016. (Divergent Ser.: 3). lib. bdg. 24.50 *(978-0-606-38141-3(4))*; lib. bdg. 24.50 *(978-0-606-38182-6(1))* Turtleback Bks.

—Carve the Mark. 2017. (YA). (gr. 9). 512p. pap. 12.99 **(978-0-06-234864-7(7))**; (ENG.). 480p. 22.99 *(978-0-06-234863-0(9))* HarperCollins Pubs. (Tegen, Katherine Bks).
—Divergent. 2013. (KOR.). **(978-89-5660-710-8(9))** Eunhaeng Namu Publishing Co.
—Divergent. Delort, Nicolas, photos by. 2014. (Divergent Ser.: 1). (ENG., Illus.). 576p. (YA). (gr. 9). pap. 12.99 *(978-0-06-238724-0(3)*, Tegen, Katherine Bks) HarperCollins Pubs.
—Divergent. 2012. (ENG.). 512p. pap. *(978-0-06-219406-0(2))* HarperCollins Pubs.
—Divergent, 3 vols. Delort, Nicolas, photos by. (Divergent Ser.: 1). (ENG., Illus.). (YA). (gr. 9-18). 2011. 496p. 17.99 *(978-0-06-202402-2(7))* 2014. 576p. 19.99 *(978-0-06-235217-0(2))* HarperCollins Pubs. (Tegen, Katherine Bks).
—Divergent. movie tie-in ed. 2014. (Divergent Ser.: Bk. 1). (ENG.). 496p. (YA). (gr. 9). 17.99 *(978-0-06-226984-1(5)*, Tegen, Katherine Bks) HarperCollins Pubs.
—Divergent. 1. 2012. (ENG.). 496p. *(978-0-00-742042-1(0))* HarperCollins Pubs. Ltd.
—Divergent. 2009. (Divergent Ser.: Bk. 1). 11.04 *(978-0-7848-3786-3(4)*, Everbind) Marco Bk. Co.
—Divergent. 2014. (Divergent Trilogy Ser.). (ENG.). (YA). (gr. 9). lib. bdg. 23.60 **(978-1-62765-593-4(X))** Perfection Learning Corp.
—Divergent. l.t. ed. 2014. (Divergent Ser.: Bk. 1). (ENG.). 530p. pap. 12.99 *(978-1-59413-745-7(5)*, Large Print Pr.) Thorndike Pr.
—Divergent. 2014. (Divergent Ser.: 1). (YA). lib. bdg. 24.50 *(978-0-606-36515-4(X))* Turtleback Bks.
—Divergent; Insurgent; Allegiant, 3 vols., Set. 2013. (Divergent Ser.: Bks. 1-3). (ENG.). (YA). (gr. 9). 55.97 *(978-0-06-227878-4(9)*, Tegen, Katherine Bks) HarperCollins Pubs.
—Divergente. 2013. (Divergent Ser.: Bk. 1).Tr. of Divergent. (SPA.). 464p. (YA). pap. 21.99 *(978-84-272-0118-7(4))* Molino, Editorial ESP. Dist: Lectorum Pubns., Inc.
—Four: A Divergent Collection: The Transfer; The Initiate; The Son; The Traitor. 2014. (Divergent Ser.). (ENG.). 304p. (J). (gr. 9). 17.99 *(978-0-06-234521-9(4))* HarperCollins Pubs.
—Insurgent. 2014. (KOR.). **(978-89-5660-758-0(3))** Eunhaeng Namu Publishing Co.
—Insurgent. 2015. pap. *(978-0-06-238845-2(2))* 2015. (Divergent Ser.: 2). (ENG.). 592p. (J). (gr. 9). pap. 12.99 *(978-0-06-202405-3(1))* 2012. (Divergent Ser.: 2). (ENG.). 544p. (YA). (gr. 9). 17.99 *(978-0-06-202404-6(3))* 2012. (Divergent Ser.: 2). 544p. (YA). (gr. 9). pap. 12.00 *(978-0-06-212784-6(5))* 2012. (Divergent Ser.: 2). (ENG.). 592p. (YA). (gr. 9). 19.99 *(978-0-06-223493-3(5))* 2015. (Divergent Ser.: 2). (ENG.). 544p. (YA). (gr. 9). 17.99 *(978-0-06-237284-0(X))* 2015. (Divergent Ser.: Bk. 2). (ENG.). 592p. (YA). (gr. 9). pap. 12.99 *(978-0-06-237285-7(8))* HarperCollins Pubs. (Tegen, Katherine Bks).
—Insurgent. 2015. (Divergent Trilogy Ser.). (ENG.). (YA). (gr. 9). lib. bdg. 23.60 **(978-1-62765-988-8(9))** Perfection Learning Corp.
—Insurgent. 2015. (Divergent Ser.: 2). (YA). lib. bdg. 24.50 *(978-0-606-36475-1(7))* Turtleback Bks.
Routley, Becky. Moon Golf. 2009. (Illus.). 28p. pap. 12.49 *(978-1-4490-4713-9(0))* AuthorHouse.
Roza, Greg. The Messy Robot. 2006. (Neighborhood Readers Ser.). (ENG., Illus.). 16p. (gr. 1-3). pap. 6.50 *(978-1-4042-7184-5(8)*, Rosen Classroom) Rosen Publishing Group, Inc., The.
Rubin, Lance. Denton Little's Deathdate. 2015. (ENG.). 352p. (YA). (gr. 9). 17.99 *(978-0-553-49696-3(4)*, Knopf Bks. for Young Readers) Random Hse. Children's Bks.
Ruby, Laura. York: The Shadow Cipher. 2017. (York Ser.: 1). (ENG.). 496p. (J). (gr. 3-7). E-Book *(978-0-06-230695-1(2)*, Waldon Pond Pr.) HarperCollins Pubs.
—York: The Shadow Cipher. Stevenson, Dave, illus. 2017. (York Ser.: 1). 496p. (J). (gr. 3-7). 17.99 *(978-0-06-230693-7(6)*, Waldon Pond Pr.) HarperCollins Pubs.
Rucka, Greg. Journey to Star Wars: The Force Awakens — Shattered Empire. 2015. (Star Wars Graphic Novels Ser.). (YA). lib. bdg. 29.40 *(978-0-606-37933-5(9))* Turtleback Bks.
Runberg, Sylvain. Orbital Vol. 1: Scars. Saincatin, Jerome, tr. from FRE. Pellé, Serge, illus. 2009. (Orbital Ser.: 1). (ENG.). 47p. pap. 11.95 *(978-1-905460-89-2(9))* CineBook GBR. Dist: National Bk. Network.
—Orbital Vol. 5: Justice. Pelle, Serge, illus. 2014. (Orbital Ser.: 5). (ENG.). 56p. pap. 13.95 *(978-1-84918-172-3(1))* CineBook GBR. Dist: National Bk. Network.
Rush, Jennifer. Altered. 2013. (Altered Ser.: 1). (ENG.). (YA). (gr. 7-17). 352p. pap. 10.00 *(978-0-316-19709-0(2))*; 336p. 18.00 *(978-0-316-19708-3(4))* Little, Brown Bks. for Young Readers.
Russell, P. M. The Wormhole Adventures: Travel Is Relative. 2007. 57p. pap. 16.95 *(978-1-60441-426-4(X))* America Star Bks.
Russell, Romina. Black Moon. 2016. (Zodiac Ser.: 3). (ENG.). 320p. (YA). (gr. 7). 18.99 *(978-1-59514-745-5(4)*, Razorbill) Penguin Young Readers Group.
—Zodiac. 2014. (Zodiac Ser.: 1). (ENG.). 336p. (YA). (gr. 7). 17.99 *(978-1-59514-740-0(3)*, Razorbill) Penguin Young Readers Group.
Russell, Romina & Loftin, Nikki. Wandering Star. 2015. (Zodiac Ser.: 2). (ENG., Illus.). 320p. (YA). (gr. 7). 18.99 *(978-1-59514-743-1(8)*, Razorbill) Penguin Young Readers Group.
—Zodiac. 2015. (Zodiac Ser.: 1). (ENG.). 480p. (YA). (gr. 7). pap. 10.99 *(978-1-59514-741-7(1)*, Razorbill) Penguin Young Readers Group.
Rust, Ned. Patrick Griffin's First Birthday on Ith. 2017. (Patrick Griffin & the Three Worlds Ser.: 2). (ENG.). 304p. (J). 16.99 *(978-1-62672-344-3(3)*, 9781626723443) Roaring Brook Pr.
Rutkoski, Marie. The Shadow Society. 2013. (ENG.). 448p. (YA). (gr. 7-12). pap. 9.99 *(978-1-250-03424-3(8))* Square Fish.
Ryan, Amy Kathleen. Flame. 2014. (Sky Chasers Ser.: 3). (ENG.). 336p. (YA). (gr. 7). 18.99 *(978-0-312-62136-0(1)*, 9780312621360, St. Martin's Griffin) St. Martin's Pr.
—Spark: A Sky Chasers Novel. 2013. (Sky Chasers Ser.: 2). (ENG.). 320p. (YA). (gr. 7). pap. 9.99 *(978-1-250-03195-2(8)*, 9781250031952, St. Martin's Griffin) St. Martin's Pr.
Ryan, Jeanne. Charisma. 2015. (ENG.). 384p. (YA). (gr. 7). 17.99 *(978-0-8037-3966-6(4)*, Dial Bks) Penguin Young Readers Group.
Ryan, Paul, et al, illus. Iron Man Epic Collection: War Games. 2014. (ENG.). 504p. (J). (gr. 4-17). pap. 39.99 *(978-0-7851-8550-5(X))* Marvel Worldwide, Inc.
—Squadron Supreme. 2013. (ENG.). 368p. (J). (gr. 4-17). pap. 34.99 *(978-0-7851-8469-0(4))* Marvel Worldwide, Inc.
Rymer, Alta M. Stars of Obron: Chambo Returns. Rymer, Alta M., illus. (Tales of Planet Artembo Ser.: Bk. 3). (Illus.). 56p. (Orig.). (J). (gr. 5-7). pap. 20.00 *(978-0-9600792-3-0(8))* Rymer Bks.
Said, S. F. Phoenix. McKean, Dave, illus. 2016. (ENG.). 496p. (J). (gr. 5). 19.99 *(978-0-7636-8850-9(9))* Candlewick Pr.
Saito, Chiho. Revolutionary Girl Utena. Be-Papas, illus. 2003. (Revolutionary Girl Utena Ser.: 3). (ENG.). 200p. pap. 9.95 *(978-1-56931-812-6(3))* Viz Media.
Sala, Richard. Cat Burglar Black. Sala, Richard, illus. 2009. (ENG., Illus.). 128p. (J). (gr. 6-9). pap. 17.99 *(978-1-59643-144-7(X)*, 9781596431447, First Second Bks.) Roaring Brook Pr.
Salwi, Dilip. Meet the Four Elements (English) 2nd ed. 2013. (ENG.). 64p. (J). (gr. 4-6). pap. 6.95 *(978-81-8332-876-0(8))* Ratna, Sagar Pvt. Ltd. IND. Dist: Midpoint Trade Bks., Inc.
—Meet the Four Elements (Hindi) 2nd ed. 2013. (ENG.). 64p. (J). (gr. 4-6). pap. 6.95 *(978-81-8332-878-4(4))* Ratna, Sagar Pvt. Ltd. IND. Dist: Midpoint Trade Bks., Inc.
Samphire, Patrick. The Emperor of Mars. Holmes, Jeremy, illus. 2017. (Secrets of the Dragon Tomb Ser.). (ENG.). 368p. (J). 16.99 *(978-0-8050-9908-9(5)*, 9780805099089, Holt, Henry & Co. Bks. For Young Readers) Holt, Henry & Co.
—Secrets of the Dragon Tomb. Holmes, Jeremy, illus. 2016. (ENG.). 336p. (J). (gr. 5-8). 16.99 *(978-0-8050-9906-5(9)*, 9780805099065, Holt, Henry & Co. Bks. For Young Readers) Holt, Henry & Co.
Sampson, Jeff. Havoc: A Deviants Novel. 2012. (Deviants Ser.: 2). (ENG.). 352p. (YA). (gr. 8). 17.99 *(978-0-06-199278-0(X))* HarperCollins Pubs.
—Ravage: A Deviants Novel. 2013. (Deviants Ser.: 3). (ENG.). 400p. (YA). (gr. 8). 17.99 *(978-0-06-199280-3(1))* HarperCollins Pubs.
—Vesper: A Deviants Novel. 2011. (Deviants Ser.: 1). (ENG.). 320p. (YA). (gr. 8). pap. 8.99 *(978-0-06-199277-3(1))* HarperCollins Pubs.
Sanderson, Brandon. Calamity. 2016. (Reckoners Ser.: Bk. 3). (ENG.). 432p. (YA). (gr. 7). lib. bdg. 21.99 *(978-0-375-99123-3(9))*; 18.99 *(978-0-385-74360-0(2))* Random Hse. Children's Bks. (Delacorte Pr.).
—Firefight. 2016. (SPA.). 432p. pap. 28.95 *(978-84-666-5836-2(X))* Ediciones B ESP. Dist: Spanish Pubs., LLC.
—Firefight. (Reckoners Ser.: Bk. 2). (ENG.). (YA). (gr. 7). 2016. 448p. pap. 10.99 *(978-0-385-74359-4(9)*, Ember) 2015. 432p. 18.99 *(978-0-385-74358-7(0)*, Delacorte Pr.) Random Hse. Children's Bks.
—Firefight. 2016. (Reckoners Ser.: 2). lib. bdg. 22.10 *(978-0-606-38447-6(2))* Turtleback Bks.
—The Reckoners, 3 vols. 2016. (ENG.). (YA). (gr. 7). 56.97 *(978-0-399-55168-0(9)*, Delacorte Pr.) Random Hse. Children's Bks.
—Steelheart. (SPA.). 416p. pap. 27.95 *(978-84-666-5296-4(5))*; 2015. pap. 14.95 *(978-84-9070-095-2(8))* Ediciones B ESP. Dist: Spanish Pubs., LLC.
—Steelheart. 2013. 386p. (YA). *(978-0-385-38371-4(1)*, Delacorte Pr) Random House Publishing Group.
—Steelheart. (Reckoners Ser.: 1). (ENG.). (YA). (gr. 7). 2014. 416p. pap. 9.99 *(978-0-385-74357-0(2)*, Ember) 2013. 400p. 18.99 *(978-0-385-74356-3(4)*, Delacorte Pr.) Random Hse. Children's Bks.
—Steelheart. 2014. (Reckoners Ser.: 1). lib. bdg. 20.85 *(978-0-606-36027-2(1))* Turtleback Bks.
Sandford, John, pseud & Cook, Michele. Outrage. 2015. (Singular Menace Ser.: Bk. 2). (ENG.). 336p. (YA). (gr. 9). 18.99 *(978-0-385-75309-8(8)*, Knopf Bks. for Young Readers) Random Hse. Children's Bks.
—Rampage. (Singular Menace Ser.: 3). (ENG.). 336p. (YA). (gr. 9). 2017. pap. 10.99 *(978-0-385-75315-9(2)*, Ember) 2016. 18.99 *(978-0-385-75313-5(6)*, Knopf Bks. for Young Readers) Random Hse. Children's Bks.
—Uncaged. (Singular Menace Ser.: Bk. 1). (ENG.). 416p. (gr. 9). 2015. (YA). pap. 10.99 *(978-0-385-75305-0(5)*, Ember) 2014. (J). 18.99 *(978-0-385-75306-7(3)*, Knopf Bks. for Young Readers) 2014. (YA). lib. bdg. 21.99 *(978-0-385-75307-4(1)*, Knopf Bks. for Young Readers) Random Hse. Children's Bks.
Sandler, Karen. Awakening. 2013. (ENG.). 400p. (YA). 18.95 *(978-1-60060-982-4(1)*, Tu Bks.) Lee & Low Bks., Inc.
—Rebellion, 1 vol. 2014. (Tankbom Trilogy Ser.). (ENG.). 400p. (YA). 18.95 *(978-1-60060-984-8(8))* Lee & Low Bks., Inc.
Sanna, Alessandro, illus. Pinocchio: The Origin Story. 2016. (ENG.). 48p. (J). (gr. k-9). 19.95 *(978-1-59270-191-9(4))* Enchanted Lion Bks., LLC.
Sant, Sharon. Runners. 2013. 286p. pap. *(978-1-907737-52-7(9))* Immanion Pr.
Santos, Ray. I Am Green Lantern. 2013. (Justice League Classic: I Can Read! Ser.). (J). lib. bdg. 13.55 *(978-0-606-32152-5(7)*, Turtleback) Turtleback Bks.
Sargent, Pamela. Farseed. 2013. (Seed Trilogy Ser.: 2). (ENG.). 288p. (YA). (gr. 8-12). pap. 9.99 *(978-0-7653-3216-5(7)*, 9780765332165, Tor Teen) Doherty, Tom Assocs., LLC.
—Homesmind (Watchstar Trilogy: Book 3) 2010. 200p. pap. 16.95 *(978-0-7592-1542-9(1))* Open Road Integrated Media, Inc.
Sarracini, Chris & Furman, Simon. Transformers: Armada Omnibus: Armada Omnibus. Raiz, James et al, illus. 2016. (Transformers Ser.). (ENG.). 416p. pap. 29.99 *(978-1-63140-563-1(2)*, 9781631405631) Idea & Design Works, LLC.
Sasaki, Chris & Wells, H. G. The War of the Worlds. Akib, Jamel, illus. 2007. (Classic Starts Ser.). 151p. (J). *(978-1-4287-4208-6(5))* Sterling Publishing Co., Inc.
Satriani, Zack. The Hidden Enemy. 2013. (ENG.). 256p. (J). (gr. 4-6). pap. 8.99 *(978-1-4449-0660-8(7))* Hodder & Stoughton GBR. Dist: Hachette Bk. Group.
—The Invasion. 2013. (ENG., Illus.). 288p. (J). (gr. 4-6). pap. 8.99 *(978-1-4449-0662-2(3))* Hodder & Stoughton GBR. Dist: Hachette Bk. Group.
Saunders, Catherine. The Story of Darth Vader. 2015. (Star Wars DK Readers Level 3 Ser.). lib. bdg. 13.55 *(978-0-606-37409-5(4))* Turtleback Bks.
Saunders, Catherine & Stock, Lisa. Are Ewoks Scared of Storm Troopers? 2013. (DK Readers Ser.). (ENG.). 32p. (J). (gr. k-4). pap. 3.99 *(978-1-4654-1415-1(0)*, DK Children) Dorling Kindersley Publishing, Inc.
—Are Ewoks Scared of Stormtroopers? 2013. (DK Readers Ser.). (ENG.). 32p. (J). (gr. k-4). 14.99 *(978-1-4654-1416-8(9)*, DK Children) Dorling Kindersley Publishing, Inc.
Saunders, Jami Lynn. Feral: Book I of the Werecat Saga. 2011. 86p. (YA). pap. 4.99 *(978-1-936307-15-9(4)*, 711Press) Vendera Publishing.
—Rabid: Book II of the Werecat Saga. 2012. 94p. (YA). pap. 4.99 *(978-1-936307-16-6(2)*, 711Press) Vendera Publishing.
Sava, Scott Christian. Hyperactive. 2008. (Illus.). 112p. 12.95 *(978-0-9789168-4-8(0))* Blue Dream Studios.
—My Grandparents Are Secret Agents. 2008. (Illus.). 112p. (J). 12.95 *(978-0-9789168-6-2(7))* Blue Dream Studios.
Savage, J. Scott. Fires of Invention. 2016. (Mysteries of Cove Ser.: 1). (Illus.). 320p. (J). pap. 7.99 *(978-1-62972-156-9(5)*, Shadow Mountain) Deseret Bk. Co.
—Gears of Revolution. 2016. (Mysteries of Cove Ser.: 2). 342p. (J). 17.99 *(978-1-62972-223-8(5)*, Shadow Mountain) Deseret Bk. Co.
Saxon, Lucy. The Almost King. 2016. (ENG., Illus.). 400p. (YA). (gr. 7-12). 17.99 *(978-1-61963-627-9(1)*, 9781619636279, Bloomsbury USA Childrens) Bloomsbury Publishing USA.
Sazaklis, John. The Biggest Little Hero, 1 vol. Baltazar, Art, illus. 2012. (DC Super-Pets Ser.). (ENG.). 56p. (gr. 2-2). pap. 4.95 *(978-1-4048-7664-4(2))*; lib. bdg. 23.99 *(978-1-4048-6490-0(3))* Picture Window Bks. (DC Super-Pets).
—Transformers: Rescue Bots: the Ghosts of Griffin Rock. 2014. (ENG., Illus.). 24p. (J). (gr. -1-3). pap. 3.99 *(978-0-316-27704-4(5))* Little, Brown Bks. for Young Readers.
Sazaklis, John, retold by. Marvel Ultimate Spider-Man: Spider-Man & His Amazing Friends. 2016. (ENG.). 80p. (J). (gr. 1-4). pap. 6.99 *(978-0-7944-3391-8(X))* Studio Fun International.
Sazaklis, John & Foxe, Steve. Transformers Robots in Disguise: Chapter Book #3. 2015. (ENG.). 144p. (J). (gr. 3-7). pap. 5.99 *(978-0-316-30192-3(2))* Little, Brown Bks. for Young Readers.
Scarborough, R. A. Starblade: The Beginning, 1 vol. 2010. 128p. pap. 19.95 *(978-1-4489-3906-0(2))* America Star Bks.
Schade, Susan. Simon's Dream. Buller, Jon, illus. 2009. (Fog Mound Ser.: 3). (ENG.). 208p. (J). (gr. 3-7). pap. 12.99 *(978-0-689-87689-9(0)*, Aladdin) Simon & Schuster Children's Publishing.
—Travels of Thelonious. Buller, Jon, illus. 2007. (Fog Mound Ser.: 1). (ENG.). 224p. (J). (gr. 3-7). pap. 11.99 *(978-0-689-87685-1(8)*, Aladdin) Simon & Schuster Children's Publishing.
Schade, Susan & Buller, Jon. Faradawn. 2008. (Fog Mound Ser.: 2). (ENG., Illus.). 208p. (J). (gr. 3-7). pap. 12.99 *(978-0-689-87687-5(4)*, Aladdin) Simon & Schuster Children's Publishing.
Schaefer, Elizabeth. The Force Awakens: Episode VII. White, Dave, illus. 2016. (LEGO Star Wars 8X8 Ser.). (ENG.). 24p. (J). (gr. -1-3). 13.55 *(978-0-606-39117-7(7))* Turtleback Bks.
—Star Wars: the Phantom Menace Read-Along Storybook & CD. Rood, Brian, illus. 2017. (Read-Along Storybook & CD Ser.). (ENG.). 32p. (J). (gr. 1-3). pap. 6.99 *(978-1-4847-8182-1(1)*, Disney Lucasfilm Press) Disney Publishing Worldwide.
Schanback, Mindy. Princess from Another Planet. 2005. (ENG.). 254p. (J). (gr. 5-9). 16.95 *(978-0-8234-1847-3(2))* Holiday Hse., Inc.
Schembra, John. A Vince Torelli Novel Book 2: Retribution. Cummins, Sandy, ed. 2007. (Shadows Trilogy). (ENG.). pap. *(978-1-876962-68-5(2)*, Writers Exchange) Writers Exchange E-Publishing.
Schindler, Roslyn. Zeon. Schindler, Roslyn, illus. 2013. (Illus.). 28p. pap. 13.95 *(978-1-61493-192-8(5))* Peppertree Pr., The.
Schleich, James J. The Sound Man. (Illus.). 64p. (J). pap. 7.00 *(978-0-615-12142-0(X))* Schleich, James.
Schmitz, James H. Trigger & Friends. 2004. (ENG.). 480p. mass mkt. 6.99 *(978-0-671-31966-3(3))* Baen Bks.
Schneider, John Lee. Extinction: Dragons of Earth: A Novel. 2005. 173p. (YA). pap. *(978-1-890109-79-0(7)*, Cross Time) Crossquarter Publishing Group.
Schoening, Dan, illus. Green Lantern, 12 vols., Set. Incl. Battle of the Blue Lanterns. Acampora, Michael V. lib. bdg. 26.65 *(978-1-4342-2608-2(5))*; Beware Our Power! Sonnebom, Scott. 26.65 *(978-1-4342-2607-5(7))*; Escape from the Orange Lanterns. Acampora, Michael Vincent. lib. bdg. 26.65 *(978-1-4342-2622-8(0))*; Fear the Shark. Sutton, Laurie S. lib. bdg. 26.65 *(978-1-4342-2620-4(4))*; Guardian of Earth. Dahl, Michael. lib. bdg. 26.65 *(978-1-4342-2611-2(5))*; High-Tech Terror. Steele, Michael A. lib. bdg. 26.65 *(978-1-4342-2609-9(3))*; Last Super Hero. Dahl, Michael. lib. bdg. 26.65 *(978-1-4342-2612-9(3))*; Light King Strikes! Sutton, Laurie S. lib. bdg. 26.65 *(978-1-4342-2610-5(7))*; Prisoner of the Ring. Sonnebom, Scott. lib. bdg. 26.65 *(978-1-4342-2624-2(7))*; Red Lanterns' Revenge. Acampora, Michael Vincent. lib. bdg. 26.65 *(978-1-4342-2623-5(9))*; Savage Sands. Bright, J. E. lib. bdg. 26.65 *(978-1-4342-2619-8(0))*; Web of Doom. Steele, Michael A. lib. bdg. 26.65 *(978-1-4342-2621-1(2))*; (Illus.). (gr. 2-3)., DC Super Heroes (Green Lantern Ser.). (ENG.). 56p. 2011. Set lib. bdg. 319.80 *(978-1-4342-3240-3(9))* Stone Arch Bks.
Scholastic & Howard, Kate. Fright Knight!, Bk. 2. 2016. (LEGO NEXO Knights Ser.). (ENG.). 80p. (J). (gr. 2-5). pap. 4.99 *(978-0-545-92555-6(X))* Scholastic, Inc.
Scholastic Editors. Space Justice! 2015. (LEGO DC Super Heroes Ser.). lib. bdg. 13.55 *(978-0-606-37077-6(3))* Turtleback Bks.
Scholastic Inc, contrib. by. The Complete Saga. 2011. (Star Wars Ser.). (ENG., Illus.). 96p. (J). (— 1). pap. 12.99 *(978-0-545-35631-2(8))* Scholastic, Inc.
Scholastic, Inc. Staff. Lightsabers: A Guide to Weapons of the Force. 2010. (Star Wars Ser.). (ENG., Illus.). 64p. (J). pap., instr.'s gde. ed. 8.99 *(978-0-545-27177-6(0))* Scholastic, Inc.
Scholastic, Inc. Staff, contrib. by. 1, 2, 3. 2012. (Star Wars Ser.). (ENG., Illus.). 26p. (J). (gr. -1-3). bds. 12.99 *(978-0-545-41878-2(X))* Scholastic, Inc.
Scholastic, Inc. Staff, ed. Chicken Soup for Little Souls: The Never Forgotten Doll. Date not set. (Star Wars Ser.). (J). pap. 4.95 *(978-0-590-39635-6(8))* Scholastic, Inc.
Scholastic, Inc. Staff & Ameet Studio Staff. NEXO Powers Rule! 2016. (LEGO NEXO Knights Ser.). (ENG.). 32p. (J). (gr. 2-5). pap., act. bk. ed. 8.99 *(978-0-545-90584-8(2))* Scholastic, Inc.
Scholastic, Inc. Staff & Fry, Jason. Darth Maul - Shadow Conspiracy. 2013. (Star Wars Ser.). (ENG.). 160p. (J). (gr. 3-7). pap. 5.99 *(978-0-545-47063-6(3))* Scholastic, Inc.
Scholastic, Inc. Staff & Howard, Kate. Ratchet & Clank. 2016. (ENG.). 144p. (J). (gr. 2-5). pap. 5.99 *(978-1-338-03041-9(8))* Scholastic, Inc.
Scholastic, Inc. Staff & Marsham, Liz. Movie Flip Book. 2016. (Batman vs. Superman: Dawn of Justice Ser.). (ENG.). 112p. (J). (gr. 3-7). pap. 9.99 *(978-0-545-91627-1(5))* Scholastic, Inc.
Scholastic, Inc. Staff & Rusu, Meredith. Ratchet & Clank: Hero Time. 2016. (ENG., Illus.). 48p. (J). (gr. -1-3). pap. 4.99 *(978-1-338-03042-6(6))* Scholastic, Inc.
Scholastic, Inc. Staff & Schmidt, Rebecca L. The Power of the Fortrex. 2016. (Scholastic Reader, Level 2 Ser.: 1). (ENG.). 32p. (J). (gr. 1-3). pap. 3.99 *(978-0-545-93338-4(2))* Scholastic, Inc.
Scholastic, Inc. Staff & West, Tracey. Graduation Day, Bk. 1. 2016. (LEGO NEXO Knights Ser.). (ENG.). 80p. (J). (gr. 2-5). pap. 4.99 *(978-0-545-92554-9(1))* Scholastic, Inc.
Scholastic, Inc. Staff & Wheeler, Alex. Hostage. 2009. (Star Wars: Rebel For Ser.: 2). (ENG.). 176p. (J). (gr. 3-7). 6.99 *(978-0-545-11218-5(4))* Scholastic, Inc.
Schoon, Christian. Under Nameless Stars. 2014. (ENG.). 368p. (J). (gr. 9). pap. 9.99 *(978-1-908844-87-3(6)*, Strange Chemistry) Watkins Media Limited GBR. Dist: Penguin Random Hse. LLC.
Schraff, Anne. Roses Red As Blood (Suspense), 1 vol. 2017. (Pageturners Ser.). (ENG.). 76p. (YA). (gr. 9-12). 8.95 **(978-1-68021-405-5(5))** Saddleback Educational Publishing, Inc.
Schwartz, Tom. Spaceship Earth: A Beginning Without End. 2010. 172p. pap. 10.99 *(978-1-57545-151-0(4))*; 19.99 *(978-1-57545-143-5(3))* RP Media. (Reagent Pr. Bks. for Young Readers).
Schweizer, Chris. The Creeps: Curse of the Attack-O-Lanterns. 2016. (Creeps Ser.: 3). (ENG., Illus.). 128p. (J). (gr. 3-7). 17.95 *(978-1-4197-2190-8(9)*, Amulet Bks.) Abrams, Inc.
Scieszka, Jon. Baloney (Henry P.) Smith, Lane, illus. 2005. (ENG.). 40p. (J). (gr. k-k). pap. 6.99 *(978-0-14-240430-0(6)*, Puffin Books) Penguin Young Readers Group.
—The Brain Turbo. Biggs, Brian, illus. 2015. (Frank Einstein Ser.). (ENG.). 192p. (J). (gr. 3-7). 13.95 *(978-1-4197-1643-0(3)*, Amulet Bks.) Abrams, Inc.
—Frank Einstein & the Antimatter Motor. Biggs, Brian, illus. 2014. (Frank Einstein Ser.: 1). (ENG.). 192p. (J). (gr. 2-6). 13.95 *(978-1-4197-1218-0(7)*, Amulet Bks.) Abrams, Inc.
—Frank Einstein & the Antimatter Motor. 2017. (Frank Einstein Ser.: 1). (J). lib. bdg. 18.40 **(978-0-606-39683-7(7))** Turtleback Bks.
—Frank Einstein & the Electro-Finger. Biggs, Brian, illus. 2015. (Frank Einstein Ser.: 2). (ENG.). 176p. (J). (gr. 3-7). 13.95 *(978-1-4197-1483-2(X)*, Amulet Bks.) Abrams, Inc.
—Frank Einstein & the Evoblaster Belt, Bk. 4. Biggs, Brian, illus. 2016. (Frank Einstein Ser.). (ENG.). 208p. (J). (gr. 3-7). pap. 7.95 *(978-1-4197-2379-7(0))* Abrams, Inc.
—Frank Einstein & the EvoBlaster Belt (Frank Einstein Series #4) Book Four. Biggs, Brian, illus. 2016. (Frank Einstein Ser.). (ENG.). 208p. (J). (gr. 3-7). 13.95 *(978-1-4197-1887-8(8)*, Amulet Bks.) Abrams, Inc.
—Frank Einstein & the EvoBlaster Belt (Frank Einstein Series #4) Book Four. Biggs, Brian, illus. 2017. (Frank Einstein Ser.). (ENG.). 224p. (J). (gr. 3-7). pap. 7.99 **(978-1-4197-2736-8(2)**, Amulet Bks.) Abrams, Inc.
Scieszka, Jon. It's All Greek to Me, No. 8. Smith, Lane, illus. 2004. (Time Warp Trio Ser.: 8). (ENG.). 80p. (J). (gr. 2-4). pap. 5.99 *(978-0-14-240116-3(1)*, Puffin Books) Penguin Young Readers Group.
Scieszka, Jon & Brian Biggs. Frank Einstein & the Electro-Finger. 2017. (Frank Einstein Ser.: 2). (J). lib. bdg. 18.40 **(978-0-606-39684-4(5))** Turtleback Bks.
Scollon, William. Doc Mcstuffins: Starry, Starry Night. 2014. (World of Reading Ser.). (Illus.). 32p. (J). lib. bdg. 13.55 *(978-0-606-35257-4(0))* Turtleback Bks.
Searles, Rachel. The Lost Planet. 2014. (Lost Planet Ser.: 1). (ENG.). 384p. (YA). (gr. 4-8). 16.99 *(978-1-250-03879-1(0)*, 9781250038791) Feiwel & Friends.
—The Stolen Moon. 2015. (Lost Planet Ser.: 2). (ENG.). 368p. (YA). (gr. 4-9). 15.99 *(978-1-250-03880-7(4)*, 9781250038807) Feiwel & Friends.
Sedgwick, Marcus. The Ghosts of Heaven. 2015. (ENG.). 336p. (YA). (gr. 7-12). 17.99 *(978-1-62672-125-8(4)*, 9781626721258) Roaring Brook Pr.
—The Ghosts of Heaven. 2016. (ENG.). 384p. (YA). pap. 9.99 *(978-1-250-07367-9(7)*, 9781250073679) Square Fish.
Seegert, Scott & Martin, John. Sci-Fi Junior High. 2017. (Sci-Fi Junior High Ser.: 1). (ENG., Illus.). 320p. (J). (gr. 3-7). 13.99 *(978-0-316-31516-6(8)*, Jimmy Patterson) Little Brown & Co.
Semionov, Vladimir & Louie, Wes, illus. Forecast from Stonehenge. 2007. (Choose Your Own Adventure Ser.: No. 19). 127p. (J). (gr. 4-7). pap. 6.99 *(978-1-933390-19-2(0))* Chooseco LLC.
Senior, Patricia. Mischief on Mumpit Mountain. 2009. 36p. pap. 14.75 *(978-1-60693-661-0(1)*, Eloquent Bks.) Strategic Book Publishing & Rights Agency (SBPRA).
Service, Pamela F. Alien Contact. Gorman, Mike, illus. (Alien Agent Ser.: 5). (ENG.). 144p. (J). (gr. 4-6). 2010. lib. bdg. 16.95 *(978-0-7613-5363-8(1)*, Carolrhoda Bks.)No. 5. 2011.

pap. 5.95 *(978-0-7613-7297-4(0)*, Darby Creek) Lerner Publishing Group.

—Alien Encounter. Gorman, Mike, illus. (Alien Agent Ser.: 4). (ENG.). 152p. (J). (gr. 4-6). 2011. pap. 5.95 *(978-0-7613-5248-8(1))* 2010. 16.95 *(978-0-8225-8873-3(0)*, Carolrhoda Bks.) Lerner Publishing Group.

—Alien Envoy. Gorman, Mike, illus. (Alien Agent Ser.). 176p. (J). (gr. 4-6). 2012. pap. 33.92 *(978-0-7613-9208-8(4)*, Darby Creek) 2012. (ENG.). pap. 5.95 *(978-0-7613-7298-1(9)*, Darby Creek) 2011. (ENG.). 16.95 *(978-0-7613-5364-5(X))* Lerner Publishing Group.

—Alien Expedition. 2010. pap. 33.92 *(978-0-7613-6958-5(9))* Lerner Publishing Group.

—Alien Expedition. Gorman, Mike, illus. (Alien Agent Ser.: 3). (ENG.). 160p. (J). (gr. 4-6). 2009. 16.95 *(978-0-8225-8870-2(6))*No. 3. 2010. pap. 5.95 *(978-0-7613-5249-5(X))* Lerner Publishing Group. (Carolrhoda Bks.).

—Camp Alien. 2010. pap. 33.92 *(978-0-7613-6955-4(4))* Lerner Publishing Group.

—Camp Alien. Gorman, Mike, illus. 2010. (Alien Agent Ser.: 2). (ENG.). 160p. (J). (gr. 4-6). pap. 5.95 *(978-0-7613-5247-1(3))* Lerner Publishing Group.

—Escape from Planet Yastol, No. 1. Gorman, Mike, illus. 2011. (Way-Too-Real Aliens Ser.: 1). (ENG.). 112p. (J). (gr. 4-6). 15.95 *(978-0-7613-7918-8(5))*; pap. 5.95 *(978-0-7613-7921-8(5))* Lerner Publishing Group. (Darby Creek).

—My Cousin, the Alien. Gorman, Mike, illus. (Alien Agent Ser.: 1). (ENG.). 160p. (J). (gr. 4-6). 2009. pap. 5.95 *(978-0-7613-4964-8(2)*, First Avenue Editions) 2008. 16.95 *(978-0-8225-7627-3(9)*, Carolrhoda Bks.) Lerner Publishing Group.

—The Not-So-Perfect Planet. Gorman, Mike, illus. (Way-Too-Real Aliens Ser.: 2). (ENG.). 120p. (J). (gr. 4-6). 2015. 34.65 *(978-1-4677-5961-8(9)*, Lerner Digital) 2012. 15.95 *(978-0-7613-7919-5(3)*, Darby Creek) 2012. pap. 6.95 *(978-0-7613-7923-2(1)*, Darby Creek) Lerner Publishing Group.

—The Wizards of Wyrd World. Gorman, Mike, illus. (Way-Too-Real Aliens Ser.: 3). (ENG.). 112p. (J). (gr. 4-6). 2015. 34.65 *(978-1-4677-5962-5(7)*, Lerner Digital) 2013. pap. 6.95 *(978-0-7613-7922-5(3)*, Darby Creek) 2012. 15.95 *(978-0-7613-7920-1(7))* Lerner Publishing Group.

—#4 Alien Encounter. Gorman, Mike, illus. 2011. (Alien Agent Ser.). 152p. (J). pap. 33.92 *(978-0-7613-7608-8(9)*, Darby Creek) Lerner Publishing Group.

—#5 Alien Contact. Gorman, Mike, illus. 2011. (Alien Agent Ser.). pap. 33.92 *(978-0-7613-8347-5(6)*, Darby Creek) Lerner Publishing Group.

Seven, John. The Alchemist War, 1 vol. Phillips, Craig, illus. 2013. (Time-Tripping Faradays Ser.). (ENG.). 160p. (gr. 4-5). 9.95 *(978-1-62370-011-9(6))*; (YA). pap. 5.95 *(978-1-4342-6438-1(6))*; (gr. 4-5). lib. bdg. 26.65 *(978-1-4342-6028-4(3))* Stone Arch Bks.

—The Dragon of Rome, 1 vol. Phillips, Craig, illus. 2013. (Time-Tripping Faradays Ser.). (ENG.). 160p. (gr. 4-5). 9.95 *(978-1-62370-012-6(4))*; lib. bdg. 26.65 *(978-1-4342-6029-1(1))* Stone Arch Bks.

—The Outlaw of Sherwood Forest, 1 vol. Hans, Stephanie, illus. 2014. (Time-Tripping Faradays Ser.). (ENG.). 192p. (gr. 4-5). lib. bdg. 26.65 *(978-1-4342-9174-5(X))* Stone Arch Bks.

—The Terror of the Tengu, 1 vol. Hans, Stephanie, illus. 2014. (Time-Tripping Faradays Ser.). (ENG.). 192p. (gr. 4-5). 26.65 *(978-1-4342-9173-8(1))* Stone Arch Bks.

—The Time-Tripping Faradays. Phillips, Craig, illus. 2013. (Time-Tripping Faradays Ser.). (ENG.). 160p. (gr. 4-5). 53.30 *(978-1-4342-8994-0(X))* Stone Arch Bks.

Seven, John & Phillips, Craig. The Dragon of Rome, 1 vol. 2013. (ENG.). 160p. (YA). pap. *(978-1-4342-6439-8(4))* Stone Arch Bks.

SFX Fantasy. Tween Tales - Robots, Dragons & the Interworld Machine. 2007. 131p. pap. 12.99 *(978-1-4303-2546-8(1))* Lulu Pr., Inc.

S.H., Addan. Guardabosque Del Ano 3000: Canis Familiaris Evolucion. 2004. (SPA., Illus.). 340p. pap. *(978-1-84401-133-9(X))* Athena Pr.

Shadow, Jak. The F. E. A. R. Agency. 2006. (F. E. A. R. Adventures S. Ser.). (ENG., Illus.). 80p. (J). 4.00 *(978-1-84046-726-0(6)*, Wizard Books) Icon Bks., Ltd. GBR. Dist: Publishers Group Canada.

Shand, Patrick. Marvel Guardians of the Galaxy: Space Riot. 2017. lib. bdg. 24.50 ***(978-0-606-40199-9(7))*** Turtleback Bks.

Shanower, Eric. Oz: Road to Oz. 2013. (ENG., Illus.). 136p. (J). (gr. -1-17). pap. 16.99 *(978-0-7851-6405-0(7))* Marvel Worldwide, Inc.

Shapiro, David R. Terra Tempo: The Four Corners of Time. Herndon, Christopher, illus. 2013. (Terra Tempo Ser.). (ENG.). 264p. (J). pap. 17.99 *(978-0-9844422-6-3(X))* Craigmore Creations.

Shea, Therese. One More Floor! 2006. (Neighborhood Readers Ser.). (ENG.). 16p. (gr. 1-3). pap. 6.50 *(978-1-4042-7244-6(5)*, Rosen Classroom) Rosen Publishing Group, Inc., The.

Shearer, Alex. The Cloud Hunters. 2013. (ENG.). 288p. (J). (gr. 6-8). 14.95 *(978-1-62636-216-1(5)*, 263216, Sky Pony Pr.) Skyhorse Publishing Co., Inc.

—Sky Run. 2014. (Cloud Hunters Ser.). (ENG.). 288p. (J). (gr. 2-7). 14.95 *(978-1-62873-593-2(7)*, Sky Pony Pr.) Skyhorse Publishing Co., Inc.

Sheehan, Anna. A Long, Long Sleep. 2011. (ENG., Illus.). 352p. (YA). (gr. 9). 16.99 *(978-0-7636-5260-9(1))* Candlewick Pr.

Shein, Erik. The Pillow Princess: Mystoryland Friends Brand. 2014. (ENG., Illus.). 32p. (J). 8.95 *(978-0-9765358-0-5(7))* Ark Watch Holdings LLC.

Sheley, Kristen. Partners in Time #4: Family Matters. 2008. 216p. pap. 15.95 *(978-0-595-51850-0(8))* iUniverse, Inc.

—Partners in Time #5: A Change of Course. 2010. 236p. 25.95 *(978-1-4502-6658-1(4))*; pap. 15.95 *(978-1-4502-6657-4(6))* iUniverse, Inc.

Shepherd, Megan. The Cage. (Cage Ser.: 1). (YA). (gr. 8). 2016. 416p. pap. 9.99 *(978-0-06-224306-5(3))* 2015. (ENG.). 400p. 17.99 *(978-0-06-224305-8(5))* HarperCollins Pubs.

—The Gauntlet. 2017. (Cage Ser.: 3). 400p. (YA). (gr. 8). 17.99 *(978-0-06-224312-6(8))* HarperCollins Pubs.

—Her Dark Curiosity. 2014. (Madman's Daughter Ser.: 2). (ENG.). 432p. (YA). (gr. 8). 17.99 *(978-0-06-212805-8(1))* HarperCollins Pubs.

—The Madman's Daughter. 2013. (Madman's Daughter Ser.: 1). (ENG.). (YA). (gr. 8). 464p. pap. 9.99 *(978-0-06-212803-4(5))*; 432p. 17.99 *(978-0-06-212802-7(7))* HarperCollins Pubs.

Shiga, Jason. Meanwhile: Pick Any Path. 3,856 Story Possibilities. 2010. (ENG., Illus.). 80p. (J). (gr. 3-7). 16.95 *(978-0-8109-8423-3(7)*, Amulet Bks.) Abrams, Inc.

Shine, Joe. I Become Shadow. 2015. (ENG.). 304p. (YA). (gr. 9). pap. 10.99 *(978-1-61695-537-3(6)*, Soho Teen) Soho Pr., Inc.

Shipton, Paul. The Games Player of Zob. McCafferty, Jan, illus. 2007. (Collins Big Cat Ser.). (ENG.). 1p. (J). (gr. 3-4). pap. 8.99 *(978-0-00-723094-5(X))* HarperCollins Pubs. Ltd. GBR. Dist: Independent Pubs. Group.

Shirvington, Jessica. Disruption. 2016. (Disruption Ser.: 01). (ENG.). 416p. (YA). (gr. 9). 9.99 *(978-0-7322-9810-4(5))* HarperCollins Pubs. Australia AUS. Dist: HarperCollins Pubs.

—One Past Midnight. 2014. (ENG.). 352p. (YA). (gr. 9). 17.99 *(978-0-8027-3702-1(1)*, 9780802737021, Bloomsbury USA Childrens) Bloomsbury Publishing USA.

Shmakov, Efim. The Return of Hezzord. 2010. 280p. pap. *(978-1-921731-15-0(X))* Zeus Pubns.

Shore, Diane Z. & Alexander, Jessica. This Is the Earth. Minor, Wendell, illus. 2016. 40p. (J). (gr. -1-3). 17.99 *(978-0-06-055526-9(2))* HarperCollins Pubs.

Shusterman, Neal. The Accelerati Trilogy Book Three Hawking's Hallway. 2017. (Accelerati Trilogy Ser.). (ENG.). 368p. (J). (gr. 5-9). pap. 8.99 *(978-1-4231-5521-8(1))* Hyperion Bks. for Children.

—The Complete Unwind Dystology: Unwind; Unwholly; Unsouled; Undivided. 2014. (Unwind Dystology Ser.). (ENG., Illus.). 1568p. (YA). (gr. 7). 73.99 *(978-1-4814-2186-7(7)*, Simon & Schuster Bks. For Young Readers) Simon & Schuster Bks. For Young Readers.

—The Dark Side of Nowhere. unabr. ed. 2004. 192p. (J). (gr. 4-7). pap. 36.00 incl. audio *(978-0-8072-8757-6(1)*, YA258SP, Listening Library) Random Hse. Audio Publishing Group.

—The Dark Side of Nowhere. 2012. (ENG.). (YA). (gr. 7). 240p. 17.99 *(978-1-4424-5812-3(7))*; 256p. pap. 9.99 *(978-1-4424-2281-0(5))* Simon & Schuster Bks. For Young Readers. (Simon & Schuster Bks. For Young Readers).

—Edison's Alley. 2016. (Accelerati Trilogy Ser.: Bk. 2). (ENG.). 256p. (J). (gr. 5-9). pap. 7.99 *(978-1-4231-5517-1(3))* Hyperion Bks. for Children.

—Scythe. 2016. (Arc of a Scythe Ser.: 1). (ENG., Illus.). 448p. (YA). (gr. 7). 18.99 *(978-1-4424-7242-6(1)*, Simon & Schuster Bks. For Young Readers) Simon & Schuster Bks. For Young Readers.

—Stories from the Unwind World. 2016. (Unwind Dystology Ser.). (ENG.). 336p. (YA). (gr. 7). pap. 11.99 *(978-1-4814-5724-8(1)*, Simon & Schuster Bks. For Young Readers) Simon & Schuster Bks. For Young Readers.

—UnBound: Stories from the Unwind World. 2015. (Unwind Dystology Ser.: 5). (ENG., Illus.). 320p. (YA). (gr. 7). 18.99 *(978-1-4814-5723-1(3)*, Simon & Schuster Bks. For Young Readers) Simon & Schuster Bks. For Young Readers.

—Undivided. 2015. (Unwind Dystology Ser.: 4). lib. bdg. 23.30 *(978-0-606-37863-5(4))* Turtleback Bks.

—UnDivided. 2014. (Unwind Dystology Ser.: Bk. 4). (ENG., Illus.). 384p. (YA). (gr. 7). 19.99 *(978-1-4814-0975-9(1)*, Simon & Schuster Bks. For Young Readers) Simon & Schuster Bks. For Young Readers.

—UnSouled. (Unwind Dystology Ser.: 3). (ENG., Illus.). (YA). (gr. 7). 2014. 432p. pap. 11.99 *(978-1-4424-2370-1(6))* 2013. 416p. 17.99 *(978-1-4424-2369-5(2))* Simon & Schuster Bks. For Young Readers. (Simon & Schuster Bks. For Young Readers).

—Unsouled. 2014. (Unwind Dystology Ser.: 3). lib. bdg. 23.30 *(978-0-606-36107-1(3))* Turtleback Bks.

—UnWholly. (Unwind Dystology Ser.: 2). (ENG.). 416p. (YA). (gr. 7). 2013. pap. 11.99 *(978-1-4424-2367-1(6)*, Simon & Schuster Bks. For Young Readers) 2012. 19.99 *(978-1-4424-2366-4(8))* Simon & Schuster Bks. For Young Readers.

—UnWholly. 2013. (Unwind Dystology Ser.: 2). lib. bdg. 23.30 *(978-0-606-32336-9(8)*, Turtleback) Turtleback Bks.

—Unwind. 2011. 10.36 *(978-0-7848-3496-1(2)*, Everbind) Marco Bk. Co.

—Unwind. (Unwind Dystology Ser.: 1). (ENG., Illus.). (YA). 2009. 384p. (gr. 8). pap. 11.99 *(978-1-4169-1205-7(3))* 2007. 352p. (gr. 7-12). 19.99 *(978-1-4169-1204-0(5))* Simon & Schuster Bks. For Young Readers. (Simon & Schuster Bks. For Young Readers).

—Unwind. 2009. (Unwind Dystology Ser.: 1). lib. bdg. 23.30 *(978-0-606-10700-6(2)*, Turtleback) Turtleback Bks.

Shusterman, Neal & Elfman, Eric. Edison's Alley. 2015. (Accelerati Trilogy Ser.: Bk. 2). (ENG.). 256p. (J). (gr. 5-9). 16.99 *(978-1-4231-4806-7(1))* Hyperion Bks. for Children.

—Hawking's Hallway. 2016. (Accelerati Trilogy Ser.: Bk. 3). (ENG.). 368p. (J). (gr. 5-9). 16.99 *(978-1-4231-4805-0(3))* Hyperion Bks. for Children.

—Tesla's Attic. 2014. (Accelerati Trilogy Ser.: Bk. 1). (ENG.). 256p. (J). (gr. 3-7). 16.99 *(978-1-4231-4803-6(7))* Hyperion Bks. for Children.

Siegel, Mark & Siegel, Alexis. The Sand Warrior. Bouma, Xanthe et al, illus. 2017. (5 Worlds Ser.: 1). (ENG.). 256p. (J). (gr. 3-7). 18.99 ***(978-1-101-93586-6(3))***; pap. 12.99 ***(978-1-101-93588-0(X))***; lib. bdg. 21.99 ***(978-1-101-93587-3(1))*** Random Hse. Children's Bks. (Random Hse. Bks. for Young Readers).

—The Sand Warrior. Bouma, Xanthe et al, illus. 2017. (5 Worlds Ser.: 1). lib. bdg. 24.50 ***(978-0-606-40243-9(8))*** Turtleback Bks.

Sierra, Donn. Candin Book 2: The Visitors. 2012. 214p. pap. 14.50 *(978-1-62212-619-4(X)*, Strategic Bk. Publishing) Strategic Book Publishing & Rights Agency (SBPRA).

Siglain, Michael. Finn & Rey Escape! 2015. (Star Wars: Force Awakens 8X8 Ser.). (J). lib. bdg. 14.75 *(978-0-606-38311-0(5))* Turtleback Bks.

—Han & Chewie Return! 2015. (Star Wars: Force Awakens 8X8 Ser.). (J). lib. bdg. 13.55 *(978-0-606-38310-3(7))* Turtleback Bks.

Sigler, Scott. Alive. 2016. (Generations Trilogy Ser.: 1). (ENG.). 384p. (gr. 9). pap. 12.00 *(978-0-553-39312-5(X)*, Del Rey) Random House Publishing Group.

Silver, Eve. Crash. 2015. (Game Ser.: 3). (ENG.). 368p. (YA). (gr. 9). 17.99 *(978-0-06-219219-6(1)*, Tegen, Katherine Bks) HarperCollins Pubs.

—Rush. (Game Ser.: 1). (ENG.). (YA). (gr. 9). 2014. 384p. pap. 9.99 *(978-0-06-219214-1(0)*, Tegen, Katherine Bks) 2013. 368p. 17.99 *(978-0-06-219213-4(2))* HarperCollins Pubs.

Silvestri, Marc & Hawkins, Matt. Cyber Force Rebirth, Vol. 1. 2013. (ENG., Illus.). 160p. (YA). pap. 9.99 *(978-1-60706-671-2(8)*, 9781607066712) Image Comics.

Simmons, Kristen. Article 5. 2012. (Article 5 Ser.: 1). (ENG.). 368p. (YA). (gr. 8-12). 17.99 *(978-0-7653-2958-5(1)*, 9780765329585, Tor Teen) Doherty, Tom Assocs., LLC.

—The Glass Arrow. (ENG.). (YA). 2016. 352p. pap. 9.99 *(978-0-7653-3664-4(2)*, 9780765336644) 2015. 336p. (gr. 8-12). 17.99 *(978-0-7653-3661-3(8)*, 9780765336613) Doherty, Tom Assocs., LLC. (Tor Teen).

—Three. 2014. (Article 5 Ser.: 3). (ENG.). 384p. (YA). (gr. 8-12). 17.99 *(978-0-7653-2960-8(3)*, 9780765329608, Tor Teen) Doherty, Tom Assocs., LLC.

Simonson, Walter. Thor by Walter Simonson Volume 3. 2013. (ENG., Illus.). 264p. (J). (gr. 4-17). pap. 29.99 *(978-0-7851-8462-1(7))* Marvel Worldwide, Inc.

Simonson, Walter, et al. Fantastic Four Epic Collection: Into the Timestream. Buckler, Rich et al, illus. 2014. (ENG.). 504p. (J). (gr. 4-17). pap. 39.99 *(978-0-7851-8895-7(9))* Marvel Worldwide, Inc.

Singer, Maurene, et al. A Place in the Sky. Marino, Natalie & Marino, Illustrator, Natalie, Natalie, illus. 2005. 52p. (J). 16.00 *(978-0-9759382-0-1(7))* Carousel Pubns., Inc.

Skillchecks for Science Fiction. rev. ed. 2005. (Fastback Ser.). 32p. (J). (gr. 6-12). pap. 5.95 *(978-0-13-024450-5(3))* Globe Fearon Educational Publishing.

Skinner, Gard. Game Slaves. 2014. (ENG.). 336p. (YA). (gr. 7). 16.99 *(978-0-547-97259-6(8))* Houghton Mifflin Harcourt Publishing Co.

Skovron, Jon. Man Made Boy. 2013. (ENG.). 384p. (YA). (gr. 7). 17.99 *(978-0-670-78620-6(9)*, Viking Books for Young Readers) Penguin Young Readers Group.

Skrimager, R. J. The Making: Volume One of the Golden Isle. 2003. 380p. (YA). pap. 20.95 *(978-0-595-26705-7(X)*, Writers Club Pr.) iUniverse, Inc.

Skrutskie, Emily. The Edge of the Abyss. 2017. (ENG.). 296p. (YA). (gr. 7-12). pap. 11.99 ***(978-1-63583-000-2(1)***, Flux) North Star Editions.

—The Edge of the Abyss. 2017. lib. bdg. 23.30 ***(978-0-606-40232-3(2))*** Turtleback Bks.

Skurzynski, Gloria. Afterwar. 2011. (ENG., Illus.). 528p. (YA). (gr. 7). pap. 9.99 *(978-1-4424-1681-9(5)*, Atheneum Bks. for Young Readers) Simon & Schuster Children's Publishing.

—The Clones Bk. 2. 2007. (ENG.). 192p. (YA). (gr. 7). pap. 10.95 *(978-1-4169-5560-3(7)*, Simon Pulse) Simon Pulse.

—Virtual War: The Virtual War Chronologs — Book 1. 2008. (ENG.). 188p. (YA). (gr. 7). pap. 10.99 *(978-1-4169-7577-9(2)*, Simon Pulse) Simon Pulse.

Skvarch, Angela & Skvarch, Jeffrey. Dinosaurs in Space. 2004. 48p. (J). per. 9.95 *(978-1-932560-35-0(1))* Aeon Publishing Inc.

Slade, Arthur. Island of Doom: Hunchback Assignments 4. 2013. (Hunchback Assignments Ser.). (ENG.). 320p. (YA). (gr. 7). pap. 9.99 *(978-0-375-85406-4(1)*, Ember) Random Hse. Children's Bks.

Slade, Arthur G. The Dark Deeps. 2011. (Hunchback Assignments Ser.: Vol. 2). (ENG.). 320p. (YA). (gr. 7). pap. 9.99 *(978-0-375-85404-0(5)*, Ember) Random Hse. Children's Bks.

—Empire of Ruins. 2012. (Hunchback Assignments Ser.). (ENG.). 300p. (YA). (gr. 7). pap. 8.99 *(978-0-375-85405-7(3)*, Ember) Random Hse. Children's Bks.

—The Hunchback Assignments. 2010. (Hunchback Assignments Ser.). (ENG.). 288p. (YA). (gr. 7). pap. 8.99 *(978-0-375-85403-3(7)*, Ember) Random Hse. Children's Bks.

Sloane, William, ed. Space, Space, Space: Stories about the Time When Men Will Be Adventuring to the Stars. 2011. 288p. 48.95 *(978-1-258-10156-5(4))* Literary Licensing, LLC.

Slott, Dan & Waid, Mark. The Amazing Spider-Man - Flying Blind. Camuncoli, Giuseppe et al, illus. 2012. (ENG.). 120p. (J). (gr. 4-17). pap. 16.99 *(978-0-7851-6002-1(7))* Marvel Worldwide, Inc.

SMARTLAB Creative Team. Space Exploration. 2010. 10p. mass mkt. 39.99 *(978-1-60380-050-1(6))* becker&mayer! books.

Smibert, Angie. The Forgetting Curve. 0 vols. 2012. (Memento Nora Ser.: 2). (ENG.). 192p. (YA). (gr. 8-12). 16.99 *(978-0-7614-6265-1(1)*, 9780761462651, Amazon Children's Publishing) Amazon Publishing.

—The Meme Plague. 0 vols. (ENG.). 240p. (YA). (gr. 7-12). 2016. pap. 9.99 *(978-1-4778-1689-9(5)*, 9781477816899, Skyscape) 2013. 16.99 *(978-1-4778-1660-8(7)*, 9781477816608, Amazon Children's Publishing) Amazon Publishing.

—Memento Nora. 0 vols. 2013. (Memento Nora Ser.: 1). (ENG.). 192p. (J). (gr. 7-10). pap. 9.99 *(978-1-4778-1624-0(0)*, 9781477816240, Amazon Children's Publishing) Amazon Publishing.

Smith, Alexander Gordon. Death Sentence. 2011. (Escape from Furnace Ser.: 3). (ENG.). 272p. (YA). (gr. 7-11). 17.99 *(978-0-374-32494-0(8)*, 9780374324940, Farrar, Straus & Giroux (BYR)) Farrar, Straus & Giroux.

—Death Sentence. 2012. (Escape from Furnace Ser.: 3). (ENG.). 288p. (YA). (gr. 7-11). pap. 10.99 *(978-0-312-67441-0(4)*, 9780312674410) Square Fish.

—Execution. 2012. (Escape from Furnace Ser.: 5). (ENG.). 320p. (YA). (gr. 7-11). 16.99 *(978-0-374-36224-9(6)*, 9780374362249, Farrar, Straus & Giroux (BYR)) Farrar, Straus & Giroux.

—Execution. 2013. (Escape from Furnace Ser.: 5). (ENG.). 336p. (YA). (gr. 7-11). pap. 10.99 *(978-1-250-02942-3(2)*, 9781250029423) Square Fish.

—Fugitives. 2012. (Escape from Furnace Ser.: 4). (ENG.). 288p. (YA). (gr. 7-11). 17.99 *(978-0-374-32484-1(0)*, 9780374324841, Farrar, Straus & Giroux (BYR)) Farrar, Straus & Giroux.

—Fugitives. 2012. (Escape from Furnace Ser.: 4). (ENG.). 304p. (YA). (gr. 7-11). pap. 10.99 *(978-1-250-00339-3(3)*, 9781250003393) Square Fish.

—Hellfighters. 2016. (Devil's Engine Ser.: 2). (ENG.). 320p. (YA). 18.99 *(978-0-374-30172-9(7)*, 9780374301729, Farrar, Straus & Giroux (BYR)) Farrar, Straus & Giroux.

—Hellraisers. 2015. (Devil's Engine Ser.: 1). (ENG.). 352p. (YA). (gr. 7). 17.99 *(978-0-374-30169-9(7)*, 9780374301699, Farrar, Straus & Giroux (BYR)) Farrar, Straus & Giroux.

—Lockdown. 2009. (Escape from Furnace Ser.: 1). (ENG.). 288p. (YA). (gr. 7-11). 17.99 *(978-0-374-32491-9(3)*, 9780374324919, Farrar, Straus & Giroux (BYR)) Farrar, Straus & Giroux.

—Lockdown. 2010. (Escape from Furnace Ser.: 1). (ENG.). 304p. (YA). (gr. 7-11). pap. 10.99 *(978-0-312-61193-4(5)*, 9780312611934) Square Fish.

—Solitary. 2010. (Escape from Furnace Ser.: 2). (ENG.). 240p. (YA). (gr. 7-11). 17.99 *(978-0-374-32492-6(1)*, 9780374324926, Farrar, Straus & Giroux (BYR)) Farrar, Straus & Giroux.

—Solitary. 2011. (Escape from Furnace Ser.: 2). (ENG.). 256p. (YA). (gr. 7-11). pap. 10.99 *(978-0-312-67476-2(7)*, 9780312674762) Square Fish.

Smith, Andrew. The Alex Crow. 2015. (ENG.). 336p. (YA). (gr. 9). 18.99 *(978-0-525-42653-0(1)*, Dutton Books for Young Readers) Penguin Young Readers Group.

—Grasshopper Jungle. 2015. (ENG.). 416p. (YA). (gr. 9). pap. 10.99 *(978-0-14-242500-8(1)*, Speak) Penguin Young Readers Group.

Smith, Clete Barrett. Alien on a Rampage. 2013. (Intergalactic Bed & Breakfast Ser.). (ENG.). 320p. (J). (gr. 3-7). pap. 6.99 *(978-1-4231-5525-6(4))* Hyperion Pr.

—Aliens in Disguise. Slade, Christian, illus. 2013. (Intergalactic Bed & Breakfast Ser.). (ENG.). 240p. (J). (gr. 3-7). 16.99 *(978-1-4231-6598-9(5))* Disney Pr.

—Aliens in Disguise. 2014. (Intergalactic Bed & Breakfast Ser.). (ENG.). 256p. (J). (gr. 3-7). pap. 6.99 *(978-1-4231-6638-2(8))* Hyperion Bks. for Children.

Smith, Geof. Everything I Need to Know I Learned from a Star Wars Little Golden Book (Star Wars) Golden Books, illus. 2016. (Little Golden Book Ser.). (ENG.). 96p. (J). (gr. k-12). 9.99 *(978-0-7364-3656-4(1)*, Golden Bks.) Random Hse. Children's Bks.

—Star Wars: Return of the Jedi (Star Wars) Cohee, Ron, illus. 2015. (Little Golden Book Ser.). (ENG.). 24p. (J). (-k). 4.99 *(978-0-7364-3548-2(4)*, Golden Bks.) Random Hse. Children's Bks.

—Star Wars: Revenge of the Sith (Star Wars) Spaziante, Patrick, illus. 2015. (Little Golden Book Ser.). (ENG.). 24p. (J). (-k). 4.99 *(978-0-7364-3540-6(9)*, Golden Bks.) Random Hse. Children's Bks.

—Star Wars: the Empire Strikes Back (Star Wars) Kennett, Chris, illus. 2015. (Little Golden Book Ser.). (ENG.). 24p. (J). (-k). 4.99 *(978-0-7364-3544-4(1)*, Golden Bks.) Random Hse. Children's Bks.

Smith, Greg Leitich. Borrowed Time. 2015. (ENG., Illus.). 192p. (J). (gr. 5-7). 16.99 *(978-0-544-23711-7(0))* Houghton Mifflin Harcourt Publishing Co.

—Chronal Engine. Henry, Blake, illus. 2013. (ENG.). 192p. (J). (gr. 5-7). pap. 6.99 *(978-0-544-02277-5(7))* Houghton Mifflin Harcourt Publishing Co.

—Ninjas, Piranhas, & Galileo. 2013. 178p. (J). pap. 14.95 *(978-1-62352-029-8(0))* IntoPrint Publishing LLC.

Smith, J. E. Complex City: All in a Day's Work. 2003. 120p. per. 12.95 *(978-0-9728070-0-5(4))* Better Comics.

Smith, Larry. Cloud Realm. 2003. (Chronicles of Ingarde: Bk. 1). 218p. (YA). pap. 15.95 *(978-0-595-30149-2(5))* iUniverse, Inc.

Smith, Mark. The Road to Winter. 2017. (Wilder Trilogy Ser.). (ENG.). 256p. (J). (gr. 8). 11.95 *(978-1-925355-12-3(8))* Text Publishing Co. AUS. Dist: Consortium Bk. Sales & Distribution.

Smith, Paul, et al, illus. Avengers: Falcon. 2014. (ENG.). 216p. (J). (gr. 4-17). pap. 24.99 *(978-0-7851-8826-1(6))* Marvel Worldwide, Inc.

Smith, Shane W. The Lesser Evil, Book 3 Comic Book. Smith, Shane W., illus. 2012. (Illus.). 114p. pap. *(978-1-927384-04-6(4))* Zeta Comics.

Smith, Sherri L. Orleans. 2013. (ENG.). 336p. (YA). (gr. 7). 17.99 *(978-0-399-25294-5(0)*, G.P. Putnam's Sons Books for Young Readers) Penguin Young Readers Group.

Snider, Brandon T. Guardians of the Galaxy: Gamora's Galactic Showdown. Marvel Press Artist, illus. 2017. (Mighty Marvel Chapter Book Ser.). (ENG.). 128p. (J). (gr. 3-7). pap. 5.99 *(978-1-4847-3213-7(8)*, Marvel Pr.) Disney Publishing Worldwide.

—Guardians of the Galaxy: Gamora's Galactic Showdown! 2017. (Mighty Marvel Chapter Bks.). (J). lib. bdg. 16.00 ***(978-0-606-39965-4(8))*** Turtleback Bks.

Snider, Brandon T. Guardians of the Galaxy Doodles. Montalvo-Lagos, Tomás, illus. 2017. (Doodle Book Ser.). (ENG.). 128p. (J). (gr. 1-3). pap. 12.99 *(978-1-4847-8767-0(6)*, Marvel Pr.) Disney Publishing Worldwide.

Sniegoski, Thomas E. Monstrous. 2017. (Savage Ser.). (ENG., Illus.). 448p. (YA). (gr. 9). 18.99 ***(978-1-4814-7718-5(8)***, Simon Pulse) Simon Pulse.

Sniegoski, Thomas E. Savage. (Savage Ser.). (ENG.). (YA). (gr. 9). 2017. 432p. pap. 9.99 *(978-1-4814-4374-6(7))* 2016. (Illus.). 416p. 17.99 *(978-1-4814-4373-9(9))* Simon Pulse. (Simon Pulse).

Sniegoski, Thomas E. & Golden, Christopher. Dragon Secrets. 2013. (Magic Zero Ser.: 2). (ENG.). 320p. (J). (gr. 3-7). pap. 6.99 *(978-1-4424-7309-6(6)*, Aladdin) Simon & Schuster Children's Publishing.

—Dragon Secrets. 2013. (Magic Zero Ser.: 2). (ENG.). 320p. (J). (gr. 3-7). 17.99 *(978-1-4424-7310-2(X)*, Simon & Schuster/Paula Wiseman Bks.) Simon & Schuster/Paula Wiseman Bks.

Sniegoski, Tom. Monstrous. 2017. (YA). pap. ***(978-1-4814-7719-2(6)***, Simon Pulse) Simon Pulse.

Sonneborn, Scott. Prisoner of the Ring, 1 vol. Schoening, Dan, illus. 2011. (Green Lantern Ser.). (ENG.). 56p. (gr. 2-3). pap. 4.95 *(978-1-4342-3410-0(X))*; lib. bdg. 26.65 *(978-1-4342-2624-2(7))* Stone Arch Bks. (DC Super Heroes).

Sorrells, Walter. The Travelers, Bk. 2. 2009. (Pendragon: 2). (ENG.). 240p. (J). (gr. 5-9). pap. 6.99 (978-1-4169-6523-7(8), Aladdin) Simon & Schuster Children's Publishing.

Souders, J. A. Rebellion. 2016. (Elysium Chronicles Ser.: 3). (ENG.). 336p. (YA). (gr. 8-12). 18.99 (978-0-7653-3247-9(7), 9780765332479, Tor Teen) Doherty, Tom Assocs., LLC.

—Renegade. 2013. (Elysium Chronicles Ser.: 1). (ENG.). 368p. (YA). (gr. 8-11). pap. 13.99 (978-0-7653-3248-6(5), 9780765332486, Tor Teen) Doherty, Tom Assocs., LLC.

—Revelations. (Elysium Chronicles Ser.: 2). (ENG.). (YA). (gr. 8-12). 2016. 368p. pap. 11.99 (978-0-7653-3249-3(3), 9780765332493) 2013. 352p. 17.99 (978-0-7653-3246-2(9), 9780765332462) Doherty, Tom Assocs., LLC. (Tor Teen).

Space Case. 2014. (Moon Base Alpha Ser.). (ENG., Illus.). 352p. (J). (gr. 3-7). 17.99 (978-1-4424-9486-2(7), Simon & Schuster Bks. For Young Readers) Simon & Schuster Bks. For Young Readers.

Space Monster Saves the Day. 2007. (Spaceboy Chapter Ser.). (J). per. 7.67 (978-1-932570-61-8(6)) Pioneer Valley Bks.

Spaceboy Chapter Books. 2007. (J). per. (978-1-932570-60-1(8)) Pioneer Valley Bks.

Sparkes, Ali. Alligator Action. Collins, Ross, illus. 2014. (S. W. I. T. C. H. Ser.: 14). (ENG.). 112p. (J). (gr. 2-5). lib. bdg. 27.93 (978-1-4677-2117-2(4), Darby Creek) Lerner Publishing Group.

—Anaconda Adventure. Collins, Ross, illus. 2014. (S. W. I. T. C. H. Ser.: 13). (ENG.). 104p. (J). (gr. 2-5). lib. bdg. 27.93 (978-1-4677-2116-5(6), Darby Creek) Lerner Publishing Group.

—Ant Attack. Collins, Ross, illus. 2013. (S. W. I. T. C. H. Ser.: 4). (ENG.). 104p. (J). (gr. 2-5). pap. 7.95 (978-1-4677-0713-8(9), Darby Creek) Lerner Publishing Group.

—Ant Attack. Collins, Ross, illus. 2013. (S. W. I. T. C. H. Ser.: 4). (ENG.). 104p. (J). (gr. 2-5). lib. bdg. 27.93 (978-0-7613-9202-6(5)) Lerner Publishing Group.

—Beetle Blast. Collins, Ross, illus. 2013. (S. W. I. T. C. H. Ser.: 6). (ENG.). 104p. (J). (gr. 2-5). pap. 7.95 (978-1-4677-0715-2(5), Darby Creek); lib. bdg. 27.93 (978-0-7613-9204-0(1)) Lerner Publishing Group.

—Chameleon Chaos. Collins, Ross, illus. 2014. (S. W. I. T. C. H. Ser.: 10). (ENG.). 112p. (J). (gr. 2-5). lib. bdg. 27.93 (978-1-4677-2113-4(1), Darby Creek) Lerner Publishing Group.

—Crane Fly Crash. Collins, Ross, illus. 2013. (S. W. I. T. C. H. Ser.: 5). (ENG.). 104p. (J). (gr. 2-5). pap. 7.95 (978-1-4677-0714-5(7), Darby Creek); lib. bdg. 27.93 (978-0-7613-9203-3(3)) Lerner Publishing Group.

—Fly Frenzy. Collins, Ross, illus. 2013. (S. W. I. T. C. H. Ser.: 2). (ENG.). 104p. (J). (gr. 2-5). pap. 7.95 (978-1-4677-0711-4(2), Darby Creek) Lerner Publishing Group.

—Fly Frenzy. Collins, Ross, illus. 2013. (S. W. I. T. C. H. Ser.: 2). (ENG.). 104p. (J). (gr. 2-5). lib. bdg. 27.93 (978-0-7613-9200-2(9)) Lerner Publishing Group.

—Frog Freakout. Collins, Ross, illus. 2014. (S. W. I. T. C. H. Ser.: 7). (ENG.). 88p. (J). (gr. 2-5). lib. bdg. 27.93 (978-1-4677-2111-0(5), Darby Creek) Lerner Publishing Group.

—Gecko Gladiator. Collins, Ross, illus. 2014. (S. W. I. T. C. H. Ser.: 12). (ENG.). 104p. (J). (gr. 2-5). lib. bdg. 27.93 (978-1-4677-2115-8(8), Darby Creek) Lerner Publishing Group.

—Grasshopper Glitch. Collins, Ross, illus. 2013. (S. W. I. T. C. H. Ser.: 3). (ENG.). 104p. (J). (gr. 2-5). pap. 7.95 (978-1-4677-0712-1(0)) Lerner Publishing Group.

—Grasshopper Glitch. Collins, Ross, illus. 2013. (S. W. I. T. C. H. Ser.: 3). (ENG.). 104p. (J). (gr. 2-5). lib. bdg. 27.93 (978-0-7613-9201-9(7)) Lerner Publishing Group.

—Lizard Loopy. Collins, Ross, illus. 2014. (S. W. I. T. C. H. Ser.: 9). (ENG.). 104p. (J). (gr. 2-5). lib. bdg. 27.93 (978-1-4677-2112-7(3), Darby Creek) Lerner Publishing Group.

—Newt Nemesis. Collins, Ross, illus. 2014. (S. W. I. T. C. H. Ser.: 8). (ENG.). 88p. (J). (gr. 2-5). lib. bdg. 27.93 (978-1-4677-3233-8(8), Darby Creek) Lerner Publishing Group.

—Spider Stampede. Collins, Ross, illus. 2013. (S. W. I. T. C. H. Ser.: 1). (ENG.). 104p. (J). (gr. 2-5). pap. 7.95 (978-1-4677-0710-7(4)) Lerner Publishing Group.

—Spider Stampede. Collins, Ross, illus. 2013. (S. W. I. T. C. H. Ser.: 1). (ENG.). 104p. (J). (gr. 2-5). lib. bdg. 27.93 (978-0-7613-9199-9(1)) Lerner Publishing Group.

—Turtle Terror. Collins, Ross, illus. 2014. (S. W. I. T. C. H. Ser.: 11). (ENG.). 104p. (J). (gr. 2-5). lib. bdg. 27.93 (978-1-4677-2114-1(X), Darby Creek) Lerner Publishing Group.

Spencer, Nick & Hickman, Jonathan. Avengers - Prelude to Infinity, Vol. 3. Caselli, Stefano, illus. 2014. (ENG.). 152p. (YA). (gr. 8-17). pap. 19.99 (978-0-7851-6654-2(8)) Marvel Worldwide, Inc.

Spiegelman, Art. Jack & the Box. Hayes, Geoffrey, illus. 2008. (ENG.). 32p. (J). (gr. -1-3). 12.95 (978-0-9799238-3-8(2)) TOON Books / RAW Junior, LLC.

Spiegelman, Nadja. Zig & Wikki in Something Ate My Homework. Loeffler, Trade, illus. 2013. (ENG.). 40p. (J). (gr. -1-3). pap. 6.99 (978-1-935179-38-2(1)) TOON Books / RAW Junior, LLC.

—Zig & Wikki in Something Ate My Homework. Mouly, Francoise, ed. Loeffler, Trade, illus. 2010. (ENG.). 40p. (J). (gr. -1-3). 12.95 (978-1-935179-02-3(0)) TOON Books / RAW Junior, LLC.

Spiegelman, Nadja & Loeffler, Trade. Zig & Wikki in Something Ate My Homework, 1 vol. 2013. (Toon Bks). (ENG.). 40p. (J). (gr. 2-3). lib. bdg. 27.07 (978-1-61479-157-7(0)) Spotlight.

—Zig & Wikki in Something Ate My Homework. 2013. (Toon Books Level 3 Ser.). lib. bdg. 14.75 (978-0-606-32252-2(3), Turtleback) Turtleback Bks.

Spoor, Mike, illus. The Emperor's Guards: Concepts of Time. 2010. (Mandrill Mountain Math Mysteries Ser.). (ENG.). 32p. (J). (gr. 2-6). pap. 10.55 (978-1-60754-927-7(1)); lib. bdg. 22.60 (978-1-60754-922-2(0)) Windmill Bks.

Spradlin, Michael P. Killer Species #4: Ultimate Attack. 2014. (Killer Species Ser.: 4). (ENG.). 192p. (J). (gr. 3-7). pap. 5.99 (978-0-545-50678-6(6), Scholastic Paperbacks) Scholastic, Inc.

—Menace from the Deep. 2013. (Killer Species Ser.: 1). lib. bdg. 16.00 (978-0-606-32447-2(X), Turtleback) Turtleback Bks.

Spring, Manda. Emerald & the Magic of Raynon. 2004. 118p. pap. 19.95 (978-1-4137-3708-0(0)) America Star Bks.

Springham, James. Earth-n-Bones: Blue Things. 2006. 54p. pap. 16.95 (978-1-4137-9738-1(5)) America Star Bks.

—Earth-n-Bones: Toxic. 2005. 56p. pap. 16.95 (978-1-4137-9755-8(5)) America Star Bks.

St. Mark Kindergarten. Kindergarten Goes to Outer Space for the Day. 2009. 28p. pap. 12.49 (978-1-4490-0587-0(X)) AuthorHouse.

Stahler, David, Jr. The Seer. 2008. 320p. (J). pap. 6.99 (978-0-06-052290-2(9), Eos) HarperCollins Pubs.

Stamps, Sarah. Our Gang & the Shrinking Machine. Workman, Paula J., illus. 2008. 33p. pap. 24.95 (978-1-60610-953-3(7)) PublishAmerica, Inc.

Stanek, Robert, pseud. Explore the Solar System. 2010. 42p. pap. 11.99 (978-1-57545-179-4(4), Reagent Pr. Bks. for Young Readers) RP Media.

—The Kingdoms & the Elves of the Reaches Iii (Reader's Choice Edition, Keeper Martin's Tales Book 3) 2008. (Illus.). 244p. pap. 15.95 (978-1-57545-198-5(0)) RP Media.

Stanford, Cody L. Sinews of the Heart. 2013. 186p. pap. 10.99 (978-1-62757-059-6(4)) Storm Moon Pr., LLC.

Stanley, Diane. Joplin, Wishing. 2017. 272p. (J). (gr. 3-7). 16.99 (978-0-06-242370-2(3)) HarperCollins Pubs.

Star Wars Staff & Valois, Rob. Sticker Storyteller. 2008. (Star Wars). (ENG.). 48p. (J). (gr. 1-3). pap. 12.99 (978-0-448-45058-2(5)) Penguin Publishing Group.

Star Wars Staff, et al. Renegade. 2009. (Star Wars: Rebel For Ser.: 3). (ENG.). 176p. (J). (gr. 3-7). pap. 6.99 (978-0-545-11211-6(7)) Scholastic, Inc.

Star Wars, Star. Star Wars - The Force Awakens Mask Book: Which Side Are You On? 2016. (ENG.). 24p. (J). (gr. -1-1). pap. 9.99 (978-0-7944-3740-4(0), Reader's Digest Children's Bks.) Studio Fun International.

Stasse, Lisa M. The Defiant. 2015. (ENG., Illus.). 352p. (YA). (gr. 7). pap. 10.99 (978-1-4424-3272-7(1)) Simon & Schuster Children's Publishing.

—The Defiant: The Forsaken Trilogy. 2014. (ENG., Illus.). 352p. (YA). (gr. 7). 17.99 (978-1-4424-3271-0(3), Simon & Schuster Bks. For Young Readers) Simon & Schuster Bks. For Young Readers.

—The Forsaken. (ENG., (YA). (gr. 7). 2013. Illus.). 400p. pap. 9.99 (978-1-4424-3266-6(7)) 2012. 384p. 16.99 (978-1-4424-3265-9(9)) Simon & Schuster Bks. For Young Readers. (Simon & Schuster Bks. For Young Readers).

—The Uprising: The Forsaken Trilogy. 2013. (ENG.). 384p. (YA). (gr. 7). 16.99 (978-1-4424-3268-0(3), Simon & Schuster Bks. For Young Readers) Simon & Schuster Bks. For Young Readers.

Steele, Andrew. The Galaxy Boys & the Sphere. 2008. (ENG.). 285p. (J). (gr. 4-7). pap. (978-1-85756-687-1(4)) Janus Publishing Co.

Steele, Michael A. Web of Doom, 1 vol. Schoening, Dan, illus. 2011. (Green Lantern Ser.). (ENG.). 56p. (gr. 2-3). lib. bdg. 26.65 (978-1-4342-2621-1(2), DC Super Heroes) Stone Arch Bks.

Steele, Michael Anthony. Web of Doom, 1 vol. Schoening, Dan, illus. 2011. (Green Lantern Ser.). (ENG.). 56p. (gr. 2-3). pap. 4.95 (978-1-4342-3407-0(X), DC Super Heroes) Stone Arch Bks.

Steinberg, D. J. Mac Attack! Smith, Brian, illus. 2008. (Daniel Boom Aka Loud Boy Ser.: 2). (ENG.). 96p. (J). (gr. 1-4). pap. 6.99 (978-0-448-44699-8(5), Grosset & Dunlap) Penguin Young Readers Group.

Stephanie. The Beginning of Gerald. 2012. 28p. pap. 24.95 (978-1-62709-212-8(9)) America Star Bks.

Stephens, Berin L. Time Gangsters. 2012. pap. 14.99 (978-1-59955-966-7(8)) Cedar Fort, Inc./CFI Distribution.

Stephens, Sarah Hines. Super-Pets Showdown, 1 vol. Baltazar, Art, illus. 2012. (DC Super-Pets Ser.). (ENG.). 56p. (gr. 2-2). pap. 4.95 (978-1-4048-7216-5(7)); lib. bdg. 23.99 (978-1-4048-6486-3(5)) Picture Window Bks. (DC Super-Pets).

Stephenson, Sasha. Iceling. 2016. (ENG.). 272p. (YA). (gr. 7). 17.99 (978-1-59514-769-1(1), Razorbill) Penguin Young Readers Group.

Steps To Literacy Staff, compiled by. The Mysterious Benedict Society Collection: Class Pack (3 titles, 6 Each) 2010. (ENG.). (J). pap. 125.82 (978-1-61267-335-6(X)) Steps To Literacy, LLC.

—The Mysterious Benedict Society Collection: Variety Pack (3 titles, 1 Each) 2010. (ENG.). (J). pap. 20.97 (978-1-61267-334-9(1)) Steps To Literacy, LLC.

Sterling, L. E. True North. 2017. (True Born Ser.: 2). (ENG.). 304p. (YA). 16.99 (978-1-63375-595-6(9), 9781633755956) Entangled Publishing, LLC.

Stern, Roger. Avengers: Absolute Vision. Akin, Ian et al, illus. 2014. (ENG.). 392p. (J). (gr. 4-17). pap. 39.99 (978-0-7851-8535-2(6)) Marvel Worldwide, Inc.

Stern, Roger & Defalco, Tom. Avengers Epic Collection: Judgement Day. Pollard, Keith et al, illus. 2014. (ENG.). 464p. (J). (gr. 4-17). pap. 34.99 (978-0-7851-8894-0(0)) Marvel Worldwide, Inc.

Stern, Roger, et al. Spider-Man by Roger Stern Omnibus. Zeck, Mike et al, illus. 2014. (ENG.). 1296p. (J). (gr. 4-17). 125.00 (978-0-7851-8827-8(4)) Marvel Worldwide, Inc.

Stevens, Eric, et al. The Menace of Metallo, 1 vol. 2013. (Superman Ser.). (ENG., Illus.). 56p. (gr. 2-3). pap. 4.95 (978-1-4342-1371-6(4), DC Super Heroes) Stone Arch Bks.

—The Revenge of Clayface, 1 vol. Schigiel, Gregg, illus. (Batman Ser.). (ENG.). 56p. (gr. 2-3). 2013. pap. 4.95 (978-1-4342-1369-3(2)) 2009. lib. bdg. 26.65 (978-1-4342-1149-1(5)) Stone Arch Bks. (DC Super Heroes).

Stevens, Noel. From the Farthest Hills of Elsewhere. 2008. 172p. pap. 13.95 (978-0-595-52835-6(X)) iUniverse, Inc.

Stevenson, Robin. Desolación, 1 vol. 2012. (Spanish Soundings Ser.). (SPA.). 160p. (YA). (gr. 8-12). pap. 9.95 (978-1-4598-0305-3(1)) Orca Bk. Pubs. USA.

Stevermer, Caroline & Collin, Francesca. River Rats. 2005. (ENG., Illus.). 320p. (YA). (gr. 7-12). pap. 19.95 (978-0-15-205554-7(1)) Houghton Mifflin Harcourt Publishing Co.

Stewart, Paul & Riddell, Chris. Mind Warp. unabr. ed. 2017. (Scavenger Ser.: 3). (ENG., Illus.). 256p. (J). (gr. 4-7). pap. 9.99 (978-1-4472-3445-6(6)) Pan Macmillan GBR. Dist: Independent Pubs. Group.

—Zoid. unabr. ed. 2016. (Scavenger Ser.: 1). (ENG., Illus.). 272p. (J). (gr. 4-7). pap. 9.99 (978-1-4472-9995-0(7)) Pan Macmillan GBR. Dist: Independent Pubs. Group.

Stewart, Trenton Lee. The Mysterious Benedict Society. Tingley, Megan, ed. Sudyka, Diana, illus. 2010. (Mysterious Benedict Society Ser.: 3). (ENG.). 400p. (J). (gr. 3-7). pap. 8.99 (978-0-316-04550-6(0)) Little, Brown Bks. for Young Readers.

—The Mysterious Benedict Society. Ellis, Carson, illus. (Mysterious Benedict Society Ser.: 1). (ENG.). (J). (gr. 3-7). 2008. 512p. pap. 9.99 (978-0-316-00395-7(6)) 2007. 496p. 19.00 (978-0-316-05777-6(0), Tingley, Megan Bks.) 2015. 512p. 12.99 (978-0-316-26501-0(2)) Little, Brown Bks. for Young Readers.

—The Mysterious Benedict Society. unabr. ed. 2007. (Mysterious Benedict Society Ser.: Bk. 1). (ENG.). (J). (gr. 3-7). 25.50 (978-0-307-28440-2(9), Listening Library (Audio)) Penguin Random House Audio Publishing Group.

—The Mysterious Benedict Society. 2009. 17.45 (978-1-60686-527-9(7)) Perfection Learning Corp.

—The Mysterious Benedict Society. 2010. (Mysterious Benedict Society Ser.: 3). (J). lib. bdg. 19.65 (978-0-606-15117-7(6), Turtleback) Turtleback Bks.

—The Mysterious Benedict Society. Ellis, Carson, illus. 2008. (Mysterious Benedict Society Ser.: 1). 485p. (J). (gr. 3-7). lib. bdg. 19.65 (978-1-4178-1817-4(4), Turtleback) Turtleback Bks.

—The Mysterious Benedict Society: 10th Anniversary Edition. Ellis, Carson, illus. 2017. (ENG.). 528p. (J). (gr. 3-7). 18.99 (978-0-316-46491-8(0)) Little, Brown Bks. for Young Readers.

—The Mysterious Benedict Society & the Perilous Journey. Sudyka, Diana, illus. 2009. (Mysterious Benedict Society Ser.: 2). (ENG.). 464p. (J). (gr. 3-7). pap. 8.99 (978-0-316-03673-3(0)) Little Brown & Co.

—The Mysterious Benedict Society & the Perilous Journey. Sudyka, Diana, illus. 2008. (Mysterious Benedict Society Ser.: 2). (ENG.). 448p. (J). (gr. 3-7). 18.99 (978-0-316-05780-6(0)) Little, Brown Bks. for Young Readers.

—The Mysterious Benedict Society & the Perilous Journey. 2009. (Mysterious Benedict Society Ser.: 2). (J). lib. bdg. 19.65 (978-0-606-07462-9(7), Turtleback) Turtleback Bks.

—The Mysterious Benedict Society & the Prisoner's Dilemma. Sudyka, Diana, illus. 2009. (Mysterious Benedict Society Ser.: 3). (ENG.). 400p. (J). (gr. 3-7). 18.99 (978-0-316-04552-0(7)) Little, Brown Bks. for Young Readers.

Stiefvater, Maggie. Ballad: A Gathering of Faerie. 2009. (Lament Novel Ser.: 2). (ENG.). 360p. (YA). (gr. 7-18). pap. 9.95 (978-0-7387-1484-4(4), Flux) North Star Editions.

Stilton, Geronimo. The Galactic Goal. 2015. (Geronimo Stilton Spacemice Ser.: 4). lib. bdg. 18.40 (978-0-606-37059-2(5)) Turtleback Bks.

—The Underwater Planet. 2016. (Geronimo Stilton Spacemice Ser.: 6). (ENG., Illus.). 128p. (J). (gr. 2-5). pap. 7.99 (978-0-545-87243-0(X), Scholastic Paperbacks) Scholastic, Inc.

Stilton, Geronimo & Pizzelli, Anna. The Underwater Planet. Facciotto, Giuseppe & Verzini, Daniele, illus. 2016. 113p. (J). **(978-1-5182-0303-9(5))** Scholastic, Inc.

Stine, Fay. Star Ship Fantasy: The New Frontier of Space. 2008. 52p. pap. 10.95 (978-1-4327-2703-1(6)) Outskirts Pr., Inc.

Stock, Lisa. Battle for Naboo. 2012. (Star Wars DK Readers Level 3 Ser.). lib. bdg. 13.55 (978-0-606-26564-5(3), Turtleback) Turtleback Bks.

Stock, Lisa. DK Readers L2: Star Wars: Rey to the Rescue! 2017. (Star Wars DK Readers Level 2 Ser.). lib. bdg. 13.55 **(978-0-606-39899-2(6))** Turtleback Bks.

Stohl, Kevin. Time Chronicles Ozone, Vol. 3. 2004. 170p. (YA). 22.95 (978-0-595-66639-3(6)) iUniverse, Inc.

Stohl, Margaret. Black Widow: Forever Red. (Black Widow Novel Ser.). (ENG.). (YA). (gr. 7-12). 2016. 432p. pap. 9.99 (978-1-4847-7645-2(3)) 2015. 416p. 17.99 (978-1-4847-2643-3(X)) Disney Publishing Worldwide. (Marvel Pr.).

—Icons. (ENG.). (YA). (gr. 7-17). 2014. (Icons Ser.: 1). 464p. pap. 24.99 (978-0-316-20519-1(2)) 2013. 448p. 18.00 (978-0-316-20518-4(4)) Little, Brown Bks. for Young Readers.

Stone, Emma. Loholt Scrimminge & the Moor-Land Quest. 2007. 140p. per. (978-1-906210-19-9(5)) Grosvenor Hse. Publishing Ltd.

Stories Beyond Time & Space. (J). pap. 15.50 (978-0-8359-0158-1(0)) Globe Fearon Educational Publishing.

Storm, Michael. Pulp7: A Sweet Deal, a Killer Calling, & a Man Inside. 2nd enl. ed. 2005. (YA). 23.95 (978-0-9744929-6-4(5)) Leeway Pubs.

Stracher, Cameron. The Water Wars. 2011. (ENG.). 256p. (YA). (gr. 7-12). pap. 10.99 (978-1-4022-6759-8(2), 9781402267598) Sourcebooks, Inc.

Straczynski, J. Michael. Ten Grand Volume 1. 2014. (ENG., Illus.). 160p. pap. 12.99 (978-1-60706-831-0(1), 9781607068310) Image Comics.

Strange, Jason. Realm of Ghosts, 1 vol. Parks, Phil, illus. 2011. (Jason Strange Ser.). (ENG.). 72p. (gr. 2-3). pap. 6.25 (978-1-4342-3096-6(1)); 25.32 (978-1-4342-2962-5(9)) Stone Arch Bks.

Strasser, Todd. The Beast of Cretacea. 2015. (ENG.). 432p. (J). (gr. 7). 18.99 (978-0-7636-6901-0(6)) Candlewick Pr.

Strathearn, Chris. Marvel's Guardians of the Galaxy: Friends & Foes. 2014. (Passport to Reading Level 2 Ser.). (ENG., Illus.). 32p. (J). (gr. -1-3). pap. 3.99 (978-0-316-29318-1(0)) Little, Brown Bks. for Young Readers.

Strickland, Brad & Fuller, Thomas E. Missing! 2004. (Mars Year One Ser.: 2). (ENG., Illus.). 176p. (J). (gr. 3-7). pap. 9.99 (978-0-689-86401-8(9), Aladdin) Simon & Schuster Children's Publishing.

Stroud, David Wayne. Wiggles the White Blood Cell. Stroud, David Wayne, illus. 2005. (Illus.). (J). 14.95 (978-0-9762835-1-5(4)) Shooting Star Publishing.

Strungis, Elaine. Sammi & Danny Learn about Jupiter. 2012. 32p. pap. 14.50 (978-1-4669-5411-3(6)) Trafford Publishing.

—Sammi & Danny Learn about Mercury. 2012. 28p. pap. 13.55 (978-1-4669-5413-7(2)) Trafford Publishing.

—Sammi & Danny Learn about the Earth. 2012. 32p. pap. 14.50 (978-1-4669-3731-4(9)) Trafford Publishing.

—Sammi & Danny Learn about Uranus. 2012. 32p. pap. 14.50 (978-1-4669-6297-2(6)) Trafford Publishing.

—Sammi & Danny Learn about Venus. 2012. 32p. pap. 14.50 (978-1-4669-3733-8(5)) Trafford Publishing.

Struyk-Bonn, Chris. Whisper, 1 vol. 2014. (ENG.). 352p. (YA). (gr. 8-12). pap. 12.95 (978-1-4598-0475-3(9)) Orca Bk. Pubs. USA.

Stupniker, Yehudit. The Remarkable Invention That Saves Zion: A Tale of Triz. 2007. 292p. 18.95 (978-1-932687-74-3(2), Devora Publishing) Simcha Media Group.

Suen, Anastasia. A Prize Inside: A Robot & Rico Story, 1 vol. Laughead, Mike, illus. 2009. (Robot & Rico Ser.). (ENG.). 32p. (gr. 1-2). pap. 6.25 (978-1-4342-1749-3(3)) Stone Arch Bks.

Sumerak, Marc. Big Trouble at the Big Top! Gurihiru Staff, illus. 2006. (X-Men Power Pack - 4 Titles Ser.). 24p. lib. bdg. 22.78 (978-1-59961-219-5(4)) Spotlight.

—Costumes On! Gurihiru Staff, illus. 2006. (X-Men Power Pack - 4 Titles Ser.). 24p. lib. bdg. 22.78 (978-1-59961-220-1(8)) Spotlight.

Sumner, M. C. Deadly Secrets. 2013. (Extreme Zone Ser.: 4). (ENG., Illus.). 192p. (YA). (gr. 11). pap. 13.99 (978-1-4814-2125-6(5), Simon Pulse) Simon Pulse.

—Lost Soul. 2013. (Extreme Zone Ser.: 7). (ENG., Illus.). 192p. (YA). (gr. 11). pap. 13.99 (978-1-4814-2117-1(4), Simon Pulse) Simon Pulse.

—Unseen Powers. 2013. (Extreme Zone Ser.: 3). (ENG., Illus.). 192p. (YA). (gr. 11). pap. 13.99 (978-1-4814-2114-0(X), Simon Pulse) Simon Pulse.

Survival Colony 9. 2014. (ENG., Illus.). 336p. (YA). (gr. 9). 18.99 (978-1-4814-0354-2(0), McElderry, Margaret K. Bks.) McElderry, Margaret K. Bks.

Sutherland, Tui T. Shadow Falling. 2007. (Avatars Ser.: Bk.2). 356p. (YA). (gr. 7-12). lib. bdg. 17.89 (978-0-06-085147-7(3), Eos) HarperCollins Pubs.

Sutton, Laurie. Stranded. Nathan, James, illus. 2017. (J). lib. bdg. **(978-1-4965-5185-6(0))** Stone Arch Bks.

Sutton, Laurie S. Night of a Thousand Doomsdays, 1 vol. Vecchio, Luciano, illus. 2013. (Man of Steel Ser.). (ENG.). 88p. (gr. 2-3). 26.65 (978-1-4342-4487-1(3)) Stone Arch Bks.

—Night of a Thousand Doomsdays. Vecchio, Luciano, illus. 2013. (Man of Steel Ser.). (ENG.). 88p. (gr. 2-3). pap. 5.95 (978-1-4342-4827-5(5)) Stone Arch Bks.

—Sinestro & the Ring of Fear, 1 vol. McManus, Shawn, illus. 2012. (DC Super-Villains Ser.). (ENG.). 56p. (gr. 2-3). pap. 5.95 (978-1-4342-3899-3(7), DC Super-villains) Stone Arch Bks.

Sutton, Laurie S. & Loughridge, Lee. Sinestro & the Ring of Fear, 1 vol. McManus, Shawn, illus. 2012. (DC Super-Villains Ser.). (ENG.). 56p. (gr. 2-3). lib. bdg. 26.65 (978-1-4342-3798-9(2), DC Super-villains) Stone Arch Bks.

Suzukaze, Ryo. Kuklo Unbound. Shibamoto, Thores, illus. 2015. (Attack on Titan Ser.). (ENG.). 298p. (J). (gr. 7). pap. 14.95 (978-1-939130-87-7(5), Vertical) Vertical, Inc.

Swain, H. A. Gifted. 2016. (ENG.). 320p. (YA). 17.99 (978-1-250-02830-3(2), 9781250028303) Feiwel & Friends.

Swanson, David. Tube World. Burke, Shane, illus. 2012. 158p. pap. 10.00 (978-0-9830830-4-7(5)) Swanson, David.

Swendson, Shanna. Rebel Mechanics. 2015. (ENG.). 320p. (YA). (gr. 7). 18.99 (978-0-374-30009-8(7), 9780374300098, Farrar, Straus & Giroux (BYR)) Farrar, Straus & Giroux.

Sweren-Becker, Daniel. The Ones, Bk. 1. 2016. (Ones Ser.: 1). (ENG.). 304p. (YA). 17.99 (978-1-250-08314-2(1), 9781250083142) Imprint IND. Dist: Macmillan.

Swindells, Robert. Timesnatch. Riley, Jon, illus. 2008. (ENG.). 176p. (YA). (gr. 7). pap. 12.99 (978-0-552-55592-0(4), Corgi) Transworld Publishers Ltd. GBR. Dist: Independent Pubs. Group.

Sykes, Harold S. The Beacon of Airport Seven. 2004. reprint ed. pap. 1.99 (978-1-4192-5375-1(1)) Kessinger Publishing, LLC.

Sylvester, Kevin. Miners. 2016. (MiNRS Ser.: 1). (ENG., Illus.). 352p. (J). (gr. 3-7). pap. 8.99 (978-1-4814-4040-0(3), McElderry, Margaret K. Bks.) McElderry, Margaret K. Bks.

—MiNRS. (MiNRS Ser.: 2). (ENG., Illus.). (J). (gr. 3-7). 2016. 352p. 17.99 (978-1-4814-4042-4(X)) 2015. 336p. 16.99 (978-1-4814-4039-4(X)) McElderry, Margaret K. Bks. (McElderry, Margaret K. Bks.).

Szpirglas, Jeff. Evil Eye. 2013. 192p. pap. (978-0-9867914-7-5(4)) Star Crossed Pr.

Takahashi, Kazuki. Yu-Gi-Oh!, Vol. 3. Sengupta, Anita, tr. Takahashi, Kazuki, illus. 2003. (ENG., Illus.). 216p. pap. 9.99 (978-1-59116-179-0(7)) Viz Media.

Tamura, Yumi. Book of Justice. Tamura, Yumi, illus. 2003. (Chicago Ser.: Vol. 2). (ENG., Illus.). 200p. pap. 15.95 (978-1-56931-829-4(8)) Viz Media.

Tan, Shaun. The Lost Thing. (Illus.). 32p. pap. (978-0-7344-0388-9(7), Lothian Children's Bks.) Hachette Australia.

Tanner, Lian. Battlesong. Szabla, Liz, ed. 2017. (Icebreaker Trilogy Ser.: 3). (ENG.). 304p. (J). 16.99 (978-1-250-05218-6(1), 9781250052186) Feiwel & Friends.

Tarkoff, Sarah. Eye of the Beholder - Revelation. 2018. (Eye of the Beholder Ser.: 1). 304p. pap. 15.99 (978-0-06-245638-0(5), Harper Voyager) HarperCollins Pubs.

Tarore, Martha. The Runaway Bubble. 2011. (ENG.). 35p. (J). pap. 16.95 (978-1-4327-5898-1(5)) Outskirts Pr., Inc.

Taylor, G. P. El Hechicero de las Sombras. Attrache, Ismael, tr. 2005. (SPA.). 328p. pap. 9.95 (978-950-511-910-3(0)) Santillana USA Publishing Co., Inc.

—Wormwood. 2004. (Illus.). 272p. (J). (gr. 3-6). 17.99 (978-1-59185-626-9(4)) Charisma Media.

Taylor, Travis S. & Nye, Jody Lynn. Moon Beam. 2017. (ENG.). 320p. (J). (gr. 5). 18.99 **(978-1-4814-8252-3(1))** Baen Bks.

TBD & Harper, Benjamin. Star Wars. 2016. (ENG., Illus.). 10p. (J). (gr. -1-1). bds. 10.99 *(978-0-7944-3589-9(0))* Studio Fun International.

Teacher Talk: Individual Title Six-Packs. (gr. -1-2). 27.00 *(978-0-7635-9477-0(6))* Rigby Education.

Teague, David. Henry Cicada's Extraordinary Elktonium Escapade. 2016. 320p. (J). (gr. 3-7). 16.99 *(978-0-06-237745-6(0))* HarperCollins Pubs.

Teague, Mark & Scholastic, Inc. Staff. The Doom Machine. Teague, Mark, illus. 2009. (ENG., Illus.). 384p. (J). (gr. 3-7). 17.99 *(978-0-545-15142-9(2),* Blue Sky Pr., The) Scholastic, Inc.

Teitelbaum, Michael. I Am Superman. 2009. (Justice League Classic: I Can Read! Ser.). (J). lib. bdg. 13.55 *(978-0-606-06951-9(8),* Turtleback) Turtleback Bks.

—The Secret Life of Black Cat. Sazaklis, John, illus. 2009. (Spider-Man Ser.). 64p. (J). (gr. 2-5). pap. 4.99 *(978-0-06-162626-5(0),* HarperFestival) HarperCollins Pubs.

Temple, Bob. Science Tales, 6 vols., Set. Horrocks, Savannah, illus. Incl. Protecting the Prairie. (ENG., Illus.). 64p. (gr. 2-4). 2008. lib. bdg. 22.65 *(978-1-4048-3651-8(9),* Chapter Readers); (Read-It! Chapter Books: Science Tales: Biome Battles Ser.). (ENG.). Illus.). 64p. 2008. Set lib. bdg. 65.97 *(978-1-4048-4374-5(4))* Picture Window Bks.

Terrell, Brandon. Limbo's Diner. 2015. (Tartan House Ser.). (ENG., Illus.). 96p. (J). (gr. 5-12). *(978-1-63235-164-7(1),* 12-Story Library) Pr. Room Editions LLC.

Terrill, Cristin. All Our Yesterdays. 2014. (All Our Yesterdays Ser.). (ENG.). 368p. (YA). (gr. 7-12). pap. 9.99 *(978-1-4231-8524-6(2))* Hyperion Bks. for Children.

—All Our Yesterdays. 2013. (All Our Yesterdays Ser.). (ENG.). 368p. (YA). (gr. 7-12). 17.99 *(978-1-4231-7637-4(5))* Hyperion Pr.

Terry, Teri. Fractured. 2014. (Slated Ser.: 2). (ENG.). 352p. (YA). (gr. 7). pap. 9.99 *(978-0-14-242504-6(4),* Speak) Penguin Young Readers Group.

—Shattered. (Slated Ser.: 3). (ENG.). (YA). (gr. 7). 2015. 336p. pap. 9.99 *(978-0-14-242507-7(9),* Speak) 2014. 320p. 17.99 *(978-0-399-16174-2(0),* Nancy Paulsen Books) Penguin Young Readers Group.

Tesler, Monica. Bounders. 2016. (Bounders Ser.: 1). (ENG., Illus.). 384p. (J). (gr. 5-9). 16.99 *(978-1-4814-4593-1(6),* Aladdin) Simon & Schuster Children's Publishing.

—The Tundra Trials. 2016. (Bounders Ser.: 2). (ENG., Illus.). 384p. (J). (gr. 5-9). 16.99 *(978-1-4814-4596-2(0),* Simon & Schuster/Paula Wiseman Bks.) Simon & Schuster/Paula Wiseman Bks.

Testa, Dom. Galahad 1: The Comet's Curse. 2005. 224p. (YA). per. 8.95 *(978-0-9760564-0-9(2))* Profound Impact Group, Inc.

—Galahad 2: The Web of Titan. 2006. (YA). per. 8.95 *(978-0-9760564-1-6(0))* Profound Impact Group, Inc.

—Galahad 3: The Cassini Code. 2008. 272p. (YA). pap. 9.95 *(978-0-9760564-4-7(5))* Profound Impact Group, Inc.

—The Galahad Archives Book One: Leaving Earth. 2016. (Galahad Ser.: 1). (ENG.). 480p. (YA). pap. 12.99 *(978-0-7653-8339-6(X),* 9780765383396, Tor Teen) Doherty, Tom Assocs., LLC.

—The Galahad Archives Book Three: A New Life. 2016. (Galahad Ser.: 3). (ENG.). 512p. (YA). pap. 16.99 *(978-0-7653-8341-9(1),* 9780765383419, Tor Teen) Doherty, Tom Assocs., LLC.

—The Galahad Archives Book Two: Into Deep Space. 2016. (Galahad Ser.: 2). (ENG.). 560p. (YA). pap. 16.99 *(978-0-7653-8340-2(3),* 9780765383402, Tor Teen) Doherty, Tom Assocs., LLC.

—The Web of Titan. 2010. (Galahad Ser.: 2). (ENG.). 272p. (YA). (gr. 8-12). pap. 8.99 *(978-0-7653-6078-6(0),* 9780765360786, Tor Teen) Doherty, Tom Assocs., LLC.

Tezuka, Osamu. Astro Boy, Vol. 20. Tezuka, Osamu, illus. 2003. (ENG., Illus.). 224p. pap. 9.95 *(978-1-56971-901-5(2))* Dark Horse Comics.

—Nextworld, Vol. 1. Tezuka, Osamu, illus. 2003. (ENG., Illus.). 168p. pap. 13.95 *(978-1-56971-866-7(0))* Dark Horse Comics.

—Phoenix, Vol. 1. Tezuka, Osamu, illus. 2003. (ENG., Illus.). 344p. pap. 15.95 *(978-1-56931-868-3(9))* Viz Media.

—Yamato/Space, Vol. 3. Tezuka, Osamu, illus. 2003. (Phoenix Ser.). (ENG., Illus.). 336p. pap. 15.95 *(978-1-59116-100-4(2))* Viz Media.

Thame, Val. Witches in Trouble. l.t. ed. 2006. 104p. per. *(978-1-905665-27-3(X))* Pollinger In Print.

The Guide Dog, Thelma. For the Love of My Pet. Hartley, Joshua, illus. 2012. (ENG.). 26p. (gr. k-5). pap. 14.95 *(978-1-61448-338-0(8))* Morgan James Publishing.

Thomas, Jane. Zioc Saves His Planet. 2009. (Illus.). 208p. pap. 14.49 *(978-1-4389-4930-7(8))* AuthorHouse.

Thomas, Leah. Nowhere near You. 2017. (ENG.). 400p. (YA). 17.99 *(978-1-68119-178-2(4),* 9781681191782, Bloomsbury USA Childrens) Bloomsbury Publishing USA.

Thomas, Lex. The Burnouts. (Quarantine Ser.: 3). (ENG.). 400p. (gr. 9-12). 2016. pap. 9.99 *(978-1-5124-0419-7(5),* Carolrhoda Bks.) 2014. (J). 17.99 *(978-1-60684-338-3(9),* Carolrhoda Lab™) Lerner Publishing Group.

—The Giant. 2016. (Quarantine Ser.: 4). (ENG.). 352p. (gr. 9-12). 17.99 *(978-1-5124-0103-5(X),* Carolrhoda Bks.); (YA). 35.99 *(978-1-5124-0159-2(5),* Carolrhoda Lab™) Lerner Publishing Group.

—The Loners. (Quarantine Ser.: No. 1). (ENG.). 416p. (gr. 9). 2013. (J). pap. 9.99 *(978-1-60684-438-0(5))* 2012. 17.99 *(978-1-60684-329-1(X))* Lerner Publishing Group. (Carolrhoda Lab™).

—Quarantine: The Saints Book 2. 2014. (Quarantine Ser.: No. 2). (ENG.). 400p. (J). (gr. 9). pap. 9.99 *(978-1-60684-540-0(3))* Lerner Publishing Group.

Thomas, Nigel. Tom Travis: The Lost People of Orion. 2006. 193p. pap. 24.95 *(978-1-4241-0382-9(7))* PublishAmerica, Inc.

Thomas, Rich. The Amazing Spider-Man: An Origin Story, 1 vol. Clark, Jeff, illus. 2012. (Marvel Origins Ser.). (ENG.). 48p. (J). (gr. -1-4). lib. bdg. 24.21 *(978-1-61479-007-5(8))* Spotlight.

—The Incredible Hulk: An Origin Story, 1 vol. Semeiks, Val, illus. 2012. (Marvel Origins Ser.). (ENG.). 48p. (J). (gr. -1-4). lib. bdg. 24.21 *(978-1-61479-009-9(4))* Spotlight.

Thompson, Colin. In the Pink. 2017. (Watch This Space Ser.: 2). (ENG.). 224p. (J). (gr. 4-7). pap. 9.99 *(978-1-74275-618-9(2))* Random Hse. Australia AUS. Dist: Independent Pubs. Group.

Thompson, Craig. Space Dumplins. 2015. (ENG.). 320p. (J). (gr. 3-7). 24.99 *(978-0-545-56541-7(3));* pap. 14.99 *(978-0-545-56543-1(X))* Scholastic, Inc. (Graphix).

—Space Dumplins. 2015. lib. bdg. 26.95 *(978-0-606-37760-7(3))* Turtleback Bks.

Thompson, Hannah. Living with the Fall. 2016. (ENG., Illus.). (J). 27.99 ***(978-1-63533-043-4(2),*** Harmony Ink Pr.) Dreamspinner Pr.

Thompson, Kirk Robert. Paradise Lost: Earth First. 2004. 384p. (YA). per. 18.95 *(978-0-9716681-3-3(2))* Magic Valley Pubs.

Thompson, Paul B. Lost Republic. 2014. 256p. (YA). (gr. 6-12). 19.95 *(978-1-62324-000-4(X))* Enslow Pubs., Inc.

Thorne, Frank. Prodigal: Egg of First Light: Egg of First Light. 2012. (ENG., Illus.). 96p. (YA). pap. 12.95 *(978-1-934944-14-1(9),* 9781934944141) Ape Entertainment.

A Thousand Pieces of You. 2014. (Firebird Ser.: 1). (ENG.). 368p. (YA). (gr. 9). 17.99 *(978-0-06-227896-8(7))* HarperCollins Pubs.

Tintera, Amy. Rebel. (Reboot Ser.: 2). 352p. (YA). (gr. 8). 2015. (ENG.). pap. 9.99 *(978-0-06-221711-0(9))* 2014. pap. 12.00 *(978-0-06-233790-0(4))* HarperCollins Pubs. (HarperTeen).

—Reboot. (Reboot Ser.: 1). (ENG.). (YA). (gr. 8). 2014. 400p. pap. 9.99 *(978-0-06-221708-0(9))* 2013. 384p. 17.99 *(978-0-06-221707-3(0))* HarperCollins Pubs. (HarperTeen).

Tipton, Scott, et al. Best of Klingons. Messina, David et al, illus. 2013. (Star Trek Ser.). (ENG.). 234p. pap. 24.99 *(978-1-61377-725-1(6),* 9781613777251) Idea & Design Works, LLC.

Tobin, Paul. The Genius Factor - How to Capture an Invisible Cat. Lafontaine, Thierry, illus. 2016. (ENG.). 272p. (J). 16.99 *(978-1-61963-840-2(1),* 9781619638402, Bloomsbury USA Childrens) Bloomsbury Publishing USA.

—How to Outsmart a Billion Robot Bees. Lafontaine, Thierry & Abey, Katie, illus. 2017. (ENG.). 320p. (J). 16.99 *(978-1-61963-897-6(5),* 9781619638976, Bloomsbury USA Childrens) Bloomsbury Publishing USA.

—Plants vs. Zombies Volume 6: Boom Boom Mushroom. Chabot, Jacob, illus. 2017. (Plants vs. Zombies Ser.: 6). (ENG.). 80p. (J). (gr. 3-7). 9.99 *(978-1-5067-0037-3(3))* Dark Horse Comics.

Tocco, John V. Meet the Gizmos: The First Kids on the International Space Station. Tocco, Douglas, illus. 2003. 32p. 16.95 *(978-0-9711665-2-3(8));* per. 9.95 *(978-0-9711665-3-0(6))* Favorite Uncle Bks., LLC.

Todd, Ilima. Remake. 2014. (Remake Ser.: 1). (ENG.). 304p. (YA). (gr. 7). 17.99 *(978-1-60907-924-6(8),* Shadow Mountain) Shadow Mountain Publishing.

Todd, Ruthven. Space Cat. 2008. (J). (gr. k-4). 27.50 *(978-0-8446-6561-0(4))* Smith, Peter Pub., Inc.

Tolar, Kathy. I Must Be from Another Planet. 2009. 20p. pap. 12.99 *(978-1-4389-9378-2(1))* AuthorHouse.

Tomizawa, Hitoshi. Alien Nine: Emulators. Pannone, Frank, ed. Jackson, Laura & Kobayashi, Yoko, trs. from JPN. Tomizawa, Hitoshi, illus. 2004. (Illus.). 248p. pap. 9.99 *(978-1-58664-924-1(8),* CMX 65004G, CPM Manga) Central Park Media Corp.

Toole, Anne. Crystal Cadets. Staffaroni, Adam, ed. 2016. (ENG., Illus.). 128p. (J). pap. 12.99 *(978-1-941302-16-3(5),* 9781941302163) Lion Forge, LLC, The.

Torday, Piers. The Last Wild. 2015. (Last Wild Ser.: 1). (ENG.). 352p. (J). (gr. 3-7). 8.99 *(978-0-14-750965-9(3),* Puffin Books) Penguin Young Readers Group.

Torres, J. Power Lunch Book 2: Seconds. 2014. (ENG., Illus.). 40p. (J). 12.99 *(978-1-62010-011-0(8),* 9781620100110) Oni Pr., Inc.

Torres, J., et al. Teen Titans Go!: Ready for Action. 2017. (ENG., Illus.). (J). (gr. 2-5). pap. 12.99 *(978-1-4012-6899-2(4))* DC Comics.

Torres, Jennifer. The Battle. 2014. (Briny Deep Mysteries Ser.: Bk. 3). (Illus.). 96p. (J). (gr. 4-9). 17.95 *(978-1-62285-186-7(2));* pap. 10.95 *(978-1-62285-187-4(0))* Enslow Pubs., Inc.

—The Disappearing. 2014. (Briny Deep Mysteries Ser.). (Illus.). 96p. (J). (gr. 4-9). 17.95 *(978-1-62285-172-0(2));* pap. 10.95 *(978-1-62285-173-7(0))* Enslow Pubs., Inc.

—The Return. 2014. (Briny Deep Mysteries Ser.: Bk. 2). (Illus.). 96p. (J). (gr. 4-9). 17.95 *(978-1-62285-181-2(1));* pap. 10.95 *(978-1-62285-182-9(X))* Enslow Pubs., Inc.

Torres, Mario J. The Incredible Adventures of Kaplan & Dylan: Book One: Present, 1 vol. 2009. 159p. pap. 24.95 *(978-1-4489-9513-4(2))* PublishAmerica, Inc.

Torrey, Michele. The Case of the Barfy Birthday. Newman, Barbara Johansen, illus. 2009. (Doyle & Fossey, Science Detectives Ser.: 4). (ENG.). 96p. (J). pap. 6.95 *(978-1-4027-4964-3(3))* Sterling Publishing Co., Inc.

—The Case of the Crooked Carnival. Newman, Barbara Johansen, illus. 2010. (Doyle & Fossey, Science Detectives Ser.). (ENG.). 96p. (J). (gr. 4-7). pap. 6.95 *(978-1-4027-4965-0(1))* Sterling Publishing Co., Inc.

—The Case of the Gasping Garbage. Torrey, Michele & Newman, Barbara Johansen, illus. 2009. (Doyle & Fossey, Science Detectives Ser.: 1). (ENG.). 96p. (J). (gr. 4-7). pap. 6.95 *(978-1-4027-4960-5(0))* Sterling Publishing Co., Inc.

—The Case of the Graveyard Ghost. Newman, Barbara Johansen, illus. 2009. (Doyle & Fossey, Science Detectives Ser.: 3). (ENG.). 96p. (J). pap. 6.95 *(978-1-4027-4963-6(5))* Sterling Publishing Co., Inc.

—The Case of the Mossy Lake Monster. Torrey, Michele & Newman, Barbara Johansen, illus. 2009. (Doyle & Fossey, Science Detectives Ser.: 2). (ENG.). 96p. (J). (gr. 4-7). pap. 6.95 *(978-1-4027-4962-9(7))* Sterling Publishing Co., Inc.

—The Case of the Terrible T. Rex. Newman, Barbara Johansen, illus. 2010. (Doyle & Fossey, Science Detectives Ser.). (ENG.). 96p. (J). (gr. 3-5). pap. 6.95 *(978-1-4027-4966-7(X))* Sterling Publishing Co., Inc.

Townsend, Kari. Fused. 2010. (ENG.). 208p. (J). (gr. 5-7). pap. 7.99 *(978-1-4022-4042-3(2),* Sourcebooks Jabberwocky) Sourcebooks, Inc.

The TrailFolk of Xunar-kun: Book Two in the Tellings of Xunar-kun. 2008. (YA). 30.95 *(978-0-9768585-3-X))*; pap. 16.95 *(978-0-9768585-4-6(1))* Howe, Tina Field.

Transformers: Rescue Bots: Team of Heroes. 2014. (Passport to Reading Level 1 Ser.). (ENG., Illus.). 32p. (J). (gr. -1-3). pap. 3.99 *(978-0-316-40557-7(4))* Little, Brown Bks. for Young Readers.

Traver, N. K. & Traver, N. K. Duplicity. 2015. (ENG.). 256p. (YA). (gr. 9-12). 18.99 *(978-1-250-05914-7(3),* 9781250059147, Dunne, Thomas Bks.) St. Martin's Pr.

Treggiari, Jo. Ashes, Ashes. (ENG.). 352p. (J). (gr. 7). 2013. pap. 9.99 *(978-0-545-25564-6(3),* Scholastic Paperbacks) 2011. 17.99 *(978-0-545-25563-9(5),* Scholastic Pr.) Scholastic, Inc.

Trevayne, Emma. Coda. 2013. (ENG.). 320p. (YA). (gr. 2-17). pap. 9.95 *(978-0-7624-4728-2(1),* Running Pr. Kids) Running Pr. Bk. Pubs.

—Gamescape - Overworld. 2016. (Gamescape Ser.: 1). 416p. (YA). (gr. 9). 17.99 *(978-0-06-240876-1(3),* Greenwillow Bks.) HarperCollins Pubs.

Trod, Mariano, et al, illus. The Brilliant Dr. Wogan. 2007. (Choose Your Own Adventure Ser.: No. 17). 112p. (J). (gr. 4-7). per. 6.99 *(978-1-933390-17-8(4),* CHC17) Chooseco LLC.

Turner, Sadie & Freedman, Colette. Anomalies. 2016. (ENG.). 336p. (J). (gr. 9-12). 17.95 *(978-1-59079-361-9(7))* Select Bks., Inc.

Tzvi, G. J. The Great Adventure of la Gang du Sept. 2008. 177p. pap. 14.95 *(978-1-4116-8291-7(2))* Lulu Pr., Inc.

Ueno, Haruki. Big Hero 6, Vol. 2. 2015. (Big Hero 6 Graphic Novel Ser.: 2). lib. bdg. 23.30 *(978-0-606-37926-7(6))* Turtleback Bks.

Ueyama, Michiro. Chaotic Century. Ueyama, Michiro, illus. (Zoids Ser.). (ENG., Illus.). Vol. 11. 2004. 82p. pap. 5.95 *(978-1-56931-858-4(1))* Vol. 12. 2003. 72p. pap. 5.95 *(978-1-56931-867-6(0))* Viz Media.

Uncle Henry. Biode. Uncle Henry, illus. 100th ed. 2005. (Illus.). 216p. pap. 7.99 *(978-1-932568-02-8(6),* UHB003) Uncle Henry Bks.

Unsworth, Tania. The One Safe Place. 2014. (ENG.). 304p. (J). (gr. 5-8). 15.95 *(978-1-61620-329-0(3),* 73329) Algonquin Bks. of Chapel Hill.

Ursula K. le Guin. 2010. (Who Wrote That? Ser.). (Illus.). 128p. (YA). (gr. 6-12). 35.00 *(978-1-60413-724-8(X),* Chelsea Hse.) Facts On File, Inc.

Valentine, James. The Past Is Gone. 2007. (TimeJumpers Ser.: 1). (ENG.). 288p. (J). (gr. 3-7). pap. 13.99 *(978-1-4169-3955-9(5),* Simon & Schuster/Paula Wiseman Bks.) Simon & Schuster/Paula Wiseman Bks.

—The Present Never Happens. 2007. (TimeJumpers Ser.: 2). (ENG.). 304p. (J). (gr. 3-7). pap. 13.99 *(978-1-4169-3956-6(3),* Simon & Schuster/Paula Wiseman Bks.) Simon & Schuster/Paula Wiseman Bks.

Van Der Watt, Tony. Balthazar, the Wolf Who Reformed. 2010. 48p. pap. 12.50 *(978-1-60911-125-0(7),* Eloquent Bks.) Strategic Book Publishing & Rights Agency (SBPRA).

Van Eekhout, Greg. The Boy at the End of the World. 2012. (ENG.). 240p. (YA). (gr. 5-8). pap. 8.99 *(978-1-59990-918-9(9),* 9781599909189, Bloomsbury USA Childrens) Bloomsbury Publishing USA.

Van Hamme, Jean. Beyond the Shadows. Rosinski, Grzegorz, illus. 2008. (Thorgal Ser.: 3). (ENG.). 96p. pap. 19.95 *(978-1-905460-45-8(7))* CineBook GBR. Dist: National Bk. Network.

van Hamme, Jean. Thorgal - City of the Lost God, Vol. 6. Rosinski, Grzegorz, illus. 2009. (Thorgal Ser.: 6). (ENG.). 96p. pap. 19.95 *(978-1-84918-001-6(6))* CineBook GBR. Dist: National Bk. Network.

Van Hamme, Jean. The Three Elders of Aran. Rosinski, illus. 2007. (Thorgal Ser.: 2). (ENG.). 96p. (J). (gr. 4-7). pap. 14.99 *(978-1-905460-31-1(7))* CineBook GBR. Dist: National Bk. Network.

Vande Velde, Vivian. Deadly Pink. (ENG.). 288p. (J). (gr. 5-7). 2013. pap. 6.99 *(978-0-544-02278-2(5))* 2012. 16.99 *(978-0-547-73850-5(1))* Houghton Mifflin Harcourt Publishing Co.

—Heir Apparent. 2004. (ENG., Illus.). 352p. (J). (gr. 5-7). reprint ed. pap. 7.99 *(978-0-15-205125-9(2))* Houghton Mifflin Harcourt Publishing Co.

Vargas, George. The Prophecy of the Ages: Of War & Choices. 2004. 458p. (YA). pap. 24.95 *(978-0-595-29607-1(6))* iUniverse, Inc.

Varma, Eric. The Orphaned Knight. 2004. (Caviant Ser.: Bk. 1). 200p. (YA). 24.95 *(978-0-595-66668-3(X))* iUniverse, Inc.

Varsell, Linda. Ends of Rainbow. Curtis, E., illus. 2003. 260p. (J). per. 8.00 *(978-0-9725479-5-6(9))* Rainbow Communications.

—The Humane Touch. Curtis, E., illus. 2003. 316p. per. 10.00 *(978-0-9728737-0-3(8))* Rainbow Communications.

—The Rainbow Breakers. Curtis, E., illus. 2003. 232p. per. 7.00 *(978-0-9725479-3-2(2))* Rainbow Communications.

—The Rainbow Circle. Curtis, E., illus. 2003. 428p. (J). per. 10.00 *(978-0-9725479-9-4(1))* Rainbow Communications.

—The Rainbow Dreamers. Curtis, E., illus. 2003. 262p. per. 8.00 *(978-0-9725479-4-9(0))* Rainbow Communications.

—The Rainbow Makers. Curtis, E., illus. 2003. 148p. per. 6.00 *(978-0-9725479-2-5(4))* Rainbow Communications.

—The Rainbow Planet. Curtis, E., illus. 2003. 162p. (J). per. 6.00 *(978-0-9725479-7-0(5))* Rainbow Communications.

—The Rainbow Remnants. Curtis, E., illus. 2003. 204p. (J). per. 7.00 *(978-0-9725479-8-7(3))* Rainbow Communications.

—The Rainbow Rescue. Curtis, E., illus. 2003. 200p. (J). per. 7.00 *(978-0-9725479-6-3(7))* Rainbow Communications.

—With a Human Touch. Curtis, E., illus. 2003. 178p. per. 6.00 *(978-0-9725479-0-1(8))* Rainbow Communications.

Vaughan, M. M. The Ability. Bruno, Iacopo, illus. (Ability Ser.). (ENG.). (YA). (gr. 3-7). 2014. 352p. pap. 6.99 *(978-1-4424-5201-5(3))* 2013. 336p. 15.99 *(978-1-4424-5200-8(5))* McElderry, Margaret K. Bks. (McElderry, Margaret K. Bks.).

—Mindscape. Bruno, Iacopo, illus. 2015. (Ability Ser.). (ENG.). 336p. (YA). (gr. 3-7). pap. 7.99 *(978-1-4424-5205-3(6),* McElderry, Margaret K. Bks.) McElderry, Margaret K. Bks.

—Six. 2015. (ENG., Illus.). 368p. (J). (gr. 3-7). 16.99 *(978-1-4814-2069-3(0),* McElderry, Margaret K. Bks.) McElderry, Margaret K. Bks.

Vaughan, M. M. & Caletti, Deb. The Last Forever. Bruno, Iacopo, illus. 2016. (ENG.). 352p. (YA). (gr. 7-7). pap. 10.99 *(978-1-4424-5002-8(9),* Simon & Schuster Bks. For Young Readers) Simon & Schuster Bks. For Young Readers.

Vaughn, C. L. I See Aliens. 2007. 15p. 10.95 *(978-1-4357-0117-5(8))* Lulu Pr., Inc.

Vaupel, Robin. Rules of the Universe. 2007. (ENG.). 192p. (J). (gr. 3-7). 16.95 *(978-0-8234-1811-4(1))* Holiday Hse., Inc.

Velvet, Black. The Adventures of Sam in Space: Planet of the Sweets. 2007. 32p. (J). pap. 8.00 *(978-0-8059-7367-9(2))* Dorrance Publishing Co., Inc.

Verba, Joan Marie. Action Alert. 2008. 176p. (YA). pap. 15.95 *(978-0-9653575-8-6(9))* FTL Pubns.

Verne, Jules. From the Earth to the Moon. 2008. (Bring the Classics to Life Ser.). (ENG., Illus.). 72p. (gr. 4-12). pap., act. bk. ed. 10.95 *(978-1-55576-181-3(X),* EDCTR-407B) EDCON Publishing Group.

—A Journey to the Center of the Earth. Kumar, Vinod, illus. 2011. (Campfire Graphic Novels Ser.). (ENG.). 72p. (YA). (gr. 5-12). pap. 9.99 *(978-93-80028-40-8(7),* Campfire) Steerforth Pr.

—Journey to the Center of the Earth. Freeberg, Eric, illus. 2011. (Classic Starts(tm) Ser.). (ENG.). 160p. (J). (gr. 2-4). 6.95 *(978-1-4027-7313-6(7))* Sterling Publishing Co., Inc.

—A Journey to the Center of the Earth, 1 vol. Fisher, Eric Scott, illus. 2011. (Calico Illustrated Classics Ser.: No. 3). (ENG.). 112p. (J). (gr. 3-6). 27.07 *(978-1-61641-104-6(X))* Magic Wagon.

—A Journey to the Interior of the Earth. 2006. 196p. per. 13.95 *(978-1-59818-461-7(X))* Aegypan.

—Topsy-Turvy. Ogilvie, J. G., tr. 2009. 108p. 22.95 *(978-1-60664-685-4(0));* pap. 9.95 *(978-1-60664-314-3(2))* Rodgers, Alan Bks.

—Voyage au Centre de la Terre.Tr. of Voyage to the Center of the Earth. (FRE.). (J). pap. 14.95 *(978-2-07-051437-3(4))* Gallimard, Editions FRA. Dist: Distribooks, Inc.

—20,000 Leagues under the Sea. D'Achille, Gino, illus. 2005. (Reader's Workshop Ser.). (ENG.). 88p. (C). pap. 17.95 *(978-0-7362-2806-0(3))* CENGAGE Learning.

—20,000 Leagues under the Sea. 2004. (Fast Track Classics Ser.). (Illus.). 48p. (J). pap. *(978-0-237-52688-7(3))* Evans Brothers, Ltd.

—20,000 Leagues under the Sea, 1 vol. Fisher, Eric Scott, illus. 2011. (Calico Illustrated Classics Ser.: No. 3). (ENG.). 112p. (YA). (gr. 3-6). 27.07 *(978-1-61641-110-7(4))* Magic Wagon.

—20,000 Leagues under the Sea: Retold from the Jules Verne Original. Andreasen, Dan, illus. 2006. (Classic Starts(tm) Ser.). (ENG.). 160p. (J). (gr. 2-4). 6.95 *(978-1-4027-2533-3(7))* Sterling Publishing Co., Inc.

Verne, Jules & Fuentes, Benny. 20,000 Leguas de Viaje Submarino, 1 vol. Smith, Tod, illus. 2010. (Classic Fiction Ser.). (SPA.). 72p. (gr. 2-3). 27.99 *(978-1-4342-2324-1(8),* Graphic Revolve en Español) Stone Arch Bks.

Vick-E & Random House Disney Staff. Wall-E. Orpinas, Jean-Paul et al, illus. 2008. (Little Golden Book Ser.). (ENG.). 24p. (J). (gr. -1-2). 3.99 *(978-0-7364-2422-6(9),* RH/Disney) Random Hse. Children's Bks.

Villeneuve, Kevin J. The Adventures of Nick the Ecologist & His Robot O-Zone: The Mystery of the Missing Trees. 2007. 96p. per. 9.95 *(978-0-595-42362-0(0))* iUniverse, Inc.

Vincent, Rachel. Brave New Girl. 2017. (ENG.). 272p. (YA). (gr. 7). 17.99 ***(978-0-399-55245-8(6),*** Delacorte Pr.) Random Hse. Children's Bks.

Vyff, Shannon. 21st Century Kids. 2007. 280p. pap. 14.95 *(978-1-886057-00-5(1))* Warren Publishing, Inc.

Wacholtz, Anthony. Can You Survive in a Dystopia? An Interactive Doomsday Adventure. Nathan, James, illus. 2016. (You Choose: Doomsday Ser.). (ENG.). 112p. (gr. 3-4). lib. bdg. 31.99 *(978-1-4914-8110-3(2),* You Choose Bks.) Capstone Press of Coughlan Cos.

Wadsworth, Kay. Daisy Moon & the Worm Armies. 2011. (Illus.). 100p. pap. 12.52 *(978-1-4567-7043-3(8))* AuthorHouse.

Wagner, John. Banzai Battalion: Just Another Bug Hunt. Bolland, Brian et al, illus. 2014. (ENG.). 160p. pap. 19.99 *(978-1-78108-218-8(9),* 2000 AD) Rebellion GBR. Dist: Simon & Schuster, Inc.

Walden, Mark. Aftershock. 2014. (H. I. V. E. Ser.: 7). (ENG., Illus.). 304p. (J). (gr. 3-7). 17.99 *(978-1-4424-9467-1(0),* Simon & Schuster Bks. For Young Readers) Simon & Schuster Bks. For Young Readers.

—Deadlock. 2015. (H. I. V. E. Ser.: 8). (ENG., Illus.). 304p. (J). (gr. 3-7). 16.99 *(978-1-4424-9470-1(0),* Simon & Schuster Bks. For Young Readers) Simon & Schuster Bks. For Young Readers.

—Dreadnought. (H. I. V. E. Ser.: 4). (ENG.). (J). (gr. 3-7). 2012. 320p. pap. 8.99 *(978-1-4424-1368-9(9))* 2011. 304p. 16.99 *(978-1-4424-2186-8(X))* Simon & Schuster Bks. For Young Readers. (Simon & Schuster Bks. For Young Readers).

—Escape Velocity. (H. I. V. E. Ser.: 3). (ENG.). (J). (gr. 3-7). 2012. 368p. pap. 8.99 *(978-1-4424-1367-2(0))* 2011. 352p. 16.99 *(978-1-4424-2185-1(1))* Simon & Schuster Bks. For Young Readers. (Simon & Schuster Bks. For Young Readers).

—H. I. V. E. Higher Institute of Villainous Education. 2007. (H. I. V. E. Ser.: 1). (ENG., Illus.). 320p. (J). (gr. 3-7). 17.99 *(978-1-4169-3571-1(1),* Simon & Schuster Bks. For Young Readers) Simon & Schuster Bks. For Young Readers.

—The Higher Institute of Villainous Education. 2008. (H. I. V. E. Ser.: 1). (ENG.). 320p. (J). (gr. 3-7). pap. 8.99 *(978-1-4169-3572-8(X),* Simon & Schuster Bks. For Young Readers) Simon & Schuster Bks. For Young Readers.

—The Overlord Protocol. (H. I. V. E. Ser.: 2). (ENG.). 384p. (J). (gr. 3-7). 2009. pap. 7.99 *(978-1-4169-3574-2(6))* 2008. 18.99 *(978-1-4169-3573-5(8))* Simon & Schuster Bks. For Young Readers. (Simon & Schuster Bks. For Young Readers).

—Retribution. 2015. (Earthfall Trilogy Ser.: 2). (ENG., Illus.). 272p. (J). (gr. 3-7). 17.99 *(978-1-4424-9418-3(2),* Simon & Schuster Bks. For Young Readers) Simon & Schuster Bks. For Young Readers.

—Rogue. (H. I. V. E. Ser.: 5). (ENG.). (J). (gr. 3-7). 2012. 320p. pap. 8.99 *(978-1-4424-1369-6(7))* 2011. 304p. 16.99 *(978-1-4424-2187-5(8))* Simon & Schuster Bks. For Young Readers. (Simon & Schuster Bks. For Young Readers).

—Zero Hour. 2012. (H. I. V. E. Ser.: 6). (ENG.). 304p. (J). (gr. 3-7). 18.99 *(978-1-4424-2188-2(6),* Simon & Schuster Bks. For Young Readers) Simon & Schuster Bks. For Young Readers.

Wallace, Daniel. Darth Vader: A 3-D Reconstruction Log. Reiff, Chris & Trevas, Chris, illus. 2011. (Star Wars Ser.). (ENG.). 24p. (J). bds. 19.99 *(978-0-545-31215-8(9))* Scholastic, Inc.

—Droid Factory. 2015. (ENG.). 24p. (J). (gr. 1-8). 19.99 *(978-0-7944-3662-9(5))* Reader's Digest Assn., Inc., The.

—Star Wars Rebels - Find It Solve It Match It. Froeb, Lori & Nathanson, Amy, eds. 2015. (ENG.). 96p. (J). (gr. k-3). pap. 8.99 *(978-0-7944-3489-2(4)*, Reader's Digest Children's Bks.) Studio Fun International.

—Star Wars: Ship Factory. 2016. (ENG.). 24p. (J). (gr. 3-8). 19.99 *(978-0-7944-3739-8(7)*, Reader's Digest Children's Bks.) Studio Fun International.

Wallach, Tommy. We All Looked Up. 2015. (ENG., Illus.). 384p. (YA). (gr. 9). 17.99 *(978-1-4814-1877-5(7)*, Simon & Schuster Bks. For Young Readers) Simon & Schuster Bks. For Young Readers.

Wallenfels, Stephen. Pod. 2012. (ENG.). 304p. (gr. 12). 7.99 *(978-1-937007-43-0(X)*, Ace Bks.) Penguin Publishing Group.

Walsh, Jill Paton. The Green Book. Bloom, Lloyd, illus. 2012. (ENG.). 80p. (J). (gr. 3-7). pap. 6.99 *(978-0-312-64122-1(2)*, 9780312641221) Square Fish.

Walters, Eric. Fight for Power. 2015. (Rule of Three Ser.: 2). (ENG.). 352p. (YA). (gr. 7). 17.99 *(978-0-374-30179-8(4)*, 9780374301798, Farrar, Straus & Giroux (BYR)) Farrar, Straus & Giroux.

—Will to Survive. 2016. (Rule of Three Ser.: 3). (ENG.). 320p. (YA). 17.99 *(978-0-374-30181-1(6)*, 9780374301811, Farrar, Straus & Giroux (BYR)) Farrar, Straus & Giroux.

Wang, Holman & Wang, Jack. Star Wars Epic Yarns: A New Hope. 2015. (ENG., Illus.). 24p. (J). (gr. -1 — 1). 9.95 *(978-1-4521-3393-5(X))* Chronicle Bks. LLC.

—Star Wars Epic Yarns: Return of the Jedi. 2015. (ENG., Illus.). 24p. (J). (gr. -1 — 1). 9.95 *(978-1-4521-3500-7(2))* Chronicle Bks. LLC.

—Star Wars Epic Yarns: The Empire Strikes Back. 2015. (ENG., Illus.). 24p. (J). (gr. -1 — 1). 9.95 *(978-1-4521-3499-4(5))* Chronicle Bks. LLC.

Ward, David. Beneath the Mask, Bk. 2. 2008. (ENG.). 272p. (YA). (gr. 5-9). 16.95 *(978-0-8109-7074-8(0)*, Amulet Bks.) Abrams, Inc.

Warrington, Dean Grey. Perfiction. 2007. 188p. per. 13.95 *(978-0-595-43758-0(3))* iUniverse, Inc.

Wasserman, Robin. Crashed. 2009. (ENG.). 448p. (YA). (gr. 9-18). 16.99 *(978-1-4169-7453-6(9)*, Simon Pulse) Simon Pulse.

—Game of Flames. 2015. (Voyager Ser.). (ENG., Illus.). 208p. (J). (gr. 3-7). 12.99 *(978-0-385-38661-6(3)*, Random Hse. Bks. for Young Readers) Random Hse. Children's Bks.

—Shattered. 2011. (Cold Awakening Ser.: 2). (ENG.). 464p. (YA). (gr. 9). pap. 9.99 *(978-1-4424-2039-7(1)*, Simon Pulse) Simon Pulse.

—Torn. 2011. (Cold Awakening Ser.: 3). (ENG.). 384p. (YA). (gr. 9). pap. 9.99 *(978-1-4169-3636-7(X)*, Simon Pulse) Simon Pulse.

—The Waking Dark. 2013. (ENG.). 464p. (YA). (gr. 9). 17.99 *(978-0-375-86877-1(1)*, Knopf Bks. for Young Readers) Random Hse. Children's Bks.

—Wired. 2010. (ENG.). 400p. (YA). (gr. 9-18). 15.99 *(978-1-4169-7454-3(7)*, Simon Pulse) Simon Pulse.

Wasserman, Robin & Carman, Patrick. Voyagers Mission Launch, 3 vols., Set, Bks. 1-3. 2016. (ENG.). 224p. (J). (gr. 3-7). 38.97 *(978-1-101-94003-7(4)*, Random Hse. Bks. for Young Readers) Random Hse. Children's Bks.

Waters, Galadriel, ed. The Plot Thickens... Harry Potter Investigated by Fans for Fans. Rogers, Melissa & Heran, Michelle, illus. 2015. (ENG.). 100p. (YA). pap. 18.95 *(978-0-9723936-3-8(3))* Wizarding World Pr.

Watson, Jacqueline. Mattie-Jo-Calico. 2003. 109p. pap. 19.95 *(978-1-59286-920-6(3))* America Star Bks.

Watson, Jude. Death on Naboo. 2006. (Star Wars Ser.: No. 4). 135p. (J). lib. bdg. 13.00 *(978-1-4242-0777-0(0))* Fitzgerald Bks.

—The Desperate Mission. 2005. (Star Wars Ser.: No. 1). 168p. (J). lib. bdg. 20.00 *(978-1-4242-0774-9(6))* Fitzgerald Bks.

—Underworld. 2005. (Star Wars Ser.: No. 3). 137p. (J). lib. bdg. 20.00 *(978-1-4242-0776-3(2))* Fitzgerald Bks.

Watson, Paul. The Robot. 2011. (ENG.). 272p. (YA). (gr. 7). E-Book *(978-1-101-54326-9(4)*, Razorbill) Penguin Young Readers Group.

Watson, Vicki. Bob & the Alien Escapade. 2013. 226p. pap. *(978-0-9574062-2-3(3))* Green, Callisto.

Waugh, Sylvia. Carrera Espacial. (SPA.). (YA). 8.95 *(978-958-04-6028-2(0))* Norma S.A. COL. Dist: Distribuidora Norma, Inc.

Webb, Philip. Six Days. 2011. (ENG.). 352p. (J). (gr. 5-9). 17.99 *(978-0-545-31767-2(3)*, Chicken Hse., The) Scholastic, Inc.

—Where the Rock Splits the Sky. 2014. (ENG.). 272p. (J). (gr. 9). 17.99 *(978-0-545-55701-6(1)*, Chicken Hse., The) Scholastic, Inc.

Weber, David & Lindskold, Jane. Fire Season. 2013. (Star Kingdom (Weber) Ser.: 2). (ENG., Illus.). 304p. (YA). (gr. 7). pap. 9.99 *(978-1-4516-3921-6(X))* Baen Bks.

Webster, Christy. Teenage Mutant Ninga Turtles: Double-Team! 2014. (Step into Reading Level 4 Ser.). lib. bdg. 13.55 *(978-0-606-36283-2(5))* Turtleback Bks.

Webster, David Scott. Book One of the Naxos Island Mages: The Grand Adventure. 2003. 200p. 24.95 *(978-0-595-75137-2(7))*; pap. 14.95 *(978-0-595-29933-1(4))* iUniverse, Inc.

Weigel, Jeff. Atomic Ace & the Robot Rampage. Weigel, Jeff, illus. 2006. (ENG., Illus.). 32p. (J). (gr. 1-5). 6.95 *(978-0-8075-0485-7(8))*; 15.95 *(978-0-8075-0484-0(X))* Whitman, Albert & Co.

Weinman, Logan & Bennett, Jeffrey. Max's Ice Age Adventure. 2007. (Science Adventures with Max the Dog Ser.). (ENG., Illus.). 32p. (J). (gr. k-2). 12.00 *(978-0-9721819-2-1(X))* Big Kid Science.

Weitz, Chris. The New Order. 2015. (Young World Ser.: 2). (ENG.). 320p. (YA). (gr. 10-17). 19.00 *(978-0-316-22630-1(0))* Little, Brown Bks. for Young Readers.

—The Young World. (Young World Ser.: 1). (ENG.). (YA). (gr. 10-17). 2015. 400p. pap. 10.99 *(978-0-316-22628-8(9))* 2014. 384p. 19.00 *(978-0-316-22629-5(7))* Little, Brown Bks. for Young Readers.

Wells, Dan. Bluescreen. 2016. (Mirador Ser.: 1). 352p. (J). (gr. 8). 17.99 *(978-0-06-234787-9(X))* HarperCollins Pubs.

—Fragments. 2013. (Partials Sequence Ser.: 2). (ENG.). 576p. (YA). (gr. 9). 17.99 *(978-0-06-207107-1(6))* HarperCollins Pubs.

—Ones & Zeroes. 2017. (Mirador Ser.: 2). 416p. (YA). (gr. 8). 17.99 *(978-0-06-234790-9(X))* HarperCollins Pubs.

—Partials. (ENG.). (YA). 2013. (Partials Sequence Ser.: 1). 528p. (gr. 9). pap. 9.99 *(978-0-06-207105-7(X))* 2012. (Partials Sequence Ser.: 1). 480p. (gr. 9). 17.99 *(978-0-06-207104-0(1))* 2012. 496p. pap. 9.99 *(978-0-06-213569-8(4))* HarperCollins Pubs.

—Ruins. 2014. (Partials Sequence Ser.: 3). (ENG.). 464p. (YA). (gr. 9). 17.99 *(978-0-06-207110-1(6))* HarperCollins Pubs.

Wells, H. G. The Invisible Man, 1 vol. Fisher, Eric Scott, illus. 2011. (Calico Illustrated Classics Ser.: No. 3). (ENG.). 112p. (YA). (gr. 3-6). 27.07 *(978-1-61641-103-9(1))* Magic Wagon.

—The Lost World. 2004. (Fast Track Classics Ser.). (Illus.). 48p. (J). pap. *(978-0-237-52404-3(X))* Evans Brothers, Ltd.

—The Time Machine. 2008. (Bring the Classics to Life Ser.). (Illus.). 72p. (gr. 4-12). pap., act. bk. ed. 10.95 *(978-0-931334-43-6(8)*, EDCTR-403B) EDCON Publishing Group.

—The Time Machine. 2004. (Fast Track Classics Ser.). (Illus.). 48p. (J). pap. *(978-0-237-52406-7(6))* Evans Brothers, Ltd.

—The Time Machine. Howell, Troy, illus. 2008. (Classic Starts(tm) Ser.). (ENG.). 160p. (J). (gr. 2-4). 6.95 *(978-1-4027-4582-9(6))* Sterling Publishing Co., Inc.

—The Time Machine. Edens, John, illus. 2005. (Reader's Workshop Ser.). (ENG.). 80p. (C). pap. 17.95 *(978-0-7362-2790-2(3))* CENGAGE Learning.

—The War of the Worlds. 2008. (Bring the Classics to Life Ser.). (ENG., Illus.). 72p. (gr. 3-12). pap., act. bk. ed. 10.95 *(978-1-55576-097-7(X)*, EDCTR-306B) EDCON Publishing Group.

—The War of the Worlds. 2003. (Saddleback Classics Ser.). (Illus.). 79p. (YA). (gr. 8-12). per. 6.95 *(978-1-56254-533-8(7)*, SP5337) Saddleback Educational Publishing, Inc.

—The War of the Worlds. 2008. 256p. (J). (gr. 3-7). 29.95 *(978-1-4344-6610-5(8))*; pap. 14.95 *(978-1-4344-6609-9(4))* Wildside Pr., LLC.

—The War of the Worlds. 2004. (Fast Track Classics Ser.). (Illus.). 48p. (J). pap. *(978-0-237-52405-0(8))* Evans Brothers, Ltd.

—War of the Worlds. Bennett, Felix, illus. 2013. (Classics of Science Fiction Ser.). (ENG.). 64p. pap. 6.95 *(978-1-906230-12-8(9))* Real Reads Ltd. GBR. Dist: Casemate Pubs. & Bk. Distributors, LLC.

—The War of the Worlds, 1 vol. Fisher, Eric Scott, illus. 2011. (Calico Illustrated Classics Ser.: No. 3). (ENG.). 112p. (YA). (gr. 3-6). 27.07 *(978-1-61641-111-4(2))* Magic Wagon.

—The War of the Worlds. Akib, Jamel, illus. 2007. (Classic Starts(tm) Ser.). (ENG.). 160p. (J). (gr. 2-4). 6.95 *(978-1-4027-3688-9(6))* Sterling Publishing Co., Inc.

Wells, H. G. & Geary, Rick. The Invisible Man. (Classics Illustrated Ser.). (Illus.). 52p. (YA). pap. 4.95 *(978-1-57209-020-0(0))* Classics International Entertainment, Inc.

Wells, H. G., et al. The Island of Doctor Moreau. (Illus.). 52p. (YA). pap. 4.95 *(978-1-57209-012-5(X))* Classics International Entertainment, Inc.

Wells, Robison. Blackout. (Blackout Ser.: 1). (ENG.). (YA). (gr. 8). 2014. 448p. pap. 9.99 *(978-0-06-202613-2(5))* 2013. 432p. 17.99 *(978-0-06-202612-5(7))* HarperCollins Pubs. (HarperTeen).

—Dead Zone. 2014. (Blackout Ser.: 2). (ENG.). 384p. (YA). (gr. 8). 17.99 *(978-0-06-227502-8(X)*, HarperTeen) HarperCollins Pubs.

—Feedback. (ENG.). (YA). 2013. (Variant Ser.: 2). 336p. (gr. 8). pap. 9.99 *(978-0-06-202611-8(9))* 2012. (Variant Ser.: 2). 320p. (gr. 8). 17.99 *(978-0-06-202610-1(0))* 2012. 320p. pap. 9.99 *(978-0-06-222830-7(7))* HarperCollins Pubs. (HarperTeen).

—Variant. (Variant Ser.: 1). (ENG.). (YA). (gr. 8). 2012. 400p. pap. 9.99 *(978-0-06-202609-5(7))* 2011. 384p. 17.99 *(978-0-06-202608-8(9))* HarperCollins Pubs. (HarperTeen).

Werlin, Nancy. Double Helix. 2005. (ENG.). 256p. (YA). (gr. 7-6). pap. 7.99 *(978-0-14-240327-3(X)*, Puffin Books) Penguin Young Readers Group.

Werner, Jane. Mickey Mouse & His Spaceship (Disney: Mickey Mouse) RH Disney, illus. 2016. (Little Golden Book Ser.). (ENG.). 24p. (J). (-k). 4.99 *(978-0-7364-3633-5(2)*, Golden/Disney) Random Hse. Children's Bks.

West, Melissa. Hover. 2013. (Taking Ser.: 2). (ENG.). 352p. (YA). (gr. 7-12). pap. 9.99 *(978-1-62266-008-7(0)*, 9781622660087) Entangled Publishing, LLC.

West, Robert. Attack of the Spider Bots, 1 vol. 2008. (Star-Fighters of Murphy Street Ser.). (ENG., Illus.). 160p. (J). (gr. 4-7). pap. 6.99 *(978-0-310-71426-2(5))* Zonderkidz.

—Escape from the Drooling Octopod!, 1 vol. 2008. (Star-Fighters of Murphy Street Ser.). (ENG., Illus.). 144p. (J). (gr. 4-7). pap. 6.99 *(978-0-310-71427-9(3))* Zonderkidz.

West, Tracey. Talent Showdown. 2017. (Pokémon Ser.). (ENG.). 96p. (J). (gr. 2-5). pap. 4.99 ***(978-1-338-17591-2(2))*** Scholastic, Inc.

West, Tracey, adapted by. Independence Day Resurgence Movie Novelization: Young Readers Edition. 2016. (ENG., Illus.). 144p. (J). (gr. 3-7). pap. 6.99 *(978-1-4814-7858-8(3)*, Simon Spotlight) Simon Spotlight.

Westerfeld, Scott. Behemoth. Thompson, Keith, illus. (Leviathan Trilogy Ser.). (ENG.). (YA). (gr. 7). 2011. 512p. pap. 12.99 *(978-1-4169-7176-4(9))* 2010. 496p. 18.99 *(978-1-4169-7175-7(0))* Simon Pulse. (Simon Pulse).

—Behemoth. Thompson, Keith, illus. l.t. ed. 2010. (Leviathan Trilogy: Bk. 2). (ENG.). 540p. 23.99 *(978-1-4104-3066-3(9))* Thorndike Pr.

—Behemoth. 2011. (Leviathan Ser.: 2). lib. bdg. 24.50 *(978-0-606-22407-9(6)*, Turtleback) Turtleback Bks.

—Blue Noon. 2008. (Midnighters Ser.: 3). (ENG., Illus.). 384p. (YA). (gr. 8-12). pap. 9.99 *(978-0-06-051959-9(2)*, HarperTeen) HarperCollins Pubs.

—Bogus to Bubbly: An Insider's Guide to the World of Uglies. Phillips, Craig, illus. 2008. (Uglies Ser.). (ENG.). 224p. (YA). (gr. 7). pap. 8.99 *(978-1-4169-7436-9(9)*, Simon Pulse) Simon Pulse.

—Extras. (Uglies Ser.: 4). (YA). 2008. 83.49 *(978-1-4281-8889-1(4))* 2007. 130.75 *(978-1-4281-7244-9(0))* 2007. 132.75 *(978-1-4281-7242-5(4))* 2007. 1.25 *(978-1-4281-7235-7(1))* 2007. 112.75 *(978-1-4281-7238-8(6))* 2007. 267.75 *(978-1-4281-7239-5(4))* 2007. 110.75 *(978-1-4281-7240-1(8))* Recorded Bks., Inc.

—Extras. 2011. (Uglies Ser.). (ENG.). 416p. (YA). (gr. 7). pap. 11.99 *(978-1-4424-1978-0(4))*; lib. bdg. 19.99 *(978-1-4424-3007-5(9))* Simon Pulse. (Simon Pulse).

—Goliath, 8 vols. 2011. (YA). 122.75 *(978-1-4618-0617-2(8))*; 124.75 *(978-1-4618-0613-4(5))*; 305.75 *(978-1-4618-0618-9(6))*; 122.75 *(978-1-4618-0614-1(3))*; 1.25 *(978-1-4640-3062-8(6))* Recorded Bks., Inc.

—Goliath. Thompson, Keith, illus. (Leviathan Trilogy Ser.). (ENG.). (YA). (gr. 7). 2012. 576p. pap. 14.99 *(978-1-4169-7178-8(5))* 2011. 560p. 19.99 *(978-1-4169-7177-1(7))* Simon Pulse. (Simon Pulse).

—Goliath. 2012. (Leviathan Ser.: 3). lib. bdg. 24.50 *(978-0-606-26355-9(1)*, Turtleback) Turtleback Bks.

—Leviathan. Thompson, Keith, illus. (Leviathan Trilogy Ser.). (ENG.). (YA). (gr. 7-18). 2010. 464p. pap. 12.99 *(978-1-4169-7174-0(2))* 2009. 448p. 19.99 *(978-1-4169-7173-3(4))* Simon Pulse. (Simon Pulse).

—Leviathan. l.t. ed. 2010. (Leviathan Trilogy: Bk. 1). (ENG.). 526p. 23.95 *(978-1-4104-2572-0(X))* Thorndike Pr.

—Leviathan. 2010. (Leviathan Ser.: 1). lib. bdg. 23.30 *(978-0-606-22393-5(2)*, Turtleback) Turtleback Bks.

—The Manual of Aeronautics: An Illustrated Guide to the Leviathan Series. Thompson, Keith, illus. 2012. (ENG.). 64p. (YA). (gr. 7). 19.99 *(978-1-4169-7179-5(3)*, Simon Pulse) Simon Pulse.

—Pretties, 10 vols. (Uglies Ser.: 2). (YA). 2008. 124.75 *(978-1-4281-1126-4(3))* 2008. 75.75 *(978-1-4281-8039-0(7))* 2007. 1.25 *(978-1-4281-1117-2(4))* 2007. 97.75 *(978-1-4281-1120-2(4))* 2006. 94.75 *(978-1-4281-1122-6(0))* 2006. 127.75 *(978-1-4281-1124-0(7))* 2006. 199.75 *(978-1-4281-1121-9(2))* Recorded Bks., Inc.

—Pretties. 2011. (Uglies Ser.). (ENG.). 368p. (YA). (gr. 7). 19.99 *(978-1-4169-3639-8(4))*; pap. 11.99 *(978-1-4424-1980-3(6))* Simon Pulse. (Simon Pulse).

—The Secret Hour. 2006. 304p. *(978-1-904233-82-4(1)*, Atom Books) Little, Brown Book Group Ltd.

—Specials. (Uglies Ser.: 3). (YA). 2010. 1.25 *(978-1-4281-3456-0(5))* 2010. 247.75 *(978-1-4281-3460-7(3))* 2008. 87.49 *(978-1-4281-8042-0(7))* 2007. 101.75 *(978-1-4281-3459-1(X))* 2007. 129.75 *(978-1-4281-3465-2(4))* 2007. 131.75 *(978-1-4281-3463-8(8))* 2007. 99.75 *(978-1-4281-3461-4(1))* Recorded Bks., Inc.

—Specials. 2011. (Uglies Ser.). (ENG.). 384p. (YA). (gr. 7). pap. 12.99 *(978-1-4424-1979-7(2))*; lib. bdg. 19.99 *(978-1-4424-3008-2(7))* Simon Pulse. (Simon Pulse).

—Touching Darkness. (Midnighters Ser.: 2). (ENG.). 336p. (YA). (gr. 8-18). 2005. 17.99 *(978-0-06-051954-4(1))* 2008. reprint ed. pap. 8.99 *(978-0-06-051956-8(8))* HarperCollins Pubs. (HarperTeen).

—Uglies. 2009. (Uglies Ser.: Bk. 1). 10.36 *(978-0-7848-3338-4(9)*, Everbind) Marco Bk. Co.

—Uglies. Fournier, Guillaume, tr. 2007. (Uglies Trilogy). (FRE.). 432p. (YA). (gr. 7-12). pap. *(978-2-266-15924-1(0))* Presses Pocket.

—Uglies. (Uglies Ser.: 1). (J). 2008. 80.49 *(978-1-4281-8028-4(1))* 2007. 199.75 *(978-1-4281-1334-3(7))* 2007. 1.25 *(978-1-4281-1330-5(4))* 2006. 127.75 *(978-1-4281-1337-4(1))* 2006. 97.75 *(978-1-4281-1333-6(9))* 2006. 124.75 *(978-1-4281-1339-8(8))* 2006. 94.75 *(978-1-4281-1335-0(5))* Recorded Bks., Inc.

—Uglies. 2011. (Uglies Ser.). (ENG.). 432p. (YA). (gr. 7). pap. 12.99 *(978-1-4424-1981-0(4))*; (Illus.). 19.99 *(978-1-4169-3638-1(6))* Simon Pulse. (Simon Pulse).

—Uglies: Uglies; Pretties; Specials; Extras. 2012. (Uglies Ser.). (ENG.). 1600p. (YA). (gr. 7). pap. 47.99 *(978-1-4424-7939-5(6)*, Simon Pulse) Simon Pulse.

Westerfeld, Scott & Grayson, Devin. Cutters. 2012. (Uglies Graphic Novel Ser.: 2). lib. bdg. 22.10 *(978-0-606-26828-8(6)*, Turtleback) Turtleback Bks.

—Shay's Story. 2012. (Uglies Graphic Novel Ser.: 1). lib. bdg. 24.50 *(978-0-606-26475-4(2)*, Turtleback) Turtleback Bks.

Westerfeld, Scott & Lanagan, Margo. Swarm. 2018. (Zeroes Ser.: 2). lib. bdg. 24.50 ***(978-0-606-40832-5(0))*** Turtleback Bks.

Westerfeld, Scott, et al. Swarm. 2016. (Zeroes Ser.: 2). (ENG., Illus.). 464p. (YA). (gr. 9). 19.99 *(978-1-4814-4339-5(9)*, Simon Pulse) Simon Pulse.

—Zeroes. (Zeroes Ser.: 1). (ENG.). (YA). (gr. 9). 2016. 576p. pap. 12.99 *(978-1-4814-4337-1(2))* 2015. (Illus.). 560p. 19.99 *(978-1-4814-4336-4(4))* Simon Pulse. (Simon Pulse).

Westlake, Donald E. The Risk Profession. 2009. 60p. pap. 7.95 *(978-1-60664-380-8(0))* Rodgers, Alan Bks.

Weston, Robert Paul. Zorgamazoo. 2010. (ENG.). 288p. (J). (gr. 3-7). 8.99 *(978-1-59514-295-5(9)*, Razorbill) Penguin Young Readers Group.

Westover, Alli. My Daddy Works at NASA. 2005. (J). 15.95 *(978-1-888237-59-7(7))* Baxter Pr.

Weyn, Suzanne. The Bar Code Prophecy. 2012. (ENG.). 208p. (J). (gr. 7). 17.99 *(978-0-545-42529-2(8)*, Scholastic Pr.) Scholastic, Inc.

—The Bar Code Tattoo. 2012. (ENG.). 256p. (J). (gr. 7). pap. 9.99 *(978-0-545-47054-4(4)*, Scholastic Paperbacks) Scholastic, Inc.

—Bionic. 2016. (ENG.). 240p. (YA). (gr. 7). 17.99 *(978-0-545-90677-7(6)*, Scholastic Pr.) Scholastic, Inc.

Whaley, John Corey. Noggin. (ENG., Illus.). (YA). (gr. 9). 2015. 368p. pap. 12.99 *(978-1-4424-5873-4(9))* 2014. 352p. 18.99 *(978-1-4424-5872-7(0))* Simon & Schuster Children's Publishing. (Atheneum Bks. for Young Readers).

Whedon, Zack. The Shepherd's Tale, Vol. 3. 2010. (ENG., Illus.). 56p. 14.99 *(978-1-59582-561-2(4))* Dark Horse Comics.

Wheeler, Kim. Even More Adventures of Jonny Plumb. 2013. 186p. pap. *(978-0-7552-1570-6(2)*, Bright Pen) Authors OnLine, Ltd.

—Jonny Plumb's New Adventures... 2013. 172p. pap. *(978-0-7552-1569-0(9)*, Bright Pen) Authors OnLine, Ltd.

Whipple, Natalie. Blindsided. 2014. (ENG.). 336p. (YA). (gr. 8). pap. 11.99 *(978-1-4714-0215-9(0))* Bonnier Publishing GBR. Dist: Independent Pubs. Group.

—Transparent. 2013. (ENG.). 368p. (YA). (gr. 8). pap. 9.99 *(978-0-06-212016-8(6)*, HarperTeen) HarperCollins Pubs.

White, Andrea. Windows on the World. 2011. 238p. (J). 18.95 *(978-1-60898-105-2(3))*; pap. 9.95 *(978-1-60898-106-9(1))* namelos llc.

White, Ruth. You'll Like It Here (Everybody Does) 2012. (ENG.). 272p. (J). (gr. 4-7). 7.99 *(978-0-375-86596-1(9)*, Yearling) Random Hse. Children's Bks.

Wiggins, Bethany. Stung. 2014. (ENG.). 320p. (YA). (gr. 9). pap. 9.99 *(978-0-8027-3589-8(4)*, 9780802735898, Bloomsbury USA Childrens) Bloomsbury Publishing USA.

Wild, Kate. Firefight. 2009. (ENG.). 352p. (J). (gr. 3-7). 16.99 *(978-0-439-87176-1(X)*, Chicken Hse., The) Scholastic, Inc.

Wiley. The Extraordinary Adventures of Ordinary Basil: Island of the Volcano Monkeys. 2007. (Ordinary Basil Ser.). (J). pap. *(978-0-439-86133-5(0))* Blue Sky Pr.

Wilkinson, Kerry. Renegade. 2015. (Silver Blackthorn Trilogy Ser.: 2). (ENG.). 368p. (YA). (gr. 8-12). 18.99 *(978-1-250-06133-1(4)*, 9781250061331, St. Martin's Griffin) St. Martin's Pr.

William H. Sadlier Staff. At Space Camp, Vol. 2. 2005. (Early Library). (gr. k-2). 24.00 net. *(978-0-8215-8945-8(8))* Sadlier, William H. Inc.

Williams, Carol Lynch. The Haven: A Novel. 2014. (ENG.). 224p. (YA). (gr. 7). 18.99 *(978-0-312-69871-3(2)*, 9780312698713, St. Martin's Griffin) St. Martin's Pr.

Williams, Carol Lynch & Earl, Cheri Pray. Sweet Secrets in Pennsylvania. Oliphant, Manelle, illus. 2013. (Just in Time Ser.: 2). (ENG.). 152p. (J). (gr. 3-7). pap. 9.95 *(978-1-938301-76-6(5))* Familius LLC.

Williams, Heather L. & Muench-Williams, Heather. Caillov Learns about Space. Storch, Ellen N., illus. l.t. ed. 2005. (HRL Board Book Ser.). (J). (gr. -1-k). bds. 10.95 *(978-1-57332-308-6(X)*, HighReach Learning, Incorporated) Carson-Dellosa Publishing, LLC.

Williams, Sean. Hollowgirl: A Twinmaker Novel. 2015. (Twinmaker Ser.: 3). (ENG.). 512p. (YA). (gr. 8). 17.99 *(978-0-06-220327-4(4))* HarperCollins Pubs.

—Twinmaker. 2013. (Twinmaker Ser.: 1). (ENG.). 496p. (YA). (gr. 8). 17.99 *(978-0-06-220321-2(5)*, HarperTeen) HarperCollins Pubs.

Williams, Suzanna. Ninety-Five Percent Human. 2013. 270p. pap. *(978-0-9574662-2-7(6))* Beresford Publishing Hse.

Williamson, Jill. Rebels, 1 vol. 2014. (Safe Lands Ser.). (ENG.). 400p. (YA). pap. 9.99 *(978-0-310-73577-9(7))* Blink.

Wills, Joseph. The World. 2013. 200p. pap. *(978-1-906954-76-5(3))* Live It Publishing.

Wilson, Daniel H. A Boy & His Bot. 2011. (ENG., Illus.). 192p. (YA). (gr. 3-7). 16.99 *(978-1-59990-280-7(X)*, 9781599902807, Bloomsbury USA Childrens) Bloomsbury Publishing USA.

Windham, Ryder. The Empire Strikes Back. novel ed. 2004. (Star Wars Ser.). (ENG., Illus.). 160p. (J). (gr. 3-7). pap. 6.99 *(978-0-439-68124-7(3))* Scholastic, Inc.

—Ezra's Gamble. 2014. (Star Wars Rebels Chapter Bks.). 154p. (J). lib. bdg. 17.20 *(978-0-606-35283-3(X))* Turtleback Bks.

—Ezra's Gamble: An Original Novel. 2014. 154p. (J). ***(978-1-4242-6296-0(8))*** Disney Publishing Worldwide.

—Galactic Crisis! 2005. (DK Readers Ser.). (ENG., Illus.). 48p. (J). (gr. 3-7). pap. 3.99 *(978-0-7566-1163-7(6)*, 1241629, DK Children) Dorling Kindersley Publishing, Inc.

—Island of Lost Masks. 2015. lib. bdg. 16.00 *(978-0-606-37793-5(X))* Turtleback Bks.

—Journey Through Space. rev. ed. 2015. (DK Readers Ser.). (ENG.). 48p. (J). (gr. 1-3). pap. 3.99 *(978-1-4654-3390-9(2)*, DK Children) Dorling Kindersley Publishing, Inc.

—LEGO(r) Bionicle. Scholastic, illus. 2016. (LEGO Bionicle Ser.: 3). (ENG.). 128p. (J). (gr. 2-5). pap. 5.99 *(978-0-545-92540-2(1))* Scholastic, Inc.

—A New Hope. novel ed. 2004. (Star Wars Ser.). (ENG., Illus.). 160p. (J). (gr. 3-7). pap. 6.99 *(978-0-439-68123-0(5))* Scholastic, Inc.

—A New Hope: The Life of Luke Skywalker. 2009. 208p. (J). *(978-0-545-16177-0(0))* Scholastic, Inc.

—The Shape-Shifter Strikes. 2003. 85p. (J). *(978-0-439-45884-9(6))* Scholastic, Inc.

—The Wrath of Darth Maul. 2012. 216p. (J). *(978-0-545-43367-9(3))* Scholastic, Inc.

Winick, Judd. The Boy Who Crashed to Earth. 2015. (Hilo Ser.: 1). (ENG., Illus.). 208p. (J). (gr. 3-7). 16.99 *(978-0-385-38618-0(4)*, Random Hse. Bks. for Young Readers) Random Hse. Children's Bks.

—Saving the Whole Wide World. 2016. (Hilo Ser.: 2). (ENG., Illus.). 208p. (J). (gr. 3-7). 16.99 *(978-0-385-38624-1(9))*;Bk. 2. 13.99 *(978-0-385-38623-4(0))* Random Hse. Children's Bks. (Random Hse. Bks. for Young Readers).

Winterfeld, Henry. Star Girl. Schabert, Kyrill, tr. from GER. Wegner, Fritz, illus. 2015. (ENG.). 192p. (J). (gr. 3-8). pap. 7.99 *(978-0-486-79468-6(7))* Dover Pubns., Inc.

Wolf, Fred Alan. Dr. Quantum in the Grandfather Paradox. 2007. (Dr. Quantum Ser.). (Illus.). 176p. (J). (gr. 4-7). per. 12.95 *(978-0-9786813-3-3(9))* Elora Media, LLC.

Wolf, Mari. An Empty Bottle. 2011. 30p. 13.95 *(978-1-4638-9995-0(5))* Rodgers, Alan Bks.

Wolfe, D. K. Flap Doodle & the Incredible Kibbil Caper 2005. (Illus.). 247p. (J). (gr. 4-6). 16.95 *(978-1-59810-031-0(9))* Jeriger Pr.

Wolff, Tracy. Book 1: Crisis. 2016. (Mars Bound Ser.). (ENG.). (J). (gr. 2-8). lib. bdg. 28.50 ***(978-1-62402-197-8(2))*** ABDO Publishing Co.

—Book 2: Sabotage. 2016. (Mars Bound Ser.). (ENG.). (J). (gr. 2-8). lib. bdg. 28.50 ***(978-1-62402-198-5(0))*** ABDO Publishing Co.

—Book 3: Restoration. 2016. (Mars Bound Ser.). (ENG.). (J). (gr. 2-8). lib. bdg. 28.50 ***(978-1-62402-199-2(9))*** ABDO Publishing Co.

Wolfman, Marv. Nova Classic Volume 3. Buscema, John et al, illus. 2014. (ENG.). 304p. (J). (gr. 4-17). pap. 34.99 *(978-0-7851-8552-9(6))* Marvel Worldwide, Inc.

Wood, Brian. Mara TP. 2013. (ENG., Illus.). 136p. (YA). pap. 12.99 *(978-1-60706-810-5(9)*, 9781607068105) Image Comics.

Wood, Dorreya. Planet Cannibal. 2009. (Illus.). 90p. (YA). pap. *(978-0-615-26795-1(5))* World Awake Bks.

Wood, Greg V. & Benchmark Education Co. Opinions about Themes in Science Fiction: Two Stories about Valerie

Logan, Interstellar Troubleshooter. Retwick, Roy, illus. 2014. (Text Connections Ser.). (J). (gr. 3). (978-1-4509-9665-5(5)) Benchmark Education Co.

Wooding, Chris. Pale. 2012. (Stoke Books Titles Ser.). (ENG.). 72p. (YA). (gr. 8-12). pap. 6.95 (978-1-78112-091-0(9)); lib. bdg. 22.60 (978-1-78112-092-7(7)) Lerner Publishing Group.

—Velocity. 2017. (ENG.). 336p. (J). (gr. 7). 18.99 (978-0-545-94494-6(5), Scholastic Pr.) Scholastic, Inc.

Wrecks, Billy. DK Adventures: DC Comics: Batman: Adventures of the Dark Knight. 2016. (DK Adventures Ser.). (ENG., Illus.). 96p. (J). (gr. 3-7). 16.99 (978-1-4654-4608-4(7), DK Children) Dorling Kindersley Publishing, Inc.

Wrede, Patricia C. Revenge of the Sith. novel ed. 2005. (Star Wars Ser.). (ENG., Illus.). 192p. (J). (gr. 3-7). pap. 6.99 (978-0-439-13929-8(5), Scholastic Paperbacks) Scholastic, Inc.

Wright Johnson, Shelli. Falcon in the Nest: A Story of Bes Adventure. 2004. 273p. pap. 27.95 (978-1-4137-5263-2(2)) America Star Bks.

Wright, Julie. Hazzardous Universe. Wasden, Kevin, illus. 2011. 242p. (J). pap. (978-1-60861-206-2(6)) Covenant Communications.

Wright, Marcus. Raincloud. 2007. 172p. pap. 9.88 (978-0-615-15579-1(0)) Digitex-U Pubns.

Wronski, Gareth. Holly Farb & the Princess of the Galaxy. 2017. (ENG., Illus.). 320p. (J). (gr. 3-7). 16.99 **(978-1-4814-7177-0(5)**, Aladdin) Simon & Schuster Children's Publishing.

Wyatt, Chris. Falcon: Fight or Flight. 2015. (Mighty Marvel Chapter Bks.). (J). lib. bdg. 16.00 (978-0-606-36905-3(8)) Turtleback Bks.

—Falcon: Fight or Flight: A Mighty Marvel Chapter Book. Grummett, Tom, illus. 2015. (Mighty Marvel Chapter Book Ser.). (ENG.). 128p. (J). (gr. 3-7). pap. 5.99 (978-1-4847-1529-1(2), Marvel Pr.) Disney Publishing Worldwide.

—Knowhere to Run: Starring Star-Lord. Lim, Ronald & Troy, Andy, illus. 2014. 117p. (J). **(978-1-4844-4394-1(2)**, Marvel Pr.) Disney Publishing Worldwide.

—Star-Lord: Knowhere to Run. 2014. (Mighty Marvel Chapter Bks.). (J). lib. bdg. 16.00 (978-0-606-35920-7(6)) Turtleback Bks.

—Star-Lord - Knowhere to Run. Lim, Ron & Troy, Andy, illus. 2014. (ENG.). 128p. (J). (gr. 3-7). pap. 5.99 (978-1-4847-1269-6(2), Marvel Pr.) Disney Publishing Worldwide.

X-Men. 2003. (J). (978-1-57657-859-9(3)) Paradise Pr., Inc.

Yager, Fred. Sound from a Star: A Novel. 2011. 150p. (YA). 31.95 (978-1-889262-90-1(0)) Hannacroix Creek Bks., Inc.

Yamamoto, Lani. Albert. Yamamoto, Lani, illus. 2004. (ENG., Illus.). 32p. (J). 10.95 (978-1-58536-251-6(4)) Sleeping Bear Pr.

Yancey, Rick. The Infinite Sea. (5th Wave Ser.: 2). (ENG.). (YA). (gr. 9-12). 2015. 336p. pap. 10.99 (978-1-101-99698-0(6), Speak) 2014. 320p. 18.99 (978-0-399-16242-8(9), G.P. Putnam's Sons Books for Young Readers) Penguin Publishing Group.

—The Infinite Sea. 2015. (5th Wave Ser.: 2). lib. bdg. 22.10 (978-0-606-38204-5(6)) Turtleback Bks.

—The Last Star. 2016. (5th Wave Ser.: 3). (ENG.). 352p. (YA). (gr. 9). 18.99 (978-0-399-16243-5(7), G.P. Putnam's Sons Books for Young Readers) Penguin Young Readers Group.

—The 5th Wave. (5th Wave Ser.: Bk. 1). (ENG.). (YA). (gr. 9). 2015. 512p. pap. 10.99 (978-0-14-242583-1(4), Speak) 2013. 480p. 18.99 (978-0-399-16241-1(0), G.P. Putnam's Sons Books for Young Readers) Penguin Publishing Group.

—The 5th Wave. movie tie-in ed. 2015. (ENG.). (YA). (gr. 9-12). (5th Wave Ser.: 1). 512p. pap. 10.99 (978-0-14-751908-5(X), Speak); (5th Wave Ser.: Bk. 1). 480p. 18.99 (978-1-101-99651-5(X), G.P. Putnam's Sons Books for Young Readers);Set. pap., pap., pap. 21.98 (978-1-101-99998-1(5), Speak) Penguin Young Readers Group.

—The 5th Wave. 2015. (5th Wave Ser.: Vol. 1). (ENG.). (YA). (gr. 9). lib. bdg. 21.60 **(978-1-62765-623-8(5))** Perfection Learning Corp.

—The 5th Wave. 2015. (5th Wave Ser.: 1). lib. bdg. 22.10 (978-0-606-36640-3(7)); lib. bdg. 22.10 (978-0-606-37680-8(1)) Turtleback Bks.

Yang, Gene Luen. The Shadow Hero. Liew, Sonny, illus. 2014. (ENG.). 176p. (YA). (gr. 7-12). pap. 17.99 (978-1-59643-697-8(2), 9781596436978, First Second Bks.) Roaring Brook Pr.

—The Shadow Hero. Liew, Sonny, illus. 2014. (YA). lib. bdg. 30.60 (978-0-606-35521-6(9)) Turtleback Bks.

Yansky, Brian. Alien Invasion & Other Inconveniences. 2010. (ENG., Illus.). 240p. (YA). (gr. 9-18). 15.99 (978-0-7636-4384-3(X)) Candlewick Pr.

Yep, Laurence. The Star Maker. 2010. (ENG.). 112p. (J). (gr. 3-7). 16.99 (978-0-06-025315-8(0)) HarperCollins Pubs.

Young, Helen Ann. Hello to Hellie's World. Young, Tim Blair, illus. 2013. 46p. pap. (978-1-908353-00-9(7)) Young Editions.

Young, Moira. Blood Red Road. (Dust Lands Ser.: 1). (ENG.). (YA). (gr. 9). 2012. 480p. pap. 10.99 (978-1-4424-2999-4(2)) 2011. (Illus.). 464p. 17.99 (978-1-4424-2998-7(4)) McElderry, Margaret K. Bks. (McElderry, Margaret K. Bks.).

—Blood Red Road, 9 vols. 2011. (YA). 122.75 (978-1-4618-0629-5(1)); 120.75 (978-1-4618-0633-2(X)); 1.25 (978-1-4640-2632-4(7)); 120.75 (978-1-4618-0630-1(5)); 286.75 (978-1-4618-0634-9(8)) Recorded Bks., Inc.

—Raging Star. (Dust Lands Ser.: 3). (ENG., Illus.). 448p. (YA). (gr. 9). 2015. pap. 10.99 (978-1-4424-3003-7(6)) 2014. 17.99 (978-1-4424-3002-0(8)) McElderry, Margaret K. Bks. (McElderry, Margaret K. Bks.).

—Rebel Heart. 2013. (Dust Lands Ser.: 2). (ENG., Illus.). 448p. (YA). (gr. 9). pap. 11.99 (978-1-4424-3001-3(X), McElderry, Margaret K. Bks.) McElderry, Margaret K. Bks.

Young, Shaun. Castor. 2016. (ENG., Illus.). 230p. (YA). pap. 14.99 (978-1-63476-886-3(8), Harmony Ink Pr.) Dreamspinner Pr.

Young, Suzanne. The Adjustment. 2017. (Program Ser.: 5). (ENG., Illus.). 416p. (YA). (gr. 9). 17.99 (978-1-4814-7132-9(5), Simon Pulse) Simon Pulse.

—The Epidemic. 2016. (Program Ser.: 4). (ENG., Illus.). 384p. (YA). (gr. 9). 17.99 (978-1-4814-4470-5(0), Simon Pulse) Simon Pulse.

—The Program. (Program Ser.: 1). (ENG., Illus.). (YA). (gr. 9). 2014. 432p. pap. 11.99 (978-1-4424-4581-9(5)) 2013. 416p. 17.99 (978-1-4424-4580-2(7)) Simon Pulse. (Simon Pulse).

—The Remedy. 2015. (Program Ser.: 3). (ENG., Illus.). 416p. (YA). (gr. 9). 17.99 (978-1-4814-3765-3(8), Simon Pulse) Simon Pulse.

—The Treatment. (ENG., Illus.). (YA). (gr. 9). 2015. (Program Ser.: 2). 368p. pap. 11.99 (978-1-4424-4584-0(X)) 2014. (Program Ser.). 352p. 18.99 (978-1-4424-4583-3(1)) Simon Pulse. (Simon Pulse).

Zachary, Alyson A. Earth Helpers: Count the Ways to Save Our Planet. 2009. (ENG.). 12p. 8.95 (978-1-58117-906-4(5), Intervisual/Piggy Toes) Bendon, Inc.

Zakour, John. Baxter Moon Galactic Scout. 2008. 198p. (J). (gr. 5-10). per. 8.95 (978-0-9768126-9-2(X)) Brown Barn Bks.

Zappa, Ahmet & Zappa, Shane Muldoon. Sage & the Journey to the Wish World. Bonatakis, Shannon & Disney Storybook Art Team, illus. 2015. (Star Darlings Ser.: 1). (ENG.). 176p. (J). (gr. 3-7). pap. 6.99 (978-1-4231-6643-6(4)) Disney Pr.

Zenescope Entertainment Staff & Brusha, Joe. Sci-Fi & Fantasy: The Perfect Mate. 2012. (Illus.). 168p. (YA). pap. 15.99 (978-1-937068-91-2(9)) Zenescope Entertainment.

Zenescope Entertainment Staff, et al. Never Underestimate a Hermit Crab. 2014. (ENG., Illus.). 48p. (J). pap. 9.99 (978-1-939683-25-0(4), 9781939683250) Zenescope Entertainment.

Zevin, Gabrielle. Because It Is My Blood, 1 vol. 2012. (Birthright Ser.: 2). (ENG.). 368p. (YA). (gr. 7). 17.99 (978-0-374-38074-8(0), 9780374380748, Farrar, Straus & Giroux (BYR)) Farrar, Straus & Giroux.

—Because It Is My Blood. 2013. (Birthright Ser.: 2). (ENG.). 384p. (YA). (gr. 7). pap. 9.99 (978-1-250-03422-9(1), 9781250034229) Square Fish.

Zhang, Kat. Echoes of Us: The Hybrid Chronicles, Book 3. 2015. (Hybrid Chronicles Ser.: 3). (ENG.). 368p. (YA). (gr. 8). pap. 9.99 (978-0-06-211494-5(8)) HarperCollins Pubs.

—Once We Were: The Hybrid Chronicles, Book 2. 2014. (Hybrid Chronicles Ser.: 2). (ENG.). 384p. (YA). (gr. 8). pap. 9.99 (978-0-06-211491-4(3)) HarperCollins Pubs.

—What's Left of Me. 2012. (Hybrid Chronicles Ser.: 1). (ENG.). 352p. (YA). (gr. 8). 17.99 (978-0-06-211487-7(5)) HarperCollins Pubs.

Zircher, Patrick, et al, illus. Captain America by Ed Brubaker - Volume 3. 2013. (ENG.). 125p. (J). (gr. 4-17). pap. 19.99 (978-0-7851-6076-2(0), Marvel Pr.) Disney Publishing Worldwide.

SCIENCE FICTION—HISTORY AND CRITICISM

Benjamin, Kathy, Lisa and Kafer & Benchmark Education Co. Staff. Opinions about Science Fiction Technology - from Fiction to Fact. 2014. (Text Connections Ser.). (J). (gr. 5). (978-1-4900-1372-5(5)) Benchmark Education Co.

Bloom, Harold, ed. Kurt Vonnegut, New Edition. 2nd rev. ed. 2008. (Bloom's Modern Critical Views Ser.). 176p. (C). (gr. 9-18). 45.00 (978-1-60413-167-3(5), Chelsea Hse.) Facts On File, Inc.

—Mary Shelley's Frankenstein. 2007. (Bloom's Guides). 150p. (YA). (gr. 9-12). 30.00 (978-0-7910-9358-0(1)) Facts On File, Inc.

Bodden, Valerie. Science Fiction. 2013. (Illus.). 48p. (J). 35.65 (978-1-60818-181-0(2), Creative Education) Creative Co., The.

Bortz, Fred. Envisioning Outer Space: Where Science & Fiction Meet. 2015. (J). (978-1-4677-6305-9(5)) Twenty First Century Bks.

Egan, Kate, et al. The World of the Hunger Games. 2012. (ENG., Illus.). 192p. (J). (gr. 7-7). 17.99 (978-0-545-42512-4(3)) Scholastic, Inc.

Friedland, Joyce, ed. Ender's Game: Novel-Ties Study Guide. 2011. 38p. pap. 16.95 (978-0-7675-4510-5(9)) Learning Links Inc.

Gagne, Tammy. The Giver. 2016. **(978-1-5105-2015-8(5))** SmartBook Media, Inc.

Hamilton, John. The Final Frontier, 1 vol. 2006. (World of Science Fiction Ser.). (ENG., Illus.). 32p. (gr. 4-7). 27.07 (978-1-59679-987-5(0), Abdo & Daughters) ABDO Publishing Co.

—Future Societies, 1 vol. 2006. (World of Science Fiction Ser.). (ENG., Illus.). 32p. (gr. 4-7). 27.07 (978-1-59679-988-2(9), Abdo & Daughters) ABDO Publishing Co.

—The Golden Age & Beyond, 1 vol. 2006. (World of Science Fiction Ser.). (ENG., Illus.). 32p. (gr. 4-7). 27.07 (978-1-59679-989-9(7), Abdo & Daughters) ABDO Publishing Co.

—Man-Made Horrors, 1 vol. 2007. (World of Horror Ser.). (ENG.). 32p. (gr. 4-8). 27.07 (978-1-59928-769-0(2), Abdo & Daughters) ABDO Publishing Co.

—Modern Masters of Science Fiction, 1 vol. 2006. (World of Science Fiction Ser.). (ENG., Illus.). 32p. (gr. 4-7). 27.07 (978-1-59679-990-5(0), Abdo & Daughters) ABDO Publishing Co.

—New Worlds, 1 vol. 2006. (World of Science Fiction - 12 Titles Ser.). (ENG., Illus.). 32p. (J). (gr. 4-7). lib. bdg. 27.07 (978-1-59679-991-2(9), Abdo & Daughter) ABDO Publishing Co.

—Pioneers of Science Fiction, 1 vol. 2006. (World of Science Fiction Ser.). (ENG.). 32p. (gr. 4-7). 27.07 (978-1-59679-992-9(7), Abdo & Daughters) ABDO Publishing Co.

—Spaceships, 1 vol. 2006. (World of Science Fiction Ser.). (ENG., Illus.). 32p. (gr. 4-7). 27.07 (978-1-59679-995-0(1), Abdo & Daughters) ABDO Publishing Co.

—Time Travel, 1 vol. 2006. (World of Science Fiction Ser.). (ENG., Illus.). 32p. (gr. 4-7). 27.07 (978-1-59679-996-7(X), Abdo & Daughters) ABDO Publishing Co.

—Weapons of Science Fiction, 1 vol. 2006. (World of Science Fiction Ser.). (ENG., Illus.). 32p. (gr. 4-7). 27.07 (978-1-59679-997-4(8), Abdo & Daughters) ABDO Publishing Co.

Hoppa, Jocelyn. Isaac Asimov: Science Fiction Trailblazer. 2009. (Authors Teens Love Ser.). (Illus.). 104p. (J). (gr. 6). lib. bdg. 33.27 (978-0-7660-2961-3(1)) Enslow Pubs., Inc.

Loos, Pamela. Reading the Giver. 2005. (Engaged Reader Ser.). (Illus.). 96p. (gr. 5-8). lib. bdg. 25.00 (978-0-7910-8830-2(8), Chelsea Hse.) Facts On File, Inc.

Nagle, Jeanne, ed. Great Authors of Science Fiction & Fantasy. 2013. (Essential Authors for Children & Teens Ser.). (Illus.). 175p. (YA). (gr. 7-12). 45.00 (978-1-62275-090-0(X)) Rosen Publishing Group, Inc., The.

Orwell, George. 1984. Orwell, George & Bloom, Harold, eds. 2nd rev. ed. 2006. (Bloom's Modern Critical Interpretations Ser.). 216p. (C). (gr. 9-18). lib. bdg. 45.00 (978-0-7910-9300-9(X), Chelsea Hse.) Facts On File, Inc.

Seife, Emily & Collins, Suzanne. The Hunger Games - Tribute Guide. 2012. (Hunger Games Ser.). (ENG., Illus.). 128p. (J). (gr. 7). pap. 7.99 (978-0-545-45782-8(3), Scholastic Pr.) Scholastic, Inc.

Throp, Claire. Exploring Other Worlds: What Is Science Fiction? 2010. (Culture in Action Ser.). (ENG.). 32p. (gr. 3-6). 30.65 (978-1-4109-3928-9(6), NA-r) Heinemann-Raintree.

SCIENCE PROJECTS

Adamick, Mike. Dad's Book of Awesome Science Experiments: 30 Inventive Experiments to Excite the Whole Family! 2014. (ENG., Illus.). 192p. pap. 18.99 (978-1-4405-7077-3(9)) Adams Media Corp.

Anderson, Maxine. Amazing Leonardo Da Vinci Inventions: You Can Build Yourself. 2006. (Build It Yourself Ser.). (ENG., Illus.). 128p. (J). (gr. 3-7). pap. 15.95 (978-0-9749344-2-6(9)) Northern Trails Pr.

Beck, Esther. Cool Odor Decoders: Fun Science Projects about Smells, 1 vol. 2008. (Cool Science Ser.). (ENG.). 32p. (YA). (gr. 2-5). 28.50 (978-1-59928-909-0(1)) ABDO Publishing Co.

—Cool Sensory Suspense: Fun Science Projects about the Senses, 1 vol. 2008. (Cool Science Ser.). (ENG.). 32p. (YA). (gr. 2-5). 28.50 (978-1-59928-910-6(5)) ABDO Publishing Co.

—Cool Spy Supplies: Fun Top Secret Science Projects, 1 vol. 2008. (Cool Science Ser.). (ENG.). 32p. (YA). (gr. 2-5). 28.50 (978-1-59928-911-3(3)) ABDO Publishing Co.

Benbow, Ann & Mably, Colin. Master the Scientific Method with Fun Life Science Projects. LaBaff, Tom, illus. 2009. (Real Life Science Experiments Ser.). 48p. (J). (gr. 2-5). lib. bdg. 25.27 (978-0-7660-3151-7(9)) Enslow Pubs., Inc.

Blobaum, Cindy. Explore Night Science! With 25 Great Projects. Stone, Bryan, illus. 2012. (Explore Your World Ser.). (ENG.). 96p. (J). (gr. k-4). pap. 12.95 (978-1-61930-156-6(3)) Open City Bks.

Bochinski, Julianne Blair. More Award-Winning Science Fair Projects. DiBiase, Judy, illus. 2003. (ENG.). 228p. (J). (gr. 6-12). pap. 22.00 (978-0-471-27337-0(6), Wiley) Wiley, John & Sons, Inc.

Bolte, Mari. Super Science Projects You Can Make & Share. 2015. (Sleepover Girls Crafts Ser.). (ENG.). 32p. (gr. 3-4). lib. bdg. 27.99 (978-1-62065-177-3(7), Snap Bks.) Capstone Press of Coughlan Cos.

Bonnet, Robert L. & Keen, Dan. Home Run! Science Projects with Baseball & Softball. 2009. (Score! Sports Science Projects Ser.). (Illus.). 104p. (J). (gr. 5-9). lib. bdg. 33.27 (978-0-7660-3365-8(1)) Enslow Pubs., Inc.

Brown, Patrica A. & Krelle, Ginger R. Classroom Hydroponic Plant Factory, Vol. 2. 2nd rev. ed. 2004. (Illus.). 102p. (YA). (gr. 7-12). pap. 19.95 (978-0-9669557-1-2(4)) Foothill-Hydroponics.

Brynie, Faith Hickman. Parent's Crash Course: Elementary School Science Fair Projects. 2005. (ENG., Illus.). 256p. pap. 16.99 (978-0-7645-9934-7(8)) Houghton Mifflin Harcourt Publishing Co.

Buczynski, Sandra. Super Smart Information Strategies: Get Ready for a Winning Science Project. 2011. (Explorer Library: Information Explorer Ser.). (ENG.). 32p. (gr. 4-8). pap. 14.21 (978-1-61080-270-3(5), 201231); lib. bdg. 28.50 (978-1-61080-124-9(5), 201134) Cherry Lake Publishing.

Burillo-Kirch, Christine. Bioengineering: Discover How Nature Inspires Human Designs. Cornell, Alexis, illus. 2016. (Build It Yourself Ser.). (ENG.). 128p. (gr. 3-7). 22.95 (978-1-61930-366-9(3)) Open City Bks.

Calhoun, Yael. Earth Science Fair Projects, Revised & Expanded Using the Scientific Method. LaBaff, Stephanie & LaBaff, Tom, illus. 2010. (Earth Science Projects Using the Scientific Method Ser.). 160p. (J). (gr. 5-18). 35.94 (978-0-7660-3425-9(9)) Enslow Pubs., Inc.

—Plant & Animal Science Fair Projects. rev. exp. ed. 2010. (Biology Science Projects Using the Scientific Method Ser.). (Illus.). 160p. (J). (gr. 5-18). 35.94 (978-0-7660-3421-1(6)) Enslow Pubs., Inc.

Candlewick Press, Candlewick. Ruff Ruffman's 44 Favorite Science Activities. WGBH, illus. 2015. (Fetch! with Ruff Ruffman Ser.). (ENG.). 132p. (J). (gr. 3-7). pap. 12.99 (978-0-7636-7432-8(X), Candlewick Entertainment) Candlewick Pr.

Carlson, Laurie M. & Carlson, Laurie. Thomas Edison for Kids: His Life & Ideas, 21 Activities. 2006. (For Kids Ser.). (ENG., Illus.). 160p. (J). (gr. 4-7). pap. 17.99 (978-1-55652-584-1(2), 1248637) Chicago Review Pr., Inc.

Carson, Mary Kay. Weather Projects for Young Scientists: Experiments & Science Fair Ideas. 2007. (ENG., Illus.). 144p. (J). (gr. 4-7). pap. 16.95 (978-1-55652-629-9(6)) Chicago Review Pr., Inc.

Cobb, Allan B. Super Science Projects about Light & Optics. 2005. (Psyched for Science Ser.). (Illus.). 48p. (YA). (gr. 5-8). lib. bdg. 29.25 (978-0-8239-3177-4(3), SCLIOP) Rosen Publishing Group, Inc., The.

—Super Science Projects about Oceans. 2005. (Psyched for Science Ser.). (Illus.). 48p. (YA). (gr. 5-8). lib. bdg. 29.25 (978-0-8239-3174-3(9), SCOCEA) Rosen Publishing Group, Inc., The.

—Super Science Projects about Sound. 2005. (Psyched for Science Ser.). (Illus.). 48p. (YA). (gr. 5-8). lib. bdg. 29.25 (978-0-8239-3176-7(5), SCSOUN) Rosen Publishing Group, Inc., The.

Cobb, Vicki. Science Experiments You Can Eat. Carpenter, Tad, illus. 2016. 256p. (J). (gr. 3-7). pap. 9.99 (978-0-06-237729-6(9)) HarperCollins Pubs.

—See for Yourself! More Than 100 Amazing Experiments for Science Fairs & School Projects. Klug, Dave, illus. 2nd ed. 2010. (ENG.). 192p. (J). (gr. 1-3). pap. 14.95 (978-1-61608-083-9(3), 608083) Skyhorse Publishing Co., Inc.

Cook, Trevor. Science Lab Set. 2009. (Illus.). (J). (gr. 4-7). 151.50 (978-1-4358-2826-1(7), PowerKids Pr.) Rosen Publishing Group, Inc., The.

Cool Science, 1 vol., Set. Incl. Cool Distance Assistants: Fun Science Projects to Propel Things. Hopwood, James. 28.50 (978-1-59928-906-9(7)); Cool Dry Ice Devices: Fun Science Projects with Dry Ice. Hopwood, James. 28.50 (978-1-59928-907-6(5)); Cool Gravity Activities: Fun Science Projects about Balance. Hopwood, James. 28.50 (978-1-59928-908-3(3)); Cool Odor Decoders: Fun Science Projects about Smells. Beck, Esther. 28.50 (978-1-59928-909-0(1)); Cool Sensory Suspense: Fun Science Projects about the Senses. Beck, Esther. 28.50 (978-1-59928-910-6(5)); Cool Spy Supplies: Fun Top Secret Science Projects. Beck, Esther. 28.50 (978-1-59928-911-3(3)); (YA). (gr. 2-5). (Cool Science Ser.: 6). (ENG.). 32p. 2008. 171.00 (978-1-59928-905-2(9), Checkerboard Library) ABDO Publishing Co.

D'Cruz, Anna-Marie. Do It Yourself Projects! Set. 2009. (Illus.). (J). (gr. 4-7). 143.70 (978-1-4358-3004-2(0), PowerKids Pr.) Rosen Publishing Group, Inc., The.

Designing a Winning Science Fair Project. 2014. (Explorer Junior Library: Information Explorer Junior Ser.). (ENG.). 24p. (J). (gr. 1-4). lib. bdg. 28.50 (978-1-63137-790-7(6), 205403) Cherry Lake Publishing.

Dorling Kindersley Publishing Staff. The Science Kit, Kit. 2011. (ENG.). 48p. (J). (gr. 3-7). 29.99 (978-0-7566-8864-6(7), DK Children) Dorling Kindersley Publishing, Inc.

Dorling Kindersley Publishing Staff & Challoner, Jack. Maker Lab: 28 Super Cool Projects. 2016. (ENG., Illus.). 160p. (J). (gr. 3-7). 19.99 (978-1-4654-5135-4(8), DK Children) Dorling Kindersley Publishing, Inc.

Doudna, Kelly. The Kid's Book of Simple Everyday Science. 2013. (ENG., Illus.). 112p. (J). (gr. k-4). pap. 13.95 (978-1-938063-34-3(1), Mighty Media Kids) Mighty Media Pr.

Duke, Shirley. Step-by-Step Experiments with the Water Cycle. Ostrom, Bob, illus. 2012. (Step-By-Step Experiments Ser.). (ENG.). 32p. (J). (gr. 1-4). lib. bdg. 29.93 (978-1-60973-615-6(X), 201241) Child's World, Inc., The.

Earth Instructional Guide. 2009. (Grade 8: Science Exit Project Kits Ser.). spiral bd. (978-1-4042-4022-3(5), Rosen Classroom) Rosen Publishing Group, Inc., The.

Ebner, Aviva. Environmental Science Experiments. 2011. (Experiments for Future Scientists Ser.). (Illus.). 160p. (gr. 5-8). 35.00 (978-1-60413-851-1(3)) Facts On File, Inc.

Ecology Experiments. 2010. (Facts on File Science Experiments Ser.). (Illus.). 184p. (J). (gr. 6-12). 40.00 (978-0-8160-8169-1(7)) Facts On File, Inc.

Edom, H. Science Activities, Vol. 1. 2010. (Science Activities Ser.). 72p. (J). 13.99 (978-0-7945-2752-5(3), Usborne) EDC Publishing.

Enz, Tammy. Dynamic Planet: Exploring Changes on Earth with Science Projects. 2015. (Discover Earth Science Ser.). (ENG., Illus.). 32p. (gr. 3-4). lib. bdg. 27.32 (978-1-4914-4815-1(6)) Capstone Press of Coughlan Cos.

—Liquid Planet: Exploring Water on Earth with Science Projects. (Illus.). 32p. 2016. (J). lib. bdg. (978-1-4747-0325-3(9)) 2015. (ENG., (gr. 3-4). lib. bdg. 27.32 (978-1-4914-4817-5(2)) Capstone Press of Coughlan Cos.

Facts on File, Inc. Staff. The Facts on File Science Handbook Set, 10-Volumes. 2009. (Science Handbook Ser.). 1824p. (gr. 6-12). 400.00 (978-0-8160-8213-1(8)) Facts On File, Inc.

Felix, Rebecca. Cool Battery & Electricity Projects: Fun & Creative Workshop Activities. 2016. (ENG., Illus.). 32p. (J). (978-1-68078-125-0(1)) ABDO Publishing Co.

—Cool Engineering Projects: Fun & Creative Workshop Activities. 2016. (ENG., Illus.). 32p. (J). (978-1-68078-127-4(8)) ABDO Publishing Co.

Friedhoffer, Bob. Everything You Need for Simple Science Fair Projects: Grades 3-5. Colon, Ernie, illus. 2006. (Scientific American Science Fair Projects Ser.). 48p. (gr. 3-5). lib. bdg. 27.00 (978-0-7910-9054-1(X)) Facts On File, Inc.

—Everything You Need for Winning Science Fair Projects: Grades 5-7. Colon, Ernie, illus. 2006. (Scientific American Science Fair Projects Ser.). 48p. (gr. 4-6). lib. bdg. 27.00 (978-0-7910-9056-5(6)) Facts On File, Inc.

—More Scientific American Winning Science Fair Projects. 2006. (Scientific American Science Fair Projects Ser.). (Illus.). 48p. (gr. 4-6). 27.00 (978-0-7910-9057-2(4)) Facts On File, Inc.

Friedhoffer, Bob & Tocci, Salvatore. Scientific American Science Fair Projects, 4 Vols., Set. 2006. (Scientific American Winning Science Fair Projects Ser.). 48p. (gr. 3-7). 108.00 (978-0-7910-9097-8(3), Chelsea Clubhouse) Facts On File, Inc.

Fulcher, Roz. Science Around the House: Simple Projects Using Household Recyclables. 2010. (Dover Children's Science Bks.). (ENG., Illus.). 80p. (J). (gr. 3-5). pap. 6.99 (978-0-486-47645-2(6)) Dover Pubns., Inc.

Gabrielson, Curt. Stomp Rockets, Catapults, & Kaleidoscopes: 30+ Amazing Science Projects You Can Build for Less Than $1. 2008. (ENG., Illus.). 176p. (J). (gr. 4-18). pap. 16.95 (978-1-55652-737-1(3)) Chicago Review Pr., Inc.

Galus, Pamela J. Science Fair Projects, Grades 5-8: An Inquiry-Based Guide. Armbrust, Janet, illus. 2003. (ENG.). 80p. (gr. 5-8). per. 16.99 (978-0-88724-949-5(3), CD-7333) Carson-Dellosa Publishing, LLC.

Gardner, Robert. Ace Your Math & Measuring Science Project: Great Science Fair Ideas. 2009. (Ace Your Physics Science Project Ser.). (Illus.). 128p. (J). (gr. 5-18). lib. bdg. 33.27 (978-0-7660-3224-8(8)) Enslow Pubs., Inc.

—Ace Your Science Project Using Chemistry Magic & Toys: Great Science Fair Ideas. 2009. (Ace Your Science Project Ser.). (Illus.). 128p. (J). (gr. 5-9). lib. bdg. 33.27 (978-0-7660-3226-2(4)) Enslow Pubs., Inc.

—Bicycle Science Projects: Physics on Wheels. 2004. (Science Fair Success Ser.). (Illus.). 112p. (J). lib. bdg. 27.94 (978-0-7660-1630-9(7)) Enslow Pubs., Inc.

—Chemistry Projects with a Laboratory You Can Build. 2007. (Build-A-Lab! Science Experiments Ser.). (Illus.). 128p. (J). (gr. 3-7). lib. bdg. 33.27 (978-0-7660-2805-0(4)) Enslow Pubs., Inc.

—Chemistry Science Fair Projects Using Acids, Bases, Metals, Salts, & Inorganic Stuff. 2004. (Chemistry! Best Science Projects Ser.). (Illus.). 128p. (J). lib. bdg. 27.94 (978-0-7660-2210-2(2)) Enslow Pubs., Inc.

—Chemistry Science Fair Projects Using Inorganic Stuff. LaBaff, Tom & LaBaff, Stephanie, illus. rev. exp. ed. 2010. (Chemistry Science Projects Using the Scientific Method Ser.). 160p. (J). (gr. 5-18). 35.94 *(978-0-7660-3413-6(5))* Enslow Pubs., Inc.

—Desert Experiments: 11 Science Experiments in One Hour or Less. 2014. (Last Minute Science Projects with Biomes Ser.). (Illus.). 48p. (gr. 5-12). (J). 25.27 *(978-0-7660-5917-7(0))*; (YA). pap. 8.95 *(978-0-7660-5918-4(9)*, Enslow Elementary) Enslow Pubs., Inc.

—Earth-Shaking Science Projects about Planet Earth. LaBaff, Tom, illus. 2007. (Rockin' Earth Science Experiments Ser.). 48p. (J). (gr. 3-4). lib. bdg. 25.27 *(978-0-7660-2733-6(3)*, Enslow Elementary) Enslow Pubs., Inc.

—Easy Genius Science Projects with Chemistry: Great Experiments & Ideas. 2008. (Easy Genius Science Projects Ser.). (Illus.). 112p. (J). (gr. 5-9). lib. bdg. 33.27 *(978-0-7660-2925-5(5))* Enslow Pubs., Inc.

—Easy Genius Science Projects with Electricity & Magnetism: Great Experiments & Ideas. 2009. (Easy Genius Science Projects Ser.). (Illus.). 128p. (J). (gr. 5-9). lib. bdg. 33.27 *(978-0-7660-2923-1(9))* Enslow Pubs., Inc.

—Easy Genius Science Projects with Light: Great Experiments & Ideas. 2008. (Easy Genius Science Projects Ser.). (Illus.). 128p. (J). (gr. 5-9). lib. bdg. 33.27 *(978-0-7660-2926-2(3))* Enslow Pubs., Inc.

—Easy Genius Science Projects with the Human Body: Great Experiments & Ideas. 2008. (Easy Genius Science Projects Ser.). (Illus.). 112p. (J). (gr. 5-9). lib. bdg. 33.27 *(978-0-7660-2927-9(1))* Enslow Pubs., Inc.

—Easy Genius Science Projects with Weather: Great Experiments & Ideas. 2009. (Easy Genius Science Projects Ser.). (Illus.). 128p. (J). (gr. 5-9). lib. bdg. 33.27 *(978-0-7660-2924-8(7))* Enslow Pubs., Inc.

—Electricity & Magnetism Science Fair Projects, Revised & Expanded Using the Scientific Method. LaBaff, Stephanie & LaBaff, Tom, illus. 2010. (Physics Science Projects Using the Scientific Method Ser.). 160p. (J). (gr. 5-18). 35.94 *(978-0-7660-3418-1(6))* Enslow Pubs., Inc.

—Electricity & Magnetism Science Fair Projects Using Batteries, Balloons, & Other Hair-Raising Stuff. 2004. (Physics! Best Science Projects Ser.). (Illus.). 128p. (J). lib. bdg. 27.94 *(978-0-7660-2127-3(0))* Enslow Pubs., Inc.

—Energy: Green Science Projects about Solar, Wind, & Water Power. 2011. (Team Green Science Projects Ser.). (Illus.). 128p. (J). (gr. 5-9). lib. bdg. 33.27 *(978-0-7660-3643-7(X))* Enslow Pubs., Inc.

—Experiments with Chemistry. 2017. (Science Whiz Experiments Ser.). 128p. (gr. 5-5). lib. bdg. 37.27 ***(978-0-7660-8676-0(3))*** Enslow Pubs., Inc.

—Far-Out Science Projects about Earth's Sun & Moon. LaBaff, Tom, illus. 2007. (Rockin' Earth Science Experiments Ser.). 48p. (J). (gr. 3-4). lib. bdg. 25.27 *(978-0-7660-2736-7(8)*, Enslow Elementary) Enslow Pubs., Inc.

—Forces & Motion Science Fair Projects, Revised & Expanded Using the Scientific Method. LaBaff, Tom & LaBaff, Stephanie, illus. 2010. (Physics Science Projects Using the Scientific Method Ser.). 160p. (J). (gr. 5-18). 35.94 *(978-0-7660-3415-0(1))* Enslow Pubs., Inc.

—Genetics & Evolution Science Fair Projects, Revised & Expanded Using the Scientific Method. LaBaff, Stephanie, illus. 2010. (Biology Science Projects Using the Scientific Method Ser.). 160p. (J). (gr. 5-18). 35.94 *(978-0-7660-3422-8(4))* Enslow Pubs., Inc.

—Grasslands Experiments: 11 Science Experiments in One Hour or Less. 2014. (Last Minute Science Projects with Biomes Ser.). (Illus.). 48p. (gr. 5-12). (J). 25.27 *(978-0-7660-5927-6(8))*; (YA). pap. 8.95 *(978-0-7660-5928-3(6)*, Enslow Elementary) Enslow Pubs., Inc.

—How Big Is Big? Science Projects with Volume. 2015. (Hot Science Experiments Ser.). 48p. (J). (gr. 3-4). 25.27 *(978-0-7660-6620-5(7))* Enslow Pubs., Inc.

—How Fast Is Fast? Science Projects with Speed. 2015. (Hot Science Experiments Ser.). 48p. (J). (gr. 3-4). 25.27 *(978-0-7660-6615-1(0))*; pap. 8.95 *(978-0-7660-6616-8(9)*, Enslow Elementary) Enslow Pubs., Inc.

—How Heavy Is Heavy? Science Projects with Weight. 2015. (Hot Science Experiments Ser.). 48p. (J). (gr. 3-4). 25.27 *(978-0-7660-6600-7(2))* Enslow Pubs., Inc.

—How High Is High? Science Projects with Height & Depth. 2015. (Hot Science Experiments Ser.). 48p. (J). (gr. 3-4). 25.27 *(978-0-7660-6595-6(2))*; pap. 8.95 *(978-0-7660-6596-3(0)*, Enslow Elementary) Enslow Pubs., Inc.

—How Hot Is Hot? Science Projects with Temperature. 2015. (Hot Science Experiments Ser.). 48p. (J). (gr. 3-4). 25.27 *(978-0-7660-6605-2(3))*; pap. 8.95 *(978-0-7660-6606-9(1)*, Enslow Elementary) Enslow Pubs., Inc.

—How Quick Is Quick? Science Projects with Time. 2015. (Hot Science Experiments Ser.). 48p. (J). (gr. 3-4). 25.27 *(978-0-7660-6610-6(X))*; pap. 8.95 *(978-0-7660-6611-3(8)*, Enslow Elementary) Enslow Pubs., Inc.

—Light, Sound, & Waves Science Fair Projects, Revised & Expanded Using the Scientific Method. 2010. (Physics Science Projects Using the Scientific Method Ser.). (Illus.). 160p. (J). (gr. 5-18). 35.94 *(978-0-7660-3416-7(X))* Enslow Pubs., Inc.

—Melting, Freezing, & Boiling Science Projects with Matter. 2006. (Fantastic Physical Science Experiments Ser.). (Illus.). 48p. (J). (gr. 4-7). lib. bdg. 25.27 *(978-0-7660-2589-9(6)*, Enslow Elementary) Enslow Pubs., Inc.

—Meteorology Projects with a Weather Station You Can Build. 2008. (Build-A-Lab! Science Experiments Ser.). (Illus.). 128p. (J). (gr. 5-18). lib. bdg. 33.27 *(978-0-7660-2807-4(0))* Enslow Pubs., Inc.

—The Physics of Sports Science Projects. 2013. (Exploring Hands-On Science Projects Ser.). 128p. (J). (gr. 5-12). pap. 10.95 *(978-1-4644-0222-7(1))*; lib. bdg. 27.94 *(978-0-7660-4146-2(8))* Enslow Pubs., Inc.

—The Physics of Toys & Games Science Projects. 2013. (Exploring Hands-On Science Projects Ser.). 128p. (J). (gr. 5-12). pap. 10.95 *(978-1-4644-0219-7(1))*; lib. bdg. 27.94 *(978-0-7660-4143-1(3))* Enslow Pubs., Inc.

—Physics Projects with a Light Box You Can Build. 2007. (Build-A-Lab! Science Experiments Ser.). (Illus.). 128p. (J). (gr. 3-7). lib. bdg. 33.27 *(978-0-7660-2810-4(0))* Enslow Pubs., Inc.

—Planet Earth Science Fair Projects, Revised & Expanded Using the Scientific Method. LaBaff, Stephanie & LaBaff, Tom, illus. 2010. (Earth Science Projects Using the Scientific Method Ser.). 160p. (J). (gr. 5-18). 35.94 *(978-0-7660-3423-5(2))* Enslow Pubs., Inc.

—Planet Earth Science Fair Projects Using the Moon, Stars, Beach Balls, Frisbees, & Other Far-Out Stuff. 2005. (Earth Science! Best Science Projects Ser.). (Illus.). 128p. (J). lib. bdg. 27.94 *(978-0-7660-2362-8(1)*, 1238538) Enslow Pubs., Inc.

—Rain Forest Experiments: 10 Science Experiments in One Hour or Less. 2014. (Last Minute Science Projects with Biomes Ser.). (Illus.). 48p. (J). (gr. 5-12). lib. bdg. 25.27 *(978-0-7660-5937-5(5))* Enslow Pubs., Inc.

—The Science Behind Magic Science Projects. 2013. (Exploring Hands-On Science Projects Ser.). 128p. (J). (gr. 5-12). pap. 10.95 *(978-1-4644-0223-4(X))*; 27.94 *(978-0-7660-4147-9(6))* Enslow Pubs., Inc.

—Science Fair Projects about Planet Earth. 2016. (Hands-On Science Ser.). 48p. (J). 27.93 *(978-0-7660-8219-9(9))* Enslow Pubs., Inc.

—Science Fair Projects about the Atmosphere. 2016. (Hands-On Science Ser.). 48p. (J). pap. 11.70 *(978-0-7660-8220-5(2))* Enslow Pubs., Inc.

—Science Fair Projects about the Properties of Matter, Revised & Expanded Using the Scientific Method. LaBaff, Stephanie, illus. 2010. (Physics Science Projects Using the Scientific Method Ser.). 160p. (J). (gr. 5-18). 35.94 *(978-0-7660-3417-4(8))* Enslow Pubs., Inc.

—Science Fair Projects about the Properties of Matter Using Marbles, Water, Balloons, & More. Tom, LaBaff, illus. 2004. (Physics! Best Science Projects Ser.). 128p. (J). lib. bdg. 27.94 *(978-0-7660-2128-0(9))* Enslow Pubs., Inc.

—Science Fair Projects about Water & Soil. 2016. (Hands-On Science Ser.). 48p. (J). pap. 11.70 *(978-0-7660-8211-3(3))* Enslow Pubs., Inc.

—Science Fair Projects about Weather. 2016. (Hands-On Science Ser.). 48p. (J). pap. 11.70 *(978-0-7660-8204-5(0))* Enslow Pubs., Inc.

—Smashing Science Projects about Earth's Rocks & Minerals. LaBaff, Tom, illus. 2007. (Rockin' Earth Science Experiments Ser.). 48p. (J). (gr. 3-4). lib. bdg. 25.27 *(978-0-7660-2731-2(7)*, Enslow Elementary) Enslow Pubs., Inc.

—Soil: Green Science Projects for a Sustainable Planet. 2011. (Team Green Science Projects Ser.). (Illus.). 128p. (J). (gr. 5-9). lib. bdg. 33.27 *(978-0-7660-3647-5(2))* Enslow Pubs., Inc.

—Solids, Liquids, & Gases Science Projects. 2013. (Exploring Hands-On Science Projects Ser.). 128p. (J). (gr. 5-12). pap. 10.95 *(978-1-4644-0221-0(3))*; lib. bdg. 27.94 *(978-0-7660-4145-5(X))* Enslow Pubs., Inc.

—Sound Projects with a Music Lab You Can Build. 2008. (Build-A-Lab! Science Experiments Ser.). (Illus.). 128p. (J). (gr. 3-7). lib. bdg. 33.27 *(978-0-7660-2809-8(7))* Enslow Pubs., Inc.

—Stellar Science Projects about Earth's Sky. LaBaff, Tom, illus. 2007. (Rockin' Earth Science Experiments Ser.). 48p. (J). (gr. 3-4). lib. bdg. 25.27 *(978-0-7660-2732-9(5)*, Enslow Elementary) Enslow Pubs., Inc.

—Super Science Projects about Earth's Soil & Water. LaBaff, Tom, illus. 2007. (Rockin' Earth Science Experiments Ser.). 48p. (J). (gr. 3-4). lib. bdg. 25.27 *(978-0-7660-2735-0(X)*, Enslow Elementary) Enslow Pubs., Inc.

—Temperate Forest Experments: 8 Science Experiments in One Hour or Less. 2014. (Last Minute Science Projects with Biomes Ser.). 48p. (J). (gr. 5-12). 25.27 *(978-0-7660-5922-1(7))* Enslow Pubs., Inc.

—Temperate Forest Experiments: 8 Science Experiments in One Hour or Less. 2014. (Last Minute Science Projects with Biomes Ser.). (Illus.). 48p. (YA). (gr. 5-12). pap. 8.95 *(978-0-7660-5923-8(5)*, Enslow Elementary) Enslow Pubs., Inc.

—Tundra Experiments: 14 Science Experiments in One Hour or Less. 2014. (Last Minute Science Projects with Biomes Ser.). (Illus.). 48p. (J). (gr. 5-12). lib. bdg. 25.27 *(978-0-7660-5942-9(1))* Enslow Pubs., Inc.

—Water: Green Science Projects for a Sustainable Planet. 2011. (Team Green Science Projects Ser.). (Illus.). 128p. (J). (gr. 5-9). lib. bdg. 33.27 *(978-0-7660-3645-1(6))* Enslow Pubs., Inc.

—Weather Science Fair Projects Using Sunlight, Rainbows, Ice Cubes, & More. 2005. (Earth Science! Best Science Projects Ser.). (Illus.). 128p. (J). lib. bdg. 27.94 *(978-0-7660-2361-1(3))* Enslow Pubs., Inc.

—Who Can Solve the Crime? Science Projects Using Detective Skills. 2010. (Who Dunnit? Forensic Science Experiments Ser.). (Illus.). 48p. (J). (gr. 2-5). 25.27 *(978-0-7660-3247-7(7))* Enslow Pubs., Inc.

—Who Forged This Document? Crime-Solving Science Projects. 2010. (Who Dunnit? Forensic Science Experiments Ser.). (Illus.). 48p. (J). (gr. 2-5). 25.27 *(978-0-7660-3246-0(9))* Enslow Pubs., Inc.

—Whose Bones Are These? Crime-Solving Science Projects. 2010. (Who Dunnit? Forensic Science Experiments Ser.). (Illus.). 48p. (J). (gr. 2-5). 25.27 *(978-0-7660-3248-4(5))* Enslow Pubs., Inc.

—Whose Fingerprints Are These? Crime-Solving Science Projects. 2010. (Who Dunnit? Forensic Science Experiments Ser.). (Illus.). 48p. (J). (gr. 2-5). 25.27 *(978-0-7660-3245-3(0))* Enslow Pubs., Inc.

—Wild Science Projects about Earth's Weather. LaBaff, Tom, illus. 2007. (Rockin' Earth Science Experiments Ser.). 48p. (J). (gr. 3-4). lib. bdg. 25.27 *(978-0-7660-2734-3(1)*, Enslow Elementary) Enslow Pubs., Inc.

Gardner, Robert & Conklin, Barbara Gardner. Ace Your Human Biology Science Project: Great Science Fair Ideas. 2009. (Ace Your Biology Science Project Ser.). (Illus.). 128p. (J). (gr. 5-9). lib. bdg. 33.27 *(978-0-7660-3219-4(1))* Enslow Pubs., Inc.

—Chemistry Science Fair Projects Using French Fries, Gumdrops, Soap, & Other Organic Stuff. 2004. (Chemistry! Best Science Projects Ser.). (Illus.). 128p. (J). lib. bdg. 27.94 *(978-0-7660-2211-9(0))* Enslow Pubs., Inc.

—Organic Chemistry Science Fair Projects, Revised & Expanded Using the Scientific Method. LaBaff, Tom & LaBaff, Stephanie, illus. 2010. (Chemistry Science Projects Using the Scientific Method Ser.). 160p. (J). (gr. 5-18). 35.94 *(978-0-7660-3414-3(3))* Enslow Pubs., Inc.

Gardner, Robert & Conklin, Joshua. Experiments for Future Chemists. 2016. (Experiments for Future STEM Professionals Ser.). 128p. (J). (gr. 6-6). lib. bdg. 37.27 *(978-0-7660-7856-7(6))* Enslow Pubs., Inc.

—Experiments for Future Engineers. 2016. (Experiments for Future STEM Professionals Ser.). 128p. (J). (gr. 6-6). 37.27 *(978-0-7660-7853-6(1))* Enslow Pubs., Inc.

—A Kid's Book of Experiments about Light. 2016. (Surprising Science Experiments Ser.). (ENG., Illus.). 48p. (J). (gr. 4-4). 27.93 *(978-0-7660-7205-3(3))* Enslow Pubs., Inc.

—A Kid's Book of Experiments about Sound. 2016. (Surprising Science Experiments Ser.). (ENG., Illus.). 48p. (J). (gr. 4-4). 27.93 *(978-0-7660-7209-1(6))* Enslow Pubs., Inc.

Gardner, Robert & Goodstein, Madeline P. Ace Your Forces & Motion Science Project: Great Science Fair Ideas. 2009. (Ace Your Physics Science Project Ser.). (Illus.). 128p. (J). (gr. 5-18). lib. bdg. 33.27 *(978-0-7660-3222-4(1))* Enslow Pubs., Inc.

—Ace Your Space Science Project: Great Science Fair Ideas. 2009. (Ace Your Science Project Ser.). (Illus.). 128p. (J). (gr. 5-9). lib. bdg. 33.27 *(978-0-7660-3230-9(2))* Enslow Pubs., Inc.

Gardner, Robert & Kemer, Eric. Easy Genius Science Projects with Temperature & Heat: Great Experiments & Ideas. 2009. (Easy Genius Science Projects Ser.). (Illus.). 128p. (J). (gr. 5-9). lib. bdg. 33.27 *(978-0-7660-2939-2(5))* Enslow Pubs., Inc.

Gardner, Robert & Shortelle, Dennis. Slam Dunk! Science Projects with Basketball. 2009. (Score! Sports Science Projects Ser.). (Illus.). 104p. (J). (gr. 5-9). lib. bdg. 33.27 *(978-0-7660-3366-5(X))* Enslow Pubs., Inc.

Gardner, Robert & Tocci, Salvatore. Ace Your Weather Science Project: Great Science Fair Ideas. 2009. (Ace Your Physics Science Project Ser.). (Illus.). 104p. (J). (gr. 5-18). lib. bdg. 33.27 *(978-0-7660-3223-1(X))* Enslow Pubs., Inc.

Gardner, Robert, et al. Ace Your Animal Science Project: Great Science Fair Ideas. 2009. (Ace Your Biology Science Project Ser.). (Illus.). 104p. (J). (gr. 5-9). lib. bdg. 33.27 *(978-0-7660-3220-0(5))* Enslow Pubs., Inc.

—Ace Your Chemistry Science Project: Great Science Fair Ideas. 2009. (Ace Your Science Project Ser.). (Illus.). 112p. (J). (gr. 5-9). mass mkt. 33.27 *(978-0-7660-3227-9(2))* Enslow Pubs., Inc.

—Ace Your Ecology & Environmental Science Project: Great Science Fair Ideas. 2009. (Ace Your Science Project Ser.). (Illus.). 112p. (J). (gr. 5-9). lib. bdg. 33.27 *(978-0-7660-3216-3(7))* Enslow Pubs., Inc.

—Ace Your Exercise & Nutrition Science Project: Great Science Fair Ideas. 2009. (Ace Your Biology Science Project Ser.). (Illus.). 128p. (J). (gr. 5-9). lib. bdg. 33.27 *(978-0-7660-3218-7(3))* Enslow Pubs., Inc.

—Ace Your Food Science Project: Great Science Fair Ideas. 2009. (Ace Your Science Project Ser.). (Illus.). 128p. (J). (gr. 5-9). lib. bdg. 33.27 *(978-0-7660-3228-6(0))* Enslow Pubs., Inc.

—Ace Your Physical Science Project: Great Science Fair Ideas. 2009. (Ace Your Physics Science Project Ser.). (Illus.). 128p. (J). (gr. 5-18). lib. bdg. 33.27 *(978-0-7660-3225-5(6))* Enslow Pubs., Inc.

—Ace Your Science Project about the Senses: Great Science Fair Ideas. 2009. (Ace Your Biology Science Project Ser.). (Illus.). 112p. (J). (gr. 5-9). lib. bdg. 33.27 *(978-0-7660-3217-0(5))* Enslow Pubs., Inc.

Goodstein, Madeline P. Goal! Science Projects with Soccer. 2009. (Score! Sports Science Projects Ser.). (Illus.). 104p. (J). (gr. 5-9). lib. bdg. 33.27 *(978-0-7660-3106-7(3))* Enslow Pubs., Inc.

—Plastics & Polymers Science Fair Projects. LaBaff, Tom & LaBaff, Stephanie, illus. rev. exp. ed. 2010. (Chemistry Science Projects Using the Scientific Method Ser.). 160p. (J). (gr. 5-18). 35.94 *(978-0-7660-3412-9(7))* Enslow Pubs., Inc.

—Wheels! Science Projects with Bicycles, Skateboards, & Skates. 2009. (Score! Sports Science Projects Ser.). (Illus.). 104p. (J). (gr. 5-9). lib. bdg. 33.27 *(978-0-7660-3107-4(1))* Enslow Pubs., Inc.

Gravois, Michael. 25 Totally Terrific Science Projects: Easy How-To's & Templates for Projects That Motivate Students to Show What They Know about Key Science Topics. 2010. (ENG.). 80p. (gr. k-6). pap. 12.99 *(978-0-545-23139-8(6)*, Teaching Resources) Scholastic, Inc.

Great Earth Science Projects. (Illus.). (J). (gr. k-5). 119.70 *(978-0-8239-7141-1(4))* Rosen Publishing Group, Inc., The.

Gregory, Josh. Experiment with Solids. 2010. (Explorer Junior Library: Science Explorer Junior Ser.). (ENG.). 32p. (J). (gr. 3-6). lib. bdg. 28.50 *(978-1-60279-845-8(1)*, 200556) Cherry Lake Publishing.

Greve, Meg. Science Projects. 2014. (ENG.). 24p. (gr. 3-5). 28.50 *(978-1-62717-690-3(X))* Rourke Educational Media.

Hagler, Gina. Electricity. 2016. (J). *(978-1-4896-5274-4(4))* Weigl Pubs., Inc.

—Magnets. 2016. (J). *(978-1-4896-5286-7(8))* Weigl Pubs., Inc.

—Sound. 2016. (J). *(978-1-4896-5292-8(2))* Weigl Pubs., Inc.

—Step-by-Step Experiments with Soils. Ostrom, Bob, illus. 2012. (Step-By-Step Experiments Ser.). (ENG.). 32p. (J). (gr. 1-4). lib. bdg. 29.93 *(978-1-60973-592-0(7)*, 201238) Child's World, Inc., The.

—Step-by-Step Experiments with Sound. Ostrom, Bob, illus. 2012. (Step-By-Step Experiments Ser.). (ENG.). 32p. (J). (gr. 1-4). lib. bdg. 29.93 *(978-1-60973-593-7(5)*, 201239) Child's World, Inc., The.

Hall, Kevin. 10 Great Makerspace Projects Using Math. 2017. (Using Makerspaces for School Projects Ser.). 64p. (gr. 11-11). 34.45 ***(978-1-4994-3846-8(X)***, Rosen Central) Rosen Publishing Group, Inc., The.

Hand, Carol. Build a Weather Station. Stewart, Roger, illus. 2016. (Earth-Friendly Projects Ser.). (ENG.). 24p. (J). (gr. 2-5). 28.50 *(978-1-5038-0789-1(4)*, 210626) Child's World, Inc., The.

Haysom, John. Science Fair Warm-Up: Learning the Practice of Scientists. 2013. (ENG., Illus.). (J). 55p. pap. *(978-1-936959-20-4(8))*; 60p. pap. *(978-1-936959-21-1(6))*; 75p. pap. ***(978-1-936959-22-8(4))*** National Science Teachers Assn.

Henneberg, Susan. Creating Science Fair Projects with Cool New Digital Tools. 2013. (Way Beyond PowerPoint: Making 21st Century Presentations Ser.). (Illus.). 48p. (J). (gr. 5-8). 29.95 *(978-1-4777-1836-0(2))*; pap. 70.50 *(978-1-4777-1848-3(6))*; pap. 11.75 *(978-1-4777-1847-6(8))* Rosen Publishing Group, Inc., The. (Rosen Reference).

Holt, Rinehart and Winston Staff. Holt Science & Technology: Long-Term Projects & Research Ideas. 5th ed. 2004. (Illus.). pap. 11.13 *(978-0-03-035191-4(X))* Holt McDougal.

—Holt Science & Technology: Science Fair Guide. 5th ed. 2004. (Illus.). pap. 11.60 *(978-0-03-035199-0(5))* Holt McDougal.

Hopwood, James. Cool Distance Assistants: Fun Science Projects to Propel Things, 1 vol. 2008. (Cool Science Ser.). (ENG.). 32p. (YA). (gr. 2-5). 28.50 *(978-1-59928-906-9(7))* ABDO Publishing Co.

—Cool Dry Ice Devices: Fun Science Projects with Dry Ice, 1 vol. 2008. (Cool Science Ser.). (ENG.). 32p. (YA). (gr. 2-5). 28.50 *(978-1-59928-907-6(5))* ABDO Publishing Co.

—Cool Gravity Activities: Fun Science Projects about Balance, 1 vol. 2008. (Cool Science Ser.). (ENG.). 32p. (YA). (gr. 2-5). 28.50 *(978-1-59928-908-3(3))* ABDO Publishing Co.

Ives, Rob. Fun Experiments with Matter: Invisible Ink, Giant Bubbles, & More. Sassin, Eva, illus. 2017. (Amazing Science Experiments Ser.). (ENG.). (J). (gr. 3-6). lib. bdg. 26.65 ***(978-1-5124-3216-9(4))*** Lerner Publishing Group.

Jacobson, Ryan. Light & Vision. 2016. (J). *(978-1-4896-5283-6(3))* Weigl Pubs., Inc.

Jones, Lorraine. Super Science Projects about Weather & Natural Forces. 2005. (Psyched for Science Ser.). (Illus.). 48p. (YA). (gr. 5-8). lib. bdg. 29.25 *(978-0-8239-3105-7(6)*, SCWENA) Rosen Publishing Group, Inc., The.

Kauffman, Dorothy. Science Lab. 2005. (Oxford Picture Dictionary for the Content Areas Ser.). (ENG., Illus.). 24p. pap. 7.56 *(978-0-19-430955-4(X))* Oxford Univ. Pr., Inc.

Kessler, Colleen. A Project Guide to Electricity & Magnetism. 2011. (Physical Science Projects for Kids Ser.). (Illus.). 48p. (J). (gr. 3-6). lib. bdg. 29.95 *(978-1-58415-966-7(9)*, 1327821) Mitchell Lane Pubs., Inc.

—A Project Guide to Reptiles & Birds. 2010. (Life Science Projects for Kids Ser.). (Illus.). 48p. (J). (gr. 4-8). lib. bdg. 29.95 *(978-1-58415-874-5(3))* Mitchell Lane Pubs., Inc.

Kjelle, Marylou Morano. A Project Guide to Wind, Weather, & the Atmosphere. 2010. (Earth Science Projects for Kids Ser.). (Illus.). 48p. (J). (gr. 4-7). lib. bdg. 29.95 *(978-1-58415-869-1(7))* Mitchell Lane Pubs., Inc.

Larson, Kirsten. Science Fair Success! 2014. (ENG.). 48p. (gr. 4-6). 35.64 *(978-1-62717-747-4(7))* Rourke Educational Media.

Latta, Sara L. All about Earth: Exploring the Planet with Science Projects. (Illus.). 32p. 2016. (J). lib. bdg. *(978-1-4747-0323-9(2))* 2015. (ENG., (gr. 3-4). lib. bdg. 27.32 *(978-1-4914-4814-4(8))* Capstone Press of Coughlan Cos.

Lee, Ji Sun & Dec, Jaymes. Tech DIY: Easy Electronics Projects for Parents & Kids. 2016. (ENG., Illus.). 192p. pap. 19.99 *(978-1-68045-177-1(4))* Maker Media, Inc.

Lockwood, Sophie. Experiment with Heat. 2010. (Explorer Junior Library: Science Explorer Junior Ser.). (ENG.). 32p. (gr. 3-6). lib. bdg. 28.50 *(978-1-60279-843-4(5)*, 200552) Cherry Lake Publishing.

—Experiment with Rocks. 2010. (Explorer Junior Library: Science Explorer Junior Ser.). (ENG.). 32p. (gr. 3-6). lib. bdg. 28.50 *(978-1-60279-836-6(2)*, 200538) Cherry Lake Publishing.

Lopez, Delano. Amazing Solar System Projects: You Can Build Yourself. 2008. (Build It Yourself Ser.). (ENG., Illus.). 128p. (J). (gr. 3-7). per. 14.95 *(978-0-9792268-1-6(3))* Octavio Publishing.

Marsico, Katie. Insects. 2016. (J). *(978-1-4896-5277-5(9))* Weigl Pubs., Inc.

—Step-by-Step Experiments with Life Cycles. Ostrom, Bob, illus. 2012. (Step-By-Step Experiments Ser.). (ENG.). 32p. (J). (gr. 1-4). lib. bdg. 29.93 *(978-1-60973-587-6(0)*, 201232) Child's World, Inc., The.

—Step-by-Step Experiments with Taste & Digestion. Ostrom, Bob, illus. 2012. (Step-By-Step Experiments Ser.). (ENG.). 32p. (J). (gr. 1-4). lib. bdg. 29.93 *(978-1-60973-614-9(1)*, 201240) Child's World, Inc., The.

McFarren, Kathleen & Graf, Mike. Science Fair Projects & Activities: Creative Ideas Using Easy-to-Find Materials. Valko, Diane & Corbin, Hillam, illus. 2005. 144p. (J). pap. 18.99 *(978-0-88160-376-7(7)*, LW407, Learning Works, The) Creative Teaching Pr., Inc.

McGill, Jordan. Earth Science Fair Projects. 2011. (gr. 3-5). pap. 12.95 *(978-1-61690-655-9(3)*, AV2 by Weigl); (Illus.). 24p. (J). 27.13 *(978-1-61690-651-1(0))* Weigl Pubs., Inc.

—Space Science Fair Projects. 2011. (J). (gr. 3-5). pap. 12.95 *(978-1-61690-657-3(X)*, AV2 by Weigl); (Illus.). 24p. 27.13 *(978-1-61690-653-5(7))* Weigl Pubs., Inc.

—Water Science Fair Projects. 2011. (J). *(978-1-61690-332-9(5))*; (gr. 3-5). pap. 12.95 *(978-1-61690-656-6(1)*, AV2 by Weigl); (Illus.). 24p. (gr. 3-6). 27.13 *(978-1-61690-652-8(9))* Weigl Pubs., Inc.

Mullins, Matt. Experiment with Liquids. 2010. (Explorer Junior Library: Science Explorer Junior Ser.). (ENG.). 32p. (gr. 3-6). lib. bdg. 28.50 *(978-1-60279-846-5(X)*, 200558) Cherry Lake Publishing.

Nash, Kimberley. Lab Reports: 10 Experiments. 2007. (ENG., Illus.). 140p. spiral bd., wbk. ed. 20.00 *(978-0-9710950-8-3(6))* Resurrection Resources LLC.

National Geographic Kids Staff, et al. Edible Science: Experiments You Can Eat. 2015. (ENG., Illus.). 80p. (J). (gr. 3-7). pap. 12.99 *(978-1-4263-2111-5(2)*, National Geographic Children's Bks.) National Geographic Society.

Neuhaus, Richard A. Science Projects: Book 1. Project Ideas in the Life Sciences, Vol. 1. Gormley, Julia Ann, illus. 2008. (ENG.). 184p. (gr. 7-12). pap. 24.95 *(978-0-9794500-1-3(2))* Gormley Publishing.

—Science Projects: Book 2. Project Ideas in Chemistry & Biochemistry, Vol. 2. Gormley, Julia Ann, illus. 2008. (ENG.).

S

196p. (gr. 7-12). pap. 24.95 (978-0-9794500-4-4(7)) Gormley Publishing.

—Science Projects: How to Collect, Analyze, & Present Your Data. Gormley, Julia Ann, illus. 2007. (ENG.). 184p. (gr. 7-12). pap. 24.95 (978-0-9794500-0-6(4)) Gormley Publishing.

O'Neal, Claire. A Project Guide to Earthquakes. 2010. (Earth Science Projects for Kids Ser.). (Illus.). 48p. (J). (gr. 4-7). lib. bdg. 29.95 (978-1-58415-870-7(0)) Mitchell Lane Pubs., Inc.

—A Project Guide to Volcanoes. 2010. (Earth Science Projects for Kids Ser.). (Illus.). 48p. (J). (gr. 4-7). lib. bdg. 29.95 (978-1-58415-868-4(9)) Mitchell Lane Pubs., Inc.

—Projects in Genetics. 2010. (Life Science Projects for Kids Ser.). (Illus.). 48p. (J). (gr. 4-8). lib. bdg. 29.95 (978-1-58415-877-6(8)) Mitchell Lane Pubs., Inc.

Orr, Tamra. Experiment with Weather. 2010. (Explorer Junior Library: Science Explorer Junior Ser.). (ENG.). 32p. (gr. 3-6). lib. bdg. 28.50 (978-1-60279-841-0(9), 200548) Cherry Lake Publishing.

Petersen, Christine. A Project Guide to Mammals. 2010. (Life Science Projects for Kids Ser.). (Illus.). 48p. (J). (gr. 4-8). lib. bdg. 29.95 (978-1-58415-875-2(1)) Mitchell Lane Pubs., Inc.

Peterson, Carol. Jump into Science: Themed Science Fairs, 1 vol. Peterson, Carol, illus. 2007. (Illus.). 152p. (C). (gr. 3-7). per. 35.00 (978-1-59158-413-1(2), TIP4132, Libraries Unlimited) ABC-CLIO, LLC.

Polinsky, Paige V. Super Simple Experiments with Elements: Fun & Innovative Science Projects. 2016. (ENG., Illus.). 32p. (J). 27.07 (978-1-68078-168-7(5)) ABDO Publishing Co.

—Super Simple Experiments with Forces: Fun & Innovative Science Projects. 2016. (ENG., Illus.). 32p. (J). (978-1-68078-169-4(3)) ABDO Publishing Co.

—Super Simple Experiments with Heat & Cold: Fun & Innovative Science Projects. 2016. (ENG., Illus.). 32p. (J). (978-1-68078-170-0(7)) ABDO Publishing Co.

—Super Simple Experiments with Light & Color: Fun & Innovative Science Projects. 2016. (ENG., Illus.). 32p. (J). (978-1-68078-171-7(5)) ABDO Publishing Co.

—Super Simple Experiments with Mass: Fun & Innovative Science Projects. 2016. (ENG.). 32p. (J). (978-1-68078-172-4(3)) ABDO Publishing Co.

Polinsky, Paige V. & Craig, Diane. Super Simple Experiments with Electricity: Fun & Innovative Science Projects. 2016. (ENG., Illus.). 32p. (978-1-68078-167-0(7)) ABDO Publishing Co.

Prize-Winning Science Fair Projects. 2015. (Prize-Winning Science Fair Projects Ser.). (ENG.). 128p. (J). (gr. 7-7). 223.62 (978-0-7660-6700-4(9)) Enslow Pubs., Inc.

Psyched for Science, 6 bks. Incl. Super Science Projects about Animals in Their Habitats. Cobb, Allan B. lib. bdg. 29.25 (978-0-8239-3175-0(7), SCADHO); Super Science Projects about Light & Optics. Cobb, Allan B. lib. bdg. 29.25 (978-0-8239-3177-4(3), SCLIOP); Super Science Projects about Oceans. Cobb, Allan B. lib. bdg. 29.25 (978-0-8239-3174-3(9), SCOCEA); Super Science Projects about Sound. Cobb, Allan B. lib. bdg. 29.25 (978-0-8239-3176-7(5), SCSOUN); Super Science Projects about Weather & Natural Forces. Jones, Lorraine. lib. bdg. 29.25 (978-0-8239-3105-7(6), SCWENA); 48p. (YA). (gr. 5-8). 2005. (Illus.). Set lib. bdg. 143.70 Rosen Publishing Group, Inc., The.

Rainis, Kenneth G. Cell & Microbe Science Fair Projects: Using Microscopes, Mold, & More. 2005. (Biology! Best Science Projects Ser.). (Illus.). 128p. (J). (gr. 6-12). lib. bdg. 27.94 (978-0-7660-2369-7(9)) Enslow Pubs., Inc.

—Microscope Science Projects & Experiments: Magnifying the Hidden World. 2003. (Science Fair Success Ser.). (Illus.). 128p. (J). lib. bdg. 26.60 (978-0-7660-2090-0(8)) Enslow Pubs., Inc.

Reilly, Kathleen M. & Takacs-Moore, Mary. Energy: 25 Projects Investigate Why We Need Power & How We Get It. Takacs-Moore, Mary, illus. 2009. (Build It Yourself Ser.). (ENG., Illus.). 128p. (J). (gr. 3-7). pap. 15.95 (978-1-934670-34-7(0)) Octavio Publishing.

Riley, Karen. Agarranderas Plasticas y Otras Cosas: Plastic Rings & Other Things. 2003. (ENG & SPA., Illus.). 16p. (J). (gr. 2-5). pap. 4.50 (978-0-9708135-2-7(X)) S.C.R.A.P. Gallery.

Robertson, Charmaine. Stephanie's Science Project. 2016. (Rosen REAL Readers: STEM & STEAM Collection). 8p. (gr. 1-k). pap. 5.46 (978-1-5081-2619-5(4), Rosen Classroom) Rosen Publishing Group, Inc., The.

Romaine, Garret. Geology Lab for Kids: 52 Projects to Explore Rocks, Gems, Geodes, Crystals, Fossils, & Other Wonders of the Earth's Surface. 2017. (Lab Ser.). (ENG., Illus.). 144p. (J). (gr. 1-7). pap. 22.99 (978-1-63159-285-0(8), Quarry Bks.) Quarto Publishing Group USA.

Rosner, Marc Alan. Science Fair Success Using the Internet. rev. ed. 2006. (Science Fair Success Ser.). (Illus.). 112p. (J). (gr. 7-12). lib. bdg. 27.94 (978-0-7660-2425-0(3)) Enslow Pubs., Inc.

Rowe, Brooke. Building a Volcano. Bane, Jeff, illus. 2016. (My Early Library: My Science Fun Ser.). (ENG.). 24p. (J). (gr. k-1). 28.50 (978-1-63471-025-1(8), 208180) Cherry Lake Publishing.

Rybolt, Thomas R. & Mebane, Robert C. Environmental Science Fair Projects: Using Water, Feathers, Sunlight, Balloons, & More. 2005. (Earth Science! Best Science Projects Ser.). (Illus.). 128p. (J). (gr. 6-13). lib. bdg. 27.94 (978-0-7660-2364-2(8)) Enslow Pubs., Inc.

—Environmental Science Fair Projects, Revised & Expanded Using the Scientific Method. LaBaff, Tom & LaBaff, Stephanie, illus. 2010. (Earth Science Projects Using the Scientific Method Ser.). 160p. (J). (gr. 5-18). 35.94 (978-0-7660-3426-6(7)) Enslow Pubs., Inc.

Rybolt, Thomas R. & Rybolt, Leah M. Smelly Science Fair Projects. 2015. (Prize-Winning Science Fair Projects Ser.). (ENG.). 128p. (J). (gr. 7-7). lib. bdg. 37.27 (978-0-7660-7022-6(0)) Enslow Pubs., Inc.

Schwartz, Heather E. Cool Engineering Activities for Girls, 1 vol. 2012. (Girls Science Club Ser.). (ENG., 32p. (gr. 3-4). Illus.). pap. 8.19 (978-1-4296-8021-9(0)); pap. 47.70 (978-1-4296-8519-1(0)); lib. bdg. 27.99 (978-1-4296-7677-9(9)) Capstone Press of Coughlan Cos. (Snap Bks.).

Slade, Suzanne. Splat! Wile E. Coyote Experiments with States of Matter, 1 vol. Cornia, Christian, illus. 2014. (Wile E. Coyote, Physical Science Genius Ser.). (ENG.). 32p. (gr. 3-4). 30.65 (978-1-4765-4224-9(4)) Capstone Press of Coughlan Cos.

—Zap! Wile E. Coyote Experiments with Energy, 1 vol. Ricci, Andrés Martínez, illus. 2014. (Wile E. Coyote, Physical Science Genius Ser.). (ENG.). 32p. (gr. 3-4). 30.65 (978-1-4765-4223-2(6)); pap. 8.95 (978-1-4765-5214-9(2)) Capstone Press of Coughlan Cos.

Sobey, Ed, ed. Electric Motor Experiments. 2011. (Cool Science Projects with Technology Ser.). (Illus.). 128p. (J). (gr. 5-18). lib. bdg. 33.27 (978-0-7660-3306-1(6)) Enslow Pubs., Inc.

—Radio-Controlled Car Experiments. 2011. (Cool Science Projects with Technology Ser.). (Illus.). 128p. (J). (gr. 5-18). lib. bdg. 33.27 (978-0-7660-3304-7(X)) Enslow Pubs., Inc.

Taylor-Butler, Christine. Experiment with Magnets. 2010. (Explorer Junior Library: Science Explorer Junior Ser.). (ENG.). 32p. (gr. 3-6). lib. bdg. 28.50 (978-1-60279-844-1(3), 200554) Cherry Lake Publishing.

—Experiment with Solar Energy. 2010. (Explorer Junior Library: Science Explorer Junior Ser.). (ENG.). 32p. (gr. 3-6). lib. bdg. 28.50 (978-1-60279-840-3(0), 200546) Cherry Lake Publishing.

—Experiments with Liquids, 1 vol. 2011. (My Science Investigations Ser.). (ENG.). 32p. (gr. 1-3). 27.32 (978-1-4329-5361-4(3), Heinemann First Library) Heinemann-Raintree.

—Experiments with Magnets & Metals, 1 vol. 2011. (My Science Investigations Ser.). (ENG.). 32p. (gr. 1-3). pap. 8.29 (978-1-4329-5365-2(6), Heinemann First Library) Heinemann-Raintree.

—Experiments with Plants, 1 vol. 2011. (My Science Investigations Ser.). (ENG.). 32p. (gr. 1-3). pap. 8.29 (978-1-4329-5368-3(0)); 27.32 (978-1-4329-5362-1(1)) Heinemann-Raintree. (Heinemann First Library).

—Experiments with Plants. 2011. (True Bk Ser.). (Illus.). 48p. (J). (ENG.). pap. 6.95 (978-0-531-26647-2(8)); lib. bdg. 29.00 (978-0-531-26347-1(9)) Scholastic Library Publishing. (Children's Pr.).

—Experiments with Rocks, 1 vol. 2011. (My Science Investigations Ser.). (ENG.). 32p. (gr. 1-3). pap. 8.29 (978-1-4329-5366-9(4)); 27.32 (978-1-4329-5360-7(5)) Heinemann-Raintree. (Heinemann First Library).

—Experiments with Soil, 1 vol. 2011. (My Science Investigations Ser.). (ENG.). 32p. (gr. 1-3). pap. 8.29 (978-1-4329-5369-0(9), Heinemann First Library) Heinemann-Raintree.

Thomas, Isabel. Experiments with Forces. 2015. (Read & Experiment Ser.). (ENG., Illus.). 32p. (gr. 2-4). 30.65 (978-1-4109-7921-6(0)) Heinemann-Raintree.

—Experiments with Magnets. 2015. (Read & Experiment Ser.). (ENG., Illus.). 32p. (gr. 2-4). 30.65 (978-1-4109-7922-3(9)) Heinemann-Raintree.

—Experiments with Materials. 2015. (Read & Experiment Ser.). (ENG., Illus.). 32p. (gr. 2-4). 30.65 (978-1-4109-7923-0(7)) Heinemann-Raintree.

—Experiments with Plants. 2015. (Read & Experiment Ser.). (ENG., Illus.). 32p. (gr. 2-4). 30.65 (978-1-4109-7924-7(5)) Heinemann-Raintree.

Tocci, Salvatore. More Simple Science Fair Projects: Grades 3-5. Wiacek, Bob, illus. 2006. (Scientific American Science Fair Projects Ser.). 48p. (J). (gr. 3-5). lib. bdg. 27.00 (978-0-7910-9055-8(8)) Facts On File, Inc.

—Science Fair Projects with Everyday Stuff. 2015. (Prize-Winning Science Fair Projects Ser.). (ENG.). 128p. (J). (gr. 7-7). lib. bdg. 37.27 (978-0-7660-7020-2(4)) Enslow Pubs., Inc.

Van Vleet, Carmella. Amazing Ben Franklin Inventions. 2007. (Build It Yourself Ser.). (ENG., Illus.). 128p. (J). (gr. 3-7). 19.95 (978-0-9792268-8-5(0)) Octavio Publishing.

—Amazing Ben Franklin Inventions: You Can Build Yourself. 2007. (Build It Yourself Ser.). (ENG., Illus.). 128p. (J). (gr. 3-7). per. 15.95 (978-0-9771294-7-8(0)) Octavio Publishing.

VanCleave, Janice. A+ Science Fair Projects. 2003. (ENG., Illus.). 164p. (gr. 7-12). pap. 14.95 (978-0-471-33102-5(3), Jossey-Bass) Wiley, John & Sons, Inc.

—A+ Science Fair Workbook & Project Journal, Grades 7-12. 2003. (ENG., Illus.). 352p. (gr. 7-12). pap. 24.95 (978-0-471-46719-9(7), Wiley) Wiley, John & Sons, Inc.

—Even More of Janice VanCleave's Wild, Wacky, & Weird Earth Science Experiments. 2017. (Janice VanCleave's Wild, Wacky, & Weird Science Experiments Ser.). 64p. (J). (gr. 10-10). 34.45 (978-1-4994-6689-8(7), Rosen Central) Rosen Publishing Group, Inc., The.

—Janice VanCleave's Big Book of Play & Find Out Science Projects. 2007. (ENG., Illus.). 224p. (gr. 3-7). per. 19.95 (978-0-7879-8928-6(2), Jossey-Bass) Wiley, John & Sons, Inc.

—Janice VanCleave's Great Science Project Ideas from Real Kids. 2006. (ENG., Illus.). 144p. (gr. 3-7). pap. 16.00 (978-0-471-47204-9(2), Wiley) Wiley, John & Sons, Inc.

—Step-by-Step Science Experiments in Astronomy. 2012. (Janice VanCleave's First-Place Science Fair Projects Ser.). (ENG., Illus.). 80p. (J). (gr. 5-8). 33.25 (978-1-4488-6978-7(1)); pap. 14.15 (978-1-4488-8461-2(6)) Rosen Publishing Group, Inc., The. (Rosen Reference).

—Step-by-Step Science Experiments in Energy. 2012. (Janice VanCleave's First-Place Science Fair Projects Ser.). (ENG., Illus.). 80p. (J). (gr. 5-8). 33.25 (978-1-4488-6979-4(X)); pap. 14.15 (978-1-4488-8471-1(3)) Rosen Publishing Group, Inc., The. (Rosen Reference).

—Super Science Challenges: Hands-On Inquiry Projects for Schools, Science Fairs, or Just Plain Fun! 2007. (ENG., Illus.). 160p. (gr. 3-7). pap. 14.95 (978-0-471-47183-7(6), Wiley) Wiley, John & Sons, Inc.

VanCleave, Janice Pratt. Janice VanCleave's Wild, Wacky, & Weird Earth Science Experiments. 2016. (Janice VanCleave's Wild, Wacky, & Weird Science Experiments Ser.). (ENG., Illus.). 64p. (J). (gr. 5-5). pap. 12.95 (978-1-4777-8973-5(1), Rosen Reference) Rosen Publishing Group, Inc., The.

VanCleave, Janice Pratt. Many More of Janice Vancleave's Wild, Wacky, & Weird Earth Science Experiments. 2017. (J). **(978-1-4994-3951-9(2)**, Rosen Reference) Rosen Publishing Group, Inc., The.

Warner, Penny. Project Book: Ideas, Tips & Techniques for School Projects. Wagner, Amy, ed. Moore, Lishia, illus. Moore, Lishia & Wagner, Amy, photos by. 2007. 80p. pap. 9.98 (978-1-887436-05-2(7)) Woodland Scenics.

Weakland, Mark. Smash! Wile E. Coyote Experiments with Simple Machines, 1 vol. Cornia, Christian, illus. 2014. (Wile E. Coyote, Physical Science Genius Ser.). (ENG.). 32p. (gr. 3-4). 30.65 (978-1-4765-4222-5(8)) Capstone Press of Coughlan Cos.

—Thud! Wile E. Coyote Experiments with Forces & Motion, 1 vol. Cornia, Christian, illus. 2014. (Wile E. Coyote, Physical Science Genius Ser.). (ENG.). 32p. (gr. 3-4). 30.65 (978-1-4765-4221-8(X)) Capstone Press of Coughlan Cos.

—Whoosh! Wile E. Coyote Experiments with Flight & Gravity. Brown, Alan, illus. 2017. (Wile E. Coyote, Physical Science Genius Ser.). (ENG.). 32p. (gr. 3-5). lib. bdg. 30.65 (978-1-5157-3732-2(2)) Capstone Press of Coughlan Cos.

Wheeler-Toppen, Jodi Lyn. Gross Science Projects, 1 vol. 2013. (Gross Guides). (ENG.). 32p. (gr. 3-4). lib. bdg. 27.99 (978-1-4296-9924-2(8), Edge Bks.) Capstone Press of Coughlan Cos.

Young, Karen Romano. Experiments to Do on Your Family. Goldin, David, illus. 2010. (Science Fair Winners Ser.). (ENG.). 80p. (J). (gr. 5-9). 24.90 (978-1-4263-0692-1(X)); pap. 12.95 (978-1-4263-0691-4(1)) National Geographic Society. (National Geographic Children's Bks.).

—Junkyard Science. Goldin, David, illus. 2010. (Science Fair Winners Ser.). (ENG.). 80p. (J). (gr. 5-9). 24.90 (978-1-4263-0690-7(3)); pap. 12.95 (978-1-4263-0689-1(X)) National Geographic Society. (National Geographic Children's Bks.).

—Try This! 50 Fun Experiments for the Mad Scientist in You. Rakola, Matthew, photos by. 2014. (ENG., Illus.). 160p. (J). (gr. 5). pap. 16.99 (978-1-4263-1711-8(5), National Geographic Children's Bks.) National Geographic Society.

SCIENCE PROJECTS—FICTION

Abdo, Kenny. Give Me Liberty or Give Me Detention!, 1 vol. Doucet, Bob, illus. 2013. (Haven't Got a Clue! Ser.). (ENG.). 80p. (J). (gr. 3-6). lib. bdg. 27.07 (978-1-61641-953-0(9), Calico Chapter Bks) Magic Wagon.

Albright, Lauren. Exit Strategy. 2017. (Max Ser.). (ENG., Illus.). 176p. (J). (gr. 4-8). 16.99 **(978-1-4814-7912-7(1)**, Aladdin) Simon & Schuster Children's Publishing.

Andersen, Jill. Tanya's Craft Project. 2016. (Rosen REAL Readers: STEM & STEAM Collection). 8p. (gr. 1-k). pap. 5.46 (978-1-5081-2586-0(4), Rosen Classroom) Rosen Publishing Group, Inc., The.

Banks, Kate & Sheldrake, Rupert. Boy's Best Friend. 2015. (ENG.). 224p. (J). (gr. 3-7). 15.99 (978-0-374-38008-3(2), 9780374380083, Farrar, Straus & Giroux (BYR)) Farrar, Straus & Giroux.

Barnes, John L. C. Clara's Clever Custard. 2010. (ENG.). 212p. (J). mass mkt. 8.99 (978-0-9566042-0-0(X)) Five Valleys Publishing GBR. Dist: Lightning Source, Inc.

Barnett, Mac. Oh No! Or How My Science Project Destroyed the World. Santat, Dan, illus. 2010. (ENG.). 40p. (J). (gr. -1-2). 16.99 (978-1-4231-2312-5(3)) Hyperion Pr.

Barrows, Annie & Blackall, Sophie. Ivy + Bean What's the Big Idea?, 1 vol. 2011. (Ivy & Bean Ser.). (ENG., Illus.). 132p. (J). (gr. 1-4). 24.21 (978-1-59961-934-7(2)) Spotlight.

Barrows, Annie, et al. Ivy + Bean What's the Big Idea? Blackall, Sophie, illus. 2010. (ENG.). 128p. (J). (gr. 1-5). 14.99 (978-0-8118-6692-7(0)) Chronicle Bks. LLC.

Bean, Raymond. Blown Away, 0 vols. unabr. ed. 2012. (Sweet Farts Ser.: 3). (ENG.). 172p. (J). (gr. 4-6). pap. 9.95 (978-1-61218-251-3(8), 9781612182513, Amazon Children's Publishing) Amazon Publishing.

—Rippin' It Old School, 0 vols. unabr. ed. 2010. (Sweet Farts Ser.: 2). (ENG.). 184p. (J). (gr. 4-6). pap. 9.95 (978-1-935597-08-7(6), 9781935597087, Two Lions) Amazon Publishing.

Birney, Betty G. Humphrey's Playful Puppy Problem. Burris, Priscilla, illus. 2014. (Humphrey's Tiny Tales Ser.: 2). (ENG.). 96p. (J). (gr. k-3). pap. 4.99 (978-0-14-751484-4(3), Puffin Books) Penguin Young Readers Group.

Boniface, William. The Extraordinary Adventures of Ordinary Boy. Gilpin, Stephen, illus. 2008. (Extraordinary Adventures of Ordinary Boy Ser.: 2). (ENG.). 368p. (J). (gr. 3-7). pap. 6.99 (978-0-06-077469-1(X)) HarperCollins Pubs.

Chabert, Jack. The Science Fair Is Freaky! Ricks, Sam, illus. 2016. (Eerie Elementary — Branches Ser.: bk.4). (ENG.). 96p. (J). (gr. 1-3). pap. 4.99 (978-0-545-87368-0(1)) Scholastic, Inc.

—The Science Fair Is Freaky! 2016. (Eerie Elementary — Branches Ser.: bk.4). (ENG.). (J). lib. bdg. 14.75 (978-0-606-38806-1(0)) Turtleback Bks.

Cheng, Andrea. The Year of the Baby. Barton, Patrice, illus. 2014. (Anna Wang Novel Ser.: 2). (ENG.). 176p. (J). (gr. 1-4). pap. 5.99 (978-0-544-22525-1(2), HMH Books For Young Readers) Houghton Mifflin Harcourt Publishing Co.

Clark, Sherryl. Kim's Super Science Day. McKenzie, Heath, illus. 2015. (J). pap. (978-1-4966-0250-3(1)) Capstone Classroom.

Clements, Andrew. Jake Drake, Know-It-All. Frazee, Marla & Pedersen, Janet, illus. 2007. (Jake Drake Ser.: Bk. 2). 88p. (gr. 2-5). 15.00 (978-0-7569-8212-6(X)) Perfection Learning Corp.

—Jake Drake, Know-It-All. Pedersen, Janet & Frazee, Marla, illus. 2007. (Jake Drake Ser.: Bk. 2). (ENG.). 112p. (J). (gr. 2-5). pap. 5.99 (978-1-4169-3931-3(8), Atheneum Bks. for Young Readers) Simon & Schuster Children's Publishing.

Cook, Eileen. Gnome Invasion. 2011. (Fourth Grade Fairy Ser.: 3). (ENG.). 160p. (J). (gr. 3-7). pap. 6.99 (978-1-4169-9813-6(6), Aladdin) Simon & Schuster Children's Publishing.

Coven, Wanda. Heidi Heckelbeck & the Secret Admirer. Burris, Priscilla, illus. 2012. (Heidi Heckelbeck Ser.: 6). (ENG.). 128p. (J). (gr. k-4). 16.99 (978-1-4424-4175-0(5)); pap. 5.99 (978-1-4424-4174-3(7)) Little Simon. (Little Simon).

Dahl, Michael. A Jar of Eyeballs. Sinkovec, Igor, illus. 2015. (Igor's Lab of Fear Ser.). (ENG.). 40p. (gr. 1-3). lib. bdg. 23.99 (978-1-4965-0455-5(0)) Stone Arch Bks.

Ecton, Emily. Project Jackalope. 2012. (ENG., Illus.). 256p. (J). (gr. 3-7). 15.99 (978-1-4521-0155-2(8)) Chronicle Bks. LLC.

Frazier, Sundee T. Brendan Buckley's Sixth-Grade Experiment. 2013. (ENG.). 288p. (J). (gr. 4-7). 6.99 (978-0-385-74051-7(4), Yearling) Random Hse. Children's Bks.

Gagnon, Mary. Are Those Your Shoes? 2008. 120p. pap. 11.95 (978-1-4357-2942-1(0)) Lulu Pr., Inc.

Gallagher, Diana G. Beware! The Complicated Life of Claudia Cristina Cortez, 1 vol. Garvey, Brann, illus. 2009. (Claudia Cristina Cortez Ser.). (ENG.). 88p. (gr. 2-3). 26.65 (978-1-4342-1575-8(X), Claudia Cristina Cortez) Stone Arch Bks.

—Mice Capades, 1 vol. Juarez, Adriana & Puglisi, Adriana, illus. 2013. (Pet Friends Forever Ser.). (ENG.). 88p. (gr. 1-3). pap. 5.95 (978-1-4795-1863-0(8)); lib. bdg. 25.32 (978-1-4048-7500-5(X)) Picture Window Bks.

Green, D. L. Zeke Meeks vs the Stinkin' Science Fair, 1 vol. Alves, Josh, illus. 2012. (Zeke Meeks Ser.). (ENG.). 128p. (gr. 2-2). pap. 5.95 (978-1-4048-7222-6(1)); lib. bdg. 22.65 (978-1-4048-6802-1(X)) Picture Window Bks. (Zeke Meeks).

Grunwell, Jeanne Marie. Mind Games. 2006. (ENG., Illus.). 144p. (J). (gr. 5-7). pap. 10.95 (978-0-618-68947-7(8)) Houghton Mifflin Harcourt Publishing Co.

Haynes, Marilee. A. K. A. Genius. 2013. (ENG.). 208p. (YA). 9.95 (978-0-8198-0830-1(X)) Pauline Bks. & Media.

Helget, Nicole. The End of the Wild. 2017. (ENG., Illus.). 272p. (J). (gr. 3-7). 16.99 (978-0-316-24511-1(9)) Little, Brown Bks. for Young Readers.

Holm, Jennifer L. & Holm, Matthew. Mad Scientist. Holm, Jennifer L. & Holm, Matthew, illus. 2011. (Babymouse Ser.: No. 14). (ENG., Illus.). 96p. (J). (gr. 2-5). pap. 6.99 (978-0-375-86574-9(8)); lib. bdg. 12.99 (978-0-375-96574-6(2)) Random Hse. Children's Bks. (Random Hse. Bks. for Young Readers).

Hughes, Alison. On a Scale of Idiot to Complete Jerk, 1 vol. 2014. (ENG., Illus.). 144p. (J). (gr. 4-7). pap. 9.95 (978-1-4598-0484-5(8)) Orca Bk. Pubs. USA.

Humphrey, Anna. Ruby Goldberg's Bright Idea. Newton, Vanessa Brantley, illus. 2013. (ENG.). 144p. (J). (gr. 3-7). 15.99 (978-1-4424-8027-8(0), Simon & Schuster Bks. For Young Readers) Simon & Schuster Bks. For Young Readers.

Johnson, Sonia M. Tyler's Third Grade Science Project. 2009. (Illus.). 20p. pap. 12.49 (978-1-4343-5553-9(5)) AuthorHouse.

Kinard, Kami. The Boy Project. 2016. (ENG.). 256p. (J). (gr. 4-7). pap. 6.99 (978-0-545-34516-3(2), Scholastic Paperbacks) Scholastic, Inc.

Komechak, Marilyn Gilbert. Paisano Pete: Snake-Killer Bird. Eckhardt, Jason C., illus. 2003. 100p. (J). (gr. 3-7). per. 11.95 (978-1-57168-770-8(X), Eakin Pr.) Eakin Pr.

Krulik, Nancy. Be Nice to Mice!, No. 20. John and Wendy Staff, illus. 2006. (Katie Kazoo, Switcheroo Ser.: 20). (ENG.). 80p. (J). (gr. 2-4). pap. 4.99 (978-0-448-44132-0(2), Grosset & Dunlap) Penguin Young Readers Group.

Krulik, Nancy & Burwasser, Amanda Elizabeth. Science No Fair! Project Droid #1. Moran, Mike, illus. 2016. (Project Droid Ser.). (ENG.). 112p. (J). (gr. 1-4). 13.99 (978-1-5107-1018-4(3), Sky Pony Pr.) Skyhorse Publishing Co., Inc.

—Soccer Shocker! Moran, Mike, illus. 2016. (Project Droid Ser.). (ENG.). 104p. (J). (gr. 1-4). pap. 4.99 (978-1-5107-1029-0(9), Sky Pony Pr.) Skyhorse Publishing Co., Inc.

Layne, Steven L. Thomas's Sheep & the Spectacular Science Project, 1 vol. Board, Perry, illus. 2004. (ENG.). 32p. (J). (gr. k-3). 16.99 (978-1-58980-210-0(1)) Pelican Publishing Co., Inc.

Manushkin, Fran. Pedro Goes Buggy. Lyon, Tammie, illus. 2016. (Pedro Ser.). (ENG.). 32p. (gr. k-2). lib. bdg. 21.32 (978-1-5158-0085-9(7)) Pedro Pubns. GBR. Dist: Capstone Pub.

—Ready, Set, Oops! 2008. pap. 34.95 (978-1-58013-762-1(8)) Kane Press, Inc.

Matlin, Marlee & Cooney, Doug. Nobody's Perfect. 2006. (ENG., Illus.). 240p. (J). (gr. 3-7). 15.95 (978-0-689-86986-0(X), Simon & Schuster Bks. For Young Readers) Simon & Schuster Bks. For Young Readers.

Mayer, Mercer. Just a School Project. Mayer, Mercer, illus. 2004. (Little Critter Ser.). (ENG., Illus.). 24p. (J). (gr. -1-2). pap. 3.99 (978-0-06-053946-7(1), HarperFestival) HarperCollins Pubs.

McCann, Jesse Leon. The Science Project. Fruchter, Jason, illus. 2003. 61p. (J). (978-0-439-56271-3(6)) Scholastic, Inc.

McElligott, Matthew & Tuxbury, Larry David. Benjamin Franklinstein Lives! McElligott, Matthew, illus. 2010. (Benjamin Franklinstein Ser.: 1). (ENG., Illus.). 128p. (J). (gr. 3-7). 12.99 (978-0-399-25229-7(0), G.P. Putnam's Sons Books for Young Readers) Penguin Young Readers Group.

McMullan, Kate. Two Good Friends. Alley, R. W., illus. 2011. (Pearl & Wagner Ser.: 2). (ENG.). 48p. (J). (gr. 1-3). pap. 3.99 (978-0-448-45690-4(7), Penguin Young Readers) Penguin Young Readers Group.

Miller, Amanda. The Library's Secret: A Hidden Adventure. 2010. 88p. pap. 10.49 (978-1-4520-7012-4(1)) AuthorHouse.

Mills, Claudia. How Oliver Olson Changed the World. Maione, Heather Harms, illus. 2009. (ENG.). 112p. (J). (gr. 2-5). 15.95 (978-0-374-33487-1(0), 9780374334871, Farrar, Straus & Giroux (BYR)) Farrar, Straus & Giroux.

—How Oliver Olson Changed the World. Maione, Heather, illus. 2011. (ENG.). 128p. (J). (gr. 2-5). pap. 6.99 (978-0-312-67282-9(9), 9780312672829) Square Fish.

Mullarkey, Lisa. The Ding Dong Ditch-A-Roo: Book 9, 1 vol. Harris, Phyllis, illus. 2012. (Katharine the Almost Great Ser.). (ENG.). 80p. (J). (gr. 1-4). 27.07 (978-1-61641-830-4(3)) Magic Wagon.

O'Ryan, Ray. Science Fair Disaster! Kraft, Jason, illus. 2016. (Galaxy Zack Ser.: 13). (ENG.). 128p. (J). (gr. k-4). pap. 5.99 (978-1-4814-5876-4(0), Little Simon) Little Simon.

Parish, Herman. Amelia Bedelia, Rocket Scientist? Sweat, Lynn, illus. (I Can Read Level 2 Ser.). 64p. (J). 2007. (ENG.). (gr. k-3). pap. 3.99 (978-0-06-051889-9(8), Greenwillow Bks.) 2005. (gr. 1-18). 15.99 (978-0-06-051887-5(1)) 2005. (gr. k-4). lib. bdg. 17.89 (978-0-06-051888-2(X), Greenwillow Bks.) HarperCollins Pubs.

—Amelia Bedelia, Rocket Scientist? Sweat, Lynn, illus. 2007. (I Can Read Ser.). 64p. 14.00 (978-0-7569-8058-0(5)) Perfection Learning Corp.

—Amelia Bedelia, Rocket Scientist? Sweat, Lynn, illus. 2007. (Amelia Bedelia: I Can Read! Ser.: 19). (J). lib. bdg. 13.55 (978-1-4177-8068-6(1), Turtleback) Turtleback Bks.

Pelletier, Cathie. The Summer Experiment. 2014. (ENG.). 288p. (J). (gr. 4-7). 16.99 *(978-1-4022-8578-3(7),* 9781402285783, Sourcebooks Jabberwocky) Sourcebooks, Inc.

Perry, Phyllis Jean. The Alien, the Giant, & Rocketman. Francis, Guy, illus. 2006. (J). pap. *(978-1-59336-723-7(6))* Mondo Publishing.

Reynolds, Paul A. Sydney & Simon: To the Moon & Beyond! Reynolds, Peter H., illus. 2017. (ENG.). 48p. (J). (gr. 1-4). lib. bdg. 12.99 *(978-1-58089-679-5(0))* Charlesbridge Publishing, Inc.

Sateren, Shelley Swanson. Max & Zoe: the Science Fair, 1 vol. Sullivan, Mary, illus. 2013. (Max & Zoe Ser.). (ENG.). 32p. (gr. k-2). pap. 5.19 *(978-1-4795-2330-6(5),* Max & Zoe) Picture Window Bks.

—The Science Fair. Sullivan, Mary, illus. 2013. (Max & Zoe Ser.). (ENG.). 32p. (gr. k-2). lib. bdg. 21.32 *(978-1-4048-7202-8(7),* Max & Zoe) Picture Window Bks.

Sierra, Judy. The Secret Science Project That Almost Ate the School. Gammell, Stephen, illus. 2006. (ENG.). 32p. (J). (gr. 1-4). 17.99 *(978-1-4169-1175-3(8),* Simon & Schuster/Paula Wiseman Bks.) Simon & Schuster/Paula Wiseman Bks.

Stadelmann, Amy Marie. The Super-Smelly Moldy Blob. Stadelmann, Amy Marie, illus. 2016. (Olive & Beatrix Ser.: 2). (ENG., Illus.). 80p. (J). (gr. k-2). 15.99 *(978-0-545-81485-0(5))* Scholastic, Inc.

Steinkraus, Kyla. Gumshoe Gang Cracks the Case. 2015. (ENG.). 64p. (gr. 3-6). 29.95 *(978-1-63430-381-1(4))* Rourke Educational Media.

Suen, Anastasia. Girls Can, Too! A Tolerence Story, 1 vol. Ebbeler, Jeff, illus. 2008. (Main Street School - Kids with Character Ser.). (ENG.). 32p. (gr. -1-4). 28.50 *(978-1-60270-271-4(3),* Looking Glass Library) ABDO Publishing Co.

Terrell, Brandon. Science Fair Sabotage. Epelbaum, Mariano, illus. 2017. (Snoops, Inc Ser.). (ENG.). 112p. (gr. 4-6). lib. bdg. 26.65 *(978-1-4965-4347-9(5))* Stone Arch Bks.

Thaler, Mike. The Science Fair from the Black Lagoon, 1 vol. Lee, Jared, illus. 2011. (Black Lagoon Adventures Ser.: No. 1). (ENG.). 64p. (gr. 3-6). 24.21 *(978-1-59961-814-2(1))* Spotlight.

SCIENTIFIC APPARATUS AND INSTRUMENTS

see also names of groups of instruments, e.g. Aeronautical Instruments; Astronomical Instruments; Chemical Apparatus; Electric Apparatus and Appliances; Meteorological Instruments

Besel, Jennifer M. Compass Roses & Directions, 1 vol. 2013. (Maps Ser.). (ENG.). 24p. (gr. k-1). pap. 6.95 *(978-1-4765-3524-1(8),* Pebble Bks.) Capstone Press of Coughlan Cos.

Bortz, Alfred B. Seven Wonders of Exploration Technology. 2010. (Seven Wonders Ser.). (YA). (gr. 5-9). lib. bdg. 33.26 *(978-0-7613-4241-0(9))* Twenty First Century Bks.

Cardenas, Ernesto & Saavedra, Patricia. El laboratorio de Ciencias. l.t. ed. 2006. (SPA., Illus.). 16p. pap. 4.95 *(978-1-933668-24-6(5))* Milo Educational Bks. & Resources.

Cardenas, Ernesto A. What Does A Scientist Use? 2009. 19.95 *(978-1-60698-020-0(3));* pap. 3.95 *(978-1-60698-018-7(1))* Milo Educational Bks. & Resources.

Cook, Trevor. Science Lab Set. 2009. (Illus.). (J). (gr. 4-7). 151.50 *(978-1-4358-2826-1(7),* PowerKids Pr.) Rosen Publishing Group, Inc., The.

Deane-Pratt, Ade. Sensors. 2012. (How Things Work Ser.). (Illus.). 32p. (YA). (gr. 3-6). lib. bdg. 26.50 *(978-1-4488-5281-9(1))* Rosen Publishing Group, Inc., The.

DeMarin, Layne. Look & Learn, 1 vol. 2011. (Wonder Readers Fluent Level Ser.). (ENG.). 32p. (gr. -1-2). pap. 5.99 *(978-1-4296-7939-8(5),* Wonder Readers) Capstone Press of Coughlan Cos.

deMarin, Layne. Look & Learn. 2011. (Wonder Readers Fluent Level Ser.). (ENG.). 16p. (gr. -1-2). pap. 35.94 *(978-1-4296-8120-9(9),* Wonder Readers) Capstone Press of Coughlan Cos.

Enz, Tammy. Build Your Own Periscope, Flashlight, & Other Useful Stuff. 2011. (Build It Yourself Ser.). (ENG.). 32p. (gr. 3-4). pap. 47.70 *(978-1-4296-6431-8(2),* Edge Bks.) Capstone Press of Coughlan Cos.

Furgang, Kathy. Science Measuring Tools & Instrumentos para medir en Ciencias: 6 English, 6 Spanish Adaptations. 2011. (ENG & SPA.). (J). 101.00 net. *(978-1-4108-5727-9(1))* Benchmark Education Co.

Goldberg, Jan. Earth Imaging Satellites. 2003. (Library of Satellites Ser.). (Illus.). 64p. (YA). (gr. 5-8). lib. bdg. 31.95 *(978-0-8239-3853-7(0),* Rosen Reference) Rosen Publishing Group, Inc., The.

Hanson, Anders. Scientist's Tools, 1 vol. 2011. (Professional Tools Ser.). (ENG., Illus.). 24p. (J). (gr. 3-5). lib. bdg. 25.65 *(978-1-61613-581-2(6),* Super SandCastle) ABDO Publishing Co.

Harris, Michael C. Spare Parts for People. 2010. (Cool Science Ser.). 48p. (J). (gr. 3-6). 28.50 *(978-1-60870-080-6(1))* Marshall Cavendish GBR. Dist: Marshall Cavendish Corp.

Helbrough, Emma. A Day in the Life of a Pirate. Firenze, Inklink, illus. 2007. (Day in the Life Ser.: Vol. 4). 32p. (J). (gr. 3-7). lib. bdg. 25.25 *(978-1-4042-3853-4(0))* Rosen Publishing Group, Inc., The.

Hicks, Kelli. Using Tools to Understand Our World. 2012. (ENG.). 24p. (gr. 3-4). pap. 8.95 *(978-1-61810-230-0(3))* Rourke Educational Media.

Holt, Rinehart and Winston Staff. Holt Science & Technology: Calculator for Biological Science Labs. 5th ed. 2004. (Illus.). pap. 14.60 *(978-0-03-035177-8(4))* Holt McDougal.

Koontz, Robin. Binoculars. 2014. (ENG.). 24p. (gr. k-3). 28.50 *(978-1-62717-640-8(3))* Rourke Educational Media.

Larson, Kirsten. Tools of the Trade: Using Scientific Equipment. 2016. (Let's Explore Science Ser.). (ENG.). 48p. (gr. 5-8). 35.64 *(978-1-68191-400-8(X))* Rourke Educational Media.

Martin, Elena. Seeing Is Believing. 2005. (Yellow Umbrella Fluent Level Ser.). (ENG., Illus.). 16p. (gr. k-1). pap. 35.70 *(978-0-7368-5299-9(9),* Yellow Umbrella Bks.) Capstone Press of Coughlan Cos.

Meredith, Susan. Using Scientific Tools. 2009. (ENG., Illus.). 48p. (gr. 4-8). pap. 10.95 *(978-1-60694-531-5(9))* Rourke Educational Media.

—Uso de Instrumentos Científicos. 2012. (SPA & ENG.). 48p. (gr. 4-8). pap. 10.95 *(978-1-61810-471-7(3))* Rourke Educational Media.

Metz, Lorijo. Using Beakers & Graduated Cylinders. 2013. (Science Tools Ser.). (ENG., Illus.). 24p. (J). (gr. 3-6). 22.60 *(978-1-4488-9685-1(1));* pap. 8.25 *(978-1-4488-9828-2(5))* Rosen Publishing Group, Inc., The. (PowerKids Pr.).

Rau, Dana Meachen. Become an Explorer: Make & Use a Compass. 2010. (Creative Adventure Guides). 48p. (J). (gr. 3-6). lib. bdg. 26.60 *(978-1-59953-383-4(9))* Norwood Hse. Pr.

Rivera, Sheila. Eyedropper. 2006. (First Step Nonfiction - Simple Tools Ser.). (ENG., Illus.). 8p. (J). (gr. -1-1). pap. 4.95 *(978-0-8225-5712-8(6),* Lerner Pubns.) Lerner Publishing Group.

—Tweezers. 2007. (First Step Nonfiction - Simple Tools Ser.). (ENG.). 8p. (gr. -1-1). pap. 4.95 *(978-0-8225-6851-3(9))* Lerner Publishing Group.

Rourke, Brigid. Tools of Science. 2013. (Rosen Readers Ser.). (ENG.). 24p. (J). (gr. 2-3). pap. 8.25 *(978-1-4777-2325-8(0));* pap. 49.50 *(978-1-4777-2326-5(9))* Rosen Publishing Group, Inc., The. (Rosen Classroom).

Salzmann, Mary Elizabeth. Doctor's Tools, 1 vol. 2011. (Professional Tools Ser.). (ENG., Illus.). 24p. (J). (gr. 3-5). lib. bdg. 25.65 *(978-1-61613-579-9(4),* Super SandCastle) ABDO Publishing Co.

Sharkawy, Azza. Observe It! 2014. (ENG., Illus.). 24p. (J). *(978-0-7787-0765-3(2))* Crabtree Publishing Co.

Smith, Paula. Measure It! 2015. (ENG., Illus.). 24p. (J). pap. *(978-0-7787-1544-3(2))* Crabtree Publishing Co.

—Model It! 2015. (ENG., Illus.). 24p. (J). pap. *(978-0-7787-1545-0(0))* Crabtree Publishing Co.

SCIENTIFIC DISCOVERIES

see Discoveries in Science

SCIENTIFIC EDUCATION

see Science—Study and Teaching

SCIENTIFIC EXPEDITIONS

see also names of regions explored, e.g. Antarctic Regions; Arctic Regions; and names of expeditions

Johnson, Rebecca L. Journey into the Deep: Discovering New Ocean Creatures. (ENG., 64p. (gr. 4-8). 2015. Illus.). 34.65 *(978-1-4677-5923-6(6),* Lerner Digital) 2010. lib. bdg. 31.93 *(978-0-7613-4148-2(X))* Lerner Publishing Group.

SCIENTIFIC EXPEDITIONS—FICTION

Brenchley, Chaz & Doyle, Arthur Conan. The Lost World. Bennett, Felix, illus. 2009. (Real Reads Ser.). 64p. (J). (gr. 4-8). pap. 13.55 *(978-1-60754-395-4(8));* lib. bdg. 29.25 *(978-1-60754-394-7(X))* Windmill Bks.

Hosler, Jay. Last of the Sandwalkers. 2015. (ENG., Illus.). 320p. (YA). (gr. 5). pap. 17.99 *(978-1-62672-024-4(X),* 9781626720244, First Second Bks.) Roaring Brook Pr.

Lane, Jean E. Lill & Mewe Journey to the Ocean of Runa. 2013. 122p. pap. 11.95 *(978-1-62212-538-8(X),* Strategic Bk. Publishing) Strategic Book Publishing & Rights Agency (SBPRA).

Sniegoski, Tom. Quest for the Spark. Smith, Jeff, illus. 2013. (BONE: Quest for the Spark Ser.). (ENG.). 288p. (J). (gr. 3-7). Bk. 3. pap. 10.99 *(978-0-545-14106-2(0))*No. 3. 22.99 *(978-0-545-14105-5(2))* Scholastic, Inc. (Graphix).

Whitmore, Andrew. Beast of the Jungle. 2007. 96p. (YA). pap. *(978-1-4207-0728-1(0))* Sundance/Newbridge Educational Publishing.

SCIENTIFIC EXPERIMENTS

see Science—Experiments

also particular branches of science with the subdivision Experiments, e.g. Chemistry—Experiments

SCIENTIFIC INSTRUMENTS

see Scientific Apparatus and Instruments

SCIENTIFIC MANAGEMENT

see Management

SCIENTIFIC METHOD

see Science—Methodology

SCIENTIFIC RECREATIONS

see also Mathematical Recreations

Blum, Raymond, et al. Giant Book of Science Fun/Giant Book of Math Fun: Flip Book. Sterling Publishing Company Staff, ed. (Illus.). 512p. pap. 9.98 *(978-1-4027-0469-7(0))* Sterling Publishing Co., Inc.

Brecher, Erwin. Are There Rainbows on the Moon? Over 200 Bizarre, Weird & Wonderful Puzzles with Science. 2013. (ENG., Illus.). 288p. 20.95 *(978-1-78097-107-0(9))* Carlton Bks., Ltd. GBR. Dist: Independent Pubs. Group.

Brown, Cynthia Light & Brown, Grace. Explore Fossils! With 25 Great Projects. Stone, Bryan, illus. 2016. (Explore Your World Ser.). (ENG.). 96p. (J). (gr. 1-5). 19.95 *(978-1-61930-331-7(0),* 1401070) Octavio Publishing.

Churchill, E. Richard, et al. 365 More Simple Science Experiments with Everyday Materials. Zweifel, Frances, illus. 2014. (ENG.). 320p. (J). (gr. -1-17). pap. 12.95 *(978-1-57912-967-5(6),* 81967, Black Dog & Leventhal Pubs. Inc.) Hachette Bks.

—365 Simple Science Experiments with Everyday Materials. Zweifel, Frances, illus. 2013. (ENG.). 306p. (J). (gr. -1-17). pap. 12.99 *(978-1-57912-927-9(7),* 81927, Black Dog & Leventhal Pubs. Inc.) Hachette Bks.

Cleary, Brian P. Mrs. Riley Bought Five Itchy Aardvarks & Other Painless Tricks for Memorizing Science Facts. Sandy, J. P., illus. 2008. (Adventures in Memory Ser.). (ENG.). 48p. (gr. 4-6). 26.60 *(978-0-8225-7819-2(0))* Lerner Publishing Group.

Cobb, Vicki & Darling, Kathy. We Dare You! Hundreds of Fun Science Bets, Challenges, & Experiments You Can Do at Home. rev. ed. 2015. (ENG., Illus.). 336p. (J). (gr. 2-7). pap. 12.95 *(978-1-62914-631-7(5),* Sky Pony Pr.) Skyhorse Publishing Co., Inc.

—We Dare You! Hundreds of Fun Science Experiments, Tricks, & Games You Can Try at Home. 2009. (ENG., Illus.). 336p. (J). (gr. 2-7). pap. 14.95 *(978-1-60239-775-0(9),* 239775) Skyhorse Publishing Co., Inc.

Dyer, Janice. Get into Wow-Factor Science. 2017. (Illus.). 32p. (J). ***(978-0-7787-3643-1(1))*** Crabtree Publishing Co.

Falk, John H., et al. Bubble Monster: And Other Science Fun. 2003. (Illus.). 176p. (J). (gr. -1-3). pap. 17.95 *(978-1-55652-301-4(7))* Chicago Review Pr., Inc.

Furgang, Kathy. A Challenging Game of True or False. 2015. (Fact or Fib? Ser.). (ENG., Illus.). 208p. (J). (gr. 3). pap. 7.95 *(978-1-4549-1588-1(9))* Sterling Publishing Co., Inc.

—Fact or Fib? A Challenging Game of True or False. 2014. (Fact or Fib? Ser.: 1). (ENG., Illus.). 208p. (J). (gr. 3). pap. 7.95 *(978-1-4549-0982-8(X))* Sterling Publishing Co., Inc.

—Fact or Fib? 2: A Challenging Game of True or False. 2014. (Fact or Fib? Ser.: 1). (ENG., Illus.). 208p. (J). (gr. 3). pap. 7.95 *(978-1-4549-0983-5(8))* Sterling Publishing Co., Inc.

—Fact or Fib? 4: A Challenging Game of True or False. 2015. (Fact or Fib? Ser.). (ENG., Illus.). 208p. (J). (gr. 3). pap. 7.95 *(978-1-4549-1589-8(7))* Sterling Publishing Co., Inc.

Gardner, Martin. Martin Gardner's Science Magic: Tricks & Puzzles. 2011. (Dover Magic Bks.). (ENG., Illus.). 96p. (gr. 4). pap. 4.99 *(978-0-486-47657-5(X))* Dover Pubns., Inc.

Hanson, Anders & Mann, Elissa. Cool String Art: Creative Activities That Make Math & Science Fun for Kids!, 1 vol. 2013. (Cool Art with Math & Science Ser.). (ENG.). 32p. (J). (gr. 3-6). lib. bdg. 28.50 *(978-1-61783-824-8(1),* Checkerboard Library) ABDO Publishing Co.

—Cool Structures: Creative Activities That Make Math & Science Fun for Kids!, 1 vol. 2013. (Cool Art with Math & Science Ser.). (ENG.). 32p. (J). (gr. 3-6). lib. bdg. 28.50 *(978-1-61783-825-5(X),* Checkerboard Library) ABDO Publishing Co.

Hickman, Pamela & Federation of Ontario Naturalists. Naturaleza Divertida. Shore, Judie, illus. (SPA.). 92p. *(978-84-9754-095-7(6),* 87821) Ediciones Oniro S.A.

—La Naturaleza y Tú. Shore, Judie, illus. (SPA.). 63p. *(978-84-9754-106-0(5),* 87822) Ediciones Oniro S.A.

El Libro de los Acertijos Científicos. (Coleccion Acertijos). (SPA.). (YA). (gr. 5-8). *(978-950-724-614-2(2),* LM8237) Lumen ARG. Dist: Lectorum Pubns., Inc.

Low, A. M. Popular Scientific Recreations - Science. 2006. 292p. per. *(978-1-4067-9717-6(0),* Hesperides Pr.) Read Bks.

Martineau, Susan. Crazy Contraptions. Ursell, Martin, illus. 2011. (Awesome Activities Ser.). (ENG.). 24p. (J). (gr. 3-6). pap. 10.60 *(978-1-61533-405-6(X));* lib. bdg. 25.25 *(978-1-61533-367-7(3))* Windmill Bks.

Press, Judy. Little Hands Sea Life Art & Activities: Creative Learning Experiences for 3-7-Year Olds. 2004. (Williamson's Little Hands Book Ser.). (Illus.). 128p. (J). pap. 12.95 *(978-1-885593-94-8(5),* Ideal Pubns.) Worthy Publishing.

Roth, Jennifer A. Backyard Laboratory. 2007. (Experiment with Science Ser.). (ENG., Illus.). 32p. (J). (gr. 3-6). 27.00 *(978-0-531-18542-1(7),* Children's Pr.) Scholastic Library Publishing.

Thomas, Lyn. 100% Pure Fake: Gross Out Your Friends & Family with 25 Great Special Effects! 2012. (ENG., Illus.). 48p. (J). (gr. 3-7). 8.95 *(978-1-55453-931-4(5))* Kids Can Pr., Ltd. CAN. Dist: Hachette Bk. Group.

VanCleave, Janice. Super Science Challenges: Hands-On Inquiry Projects for Schools, Science Fairs, or Just Plain Fun! 2007. (ENG., Illus.). 160p. (gr. 3-7). pap. 14.95 *(978-0-471-47183-7(6),* Wiley) Wiley, John & Sons, Inc.

SCIENTISTS

see also Science—Vocational Guidance

also classes of scientists, e.g. Astronomers; Chemists; Geologists; Mathematicians; Naturalists; Physicists, etc.; and names of scientists

Abbey, Cherie D., ed. Biography Today: Profiles of People of Interest to Young Readers. 2003. (Biography Today Subject Ser.: 8). 200p. lib. bdg. 44.00 *(978-0-7808-0656-6(5))* Omnigraphics, Inc.

Abbey, Cherie D. & Hillstrom, Kevin, eds. Biography Today: Scientists & Inventors Volume 9. 2004. (Biography Today Subject Ser.: Vol. 9). (Illus.). 200p. (gr. 4-7). 44.00 *(978-0-7808-0711-2(1))* Omnigraphics, Inc.

ABDO Publishing. Great Moments in Science. 2016. (Great Moments in Science Ser.: 6). (ENG.). 48p. (J). (gr. 3-6). lib. bdg. 196.74 *(978-1-68078-014-7(X))* ABDO Publishing Co.

ABDO Publishing Company Staff. Conservationists. 2014. (Conservationists Ser.: 6). (ENG.). 32p. (gr. 3-6). lib. bdg. 162.42 *(978-1-62403-091-8(2),* Checkerboard Library) ABDO Publishing Co.

—Great Minds of Science. 2014. (Great Minds of Science Ser.: 6). (ENG.). 48p. (gr. 8-12). lib. bdg. 196.74 *(978-1-62403-376-6(8))* ABDO Publishing Co.

Ackerman, Jane. Louis Pasteur & the Founding of Microbiology. 2004. (Profiles in Science Ser.). (Illus.). 144p. (YA). (gr. 6-12). 26.95 *(978-1-931798-13-6(3))* Reynolds, Morgan Inc.

Adams, Colleen. Benjamin Franklin: American Inventor. 2009. (Reading Room Collection 2 Ser.). 24p. (gr. 3-4). 42.50 *(978-1-60851-959-0(7),* PowerKids Pr.) Rosen Publishing Group, Inc., The.

Adler, David A. A Picture Book of Benjamin Franklin. Wallner, John & Wallner, Alexandra, illus. 2008. (Picture Book Biography Ser.). (J). (gr. k-3). 28.95 incl. audio compact disk *(978-1-4301-0340-0(X));*Set. pap. 37.95 incl. audio *(978-1-4301-0338-7(8))* Live Oak Media.

—A Picture Book of George Washington Carver. Brown, Dan, illus. 2008. (Picture Book Biography Ser.). (J). (gr. -1-2). 28.95 incl. audio compact disk *(978-1-4301-0348-6(5))* Live Oak Media.

Allen, John. Robert Boyle: Father of Chemistry. 2005. (Giants of Science Ser.). (ENG., Illus.). 64p. (J). (gr. 3-7). lib. bdg. 28.35 *(978-1-56711-887-2(9),* Blackbirch Pr., Inc.) Cengage Gale.

Alphin, Elaine Marie. Germ Hunter: A Story about Louis Pasteur. Verstraete, Elaine, illus. 2003. (Creative Minds Biography Ser.). 64p. (J). lib. bdg. 22.60 *(978-1-57505-179-6(6));* (ENG.). (gr. 4-8). per. 8.95 *(978-0-87614-929-4(8))* Lerner Publishing Group. (Carolrhoda Bks.).

Anastasio, Dina & dePaola, Tomie. Who Was Steve Irwin? Eldridge, Jim, illus. 2015. (Who Was? Ser.). (ENG.). 112p. (J). (gr. 3-7). 5.99 *(978-0-448-48838-7(8),* Grosset & Dunlap) Penguin Young Readers Group.

Anderson, Margaret J. & Stephenson, Karen F. Aristotle: Genius Philosopher & Scientist. 2015. (Genius Scientists & Their Genius Ideas Ser.). 96p. (J). (gr. 5-12). 27.94 *(978-0-7660-6535-2(9));* pap. 10.95 *(978-0-7660-6536-9(7))* Enslow Pubs., Inc.

—Aristotle: Philosopher & Scientist. 2004. (Great Minds of Science Ser.). (Illus.). 112p. (J). lib. bdg. 27.94 *(978-0-7660-2096-2(7))* Enslow Pubs., Inc.

Anderson, Michael, ed. Pioneers of the Green Movement: Environmental Solutions. 2012. (Inventors & Innovators Ser.). (ENG., Illus.). 112p. (gr. 7-12). (J). 32.90 *(978-1-61530-698-5(6));* (YA). 65.80 *(978-1-61530-788-3(5))* Rosen Publishing Group, Inc., The.

Anniss, Matt. James Watson & Francis Crick. 2014. (Dynamic Duos of Science Ser.). 48p. (YA). (gr. 5-8). pap. 84.30 *(978-1-4824-1282-6(9))* Stevens, Gareth Publishing LLLP.

Apel, Melanie Ann. Virginia Apgar: Innovative Female Physician & Inventor of the Apgar Score. (Women Hall of Famers in Mathematics & Science Ser.). 112p. (gr. 5-8). 2009. 63.90 *(978-1-60854-815-6(5))* 2004. (Illus.). lib. bdg. 34.60 *(978-0-8239-3880-3(8))* Rosen Publishing Group, Inc., The. (Rosen Reference).

Bailey, Gerry & Foster, Karen. Galileo's Telescope. Noyes, Leighton & Radford, Karen, illus. 2008. (Stories of Great People Ser.). (ENG.). 40p. (J). (gr. 3-6). lib. bdg. *(978-0-7787-3694-3(6));* pap. *(978-0-7787-3716-2(0))* Crabtree Publishing Co.

Balchin, Jon. Science: 100 Scientists Who Changed the World. 2003. (Illus.). 224p. 18.95 *(978-1-59270-017-2(9))* Enchanted Lion Bks., LLC.

Bankston, John. Gregor Mendel & the Discovery of the Gene. 2004. (Uncharted, Unexplored, & Unexplained Ser.). (Illus.). 48p. (J). (gr. 4-8). lib. bdg. 29.95 *(978-1-58415-266-8(4))* Mitchell Lane Pubs., Inc.

Bardoe, Cheryl. Gregor Mendel: The Friar Who Grew Peas. Smith, Jos. A., illus. 2015. (ENG.). 32p. (J). (gr. k-4). pap. 9.95 *(978-1-4197-1840-3(1),* Abrams Bks. for Young Readers) Abrams, Inc.

Barnham, Kay, et al. Science Biographies, 1 vol. 2014. (Science Biographies Ser.). (ENG.). 32p. (gr. 2-4). lib. bdg. 183.90 *(978-1-4109-6241-6(5),* Raintree Perspectives) Heinemann-Raintree.

Baxter, Roberta. Skeptical Chemist: The Story of Robert Boyle. 2006. (Profiles in Science Ser.). (Illus.). 128p. (gr. 6-12). lib. bdg. 27.95 *(978-1-59935-025-7(4))* Reynolds, Morgan Inc.

Be a Scientist! 2014. (Be a Scientist! Ser.). 32p. (J). (gr. 3-6). 159.60 *(978-1-4824-1177-5(6));* pap. 63.00 *(978-1-4824-1553-7(4))* Stevens, Gareth Publishing LLLP.

Bedell, J. M. So, You Want to Work with Animals? Discover Fantastic Ways to Work with Animals, from Veterinary Science to Aquatic Biology. 2017. (Be What You Want Ser.). (ENG., Illus.). 256p. (J). (gr. 3-7). 19.99 *(978-1-58270-596-5(8))* Aladdin/Beyond Words.

Belton, Blair. Be a Zoologist. 2014. (Be a Scientist! Ser.). 32p. (J). (gr. 3-6). pap. 10.50 *(978-1-4824-1286-4(1));* pap. 63.00 *(978-1-4824-1188-1(1))* Stevens, Gareth Publishing LLLP.

Bendick, Jeanne. Archimedes & the Door of Science: Immortals of Science. 2011. 154p. (gr. 5-8). 41.95 *(978-1-258-01488-9(2))* Literary Licensing, LLC.

Benge, Janet & Benge, Geoff. Heroes of History - Benjamin Franklin: Live Wire. 2005. (Heroes of History Ser.). (ENG., Illus.). 208p. (YA). (gr. 5). pap. 9.99 *(978-1-932096-14-9(0))* Emerald Bks.

Bennett, Doraine & Scott, Clark C. Benjamin Franklin. 2012. (Illus.). 24p. (J). *(978-1-935884-38-5(7));* pap. *(978-1-935884-47-7(6))* State Standards Publishing, LLC.

Biskup, Agnieszka. The Amazing Work of Scientists with Max Axiom, Super Scientist, 1 vol. Baez, Marcelo, illus. 2013. (Graphic Science & Engineering in Action Ser.). (ENG.). 32p. (gr. 3-4). pap. 8.10 *(978-1-62065-701-0(5));* lib. bdg. 30.65 *(978-1-4296-9936-5(1))* Capstone Press of Coughlan Cos. (Graphic Library).

Boekhoff, P. M. Galileo. 2003. (Inventors & Creators Ser.). (Illus.). 48p. (J). 23.70 *(978-0-7377-1891-1(9),* Greenhaven Pr., Inc.) Cengage Gale.

Boekhoff, P. M. & Kallen, Stuart A. Benjamin Franklin. 2006. (Illus.). 48p. (J). (gr. 4-8). 17.00 *(978-1-4223-5322-6(2))* DIANE Publishing Co.

Bortz, Fred. The Laws of Genetics & Gregor Mendel. 2013. (Revolutionary Discoveries of Scientific Pioneers Ser.). (Illus.). 80p. (J). (gr. 7-12). 33.25 *(978-1-4777-1806-3(0))* Rosen Publishing Group, Inc., The.

BourkeKenna. JEFF CORWIN: WILD MAN BEGINNING BOOK WITH ONLINE ACCESS. 2014. (ENG.). 24p. pap. 9.50 *(978-1-107-68039-5(5))* Cambridge Univ. Pr.

Bozzone, Donna M. Famous Immigrant Computer Scientists. 2017. (YA). ***(978-0-7660-9246-4(1))*** Enslow Pubs., Inc.

Brasch, Nicholas. Leonardo Da Vinci. 2013. (Discovery Education: Discoveries & Inventions Ser.). 32p. (J). (gr. 3-6). 25.25 *(978-1-4777-1330-3(1),* PowerKids Pr.) Rosen Publishing Group, Inc., The.

—Leonardo Da Vinci: The Greatest Inventor. 2013. (Discovery Education: Discoveries & Inventions Ser.). 32p. (J). (gr. 3-6). pap. 60.00 *(978-1-4777-1503-1(7),* PowerKids Pr.) Rosen Publishing Group, Inc., The.

Brasch, Nicolas. Leonardo Da Vinci: The Greatest Inventor. 2013. (Discovery Education: Discoveries & Inventions Ser.). (ENG., Illus.). 32p. (J). (gr. 3-6). pap. 10.00 *(978-1-4777-1502-4(9),* PowerKids Pr.) Rosen Publishing Group, Inc., The.

Brezina, Corona. Careers as a Medical Examiner. (Careers in Forensics Ser.). 64p. 2009. (gr. 5-5). 58.50 *(978-1-61511-799-4(7),* Rosen Reference) 2008. (Illus.). (J). (gr. 3-7). lib. bdg. 31.95 *(978-1-4042-1347-0(3))* Rosen Publishing Group, Inc., The.

Brinkerhoff, Shirley. Research Scientist. Riggs, Ernestine G. & Gholar, Cheryl, eds. 2013. (Careers with Character Ser.: 18). 96p. (J). (gr. 7-18). 22.95 *(978-1-4222-2765-7(0))* Mason Crest.

Burling, Alexis. Robert Boyle. 2017. (Leaders of the Scientific Revolution Ser.). 112p. (gr. 12-13). 37.10 ***(978-1-5081-7476-9(8),*** Rosen Young Adult) Rosen Publishing Group, Inc., The.

Byman, Jeremy. Carl Sagan: In Contact with the Cosmos. 2004. (Great Scientists Ser.). (Illus.). 112p. (YA). (gr. 6-12). 21.95 *(978-1-883846-55-8(2),* First Biographies) Reynolds, Morgan Inc.

Byrd, Robert. Electric Ben: The Amazing Life & Times of Benjamin Franklin. 2012. (ENG.). 40p. (J). (gr. k-3). 17.99 *(978-0-8037-3749-5(1),* Dial Bks) Penguin Young Readers Group.

Calkhoven, Laurie. Women Who Launched the Computer Age. Petersen, Alyssa, illus. 2016. (You Should Meet Ser.). (ENG.). 48p. (J). (gr. 1-3). pap. 3.99 *(978-1-4814-7046-9(9),* Simon Spotlight) Simon Spotlight.

S

Capstone Press Staff & Rustad, Martha E. H. Little Scientist, 1 vol. 2014. (Little Scientist Ser.). (ENG.). 32p. (gr. 1-2). 55.98 *(978-1-4914-0801-8(4))* Capstone Press of Coughlan Cos.

Carson, Mary Kay. The Bat Scientists. Uhlman, Tom, photos by. (Scientists in the Field Ser.). (ENG., Illus.). 80p. (J). (gr. 5-7). 2013. pap. 9.99 *(978-0-544-10493-8(5))* 2010. 18.99 *(978-0-547-19956-6(2))* Houghton Mifflin Harcourt Publishing Co.

Challoner, Jack. Exploring the Mysteries of Genius & Invention. 2016. (STEM Guide to the Universe Ser.). (ENG.). 96p. (J). (gr. 9-9). lib. bdg. 46.10 *(978-1-4994-6410-8(X))* Rosen Publishing Group, Inc., The.

Chambers, Mary & Meinking, Mary. Who Counts the Penguins? Working in Antarctica. 2010. (Wild Work Ser.). (ENG.). 32p. (gr. 1-2). 29.99 *(978-1-4109-3855-8(7),* Read Me!) Heinemann-Raintree.

Ciovacco, Justine. Leonardo Da Vinci, 1 vol. 2015. (ENG., Illus.). 32p. (J). 23.45 *(978-1-62275-677-3(0),* Britannica Educational Publishing) Rosen Publishing Group, Inc., The.

Cohen, Sheila & Terman Cohen, Sheila. Gaylord Nelson: Champion for Our Earth. 2010. (Badger Biographies Ser.). (ENG., Illus.). 120p. (J). pap. 12.95 *(978-0-87020-443-2(2))* Wisconsin Historical Society.

Cohn, Jessica. Parasite Collector. 2010. (Benchmark Rockets: Dirty & Dangerous Jobs Ser.). 32p. (J). (gr. 3-6). 28.50 *(978-1-60870-175-9(1))* Marshall Cavendish Corp.

Colbert, David. Benjamin Franklin. 2008. (10 Days Ser.). (ENG.). 160p. (J). (gr. 3-8). pap. 8.99 *(978-1-4169-6446-9(0),* Simon & Schuster/Paula Wiseman Bks.) Simon & Schuster/Paula Wiseman Bks.

Coleman, Miriam. Mujeres en Las Ciencias (Women in Science) 2015. (Ellas Abrieron Camino (Women Groundbreakers) Ser.). (ENG & SPA.). 32p. (J). (gr. 4-5). 26.25 *(978-1-4994-0539-2(1),* PowerKids Pr.) Rosen Publishing Group, Inc., The.

Collins, Luke. Mae Jemison, 1 vol. 2014. (Great African-Americans Ser.). (ENG.). 24p. (gr. k-1). lib. bdg. 21.99 *(978-1-4765-3954-6(5),* Pebble Bks.) Capstone Press of Coughlan Cos.

Collard, Sneed B., III. Benjamin Franklin: The Man Who Could Do Just about Anything. 2006. (American Heroes Ser.). (Illus.). 48p. (gr. 3-7). lib. bdg. 29.93 *(978-0-7614-2161-0(0),* Benchmark Bks.) Marshall Cavendish Corp.

—Science Adventures, 4 bks., Set. Incl. In the Deep Sea. 44p. (YA). (gr. 3-6). lib. bdg. 29.93 *(978-0-7614-1952-5(7));* In the Rain Forest Canopy. 44p. (J). (gr. 3-7). lib. bdg. 29.93 *(978-0-7614-1954-9(3),* Benchmark Bks.); In the Wild. 48p. (gr. 4-7). lib. bdg. 29.93 *(978-0-7614-1955-6(1),* Benchmark Bks.); On the Coral Reefs. 43p. (YA). (gr. 3-6). lib. bdg. 29.93 *(978-0-7614-1953-2(5));* (Illus.). 2005. 119.71 *(978-0-7614-1951-8(9),* Benchmark Bks.) Marshall Cavendish Corp.

Conklin, Wendy. 16th Century Superstar: Da Vinci. 2017. (TIME for KIDS(r) Nonfiction Readers Ser.). (Illus.). 32p. (J). (gr. 7-7). pap. 8.99 *(978-1-4938-3630-7(7))* Teacher Created Materials, Inc.

Conlan, Kathy & Canadian Museum of Nature Staff. Under the Ice: A Marine Biologist at Work. 2004. (ENG., Illus.). 56p. (J). (gr. 4-6). 11.95 *(978-1-55337-060-4(0))* Kids Can Pr., Ltd. CAN. Dist: Hachette Bk. Group.

Cornell, Kari. Urban Biologist Danielle Lee. 2016. (STEM Trailblazer Bios Ser.). (ENG., Illus.). 32p. (J). (gr. 2-5). 26.65 *(978-1-4677-9529-6(1),* Lerner Pubns.) Lerner Publishing Group.

Corwin, Jeff. A Wild Life: The Authorized Biography. 2009. (Jeff Corwin Ser.). (ENG.). 112p. (J). (gr. 3-7). 6.99 *(978-0-14-241403-3(4),* Puffin Books) Penguin Young Readers Group.

Crawford, Laura. Benjamin Franklin from A to Z, 1 vol. Hierstein, Judith, illus. 2013. (ENG.). 32p. (J). (gr. k-3). 16.99 *(978-1-4556-1713-5(X))* Pelican Publishing Co., Inc.

Cregan, Elizabeth R. C. Pioneers in Cell Biology, 1 vol. 2007. (Science Readers Ser.). (ENG.). 32p. (J). (gr. 3-3). pap. 8.99 *(978-0-7439-0586-2(5))* Shell Educational Publishing.

Crompton, Samuel Willard. Emanuel Swedenborg. 2004. (Spiritual Leaders & Thinkers Ser.). (Illus.). 120p. (J). (gr. 9-13). 30.00 *(978-0-7910-8102-0(8),* Chelsea Hse.) Facts On File, Inc.

Crompton, Samuel Willard. Thomas Paine: Fighting for American Independence. 2017. (Rebels with a Cause Ser.). 128p. (gr. 8-8). lib. bdg. 37.27 ***(978-0-7660-8515-2(5))*** Enslow Pubs., Inc.

Cullen, J. Heather. Barbara McClintock. 2003. (Women in Science Ser.). (Illus.). 112p. (gr. 6-12). 30.00 *(978-0-7910-7248-6(7),* Chelsea Hse.) Facts On File, Inc.

Cullen, Katherine. Science, Technology, & Society: The People Behind the Science. 2005. (Pioneers in Science Ser.). (Illus.). 172p. (gr. 6-12). 29.95 *(978-0-8160-5468-8(1))* Facts On File, Inc.

Cullen, Katherine, et al. Pioneers in Science Set. 2005. (Pioneers in Science Ser.). 192p. (gr. 6-12). 179.70 *(978-0-8160-5460-2(6))* Facts On File, Inc.

Curtis, Suzanne. John Wesley Powell: American Hero. 2013. (ENG & SPA., Illus.). 78p. (J). pap. 8.95 *(978-0-86541-178-4(6))* Filter Pr., LLC.

Dakers, Diane. Dian Fossey: Animal Rights Activist & Protector of Mountain Gorillas. 2016. (ENG., Illus.). 112p. (J). lib. bdg. *(978-0-7787-2563-3(4))* Crabtree Publishing Co.

Davis, Lynn. Thomas Edison, 1 vol. 2016. (ENG., Illus.). 24p. (J). 25.65 *(978-1-62403-723-8(2))* ABDO Publishing Co.

De Angelis, Gina & Bianco, David J. Computers: Processing the Data. 2005. (Innovators Ser.: Vol. 13). (Illus.). 144p. (J). (gr. 5-18). lib. bdg. 24.95 *(978-1-881508-87-8(0))* Oliver Pr., Inc.

deMarin, Layne. What Scientists Do. 2011. (Wonder Readers Fluent Level Ser.). (ENG.). (gr. -1-2). 16p. pap. 35.94 *(978-1-4296-8205-3(1));* 32p. pap. 5.99 *(978-1-4296-7945-9(X))* Capstone Press of Coughlan Cos. (Wonder Readers).

Di Piazza, Domenica. NASA Computer Scientist Margaret Hamilton. 2017. (STEM Trailblazer Bios Ser.). (ENG.). 32p. (J). (gr. 2-5). 26.65 ***(978-1-5124-3450-7(7))*** Lerner Publishing Group.

Dolan, Ellen M. Thomas Alva Edison: American Inventor & Businessman. 2015. (Legendary American Biographies Ser.). 96p. (J). (gr. 6-12). 27.94 *(978-0-7660-6510-9(3));* pap. 10.95 *(978-0-7660-6511-6(1))* Enslow Pubs., Inc.

Don Nardo. The Trial of Galileo. 2003. (Famous Trials Ser.). (ENG., Illus.). 112p. (J). 29.95 *(978-1-59018-423-3(8))* Cengage Gale.

Dorling Kindersley Publishing Staff. Look I'm a Scientist. 2017. (ENG., Illus.). 48p. (J). (gr. -1-2). 12.99 ***(978-1-4654-5963-3(4),*** DK Children) Dorling Kindersley Publishing, Inc.

Dorling Kindersley Publishing Staff & Moulds, Steve. How to Be a Scientist. 2017. (ENG., Illus.). 144p. (J). (gr. 2-4). 19.99 *(978-1-4654-6121-6(3),* DK Children) Dorling Kindersley Publishing, Inc.

Dorling Kindersley Publishing Staff, et al. Jungle Adventure. 2015. (DK Adventures Ser.). (ENG., Illus.). 128p. (J). (gr. 3-7). pap. 5.99 *(978-1-4654-2931-5(X),* DK Children) Dorling Kindersley Publishing, Inc.

—Jungle Adventures. 2015. (DK Adventures Ser.). (ENG., Illus.). 128p. (J). (gr. 3-7). 16.99 *(978-1-4654-2930-8(1),* DK Children) Dorling Kindersley Publishing, Inc.

Driscoll, Laura. George Washington Carver: The Peanut Wizard. Weber, Jill, illus. 2003. (Smart about History Ser.). (ENG.). 32p. (J). (gr. k-4). mass mkt. 5.99 *(978-0-448-43243-4(9),* Grosset & Dunlap) Penguin Young Readers Group.

Duignan, Brian, ed. The Britannica Guide to the World's Most Influential People (Print/eBook Combo Set), 8 vols., Set. Incl. 100 Most Influential Philosophers of All Time. 368p. (YA). (gr. 9-12). 2009. E-Book 106.00 *(978-1-61530-072-3(4));* (Britannica Guide to the World's Most Influential People Ser.). 384p. 2009. Set E-Book 848.00 *(978-1-61530-165-2(8))* Rosen Publishing Group, Inc., The.

Dynamic Duos of Science. 2014. (Dynamic Duos of Science Ser.). 48p. (YA). (gr. 5-8). 191.70 *(978-1-4824-1183-6(0))* Stevens, Gareth Publishing LLLP.

Eamer, Claire. Before the World Was Ready: Stories of Daring Genius in Science. Boothroyd, Sa, illus. 2013. (ENG.). 128p. (J). (gr. 4-7). pap. 14.95 *(978-1-55451-535-6(1),* 9781554515356) Annick Pr., Ltd. CAN. Dist: Publishers Group West (PGW).

Edwards, Linda McMurry. George Washington Carver: The Life of the Great American Agriculturist. 2009. (Library of American Lives & Times Ser.). 112p. (gr. 5-5). 69.20 *(978-1-60853-485-2(5))* Rosen Publishing Group, Inc., The.

Elliot, Henry. John Muir: Protecting & Preserving the Environment. 2009. (Voices for Green Choices Ser.). (ENG., Illus.). 48p. (J). (gr. 5-9). lib. bdg. *(978-0-7787-4668-3(2))* Crabtree Publishing Co.

Endres, Hollie J. & Endres, Hollie. Scientists Try, Try Again. 2007. (Shockwave: Life Stories Ser.). (ENG., Illus.). 36p. (J). (gr. 3-5). 25.00 *(978-0-531-17744-0(0),* Children's Pr.) Scholastic Library Publishing.

Endsley, Kezia, et al. Inventors of Computer Technology. 2015. 144p. (J). lib. bdg. 36.95 *(978-1-5026-0654-9(2))* Musa Publishing.

Environment & Natural Resources. 2010. (Green Careers Ser.). (Illus.). 184p. (C). (gr. 9-18). 32.95 *(978-0-8160-8151-6(4),* Ferguson Publishing Co.) Facts On File, Inc.

Espinosa, Rod. Benjamin Franklin, 1 vol. Espinosa, Rod, illus. 2007. (Bio-Graphics Ser.). (ENG., Illus.). 32p. (gr. 3-6). 28.50 *(978-1-60270-066-6(4),* Graphic Planet- Nonfiction) ABDO Publishing Co.

Fandel, Jennifer. Louis Pasteur. 2003. (World Was Never the Same Ser.). (J). *(978-1-58417-266-6(5))* Lake Street Pubs.

Farndon, John. Great Scientists. 2010. (Science Library). 40p. (J). (gr. 3-18). lib. bdg. 19.95 *(978-1-4222-1549-4(0))* Mason Crest.

Farndon, John & Woolf, Alex. Great Scientists. 2012. (Great People in History Ser.). (ENG.). 128p. (YA). (gr. 8-12). 34.60 *(978-1-4777-0405-9(1))* Rosen Publishing Group, Inc., The.

Feinstein, Stephen. Louis Pasteur: The Father of Microbiology. 2008. (Inventors Who Changed the World Ser.). (Illus.). 128p. (J). (gr. 6-18). lib. bdg. 34.60 *(978-1-59845-078-1(6),* MyReportLinks.com Bks.) Enslow Pubs., Inc.

—Read about Benjamin Franklin. 2006. (I Like Biographies! Ser.). (Illus.). 24p. (J). (gr. 1-3). lib. bdg. 22.60 *(978-0-7660-2596-7(9),* Enslow Elementary) Enslow Pubs., Inc.

Fekany Lee, Kimberly. Cell Scientists: Discovering How Cells Work, 1 vol. 2007. (Science Readers Ser.). (ENG.). 32p. (J). (gr. 3-3). pap. 8.99 *(978-0-7439-0584-8(9))* Shell Educational Publishing.

Flath, Camden. Tomorrow's Enterprising Scientists: Computer Software Designers & Specialists. 2010. (New Careers for the 21st Century Ser.). 64p. (YA). (gr. 7-18). pap. 9.95 *(978-1-4222-2043-6(5));* lib. bdg. 22.95 *(978-1-4222-1822-8(8))* Mason Crest.

Fleming, Candace. Ben Franklin's Almanac: Being a True Account of the Good Gentleman's Life. 2003. (ENG., Illus.). 128p. (J). (gr. 5-9). 21.99 *(978-0-689-83549-0(3),* Atheneum Bks. for Young Readers) Simon & Schuster Children's Publishing.

Fleming, Thomas. Ben Franklin: Inventing America. (Great Leaders & Events Ser.). (ENG.). 208p. (J). (gr. 4-8). 2017. lib. bdg. 35.99 ***(978-1-942875-23-9(1))*** 2016. (Illus.). pap. 12.99 *(978-0-7603-5228-1(3))* Quarto Publishing Group USA. (Voyageur Pr.).

Forbes, Charlotte & Forbes, Charlotte. Those Amazing Scientists. Pillion, Dean, illus. 2007. 26p. (J). *(978-0-9772799-1-3(X))* Trilogy Pubns. LLC.

Fortey, Jacqueline & Dorling Kindersley Publishing Staff. Great Scientists. 2007. (DK Eyewitness Bks.). (ENG., Illus.). 72p. (J). (gr. 3-7). 16.99 *(978-0-7566-2974-8(8),* DK Children) Dorling Kindersley Publishing, Inc.

Foster, Leila Merrell. Benjamin Franklin: Statesman & Inventor. 2015. (Legendary American Biographies Ser.). 96p. (J). (gr. 6-12). 27.94 *(978-0-7660-6445-4(X))* Enslow Pubs., Inc.

Fradin, Dennis Brindell. Nicolaus Copernicus: The Earth Is a Planet. von Buhler, Cynthia, tr. von Buhler, Cynthia, illus. 2003. 32p. (J). (gr. 2-6). 15.95 *(978-1-59336-006-1(1));* pap. *(978-1-59336-007-8(X))* Mondo Publishing.

—Who Was Ben Franklin? O'brien, John, illus. 2003. (Who Was...? Ser.). 105p. (gr. 4-7). 15.00 *(978-0-7569-1589-6(9))* Perfection Learning Corp.

Franco, Michou. I Can Be a Scientist. 2017. (I Can Be Anything! Ser.). 24p. (gr. k-k). pap. 8.15 ***(978-1-4824-6329-3(6))*** Stevens, Gareth Publishing LLLP.

Franklin, Benjamin. Benjamin Franklin's Wise Words. Harper, Fred, illus. 2017. (ENG.). 128p. (J). (gr. 3-7). 16.99 *(978-1-4263-2699-8(8));* lib. bdg. 26.90 *(978-1-4263-2700-1(5))* National Geographic Society. (National Geographic Children's Bks.).

Freedman, Claire. Monstersaurus. Cort, Ben, illus. 2013. (J). *(978-1-4351-4952-6(1))* Barnes & Noble, Inc.

Freedman, Russell. Becoming Ben Franklin: How a Candle-Maker's Son Helped Light the Flame of Liberty. 2013. (ENG.). 96p. (J). (gr. 5). 24.95 *(978-0-8234-2374-3(3))* Holiday Hse., Inc.

Fries-Gaither, Jessica. Notable Notebooks: Scientists & Their Writings. 2017. (ENG., Illus.). 32p. (J). (gr. 2-4). 18.95 *(978-1-68140-379-3(X));* pap. 12.95 *(978-1-68140-307-6(2))* National Science Teachers Assn.

Frisch, Aaron. Albert Einstein. 2005. (Genius Ser.). (Illus.). 48p. (J). (gr. 5-9). lib. bdg. 21.95 *(978-1-58341-328-9(6),* Creative Education) Creative Co., The.

Frydenborg, Kay. Wild Horse Scientists. (Scientists in the Field Ser.). (ENG., Illus.). 80p. (J). (gr. 5-7). 2014. pap. 9.99 *(978-0-544-25746-7(4),* HMH Books For Young Readers) 2012. 18.99 *(978-0-547-51831-2(5))* Houghton Mifflin Harcourt Publishing Co.

Ganeri, Anita. Ocean Divers, 1 vol. 2011. (Landform Adventurers Ser.). (ENG.). 32p. (J). (gr. 1-2). 29.99 *(978-1-4109-4140-4(X),* Read Me!) Heinemann-Raintree.

Gaustad, Edwin S. Benjamin Franklin: Inventing America. 2006. 143p. (J). (gr. 4-8). reprint ed. 22.00 *(978-1-4223-5227-4(7))* DIANE Publishing Co.

Gazlay, Suzy. David Suzuki: Doing Battle with Climate Change. 2009. (Voices for Green Choices Ser.). (ENG., Illus.). 48p. (J). (gr. 5-9). lib. bdg. *(978-0-7787-4665-2(8))* Crabtree Publishing Co.

Giblin, James Cross. The Amazing Life of Benjamin Franklin. Dooling, Michael, illus. 2006. 48p. (gr. -1-3). 18.00 *(978-0-7569-6551-8(9))* Perfection Learning Corp.

Gibson, Brylee. Extreme Scientists. 2007. (Connectors Ser.). (gr. 2-5). pap. *(978-1-877453-08-3(0))* Global Education Systems Ltd.

Gilman, Sarah. Ben Franklin. 2016. (Explore Colonial America Ser.). (Illus.). 48p. (J). (gr. 5-4). 27.93 *(978-0-7660-7873-4(6))* Enslow Pubs., Inc.

Glass, Maya. Benjamin Franklin: Early American Genius. (Primary Sources of Famous People in American History Ser.). 32p. 2009. (gr. 2-3). 47.90 *(978-1-60851-654-4(7))* 2004. (ENG., Illus.). (gr. 4-8). pap. 10.00 *(978-0-8239-4175-9(2))* Rosen Publishing Group, Inc., The.

—Benjamin Franklin: Early American Genius / Político e inventor Estadounidense. 2009. (Famous People in American History/Grandes personajes en la historia de los Estados Unidos Ser.). (ENG & SPA.). 32p. (gr. 2-3). 47.90 *(978-1-61512-538-8(8),* Editorial Buenas Letras) Rosen Publishing Group, Inc., The.

—Benjamin Franklin: Político e inventor Estadounidense. 2004. (Grandes personajes en la historia de los Estados Unidos Ser.). (SPA.). 32p. (gr. 5-8). pap. 10.00 *(978-0-8239-4221-3(X),* Rosen Classroom) Rosen Publishing Group, Inc., The.

—Benjamin Franklin: Político e inventor estadounidense (Benjamin Franklin: Early American Genius) 2009. (Grandes personajes en la historia de los Estados Unidos (Famous People in American History) Ser.). (SPA.). 32p. (gr. 2-3). 47.90 *(978-1-61512-790-0(9),* Editorial Buenas Letras) Rosen Publishing Group, Inc., The.

Goldsmith, Mike. Eureka! The Most Amazing Scientific Discoveries of All Time. 2014. (ENG., Illus.). 96p. (J). (gr. 4-7). 19.95 *(978-0-500-65025-7(X),* 565025) Thames & Hudson.

Goldsmith, Mike & Gifford, Clive. Eureka: The Most Amazing Scientific Discoveries of All Time. 2016. (ENG., Illus.). 96p. (J). (gr. 4-6). pap. 13.95 *(978-0-500-29227-3(2),* 529227) Thames & Hudson.

Gomez, Rebecca. Albert Einstein, 1 vol. 2003. (First Biographies Ser.). (ENG., Illus.). 32p. (J). (gr. 1-4). 27.07 *(978-1-57765-946-4(5))* ABDO Publishing Co.

Goodridge, Catherine. Jane Goodall (Spanish) 2011. (SPA.). (J). pap. 40.00 net. *(978-1-4108-2426-4(8),* A24268) Benchmark Education Co.

Gosman, Gillian. Benjamin Franklin. 2011. (Life Stories Ser.). (Illus.). 24p. (J). pap. 8.25 *(978-1-4488-2759-6(0));* (gr. 1-4). lib. bdg. 22.60 *(978-1-4488-2585-1(7))* Rosen Publishing Group, Inc., The. (PowerKids Pr.).

—Benjamin Franklin. 2011. (Life Stories / Biografías Ser.). (ENG & SPA., Illus.). 24p. (J). (gr. 1-4). lib. bdg. 22.60 *(978-1-4488-3219-4(5))* Rosen Publishing Group, Inc., The.

Gould, Jane H. Benjamin Franklin. 2012. (Jr. Graphic Founding Fathers Ser.). (ENG., Illus.). 24p. (J). (gr. 3-6). pap. 10.60 *(978-1-4488-7990-8(6));* lib. bdg. 25.25 *(978-1-4488-7896-3(9))* Rosen Publishing Group, Inc., The. (PowerKids Pr.).

—George Washington Carver. 2013. (Jr. Graphic American Inventors Ser.). (ENG., Illus.). 24p. (J). (gr. 3-6). pap. 10.60 *(978-1-4777-0141-6(9));* lib. bdg. 25.25 *(978-1-4777-0078-5(1))* Rosen Publishing Group, Inc., The. (PowerKids Pr.).

Gow, Mary. The Great Thinker: Aristotle & the Foundations of Science. 2010. (Great Minds of Ancient Science & Math Ser.). 128p. (J). (gr. 4-7). 33.27 *(978-0-7660-3121-0(7))* Enslow Pubs., Inc.

—Robert Boyle: Pioneer of Experimental Chemistry. 2005. (Great Minds of Science Ser.). (Illus.). 128p. (J). lib. bdg. 27.94 *(978-0-7660-2501-1(2))* Enslow Pubs., Inc.

—Robert Hooke: Creative Genius, Scientist, Inventor. 2006. (Great Minds of Science Ser.). (Illus.). 128p. (J). (gr. 6-10). lib. bdg. 31.93 *(978-0-7660-2547-9(0))* Enslow Pubs., Inc.

Graham, Amy. Astonishing Ancient World Scientists: Eight Great Brains. 2009. (Great Scientists & Famous Inventors Ser.). (Illus.). 128p. (J). (gr. 5-9). lib. bdg. 34.60 *(978-1-59845-079-8(4))* Enslow Pubs., Inc.

—Thomas Edison: Wizard of Light & Sound. 2007. (Inventors Who Changed the World Ser.). (Illus.). 128p. (J). (gr. 5-9). lib. bdg. 34.60 *(978-1-59845-052-1(2),* MyReportLinks.com Bks.) Enslow Pubs., Inc.

Gray, Leon. Animal Scientists. 2015. (Animal Scientists Ser.). (ENG.). 32p. (gr. 3-4). 136.60 *(978-1-4914-7010-7(0),* Fact Finders) Capstone Press of Coughlan Cos.

Grayson, Robert. Ed Begley, Jr. Living Green. 2009. (Voices for Green Choices Ser.). (ENG., Illus.). 48p. (J). (gr. 5-9). lib. bdg. *(978-0-7787-4667-6(4))* Crabtree Publishing Co.

Great Scientific Questions & the Scientists Who Answered Them. 2005. (Illus.). 112p. (gr. 7-12). lib. bdg. 319.20 *(978-1-4042-0356-3(7))* Rosen Publishing Group, Inc., The.

Green, Dan. Rebel Science. Lyttleton, David, illus. 2016. (ENG.). 80p. (J). (gr. 3). 14.95 *(978-1-4549-1945-2(0),* 1402430) Sterling Publishing Co., Inc.

Gregory, Josh. Hydrologist. 2013. (21st Century Skills Library: Cool STEM Careers Ser.). (ENG., Illus.). 32p. (J). (gr. 4-8). 28.50 *(978-1-62431-001-0(X),* 202455); pap. 14.21 *(978-1-62431-025-6(7),* 202457) Cherry Lake Publishing.

Greve, Tom. Botanists. 2015. (ENG.). 48p. (gr. 3-6). 35.64 *(978-1-63430-412-2(8))* Rourke Educational Media.

Haldy, Emma E. Benjamin Franklin. Bane, Jeff, illus. 2016. (My Early Library: My Itty-Bitty Bio Ser.). (ENG.). 24p. (J). (gr. k-1). 28.50 *(978-1-63470-478-6(9),* 207643) Cherry Lake Publishing.

Hall, Derek. Chemistry, Earth, & Space Sciences. 2010. (Facts at Your Fingertips Ser.). (YA). (gr. 7-12). 35.65 *(978-1-933834-47-4(1))* Brown Bear Books.

—Life Sciences. 2009. (FAYFT: Great Scientists Ser.). 64p. (gr. 4-10). 39.95 *(978-1-933834-45-0(5))* Brown Bear Bks.

—Physical Sciences. 2009. (FAYFT: Great Scientists Ser.). 64p. (gr. 4-10). 39.95 *(978-1-933834-46-7(3))* Brown Bear Bks.

Hall, Derek, ed. Philosophy, Invention, & Engineering. 2009. (FAYFT: Great Scientists Ser.). 64p. (gr. 4-10). 39.95 *(978-1-933834-48-1(X))* Brown Bear Bks.

Hamilton, Janet. James Watson: Solving the Mystery of DNA. 2004. (Nobel Prize-Winning Scientists Ser.). (Illus.). 104p. (J). lib. bdg. 27.94 *(978-0-7660-2258-4(7))* Enslow Pubs., Inc.

Hand, Carol. Jane Goodall. 2014. (Great Science Writers Ser.). (Illus.). 112p. (J). (gr. 7-12). 35.60 *(978-1-4777-7685-8(0))* Rosen Publishing Group, Inc., The.

Hansen, Grace. Jane Goodall: Chimpanzee Expert & Activist, 1 vol. 2014. (History Maker Biographies Ser.). (ENG., Illus.). 24p. (J). (gr. 2-4). lib. bdg. 28.50 *(978-1-62970-702-0(3))* ABDO Publishing Co.

Hanson, Anders. Scientist's Tools, 1 vol. 2011. (Professional Tools Ser.). (ENG., Illus.). 24p. (J). (gr. 3-5). lib. bdg. 25.65 *(978-1-61613-581-2(6),* Super SandCastle) ABDO Publishing Co.

Hantula, Richard. Jonas Salk. 2004. (Trailblazers of the Modern World Ser.). (Illus.). 48p. (gr. 5-12). lib. bdg. 31.00 *(978-0-8368-5100-7(5),* Gareth Stevens Secondary Library) Stevens, Gareth Publishing LLLP.

Harness, Cheryl. The Remarkable Benjamin Franklin. (ENG., Illus.). 48p. (J). (gr. 2-5). 2008. 7.95 *(978-1-4263-0297-8(5))* 2005. 27.90 *(978-0-7922-7884-9(4))* National Geographic Society. (National Geographic Children's Bks.).

—The Remarkable Benjamin Franklin. Harness, Cheryl, illus. 2005. (National Geographic Ser.). (ENG., Illus.). 48p. (J). (gr. 2-5). 17.95 *(978-0-7922-7882-5(8),* National Geographic Children's Bks.) National Geographic Society.

Harris, Godfrey, et al. The Life & Contributions of Leonardo Da Vinci. 2006. 58p. (J). pap. *(978-0-935047-60-8(3))* Americas Group, The.

Harris, Laurie Lanzen. Biography for Beginners: Inventors. 2006. (J). lib. bdg. 55.00 *(978-1-931360-27-2(8))* Favorable Impressions.

Hartman, Eve & Meshbesher, Wendy. Do Scientists Care about Animal Welfare?, 1 vol. 2012. (Sci-Hi: Science Issues Ser.). (ENG., Illus.). 48p. (gr. 4-4). lib. bdg. 33.32 *(978-1-4109-4462-7(X),* Sci-Hi) Heinemann-Raintree.

—The Scientists Behind Medical Advances, 1 vol. 2011. (Sci-Hi: Scientists Ser.). (ENG.). 48p. (gr. 4-4). pap. 9.95 *(978-1-4109-4055-1(1),* Sci-Hi) Heinemann-Raintree.

Hasday, Judy L. Albert Einstein: The Giant of 20th Century Science. 2004. (Nobel Prize-Winning Scientists Ser.). (Illus.). 128p. (J). lib. bdg. 26.60 *(978-0-7660-2185-3(8))* Enslow Pubs., Inc.

Haven, Kendall F. Women at the Edge of Discovery: 40 True Science Adventures, 1 vol. 2003. 296p. (C). (gr. 4-9). pap. 35.00 *(978-1-59158-015-7(3),* LU0153, Libraries Unlimited) ABC-CLIO, LLC.

Haynie, Rachel. First, You Explore: The Story of Young Charles Townes. Cook, Trahern, illus. 2014. (Young Palmetto Bks.). (ENG.). 40p. (J). 29.95 *(978-1-61117-343-7(4))* Univ. of South Carolina Pr.

Heinrichs, Ann. Nanotechnologist. 2009. (21st Century Skills Library: Cool Science Careers Ser.). (ENG.). 32p. (gr. 4-8). lib. bdg. 28.50 *(978-1-60279-307-1(7),* 200203) Cherry Lake Publishing.

Heitkamp, Kristina Lyn. Rachel Carson: Pioneering Environmental Activist. 2017. (J). ***(978-1-5383-8075-8(7));*** pap. ***(978-1-5383-8074-1(9))*** Rosen Publishing Group, Inc., The.

Heller, Esther Susan. Menorah under the Sea. Ginsburg, David, photos by. 2009. (Hanukkah Ser.). (Illus.). 32p. (J). (gr. k-2). 17.95 *(978-0-8225-7386-9(5),* Kar-Ben Publishing) Lerner Publishing Group.

—Menorah under the Sea. 2009. (Hanukkah Ser.). (ENG.). 32p. (J). (gr. k-3). pap. 7.95 *(978-0-8225-7390-6(3),* Kar-Ben Publishing) Lerner Publishing Group.

Heos, Bridget. Stronger Than Steel: Spider Silk DNA & the Quest for Better Bulletproof Vests, Sutures, & Parachute Rope. Comins, Andy, illus. 2013. (Scientists in the Field Ser.). (ENG.). 80p. (J). (gr. 5-7). 18.99 *(978-0-547-68126-9(7))* Houghton Mifflin Harcourt Publishing Co.

Hesleden, Michael. Benjamin Franklin: American Diplomat. 2015. (Spotlight on American History Ser.). (ENG., Illus.). 24p. (J). (gr. 4-6). pap. 10.00 *(978-1-4994-1782-1(9),* PowerKids Pr.) Rosen Publishing Group, Inc., The.

Hilliam, Rachel. Galileo Galilei: Father of Modern Science. 2009. (Rulers, Scholars, & Artists of the Renaissance Ser.). 112p. (gr. 5-8). 66.50 *(978-1-60852-941-4(X),* Rosen Reference) Rosen Publishing Group, Inc., The.

Holmes, Parker. Oceanographers, 01 vols., 1. 2016. (Out of the Lab: Extreme Jobs in Science Ser.). (ENG., Illus.). 32p. (J). pap. 10.00 *(978-1-5081-4517-2(2),* PowerKids Pr.) Rosen Publishing Group, Inc., The.

Hoppa, Jocelyn. Isaac Asimov: Science Fiction Trailblazer. 2009. (Authors Teens Love Ser.). (Illus.). 104p. (J). (gr. 6). lib. bdg. 33.27 *(978-0-7660-2961-3(1))* Enslow Pubs., Inc.

Horvath, Joan. What Scientists Actually Do. 2008. (Illus.). 208p. (YA). pap. 16.95 *(978-1-933277-08-0(4))* Stargazer Publishing Co.
Houran, Lori Haskins. How to Spy on a Shark. Marquez, Francisca, illus. 2015. (ENG.). 24p. (J). (gr. -1-3). 15.99 *(978-0-8075-3402-1(1))* Whitman, Albert & Co.
Housel, Debra J. Pioneering Ecologists, 1 vol. 2007. (Science Readers Ser.). (SPA & ENG.). 32p. (J). (gr. 3-3). pap. 8.99 *(978-0-7439-0592-3(X))* Shell Educational Publishing.
Hunter, Dru. How Do We Apply Science? 2015. (Illus.). 48p. (J). *(978-1-60818-592-4(3)*, Creative Education) Creative Co., The.
—How Does It Work? 2015. (Illus.). 48p. (J). *(978-1-60818-593-1(1)*, Creative Education) Creative Co., The.
—How Does It Work? Think Like a Scientist. 2016. (Think Like a Scientist Ser.). (ENG.). 48p. (J). (gr. 5-9). pap. 12.00 *(978-1-62832-198-2(9)*, Creative Paperbacks) Creative Co., The.
—What Is Out There? 2015. (Illus.). 48p. (J). *(978-1-60818-594-8(X)*, Creative Education) Creative Co., The.
—What Is the Reason? 2015. (Illus.). 48p. (J). *(978-1-60818-595-5(8)*, Creative Education) Creative Co., The.
—Where Do We Look for Life? 2015. (Illus.). 48p. (J). *(978-1-60818-596-2(6)*, Creative Education) Creative Co., The.
—Where Do We Look for Life? Think Like a Scientist. 2016. (Think Like a Scientist Ser.). (ENG.). 48p. (J). (gr. 5-9). pap. 12.00 *(978-1-62832-201-9(2)*, Creative Paperbacks) Creative Co., The.
Hunter, Nick. Louis Pasteur, 1 vol. 2014. (Science Biographies Ser.). (ENG.). 32p. (gr. 2-4). lib. bdg. 30.65 *(978-1-4109-6236-2(9)*, Raintree Perspectives) Heinemann-Raintree.
Ignotofsky, Rachel. Women in Science. (ENG., Illus.). 2017. 100p. 20.00 *(978-1-60774-981-3(5)*, Clarkson Potter) 2016. 128p. (gr. 5). 16.99 *(978-1-60774-976-9(9)*, Ten Speed Pr.) Potter/TenSpeed/Harmony.
Indovino, Shaina. Women in Anthropology. Lee-Karlon, Ann, ed. 2013. (Major Women in Science Ser.: 10). 64p. (J). (gr. 7-18). 22.95 *(978-1-4222-2924-8(6))* Mason Crest.
—Women in Information Technology. Lee-Karlon, Ann, ed. 2013. (Major Women in Science Ser.: 10). 64p. (J). (gr. 7-18). 22.95 *(978-1-4222-2928-6(9))* Mason Crest.
Ingram, Scott. Nicolaus Copernicus: Father of Modern Astronomy. 2004. (Illus.). 64p. (J). 26.20 *(978-1-56711-489-8(X)*, Blackbirch Pr., Inc.) Cengage Gale.
Isaac Newton: Organizing the Universe. 2004. (Great Scientists Ser.). (Illus.). 144p. (YA). (gr. 6-12). 26.95 *(978-1-931798-01-3(X))* Reynolds, Morgan Inc.
Isle, Mick. Aristotle: Pioneering Philosopher & Founder of the Lyceum. 2009. (Library of Greek Philosophers Ser.). 112p. (gr. 6-6). 66.50 *(978-1-60853-658-0(0)*, Rosen Reference) Rosen Publishing Group, Inc., The.
Jackson, Donna M. The Bug Scientists. 2004. (Illus.). 48p. (J). lib. bdg. 13.60 *(978-0-7569-5192-4(5))* Perfection Learning Corp.
Jackson, Donna M. & O'Connell, Caitlin. The Elephant Scientist. 2016. (Scientists in the Field Ser.). lib. bdg. 20.85 *(978-0-606-37983-0(5))* Turtleback Bks.
James, Emily. Great Scientists & Inventors. 2017. (Great Scientists & Inventors Ser.). (ENG.). 24p. (gr. k-1). 159.90 *(978-1-5157-3910-4(4)*, Pebble Plus) Capstone Press of Coughlan Cos.
—Rachel Carson. 2017. (Great Scientists & Inventors Ser.). (ENG., Illus.). 24p. (gr. k-1). lib. bdg. 26.65 *(978-1-5157-3881-7(7))* Capstone Press of Coughlan Cos.
James, Wayan. Scientists Look for Patterns & Rules. 2016. (Rosen REAL Readers: STEM & STEAM Collection). 12p. (gr. 1-k). pap. 6.33 *(978-1-5081-2431-3(0)*, Rosen Classroom) Rosen Publishing Group, Inc., The.
Jankowski, Connie. Jane Goodall: Animal Scientist & Friend, 1 vol. 2007. (Science Readers Ser.). (SPA & ENG.). 32p. (J). (gr. 3-3). pap. 8.99 *(978-0-7439-0594-7(6))* Shell Educational Publishing.
—Pioneers of Light & Sound, 1 vol. 2007. (Science Readers Ser.). (ENG.). 32p. (J). (gr. 3-3). pap. 8.99 *(978-0-7439-0580-0(6))* Shell Educational Publishing.
Jeffrey, Gary. Hurricane Hunters & Tornado Chasers. Garofalo, Gianluca, illus. 2008. (Graphic Careers Ser.). (ENG.). 48p. (gr. 5-8). per. 14.05 *(978-1-4042-1459-0(3))*; (YA). lib. bdg. 31.95 *(978-1-4042-1458-3(5))* Rosen Publishing Group, Inc., The.
Jenner, Caryn & Dorling Kindersley Publishing Staff. Thomas Edison - The Great Inventor, Level 4. 2007. (DK Readers Ser.). (ENG.). 48p. (J). (gr. 3-7). pap. 3.99 *(978-0-7566-2946-5(2)*, DK Children) Dorling Kindersley Publishing, Inc.
Kamberg, Mary-Lane. Stephen Hawking. 2014. (Great Science Writers Ser.). (Illus.). 112p. (J). (gr. 7-12). 35.60 *(978-1-4777-7683-4(4))* Rosen Publishing Group, Inc., The.
Kawa, Katie. Forensic Detectives, 01 vols., 1. 2016. (Out of the Lab: Extreme Jobs in Science Ser.). (ENG., Illus.). 32p. (J). pap. 10.00 *(978-1-5081-4521-9(0)*, PowerKids Pr.) Rosen Publishing Group, Inc., The.
Kelly, Jack. Benjamin Franklin. Tafalla, Ortiz, illus. 2005. (Heroes of America Ser.). 239p. (gr. 3-8). 27.07 *(978-1-59679-257-9(4)*, Abdo & Daughters) ABDO Publishing Co.
Kennon, Caroline. Leonardo Da Vinci in His Own Words. 2016. (Eyewitness to History Ser.). (ENG.). 32p. (J). (gr. 4-5). pap. 10.50 *(978-1-4824-4074-4(1))* Stevens, Gareth Publishing LLLP.
Kent, Deborah. Mario Molina: Chemist & Nobel Prize Winner. 2004. (Proud Heritage: the Hispanic Library). (ENG., Illus.). 40p. (J). (gr. 3-6). 29.93 *(978-1-59296-170-2(3)*, 200011) Child's World, Inc., The.
Kepnes, Caroline. Stephen Crane. 2004. (Classic Storytellers Ser.). (Illus.). 48p. (J). (gr. 4-8). lib. bdg. 29.95 *(978-1-58415-272-9(9))* Mitchell Lane Pubs., Inc.
Knowles, Johanna. Jacques Cousteau. 2011. (Conservation Heroes Ser.). (Illus.). 120p. (YA). (gr. 6-12). 35.00 *(978-1-60413-947-1(1)*, Chelsea Hse.) Facts On File, Inc.
Koontz, Robin Michal. Entomologists. 2015. (ENG.). 48p. (gr. 3-6). 35.64 *(978-1-63430-410-8(1))* Rourke Educational Media.
—Marine Biologists. 2015. (ENG.). 48p. (gr. 3-6). 35.64 *(978-1-63430-408-5(X))* Rourke Educational Media.
—Volcanologists. 2015. (ENG.). 48p. (gr. 3-6). 35.64 *(978-1-63430-409-2(8))* Rourke Educational Media.
Kortemeier, Todd. Unsung Heroes of Science. 2017. (Unsung Heroes Ser.). (ENG.). 32p. (J). (gr. 3-6). 21.95 *(978-1-63235-309-2(1))* Pr. Room Editions LLC.
Kraft Rector, Rebecca. Alan Turing, 01 vols., 1. 2016. (Tech Pioneers Ser.). (ENG.). 112p. (J). 35.60 *(978-1-4994-6280-7(8)*, Rosen Young Adult) Rosen Publishing Group, Inc., The.
Krensky, Stephen & Dorling Kindersley Publishing Staff. Benjamin Franklin. 2007. (DK Biography Ser.). (ENG., Illus.). 128p. (J). (gr. 5-12). pap. 6.99 *(978-0-7566-3528-2(4)*, DK Children) Dorling Kindersley Publishing, Inc.
Krull, Kathleen. Benjamin Franklin. Kulikov, Boris, illus. 2014. (Giants of Science Ser.). (ENG.). 128p. (J). (gr. 3-7). pap. 7.99 *(978-0-14-751178-2(X)*, Puffin Books) Penguin Young Readers Group.
—Leonardo Da Vinci. Kulikov, Boris, illus. 2008. (Giants of Science Ser.). (ENG.). 128p. (J). (gr. 3-7). 7.99 *(978-0-14-240821-6(2)*, Puffin Books) Penguin Young Readers Group.
—Lives of the Scientists: Experiments, Explosions (and What the Neighbors Thought) Hewitt, Kathryn, illus. 2016. (Lives Of ... Ser.). (ENG.). 96p. (J). (gr. 5-7). 8.99 *(978-0-544-81087-7(2)*, HMH Books For Young Readers) Houghton Mifflin Harcourt Publishing Co.
—Lives of the Scientists: Experiments, Explosions (And What the Neighbors Thought) Hewitt, Kathryn, illus. 2013. (ENG.). 96p. (J). (gr. 5-7). 20.99 *(978-0-15-205909-5(1))* Houghton Mifflin Harcourt Publishing Co.
Kurtz, Jane. Mister Bones: Dinosaur Hunter. Haverfield, Mary, illus. 2004. (Ready-To-Reads Ser.). (ENG.). 32p. (J). (gr. -1-1). pap. 3.99 *(978-0-689-85960-1(0)*, Simon Spotlight) Simon Spotlight.
Lace, William W. Benjamin Franklin. 2010. (Leaders of the Colonial Era Ser.). (Illus.). 120p. (gr. 5-8). 35.00 *(978-1-60413-737-8(1)*, Chelsea Hse.) Facts On File, Inc.
Lachner, Elizabeth, ed. Top 101 Scientists. 2016. (People You Should Know Ser.). 184p. (J). (gr. 8-8). lib. bdg. 36.25 *(978-1-68048-510-3(5))* Rosen Publishing Group, Inc., The.
Landau, Elaine. Meet Ben Franklin with Elaine Landau. 2006. (Explore Colonial America with Elaine Landau Ser.). (Illus.). 48p. (J). (gr. 3-4). lib. bdg. 25.27 *(978-0-7660-2555-4(1)*, Enslow Elementary) Enslow Pubs., Inc.
Lantier, Patricia. Rachel Carson: Fighting Pesticides & Other Chemical Pollutants. 2009. (Voices for Green Choices Ser.). (ENG., Illus.). 48p. (J). (gr. 5-9). lib. bdg. *(978-0-7787-4663-8(1))* Crabtree Publishing Co.
Larson, Kirsten. Tools of the Trade: Using Scientific Equipment. 2016. (Let's Explore Science Ser.). (ENG.). 48p. (gr. 5-8). 35.64 *(978-1-68191-400-8(X))* Rourke Educational Media.
Latta, Sara L. Ice Scientist: Careers in the Frozen Antarctic. 2009. (Wild Science Careers Ser.). (Illus.). 128p. (J). (gr. 5-9). lib. bdg. 33.27 *(978-0-7660-3048-0(2))* Enslow Pubs., Inc.
—Polar Scientists: Studying the Antarctic. 2015. (Extreme Science Careers Ser.). (ENG., Illus.). 128p. (J). (gr. 7-7). 37.27 *(978-0-7660-6966-4(4))* Enslow Pubs., Inc.
—Who Fixed Babies' Hearts? Vivien Thomas. 2012. (I Like Inventors! Ser.). (Illus.). 24p. (J). (gr. k-3). pap. 7.95 *(978-1-4644-0130-5(6)*, Enslow Elementary) Enslow Pubs., Inc.
Lawlor, Laurie. Rachel Carson & Her Book That Changed the World. Beingessner, Laura, illus. 2014. (ENG.). 32p. (J). (gr. k-5). 7.99 *(978-0-8234-3193-9(2))* Holiday Hse., Inc.
Leaders of the Scientific Revolution. 2017. (Leaders of the Scientific Revolution Ser.). 112p. (gr. 12-13). 296.80 ***(978-1-4994-6634-8(X)**, Rosen Young Adult)* Rosen Publishing Group, Inc., The.
Leavitt, Amie Jane. Becoming a Software Engineer. 2017. (Tech Track: Building Your Career in IT Ser.). 80p. (J). (gr. 12-12). 35.75 ***(978-1-5081-7554-4(3)**,* Rosen Young Adult) Rosen Publishing Group, Inc., The.
Leavitt, Amie Jane. Who Really Discovered Electricity?, 1 vol. 2011. (Race for History Ser.). (ENG.). 48p. (gr. 3-4). Illus.). pap. 8.10 *(978-1-4296-6248-2(4))*; pap. 47.70 *(978-1-4296-6416-5(9))* Capstone Press of Coughlan Cos. (Fact Finders).
Lee, Sally. Mad Scientists: The Not-So-Crazy Work of Amazing Scientists, 1 vol. 2014. (Scary Science Ser.). (ENG.). 32p. (gr. 3-4). lib. bdg. 27.32 *(978-1-4765-3928-7(6)*, Fact Finders) Capstone Press of Coughlan Cos.
Levine, Ellen. Rachel Carson. 2008. (Up Close Ser.). (ENG., Illus.). 224p. (YA). (gr. 7-18). 7.99 *(978-0-14-241046-2(2)*, Puffin Books) Penguin Young Readers Group.
Liebman, Daniel. I Want to Be a Scientist. 2016. (I Want to Be Ser.). (ENG., Illus.). 24p. (J). (gr. -1-2). pap. 3.99 *(978-1-77085-789-6(3)*, 9781770857896) Firefly Bks., Ltd.
Liebman, Daniel & Mlawer, Teresa. Quiero Ser Científico. 2016. (Quiero Ser). (SPA., Illus.). 24p. (J). (gr. -1-2). pap. 6.99 *(978-1-77085-865-7(2)*, 9781770858657) Firefly Bks., Ltd.
Little Scientist, 1 vol. 2014. (Little Scientist Ser.). (ENG.). 32p. (gr. 1-2). pap. 13.90 *(978-1-4914-0803-2(0))* Capstone Press of Coughlan Cos.
Llanas, Sheila. Jonas Salk: Medical Innovator & Polio Vaccine Developer, 1 vol. 2013. (Essential Lives Set 8 Ser.). (ENG., Illus.). 112p. (J). (gr. 6-12). lib. bdg. 35.64 *(978-1-61783-896-5(9)*, Essential Library) ABDO Publishing Co.
Lo Bosco, Maryellen. Famous Immigrant Scientists. 2017. (J). ***(978-0-7660-9244-0(5))*** Enslow Pubs., Inc.
Lourie, Peter. The Manatee Scientists: Saving Vulnerable Species. (Scientists in the Field Ser.). (ENG., Illus.). 80p. (J). (gr. 5-7). 2016. pap. 9.99 *(978-0-544-22529-9(5)*, HMH Books For Young Readers) 2011. 18.99 *(978-0-547-15254-7(X))* Houghton Mifflin Harcourt Publishing Co.
—The Manatee Scientists: The Science of Saving the Vulnerable. 2016. (Scientists in the Field Ser.). lib. bdg. 20.85 *(978-0-606-37985-4(1))* Turtleback Bks.
MacBain, Jennifer. Gertrude Elion: Nobel Prize Winner in Physiology & Medicine. (Women Hall of Famers in Mathematics & Science Ser.). 112p. (gr. 5-8). 2009. 63.90 *(978-1-60854-811-8(2))* 2004. (Illus.). (YA). lib. bdg. 34.60 *(978-0-8239-3876-6(X))* Rosen Publishing Group, Inc., The. (Rosen Reference).
Mahoney, Emily. Antarctic Researchers, 01 vols., 1. 2016. (Out of the Lab: Extreme Jobs in Science Ser.). (ENG., Illus.). 32p. (J). pap. 10.00 *(978-1-5081-4505-9(9)*, PowerKids Pr.) Rosen Publishing Group, Inc., The.
Malnor, Bruce & Malnor, Carol. Earth Heroes, Champions of the Wilderness, 1 vol. Hovemann, Anisa Claire, illus. 2009. (ENG.). 144p. (J). (gr. 5-9). pap. 11.95 *(978-1-58469-116-7(6))* Dawn Pubns.
Maloof, Torrey. Analyze It!, 1 vol. rev. ed. 2014. (Science Readers: Content & Literacy Ser.). (ENG.). 32p. (gr. 2-2). pap. 8.99 *(978-1-4807-4613-8(4))* Teacher Created Materials, Inc.
Mara, Wil. Benjamin Franklin. (Rookie Biographies(r) Ser.). (Illus.). (J). 2014. (ENG.). 32p. pap. 5.95 *(978-0-531-21201-1(7))* 2014. (ENG., 32p. lib. bdg. 25.00 *(978-0-531-20558-7(4))* 2007. 31p. (gr. 1-2). pap. 4.95 *(978-0-531-12591-5(2)*, Children's Pr.) Scholastic Library Publishing.
Marcovitz, Hal. Benjamin Franklin: Scientist, Inventor, Printer, & Statesman. 2006. (Leaders of the American Revolution Ser.). (Illus.). 100p. (gr. 5-8). lib. bdg. 30.00 *(978-0-7910-9219-4(4)*, Chelsea Hse.) Facts On File, Inc.
Marrin, Albert. Thomas Paine: Crusader for Liberty: How One Man's Ideas Helped Form a New Nation. 2016. (ENG.). 144p. (YA). (gr. 7). pap. 15.99 *(978-0-375-85969-4(1)*, Ember) Random Hse. Children's Bks.
Marsh, Carole. Marie Curie, Nobel Prize Winning Scientist. 2004. 12p. (gr. k-4). 2.95 *(978-0-635-02374-2(1))* Gallopade International.
Martin, Jacqueline Briggs. Snowflake Bentley. Azarian, Mary, illus. 2009. (ENG.). 32p. (J). (gr. -1-3). pap. 7.99 *(978-0-547-24829-5(6))* Houghton Mifflin Harcourt Publishing Co.
—Snowflake Bentley. 2004. (Illus.). (J). (gr. -1-3). spiral bd. *(978-0-616-01714-2(6))* Canadian National Institute for the Blind/Institut National Canadien pour les Aveugles.
Mason, Paul. Bonkers Boffins, Inventors & Other Eccentric Eggheads. 2017. (Barmy Biogs Ser.). (ENG., Illus.). 96p. (J). (gr. 4-6). pap. 7.99 ***(978-0-7502-8391-5(2)**,* Wayland) Hachette Children's Group GBR. Dist: Hachette Bk. Group.
Maxwell, Cassandre. Fur, Fins, & Feathers: Abraham Dee Bartlett & the Invention of the Modern Zoo. 2015. (ENG., Illus.). 34p. (J). 17.00 *(978-0-8028-5432-2(X)*, Eerdmans Bks For Young Readers) Eerdmans, William B. Publishing Co.
Maynard, Charles W. John Wesley Powell: Soldier, Scientist, & Explorer. 2009. (Famous Explorers of the American West Ser.). 24p. (gr. 3-4). 42.50 *(978-1-61512-505-0(1)*, PowerKids Pr.) Rosen Publishing Group, Inc., The.
McCartin, Brain. Thomas Paine: "Common Sense" & Revolutionary Pamphleteering. 2005. (Library of American Lives & Times). (Illus.). 112p. (J). (gr. 4-8). lib. bdg. 34.60 *(978-0-8239-5729-3(2))* Rosen Publishing Group, Inc., The.
McCully, Emily Arnold. Caroline's Comets: A True Story. 2017. (ENG.). 40p. (J). (gr. -1-3). 16.95 *(978-0-8234-3664-4(0))* Holiday Hse., Inc.
McCurdy, Michael. So Said Ben. 2007. (ENG., Illus.). 32p. (J). (gr. 1-3). 17.95 *(978-1-56846-147-2(X)*, Creative Editions) Creative Co., The.
McDaniel, Jequita Potts. Mardy Murie Did! Grandmother of Conservation. Van Zyle, Jon, illus. 2011. (J). *(978-1-58979-525-9(3))* Taylor Trade Publishing.
McDaniel, Jequite Po & Van Zyle, Jon. Mardi Murie Did! Grandmother of Conservation. 2011. (ENG., Illus.). 32p. (J). (gr. -1-2). 15.95 *(978-1-58979-565-5(2))* Taylor Trade Publishing.
McDowell, Pamela. Benjamin Franklin. 2013. *(978-1-62127-307-3(5))*; pap. *(978-1-62127-313-4(X))* Weigl Pubs., Inc.
McGowan, Joe. Al Gore. 2009. (People We Should Know Ser.). (ENG.). 48p. (J). (gr. 3-5). pap. 10.50 *(978-1-4339-2146-9(4)*, Gareth Stevens Learning Library) Stevens, Gareth Publishing LLLP.
McGowan, Joseph. Al Gore. 2009. (People We Should Know Ser.). (ENG.). 48p. (J). (gr. 3-5). lib. bdg. 31.00 *(978-1-4339-1947-3(8)*, Gareth Stevens Learning Library) Stevens, Gareth Publishing LLLP.
McLeese, Don. Benjamin Franklin. 2005. (Heroes of the American Revolution Ser.). (Illus.). 32p. (gr. 2-5). 19.95 *(978-1-59515-216-9(4))* Rourke Educational Media.
McNeil, Niki, et al. HOCPP 1107 Steve Irwin. 2006. spiral bd. 21.00 *(978-1-60308-107-8(0))* In the Hands of a Child.
McPherson, Stephanie Sammartino. Tim Berners-Lee: Inventor of the World Wide Web. 2009. (USA TODAY Lifeline Biographies Ser.). (ENG., Illus.). 112p. (J). (gr. 6-12). lib. bdg. 34.60 *(978-0-8225-7273-2(7))* Lerner Publishing Group.
Medina, Nico & Putra, Dede. Who Was Jacques Cousteau? 2015. (Who Was... ? Ser.). lib. bdg. 16.00 *(978-0-606-36599-4(0))* Turtleback Bks.
Meltzer, Brad. I Am Jane Goodall. Eliopoulos, Christopher, illus. 2016. (Ordinary People Change the World Ser.). (ENG.). 40p. (J). (gr. k-3). 14.99 *(978-0-525-42849-7(6)*, Dial Bks) Penguin Young Readers Group.
Miller, Brandon Marie. Benjamin Franklin, American Genius: His Life & Ideas with 21 Activities. 2009. (For Kids Ser.). (ENG., Illus.). 144p. (J). (gr. 4-7). pap. 16.95 *(978-1-55652-757-9(8))* Chicago Review Pr., Inc.
Miller, Marie-Therese. Rachel Carson. 2011. (Conservation Heroes Ser.). (Illus.). 136p. (YA). (gr. 6-12). 35.00 *(978-1-60413-950-1(1)*, Chelsea Hse.) Facts On File, Inc.
Montgomery, Sy. The Great White Shark Scientist. Ellenbogen, Keith, photos by. 2016. (Scientists in the Field Ser.). (ENG., Illus.). 80p. (J). (gr. 5-7). 18.99 *(978-0-544-35298-8(X)*, HMH Books For Young Readers) Houghton Mifflin Harcourt Publishing Co.
Montgomery, Sy & Grandin, Temple. Temple Grandin: How the Girl Who Loved Cows Embraced Autism & Changed the World. 2012. (ENG., Illus.). 160p. (J). (gr. 5-7). 18.99 *(978-0-547-44315-7(3))* Houghton Mifflin Harcourt Publishing Co.
Mullins, Matt. Geoscientist. 2013. (21st Century Skills Library: Cool STEM Careers Ser.). (ENG.). 32p. (J). (gr. 4-8). 28.50 *(978-1-62431-004-1(4)*, 202467); pap. 14.21 *(978-1-62431-028-7(1)*, 202469) Cherry Lake Publishing.
Nelson, Maria. The Life of Ben Franklin. 2012. (Famous Lives Ser.). (ENG.). 24p. (J). (gr. k-3). lib. bdg. 22.60 *(978-1-4339-6345-2(0))*; (gr. 1-4). pap. 8.15 *(978-1-4339-6347-6(7))* Stevens, Gareth Publishing LLLP.
—The Life of Ben Franklin / la Vida de BenjamiN Franklin. 2012. (Famous Lives / Vidas extraordinarias Ser.). (ENG & SPA., Illus.). 24p. (J). (gr. k-3). 22.60 *(978-1-4339-6653-8(0))* Stevens, Gareth Publishing LLLP.
Nelson, Robin. George Washington Carver: A Life of Devotion. 2007. (Pull Ahead Books-Biographies Ser.). (ENG.). 32p. (gr. k-3). pap. 7.95 *(978-0-8225-6455-3(6))* Lerner Publishing Group.
Newman, Patricia. Zoo Scientists to the Rescue. Crawley, Annie, photos by. 2017. (ENG., Illus.). (J). (gr. 4-8). lib. bdg. 33.32 ***(978-1-5124-1571-1(5)**,* Millbrook Pr.) Lerner Publishing Group.
Nichols, Catherine. Leonardo Da Vinci. 2006. (Primary Source Library of Famous Artists Ser.). (Illus.). 32p. (J). (gr. -1-3). lib. bdg. 23.95 *(978-1-4042-2762-0(8)*, PowerKids Pr.) Rosen Publishing Group, Inc., The.
—Leonardo da Vinci. 2009. (Primary Source Library of Famous Artists Ser.). 32p. (gr. 3-4). 42.50 *(978-1-60854-101-0(0)*, PowerKids Pr.) Rosen Publishing Group, Inc., The.
Norlander, Britt. I've Discovered Electricity! 2008. (Eureka! Ser.). 32p. (gr. 4-18). lib. bdg. 28.50 *(978-0-7614-3195-4(0)*, Benchmark Bks.) Marshall Cavendish Corp.
Northrup, Mary. Pioneering American Computer Geniuses. 2013. (Inspiring Collective Biographies Ser.). 112p. (J). (gr. 5-18). lib. bdg. 33.27 *(978-0-7660-4167-7(0))* Enslow Pubs., Inc.
Notable Scientists Set. 2005. (Notable Scientists Ser.). 400p. (gr. 6-12). 300.00 *(978-0-8160-5967-6(5))* Facts On File, Inc.
Novelli, Luca. Leonardo Da Vinci & the Pen That Drew the Future. 2017. (Flashes of Genius Ser.). (ENG.). 112p. (J). (gr. 3). pap. 9.99 ***(978-1-61373-869-6(2))*** Chicago Review Pr., Inc.
O'Connell, Caitlin & Jackson, Donna M. The Elephant Scientist. Rodwell, Timothy, illus. 2016. (Scientists in the Field Ser.). (ENG.). 80p. (J). (gr. 5-7). 9.99 *(978-0-544-66830-0(8)*, HMH Books For Young Readers) Houghton Mifflin Harcourt Publishing Co.
O'Donnell, Kerri. Galileo: Man of Science. 2009. (Reading Room Collection 2 Ser.). 24p. (gr. 3-4). 42.50 *(978-1-60851-964-4(3)*, PowerKids Pr.) Rosen Publishing Group, Inc., The.
Ollhoff, Jim. Jacques Cousteau. 2013. (Great Explorers Ser.). (Illus.). 32p. (J). (gr. 5-9). lib. bdg. 27.07 *(978-1-61783-966-5(3)*, Abdo & Daughters) ABDO Publishing Co.
Olsen, Alana. A Day at Work with a Molecular Biologist, 01 vols., 1. 2016. (Super STEM Careers Ser.). (ENG., Illus.). 24p. (J). pap. 8.25 *(978-1-5081-4410-6(9)*, PowerKids Pr.) Rosen Publishing Group, Inc., The.
Orozco, Julia & Mulfinger, George. Christian Men of Science. 2004. (Illus.). 304p. (YA). pap. 14.99 *(978-1-932307-22-1(2)*, Ambassador-Emerald, International) Emerald Hse. Group, Inc.
Owen, Ruth. Marine Biologists. 2013. (Out of the Lab: Extreme Jobs in Science Ser.). 32p. (J). (gr. 3-6). pap. 60.00 *(978-1-4777-1386-0(7))*; pap. 10.00 *(978-1-4777-1381-5(6))*; lib. bdg. 25.25 *(978-1-4777-1291-7(7))* Rosen Publishing Group, Inc., The. (PowerKids Pr.).
Owens, L. L. Benjamin Franklin, 1 vol. 2007. (Essential Lives Set 1 Ser.). (ENG., Illus.). 112p. (J). (gr. 6-12). lib. bdg. 35.64 *(978-1-59928-840-6(0))* ABDO Publishing Co.
Patent, Dorothy Hinshaw. The Call of the Osprey. Muñoz, William, illus. Muñoz, William, photos by. 2015. (Scientists in the Field Ser.). (ENG.). 80p. (J). (gr. 5-7). 18.99 *(978-0-544-23268-6(2)*, HMH Books For Young Readers) Houghton Mifflin Harcourt Publishing Co.
Payment, Simone. Biologists at Work. 2017. (Scientists at Work Ser.). 32p. (J). (gr. 6-8). pap. 12.90 ***(978-1-68048-749-7(3)**,* Britannica Educational Publishing) Rosen Publishing Group, Inc., The.
Peterson, Judy Monroe. Underwater Explorers: Marine Biologists. 2009. (Extreme Scientists Ser.). 24p. (gr. 2-3). 42.50 *(978-1-61512-453-4(5)*, PowerKids Pr.); (Illus.). (YA). lib. bdg. 22.60 *(978-1-4042-4526-6(X))* Rosen Publishing Group, Inc., The.
Peterson, Megan Cooley & Rustad, Martha E. H. Little Scientists. 2013. (Little Scientist Ser.). (ENG.). 32p. (gr. 1-2). 41.70 *(978-1-4765-3731-3(3))*; pap. 41.70 *(978-1-4765-3729-0(1))*; lib. bdg. 167.94 *(978-1-4765-0466-7(0))* Capstone Press of Coughlan Cos.
Petrie, Kristin. Jacques Cousteau, 1 vol. 2004. (Explorers Set 1 Ser.). (ENG.). 32p. (gr. k-6). 27.07 *(978-1-59197-599-1(9)*, Checkerboard Library) ABDO Publishing Co.
Pezzi, Bryan. David Suzuki. 2010. (Illus.). 24p. *(978-1-77071-595-0(9))*; pap. *(978-1-77071-601-8(7))* Weigl Educational Pubs. Ltd.
Phillips, Dee. Rachel Carson: Environmental Pioneer. 2013. (Rosen Readers Ser.). (ENG.). 24p. (J). (gr. 3-4). pap. 8.25 *(978-1-4777-2465-1(6)*, Rosen Classroom) Rosen Publishing Group, Inc., The.
Phillips, Dorian. Rachel Carson: Environmental Pioneer. 2013. (Rosen Readers Ser.). (ENG.). 24p. (J). (gr. 3-4). pap. 49.50 *(978-1-4777-2466-8(4)*, Rosen Classroom) Rosen Publishing Group, Inc., The.
Phillips, John & National Geographic Kids Staff. Leonardo Da Vinci: The Genius Who Defined the Renaissance. 2008. (National Geographic World History Biographies Ser.). (ENG., Illus.). 64p. (J). (gr. 3-7). pap. 7.99 *(978-1-4263-0248-0(7)*, National Geographic Children's Bks.) National Geographic Society.
Physicians, Scientists, & Mathematicians of the Islamic World. 2016. (Physicians, Scientists, & Mathematicians of the Islamic World Ser.). 112p. (gr. 6-6). 259.70 *(978-1-4777-8547-8(7)*, Rosen Young Adult) Rosen Publishing Group, Inc., The.
Piddock, Charles. Rachel Carson: A Voice for the Natural World. 2009. (Life Portraits Ser.). (Illus.). 112p. (YA). (gr. 7-12). lib. bdg. 36.00 *(978-1-4339-0058-7(0))* Stevens, Gareth Publishing LLLP.

S

Polcovar, Jane. Rosalind Franklin & the Structure of Life. 2006. (Profiles in Science Ser.). (Illus.). 144p. (J). (gr. 3-7). lib. bdg. 27.95 *(978-1-59935-022-6(X))* Reynolds, Morgan Inc.

Porterfield, Jason. Tim Berners-Lee, 01 vols., 1. 2016. (Tech Pioneers Ser.). (ENG.). 112p. (J). 35.60 *(978-1-4994-6290-6(5)*, Rosen Young Adult) Rosen Publishing Group, Inc., The.

Puerta, Germán. Galileo Galilei - Y Sin Embargo se Mueve. 2005. (SPA.). 108p. (YA). *(978-958-30-1700-1(0))* Panamericana Editorial.

Rabinowitz, Alan. A Boy & a Jaguar. Chien, Catia, illus. 2014. (ENG.). 32p. (J). (gr. -1-3). 17.99 *(978-0-547-87507-1(X)*, HMH Books For Young Readers) Houghton Mifflin Harcourt Publishing Co.

Randolph, Ryan P. Benjamin Franklin: Inventor, Writer & Patriot. 2005. (Library of American Lives & Times). (Illus.). 112p. (YA). (gr. 4-8). lib. bdg. 34.60 *(978-0-8239-5751-4(9))* Rosen Publishing Group, Inc., The.

—Benjamin Franklin: Inventor, Writer, & Patriot. 2009. (Library of American Lives & Times Ser.). 112p. (gr. 5-5). 69.20 *(978-1-60853-472-2(3))* Rosen Publishing Group, Inc., The.

Rauf, Don. Thomas Paine: Author of Common Sense. 2017. (J). ***(978-1-5383-8100-7(1))*** Rosen Publishing Group, Inc., The.

Rausch, Monica. Benjamín Franklin. 2007. (Grandes personajes (Spanish- Great Americans) Ser.). 24p. (gr. 1-4). (ENG & SPA.). pap. 8.15 *(978-0-8368-7988-9(0))*; (Illus.). pap. 8.15 *(978-0-8368-7689-5(X))*; (Illus.). lib. bdg. 22.00 *(978-0-8368-7682-6(2))* Stevens, Gareth Publishing LLLP. (Weekly Reader Leveled Readers).

Rausch, Monica L. Benjamin Franklin. 2007. (Grandes personajes (Great Americans) Ser.). (ENG & SPA., Illus.). 24p. (gr. 1-4). lib. bdg. 22.00 *(978-0-8368-7981-0(3)*, Weekly Reader Leveled Readers) Stevens, Gareth Publishing LLLP.

Raynham, Alex. Factfiles Leonardo da Vinci. 3rd ed. 2013. (ENG., Illus.). 64p. pap. 10.00 *(978-0-19-423670-6(6))* Oxford Univ. Pr., Inc.

Reed, Jennifer. Leonardo da Vinci: Genius of Art & Science. 2005. (Great Minds of Science Ser.). (Illus.). 128p. (J). lib. bdg. 27.94 *(978-0-7660-2500-4(4))* Enslow Pubs., Inc.

Reid, Struan & Fara, Patricia. El Libro de los Cientificos: Desde Arquimedes a Einstein. (SPA.). (YA). (gr. 5-8). pap. *(978-950-724-272-4(4)*, LMA8234) Lumen ARG. Dist: Lectorum Pubns., Inc.

Revolutionary Discoveries of Scientific Pioneers. 2013. (Revolutionary Discoveries of Scientific Pioneers Ser.). 80p. (YA). (gr. 7-12). 266.00 *(978-1-4777-1818-6(4))* Rosen Publishing Group, Inc., The.

Rice, Dona Herweck. What a Scientist Sees. 2015. (Science Readers: Content & Literacy Ser.). (ENG.). 32p. (gr. 4-4). pap. 8.99 *(978-1-4807-4691-6(6))* Teacher Created Materials, Inc.

—What the Evidence Shows. 2015. (Science Readers: Content & Literacy Ser.). (Illus.). 32p. (gr. 5-5). pap. 8.99 *(978-1-4807-4730-2(0))* Teacher Created Materials, Inc.

Rice, William B. The First Geologists, 1 vol. 2007. (Science Readers Ser.). (ENG.). 32p. (J). (gr. 3-3). pap. 8.99 *(978-0-7439-0554-1(7))* Shell Educational Publishing.

—Jane Goodall, 1 vol. 2nd rev. ed. 2012. (TIME for KIDS(r) Nonfiction Readers Ser.). (ENG.). 32p. (J). (gr. 3-3). pap. 8.99 *(978-1-4333-3684-3(7))* Teacher Created Materials, Inc.

Rich, Mari. Computer Science, Vol. 10. Gilmore, Malinda & Pouson, Mel, eds. 2016. (Black Achievement in Science Ser.). (Illus.). 64p. (J). (gr. 7). 23.95 *(978-1-4222-3557-7(2))* Mason Crest.

—Technology, Vol. 10. Gilmore, Malinda & Pouson, Mel, eds. 2016. (Black Achievement in Science Ser.). (Illus.). 64p. (J). (gr. 7). 23.95 *(978-1-4222-3564-5(5))* Mason Crest.

Richard, Orlin. 12 Scientists Who Changed the World. 2016. (Change Makers Ser.). (ENG., Illus.). 32p. (J). (gr. 3-6). 19.95 *(978-1-63235-149-4(8)*, 12-Story Library) Pr. Room Editions LLC.

Ridley, Sarah. Charles Darwin. 2017. (Super Scientists Ser.). (ENG., Illus.). 24p. (J). (gr. 1-3). pap. 9.99 ***(978-1-4451-5355-1(6)***, Franklin Watts) Hachette Children's Group GBR. Dist: Hachette Bk. Group.

—Galileo Galilei. 2017. (Super Scientists Ser.). (ENG., Illus.). 24p. (J). (gr. 1-3). pap. 9.99 ***(978-1-4451-5358-2(0)***, Franklin Watts) Hachette Children's Group GBR. Dist: Hachette Bk. Group.

Riley, Gail Blasser. Benjamin Franklin & Electricity. 2004. (Cornerstones of Freedom Ser.). (ENG., Illus.). 48p. (YA). (gr. 4-7). 26.00 *(978-0-516-24240-8(7))* Scholastic Library Publishing.

Riley, John B. Benjamin Franklin: A Photo Biography. l.t. ed. 2004. (First Biographies Ser.). (Illus.). 24p. (YA). (gr. 5-18). 16.95 *(978-1-883846-64-0(1)*, First Biographies) Reynolds, Morgan Inc.

Rinaldo, Denise. Jane Goodall: With a Discussion of Responsibility. 2003. (Values in Action Ser.). (J). *(978-1-59203-062-0(9))* Learning Challenge, Inc.

—Leonardo Da Vinci: With a Discussion of Imagination. 2003. (Values in Action Ser.). (J). *(978-1-59203-066-8(1))* Learning Challenge, Inc.

Ring, Susan. Scientists at Work. 2005. (Yellow Umbrella Fluent Level Ser.). (ENG., Illus.). 16p. (gr. k-1). pap. 35.70 *(978-0-7368-5303-3(0)*, Yellow Umbrella Bks.) Capstone Press of Coughlan Cos.

Rock, Meghan. Rachel Carson: Marine Biologist & Winner of the National Book Award. 2016. (Women in Science Ser.). 128p. (J). 45.64 *(978-1-5026-2319-5(6))* Cavendish Square Publishing.

Romero, Libby. Ibn Al-Haytham. 2016. (Illus.). 48p. (J). *(978-1-4263-2616-5(5))* National Geographic Society.

—Ibn Al-Haytham: The Man Who Discovered How We See. 2016. (Readers Bios Ser.). (ENG., Illus.). 48p. (J). (gr. 1-4). pap. 3.99 *(978-1-4263-2500-7(2)*, National Geographic Children's Bks.) National Geographic Society.

Roscoe, Kelly & Isle, Mick. Aristotle: The Father of Logic. 2015. (Greatest Greek Philosophers Ser.). (ENG.). 112p. (J). (gr. 7-8). 35.60 *(978-1-4994-6126-8(7)*, Rosen Young Adult) Rosen Publishing Group, Inc., The.

Roselli, Stephanie. The Budding Scientist. 2012. (Budding Ser.). (ENG., Illus.). 72p. pap. 9.95 *(978-0-87659-385-1(6)*, Gryphon House Inc) Gryphon Hse., Inc.

Ross, Val. The Road to There: Mapmakers & Their Stories. 2009. (ENG., Illus.). 152p. (J). (gr. 5). pap. 15.95 *(978-0-88776-933-7(0)*, Tundra Bks.) Tundra Bks. CAN. Dist: Penguin Random Hse. LLC.

Rubin, Elizabeth. The Curies & Radium. Moyler, Alan, illus. 2011. 122p. 40.95 *(978-1-258-09479-9(7))* Literary Licensing, LLC.

Rustad, Martha E. H. Little Scientists, 1 vol. 2014. (Little Scientist Ser.). (ENG.). 32p. (gr. 1-2). pap. 27.80 *(978-1-4765-6898-0(7))* Capstone Press of Coughlan Cos.

Saddleback Educational Publishing Staff, ed. Albert Einstein, 1 vol. unabr. ed. 2008. (Graphic Biographies Ser.). (ENG., Illus.). 25p. (YA). (gr. 9-12). pap. 7.95 *(978-1-59905-212-0(1))* Saddleback Educational Publishing, Inc.

Salas, Laura Purdie. Discovering Nature's Laws: A Story about Isaac Newton. Reynolds, Emily C. S., tr. Reynolds, Emily C. S., illus. 2003. (Creative Minds Biographies Ser.). (ENG.). 64p. (gr. 4-8). pap. 8.95 *(978-1-57505-606-7(2))*; lib. bdg. 22.60 *(978-1-57505-183-3(4))* Lerner Publishing Group.

Salzmann, Mary Elizabeth. Benjamin Franklin, 1 vol. 2016. (ENG., Illus.). 24p. (J). *(978-1-68078-157-1(X))* ABDO Publishing Co.

Sammons, Sandra Wallus. Marjory Stoneman Douglas & the Florida Everglades. 2010. (Pineapple Press Biography Ser.). (ENG.). 72p. (J). (gr. 4-7). pap. 7.95 *(978-1-56164-471-1(4))*; 11.95 *(978-1-56164-470-4(6))* Pineapple Pr., Inc.

Satterfield, Kathryn Hoffman. Benjamin Franklin A Man of Many Talents. 2005. 44p. (J). lib. bdg. 15.00 *(978-1-4242-0846-3(7))* Fitzgerald Bks.

Scheppler, Bill. Al-Biruni: Master Astronomer & Muslim Scholar of the Eleventh Century. 2009. (Great Muslim Philosophers & Scientists of the Middle Ages Ser.). 112p. (gr. 6-6). 66.50 *(978-1-61513-177-8(9)*, Rosen Reference) Rosen Publishing Group, Inc., The.

Scherer, Glenn & Fletcher, Marty. Who on Earth Is Rachel Carson? Mother of the Environmental Movement. 2009. (Scientists Saving the Earth Ser.). (Illus.). 112p. (J). (gr. 5-9). lib. bdg. 33.27 *(978-1-59845-116-0(2))* Enslow Pubs., Inc.

Schraff, Anne. Charles Drew: Pioneer in Medicine. 2003. (Famous Inventors Ser.). (Illus.). 32p. (J). (gr. 1-4). lib. bdg. 22.60 *(978-0-7660-2008-5(8))* Enslow Pubs., Inc.

Sci-Hi - Scientists, 6 vols., Set. Incl. Scientists Behind Earth's Processes. Solway, Andrew. pap. 9.95 *(978-1-4109-4051-3(9))*; Scientists Behind Energy. Solway, Andrew. pap. 9.95 *(978-1-4109-4052-0(7))*; Scientists Behind Living Things. Snedden, Robert. pap. 9.95 *(978-1-4109-4054-4(3))*; Scientists Behind Medical Advances. Hartman, Eve & Meshbesher, Wendy. pap. 9.95 *(978-1-4109-4055-1(1))*; Scientists Behind Space. Hartman, Eve & Meshbesher, Wendy. pap. 9.95 *(978-1-4109-4056-8(X))*; Scientists Behind the Environment. Snedden, Robert. pap. 9.95 *(978-1-4109-4053-7(5))*; (gr. 4-4). (Sci-Hi: Scientists Ser.). (ENG.). 48p. 2011. Set pap. 53.94 *(978-1-4109-4057-5(8))*; Set lib. bdg. 133.28 *(978-1-4109-4050-6(0))* Heinemann-Raintree. (Sci-Hi).

Scientists at Work. 2017. (Scientists at Work Ser.). 32p. (gr. 6-8). 146.70 ***(978-1-5081-0544-2(8))***; pap. 77.40 ***(978-1-5081-0546-6(4))*** Rosen Publishing Group, Inc., The. (Britannica Educational Publishing).

Scott, Celicia. YouTube: How Steve Chen Changed the Way We Watch Videos. 2014. (Wizards of Technology Ser.: 10). (Illus.). 64p. (J). (gr. 7-18). 23.95 *(978-1-4222-3188-3(7))* Mason Crest.

Sepahban, Lois. Temple Grandin: Inspiring Animal-Behavior Scientist, 1 vol. 2014. (Great Minds of Science Ser.). (ENG.). 48p. (gr. 8-12). lib. bdg. 32.79 *(978-1-62403-380-3(6))* ABDO Publishing Co.

Shetty, B. Vithal. World as Seen under the Lens of a Scientist: Negro Zero to American Hero Who Changed United States from American Hypocrisy to Greatest Democracy. 2009. 552p. 34.99 *(978-1-4415-0472-2(9))*; pap. 23.99 *(978-1-4415-0471-5(0))* Xlibris Corp.

Simon, Samantha. Clinical & Medical Laboratory Scientists. 2017. (Careers in Healthcare Ser.: Vol. 13). (ENG.). (YA). (gr. 7-12). 23.95 ***(978-1-4222-3796-0(6))*** Mason Crest.

Slade, Suzanne. The Inventor's Secret: What Thomas Edison Told Henry Ford. Reinhardt, Jennifer Black, illus. 2015. (ENG.). 48p. (J). (gr. 1-4). lib. bdg. 16.95 *(978-1-58089-667-2(7))* Charlesbridge Publishing, Inc.

Small, Cathleen. Barbara Mcclintock: Cytogeneticist & Discoverer of Mobile Genetic Elements. 2016. (Women in Science Ser.). 128p. (J). lib. bdg. 45.64 *(978-1-5026-2311-9(0))* Cavendish Square Publishing.

Smith, Linda Wasmer. Louis Pasteur: Disease Fighter. rev. ed. 2007. (Great Minds of Science Ser.). (Illus.). 128p. (J). (gr. 4-10). lib. bdg. 33.27 *(978-0-7660-2792-3(9))* Enslow Pubs., Inc.

—Louis Pasteur: Genius Disease Fighter. 2015. (Genius Scientists & Their Genius Ideas Ser.). 96p. (J). (gr. 5-12). 27.94 *(978-0-7660-6575-8(8))*; pap. 10.95 *(978-0-7660-6576-5(6))* Enslow Pubs., Inc.

Smith, Paula. Measure It! 2015. (ENG., Illus.). 24p. (J). pap. *(978-0-7787-1544-3(2))* Crabtree Publishing Co.

—Model It! 2015. (ENG., Illus.). 24p. (J). pap. *(978-0-7787-1545-0(0))* Crabtree Publishing Co.

—Plan & Investigate It! 2015. (ENG., Illus.). 24p. (J). pap. *(978-0-7787-1546-7(9))* Crabtree Publishing Co.

—Prove It! 2015. (ENG., Illus.). 24p. (J). pap. *(978-0-7787-1547-4(7))* Crabtree Publishing Co.

Snedden, Robert. The Scientists Behind the Environment, 1 vol. 2011. (Sci-Hi: Scientists Ser.). (ENG.). 48p. (gr. 4-4). pap. 9.95 *(978-1-4109-4053-7(5))*; lib. bdg. 33.32 *(978-1-4109-4046-9(2))* Heinemann-Raintree. (Sci-Hi).

Somervill, Barbara. Marine Biologist. 2009. (21st Century Skills Library: Cool Science Careers Ser.). (ENG.). 32p. (gr. 4-8). lib. bdg. 28.50 *(978-1-60279-504-4(5)*, 200306) Cherry Lake Publishing.

Souza, Dorothy M. John Wesley Powell. 2004. (Watts Library). (ENG., Illus.). 64p. (J). (gr. 5-7). pap. 8.95 *(978-0-531-16653-6(8)*, Watts, Franklin) Scholastic Library Publishing.

Spangenburg, Ray, et al. Makers of Modern Science, 10 vols., Set. 2011. (Makers of Modern Science Ser.). 160p. (gr. 6-12). 350.00 *(978-0-8160-6170-9(X)*, Chelsea Hse.) Facts On File, Inc.

—Rita Levi-Montalcini: Discoverer of Nerve Growth Factor. 2009. (Makers of Modern Science Ser.). (Illus.). 176p. (gr. 6-12). 35.00 *(978-0-8160-6171-6(8)*, Chelsea Hse.) Facts On File, Inc.

Spilsbury, Louise. Zoologists in the Field. 2010. (Big Picture: People & Culture Ser.). (ENG.). 24p. (gr. 1-2). pap. 41.70 *(978-1-4296-5822-5(3)*, First Facts) Capstone Press of Coughlan Cos.

Spotlight on Kids Can Code: Set 3. 2017. (Spotlight on Kids Can Code Ser.). 24p. (gr. 8-10). 315.00 ***(978-1-5081-5590-4(9))***; pap. 141.00 ***(978-1-5081-5591-1(7))*** Rosen Publishing Group, Inc., The. (PowerKids Pr.).

Squire, Ann O. Extreme Science Careers. 2014. (True Book(tm), a — Extreme Science Ser.). (ENG.). 48p. (J). lib. bdg. 31.00 *(978-0-531-20744-4(7))* Scholastic Library Publishing.

Sterling, Kristin. Jane Goodall: A Life of Loyalty. 2008. (Pull Ahead Books-Biographies Ser.). (ENG.). 32p. (gr. k-3). pap. 7.95 *(978-0-8225-8728-6(9))* Lerner Publishing Group.

Strauss, Holden. Jobs in Science: Solve Problems Involving Measurement & Estimation. 2014. (Rosen Common Core Math Readers Ser.). (ENG.). 24p. (J). (gr. 3-4). pap. 8.25 *(978-1-4777-4912-8(8)*, PowerKids Pr.) Rosen Publishing Group, Inc., The.

Streissguth, Tom. Benjamin Franklin. 2005. (Bios for Challenged Readers Ser.). (Illus.). 112p. (J). (gr. 6-12). lib. bdg. 27.93 *(978-0-8225-2210-2(1))* Lerner Publishing Group.

Strom, Laura Layton. Leonardo Da Vinci. 2007. (Shockwave: Life Stories Ser.). (ENG., Illus.). 36p. (J). (gr. 3-5). 25.00 *(978-0-531-17771-6(8)*, Children's Pr.) Scholastic Library Publishing.

Sullivan, Anne Marie. Sir Isaac Newton: Famous English Scientist. 2004. (Great Names Ser.). (Illus.). 32p. (J). (gr. 3-18). lib. bdg. 19.95 *(978-1-59084-139-6(5))* Mason Crest.

Superheroes of Science. 2015. (Superheroes of Science Ser.). (ENG.). 48p. (J). (gr. 6-6). pap., pap., pap. 505.80 *(978-1-4824-3507-8(1))* Stevens, Gareth Publishing LLLP.

Teacher Created Materials Staff, ed. Biographies III Science Pioneers: Themed Classroom Readers- 2007. (Themed Reader Sets Ser.). pap. 439.99 *(978-1-4333-0157-5(1))* Teacher Created Materials, Inc.

Thayer, William Makepeace. From Boyhood to Manhood: Life of Benjamin Franklin. 2006. pap. *(978-1-4068-0906-0(3))* Echo Library.

Thomas, William David. Marine Biologist. 2009. (Cool Careers: Cutting Edge Ser.). 32p. (J). (gr. 5-8). pap. 10.50 *(978-1-4339-2156-8(1))*; lib. bdg. 26.00 *(978-1-4339-1957-2(5))* Stevens, Gareth Publishing LLLP.

Thompson, Clifford. Climatologists!, Vol. 10. 2015. (Scientists in Action Ser.). (Illus.). 48p. (J). (gr. 5). 20.95 *(978-1-4222-3422-8(3))* Mason Crest.

Time for Kids Editors. Benjamin Franklin - A Man of Many Talents. 2005. (Time for Kids Ser.). (ENG., Illus.). 48p. (J). (gr. 2-4). pap. 3.99 *(978-0-06-057609-7(X))* HarperCollins Pubs.

Todd, Kim D. Jean Jennings Bartik: Computer Pioneer. 2015. (Notable Missourians Ser.). (ENG., Illus.). 48p. (J). pap. 24.00 *(978-1-61248-145-6(0))* Truman State Univ. Pr.

Tracy, Kathleen. Leonardo Da Vinci. 2008. (Art Profiles for Kids Ser.). (Illus.). 48p. (YA). (gr. 4-7). lib. bdg. 29.95 *(978-1-58415-711-3(9))* Mitchell Lane Pubs., Inc.

—Robert Koch & the Study of Anthrax. 2004. (Uncharted, Unexplored, & Unexplained Ser.). (Illus.). 48p. (J). (gr. 4-8). lib. bdg. 29.95 *(978-1-58415-261-3(3))* Mitchell Lane Pubs., Inc.

Tremblay, E. A. Rachel Carson. 2003. (Women in Science Ser.). (Illus.). 112p. (gr. 6-12). 30.00 *(978-0-7910-7244-8(4)*, Chelsea Hse.) Facts On File, Inc.

Tuffen, Hugh & Waldron, Melanie. Volcanologist: The Coolest Jobs on the Planet, 1 vol. HL Studios Staff, illus. 2014. (Coolest Jobs on the Planet Ser.). (ENG.). 48p. (gr. 6-6). 32.65 *(978-1-4109-6643-8(7))*; pap. 8.99 *(978-1-4109-6649-0(6))* Heinemann-Raintree.

Tupper, Susan. Fran & Frederick Hamerstrom: Wildlife Conservation Pioneers. 2016. (Badger Biographies Ser.). (Illus.). 136p. (J). (gr. 4-6). pap. 12.95 *(978-0-87020-732-7(6))* Wisconsin Historical Society.

Unlocking the Secrets of Science: Set of 15 Scientists. (Illus.). (gr. 4-10). lib. bdg. *(978-1-58415-233-0(8))* Mitchell Lane Pubs., Inc.

Van Gorp, Lynn. Gregor Mendel: Genetics Pioneer, 1 vol. 2007. (Science Readers Ser.). (ENG.). 32p. (J). (gr. 3-3). pap. 8.99 *(978-0-7439-0598-5(9))* Shell Educational Publishing.

Vander Hook, Sue. Louis Pasteur: Groundbreaking Chemist & Biologist, 1 vol. 2011. (Essential Lives Set 6 Ser.). (ENG., Illus.). 112p. (J). (gr. 6-12). lib. bdg. 35.64 *(978-1-61714-783-8(4)*, Essential Library) ABDO Publishing Co.

Venezia, Mike. Benjamin Franklin: Electrified the World with New Ideas. Venezia, Mike, illus. 2009. (Getting to Know the World's Greatest Inventors & Scientists Ser.). (ENG., Illus.). 32p. (J). (gr. 2-5). 28.00 *(978-0-531-23701-4(X))* Scholastic Library Publishing.

—Getting to Know the World's Greatest Inventors & Scientists, 4 vols., Set. Venezia, Mike, illus. Incl. Charles Drew: Doctor Who Got the World Pumped up to Donate Blood. 28.00 *(978-0-531-23725-0(7))*; Henry Ford: Big Wheel in the Auto Industry. 28.00 *(978-0-531-23726-7(5))*; Mary Leakey - Archaeologist Who Really Dug Her Work. 28.00 *(978-0-531-23727-4(3))*; Stephen Hawking: Cosmologist Who Gets a Big Bang Out of the Universe. 28.00 *(978-0-531-23728-1(1))*; 32p. (J). (gr. 2-5). 2009. (Illus.). 2009. Set lib. bdg. 112.00 *(978-0-531-26130-9(1)*, Watts, Franklin) Scholastic Library Publishing.

—Leonardo Davinci. Venezia, Mike, illus. rev. ed. 2015. (Getting to Know the World's Greatest Artists Ser.). (ENG., Illus.). 40p. (J). pap. 7.95 *(978-0-531-21289-9(0))* Scholastic Library Publishing.

—Rachel Carson: Clearing the Way for Environmental Protection. Venezia, Mike, illus. (Getting to Know the World's Greatest Inventors & Scientists Ser.). (ENG., Illus.). 32p. (J). 2010. (gr. 3-4). pap. 6.95 *(978-0-531-20778-9(1)*, Children's Pr.) 2009. (gr. 2-5). 28.00 *(978-0-531-23704-5(4))* Scholastic Library Publishing.

Verstraete, Larry. S Is for Scientists: A Discovery Alphabet. Geister, David, illus. 2010. (Science Alphabet Ser.). (ENG & ABK.). 40p. (J). (gr. 1-4). 16.95 *(978-1-58536-470-1(3)*, 202189) Sleeping Bear Pr.

Wallace, Ian. The Slippers' Keeper, 1 vol. 2015. (ENG., Illus.). 36p. (J). (gr. k-3). 18.95 *(978-1-55498-414-5(9))* Groundwood Bks. CAN. Dist: Publishers Group West (PGW).

Waxman, Laura Hamilton. Genetics Expert Joanna L. Kelley. 2015. (STEM Trailblazer Bios Ser.). (ENG., Illus.). 32p. (J). (gr. 2-5). pap. 7.95 *(978-1-4677-6120-8(6))*; lib. bdg. 26.60 *(978-1-4677-5795-9(0))* Lerner Publishing Group. (Lerner Pubns.).

Webster, Christine. Who on Earth Is Archie Carr? Protector of Sea Turtles. 2009. (Scientists Saving the Earth Ser.). (Illus.). 112p. (J). (gr. 5-9). lib. bdg. 33.27 *(978-1-59845-120-7(0))* Enslow Pubs., Inc.

Wendinger, Jennifer. Unusual & Awesome Jobs Using Science: Hollywood Animal Trainer, Cave Diver, & More. 2015. (You Get Paid for THAT? Ser.). (ENG.). 32p. (gr. 3-4). 27.99 *(978-1-4914-2031-7(6))* Capstone Press of Coughlan Cos.

Weston Woods Staff, creator. Snowflake Bentley. 2004. 29.95 *(978-1-55592-624-3(X))* Weston Woods Studios, Inc.

What Do Scientists Do? Big Book: Level E. 8p. 20.95 *(978-0-322-00346-0(6))* Wright Group/McGraw-Hill.

Wheeler, Jill C. Rachel Carson: Extraordinary Environmentalist, 1 vol. 2012. (Women in Science Ser.). (ENG., Illus.). 32p. (J). (gr. 3-6). lib. bdg. 27.07 *(978-1-61783-446-2(7)*, Checkerboard Library) ABDO Publishing Co.

Whiting, Jim. Benjamin Franklin. 2006. (Profiles in American History Ser.). (Illus.). 48p. (J). (gr. 3-7). lib. bdg. 29.95 *(978-1-58415-435-8(7))* Mitchell Lane Pubs., Inc.

Williams, Judith. Exploring the Rain Forest Treetops with a Scientist. 2004. (I Like Science! Ser.). (Illus.). 24p. (J). lib. bdg. 22.60 *(978-0-7660-2294-2(3))* Enslow Pubs., Inc.

—Forensic Scientist: Careers Solving Crimes & Scientific Mysteries. 2009. (Wild Science Careers Ser.). (Illus.). 128p. (J). (gr. 5-9). lib. bdg. 33.27 *(978-0-7660-3051-0(2))* Enslow Pubs., Inc.

—Saving Endangered Animals with a Scientist. 2004. (I Like Science! Ser.). (Illus.). 24p. (J). (gr. 2-4). lib. bdg. 21.26 *(978-0-7660-2276-8(5))* Enslow Pubs., Inc.

Wilson, Janet. Severn & the Day She Silenced the World, 1 vol. 2014. (Kids' Power Book Ser.: 5). (ENG., Illus.). 184p. (J). (gr. 6-8). pap. 14.95 *(978-1-927583-23-4(3))* Second Story Pr. CAN. Dist: Orca Bk. Pubs. USA.

Wilson, Janet & Second Story Press Staff. Our Earth: How Kids Are Saving the Planet, 1 vol. 2010. (ENG., Illus.). 32p. (J). (gr. 3-5). lib. bdg. 18.95 *(978-1-897187-84-5(X))* Second Story Pr. CAN. Dist: Orca Bk. Pubs. USA.

Winter, Jeanette. The Watcher: Jane Goodall's Life with the Chimps. Winter, Jeanette, illus. 2011. (ENG., Illus.). 48p. (J). (gr. -1-3). 17.99 *(978-0-375-86774-3(0)*, Schwartz & Wade Bks.) Random Hse. Children's Bks.

Wolny, Philip. Geologists at Work. 2017. (Scientists at Work Ser.). 32p. (gr. 6-8). pap. 12.90 ***(978-1-68048-760-2(4)***, Britannica Educational Publishing) Rosen Publishing Group, Inc., The.

World Book's Biographical Encyclopedia of Scientists, 8 vols. 2005. 1,536p. (YA). (gr. 6-18). 329.00 *(978-0-7166-7601-0(X)*, 20170) World Bk., Inc.

Wright, A. Gilbert. In the Steps of the Great American Herpetologist. Kalmenoff, Matthew, illus. 2014. (ENG.). 128p. (J). (gr. 2-6). pap. 11.95 *(978-1-59077-360-4(8))* Evans, M. & Co., Inc.

Wyborny, Sheila. Nikola Tesla. 2012. (Innovators Ser.). (ENG., Illus.). 64p. (gr. 4-8). lib. bdg. 29.60 *(978-0-7377-5528-2(8)*, Kidhaven) Cengage Gale.

Yasuda, Anita. Forensics: Cool Women Who Investigate. Bruce, Allison, illus. 2016. (Girls in Science Ser.). (ENG.). 112p. (J). (gr. 3-7). 19.95 *(978-1-61930-346-1(9)*, 1401408) Open City Bks.

Yount, Lisa. Antoni Van Leeuwenhoek: First to See Microscopic Life. rev. ed. 2008. (Great Minds of Science Ser.). (Illus.). 128p. (J). (gr. k-5). lib. bdg. 33.27 *(978-0-7660-3012-1(1))* Enslow Pubs., Inc.

Zannos, Susan. Dmitri Mendeleyev & the Periodic Table. 2004. (Uncharted, Unexplored, & Unexplained Ser.). (Illus.). 48p. (J). (gr. 4-8). lib. bdg. 29.95 *(978-1-58415-267-5(2))* Mitchell Lane Pubs., Inc.

—The Life & Times of Archimedes. 2004. (Biography from Ancient Civilizations Ser.). (Illus.). 48p. (J). (gr. 4-8). lib. bdg. 29.95 *(978-1-58415-242-2(7))* Mitchell Lane Pubs., Inc.

SCIENTISTS—FICTION

Abela, Deborah. In Search of the Time & Space Machine. Murphy, Jobi, illus. 2005. (Spy Force Ser.). 256p. (Orig.). (J). 14.95 *(978-1-74051-765-2(2)*, Simon & Schuster Bks. For Young Readers) Simon & Schuster Bks. For Young Readers.

Amo, Montserrat del. Montes, Pájaros y Amigos. 2007. (SPA.). 104p. (gr. 5-8). pap. 13.99 *(978-84-207-2788-2(1)*, GS6293) Grupo Anaya, S.A. ESP. Dist: Lectorum Pubns., Inc.

Anderson, M. T. Whales on Stilts! Cyrus, Kurt, illus. 2010. (Pals in Peril Tale Ser.). (ENG.). (J). (gr. 5-9). 208p. 17.99 *(978-1-4424-0695-7(X))*; 224p. pap. 7.99 *(978-1-4424-0701-5(8))* Beach Lane Bks. (Beach Lane Bks.).

—Whales on Stilts! Cyrus, Kurt, illus. 2006. (M. T. Anderson's Thrilling Tales Ser.). 188p. (gr. 5-9). 15.95 *(978-0-7569-7213-4(2))* Perfection Learning Corp.

Atkins, Jeannine. Finding Wonders: A Verse History of Girls & Science. 2017. (ENG., Illus.). 208p. (J). (gr. 5). pap. 7.99 *(978-1-4814-6566-3(X))* Simon & Schuster Children's Publishing.

—Finding Wonders: Three Girls Who Changed Science. 2016. (ENG., Illus.). 208p. (J). (gr. 5). 17.99 *(978-1-4814-6565-6(1)*, Atheneum Bks. for Young Readers) Simon & Schuster Children's Publishing.

Avery, Ben G. Pyramid Peril, 1 vol. Gaudiamo, Adi Darda, illus. 2007. (Z Graphic Novels / TimeFlyz Ser.). (ENG.). 160p. (J). (gr. 3-7). pap. 6.99 *(978-0-310-71361-6(7))* Zondervan.

Baker, Chandler. Teen Frankenstein. 2016. (High School Horror Ser.: 1). (ENG.). 368p. (YA). 17.99 *(978-1-250-05874-4(0)*, 9781250058744) Feiwel & Friends.

—Teen Frankenstein. 2017. (High School Horror Ser.: 1). (ENG.). 336p. (YA). pap. 9.99 *(978-1-250-06887-3(8)*, 9781250068873) Square Fish.

Bass, Guy. The Ghost of Grotteskew, 1 vol. Williamson, Pete, illus. 2014. (Stitch Head Ser.). (ENG.). 208p. (gr. 3-4). 10.95 *(978-1-62370-030-0(2))* Capstone Young Readers of Coughlan Cos.

—The Pirate's Eye, 1 vol. Williamson, Pete, illus. 2013. (Stitch Head Ser.). (ENG.). 208p. (gr. 3-4). 10.95 *(978-1-62370-008-9(6))* Capstone Young Readers of Coughlan Cos.

—Stitch Head, 1 vol. Williamson, Pete, illus. 2013. (Stitch Head Ser.). (ENG.). 192p. (gr. 3-4). 10.95 *(978-1-62370-007-2(8))*; pap. 262.80 *(978-1-62370-161-1(9))* Capstone Young Readers of Coughlan Cos.

Beaty, Andrea. Ada Twist, Scientist. Roberts, David, illus. 2016. (ENG.). 32p. (J). (gr. k-2). 17.95 *(978-1-4197-2137-3(2),* Abrams Bks. for Young Readers) Abrams, Inc.

Bennett, Sandra. Gingerbread Aliens. Welsh, Hayley, illus. 2012. (ENG.). 56p. (J). pap. *(978-0-9872356-4-0(8))* Australian Self Publishing Group/ Inspiring Pubs.

Benton, Jim. Attack of the 50-Ft. Cupid. Benton, Jim, illus. 2005. (Franny K. Stein, Mad Scientist Ser.: 2). (ENG., Illus.). 112p. (J). (gr. 2-5). pap. 5.99 *(978-0-689-86296-0(2),* Simon & Schuster Bks. For Young Readers) Simon & Schuster Bks. For Young Readers.

—The Complete Franny K. Stein, Mad Scientist: Lunch Walks among Us; Attack of the 50-Ft. Cupid - The Invisible Fra - The Fran That Time Forgot - Frantastic Voyage - The Fran with Four Brains - The Frandidate. Benton, Jim, illus. 2012. (Franny K. Stein, Mad Scientist Ser.). (ENG., Illus.). 784p. (J). (gr. 2-5). pap. 41.99 *(978-1-4424-7424-6(6),* Simon & Schuster Bks. For Young Readers) Simon & Schuster Bks. For Young Readers.

Biskup, Agnieszka & Sohn, Emily. Ciencia Gráfica. Martin, Cynthia & Dominguez, Richard, illus. 2013. (Ciencia Gráfica Ser.). (SPA.). 32p. (gr. 3-4). lib. bdg. 245.20 *(978-1-62065-186-5(6))* Capstone Press of Coughlan Cos.

—Ciencia Gráfica. Martin, Cynthia & Dominguez, Richard, illus. 2013. (Ciencia Gráfica Ser.). (SPA.). 32p. (gr. 3-4). lib. bdg. 122.60 *(978-1-62065-185-8(8))* Capstone Press of Coughlan Cos.

Blaine, John. The Caves of Fear: A Rick Brant Science Adventure Story. 2011. 220p. 44.95 *(978-1-258-09271-9(9))* Literary Licensing, LLC.

—Smuggler's Reef: A Rick Brant Science Adventure Story. 2011. 220p. 44.95 *(978-1-258-04085-7(9))* Literary Licensing, LLC.

Blaine, John & Goodwin, Harold Leland. The Caves of Fear. 2011. 150p. 24.95 *(978-1-4638-9614-0(X))*; pap. 13.95 *(978-1-4638-0073-4(8))* Rodgers, Alan Bks.

Bradley, Timothy. Ripple Effect. rev. ed. 2014. (Sci Hi Ser.). (ENG., Illus.). 176p. (J). (gr. 3-6). lib. bdg. 26.96 *(978-1-4807-4216-1(3))* Teacher Created Materials, Inc.

Briner, Karen. Snowize & Snitch: Highly Effective Defective Detectives. Rivas, Victor, illus. 2016. (ENG.). 272p. (J). 16.95 *(978-0-8234-3567-8(9))* Holiday Hse., Inc.

Brinley, Bertrand R. The Big Chunk of Ice: The Last Known Adventure of the Mad Scientists' Club. Geer, Charles, illus. 2005. (Mad Scientist Club Ser.). 275p. (J). (gr. 3-7). 18.95 *(978-1-930900-29-5(5))* Purple Hse. Pr.

—The Mad Scientists' Club Complete Collection. Geer, Charles, illus. 2010. 619p. (YA). pap. 29.99 *(978-1-930900-51-6(1))* Purple Hse. Pr.

Broad, Michael. Ghost Diamond!, No. 1. Broad, Michael, illus. 2011. (Agent Amelia Ser.: 1). (ENG., Illus.). 144p. (J). (gr. 2-5). pap. 5.95 *(978-0-7613-8060-3(4),* Darby Creek); lib. bdg. 22.60 *(978-0-7613-8056-6(6))* Lerner Publishing Group.

—Hypno Hounds!, No. 3. Broad, Michael, illus. 2011. (Agent Amelia Ser.: 3). (ENG., Illus.). 144p. (J). (gr. 2-5). pap. 5.95 *(978-0-7613-8062-7(0),* Darby Creek); lib. bdg. 22.60 *(978-0-7613-8058-0(2))* Lerner Publishing Group.

—#1 Ghost Diamond! 2011. (Agent Amelia Ser.). pap. 33.92 *(978-0-7613-8341-3(7),* Darby Creek) Lerner Publishing Group.

—#3 Hypno Hounds! 2011. (Agent Amelia Ser.). pap. 33.92 *(978-0-7613-8343-7(3),* Darby Creek) Lerner Publishing Group.

Brouwer, Sigmund. Ambush. 2009. (Robot Wars Ser.: 3). (ENG.). 304p. (YA). pap. 7.99 *(978-1-4143-2311-4(5),* Tyndale Kids) Tyndale Hse. Pubs.

Bryers, Paul. Kobal. 2009. 1.00 *(978-1-4074-4320-1(8))* Recorded Bks., Inc.

Campbell, Howard. A Dog Named Pavlov: Un Perro Llamado Pavlov. McCloskey, Kevin, illus. 2010. 44p. (J). pap. *(978-0-9790350-4-3(X))* Star Fire.

Castle, M. E. Game of Clones. (Clone Chronicles Ser.: No. 3). (ENG.). 256p. (J). (gr. 3-7). 2014. 15.99 *(978-1-60684-234-8(X))*No. 3. 2015. pap. 6.99 *(978-1-60684-538-7(1))* Lerner Publishing Group. (Darby Creek).

Catlow, Nikalas & Wesson, Tim. Aliens vs. Mad Scientists under the Ocean. Catlow, Nikalas & Wesson, Tim, illus. 2011. (Mega Mash-Up Ser.). (ENG., Illus.). 96p. (J). (gr. 2-5). pap. 6.99 *(978-0-7636-5874-8(X),* Nosy Crow) Candlewick Pr.

Chabert, Jack. Sam Battles the Machine! Ricks, Sam, illus. 2017. (Eerie Elementary — Branches Ser.: bk.6). (ENG.). 96p. (J). (gr. 1-3). pap. 4.99 ***(978-0-545-87378-9(9))*** Scholastic, Inc.

—Sam Battles the Machine! 2017. (Eerie Elementary — Branches Ser.: bk.6). (ENG.). (J). lib. bdg. 14.75 ***(978-0-606-40191-3(1))*** Turtleback Bks.

Chabert, Jack. The Science Fair Is Freaky! Ricks, Sam, illus. 2016. (Eerie Elementary — Branches Ser.: bk.4). (ENG.). 96p. (J). (gr. 1-3). pap. 4.99 *(978-0-545-87368-0(1))* Scholastic, Inc.

—The Science Fair Is Freaky! 2016. (Eerie Elementary — Branches Ser.: bk.4). (ENG.). (J). lib. bdg. 14.75 *(978-0-606-38806-1(0))* Turtleback Bks.

Chapman, Karen B. The Marino Mission: One Girl, One Mission, One Thousand Words - 1,000 Need-to-Know New 'SAT Vocabulary Words. 2004. (ENG.). 336p. pap. 15.99 *(978-0-7645-7831-1(6))* Houghton Mifflin Harcourt Publishing Co.

Clenott, Peter. Devolution. 2013. 280p. pap. *(978-1-927792-14-8(2))* Imajin Bks.

Cole, Joanna. The Science Fair Expedition. Degen, Bruce, illus. 2006. (Magic School Bus Ser.). (ENG.). 56p. (J). (gr. 2-5). 17.99 *(978-0-590-10824-9(7),* Scholastic) Scholastic, Inc.

Collins, Janet Ann. The Peril of the Sinister Scientist. 2009. 98p. pap. 7.95 *(978-1-935137-79-5(4))* Guardian Angel Publishing, Inc.

Collins Staff. Amazing Mathematicians, Level 2. 2014. (Collins English Readers Ser.). (ENG.). 80p. pap. 13.95 incl. audio compact disk *(978-0-00-754503-2(7))* HarperCollins Pubs. Ltd. GBR. Dist: Independent Pubs. Group.

Colvin, S. R. R. The Krybosian Stairpath: Magnetic Reversal. 2009. 200p. pap. 14.95 *(978-1-4401-5927-5(0))* iUniverse, Inc.

Cowan, Jennifer. Earthgirl. 2013. 272p. pap. *(978-1-4596-6502-6(3))* ReadHowYouWant.com, Ltd.

Cummings, Troy. Sneeze of the Octo-Schnozz. 2016. (Notebook of Doom Ser.: 11). lib. bdg. 14.75 ***(978-0-606-39714-8(0))*** Turtleback Bks.

Dean, Ramsey. Riding on a Beam of Light: Albert Einstein. Hamdan, Noah, illus. 2013. 48p. pap. 10.48 *(978-0-9893372-1-2(9))* Ramsey Dean, Inc.

Del Toro, Gladys. The Mutation of Black Cat, 1 vol. 2009. 76p. pap. 16.95 *(978-1-61546-487-6(5))* PublishAmerica, Inc.

Dexter & Missy the Kitten. 2004. (J). per. 15.99 *(978-0-9753533-1-8(4))* Golden Eagle Publishing Hse., Inc.

Dexter Rescues Matt the Duckling. 2004. (J). per. 15.99 *(978-0-9753533-3-2(0))* Golden Eagle Publishing Hse., Inc.

Dexter the Hamster Gets Lost. 2004. (J). per. 15.99 *(978-0-9753533-2-5(2))* Golden Eagle Publishing Hse., Inc.

Duncan, Alexandra. Sound. 2015. (Salvage Ser.: 2). (ENG.). 496p. (YA). (gr. 8). 17.99 *(978-0-06-222017-2(9),* Greenwillow Bks.) HarperCollins Pubs.

Durst, Sarah Beth. Ice. (ENG.). (YA). (gr. 7). 2010. 336p. pap. 8.99 *(978-1-4169-8644-7(8))* 2009. 320p. 16.99 *(978-1-4169-8643-0(X))* McElderry, Margaret K. Bks. (McElderry, Margaret K. Bks.).

Ferrie, Chris. Goodnight Lab. 2017. (ENG.). 32p. (J). (-3). 17.99 ***(978-1-4926-5617-3(8)***, Sourcebooks Jabberwocky) Sourcebooks, Inc.

Furlong, C. T. Killer Genes. 2012. (Arctic6 Adventure Ser.). 192p. (YA). (gr. 4-6). pap. 45.54 *(978-0-7613-9209-5(2))* Lerner Publishing Group.

—Killer Strangelets. 2011. (Arctic6 Ser.). 208p. (J). pap. *(978-0-9562315-6-7(X))* Inside Pocket Publishing, Ltd.

Furlong, Carol T. Killer Genes. 2012. (Arctic6 Adventure Ser.). 192p. (YA). (gr. 4-6). pap. 7.99 *(978-0-9562315-7-4(8))* Lerner Publishing Group.

Graves, Annie. Frankenkids. 2015. (Nightmare Club Ser.: 5). (ENG., Illus.). 64p. (J). (gr. 2-5). pap. 6.99 *(978-1-4677-6043-0(9))* Lerner Publishing Group.

—Frankenkids. McElhinney, Glenn, illus. 2015. (Nightmare Club Ser.: 5). (ENG.). 64p. (J). (gr. 2-5). lib. bdg. 25.32 *(978-1-4677-4352-5(6))* Lerner Publishing Group.

Hamilton, Kersten. The Tick-Tock Man. Hamilton, James, illus. 2016. (Gadgets & Gears Ser.: 3). (ENG.). 144p. (J). (gr. 2-5). 16.99 *(978-0-544-43300-7(9))* Houghton Mifflin Harcourt Publishing Co.

Hawking, Stephen W. & Hawking, Lucy. George's Secret Key to the Universe. Parsons, Garry, illus. 2009. (George's Secret Key Ser.). (ENG.). 336p. (J). (gr. 3-7). pap. 12.99 *(978-1-4169-8584-6(0),* Simon & Schuster Bks. For Young Readers) Simon & Schuster Bks. For Young Readers.

Hawkins, Matt. Think Tank, Vol. 1. 2012. (ENG., Illus.). 120p. (YA). pap. 14.99 *(978-1-60706-660-6(2),* 9781607066606) Image Comics.

Holm, Jennifer L. The Fourteenth Goldfish. 2015. (CHI.). 264p. (J). pap. *(978-986-320-783-2(7))* Commonwealth Publishing Co., Ltd.

—The Fourteenth Goldfish. (ENG.). (J). (gr. 3-7). 2016. 240p. 7.99 *(978-0-375-87114-6(4),* Yearling) 2014. 208p. 16.99 *(978-0-375-87064-4(4),* Random Hse. Bks. for Young Readers) 2014. 208p. lib. bdg. 19.99 *(978-0-375-97064-1(9),* Random Hse. Bks. for Young Readers) Random Hse. Children's Bks.

—The Fourteenth Goldfish. 2016. lib. bdg. 18.40 *(978-0-606-38465-0(0))* Turtleback Bks.

Jayasuriya, Michael. The Time MacHine. 2011. 66p. pap. 15.99 *(978-1-4653-3741-2(5))* Xlibris Corp.

Jones, C. B. The Cats' Meow. Green, Chris, illus. 2017. (Bog Hollow Boys Ser.). (ENG.). 72p. (gr. 4-5). lib. bdg. 25.32 *(978-1-4965-4057-7(3))* Stone Arch Bks.

Kelly, Jacqueline. La Evolución de Calpurnia Tate. 2010.Tr. of Evolution of Calpurnia Tate. (SPA.). 272p. (YA). pap. 20.95 *(978-84-9918-103-5(1))* Roca Editorial ESP. Dist: Spanish Pubs., LLC.

—La Evolucion de Calpurnia Tate, Vol. 2. 2011.Tr. of Evolution of Calpurnia Tate. (SPA.). 272p. pap. 12.95 *(978-84-92833-15-3(7))* Roca Editorial ESP. Dist: Spanish Pubs., LLC.

—The Evolution of Calpurnia Tate. 2009. (Calpurnia Tate Ser.: 1). (ENG.). 352p. (J). (gr. 4-7). 17.99 *(978-0-8050-8841-0(5),* 9780805088410, Holt, Henry & Co. Bks. For Young Readers) Holt, Henry & Co.

—The Evolution of Calpurnia Tate. 2010. 340p. 18.00 *(978-1-60686-849-2(7))* Perfection Learning Corp.

—The Evolution of Calpurnia Tate. 2011. (Calpurnia Tate Ser.: 1). (ENG.). 368p. (J). (gr. 4-7). pap. 7.99 *(978-0-312-65930-1(X),* 9780312659301) Square Fish.

—The Evolution of Calpurnia Tate. 2011. (Calpurnia Tate Ser.: 1). (J). lib. bdg. 18.40 *(978-0-606-20974-8(3),* Turtleback) Turtleback Bks.

King, J. Eric & Graham, Greg. Byron Carmichael Book One: The Human Corpse Trade. Mizer, Lindsay, ed. Warner, Michael, illus. 2008. (ENG.). 408p. (gr. 8-12). 18.95 *(978-0-615-15770-2(X))* G & K Publishing.

Kirby, Matthew J. The Arctic Code. 2015. (Dark Gravity Sequence Ser.: 1). (ENG.). 336p. (J). (gr. 3-7). 16.99 *(978-0-06-222487-3(5))* HarperCollins Pubs.

Klages, Ellen. The Green Glass Sea. 2008. (ENG.). 368p. (J). (gr. 3-7). 8.99 *(978-0-14-241149-0(3),* Puffin Books) Penguin Young Readers Group.

—The Green Glass Sea. 2008. 321p. (gr. 4-7). 19.00 *(978-0-7569-8931-6(0))* Perfection Learning Corp.

Langdale, Mark Roland. Professor Doppelganger & the Fantastical Cloud Factory. 2012. 106p. pap. *(978-1-78003-267-2(6))* Pen Pr. Pubs., Ltd.

Larry, H. I. Poison Island. Oswald, Ash, illus. 2008. (Zac Power Ser.: 1). (ENG.). 96p. (J). (gr. 3-6). pap. 5.99 *(978-0-312-34659-1(X),* 9780312346591) Square Fish.

Lassiter, Rhiannon. Shadows. 2011. (Hex Ser.: 2). (ENG.). 272p. (YA). (gr. 7). pap. 12.99 *(978-1-4424-3103-4(2),* Simon Pulse) Simon Pulse.

Latham, Jean Lee. Carry on, Mr. Bowditch. 2003. (ENG., Illus.). 256p. (YA). (gr. 7). pap. 7.99 *(978-0-618-25074-5(3))* Houghton Mifflin Harcourt Publishing Co.

Linke, Glenn Colin. The Gargantuan Boy. 2011. 102p. pap. 30.50 *(978-1-60976-079-3(4),* Eloquent Bks.) Strategic Book Publishing & Rights Agency (SBPRA).

Lopuszynski, Barbara. Angel & Brie. 2013. (ENG.). 246p. (YA). pap. 14.95 *(978-1-4787-0886-5(7))* Outskirts Pr., Inc.

Lumry, Amanda & Hurwitz, Laura. Operation Orangutan. 2007. (Adventures of Riley (Unnumbered) Ser.). (Illus.). 36p. (J). (gr. -1-3). 15.95 *(978-0-9748411-4-4(5))* Eaglemont Pr.

Lyga, Barry. The Secret Sea. 2016. (ENG.). 448p. (J). 16.99 *(978-1-250-07283-2(2),* 9781250072832) Feiwel & Friends.

MacDonald, Tom. Secret of the Tree: Marcus Speer's Ecosentinel. Stieber, Joel, illus. 2009. 300p. pap. 18.95 *(978-0-595-52402-0(8))* iUniverse, Inc.

The Mad Scientist, 6 vols. (Woodland Mysteriestm Ser.). 133p. (gr. 3-7). 42.50 *(978-0-7802-7928-5(X))* Wright Group/McGraw-Hill.

Manga University Staff. My First PC: The Comic Book That Teaches You about the Internet. 2012. 128p. (J). pap. 9.99 *(978-4-921205-28-7(0))* Japanime Co., Ltd. JPN. Dist: Diamond Bk. Distributors.

Marsh, Carole. The Behemoth Blizzard Mystery. (Masters of Disasters Ser.). (Illus.). 118p. (J). (gr. 3-5). 2008. per. 5.99 *(978-0-635-06464-6(2))* 2007. 14.95 *(978-0-635-06467-7(7))* Gallopade International.

—The Earthshaking Earthquake Mystery! 2007. (Masters of Disasters Ser.). (Illus.). 118p. (J). (gr. 2-9). per. 5.99 *(978-0-635-06339-7(5))* Gallopade International.

—The Ferocious Forest Fire Mystery. 2008. (Masters of Disasters Ser.). (Illus.). 118p. (J). (gr. 3-5). 14.95 *(978-0-635-06468-4(5))*; per. 5.99 *(978-0-635-06465-3(0))* Gallopade International.

—The Horrendous Hurricane Mystery. 2007. (Masters of Disasters Ser.). (Illus.). 118p. (J). (gr. 2-9). 14.95 *(978-0-635-06396-0(4))*; per. 7.99 *(978-0-635-06340-3(9))* Gallopade International.

—The Treacherous Tornado Mystery. 2007. (Masters of Disasters Ser.). (Illus.). 118p. (J). (gr. 2-9). 14.95 *(978-0-635-06394-6(8))*; per. 5.99 *(978-0-635-06338-0(7))* Gallopade International.

—The Voracious Volcano Mystery. 2008. (Masters of Disasters Ser.). (Illus.). 118p. (J). (gr. 3-5). 14.95 *(978-0-635-06466-0(9))*; per. 5.99 *(978-0-635-06463-9(4))* Gallopade International.

Mazzola, Lori E. The Forbidden Forest: Tales of the Tree People, 1 vol. 2009. 151p. pap. 24.95 *(978-1-4489-2656-5(4))* America Star Bks.

McElligott, Matthew & Tuxbury, Larry David. Benjamin Franklinstein Lives! McElligott, Matthew, illus. 2010. (Benjamin Franklinstein Ser.: 1). (ENG., Illus.). 128p. (J). (gr. 3-7). 12.99 *(978-0-399-25229-7(0),* G.P. Putnam's Sons Books for Young Readers) Penguin Young Readers Group.

—Benjamin Franklinstein Meets the Fright Brothers. McElligott, Matthew, illus. 2011. (Benjamin Franklinstein Ser.). (ENG., Illus.). 176p. (J). (gr. 3-7). E-Book *(978-1-101-53556-1(3),* Puffin Books) Penguin Young Readers Group.

Mead, Richelle. Silver Shadows. 2015. (Bloodlines Ser.: 5). (ENG.). 416p. (YA). (gr. 7). pap. 9.99 *(978-1-59514-632-8(6),* Razorbill) Penguin Young Readers Group.

Melville, V. H. Livia the Scientist. 2007. 20p. per. 24.95 *(978-1-4241-8547-4(5))* America Star Bks.

Mills, Rachel. Wraiths. 2010. 269p. pap. 18.95 *(978-1-4461-4326-1(0))* Lulu Pr., Inc.

Miss Gomez's Third Grade Class Staff. Wacky Stories from Wisdom Academy for Young Scientists. 2013. (ENG.). 63p. (YA). pap. 16.95 *(978-1-4787-1103-2(5))* Outskirts Pr., Inc.

Montgomery, R. A. The Brilliant Dr. Wogan. 2005. (Choose Your Own Adventure Ser.). (Illus.). 112p. (gr. 4-8). pap. 5.50 *(978-0-7608-9705-8(0))* Sundance/Newbridge Educational Publishing.

Munday, Dj. The Secret Dummy of Joshua Bean. 2008. 84p. pap. *(978-1-84923-029-2(3))* YouWriteOn.

Nye, Bill & Mone, Gregory. Jack & the Geniuses: At the Bottom of the World. Iluzada, Nicholas, illus. 2017. (ENG.). 256p. (J). (gr. 3-7). 13.95 *(978-1-4197-2303-2(0),* Amulet Bks.) Abrams, Inc.

Onion Head Monster Attacks. 2007. (YA). per. 12.95 *(978-0-9793676-0-1(3))* Friedrich, Paul.

Onion Head Monster Attacks (XL) 2006. per. 19.99 *(978-0-9793676-3-2(8))* Friedrich, Paul.

Osorio, Rick. The Great Adventure of Sally Rock & el Lobo. 2007. (ENG.). 96p. per. 19.95 *(978-1-4241-5869-0(9))* America Star Bks.

The Perfect Person, 6 Packs. (Bookweb Ser.). 32p. (gr. 4-18). 34.00 *(978-0-7635-3734-0(9))* Rigby Education.

The Perfect Pet, 6 Packs. (Bookweb Ser.). 32p. (gr. 5-18). 34.00 *(978-0-7635-3781-4(0))* Rigby Education.

Perritano, John. The Comet of Doom, 1 vol. Laughead, Mike, illus. 2014. (Kid Squad Saves the World Ser.). (ENG.). 112p. (J). (gr. 8-12). 27.07 *(978-1-62402-038-4(0))* Magic Wagon.

—Madness of Captain Cyclops, 1 vol. 2014. (Kid Squad Saves the World Ser.). (ENG.). 112p. (J). (gr. 8-12). lib. bdg. 27.07 *(978-1-62402-040-7(2),* Calico Chapter Bks) Magic Wagon.

—The Snickerblooms & the Age Bug, 1 vol. Laughead, Mike, illus. 2014. (Kid Squad Saves the World Ser.). (ENG.). 112p. (J). (gr. 8-12). 27.07 *(978-1-62402-041-4(0))* Magic Wagon.

Peterfreund, Diana. Omega City. 2015. (Omega City Ser.: 1). (ENG.). 336p. (J). (gr. 3-7). 16.99 *(978-0-06-231085-9(2))* HarperCollins Pubs.

Rand, Johnathan. American Chillers #23 Wicked Velociraptors of West Virginia. 2008. 208p. (J). pap. 5.99 *(978-1-893699-94-6(3))* AudioCraft Publishing, Inc.

Random House Staff. Monkey Business (Teenage Mutant Ninja Turtles) Random House Staff & Spaziante, Patrick, illus. 2013. (Pictureback(R) Ser.). (ENG.). 16p. (J). (gr. -1-2). 3.99 *(978-0-449-81852-7(7),* Random Hse. Bks. for Young Readers) Random Hse. Children's Bks.

Reiche, Dietlof & Brownjohn, John. Freddy in Peril: Book Two in the Golden Hamster Saga. Cepeda, Joe, illus. 2004. 202p. (J). pap. *(978-0-439-64984-1(6))* Scholastic, Inc.

Reid, Roger. Space. 2008. (ENG.). 160p. (J). 19.95 *(978-1-58838-230-6(3),* NewSouth Bks.) NewSouth, Inc.

Richards, C. J. Battle of the Bots. Fujita, Goro, illus. (Robots Rule Ser.: 3). (ENG.). 240p. (J). (gr. 2-5). 2017. pap. 6.99 *(978-0-544-93524-2(1))* 2015. 13.99 *(978-0-544-33932-3(0))* Houghton Mifflin Harcourt Publishing Co. (HMH Books For Young Readers).

—Battle of the Bots. 2017. (Robots Rule Ser.: 3). (ENG.). (J). (gr. 2-5). lib. bdg. 17.20 ***(978-0-606-39811-4(2))*** Turtleback Bks.

Rogers, Buddy & Avery, Ben. Power Play, 1 vol. Wong, Scott, illus. 2008. (Z Graphic Novels / TimeFlyz Ser.). (ENG.). 160p. (J). pap. 6.99 *(978-0-310-71365-4(X))* Zondervan.

Rose, John. Wikker. 2007. 248p. pap. 17.95 *(978-1-4303-1523-0(7))* Lulu Pr., Inc.

Rossiter, Nan Parson. The Fo'c'sle: Henry Beston's Outermost House. 2012. (Illus.). 32p. (J). (gr. 5-18). 17.95 *(978-1-56792-433-6(6))* Godine, David R. Pub.

Roy, Philip. Me & Mr. Bell: A Novel, 1 vol. 2013. (ENG.). 140p. pap. *(978-1-927492-55-0(6))* Cape Breton Univ. Pr.

Schwartz, Tom. Spaceship Earth: A Beginning Without End. 2010. 172p. pap. 10.99 *(978-1-57545-151-0(4))*; 19.99 *(978-1-57545-143-5(3))* RP Media. (Reagent Pr. Bks. for Young Readers).

Shelley, Mary. Frankenstein. Irving, Frazer, illus. 2005. 176p. (gr. 3-7). 21.00 *(978-0-7569-5809-1(1))* Perfection Learning Corp.

—Frankenstein. 2010. (ENG., Illus.). 28p. 29.95 *(978-0-7893-2085-8(1))* Universe Publishing.

—Frankenstein: The Graphic Novel. 2010. (Classic Graphic Novel Collection). (ENG., Illus.). 144p. (YA). (gr. 7-12). 34.80 *(978-1-4205-0374-6(X))* Cengage Gale.

Shreve, Steve. Stan & the Toilet Monster, 0 vols. 2011. (ENG.). 164p. (J). (gr. 2-6). 12.99 *(978-0-7614-5977-4(4),* 9780761459774, Amazon Children's Publishing) Amazon Publishing.

Simonson, Louise. Snow White & the Seven Robots. Sanchez, Jimena, illus. 2015. (Far Out Fairy Tales Ser.). (ENG.). 40p. (gr. 3-4). lib. bdg. 25.32 *(978-1-4342-9648-1(2))* Stone Arch Bks.

Sipperley, Keli. Ice Cream with Albert Einstein. 2016. (Time Hop Sweets Shop Ser.). (ENG.). 32p. (gr. k-3). 25.65 *(978-1-68191-376-6(3))* Rourke Educational Media.

Smith, Roland. Tentacles. 2009. (ENG.). 336p. (J). (gr. 3-7). 16.99 *(978-0-545-16688-1(8),* Scholastic Pr.) Scholastic, Inc.

Sonnebom, Scott. Feet First. Banks, Timothy, illus. 2014. (Frankenstein Journals). (ENG.). 80p. (gr. 2-3). 22.65 *(978-1-4342-8999-5(0))* Stone Arch Bks.

—The Frankenstein Journals, 1 vol. Banks, Timothy, illus. 2014. (Frankenstein Journals). (ENG.). 160p. (gr. 2-3). 9.95 *(978-1-4342-9130-1(8))* Stone Arch Bks.

—No Guts, No Gloria. Banks, Timothy, illus. 2015. (Frankenstein Journals). (ENG.). 80p. (gr. 2-3). 22.65 *(978-1-4965-0221-6(3))* Stone Arch Bks.

—A Pain in the Butt. Banks, Timothy, illus. 2015. (Frankenstein Journals). (ENG.). 80p. (gr. 2-3). 22.65 *(978-1-4965-0222-3(1))* Stone Arch Bks.

Spradlin, Michael P. Menace from the Deep. 2013. (Killer Species Ser.: 1). lib. bdg. 16.00 *(978-0-606-32447-2(X),* Turtleback) Turtleback Bks.

Springham, James. Earth-n-Bones: Toxic. 2005. 56p. pap. 16.95 *(978-1-4137-9755-8(5))* America Star Bks.

Stine, R. L. Frankenstein's Dog. 2013. (Goosebumps Most Wanted Ser.: 4). (ENG.). 160p. (J). (gr. 3-7). pap. 6.99 *(978-0-545-41801-0(1),* Scholastic Paperbacks) Scholastic, Inc.

—Frankenstein's Dog. 2013. (Goosebumps Most Wanted Ser.: 4). 136p. (J). lib. bdg. 17.20 *(978-0-606-32006-1(7),* Turtleback) Turtleback Bks.

Tatulli, Mark, et al. Lio: Making Friends. 2013. (Lio Ser.: 8). (ENG., Illus.). 224p. (J). pap. 9.99 *(978-1-4494-2558-6(5))* Andrews McMeel Publishing.

Thomas, Carroll, creator. Under the Open Sky: A Matty Trescott Novel. 2005. (Illus.). 184p. (J). per. 12.95 *(978-0-9762091-2-6(8))* Antrim Hse.

Thomas, Rich. The Incredible Hulk: An Origin Story, 1 vol. Semeiks, Val, illus. 2012. (Marvel Origins Ser.). (ENG.). 48p. (J). (gr. -1-4). lib. bdg. 24.21 *(978-1-61479-009-9(4))* Spotlight.

Thrasher, Amanda M. A Fairy Match in the Mushroom Patch. 2013. (ENG., Illus.). 162p. (J). (gr. 2-4). pap. 7.99 *(978-0-9888568-1-3(6))* Rising Phoenix Pr.

Torres, Mario J. The Incredible Adventures of Kaplan & Dylan: Book One: Present, 1 vol. 2009. 159p. pap. 24.95 *(978-1-4489-9513-4(2))* PublishAmerica, Inc.

Torrey, Michele. The Case of the Terrible T. Rex. Newman, Barbara Johansen, illus. 2010. (Doyle & Fossey, Science Detectives Ser.). (ENG.). 96p. (J). (gr. 3-5). pap. 6.95 *(978-1-4027-4966-7(X))* Sterling Publishing Co., Inc.

Toufexis, George. MONSTER MASH-Up — Rise of the Predators. 2014. (ENG., Illus.). 48p. (J). (gr. 4). pap. 4.99 *(978-0-486-49224-7(9))* Dover Pubns., Inc.

—MONSTER MASH-Up — Robots' Revenge. 2014. (ENG., Illus.). 48p. (J). (gr. 4). pap. 4.99 *(978-0-486-49225-4(7))* Dover Pubns., Inc.

Trent, Tiffany. The Unnaturalists. 2013. (ENG., Illus.). 336p. (YA). (gr. 7). pap. 9.99 *(978-1-4424-2207-0(6),* Simon & Schuster Bks. For Young Readers) Simon & Schuster Bks. For Young Readers.

Trine, Greg. Attack of the Valley Girls. Montijo, Rhode, illus. 6th ed. 2008. (Melvin Beederman, Superhero Ser.: 6). (ENG.). 144p. (J). (gr. 2-5). pap. 8.99 *(978-0-8050-8161-9(5),* 9780805081619) Square Fish.

Trod, Mariano, et al, illus. The Brilliant Dr. Wogan. 2007. (Choose Your Own Adventure Ser.: No. 17). 112p. (J). (gr. 4-7). per. 6.99 *(978-1-933390-17-8(4),* CHC:17) Chooseco LLC.

Villeneuve, Kevin J. The Adventures of Nick the Ecologist & His Robot O-Zone: The Mystery of the Missing Trees. 2007. 96p. per. 9.95 *(978-0-595-42362-0(0))* iUniverse, Inc.

Walsh, Ann. Flower Power. 2006. (Orca Currents Ser.). 107p. (gr. 5-9). 19.95 *(978-0-7569-6874-8(7))* Perfection Learning Corp.

Walters, Eric. Visions. 2011. (ENG.). 208p. (J). pap. *(978-1-55455-122-4(6))* Fitzhenry & Whiteside, Ltd.

Wells, H. G. The Invisible Man. Calero, Dennis, illus. 2010. (Classic Fiction Ser.). 72p. pap. 0.60 *(978-1-4342-3208-3(5)*, Graphic Revolve) Stone Arch Bks.

SCIENTISTS, AFRICAN AMERICAN

see African American Scientists

SCILLY, ISLES OF (ENGLAND)—FICTION

Morpurgo, Michael. Why the Whales Came. 2nd ed. 2017. (ENG., Illus.). 192p. (J). (gr. 5-7). pap. 9.99 ***(978-1-4052-2925-8(X))*** Egmont Bks., Ltd. GBR. Dist: Independent Pubs. Group.

SCOOBY-DOO (FICTITIOUS CHARACTER)—FICTION

ABDO Publishing. Scooby-Doo Comic Readers. 2016. (Scooby-Doo Comic Readers Ser.: 6). (ENG.). 32p. (J). (gr. k-3). lib. bdg. 145.26 *(978-1-61479-450-9(2)*, Graphic Planet) Magic Wagon.

Abdo Publishing. Scooby-Doo Graphic Novels Set 3, 1 vol. 2013. (Scooby-Doo Graphic Novels Set 3 Ser.: 6). (ENG.). 24p. (J). (gr. 2-6). lib. bdg. 145.26 *(978-1-61479-048-8(5)*, Essential Library) ABDO Publishing Co.

—Scooby-Doo Mysteries Set 2, 1 vol. 2013. (Scooby-Doo Mysteries Set 2 Ser.: 6). (ENG.). 64p. (J). (gr. 3-6). lib. bdg. 145.26 *(978-1-61479-041-9(8)*, Essential Library) ABDO Publishing Co.

—Scooby-Doo! Picture Clue Books, 1 vol. 2013. (Scooby-Doo! Picture Clue Bks.: 6). (ENG.). 24p. (J). (gr. -1-1). lib. bdg. 145.26 *(978-1-61479-034-1(5))* ABDO Publishing Co.

ABDO Publishing Company Staff & Howard, Lee. Scooby-Doo Comic Storybook. Alcadia SNC Staff, illus. 2014. (Scooby-Doo Comic Storybook Ser.: 4). (ENG.). 32p. (J). (gr. 5-9). lib. bdg. 96.84 *(978-1-61479-280-2(1)*, Graphic Planet) Magic Wagon.

Adamson, Heather & Adamson, Thomas K. Scooby-Doo! a Time Mystery: The Case of the Spinning Spook. Neely, Scott, illus. 2017. (Solve It with Scooby-Doo!: Math Ser.). (ENG.). 24p. (gr. k-2). lib. bdg. 27.99 ***(978-1-5157-7910-0(6))*** Capstone Press of Coughlan Cos.

—Scooby-Doo! an Estimation Mystery: The Case of the Greedy Ghost. Neely, Scott, illus. 2017. (Solve It with Scooby-Doo!: Math Ser.). (ENG.). 24p. (gr. k-2). lib. bdg. 27.99 ***(978-1-5157-7905-6(X))*** Capstone Press of Coughlan Cos.

Auerbach, Annie. Scooby-Doo in the Coolsville Contraption Contest, 1 vol. 2016. (Scooby-Doo! Set 3 Ser.). (ENG., Illus.). 32p. (J). (gr. k-4). lib. bdg. 24.21 *(978-1-61479-409-7(X))* Spotlight.

—Scooby-Doo in the Mystery Mansion, 1 vol. 2016. (Scooby-Doo! Set 3 Ser.). (ENG., Illus.). 32p. (J). (gr. k-4). lib. bdg. 24.21 *(978-1-61479-411-0(1)*, 1401187) Spotlight.

Balaban, Mariah. Scooby-Doo! & the Haunted Diner. 2010. (Illus.). 31p. (J). *(978-0-545-20882-6(3))* Scholastic, Inc.

—Scooby-Doo & the Rotten Robot, 1 vol. Duendes Del Sur Staff, illus. 2012. (Scooby-Doo! Set 2 Ser.: No. 2). (ENG.). 24p. (J). (gr. k-3). lib. bdg. 24.21 *(978-1-59961-868-5(0))* Spotlight.

—Scooby-Doo & the Scary Snowman, 1 vol. Duendes Del Sur Staff, illus. 2012. (Scooby-Doo! Set 2 Ser.: No. 2). (ENG.). 24p. (J). (gr. k-3). lib. bdg. 24.21 *(978-1-59961-869-2(9))* Spotlight.

—Scooby-Doo & the Thanksgiving Terror, 1 vol. Duendes Del Sur Staff, illus. 2012. (Scooby-Doo! Set 2 Ser.: No. 2). (ENG.). 24p. (J). (gr. k-3). lib. bdg. 24.21 *(978-1-59961-870-8(2))* Spotlight.

Barbo, Maria S. Catnapped Caper, 1 vol. 2013. (Scooby-Doo! Picture Clue Bks.). (ENG.). 24p. (J). (gr. -1-1). lib. bdg. 24.21 *(978-1-61479-035-8(3)*, Essential Library) ABDO Publishing Co.

—Treasure Hunt, 1 vol. 2013. (Scooby-Doo! Picture Clue Bks.). (ENG.). 24p. (J). (gr. -1-1). lib. bdg. 24.21 *(978-1-61479-040-2(X)*, Essential Library) ABDO Publishing Co.

Bird, Benjamin. Scooby-Doo! Little Mysteries. 2015. (Scooby-Doo! Little Mysteries Ser.). (ENG.). 20p. (gr. -1 — 1). bds. 31.96 *(978-1-62370-449-0(9))* Capstone Press of Coughlan Cos.

—Scooby-Doo's 1-2-3 Mystery. 2015. (Scooby-Doo! Little Mysteries Ser.). (ENG., Illus.). 20p. (gr. -1 — 1). bds. 7.99 *(978-1-62370-177-2(5))* Capstone Press of Coughlan Cos.

—Scooby-Doo's ABC Mystery. 2015. (Scooby-Doo! Little Mysteries Ser.). (ENG., Illus.). 20p. (gr. -1 — 1). bds. 7.99 *(978-1-62370-175-8(9))* Capstone Press of Coughlan Cos.

—Scooby-Doo's Color Mystery. 2015. (Scooby-Doo! Little Mysteries Ser.). (ENG., Illus.). 20p. (gr. -1 — 1). bds. 7.99 *(978-1-62370-176-5(7))* Capstone Press of Coughlan Cos.

—Scooby-Doo's Shape Mystery. 2015. (Scooby-Doo! Little Mysteries Ser.). (ENG., Illus.). 20p. (gr. -1 — 1). bds. 7.99 *(978-1-62370-178-9(3))* Capstone Press of Coughlan Cos.

Bright, J. E. The Case of the Cheese Thief, 1 vol. Neely, Scott, illus. 2014. (You Choose Stories: Scooby-Doo Ser.). (ENG.). 112p. (gr. 2-3). pap. 6.95 *(978-1-4342-7927-9(8)*, You Choose Bks.) Capstone Press of Coughlan Cos.

Bright, J. E., et al. You Choose Stories: Scooby-Doo. 2016. (You Choose Stories: Scooby-Doo Ser.). (ENG.). 112p. (gr. 2-3). 391.80 *(978-1-4965-2669-4(4)*, You Choose Bks.) Capstone Press of Coughlan Cos.

Busch, Robbie. Scooby-Doo in Barnstormin' Banshee, 1 vol. Williams, Anthony, illus. 2010. (Scooby-Doo Graphic Novels Ser.: No. 1). (ENG.). 24p. (J). (gr. 2-5). 24.21 *(978-1-59961-691-9(2))* Spotlight.

—Scooby-Doo in Don't Play Dummy with Me, 1 vol. Deporter, Vincent, illus. 2010. (Scooby-Doo Graphic Novels Ser.: No. 1). (ENG.). 24p. (J). (gr. 2-5). 24.21 *(978-1-59961-693-3(9))* Spotlight.

—Scooby-Doo in Ready-to-Werewolf, 1 vol. Matchette, Karen, illus. 2010. (Scooby-Doo Graphic Novels Ser.: No. 1). (ENG.). 24p. (J). (gr. 2-5). 24.21 *(978-1-59961-696-4(3))* Spotlight.

—Scooby-Doo in the Agony of de Feet!, 1 vol. Pope, Robert, illus. 2010. (Scooby-Doo Graphic Novels Ser.: No. 1). (ENG.). 24p. (J). (gr. 2-5). 24.21 *(978-1-59961-690-2(4))* Spotlight.

Class 1-208. Pizza Place Ghost, 1 vol. 2013. (Scooby-Doo! Picture Clue Bks.). (ENG.). 24p. (J). (gr. -1-1). lib. bdg. 24.21 *(978-1-61479-038-9(8)*, Essential Library) ABDO Publishing Co.

Collins, Terry & Weakland, Mark. Unmasking Monsters with Scooby-Doo! Cornia, Christian et al, illus. 2015. (Unmasking Monsters with Scooby-Doo! Ser.). (ENG.). 24p. (gr. 1-2). lib. bdg. 155.94 *(978-1-4914-1797-3(8))* Capstone Press of Coughlan Cos.

Cooley Peterson, Megan. Scooby-Doo Solves It with S. T. E. M. Brizuela, Dario & Cornia, Christian, illus. 2016. (Scooby-Doo Solves It with S. T. E. M. Ser.). (ENG.). 32p. (gr. 3-4). 111.96 *(978-1-5157-2663-0(0))* Capstone Press of Coughlan Cos.

Cunningham, Scott. Scooby-Doo & the Hungry Ghost. Duendes Del Sur Staff, illus. 2005. (Scooby Doo Ser.). (ENG.). 12p. (J). (gr. -1-3). 8.99 *(978-0-439-74882-7(8))* Scholastic, Inc.

—Scooby-Doo in Terror Is Afoot!, 1 vol. Neely, Scott, illus. 2010. (Scooby-Doo Graphic Novels Ser.: No. 1). (ENG.). 24p. (J). (gr. 2-5). 24.21 *(978-1-59961-698-8(X))* Spotlight.

Cunningham, Scott & Barrios, Roberto. Scooby-Doo & the Shadow Goblin, 1 vol. 2012. (Scooby-Doo Graphic Novels Ser.: No. 2). (ENG., Illus.). 24p. (J). (gr. 2-5). 24.21 *(978-1-59961-917-0(2))* Spotlight.

Dahl, Michael. Scooby Doo Joke Books. Jeralds, Scott, illus. 2015. (Scooby-Doo Joke Bks.). (ENG.). 64p. (gr. 2-3). lib. bdg. 90.60 *(978-1-4965-0300-8(7)*, Scooby-Doo) Stone Arch Bks.

Fertig, Michael P. Musical Mystery Scooby Doo! McKee, Darren, illus. 2007. (Scooby Doo Ser.). (J). (gr. -1-3). 12.98 *(978-1-4127-7429-1(2))* Publications International, Ltd.

Fisch, Sholly. Scooby-Doo in Fangs, but No Fangs!, 1 vol. 2013. (Scooby-Doo Graphic Novels Set 3 Ser.). (ENG.). 24p. (J). (gr. 2-6). lib. bdg. 24.21 *(978-1-61479-051-8(5)*, Essential Library) ABDO Publishing Co.

—Scooby-Doo in Trick or Treat!, 1 vol. Staton, Joe, illus. 2010. (Scooby-Doo Graphic Novels Ser.: No. 1). (ENG.). 24p. (J). (gr. 2-5). 24.21 *(978-1-59961-699-5(8))* Spotlight.

Gelsey, James. The Baseball Boogeyman. 2004. (Illus.). 44p. (J). *(978-0-439-55713-9(5))* Scholastic, Inc.

—Scooby-Doo! & the Carnival Creeper, 1 vol. 2013. (Scooby-Doo Mysteries Set 2 Ser.). (ENG.). 64p. (J). (gr. 3-6). lib. bdg. 24.21 *(978-1-61479-042-6(6))* ABDO Publishing Co.

—Scooby-Doo! & the Frankenstein Monster, 1 vol. 2013. (Scooby-Doo Mysteries Set 2 Ser.). (ENG.). 64p. (J). (gr. 3-6). lib. bdg. 24.21 *(978-1-61479-043-3(4))* ABDO Publishing Co.

—Scooby-Doo! & the Groovy Ghost, 1 vol. 2013. (Scooby-Doo Mysteries Set 2 Ser.). (ENG.). 64p. (J). (gr. 3-6). lib. bdg. 24.21 *(978-1-61479-044-0(2))* ABDO Publishing Co.

—Scooby-Doo! & the Gruesome Goblin, 1 vol. 2013. (Scooby-Doo Mysteries Set 2 Ser.). (ENG.). 64p. (J). (gr. 3-6). lib. bdg. 24.21 *(978-1-61479-045-7(0))* ABDO Publishing Co.

—Scooby-Doo! & the Howling Wolfman, 1 vol. 2013. (Scooby-Doo Mysteries Set 2 Ser.). (ENG.). 64p. (J). (gr. 3-6). lib. bdg. 24.21 *(978-1-61479-046-4(9))* ABDO Publishing Co.

—Scooby-Doo! & the Spooky Strikeout, 1 vol. 2013. (Scooby-Doo Mysteries Set 2 Ser.). (ENG.). 64p. (J). (gr. 3-6). lib. bdg. 24.21 *(978-1-61479-047-1(7))* ABDO Publishing Co.

Gelsey, James & Duendes Del Sur Staff. Scooby-Doo & the Karate Caper, 1 vol. 2011. (Scooby-Doo Mysteries Ser.). (ENG., Illus.). 64p. (J). (gr. 3-6). 24.21 *(978-1-59961-891-3(5))* Spotlight.

—Scooby-Doo & the Sunken Ship, 1 vol. 2011. (Scooby-Doo Mysteries Ser.). (ENG., Illus.). 64p. (J). (gr. 3-6). 24.21 *(978-1-59961-893-7(1))* Spotlight.

—Scooby-Doo & the Witch Doctor, 1 vol. 2011. (Scooby-Doo Mysteries Ser.). (ENG., Illus.). 64p. (J). (gr. 3-6). 24.21 *(978-1-59961-895-1(8))* Spotlight.

—Scooby-Doo & the Zombie's Treasure, 1 vol. 2011. (Scooby-Doo Mysteries Ser.). (ENG., Illus.). 64p. (J). (gr. 3-6). 24.21 *(978-1-59961-896-8(6))* Spotlight.

Giffen, Keith. Scooby Apocalypse Vol. 1. 2017. lib. bdg. 29.40 ***(978-0-606-39806-0(6))*** Turtleback Bks.

Griep, Heinrich & Laguna, Fabio. Scooby-Doo in Sumo A-Go-Go, 1 vol. 2012. (Scooby-Doo Graphic Novels Ser.: No. 2). (ENG., Illus.). 24p. (J). (gr. 2-5). 24.21 *(978-1-59961-923-1(7))* Spotlight.

Griep, Terrance & Batic, Leo. Scooby-Doo in Chills & Spills!, 1 vol. 2012. (Scooby-Doo Graphic Novels Ser.: No. 2). (ENG., Illus.). 24p. (J). (gr. 2-5). 24.21 *(978-1-59961-919-4(9))* Spotlight.

Griep, Terrence, Jr. Scooby-Doo in Screechy Keen, 1 vol. Matchette, Karen, illus. 2010. (Scooby-Doo Graphic Novels Ser.: No. 1). (ENG.). 24p. (J). (gr. 2-5). 24.21 *(978-1-59961-697-1(1))* Spotlight.

Gross, Scott. Scooby-Doo & the Aliens of Area 49, 1 vol. 2013. (Scooby-Doo Graphic Novels Set 3 Ser.). (ENG.). 24p. (J). (gr. 2-6). lib. bdg. 24.21 *(978-1-61479-049-5(3)*, Essential Library) ABDO Publishing Co.

Herman, Gail. Fall Fright. Duendes Del Sur Staff, illus. 2005. (Hello Reader! Ser.). 32p. (J). pap. *(978-0-439-78358-3(5))* Scholastic, Inc.

—Scooby-Doo: A Scooby-Rific Reader. 2012. (Illus.). (J). *(978-1-4351-3986-2(0))* Scholastic, Inc.

—Scooby-Doo in the Lighthouse Mystery, 1 vol. 2016. (Scooby-Doo! Set 3 Ser.). (ENG., Illus.). 32p. (J). (gr. k-4). lib. bdg. 24.21 *(978-1-61479-410-3(3))* Spotlight.

—Scooby-Doo in up, up, & Away!, 1 vol. 2016. (Scooby-Doo! Set 3 Ser.). (ENG., Illus.). 32p. (J). (gr. k-4). lib. bdg. 24.21 *(978-1-61479-412-7(X))* Spotlight.

—A Scooby-Rific Reader. Duendes Del Sur Staff, illus. 2005. (Scooby Doo Ser.). 290p. (J). *(978-0-681-15349-3(0))* Scholastic, Inc.

Hinkler Books, ed. Scooby Doo! & the Gang's Spooky Snacks. 2012. 48p. (J). 19.99 *(978-1-74308-544-8(3))* Hinkler Bks. Pty, Ltd. AUS. Dist: Ideals Pubns.

Howard, Kate. Hotel of Horrors. 2012. (Scooby Doo 8X8 Ser.). lib. bdg. 14.75 *(978-0-606-31559-3(4)*, Turtleback) Turtleback Bks.

Howard, Lee. Scooby-Doo & the High Tech House of the Future, 1 vol. 2016. (Scooby-Doo Comic Readers Ser.). (ENG.). 32p. (J). (gr. k-3). lib. bdg. 24.21 *(978-1-61479-452-3(9)*, Graphic Planet) Magic Wagon.

—Scooby-Doo & the Unnatural, 1 vol. 2016. (Scooby-Doo Comic Readers Ser.). (ENG.). 32p. (J). (gr. k-3). lib. bdg. 24.21 *(978-1-61479-453-0(7)*, Graphic Planet) Magic Wagon.

—Scooby-Doo in Bake-Off Mayhem, 1 vol. 2016. (Scooby-Doo Leveled Readers Ser.). (ENG., Illus.). 32p. (J). (gr. k-4). lib. bdg. 24.21 *(978-1-61479-418-9(9))* Spotlight.

—Scooby-Doo in Mummy Scares Best, 1 vol. 2016. (Scooby-Doo Comic Readers Ser.). (ENG.). 32p. (J). (gr. k-3). lib. bdg. 24.21 *(978-1-61479-455-4(3)*, Graphic Planet) Magic Wagon.

—Scooby-Doo in There's No Creature Like Snow Creature, 1 vol. 2016. (Scooby-Doo Comic Readers Ser.). (ENG.). 32p. (J). (gr. k-3). lib. bdg. 24.21 *(978-1-61479-456-1(1)*, Graphic Planet) Magic Wagon.

Hurley, Jo. Scooby-Doo! & the Phantom Prankster. 2005. (Illus.). 44p. *(978-0-439-73708-1(7))* Scholastic, Inc.

Ip, Ivy S. Clues at the Carnival, 1 vol. 2013. (Scooby-Doo! Picture Clue Bks.). (ENG.). 24p. (J). (gr. -1-1). lib. bdg. 24.21 *(978-1-61479-036-5(1)*, Essential Library) ABDO Publishing Co.

Korte, Steve. Curse of the Stage Fright. Neely, Scott, illus. 2016. (Scooby-Doo Comic Chapter Bks.). (ENG.). 88p. (gr. 3-7). pap. 5.95 *(978-1-4965-3587-0(1))*; lib. bdg. 27.32 *(978-1-4965-3583-2(9))* Capstone Press of Coughlan Cos.

Korte, Steve, et al. Scooby-Doo Comic Chapter Books. Neely, Scott, illus. 2016. (Scooby-Doo Comic Chapter Bks.). (ENG.). 88p. (gr. 3-7). 109.28 *(978-1-4965-3603-7(7))* Capstone Press of Coughlan Cos.

Kravitz, Darryl Taylor & Pope, Robert. Scooby-Doo in Nothing S'More Terrifying!, 1 vol. 2012. (Scooby-Doo Graphic Novels Ser.: No. 2). (ENG., Illus.). 24p. (J). (gr. 2-5). 24.21 *(978-1-59961-921-7(0))* Spotlight.

Kress, Earl. Scooby-Doo in Hear No Evil, 1 vol. Delaney, John, illus. 2010. (Scooby-Doo Graphic Novels Ser.: No. 1). (ENG.). 24p. (J). (gr. 2-5). 24.21 *(978-1-59961-694-0(7))* Spotlight.

Kupperberg, Paul. Scooby-Doo & the Night of the Undead!, 1 vol. 2013. (Scooby-Doo Graphic Novels Set 3 Ser.). (ENG.). 24p. (J). (gr. 2-6). lib. bdg. 24.21 *(978-1-61479-050-1(7)*, Essential Library) ABDO Publishing Co.

—Scooby-Doo in over the Boardwalk, 1 vol. 2013. (Scooby-Doo Graphic Novels Set 3 Ser.). (ENG., Illus.). 24p. (J). (gr. 2-6). lib. bdg. 24.21 *(978-1-61479-052-5(3)*, Essential Library) ABDO Publishing Co.

—Scooby-Doo in Read All about It!, 1 vol. 2013. (Scooby-Doo Graphic Novels Set 3 Ser.). (ENG.). 24p. (J). (gr. 2-6). lib. bdg. 24.21 *(978-1-61479-053-2(1)*, Essential Library) ABDO Publishing Co.

Kupperberg, Paul & Laguna, Fabio. Scooby-Doo Versus Them!, 1 vol. 2012. (Scooby-Doo Graphic Novels Ser.: No. 2). (ENG., Illus.). 24p. (J). (gr. 2-5). 24.21 *(978-1-59961-926-2(1))* Spotlight.

Manning, Matthew K. The Mystery of the Mayhem Mansion. Neely, Scott, illus. 2016. (You Choose Stories: Scooby-Doo Ser.). (ENG.). 112p. (gr. 2-3). lib. bdg. 32.65 *(978-1-4965-2661-8(9)*, You Choose Bks.) Capstone Press of Coughlan Cos.

—Mystery of the Mist Monster. Neely, Scott, illus. 2016. (Scooby-Doo Comic Chapter Bks.). (ENG.). 88p. (gr. 3-7). pap. 5.95 *(978-1-4965-3590-0(1))*; lib. bdg. 27.32 *(978-1-4965-3586-3(3))* Capstone Press of Coughlan Cos.

—The Salem Witch Showdown. Neely, Scott, illus. 2017. (You Choose Stories: Scooby-Doo Ser.). (ENG.). 112p. (gr. 2-3). lib. bdg. 32.65 *(978-1-4965-4334-9(3)*, You Choose Bks.) Capstone Press of Coughlan Cos.

—Secret of the Haunted Cave. Neely, Scott, illus. 2016. (Scooby-Doo Comic Chapter Bks.). (ENG.). 88p. (gr. 3-7). pap. 5.95 *(978-1-4965-3589-4(8))*; lib. bdg. 27.32 *(978-1-4965-3585-6(5))* Capstone Press of Coughlan Cos.

Manning, Matthew K. & Steele, Michael Anthony. You Choose Stories: Scooby-Doo. 2016. (You Choose Stories: Scooby-Doo Ser.). (ENG.). 112p. (gr. 2-3). pap. 13.90 *(978-1-4965-2670-0(8)*, You Choose Bks.) Capstone Press of Coughlan Cos.

Manning, Matthew K. & Sutton, Laurie S. You Choose Stories: Scooby-Doo. Neely, Scott, illus. 2017. (You Choose Stories: Scooby-Doo Ser.). (ENG.). 112p. (gr. 2-3). 457.10 *(978-1-4965-4341-7(6)*, You Choose Bks.) Capstone Press of Coughlan Cos.

McCann, Jesse Leon. Scooby-Doo & Museum Madness, 1 vol. Duendes Del Sur Staff, illus. 2012. (Scooby-Doo! Set 2 Ser.: No. 2). (ENG.). 24p. (J). (gr. k-3). lib. bdg. 24.21 *(978-1-59961-867-8(2))* Spotlight.

—Scooby-Doo & the Fishy Phantom, 1 vol. Duendes Del Sur Staff, illus. 2012. (Scooby-Doo! Set 2 Ser.: No. 2). (ENG.). 24p. (J). (gr. k-3). lib. bdg. 24.21 *(978-1-59961-866-1(4))* Spotlight.

Musacchia, Vince, illus. Scooby-Doo! The Case of the Disappearing Scooby Snacks. 2005. (Media Favorites!! Ser.). 22p. (J). 9.95 *(978-1-58117-214-0(1)*, Intervisual/Piggy Toes) Bendon, Inc.

Panini Publishing, creator. Scooby Doo! Summer Annual. 2011. (Illus.). 63p. (J). (gr. 4-7). pap. *(978-1-84653-145-3(4))* Panini Publishing.

Penney, Shannon. Decodes a Mystery. 2005. 22p. *(978-0-439-67841-4(2))* Scholastic, Inc.

Peterson, Megan Cooley. Scooby-Doo! a Science of Chemical Reactions Mystery: The over-Reacting Ghost. Brizuela, Dario, illus. 2017. (Scooby-Doo Solves It with S. T. E. M. Ser.). (ENG.). 32p. (gr. 3-4). lib. bdg. 27.99 *(978-1-5157-3697-4(0))* Capstone Press of Coughlan Cos.

—Scooby-Doo! a Science of Electricity Mystery: The Mutant Crocodile. Cornia, Christian, illus. 2017. (Scooby-Doo Solves It with S. T. E. M. Ser.). (ENG.). 32p. (gr. 3-4). lib. bdg. 27.99 *(978-1-5157-3698-1(9))* Capstone Press of Coughlan Cos.

—Scooby-Doo! a Science of Light Mystery: The Angry Alien. Brizuela, Dario, illus. 2017. (Scooby-Doo Solves It with S. T. E. M. Ser.). (ENG.). 32p. (gr. 3-4). lib. bdg. 27.99 *(978-1-5157-3700-1(4))* Capstone Press of Coughlan Cos.

—Scooby-Doo! a Science of Magnetism Mystery: The Magnetic Monster. Cornia, Christian, illus. 2017. (Scooby-Doo Solves It with S. T. E. M. Ser.). (ENG.). 32p. (gr. 3-4). lib. bdg. 27.99 *(978-1-5157-3699-8(7))* Capstone Press of Coughlan Cos.

—Scooby-Doo Solves It with S. T. E. M. Brizuela, Dario, illus. 2017. (Scooby-Doo Solves It with S. T. E. M. Ser.). (ENG.). 32p. (gr. 3-4). 223.92 *(978-1-5157-3717-9(9))* Capstone Press of Coughlan Cos.

Publications International Ltd. Staff, ed. Scooby Doo Message in a Bottle Sound Book. 2004. (Illus.). 24p. 15.98 *(978-1-4127-0600-1(9)*, 7222600) Publications International, Ltd.

—Scooby Doo: Spooky Shadows: Flashlight Adventure Sound Book. 2013. 14p. (J). (gr. 1-3). 17.98 *(978-1-4508-6598-2(4)*, f7a3c6e7-aa63-4615-8fc2-d9e099fdce9c) Publications International, Ltd.

Rozum, Fred & Gross, Scott. Scooby-Doo & Those Meddling Kids, 1 vol. 2012. (Scooby-Doo Graphic Novels Ser.: No. 2). (ENG., Illus.). 24p. (J). (gr. 2-5). 24.21 *(978-1-59961-918-7(0))* Spotlight.

Rozum, John. Scooby-Doo in Yankee Doodle Danger, 1 vol. 2013. (Scooby-Doo Graphic Novels Set 3 Ser.). (ENG.). 24p. (J). (gr. 2-6). lib. bdg. 24.21 *(978-1-61479-054-9(X)*, Essential Library) ABDO Publishing Co.

Rozum, John & Pope, Robert. Scooby-Doo & the Monster of a Thousand Faces!, 1 vol. 2012. (Scooby-Doo Graphic Novels Ser.: No. 2). (ENG., Illus.). 24p. (J). (gr. 2-5). 24.21 *(978-1-59961-916-3(4))* Spotlight.

Sander, Sonia. Big-Top Scooby-Doo! Movie Reader. 2012. (Scooby Doo Reader Ser.). lib. bdg. 13.55 *(978-0-606-26542-3(2)*, Turtleback) Turtleback Bks.

—Chill Out, Scooby-Doo!, 1 vol. Duendes Del Sur Staff, illus. 2012. (Scooby-Doo! Set 2 Ser.: No. 2). (ENG.). 32p. (J). (gr. k-3). lib. bdg. 24.21 *(978-1-59961-865-4(6))* Spotlight.

—Scooby-Doo & the Chocolate Phantom, 1 vol. 2016. (Scooby-Doo Comic Readers Ser.). (ENG.). 32p. (J). (gr. k-3). lib. bdg. 24.21 *(978-1-61479-451-6(0)*, Graphic Planet) Magic Wagon.

—Scooby-Doo & the International Express. 2009. (Illus.). 32p. (J). pap. *(978-0-545-16283-8(1))* Scholastic, Inc.

—Scooby-Doo in Food Fight!, 1 vol. 2016. (Scooby-Doo Comic Readers Ser.). (ENG.). 32p. (J). (gr. k-3). lib. bdg. 24.21 *(978-1-61479-454-7(5)*, Graphic Planet) Magic Wagon.

—Scooby-Doo in Keepaway Camp, 1 vol. 2016. (Scooby-Doo! Set 3 Ser.). (ENG., Illus.). 32p. (J). (gr. k-3). lib. bdg. 24.21 *(978-1-61479-407-3(3)*, 1401183) Spotlight.

—Scooby-Doo in Raging River Adventure, 1 vol. 2016. (Scooby-Doo Leveled Readers Ser.). (ENG., Illus.). 32p. (J). (gr. k-4). lib. bdg. 24.21 *(978-1-61479-420-2(0))* Spotlight.

—Scooby-Doo in Shiver Me Timbers, 1 vol. 2016. (Scooby-Doo! Set 3 Ser.). (ENG., Illus.). 32p. (J). (gr. k-4). lib. bdg. 24.21 *(978-1-61479-408-0(1)*, 1401184) Spotlight.

—Scooby-Doo Steals the Dog Show, 1 vol. 2016. (Scooby-Doo Leveled Readers Ser.). (ENG., Illus.). 32p. (J). (gr. k-4). lib. bdg. 24.21 *(978-1-61479-421-9(9))* Spotlight.

—Werewolf Watch. 2012. (Scooby Doo Reader Ser.). lib. bdg. 13.55 *(978-0-606-23961-5(8)*, Turtleback) Turtleback Bks.

—Witching Hour. 2009. (Scooby Reader 25 Ser.). (ENG., Illus.). 32p. (J). (gr. -1-3). pap. 3.99 *(978-0-545-16106-0(1))* Scholastic, Inc.

Sazaklis, John. The Mystery of the Maze Monster, 1 vol. Neely, Scott, illus. 2014. (You Choose Stories: Scooby-Doo Ser.). (ENG.). 112p. (gr. 2-3). pap. 6.95 *(978-1-4342-7928-6(6)*, You Choose Bks.) Capstone Press of Coughlan Cos.

Scholastic, Inc. Staff. Scooby-Doo: Frankencreepy Movie Reader. 2014. (Scooby Doo Reader Ser.). lib. bdg. 13.55 *(978-0-606-36270-2(3))* Turtleback Bks.

Scholastic, Inc. Staff & Duendes Del Sur Staff, contrib. by. Scooby-Doo! & the Mummy's Curse. 2005. (Illus.). 24p. (J). *(978-1-4156-3913-9(2))* Scholastic, Inc.

Scooby-Do! Scooby. . . Don't! 2005. (Media Favorites!! Ser.). 14p. (J). 10.95 *(978-1-58117-215-7(X)*, Intervisual/Piggy Toes) Bendon, Inc.

Scooby-Doo & the Case of the Disappearing Scooby Snacks. 2004. (Media Favorites!! Ser.). 12p. (J). 4.95 *(978-1-58117-329-1(6)*, Intervisual/Piggy Toes) Bendon, Inc.

Scooby-Doo! el caso de las Scooby-galletas Misteriosas. 2005.Tr. of Scooby Doo! The Case of the Disappearing Scooby Snacks. (SPA.). 12p. (J). 4.95 *(978-1-58117-330-7(X)*, Intervisual/Piggy Toes) Bendon, Inc.

Simmons, Alex. Scooby-Doo in Dead & Let Spy, 1 vol. Pope, Robert, illus. 2010. (Scooby-Doo Graphic Novels Ser.: No. 1). (ENG.). 24p. (J). (gr. 2-5). 24.21 *(978-1-59961-692-6(0))* Spotlight.

Steele, Michael Anthony. The Case of the Fright Flight. Neely, Scott, illus. 2016. (You Choose Stories: Scooby-Doo Ser.). (ENG.). 112p. (gr. 2-3). lib. bdg. 32.65 *(978-1-4965-2662-5(7)*, You Choose Bks.) Capstone Press of Coughlan Cos.

—Creepy Cowboy Caper. Jeralds, Scott, illus. 2017. (Scooby-Doo! Beginner Mysteries Ser.). (ENG.). 112p. (gr. 2-3). lib. bdg. 22.65 ***(978-1-4965-4768-2(3))*** Capstone Press of Coughlan Cos.

—Monster Mutt Madness. Jeralds, Scott, illus. 2017. (Scooby-Doo! Beginner Mysteries Ser.). (ENG.). 112p. (gr. 2-3). lib. bdg. 22.65 ***(978-1-4965-4767-5(5))*** Capstone Press of Coughlan Cos.

—Skeleton Crew Showdown. Jeralds, Scott, illus. 2017. (Scooby-Doo! Beginner Mysteries Ser.). (ENG.). 112p. (gr. 2-3). lib. bdg. 22.65 ***(978-1-4965-4769-9(1))*** Capstone Press of Coughlan Cos.

—Vampire Zoo Hullabaloo. Jeralds, Scott, illus. 2017. (Scooby-Doo! Beginner Mysteries Ser.). (ENG.). 112p. (gr. 2-3). lib. bdg. 22.65 ***(978-1-4965-4770-5(5))*** Capstone Press of Coughlan Cos.

Strom, Frank. Scooby-Doo & the Mystery Date, 1 vol. Deporter, Vincent, illus. 2010. (Scooby-Doo Graphic Novels Ser.: No. 1). (ENG.). 24p. (J). (gr. 2-5). 24.21 *(978-1-59961-689-6(0))* Spotlight.

Strom, Frank & Barrios, Roberto. Scooby-Doo in Welcome to the Jungle, 1 vol. 2012. (Scooby-Doo Graphic Novels Ser.: No. 2). (ENG., Illus.). 24p. (J). (gr. 2-5). 24.21 *(978-1-59961-925-5(3))* Spotlight.

Sturk, Karl. Movie Star Mystery. 2010. (Scooby Doo Reader Ser.: 24). lib. bdg. 13.55 *(978-0-606-07085-0(0)*, Turtleback) Turtleback Bks.

Sutton, Laurie S. The Case of the Clown Carnival. Neely, Scott, illus. 2017. (You Choose Stories: Scooby-Doo Ser.). (ENG.). 112p. (gr. 2-3). lib. bdg. 32.65 *(978-1-4965-4333-2(5)*, You Choose Bks.) Capstone Press of Coughlan Cos.

—The Curse of Atlantis. Neely, Scott, illus. 2015. (You Choose Stories: Scooby-Doo Ser.). (ENG.). 112p. (gr. 2-3). lib. bdg. 32.65 *(978-1-4965-0477-7(1))* Stone Arch Bks.

—The Fright at Zombie Farm. Neely, Scott, illus. 2015. (You Choose Stories: Scooby-Doo Ser.). (ENG.). 112p. (gr. 2-3). lib. bdg. 32.65 *(978-1-4342-9713-6(6)*, You Choose Bks.) Capstone Press of Coughlan Cos.
—The Ghost of the Bermuda Triangle, 1 vol. Neely, Scott, illus. 2014. (You Choose Stories: Scooby-Doo Ser.). (ENG.). 112p. (gr. 2-3). 32.65 *(978-1-4342-9126-4(X)*, You Choose Bks.) Capstone Press of Coughlan Cos.
—The House on Spooky Street. Neely, Scott, illus. 2015. (You Choose Stories: Scooby-Doo Ser.). (ENG.). 112p. (gr. 2-3). lib. bdg. 32.65 *(978-1-4342-9714-3(4)*, You Choose Bks.) Capstone Press of Coughlan Cos.
—Legend of the Gator Man. Neely, Scott, illus. 2016. (Scooby-Doo Comic Chapter Bks.). (ENG.). 88p. (gr. 3-7). pap. 5.95 *(978-1-4965-3588-7(X))*; lib. bdg. 27.32 *(978-1-4965-3584-9(7))* Capstone Press of Coughlan Cos.
—The Mystery of the Aztec Tomb, 1 vol. Neely, Scott, illus. 2014. (You Choose Stories: Scooby-Doo Ser.). (ENG.). 112p. (gr. 2-3). 32.65 *(978-1-4342-9127-1(8)*, You Choose Bks.) Capstone Press of Coughlan Cos.
—The Secret of the Flying Saucer. Neely, Scott, illus. 2015. (You Choose Stories: Scooby-Doo Ser.). (ENG.). 112p. (gr. 2-3). lib. bdg. 32.65 *(978-1-4965-0478-4(X))* Stone Arch Bks.
—The Secret of the Sea Creature, 1 vol. Neely, Scott, illus. 2014. (You Choose Stories: Scooby-Doo Ser.). (ENG.). 112p. (gr. 2-3). pap. 6.95 *(978-1-4342-7925-5(1)*, You Choose Bks.) Capstone Press of Coughlan Cos.
—The Terror of the Bigfoot Beast, 1 vol. Neely, Scott, illus. 2014. (You Choose Stories: Scooby-Doo Ser.). (ENG.). 112p. (gr. 2-3). pap. 6.95 *(978-1-4342-7926-2(X)*, You Choose Bks.) Capstone Press of Coughlan Cos.
—The History of the Maze Monster. 2014. (You Choose Stories: Scooby-Doo Ser.). (ENG.). 112p. (gr. 2-3). 130.60 *(978-1-4342-8458-7(1)*, You Choose Bks.) Capstone Press of Coughlan Cos.
—You Choose: Scooby-Doo. 2013. (You Choose Stories: Scooby Doo Ser.). (ENG.). 112p. pap. 166.80 *(978-1-4342-9604-7(0))* Stone Arch Bks.
Wasserman, Robin. Search for Scooby Snacks, 1 vol. 2013. (Scooby-Doo! Picture Clue Bks.). (ENG.). 24p. (J). (gr. -1-1). lib. bdg. 24.21 *(978-1-61479-039-6(6)*, Essential Library) ABDO Publishing Co.

SCOPES, JOHN THOMAS, 1900-1970

Crewe, Sabrina & Uschan, Michael V. The Scopes "Monkey" Trial. 2005. (Events That Shaped America Ser.). (Illus.). 32p. (gr. 3-6). lib. bdg. 26.00 *(978-0-8368-3415-4(1)*, Gareth Stevens Learning Library) Stevens, Gareth Publishing LLLP.
Johnson, Anne Janette. The Scopes Monkey Trial. 2006. (Defining Moments Ser.). (Illus.). 246p. (gr. 9-18). 55.00 *(978-0-7808-0955-0(6))* Omnigraphics, Inc.
Kowalski, Kathiann M. Evolution on Trial: From the Scopes Monkey Case to Inherit the Wind. 2009. (Famous Court Cases That Became Movies Ser.). (Illus.). 112p. (J). (gr. 7-12). lib. bdg. 33.27 *(978-0-7660-3056-5(3))* Enslow Pubs., Inc.
The Scopes Monkey Trial: Debate over Evolution. 2010. (Milestones in American History Ser.). (Illus.). 128p. (J). (gr. 6-12). 35.00 *(978-1-60413-679-1(0)*, Chelsea Hse.) Facts On File, Inc.
Uschan, Michael V. The Scopes "Monkey" Trial. 2004. (Landmark Events in American History Ser.). (Illus.). 48p. (gr. 5-12). pap. 14.05 *(978-0-8368-5424-4(1))*; lib. bdg. 31.00 *(978-0-8368-5396-4(2))* Stevens, Gareth Publishing LLLP. (Gareth Stevens Secondary Library).

SCORPIONS

Bodden, Valerie. Scorpions. 2011. (Creepy Creatures Ser.). 24p. (J). (gr. 1-3). (ENG.). pap. 8.99 *(978-0-89812-568-9(5)*, Creative Paperbacks); 24.25 *(978-1-58341-995-3(0)*, Creative Education) Creative Co., The.
—Scorpions. 2010. (ENG., Illus.). 24p. (J). 8.95 *(978-1-926853-75-8(X))* Saunders Bk. Co. CAN. Dist: Creative Co., The.
Bright, Michael. Build the Scorpion. 2015. (Build It Ser.). (ENG., Illus.). 32p. (J). (gr. k). 19.95 *(978-1-62686-204-3(4)*, Silver Dolphin Bks.) Readerlink Distribution Services, LLC.
Davin, Rose. Scorpions. 2017. (Meet Desert Animals Ser.). (ENG., Illus.). 24p. (gr. k-1). lib. bdg. 26.65 *(978-1-5157-4601-0(1)*, Pebble Plus) Capstone Press of Coughlan Cos.
Feltes Taylor, Kimberly. Scorpion vs. Centipede: Duel to the Death. 2016. (Bug Wars Ser.). (ENG., Illus.). 32p. (gr. 3-4). lib. bdg. 27.99 *(978-1-4914-8066-3(1)*, Edge Bks.) Capstone Press of Coughlan Cos.
Franchino, Vicky. Scorpions. 2015. (ENG.). 48p. (J). pap. 6.95 *(978-0-531-21188-5(6)*, Orchard Bks.) Scholastic Library Publishing.
Ganeri, Anita. Scorpion, 1 vol. 2011. (Day in the Life: Desert Animals Ser.). (ENG.). 24p. (gr. k-2). pap. 6.79 *(978-1-4329-4785-9(0))*; (Illus.). 23.32 *(978-1-4329-4776-7(1))* Heinemann-Raintree. (Heinemann Read & Learn).
Goldish, Meish. Bark Scorpion. 2015. (Desert Animals Searchin' for Shade Ser.). (ENG.). 24p. (J). (gr. -1-3). lib. bdg. 23.93 *(978-1-62724-535-7(9))* Bearport Publishing Co., Inc.
Gonzales, Doreen. Scorpions in the Dark. 2009. 24p. (YA). pap. 8.25 *(978-1-4358-3257-2(4))*; (Illus.). (J). (gr. 1-3). 22.60 *(978-1-4042-8100-4(2))* Rosen Publishing Group, Inc., The.
Lunis, Natalie. Stinging Scorpions. 2009. (No Backbone! Ser.). (Illus.). 24p. (J). (gr. k-3). lib. bdg. 21.28 *(978-1-59716-756-7(8))* Bearport Publishing Co., Inc.
Lynette, Rachel. Scorpions. 2013. (Monsters of the Animal Kingdom Ser.). (ENG., Illus.). 24p. (J). (gr. k-5). pap. 8.25 *(978-1-4488-9722-3(X))*; lib. bdg. 22.60 *(978-1-4488-9633-2(9))* Rosen Publishing Group, Inc., The. (PowerKids Pr.).
Markle, Sandra. Scorpions: Armored Stingers. 2011. (Arachnid World Ser.). (ENG., Illus.). 48p. (gr. 4-8). lib. bdg. 29.27 *(978-0-7613-5037-8(3))* Lerner Publishing Group.
—Wind Scorpions: Killer Jaws. 2012. (Arachnid World Ser.). (ENG., Illus.). 48p. (J). (gr. 4-8). lib. bdg. 29.27 *(978-0-7613-5048-4(9))* Lerner Publishing Group.
Markovics, Joyce. MIS Pinzas Son Negras y Enormes (Scorpion) 2016. (Pistas de Animales 2 Ser.). (SPA.). 24p. (J). (gr. -1-3). 17.95 *(978-1-944102-78-4(7))* Bearport Publishing Co., Inc.
Markovics, Joyce L. My Claws Are Huge & Black. 2016. (Zoo Clues 2 Ser.). (ENG & SPA.). 24p. (J). (gr. -1-3). lib. bdg. 17.95 *(978-1-944102-60-9(4))* Bearport Publishing Co., Inc.
McAneney, Caitie. Scorpion vs. Black Widow. 2015. (Bizarre Beast Battles Ser.). (ENG., Illus.). 24p. (J). (gr. 2-3). pap. 8.15 *(978-1-4824-2792-9(3))* Stevens, Gareth Publishing LLLP.
McFee, Shane. Scorpions. (Poison! Ser.). 24p. (gr. 2-3). 2009. 42.50 *(978-1-60851-325-3(4)*, PowerKids Pr.) 2007. (Illus.). (J). lib. bdg. 22.60 *(978-1-4042-3794-0(1)*, 1270815) Rosen Publishing Group, Inc., The.
Otfinoski, Steven. Scorpions. 2011. (Animals Animals 12 Ser.). (Illus.). 48p. (J). (gr. 3). 23.95 *(978-0-7614-4878-5(0))* Marshall Cavendish Corp.
Owings, Lisa. The Deathstalker Scorpion. 2013. (Nature's Deadliest Ser.). (ENG., Illus.). 24p. (J). (gr. 3-8). lib. bdg. 25.95 *(978-1-60014-879-8(4)*, Pilot Bks.) Bellwether Media.
Pallotta, Jerry. Tarantula vs. Scorpion. Bolster, Robert, illus. 2016. (Who Would Win? Ser.). (ENG.). 32p. (J). (gr. 1-3). pap. 3.99 *(978-0-545-30172-5(6))* Scholastic, Inc.
Porter, Esther. Scorpions, 1 vol. 2013. (Creepy Crawlers Ser.). (ENG., Illus.). 24p. (J). (gr. k-1). lib. bdg. 26.65 *(978-1-4765-2064-3(X)*, Pebble Plus) Capstone Press of Coughlan Cos.
Pringle, Laurence. Scorpion Man: Exploring the World of Scorpions. Polis, Gary A., illus. 2008. (ENG.). 48p. (J). (gr. 1-3). 11.99 *(978-1-4169-7574-8(8)*, Simon & Schuster/Paula Wiseman Bks.) Simon & Schuster/Paula Wiseman Bks.
—Scorpions! Strange & Wonderful. Henderson, Meryl, illus. 2013. (Strange & Wonderful Ser.). (ENG.). 32p. (J). (gr. 3-5). 16.95 *(978-1-59078-473-0(1))* Boyds Mills Pr.
Raum, Elizabeth. Scorpions. 2015. (Poisonous Animals Ser.). (ENG., Illus.). 32p. (J). (gr. 2-4). 19.95 *(978-1-60753-788-5(5))* Amicus Publishing.
Roza, Greg. Sting! The Scorpion & Other Animals That Sting. 2011. (Armed & Dangerous Ser.). (Illus.). 24p. (J). pap. 8.25 *(978-1-4488-2680-3(2)*, PowerKids Pr.); (gr. 1-4). 22.60 *(978-1-4488-2548-6(2))* Rosen Publishing Group, Inc., The.
Schuetz, Kari. Scorpions. 2015. (Creepy Crawlies Ser.). (ENG., Illus.). 24p. (J). (gr. k-3). lib. bdg. 25.95 *(978-1-62617-226-5(9)*, Blastoff! Readers) Bellwether Media.
Shea, Therese. Scorpions. 2015. (Things That Sting Ser.). (ENG., Illus.). 24p. (J). (gr. 2-3). lib. bdg. 22.60 *(978-1-4824-1714-2(6))* Stevens, Gareth Publishing LLLP.
Sullivan, Laura L. The Deathstalker Scorpion. 2017. (J). ***(978-1-5026-2577-9(6))*** Cavendish Square Publishing.
Thomas, Isabel. Scorpion vs. Tarantula. 2017. (Animal Rivals Ser.). (ENG.). 24p. (J). (gr. k-2). lib. bdg. 23.32 ***(978-1-4846-4070-8(5)***, Heinemann Read & Learn) Heinemann-Raintree.

SCOTLAND

Bodden, Valerie. To the Heart of Africa. 2011. (Illus.). 48p. (J). 35.65 *(978-1-60818-066-0(2)*, Creative Education) Creative Co., The.
Carr, Simonetta. John Knox. Abraxas, Matt, illus. 2014. (ENG.). 64p. (J). 18.00 *(978-1-60178-289-2(6))* Reformation Heritage Bks.
Gifford, Clive. Andy Murray. 2017. (Inspirational Lives Ser.). (ENG., Illus.). 32p. (J). (gr. 4-6). pap. 11.99 *(978-0-7502-9495-9(7)*, Wayland) Hachette Children's Group GBR. Dist: Hachette Bk. Group.
Kirkby, Mandy. Pick Your Brains about Scotland. Williams, Caspar, illus. 2005. (Pick Your Brains Ser.). 128p. pap. 9.95 *(978-1-86011-223-2(4))* Cadogan Guides GBR. Dist: Globe Pequot Pr., The.
MacDonald, Fiona. Meet a Body Snatcher! Criminals & Murderers You'D Rather Avoid. 2009. (You Wouldn't Want to Ser.). (ENG., Illus.). 32p. (J). (gr. 3-18). 29.00 *(978-0-531-20822-9(2)*, Watts, Franklin) Scholastic Library Publishing.
MacKenzie, Catherine. Scottish Highland. 2007. (Adventure Ser.). (ENG., Illus.). 96p. (J). per. 8.99 *(978-1-84550-281-2(7)*, beeaf3cf-4408-4d2c-89dc-81ff3e31e46b) Christian Focus Pubns. GBR. Dist: Bookmasters Distribution.
Zocchi, Judy. In Scotland. Brodie, Neale, illus. 2005. (Global Adventures II Ser.). 32p. (J). per. 10.95 *(978-1-59646-149-9(7))* Dingles & Co.
—In Scotland/en Escocia. Brodie, Neale, illus. 2005. (Global Adventures II Ser.).Tr. of En Escocia. (ENG & SPA.). 32p. (J). per. 10.95 *(978-1-59646-151-2(9))* Dingles & Co.

SCOTLAND—FICTION

Alexander, Sarah. The Art of Not Breathing. (ENG.). 288p. (YA). (gr. 9). 2017. pap. 9.99 *(978-0-544-93687-4(6))* 2016. 17.99 *(978-0-544-63388-9(1))* Houghton Mifflin Harcourt Publishing Co. (HMH Books For Young Readers).
Anderson, Sandra. Rockcliffe. 2007. 156p. per. 8.95 *(978-1-59800-893-7(5))* Outskirts Pr., Inc.
Atkin, Jean. The Crow House. 2013. 270p. pap. *(978-1-78299-650-7(8))* FeedARead.com.
Baccalario, P. D. Suitcase of Stars, 1 vol. Bruno, Iacopo, illus. 2014. (Enchanted Emporium Ser.). (ENG.). 240p. (gr. 4-8). pap. 9.25 *(978-1-4342-6519-7(6))* Stone Arch Bks.
—Suitcase of Stars, 1 vol. Pernigotti, Chiara, tr. from ITA. Bruno, Iacopo, illus. 2014. (Enchanted Emporium Ser.). (ENG.). 240p. (gr. 4-8). 26.65 *(978-1-4342-6516-6(1))* Stone Arch Bks.
Baccalario, Pierdomenico. Compass of Dreams, 1 vol. Pernigotti, Chiara, tr. from ITA. Bruno, Iacopo, illus. 2014. (Enchanted Emporium Ser.). (ENG.). 240p. (gr. 4-8). 26.65 *(978-1-4342-6517-3(X))* Stone Arch Bks.
—Map of the Passages. McGuinness, Nanette, tr. from ITA. Bruno, Iacopo, illus. 2015. (Enchanted Emporium Ser.). (ENG.). 240p. (gr. 4-8). 12.95 *(978-1-62370-204-5(6))* Stone Arch Bks.
—Suitcase of Stars, 1 vol. Bruno, Iacopo, illus. 2014. (Enchanted Emporium Ser.). (ENG.). 240p. (gr. 4-8). 12.95 *(978-1-62370-039-3(6))* Capstone Young Readers of Coughlan Cos.
Baccalario, Pierdomenico & McGuinness, Nanette. The Thief of Mirrors. Pernigotti, Chiara, tr. from ITA. Bruno, Iacopo, illus. 2015. (Enchanted Emporium Ser.). (ENG.). 240p. (gr. 4-8). lib. bdg. 26.65 *(978-1-4965-0516-3(6))* Stone Arch Bks.
Bach, Ari. Valhalla. 2nd ed. 2016. (ENG., Illus.). (YA). (gr. 9-12). 29.99 ***(978-1-63477-990-6(8))*** 2014. 330p. pap. 17.99 *(978-1-62798-718-9(5))* Dreamspinner Pr. (Harmony Ink Pr.).
Barrowman, John & Barrowman, Carole E. Bone Quill. 2014. (Hollow Earth Ser.). (ENG., Illus.). 304p. (J). (gr. 3-7). pap. 8.99 *(978-1-4424-8929-5(4)*, Aladdin) Simon & Schuster Children's Publishing.
—Hollow Earth. 2012. (Hollow Earth Ser.). (ENG.). 400p. (J). (gr. 3-7). 16.99 *(978-1-4424-5852-9(6)*, Aladdin) Simon & Schuster Children's Publishing.
Bayham, Dalan J. The Loch Ness Monster Incident - Junior Explorers Society Episode 2. 2007. 160p. pap. 12.95 *(978-1-4303-2291-7(8))* Lulu Pr., Inc.
Bell, Alex. Frozen Charlotte. 2016. (ENG.). 304p. (J). (gr. 7). 18.99 *(978-0-545-94108-2(3)*, Scholastic Pr.) Scholastic, Inc.
Bennett, Paul. Freddie, Bill & Irving. Shannon, Kate, illus. 2009. 112p. (gr. 2-2). pap. 25.16 *(978-1-4251-7692-1(5))* Trafford Publishing.
Black, Sean. Extolziby Gruff & the 39th College. 2013. 236p. pap. *(978-1-909062-25-2(1))* Sean Black Digital.
Blackford. The Eskdale Herd-boy. l.t. ed. 2007. (ENG.). 146p. pap. 19.99 *(978-1-4264-8722-4(3))* Creative Media Partners, LLC.
—The Eskdale Herd-boy: The Eskdale Herd-boy. 2007. (ENG.). 134p. pap. 18.99 *(978-1-4264-8667-8(7))* Creative Media Partners, LLC.
—The Eskdale Herd Boy A Scottish Tale for the Instruction & Amusement of Young Persons. 2004. reprint ed. pap. 15.95 *(978-1-4191-6125-4(3))* Kessinger Publishing, LLC.
Bold, Emily. Breath of Yesterday, 0 vols. Bell, Katja, tr. from GER. 2014. (Curse Ser.: 2). (ENG.). 376p. (YA). (gr. 9-12). pap. 9.99 *(978-1-4778-4714-5(6)*, 9781477847145) Amazon Publishing.
—The Curse: Touch of Eternity, 0 vols. Heron, Jeanette, tr. from GER. 2013. (Curse Ser.: 1). (ENG.). 318p. (YA). (gr. 9-12). pap. 9.99 *(978-1-4778-0735-4(7)*, 9781477807354) Amazon Publishing.
Bond, Doug. Crown & Covenant, 3 bks. Bird, Matthew, illus. 2004. (Crown & Covenant Ser.). (J). per. 26.99 *(978-0-87552-671-3(3))* P & R Publishing.
Brown, Hazel. Prince Henry St. Clair Earl of Orkney. Bramadat, Dawn, ed. Brown, Hazel, illus. 2013. (Illus.). 106p. pap. 25.95 *(978-1-935786-57-3(1))* St. Clair Pubns.
Brown, Kathryn. Adventures at Aaron Loch Farm. 2009. 50p. pap. 23.50 *(978-1-4092-6961-8(2))* Lulu Pr., Inc.
Bruce Clarke, Margaret. Hunter's Marjory. 2007. 244p. 27.95 *(978-1-4218-4203-5(3))*; per. 12.95 *(978-1-4218-4301-8(3))* 1st World Publishing, Inc. (1st World Library - Literary Society).
Bunting, Eve. Forbidden. 2017. (ENG.). 224p. (YA). (gr. 7). pap. 9.99 *(978-0-544-93881-6(X)*, HMH Books For Young Readers) Houghton Mifflin Harcourt Publishing Co.
Butler, Berwyn. Dinky the Doorknob: The Adventures of Sir Dinkum Wilhelm, the Third Earl of Surridge. 2005. (J). per. 11.95 *(978-1-933732-02-2(4))* Big Ransom Studio.
Butler, Berwyn & McClean, Shorty. Dinky the Doorknob. 2006. (J). lib. bdg. 21.95 *(978-1-933732-04-6(0))* Big Ransom Studio.
Campbell, Angus Peter. Archie & the North Wind. 2010. (ENG.). 192p. pap. 17.95 *(978-1-906817-38-1(3)*, 9781906817381) Luath Pr. Ltd. GBR. Dist: Midpoint Trade Bks., Inc.
Clarke, Margaret Bruce. Hunter's Marjory. 2007. 148p. per. *(978-1-4068-4613-3(9))* Echo Library.
Cohen, Rosalind. Scotland Yard, Us. 2008. 28p. pap. 13.99 *(978-1-4389-4328-2(8))* AuthorHouse.
Cole, Steve. Z. Rex. 2010. (ENG.). 256p. (J). (gr. 5-18). 8.99 *(978-0-14-241712-6(2)*, Puffin Books) Penguin Young Readers Group.
Collins, Tim. Fangs a Lot: Final Notes from a Totally Lame Vampire. Pinder, Andrew, illus. 2014. (ENG.). 320p. (J). (gr. 5-9). 13.99 *(978-1-4814-2134-8(4)*, Aladdin) Simon & Schuster Children's Publishing.
Cooper, Susan. The Boggart. 2004. 196p. (gr. 3-7). 17.00 *(978-0-7569-3932-8(1))* Perfection Learning Corp.
Cummings, Mag. Fishplates & Frogs. 2007. 272p. per. *(978-1-905529-99-5(6))* Grosvenor Hse. Publishing Ltd.
Dawley, Linda. Wee Mac. 2014. (ENG.). 146p. (J). pap. *(978-0-9941011-8-1(X)*, The Little Red Hen Community Pr.) CCB Publishing.
De Saulles, Tony. The Loch Ness Monster Spotters. 2017. (Early Reader Ser.). (ENG., Illus.). 64p. (J). (gr. 1-3). 4.99 ***(978-1-5101-0185-2(3)***, Orion Children's Bks.) Hachette Children's Group GBR. Dist: Hachette Bk. Group.
Derwent, Lavinia. Sula, 1 vol. (ENG., Illus.). 144p. 10.00 *(978-0-86315-487-4(5))* Floris Bks. GBR. Dist: SteinerBooks, Inc.
Destiny, A. & Helms, Rhonda. Sparks in Scotland. 2015. (Flirt Ser.). (ENG.). 224p. (YA). (gr. 7). pap. 9.99 *(978-1-4814-2121-8(2)*, Simon Pulse) Simon Pulse.
Dickinson, Peter. Emma Tupper's Diary. 2014. (ENG.). 212p. (J). (gr. 4). pap. 12.00 *(978-1-61873-063-3(0)*, Big Mouth Hse.) Small Beer Pr.
Don, Lari. First Aid for Fairies & Other Fabled Beasts. 2008. (ENG.). 224p. (J). pap. *(978-0-86315-636-6(3))* Floris Bks.
Douglas, Margaret. Spirit of Meradoon. 2012. 192p. (gr. 2-2). 30.95 *(978-1-4497-6471-5(1))*; pap. 13.95 *(978-1-4497-6470-8(3))* Author Solutions, Inc. (WestBow Pr.).
Downer, Ann. The Dragon of Never-Was. Rayyan, Omar, illus. 2008. (ENG.). 320p. (J). (gr. 3-6). pap. 14.99 *(978-1-4169-5453-8(8)*, Atheneum Bks. for Young Readers) Simon & Schuster Children's Publishing.
Duckers, John. The Amazing Adventures of the Silly Six. 2013. (Illus.). 188p. pap. *(978-1-78148-626-9(3))* Grosvenor Hse. Publishing Ltd.
Ehrenhaft, Daniel. Drawing a Blank: Or How I Tried to Solve a Mystery, End a Feud, & Land the Girl of My Dreams. Ristow, Trevor, illus. 2009. (ENG.). 352p. (J). pap. 8.99 *(978-0-06-075254-5(8)*, HarperTeen) HarperCollins Pubs.
Farmer, Nancy. The Islands of the Blessed. 2012. (ENG., Illus.). 496p. (YA). (gr. 7). pap. 11.99 *(978-1-4169-0738-1(6)*, Atheneum Bks. for Young Readers) Simon & Schuster Children's Publishing.
—The Islands of the Blessed. Foster, Jon, illus. 2009. (ENG.). 496p. (YA). (gr. 7-9). 18.99 *(978-1-4169-0737-4(8)*, Atheneum/Richard Jackson Bks.) Simon & Schuster Children's Publishing.
—The Islands of the Blessed. l.t. ed. 2010. (Sequel to the Land of the Silver Apples Ser.). (ENG.). 520p. (J). 23.95 *(978-1-4104-2253-8(4))* Thorndike Pr.
Ferchaud, Steve, illus. Glen Robbie: A Scottish Fairy Tale. 2006. (J). 22.95 *(978-1-58478-013-7(4)*, Highland Children's Pr.) Heather & Highlands Publishing.
—The Man Who Spoke with Cats. 2006. (ENG.). 48p. (J). 18.95 *(978-1-58478-019-9(3)*, Highland Children's Pr.) Heather & Highlands Publishing.
Flitcroft, Jean. The Loch Ness Monster. 2014. (Cryptid Files Ser.: No. 1). 192p. (gr. 4-8). (J). lib. bdg. 27.93 *(978-1-4677-2602-3(8))*; (ENG.). (YA). pap. 7.95 *(978-1-4677-3481-3(0))* Lerner Publishing Group. (Darby Creek).
—The Loch Ness Monster. 2010. (Cryptid Files Ser.: No. 1). xii, 176p. (J). pap. *(978-1-84840-940-8(0))* Little Island.
Foreman, Colin. A Moment Comes. Colin Foreman. 2007. (Keepers & Seekers Ser.). (ENG., Illus.). 320p. pap. *(978-0-9548949-2-4(8))* Myroy Bks. Ltd.
Forest, Heather. The Woman Who Flummoxed the Fairies. Gaber, Susan, illus. 2013. (ENG.). 32p. (J). (gr. -1-3). 8.95 *(978-1-939160-71-3(5))* August Hse. Pubs., Inc.
Forster, David. Dreamer in the Snows. 2017. (ENG.). 312p. pap. 15.95 ***(978-1-78629-823-2(6)***, 44efd4ae-c88b-4fbf-af8b-a77e619889dd) Austin, Stan AUS. Dist: Bookmasters Distribution.
Galer, Chris. Ross Gang. 2006. 136p. per. *(978-1-905529-84-1(8))* Grosvenor Hse. Publishing Ltd.
Glori, Debi. The Tobermory Cat. 2013. (ENG., Illus.). 32p. (J). (gr. k). *(978-1-78027-099-9(2))* Birlinn, Ltd.
Graham, H. P. & De Bats, M. On the Heels of the Hunted. 2013. 346p. pap. *(978-1-78148-067-0(2))* Grosvenor Hse. Publishing Ltd.
Grant, Michael. The Key. (Magnificent 12 Ser.: 3). (ENG.). (J). (gr. 3-7). 2013. 304p. pap. 5.99 *(978-0-06-183371-7(1))* 2012. (Illus.). 288p. 16.99 *(978-0-06-183370-0(3))* HarperCollins Pubs. (Tegen, Katherine Bks).
Gray, Keith. Ostrich Boys. 2011. (ENG.). 304p. (YA). (gr. 7). pap. 9.99 *(978-0-375-85844-4(X)*, Random Hse. Bks. for Young Readers) Random Hse. Children's Bks.
Hartley, James. The Invisible Hand: Shakespeare's Moon, Act I. 2017. (ENG.). 168p. (J). (gr. 6-12). pap. 11.95 *(978-1-78535-498-4(1)*, Lodestone Bks.) Hunt, John Publishing Ltd. GBR. Dist: National Bk. Network.
Hawkins, Rachel. Journey's End. 2016. (ENG.). 304p. (J). (gr. 3-7). 16.99 *(978-0-399-16960-1(1)*, G.P. Putnam's Sons Books for Young Readers) Penguin Young Readers Group.
Henderson, Lauren. Kiss of Death. 2012. (ENG.). 318p. (YA). (gr. 9). pap. 9.99 *(978-0-385-73780-7(7)*, Ember) Random Hse. Children's Bks.
Hendry, Frances. Quest for a Kelpie. l.t. ed. 2007. 248p. per. *(978-1-905665-17-4(2))* Pollinger In Print.
Hergé. The Black Island. (Illus.). 62p. (J). 19.95 *(978-0-8288-5012-4(7))* French & European Pubns., Inc.
—L' Ile Noire.Tr. of Black Island. (FRE., Illus.). (J). (gr. 7-9). ring bd. 19.95 *(978-0-8288-5039-1(9))* French & European Pubns., Inc.
Hinds, Gareth. Macbeth. Hinds, Gareth, illus. 2015. (ENG., Illus.). 152p. (YA). (gr. 7). 21.99 *(978-0-7636-6943-0(1))* Candlewick Pr.
Hood, Ann. Alexander Graham Bell: Master of Sound. Zilber, Denis, illus. 2013. (Treasure Chest Ser.: 7). (ENG.). 192p. (J). (gr. 3-7). 6.99 *(978-0-448-45730-7(X)*, Grosset & Dunlap) Penguin Young Readers Group.
Howell, Gill. Selkie Child. Keen, Sophie, illus. 2005. (ENG.). 24p. (J). lib. bdg. 23.65 *(978-1-59646-750-7(9))* Dingles & Co.
Hunter, Donna K. Hunterston Happenings: Kilts, Casts & Castles. 2013. (Illus.). 60p. pap. 24.99 *(978-1-4772-2400-7(9))* AuthorHouse.
Jakobsen, Lars. The Mysterious Manuscript. Jakobsen, Lars, illus. 2012. (Mortensen's Escapades Ser.: 1). (ENG., Illus.). 48p. (gr. 6-12). pap. 6.95 *(978-0-8225-9409-3(9))*; lib. bdg. 27.93 *(978-0-7613-7883-9(9))* Lerner Publishing Group. (Graphic Universe™).
Johnson, Alaya. The Goblin King. Gandy, Meg, illus. 2009. (Twisted Journeys (r) Ser.: 10). (ENG.). 112p. (J). (gr. 4-7). pap. 7.95 *(978-0-8225-9259-4(2))* Lerner Publishing Group.
Johnson, Alaya Dawn. The Goblin King, No. 10. Gandy, Meg & Olson, Meagan, illus. 2009. (Twisted Journeys (r) Ser.: 10). (ENG.). 112p. (J). (gr. 4-7). 27.93 *(978-0-8225-9253-2(3)*, Graphic Universe™) Lerner Publishing Group.
Johnson, C. Homecoming. 2007. (Illus.). 64p. per. 10.00 *(978-1-4251-1358-2(3))* Trafford Publishing.
Jordan, Apple. Oh, Brother! Random House Disney Staff, illus. 2012. (Step into Reading Ser.). (ENG.). 32p. (J). (gr. -1-1). pap. 3.99 *(978-0-7364-2887-3(9)*, RH/Disney) Random Hse. Children's Bks.
Kane, James. Tom & Katie's Greatest Adventure. 2005. 73p. pap. 14.95 *(978-1-4241-0776-6(8))* PublishAmerica, Inc.
Kay, Susan. Abby & Gabby Tales. 2009. 16p. pap. 9.99 *(978-1-4389-6467-6(6))* AuthorHouse.
Kellerhals-Stewart, Heather. Brave Highland Heart. 2004. (Illus.). (J). (gr. k-3). spiral bd. *(978-0-616-01688-6(3))* Canadian National Institute for the Blind/Institut National Canadien pour les Aveugles.
King-smith, Dick. The Water Horse. Parkins, David, illus. 2007. (ENG.). 128p. (J). (gr. 1-4). 5.99 *(978-0-375-84231-3(4)*, Yearling) Random Hse. Children's Bks.
Klise, Kate. The Loch Ness Punster. Klise, M. Sarah, illus. 2016. (43 Old Cemetery Road Ser.: 7). (ENG.). 144p. (J). (gr. 2-5). pap. 6.99 *(978-0-544-81085-3(6)*, HMH Books For Young Readers) Houghton Mifflin Harcourt Publishing Co.
Knight, Eric. Lassie Come-Home. Kirmse, Marguerite, illus. rev. ed. 2003. (ENG.). 256p. (J). (gr. 3-7). 24.99 *(978-0-8050-7206-8(3)*, 9780805072068, Holt, Henry & Co. Bks. For Young Readers) Holt, Henry & Co.
Krech, Bob & Krecht, R.J. Love Puppies & Corner Kicks. 2011. (ENG.). 224p. (J). (gr. 5-18). 7.99 *(978-0-14-241783-6(1)*, Puffin Books) Penguin Young Readers Group.
Krumm, Brian & Kortenkamp, Steve. Exploring Space & Beyond. 2015. (Exploring Space & Beyond Ser.). (ENG.). (gr. 3-4). 114.61 *(978-1-4914-6659-9(6)*, Connect) Stone Arch Bks.
Kudina Steinberg, Ganna V. The Princess Conspiracy: an Inspector Poopchyk Mystery. 2009. 143p. 30.00 *(978-0-557-08936-9(0))* Lulu Pr., Inc.

S

Lang, Andrew. Prince Ricardo of Pantouflia. 2006. (Illus.). pap. 24.95 (978-1-4286-0645-6(9)) Kessinger Publishing, LLC.

Laurel Associates. Kidnapped Study Guide: The Complete Adventures of David Balfour. 2006. (Classics Ser.). (Illus.). 48p. (YA). per. 17.95 (978-1-56254-874-2(3)) Saddleback Educational Publishing, Inc.

Leaf, Munro. Wee Gillis. Lawson, Robert, illus. 2006. (New York Review Children's Collection). (ENG.). 80p. (J). (gr. -1-2). 15.95 (978-1-59017-206-3(X), NYR Children's Collection) New York Review of Bks., Inc., The.

Lemley, Ronald W. The Wee Bannock: A Scottish Fairy Tale. 2008. 43p. pap. 24.95 (978-1-60610-122-3(6)) America Star Bks.

Lester, Helen. The Loch Mess Monster. Munsinger, Lynn, illus. 2014. (ENG.). 32p. (J). (gr. -1-3). 16.99 (978-0-544-09990-6(7), HMH Books For Young Readers) Houghton Mifflin Harcourt Publishing Co.

Lewis, Gill. Wild Wings. Onoda, Yuta, illus. (ENG.). 304p. (J). (gr. 3-7). 2012. pap. 7.99 (978-1-4424-1446-4(4)) 2011. 18.99 (978-1-4424-1445-7(6)) Simon & Schuster Children's Publishing. (Atheneum Bks. for Young Readers).

Lindenbaum, Pija. Mini Mia & Her Darling Uncle. Dyssegaard, Elisabeth Kallick, tr. from SWE. 2007. (Illus.). 40p. (J). (gr. -1-3). 16.00 (978-91-29-66734-9(8)) R & S Bks. SWE. Dist: Macmillan.

Linklater, Eric. The Pirates in the Deep Green Sea. 2013. (ENG.). 314p. (YA). pap. 16.99 (978-1-4482-0582-0(4), 9781448205820, Bloomsbury Reader) Bloomsbury Publishing Plc GBR. Dist: Macmillan.

Lund, Celia. Square Sails & Dragons. 2006. 284p. per. 19.95 (978-1-4120-5758-5(2)) Trafford Publishing.

Lunetta, Demitria. Bad Blood. 2017. (ENG.). 272p. (YA). (gr. 7). 17.99 (978-1-101-93805-8(6), Delacorte Pr.) Random Hse. Children's Bks.

MacDonald, George. A Double Story. 2008. 108p. 22.95 (978-1-60664-983-1(3)) Aegypan.

—The Elect Lady. 2008. 148p. 24.95 (978-1-60664-792-9(X)) Aegypan.

—The History of Gutta-Percha Willie. 2006. 116p. per. 9.95 (978-1-59818-578-2(0)) Aegypan.

—The History of Gutta-Percha Willie. 2007. 136p. per. (978-1-4065-2998-2(2)) Dodo Pr.

—Ranald Bannermans Boyhood. 2006. 168p. per. 13.95 (978-1-59818-238-5(2)) Aegypan.

MacKenzie, C. A. The Search for a Golden Eagle. 2013. (Illus.). 48p. pap. 10.95 (978-0-7552-0712-1(2)) Authors OnLine, Ltd. GBR. Dist: Printondemand-worldwide.com.

MacKie, Ian. The Adventures of Hamish the Sea Eagle. Mackie, Marie-Anne, illus. 2013. 24p. (978-1-78148-614-6(X)) Grosvenor Hse. Publishing Ltd.

Matthews, Rodney, illus. Tales of King Arthur. rev. ed. 2007. (Usborne Classics Retold Ser.). 139p. (J). (gr. 4-7). per. 4.99 (978-0-7945-1483-9(9), Usborne) EDC Publishing.

May, Elizabeth. The Vanishing Throne. 2016. (Falconer Ser.: 2). (ENG., Illus.). 458p. (YA). (gr. 7-12). 17.99 (978-1-4521-2882-5(0)) Chronicle Bks. LLC.

—The Vanishing Throne: Book Two of the Falconer Trilogy. 2017. (Falconer Ser.: 2). (ENG.). 480p. (YA). pap. 10.99 (978-1-4521-6140-2(2)) Chronicle Bks. LLC.

McCartney, Tania. A Scottish Year: Twelve Months in the Life of Scotland's Kids. Snerling, Tina, illus. 2015. (Kids' Year Ser.). (ENG.). 32p. (J). (gr. -1-3). 17.99 (978-1-921966-87-3(4), EK Bks.) Exisle Publishing Pty Ltd. AUS. Dist: Hachette Bk. Group.

McKay, Kirsty. Undead. 2013. (ENG.). 288p. (J). (gr. 7). pap. 9.99 (978-0-545-38189-5(4), Chicken Hse., The) Scholastic, Inc.

—Unfed. 2015. (Undead Ser.: 2). (YA). 1.25 (978-1-4906-3511-8(4)) Recorded Bks., Inc.

—Unfed. 2013. (YA). (978-0-545-53674-5(X)); (ENG.). 288p. (J). (gr. 9). 17.99 (978-0-545-53672-1(3)) Scholastic, Inc. (Chicken Hse., The).

McLean, Allan Campbell. The Hill of the Red Fox. 2nd ed. 2006. (Kelpies Ser.). (ENG.). 272p. (J). 11.95 (978-0-86315-556-7(1)) Floris Bks. GBR. Dist: SteinerBooks, Inc.

Miles, Cindy. Forevermore. 2013. (ENG.). 288p. (J). (gr. 7). pap. 9.99 (978-0-545-42622-0(7)) Scholastic, Inc.

Millar, Martin. Lonely Werewolf Girl. 2008. (ENG.). 560p. per. (978-0-9796636-6-6(0)) CSA Telltapes, Ltd.

Moore, Meredith. Fiona. 2016. (ENG.). 384p. (YA). (gr. 7). 17.99 (978-1-59514-784-4(5), Razorbill) Penguin Young Readers Group.

Nicholson, Mike. Catscape, 1 vol. 2006. (ENG.). 176p. (YA). 9.99 (978-0-86315-531-4(6)) Floris Bks. GBR. Dist: SteinerBooks, Inc.

Paterson, Judy. Scottish Folk Tales for Children. 2017. (Folk Tales for Children Ser.). (ENG., Illus.). 192p. (J). (gr. 2-4). pap. 16.99 (978-0-7509-6844-7(3)) History Pr. Ltd.,The GBR. Dist: Independent Pubs. Group.

Paul, Colette. Whoever You Chose to Love. 2004. 256p. pap. (978-0-297-84717-5(1), Weidenfeld & Nicolson) Orion Publishing Group, Ltd.

Pelley, Kathleen. The Giant King. Manning, Maurie J., tr. Manning, Maurie J., illus. 2003. (New Child & Family Press Titles Ser.). 32p. (gr. -1-4). 14.95 (978-0-87868-880-7(3), 8803, Child & Family Pr.) Child Welfare League of America, Inc.

Perkins, Lucy Fitch. The Scotch Twins. 2004. reprint ed. pap. 15.95 (978-1-4191-8160-3(2)); pap. 1.99 (978-1-4192-8160-0(7)) Kessinger Publishing, LLC.

Peyton, K. M. Stealaway. Wyatt, David, illus. 2004. (ENG.). 96p. (J). 12.95 (978-0-8126-2722-0(9)) Cricket Bks.

Poulsen, David A. Shivers & Shakes. 2009. (Salt & Pepper Chronicles Ser.). (ENG.). 176p. (J). (gr. 3-7). pap. (978-1-55470-144-5(9)) Me to We.

Pow, Tom. Sixteen String Jack & the Garden of Adventure. Andrew, Ian, illus. 2016. (ENG.). 32p. (J). (gr. -1-k). (978-1-78027-226-9(X)) Birlinn, Ltd.

Rae, Milne. Geordie's Tryst. 2007. 72p. per. (978-1-4068-3682-0(6)) Echo Library.

Random House Disney Staff. Big Bear, Little Bear. Random House Disney Staff, illus. 2012. (Step into Reading Ser.). (ENG., Illus.). 32p. (J). (gr. -1-1). pap. 3.99 (978-0-7364-2915-3(8), RH/Disney) Random Hse. Children's Bks.

—Brave Big Golden Book (Disney/Pixar Brave) Random House Disney Staff, illus. 2012. (Big Golden Book Ser.). (ENG., Illus.). 64p. (J). (gr. -1-2). 9.99 (978-0-7364-2918-4(2), Golden/Disney) Random Hse. Children's Bks.

Ransome, Arthur. Great Northern? 2003. (Swallows & Amazons Ser.). (ENG., Illus.). 352p. (J). pap. 14.95 (978-1-56792-259-2(7)) Godine, David R. Pub.

Rees, Gwyneth. Fairy Dust. 2016. (Fairy Ser.: 1). (ENG., Illus.). 160p. (J). (gr. 2-4). pap. 9.99 (978-1-5098-1867-9(7)) Pan Macmillan GBR. Dist: Independent Pubs. Group.

RH Disney Staff. Brave Little Golden Book (Disney/Pixar Brave) RH Disney Staff, illus. 2012. (Little Golden Book Ser.). (ENG., Illus.). 24p. (J). (gr. k-k). 4.99 (978-0-7364-2901-6(8), Golden/Disney) Random Hse. Children's Bks.

Richardson, Alex. Gladigator & the Legend of Auchinle. 2009. (Illus.). 96p. pap. 31.99 (978-1-4490-1968-6(4)) AuthorHouse.

—Gladigator & the legend of Auchinlea. 2010. (Illus.). 96p. pap. 11.99 (978-1-4520-3324-2(2)) AuthorHouse.

Roberts, Scott A. The Rollicking Adventures of Tam O'Hare. Roberts, Scott A., illus. 2007. (ENG., Illus.). 228p. (J). (gr. 4-7). per. 16.95 (978-1-60037-289-6(9)) Morgan James Publishing.

Rooney-Freedman, Isabelle. Angus MacDream & the Roktopus Rogue. 2011. 206p. pap. 11.95 (978-0-9843064-3-5(9)) Word with You Pr., A.

Runholt, Susan. Rescuing Seneca Crane. 2009. (Kari & Lucas Mystery Ser.). (ENG.). 288p. (J). (gr. 5-18). 16.99 (978-0-670-06291-1(X), Viking Books for Young Readers) Penguin Young Readers Group.

Russel, Mary. Flickertail & Paint, Barnyard Sleuths, 1 vol. 2010. 96p. pap. 19.95 (978-1-4489-7248-7(5)) America Star Bks.

Scribner, Meagen & Jensen, Angelina. Princess & the Peasant. 2013. 40p. pap. (978-1-4602-3308-5(5)) FriesenPress.

Shakespeare, William. Macbeth, 1 vol. Pérez, Daniel & Ferran, Daniel, illus. 2011. (Shakespeare Graphics Ser.). (ENG.). 88p. (gr. 2-3). pap. 7.15 (978-1-4342-3447-6(9), Shakespeare Graphics) Stone Arch Bks.

—Macbeth, 1 vol. Ferran, Daniel, illus. 2011. (Shakespeare Graphics Ser.). (ENG.). 88p. (gr. 2-3). lib. bdg. 27.99 (978-1-4342-2506-1(2), Shakespeare Graphics) Stone Arch Bks.

Shaw, Murray & Cosson, M. J. Sherlock Holmes & the Adventure at the Abbey Grange. Rohrbach, Sophie, illus. 2010. (On the Case with Holmes & Watson Ser.: 2). (ENG.). 48p. (J). (gr. 4-6). pap. 6.95 (978-0-7613-6200-5(2), Graphic Universe™) Lerner Publishing Group.

—Sherlock Holmes & the Adventure of the Speckled Band. Rohrbach, Sophie, illus. 2010. (On the Case with Holmes & Watson Ser.: 5). (ENG.). 48p. (J). (gr. 4-6). pap. 6.95 (978-0-7613-6198-5(7), Graphic Universe™) Lerner Publishing Group.

Simons, D. M. Keep Her Safe. 2011. (ENG.). 232p. pap. (978-1-84876-697-6(1)) Troubador Publishing Ltd.

Spirn, Michele Sobel. The Bridges in Edinburgh. 2004. (Going to Ser.). 144p. (J). pap. 6.95 (978-1-893577-11-4(2)) Fruitbearer Publishing, LLC.

Stevenson, Robert Louis. Kidnapped. Kennedy, Cam, illus. 2007. (ENG.). 64p. (YA). (gr. 5). pap. 11.95 (978-0-88776-843-9(1), Tundra Bks.) Tundra Bks. CAN. Dist: Penguin Random Hse. LLC.

—Kidnapped. 2006. per. 8.95 (978-1-57646-970-5(0)) Quiet Vision Publishing.

—Kidnapped. 2006. (Classics Ser.). (Illus.). 80p. (YA). (gr. 4-7). per. 8.95 (978-1-56254-873-5(5)) Saddleback Educational Publishing, Inc.

—Kidnapped: Adapted for Young Readers. Kliros, Thea, illus. abr. ed. 2011. (Dover Children's Thrift Classics Ser.). (ENG.). 96p. (J). (gr. 3-8). reprint ed. pap. 4.00 (978-0-486-29354-7(8)) Dover Pubns., Inc.

—Kidnapped: Bring the Classics to Life. 2008. (Bring the Classics to Life Ser.). (ENG., Illus.). 72p. (gr. 3-12). pap., act. bk. ed. 10.95 (978-0-931334-65-8(9), EDCTR-303B) EDCON Publishing Group.

Stevenson, Steve. The King of Scotland's Sword. 2013. (Agatha Girl of Mystery Ser.: 3). lib. bdg. 16.00 (978-0-606-31688-0(4), Turtleback) Turtleback Bks.

Stilton, Geronimo & Stilton, Thea. Thea Stilton & the Secret of the Old Castle. 2012. (Thea Stilton Ser.: 10). (ENG., Illus.). 176p. (J). (gr. 2-5). pap. 8.99 (978-0-545-34107-3(8), Scholastic Paperbacks) Scholastic, Inc.

Stilton, Thea. Thea Stilton & the Secret of the Old Castle. 2012. (Thea Stilton Ser.: 10). lib. bdg. 19.65 (978-0-606-23930-1(8), Turtleback) Turtleback Bks.

Stoddart, Lady. The Eskdale Herd Boy: A Scottish Tale for the Instruction & Amusement of Young Persons. 2005. reprint ed. pap. 20.95 (978-1-4179-6691-2(2)) Kessinger Publishing, LLC.

Strachan, Linda. Hamish Mchaggis & the Ghost of Glamis. Collins, Sally J., illus. 2005. (Hamish Mchaggis Ser.). 26p. (J). per. 9.00 (978-0-9546701-9-1(1)) GW Publishing GBR. Dist: Wilson & Assocs.

—Hamish Mchaggis & the Search for the Loch Ness Monster. Collins, Sally J., illus. 2005. 32p. (J). pap. 9.00 (978-0-9546701-5-3(9)) GW Publishing GBR. Dist: Wilson & Assocs.

—Hamish Mchaggis & the Skye Surprise. Collins, Sally J., illus. 2005. (Hamish Mchaggis Ser.). 26p. (J). pap. 9.00 (978-0-9546701-8-4(3)) GW Publishing GBR. Dist: Wilson & Assocs.

Sutcliff, Rosemary. The Mark of the Horse Lord. 2015. (Rediscovered Classics Ser.). (ENG.). 296p. (YA). (gr. 7). pap. 12.95 (978-1-61373-154-3(X)) Chicago Review Pr., Inc.

—Sword Song. 2005. (ENG., Illus.). 288p. (YA). (gr. 7-12). per. 11.99 (978-0-374-46984-9(9), Farrar, Straus & Giroux (BYR)) Farrar, Straus & Giroux.

Taylor, Janet B. Into the Dim. 2017. lib. bdg. 20.85 **(978-0-606-39929-6(1))** Turtleback Bks.

Thompson, Emma. The Further Tale of Peter Rabbit. Taylor, Eleanor, illus. 2012. (Peter Rabbit Ser.). (ENG.). 72p. (J). (gr. -1-2). 20.00 (978-0-7232-6910-6(6), Warne) Penguin Young Readers Group.

Thomson, Kerr. Washed Ashore. 2017. (ENG.). 320p. (J). (gr. 7). 17.99 **(978-0-545-90420-9(X)**, Chicken Hse., The) Scholastic, Inc.

Tracey, Rhian. When Isla Meets Luke Meets Isla. 2003. (ENG.). 224p. (YA). (gr. 7). pap. 12.95 (978-0-7475-6344-0(6)) Bloomsbury Publishing Plc GBR. Dist: Independent Pubs. Group.

Tuxford, Jenny & Brazier, Jenny. Fredd Boggitt & the Loch Ness Monster. 2009. 152p. pap. 11.99 (978-1-4389-9593-9(8)) AuthorHouse.

Vanderwal, Andrew H. The Battle for Duncragglin. 2009. (ENG.). 320p. (YA). (gr. 5-18). 19.95 (978-0-88776-886-6(5), Tundra Bks.) Tundra Bks. CAN. Dist: Penguin Random Hse. LLC.

Wallace, Karen. Flash Harriet & the Loch Ness Monster. Nayler, Sarah, illus. 2007. (Collins Big Cat Ser.). (ENG.). 160p. (J). (gr. 2-4). pap. 8.99 (978-0-00-723082-2(6)) HarperCollins Pubs. Ltd. GBR. Dist: Independent Pubs. Group.

Walton, O. F. Saved at Sea: A Young Boy in a Dramatic Rescue. 2007. (Classic Stories Ser.). (ENG., Illus.). 144p. (J). mass mkt. 7.99 (978-1-85792-795-5(8), 9781857927955) Christian Focus Pubns. GBR. Dist: Bookmasters Distribution.

Watson, Sally. Witch of the Glens. 2004. (YA). pap. 12.95 (978-1-59511-001-5(1), 800-691-7779) Image Cascade Publishing.

Weatherstone, Hollie. When the Pandas Came to Scotland. 2012. (Illus.). 20p. pap. 19.82 (978-1-4772-3528-7(0)) AuthorHouse.

Wein, Elizabeth. The Pearl Thief. 2017. (ENG.). 336p. (YA). (gr. 7-12). 18.99 (978-1-4847-1716-5(3)) Hyperion Bks. for Children.

Weyn, Suzanne. Dr. Frankenstein's Daughters. 2013. (ENG.). 256p. (J). (gr. 7). 17.99 (978-0-545-42533-9(6), Scholastic Pr.) Scholastic, Inc.

Wiggin, Kate Douglas. Penelope's Experiences in Scotland. 2008. 156p. (gr. 4-7). pap. 13.95 (978-1-60664-127-9(1)) Aegypan.

—Penelope's Experiences in Scotland. 2004. reprint ed. pap. 1.99 (978-1-4192-4071-3(4)); pap. 21.95 (978-1-4191-4071-6(X)) Kessinger Publishing, LLC.

Wightman, Jillian C. The Adventures of Erin Mctavitt. 2008. 68p. pap. 19.95 (978-1-4327-3164-9(5)) Outskirts Pr., Inc.

Wiley, Melissa. Little House in the Highlands. 2007. (Little House Prequel Ser.). (ENG.). 160p. (J). (gr. 3-7). pap. 6.99 (978-0-06-114817-0(2)) HarperCollins Pubs.

Wilson, Barbara-Ann. The Faerie Hill. 2008. 124p. pap. 20.95 (978-1-4092-1845-6(7)) Lulu Pr., Inc.

Wilson, Db. Teale Tales: Wyv Land of Magik. 2012. 266p. pap. (978-1-78176-345-2(3)) FeedARead.com.

Yolen, Jane & Stemple, Adam. Stone Cold. Zangara, Orion, illus. 2016. (Stone Man Mysteries Ser.: 1). (ENG.). 80p. (J). (gr. 7-12). pap. 8.99 (978-1-5124-1155-3(8)); lib. bdg. 29.32 (978-1-4677-4196-5(5)); E-Book 21.99 (978-1-5124-0903-1(0), 9781512409031) Lerner Publishing Group. (Graphic Universe™).

Young, Francis Kerr. The Paperweight. Steele, Andrew & Clement, Devyn, illus. 2008. 39p. pap. 24.95 (978-1-60610-034-9(3)) America Star Bks.

Young, Jessica. Howl at the Moon: a Branches Book (Haggis & Tank Unleashed #3) Burks, James, illus. 2017. (Haggis & Tank Unleashed Ser.: 3). (ENG.). 80p. (J). (gr. k-2). pap. 4.99 **(978-1-338-04525-3(3))** Scholastic, Inc.

SCOTLAND—HISTORY

Burnett, Allan. Macbeth & All That. Anderson, Scoular, illus. 2007. (ENG.). 128p. (gr. 4-7). per. (978-1-84158-574-1(2)) Birlinn, Ltd.

—Robert the Bruce. Anderson, Scoular, illus. 2006. (ENG.). 105p. pap. (978-1-84158-497-3(5)) Birlinn, Ltd.

—The Story of Scotland: Inspired by the Great Tapestry of Scotland. 2015. (ENG., Illus.). 128p. (J). (gr. 4-7). pap. (978-1-78027-241-2(3)) Birlinn, Ltd.

—William Wallace & All That. Anderson, Scoular, illus. 2006. (ENG.). 128p. pap. (978-1-84158-498-0(3)) Birlinn, Ltd.

Capt, E. Raymond. Isle of Iona. 2003. 160p. per. 11.95 (978-0-934666-58-9(X)) Artisan Pubs.

Carruth, J. A., text. Mary Queen of Scots. (Scotland in Words & Pictures Ser.). (Illus.). 32p. pap. 3.95 (978-0-7117-0147-2(4)) Jarrold Publishing GBR. Dist: 7 Hills Bk. Distributors.

Gagne, Tammy. My Home Is My Castle Glamis Castle: Glamis. 2015. (ENG., Illus.). 48p. (J). 29.95 (978-1-62469-134-8(X)) Purple Toad Publishing, Inc.

Ganeri, Anita. Scotland. Isik, Semur, illus. 2015. (Country Guides, with Benjamin Blog & His Inquisitive Dog Ser.). (ENG.). 32p. (gr. 1-3). 29.99 (978-1-4109-6850-0(2), Read Me!) Heinemann-Raintree.

Harman, Alice. Scotland. 2016. (Fact Cat: United Kingdom Ser.). (ENG., Illus.). 24p. (J). (gr. k-2). pap. 9.99 (978-0-7502-8928-3(7), Wayland) Hachette Children's Group GBR. Dist: Hachette Bk. Group.

Kelly, Terri B. Mary Slessor: Missionary Mother. 2014. (Illus.). 164p. (J). (978-1-60682-630-0(1)) BJU Pr.

Kiehm, Eve Begley. B Is for Bagpipes: A Scotland Alphabet. Rutherford, Alexa, illus. 2010. (Discover the World Ser.). (ENG.). 40p. (J). 17.95 (978-1-58536-453-4(3)) Sleeping Bear Pr.

Knox, Barbara. Edinburgh Castle: Scotland's Haunted Fortress. 2006. (Castles, Palaces, & Tombs Ser.). (Illus.). 32p. (YA). (gr. 2-5). lib. bdg. 25.27 (978-1-59716-248-7(5)) Bearport Publishing Co., Inc.

Leavitt, Amie Jane. My Home Is My Castle Balmoral Castle: Balmoral Castle. 2015. (ENG., Illus.). 48p. (J). 29.95 (978-1-62469-136-2(6)) Purple Toad Publishing, Inc.

Levy, P., et al. Scotland. 2nd rev. ed. 2010. (Cultures of the World 21 Ser.). 144p. (gr. 6). lib. bdg. 42.79 (978-1-60870-218-3(9)) Marshall Cavendish Corp.

Lynch, Annabelle. Living in Scotland. 2017. (Living in the UK Ser.). (ENG., Illus.). 24p. (J). (gr. k-2). pap. 11.99 (978-1-4451-4819-9(6), Franklin Watts) Hachette Children's Group GBR. Dist: Hachette Bk. Group.

—Scotland. 2017. (Let's Visit Ser.). (ENG., Illus.). 24p. (J). (gr. k-2). pap. 10.99 (978-1-4451-3703-2(8), Franklin Watts) Hachette Children's Group GBR. Dist: Hachette Bk. Group.

MacAndrew, Richard. Scotland. 2009. (ENG., Illus.). 80p. pap. 12.75 (978-84-8323-579-9(X)) Cambridge Univ. Pr.

MacDonald, Fiona. You Wouldn't Want to Meet a Body Snatcher! Criminals & Murderers You'd Rather Avoid. 2009. (You Wouldn't Want to... Ser.). (ENG., Illus.). 32p. (J). (gr. 3-18). pap. 9.95 (978-0-531-21046-8(4), Children's Pr.) Scholastic Library Publishing.

Marshall, H. E. Scotland's Story. rev. ed. 2006. (Illus.). 352p. (978-1-902984-77-3(3), Galore Park) Hodder Education Group.

—Scotland's Story (Yesterday's Classics) Skelton, J. R. et al, illus. 2005. 552p. (J). per. 17.95 (978-1-59915-056-7(5)) Yesterday's Classics.

Rodgers, Alan & Streluk, Angella. Scotland. 2013. (Step up Geography Ser.). (ENG., Illus.). 32p. (J). pap. 12.99 (978-0-237-54377-8(X)) Evans Brothers, Ltd. GBR. Dist: Independent Pubs. Group.

Rudolph, Jessica. Scotland. 2017. (Countries We Come From Ser.). (ENG.). 32p. (J). (gr. k-3). 19.95 **(978-1-68402-255-7(X))** Bearport Publishing Co., Inc.

Waldron, Melanie. Scotland, 1 vol. 2011. (Countries Around the World Ser.). (ENG.). 48p. (gr. 3-6). pap. 9.95 (978-1-4329-5241-9(2), NA-h) Heinemann-Raintree.

Yomtov, Nelson. Scotland. 2014. (ENG.). 144p. (J). lib. bdg. 40.00 (978-0-531-20794-9(3)) Scholastic Library Publishing.

Zobel, Derek. Scotland. 2012. (Exploring Countries Ser.). (ENG., Illus.). 32p. (J). (gr. 3-7). lib. bdg. 26.95 (978-1-60014-734-0(8), Blastoff! Readers) Bellwether Media.

Zocchi, Judy. In Scotland. Brodie, Neale, illus. 2005. (Global Adventures I Ser.). 32p. (J). pap. 10.95 (978-1-59646-147-5(0)); lib. bdg. 21.65 (978-1-59646-012-6(1)) Dingles & Co.

—In Scotland/en Escocia. Brodie, Neale, illus. 2005. (Global Adventures I Ser.).Tr. of En Escocia. (ENG & SPA.). 32p. (J). pap. 10.95 (978-1-59646-150-5(0)); lib. bdg. (978-1-59646-013-3(X)) Dingles & Co.

SCOTLAND—HISTORY—FICTION

Bond, Douglas. King's Arrow. Bird, Matthew, illus. 2003. (Crown & Covenant Ser.). 208p. (J). per. 10.99 (978-0-87552-743-7(4)) P & R Publishing.

—Rebel's Keep. Bird, Matthew, illus. 2004. (Crown & Covenant Ser.). 285p. (J). per. 9.99 (978-0-87552-744-4(2)) P & R Publishing.

Burack, Emilie Christie. The Runaway's Gold. 2015. (ENG., Illus.). 320p. (YA). (gr. 3-9). 16.95 (978-1-4197-1369-9(8), Amulet Bks.) Abrams, Inc.

Cameron, Ian. Stirling Bridge. (Illus.). 32p. pap. 6.95 (978-1-899827-07-7(2)) Scottish Children's Pr. GBR. Dist: Wilson & Assocs.

Cooney, Caroline B. Enter Three Witches: A Story of Macbeth. l.t. ed. 2007. (Thorndike Literacy Bridge Young Adult Ser.). 343p. (YA). (gr. 8-12). 22.95 (978-0-7862-9889-1(8)) Thorndike Pr.

Cooney, Caroline B. & Shakespeare, William. Enter Three Witches: A Story of Macbeth. 2007. 281p. (YA). pap. (978-0-545-01972-9(9)) Scholastic, Inc.

Cremer, Andrea. Rift. 2013. (Nightshade Ser.). (ENG.). 480p. (YA). (gr. 9). pap. 9.99 (978-0-14-242493-3(5), Speak) Penguin Young Readers Group.

Davidson, Jenny. The Explosionist. 2008. 464p. (YA). (gr. 7-18). lib. bdg. 18.89 (978-0-06-123976-2(3), HarperTeen) HarperCollins Pubs.

Hendry, Frances. Quest for a Queen: The Falcon. 2006. pap. (978-1-905665-06-8(7)) Pollinger In Print.

Henty, George Alfred. Bonnie Prince Charlie: A Tale of Fontenoy & Culloden. 2007. (ENG.). 280p. pap. 21.99 (978-1-4264-2121-1(4)); 268p. pap. 23.99 (978-1-4264-2189-1(3)) Creative Media Partners, LLC.

—In Freedom's Cause: A Story of Wallace & Bruce. 2004. reprint ed. pap. 1.99 (978-1-4192-2572-7(3)) Kessinger Publishing, LLC.

—In Freedom's Cause: A Story of Wallace & Bruce. 2004. 176p. (YA). pap. 8.95 (978-1-57646-886-9(0)) Quiet Vision Publishing.

—In Freedom's Cause: A Tale of Wallace & Bruce. 2011. 372p. pap. 19.95 (978-1-61179-152-5(9)) Fireship Pr.

Jenkins, Sara D. The Prose Marmion a Tale of the Scottish. 2004. reprint ed. pap. 15.95 (978-1-4191-7925-9(X)) Kessinger Publishing, LLC.

—The Prose Marmion A Tale of the Scottish Border. 2004. reprint ed. pap. 1.99 (978-1-4192-7925-6(4)) Kessinger Publishing, LLC.

Laird, Elizabeth. The Betrayal of Maggie Blair. 2011. (ENG.). 432p. (YA). (gr. 7-18). 16.99 (978-0-547-34126-2(1)) Houghton Mifflin Harcourt Publishing Co.

Lennon, Joan. Silver Skin. 2015. (ENG.). 224p. (J). pap. (978-1-78027-284-9(7)) Birlinn, Ltd.

Lightwood, Donald. The Long Revenge. 128p. pap. 7.95 (978-1-899827-94-7(3)) Scottish Children's Pr. GBR. Dist: Wilson & Assocs.

Lockwood, Vicki. The Magnificent Lizzie Brown & the Fairy Child. Hans, Stephanie, illus. 2015. (Magnificent Lizzie Brown Ser.). (ENG.). 200p. (gr. 5-9). 10.95 (978-1-62370-210-6(0)) Stone Arch Bks.

Maclean, Fiona. Death or Victory: Tales of the Clan Maclean. Turnbull, Brian, illus. 2011. 128p. (YA). pap. (978-2-930583-06-8(1)) White & MacLean Publishing BEL. Dist: Gardners Bks. Ltd.

Marston, Hope Irvin. Against the Tide: The Valor of Margaret Wilson. 2007. (Chosen Daughters Ser.). 219p. (J). (gr. 3-7). per. 11.99 (978-1-59638-061-5(6)) P & R Publishing.

Meyer, Carolyn. The Wild Queen: The Days & Nights of Mary, Queen of Scots. 2013. (Young Royals Ser.). (ENG.). 432p. (YA). (gr. 7). pap. 8.99 (978-0-544-02219-5(X)) Houghton Mifflin Harcourt Publishing Co.

Morgan, Nicola. Fleshmarket. 2003. (ENG.). 272p. (J). (gr. 7-17). pap. 9.99 (978-0-340-85557-7(6)) Hodder & Stoughton GBR. Dist: Hachette Bk. Group.

—The Highwayman's Curse. 2009. (J). (978-0-7636-4066-8(2)) Candlewick Pr.

Shakespeare, William. Macbeth. Deas, Robert, illus. 2008. (ENG.). 208p. (YA). (gr. 7-11). pap. 12.95 (978-0-8109-7073-1(2), Amulet Bks.) Abrams, Inc.

—Macbeth: The Graphic Novel. 2010. (Classic Graphic Novel Collection). 144p. (YA). (gr. 7-12). 34.80 (978-1-4205-0373-9(1)) Cengage Gale.

Silverthorne, Judith. The Secret of the Stone Circle, 1 vol. 2010. (From Many Peoples Ser.). (ENG.). 224p. (J). (gr. 4-8).

pap. 8.95 *(978-1-55050-431-6(2))* Coteau Bks. CAN. Dist: Orca Bk. Pubs. USA.

Stevenson, Robert Louis. Kidnapped. 2009. (Puffin Classics Ser.). (ENG.). 352p. (J). (gr. 5-7). 5.99 *(978-0-14-132602-3(6),* Puffin Books) Penguin Young Readers Group.

—Kidnapped. Kumar, Naresh, illus. 2011. (Campfire Graphic Novels Ser.). (ENG.). 72p. (YA). (gr. 3-7). pap. 9.99 *(978-93-80028-52-1(0),* Campfire) Steerforth Pr.

—Kidnapped, 1 vol. Fisher, Eric Scott, illus. 2011. (Calico Illustrated Classics Ser.: No. 3). (ENG.). 112p. (YA). (gr. 3-6). 27.07 *(978-1-61641-105-3(8))* Magic Wagon.

—Kidnapped & Catriona. 2007. (ENG.). 496p. per. *(978-1-84697-033-7(4))* Birlinn, Ltd.

Stevenson, Robert Louis & Wyeth, N. C. Kidnapped. Wyeth, N. C., illus. 2004. (Scribner Storybook Classics Ser.). (ENG., Illus.). 64p. (J). (gr. 3-7). 19.99 *(978-0-689-86542-8(2),* Atheneum Bks. for Young Readers) Simon & Schuster Children's Publishing.

Strachan, Linda. Hamish Mchaggis & the Edinburgh Adventure. Collins, Sally J., illus. 2005. (Hamish Mchaggis Ser.). 26p. (J). per. 9.00 *(978-0-9546701-7-7(5))* GW Publishing GBR. Dist: Wilson & Assocs.

Sutcliff, Rosemary. The Mark of the Horse Lord. 2006. (ENG.). 289p. (YA). (gr. 12). per. 10.95 *(978-1-932425-62-8(4),* Lemniscaat) Boyds Mills Pr.

Thomas, Roy & Stevenson, Robert Louis. Death in the Forest, 1 vol., Vol. 4. Gully, Mario, illus. 2011. (Kidnapped! Ser.). (ENG.). 24p. (J). (gr. 5-9). 24.21 *(978-1-59961-784-8(6))* Spotlight.

—The End of the Quest, 1 vol., Vol. 5. Gully, Mario, illus. 2011. (Kidnapped! Ser.). (ENG.). 24p. (YA). (gr. 5-9). 24.21 *(978-1-59961-785-5(4))* Spotlight.

—I Go to Sea, 1 vol., Vol. 2. Gully, Mario, illus. 2011. (Kidnapped! Ser.). (ENG.). 24p. (J). (gr. 5-9). 24.21 *(978-1-59961-782-4(X))* Spotlight.

—The Loss of the Brig, 1 vol., Vol. 3. Gully, Mario, illus. 2011. (Kidnapped! Ser.). (ENG.). 24p. (YA). (gr. 5-9). 24.21 *(978-1-59961-783-1(8))* Spotlight.

Vanderwal, Andrew H. Death of a King. 2013. (ENG., Illus.). 290p. (YA). (gr. 5). 19.95 *(978-1-77049-398-8(0),* Tundra Bks.) Tundra Bks. CAN. Dist: Penguin Random Hse. LLC.

Weigand, Edith S. If Mandy Ruled the World. 2003. (Illus.). 16p. 7.95 *(978-0-9618904-9-0(5))* Zhera Pubns.

Whitney, Gary & Whitney, Molly. Thistle Downe. 2016. (ENG., Illus.). 128p. (J). 22.95 *(978-1-942945-14-7(0),* 9781942945147) Bright Sky Pr.

Wiley, Melissa. Beyond the Heather Hills. Graef, Renee, illus. 2003. (Little House Ser.). 189p. (J). (gr. 3-7). 14.65 *(978-0-7569-3467-5(2))* Perfection Learning Corp.

Wright, Peter M. The Stone Prince, 1 vol. 2009. 48p. pap. 16.95 *(978-1-4489-2591-9(6))* America Star Bks.

Yolen, Jane & Harris, Robert J. Girl in a Cage. 2004. 234p. (gr. 5-9). 17.00 *(978-0-7569-2946-6(6))* Perfection Learning Corp.

SCOTLAND—HISTORY—WAR OF INDEPENDENCE, 1285-1371

Clare, John. Braveheart. 2009. (Hodder History: Concepts & Processes Ser.). (Illus.). 48p. pap. 23.50 *(978-0-340-95771-4(9))* Hodder Education Group GBR. Dist: Trans-Atlantic Pubns., Inc.

SCOTLAND—KINGS AND RULERS

Burnett, Allan. Macbeth & All That. Anderson, Scoular, illus. 2007. (ENG.). 128p. (gr. 4-7). per. *(978-1-84158-574-1(2))* Birlinn, Ltd.

SCOTS—UNITED STATES—FICTION

Gratz, Alan. Something Wicked. 2009. (ENG.). 288p. (YA). (gr. 7-18). 7.99 *(978-0-14-241496-5(4),* Puffin Books) Penguin Young Readers Group.

Namioka, Lensey. Half & Half. 2005. 136p. (gr. 3-7). 16.00 *(978-0-7569-5680-6(3))* Perfection Learning Corp.

Wibberley, Leonard. Peter Treegate's War. 2009. 134p. (YA). pap. 12.95 *(978-1-932350-21-0(7))* Bethlehem Bks.

SCOTT, DRED, 1809-1858

Blue, Rose & Naden, Corinne J. Dred Scott: Person or Property? 2004. (Supreme Court Milestones Ser.). (Illus.). 128p. (J). 37.07 *(978-0-7614-1841-2(5),* Benchmark Bks.) Marshall Cavendish Corp.

Gunderson, Cory Gideon. Dred Scott Decision, 1 vol. 2004. (American Moments Ser.). (ENG.). 48p. (gr. 4-8). 27.07 *(978-1-59197-283-9(3),* Abdo & Daughters) ABDO Publishing Co.

Herda, D. J. The Dred Scott Case: Slavery & Citizenship. rev. ed. 2010. (Landmark Supreme Court Cases, Gold Edition Ser.). (Illus.). 104p. (J). (gr. 6-18). 33.27 *(978-0-7660-3427-3(5))* Enslow Pubs., Inc.

—Slavery & Citizenship: The Dred Scott Case. 2016. (US Supreme Court Landmark Cases Ser.). 128p. (J). 37.27 *(978-0-7660-8426-1(4))* Enslow Pubs., Inc.

McNeese, Tim. Dred Scott V. Sandford: The Pursuit of Freedom. 2006. (Great Supreme Court Decisions Ser.). (Illus.). 120p. (YA). (gr. 5-9). lib. bdg. 32.95 *(978-0-7910-9236-1(4))* Facts On File, Inc.

Rosen, Daniel. Dred Scott & the Supreme Court: Set Of 6. 2011. (Navigators Ser.). (J). pap. 48.00 net. *(978-1-4108-6258-7(5))* Benchmark Education Co.

—Dred Scott & the Supreme Court: Text Pairs. 2008. (Bridges/Navigators Ser.). (J). (gr. 5). 94.00 *(978-1-4108-8413-8(9))* Benchmark Education Co.

Skog, Jason. The Dred Scott Decision. 2006. (We the People: Civil War Era Ser.). (ENG., Illus.). 48p. (gr. 5-6). 7.95 *(978-0-7565-2038-0(X),* We the People) Compass Point Bks.

Swain, Gwenyth. Dred & Harriet Scott: A Family's Struggle for Freedom. 2004. (ENG., Illus.). 112p. (J). 22.95 *(978-0-87351-482-8(3));* pap. 14.95 *(978-0-87351-483-5(1))* Minnesota Historical Society Pr. (Borealis Bk.).

SCOTT, ROBERT FALCON, 1868-1912

Dowdeswell, Evelyn, et al. Scott of the Antarctic. 2012. (ENG., Illus.). 32p. (gr. 1-3). 26.65 *(978-1-4329-6890-8(4));* pap. 6.49 *(978-1-4329-6891-5(2))* Heinemann-Raintree. (Heinemann First Library).

Grochowicz, Joanna. Into the White: Scott's Antarctic Odyssey. 2017. (ENG.). 288p. (J). (gr. 5-9). pap. 12.99 ***(978-1-76029-365-9(2))*** Allen & Unwin AUS. Dist: Independent Pubs. Group.

Llanas, Sheila Griffin. Who Reached the South Pole First? (Race for History Ser.). (ENG.). 32p. (gr. 3-4). 2011. pap. 47.70 *(978-1-4296-6413-4(4))* 2010. lib. bdg. 27.32 *(978-1-4296-3344-4(1))* Capstone Press of Coughlan Cos. (Fact Finders).

McNeil, Niki, et al. HOCPP 1132 Robert Falcon Scott. 2006. spiral bd. 18.50 *(978-1-60308-132-0(1))* In the Hands of a Child.

Riddle, John. Robert F. Scott: British Explorer of the South. 2004. (Great Names Ser.). (Illus.). 32p. (J). (gr. 3-18). lib. bdg. 19.95 *(978-1-59084-146-4(8))* Mason Crest.

SCOTTISH POETRY

Aigner-Clark, Julie. Baby Einstein Poemas Preciosos: Pretty Poems & Wonderful Words. Zaidi, Nadeem, illus. 2004. (SPA.). 10p. (J). 9.95 *(978-970-718-210-3(5),* Silver Dolphin Bks.) Readerlink Distribution Services, LLC.

Stevenson, Robert Louis. A Child's Garden of Verses. McClintock, Barbara, illus. 2011. (ENG.). 80p. (J). (gr. -1-3). 17.99 *(978-0-06-028228-8(2))* HarperCollins Pubs.

—A Child's Garden of Verses: A Collection of Scriptures, Prayers & Poems, 1 vol. Wildsmith, Brian, illus. 2008. (ENG.). 32p. (J). 19.95 *(978-1-59572-057-3(X))* Star Bright Bks., Inc.

—Poetry For Young People: Robert Louis Stevenson. 2003. cd-rom 19.00 *(978-0-931968-62-4(3))* Samizdat Express.

SCOUTS AND SCOUTING

see also Boy Scouts; Girl Scouts

Buckley, James. Coaching & Scouting, Vol. 10. Ferrer, Al, ed. 2015. (Careers off the Field Ser.). (Illus.). 64p. (J). (gr. 7). lib. bdg. 23.95 *(978-1-4222-3267-5(0))* Mason Crest.

Calvert, Patricia. Kit Carson: He Led the Way. 2006. (Great Explorations Ser.). (Illus.). 80p. (gr. 6-7). lib. bdg. 22.95 *(978-0-7614-2223-5(4),* Benchmark Bks.) Marshall Cavendish Corp.

Girl Scouts of the USA, creator. The Senior Girl's Guide to Girl Scouting. 2011. spiral bd. 22.50 *(978-0-88441-779-8(4))* Girl Scouts of the USA.

Kalar, Bonnie. The Scouts. Spreen, Kathe, illus. Date not set. 8p. (J). (gr. -1-2). pap. *(978-1-891619-26-7(8))* Corona Pr.

Russell, Wendy Thomas & Goodman, Sarah. MEdia. 2010. (Illus.). 96p. (J). *(978-0-88441-752-1(2))* Girl Scouts of the USA.

Sanford, William R. & Green, Carl R. Kit Carson: Courageous Mountain Man. 2012. (Courageous Heroes of the American West Ser.). 48p. (J). pap. 8.95 *(978-1-4644-0094-0(6));* (Illus.). (gr. 5-18). 22.60 *(978-0-7660-4011-3(9))* Enslow Pubs., Inc.

Savage, Jeff. Fearless Scouts: True Tales of the Wild West. 2012. (True Tales of the Wild West Ser.). (Illus.). 48p. (J). (gr. 5-18). pap. 8.95 *(978-1-4644-0032-2(6));* lib. bdg. 22.60 *(978-0-7660-4024-3(0))* Enslow Pubs., Inc.

Studio 2b: Focus - Express It. 2004. (YA). pap. *(978-0-88441-671-5(2))* Girl Scouts of the USA.

Studio 2b Focus - Don't Sweat It. 2004. (YA). pap. *(978-0-88441-669-2(0))* Girl Scouts of the USA.

Studio 2b Focus - Mind Your Own Business. 2004. (YA). pap. *(978-0-88441-668-5(2))* Girl Scouts of the USA.

STUDIO 2B Guide for Councils Phase II: Strategies & Models. 2004. (YA). *(978-0-88441-686-9(0))* Girl Scouts of the USA.

Tuchman, Laura. Welcome to the Daisy Flower Garden. Kalis, Jennifer, illus. 2008. 88p. (J). *(978-0-88441-709-5(3))* Girl Scouts of the USA.

Vander Pluym, Andrea. Mission: Sisterhood. Waters, Susy Pilgrim, illus. 2010. 80p. (YA). *(978-0-88441-753-8(0))* Girl Scouts of the USA.

Warren, Andrea. The Boy Who Became Buffalo Bill: Growing up Billy Cody in Bleeding Kansas, 0 vols. 2015. (ENG., Illus.). 256p. (J). 19.99 *(978-1-4778-2718-5(8),* 9781477827185, Two Lions) Amazon Publishing.

Wiese, Jim & Melton, H. Keith. The Spy's Guide to Scouting & Reconnaissance. 2003. (Illus.). 48p. (J). *(978-0-439-33647-5(3))* Scholastic, Inc.

SCOUTS AND SCOUTING—FICTION

Appelt, Kathi. The True Blue Scouts of Sugar Man Swamp. 2014. (ENG., Illus.). 352p. (J). (gr. 3-7). pap. 8.99 *(978-1-4424-2108-0(8),* Atheneum Bks. for Young Readers) Simon & Schuster Children's Publishing.

—The True Blue Scouts of Sugar Man Swamp. Bricking, Jennifer, illus. 2013. (ENG.). 336p. (J). (gr. 3-7). 16.99 *(978-1-4424-2105-9(3))* Simon & Schuster Children's Publishing.

Berenstain, Jan & Berenstain, Mike. Help the Homeless, 1 vol. 2012. (I Can Read! / Berenstain Bears / Good Deed Scouts / Living Lights Ser.). (ENG., Illus.). 32p. (J). pap. 3.99 *(978-0-310-72102-4(4))* Zonderkidz.

—Honey Hunt Helpers, 1 vol. 2012. (I Can Read! / Berenstain Bears / Good Deed Scouts / Living Lights Ser.). (ENG., Illus.). 32p. (J). pap. 3.99 *(978-0-310-72101-7(6))* Zonderkidz.

—Let the Bible Be Your Guide. 2011. (Berenstain Bears/Living Lights Ser.). (ENG., Illus.). 40p. (J). 6.99 *(978-0-310-72714-9(6))* Zonderkidz.

Bowen, Robert Sidney. Dave Dawson, Flight Lieutenant. 2011. 248p. 46.95 *(978-1-258-01820-7(9))* Literary Licensing, LLC.

D'Ath, Justin. Grizzly Trap. 2015. (ENG.). 144p. (J). pap. 4.99 *(978-1-61067-359-4(X))* Kane Miller.

Dillard, Sarah. Mouse Scouts. 2016. (Mouse Scouts Ser.). (ENG., Illus.). 128p. (J). (gr. 2-5). 12.99 *(978-0-385-75599-3(6),* Knopf Bks. for Young Readers) Random Hse. Children's Bks.

—Mouse Scouts: Make a Difference. 2016. (Mouse Scouts Ser.). (ENG., Illus.). 144p. (J). (gr. 2-5). 12.99 *(978-0-385-75603-7(8),* Knopf Bks. for Young Readers) Random Hse. Children's Bks.

Disney Book Group Staff. Doc Mcstuffins Training Army Al. Disney Storybook Art Team, illus. 2014. (ENG.). 24p. (J). (gr. -1-k). pap. 3.99 *(978-1-4847-1419-5(9))* Disney Pr.

Emerson, Carl. Monster Boy & the Scary Scouts, 1 vol. Levin, Lon, illus. 2010. (Monster Boy Set 2 Ser.). (ENG.). 32p. (J). (gr. k-3). 28.50 *(978-1-60270-778-8(2))* ABDO Publishing Co.

Garis, Lilian C. The Girl Scout Pioneers; or, Winning the First B C. 2007. 148p. per. *(978-1-4065-2775-9(0))* Dodo Pr.

Gatewood, June S. Mandy Miller & the Brownie Troop. Connors, Mary, illus. 2009. 48p. pap. 17.49 *(978-1-4389-1727-6(9))* AuthorHouse.

Hapka, Catherine, pseud. Pony Crazy. Kennedy, Anne, illus. 2009. (I Can Read Level 2 Ser.). (ENG.). 32p. (J). (gr. -1-3). 16.99 *(978-0-06-125533-5(5))* HarperCollins Pubs.

Hawke, Jay Jordan. A Scout Is Brave. 2nd ed. 2016. (ENG., Illus.). (J). 24.99 ***(978-1-63477-929-6(0),*** Harmony Ink Pr.) Dreamspinner Pr.

Kipling, Rudyard. Land & Sea Tales for Scouts & Scout. 2005. pap. 30.95 *(978-1-885529-84-8(8))* Stevens Publishing.

Mccormick, Scott. Camping Catastrophe! Lazzell, R. H., illus. 2016. (Mr. Pants Ser.: 4). (ENG.). 128p. (J). (gr. k-3). 12.99 *(978-0-525-42812-1(7),* Dial Bks) Penguin Young Readers Group.

McCormick, Wilfred. Eagle Scout: A Bronc Burnett Story. 2011. 192p. 42.95 *(978-1-258-07309-1(9))* Literary Licensing, LLC.

Osmond, Joanne H. A Fishy Adventure. Osmond, Jack, illus. 2013. 152p. pap. 12.99 *(978-1-933334-26-4(6))* Vision Tree, Ltd., The.

Ralphson, G. Harvey. Boy Scouts on the Open Plain. 2005. pap. 27.95 *(978-1-885529-55-8(4))* Stevens Publishing.

Rubino, Tony. Who Ate the Brownies. 2013. 28p. pap. 24.95 *(978-1-63004-481-7(4))* America Star Bks.

Welcom to the Nature Scouts. 2003. (J). per. *(978-1-57657-874-2(7))* Paradise Pr., Inc.

Wilson, John. Victorio's War, 1 vol. 2012. (Desert Legend Trilogy Ser.: 3). (ENG.). 176p. (YA). (gr. 8-12). pap. 12.95 *(978-1-55469-882-0(0))* Orca Bk. Pubs. USA.

SCRIPTURES, HOLY

see Bible

SCREEN PROCESS PRINTING

Luidens, Lyz, et al. Silk Screening. 2015. (21st Century Skills Innovation Library: Makers As Innovators Ser.). (ENG., Illus.). 32p. (J). (gr. 4-8). 29.93 *(978-1-63362-379-8(3),* 206936) Cherry Lake Publishing.

SCROOGE, EBENEZER (FICTITIOUS CHARACTER)—FICTION

Block, Shelly, et al. Uncle Scrooge, No. 351. Clark, John, ed. 2006. (ENG., Illus.). 64p. pap. 6.95 *(978-1-888472-15-8(4),* 9781888472158) Gemstone Publishing, Inc.

A Christmas Carol. 2004. (J). cd-rom 7.99 *(978-0-9740847-9-4(4))* GiGi Bks.

A Christmas Carol. 2003. (Illus.). 32p. (J). 9.98 *(978-1-4054-0997-1(5));* 4.98 *(978-1-4054-0980-3(0))* Parragon, Inc.

Dickens, Charles. A Christmas Carol. 2008. (Illus.). 116p. (Orig.). pap. 7.99 *(978-1-60450-545-0(1),* Serenity Pubs.) Arc Manor.

—A Christmas Carol. Bryant, Clive, ed. Collins, Mike & Offredi, James, illus. 2012. (ENG.). 160p. (Orig.). (gr. 6). lib. bdg. 24.95 *(978-1-907127-40-3(2))* Classical Comics GBR. Dist: Publishers Group West (PGW).

—A Christmas Carol. Howell, Keith, tr. Roach, David & Offredi, James, illus. 2008. (ENG.). 144p. (Orig.). (gr. 4-18). pap. 16.95 *(978-1-906332-52-5(5));* pap. 16.95 *(978-1-906332-51-8(7))* Classical Comics GBR. (Classical Comics, Ltd.). Dist: Publishers Group West (PGW).

—A Christmas Carol. 2008. 160p. (Orig.). (gr. 5-6). pap. 11.95 *(978-1-4341-0214-0(9))* Editorium, The.

—A Christmas Carol. 2006. (Illus.). 61p. (Orig.). (J). lib. bdg. 30.77 *(978-1-4242-1016-9(X))* Fitzgerald Bks.

—A Christmas Carol. 2009. 84p. (Orig.). (gr. -1-18). pap. 19.99 *(978-1-4432-6003-9(7))* General Bks. LLC.

—A Christmas Carol. Helquist, Brett, illus. 2009. (ENG.). 40p. (Orig.). (J). (gr. k). 17.99 *(978-0-06-165099-4(4))* HarperCollins Pubs.

—A Christmas Carol. 2008. (Puffin Classics Ser.). (ENG., Illus.). 160p. (Orig.). (J). (gr. 5-7). 5.99 *(978-0-14-132452-4(X),* Puffin Books) Penguin Young Readers Group.

—A Christmas Carol. 2004. 224p. (Orig.). (YA). pap. 29.00 incl. audio *(978-1-4000-9005-1(9),* Listening Library) Random Hse. Audio Publishing Group.

—A Christmas Carol. Donnelly, Karen, illus. 2013. (Charles Dickens Ser.). (ENG.). 64p. (Orig.). pap. 6.95 *(978-1-906230-02-9(1))* Real Reads Ltd. GBR. Dist: Casemate Pubs. & Bk. Distributors, LLC.

—A Christmas Carol. Andrews, Gary, illus. 2008. (Fast Track Classics Ser.). 46p. (Orig.). (J). (gr. 4-7). pap. 10.00 *(978-1-4190-5087-9(7))* Steck-Vaughn.

—A Christmas Carol. McKowen, Scott, illus. 2009. (Sterling Unabridged Classics Ser.). (ENG.). 96p. (Orig.). (J). (gr. 5). 9.95 *(978-1-4027-6690-9(4))* Sterling Publishing Co., Inc.

—Christmas Carol. Innocenti, Roberto, illus. 2005. 152p. (J). (gr. 4-6). 35.00 *(978-1-56846-182-3(8))* Creative Co., The.

—A Christmas Carol. 2009. (Foundation Classics Ser.). 56p. (J). (gr. 5-9). lib. bdg. 27.95 *(978-1-60754-850-8(X))* Windmill Bks.

—A Christmas Carol. Blake, Quentin, illus. unabr. ed. 2004. (Chrysalis Childrens Classics Ser.). 190p. (Orig.). (YA). pap. *(978-1-84365-063-8(0),* Pavilion Children's Books) Pavilion Bks.

—A Christmas Carol, 1 vol. 2010. (Illustrated Classics Ser.). (ENG., Illus.). 64p. (Orig.). (YA). (gr. 9-12). pap. 9.95 *(978-1-56254-890-2(5))* Saddleback Educational Publishing, Inc.

—A Christmas Carol the Graphic Novel - Original Text: British Edition. Collins, Mike et al, illus. 2008. 160p. (Orig.). pap. *(978-1-906332-17-4(7))* Classical Comics.

—Quentin Blake's a Christmas Carol. Blake, Quentin, illus. 2012. (ENG.). 150p. (J). (gr. 2-4). 16.99 *(978-1-84365-165-9(3),* Pavilion Children's Books) Pavilion Bks. GBR. Dist: Independent Pubs. Group.

Marks, Alan, illus. A Christmas Carol. 2013. (ENG.). 24p. (J). 18.99 *(978-0-7945-2910-9(0),* Usborne) EDC Publishing.

Wilson, Matthew. Scrooge & Santa GN. 2011. (Illus.). 100p. pap. 14.95 *(978-1-897548-98-1(2))* Arcana Studio, Inc.

SCUBA DIVING

Here are entered works on free diving with the use of a self-contained underwater breathing apparatus. Works on free diving with the use of mask, fins and snorkel are entered under Skin Diving.

Arroyo, Sheri, et al. How Deep Sea Divers Use Math. 2009. (Math in the Real World Ser.). 32p. (gr. 4-6). 28.00 *(978-1-60413-611-1(1),* Chelsea Clubhouse) Facts On File, Inc.

Bodden, Valerie. Scuba Diving. 2009. (Active Sports Ser.). (J). (gr. 1-5). 24.25 *(978-1-58341-701-0(X),* Creative Education) Creative Co., The.

Broadbent, Paul. Scuba Diving. 2007. (Trackers-Math Ser.). (gr. 2-5). pap. 5.00 *(978-1-59055-938-3(X))* Pacific Learning, Inc.

Gilkerson, Patricia. My Adventure Scuba Diving. 2006. (My Adventure Ser.). 44p. (J). (gr. -1-3). pap. 8.99 *(978-1-59092-286-6(7))* Blue Forge Pr.

Huntrods, David. For the Love of Scuba. 2006. (For the Love of Sports Ser.). (Illus.). 24p. lib. bdg. 24.45 *(978-1-59036-382-9(5));* per. 8.95 *(978-1-59036-383-6(3))* Weigl Pubs., Inc.

—Scuba. 2013. (J). *(978-1-62127-320-2(2));* pap. *(978-1-62127-325-7(3))* Weigl Pubs., Inc.

Lopatka, Michael. Scuba Divers Sign Language: A Guide to Underwater Communications of Tropical Reef Inhabitants. 2003. (Illus.). 75p. 12.95 *(978-0-9723218-9-1(6),* 0-9723218-9-6) Awesome Guides, Inc.

McFee, Shane. Scuba Diving. (Living on the Edge Ser.). 24p. (gr. 2-3). 2009. 42.50 *(978-1-61514-298-9(3),* PowerKids Pr.) 2008. (Illus.). (J). lib. bdg. 22.60 *(978-1-4042-4217-3(1))* Rosen Publishing Group, Inc., The.

Nagelhout, Ryan. Diving with Sharks. 2014. (Illus.). 32p. (J). *(978-1-4824-3287-9(0))* Stevens, Gareth Publishing LLLP.

Ryback, Carol. Scuba Diving. 2005. (Extreme Sports Ser.). (Illus.). 24p. (gr. 2-5). pap. 8.15 *(978-0-8368-4549-5(8));* lib. bdg. 23.00 *(978-0-8368-4542-6(0))* Stevens, Gareth Publishing LLLP. (Gareth Stevens Learning Library).

Teitelbaum, Michael. Scuba Diving. 2011. (Extreme Sports Ser.). (ENG., Illus.). 32p. (J). (gr. 2-5). lib. bdg. 28.50 *(978-1-60973-182-3(4),* 201131) Child's World, Inc., The.

Woolf, Alex. Sailing the Great Barrier Reef. 2014. (Traveling Wild Ser.). 32p. (J). (gr. 3-6). pap. 63.00 *(978-1-4824-1252-9(7))* Stevens, Gareth Publishing LLLP.

SCULLING

see Rowing

SCULPTORS

Coury, Tina Nichols. Hanging off Jefferson's Nose: Growing up on Mount Rushmore. Comport, Sally Wern, illus. 2012. (ENG.). 40p. (J). (gr. k-3). 16.99 *(978-0-8037-3731-0(9),* Dial Bks) Penguin Young Readers Group.

Di Cagno, Gabriella. Michelangelo. 2008. (Art Masters Ser.). 64p. (YA). (gr. 6-18). lib. bdg. 24.95 net. *(978-1-934545-01-0(5))* Oliver Pr., Inc.

Dunn, L. Kerr. Dreaming with Animals: Anna Hyatt Huntington & Brookgreen Gardens. Wyrick, Monica, illus. 2017. (Young Palmetto Bks.). (ENG.). 40p. (J). 18.99 *(978-1-61117-820-3(7))* Univ. of South Carolina Pr.

FitzGerald, Dawn. Vinnie & Abraham. Stock, Catherine, illus. 2007. (ENG.). 48p. (J). (gr. k-3). lib. bdg. 16.95 *(978-1-57091-658-8(6))* Charlesbridge Publishing, Inc.

Geis Conti, Patricia. Alexander Calder. 2010. (¡Mira Qué Artista! Ser.). (SPA.). 18p. (J). (gr. 2-4). 21.95 *(978-84-9825-375-7(6))* Combel Editorial, S.A. ESP. Dist: Independent Pubs. Group.

Geis, Patricia. Alexander Calder. 2014. (Meet the Artist Ser.). (ENG., Illus.). 18p. (J). (gr. 2-7). 24.95 *(978-1-61689-225-8(0))* Princeton Architectural Pr.

Kuiper, Kathleen, ed. The 100 Most Influential Painters & Sculptors of the Renaissance. 2009. (Britannica Guide to the World's Most Influential People Ser.). (Illus.). 376p. (YA). (gr. 9-12). lib. bdg. 53.00 *(978-1-61530-004-4(X))* Rosen Publishing Group, Inc., The.

Morrison, Taylor. The Buffalo Nickel. Morrison, Taylor, illus. 2006. (Illus.). 32p. (J). (gr. 4-8). reprint ed. 16.00 *(978-1-4223-5858-0(5))* DIANE Publishing Co.

O'Reilly, Sally. Henry Moore. 2003. (Artists in Their Time Ser.). (ENG., Illus.). 48p. (J). 24.00 *(978-0-531-12241-9(7),* Watts, Franklin) Scholastic Library Publishing.

Schroeder, Alan & National Geographic Learning Staff. In Her Hands: The Story of Sculptor Augusta Savage. Bereal, JaeMe, illus. 2009. (ENG.). 48p. (C). pap. 16.95 *(978-1-60060-989-3(9))* National Geographic School Publishing, Inc.

Stock, Catherine. Vinnie & Abraham. unabr. ed. 2008. (J). (gr. 2-5). 29.95 incl. audio compact disk *(978-0-8045-4190-9(6));* 27.95 incl. audio *(978-0-8045-6967-5(3))* Spoken Arts, Inc.

Stone, Tanya Lee. Sandy's Circus: A Story about Alexander Calder. Kulikov, Boris, illus. 2008. (ENG.). 40p. (J). (gr. 1-3). 16.99 *(978-0-670-06268-3(5),* Viking Books for Young Readers) Penguin Young Readers Group.

Tiger, Caroline. Isamu Noguchi. 2007. (Asian Americans of Achievement Ser.). (Illus.). 112p. (YA). (gr. 7-12). lib. bdg. 35.00 *(978-0-7910-9276-7(3))* Facts On File, Inc.

Wenzel, Angela. 13 Sculptures Children Should Know. 2010. (ENG., Illus.). 48p. (J). (gr. 3-7). 14.95 *(978-3-7913-7010-1(3))* Prestel Verlag GmbH & Co KG. DEU. Dist: Penguin Random Hse. LLC.

SCULPTORS—FICTION

Arnold, Elana K. Infandous. 2015. (ENG.). 200p. (YA). (gr. 8-12). 18.99 *(978-1-4677-3849-1(2))* Lerner Publishing Group.

Aston, Dianna Hutts. Dream Something Big: The Story of the Watts Towers. Roth, Susan L., illus. 2011. (ENG.). 40p. (J). (gr. k-3). 17.99 *(978-0-8037-3245-2(7),* Dial Bks) Penguin Young Readers Group.

Atkins, Jeannine. Stone Mirrors: The Sculpture & Silence of Edmonia Lewis. 2017. (ENG., Illus.). 176p. (J). (gr. 7). 17.99 *(978-1-4814-5905-1(8),* Atheneum Bks. for Young Readers) Simon & Schuster Children's Publishing.

Bedard, Michael. The Clay Ladies. braille ed. 2004. (J). (gr. k-3). spiral bd. *(978-0-616-01544-5(5))* Canadian National Institute for the Blind/Institut National Canadien pour les Aveugles.

Bradbury, Jennifer. Outside In. 2017. (ENG., Illus.). 288p. (J). (gr. 3-7). 16.99 ***(978-1-4424-6827-6(0),*** Atheneum/Caitlyn Dlouhy Books) Simon & Schuster Children's Publishing.

Carmichael, Clay. Wild Things. (ENG.). (J). 2012. 248p. (gr. 5-8). pap. 9.95 *(978-1-59078-914-8(8))* 2009. 248p. (gr. 4-6). 18.95 *(978-1-59078-627-7(0),* Front Street) Boyds Mills Pr.

—Wild Things, 6 vols. 2010. (J). 77.75 *(978-1-4498-0632-3(5))* Recorded Bks., Inc.

Daly, Jude. Sivu's Six Wishes: A Taoist Tale. 2010. (ENG., Illus.). 36p. (J). (gr. 1-5). 17.00 *(978-0-8028-5369-1(2),*

S

Eerdmans Bks For Young Readers) Eerdmans, William B. Publishing Co.

Stanley, Diane. The Trouble with Wishes. Stanley, Diane, illus. 2007. (Illus.). 32p. (J). (gr. k-3). lib. bdg. 17.89 *(978-0-06-055452-1(5))* HarperCollins Pubs.

Ziarnik, Natalie. Madeleine's Light: A Story of Camille Claudel. Dunn, Robert, illus. 2012. (ENG.). 32p. (J). (gr. k-2). 17.95 *(978-1-59078-855-4(9))* Boyds Mills Pr.

SCULPTURE

see also Mobiles (Sculpture); Modeling; Monuments; Soap Sculpture

Alexander, Heather & Hamilton, Meredith. A Child's Introduction to Art: The World's Greatest Paintings & Sculptures. Hamilton, Meredith, illus. 2014. (ENG., Illus.). 96p. (J). (gr. -1-17). 19.99 *(978-1-57912-956-9(0)*, 81956, Black Dog & Leventhal Pubs. Inc.) Hachette Bks.

Beak, Nick Huckleberry. How to Bend Balloons. 2013. (ENG., Illus.). 64p. (J). (gr. 3-7). 9.99 *(978-1-84322-864-6(5)*, Armadillo) Anness Publishing GBR. Dist: National Bk. Network.

Briggs, Paula. Make Build Create: Sculpture Projects for Children. 2016. (ENG., Illus.). 144p. pap. 24.95 *(978-1-910433-70-6(5))* Black Dog Publishing Ltd. GBR. Dist: Two Rivers Distribution.

Capek, Michael. Secrets of the Terracotta Army: Tomb of an Ancient Chinese Emperor, 1 vol. 2014. (Archaeological Mysteries Ser.). (ENG.). 32p. (gr. 3-4). lib. bdg. 27.99 *(978-1-4765-9917-5(3))* Capstone Press of Coughlan Cos.

deMarin, Layne. Built from Stone, 1 vol. 2011. (Wonder Readers Fluent Level Ser.). (ENG.). 32p. (gr. -1-2). pap. 5.99 *(978-1-4296-7911-4(5)*, Wonder Readers) Capstone Press of Coughlan Cos.

Hill, Isabel T. Urban Animals, 1 vol. Hill, Isabel T., photos by. 2009. (ENG., Illus.). 32p. (J). (gr. 2-7). 17.95 *(978-1-59572-209-6(2))* Star Bright Bks., Inc.

Howse, Jennifer. Totem Poles: Canadian Icons. 2010. (Illus.). 24p. *(978-1-77071-574-5(6))*; pap. *(978-1-77071-581-3(9))* Weigl Educational Pubs. Ltd.

James, Sara. Sculpting. 2014. (Art Today! Ser.: 10). (Illus.). 64p. (J). (gr. 7-18). 23.95 *(978-1-4222-3176-0(3))* Mason Crest.

Jiang, Helga. Clay Charm Magic! 25 Amazing, Teeny-Tiny Projects to Make with Polymer Clay. 2014. (ENG.). 128p. (J). (gr. k). 12.95 *(978-1-63220-398-4(7)*, Sky Pony Pr.) Skyhorse Publishing Co., Inc.

Kallen, Stuart. Sculpture. 2014. (Discovering Art). (ENG., Illus.). 80p. (J). lib. bdg. *(978-1-60152-678-6(4))* ReferencePoint Pr., Inc.

Krempel, Ulrich. Niki's World: Niki de Saint Phalle. 2004. (Adventures in Art Ser.). (Illus.). 30p. (J). 14.95 *(978-3-7913-3068-6(3))* Prestel Publishing.

Kuiper, Kathleen, ed. The 100 Most Influential Painters & Sculptors of the Renaissance. 2009. (Britannica Guide to the World's Most Influential People Ser.). (Illus.). 376p. (YA). (gr. 9-12). lib. bdg. 53.00 *(978-1-61530-004-4(X))* Rosen Publishing Group, Inc., The.

May, Susie & Whitely, Heather. Shape. 2006. (Children's Art Ser. from the National Gallery of Victoria Ser.). (Illus.). 28p. pap. 9.95 *(978-0-7241-0239-6(6))* National Gallery of Victoria AUS. Dist: Antique Collectors' Club.

Nardo, Don. Sculpture. 2006. (Eye on Art Ser.). (ENG., Illus.). 104p. (J). (gr. 3-7). lib. bdg. 34.80 *(978-1-59018-966-5(3)*, Lucent Bks.) Cengage Gale.

Nelson, Robin. From Wax to Crayon. 2013. (Start to Finish, Second Series: Everyday Products Ser.). (ENG., Illus.). 24p. (gr. k-3). pap. 6.95 *(978-1-4677-0798-5(8))*; lib. bdg. 23.93 *(978-0-7613-9183-8(5)*, Lerner Pubns.) Lerner Publishing Group.

Pitamic, Maja & Laidlaw, Jill. Three-Dimensional Art Adventures: 36 Creative, Artist-Inspired Projects in Sculpture, Ceramics, Textiles, & More. 2016. (Art Adventures Ser.). (ENG., Illus.). 144p. (J). (gr. 1). pap. 19.99 *(978-1-61373-659-3(2))* Chicago Review Pr., Inc.

Pym, Tasha. Super Sculptures. Elworthy, Antony, photos by. 2006. (Collins Big Cat Ser.). (ENG., Illus.). 24p. (J). (gr. 1-1). pap. 6.99 *(978-0-00-718686-0(X))* HarperCollins Pubs. Ltd. GBR. Dist: Independent Pubs. Group.

QEB Let's Start! Art National Book Stores Edition: Sculpture. 2006. (J). per. *(978-1-59566-302-3(9))* QEB Publishing Inc.

Raczka, Bob. 3-D ABC: A Sculptural Alphabet. 2006. (Bob Raczka's Art Adventures Ser.). (ENG., Illus.). 32p. (J). (gr. k-12). lib. bdg. 25.26 *(978-0-7613-9456-3(7)*, Millbrook Pr.) Lerner Publishing Group.

Taylor, Terry. Sand Play! 20+ SANDsational Ideas. 2014. (ENG.). 48p. (J). (gr. 2-6). pap. 7.99 *(978-0-486-79479-2(2))* Dover Pubns., Inc.

Tullet, Hervé. The Game of Sculpture. 2012. (Tullet Game Ser.). (ENG.). 14p. (gr. -1-1). 12.95 *(978-0-7148-6489-1(7))* Phaidon Pr., Inc.

—The Giant Game of Sculpture. 2014. (ENG., Illus.). 16p. (gr. k-3). 29.95 *(978-0-7148-6800-4(0))* Phaidon Pr., Inc.

VanVoorst, Jenny Fretland. La Escultura. 2016. (El Estudio del Artista (Artist's Studio)).Tr. of Scupture. (SPA.). 24p. (J). (gr. k-2). lib. bdg. 25.65 *(978-1-62031-323-7(5)*, Bullfrog Bks.) Jump! Inc.

—Sculpture. 2016. (Artist's Studio Ser.). 24p. (J). (gr. k-2). lib. bdg. 25.65 *(978-1-62031-284-1(0)*, Bullfrog Bks.) Jump! Inc.

Weill, Cynthia. Mi Familia Calaca / My Skeleton Family. Zarate, Jesus, illus. 2016. (First Concepts in Mexican Folk Art Ser.). (ENG.). 32p. (J). (gr. -1-2). pap. 7.95 *(978-1-941026-34-2(6))* Cinco Puntos Pr.

Wenzel, Angela. 13 Sculptures Children Should Know. 2010. (ENG., Illus.). 48p. (J). (gr. 3-7). 14.95 *(978-3-7913-7010-1(3))* Prestel Verlag GmbH & Co KG. DEU. Dist: Penguin Random Hse. LLC.

SCULPTURE—FICTION

Balliett, Blue. The Calder Game. Helquist, Brett, illus. (ENG.). (J). (gr. 3-7). 2010. 416p. 7.99 *(978-0-439-85208-1(0)*, Scholastic Paperbacks) 2008. 400p. 17.99 *(978-0-439-85207-4(2)*, Scholastic Pr.) Scholastic, Inc.

Brezenoff, Steven. The Case of the Stolen Sculpture. Weber, Lisa K., illus. 2015. (Museum Mysteries Ser.). (ENG.). 128p. (gr. 2-3). lib. bdg. 26.65 *(978-1-4342-9686-3(5))* Stone Arch Bks.

Campos, Tito. Muffler Man el Hombre Mofle. Alvarez, Lamberto, illus. 2009. 32p. (J). pap. 7.95 *(978-1-55885-557-1(2)*, Piñata Books) Arte Publico Pr.

Howse, Jennifer. Les Totems: Les Emblèmes Canadiens. McMann, Julie, tr. from ENG. 2011. (FRE.). 24p. (YA). (gr. 2-4). *(978-1-77071-412-0(X))* Weigl Educational Pubs. Ltd.

Kusmierski, Janet & Colin, Paul. Snowman's Big Job. 2004. (Illus.). (J). *(978-0-439-58392-3(6))* Scholastic, Inc.

Lee, Ingrid. Dragon Tide, 1 vol. Meister, Soizick, illus. 2006. (ENG.). 32p. (J). (gr. -1-3). 17.95 *(978-1-55143-352-3(4))* Orca Bk. Pubs. USA.

Marsoli, Lisa Ann & Bridwell, Norman. The Snow Dog. Haefele, Steve, illus. 2004. (Big Red Reader Ser.). (J). pap. *(978-0-439-58559-0(7))* Scholastic, Inc.

Parker, Emma. The Snowman Olympics. 2010. (Illus.). 20p. pap. *(978-1-877561-36-8(3))* First Edition Ltd.

Pinkney, Jeff. Soapstone Signs, 1 vol. Gait, Darlene, illus. 2014. (Orca Echoes Ser.). (ENG.). 64p. (J). (gr. 2-3). pap. 6.95 *(978-1-4598-0400-5(7))* Orca Bk. Pubs. USA.

Reynolds, Aaron. Metal Man. Hoppe, Paul, illus. 2010. (ENG.). 32p. (J). (gr. k-3). pap. 7.95 *(978-1-58089-151-6(9))* Charlesbridge Publishing, Inc.

Rider, Cynthia. Our Snowman. Evans, Nicola, illus. 2013. (Start Reading Ser.). (ENG.). 24p. (gr. k-1). pap. 41.94 *(978-1-4765-3229-5(X))*; pap. 7.95 *(978-1-4765-3196-0(X))* Capstone Press of Coughlan Cos.

Styles, Walker. The Case of the Missing Tiger's Eye. Whitehouse, Ben, illus. 2016. (Rider Woofson Ser.: 1). (ENG.). 128p. (J). (gr. k-4). 16.99 *(978-1-4814-5738-5(1)*, Little Simon) Little Simon.

Sullivan, Kate. On Linden Square. Sullivan, Kate, illus. 2013. (ENG., Illus.). 40p. 15.99 *(978-1-58536-832-7(6))* Sleeping Bear Pr.

Tegen, Katherine Brown. Snowman Magic. Dorman, Brandon, illus. 2012. (ENG.). 32p. (J). (gr. -1-3). 12.99 *(978-0-06-201445-0(5))* HarperCollins Pubs.

Thielbar, Melinda. The Book Bandit: A Mystery with Geometry. Grandt, Eve et al, illus. 2010. (Manga Math Mysteries Ser.: 7). (ENG.). 48p. (gr. 3-5). 29.27 *(978-0-7613-4909-9(X))* Lerner Publishing Group.

—The Book Bandit No. 7: A Mystery with Geometry. Lee, Jenn Manley & Chow, Candice, illus. 2011. (Manga Math Mysteries Ser.: 7). (ENG.). 48p. (gr. 3-5). pap. 6.95 *(978-0-7613-8136-5(8)*, Graphic Universe™) Lerner Publishing Group.

—#7 the Book Bandit: A Mystery with Geometry. Lee, Jenn Manley & Chow, Candice, illus. 2011. (Manga Math Mysteries Set II Ser.). pap. 39.62 *(978-0-7613-8364-2(6)*, Graphic Universe™) Lerner Publishing Group.

Trice, Linda. Kenya's Art. Mitchell, Hazel, illus. 2016. (ENG.). 32p. (J). (gr. -1-3). 16.95 *(978-1-57091-848-3(1))* Charlesbridge Publishing, Inc.

Wallace, Nancy Elizabeth & Friedlaender, Linda. Look! Look! Look! at Sculpture, 0 vols. 2012. (ENG.). 40p. (J). (gr. k-3). 17.99 *(978-0-7614-6132-6(9)*, 9780761461326, Amazon Children's Publishing) Amazon Publishing.

SCULPTURE—HISTORY

Carter, David A. & Diaz, James. You Call That Art?! Learn about Modern Sculpture & Make Your Own. 2014. (ENG., Illus.). 48p. (J). (gr. 3-7). 24.95 *(978-1-4197-1307-1(8)*, Abrams Bks. for Young Readers) Abrams, Inc.

Osier, Peter. The History of Western Sculpture. 2015. (Britannica Guide to the Visual & Performing Arts Ser.). (ENG., Illus.). 128p. (J). (gr. 9-10). 45.00 *(978-1-68048-085-6(5)*, Britannica Educational Publishing) Rosen Publishing Group, Inc., The.

Osier, Peter, ed. The History of Western Sculpture. 2015. (Britannica Guide to the Visual & Performing Arts Ser.). (ENG.). 128p. (YA). (gr. 9-10). 90.00 *(978-1-68048-086-3(3)*, Britannica Educational Publishing) Rosen Publishing Group, Inc., The.

Spilsbury, Richard. Stories Behind the Art - Sculpture. 2017. (Stories in Art Ser.). (ENG., Illus.). 32p. (J). (gr. 4-6). pap. 11.99 *(978-0-7502-9486-7(8)*, Wayland) Hachette Children's Group GBR. Dist: Hachette Bk. Group.

SCULPTURE, RELIGIOUS

see Christian Art and Symbolism

SCULPTURE—TECHNIQUE

see also Modeling

Hanson, Anders. Cool Sculpture: The Art of Creativity for Kids, 1 vol. 2009. (Cool Art Ser.). (ENG.). 32p. (gr. 3-6). 28.50 *(978-1-60453-144-2(4)*, Checkerboard Library) ABDO Publishing Co.

Kuhtz, Cleo, ed. Sculpture: Materials, Technique, Styles, & Practice. 2016. (Britannica's Practical Guide to the Arts Ser.). 128p. (J). (gr. 10-10). lib. bdg. 36.25 *(978-1-68048-375-8(7))* Rosen Publishing Group, Inc., The.

Luxbacher, Irene. 123 I Can Sculpt! Luxbacher, Irene, illus. 2007. (Starting Art Ser.). (ENG., Illus.). 24p. (J). (gr. -1-2). pap. 5.95 *(978-1-55453-151-6(9))* Kids Can Pr., Ltd. CAN. Dist: Hachette Bk. Group.

Reid, Emily. Space Claymation. 2016. (Claymation Sensation Ser.). 32p. (gr. 3-3). pap. 11.75 *(978-1-4994-8100-6(4)*, Windmill Bks.) Rosen Publishing Group, Inc., The.

—Sports Claymation. 2016. (Claymation Sensation Ser.). 32p. (gr. 3-3). pap. 11.75 *(978-1-4994-8104-4(7)*, Windmill Bks.) Rosen Publishing Group, Inc., The.

Schwake, Susan. 3D Art Lab for Kids: 32 Hands-On Adventures in Sculpture & Mixed Media - Including Fun Projects Using Clay, Plaster, Cardboard, Paper, Fiber Beads & More! Schwake, Rainer, photos by. 2013. (Lab Ser.). (ENG., Illus.). 144p. pap. 24.99 *(978-1-59253-815-7(0)*, 1592538150, Quarry Books) Quarto Publishing Group USA.

Spilsbury, Richard. Sculpture. 2009. (Stories in Art Ser.). (Illus.). 30p. (J). lib. bdg. 26.50 *(978-1-4042-4435-1(2)*, PowerKids Pr.) Rosen Publishing Group, Inc., The.

Thomas, Isabel. Sculptures, 1 vol. 2011. (Start with Art Ser.). (ENG.). 24p. (gr. k-2). 23.32 *(978-1-4329-5017-0(7)*, Heinemann Read & Learn) Heinemann-Raintree.

Watt, Fiona. Complete Book of Art Ideas. 2005. (Art Ideas Ser.). 288p. (J). 39.95 *(978-0-7945-0900-2(2))*, Usborne) EDC Publishing.

SEA

see Ocean

SEA ANIMALS

see Marine Animals

SEA FISHERIES

see Fisheries

SEA HORSES

Bell, Samantha. Sea Horses. 2014. (21st Century Skills Library: Exploring Our Oceans Ser.). (ENG., Illus.). 32p. (J). (gr. 3-6). 28.50 *(978-1-62431-604-3(2)*, 203200) Cherry Lake Publishing.

Berger, Melvin & Berger, Gilda. Caballitos de Mar: Sea Horses. 2006. (SPA & ENG., Illus.). (J). *(978-0-439-87988-0(4))* Scholastic, Inc.

Butterworth, Christine. Sea Horse: The Shyest Fish in the Sea. Lawrence, John, illus. 2010. (Read, Listen, & Wonder Ser.). (ENG.). 32p. (J). (gr. -1-3). pap. 9.99 *(978-0-7636-4868-8(X))* Candlewick Pr.

—Sea Horse: The Shyest Fish in the Sea. Lawrence, John, illus. 2009. (Read & Wonder Ser.). (ENG.). 32p. (J). (gr. -1-3). pap. 6.99 *(978-0-7636-4140-5(5))* Candlewick Pr.

Clinging Sea Horses 6-Pack. 2004. (Illus.). (J). lib. bdg. 39.99 *(978-0-8225-5192-8(6))* Lerner Publishing Group.

Coldiron, Deborah. Sea Horses, 1 vol. 2007. (Underwater World Ser.). (ENG.). 32p. (gr. k-3). 27.07 *(978-1-59928-821-5(4)*, Buddy Bks.) ABDO Publishing Co.

Curtis, Jennifer Keats. Seahorses. Wallace, Chad, illus. 2012. (ENG.). 32p. (J). (gr. -1-3). 18.99 *(978-0-8050-9239-4(0)*, 9780805092394, Holt, Henry & Co. Bks. For Young Readers) Holt, Henry & Co.

George, Twig C. Seahorses. (gr. k-3). 2005. (Illus.). 31p. (J). per. 8.95 *(978-0-8225-3390-0(1))* 2003. 32p. lib. bdg. 24.90 *(978-0-7613-2869-8(6)*, Millbrook Pr.) Lerner Publishing Group.

Gibbs, Maddie. Sea Horses. 2013. (PowerKids Readers: Fun Fish Ser.). 24p. (J). (gr. k-2). 22.60 *(978-1-4777-0761-6(1))*; pap. 49.50 *(978-1-4777-0856-9(1))*; (ENG., Illus.). pap. 8.25 *(978-1-4777-0855-2(3))* Rosen Publishing Group, Inc., The. (PowerKids Pr.).

—Sea Horses / Los Caballos de Mar. De La Vega, Eida, ed. 2013. (PowerKids Readers: Fun Fish / Peces Divertidos Ser.). (ENG & SPA.). 24p. (J). (gr. k-2). 22.60 *(978-1-4777-1219-1(4)*, PowerKids Pr.) Rosen Publishing Group, Inc., The.

Gilkerson, Patricia. My Adventure with Sea Horses. 2009. (ENG.). 44p. (J). 8.99 *(978-1-59092-465-5(7))* Blue Forge Pr.

Gish, Melissa. Living Wild: Seahorses. 2017. (Living Wild Ser.). (ENG.). 48p. (J). (gr. 5-7). pap. 12.00 ***(978-1-62832-437-2(6)***, Creative Paperbacks) Creative Co., The.

—Seahorses. 2017. (J). ***(978-1-60818-834-5(5)***, Creative Education) Creative Co., The.

Hansen, Grace. Seahorses, 1 vol. 2014. (Ocean Life Ser.). (ENG.). 24p. (J). (gr. 2-4). lib. bdg. 28.50 *(978-1-62970-711-2(2))* ABDO Publishing Co.

Heller, Ruth. Sea Life. Heller, Ruth, illus. 2009. (Designs for Coloring Ser.). (ENG., Illus.). 64p. (J). (gr. 1-3). 6.99 *(978-0-448-45204-3(9)*, Grosset & Dunlap) Penguin Young Readers Group.

Is it a Fish? 6 Each of 1, 6 vols. (Sunshinetm Science Ser.). 24p. (gr. 1-2). 41.95 *(978-0-7802-1428-6(5))* Wright Group/McGraw-Hill.

Is it a Fish? Big Book. (Sunshinetm Science Ser.). 24p. (gr. 1-2). 37.50 *(978-0-7802-1429-3(3))* Wright Group/McGraw-Hill.

James, Helen Foster. Discover Sea Horses. 2015. (21st Century Basic Skills Library: Splash! Ser.). (ENG., Illus.). 24p. (J). (gr. 2-4). 24.21 *(978-1-63362-605-8(9)*, 206604) Cherry Lake Publishing.

Jango-Cohen, Judith. Clinging Sea Horses. 2005. (Pull Ahead Bks.). (Illus.). 32p. (gr. k-3). lib. bdg. 22.60 *(978-0-8225-3764-9(8))* Lerner Publishing Group.

Kalman, Bobbie. Les Hippocampes. 2010. (FRE., Illus.). 32p. (J). pap. 9.95 *(978-2-89579-286-4(0))* Bayard Canada Livres CAN. Dist: Crabtree Publishing Co.

—The Life Cycle of a Sea Horse. 2003. (Life Cycle Ser.). (ENG., Illus.). 32p. (J). pap. *(978-0-7787-0693-9(1))*; lib. bdg. *(978-0-7787-0663-2(X))*; lib. bdg. *(978-0-7787-0663-2(X))* Crabtree Publishing Co.

Laughlin, Kara L. Sea Horses. 2017. (In the Deep Blue Sea Ser.). (ENG.). 24p. (J). (gr. k-3). lib. bdg. 27.07 *(978-1-5038-1688-6(5)*, 211524) Child's World, Inc., The.

Leaf, Christina. Sea Horses. (Ocean Life Up Close Ser.). 24p. (J). (gr. k-3). 2017. pap. 6.99 ***(978-1-61891-267-1(4))*** 2016. (ENG., Illus.). 25.95 *(978-1-62617-420-7(2))* Bellwether Media. (Blastoff! Readers).

Meister, Cari. Sea Horses. 2013. (ENG., Illus.). 24p. (J). lib. bdg. 25.65 *(978-1-62031-033-5(3))* Jump! Inc.

Otfinoski, Steven. Seahorses. 2007. (Animals Animals Ser.). (Illus.). 48p. (gr. 3-3). lib. bdg. 29.93 *(978-0-7614-2529-8(2))* Marshall Cavendish Corp.

Owen, Ruth. Seahorse Fry. 2012. (Water Babies Ser.). 24p. (J). (gr. -1-3). lib. bdg. 21.32 *(978-1-61772-604-0(4))* Bearport Publishing Co., Inc.

Rabe, Tish. King Cecil the Sea Horse (Dr. Seuss/Cat in the Hat) Moroney, Christopher, illus. 2013. (Little Golden Book Ser.). (ENG.). 24p. (J). (-k). 3.99 *(978-0-449-81010-1(0)*, Golden Bks.) Random Hse. Children's Bks.

Rhodes, Mary Jo & Hall, David. Seahorses & Sea Dragons. Hall, David, photos by. 2005. (Undersea Encounters Ser.). (ENG., Illus.). 48p. (J). (gr. 3-7). lib. bdg. 27.00 *(978-0-516-24393-1(4)*, Children's Pr.) Scholastic Library Publishing.

Sexton, Colleen. The Life Cycle of a Sea Horse. 2010. (Life Cycles Ser.). (ENG., Illus.). 24p. (J). (gr. k-3). lib. bdg. 25.95 *(978-1-60014-312-0(1)*, Blastoff! Readers) Bellwether Media.

Shaskan, Trisha Speed. I Am a Sea Horse: The Life of a Dwarf Sea Horse, 1 vol. Ouren, Todd, illus. 2008. (I Live in the Ocean Ser.). (ENG.). 24p. (gr. -1-2). lib. bdg. 26.65 *(978-1-4048-4726-6(6))* Picture Window Bks.

Shofner, Melissa Raé. Sea Horses. 2017. (Freaky Fish Ser.). 24p. (J). (gr. 2-3). pap. 48.90 ***(978-1-5382-0250-0(6))*** Stevens, Gareth Publishing LLLP.

Turner, Pamela S. Project Seahorse. Tuason, Scott, illus. 12th ed. 2010. (Scientists in the Field Ser.). (ENG.). 64p. (J). (gr. 5-7). 18.99 *(978-0-547-20713-1(1))* Houghton Mifflin Harcourt Publishing Co.

Walker, Sally M. Sea Horses. 2004. (Early Bird Nature Bks.). (Illus.). 47p. (J). 25.26 *(978-0-8225-3051-0(1)*, Lerner Pubns.) Lerner Publishing Group.

Wearing, Judy. Seahorses. 2009. (World of Wonder Ser.). (Illus.). 24p. (J). (gr. 2-4). lib. bdg. 24.45 *(978-1-60596-102-6(7))* Weigl Pubs., Inc.

—Seahorses: World of Wonder: Underwater Life. 2009. (Illus.). 24p. (J). pap. 8.95 *(978-1-60596-103-3(5))* Weigl Pubs., Inc.

Weber, Valerie J. Sea Horses. 2008. (Animals That Live in the Ocean Ser.). (Illus.). 24p. (gr. -1-3). pap. 8.15 *(978-0-8368-9342-7(5)*, Weekly Reader Leveled Readers) Stevens, Gareth Publishing LLLP.

—Sea Horses/Caballitos de Mar. 2008. (Animals That Live in the Ocean/Animales Que Viven en el Oceano Ser.). (SPA & ENG.). 24p. (J). (gr. -1-3). lib. bdg. 22.60 *(978-0-8368-9249-9(6)*, Weekly Reader Leveled Readers) Stevens, Gareth Publishing LLLP.

Weber, Valerie J. & Weber, Valerie J. Sea Horses. 2008. (Animals That Live in the Ocean Ser.). (Illus.). 24p. (J). (gr. -1-3). lib. bdg. 22.60 *(978-0-8368-9243-7(7)*, Weekly Reader Leveled Readers) Stevens, Gareth Publishing LLLP.

—Sea Horses: Caballitos de Mar. 2008. (Animals That Live in the Ocean/Animales Que Viven en el Oceano Ser.). (SPA & ENG.). 24p. (gr. -1-3). pap. 8.15 *(978-0-8368-9348-9(4)*, Weekly Reader Leveled Readers) Stevens, Gareth Publishing LLLP.

SEA HORSES—FICTION

Bise, Jr. J. David & Bise, Jr. In Search of a Name a Seahorse Story. 2011. 44p. pap. 15.50 *(978-1-60976-288-9(6)*, Strategic Bk. Publishing) Strategic Book Publishing & Rights Agency (SBPRA).

Carle, Eric. Mister Seahorse. Carle, Eric, illus. (ENG., Illus.). (J). (gr. -1 — 1). 2011. 64p. bds. 8.99 *(978-0-399-25490-1(0))* 2004. 32p. 18.99 *(978-0-399-24269-4(4))* Penguin Young Readers Group. (Philomel Bks.).

Dadey, Debbie. The Secret Sea Horse. Avakyan, Tatevik, illus. 2013. (Mermaid Tales Ser.: 6). (ENG.). 112p. (J). (gr. 1-4). 15.99 *(978-1-4424-8261-6(3))*; pap. 5.99 *(978-1-4424-8260-9(5))* Simon & Schuster Children's Publishing. (Aladdin).

Dadey, Debby & Dadey, Debbie. Secret Sea Horse, 1 vol., Bk. 6. 2015. (Mermaid Tales Ser.). (ENG.). 96p. (J). (gr. 2-4). 24.21 *(978-1-61479-327-4(1)*, Spotlight) ABDO Publishing Co.

Davies, Caroline, illus. Seahorse. 2017. (Shake & Play Bath Bks.). (ENG.). 8p. (J). (gr. -1 — 1). 5.99 ***(978-1-4380-7842-7(0))*** Barron's Educational Series, Inc.

Dean, James. Pete the Cat: Scuba-Cat. Dean, James, illus. 2016. (My First I Can Read Ser.). (Illus.). 32p. (J). (gr. -1-3). pap. 3.99 *(978-0-06-230388-2(0))* HarperCollins Pubs.

Dean, James, illus. Pete the Cat: Scuba-Cat. 2016. 31p. (J). *(978-1-4844-7052-7(4))* Harper & Row Ltd.

Giulieri, Anne. Little Sea Horse & the Big Crab, 1 vol. Aranda, Omar, illus. 2012. (Engage Literacy Yellow Ser.). (ENG.). 32p. (gr. k-2). pap. 5.99 *(978-1-4296-8968-7(4)*, Engage Literacy) Capstone Press of Coughlan Cos.

—Little Sea Horse & the Big Storm, 1 vol. Aranda, Omar, illus. 2012. (Engage Literacy Blue Ser.). (ENG.). 32p. (gr. k-2). pap. 5.99 *(978-1-4296-8992-2(7)*, Engage Literacy) Capstone Press of Coughlan Cos.

Hendra, Sue. Barry the Fish with Fingers & the Hairy Scary Monster. 2011. 32p. *(978-1-74276-025-4(2)*, Koala Books) Scholastic Australia.

King, Karen. Sparkle the Seahorse. Hicks, Angie, illus. 2012. (ENG.). 24p. (J). 9.95 *(978-1-84135-879-6(7))* Award Pubns. Ltd. GBR. Dist: Parkwest Pubns., Inc.

Krosoczka, Jarrett J. Peanut Butter & Jellyfish. 2014. (ENG.). 40p. (J). (gr. -1-2). 16.99 *(978-0-375-87036-1(9)*, Knopf Bks. for Young Readers) Random Hse. Children's Bks.

Lee, Julia Elizabeth. Seahorses Down Under. Weiser, Robert, ed. (Defenders of Wildlife Ser.). (Illus.). 50+p. (J). (gr. k-3). lib. bdg. 9.95 *(978-0-9666857-0-1(9))* Dawn of Day Childrens Publishing Co., Inc.

Meadows, Daisy. Rihanna the Seahorse Fairy. 2012. (Illus.). 65p. (J). *(978-0-545-42599-5(9))* Scholastic, Inc.

Opal, Paola. Pippy. 2013. (Simply Small Ser.: 12). (ENG., Illus.). 24p. (J). bds. 7.95 *(978-1-897476-92-5(2))* Simply Read Bks. CAN. Dist: Ingram Publisher Services.

Salzmann, Mary Elizabeth. Sea Horse Races, 1 vol. 2007. (Critter Chronicles Ser.). (ENG., Illus.). 24p. (J). (gr. k-3). lib. bdg. 24.21 *(978-1-59928-468-2(5)*, SandCastle) ABDO Publishing Co.

Spickett, D. M. The Adventures of Sarah the Seahorse, 1 vol. 2009. 21p. pap. 24.95 *(978-1-61546-205-6(8))* America Star Bks.

Steele, Margaret. Wuz Da Nite Befo: A Pidgin Christmas Story in Hawaii. Chang, Roy, illus. 2005. 24p. 10.95 *(978-1-56647-750-5(6))* Mutual Publishing LLC.

Voyage to Shelter Cove. 2006. (Illus.). (J). pap., act. bk. ed. 2.00 *(978-0-9724425-5-8(3)*, White Tiger Pr.) Homes for the Homeless Institute, Inc.

Walker, Sally M. Seahorse Reef: A Story of the South Pacific. Petruccio, Steven James, illus. 2005. (ENG.). 32p. (J). (gr. -1-2). pap. 6.95 *(978-1-56899-938-8(0)*, S4020) Soundprints.

Wyllie, Jim & Wyllie, Miggie. Cedric's Day at the Castle. 2003. (Illus.). 24p. (J). (gr. -1-1). pap. 7.95 *(978-1-85149-712-6(9))* Antique Collectors' Club.

SEA IN ART

Baumbusch, Brigitte. Oceans in Art. 2005. (What Makes a Masterpiece? Ser.). (Illus.). 32p. (gr. 1-4). lib. bdg. 23.00 *(978-0-8368-4782-6(2)*, Gareth Stevens Learning Library) Stevens, Gareth Publishing LLLP.

Harbo, Christopher L. Easy Ocean Origami, 1 vol. 2010. (Easy Origami Ser.). (ENG.). 24p. (gr. 1-2). lib. bdg. 25.32 *(978-1-4296-5385-5(X)*, First Facts) Capstone Press of Coughlan Cos.

Montgomery, Kelly & Creative Haven Staff. Sea Life Designs Coloring Book. 2012. (Adult Coloring Ser.). (ENG., Illus.). 64p. (gr. 3). pap. 5.99 *(978-0-486-49088-5(2))* Dover Pubns., Inc.

SEA LIFE

see Seafaring Life

also names of countries with the subhead Navy, e.g., United States—Navy

SEA LIONS

see Seals (Animals)

SEA MOSSES

see Algae

SEA POETRY

Coombs, Kate. Water Sings Blue: Ocean Poems. So, Meilo, illus. 2012. (ENG.). 36p. (J). (gr. -1-3). 16.99 *(978-0-8118-7284-3(X))* Chronicle Bks. LLC.

Hughes, Langston. Sail Away. Bryan, Ashley, illus. 2015. (ENG.). 40p. (J). (gr. -1-3). 17.99 *(978-1-4814-3085-2(8))* Simon & Schuster Children's Publishing.

SEA POWER

see also Disarmament; Naval History; Warships

also names of countries with the subhead Navy or the subdivision History, Naval, e.g. United States—Navy; United States—History, Naval, etc.

Dougherty, Martin J. Sea Warfare. 2010. (Modern Warfare Ser.). (Illus.). 32p. (J). (gr. 2-5). lib. bdg. 26.00 *(978-1-4339-2734-8(9))* Stevens, Gareth Publishing LLLP.

Mueller, Richard. Naval Warfare of the Future. (Library of Future Weaponry Ser.). 64p. 2009. (gr. 6-6). 58.50 *(978-1-60853-640-5(8))* 2005. (Illus.). (J). (gr. 2-7). lib. bdg. 31.95 *(978-1-4042-0526-0(8))* Rosen Publishing Group, Inc., The.

SEA ROUTES

see Trade Routes

SEA SHELLS

see Shells

SEA SHORE

see Seashore

SEA STORIES

Anton, Amy Way. Ina the Octopus & Her Shipwreck Adventure. Way, MaryFaye, illus. 2008. 28p. pap. 13.99 *(978-1-4389-2177-8(2))* AuthorHouse.

Ardizzone, Edward. Tim All Alone. 2015. (Little Tim Ser.). (ENG., Illus.). 56p. (J). (gr. k-3). 18.99 *(978-1-84780-628-4(7),* Frances Lincoln) Quarto Publishing Group UK GBR. Dist: Hachette Bk. Group.

—Tim to the Rescue. 2015. (Little Tim Ser.). (ENG., Illus.). 56p. (J). (gr. k-3). 18.99 *(978-1-84780-630-7(9),* Frances Lincoln) Quarto Publishing Group UK GBR. Dist: Hachette Bk. Group.

—Tim's Friend Towser. 2015. (Little Tim Ser.). (ENG., Illus.). 56p. (J). (gr. -1-2). 18.99 *(978-1-84780-631-4(7),* Frances Lincoln) Quarto Publishing Group UK GBR. Dist: Hachette Bk. Group.

Avi. The True Confessions of Charlotte Doyle. 2012. (ENG.). 240p. (J). (gr. 3-7). pap. 6.99 *(978-0-545-47711-6(5),* Scholastic Paperbacks) Scholastic, Inc.

—The True Confessions of Charlotte Doyle. l.t. ed. 2005. 337p. pap. 10.95 *(978-0-7862-7252-5(X),* Large Print Pr.) Thorndike Pr.

—The True Confessions of Charlotte Doyle. 2012. lib. bdg. 17.20 *(978-0-606-26779-3(4),* Turtleback) Turtleback Bks.

Babbitt, Natalie. The Eyes of the Amaryllis. 2007. (ENG.). 144p. (J). (gr. 5-8). per. 7.99 *(978-0-312-37008-4(3),* 9780312370084) Square Fish.

Beck, Patricia. Prince Hasmir's High Seas Adventure. 2011. 24p. pap. 15.99 *(978-1-4628-6151-4(2))* Xlibris Corp.

Bently, Peter. Captain Jack & the Pirates. Oxenbury, Helen, illus. 2016. (ENG.). 32p. (J). (-k). 17.99 *(978-0-525-42950-0(6),* Dial Bks) Penguin Young Readers Group.

Blade, Adam. Deep Dive #3: Manak the Manta Ray. 2013. (Deep Dive Ser.: 3). (ENG.). 128p. (J). (gr. 2-5). pap. 4.99 *(978-0-545-42769-2(X),* Scholastic Paperbacks) Scholastic, Inc.

Bleu, Kennedy. Cotter Otter in Treasure Water. Goembel, Ponder, illus. 2014. (ENG.). 24p. (J). pap. 24.95 *(978-1-63004-814-3(3))* America Star Bks.

Bodeen, S. A. The Raft. 2013. (ENG.). 256p. (YA). (gr. 7-12). pap. 9.99 *(978-1-250-02739-9(X),* 9781250027399) Square Fish.

Bringsvaerd, Tor Age. Ruffen: The Escape to Loch Ness. Hansen, Thore, illus. 2009. (Ruffen Ser.). 72p. (J). (gr. 1-4). 16.95 *(978-0-9815761-2-1(5))* Mackenzie Smiles, LLC.

Collingwood, Harry. The Castaways. 2008. 172p. 25.95 *(978-1-60664-710-3(5));* pap. 13.95 *(978-1-60664-209-2(X))* Rodgers, Alan Bks.

—The Rover's Secret. 2011. 274p. 29.95 *(978-1-4638-9505-1(4))* Rodgers, Alan Bks.

—Under the Chilean Flag. 2009. 184p. 26.95 *(978-1-60664-598-7(6));* pap. 13.95 *(978-1-60664-330-3(4))* Rodgers, Alan Bks.

Cooper, Susan. Victory. 2013. (ENG., Illus.). 224p. (J). (gr. 5-9). 17.99 *(978-1-4424-8079-7(3));* pap. 6.99 *(978-1-4424-8080-3(7))* McElderry, Margaret K. Bks. (McElderry, Margaret K. Bks.).

Croce, Pat & Slutsky, Adam. Plunder. 2015. (Plunder Ser.: 1). (ENG.). 336p. 31.95 *(978-1-68162-373-3(0));* 338p. (J). pap. 16.95 *(978-1-63026-893-0(3))* Turner Publishing Co.

Cummings, Mary. And the Baker's Boy Went to Sea. 2006. (Illus.). 195p. (YA). 16.95 *(978-0-9774855-0-5(1))* Sparkling Pr.

Dalmatian Press Staff, adapted by. Moby Dick. (J). 9.95 *(978-1-56156-308-1(0))* Kidsbooks, LLC.

De Valor, Diana. The Great Adventures of Sea Worthy with the I Can Crew: The Treasure of Captain Blue Beard. 2011. 32p. pap. 19.95 *(978-1-4269-6627-9(X))* Trafford Publishing.

Duncan, Daniel. South. 2017. (ENG., Illus.). 40p. (J). (gr. k-2). 17.95 *(978-1-4197-2299-8(9),* Abrams Bks. for Young Readers) Abrams, Inc.

Eames, Brian. The Dagger Quick. (Dagger Chronicles Ser.). (ENG., (J). (gr. 3-7). 2013. Illus.). 352p. pap. 6.99 *(978-1-4424-8368-2(7))* 2011. 336p. 15.99 *(978-1-4424-2311-4(0))* Simon & Schuster/Paula Wiseman Bks. (Simon & Schuster/Paula Wiseman Bks.).

Eisner, Will & Melville, Herman. Moby Dick. 2003. (ENG., Illus.). 32p. (J). pap. 7.95 *(978-1-56163-294-7(5))* NBM Publishing Co.

Else, Barbara. The Traveling Restaurant: Jasper's Voyage in Three Parts. 2012. (Gecko Press Titles Ser.). (ENG.). 304p. (J). (gr. 5-8). 17.95 *(978-1-877579-03-5(3))* Gecko Pr. NZL. Dist: Lerner Publishing Group.

Faiella, Graham. Moby Dick & the Whaling Industry of the 19th Century. 2009. (Looking at Literature Through Primary Sources Ser.). 64p. (gr. 5-8). 58.50 *(978-1-61514-305-4(X))* Rosen Publishing Group, Inc., The.

Fenton, Geleta. Joel's Adventure at Sea. Siniard, Ricky, illus. 2013. 50p. (J). mass mkt. 9.95 *(978-0-9824433-2-3(3))* Octopus Publishing Co.

Flanagan, John. The Ghostfaces. 2016. (Brotherband Chronicles Ser.: 6). (ENG.). 400p. (J). (gr. 5). 18.99 *(978-0-399-16357-9(3),* Philomel Bks.) Penguin Young Readers Group.

Fultz, Steven D. The Adventures of the Barnyard Detectives: Where's Mr. Peacock, 1 vol. 2009. 79p. pap. 19.95 *(978-1-60749-965-7(7))* America Star Bks.

Garland, Michael. Miss Smith under the Ocean. Garland, Michael, illus. 2011. (ENG., Illus.). 32p. (J). (gr. -1-2). 16.99 *(978-0-525-42342-3(7),* Dutton Books for Young Readers) Penguin Young Readers Group.

Gilkerson, William. Pirate's Passage. 2014. (ENG., Illus.). 376p. (J). (gr. 4-7). pap. 16.95 *(978-1-61180-247-4(4),* Trumpeter) Shambhala Pubns., Inc.

Golden, Christopher & Lebbon, Tim. The Sea Wolves Bk. 2, Bk. 2. Ruth, Greg, illus. 2012. (Secret Journeys of Jack London Ser.: 2). (ENG.). 400p. (YA). (gr. 8). 16.99 *(978-0-06-186320-2(3),* HarperTeen) HarperCollins Pubs.

Hart, Alison. Leo, Dog of the Sea, 1 vol. Montgomery, Michael G., illus. 2017. (Dog Chronicles Ser.: 5). (ENG.). 176p. (J). (gr. 2-5). 12.95 *(978-1-56145-964-3(X))* Peachtree Pubs.

Hastings, Brian. Merryn's Journey. 2016. (ENG., Illus.). 40p. (J). (gr. -1). 14.95 *(978-1-4549-2161-5(7))* Sterling Publishing Co., Inc.

Hawes, Charles Boardman. The Dark Frigate. 2005. pap. 27.95 *(978-1-4179-3209-2(0))* Kessinger Publishing, LLC.

Hesse, Karen. Stowaway. unabr. ed. 2004. 328p. (J). (gr. 5-9). pap. 48.00 incl. audio *(978-0-8072-8760-6(1),* LYA 259 SP, Listening Library) Random Hse. Audio Publishing Group.

Hodgson, William Hope. The Sea Horses. 2004. reprint ed. pap. 1.99 *(978-1-4192-8166-2(6))* Kessinger Publishing, LLC.

Hopkins, William J. The Sandman: His Sea Stories (Yesterday's Classics) Horne, Diantha W., illus. 2009. 188p. pap. 9.95 *(978-1-59915-303-2(3))* Yesterday's Classics.

Horrigan, David J. The Spark in the Sea: Adventures in Marine Science, 1. 2003. 152p. pap. 24.00 *(978-0-9743712-0-7(3),* 001) Home Planet Bks.

Jacobson, Bonny B. Whale Fables. 2011. 68p. pap. 31.99 *(978-1-4535-9956-3(8))* Xlibris Corp.

Jobling, Curtis. Storm of Sharks. 2013. (Wereworld Ser.: 5). (ENG.). 480p. (J). (gr. 5). 16.99 *(978-0-670-78558-2(X),* Viking Books for Young Readers) Penguin Young Readers Group.

Katar, Al. Captain Scratch: The Island of Sirmarj. 2008. 48p. pap. 21.99 *(978-1-4363-4188-2(4))* Xlibris Corp.

Kipling, Rudyard. Land & Sea Tales for Scouts & Scout. 2005. pap. 30.95 *(978-1-885529-84-8(8))* Stevens Publishing.

Kirker, Solveig. The Florida Pod. 2009. 32p. pap. 12.99 *(978-1-4389-3137-1(9))* AuthorHouse.

Kositsky, Lynne. Minerva's Voyage. 2009. (ENG., Illus.). 240p. (YA). (gr. 6-18). pap. 10.99 *(978-1-55488-439-1(X),* Dundurn Pr.) Dundurn CAN. Dist: Ingram Publisher Services.

LaBaff, Stephanie. Draw Pirates in 4 Easy Steps: Then Write a Story. LaBaff, Tom, illus. 2012. (Drawing in 4 Easy Steps Ser.). 48p. (J). (gr. 3-18). pap. 8.95 *(978-1-4644-0012-4(1),* Enslow Elementary) Enslow Pubs., Inc.

Langridge, Roger. Snarked, Vol. 3. 2013. (Snarked Ser.). (ENG., Illus.). 112p. (J). (gr. 4). pap. 14.99 *(978-1-60886-295-5(X))* Boom! Studios.

Lasky, Kathryn. Pirate Bob. Clark, David, illus. alt. ed. 2008. (ENG.). 32p. (J). (gr. k-3). per. 8.95 *(978-1-57091-647-2(0))* Charlesbridge Publishing, Inc.

Lawrence, Iain. The Buccaneers. 2003. (High Seas Trilogy). (Illus.). 244p. (gr. 5-9). 16.50 *(978-0-7569-1454-7(X))* Perfection Learning Corp.

Lawrence, L. S. Escape by Sea. 2009. 208p. (J). (gr. 3-7). 16.95 *(978-0-8234-2217-3(8))* Holiday Hse., Inc.

LeBrun, Barbie. Porter Horse Finds Blackbeard's Treasure. 2013. (ENG.). 24p. (J). pap. 21.95 *(978-1-4787-1604-4(5))* Outskirts Pr., Inc.

Lees, Caroline. Silly Sea Stories. 2010. (Illus.). 48p. pap. 19.49 *(978-1-4389-0701-7(X))* AuthorHouse.

Lindgren, Astrid. Pippi in the South Seas. (Pippi Longstocking Ser.). 125p. (J). (gr. 3-5). pap. 3.99 *(978-0-8072-1392-6(6),* Listening Library) Random Hse. Audio Publishing Group.

Liora, Iimma. Flick Goes under the Sea! 2012. 32p. (-18). pap. 16.95 *(978-1-4525-0663-0(9))* Balboa Pr.

little bee books, little bee. Dive into the Sea! Llewhellin, Gareth, illus. 2016. (ENG.). 12p. (J). (gr. -1 — 1). bds. 7.99 *(978-1-4998-0297-9(8))* Little Bee Books Inc.

Lloyd, Michael. The Pirate Children. 2017. (ENG.). 334p. (J). pap. 15.95 ***(978-1-78693-666-0(6),*** c1ba7a42-0295-4a40-bb92-9690da2fc058) Austin, Stan AUS. Dist: Bookmasters Distribution.

LoDolce, Jodi. Johnny's Adventure at Sea. 2013. 18p. pap. 8.99 *(978-1-62839-102-2(2))* Salem Author Services.

London, Jack. The Mutiny of the 'ElsinoreApos. 2006. 264p. per. 15.95 *(978-1-59818-834-9(8))* Aegypan.

—Sea Wolf, Vol. 3. 2008. (Bring the Classics to Life Ser.). (ENG., Illus.). 72p. (gr. 3-12). pap., act. bk. ed. 10.95 *(978-1-55576-180-6(1),* EDN307B) EDCON Publishing Group.

Lunn, John. The Mariner's Curse. 2004. (ENG.). 216p. (J). (gr. 4-7). pap. 8.95 *(978-0-88776-672-5(2),* Tundra Bks.) Tundra Bks. CAN. Dist: Penguin Random Hse. LLC.

MacFarlane, John. Stormstruck! 2015. (ENG.). 160p. (J). (gr. 3-7). 16.95 *(978-0-8234-3394-0(3))* Holiday Hse., Inc.

Mahy, Margaret. The Man Whose Mother Was a Pirate. Chamberlain, Margaret, illus. 2013. (Early Reader Ser.). (ENG.). 64p. (J). (gr. k-2). pap. 7.99 *(978-1-4440-0925-5(7),* Orion Children's Bks.) Hachette Children's Group GBR. Dist: Hachette Bk. Group.

Mariconda, Barbara. Lucy at Sea. 2013. (Voyage of Lucy P. Simmons Ser.: 2). (ENG.). 320p. (J). (gr. 3-7). 16.99 *(978-0-06-211993-3(1),* Tegen, Katherine Bks) HarperCollins Pubs.

Martin, Ann M. & Godwin, Laura. The Doll People Set Sail. Helquist, Brett, illus. 2014. (Doll People Ser.: Bk. 4). (ENG.). 304p. (J). (gr. 3-7). 17.99 *(978-1-4231-3683-5(7))* Hyperion Bks. for Children.

McCall Smith, Alexander. School Ship Tobermory. 2016. (School Ship Tobermory Ser.). (ENG., Illus.). 224p. (J). (gr. 3-7). 15.99 *(978-0-399-55261-8(8),* Delacorte Bks. for Young Readers) Random Hse. Children's Bks.

McDonnell, Vincent. The Catalpa Adventure: Escape to Freedom. 2010. (ENG.). 128p. (J). pap. 12.95 *(978-1-84889-038-1(9))* Collins Pr., The IRL. Dist: Dufour Editions, Inc.

Meadows, Daisy. Courtney the Clownfish Fairy. 2011. (Illus.). 62p. (J). *(978-0-545-28877-4(0))* Scholastic, Inc.

—Stephanie the Starfish Fairy. 2011. (Illus.). 65p. (J). *(978-0-545-28875-0(4))* Scholastic, Inc.

—Tess the Sea Turtle Fairy. 2011. (Illus.). 65p. (J). *(978-0-545-28874-3(6))* Scholastic, Inc.

—Whitney the Whale Fairy. 2011. (Illus.). 64p. (J). *(978-0-545-28876-7(2))* Scholastic, Inc.

Melville, Herman. Cities of the Fantastic: Brusel. Eisner, Will, illus. 2003. (Cities of the Fantastic Ser.). (ENG.). 120p. 19.95 *(978-1-56163-291-6(0))* NBM Publishing Co.

—Moby Dick. Eisner, Will, illus. 2003. (ENG.). 32p. (J). (gr. 4-7). 15.95 *(978-1-56163-293-0(7))* NBM Publishing Co.

—Moby Dick. 2008. (Bring the Classics to Life Ser.). (Illus.). 72p. (gr. 5-12). pap., act. bk. ed. 10.95 *(978-1-55576-326-8(X),* EDCTR-508B) EDCON Publishing Group.

—Moby Dick. Elphinstone, Katy, illus. 2014. (Travel & Adventure Ser.). (ENG.). 64p. pap. 6.95 *(978-1-906230-72-2(2))* Real Reads Ltd. GBR. Dist: Casemate Pubs. & Bk. Distributors, LLC.

—Moby Dick. 2003. (Historias de Siempre Ser.). (SPA., Illus.). 92p. (J). (gr. 5-8). pap. 9.95 *(978-84-204-5732-1(9))* Santillana USA Publishing Co., Inc.

—Moby-Dick. Freeberg, Eric, illus. 2010. (Classic Starts(tm) Ser.). (ENG.). 160p. (J). (gr. 2-4). 6.95 *(978-1-4027-6644-2(0))* Sterling Publishing Co., Inc.

—Moby Dick, Grades 5-12. adapted ed. pap., tchr. ed. 4.95 *(978-0-8359-0123-9(8))* Globe Fearon Educational Publishing.

Melville, Herman, et al. Moby Dick. (Classics Illustrated Ser.). (Illus.). 52p. (YA). pap. 4.95 *(978-1-57209-003-3(0))* Classics International Entertainment, Inc.

Meyer, L. A. The Mark of the Golden Dragon: Being an Account of the Further Adventures of Jacky Faber, Jewel of the East, Vexation of the West & Pearl of the South China Sea. (Bloody Jack Adventures Ser.: 9). (ENG.). (YA). (gr. 9). 2013. 400p. pap. 9.99 *(978-0-544-00328-6(4))* 2011. 384p. 16.99 *(978-0-547-51764-3(5))* Houghton Mifflin Harcourt Publishing Co.

—Under the Jolly Roger: Being an Account of the Further Nautical Adventures of Jacky Faber. 2010. (Bloody Jack Adventures Ser.: 3). (ENG., Illus.). 528p. (YA). (gr. 7). pap. 9.99 *(978-0-15-205873-9(7))* Houghton Mifflin Harcourt Publishing Co.

—The Wake of the Lorelei Lee: Being an Account of the Further Adventures of Jacky Faber, on Her Way to Botany Bay. 2010. (Bloody Jack Adventures Ser.: Bk. 8). audio compact disk 29.95 *(978-1-59316-484-3(X))* Listen & Live Audio, Inc.

Milbourne, Anna. How Deep Is the Sea? Riglietti, Serena, illus. 2010. (Picture Bks). 24p. (J). 10.99 *(978-0-7945-2311-4(0))* EDC Publishing.

Milford, Kate. The Left-Handed Fate. Wheeler, Eliza, illus. 2016. (ENG.). 384p. (J). 16.99 *(978-0-8050-9800-6(3),* 9780805098006, Holt, Henry & Co. Bks. For Young Readers) Holt, Henry & Co.

—The Left-Handed Fate. Wheeler, Eliza, illus. 2017. (ENG.). 384p. (J). pap. 7.99 *(978-1-250-12183-7(3),* 9781250121837) Square Fish.

Moniz, Michael. The Whalemaster. 2016. (ENG., Illus.). 235p. (J). (gr. 4-7). pap. 9.95 *(978-1-927018-79-8(X))* Simply Read Bks. CAN. Dist: Ingram Publisher Services.

Mowat, Farley. The Black Joke. 2009. (ENG.). 192p. pap. 9.95 *(978-0-7710-6469-2(1),* Emblem Editions) McClelland & Stewart CAN. Dist: Random Hse., Inc.

Niedworok, Claudio O. Seafarers: Chronicles of the Suspense & Romance of the Sea. Knight, Tori, ed. Cooper, Paul, illus. Date not set. 80p. (Orig.). (YA). pap. 11.95 *(978-1-882133-05-5(6))* Barefoot Pr.

Ocean, Davy. The Boy Who Cried Shark. Blecha, Aaron, illus. 2015. (Shark School Ser.: 4). (ENG.). 144p. (J). (gr. 1-4). 16.99 *(978-1-4814-0689-5(2),* Aladdin) Simon & Schuster Children's Publishing.

—A Fin-Tastic Finish. Blecha, Aaron, illus. 2015. (Shark School Ser.: 5). (ENG.). 160p. (J). (gr. 1-4). 16.99 *(978-1-4814-0692-5(2),* Aladdin) Simon & Schuster Children's Publishing.

O'Rourke, Ryan. Bella Lost & Found. O'Rourke, Ryan, illus. 2014. (ENG., Illus.). 40p. (J). (gr. -1-3). 17.99 *(978-0-06-221861-2(1))* HarperCollins Pubs.

Penrose, Margaret. The Motor Girls on the Coast or the Waif from the Se. 2011. 140p. pap. 9.99 *(978-1-61203-219-1(2))* Bottom of the Hill Publishing.

Pfister, Marcus. Rainbow Fish Deep Sea Adventure Sticker & Coloring Storybook. 2010. (Rainbow Fish Ser.). (ENG.). 24p. (gr. -1-2). 5.95 *(978-0-7358-2318-1(9))* North-South Bks., Inc.

Priestley, Chris. Tales of Terror from the Black Ship. Roberts, David, illus. 2008. (Tales of Terror Ser.: 1). (ENG.). 256p. (YA). (gr. 3-6). 12.99 *(978-1-59990-290-6(7),* 9781599902906, Bloomsbury USA Childrens) Bloomsbury Publishing USA.

Pryor, Bonnie. Captain Hannah Pritchard: The Hunt for Pirate Gold. 2011. (Historical Fiction Adventures (HFA) Ser.). (Illus.). 160p. (J). (gr. 3-18). pap. 10.95 *(978-1-59845-283-9(5));* (gr. 4-7). lib. bdg. 29.27 *(978-0-7660-3817-2(3))* Enslow Pubs., Inc.

—Hannah Pritchard: Pirate of the Revolution. 2008. (Historical Fiction Adventures (HFA) Ser.). (Illus.). 160p. (J). (gr. 3-7). lib. bdg. 29.27 *(978-0-7660-2851-7(8))* Enslow Pubs., Inc.

Ransome, Arthur. We Didn't Mean to Go to Sea. 2010. (ENG.). 100p. (gr. 2). pap. 22.95 *(978-1-906582-05-0(X))* Aurora Metro Pubns. Ltd. GBR. Dist: Consortium Bk. Sales & Distribution.

Rees, Celia. Pirates! The True & Remarkable Adventures of Minerva Sharpe & Nancy Kington, Female Pirates. 2005. (Illus.). 379p. (YA). (gr. 9-12). 16.60 *(978-0-7569-6304-0(4))* Perfection Learning Corp.

RH Disney. Beware the Kakamora! RH Disney, illus. 2016. (Pictureback(R) Ser.). (ENG., Illus.). 24p. (J). (gr. -1-2). 4.99 *(978-0-7364-3601-4(4),* RH/Disney) Random Hse. Children's Bks.

—Moana Big Golden Book (Disney Moana) RH Disney, illus. 2016. (Big Golden Book Ser.). (ENG., Illus.). 48p. (J). (gr. -1-2). 9.99 *(978-0-7364-3602-1(2),* Golden/Disney) Random Hse. Children's Bks.

—Moana Junior Novelization. RH Disney, illus. 2016. (Junior Novel Ser.). (ENG., Illus.). 144p. (J). (gr. 2-5). 6.99 *(978-0-7364-3600-7(6),* RH/Disney) Random Hse. Children's Bks.

—Moana: the Deluxe Junior Novelization (Disney Moana) RH Disney, illus. 2016. (Deluxe Junior Novel Ser.). (ENG., Illus.). 144p. (J). (gr. 2-5). 9.99 *(978-0-7364-3574-1(3),* RH/Disney) Random Hse. Children's Bks.

—Quest for the Heart. RH Disney, illus. 2016. (Step into Reading Ser.). (ENG., Illus.). 32p. (J). (gr. -1-1). lib. bdg. 12.99 *(978-0-7364-8226-4(1),* RH/Disney) Random Hse. Children's Bks.

Rockwood, Roy. The Wizard of the Sea. 2007. 84p. per. *(978-1-4068-3969-2(8))* Echo Library.

Roop, Connie & Roop, Peter. Good-Bye for Today: The Diary of a Young Girl at Sea. Allen, Thomas B., illus. 2008. (ENG.). 48p. (J). (gr. 4-6). 11.99 *(978-1-4169-7573-1(X),* Simon & Schuster/Paula Wiseman Bks.) Simon & Schuster/Paula Wiseman Bks.

Rosen, Michael J. Sailing the Unknown: Around the World with Captain Cook. Pritelli, Maria Cristina, illus. 2012. (ENG.). 40p. (J). (gr. 1-3). 19.99 *(978-1-56846-216-5(6),* Creative Editions) Creative Co., The.

Ruby, Anne. Children of the Sea. Meier, Ty, illus. 2007. (YA). per. *(978-0-9787881-0-0(9))* Seachild.

Sante, Andrew R. The Silver Heart Chronicles: The Voyage. 2012. 50p. 24.99 *(978-1-4771-4700-9(4));* pap. 15.99 *(978-1-4771-4699-6(7))* Xlibris Corp.

Scollon, Bill. Moana Guide Book (Disney Moana) Random House Disney Staff, illus. 2016. (Essential Guide Ser.). (ENG.). 64p. (J). (gr. 4-7). pap. 7.99 *(978-0-7364-3673-1(1),* RH/Disney) Random Hse. Children's Bks.

Shelton, Dave. A Boy & a Bear in a Boat. 2013. (ENG.). 304p. (J). (gr. 2-5). 6.99 *(978-0-449-81060-6(7),* Yearling) Random Hse. Children's Bks.

Smith, Barbara. Ghost Stories of the Sea, 1 vol., Vol. 1. rev. ed. 2003. (Ghost Stories Ser.). (ENG., Illus.). 224p. (gr. 4). pap. 12.95 *(978-1-894877-23-7(3),* 1894877233, Ghost Hse. Bks.) Lone Pine Publishing USA.

Soundprints Staff. Ocean Adventures: Story-Time Treasury. 2005. (Smithsonian Institution Story-Time Treasures Ser.). (Illus.). 256p. (J). (gr. -1-2). 14.95 *(978-1-59069-226-4(8),* HT1001) Studio Mouse LLC.

Squid-Napped! 2014. (Shark School Ser.: 3). (ENG., Illus.). 144p. (J). (gr. 1-4). pap. 5.99 *(978-1-4814-0684-0(1),* Aladdin) Simon & Schuster Children's Publishing.

Stevenson, Robert Louis. Secuestrado. 3rd ed. (Coleccion Clasicos en Accion).Tr. of Kidnapped. (SPA., Illus.). 80p. (YA). (gr. 5-8). 15.95 *(978-84-241-5781-4(8),* EV1487) Everest Editora ESP. Dist: Lectorum Pubns., Inc.

Taylor, Theodore. The Odyssey of Ben O'Neal. 2004. (ENG., Illus.). 264p. (J). (gr. 2-5). pap. 15.95 *(978-0-15-205295-9(X))* Houghton Mifflin Harcourt Publishing Co.

Terry, Alana. What Hurricane? My Solar-Powered History on a Supply Ship to the Jamestown Colony. Steffen, Jeremy, illus. 2013. 136p. pap. 12.99 *(978-1-937848-05-7(1))* Do Life Right, Inc.

Thomas, David, ed. Teenage Sea Stories. 2011. 252p. 46.95 *(978-1-258-10166-4(1))* Literary Licensing, LLC.

Troncale, Steven L. Yankee Boys of War. 2003. 171p. pap. 24.95 *(978-1-59286-879-7(7))* America Star Bks.

Tweed, Susan Larned. A Sailor's Adventure: Sailing Stormy Seas. 2012. 24p. pap. 11.50 *(978-1-61897-522-5(6),* Strategic Bk. Publishing) Strategic Book Publishing & Rights Agency (SBPRA).

Valor, De. Pirate Adventures of Sea Worthy: Featuring: the Treasure of Captain Blue Beard & the Return of Captain Blue Beard. 2013. 150p. (gr. 2-2). 20.35 *(978-1-4669-7483-8(4));* pap. 10.35 *(978-1-4269-9551-4(2))* Trafford Publishing.

Verne, Jules. Dick Sand. Munro, George, tr. 2008. 296p. 29.95 *(978-1-60664-752-3(0))* Rodgers, Alan Bks.

—Twenty Thousand Leagues under the Sea. l.t. ed. 2006. 592p. pap. *(978-1-84702-222-6(7))* Echo Library.

—20,000 Leagues under the Sea. D'Achille, Gino, illus. 2005. (Reader's Workshop Ser.). (ENG.). 88p. (C). pap. 17.95 *(978-0-7362-2806-0(3))* CENGAGE Learning.

—20,000 Leagues under the Sea, 1 vol. Fisher, Eric Scott, illus. 2011. (Calico Illustrated Classics Ser.: No. 3). (ENG.). 112p. (YA). (gr. 3-6). 27.07 *(978-1-61641-110-7(4))* Magic Wagon.

—20,000 Leagues under the Sea: Retold from the Jules Verne Original. Andreasen, Dan, illus. 2006. (Classic Starts(tm) Ser.). (ENG.). 160p. (J). (gr. 2-4). 6.95 *(978-1-4027-2533-3(7))* Sterling Publishing Co., Inc.

Weston Woods Staff, creator. Burt Dow: Deep Water Man. 2004. (J). 18.95 *(978-1-55592-374-7(7));* 38.75 *(978-1-55592-376-1(3))* Weston Woods Studios, Inc.

Wheeler, Lisa. Seadogs: An Epic Ocean Operetta. Siegel, Mark, illus. 2006. (ENG.). 40p. (J). (gr. 2-5). reprint ed. 7.99 *(978-1-4169-4103-3(7),* Atheneum Bks. for Young Readers) Simon & Schuster Children's Publishing.

Whistler, Charles W. A Sea-Queen's Sailing. Groome, W. H. C., illus. 2011. 346p. 24.95 *(978-1-934671-42-9(8))* Salem Ridge Press LLC.

Williams, Geoffrey T. The Great White Red Alert. Artful Doodlers, illus. Campbell, Tom, photos by. 2008. (Save Our Seas Adventure Bks.). (ENG.). 64p. (J). (gr. 4-7). 8.95 *(978-0-9800444-0-9(5))* Save Our Seas, Ltd.

Zuhdi, Darla. A South Sea Adventure, Vol. 4. 2005. (Cat Detectives Present Ser.: 4). (Illus.). 104p. (J). per. 6.99 *(978-0-9706062-6-6(5))* catBOX Entertainment, Inc.

2nd and 7 Foundation. The Hog Mollies & the Amazing Aquatic Adventure (Soft Cover) rev. ed. 2011. (ENG.). 32p. pap. 6.95 *(978-0-7575-9147-1(7))* Kendall Hunt Publishing Co.

2nd and 7 Foundation Staff. The Hog Mollies & the Amazing Aquatic Adventure. rev. ed. 2011. 32p. pap. 12.95 *(978-0-7575-9148-8(5))* Kendall Hunt Publishing Co.

SEA WAVES

see Ocean Waves

SEAFARING LIFE

Baum, L. Frank. Navy Alphabet Book. 2004. (ENG., Illus.). 60p. (J). (gr. -1-3). per. 14.95 *(978-1-55709-570-1(1))* Applewood Bks.

Branse, J. L. A Day in the Life of a Colonial Sea Captain. 2009. (Library of Living & Working in Colonial Times Ser.). 24p. (gr.

3-3). 42.50 *(978-1-60853-737-2(4),* PowerKids Pr.) Rosen Publishing Group, Inc., The.
Brewster, Joy. El mundo bajo las Olas. Hanner, Albert, illus. 2011. (SPA.). 32p. (J). pap. 49.00 net. *(978-1-4108-2339-7(3),* A23393) Benchmark Education Co.
Brook, Henry. Sea Adventures. 2008. (True Adventure Stories Ser.). 153p. (J). pap. 4.99 *(978-0-7945-2195-0(9),* Usborne) EDC Publishing.
Bruce, Julia. Sail! Can You Command a Sea Voyage? Dennis, Peter, illus. 2009. (Step into History Ser.). 32p. (J). (gr. 2-5). lib. bdg. 23.94 *(978-0-7660-3477-8(1))* Enslow Pubs., Inc.
Crompton, Samuel Willard. Francis Drake & the Oceans of the World. Goetzmann, William H., ed. 2005. (Explorers of New Worlds Ser.). (Illus.). 160p. (J). (gr. 5-8). lib. bdg. 30.00 *(978-0-7910-8615-5(1))* Facts On File, Inc.
Dover & Printworks KMG Staff. Sea Life Field Guide. 2013. (ENG.). 48p. (J). (gr. 3-8). pap. 5.99 *(978-0-486-49157-8(9))* Dover Pubns., Inc.
Duder, Tessa, ed. Down to the Sea Again: True Sea Stories for Young Newzealanders. 2005. 256p. (J). *(978-1-86950-476-2(3))* HarperCollins Pubs. New Zealand NZL. Dist: HarperCollins Pubs. Australia.
Hirschi, Ron. Swimming with Humuhumu: A Young Snorkeler's First Guide to Hawaiian Sea Life. Yee, Tammy, illus. 32p. (J). 14.99 *(978-0-931548-67-3(5),* 25098-000) Island Heritage Publishing.
Meredith, Susan Markowitz. Hiding in the Sea: Set Of 6. 2011. (Early Connections Ser.). (J). pap. 37.00 net. *(978-1-4108-1080-9(1))* Benchmark Education Co.
Meyer, L. A. The Wake of the Lorelei Lee: Being an Account of the Further Adventures of Jacky Faber, on Her Way to Botany Bay. (Bloody Jack Adventures Ser.: 8). (ENG.). (YA). (gr. 9). 2012. 576p. pap. 9.99 *(978-0-547-72194-1(3))* 2010. 560p. 17.00 *(978-0-547-32768-6(4))* Houghton Mifflin Harcourt Publishing Co.
Noe, Ida, et al. Zendoodle Color-By-Number: Sea Life: Underwater Worlds to Color & Display. 2017. (ENG., Illus.). 128p. pap. 13.99 ***(978-1-250-14074-6(9),*** 9781250140746, St. Martin's Griffin) St. Martin's Pr.
O'Donnell, Liam. Crack the Pirate Code. 2017. (Pirates! Ser.). (ENG.). 32p. (gr. 1-3). lib. bdg. 29.99 ***(978-1-4109-8706-8(X),*** Read Me!) Heinemann-Raintree.
—Get into Pirate Gear. 2017. (Pirates! Ser.). (ENG.). 32p. (gr. 1-3). lib. bdg. 29.99 ***(978-1-4109-8705-1(1),*** Read Me!) Heinemann-Raintree.
—Hop on the Pirate History Boat. 2017. (Pirates! Ser.). (ENG.). 32p. (gr. 1-3). lib. bdg. 29.99 ***(978-1-4109-8703-7(5),*** Read Me!) Heinemann-Raintree.
Petrillo, Valerie. Sailors, Whalers, Fantastic Sea Voyages: An Activity Guide to North American Sailing Life. 2003. (ENG., Illus.). 224p. (J). (gr. 4-7). pap. 14.95 *(978-1-55652-475-2(7))* Chicago Review Pr., Inc.
Rice, Dona Herweck. Sea Life, 1 vol. 2nd rev. ed. 2011. (Nonfiction Readers Ser.). (ENG.). 20p. (J). (gr. 1-1). pap. 4.99 *(978-1-4333-3590-7(5))* Teacher Created Materials, Inc.
Soffer, Ruth, et al. Big Book of Sea Life to Color. 2008. (Dover Nature Coloring Book Ser.). (ENG., Illus.). 144p. (J). (gr. 3-5). 8.95 *(978-0-486-46681-1(7))* Dover Pubns., Inc.
Sohl, Marcia & Dackerman, Gerald. Two Years Before the Mast: Student Activity Book. Cruz, Ernesto R, illus. (Now Age Illustrated Ser.). (J). (gr. 4-12). stu. ed. 1.25 *(978-0-88301-294-9(4))* Pendulum Pr., Inc.
Steele, Philip. The Amazing History of Pirates: See What a Buccaneer's Life Was Really Like, with over 350 Exciting Pictures. 2016. (ENG., Illus.). 64p. 12.99 *(978-1-86147-711-8(2),* Armadillo) Anness Publishing GBR. Dist: National Bk. Network.
Walker, Pam & Wood, Elaine. Life in the Sea Set, 6 vols. 2005. (Life in the Sea Ser.). 472p. (gr. 5-8). 175.00 *(978-0-8160-5700-9(1))* Facts On File, Inc.
West, David. Ten of the Best Adventures on the Seas. 2015. (Ten of the Best: Stories of Exploration & Adventure Ser.). (ENG., Illus.). 24p. (J). (gr. 3-6). *(978-0-7787-1839-0(5))* Crabtree Publishing Co.

SEALS (ANIMALS)

Adamson, Heather. Sea Lions. 2017. (Ocean Life up Close Ser.). (ENG., Illus.). 24p. (J). (gr. k-3). lib. bdg. 25.95 ***(978-1-62617-645-4(0),*** Blastoff! Readers) Bellwether Media.
Blake, Jason. Focas Fabulosas. 2008. (SPA., Illus.). 24p. (J). pap. *(978-0-545-02283-5(5))* Scholastic, Inc.
Bloom, Paul. Seal or Sea Lion? 2015. (Animal Look-Alikes Ser.). (ENG., Illus.). 24p. (J). (gr. 1-2). lib. bdg. 22.60 *(978-1-4824-2726-4(5))* Stevens, Gareth Publishing LLLP.
Butterworth, Christine. See What a Seal Can Do. Nelms, Kate, illus. 2015. (Read & Wonder Ser.). (ENG.). 32p. (J). (gr. -1-3). 6.99 *(978-0-7636-7649-0(7))* Candlewick Pr.
Coleman, Miriam. Swimming with Sea Lions. 2009. (Flippers & Fins Ser.). (Illus.). 24p. (J). (ENG.). pap. 8.25 *(978-1-4358-3247-3(7),* PowerKids Pr.); (gr. 1-3). lib. bdg. 22.60 *(978-1-4042-8095-3(2))* Rosen Publishing Group, Inc., The.
Crossingham, John & Kalman, Bobbie. Seals & Sea Lions. 2005. (Living Ocean Ser.). (ENG., Illus.). 32p. (J). (gr. -1-3). lib. bdg. *(978-0-7787-1301-2(6));* (gr. 3-4). pap. *(978-0-7787-1323-4(7))* Crabtree Publishing Co.
Dessen, Maci. Elephant Seals, 01 vols., 1. 2016. (Ocean Friends Ser.). (ENG., Illus.). 24p. (J). pap. 8.25 *(978-1-5081-4168-6(1),* PowerKids Pr.) Rosen Publishing Group, Inc., The.
Drumlin, Sam. Harp Seals. 2013. (PowerKids Readers: Sea Friends Ser.). (ENG., Illus.). 24p. (J). (gr. k-2). pap. 8.25 *(978-1-4488-9750-6(5));* lib. bdg. 22.60 *(978-1-4488-9646-2(0))* Rosen Publishing Group, Inc., The. (PowerKids Pr.).
—Harp Seals: Las Focas de Groenlandia. Alamán, Eduardo, tr. from ENG. 2013. (PowerKids Readers: Sea Friends / Los Amigos Del Mar Ser.). (SPA & ENG., Illus.). 24p. (J). (gr. k-2). lib. bdg. 22.60 *(978-1-4488-9973-9(7),* PowerKids Pr.) Rosen Publishing Group, Inc., The.
Emily Rose Townsend. Seals [Scholastic]. 2009. (Polar Animals Ser.). 24p. (gr. k-1). pap. 0.34 *(978-1-4296-4226-2(2),* Pebble Bks.) Capstone Press of Coughlan Cos.
Feldman, Thea. Kingfisher Readers L1: Seals. 2015. (Kingfisher Readers Ser.). (ENG., Illus.). 32p. (gr. k-3). 12.99 *(978-0-7534-7223-1(6),* 9780753472231, Kingfisher) Roaring Brook Pr.
Fetty, Margaret. Sea Lions. 2006. (Smart Animals! Ser.). (Illus.). 32p. (J). (gr. 2-5). lib. bdg. 25.27 *(978-1-59716-274-6(4))* Bearport Publishing Co., Inc.
Franks, Katie. Sea Lions. 2014. (Zoo's Who's Who Ser.). (Illus.). 24p. (J). (gr. k-2). pap. 8.25 *(978-1-4777-6585-2(9),* PowerKids Pr.) Rosen Publishing Group, Inc., The.
Gallagher, Debbie. Seals & Sea Lions. 2009. (Zoo Animals 2 Ser.). 32p. (gr. 2). lib. bdg. 18.56 *(978-0-7614-4748-1(2))* Marshall Cavendish GBR. Dist: Marshall Cavendish Corp.
Gish, Melissa. Living Wild: Sea Lions. 2013. (Living Wild Ser.). (ENG., Illus.). 48p. (J). (gr. 4-7). pap. 12.00 *(978-0-89812-776-8(9),* Creative Paperbacks) Creative Co., The.
—Sea Lions. 2012. (Living Wild Ser.). 48p. (gr. 5-12). 23.95 *(978-1-60818-169-8(3),* Creative Education) Creative Co., The.
Goldish, Meish. Sea Lions in the Navy. 2012. (America's Animal Soldiers Ser.). 24p. (J). (gr. 1-6). lib. bdg. 23.93 *(978-1-61772-450-3(5))* Bearport Publishing Co., Inc.
—Southern Elephant Seal: The Biggest Seal in the World. 2010. (More SuperSized! Ser.). (Illus.). 24p. (J). (gr. k-3). lib. bdg. 22.61 *(978-1-936087-26-6(X))* Bearport Publishing Co., Inc.
Gray, Susan H. Elephant Seal. 2007. (21st Century Skills Library: Road to Recovery Ser.). (ENG.). 32p. (gr. 4-8). lib. bdg. 28.50 *(978-1-60279-038-4(8),* 200078) Cherry Lake Publishing.
Green, Jen. California Sea Lion. 2013. (Science Slam: the Deep End-Animal Life Underwater Ser.). 24p. (J). (gr. -1-3). lib. bdg. 23.93 *(978-1-61772-919-5(1))* Bearport Publishing Co., Inc.
—Sea Lions. 2008. (Illus.). 52p. (J). *(978-0-7172-6285-4(5))* Grolier, Ltd.
Haller, Christine A. Chippy: The sea lion that lost its Way. Lund, Nancy M., illus. 2006. 20p. (J). 11.95 *(978-0-9771129-0-6(X))* Oxbow Bks.
Haney, Johannah & Haney-Withrow, Anna. Seals. 2010. (Endangered! 2 Ser.). 48p. (gr. 3). lib. bdg. 29.93 *(978-0-7614-4053-6(4))* Marshall Cavendish Corp.
Harvey, Jeanne Walker. Astro: The Steller Sea Lion, 1 vol. Bersani, Shennen, illus. 2010. (ENG.). 32p. (J). (gr. -1-4). pap. 9.95 *(978-1-60718-874-2(0))* Arbordale Publishing.
—Honey Girl: The Hawaiian Monk Seal. Bersani, Shennen, illus. 2017. (ENG.). 32p. (J). (gr. k-3). pap. 9.95 *(978-1-62855-922-4(9))* Arbordale Publishing.
Hendrix, Emilia. Seals & Pups. 2016. (Animal Family Ser.). (ENG., Illus.). 24p. (J). (gr. k-k). pap. 8.15 *(978-1-4824-3787-4(2))* Stevens, Gareth Publishing LLLP.
Hengel, Katherine. It's a Baby Australian Fur Seal!, 1 vol. 2010. (Baby Australian Animals Ser.). (ENG., Illus.). 24p. (J). (gr. k-3). lib. bdg. 24.21 *(978-1-60453-574-7(1),* SandCastle) ABDO Publishing Co.
Jackson, Tom. Seals. 2008. (Nature's Children Ser.). (Illus.). 52p. (J). *(978-0-7172-6243-4(X))* Grolier, Ltd.
Johnson, Elizabeth R. Sea Lion. 2016. (Sea Life Ser.). (ENG., Illus.). 24p. (gr. k-1). lib. bdg. 26.65 *(978-1-5157-2082-9(9),* Pebble Plus) Capstone Press of Coughlan Cos.
Kalman, Bobbie. Endangered Monk Seals. 2004. (Earth's Endangered Animals Ser.). (ENG., Illus.). 32p. (J). pap. *(978-0-7787-1897-0(2))* Crabtree Publishing Co.
Kalman, Bobbie & Crossingham, John. Les Phoques et les Otaries. Briere, Marie-Josee, tr. from ENG. 2007. (Petit Monde Vivant Ser.). (FRE., Illus.). 32p. (J). pap. 9.95 *(978-2-89579-165-2(1))* Bayard Canada Livres CAN. Dist: Crabtree Publishing Co.
Kawa, Katie. Baby Seals. 2011. (Cute & Cuddly: Baby Animals Ser.). (Illus.). 24p. (gr. k-2). (J). pap. 8.15 *(978-1-4339-5536-5(9));* (J). lib. bdg. 22.60 *(978-1-4339-5534-1(2));* 69.20 *(978-1-4339-6894-5(0))* Stevens, Gareth Publishing LLLP.
Keller, Susanna. Meet the Sea Lion. 2010. (At the Zoo Ser.). 24p. (J). (ENG.). pap. 8.25 *(978-1-4358-9728-1(5));* (Illus.). (gr. -1-1). lib. bdg. 22.60 *(978-1-4358-9308-5(5))* Rosen Publishing Group, Inc., The. (PowerKids Pr.).
King, Aven. Harp Seals, 01 vols., 1. 2016. (Ocean Friends Ser.). (ENG., Illus.). 24p. (J). pap. 8.25 *(978-1-5081-4172-3(X),* PowerKids Pr.) Rosen Publishing Group, Inc., The.
King, Zelda. Seals. 2012. (Illus.). 24p. (J). 49.50 *(978-1-4488-5144-7(0),* PowerKids Pr.); pap. 8.25 *(978-1-4488-5143-0(2),* PowerKids Pr.); lib. bdg. 22.60 *(978-1-4488-5006-8(1))* Rosen Publishing Group, Inc., The.
Lamm, Drew. Sea Lion Swims. Cohen, Jessie, photos by. 2005. (Let's Go to the Zoo! Ser.). (ENG., Illus.). 16p. (J). (gr. -1-k). 5.95 *(978-1-56899-976-0(3),* B9010) Soundprints.
Landau, Elaine. Harp Seals: Animals of the Snow & Ice. 2010. (Animals of the Snow & Ice Ser.). (Illus.). 32p. (J). (gr. 1-3). 23.94 *(978-0-7660-3460-0(7))* Enslow Pubs., Inc.
Laughlin, Kara L. Seals. 2017. (In the Deep Blue Sea Ser.). (ENG.). 24p. (J). (gr. k-3). lib. bdg. 27.07 *(978-1-5038-1691-6(5),* 211525) Child's World, Inc., The.
Leaf, Christina. Baby Seals. 2014. (Super Cute! Ser.). (ENG., Illus.). 24p. (J). (gr. k-3). lib. bdg. 25.95 *(978-1-60014-977-1(4),* Blastoff! Readers) Bellwether Media.
León, Vicki. A Colony of Seals: The Captivating Life of a Deep Sea Diver. 2nd ed. 2005. (Jean-Michel Cousteau Presents Ser.). (ENG., Illus.). 48p. (J). (gr. 4). per. 9.95 *(978-0-9766134-0-4(9))* London Town Pr.
Lunis, Natalie. California Sea Lion: Fast & Smart! 2010. (Blink of an Eye: Superfast Animals Ser.). 24p. (J). (gr. k-3). lib. bdg. 22.61 *(978-1-936088-08-9(8))* Bearport Publishing Co., Inc.
Macheske, Felicia. Sunny Swimmers: Monk Seal. 2017. (Guess What Ser.). (ENG., Illus.). 24p. (J). (gr. k-2). lib. bdg. 28.50 *(978-1-63472-175-2(6),* 209272) Cherry Lake Publishing.
Markle, Sandra. Leopard Seals. 2009. (Animal Predators Ser.). (ENG.). 40p. (gr. 3-6). 26.60 *(978-1-58013-540-5(4))* Lerner Publishing Group.
Markovics, Joyce L. Weddell Seal: Fat & Happy. 2008. (Uncommon Animals Ser.). (Illus.). 32p. (YA). (gr. 2-5). lib. bdg. 25.27 *(978-1-59716-734-5(7),* 1284362) Bearport Publishing Co., Inc.
Marsico, Katie. Leopard Seal, 1 vol. 2011. (Day in the Life: Polar Animals Ser.). (ENG.). 24p. (gr. k-2). pap. 6.79 *(978-1-4329-5338-6(9),* Heinemann Read & Learn) Heinemann-Raintree.
Martin-James, Kathleen. Harp Seals. 2008. (Early Bird Nature Bks.). (ENG.). 48p. (gr. 2-5). 26.60 *(978-0-8225-7889-5(1))* Lerner Publishing Group.
Meinking, Mary. Polar Bear vs. Seal, 1 vol. 2011. (Predator vs. Prey Ser.). (ENG., Illus.). 32p. (gr. 1-2). pap. 8.29 *(978-1-4109-3948-7(0),* Read Me!) Heinemann-Raintree.
Meister, Cari. Seals. 2012. (ENG., Illus.). 24p. (J). lib. bdg. 25.65 *(978-1-62031-011-3(2))* Jump! Inc.
Metz, Lorijo. Discovering Sea Lions. 2012. (Along the Shore Ser.). (Illus.). 24p. (J). (gr. k-3). lib. bdg. 22.60 *(978-1-4488-4992-5(6))* Rosen Publishing Group, Inc., The.
Miller, Sara Swan. Seals of the Antarctic. 2009. (Brrr! Polar Animals Ser.). (Illus.). 24p. (J). (gr. k-5). pap. 8.25 *(978-1-4358-3149-0(7),* PowerKids Pr.); 24p. (gr. 2-3). 42.50 *(978-1-61511-754-3(7),* PowerKids Pr.); (J). (gr. k-3). lib. bdg. 22.60 *(978-1-4358-2745-5(7))* Rosen Publishing Group, Inc., The.
Owen, Ruth. Seal Pups. 2012. (Water Babies Ser.). 24p. (J). (gr. -1-3). lib. bdg. 21.32 *(978-1-61772-605-7(2))* Bearport Publishing Co., Inc.
Owings, Lisa. Elephant Seal. 2014. (Extremely Weird Animals Ser.). (ENG., Illus.). 24p. (J). (gr. 3-8). lib. bdg. 25.95 *(978-1-62617-074-2(6),* Pilot Bks.) Bellwether Media.
Peterson, Brenda. Leopard & Silkie: One Boy's Quest to Save the Seal Pups. Lindsey, Robin, photos by. 2012. (My Readers Ser.). (ENG., Illus.). 32p. (J). (gr. -1-3). 17.99 *(978-0-8050-9167-0(X),* 9780805091670, Holt, Henry & Co. Bks. For Young Readers) Holt, Henry & Co.
—Seal Pup Rescue. Lindsey, Robin, photos by. 2013. (My Readers Ser.). (ENG., Illus.). 32p. (J). (gr. k-2). pap. 4.99 *(978-1-250-02776-4(4),* 9781250027764) Square Fish.
Peterson, Megan Cooley & Rustad, Martha E. H. California Sea Lions, 1 vol. 2012. (Marine Mammals Ser.). (ENG., Illus.). 24p. (gr. k-1). lib. bdg. 26.65 *(978-1-4296-8573-3(5),* Pebble Plus) Capstone Press of Coughlan Cos.
—Elephant Seals, 1 vol. 2012. (Marine Mammals Ser.). (ENG., Illus.). 24p. (gr. k-1). lib. bdg. 26.65 *(978-1-4296-8574-0(3),* Pebble Plus) Capstone Press of Coughlan Cos.
Pettiford, Rebecca. Seals. 2017. (Ocean Life up Close Ser.). (ENG., Illus.). 24p. (J). (gr. k-3). lib. bdg. 25.95 *(978-1-62617-574-7(8),* Blastoff! Readers) Bellwether Media.
Phillips, Dee. Harp Seal. 2015. (Arctic Animals: Life Outside the Igloo Ser.). (ENG.). 24p. (J). (gr. -1-3). lib. bdg. 23.93 *(978-1-62724-531-9(6))* Bearport Publishing Co., Inc.
Read, Tracy C. Exploring the World of Seals & Walruses. 2011. (Exploring the World Of Ser.). (ENG., Illus.). 24p. (J). (gr. 3-7). 16.95 *(978-1-55407-784-7(2),* 9781554077847); pap. 6.95 *(978-1-55407-797-7(4),* 9781554077977) Firefly Bks., Ltd.
Riggs, Kate. Amazing Animals: Sea Lions. 2014. (Amazing Animals Ser.). (ENG.). 24p. (J). (gr. 1-3). pap. 8.99 *(978-0-89812-928-1(1),* Creative Paperbacks) Creative Co., The.
—Sea Lions. (J). 2015. *(978-1-60818-516-0(8))* 2014. 25.65 *(978-1-60818-349-4(1))* Creative Co., The. (Creative Education).
—Seedlings: Sea Lions. 2015. (Seedlings Ser.). (ENG.). 24p. (J). (gr. -1-1). pap. 7.99 *(978-1-62832-116-6(4),* Creative Paperbacks) Creative Co., The.
Rockwood, Leigh. Tell Me the Difference Between a Seal & a Sea Lion. 2013. (How Are They Different? Ser.). (ENG., Illus.). 24p. (J). (gr. k-5). pap. 8.25 *(978-1-4488-9738-4(6));* lib. bdg. 22.60 *(978-1-4488-9640-0(1))* Rosen Publishing Group, Inc., The. (PowerKids Pr.).
Rustad, Martha E. H. A Baby Seal Story. 2011. (Baby Animals Ser.). (ENG.). 24p. (gr. k-1). pap. 41.70 *(978-1-4296-7102-6(5),* Pebble Plus) Capstone Press of Coughlan Cos.
Seals. 2014. (ENG.). 48p. (J). lib. bdg. 28.00 *(978-0-531-20666-9(1))* Scholastic Library Publishing.
Sellers, Charles. Subtracting with Seals. 2011. (Animal Math Ser.). 24p. (J). (gr. 1-3). pap. 8.15 *(978-1-4339-5672-0(1));* lib. bdg. 22.60 *(978-1-4339-5670-6(5))* Stevens, Gareth Publishing LLLP.
Sexton, Colleen. Sea Lions. 2008. (Oceans Alive Ser.). (ENG., Illus.). 24p. (J). (gr. k-3). lib. bdg. 25.95 *(978-1-60014-174-4(9))* Bellwether Media.
—Seal Pups. 2008. (Watch Animals Grow Ser.). (ENG., Illus.). 24p. (J). (gr. k-3). lib. bdg. 25.95 *(978-1-60014-171-3(4))* Bellwether Media.
—Seals. 2007. (Oceans Alive Ser.). (ENG., Illus.). 24p. (J). (gr. k-3). lib. bdg. 25.95 *(978-1-60014-056-3(4))* Bellwether Media.
Shivley, Julie. Baby Seal. Sharp, Chris & Seaworld, Chris, illus. Seaworld, Chris, photos by. 2005. (Seaworld Animal Library: Vol. 3). 26p. (J). (gr. -1-k). bds. 6.95 *(978-0-8249-6617-1(1),* Ideal Pubns.) Worthy Publishing.
Silverman, Buffy. Can You Tell a Seal from a Sea Lion? 2012. (Animal Look-Alikes Ser.). 32p. (gr. k-2). pap. 45.32 *(978-0-7613-9257-6(2));* (ENG.). pap. 7.95 *(978-0-7613-8556-1(8));* (ENG., Illus.). lib. bdg. 26.60 *(978-0-7613-6738-3(1),* Lerner Pubns.) Lerner Publishing Group.
Soundprints Staff, ed. Oceanic Collection III: Beluga Whale, Harp Seal, Walrus & Lobster Books, 4 micro bks. (Smithsonian Oceanic Collection). (Illus.). 128p. (J). (gr. -1-2). 18.95 *(978-1-56899-633-2(0))* Soundprints.
Spilsbury, Louise. Seal, 1 vol. 2010. (Day in the Life: Sea Animals Ser.). (ENG.). 24p. (gr. k-2). 23.32 *(978-1-4329-4002-7(3));* pap. 6.79 *(978-1-4329-4009-6(0))* Heinemann-Raintree. (Heinemann Read & Learn).
Stearns, Precious. Steller Sea Lions. 2009. (Eye to Eye with Endangered Species Ser.). (Illus.). 24p. (gr. 3-6). (J). lib. bdg. 27.07 *(978-1-60694-402-8(9));* (ENG.). pap. 8.95 *(978-1-60694-841-5(5))* Rourke Educational Media.
The Story of Small Fry: Individual Title Six-Packs. (Action Packs Ser.). 104p. (gr. 3-5). 44.00 *(978-0-7635-8405-4(3))* Rigby Education.
Taylor, Trace & Sanchez, Lucia M. Focas (Seals) 2011. (poder de 100 - Animales marinos Ser.). (SPA.). 12p. pap. 39.62 *(978-1-61541-277-8(8))* American Reading Co.
Throp, Claire. Seals, 1 vol. 2013. (Living in the Wild: Sea Mammals Ser.). (ENG.). 48p. (gr. 4-6). pap. 9.95 *(978-1-4329-7071-0(2));* lib. bdg. 33.32 *(978-1-4329-7064-2(X))* Heinemann-Raintree. (Heinemann InfoSearch).
Tourville, Amanda Doering. Sunning Sea Lions: Discovering Even Numbers, 1 vol. Holm, Sharon Lane, illus. 2008. (Count the Critters Ser.). (ENG.). 24p. (J). (gr. k-3). 27.07 *(978-1-60270-267-7(5))* Magic Wagon.
Townsend, Emily Rose. Seals, 1 vol. 2004. (Polar Animals Ser.). (ENG., Illus.). 24p. (gr. k-1). 21.32 *(978-0-7368-2359-3(X),* Pebble Bks.) Capstone Press of Coughlan Cos.
Twine, Alice. Seals. (Baby Animals Ser.). 24p. 2009. (gr. 1-1). 42.50 *(978-1-61511-496-2(3),* PowerKids Pr.) 2007. (Illus.). (J). (gr. 3-7). lib. bdg. 22.60 *(978-1-4042-3773-5(9))* Rosen Publishing Group, Inc., The.
—Seals/Focas. 2009. (Baby Animals/Animales bebé Ser.). (ENG & SPA.). 24p. (gr. 1-1). 42.50 *(978-1-61511-508-2(0),* Editorial Buenas Letras) Rosen Publishing Group, Inc., The.
—Seals/Focas. Obregon, Jose Maria, tr. 2007. (Baby Animals / Animales Bebé Ser.). (ENG & SPA., Illus.). 24p. (J). (gr. -1-3). lib. bdg. 22.60 *(978-1-4042-7632-1(7),* Editorial Buenas Letras) Rosen Publishing Group, Inc., The.
Walker, Harvey Jeanne. Honey Girl: The Hawaiian Monk Seal. Bersani, Shennen, illus. 2017. (ENG.). 32p. (J). (gr. k-3). 17.95 *(978-1-62855-921-7(7))* Arbordale Publishing.
Wexo, John Bonnett. Seals & Sea Lions. rev. ed. 2003. (Illus.). 24p. (J). (gr. 1-7). 10.95 *(978-1-932396-00-3(4),* Zoo Bks.) Wildlife Education, Ltd.
Wildlife Education, compiled by. Seals. 2007. (Illus.). 12p. (J). 5.99 *(978-1-932396-41-6(1),* Critters Up Close) Wildlife Education, Ltd.
Wilsdon, Christina. Seals. 2010. (Amazing Animals Ser.). (ENG.). 48p. (J). (gr. 2-6). pap. 10.50 *(978-1-4339-4026-2(4));* lib. bdg. 28.00 *(978-1-4339-4025-5(6))* Stevens, Gareth Publishing LLLP. (Gareth Stevens Learning Library).
—Seals. 2007. (J). *(978-1-59939-127-4(9),* Reader's Digest Young Families, Inc.) Studio Fun International.

SEALS (ANIMALS)—FICTION

Aronson, Rosy. A Tale of Serendipity: the Adventure Begins! 2010. 370p. pap. 24.84 *(978-0-557-12641-5(X))* Lulu Pr., Inc.
Brezenoff, Steve. The Seals That Wouldn't Swim, 1 vol. Calo, Marcos, illus. 2011. (Field Trip Mysteries Ser.). (ENG.). 88p. (gr. 2-3). pap. 6.10 *(978-1-4342-3428-5(2));* lib. bdg. 25.32 *(978-1-4342-3225-0(5))* Stone Arch Bks.
Butterworth, Chris. See What a Seal Can Do. Nelms, Kate, illus. 2013. (ENG.). 32p. (J). (gr. k-4). 14.99 *(978-0-7636-6574-6(6))* Candlewick Pr.
Call of the Selkie: Individual Title Six-Packs. (Action Packs Ser.). 104p. (gr. 3-5). 44.00 *(978-0-7635-2991-8(5))* Rigby Education.
Cobb, Amelia. Silky Seal Pup. 2016. (Zoe's Rescue Zoo Ser.: 3). (ENG.). 128p. (J). (gr. 2-5). pap. 4.99 *(978-0-545-84224-2(7),* Scholastic Paperbacks) Scholastic, Inc.
Cook, Sherry & Johnson, Terri. Susie Sound, 26. Kuhn, Jesse, illus. Lt. ed. 2006. 32p. (J). 7.99 *(978-1-933815-18-3(3),* Quirkles, The) Creative 3, LLC.
Cosgrove, Stephen. Pickles & the P-Flock Bullies. James, Robin, illus. 2014. (ENG.). 32p. (J). (gr. k-3). 16.99 *(978-1-57061-887-1(9),* Little Bigfoot) Sasquatch Bks.
Crowley, Peter. J T Seavey. 2012. (ENG.). 35p. (J). pap. 18.95 *(978-1-4327-8712-7(8))* Outskirts Pr., Inc.
Dombey, Elizabeth & Muldrow, Diane. How Do Penguins Play? Walker, David, illus. 2011. (Little Golden Book Ser.). (ENG.). 24p. (J). (gr. -1-k). 4.99 *(978-0-375-86501-5(2),* Golden Bks.) Random Hse. Children's Bks.
Don, Lari. Never Trust a Tiger: A Story from Korea. Williamson, Melanie, illus. 2012. (Animal Stories Ser.). (ENG.). 48p. (J). (gr. 1-4). pap. 8.99 *(978-1-84686-776-7(2))* Barefoot Bks., Inc.
Dynamo. Googly Eyes: Flipper the Seal Makes a Discovery! 2014. (ENG., Illus.). 12p. (J). (gr. -1-2). bds. 6.99 *(978-1-84322-905-6(6),* Armadillo) Anness Publishing GBR. Dist: National Bk. Network.
Foreman, Michael. Seal Surfer. Foreman, Michael, illus. 2007. (ENG., Illus.). 36p. (J). (gr. k-4). pap. 12.99 *(978-1-84270-578-0(4))* Andersen Pr. GBR. Dist: Independent Pubs. Group.
French, Sarah. Summer Friends. 2011. (ENG., Illus.). 32p. (J). 17.95 *(978-0-9827146-5-2(3))* Vineyard Stories.
George, Elisabeth. The Edge of the Water. 2014. (Edge of Nowhere Ser.). (ENG.). 448p. (YA). (gr. 7). 18.99 *(978-0-670-01297-8(1),* Viking Books for Young Readers) Penguin Young Readers Group.
George, Elizabeth. The Edge of the Water. 2015. (Edge of Nowhere Ser.). (ENG.). 464p. (YA). (gr. 7). pap. 9.99 *(978-0-14-242674-6(1),* Speak) Penguin Young Readers Group.
Harris, Sue. Little Seal Finds a Friend. Boey, Stephanie, illus. 2007. (ENG.). 24p. (J). *(978-1-55168-295-2(8))* Fenn, H. B. & Co., Ltd.
He Who Listens: Individual Title Six-Packs. (Literatura 2000 Ser.). (gr. 2-3). 33.00 *(978-0-7635-0171-6(9))* Rigby Education.
Hoff, Syd. Sammy the Seal. Hoff, Syd, illus. 2017. (I Can Read Level 1 Ser.). (Illus.). 72p. (J). (gr. -1-3). 9.99 *(978-0-06-257274-5(1))* HarperCollins Pubs.
Holden, Pam. Seal on the Loose. Hatam, Samer, illus. 2015. (ENG.). 16p. (-1). pap. *(978-1-77654-134-8(0),* Red Rocket Readers) Flying Start Bks.
Hollenbeck, Kathleen M. Islands of Ice: The Story of a Harp Seal. Genzo, John Paul, illus. (Smithsonian Oceanic Collection Ser.). (ENG.). 32p. (J). (gr. -1-3). 2011. 19.95 *(978-1-60727-652-4(6))* 2005. 19.95 *(978-1-56899-967-8(4),* BC4021) 2005. 4.95 *(978-1-56899-966-1(6),* B4071) 2005. 9.95 *(978-1-56899-970-8(4),* PB4071) 2005. 15.95 *(978-1-56899-965-4(8),* B4021) Soundprints.
Holloway, Christina. Irish Selkie. 2008. 12p. pap. 24.95 *(978-1-60610-693-8(7))* America Star Bks.
Horn, Sandra. Silkie. (Illus.). 89p. pap. 7.95 *(978-0-340-67265-5(X))* Hodder & Stoughton GBR. Dist: Trafalgar Square Publishing.
Howell, Gill. Selkie Child. Keen, Sophie, illus. 2005. (ENG.). 24p. (J). lib. bdg. 23.65 *(978-1-59646-750-7(9))* Dingles & Co.
Image Books Staff. Little Seal: Finger Puppet Book. Put, Klaartje van der, illus. 2012. (Little Finger Puppet Board Bks.:

FING). (ENG.). 12p. (J). (gr. -1 — 1). bds. 6.99 *(978-1-4521-0812-4(9))* Chronicle Bks. LLC.
Kaczka, Fallon. What about Oysters. 2010. 24p. 13.00 *(978-1-4520-2066-2(3))* AuthorHouse.
Kipling, Rudyard. The White Seal. Jones, Chuck, illus. 2006. (ENG.). 32p. (J). (gr. -1-3). 8.95 *(978-0-8249-6598-3(1),* Ideal Pubns.) Worthy Publishing.
LaFaye, A. Water Steps. 2009. (ENG., Illus.). 208p. (J). (gr. 2-7). 16.95 *(978-1-57131-687-5(6));* pap. 6.95 *(978-1-57131-686-8(8))* Milkweed Editions.
Lanagan, Margo. The Brides of Rollrock Island. 2012. (ENG.). 320p. (YA). (gr. 9). 17.99 *(978-0-375-86919-8(0),* Knopf Bks. for Young Readers) Random Hse. Children's Bks.
Lawton, Diana. Paulie the Penguin Meets Sammy the Seal. 2012. 30p. 24.95 *(978-1-4626-6782-6(1))* America Star Bks.
Leach, Cheryl. Sally to the Rescue. 2012. 36p. pap. 20.99 *(978-1-4772-9974-6(2))* AuthorHouse.
London, C. Alexander. Honor Bound. 2014. (Tides of War Ser.: 2). (ENG.). 224p. (J). (gr. 5-9). pap. 5.99 *(978-0-545-66301-4(6),* Scholastic Paperbacks) Scholastic, Inc.
MacGregor, Jill. Swim Safe Little Seals. 2006. (Illus.). 31p. (J). 14.95 *(978-0-9774062-0-3(2))* Seal Publishing, LLC.
Marsaw, Roy. Swim, Swam, Swum. Harris, Phyllis, illus. 2007. 32p. (J). pap. 14.95 *(978-0-9744446-8-0(5))* All About Kids Publishing.
McDoogle, Farrah. OLIVIA & the Sea Lions. Spaziante, Patrick, illus. 2013. (Olivia TV Tie-In Ser.). (ENG.). 16p. (J). (gr. -1-1). pap. 5.99 *(978-1-4424-7364-5(9),* Simon Spotlight) Simon Spotlight.
Medina, Larry. The Adventures of Peek a Boo the Sea Lion. 2010. 40p. 21.00 *(978-1-4520-1499-9(X))* AuthorHouse.
Murphy, T. M. Saving Santa's Seals. Taylor, Adam, illus. 2009. (LeapKids Ser.). (ENG.). 170p. (J). (gr. 1-5). pap. 10.95 *(978-0-9815148-8-8(X))* Leapfrog Pr.
Papish, Ram. The Little Seal: An Alaska Adventure. 2009. (ENG., Illus.). 24p. (J). 15.95 *(978-1-60223-068-2(4))* Univ. of Alaska Pr.
Patterson, Ellie. Baby Bear & the Big, Wide World. Kolanovic, Dubravka, illus. 2013. (J). *(978-1-4351-4929-8(7))* Barnes & Noble, Inc.
Patterson, Sherri, et al. No-No & the Secret Touch: The Gentle Story of a Little Seal Who Learns to Stay Safe, Say "No" & Tell! Krupp, Marian N., illus. unabr. ed. 70p. (J). (gr. 1-6). pap. 14.95 incl. audio *(978-0-9632276-2-1(9))* National Self-Esteem Resources & Development Ctr.
Resnicoff, Stan. Stanley, the Seal of Approval. 2012. (ENG.). (J). pap. *(978-1-4675-1535-1(3))* Independent Pub.
Rylant, Cynthia. The Sea Lion. McDaniels, Preston, illus. 2017. (Lighthouse Family Ser.: 7). (ENG.). 48p. (J). (gr. 1-5). 15.99 *(978-1-4814-6025-5(0),* Beach Lane Bks.) Beach Lane Bks.
Salzmann, Mary Elizabeth. Presidential Seal, 1 vol. 2007. (Critter Chronicles Ser.). (ENG., Illus.). 24p. (J). (gr. k-3). lib. bdg. 24.21 *(978-1-59928-464-4(2),* SandCastle) ABDO Publishing Co.
Seeger, Laura Vaccaro. What If? Seeger, Laura Vaccaro, illus. 2010. (ENG., Illus.). 32p. (J). (gr. -1-2). 17.99 *(978-1-59643-398-4(1),* 9781596433984) Roaring Brook Pr.
Sherrow, Victoria. Galapagos Fur Seal. 2012. (ENG.). 24p. (J). pap. 3.95 *(978-1-60727-725-5(5))* Soundprints.
—Galapagos Fur Seal: At Home in the Tropics. Wertheim, Anne, illus. 2011. (ENG.). 32p. (J). pap. 8.95 *(978-1-60727-613-5(5))* Soundprints.
Sobel, Deane. Philip the Sea Lion. 2012. (ENG.). (J). pap. *(978-1-4675-2347-9(X))* Independent Pub.
Spalding, Andrea. Seal Song, 1 vol. Milelli, Pascal, illus. 2011. (ENG.). 32p. (J). (gr. -1-3). 19.95 *(978-1-55469-242-2(3))* Orca Bk. Pubs. USA.
Sue-A-Quan, Goomatie. A Seal Fascination at Sea: A Fascinating Seal. 2008. (Illus.). 38p. (J). pap. 19.00 *(978-0-8059-7517-8(9))* Dorrance Publishing Co., Inc.
Sundaram, Renuka. Sammy, the Galapagos Sea Lion. 2011. 32p. pap. 15.00 *(978-1-61286-015-2(X))* Avid Readers Publishing Group.
Thomas, Shelley Moore. Secrets of Selkie Bay. 2015. (ENG.). 208p. (J). (gr. 3-7). 15.99 *(978-0-374-36749-7(3),* 9780374367497, Farrar, Straus & Giroux (BYR)) Farrar, Straus & Giroux.
Virgo, Seán. The Shadow Mother, 1 vol. Pérez, Javier Serrano, illus. 2014. (ENG.). 64p. (J). (gr. 6). 21.95 *(978-0-88899-971-9(2))* Groundwood Bks. CAN. Dist: Publishers Group West (PGW).
Waters, Summer. Stormy Skies. 2010. (Silver Dolphins Ser.: 8). (ENG.). 176p. (J). (gr. 2-4). pap. 7.99 *(978-0-00-734813-8(4),* HarperCollins Children's Bks.) HarperCollins Pubs. Ltd. GBR. Dist: HarperCollins Pubs.
Zoehfeld, Kathleen Weidner. Seal Pup Grows Up: The Story of a Harbor Seal. Bonforte, Lisa, illus. 2011. (Smithsonian Oceanic Collection Ser.). (ENG.). 32p. (J). (gr. -1-3). 19.95 *(978-1-60727-663-0(1))* Soundprints.

SEAMANSHIP

see also Navigation

Mosenthal, Basil, et al. Getting Afloat: All You Need to Know about Sailing Small Boats. 2003. (ENG., Illus.). 80p. pap. *(978-0-7136-5278-9(0),* Adlard Coles) Bloomsbury Publishing Plc.

SEAMEN

see Sailors

SEARCH AND RESCUE OPERATIONS

see Rescue Work

SEASHORE

Allaire, Caroline & Broutin, Christian. Let's Look at the Seashore. Broutin, Christian, illus. 2012. (ENG., Illus.). 38p. (J). (gr. 1-4). pap. 11.99 *(978-1-85103-341-6(6))* Moonlight Publishing, Ltd. GBR. Dist: Independent Pubs. Group.
Amery, Heather. The Seaside. Cartwright, Stephen, illus. 2008. (Usborne Talkabout Bks.). 12p. (J). bds. 8.99 *(978-0-7945-1794-6(3),* Usborne) EDC Publishing.
—What's Happening at the Seaside? Cartwright, Stephen, illus. rev. ed. 2006. (What's Happening Ser.). 16p. (J). (gr. -1-3). 5.99 *(978-0-7945-1290-3(9),* Usborne) EDC Publishing.
Anderson, Sheila. Coasts. 2008. (First Step Nonfiction - Landforms Ser.). (Illus.). 23p. (J). (gr. -1). lib. bdg. 18.60 *(978-0-8225-8595-4(2),* Lerner Pubns.); pap. 34.95 *(978-0-8225-9935-7(X))* Lerner Publishing Group.
Andrews, Alexa. At the Beach. Keimig, Candice, illus. 2013. (Penguin Young Readers, Level 1 Ser.). (ENG.). 32p. (J). (gr. k-1). 14.99 *(978-0-448-46570-8(1));* pap. 3.99 *(978-0-448-46471-8(3))* Penguin Young Readers Group. (Penguin Young Readers).
Arnosky, Jim. Beachcombing: Exploring the Seashore. 2014. (ENG.). 32p. (J). (gr. 2-5). 8.99 *(978-0-14-751163-8(1),* Puffin Books) Penguin Young Readers Group.
Beckett-Bowman, Lucy. Seashore. Donaera, Patrizia & Haggerty, Tim, illus. 2008. (Beginners Nature Ser.). 32p. (J). (gr. -1-3). 4.99 *(978-0-7945-2061-8(8),* Usborne) EDC Publishing.
Benjamin, Tina. Let's Visit the Beach. 2015. (Let's Go Outdoors! Ser.). (ENG., Illus.). 24p. (J). (gr. k-k). lib. bdg. 22.60 *(978-1-4824-2631-1(5))* Stevens, Gareth Publishing LLLP.
Berne, Emma Carlson. Bays. 2008. (Geography Zone: Landforms Ser.). (Illus.). 24p. (J). (gr. 2-5). lib. bdg. 22.60 *(978-1-4042-4206-7(6))* Rosen Publishing Group, Inc., The.
Beylon, Cathy. At the Beach. 2004. (Dover Coloring Bks.). (ENG., Illus.). 32p. (J). (gr. -1-2). pap. 3.99 *(978-0-486-43643-2(8))* Dover Pubns., Inc.
Bluemel Oldfield, Dawn. Patterns at the Seashore. 2014. (Math Blast!: Seeing Patterns All Around Ser.). (ENG.). 32p. (J). (gr. -1-3). lib. bdg. 26.60 *(978-1-62724-335-3(6))* Bearport Publishing Co., Inc.
Brown, Carron. Secrets of the Seashore. Nassner, Alyssa, illus. 2014. (ENG.). 36p. (J). (gr. 1). 12.99 *(978-1-61067-309-9(3))* Kane Miller.
Burgess, Thornton W. Burgess Sea Shore Book for Children. (J). 26.95 *(978-0-8488-0403-9(1))* Amereon Ltd.
Burton, Margie, et al. Clean Beaches. 2011. (Early Connections Ser.). (J). *(978-1-61672-518-1(4))* Benchmark Education Co.
—Clean Beaches & Playas Limpias: 6 English, 6 Spanish Adaptations. 2011. (J). spiral bd. 75.00 net. *(978-1-4108-5625-8(9))* Benchmark Education Co.
Carlson Berne, Emma. Bays. 2009. (Geography Zone: Landforms Ser.). 24p. (gr. 2-3). 42.50 *(978-1-61512-690-3(2),* PowerKids Pr.) Rosen Publishing Group, Inc., The.
Carlson-Berne, Emma. Beaches. 2008. (Geography Zone: Landforms Ser.). (Illus.). 24p. (J). (gr. 2-5). lib. bdg. 22.60 *(978-1-4042-4205-0(8))* Rosen Publishing Group, Inc., The.
Carlson Berne, Emma. Beaches. 2009. (Geography Zone: Landforms Ser.). 24p. (gr. 2-3). 42.50 *(978-1-61512-691-0(0),* PowerKids Pr.) Rosen Publishing Group, Inc., The.
Carolan. B Is for Beach: An Alphabet Book. 2007. 64p. 18.95 incl. audio compact disk *(978-0-9715333-8-7(5))* Banana Patch Pr.
Crossingham, John & Kalman, Bobbie. Cadenas Alimentarias de la Costa Marina. 2006. (Cadenas Alimentarias Ser.). (SPA., Illus.). 32p. (J). (gr. 3-7). pap. *(978-0-7787-8547-7(5))* Crabtree Publishing Co.
Crow, Marilee. Down by the Shore. Roberts, Mary Sue, photos by. 2011. (Illus.). 30p. 19.95 *(978-1-61633-087-3(2))* Guardian Angel Publishing, Inc.
Davidson, Avelyn. Beach Biology. 2007. (Shockwave: Life Science & Medicine Ser.). (Illus.). 36p. (J). (gr. 4-6). pap. 6.95 *(978-0-531-15495-3(5),* Children's Pr.) Scholastic Library Publishing.
Day, Amelia. Olivia's Ocean Adventure. 2013. (Core Math Skills: Numbers & Operations in Base 10 Ser.). 24p. (J). (gr. 1-2). 22.60 *(978-1-4777-2222-0(X),* Rosen Classroom) Rosen Publishing Group, Inc., The.
—Olivia's Ocean Adventure: Understand Place Value. 2013. (Rosen Math Readers Ser.). (ENG.). 24p. (J). (gr. 1-2). pap. 8.25 *(978-1-4777-2037-0(5));* pap. 49.50 *(978-1-4777-2038-7(3))* Rosen Publishing Group, Inc., The. (Rosen Classroom).
Dorling Kindersley Publishing Staff. Seashore. 2017. (ENG., Illus.). 64p. (J). (gr. 1-3). 9.99 *(978-1-4654-5756-1(9),* DK Children) Dorling Kindersley Publishing, Inc.
Dunn, Mary. My Adventure Building the Eiffel Tower. 2007. 44p. (J). 8.99 *(978-1-59092-413-6(4))* Blue Forge Pr.
ETA/Cuisenaire Staff. At the Beach. 2003. (SunSprouts Ser.). (ENG.). (gr. -1-3). pap. 4.95 *(978-0-7406-2008-9(8),* SunSprouts) ETA hand2mind.
Evans, Shira. At the Beach. 2017. (Readers Ser.). (ENG., Illus.). 24p. (J). (-k). pap. 3.99 *(978-1-4263-2807-7(9),* National Geographic Children's Bks.) National Geographic Society.
—National Geographic Readers: at the Beach. 2017. (Readers Ser.). (ENG., Illus.). 24p. (J). (-k). lib. bdg. 13.90 *(978-1-4263-2808-4(7),* National Geographic Children's Bks.) National Geographic Society.
Felix, Rebecca. Visiting the Beach in Summer. 2014. (21st Century Basic Skills Library: Let's Look at Summer Ser.). (ENG., Illus.). 24p. (J). (gr. k-3). 22.79 *(978-1-63137-598-9(9),* 205175) Cherry Lake Publishing.
Foxxe, Ellen. The Rising Seas: Shorelines under Threat. 2009. (Extreme Environmental Threats Ser.). 64p. (gr. 6-6). 58.50 *(978-1-61512-436-7(5))* Rosen Publishing Group, Inc., The.
Fretland VanVoorst, Jenny. Las Formas en la Playa. 2015.Tr. of Shapes by the Sea. (SPA., Illus.). 24p. (J). lib. bdg. *(978-1-62031-249-0(2),* Bullfrog Bks.) Jump! Inc.
—Shapes by the Sea. 2015. (Illus.). 24p. (J). lib. bdg. *(978-1-62031-202-5(6),* Bullfrog Bks.) Jump! Inc.
From Rocks to Sand: Level L, 6 vols. (Wonder Worldtm Ser.). 16p. 34.95 *(978-0-7802-4575-4(X))* Wright Group/McGraw-Hill.
Ganeri, Anita. Exploring Coasts: A Benjamin Blog & His Inquisitive Dog Investigation. 1 vol. 2014. (Exploring Habitats with Benjamin Blog & His Inquisitive Dog Ser.). (ENG., Illus.). 32p. (gr. 1-3). lib. bdg. 29.99 *(978-1-4329-8777-0(1),* NA-h) Heinemann-Raintree.
—Exploring Habitats, with Benjamin Blog & His Inquisitive Dog, 1 vol. 2014. (Exploring Habitats with Benjamin Blog & His Inquisitive Dog Ser.). (ENG.). 32p. (gr. 1-3). lib. bdg. 179.94 *(978-1-4329-8781-7(X),* NA-h) Heinemann-Raintree.
Geatches, Hazel, ed. At the Beach. 2012. (ENG., Illus.). 32p. 9.38 *(978-0-19-464628-4(9))* Oxford Univ. Pr., Inc.
Grandma Fudgie. A Day at the Beach. 2011. 24p. pap. 14.99 *(978-1-4567-5548-5(X))* AuthorHouse.
Grassby, Donna. A Seaside Alphabet. Tooke, Susan, illus. 2009. (ABC Our Country Ser.). (ENG.). 32p. (J). (gr. 1-4). pap. 7.95 *(978-0-88776-938-2(1),* Tundra Bks.) Tundra Bks. CAN. Dist: Penguin Random Hse. LLC.
Green, Jen. Coastlines Around the World. 2009. (Geography Now! Ser.). (ENG., Illus.). 32p. (J). (gr. 4-6). pap. 10.00 *(978-1-4358-2957-2(3),* PowerKids Pr.); (YA). (gr. 3-6). lib. bdg. 26.50 *(978-1-4358-2871-1(2))* Rosen Publishing Group, Inc., The.
—Coasts. 2011. (Geography Wise Ser.). (Illus.). 32p. (YA). (gr. 2-5). lib. bdg. 26.50 *(978-1-4488-3279-8(9))* Rosen Publishing Group, Inc., The.
—Projects with the Seaside. 2014. (Make & Learn Ser.). (Illus.). 32p. (J). (gr. 3-6). lib. bdg. 27.50 *(978-1-4777-7173-0(5),* PowerKids Pr.) Rosen Publishing Group, Inc., The.
Greenaway, Theresa, ed. Ocean: A Foldout Book & Wall Chart. 2005. (Illus.). 12p. (J). (gr. k-4). reprint ed. 10.00 *(978-0-7567-8533-8(2))* DIANE Publishing Co.
Gregoire, Maryellen. At the Beach. 2012. (Wonder Readers Emergent Level Ser.). (ENG.). (gr. -1-k). 16p. pap. 35.94 *(978-1-4296-9205-2(7));* 32p. pap. 5.99 *(978-1-4296-9195-6(6))* Capstone Press of Coughlan Cos. (Wonder Readers).
—En la Playa (at the Beach) 2012. (Wonder Readers Spanish Emergent Ser.). (SPA.). 16p. (gr. -1-1). pap. 35.94 *(978-1-62065-566-5(7))* Capstone Press of Coughlan Cos.
Hainnu, Rebecca. A Walk on the Shoreline, 1 vol. Leng, Qin, illus. 2015. (ENG.). 32p. (J). (gr. k-2). 16.95 *(978-1-77227-024-2(5))* Inhabit Media Inc. CAN. Dist: Independent Pubs. Group.
Halpern, Monica. All about Tide Pools. 2007. (Science Chapters Ser.). (ENG., Illus.). 48p. (J). (gr. 1-4). 17.90 *(978-1-4263-0184-1(7),* National Geographic Children's Bks.) National Geographic Society.
Harvey, Stephanie, et al. Living on the Coast. 2014. (Ladders Social Studies). (ENG.). 24p. 8.95 *(978-1-285-34802-5(8));* 8.95 *(978-1-285-34803-2(6))* National Geographic School Publishing, Inc.
Hewitt, Sally. By the Sea. 2010. (Starting Geography Ser.). 32p. (J). (gr. 2-5). 28.50 *(978-1-60753-123-4(2))* Amicus Publishing.
—By the Sea. 2012. (Deadly & Incredible Animals Ser.). 32p. (gr. 2-6). 27.10 *(978-1-59920-409-3(6))* Black Rabbit Bks.
Holland, Gini. I Live near the Ocean. 2004. (Weekly Reader Early Learning Library). (Illus.). 24p. (gr. k-3). pap. 8.15 *(978-0-8368-4089-6(5),* Weekly Reader Leveled Readers) Stevens, Gareth Publishing LLLP.
—I Live near the Ocean/Vivo cerca del Mar. Coffey, Colleen & Carrillo, Consuelo, trs. 2004. (Weekly Reader Early Learning Library). (SPA & ENG., Illus.). 24p. (gr. k-3). pap. 8.15 *(978-0-8368-4137-4(9));* lib. bdg. 22.00 *(978-0-8368-4130-5(1))* Stevens, Gareth Publishing LLLP. (Weekly Reader Leveled Readers).
I Feel Hot, 6 Packs. (gr. -1-2). 23.00 *(978-0-7635-9014-7(2))* Rigby Education.
Johansson, Philip. The Seashore: A Saltwater Web of Life. 2007. (Wonderful Water Biomes Ser.). (Illus.). 48p. (J). (gr. 3-7). lib. bdg. 25.27 *(978-0-7660-2811-1(9),* Enslow Elementary) Enslow Pubs., Inc.
Kalman, Bobbie. Earth's Coasts. 2008. (Looking at Earth Ser.). (ENG., Illus.). 32p. (J). (gr. 1-4). lib. bdg. *(978-0-7787-3206-8(1))* Crabtree Publishing Co.
—Las Costas de la Tierra. 2009. (SPA.). 32p. (J). *(978-0-7787-8237-7(9));* pap. *(978-0-7787-8254-4(9))* Crabtree Publishing Co.
Kawa, Katie. My First Trip to the Beach. 2012. (My First Adventures Ser.). (Illus.). 24p. (gr. k-2). 69.20 *(978-1-4339-8049-7(5));* (J). pap. 8.15 *(978-1-4339-7309-3(X));* (J). lib. bdg. 22.60 *(978-1-4339-7308-6(1))* Stevens, Gareth Publishing LLLP.
—My First Trip to the Beach: Mi Primer Viaje a la Playa. 2012. (My First Adventures / Mis primeras aventuras Ser.). (SPA., Illus.). 24p. (J). (gr. k-2). lib. bdg. 22.60 *(978-1-4339-7376-5(6))* Stevens, Gareth Publishing LLLP.
Kent, Lorna, illus. At the Beach. 2004. 8p. (J). bds. 3.99 *(978-1-85854-087-0(9))* Brimax Books Ltd. GBR. Dist: Byeway Bks.
Kerrigan, Michael. Coastlines. 2004. (Geography Fact Files Ser.). (J). lib. bdg. 28.50 *(978-1-58340-424-9(4))* Black Rabbit Bks.
King, Zelda. Examining Tide Pool Habitats. 2009. (Graphic Organizers: Habitats Ser.). 24p. (gr. 2-3). 42.50 *(978-1-61513-103-7(5));* (J). lib. bdg. 22.60 *(978-1-4358-2719-6(8))* Rosen Publishing Group, Inc., The. (PowerKids Pr.).
Kingsley, Charles. Glaucus or the Wonders of the Shore. 2004. reprint ed. pap. 15.95 *(978-1-4191-2183-8(9));* pap. 1.99 *(978-1-4192-2183-5(3))* Kessinger Publishing, LLC.
Kittinger, Jo S. Going to the Beach. Warren, Shari, illus. 2011. (Rookie Ready to Learn Ser.). 32p. (J). (ENG.). pap. 5.95 *(978-0-531-26801-8(2));* (gr. -1-k). lib. bdg. 23.00 *(978-0-531-25641-1(3))* Scholastic Library Publishing. (Children's Pr.).
Kochanoff, Peggy. Be a Beach Detective: Solving the Mysteries of Seas, Sands & Surf, 1 vol. 2015. (ENG., Illus.). 40p. (J). (gr. k-3). pap. 14.95 *(978-1-77108-267-9(4))* Nimbus Publishing, Ltd. CAN. Dist: Orca Bk. Pubs. USA.
Koeppel, Ruth. At the Seashore. McBee, Scott, illus. 2009. (ENG.). 10p. (J). (gr. -1-1). 12.99 *(978-1-58476-817-3(7))* Innovative Kids.
Kopp, Megan. What Do You Find in a Tide Pool? 2016. (ENG., Illus.). 24p. (J). *(978-0-7787-2263-2(5))* Crabtree Publishing Co.
Laber-Warren, Emily & Goldman, Laurie. A Walk on the Beach: Into the Field Guide. 2013. (ENG.). 112p. (J). (gr. k). 19.99 *(978-1-935703-24-2(2))* Downtown Bookworks.
Labrecque, Ellen. Living Beside the Ocean. 2015. (Places We Live Ser.). (ENG., Illus.). 32p. (gr. 1-3). 27.32 *(978-1-4846-0803-6(8),* Heinemann First Library) Heinemann-Raintree.
Lantz, Peggy Sias & Hale, Wendy A. The Coastlines of Florida. 2014. (Florida Water Story Ser.). (ENG., Illus.). 34p. (J). (gr. 4). pap. 6.95 *(978-1-56164-702-6(0))* Pineapple Pr., Inc.
Laughing Elephant Staff, compiled by. By the Sea. 2013. (Shape Bks.). (ENG., Illus.). 16p. pap. 9.95 *(978-1-59583-702-8(7))* Laughing Elephant.
Lennon, Liz. What I Like: The Seaside. 2017. (Little Stars Ser.). (ENG., Illus.). 24p. (J). (gr. -1-k). pap. 6.99 *(978-1-4451-4767-3(X),* Franklin Watts) Hachette Children's Group GBR. Dist: Hachette Bk. Group.
Lindeen, Mary. At the Beach. 2015. (BeginningtoRead Ser.). (ENG.). 32p. (J). (gr. k-2). pap. 11.94 *(978-1-60357-758-8(0));* lib. bdg. 22.60 *(978-1-59953-698-9(6))* Norwood Hse. Pr.
Litchfield, Jo. Beach. 2004. (Look & Say Board Books Ser.). (ENG., Illus.). 12p. (J). bds. 7.95 *(978-0-7945-0703-9(4),* Usborne) EDC Publishing.
Lynch, Annabelle. The Seaside, 01 vols., 1. 2016. (Nature Explorers Ser.). (ENG., Illus.). 24p. (J). pap. 8.25 *(978-1-5081-9073-8(9),* Windmill Bks.) Rosen Publishing Group, Inc., The.
Macken, JoAnn Early. Beaches. 2005. (Water Habitats Ser.). (Illus.). 24p. (gr. k-3). lib. bdg. 22.00 *(978-0-8368-4882-3(9),* Weekly Reader Leveled Readers) Stevens, Gareth Publishing LLLP.
Macken, JoAnn Early & Early Macken, JoAnn. Beaches (Playas) 2005. (Water Habitats/ Habitats acuaticos Ser.). (SPA., Illus.). 24p. (gr. k-3). pap. 8.15 *(978-0-8368-6034-4(9),* Weekly Reader Leveled Readers) Stevens, Gareth Publishing LLLP.
—Beaches/Playas. 2005. (Water Habitats/ Habitats acuaticos Ser.). (SPA., Illus.). 24p. (gr. k-3). lib. bdg. 22.00 *(978-0-8368-6027-6(6),* Weekly Reader Leveled Readers) Stevens, Gareth Publishing LLLP.
Meachen Rau, Dana. At the Beach. 2007. (Fun Time Ser.). (Illus.). 24p. (gr. k-1). lib. bdg. 15.95 *(978-0-7614-2609-7(4),* Benchmark Bks.) Marshall Cavendish Corp.
—En la Playa. 2007. (¡A Divertirnos! Ser.). (SPA., Illus.). 24p. (gr. k-1). lib. bdg. 15.95 *(978-0-7614-2748-3(1),* Benchmark Bks.) Marshall Cavendish Corp.
Meredith, Susan Markowitz. Patterns at the Beach. 2011. (Early Connections Ser.). (J). *(978-1-61672-371-2(8))* Benchmark Education Co.
Michaels, Chris. Finding Stripes. 2010. (Sight Word Readers Ser.). (J). 3.49 *(978-1-60719-626-6(3))* Newmark Learning LLC.
Milbourne, Anna. On the Seashore. Waters, Erica-Jane, illus. 2006. 24p. (J). (gr. -1-3). 9.99 *(978-0-7945-1069-5(8),* Usborne) EDC Publishing.
Mis, Melody S. Exploring Peninsulas. 2009. (Geography Zone: Landforms Ser.). 24p. (J). (gr. 2-4). pap. 8.25 *(978-1-4358-3109-4(8),* PowerKids Pr.) Rosen Publishing Group, Inc., The.
Moses, Jessie. My Day at the Beach. Boyer, Lyn, illus. 2017. (Text Connections Guided Close Reading Ser.). (J). (gr. k). *(978-1-4900-1769-3(0))* Benchmark Education Co.
Murray, W. On the Beach. (Sunstart Ser.: No. 747-2). (Illus.). 50p. (J). (gr. -1-5). 3.50 *(978-0-7214-8001-5(2),* Dutton Juvenile) Penguin Publishing Group.
On the Beach: Individual Title Six Packs. (Chiquilibros Ser.). (gr. k-1). 23.00 *(978-0-7635-0448-9(3))* Rigby Education.
Owen, Ruth. Welcome to the Seashore. 2016. (Nature's Neighborhoods: All about Ecosystems Ser.). (ENG.). 32p. (J). (gr. -1-3). lib. bdg. 19.95 *(978-1-910549-68-1(1))* Bearport Publishing Co., Inc.
Parker, Steve. The Seashore. 2010. (Unpredictable Nature Ser.). (Illus.). 48p. (J). (gr. 3-18). lib. bdg. 19.95 *(978-1-4222-2006-1(0))* Mason Crest.
—Seashore. Dorling Kindersley Publishing Staff, ed. 2004. (DK Eyewitness Bks.). (ENG., Illus.). 72p. (J). (gr. 3-7). 16.99 *(978-0-7566-0721-0(3),* DK Children) Dorling Kindersley Publishing, Inc.
Patrizzi, Barbara. O Is for Oystercatcher: A Book of Seaside ABCs. Patrizzi, Barbara, illus. 2003. (Illus.). 55p. 15.95 *(978-1-59322-008-2(1))* Down The Shore Publishing Corp.
Phillips, Clifton. Waterworld Wonderways. 2007. 36p. 9.99 *(978-0-9797106-2-9(6))* Avid Readers Publishing Group.
La Playa: Individual Title Six-Packs. (Literatura 2000 Ser.). (SPA.). (gr. -1-1). 28.00 *(978-0-7635-1001-5(7))* Rigby Education.
Randall, Jory. My Day at the Beach. 2009. (Kid's Life! Ser.). 24p. (J). (ENG.). pap. 8.25 *(978-1-4358-2467-6(9));* (Illus.). lib. bdg. 22.60 *(978-1-4042-8074-8(X))* Rosen Publishing Group, Inc., The. (PowerKids Pr.).
Rau, Dana Meachen. Think Like a Scientist at the Beach. 2011. (Explorer Junior Library: Science Explorer Junior Ser.). (ENG.). 32p. (gr. 4-8). lib. bdg. 28.50 *(978-1-61080-168-3(7),* 201106) Cherry Lake Publishing.
Richter, A. By the Ocean: Learning the Long O Sound. 2009. (PowerPhonics Ser.). 24p. (gr. 1-1). 39.90 *(978-1-60851-436-6(6),* PowerKids Pr.) Rosen Publishing Group, Inc., The.
Rigby Education Staff. Look up, Look down, Look All Around. (Illus.). 8p. (J). bds. 3.95 *(978-0-7635-6504-6(0),* 765040C99) Rigby Education.
Rissman, Rebecca. Going to a Beach, 1 vol. 2012. (World of Field Trips Ser.). (ENG.). 24p. (gr. -1-1). lib. bdg. 22.65 *(978-1-4329-6064-3(4),* Acorn) Heinemann-Raintree.
A Seaside Ecosystem. 2012. (Nature Trail Ser.). (ENG., Illus.). 32p. (J). (gr. k-5). 23.95 *(978-1-4488-6628-1(6),* PowerKids Pr.) Rosen Publishing Group, Inc., The.
Serafini, Frank. Looking Closely along the Shore. Serafini, Frank, illus. 2008. (Looking Closely Ser.). (ENG., Illus.). 40p. (J). (gr. -1-2). 16.95 *(978-1-55453-141-7(1))* Kids Can Pr., Ltd. CAN. Dist: Hachette Bk. Group.
Sévigny, Eric, illus. Caillou - At the Beach. 2012. (Clubhouse Ser.). (ENG.). 24p. (J). (gr. -1-1). pap. 3.99 *(978-2-89450-942-5(1))* Caillouet, Gerry.
Sexton, Colleen. Tide Pools. 2008. (Learning about the Earth Ser.). (ENG., Illus.). 24p. (J). (gr. k-3). lib. bdg. 25.95 *(978-1-60014-231-4(1))* Bellwether Media.
—Tide Pools. 2011. (Blastoff! Readers Ser.). 24p. (J). pap. 5.95 *(978-0-531-26037-1(2),* Children's Pr.) Scholastic Library Publishing.
Shah, Kieran. Math by the Ocean. 2016. (Math Is Everywhere! Ser.). 00024p. (J). pap. 8.15 *(978-1-4824-5508-3(0))* Stevens, Gareth Publishing LLLP.
Smith, Alastair & Howell, Laura. On the Beach. 2004. (Luxury Lift-the-Flap Ser.). 16p. (J). (gr. 1-18). 11.95 *(978-0-7945-0740-4(9),* Usborne) EDC Publishing.
Smith, Carrie & Swain, Cameron. Fun at the Beach. 2006. (Early Explorers Ser.). (J). pap. *(978-1-4108-6021-7(3))* Benchmark Education Co.

S

Spilsbury, Louise & Spilsbury, Richard. A Nature Walk on the Beach, 1 vol. 2014. (Nature Walks Ser.). (ENG., Illus.). 24p. (gr. k-2). 23.32 (978-1-4846-0400-7(8), Heinemann Read & Learn) Heinemann-Raintree.

Steele, Phillip W. Changing Coastlines. 2004. (Earth's Changing Landscape Ser.). (Illus.). 46p. (J). lib. bdg. 28.50 (978-1-58340-476-8(7)) Black Rabbit Bks.

Sterling Children's, Sterling. A Day at the Beach: A Book Of 123s. 2016. (ENG., Illus.). 28p. (J). (— 1). bds. 6.95 (978-1-4114-7588-5(7), Spark Publishing Group) Sterling Publishing Co., Inc.

Taylor, Barbara. Coastal Habitats. 2006. (Exploring Habitats Ser.). (Illus.). 36p. (gr. 3-7). lib. bdg. 26.00 (978-0-8368-7252-1(5), Gareth Stevens Learning Library) Stevens, Gareth Publishing LLLP.

Taylor, Trace & Zorzi, Gina. At the Beach. 2006. (1-3Y in My World Ser.). (ENG., Illus.). 20p. (J). (gr. k-1). pap. 5.99 (978-1-59301-261-8(6)) American Reading Co.

Thomas, M. Summer at the Beach: Learning the EA Sound. 2009. (PowerPhonics Ser.). 24p. (gr. 1-1). 39.90 (978-1-60851-472-4(2), PowerKids Pr.) Rosen Publishing Group, Inc., The.

Thomson, Ruth. Coasts. 2012. (Geography Corner Ser.). (ENG., Illus.). 24p. (J). (gr. k-3). 21.25 (978-1-4488-6616-8(2), PowerKids Pr.) Rosen Publishing Group, Inc., The.

Unstead, Sue. Seashore. 2006. (Illus.). 32p. (J). (978-0-439-91178-8(8), Scholastic) Scholastic, Inc.

Vogel, Carole G. Shifting Shores. 2003. (Restless Sea Ser.). (ENG.). 80p. (gr. 5-8). pap. 12.95 (978-0-531-16683-3(X)); (Illus.). (J). 30.50 (978-0-531-12322-5(7)) Scholastic Library Publishing. (Watts, Franklin).

Watt, Fiona. Seaside Stroller Book. Baggott, Stella, illus. 2010. 8p. (J). 7.99 (978-0-7945-2810-2(4), Usborne) EDC Publishing.

When the Tide Goes Out: Individual Title, 6 packs. (Story Steps Ser.). (gr. k-2). 20.00 (978-0-7635-9590-6(X)) Rigby Education.

Woodward, John. Along the Shore. 2010. (Oceans Alive! Ser.). 32p. lib. bdg. 28.50 (978-1-933834-61-0(7)) Brown Bear Bks.

Wynne, Patricia J. BOOST Seashore Activity Book. 2013. (BOOST Educational Ser.). (ENG.). 48p. (J). (gr. 1-2). pap. 5.99 (978-0-486-49408-1(X)) Dover Pubns., Inc.

—Seashore Activity Book. 2005. (Dover Children's Activity Bks.). (ENG., Illus.). 48p. (J). (gr. 3-8). per., act. bk. ed. 4.99 (978-0-486-44434-5(1)) Dover Pubns., Inc.

Yoon, Salina. At the Beach. 2011. (ENG., Illus.). 12p. (J). (gr. -1 — 1). bds. 6.99 (978-0-312-66303-2(X), 9780312663032) Feiwel & Friends.

SEASHORE—FICTION

Adler, David A. Young Cam Jansen & the Double Beach Mystery. Natti, Susanna, illus. 2003. (Young Cam Jansen Ser.: 8). (ENG.). 32p. (J). (gr. 1-3). mass mkt. 3.99 (978-0-14-250079-8(8), Penguin Young Readers) Penguin Young Readers Group.

Adrian, Mikel. Iza & Her Magic Seashell. Cotton, Sue Lynn, illus. 2012. 28p. 24.95 (978-1-61493-077-8(5)) Peppertree Pr., The.

Albert, Burton. Where Does the Trail Lead? Pinkney, Brian, illus. 2008. (ENG.). 40p. (J). (gr. -1-3). 13.99 (978-1-4169-7138-2(6), Aladdin) Simon & Schuster Children's Publishing.

Alley, R. W. Gretchen over the Beach. 2016. (ENG., Illus.). 32p. (J). (gr. -1-3). 14.99 (978-0-547-90708-6(7)) Houghton Mifflin Harcourt Publishing Co.

Anderson, Sorrel. Make a Mess of the Seaside, 2. 2010. (Clumsies Ser.: 2). (ENG., Illus.). 112p. (J). pap. 5.99 (978-0-00-733935-8(6), HarperCollins Children's Bks.) HarperCollins Pubs. Ltd. GBR. Dist: HarperCollins Pubs.

Arena, Felice & Kettle, Phil. Hit the Beach. Vane, Mitch, illus. 2004. (J). pap. (978-1-59336-361-1(3)) Mondo Publishing.

At the Beach. 2004. (Out & about Ser.). 12p. (J). bds. 4.99 (978-1-85997-807-8(X)) Byeway Bks.

Avery, Tom. Not As We Know It. 2016. (ENG.). 176p. (J). (gr. 4-7). 16.99 (978-0-553-53509-9(9), Schwartz & Wade Bks.) Random Hse. Children's Bks.

Bancks, Tristan. Mac Slater Hunts the Cool. (Mac Slater Hunts the Cool Ser.). (ENG.). 224p. (J). (gr. 3-7). 2011. pap. 6.99 (978-1-4169-8575-4(1)) 2010. 15.99 (978-1-4169-8574-7(3)) Simon & Schuster Bks. For Young Readers. (Simon & Schuster Bks. For Young Readers).

Barefoot Books Staff. Out of the Blue. Alison, Jay & Jay, Alison, illus. 2014. 32p. (J). (gr. -1-k). 14.99 (978-1-78285-042-7(2)) Barefoot Bks., Inc.

Barkley, Callie. Liz & the Sand Castle Contest. Riti, Marsha, illus. 2015. (Critter Club Ser.: 11). (ENG.). 128p. (J). (gr. k-4). pap. 5.99 (978-1-4814-2405-9(X), Little Simon) Little Simon.

Barron, T. A. The Lost Years of Merlin. unabr. ed. 2004. (Lost Years of Merlin Ser.: Bk. 1). 284p. (J). (gr. 5-9). pap. 46.00 incl. audio (978-0-8072-8766-8(0), YA261SP, Listening Library) Random Hse. Audio Publishing Group.

Beam, Emily. Tumtum & Nutmeg: Adventures Beyond Nutmouse Hall. 2011. (Tumtum & Nutmeg Ser.: 1). (ENG., Illus.). 512p. (J). (gr. 3-7). pap. 10.00 (978-0-316-07574-9(4)) Little, Brown Bks. for Young Readers.

—Tumtum & Nutmeg: the Rose Cottage Adventures. Price, Nick, illus. 2013. (Tumtum & Nutmeg Ser.: 2). (ENG.). 416p. (J). (gr. 3-7). pap. 10.99 (978-0-316-08598-4(7)) Little, Brown Bks. for Young Readers.

Beil, Michael D. Summer at Forsaken Lake. Kneen, Maggie, illus. 2013. (ENG.). 336p. (J). (gr. 5). pap. 8.99 (978-0-375-86496-4(2), Yearling) Random Hse. Children's Bks.

Bentley, Sue. Seaside Mystery. 2013. (Magic Kitten Ser.: 9). lib. bdg. 16.00 (978-0-606-32121-1(7), Turtleback) Turtleback Bks.

—A Splash of Magic #3. Swan, Angela, illus. 2013. (Magic Bunny Ser.: 3). (ENG.). 128p. (J). (gr. 1-3). pap. 5.99 (978-0-448-46729-0(1), Grosset & Dunlap) Penguin Young Readers Group.

Berenstain, Jan, et al. The Berenstain Bears Go on Vacation. Berenstain, Jan & Berenstain, Mike, illus. 2010. (Berenstain Bears Ser.). (ENG.). 32p. (J). (gr. -1-3). pap. 6.99 (978-0-06-057433-8(X)) HarperCollins Pubs.

Berenstain, Stan & Berenstain, Jan. The Berenstain Bears' Seashore Treasure. Berenstain, Jan, illus. 2005. (I Can Read Level 1 Ser.). (ENG., Illus.). 32p. (J). (gr. k-3). pap. 3.99 (978-0-06-058341-5(X)) HarperCollins Pubs.

Blackaby, Susan. El Lugar de Luis, 1 vol. Ruíz, Carlos, tr. from ENG. Gallagher-Cole, Mernie, illus. 2006. (Read-It! Readers en Español: Story Collection).Tr. of Place for Mike. (SPA.). 24p. (gr. -1-3). 21.32 (978-1-4048-1688-6(7), Easy Readers) Picture Window Bks.

Blackstone, Stella. Secret Seahorse. Beaton, Clare, illus. 2005. (J). (gr. -1-2). 24p. bds. 7.99 (978-1-905236-15-2(8)); 24p. 15.99 (978-1-84148-704-5(X)); 32p. pap. 7.99 (978-1-84148-937-7(9)) Barefoot Bks., Inc.

Bles, Riemke. Beene & What He Learned about the Atlantic Ocean. 2011. 32p. pap. 28.99 (978-1-4634-1633-1(4)) AuthorHouse.

Blumberg, Margie. Sunny Bunnies. Goulding, June, illus. 2008. (ENG.). 32p. (gr. -1-k). 15.95 (978-0-9624166-4-4(9)) MB Publishing, LLC.

Blumenthal, Deborah. The Lifeguard. (ENG.). 288p. (YA). (gr. 8-12). 2013. 9.99 (978-0-8075-4536-2(8)) 2012. 16.99 (978-0-8075-4535-5(X)) Whitman, Albert & Co.

Bonacci, Ross. Rossi & Lucy Go to the Beach. Karla, Nicolee, illus. 2013. 38p. pap. (978-0-9873831-2-9(4)) Bonacci Publishing.

Bond, Michael. Paddington at the Beach. Alley, R. W., illus. 2015. (Paddington Ser.). 32p. (J). (gr. -1-3). 17.99 (978-0-06-231720-9(2)) HarperCollins Pubs.

—Paddington Sets Sail. Alley, R. W., illus. 2016. (I Can Read Level 1 Ser.). 32p. (J). (gr. -1-3). pap. 3.99 (978-0-06-243064-9(5)) HarperCollins Pubs.

Bourke, Debra. First Day at Bouddi School. Cowley, Ray B., illus. 2012. 32p. pap. 18.00 (978-1-4349-8469-2(9), RoseDog Bks.) Dorrance Publishing Co., Inc.

Branford, Henrietta & Beardshaw, Rosalind. Splash! (Illus.). 32p. (J). 19.99 (978-0-340-85550-8(9)) Macmillan Pubs., Ltd. GBR. Dist: Trafalgar Square Publishing.

Broach, Elise. Seashore Baby. 2010. (Baby Seasons Ser.). (ENG., Illus.). 14p. (J). (gr. -1 — 1). bds. 7.99 (978-0-316-04303-8(6)) Little, Brown Bks. for Young Readers.

Brooks, Brian. Oopsy Daisy's Bad Day. Brooks, Brian, illus. 2007. (Illus.). 62p. (J). reprint ed. 13.00 (978-1-4223-9004-7(7)) DIANE Publishing Co.

Brouillette, Kathy. What Makes me Smile. 2010. 16p. 8.99 (978-1-4520-1112-7(5)) AuthorHouse.

Bubble Guppies, Bubble. Bubble Guppies: Let's Play, Bubble Puppy! A PeekABoo Book. 2015. (ENG.). 10p. (J). (gr. -1-k). bds. 10.99 (978-0-7944-3470-0(3), Reader's Digest Children's Bks.) Studio Fun International.

Buggs, Matthews. Beach Party. 2006. (J). 10.00 (978-0-9790515-3-1(3)) Pinkston, Anastasia.

Bulion, Leslie. Uncharted Waters, 1 vol. (ENG.). 192p. (J). (gr. 3-7). 2009. pap. 7.95 (978-1-56145-485-3(0)) 2006. 14.95 (978-1-56145-365-8(X)) Peachtree Pubs.

The Busy Beach. 2003. (J). 12.75 (978-0-89610-768-7(X)) Island Heritage Publishing.

Byars, Betsy. The Animal, the Vegetable, & John D. Jones. 150p. (J). (gr. 4-6). pap. 3.50 (978-0-8072-1414-5(0), Listening Library) Random Hse. Audio Publishing Group.

Caine, Paul. Jake's Journey. 2010. 68p. pap. 10.49 (978-1-4520-0508-9(7)) AuthorHouse.

Canale, Suzie Hearl. The Candy Roses of Cape Care. Coffey, Kevin, illus. 2012. 38p. (J). 14.95 (978-1-937406-67-7(9)) Mascot Bks., Inc.

Candlewick Press Staff. Peppa Pig & the Great Vacation. 2014. (Peppa Pig Ser.). (ENG.). 32p. (J). (-k). 12.99 (978-0-7636-6986-7(5), Candlewick Entertainment) Candlewick Pr.

Carestio, Michael A. Black Jack Jetty: A Boy's Journey Through Grief. 2010. (Illus.). 64p. (J). (gr. 3-8). 14.95 (978-1-4338-0784-8(X)); pap. 9.95 (978-1-4338-0786-2(6)) American Psychological Assn. (Magination Pr.).

Case, Julie. Emma & the Whale. White, Lee, illus. 2017. (ENG.). 40p. (J). (gr. -1-3). 17.99 (978-0-553-53847-2(0), Schwartz & Wade Bks.) Random Hse. Children's Bks.

Caswell, Deanna. Beach House. Bates, Amy June, illus. 2015. (ENG.). 32p. (J). (gr. -1-k). 16.99 (978-1-4521-2408-7(6)) Chronicle Bks. LLC.

Catrow, David. Fun in the Sun. Catrow, David, illus. 2016. (ENG., Illus.). 32p. (J). 6.99 (978-0-8234-3569-2(5)) Holiday Hse., Inc.

—Fun in the Sun. 2015. (ENG., Illus.). 32p. (J). (gr. -1-1). 16.95 (978-0-8234-2945-5(8)) Holiday Hse., Inc.

Chapman, Carlene. Jackson Goes to the Beach. 2010. 24p. pap. 11.95 (978-1-4490-9768-4(5)) AuthorHouse.

Chichester Clark, Emma. Beside the Sea. Chichester Clark, Emma, illus. 2007. (Melrose & Croc Ser.). (ENG., Illus.). 32p. (J). (gr. -1-2). pap. 8.95 (978-0-00-718244-2(9), HarperCollins Children's Bks.) HarperCollins Pubs. Ltd. GBR. Dist: HarperCollins Pubs.

Child's Play. Off to the Beach! Cocoretto, illus. 2016. (Tactile Bks.). (ENG.). 12p. (J). (978-1-84643-923-0(X)) Child's Play International Ltd.

Clark, Joyce. Katie. 2006. 196p. 27.43 (978-1-4122-0067-7(9)) Trafford Publishing.

Clements, Andrew. Because Your Daddy Loves You. Alley, R. W., illus. 2009. (ENG.). 32p. (J). (gr. -1-3). pap. 6.99 (978-0-547-23764-0(2)) Houghton Mifflin Harcourt Publishing Co.

—Because Your Daddy Loves You. Alley, R. W., tr. Alley, R. W., illus. 2005. (ENG.). 32p. (J). (gr. -1-3). 16.99 (978-0-618-00361-7(4)) Houghton Mifflin Harcourt Publishing Co.

Collins, Izola. Pip, Squeak, & Zoom. 2009. 68p. pap. 23.49 (978-1-4490-0717-1(1)) AuthorHouse.

Collins, Renee. Until We Meet Again. 2015. (ENG.). 336p. (YA). (gr. 8-12). 16.99 (978-1-4926-2116-4(1), 9781492621164) Sourcebooks, Inc.

Condra, Estelle. See the Ocean. 7.95 (978-1-57102-178-6(7), Ideal Pubns.) Worthy Publishing.

Cooper, Elisha. Beach. Cooper, Elisha, illus. 2006. (ENG., Illus.). 40p. (J). (gr. -1-k). 17.99 (978-0-439-68785-0(3), Orchard Bks.) Scholastic, Inc.

Coste, Marion. Wild Beach. Gray, Cissy, illus. 2005. 32p. (J). pap. 8.25 (978-0-89317-062-2(3), WW-623); lib. bdg. 17.95 (978-0-89317-061-5(5), WW-0615) Finney Co., Inc. (Windward Publishing).

Couloumbis, Audrey. Lexie. Denos, Julia, illus. 2012. (ENG.). 208p. (J). (gr. 3-7). pap. 6.99 (978-0-375-85633-4(1), Yearling) Random Hse. Children's Bks.

Cousins, Lucy. Maisy Goes on Vacation. Cousins, Lucy, illus. 2012. (Maisy Ser.). (ENG., Illus.). 32p. (J). (gr. -1-2). pap. 6.99 (978-0-7636-6039-0(6)) Candlewick Pr.

Cowley, Joy. Freddy Bear & the Beach. Webb, Philip, illus. 2016. (Freddy Bear Ser.). (ENG.). 20p. (J). (gr. -1-k). bds. 12.99 (978-1-927262-56-6(9)) Upstart Pr. NZL. Dist: Independent Pubs. Group.

—Mrs. WishyWashy & the Big Tub. 2009. pap. 8.25 (978-1-60559-233-6(1)) Hameray Publishing Group, Inc.

Crimi, Carolyn. There Might Be Lobsters. Molk, Laurel, illus. 2017. (ENG.). 32p. (J). (gr. -1-2). 16.99 (978-0-7636-7542-4(3)) Candlewick Pr.

Crockett-Blassingame, Linda, illus. See the Ocean. 2006. 32p. (J). 14.95 (978-0-9778143-0-5(0)) Inclusive Books LLC.

Crupi, Jaclyn. Theo at the Beach. Verdoux, Aurélia, illus. 2013. (J). (978-1-4351-4722-5(7)) Barnes & Noble, Inc.

Daffney. The Birthday Fairy. 2009. 16p. pap. 8.49 (978-1-4490-0095-0(9)) AuthorHouse.

Davis, Jacky & Soman, David. Ladybug Girl at the Beach. Soman, David, illus. 2010. (Ladybug Girl Ser.). (ENG., Illus.). 36p. (J). (gr. -1-k). 17.99 (978-0-8037-3416-6(6), Dial Bks) Penguin Young Readers Group.

Dean, James. Pete at the Beach. Dean, James, illus. 2013. (My First I Can Read Ser.). (ENG., Illus.). 32p. (J). (gr. -1-3). pap. 3.99 (978-0-06-211072-5(1)) HarperCollins Pubs.

deGroat, Diane. Gilbert, the Surfer Dude. 2009. (Illus.). 31p. (J). lib. bdg. 18.89 (978-0-06-125212-9(3)) HarperCollins Pubs.

Dessen, Sarah. The Moon & More. 2013. (ENG.). 384p. (J). (gr. 7). 19.99 (978-0-670-78560-5(1), Viking Books for Young Readers) Penguin Young Readers Group.

Disney Book Group Staff. Teen Beach 2. 2015. (ENG.). 128p. (J). (gr. 5-9). pap. 5.99 (978-1-4847-1077-7(0)) Disney Pr.

Dubose, Sarah. Uncharted Waters. 2013. 440p. pap. (978-1-4596-6282-7(2)) ReadHowYouWant.com, Ltd.

Dudar, Judy. I Spy a Bunny, 1 vol. Rudnicki, Richard, illus. 2009. (ENG.). 32p. (J). (gr. -1-2). 17.95 (978-1-55109-700-8(1)) Nimbus Publishing, Ltd. CAN. Dist: Orca Bk. Pubs. USA.

Durk, Jim, illus. Rabbid of the Sea. 2015. (Rabbids Invasion Ser.). (ENG.). 40p. (J). (gr. 1-3). pap. 3.99 (978-1-4814-3545-1(0), Simon Spotlight) Simon Spotlight.

Dyan, Penelope. Courtney's Beach. Dyan, Penelope, illus. 2008. (Illus.). 44p. pap. 11.95 (978-1-935118-35-0(8)) Bellissima Publishing, LLC.

Eastman, Peter. Fred & Ted Like to Fly. Eastman, Peter, illus. 2007. (Beginner Books Ser.). (ENG., Illus.). 48p. (J). (gr. -1-2). 8.99 (978-0-375-84064-7(8), Random Hse. Bks. for Young Readers) Random Hse. Children's Bks.

Edelson, Madelyn. The Proud Beech: A Long Island Folk Tale. Tucker, Diane, illus. 2004. 48p. (J). pap. 14.95 (978-0-9658920-7-0(7)) Edelson, Madelyn.

Edwards, Meinir Wyn. Maelgwn, King of Gwynedd. Wade, Gini, illus. 2008. (ENG.). 24p. (J). pap. 4.95 (978-1-84771-024-6(7)) Y Lolfa GBR. Dist: Dufour Editions, Inc.

Eliot, Margaret. Cat & Tiger Go to the Seaside. 2012. 24p. pap. 28.03 (978-1-4691-7674-1(2)) Xlibris Corp.

Ellis, Dianne. Rusty Rumble's Day at the Beach. 2012. 40p. pap. 32.70 (978-1-4797-0360-9(5)) Xlibris Corp.

Elmquist, Laurie. Beach Baby, 1 vol. MacKay, Elly, illus. 2016. (ENG.). 24p. (J). (gr. -1-k). bds. 9.95 (978-1-4598-0954-3(8)) Orca Bk. Pubs. USA.

Everett, Reese. Monster in the Mangroves. 2015. (ENG.). 48p. (gr. k-3). 27.07 (978-1-63430-377-4(6)) Rourke Educational Media.

Fernandez, Joy C. Rockman. 2010. 36p. pap. 16.45 (978-1-4520-6751-3(1)) AuthorHouse.

Ferrante, Elena. The Beach at Night. Goldstein, Ann, tr. from ITA. Cerri, Mara, illus. 2016. (ENG.). 38p. 13.00 (978-1-60945-370-1(0)) Europa Editions, Inc.

Fineman, Kelly Ramsdell. At the Boardwalk. Armino, Monica, illus. 2012. (ENG.). 32p. (J). (978-1-58925-104-5(0)); pap. (978-1-58925-431-2(7)) Tiger Tales.

Finn, Rebecca, illus. Busy Beach. 2016. (Busy Bks.). (ENG.). 10p. (J). (gr. -1). bds. 8.95 (978-1-4549-1941-4(8)) Sterling Publishing Co., Inc.

Fleming, Candace. Tippy-Tippy-Tippy, Splash! Karas, G. Brian, illus. 2014. (ENG.). 40p. (J). (gr. -1-3). 16.99 (978-1-4169-5403-3(1), Atheneum Bks. for Young Readers) Simon & Schuster Children's Publishing.

Forton-Barnes, Therese. Zaki & Venus. 2007. 13.95 (978-1-59526-388-9(8)) Aeon Publishing Inc.

Frazee, Marla. A Couple of Boys Have the Best Week Ever. 2008. (ENG., Illus.). 40p. (J). (gr. 1-4). 17.99 (978-0-15-206020-6(0)) Houghton Mifflin Harcourt Publishing Co.

French, Sarah. Summer Friends. 2011. (ENG., Illus.). 32p. (J). 17.95 (978-0-9827146-5-2(3)) Vineyard Stories.

Fry, Sonali & Knight, Hilary. Eloise Goes to the Beach. Lyon, Tammie Speer & Lyon, Tammie, illus. 2007. (Eloise Ser.). (ENG.). 12p. (J). (gr. -1-2). 9.99 (978-1-4169-3344-1(1), Little Simon) Little Simon.

Gall, Chris. Dinotrux Dig the Beach. 2015. (Dinotrux Ser.: 3). (ENG., Illus.). 32p. (J). (gr. -1-3). 17.00 (978-0-316-37553-5(5)) Little Brown & Co.

Gallup, Zd. Nap Time at the Beach. 2013. 34p. pap. 14.95 (978-1-4575-2129-4(6)) Dog Ear Publishing, LLC.

Gamble, Adam. Good Night Beach. Kelly, Cooper, illus. 2007. (Good Night Our World Ser.). (ENG.). 28p. (J). (gr. k — 1). bds. 9.95 (978-1-60219-002-3(X)) Good Night Bks.

Garcia, Jesus E. Tim & Ann's First Day at the Beach. 2013. 24p. pap. 24.95 (978-1-62709-341-5(9)) America Star Bks.

Gateley, Edwina. God Goes on Vacation. Gateley, Edwina, illus. 2009. (Illus.). 32p. (Orig.). (J). pap. 9.95 (978-0-8091-6747-0(6)) Paulist Pr.

Gay, Marie-Louise. Stella, Star of the Sea, 1 vol. (Stella & Sam Ser.). (ENG., Illus.). 32p. (J). (gr. k-k). 2010. pap. 7.95 (978-0-88899-992-4(5)) 2004. 7.95 (978-0-88899-572-8(5)) Groundwood Bks. CAN. Dist: Publishers Group West (PGW).

Geraldi, Michele J. A Shell Story. 2009. 28p. pap. 13.99 (978-1-4389-2827-2(0)) AuthorHouse.

Gibson, Mary, illus. Buried Treasure. 2007. 12p. (J). 5.95 (978-0-9801269-0-7(8)) Scribe's Closet Pubns., The.

Gillespie, Elizabeth. Robbie's Beach Adventure. 2011. 28p. pap. 15.99 (978-1-4628-7992-2(6)) Xlibris Corp.

Gillingham, Sara. On My Beach. Siminovich, Lorena, illus. 2015. (ENG.). 12p. (J). (gr. -1 — 1). bds. 8.99 (978-1-4521-0640-3(1)) Chronicle Bks. LLC.

Gompper, Gail. Every Day by the Bay. Gompper, Gail, illus. 2011. (ENG., Illus.). 24p. (J). bds. 9.95 (978-0-9726487-7-6(1)) Puddle Jump Pr., Ltd.

Gorbachev, Valeri. Not Me! Gorbachev, Valeri, illus. 2016. (ENG., Illus.). 24p. (J). 14.95 (978-0-8234-3546-3(6)); pap. 6.99 (978-0-8234-3547-0(4)) Holiday Hse., Inc.

Gordon, Marie Elaina. My Grand-Mom Told Me-down by the Sea. 2008. 108p. pap. 19.95 (978-1-4241-9095-9(9)) America Star Bks.

Gow, Kailin. Loving Summer. 2012. 250p. (-18). pap. 9.99 (978-1-59748-044-4(4), The Edge) Sparklesoup LLC.

Green, Judy. The Little Blue Octopus. 2009. 28p. pap. 21.99 (978-1-4415-3393-7(1)) Xlibris Corp.

Greenwald, Lisa. Dog Beach Unleashed. 2015. (Seagate Summers Ser.). (ENG., Illus.). 240p. (YA). (gr. 5-9). 15.95 (978-1-4197-1481-8(3), Amulet Bks.) Abrams, Inc.

—Welcome to Dog Beach. (Seagate Summers Ser.). (ENG.). (YA). (gr. 3-7). 2015. 288p. pap. 6.95 (978-1-4197-1497-9(X)) 2014. 272p. 15.95 (978-1-4197-1018-6(4)) Abrams, Inc. (Amulet Bks.).

Grey, Mini. Traction Man & the Beach Odyssey. 2012. (ENG., Illus.). 32p. (J). (gr. k-3). 16.99 (978-0-375-86952-5(2), Knopf Bks. for Young Readers) Random Hse. Children's Bks.

Guerras Safia. Lou Lou. Kemble, Mai S., illus. 2013. (ENG.). 24p. (J). pap. 16.95 (978-1-4787-2359-2(9)) Outskirts Pr., Inc.

H & T Imaginations Unlimited, Inc. Sand Castles with Professor Woodpecker. 2009. 12p. pap. 8.49 (978-1-4389-7262-6(8)) AuthorHouse.

Han, Jenny. The Complete Summer I Turned Pretty Trilogy: The Summer I Turned Pretty; It's Not Summer Without You; We'll Always Have Summer. 2013. (Summer I Turned Pretty Ser.). (ENG., Illus.). 928p. (YA). (gr. 7). pap. 32.99 (978-1-4424-9832-7(3), Simon & Schuster Bks. For Young Readers) Simon & Schuster Bks. For Young Readers.

—It's Not Summer Without You, 6 vols. 2010. (Summer I Turned Pretty Ser.: 2). (YA). 90.75 (978-1-4498-2018-3(2)); 88.75 (978-1-4498-2020-6(4)); 1.25 (978-1-4498-2022-0(0)); 73.75 (978-1-4498-2016-9(6)); 230.75 (978-1-4498-2015-2(8)) Recorded Bks., Inc.

—It's Not Summer Without You. (Summer I Turned Pretty Ser.). (ENG.). (YA). (gr. 7). 2011. 320p. pap. 10.99 (978-1-4169-9556-2(0)) 2010. 288p. 18.99 (978-1-4169-9555-5(2)) Simon & Schuster Bks. For Young Readers. (Simon & Schuster Bks. For Young Readers).

—The Summer I Turned Pretty. (Summer I Turned Pretty Ser.). (ENG.). (YA). (gr. 7). 2010. 304p. pap. 10.99 (978-1-4169-6829-0(6)) 2009. 288p. 19.99 (978-1-4169-6823-8(7)) Simon & Schuster Bks. For Young Readers. (Simon & Schuster Bks. For Young Readers).

—The Summer I Turned Pretty. 2010. lib. bdg. 22.10 (978-0-606-14529-9(X), Turtleback) Turtleback Bks.

—We'll Always Have Summer. 2011. (YA). 1.25 (978-1-4640-1977-7(0)) Recorded Bks., Inc.

—We'll Always Have Summer. (Summer I Turned Pretty Ser.). (ENG.). (YA). (gr. 7). 2012. 320p. pap. 10.99 (978-1-4169-9559-3(5)) 2011. 304p. 17.99 (978-1-4169-9558-6(7)) Simon & Schuster Bks. For Young Readers. (Simon & Schuster Bks. For Young Readers).

Hanson, Warren. Sea of Sleep. LaMarche, Jim, illus. 2010. (ENG.). 32p. (J). (gr. -1-3). 16.99 (978-0-439-69735-4(2), Scholastic Pr.) Scholastic, Inc.

Hatton, Jenny. Swimming in the Sun. Rankin, Joan, illus. 2012. (Lucy Bks.). (ENG.). 32p. (J). (gr. -1-k). pap. 6.95 (978-1-4314-0218-2(4)) Jacana Media ZAF. Dist: Independent Pubs. Group.

Heady, Heather. What's at the Beach? Storch, Ellen N., illus. l.t. ed. 2005. 10p. (J). (gr. -1-k). pap. 10.95 (978-1-57332-355-0(1), HighReach Learning, Incorporated) Carson-Dellosa Publishing, LLC.

Henkes, Kevin. Junonia. Henkes, Kevin, illus. (Illus.). 192p. (J). (gr. 3-7). 2012. (ENG.). pap. 6.99 (978-0-06-196419-0(0)) 2011. (ENG., 15.99 (978-0-06-196417-6(4)) 2011. lib. bdg. 16.89 (978-0-06-196418-3(2)) HarperCollins Pubs. (Greenwillow Bks.).

Hennessy, B. G. Corduroy Goes to the Beach. McCue, Lisa, illus. 2006. (Corduroy Ser.). (ENG.). 20p. (J). (gr. 1-k). 11.99 (978-0-670-06052-8(6), Viking Books for Young Readers) Penguin Young Readers Group.

Hillert, Margaret. Dear Dragon Goes to the Beach. Pullan, Jack, illus. 2015. (BeginningtoRead Ser.). (ENG.). 32p. (J). (gr. k-2). lib. bdg. 22.60 (978-1-59953-704-7(4)) Norwood Hse. Pr.

—Let's Go, Dear Dragon. Pullan, Jack, illus. 2016. (BeginningtoRead Ser.). (ENG.). 32p. (J). (-2). lib. bdg. 22.60 (978-1-59953-774-0(5)) Norwood Hse. Pr.

Hills, Tad. Duck & Goose Go to the Beach. 2014. (Duck & Goose Ser.). (ENG., Illus.). 40p. (J). (gr. -1-2). 17.99 (978-0-385-37235-0(3), Schwartz & Wade Bks.) Random Hse. Children's Bks.

Hochman, Marisa. A Walk in Pirate's Cove. Woodland, Bette, illus. 2012. (ENG.). 32p. (J). (978-0-9865679-0-2(6)) Fitzhenry & Whiteside, Ltd.

Hofmeister, Alan, et al. The Shell. (Reading for All Learners Ser.). (Illus.). (J). pap. (978-1-56861-103-7(X)) Swift Learning Resources.

Holland, Amy L. The Adventures of Bubba & Sis: Book One. 2009. 16p. pap. 8.49 (978-1-4389-5941-2(9)) AuthorHouse.

Holm, Jennifer L. & Holm, Matthew. Beach Babe. 2008. (Babymouse Ser.: No. 3). (Illus.). 91p. (gr. 2-5). 17.00 (978-0-7569-8345-1(2)) Perfection Learning Corp.

—Beach Babe. 2006. (Babymouse Ser.: 3). (ENG., Illus.). 96p. (J). (gr. 2-5). pap. 6.99 (978-0-375-83231-4(9), Random Hse. Bks. for Young Readers) Random Hse. Children's Bks.

Hope, Laura Lee. The Bobbsey Twins at the Seashore. 2005. 26.95 (978-1-4218-1070-6(0)); 176p. pap. 11.95 (978-1-4218-1170-3(7)) 1st World Publishing, Inc. (1st World Library - Literary Society).

Hoppner, Gabi. Beach Fun. 2004. (What A Series of Fun! Ser.). (Illus.). 10p. (J). bds. 3.99 *(978-1-59384-053-2(5))* Parklane Publishing.

Horvath, Polly. My One Hundred Adventures. 2010. (My One Hundred Adventures Ser.). (ENG., Illus.). 272p. (J). (gr. 3-7). 7.99 *(978-0-375-85526-9(2)*, Yearling) Random Hse. Children's Bks.

Howell, Gail L. Sarah's World: Sarah Meets her Cousins by the Sea. 2009. 24p. pap. 11.49 *(978-1-4389-4864-5(6))* AuthorHouse.

Hughes, Shirley. Lucy & Tom at the Seaside. 2016. (ENG., Illus.). 32p. (J). (-k). pap. 12.99 *(978-1-78295-516-0(X)*, Red Fox) Random House Children's Books GBR. Dist: Independent Pubs. Group.

Hurley, Jorey. Fetch. Hurley, Jorey, illus. 2015. (ENG., Illus.). 40p. (J). (gr. -1-2). 17.99 *(978-1-4424-8969-1(3)*, Simon & Schuster Bks. For Young Readers) Simon & Schuster Bks. For Young Readers.

Hutchings, Tony, illus. A Week at the Seaside. 2014. (J). *(978-1-4351-5464-3(9))* Barnes & Noble, Inc.

Hutton, John. Beach: Baby Unplugged. Kang, Andrea, illus. 2012. (Baby Unplugged Ser.). (ENG.). 14p. (J). (— 1). bds. 7.99 *(978-1-936669-07-3(2))* Blue Manatee Press.

Idle, Molly. Sea Rex. Idle, Molly, illus. 2015. (ENG., Illus.). 34p. (J). (-k). 16.99 *(978-0-670-78574-2(1)*, Viking Books for Young Readers) Penguin Young Readers Group.

Jackson, Byron & Jackson, Kathryn. A Day at the Seashore. 2010. (Little Golden Book Ser.). (ENG., Illus.). 24p. (J). (gr. -1-2). 4.99 *(978-0-375-85425-5(8)*, Golden Bks.) Random Hse. Children's Bks.

Jeanba, Malahkee. Makeda Goes to the Beach. 2012. 24p. pap. 15.99 *(978-1-4691-9129-4(6))* Xlibris Corp.

Jessell, Tim. The Boardwalk Mystery. Dunn, Robert, illus. 2013. (Boxcar Children Mysteries Ser.: 131). (ENG.). 144p. (J). (gr. 1-5). 15.99 *(978-0-8075-0802-2(0))*; pap. 5.99 *(978-0-8075-0803-9(9))* Whitman, Albert & Co.

Johnson, C. Homecoming. 2007. (Illus.). 64p. per. 10.00 *(978-1-4251-1358-2(3))* Trafford Publishing.

Jules, Jacqueline. The Beach Trip. Smith, Kim, illus. 2016. (Sofia Martinez Ser.). (ENG.). 32p. (gr. k-2). lib. bdg. 21.32 *(978-1-4795-8719-3(2)*, Sofia Martinez) Picture Window Bks.

Kalar, Bonnie. A Trip to the Beach. Spreen, Kathe, illus. Date not set. 12p. (J). (gr. -1-2). pap. *(978-1-891619-42-7(X))* Corona Pr.

Kann, Victoria. Aqualicious. Kann, Victoria, illus. 2015. (ENG., Illus.). 40p. (J). (gr. -1-3). 17.99 *(978-0-06-233016-1(0))* HarperCollins Pubs.

Katz, Karen. Where Is Baby's Beach Ball? Katz, Karen, illus. 2009. (ENG., Illus.). 14p. (J). (gr. -1 — 1). bds. 6.99 *(978-1-4169-4962-6(3)*, Little Simon) Little Simon.

Keller, Holly. Miranda's Beach Day. Keller, Holly, illus. 2009. (Illus.). 32p. (J). (gr. -1). lib. bdg. 18.89 *(978-0-06-158300-1(6))*; (ENG., 17.99 *(978-0-06-158298-1(0))* HarperCollins Pubs. (Greenwillow Bks.).

Kettle, Shey. Surf Girls. Thomas, Meredith, illus. 2005. (Girlz Rock! Ser.). (J). pap. *(978-1-59336-708-4(2))* Mondo Publishing.

Kirby, Jessi. Moonglass. 2012. (ENG.). 256p. (YA). (gr. 7). pap. 9.99 *(978-1-4424-1695-6(5)*, Simon & Schuster Bks. For Young Readers) Simon & Schuster Bks. For Young Readers.

Konagaya, Kiyomi. Beach Feet. Saito, Masamitsu, illus. 2012. (Being in the World Ser.). (ENG.). 32p. (J). (gr. k-k). 14.95 *(978-1-59270-121-6(3))* Enchanted Lion Bks., LLC.

Kondrchek, Jamie & Rasemas, Joe. What Day Is It? (Que Dia Es Hoy?) Vega, Eida de la, tr. Rasemas, Joe, illus. 2009. (Day in the Life Ser.). (SPA & ENG., Illus.). 32p. (J). (gr. -1-1). 25.70 *(978-1-58415-838-7(7))* Mitchell Lane Pubs., Inc.

Koss, Amy Goldman. Kailey. Howe, Philip, illus. 2003. (American Girl of Today Ser.). (ENG.). 160p. (J). pap. 6.95 *(978-1-58485-591-0(6))* American Girl Publishing, Inc.

Krulik, Nancy. Catch That Wave. Braun, Sebastien, illus. 2013. (Magic Bone Ser.: 2). (ENG.). 128p. (J). (gr. 1-3). pap. 5.99 *(978-0-448-46444-2(6)*, Grosset & Dunlap) Penguin Young Readers Group.

—Catch That Wave. 2013. (Magic Bone Ser.: 2). lib. bdg. 14.75 *(978-0-606-31681-1(7)*, Turtleback) Turtleback Bks.

Kurtz, Carmen. Veva y el Mar.Tr. of Veva & the Sea. (SPA.). 144p. (J). (gr. 3-5). *(978-84-279-3129-9(8))* Noguer y Caralt Editores, S. A. ESP. Dist: Lectorum Pubns., Inc.

Laberje, Reji. Max Explores the Beach. Fenech, Liza, illus. 2015. (Max Explores Ser.). (ENG.). 20p. (J). (— 1). bds. 9.95 *(978-1-62937-101-6(7))* Triumph Bks.

Lantz, Frances L. Sea for Yourself. 2004. (Luna Bay Ser.: No. 8). 176p. mass mkt. 4.99 *(978-0-06-059520-3(5)*, Harper Entertainment) HarperCollins Pubs.

Lasaracina, Barbara. Mermaid Tears: A Magical Sea Tale. Peer, Nancy, illus. 2010. 28p. pap. 11.99 *(978-1-60844-451-9(1))* Dog Ear Publishing, LLC.

Le Clézio, J. M. G. Lullaby. Lemoine, Georges, illus. 2007. (FRE.). 72p. (J). (gr. 5-10). pap. *(978-2-07-061258-1(9))* Gallimard, Editions.

LeapFrog Staff. Imagination Desk Counting Day at the Beach. 2003. (Illus.). 9.99 *(978-1-59319-025-5(5))* LeapFrog Enterprises, Inc.

Leblanc, A. J. Donnie the Little Knee Boarder. 2012. 28p. pap. 24.95 *(978-1-4626-8313-0(4))* PublishAmerica, Inc.

Lee, Quinlan B. Beach Day. Haefele, Steve, illus. 2006. (J). *(978-0-439-81618-2(1))* Scholastic, Inc.

Lee, Suzy. Wave. 2008. (ENG., Illus.). 40p. (J). (gr. -1-17). 15.99 *(978-0-8118-5924-0(X))* Chronicle Bks. LLC.

Lester, Alison. Magic Beach. Lester, Alison, illus. 2006. (ENG., Illus.). 32p. (J). (gr. -1-k). pap. 11.99 *(978-1-74114-488-8(4))* Allen & Unwin AUS. Dist: Independent Pubs. Group.

—Noni the Pony Goes to the Beach. Lester, Alison, illus. 2015. (ENG., Illus.). 32p. (J). (gr. -1-3). 17.99 *(978-1-4814-4625-9(8)*, Beach Lane Bks.) Beach Lane Bks.

Lewis, Gill. One White Dolphin. Aparicio, Raquel, illus. 2013. (ENG.). 368p. (J). (gr. 3-7). pap. 8.99 *(978-1-4424-1448-8(0)*, Atheneum Bks. for Young Readers) Simon & Schuster Children's Publishing.

Lies, Brian. Bats at the Beach. (Bat Book Ser.). (ENG., Illus.). 32p. (J). (gr. -1 — 1). 2011. bds. 11.99 *(978-0-547-55437-2(0))* 2006. 17.99 *(978-0-618-55744-8(X))* Houghton Mifflin Harcourt Publishing Co.

Lilienstein, Jennel. Day at the Beach. 2003. (Illus.). 36p. (J). 8.99 *(978-0-9741215-1-2(7))* Stories of My Life, The.

Linder, Karen A. Jack the Curly Black Dog: Goes to the Beach. 2010. 20p. 13.80 *(978-1-4520-3434-8(6))* AuthorHouse.

Logan, Dottie Colegrove. Picnic on the Beach: Nana & Me Series, Book Three. 2010. 16p. 12.99 *(978-1-4490-3689-8(9))* AuthorHouse.

Lorimer, Janet. Ring of Fear, 1 vol. unabr. ed. 2010. (Q Reads Ser.). (ENG.). 32p. (YA). (gr. 9-12). pap. 6.95 *(978-1-61651-194-4(X))* Saddleback Educational Publishing, Inc.

Lubar, David. Dunk. 2004. (ENG.). 272p. (YA). (gr. 7-18). reprint ed. pap. 7.99 *(978-0-618-43909-6(9))* Houghton Mifflin Harcourt Publishing Co.

Lucas, Sally. Dancing Dinos at the Beach. Lucas, Margeaux, illus. 2010. (Step into Reading Ser.). (ENG.). 32p. (J). (gr. -1-1). pap. 3.99 *(978-0-375-85640-2(4)*, Random Hse. Bks. for Young Readers) Random Hse. Children's Bks.

Lynch, Chris. The Gravedigger's Cottage. 2004. (ENG.). 208p. (J). (gr. 7-18). 15.99 *(978-0-06-623940-8(0))* HarperCollins Pubs.

Macveety, Sue Maney. Singing Sea/el Mar Que Canta. Zantay, Valerie, tr. 2005. (SPA., Illus.). 33p. per. 15.99 *(978-1-4134-7275-2(3))* Xlibris Corp.

Maddox, Tony & Wen, Dref. Ffred Ar y Môr: Cyfres Ffred Ci'r Fferm. 2005. (WEL., Illus.). 32p. pap. *(978-1-85596-666-6(2))* Dref Wen.

Magill, Sharon L. Chloe Madison & the Beach Heists. 2009. 60p. pap. 10.49 *(978-1-4389-4191-2(9))* AuthorHouse.

Magnuson, James. Emma's First Agate, 1 vol. LeMay, Meagan, illus. 2014. (ENG.). 32p. (J). (gr. 1-2). pap. 7.95 *(978-1-59193-443-1(5))* Adventure Pubns.

Mann, Jennifer K. Sam & Jump. Mann, Jennifer K., illus. 2016. (ENG., Illus.). 32p. (J). (gr. -1-2). 15.99 *(978-0-7636-7947-7(X))* Candlewick Pr.

Manushkin, Fran & Lyon, Tammie. La Jefa Del Mundo, 1 vol. Lyon, Tammie, illus. 2012. (Katie Woo en Español Ser.). (SPA., Illus.). 32p. (gr. k-2). pap. 6.95 *(978-1-4048-7679-8(0))*; lib. bdg. 21.32 *(978-1-4048-7523-4(9))* Picture Window Bks.

Marquess, Dana. Night of the Lighted Freedom - A Firefly Fantasy. 2006. (ENG., Illus.). 32p. (J). 19.95 *(978-1-932278-06-4(0))* Mayhaven Publishing, Inc.

Matheson, Shirlee Smith. Fastback Beach, 1 vol. 2003. (Orca Soundings Ser.). (ENG.). 128p. (YA). (gr. 8-12). pap. 9.95 *(978-1-55143-267-0(6))* Orca Bk. Pubs. USA.

May, Eleanor. A Beach for Albert. Melmon, Deborah, illus. 2013. (Mouse Math Ser.). 32p. (gr. -1-1). (ENG.). pap. 7.95 *(978-1-57565-531-4(4))*; lib. bdg. 22.60 *(978-1-57565-530-7(6))* Kane Press, Inc.

Mayer, Mercer. Just Grandma, Grandpa, & Me. 2016. (Pictureback(R) Ser.). (ENG., Illus.). 48p. (J). (gr. -1-2). 5.99 *(978-0-553-53986-8(8)*, Random Hse. Bks. for Young Readers) Random Hse. Children's Bks.

—Just Grandma, Grandpa, & Me. 2016. (Little Critter Ser.). lib. bdg. 16.00 *(978-0-606-38482-7(0))* Turtleback Bks.

McCarty, Peter. Hondo & Fabian. unabr. ed. 2006. (Illus.). (J). (gr. -1-3). 29.95 *(978-0-439-84906-7(3)*, WHCD688) Weston Woods Studios, Inc.

McClure, Nikki. Waiting for High Tide. 2016. (ENG., Illus.). 48p. (J). (gr. k-2). 19.95 *(978-1-4197-1656-0(5)*, Abrams Bks. for Young Readers) Abrams, Inc.

McDonald, Kirsten. The Sandy Weekend, 1 vol. Meza, Erika, illus. 2016. (ENG.). 32p. (J). 27.07 *(978-1-62402-142-8(5))* Magic Wagon.

McHeffey, Adam. Asiago, 0 vols. McHeffey, Adam, illus. 2012. (ENG., Illus.). 32p. (J). (gr. k-3). 16.99 *(978-0-7614-6138-8(8)*, 9780761461388, Amazon Children's Publishing) Amazon Publishing.

McKay, Hilary. Lulu & the Dog from the Sea. Lamont, Priscilla, illus. 2013. (Lulu Ser.: Book 2). (ENG.). 112p. (J). (gr. 1-5). 13.99 *(978-0-8075-4820-2(0))* Whitman, Albert & Co.

McNamara, Margaret. Summer Treasure. Gordon, Mike, illus. 2012. (Robin Hill School Ser.). (ENG.). 32p. (J). (gr. -1-1). 15.99 *(978-1-4424-3646-6(8))*; pap. 3.99 *(978-1-4424-3645-9(X))* Simon Spotlight. (Simon Spotlight).

Meadows, Daisy. Nicole the Beach Fairy. 2014. (Rainbow Magic — the Earth Fairies Ser.). lib. bdg. 14.75 *(978-0-606-35830-9(7))* Turtleback Bks.

Meckel, Jamie & BeachHouse Publishing. Down at the Beach. 2011. (ENG.). 16p. (J). (gr. -1-1). bds. 7.95 *(978-1-933067-41-4(1))* Beachhouse Publishing, LLC.

Meister, Cari. Moopy on the Beach, 1 vol. Messner, Dennis, illus. 2010. (Monster Friends Ser.). (ENG.). 32p. (gr. 2-3). pap. 6.25 *(978-1-4342-2304-3(3))*; lib. bdg. 22.65 *(978-1-4342-1874-2(0))* Stone Arch Bks.

Merveille, David. Mr Hulot on the Beach. 2016. (ENG., Illus.). 32p. (J). 18.95 *(978-0-7358-4254-0(X))* North-South Bks., Inc.

Militello, Vincent. Nicholas the Naked Sicilian, & Other Stories. 2007. 140p. pap. 3.95 *(978-1-4259-6966-0(6))* AuthorHouse.

Miller, Pam, et al. The Beach Box: Going to the Beach/Sand/Shells. Warren, Shari et al, illus. 2008. (Rookie Reader Ser.). (ENG.). 88p. (J). (gr. k-3). pap. 9.95 *(978-0-516-29687-6(6)*, Children's Pr.) Scholastic Library Publishing.

Miller, Suzanne. Pirates! That Is Who We Be! 2010. 28p. pap. 13.50 *(978-1-4490-6362-7(4))* AuthorHouse.

Mills-Darlow, Beryl C. My Beach Granny. 2012. 36p. pap. 14.50 *(978-1-61897-681-9(8)*, Strategic Bk. Publishing) Strategic Book Publishing & Rights Agency (SBPRA).

Milord, Susan. Pebble: A Story about Belonging. Milord, Susan, illus. 2007. (ENG., Illus.). 32p. (J). (gr. -1-2). 15.99 *(978-0-06-085807-0(9))* HarperCollins Pubs.

Montgomery, L. M. Along the Shore: Tales by the Sea. (YA). 22.95 *(978-0-8488-2655-0(8))* Amereon Ltd.

Moon, Jonny. The Beach Buoy. 2011. (GUNK Aliens Ser.). (ENG., Illus.). 112p. (J). (gr. 2-4). 7.99 *(978-0-00-732616-7(5))* HarperCollins Pubs. Ltd. GBR. Dist: Independent Pubs. Group.

Moore, Jodi. When a Dragon Moves In. McWilliam, Howard, illus. 2011. (When a Dragon Moves In Ser.). (ENG.). 32p. (J). (gr. k-2). 16.95 *(978-0-9799746-7-0(4))* Flashlight Pr.

Moskowitz, Hannah. Invincible Summer. 2011. (ENG.). 288p. (YA). (gr. 9-18). pap. 9.99 *(978-1-4424-0751-0(4)*, Simon Pulse) Simon Pulse.

Munsch, Robert. The Sandcastle Contest. 2007. 15.00 *(978-0-7569-7690-3(1))* Perfection Learning Corp.

Murphy, Stuart J. Camille y Su Equipo. 2012. (I See I Learn Ser.). (SPA & ENG., Illus.). 32p. (J). (-k). 14.95 *(978-1-58089-490-6(9))*; pap. 6.95 *(978-1-58089-491-3(7))* Charlesbridge Publishing, Inc.

—Camille's Team. 2011. (I See I Learn Ser.). (ENG., Illus.). 32p. (J). (gr. -1-k). 14.95 *(978-1-58089-458-6(5))*; pap. 6.95 *(978-1-58089-459-3(3))* Charlesbridge Publishing, Inc.

Nesbit, E. Wet Magic. 2006. 188p. (gr. -1-7). 26.95 *(978-1-59818-174-6(2))* Aegypan.

Nicoll, David. Bean at the Beach. 2012. 24p. pap. 15.99 *(978-1-4691-7042-8(6))* Xlibris Corp.

Nosy Crow Staff. Noodle Loves the Beach. Billet, Marion, illus. 2012. (Noodle Ser.). (ENG.). 10p. (J). (gr. k — 1). bds. 8.99 *(978-0-7636-5898-4(7)*, Nosy Crow) Candlewick Pr.

Nugent, Cynthia. Fred & Pete at the Beach, 1 vol. 2009. (ENG., Illus.). 32p. (J). (gr. -1-3). 19.95 *(978-1-55469-126-5(5))* Orca Bk. Pubs. USA.

O'Connor, Jane. Sand Castles & Sand Palaces. Glasser, Robin Preiss, illus. 2014. (Fancy Nancy Ser.). (ENG.). 24p. (J). (gr. -1-3). pap. 4.99 *(978-0-06-226954-6(2)*, HarperFestival) HarperCollins Pubs.

—Sand Castles & Sand Palaces. 2014. (Fancy Nancy Picture Bks.). (J). lib. bdg. 14.75 *(978-0-606-36477-5(3))* Turtleback Bks.

Olker, Constance. The Punctuation Pals Go to the Beach. Guzman, Minerva, illus. 2005. (Punctuation Pals Ser.). 36p. (J). per. 18.95 *(978-1-933449-12-8(8))* Nightengale Pr.

O'Reilly, Sean. Monster Beach, 1 vol. Arcana Studio Staff, illus. 2012. (Mighty Mighty Monsters Ser.). (ENG.). 48p. (gr. 2-3). pap. 6.10 *(978-1-4342-4608-0(6))* Stone Arch Bks.

Oud, Pauline. Going to the Beach with Lily & Milo. Oud, Pauline, illus. 2011. (Lily & Milo Ser.). (ENG., Illus.). 28p. (J). (gr. k — 1). 12.95 *(978-1-60537-094-1(0))* Cobblestone Publishing Co.

Pace, Anne Marie. Vampirina at the Beach. Pham, LeUyen, illus. 2017. (Vampirina Ser.). (ENG.). 40p. (J). (gr. -1-k). 16.99 *(978-1-4847-7342-0(X))* Disney Pr.

Palka, Yvonne. Dragon Fire Ocean Mist. 2009. pap. 12.95 *(978-0-9817668-0-5(3))* Heartrock Pr.

Paquette, Ammi-Joan. The Tiptoe Guide to Tracking Mermaids. LeTourneau, Marie, illus. 2012. (ENG.). 32p. (J). (gr. -1-3). 16.95 *(978-1-933718-59-0(5))* Tanglewood Pr.

Parish, Herman. Amelia Bedelia Digs In. 2017. (Amelia Bedelia Chapter Book Ser.: 12). lib. bdg. 14.75 ***(978-0-606-40061-9(3))*** Turtleback Bks.

—Amelia Bedelia Sets Sail. Avril, Lynne, illus. 2015. (Amelia Bedelia Ser.). (ENG.). 160p. (J). (gr. 1-5). pap. 4.99 *(978-0-06-233404-6(2)*, Greenwillow Bks.) HarperCollins Pubs.

—Sets Sail. Avril, Lynne, illus. 2015. (Amelia Bedelia Ser.). (ENG.). 160p. (J). (gr. 1-5). 15.99 *(978-0-06-233405-3(0)*, Greenwillow Bks.) HarperCollins Pubs.

Parr, Todd. Otto Goes to the Beach. 2014. (Passport to Reading Level 1 Ser.). (ENG., Illus.). 32p. (J). (gr. -1-1). 3.99 *(978-0-316-24602-6(6))* Little, Brown Bks. for Young Readers.

Parvensky Barwell, Catherine A. Tommi Goes to the Beach, 4 vols. Barwell, Matthew W. & Parvensky, Mary T., eds. 2006. (Illus.). 40p. (J). *(978-0-9774409-2-4(3)*, TL003) ILT Publishing.

Patterson, Sandra Jean. Crabby Crab. 2006. bds. 12.95 *(978-1-59700-246-2(1))* Island Heritage Publishing.

Paulsen, Gary. The Voyage of the Frog. 2009. (ENG.). 160p. (J). (gr. 7). 5.99 *(978-0-545-08535-9(7)*, Scholastic Paperbacks) Scholastic, Inc.

Perry, Robert. Down at the Seaweed Cafe. Guzek, Greta, illus. unabr. ed. 2010. (ENG.). 32p. (J). pap. 9.95 *(978-0-88971-246-1(8))* Nightwood Editions CAN. Dist: Midpoint Trade Bks., Inc.

Pfister, Marcus. Rainbow Fish Colors. 2013. (Rainbow Fish Ser.). (ENG., Illus.). 12p. (J). (gr. 1-1). bds. 7.95 *(978-0-7358-4147-5(0))* North-South Bks., Inc.

Pliscou, Lisa. Dude: Fun with Dude & Betty. Dunne, Tom, illus. 2011. (ENG.). 40p. (J). (gr. 1-3). 14.99 *(978-0-06-175690-0(3))* HarperCollins Pubs.

Priddy, Roger. Seaside. 2014. (Toddler Town Ser.). (ENG.). 10p. (J). (gr. -1 — 1). bds. 7.99 *(978-0-312-51670-3(3)*, 9780312516703, Priddy Bks.) St. Martin's Pr.

Pryor, Bonnie. Lottie's Dream. 2013. (ENG.). 36p. (J). (gr. -1-3). 14.99 *(978-1-4424-8878-6(6)*, Atheneum Bks. for Young Readers) Simon & Schuster Children's Publishing.

Puck. 123 Beach. 2012. (Cool Counting Bks.). (ENG., Illus.). 22p. (J). (gr. k — 1). bds. 7.95 *(978-0-9838121-1-1(X))* Duo Pr. LLC.

Raven, Margot Theis. Circle Unbroken. Lewis, E. B., illus. 2007. (ENG.). 48p. (J). (gr. -1-3). per. 8.99 *(978-0-312-37603-1(0)*, 9780312376031) Square Fish.

Reasoner, Charles. Shapes at the Beach. Pitt, Sarah, illus. 2009. (3D Board Bks.). 12p. (J). (gr. -1-k). bds. 9.99 *(978-1-934650-36-3(6))* Just For Kids Pr., LLC.

Rebello, Kevin. Julia & Mckinley's Day at the Beach. 2009. 32p. pap. 12.99 *(978-1-4389-7330-2(6))* AuthorHouse.

Redbank, Tennant. The Beach Bandit. 2016. (Barbie Chapters Ser.). (ENG., Illus.). 64p. (J). (gr. 1-4). lib. bdg. 12.99 *(978-0-375-97413-7(X)*, Random Hse. Bks. for Young Readers) Random Hse. Children's Bks.

Rees, Margaret. Primrose & the Mystery of Frangipani Bay. 2015. (ENG., Illus.). 45p. (J). (gr. 3-4). pap. 11.95 *(978-1-78455-832-1(X)*, 18de55dc-6e2c-45a7-b765-ce2b58e00c12) Austin, Stan AUS. Dist: Bookmasters Distribution.

Reid, Hunter. Beach Day! Hinton, Stephanie, illus. 2016. (Fluorescent Pop! Ser.). (ENG.). 14p. (J). (gr. -1-k). bds. 5.99 *(978-1-4998-0219-1(6))* Little Bee Books Inc.

Renaud, Anne. How the Sea Came to Marissa. Durland, Maud, illus. 2006. 32p. (J). *(978-1-58270-129-5(6))* Beyond Words Publishing, Inc.

Resnicoff, Stan. Stanley, the Seal of Approval. 2012. (ENG.). (J). pap. *(978-1-4675-1535-1(3))* Independent Pub.

Rey, Margret & Rey, H. A. Curious George Goes to the Beach. 2014. (Curious George 8x8 Ser.). (gr. k-3). lib. bdg. 13.55 *(978-0-613-21392-9(0)*, Turtleback) Turtleback Bks.

Ricchiazzi, Lisa Gail. The Little Lost Seashell: (Never Lose Hope) 2011. 20p. (gr. -1). 11.59 *(978-1-4269-6505-0(2))* Trafford Publishing.

Richburg, Sheila. The Story of Panhandle Pete Part One. 2010. 19p. 16.95 *(978-0-557-15382-4(4))* Lulu Pr., Inc.

Riley, J. D. Axel the Truck: Beach Race. 2013. (My First I Can Read Ser.). (J). lib. bdg. 13.55 *(978-0-606-31812-9(7)*, Turtleback) Turtleback Bks.

Roberts, Roxanne. Angel Wings, Faery Dust & Other Magical Things: A Story about Merpeople. 2011. 24p. pap. 11.50 *(978-1-61204-588-7(X)*, Strategic Bk. Publishing) Strategic Book Publishing & Rights Agency (SBPRA).

Rockwell, Anne. At the Beach. Rockwell, Harlow, illus. 2016. (ENG.). 24p. (J). (gr. -1-3). lib. bdg. 17.20 *(978-0-606-39423-9(0))* Turtleback Bks.

Rockwell, Anne F. At the Beach. Rockwell, Harlow & Rockwell, Lizzy, illus. 2014. (ENG.). 24p. (J). (gr. -1-3). 14.99 *(978-1-4814-1133-2(0)*, Aladdin) Simon & Schuster Children's Publishing.

Rogers, Lauren. Skyler & the Se. Sexton, Jessa, ed. Keaggy, Sarah, illus. 2012. 36p. pap. 8.00 *(978-0-9860150-1-4(6))* O'More Publishing.

Romolino, Kimberly. A Day at Sea. 2009. 15p. pap. 24.95 *(978-1-60813-803-6(8))* America Star Bks.

Rotner, Shelley. Senses at the Seashore. Rotner, Shelley, photos by. (Shelley Rotner's Early Childhood Library Ser.). (ENG., Illus.). 32p. (J). (gr. -1-2). 2010. pap. 7.95 *(978-0-7613-6530-3(3))* 2006. lib. bdg. 22.60 *(978-0-7613-2897-1(1))* Lerner Publishing Group.

Rouncville, Bibi. Sea Bugs & Moose Eggs. 2009. 52p. pap. 9.50 *(978-1-4357-4004-4(1))* Lulu Pr., Inc.

Rylant, Cynthia. The Octopus. McDaniels, Preston, illus. 2005. (Lighthouse Family Ser.: 5). (ENG.). 64p. (J). (gr. 1-5). 15.99 *(978-0-689-86246-5(6)*, Simon & Schuster Bks. For Young Readers) Simon & Schuster Bks. For Young Readers.

—The Otter. McDaniels, Preston, illus. 2016. (Lighthouse Family Ser.: 6). (ENG.). 48p. (J). (gr. 1-5). 15.99 *(978-1-4814-6045-3(5)*, Beach Lane Bks.) Beach Lane Bks.

—The Sea Lion. McDaniels, Preston, illus. 2017. (Lighthouse Family Ser.: 7). (ENG.). 48p. (J). (gr. 1-5). 15.99 *(978-1-4814-6025-5(0)*, Beach Lane Bks.) Beach Lane Bks.

Sage, Molly. At the Beach. Sage, Molly, illus. 2007. (ENG., Illus.). 6p. (J). (gr. k — 1). 6.99 *(978-1-85602-497-6(0))* Pavilion Bks. GBR. Dist: Independent Pubs. Group.

Sanders, Jane. Seashore Stroll, 1 vol. 2017. (ENG., Illus.). 22p. (J). bds. 9.99 *(978-1-4236-4712-6(2))* Gibbs Smith, Publisher.

Santillo, LuAnn. The Snack Shack. Santillo, LuAnn, ed. 2003. (Half-Pint Kids Readers Ser.). (Illus.). 7p. (J). (gr. -1-1). pap. 1.00 *(978-1-59256-086-8(5))* Half-Pint Kids, Inc.

Sattler, Jennifer. Pig Kahuna Pirates! 2014. (Pig Kahuna Ser.). (ENG., Illus.). 32p. (J). (gr. -1-1). 16.99 *(978-1-61963-200-4(4)*, 9781619632004, Bloomsbury USA Childrens) Bloomsbury Publishing USA.

—Who's That Pig? 2015. (Pig Kahuna Ser.). (ENG., Illus.). 32p. (J). (gr. -1-1). 16.99 *(978-1-61963-632-3(8)*, 9781619636323, Bloomsbury USA Childrens) Bloomsbury Publishing USA.

Sattler, Jennifer Gordon, illus. Pig Kahuna Pirates! 2014. (J). *(978-1-61963-203-5(9))* Bloomsbury Pr.

Schroder, Jack. A Fun Day at the Beach. 2005. 170p. (YA). per. 6.95 net. *(978-0-9763810-0-6(1))* Catalpa Pr.

Schroeder, Lisa. The Day Before. 2012. (ENG.). 336p. (YA). (gr. 9). pap. 9.99 *(978-1-4424-1744-1(7)*, Simon Pulse) Simon Pulse.

Schueler, M. A. Penny the Beach Westie Big Trouble for a Little Dog. 2009. 24p. pap. 16.50 *(978-1-60860-424-1(1)*, Eloquent Bks.) Strategic Book Publishing & Rights Agency (SBPRA).

Schwartz, Joanne. Pinny in Summer, 1 vol. Malenfant, Isabelle, illus. 2016. (ENG.). 32p. (J). (gr. -1-2). 16.95 *(978-1-55498-782-5(2))* Groundwood Bks. CAN. Dist: Publishers Group West (PGW).

—Town Is by the Sea, 1 vol. Smith, Sydney, illus. 2017. (ENG.). 52p. (J). (gr. k-4). 19.95 *(978-1-55498-871-6(3))* Groundwood Bks. CAN. Dist: Publishers Group West (PGW).

Scotton, Rob. A Whale of a Tale. 2013. (Splat the Cat: I Can Read Ser.). (J). lib. bdg. 13.55 *(978-0-606-31814-3(3)*, Turtleback) Turtleback Bks.

Seashore Touch & See Hi? 2004. (J). 11.95 *(978-0-89610-999-5(2))* Island Heritage Publishing.

Seuss, Dr. Sneetches on Beaches. 2011. (Dr. Seuss Nursery Collection). (ENG., Illus.). 14p. (J). (— 1). 10.99 *(978-0-375-87318-8(X)*, Random Hse. Bks. for Young Readers) Random Hse. Children's Bks.

Shemock, Judith. Sammi the Seahorse. 2012. 28p. pap. 15.99 *(978-1-4691-3293-8(1))* Xlibris Corp.

Shortcake 99. The Beach Day. 2011. 24p. pap. 13.00 *(978-1-4634-1337-8(8))* AuthorHouse.

Skewes, John & Ode, Eric. Elliott the Otter: The Totally Untrue Story of Elliott Bay. Skewes, John, illus. 2015. (ENG., Illus.). 32p. (J). (gr. -1-2). 16.99 *(978-1-57061-952-6(2)*, Little Bigfoot) Sasquatch Bks.

Slate, Kelly. The Adventures of Santa Claws: At Amelia Island. 2012. 28p. pap. 16.99 *(978-1-4772-2093-1(3))* AuthorHouse.

Smallman, Steve. Santa Is Coming to the Beach. Dunn, Robert, illus. 2015. (ENG.). 32p. (J). (-3). 9.99 *(978-1-4926-2846-0(8)*, Sourcebooks Jabberwocky) Sourcebooks, Inc.

Smith, Alex T. Claude at the Beach, 1 vol. Smith, Alex T., illus. (Claude Ser.). (ENG., Illus.). 96p. (J). (gr. 1-3). 2016. pap. 7.95 *(978-1-56145-919-3(4))* 2014. 12.95 *(978-1-56145-703-8(5))* Peachtree Pubs.

Smith, Carrie. Going to the Beach: Small Book. 2004. (Shared Connections Ser.). (J). pap. *(978-1-4108-1639-9(7))* Benchmark Education Co.

Smith, John D. H. The Whale Whisperers, 1 vol. Smith, Anne, illus. 2009. 17p. pap. 24.95 *(978-1-60749-211-5(3))* America Star Bks.

Snow, Carol. Switch. 2009. (ENG.). 240p. (YA). (gr. 8). pap. 8.99 *(978-0-06-145210-9(6)*, HarperTeen) HarperCollins Pubs.

Spinelli, Eileen. Summerhouse Time. Lew-Vriethoff, Joanne, illus. 2009. (ENG.). 224p. (J). (gr. 3-7). 6.99 *(978-0-440-42224-2(8)*, Yearling) Random Hse. Children's Bks.

S

Spinelli, Patti. Mackenzie & Emma Visit York Beach. Spinelli, Patti, illus. 2003. (Illus.). (J). *(978-0-9742328-0-5(7))* Spinelli, Patti.

Spohn, Kate. Turtle & Snake's Day at the Beach. Spohn, Kate, illus. 2004. (Puffin Easy-to-Read Ser.). (Illus.). 32p. (gr. k-3). 14.00 *(978-0-7569-2826-1(5))* Perfection Learning Corp.

Sprenger, Luke. Sommer in Canvas Bay. 2008. 92p. pap. 13.95 *(978-1-4092-3213-1(1))* Lulu Pr., Inc.

Spurr, Elizabeth. At the Beach, 1 vol. Oliphant, Manelle, illus. 2013. (ENG.). 22p. (J). (gr. -1 — 1). bds. 6.95 *(978-1-56145-583-6(0))* Peachtree Pubs.

Spykman, E. C. Terrible, Horrible Edie. 2010. (ENG.). 232p. (J). (gr. 4-7). 16.95 *(978-1-59017-353-4(8))*, NYR Children's Collection) New York Review of Bks., Inc., The.

Stella, Lennon & Stella, Maisy. In the Waves. Björkman, Steve, illus. 2015. (ENG.). 40p. (J). (gr. -1-3). 17.99 *(978-0-06-235939-1(8))* HarperCollins Pubs.

Stewart, Nancy. Bella Saves the Beach. Bell, Samantha, illus. 2013. 24p. 19.95 *(978-1-61633-370-6(7))*; pap. 11.95 *(978-1-61633-371-3(5))* Guardian Angel Publishing, Inc.

—One Pelican at a Time: A Story of the Gulf Oil Spill. Bell, Samantha, illus. 2011. 26p. (J). 19.95 *(978-1-61633-138-2(0))*; pap. 11.95 *(978-1-61633-139-9(9))* Guardian Angel Publishing, Inc.

Stine, R. L. Attack of the Jack. 2017. (Goosebumps SlappyWorld Ser.: 2). lib. bdg. 17.20 ***(978-0-606-40169-2(5))*** Turtleback Bks.

—Attack of the Jack (Goosebumps SlappyWorld #2) 2017. (Goosebumps SlappyWorld Ser.: 2). (ENG.). 160p. (J). (gr. 3-7). pap. 6.99 ***(978-1-338-06836-8(9)***, Scholastic Paperbacks) Scholastic, Inc.

Stoddart, Heidi Jardine. Back to the Beach, 1 vol. 2009. (ENG., Illus.). 32p. (J). (gr. -1-3). 10.95 *(978-1-55109-702-2(8))* Nimbus Publishing, Ltd. CAN. Dist: Orca Bk. Pubs. USA.

—East to the Sea, 1 vol. 2007. (ENG., Illus.). 32p. (J). (gr. -1-2). pap. 10.95 *(978-1-55109-577-6(7))* Nimbus Publishing, Ltd. CAN. Dist: Orca Bk. Pubs. USA.

Strasser, Todd & Thacker, Nola. The Shore: Shirt & Shoes Not Required; LB (Laguna Beach) 2011. (ENG.). 480p. (YA). (gr. 9). pap. 9.99 *(978-1-4424-1970-4(9)*, Simon Pulse) Simon Pulse.

Takhar, Jodi. Four Seasons of Fun. Takhar, Jodi & Jones, Paul, illus. 14p. (J). (gr. -1-3). 19.95 *(978-1-886000-02-5(6))* Takhar's, Jodi Spilt Milk Collection.

Tarshis, Lauren. I Survived the Shark Attacks of 1916. 2010. (I Survived Ser.: 2). (ENG.). 112p. (J). (gr. 3-7). pap. 4.99 *(978-0-545-20695-2(2)*, Scholastic Paperbacks) Scholastic, Inc.

—I Survived the Shark Attacks of 1916. 2010. (I Survived . Ser.: No. 2). lib. bdg. 14.75 *(978-0-606-23742-0(9)*, Turtleback) Turtleback Bks.

Telma, Tante. Telma's Day at Magens Bay. 2012. 16p. pap. 15.99 *(978-1-4772-7776-8(5))* AuthorHouse.

Thrasher, Grady. Tim & Sally's Beach Adventure. Rabon, Elaine Hearn, illus. 2008. 48p. (J). (gr. -1-3). 18.95 *(978-1-58818-161-9(8))* Hill Street Pr., LLC.

Torres, J. Checkers & Dot at the Beach. Lum, J., illus. 2013. (J). E-Book *(978-1-77049-448-0(0))* Tundra Bks.

—Checkers & Dot at the Beach. Lum, J., illus. 2013. (Checkers & Dot Ser.). (ENG.). 16p. (J). (— 1). bds. 7.95 *(978-1-77049-444-2(8)*, Tundra Bks.) Tundra Bks. CAN. Dist: Penguin Random Hse. LLC.

Tucker, Valerie Nell. The Hermit's Box. 2009. 36p. pap. 15.49 *(978-1-4490-2285-3(5))* AuthorHouse.

Tunks, Karyn. Jubilee!, 1 vol. Buckner, Julie, illus. 2012. (ENG.). 32p. (J). (gr. k-3). 16.99 *(978-1-58980-880-5(0))* Pelican Publishing Co., Inc.

Twitty, Mary F. Ashley Visits Urchin Village. 2008. 92p. pap. 51.99 *(978-1-4363-5578-0(8))* Xlibris Corp.

Tyler, Jenny & Cartwright, S. Duck by the Sea. 2004. (SPA.). 6p. (J). vinyl bd. 7.95 *(978-0-7945-0569-1(4))* EDC Publishing.

Valentin, Karen. When Are We Going to the Beach? 2009. 32p. 6.95 *(978-1-60349-020-7(5)*, Marimba Bks.) Hudson Publishing Group, The.

Van Dusen, Chris. Down to the Sea with Mr. Magee. 2006. (ENG., Illus.). 36p. (J). (gr. -1-7). pap. 6.99 *(978-0-8118-5225-8(3))* Chronicle Bks. LLC.

Van Eekhout, Greg. Kid vs. Squid. 2010. (ENG.). 208p. (YA). (gr. 3-6). 16.99 *(978-1-59990-489-4(6)*, 9781599904894, Bloomsbury USA Childrens) Bloomsbury Publishing USA.

Vasiliu, Mircea. A Day at the Beach. 2007. (Illus.). 36p. (J). 7.95 *(978-1-59091-068-9(0))* Eastern National.

Veranda, Molly. Molly & Tucker get Shanghaied. 2009. 41p. pap. 9.96 *(978-0-557-04210-4(0))* Lulu Pr., Inc.

Voake, Steve. Daisy Dawson at the Beach. Meserve, Jessica, illus. (Daisy Dawson Ser.: 4). (ENG.). (J). (gr. 1-4). 2012. 96p. pap. 5.99 *(978-0-7636-5946-2(0))* 2011. 87p. 14.99 *(978-0-7636-5306-4(3))* Candlewick Pr.

Wade, Judith. Faeleri, the Horse from the Sea. 2007. 107p. (J). mass mkt. 5.99 *(978-0-9728958-5-9(X))* Riley Pr.

Wagner, Jenny. High Hopes on Sea. Rogers, Gregory, illus. 2005. (UQP Children's Fiction Ser.). 80p. (Orig.). (J). pap. *(978-0-7022-3525-2(3))* Univ. of Queensland Pr.

Waite, Lance. A Day with Dad at the Beach. 2008. (J). 17.99 *(978-1-60131-016-3(1)*, Parents Publishing Group) Big Tent Bks.

Walker, Anna. I Love Vacations. Walker, Anna, illus. 2011. (ENG., Illus.). 32p. (J). (gr. -1-1). 9.99 *(978-1-4169-8321-7(X)*, Simon & Schuster Bks. For Young Readers) Simon & Schuster Bks. For Young Readers.

Walker, Jorge. Little Winston's Desire. 2011. 20p. pap. 9.49 *(978-1-4567-2396-5(0))* AuthorHouse.

Wallace, Nancy Elizabeth. Shells! Shells! Shells!, 0 vols. 2013. (ENG.). 40p. (J). (gr. k-3). pap. 9.99 *(978-1-4778-1679-0(8)*, 9781477816790, Amazon Children's Publishing) Amazon Publishing.

Webb, Jane K. My Super Stupendous Day at the Beach. Cupolo, Eileen, illus. 2012. 24p. pap. 12.95 *(978-1-61493-044-0(9))* Peppertree Pr., The.

Wells, Carolyn. Marjorie at Seacote. 2011. 296p. 48.95 *(978-1-258-08998-6(X))* Literary Licensing, LLC.

—Marjorie at Seacote. 2006. 29.95 *(978-1-55742-656-7(2))*; pap. 14.95 *(978-1-55742-653-6(8))* Wildside Pr., LLC.

—Patty's Butterfly Days. 2005. 28.95 *(978-1-4218-0309-8(7)*, 1st World Library - Literary Society) 1st World Publishing, Inc.

Wen, Dref. Traeth Prysur. 2005.Tr. of Busy Beach. (WEL., Illus.). 12p. *(978-1-85596-661-1(1))* Dref Wen.

White, Amanda. Sand Sister. 2016. (ENG.). 32p. (J). (gr. -1-2). pap. 8.99 *(978-1-78285-279-7(4))* Barefoot Bks., Inc.

—Sand Sister. Morales, Yuyi, illus. 2004. 32p. (J). 16.99 *(978-1-84148-617-8(5))* Barefoot Bks., Inc.

White, Pam. Buddy Goes to the Beach. 2010. 20p. 12.50 *(978-1-4520-3065-4(0))* AuthorHouse.

Williams, Karen Lynn. A Beach Tail. Cooper, Floyd, illus. 2010. (ENG.). 32p. (J). (gr. -1-2). 17.95 *(978-1-59078-712-0(9))* Boyds Mills Pr.

Wright, Kiyah. Vacation Fun. 2011. 24p. pap. 14.95 *(978-1-4634-4055-8(3))* AuthorHouse.

Yasuda, Anita. The Beach Bandit, 1 vol. Harpster, Steve, illus. 2013. (Dino Detectives Ser.). (ENG.). 32p. (gr. 1-2). pap. 5.95 *(978-1-4342-4830-5(5))*; lib. bdg. 22.65 *(978-1-4342-4154-2(8))* Stone Arch Bks.

Yoon, Salina. Penguin on Vacation. Yoon, Salina, illus. (Penguin Ser.). (ENG., Illus.). (J). (gr. -1-1). 2015. 34p. bds. 7.99 *(978-0-8027-3837-0(0)*, 9780802738370) 2013. 40p. 14.99 *(978-0-8027-3397-9(2)*, 9780802733979) Bloomsbury Publishing USA. (Bloomsbury USA Childrens).

Young, Ruth. Aunty Marmalade. 2009. 218p. pap. 13.78 *(978-1-60693-893-5(2)*, Eloquent Bks.) Strategic Book Publishing & Rights Agency (SBPRA).

Zadunajsky, Donna M. Tayla's Day at the Beach. Bicking, Judith, illus. 2013. (ENG.). 26p. pap. 6.99 *(978-1-938037-34-4(0))* Zadunajsky, Donna M.

Zeigler, Robbie. Down by the Se. 2011. 16p. pap. 13.99 *(978-1-4634-2056-7(0))* AuthorHouse.

Zolotow, Charlotte. The Seashore Book. Minor, Wendell, illus. 2004. (Reading Rainbow Bks.). (gr. -1-3). 17.00 *(978-0-7569-4234-2(9))* Perfection Learning Corp.

Zolotow, Charlotte & Minor, Wendell. The Seashore Book. 2017. (ENG., Illus.). 32p. (J). (-k). lib. bdg. 16.99 *(978-1-58089-787-7(8))* Charlesbridge Publishing, Inc.

SEASONS

see also names of the seasons, e.g. Autumn, etc.

Algarra, Alejandro & Bonilla, Rocio. What Causes Weather & Seasons? 2016. (Curious Young Minds Ser.). (ENG.). 36p. (J). (gr. -1-2). pap. 7.99 *(978-1-4380-0892-9(9))* Barron's Educational Series, Inc.

Aloian, Molly. How Do We Know It Is Spring? 2013. (ENG., Illus.). 24p. (J). *(978-0-7787-0959-6(0))*; pap. *(978-0-7787-0963-3(9))* Crabtree Publishing Co.

—How Do We Know It Is Summer? 2013. (ENG., Illus.). 24p. (J). *(978-0-7787-0960-2(4))*; pap. *(978-0-7787-0964-0(7))* Crabtree Publishing Co.

—How Do We Know It Is Winter? 2013. (ENG., Illus.). 24p. (J). *(978-0-7787-0962-6(0))* Crabtree Publishing Co.

—How Do We Know It's Fall? 2013. (ENG., Illus.). 24p. (J). *(978-0-7787-0961-9(2))*; pap. *(978-0-7787-0965-7(5))* Crabtree Publishing Co.

—How Do We Know It's Winter? 2013. (ENG., Illus.). 24p. (J). pap. *(978-0-7787-0966-4(3))* Crabtree Publishing Co.

Anderson, Sheila. Lightning Bolt Books: Our Four Seasons, 4 vols., Set. Incl. Are You Ready for Fall? lib. bdg. 26.60 *(978-0-7613-4586-2(8))*; Are You Ready for Spring? lib. bdg. 26.60 *(978-0-7613-4584-8(1))*; Are You Ready for Summer? lib. bdg. 26.60 *(978-0-7613-4585-5(X))*; Are You Ready for Winter? lib. bdg. 26.60 *(978-0-7613-4583-1(3))*; 32p. (gr. k-2). 2010. 2009. Set lib. bdg. 101.04 *(978-0-7613-4582-4(5)*, Lerner Pubns.) Lerner Publishing Group.

Appleby, Alex. Qu Sucede en Invierno? / What Happens in Winter?, Vol. 1. 2014. (Cuatro Estaciones Estupendas / Four Super Seasons Ser.). (SPA & BYN.). 24p. (J). (gr. k-k). 22.60 *(978-1-4824-0132-5(0))* Stevens, Gareth Publishing LLLP.

—Qu Sucede en Otoo? / What Happens in Fall?, Vol. 1. 2014. (Cuatro Estaciones Estupendas / Four Super Seasons Ser.). (SPA & BYN.). 24p. (J). (gr. k-k). 22.60 *(978-1-4824-0101-1(0))* Stevens, Gareth Publishing LLLP.

—Qu Sucede en Primavera? / What Happens in Spring?, Vol. 1. 2014. (Cuatro Estaciones Estupendas / Four Super Seasons Ser.). (SPA & BYN.). 24p. (J). (gr. k-k). 22.60 *(978-1-4824-0119-6(3))* Stevens, Gareth Publishing LLLP.

—Qu Sucede en Verano? / What Happens in Summer?, Vol. 1. 2014. (Cuatro Estaciones Estupendas / Four Super Seasons Ser.). (SPA & BYN.). 24p. (J). (gr. k-k). 22.60 *(978-1-4824-0128-8(2))* Stevens, Gareth Publishing LLLP.

Aspen-Baxter, Linda & Kissock, Heather. Las Estaciones. 2012. (Mirando Al Cielo Ser.). (SPA., Illus.). 24p. (J). (gr. k-2). lib. bdg. 27.13 *(978-1-61913-217-7(6)*, AV2 by Weigl) Weigl Pubs., Inc.

Baker, Chris. A Year in Barrowswold Forest: Band 15/Emerald. 2017. (ENG.). 48p. (J). pap. 8.99 ***(978-0-00-820886-8(7))*** HarperCollins Pubs. Ltd. GBR. Dist: Independent Pubs. Group.

Barraclough, Sue. Seasons. 2009. (Me & My World Ser.). (Illus.). 24p. (J). (gr. -1-2). pap. 8.15 *(978-1-60754-066-3(5))*; lib. bdg. 22.60 *(978-1-60754-059-5(2))* Windmill Bks.

Beckett, Sydney. My Favorite Season. 2012. (InfoMax Readers Ser.). (ENG., Illus.). 16 pp.p. (J). (gr. k-1). pap. 7.00 *(978-1-4488-8914-3(6)*, Rosen Classroom) Rosen Publishing Group, Inc., The.

Benchmark Education Company. Weather & Climate (Teacher Guide) 2005. *(978-1-4108-4635-8(0))* Benchmark Education Co.

Benchmark Education Company, LLC Staff, compiled by. Weather & Seasons. 2006. (J). 265.00 *(978-1-4108-7031-5(6))* Benchmark Education Co.

Branley, Franklyn M. Sunshine Makes the Seasons. Rex, Michael, illus. 2005. (Let's-Read-And-Find-Out Science 2 Ser.). (ENG.). 40p. (J). (gr. k-4). pap. 5.99 *(978-0-06-059205-9(2)*, Collins) HarperCollins Pubs.

—Sunshine Makes the Seasons. Rex, Michael, illus. 2016. (Let's-Read-And-Find-Out Science 2 Ser.). 40p. (J). (gr. -1-3). pap. 6.99 *(978-0-06-238209-2(8))* HarperCollins Pubs.

Branley, Franklyn Mansfield. Sunshine Makes the Seasons. Rex, Michael, illus. 2005. (Let's-Read-and-Find-Out-Science Ser.). (ENG.). 40p. (J). (gr. -1 — 1). 15.99 *(978-0-06-059203-5(6))* HarperCollins Pubs.

Braun, Eric. Curious Pearl Identifies the Reason for Seasons: 4D an Augmented Reality Science Experience. Dehennin, Stephanie, illus. 2017. (Curious Pearl, Science Girl 4D Ser.). (ENG.). 24p. (gr. k-2). lib. bdg. 20.65 ***(978-1-5158-1343-9(6))*** Picture Window Bks.

Brennan, Linda Crotta. Leaves Change Color. 2014. (Tell Me Why Library). (ENG., Illus.). 24p. (J). (gr. 2-5). 25.64 *(978-1-63188-008-7(X)*, 205439) Cherry Lake Publishing.

Brocket, Jane. Rainy, Sunny, Blowy, Snowy - What Are Seasons? Brocket, Jane, photos by. 2014. (Jane Brocket's Clever Concepts Ser.). (ENG., Illus.). 32p. (J). (gr. -1-2). lib. bdg. 26.60 *(978-1-4677-0231-7(5)*, Millbrook Pr.) Lerner Publishing Group.

Brown, Janet Allison & Brown, Janet Allison. Seasons, Vol. 4. 2005. (Our Seasons & Weather Ser.). (YA). (gr. k-3). 118.80 *(978-0-7368-4201-3(2)*, Pebble Bks.) Capstone Press of Coughlan Cos.

Brown, Jeremy. God Makes the Seasons. 2011. 28p. pap. 14.93 *(978-1-4269-4946-3(4))* Trafford Publishing.

Burningham, John. Las Estaciones. (SPA., Illus.). (J). (gr. k-3). *(978-84-88342-14-0(4)*, KK7662) S.A. Kokinos ESP. Dist: Lectorum Pubns., Inc.

Cannon, Shannon. The Seasons, 6 vols., Set. 2003. (Phonics Readers 1-36 Ser.). (ENG.). 8p. (gr. k-1). pap. 29.70 *(978-0-7368-3204-5(1)*, Phonics Readers) Capstone Press of Coughlan Cos.

Capstone Press. First Graphics: Seasons, 1 vol. 2010. (First Graphics: Seasons Ser.). (ENG.). 32p. lib. bdg. 106.60 *(978-1-4296-5936-9(X))* Capstone Press of Coughlan Cos.

Cardenas, Ernesto A. The Four Seasons of the Year. 2009. pap. 4.95 *(978-1-60698-092-7(0))* Milo Educational Bks. & Resources.

—Spring, Summer, Fall, & Winter. 2009. 19.95 *(978-1-60698-011-8(4))*; pap. 3.95 *(978-1-60698-009-5(2))* Milo Educational Bks. & Resources.

Carole, Bonnie. Orange & Brown in Fall. 2015. (ENG.). 24p. (gr. -1-1). pap. 8.95 *(978-1-63430-080-3(7))* Rourke Educational Media.

Carr, Aaron. Spring. 2013. 25.00 *(978-1-62127-493-3(4))* Weigl Pubs., Inc.

—Summer. 2013. 25.00 *(978-1-62127-494-0(2))* Weigl Pubs., Inc.

—Winter. 2013. pap. 17.95 *(978-1-62127-495-7(0))* Weigl Pubs., Inc.

Carroll. Lbd Gka Nf Fun for All Seasons. 2009. (C). pap. 8.53 *(978-1-4189-3337-1(6))* Rigby Education.

Ceanadach, Siusaidh. Let's Talk about Elements & the Pagan Wheel. 2013. (ENG.). 73p. pap. 9.95 *(978-1-78099-561-8(X)*, Moon Bks.) Hunt, John Publishing Ltd. GBR. Dist: National Bk. Network.

Children's Press, contrib. by. Sing a Song of Seasons. 2009. (Rookie Preschool Ser.). (ENG.). 24p. (J). (gr. -1). lib. bdg. 23.00 *(978-0-531-24409-8(1)*, Children's Pr.) Scholastic Library Publishing.

Colorful Days. 2014. (DK Readers Ser.). (ENG.). 32p. (J). (gr. -1-1). pap. 3.99 *(978-1-4654-1674-2(9)*, DK Children) Dorling Kindersley Publishing, Inc.

DeGezelle, Terri. Exploring the Seasons. 2012. (Exploring the Seasons Ser.). (ENG.). 24p. (gr. k-1). pap. 27.80 *(978-1-4296-8354-8(6))*; pap. 166.80 *(978-1-4296-8355-5(4))*; lib. bdg. 53.30 *(978-1-4296-8141-4(1))* Capstone Press of Coughlan Cos. (Pebble Plus).

deMarin, Layne. Desert Seasons. 2011. (Wonder Readers Fluent Level Ser.). (ENG.). 16p. (gr. -1-2). pap. 35.94 *(978-1-4296-8082-0(2)*, Wonder Readers) Capstone Press of Coughlan Cos.

Dickmann, Nancy. Las Estaciones en la Granja. 2011. (Mundo de la Granja Ser.). 24p. (gr. -1-1). (SPA & ENG.). 22.65 *(978-1-4329-5311-9(7))*; (ENG & SPA.). pap. 6.29 *(978-1-4329-5318-8(4))* Heinemann-Raintree. (Bellota).

—El Mundo de la Granja, 6 vols., Set. Incl. Alimentos de la Granja. pap. 6.29 *(978-1-4329-5315-7(X))*; Animales de la Granja. pap. 6.29 *(978-1-4329-5313-3(3))*; Estaciones en la Granja. pap. 6.29 *(978-1-4329-5318-8(4))*; Las Plantas de la Granja. (Illus.). pap. 6.29 *(978-1-4329-5317-1(6))*; Máquinas de la Granja. pap. 6.29 *(978-1-4329-5314-0(1))*; Trabajos en la Granja. pap. 6.29 *(978-1-4329-5316-4(8))*; (gr. -1-1). (Mundo de la Granja Ser.). (SPA.). 24p. 2011. Set pap. 35.94 *(978-1-4329-5319-5(2)*, Bellota) Heinemann-Raintree.

—Seasons on a Farm, 1 vol. 2010. (World of Farming Ser.). 24p. (ENG.). (gr. -1-1). pap. 6.29 *(978-1-4329-3953-3(X))*; pap. 32.35 *(978-1-4329-3944-1(0))* Heinemann-Raintree. (Acorn).

Dolphin, Colleen. Signs of Autumn, 1 vol. 2012. (Signs of the Seasons Ser.). (ENG.). 24p. (J). (gr. k-3). lib. bdg. 24.21 *(978-1-61783-392-2(4)*, SandCastle) ABDO Publishing Co.

—Signs of Spring, 1 vol. 2012. (Signs of the Seasons Ser.). (ENG.). 24p. (J). (gr. k-3). lib. bdg. 24.21 *(978-1-61783-393-9(2)*, SandCastle) ABDO Publishing Co.

—Signs of Summer, 1 vol. 2012. (Signs of the Seasons Ser.). (ENG.). 24p. (J). (gr. k-3). lib. bdg. 24.21 *(978-1-61783-394-6(0)*, SandCastle) ABDO Publishing Co.

—Signs of Winter, 1 vol. 2012. (Signs of the Seasons Ser.). (ENG.). 24p. (J). (gr. k-3). lib. bdg. 24.21 *(978-1-61783-395-3(9)*, SandCastle) ABDO Publishing Co.

Dompierre, Judith E. No More Than Four of a Kind. 2012. 36p. pap. 24.95 *(978-1-4626-9329-0(6))* America Star Bks.

Droop, Constanza. Que? Como? Por Que?: Las Estaciones del Ano. Caballero, D., tr. Droop, Constanza, illus. 2007. (Junior (Silver Dolphin) Ser.). (Illus.). 16p. (J). (gr. -1). *(978-970-718-492-3(2)*, Silver Dolphin en Español) Advanced Marketing, S. de R. L. de C. V.

Eckart, Edana. Watching the Seasons. 2004. (Wel-Watching Nature Ser.). (J). 19.00 *(978-0-516-27600-7(X))*; (ENG.). 24p. (gr. -1-2). pap. 4.95 *(978-0-516-25937-6(7))* Scholastic Library Publishing. (Children's Pr.).

Education.com. Celebrate the Seasons: A Workbook of Seasons, Holidays, Weather, & Time. 2015. (ENG.). 128p. (J). (gr. -1-k). pap. 7.99 *(978-0-486-80257-2(4))* Dover Pubns., Inc.

Las Estaciones del Ano, 4 vols. 2006. (SPA.). (J). (gr. k-2). 69.08 *(978-0-8225-3322-1(7)*, Ediciones Lerner) Lerner Publishing Group.

Evan-Moor. Art for All Seasons: Grades 1-4. 2004. (ENG., Illus.). 208p. (J). pap. 24.99 *(978-1-55799-953-5(8)*, EMC 2001) Evan-Moor Educational Pubs.

Evans, David & Williams, Claudette. Seasons & Weather. (Let's Explore Science Ser.). (Illus.). (J). 12.95 *(978-0-590-74592-5(1))* Scholastic, Inc.

Feeney, Stephanie. Sun & Rain: Exploring Seasons in Hawai'i. 2008. (Latitude 20 Bks.). (Illus.). 48p. (J). (gr. -1-3). 15.99 *(978-0-8248-3088-5(1))* Univ. of Hawaii Pr.

Feldman, Thea. Seasons. 2013. (Kingfisher Readers Ser.). (ENG., Illus.). 32p. (J). (gr. k-3). pap. 3.99 *(978-0-7534-6898-2(0)*, 9780753468982, Kingfisher) Roaring Brook Pr.

Ferguson, Gloria. What Season Is It? Weir, Carrie & Weir, Nolet, illus. Frigon, Kerry, photos by. 2011. 28p. pap. 24.95 *(978-1-4626-4136-9(9))* America Star Bks.

Ferris, Diane J. Weather Watcher. 2009. (Illus.). 20p. pap. 13.00 *(978-1-4490-1218-2(3))* AuthorHouse.

First Graphics - Seasons. 2010. (First Graphics: Seasons Ser.). (ENG.). 24p. (gr. 1-2). pap. 18.87 *(978-1-4296-5696-2(4))*; pap. 142.80 *(978-1-4296-5698-6(0))* Capstone Press of Coughlan Cos.

First Graphics: Seasons Collection. 2010. (First Graphics: Seasons Ser.). (ENG.). 24p. (gr. 1-2). pap. 18.87 *(978-1-4296-5697-9(2))* Capstone Press of Coughlan Cos.

Fisher, Valorie. Everything I Need to Know Before I'm Five. Fisher, Valorie, illus. 2011. (ENG., Illus.). 40p. (J). (gr. k-k). 17.99 *(978-0-375-86865-8(8)*, Schwartz & Wade Bks.) Random Hse. Children's Bks.

Fort, Holli, et al. Teachers' Favorites Fun Activities for Fall! Hamblin, George, illus. 2010. 96p. (J). *(978-1-4508-2765-2(9))* Publications International, Ltd.

The Four Seasons. 16.95 incl. audio compact disk *(978-0-9700489-5-0(5))* Little Fiddle Co., Inc., The.

Fun in Fall. 2015. (Fun in Fall Ser.). (ENG.). 24p. (J). (gr. k-k). 135.60 *(978-1-4824-1631-2(X))* Stevens, Gareth Publishing LLLP.

George, Jean Craighead. Spring Moon. 2003. (J). (gr. 3-7). 20.75 *(978-0-8446-7242-7(4))* Smith, Peter Pub., Inc.

Ghigna, Charles. Hail to Spring! Watson, Laura, illus. 2015. (Springtime Weather Wonders Ser.). (ENG.). 24p. (gr. -1-2). lib. bdg. 21.99 *(978-1-4795-6029-5(4))* Picture Window Bks.

Glaser, Linda. It's Fall! Swan, Susan, illus. 2003. (Celebrate the Seasons! Ser.). (ENG.). 32p. (gr. k-3). pap. 7.95 *(978-0-7613-1342-7(7))* Lerner Publishing Group.

Gold, Kimberley. Four Seasons. (Flip Flap Fun Book Ser.). (Illus.). 10p. (J). bds. *(978-2-89393-934-6(1))* Phidal Publishing, Inc./Editions Phidal, Inc.

Green, Jen. Weather & Seasons. 2008. (Our Earth Ser.). (Illus.). 24p. (J). (gr. 1-4). lib. bdg. 22.60 *(978-1-4042-4272-2(4))* Rosen Publishing Group, Inc., The.

Gürth, Per-Henrik. Canada All Year. Gürth, Per-Henrik, illus. 2011. (ENG., Illus.). 32p. (J). (gr. -1-1). 14.95 *(978-1-55453-709-9(6))* Kids Can Pr., Ltd. CAN. Dist: Hachette Bk. Group.

Guy, Ginger Foglesong. Dias y Dias: Days & Days. Moreno, Rene King, illus. 2011. (SPA & ENG.). (J). 16.99 *(978-0-06-173182-2(X)*, Greenwillow Bks.) HarperCollins Pubs.

Haelle, Tara. Seasons, Tides, & Lunar Phases. 2016. (Let's Explore Science Ser.). (ENG., Illus.). 48p. (gr. 5-8). 35.64 *(978-1-68191-395-7(X))* Rourke Educational Media.

Hansen, Amy S. Where Does the Sun Go at Night? An Earth Science Mystery, 1 vol. Scott, Korey, illus. 2011. (First Graphics: Science Mysteries Ser.). (ENG.). 24p. (gr. 1-2). pap. 6.29 *(978-1-4296-7176-7(9))*; pap. 35.70 *(978-1-4296-7180-4(7))*; lib. bdg. 23.99 *(978-1-4296-6098-3(8))* Capstone Press of Coughlan Cos.

Hedlund, Stephanie. Seasons. Bauer, Stephanie, illus. 2013. (Seasons Ser.: 4). 24p. (J). (gr. k-4). lib. bdg. 108.28 *(978-1-61641-991-2(1)*, Looking Glass Library- Nonfiction) Magic Wagon.

Helenek, Sophie. My First Book FRUITS: GOLD Mom's Choice Awards. 2014. (My First Book Ser.). (ENG., Illus.). 16p. (J). (gr. -1-k). bds. 5.99 *(978-0-9894505-0-8(3))* Nursery Bks.

Heuninck, Ronald. Rain or Shine. Heuninck, Ronald, illus. Orig. Title: Buiten Spelen. (Illus.). 12p. (J). pap. 5.50 *(978-0-86315-089-0(6)*, 20269) Floris Bks. GBR. Dist: Gryphon Hse., Inc.

Highlights for Children Editorial Staff, creator. All about Spring. 2017. (All about Activity Bks.). (ENG.). 32p. (J). (gr. -1-k). pap. 4.99 *(978-1-62979-696-3(4)*, Highlights) Boyds Mills Pr.

Hirschi, Ron. Winter Is for Whales: A Book of Hawaiian Seasons. Green, Yuko, illus. 2007. (ENG.). 36p. (J). (gr. -1-3). *(978-1-59700-504-3(5))* Island Heritage Publishing.

Hudson, Cheryl Willis. Book of Seasons. Simpson, Howard, illus. (Afro-Bets Ser.). (J). pap. 4.95 *(978-0-940975-15-6(7))* Just Us Bks., Inc.

Hunt, Jeanne. Celebrating Saints & Seasons: Hundreds of Activities for Catholic Children. 2010. (ENG.). 192p. pap. 12.99 *(978-0-86716-959-1(1))* Franciscan Media.

Jackson, Ellen B. The Spring Equinox: The Greening of the Earth. 2003. (Illus.). 32p. (J). (gr. 3-6). pap. 7.95 *(978-0-7613-1983-2(2)*, Millbrook Pr.) Lerner Publishing Group.

James, Wayan. Daylight in Winter, Summer, Fall, & Spring. 2016. (Rosen REAL Readers: STEM & STEAM Collection). 12p. (gr. 1-k). pap. 6.33 *(978-1-5081-2446-7(9)*, Rosen Classroom) Rosen Publishing Group, Inc., The.

Johnson, T. Seasons of the Year. 2010. 16p. (J). pap. 13.95 *(978-1-4327-5070-1(4))* Outskirts Pr., Inc.

Jones, Tammy. Look at the Weather. 2009. (Sight Word Readers Set A Ser.). (J). *(978-1-60719-140-7(7))* Newmark Learning LLC.

Kalman, Bobbie. ¿Qué Es el Tiempo? 2009. (SPA.). 24p. (J). *(978-0-7787-8703-7(6))*; pap. *(978-0-7787-8742-6(7))* Crabtree Publishing Co.

—What Time Is It? 2008. (Looking at Nature Ser.). (ENG., Illus.). 24p. (J). (gr. -1-2). pap. *(978-0-7787-3345-4(9))*; lib. bdg. *(978-0-7787-3325-6(4))* Crabtree Publishing Co.

—Which Season Is It? 2011. (ENG.). 16p. (J). *(978-0-7787-9553-7(5))*; pap. *(978-0-7787-9578-0(0))* Crabtree Publishing Co.

Kalman, Bobbie & MacAulay, Kelley. Changing Seasons. 2005. (ENG., Illus.). 32p. (J). pap. *(978-0-7787-2309-7(7))* Crabtree Publishing Co.

Kissock, Heather. Seasons. 2011. (J). 27.13 *(978-1-61690-956-7(0))*; *(978-1-61690-602-3(2))* Weigl Pubs., Inc.

Kniffke, Sophie, et al. El Tiempo. (Coleccion Mundo Maravilloso).Tr. of Seasons & Weather. (SPA., Illus.). 40p.

(J). (gr. 2-4). *(978-84-348-3470-5(7)*, SM5473) SM Ediciones.

Lane, Bonnie. Bob the Inchworm & the Four Seasons. 2009. 20p. pap. 11.00 *(978-1-4389-9833-6(3))* AuthorHouse.

Latta, Sara L. ¿Qué Pasa en el Invierno? What Happens in Winter? 2010. (SPA.). (J). 23.94 *(978-0-7660-3244-6(2)*, Enslow Elementary) Enslow Pubs., Inc.

—¿Qué Pasa en el Otoño? What Happens in Fall? 2010. (SPA.). (J). 23.94 *(978-0-7660-3241-5(8)*, Enslow Elementary) Enslow Pubs., Inc.

—¿Qué Pasa en el Verano? What Happens in Summer? 2010. (SPA.). (J). 23.94 *(978-0-7660-3243-9(4)*, Enslow Elementary) Enslow Pubs., Inc.

—¿Qué Sucede en la Primavera? What Happens in Spring? 2010. (SPA.). (J). 23.94 *(978-0-7660-3242-2(6)*, Enslow Elementary) Enslow Pubs., Inc.

—What Happens in Fall? 2006. (I Like the Seasons! Ser.). (Illus.). 24p. (J). (gr. 1-3). lib. bdg. 22.60 *(978-0-7660-2417-5(2)*, Enslow Elementary) Enslow Pubs., Inc.

—What Happens in Spring? 2006. (I Like the Seasons! Ser.). (Illus.). 24p. (J). (gr. 1-3). lib. bdg. 22.60 *(978-0-7660-2419-9(9)*, Enslow Elementary) Enslow Pubs., Inc.

—What Happens in Summer? 2006. (I Like the Seasons! Ser.). (Illus.). 24p. (J). (gr. 1-3). lib. bdg. 22.60 *(978-0-7660-2416-8(4)*, Enslow Elementary) Enslow Pubs., Inc.

—What Happens in Winter? 2006. (I Like the Seasons! Ser.). (Illus.). 24p. (J). (gr. 1-3). lib. bdg. 22.60 *(978-0-7660-2418-2(0)*, Enslow Elementary) Enslow Pubs., Inc.

—Why Is It Fall? 2012. (Why Do We Have Seasons? Ser.). (Illus.). 24p. (J). (gr. k-18). pap. 7.95 *(978-1-59845-388-1(2)*, Enslow Elementary) Enslow Pubs., Inc.

—Why Is It Spring? 2012. (Why Do We Have Seasons? Ser.). (Illus.). 24p. (J). (gr. k-18). pap. 7.95 *(978-1-59845-389-8(0)*, Enslow Elementary); 22.60 *(978-0-7660-3986-5(2))* Enslow Pubs., Inc.

—Why Is It Summer? 2012. (Why Do We Have Seasons? Ser.). (Illus.). 24p. (J). (gr. k-18). pap. 7.95 *(978-1-59845-390-4(4)*, Enslow Elementary) Enslow Pubs., Inc.

—Why Is It Winter? 2012. (Why Do We Have Seasons? Ser.). (Illus.). 24p. (J). (gr. k-18). pap. 7.95 *(978-1-59845-391-1(2)*, Enslow Elementary); 22.60 *(978-0-7660-3988-9(9))* Enslow Pubs., Inc.

LernerClassroom Editors. First Step Nonfiction-Seasons Teaching Guide. 2009. pap. 7.95 *(978-0-8225-5628-2(6))* Lerner Publishing Group.

Lin, Grace & Mckneally, Ranida T. Our Seasons. Lin, Grace, illus. 2007. (ENG., Illus.). 32p. (J). (gr. k-3). pap. 7.95 *(978-1-57091-361-7(7))* Charlesbridge Publishing, Inc.

Linde, Barbara M. Weather & Climate. 2005. (J). pap. *(978-1-4108-4587-0(7))* Benchmark Education Co.

Linus, Benjamin. Spring, Summer, Fall, Winter. 2012. (InfoMax Readers Ser.). (ENG., Illus.). 16 pp.p. (J). (gr. k-1). pap. 7.00 *(978-1-4488-8959-4(6)*, Rosen Classroom) Rosen Publishing Group, Inc., The.

MacDonald, Margaret. What Season Is It? 2011. (Learn-Abouts Ser.). (Illus.). 16p. (J). pap. 7.95 *(978-1-59920-617-2(X))* Black Rabbit Bks.

Maguire, Kay. Nature's Day. Kroll, Danielle, illus. 2016. (Nature's Day Ser.). (ENG.). 80p. (J). (gr. k-3). 24.99 *(978-1-84780-707-6(0)*, Wide Eyed Editions) Quarto Publishing Group UK GBR. Dist: Hachette Bk. Group.

—Nature's Day: Discover the World of Wonder on Your Doorstep. Kroll, Danielle, illus. 2015. (Nature's Day Ser.). (ENG.). 80p. (J). 24.99 *(978-1-84780-608-6(2)*, Wide Eyed Editions) Quarto Publishing Group UK GBR. Dist: Littlehampton Bk Services, Ltd.

—Out & About. Kroll, Danielle, illus. 2016. (Nature's Day Ser.). (ENG.). 56p. (J). pap. 10.99 *(978-1-84780-800-4(X)*, Wide Eyed Editions) Quarto Publishing Group UK GBR. Dist: Littlehampton Bk Services, Ltd.

Maguire, Kay & Kroll, Danielle. Nature's Day: Out & About: Spotting, Making & Collecting Activities. 2016. (ENG.). 56p. (J). (gr. k-3). pap. 9.99 *(978-1-84780-836-3(0)*, Wide Eyed Editions) Quarto Publishing Group UK GBR. Dist: Hachette Bk. Group.

Manushkin, Fran. Katie Woo Spring 2010, 6 vols., Set. Lyon, Tammie, illus. Incl. Best Season Ever. lib. bdg. 21.32 *(978-1-4048-5730-8(3))*; Katie Goes Camping. lib. bdg. 21.32 *(978-1-4048-5731-5(1))*; Katie in the Kitchen. lib. bdg. 21.32 *(978-1-4048-5724-7(9))*; Make-Believe Class. lib. bdg. 21.32 *(978-1-4048-5732-2(X))*; Moving Day. lib. bdg. 21.32 *(978-1-4048-5733-9(8))*; Nervous Night. lib. bdg. 21.32 *(978-1-4048-5725-4(7))*; (gr. k-2). (Katie Woo Ser.). (ENG., Illus.). 32p. 2010. Set lib. bdg. 127.92 *(978-1-4048-5973-9(X))* Picture Window Bks.

Markovics, Joyce L. Los Colores de Las Estaciones: Cómo Cambian. 2014. (Los Colores Cuentan una Historia Ser.). (SPA.). 24p. (J). (gr. -1-3). lib. bdg. 23.93 *(978-1-62724-469-5(7))* Bearport Publishing Co., Inc.

—The Seasons' Colors: How They Change. 2015. (Illus.). 24p. (J). lib. bdg. *(978-1-62724-327-8(5))* Bearport Publishing Co., Inc.

McCarroll, Tolbert. A Winter Walk. Beebee, Dorothy, illus. 2006. (ENG.). 160p. 14.95 *(978-0-8245-2416-6(0))* Crossroad Publishing Co., The.

Meachen Rau, Dana. Space & Time. 2008. (Earth Matters Ser.). 32p. (gr. 1-2). lib. bdg. 15.95 *(978-0-7614-3049-0(0)*, Benchmark Bks.) Marshall Cavendish Corp.

—Space & Time/El Tiempo y Espacio. 2008. (Earth Matters/El Planeta Es Importante Ser.). (SPA & ENG.). 32p. (gr. k-1). lib. bdg. 15.95 *(978-0-7614-3496-2(8)*, Benchmark Bks.) Marshall Cavendish Corp.

—El Tiempo y el Espacio. 2008. (Planeta Es Importante Ser.). (SPA.). 32p. (gr. 1-2). lib. bdg. 15.95 *(978-0-7614-3470-2(4)*, Benchmark Bks.) Marshall Cavendish Corp.

Meister, Cari. First Graphics - Seasons, Set. Lingenfelter, Jim, illus. Incl. Fall Is Fun. lib. bdg. 23.99 *(978-1-4296-4731-1(0))*; Spring Is Special. lib. bdg. 23.99 *(978-1-4296-4729-8(9))*; Summer Is Super. lib. bdg. 23.99 *(978-1-4296-4730-4(2))*; Winter Is Wonderful. lib. bdg. 23.99 *(978-1-4296-4732-8(9))*; (Illus.). (gr. 1-2). (First Graphics: Seasons Ser.). (ENG.). 24p. 2010. Set lib. bdg. 95.96 *(978-1-4296-4733-5(7))* Capstone Press of Coughlan Cos.

Miller, Derek L. Earth, Sun, & Moon: Cyclic Patterns of Lunar Phases, Eclipses, & the Seasons. 2016. (Space Systems Ser.). 112p. (J). 42.79 *(978-1-5026-2291-4(2))* Cavendish Square Publishing.

Mills, Nathan & Rodgers, Katherine. What Season Is It? 2012. (Rosen Readers Ser.). (ENG., Illus.). 16p. (J). (gr. k-1). pap. 7.00 *(978-1-4488-8695-1(3)*, Rosen Classroom) Rosen Publishing Group, Inc., The.

Moon, Walt K. ¡El Otoño Es Divertido! 2017. (Bumba Books (tm) en Español — Diviértete con Las Estaciones (Season Fun) Ser.). (SPA., Illus.). 24p. (J). (gr. -1-1). 25.32 *(978-1-5124-2860-5(4))* Lerner Publishing Group.

—¡El Verano Es Divertido! 2017. (Bumba Books (tm) en Español — Diviértete con Las Estaciones (Season Fun) Ser.). (SPA., Illus.). 24p. (J). (gr. -1-1). 25.32 *(978-1-5124-2862-9(0))* Lerner Publishing Group.

—Fall Is Fun! 2016. (Bumba Books (tm) — Season Fun Ser.). (ENG., Illus.). 24p. (J). (gr. -1-1). 25.32 *(978-1-5124-1409-7(3))* Lerner Publishing Group.

—¡La Primavera Es Divertida! 2017. (Bumba Books (tm) en Español — Diviértete con Las Estaciones (Season Fun) Ser.). (SPA., Illus.). 24p. (J). (gr. -1-1). 25.32 *(978-1-5124-2861-2(2))* Lerner Publishing Group.

—Spring Is Fun! 2016. (Bumba Books (tm) — Season Fun Ser.). (ENG., Illus.). 24p. (J). (gr. -1-1). 25.32 *(978-1-5124-1411-0(5))* Lerner Publishing Group.

—Summer Is Fun! 2016. (Bumba Books (tm) — Season Fun Ser.). (ENG., Illus.). 24p. (J). (gr. -1-1). 25.32 *(978-1-5124-1412-7(3))* Lerner Publishing Group.

Morgan, Sally. Seasons. 2011. (Earth Cycles Ser.). 32p. (YA). (gr. 3-6). lib. bdg. 28.50 *(978-1-59920-526-7(2))* Black Rabbit Bks.

Murray, Julie. Fall, 1 vol. 2016. (ENG., Illus.). 24p. (J). *(978-1-62970-919-2(0)*, 1391198) ABDO Publishing Co.

—Spring, 1 vol. 2016. (ENG., Illus.). 24p. *(978-1-62970-920-8(4)*, 1391200) ABDO Publishing Co.

—Summer, 1 vol. 2016. (ENG., Illus.). 24p. ***(978-1-62970-921-5(2)***, 1391201) ABDO Publishing Co.

—Winter, 1 vol. 2016. (ENG., Illus.). 24p. ***(978-1-62970-922-2(0)***, 1391203) ABDO Publishing Co.

My First Book of Seasons. (Butterfly Bks.). (ARA., Illus.). (J). 14.95 *(978-0-86685-711-6(7))* International Bk. Ctr., Inc.

National Geographic Learning Staff. Why Do the Seasons Change? 2010. (ENG., Illus.). 32p. (C). (gr. -1-3). pap. 12.95 *(978-0-7614-3367-5(8))* National Geographic School Publishing, Inc.

Nelson, Robin. Estaciones (Seasons) 2012. (Mi Primer Paso Al Mundo Real - Descubriendo Los Ciclos de la Naturaleza (First Step Nonfiction - Discovering Nature's Cycles) Ser.). (Illus.). 24p. (gr. k-2). (ENG & SPA.). pap. 6.95 *(978-0-7613-9357-3(9))*; (SPA., lib. bdg. 23.93 *(978-0-7613-9339-9(0))* Lerner Publishing Group. (Ediciones Lerner).

—Seasons. 2010. pap. 33.92 *(978-0-7613-6916-5(3))*; (ENG.). 24p. pap. 6.95 *(978-0-7613-5684-4(3))*; (ENG., Illus.). 24p. lib. bdg. 23.93 *(978-0-7613-4578-7(7))* Lerner Publishing Group.

Nunn, Daniel. The Seasons. 2013. (True or False? Ser.). (ENG.). 24p. (gr. -1-1). pap. 6.29 *(978-1-4109-5074-1(3)*, NA-r) Heinemann-Raintree.

—The Seasons - True or False? 2013. (True or False? Ser.). (ENG.). 24p. (gr. -1-1). lib. bdg. 22.65 *(978-1-4109-5068-0(9)*, NA-r) Heinemann-Raintree.

O'Mara, Mary. Monsoon! An Extreme Weather Season. 2009. (Science Kaleidoscope Ser.). (J). lib. bdg. 25.25 *(978-1-4358-2988-6(3)*, PowerKids Pr.) Rosen Publishing Group, Inc., The.

Pebble Books: Our Seasons & Weather. 2005. (YA). (gr. k-3). 712.80 *(978-0-7368-4219-8(5)*, Pebble Bks.) Capstone Press of Coughlan Cos.

Pendergast, George. A Year of Seasons. 2015. (Cycles in Nature Ser.). (ENG., Illus.). 24p. (J). (gr. 1-2). lib. bdg. 22.60 *(978-1-4824-1654-1(9))* Stevens, Gareth Publishing LLLP.

Perez, Marlene. Colors of the Seasons. 2004. (Shared Connections Ser.). (J). pap. *(978-1-4108-1628-3(1))* Benchmark Education Co.

—Colors of the Seasons (Big Book) 2004. (Shared Connections Ser.). (J). pap., instr.'s gde. ed. 27.00 *(978-1-4108-1604-7(4))* Benchmark Education Co.

Powell, Jillian. Projects with Weather & Seasons. 2014. (Make & Learn Ser.). (Illus.). 32p. (J). (gr. 3-6). lib. bdg. 27.50 *(978-1-4777-7181-5(6)*, PowerKids Pr.) Rosen Publishing Group, Inc., The.

Priddy, Roger. Fall. 2010. (Bright Baby Touch & Feel Ser.). (ENG., Illus.). 12p. (J). (gr. -1 — 1). bds. 4.95 *(978-0-312-50922-4(7)*, 9780312509224, Priddy Bks.) St. Martin's Pr.

Provensen, Alice & Provensen, Martin. A Book of Seasons. 32p. (J). Random Hse. Children's Bks.

Radtke, Becky J. Four Seasons of Fun Activity Book. 2013. (ENG.). 48p. (J). (gr. 1-4). pap. 4.99 *(978-0-486-49894-2(8))* Dover Pubns., Inc.

Randolph, Joanne. All about the Seasons. (It's about Time Ser.). 24p. 2009. (gr. 1-1). 42.50 *(978-1-61513-633-9(9)*, PowerKids Pr.) 2007. (Illus.). (J). (gr. k-2). lib. bdg. 22.60 *(978-1-4042-3768-1(2))* Rosen Publishing Group, Inc., The.

—All about the Seasons/Las Estaciones. 2009. (It's about Time/Los libros del tiempo Ser.). (ENG & SPA.). 24p. (gr. 1-1). 42.50 *(978-1-61513-629-2(0)*, Editorial Buenas Letras) Rosen Publishing Group, Inc., The.

—All about the Seasons/Las Estaciones. Brusca, Maria Cristina, tr. 2007. (It's about Time / Los Libros Del Tiempo Ser.). (ENG & SPA., Illus.). 24p. (J). (gr. k-2). lib. bdg. 22.60 *(978-1-4042-7629-1(7))* Rosen Publishing Group, Inc., The.

Rau, Dana Meachen. Seasons. 2009. (Bookworms Ser.). 32p. (gr. 1-2). 15.95 *(978-0-7614-4098-7(4))* Marshall Cavendish Corp.

—Seasons/Las Estaciones. 2009. (Bookworms Ser.). (SPA & ENG.). 32p. (gr. 1-2). lib. bdg. 15.95 *(978-0-7614-4791-7(1))* Marshall Cavendish Corp.

Rey, H. A. Curious George Discovers the Seasons. 2016. (Curious George Ser.). (ENG., Illus.). 32p. (J). (gr. -1-3). pap. 6.99 *(978-0-544-78509-0(6)*, HMH Books For Young Readers) Houghton Mifflin Harcourt Publishing Co.

Rice, William. The Seasons, 1 vol. (Science Readers: Content & Literacy Ser.). (ENG., Illus.). 24p. (gr. 1-1). 2015. (J). 22.96 *(978-1-4938-1156-4(8))* 2014. pap. 8.99 *(978-1-4807-4569-8(3))* Teacher Created Materials, Inc.

Richard, Orlin. Investigating Seasons. 2015. (ENG., Illus.). 40p. (J). (gr. 3-5). 29.32 *(978-1-4677-8059-9(6)*, Lerner Pubns.) Lerner Publishing Group.

Rigby Education Staff. Discovery World Yel Seasons. (Discovery World Ser.). (Illus.). 12p. (gr. k-1). 23.00 *(978-0-7635-2694-8(0))* Rigby Education.

Riley, Peter. Seasons. 2017. (Ways into Science Ser.). (ENG., Illus.). 32p. (J). (gr. k-2). pap. 11.99 *(978-1-4451-3481-9(0)*, Franklin Watts) Hachette Children's Group GBR. Dist: Hachette Bk. Group.

Rissman, Rebecca. Seasons, 1 vol. 2013. (Picture This! Ser.). (ENG.). 24p. (gr. -1-k). pap. 9.95 *(978-1-4109-5257-8(6)*, NA-r) Heinemann-Raintree.

Rock, Lois. Thank You, God. Widdowson, Kay, illus. 2nd ed. 2013. (Prayers for Little Hands Ser.). (ENG.). 8p. (J). (— 1). 8.99 *(978-0-7459-6377-8(3))* Lion Hudson PLC GBR. Dist: Independent Pubs. Group.

Rockwell, Anne F. Four Seasons Make a Year. Halsey, Megan, illus. 2004. (ENG.). 32p. (J). (gr. k-3). 17.99 *(978-0-8027-8883-2(1)*, 9780802788832, Bloomsbury USA Childrens) Bloomsbury Publishing USA.

Rookie Ready to Learn - Seasons & Weather, 5 vols., Set. Incl. Animal Babies. Hamsa, Bobbie. Dunnington, Tom, illus. 40p. lib. bdg. 23.00 *(978-0-531-25640-4(5))*; Going to the Beach. Kittinger, Jo S. Warren, Shari, illus. 32p. lib. bdg. 23.00 *(978-0-531-25641-1(3))*; Pumpkin Fever. Simon, Charnan. Bryan-Hunt, Jan, illus. 40p. lib. bdg. 23.00 *(978-0-531-25643-5(X))*; Snow Joe. Greene, Carol. Sharp, Paul, illus. 40p. lib. bdg. 23.00 *(978-0-531-25644-2(8))*; (J). (gr. -1-k). (Rookie Ready to Learn Ser.). 2011. Set lib. bdg. 115.00 *(978-0-531-26724-0(5)*, Children's Pr.) Scholastic Library Publishing.

Royston, Angela. Looking at Weather & Seasons: How Do They Change? 2008. (Looking at Science: How Things Change Ser.). (Illus.). 32p. (J). (gr. 3-7). lib. bdg. 23.94 *(978-0-7660-3093-0(8)*, Enslow Elementary) Enslow Pubs., Inc.

Sayre, April Pulley. Full of Fall. 2017. (ENG., Illus.). 40p. (J). (gr. -1-3). 17.99 ***(978-1-4814-7984-4(9)***, Beach Lane Bks.) Beach Lane Bks.

Scheunemann, Pam. Time to Learn about Seasons & Years, 1 vol. 2008. (Time Ser.). (ENG., Illus.). 24p. (J). (gr. k-3). lib. bdg. 24.21 *(978-1-60453-018-6(9))* ABDO Publishing Co.

Scholastic, Inc. Staff. Seasons & Holidays: 40 Instant & Adorable Patterns for Bulletin Boards, Class Books, Newsletters, Stationery, & More. 2004. (Biggie Patterns Ser.). (ENG.). 48p. (gr. -1-3). pap. 10.99 *(978-0-439-46840-4(X))* Scholastic, Inc.

Schuh, Mari C. Crayola Fall Colors. 2017. (Crayola (r) Seasons Ser.). (ENG.). 24p. (J). (gr. -1-3). 26.65 ***(978-1-5124-3291-6(1))*** Lerner Publishing Group.

—Crayola Summer Colors. 2017. (Crayola (r) Seasons Ser.). (ENG.). 24p. (J). (gr. -1-3). 26.65 ***(978-1-5124-3290-9(3))*** Lerner Publishing Group.

Schuh, Mari C. I Feel Fall Weather. 2016. (First Step Nonfiction — Observing Fall Ser.). (ENG., Illus.). 24p. (J). (gr. k-2). 23.99 *(978-1-5124-0797-6(6))* Lerner Publishing Group.

Seasons: Individual Title, 6 packs. (Discovery World Ser.). 12p. (gr. k-1). 28.00 *(978-0-7635-8445-0(2))* Rigby Education.

The Seasons: Individual Title Two-Packs. (Chiquilibros Ser.). (gr. -1-1). 12.00 *(978-0-7635-8543-3(2))* Rigby Education.

Seasons of the Year. 2017. (Seasons of the Year Ser.). 24p. (gr. 5-6). 98.40 ***(978-1-4994-8274-4(4))***; pap. 33.00 ***(978-1-4994-8411-3(9))*** Rosen Publishing Group, Inc., The. (Windmill Bks.).

Seelig, Renate, illus. Mein Kleiner Brockhaus: Jahreszeiten. (GER.). 28p. (J). (gr. -1-18). *(978-3-7653-2571-7(6))* Brockhaus, F. A., GmbH DEU. Dist: International Bk. Import Service, Inc.

Serio, Marie L. Hello Autumn Goodbye Autumn. 2011. (Illus.). 16p. (gr. 1-2). pap. 9.75 *(978-1-4634-0215-0(5))* AuthorHouse.

Sesame Workshop. Toddler Time Explore Seasons with Cookie Monster. 2011. (J). (gr. k-1). pap. 3.99 *(978-1-59922-883-9(1))* Twin Sisters IP, LLC.

Shapiro, Sara. What Do You See? A Book about the Seasons. 2009. (Illus.). 16p. (J). pap. *(978-0-545-16154-1(1))* Scholastic, Inc.

Shepherd, Jodie. Crayola Spring Colors. 2017. (Crayola (r) Seasons Ser.). (ENG.). 24p. (J). (gr. -1-3). 26.65 ***(978-1-5124-3292-3(X))*** Lerner Publishing Group.

—Crayola Winter Colors. 2017. (Crayola (r) Seasons Ser.). (ENG.). 24p. (J). (gr. -1-3). 26.65 ***(978-1-5124-3293-0(8))*** Lerner Publishing Group.

Slade, Suzanne. The Four Seasons. (Cycles in Nature Ser.). (gr. 3-3). 2009. 24p. 42.50 *(978-1-61512-111-3(0))* 2007. 28p. pap. 21.25 *(978-1-4358-3827-7(0))* Rosen Publishing Group, Inc., The. (PowerKids Pr.).

Smith, Ian. Scholastic Clubs Animal Kingdom Pack (5 x PB QAL Titles) 2004. (QEB Start Talking Ser.). (Illus.). 24p. (J). per. 15.95 *(978-1-59566-162-3(X))* QEB Publishing Inc.

Smith, Sian. Seasons. 2014. (Seasons Ser.). (ENG.). 24p. (gr. -1-1). 26.00 *(978-1-4846-0358-1(3)*, Acorn) Heinemann-Raintree.

Stark, Ryan. Why Do Seasons Change? 2013. (Nature's Super Secrets Ser.). (Illus.). 24p. (J). (gr. 1-3). 22.60 *(978-1-4339-8185-2(8))*; pap. 8.15 *(978-1-4339-8186-9(6))* Stevens, Gareth Publishing LLLP.

Steffora, Tracey. Estaciones del Año. 2011. (Medir el Tiempo Ser.). (SPA.). 24p. (gr. -1-1). 22.65 *(978-1-4329-5632-5(9))*; pap. 6.29 *(978-1-4329-5639-4(6))* Heinemann-Raintree. (Bellota).

—Seasons of the Year, 1 vol. 2011. (Measuring Time Ser.). (ENG.). 24p. (gr. -1-1). pap. 6.29 *(978-1-4329-4909-9(8)*, Acorn) Heinemann-Raintree.

Stewart, Melissa. Why Do the Seasons Change? 2006. (Tell Me Why, Tell Me How Ser.). (Illus.). 32p. (gr. 3-7). lib. bdg. 29.93 *(978-0-7614-2112-2(2)*, Benchmark Bks.) Marshall Cavendish Corp.

Storad, Conrad J. Earth Is Tilting! 2011. (ENG., Illus.). 24p. (gr. 2-3). pap. 8.95 *(978-1-61741-952-2(4))* Rourke Educational Media.

Strudwick, Leslie. The Science of Seasons. 2003. (Living Science Ser.). (Illus.). 32p. (J). (gr. 1-3). pap. 9.95 *(978-1-930954-16-8(6))* Weigl Pubs., Inc.

Sundance/Newbridge LLC Staff. The Four Seasons. 2007. (Early Science Ser.). (gr. k-3). 18.95 *(978-1-4007-6143-2(3))*; pap. 6.10 *(978-1-4007-6139-5(5))* Sundance/Newbridge Educational Publishing.

Thornborough, Kathy. Seasons. Petelinsek, Kathleen, illus. 2014. (Talking Hands Ser.). (ENG.). 24p. (J). (gr. k-3). 25.64 *(978-1-62687-323-0(2)*, 207163) Child's World, Inc., The.

Thornhill, Jan. Is This Panama? A Migration Story. Kim, Soyeon & Owlkids Books Inc. Staff, illus. 2013. (ENG.). 40p. (J). (gr. k-4). 16.95 *(978-1-926973-88-3(7)*, Owlkids) Owlkids Bks. Inc. CAN. Dist: Publishers Group West (PGW).

Trumbauer, Lisa. A Year in the Desert, 6 vols., Set. 2005. (Yellow Umbrella Fluent Level Ser.). (ENG., Illus.). 16p. (gr. k-1). pap. 35.70 *(978-0-7368-5302-6(2)*, Yellow Umbrella Bks.) Capstone Press of Coughlan Cos.

Ventura, Marne. Why Does Earth Have Seasons? 2016. (Everyday Earth Science Ser.). (ENG.). 24p. (J). (gr. k-3). 27.07 *(978-1-5038-0798-3(3)*, 210634) Child's World, Inc., The.

Walpole, Brenda. I Wonder Why the Sun Rises: And Other Questions about Time & Seasons. 2011. (I Wonder Why Ser.). (ENG., Illus.). 32p. (J). (gr. k-3). pap. 6.99 *(978-0-7534-6529-5(9)*, 9780753465295, Kingfisher) Roaring Brook Pr.

—I Wonder Why the Sun Rises & Other Questions about Time & Seasons. 2008. (I Wonder Why Ser.). (Illus.). 32p. (gr. k-3). 17.00 *(978-0-7569-9054-1(8))* Perfection Learning Corp.

Watt, Fiona. Rainy Day Stroller Book. Baggott, Stella, illus. 2010. 8p. (J). 7.99 *(978-0-7945-2850-8(3)*, Usborne) EDC Publishing.

Weather & Seasons Classroom Library. (gr. k-2). lib. bdg. 128.95 *(978-0-7368-1828-5(6))* Red Brick Learning.

Weather & Seasons Complete Program. (gr. k-2). 642.95 *(978-0-7368-1829-2(4))* Red Brick Learning.

Weiner, Miriam. Shakespeare's Seasons. Whitt, Shannon, illus. 2012. (ENG.). 32p. (J). (gr. -1). 16.99 *(978-1-935703-57-0(9))* Downtown Bookworks.

Welzen, Jon. I Know the Seasons. 2016. (What I Know Ser.). 00024p. (J). pap. 8.15 *(978-1-4824-5473-4(4))* Stevens, Gareth Publishing LLLP.

White, Teagan. Adventures with Barefoot Critters. (ENG., Illus.). (J). 2017. 30p. (— 1). bds. 7.99 *(978-1-101-91913-2(2))* 2014. 32p. (gr. -1-3). 16.99 *(978-1-77049-624-8(6))* Tundra Bks. CAN. (Tundra Bks.). Dist: Penguin Random Hse. LLC.

World Book, Inc Staff, contrib. by. Seasonal Forests. 2012. (J). *(978-0-7166-0444-0(2))* World Bk., Inc.

Ziefert, Harriet. One Red Apple. Gudeon, Karla, illus. 2009. 36p. (J). 15.99 *(978-1-934706-46-6(9))* Blue Apple Bks.

Zoehfeld, Kathleen Weidner. Secrets of the Seasons: Orbiting the Sun in Our Backyard. 2014. (ENG., Illus.). 40p. (J). (gr. k-3). 16.99 *(978-0-517-70994-8(5))*; lib. bdg. 19.99 *(978-0-517-70995-5(3))* Random Hse. Children's Bks. (Knopf Bks. for Young Readers).

SEASONS—FICTION

Adler, David A. It's Time to Sleep, It's Time to Dream. Chorao, Kay, illus. 2009. (ENG.). 32p. (J). (gr. -1-k). 16.95 *(978-0-8234-1924-1(X))* Holiday Hse., Inc.

Allen, Elise & Stanford, Halle. Autumn's Secret Gift. Pooler, Paige, illus. 2014. (Enchanted Sisters Ser.). (ENG.). 128p. (J). (gr. 2-4). pap. 5.99 *(978-1-61963-254-7(3)*, 9781619632547, Bloomsbury USA Childrens) Bloomsbury Publishing USA.

—Autumn's Secret Gift. Pooler, Paige, illus. 2014. (Enchanted Sisters Ser.: 1). lib. bdg. 16.00 *(978-0-606-35519-3(7))* Turtleback Bks.

—Spring's Sparkle Sleepover. Pooler, Paige, illus. 2015. (Enchanted Sisters Ser.). (ENG.). 128p. (J). (gr. 2-4). 15.99 *(978-1-61963-296-7(9)*, 9781619632967); pap. 5.99 *(978-1-61963-269-1(1)*, 9781619632691) Bloomsbury Publishing USA. (Bloomsbury USA Childrens).

—Summer's Friendship Games. Pooler, Paige, illus. 2015. (Enchanted Sisters Ser.). (ENG.). 128p. (J). (gr. 2-4). 15.99 *(978-1-61963-271-4(3)*, 9781619632714, Bloomsbury USA Childrens) Bloomsbury Publishing USA.

—Winter's Flurry Adventure. Pooler, Paige, illus. 2014. (Enchanted Sisters Ser.). (ENG.). 128p. (YA). (gr. 2-4). pap. 5.99 *(978-1-61963-267-7(5)*, 9781619632677, Bloomsbury USA Childrens) Bloomsbury Publishing USA.

—Winter's Flurry Adventure. Pooler, Paige, illus. 2014. (Enchanted Sisters Ser.: 2). (YA). lib. bdg. 16.00 *(978-0-606-36217-7(7))* Turtleback Bks.

Allred, Sylvester. Rascal, the Tassel-Eared Squirrel. Iverson, Diane, illus. 2007. (ENG.). 64p. 16.95 *(978-0-938216-88-9(0))* Grand Canyon Assn.

Allred, Sylvester & Iverson, Diane. Rascal, the Tassel-Eared Squirrel. 2007. (ENG., Illus.). 64p. pap. 9.95 *(978-0-938216-44-5(9))* Grand Canyon Assn.

Anderson, Derek. Blue Burt & Wiggles. Anderson, Derek, illus. 2014.Tr. of Signed in American Sign Language. (ENG., Illus.). 32p. (J). (gr. -1-3). 16.99 *(978-1-4814-1933-8(1)*, Simon & Schuster Bks. For Young Readers) Simon & Schuster Bks. For Young Readers.

Ashburn, Boni. I Had a Favorite Hat. Ng, Robyn, illus. 2015. (ENG.). 32p. (J). (gr. -1-3). 16.95 *(978-1-4197-1462-7(7)*, Abrams Bks. for Young Readers) Abrams, Inc.

AZ Books Staff. Our Cozy Forest. Zayceva, Irina, ed. 2012. (Hook-And-Loop-Pictures Ser.). (ENG.). 8p. (J). (-k). bds. 11.95 *(978-1-61889-157-0(X))* AZ Bks. LLC.

Baker, Keith. Hap-Pea All Year! Baker, Keith, illus. 2016. (Peas Ser.). (ENG., Illus.). 40p. (J). (gr. -1-3). 17.99 *(978-1-4814-5854-2(X)*, Beach Lane Bks.) Beach Lane Bks.

Barklem, Jill. Spring Story. Barklem, Jill, illus. 2011. (Brambly Hedge Ser.). (ENG., Illus.). 32p. (J). 9.99 *(978-0-00-183922-9(5)*, HarperCollins Children's Bks.) HarperCollins Pubs. Ltd. GBR. Dist: HarperCollins Pubs.

—Summer Story. Barklem, Jill, illus. 2011. (Brambly Hedge Ser.). (ENG., Illus.). 32p. (J). 9.99 *(978-0-00-183923-6(3)*, HarperCollins Children's Bks.) HarperCollins Pubs. Ltd. GBR. Dist: HarperCollins Pubs.

Berger, Carin. Finding Spring. Berger, Carin, illus. 2015. (ENG., Illus.). 40p. (J). (gr. -1-3). 17.99 *(978-0-06-225019-3(1)*, Collins Design) HarperCollins Pubs.

S

—Forever Friends. Berger, Carin, illus. 2010. (ENG., Illus.). 40p. (J). (gr. -1-1). 16.99 *(978-0-06-191528-4(9),* Greenwillow Bks.) HarperCollins Pubs.

Berger, Samantha & Chanko, Pamela. It's Spring! Sweet, Melissa, illus. 2003. (ENG.). 30p. (J). (gr. -1-3). bds. 6.99 *(978-0-439-44238-1(9),* Cartwheel Bks.) Scholastic, Inc.

Bergren, Lisa Tawn. God Gave Us Thankful Hearts. Hohn, David, illus. 2016. (ENG.). 40p. (J). (gr. -1-2). 10.99 *(978-1-60142-874-5(X),* WaterBrook Pr.) Crown Publishing Group.

Berner, Rotraut Susanne. In the Town All Year 'Round. Konings, Neeltje & Elliott, Nick, trs. from GER. 2008. (ENG., Illus.). 72p. (J). (gr. -1-k). 16.99 *(978-0-8118-6474-9(X))* Chronicle Bks. LLC.

Beskow, Elsa. Children of the Forest. gif. ed. 2005. (ENG., Illus.). 32p. (J). (gr. -1-3). *(978-0-86315-497-3(2))* Floris Bks.

Birnbaum, A. Green Eyes. Birnbaum, A., illus. 2011. (Family Storytime Ser.). (ENG., Illus.). 48p. (J). (gr. -1-2). pap. 7.99 *(978-0-375-86201-4(3),* Dragonfly Bks.) Random Hse. Children's Bks.

Bishop, Celeste. It's Fall. 2016. (Four Seasons Ser.). (ENG., Illus.). 24p. (gr. 1-1). pap. 8.25 *(978-1-5081-5179-1(2),* PowerKids Pr.) Rosen Publishing Group, Inc., The.

—It's Raining. 2016. (What's the Weather Like? Ser.). 24p. (gr. 1-1). pap. 8.25 *(978-1-4994-2351-8(9),* PowerKids Pr.) Rosen Publishing Group, Inc., The.

Bissonette, Aimee M. North Woods Girl. McGehee, Claudia, illus. 2015. (ENG.). 32p. (J). 16.95 *(978-0-87351-966-3(3))* Minnesota Historical Society Pr.

Blackford, Cheryl. Hungry Coyote. Caple, Laurie, illus. 2015. (ENG.). 32p. (J). (gr. -1-2). 16.95 *(978-0-87351-964-9(7))* Minnesota Historical Society Pr.

Blackstone, Stella. On y Danse les Saisons. Carluccio, Maria, illus. 2016. (FRE.). (J). pap. *(978-1-78285-298-8(0))* Barefoot Bks., Inc.

—Skip Through the Seasons. Carluccio, Maria, illus. 2009. (ENG.). 32p. (J). 16.99 *(978-1-84686-293-9(0))* Barefoot Bks., Inc.

Blexbolex. Seasons. Bedrick, Claudia Z., tr. from FRE. 2010.Tr. of Saisons. (ENG., Illus.). 180p. (J). (gr. -1-2). 22.95 *(978-1-59270-095-0(0))* Enchanted Lion Bks., LLC.

Boom Boom. 2014. (ENG., Illus.). 40p. (J). (gr. -1-3). 17.99 *(978-1-4424-3412-7(0),* Beach Lane Bks.) Beach Lane Bks.

Brennan, Martin. I Saw It in the Garden. Monroe, Michael Glenn, illus. 2006. 32p. (J). (gr. -1-3). 17.95 *(978-1-58726-296-8(7),* Mitten Pr.) Ann Arbor Editions LLC.

Broach, Elise. Barnyard Baby. Doerrfeld, Cori, illus. 2013. (Baby Seasons Ser.). (ENG.). 14p. (J). (gr. -1 — 1). bds. 7.99 *(978-0-316-21203-8(2))* Little, Brown Bks. for Young Readers.

Brown, Kimberly. Autumn Castles. 2012. 28p. pap. 12.50 *(978-1-61897-032-9(1),* Strategic Bk. Publishing) Strategic Book Publishing & Rights Agency (SBPRA).

Bruel, Nick. A Wonderful Year. Bruel, Nick, illus. 2015. (ENG., Illus.). 40p. (J). (gr. -1-1). 17.99 *(978-1-59643-611-4(5),* 9781596436114) Roaring Brook Pr.

Bush, Leanne. Sarah's Happy Harvest Time, 1 vol. Briggs, Charlotte, illus. 2009. 32p. pap. 24.95 *(978-1-60813-818-0(6))* America Star Bks.

Camden, Marian Louise. An Earth Child's Book of the Year. Wright, Diane Beem, illus. 2011. 32p. pap. *(978-1-77067-742-5(9))* FriesenPress.

Candlewick Press, Candlewick. Peppa Pig & the Year of Family Fun. 2016. (Peppa Pig Ser.). (ENG., Illus.). 10p. (J). (gr. -1-2). 17.99 *(978-0-7636-8739-7(1),* Candlewick Entertainment) Candlewick Pr.

Capucilli, Alyssa Satin. My Mom & Me. Mitchell, Susan, illus. 2009. (ENG.). 16p. (J). (gr. -1-1). 7.99 *(978-1-4169-5829-1(0),* Little Simon) Little Simon.

Carter, David A. Snow Bugs: A Wintery Pop-Up Book. Carter, David A., illus. 2009. (David Carter's Bugs Ser.). (ENG., Illus.). 20p. (J). (gr. -1-3). 11.99 *(978-1-4169-5054-7(0),* Little Simon) Little Simon.

Chernesky, Felicia Sanzari. Pick a Circle, Gather Squares: A Fall Harvest of Shapes. Swan, Susan, illus. 2013. (ENG.). 32p. (J). (gr. -1-3). 16.99 *(978-0-8075-6538-4(5))* Whitman, Albert & Co.

Cherobin. Zoomy Boomy, the Moon, & the Earth: All in its Season, & Seasons Change. 2010. 24p. pap. 14.99 *(978-1-4490-2658-5(3))* AuthorHouse.

Child's Play. Fall. Busby, Ailie, illus. 2015. (Seasons Ser.: 4). (ENG.). 12p. (J). (gr. 1-1). bds. *(978-1-84643-744-1(X))* Child's Play International Ltd.

Child's Play Staff. Spring. Busby, Ailie, illus. 2015. (Seasons Ser.: 4). (ENG.). 12p. (J). (gr. 1-1). bds. *(978-1-84643-741-0(5))* Child's Play International Ltd.

Christenson, Lisa & Christenson, Emme Jo. Seasons on the Sofa. Christenson, Lisa & Christenson, Emme Jo, illus. 2006. (Illus.). per. *(978-0-9725311-3-9(0),* Pickled Eggs Press (TM)) Lisa Loucks Christenson Publishing, LLC.

Cochran, Jean M. Off I Go! Gullens, Lee M., illus. 2008. (ENG.). 32p. (J). (gr. -1-k). 16.95 *(978-0-9792035-1-0(1))* Pleasant St. Pr.

Cook, Maureen McNamee. Is There Magic in the Mountains, Mamma? Connell, Jacqueline, illus. 2008. 23p. pap. 24.95 *(978-1-60672-673-0(0))* America Star Bks.

Costa, Nicoletta. The Little Tree That Would Not Share. Costa, Nicoletta, illus. 2016. (ENG., Illus.). 32p. (J). 16.95 *(978-0-8234-3549-4(0))* Holiday Hse., Inc.

Crayton, Tina Anderson. Sniffles: Each Season Brings New Sniffles. 2012. 12p. pap. 15.99 *(978-1-4772-8454-4(0))* AuthorHouse.

Crilley, Mark. Autumn. Crilley, Mark, illus. 2007. (Miki Falls Ser.: 3). (ENG., Illus.). 176p. (YA). (gr. 8-12). pap. 8.99 *(978-0-06-084618-3(6))* HarperCollins Pubs.

Davis, Jim & Michiels, Cedric. Unfair Weather. Dargaud Media Staff & Ellipsanime Staff, illus. 2013. (Garfield Show Ser.). (ENG.). 64p. (J). (gr. 1-5). 11.99 *(978-1-59707-433-9(0),* 9781597074339) Papercutz.

de Brunhoff, Laurent & Rose, Phyllis. Babar & His Family. 2012. (ENG., Illus.). 24p. (J). (gr. -1 — 1). bds. 7.95 *(978-1-4197-0263-1(7),* Abrams Appleseed) Abrams, Inc.

Deady, Kathleen W. All Year Long. Bronson, Linda, illus. 2004. (Carolrhoda Picture Books Ser.). 32p. (J). (gr. -1-3). 15.95 *(978-1-57505-537-4(6))* Lerner Publishing Group.

dePaola, Tomie. Four Friends in Autumn. dePaola, Tomie, illus. 2004. (ENG., Illus.). 32p. (J). (gr. -1-3). 17.99 *(978-0-689-85980-9(5),* Simon & Schuster Bks. For Young Readers) Simon & Schuster Bks. For Young Readers.

Derby, Sally & Burrowes, Adjoa J. My Steps. 2005. (Sally, Illus.). 32p. (J). (gr. 1-4). pap. 9.95 *(978-1-880000-84-7(9))* Lee & Low Bks., Inc.

Desrochers, Diane O. The Little Tree That Would Be Great. Boucher, Julie, illus. 2009. 36p. pap. 14.95 *(978-0-9819727-7-0(2))* Fiction Publishing, Inc.

Dierenfeldt, Jane. A Time for Everything. Hanawalt, Josh, illus. 2012. 36p. 24.95 *(978-1-4626-6146-6(7))* America Star Bks.

Diesen, Deborah. Bloom. Lundquist, Mary, illus. 2017. (ENG.). 32p. (J). 16.99 *(978-0-374-30250-4(2),* 9780374302504, Farrar, Straus & Giroux (BYR)) Farrar, Straus & Giroux.

Disney Publishing Staff. My Favorite Season, 15 vols. 2003. (It's Fun to Learn Ser.). (Illus.). 32p. (J). (gr. -1-3). 3.99 *(978-1-57973-129-8(5))* Advance Pubs. LLC.

Doty, Linda. In Search of the Robin. 2003. 35p. pap. 24.95 *(978-1-4137-0231-6(7))* PublishAmerica, Inc.

Drescher, Daniela. In the Land of Elves, 1 vol. Orig. Title: Im Zwergenland. (ENG., Illus.). 24p. 14.95 *(978-0-86315-484-3(0))* Floris Bks. GBR. Dist: SteinerBooks, Inc.

Dubuc, Marianne, creator. The Lion & the Bird. 2014. (ENG., Illus.). 64p. (J). (gr. -1). 17.95 *(978-1-59270-151-3(5))* Enchanted Lion Bks., LLC.

Duval, Kathy. A Bear's Year. Turley, Gerry, illus. 2015. (ENG.). 40p. (J). (gr. -1-2). 17.99 *(978-0-385-37011-0(3),* Schwartz & Wade Bks.) Random Hse. Children's Bks.

Eastman, P. D. Aaron Loves Apples & Pumpkins. 2015. (Step into Reading Ser.). (ENG., Illus.). 32p. (J). (gr. -1-1). 12.99 *(978-0-553-51235-9(8),* Random Hse. Bks. for Young Readers) Random Hse. Children's Bks.

Ehlert, Lois. Leaf Man. 2014. (ENG., Illus.). 40p. (J). (gr. -1-3). 26.99 *(978-0-544-33916-3(9),* HMH Books For Young Readers) Houghton Mifflin Harcourt Publishing Co.

Emanuel, Effie Ann. Charles Chameleon. 2007. 32p. per. 24.95 *(978-1-4241-8621-1(8))* America Star Bks.

Espluga, Maria. I, Farmer: Yo, Campesino. 2009. (SPA & ENG.). 28p. (J). 13.95 *(978-1-931398-54-1(2))* Me+Mi Publishing.

Estes, Don. Willy & Friends traveling through the Seasons: The continuing story of Willy the little fire Jeep. Glass, Eric, illus. 2006. (J). *(978-1-883551-75-9(7),* Maple Corners Press) Attic Studio Publishing Hse.

Félix, Lucie. Apples & Robins. 2016. (ENG., Illus.). 56p. (J). (gr. k-3). 16.99 *(978-1-4521-3264-8(X))* Chronicle Bks. LLC.

Ferrier, Fhiona, et al. Wake up, Spring. Ferrier, Katherine, illus. 2015. (ENG.). 40p. (J). (gr. 2-5). 26.65 *(978-1-4677-8584-6(9),* Graphic Universe™) Lerner Publishing Group.

Finch, Keith. Poppy Cat's Garden. Jones, Lara, illus. 2008. (ENG.). 8p. (J). (gr. 3-6). bds. 16.95 *(978-0-230-01715-3(0),* Macmillan) Pan Macmillan GBR. Dist: Trans-Atlantic Pubns., Inc.

Florian, Douglas. The Curious Cares of Bears. Sánchez, Sonia, illus. 2017. (ENG.). 32p. (J). (gr. -1-3). 16.99 ***(978-1-4998-0462-1(8))*** Little Bee Books Inc.

The Four Seasons. 2016. (Four Seasons Ser.). 24p. (gr. 1-1). 94.40 *(978-1-4994-2436-2(1));* pap. 33.00 *(978-1-4994-2490-4(6))* Rosen Publishing Group, Inc., The. (PowerKids Pr.).

Fraggalosch, Audrey. Let's Explore, Moose! Forest, Crista, illus. 2005. (ENG.). 32p. (J). (gr. -1-1). pap. 3.95 *(978-1-59249-151-3(0),* S2017) Soundprints.

Fritz, Jean & dePaola, Tomie. Bunny Hopwell's First Spring. Dixon, Rachel, illus. 2015. (G&d Vintage Ser.). (ENG.). 32p. (J). (gr. -1-k). bds. 7.99 *(978-0-448-48463-1(3),* Grosset & Dunlap) Penguin Young Readers Group.

Frost, Helen. Applesauce Weather. Bates, Amy June, illus. 2016. (ENG.). 112p. (J). (gr. 3-7). 14.99 *(978-0-7636-7576-9(8))* Candlewick Pr.

George, Lynn. The Leaf Pile. 2006. (Neighborhood Readers Ser.). (ENG.). 16p. (gr. 1-3). pap. 6.50 *(978-1-4042-7120-3(1),* Rosen Classroom) Rosen Publishing Group, Inc., The.

Gershator, Phillis. Listen, Listen. Jay, Alison, illus. 2007. (ENG.). 32p. (J). (gr. -1-3). 16.99 *(978-1-84686-084-3(9))* Barefoot Bks., Inc.

Giuliano, Kevin. When I Was Young. 2010. 36p. pap. 18.99 *(978-1-4520-6314-0(1))* AuthorHouse.

Gravett, Emily. The Rabbit Problem. Gravett, Emily, illus. 2010. (ENG., Illus.). 32p. (J). (gr. -1-3). 17.99 *(978-1-4424-1255-2(0),* Simon & Schuster Bks. For Young Readers) Simon & Schuster Bks. For Young Readers.

Griffin, Adele & Sheinmel, Courtney. Agnes & Clarabelle. Palacios, Sara, illus. 2017. (Agnes & Clarabelle Ser.). (ENG.). 80p. (J). 9.99 *(978-1-61963-137-3(7),* 9781619631373, Bloomsbury USA Childrens) Bloomsbury Publishing USA.

Hall, Kirsten. Good Times: All about the Seasons. Luedecke, Bev, illus. 2004. (Beastieville Ser.). (J). 19.50 *(978-0-516-23648-3(2),* Children's Pr.) Scholastic Library Publishing.

Hall, Michael. Wonderfall. Hall, Michael, illus. 2016. (Illus.). 40p. (J). (gr. -1-3). 17.99 *(978-0-06-238298-6(5),* Greenwillow Bks.) HarperCollins Pubs.

Halperin, Wendy Anderson, et al. Peace. Halperin, Wendy Anderson, illus. 2013. (ENG., Illus.). 40p. (J). (gr. -1-3). 17.99 *(978-0-689-82552-1(8),* Atheneum Bks. for Young Readers) Simon & Schuster Children's Publishing.

Harris, Harris. Union Cross: New Seasons. 2013. 234p. (J). pap. 9.00 *(978-1-60039-202-3(4))* Lamp Post Inc.

Harris, Nicholas. A Year at a Farm. 2008. (Time Goes By Ser.). (ENG., Illus.). 24p. (gr. k-3). lib. bdg. 22.60 *(978-1-58013-553-5(6))* Lerner Publishing Group.

Harrison, Nicholas. A Year at a Farm. 2008. (Time Goes By Ser.). (ENG.). (gr. k-3). pap. 39.62 *(978-0-7613-4713-2(5))* Lerner Publishing Group.

Harshman, Marc & Ryan, Cheryl. Red Are the Apples. Zahares, Wade, illus. 2007. (ENG.). 32p. (J). (gr. -1-3). pap. 6.99 *(978-0-15-206065-7(0))* Houghton Mifflin Harcourt Publishing Co.

Henkes, Kevin. In the Middle of Fall. Dronzek, Laura, illus. 2017. 40p. (J). (gr. -1-3). 17.99 ***(978-0-06-257311-7(X),*** Collins Design) HarperCollins Pubs.

—Old Bear. Henkes, Kevin, illus. 2008. (Illus.). 32p. (J). (gr. -1-5). (ENG.). 17.99 *(978-0-06-155205-2(4));* lib. bdg. 18.89 *(978-0-06-155206-9(2))* HarperCollins Pubs. (Greenwillow Bks.).

—Old Bear Board Book. Henkes, Kevin, illus. 2011. (ENG., Illus.). 28p. (J). (gr. -1 — 1). bds. 7.99 *(978-0-06-208963-2(3),* Greenwillow Bks.) HarperCollins Pubs.

—When Spring Comes. Dronzek, Laura, illus. 2016. 40p. (J). (gr. -1-3). 18.89 *(978-0-06-233140-3(X),* Collins Design) HarperCollins Pubs.

Hensel, Rita. Humble Stew in Going Country. 2008. 41p. pap. 24.95 *(978-1-60563-219-3(8))* America Star Bks.

Hillert, Margaret. It's Fall, Dear Dragon. Schimmell, David, illus. 2009. (BeginningtoRead Ser.). 32p. (J). (gr. k-2). lib. bdg. 22.60 *(978-1-59953-311-7(1))* Norwood Hse. Pr.

Holland, Loretta. Fall Leaves. MacKay, Elly, illus. 2014. (ENG.). 32p. (J). (gr. -1-3). 16.99 *(978-0-544-10664-2(4),* HMH Books For Young Readers) Houghton Mifflin Harcourt Publishing Co.

Holloway, Jamie. Let's Go Pumpkin Picking. 2015. (Rosen REAL Readers: STEM & STEAM Collection). (ENG.). 8p. pap. 5.46 *(978-1-4994-9542-3(0),* Rosen Classroom) Rosen Publishing Group, Inc., The.

Holmes, Ardy. 4 Seasons of Color. 2007. 48p. per. 16.95 *(978-1-4241-7249-8(7))* America Star Bks.

Horácek, Petr. A Surprise for Tiny Mouse. Horácek, Petr, illus. 2015. (ENG., Illus.). 16p. (J). (— 1). bds. 8.99 *(978-0-7636-7967-5(4))* Candlewick Pr.

Huisingh, Rosemary. Vocabulary Stories for Toddlers: Seasons. 2012. (Illus.). *(978-0-7606-1348-1(6))* LinguiSystems, Inc.

Hurst, Elva. Autumn Days: Based on a True Story. 2015. (Farm Life Ser.). (ENG., Illus.). 80p. (J). pap. 6.99 *(978-0-7369-6094-6(5))* Harvest Hse. Pubs.

—When School Bells Call: Based on a True Story. 2015. (Farm Life Ser.). (ENG.). 80p. (J). pap. 6.99 *(978-0-7369-6092-2(9))* Harvest Hse. Pubs.

Igl, Janeane. Winter, Spring, Summer, Fall: (A Sing-Song Book) 2008. 20p. pap. 24.95 *(978-1-60563-279-7(1))* America Star Bks.

Iwamuara, Kazuo. Hooray for Fall! Iwamuara, Kazuo, illus. 2009. (ENG., Illus.). 32p. (J). (gr. -1-3). 16.95 *(978-0-7358-2252-8(2))* North-South Bks., Inc.

Jay, Alison & Gershator, Phillis. Listen, Listen. 2008. (ENG., Illus.). 32p. (J). (gr. -1-k). 14.99 *(978-1-84686-201-4(9))* Barefoot Bks., Inc.

Jones, Francesca & Jones, Frankie. Where's the Pumpkin? Galloway, Fhiona, illus. 2015. (ENG.). 16p. (J). (gr. -1 — 1). bds. 5.99 *(978-1-4998-0097-5(5))* Little Bee Books Inc.

Jones, Frankie. Fall Is Here! Galloway, Fhiona, illus. 2015. (ENG.). 16p. (J). (gr. -1-k). bds. 5.99 *(978-1-4998-0110-1(6))* Little Bee Books Inc.

Jordan, Apple. A Fairy-Tale Fall. Legramandi, Francesco, illus. 2010. (Step into Reading Ser.). (ENG.). 32p. (J). (gr. k-3). pap. 3.99 *(978-0-7364-2674-9(4),* RH/Disney) Random Hse. Children's Bks.

—A Fairy-Tale Fall. 2010. (Disney Princess Step into Reading Ser.). lib. bdg. 13.55 *(978-0-606-14879-5(5),* Turtleback) Turtleback Bks.

Katz, Karen. Baby Loves Fall! A Karen Katz Lift-The-Flap Book. Katz, Karen, illus. 2013. (ENG., Illus.). 14p. (J). (gr. -1 — 1). bds. 6.99 *(978-1-4424-5209-1(9),* Little Simon) Little Simon.

Keeler, Renee, illus. Seasons. 2006. (Learn to Write Ser.). 8p. (J). (gr. k-2). pap. 3.49 *(978-1-59198-291-3(X),* 6185) Creative Teaching Pr., Inc.

King-Chai, Sharon. Lucy Ladybug. 2016. (ENG., Illus.). 32p. (J). (gr. -1-2). 16.99 *(978-0-553-51005-8(3),* Random Hse. Bks. for Young Readers) Random Hse. Children's Bks.

Kirk, Daniel. The Thing about Spring. 2015. (ENG., Illus.). 32p. (J). (gr. -1-3). 16.95 *(978-1-4197-1492-4(9),* Abrams Bks. for Young Readers) Abrams, Inc.

Kondrchek, Jamie & Rasemas, Joe. What Should I Wear Today? (Que Ropa Me Pondre Hoy?) Vega, Eida de la, tr. Rasemas, Joe, illus. 2009. (Day in the Life Ser.). (ENG & SPA., Illus.). 32p. (J). (gr. -1-1). 25.70 *(978-1-58415-839-4(5))* Mitchell Lane Pubs., Inc.

Koopmans, Loek. Frog, Bee & Snail Look for Snow, 1 vol. 2006. Orig. Title: Samen Op Zoek. (ENG., Illus.). 28p. (J). (gr. -1-3). 15.95 *(978-0-86315-559-8(6))* Floris Bks. GBR. Dist: SteinerBooks, Inc.

Kosinski, Colleen Rowan, illus. Lilla's Sunflowers. 2016. (ENG.). 32p. (J). (gr. -1-k). 16.99 *(978-1-5107-0464-0(7),* Sky Pony Pr.) Skyhorse Publishing Co., Inc.

Kroner, David & Du Houx, Ramona. Seasons. Du Houx, E. M. Cornell, illus. 2007. 70p. (J). per. 6.95 *(978-1-882190-54-6(8))* Polar Bear & Co.

Kruusval, Catarina. Ellen's Apple Tree. Sandin, Joan, tr. from SWE. 2008. (Illus.). 32p. (J). (gr. -1-3). 16.00 *(978-91-29-66905-3(7))* R & S Bks. SWE. Dist: Macmillan.

LaMarche, Jim. Pond. LaMarche, Jim, illus. 2016. (ENG., Illus.). 40p. (J). (gr. -1-3). 17.99 *(978-1-4814-4735-5(1),* Simon & Schuster/Paula Wiseman Bks.) Simon & Schuster/Paula Wiseman Bks.

Las Cuatro Estaciones / the Four Seasons. 2016. (Las Cuatro Estaciones / the Four Seasons Ser.). (ENG & SPA.). 24p. (gr. 1-1). 94.40 *(978-1-4994-2467-6(1),* PowerKids Pr.) Rosen Publishing Group, Inc., The.

Leahy, Sandy & Tarentino, Kathy. The Hibernating House. 2013. 26p. 19.95 *(978-1-4575-1753-2(1));* pap. 12.95 *(978-1-4575-1670-2(5))* Dog Ear Publishing, LLC.

Lee, Nancy. Hoover's Funny Little Kids. 2005. (J). spiral bd. 8.95 *(978-0-9748087-8-9(4))* Journey Pubns., LLC.

Lenart, Claudia, illus. Seasons of Joy: Every Day Is for Outdoor Play. 2017. (J). pap. ***(978-1-61599-317-8(7))*** Loving Healing Pr., Inc.

Levine, Rhoda. Arthur. Alison, Everett, illus. 2015. (ENG.). 48p. (J). (gr. -1-2). 15.95 *(978-1-59017-935-2(8),* NYR Children's Collection) New York Review of Bks., Inc., The.

Lin, Grace. Ling & Ting: Together in All Weather. 2015. (ENG., Illus.). 48p. (J). (gr. 1-4). 16.00 *(978-0-316-33549-2(5))* Little Brown & Co.

—Ling & Ting: Together in All Weather. 2016. (Passport to Reading Level 3 Ser.). (J). lib. bdg. 14.75 *(978-0-606-39187-0(8))* Turtleback Bks.

—Ling & Ting: Together in All Weather. 2016. (ENG.). 48p. (J). (gr. 1-4). pap. 4.99 *(978-0-316-33548-5(7))* Little, Brown Bks. for Young Readers.

Lister, Mary. Winter King, Summer Queen. Mayo, Diana, illus. 2007. (ENG.). 32p. (J). (gr. -1-3). pap. 7.99 *(978-1-84686-080-5(6));* pap. 9.99 *(978-1-84686-009-6(1))* Barefoot Bks., Inc.

Lloyd-Jones, Sally. Bunny's First Spring, 1 vol. McPhail, David, illus. 2015. (ENG.). 32p. (J). 16.99 *(978-0-310-73386-7(3))* Zonderkidz.

Long, Loren. Little Tree. Long, Loren, illus. 2015. (ENG., Illus.). 40p. (J). (gr. k-3). 17.99 *(978-0-399-16397-5(2),* Philomel Bks.) Penguin Young Readers Group.

Maass, Robert. A Is for Autumn. Maass, Robert, photos by. 2011. (ENG., Illus.). 32p. (J). (gr. -1-1). 16.99 *(978-0-8050-9093-2(2),* 9780805090932, Holt, Henry & Co. Bks. For Young Readers) Holt, Henry & Co.

Mackall, Dandi. Wonderful Gifts of Winter. Blackmore, Katherine, illus. (Seasons Ser.). (ENG.). 32p. (gr. -1-3). 2017. (J). pap. 3.99 ***(978-1-4627-4524-1(5))*** 2014. 9.99 *(978-1-4336-8239-1(7))* B&H Publishing Group. (B&H Kids).

Mahoney, Liana. Forest Green: A Walk Through the Adirondack Seasons. Henry, Maggie, illus. 2014. (J). *(978-1-59531-047-7(9))* North Country Bks., Inc.

Manushkin, Fran. Best Season Ever, 1 vol. Lyon, Tammie, illus. 2010. (Katie Woo Ser.). (ENG.). 32p. (gr. k-2). lib. bdg. 21.32 *(978-1-4048-5730-8(3))* Picture Window Bks.

Marino Walters, Jennifer. Amazing Autumn. Nez, John, illus. 2016. (Seasons Ser.). (ENG.). 24p. (J). (gr. -1-1). lib. bdg. 25.32 *(978-1-63440-045-9(3))* Red Chair Pr.

Martin, David. Shh! Bears Sleeping. Johnson, Steve & Fancher, Lou, illus. 2016. (ENG.). 32p. (J). (gr. -1-2). 16.99 *(978-0-670-01718-8(3),* Viking Books for Young Readers) Penguin Young Readers Group.

Matheson, Christie. Tap the Magic Tree. Matheson, Christie, illus. 2013. (ENG., Illus.). 40p. (J). (gr. -1-3). 16.99 *(978-0-06-227445-8(7),* Greenwillow Bks.) HarperCollins Pubs.

Mayer, Mercer. The Fall Festival. 2012. (Illus.). 32p. (J). *(978-0-06-222992-2(3)); (978-1-4351-4384-5(1))* HarperCollins Pubs.

McAllister, Angela. Winter's Child. Baker-Smith, Grahame, illus. 2015. (ENG.). 40p. (J). (gr. -1-2). 16.99 *(978-0-7636-7964-4(X),* Templar) Candlewick Pr.

McBratney, Sam. Guess How Much I Love You All Year Round. Jeram, Anita, illus. 2010. (Guess How Much I Love You Ser.). (ENG.). 72p. (J). (gr. -1-2). 16.99 *(978-0-7636-4654-7(7))* Candlewick Pr.

—Guess How Much I Love You Coloring Book. Jeram, Anita, illus. 2017. (Guess How Much I Love You Ser.). (ENG.). 96p. (J). (gr. k-12). pap. 7.99 *(978-0-7636-9467-8(3))* Candlewick Pr.

—A Surprise for the Nutbrown Hares. Jeram, Anita, illus. 2009. (J). *(978-0-7636-4903-6(1))* Candlewick Pr.

McCarty, Peter. Fall Ball. McCarty, Peter, illus. 2013. (ENG., Illus.). 32p. (J). (gr. -1-3). 16.99 *(978-0-8050-9253-0(6),* 9780805092530, Holt, Henry & Co. Bks. For Young Readers) Holt, Henry & Co.

Mcghee, Alison. Making a Friend. Rosenthal, Marc, illus. 2011. (ENG.). 40p. (J). (gr. -1-3). 16.99 *(978-1-4169-8998-1(6),* Atheneum Bks. for Young Readers) Simon & Schuster Children's Publishing.

McNamara, Margaret. Fall Leaf Project. Gordon, Mike, illus. 2006. (Robin Hill School Ser.). (ENG.). 32p. (J). (gr. -1-1). pap. 3.99 *(978-1-4169-1537-9(0),* Simon Spotlight) Simon Spotlight.

Menge, Dawn & Rhoades, Heath. Queen Vernita Meets Sir HeathyBean the Astronomer. 2010. 33p. (J). pap. 19.95 *(978-1-4327-3120-5(3))* Outskirts Pr., Inc.

Messersmith, Heather. Seasons. 2005. pap. 23.50 *(978-1-4208-6698-8(2))* AuthorHouse.

Metzger, Steve. I Love You All Year Long. Keay, Claire, illus. 2009. 20p. (J). (gr. -1-k). 8.95 *(978-1-58925-847-1(9))* Tiger Tales.

—We're Going on a Leaf Hunt. Sakamoto, Miki, illus. 2005. (J). pap. *(978-0-439-77361-4(X))* Scholastic, Inc.

Micklos, John. One Leaf, Two Leaves, Count with Me! McFarland, Clive, illus. 2017. (ENG.). 32p. (J). (— 1). 16.99 ***(978-0-399-54471-2(2),*** Nancy Paulsen Books) Penguin Young Readers Group.

Mills, Nathan & Francis, Bill. Hannah's Four Seasons. 2012. (Rosen Readers Ser.). (ENG., Illus.). 16p. (J). (gr. k-1). pap. 7.00 *(978-1-4488-8740-8(2),* Rosen Classroom) Rosen Publishing Group, Inc., The.

Mioduchowska, Anna. In Between Season. 67p. (J). 12.95 *(978-1-895836-56-1(5))* River Bks. CAN. Dist: Coteau Bks.

Moonah, Karen. Spring into Summer! 2012. (Cat in the Hat Knows a Lot about That Ser.). lib. bdg. 14.75 *(978-0-606-23849-6(2),* Turtleback) Turtleback Bks.

Moreel, Yvette. Whirly's Autumn Surprise. 2011. 44p. pap. 21.99 *(978-1-4628-9686-8(3))* Xlibris Corp.

Moroney, Tracey, illus. Little Fox's Surprise. 2015. (J). ***(978-0-545-84956-2(X))*** Scholastic, Inc.

Moss, Marissa. Amelia's 5th-Grade Notebook. Moss, Marissa, illus. 2006. (Amelia Ser.). (ENG., Illus.). 40p. (J). (gr. 2-5). 12.99 *(978-1-4169-0912-5(5),* Simon & Schuster/Paula Wiseman Bks.) Simon & Schuster/Paula Wiseman Bks.

Nettrour, Nelani. Jodi & the Seasons. Nettrour, Heather, illus. l.t. ed. 2004. 88p. pap. 11.95 *(978-1-932657-16-6(9))* Third Millennium Pubns.

Nicholas, Nicki. Peter & Lil's Amazing Autumn Day. 2011. 24p. (gr. 1-2). pap. 15.50 *(978-1-4269-6047-5(6))* Trafford Publishing.

O'Brien, Anne Sibley. Abracadabra, It's Spring! Gal, Susan, illus. 2016. (Seasonal Magic Ser.). (ENG.). 24p. (J). (gr. -1-k). 14.95 *(978-1-4197-1891-5(6),* Abrams Appleseed) Abrams, Inc.

—Hocus Pocus, It's Fall! Gal, Susan, illus. 2016. (ENG.). 24p. (J). (gr. -1-k). 12.95 *(978-1-4197-2125-0(9),* Abrams Appleseed) Abrams, Inc.

O'Connor, Jane. Fancy Nancy & the Fall Foliage. Glasser, Robin Preiss, illus. 2014. (Fancy Nancy Ser.). (ENG.). 24p. (J). (gr. -1-3). pap. 4.99 *(978-0-06-208630-3(8),* HarperFestival) HarperCollins Pubs.

O'Garden, Irene. Forest, What Would You Like? Schories, Pat, illus. 2013. (ENG.). 32p. (J). (gr. -1-3). 16.95 *(978-0-8234-2322-4(0))* Holiday Hse., Inc.

Owens, Katherine. Tree Seasons Ball, 1 bk. l.t. ed. 2004. (Illus.). 40p. (J). per. 19.99 *(978-0-9760419-0-0(1),* TREESEASONSBALL) ThatsMyLife Co.

Pak, Kenard. Goodbye Autumn, Hello Winter. Pak, Kenard, illus. 2017. (ENG., Illus.). 32p. (J). 17.99 **(978-1-62779-416-9(6)**, 9781627794169, Holt, Henry & Co. Bks. For Young Readers) Holt, Henry & Co.

Pak, Kenard. Goodbye Summer, Hello Autumn. Pak, Kenard, illus. 2016. (ENG., Illus.). 32p. (J). 17.99 *(978-1-62779-415-2(8)*, 9781627794152, Holt, Henry & Co. Bks. For Young Readers) Holt, Henry & Co.

Paradis, Anne. Baby Caillou Looks Around - The Seasons. 2014. (Baby Caillou Ser.). (ENG., Illus.). 10p. (J). bds. 6.99 *(978-2-89718-154-3(0))* Caillouet, Gerry.

Parker, Amy. Tiny Blessings: for All Seasons. Walsh, Sarah, illus. 2017. (ENG.). 10p. (J). (gr. -1 — 1). bds. 7.99 *(978-0-7624-6180-6(2)*, Running Pr.) Running Pr. Bk. Pubs.

Peschke, Marci. Daisy's Fall Festival, 1 vol., Bk. 4. Pilz, M. H., illus. 2011. (Growing up Daisy Ser.). (ENG.). 80p. (gr. 3-8). 27.07 *(978-1-61641-117-6(1)*, Calico Chapter Bks) Magic Wagon.

Plourde, Lynn. Bella's Fall Coat. Gal, Susan, illus. 2016. (ENG.). 40p. (J). (gr. -1-k). 17.99 *(978-1-4847-2697-6(9))* Disney Pr.

—Wild Child. 2003. 18.40 *(978-0-613-69321-9(3)*, Turtleback) Turtleback Bks.

Plourde, Lynn & Couch, Greg. Wild Child. 2003. (ENG., Illus.). 32p. (J). (gr. -1-3). 7.99 *(978-0-689-86349-3(7)*, Aladdin) Simon & Schuster Children's Publishing.

Polacco, Patricia. For the Love of Autumn. Polacco, Patricia, illus. 2008. (ENG., Illus.). 40p. (J). (gr. 1-4). 17.99 *(978-0-399-24541-1(3)*, Philomel Bks.) Penguin Young Readers Group.

Posner, Renee & Quinton, Sasha. Suzy Season Loves Spring. D'Argo, Laura, illus. (Be Mine Bears Ser.). (J). bds. 4.99 *(978-1-58209-350-5(4))* Bks. Are Fun, Ltd.

Precious Moments, Precious. Precious Moments: Happy Harvest, 1 vol. 2016. (ENG., Illus.). 32p. (J). bds. 9.99 *(978-0-7180-3241-8(1))* Nelson, Thomas Inc.

Prochovnic, Dawn Babb. Four Seasons! Five Senses! Sign Language for the Seasons & Senses, 1 vol. Bauer, Stephanie, illus. 2012. (ENG.). 32p. 28.50 *(978-1-61641-836-6(2)*, Looking Glass Library) Magic Wagon.

Pugliano-Martin, Carol. Glooscap Makes the Seasons: A Canadian Legend. 2006. (J). pap. *(978-1-4108-7159-6(2))* Benchmark Education Co.

—Ready for Fall! 2006. (Early Explorers Ser.). (J). pap. *(978-1-4108-6103-0(1))* Benchmark Education Co.

Quinlan, Nigel. The Weatherman. 2015. (ENG.). 320p. (J). (gr. 4-7). 16.99 *(978-1-62672-033-6(9)*, 9781626720336) Roaring Brook Pr.

Raczka, Bob. Fall Mixed Up. Cameron, Chad, illus. 2011. (Carolrhoda Picture Books Ser.). (ENG.). 40p. (J). (gr. -1-3). lib. bdg. 17.95 *(978-0-7613-4606-7(6)*, Carolrhoda Bks.) Lerner Publishing Group.

Rawlinson, Julia. Fletcher & the Falling Leaves. 2011. (J). (gr. -1-2). 18.95 *(978-0-545-19705-2(8))*; 29.95 *(978-0-545-19699-4(X))* Weston Woods Studios, Inc.

Remenar, Kristen. Groundhog's Dilemma. Faulkner, Matt, illus. 2015. (ENG.). 32p. (J). (gr. -1-2). lib. bdg. 16.95 *(978-1-58089-600-9(6))* Charlesbridge Publishing, Inc.

Rey, H. A. & Rey, Margret. Seasons. 2008. (Curious George Ser.). (ENG., Illus.). 10p. (J). (gr. -1 — 1). bds. 6.99 *(978-0-618-99848-7(9))* Houghton Mifflin Harcourt Publishing Co.

Rhode, Paul. Presents for Phoebe: Growing Independent. Margolis, Al, illus. 2011. 24p. (YA). pap. 9.95 *(978-1-935706-05-2(5))* Wiggles Pr.

Riggs, Kate. Colors of Nature. Domeniconi, Paolo, illus. 2017. (ENG.). 14p. (J). (gr. -1 — 1). bds. 8.99 *(978-1-56846-299-8(9)*, Creative Education) Creative Co., The.

Rim, Sujean. Birdie's Happiest Halloween. 2016. (ENG., Illus.). 40p. (J). (gr. -1-3). 16.99 *(978-0-316-40746-5(1))* Little Brown & Co.

Ringler, Matt. It's Fall! Shearing, Leonie, illus. 2006. 28p. (J). pap. *(978-0-439-87146-4(8))* Scholastic, Inc.

—One Little, Two Little, Three Little Apples. Kennedy, Anne, illus. 2005. (J). pap. *(978-0-439-77500-7(0))* Scholastic, Inc.

Rockwell, Anne. Apples & Pumpkins. Rockwell, Lizzy, illus. 2014. (Classic Board Bks.). (ENG.). 28p. (J). (gr. -1-k). bds. 7.99 *(978-1-4424-9977-5(X)*, Little Simon) Little Simon.

Rockwell, Anne F. Apples & Pumpkins. Rockwell, Lizzy, illus. 2012. (ENG.). 24p. (J). (gr. -1-3). 5.99 *(978-1-4424-7656-1(7)*, Aladdin) Simon & Schuster Children's Publishing.

Rodhe, Paul & Wallas Reidy, Sarah. The Little Plum Tree. Margolis, Al & Young, Bill, illus. 2010. 24p. (J). pap. 9.95 *(978-1-935706-06-9(3))* Wiggles Pr.

Rohmann, Eric. A Kitten Tale. 2012. (ENG.). 32p. (J). (gr. -1-2). pap. 7.99 *(978-0-307-97774-8(9)*, Dragonfly Bks.) Random Hse. Children's Bks.

Rosas, Heather. Red Riding Hood's Rainbow. 2009. (ENG.). 16p. (J). bds. 8.95 *(978-1-58117-863-0(8)*, Intervisual/Piggy Toes) Bendon, Inc.

Rosen, Michael J. The Forever Flowers. Danowski, Sonja, illus. 2014. (ENG.). 32p. (J). (gr. 1-3). 18.99 *(978-1-56846-273-8(5)*, Creative Editions) Creative Co., The.

Rosenstiehl, Agnes. Silly Lilly & the Four Seasons, 1 vol. 2013. (Toon Bks). (ENG.). 36p. (J). (gr. k-1). lib. bdg. 27.07 *(978-1-61479-155-3(4))* Spotlight.

—Silly Lilly & the Four Seasons. 2013. (ENG., Illus.). 32p. (J). (gr. -1-3). pap. 4.99 *(978-1-935179-23-8(3))* TOON Books / RAW Junior, LLC.

—Silly Lilly & the Four Seasons. Mouly, Francoise, ed. 2008. (ENG., Illus.). 36p. (J). (gr. -1-3). 12.95 *(978-0-9799238-1-4(6))* TOON Books / RAW Junior, LLC.

Rossiter, Nan Parson. The Fo'c'sle: Henry Beston's Outermost House. 2012. (Illus.). 32p. (J). (gr. 5-18). 17.95 *(978-1-56792-433-6(6))* Godine, David R. Pub.

Ruffenach, Jessie, ed. Baby Learns about Seasons. Thomas, Peter, tr. from ENG. Blacksheep, Beverly, illus. 2005. (NAV & ENG.). 16p. (J). (gr. 4-7). 7.95 *(978-1-893354-61-6(X))* Salina Bookshelf Inc.

Rylant, Cynthia. In November. Kastner, Jill, illus. 2014. 32p. pap. 7.00 *(978-1-61003-180-6(6))* Center for the Collaborative Classroom.

—In November. Kastner, Jill, illus. 2008. (ENG.). 32p. (J). (gr. -1-3). pap. 6.99 *(978-0-15-206342-9(0))* Houghton Mifflin Harcourt Publishing Co.

—Mr. Putter & Tabby Ring the Bell. Howard, Arthur, illus. (Mr. Putter & Tabby Ser.). (ENG.). 44p. (J). (gr. 1-4). 2012. pap. 5.99 *(978-0-547-85075-7(1))* 2011. 14.99 *(978-0-15-205071-9(X))* Houghton Mifflin Harcourt Publishing Co.

Rylant, Cynthia & Siegel, Mark. Long Night Moon. Siegel, Mark, illus. 2004. (ENG., Illus.). 32p. (J). (gr. -1-3). 17.99 *(978-0-689-85426-2(9)*, Simon & Schuster Bks. For Young Readers) Simon & Schuster Bks. For Young Readers.

Ryski, Dawid. My Four Seasons. 2017. (ENG., Illus.). 32p. (J). (gr. -1-3). 19.95 **(978-3-89955-784-8(0))** Die Gestalten Verlag DEU. Dist: Penguin Random Hse. LLC.

Sanna, Alessandro, creator. The River. 2014. (ENG., Illus.). 110p. (J). (gr. k). 22.95 *(978-1-59270-149-0(3))* Enchanted Lion Bks., LLC.

Sargent, David M., Jr. Autumn's Emergency. Huff, Jeane Lirley, illus. 2003. (Doggie Tails Ser.). 32p. (J). lib. bdg. 19.95 *(978-1-56763-845-5(7))* Ozark Publishing.

Savard, Remi, et al. First Spring: An Innu Tale of North America. 2006. (ENG., Illus.). 44p. (J). (gr. -1-k). 16.95 *(978-1-894965-34-7(5))* Simply Read Bks. CAN. Dist: Ingram Publisher Services.

Scarry, Richard. Richard Scarry's Best Busy Year Ever. 2011. (ENG., Illus.). 72p. (J). (gr. -1-2). 12.95 *(978-1-4027-7219-1(X))* Sterling Publishing Co., Inc.

Schertle, Alice. Such a Little Mouse. Yue, Stephanie, illus. 2015. (ENG.). 32p. (J). (gr. -1-k). 16.99 *(978-0-545-64929-2(3))* Scholastic, Inc.

—Very Hairy Bear. Phelan, Matt, illus. 2012. lib. bdg. 17.20 *(978-0-606-26605-5(4)*, Turtleback) Turtleback Bks.

Scholastic, Inc. Staff. Peppa's Windy Fall Day. 2015. (Peppa Pig 8X8 Ser.). (Illus.). (J). lib. bdg. 13.55 *(978-0-606-37088-2(9))* Turtleback Bks.

Scholastic, Inc. Staff, contrib. by. The Seasons. 2014. (Rookie Toddler(r) Ser.). (ENG.). 12p. (J). bds. 6.95 *(978-0-531-20914-1(8))* Scholastic Library Publishing.

Schram, Peninnah & Davis, Rachayl Eckstein. The Apple Tree's Discovery. Lee, Wendy W., illus. 2012. (Kar-Ben Favorites Ser.). (ENG.). 24p. (J). (gr. -1-2). pap. 7.95 *(978-0-7613-5132-0(9))*; lib. bdg. 16.95 *(978-0-7613-5130-6(2))* Lerner Publishing Group. (Kar-Ben Publishing).

Singleton, Linda Joy. Snow Dog, Sand Dog. Golden, Jess, illus. 2014. (ENG.). 32p. (J). (gr. -1-3). 16.99 *(978-0-8075-7536-9(4))* Whitman, Albert & Co.

Slegers, Liesbet. Fall Leaves. 2012. (Clavis Toddler: Daily Life Ser.). (ENG.). 12p. (J). (gr. k — 1). bds. 5.95 *(978-1-60537-122-1(X))* Cobblestone Publishing Co.

Spinelli, Eileen. I Know It's Autumn. Hayashi, Nancy, tr. Hayashi, Nancy, illus. 2004. 32p. (J). (gr. -1-2). lib. bdg. 17.89 *(978-0-06-029423-6(X))* HarperCollins Pubs.

—Now It Is Summer. DePalma, Mary Newell, illus. 2011. (ENG.). 36p. (YA). (gr. -1-3). 16.00 *(978-0-8028-5340-0(4)*, Eerdmans Bks For Young Readers) Eerdmans, William B. Publishing Co.

Spinelli, Eileen & Spinelli. I Know It's Autumn. Hayashi, Nancy, tr. Hayashi, Nancy, illus. 2004. (ENG.). 32p. (J). (gr. -1-2). 16.99 *(978-0-06-029422-9(1))* HarperCollins Pubs.

Steers, Billy. Tractor Mac Harvest Time. 2015. (Tractor Mac Ser.). (ENG., Illus.). 32p. (J). (gr. -1-2). 8.99 *(978-0-374-30111-8(5)*, 9780374301118, Farrar, Straus & Giroux (BYR)) Farrar, Straus & Giroux.

Steggall, Susan. Following the Tractor. 2015. (ENG., Illus.). 32p. (J). pap. 8.99 *(978-1-84780-657-4(0)*, Frances Lincoln) Quarto Publishing Group UK GBR. Dist: Littlehampton Bk Services, Ltd.

Stein, David Ezra. Leaves. Stein, David Ezra, illus. (ENG., Illus.). (J). (gr. -1 — 1). 2010. 30p. bds. 6.99 *(978-0-399-25497-0(8))* 2007. 32p. 16.99 *(978-0-399-24636-4(3))* Penguin Young Readers Group. (G.P. Putnam's Sons Books for Young Readers).

Stringer, Lauren. Winter Is the Warmest Season. 2006. (ENG., Illus.). 40p. (J). (gr. -1-3). 16.99 *(978-0-15-204967-6(3))* Houghton Mifflin Harcourt Publishing Co.

Stringer, Lauren, illus. Yellow Time. 2016. (ENG.). 40p. (J). (gr. -1-3). 17.99 *(978-1-4814-3156-9(0)*, Beach Lane Bks.) Beach Lane Bks.

SungJa, Cho. Bubbly & Grumpy. SukWon, Sa, illus. rev. ed. 2014. (MySELF Bookshelf Ser.). (ENG.). 32p. (J). (gr. k-2). pap. 11.94 *(978-1-60357-660-4(6))* Norwood Hse. Pr.

Symons, Brandy. Lemonade Kisses. 2009. 24p. pap. 12.95 *(978-1-4389-7251-0(2))* AuthorHouse.

Teckentrup, Britta. Tree: A Peek-Through Picture Book. 2016. (ENG.). 32p. (J). (gr. -1-2). 14.99 *(978-1-101-93242-1(2)*, Doubleday Bks. for Young Readers) Random Hse. Children's Bks.

Thompson, Lauren. Mouse's First Fall. Erdogan, Buket, illus. 2010. (Classic Board Bks.). (ENG.). 34p. (J). (gr. -1 — 1). bds. 7.99 *(978-1-4169-9477-0(7)*, Little Simon) Little Simon.

Thornhill, Jan. Winter's Coming: A Story of Seasonal Change. Bisaillon, Josée, illus. 2014. (ENG.). 32p. (J). (gr. k-4). 16.95 *(978-1-77147-002-5(X)*, Owlkids) Owlkids Bks. Inc. CAN. Dist: Publishers Group West (PGW).

Tickle, Jessica Courtney, illus. Four Seasons in One Day. 2016. (Story Orchestra Ser.). (ENG.). 24p. (J). (gr. 1-4). 22.99 *(978-1-84780-877-6(8)*, Frances Lincoln Children's Bks.) Quarto Publishing Group UK GBR. Dist: Hachette Bk. Group.

Trinco, Trish. The Leaf That Wouldn't Leave. Langdo, Bryan, illus. 2008. (ENG.). 32p. (J). 16.95 *(978-0-931674-90-7(5)*, Waldman House Pr.) TRISTAN Publishing, Inc.

Wallace, Nancy Elizabeth. Leaves! Leaves! Leaves!, 1 vol. 2003. (ENG., Illus.). 32p. (J). 16.95 *(978-0-7614-5140-2(4))* Marshall Cavendish Corp.

Walsh, Susanne. My Very Favorite Time of Year: Featuring the Whimsy Kids. 2007. 34p. pap. 24.95 *(978-1-4241-9090-4(8))* America Star Bks.

Walters, Jennifer Marino. Amazing Autumn. Nez, John, illus. 2016. (Seasons Ser.). (ENG.). 24p. (J). (gr. -1-1). pap. 6.99 *(978-1-63440-120-3(4))* Red Chair Pr.

Waters, Tony. Cinnamon's Busy Year. Waters, Tony, illus. 2003. (Illus.). 32p. (J). (gr. -1-3). pap. 5.95 *(978-0-9710278-2-4(X))* All About Kids Publishing.

Watt, Fiona. Hide-and-Seek Bunnies. Danson, Lesley, illus. 2007. (Touchy-Feely Flap Bks). 10p. (J). (gr. -1-k). bds. 16.99 *(978-0-7945-1566-9(5)*, Usborne) EDC Publishing.

Wayne, Viv. Bloom Where You Are Planted: A garden story about overcoming your Challenges. 2012. 28p. pap. 19.99 *(978-1-4685-4791-7(7))* AuthorHouse.

Weiss, Ellen. Winter Spring Summer Fall: A Touch-and-Feel Seasons Book. Bennett, Andy, illus. 2006. (PBS Kids Ser.). 8p. (J). (gr. -1-k). bds. 6.95 *(978-1-57791-312-2(4))* Brighter Minds Children's Publishing.

Wellington, Monica. My Leaf Book. 2015. (ENG., Illus.). 32p. (J). (gr. -1-k). 16.99 *(978-0-8037-4141-6(3)*, Dial Bks) Penguin Young Readers Group.

Weston Woods Staff, creator. Fletcher & the Falling Leaves. 2011. 38.75 *(978-0-545-19710-6(4))* Weston Woods Studios, Inc.

—In the Small, Small Pond. 2011. 38.75 *(978-0-439-84578-6(5))* Weston Woods Studios, Inc.

—Inch by Inch. 2011. 38.75 *(978-0-439-90543-5(5))* Weston Woods Studios, Inc.

Williams, Rozanne Lanczak. Seasons. Maio, Barbara & Faulkner, Stacey, eds. 2006. (J). per. 6.99 *(978-1-59198-342-2(8))* Creative Teaching Pr., Inc.

Wilson, Pamela J. Tales from Tubblewood Too. 2009. (Illus.). 164p. 23.50 *(978-1-4389-4064-9(5))* AuthorHouse.

—Tales from Tubblewood Too: Miss Duck to the Rescue. 2009. (Illus.). 164p. pap. 13.50 *(978-1-4389-4063-2(7))* AuthorHouse.

Wilson, Steve. Hedgehugs: Autumn Hide-And-Squeak. Tapper, Lucy, illus. 2017. (Hedgehugs Ser.). (ENG.). 32p. (J). 16.99 **(978-1-250-11248-4(6)**, 9781250112484, Holt, Henry & Co. Bks. For Young Readers) Holt, Henry & Co.

Wright, Maureen. Sneeze, Big Bear, Sneeze!, 0 vols. Hillenbrand, Will, illus. 2011. (ENG.). 32p. (J). (gr. -1-3). 16.99 *(978-0-7614-5959-0(6)*, 9780761459590, Amazon Children's Publishing) Amazon Publishing.

Yee, Wong Herbert. My Autumn Book. Yee, Wong Herbert, illus. 2015. (ENG., Illus.). 32p. (J). (gr. -1-1). 14.99 *(978-0-8050-9922-5(0)*, 9780805099225, Holt, Henry & Co. Bks. For Young Readers) Holt, Henry & Co.

Yolen, Jane. Sing a Season Song. Ashlock, Lisel Jane, illus. 2015. (ENG.). 48p. (J). (gr. 1-3). 19.99 *(978-1-56846-255-4(7)*, Creative Editions) Creative Co., The.

Yoon, Salina. Penguin & Pumpkin. 2014. (Penguin Ser.). (ENG., Illus.). 40p. (J). (gr. -1-1). 14.99 *(978-0-8027-3732-8(3)*, 9780802737328, Bloomsbury USA Childrens) Bloomsbury Publishing USA.

—Penguin & Pumpkin. 2014. (Illus.). (J). *(978-0-8027-3770-0(6))* Walker & Co.

Zolotow, Charlotte. Say It! Voake, Charlotte, illus. 2015. (ENG.). 32p. (J). (-k). 15.99 *(978-0-7636-8115-9(6))* Candlewick Pr.

SEASONS—POETRY

Diaz, David, illus. Sharing the Seasons: A Book of Poems. 2010. (ENG.). 96p. (J). (gr. 3-7). 24.99 *(978-1-4169-0210-2(4)*, McElderry, Margaret K. Bks.) McElderry, Margaret K. Bks.

Franco, Betsy & Salerno, Steven. Mathematickles! 2006. (Illus.). (gr. k-5). 18.00 *(978-0-7569-6709-3(0))* Perfection Learning Corp.

Giovanni, Nikki. The Sun Is So Quiet. Bryan, Ashley, illus. 2014. (ENG.). 32p. (J). (gr. -1-3). 8.99 *(978-1-250-04669-7(6)*, 9781250046697) Square Fish.

Jenkins, Ellie, illus. Poems for the Seasons. 2017. (Poems Just for Me Ser.). 32p. (gr. 7-8). 27.25 **(978-1-4994-8387-1(2)**, Windmill Bks.) Rosen Publishing Group, Inc., The.

Low, Elizabeth Cothen. Big Book of Seasons, Holidays, & Weather: Rhymes, Fingerplays, & Songs for Children. 2011. (ENG., Illus.). 156p. E-Book *(978-1-59884-624-9(8)*, Libraries Unlimited) ABC-CLIO, LLC.

Mackall, Dandi. The Fantastic Gifts of Fall. 2014. (Seasons Ser.). (ENG., Illus.). 32p. (J). (gr. -1-3). 9.99 *(978-1-4336-8237-7(0)*, B&H Kids) B&H Publishing Group.

Muth, Jon J. Hi, Koo! A Year of Seasons. 2014. (ENG., Illus.). 32p. (J). (gr. -1-3). 17.99 *(978-0-545-16668-3(3)*, Scholastic Pr.) Scholastic, Inc.

O'Rourke, Ryan, illus. One Big Rain: Poems for Every Season. 2014. (ENG.). 32p. (J). (gr. 2-5). pap. 7.95 *(978-1-57091-717-2(5))* Charlesbridge Publishing, Inc.

Raczka, Bob & Reynolds, Peter H. Guyku: A Year of Haiku for Boys. Reynolds, Peter H., illus. 2010. (ENG., Illus.). 48p. (J). (gr. -1-3). 16.99 *(978-0-547-24003-9(1))* Houghton Mifflin Harcourt Publishing Co.

Seasons Come Seasons Go. 2nd ed. 2005. per. *(978-0-9763958-0-5(0))* Aceybee Publishing.

Sidman, Joyce. Red Sings from Treetops: A Year in Colors. Zagarenski, Pamela, illus. 2009. (ENG.). 32p. (J). (gr. -1-3). 17.99 *(978-0-547-01494-4(5))* Houghton Mifflin Harcourt Publishing Co.

—Red Sings from Treetops: A Year in Colors. 2010. (J). 38.75 *(978-1-4498-2608-6(3))*; 36.75 *(978-1-4498-2606-2(7))*; 184.75 *(978-1-4498-2605-5(9))*; 36.75 *(978-1-4498-2610-9(5))* Recorded Bks., Inc.

Siebert, Diane. Spring, Summer, Autumn, Winter. Burckhardt, Marc, illus. 2005. (J). *(978-1-59336-299-7(4))*; pap. *(978-1-59336-300-0(1))* Mondo Publishing.

Thomas, Patricia. Nature's Paintbox: A Seasonal Gallery of Art & Verse. Orback, Craig, illus. 2007. (Millbrook Picture Books Ser.). (ENG.). 32p. (J). (gr. 2-4). lib. bdg. 16.95 *(978-0-8225-6807-0(1)*, Millbrook Pr.) Lerner Publishing Group.

Zolotow, Charlotte. Changes: A Child's First Poetry Collection. Beeke, Tiphanie, illus. 2015. (ENG.). 40p. (J). (-2). 16.99 *(978-1-4926-0168-5(3)*, Sourcebooks Jabberwocky) Sourcebooks, Inc.

SEATTLE, CHIEF, 1790-1866

Carew-Miller, Anna. Chief Seattle: Great Chief. 2004. (Great Names Ser.). (Illus.). 32p. (J). (gr. 3-18). lib. bdg. 19.95 *(978-1-59084-154-9(9))* Mason Crest.

SEATTLE (WASH.)

Dyan, Penelope. Smile Seattle! a Kid's Guide to Seattle, Washington. Weigand, John D., photos by. 2013. (Illus.). 34p. pap. 11.95 *(978-1-61477-109-8(X))* Bellissima Publishing, LLC.

Filer, Patricia & Fulton, Cathy. Welcome to the Greenland: A Children's Activity Guide to the Birthplace of Seattle. 2003. (Illus.). 40p. (J). spiral bd. 24.95 *(978-0-9727759-5-3(1))* Capturing Memories.

Laberje, Reji. Max Explores Seattle. Fenech, Liza, illus. 2015. (Max Explores Ser.). (ENG.). 20p. (J). (— 1). bds. 9.95 *(978-1-62937-103-0(3))* Triumph Bks.

Patent, Dorothy Hinshaw & Young, Jeffrey. Dog on Board: The True Story of Eclipse, the Bus-Riding Dog. Munoz, William, illus. 2016. (ENG.). 40p. (J). (gr. -1-3). 16.99 *(978-0-399-54988-5(9)*, Crown Books For Young Readers) Random Hse. Children's Bks.

Price, Roger & Mad Libs Staff. I Love Seattle Mad Libs. 2015. (Mad Libs Ser.). (ENG.). 48p. (J). (gr. 3-7). bds. 4.99 *(978-0-8431-8268-2(7)*, Mad Libs) Penguin Young Readers Group.

Skewes, John. Seattle ABC: a Larry Gets Lost Book. 2017. (Larry Gets Lost Ser.). (ENG., Illus.). 32p. (J). (-k). 14.99 *(978-1-63217-093-4(0)*, Little Bigfoot) Sasquatch Bks.

Tracy, Kathleen. Seattle. 2010. (Class Trip Ser.). (Illus.). 48p. (J). (gr. 2-5). lib. bdg. 29.95 *(978-1-58415-880-6(8))* Mitchell Lane Pubs., Inc.

SEATTLE (WASH.)—FICTION

Anonymous. Calling Maggie May. 2015. (ENG., Illus.). 272p. (YA). (gr. 9). pap. 10.99 *(978-1-4814-3901-5(4)*, Simon Pulse) Simon Pulse.

Bacho, Peter. Leaving Yesler. 2010. 285p. (YA). pap. 16.00 *(978-1-929355-57-0(2))* Pleasure Boat Studio: A Literary Pr.

Barden, Stephanie. Cinderella Smith. Goode, Diane, illus. (Cinderella Smith Ser.: 1). (ENG.). (J). 2011. 160p. (gr. 3-7). 16.99 *(978-0-06-196423-7(9))* Vol. 3. 2013. 144p. (gr. 1-5). 16.99 *(978-0-06-200443-7(3))* HarperCollins Pubs.

—The More the Merrier. Goode, Diane, illus. (Cinderella Smith Ser.: 2). (ENG.). (J). (gr. 3-7). 2013. 160p. pap. 5.99 *(978-0-06-200442-0(5))* 2012. 144p. 15.99 *(978-0-06-200440-6(9))* HarperCollins Pubs.

Brockenbrough, Martha. The Game of Love & Death. 2015. (ENG.). 336p. (J). (gr. 7). 17.99 *(978-0-545-66834-7(4))* Scholastic, Inc.

Caletti, Deb. The Nature of Jade. 2008. (ENG.). 320p. (YA). (gr. 7-12). pap. 10.99 *(978-1-4169-1006-0(9)*, Simon Pulse) Simon Pulse.

Colbert, Cory. Sammy the Sea Otter Makes New Friends: Adventures of Sammy the Sea Otter. 2011. 18p. pap. 11.95 *(978-1-4327-7648-0(7))* Outskirts Pr., Inc.

Cosgrove, Stephen. Good Night, Wheedle. James, Robin, illus. 2016. (ENG.). 20p. (J). (— 1). bds. 9.99 *(978-1-63217-075-0(2)*, Little Bigfoot) Sasquatch Bks.

—Pickles & the P-Flock Bullies. James, Robin, illus. 2014. (ENG.). 32p. (J). (gr. k-3). 16.99 *(978-1-57061-887-1(9)*, Little Bigfoot) Sasquatch Bks.

—Wheedle on the Needle. James, Robin, illus. 2009. (ENG.). 32p. (J). (gr. -1-2). 17.99 *(978-1-57061-628-0(0)*, Little Bigfoot) Sasquatch Bks.

Cupala, Holly. Don't Breathe a Word. 2012. (ENG.). 320p. (YA). (gr. 9). pap. 8.99 *(978-0-06-176669-5(0)*, HarperTeen) HarperCollins Pubs.

—Tell Me a Secret. 2010. (ENG.). 304p. (YA). (gr. 9-18). 16.99 *(978-0-06-176666-4(6)*, HarperTeen) HarperCollins Pubs.

Dokey, Cameron. How Not to Spend Your Senior Year. 2012. (Romantic Comedies Ser.). (ENG.). 304p. (YA). (gr. 9). pap. 14.99 *(978-1-4424-6056-0(3)*, Simon Pulse) Simon Pulse.

Hobbs, Will. Jackie's Wild Seattle. (ENG.). 208p. (J). (gr. 5-18). 2004. pap. 6.99 *(978-0-380-73311-8(0))* 2003. 19.99 *(978-0-688-17474-3(4))* HarperCollins Pubs.

Holtzen, Mark. A Ticket to the Pennant: A Tale of Baseball in Seattle. Skewes, John, illus. 2016. (ENG.). 32p. (J). (gr. -1-3). 17.99 *(978-1-63217-003-3(5)*, Little Bigfoot) Sasquatch Bks.

Hudspeth, Jodi. Unconditional Love. 2009. 80p. pap. 28.99 *(978-1-4343-6383-1(X))* AuthorHouse.

Ingold, Jeanette. Paper Daughter. 2013. (ENG.). 224p. (YA). (gr. 7). pap. 7.99 *(978-0-544-10484-6(6))* Houghton Mifflin Harcourt Publishing Co.

James, Wilson. SONS & BROTHERS in SEATTLE. 2009. 158p. pap. 14.95 *(978-0-557-07436-5(3))* Lulu Pr., Inc.

Kehret, Peg. Abduction! 2006. (ENG.). 224p. (J). (gr. 5-18). 6.99 *(978-0-14-240617-5(1)*, Puffin Books) Penguin Young Readers Group.

—Abduction! 2007. 215p. (gr. 3-7). 17.00 *(978-0-7569-8282-9(0))* Perfection Learning Corp.

Lockhart, E. The Boyfriend List: 15 Guys, 11 Shrink Appointments, 4 Ceramic Frogs & Me, Ruby Oliver. 2006. (Ruby Oliver Quartet Ser.). (ENG.). 256p. (YA). (gr. 7-12). reprint ed. pap. 9.99 *(978-0-385-73207-9(4)*, Ember) Random Hse. Children's Bks.

—Real Live Boyfriends: Yes. Boyfriends, Plural. If My Life Weren't Complicated, I Wouldn't Be Ruby Oliver. 2011. (Ruby Oliver Quartet Ser.). (ENG.). 240p. (J). (gr. 7). pap. 8.99 *(978-0-385-73429-5(8)*, Ember) Random Hse. Children's Bks.

—The Treasure Map of Boys: Noel, Jackson, Finn, Hutch, Gideon - And Me, Ruby Oliver. 2010. (Ruby Oliver Quartet Ser.). (ENG.). 256p. (J). (gr. 7). pap. 8.99 *(978-0-385-73427-1(1)*, Delacorte Pr.) Random Hse. Children's Bks.

Loyd, Mark. Big Ben: A Little Known Story. Loyd, Mark, illus. 2005. (Illus.). (J). *(978-0-9773317-1-0(7))* Too Fun Publishing.

Marsh, Carole. Mystery at the Space Needle. 2016. (Real Kids, Real Places Ser.). (ENG.). (J). (gr. 3-7). pap. 7.99 *(978-0-635-12432-6(7)*, Marsh, Carole Mysteries) Gallopade International.

Mathieson, Karen. Liza, Elizabeth: Book Three of the Rosemary Ridge Trilogy. 2013. 164p. (J). pap. 7.99 *(978-1-940350-08-0(5))* Portable COO, The.

McBride, Lish. Hold Me Closer, Necromancer. 2010. (Necromancer Ser.: 1). (ENG.). 352p. (YA). (gr. 9-13). 16.99 *(978-0-8050-9098-7(3)*, 9780805090987, Holt, Henry & Co. Bks. For Young Readers) Holt, Henry & Co.

—Necromancing the Stone. 2013. (Necromancer Ser.: 2). (ENG.). 368p. (YA). (gr. 9-13). pap. 9.99 *(978-1-250-03415-1(9)*, 9781250034151) Square Fish.

McKernan, Victoria. The Devil's Paintbox. (ENG.). (YA). (gr. 9). 2013. 384p. pap. 9.99 *(978-0-449-81655-4(9)*, Ember) 2010. 368p. mass mkt. 8.99 *(978-0-440-23962-8(1)*, Laurel Leaf) Random Hse. Children's Bks.

Meyer, Stephenie. The Short Second Life of Bree Tanner. 2012. (Twilight Saga Ser.). (ENG.). 224p. (YA). (gr. 7-17).

S

pap. 8.99 *(978-0-316-22852-7(4))* Little, Brown Bks. for Young Readers.

Mochizuki, Ken. Beacon Hill Boys. 2004. 200p. 16.00 *(978-0-7569-4281-6(0))* Perfection Learning Corp.

Papp, Robert, illus. The Seattle Puzzle. 2007. (Boxcar Children Mysteries Ser.: 111). (ENG.). 128p. (J). (gr. 1-5). lib. bdg. 14.99 *(978-0-8075-5560-6(6))*; per. 5.99 *(978-0-8075-5561-3(4))* Whitman, Albert & Co.

Powell, Randy. Tribute to Another Dead Rock Star. 2003. (ENG.). 224p. (YA). (gr. 7-12). pap. 14.99 *(978-0-374-47968-8(2)*, Sunburst) Farrar, Straus & Giroux.

Reed, Amy. Beautiful. 2010. (ENG.). 256p. (YA). (gr. 9). pap. 10.99 *(978-1-4169-7831-2(3)*, Simon Pulse) Simon Pulse.

—Clean. (ENG.). (YA). (gr. 9). 2012. 304p. pap. 10.99 *(978-1-4424-1345-0(X))* 2011. 288p. 16.99 *(978-1-4424-1344-3(1))* Simon Pulse. (Simon Pulse).

Reed, Amy Lynn. Beautiful. 2009. (ENG.). 240p. (YA). (gr. 9-18). 16.99 *(978-1-4169-7830-5(5)*, Simon Pulse) Simon Pulse.

Renn, Diana. Tokyo Heist. 2013. (ENG.). 384p. (YA). (gr. 7). pap. 8.99 *(978-0-14-242654-8(7)*, Speak) Penguin Young Readers Group.

Savage, J. Scott. Gears of Revolution. 2016. (Mysteries of Cove Ser.: 2). 342p. (J). 17.99 *(978-1-62972-223-8(5)*, Shadow Mountain) Deseret Bk. Co.

Skewes, John & Ode, Eric. Larry Gets Lost in Seattle: 10th Anniversary Edition. 10th ed. 2017. (Larry Gets Lost Ser.). (ENG., Illus.). 32p. (J). (gr. -1-2). 17.99 *(978-1-63217-092-7(2)*, Little Bigfoot) Sasquatch Bks.

Skovron, Jon. Misfit. 2011. (ENG.). 384p. (YA). (gr. 9-17). 16.95 *(978-1-4197-0021-7(9)*, Amulet Bks.) Abrams, Inc.

Smallman, Steve. Santa Is Coming to Seattle. Dunn, Robert, illus. 2015. (ENG.). 32p. (J). (-3). 9.99 *(978-1-4926-2649-7(X)*, Sourcebooks Jabberwocky) Sourcebooks, Inc.

Steere, Jay & Gamble, Adam. Good Night Seattle. Veno, Joe, illus. 2007. (Good Night Our World Ser.). (ENG.). 20p. (J). (gr. k — 1). bds. 9.95 *(978-1-60219-014-6(3))* Good Night Bks.

Thomas, Terri. The Barge Ghost, 1 vol. unabr. ed. 2010. (Q Reads Ser.). (ENG.). 32p. (YA). (gr. 9-12). pap. 6.95 *(978-1-61651-211-8(3))* Saddleback Educational Publishing, Inc.

Trueman, Terry. Life Happens Next. 2012. (Stuck in Neutral Ser.: 3). (ENG.). 144p. (YA). (gr. 9). 17.99 *(978-0-06-202803-7(0)*, HarperTeen) HarperCollins Pubs.

SEATTLE MARINERS (BASEBALL TEAM)

Freedman, Lew. Seattle Mariners, 1 vol. (Inside MLB Ser.). (ENG., Illus.). 48p. (gr. 3-6). 2011. (YA). lib. bdg. 32.79 *(978-1-61714-059-4(7))* 2014. (J). lib. bdg. 32.79 *(978-1-62403-485-5(3)*, SportsZone) ABDO Publishing Co.

LeBoutillier, Nate. The Story of the Seattle Mariners. 2011. (Baseball: the Great American Game Ser.). (Illus.). 48p. (J). (gr. 5-8). lib. bdg. 34.25 *(978-1-60818-056-1(5)*, Creative Education) Creative Co., The.

Peterson, Sheryl. The Story of the Seattle Mariners. 2007. (Baseball, the Great American Game Ser.). (Illus.). 48p. (YA). (gr. 4-7). lib. bdg. 32.80 *(978-1-58341-500-9(9))* Creative Co., The.

Stewart, Mark. The Seattle Mariners. 2012. (Team Spirit Ser.). 48p. (J). (gr. 3-6). lib. bdg. 29.27 *(978-1-59953-497-8(5))* Norwood Hse. Pr.

SEATTLE SEAHAWKS (FOOTBALL TEAM)

Adamson, Thomas K. The Seattle Seahawks Story. 2016. (NFL Teams Ser.). (ENG., Illus.). 32p. (J). (gr. 3-7). lib. bdg. 26.95 *(978-1-62617-382-8(6)*, Torque Bks.) Bellwether Media.

Burgess, Zack. Meet the Seattle Seahawks. 2016. (Big Picture Sports Ser.). (ENG., Illus.). 24p. (J). (gr. k-3). lib. bdg. 22.60 *(978-1-59953-748-1(6))* Norwood Hse. Pr.

Gilbert, Sara. The History of the Seattle Seahawks. 2004. (NFL Today Ser.). (Illus.). 32p. (YA). (gr. 5-9). 18.95 *(978-1-58341-314-2(6))* Creative Co., The.

—The Story of the Seattle Seahawks. 2009. (NFL Today Ser.). 48p. (YA). (gr. 5-9). 22.95 *(978-1-58341-771-3(0))* Creative Co., The.

Lester, Brian. Seattle Seahawks, 1 vol. 2010. (Inside the NFL Ser.). (ENG.). 48p. (YA). (gr. 3-6). lib. bdg. 32.79 *(978-1-61714-028-0(7))* ABDO Publishing Co.

Monnig, Alex. Seattle Seahawks. 2015. (Insider's Guide to Pro Football Ser.). (ENG.). 32p. (J). (gr. k-3). 28.50 *(978-1-63407-017-1(8)*, 208852) Child's World, Inc., The.

Sandler, Michael. Malcolm Smith & the Seattle Seahawks: Super Bowl XLVIII. 2015. (Illus.). 24p. (J). lib. bdg. *(978-1-62724-295-0(3))* Bearport Publishing Co., Inc.

Stewart, Mark. The Seattle Seahawks. rev. ed. 2012. (Team Spirit Ser.). (ENG.). 48p. (J). (gr. 3-6). lib. bdg. 29.27 *(978-1-59953-539-5(4))* Norwood Hse. Pr.

Whiting, Jim. NFL Today: Seattle Seahawks. 2013. (NFL Today Ser.). (ENG., Illus.). 48p. (J). (gr. 4-7). pap. 12.00 *(978-0-89812-873-4(0)*, Creative Paperbacks) Creative Co., The.

—The Story of the Seattle Seahawks. 2013. (Illus.). 48p. (J). 35.65 *(978-1-60818-320-3(3)*, Creative Education) Creative Co., The.

Wyner, Zach. Seattle Seahawks. 2015. (Illus.). 32p. (J). pap. *(978-1-4896-0891-8(5))* Weigl Pubs., Inc.

Zappa, Marcia. Seattle Seahawks, 1 vol. 2014. (NFL's Greatest Teams Set 2 Ser.). (ENG.). 32p. (gr. 2-5). 28.50 *(978-1-62403-591-3(4))* ABDO Publishing Co.

SEAWEED

see Algae

SECONDARY EDUCATION

see Education, Secondary

SECONDARY SCHOOLS

see Education, Secondary; High Schools; Public Schools

SECRET SERVICE

see also Detectives; Spies

also subdivision Secret Service under individual wars, e.g. World War, 1939-1945—Secret Service.

Bascomb, Neal. The Nazi Hunters: How a Team of Spies & Survivors Captured the World's Most Notorious Nazi. 2013. (ENG., Illus.). 256p. (J). (gr. 7). 17.99 *(978-0-545-43099-9(2)*, Levine, Arthur A. Bks.) Scholastic, Inc.

Caravantes, Peggy. Petticoat Spies: Six Women Spies of the US Civil War. 2004. (Notable Americans Ser.). (Illus.). 112p. (YA). (gr. 6-12). 23.95 *(978-1-883846-88-6(9)*, First Biographies) Reynolds, Morgan Inc.

Costain, Meredith. Spies Revealed. 2013. (Discovery Education: Sensational True Stories Ser.). (ENG., Illus.). 32p. (J). (gr. 3-6). pap. 10.00 *(978-1-4777-0103-4(6))*; lib. bdg. 25.25 *(978-1-4777-0059-4(5))* Rosen Publishing Group, Inc., The. (PowerKids Pr.).

Croce, Nicholas. Detectives: Life Investigating Crime. 2009. (Extreme Careers Ser.). 64p. (gr. 5-5). 58.50 *(978-1-61512-390-2(3)*, Rosen Reference) Rosen Publishing Group, Inc., The.

Gilbert, Adrian. Spy School. 2009. (Spy Files Ser.). (ENG., Illus.). 32p. (J). (gr. 3-12). pap. 6.95 *(978-1-55407-575-1(0)*, 9781554075751) Firefly Bks., Ltd.

Larson, Kirsten W. The Secret Service. 2016. (Protecting Our People Ser.). (ENG., Illus.). 32p. (J). (gr. 1-4). 20.95 *(978-1-60753-987-2(X))* Amicus Publishing.

Newcomb, Tim. Secret Service Agent, Vol. 12. 2015. (On a Mission Ser.). (Illus.). 48p. (J). (gr. 5). 20.95 *(978-1-4222-3400-6(2))* Mason Crest.

Polisar, Patti. Inside France's DGSE: The General Directorate for External Security. 2005. (Illus.). 63p. (gr. 4-8). reprint ed. 20.00 *(978-0-7567-8670-0(3))* DIANE Publishing Co.

Ryan, Bernard. The Secret Service. 2010. (Law Enforcement Agencies Ser.). (Illus.). 128p. (gr. 6-12). 35.00 *(978-1-60413-623-4(5)*, Chelsea Hse.) Facts On File, Inc.

Shea, Therese. A Career As a Secret Service Agent. 2015. (Federal Forces: Careers As Federal Agents Ser.). (ENG., Illus.). 32p. (J). (gr. 4-5). 26.25 *(978-1-4994-1117-1(0)*, PowerKids Pr.) Rosen Publishing Group, Inc., The.

Souter, Gerry. Secret Service Agent: And Careers in Federal Protection. 2006. (Homeland Security & Counterterrorism Careers Ser.). (Illus.). 128p. (J). (gr. 5-9). lib. bdg. 33.27 *(978-0-7660-2651-3(5))* Enslow Pubs., Inc.

Woog, Adam. Careers in the Secret Service. 2014. 96p. 39.92 *(978-1-62712-434-8(9))* Cavendish Square Publishing.

—Careers in the Secret Service. 2013. (J). 34.21 *(978-1-60870-960-1(4))* Marshall Cavendish Corp.

SECRET SERVICE—FICTION

Blum, Paul. Alien Implants. 2007. (Extraordinary Files Ser.). (ENG., Illus.). 48p. (J). (gr. 4-7). pap. 11.99 *(978-1-84680-181-5(8))* Evans Brothers, Ltd. GBR. Dist: Independent Pubs. Group.

—Dawn of the Zombies. 2007. (Extraordinary Files Ser.). (ENG., Illus.). 48p. (J). (gr. 4-7). pap. 10.99 *(978-1-84680-250-8(4))* Evans Brothers, Ltd. GBR. Dist: Independent Pubs. Group.

—Day of Judgement. 2007. (Extraordinary Files Ser.). (ENG., Illus.). 48p. (J). (gr. 4-7). pap. 11.99 *(978-1-84680-251-5(2))* Evans Brothers, Ltd. GBR. Dist: Independent Pubs. Group.

—Gene Machine. 2007. (Extraordinary Files Ser.). (ENG., Illus.). 48p. (J). (gr. 4-7). pap. 10.99 *(978-1-84680-252-2(0))* Evans Brothers, Ltd. GBR. Dist: Independent Pubs. Group.

—Killer Robot. 2007. (Extraordinary Files Ser.). (ENG., Illus.). 48p. (J). (gr. 4-7). pap. 10.99 *(978-1-84680-178-5(8))* Evans Brothers, Ltd. GBR. Dist: Independent Pubs. Group.

—Puppet Master. 2007. (Extraordinary Files Ser.). (ENG., Illus.). 48p. (J). (gr. 4-7). pap. 10.99 *(978-1-84680-182-2(6))* Evans Brothers, Ltd. GBR. Dist: Independent Pubs. Group.

—Secrets & Lies. 2007. (Extraordinary Files Ser.). (ENG., Illus.). 48p. (J). (gr. 4-7). pap. 10.99 *(978-1-84680-249-2(0))* Evans Brothers, Ltd. GBR. Dist: Independent Pubs. Group.

—Sleep Walker. 2007. (Extraordinary Files Ser.). (ENG., Illus.). 48p. (J). (gr. 4-7). pap. 10.99 *(978-1-84680-174-7(5))* Evans Brothers, Ltd. GBR. Dist: Independent Pubs. Group.

—Spider Invasion. 2007. (Extraordinary Files Ser.). (ENG., Illus.). 48p. (J). (gr. 4-7). pap. 10.99 *(978-1-84680-183-9(4))* Evans Brothers, Ltd. GBR. Dist: Independent Pubs. Group.

—Werewolf Eclipse. 2007. (Extraordinary Files Ser.). (ENG., Illus.). 48p. (J). (gr. 4-7). pap. 10.99 *(978-1-84680-180-8(X))* Evans Brothers, Ltd. GBR. Dist: Independent Pubs. Group.

Cox, Joseph J. Grobar & the Mind Control Potion. Becker, Rebecca J., illus. 2005. 168p. (J). per. 9.95 *(978-0-9764659-3-5(0))* Suckerfish Bks.

Dautel, Daniel. Mission to Mount Everest. 2009. 90p. pap. 9.96 *(978-0-557-09695-4(2))* Lulu Pr., Inc.

de Groot, Bob. Clifton Vol. 6: Kidnapping. 2009. (Clifton Ser.: 6). (ENG., Illus.). 48p. (J). (gr. 3-17). pap. 11.95 *(978-1-905460-87-8(2))* CineBook GBR. Dist: National Bk. Network.

Goldsmann, Henri. Secret Agent Spanky Sheep in the mystery of: the Pooperous Pizza Plunderer. 2006. 140p. pap. 11.99 *(978-1-4116-8094-4(4))* Lulu Pr., Inc.

Groot, Bob de. Jade Vol. 5. Rodrigue. illus. 2008. (Clifton Ser.: 5). (ENG.). 48p. pap. 11.95 *(978-1-905460-52-6(X))* CineBook GBR. Dist: National Bk. Network.

Groot, De. Black Moon. Spear, Luke, tr. from FRE. Rodrigue, illus. 2007. (Clifton Ser.: 4). (ENG.). 48p. (J). (gr. 4-7). pap. 9.99 *(978-1-905460-30-4(9))* CineBook GBR. Dist: National Bk. Network.

Harvey, Paul E., Jr. The Adventures of Shamus the Leprechaun. 2009. 48p. pap. 15.50 *(978-1-60693-924-6(6)*, Strategic Bk. Publishing) Strategic Book Publishing & Rights Agency (SBPRA).

Hunt, Elizabeth Singer. The Puzzle of the Missing Panda, Bk. 7. Williamson, Brian, illus. 2008. (Secret Agent Jack Stalwart Ser.: 7). (ENG.). 128p. (J). (gr. 1-4). pap. 5.99 *(978-1-60286-020-9(3)*, Weinstein Bks.) Perseus Bks. Group.

—The Secret of the Sacred Temple. Williamson, Brian, illus. 2008. (Secret Agent Jack Stalwart Ser.: 5). (ENG.). 128p. (J). (gr. 1-4). per. 5.99 *(978-1-60286-003-2(3)*, Weinstein Bks.) Perseus Bks. Group.

Payson, Howard. The Boy Scouts under Sealed Orders. 2005. (Illus.). pap. 30.95 *(978-1-885529-57-2(0))* Stevens Publishing.

Richards, Justin. Sorted! 2009. (Agent Alfie Ser.: 2). (ENG., Illus.). 176p. (J). (gr. 2-4). pap. 6.99 *(978-0-00-727358-4(4)*, HarperCollins Children's Bks.) HarperCollins Pubs. Ltd. GBR. Dist: HarperCollins Pubs.

Smith, Roland. Independence Hall. (I, Q Ser.: Bk. 1). (ENG., 312p. (gr. 5-9). 2009. Illus.). (J). 15.95 *(978-1-58536-468-8(1))* 2008. (YA). pap. 8.95 *(978-1-58536-325-4(1))* Sleeping Bear Pr.

Turk, Judy Vanslyke, et al. Laughing Thief. 2007. (Clifton Ser.: 2). (ENG., Illus.). 48p. (J). (gr. 4-7). per. 9.99 *(978-1-905460-07-6(4))* CineBook GBR. Dist: National Bk. Network.

Van Draanen, Wendelin. Sammy Keyes & the Dead Giveaway. 2008. (Sammy Keyes Ser.: Bk. 10). (J). 64.99 *(978-1-60640-639-7(6))* Findaway World, LLC.

—Sammy Keyes & the Dead Giveaway. unabr. ed. 2006. (Sammy Keyes Ser.: Bk. 10). (J). (gr. 5-7). pap. 54.95 incl. audio compact disk *(978-1-59519-771-9(0))*; pap. 36.95 incl. audio *(978-1-59519-770-2(2))* Live Oak Media.

—Sammy Keyes & the Dead Giveaway. 2007. (Sammy Keyes Ser.: Bk. 10). (ENG., Illus.). 304p. (J). (gr. 5-7). per. 7.99 *(978-0-440-41911-2(5)*, Yearling) Random Hse. Children's Bks.

SECRET WRITING

see Cryptography

SECRETARIES

Kidde, Rita. What Do School Secretaries Do? 2014. (Jobs in My School Ser.). (Illus.). 24p. (J). (gr. k-2). pap. 8.25 *(978-1-4777-6538-8(7)*, PowerKids Pr.) Rosen Publishing Group, Inc., The.

—What Do School Secretaries Do? (¿Qué Hacen los Secretarios de la Escuela?) de la Vega, Eida, ed. 2014. (Oficios en Mi Escuela / Jobs in My School Ser.). (SPA & ENG.). 24p. (J). (gr. k-2). lib. bdg. 23.60 *(978-1-4777-6795-5(9)*, PowerKids Pr.) Rosen Publishing Group, Inc., The.

Syrewicz, Connor. Personal Assistant. 2013. (Earning $50,000 - $100,000 with a High School Diploma or Less Ser.: 14). 64p. (J). (gr. 7-18). 22.95 *(978-1-4222-2897-5(5))* Mason Crest.

SECRETARIES—FICTION

Stockton, Frank Richard. What Might Have Been Expected. 2009. 128p. 23.95 *(978-1-60664-676-2(1))*; pap. 10.95 *(978-1-60664-305-1(3))* Rodgers, Alan Bks.

Thaler, Mike. The School Secretary from the Black Lagoon. Lee, Jared, illus. 2006. (J). *(978-0-439-80077-8(3))* Scholastic, Inc.

SECTS

see also names of churches and sects, e.g. Methodist Church, etc.

Calvert, John. Divisions in Islam. 2010. (World of Islam Ser.). (Illus.). 64p. (YA). (gr. 4-7). lib. bdg. 22.95 *(978-1-4222-0533-4(9))* Mason Crest.

Erdreich, Sarah. Cults. Espejo, Roman, ed. 2012. (Opposing Viewpoints Ser.). (ENG., Illus.). 240p. (gr. 10-12). 42.95 *(978-0-7377-3994-7(0))*; pap. 29.45 *(978-0-7377-3995-4(9))* Cengage Gale. (Greenhaven Pr., Inc.).

Kiesbye, Stefan. Drunk Driving. 2008. (Social Issues Firsthand Ser.). (ENG., Illus.). 192p. (gr. 10-12). lib. bdg. 38.30 *(978-0-7377-4031-8(0)*, LML02109-239990, Greenhaven Pr., Inc.) Cengage Gale.

Person, Stephen. Voodoo in New Orleans. 2010. (HorrorScapes Ser.). 32p. (YA). (gr. 4-7). lib. bdg. 25.27 *(978-1-936087-99-0(5))* Bearport Publishing Co., Inc.

Piehl, Norah. Cults. 2012. (Issues That Concern You Ser.). (ENG., Illus.). 144p. (gr. 7-10). lib. bdg. 42.00 *(978-0-7377-6286-0(1))* Cengage Gale.

Schauer, Peter J. The People Behind Cult Murders. 2016. (Psychology of Mass Murderers Ser.). (Illus.). 144p. (J). (gr. 8-8). 37.27 *(978-0-7660-7610-5(5))* Enslow Pubs., Inc.

SECURITIES EXCHANGE

see Stock Exchanges

SECURITY (PSYCHOLOGY)

Hunter, Nick. Terrorism & Security, 1 vol. 2011. (Hot Topics Ser.). (ENG.). 56p. (gr. 7-8). pap. 10.95 *(978-1-4329-6207-4(8)*, NA-h) Heinemann-Raintree.

Schulz, Charles. Seguridad es un Pulgar y una Manta. (SPA.). (J). 7.00 *(978-84-7655-664-1(0)*, PI3929) Plaza Joven, S.A. ESP. Dist: Lectorum Pubns., Inc.

SECURITY (PSYCHOLOGY)—FICTION

Benton, Jim. School. Hasn't This Gone on Long Enough? Benton, Jim, illus. 2012. (Dear Dumb Diary Year Two Ser.: 1). (ENG., Illus.). 160p. (J). (gr. 3-7). pap. 5.99 *(978-0-545-37761-4(7)*, Scholastic Paperbacks) Scholastic, Inc.

Harris, Robie H. Turtle & Me. Freeman, Tor, illus. 2015. (ENG.). 40p. (J). (gr. -1-3). 16.99 *(978-1-4998-0046-3(0))* Little Bee Books Inc.

Littman, Sarah Darer. Want to Go Private? (ENG.). 336p. (J). 2013. (gr. 7). pap. 10.99 *(978-0-545-15147-4(3))* 2011. (gr. 9-9). 17.99 *(978-0-545-15146-7(5)*, Scholastic Pr.) Scholastic, Inc.

Rylant, Cynthia. The Stars Will Still Shine. Beeke, Tiphanie, illus. 2005. 40p. (J). lib. bdg. 17.89 *(978-0-06-054640-3(9))*; (ENG.). (gr. -1-3). 17.99 *(978-0-06-054639-7(5))* HarperCollins Pubs.

Shaw, Susan. Safe. 2007. (ENG.). 176p. (YA). (gr. 9-18). pap. 14.00 *(978-0-525-47829-4(9)*, Dutton Books for Young Readers) Penguin Young Readers Group.

Simon, Coco. Katie Starting from Scratch. 2014. (Cupcake Diaries: 21). (ENG., Illus.). 160p. (J). (gr. 3-7). pap. 5.99 *(978-1-4814-0471-6(7)*, Simon Spotlight) Simon Spotlight.

Spinelli, Jerry. Eggs. 2008. (ENG., Illus.). 240p. (J). (gr. 3-7). pap. 8.99 *(978-0-316-16647-8(2))* Little, Brown Bks. for Young Readers.

SECURITY, INTERNATIONAL

see also Disarmament; International Organization

Bauder, Julia. Is Iran a Threat to Global Security? (At Issue Ser.). (ENG., Illus.). 114p. (J). (gr. 10-12). 2006. pap. 31.80 *(978-0-7377-3526-0(0))* 2004. 22.50 *(978-0-7377-3527-7(9))* Cengage Gale. (Greenhaven Pr., Inc.).

Cahill, Bryon. Freedom from Fear. 2013. (Four Freedoms Ser.). (ENG., Illus.). 32p. (J). (gr. 3-6). pap. 8.95 *(978-1-937529-86-4(X))*; lib. bdg. 19.95 net. *(978-1-937529-94-9(0))* Red Chair Pr.

Hudak, Heather C. McCarthyism & the Red Scare. 2017. 48p. (J). ***(978-0-7787-3939-5(2))*** Crabtree Publishing Co.

Van Dijk, Ruud. The Making of the Modern World: 1945 to the Present: Governance & the Quest for Security, Vol. 9. 2016. (Making of the Modern World: 1945 to the Present Ser.: Vol. 9). (ENG., Illus.). 64p. (J). (gr. 7-12). 23.95 *(978-1-4222-3638-3(2))* Mason Crest.

SEDITION

see Political Crimes and Offenses; Revolutions

SEEDS

Allyn, Daisy. Seeds & Plants. 2012. (InfoMax Readers Ser.). (ENG., Illus.). 16 pp.p. (J). (gr. k-1). pap. 7.00 *(978-1-4488-8932-7(4)*, Rosen Classroom) Rosen Publishing Group, Inc., The.

Aloian, Molly. What Are Seeds? 2012. (ENG., Illus.). 24p. (J). *(978-0-7787-4221-0(0))*; pap. *(978-0-7787-4226-5(1))* Crabtree Publishing Co.

Amstutz, Lisa J. Which Seed Is This?, 1 vol. 2012. (Nature Starts Ser.). (ENG.). 32p. (gr. 1-2). pap. 8.10 *(978-1-4296-7851-3(8))*; pap. 47.70 *(978-1-4296-8297-8(3))*; lib. bdg. 27.32 *(978-1-4296-7552-9(7))* Capstone Press of Coughlan Cos. (Aplus Bks.).

Aston, Dianna Hutts. A Seed Is Sleepy. Long, Sylvia, illus. 2007. (ENG.). 40p. (J). (gr. k-5). 16.99 *(978-0-8118-5520-4(1))* Chronicle Bks. LLC.

—A Seed Is Sleepy. 2014. (J). lib. bdg. 18.40 *(978-0-606-35291-8(0))* Turtleback Bks.

Austen, Elizabeth. Seeds, 1 vol. rev. ed. 2014. (Science Readers: Content & Literacy Ser.). (ENG., Illus.). 24p. (gr. k-k). (J). 22.96 *(978-1-4938-1132-8(0))*; pap. 8.99 *(978-1-4807-4522-3(7))* Teacher Created Materials, Inc.

Balsavar, Deepa & Kaushal, Tara. The Seed. 2005. (HIN & ENG., Illus.). (J). *(978-81-8146-110-0(X))* Tulika Pubs.

Benbow, Ann & Mably, Colin. Sprouting Seed Science Projects. Labaff, Tom, illus. 2009. (Real Life Science Experiments Ser.). 48p. (J). (gr. 2-5). lib. bdg. 25.27 *(978-0-7660-3147-0(0))* Enslow Pubs., Inc.

Benchmark Education Co., LLC. We Need a Seed Big Book. 2014. (Shared Reading Foundations Ser.). (J). (gr. -1). *(978-1-4509-9449-1(0))* Benchmark Education Co.

Bishop, Celeste. ¿Por Qué Las Plantas Tienen Flores? / Why Do Plants Have Flowers?, 01 vols., 1. 2016. (Partes de la Planta / Plant Parts Ser.). (ENG & SPA., Illus.). 24p. (J). 23.60 *(978-1-5081-4739-8(6)*, PowerKids Pr.) Rosen Publishing Group, Inc., The.

—¿Por Qué Las Plantas Tienen Frutas? / Why Do Plants Have Fruits?, 01 vols., 1. 2016. (Partes de la Planta / Plant Parts Ser.). (ENG & SPA., Illus.). 24p. (J). 23.60 *(978-1-5081-4740-4(X)*, PowerKids Pr.) Rosen Publishing Group, Inc., The.

—¿Por Qué Las Plantas Tienen Semillas? / Why Do Plants Have Seeds?, 01 vols., 1. 2016. (Partes de la Planta / Plant Parts Ser.). (ENG & SPA., Illus.). 24p. (J). 23.60 *(978-1-5081-4732-9(9)*, PowerKids Pr.) Rosen Publishing Group, Inc., The.

—Why Do Plants Have Flowers?, 01 vols., 1. 2016. (Plant Parts Ser.). (ENG., Illus.). 24p. (J). pap. 8.25 *(978-1-5081-4213-3(0)*, PowerKids Pr.) Rosen Publishing Group, Inc., The.

—Why Do Plants Have Fruits?, 01 vols., 1. 2016. (Plant Parts Ser.). (ENG., Illus.). 24p. (J). pap. 8.25 *(978-1-5081-4217-1(3)*, PowerKids Pr.) Rosen Publishing Group, Inc., The.

—Why Do Plants Have Seeds?, 01 vols., 1. 2016. (Plant Parts Ser.). (ENG., Illus.). 24p. (J). pap. 8.25 *(978-1-5081-4229-4(7)*, PowerKids Pr.) Rosen Publishing Group, Inc., The.

Blackaby, Susan. Plant Packages: A Book about Seeds, 1 vol. Delage, Charlene, illus. 2003. (Growing Things Ser.). (ENG.). 24p. (gr. -1-2). per. 8.95 *(978-1-4048-0384-8(X))* Picture Window Bks.

Blanchard, Emma. Seeds I See: Work with 11-19 to Gain Foundations for Place Value. 2013. (Rosen Math Readers Ser.). (ENG.). 16p. (J). (gr. k-1). pap. 42.00 *(978-1-4777-1606-9(8))*; (Illus.). pap. 7.00 *(978-1-4777-1605-2(X))* Rosen Publishing Group, Inc., The. (Rosen Classroom).

Bodach, Vijaya K. Seeds [Scholastic]. 2010. (Plant Parts Ser.). 24p. pap. 0.52 *(978-1-4296-5060-1(5)*, Pebble Plus) Capstone Press of Coughlan Cos.

Bodach, Vijaya Khisty. Seeds. 2016. (Plant Parts Ser.). (ENG.). 24p. (gr. k-1). pap. 7.29 *(978-1-5157-4246-3(6)*, Pebble Plus) Capstone Press of Coughlan Cos.

Buchanan, Shelly. Plant Reproduction. 2015. (Science Readers: Content & Literacy Ser.). (ENG., Illus.). 32p. (J). (gr. 4-4). pap. 8.99 *(978-1-4807-4676-3(2))* Teacher Created Materials, Inc.

Carle, Eric. The Tiny Seed. Carle, Eric, illus. 2015. (World of Eric Carle Ser.). (ENG., Illus.). 32p. (J). (gr. k-2). pap. 3.99 *(978-1-4814-3575-8(2)*, Simon Spotlight) Simon Spotlight.

Cartw, Paul. Where Are the Seeds/Ww/E. (Wonder Worldtm Ser.). 16p. 29.95 *(978-0-7802-2042-3(0))* Wright Group/McGraw-Hill.

Clay, Kathryn. Planting Seeds. 2016. (Celebrate Spring Ser.). (ENG., Illus.). 24p. (gr. k-1). lib. bdg. 21.99 *(978-1-4914-8305-3(9)*, Pebble Bks.) Capstone Press of Coughlan Cos.

Dybvik, Tina. Sadie's Seed Adventures: Learning about Seeds, 1 vol. Record, Adam, illus. 2013. (Take It Outside Ser.). (ENG.). 24p. (gr. k-2). 27.32 *(978-1-4048-8316-1(9))*; pap. 8.95 *(978-1-4795-1937-8(5))* Picture Window Bks.

Galbraith, Kathryn O. Planting the Wild Garden, 1 vol. Halperni, Wendy Anderson, illus. 2015. (ENG.). 32p. (J). (gr. 1-3). pap. 7.95 *(978-1-56145-791-5(4))* Peachtree Pubs.

—Planting the Wild Garden, 1 vol. Halperin, Wendy, illus. 2011. (ENG.). 32p. (J). (gr. -1-3). 15.95 *(978-1-56145-563-8(6))* Peachtree Pubs.

Gibbons, Gail. From Seed to Plant. Gibbons, Gail, illus. 2012. (Illus.). audio compact disk 18.95 *(978-1-4301-1079-8(1))* Live Oak Media.

Glaser, Rebecca. Seeds. 2012. (ENG., Illus.). 24p. (J). lib. bdg. 25.65 *(978-1-62031-029-8(5))* Jump! Inc.

Gray, Susan H. Experiment with Seeds. 2010. (Explorer Junior Library: Science Explorer Junior Ser.). (ENG.). 32p. (gr. 3-6). lib. bdg. 28.50 *(978-1-60279-835-9(4)*, 200536) Cherry Lake Publishing.

—Super Cool Science Experiments: Seeds. 2009. (Explorer Library: Science Explorer Ser.). (ENG.). 32p. (gr. 4-8). lib. bdg. 28.50 *(978-1-60279-514-3(2)*, 200293) Cherry Lake Publishing.

Gregory, Josh. From Thistle Burrs to... Velcro. 2012. (21st Century Skills Innovation Library: Innovations from Nature Ser.). (ENG.). 32p. (gr. 4-8). 28.50 *(978-1-61080-494-3(5)*, 202104); pap. 14.21 *(978-1-61080-668-8(9)*, 202278) Cherry Lake Publishing.

Haakonsen, Jens. What Are Seeds? 2017. (Plants in My World Ser.). 24p. (gr. 4-6). pap. 8.25 **(978-1-5081-6155-4(0),** PowerKids Pr.) Rosen Publishing Group, Inc., The.
Hayes, Amy. A Seed Becomes a Dandelion. 2016. (Transformations in Nature Ser.). (ENG., Illus.). 24p. (J). (gr. 1-1). pap. 8.22 (978-1-5026-0826-0(X)) Cavendish Square Publishing.
Heller, Ruth. The Reason for a Flower. (FRE.). (J). 6.99 (978-0-590-71999-5(8)) Scholastic, Inc.
Jordan, Helene J. Cómo Crece una Semilla, 1 vol. Fiol, Maria A., tr. Krupinski, Loretta, illus. 2006. (Let's-Read-And-Find-Out Science 1 Ser.).Tr. of How a Seed Grows. (SPA.). 32p. (J). (gr. -1-3). pap. 6.99 (978-0-06-088716-2(8)) HarperCollins Pubs.
Juettner, Bonnie. The Seed Vault. 2009. (Great Idea Ser.). (Illus.). 48p. (J). (gr. 4-6). lib. bdg. 26.60 (978-1-59953-343-8(X)) Norwood Hse. Pr.
Kababik, Dana. From Seed to Flower. 2003. (Grow up! Ser.). (J). (978-1-58417-170-6(7)); pap. (978-1-58417-176-8(6)) Lake Street Pubs.
Kim, Sue. How Does a Seed Grow? A Book with Foldout Pages. Tilde, photos by. 2010. (ENG., Illus.). 14p. (J). (gr. -1-1). bds. 8.99 (978-1-4169-9435-0(1), Little Simon) Little Simon.
Lawrence, Ellen. From Bird Poop to Wind: How Seeds Get Around. 2012. (Science Slam: Plant-Ology Ser.). (Illus.). 24p. (J). (gr. -1-3). lib. bdg. 23.93 (978-1-61772-585-2(4)) Bearport Publishing Co., Inc.
Macken, JoAnn Early. Flip, Float, Fly: Seeds on the Move. Paparone, Pam, illus. 2008. (ENG.). 32p. (J). (gr. 1-5). 17.95 (978-0-8234-2043-8(4)) Holiday Hse., Inc.
—Flip, Float, Fly: Seeds on the Move. Paparone, Pam, illus. 2016. (ENG.). 32p. (J). 7.99 (978-0-8234-3758-0(2)) Holiday Hse., Inc.
Mann, Rachel. Plants Grow from Seeds, 6 vols., Set. 2003. (Phonics Readers 1-36 Ser.). (ENG.). 8p. (gr. k-1). pap. 29.70 (978-0-7368-3207-6(6), Phonics Readers) Capstone Press of Coughlan Cos.
Mitchell, Melanie. Seeds. 2015. (First Step Nonfiction - Parts of Plants Ser.). (ENG., Illus.). 8p. (gr. -1-1). 11.99 (978-1-5124-1052-5(7)) Lerner Publishing Group.
Mitchell, Melanie S. Seeds. 2004. (First Step Nonfiction - Parts of Plants Ser.). (ENG., Illus.). 8p. (gr. -1-1). pap. 4.95 (978-0-8225-3920-9(9), Lerner Pubns.) Lerner Publishing Group.
Moore, David. Expl on Your Own Trees Seeds & Leaves. 2009. (Explore on Your Own Ser.). (ENG.). (C). pap. 7.95 (978-0-7362-5563-9(X)) National Geographic School Publishing, Inc.
Morgan, Emily R. Next Time You See a Maple Seed. 2014. (Next Time You See Ser.). (ENG.). 32p. (J). (gr. k-5). 12.95 (978-1-938946-35-6(9)) National Science Teachers Assn.
Morgan, Sally. Flowers, Fruits & Seeds. (Looking at Plants Ser.). (Illus.). 32p. (J). lib. bdg. 24.25 (978-1-931983-10-5(0)) Chrysalis Education.
Morley, Margaret W. Little Wanderers. 2009. (Illus.). 116p. pap. 8.95 (978-1-59915-317-9(3)) Yesterday's Classics.
—Seed-Babies. 2009. (Illus.). 88p. pap. 7.95 (978-1-59915-316-2(5)) Yesterday's Classics.
O'Donnell, K. So Many Seeds: Learning the S Sound. 2009. (PowerPhonics Ser.). 24p. (gr. 1-1). 39.90 (978-1-60851-471-7(4), PowerKids Pr.) Rosen Publishing Group, Inc., The.
Ohanesian, Diane C. Seeds & Plants: Grades 2 & 3. (Illus.). (J). pap., wbk. ed. 4.99 (978-0-88743-961-2(6)) School Zone Publishing Co.
Owen, Ruth. How Do Plants Make & Spread Their Seeds? 2014. (World of Plants Ser.). 32p. (J). (gr. 2-5). lib. bdg. 26.25 (978-1-4777-7145-7(X), PowerKids Pr.) Rosen Publishing Group, Inc., The.
—Science & Craft Projects with Plants & Seeds. 2013. (Get Crafty Outdoors Ser.). (ENG., Illus.). 32p. (J). (gr. k-3). 26.50 (978-1-4777-0247-5(4)); pap. 11.75 (978-1-4777-0257-4(1)) Rosen Publishing Group, Inc., The. (PowerKids Pr.).
Pallotta, Jerry. Who Will Plant a Tree? Leonard, Tom, illus. 2010. (ENG.). 32p. (J). (gr. -1-2). 15.95 (978-1-58536-502-9(5)) Sleeping Bear Pr.
Peterson, Cris. Seed, Soil, Sun: Earth's Recipe for Food. Lundquist, David R., photos by. 2012. (ENG., Illus.). 32p. (J). (gr. k-4). pap. 7.95 (978-1-59078-947-6(4)) Boyds Mills Pr.
Plants & Seeds, 6 vols. (Sunshinetm Science Ser.). 24p. (gr. 1-2). 31.50 (978-0-7802-0291-7(0)) Wright Group/McGraw-Hill.
Prokos, Anna. Seed Power: Discovering How Plants Grow. Clegg, Dave, illus. 2017. (Imagine That! Ser.). (ENG.). 32p. (J). (gr. 2-4). lib. bdg. 26.65 (978-1-63440-151-7(4)); 39.99 **(978-1-63440-163-0(8))** Red Chair Pr.
Puri, Devi. Seeds, Bulbs, & Sprouts. 2015. (Garden Squad! Ser.). (ENG., Illus.). 24p. (J). (gr. 3-4). pap. 8.25 (978-1-4994-0977-2(X), PowerKids Pr.) Rosen Publishing Group, Inc., The.
Reid, Barbara. Seed to Sunflower: A First Look Board Book. Crysler, Ian, photos by. 2004. (Illus.). 12p. (J). (gr. k-2). reprint ed. 10.00 (978-0-7567-7853-8(0)) DIANE Publishing Co.
Relf, Patricia. Magic School Plants Seeds. 2014. 14.00 (978-1-63419-672-7(4)) Perfection Learning Corp.
Rhodes, Evan. How Do Seeds Sprout? 2013. (Nature's Super Secrets Ser.). (Illus.). 24p. (J). (gr. 1-3). pap. 8.15 (978-1-4339-8166-1(1)); lib. bdg. 22.60 (978-1-4339-8165-4(3)) Stevens, Gareth Publishing LLLP.
Richards, Jean. A Fruit Is a Suitcase for Seeds. Hariton, Anca, illus. 2006. (ENG.). 32p. (J). (gr. -1-3). pap. 6.95 (978-0-8225-5991-7(9), First Avenue Editions) Lerner Publishing Group.
Rigby Education Staff. From Here to There. (Sails Literacy Ser.). (Illus.). 16p. (gr. 2-3). 27.00 (978-0-7635-9958-4(1), 699581C99) Rigby Education.
Riggs, Kate. A Seed Needs Sun. Dogi, Fiammetta, illus. 2014. (ENG.). 14p. (J). (gr. -1-k). 7.99 (978-1-56846-254-7(9), Creative Editions) Creative Co., The.
—Sunflower. 2012. (Grow with Me Ser.). (Illus.). 32p. (J). (gr. 3-8). 19.95 (978-1-60818-218-3(5), Creative Education) Creative Co., The.
Robbins, Ken. Seeds. Robbins, Ken, illus. 2005. (ENG., Illus.). 32p. (J). (gr. 1-4). 17.99 (978-0-689-85041-7(7), Atheneum Bks. for Young Readers) Simon & Schuster Children's Publishing.
Rockwell, Anne. One Bean. 2014. 17.00 (978-1-63419-723-6(2)) Perfection Learning Corp.
Roemer, Heidi. What Kind of Seeds Are These? Kassian, Olena, illus. 2006. (ENG.). 32p. (J). (gr. k-1). 16.95 (978-1-55971-955-1(9)) Cooper Square Publishing Llc.
Sayre, April Pulley. Let's Go Nuts! Seeds We Eat. Sayre, April Pulley, illus. 2013. (ENG., Illus.). 32p. (J). (gr. -1-3). 16.99 (978-1-4424-6728-6(2), Beach Lane Bks.) Beach Lane Bks.
Schaefer, Lola M. Pick, Pull, Snap! Where Once a Flower Bloomed. George, Lindsay Barrett, illus. 2003. (ENG.). 32p. (J). (gr. k-5). 17.99 (978-0-688-17834-5(0), Greenwillow Bks.) HarperCollins Pubs.
Scholastic, Inc. Staff, contrib. by. What Happens Next? Seed to Plant. 2013. (ENG.). 12p. (J). bds. 6.95 (978-0-531-27255-8(9)) Scholastic Library Publishing.
School Zone Publishing Company Staff. Seeds & Plants. (Illus.). (J). 19.99 incl. audio compact disk (978-0-88743-922-3(5)) School Zone Publishing Co.
Scraper, Katherine. A Seed Needs Help. 2006. (Early Explorers Ser.). (J). pap. (978-1-4108-6026-2(4)) Benchmark Education Co.
Seeds. (Early Intervention Levels Ser.). 23.10 (978-0-7362-0011-0(8)) CENGAGE Learning.
Seeds Grow, 6 vols. (Sunshinetm Science Ser.). 24p. (gr. 1-2). 31.50 (978-0-7802-0290-0(2)); 36.95 (978-0-7802-0541-3(3)) Wright Group/McGraw-Hill.
Seeds, Seeds, Seeds, 6 vols. (Sunshinetm Science Ser.). 24p. (gr. 1-2). 31.50 (978-0-7802-0289-4(9)) Wright Group/McGraw-Hill.
Sian revision seed Mysteries. 2004. (J). (978-1-59242-065-0(6)) Delta Education, LLC.
Sterling, Kristin. Exploring Seeds. 2011. (First Step Nonfiction / Let's Look at Plants Ser.). pap. 33.92 (978-0-7613-8617-9(3)); lib. bdg. 21.27 (978-0-7613-5782-7(3)); (ENG.). 24p. pap. 6.95 (978-0-7613-7835-8(9)) Lerner Publishing Group.
Stewart, Melissa. How Does a Seed Sprout? And Other Questions about Plants. Schwartz, Carol, illus. 2014. (Good Question! Ser.). (ENG.). 32p. (J). (gr. 1). pap. 5.95 (978-1-4549-0671-1(5)) Sterling Publishing Co., Inc.
Stone, Lynn. Seeds. 2007. (ENG., Illus.). 24p. (gr. 2-3). per. 8.95 (978-1-60044-695-5(7)) Rourke Educational Media.
Sundance/Newbridge LLC Staff. Seeds Get Around. 2007. (Early Science Ser.). (gr. k-3). 18.95 (978-1-4007-6341-2(X)); pap. 6.10 (978-1-4007-6337-5(1)) Sundance/Newbridge Educational Publishing.
Thomson, Ruth. The Life Cycle of a Bean. 2007. (Learning about Life Cycles Ser.). (Illus.). 24p. (J). (gr. 4-7). lib. bdg. 22.60 (978-1-4042-3714-8(3), PowerKids Pr.) Rosen Publishing Group, Inc., The.
Throp, Claire. All about Seeds. (All about Plants Ser.). (ENG.). 24p. (gr. -1-1). 2016. pap. 5.99 (978-1-4846-3849-1(2)) 2014. 22.65 (978-1-4846-0509-7(8)) Heinemann-Raintree. (Acorn).
Wade, Mary Dodson. Seeds Sprout! 2009. (I Like Plants! Ser.). (Illus.). 24p. (J). (gr. k-3). lib. bdg. 22.60 (978-0-7660-3154-8(3)); (gr. 1-3). pap. 7.95 (978-0-7660-3614-7(6), Enslow Elementary) Enslow Pubs., Inc.
Waldron, Melanie. Seeds & Fruits, 1 vol. 2014. (Plant Parts Ser.). (ENG.). 32p. (gr. 2-4). lib. bdg. 30.65 (978-1-4109-5423-7(4), Raintree Perspectives) Heinemann-Raintree.
Ward, Jennifer. What Will Grow? Ghahremani, Susie, illus. 2017. (ENG.). 40p. (J). 16.99 (978-1-68119-030-3(3), 9781681190303, Bloomsbury USA Childrens) Bloomsbury Publishing USA.
Weakland, Mark. Seeds Go, Seeds Grow, 1 vol. 2011. (Science Starts Ser.). (ENG., 32p. (gr. 1-2). Illus.). pap. 8.10 (978-1-4296-6145-4(3)); pap. 47.70 (978-1-4296-6146-1(1)) Capstone Press of Coughlan Cos. (Aplus Bks.).
Whitehouse, Patricia. Las Semillas. 2nd ed. 2010. (Las Plantas Ser.). (ENG & SPA.). 24p. (gr. k-2). 23.32 (978-1-4329-4189-5(5)); pap. 6.79 (978-1-4329-4194-9(1)) Heinemann-Raintree.

SEEING EYE DOGS

see Guide Dogs

SEGHERS, CHARLES JOHN, 1839-1886

Bosco, Antoinette. Charles John Seghers: Pioneer in Alaska. Kalmenoff, Matthew, illus. 2011. 194p. 42.95 (978-1-258-01868-9(3)) Literary Licensing, LLC.

SEGREGATION IN EDUCATION

see also Discrimination in Education

Aretha, David. Brown V. Board of Education. 2013. (The Civil Rights Movement Ser.). (Illus.). 128p. (YA). 28.95 (978-1-59935-370-8(9)) Reynolds, Morgan Inc.
—With All Deliberate Speed: Court-Ordered Busing & American Schools. 2012. (Civil Rights Movement Ser.). (YA). (gr. 7-12). 28.95 (978-1-59935-181-0(1)) Reynolds, Morgan Inc.
Bridges, Ruby. Ruby Bridges Goes to School: My True Story. 2009. (Scholastic Reader Level 2 Ser.). (ENG.). 32p. (J). (gr. -1-3). pap. 3.99 (978-0-545-10855-3(1)) Scholastic, Inc.
—Ruby Bridges Goes to School: My True Story. 2009. (Scholastic Reader Level 2 Ser.). lib. bdg. 13.55 (978-0-606-06808-6(2), Turtleback) Turtleback Bks.
Bridges, Ruby & Maccarone, Grace. Let's Read About — Ruby Bridges. Van Wright, Cornelius & Hu, Ying-Hwa, illus. 2003. (Scholastic First Biographies Ser.). (J). (978-0-439-51362-3(6)) Scholastic, Inc.
Coles, Robert. The Story of Ruby Bridges. 2009. 8.44 (978-0-7848-3016-1(9), Everbind) Marco Bk. Co.
—The Story of Ruby Bridges. 2011. 17.00 (978-1-61383-173-1(0)) Perfection Learning Corp.
—The Story of Ruby Bridges. Ford, George, illus. 50th anniv. ed. 2010. (ENG.). 32p. (J). (gr. -1-3). pap. 6.99 (978-0-439-47226-5(1), Scholastic Paperbacks) Scholastic, Inc.
—The Story of Ruby Bridges. 2010. lib. bdg. 17.20 (978-0-606-23189-3(7), Turtleback) Turtleback Bks.
Donaldson, Madeline. Ruby Bridges. 2009. (History Maker Biographies Ser.). (ENG., Illus.). 48p. (gr. 3-6). 27.93 (978-0-7613-4220-5(6), Lerner Pubns.) Lerner Publishing Group.
Furgang, Kathy. Brown V. Board of Education. 2017. (J). pap. **(978-1-5383-8021-5(8))** Rosen Publishing Group, Inc., The.
Garbus, Julia. Brown vs the Board of Education Trial. Greenhaven Press Staff, ed. 2014. (Perspectives on Modern World History Ser.). (ENG., Illus.). 224p. (gr. 10-12). lib. bdg. 47.80 (978-0-7377-7307-1(3), Greenhaven Pr., Inc.) Cengage Gale.
Gold, Susan Dudley. Brown V. Board of Education: Separate but Equal? 2004. (Supreme Court Milestones Ser.). (Illus.). 143p. (J). 37.07 (978-0-7614-1842-9(3), Benchmark Bks.) Marshall Cavendish Corp.
Goodman, Susan E. The First Step: How One Girl Put Segregation on Trial. Lewis, E. B., illus. 2016. (J). (978-0-8027-3741-0(2)) Bloomsbury Pr.
—The First Step: How One Girl Put Segregation on Trial. Lewis, E. B., illus. 2016. (ENG.). 40p. (J). 17.99 (978-0-8027-3739-7(0), 9780802737397, Bloomsbury USA Childrens) Bloomsbury Publishing USA.
Hinton, KaaVonia. Brown V. Board of Education, Topeka, KS, 1954. 2009. (Monumental Milestones Ser.). 48p. (YA). (gr. 4-7). lib. bdg. 29.95 (978-1-58415-738-0(0)) Mitchell Lane Pubs., Inc.
—Desegregating America's Schools. 2009. (Monumental Milestones Ser.). 48p. (YA). (gr. 4-7). lib. bdg. 29.95 (978-1-58415-737-3(2)) Mitchell Lane Pubs., Inc.
Kanefield, Teri. The Girl from the Tar Paper School: Barbara Rose Johns & the Advent of the Civil Rights Movement. 2014. (ENG., Illus.). 56p. (J). (gr. 3-7). 19.95 (978-1-4197-0796-4(5), Abrams Bks. for Young Readers) Abrams, Inc.
Klein, Rebecca T. School Integration: Brown V. Board of Education of Topeka. 2014. (Celebration of the Civil Rights Movement Ser.). (Illus.). 80p. (J). (gr. 7-12). 34.25 (978-1-4777-7743-5(1)) Rosen Publishing Group, Inc., The.
—Your Legal Rights in School, 1 vol. 2015. (ENG., Illus.). 64p. (J). 33.25 (978-1-4777-8048-0(3), Rosen Reference) Rosen Publishing Group, Inc., The.
Krumm, Brian. The Little Rock Nine: A Primary Source Exploration of the Battle for School Integration, 1 vol. 2014. (We Shall Overcome Ser.). (ENG.). 32p. (gr. 3-4). lib. bdg. 27.32 (978-1-4914-0225-2(3)) Capstone Press of Coughlan Cos.
Looye, Juliette. Ruby Bridges. (Voices Reading Ser.). (Illus.). 16p. (J). pap. (978-0-7367-2913-0(5)) Zaner-Bloser, Inc.
Lucas, Eileen. Cracking the Wall: The Struggles of the Little Rock Nine. Anthony, Mark, illus. 2007. pap. 37.95 incl. audio (978-1-59519-939-3(X)); pap. 39.95 incl. audio compact disk (978-1-59519-943-0(8)) Live Oak Media.
—The Little Rock Nine Stand up for Their Rights. Gustavson, Adam, illus. 2011. 48p. pap. 9.95 (978-0-7613-7118-2(4)); pap. 56.72 (978-0-7613-7634-7(8)) Lerner Publishing Group.
Magoon, Kekla. Today the World Is Watching You: The Little Rock Nine & the Fight for School Integration 1957. 2011. (Civil Rights Struggles around the World Ser.). (ENG., Illus.). 160p. (gr. 9-12). 38.60 (978-0-7613-5767-4(X)) Lerner Publishing Group.
Miller, Mara. School Desegregation & the Story of the Little Rock Nine. 2008. (From Many Cultures, One History Ser.). (Illus.). 128p. (J). (gr. 3-7). lib. bdg. 33.27 (978-0-7660-2835-7(6)) Enslow Pubs., Inc.
Morretta, Alison. Rosa Parks & Civil Disobedience. 2016. (Primary Sources of the Civil Rights Movement Ser.). (Illus.). 64p. (J). (gr. 6-6). 34.21 (978-1-5026-1870-2(2)) Cavendish Square Publishing.
Ribke, Simone T. Ruby Bridges. 2015. (Rookie Biographies(r) Ser.). (ENG., Illus.). 32p. (J). pap. 5.95 (978-0-531-20993-6(8)) Scholastic Library Publishing.
Rubin, Susan Goldman. Brown V. Board of Education: A Fight for Simple Justice. 2016. (ENG., Illus.). 144p. (J). (gr. 5-8). 18.95 (978-0-8234-3646-0(2)) Holiday Hse., Inc.
Taylor, Charlotte & Miller, Mara. The Little Rock Nine & School Desegregation. 2015. (Our Shared History Ser.). (ENG., Illus.). 128p. (J). (gr. 7-7). lib. bdg. 37.27 (978-0-7660-7010-3(7)) Enslow Pubs., Inc.
Tisdale, Rachel. Brown V. Board of Education, 1 vol., 1. 2014. (We Shall Overcome Ser.). (ENG.). 32p. (J). (gr. 3-6). 26.25 (978-1-4777-6073-4(3), PowerKids Pr.) Rosen Publishing Group, Inc., The.
—The Little Rock Nine, 1 vol., 1. 2014. (We Shall Overcome Ser.). (ENG.). 32p. (J). (gr. 3-6). 26.25 (978-1-4777-6057-4(1), PowerKids Pr.) Rosen Publishing Group, Inc., The.
Tonatiuh, Duncan. Separate Is Never Equal: Sylvia Mendez & Her Family's Fight for Desegregation. 2014. (ENG., Illus.). 40p. (J). (gr. 1-4). 18.95 (978-1-4197-1054-4(0), Abrams Bks. for Young Readers) Abrams, Inc.
Tougas, Shelley. Little Rock Girl 1957: How a Photograph Changed the Fight for Integration, 1 vol. 2011. (Captured History Ser.). (ENG.). 64p. (gr. 5-7). pap. 9.10 (978-0-7565-4512-3(9)); lib. bdg. 34.65 (978-0-7565-4440-9(8)) Compass Point Bks. (CPB Grades 4-8).
Walker, Paul Robert. Remember Little Rock: The Time, the People, the Stories. 2009. (Remember Ser.). (ENG., Illus.). 64p. (J). (gr. 5). 17.95 (978-1-4263-0402-6(1)); lib. bdg. 27.90 (978-1-4263-0403-3(X)) National Geographic Society. (National Geographic Children's Bks.).

SEGREGATION IN EDUCATION—FICTION

Conkling, Winifred. Sylvia & Aki. (ENG.). 160p. (J). 2013. (gr. 4-7). 6.99 (978-1-58246-345-2(X), Yearling) 2011. (Illus.). (gr. 3-7). 16.99 (978-1-58246-337-7(9), Tricycle Pr.) Random Hse. Children's Bks.
Sharenow, Robert. My Mother the Cheerleader. 2007. 304p. (J). (gr. 7-18). 16.99 (978-0-06-114896-5(2)); lib. bdg. 17.89 (978-0-06-114897-2(0)) HarperCollins Pubs. (Geringer, Laura Book).
Walvoord, Linda & Walvoord. Rosetta, Rosetta, Sit by Me!, 0 vols. Velasquez, Eric, illus. 2004. (ENG.). 80p. (J). (gr. 3-6). 14.95 (978-0-7614-5171-6(4), 9780761451716, Amazon Children's Publishing) Amazon Publishing.

SEISMOGRAPHY

see Earthquakes

SEISMOLOGY

see Earthquakes

SELECTION, NATURAL

see Natural Selection

SELECTIVE SERVICE

see Draft

SELF-ACCEPTANCE

Beaupré, Nathalie. Why Am I Perfect? An Empowering Book Written for Children First. 2012. 72p. 24.99 (978-1-4797-1114-7(4)); pap. 15.99 (978-1-4797-1113-0(6)) Xlibris Corp.
Conway, Celeste. Body Image & the Media. 2013. (Hot Topics in Media EBook Ser.). (ENG.). 48p. (J). pap. 15.64 (978-1-61783-782-1(2)); (gr. 3-6). lib. bdg. 32.79 (978-1-61783-732-6(6)) ABDO Publishing Co.
Esherick, Joan. Physical Challenges. Albers, Lisa et al, eds. 2014. (Living with a Special Need Ser.: 16). 128p. (J). (gr. 7-18). 25.95 (978-1-4222-3041-1(4)) Mason Crest.
Freeland, Claire A.B. & Toner, Jacqueline B. What to Do When Mistakes Make You Quake: A Kid's Guide to Accepting Imperfection. McDonnell, Janet, illus. 2015. 96p. (J). (978-1-4338-1930-8(9), Magination Pr.) American Psychological Assn.
Greitens, Eric. The Warrior's Heart: Becoming a Man of Compassion & Courage. (ENG., Illus.). (YA). (gr. 7). 2015. 288p. pap. 9.99 (978-0-544-10481-5(1), HMH Books For Young Readers) 2012. 272p. 16.99 (978-0-547-86852-3(9)) Houghton Mifflin Harcourt Publishing Co.
Grossman, Laurie, et al. Master of Mindfulness: How to Be Your Own Superhero in Times of Stress. 2016. (ENG., Illus.). 72p. (J). (gr. k-5). pap. 14.95 (978-1-62625-464-0(8)) New Harbinger Pubns.
Jones, Viola & Willett, Edward. Conquering Negative Body Image, 01 vols., 1. 2016. (Conquering Eating Disorders Ser.). (ENG.). 64p. (J). 32.95 (978-1-4994-6205-0(0), Rosen Young Adult) Rosen Publishing Group, Inc., The.
Kelly, Dorothy A. Developing a Sense of Self: A Workbook of Tenets & Tactics for Adolescent Girls. 2006. (Illus.). 146p. (J). pap. 29.99 (978-0-87101-366-8(5), NASW Pr.) National Assn. of Social Workers/NASW Pr.
Lite, Lori. Affirmation Weaver: A Believe in Yourself Story Designed to Help Children Increase Self-Esteem While Decreasing Stress & Anxiety. 2nd ed. 2011. 24p. pap. 14.95 (978-0-9836256-9-8(7)) Stress Free Pubs.
—Angry Octopus: An Anger Management Story Introducing Active Progressive Muscular Relaxation & Deep Breathing. 2011. (Illus.). 30p. (gr. -1-3). pap. 14.95 (978-0-9836256-8-1(9)) Stress Free Pubs.
—A Boy & a Turtle: A Relaxation Story Teaching Young Children Visualization Techniques to Increase Creativity While Lowering Stress & Anxiety Lev. 3rd ed. 2012.Tr. of niño y una Tortuga. (ENG.). 16p. (J). pap. 12.95 (978-1-937985-13-4(X)) Stress Free Pubs.
—Bubble Riding: A Relaxation Story Designed to Teach Children Visualization Techniques to Increase Creativity While Lowering Stress & Anxiety. 2012.Tr. of Montando Burbujas. (ENG.). (J). pap. 14.95 (978-1-937985-03-5(2)) Stress Free Pubs.
—Buenas Noches Oruga: Una Historia para la Relajación Que Ayuda a Los Niños a Controlar la Ira y el Estrés para Que Se Queden Dormidos Sosegadamente. 2012.Tr. of Goodnight Caterpillar. (SPA., Illus.). 16p. (J). pap. 12.95 (978-1-937985-16-5(4)) Stress Free Pubs.
—Caleta de la Nutria Marina: Un Cuento para la Ansiedad Infantil, Enseña la Relajación, la Respiración Profunda para Reducir la Ansiedad, el Estrés y la Ira, a la Vez Que Fomenta el Sueño Sosegado. 2011.Tr. of Sea Otter Cove. (SPA., Illus.). 28p. (J). pap. 14.95 (978-1-937985-11-0(3)) Stress Free Pubs.
—The Goodnight Caterpillar: A Children's Relaxation Story to Improve Sleep, Manage Stress, Anxiety, Anger. 3rd abr. ed. 2011.Tr. of Buenas Noches, Oruga. (ENG.). 18p. (J). pap. 12.95 (978-1-937985-00-4(8)) Stress Free Pubs.
—Montando Burbujas: Un Cuento con Ejercicios de Relajación para Niños, Diseñada para Enseñar a Los Niños Técnicas de Visualización para Aumentar la Creatividad Mientras Disminuyen Sus Niveles de Ansiedad y de Estrés. 2012.Tr. of Bubble Riding. (SPA., Illus.). 32p. (J). pap. 14.95 (978-1-937985-12-7(1)) Stress Free Pubs.
—El Niño y la Tortuga: Un Cuento para Promover la Relajación. 2012.Tr. of Boy & a Turtle. (SPA., Illus.). 16p. (J). pap. 12.95 (978-1-937985-17-2(2)) Stress Free Pubs.
—El Pulpo Enojado: Un Cuento Sobre Cómo Controlar la Ira Que Enseña la Relajación Muscular Activa y Progresiva, y la Respiración: un Cuento Sobre Cómo Controlar la Ira Que Enseña la Relajación Muscular Activa y Progresiva, y la Respiración. 2012.Tr. of Angry Octopus. (SPA., Illus.). 30p. (J). pap. 14.95 (978-1-937985-01-1(6)) Stress Free Pubs.
—Sea Otter Cove: A Relaxation Story, Introducing Deep Breathing to Decrease Anxiety, Stress & Anger While Promoting Peaceful Sleep. 2nd ed. 2012.Tr. of Caleta de la Nutria Marina. (SPA & ENG., Illus.). 24p. (J). 14.95 (978-1-937985-08-0(3)) Stress Free Pubs.
—Tejedor de Afirmaciones: Un Cuento Que Aumenta la Autoestima en Los Niños, Creer en Ellos Mismos, Mientras Que Reducen Su Estrés y Su Ansiedad. 2012.Tr. of Affirmation Weaver. (SPA., Illus.). 24p. (J). pap. 14.95 (978-1-937985-02-8(4)) Stress Free Pubs.
Mastromarino, Diane, ed. The Girl's Guide to Loving Yourself: A Book about Falling in Love with the One Person Who Matters Most - You. (ENG.). 64p. pap. 9.95 (978-0-88396-751-5(0), Blue Mountain Pr.) Blue Mountain Arts Inc.
Miller, Ruth L. The Power of Self Ralph Waldo Emerson's Wonder Filled Life. Shonkwiler, Martha, illus. 2013. 66p. pap. 12.00 (978-0-945385-85-1(4)) WiseWoman Pr.
Ottaviano, Patricia. Girl World: How to Ditch the Drama & Find Your Inner Amazing. 2015. (ENG.). 160p. (YA). (gr. 6-12). pap. 9.99 (978-1-4926-0912-4(9), 9781492609124) Sourcebooks, Inc.
Palmer, Pat. Liking Myself. Shondeck, Betty, illus. 2010. 102p. (J). pap. 12.99 (978-0-9622834-2-0(8)) Uplift Pr.
Parr, Todd. The Okay Book. 2004. (ENG., Illus.). 24p. (J). (gr. -1 — 1). bds. 6.99 (978-0-316-90809-2(6)) Little, Brown Bks. for Young Readers.
Payne, Lauren Murphy. Just Because I Am: A Child's Book of Affirmation. Iwai, Melissa, illus. 2nd rev. ed. 2015. (ENG.). 36p. (J). (gr. -1-2). 14.99 (978-1-63198-051-0(3)) Free Spirit Publishing, Inc.
Tool Kits for Kids LLC Staff, creator. Outsmart Your Worry - Tool Kit for Kids: Elementary School Edition. 2008. (Illus.). 23p. (J). 39.95 (978-0-9819483-0-0(8)) Tool Kits For Kids LLC.

—Outsmart Your Worry - Tool Kit for Kids: High School / Middle School Edition. 2008. (Illus.). (J). 39.95 *(978-0-9819483-1-7(6))* Tool Kits For Kids LLC.

SELF-ACCEPTANCE—FICTION

Al-Ghani, K. I. Baby Blue Has the Blues, 1 vol. Al-Ghani, Haitham, illus. 2011. (ENG.). 32p. (J). 16.99 *(978-0-7643-3732-1(7)*, 9780764337321, Schiffer Publishing Ltd) Schiffer Publishing, Ltd.

Anderson, M. T. Burger Wuss. 2008. (ENG., Illus.). 192p. (YA). (gr. 9). per. 8.99 *(978-0-7636-3178-9(7))* Candlewick Pr.

Archambault, Marc. Teevert the Little Green Leaf. 2010. 31p. 18.98 *(978-0-557-17967-1(X))* Lulu Pr., Inc.

Arkangel, Brian. Cow Story. Moffat, Ross, illus. 2009. 24p. pap. 24.95 *(978-1-60703-272-4(4))* America Star Bks.

Atamer, Billie. The Little Purple Pumpkin. 2013. 28p. (gr. -1-3). pap. 11.95 *(978-1-61244-235-8(8))* Halo Publishing International.

Ayton, Shalanna. The Adventures of Missy the Moose. 2009. 68p. pap. 26.99 *(978-1-4389-7827-7(8))* AuthorHouse.

Baird, Noah. Southpaw. McMaugh, Kimberly, illus. 2013. 40p. pap. 13.95 *(978-1-938101-35-9(9))* Indigo Sea Pr., LLC.

Baker, Keith. Sometimes. 2003. (Green Light Readers Level 1 Ser.). (ENG., Illus.). 24p. (J). (gr. -1-3). pap. 3.95 *(978-0-15-204847-1(2))* Houghton Mifflin Harcourt Publishing Co.

—Sometimes. 2003. (Green Light Readers — Level 1 Ser.). (gr. -1-2). lib. bdg. 13.50 *(978-0-613-64597-3(9)*, Turtleback) Turtleback Bks.

—Sometimes/Algunas Veces. Flor Ada, Alma & Campoy, F. Isabel, trs. from ENG. 2007. (Green Light Readers Level 1 Ser.). (ENG & SPA., Illus.). 28p. (J). (gr. -1-3). pap. 3.95 *(978-0-15-205961-3(X))* Houghton Mifflin Harcourt Publishing Co.

Bar-el, Dan. Not Your Typical Dragon. Bowers, Tim, illus. 2013. (ENG.). 40p. (J). (gr. -1-k). 16.99 *(978-0-670-01402-6(8)*, Viking Books for Young Readers) Penguin Young Readers Group.

Beaumont, Karen. Wild about Us! Stevens, Janet, illus. 2015. (ENG.). 40p. (J). (gr. -1-3). 17.99 *(978-0-15-206294-1(7)*, HMH Books For Young Readers) Houghton Mifflin Harcourt Publishing Co.

Beck, Rachel. Bella & the Little Gray Kitten. 2011. 40p. (gr. -1). pap. 18.50 *(978-1-4567-3365-0(6))* AuthorHouse.

Benedetto, K. & Barlow, J. I See the World. 2009. pap. *(978-1-61584-125-7(3))* Independent Pub.

Berenstain, Stan, et al. God Loves You!, 1 vol. 2008. (Berenstain Bears/Living Lights Ser.). (ENG., Illus.). 32p. (J). pap. 3.99 *(978-0-310-71250-3(5))* Zonderkidz.

Bergen, Lara. Sophie the Awesome. Tallardy, Laura, illus. 2010. 99p. (J). *(978-0-545-24231-8(2))* Scholastic, Inc.

Bingham, Kelly. Shark Girl. (ENG., Illus.). 288p. (YA). (gr. 7). 2010. pap. 8.99 *(978-0-7636-4627-1(X))* 2007. 16.99 *(978-0-7636-3207-6(4))* Candlewick Pr.

Bloom, Denise. More Than a Spoonful. 2007. 28p. (J). (gr. -1-2). pap. 5.95 *(978-0-9778113-2-8(8))* HeartFelt Stories LLC.

Bloom, Denise, et al. More Than a Spoonful. 2007. (Heartfelt Stories Ser.). (Illus.). 28p. (J). 12.95 *(978-0-9778113-0-4(1))* HeartFelt Stories LLC.

Blume, Judy. Otherwise Known as Sheila the Great. 2007. (ENG.). 176p. (J). (gr. 3-7). 7.99 *(978-0-14-240879-7(4)*, Puffin Books) Penguin Young Readers Group.

—Otherwise Known as Sheila the Great. 2007. 154p. (gr. 4-7). 16.00 *(978-0-7569-7915-7(3))* Perfection Learning Corp.

—Otherwise Known as Sheila the Great. 2007. (Fudge Bks.: 2). 138p. (gr. 4-7). lib. bdg. 18.40 *(978-1-4177-8370-0(2)*, Turtleback) Turtleback Bks.

Boulden, James. Buddy Learns from His Mistakes: Student Involvement Pack. 2003. (Illus.). 21p. (J). 24.95 *(978-1-892421-78-4(X))* Boulden Publishing.

Briceno, Carole. Turtle's Journey, 1 vol. White, Tina Jorgenson, illus. 2009. 28p. pap. 24.95 *(978-1-60813-934-7(4))* America Star Bks.

Brown, Peter. Mr. Tiger Goes Wild. 2013. (ENG.). 48p. (J). 126.00 *(978-0-316-25551-6(3))*; (Illus.). (gr. -1-1). 18.00 *(978-0-316-20063-9(8))* Little, Brown Bks. for Young Readers.

Burch, Christian. Hit the Road, Manny: A Manny Files Novel. 2008. (ENG.). 240p. (J). (gr. 3-7). 16.99 *(978-1-4169-2812-6(X)*, Atheneum Bks. for Young Readers) Simon & Schuster Children's Publishing.

Burkhart, Kiersi, et al. The Long Trail Home. 2017. (Quartz Creek Ranch Ser.). (ENG.). 240p. (gr. 4-8). 6.99 *(978-1-5124-3090-5(0)*, Darby Creek) Lerner Publishing Group.

Burn, Doris. Andrew Henry's Meadow. Burn, Doris, illus. 2012. (ENG., Illus.). 48p. (J). (gr. 1-4). 16.99 *(978-0-399-25608-0(3)*, Philomel Bks.) Penguin Young Readers Group.

Burns, Marilyn. The Greedy Triangle. Silveria, Gordon, illus. 2008. (Scholastic Bookshelf Ser.). (ENG.). 32p. (J). (gr. -1-3). pap. 6.99 *(978-0-545-04220-8(8)*, Scholastic Paperbacks) Scholastic, Inc.

Cabral, Noel. Rachel's Four-Legged Friend. 2012. 24p. 24.95 *(978-1-4626-6089-6(4))* America Star Bks.

Caminada, Janet Barnett. Yoga, the Kid & the Cricket: A fun & easy illustrated guide to beginner's yoga. A complete yoga workout that follows along with the story. Written. 2011. 36p. pap. 22.88 *(978-1-4634-4478-5(8))* AuthorHouse.

Campbell, Jennifer. Elise the Elephant. Cox, Nancy, illus. 2012. 32p. pap. 16.99 *(978-1-4567-9920-5(7))* AuthorHouse.

Cardin, Jodi. Bernice's Bad Hair Days. Chin, Todd, illus. 2009. 56p. (J). pap. *(978-1-60800-004-3(4))* LifeReloaded Specialty Publishing LLC.

Carter, Catherine. Anna's Choice. Pittman, Gail, illus. 2005. 24p. (J). (gr. 3-7). 12.95 *(978-1-893062-79-5(1))* Quail Ridge Pr., Inc.

Cavanaugh, Nancy J. This Journal Belongs to Ratchet. 2014. (ENG.). 320p. (J). (gr. 3-6). pap. 6.99 *(978-1-4926-0109-8(8)*, 9781492601098, Sourcebooks Jabberwocky) Sourcebooks, Inc.

Cento, Nucci. Maverick & Miss Murphy at Rascal's Rescue Ranch. 2009. 48p. pap. 12.50 *(978-1-60860-388-6(1)*, Eloquent Bks.) Strategic Book Publishing & Rights Agency (SBPRA).

Ciddor, Anna. Runestone: The First Book about the Adventures of Oddo & Thora. 2007. (Viking Magic Ser.). (ENG., Illus.). 192p. (Orig.). (J). (gr. 4-7). pap. 11.99 *(978-1-86508-689-7(4))* Allen & Unwin AUS. Dist: Independent Pubs. Group.

Claverie, Jean & Chapouton, Anne Marie. Julian. 2003. (SPA., Illus.). 28p. *(978-84-85334-71-1(X))* Lóguez Ediciones ESP. Dist: Lectorum Pubns., Inc.

Cocca-Leffler, Maryann. Janine. Cocca-Leffler, Maryann, illus. 2015. (ENG., Illus.). 32p. (J). (gr. -1-3). 16.99 *(978-0-8075-3754-1(3))* Whitman, Albert & Co.

Cole, Hana. Hooray! I'm Catholic. Steege, Joanna, illus. 2010. 32p. (J). 14.95 *(978-0-8091-6746-3(8)*, Ambassador Bks.) Paulist Pr.

Colfer, Chris. The Curvy Tree. Dorman, Brandon, illus. 2015. (ENG.). 32p. (J). (gr. -1-3). 17.00 *(978-0-316-40685-7(6))* Little Brown & Co.

Collins, Ross. Medusa Jones. 2008. (J). *(978-0-439-90101-7(4)*, Levine, Arthur A. Bks.) Scholastic, Inc.

Cooner, Donna. Skinny. (ENG.). 272p. (J). (gr. 7). 2014. pap. 9.99 *(978-0-545-42764-7(9))* 2012. 17.99 *(978-0-545-42763-0(0))* Scholastic, Inc.

Cooper, Abby. Sticks & Stones. 2017. (J). lib. bdg. 18.40 ***(978-0-606-39950-0(X))*** Turtleback Bks.

Cotterill, Colin. Average Alan. 2013. 150p. pap. *(978-616-7503-18-9(4))* Asia Document Bureau, Ltd.

Coven, Wanda. Heidi Heckelbeck Gets Glasses. Burris, Priscilla, illus. 2012. (Heidi Heckelbeck Ser.: 5). (ENG.). 128p. (J). (gr. k-2). pap. 5.99 *(978-1-4424-4171-2(2))*; 15.99 *(978-1-4424-4172-9(0))* Little Simon. (Little Simon).

—Heidi Heckelbeck Gets Glasses. 2012. (Heidi Heckelbeck Ser.: 5). lib. bdg. 16.00 *(978-0-606-26888-2(X)*, Turtleback) Turtleback Bks.

Cuevas, Michelle. Beyond the Laughing Sky. Morstad, Julie, illus. 2014. (ENG.). 160p. (J). (gr. 3-7). 16.99 *(978-0-8037-3867-6(6)*, Dial Bks) Penguin Young Readers Group.

Cuthand, Beth. Sikihpsis. Cuthand, Stan, tr. Longman, Mary, illus. ed. 2007. (Little Duck Ser.). (CRE & ENG.). 28p. 17.00 *(978-1-894778-44-2(8))* Theytus Bks., Ltd. CAN. Dist: Univ. of Toronto Pr.

Dakos, Kalli. Why Am I Blue? A Story about Being Yourself. Garófoli, Viviana, illus. 2017. 32p. (J). 15.95 ***(978-1-4338-2734-1(4)***, Magination Pr.) American Psychological Assn.

De la Peña, Matt. Mexican WhiteBoy. 2010. (ENG.). 256p. (YA). (gr. 9). pap. 9.99 *(978-0-440-23938-3(9)*, Ember) Random Hse. Children's Bks.

—Mexican WhiteBoy. 2010. lib. bdg. 20.85 *(978-0-606-12316-7(4)*, Turtleback) Turtleback Bks.

Demonia, Lori. Leah's Voice. 2013. 28p. 16.95 *(978-1-61244-240-2(4))* Halo Publishing International.

Denton, Kiwi. Freddie's Magical Glasses, 1 vol. 2010. 18p. 24.95 *(978-1-4489-3309-9(9))* PublishAmerica, Inc.

Deuker, Carl. On the Devil's Court. 2008. (ENG.). 208p. (YA). (gr. 7-17). pap. 10.99 *(978-0-316-06727-0(X))* Little, Brown Bks. for Young Readers.

Dickey, R. A. Knuckleball Ned. Bowers, Tim, illus. 2014. (ENG.). 32p. (J). (gr. -1-k). 17.99 *(978-0-8037-4038-9(7)*, Dial Bks) Penguin Young Readers Group.

Diggs, Taye. Chocolate Me! Evans, Shane W., illus. 2011. (ENG.). 40p. (J). (gr. -1-3). 17.99 *(978-0-312-60326-7(6)*, 9780312603267) Feiwel & Friends.

Disney & Sisler, Celeste. Disney Fairies: Meet Tinker Bell. 2014. (Passport to Reading Level 1 Ser.). (ENG., Illus.). 32p. (J). (gr. -1-3). 3.99 *(978-0-316-28327-4(4))* Little, Brown Bks. for Young Readers.

Dole, Mayra Lazara. Down to the Bone. 2008. 384p. (J). (gr. 9). lib. bdg. 17.89 *(978-0-06-084311-3(X)*, HarperTeen) HarperCollins Pubs.

Doren, Greg Van. Obleo. 2010. 24p. pap. 11.49 *(978-1-4490-8811-8(2))* AuthorHouse.

Doyle, Marissa. Courtship & Curses. 2013. (ENG.). 368p. (YA). (gr. 9-13). pap. 10.99 *(978-1-250-02744-3(6))* Square Fish.

Drachman, Eric. A Frog Thing. Muscarello, James, illus. 2006. (ENG.). 32p. (J). (gr. -1-2). 18.95 incl. audio compact disk *(978-0-9703809-3-7(3))* Kidwick Bks.

Driskell, Cheryl. Child & Youth Reiki Program: Mount Kurama & the Emerald Lake. 2005. 84p. (J). pap. 15.95 *(978-1-4116-3900-3(6))* Lulu Pr., Inc.

Duvoisin, Roger. Donkey-Donkey. 2016. (ENG., Illus.). 56p. (J). (-k). 16.95 *(978-1-59017-964-2(1)*, NYR Children's Collection) New York Review of Bks., Inc., The.

Ebeling, Vicki. The Winners Group. 2007. (J). per. 7.95 *(978-0-9779768-0-5(7))* Ebeling, Vicki.

Eland, Lindsay. A Summer of Sundays. (ENG.). 336p. (J). (gr. 3-7). 2014. pap. 8.99 *(978-1-60684-541-7(1))* 2013. 16.99 *(978-1-60684-030-6(4))* Lerner Publishing Group. (Carolrhoda Bks.).

Elliott, Sherria L. My Shaking Eyes. Moore, Sasha & Tilak, Brian, illus. 2013. 30p. pap. 12.99 *(978-0-9846963-2-1(6))* 4Elliott Publishing, Inc.

Emerson, Carl. Falling Freddy the Fainting Goat, 1 vol. Trover, Zachary, illus. 2007. (Animal Underdogs Ser.). (ENG.). 32p. (gr. -1-4). 28.50 *(978-1-60270-015-4(X)*, Looking Glass Library) ABDO Publishing Co.

Erskine, Kathryn. The Absolute Value of Mike. 2012. (ENG.). 272p. (J). (gr. 5-18). pap. 7.99 *(978-0-14-242101-7(4)*, Puffin Books) Penguin Young Readers Group.

Escott, Maria. Green Anole Meets Brown Anole, a Love Story. Wigal, Mike, illus. 2010. 28p. pap. 12.95 *(978-1-936051-82-3(6))* Peppertree Pr., The.

Feldman, Thea. Rudolph the Red-Nosed Reindeer. Madrid, Erwin, illus. 2016. (ENG.). 22p. (J). bds. 10.99 *(978-1-250-12323-7(2)*, 9781250123237, Holt, Henry & Co. Bks. For Young Readers) Holt, Henry & Co.

Ferguson, Terrence. Stuttering Sammie: I'm Just Like You, I Just Repeat Some Letters or Words When I Talk. 2012. 24p. 24.95 *(978-1-4626-6267-8(6))*; pap. 24.95 *(978-1-4626-8326-0(6))* America Star Bks.

Flesher, Vivienne. Alfred's Nose. Flesher, Vivienne, illus. 2008. (Illus.). 32p. (J). (gr. -1-2). lib. bdg. 17.89 *(978-0-06-084314-4(4))* HarperCollins Pubs.

Folz, Alexandra. Indigo's Bracelet. 2010. 84p. pap. 9.95 *(978-1-4525-0058-4(4))* Get Published.

Forester, Victoria. The Boy Who Knew Everything. 2015. (ENG.). 416p. (J). (gr. 4-7). 16.99 *(978-0-312-62600-6(2)*, 9780312626006) Feiwel & Friends.

—The Girl Who Could Fly. 2008. (ENG.). 336p. (J). (gr. 4-7). 16.95 *(978-0-312-37462-4(3)*, 9780312374624) Feiwel & Friends.

—The Girl Who Could Fly. Barcellona, Christine, ed. 2015. (ENG.). 352p. (J). (gr. 4-7). pap. 7.99 *(978-1-250-07246-7(8)*, 9781250072467) Square Fish.

Frank, E. R. Wrecked. (ENG., (YA). 2015. Illus.). 336p. (gr. 9). pap. 10.99 *(978-1-4814-5137-6(5))* 2007. 256p. (gr. 7-12). pap. 9.99 *(978-0-689-87384-3(0))* Simon & Schuster Children's Publishing. (Atheneum Bks. for Young Readers).

Friend, Natasha. My Life in Black & White. 2012. (ENG.). 304p. (YA). (gr. 7-18). pap. 8.99 *(978-0-670-78494-3(X)*, Viking Books for Young Readers) Penguin Young Readers Group.

Frye, Karen. Flake, 1 vol. 2010. 16p. 24.95 *(978-1-4489-4935-9(1))* PublishAmerica, Inc.

Furrow, Eva & Napoli, Donna Jo. Take Your Time: A Tale of Harriet, the Galápagos Tortoise. Molk, Laurel, illus. 2017. (ENG.). 32p. (J). 16.99 *(978-0-8050-9521-0(7)*, 9780805095210, Holt, Henry & Co. Bks. For Young Readers) Holt, Henry & Co.

Furukawa, Masumi, illus. The Ugly Duckling. 2007. (Flip-Up Fairy Tales Ser.). (ENG.). 24p. (J). (gr. -1-2). audio compact disk *(978-1-84643-095-4(X))* Child's Play International Ltd.

Garland, Michael. Fish Had a Wish. Garland, Michael, illus. (I Like to Read(r) Ser.). (ENG., Illus.). 24p. (J). 2013. pap. 6.99 *(978-0-8234-2757-4(9))* 2012. 14.95 *(978-0-8234-2394-1(8))* Holiday Hse., Inc.

Gawade, Akansha A. This Is Who I Am. 2006. (J). pap. 8.00 *(978-0-8059-6886-6(5))* Dorrance Publishing Co., Inc.

Genhart, Michael. Mac & Geeeez! ...being Real Is What It's All About. Mack, Steve, illus. 2017. (J). ***(978-1-4338-2723-5(9)***, Magination Pr.) American Psychological Assn.

Gibney, Shannon. See No Color. 2015. (ENG.). 192p. (YA). (gr. 7-12). 18.99 *(978-1-4677-8814-4(7)*, Carolrhoda Lab™); 18.99 *(978-1-4677-7682-0(3))* Lerner Publishing Group.

Giff, Patricia Reilly. All the Way Home. 2003. (ENG., Illus.). 176p. (J). (gr. 3-7). pap. 7.99 *(978-0-440-41182-6(3)*, Yearling) Random Hse. Children's Bks.

Gil, Carmen. Story of a Cockroach. 2012. (Mini-Animalist Ser.). (ENG., Illus.). 32p. (J). (gr. -1-2). *(978-84-15241-22-5(4))* D P & G Military Pubs.

Glickman, Susan. Bernadette & the Lunch Bunch, 1 vol. Allard, Melanie, illus. 2009. (Lunch Bunch Ser.). (ENG.). 123p. (J). (gr. 1-4). pap. 6.95 *(978-1-897187-51-7(3))* Second Story Pr. CAN. Dist: Orca Bk. Pubs. USA.

Golden, Laura. Every Day After. 2014. (ENG.). 224p. (J). (gr. 4-7). 6.99 *(978-0-307-98314-5(5)*, Yearling) Random Hse. Children's Bks.

Goobie, Beth & Fernández, Queta. Ni un Día Más, 1 vol. 2009. (Spanish Soundings Ser.). (SPA.). 112p. (YA). (gr. 8-12). pap. 9.95 *(978-1-55469-137-1(0))* Orca Bk. Pubs. USA.

Goss, Leon. I'm Good, I'm Beautiful, I'm Smart. Mailey, Maria C. & Neuburger, Jenny, illus. 2005. (J). per. *(978-1-933156-02-6(3)*, VisionQuest Kids) GSVQ Publishing.

Gottfred, B. T. The Nerdy & the Dirty. 2016. (ENG.). 304p. (YA). 17.99 *(978-1-62779-850-1(1)*, 9781627798501, Holt, Henry & Co. Bks. For Young Readers) Holt, Henry & Co.

Grammy Sunshine. The Adventures of Mouse: The Mouse Who Wanted to Be A Pig. 2009. 20p. pap. 12.49 *(978-1-4389-9268-6(8))* AuthorHouse.

Grateful Steps Publishing & Tipton, Angela. Butterflies Don't Crawl. Irvine, Wil, illus. 2009. 32p. (J). 16.95 *(978-1-935130-14-7(5))* Grateful Steps.

Gray, Diane. The Bears with Unruly Hairs. 2011. 28p. pap. 15.99 *(978-1-4568-8129-0(9))* Xlibris Corp.

Green, George & Brooke, Amy/ J. George Green's, the Lion Who Couldn't Roar. 2008. (Illus.). (J). per. 16.99 *(978-1-933156-14-9(7)*, Visikid Bks.) GSVQ Publishing.

Haber, Tiffany Strelitz. The Monster Who Lost His Mean. Edmunds, Kirstie, illus. 2012. (ENG.). 40p. (J). (gr. -1-3). 17.99 *(978-0-8050-9375-9(3)*, 9780805093759, Holt, Henry & Co. Bks. For Young Readers) Holt, Henry & Co.

Harrison, Hannah E. Extraordinary Jane. 2014. (ENG.). 40p. (J). (gr. -1-k). 16.99 *(978-0-8037-3914-7(1)*, Dial Bks) Penguin Young Readers Group.

Haworth-Attard, Barbara. My Life from Air-Bras to Zits. 2009. (ENG.). 288p. (YA). (gr. 7-10). pap. 9.95 *(978-0-7387-1483-7(6)*, Flux) North Star Editions.

Headley, Justina Chen. The Patch. Vane, Mitch, illus. 2007. (ENG.). 32p. (J). (gr. k-3). pap. 7.95 *(978-1-58089-170-7(5))* Charlesbridge Publishing, Inc.

Henshon, Suzanna E. Spiders on the Ceiling. 2006. (J). *(978-0-88092-614-0(7))* Royal Fireworks Publishing Co.

Hofmann-Maniyar, Ariane. That's NOT How You Do It! Hofmann-Maniyar, Ariane, illus. 2017. (Child's Play Library). (ENG., Illus.). 32p. (J). *(978-1-84643-929-2(9))* Child's Play International Ltd.

Hogan, Mary. Pretty Face. (ENG.). 224p. (J). 2009. pap. 8.99 *(978-0-06-084113-3(3))* 2008. (gr. 9-18). 16.99 *(978-0-06-084111-9(7))* HarperCollins Pubs. (HarperTeen).

Howe, James. Addie on the Inside. 2011. (Misfits Ser.). (ENG., Illus.). 224p. (J). (gr. 5-9). 16.99 *(978-1-4169-1384-9(X)*, Atheneum Bks. for Young Readers) Simon & Schuster Children's Publishing.

Hudson, Katy. Bear & Duck. Hudson, Katy, illus. 2015. (ENG., Illus.). 32p. (J). (gr. -1-3). 17.99 *(978-0-06-232051-3(3))* HarperCollins Pubs.

Jakubowski, Michele. Ashley Small & Ashlee Tall, 4 vols. Fekete, H., illus. 2016. (Ashley Small & Ashlee Tall Ser.). (ENG.). 64p. (gr. 1-3). 82.60 *(978-1-5158-0021-7(0))* Picture Window Bks.

Jerry, Spinelli. Loser. 2014. (ENG.). 224p. (J). (gr. 7-7). 11.24 *(978-1-63245-207-8(3))* Lectorum Pubns., Inc.

Jovanovic, Katarina. The King Has Goat Ears, 1 vol. Beha, Philippe, illus. 2008. (ENG.). 32p. (J). (gr. k-2). 16.95 *(978-1-896580-22-7(X))* Tradewind Bks. CAN. Dist: Orca Bk. Pubs. USA.

Kaiser, Lori. Megan the Moody Moose. Kaiser, Lori, illus. 2013. (Illus.). 26p. pap. *(978-0-9883770-5-9(5))* Roxby Media Ltd.

Katrana, Carol. Charlie, the Christmas Camel: A Christmas Story to Remember. 2012. 120p. (gr. 4-6). pap. 16.95 *(978-1-4772-7710-2(2))* AuthorHouse.

Keith, Brooke. Chrissie's Shell. Bausman, Mary, illus. 2010. 32p. (J). 14.99 *(978-1-59317-398-2(9))* Warner Pr., Inc.

Kent, Renee Holmes. Robyn Flies Home, Vol. 4. 2004. (Adventures in Misty Falls Ser.: Vol. 4). (Illus.). 100p. (gr. 4-7). pap. 4.99 *(978-1-56309-764-5(8)*, N007106) New Hope Pubs.

Kessler, Jackie Morse. Rage. 2011. (Riders of the Apocalypse Ser.: 2). (ENG.). 240p. (YA). (gr. 7-18). pap. 9.99 *(978-0-547-44528-1(8))* Houghton Mifflin Harcourt Publishing Co.

Keyser, Amber J. & Burkhart, Kiersi. The Long Trail Home. 2017. (Quartz Creek Ranch Ser.). (ENG.). 240p. (gr. 4-8). lib. bdg. 27.99 *(978-1-4677-9256-1(X))*; 35.99 ***(978-1-5124-2698-4(9))*** Lerner Publishing Group. (Darby Creek).

Kimmel, Elizabeth Cody. Lily B. on the Brink of Love. 2005. (ENG.). 192p. (J). 15.99 *(978-0-06-075541-6(5))* HarperCollins Pubs.

—Suddenly Supernatural: Scaredy Kat. 2010. (Suddenly Supernatural Ser.: 2). (ENG.). 272p. (J). (gr. 3-7). pap. 5.99 *(978-0-316-08745-2(9))* Little, Brown Bks. for Young Readers.

King-Chai, Sharon. Lucy Ladybug. 2016. (ENG., Illus.). 32p. (J). (gr. -1-2). 16.99 *(978-0-553-51005-8(3)*, Random Hse. Bks. for Young Readers) Random Hse. Children's Bks.

Kittle, Katrina. Reasons to Be Happy. 2011. (ENG.). 288p. (J). (gr. 6-8). pap. 10.99 *(978-1-4022-6020-9(2)*, Sourcebooks Jabberwocky) Sourcebooks, Inc.

Knapp, J. Richard. Bobby's Story: An Amazing Story of Teen Courage. 2006. (ENG.). 224p. (YA). per. 14.95 *(978-0-9774761-7-6(0)*, Books To Believe In) Thornton Publishing, Inc.

Knight, Chris. Karen Bighead: The Story of a Little Girl with a Big Head. 2011. (Illus.). 24p. 12.12 *(978-1-4520-7730-7(4))* AuthorHouse.

Koertge, Ron. Now Playing: Stoner & Spaz II. 2011. (ENG., Illus.). 224p. (YA). (gr. 9-18). 16.99 *(978-0-7636-5081-0(1))* Candlewick Pr.

—Stoner & Spaz. 2011. (ENG., Illus.). 192p. (YA). (gr. 9). pap. 7.99 *(978-0-7636-5757-4(3))* Candlewick Pr.

Koffman, Donna Carol. Different Kinds of Special. Biggar, Breanne, illus. 2011. 36p. pap. *(978-1-55483-897-4(5))* Insomniac Pr.

Kogler, Jennifer. The Otherworldlies. 2008. 400p. (J). lib. bdg. 17.89 *(978-0-06-073960-7(6))*; (ENG.). (gr. 5-18). 16.99 *(978-0-06-073959-1(2))* HarperCollins Pubs. (Eos).

Kogler, Jennifer Anne & Kogler, Jennifer A. The Otherworldlies. 2009. (ENG.). 400p. (YA). (gr. 8). pap. 8.99 *(978-0-06-073961-4(4)*, HarperTeen) HarperCollins Pubs.

Kowalski, Bernard. Alexis & Ralph the Dragon, 1 vol. 2010. 32p. 24.95 *(978-1-4512-1008-6(8))* PublishAmerica, Inc.

Kranz, Linda. You Be You. Mlawer, Teresa, tr. from ENG. 2014. (ENG & SPA., Illus.). 32p. (J). (gr. -1-1). 12.95 *(978-1-63076-021-2(8))* Taylor Trade Publishing.

—You Be You. (J). 2011. *(978-1-58979-667-6(5))* 2011. (ENG., Illus.). 32p. (gr. -1-1). 12.95 *(978-1-58979-666-9(7))* Vol. 2013. (ENG., Illus.). 32p. (gr. -1 — 1). 7.95 *(978-1-58979-747-5(7))* Taylor Trade Publishing.

Krupic, Janice. Felicia's Family Divorces. 2004. 72p. *(978-0-9745219-0-9(6))* Children Concept Publishing.

Kwaymullina, Ezekiel. Colour Me. 2017. (ENG.). 32p. (J). (gr. -1-1). 16.99 ***(978-1-925164-65-7(9))*** Fremantle Pr. AUS. Dist: Independent Pubs. Group.

Laubenstein, Sharon. Something about Sally. 2013. 24p. pap. 10.95 *(978-1-4908-0723-2(3)*, WestBow Pr.) Author Solutions, Inc.

Le Guin, Ursula K. Very Far Away from Anywhere Else. 2004. (ENG.). 144p. (YA). (gr. 7-12). pap. 6.95 *(978-0-15-205208-9(9))* Houghton Mifflin Harcourt Publishing Co.

Leppard, Laura Jennifer. The Duchess of Sao Paulo. 2006. 49p. (J). pap. 17.89 *(978-1-4116-6635-1(6))* Lulu Pr., Inc.

Levine, Gail Carson. Fairest. 2006. 326p. (J). (gr. 3-7). lib. bdg. 18.89 *(978-0-06-073409-1(4))* HarperCollins Pubs.

—Fairest. l.t. rev. ed. 2007. (Literacy Bridge Young Adult Ser.). 349p. (J). (gr. 3-7). 23.95 *(978-0-7862-9270-7(9))* Thorndike Pr.

Levine, Gail Carson & Levine, Gail C. Fairest. 2012. (ENG.). 352p. (J). (gr. 3-7). pap. 6.99 *(978-0-06-073410-7(8))* HarperCollins Pubs.

Licker, Laura. Frogs & Dragons, 1 vol. 2009. 28p. pap. 24.95 *(978-1-60836-475-6(5))* America Star Bks.

López, Diana. Choke. 2012. (ENG.). 240p. (J). (gr. 7). 17.99 *(978-0-545-41822-5(4))* Scholastic, Inc.

Louise, Kate. Tough Cookie. Sandford, Grace, illus. 2015. (ENG.). 32p. (J). (gr. -1-k). 16.99 *(978-1-63450-197-2(7)*, Sky Pony Pr.) Skyhorse Publishing Co., Inc.

—The Upside-Down Fish. Matine, Laura, illus. 2015. (ENG.). 32p. (J). (gr. -1-k). 16.95 *(978-1-62914-628-7(5)*, Sky Pony Pr.) Skyhorse Publishing Co., Inc.

Love, Katie. Fruit to Live By..., 1 vol. 2009. 62p. pap. 16.95 *(978-1-60836-122-9(5))* PublishAmerica, Inc.

Lucado, Max. Punchinello & the Most Marvelous Gift: And, Your Special Gift. Martinez, Sergio, illus. 2007. (J). *(978-1-58134-877-4(0))* Crossway.

Lucado, Max, et al. Your Special Gift. Wenzel, David T. & Wenzel, David, illus. 2006. (Max Lucado's Wemmicks Ser.: 6). 32p. (J). (gr. -1-3). 16.99 *(978-1-58134-698-5(0))* Crossway.

Ludwig, Trudy. Too Perfect. Fields, Lisa, illus. 2009. (ENG.). 32p. (J). (gr. 1-4). 15.99 *(978-1-58246-258-5(5)*, Tricycle Pr.) Random Hse. Children's Bks.

Lytton, Deborah. Silence. 2015. (ENG.). 320p. (YA). (gr. 7). 17.99 *(978-1-60907-945-1(0)*, Shadow Mountain) Shadow Mountain Publishing.

MacDonald, Alan. The Pig in a Wig. Hess, Paul, illus. 2003. 32p. (J). (gr. k-3). pap. 6.95 *(978-1-56145-299-6(8)*, Q32523) Peachtree Pubs.

MacHale, D. J. The Monster Princess. Boiger, Alexandra, illus. 2010. (ENG.). 40p. (J). (gr. -1-1). 17.99 *(978-1-4169-4809-4(0)*, Aladdin) Simon & Schuster Children's Publishing.

Make Believe Ideas. Paulette the Pinkest Puppy. 2014. (ENG.). 32p. (J). 15.99 *(978-1-78235-975-3(3))* Make Believe Ideas GBR. Dist: Nelson, Thomas Inc.

—Paulette the Pinkest Puppy in the World. 2014. (ENG.). 32p. (J). pap. 6.99 *(978-1-78235-974-6(5))* Make Believe Ideas GBR. Dist: Nelson, Thomas Inc.

Malik, Katherine. Giselle's Magical World, 1 vol. 2009. 150p. pap. 24.95 *(978-1-4489-1902-4(9))* America Star Bks.

Manning, Jane. Millie Fierce. Manning, Jane, illus. 2012. (Millie Fierce Ser.). (ENG., Illus.). 32p. (J). (gr. -1-2). 16.99 *(978-0-399-25642-4(3),* Philomel Bks.) Penguin Young Readers Group.

Markes, Julie & Markes. Good Thing You're Not an Octopus! Smith, Maggie, illus. 2006. (ENG.). 40p. (J). (gr. -1-3). pap. 6.99 *(978-0-06-443586-4(5))* HarperCollins Pubs.

Marlowe, Sara. My New Best Friend. Salom, Ivette, illus. 2016. (ENG.). 32p. (J). 15.95 *(978-1-61429-353-8(8))* Wisdom Pubns.

Massie, Felix. Terry Perkins & His Upside down Frown. 2018. (ENG., Illus.). 32p. (J). 17.99 *(978-1-84780-620-8(1),* Frances Lincoln Children's Bks.) Quarto Publishing Group UK GBR. Dist: Littlehampton Bk Services, Ltd.

McClure, Brian D. The Up down Day. Plumlee, Buddy, illus. 2009. (Brian D. Mcclure Childrens Book Collection). 47p. (J). (gr. -1-3). 14.95 *(978-1-933426-07-5(1))* Universal Flag Publishing.

McDonald, Fiona. Ghost Doll & Jasper. 2012. (ENG., Illus.). 112p. (J). (gr. 2-7). 12.95 *(978-1-62087-174-4(2),* 620174, Sky Pony Pr.) Skyhorse Publishing Co., Inc.

McGann, Amber Ann. Windrush the Crooked Llama. 2008. 34p. pap. 24.95 *(978-1-60563-728-0(9))* PublishAmerica, Inc.

McGregor, Janet C. Happy for a Honk & a Wave. Craft, Donna, illus. 2010. 20p. pap. 12.95 *(978-1-936343-04-1(5))* Peppertree Pr., The.

Midden, Maribeth Grubb. Rosie: The Patchwork Bunny. Techau, Ashlyn, illus. 2011. 24p. (gr. 1-2). pap. 12.99 *(978-1-4269-5671-3(1))* Trafford Publishing.

Mith with an Itch. 2008. (Illus.). 34p. (J). 10.95 *(978-0-9800259-0-3(7))* Dream Weaver Ministries, Inc.

Moore, Julianne. Best Friends Forever. Pham, LeUyen, illus. (Freckleface Strawberry Ser.). (ENG.). 40p. (J). (gr. -1-8). 2011. 16.99 *(978-1-59990-551-8(5),* 9781599905518) 2007. 17.99 *(978-1-59990-107-7(2),* 9781599901077) Bloomsbury Publishing USA. (Bloomsbury USA Childrens).

—Best Friends Forever. 2015. (CHI.). 40p. (J). (gr. -1-8). pap. *(978-7-5133-1778-8(X))* New Star Publishing Hse.

—Best Friends Forever. Pham, LeUyen, illus. (Step into Reading Ser.). (ENG.). 32p. (J). (gr. -1-1). 2017. 15.99 *(978-0-375-97369-7(9),* Random Hse. Bks. for Young Readers) 2016. 12.99 *(978-0-385-39198-6(6),* Doubleday Bks. for Young Readers) 2016. pap. 3.99 *(978-0-385-39197-9(8),* Random Hse. Bks. for Young Readers) Random Hse. Children's Bks.

—Freckleface Strawberry: Monster Time! Pham, LeUyen, illus. 2017. (Step into Reading Ser.). (ENG.). 32p. (J). (gr. -1-1). pap. 3.99 *(978-0-385-39200-6(1),* Random Hse. Bks. for Young Readers) Random Hse. Children's Bks.

Moore, Leslie. Right Left: A Boy Named Grey. 2013. 48p. pap. 20.45 *(978-1-4497-8649-6(9),* WestBow Pr.) Author Solutions, Inc.

Moulton, Erin E. Tracing Stars. 2013. (ENG.). 256p. (J). (gr. 3-7). pap. 6.99 *(978-0-14-242653-1(9),* Puffin Books) Penguin Young Readers Group.

Murray, Lisa A. Portend Learns That We Need Each Other. 2011. 32p. pap. 15.99 *(978-1-4634-0132-0(9))* AuthorHouse.

Murray, Martine. Molly & Pim & the Millions of Stars. 2017. (ENG., Illus.). 192p. (J). (gr. 3-7). 16.99 *(978-0-399-55040-9(2),* Knopf Bks. for Young Readers) Random Hse. Children's Bks.

Murrell, Diane. Oliver Onion: The Onion Who Learns to Accept & Be Himself. Murrell, Diane, illus. 2004. (Illus.). 40p. (J). (gr. -1-4). 16.95 *(978-1-931282-64-2(1))* Autism Asperger Publishing Co.

Nanette. Little Red. 2004. (Life on Granny's Farm Ser.). (J). 12.95 *(978-0-9741269-1-3(8))* St. Bernard Publishing, LLC.

—Oinky the Yellow Pig. 2004. (Life on Granny's Farm Ser.). (J). 12.95 *(978-0-9741269-4-4(2))* St. Bernard Publishing, LLC.

Nasser, Amal. Falfoul's Trunk. Abul-Maati, Rania, illus. 2016. (Stories & Fables from Around the World Ser.). (ENG.). 24p. (J). (gr. 2-1). lib. bdg. 24.60 *(978-1-4777-5693-5(0),* Windmill Bks.) Rosen Publishing Group, Inc., The.

Nevers, Merri B. Lonely Lucille. 2012. 28p. pap. 16.95 *(978-1-4497-4246-1(7),* WestBow Pr.) Author Solutions, Inc.

Norman, Kim. Still a Gorilla! Geran, Chad, illus. 2016. (ENG.). 32p. (J). (gr. -1-k). 16.99 *(978-0-545-75791-1(6))* Scholastic, Inc.

Oliver, Amanda Eaddy. Cheyenne the Cat. 2010. 28p. 13.99 *(978-1-4520-6218-1(8))* AuthorHouse.

Palacio, R. J. Wonder. 2015. (JPN.). 420p. (J). *(978-4-593-53495-1(X))* Holp Shuppan, Publishing.

—Wonder. 2015. (SPA.). 160p. (J). (gr. 3-7). pap. 9.95 *(978-607-31-3242-8(5))* Penguin Random House Grupo Editorial, S.A. de C.V. MEX. Dist: Two Rivers Distribution.

—Wonder. (ENG.). (J). (gr. 3-7). 2015. 176p. 12.99 *(978-0-553-49907-0(6))* 2012. 320p. 16.99 *(978-0-375-86902-0(6))* 2012. 320p. lib. bdg. 19.99 *(978-0-375-96902-7(0))* Random Hse. Children's Bks. (Knopf Bks. for Young Readers).

—Wonder. l.t. ed. 2013. (ENG.). 482p. 23.99 *(978-1-4104-5741-7(9))* Thorndike Pr.

—Wonder. 2012. lib. bdg. 29.40 *(978-0-606-36646-5(6))* Turtleback Bks.

Paley, Sasha. Huge. 2008. (ENG.). 272p. (YA). (gr. 7-12). pap. 8.99 *(978-1-4169-5795-9(2),* Simon & Schuster Bks. For Young Readers) Simon & Schuster Bks. For Young Readers.

Petty, Dev. I Don't Want to Be a Frog. Boldt, Mike, illus. 2015. (ENG.). 32p. (J). (gr. -1-2). lib. bdg. 19.99 *(978-0-375-97334-5(6),* Doubleday Bks. for Young Readers) Random Hse. Children's Bks.

Petty, Dini. The Queen, the Bear & the Bumblebee. Cowles, Rose, illus. 32p. (J). 19.95 *(978-1-55285-151-7(6))* Whitecap Bks., Ltd. CAN. Dist: Graphic Arts Ctr. Publishing Co.

Phyllarry (Rittmueller), Kathryn. Beauregart the Bear. 2009. (ENG., Illus.). 64p. (J). 12.95 *(978-0-943972-80-0(9))* Homestead Publishing.

Pitino, Donna Marie. Too-Tall Tina. Woodruff, Liza, illus. 2005. (Math Matters Ser.). (ENG.). 32p. (J). (gr. -1-3). pap. 5.95 *(978-1-57565-150-7(5))* Kane Press, Inc.

Polonsky, Ami. Gracefully Grayson. 2016. (ENG., Illus.). 250p. (J). (gr. 5-9). pap. 8.99 *(978-1-4847-2365-4(1))* Hyperion Bks. for Children.

Pride, Wallace. The Mighty Christmas Oak. 2008. 19p. pap. 24.95 *(978-1-60672-752-2(4))* PublishAmerica, Inc.

Purkapile, Susan & Peck, Amy. Mumbles the Bumble Bee: The Bee Who Couldn't Buzz. Ducommun, Barbara, illus. 2008. (J). *(978-1-930596-87-0(1))* Amherst Pr.

Raschka, Chris. Crabby Crab. 2014. (Thingy Things Ser.). (ENG., Illus.). 24p. (J). (gr. -1-k). 6.95 *(978-1-4197-1056-8(7),* Abrams Appleseed) Abrams, Inc.

Reade, O. K. The Little Girl & Her Shadow. 2015. (Illus.). (J). 12.99 *(978-1-4621-1618-8(3))* Cedar Fort, Inc./CFI Distribution.

Redbank, Tennant & Jackson, Kathryn. The Saggy Baggy Elephant. DiCicco, Sue & Hathi, Garva, illus. 2016. (Step into Reading Ser.). (ENG.). 32p. (J). (gr. -1-1). pap. 3.99 *(978-0-553-53588-4(9),* Random Hse. Bks. for Young Readers) Random Hse. Children's Bks.

Regan, Anne, ed. First Time for Everything. 2016. (ENG., Illus.). (J). 32.99 ***(978-1-63533-015-1(7),*** Harmony Ink Pr.) Dreamspinner Pr.

Ritter, John H. Choosing up Sides. 2004. 166p. (gr. 5-9). 16.00 *(978-0-7569-4094-2(X))* Perfection Learning Corp.

Romig, Hilary. Meet Ruby & Louise. 2009. 16p. pap. 8.49 *(978-1-4389-4609-2(0))* AuthorHouse.

Roos, Stephen. The Gypsies Never Came. Liepke, Peter, photos by. 2010. (ENG., Illus.). 128p. (J). (gr. 3-7). pap. 7.99 *(978-1-4424-2940-6(2),* Simon & Schuster Bks. For Young Readers) Simon & Schuster Bks. For Young Readers.

Rosenthal, Amy Krouse & Lichtenheld, Tom. The OK Book. Rosenthal, Amy Krouse & Lichtenheld, Tom, illus. 2007. (Illus.). 40p. (J). (gr. -1-3). lib. bdg. 14.89 *(978-0-06-115256-6(0))* HarperCollins Pubs.

—The Ok Book. Rosenthal, Amy Krouse & Lichtenheld, Tom, illus. 2007. (ENG., Illus.). 40p. (J). (gr. -1-2). 12.99 *(978-0-06-115255-9(2))* HarperCollins Pubs.

Rudolph, Shaina & Royer, Danielle. All My Stripes: A Story for Children with Autism. Zivoin, Jennifer, illus. 2014. (J). pap. *(978-1-4338-1917-9(1),* Magination Pr.) American Psychological Assn.

Ryan, P E. Saints of Augustine. 2007. 308p. (YA). (gr. 7-18). 16.99 *(978-0-06-085810-0(9));* lib. bdg. 17.89 *(978-0-06-085811-7(7))* HarperCollins Pubs. (HarperTeen).

Salter, Sydney. My Big Nose & Other Natural Disasters. 2009. (ENG., Illus.). 352p. (J). (gr. 7-18). pap. 19.95 *(978-0-15-206643-7(8))* Houghton Mifflin Harcourt Publishing Co.

Savageau, Cheryl & Hynes, Robert. Muskrat Will Be Swimming, 1 vol. 2006. (ENG., Illus.). 32p. (gr. 3-7). 7.95 *(978-0-88448-280-2(4),* 884280) Tilbury Hse. Pubs.

Scanlon, Liz Garton. Noodle & Lou. Howard, Arthur, illus. 2011. (ENG.). 32p. (J). (gr. -1-1). 15.99 *(978-1-4424-0288-1(1),* Beach Lane Bks.) Beach Lane Bks.

Scheier, Leah. Your Voice Is All I Hear. 2015. (ENG.). 336p. (YA). (gr. 8-12). pap. 9.99 *(978-1-4926-1441-8(6))* Sourcebooks, Inc.

Schmidt, Tiffany. Bright Before Sunrise. 2015. (ENG.). 304p. (YA). (gr. 7). pap. 9.99 *(978-0-8027-3502-7(9),* 9780802735027, Bloomsbury USA Childrens) Bloomsbury Publishing USA.

Schoonmaker, Elizabeth. Square Cat. Schoonmaker, Elizabeth, illus. 2011. (ENG., Illus.). 32p. (J). (gr. -1-3). 16.99 *(978-1-4424-0619-3(4),* Aladdin) Simon & Schuster Children's Publishing.

Schram, Peninnah & Davis, Rachayl Eckstein. The Apple Tree's Discovery. Lee, Wendy W., illus. 2012. (Kar-Ben Favorites Ser.). (ENG.). 24p. (J). (gr. -1-2). pap. 7.95 *(978-0-7613-5132-0(9));* lib. bdg. 16.95 *(978-0-7613-5130-6(2))* Lerner Publishing Group. (Kar-Ben Publishing).

Shelton, Crystal G. Theodore's Rings. 2013. 24p. pap. 24.95 *(978-1-62709-378-1(8))* America Star Bks.

Shimberg, Elaine Fantle. Helga, the Hippopotamouse. Walling, Sandy Seeley, illus. 2008. (ENG.). 36p. (J). 7.95 *(978-0-9741940-4-2(2))* Abernathy Hse. Publishing.

Silverstein, Shel. The Missing Piece Meets the Big O. Silverstein, Shel, illus. 2006. (ENG., Illus.). 104p. (J). (gr. -1-3). 16.99 *(978-0-06-025657-9(5))* HarperCollins Pubs.

—The Missing Piece Meets the Big O. 2005. (CHI., Illus.). 60p. (J). *(978-7-5442-2517-5(8))* Nanhai Publishing Co.

Simon, Coco. Alexis: The Icing on the Cupcake. 2014. (Cupcake Diaries: 20). lib. bdg. 17.20 *(978-0-606-35786-9(6))* Turtleback Bks.

—Alexis the Icing on the Cupcake. 2014. (Cupcake Diaries: 20). (ENG., Illus.). 160p. (J). (gr. 3-7). pap. 6.99 *(978-1-4814-0468-6(7),* Simon Spotlight) Simon Spotlight.

—Mia: A Matter of Taste. 2013. (Cupcake Diaries: 14). lib. bdg. 16.00 *(978-0-606-32042-9(3),* Turtleback) Turtleback Bks.

—Mia a Matter of Taste. 2013. (Cupcake Diaries: 14). (ENG., Illus.). 160p. (J). (gr. 3-7). 15.99 *(978-1-4424-7480-2(7));* pap. 6.99 *(978-1-4424-7435-2(1))* Simon Spotlight. (Simon Spotlight).

Sloan, Holly Goldberg. Short. 2017. (ENG.). 304p. (J). (gr. 3-7). 16.99 *(978-0-399-18621-9(2),* Dial Bks) Penguin Young Readers Group.

Smith, Bryan. Is There an App for That? Wish, Katia, illus. 2015. (ENG.). 32p. (J). pap. 10.95 *(978-1-934490-74-7(1))* Boys Town Pr.

Smithem, Beth. Cocoa Bean & Squirt. 2010. 68p. pap. 10.49 *(978-1-4520-1929-1(0))* AuthorHouse.

Sommer, Carl. If Only I Were- James, Kennon, illus. 2014. (J). pap. *(978-1-57537-954-8(6))* Advance Publishing, Inc.

—If Only I Were...(Si Yo Fuese...) James, Kennon, illus. 2009. (Another Sommer-Time Story Bilingual Ser.). (SPA & ENG.). 48p. (J). lib. bdg. 16.95 *(978-1-57537-154-2(5))* Advance Publishing, Inc.

Spinelli, Eileen. Another Day As Emily. Lew-Vriethoff, Joanne, illus. 2015. (ENG.). 240p. (J). (gr. 3-7). 6.99 *(978-0-449-80989-1(7),* Yearling) Random Hse. Children's Bks.

Spinelli, Jerry. Loser. 2003. (ENG.). 224p. (J). (gr. 3-7). pap. 6.99 *(978-0-06-054074-6(5))* HarperCollins Pubs.

—Loser. 2003. (J). (gr. 3-6). lib. bdg. 17.20 *(978-0-613-66899-6(5),* Turtleback) Turtleback Bks.

Stanton, Elizabeth Rose. Henny. Stanton, Elizabeth Rose, illus. 2014. (ENG., Illus.). 40p. (J). (gr. -1-3). 17.99 *(978-1-4424-8436-8(5),* Simon & Schuster/Paula Wiseman Bks.) Simon & Schuster/Paula Wiseman Bks.

Steers, Billy. Tractor Mac Learns to Fly. (Tractor Mac Ser.). (ENG., Illus.). (J). 2016. 24p. pap. 4.99 *(978-0-374-30537-6(4),* 9780374305376) 2015. 32p. (gr. -1-2). 8.99 *(978-0-374-30103-3(4),* 9780374301033) Farrar, Straus & Giroux. (Farrar, Straus & Giroux (BYR)).

—Tractor Mac Learns to Fly. 2016. (Tractor Mac Ser.). (J). lib. bdg. 14.75 *(978-0-606-39558-8(X))* Turtleback Bks.

Steers, Billy, illus. Tractor Mac Learns to Fly. 2007. (J). 7.95 *(978-0-9788496-2-7(0))* Tractor Mac Inc.

Stevens, Janet & Crummel, Susan Stevens. Jackalope. 2003. (ENG., Illus.). 56p. (J). (gr. -1-3). 17.00 *(978-0-15-216736-3(6))* Houghton Mifflin Harcourt Publishing Co.

Stone, Tamara Ireland. Every Last Word. 2015. (ENG.). 368p. (YA). (gr. 7-12). 17.99 *(978-1-4847-0527-8(0))* Hyperion Bks. for Children.

—Every Last Word. 2017. (ENG.). (YA). (gr. 7-12). lib. bdg. 20.85 ***(978-0-606-39885-5(6))*** Turtleback Bks.

Stuart, Tara. Tara's Tales: Trees. 2013. 60p. pap. 17.99 *(978-1-4575-2186-7(5))* Dog Ear Publishing, LLC.

Sullivan, Candida. Zippy & the Stripes of Courage. 2011. (J). pap. 13.99 *(978-1-937331-08-5(3))* ShadeTree Publishing, LLC.

Taylor-Chiarello, Robin. The Blue Lobster. Bohart, Lisa, illus. 2011. 36p. pap. 15.95 *(978-1-936343-84-3(3))* Peppertree Pr., The.

Taylor, Helen. Emu Can't Fly. Gilles-Gray, Carolyn, illus. 2013. 24p. pap. *(978-1-921883-39-2(1),* MBS Pr.) Pick-a-Woo Woo Pubs.

Terry, Michael. Rhinos Horns. 2003. (Illus.). (J). *(978-1-58234-796-7(4),* Bloomsbury USA Childrens) Bloomsbury Publishing USA.

Thurston, Alecia Frances. Shumalady's Butterfly Tree. 2010. 40p. pap. 18.49 *(978-1-4490-5609-4(1))* AuthorHouse.

Todd, Ilima. Remake. 2014. (Remake Ser.: 1). (ENG.). 304p. (YA). (gr. 7). 17.99 *(978-1-60907-924-6(8),* Shadow Mountain) Shadow Mountain Publishing.

Tokio, Marnelle. More Than You Can Chew. 2003. (ENG., Illus.). 240p. (J). (gr. 9-18). pap. 12.95 *(978-0-88776-639-8(0),* Tundra Bks.) Tundra Bks. CAN. Dist: Penguin Random Hse. LLC.

Townsend, Wendy. Lizard Love. 2013. 198p. 18.95 *(978-1-60898-151-9(7))* namelos llc.

Ungerer, Tomi. Adelaide: The Flying Kangaroo. 2011. (ENG., Illus.). 40p. (gr. -1-3). 16.95 *(978-0-7148-6083-1(2))* Phaidon Pr., Inc.

Ure, Daylene Mary. Today I'm Going to be a Hedgehog. 2008. 36p. 16.50 *(978-0-615-25326-8(1))* Ure, Daylene.

Vezeau, Sheila. Sky, the Blue Bunny. Ostrowski, Justin, illus. 2012. 16p. pap. 24.95 *(978-1-4626-7533-3(6))* America Star Bks.

Walter, Debbie. Introducing Russell. Walter, Debbie, illus. 2007. (Illus.). 68p. (J). per. 6.95 *(978-0-9766315-2-1(0))* Moose Run Productions.

White, Pamela. Poppa Full of Pictures. 2012. 16p. pap. 15.99 *(978-1-4772-9223-5(3))* AuthorHouse.

Williams, Bonnie. Pete Can Fly! Gordon, John, illus. 2014. (Dino School Ser.). (ENG.). 24p. (J). (gr. -1-1). pap. 3.99 *(978-1-4814-0465-5(2),* Simon Spotlight) Simon Spotlight.

Williams, Laura E. Slant. 2008. (ENG.). 160p. (J). (gr. 2-8). pap. 6.95 *(978-1-57131-682-0(5))* Milkweed Editions.

Wilson, Diane Lee. Black Storm Comin' 2006. (ENG.). 240p. (J). (gr. 5-9). pap. 7.99 *(978-0-689-87138-2(4),* McElderry, Margaret K. Bks.) McElderry, Margaret K. Bks.

—Black Storm Comin' 2006. (Illus.). 291p. (gr. 5-9). 17.00 *(978-0-7569-6908-0(5))* Perfection Learning Corp.

Winter, Laurel. Growing Wings. 2010. (ENG.). 208p. (J). (gr. 2-5). pap. 13.95 *(978-0-547-24904-9(7))* Houghton Mifflin Harcourt Publishing Co.

Wojtowicz, Jen. The Boy Who Grew Flowers. Adams, Steve, illus. 2012. (ENG.). 32p. (J). (gr. k-5). 8.99 *(978-1-84686-749-1(5))* Barefoot Bks., Inc.

Wojtowicz, Jen & Wojzowitz, Jen. The Boy Who Grew Flowers. Adams, Steve, illus. 2005. (ENG.). 32p. (J). (gr. -1-3). 16.99 *(978-1-84148-686-4(8))* Barefoot Bks., Inc.

Wonder, 2 vols., Set. 2014. (ENG.). 432p. (J). (gr. 3-7). 31.98 *(978-0-553-49906-3(8),* Knopf Bks. for Young Readers) Random Hse. Children's Bks.

Yee, Paul. Money Boy. 2013. 192p. pap. *(978-1-4596-6450-0(7))* ReadHowYouWant.com, Ltd.

Zeitlin, Meredith. Freshman Year & Other Unnatural Disasters. 2013. (ENG.). 288p. (YA). (gr. 7). pap. 8.99 *(978-0-14-242421-6(8),* Speak) Penguin Young Readers Group.

Zia, Farhana. The Garden of My Imaan, 1 vol. (ENG.). (J). (gr. 3-6). 2016. 232p. pap. 7.95 *(978-1-56145-921-6(6))* 2013. 192p. 15.95 *(978-1-56145-698-7(5))* Peachtree Pubs.

SELF-CONFIDENCE

see also Self-reliance

Calland, Chris & Hutchinson, Nicky. Minnie & Max are Ok! Smid, Emmi, illus. 2017. (ENG.). 40p. (J). 17.95 ***(978-1-78592-233-6(5),*** 8631) Kingsley, Jessica Pubs. GBR. Dist: Macmillan Distribution Ltd.

Chinn, Jacqueline. How Can I Be Special? Mondragon, Manny, illus. 2003. (J). pap. 15.95 *(978-0-929526-55-3(4))* Double B Pubns.

Devon, Natasha, et al. The Self-Esteem Team's Guide to Sex, Drugs & WTFs?!! 2016. (ENG., Illus.). 288p. (YA). (gr. 7). pap. 15.95 *(978-1-78418-642-5(2))* Blake, John Publishing, Ltd. GBR. Dist: Independent Pubs. Group.

Domoney, Cathy. Madeleine, Maddy & Midge: Positive Thinking for Children. 2012. 36p. pap. 15.95 *(978-1-4525-0761-3(9))* Balboa Pr.

Dreaming Bigger Dreams. 2005. (YA). per. *(978-1-59872-127-0(5))* Instant Pub.

Etingoff, Kim. Confidence. 2013. (Junior Martial Arts Ser.: 9). 32p. (J). (gr. 4-18). 19.95 *(978-1-4222-2734-3(0))* Mason Crest.

Everly, Nita. Early Social Behavior Books Can You Keep Trying? 2007. (J). spiral bd. 11.95 *(978-0-7606-0738-1(9))* LinguiSystems, Inc.

Fox, Annie. Be Confident in Who You Are, Vol. 1. Kindt, Matt, illus. 2008. (Middle School Confidential Ser.: Bk. 1). (ENG.). 96p. (YA). (gr. 6-18). pap. 9.99 *(978-1-57542-302-9(2),* 1285958) Free Spirit Publishing, Inc.

Frankel, Erin. Weird! Heaphy, Paula, illus. 2013. (Weird! Ser.). (ENG.). 48p. (J). (gr. k-4). pap. 9.99 *(978-1-57542-437-8(1))* Free Spirit Publishing, Inc.

Free Spirit Publishing Staff & Stein, Deborah Jiang. Kids' Attitude. 2009. (In a Jar(r) Ser.). (ENG.). (J). (gr. 3). 9.99 *(978-1-57542-921-2(7))* Free Spirit Publishing, Inc.

Green, Edna. My Special Thoughts. 2003. (J). (gr. -1-5). bds. 11.95 *(978-0-9743019-0-7(6))* My Special Thoughts.

Harris, Destiny. Beauty Secrets for Girls. 2004. (J). per. *(978-0-9754380-2-2(6),* 100) Harris, Pleshette Communications Inc. Publishing.

Jeffers, Susan & Gradstein, Donna. I Can Handle It! 50 Confidence-Building Stories to Empower Your Child. 2006. (ENG., Illus.). 160p. per. 9.95 *(978-0-9777618-0-7(0))* Jeffers Pr.

Meiners, Cheri J. Feel Confident! Allen, Elizabeth, illus. 2013. (Being the Best Me Ser.). (ENG.). 40p. (J). (gr. -1-3). 14.99 *(978-1-57542-453-8(3));* pap. 11.99 *(978-1-57542-442-2(8))* Free Spirit Publishing, Inc.

Miller, Ruth L. The Power of Self Ralph Waldo Emerson's Wonder Filled Life. Shonkwiler, Martha, illus. 2013. 66p. pap. 12.00 *(978-0-945385-85-1(4))* WiseWoman Pr.

Moss, Wendy. Being Me: A Kid's Guide to Boosting Confidence & Self-Esteem. 2010. (Illus.). 112p. (J). (gr. 3-8). 14.95 *(978-1-4338-0883-8(8));* pap. 9.95 *(978-1-4338-0884-5(6))* American Psychological Assn. (Magination Pr.).

Payne, Lauren Murphy. Just Because I Am. 2015. lib. bdg. 20.85 *(978-0-606-37402-6(7))* Turtleback Bks.

Rice, Ashley. Girls Rule: A very special book created especially for girls — UPDATED EDITION —, 1 vol. 2011. 64p. pap. 12.95 *(978-1-59842-598-7(6))* Blue Mountain Arts Inc.

Rotner, Shelley. We All Do Something Well. 2013. (Shelley Rotner's World Ser.). (ENG.). 24p. (gr. 1-2). pap. 47.70 *(978-1-62065-755-3(4),* Aplus Bks.) Capstone Press of Coughlan Cos.

—We All Do Something Well, 1 vol. Rotner, Shelley, photos by. 2013. (Shelley Rotner's World Ser.). (ENG., Illus.). 24p. (gr. 1-2). pap. 8.10 *(978-1-62065-754-6(6));* lib. bdg. 27.32 *(978-1-62065-067-7(3))* Capstone Press of Coughlan Cos. (Aplus Bks.).

Schab, Lisa M. Cool, Calm, & Confident: A Workbook to Help Kids Learn Assertiveness Skills. 2009. (Instant Help Ser.). (ENG.). 184p. (J). (gr. k-5). pap. 18.95 *(978-1-57224-630-0(8),* Instant Help Books) New Harbinger Pubns.

Shipp, Josh. The Teen's Guide to World Domination: Advice on Life, Liberty, & the Pursuit of Awesomeness. 2010. (ENG.). 304p. (YA). (gr. 8-18). pap., instr.'s gde. ed. 15.99 *(978-0-312-64154-2(0),* 9780312641542, St. Martin's Griffin) St. Martin's Pr.

Straight Talk about Self-Confidence. (YA). (gr. 6-8). 69.95 *(978-1-55942-197-3(5),* 9239V9) Witcher Productions.

Summers, Barbara, ed. Open the Unusual Door: True Life Stories of Challenge, Adventure, & Success by Black Americans. 2005. (ENG., Illus.). 224p. (YA). (gr. 7-18). pap. 12.99 *(978-0-618-58531-1(1))* Houghton Mifflin Harcourt Publishing Co.

Tool Kits for Kids LLC Staff, creator. Charge up Your Confidence - Tool Kit for Kids: Elementary School Edition. 2008. (Illus.). (J). 39.95 *(978-0-9819483-2-4(4))* Tool Kits For Kids LLC.

—Charge up Your Confidence - Tool Kit for Kids: High School / Middle School Edition. 2009. (Illus.). (J). 39.95 *(978-0-9819483-3-1(2))* Tool Kits For Kids LLC.

Van Wagenen, Maya. Popular: A Memoir. (ENG.). 272p. (YA). (gr. 7). 2015. pap. 10.99 *(978-0-14-751254-3(9),* Speak) 2014. (Illus.). 18.99 *(978-0-525-42681-3(7),* Dutton Books for Young Readers) Penguin Young Readers Group.

—Popular: A Memoir. 2015. lib. bdg. 22.10 *(978-0-606-36796-7(9))* Turtleback Bks.

Yankee, Kris & Nelson, Marian. Are You Confident Today? 2014. (ENG., Illus.). 32p. (J). pap. 9.95 *(978-1-938326-24-0(5),* Ferne Pr.) Nelson Publishing & Marketing.

SELF-CONFIDENCE—FICTION

Aisha. Parsley, Sage, Rosemary & Thyme. 2012. 24p. 24.95 *(978-1-4626-5122-1(4))* America Star Bks.

Alexander, Jill S. The Sweetheart of Prosper County. 2010. (ENG.). 240p. (YA). (gr. 7-12). pap. 18.99 *(978-0-312-54857-5(5),* 9780312548575) Square Fish.

Allen, Debbie. Dancing in the Wings. Nelson, Kadir, illus. 2003. (ENG.). 32p. (J). (gr. -1-3). 7.99 *(978-0-14-250141-2(7),* Puffin Books) Penguin Young Readers Group.

—Dancing in the Wings. Nelson, Kadir, illus. 2003. (J). (gr. -1-3). 14.65 *(978-0-7569-7022-2(9))* Perfection Learning Corp.

Anderson, Jodi Lynn. Among the Stars. 2014. (May Bird Ser.: 2). (ENG., Illus.). 304p. (J). (gr. 3-7). pap. 6.99 *(978-1-4424-9578-4(2),* Aladdin) Simon & Schuster Children's Publishing.

—Among the Stars. 2014. (May Bird Ser.: 2). (ENG., Illus.). 304p. (J). (gr. 3-7). 17.99 *(978-1-4424-9579-1(0),* Simon & Schuster/Paula Wiseman Bks.) Simon & Schuster/Paula Wiseman Bks.

Anderson, John David. Sidekicked. 2013. (ENG.). 384p. (J). (gr. 3-7). 16.99 *(978-0-06-213314-4(4),* Waldon Pond Pr.) HarperCollins Pubs.

Applegate, Katherine. Don't Tap-Dance on Your Teacher. Biggs, Brian, illus. 2009. (Roscoe Riley Rules Ser.: 5). (ENG.). 96p. (J). (gr. 1-5). pap. 4.99 *(978-0-06-114889-7(X))* HarperCollins Pubs.

—Don't Tap-Dance on Your Teacher. Biggs, Brian, illus. 2016. (Roscoe Riley Rules Ser.: 5). (ENG.). 112p. (J). (gr. 1-5). 14.75 *(978-0-606-39252-5(1))* Turtleback Bks.

—Don't Tap-Dance on Your Teacher. 2009. (Roscoe Riley Rules Ser.: 5). (J). lib. bdg. 14.75 *(978-0-606-05007-4(8),* Turtleback) Turtleback Bks.

Aronson, Sarah. Beyond Lucky. 2011. (ENG.). 256p. (J). (gr. 3-7). 16.99 *(978-0-8037-3520-0(0),* Dial Bks) Penguin Young Readers Group.

Arreola, Perla. Weenz the Cat: What about Me? Arreola, Manuel, illus. 2013. 30p. 14.99 *(978-0-9859298-7-9(1))* Dream&Achieve Bks.

Bandsuh, Jim. Helmet Hank. 2007. (Illus.). (J). per. 15.99 *(978-1-933156-19-4(8),* Visikid Bks.) GSVQ Publishing.

S

Barnes, Derrick. Crown: An Ode to the Fresh Cut. James, Gordon C., illus. 2017. (Denene Millner Bks.). (ENG.). 32p. (J). (gr. -1-3). 17.95 **(978-1-57284-224-3(5))** Agate Publishing, Inc.

Bartha, Alysa. Petal's Wish. 2010. 32p. 14.99 (978-1-4490-7417-3(0)) AuthorHouse.

Bee, Sarah. The Yes. Kitamura, Satoshi, illus. 2015. (ENG.). 32p. (J). 16.00 (978-0-8028-5449-0(4), Eerdmans Bks For Young Readers) Eerdmans, William B. Publishing Co.

Belavilas, Charlotte. Walter, the Carpenter Bee. 2007. pap. 9.00 (978-0-8059-8504-7(2)) Dorrance Publishing Co., Inc.

Bell, Krista & Smith, Craig. If the Shoe Fits. 2008. (Illus.). 60p. (Orig.). (J). (gr. -1-3). 14.95 (978-1-58089-338-1(4)) Charlesbridge Publishing, Inc.

Benedetto, K. & Barlow, J. I See the World. 2009. pap. (978-1-61584-125-7(3)) Independent Pub.

Benton, Jim. Howard Hubbins Half Hour Hero. 2008. (J). pap. 4.99 (978-0-06-059774-0(7)) HarperCollins Pubs.

Berkowitz, Barbara. The Talent Show. 2009. 108p. 21.49 (978-1-4389-9826-8(0)); pap. 10.99 (978-1-4389-9825-1(2)) AuthorHouse.

Bertrand, Diane Gonzales. The F Factor. 2010. 256p. (YA). (gr. 6-18). pap. 12.95 (978-1-55885-598-4(X), Piñata Books) Arte Publico Pr.

Blevins, Wiley. Go, Billy, Go! Being Yourself. Gordon, John, illus. 2015. (ENG.). 24p. (J). (gr. k-2). lib. bdg. 19.99 (978-1-63440-003-9(8)) Red Chair Pr.

—Stella... Almost: Self-Confidence. Nez, John Abbott, illus. 2015. (ENG.). 24p. (J). (gr. k-2). lib. bdg. 19.99 (978-1-63440-006-0(2), 1392169) Red Chair Pr.

Bloom, Stephanie. The Drummer Who Lost His Beat. Keylon, Joe, illus. 2005. 40p. (J). lib. bdg. 16.95 (978-1-931969-47-5(7)) Bloom & Grow Bks.

Blume, Lesley M. M. Cornelia & the Audacious Escapades of the Somerset Sisters. (ENG.). 272p. (J). (gr. 3-7). 2008. 7.99 (978-0-440-42110-8(1), Yearling) 2006. 15.95 (978-0-375-83523-0(7), Knopf Bks. for Young Readers) Random Hse. Children's Bks.

Bowe, Julie. Pompom Problems. 2015. (Victoria Torres, Unfortunately Average Ser.). (ENG.). 160p. (gr. 4-4). lib. bdg. 26.65 (978-1-4965-0532-3(8)) Stone Arch Bks.

Bowen, Carl. Fire Front. Lee, Marc, illus. 2016. (Firestormers Ser.). (ENG.). 112p. (gr. 4-8). lib. bdg. 26.65 (978-1-4965-3308-1(9)) Stone Arch Bks.

—Quarterback Rush, 1 vol. Garcia, Eduardo, illus. 2014. (Sports Illustrated Kids Graphic Novels Ser.). (ENG.). 72p. (gr. 2-5). 26.65 (978-1-4342-6489-3(0)) Stone Arch Bks.

Bowen, Carl & Fuentes, Benny. BMX Breakthrough, 1 vol. Sandoval, Gerardo, illus. 2011. (Sports Illustrated Kids Graphic Novels Ser.). (ENG.). 56p. (gr. 2-3). pap. 7.19 (978-1-4342-3401-8(0)); lib. bdg. 26.65 (978-1-4342-2240-4(3)) Stone Arch Bks.

Bowen, Fred. Full Court Fever, 1 vol. 2009. (All-Star Sports Story Ser.). (ENG., Illus.). 112p. (J). pap. 5.95 (978-1-56145-508-9(3)) Peachtree Pubs.

—The Golden Glove, 1 vol. 2009. (Fred Bowen Sports Story Ser.). (ENG., Illus.). 112p. (J). (gr. 3). pap. 6.95 (978-1-56145-505-8(9)) Peachtree Pubs.

—Hardcourt Comeback, 1 vol. 2010. (Fred Bowen Sports Stories Ser.). (ENG., Illus.). 144p. (J). (gr. 2-7). pap. 5.95 (978-1-56145-516-4(4), Peachtree Junior) Peachtree Pubs.

—On the Line, 1 vol. 2nd ed. 2009. (Fred Bowen Sports Story Ser.). (ENG., Illus.). 112p. (J). pap. 6.95 (978-1-56145-511-9(3)) Peachtree Pubs.

Brantz, Loryn, illus. Not Just a Dot. 2014. (ENG.). 32p. (J). (-k). 16.95 (978-1-62914-622-5(6), Sky Pony Pr.) Skyhorse Publishing Co., Inc.

Braunstein, M. & Braunstein, J. Don't I Look Smart. 2009. (978-1-61584-845-4(2)) Independent Pub.

—Don't Look Smart?! 2009. (J). pap. (978-1-61623-138-5(6)) Independent Pub.

Brennan-Nelson, Denise. Buzzy the Bumblebee. Monroe, Michael Glenn, illus. 2003. (ENG.). 32p. (J). (gr. k-6). pap. 6.95 (978-1-58536-166-3(6)) Sleeping Bear Pr.

Brian, Kate, pseud. Megan Meade's Guide to the McGowan Boys. 2006. (ENG.). 288p. (YA). (gr. 7-12). pap. 9.99 (978-1-4169-0031-3(4), Simon & Schuster Bks. For Young Readers) Simon & Schuster Bks. For Young Readers.

Bright, Rachel. The Lion Inside. Field, Jim, illus. 2016. (ENG.). 32p. (J). (gr. -1-k). 16.99 (978-0-545-87350-5(9), Scholastic Pr.) Scholastic, Inc.

Brightwood, Laura, illus. The Woodsman & His Ax. Brightwood, Laura, . 2007. (J). DVD (978-1-934409-07-7(3)) 3-C Institute for Social Development.

Britton, Faith. If You'D Only Believe. 2009. 24p. pap. 12.99 (978-1-4490-1741-5(X)) AuthorHouse.

Brown, Tricia. Charlie & the Blanket Toss. Martinsen, Sarah, illus. 2015. (ENG.). 32p. (J). pap. 10.99 (978-1-941821-66-4(9), Alaska Northwest Bks.) Graphic Arts Ctr. Publishing Co.

Brown-Wood, Janay. Imani's Moon. Mitchell, Hazell, illus. 2014. (ENG.). 32p. (J). (gr. 1-4). pap. 7.95 (978-1-934133-58-3(2), Mackinac Island Press, Inc.) Charlesbridge Publishing, Inc.

Bruchac, Joseph. The Way. 2013. (ENG.). 160p. (YA). (gr. 6-12). pap. 9.95 (978-1-4677-0862-3(3)) 2007. 156p. (J). (gr. 4-7). 16.95 (978-1-58196-062-4(X)) Lerner Publishing Group. (Darby Creek).

Bruel, Nick. Little Red Bird. Bruel, Nick, illus. 2008. (ENG., Illus.). 32p. (J). (gr. -1-1). 17.99 (978-1-59643-339-7(6), 9781596433397) Roaring Brook Pr.

Brun, Laura. Frosty the Craft Maker. 2012. 24p. pap. 24.95 (978-1-62709-700-0(7)) America Star Bks.

Bryant, Annie. Time's Up. 2008. (Beacon Street Girls Ser.: 12). (ENG.). 208p. (J). (gr. 4-8). pap. 7.99 (978-1-4169-6422-3(3), Aladdin) Simon & Schuster Children's Publishing.

Bunting, Eve. I Don't Want to Go to Camp. Cocca-Leffler, Maryann, illus. 2003. (ENG.). 32p. (J). (gr. -1-1). pap. 8.95 (978-1-59078-074-9(4)) Boyds Mills Pr.

Burch, Christian. The Manny Files. 2008. (Mix Ser.). (ENG.). 304p. (J). (gr. 4-8). pap. 14.99 (978-1-4169-5534-4(8), Aladdin) Simon & Schuster Children's Publishing.

Burk, Josh. The Summer of Saint Nick. 2007. (ENG.). 152p. (YA). per. 12.95 (978-0-9768042-2-2(0)) Maven Of Memory Publishing.

Burrows, Mark. I'll Take My Chances, 1 vol. Springer, Sally, illus. 2015. (ENG.). 32p. (J). (gr. -1-3). 16.99 (978-1-4556-2106-4(4)) Pelican Publishing Co., Inc.

Cabot, Meg. Princess Mia. (ENG.). 2008. (Princess Diaries: Vol. 9). 256p. (J). (gr. 7-18). 16.99 (978-0-06-072461-0(7)) Vol. 9. 2009. (Princess Diaries: 9). 304p. (YA). (gr. 8). pap. 9.99 (978-0-06-072463-4(3), HarperTeen) HarperCollins Pubs.

—Princess Mia. 2009. (Princess Diaries: 9). (YA). lib. bdg. 20.85 (978-0-606-02178-4(7), Turtleback) Turtleback Bks.

Calabrese, Dianne. The Inspirational Guide, 1 vol. 2010. 24p. 24.95 (978-1-4489-4844-4(4)) PublishAmerica, Inc.

Caruso, Rosalie. How I taught my mom... the Law of Attraction. 2010. 48p. 17.45 (978-1-4525-0135-2(1)) Get Published.

Castle, M. E. Popular Clone. 2012. (Clone Chronicles Ser.: No. 1). (ENG.). 320p. (J). (gr. 3-7). 15.99 (978-1-60684-232-4(3), Darby Creek) Lerner Publishing Group.

Cellucci, Lucy Lemay. True Colours. 2010. (ENG., Illus.). 240p. (YA). (gr. 7-10). pap. 9.95 (978-1-926607-13-9(9), Napoleon & Co.) Dundurn CAN. Dist: Ingram Publisher Services.

Cervantes, Angela. Allie, First at Last. 2016. (ENG.). 208p. (J). (gr. 3-7). 16.99 (978-0-545-81223-8(2), Scholastic Pr.) Scholastic, Inc.

Chandler, Bill & Chandler, Marie. The Reindeer That Couldn't Fly. Kling, Leslie, illus. 2009. 48p. pap. 19.99 (978-1-933817-40-8(2)) Profits Publishing.

Chapman, Lara. Flawless. 2011. (ENG.). 272p. (YA). (gr. 7-12). 16.99 (978-1-59990-631-7(7), 9781599906317); pap. 9.99 (978-1-59990-596-9(5), 9781599905969) Bloomsbury Publishing USA. (Bloomsbury USA Childrens).

Chidebelu-Eze / Dove Publishing, Chibueze Obi. The Lion That Finally Roared: Inspirational Story of Purpose & Destiny. Newborne, David / F., illus. 2008. 80p. (J). 17.99 (978-0-9766578-5-9(6)); pap. 11.99 (978-0-9766578-6-6(4)) Dove Publishing, Inc.

Chin, Oliver. Year of the Rooster. Calle, Juan, illus. 2016. (Tales from the Chinese Zodiac Ser.: 12). (ENG.). 40p. (J). (gr. -1). 15.95 (978-1-59702-125-8(3)) Immedium.

Choyce, Lesley. Carrie Loses Her Nerve, 1 vol. Thurman, Mark, illus. 2003. (Formac First Novels Ser.: 26). (ENG.). 64p. (J). (gr. 1-5). 4.95 (978-0-88780-591-2(4), 9780887805912); 14.95 (978-0-88780-592-9(2), 9780887805929) Formac Publishing Co., Ltd. CAN. Dist: Casemate Pubs. & Bk. Distributors, LLC.

Christopher, Matt. The Dog That Pitched a No-Hitter. 2013. (Passport to Reading Level 3 Ser.). (ENG., Illus.). 48p. (J). (gr. 1-4). 4.99 (978-0-316-21848-1(0)) Little, Brown Bks. for Young Readers.

—Fairway Phenom. 2003. (Matt Christopher Sports Bio Bookshelf Ser.). 132p. (J). (gr. 4-7). 12.65 (978-0-7569-1605-3(4)) Perfection Learning Corp.

—Hook Shot Hero: A Nothin' but Net Sequel. 2011. (ENG.). 144p. (J). (gr. 3-7). pap., pap. 5.99 (978-0-316-10296-4(2)) Little, Brown Bks. for Young Readers.

—The Lucky Baseball Bat. Henneberger, Robert, illus. 2005. 123p. (gr. -1-3). 16.00 (978-0-7569-4890-0(8)) Perfection Learning Corp.

—The Lucky Baseball Bat: 50th Anniversary Commemorative Edition. Henneberger, Robert, illus. anniv. ed. 2004. (ENG.). 128p. (J). (gr. -1-17). pap. 5.99 (978-0-316-01012-2(X)) Little, Brown Bks. for Young Readers.

—Man Out at First. Beier, Ellen, illus. 2009. (New Peach Street Mudders Sports Library). 64p. (J). (gr. 2-4). lib. bdg. 23.93 (978-1-59953-319-3(7)) Norwood Hse. Pr.

Ciencin, Scott, et al. Snowboard Standoff, 1 vol. Esparza, Andres et al, illus. 2011. (Sports Illustrated Kids Graphic Novels Ser.). (ENG.). 56p. (gr. 2-3). pap. 7.19 (978-1-4342-3403-2(7)) Stone Arch Bks.

—Snowboard Standoff, 1 vol. Aburto, Jesus et al, illus. 2011. (Sports Illustrated Kids Graphic Novels Ser.). (ENG.). 56p. (gr. 2-3). lib. bdg. 26.65 (978-1-4342-2242-8(X)) Stone Arch Bks.

Clark, Ruth. Airport Mouse Works the Nightshift. 2008. (ENG.). 32p. (J). 15.95 (978-0-9792963-3-8(1)) Hollywood Operating System.

Clough, Paige. The Jumping Orie Story. Yates, Bridget & Ward, Karen, illus. 2015. (J). (978-1-942945-24-6(8)) Bright Sky Pr.

—The Jumping Orie Story. Yates, Bridget & Ward, Karen, illus. 2015. (J). **(978-0-9915511-2-5(5))** Rule 2 Bks.

Cohen, Miriam. Layla's Head Scarf, 1 vol. Himler, Ronald, illus. 2009. (ENG.). 32p. (J). (gr. -1-3). 15.95 (978-1-59572-177-8(0)); pap. 5.95 (978-1-59572-178-5(9)) Star Bright Bks., Inc.

Cooner, Donna. Worthy. 2017. (ENG.). 288p. (J). (gr. 7). 17.99 (978-0-545-90393-6(9)) Scholastic, Inc.

Copeland, Misty. Firebird. Myers, Christopher, illus. 2014. (ENG.). 40p. (J). (gr. k-3). 17.99 (978-0-399-16615-0(7), G.P. Putnam's Sons Books for Young Readers) Penguin Young Readers Group.

Cornish, D. M. Foundling. Cornish, D. M., illus. 2007. (Monster Blood Tattoo Ser.). (Illus.). 434p. (gr. 7-12). 20.00 (978-0-7569-7957-7(9)) Perfection Learning Corp.

Cosgrove, Stephen. Mizz Buggly: Doing Your Best. Arroyo, Fian, illus. 2004. (J). (978-1-58804-380-1(0)) P C I Education.

Cowing, Sue. Call Me Drog. 2014. (ENG.). 320p. (J). 13.99 (978-0-00-757804-7(0)) HarperCollins Pubs. Ltd. GBR. Dist: Independent Pubs. Group.

—You Will Call Me Drog. 2011. (Exceptional Reading & Language Arts Titles for Intermediate Grades Ser.). (ENG.). 288p. (J). (gr. 4-7). 16.95 (978-0-7613-6076-6(X), Carolrhoda Bks.) Lerner Publishing Group.

Curtis, Kelli. Amber & the Fallen Bridge. 2009. 32p. pap. 13.00 (978-1-60860-631-3(7), Strategic Bk. Publishing) Strategic Book Publishing & Rights Agency (SBPRA).

Cushman, Karen. Grayling's Song. 2016. (ENG.). 224p. (J). (gr. 5-7). 16.99 (978-0-544-30180-1(3), Clarion Bks.) Houghton Mifflin Harcourt Trade & Reference Pubs.

Darby, Kim. I Wish I May I Wish I Might. 2009. 16p. pap. 8.49 (978-1-4490-3404-7(7)) AuthorHouse.

Davis, Jacky. Black Belt Bunny. Fleck, Jay, illus. 2017. (ENG.). 40p. (J). (-k). 16.99 **(978-0-525-42902-9(6)**, Dial Bks) Penguin Young Readers Group.

Defillippo, Steve. Growing up Nicely! Grammy Helps Adam Grow up & Develop Social Skills & Moral Values. 2012. 24p. (-18). pap. 15.99 (978-1-4797-0957-1(3)) Xlibris Corp.

Delaney, Michael. Obi, Gerbil on the Loose! 2008. (ENG.). 208p. (J). (gr. 5-18). 16.99 (978-0-525-47890-4(6), Dutton Books for Young Readers) Penguin Young Readers Group.

Desir, C. & Perry, Jolene. Love Blind. 2016. (ENG., Illus.). 320p. (YA). (gr. 9). 17.99 (978-1-4814-1693-1(6), Simon Pulse) Simon Pulse.

Diesen, Deborah. The Pout-Pout Fish Goes to School. Hanna, Dan, illus. 2014. (Pout-Pout Fish Adventure Ser.). (ENG.). 32p. (J). (gr. -1-k). 16.99 (978-0-374-36095-5(2), 9780374360955, Farrar, Straus & Giroux (BYR)) Farrar, Straus & Giroux.

Diggle, David Mark. Barbara: A Sssslithering Adventure of Self Discovery. Diggle, Daniel James, illus. 2011. 24p. (J). pap. (978-0-9871657-9-4(8)) Diggle de Doo Productions Pty, Ltd.

Dinolfo, Louann S. The Calico Kite. 2011. 28p. pap. 15.99 (978-1-4628-6356-3(6)) Xlibris Corp.

Dion. Fishing with Balloons. 2004. (Illus.). 57p. (J). pap. 4.95 (978-1-881929-34-5(5)) Oxton Hse., Pubs.

Dionne, Erin. The Total Tragedy of a Girl Named Hamlet. 2011. (ENG.). 304p. (J). (gr. 3-7). 8.99 (978-0-14-241748-5(3), Puffin Books) Penguin Young Readers Group.

Double Reverse, 1 vol. 2014. (Sports Stories Ser.). (ENG.). 128p. (J). (gr. 2-6). pap. 5.95 (978-1-56145-807-3(4)) Peachtree Pubs.

Dowell, Frances O'Roark. The Second Life of Abigail Walker. (ENG., Illus.). (J). (gr. 3-7). 2013. 272p. pap. 5.99 (978-1-4424-0594-3(5)) 2012. 240p. 16.99 (978-1-4424-0593-6(7)) Simon & Schuster Children's Publishing. (Atheneum Bks. for Young Readers).

Dower, Laura. Gabi & the Great Big Bakeover. Lazuli, Lilly, illus. 160p. 2017. (J). (978-1-4747-2213-1(X)) 2016. (ENG.). (gr. 4-5). lib. bdg. 26.65 (978-1-4965-3119-3(1)) Stone Arch Bks.

Drachman, Eric. Leo the Lightning Bug. Muscarello, James, illus. l.t. ed. 2005. (ENG.). 32p. (J). (gr. -1-2). 18.95 incl. audio compact disk (978-0-9703809-0-6(9)) Kidwick Bks.

Drouhard, Brianne. Billie the Unicorn. 2011. (ENG., Illus.). 36p. (J). (gr. -1-3). 15.95 (978-1-59702-024-4(9)) Immedium.

Duchess of York Staff & Ferguson, Sarah. Ballerina Rosie. Goode, Diane, illus. 2012. (ENG.). 32p. (J). (gr. -1-3). 16.99 (978-1-4424-3066-2(4), Simon & Schuster/Paula Wiseman Bks.) Simon & Schuster/Paula Wiseman Bks.

Dunlap, Sonya K. Responza the Bull Learns the Ropes. 2008. 24p. pap. 17.95 (978-0-9815245-5-9(9)) Accelerator Bks.

Durso, Diana T. Did You Know That's Not My Name? 2009. 52p. pap. 19.95 (978-1-4389-3182-1(4)) AuthorHouse.

Dyan, Penelope. Mikey & Me & the Se. 2011. 36p. pap. 11.95 (978-1-935630-63-0(6)) Bellissima Publishing, LLC.

Easton, Kelly. To Be Mona. (ENG.). 224p. (YA). (gr. 7). 2009. pap. 7.99 (978-1-4169-0055-9(1)) 2008. 16.99 (978-1-4169-0054-2(3)) McElderry, Margaret K. Bks. (McElderry, Margaret K. Bks.).

Efaw, Amy. Battle Dress. 2003. 400p. (J). (gr. 7-18). pap. 6.99 (978-0-06-053520-9(2)) HarperCollins Pubs.

—Battle Dress. 2010. (ENG.). 304p. (YA). (gr. 7-18). 8.99 (978-0-14-241397-5(6), Speak) Penguin Young Readers Group.

Ering, Timothy Basil. Necks Out for Adventure! Ering, Timothy Basil, illus. 2008. (ENG., Illus.). 48p. (J). (gr. -1-3). 16.99 (978-0-7636-2355-5(5)) Candlewick Pr.

Fagan, Cary. I Wish I Could Draw, 1 vol. 2014. (ENG., Illus.). 32p. (J). (gr. k-3). 12.95 (978-1-55498-318-6(5)) Groundwood Bks. CAN. Dist: Publishers Group West (PGW).

Flinn, Alex. Diva. 2013. (ENG.). 304p. (YA). (gr. 9). pap. 9.99 (978-0-06-212434-0(X)) 2007. (ENG.). 288p. (J). (gr. 9-12). pap. 8.99 (978-0-06-056846-7(1), HarperTeen) 2006. 263p. (YA). (gr. 7-12). 16.99 (978-0-06-056843-6(7), HarperTeen) 2006. 263p. (YA). (gr. 7-12). lib. bdg. 18.89 (978-0-06-056845-0(3), HarperTeen) HarperCollins Pubs.

Foard, Sheila Wood. Harvey Girl. 2006. (ENG., Illus.). 176p. (YA). (gr. 7-12). per. 18.95 (978-0-89672-570-6(7)) Texas Tech Univ. Pr.

Ford, Adam B. Jam-Bo, Litta-Girl, & the Bullies. Huddleston, Courtney, illus. 2013. 44p. pap. 12.95 (978-0-9794104-9-9(5)) H Bar Pr.

Forman, Gayle. Sisters in Sanity. (YA). 2016. (ENG.). 304p. (gr. 8). pap. 9.99 (978-0-06-088749-0(4)) 2007. 290p. (gr. 7-12). lib. bdg. 17.89 (978-0-06-088748-3(6)) 2007. (ENG.). 304p. (gr. 7-18). 16.99 (978-0-06-088747-6(8)) HarperCollins Pubs. (HarperTeen).

Friedman, Aimee. Two Summers. 2016. (ENG.). 368p. (J). (gr. 7). 17.99 (978-0-545-51807-9(5)) Scholastic, Inc.

Friedman, Laurie B. Game Time, Mallory! Kalis, Jennifer, illus. 2015. (J). 15.99 (978-1-4677-6188-8(5)) Lerner Publishing Group.

Galante, Cecilia. The World from up Here. (ENG.). 320p. (J). (gr. 3-7). 2017. pap. 6.99 **(978-0-545-84846-6(6))** 2016. 16.99 (978-0-545-84845-9(8), Scholastic Pr.) Scholastic, Inc.

Gassman, Julie A. I Am on Strike Against Softball, 1 vol. Santillan, Jorge H., illus. 2012. (Sports Illustrated Kids Victory School Superstars Ser.). (ENG.). 56p. (gr. 1-3). pap. 5.95 (978-1-4342-3870-2(9)); lib. bdg. 26.65 (978-1-4342-2247-3(0)) Stone Arch Bks.

Gelin, Antoinette. Captain Underfish: Superhero for the Underworld. 2011. 40p. pap. 25.95 (978-1-4634-2662-0(3)) AuthorHouse.

Gervay, Susanne. Being Jack. Wilcox, Cathy, illus. 2015. 167p. (J). (978-1-61067-455-3(3)) Kane Miller.

—I Am Jack. Cathy, Wilcox, illus. 2013. (ENG.). 144p. (J). pap. 5.99 (978-1-61067-128-6(7)) Kane Miller.

Gibbs, Lynne. Molly Mouse Is Shy: A Story of Shyness. Mitchell, Melanie, illus. 2009. (Let's Grow Together Ser.). 32p. (J). (gr. -1-2). pap. 10.55 (978-1-60754-761-7(9)); lib. bdg. 22.60 (978-1-60754-756-3(2)) Windmill Bks.

Giff, Patricia Reilly. The Number One Kid. Bright, Alasdair, illus. 2010. (Zigzag Kids Ser.). (ENG.). 80p. (J). (gr. 1-4). pap. 4.99 (978-0-553-49468-6(6), Yearling) Random Hse. Children's Bks.

Glassman, Miriam. Call Me Oklahoma! 2013. (ENG.). 128p. (J). (gr. 2-7). 16.95 (978-0-8234-2742-0(0)) Holiday Hse., Inc.

Going, K. L. The Liberation of Gabriel King. 2007. (ENG.). 160p. (J). (gr. 3-7). 6.99 (978-0-14-240766-0(6), Puffin Books) Penguin Young Readers Group.

—The Liberation of Gabriel King. 2007. 151p. (gr. 3-7). 17.00 (978-0-7569-7762-7(2)) Perfection Learning Corp.

Goobie, Beth. Kicked Out. 2004. (Orca Soundings Ser.). 92p. 19.95 (978-0-7569-4309-7(4)) Perfection Learning Corp.

Goobie, Beth & Fernández, Queta. El Que Dirán, 1 vol. 2008. (Spanish Soundings Ser.). (SPA.). 112p. (YA). (gr. 8-12). pap. 9.95 (978-1-55143-973-0(5)) Orca Bk. Pubs. USA.

Goss, Michael Anthony. The Bat Who Wore Glasses. Longabough, Kristen, illus. 2005. (J). pap. (978-1-933156-13-2(9)); per. 16.99 (978-1-933156-06-4(6)) GSVQ Publishing. (VisionQuest Kids).

Grannis, Greg. Lottie Bright & the Starmaker's Universe. Vargas, Robert, illus. 2006. (ENG.). 280p. (J). per. (978-0-9778205-9-7(9)) Helm Publishing.

Grant, Crystal. Warrior Boy. 2007. (ENG.). 92p. per. 16.95 (978-1-4241-3978-1(3)) PublishAmerica, Inc.

Greene, Stephanie. Queen Sophie Hartley. 2011. (ENG.). 144p. (J). (gr. 2-5). pap. 5.99 (978-0-547-55021-3(9)) Houghton Mifflin Harcourt Publishing Co.

Griffie, Sandra. The Snow Dancer. 2012. 28p. 24.95 (978-1-4626-6777-2(5)) America Star Bks.

Groeneweg, Nicole. One Word Pearl. Mitchell, Hazel, illus. 2013. (ENG.). 32p. (J). (gr. k-3). 17.95 (978-1-934133-53-8(1)); pap. 7.95 (978-1-934133-54-5(X)) Charlesbridge Publishing, Inc.

Guanci, Anne Marie. David & the Worry Beast: Helping Children Cope with Anxiety. Attia, Caroline, illus. 2007. (ENG.). 48p. (J). (gr. -1-4). pap. 9.95 (978-0-88282-275-4(6)) New Horizon Pr. Pubs., Inc.

Gurevich, Margaret. Design Disaster. Hagel, Brooke, illus. 2015. (Chloe by Design Ser.). (ENG.). 96p. (gr. 5-8). 25.32 (978-1-4965-0505-7(0)) Stone Arch Bks.

—Gina's Balance. 2016. (What's Your Dream? Ser.). (ENG., Illus.). 96p. (gr. 3-4). lib. bdg. 25.32 (978-1-4965-3443-9(3)) Capstone Press of Coughlan Cos.

—Unraveling, 1 vol. Hagel, Brooke, illus. 2014. (Chloe by Design Ser.). (ENG.). 96p. (gr. 5-8). 25.32 (978-1-4342-9179-0(0)) Stone Arch Bks.

Hale, Shannon. The Forgotten Sisters. 2015. (Princess Academy Ser.: 3). (ENG.). 336p. (YA). (gr. 5-8). 17.99 (978-1-61963-485-5(6), 9781619634855, Bloomsbury USA Childrens) Bloomsbury Publishing USA.

—Palace of Stone. (Princess Academy Ser.: 2). (ENG.). (YA). (gr. 5-8). 2015. 352p. pap. 7.99 (978-1-61963-257-8(8), 9781619632578) 2012. 336p. 17.99 (978-1-59990-873-1(5), 9781599908731) Bloomsbury Publishing USA. (Bloomsbury USA Childrens).

—Palace of Stone. 2015. (Princess Academy Ser.: 2). (YA). lib. bdg. 18.40 (978-0-606-36439-3(0)) Turtleback Bks.

—Princess Academy. (Princess Academy Ser.: 1). (ENG.). (YA). (gr. 5-8). 2005. 320p. 17.99 (978-1-58234-993-0(2), 9781582349930) 2nd ed. 2015. 336p. pap. 7.99 (978-1-61963-613-2(1), 9781619636132) Bloomsbury Publishing USA. (Bloomsbury USA Childrens).

—Princess Academy. 2009. (Princess Academy Ser.: No. 1). 8.86 (978-0-7848-2867-0(9), Everbind) Marco Bk. Co.

—Princess Academy. 2007. (Princess Academy Ser.: No. 1). 314p. (gr. 5-9). 18.00 (978-0-7569-8180-8(8)) Perfection Learning Corp.

—Princess Academy. (Princess Academy Ser.: No. 1). (978-0-439-88811-0(5), Scholastic) Scholastic, Inc.

—Princess Academy. l.t. ed. 2006. (Princess Academy Ser.: No. 1). 339p. (J). (gr. 5-9). 23.95 (978-0-7862-8733-8(0)) Thorndike Pr.

—Princess Academy. 2015. (Princess Academy Ser.: 1). (YA). lib. bdg. 18.40 (978-0-606-36438-6(2)) Turtleback Bks.

—Princess Academy - The Forgotten Sisters. 2016. (Princess Academy Ser.: 3). (ENG.). 352p. (J). pap. 7.99 (978-1-61963-933-1(5), 9781619639331, Bloomsbury USA Childrens) Bloomsbury Publishing USA.

Harkness, Karen. Coralee's Best Run Yet. 2007. (Illus.). 40p. (J). per. 7.99 net. (978-0-9800934-0-7(6)) H&W Publishing Inc.

Hart, Lauri J. A Day in the Life of Nicholas B. 2009. 28p. pap. 14.99 (978-1-4490-1935-8(8)) AuthorHouse.

Hartt-Sussman, Heather. Noni Says No. Côté, Geneviève, illus. 2011. (ENG.). 24p. (J). (gr. -1-2). 17.95 (978-1-77049-233-2(X), Tundra Bks.) Tundra Bks. CAN. Dist: Penguin Random Hse. LLC.

Haynes, Marilee. Pictures of Me. 2016. 149p. (J). pap. (978-0-8198-6019-4(0)) Pauline Bks. & Media.

Hector, Julian. The Gentleman Bug. Hector, Julian, illus. 2010. (ENG., Illus.). 40p. (J). (gr. -1-k). 16.99 (978-1-4169-9467-1(X), Atheneum Bks. for Young Readers) Simon & Schuster Children's Publishing.

Heller, Alyson. After-School Sports Club Adventures. Björkman, Steve, illus. 2016. (J). **(978-1-4814-7741-3(2))** Simon & Schuster Children's Publishing.

Hobbs, Valerie. Minnie McClary Speaks Her Mind. 2013. (ENG.). 240p. (J). (gr. 4-8). pap. 9.99 (978-1-250-03408-3(6), 9781250034083) Square Fish.

Hoblin, Paul. The Clutch. 2017. (Gridiron Ser.). (ENG.). 120p. (YA). (gr. 6-12). 26.65 **(978-1-5124-3980-9(0))** Lerner Publishing Group.

Hoffman, Mary. City of Secrets. (Stravaganza Ser.). (ENG.). (YA). 2010. 416p. (gr. 7). pap. 8.99 (978-1-59990-451-1(9), 9781599904511) 2008. 400p. (gr. 5-18). 17.99 (978-1-59990-202-9(8), 9781599902029) Bloomsbury Publishing USA. (Bloomsbury USA Childrens).

—City of Ships. 2010. (Stravaganza Ser.). (ENG.). 368p. (YA). (gr. 7-18). 17.99 (978-1-59990-491-7(8), 9781599904917, Bloomsbury USA Childrens) Bloomsbury Publishing USA.

—Stravaganza: City of Ships. 2012. (Stravaganza Ser.). (ENG.). 384p. (YA). (gr. 7). pap. 9.99 (978-1-59990-832-8(8), 9781599908328, Bloomsbury USA Childrens) Bloomsbury Publishing USA.

Hopkins, Cathy. Mates, Dates, & Chocolate Cheats. 2011. (Mates, Dates Ser.). (ENG.). 224p. (YA). (gr. 7). pap. 10.99 (978-1-4424-3081-5(8), Simon Pulse) Simon Pulse.

Howling, Eric. Drive, 1 vol. 2008. (Lorimer Sports Stories Ser.). (ENG.). 120p. (J). (gr. 4-8). 9.95 (978-1-55277-009-2(5), 9781552770092); 16.95 (978-1-55277-010-8(9), 9781552770108) Lorimer, James & Co., Ltd., Pubs. CAN. Dist: Casemate Pubs. & Bk. Distributors, LLC.

Hueller, Andy. Dizzy Fantastic & Her Flying Bicycle. 2010. (Illus.). 155p. (J). pap. 8.99 (978-1-59955-395-5(3)) Cedar Fort, Inc./CFI Distribution.

Hurwitz, Johanna. Mighty Monty: More First-Grade Adventures. McGrory, Anik, illus. 2010. (Monty Ser.). (ENG.).

112p. (J). (gr. 1-4). pap. 5.99 *(978-0-7636-4786-5(1))* Candlewick Pr.

Hurwitz, Michele Weber. Calli Be Gold. 2012. (ENG.). 208p. (J). (gr. 3-7). 6.99 *(978-0-375-86528-2(4),* Yearling) Random Hse. Children's Bks.

Jakubowski, Michele. The Big Bike. Waters, Erica-Jane, illus. 2015. (Perfectly Poppy Ser.). (ENG.). 32p. (gr. k-2). 22.65 *(978-1-4795-5801-8(X))* Picture Window Bks.

Jellen, Michelle. Spain or Shine. 2005. (S. A. S. S. Ser.). (ENG., Illus.). 224p. (YA). (gr. 7-7). 7.99 *(978-0-14-240368-6(7),* Speak) Penguin Young Readers Group.

Johnson, Kathleen A. A Voice Came to Me. 2006. lib. bdg. 17.95 *(978-0-9785623-0-4(5))* Voice of Light Pubns.

Johnson, Lauren. Beastly Basketball, 1 vol. Garcia, Eduardo, illus. 2014. (Sports Illustrated Kids Graphic Novels Ser.). (ENG.). 72p. (gr. 2-5). lib. bdg. 26.65 *(978-1-4342-6490-9(4))* Stone Arch Bks.

Johnston, Tony. A Small Thing ... but Big. Hooper, Hadley, illus. 2016. (ENG.). 40p. (J). 17.99 *(978-1-62672-256-9(0),* 9781626722569) Roaring Brook Pr.

Jones, Christianne. Fuchsia Fierce. Canby, Kelly, illus. 2016. (Fiction Picture Bks.). (ENG.). 32p. (gr. 1-2). lib. bdg. 22.65 *(978-1-5158-0553-3(0),* Fiction Picture Bks.) Picture Window Bks.

Jones, Christianne C. Fuchsia Fierce. Canby, Kelly, illus. 2016. (ENG.). 32p. (gr. 1-2). 15.95 *(978-1-62370-786-6(2))* Capstone Young Readers of Coughlan Cos.

Jones, Debra M. What in the World Should I Be. Collier, Kevin, illus. 2010. 16p. pap. 9.95 *(978-1-61633-037-8(6))* Guardian Angel Publishing, Inc.

Jones, Diana Wynne & Jones, Ursula. The Islands of Chaldea. 368p. (J). (gr. 3-7). 2015. pap. 9.99 *(978-0-06-229508-8(X))* 2014. 17.99 *(978-0-06-229507-1(1))* HarperCollins Pubs. (Greenwillow Bks.).

Jones, Janey Louise. Dancer the Wild Pony. Poh, Jennie, illus. 2016. (Superfairies Ser.). (ENG.). 56p. (gr. k-3). lib. bdg. 23.99 *(978-1-4795-8642-4(0))* Picture Window Bks.

Jones, Jen. Brooke's Quest for Captain, No. 2. 2011. (Team Cheer Ser.). (ENG.). 112p. (gr. 4-4). lib. bdg. 25.32 *(978-1-4342-2995-3(5),* Team Cheer) Stone Arch Bks.

Jones, Traci L. Standing Against the Wind. 2010. (ENG.). 208p. (YA). (gr. 7-9). pap. 11.99 *(978-0-312-62293-0(7),* 9780312622930) Square Fish.

Jordan, Apple. A Princess Can! (Disney Princess) RH Disney Staff et al, illus. 2015. (Step into Reading Ser.). (ENG.). 24p. (J). (gr. -1-1). 4.99 *(978-0-7364-3341-9(4),* RH/Disney) Random Hse. Children's Bks.

Jordan, Deloris. Michael's Golden Rules. Nelson, Kadir, illus. 2007. (ENG.). 32p. (J). (gr. 1-5). 17.99 *(978-0-689-87016-3(7),* Simon & Schuster/Paula Wiseman Bks.) Simon & Schuster/Paula Wiseman Bks.

Jordan, Dream. Bad Boy. 2012. (ENG.). 208p. (YA). (gr. 6-11). pap. 17.99 *(978-0-312-54997-8(0),* 9780312549978, St. Martin's Griffin) St. Martin's Pr.

Jungle Crossing. 2011. (ENG.). 228p. (J). (gr. 5-7). pap. 13.99 *(978-0-547-55009-1(X))* Houghton Mifflin Harcourt Publishing Co.

Kakakios, Melissa. I Love Taekwondo: My First Taekwondo Books. 2013. 28p. pap. 16.95 *(978-1-4525-7668-8(8),* Balboa Pr.) Author Solutions, Inc.

Kay, Karin. Floppy Cat. 2009. (J). 16.95 *(978-0-9823818-0-9(8))* Floppy Cat Co.

Kelley, Jane. Nature Girl. 2011. (ENG., Illus.). 256p. (J). (gr. 3-7). pap. 6.99 *(978-0-375-85635-8(8),* Yearling) Random Hse. Children's Bks.

Kim, YeShil. We Are Proud of You. The Pope Twins, illus. rev. ed. 2014. (MySELF Bookshelf Ser.). (ENG.). 32p. (J). (gr. k-2). pap. 11.94 *(978-1-60357-651-2(7));* lib. bdg. 25.27 *(978-1-59953-642-2(0))* Norwood House Pr.

King, A. S. Everybody Sees the Ants. 2011. (ENG.). 288p. (YA). (gr. 10-17). 18.00 *(978-0-316-12928-2(3))* Little Brown & Co.

—Everybody Sees the Ants. 2012. (ENG.). 320p. (YA). (gr. 10-17). pap. 10.00 *(978-0-316-12927-5(5))* Little, Brown Bks. for Young Readers.

Kinra, Richa, illus. The Princess Panda Tea Party: A Cerebral Palsy Fairy Tale. 2014. 45p. (J). pap. 14.95 *(978-1-61599-219-5(7))* Loving Healing Pr., Inc.

Kirby, Matthew J. Icefall. (ENG.). 336p. (J). (gr. 3-7). 2013. pap. 6.99 *(978-0-545-27425-8(7),* Scholastic Paperbacks) 2011. 17.99 *(978-0-545-27424-1(9),* Scholastic Pr.) Scholastic, Inc.

Kirouac Bn, Nicole. I Am Unique. 2013. 32p. pap. 13.99 *(978-1-4525-7594-0(0),* Balboa Pr.) Author Solutions, Inc.

Knight, Richard, et al. Finn at Clee Point. Hurst, Oliver, illus. 2012. (ENG.). 128p. (J). pap. 12.99 *(978-1-84686-401-8(1))* Barefoot Bks., Inc.

Knudson, Mike & Wilkinson, Steve. Raymond & Graham Rule the School. Curtis, Stacy, illus. 2009. (Raymond & Graham Ser.). (ENG.). 144p. (J). (gr. 3-7). 6.99 *(978-0-14-241426-2(3),* Puffin Books) Penguin Young Readers Group.

Konigsburg, E. L. The View from Saturday. 280p. (YA). (gr. 5-18). pap. 4.95 *(978-0-8072-1511-1(2),* Listening Library) Random Hse. Audio Publishing Group.

Kravitz, Danny. Tommy Mcknight & the Great Election. 2016. (Presidential Politics Ser.). (ENG.). 96p. (gr. 3-4). lib. bdg. 26.65 *(978-1-4965-2585-7(X),* Connect) Stone Arch Bks.

—Tommy McKnight & the Great Election. 2016. (J). pap. *(978-1-4965-2752-3(6))* Stone Arch Bks.

Kreloff, Elliot. Please Don't Make Me Fly! A Growing-Up Story of Self-Confidence. Kreloff, Elliot, illus. 2017. (Growing Up Ser.). (ENG., Illus.). 32p. (gr. -1-1). lib. bdg. 19.99 ***(978-1-63440-179-1(4));*** 30.65 ***(978-1-63440-183-8(2))*** Red Chair Pr.

Krishnaswami, Uma. El árbol Más Feliz: Un Cuento Sobre Yoga. Jeyaveeran, Ruth, illus. 2008.Tr. of Happiest Tree: a Yoga Story. (SPA.). 32p. (J). pap. 10.95 *(978-1-62014-149-6(3))* Lee & Low Bks., Inc.

Kroll, Steven. When I Dream of Heaven: Angelina's Story. 2004. 156p. (J). lib. bdg. 16.92 *(978-1-4242-0770-1(3))* Fitzgerald Bks.

Kylie's Song: Evaluation Guide. 2006. (J). *(978-1-55942-414-1(1))* Witcher Productions.

Lamb, Bianca the Dancing Crocodile. Skon, Sandy, illus. 2008. 30p. pap. 24.95 *(978-1-60563-447-0(6))* America Star Bks.

Lamb, Anne. Beat Bugs. 2017. (Beat Bugs Ser.). 32p. (J). (gr. -1-3). 9.99 *(978-0-06-264076-5(3),* HarperFestival) HarperCollins Pubs.

Landry, Cristy. Snowboarding with Courage. 2016. 98p. (YA). (gr. 8-12). pap. 10.95 *(978-0-9963756-0-3(0))* All About Kids Publishing.

Langston, Laura. Exit Point, 1 vol. 2006. (Orca Soundings Ser.). (ENG.). 136p. (YA). (gr. 8-12). per. 9.95 *(978-1-55143-505-3(5))* Orca Bk. Pubs. USA.

Larsen, Ramonita. Yes, I Can Do It/Si, lo Puedo Hacer. Larsen, Ramonita, illus. l.t. ed. 2006. (Illus.). 18p. (J). per. 10.99 *(978-1-59879-292-8(X))* Lifevest Publishing, Inc.

Law, Felicia. Alice the Armadillo: A Tale of Self Discovery. Messina, Lilli, illus. 2010. (Animal Fair Values Ser.). 32p. (J). (gr. -1-3). pap. 10.55 *(978-1-60754-809-6(7));* lib. bdg. 22.60 *(978-1-60754-805-8(4))* Windmill Bks.

Levine, Gail Carson. The Two Princesses of Bamarre. (J). 2012. (ENG.). 272p. (gr. 3-7). pap. 6.99 *(978-0-06-440966-7(X))* 2004. (Illus.). 304p. (gr. 7-18). reprint ed. pap. 6.99 *(978-0-06-057580-9(8))* HarperCollins Pubs.

Levy, Debbie. Underwater. 2007. (Darby Creek Exceptional Titles Ser.). 155p. (J). (gr. 4-7). 16.95 *(978-1-58196-053-2(0),* Darby Creek) Lerner Publishing Group.

Lewin, Betsy. You Can Do It! Lewin, Betsy, illus. 2014. (I Like to Read(r) Ser.). (ENG., Illus.). 24p. (J). (gr. -1-3). 6.99 *(978-0-8234-3055-0(3))* Holiday Hse., Inc.

—You Can Do It! 2013. (I Like to Read(r) Ser.). (ENG.). 24p. (J). 14.95 *(978-0-8234-2522-8(3))* Holiday Hse., Inc.

Lichtenheld, Tom. Bridget's Beret. Lichtenheld, Tom, illus. 2010. (ENG., Illus.). 40p. (J). (gr. -1-2). 16.99 *(978-0-8050-8775-8(3),* 9780805087758, Holt, Henry & Co. Bks. For Young Readers) Holt, Henry & Co.

Lippmann, Wilfried. The Gift of Eye. 2008. 140p. (gr. 7-12). pap. 11.95 *(978-0-595-52251-4(3))* iUniverse, Inc.

Litz, Amanda. Sam & Pam Can & You Can Too! We Can Count. Garcia, Cynthia, illus. 2011. 32p. (J). pap. 3.99 *(978-0-9841496-3-6(5))* Traveler's Trunk Publishing LLC.

Lombardo, Constance. Stunt Cat to the Stars. Lombardo, Constance, illus. 2015. (Mr. Puffball Ser.: 1). (ENG., Illus.). 240p. (J). (gr. 3-7). 12.99 *(978-0-06-232065-0(3))* HarperCollins Pubs.

Lonczak, Heather Suzanne. Mookey the Monkey Gets over Being Teased. Ramsey, Marcy Dunn, illus. 2006. 32p. (J). (gr. -1-3). 14.95 *(978-1-59147-479-1(5));* 9.95 *(978-1-59147-480-7(9))* American Psychological Assn. (Magination Pr.).

Look, Lenore. Alvin Ho: Allergic to Birthday Parties, Science Projects, & Other Man-Made Catastrophes. Pham, LeUyen, illus. 2011. (Alvin Ho Ser.). (ENG.). 192p. (J). (gr. 1-4). 6.99 *(978-0-375-87369-0(4),* Yearling) Random Hse. Children's Bks.

—Alvin Ho: Allergic to Camping, Hiking, & Other Natural Disasters. Pham, LeUyen, illus. 2010. (Alvin Ho Ser.). (ENG.). 192p. (J). (gr. 1-4). 6.99 *(978-0-375-85750-8(8),* Yearling) Random Hse. Children's Bks.

—Alvin Ho: Allergic to Dead Bodies, Funerals, & Other Fatal Circumstances. Pham, LeUyen, illus. 2012. (Alvin Ho Ser.). (ENG.). 208p. (J). (gr. 1-4). 6.99 *(978-0-307-97695-6(5),* Yearling) Random Hse. Children's Bks.

Lord, Michelle. The Quick Quarterback, 1 vol. Harpster, Steve, illus. 2012. (My First Graphic Novel Ser.). (ENG.). 32p. (gr. k-2). pap. 6.25 *(978-1-4342-3861-0(X),* My First Graphic Novel) Stone Arch Bks.

Lubar, David. My Rotten Life. 2009. (Nathan Abercrombie, Accidental Zombie Ser.: 1). (ENG., Illus.). 160p. (J). (gr. 3-7). pap. 8.99 *(978-0-7653-1634-9(X),* 9780765316349, Starscape) Doherty, Tom Assocs., LLC.

—Sleeping Freshmen Never Lie. 2007. (ENG.). 288p. (YA). (gr. 7-18). 10.99 *(978-0-14-240780-6(1),* Speak) Penguin Young Readers Group.

—Sophomores & Other Oxymorons. 2015. (ENG.). 432p. (YA). (gr. 7). 17.99 *(978-0-525-42970-8(0),* Dutton Books for Young Readers) Penguin Young Readers Group.

Ludwig, Trudy. Just Kidding. Gustavson, Adam, illus. 2006. (ENG.). 32p. (J). (gr. 1-4). 15.99 *(978-1-58246-163-2(5),* Tricycle Pr.) Random Hse. Children's Bks.

Lukachko, Mary Louise. Peter the Blue Penguin. 2012. 28p. pap. 24.95 *(978-1-4626-8186-0(7))* America Star Bks.

Lupica, Mike. Long Shot, 1 vol. 2012. (Comeback Kids Ser.). (ENG.). 192p. (J). (gr. 4-8). lib. bdg. 27.07 *(978-1-59961-176-1(7))* Spotlight.

—Qb 1. 2013. (ENG.). 272p. (J). (gr. 5). 17.99 *(978-0-399-25228-0(2),* Philomel Bks.) Penguin Publishing Group.

—Qb 1. 2014. (ENG.). 288p. (J). (gr. 5). pap. 7.99 *(978-0-14-751152-2(6),* Puffin Books) Penguin Young Readers Group.

—Safe at Home, 1 vol. 2012. (Comeback Kids Ser.). (ENG.). 192p. (J). (gr. 4-8). lib. bdg. 27.07 *(978-1-59961-177-8(5))* Spotlight.

Lyssenko, Taras. Wendy's Fear of Heights. 2003. 14p. (J). *(978-0-9740542-0-9(8))* Prairie Shore Creative, Inc.

Mabille, Christine. Potato-Kid & the Adventure: Treasures Within, 1 vol. 2009. 76p. pap. 19.95 *(978-1-61582-981-1(4))* America Star Bks.

MacHale, D. J. Pendragon: The Merchant of Death; The Lost City of Fear; The Never War; The Reality Bug; Black Water. 2013. (Pendragon Ser.). (ENG., Illus.). 1968p. (J). (gr. 5-9). pap. 49.99 *(978-1-4424-9926-3(5),* Simon & Schuster/Paula Wiseman Bks.) Simon & Schuster/Paula Wiseman Bks.

Mack, Winnie. After All, You're Callie Boone. 2013. (ENG.). 192p. (J). (gr. 4-7). pap. 14.99 *(978-1-250-02735-1(7),* 9781250027351) Square Fish.

Mackler, Carolyn. Tangled. (ENG.). (YA). (gr. 9). 2011. 336p. pap. 9.99 *(978-0-06-173106-8(4))* 2009. 320p. 16.99 *(978-0-06-173104-4(8))* HarperCollins Pubs. (HarperTeen).

Maddox, Jake. Bad-Luck Basketball, 1 vol. Ray, Mike, illus. 2014. (Jake Maddox JV Ser.). (ENG.). 96p. (gr. 3-4). 25.99 *(978-1-4342-9156-1(1))* Stone Arch Bks.

—Basketball Breakdown. 2016. (Jake Maddox JV Girls Ser.). (ENG.). 96p. (gr. 3-4). lib. bdg. 25.99 *(978-1-4965-3166-7(3))* Stone Arch Bks.

—BMX Bravery. 2016. (Jake Maddox JV Ser.). (ENG.). 96p. (gr. 3-4). lib. bdg. 25.99 *(978-1-4965-2630-4(9))* Stone Arch Bks.

—BMX Challenge, 1 vol. Tiffany, Sean, illus. 2011. (Jake Maddox Sports Stories Ser.). (ENG.). 72p. (gr. 2-3). pap. 5.95 *(978-1-4342-3423-0(1))* Stone Arch Bks.

—Cowboy Up, 1 vol. Tiffany, Sean, illus. 2011. (Jake Maddox Sports Stories Ser.). (ENG.). 72p. (gr. 2-3). pap. 5.95 *(978-1-4342-3425-4(8));* lib. bdg. 25.32 *(978-1-4342-2989-2(0))* Stone Arch Bks.

—Dancing Solo, 1 vol. Wood, Katie, illus. 2014. (Jake Maddox Girl Sports Stories Ser.). (ENG.). 72p. (gr. 2-3). 25.32 *(978-1-4342-4142-9(4))* Stone Arch Bks.

—Double-Axel Doubt, 1 vol. 2011. (Jake Maddox Girl Sports Stories Ser.). (ENG.). 72p. (gr. 2-3). lib. bdg. 25.32 *(978-1-4342-2499-6(6))* Stone Arch Bks.

—En la línea de Ataque. Heck, Claudia M., tr. from ENG. Tiffany, Sean, illus. 2012. (Jake Maddox en Español Ser.). (SPA.). 72p. (gr. 2-3). 25.32 *(978-1-4342-3813-9(X))* Stone Arch Bks.

—Heavyweight Takedown. 2015. (Jake Maddox JV Ser.). (ENG.). 96p. (gr. 3-4). lib. bdg. 25.99 *(978-1-4342-9638-2(5))* Stone Arch Bks.

—Hoop Hustle. Aburto, Jesus, illus. 2015. (Jake Maddox Sports Stories Ser.). (ENG.). 72p. (gr. 2-3). lib. bdg. 25.32 *(978-1-4965-0494-4(1))* Stone Arch Bks.

—On the Line, 1 vol. Tiffany, Sean, illus. 2006. (Jake Maddox Sports Stories Ser.). (ENG.). 72p. (gr. 2-3). 25.32 *(978-1-59889-062-4(X));* pap. 5.95 *(978-1-59889-240-6(1))* Stone Arch Bks.

—Over the Net, 1 vol. Mourning, Tuesday, illus. 2009. (Jake Maddox Girl Sports Stories Ser.). (ENG.). 72p. (gr. 2-3). 25.32 *(978-1-4342-1213-9(0))* Stone Arch Bks.

—Pool Panic. Wood, Katie, illus. 2016. (Jake Maddox Girl Sports Stories Ser.). (ENG.). 72p. (gr. 2-3). lib. bdg. 25.32 *(978-1-4965-2618-2(X))* Stone Arch Bks.

—Slam Dunk Shoes, 1 vol. Tiffany, Sean, illus. 2007. (Jake Maddox Sports Stories Ser.). (ENG.). 72p. (gr. 2-3). 25.32 *(978-1-59889-842-2(6));* per. 5.95 *(978-1-59889-894-1(9))* Stone Arch Bks.

—Slap-Shot Slump. 2015. (Jake Maddox JV Ser.). (ENG.). 96p. (gr. 3-4). lib. bdg. 25.99 *(978-1-4342-9635-1(0))* Stone Arch Bks.

—Soccer Step-Up. 2016. (Jake Maddox JV Girls Ser.). (ENG.). 96p. (gr. 3-4). lib. bdg. 25.99 *(978-1-4965-3675-4(4))* Stone Arch Bks.

—Squad Struggles. Wood, Katie, illus. 2017. (Jake Maddox Girl Sports Stories Ser.). (ENG.). 72p. (gr. 2-3). lib. bdg. 25.32 ***(978-1-4965-4971-6(6))*** Stone Arch Bks.

Maddox, Jake. Storm Surfer, 1 vol. Mourning, Tuesday, illus. 2008. (Jake Maddox Girl Sports Stories Ser.). (ENG.). 72p. (gr. 2-3). lib. bdg. 25.32 *(978-1-4342-0471-4(5));* per. 5.95 *(978-1-4342-0521-6(5))* Stone Arch Bks.

Maddox, Jake & Berne, Emma Carlson. Horseback Hurdles, 1 vol. Wood, Katie, illus. 2012. (Jake Maddox Girl Sports Stories Ser.). (ENG.). 72p. (gr. 2-3). pap. 5.95 *(978-1-4342-3905-1(5));* lib. bdg. 25.32 *(978-1-4342-3294-6(8))* Stone Arch Bks.

Madkins, Dorenda W. Smiley Face: A Smile a Day Takes the Frown Away. 2012. 28p. pap. 24.95 *(978-1-4626-6553-2(5))* America Star Bks.

Magnus, Kellie. Little Lion Goes to School. Robinson, Michael, illus. l.t. ed. 2003. 16p. (J). 9.99 *(978-0-9744211-0-0(3))* Media Magic New York.

Mahoney, Daniel J. Monstergarten. Kaminsky, Jef, illus. 2013. (ENG.). 40p. (J). (gr. -1-k). 16.99 *(978-1-250-01441-2(7),* 9781250014412) Feiwel & Friends.

Mahony, Mary. Harry Scores A Hat Trick, Pawns, Pucks, & Scoliosis: The Sequel to Stand Tall, Harry. Pasternack, Susan, ed. Larkin, Catherine, illus. 2003. 130p. (YA). (gr. 5-8). per. 14.95 *(978-0-9658879-3-9(6))* Redding Pr.

Maier, Inger M. When Lizzie Was Afraid: Of Trying New Things. Candon, Jennifer, illus. 2004. 32p. (J). 14.95 *(978-1-59147-170-7(2));* pap. 9.95 *(978-1-59147-171-4(0))* American Psychological Assn. (Magination Pr.).

Markey, Kevin. Rainmaker. 2012. (Illus.). (J). 230p. lib. bdg. 16.89 *(978-0-06-115229-0(3));* (ENG., 240p. (gr. 3-7). 15.99 *(978-0-06-115228-3(5))* HarperCollins Pubs.

—Slumpbuster. Fitzgerald, Royce, illus. 2010. (Super Sluggers Ser.). (ENG.). 208p. (J). (gr. 3-7). pap. 6.99 *(978-0-06-115220-7(X))* HarperCollins Pubs.

—Wing Ding. 2012. (Super Sluggers Ser.). (ENG.). 224p. (J). (gr. 3-7). pap. 5.99 *(978-0-06-115227-6(7))* HarperCollins Pubs.

Marshall, Joseph. In the Footsteps of Crazy Horse. Yellowhawk, James Mark, illus. 2015. (ENG.). 176p. (J). (gr. 5-9). 16.95 *(978-1-4197-0785-8(X),* Amulet Bks.) Abrams, Inc.

Martin, Sheila. Muddy Water. 2005. pap. 16.95 *(978-1-4137-8551-7(4))* PublishAmerica, Inc.

Masino, Brian. Cabbage Patch Kids: We Are All Best Friends. Karl, Linda, illus. 2006. (J). pap. *(978-0-439-76820-7(9))* Scholastic, Inc.

McAnulty, Stacy. Beautiful. Lew-Vriethoff, Joanne, illus. 2016. (ENG.). 32p. (J). (gr. -1-17). 16.95 *(978-0-7624-5781-6(3),* Running Pr. Kids) Running Pr. Bk. Pubs.

McClure, Kim. Edgar the Seagull who was Afraid to Fly. 2009. 34p. pap. 16.70 *(978-0-557-05920-1(8))* Lulu Pr., Inc.

McCrimmon, Linda. Can You Please tie My Shoes? 2007. (J). 10.95 *(978-0-9796978-2-1(4))* G Publishing LLC.

McGowan, Keith. The Witch's Guide to Cooking with Children. Tanaka, Yoko, illus. 2011. (ENG.). 192p. (J). (gr. 4-7). pap. 8.99 *(978-0-312-67486-1(4),* 9780312674861) Square Fish.

McKay, Hilary. Permanent Rose. 2006. (ENG.). 256p. (J). (gr. 3-7). reprint ed. per. 7.99 *(978-1-4169-2804-1(9),* McElderry, Margaret K. Bks.) McElderry, Margaret K. Bks.

McKissack, Robert L. Try Your Best. Cepeda, Joe, illus. 2004. (Green Light Readers Level 2 Ser.). (ENG.). 24p. (J). (gr. -1-3). pap. 3.95 *(978-0-15-205090-0(6))* Houghton Mifflin Harcourt Publishing Co.

—Try Your Best. Cepeda, Joe, illus. 2005. (Green Light Readers Level 2 Ser.). (gr. k-2). 13.95 *(978-0-7569-5630-1(7))* Perfection Learning Corp.

McKnight, Marty. Jim Nasium. 2015. (Jim Nasium Ser.). (ENG.). 88p. (gr. 2-3). 101.28 *(978-1-4965-2010-4(6))* Stone Arch Bks.

—Jim Nasium Is a Basket Case. Jones, Chris B., illus. 2015. (Jim Nasium Ser.). (ENG.). 88p. (gr. 2-3). pap. 5.95 *(978-1-4965-0526-2(3))* Stone Arch Bks.

—Jim Nasium Is a Football Fumbler. Jones, Chris B., illus. 2015. (Jim Nasium Ser.). (ENG.). 88p. (gr. 2-3). lib. bdg. 25.32 *(978-1-4965-0522-4(0))* Stone Arch Bks.

—Jim Nasium Is a Hockey Hazard. Jones, Chris B., illus. 2015. (Jim Nasium Ser.). (ENG.). 88p. (gr. 2-3). pap. 5.95 *(978-1-4965-0524-8(7))* Stone Arch Bks.

—Jim Nasium Is a Soccer Goofball. Jones, Chris B., illus. 2015. (Jim Nasium Ser.). (ENG.). 88p. (gr. 2-3). pap. 5.95 *(978-1-4965-0525-5(5))* Stone Arch Bks.

—Jim Nasium Is a Strikeout King. Jones, Chris, illus. 2016. (Jim Nasium Ser.). (ENG.). 88p. (gr. 2-3). lib. bdg. 25.32 *(978-1-4965-3025-7(X))* Stone Arch Bks.

—Jim Nasium Is a Tennis Mismatch. Jones, Chris, illus. 2016. (Jim Nasium Ser.). (ENG.). 88p. (gr. 2-3). lib. bdg. 25.32 *(978-1-4965-3026-4(8))* Stone Arch Bks.

McMann, Lisa. Island of Silence. (Unwanteds Ser.: 2). (ENG., (J). (gr. 3-7). 2013. Illus.). 432p. pap. 8.99 *(978-1-4424-0772-5(7))* 2012. 416p. 18.99 *(978-1-4424-0771-8(9))* Simon & Schuster Children's Publishing. (Aladdin).

—Island of Silence. 2013. (Unwanteds Ser.: 2). lib. bdg. 18.40 *(978-0-606-32044-3(X),* Turtleback) Turtleback Bks.

McMullan, Akilah. The Best Me I Can Be. 2010. 28p. pap. 13.99 *(978-1-4490-1840-5(8))* AuthorHouse.

McNamara, Margaret. A Poem in Your Pocket. Karas, G. Brian, illus. 2015. (Mr. Tiffin's Classroom Ser.). (ENG.). 40p. (J). (gr. -1-3). 16.99 *(978-0-307-97947-6(4),* Schwartz & Wade Bks.) Random Hse. Children's Bks.

McStay, Moriah. Everything That Makes You. 2015. (ENG.). 352p. (YA). (gr. 8). 17.99 *(978-0-06-229548-4(9),* Tegen, Katherine Bks) HarperCollins Pubs.

McVoy, Terra Elan. Being Friends with Boys. (ENG., (YA). (gr. 9). 2013. Illus.). 384p. pap. 10.99 *(978-1-4424-2160-8(6))* 2012. 368p. 16.99 *(978-1-4424-2159-2(2))* Simon Pulse. (Simon Pulse).

Meister, Cari. The Fancy Octopus, 1 vol. Harpster, Steve, illus. 2011. (Ocean Tales Ser.). (ENG.). 32p. (gr. 2-3). pap. 6.25 *(978-1-4342-3392-9(8));* lib. bdg. 22.65 *(978-1-4342-3201-4(8))* Stone Arch Bks.

Merschel, Michael. Revenge of the Star Survivors. 2017. (ENG.). 320p. (J). (gr. 5-8). 17.95 *(978-0-8234-3667-5(5))* Holiday Hse., Inc.

Messner, Kate. All the Answers. (ENG.). 2016. 272p. (J). pap. 7.99 *(978-1-68119-020-4(6),* 9781681190204) 2015. 256p. (YA). (gr. 3-6). 16.99 *(978-1-61963-374-2(4),* 9781619633742) Bloomsbury Publishing USA. (Bloomsbury USA Childrens).

Miles, Brenda & Sweet, Susan D. Cinderstella: A Tale of Planets Not Princes. Docampo, Valeria, illus. 2016. (J). *(978-1-4338-2270-4(9),* Magination Pr.) American Psychological Assn.

Mills, Joyce C. & Crowley, Richard J. Sammy the Elephant & Mr. Camel: A Story to Help Children Overcome Bedwetting. Pillo, Cary, illus. 2nd ed. 2005. 32p. (J). 14.95 *(978-1-59147-247-6(4));* pap. 9.95 *(978-1-59147-248-3(2))* American Psychological Assn. (Magination Pr.).

Minou: Evaluation Guide. 2006. (J). *(978-1-55942-416-5(8))* Witcher Productions.

Monteiro, Francelina. The Star That Couldn't Shine. 2009. 24p. pap. 12.99 *(978-1-4490-3775-8(5))* AuthorHouse.

Morgan, Alex. Shaken Up. 2015. (Kicks Ser.). (ENG., Illus.). 128p. (J). (gr. 3-7). 16.99 *(978-1-4814-5100-0(6),* Simon & Schuster Bks. For Young Readers) Simon & Schuster Bks. For Young Readers.

Morgan, Melissa J. Sunrise. 2009. (Summer Confidential Ser.: 1). (ENG.). 240p. (J). (gr. 5-6). pap. 7.99 *(978-0-448-44988-3(9),* Grosset & Dunlap) Penguin Young Readers Group.

—Twilight. 2009. (Summer Confidential Ser.: 3). (ENG.). 240p. (J). (gr. 5-18). pap. 7.99 *(978-0-448-44990-6(0),* Grosset & Dunlap) Penguin Young Readers Group.

Ms. Sue. Where Is Your Name? Ducy, George, illus. 2009. 24p. pap. 24.95 *(978-1-60672-711-9(7))* America Star Bks.

Mullarkey, Lisa. Daniela, 1 vol. Franco, Paula, illus. 2016. (Pony Girls Ser.). (ENG.). 112p. (J). (gr. 1-4). 27.07 *(978-1-62402-128-2(X))* Magic Wagon.

Murray, Stuart A. P. Matty in the Goal. 2012. (Champion Sports Story Ser.). 104p. (J). (gr. 3-18). pap. 10.95 *(978-1-4644-0003-2(2));* 27.94 *(978-0-7660-3877-6(7))* Enslow Pubs., Inc.

Nanette. Blue the Frog. 2004. (Life on Granny's Farm Ser.). (J). 12.95 *(978-0-9741269-2-0(6))* St. Bernard Publishing, LLC.

Naylor, Phyllis Reynolds. Including Alice. 2005. (Alice McKinley Ser.: No. 16). 277p. (J). (gr. 4-7). 13.65 *(978-0-7569-5460-4(6))* Perfection Learning Corp.

Neilly, Lori Ann. The Oracle & the Mirror. 2013. 56p. pap. 24.20 *(978-1-4669-8403-5(1))* Trafford Publishing.

Newman, Lesléa. Miss Tutu's Star. Armstrong-Ellis, Carey, illus. 2010. (ENG.). 32p. (J). (gr. k-2). 17.95 *(978-0-8109-8396-0(6),* Abrams Bks. for Young Readers) Abrams, Inc.

Newman, Patrice Tomasetti. Where Oh Where? It's in My Hair! 2012. 26p. 24.95 *(978-1-4626-6284-5(6))* America Star Bks.

Oates, Joyce Carol. Sexy. 2005. 272p. (J). (gr. 7-18). 16.99 *(978-0-06-054149-1(0),* HarperTeen) HarperCollins Pubs.

O'Dell, Kathleen. Agnes Parker... Keeping Cool in Middle School. 2008. (ENG.). 160p. (J). (gr. 3-7). 6.99 *(978-0-14-241181-0(7),* Puffin Books) Penguin Young Readers Group.

Oliver, Sarah. Be the Best. 2008. (Illus.). 104p. pap. 25.50 *(978-0-9559820-0-2(6))* Oliver, Sarah GBR. Dist: Lulu Pr., Inc.

Osburn, Jacquelyn. Willy, the Worried Worm. 2008. 24p. pap. 12.99 *(978-1-4343-8183-5(8))* AuthorHouse.

Parr, Todd. Be Who You Are! 2016. (ENG., Illus.). 32p. (J). (gr. -1-1). 17.99 *(978-0-316-26523-2(3))* Little, Brown Bks. for Young Readers.

Paulsen, Gary. Molly Mcginty Has a Really Good Day. 2006. (Illus.). 105p. (J). (gr. 3-7). 13.15 *(978-0-7569-6621-8(3))* Perfection Learning Corp.

—Notes from the Dog. 2011. (ENG.). 144p. (YA). (gr. 7). pap. 6.99 *(978-0-375-85542-9(4),* Ember) Random Hse. Children's Bks.

Pearsall, Shelley. All of the Above. Steptoe, Javaka, illus. 2008. (ENG.). 256p. (J). (gr. 3-7). per. 8.00 *(978-0-316-11526-1(6))* Little, Brown Bks. for Young Readers.

Pennington, Beverly A. Jonathan's Discovery. Pennington, Beverly A., illus. 2006. (Illus.). 29p. (J). (gr. -1-3). pap. 12.95 (978-1-56167-920-1(8)) American Literary Pr.

Pequeña the Burro: Evaluation Guide. 2006. (J). (978-1-55942-420-2(6)) Witcher Productions.

Perl, Erica S. When Life Gives You O. J. (ENG.). 224p. (J). (gr. 3-7). 2013. 6.99 (978-0-375-85902-1(0), Yearling) 2011. 15.99 (978-0-375-85924-3(1), Knopf Bks. for Young Readers) Random Hse. Children's Bks.

Perry, Gina. Small. 2017. (ENG.). 40p. (J). (gr. -1-3). 17.99 **(978-1-4998-0401-0(6))** Little Bee Books Inc.

Perry, Laurie. Brown Bear, 1 vol. Mackay, Hugh, illus. 2010. 22p. pap. 24.95 (978-1-4489-5702-6(8)) PublishAmerica, Inc.

Peterson, Tina L. Oscar & the Amazing Gravity Repellent. Bonet, Xavier, illus. 2015. (Middle-Grade Novels Ser.). (ENG.). 224p. (gr. 4-7). lib. bdg. 26.65 (978-1-4965-0000-7(8)) Stone Arch Bks.

Phipps, Ben. I'm a Winner You're a Winner: Remembering How Great You Are. 2006. (J). per. 9.95 (978-0-9779374-0-0(2)) One Source Publishing, LLC.

Piper, Deb. From A— to Zulinski. 2008. (J). pap. (978-0-88092-713-0(5)); lib. bdg. (978-0-88092-712-3(7)) Royal Fireworks Publishing Co.

Pitchford, Dean. Captain Nobody. 2010. (ENG.). 208p. (J). (gr. 3-7). 6.99 (978-0-14-241667-9(3), Puffin Books) Penguin Young Readers Group.

Poulsen, David A. Numbers. 2nd ed. 2015. (ENG.). 200p. (YA). pap. 12.99 (978-1-4597-3248-3(0)) Dundurn CAN. Dist: Ingram Publisher Services.

—Numbers. 2008. (ENG.). 232p. (YA). (gr. 6-18). (978-1-55470-095-0(7)) Me to We.

Powers, David M. F. Ein Schmetterling Ohne Flügel. Vail, Sue, tr. Nesterova, Natalia, illus. 2013. 42p. pap. 9.99 (978-0-9860373-3-7(8)) Pants On Fire Pr.

Priebe, Val. Basketball Breakdown. 2016. (Jake Maddox JV Girls Ser.). (ENG.). 96p. (gr. 3-4). pap. 5.95 (978-1-4965-3676-1(2)) Stone Arch Bks.

Queen Latifah. Queen of the Scene. Morrison, Frank, illus. 2006. 32p. (J). (gr. -1-3). 17.89 incl. audio compact disk (978-0-06-077857-6(1), Geringer, Laura Book) HarperCollins Pubs.

Raskin, Joyce. My Misadventures As a Teenage Rock Star. Chu, Carol, illus. 2011. (ENG.). 112p. (YA). (gr. 7-18). pap. 8.99 (978-0-547-39311-7(3)) Houghton Mifflin Harcourt Publishing Co.

Reichman, Justin. The Green. 2005. (Dream Ser.: Vol. 9). 150p. (gr. 3-8). pap. 9.95 (978-0-9708992-9-3(7)) Scobre Pr. Corp.

Reinhardt, Jennifer Black. Blue Ethel. Reinhardt, Jennifer Black, illus. 2017. (ENG., Illus.). 40p. (J). 17.99 (978-0-374-30382-2(7), 9780374303822, Farrar, Straus & Giroux (BYR)) Farrar, Straus & Giroux.

Rennison, Louise. Withering Tights. (Misadventures of Tallulah Casey Ser.: 1). (ENG.). (YA). (gr. 8). 2012. 304p. pap. 8.99 (978-0-06-179933-4(5)) 2011. 288p. 16.99 (978-0-06-179931-0(9)) HarperCollins Pubs. (HarperTeen).

Resau, Laura. Red Glass. 2009. (ENG.). 304p. (YA). (gr. 7). pap. 8.99 (978-0-440-24025-9(5), Delacorte Bks. for Young Readers) Random Hse. Children's Bks.

Reynolds, Peter H. The Dot. Reynolds, Peter H., illus. 2003. (Creatrilogy Ser.). (ENG., Illus.). 32p. (J). (gr. k-12). 15.00 (978-0-7636-1961-9(2), 53509533) Candlewick Pr.

Reynolds, Peter H. & Reynolds, Peter. Ish. Reynolds, Peter H. & Reynolds, Peter, illus. 2004. (Creatrilogy Ser.). (ENG., Illus.). 32p. (J). (gr. k-12). 15.00 (978-0-7636-2344-9(X)) Candlewick Pr.

Rigby, Jill. I Put It Right There! I Swear! The story of one boy's master plan to overcome executive functioning Difficulties! 2011. 28p. pap. 12.77 (978-1-4634-3710-7(2)) AuthorHouse.

Riley, Zach. Surprise Kick. Ricci, Andrés, illus. 2012. (Zach Riley Ser.). 80p. (J). (gr. 3-6). lib. bdg. 27.07 (978-1-61783-536-0(6)) Magic Wagon.

Ripken, Cal. Wild Pitch. Cowherd, Kevin, illus. 2014. (Cal Ripken, Jr. 's All Stars Ser.). (ENG.). 224p. (J). (gr. 3-7). pap. 6.99 (978-1-4231-4005-4(2)) Hyperion Bks. for Children.

Ripken, Cal, et al. Cal Ripken, Jr. 's All-Stars the Closer. 2016. (Cal Ripken, Jr. 's All Stars Ser.). (ENG.). 208p. (J). (gr. 3-7). 16.99 (978-1-4231-7868-2(8)) Hyperion Bks. for Children.

Ripken Jr., Cal. Cal Ripken, Jr. 's All Stars the Closer. 2017. (Cal Ripken, Jr. 's All Stars Ser.). (ENG.). 208p. (J). (gr. 3-7). pap. 6.99 (978-1-4847-2788-1(6)) Hyperion Bks. for Children.

Robinson, Gary. Tribal Journey. 2013. (YA). 111p. (978-1-939053-87-9(0)); (ENG.). 120p. pap. 9.95 (978-1-939053-01-5(3), 7th Generation) Book Publishing Co.

Rodda, Emily. The Flower Fairies. Vitale, Raoul, illus. 2003. (Fairy Realm Ser.). 128p. (J). 8.99 (978-0-06-009586-4(5)) HarperCollins Pubs.

Root, Phyllis. Lilly & the Pirates. Shepperson, Rob, illus. 2010. (ENG.). 116p. (J). (gr. 4-6). 16.95 (978-1-59078-583-6(5), Front Street) Boyds Mills Pr.

Rosciti, Donna. The Birthday Train: Book 1. 2013. (ENG.). 48p. (J). 24.95 (978-1-4787-2236-6(3)) Outskirts Pr., Inc.

Rosenlund, Ranee. Benny the Frog's Leap of Faith. 2010. 16p. 8.49 (978-1-4490-5408-3(0)) AuthorHouse.

Roth, Sarra J. Not the Quitting Kind. Bishop, Tracy, illus. 2014. 32p. pap. 16.99 (978-1-4413-1415-4(6)) Peter Pauper Pr. Inc.

Ryder, Chloe. Princess Ponies 8: a Singing Star. 2015. (Princess Ponies Ser.). (ENG., Illus.). 128p. (J). (gr. 2-4). pap. 5.99 (978-1-61963-567-8(4), 9781619635678, Bloomsbury USA Childrens) Bloomsbury Publishing USA.

Saltzberg, Barney. Star of the Week. Saltzberg, Barney, illus. 2010. (ENG., Illus.). 32p. (J). (gr. k-3). pap. 6.99 (978-0-7636-3076-8(4)) Candlewick Pr.

Schafer, Milton. I'm Big! Lew-Vriethoff, Joanne, illus. 2006. (J). (978-1-4156-8150-3(3), Dial) Penguin Publishing Group.

Schraff, Anne. I Am Underdog. 2014. (Red Rhino Ser.). (J). lib. bdg. 18.40 (978-0-606-36198-9(7)) Turtleback Bks.

Schroeder, Lisa. Keys to the City. 2017. (ENG.). 240p. (J). (gr. 3-7). 16.99 **(978-0-545-90738-5(1)**, Scholastic Pr.) Scholastic, Inc.

Scieszka, Jon. The Great Truck Rescue. Shannon, David et al, illus. 2010. (Jon Scieszka's Trucktown Ser.). (ENG.). 40p. (J). (gr. -1-3). pap. 3.99 (978-1-4424-0932-3(0), Simon & Schuster Bks. For Young Readers) Simon & Schuster Bks. For Young Readers.

Sebra, Diane. Making Mountains Out of Moles. 2003. 120p. pap. 9.95 (978-1-55517-712-6(3), 77123) Cedar Fort, Inc./CFI Distribution.

Serluca-Foster, Rosemary. Genevieve's Gift: A Child's Joyful Tale of Connecting with Her Intuitive Heart. 2007. (ENG.). 32p. pap. 11.99 (978-1-4196-7321-4(1)) CreateSpace Independent Publishing Platform.

Sheldon, Dyan. Sophie Pitt-Turnbull Discovers America. 2007. (ENG.). 192p. (YA). (gr. 7-12). per. 7.99 (978-0-7636-3295-3(3)) Candlewick Pr.

Shevah, Emma. Dara Palmer's Major Drama. 2016. (ENG.). 288p. (J). (gr. 3-7). 16.99 (978-1-4926-3138-5(8), 9781492631385, Sourcebooks Jabberwocky) Sourcebooks, Inc.

Sileo, Frank J. Don't Put Yourself down in Circus Town: A Story about Self-Confidence. Cornelison, Sue, illus. 2014. (J). pap. (978-1-4338-1914-8(7), Magination Pr.) American Psychological Assn.

Skovron, Jon. Struts & Frets. (ENG.). 304p. (YA). 2011. (gr. 9-17). pap. 7.95 (978-1-4197-0028-6(6)) 2009. (gr. 7-11). 16.95 (978-0-8109-4174-8(0)) Abrams, Inc. (Amulet Bks.).

Small Acts of Amazing Courage. 2013. (ENG., Illus.). 240p. (J). (gr. 4-7). pap. 6.99 (978-1-4424-9495-4(6), Simon & Schuster/Paula Wiseman Bks.) Simon & Schuster/Paula Wiseman Bks.

Small, Lily. Bella the Bunny. 2015. (Fairy Animals of Misty Wood Ser.: 2). (ENG., Illus.). 144p. (J). (gr. k-3). pap. 5.99 (978-1-62779-142-7(6), 9781627791427, Holt, Henry & Co. Bks. For Young Readers) Holt, Henry & Co.

Small, Tanya. What You Say Is What You Are. 2007. pap. 7.50 (978-0-9705090-1-7(4)) MorningGlory Publishing.

Sorenson, Margo. Ambrose & the Cathedral Dream. Szegedi, Katalin, illus. 2006. (ENG.). 32p. (J). (gr. -1-3). 4.24 (978-0-8146-3004-4(9)) Liturgical Pr.

Standish, Burt L. Frank Merriwell's Confidence. Rudman, Jack, ed. 2003. (Frank Merriwell Ser.). 29.95 (978-0-8373-9349-0(3)); pap. 9.95 (978-0-8373-9049-9(4)) Merriwell, Frank Inc.

Steers, Billy. Tractor Mac New Friend. 2015. (Tractor Mac Ser.). (ENG., Illus.). 32p. (J). (gr. -1-k). 8.99 (978-0-374-30110-1(7), 9780374301101, Farrar, Straus & Giroux (BYR)) Farrar, Straus & Giroux.

Stein, David Ezra. Pouch! Stein, David Ezra, illus. 2010. (Rise & Shine Ser.). (ENG., Illus.). 32p. (C). (gr. -1-k). 25.95 (978-0-399-25051-4(4)) National Geographic School Publishing, Inc.

—Pouch! Stein, David Ezra, illus. 2012. (ENG., Illus.). 32p. (J). (gr. -1 — 1). bds. 7.99 (978-0-399-25738-4(1), Nancy Paulsen Books) Penguin Young Readers Group.

Stevens, Elizabeth. Mister D. Frongia, Daniela, illus. 2012. 24p. (J). 16.95 (978-1-60131-114-6(1)) Big Tent Bks.

Stone, Phoebe. Paris for Two. 2016. (ENG.). 272p. (J). (gr. 3-7). 16.99 (978-0-545-44362-3(8), Levine, Arthur A. Bks.) Scholastic, Inc.

Strasser, Todd. Con-Fidence. 2006. (ENG.). 164p. (J). (gr. 4-7). pap. 6.95 (978-0-8234-2061-2(2)) Holiday Hse., Inc.

Struyk-Bonn, Chris. Nice Girls Endure. 2016. (ENG.). 256p. (gr. 9-12). 16.95 (978-1-63079-047-9(8)) Switch Pr.

Supplee, Suzanne. Somebody Everybody Listens To. 2011. (ENG.). 288p. (YA). (gr. 7-18). 8.99 (978-0-14-241886-4(2), Speak) Penguin Young Readers Group.

Susanne, Gervay & Gervay, Susanne. Being Jack. Wilcox, Cathy, illus. 2016. (ENG.). 192p. (J). pap. 5.99 (978-1-61067-379-2(4)) Kane Miller.

Swift, Amanda. Big Bones. 2005. (ENG.). 144p. (J). (gr. 4-7). per. 9.95 (978-0-689-87547-2(9)) Simon & Schuster, Ltd. GBR. Dist: Simon & Schuster, Inc.

Tashjian, Janet. Sticker Girl. Wilmink, Inga, illus. 2016. (Sticker Girl Ser.). (ENG.). 176p. (J). 13.99 (978-1-62779-335-3(6), 9781627793353, Holt, Henry & Co. Bks. For Young Readers) Holt, Henry & Co.

Taylor-Butler, Christine. I Am Smart. Borlasca, Hector, illus. (My First Reader Ser.). (ENG.). 32p. (J). (gr. k-1). 2006. per. 3.95 (978-0-516-24971-1(1)) 2005. lib. bdg. 18.50 (978-0-516-25176-9(7)) Scholastic Library Publishing. (Children's Pr.).

Taylor, Helen. Emu Can't Fly. Gilles-Gray, Carolyn, illus. 2013. 24p. pap. (978-1-921883-39-2(1), MBS Pr.) Pick-a-Woo Woo Pubs.

Terrell, Brandon. Double Scribble. 2017. (Jake Maddox Graphic Novels Ser.). (ENG., Illus.). 72p. (gr. 2-5). lib. bdg. 26.65 (978-1-4965-3701-0(7)) Stone Arch Bks.

—Fearless, 1 vol. Cano, Fernando, illus. 2014. (Tony Hawk: Live2Skate Ser.). (ENG.). 72p. (gr. 4-5). 25.32 (978-1-4342-9141-7(3), Tony Hawk's 900 Revolution) Stone Arch Bks.

—8-Bit Baseball, 1 vol. Ferrara, Eduardo, illus. 2014. (Sports Illustrated Kids Graphic Novels Ser.). (ENG.). 72p. (gr. 2-5). 26.65 (978-1-4342-4164-1(5)) Stone Arch Bks.

Terrell, Brandon & Fuentes, Benny. Quarterback Scramble, 1 vol. Sandoval, Gerardo, illus. 2011. (Sports Illustrated Kids Graphic Novels Ser.). (ENG.). 56p. (gr. 2-3). pap. 7.19 (978-1-4342-3070-6(8)); lib. bdg. 26.65 (978-1-4342-2220-6(9)) Stone Arch Bks.

Thompson, Carol. Run! Thompson, Carol, illus. 2013. (Little Movers Ser.). (ENG., Illus.). 12p. (J). bds. (978-1-84643-616-1(8)) Child's Play International Ltd.

Thompson, Colin & Lissiat, Amy. Norman & Brenda. 2009. (ENG., Illus.). 32p. (J). 6.99 (978-1-933605-86-9(3)) Kane Miller.

Thompson, Lauren. Wee Little Chick. Butler, John, illus. 2008. (Wee Little Ser.). (ENG.). 32p. (J). (gr. -1-1). 15.99 (978-1-4169-3468-4(5), Simon & Schuster Bks. For Young Readers) Simon & Schuster Bks. For Young Readers.

Tracy, Roseann. Do You Love Me When I Am Upside Down? 2008. 28p. pap. 12.99 (978-1-4389-0503-7(3)) AuthorHouse.

Vail, Rachel. Piggy Bunny. Tankard, Jeremy, illus. 2012. (ENG.). 32p. (J). (gr. -1-1). 14.99 (978-0-312-64988-3(6), 9780312649883) Feiwel & Friends.

van Genechten, Guido. Kangaroo Christine. van Genechten, Guido, illus. 2005. (Illus.). 24p. (J). (gr. 3-7). pap. 6.95 (978-1-58925-396-4(5)) Tiger Tales.

VanDenberg, Saidat. Tadias & the Pitbully Tree. 2012. 36p. pap. 21.99 (978-1-4797-0172-8(6)) Xlibris Corp.

Vega, Denise. Rock On: A Story of Guitars, Gigs, Girls, & a Brother (Not Necessarily in That Order) 2012. (ENG., Illus.). 304p. (YA). (gr. 7-17). 17.99 (978-0-316-13310-4(8)) Little, Brown Bks. for Young Readers.

—Rock On: A Story of Guitars, Gigs, Girls, & a Brother (not Necessarily in That Order) 2013. (ENG., Illus.). 304p. (YA). (gr. 7-17). pap. 8.99 (978-0-316-13309-8(4)) Little, Brown Bks. for Young Readers.

Ventura, Marne. Edgy Estella Aces the Sleepover Party. Trinidad, Leo, illus. 2016. (Worry Warriors Ser.). (ENG.). 96p. (gr. 2-4). lib. bdg. 25.99 (978-1-4965-3610-5(X)) Stone Arch Bks.

Vision, David & Vision, Mutiya Sahar. If Only I Could! Alcantara, Ignacio, illus. 2009. 32p. 17.00 (978-0-9659538-8-7(2)) Von Curtis Publishing.

Vivian, Siobhan. Same Difference. 2014. (ENG.). 304p. (J). pap. 9.99 (978-0-545-75802-4(5)) Scholastic, Inc.

Vizzini, Med. Be More Chill. 2011. 9.68 (978-0-7848-3414-5(8), Everbind) Marco Bk. Co.

Vizzini, Ned. Be More Chill. 2005. (ENG.). 304p. (J). (gr. 5-9). per. 8.99 (978-0-7868-0996-7(5)) Disney Publishing Worldwide.

Wade, Rebecca. The Theft & the Miracle. 2007. 351p. (J). (gr. 4-7). lib. bdg. 17.89 (978-0-06-077495-0(9)) HarperCollins Pubs.

Walker, Melissa. Small Town Sinners. (ENG.). (YA). (gr. 9-12). 2013. 304p. pap. 9.99 (978-1-59990-982-0(0), 9781599909820) 2011. 288p. 16.99 (978-1-59990-527-3(2), 9781599905273) Bloomsbury Publishing USA. (Bloomsbury USA Childrens).

Wallace, Rich. Between the Sticks, 1 vol. Heitz, Tim, illus. 2016. (Game Face Ser.). (ENG.). 112p. (J). (gr. 3-7). 27.07 (978-1-62402-132-9(8)) Magic Wagon.

—Dunk under Pressure, Vol. 7. 7th ed. 2007. (Winning Season Ser.). (ENG.). 120p. (J). (gr. 3-7). 5.99 (978-0-14-240858-2(1), Puffin Books) Penguin Young Readers Group.

—Pressure Point, 1 vol. Heitz, Tim, illus. 2016. (Game Face Ser.). (ENG.). 112p. (J). (gr. 3-7). 27.07 (978-1-62402-135-0(2)) Magic Wagon.

—The Roar of the Crowd. 2005. (Winning Season Ser.). (ENG.). 128p. (J). (gr. 3-7). pap. 5.99 (978-0-14-240443-0(8), Puffin Books) Penguin Young Readers Group.

—Roar of the Crowd. 2004. 101p. (J). lib. bdg. 15.38 (978-1-4242-2165-3(X)) Fitzgerald Bks.

—Second-String Center. 2008. (Winning Season Ser.: 10). (ENG.). 128p. (J). (gr. 3-7). 5.99 (978-0-14-241216-9(3), Puffin Books) Penguin Young Readers Group.

Warren, Dotti M. Dreama Lynn & the Magic Tu Tu. 2008. 16p. pap. 9.49 (978-1-4389-2983-5(8)) AuthorHouse.

Weinberger, Justin. Reformed. 2017. (ENG.). 208p. (J). (gr. 3-7). 16.99 (978-0-545-90252-6(5), Scholastic Pr.) Scholastic, Inc.

Weston, Carol. Ava XOX. 2016. (Ava & Pip Ser.: 3). (ENG.). 208p. (J). (gr. 5-8). 15.99 (978-1-4926-2077-8(7), 9781492620778, Sourcebooks Jabberwocky) Sourcebooks, Inc.

Weston Woods Staff, creator. Casi. 2011. (SPA.). 29.95 (978-0-439-90592-3(3)) Weston Woods Studios, Inc.

Whelan, Gloria. Small Acts of Amazing Courage. 2011. (ENG.). 224p. (J). (gr. 4-7). 15.99 (978-1-4424-0931-6(2), Simon & Schuster/Paula Wiseman Bks.) Simon & Schuster/Paula Wiseman Bks.

Whelen-Banks, Jane. Liam Goes Poo in the Toilet: A Story about Trouble with Toilet Training. 2008. (ENG., Illus.). 32p. 12.95 (978-1-84310-900-6(X), 5371) Kingsley, Jessica Pubs. GBR. Dist: Macmillan Distribution Ltd.

—Liam Says "Hi" Learning to Greet a Friend. 2008. (ENG., Illus.). 32p. 12.95 (978-1-84310-901-3(8), 5372) Kingsley, Jessica Pubs. GBR. Dist: Macmillan Distribution Ltd.

Wigington, Patti. Summer's Ashes. 2007. (ENG.). 208p. (gr. 8-12). per. 15.00 (978-0-9766805-9-8(9)) Keene Publishing.

Wilkerson, L. Kobie, 3rd, reader. Fred & Mary. 2008. (Illus.). 32p. (J). 24.95 incl. DVD, audio compact disk (978-0-9796679-0-9(9)) Love II Learn Bks.

Williams, Laura E. Slant. 2008. (ENG.). 160p. (J). (gr. 2-8). pap. 6.95 (978-1-57131-682-0(5)) Milkweed Editions.

Willow, Bim. I-Can't & I-Can! Morales, Jose, illus. 2012. 28p. pap. 8.99 (978-0-9853574-3-6(6)) Mountan Creek Pubns.

Wong, Janet S. & Wong, Janet G. Minn & Jake. Cote, Genevieve, illus. 2008. (ENG.). 160p. (J). (gr. 2-5). pap. 9.99 (978-0-374-40021-7(0), 9780374400217, Farrar, Straus & Giroux (BYR)) Farrar, Straus & Giroux.

Wood, David & Wood, Aimee. The Beautiful Swan. 2008. 24p. pap. 14.95 (978-1-59858-624-4(6)) Dog Ear Publishing, LLC.

Woods, Brenda. Zoe in Wonderland. 2017. (ENG.). 224p. (J). (gr. 3-7). 8.99 **(978-0-425-28891-7(9)**, Puffin Books) Penguin Young Readers Group.

Woods, Brenda & Airgood, Ellen. Zoe in Wonderland. 2016. (ENG.). 208p. (J). (gr. 3-7). 16.99 (978-0-399-17097-3(9), Nancy Paulsen Books) Penguin Young Readers Group.

Wright, Johanna. Bunnies on Ice. Wright, Johanna, illus. 2013. (ENG., Illus.). 32p. (J). (gr. -1-1). 16.99 (978-1-59643-404-2(X), 9781596434042) Roaring Brook Pr.

Wright-McAdoo, Joyce & Wright-Mcadoo, Joyce. Zimb: Believe. 2009. (Illus.). 28p. pap. 15.99 (978-1-4415-8051-1(4)) Xlibris Corp.

Wrong Way, Mallory! 2015. (Mallory Ser.: 23). (ENG., Illus.). 160p. (J). (gr. 2-5). 15.95 (978-1-4677-0923-1(9)) Lerner Publishing Group.

Wyley, Enda. Boo & Bear. Massardier, Greg, tr. Massardier, Greg, illus. 2003. (Panda Cubs Ser.: 01). (ENG.). 48p. (J). pap. 9.95 (978-0-86278-806-3(4)) O'Brien Pr., Ltd., The IRL. Dist: Dufour Editions, Inc.

Yaccarino, Dan. Morris Mole. Yaccarino, Dan, illus. 2017. (Illus.). 40p. (J). (gr. -1-3). 17.99 (978-0-06-241107-5(1)) HarperCollins Pubs.

You Can Be Anything! 2006. (Illus.). 32p. (J). 14.95 (978-0-9786813-1-9(2)) Elora Pr.

Zobel-Nolan, Allia. What I Like about Me! Sakamoto, Miki, illus. 2009. (What I Like about Me Ser.). (ENG.). 14p. (J). (gr. -1-2). 6.99 (978-0-7944-1945-5(3), Reader's Digest Children's Bks.) Studio Fun International.

Zuppardi, Sam. Jack's Worry. Zuppardi, Sam, illus. 2016. (ENG., Illus.). 32p. (J). (gr. -1-3). 16.99 (978-0-7636-7845-6(7)) Candlewick Pr.

SELF-CONTROL

Antill, Sara. Self-Control. 2013. (Character Strength Ser.). 24p. (J). (gr. 3-6). pap. 49.50 (978-1-4488-9817-6(X)); pap. 8.25 (978-1-4488-9816-9(1)); lib. bdg. 22.60 (978-1-4488-9679-0(7)) Rosen Publishing Group, Inc., The. (PowerKids Pr.).

Baruch-Feldman, Caren. The Grit Guide for Teens: A Workbook to Help You Build Perseverance, Self-Control, & a Growth Mindset. 2017. (ENG.). 152p. (YA). (gr. 6-12). pap. 16.95 (978-1-62625-856-3(2)) New Harbinger Pubns.

Brukner, Lauren. How to Be a Superhero Called Self-Control! Super Powers to Help Younger Children to Regulate Their Emotions & Senses. Phillips-Smith, Anthony & Apsley House, London Staff, illus. 2015. (ENG.). 112p. 19.95 (978-1-84905-717-2(6), 8140) Kingsley, Jessica Pubs. GBR. Dist: Macmillan Distribution Ltd.

Doron. Look in the Mirror... 2005. 228p. pap. 15.00 (978-1-4116-0109-3(2)) Lulu Pr., Inc.

—Look in the Mirror. 2nd ed. 2005. 335p. pap. 16.56 (978-1-4116-0197-0(1)) Lulu Pr., Inc.

Doudna, Kelly. Keep Your Cool!, 1 vol. 2007. (Character Concepts Ser.). (ENG., Illus.). 24p. (J). (gr. k-3). lib. bdg. 24.21 (978-1-59928-736-2(6), SandCastle) ABDO Publishing Co.

Esherick, Joan. Physical Challenges. Albers, Lisa et al, eds. 2014. (Living with a Special Need Ser.: 16). 128p. (J). (gr. 7-18). 25.95 (978-1-4222-3041-1(4)) Mason Crest.

Hansen, Sharon A. The Executive Functioning Workbook for Teens: Help for Unprepared, Late, & Scattered Teens. 2013. (ENG.). 144p. (YA). (gr. 6-12). pap. 17.95 (978-1-60882-656-8(2)) New Harbinger Pubns.

James, Sara. Self-Discipline. 2013. (Junior Martial Arts Ser.: 9). 32p. (J). (gr. 4-18). 19.95 (978-1-4222-2739-8(1)) Mason Crest.

Lisbona, Margie Taylor. Rock & Rhino Learn Responsibility. Roberts, J. P., illus. 2011. 48p. pap. (978-1-77067-530-8(2)) FriesenPress.

Manolis, Kay & Todd, Anne. George Washington: A Life of Self-Discipline. 2007. (People of Character Ser.). (ENG., Illus.). 24p. (J). (gr. 2-5). lib. bdg. 25.95 (978-1-60014-094-5(7)) Bellwether Media.

Phelan,, Thomas W. & Lee, Tracy M. 1-2-3 Magic for Kids: Helping Your Kids Understand the New Rules. 2nd ed. 2017. (ENG., Illus.). 128p. pap. 9.99 (978-1-4926-4786-7(1), 9781492647867) Sourcebooks, Inc.

Pryor, Kimberley Jane. Self-Discipline. 2010. (Values 2 Ser.). 32p. (gr. 1). 18.56 (978-1-60870-147-6(6)) Marshall Cavendish GBR. Dist: Marshall Cavendish Corp.

Purcell, Sherry L. Using Assistive Technology. 2004. 325p. (gr. 4-6). spiral bd. 29.00 incl. audio compact disk (978-1-57861-493-6(7), IEP Resources) Attainment Co., Inc.

Regan, Lisa. Don't Get Angry, Annie: Stay Calm. 2017. (You Choose Ser.). 32p. (J). (gr. 2-2). lib. bdg. 25.27 **(978-0-7660-8700-2(X))** Enslow Pubs., Inc.

Siddoway, Ramona. Self-Control. 2013. (7 Character Strengths of Highly Successful Students Ser.). 64p. (J). (gr. 5-8). pap. 77.70 (978-1-4488-9564-9(2)); (ENG., Illus.). pap. 12.95 (978-1-4488-9563-2(4), Rosen Classroom); (ENG., Illus.). lib. bdg. 31.95 (978-1-4488-9543-4(X), Rosen Classroom) Rosen Publishing Group, Inc., The.

SELF-CULTURE

see also Books and Reading

Asugha, Ruby. Little Sisters, Listen Up! A Message of Hope for Girls Growing up in Poverty Racism, & Despair. 2004. 138p. 9.95 (978-1-889322-61-2(X), 25-017) Boys Town Pr.

Bishop, John. Goal Setting for Students: Winner of three national parenting book Awards. 2003. (Illus.). (YA). pap. 11.95 (978-0-9743700-0-2(2)) Accent On Success.

Bright Ideas: Level O, 6 vols. (Explorers Ser.). 32p. (gr. 3-6). 44.95 (978-0-7699-0598-3(6)) Shortland Pubns. (U. S. A.) Inc.

Cox, Scott, Sr. Love Your Ego As Your SELF. 2004. (J). per. 12.95 (978-0-9753817-1-7(7)) Unlimited Horizons.

Douglas, Marianne. How to Deal When Your Middle Name Is Stress: Real Teens - Real Advice. 2004. (J). per. 4.95 (978-1-59196-643-2(4)) Instant Pub.

Renaud, Andrea. The Goal Keeper Journal. 2003. (Illus.). 160p. (YA). per. (978-0-9717041-1-4(2)) A Happy Friend, Inc.

Stone, Penny. Complicated Mourning & Grief Blocks: How to Move Forward Past Our Pain. 2004. (New Line of Grief Guides). 64p. pap. 15.00 (978-1-891400-10-0(X)) Sourcebooks, Inc.

—My World Is Upside Down: Making Sense of Life after Confronting Death. 2004. (New Line of Grief Guides). 9.95 (978-1-891400-24-7(X)) Sourcebooks, Inc.

—Surviving the Loss of a Parent. 2005. (New Line of Grief Guides). 9.95 (978-1-891400-57-5(6)) Sourcebooks, Inc.

—Taste of Cultures: Italy. 2004. (New Line of Grief Guides). 9.95 (978-1-891400-76-6(2)) Sourcebooks, Inc.

Thayer, William Makepeace. The Bobbin Boy: Or, How Nat Got His Learning. 2007. (ENG.). 210p. pap. 20.99 (978-1-4346-3420-7(5)); 228p. pap. 22.99 (978-1-4346-3421-4(3)) Creative Media Partners, LLC.

Wolff, Ariana. Khan Academy & Salman Khan, 1 vol. 2015. (ENG.). 128p. (YA). 35.60 (978-1-4777-7927-9(2), Rosen Young Adult) Rosen Publishing Group, Inc., The.

SELF-DEFENSE

see also Boxing; Judo; Karate

Berry, Joy. Help Me Be Good Fighting. Bartholomew, illus. 2010. (Help Me Be Good Ser.). (ENG.). 32p. (J). (gr. -1-2). pap. 4.99 (978-1-60577-135-9(X)) Berry, Joy Enterprises.

Chaline, Eric. Martial Arts for Women: Winning Ways. James, Adam, ed. 2015. (Mastering Martial Arts Ser.). (Illus.). 96p. (J). (gr. 5). lib. bdg. 24.95 (978-1-4222-3243-9(3)) Mason Crest.

Feigh, Alison. I Can Play It Safe. Logan, Laura, illus. 2008. (ENG.). 32p. (J). (gr. -1-3). 14.99 (978-1-57542-285-5(9)) Free Spirit Publishing, Inc.

Holt, Rinehart and Winston Staff. Holt Science & Technology Chapter 27: Life Science: Body Defenses. 5th ed. 2004. (Illus.). pap. 12.86 (978-0-03-030256-5(0)) Holt McDougal.

James, Sara. Self-Defense. 2013. (Junior Martial Arts Ser.: 9). 32p. (J). (gr. 4-18). 19.95 *(978-1-4222-2738-1(3))* Mason Crest.

McNab, Chris. Martial Arts for People with Disabilities. 2004. (Martial & Fighting Arts Ser.). (Illus.). 96p. (YA). (gr. 7). lib. bdg. 22.95 *(978-1-59084-399-4(1))* Mason Crest.

Mitchell, Susan K. Animal Chemical Combat: Poisons, Smells, & Slime. 2008. (Amazing Animal Defenses Ser.). (Illus.). 48p. (J). (gr. 5-9). lib. bdg. 25.27 *(978-0-7660-3294-1(9))* Enslow Pubs., Inc.

Ollhoff, Jim. Grappling, 1 vol. 2008. (World of Martial Arts Ser.). (ENG., Illus.). 32p. (gr. 4-8). 27.07 *(978-1-59928-976-2(8),* Abdo & Daughters) ABDO Publishing Co.

Richardson, Kimberly Stanton. Gus Learns to Fly: Self-Defense Is Self-Discovery. Crowley, Adam A., photos by. 2012. (ENG., Illus.). 44p. (J). (gr. k). pap. 18.00 *(978-0-939165-64-3(3))* NewSage Pr., LLC.

Safe Kids USA Staff. Self-Defense for Kids: Learn Practical & Effective Techniques to Help You Defend Yourself. 2004. (Illus.). 47p. (J). (gr. -1-12). pap. 6.95 *(978-0-9718609-5-7(5))* High Mountain Publishing.

Thompson, Tamara. Self-Defense Laws. Greenhaven Press Editors & Gale, A. G., eds. 2014. (At Issue Ser.). (ENG.). 128p. (gr. 10-12). pap. 27.80 *(978-0-7377-6855-8(X),* Greenhaven Pr., Inc.) Cengage Gale.

—Self-Defense Laws. Greenhaven Press Editors, ed. 2014. (At Issue Ser.). (ENG.). 128p. (gr. 10-12). lib. bdg. 39.40 *(978-0-7377-6854-1(1),* Greenhaven Pr., Inc.) Cengage Gale.

Williamson, Wendy. Christian Martial Arts 101. 2004. (ENG.). 256p. per. 29.95 *(978-0-9721328-1-7(3))* Agapy LLC.

—Christian Martial Arts 101 (Instructor's Edition) 2004. (ENG.). 288p. per. 18.95 *(978-0-9721328-2-4(1))* Agapy LLC.

Wood, Alix. Aikido. 2013. (Kid's Guide to Martial Arts Ser.). (ENG., Illus.). 32p. (J). (gr. 3-6). pap. 11.75 *(978-1-4777-0352-6(7));* lib. bdg. 26.50 *(978-1-4777-0315-1(2))* Rosen Publishing Group, Inc., The. (PowerKids Pr.).

SELF-ESTEEM

Apel, Melanie Ann. Let's Talk about When You Think Nobody Likes You. 2009. (Let's Talk Library). 24p. (gr. 2-3). 42.50 *(978-1-60853-449-4(9),* PowerKids Pr.) Rosen Publishing Group, Inc., The.

Asgedom, Mawi. The Code: The 5 Secrets of Teen Success. 2003. (ENG., Illus.). 160p. (YA). (gr. 7-17). pap. 10.00 *(978-0-316-73689-3(9))* Little, Brown Bks. for Young Readers.

Becnel, Barbara, ed. Gangs & Self-Esteem: Stanley Tookie Williams Street Peace Series, 8 bks., Vol. 1, Bk. 4. 2008. 24p. (J). 6.95 *(978-0-9753584-1-2(3))* Damamli Publishing Co.

Bell, Latarcia. The Looking Glass. 2011. 28p. pap. 24.95 *(978-1-4626-3234-3(3))* America Star Bks.

Bender, Alexandra Sabina. Alana's Advice... When There's a Clique, You've Got to Think Quick. 2007. (Illus.). 152p. (J). (gr. 4-10). per. 14.95 *(978-1-84590-075-5(8))* Crown Hse. Publishing.

Bolden, Tanisha N. This Is Why I Rock: A Self-Empowerment Journal for Youth. 2011. 112p. pap. 11.95 *(978-0-9831743-2-5(6))* Second Time Media & Communications.

Bowen, Shane. Out of the Darkness. 2010. 220p. pap. 21.95 *(978-0-557-26249-6(6))* Lulu Pr., Inc.

Box, Su. You Are Very Special: With a Special Surprise for You Inside! Poole, Susie, illus. 2011. (ENG.). 12p. (J). (gr. -1-k). bds. 7.99 *(978-0-7459-6300-6(5))* Lion Hudson PLC GBR. Dist: Independent Pubs. Group.

Boyd, Beverly L. I Am a Blessing in Disguise Journal for Children. 2012. (Illus.). 65p. (J). per. 14.95 *(978-0-9742367-8-0(0))* ABR Pubns.

Bozzi, Riccardo. The World Belongs to You. Zagnoli, Olimpia, illus. 2013. (ENG.). 40p. (J). (gr. 3-7). 14.99 *(978-0-7636-6488-6(X),* Templar) Candlewick Pr.

Cain, Susan, et al. Quiet Power: The Secret Strengths of Introverts. Snider, Grant, illus. (ENG.). 288p. (J). (gr. 5). 2017. 9.99 *(978-0-14-750992-5(0),* Puffin Books) 2016. 17.99 *(978-0-8037-4060-0(3),* Dial Bks) 2016. lib. bdg. 20.99 *(978-0-399-18672-1(7),* Dial Bks) Penguin Young Readers Group.

Calhoun, Dorothy Sweet. Six Bees for Children: A Collection of Educational Wisdoms for Children. 2012. (ENG.). 30p. (J). pap. 14.95 *(978-1-4327-8870-4(1))* Outskirts Pr., Inc.

Cassius, Sonya. My Beautiful World. 2009. (Illus.). 32p. pap. 12.99 *(978-1-4343-0061-4(7))* AuthorHouse.

Cavell-Clarke, Steffi. Respecting Others. 2017. (Illus.). 24p. (J). ***(978-0-7787-3263-1(0))*** Crabtree Publishing Co.

Chargualaf, Cathy. Animal Storybook No. 1: Building Self-Esteem Through Animal Stories. 2013. 32p. pap. 13.99 *(978-1-4525-7575-9(4),* Balboa Pr.) Author Solutions, Inc.

—Animal Storybook No. 2: Building Self-Esteem Through Animal Stories. 2013. 32p. pap. 13.99 *(978-1-4525-7583-4(5),* Balboa Pr.) Author Solutions, Inc.

Child, Maria. Girls Own Book 1834. 2006. 292p. per. *(978-1-4067-9133-4(4),* Pomona Pr.) Read Bks.

Chinn, Jacqueline. How Can I Be Special? Mondragon, Manny, illus. 2003. (J). pap. 15.95 *(978-0-929526-55-3(4))* Double B Pubns.

Collins-Donnelly, Kate. Banish Your Self-Esteem Thief: A Cognitive Behavioural Therapy Workbook on Building Positive Self-Esteem for Young People. 2014. (Gremlin & Thief CBT Workbooks Ser.). (ENG., Illus.). 240p. (C). pap. 24.95 *(978-1-84905-462-1(2),* 2412) Kingsley, Jessica Pubs. GBR. Dist: Macmillan Distribution Ltd.

Costanzo, Charlene A. & Costanzo, Charlene. The Twelve Gifts of Birth. Ackison, Wendy Wassink, illus. Reger, Jill, photos by. 2011. (Twelve Gifts Ser.: 1). (ENG.). 64p. 22.99 *(978-0-06-621104-6(2),* Morrow, William & Co.) HarperCollins Pubs.

Devon, Natasha, et al. The Self-Esteem Team's Guide to Sex, Drugs & WTFs?!! 2016. (ENG., Illus.). 288p. (YA). (gr. 7). pap. 15.95 *(978-1-78418-642-5(2))* Blake, John Publishing, Ltd. GBR. Dist: Independent Pubs. Group.

Domoney, Cathy. Madeleine, Maddy & Midge: Positive Thinking for Children. 2012. 36p. pap. 15.95 *(978-1-4525-0761-3(9))* Balboa Pr.

Doron. Look in the Mirror... 2005. 228p. pap. 15.00 *(978-1-4116-0109-3(2))* Lulu Pr., Inc.

—Look in the Mirror. 2nd ed. 2005. 335p. pap. 16.56 *(978-1-4116-0197-0(1))* Lulu Pr., Inc.

Dunn, Michael P. What's the Big Secret? 2003. (Illus.). 192p. per. 13.95 *(978-0-9724924-3-0(7))* Big Secret, The.

Dyer, Wayne & Tracy, Kristina. No Excuses! How What You Say Can Get in Your Way. Budnick, Stacy Heller, illus. 2009. (ENG.). 32p. 15.99 *(978-1-4019-2583-3(9),* 1060) Hay Hse., Inc.

Elisha, . & Elyssa. I Love Me: Self-Esteem in Seven Easy Steps. 2014. (ENG., Illus.). 72p. pap. 9.95 *(978-1-63047-140-8(2))* Morgan James Publishing.

Espeland, Pamela & Verdick, Elizabeth. Proud to Be You: The Positive Identity Assets. 2006. (Adding Assets Series for Kids Ser.). (ENG., Illus.). 80p. (J). (gr. 3-7). pap. 7.99 *(978-1-57542-202-2(6))* Free Spirit Publishing, Inc.

Falconer, Ian & Jordom, Deloris M. Dream Big: Starring Olivia. 2006. (ENG., Illus.). 64p. 9.99 *(978-0-7407-5818-8(7))* Andrews McMeel Publishing.

Ferguson, Addy. Group Bullying: Exclusion & Ganging Up. 2013. (Stand up: Bullying Prevention Ser.). (ENG., Illus.). 24p. (J). (gr. 3-6). pap. 8.25 *(978-1-4488-9796-4(3));* lib. bdg. 22.60 *(978-1-4488-9669-1(X))* Rosen Publishing Group, Inc., The. (PowerKids Pr.).

—What to Do When You Are Bullied for Being Different. 2014. (Stand up: Bullying Prevention Ser.). 24p. (J). (gr. k-3). lib. bdg. 23.60 *(978-1-4777-6892-1(0),* PowerKids Pr.) Rosen Publishing Group, Inc., The.

Fixman, Jennifer. Make a Difference with Miss Jenny. 2009. 64p. 19.99 *(978-1-930979-14-7(2))* Edutunes.

Forche, Carolyn A. Colors Come from God ... Just Like Me! 2015. 32p. pap. 9.99 *(978-1-5018-0838-8(9))* Abingdon Pr.

Foudy, Julie. Choose to Matter. 2017. (ENG.). 304p. (YA). (gr. 7-12). 17.99 *(978-1-368-00338-4(9))* Disney Pr.

Girard, Vanessa, DM. Diversity Is U & Me (high school survival Guide) 2010. 92p. pap. 10.99 *(978-0-557-54094-5(1))* Lulu Pr., Inc.

Harper, Hill. Letters to a Young Sister: DeFINE Your Destiny. 2009. (ENG.). 304p. (gr. 12-18). 17.00 *(978-1-59240-459-9(6),* Avery) Penguin Publishing Group.

How to Be a S. T. A. R. The Young Person's Guide to Finding Success & Living Your Dreams. 2nd ed. 2003. (J). *(978-0-9728626-0-8(9))* Gems International, LLC.

James, Sara. Self-Esteem. 2013. (Junior Martial Arts Ser.: 9). 32p. (J). (gr. 4-18). 19.95 *(978-1-4222-2740-4(5))* Mason Crest.

Kalman, Izzy C. Bullies to Buddies - How to Turn Your Enemies into Friends! How to Turn Your Enemies into Friends! Kalman, Lola, illus. 2005. (ENG.). 128p. (YA). per. 15.00 *(978-0-9706482-1-1(9))* The Wisdom Pages, Inc.

Kaufman, Gershen, et al. Defiendete! Desarrolla Tu Poder Personal y Autoestima. 2005. (SPA & ENG., Illus.). 112p. (J). (gr. 4-7). per. 11.95 *(978-968-860-226-3(4))* Editorial Pax MEX. Dist: Independent Pubs. Group.

Keep Empowering Yourself Successfully: Raising Your Self Esteem. 2004. (YA). *(978-0-9762009-1-8(0))* Keep Empowering Yourself Successfully.

Kent, Susan. Learning How to Feel Good about Yourself. 2009. (Violence Prevention Library). 24p. (gr. 2-3). 42.50 *(978-1-60854-265-9(3),* PowerKids Pr.) Rosen Publishing Group, Inc., The.

Kunjufu, Jawanza & Prescott, Folami. Kindergarten: Self-Esteem Through Culture Leads to Academic Excellence. 2003. (ENG.). 60p. (J). (gr. k). pap. 9.95 *(978-0-913543-85-6(3))* African American Images.

—Self-Esteem Through Culture Leads to Academic Excellence. 2003. (ENG.). 60p. (J). (gr. 8). pap. 9.95 *(978-0-913543-93-1(4));* (gr. 9-12). pap. 14.95 *(978-0-913543-94-8(2))* African American Images.

—SETCLAE, Fifth Grade: Self-Esteem Through Culture Leads to Academic Excellence. 2003. (ENG.). 60p. (J). (gr. 5). pap. 9.95 *(978-0-913543-90-0(X))* African American Images.

—SETCLAE, First Grade: Self-Esteem Through Culture Leads to Academic Excellence. 2003. (ENG.). 60p. (J). (gr. 1). pap. 9.95 *(978-0-913543-86-3(1))* African American Images.

—SETCLAE, Fourth Grade: Self-Esteem Through Culture Leads to Academic Excellence. 2003. (ENG.). 60p. (J). (gr. 4). pap. 9.95 *(978-0-913543-89-4(6))* African American Images.

—SETCLAE, Second Grade: Self-Esteem Through Culture Leads to Academic Excellence. 2003. (ENG.). 60p. (J). (gr. 2). pap. 9.95 *(978-0-913543-87-0(X))* African American Images.

—SETCLAE, Seventh Grade: Self-Esteem Through Culture Leads to Academic Excellence. 2003. (ENG.). 60p. (J). (gr. 7). pap. 9.95 *(978-0-913543-92-4(6))* African American Images.

—SETCLAE, Sixth Grade: Self-Esteem Through Culture Leads to Academic Excellence. 2003. (ENG.). 60p. (J). (gr. 6). pap. 9.95 *(978-0-913543-91-7(8))* African American Images.

—SETCLAE, Third Grade: Self-Esteem Through Culture Leads to Academic Excellence. 2003. (ENG.). 60p. (J). (gr. 3). pap. 9.95 *(978-0-913543-88-7(8))* African American Images.

Landau, Jennifer. Teens Talk about Self-Esteem & Self-Confidence. 2017. ***(978-1-5081-7637-4(X))*** Rosen Publishing Group, Inc., The.

Lishinski, Ann King. Let Your Light Shine. Morello, Charles, ed. Lishinski, Jamie, illus. 2003. (J). pap. 9.95 *(978-0-9709575-0-4(5))* Singing River Pubns.

Lite, Lori. Affirmation Weaver: A Believe in Yourself Story, Designed to Help Children Boost Self-Esteem While Decreasing Stress & Anxiety (Indigo Dreams) 2008. (Illus.). 35p. (J). 14.95 *(978-0-9787781-5-6(4))* Stress Free Pubs.

—Affirmation Weaver: A Believe in Yourself Story Designed to Help Children Increase Self-Esteem While Decreasing Stress & Anxiety. 2nd ed. 2011. 24p. pap. 14.95 *(978-0-9836256-9-8(7))* Stress Free Pubs.

—Angry Octopus: An Anger Management Story Introducing Active Progressive Muscular Relaxation & Deep Breathing. 2011. (Illus.). 30p. (gr. -1-3). pap. 14.95 *(978-0-9836256-8-1(9))* Stress Free Pubs.

—A Boy & a Turtle: A Relaxation Story Teaching Young Children Visualization Techniques to Increase Creativity While Lowering Stress & Anxiety Lev. 3rd ed. 2012.Tr. of niño y una Tortuga. (ENG.). 16p. (J). pap. 12.95 *(978-1-937985-13-4(X))* Stress Free Pubs.

—Bubble Riding: A Relaxation Story Designed to Teach Children Visualization Techniques to Increase Creativity While Lowering Stress & Anxiety. 2012.Tr. of Montando Burbujas. (ENG.). (J). pap. 14.95 *(978-1-937985-03-5(2))* Stress Free Pubs.

—Buenas Noches Oruga: Una Historia para la Relajación Que Ayuda a Los Niños a Controlar la Ira y el Estrés para Que Se Queden Dormidos Sosegadamente. 2012.Tr. of Goodnight Caterpillar. (SPA., Illus.). 16p. (J). pap. 12.95 *(978-1-937985-16-5(4))* Stress Free Pubs.

—Caleta de la Nutria Marina: Un Cuento para la Ansiedad Infantil, Enseña la Relajación, la Respiración Profunda para Reducir la Ansiedad, el Estrés y la Ira, a la Vez Que Fomenta el Sueño Sosegado. 2011.Tr. of Sea Otter Cove. (SPA., Illus.). 28p. (J). pap. 14.95 *(978-1-937985-11-0(3))* Stress Free Pubs.

—Children's Wellness Curriculum: Lessons, Stories & Techniques Designed to Decrease Bullying, Anxiety, Anger & Obesity While Promoting Self-Esteem & Healthy Food Choices. 2007. (J). (gr. k-5). 89.95 incl. audio compact disk *(978-0-9787781-2-5(X),* 5) Stress Free Pubs.

—The Goodnight Caterpillar: A Children's Relaxation Story to Improve Sleep, Manage Stress, Anxiety, Anger. 3rd abr. ed. 2011.Tr. of Buenas Noches, Oruga. (ENG.). 18p. (J). pap. 12.95 *(978-1-937985-00-4(8))* Stress Free Pubs.

—Montando Burbujas: Un Cuento con Ejercicios de Relajación para Niños, Diseñada para Enseñar a Los Niños Técnicas de Visualización para Aumentar la Creatividad Mientras Disminuyen Sus Niveles de Ansiedad y de Estrés. 2012.Tr. of Bubble Riding. (SPA., Illus.). 32p. (J). pap. 14.95 *(978-1-937985-12-7(1))* Stress Free Pubs.

—El Niño y la Tortuga: Un Cuento para Promover la Relajación. 2012.Tr. of Boy & a Turtle. (SPA., Illus.). 16p. (J). pap. 12.95 *(978-1-937985-17-2(2))* Stress Free Pubs.

—El Pulpo Enojado: Un Cuento Sobre Cómo Controlar la Ira Que Enseña la Relajación Muscular Activa y Progresiva, y la Respiración: un Cuento Sobre Cómo Controlar la Ira Que Enseña la Relajación Muscular Activa y Progresiva, y la Respiración. 2012.Tr. of Angry Octopus. (SPA., Illus.). 30p. (J). pap. 14.95 *(978-1-937985-01-1(6))* Stress Free Pubs.

—Sea Otter Cove: A Relaxation Story, Introducing Deep Breathing to Decrease Anxiety, Stress & Anger While Promoting Peaceful Sleep. 2nd ed. 2012.Tr. of Caleta de la Nutria Marina. (SPA & ENG., Illus.). 24p. (J). 14.95 *(978-1-937985-08-0(3))* Stress Free Pubs.

—Tejedor de Afirmaciones: Un Cuento Que Aumenta la Autoestima en Los Niños, Creer en Ellos Mismos, Mientras Que Reducen Su Estrés y Su Ansiedad. 2012.Tr. of Affirmation Weaver. (SPA., Illus.). 24p. (J). pap. 14.95 *(978-1-937985-02-8(4))* Stress Free Pubs.

Markowitz, Siri. HELP with RAISING YOUR NURSERY or PRESCHOOL CHILDREN - 26 great ideas for parents & preschool Teachers. 2009. 44p. pap. 19.99 *(978-0-557-09610-7(3))* Lulu Pr., Inc.

Mastromarino, Diane, ed. The Girl's Guide to Loving Yourself: A Book about Falling in Love with the One Person Who Matters Most - You. (ENG.). 64p. pap. 9.95 *(978-0-88396-751-5(0),* Blue Mountain Pr.) Blue Mountain Arts Inc.

McCloud, Carol. Growing up with a Bucket Full of Happiness: Three Rules for a Happier Life. Weber, Penny, illus. 2010. (ENG.). 86p. (J). (gr. 4). pap. 9.95 *(978-1-933916-57-6(5))* Bucket Fillers, Inc.

—Have You Filled a Bucket Today? A Guide to Daily Happiness for Kids. Messing, David, illus. 2006. (ENG.). 32p. (J). (gr. -1-3). pap. 9.95 *(978-0-9785075-1-0(7),* Ferne Pr.) Nelson Publishing & Marketing.

Mccloud, Carol. Have You Filled a Bucket Today: A Guide to Daily Happiness for Kids. 2015. lib. bdg. 20.80 *(978-0-606-38236-6(4))* Turtleback Bks.

McCloud, Carol & Martin, Katherine. Fill a Bucket: A Guide to Daily Happiness for Young Children. David, Messing, illus. 2009. (ENG.). 26p. (J). (-2). 9.95 *(978-1-933916-43-9(5))* Bucket Fillers, Inc.

McNulty John. I Am Your Self-Esteem. Gilmour, Karen, illus. 2006. 32p. (J). *(978-0-9769580-5-5(8))* I Am Your Playground LLC.

Mitchell-Tulloss, Delores. ABCs of Character for People Around the World. Hardison, Brian, illus. 2007. 32p. (J). pap. *(978-0-9670712-6-8(7))* zReyomi Publishing.

Moe, Barbara. Understanding Negative Body Image. 2009. (Teen Eating Disorder Prevention Book Ser.). 192p. (gr. 7-12). 63.90 *(978-1-61511-242-5(1))* Rosen Publishing Group, Inc., The.

Morse, Philip C. Kick Out Stress - Teen Stress Reduction Program: Improving Self-Esteem, Optimizing Performance in School & Sports & Improving Physical & Emotional Health. 2004. (YA). (gr. 8-12). pap. *(978-0-9748548-0-9(8))* Mind/Body Workshops.

Moss, Wendy. Being Me: A Kid's Guide to Boosting Confidence & Self-Esteem. 2010. (Illus.). 112p. (J). (gr. 3-8). 14.95 *(978-1-4338-0883-8(8));* pap. 9.95 *(978-1-4338-0884-5(6))* American Psychological Assn. (Magination Pr.).

Mulcahy, William. Zach Hangs in There. McKee, Darren, illus. 2017. (Zach Rules Ser.). (ENG.). 32p. (J). (gr. k-3). 12.99 ***(978-1-63198-162-3(5))*** Free Spirit Publishing, Inc.

Naik, Anita. Think Yourself Gorgeous: How to Feel Good - Inside & Out. 2012. (ENG., Illus.). 176p. (YA). (gr. 7). pap. 11.99 *(978-0-7499-5244-0(X),* Piatkus Bks.) Little, Brown Book Group Ltd. GBR. Dist: Independent Pubs. Group.

Noah, Michal Y. A-Z the Universe in Me. 2012. 18.95 *(978-0-7414-7841-2(2));* pap. 13.95 *(978-0-7414-7840-5(4))* Infinity Publishing.

O'Keefe, Susan Heyboer. Be the Star That You Are: A Book for Kids Who Feel Different. Alley, R. W., illus. 2005. (Elf-Help Books for Kids). (J). per. 7.95 *(978-0-87029-391-7(5))* Abbey Pr.

Onuoha-Ezemma, Glory. Don't Make Fun of My Name: My Name Is Special to My Parents & Me. unabr. ed. 2003. (Illus.). 47p. (J). (gr. k-6). pap. 9.95 *(978-0-9661598-6-8(1))* Ekwike Bks. & Publishing.

Onyett, Nicola & Williams, Tennessee. A Streetcar Named Desire. 2011. (Philip Allan Literature Guide for A-Level Ser.). (Illus.). 96p. (gr. 10-12). pap. 24.95 *(978-1-4441-2156-8(1))* Trans-Atlantic Pubns., Inc.

Ornelas, Lourdes. So Can I. 2013. 32p. 25.99 *(978-1-4808-0189-9(5));* pap. 16.99 *(978-1-4808-0187-5(9))* Archway Publishing.

Orr, Tamra. Beautiful Me: Finding Personal Strength & Self Acceptance, 1 vol. 2008. (Essential Health: a Guy's Guide Ser.). (ENG.). 112p. (J). (gr. 6-12). lib. bdg. 35.64 *(978-1-60453-098-8(7))* ABDO Publishing Co.

Ottaviano, Patricia. Girl World: How to Ditch the Drama & Find Your Inner Amazing. 2015. (ENG.). 160p. (YA). (gr. 6-12). pap. 9.99 *(978-1-4926-0912-4(9),* 9781492609124) Sourcebooks, Inc.

Rice, Ashley. Make Your Dreams Come True: A Girl's Guide to Always Believing in Yourself. 2015. 96p. pap. ***(978-1-59842-865-0(9)***, Blue Mountain Pr.) Blue Mountain Arts Inc.

Rodi, Robert & Ross, Laura. Staying Mentally Healthy, Vol. 10. Jennings, Kevin, ed. 2016. (Living Proud! Growing up LGBTQ Ser.). (Illus.). 64p. (J). (gr. 7). 23.95 *(978-1-4222-3510-2(6))* Mason Crest.

Rogers, Jennifer. While the Stars Are at Play. 2013. 30p. pap. 13.99 *(978-1-4525-6681-8(X))* Balboa Pr.

Rothenberg, B. Annye. Mommy & Daddy Are Always Supposed to Say Yes — Aren't They? Eldridge, Marion, illus. 2007. 40p. (J). pap. 9.95 *(978-0-9790420-0-3(3))* Perfecting Parenting Pr.

Rue, Nancy N. Everybody Tells Me to Be Myself but I Don't Know Who I Am. 2007. (Faithgirlz! Ser.). (ENG., Illus.). 144p. (J). (gr. 3-7). pap. 7.99 *(978-0-310-71295-4(5))* Zonderkidz.

Schab, Lisa M. Cool, Calm, & Confident: A Workbook to Help Kids Learn Assertiveness Skills. 2009. (Instant Help Ser.). (ENG.). 184p. (J). (gr. k-5). pap. 18.95 *(978-1-57224-630-0(8),* Instant Help Books) New Harbinger Pubns.

—Self-Esteem for Teens: Six Principles for Creating the Life You Want. 2016. (Instant Help Solutions Ser.). (ENG.). 184p. (YA). (gr. 6-12). pap. 16.95 *(978-1-62625-419-0(2))* New Harbinger Pubns.

—The Self-Esteem Workbook for Teens: Activities to Help You Build Confidence & Achieve Your Goals. 2013. (ENG.). 200p. (YA). (gr. 6-12). pap. 15.95 *(978-1-60882-582-0(5),* Instant Help Books) New Harbinger Pubns.

Schoenberg, Jill. Journal Buddies: A Girl's Journal for Sharing & Celebrating Magnificence. 2nd ed. 2007. (J). per. 16.95 *(978-0-9768623-0-7(1))* Blue Sky at Night Publishing.

Self-Esteem Garden. 2003. *(978-1-57543-116-1(5))* MAR*CO Products, Inc.

The Self-Esteem Handbook for Kids. 2004. (J). 24.95 *(978-0-9725836-0-2(2))* Long Life Publishing Co.

Snow, Todd. You Are Important. Strong, Melodee, illus. 2007. (You Are Important Ser.). (ENG.). 24p. (J). (gr. -1-k). bds. 7.99 *(978-1-934277-06-5(1))* Maren Green Publishing, Inc.

Sommer, Carl. If Only I Were. . . 2003. (Another Sommer-Time Story Ser.). (Illus.). 48p. (J). (gr. 1-4). 16.95 incl. audio *(978-1-57537-551-9(6))* Advance Publishing, Inc.

—If Only I Were. . . James, Kennon, illus. 2003. (Another Sommer-Time Story Ser.). (ENG.). 48p. (J). 16.95 incl. audio compact disk *(978-1-57537-502-1(8))* Advance Publishing, Inc.

St. Stephen's Community House Staff. It's Not All Black & White: Multiracial Youth Speak Out. 2012. (ENG., Illus.). 120p. (YA). (gr. 7-12). pap. 12.95 *(978-1-55451-380-2(4),* 9781554513802) Annick Pr., Ltd. CAN. Dist: Publishers Group West (PGW).

Standard Publishing Staff. Self Esteem. 2006. cd-rom 24.99 *(978-0-7847-1886-5(5))* Standard Publishing.

Stewart, Sheila. I Like Me. (Kids Have Troubles Too Ser.). 48p. (YA). (gr. 5-18). 2010. lib. bdg. 19.95 *(978-1-4222-1699-6(3))* 2009. pap. 7.95 *(978-1-4222-1912-6(7))* Mason Crest.

Sunderland, Margot, et al. Helping Children Who Think They Are Worthless. 2017. (Helping Children with Feelings Ser.). (ENG., Illus.). 96p. (C). pap. 34.95 *(978-0-86388-466-5(0),* Y329814, Routledge) Taylor & Francis Group GBR. Dist: Taylor & Francis Group.

Swan, Richard. The Pardoner's Prologue & Tale. 2011. (Philip Allan Literature Guide for A-Level Ser.). (Illus.). 96p. (gr. 10-12). pap. 24.95 *(978-1-4441-2159-9(6))* Trans-Atlantic Pubns., Inc.

Tammen, Christina. C h u m P. 2010. 42p. pap. 13.95 *(978-1-935268-21-5(X))* Halo Publishing International.

Telgemeier, Raina. Smile. 2010. 21.00 *(978-1-60686-896-6(9))* Perfection Learning Corp.

—Smile. 2010. (ENG.). 224p. (J). (gr. 3-7). 24.99 *(978-0-545-13205-3(3));* (Illus.). pap. 10.99 *(978-0-545-13206-0(1))* Scholastic, Inc. (Graphix).

—Smile. 2010. lib. bdg. 22.10 *(978-0-606-14082-9(4),* Turtleback) Turtleback Bks.

Thomas, Natasha. Mommy & Daddy Is There Really Greatness in Me? 2013. (ENG.). 24p. (J). pap. 34.95 *(978-1-4327-8767-7(5))* Outskirts Pr., Inc.

Tool Kits for Kids LLC Staff, creator. Charge up Your Confidence - Tool Kit for Kids: Elementary School Edition. 2008. (Illus.). (J). 39.95 *(978-0-9819483-2-4(4))* Tool Kits For Kids LLC.

—Charge up Your Confidence - Tool Kit for Kids: High School / Middle School Edition. 2009. (Illus.). (J). 39.95 *(978-0-9819483-3-1(2))* Tool Kits For Kids LLC.

Van Leeuwen, Michele D., creator. Summer Bridge Activities: Grades PK to K. 2012. (Summer Bridge Activities Ser.). (ENG., Illus.). 150p. pap. 14.95 *(978-1-60996-440-5(3))* Carson-Dellosa Publishing, LLC.

Vaughn, Wendy. For Children of the World with Love. 2003. 63p. pap. 19.95 *(978-1-4137-0124-1(8))* America Star Bks.

Viglione, Steve. The I AM! Affirmation Book (English-Spanish Edition) Discovering the Value of Who You Are. 2007. (Love - Wisdom Ser.). (Illus.). (J). 6.95 *(978-0-9645224-7-3(0))* I AM Foundation, The.

Vinci, Daniela V. Hi, My Name Is Daniela & I Want to Be a Great Woman: How I Found Me. 2008. 72p. pap. 10.95 *(978-0-595-52116-6(9))* iUniverse, Inc.

Weiss, S. I. Coping with the Beauty Myth: A Guide for Real Girls. 2009. (Coping Ser.). 192p. (gr. 7-12). 63.90 *(978-1-61512-014-7(9))* Rosen Publishing Group, Inc., The.

Weiss, Stefanie Iris. Coping with the Beauty Myth: A Guide for Real Girls. 2005. (Coping Ser.). (Illus.). 192p. (YA). (gr. 7-12). lib. bdg. 34.60 *(978-0-8239-3757-8(7))* Rosen Publishing Group, Inc., The.

S

West, Lorraine, illus. The Mirror & Me. 2005. 40p. (J). per. 12.95 (978-0-9768674-0-1(0)) Hit Records, LLC.

Wilde, Jerry. Hot Stuff to Help Kids Cheer Up: The Depression & Self-Esteem Workbook. 2007. (ENG.). 80p. (J). (gr. 4-7). pap. 9.95 (978-1-4022-0926-0(6), Sourcebooks Jabberwocky) Sourcebooks, Inc.

Wiley, Judith Gupton. Something More Special. 2011. 16p. 8.32 (978-1-4567-4283-6(3)) AuthorHouse.

Woods, Earl & Tiger Woods Foundation Staff. Start Something: You Can Make a Difference. 2006. (ENG., Illus.). 144p. (gr. 4-7). pap. 14.00 (978-1-4165-3704-5(X)) Simon & Schuster.

Yankee, Kris & Nelson, Marian. Are You Confident Today? 2014. (ENG., Illus.). 32p. (J). pap. 9.95 (978-1-938326-24-0(5), Ferne Pr.) Nelson Publishing & Marketing.

SELF-ESTEEM—FICTION

Abromovitz, Jaime. Baby Dreamer Ding-A-Ling: Ding-A-Lings. 2004. (Illus.). (J). per. 9.95 (978-0-9762587-1-1(4)) StoryGirl Productions, LLC.

—Dreamer Ding-A-Ling: Ding-A-Lings: the Banana Phone. 2004. (Illus.). (J). per. 9.95 (978-0-9762587-0-4(6)) StoryGirl Productions, LLC.

—Zazzy-Q Ding-A-Ling: Ding-A-Lings: the Magic Wand. 2004. (Illus.). (J). per. 9.95 (978-0-9762587-2-8(2)) StoryGirl Productions, LLC.

Akerson, Julie Chicos. The Life of Riley the Cat. Taylor, Jennifer, illus. 2005. 28p. (J). 15.50 (978-1-4120-5858-2(9)) Trafford Publishing.

Aldrich, Jodi. Bee Mumble & Wug. 2011. 36p. (J). pap. 20.95 (978-1-4327-6808-9(5)) Outskirts Pr., Inc.

Alexander, Kwame. Booked. 2016. (ENG.). 320p. (J). (gr. 5-7). 16.99 (978-0-544-57098-6(7), HMH Books For Young Readers) Houghton Mifflin Harcourt Publishing Co.

—Booked. 2016. lib. bdg. 29.40 (978-0-606-37992-2(4)) Turtleback Bks.

Almada, Ariel Andres. Walking Through a World of Aromas. 2013. (ENG., Illus.). 24p. (J). (gr. k-2). 16.95 (978-84-15619-48-2(0)) Eastern National.

Amenii, Nehprii. Memories of the Little Elephant. 2008. (Illus.). 60p. (J). 24.95 (978-0-9797010-0-9(7)) Khunum Productions, Inc.

Appelt, Kathi. Incredible Me! Karas, G. Brian, illus. 2003. (ENG.). 32p. (J). (gr. -1-3). 16.99 (978-0-06-028622-4(9)) HarperCollins Pubs.

Applehead, Zippy. You Are Who You Be. 2012. 28p. pap. 24.95 (978-1-4626-6505-1(5)) America Star Bks.

Attaway-Young, Andrea & Lane Durbin, Deborah. The Secret Treasure - A Fairy Tale. 2010. (ENG.). 40p. 9.95 (978-1-934363-70-6(7)) Zoe Life Publishing.

Azore, Barbara. Wanda's Freckles. Graham, Georgia, illus. 2009. (ENG.). 24p. (J). (gr. -1-2). 19.95 (978-0-88776-862-0(8), Tundra Bks.) Tundra Bks. CAN. Dist: Penguin Random Hse. LLC.

Bailey, Mark & Oatman, Michael. Tiny Pie. Hemingway, Edward, illus. 2013. (ENG.). 32p. (J). (gr. -1-17). 15.95 (978-0-7624-4482-3(7), Running Pr. Kids) Running Pr. Bk. Pubs.

Bakker, Merel. Maks & Mila on a Special Journey. Mini Pois Etc, illus. 2013. 54p. (978-2-9700865-0-5(6)) Mila Publishing, Merel Bakker.

Balash, Sue Beth. Mimi the Inchworm. 2009. (ENG.). 32p. pap. 10.95 (978-1-933916-44-6(3), Ferne Pr.) Nelson Publishing & Marketing.

Banks, Piper. Geek Abroad, 2 vols. 2008. (Geek High Ser.: 2). (ENG.). 256p. (YA). (gr. 9-18). 9.99 (978-0-451-22393-7(4), Berkley) Penguin Publishing Group.

—Revenge of the Geek. 2010. (Geek High Ser.: 4). (ENG.). 256p. (gr. 12-18). 9.99 (978-0-451-23134-5(1), Berkley) Penguin Publishing Group.

—Summer of the Geek. 2010. (Geek High Ser.: 3). (ENG.). 256p. (YA). (gr. 5-18). 9.99 (978-0-451-22984-7(3), Berkley) Penguin Publishing Group.

Banting, Celia. I Only Said Yes So That They'd Like Me. 2006. (Illus.). 224p. (YA). per. 14.99 (978-0-9786648-1-7(7)) Wighita Pr.

Baratz-Logsted, Lauren. Me, in Between. 2008. (ENG.). 208p. (J). (gr. 4-8). pap. 5.99 (978-1-4169-5068-4(0), Simon & Schuster/Paula Wiseman Bks.) Simon & Schuster/Paula Wiseman Bks.

Beaumont, Karen. I Like Myself! Catrow, David, illus. (ENG.). 32p. (J). (gr. -1 — 1). 2010. bds. 11.99 (978-0-547-40163-8(9)) 2004. 17.99 (978-0-15-202013-2(6)) Houghton Mifflin Harcourt Publishing Co.

—I Like Myself! (board Book) Catrow, David, illus. 2016. (ENG.). 32p. (J). (— 1). bds. 7.99 (978-0-544-64101-3(9), HMH Books For Young Readers) Houghton Mifflin Harcourt Publishing Co.

Beck, Nina. This Book Isn't Fat, It's Fabulous. 2009. (ENG.). 256p. (J). (gr. 9). pap. 8.99 (978-0-545-01704-6(1)) Scholastic, Inc.

Bellingham, Brenda. Lilly Takes the Lead. MacDonald, Clarke, illus. 2006. (Formac First Novels Ser.: 34). (ENG.). 64p. (gr. 2-5). 14.95 (978-0-88780-703-9(8), 9780887807039) Formac Publishing Co., Ltd. CAN. Dist: Casemate Pubs. & Bk. Distributors, LLC.

Benoff-Nadel, Phyllis. The Magical Garden. 2013. 32p. pap. 16.99 (978-1-4525-7445-5(6), Balboa Pr.) Author Solutions, Inc.

Biancakrystal. Clap to Beauty: A toddler self-esteem Book. 2011. 16p. pap. 10.00 (978-1-4634-1693-5(8)) AuthorHouse.

Binkow, Howard. Howard B. Wigglebottom Listens to His Heart. Cornelison, Susan F., illus. 2nd ed. 2008. (ENG.). 32p. (J). 15.00 (978-0-9715390-2-0(2)) We Do Listen Foundation.

Birkholz, Gay Lyn. Veneti: Lake Michigan's Treasure. Williamson, Linda K., illus. 2010. 52p. pap. 17.00 (978-1-60860-129-5(3), Strategic Bk. Publishing) Strategic Book Publishing & Rights Agency (SBPRA).

Black, Cassandra. Twinkle: The Only Firefly Who Couldn't Light Up. Kirk, Tim, illus. 3rd ed. 2012. (ENG.). 111p. (J). (gr. 4-7). pap. 12.99 (978-0-9742739-3-8(7)) Lavender Bks.

Bowe, Julie. Pompom Problems. 2015. (Victoria Torres, Unfortunately Average Ser.). (ENG.). 160p. (gr. 4-4). lib. bdg. 26.65 (978-1-4965-0532-3(8)) Stone Arch Bks.

Bowser, Ken. Bobbi's Big Brake. Bowser, Ken, illus. 2016. (Funny Bone Readers: Truck Pals on the Job Ser.). (ENG., Illus.). 24p. (gr. k-2). lib. bdg. 19.99 (978-1-63440-062-6(3)) Red Chair Pr.

—Bobbi's Big Brake: Self-Confidence. Bowser, Ken, illus. 2016. (Funny Bone Readers: Truck Pals on the Job Ser.). (ENG., Illus.). 24p. (gr. k-2). 30.65 (978-1-63440-064-0(X)) Red Chair Pr.

—Lawni Takes the Field: Teamwork. Bowser, Ken, illus. 2016. (Funny Bone Readers: Truck Pals on the Job Ser.). (ENG., Illus.). 24p. (gr. k-2). 30.65 (978-1-63440-076-3(3)) Red Chair Pr.

Briggs, Mayke Beckmann. Here You Are. Briggs, Mayke Beckmann, illus. 2007. (Illus.). 44p. (J). 16.95 (978-0-9776469-1-3(2)) BoathouseBooks.

Brosgol, Vera. Anya's Ghost. Brosgol, Vera, illus. 2011. (ENG., Illus.). 224p. (YA). (gr. 7-12). 22.99 (978-1-59643-713-5(8), 9781596437135, First Second Bks.) Roaring Brook Pr.

—Anya's Ghost. Brosgol, Vera, illus. 2014. (ENG., Illus.). 240p. (YA). (gr. 7). pap. 10.99 (978-1-250-04001-5(9), 9781250040015) Square Fish.

Broski, Julie. Being Me. Vigla, Vincent, illus. 2011. (Rookie Ready to Learn Ser.). 40p. (J). (ENG.). pap. 5.95 (978-0-531-26653-3(2)); (gr. -1-k). lib. bdg. 23.00 (978-0-531-26428-7(9)) Scholastic Library Publishing. (Children's Pr.).

Brown, Ayanna. I Am Beautiful, for All the Children of the World, 1 vol. Elliot, Lee, photos by. 2010. (Illus.). 20p. pap. 24.95 (978-1-4489-8112-0(3)) PublishAmerica, Inc.

Brown, Corinne. Wishful Watoosi: The Horse That Wished He Wasn't. 2012. (ENG., Illus.). 32p. (J). 16.95 (978-0-9721057-2-9(7), 3000) Cowgirl Peg Enterprises.

Brudos, Susan E. & Rubino, Alisa A., illus. Wayne's Trail. 2004. (J). pap. (978-0-932991-62-1(9)) Place In The Woods, The.

Bryant, Annie. The Great Scavenger Hunt. 2009. (Beacon Street Girls Ser.: 15). (ENG.). 304p. (J). (gr. 4-8). pap. 8.99 (978-1-4169-6442-1(8), Aladdin) Simon & Schuster Children's Publishing.

—Green Algae & Bubble Gum Wars. 2008. (Beacon Street Girls Ser.: 13). (ENG.). 256p. (J). (gr. 4-8). pap. 7.99 (978-1-4169-6429-2(0), Aladdin) Simon & Schuster Children's Publishing.

—Isabel's Texas Two-Step. 2008. (Beacon Street Girls Ser.: No. 5). (ENG.). 256p. (J). (gr. 4-8). pap. 7.99 (978-1-4169-6423-0(1), Aladdin) Simon & Schuster Children's Publishing.

Burk, Josh. The Summer of Saint Nick. 2007. (ENG.). 152p. (YA). per. 12.95 (978-0-9768042-2-2(0)) Maven Of Memory Publishing.

Byrd, Jeff, illus. A Tale of Two Tails, el Perro con Dos Colas: A children's story in English & Spanish. 2004. Tr. of Perro con Dos Colas. (SPA.). (J). (gr. -1-3). per. 14.95 (978-0-9746024-0-0(X)) One Arm Publishing.

Campisi, Stephanie. The Ugly Dumpling. Kober, Shahar, illus. 2016. (ENG.). 32p. (J). (-3). 15.95 (978-1-938063-67-1(8), Mighty Media Kids) Mighty Media Pr.

Carlson, Nancy. ¡Piensa en Grande! 2005. (Libros Ilustrados (Picture Bks.)). (SPA., Illus.). 32p. (J). (gr. k-2). lib. bdg. 15.95 (978-0-8225-3192-0(5), Ediciones Lerner) Lerner Publishing Group.

—Think Big! 2005. (Illus.). 28p. (J). (gr. -1-3). 15.95 (978-1-57505-622-7(4), Carolrhoda Bks.) Lerner Publishing Group.

Carman, Debby. I'm Maximum Cat, That's a Fact! 2007. (Illus.). 28p. (J). 14.99 (978-0-9777340-2-3(1)) Faux Paw Media Group.

—Kittywimpuss Got Game. Carman, Debby, illus. 2007. (Illus.). 28p. (J). (gr. -1-1). 14.99 (978-0-9777340-4-7(8)) Faux Paw Media Group.

Caruso, Rosalie. How I taught my mom... the Law of Attraction. 2010. 48p. 17.45 (978-1-4525-0135-2(1)) Get Published.

Cattanach, Ann. Malpas the Dragon. Renouf, Michael, illus. 2007. (ENG.). 28p. (J). (gr. 3-7). per. 15.95 (978-1-84310-572-5(1), 1774) Kingsley, Jessica Pubs. GBR. Dist: Macmillan Distribution Ltd.

Chandler Goldstein. Georgette: A Little Frog Discovers the Value in Revealing Her True Self! 2012. 20p. pap. 15.99 (978-1-4772-0835-9(6)) AuthorHouse.

Charaipotra, Sona & Clayton, Dhonielle. Shiny Broken Pieces. 2017. 384p. (YA). (gr. 9). pap. 9.99 **(978-0-06-234243-0(6)**, HarperTeen) HarperCollins Pubs.

Chen, Justina. Nothing but the Truth (And a Few White Lies) 2007. (Justina Chen Novel Ser.). (ENG.). 256p. (J). (gr. 7-17). per. 9.99 (978-0-316-01131-0(2)) Little, Brown Bks. for Young Readers.

Clarissa - Evaluation Guide: Evaluation Guide. 2006. (J). (978-1-55942-402-8(8)) Witcher Productions.

Clarke, Jane. Plodney Creeper, Supersloth. 2006. (Blue Bananas Ser.). (ENG., Illus.). 48p. (J). (gr. -1-3). (978-0-7787-0896-4(9)) Crabtree Publishing Co.

Clevenger, Lee. IncrediBoy: Be Careful What You Wish. 2004. 267p. (J). pap. 12.95 (978-0-9764052-0-7(2)) Thomas Max Publishing.

Codell, Esmé Raji. Sahara Special. 2003. (ENG., Illus.). 208p. (J). (gr. 3-7). pap. 16.49 (978-0-7868-2627-8(4)) Hyperion Bks. for Children.

—Sahara Special. 2004. (ENG.). 192p. (J). (gr. 3-7). pap. 6.99 (978-0-7868-1611-8(2)) Hyperion Pr.

Cohn, Rachel. You Know Where to Find Me. (ENG.). (YA). (gr. 7). 2009. 224p. pap. 8.99 (978-0-689-87860-2(5)) 2008. 208p. 16.99 (978-0-689-87859-6(1)) Simon & Schuster Bks. For Young Readers. (Simon & Schuster Bks. For Young Readers).

Cole, Kathryn. Never Give Up: A Story about Self-Esteem, 1 vol. Leng, Qin, illus. 2015. (I'm a Great Little Kid Ser.). (ENG.). 24p. (J). (gr. 1-3). 15.95 (978-1-927583-60-9(8)) Second Story Pr. CAN. Dist: Orca Bk. Pubs. USA.

Conner, Wendy Simpson. Princess of the Moon. (Illus.). (J). 16.95 (978-1-889599-20-5(4)) Interstellar Publishing Co.

Conway, David. Errol & His Extraordinary Nose. Angaramo, Roberta, illus. 2010. (ENG.). 32p. (J). (gr. -1-3). 16.95 (978-0-8234-2262-3(3)) Holiday Hse., Inc.

Cook, Julia. Cliques Just Don't Make Cents. DuFalla, Anita, illus. 2012. (ENG.). 32p. (J). pap. 10.95 (978-1-934490-39-6(3)) Boys Town Pr.

Cottswold, Wooley. Rose & the Bald-Headed Elephant. 2009. (Illus.). 28p. (J). 16.95 (978-0-9779064-0-6(X)) Archie Publishing.

Crane, Stephen. The Red Badge of Courage: With a Discussion of Self-Esteem. Clift, Eva, illus. 2003. (Values in Action Illustrated Classics Ser.). 190p. (J). (978-1-59203-034-7(3)) Learning Challenge, Inc.

Crowley, Cath. A Little Wanting Song. 2011. (ENG.). 288p. (YA). (gr. 9). pap. 8.99 (978-0-375-85449-1(5), Ember) Random Hse. Children's Bks.

CUNNINGHAM, WHO AM I SAUNDA. Who am I? 2008. 75p. pap. 14.95 (978-1-4357-0475-6(4)) Lulu Pr., Inc.

Curtis, Jamie Lee. I'm Gonna Like Me: Letting off a Little Self-Esteem. Cornell, Laura, illus. 2007. (ENG.). 32p. (J). (gr. -1-3). 16.99 (978-0-06-028761-0(6)) HarperCollins Pubs.

Dahl, Michael. A Jar of Eyeballs. Sinkovec, Igor, illus. 2015. (Igor's Lab of Fear Ser.). (ENG.). 40p. (gr. 1-3). lib. bdg. 23.99 (978-1-4965-0455-5(0)) Stone Arch Bks.

Dahnke, Julie. I'm Not Perfect So What? 2012. 20p. pap. 15.99 (978-1-4772-5662-6(8)) AuthorHouse.

Danziger, Paula. I, Amber Brown. Ross, Tony, illus. 2011. (Amber Brown Ser.: 8). (ENG.). 160p. (J). (gr. 2-5). 5.99 (978-0-14-241965-6(6), Puffin Books) Penguin Young Readers Group.

—I, Amber Brown. 2004. (Amber Brown Ser.: No. 8). 144p. (J). (gr. 2-4). pap. 17.00 incl. audio (978-0-8072-2064-1(7), Listening Library) Random Hse. Audio Publishing Group.

Darden, Hunter. Pete's Angel. Vaca, Sally, illus. 2008. 44p. pap. 12.00 (978-1-60693-264-3(0), Strategic Bk. Publishing) Strategic Book Publishing & Rights Agency (SBPRA).

Debeer, Kristen. I Believe in You: A Mother's Message to Her Son with Learning Differences. Santy, Elizabeth & Fisher, Jessie, illus. 2012. 32p. pap. 12.97 (978-1-61897-802-8(0), Strategic Bk. Publishing) Strategic Book Publishing & Rights Agency (SBPRA).

Defillippo, Steve. Growing up Nicely! Grammy Helps Adam Grow up & Develop Social Skills & Moral Values. 2012. 24p. (-18). pap. 15.99 (978-1-4797-0957-1(3)) Xlibris Corp.

DelleCava, Karen. A Closer Look. 2011. 304p. (YA). (gr. 9-18). 16.95 (978-1-934813-49-2(4)) Westside Bks.

Dewdney, Anna. Little Excavator. 2017. (ENG., Illus.). 44p. (J). (-k). 17.99 (978-1-101-99920-2(9), Viking Books for Young Readers) Penguin Young Readers Group.

Diggle, David Mark. Barbara: A Sssslithering Adventure of Self Discovery. Diggle, Daniel James, illus. 2011. 24p. (J). pap. (978-0-9871657-9-4(8)) Diggle de Doo Productions Pty. Ltd.

Dionne, Erin. Models Don't Eat Chocolate Cookies. 2009. (ENG.). 256p. (J). (gr. 3-7). pap. 6.99 (978-0-8037-3296-4(1), Dial Bks) Penguin Young Readers Group.

Dipucchio, Kelly. Clink. Myers, Matthew, illus. 2011. (ENG.). 32p. (J). (gr. -1-2). 16.99 (978-0-06-192928-1(X)) HarperCollins Pubs.

Dixon, Tiffany. Everyone Is Special. 2008. 16p. per. 24.95 (978-1-60441-231-4(3)) America Star Bks.

Donovan, Rebecca. Out of Breath, 0 vols. unabr. ed. 2013. (Breathing Ser.: 3). (ENG.). 432p. (YA). (gr. 10-12). pap. 9.99 (978-1-4778-1718-6(2), 9781477817186, Amazon Children's Publishing) Amazon Publishing.

Douglas, Babette. Curly Hare Gets It Straight. Williams, Ted, illus. 2006. (Kiss a Me Teacher Creature Stories Ser.). (J). (gr. -1-3). (978-1-890343-35-4(8)) Kiss A Me Productions, Inc.

Dowell, Frances O'Roark. Chicken Boy. Krause, George, photos by. 2007. (ENG., Illus.). 224p. (J). (gr. 5-9). pap. 6.99 (978-1-4169-3482-0(0), Atheneum Bks. for Young Readers) Simon & Schuster Children's Publishing.

—Chicken Boy. 2005. (ENG., Illus.). 208p. (J). (gr. 5-9). 17.99 (978-0-689-85816-1(7), Atheneum Bks. for Young Readers) Simon & Schuster Children's Publishing.

Doyle, Malachy. Long Gray Norris. 2006. (Yellow Bananas Ser.). (ENG., Illus.). 48p. (J). (gr. -1-3). (978-0-7787-1002-8(5)) Crabtree Publishing Co.

Dreiling, Christy. Holes in My Socks. 2005. pap. 16.95 (978-0-9771891-0-6(4)) Holes In My Socks Publishing.

Dubovoy, Silvia. Turquesita. (SPA.). (J). pap. (978-968-6465-18-1(9)) Casa de Estudios de Literatura y Talleres Artisticos Amaquemecan A.C. MEX. Dist: Lectorum Pubns., Inc.

Dyan, Penelope. You Are Okay! Dyan, Penelope, illus. 2013. (Illus.). 34p. pap. 11.95 (978-1-61477-070-1(0)) Bellissima Publishing, LLC.

Echols, Jennifer. The One That I Want. 2012. (ENG.). 288p. (YA). (gr. 7). pap. 9.99 (978-1-4424-5236-7(6), Simon Pulse) Simon Pulse.

Emerson, Carl. Nosy Arnie the Anteater, 1 vol. Trover, Zachary, illus. 2007. (Animal Underdogs Ser.). (ENG.). 32p. (gr. -1-4). 28.50 (978-1-60270-016-1(8), Looking Glass Library) ABDO Publishing Co.

—Opie the Opossum Wakes Up, 1 vol. Trover, Zachary, illus. 2007. (Animal Underdogs Ser.). (ENG.). 32p. (gr. -1-4). 28.50 (978-1-60270-017-8(6), Looking Glass Library) ABDO Publishing Co.

Ewart, Franzeska G. Speak up, Spike. Oliver, Mark, illus. 2005. (Yellow Go Bananas Ser.). (ENG.). 48p. (J). (gr. 3-4). (978-0-7787-2744-6(0)); lib. bdg. (978-0-7787-2722-4(X)) Crabtree Publishing Co.

Flake, Sharon G. The Skin I'm In. Disney Press Staff, illus. rev. ed. 2007. (ENG.). 176p. (J). (gr. 5-9). pap. 8.99 (978-1-4231-0385-1(8), Jump at the Sun) Hyperion Bks. for Children.

—The Skin I'm In. 2007. (J). lib. bdg. 19.65 (978-1-4178-0860-1(8), Turtleback) Turtleback Bks.

Fleischman, Paul. Breakout. 2003. (ENG.). 160p. (J). 15.95 (978-0-8126-2696-4(6)) Cricket Bks.

—Breakout. 2005. (ENG.). 144p. (YA). (gr. 7). reprint ed. pap. 6.99 (978-0-689-87189-4(9), Simon Pulse) Simon Pulse.

Foltz, Joanna "Gwen". The Owl Tree. 2011. 28p. pap. 13.59 (978-1-4634-1199-2(5)) AuthorHouse.

Folz, Alexandra. Indigo's Bracelet. 2010. 84p. pap. 9.95 (978-1-4525-0058-4(4)) Get Published.

Frankel, Erin. Nobody! A Story about Overcoming Bullying in Schools. Heaphy, Paula, illus. 2015. (ENG.). 48p. (J). (gr. k-4). 15.99 (978-1-57542-495-8(9)) Free Spirit Publishing, Inc.

Franklin, Shirley A. Lupita's Quinciner: A Celebration to Remember. 2008. 48p. pap. 8.95 (978-1-4401-0234-9(1)) iUniverse, Inc.

Fredericks, Mariah. Life. Watkins, Liselotte, illus. 2009. (In the Cards Ser.: No. 3). (ENG.). 272p. (J). pap. 5.99 (978-0-689-87659-2(9), Simon & Schuster/Paula Wiseman Bks.) Simon & Schuster/Paula Wiseman Bks.

Furtado, Sierra. Life Uploaded. 2016. 242p. (YA). pap. **(978-1-5011-4396-0(4)**, Gallery Bks.) Gallery Bks.

Fusco, Kimberly Newton. Beholding Bee. 2015. (ENG.). 336p. (J). (gr. 3-7). 7.99 (978-0-375-86808-5(9), Yearling) Random Hse. Children's Bks.

Gallucci, Susie. Believe I-Can. Sellers, Amy, illus. 2006. (J). (978-0-9776074-1-9(0)) Pounce To Success International, Inc.

—Dream I-Can. Sellers, Amy, illus. 2006. (J). (978-0-9776074-2-6(9)) Pounce To Success International, Inc.

Gano, Debra. Beauty's Secret. Pitre, Dawn, illus. 2008. (Heartlight Girls Ser.). 54p. (J). 17.95 (978-0-9787689-0-4(6)) Heartlight Girls.

Garcia, Mary. Play with Me: Togetherness Time for Your Preschooler & You. (J). 2007. 16.95 (978-0-9790931-2-8(0)) 2006. 16.95 (978-0-9790931-0-4(4)) SMARTseeds Co., LLC, The.

—Play with Me: Togetherness Time for Your Preschooler & You: St. Valentine's Day. 2007. (J). (978-0-9790931-1-1(2)) SMARTseeds Co., LLC, The.

Gayle, Sherri. Bubbles of Faith. 2013. 48p. pap. 11.95 (978-1-61244-076-7(2)) Halo Publishing International.

Gervay, Susanne. Butterflies. 2012. (Fiction Ser.). (ENG.). 256p. (J). pap. 4.99 (978-1-61067-043-2(4)) Kane Miller.

Gifaldi, David. Toby Scudder, King of the School. 2005. (ENG.). 208p. (J). (gr. 5-7). pap. 12.95 (978-0-618-55158-3(1)) Houghton Mifflin Harcourt Publishing Co.

Going, K. L. King of the Screwups. 2010. (ENG., Illus.). 320p. (YA). (gr. 7). pap. 9.99 (978-0-547-33166-9(5)) Houghton Mifflin Harcourt Publishing Co.

Goobie, Beth. Something Girl, 1 vol. 2005. (Orca Soundings Ser.). (ENG.). 128p. (YA). (gr. 8-12). per. 9.95 (978-1-55143-347-9(8)) Orca Bk. Pubs. USA.

Goodman, Shawn. Kindness for Weakness. 2015. (ENG.). 272p. (YA). (gr. 9). pap. 9.99 (978-0-385-74325-9(4), Ember) Random Hse. Children's Bks.

Gordon, David. The Ugly Truckling. Gordon, David, illus. 2004. (Illus.). 32p. (J). (gr. -1-2). lib. bdg. 16.89 (978-0-06-054601-4(8), Geringer, Laura Book) HarperCollins Pubs.

Goss, Leon. Selfus Esteemus Personalitus Low. Tunell, Ken, illus. 2005. (J). pap. (978-1-933156-08-8(2), VisionQuest Kids) GSVQ Publishing.

Goss, Leon, 3rd. Selfus Esteemus Personalitus Low. Tunell, Ken, illus. 2005. 32p. (J). per. 16.99 (978-1-933156-00-2(7), VisionQuest Kids) GSVQ Publishing.

Graff, Lisa. Absolutely Almost. 2014. (ENG.). 304p. (J). (gr. 3-7). 16.99 (978-0-399-16405-7(7), Philomel Bks.) Penguin Young Readers Group.

Gray, Kes. Worries Go Away! Wildish, Lee, illus. 2015. (ENG.). 32p. (J). (gr. -1-k). pap. 9.99 (978-1-4449-0017-0(X)) Hodder & Stoughton GBR. Dist: Hachette Bk. Group.

Greene, Bette. Summer of My German Soldier. 2006. (Puffin Modern Classics Ser.). (ENG.). 240p. (J). (gr. 5-18). 7.99 (978-0-14-240651-9(1), Puffin Books) Penguin Young Readers Group.

Griffin, Saundra J. Which Should I Be? 2004. 21p. pap. 24.95 (978-1-4137-3167-5(8)) PublishAmerica, Inc.

Hairston, Lisa Lee. Victoria Has A Secret. 2011. 36p. 23.00 (978-1-4269-4994-4(4)) Trafford Publishing.

Hale, Shannon. Forest Born. (Books of Bayern Ser.). (ENG.). (YA). 2017. 400p. pap. 9.99 (978-1-68119-319-9(1), 9781681193199) 2011. 400p. (gr. 7). pap. 9.99 (978-1-59990-692-8(9), 9781599906928) 2009. (Illus.). 400p. (gr. 7-18). 18.99 (978-1-59990-167-1(6), 9781599901671) 2011. 416p. (gr. 7-12). 19.99 (978-1-59990-691-1(0), 9781599906911) Bloomsbury Publishing USA. (Bloomsbury USA Childrens).

—River Secrets. (Books of Bayern Ser.). (ENG., Illus.). (YA). (gr. 7). 2008. 320p. 9.99 (978-1-59990-293-7(1), 9781599902937) 2006. 304p. 18.99 (978-1-58234-901-5(0), 9781582349015) Bloomsbury Publishing USA. (Bloomsbury USA Childrens).

Halley, Marilyn. Apple-Green Eyes. 2005. pap. 8.00 (978-0-8059-6681-7(1)) Dorrance Publishing Co., Inc.

Hallmark, Danna G. How Do I Feel Happy? How Do I Feel Sad? 2008. 36p. pap. 24.95 (978-1-4241-9178-9(5)) PublishAmerica, Inc.

Han, Jenny. Shug. (ENG.). 256p. 2007. (J). (gr. 4-8). pap. 7.99 (978-1-4169-0943-9(5), Simon & Schuster/Paula Wiseman Bks.) 2006. (Illus.). (YA). (gr. 7-7). 16.99 (978-1-4169-0942-2(7), Simon & Schuster Bks. For Young Readers) Simon & Schuster Bks. For Young Readers.

Hansen, MaryAnn Shelley. Sam the Second. 2010. 32p. 14.49 (978-1-4520-2408-0(1)) AuthorHouse.

Harper, Charise Mericle. Cupcake. Harper, Charise Mericle, illus. 2010. (ENG., Illus.). 32p. (J). (gr. -1-1). 14.99 (978-1-4231-1897-8(9)) Hyperion Pr.

Harris, Devon D. Yes I Can. 2006. (Illus.). 48p. (J). (978-0-9764082-4-6(4)) Waterhouse Publishing.

Hartnett, Sonya. Butterfly. (ENG.). 240p. (YA). (gr. 9). 2013. pap. 7.99 (978-0-7636-6334-6(4)) 2010. (Illus.). 16.99 (978-0-7636-4760-5(8)) Candlewick Pr.

Hawley, Bobby. By Golly, Molly, You're Right. 2006. 48p. pap. 16.95 (978-1-4241-2085-7(3)) PublishAmerica, Inc.

Hayes, Sonia. Ms. Thang. 2009. (ENG.). 200p. (YA). per. 9.95 (978-0-9777573-0-5(7)) NUA Multimedia.

—Urban Goddess. 2007. 224p. (YA). per. 9.95 (978-0-9777573-1-2(5)) NUA Multimedia.

Haynes, Marilee. A. K. A. Genius. 2013. (ENG.). 208p. (YA). 9.95 (978-0-8198-0830-1(X)) Pauline Bks. & Media.

Hearth, Liese. My Dog Burps. 2008. 14p. pap. 24.95 (978-1-4241-9608-1(6)) America Star Bks.

Heinz, Renata Perpetua. Nali's Life. 2008. 17p. pap. 24.95 (978-1-4241-9245-8(5)) America Star Bks.

Helen, Grace. Vicky Sticky Lips: Putting Others to the Test. 2012. 24p. 24.95 (978-1-4626-5975-3(6)) America Star Bks.

Heling, Kathryn & Hembrook, Deborah. I Wish I Had Freckles Like Abby. Adamson, Bonnie, illus. 2010. (I Wish Ser.). (ENG.). 32p. (J). (gr. 4-7). pap. 7.95 (978-1-934960-47-9(0), Raven Tree Pr.,Csi) Continental Sales, Inc.

—I Wish I Had Freckles Like Abby/Quisiera Tener Pecas Como Abby. Adamson, Bonnie, illus. 2007. (SPA & ENG.).

32p. (J). (gr. -1-3). pap. 7.95 *(978-0-9770906-6-2(3)*, Raven Tree Pr.,Csi) Continental Sales, Inc.

—I Wish I Had Glasses Like Rosa. Adamson, Bonnie, illus. 2010. (I Wish Ser.). (ENG.). 32p. (J). (gr. 4-7). pap. 7.95 *(978-1-934960-49-3(7)*, Raven Tree Pr.,Csi) Continental Sales, Inc.

Heling, Kathryn, et al. I Wish I Had Freckles Like Abby/Quisiera Tener Pecas Como Abby. de La Vega, Eida, tr. Adamson, Bonnie, illus. 2007. (I Wish Ser.). (SPA & ENG.). 32p. (J). (gr. -1-3). 16.95 *(978-0-9724973-8-1(2)*, 626999, Raven Tree Pr.,Csi) Continental Sales, Inc.

Hernandez, Jo Ann Yolanda. The Throwaway Piece. 2006. 246p. (J). (gr. 6). per. 9.95 *(978-1-55885-353-9(7)*, Piñata Books) Arte Publico Pr.

Herrndorf, Wolfgang. Why We Took the Car. Mohr, Tim, tr. from GER. 2014. (ENG.). 256p. (J). (gr. 9). 17.99 *(978-0-545-48180-9(5)*, Levine, Arthur A. Bks.) Scholastic, Inc.

—You, Me, & a Russian Jeep. 2013. (YA). pap. *(978-0-545-48181-6(3)*, Levine, Arthur A. Bks.) Scholastic, Inc.

Hill, Janet Muirhead. Kendall's Storm. Leonhard, Herb, illus. 2011. (J). pap. 12.00 *(978-0-9820893-0-9(9))* Raven Publishing Inc. of Montana.

—Kyleah's Tree. Leonhard, Herb, illus. 2011. (J). pap. 12.00 *(978-0-9827377-9-8(3))* Raven Publishing Inc. of Montana.

Holder, Amy. The Lipstick Laws. 2011. (ENG.). 240p. (YA). (gr. 7-18). pap. 13.99 *(978-0-547-36306-6(0))* Houghton Mifflin Harcourt Publishing Co.

Homzie, Hillary. Things Are Gonna Get Ugly. 2009. (Mix Ser.). (ENG.). 272p. (J). (gr. 4-8). pap. 5.99 *(978-1-4169-7563-2(2)*, Aladdin) Simon & Schuster Children's Publishing.

Honsinger, Linda. Leonard Lou: Beautiful, Brave, Strong, & True. Honsinger, Alise, illus. 2012. 38p. 24.95 *(978-1-4626-6872-4(0))* America Star Bks.

Hoog, Mark. Your Song: A Growing Field Adventure. Aukerman, Robert J., illus. 2007. (ENG.). 43p. (J). (gr. -1-3). 16.95 *(978-0-9770391-2-8(9))* Growing Field Bks.

Hoog, Mark E. Dream Machine: A Growing Field Adventure. Aukerman, Robert J., illus. 2007. (Growing Field Adventure Ser.). (ENG.). 35p. (J). (gr. -1-3). 16.95 *(978-0-9770391-1-1(0)*, 5000) Growing Field Bks.

Hopkins, Ellen. Perfect. (ENG., (YA). (gr. 9). 2013. Illus.). 656p. pap. 12.99 *(978-1-4169-8325-5(2))* 2011. 640p. 18.99 *(978-1-4169-8324-8(4))* McElderry, Margaret K. Bks. (McElderry, Margaret K. Bks.).

Houghton Mifflin Harcourt Publishing Company Staff. Girl Power 5-Minute Stories. 2015. (5-Minute Stories Ser.). (ENG., Illus.). 224p. (J). (gr. -1-3). 12.99 *(978-0-544-33925-5(8)*, HMH Books For Young Readers) Houghton Mifflin Harcourt Publishing Co.

Howland, Leila. Hello, Sunshine. 2017. (ENG.). 368p. (YA). (gr. 9-17). 17.99 ***(978-1-4847-2545-0(X))*** Hyperion Bks. for Children.

Jacono, Mary Kaye. Lenny's Gift. 2005. 27p. pap. 10.95 *(978-0-7414-2602-4(1))* Infinity Publishing.

Jenkins, Toye L. The Way God Made Me: A Self Image Book for Girls. 2009. 28p. pap. 12.49 *(978-1-4389-9363-8(3))* AuthorHouse.

Jiries, Nariman. Grace-A-Lena Learns the Meaning of Self-Esteem. 2012. 36p. pap. 21.99 *(978-1-4771-0476-7(3))* Xlibris Corp.

Johnson, Felicia P. Shuck Shuck Shuck. 2011. 28p. pap. 21.99 *(978-1-4568-6343-2(6))* Xlibris Corp.

Johnson, Harvell. What about Johnson? Howard, Vanetta, ed. Clark, Donna Osborn, illus. 2013. 132p. pap. 11.95 *(978-0-9885056-0-5(6))* Word on Da Street Publishing.

Johnson, Kathleen A. A Voice Came to Me. 2006. lib. bdg. 17.95 *(978-0-9785623-0-4(5))* Voice of Light Pubns.

Johnson, Maerryane. I Am Still the Same Aubrey! 2013. 24p. pap. 24.95 *(978-1-4626-9878-3(6))* America Star Bks.

Jones, Patrick. Pass It Forward. 2016. (Bounce Ser.). (ENG.). 104p. (YA). (gr. 6-12). lib. bdg. 26.65 *(978-1-5124-1125-6(6)*, Darby Creek) Lerner Publishing Group.

Jones, Patrick & Chartier, Brent. The Franchise. 2015. (Opportunity Ser.). (ENG.). 104p. (YA). (gr. 6-12). 34.65 *(978-1-4677-6015-7(3)*, Lerner Digital) Lerner Publishing Group.

—The Franchise. 2013. (Opportunity Ser.). (ENG.). 104p. (YA). (gr. 6-12). pap. 7.95 *(978-1-4677-1496-9(8))*; lib. bdg. 27.93 *(978-1-4677-1375-7(9))* Lerner Publishing Group. (Darby Creek).

K. Elizabeth, Sterling. Austin's First Puppy. 2007. 48p. (J). pap. 10.95 *(978-0-7414-3263-6(3))* Infinity Publishing.

Kamins, Julie Firstenberg. Why Am I at the Red Table? Long, Carlos, illus. 2008. 32p. (J). 13.95 *(978-0-9771566-9-6(9))* Librujas.

Kares, P. S. The Prairie Orphans' Journey. 2008. 32p. per. 24.95 *(978-1-4241-8396-8(0))* America Star Bks.

Kath, Natalie. The Summer I Lost It, 1 vol. (Stone Arch Novels Ser.). (ENG.). 128p. (gr. 4-8). 2012. pap. 6.95 *(978-1-4342-4067-5(3))* 2011. lib. bdg. 26.65 *(978-1-4342-3316-5(2))* Stone Arch Bks. (Stone Arch Novels).

Katie, Byron & Wilhelm, Hans. Tiger-Tiger, Is It True? Four Questions to Make You Smile Again. 2009. (ENG., Illus.). 32p. 14.95 *(978-1-4019-2560-4(X)*, 1076) Hay Hse., Inc.

Kelly, Erin Entrada. Blackbird Fly. Peterschmidt, Betsy, illus. 2016. 320p. (J). (gr. 3-7). pap. 6.99 *(978-0-06-223862-7(0)*, Greenwillow Bks.) HarperCollins Pubs.

Kessler, Jackie Morse. Loss. 2012. (Riders of the Apocalypse Ser.: 3). (ENG.). 272p. (YA). (gr. 7). pap. 8.99 *(978-0-547-71215-4(4))* Houghton Mifflin Harcourt Publishing Co.

—Loss. 2012. (Riders of the Apocalypse Ser.: 3). lib. bdg. 19.65 *(978-0-606-24742-9(4)*, Turtleback) Turtleback Bks.

Kirouac Bn, Nicole. I Am Unique. 2013. 32p. pap. 13.99 *(978-1-4525-7594-0(0)*, Balboa Pr.) Author Solutions, Inc.

Knowles, Alison. Ollie & the Silver Stripe. Wiltshire, Sophie, illus. 2017. (ENG.). 64p. (J). 17.95 *(978-1-78592-241-1(6)*, 9041) Kingsley, Jessica Pubs. GBR. Dist: Macmillan Distribution Ltd.

Kobert, Michael Gilead & Donato, Dona. Who Goes with That Nose? The Wild Adventures of Juicy Coppertoes. Fuller, Laurie, illus. 2005. 40p. (J). per. 9.95 *(978-0-9770700-0-8(X))* Giggling Gorilla Productions, LLC.

Koehler, Lora. The Little Snowplow. Parker, Jake, illus. 2015. (ENG.). 32p. (J). (gr. -1-2). 15.99 *(978-0-7636-7074-0(X))* Candlewick Pr.

Koller, Jackie French. A Wizard Named Nell. Guay, Rebecca, illus. 2003. (ENG.). 208p. (J). (gr. 3-7). pap. 11.95 *(978-0-689-85591-7(5)*, Aladdin) Simon & Schuster Children's Publishing.

Krauss, Trisha. Charlotte's Very Own Dress. 2016. (ENG., Illus.). 40p. (J). (gr. -1-2). 16.99 *(978-0-553-52095-8(4)*, Random Hse. Bks. for Young Readers) Random Hse. Children's Bks.

Kreloff, Elliot. Worth the Wait: A Growing-Up Story of Self-Esteem. Kreloff, Elliot, illus. 2017. (Growing Up Ser.). (ENG., Illus.). 32p. (gr. -1-1). lib. bdg. 19.99 ***(978-1-63440-180-7(8))***; 30.65 ***(978-1-63440-184-5(0))*** Red Chair Pr.

Krohberger, Dawn. Jack Out of the Box: Self-Esteem Elevation for Children. 2013. 24p. pap. 12.99 *(978-1-4525-8253-5(X)*, Balboa Pr.) Author Solutions, Inc.

Lakes, Lofton & Metu, illus. The Dream Team. 2007. 48p. (YA). pap. *(978-0-9799320-0-7(9))* Pinkney, Gail.

Lane, Deborah Jean. I Am an Individual. 2004. pap. 8.00 *(978-0-8059-6527-8(0))* Dorrance Publishing Co., Inc.

Lane, Melaina. Chubs. . Another Day at School. 2011. 20p. 9.14 *(978-1-4251-7330-2(6))* Trafford Publishing.

Larsen, Jen. Future Perfect. 2015. (ENG.). 320p. (YA). (gr. 8-12). 17.99 *(978-0-06-232123-7(4)*, HarperTeen) HarperCollins Pubs.

Larsen, Ramonita. Yes, I Can Do It/Si, lo Puedo Hacer. Larsen, Ramonita, illus. l.t. ed. 2006. (Illus.). 18p. (J). per. 10.99 *(978-1-59879-292-8(X))* Lifevest Publishing, Inc.

Lea, Audry. Scott the Dot. 2005. (Illus.). 32p. (J). 16.00 *(978-1-4120-4927-6(X))* Trafford Publishing.

Lechelt, Karen. What Do You Love about You? 2016. (ENG., Illus.). 32p. (J). 16.99 *(978-1-68119-093-8(1)*, 9781681190938, Bloomsbury USA Childrens) Bloomsbury Publishing USA.

Lee, Jeffrey Lyndon. Locked in the Box. 2013. 40p. pap. 24.95 *(978-1-4626-6218-0(8))* America Star Bks.

Leveen, Tom. Zero. 2013. (ENG.). 320p. (YA). (gr. 9). pap. 9.99 *(978-0-375-87337-9(6)*, Ember) Random Hse. Children's Bks.

Levy, Joanne. Crushing It. 2017. (Mix Ser.). (ENG., Illus.). 240p. (J). (gr. 4-8). pap. 7.99 *(978-1-4814-6473-4(6)*, Aladdin) Simon & Schuster Children's Publishing.

Lewis-Cook, Ashley. Beautiful Me! 2012. (Illus.). 16p. pap. 15.99 *(978-1-4772-1291-2(4))* AuthorHouse.

Lockhart, Kendra. Marvelous Misadventures of Magnificent Madelaine. 2010. (Illus.). 24p. (J). pap. 14.95 *(978-0-9843883-4-9(6)*, Green Lady Pr., The) RealityIsBooks.com, Inc.

London, Adam. Lucky the Rubber Ducky. Atherton, Jim, illus. 2009. 14p. (J). pap. 14.95 *(978-0-578-00865-3(3))* AthertonCustoms.

London, Kelli. Star Power. 2013. (Charly's Epic Fiascos Ser.). (ENG., Illus.). 224p. (YA). (gr. 9). pap. 9.95 *(978-0-7582-8699-4(6)*, K-Teen/Dafina) Kensington Publishing Corp.

Lotorto-Soroka, Mary. Who Needs Spots Anyways? 2009. 24p. pap. 12.99 *(978-1-4490-3947-9(2))* AuthorHouse.

Love, D. Anne. Defying the Diva. 2008. (ENG., Illus.). 272p. (YA). (gr. 7-12). 17.99 *(978-1-4169-3481-3(2)*, McElderry, Margaret K. Bks.) McElderry, Margaret K. Bks.

Lucado, Max. The Tallest of Smalls, 1 vol. Monescillo, Maria, illus. 2009. (ENG.). 32p. (gr. -1-2). 16.99 *(978-1-4003-1514-7(X))* Nelson, Thomas Inc.

—You Are Special. Martinez, Sergio, illus. rev. ed. 2007. 32p. (J). (gr. -1-3). 19.99 *(978-1-58134-894-1(0))* Crossway.

Ludwig, Trudy. Better Than You. Gustavson, Adam, illus. 2011. (ENG.). 32p. (J). (gr. 1-4). 15.99 *(978-1-58246-380-3(8)*, Knopf Bks. for Young Readers) Random Hse. Children's Bks.

Lüftner, Kai. Lily Loves. Drews, Judith, illus. 2012. (ENG.). 32p. (J). (gr. -1-3). pap. 16.95 *(978-1-897476-94-9(9))* Simply Read Bks. CAN. Dist: Ingram Publisher Services.

Lyga, Barry. Hero Type. 2009. (ENG.). 312p. (YA). (gr. 7). pap. 8.99 *(978-0-547-24877-6(6))* Houghton Mifflin Harcourt Publishing Co.

MacMillan, Ian C. Khala Maninge - the Little Elephant That Cried a Lot: An African Fable. MacMillan, Eric G., illus. 2nd ed. 2003. lib. bdg. 5.00 *(978-0-9729698-0-2(2))* Maninge Mali.

Madonna, Lenae. Lost & Found. Conde, Manuel, illus. 2012. 38p. (J). 16.95 *(978-1-60131-115-3(X)*, Castlebridge Bks.) Big Tent Bks.

Maier, Inger M. When Lizzie Was Afraid: Of Trying New Things. Candon, Jennifer, illus. 2004. 32p. (J). 14.95 *(978-1-59147-170-7(2))*; pap. 9.95 *(978-1-59147-171-4(0))* American Psychological Assn. (Magination Pr.).

Maner, Dee. Artie: The First Artificial Christmas Tree. 2016. (ENG.). 32p. (J). 19.95 *(978-1-942945-28-4(0)*, 9781942945284) Bright Sky Pr.

Mangum, Kay Lynn. When the Bough Breaks. 2007. 352p. (YA). pap. 15.95 *(978-1-59038-748-1(1))* Deseret Bk. Co.

Mann, Gerre. Cora the Caterpillar. Brody, Joyce, illus. 2012. 20p. pap. 14.99 *(978-1-61170-088-6(4))* Robertson Publishing.

Marchese, Stephen, illus. The Flights of Marceau: Week Two. 2007. (ENG.). 60p. (J). 16.95 *(978-0-9797495-1-3(4))* Majestic Eagle Publishing.

Marino, Peter. Dough Boy. 2007. (ENG.). 176p. (YA). (gr. 7-12). pap. 6.95 *(978-0-8234-2096-4(5))* Holiday Hse., Inc.

Mauzy, Barbara E. Don't Be a Schwoe: Fitness, 1 vol. Stuhmer, Bob, illus. 2013. (ENG.). 64p. (J). 16.99 *(978-0-7643-4295-0(9)*, 9780764342950) Schiffer Publishing, Ltd.

McBratney, Sam. You're All My Favorites. Jeram, Anita, illus. 2008. (ENG.). 32p. (J). (gr. k-k). bds. 7.99 *(978-0-7636-4297-6(5))* Candlewick Pr.

McVay, Kinsy. Just Line Around. 2009. 52p. pap. 18.50 *(978-1-60860-423-4(3)*, Eloquent Bks.) Strategic Book Publishing & Rights Agency (SBPRA).

Michelle, Nelson-Schmidt. Jonathan James & Whatif Monster. Michelle, Nelson-Schmidt, illus. 2012. (ENG., Illus.). (J). 12.99 *(978-1-61067-131-6(7))* Kane Miller.

Michie, Brandon J. Andie the Ant: Animal Lessons. 2012. 16p. pap. 14.97 *(978-1-4670-2585-0(2))* AuthorHouse.

Mills, Joyce C. Little Tree: A Story for Children with Serious Medical Illness. Sebern, Brian, illus. 2nd ed. 2003. 32p. (J). pap. 9.95 *(978-1-59147-042-7(0))*; 14.95 *(978-1-59147-041-0(2))* American Psychological Assn. (Magination Pr.).

Mitchell, P. S. I Don't Wanna Be Me. 2013. 48p. 15.95 *(978-0-615-80354-8(7))* Mitchell, P. S.

Moger, Susan. Of Better Blood. 2016. (ENG.). 304p. (YA). (gr. 8-12). 16.99 *(978-0-8075-4774-8(3))* Whitman, Albert & Co.

Montgomery, L. M. Mistress Pat: From the Author of Anne of Green Gables. 2014. (ENG.). 384p. (YA). (gr. 5-12). pap. 8.99 *(978-1-4022-8927-9(8))* Sourcebooks, Inc.

Moore, Stephanie Perry. Icing on the Cake. 2014. (Sharp Sisters Ser.: 5). (ENG.). 160p. (YA). (gr. 6-12). pap. 7.95 *(978-1-4677-4487-4(5)*, Darby Creek); lib. bdg. 27.93 *(978-1-4677-3728-9(3))* Lerner Publishing Group.

Morgan, Dennis W. Stubby the Giraffe Who Wouldn't Take Chances. 2013. 40p. pap. 14.99 *(978-0-9892295-0-0(5))* Dreamstreet Studios, Inc. (A Div. of DSMV Industries, Inc.).

Mosier, Paul. Train I Ride. 2017. 192p. (J). (gr. 3-7). 16.99 *(978-0-06-245573-4(7))* HarperCollins Pubs.

Ms. Sue. Where Is Your Name? Ducy, George, illus. 2009. 24p. pap. 24.95 *(978-1-60672-711-9(7))* America Star Bks.

Mucklow, Hope. Rojo the Baby Red Panda at the Zoo: An Allegory about Self-Worth Through a Red Panda & Giant Panda Comparison. 2014. (ENG., Illus.). 32p. (J). (gr. -1-3). 14.95 *(978-1-62086-593-4(9))* Mascot Bks., Inc.

Murcray, Rod. Tuttle Stories. McDaniel, Rick, illus. 2012. 40p. pap. 14.95 *(978-1-61897-654-3(0)*, Strategic Bk. Publishing) Strategic Book Publishing & Rights Agency (SBPRA).

Murdoch, Patricia. Exposure, 1 vol. 2006. (Orca Soundings Ser.). (ENG.). 128p. (YA). (gr. 8-12). per. 9.95 *(978-1-55143-493-3(8))* Orca Bk. Pubs. USA.

Murphy, Julie. Dumplin. (YA). (gr. 8). 2017. 400p. pap. 9.99 *(978-0-06-232719-2(4))* 2015. (ENG.). 384p. 17.99 *(978-0-06-232718-5(6))* HarperCollins Pubs.

—Dumplin. 2017. (YA). lib. bdg. 20.85 ***(978-0-606-39647-9(0))*** Turtleback Bks.

Murray, Fisher C & Murray, Colleen O. One & Only Bernadette P. McMull. 2009. (ENG.). 32p. pap. 10.95 *(978-1-933916-52-1(4)*, Ferne Pr.) Nelson Publishing & Marketing.

Myers, Lily. This Impossible Light. 2017. (ENG.). 352p. (YA). (gr. 7). 17.99 *(978-0-399-17372-1(2)*, Philomel Bks.) Penguin Young Readers Group.

Mystic. Talon Hawke: A Journey Through Darkness. 2007. 228p. per. 15.95 *(978-0-595-46386-2(X))* iUniverse, Inc.

Nanette. The Black Alligator. 2004. (Life on Granny's Farm Ser.). (J). 12.95 *(978-0-9741269-3-7(4))* St. Bernard Publishing, LLC.

Naylor, Phyllis Reynolds. I Like Him, He Likes Her: Alice Alone; Simply Alice; Patiently Alice. 2010. (Alice Ser.). (ENG.). 640p. (YA). (gr. 7). pap. 12.99 *(978-1-4424-0978-1(9)*, Atheneum Bks. for Young Readers) Simon & Schuster Children's Publishing.

Nelson, Jacob. And Then There Was Jake. 2012. (ENG.). (YA). pap. *(978-1-4675-4158-9(3))* Independent Pub.

Nelson-Schmidt, Michelle. Jonathan James & the Whatif Monster. Nelson-Schmidt, Michelle, illus. 2013. (ENG., Illus.). 32p. (J). pap. 6.99 *(978-1-61067-118-7(X))* Kane Miller.

—Jonathan James & the Whatif Monster. 2013. (ENG., Illus.). (J). 26.99 *(978-1-61067-194-1(5))* Kane Miller.

Newman, Patrice Tomasetti. Where Oh Where? It's in My Hair! 2012. 26p. 24.95 *(978-1-4626-6284-5(6))* America Star Bks.

Nolan, Lucy & Nolan. Jack Quack, 1 vol. Wesson, Andrea, illus. 2003. (ENG.). 32p. (J). (gr. k-3). pap. 5.95 *(978-0-7614-5153-2(6))* Marshall Cavendish Corp.

Oates, Joyce Carol. Two or Three Things I Forgot to Tell You. (ENG.). (YA). (gr. 9). 2013. 304p. pap. 9.99 *(978-0-06-211048-0(9))* 2012. 288p. 17.99 *(978-0-06-211047-3(0))* HarperCollins Pubs. (HarperTeen).

Ostrovski, Emil. Away We Go. 2016. 272p. (YA). (gr. 9). 17.99 *(978-0-06-223855-9(8)*, Greenwillow Bks.) HarperCollins Pubs.

Owens, Connie S. I know I am Special! 2003. pap. 5.99 *(978-1-59317-010-3(6))* Warner Pr., Inc.

Paige, D. M. Going to Press. (Opportunity Ser.). (ENG.). 104p. (YA). (gr. 6-12). 2015. 34.65 *(978-1-4677-6016-4(1)*, Lerner Digital) 2013. pap. 7.95 *(978-1-4677-1495-2(X)*, Darby Creek) 2013. lib. bdg. 27.93 *(978-1-4677-1373-3(2)*, Darby Creek) Lerner Publishing Group.

Paley, Sasha & Greenwald, Lisa. Huge. 2007. (ENG.). 272p. (YA). (gr. 9-12). 15.99 *(978-1-4169-3517-9(7)*, Simon & Schuster Bks. For Young Readers) Simon & Schuster Bks. For Young Readers.

Parr, Todd. Be Who You Are! 2016. (ENG., Illus.). 32p. (J). (gr. -1-1). 17.99 *(978-0-316-26523-2(3))* Little, Brown Bks. for Young Readers.

—It's Okay to Be Different. 2009. (ENG., Illus.). 32p. (J). (gr. -1-1). pap. 8.00 *(978-0-316-04347-2(8))* Little Brown & Co.

—It's Okay to Make Mistakes. 2014. (ENG., Illus.). 32p. (J). (gr. -1-1). 17.99 *(978-0-316-23053-7(7))* Little, Brown Bks. for Young Readers.

Patel, Sonia. Rani Patel in Full Effect. 2016. (ENG.). 224p. (J). (gr. 6). 16.95 *(978-1-941026-49-6(4))* Cinco Puntos Pr.

Pearce, Jackson. As You Wish. (ENG.). 304p. (YA). (gr. 8). 2010. pap. 8.99 *(978-0-06-166154-9(6))* 2009. 16.99 *(978-0-06-166152-5(X))* HarperCollins Pubs. (HarperTeen).

Penn, Audrey. A Kiss Goodbye. Gibson, Barbara Leonard, illus. 2007. (Kissing Hand Ser.). (ENG.). 32p. (J). (gr. -1-3). 16.95 *(978-1-933718-04-0(8))* Tanglewood Pr.

Penn, Audrey & Cosgrove, Stephen. Sassafras. Harper, Ruth E. & James, Robin, illus. 2006. (ENG.). 32p. (J). (gr. -1-3). 16.95 *(978-1-933718-03-3(X))* Tanglewood Pr.

Phillips, Dee. Mirror, 1 vol. 2014. (Right Now! Ser.). (ENG.). 48p. (YA). (gr. 9-12). pap. 8.95 *(978-1-62250-879-2(3))* Saddleback Educational Publishing, Inc.

Pilling, Ann. The Year of the Worm. 172p. (J). (gr. 4-7). pap. 7.50 *(978-0-7459-4294-0(6)*, Lion Books) Lion Hudson PLC GBR. Dist: Trafalgar Square Publishing.

Plummer, Deborah. The Adventures of the Little Tin Tortoise: A Self-Esteem Story with Activities for Teachers, Parents & Carers. Serrurier, Jane, illus. 2005. (ENG.). 144p. (J). per. 32.95 *(978-1-84310-406-3(7)*, 4496) Kingsley, Jessica Pubs. GBR. Dist: Macmillan Distribution Ltd.

Pokeberry, P. J. The Huckenpuck Papers: The Tales of a Family's Secret & a Young Girls Search for Self-Esteem. 2003. (Illus.). 87p. (J). pap. 8.95 *(978-0-943962-03-0(X))* Viewpoint Pr.

Polacco, Patricia. The Junkyard Wonders. Polacco, Patricia, illus. 2010. (ENG., Illus.). 48p. (J). (gr. 1-4). 17.99 *(978-0-399-25078-1(6)*, Philomel Bks.) Penguin Young Readers Group.

Poland, Pitch & Poland, Inglan. Lost & Found. Rose, Drew, illus. 2013. 30p. (J). *(978-0-9853430-0-2(1))* Little P Pr. Co.

Pressler, Mirjam. Let Sleeping Dogs Lie. Macki, Erik J., tr. from GER. 2007. (ENG.). 208p. (J). (gr. 9-12). 16.95 *(978-1-932425-84-0(5)*, Front Street) Boyds Mills Pr.

Provenzano, Stella Marie. How Rusty Rooster Found His Do. 2008. 16p. per. 24.95 *(978-1-4241-9362-2(1))* America Star Bks.

Pukac, Michael & Stephen, Marchesi, illus. The Flights of Marceau: Week Three. 2008. (ENG.). 64p. (J). 16.95 *(978-0-9797495-2-0(2))* Majestic Eagle Publishing.

Pulley, Kelly. Ten Unusual Features of Lulu McDunn. Pulley, Kelly, illus. 2010. (Illus.). 32p. (J). (gr. -1). 16.95 *(978-0-9820812-7-3(8)*, Frog Legs Ink) Gauthier Pubns. Inc.

Rainey. School Is Cool. Huggens, Karin, illus. 2004. (J). *(978-0-9666199-9-7(4))* DreamDog Pr.

Rankin, Heather & Rankin, Heather. All It Takes Is One Friend. 2012. 46p. pap. *(978-0-9878945-0-2(1))* Our Farm Bks.

Rayburn, Tricia. Maggie Bean Stays Afloat. 2008. (ENG.). 320p. (J). (gr. 4-8). pap. 6.99 *(978-1-4169-3347-2(6)*, Aladdin) Simon & Schuster Children's Publishing.

—The Melting of Maggie Bean. 2007. (ENG.). 256p. (J). (gr. 4-8). pap. 6.99 *(978-1-4169-3348-9(4)*, Aladdin) Simon & Schuster Children's Publishing.

Redmond, Valerie. Emma & the African Wishing Bead. Victoria, Kirton, illus. 2013. 28p. pap. 13.95 *(978-1-61244-115-3(7))* Halo Publishing International.

Reed, Amy. Beautiful. 2010. (ENG.). 256p. (YA). (gr. 9). pap. 10.99 *(978-1-4169-7831-2(3)*, Simon Pulse) Simon Pulse.

Reed, Amy Lynn. Beautiful. 2009. (ENG.). 240p. (YA). (gr. 9-18). 16.99 *(978-1-4169-7830-5(5)*, Simon Pulse) Simon Pulse.

Reisfeld, Randi. Rehab. 2008. (ENG.). 256p. (YA). (gr. 9-18). pap. 8.99 *(978-1-4169-6121-5(6)*, Simon Pulse) Simon Pulse.

Reynolds, Cynthia Furlong. Grammie's Secret Cupboard. Dodson, Bert, illus. 2007. 32p. (J). (gr. -1-3). 17.95 *(978-1-58726-310-1(6)*, Mitten Pr.) Ann Arbor Editions LLC.

Richards, Arlene. That's Bingzy! Busy Building Self-Esteem. Zimmerman, Louis, illus. 2007. 32p. (J). (gr. -1-3). 19.95 incl. audio compact disk *(978-0-9794323-4-7(0))* Bing Note, Inc.

Richardson, Charisse K. & Richardson, Charisse. The Real Lucky Charm. Velasquez, Eric, illus. 2005. (ENG.). 80p. (J). (gr. 2-5). 5.99 *(978-0-14-240431-7(4)*, Puffin Books) Penguin Young Readers Group.

Richmond, Marianne. Hooray for You! A Celebration Of "You-Ness" 2015. (Marianne Richmond Ser.: 0). (ENG.). 24p. (J). (-2). bds. 7.99 *(978-1-4926-1555-2(2))* Sourcebooks, Inc.

Robinson, Gary. Tribal Journey. 2013. (YA). 111p. *(978-1-939053-87-9(0))*; (ENG.). 120p. pap. 9.95 *(978-1-939053-01-5(3)*, 7th Generation) Book Publishing Co.

Rodriguez, Grisell. Chaka the Cow. 2010. 32p. pap. 13.99 *(978-1-60844-153-2(9))* Dog Ear Publishing, LLC.

Rollins, Danielle. Breaking. 2017. (ENG.). 304p. (YA). 17.99 *(978-1-61963-740-5(5)*, 9781619637405, Bloomsbury USA Childrens) Bloomsbury Publishing USA.

Roy, Wendy. Kelly Confident Shows You Why... It's POWERFUL to be a GIRL! It's POWERFUL to be a GIRL! 2012. (ENG.). 34p. (J). pap. 10.95 *(978-0-615-59502-3(2))* Roy, Wendy.

Salter, Sydney. My Big Nose & Other Natural Disasters. 2009. (ENG., Illus.). 352p. (J). (gr. 7-18). pap. 19.95 *(978-0-15-206643-7(8))* Houghton Mifflin Harcourt Publishing Co.

Salvatus, Mark & Olizon-Chikiamco, Norma. Pan de Sal Saves the Day: An Award-Winning ChildrenAEs Story from the Philippines [New Bilingual English & Tagalog Edition]. 2017. (ENG., Illus.). 28p. (J). (gr. -1-6). pap. 8.95 *(978-0-8048-4754-4(1))* Tuttle Publishing.

Samuels, Arthur. Old Flames: Teen Bullies & Prep School Cruelty. 2013. 238p. pap. 14.00 *(978-0-9882394-4-9(2))* Dr. Joyce STARR Publishing.

Santomero, Angela C., adapted by. You Are Special, Daniel Tiger! 2014. (Daniel Tiger's Neighborhood Ser.). (ENG., Illus.). 26p. (J). (gr. -1-2). 12.99 *(978-1-4814-1915-4(3)*, Simon Spotlight) Simon Spotlight.

Schraff, Anne. Outrunning the Darkness, 1 vol. unabr. ed. 2010. (Urban Underground Ser.). (ENG.). 191p. (YA). (gr. 9-12). pap. 9.95 *(978-1-61651-000-8(5))* Saddleback Educational Publishing, Inc.

—To Be Somebody. 2008. (Passages Ser.). 120p. (J). (gr. 4-6). lib. bdg. 13.95 *(978-0-7569-8390-1(8))* Perfection Learning Corp.

—To Catch a Dream, 1 vol. unabr. ed. 2011. (Urban Underground Ser.). (ENG.). 198p. (YA). (gr. 9-12). pap. 9.95 *(978-1-61651-269-9(5))* Saddleback Educational Publishing, Inc.

Schraff, Anne E. Hurting Time. 2012. (Urban Underground — Cesar Chavez High School Ser.: 27). (YA). lib. bdg. 20.80 *(978-0-606-26597-3(X)*, Turtleback) Turtleback Bks.

Serluca-Foster, Rosemary. Genevieve's Gift: A Child's Joyful Tale of Connecting with Her Intuitive Heart. 2007. (ENG.). 32p. pap. 11.99 *(978-1-4196-7321-4(1))* CreateSpace Independent Publishing Platform.

Sesame Workshop. Just One You! 2015. (Sesame Street Scribbles Elmo Ser.: 0). (ENG.). 32p. (J). (-3). 10.99 *(978-1-4022-9735-9(1)*, Sourcebooks Jabberwocky) Sourcebooks, Inc.

Small, Tanya. What You Say Is What You Are. 2007. pap. 7.50 *(978-0-9705090-1-7(4))* MorningGlory Publishing.

Smillie, Bryan. A Time for Evron. Rooth, Mike, illus. 2004. 190p. 11.95 *(978-0-9689516-0-6(0))* Shabrya Publishing CAN. Dist: Hushion Hse. Publishing, Ltd.

Smith, Bryan. Is There an App for That? Wish, Katia, illus. 2015. (ENG.). 32p. (J). pap. 10.95 *(978-1-934490-74-7(1))* Boys Town Pr.

Smith, Bryan. Mindset Matters. Griffin, Lisa, illus. 2017. (Without Limits Ser.: 2). (ENG.). 32p. (J). (gr. k-5). pap. 10.95 ***(978-1-944882-12-9(X))*** Boys Town Pr.

Smith, M. Jane. The First Fry Bread: A Gitxsan Story. Wheeler, Jordan, ed. Mowatt, Ken N., illus. 2012. 32p. pap. (978-1-4602-0226-5(0)) FriesenPress.

Smith, Suzanne C. Peter Cottontail & the Easter Bunny Imposter. Brittingham, Geoffrey, illus. 24p. (J). pap. 3.25 (978-0-8249-5372-0(X), Ideal Pubns.) Worthy Publishing.

Sohaili, Monira. Stories from Earth & Beyond: Enchanting & Inspirational Stories. 2006. (Illus.). 94p. per. 9.95 (978-1-60002-044-5(5), 2833) Mountain Valley Publishing, LLC.

Sommer, Carl. The Eagle & the Chickens. Noé, illus. 2016. (J). (978-1-57537-945-6(7)) Advance Publishing, Inc.

—The Ugly Princess. Martinez, Jorge, illus. 2016. 32p. (J). (978-1-57537-948-7(1)) Advance Publishing, Inc.

Sones, Sonya. What My Girlfriend Doesn't Know. 2011. 9.68 (978-0-7848-3389-6(3), Everbind) Marco Bk. Co.

—What My Girlfriend Doesn't Know. 2013. (ENG., Illus.). 320p. (YA). (gr. 7). pap. 9.99 (978-1-4424-9384-1(4), Simon & Schuster Bks. For Young Readers) Simon & Schuster Bks. For Young Readers.

Spencer, Mignon. I'm Living My Dream: An inspirationsl Rhyme for all Ages in English & Spanish. Mack, Travis, illus. 2008.Tr. of Hago mi sueno Realidad. (ENG & SPA.). 32p. (J). 12.99 (978-0-9763871-2-1(3)) Solomon's Bks.

Spero, Mitch & Spero, Maria. Florida the Turtle: Who Thinks He's a Dog Finds His Feelings. 2012. 28p. pap. 21.99 (978-1-4771-0184-1(5)) Xlibris Corp.

Springer, Nancy. Somebody. 2009. (ENG.). 128p. (YA). (gr. 7-18). 16.95 (978-0-8234-2099-5(X)) Holiday Hse., Inc.

Starcher, Michele. The Ornery Angel. 2005. 68p. per. 13.95 (978-1-59858-039-6(6)) Dog Ear Publishing, LLC.

Stevenson, Robin. Out of Order, 1 vol. 2007. (ENG.). 232p. (YA). (gr. 7-12). per. 9.95 (978-1-55143-693-7(0)) Orca Bk. Pubs. USA.

Stoehr, Shelley. Crosses. 2003. 161p. (YA). pap. 13.95 (978-0-595-26952-5(4), Writers Club Pr.) iUniverse, Inc.

Storti, Jill. Keiko the Koala. 2011. 24p. (gr. -1 — 1). pap. 12.95 (978-1-4567-3110-6(6)) AuthorHouse.

Strasnick, Lauren. Nothing Like You. 2010. (ENG.). 240p. (YA). (gr. 9). pap. 8.99 (978-1-4169-8265-4(5), Simon Pulse) Simon Pulse.

StVil, Lola. Girls Like Me. 2016. (ENG.). 320p. (YA). (gr. 7). 17.99 (978-0-544-70674-3(9), HMH Books For Young Readers) Houghton Mifflin Harcourt Publishing Co.

Sue. The Whinermans. 2010. 72p. (gr. 1-2). pap. 8.95 (978-1-4502-4998-0(1)) iUniverse, Inc.

Sunderland, Margot & Hancock, Nicky. Ruby & the Rubbish Bin. Armstrong, Nicky, tr. Armstrong, Nicky, illus. 2017. (Helping Children with Feelings Ser.). (ENG.). 32p. (C). pap. 15.95 (978-0-86388-462-7(8), Y329066, Routledge) Taylor & Francis Group GBR. Dist: Taylor & Francis Group.

Supplee, Suzanne. Artichoke's Heart. 2009. (ENG.). 288p. (YA). (gr. 7-18). 8.99 (978-0-14-241427-9(1), Speak) Penguin Young Readers Group.

Tanaka, Usa. Give Me That! Tanaka, Usa, illus. 2007. (ENG., Illus.). 32p. (J). 15.95 (978-0-9741319-0-0(3)) 4N Publishing LLC.

Taylor, Carol K. Behind the Fence. 2009. 24p. pap. 12.99 (978-1-4389-4352-7(0)) AuthorHouse.

Taylor, Helen. Emu Can't Fly. Gilles-Gray, Carolyn, illus. 2013. 24p. pap. (978-1-921883-39-2(1), MBS Pr.) Pick-a-Woo Woo Pubs.

Tennant, Kim. Thin Club. 2007. 52p. per. 10.00 (978-1-4257-2619-5(4)) Xlibris Corp.

Terrill Holdman, Shirley. The Adventures of Giggles & Owen: Adventure Three - Unlimited Pawsibilities. Leeds, Marjorie M., illus. 2013. 50p. pap. 17.95 (978-1-4575-2175-1(X)) Dog Ear Publishing, LLC.

Thomas, E. J. Brooster Rooster: King of the Farmyard, 1 vol. 2009. 22p. pap. 24.95 (978-1-60813-936-1(0)) America Star Bks.

Thompson, Kay. Eloise's What I Absolutely Love Love Love. 2005. (Eloise Ser.). (ENG., Illus.). 32p. (J). 12.99 (978-0-689-84965-7(6), Simon & Schuster Bks. For Young Readers) Simon & Schuster Bks. For Young Readers.

Thurman, Carol. Molly's Field of Dreams. 2011. 24p. pap. 11.99 (978-1-4567-3101-4(7)) AuthorHouse.

Tillman, Nancy. The Crown on Your Head. Tillman, Nancy, illus. (ENG., Illus.). (J). (gr. -1-3). 2014. 34p. 7.99 (978-1-250-04045-9(0), 9781250040459) 2011. 32p. 17.99 (978-0-312-64521-2(X), 9780312645212) Feiwel & Friends.

—On the Night You Were Born. Tillman, Nancy, illus. 2006. (ENG., Illus.). 32p. (J). (gr. -1 — 1). 16.95 (978-0-312-34606-5(9), 9780312346065) Feiwel & Friends.

—You're Here for a Reason. 2015. (ENG., Illus.). 32p. (J). (gr. -1-3). 17.99 (978-1-250-05626-9(8), 9781250056269) Feiwel & Friends.

Treasure Island: A Growing Field Adventure. 2011. (Illus.). 64p. (J). 16.95 (978-0-9770391-4-2(5)) Growing Field Bks.

Vail, Rachel. Gorgeous. (Avery Sisters Trilogy Ser.: 2). (ENG.). (YA). (gr. 8). 2010. 304p. pap. 9.99 (978-0-06-089048-3(7)) 2009. 288p. 16.99 (978-0-06-089046-9(0)) HarperCollins Pubs.

—What Are Friends For? 2014. (Friendship Ring Ser.: 4). (ENG.). 176p. (J). (gr. 5). pap. 7.99 (978-0-14-751121-8(6), Puffin Books) Penguin Young Readers Group.

Vawter, Vince. Paperboy. 2013. (ENG.). 240p. (J). (gr. 5). 16.99 (978-0-385-74244-3(4)); lib. bdg. 19.99 (978-0-375-99058-8(5)) Random Hse. Children's Bks. (Delacorte Bks. for Young Readers).

Viknesh, R. My Fantasy Your Treat. 2012. 32p. pap. 28.55 (978-1-4669-2733-9(X)) Trafford Publishing.

Vivian, Siobhan. The List. (ENG.). 336p. (J). (gr. 9). 2014. pap. 9.99 (978-0-545-16918-9(6), Scholastic Paperbacks) 2012. 17.99 (978-0-545-16917-2(8), PUSH) Scholastic, Inc.

Wagele, Elizabeth. Finding the Birthday Cake: Helping Children Raise Their Self-Esteem. Wagele, Elizabeth, illus. 2007. (ENG., Illus.). 48p. (J). (gr. k-4). per. 8.95 (978-0-88282-277-8(2)) New Horizon Pr. Pubs., Inc.

Walton, K. M. Cracked. 2012. (ENG.). (YA). (gr. 9). 336p. pap. 11.99 (978-1-4424-2917-8(8)); 320p. 16.99 (978-1-4424-2916-1(X)) Simon Pulse. (Simon Pulse).

—Empty. 2013. (ENG., (YA). (gr. 9). Illus.). 272p. pap. 10.99 (978-1-4424-5358-6(3)); 256p. 16.99 (978-1-4424-5359-3(1)) Simon Pulse. (Simon Pulse).

Webster, Wendy. Magicus Perfecticum. 2009. (Illus.). 60p. pap. 11.49 (978-1-4490-0765-2(1)) AuthorHouse.

Weeks, Sarah. I'm a Pig. Berry, Holly, illus. 2005. 32p. (J). (gr. -1-2). lib. bdg. 16.89 (978-0-06-074344-4(1), Geringer, Laura Book) HarperCollins Pubs.

—Oggie Cooder. 2009. (Oggie Cooder Ser.: Vol. 1). (ENG.). 176p. (J). (gr. 2-5). 5.99 (978-0-439-92794-9(3), Scholastic Paperbacks) Scholastic, Inc.

Weinberger, Kimberly. Dolphin's Big Leap. Ziss, Debra, illus. 2003. (Hello Reader! Ser.). 30p. (J). (978-0-439-44159-9(5)) Scholastic, Inc.

Weiner, Marcella Bakur & Neimark, Jill. I Want Your Moo: A Story for Children about Self-Esteem. Adinolfi, JoAnn, illus. 2nd ed. 2009. 32p. (J). (gr. -1-3). 14.95 (978-1-4338-0542-4(1)); pap. 9.95 (978-1-4338-0552-3(9)) American Psychological Assn. (Magination Pr.).

Werlin, Nancy. Extraordinary. 2011. (ENG.). 416p. (YA). (gr. 7-18). 9.99 (978-0-14-241974-8(5), Speak) Penguin Young Readers Group.

What Do You See When You Look at Me? 2003. (J). 12.00 (978-0-9724442-7-9(0)) LightHouse Pr.

White, Tracy. How I Made It to Eighteen: A Mostly True Story. White, Tracy, illus. 2010. (ENG., Illus.). 160p. (YA). (gr. 9-13). 23.99 (978-1-59643-454-7(6), 9781596434547) Roaring Brook Pr.

Wild, Margaret. Fox. Brooks, Ron, illus. 2006. (ENG.). 32p. (J). (gr. 1). pap. 7.99 (978-1-933605-15-9(4)) Kane Miller.

Wilkerson, L. Kobie, 3rd, reader. Fred & Mary. 2008. (Illus.). 32p. (J). 24.95 incl. DVD, audio compact disk (978-0-9796679-0-9(9)) Love II Learn Bks.

Wilson, Jacqueline. Cookie. Sharratt, Nick, illus. 2010. (ENG.). 352p. (J). (gr. 4-7). pap. 11.99 (978-0-312-64290-7(3), 9780312642907) Square Fish.

Wilson, Troy. Perfect Man, 1 vol. Griffiths, Dean, illus. 2005. (ENG.). 32p. (J). (gr. -1-3). per. 9.95 (978-1-55143-435-3(0)) Orca Bk. Pubs. USA.

Witherow, Wendy. Miranda's Makeover. Pulley, Kelly, illus. 2007. 93p. (J). (978-1-934306-11-6(8)) Mission City Pr., Inc.

Withers, Pam. Breathless, 1 vol. 2005. (Orca Soundings Ser.). (ENG.). 128p. (YA). (gr. 8-12). per. 9.95 (978-1-55143-480-3(6)) Orca Bk. Pubs. USA.

Woik, Julie. The Life & Times of Lilly the Lash: The Garden Gathering. Tobin, Marc, illus. 2009. (ENG.). 48p. (J). 19.95 (978-0-9663335-7-2(8)) Snow In Sarasota Publishing.

Wright-McAdoo, Joyce & Wright-Mcadoo, Joyce. Zimb: Believe. 2009. (Illus.). 28p. pap. 15.99 (978-1-4415-8051-1(4)) Xlibris Corp.

Yamada, Kobi. What Do You Do with an Idea? Besom, Mae, illus. 2014. (ENG.). 36p. (J). (gr. -1-3). 16.95 (978-1-938298-07-3(1)) Compendium, Inc., Publishing & Communications.

Yep, Laurence. When the Circus Came to Town. Wang, Suling, illus. 2004. 112p. (J). (gr. 3-5). 13.65 (978-0-7569-2969-5(5)) Perfection Learning Corp.

Young, Karen Romano. Cobwebs. 400p. 2005. (ENG.). (YA). pap. 7.99 (978-0-06-441028-1(5), HarperTeen) 2004. (J). (gr. 7-18). lib. bdg. 16.89 (978-0-06-029762-6(X)) HarperCollins Pubs.

Zarr, Sara. Story of a Girl. 2008. (ENG.). 224p. (YA). (gr. 7-17). per. 10.99 (978-0-316-01454-0(0)) Little, Brown Bks. for Young Readers.

Zevgolis, Irene, illus. The Dreamer & the Moon: An Inspirational Story with a Ballet Theme. 2008. (J). (978-0-615-17590-4(2)) E-City Publishing.

Zoehfeld, Kathleen Weidner & Rey, H. A. Curious You on Your Way! 2008. (Curious George Ser.). (ENG., Illus.). 32p. (J). (gr. -1-3). 12.95 (978-0-618-91975-8(9)) Houghton Mifflin Harcourt Publishing Co.

Zusak, Markus. Cartas Cruzadas. 2012. (Vintage Espanol Ser.). (SPA.). 384p. (YA). (gr. 7). pap. 14.95 (978-0-307-95145-8(6), Vintage Espanol) Knopf Doubleday Publishing Group.

—I Am the Messenger. 2009. 10.52 (978-0-7848-2491-7(6), Everbind) Marco Bk. Co.

—I Am the Messenger. 2006. 21.00 (978-0-7569-7034-5(2)) Perfection Learning Corp.

—I Am the Messenger. (ENG.). 368p. (YA). (gr. 7). 2005. 16.95 (978-0-375-83099-0(5)) 2006. (Illus.). reprint ed. pap. 10.99 (978-0-375-83667-1(5)) Random Hse. Children's Bks. (Knopf Bks. for Young Readers).

—I Am the Messenger. (J). 2007. 1.25 (978-1-4281-2308-3(3)) 2007. 77.75 (978-1-4281-2309-0(1)) 2006. 74.75 (978-1-4281-2311-3(3)) Recorded Bks., Inc.

SELF-GOVERNMENT

see Democracy

SELF-INSTRUCTION

see Self-Culture

SELF-MUTILATION

Allman, Toney. Self-Harm. 2017. (Hot Topics Ser.). 112p. (YA). (gr. 7-7). lib. bdg. 39.40 **(978-1-5345-6017-8(3)**, Lucent Pr.) Greenhaven Publishing LLC.

Eagen, Rachel. Cutting & Self-Injury. 2010. (ENG.). 48p. (J). pap. (978-0-7787-2137-6(X)); lib. bdg. (978-0-7787-2130-7(2)) Crabtree Publishing Co.

Parks, Peggy J. Self-Injury Disorder. 2010. (Compact Research Ser.). (YA). (gr. 7-12). 26.95 (978-1-60152-112-5(X)) ReferencePoint Pr., Inc.

—Teens, Cuttung, & Self-Injury. 2015. (ENG., Illus.). 96p. (J). lib. bdg. (978-1-60152-770-7(5)) ReferencePoint Pr., Inc.

Pomere, Jonas. Frequently Asked Questions about Self Mutilation & Cutting. 2009. (FAQ: Teen Life Ser.). 64p. (gr. 5-6). 58.50 (978-1-61512-587-6(6)) Rosen Publishing Group, Inc., The.

Shapiro, Lawrence E. Stopping the Pain: A Workbook for Teens Who Cut & Self-Injure. 2008. (Instant Help Ser.). (ENG., Illus.). 168p. (YA). (gr. 6-12). pap. 16.95 (978-1-57224-602-7(2), Instant Help Books) New Harbinger Pubns.

Shea, John M. Self-Injury & Cutting: Stopping the Pain. 2013. (Helpline: Teen Issues & Answers Ser.). (ENG., Illus.). 80p. (YA). (gr. 7-12). lib. bdg. 33.25 (978-1-4488-9448-2(4), Rosen Classroom) Rosen Publishing Group, Inc., The.

Williams, Mary E. Self-Injury. 2013. (Introducing Issues with Opposing Viewpoints Ser.). (ENG., Illus.). 144p. (gr. 7-10). lib. bdg. 42.00 (978-0-7377-6280-8(2), Greenhaven Pr., Inc.) Cengage Gale.

—Self-Mutilation. 2008. (Introducing Issues with Opposing Viewpoints Ser.). (ENG., Illus.). 112-144p. (gr. 7-10). 36.95 (978-0-7377-4173-5(2), Greenhaven Pr., Inc.) Cengage Gale.

Winkler, Kathleen. Cutting & Self-Mutilation: When Teens Injure Themselves. 2003. (Teen Issues Ser.). (Illus.). 64p. (YA). (gr. 6-12). lib. bdg. 22.60 (978-0-7660-1956-0(X)) Enslow Pubs., Inc.

SELF-MUTILATION—FICTION

Dzidrums, Christine. Cutters Don't Cry. Allison, Elizabeth, ed. Dzidrums, Joseph, photos by. 2010. (Illus.). 132p. (YA). 24.99 (978-0-9826435-2-5(7)); pap. 14.99 (978-0-9826435-1-8(9)) Creative Media Publishing.

Glasgow, Kathleen. Girl in Pieces. 2016. (ENG.). 416p. (YA). (gr. 9). lib. bdg. 21.99 (978-1-101-93473-9(5), Delacorte Pr.) Random House Publishing Group.

—Girl in Pieces. 2016. (ENG.). 416p. (YA). (gr. 9). 18.99 (978-1-101-93471-5(9), Delacorte Pr.) Random Hse. Children's Bks.

Hoban, Julia. Willow. 2010. (ENG.). 336p. (YA). (gr. 9-18). 8.99 (978-0-14-241666-2(5), Speak) Penguin Young Readers Group.

Jablonski, Carla. Thicker Than Water. 2007. (ENG.). 272p. (YA). (gr. 9-12). 8.99 (978-1-59514-123-1(5), Razorbill) Penguin Young Readers Group.

Kessler, Jackie Morse. Rage. 2011. (Riders of the Apocalypse Ser.: 2). (ENG.). 240p. (YA). (gr. 7-18). pap. 9.99 (978-0-547-44528-1(8)) Houghton Mifflin Harcourt Publishing Co.

Lancett, Peter. Seeing Red, 1 vol. unabr. ed. 2012. (Cutting Edge Ser.). (ENG.). 221p. (YA). (gr. 9-12). pap. 9.95 (978-1-61651-759-5(X)) Saddleback Educational Publishing, Inc.

McCormick, Patricia. Cut. unabr. ed. 2004. 168p. (J). (gr. 7-18). pap. 36.00 incl. audio (978-0-8072-0868-7(X), LYA 320 SP, Listening Library) Random Hse. Audio Publishing Group.

—Cut. 2011. (ENG.). 176p. (J). (gr. 7-7). pap. 8.99 (978-0-545-29079-1(1), PUSH) Scholastic, Inc.

—Cut. 2011. (gr. 7-12). lib. bdg. 19.65 (978-0-613-49394-9(X), Turtleback) Turtleback Bks.

Rainfield, Cheryl. Scars. 2011. 8.67 (978-0-7848-3439-8(3), Everbind) Marco Bk. Co.

Stoehr, Shelley. Crosses. 2003. 161p. (YA). pap. 13.95 (978-0-595-26952-5(4), Writers Club Pr.) iUniverse, Inc.

White, Tracy. How I Made It to Eighteen: A Mostly True Story. White, Tracy, illus. 2010. (ENG., Illus.). 160p. (YA). (gr. 9-13). 23.99 (978-1-59643-454-7(6), 9781596434547) Roaring Brook Pr.

SELF-PERCEPTION

Adson, Patricia R. A Princess & Her Garden: A Fable of Awakening & Arrival. 2nd ed. 2011. (J). (978-0-935652-93-2(0)) Center for Applications of Psychological Type, Inc.

Apel, Melanie Ann. Let's Talk about When You Think Nobody Likes You. 2009. (Let's Talk Library). 24p. (gr. 2-3). 42.50 (978-1-60853-449-4(9), PowerKids Pr.) Rosen Publishing Group, Inc., The.

Carlson, Dale. Understand Your Self: Teen Manual for the Understanding of Oneself. 2013. (ENG., Illus.). 192p. (gr. 9-13). pap. 14.95 (978-1-884158-36-0(6), 21540f59-9618-4de6-80e4-f5fe89e31805) Team Kreskin Productions, LLC.

Conway, Celeste. Body Image & the Media. 2013. (Hot Topics in Media EBook Ser.). (ENG.). 48p. (J). pap. 15.64 (978-1-61783-782-1(2)); (gr. 3-6). lib. bdg. 32.79 (978-1-61783-732-6(6)) ABDO Publishing Co.

Espeland, Pamela. Knowing Me, Knowing You: The I-Sight Way to Understand Yourself & Others. 2004. (Illus.). 128p. (YA). (gr. 8-12). pap. 13.95 (978-1-57542-090-5(2)) Free Spirit Publishing, Inc.

Gitlin, Martin. I'm Being Targeted by a Gang. Now What? 2016. (Teen Life 411 Ser.). 00112p. (J). (gr. 7-7). 37.10 (978-1-5081-7191-1(2), Rosen Young Adult) Rosen Publishing Group, Inc., The.

Hawkins, Frank C. & Laube, Greta L. B. The Book of Bad Habits for Young (and Not So Young!) Men & Women: How to Chuck the Worst & Turn the Rest to Your Advantage. Hong, Richard, illus. 2010. (ENG.). 148p. (J). (gr. 7). pap. 12.95 (978-0-9793219-3-1(X)) Big Book Pr., LLC.

Higginbotham, Anastasia, illus. Tell Me about Sex, Grandma. 2017. (Ordinary Terrible Things Ser.). (ENG.). 64p. (J). (gr. -1-3). 17.95 (978-1-55861-419-2(2)) Feminist Pr. at The City Univ. of New York.

Kelly, Dorothy A. Developing a Sense of Self: A Workbook of Tenets & Tactics for Adolescent Girls. 2006. (Illus.). 146p. (J). pap. 29.99 (978-0-87101-366-8(5), NASW Pr.) National Assn. of Social Workers/NASW Pr.

Lazear, Jonathon. Come On, Get Happy. 2004. (ENG., Illus.). 384p. (978-0-00-717532-1(9), HarperElement) HarperCollins Pubs. Ltd.

Lindsey, Brooklyn. Confessions of a Not-So-Supermodel: Faith, Friends, & Festival Queens, 1 vol. 2008. (Invert Ser.). (ENG., Illus.). 176p. (YA). (gr. 7-14). pap. 9.99 (978-0-310-27753-8(1)) Zondervan.

Madison, Lynda. All about You Quiz Book: Discover More about Yourself & How to Be Your Best! Laskey, Shannon, illus. 2009. (ENG.). 64p. (YA). (gr. 3-18). spiral bd. 9.95 (978-1-59369-598-9(5)) American Girl Publishing, Inc.

Meister, Cari. What Can I Be? 2004. (Rookie Reader Skill Set Ser.). (ENG.). 24p. (J). (gr. k-2). pap. 4.95 (978-0-516-27810-0(X), Children's Pr.) Scholastic Library Publishing.

Mills, J. Elizabeth. Expectations for Women: Confronting Stereotypes. 2010. (Young Woman's Guide to Contemporary Issues Ser.). 112p. (YA). (gr. 9-12). lib. bdg., E-Book 63.90 (978-1-61532-907-6(2)) Rosen Publishing Group, Inc., The.

Mirriam-Goldberg, Caryn. Write Where You Are: How to Use Writing to Make Sense of Your Life: A Guide for Teens. 2004. (Illus.). 168p. (YA). (gr. 7-12). pap. 14.95 (978-1-57542-060-8(0)) Free Spirit Publishing, Inc.

Moe, Barbara. Understanding Negative Body Image. 2009. (Teen Eating Disorder Prevention Book Ser.). 192p. (gr. 7-12). 63.90 (978-1-61511-242-5(1)) Rosen Publishing Group, Inc., The.

Monchamp, Genny. God Made Wonderful Me! Kaminski, Karol, illus. 2008. 14p. (J). (gr. -1). 8.95 (978-0-8198-3108-8(5)) Pauline Bks. & Media.

Payne, Lauren Murphy. Just Because I Am: A Child's Book of Affirmation. Iwai, Melissa, illus. 2nd rev. ed. 2015. (ENG.). 36p. (J). (gr. -1-2). 14.99 (978-1-63198-051-0(3)) Free Spirit Publishing, Inc.

Strickland, Jennifer. Pretty from the Inside Out: Discover All the Ways God Made You Special. 2015. (ENG.). 128p. (J). pap. 10.99 (978-0-7369-5634-5(4)) Harvest Hse. Pubs.

Weiss, S. I. Coping with the Beauty Myth: A Guide for Real Girls. 2009. (Coping Ser.). 192p. (gr. 7-12). 63.90 (978-1-61512-014-7(9)) Rosen Publishing Group, Inc., The.

Willett, Edward. Negative Body Image. (Danger Zone: Dieting & Eating Disorders Ser.). 64p. 2009. (gr. 5-6). 55.90 (978-1-61512-125-0(0)) 2006. (Illus.). (YA). (gr. 7-12). lib. bdg. 31.95 (978-1-4042-1995-3(1)) Rosen Publishing Group, Inc., The.

Wooster, Patricia. Ignite Your Spark: Discovering Who You Are from the Inside Out. 2017. (ENG., Illus.). 224p. (J). (gr. 7). pap. 12.99 (978-1-58270-564-4(X)) Simon Pulse/Beyond Words.

SELF-PERCEPTION—FICTION

Alcott, Jessica. Even When You Lie to Me. 2015. (ENG.). 352p. (YA). (gr. 9). 17.99 (978-0-385-39116-0(1), Crown Books For Young Readers) Random Hse. Children's Bks.

Alfonsi, Alice, adapted by. Face-off. 2006. (Hannah Montana Ser.). (Illus.). 126p. (J). (gr. 3-7). 12.65 (978-0-7569-8315-4(0)) Perfection Learning Corp.

Allen, Crystal. The Laura Line. (J). (gr. 3-7). 2016. 352p. pap. 6.99 (978-0-06-249021-6(4)) 2013. (ENG.). 336p. 16.99 (978-0-06-199274-2(7)) HarperCollins Pubs.

Andrews, Julie & Hamilton, Emma Walton. The Very Fairy Princess. Davenier, Christine, illus. 2010. (Very Fairy Princess Ser.). (ENG.). 32p. (J). (gr. -1-3). 18.00 (978-0-316-04050-1(9)) Little, Brown Bks. for Young Readers.

Angelou, Maya. Cedric of Jamaica. Rockwell, Lizzy, illus. 2005. (Random House Pictureback Book Ser.). (J). (978-0-375-83269-7(6)) Random Hse., Inc.

Anonymous. Letting Ana Go. 2013. (ENG.). 304p. (YA). (gr. 9). 17.99 (978-1-4424-7223-5(5)); (Illus.). pap. 10.99 (978-1-4424-7213-6(8)) Simon Pulse. (Simon Pulse).

Auerbach, Annie. Spongebob Superstar, Vol. 5. 2004. 64p. (J). (gr. 2-5). pap. 17.00 incl. audio (978-1-4000-8628-3(0), Listening Library) Random Hse. Audio Publishing Group.

Avi. The True Confessions of Charlotte Doyle. 2012. (ENG.). 240p. (J). (gr. 3-7). pap. 6.99 (978-0-545-47711-6(5), Scholastic Paperbacks) Scholastic, Inc.

—The True Confessions of Charlotte Doyle. 2012. lib. bdg. 17.20 (978-0-606-26779-3(4), Turtleback) Turtleback Bks.

Ballard, Alexandra. What I Lost. 2017. (ENG., Illus.). 400p. (YA). 17.99 (978-0-374-30463-8(7), 9780374304638, Farrar, Straus & Giroux (BYR)) Farrar, Straus & Giroux.

Barnwell, Ysaye M. No Mirrors in My Nana's House. Saint James, Synthia, illus. 2005. (ENG.). 32p. (J). (gr. -1-3). reprint ed. 10.99 (978-0-15-205243-0(7)) Houghton Mifflin Harcourt Publishing Co.

Barson, Kelly. Charlotte Cuts It Out. 2016. (ENG.). 368p. (YA). (gr. 7). 17.99 (978-0-451-46893-2(7), Viking Books for Young Readers) Penguin Young Readers Group.

Base, Graeme. The Last King of Angkor Wat. 2014. (ENG., Illus.). 36p. (J). (gr. k-2). 17.95 (978-1-4197-1354-5(X), Abrams Bks. for Young Readers) Abrams, Inc.

Becker Holstein, Barbara. Secrets: Diary of a Gutsy Teen. 2015. (ENG.). 144p. (J). (gr. 2-7). 12.95 (978-1-62914-626-3(9), Sky Pony Pr.) Skyhorse Publishing Co., Inc.

Bencastro, Mario. A Promise to Keep. Giersbach-Rascon, Susan, tr. from SPA. 2005. 134p. (J). (gr. 3-7). pap. 9.95 (978-1-55885-457-4(6), Piñata Books) Arte Publico Pr.

Billingsley, Franny. Chime. 2011. (Playaway Young Adult Ser.). (YA). 59.99 (978-1-61707-143-0(9)) Findaway World, LLC.

—Chime. 2012. (ENG.). 384p. (YA). (gr. 7-18). 8.99 (978-0-14-242092-8(1), Speak) Penguin Young Readers Group.

Bloom, Denise. More Than a Spoonful. 2007. 28p. (J). (gr. -1-2). pap. 5.95 (978-0-9778113-2-8(8)) HeartFelt Stories LLC.

Bloom, Denise, et al. More Than a Spoonful. 2007. (Heartfelt Stories Ser.). (Illus.). 28p. (J). 12.95 (978-0-9778113-0-4(1)) HeartFelt Stories LLC.

Bolden, Tonya. Finding Family. (ENG., Illus.). 192p. (YA). (gr. 3-12). 2012. pap. 7.99 (978-1-59990-830-4(1), 9781599908304) 2010. 15.99 (978-1-59990-318-7(0), 9781599903187) Bloomsbury Publishing USA. (Bloomsbury USA Childrens).

Brian, Kate, pseud. Sweet 16. 2007. (ENG.). 288p. (YA). (gr. 7-12). pap. 9.99 (978-1-4169-0033-7(0), Simon & Schuster Bks. For Young Readers) Simon & Schuster Bks. For Young Readers.

Brightwood, Laura, illus. Look What You've Done. Brightwood, Laura, . 2007. (J). DVD (978-1-934409-03-9(0)) 3-C Institute for Social Development.

Broski, Julie. Being Me. Vigla, Vincent, illus. 2011. (Rookie Ready to Learn Ser.). 40p. (J). (ENG.). pap. 5.95 (978-0-531-26653-3(2)); (gr. -1-k). lib. bdg. 23.00 (978-0-531-26428-7(9)) Scholastic Library Publishing. (Children's Pr.).

Brown, Devin. Not Exactly Normal. 2006. 234p. (J). (gr. 4). per. 8.00 (978-0-8028-5287-8(4), Eerdmans Bks For Young Readers) Eerdmans, William B. Publishing Co.

Brown, Lisa. How to Be. Brown, Lisa, illus. 2006. (ENG., Illus.). 32p. (J). (gr. -1 — 1). 17.99 (978-0-06-054635-9(2)) HarperCollins Pubs.

Burns, Suzanne. The Moon Painters. 2003. 192p. 14.00 (978-1-894942-36-2(1)) Zumaya Pubns. LLC.

Bush, Penelope. Alice in Time. 2011. (ENG., Illus.). 208p. (YA). (gr. 7-18). 17.95 (978-0-8234-2329-3(8)) Holiday Hse., Inc.

Caletti, Deb. Honey, Baby, Sweetheart. 2008. (ENG.). 336p. (YA). (gr. 7-12). pap. 9.99 (978-1-4169-5783-6(9), Simon Pulse) Simon Pulse.

Cameron, Ann. The Secret Life of Amanda K. Woods. 2014. (ENG.). 208p. (J). (gr. 5-9). pap. 6.99 (978-1-250-04419-8(7), 9781250044198) Square Fish.

Cameron, Peter. Someday This Pain Will Be Useful to You. 2009. (ENG.). 240p. (YA). (gr. 9-13). pap. 16.00 (978-0-312-42816-7(2), 9780312428167) Picador.

Cash, M. A. Edward of Canterbury & the King of Red. Adams, Craig, illus. 2003. (J). (978-0-9772711-0-8(2)) Jama Kids.

Castellucci, Cecil. Beige. (ENG., 320p. (YA). 2009. Illus.). (gr. 9). pap. 8.99 *(978-0-7636-4232-7(0))* 2007. (Illus.). (gr. 9-18). 16.99 *(978-0-7636-3066-9(7))* 2007. 25.66 *(978-1-4287-4767-8(2))* Candlewick Pr.
Chambers, Aidan. The Toll Bridge. 2009. (ENG.). 288p. (YA). (gr. 9-17). pap. 9.95 *(978-0-8109-8358-8(3),* Amulet Bks.) Abrams, Inc.
Christopher, Matt. Center Court Sting. 2005. (Sports Classics II Ser.). 140p. (J). lib. bdg. 15.00 *(978-1-59054-749-6(7))* Fitzgerald Bks.
—Center Court Sting. l.t. ed. 2007. (New Matt Christopher Sports Library). 160p. (J). (gr. 4-6). lib. bdg. 26.60 *(978-1-59953-106-9(2))* Norwood Hse. Pr.
—Slam Dunk. 2004. (ENG., Illus.). 128p. (J). (gr. 3-7). pap. 5.99 *(978-0-316-60762-9(2))* Little, Brown Bks. for Young Readers.
Coburn, Jake. Prep. 2005. (ENG.). 192p. (YA). (gr. 7-7). 6.99 *(978-0-14-240307-5(5),* Speak) Penguin Young Readers Group.
Connelly, Wendy. Fiona the Firefly! 2003. (Illus.). (J). 12.95 *(978-1-929039-16-6(6))* Ambassador Bks., Inc.
Conrad, Lauren. L. A. Candy. (L. A. Candy Ser.: 1). (ENG.). (YA). (gr. 9-18). 2010. 352p. pap. 9.99 *(978-0-06-176759-3(X))* 2009. 336p. 17.99 *(978-0-06-176758-6(1))* HarperCollins Pubs.
Conway, Celeste. When You Open Your Eyes. 2012. (ENG.). 320p. (YA). (gr. 9). 16.99 *(978-1-4424-4229-0(8));* pap. 9.99 *(978-1-4424-3031-0(1))* Simon Pulse. (Simon Pulse).
Cook, Eileen. The Education of Hailey Kendrick. 2011. (ENG.). (YA). (gr. 9). 288p. pap. 9.99 *(978-1-4424-1326-9(3));* 272p. 16.99 *(978-1-4424-1325-2(5))* Simon Pulse. (Simon Pulse).
Copeland, Cynthia L. The 15 Best Things about Being the New Kid. Vargo, Sharon, illus. 2006. (Silly Millies Ser.). 32p. (J). (gr. -1-3). lib. bdg. 21.27 *(978-0-7613-2889-6(0),* Millbrook Pr.); (gr. 2). per. 5.95 *(978-0-8225-6473-7(4),* First Avenue Editions) Lerner Publishing Group.
Coyle, Carmela Lavigna. Do Princesses Wear Hiking Boots? Gordon, Mike & Gordon, Carl, illus. 2003. (ENG.). 32p. (J). (gr. -1-2). 15.95 *(978-0-87358-828-7(2))* Cooper Square Publishing Llc.
Crutcher, Chris. Deadline. (ENG.). (YA). (gr. 9). 2009. 336p. pap. 9.99 *(978-0-06-085091-3(4))* 2007. 320p. 17.99 *(978-0-06-085089-0(2))* HarperCollins Pubs. (Greenwillow Bks.).
—Deadline. 2011. 10.36 *(978-0-7848-3487-9(3),* Everbind) Marco Bk. Co.
Culbertson, Kim. The Possibility of Now. 2016. (Point Ser.). (ENG.). 304p. (J). (gr. 7). 17.99 *(978-0-545-73146-1(1))* Scholastic, Inc.
Cumyn, Alan. Hot Pterodactyl Boyfriend. 2016. (ENG., Illus.). 416p. (YA). (gr. 9). 17.99 *(978-1-4814-3980-0(4),* Atheneum/Caitlyn Dlouhy Books) Simon & Schuster Children's Publishing.
Cuyler, Margery. Bullies Never Win. Howard, Arthur, illus. 2009. (ENG.). 32p. (J). (gr. k-3). 17.99 *(978-0-689-86187-1(7),* Simon & Schuster Bks. For Young Readers) Simon & Schuster Bks. For Young Readers.
Daily, Lisa. Beauty. 2012. (ENG.). 288p. (YA). (gr. 7-18). pap. 9.99 *(978-1-59514-380-8(7),* Razorbill) Penguin Young Readers Group.
Dean, Myers Walter. Monster. 2014. (ENG.). 304p. (J). (gr. 12-12). 14.24 *(978-1-63245-060-9(7))* Lectorum Pubns., Inc.
Dessen, Sarah. Saint Anything. (ENG.). (YA). (gr. 7). 2016. 448p. pap. 10.99 *(978-0-14-751603-9(X),* Speak) 2015. 432p. 19.99 *(978-0-451-47470-4(8),* Viking Books for Young Readers) Penguin Young Readers Group.
—Saint Anything. 2016. lib. bdg. 22.10 *(978-0-606-38833-7(8))* Turtleback Bks.
Devore, Laurie. How to Break a Boy. 2017. (ENG.). 352p. (YA). 17.99 *(978-1-250-08286-2(2),* 9781250082862) Imprint IND. Dist: Macmillan.
Doktorski, Jennifer Salvato. Famous Last Words. 2013. (ENG.). 288p. (YA). (gr. 7). 17.99 *(978-0-8050-9367-4(2),* 9780805093674, Holt, Henry & Co. Bks. For Young Readers) Holt, Henry & Co.
Durrant, George D. Shakespeare's Best Work: A Novel of Unexpected Family Ties & Uncommon Faith. 2003. 130p. pap. 10.95 *(978-1-55517-709-6(3),* 77093) Cedar Fort, Inc./CFI Distribution.
Echols, Jennifer. Biggest Flirts. 2014. (Superlatives Ser.). (ENG., Illus.). 336p. (YA). (gr. 9). pap. 9.99 *(978-1-4424-7445-1(9),* Simon Pulse) Simon Pulse.
Emerson, Carl. Sally the Salamander's Lost Tail, 1 vol. Trover, Zachary, illus. 2007. (Animal Underdogs Ser.). (ENG.). 32p. (gr. -1-4). 28.50 *(978-1-60270-018-5(4),* Looking Glass Library) ABDO Publishing Co.
Fisher, Dorothy Canfield. Understood Betsy. 2004. reprint ed. pap. 1.99 *(978-1-4192-9201-9(3));* pap. 24.95 *(978-1-4179-0955-1(2))* Kessinger Publishing, LLC.
Fox, Mem. The Goblin & the Empty Chair. Dillon, Leo & Dillon, Diane, illus. 2009. (ENG.). 32p. (J). (gr. k-3). 17.99 *(978-1-4169-8585-3(9),* Beach Lane Bks.) Beach Lane Bks.
Galante, Cecilia. The Sweetness of Salt. 2012. (ENG.). 320p. (YA). (gr. 7). pap. 9.99 *(978-1-59990-853-3(0),* 9781599908533, Bloomsbury USA Childrens) Bloomsbury Publishing USA.
Gantos, Jack. Best in Show for Rotten Ralph. Rubel, Nicole, illus. 2008. (Rotten Ralph Rotten Readers Ser.). (J). 25.95 incl. audio *(978-1-4301-0448-3(1));* 28.95 incl. audio compact disk *(978-1-4301-0451-3(1))* Live Oak Media.
Gerber, Linda. Now & Zen. 2006. (S. A. S. S. Ser.). (ENG., Illus.). 224p. (YA). (gr. 7-18). 7.99 *(978-0-14-240657-1(0),* Speak) Penguin Young Readers Group.
Gologan, Trena. Esther's Younique Crown. 2008. 32p. pap. 16.25 *(978-1-4357-3544-6(7))* Lulu Pr., Inc.
Goss, Leon. Selfus Esteemus Personalitus Low. Tunell, Ken, illus. 2005. (J). pap. *(978-1-933156-08-8(2),* VisionQuest Kids) GSVQ Publishing.
Goss, Leon, 3rd. Selfus Esteemus Personalitus Low. Tunell, Ken, illus. 2005. 32p. (J). per. 16.99 *(978-1-933156-00-2(7),* VisionQuest Kids) GSVQ Publishing.
Green, John. An Abundance of Katherines. 2008. (J). 69.99 *(978-1-60514-809-0(1))* Findaway World, LLC.
—An Abundance of Katherines. 2009. 9.68 *(978-0-7848-1947-0(5),* Everbind) Marco Bk. Co.
—An Abundance of Katherines. (ENG., Illus.). (YA). 2008. 272p. (gr. 7-18). 10.99 *(978-0-14-241070-7(5),* Speak) 2006. 240p. (gr. 9-18). 18.99 *(978-0-525-47688-7(1),* Dutton Books for Young Readers) Penguin Young Readers Group.
—An Abundance of Katherines. 2008. 20.00 *(978-1-60686-090-8(9))* Perfection Learning Corp.
—El Teorema Katherine. 2015.Tr. of An Abundance of Katherines. (SPA.). 320p. (YA). (gr. 7). pap. 12.95 *(978-1-101-91056-6(9),* Vintage Espanol) Knopf Doubleday Publishing Group.
Greene, Stephanie. Moose's Big Idea, 0 vols. Mathieu, Joe, illus. 2010. (Moose & Hildy Ser.: 0). (ENG.). 64p. (J). (gr. 1-4). pap. 6.99 *(978-0-7614-5698-8(8),* 9780761456988, Amazon Children's Publishing) Amazon Publishing.
Grover, Lorie Ann. On Pointe. 2008. (ENG.). 320p. (J). (gr. 3-7). pap. 14.99 *(978-1-4169-7826-8(7),* McElderry, Margaret K. Bks.) McElderry, Margaret K. Bks.
Hall, Angela Marie. Priscilla Pennybrook: Hello World, I Have Arrived!, 1 vol. 2009. 55p. pap. 16.95 *(978-1-61582-899-9(0))* America Star Bks.
Halpern, Julie. Get Well Soon. 2009. (ENG.). 224p. (YA). (gr. 7-12). pap. 9.99 *(978-0-312-58148-0(3),* 9780312581480) Square Fish.
—Have a Nice Day. 2013. (ENG.). 352p. (YA). (gr. 7-12). pap. 10.99 *(978-1-250-03420-5(5),* 9781250034205) Square Fish.
Harris-Wyrick, Wayne. Why Am I Me? Macquignon, Stephen, illus. 2011. 32p. pap. 17.99 *(978-0-9828346-2-6(4))* 4RV Publishing, LLC.
Hartt-Sussman, Heather. Noni Says No. Côté, Geneviève, illus. 2011. (ENG.). 24p. (J). (gr. -1-2). 17.95 *(978-1-77049-233-2(X),* Tundra Bks.) Tundra Bks. CAN. Dist: Penguin Random Hse. LLC.
Hayes, Sonia. Ms. Thang. 2009. (ENG.). 200p. (YA). per. 9.95 *(978-0-9777573-0-5(7))* NUA Multimedia.
—Urban Goddess. 2007. 224p. (YA). per. 9.95 *(978-0-9777573-1-2(5))* NUA Multimedia.
Henkes, Kevin. Olive's Ocean. (ENG.). 224p. (J). (gr. 3-7). 2003. 16.99 *(978-0-06-053543-8(1),* 53396925) 2005. reprint ed. pap. 6.99 *(978-0-06-053545-2(8))* HarperCollins Pubs. (Greenwillow Bks.).
Hijuelos, Óscar. Dark Dude. 2009. (ENG., Illus.). 464p. (YA). (gr. 8-18). pap. 12.99 *(978-1-4169-4945-9(3),* Atheneum Bks. for Young Readers) Simon & Schuster Children's Publishing.
Hijuelos, Óscar & Óscar, Hijuelos. Dark Dude. Roja, Alberto Jimenez, tr. 2010. (SPA.). 430p. (YA). (gr. 9-18). 19.99 *(978-84-441-4316-3(2))* Everest Editora ESP. Dist: Lectorum Pubns., Inc.
Hoffman, Alice. Indigo. 2003. (ENG.). 96p. (J). (gr. 3-7). pap. 6.99 *(978-0-439-25636-0(4),* Scholastic Paperbacks) Scholastic, Inc.
Holm, Jennifer L. An Adventure. 2010. (Boston Jane Ser.: No. 1). (ENG.). 272p. (J). (gr. 3-7). 7.99 *(978-0-375-86204-5(8),* Yearling) Random Hse. Children's Bks.
—Wilderness Days. unabr. ed. 2004. (Boston Jane Ser.: No. 2). 288p. (J). (gr. 5-9). pap. 38.00 incl. audio *(978-0-8072-0787-1(X),* S YA 307 SP, Listening Library) Random Hse. Audio Publishing Group.
Humphrey, Anna. Mission (un)Popular. 2013. (ENG.). 416p. (J). (gr. 5-9). pap. 6.99 *(978-1-4231-2321-7(2))* Hyperion Pr.
Hundal, Nancy. Kaleidoscopes & Butterfly Dreams. 2009. (ENG.). 112p. (YA). (gr. 5-9). pap. 12.95 *(978-0-88982-256-6(5))* Oolichan Bks. CAN. Dist: Univ. of Toronto Pr.
Jaffe, Gail Lois. The Enchanted Mirror. Holmes, Jon, ed. 32p. (YA). (gr. 6-18). 24.95 *(978-0-9667476-0-7(7))* Papillon Pr., Inc.
Jenkins, A. M. Out of Order. 2003. 256p. (J). lib. bdg. 16.89 *(978-0-06-623969-9(9))* HarperCollins Pubs.
Johnson, LouAnne. Muchacho. 2011. (ENG.). 208p. (YA). (gr. 7). pap. 9.99 *(978-0-375-85903-8(9),* Ember) Random Hse. Children's Bks.
Johnson, Vincent L. Of Corn Silk & Black Braids. Crockett, Linda, illus. 2005. 32p. (J). (gr. k-3). 17.95 *(978-0-9657033-2-1(0))* Marzetta Bks.
Jones, Diana Wynne. The Merlin Conspiracy. 480p. (J). 2004. (Magids Ser.: 2). (gr. 3-7). pap. 9.99 *(978-0-06-052320-6(4),* Greenwillow Bks.) 2003. (gr. 5-18). 17.89 *(978-0-06-052319-0(0))* HarperCollins Pubs.
Kazmierczak, Jean. National Chrome 2: The Good, the Bad & the Indifferent. 2008. 76p. pap. 16.95 *(978-1-60703-641-8(X))* PublishAmerica, Inc.
Kephart, Beth. The Heart Is Not a Size. 2010. (ENG.). 256p. (YA). (gr. 8-18). 16.99 *(978-0-06-147048-6(1),* HarperTeen) HarperCollins Pubs.
Keplinger, Kody. The DUFF: Designated Ugly Fat Friend. (ENG.). (YA). (gr. 10-17). 2011. 304p. pap., pap. 10.99 *(978-0-316-08424-6(7))* 2015. 320p. pap. 10.00 *(978-0-316-38180-2(2))* Little, Brown Bks. for Young Readers. (Poppy).
Khorana, Aditi. Mirror in the Sky. 2016. (ENG.). 352p. (YA). (gr. 7). 17.99 *(978-1-59514-856-8(6),* Razorbill) Penguin Young Readers Group.
Kimmel, Elizabeth Cody. The Reinvention of Moxie Roosevelt. 2011. (ENG.). 256p. (J). (gr. 5-18). 6.99 *(978-0-14-241870-3(6),* Puffin Books) Penguin Young Readers Group.
Kipling, Rudyard. Captains Courageous. 2006. (Classics Ser.). (Illus.). 48p. (YA). per. 17.95 *(978-1-56254-869-8(7));* 80p. (J). (gr. 4-7). per. *(978-1-56254-868-1(9))* Saddleback Educational Publishing, Inc.
Kishimoto, Masashi. Naruto: Chapter Book, Vol. 1. Kishimoto, Masashi, illus. 2008. (ENG., Illus.). 80p. (J). (gr. 1-5). pap. 4.99 *(978-1-4215-2056-8(7))* Viz Media.
Klass, David. You Don't Know Me. 2010. (ENG.). 288p. (YA). (gr. 9-12). pap. 9.99 *(978-0-312-65302-6(6))* Square Fish.
Klimo, Kate. Twinky the Dinky Dog. Fleming, Michael, illus. 2013. (Step into Reading Ser.). (ENG.). 48p. (J). (gr. k-3). pap. 3.99 *(978-0-307-97667-3(X),* Random Hse. Bks. for Young Readers) Random Hse. Children's Bks.
Koertge, Ronald. Boy Girl Boy. 2007. (ENG., Illus.). 180p. (YA). (gr. 9-18). pap. 12.95 *(978-0-15-205865-4(6))* Houghton Mifflin Harcourt Publishing Co.
Kogler, Jennifer Anne. Ruby Tuesday. 2005. (ENG.). 320p. (J). (gr. 7-18). 15.99 *(978-0-06-073956-0(8))* HarperCollins Pubs.
Koja, Kathe. Talk. 2008. (ENG.). 144p. (YA). (gr. 7-12). per. 16.99 *(978-0-312-37605-5(7),* 9780312376055) Square Fish.
Kottaras, E. Katherine. The Best Possible Answer. 2016. (ENG.). 272p. (YA). 18.99 *(978-1-250-07281-8(6),* 9781250072818, St. Martin's Griffin) St. Martin's Pr.
LaFaye, A. Nissa's Place. 2010. (ENG.). 256p. (J). (gr. 2-8). pap. 8.00 *(978-1-57131-697-4(3))* Milkweed Editions.
Leavy, Patricia. Blue. 2015. (ENG., Illus.). 168p. pap. *(978-94-6300-353-7(3))* Sense Pubs.
Leveen, Tom. Party. 2011. (ENG.). 240p. (YA). (gr. 9). pap. 8.99 *(978-0-375-86392-9(3),* Ember) Random Hse. Children's Bks.
Littman, Sarah Darer. Purge. 2010. (ENG.). 240p. (J). (gr. 7). 8.99 *(978-0-545-05237-5(8),* Scholastic Paperbacks) Scholastic, Inc.
Lockhart, E. Real Live Boyfriends: Yes. Boyfriends, Plural. If My Life Weren't Complicated, I Wouldn't Be Ruby Oliver. 2011. (Ruby Oliver Quartet Ser.). (ENG.). 240p. (J). (gr. 7). pap. 8.99 *(978-0-385-73429-5(8),* Ember) Random Hse. Children's Bks.
Lowry, Brigid. Follow the Blue. 2004. (ENG.). 205p. (J). (gr. 7-18). tchr. ed. 16.95 *(978-0-8234-1827-5(8))* Holiday Hse., Inc.
—Follow the Blue. 2006. (ENG.). 208p. (YA). (gr. 8-12). pap. 18.99 *(978-0-312-34297-5(7),* 9780312342975, St. Martin's Griffin) St. Martin's Pr.
Lyga, Barry. The Astonishing Adventures of Fanboy & Goth Girl. 2007. (ENG.). 320p. (YA). (gr. 7-12). pap. 9.99 *(978-0-618-91652-8(0))* Houghton Mifflin Harcourt Publishing Co.
Lynch, Chris. Me, Dead Dad, & Alcatraz. 3rd ed. 2005. (ENG.). 240p. (J). 15.99 *(978-0-06-059709-2(7))* HarperCollins Pubs.
Mackler, Carolyn. Guyaholic. 2009. (ENG., Illus.). 192p. (YA). (gr. 9). pap. 7.99 *(978-0-7636-2801-7(8))* Candlewick Pr.
Marchetta, Melina. Jellicoe Road. 2008. (ENG.). 432p. (YA). (gr. 9-18). 17.99 *(978-0-06-143183-8(4),* HarperTeen) HarperCollins Pubs.
May, Eleanor. The Real Me. Gott, Barry, illus. 2006. (Social Studies Connects). 32p. (J). (gr. k-2). pap. 5.95 *(978-1-57565-186-6(6))* Kane Press, Inc.
McDonald, Abby. Boys, Bears, & a Serious Pair of Hiking Boots. (ENG., Illus.). 304p. (YA). (gr. 9). 2011. pap. 7.99 *(978-0-7636-4994-4(5))* 2010. 16.99 *(978-0-7636-4382-9(3))* Candlewick Pr.
McHay, Micki. The Ugly Snowflake (children's hard cover book with musical C. D.) 2006. (J). 15.95 *(978-0-9786826-0-6(2))* McHay, Micki.
McNamara, Margaret. How Many Seeds in a Pumpkin? Karas, G. Brian, illus. 2007. (Mr. Tiffin's Classroom Ser.). (ENG.). 40p. (J). (gr. -1-2). 17.99 *(978-0-375-84014-2(1),* Schwartz & Wade Bks.) Random Hse. Children's Bks.
Messer, Celeste M. Andi's Choice. Hoeffner, Deb, illus. 2004. 82-92p. 4.95 *(978-0-9702171-6-5(1))* AshleyAlan Enterprises.
Mohler, Marie. Leonard's Song. 2008. 32p. 18.95 *(978-1-4357-1372-7(9))* Lulu Pr., Inc.
Montgomery, L. M. Anne of the Island. 2006. (ENG.). pap. *(978-1-4068-2171-0(3));* pap. *(978-1-4068-3175-7(1))* Echo Library.
—Anne of the Island. 2004. reprint ed. pap. 1.99 *(978-1-4192-0718-1(0));* pap. 30.95 *(978-1-4179-0885-1(8))* Kessinger Publishing, LLC.
—Anne of the Island. l.t. ed. 2004. 396p. 26.00 *(978-1-58287-640-5(1))* North Bks.
—Anne of the Island. 2010. (Puffin Classics Ser.). (ENG.). 368p. (J). (gr. 5-7). pap. 5.99 *(978-0-14-132736-5(7),* Puffin Books) Penguin Young Readers Group.
Moranville, Sharelle Byars. 27 Magic Words. 2016. (ENG.). 208p. (J). (gr. 3-7). 16.95 *(978-0-8234-3657-6(8))* Holiday Hse., Inc.
Moss, Marissa. The All-New Amelia. Moss, Marissa, illus. (ENG., Illus.). (J). 2013. 5.99 *(978-1-4169-1289-7(4))* 2007. 40p. (gr. 2-5). 12.99 *(978-1-4169-0908-8(7))* Simon & Schuster/Paula Wiseman Bks. (Simon & Schuster/Paula Wiseman Bks.).
—Amelia's Cross-My-Heart, Hope-to-Die Guide to the Real, True You! Moss, Marissa, illus. 2010. (Amelia Ser.). (ENG., Illus.). 64p. (J). (gr. 5-8). 9.99 *(978-1-4169-8710-9(X),* Simon & Schuster/Paula Wiseman Bks.) Simon & Schuster/Paula Wiseman Bks.
Munsch, Robert. Makeup Mess. 2004. (Illus.). (J). (gr. k-3). spiral bd. *(978-0-616-11125-3(8))* Canadian National Institute for the Blind/Institut National Canadien pour les Aveugles.
—Makeup Mess. Martchenko, Michael, illus. 2004. (J). (gr. k-3). spiral bd. *(978-0-616-11124-6(X))* Canadian National Institute for the Blind/Institut National Canadien pour les Aveugles.
Myers, Walter Dean. Lockdown. (YA). (gr. 8). 2011. (ENG.). 272p. pap. 9.99 *(978-0-06-121482-0(5))* 2010. 256p. lib. bdg. 17.89 *(978-0-06-121481-3(7))* 2010. (ENG.). 256p. 16.99 *(978-0-06-121480-6(9))* HarperCollins Pubs. (Amistad).
—Monster. Myers, Christopher, illus. 2004. (Monster Ser.). (ENG.). 304p. (YA). (gr. 8). reprint ed. pap. 9.99 *(978-0-06-440731-1(4),* Amistad) HarperCollins Pubs.
Myracle, Lauren. Ten. (Winnie Years Ser.). (ENG.). (J). (gr. 3-7). 2012. 240p. pap. 7.99 *(978-0-14-242134-5(0),* Puffin Books) 2011. 272p. 16.99 *(978-0-525-42356-0(7),* Dutton Books for Young Readers) Penguin Young Readers Group.
—Twelve. 2008. (Winnie Years Ser.). (ENG.). 224p. (J). (gr. 5-18). 7.99 *(978-0-14-241091-2(8),* Puffin Books) Penguin Young Readers Group.
Nash, Andy. Tatum & Her Tiger: For Kids Blessed with Passion. 2007. (Illus.). (J). 9.99 *(978-0-8127-0451-8(7))* Autumn Hse. Publishing Co.
Naylor, Phyllis Reynolds. Dangerously Alice. 2007. (Alice Ser.: 19). (ENG.). 304p. (YA). (gr. 9-12). 15.99 *(978-0-689-87094-1(9),* Atheneum Bks. for Young Readers) Simon & Schuster Children's Publishing.
—Dangerously Alice. 2008. (Alice Ser.: No. 19). (ENG.). 320p. (YA). mass mkt. 6.99 *(978-0-689-87095-8(7),* Simon Pulse) Simon Pulse.
—The Grooming of Alice. 2012. (Alice Ser.: 12). (ENG., Illus.). 240p. (J). (gr. 5-9). pap. 6.99 *(978-1-4424-3496-7(1),* Atheneum Bks. for Young Readers) Simon & Schuster Children's Publishing.
—Please Don't Be True: Dangerously Alice; Almost Alice; Intensely Alice. 2011. (Alice Ser.). (ENG., Illus.). 768p. (YA). (gr. 9). pap. 12.99 *(978-1-4424-1721-2(8),* Atheneum Bks. for Young Readers) Simon & Schuster Children's Publishing.
Neasi, Barbara J. So Many Me's. 2004. (Rookie Reader Español Ser.). (ENG.). 32p. (J). (gr. k-2). pap. 4.95 *(978-0-516-27786-8(3),* Children's Pr.) Scholastic Library Publishing.
Nolan, Han. Send Me down a Miracle. 2003. (ENG.). 276p. (YA). (gr. 7-12). pap. 15.95 *(978-0-15-204680-4(1))* Houghton Mifflin Harcourt Publishing Co.
Oliver, Lauren. Before I Fall. (ENG.). (YA). (gr. 9). 2016. 544p. pap. 10.99 *(978-0-06-172681-1(8))* 2010. 480p. 17.99 *(978-0-06-172680-4(X))* HarperCollins Pubs.
—Before I Fall. 2010. 368p. pap. *(978-0-340-98090-3(7),* Hodder Paperbacks) Hodder & Stoughton.
—Before I Fall. 2016. (YA). lib. bdg. 22.10 *(978-0-606-23576-1(0),* Turtleback) Turtleback Bks.
Palatini, Margie. The Zoey Zone. Palatini, Margie, illus. 2010. (ENG., Illus.). 192p. (J). (gr. 3-6). pap. 6.99 *(978-0-06-113900-0(9),* Tegen, Katherine Bks) HarperCollins Pubs.
Paulsen, Gary. Dogsong. 2007. (ENG.). 192p. (J). (gr. 5-9). pap. 7.99 *(978-1-4169-3962-7(8),* Simon & Schuster Bks. For Young Readers) Simon & Schuster Bks. For Young Readers.
—Dogsong. 2007. (ENG.). 192p. (YA). (gr. 7). mass mkt. 7.99 *(978-1-4169-3919-1(9),* Simon Pulse) Simon Pulse.
Pearson, Mary E. The Adoration of Jenna Fox. 2008. (Jenna Fox Chronicles Ser.: 1). (ENG.). 272p. (YA). (gr. 7-12). 24.99 *(978-0-8050-7668-4(9),* Holt, Henry & Co. Bks. For Young Readers) Holt, Henry & Co.
—The Adoration of Jenna Fox. 2011. 9.46 *(978-0-7848-3478-7(4),* Everbind) Marco Bk. Co.
—The Adoration of Jenna Fox. 2009. (Jenna Fox Chronicles Ser.: 1). (ENG.). 288p. (YA). (gr. 7-12). pap. 10.99 *(978-0-312-59441-1(0),* 9780312594411) Square Fish.
Pelley, Kathleen T. Raj the Bookstore Tiger. Keiser, Paige, illus. 2011. (ENG.). 32p. (J). (gr. -1-3). 15.95 *(978-1-58089-230-8(2))* Charlesbridge Publishing, Inc.
Pennypacker, Sara. The Talented Clementine. Frazee, Marla, illus. (Clementine Book Ser.). (ENG.). (J). 2008. 160p. (gr. 1-3). pap. 5.99 *(978-0-7868-3871-4(X))* 2007. 144p. (gr. 2-5). 14.99 *(978-0-7868-3870-7(1))* Hyperion Pr.
Peters, Julie Anne. Pretend You Love Me. 2011. (ENG.). 304p. (YA). (gr. 10-17). pap. 10.99 *(978-0-316-12741-7(8))* Little, Brown Bks. for Young Readers.
Polacco, Patricia. Gracias, Senor Falker. 2006. (SPA., Illus.). 34p. (J). (gr. 2-3). per. 7.99 *(978-1-933032-02-3(2),* LC34004) Lectorum Pubns., Inc.
—Thank You, Mr. Falker. Polacco, Patricia, illus. 2012. (ENG., Illus.). 40p. (J). (gr. k-3). 12.99 *(978-0-399-25762-9(4),* Philomel Bks.) Penguin Young Readers Group.
Proimos, James. 12 Things to Do Before You Crash & Burn. 2011. (ENG.). 128p. (YA). (gr. 9-13). 14.99 *(978-1-59643-595-7(X))* Roaring Brook Pr.
Queen Latifah. Queen of the Scene. Morrison, Frank, illus. 2006. 32p. (J). (gr. -1-3). 17.89 incl. audio compact disk *(978-0-06-077857-6(1),* Geringer, Laura Book) HarperCollins Pubs.
Quick, Matthew. Every Exquisite Thing. 2016. (ENG.). 272p. (YA). (gr. 10-17). 17.99 *(978-0-316-37959-5(X))* Little Brown & Co.
Rahlens, Holly-Jane. Prince William, Maximilian Minsky, & Me. 2007. (ENG.). 320p. (YA). (gr. 7-11). per. 7.99 *(978-0-7636-3299-1(6))* Candlewick Pr.
Randle, Kristen D. Slumming. 2003. (Illus.). 240p. (J). lib. bdg. 16.89 *(978-0-06-001023-2(1),* HarperTeen) HarperCollins Pubs.
Raschke, Erik. The Book of Samuel: A Novel. 2009. (ENG.). 256p. (YA). (gr. 4-7). pap. 18.99 *(978-0-312-37969-8(2),* 9780312379698, St. Martin's Griffin) St. Martin's Pr.
Ratzlaff, Aaron J. Quills. 2011. (ENG.). 40p. (J). pap. 13.99 *(978-0-8361-9509-5(4))* Herald Pr.
Resau, Laura. What the Moon Saw. 2008. (ENG.). 272p. (J). (gr. 3-7). pap. 7.99 *(978-0-440-23957-4(5),* Yearling) Random Hse. Children's Bks.
Reynolds, Peter H. Peter Reynolds Creatrilogy Box Set (Dot, Ish, Sky Color) 2012. (ENG.). (J). (gr. k-4). 40.00 *(978-0-7636-6327-8(1))* Candlewick Pr.
—So Few of Me. Reynolds, Peter H., illus. 2006. (ENG., Illus.). 32p. (J). (gr. k-12). 15.00 *(978-0-7636-2623-5(6))* Candlewick Pr.
Rivers, Karen. The Girl in the Well Is Me. (ENG.). 224p. (J). (gr. 5-8). 2017. pap. 6.95 *(978-1-61620-696-3(9))* 2016. 16.95 *(978-1-61620-569-0(5))* Algonquin Bks. of Chapel Hill.
Rue, Ginger. Rock 'n' Roll Rebel. 2016. (Tig Ripley Ser.). (ENG.). 349p. (J). (gr. 4-7). 16.99 *(978-1-58536-945-4(4),* 204106) Sleeping Bear Pr.
Ryan, Amy Kathleen. Vibes. 2010. (ENG.). 264p. (YA). (gr. 9). pap. 14.95 *(978-0-547-24889-9(X))* Houghton Mifflin Harcourt Publishing Co.
Salm, Arthur. Anyway: A Story about Me with 138 Footnotes, 27 Exaggerations, & 1 Plate of Spaghetti. 2012. (ENG., Illus.). 192p. (J). (gr. 3-7). 15.99 *(978-1-4424-2930-7(5),* Simon & Schuster Bks. For Young Readers) Simon & Schuster Bks. For Young Readers.
—Anyway* *a Story about Me with 138 Footnotes, 27 Exaggerations, & 1 Plate of Spaghetti. 2013. (ENG., Illus.). 192p. (J). (gr. 3-7). pap. 7.99 *(978-1-4424-2931-4(3),* Simon & Schuster Bks. For Young Readers) Simon & Schuster Bks. For Young Readers.
Scheunemann, Pam. Crocodile Tears, 1 vol. Chawla, Neena, illus. 2007. (Critter Chronicles Ser.). (ENG.). 24p. (J). (gr. k-3). lib. bdg. 24.21 *(978-1-59928-436-1(7),* SandCastle) ABDO Publishing Co.
Schraff, Anne. To Be Somebody. 2008. (Passages Ser.). 120p. (J). (gr. 4-6). lib. bdg. 13.95 *(978-0-7569-8390-1(8))* Perfection Learning Corp.
Schulte, Mary. Who Do I Look Like? Roos, Maryn, illus. 2006. (Rookie Reader Skill Set Ser.). (ENG.). 32p. (J). (gr. k-2). pap. 4.95 *(978-0-516-24758-8(1),* Children's Pr.) Scholastic Library Publishing.
Scott, Elizabeth. Between Here & Forever. (ENG.). (YA). (gr. 9). 2012. 272p. pap. 9.99 *(978-1-4169-9485-5(8))* 2011. 256p. 16.99 *(978-1-4169-9484-8(X))* Simon Pulse. (Simon Pulse).

S

—Love You Hate You Miss You. (ENG.). (YA). (gr. 8). 2010. 304p. pap. 8.99 *(978-0-06-112285-9(8))* 2009. 288p. 16.99 *(978-0-06-112283-5(1))* HarperCollins Pubs. (HarperTeen).
Scott, Lisa Ann. School of Charm. 2014. (ENG.). 304p. (J). (gr. 3-7). 16.99 *(978-0-06-220758-6(X),* Tegen, Katherine Bks) HarperCollins Pubs.
Sedoti, Chelsea. The Hundred Lies of Lizzie Lovett. 2017. (ENG.). 400p. (YA). (gr. 8-12). 17.99 *(978-1-4926-3608-3(8),* 9781492636083) Sourcebooks, Inc.
Sharif, Medeia. Bestest. Ramadan. Ever. 2011. (ENG.). 312p. (YA). pap. 9.95 *(978-0-7387-2323-5(1),* Flux) North Star Editions.
Sharp, Michael. Vayda Jane Bean - Chocolate. Van Tine, Laura, illus. 2007. 20p. pap. *(978-1-897455-70-8(4))* Avatar Pubns., Inc.
Shusterman, Neal. Full Tilt. 2009. (ENG.). 224p. (YA). (gr. 7). pap. 10.99 *(978-1-4169-9748-1(2),* Simon & Schuster Bks. For Young Readers) Simon & Schuster Bks. For Young Readers.
—Full Tilt. 2004. (ENG.). 208p. (YA). (gr. 7). mass mkt. 8.99 *(978-0-689-87325-6(5),* Simon Pulse) Simon Pulse.
—The Schwa Was Here. 2006. (ENG.). 240p. (YA). (gr. 7-18). reprint ed. 6.99 *(978-0-14-240577-2(9),* Puffin Books) Penguin Young Readers Group.
Sims, Guy A. & Myers, Walter Dean. Monster. Anyabwile, Dawud, illus. 2015. (Monster Ser.). (ENG.). 160p. (YA). (gr. 8). pap. 9.99 *(978-0-06-227499-1(6))* HarperCollins Pubs.
Skilton, Sarah. Bruised. 2013. (ENG.). 288p. (YA). (gr. 7-17). 18.95 *(978-1-4197-0387-4(0),* Amulet Bks.) Abrams, Inc.
Smallman, Steve. Bumbletum. Warnes, Tim, illus. 2006. 24p. (J). (gr. -1-3). 15.95 *(978-1-58925-060-4(5))* Tiger Tales.
Snider, Cindy Gay. Finding Anna Bee. Chambers, Mary, illus. 2007. 163p. (J). (gr. 3-7). per. 9.99 *(978-0-8361-9392-3(X))* Herald Pr.
Sonnenblick, Jordan. Notes from the Midnight Driver. 2009. 265p. 18.00 *(978-1-60686-516-3(1))* Perfection Learning Corp.
—Notes from the Midnight Driver. 2007. (ENG.). 288p. (J). (gr. 7-12). pap. 9.99 *(978-0-439-75781-2(9),* Scholastic Paperbacks) Scholastic, Inc.
Steig, William. Toby, Who Are You? Euvremer, Teryl, illus. 2004. 32p. (J). (gr. -1-3). lib. bdg. 15.89 *(978-0-06-000706-5(0),* Cotler, Joanna Books) HarperCollins Pubs.
Stein, Gertrude & Hurd, Thacher. The World Is Round. Hurd, Clement, illus. 75th ed. 2013. (ENG.). 128p. 19.99 *(978-0-06-220307-6(X),* Collins Design) HarperCollins Pubs.
Stevenson, Robin. Out of Order, 1 vol. 2007. (ENG.). 232p. (YA). (gr. 7-12). per. 9.95 *(978-1-55143-693-7(0))* Orca Bk. Pubs. USA.
Talley, Gigi T. Fairest Florabell. 2012. 34p. 24.95 *(978-1-4560-0628-0(2))* America Star Bks.
Tamaki, Mariko. Saving Montgomery Sole. 2016. (ENG.). 240p. (YA). 17.99 *(978-1-62672-271-2(4),* 9781626722712) Roaring Brook Pr.
—Saving Montgomery Sole. 2017. (ENG.). 240p. (YA). pap. 9.99 *(978-1-250-10440-3(8),* 9781250104403) Square Fish.
—Saving Montgomery Sole. 2017. (YA). lib. bdg. 20.85 ***(978-0-606-39584-7(9))*** Turtleback Bks.
Thompson, Alicia. Psych Major Syndrome. 2010. (ENG.). 336p. pap. 8.99 *(978-1-4231-1549-6(X))* Disney Pr.
Tracy, Kristen. The Reinvention of Bessica Lefter. 2012. (ENG.). 320p. (J). (gr. 5). 7.99 *(978-0-375-84547-5(X),* Yearling) Random Hse. Children's Bks.
Vail, Rachel. Not That I Care. 2014. (Friendship Ring Ser.: 3). (ENG.). 176p. (J). (gr. 5). pap. 7.99 *(978-0-14-751120-1(8),* Puffin Books) Penguin Young Readers Group.
Van Draanen, Wendelin. Flipped. 2003. (ENG.). 256p. (YA). (gr. 7-9). pap. 9.99 *(978-0-375-82544-6(4),* Ember) Random Hse. Children's Bks.
Van Dusen, Chris. King Hugo's Huge Ego. 2011. (ENG., Illus.). 40p. (J). (gr. -1-2). 16.99 *(978-0-7636-5004-9(8))* Candlewick Pr.
Vande Velde, Vivian. Frogged. 2013. (ENG., Illus.). 208p. (J). (gr. 5-7). 16.99 *(978-0-547-94215-5(X))* Houghton Mifflin Harcourt Publishing Co.
Velmans, Hester. Isabel of the Whales. 2006. (ENG.). 192p. (J). (gr. 3-7). per. 6.99 *(978-0-440-42025-5(3),* Yearling) Random Hse. Children's Bks.
Vipont, Elfrida. The Lark in the Morn. Freeman, T. R., illus. 2007. 196p. (YA). pap. 12.95 *(978-1-932350-22-7(5))* Bethlehem Bks.
Vision, Mutiya Sahar. Disabilities. Alcantara, Ignacio, illus. 2009. 32p. 17.00 *(978-0-9659538-9-4(0))* Von Curtis Publishing.
Vivian, Siobhan. The List. (ENG.). 336p. (J). (gr. 9). 2014. pap. 9.99 *(978-0-545-16918-9(6),* Scholastic Paperbacks) 2012. 17.99 *(978-0-545-16917-2(8),* PUSH) Scholastic, Inc.
Vizzini, Med. Be More Chill. 2011. 9.68 *(978-0-7848-3414-5(8),* Everbind) Marco Bk. Co.
Vizzini, Ned. Be More Chill. 2005. (ENG.). 304p. (J). (gr. 5-9). per. 8.99 *(978-0-7868-0996-7(5))* Disney Publishing Worldwide.
Vrettos, Adrienne Maria. Skin. (ENG.). (YA). (gr. 7-12). 2007. 272p. pap. 9.99 *(978-1-4169-0656-8(8))* 2006. (Illus.). 240p. 16.95 *(978-1-4169-0655-1(X))* McElderry, Margaret K. Bks. (McElderry, Margaret K. Bks.).
Waldron, Kevin. Mr. Peek & the Misunderstanding at the Zoo. Waldron, Kevin, illus. 2010. (ENG., Illus.). 48p. (J). (gr. k-12). 15.99 *(978-0-7636-4549-6(4),* Templar) Candlewick Pr.
Wild, Margaret. Jinx. Gould, Jason, photos by. 2004. (ENG., Illus.). 224p. (YA). (gr. 9). reprint ed. pap. 11.95 *(978-0-689-86541-1(4),* Simon Pulse) Simon Pulse.
Witherow, Wendy. Miranda's Makeover. Pulley, Kelly, illus. 2007. 93p. (J). *(978-1-934306-11-6(8))* Mission City Pr., Inc.
Wolcott, P. A. The Fox, the Badger, & the Bunny: A Dales Tale. Wolcott, K. Hannah, ed. Schweitzer, Patty, illus. 2009. 20p. pap. 24.95 *(978-1-60749-525-3(2))* America Star Bks.
Wolfson, Jill. What I Call Life. 2008. (ENG.). 288p. (J). (gr. 5-9). pap. 19.99 *(978-0-312-37752-6(5),* 9780312377526) Square Fish.
Wong, Joyce Lee. Seeing Emily. 2005. (ENG., Illus.). 288p. (J). (gr. 7-11). 16.95 *(978-0-8109-5757-2(4),* Abrams Bks. for Young Readers) Abrams, Inc.
Yaccarino, Dan. Unlovable. Yaccarino, Dan, illus. rev. ed. 2004. (ENG., Illus.). 32p. (J). (gr. -1-1). reprint ed. pap. 7.99 *(978-0-8050-7532-8(1),* 9780805075328) Square Fish.
Yovanoff, Brenna. Places No One Knows. 2016. (ENG.). 384p. (YA). (gr. 9). 17.99 *(978-0-553-52263-1(9),* Delacorte Pr.) Random Hse. Children's Bks.
Zadoff, Allen. Food, Girls, & Other Things I Can't Have. 2011. (ENG., Illus.). 320p. (gr. 9). pap. 9.99 *(978-1-60684-151-8(3),* Carolrhoda Lab™) Lerner Publishing Group.
Zeitlin, Meredith. Freshman Year & Other Unnatural Disasters. 2013. (ENG.). 288p. (YA). (gr. 7). pap. 8.99 *(978-0-14-242421-6(8),* Speak) Penguin Young Readers Group.

SELF-RELIANCE

see also Self-confidence

Berry, Joy. Getting Dressed. 2009. (ENG.). 40p. (J). (gr. k — 1). bds. 7.95 *(978-1-60577-009-3(4))* Berry, Joy Enterprises.
Child, Maria. Girls Own Book 1834. 2006. 292p. per. *(978-1-4067-9133-4(4),* Pomona Pr.) Read Bks.
Dyer, Wayne & Dyer, Summer. 10 Secrets for Success & Inner Peace for Teens. 2004. 12.95 *(978-1-4019-0270-4(7),* 2707, Hay Hse. Lifestyles) Hay Hse., Inc.
Falconer, Ian & Jordom, Deidre M. Dream Big: Starring Olivia. 2006. (ENG., Illus.). 64p. 9.99 *(978-0-7407-5818-8(7))* Andrews McMeel Publishing.
McCloud, Carol. Growing up with a Bucket Full of Happiness: Three Rules for a Happier Life. Weber, Penny, illus. 2010. (ENG.). 86p. (J). (gr. 4). pap. 9.95 *(978-1-933916-57-6(5))* Bucket Fillers, Inc.
Noah, Michal Y. A-Z the Universe in Me. 2012. 18.95 *(978-0-7414-7841-2(2));* pap. 13.95 *(978-0-7414-7840-5(4))* Infinity Publishing.

SELF-RELIANCE—FICTION

Adams, Diane. I Can Do It Myself!, 1 vol. Hayashi, Nancy, illus. (ENG.). 32p. (J). (gr. -1-1). 2013. 7.95 *(978-1-56145-725-0(6))* 2009. 15.95 *(978-1-56145-471-6(0))* Peachtree Pubs.
—Teacher's Little Helper, 1 vol. Hayashi, Nancy, illus. 2012. (ENG.). 32p. (J). 15.95 *(978-1-56145-630-7(6))* Peachtree Pubs.
Alger, Horatio. Frank & Fearless or the Fortunes of Jasper Kent. 2007. 228p. 20.99 *(978-1-4280-7465-1(1));* per. 14.99 *(978-1-4280-7470-5(8))* IndyPublish.com.
Aliki. All by Myself! Aliki, illus. 2003. (ENG., Illus.). 32p. (J). (gr. -1-1). pap. 6.99 *(978-0-06-446253-2(6))* HarperCollins Pubs.
—All by Myself! 2003. (J). (gr. k-3). lib. bdg. 17.20 *(978-0-613-65685-6(7),* Turtleback) Turtleback Bks.
Auch, M. J. One-Handed Catch. 2009. (ENG.). 272p. (J). (gr. 5-9). pap. 6.99 *(978-0-312-53575-9(9),* 9780312535759) Square Fish.
Auch, Mary Jane. One-Handed Catch. 2009. 272p. (J). (gr. 5-9). pap. 6.99 *(978-0-312-58002-5(9))* Square Fish.
Badescu, Ramona. Pomelo's Big Adventure. Chaud, Benjamin, illus. 2014. (Pomelo the Garden Elephant Ser.). (ENG.). 40p. (J). (gr. -1-3). 17.95 *(978-1-59270-158-2(2))* Enchanted Lion Bks., LLC.
Baratz-Logsted, Lauren. Me, in Between. 2008. (ENG.). 208p. (J). (gr. 4-8). pap. 5.99 *(978-1-4169-5068-4(0),* Simon & Schuster/Paula Wiseman Bks.) Simon & Schuster/Paula Wiseman Bks.
Bea, Holly. Lucy Goose Goes to Texas. Boddy, Joe, illus. 2005. (ENG.). 32p. (J). (gr. -1-5). 15.95 *(978-1-932073-15-7(9))* New World Library.
Becker Holstein, Barbara. The Truth: Diary of a Gutsy Tween. 2014. (ENG.). 176p. (J). (gr. 2-7). 12.95 *(978-1-62873-611-3(9),* Sky Pony Pr.) Skyhorse Publishing Co., Inc.
Best, Cari. Sally Jean, the Bicycle Queen. Davenier, Christine, illus. 2006. (ENG.). 32p. (J). (gr. -1-3). 17.99 *(978-0-374-36386-4(2),* 9780374363864, Farrar, Straus & Giroux (BYR)) Farrar, Straus & Giroux.
Block, Francesca Lia. Pink Smog: Becoming Weetzie Bat. 2012. (Weetzie Bat Ser.: 6). (ENG.). 208p. (YA). (gr. 9). 17.99 *(978-0-06-156598-4(9),* HarperTeen) HarperCollins Pubs.
Boochever, Annie. Bristol Bay Summer. 2014. (ENG., Illus.). 258p. (J). (gr. 3-7). 28.99 *(978-1-941821-27-5(8));* pap. 12.99 *(978-0-88240-994-8(8))* Graphic Arts Ctr. Publishing Co. (Alaska Northwest Bks.).
Cameron, Ann. Gloria Rising. 2004. (Stepping Stone Book Ser.). (ENG.). 112p. (J). (gr. 1-4). 4.99 *(978-0-440-41998-3(0),* Random Hse. Bks. for Young Readers) Random Hse. Children's Bks.
Carmichael, Clay. Wild Things. (ENG.). (J). 2012. 184p. (gr. 5-8). pap. 9.95 *(978-1-59078-914-8(8))* 2009. 248p. (gr. 4-6). 18.95 *(978-1-59078-627-7(0),* Front Street) Boyds Mills Pr.
—Wild Things, 6 vols. 2010. (J). 77.75 *(978-1-4498-0632-3(5))* Recorded Bks., Inc.
Clements, Andrew. Because Your Mommy Loves You. Alley, R. W., illus. 2012. (ENG.). 32p. (J). (gr. -1-3). 16.99 *(978-0-547-25522-4(5))* Houghton Mifflin Harcourt Publishing Co.
Climo, Liz. Rory the Dinosaur: Me & My Dad. 2015. (ENG., Illus.). 40p. (J). (gr. -1-3). 17.00 *(978-0-316-27728-0(2))* Little Brown & Co.
Coles, Michael Joseph, et al. The Land of Caring Bou. Banks, Timothy, illus. 2006. (J). *(978-0-87483-814-5(2))* August Hse. Pubs., Inc.
Connor, Leslie. Crunch. 2012. (ENG.). 336p. (J). (gr. 5). pap. 6.99 *(978-0-06-169234-5(4),* Tegen, Katherine Bks) HarperCollins Pubs.
—Waiting for Normal. (ENG.). (J). (gr. 5). 2010. 320p. pap. 6.99 *(978-0-06-089090-2(8))* 2008. 304p. 16.99 *(978-0-06-089088-9(6))* HarperCollins Pubs. (Tegen, Katherine Bks).
Decker, Tim. The Punk Ethic. Decker, Tim, illus. 2012. (ENG., Illus.). 188p. (YA). 18.95 *(978-1-60898-120-5(7));* pap. 9.95 *(978-1-60898-121-2(5))* namelos llc.
Denise, Carolyn. I Can Do It Myself! Chatterji, Somnath, illus. 2012. (ENG.). 16p. (J). (gr. -1-3). pap. 19.95 *(978-0-9835651-4-7(7))* Levi Bass Publishing.
Deshone, Jerry Michael. Bear in Mind. 2011. 24p. pap. 24.95 *(978-1-4626-2973-2(3))* America Star Bks.
Diesen, Deborah. The Pout-Pout Fish, Far, Far from Home. Hanna, Dan, illus. 2017. (Pout-Pout Fish Adventure Ser.). (ENG.). 32p. (J). 16.99 *(978-0-374-30194-1(8),* 9780374301941, Farrar, Straus & Giroux (BYR)) Farrar, Straus & Giroux.
Dorfman, Craig. I Knew You Could! A Book for All the Stops in Your Life. Ong, Cristina, illus. 2003. (Little Engine That Could Ser.). (ENG.). 32p. (J). (gr. -1-2). 11.99 *(978-0-448-43148-2(3),* Grosset & Dunlap) Penguin Young Readers Group.
Duey, Kathleen. Korow: A Baby Chimpanzee's Story. Gurin, Lara, illus. 2008. (My Animal Family Ser.). (ENG.). 32p. (J). (gr. -1-3). 12.99 *(978-0-8249-1816-3(9),* Ideal Pubns.) Worthy Publishing.
—Leo: A Baby Lion's Story. Gurin, Lara, illus. 2008. (My Animal Family Ser.). 32p. (J). (gr. -1-3). 12.99 *(978-0-8249-1817-0(7),* Ideal Pubns.) Worthy Publishing.
—Nanuq: A Baby Polar Bear's Story. Gurin, Lara, illus. 2008. (ENG.). 32p. (J). (gr. -1-3). 12.99 *(978-0-8249-1818-7(5),* Ideal Pubns.) Worthy Publishing.
Duncan, Alexandra. Salvage. 2014. (Salvage Ser.: 1). (ENG.). 528p. (YA). (gr. 8). 17.99 *(978-0-06-222014-1(4),* Greenwillow Bks.) HarperCollins Pubs.
Ellis, Edward Sylvester. Through Forest & Fire. 2005. pap. 14.95 *(978-1-59224-221-4(9))* Wildside Pr., LLC.
Fleming, Candace. Imogene's Last Stand. Carpenter, Nancy, illus. (ENG.). 40p. (J). (gr. -1-3). 2014. 7.99 *(978-0-385-38654-8(0),* Dragonfly Bks.) 2009. 16.99 *(978-0-375-83607-7(1),* Schwartz & Wade Bks.) Random Hse. Children's Bks.
Giff, Patricia Reilly. Genevieve's War. Stadtlander, Becca, illus. 2017. (ENG.). 240p. (J). (gr. 3-7). 16.95 *(978-0-8234-3800-6(7))* Holiday Hse., Inc.
—R My Name Is Rachel. 2012. (ENG.). 176p. (J). (gr. 4-7). pap. 6.99 *(978-0-440-42176-4(4),* Yearling) Random Hse. Children's Bks.
Golden, Laura. Every Day After. 2013. (ENG.). 224p. (J). (gr. 4-7). 15.99 *(978-0-385-74326-6(2),* Delacorte Bks. for Young Readers) Random Hse. Children's Bks.
Harazin, S. A. Painless. 2015. (ENG.). 304p. (YA). (gr. 8-12). 16.99 *(978-0-8075-6288-8(2))* Whitman, Albert & Co.
Henderson, Leah. One Shadow on the Wall. 2017. (ENG., Illus.). 448p. (J). (gr. 3-7). 16.99 *(978-1-4814-6295-2(4),* Atheneum Bks. for Young Readers) Simon & Schuster Children's Publishing.
Hengel, Katherine. Taking Control, 1 vol. unabr. ed. 2011. (District 13 Ser.). (ENG.). 48p. (YA). (gr. 9-12). pap. 7.95 *(978-1-61651-276-7(8))* Saddleback Educational Publishing, Inc.
Horvath, Polly. Everything on a Waffle, 1 vol. (ENG., Illus.). 160p. (J). pap. 8.95 *(978-0-88899-442-4(7))* Groundwood Bks. CAN. Dist: Publishers Group West (PGW).
—Everything on a Waffle. 2008. (Illus.). 154p. (gr. 5-9). 18.00 *(978-0-7569-8776-3(8))* Perfection Learning Corp.
—Everything on a Waffle. 2008. (ENG., Illus.). 176p. (J). (gr. 5-9). pap. 7.99 *(978-0-312-38004-5(6),* 9780312380045) Square Fish.
—One Year in Coal Harbor. 2014. (ENG.). 224p. (J). (gr. 4-7). 7.99 *(978-0-385-38653-1(2),* Yearling) Random Hse. Children's Bks.
Howard, Elizabeth Fitzgerald. The Train to Lulu's. Casilla, Robert, illus. 2007. (ENG.). 36p. (J). (gr. -1-3). 10.99 *(978-1-4169-6161-1(5),* Simon & Schuster/Paula Wiseman Bks.) Simon & Schuster/Paula Wiseman Bks.
Hsiao, Christie. Journey to Rainbow Island. 2013. (ENG., Illus.). 400p. (J). (gr. 2-7). 17.95 *(978-1-939529-24-4(7))* BenBella Bks.
Hubbard, Kirsten. Watch the Sky. 2015. (ENG.). 272p. (J). (gr. 3-7). 16.99 *(978-1-4847-0833-0(4))* Hyperion Bks. for Children.
Jacobson, Jennifer Richard. Small as an Elephant. 2011. (ENG., Illus.). 288p. (J). (gr. 4-7). 15.99 *(978-0-7636-4155-9(3))* Candlewick Pr.
Katherine, Paterson. Lyddie. 2014. (Puffin Modern Classics Ser.). (ENG.). 192p. (J). (gr. 1-4). 11.24 *(978-1-63245-221-7(2))* Lectorum Pubns., Inc.
Killion, Bette. Little Lek Longtail Learns to Sleep. Vidal, Beatriz, illus. 2016. (ENG.). 28p. (J). (gr. k-3). 17.95 *(978-1-937786-63-2(3),* Wisdom Tales) World Wisdom, Inc.
Larson, Kirby. Hattie Big Sky. (ENG.). (YA). (gr. 7-7). 2008. 304p. 7.99 *(978-0-385-73595-7(2),* Yearling) 2007. 320p. pap. 8.99 *(978-0-440-23941-3(9),* Ember) Random Hse. Children's Bks.
—Hattie Big Sky. l.t. ed. 2007. (Literacy Bridge Young Adult Ser.). 381p. (YA). (gr. 7-12). 23.95 *(978-0-7862-9697-2(6))* Thorndike Pr.
—Hattie Ever After. 2014. (ENG.). 256p. (YA). (gr. 7). pap. 8.99 *(978-0-375-85090-5(2),* Ember) Random Hse. Children's Bks.
Law, Felicia. Kimberly the Koala: A Tale of Independence. Danson, Lesley, illus. 2010. (Animal Fair Values Ser.). (ENG.). 32p. (J). (gr. -1-3). pap. 10.55 *(978-1-60754-909-3(3));* lib. bdg. 22.60 *(978-1-60754-902-4(6))* Windmill Bks.
—Limpopo the Lion: A Tale of Laziness & Lethargy. Messina, Lilli, illus. 2010. (Animal Fair Values Ser.). 32p. (J). (gr. -1-3). pap. 10.55 *(978-1-60754-808-9(9));* lib. bdg. 22.60 *(978-1-60754-804-1(6))* Windmill Bks.
Le Guin, Ursula K. Jane on Her Own. Schindler, S. D., illus. 2003. (Catwings Ser.: No. 4). (ENG.). 48p. (J). (gr. -1-3). 5.99 *(978-0-439-55192-2(7))* Scholastic, Inc.
MacColl, Michaela & Chronicle Books Staff. A Novel of Intrigue & Romance. 2010. (ENG., Illus.). 368p. (YA). (gr. 7-17). 16.99 *(978-0-8118-7300-0(5))* Chronicle Bks. LLC.
Maddox, Jake. Skateboard Struggle, 1 vol. Tiffany, Sean, illus. 2011. (Jake Maddox Sports Stories Ser.). (ENG.). 72p. (gr. 2-3). pap. 5.95 *(978-1-4342-3424-7(X))* Stone Arch Bks.
Maggiore, Lisa. Ava the Monster Slayer. Felten, Ross, illus. 2015. (ENG.). 32p. (J). (gr. -1-k). 16.99 *(978-1-63450-151-4(9),* Sky Pony Pr.) Skyhorse Publishing Co., Inc.
Mary-Todd, Jonathan. The Giant. 2014. (Bareknuckle Ser.). 104p. (YA). (gr. 6-12). lib. bdg. 27.93 *(978-1-4677-1457-0(7),* Darby Creek) Lerner Publishing Group.
Matson, Morgan. Since You've Been Gone. 2015. (ENG., Illus.). 480p. (YA). (gr. 7). pap. 9.99 *(978-1-4424-3501-8(1),* Simon & Schuster Bks. For Young Readers) Simon & Schuster Bks. For Young Readers.
Mayer, Mercer. All by Myself. 2014. 24p. pap. 4.00 *(978-1-61003-371-8(X))* Center for the Collaborative Classroom.
McGinnis, Mindy. In a Handful of Dust. 2014. (ENG.). 384p. (YA). (gr. 9). 17.99 *(978-0-06-219853-2(X),* Tegen, Katherine Bks) HarperCollins Pubs.
—Not a Drop to Drink. 2013. (ENG.). 320p. (YA). (gr. 9). 17.99 *(978-0-06-219850-1(5),* Tegen, Katherine Bks) HarperCollins Pubs.
Mikaelsen, Ben. Stranded. 2010. (ENG.). 288p. (J). (gr. 3-7). pap. 5.99 *(978-1-4231-3362-9(5))* Hyperion Pr.
Mlynowski, Sarah. Ten Things We Did (and Probably Shouldn't Have) (YA). (gr. 9). 2017. 384p. pap. 9.99 ***(978-0-06-268303-8(9))*** 2012. (ENG.). 368p. pap. 9.99 *(978-0-06-170126-9(2),* HarperTeen) 2011. (ENG.). 368p. 16.99 *(978-0-06-170124-5(6),* HarperTeen) HarperCollins Pubs.
Mothershead, Martha Fulford. Petoskey Stone Soup. Clarkson, Janet M., illus. 2006. 32p. (J). 18.95 *(978-0-9785465-0-2(4))* Leelanau Pr.
Munsch, Robert. The Paper Bag Princess: The Story Behind the Story. Martchenko, Michael, illus. 3rd anniv. ed. 2005. (ENG.). 64p. (J). (gr. -1-12). 19.95 *(978-1-55037-915-0(1),* 9781550379150) Annick Pr., Ltd. CAN. Dist: Publishers Group West (PGW).
Parrott, Darcie. Ladybug's Walk. 2007. (ENG.). 32p. (J). (gr. -1-k). 10.95 *(978-0-9772692-8-0(0))* Birch Island.
Paterson, Katherine. The Same Stuff As Stars. 2015. (ENG.). 256p. (J). (gr. 5-7). pap. 7.99 *(978-0-544-54030-9(1),* HMH Books For Young Readers) Houghton Mifflin Harcourt Publishing Co.
—The Same Stuff as Stars. 2004. 270p. (gr. 3-7). 17.00 *(978-0-7569-2801-8(X))* Perfection Learning Corp.
Patterson, James & Tebbetts, Chris. Save Rafe! Park, Laura, illus. 2014. (Middle School Ser.: 6). (ENG.). 288p. (J). (gr. 3-7). 13.99 *(978-0-316-32212-6(1),* Jimmy Patterson) Little Brown & Co.
Patterson, James & Tebbetts, Christopher. Save Rafe! Park, Laura, illus. 2014. 269p. (J). *(978-0-316-28629-9(X))* Little Brown & Co.
Paulsen, Gary. Brian's Return. unabr. ed. 2004. (Middle Grade Cassette Librariestm Ser.). 115p. (J). (gr. 5-9). pap. 29.00 incl. audio *(978-0-8072-0658-4(X),* S YA 292 SP, Listening Library) Random Hse. Audio Publishing Group.
—Brian's Return. 2012. (Hatchet Adventure Ser.). (ENG.). 160p. (YA). (gr. 5). pap. 9.99 *(978-0-307-92960-0(4),* Ember) Random Hse. Children's Bks.
—Fishbone's Song. 2016. (ENG., Illus.). 160p. (J). (gr. 5). 16.99 *(978-1-4814-5226-7(6),* Simon & Schuster Bks. For Young Readers) Simon & Schuster Bks. For Young Readers.
—The River. unabr. ed. 2004. (Middle Grade Cassette Librariestm Ser.). 132p. (J). (gr. 5-9). pap. 29.00 incl. audio *(978-0-8072-8704-0(0),* S YA 241 SP, Listening Library) Random Hse. Audio Publishing Group.
—The River. 2012. (Hatchet Adventure Ser.). (ENG.). 176p. (YA). (gr. 5). pap. 9.99 *(978-0-307-92961-7(2),* Ember) Random Hse. Children's Bks.
—The River. 2012. lib. bdg. 20.85 *(978-0-606-23880-9(8),* Turtleback) Turtleback Bks.
Peralta, Joaquin. Emma Snow: At the Edge of the World. 2009. 206p. (J). pap. 17.00 *(978-1-934376-19-5(1))* Balona Bks.
Pérez, Ashley Hope. What Can't Wait. 2011. (Carolrhoda YA Ser.). (ENG.). 240p. (YA). (gr. 9-12). 17.95 *(978-0-7613-6155-8(3),* Carolrhoda Bks.) Lerner Publishing Group.
Petrillo, Genevieve & Lyon, Lea. Keep Your Ear on the Ball, 1 vol. Lyon, Lea, illus. 2007. (ENG., Illus.). 32p. (J). (gr. -1-3). 16.95 *(978-0-88448-296-3(0))* Tilbury Hse. Pubs.
Polette, Keith. Isabel & the Hungry Coyote. 2009. (ENG.). 32p. (J). (gr. 4-7). 16.95 *(978-1-934960-72-1(1),* Raven Tree Pr.,Csi) Continental Sales, Inc.
Porter, Gene Stratton-. A Girl of the Limberlost. 2011. 266p. pap. 17.99 *(978-1-61279-071-8(2))* Publishing in Motion.
Pratt, Drusilla. What Do I Love. 2012. 28p. pap. 13.00 *(978-1-105-73983-5(X))* Lulu Pr., Inc.
Rinaldi, Ann. Juliet's Moon. 2010. (ENG., Illus.). 256p. (YA). (gr. 7). pap. 14.99 *(978-0-547-25874-4(7))* Houghton Mifflin Harcourt Publishing Co.
Robaard, Jedda. Stanley the Sock Monster Goes to the Moon. 2015. (ENG.). 40p. (J). (gr. -1-2). 16.99 *(978-1-4998-0012-8(6))* Little Bee Books Inc.
Ross, Tony. I Want to Do It Myself! Ross, Tony, illus. 2011. (Andersen Press Picture Bks). (ENG., Illus.). 32p. (J). (gr. -1-3). 16.95 *(978-0-7613-7412-1(4))* Lerner Publishing Group.
Sarno-Doyle, Christine. Your Inside Shape. 2012. (ENG., Illus.). 32p. (J). 17.95 *(978-0-9824461-0-2(1))* SDP Publishing.
Schulz, Kathy. I Need a Little Help. Iosa, Ann, illus. 2011. (Rookie Ready to Learn — All about Me! Ser.). 32p. (J). (gr. -1-k). lib. bdg. 25.00 *(978-0-531-26526-0(9),* Children's Pr.) Scholastic Library Publishing.
—Necesito una Ayudita. Iosa, Ann, illus. 2011. (Rookie Ready to Learn Español Ser.). (SPA.). 32p. (J). pap. 5.95 *(978-0-531-26782-0(2));* lib. bdg. 23.00 *(978-0-531-26114-9(X))* Scholastic Library Publishing. (Children's Pr.).
Shank, Marilyn Sue. Child of the Mountains. 2013. (ENG.). 272p. (J). (gr. 4-7). 6.99 *(978-0-375-87331-7(7),* Yearling) Random Hse. Children's Bks.
Sharafeddine, Fatima. The Servant, 1 vol. 2017. (ENG.). 160p. (J). (gr. 6). pap. 9.95 *(978-1-55498-308-7(8))* Groundwood Bks. CAN. Dist: Publishers Group West (PGW).
Shields, Gillian. DogFish. Taylor, Dan, illus. 2008. (ENG.). 32p. (J). (gr. -1-2). 16.99 *(978-1-4169-7127-6(0),* Atheneum Bks. for Young Readers) Simon & Schuster Children's Publishing.
Smith, Bryan. Mindset Matters. Griffin, Lisa, illus. 2017. (Without Limits Ser.: 2). (ENG.). 32p. (J). (gr. k-5). pap. 10.95 ***(978-1-944882-12-9(X))*** Boys Town Pr.
Sternberg, Julie. Like Pickle Juice on a Cookie. Cordell, Matthew, illus. 2011. (Eleanor Ser.). (ENG.). 128p. (J). (gr. 3-7). 15.95 *(978-0-8109-8424-0(5),* Amulet Bks.) Abrams, Inc.
Stott, Ann. I'll Be There. Phelan, Matt, illus. 2011. (ENG.). 32p. (J). (gr. -1-2). 14.99 *(978-0-7636-4711-7(X))* Candlewick Pr.
Stratton-Porter, Gene. A Girl of the Limberlost. (J). reprint ed. lib. bdg. 33.95 *(978-0-89190-948-4(6),* Rivercity Pr.) Amereon Ltd.
—A Girl of the Limberlost. Benda, Wladyslaw T., illus. 2005. reprint ed. pap. 38.95 *(978-0-7661-9424-3(8))* Kessinger Publishing, LLC.

—A Girl of the Limberlost. 2006. 336p. (YA). 21.95 *(978-1-934169-30-8(7))*; pap. 10.95 *(978-1-934169-31-5(5))* Norilana Bks.
—A Girl of the Limberlost. (Twelve-Point Ser.). 2003. (J). lib. bdg. 25.00 *(978-1-58287-232-2(5))* 2004. 463p. 26.00 *(978-1-58287-716-7(5))* North Bks.
Tennant, Kim. Thin Club. 2007. 52p. per. 10.00 *(978-1-4257-2619-5(4))* Xlibris Corp.
Trigiani, Adriana. Viola in Reel Life. (Viola Ser.: 1). (ENG.). (YA). (gr. 8). 2011. 304p. pap. 8.99 *(978-0-06-145104-1(5))* 2009. 288p. 17.99 *(978-0-06-145102-7(9))* HarperCollins Pubs. (HarperTeen).
van Genechten, Guido. Alex & the Tart. 2005. (Von Hamm Family Ser.). (Illus.). 32p. (J). (gr. -1-2). 6.95 *(978-1-58925-393-3(0))* Tiger Tales.
Van Leeuwen, Jean. Cabin on Trouble Creek. 2008. (ENG.). 224p. (J). (gr. 3-7). 7.99 *(978-0-14-241164-3(7))*, Puffin Books) Penguin Young Readers Group.
Voigt, Cynthia. The Book of Lost Things. Bruno, Iacopo, illus. 2013. (Mister Max Ser.: Bk. 1). (ENG.). 400p. (J). (gr. 3-7). 16.99 *(978-0-307-97681-9(5))*, Knopf Bks. for Young Readers) Random Hse. Children's Bks.
—Mister Max: the Book of Kings: Mister Max 3. Bruno, Iacopo, illus. 2016. (Mister Max Ser.). (ENG.). 352p. (J). (gr. 3-7). 7.99 *(978-0-307-97688-8(2))*, Yearling) Random Hse. Children's Bks.
—Mister Max: the Book of Lost Things: Mister Max 1. Bruno, Iacopo, illus. 2014. (Mister Max Ser.). (ENG.). 400p. (J). (gr. 3-7). 7.99 *(978-0-307-97682-6(3))*, Yearling) Random Hse. Children's Bks.
—Mister Max: the Book of Secrets. Bruno, Iacopo, illus. 2014. (Mister Max Ser.). (ENG.). 384p. (J). (gr. 3-7). 16.99 *(978-0-307-97684-0(X))*, Knopf Bks. for Young Readers) Random Hse. Children's Bks.
—The Book of Kings. Bruno, Iacopo, illus. 2015. (Mister Max Ser.). (ENG.). 352p. (J). (gr. 3-7). 16.99 *(978-0-307-97687-1(4))*, Knopf Bks. for Young Readers) Random Hse. Children's Bks.
Vrabel, Beth. A Blind Guide to Stinkville. 2015. (ENG.). 264p. (J). (gr. 2-7). 16.99 *(978-1-63450-157-6(8))*, Sky Pony Pr.) Skyhorse Publishing Co., Inc.
Waber, Bernard. Betty's Day Off. Date not set. (J). *(978-0-618-46875-1(7))* Houghton Mifflin Harcourt Publishing Co.
Weston Woods Staff, creator. I Like Me! 2011. 29.95 *(978-0-545-23373-6(9))*; 38.75 *(978-0-545-23378-1(X))*; 18.95 *(978-0-545-23376-7(3))* Weston Woods Studios, Inc.
Wiles, Deborah. Love, Ruby Lavender. 2005. (ENG., Illus.). 240p. (J). (gr. 2-5). reprint ed. pap. 7.99 *(978-0-15-205478-6(2))* Houghton Mifflin Harcourt Publishing Co.
—Love, Ruby Lavender. 2004. 216p. (J). (gr. 3-7). pap. 36.00 incl. audio *(978-0-8072-2096-2(5))*, Listening Library) Random Hse. Audio Publishing Group.
Young, Rebecca. Teacup. Ottley, Matt, illus. 2016. (ENG.). 40p. (J). (gr. -1-3). 17.99 *(978-0-7352-2777-4(2))*, Dial Bks) Penguin Young Readers Group.

SELF-RESPECT

Asher, Sandy, ed. With All My Heart, with All My Mind: Thirteen Stories about Growing up Jewish. 2004. Orig. Title: Today I Am. 164p. (J). (gr. 4-8). reprint ed. pap. 18.00 *(978-0-7567-7692-3(9))* DIANE Publishing Co.
Greene, Ida. Looking for Love in All the Wrong Places. 2013. 90p. (Orig.). (gr. 10-18). pap. 19.95 *(978-1-881165-05-7(1))* People Skills International.
The Need to Know Library: Guidance for Today's Problems, 8 bks. Incl. Everything You Need to Know about Bipolar Disorder & Manic Depressive Illness. Sommers, Michael A. (J). (gr. 4-6). 2000. lib. bdg. 25.25 *(978-0-8239-3106-4(4))*, NTBIDI); Everything You Need to Know about Deafness. Basinger, Carol. (J). (gr. 7-12). 2005. lib. bdg. 31.95 *(978-0-8239-3165-1(X))*, NTDEAF); Everything You Need to Know about Diabetes. Apel, Melanie Ann. (YA). (gr. 7-12). 2005. lib. bdg. 31.95 *(978-0-8239-3090-6(4))*, NTDIAB); Everything You Need to Know about Family Court. Bianchi, Anne. (YA). (gr. 7-12). 2005. lib. bdg. 31.95 *(978-0-8239-3163-7(3))*, NTFACO); Everything You Need to Know about Hepatitis. Aronson, Virginia. (YA). (gr. 7-12). 2005. lib. bdg. 31.95 *(978-0-8239-3100-2(5))*, NTHEPA); Everything You Need to Know about Media Violence. Edgar, Kathleen J. (YA). (gr. 4-6). 2000. lib. bdg. 31.95 *(978-0-8239-3108-8(0))*, NTMEVI); Everything You Need to Know about Schizophrenia. Friedman, Michelle S. (YA). (gr. 7-12). 2005. lib. bdg. 31.95 *(978-0-8239-3091-3(2))*, NTSCHI); 64p. (Illus.). Set lib. bdg. 202.00 *(978-0-8239-9282-9(9))* Rosen Publishing Group, Inc., The.
Story Rhyme Staff. Self-Esteem: Stories, Poetry & Activity Pages. Story Rhyme Staff, illus. Date not set. (Illus.). 28p. (YA). (gr. 4-9). ring bd. 19.95 *(978-1-56820-107-8(9))* Story Time Stories That Rhyme.

SELLING

see Sales Personnel

SEMANTICS

Carr, Aaron. Opposites, with Code. 2012. (Science Kids Ser.). (ENG., Illus.). 24p. (J). (gr. -1-1). pap. 12.95 *(978-1-61913-308-2(3))*; lib. bdg. 27.13 *(978-1-61913-085-2(8))* Weigl Pubs., Inc. (AV2 by Weigl).

SEMMES, RAPHAEL, 1809-1877

Bailey, Tom. Raphael Semmes: Commander of the Alabama. 2011. (Illus.). 120p. (J). *(978-1-59421-062-4(4))* Seacoast Publishing, Inc.

SENATORS—UNITED STATES

see Legislators—United States; United States—Congress—Senate—Biography

SENEGAL

Berg, Elizabeth & Lau, Ruth. Senegal. 2nd rev. ed. 2009. (Cultures of the World 17 Ser.). 144p. (gr. 6). 42.79 *(978-0-7614-4481-7(5))* Marshall Cavendish Corp.
Mulroy, Tanya. Senegal. 2012. (J). pap. *(978-1-4222-2229-4(2))* Mason Crest.
—Senegal. Rotberg, Robert I., ed. 2012. (Evolution of Africa's Major Nations Ser.). (Illus.). 80p. (J). (gr. 7). 22.95 *(978-1-4222-2201-0(2))* Mason Crest.
Streissguth, Thomas & Streissguth, Tom. Senegal in Pictures. 2009. (Visual Geography Series, Second Ser.). (ENG., Illus.). 80p. (J). (gr. 5-12). 31.93 *(978-1-57505-951-8(7))* Lerner Publishing Group.

SENSES AND SENSATION

see also Hearing; Smell; Touch; Vision

Alda, Arlene. Except the Color Grey. 2011. (ENG., Illus.). 24p. (J). (gr. k-k). 16.95 *(978-1-77049-284-4(4))*, Tundra Bks.) Tundra Bks. CAN. Dist: Penguin Random Hse. LLC.
Algarra, Alejandro. How Do Animals Use Their Five Senses? Bonilla, Rocio, illus. 2016. 35p. (J). ***(978-1-5182-3150-6(0))*** Barron's Educational Series, Inc.
Algarra, Alejandro & Bonilla, Rocio. How Do Animals Use Their Five Senses? 2016. (Curious Young Minds Ser.). (ENG., Illus.). 36p. (J). (gr. -1-2). pap. 7.99 *(978-1-4380-0891-2(0))* Barron's Educational Series, Inc.
Aliki. My Five Senses. Aliki, illus. 2015. (Let's-Read-And-Find-Out Science 1 Ser.). (ENG., Illus.). 32p. (J). (gr. -1-3). 17.99 *(978-0-06-238191-0(1))* HarperCollins Pubs.
—My Five Senses. 2014. (Let's-Read-And-Find-Out Science 1 Ser.). (ENG.). 32p. (J). (gr. k-3). 10.24 *(978-1-63245-272-6(3))* Lectorum Pubns., Inc.
All about My Senses. 2017. (All about My Senses Ser.). 24p. (gr. k-1). pap. 56.10 ***(978-0-7660-8813-9(8))***; lib. bdg. 135.60 ***(978-0-7660-8601-2(1))*** Enslow Pubs., Inc.
Aloian, Molly. What Is Taste? 2013. (ENG., Illus.). 24p. (J). *(978-0-7787-0967-1(1))*; pap. *(978-0-7787-0972-5(8))* Crabtree Publishing Co.
Appleby, Alex. Dinosaur's Five Senses. 2013. (Dinosaur School Ser.). 24p. (J). (gr. k-1). pap. 48.90 *(978-1-4339-9051-9(2))*; pap. 8.15 *(978-1-4339-9050-2(4))*; (ENG., Illus.). lib. bdg. 22.60 *(978-1-4339-9049-6(0))* Stevens, Gareth Publishing LLLP.
—Lo Que Oigo / What I Hear. 2014. (Mis Cinco Sentidos / My Five Senses Ser.). (SPA.). 24p. (J). (gr. k-2). 22.60 *(978-1-4824-0869-0(4))* Stevens, Gareth Publishing LLLP.
—Lo Que Toco / What I Touch. 2014. (Mis Cinco Sentidos / My Five Senses Ser.). (SPA.). 24p. (J). (gr. k-2). 22.60 *(978-1-4824-0877-5(5))* Stevens, Gareth Publishing LLLP.
—My Five Senses. 2014. (My Five Senses Ser.). 24p. (J). (gr. k-2). 113.00 *(978-1-4824-1036-5(2))* Stevens, Gareth Publishing LLLP.
—What I Hear. 2014. (My Five Senses Ser.). (Illus.). 24p. (J). (gr. k-2). pap. 8.15 *(978-1-4824-0776-1(0))* Stevens, Gareth Publishing LLLP.
—What I See. 2014. (My Five Senses Ser.). 24p. (J). (gr. k-2). 22.60 *(978-1-4824-0808-9(2))* Stevens, Gareth Publishing LLLP.
—What I Smell. 2014. (My Five Senses Ser.). 24p. (J). (gr. k-2). 22.60 *(978-1-4824-0813-3(9))*; pap. 8.15 *(978-1-4824-0814-0(7))* Stevens, Gareth Publishing LLLP.
—What I Taste. 2014. (My Five Senses Ser.). (Illus.). 24p. (J). (gr. k-2). 22.60 *(978-1-4824-0818-8(X))* Stevens, Gareth Publishing LLLP.
—What I Touch. 2014. (My Five Senses Ser.). 24p. (J). (gr. k-2). pap. 48.90 *(978-1-4824-0824-9(4))*; pap. 8.15 *(978-1-4824-0823-2(6))* Stevens, Gareth Publishing LLLP.
Baby Shakespeare. (Baby Einstein Ser.). (Illus.). 28p. (J). (gr. -1). pap. 19.98 incl. audio, VHS *(978-1-892309-15-0(7))* Baby Einstein Co., LLC, The.
Bailey, Jacqui. What Happens When You Use Your Senses? 2009. 32p. (gr. k-5). pap. 10.60 *(978-1-4358-2616-8(7))*, Rosen Classroom) 2008. (Illus.). 30p. (J). (gr. -1-2). lib. bdg. 26.50 *(978-1-4042-4427-6(1))* Rosen Publishing Group, Inc., The.
Ballard, Carol. Understanding the Senses. 2010. (Understanding the Human Body Ser.). (Illus.). 48p. (J). pap. 11.75 *(978-1-4358-9689-5(0))*; (YA). (gr. 5-8). lib. bdg. 29.25 *(978-1-4358-9683-3(1))* Rosen Publishing Group, Inc., The. (Rosen Reference).
—Your Sense of Touch. 2010. (Your Body at Work Ser.). (ENG.). 32p. (YA). (gr. 2-5). lib. bdg. 26.60 *(978-1-4339-4115-3(5))* Stevens, Gareth Publishing LLLP.
Barnham, Kay. Taste. 2005. (Our Senses Ser.). (Illus.). 24p. (gr. k-3). lib. bdg. 23.00 *(978-0-8368-4409-2(2))*, Gareth Stevens Learning Library) Stevens, Gareth Publishing LLLP.
Barraclough, Sue. What Can I Taste? 2005. (J). *(978-1-4034-7081-2(2))*; (ENG.). 32p. pap. *(978-1-4034-7087-4(1))* Steck-Vaughn.
Beattie, Steven M., II. These Are My Sensors. Beattie, Steven M., II, illus. 2007. (Illus.). 32p. (gr. -1-k). 19.99 *(978-1-59879-310-9(1))* Lifevest Publishing, Inc.
Beaumont, Susanna. Baby Senses Taste. 2005. (Baby Senses Ser.). (Illus.). 12p. (gr. -1-k). per., bds. *(978-1-905051-50-2(6))* Make Believe Ideas.
Beck, Esther. Cool Sensory Suspense: Fun Science Projects about the Senses, 1 vol. 2008. (Cool Science Ser.). (ENG.). 32p. (YA). (gr. 2-5). 28.50 *(978-1-59928-910-6(5))* ABDO Publishing Co.
Bellamy, Adam. What's Intuition? 2017. (All about My Senses Ser.). 24p. (J). (gr. k-1). lib. bdg. 22.60 ***(978-0-7660-8722-4(0))*** Enslow Pubs., Inc.
—What's That I Feel? 2017. (All about My Senses Ser.). 24p. (J). (gr. k-1). lib. bdg. 22.60 ***(978-0-7660-8720-0(4))*** Enslow Pubs., Inc.
—What's That I Hear? 2017. (All about My Senses Ser.). 24p. (J). (gr. k-1). lib. bdg. 22.60 ***(978-0-7660-8603-6(8))*** Enslow Pubs., Inc.
—What's That Smell? 2017. (All about My Senses Ser.). 24p. (J). (gr. k-1). lib. bdg. 22.60 ***(978-0-7660-8607-4(0))*** Enslow Pubs., Inc.
—What's That Taste? 2017. (All about My Senses Ser.). 24p. (J). (gr. k-1). lib. bdg. 22.60 ***(978-0-7660-8609-8(7))*** Enslow Pubs., Inc.
Benbow, Ann & Mably, Colin. Sensational Human Body Science Projects. LaBaff, Tom, illus. 2009. (Real Life Science Experiments Ser.). 48p. (J). (gr. 2-5). lib. bdg. 25.27 *(978-0-7660-3149-4(7))* Enslow Pubs., Inc.
Benchmark Education Company, LLC Staff, compiled by. Senses. 2006. (J). 91.00 *(978-1-4108-7033-9(2))* Benchmark Education Co.
Bentley, Joyce. Soft. 2006. (Things Around Us Ser.). (J). *(978-1-59389-278-4(0))* Chrysalis Education.
—Wet. 2006. (Things Around Us Ser.). (J). *(978-1-59389-279-1(9))* Chrysalis Education.
Bjorklund, Ruth. The Senses. 2009. (Amazing Human Body 2 Ser.). 80p. (gr. 5). lib. bdg. 34.21 *(978-0-7614-4043-7(7))* Marshall Cavendish GBR. Dist: Marshall Cavendish Corp.
Bodach, Vijaya Khisty. Making Observations. 2008. (Discovering & Exploring Science Ser.). (Illus.). 16p. (J). (gr. -1-3). lib. bdg. 12.95 *(978-0-7569-8431-1(9))* Perfection Learning Corp.
Boothroyd, Jennifer. Lightning Bolt Books: Your Amazing Senses, 5 vols., Set. Incl. What Is Hearing? (Illus.). (J). 26.60 *(978-0-7613-4250-2(8))*; What Is Sight? 26.60 *(978-0-7613-4248-9(6))*; What Is Smell? 26.60 *(978-0-7613-4253-3(2))*; What Is Taste? 26.60 *(978-0-7613-4251-9(6))*; What Is Touch? 26.60 *(978-0-7613-4252-6(4))*; 32p. (gr. k-2). 2009. Set lib. bdg. 126.30 *(978-0-7613-4246-5(X))*, Lerner Pubns.) Lerner Publishing Group.
—What Is Taste? 2009. (Lightning Bolt Books (tm) — Your Amazing Senses Ser.). (ENG.). 32p. (gr. k-2). 26.60 *(978-0-7613-4251-9(6))*, Lerner Pubns.); pap. 7.95 *(978-0-7613-5017-0(9))* Lerner Publishing Group.
Boynton, Jeannette. God Loves Variety. Boynton, Jeannette & Holdeen, Bonnie, illus. 2007. (J). per. 10.99 *(978-1-59879-264-5(4))* Lifevest Publishing, Inc.
Brocket, Jane. Cold, Crunchy, Colorful: Using Our Senses. Brocket, Jane, photos by. 2014. (Jane Brocket's Clever Concepts Ser.). (ENG., Illus.). 32p. (gr. -1-2). lib. bdg. 26.60 *(978-1-4677-0233-1(1))*, Millbrook Pr.) Lerner Publishing Group.
Buchanan, Shelly. Animal Senses. 2015. (Science Readers: Content & Literacy Ser.). (ENG.). 32p. (J). (gr. 4-4). pap. 8.99 *(978-1-4807-4678-7(9))* Teacher Created Materials, Inc.
Burstein, John. Patterns: What's on the Wall? 2003. (Weekly Reader Early Learning Library). (Illus.). 24p. (J). (gr. k-4). pap. 8.15 *(978-0-8368-3831-2(9))*, Weekly Reader Leveled Readers) Stevens, Gareth Publishing LLLP.
Burton, Margie, et al. My Five Senses. 2011. (Early Connections Ser.). (J). *(978-1-61672-263-0(0))* Benchmark Education Co.
Canavan, Thomas. Do You Really Taste with Your Nose? Questions about the Senses. 2016. (Human Body FAQ Ser.). 0032p. (J). (gr. 3-3). pap. 10.00 *(978-1-4994-3163-6(5))*, PowerKids Pr.) Rosen Publishing Group, Inc., The.
Cardenas, Ernesto A. The Five Senses. 2009. pap. 4.95 *(978-1-60698-074-3(2))* Milo Educational Bks. & Resources.
—With My Senses. 2009. 19.95 *(978-1-60698-029-3(7))*; pap. 3.95 *(978-1-60698-027-9(0))* Milo Educational Bks. & Resources.
Carr, Aaron. El Gusto. 2013. (Mis Sentidos Ser.). (SPA., Illus.). 24p. (J). (gr. 3-7). lib. bdg. 27.13 *(978-1-62127-581-7(7))*, AV2 by Weigl) Weigl Pubs., Inc.
—El Oido. 2013. (Mis Sentidos Ser.). (SPA., Illus.). 24p. (J). (gr. -1-3). lib. bdg. 27.13 *(978-1-62127-575-6(2))*, AV2 by Weigl) Weigl Pubs., Inc.
—El Olfato. 2013. (Mis Sentidos Ser.). (SPA., Illus.). 24p. (J). (gr. 3-7). lib. bdg. 27.13 *(978-1-62127-579-4(5))*, AV2 by Weigl) Weigl Pubs., Inc.
—Tacto. 2014. (SPA., Illus.). 24p. (J). *(978-1-62127-583-1(3))* Weigl Pubs., Inc.
—Vista. 2014. (SPA., Illus.). 24p. (J). *(978-1-62127-577-0(9))* Weigl Pubs., Inc.
Casado, Dami & Casado, Alicia. El Gusto. 2005. (Sentidos y Algo Más). (SPA.). 10p. *(978-84-272-6414-4(3))* Molino, Editorial.
—El Oido. 2005. (Sentidos y Algo Más). (SPA & ESP.). 16p. 8.99 *(978-84-272-6412-0(7))* Molino, Editorial ESP. Dist: Santillana USA Publishing Co., Inc.
—La Palabra. 2005. (Sentidos y Algo Más). (SPA & ESP.). 16p. 8.99 *(978-84-272-6416-8(X))* Molino, Editorial ESP. Dist: Santillana USA Publishing Co., Inc.
—El Tacto. 2005. (Sentidos y Algo Más). (SPA & ESP.). 16p. 8.99 *(978-84-272-6415-1(1))* Molino, Editorial ESP. Dist: Santillana USA Publishing Co., Inc.
—La Vista. 2005. (Sentidos y Algo Más). (SPA & ESP.). 16p. 8.99 *(978-84-272-6411-3(9))* Molino, Editorial ESP. Dist: Santillana USA Publishing Co., Inc.
Chara, Kathleen A. & Chara, Paul J. Sensory Smarts: A Book for Kids with ADHD or Autism Spectrum Disorders Struggling with Sensory Integration Problems. Bems, Joel M., illus. 2004. (ENG.). 80p. (J). pap. *(978-1-84310-783-5(X))* Kingsley, Jessica Pubs.
Claymation Sensation. 2016. (Claymation Sensation Ser.). 32p. (gr. 3-3). 171.00 *(978-1-4994-8096-2(2))*; pap. 70.50 *(978-1-5081-9271-8(5))* Rosen Publishing Group, Inc., The. (Windmill Bks.).
Coan, Sharon. Message Received!, 1 vol. (Science Readers: Content & Literacy Ser.). (ENG., Illus.). 24p. (gr. 1-1). 2015. (J). 22.96 *(978-1-4938-1152-6(5))* 2014. pap. 8.99 *(978-1-4807-4565-0(0))* Teacher Created Materials, Inc.
Cobb, Vicki. Perk up Your Ears: Discover Your Sense of Hearing. Lewis, Cynthia, illus. 2003. (Five Senses Ser.). (ENG.). 32p. (gr. 3-5). pap. 7.95 *(978-0-7613-1981-8(6))*, Millbrook Pr.) Lerner Publishing Group.
Colligan, L. H. Pain Treatments. 2013. (Advances in Medicine Ser.). 64p. (J). (gr. 6-9). pap. 15.28 *(978-1-62712-011-1(4))*; (Illus.). 34.21 *(978-1-60870-468-2(8))* Cavendish Square Publishing.
Collins, Andrew. See, Hear, Smell, Taste, & Touch: Using Your Five Senses. 2006. (Science Chapters Ser.). (ENG., Illus.). 48p. (J). (gr. 1-4). lib. bdg. 17.90 *(978-0-7922-5943-5(2))*, National Geographic Children's Bks.) National Geographic Society.
Como Funcionan Nuestros Sentidos. (SPA.). 92p. (J). 10.00 *(978-84-342-1809-3(7))* Parramon Ediciones S.A. ESP. Dist: Distribuidora Norma, Inc.
Cornell, Kari. Our Senses. 2016. (Illus.). 16p. (J). *(978-0-87659-701-9(0))* Gryphon Hse., Inc.
Dalmatian Press Staff. Pop & Sniff Fruit. 2008. (ENG.). 12p. (J). 10.95 *(978-1-58117-676-6(7))*, Intervisual/Piggy Toes) Bendon, Inc.
Dayton, Connor. El Gusto / Taste, 1 vol., 1. De La Vega, Eida, ed. 2014. (Tus Cinco Sentidos y Tu Sexto Sentido / Your Five Senses & Your Sixth Sense Ser.). (SPA & BYN.). 24p. (J). (gr. k-2). 23.60 *(978-1-4777-3274-8(8))*, PowerKids Pr.) Rosen Publishing Group, Inc., The.
—El Odo / Hearing. De La Vega, Eida, ed. 2014. (Tus Cinco Sentidos y Tu Sexto Sentido / Your Five Senses & Your Sixth Sense Ser.). (SPA & BYN.). 24p. (J). (gr. k-2). 23.60 *(978-1-4777-3268-7(3))*, PowerKids Pr.) Rosen Publishing Group, Inc., The.
—Taste, 1 vol., 1. 2014. (Your Five Senses & Your Sixth Sense Ser.). (ENG.). 24p. (J). (gr. k-2). 23.60 *(978-1-4777-2856-7(2))*, PowerKids Pr.) Rosen Publishing Group, Inc., The.
—Touch, 1 vol., 1. 2014. (Your Five Senses & Your Sixth Sense Ser.). (ENG.). 24p. (J). (gr. k-2). pap. 8.25 *(978-1-4777-2948-9(8))*, PowerKids Pr.) Rosen Publishing Group, Inc., The.
Del Moral, Susana. Que Flota? Un Libro para Banarse y Disfrutar. Zaidi, Nadeem, illus. 2006. (Baby Einstein Ser.). (SPA.). 8p. (J). (gr. -1). *(978-970-718-453-4(1))*, Silver Dolphin en Español) Advanced Marketing, S. de R. L. de C. V.
Dell, J. A. The Gateways of Knowledge: An Introduction to the Study of the Senses. 2013. (ENG.). 186p. pap. 35.99 *(978-1-107-65583-6(8))* Cambridge Univ. Pr.
Dorling Kindersley Publishing Staff. Baby Loves Peekaboo! Quasha, Jennifer, ed. King, Dave, photos by. 2008. (ENG., Illus.). 12p. (J). (gr. -1-k). bds. 6.99 *(978-0-7566-3486-5(5))*, DK Children) Dorling Kindersley Publishing, Inc.
—I Love You. 2016. (Baby Touch & Feel Ser.). (ENG.). 14p. (J). (— 1). bds. 5.99 *(978-1-4654-5763-9(1))*, DK Children) Dorling Kindersley Publishing, Inc.
—Look I'm a Cook. 2017. (ENG.). 48p. (J). (gr. -1-2). 12.99 ***(978-1-4654-5964-0(2))***, DK Children) Dorling Kindersley Publishing, Inc.
Dorling Kindersley Publishing Staff. SENSEational Illusions. 2015. (ENG., Illus.). 32p. (J). (gr. 3-7). 19.99 *(978-1-4654-3829-4(7))*, DK Children) Dorling Kindersley Publishing, Inc.
Douglas, Lloyd G. My Ears. 2004. (Wel-My Body Ser.). (J). 19.00 *(978-0-516-24062-6(5))*, Children's Pr.) Scholastic Library Publishing.
—My Eyes. 2004. (Wel-My Body Ser.). (J). 19.00 *(978-0-516-24060-2(9))*, Children's Pr.) Scholastic Library Publishing.
Durrie, Karen. Taste. 2012. (J). *(978-1-61913-312-9(1))*; pap. 12.95 *(978-1-61913-317-4(2))* Weigl Pubs., Inc.
Editions Phidal Staff, ed. Senses. (Jump Ser.). (Illus.). 32p. (J). (gr. 2-7). pap. 4.95 *(978-1-882210-30-5(1))* Action Publishing, Inc.
—Senses. 2004. (Illus.). lib. bdg. 7.95 *(978-0-8225-5162-1(4))* Lerner Publishing Group.
Equipo Staff & Delafosse, Claude. El Tacto. (Coleccion Mundo Maravilloso). (SPA., Illus.). 42p. (J). (gr. 2-4). *(978-84-348-5207-5(1))*, SM8406) SM Ediciones.
Farndon, John. Stickmen's Guide to Your Brilliant Brain. Dean, Venitia, illus. 2017. (Stickmen's Guides to Your Awesome Body Ser.). (ENG.). 32p. (J). (gr. 3-6). 26.65 ***(978-1-5124-3213-8(X))*** Lerner Publishing Group.
Feldman, Jean R. & Karapetkova, Holly. Five Senses (Lap Book) 2010. (ENG., Illus.). 12p. (gr. -1-k). 9.95 *(978-1-61590-176-0(0))* Rourke Educational Media.
Furgang, Kathy. My Eyes. 2009. (My Body Ser.). 24p. (gr. 3-3). 42.50 *(978-1-61514-688-8(1))*, PowerKids Pr.) Rosen Publishing Group, Inc., The.
—My Nose. 2009. (My Body Ser.). 24p. (gr. 3-3). 42.50 *(978-1-61514-691-8(1))*, PowerKids Pr.) Rosen Publishing Group, Inc., The.
Ganeri, Anita. Taste. 2013. (Senses Ser.). (Illus.). 24p. (gr. k-3). 28.50 *(978-1-59920-854-1(7))* Black Rabbit Bks.
Gardner, Robert, et al. Ace Your Science Project about the Senses: Great Science Fair Ideas. 2009. (Ace Your Biology Science Project Ser.). (Illus.). 112p. (J). (gr. 5-9). lib. bdg. 33.27 *(978-0-7660-3217-0(5))* Enslow Pubs., Inc.
George, Patrick. I Taste... George, Patrick, illus. 2013. (ENG., Illus.). 36p. (J). (gr. -1-k). 12.99 *(978-1-908473-06-6(1))* PatrickGeorge GBR. Dist: Independent Pubs. Group.
Gibson, Brylee. Keeping in Touch. 2007. (Connectors Ser.). (gr. 2-5). pap. *(978-1-877453-05-2(6))* Global Education Systems Ltd.
Glover, David & Glover, Penny. Senses. 2005. (Humans & Animals Ser.). (Illus.). 30p. (J). (gr. 2-4). lib. bdg. 27.10 *(978-1-58340-692-2(1))* Black Rabbit Bks.
Gregoire, Maryellen. Your Five Senses. 2011. (Wonder Readers Emergent Level Ser.). (ENG.). (gr. -1-1). 16p. pap. 35.94 *(978-1-4296-8211-4(6))*; 32p. pap. 5.99 *(978-1-4296-7880-3(1))* Capstone Press of Coughlan Cos. (Wonder Readers).
Group/McGraw-Hill, Wright. Nuestros Cinco Sentidos, 6 vols. (First Explorers. Primeros Exploradores Nonfiction Sets Ser.). (SPA.). (gr. 1-2). 29.95 *(978-0-7699-1476-3(4))* Shortland Pubns. (U. S. A.) Inc.
Haddon, Jean. Make Sense! DiRocco, Carl, illus. 2006. (Silly Millies Ser.). 32p. (J). (gr. 3-7). per. 5.95 *(978-0-8225-6472-0(6))*, First Avenue Editions); (ENG.). (gr. k-2). lib. bdg. 21.27 *(978-0-7613-3403-3(3))*, Millbrook Pr.) Lerner Publishing Group.
Hall, Kirsten. Animal Taste. 2005. (Animals & Their Senses Ser.). (Illus.). 24p. (gr. k-3). lib. bdg. 22.00 *(978-0-8368-4805-2(5))*, Weekly Reader Leveled Readers) Stevens, Gareth Publishing LLLP.
—Animal Taste (El Gusto en los Animales) 2005. (Animals & Their Senses/ Los sentidos de los animales (bilingual) Ser.). (ENG & SPA., Illus.). 24p. (gr. k-3). pap. 8.15 *(978-0-8368-4823-6(3))*, Weekly Reader Leveled Readers) Stevens, Gareth Publishing LLLP.
—Animal Taste (el Gusto en los Animales) 2005. (Animals & Their Senses/ Los sentidos de los animales Ser.). (ENG & SPA., Illus.). 24p. (gr. k-3). lib. bdg. 22.00 *(978-0-8368-4817-5(9))*, Weekly Reader Leveled Readers) Stevens, Gareth Publishing LLLP.
—Animal Touch (El Tacto en los Animales) 2005. (Animals & Their Senses/ Los sentidos de los animales (bilingual) Ser.). (ENG & SPA., Illus.). 24p. (gr. k-3). pap. 8.15 *(978-0-8368-4824-3(1))*; lib. bdg. 22.00 *(978-0-8368-4818-2(7))* Stevens, Gareth Publishing LLLP. (Weekly Reader Leveled Readers).
Hanel, Rachael. Smell. 2003. 24p. (J). lib. bdg. 21.35 *(978-1-58340-306-8(X))* Black Rabbit Bks.
Hartley Steiner. This Is Gabriel Making Sense of School: A Book about Sensory Processing Disorder. 2010. 28p. pap. 13.95 *(978-1-4269-2777-5(0))* Trafford Publishing.
Helenek, Sophie. My First Book MUSICAL INSTRUMENTS: GOLD Mom's Choice Awards Recipient. 2014. (My First Book Ser.). (ENG., Illus.). 16p. (J). (gr. -1 — 1). bds. 5.99 *(978-0-9894505-2-2(X))* Nursery Bks.

S

Hengel, Katherine. Ears Are for Earrings: The Sense of Hearing, 1 vol. 2012. (All about Your Senses Ser.) (ENG.). 24p. (J). (gr. k-3). lib. bdg. 24.21 *(978-1-61783-196-6(4),* SandCastle) ABDO Publishing Co.

—Eyes Are for Winking: The Sense of Sight, 1 vol. 2012. (All about Your Senses Ser.). (ENG.). 24p. (J). (gr. k-3). lib. bdg. 24.21 *(978-1-61783-197-3(2),* SandCastle) ABDO Publishing Co.

—Hands Are for Holding: The Sense of Touch, 1 vol. 2012. (All about Your Senses Ser.). (ENG.). 24p. (J). (gr. k-3). lib. bdg. 24.21 *(978-1-61783-198-0(0),* SandCastle) ABDO Publishing Co.

—Mouths Are for Smiling: The Sense of Taste, 1 vol. 2012. (All about Your Senses Ser.). (ENG.). 24p. (J). (gr. k-3). lib. bdg. 24.21 *(978-1-61783-199-7(9),* SandCastle) ABDO Publishing Co.

—Noses Are for Picking: The Sense of Smell, 1 vol. 2012. (All about Your Senses Ser.). (ENG.). 24p. (J). (gr. k-3). lib. bdg. 24.21 *(978-1-61783-200-0(6),* SandCastle) ABDO Publishing Co.

—Senses Are for Everything: The Five Senses, 1 vol. 2012. (All about Your Senses Ser.). (ENG.). 24p. (J). (gr. k-3). lib. bdg. 24.21 *(978-1-61783-201-7(4),* SandCastle) ABDO Publishing Co.

Hewitt, Sally. Tastes Good! 2008. (Let's Start Science Ser.). (ENG., Illus.). 24p. (J). (gr. 3-7). pap. *(978-0-7787-4061-2(7))* Crabtree Publishing Co.

Hickman, Pamela. How Animals Use Their Senses. Stephens, Pat, illus. 2006. (Kids Can Read Ser.). (ENG.). 32p. (J). (gr. 1-3). 3.95 *(978-1-55337-903-4(9));* 14.95 *(978-1-55337-902-7(0))* Kids Can Pr., Ltd. CAN. Dist: Hachette Bk. Group.

Hidalgo, Maria. Taste. 2003. 24p. (J). lib. bdg. 21.35 *(978-1-58340-305-1(1))* Black Rabbit Bks.

—Touch. 2003. 24p. (J). lib. bdg. 21.35 *(978-1-58340-307-5(8))* Black Rabbit Bks.

Hilton, Jennifer Sue & McCurry, Kristen. El Mundo Maravilloso de Dios. Rimmington, Natasha, illus. 2016. (SPA.). (J). *(978-1-5064-2094-3(X))* Augsburg Fortress, Pubs.

Honders, Christine. How Sharks & Other Animals Sense Electricity. 2015. (Superior Animal Senses Ser.). (ENG., Illus.). 24p. (J). (gr. 3-4). pap. 8.25 *(978-1-4994-0994-9(X),* PowerKids Pr.) Rosen Publishing Group, Inc., The.

Howells, Shelley. Making Sense of Your Senses: Set Of 6. 2011. (Navigators Ser.). (J). pap. 44.00 net. *(978-1-4108-0407-5(0))* Benchmark Education Co.

—Making Sense of Your Senses & Tus sentidos tienen Sentido: 6 English, 6 Spanish Adaptations. 2011. (ENG & SPA.). (J). 89.00 net. *(978-1-4108-5677-7(1))* Benchmark Education Co.

Hutmacher, Kimberly M. Your Senses at the Dentist's Office. 2011. (Out & about with Your Senses Ser.). (ENG.). 24p. (J). (gr. k-1). lib. bdg. 26.65 *(978-1-4296-6664-0(1),* Pebble Plus) Capstone Press of Coughlan Cos.

—Your Senses at the Fire Station, 1 vol. 2011. (Out & about with Your Senses Ser.). (ENG.). 24p. (J). (gr. k-1). lib. bdg. 26.65 *(978-1-4296-6667-1(6),* Pebble Plus) Capstone Press of Coughlan Cos.

Ikids Staff. The Five Senses. 2009. (ENG., Illus.). 20p. (J). (gr. -1-1). 6.99 *(978-1-58476-812-8(6))* Innovative Kids.

Issa, Joanna. These Are My Senses, 1 vol. 2014. (These Are My Senses Ser.). (ENG.). 24p. (gr. -1-1). pap. 29.95 *(978-1-4846-0435-9(0),* Acorn) Heinemann-Raintree.

—What Can I Taste?, 1 vol. 2014. (These Are My Senses Ser.). (ENG., Illus.). 24p. (gr. -1-1). pap. 5.99 *(978-1-4846-0430-4(X),* Acorn) Heinemann-Raintree.

Jones, Ayesha. Allah Gave Me a Tongue to Taste. Stratford, Stevan, illus. 2016. (ENG.). 32p. (J). 8.95 *(978-0-86037-338-4(X))* Kube Publishing Ltd. GBR. Dist: Consortium Bk. Sales & Distribution.

Kalman, Bobbie. How Does It Feel? 2007. (Looking at Nature Ser.). (ENG., Illus.). 24p. (J). (gr. -1-2). pap. *(978-0-7787-3334-8(3));* lib. bdg. *(978-0-7787-3314-0(9))* Crabtree Publishing Co.

—MIS Sentidos Me Ayudan. 2010. (SPA & ENG.). 16p. (J). pap. *(978-0-7787-8584-2(X))* Crabtree Publishing Co.

—My Senses Help Me. 2010. (My World Ser.). (ENG., Illus.). 16p. (J). (gr. k-2). *(978-0-7787-9428-8(8));* pap. *978-0-7787-9472-1(5))* Crabtree Publishing Co.

—What Senses Do Animals Have? 2009. (Big Science Ideas Ser.). (ENG., Illus.). 32p. (J). (gr. 1-4). pap. *(978-0-7787-3305-8(X));* (gr. 2-4). *(978-0-7787-3285-3(1))* Crabtree Publishing Co.

Karim, Joseph & Karim, Silvana. What Does Happy Look Like? Karim, Joseph & Karim, Silvana, illus. 2009. (Illus.). 47p. (J). pap. 18.95 *(978-1-934575-54-3(2))* Autism Asperger Publishing Co.

Kashman, Nancy & Mora, Janet. The Sensory Connection: Sensory & Communication Strategies That Work, 1. 2nd ed. 2005. Orig. Title: An OT & SLP Team Approach. (Illus.). 192p. per. 19.95 *(978-1-931615-21-1(7))* Sensory Resources.

Katz, Karen. A Potty for Me! Katz, Karen, illus. 2005. (ENG., Illus.). 26p. (J). (gr. -1-k). tchr. ed. 7.99 *(978-0-689-87423-9(5),* Little Simon) Little Simon.

—Wiggle Your Toes: A Karen Katz Book to Pull, Fluff, & Wiggle. Katz, Karen, illus. 2006. (ENG., Illus.). 14p. (J). (gr. -1-k). bds. 11.99 *(978-1-4169-0365-9(8),* Little Simon) Little Simon.

Kauffman, Dorothy. Use Your Senses. 2005. (Oxford Picture Dictionary for the Content Areas Ser.). (ENG., Illus.). 24p. pap. 7.56 *(978-0-19-430954-7(1))* Oxford Univ. Pr., Inc.

Kirk, Bill. Great Gobs of Gustation- the Sum of Our Parts. Ruble, Eugene, illus. 2013. 24p. pap. 10.95 *(978-1-61633-358-4(8))* Guardian Angel Publishing, Inc.

Klingel, Cynthia & Noyed, Robert B. Nose. 2010. (Let's Read about Our Bodies Ser.). (Illus.). 24p. (gr. k-3). pap. 8.15 *(978-1-4339-3372-1(1));* (J). lib. bdg. 22.00 *(978-1-4339-3371-4(3))* Stevens, Gareth Publishing LLLP.

—Nose / la Nariz. 2010. (Let's Read about Our Bodies / Hablemos del cuerpo humano Ser.). (SPA., Illus.). 24p. (gr. k-3). pap. 8.15 *(978-1-4339-3748-4(4))* Stevens, Gareth Publishing LLLP.

—Nose/la Nariz. 2010. (Let's Read about Our Bodies / Hablemos del cuerpo humano Ser.). (SPA., Illus.). 24p. (J). (gr. k-3). lib. bdg. 22.00 *(978-1-4339-3747-7(6))* Stevens, Gareth Publishing LLLP.

Kopp, Megan. Senses. 2016. (Illus.). 24p. (J). *(978-1-5105-0939-9(9))* SmartBook Media, Inc.

Kroneberger, Abigail Grace. The Sensory Room Kids Get in Sync. Kroneberger, Abigail Grace, illus. 2008. (Illus.). 24p. per. 12.95 *(978-1-934246-98-6(0))* Peppertree Pr., The.

Kurtz, John. The World Around Us! Tasting. 2011. (Dover Coloring Bks.). (ENG.). 32p. (J). (gr. k-3). pap. 4.99 *(978-0-486-48037-4(2))* Dover Pubns., Inc.

Larson, Kirsten W. Super Powers in Nature. 2015. (Freaky Nature Ser.). (ENG., Illus.). 32p. (J). (gr. 2-4). 19.95 *(978-1-60753-781-6(8))* Amicus Publishing.

Lay, Kathryn. Extreme Senses: Animals with Unusual Senses for Hunting Prey. Wald, Christina, illus. 2012. pap. 28.50 *(978-1-61478-860-7(X))* ABDO Publishing Co.

—Extreme Senses: Animals with Unusual Senses for Hunting Prey, 1 vol. Wald, Christina, illus. 2012. (Sensing Their Prey Ser.). (ENG.). 32p. (J). (gr. -1-4). lib. bdg. 28.50 *(978-1-61641-865-6(6),* Looking Glass Library) Magic Wagon.

—Tasting Their Prey: Animals with an Amazing Sense of Taste, 1 vol. Wald, Christina, illus. 2012. (Sensing Their Prey Ser.). (ENG.). 32p. (J). (gr. -1-4). lib. bdg. 28.50 *(978-1-61641-869-4(9),* Looking Glass Library) Magic Wagon.

Layton, Neil. Go Wild with Noises. 2004. (Illus.). 12p. (J). bds. *(978-1-84458-043-9(1),* Pavilion Children's Books) Pavilion Bks.

LernerClassroom Editors. First Step Nonfiction-Senses Teaching Guide. 2009. pap. 7.95 *(978-0-8225-5973-3(0))* Lerner Publishing Group.

Libra, Anna. Why Does Loud Music Hurt My Ears? An Inside Look at the Ear. 2003. (J). pap. *(978-1-58417-072-3(7));* lib. bdg. *(978-1-58417-009-9(3))* Lake Street Pubs.

—Why Does That Taste Bad? An Inside Look at the Tongue. 2003. (J). pap. *(978-1-58417-069-3(7));* lib. bdg. *(978-1-58417-006-8(9))* Lake Street Pubs.

Light, Douglas. The Senses. 2009. (Human Body: How It Works Ser.). (Illus.). 168p. (C). (gr. 9-18). 35.00 *(978-1-60413-362-2(7),* Chelsea Hse.) Facts On File, Inc.

Llewellyn, Claire. Our Senses Red Band. 2016. (Cambridge Reading Adventures Ser.). (ENG.). 16p. pap. 6.56 *(978-1-316-60568-4(X))* Cambridge Univ. Pr.

Llewellyn, Claire & Feldman, Thea. Kingfisher Readers L2: Amazing Animal Senses. 2014. (Kingfisher Readers Ser.). (ENG., Illus.). 32p. (J). (gr. k-3). 12.99 *(978-0-7534-7173-9(6),* 9780753471739, Kingfisher) Roaring Brook Pr.

Loh-Hagan, Virginia. Top 10: Super Senses. 2017. (Wild Wicked Wonderful Ser.). (ENG., Illus.). 32p. (J). (gr. 4-8). lib. bdg. 29.93 *(978-1-63472-141-7(1),* 209136, 45th Parallel Press) Cherry Lake Publishing.

Lowery, Lawrence F. Fragrant As a Flower: I Wonder Why. 2017. (I Wonder Why Ser.). (ENG., Illus.). 36p. (J). (gr. k-2). pap. 11.95 *(978-1-68140-353-3(6))* National Science Teachers Assn.

—Look & See: I Wonder Why. 2017. (I Wonder Why Ser.). (ENG., Illus.). 36p. (J). (gr. k-2). pap. 11.95 *(978-1-68140-355-7(2))* National Science Teachers Assn.

—Quiet As a Butterfly. 2017. (I Wonder Why Ser.). (ENG., Illus.). 36p. (J). (gr. k-2). pap. 11.95 *(978-1-68140-354-0(4))* National Science Teachers Assn.

MacKenzie, Catherine. Smell. 2010. (Senses (Board Books) Ser.). (ENG.). 16p. (J). (gr. -1-3). bds. 3.99 *(978-1-85792-564-7(5),* 9781857925647) Christian Focus Pubns. GBR. Dist: Bookmasters Distribution.

—Taste. 2010. (Senses (Board Books) Ser.). (ENG.). 16p. (J). (gr. -1-3). bds. 3.99 *(978-1-85792-561-6(0),* 9781857925616) Christian Focus Pubns. GBR. Dist: Bookmasters Distribution.

Macnair, Patricia. Sensational Senses. Watson, Richard, illus. 2016. (ENG.). 14p. (J). (gr. k-2). 14.99 *(978-1-4052-7163-9(9))* Egmont Bks., Ltd. GBR. Dist: Independent Pubs. Group.

—Senses. Watson, Richard, illus. 2016. (Reading Ladder Ser.). (ENG.). 32p. (J). (gr. 1-3). pap. 7.99 *(978-1-4052-8041-9(7))* Egmont Bks., Ltd. GBR. Dist: Independent Pubs. Group.

Marchesani, Laura & Grosset and Dunlap Staff. Baby's World: A First Book of Senses. Aikins, Dave, illus. 2013. (Sassy Ser.). (ENG.). 12p. (J). (gr. -1 — 1). bds. 7.99 *(978-0-448-47788-6(2),* Grosset & Dunlap) Penguin Young Readers Group.

Martineau, Susan. Understanding Feelings. 2011. (Positive Steps Ser.). 32p. (gr. 2-5). lib. bdg. 31.35 *(978-1-59920-494-9(0))* Black Rabbit Bks.

Mason, Paul. Out & about with Your Senses. 2011. (Out & about with Your Senses Ser.). (ENG.). 24p. (gr. k-1). lib. bdg. 53.30 *(978-1-4296-6668-8(4),* Pebble Plus) Capstone Press of Coughlan Cos.

McAneney, Caitlin. How Elephants & Other Animals Hear the Earth. 2015. (Superior Animal Senses Ser.). (ENG., Illus.). 24p. (J). (gr. 3-4). pap. 8.25 *(978-1-4994-0991-8(5),* PowerKids Pr.) Rosen Publishing Group, Inc., The.

McKendry, Sam. Are You Ticklish?/Tienes Cosquillas? Mitchell, Melanie, illus. 2005. (ENG.). 12p. (gr. -1-k). 10.95 *(978-1-58117-472-4(1),* Intervisual/Piggy Toes) Bendon, Inc.

McNeil, Niki, et al. HOCPP 1067 the Five Senses. 2006. spiral bd. 15.50 *(978-1-60308-067-5(8))* In the Hands of a Child.

Merer, Laura, illus. My Five Senses. 2010. (My World Ser.). (ENG.). 24p. (J). (gr. -1-1). pap. 8.15 *(978-1-61533-029-4(1))* Windmill Bks.

Merer, Laura Blanken, illus. My Five Senses. 2010. (My World Ser.). (ENG.). 24p. (J). (gr. -1-1). lib. bdg. 22.60 *(978-1-60754-948-2(4))* Windmill Bks.

Michael, Joan, illus. The Five Senses/Opposites & Position Words, 4 bks., Set. Incl. Let's Play a Five Senses Guessing Game. Miller, Amanda. 18.00 *(978-0-531-14871-6(8));* Let's Talk about Opposites, Morning to Night. Falk, Laine. Larsen, Eric, illus. 18.00 *(978-0-531-14872-3(6));* 24p. (J). (gr. -1-3). 2007. (Let's Find Out Early Learning Bks.). 2007. 72.00 o.p. *(978-0-531-17574-3(X),* Children's Pr.) Scholastic Library Publishing.

Miller, Amanda. Let's Play a Five Senses Guessing Game. Michael, Joan, illus. 2007. (Let's Find Out Early Learning Bks.). (ENG.). 24p. (J). (gr. -1-3). 18.00 *(978-0-531-14871-6(8),* Children's Pr.) Scholastic Library Publishing.

Miller-Schroeder, Patricia. Senses. 2007. (Life Science (Weigl Hardcover) Ser.). (Illus.). 32p. (J). (gr. 4-7). lib. bdg. 26.00 *(978-1-59036-715-5(4));* per. 9.95 *(978-1-59036-716-2(2))* Weigl Pubs., Inc.

Mills, Nathan & Diggory, Nikki. Our Five Senses. 2012. (Rosen Readers Ser.). (ENG., Illus.). 16p. (J). (gr. k-1). pap. 7.00 *(978-1-4488-8686-9(4),* Rosen Classroom) Rosen Publishing Group, Inc., The.

Mis Cinco Sentidos / My Five Senses. 2014. (Mis Cinco Sentidos / My Five Senses Ser.). (SPA.). 24p. (J). (gr. k-2). 113.00 *(978-1-4824-1040-2(0))* Stevens, Gareth Publishing LLLP.

Mitchell, Melanie S. Ears. 2008. (First Step Nonfiction - Animal Traits Ser.). (ENG., Illus.). 8p. (gr. -1-1). pap. 4.95 *(978-0-8225-3910-0(1),* Lerner Pubns.) Lerner Publishing Group.

Mlawer, Teresa, tr. What Do I Feel? / ¿Qué Siento? Kubler, Annie, illus. 2015. (Small Senses Bilingual Ser.: 5). (ENG & SPA.). 12p. (J). bds. *(978-1-84643-721-2(0))* Child's Play International Ltd.

—What Do I Hear? / ¿Qué Oigo? Kubler, Annie, illus. 2015. (Small Senses Bilingual Ser.: 5). (ENG & SPA.). 12p. (J). bds. *(978-1-84643-724-3(5))* Child's Play International Ltd.

—What Do I See? / ¿Qué Veo? Kubler, Annie, illus. 2015. (Small Senses Bilingual Ser.: 5). (ENG & SPA.). 12p. (J). bds. *(978-1-84643-725-0(3))* Child's Play International Ltd.

—What Do I Smell? / ¿Qué Huelo? Kubler, Annie, illus. 2015. (Small Senses Bilingual Ser.: 5). (ENG & SPA.). 12p. (J). bds. *(978-1-84643-723-6(7))* Child's Play International Ltd.

—What Do I Taste? / ¿Qué Saboreo? Kubler, Annie, illus. 2015. (Small Senses Bilingual Ser.: 5). (ENG & SPA.). 12p. (J). bds. *(978-1-84643-722-9(9))* Child's Play International Ltd.

Morgan, Philip. Sending Messages. 2010. (How Your Body Works). 32p. (YA). (gr. 4-7). 28.50 *(978-1-60753-056-5(2))* Amicus Publishing.

—Sensing the World. 2012. (Illus.). 32p. (gr. 4-7). pap. 8.95 *(978-1-926722-66-5(3))* Saunders Bk. Co. CAN. Dist: RiverStream Publishing.

Morgan, Sally. How Taste Works. 2010. (Our Senses Ser.). 24p. (J). (gr. k-2). pap. 8.25 *(978-1-61532-563-4(8),* PowerKids Pr.); (Illus.). (gr. -1-2). lib. bdg. 22.60 *(978-1-61532-555-9(7))* Rosen Publishing Group, Inc., The.

—Our Senses, 5 vols., Set. Incl. How Hearing Works. lib. bdg. 22.60 *(978-1-61532-552-8(2));* How Sight Works. lib. bdg. 22.60 *(978-1-61532-553-5(0));* How Smell Works. lib. bdg. 22.60 *(978-1-61532-554-2(9));* How Taste Works. lib. bdg. 22.60 *(978-1-61532-555-9(7));* How Touch Works. lib. bdg. 22.60 *(978-1-61532-556-6(5));* (J). (gr. -1-2). (Illus.). 24p. 2010. Set lib. bdg. 106.25 *(978-1-61532-845-1(9),* PowerKids Pr.) Rosen Publishing Group, Inc., The.

Mucklow, Nancy. The Sensory Team Handbook: A Hands-on Tool to Help Young People Make Sense of Their Senses & Take Charge of Their Sensory Processing. 2nd ed. 2009. (Illus.). 180p. (YA). pap. *(978-0-9811439-2-7(X))* Grass, Michael Hse.

Murphy, Glenn & Muprhy, Lorna. Poo! What Is That Smell? Everything You Ever Needed to Know about the Five Senses. unabr. ed. 2014. (ENG., Illus.). 176p. (J). (gr. 2-4). pap. 9.99 *(978-0-330-53852-7(7))* Pan Macmillan GBR. Dist: Independent Pubs. Group.

Murphy, Patricia J. Taste. 2003. (True Bks.). (ENG.). 48p. (gr. 3-5). pap. 6.95 *(978-0-516-26971-9(2),* Children's Pr.) Scholastic Library Publishing.

Murray, Julie. The Five Senses, 1 vol. 2016. (ENG., Illus.). 24p. (J). *(978-1-62970-924-6(7),* 1391204) ABDO Publishing Co.

—I Can See, 1 vol. 2016. (ENG., Illus.). 24p. (J). *(978-1-62970-926-0(3),* 1391207) ABDO Publishing Co.

—I Can Taste, 1 vol. 2016. (ENG., Illus.). 24p. (J). *(978-1-62970-928-4(X))* ABDO Publishing Co.

Nagelhout, Ryan. How Pigeons & Other Animals Sense Magnetic Fields. 2015. (Superior Animal Senses Ser.). (ENG., Illus.). 24p. (J). (gr. 3-4). pap. 8.25 *(978-1-4994-0992-5(3),* PowerKids Pr.) Rosen Publishing Group, Inc., The.

Nelson, Robin. El Gusto. Translations.com Staff, tr. from ENG. 2006. (Mi Primer Paso Al Mundo Real - Los Sentidos (First Step Nonfiction - Senses) Ser.). (SPA., Illus.). 24p. (gr. k-2). lib. bdg. 23.93 *(978-0-8225-6224-5(3),* Ediciones Lerner) Lerner Publishing Group.

—Hearing. 2005. (First Step Nonfiction Ser.). (Illus.). 24p. (gr. k-2). lib. bdg. 17.27 *(978-0-8225-1264-6(5))* Lerner Publishing Group.

—Tasting. 2005. (Senses Ser.). (Illus.). 24p. (gr. k-2). lib. bdg. 17.27 *(978-0-8225-1265-3(3))* Lerner Publishing Group.

—Touching. 2005. (First Step Nonfiction Ser.). (Illus.). 24p. (gr. k-2). lib. bdg. 17.27 *(978-0-8225-1266-0(1))* Lerner Publishing Group.

The Nervous System/The Senses/The Skin. 2006. (World Book's Human Body Works). (Illus.). 48p. (J). *(978-0-7166-4430-9(4))* World Bk., Inc.

Nettleton, Pamela Hill. Look, Listen, Taste, Touch, & Smell: Learning about Your Five Senses. Shipe, Becky, illus. 2004. (Amazing Body Ser.). (ENG.). 24p. (gr. k-3). per. 8.95 *(978-1-4048-0508-8(7))* Picture Window Bks.

O'Hara, Nicholas. Textura / Sort It by Texture. de la Vega, Eida, tr. 2015. (Vamos a Agrupar Por... / Sort It Out! Ser.). (ENG & SPA.). 24p. (J). (gr. k-1). lib. bdg. 22.60 *(978-1-4824-3223-7(4))* Stevens, Gareth Publishing LLLP.

Oliendo. (Coleccion Mil Preguntas). (SPA., Illus.). 24p. (J). pap. 4.50 *(978-950-11-0659-6(4),* SGM628) Sigmar ARG. Dist: Continental Bk. Co., Inc.

Olson, Karen W. Eyes, Ears, Nose & Mouth. George, Leonard, Jr., illus. 2005. (ENG.). 20p. (J). pap. 10.95 *(978-1-894778-34-3(0))* Theytus Bks., Ltd. CAN. Dist: Univ. of Toronto Pr.

Our Senses. (Early Intervention Levels Ser.). 23.10 *(978-0-7362-0030-1(4));* Vol. 4. 3.85 *(978-1-56334-978-2(7))* CENGAGE Learning.

Oyendo. (Coleccion Mil Preguntas). (SPA., Illus.). 24p. (J). pap. 5.50 *(978-950-11-0662-6(4),* SGM624) Sigmar ARG. Dist: Continental Bk. Co., Inc.

Page, Robin & Jenkins, Steve. What Do You Do with a Tail Like This? 2008. (ENG., Illus.). 32p. (J). (gr. -1-3). pap. 7.95 *(978-0-618-99713-8(X))* Houghton Mifflin Harcourt Publishing Co.

Paine, Penelope C. Gift of Taste. Maeno, Itoko, illus. 2006. 24p. per. 5.95 *(978-0-9707944-6-8(0))* Paper Posie.

Pat Them Gently w/ Plush. 2007. 14.95 *(978-1-58117-626-1(0),* Intervisual/Piggy Toes) Bendon, Inc.

Petersen, Christine. Does Everyone Have ADHD? A Teen's Guide to Diagnosis & Treatment. (ENG., Illus.). 144p. (YA). (gr. 9-13). 2007. pap. 17.95 *(978-0-531-17975-8(3))* 2006. 30.50 *(978-0-531-16794-6(1),* Watts, Franklin) Scholastic Library Publishing.

Phidal Publishing Staff, ed. Senses. (Turn & Learn Ser.). 12p. (J). *(978-2-7643-0140-1(5))* Phidal Publishing, Inc./Editions Phidal, Inc.

Piggy Toes Press Staff. Dog Walk. 2006. (ENG.). 14p. 9.95 *(978-1-58117-481-6(0),* Intervisual/Piggy Toes) Bendon, Inc.

Priddy, Roger. Bright Baby Touch & Feel Hugs & Kisses. 2009. (Bright Baby Touch & Feel Ser.). (ENG.). 12p. (J). (gr. -1 — 1). bds. 4.95 *(978-0-312-50827-2(1),* 9780312508272, Priddy Bks.) St. Martin's Pr.

—Quack! Quack! These Baby Animals Can't Wait to Meet You! rev. ed. 2004. (Baby Touch & Feel Ser.). (ENG., Illus.). 12p. (J). (gr. -1 — 1). bds. 8.95 *(978-0-312-49250-2(2),* 9780312492502, Priddy Bks.) St. Martin's Pr.

Prior, Jennifer. The Five Senses, 1 vol. 2nd rev. ed. 2013. (Nonfiction Readers Ser.). (ENG., Illus.). 32p. (J). (gr. 3-3). pap. 25.96 *(978-1-4807-1085-6(7))* Shell Educational Publishing.

—The Five Senses, 1 vol. 2nd rev. ed. 2012. (Nonfiction Readers Ser.). (ENG.). 32p. (J). (gr. 3-3). pap. 8.99 *(978-1-4333-3676-8(6))* Teacher Created Materials, Inc.

Pryor, Kimberley Jane. Hearing. 2003. (Senses Ser.). (Illus.). 32p. (gr. 2-4). 23.00 *(978-0-7910-7554-8(0),* Chelsea Hse.) Facts On File, Inc.

—Seeing. 2003. (Senses Ser.). (Illus.). 32p. (gr. 2-4). 23.00 *(978-0-7910-7555-5(9),* Chelsea Hse.) Facts On File, Inc.

—Smelling. 2003. (Senses Ser.). (Illus.). 32p. (gr. 2-4). 23.00 *(978-0-7910-7556-2(7),* Chelsea Hse.) Facts On File, Inc.

—Tasting. 2003. (Senses Ser.). (Illus.). 32p. (gr. 2-4). 23.00 *(978-0-7910-7557-9(5),* Chelsea Hse.) Facts On File, Inc.

—Touching. 2003. (Senses Ser.). (Illus.). 32p. (gr. 2-4). 23.00 *(978-0-7910-7558-6(3),* Chelsea Hse.) Facts On File, Inc.

—Your Senses. 2003. (Senses Ser.). (Illus.). 32p. (gr. 2-4). 23.00 *(978-0-7910-7559-3(1),* Chelsea Hse.) Facts On File, Inc.

Rajczak, Kristen. How Snakes & Other Animals Taste the Air. 2015. (Superior Animal Senses Ser.). (ENG., Illus.). 24p. (J). (gr. 3-4). pap. 8.25 *(978-1-4994-0995-6(8),* PowerKids Pr.) Rosen Publishing Group, Inc., The.

Ramos, et al. El Pastel de Chocolate. (SPA.). 32p. (J). 10.00 *(978-84-342-2515-2(8))* Parramon Ediciones S.A. ESP. Dist: Distribuidora Norma, Inc.

Randolph, Joanne, ed. Taste & Digestion. 2017. (Amazing Human Body Ser.). 48p. (J). (gr. 6-6). pap. 11.70 ***(978-0-7660-8989-1(4))*** Enslow Pubs., Inc.

Rappaport, Carrie, et al. The Best Sense for Safety. 2017. (Text Connections Guided Close Reading Ser.). (J). (gr. 1). *(978-1-4900-1828-7(X))* Benchmark Education Co.

Rauf, Don. The Senses. 2017. (Freaky Phenomena Ser.: Vol. 8). (ENG., Illus.). (YA). (gr. 5-8). 20.95 ***(978-1-4222-3780-9(X))*** Mason Crest.

Rešcek, Sanja, illus. Bounce & Jiggle. 2007. (Baby Gym Ser.). (ENG.). 12p. (J). (gr. -1). bds. *(978-1-84643-131-9(X))* Child's Play International Ltd.

—Calm & Soothe. 2007. (Baby Gym Ser.). (ENG.). 12p. (J). (gr. -1). bds. *(978-1-84643-133-3(6))* Child's Play International Ltd.

—Touch & Tickle. 2007. (Baby Gym Ser.). (ENG.). 12p. (J). (gr. -1). bds. *(978-1-84643-130-2(1))* Child's Play International Ltd.

—Wiggle & Move. 2007. (Baby Gym Ser.). (ENG.). 12p. (J). (gr. -1). bds. *(978-1-84643-132-6(8))* Child's Play International Ltd.

Riley, Peter. Your Body, Your Senses. 2016. (Ways into Science Ser.). (ENG., Illus.). 32p. (J). (gr. k-2). pap. 11.99 *(978-1-4451-3479-6(9),* Franklin Watts) Hachette Children's Group GBR. Dist: Hachette Bk. Group.

Rissman, Rebecca. Using Your Senses, 1 vol. 2011. (ENG.). 24p. (gr. -1-1). pap. 9.95 *(978-1-4329-5495-6(4));* 25.99 *(978-1-4329-5350-8(8))* Heinemann-Raintree. (Acorn Read-Aloud).

Robert, Na'ima Bint & Petrova-Browning, Nina. Welcome to the World Baby. Brazell, Derek, illus. 2005. (ENG & BUL.). 32p. (J). pap. *(978-1-84444-721-3(9))* Mantra Lingua.

Roca, Nuria. The 5 Senses. Curto, Rosa Maria, illus. 2006. (Let's Learn About Ser.). (ENG.). 36p. (J). (gr. -1-3). per. 7.99 *(978-0-7641-3312-1(8))* Barron's Educational Series, Inc.

Rofé, April, illus. The SENSEational Alphabet: See-Read, Touch-Feel, Scratch & Smell, Hear-Learn, Have Fun! 2006. (J). *(978-0-9779189-1-1(2))* Waldenhouse Pubs., Inc.

Romanek, Trudee. Wow! The Most Interesting Book You'll Ever Read about the Five Senses. Cowles, Rose, illus. 2004. (Mysterious You Ser.). (ENG.). 40p. (J). (gr. 4-9). 7.95 *(978-1-55337-630-9(7))* Kids Can Pr., Ltd. CAN. Dist: Hachette Bk. Group.

Rosa-Mendoza, Gladys. My Senses/Mis Sentidos. Merer, Laura, illus. 2007. (English Spanish Foundations Ser.). (ENG & SPA.). 20p. (J). (gr. -1-k). bds. 6.95 *(978-1-931398-21-3(6))* Me+Mi Publishing.

Rotner, Shelley. Senses in the City. Rotner, Shelley, photos by. 2008. (Shelley Rotner's Early Childhood Library Ser.). (ENG., Illus.). 32p. (gr. -1-2). lib. bdg. 23.93 *(978-0-8225-7502-3(7))* Lerner Publishing Group.

—Senses on the Farm. 2008. (Illus.). 32p. (J). (gr. -1-2). 23.93 *(978-0-8225-8623-4(1),* Millbrook Pr.) Lerner Publishing Group.

Royston, Angela. Senses. 2011. (Your Body Inside & Out Ser.). (Illus.). 32p. (J). (gr. 3-6). lib. bdg. 28.50 *(978-1-59771-267-5(1))* Sea-To-Sea Pubns.

Rustad, Martha E. H. Touching. 2014. (Illus.). 24p. (J). lib. bdg. 25.65 *(978-1-62031-119-6(4),* Bullfrog Bks.) Jump! Inc.

Saab, Carl Y. Seeing, Hearing, & Smelling the World. 2007. (Brain Works). (Illus.). 101p. (YA). (gr. 5-9). lib. bdg. 32.95 *(978-0-7910-8945-3(2))* Facts On File, Inc.

Salas, Laura Purdie. I'm Exploring with My Senses: A Song about the Five Senses, 1 vol. De Giorgi, Sergio, illus. 2010. (Science Songs Ser.). (ENG.). 24p. (gr. 1-3). lib. bdg. 26.65 *(978-1-4048-5764-3(8))* Picture Window Bks.

SAMI Staff. Look, Baby! 2009. (ENG., Illus.). 20p. (J). (— 1). 9.95 *(978-1-934706-26-8(4))* Blue Apple Bks.

Scholastic Clubs US Five Senses Pack: Let's Start Science. 2006. (J). 34.75 *(978-1-59566-323-8(1))* QEB Publishing Inc.

Schuh, Mari. The Sense of Hearing. 2007. (Senses Ser.). (ENG., Illus.). 24p. (J). (gr. 2-5). lib. bdg. 25.95 *(978-1-60014-070-9(X))* Bellwether Media.

—The Sense of Sight. 2007. (Senses Ser.). (ENG., Illus.). 24p. (J). (gr. 2-5). lib. bdg. 25.95 *(978-1-60014-071-6(8))* Bellwether Media.

—The Sense of Smell. 2007. (Senses Ser.). (ENG., Illus.). 24p. (J). (gr. 2-5). lib. bdg. 25.95 *(978-1-60014-072-3(6))* Bellwether Media.

—The Sense of Touch. 2007. (Senses Ser.). (ENG., Illus.). 24p. (J). (gr. 2-5). lib. bdg. 25.95 *(978-1-60014-074-7(2))* Bellwether Media.

Sensational!, 6 Pack. (Bookweb Ser.). 32p. (gr. 3-18). 34.00 *(978-0-7635-3949-8(X))* Rigby Education.

The Senses, 6 vols., Set. 2005. (Senses Ser.). (Illus.). 32p. (gr. 2-4). 138.00 *(978-0-7910-7553-1(2),* Chelsea Hse.) Facts On File, Inc.

Shea, Therese. How Dolphins & Other Animals Use Sonar. 2015. (Superior Animal Senses Ser.). (ENG., Illus.). 24p. (J). (gr. 3-4). pap. 8.25 *(978-1-4994-0988-8(5),* PowerKids Pr.) Rosen Publishing Group, Inc., The.

Sian revision smell taste Touch. 2004. (J). *(978-1-59242-069-8(9))* Delta Education, LLC.

Sights & Sounds. (YA). (gr. 8). 48.95 *(978-0-673-72661-2(4),* Scott Foresman) Addison Wesley Schl.

Silver Dolphin en Español Staff, creator. El Gusto. 2007. (Baby Senses (Silver Dolphin en Espanol) Ser.). (Illus.). 10p. (J). (gr. -1). bds. *(978-970-718-473-2(6),* Silver Dolphin en Español) Advanced Marketing, S. de R. L. de C. V.

—El Olfato. 2007. (Baby Senses (Silver Dolphin en Espanol) Ser.). (Illus.). 10p. (J). (gr. 5). bds. *(978-970-718-471-8(X),* Silver Dolphin en Español) Advanced Marketing, S. de R. L. de C. V.

—La Vista. 2007. (Baby Senses (Silver Dolphin en Espanol) Ser.). (Illus.). 8p. (J). (gr. -1). bds. *(978-970-718-472-5(8),* Silver Dolphin en Español) Advanced Marketing, S. de R. L. de C. V.

Simon, Seymour. Eyes & Ears. (ENG., Illus.). 32p. (J). (gr. k-5). 2005. pap. 6.99 *(978-0-06-073302-5(0))* 2003. 15.99 *(978-0-688-15303-8(8))* HarperCollins Pubs.

—Eyes & Ears. 2005. (Illus.). (gr. k-3). 17.00 *(978-0-7569-5398-0(7))* Perfection Learning Corp.

Slegers, Liesbet. Que Veo?/ What Do I See? 2008. 24p. bds. 11.95 *(978-84-263-6705-1(4))* Vives, Luis Editorial (Edelvives) ESP. Dist: Baker & Taylor Bks.

Smart Kids Publishing Staff. What's That Sound. Sharp, Chris, illus. 2005. 10p. (J). (gr. -1-k). 12.95 *(978-0-8249-6624-9(4),* Ideal Pubns.) Worthy Publishing.

Sounds & Hearing. 2005. (J). *(978-0-9767850-0-2(5))* Success for All Foundation.

Spilsbury, Louise & Spilsbury, Richard. The Science of the Senses. 2017. (Flowchart Smart Ser.). 48p. (gr. 4-5). pap. 84.30 ***(978-1-5382-0685-0(4))*** Stevens, Gareth Publishing LLLP.

Squier, Robert, illus. Sensational Senses, 5 vols., Set. Incl. Your Sensational Sense of Hearing. Vogel, Julia. lib. bdg. 27.07 *(978-1-60954-286-3(X),* 200815); Your Sensational Sense of Sight. Vogel, Julie. lib. bdg. 27.07 *(978-1-60954-287-0(8),* 200816); Your Sensational Sense of Smell. Vogel, Julie & Vogel, Julia. lib. bdg. 27.07 *(978-1-60954-288-7(6),* 200817); Your Sensational Sense of Taste. Vogel, Julie & Vogel, Julia. lib. bdg. 27.07 *(978-1-60954-289-4(4),* 200818); Your Sensational Sense of Touch. Vogel, Julie & Vogel, Julia. lib. bdg. 27.07 *(978-1-60954-290-0(8),* 200819); (Illus.). 32p. (J). (gr. k-3). (Sensational Senses Ser.). (ENG.). 2011. 135.35 *(978-1-60954-400-3(5),* 200814) Child's World, Inc., The.

Steffora, Tracey. My Five Senses, 1 vol. 2014. (These Are My Senses Ser.). (ENG., Illus.). 24p. (J). (gr. -1-1). 26.00 *(978-1-4846-0442-7(3),* Acorn) Heinemann-Raintree.

Steps To Literacy Staff, compiled by. Read about the Five Sense Collection: Lib052. 2005. (ENG., Illus.). (J). pap. *(978-1-60015-011-1(6))* Steps To Literacy, LLC.

Stewart, Melissa. How Does the Ear Hear? And Other Questions about the Five Senses. Madsen, Jim, illus. 2014. (Good Question! Ser.). (ENG.). 40p. (J). (gr. 1). 12.95 *(978-1-4549-0672-8(3))* Sterling Publishing Co., Inc.

Stihler, Cherie B. Squishy, Squishy: A Book about My Five Senses. Rose, Heidi, illus. 2005. 23p. (J). pap. 5.95 *(978-0-8198-7078-0(1),* 332-374) Pauline Bks. & Media.

Stradling, Jan. Sense This: Level I, 6 vols. (First Explorers Ser.). 24p. (gr. 1-2). 29.95 *(978-0-7699-1452-7(7))* Shortland Pubns. (U. S. A.) Inc.

Studio Mouse Staff. Learn about Five Senses with JoJo! - My Five Senses. 2006. (ENG., Illus.). 60p. (J). (gr. -1-3). 12.99 *(978-1-59069-478-7(3))* Studio Mouse LLC.

Sundance/Newbridge LLC Staff. See, Hear, Touch, Taste, Smell. 2007. (Early Science Ser.). (gr. k-3). 18.95 *(978-1-4007-6197-5(2));* pap. 6.10 *(978-1-4007-6193-7(X))* Sundance/Newbridge Educational Publishing.

Superior Animal Senses. 2015. (Superior Animal Senses Ser.). (ENG.). 24p. (J). (gr. 3-4). pap., pap., pap. 297.00 *(978-1-4994-1317-5(3),* PowerKids Pr.) Rosen Publishing Group, Inc., The.

Tatchell, Judy. How Do Your Senses Work? Wheatley, Maria, illus. rev. ed. 2004. (Flip Flaps Ser.). 16p. (J). (gr. 2-18). pap. 7.95 *(978-0-7945-0642-1(9),* Usborne) EDC Publishing.

Taylor, Kristen Fitz & McDonald, Cheryl. Danceland: Fun Songs & Activities to Improve Sensory Skills. 2nd ed. 2008. 32p. (gr. -1-k). audio 19.95 *(978-1-931615-04-4(7))* Sensory Resources.

Thames, Susan. Our Senses. 2007. (ENG., Illus.). 24p. (gr. k-1). 28.50 *(978-1-60472-112-6(X));* pap. 8.95 *(978-1-60044-674-0(4))* Rourke Educational Media.

Todoro, Carlie. Is It Rough? Is It Smooth? 2008. (Rosen Real Readers: Upper Emergent Ser.). (ENG., Illus.). 12p. (gr. 1-2). pap. 5.90 *(978-0-8239-8206-6(8))* Rosen Publishing Group, Inc., The.

Townsend, John. Amazing Animal Senses, 1 vol. 2012. (Animal Superpowers Ser.). (ENG.). 32p. (gr. 1-3). lib. bdg. 29.99 *(978-1-4109-4747-5(5),* Read Me!) Heinemann-Raintree.

Treays, Rebecca. Understanding Your Senses. 2005. (Illus.). 31p. (J). pap. *(978-0-439-79805-1(1))* Scholastic, Inc.

Troupe, Thomas Kingsley. You Call That a Nose? Learning about Human Senses with the Garbage Gang. Toye, Derek, illus. 2015. (Garbage Gang's Super Science Questions Ser.). (ENG.). 24p. (gr. k-2). lib. bdg. 26.65 *(978-1-4795-7058-4(3))* Picture Window Bks.

Tullet, Hervé. The Five Senses. 2005. (ENG., Illus.). 144p. (J). (gr. -1-3). pap. 19.95 *(978-1-85437-581-0(4))* Tate Publishing, Ltd. GBR. Dist: Abrams, Inc.

Tyler, Jenny. Jugamos Al Escondite? 2004. (Titles in Spanish Ser.). (SPA., Illus.). 10p. (J). 15.95 *(978-0-7460-6114-5(5),* Usborne) EDC Publishing.

Vogel, Julie & Vogel, Julia. Your Sensational Sense of Taste. Squier, Robert, illus. 2011. (Sensational Senses Ser.). (ENG.). 32p. (J). (gr. k-3). lib. bdg. 27.07 *(978-1-60954-289-4(4),* 200818) Child's World, Inc., The.

Walt & Wells. Este No Es Mi Dinosaurio. 2004. (Touchy-Feely Board Bks.).Tr. of This Is Not My Dinosaur. (SPA., Illus.). 12p. (J). (gr. -1-18). 7.99 *(978-0-7460-5079-8(8))* EDC Publishing.

Wang, Margaret. Baby Mine Touch & Feel Flashcards. 2006. (ENG.). 10p. 12.95 *(978-1-58117-502-8(7),* Intervisual/Piggy Toes) Bendon, Inc.

Waters, John F. Sharks Have Six Senses. Barner, Bob, illus. 2015. (Let's-Read-And-Find-Out Science 2 Ser.). (ENG.). 40p. (J). (gr. -1-3). 17.99 *(978-0-06-028140-3(5))* HarperCollins Pubs.

Watt, Fiona. Baby Monster Cloth Book. Wells, Rachel, illus. 2007. (Usborne Cloth Bks.). 10p. (J). (gr. -1-k). 10.99 *(978-0-7945-1428-0(6),* Usborne) EDC Publishing.

—Cuddly Baby: Snuggletime. MacKinnon, Catherine-Anne, illus. 2006. 10p. (J). (gr. -1-k). bds. 8.99 *(978-0-7945-1070-1(1),* Usborne) EDC Publishing.

—Esta No Es Mi Muneca. Wells, Rachel, illus. 2005. (Titles in Spanish Ser.). (SPA.). 10p. (J). 7.95 *(978-0-7460-6102-2(1),* Usborne) EDC Publishing.

—Este No es Mi Sirenita. 2006. 10p. (J). bds. 9.99 *(978-0-7460-7386-5(0),* Usborne) EDC Publishing.

—Hide-and-seek baby board Book. 2005. 10p. (J). 8.99 *(978-0-7945-1055-8(6),* Usborne) EDC Publishing.

—Snuggletime Busy Baby. MacKinnon, Catherine-Anne, illus. 2005. 10p. (J). (gr. -1-k). per., bds. 8.99 *(978-0-7945-1054-1(X),* Usborne) EDC Publishing.

—That's Not My Mermaid: Her Hair Is Too Fluffy. Wells, Rachel, illus. 2006. (Usborne Touchy-Feely Board Bks.). 10p. (J). (gr. -1-k). bds. 9.99 *(978-0-7945-1083-1(3),* Usborne) EDC Publishing.

—That's Not My Robot... Wells, Rachel, illus. 2005. (Usborne Touchy-Feely Board Bks.). 10p. (J). (gr. -1-k). bds. 7.95 *(978-0-7945-1169-2(4),* Usborne) EDC Publishing.

Wearing, Judy. Taste. 2009. (World of Wonder Ser.). (Illus.). 24p. (J). (gr. 2-4). pap. 8.95 *(978-1-60596-057-9(8));* lib. bdg. 24.45 *(978-1-60596-056-2(X))* Weigl Pubs., Inc.

Weiss, Ellen. The Sense of Taste. 2008. (True Book(tm), a — Health & the Human Body Ser.). (ENG., Illus.). 48p. (J). (gr. 2-5). 31.00 *(978-0-531-16873-8(5))* Scholastic Library Publishing.

Wheeler-Toppen, Jodi Lyn. Our Ears Can Hear. 2017. (Our Amazing Senses Ser.). (ENG.). 24p. (gr. k-1). lib. bdg. 21.99 ***(978-1-5157-6713-8(2),*** Pebble Bks.) Capstone Press of Coughlan Cos.

—Our Eyes Can See. 2017. (Our Amazing Senses Ser.). (ENG.). 24p. (gr. k-1). lib. bdg. 21.99 ***(978-1-5157-6714-5(0),*** Pebble Bks.) Capstone Press of Coughlan Cos.

—Our Mouths Can Taste. 2017. (Our Amazing Senses Ser.). (ENG.). 24p. (gr. k-1). lib. bdg. 21.99 ***(978-1-5157-6707-7(8),*** Pebble Bks.) Capstone Press of Coughlan Cos.

—Our Noses Can Smell. 2017. (Our Amazing Senses Ser.). (ENG.). 24p. (gr. k-1). lib. bdg. 21.99 ***(978-1-5157-6711-4(6),*** Pebble Bks.) Capstone Press of Coughlan Cos.

—Our Skin Can Touch. 2017. (Our Amazing Senses Ser.). (ENG.). 24p. (gr. k-1). lib. bdg. 21.99 ***(978-1-5157-6715-2(9))*** Capstone Press of Coughlan Cos.

World of Wonder: Senses, 6 vols., Set. Incl. Common Sense. De Medeiros, Michael. lib. bdg. 24.45 *(978-1-60596-062-3(4));* Hearing. Winnick, Nick. lib. bdg. 24.45 *(978-1-60596-054-8(3));* Sight. Bekkering, Annalise. lib. bdg. 24.45 *(978-1-60596-052-4(7));* Smell. Wearing, Judy. lib. bdg. 24.45 *(978-1-60596-060-9(8));* Taste. Wearing, Judy. lib. bdg. 24.45 *(978-1-60596-056-2(X));* Touch. DeMedeiros, James. lib. bdg. 24.45 *(978-1-60596-058-6(6));* (Illus.). 24p. (J). (gr. 2-4). 2009. 2010. Set lib. bdg. 146.70 *(978-1-60596-668-7(1))* Weigl Pubs., Inc.

Young, Laurie. I See a Monster! Mahoney, Daniel J. & Mahoney, Daniel, illus. 2006. (ENG.). 12p. (J). (gr. -1-k). bds. 10.95 *(978-1-58117-483-0(7),* Intervisual/Piggy Toes) Bendon, Inc.

SENSES AND SENSATION—FICTION

Almada, Ariel Andres. Walking Through a World of Aromas. 2013. (ENG., Illus.). 24p. (J). (gr. k-2). 16.95 *(978-84-15619-48-2(0))* Eastern National.

Baker, Keith. Sometimes. 2003. (Green Light Readers Level 1 Ser.). (ENG., Illus.). 24p. (J). (gr. -1-3). pap. 3.95 *(978-0-15-204847-1(2))* Houghton Mifflin Harcourt Publishing Co.

—Sometimes. 2003. (Green Light Readers — Level 1 Ser.). (gr. -1-2). lib. bdg. 13.50 *(978-0-613-64597-3(9),* Turtleback) Turtleback Bks.

—Sometimes/Algunas Veces. Flor Ada, Alma & Campoy, F. Isabel, trs. from ENG. 2007. (Green Light Readers Level 1 Ser.). (ENG & SPA., Illus.). 28p. (J). (gr. -1-3). pap. 3.95 *(978-0-15-205961-3(X))* Houghton Mifflin Harcourt Publishing Co.

Beavin, John. The Parable of the Stars. 2009. 24p. pap. 11.50 *(978-1-60693-368-8(X),* Strategic Bk. Publishing) Strategic Book Publishing & Rights Agency (SBPRA).

Blackstone, Stella. La Familia Ocupada de Oso. 2012. (ENG & SPA.). (J). 6.99 *(978-1-84686-771-2(1))* Barefoot Bks., Inc.

—La Famille Active de l'Ours. 2012.Tr. of Bear's Busy Family. (FRE & ENG.). (J). pap. 6.99 *(978-1-84686-772-9(X))* Barefoot Bks., Inc.

Book Company Staff. Are You a Dinosaur? 2003. (Novelty Bks.). (J). 12.95 *(978-1-74047-319-4(1))* Book Co. Publishing Pty, Ltd., The AUS. Dist: Penton Overseas, Inc.

—Are You a Frog? 2003. (Novelty Bks.). (Illus.). (J). 12.95 *(978-1-74047-318-7(3))* Book Co. Publishing Pty, Ltd., The AUS. Dist: Penton Overseas, Inc.

Boynton, Sandra. Tickle Time! 2012. (ENG., Illus.). 24p. (J). (gr. k-1). bds. 6.95 *(978-0-7611-6883-6(4),* 16883) Workman Publishing Co., Inc.

Brown, Gina Bates. Zen & Bodhi's Snowy Day. Hinder, Sarah Jane, illus. 2014. (ENG.). 24p. (J). 15.95 *(978-1-61429-165-7(9))* Wisdom Pubns.

Coll, Ivar Da. Cinco Amigos. (SPA.). (J). bds. *(978-958-04-4909-6(0))* Norma S.A. COL. Dist: Lectorum Pubns., Inc.

Crupi, Jaclyn. Theo at the Beach. Verdoux, Aurélia, illus. 2013. (J). *(978-1-4351-4722-5(7))* Barnes & Noble, Inc.

Del Moral, Susana. La Casa de Violet. Zaidi, Nadeem, illus. 2005. (Baby Einstein: Libros de Carton Ser.). (SPA.). 10p. (J). (gr. -1). bds. *(978-970-718-305-6(5),* Silver Dolphin en Español) Advanced Marketing, S. de R. L. de C. V.

Derubertis, Barbara. Sammy Skunk's Super Sniffer. Alley, R. W., illus. 2011. (Animal Antics A to Z Set III Ser.). pap. 45.32 *(978-0-7613-8428-1(6))* Kane Press, Inc.

deRubertis, Barbara. Sammy Skunk's Super Sniffer. Alley, R. W., illus. 2011. (Animal Antics A to Z Ser.). pap. 7.95 *(978-1-57565-344-0(3));* lib. bdg. 22.60 *(978-1-57565-352-5(4))* Kane Press, Inc.

Doudna, Kelly. Rabbit Ears. Nobens, C. A., illus. 2006. (Fact & Fiction Ser.). 24p. (J). pap. 48.42 *(978-1-59679-962-2(5))* ABDO Publishing Co.

Emma Treehouse Ltd. My Pets. Davis, Caroline, illus. 2007. (Easy Flaps Ser.). 10p. (J). (gr. -1). bds. 6.95 *(978-1-58925-824-2(X))* Tiger Tales.

Farrington Wilson, Lynda. Squirmy Wormy: How I Learned to Help Myself. 2009. (ENG., Illus.). 32p. (gr. 1). pap. 14.95 *(978-1-935567-18-9(7),* 9781935567189) Sensory Resources.

Flesher, Vivienne. Alfred's Nose. Flesher, Vivienne, illus. 2008. (Illus.). 32p. (J). (gr. -1-2). lib. bdg. 17.89 *(978-0-06-084314-4(4))* HarperCollins Pubs.

Grau, Sheila. The Boy with Seventeen Senses. 2016. (ENG.). 256p. (J). (gr. 3-7). 16.95 *(978-1-4197-2119-9(4),* Amulet Bks.) Abrams, Inc.

Hall, Kirsten. A Perfect Day: All about the Five Senses. Luedecke, Bev, illus. (Beastieville Ser.). (J). (gr. k-1). 2005. (ENG.). 32p. pap. 3.95 *(978-0-516-25521-7(5))* 2004. 19.50 *(978-0-516-24437-2(X))* Scholastic Library Publishing. (Children's Pr.).

Hamilton, Robert M. Mia's Five Senses. 2012. (InfoMax Readers Ser.). (ENG., Illus.). 16 pp.p. (J). (gr. k-1). pap. 7.00 *(978-1-4488-8905-1(7),* Rosen Classroom) Rosen Publishing Group, Inc., The.

Harris, Marie. The Girl Who Heard Colors. Newton, Vanessa Brantley, illus. 2013. (ENG.). 32p. (J). (gr. -1-k). 16.99 *(978-0-399-25643-1(1),* Nancy Paulsen Books) Penguin Young Readers Group.

Hayward, Mark Brauner. I See Without My Eyes. Hartman, Nancy Lee, illus. 2009. 32p. pap. 12.99 *(978-1-4343-3823-5(1))* AuthorHouse.

Hopgood, Tim. Hooray for Hoppy! 2015. (ENG., Illus.). 32p. (J). (gr. -1-k). 16.99 *(978-0-374-30129-3(8),* 9780374301293, Farrar, Straus & Giroux (BYR)) Farrar, Straus & Giroux.

Hughes, Jack. Rex's Specs. 2014. (Dinosaur Friends Ser.). (Illus.). 32p. (J). (gr. k-3). lib. bdg. 26.25 *(978-1-4777-9226-1(0))* Windmill Bks.

Isadora, Rachel. I Hear a Pickle: And Smell, See, Touch, & Taste It, Too! Isadora, Rachel, illus. 2016. (ENG., Illus.). 32p. (J). (-k). 16.99 *(978-0-399-16049-3(3),* Nancy Paulsen Books) Penguin Young Readers Group.

Jeffers, Oliver. The Incredible Book Eating Boy. Jeffers, Oliver, illus. (ENG., Illus.). 32p. pap. *(978-0-00-718231-2(7),* HarperCollins Children's Bks.) HarperCollins Pubs. Ltd.

Kranowitz, Carol Stock. The Goodenoughs Get in Sync: A Story for Kids about the Tough Day When Filibuster Grabbed Darwin's Rabbit's Foot... Wylie, T. J., illus. 2004. 86p. (J). 14.95 *(978-1-931615-17-4(9),* 978-1-931615-17-4) Sensory Resources.

Ladd, Debbie. Don't Pick Your Nose, one. 2003. (Illus.). 24p. (J). 12.95 *(978-0-9727615-1-2(9))* Deb on Air Bks.

Lloyd, Megan Wagner. Finding Wild. Halpin, Abigail, illus. 2016. (ENG.). 32p. (J). (gr. -1-2). 16.99 *(978-1-101-93281-0(3),* Knopf Bks. for Young Readers) Random Hse. Children's Bks.

Mandy and Ness Staff, et al. Hattie's House: A First Book about Sound. 2005. (Senses Ser.). (URD, ENG, VIE, CHI & BEN., Illus.). 16p. (J). pap. 9.95 *(978-1-84059-156-9(0))* Milet Publishing.

Marshall, Rita. Taste the Clouds. Domeniconi, Paolo, illus. 2016. (ENG.). 14p. (J). (gr. -1-k). bds. 8.99 *(978-1-56846-285-1(9),* Creative Editions) Creative Co., The.

Mass, Wendy. A Mango-Shaped Space. 2005. (ENG.). 240p. (YA). (gr. 3-7). per. 8.99 *(978-0-316-05825-4(4))* Little, Brown Bks. for Young Readers.

McKendry, Sam. Are You Ticklish? A Touch & Tickle Book. Mitchell, Melanie, illus. 2007. 15.95 *(978-1-58117-571-4(X),* Intervisual/Piggy Toes) Bendon, Inc.

Melling, David. Two by Two & a Half. Melling, David, illus. 2008. (ENG., Illus.). 32p. (J). (gr. -1-k). pap. 9.99 *(978-0-340-90311-7(2))* Hodder & Stoughton GBR. Dist: Hachette Bk. Group.

Miller, Sara F. Pooh's Honey Trouble. 2012. (ENG.). 16p. (J). (gr. -1-1). bds. 6.99 *(978-1-4231-3579-1(2))* Disney Pr.

Moore, Ann C. Looking for a Place to Take a Long Winter Nap. 2009. 32p. pap. 14.49 *(978-1-4490-0852-9(6))* AuthorHouse.

Muntean, Michaela. Elmo Can... Taste! Touch! Smell! See! Hear! (Sesame Street) Swanson, Maggie, illus. 2013. (Big Bird's Favorites Board Bks.). (ENG.). 24p. (J). (— 1). bds. 4.99 *(978-0-307-98078-6(2),* Random Hse. Bks. for Young Readers) Random Hse. Children's Bks.

Nelson, N. A. Bringing the Boy Home. 2008. (ENG.). 224p. (J). (gr. 3-7). 16.99 *(978-0-06-088698-1(6))* HarperCollins Pubs.

Nex, Anthony, photos by. Little Feet Love. 2009. (Illus.). 12p. 7.95 *(978-1-58117-881-4(6),* Intervisual/Piggy Toes) Bendon, Inc.

Nichols, Kathleen. My Five Senses. 2008. (ENG., Illus.). 12p. (J). (gr. k-k). bds. *(978-1-59700-581-4(9))* Island Heritage Publishing.

O'Brien, Gerry. Bubba Begonia, You'll Be Sorry. Jones, Brenda, illus. 2006. (ENG.). 80p. (J). per. 6.95 *(978-1-894838-23-8(8))* Acorn Pr., The CAN. Dist: Univ. of Toronto Pr.

Patricelli, Leslie. Binky. Patricelli, Leslie, illus. 2005. (Leslie Patricelli Board Bks.). (ENG., Illus.). 24p. (J). (— 1). bds. 6.99 *(978-0-7636-2364-7(4))* Candlewick Pr.

—Blankie. Patricelli, Leslie, illus. 2005. (Leslie Patricelli Board Bks.). (ENG., Illus.). 24p. (J). (— 1). bds. 6.99 *(978-0-7636-2363-0(6))* Candlewick Pr.

—Yummy Yucky/¡Ñam! ¡Puaj! Patricelli, Leslie, illus. 2016. (Leslie Patricelli Board Bks.). (ENG & SPA., Illus.). (J). (— 1). bds. 6.99 *(978-0-7636-8776-2(6))* Candlewick Pr.

Payne, Laurie. Mush & the Big Blue Flower. Campbell, Ruth, illus. 2007. (ENG.). 104p. (J). (gr. -1). pap. 12.95 *(978-0-88982-242-9(5))* Oolichan Bks. CAN. Dist: Univ. of Toronto Pr.

Piggy Toes Press Staff, creator. Little Feet Like: A Tiny Tootsie Touch & Feel Book. 2008. (ENG., Illus.). 12p. (gr. -1-k). 9.95 *(978-1-58117-692-6(9),* Intervisual/Piggy Toes) Bendon, Inc.

Prochovnic, Dawn Babb. Four Seasons! Five Senses! Sign Language for the Seasons & Senses, 1 vol. Bauer, Stephanie, illus. 2012. (ENG.). 32p. 28.50 *(978-1-61641-836-6(2),* Looking Glass Library) Magic Wagon.

Quinton, Sasha, text. Ears. 2010. (Illus.). 10p. (J). *(978-1-936199-15-0(7))* Book Shop, Ltd., The.

—Noses. 2010. (Illus.). 10p. (J). *(978-1-936199-17-4(3))* Book Shop, Ltd., The.

—Paws. 2010. (Illus.). 10p. (J). *(978-1-936199-16-7(5))* Book Shop, Ltd., The.

Raschka, Chris. Five for a Little One. Raschka, Chris, illus. 2006. (ENG., Illus.). 48p. (J). (gr. -1-2). 17.99 *(978-0-689-84599-4(5),* Atheneum/Richard Jackson Bks.) Simon & Schuster Children's Publishing.

Rey, H. A. Curious George Discovers the Senses. 2015. (Curious George Ser.). (ENG., Illus.). 32p. (J). (gr. -1-3). 6.99 *(978-0-544-50023-5(7),* HMH Books For Young Readers) Houghton Mifflin Harcourt Publishing Co.

Roth, Judith L. & Rothshank, Brooke, illus. Julia's Words. 2008. (J). (gr. -1-3). pap. 12.99 *(978-0-8361-9417-3(9))* Herald Pr.

Rotner, Shelley. Senses at the Seashore. Rotner, Shelley, photos by. (Shelley Rotner's Early Childhood Library Ser.). (ENG., Illus.). 32p. (J). (gr. -1-2). 2010. pap. 7.95 *(978-0-7613-6530-3(3))* 2006. lib. bdg. 22.60 *(978-0-7613-2897-1(1))* Lerner Publishing Group.

Ruffenach, Jessie, ed. Baby Learns about Senses. Thomas, Peter, tr. from ENG. Blacksheep, Beverly, illus. 2005. (NAV & ENG.). 16p. (J). (gr. 4-7). 7.95 *(978-1-893354-63-0(6))* Salina Bookshelf Inc.

Rummel, Verna. I Can Too, 1 vol. 2009. 12p. pap. 24.95 *(978-1-60836-089-5(X))* America Star Bks.

Ryan, Pam Muñoz. Hello Ocean. Astrella, Mark, illus. 2014. 32p. pap. 8.00 *(978-1-61003-319-0(1))* Center for the Collaborative Classroom.

—Hello, Ocean / Hola Mar. Canetti, Yanitzia, tr. from ENG. Astrella, Mark, illus. 2003. (ENG & SPA.). 32p. (J). (gr. -1-2). pap. 7.95 *(978-1-57091-372-3(2))* Charlesbridge Publishing, Inc.

Shannon, David. David Smells! Shannon, David, illus. 2005. (David Smells! Ser.). (ENG., Illus.). 12p. (J). (gr. -1-k). bds. 6.99 *(978-0-439-69138-3(9),* Blue Sky Pr., The) Scholastic, Inc.

Steiner, Hartley. This Is Gabriel - Making Sense of School: A Book about Sensory Processing Disorder. 2nd rev. ed. 2012. (ENG., Illus.). 32p. pap. 9.95 *(978-1-935567-34-9(9))* Sensory Resources.

Stojic, Manya. Rain. Stojic, Manya, illus. 2009. (Rise & Shine Ser.). (ENG., Illus.). 32p. (J). (gr. -1-2). pap. 7.99 *(978-0-385-73729-6(7),* Dragonfly Bks.) Random Hse. Children's Bks.

Taylor, Alastair. Mr. Blewitt's Nose. 2005. (J). (gr. k-3). 16.00 *(978-0-618-58111-5(1))* Houghton Mifflin Harcourt Trade & Reference Pubs.

Tildes, Phyllis Limbacher. The Magic Babushka. Tildes, Phyllis Limbacher, illus. 2009. (ENG., Illus.). 32p. (J). (gr. k-3). pap. 7.95 *(978-1-58089-225-4(6))* Charlesbridge Publishing, Inc.

Van Fleet, Matthew. Lick! Van Fleet, Matthew, illus. 2013. (ENG., Illus.). 14p. (J). (gr. -1-1). 9.99 *(978-1-4424-6049-2(0),* Simon & Schuster/Paula Wiseman Bks.) Simon & Schuster/Paula Wiseman Bks.

—Sniff! Van Fleet, Matthew, illus. 2012. (ENG., Illus.). 14p. (J). (gr. -1-1). 9.99 *(978-1-4424-6050-8(4),* Simon & Schuster/Paula Wiseman Bks.) Simon & Schuster/Paula Wiseman Bks.

Veenendall, Jennifer. Why Does Izzy Cover Her Ears? Dealing with Sensory Overload. 2009. (Illus.). 39p. (J). 18.95 *(978-1-934575-46-8(1))* Autism Asperger Publishing Co.

Vonthron, Satanta C. Marsy's Perfect Eyesight. Teeple, Jackie, illus. I.t. ed. 2005. (J). (gr. -1-k). pap. 10.95 *(978-1-57332-345-1(4));* pap. 10.95 *(978-1-57332-344-4(6))* Carson-Dellosa Publishing, LLC. (HighReach Learning, Incorporated).

Wagner, Brian. 10 Things Not to Do with Your Eyeball. 2005. 20p. 9.99 *(978-1-4116-5977-3(5))* Lulu Pr., Inc.

Watt, Fiona. That's Not My Hamster. 2012. (Touchy-Feely Board Bks). 10p. (J). bds. 8.99 *(978-0-7945-3277-2(2),* Usborne) EDC Publishing.

—That's Not My Train. rev. ed. 2008. (Touchy-Feely Board Bks). 10p. (J). bds. 8.99 *(978-0-7945-2168-4(1),* Usborne) EDC Publishing.

Watt, Fiona & Wells, Rachel. That's Not My Train: Its Wheels Are Too Slippery. 2004. (Touchy-Feely Board Bks.). (SPA & ENG., Illus.). 1p. (J). (gr. -1-18). bds. 7.95 *(978-0-7460-3779-9(1))* EDC Publishing.

Wax, Wendy. Look Who's Buzzing. 2009. 12p. 9.95 *(978-1-58117-911-8(1),* Intervisual/Piggy Toes) Bendon, Inc.

Werber, Yael. Spring for Sophie. Hill, Jen, illus. 2017. (ENG.). 32p. (J). (gr. -1-3). 17.99 *(978-1-4814-5134-5(0),* Simon & Schuster Bks. For Young Readers) Simon & Schuster Bks. For Young Readers.

Whose Ears. 2005. (J). bds. 5.99 *(978-1-933200-06-4(5))* Family Bks. at Home.

Whose Feet. 2005. (J). bds. 5.99 *(978-1-933200-02-6(2))* Family Bks. at Home.

Whose Nose. 2005. (J). bds. 5.99 *(978-1-933200-03-3(0))* Family Bks. at Home.

S

Wood, Douglas. No One but You. Lynch, P. J., illus. 2011. (ENG.). 32p. (J). (gr. 1-4). 17.99 (978-0-7636-3848-1(X)) Candlewick Pr.

Zaidi, Nadeem, illus. Baby Mozart: Musica Por Todas Partes. 2005. (Baby Einstein: Libros de Carton Ser.). (SPA.). 16p. (J). (gr. -1). bds. (978-970-718-309-4(8), Silver Dolphin en Español) Advanced Marketing, S. de R. L. de C. V.

SEPARATION (LAW)

see Divorce

SEPARATION ANXIETY

Berry, Joy. Let's Talk about Being Away from Your Parents. Smith, Maggie, illus. 2010. (Let's Talk About Ser.). (ENG.). 32p. (J). (gr. -1-k). pap. 4.99 (978-1-60577-202-8(X)) Berry, Joy Enterprises.

Lavallee, Kristen & Schneider, Silvia. What to Do When You Don't Want to Be Apart: A Kid's Guide to Overcoming Separation Anxiety. McDonnell, Janet, illus. 2017. (J). pap. **(978-1-4338-2713-6(1)**, Magination Pr.) American Psychological Assn.

SEPARATION ANXIETY—FICTION

Barclift, Betty. Gypsy Summer: A Novel. 2003. 160p. (J). pap. 7.99 (978-0-8254-2038-2(5)) Kregel Pubns.

Dewdney, Anna. Llama Llama Misses Mama. 2009. (Llama Llama Ser.). (ENG., Illus.). 40p. (J). (gr. -1-k). 17.99 (978-0-670-06198-3(0), Viking Books for Young Readers) Penguin Young Readers Group.

Dowell, Frances O'Roark. Shooting the Moon. 2008. (ENG., Illus.). 176p. (J). (gr. 5-9). 16.99 (978-1-4169-2690-0(9), Atheneum Bks. for Young Readers) Simon & Schuster Children's Publishing.

Edwards, Becky. My First Day at Nursery School. Flintoft, Anthony, illus. 2004. (ENG.). 32p. (J). (gr. -1-1). pap. 7.99 (978-1-58234-909-1(6), 9781582349091, Bloomsbury USA Childrens) Bloomsbury Publishing USA.

Freeman, Suzanne. The Cuckoo's Child. 249p. (YA). (gr. 5-8). pap. 5.95 (978-0-8072-1510-4(4), Listening Library) Random Hse. Audio Publishing Group.

Greene, Marjorie. Cassie's Big Day. 2003. (Illus.). (J). 16.95 (978-0-9741764-0-6(0)) Greene, Marjorie A.

Haughton, Chris. Little Owl Lost. Haughton, Chris, illus. 2010. (ENG., Illus.). 32p. (J). (gr. -1-k). 14.99 (978-0-7636-5022-3(6)) Candlewick Pr.

Hughes, Shirley. Don't Want to Go! Hughes, Shirley, illus. 2010. (ENG., Illus.). 32p. (J). (gr. -1-2). 16.99 (978-0-7636-5091-9(9)) Candlewick Pr.

Kaufmann, Nancy. Bye, Bye! Spetter, Jung-Hee, illus. 2004. (ENG.). 32p. (J). (gr. -1-1). 14.95 (978-1-886910-95-9(2), Lemniscaat) Boyds Mills Pr.

Maier, Inger M. When Fuzzy Was Afraid: Of Losing His Mother. Candon, Jennifer, illus. 2004. 32p. (J). 14.95 (978-1-59147-168-4(0)); pap. 9.95 (978-1-59147-169-1(9)) American Psychological Assn. (Magination Pr.).

Maturana, Andrea. Life Without Nico. Olea, Francisco Javier, illus. 2016. (ENG.). 40p. (J). (gr. -1-2). 16.95 (978-1-77138-611-1(8)) Kids Can Pr., Ltd. CAN. Dist: Hachette Bk. Group.

Pando, Nancy J. I Don't Want to Go to School: Helping Children Cope with Separation Anxiety. Voerg, Kathy, illus. 2005. (Let's Talk Ser.). (ENG.). 48p. (J). (gr. -1-1). per. 9.95 (978-0-88282-254-9(3)) New Horizon Pr. Pubs., Inc.

Peck, Judith. The Bright Blue Button & the Button-Hole. Stasolla, Mario, illus. 2004. 28p. (J). 18.95 (978-0-9746119-5-2(6)) Imagination Arts Pubns.

Penn, Audrey. Un Beso en Mi Mano. Harper, Ruth E. & Leak, Nancy M., illus. 2006. (Kissing Hand Ser.). (SPA & ENG.). 32p. (J). (gr. -1-3). 16.95 (978-1-933718-01-9(3)) Tanglewood Pr.

—The Kissing Hand. Gibson, Barbara Leonard, illus. 2014. (Kissing Hand Ser.). (ENG.). 14p. (J). (-k). bds. 7.99 (978-1-933718-77-4(3)) Tanglewood Pr.

—The Kissing Hand. Harper, Ruth E. & Leak, Nancy M., illus. 2007. (Kissing Hand Ser.). (ENG.). 32p. (J). (gr. -1-3). 28.95 (978-1-933718-07-1(2)); 12.95 (978-1-933718-10-1(2)) Tanglewood Pr.

Penn, Audrey, et al, illus. The Kissing Hand. 2010. 23.05 (978-0-7569-9299-6(0)) Natl Bk. Network.

Potvin, Amy K. I Miss Daddy. 2009. 28p. pap. 13.99 (978-1-4259-1705-0(4)) AuthorHouse.

Sederman, Marty & Epstein, Seymour. The Magic Box: When Parents Can't Be There to Tuck You In. Brooks, Karen Stormer, illus. 2003. 32p. (J). (gr. -1-3). 14.95 (978-1-55798-807-2(2), Magination Pr.) American Psychological Assn.

Stratford, Anne Margaret. My Daddy Is A Soldier. 2008. (Illus.). 40p. (J). 17.99 (978-0-9817938-0-1(0)) Diamond Fly Publishing, Inc.

Verburg, Bonnie. The Kiss Box. Cole, Henry, illus. 2011. (ENG.). 32p. (J). (gr. -1-k). 16.99 (978-0-545-11284-0(2), Orchard Bks.) Scholastic, Inc.

Wells, Rosemary. Love Waves: Midi Edition. Wells, Rosemary, illus. 2012. (ENG., Illus.). 32p. (J). (gr. k — 1). 8.99 (978-0-7636-6224-0(0)) Candlewick Pr.

Woodson, Jacqueline. Coming on Home Soon. Lewis, Earl & Lewis, E. B., illus. 2004. (ENG.). 32p. (J). (gr. k-3). 17.99 (978-0-399-23748-5(8), G.P. Putnam's Sons Books for Young Readers) Penguin Young Readers Group.

SEPTEMBER 11 TERRORIST ATTACKS, 2001

Anderson, Dale. The Terrorist Attacks of September, 11, 2001. 2003. (Landmark Events in American History Ser.). (Illus.). 48p. (gr. 5-12). pap. 14.05 (978-0-8368-5408-4(X), Gareth Stevens Secondary Library) Stevens, Gareth Publishing LLLP.

Andryszewski, Tricia. Terrorism in America. 2003. (Headliners Ser.). (Illus.). 64p. (J). (gr. 5-8). lib. bdg. 25.90 (978-0-7613-2803-2(3), Millbrook Pr.) Lerner Publishing Group.

Baurys, Tamra. The World Will Never Forget. Bouchal, Renee', illus. 2011. 34p. pap. 12.95 (978-0-9833354-2-9(7)) Amira Rock Publishing.

Benoit, Peter. September 11, 2001: The 10th Anniversary. 2011. (Cornerstones of Freedom, Third Ser.). (Illus.). 64p. (J). (gr. 4-6). lib. bdg. 30.00 (978-0-531-25040-2(7), Children's Pr.) Scholastic Library Publishing.

—September 11 Then & Now. 2011. (True Bk Ser.). (ENG., Illus.). 48p. (J). pap. 6.95 (978-0-531-26629-8(X)); (gr. 3-5). lib. bdg. 29.00 (978-0-531-25424-0(0)) Scholastic Library Publishing. (Children's Pr.).

—September 11 We Will Never Forget No. 11. 2011. (Cornerstones of Freedom, Third Ser.). (ENG., Illus.). 64p. (J). pap. 8.95 (978-0-531-26565-9(X), Children's Pr.) Scholastic Library Publishing.

Bodden, Valerie. The 9/11 Terror Attacks. 2007. (Days of Change Ser.). (Illus.). 48p. (J). (gr. 4-7). lib. bdg. 31.35 (978-1-58341-549-8(1), Creative Education) Creative Co., The.

—The 9/11 Terror Attacks: Days of Change. 2015. (Illus.). 80p. (J). (978-1-60818-529-0(X), Creative Education) Creative Co., The.

—The 9/11 Terror Attacks: Odysseys in History. 2016. (Odysseys in History Ser.). (ENG.). 80p. (J). (gr. 7-10). pap. 14.99 (978-1-62832-130-2(X), Creative Paperbacks) Creative Co., The.

Brewer, Paul. September 11 & Radical Islamic Terrorism. 2006. (Terrorism in Today's World Ser.). (Illus.). 48p. (gr. 5-12). pap. 14.05 (978-0-8368-6567-7(7)); lib. bdg. 31.00 (978-0-8368-6560-8(X)) Stevens, Gareth Publishing LLLP. (Gareth Stevens Secondary Library).

Brown, Don. America Is under Attack: September 11, 2001: the Day the Towers Fell. 2014. (Actual Times Ser.: 4). (ENG., Illus.). 64p. (J). (gr. 1-5). pap. 9.99 (978-1-250-04415-0(4), 9781250044150) Square Fish.

—America Is under Attack Vol. 4: The Day the Towers Fell - September 11, 2001. 2011. (Actual Times Ser.: 4). (ENG., Illus.). 64p. (J). (gr. 1-5). 16.99 (978-1-59643-694-7(8), 9781596436947) Roaring Brook Pr.

Buell, Tonya. The Crash of United Flight 93 on September 11, 2001. 2005. (Terrorist Attacks Ser.). (Illus.). 64p. (YA). (gr. 7-12). lib. bdg. 31.95 (978-0-8239-3857-5(3)) Rosen Publishing Group, Inc., The.

Casil, Amy Sterling. Coping with Terrorism. 2005. (Coping Ser.). 192p. (YA). (gr. 7-12). lib. bdg. 34.60 (978-0-8239-4484-2(0)) Rosen Publishing Group, Inc., The.

Challen, Paul C. Surviving 9/11. 2015. (Surviving Disaster Ser.). (ENG., Illus.). 48p. (J). (gr. 5-6). 30.25 (978-1-4994-3657-0(2), Rosen Central) Rosen Publishing Group, Inc., The.

Corrigan, Jim. Causes of the War on Terrorism. 2009. (J). lib. bdg. (978-1-59556-035-3(1)) OTTN Publishing.

Deedy, Carmen Agra. 14 Cows for America, 1 vol. González, Thomas, illus. 2009. (ENG.). 36p. (J). (gr. 1-5). 17.95 (978-1-56145-490-7(7)) Peachtree Pubs.

—14 Cows for America. Gonzalez, Thomas, illus. 2016. (ENG.). 36p. (J). (gr. -1-3). lib. bdg. 19.60 (978-0-606-39065-1(0)) Turtleback Bks.

—14 Vacas para América, 1 vol. González, Thomas, illus. 2010.Tr. of 14 Cows for America. (SPA.). 36p. (J). pap. 8.95 (978-1-56145-555-3(5)) Peachtree Pubs.

—14 Vacas para América, 1 vol. De la Torre, Cristina, tr. from ENG. González, Thomas, illus. 2010.Tr. of 14 Cows for America. (SPA.). 36p. (J). (gr. 1-5). 17.95 (978-1-56145-550-8(4)) Peachtree Pubs.

Deedy, Carmen Agra & Naiyomah, Wilson Kimeli. 14 Cows for America, 1 vol. González, Thomas, illus. 2016. (ENG.). 36p. (J). (gr. 1-5). pap. 8.95 (978-1-56145-961-2(5)) Peachtree Pubs.

Doeden, Matt. Impact: The Story of the September 11 Terrorist Attacks. 2015. (Tangled History Ser.). (ENG.). 112p. (gr. 3-4). lib. bdg. 31.99 (978-1-4914-7079-4(8)) Capstone Press of Coughlan Cos.

Fradin, Dennis Brindell. September 11, 2001. 2009. (Turning Points in U. S. History Ser.). 48p. (gr. 3-6). 31.36 (978-0-7614-4259-2(6)) Marshall Cavendish Corp.

Gard, Carolyn. The Attack on the Pentagon on September 11, 2001. 2005. (Terrorist Attacks Ser.). (Illus.). 64p. (YA). (gr. 7-12). lib. bdg. 31.95 (978-0-8239-3858-2(1)) Rosen Publishing Group, Inc., The.

—The Attack on the Pentagon on September 11 2001. 2009. (Terrorist Attacks Ser.). 64p. (gr. 5-5). 58.50 (978-1-60853-310-7(7)) Rosen Publishing Group, Inc., The.

—The Attacks on the World Trade Center: February 26, 1993, & September 11, 2001. 2005. (Terrorist Attacks Ser.). (Illus.). 64p. (YA). (gr. 5-9). lib. bdg. 31.95 (978-0-8239-3657-1(0)) Rosen Publishing Group, Inc., The.

Gassman, Julie. Saved by the Boats: The Heroic Sea Evacuation of September 11. Moors, Steve, illus. 2016. (Encounter: Narrative Nonfiction Picture Bks.). (ENG.). 32p. (gr. 3-4). lib. bdg. 27.32 (978-1-5157-0269-6(3)) Encounter Bks.

Goldish, Meish. Ground Zero Dogs. 2012. (Dog Heroes Ser.). 32p. (J). (gr. 2-7). lib. bdg. 25.27 (978-1-61772-576-0(5)) Bearport Publishing Co., Inc.

Green, Robert. Cause & Effect the September 11 Attacks: The September 11 Attacks. 2015. (ENG., Illus.). 80p. (J). lib. bdg. (978-1-60152-788-2(8)) ReferencePoint Pr., Inc.

Greene, Jacqueline Dembar. The 2001 World Trade Center Attack. 2007. (Code Red Ser.). (Illus.). 32p. (YA). (gr. 2-5). lib. bdg. 25.27 (978-1-59716-365-1(1)) Bearport Publishing Co., Inc.

Halberstam, David. Firehouse. 2003. (ENG., Illus.). 208p. (gr. 8-17). pap. 16.00 (978-0-7868-8851-1(2)) Hyperion Pr.

Hampton, Wilborn. September 11, 2001: Attack on New York City. 2011. (ENG., Illus.). 160p. (J). (gr. 5). pap. 12.99 (978-0-7636-5767-3(0)) Candlewick Pr.

Hauley, Fletcher. Critical Perspectives on 9/11. 2005. (Critical Anthologies of Nonfiction Writing Ser.). 176p. (J). (gr. 7-12). lib. bdg. 37.95 (978-1-4042-0060-9(6)) Rosen Publishing Group, Inc., The.

Hauley, Fletcher, ed. Critical Perspectives On 9/11. 2009. (Critical Anthologies of Nonfiction Writing Ser.). 176p. (gr. 8-8). 63.90 (978-1-61512-072-7(6)) Rosen Publishing Group, Inc., The.

Hirsch, Judd, reader. Fireboat: The Heroic Adventures of the John J. Harvey. (Illus.). (J). 2006. pap. incl. audio (978-1-59112-985-1(0)) 2004. pap. 39.95 incl. audio compact disk (978-1-59112-989-9(3)) Live Oak Media.

Johnson, Linda Carlson & Johnson, Keri. 9.11 Helping the Heroes: A Salvation Army Story. 2011. (Illus.). (J). (978-0-89216-130-0(2)) Salvation Army.

Kalman, Maira. Fireboat: The Heroic Adventures of the John J. Harvey. Kalman, Maira, illus. 2005. (ENG., Illus.). 48p. (J). (gr. -1-3). reprint ed. pap. 6.99 (978-0-14-240362-4(8), Puffin Books) Penguin Young Readers Group.

Kowalski, Kathiann M. A Pro/con Look at Homeland Security: Safety vs. Liberty After 9/11. 2008. (Issues in Focus Today Ser.). (Illus.). 112p. (J). (gr. 3-7). lib. bdg. 33.27 (978-0-7660-2914-9(X)) Enslow Pubs., Inc.

Koya, Lena & Buell, Tonya. Investigating the Crash of Flight 93. 2017. (Terrorism in the 21st Century: Causes & Effects Ser.). 64p. (gr. 12-11). 34.45 **(978-1-5081-7459-2(8)**, Rosen Young Adult) Rosen Publishing Group, Inc., The.

Koya, Lena & Gard, Carolyn. Investigating the Attack on the Pentagon. 2017. (Terrorism in the 21st Century: Causes & Effects Ser.). 64p. (J). (gr. 12-11). 34.45 **(978-1-5081-7453-0(9)**, Rosen Young Adult) Rosen Publishing Group, Inc., The.

—Investigating the Attacks on the World Trade Center. 2017. (Terrorism in the 21st Century: Causes & Effects Ser.). 64p. (J). (gr. 12-11). 34.45 **(978-1-5081-7455-4(5)**, Rosen Young Adult) Rosen Publishing Group, Inc., The.

Lynch, Kelly Ann. He Said Yes: The Story of Father Mychal Judge. Oatman, M. Scott, illus. 2007. 32p. (J). (gr. -1-3). 12.95 (978-0-8091-6740-1(9), 6740-1) Paulist Pr.

Margulies, Philip. Al-Qaeda: Osama Bin Laden's Army of Terrorists. 2005. (Inside the World's Most Infamous Terrorist Organizations Ser.). (Illus.). 64p. (YA). (gr. 7-12). lib. bdg. 31.95 (978-0-8239-3817-9(4)) Rosen Publishing Group, Inc., The.

Margulies, Phillip. Al Qaeda: Osama bin Laden's Army of Terrorists. 2009. (Inside the World's Most Infamous Terrorist Organizations Ser.). 64p. (gr. 5-5). 58.50 (978-1-61513-573-8(1)) Rosen Publishing Group, Inc., The.

Marin, Dale Diane. Rachel Beth & the Day the Towers Came Down, 1 vol. Marin, Liz, illus. 2009. 27p. pap. 24.95 (978-1-60813-328-4(1)) America Star Bks.

McNeil, Niki, et al. HOCPP 1105 September 11th 2001. 2006. spiral bd. 21.00 (978-1-60308-105-4(4)) In the Hands of a Child.

Miller, Mara. Remembering September 11, 2001: What We Know Now. 2010. (Issues in Focus Today Ser.). 112p. (J). (gr. 7-12). 33.27 (978-0-7660-2931-6(X)) Enslow Pubs., Inc.

Murdico, Suzanne J. Osama Bin Laden. 2007. (Middle East Leaders Ser.). (Illus.). 112p. (J). (gr. 3-7). lib. bdg. 34.60 (978-1-4042-0875-9(5), Rosen Reference) Rosen Publishing Group, Inc., The.

—Osama bin Laden. 2009. (Middle East Leaders Ser.). 112p. (gr. 5-8). 66.50 (978-1-61514-647-5(4), Rosen Reference) Rosen Publishing Group, Inc., The.

Murray, Laura K. The 9/11 Terror Attacks. 2016. 48p. (J). (978-1-60818-750-8(0), Creative Education) Creative Co., The.

Nolan, Janet. Seven & a Half Tons of Steel, 1 vol. González, Thomas, illus. 2016. (ENG.). 36p. (J). (gr. 1-5). 17.95 (978-1-56145-912-4(7)) Peachtree Pubs.

Pierce, Alan. September 11 2001, 1 vol. 2005. (American Moments Set li Ser.). (ENG.). 48p. (gr. 4-8). 27.07 (978-1-59197-735-3(5), Abdo & Daughters) ABDO Publishing Co.

Ringgold, Faith, intro. What Will You Do for Your Peace? Impact of 9/11 on New York City Youth. 2004. (Illus.). 32p. (YA). 16.95 net. (978-0-9761753-0-8(4)) InterRelations Collaborative, Inc.

Roleff, Tamara L., ed. The World Trade Center Attack. 2003. (History Firsthand Ser.). (Illus.). 202p. (YA). (gr. 7-10). pap. 21.20 (978-0-7377-1469-2(7), Greenhaven Pr., Inc.) Cengage Gale.

Santora, Maureen Crethan. The Day the Towers Fell: The Story of September 11, 2001. 2008. 36p. (J). pap. 21.99 (978-1-4257-7869-9(0)) Xlibris Corp.

—The Day the Towers Fell: The Story of September 11, 2001. Santora, Maureen Crethan, illus. 2008. (Illus.). 32p. (J). 31.99 (978-1-4257-7872-9(0)) Xlibris Corp.

—My Son Christopher: A 9/11 Mother's Tale of Remembrance. 2008. 36p. 31.99 (978-1-4363-3044-2(0)) Xlibris Corp.

Scheppler, Bill. Guantánamo Bay & Military Tribunals: The Detention & Trial of Suspected Terrorists. 2009. (Frontline Coverage of Current Events Ser.). 48p. (gr. 5-5). 53.00 (978-1-61512-655-2(4)) Rosen Publishing Group, Inc., The.

Smith, Katrina M. This Is My Flag. 2011. 44p. pap. 18.46 (978-1-4634-4785-4(X)) AuthorHouse.

The\September 11 Generation. Freedom's Answer: When the Twin Towers Fell, the Next Generation Rose! 2004. 160p. pap. (978-0-9720227-7-4(5)) Little Moose Pr.

Whiting, Jim & Murray, Laura K. The 9/11 Attacks. 2017. (Turning Points Ser.). (ENG.). 48p. (J). (gr. 1-3). pap. 12.00 (978-1-62832-346-7(9), Creative Paperbacks) Creative Co., The.

Williams, Brian. America under Attack. 2003. (Dates with History Ser.). 45p. (J). lib. bdg. 28.50 (978-1-58340-406-5(6)) Black Rabbit Bks.

Yeager, Allison Blair. If I Could Change the World. Mesch, Kate, ed. (Illus.). 32p. (YA). (gr. 1-18). pap. 8.95 (978-0-9715322-0-5(6), LUBOITCCW) Luv U Bks.

Zullo, Allan. Heroes of 9/11. 2011. (Illus.). 181p. (J). pap. (978-0-545-25506-6(6)) Scholastic, Inc.

—10 True Tales: Heroes Of 9/11. 2015. (Ten True Tales Ser.). (ENG.). 192p. (J). (gr. 3-7). pap. 5.99 (978-0-545-81813-1(3), Scholastic Nonfiction) Scholastic, Inc.

13 Unknown Souls. 2003. (YA). 13.00 (978-0-9745360-0-2(8)) Burney Enterprises Unlimited.

SEQUOIA NATIONAL FOREST (CALIF.)

Nicholas, Jeff D. Sequoia & Kings Canyon. 2004. (Illus.). per. 4.95 (978-1-58071-054-1(9), Wish You Were Here) Sierra Pr.

SEQUOYAH, 1770?-1843

Bennett, Doraine. Sequoyah. 2008. (978-1-935077-05-3(8)); pap. (978-1-935077-12-1(0)) State Standards Publishing, LLC.

Levine, Michelle. Sequoyah. 2004. (History Maker Bios Ser.). (J). pap. 8.95 (978-0-8225-2071-9(0)) Lerner Publishing Group.

Marsh, Carole. Sequoyah. 2003. 12p. (gr. k-4). 2.95 (978-0-635-02363-6(6)) Gallopade International.

Rodgers, Kelly. Sequoyah & the Written Word. 2016. (Primary Source Readers Ser.). (Illus.). 32p. (gr. 2-2). 8.99 (978-1-4938-2554-7(2)) Teacher Created Materials, Inc.

Rumford, James. Sequoyah: The Cherokee Man Who Gave His People Writing. Huckaby, Anna Sixkiller, tr. 2010. (ENG & CHR., Illus.). 32p. (C). (gr. -1-3). tchr. ed. 26.95 (978-0-618-36947-8(3)) National Geographic School Publishing, Inc.

Summitt, April R. Sequoyah & the Invention of the Cherokee Alphabet, 1 vol. 2012. (Landmarks of the American Mosaic Ser.). (Illus.). 164p. (C). 41.00 (978-0-313-39177-4(7), A3212C, Greenwood) ABC-CLIO, LLC.

Townsend, Dana E. Sequoyah & the Cherokee Alphabet. Gabriel, Andrea, illus. 2005. (Voices Reading Ser.). 32p. (J). (978-0-7367-2953-6(4)) Zaner-Bloser, Inc.

Waxman, Laura Hamilton. Sequoyah. 2004. (History Maker Biographies Ser.). (ENG., Illus.). 48p. (gr. 3-6). 27.93 (978-0-8225-0697-3(1), Carolrhoda Bks.) Lerner Publishing Group.

Waya, Joe. We Should Honor Sequoyah. 2017. (Text Connections Guided Close Reading Ser.). (J). (gr. 2). (978-1-4900-1856-0(5)) Benchmark Education Co.

SEQUOYAH, 1770?-1843—FICTION

Brown, Frances Williams. Captured Words: The Story of A Great Indian. Bjorklund, L. F., illus. 2011. 192p. 42.95 (978-1-258-09914-5(4)) Literary Licensing, LLC.

Bruchac, Joseph. Talking Leaves. (ENG.). (J). (gr. 5). 2017. 288p. pap. 8.99 **(978-0-14-242298-4(3)**, Puffin Books) 2016. 256p. 16.99 (978-0-8037-3508-8(1), Dial Bks) Penguin Young Readers Group.

SERIALS (PUBLICATIONS)

see Periodicals

SERIGRAPHY

see Screen Process Printing

SERMON ON THE MOUNT

Gortler, Rosemarie & Piscitelli, Donna. The Beatitudes for Children. Sternhagen, Mimi, illus. 2009. 64p. (J). (gr. -1-3). pap. 6.95 (978-1-59276-545-4(9)) Our Sunday Visitor, Publishing Div.

Halpin, D. Thomas. The Beatitudes Coloring & Activity Book. Richards, Virginia Helen, illus. 2006. (J). 1.95 (978-0-8198-2359-5(7)) Pauline Bks. & Media.

Larsen, Carolyn. Teachings of Jesus. 2012. (Standard Bible Storybook Ser.). (ENG., Illus.). 32p. (J). 7.99 (978-0-7847-3565-7(4)) Standard Publishing.

SERMONS

Beeching, Henry Charles. Seven Sermons to Schoolboys. 2006. pap. 20.95 (978-1-4286-3591-3(2)) Kessinger Publishing, LLC.

Dyan, Penelope. Beatitudes Are Attitudes. 2011. 34p. pap. 11.95 (978-1-935630-90-6(3)) Bellissima Publishing, LLC.

Ewald, Thomas & Carson-Dellosa Publishing Staff. Five-Minute Sermons for Children: 56 Invitations to Grow in Grace. 2004. (ENG., Illus.). 64p. (gr. k-5). pap. 9.99 (978-0-88724-215-1(4), CD-2029) Carson-Dellosa Publishing, LLC.

Group Publishing Staff, ed. Quick Children's Sermons: Did Adam & Eve Have Bellybuttons? 2004. (Illus.). 96p. (gr. -1-6). pap. 17.99 (978-0-7644-2296-6(0), Flagship Church Resources) Group Publishing, Inc.

Hewitt, Beth Edington. Sermones Que Cautivan A los Ninos: Como Preparar y Presentar Sermones Infantiles Poderosos. Ballesta, Alfredo, tr. 2006. (SPA.). 208p. pap. 9.50 (978-0-311-43030-7(9), Editorial Mundo Hispano) Casa Bautista de Publicaciones.

Newton, Richard. Bible Promises: Sermons for Children on. 2006. pap. 15.99 (978-1-59925-057-1(8)) Solid Ground Christian Bks.

—Bible Warnings: Sermons to Children. 2006. pap. 25.00 (978-1-59925-083-0(7)) Solid Ground Christian Bks.

—Leaves from the Tree of Life: Sermons for Children. 2011. 164p. pap. 17.00 (978-1-59925-150-9(7)) Solid Ground Christian Bks.

—Pebbles from the Brook: Sermons for Children Fighting the Good Fight of Faith. 2011. 316p. pap. 23.00 (978-1-59925-151-6(5)) Solid Ground Christian Bks.

Phillips, Mary. Children'S Sermons with Humor. 2009. 56p. pap. 15.99 (978-1-4415-1156-0(3)) Xlibris Corp.

Smith, Rodney Gipsy. The Lost Christ. 2003. (Illus.). 32p. 2.99 (978-1-931393-05-8(2)) Christian Life Bks.

Staf, Edie. Christmas Novena: For Home or Classroom. 22p. (J). (gr. 2-8). pap. 1.50 (978-0-8198-1456-2(3), 332-032) Pauline Bks. & Media.

Vanissery, Matthew. Awesome Homilies: The Power of His Word. 2004. 236p. pap. 29.95 (978-0-9759906-0-5(8)) Vanissery, Matthew.

Wehrheim, Carol A. Feasting on the Word Childrens's Sermons for Year A. 2016. (ENG.). 128p. pap. 20.00 (978-0-664-26107-8(8)) Westminster John Knox Pr.

Wezeman, Phyllis Vos & Liechty, Anna L. Tell Me a Story: 30 Children's Sermons Based on Best-Loved Books. 2005. (New Brown Bag Ser.). (Illus.). 96p. pap. 12.00 (978-0-8298-1635-8(6)) Pilgrim Pr., The/United Church Pr.

Wezeman, Phyllis Vos, et al. Wipe the Tears: 30 Children's Sermons on Death. 2005. (New Brown Bag Ser.). (Illus.). 96p. 10.00 (978-0-8298-1520-7(1)) Pilgrim Pr., The/United Church Pr.

SERPENTS

see Snakes

SERRA, JUNIPERO, 1713-1784

Améz, Lynda. Father Junipero Serra: Founder of the California Missions. 2015. (Exceptional Latinos Ser.). (ENG.). 24p. (J). (gr. 3-4). pap. 9.35 (978-0-7660-6710-3(6)) Enslow Pubs., Inc.

Gasnick, Roy M. & Grycan, Julien. Serra: American Founding Father. 2010. (ENG., Illus.). 35p. pap. 2.95 (978-0-86716-942-3(7)) Franciscan Media.

Marsh, Carole. Father Junipero Serra: California Missions Founder: California Missions Founder. 2003. 12p. (gr. k-4). 2.95 (978-0-635-02136-6(6)) Gallopade International.

Nussbaum, Ben. Junipero Serra: A Spanish Missionary. 2017. (Primary Source Readers Ser.). (Illus.). 32p. (gr. 4-4). 9.99 **(978-1-4258-3235-3(0))** Teacher Created Materials, Inc.

SERVICE, COMPULSORY MILITARY

see Draft

SET THEORY

see also Arithmetic; Number Theory

Aboff, Marcie. If You Were a Set, 1 vol. Dillard, Sarah, illus. 2008. (Math Fun Ser.). (ENG.). 24p. (gr. 2-4). 27.99 (978-1-4048-4799-6(5)); pap. 7.95 (978-1-4048-4800-9(2)) Picture Window Bks.

—If You Were a Set [LTD Commodities]. Dillard, Sarah, illus. 2010. (Math Fun Ser.). 24p. pap. 3.50 *(978-1-4048-6258-6(7),* Nonfiction Picture Bks.) Picture Window Bks.
—Sorting Fur, Feathers, Tails, & Scales. (Data Mania Ser.). (ENG & ABK.). 24p. (gr. 1-2). 2011. pap. 41.70 *(978-1-4296-6467-7(3))* 2010. lib. bdg. 25.32 *(978-1-4296-4526-3(1))* Capstone Press of Coughlan Cos. (First Facts).
Alexander, Emmett. Sort It by Size. 2015. (Sort It Out! Ser.). (ENG., Illus.). 24p. (J). (gr. k-1). pap. 8.15 *(978-1-4824-2573-4(4))* Stevens, Gareth Publishing LLLP.
Atwood, Megan. Busy Beavers: Counting By 5s, 1 vol. Holm, Sharon, illus. 2012. (Count the Critters Ser.). (ENG.). 24p. (J). (gr. k-3). 27.07 *(978-1-61641-852-6(4))* Magic Wagon.
—Monarch Migration: Counting by 10s, 1 vol. Holm, Sharon, illus. 2012. (Count the Critters Ser.). (ENG.). 24p. (J). (gr. k-3). 27.07 *(978-1-61641-854-0(0))* Magic Wagon.
Becker, Ann & Peppas, Lynn. Sorting. 2009. (ENG.). 24p. (J). lib. bdg. *(978-0-7787-4349-1(7));* pap. *(978-0-7787-4367-5(5))* Crabtree Publishing Co.
Corcorane, Ann. Sorting, 1 vol. 2011. (Wonder Readers Emergent Level Ser.). (ENG.). (gr. -1-1). 32p. pap. 5.99 *(978-1-4296-7870-4(4));* 16p. pap. 35.94 *(978-1-4296-8151-3(9))* Capstone Press of Coughlan Cos. (Wonder Readers).
Coss, Lauren. Let's Sort by Color. 2014. (21st Century Basic Skills Library: Sorting Ser.). (ENG., Illus.). 24p. (J). (gr. k-3). 22.79 *(978-1-63137-634-4(9),* 205319) Cherry Lake Publishing.
—Let's Sort by Size. 2014. (21st Century Basic Skills Library: Sorting Ser.). (ENG., Illus.). 24p. (J). (gr. k-3). 22.79 *(978-1-63137-635-1(7),* 205323) Cherry Lake Publishing.
—Let's Sort Money. 2014. (21st Century Basic Skills Library: Sorting Ser.). (ENG.). 24p. (J). (gr. k-3). 22.79 *(978-1-63137-633-7(0),* 205315) Cherry Lake Publishing.
—Let's Sort Shapes. 2014. (21st Century Basic Skills Library: Sorting Ser.). (ENG.). 24p. (J). (gr. k-3). 22.79 *(978-1-63137-632-0(2),* 205311) Cherry Lake Publishing.
Day, Nancy Raines. What in the World? Sets in Nature. Cyrus, Kurt, illus. 2015. (ENG.). 32p. (J). (gr. -1-3). 17.99 *(978-1-4814-0060-2(6),* Beach Lane Bks.) Beach Lane Bks.
Doudna, Kelly. Use Your Eye, Let's Classify!, 1 vol. 2007. (Science Made Simple Ser.). (ENG., Illus.). 24p. (J). (gr. k-3). lib. bdg. 24.21 *(978-1-59928-620-4(3),* SandCastle) ABDO Publishing Co.
GER Set Square. 2006. (J). 2.90 *(978-1-934046-11-1(6))* Global Education Resources, LLC.
Hawley, Ella. The Number 1. 2010. (Numbers in My World Ser.). (ENG.). 16p. (J). bds. 11.95 *(978-1-4358-9319-1(0),* PowerKids Pr.) Rosen Publishing Group, Inc., The.
—The Number 2. 2010. (Numbers in My World Ser.). (ENG.). 16p. (J). bds. 11.95 *(978-1-4358-9320-7(4),* PowerKids Pr.) Rosen Publishing Group, Inc., The.
—The Number 3. 2010. (Numbers in My World Ser.). (ENG.). 16p. (J). bds. 11.95 *(978-1-4358-9321-4(2),* PowerKids Pr.) Rosen Publishing Group, Inc., The.
—The Number 4. 2010. (Numbers in My World Ser.). (ENG.). 16p. (J). bds. 11.95 *(978-1-4358-9322-1(0),* PowerKids Pr.) Rosen Publishing Group, Inc., The.
—The Number 5. 2010. (Numbers in My World Ser.). (ENG.). 16p. (J). bds. 11.95 *(978-1-4358-9323-8(9),* PowerKids Pr.) Rosen Publishing Group, Inc., The.
—Numbers 1, 2, 3, 4, 5. 2010. (Numbers in My World Ser.). (ENG.). 16p. (J). bds. 11.95 *(978-1-4358-9324-5(7),* PowerKids Pr.) Rosen Publishing Group, Inc., The.
Jocelyn, Marthe. Same Same. Slaughter, Tom, illus. (ENG.). (J). (gr. k-k). 2010. 16p. bds. 7.95 *(978-0-88776-987-0(X))* 2009. 24p. 15.95 *(978-0-88776-885-9(7))* Tundra Bks. CAN. (Tundra Bks.). Dist: Penguin Random Hse. LLC.
Kompelien, Tracy. There Is Order on the Border!, 1 vol. 2007. (Math Made Fun Ser.). (ENG., Illus.). 24p. (J). (gr. k-3). lib. bdg. 24.21 *(978-1-59928-547-4(9),* SandCastle) ABDO Publishing Co.
Loughran, Donna & Brunner-Jass, Renata. Hidden Ducks: Describing & Interpreting Data. 2013. (IMath Ser.). (Illus.). 48p. (J). (gr. 5-6). pap. 11.94 *(978-1-60357-511-9(1));* lib. bdg. 23.94 *(978-1-59953-572-2(6))* Norwood Hse. Pr.
Marks, Jennifer L. Clasificar Juguetes/Sorting Toys, 1 vol. 2012. (Vamos a Ordenar / Sorting Ser.). (ENG, SPA & MUL.). 32p. (gr. 1-2). lib. bdg. 27.32 *(978-1-4296-8254-1(X),* A+ Bilingue/Bilingual) Capstone Press of Coughlan Cos.
McDonnell, Mary Rose. Sorting with Snakes. 2013. (Animal Math Ser.). 24p. (J). (gr. 1-3). 22.60 *(978-1-4339-9328-2(7))* Stevens, Gareth Publishing LLLP.
Miller, Reagan & Berry, Minta. What Comes in Sets? Crabtree Publishing Staff, ed. 2011. (My Path to Math Ser.: No. 38). (ENG., Illus.). 24p. (J). (gr. k-3). pap. *(978-0-7787-5268-4(2))* Crabtree Publishing Co.
—What Comes in Sets? 2011. (ENG., Illus.). 24p. (J). lib. bdg. *(978-0-7787-5279-0(8))* Crabtree Publishing Co.
Mineo, Kate. Compare with Bears. 2011. (Animal Math Ser.). (Illus.). 24p. (J). (gr. 1-3). pap. 8.15 *(978-1-4339-5660-7(8));* lib. bdg. 22.60 *(978-1-4339-5658-4(6))* Stevens, Gareth Publishing LLLP.
Murphy, Stuart J. 3 Little Firefighters. 2003. (MathStart Level 1 Ser.). (J). (gr. k-3). 16.00 *(978-0-613-68469-9(9),* Turtleback) Turtleback Bks.
Nations, Susan & Weekly Reader Editorial Staff. I Know Same & Different (Igual y Diferente) 2006. (I'm Ready for Math/YA Puedo Aprender Matematicas Ser.). (ENG & SPA., Illus.). 16p. (gr. -1-2). lib. bdg. 19.00 *(978-0-8368-6486-1(7),* Weekly Reader Leveled Readers) Stevens, Gareth Publishing LLLP.
Ribke, Simone T. Grouping at the Dog Show. 2006. (Rookie Read-About Math Ser.). (ENG., Illus.). 32p. (J). (gr. 1-2). lib. bdg. 20.50 *(978-0-516-24959-9(2),* Children's Pr.) Scholastic Library Publishing.
Roy, Jennifer Rozines & Roy, Gregory. Sorting at the Ocean. 2005. (Math All Around Ser.). (Illus.). 32p. (gr. 2-7). lib. bdg. 29.93 *(978-0-7614-1998-3(5),* Benchmark Bks.) Marshall Cavendish Corp.
Shepherd, Jodie. The Crayola Sorting Book. 2017. (Crayola (r) Concepts Ser.). (ENG.). 24p. (J). (gr. -1-3). 26.65 ***(978-1-5124-3286-2(5))*** Lerner Publishing Group.
Snyder, Jane. Days of the Week: Learning Ordinal Numbers. 2009. (Math for the REAL World Ser.). 12p. (gr. 1-2). pap. 5.90 *(978-0-8239-8913-3(5),* Rosen Classroom) Rosen Publishing Group, Inc., The.
Steffora, Tracey. Sorting at the Market, 1 vol. 2011. (Math Around Us Ser.). (ENG.). 24p. (gr. -1-1). 22.65 *(978-1-4329-4927-3(6));* pap. 6.29 *(978-1-4329-4935-8(7))* Heinemann-Raintree. (Acorn).
Tang, Greg. Math-Terpieces: The Art of Problem-Solving. Paprocki, Greg, illus. 2003. (ENG.). 32p. (J). (gr. 2-5). 18.99 *(978-0-439-44388-3(1))* Scholastic, Inc.
Weekly Reader Editorial Staff. I Know Same & Different. 2006. (I'm Ready for Math Ser.). (Illus.). 16p. (gr. -1-2). pap. 5.30 *(978-0-8368-6481-6(6),* Weekly Reader Leveled Readers) Stevens, Gareth Publishing LLLP.
—I Know Same & Different. 2006. (I'm Ready for Math Ser.). (Illus.). 16p. (gr. -1-2). lib. bdg. 19.00 *(978-0-8368-6476-2(X),* Weekly Reader Leveled Readers) Stevens, Gareth Publishing LLLP.
Weekly Reader Editorial Staff, contrib. by. I Know Same & Different (Igual y Diferente) 2006. (I'm Ready for Math/ Ya puedo aprender matematicas Ser.). (ENG & SPA., Illus.). 16p. (gr. -1-2). pap. 5.30 *(978-0-8368-6491-5(3),* Weekly Reader Leveled Readers) Stevens, Gareth Publishing LLLP.

SETS (MATHEMATICS)
see Set Theory

SETTLEMENTS, SOCIAL
see Social Settlements

SEUSS, DR., 1904-1991
Anderson, Tanya. Dr. Seuss (Theodor Geisel) 2nd rev. ed. 2011. (Who Wrote That? Ser.). (Illus.). 128p. (gr. 6-12). 35.00 *(978-1-60413-750-7(9),* Chelsea Hse.) Facts On File, Inc.
Carlson, Cheryl. Dr. Seuss [Scholastic]. 2011. (First Biographies - Writers, Artists, & Athletes Ser.). 24p. pap. 0.50 *(978-1-4296-6317-5(0),* Pebble Bks.) Capstone Press of Coughlan Cos.
Foran, Jill. Dr. Seuss. 2012. (J). 13.95 *(978-1-61913-059-3(9));* pap. 28.55 *(978-1-61913-595-6(7))* Weigl Pubs., Inc.
Grahame-Smith, Deborah. Dr. Seuss. 2014. (Spotlight on Children's Authors Ser.). 48p. (J). (gr. 4-6). lib. bdg. 29.93 *(978-1-62712-846-9(8))* Cavendish Square Publishing.
Guillain, Charlotte. Dr. Seuss, 1 vol. 2012. (Author Biographies Ser.). (ENG.). 24p. (gr. 1-2). 23.32 *(978-1-4329-5959-3(X));* pap. 6.79 *(978-1-4329-5965-4(4))* Heinemann-Raintree. (Heinemann Read & Learn).
Klimo, Kate. Dr. Seuss: the Great Doodler. 2016. (Step into Reading Ser.). (ENG., Illus.). 48p. (J). (gr. k-3). lib. bdg. 15.99 *(978-0-375-97376-5(1),* Random Hse. Bks. for Young Readers) Random Hse. Children's Bks.
Krull, Kathleen. The Boy on Fairfield Street: How Ted Geisel Grew up to Become Dr. Seuss. Johnson, Steve & Fancher, Lou, illus. 2010. (ENG.). 48p. (J). (gr. k-4). pap. 7.99 *(978-0-375-85550-4(5),* Dragonfly Bks.) Random Hse. Children's Bks.
—The Boy on Fairfield Street: How Ted Geisel Grew up to Become Dr. Seuss. 2010. lib. bdg. 18.40 *(978-0-606-12416-4(0),* Turtleback) Turtleback Bks.
Kudlinski, Kathleen. Dr. Seuss: Young Author & Artist. Henderson, Meryl, illus. 2005. 184p. (J). lib. bdg. 18.46 *(978-1-4242-2201-8(X))* Fitzgerald Bks.
Landau, Jennifer. Dr. Seuss, 01 vols., 1. 2016. (Britannica Beginner Bios Ser.). (ENG., Illus.). 32p. (J). pap. 12.90 *(978-1-5081-0063-8(2),* Britannica Educational Publishing) Rosen Publishing Group, Inc., The.
Miklowitz, Gloria D. Dr. Seuss. 2004. (ENG., Illus.). 26p. (J). (gr. 2-5). pap. 7.33 *(978-0-7685-1217-5(4),* Dominie Elementary) Pearson Schl.
Pascal, Janet. Who Was Dr. Seuss? Harrison, Nancy, illus. 2011. (Who Was? Ser.). (ENG.). 112p. (J). (gr. 3-7). pap. 5.99 *(978-0-448-45585-3(4),* Grosset & Dunlap) Penguin Young Readers Group.
Schuetz, Kari. Dr. Seuss. 2015. (Children's Storytellers Ser.). (ENG., Illus.). 24p. (J). (gr. 2-5). lib. bdg. 25.95 *(978-1-62617-265-4(X),* Blastoff! Readers) Bellwether Media.
Waxman, Laura Hamilton. Dr. Seuss. 2010. (History Maker Biographies Ser.). (ENG.). 48p. (gr. 3-6). lib. bdg. 27.93 *(978-0-7613-5206-8(6),* Lerner Pubns.) Lerner Publishing Group.

SEVEN WONDERS OF THE WORLD
Benchmark Education Company. The Seven Wonders of the Ancient World (Teacher Guide) 2004. *(978-1-4108-2582-7(5))* Benchmark Education Co.
Collins. Collins Fascinating Facts - Amazing Places. rev. ed. 2016. (Collins Fascinating Facts Ser.). (ENG.). 72p. (J). (gr. 1-3). pap. 10.99 *(978-0-00-816919-0(5))* HarperCollins Pubs. Ltd. GBR. Dist: Independent Pubs. Group.
Gonzales, Doreen. Seven Wonders of the Modern World: A MyReportLinks. com Book. 2005. (Seven Wonders of the World Ser.). (Illus.). 48p. (J). lib. bdg. 25.26 *(978-0-7660-5292-5(3),* MyReportLinks.com Bks.) Enslow Pubs., Inc.
—What Are the 7 Wonders of the Modern World? 2013. (What Are the Seven Wonders of the World? Ser.). 48p. (J). (gr. 4-10). pap. 8.95 *(978-1-4644-0231-9(0));* 25.27 *(978-0-7660-4152-3(2))* Enslow Pubs., Inc.
Gonzales, Doreen & Graham, Amy. What Are the 7 Wonders of the Natural World? 2013. (What Are the Seven Wonders of the World? Ser.). 48p. (J). (gr. 4-18). 25.27 *(978-0-7660-4153-0(0))* Enslow Pubs., Inc.
Graham, Amy. What Are the 7 Wonders of the Natural World? 2013. (What Are the Seven Wonders of the World? Ser.). 48p. (J). (gr. 4-10). pap. 8.95 *(978-1-4644-0232-6(9))* Enslow Pubs., Inc.
HarrisNic. WONDERS OF THE WORLD HIGH BEGINNING BOOK WITH ONLINE ACCESS. 2014. (ENG.). 24p. (J). pap. 9.50 *(978-1-107-64298-0(1))* Cambridge Univ. Pr.
Hibbert, Adam. World Wonders. 2010. (Unpredictable Nature Ser.). 48p. (J). (gr. 3-18). lib. bdg. 19.95 *(978-1-4222-2008-5(7))* Mason Crest.
Kenah, Katharine. Amazing Creations. 2006. (Extreme Readers: Level 2 Ser.). (Illus.). 32p. (gr. 4-7). 13.95 *(978-0-7569-6844-1(5))* Perfection Learning Corp.
Koll, Hilary & Mills, Steve. A Math Journey Around the Wonders of the World. 2016. (ENG., Illus.). 32p. (J). *(978-0-7787-2321-9(6))* Crabtree Publishing Co.
Laliberte, Michelle. Seven Wonders of the Ancient World: A MyReportLinks.com Book. Johnson, Howard David, illus. 2005. (Seven Wonders of the World Ser.). 48p. (J). (gr. 4-10). lib. bdg. 26.60 *(978-0-7660-5293-2(1),* MyReportLinks.com Bks.) Enslow Pubs., Inc.
—What Are the 7 Wonders of the Ancient World? 2013. (What Are the Seven Wonders of the World? Ser.). 48p. (J). (gr. 4-10). pap. 8.95 *(978-1-4644-0230-2(2));* 25.27 *(978-0-7660-4151-6(4))* Enslow Pubs., Inc.
Mchugh, Arianne. Seven Wonders of the Ancient World. 2015. (Red Rhino Nonfiction Ser.). (J). lib. bdg. 20.80 *(978-0-606-37197-1(4))* Turtleback Bks.
Piano, Maureen. My Adventure to the Wonders of the World. 2006. 44p. (J). 8.99 *(978-1-59092-445-7(2))* Blue Forge Pr.
Seven Wonders, 7 vols., Set. Incl. Seven Wonders Beyond the Solar System. Miller, Ron. (Illus.). 33.26 *(978-0-7613-5454-3(9));* Seven Wonders of Asteroids, Comets, & Meteors. Miller, Ron. lib. bdg. 33.26 *(978-0-7613-5451-2(4));* Seven Wonders of Space Phenomena. Ward, D. J. 33.26 *(978-0-7613-5452-9(2));* Seven Wonders of Space Technology. Bortz, Fred. (Illus.). 33.26 *(978-0-7613-5453-6(0));* Seven Wonders of the Gas Giants & Their Moons. Miller, Ron. lib. bdg. 33.26 *(978-0-7613-5449-9(2));* Seven Wonders of the Rocky Planets & Their Moons. Miller, Ron. lib. bdg. 33.26 *(978-0-7613-5448-2(4));* Seven Wonders of the Sun & Other Stars. Hansen, Rosanna. 33.26 *(978-0-7613-5450-5(6));* 80p. (gr. 5-8). 2011. 2011. Set lib. bdg. 232.82 *(978-0-7613-7469-5(8),* Twenty-First Century Bks.) Lerner Publishing Group.
Sullivan, Erin Ash. The Seven Wonders of the Ancient World. 2011. (Navigators Ser.). (J). pap. 50.00 net. *(978-1-4108-2567-4(1))* Benchmark Education Co.
—The Seven Wonders of the Ancient World & Las siete maravillas del mundo Antiguo: 6 English, 6 Spanish Adaptations. 2011. (ENG & SPA.). (J). 101.00 net. *(978-1-4108-5728-6(X))* Benchmark Education Co.
Top That Publishing Staff, ed. 7 Wonders of World. 2004. (Know How Know Why Ser.). (Illus.). 48p. (J). pap. *(978-1-84510-073-5(5))* Top That! Publishing PLC.
Van Vleet, Carmella. Seven Wonders of the World: Discover Amazing Monuments to Civilization with 20 Projects. Rizvi, Farah, illus. 2011. (Build It Yourself Ser.). (ENG.). 128p. (J). (gr. 3-7). 21.95 *(978-1-934670-82-8(0));* pap. 15.95 *(978-1-936313-73-0(1))* Open City Bks.
Woods, Michael & Woods, Mary B. Seven Wonders of the Ancient World. 2008. (Seven Wonders Ser.). (ENG., Illus.). 80p. (gr. 5-8). lib. bdg. 33.26 *(978-0-8225-7568-9(X))* Lerner Publishing Group.
World Book, Inc Staff, contrib. by. Wonders of the World. 2011. (J). *(978-0-7166-1794-5(3))* World Bk., Inc.

SEWAGE DISPOSAL
see also Refuse and Refuse Disposal; Water—Pollution
Furgang, Kathy. Zoom in on Water & Sewage Systems. 2017. (Zoom in on Engineering Ser.). 24p. (J). (gr. 2-2). pap. 9.35 ***(978-0-7660-8840-5(5));*** lib. bdg. 22.60 ***(978-0-7660-8714-9(X))*** Enslow Pubs., Inc.
Laplante, Walter. What Happens When I Flush the Toilet? 2016. (Everyday Mysteries Ser.). (ENG.). 24p. (J). (gr. 1-2). pap. 8.15 *(978-1-4824-3825-3(9))* Stevens, Gareth Publishing LLLP.
Mahoney, Emily. Wasted Waters. 2017. (Unnatural Disasters Ser.). 32p. (J). (gr. 4-5). pap. 10.50 ***(978-1-5382-0527-3(0))*** Stevens, Gareth Publishing LLLP.
Newman, Patricia. Plastic, Ahoy! Investigating the Great Pacific Garbage Patch. Crawley, Annie, illus. 2014. (ENG.). 48p. (gr. 3-6). lib. bdg. 30.60 *(978-1-4677-1283-5(3),* Millbrook Pr.) Lerner Publishing Group.
Porter, Esther. What's Sprouting in My Trash? A Book about Composting. 2013. (Earth Matters Ser.). (ENG.). 32p. (gr. 1-2). pap. 47.70 *(978-1-62065-746-1(5));* lib. bdg. 27.32 *(978-1-62065-047-9(9))* Capstone Press of Coughlan Cos. (Aplus Bks.).
Rhatigan, Joe. Get a Job at the Garbage Dump. 2016. (Bright Futures Press: Get a Job Ser.). (ENG.). 32p. (J). (gr. 4-6). 29.93 *(978-1-63471-905-6(0),* 208941) Cherry Lake Publishing.
Roza, Greg. How Do Sewers Work? 2016. (STEM Waterworks Ser.). 32p. (J). (gr. 5-5). pap. 11.75 *(978-1-4994-2003-6(X),* PowerKids Pr.) Rosen Publishing Group, Inc., The.

SEWING
see also Dressmaking; Embroidery; Needlework
Blake, Susannah. Crafts for Styling Your Wardrobe. 2013. (Eco Chic Ser.). 32p. (J). lib. bdg. 23.94 *(978-0-7660-4316-9(9))* Enslow Pubs., Inc.
Butcher, Alice & Farquhar, Ginny. Sewing for Kids: Easy Projects to Sew at Home. 2013. (ENG., Illus.). 80p. pap. 14.99 *(978-1-4463-0261-3(X))* David & Charles Pubs. GBR. Dist: F&W Media, Inc.
Carlson, Laurie M. Queen of Inventions: How the Sewing Machine Changed the World. 2003. (Illus.). 32p. lib. bdg. 22.90 *(978-0-7613-2706-6(1),* Millbrook Pr.) Lerner Publishing Group.
Cherry, Winky. My First Doll Book: Hand Sewing. 2nd ed. 2011. (My First Sewing Book Kit Ser.). (ENG.). 40p. (J). (gr. 3-7). pap. 16.95 *(978-0-935278-87-3(7))* Palmer-Pletsch Assocs.
—My First Machine Sewing Book: Straight Stitching. 2nd ed. 2011. (My First Sewing Book Kit Ser.). (ENG.). 40p. (J). (gr. 3-7). pap. 16.95 *(978-0-935278-88-0(5))* Palmer-Pletsch Assocs.
—My First Quilt Book: Machine Sewing. 2nd ed. 2011. (My First Sewing Book Kit Ser.). (ENG., Illus.). 40p. (J). (gr. 2). pap. 16.95 *(978-0-935278-90-3(7))* Palmer-Pletsch Assocs.
—My First Sewing Book: Hand Sewing. 2nd ed. 2011. (My First Sewing Book Kit Ser.). (ENG.). 40p. (J). (gr. 3-7). pap. 16.95 *(978-0-935278-85-9(0))* Palmer-Pletsch Assocs.
CICO Kidz Staff, compiled by. My First Stitching & Sewing Book: Learn How to Sew with These 35 Cute & Easy Projects: Simple Stitches, Sweet Embroidery,pretty Applique. 2016. (ENG., Illus.). 128p. (J). (gr. 7-11). pap. 14.95 *(978-1-78249-334-1(4),* CICO Books) Ryland Peters & Small GBR. Dist: WIPRO.
Cook, Deanna F. Teddy Bear Doctor: Fix the Boo-Boos & Heal the Ouchies of Your Favorite Stuffed Animals. 2015. (ENG., Illus.). 64p. (J). (gr. -1). pap. 10.95 *(978-1-61212-402-5(X),* 622402) Storey Publishing, LLC.
Curto, Rosa M. Super Simple Sewing for Kids. 2016. (Super Simple... Bks.). (ENG.). 96p. (J). (gr. 2-6). pap. 11.99 *(978-1-4380-0825-7(2))* Barron's Educational Series, Inc.
Davis, Tina. See & Sew: A Sewing Book for Children. 2006. (ENG., Illus.). 150p. (gr. 8-17). 19.95 *(978-1-58479-491-2(7))* Stewart, Tabori & Chang.
Dorling Kindersley Publishing Staff. Let's Sew. 2016. (ENG., Illus.). 64p. (J). (gr. 1-4). 15.99 *(978-1-4654-4508-7(0),* DK Children) Dorling Kindersley Publishing, Inc.
Fryer, Jane Eayre. The Mary Frances Sewing Book 100th Anniversary Edition: A Childrens Story-Instruction Sewing Book with Doll Clothes Patterns for American Girl & Other 18-Inch Dolls. 2011. (ENG., Illus.). 284p. (J). pap. 19.95 *(978-1-937564-01-8(0),* Classic Bookwrights) Lindaloo Enterprises.
Hardy, Emma. My First Sewing Machine Book: 35 Fun & Easy Projects for Children Aged 7 Years + 2014. (ENG., Illus.). 128p. (J). (gr. 7-11). pap. 14.95 *(978-1-78249-101-9(5),* CICO Books) Ryland Peters & Small GBR. Dist: WIPRO.
Kachidurian, Debbie, et al. Accessorize Yourself! 77 Projects to Personalize Your Look. 2016. (Craft It Yourself Ser.). (ENG., Illus.). 144p. (gr. 3-4). pap. 14.95 *(978-1-62370-645-6(9))* Capstone Young Readers of Coughlan Cos.
Kerr, Sophie. A Kid's Guide to Sewing: 16 Projects You'll Love to Make & Use. 2013. (ENG., Illus.). 144p. (J). (gr. 6-9). pap. 21.95 *(978-1-60705-751-2(4),* FunStitch Studio) C & T Publishing.
Kuskowski, Alex. Cool Sewing for Kids: A Fun & Creative Introduction to Fiber Art, 1 vol. 2014. (Cool Fiber Art Ser.). (ENG.). 32p. (gr. 8-12). lib. bdg. 28.50 *(978-1-62403-311-7(3),* Checkerboard Library) ABDO Publishing Co.
Lan, Angela. #OOTD Sew & Style: Make Your Dream Wardrobe with Angela. 2016. (ENG., Illus.). 128p. (J). (gr. 6-12). pap. 24.95 *(978-1-61745-136-2(3),* Stash Bks.) C & T Publishing.
Lisle, Andria & Plumley, Amie Petronis. Sewing School 2: Lessons in Machine Sewing; 20 Projects Kids Will Love to Make. 2013. (Sewing School Ser.). (ENG., Illus.). 160p. (J). (gr. 3-8). pap. 18.95 *(978-1-61212-049-2(0),* 622049) Storey Publishing, LLC.
Low, Rachel. Girl's Guide to DIY Fashion: Design & Sew 5 Complete Outfits * Mood Boards * Fashion Sketching * Choosing Fabric * Adding Style. 2015. (ENG., Illus.). 192p. (J). (gr. 2-8). pap. 19.95 *(978-1-60705-995-0(9),* FunStitch Studio) C & T Publishing.
Maloney, Brenna. This Is Mouse - An Adventure in Sewing: Make Mouse & Friends * Travel with Them from Africa to Outer Space. 2015. (ENG., Illus.). 112p. pap. 16.95 *(978-1-60705-977-6(0),* FunStitch Studio) C & T Publishing.
McNicol, Alison. My First Learn to Sew Book. 2012. (Illus.). 42p. pap. *(978-1-908707-04-8(6))* Kyle Craig Publishing.
—My First Sewing Machine Book: Learn to Sew Kids. 2011. (ENG., Illus.). 40p. pap. *(978-1-908707-00-0(3))* Kyle Craig Publishing.
Meyer, Carolyn. Miss Patch's Learn-To-Sew Book. Suzuki, Mary, illus. 2014. (ENG.). 96p. (J). (gr. 1-4). pap. 9.99 *(978-0-544-33905-7(3),* HMH Books For Young Readers) Houghton Mifflin Harcourt Publishing Co.
Milligan, Lynda & Smith, Nancy. The Best of Sewing Machine Fun for Kids: Ready, Set, Sew - 37 Projects & Activities. 2nd ed. 2016. (ENG., Illus.). 128p. (J). (gr. 4-9). pap. 16.95 *(978-1-61745-263-5(7),* FunStitch Studio) C & T Publishing.
Nicoll, Allison. Sew It! Make 17 Projects with Yummy Precut Fabric - Jelly Rolls, Layer Cakes, Charm Packs & Fat Quarters. 2014. (ENG., Illus.). 128p. (J). (gr. 1). pap. 19.95 *(978-1-60705-874-8(X),* FunStitch Studio) C & T Publishing.
O'Donoghue, Sean. Create a Quilt: Understand Concepts of Area. 2014. (Rosen Common Core Math Readers Ser.). (ENG., Illus.). 24p. (J). (gr. 3-4). pap. 8.25 *(978-1-4777-4894-7(6),* Rosen Classroom) Rosen Publishing Group, Inc., The.
Petelinsek, Kathleen. Learning to Sew. Petelinsek, Kathleen, illus. 2014. (How-To Library). (ENG., Illus.). 32p. (J). (gr. 3-6). 28.50 *(978-1-63137-780-8(9),* 205363) Cherry Lake Publishing.
Phillips, Jennifer. Picture Perfect! Glam Scarves, Belts, Hats, & Other Fashion Accessories for All Occassions. 2016. (Accessorize Yourself! Ser.). (ENG., Illus.). 48p. (gr. 4-5). lib. bdg. 34.65 *(978-1-4914-8229-2(X))* Capstone Press of Coughlan Cos.
Pittman, Janet. Colourful Quilts for Playful Kids. 2012. (Illus.). 96p. pap. *(978-1-935726-25-8(0))* Landauer Publishing, LLC.
Ross, Kathy. Things to Make for Your Doll. Garvin, Elaine, illus. (Girl Crafts Ser.). 48p. 2005. (ENG.). (gr. 2-5). lib. bdg. 26.60 *(978-0-7613-2861-2(0),* Millbrook Pr.) 2003. (J). (gr. k-2). pap. 7.95 *(978-0-7613-1781-4(3),* First Avenue Editions) Lerner Publishing Group.
Sadler, Ann. Sewing.Tr. of Couture. (FRE., Illus.). (J). (gr. k-5). pap. 7.99 *(978-0-590-24055-0(2))* Scholastic, Inc.
Sadler, Judy Ann & Sadler, Judy. Simply Sewing. Kurisu, Jane, illus. 2004. (Kids Can Do It Ser.). (ENG.). 48p. (J). (gr. 3-7). pap. 7.95 *(978-1-55337-660-6(9))* Kids Can Pr., Ltd. CAN. Dist: Hachette Bk. Group.
Sadler, Judy Ann, et al. The Jumbo Book of Needlecrafts. Bradford, June et al, illus. 2005. (Jumbo Bks.). (ENG.). 208p. (J). (gr. 3-7). 16.95 *(978-1-55337-793-1(1))* Kids Can Pr., Ltd. CAN. Dist: Hachette Bk. Group.
Scholastic & Klutz Editors. Sew Mini Animals. 2017. (ENG.). 48p. (J). (gr. 3-7). 21.99 *(978-1-338-10644-2(9))* Klutz.
Scott-Smith, Louise & Vaux, Georgia. I Can Make Dolls' Clothes. 2015. (ENG., Illus.). 176p. (J). (gr. 3-5). 19.95 *(978-0-500-65051-6(9),* 565051) Thames & Hudson.
Stephens, Sarah Hines. Show Off: How to Do Absolutely Everything. One Step at a Time. Mann, Bethany, illus. 2009. (ENG.). 224p. (J). (gr. 5-9). pap. 18.99 *(978-0-7636-4599-1(0))* Candlewick Pr.
Thomas Nelson. My Fabulous Fox Sewing Kit. 2015. (ENG.). 12p. (J). (gr. -1-2). *(978-1-78393-463-8(8))* Make Believe Ideas.
—My Olivia Owl Sewing Kit. 2015. (ENG.). 12p. (J). (gr. 1-5). *(978-1-78393-703-5(3))* Make Believe Ideas.
—My Pepper Puppy Sewing Kit. 2015. (ENG.). 12p. (J). (gr. 1-5). *(978-1-78393-878-0(1))* Make Believe Ideas.
Trail, Sara. Sew with Sara: Fun Stuff to Keep, Give, Sell! 2009. (ENG., Illus.). 112p. pap. 19.95 *(978-1-57120-603-9(5))* C & T Publishing.

S

Turnbull, Stephanie. Cool Stuff to Sew. 2014. (Cool Stuff Ser.). 32p. (gr. 2-5). 31.35 *(978-1-62588-191-5(6))* Black Rabbit Bks.

—Sewing. 2015. (Try This! Ser.). (ENG., Illus.). 24p. (J). (gr. 2-6). 27.10 *(978-1-62588-375-9(7)*, 1389476) Black Rabbit Bks.

Vagts, Carolyn, ed. I Can Quilt. 2012. (I Can Ser.). (ENG., Illus.). 32p. (J). (gr. 4-7). pap. 7.95 *(978-1-59217-460-7(4)*, Annie's) Annie's Publishing, LLC.

Warwick, Ellen. Stuff to Hold Your Stuff. Lum, Bernice, illus. 2006. (Planet Girl Ser.). (ENG.). 80p. (J). (gr. 5-9). 12.95 *(978-1-55337-745-0(1))* Kids Can Pr., Ltd. CAN. Dist: Hachette Bk. Group.

Weglarz, Lynn. I Can Sew. Frank, Sharon, ed. 2012. (I Can Ser.). (ENG., Illus.). 32p. (J). (gr. 4-7). pap. 7.95 *(978-1-59217-390-7(X)*, Annie's) Annie's Publishing, LLC.

Wrigley, Annabel. We Love to Sew: 28 Pretty Things to Make. 2013. (ENG., Illus.). 176p. pap. 22.95 *(978-1-60705-632-4(1))* C & T Publishing.

—We Love to Sew — Bedrooms: 23 Projects, Cool Stuff for Your Space. 2014. (ENG., Illus.). 176p. (J). (gr. 2-8). pap. 21.95 *(978-1-60705-824-3(3)*, FunStitch Studio) C & T Publishing.

SEX

see also Reproduction

also headings beginning with the word Sexual

Ascension Press, creator. Theology of the Body for Teens Student Workbook: Discovering God's Plan for Love & Life. 2006. (Illus.). 210p. per. 14.95 *(978-1-932927-86-3(7))* Ascension Pr.

Attwood, Sarah. Making Sense of Sex: A Forthright Guide to Puberty, Sex & Relationships for People with Asperger's Syndrome. Powell, Jonathan, illus. 2008. (ENG.). 320p. (J). (gr. 4-12). pap. 21.95 *(978-1-84310-374-5(5)*, 1254) Kingsley, Jessica Pubs. GBR. Dist: Macmillan Distribution Ltd.

Bailey, Jacqui. Sex, Puberty, & All That Stuff: A Guide to Growing Up. McCafferty, Jan, illus. 2004. (ENG.). 112p. (YA). pap. 12.99 *(978-0-7641-2992-6(9))* Barron's Educational Series, Inc.

Cart, Michael. Necessary Noise: Stories about Our Families as They Really Are. Noruzi, Charlotte, illus. 2003. 256p. (J). (gr. 12-18). lib. bdg. 16.89 *(978-0-06-027500-6(6))* HarperCollins Pubs.

Choosing the Best Path. 3rd ed. 2004. *(978-0-9724890-2-7(9))* Choosing The Best Publishing.

Crabtree Publishing Company Staff & Bow, James. Sex. 2012. (ENG., Illus.). 48p. (J). *(978-0-7787-2186-4(8))*; pap. *(978-0-7787-2193-2(0))* Crabtree Publishing Co.

Craig, Joe. A Guy's Guide to Sexuality & Sexual Identity in the 21st Century. 2011. (Young Man's Guide to Contemporary Issues Ser.). (ENG.). 104p. (YA). (gr. 9-12). lib. bdg. 34.60 *(978-1-4488-5524-7(1))* Rosen Publishing Group, Inc., The.

Cross, Craig, et al. Questions You Can't Ask Your Mama about Sex. 1 vol. 2005. (Invert Ser.). (ENG.). 128p. (YA). pap. 9.99 *(978-0-310-25812-4(X))* Zondervan.

Culp, Jennifer. Dating Etiquette & Sexual Respect. 2016. (Etiquette Rules! Ser.). 00048p. (J). (gr. 6-6). pap. 11.75 *(978-1-4994-6492-4(4))* Rosen Publishing Group, Inc., The.

Custom Curricul Staff. What about Sex, Drugs, And... ? 2004. (Custom Curriculum Ser.). 256p. pap., pap. 19.99 *(978-0-7814-4093-6(9)*, 0781440939) Cook, David C.

Ferguson, Olivia & Haugen, Hayley Mitchell. Is Childhood Becoming Too Sexualized? 2010. (At Issue Ser.). (ENG.). 114p. pap. 24.45 *(978-0-7377-4885-7(0)*, Greenhaven Pr., Inc.) Cengage Gale.

Ferguson, Olivia, et al. Is Childhood Becoming Too Sexualized? 2010. (At Issue Ser.). (ENG.). 128p. (gr. 10-12). 39.40 *(978-0-7377-4884-0(2))* Cengage Gale.

Friedman, Lauri S., ed. Sexual Orientation. 2012. (Introducing Issues with Opposing Viewpoints Ser.). (ENG., Illus.). 144p. (J). (gr. 7-10). lib. bdg. 36.95 *(978-0-7377-6281-5(0)*, Greenhaven Pr., Inc.) Cengage Gale.

Gay & Lesbian Writers. (Illus.). (gr. 9-13). pap. *(978-0-7910-8395-6(0))*; 2005. 144p. (gr. 6-12). 175.00 *(978-0-7910-8477-9(9))* Facts On File, Inc. (Chelsea Hse.).

Gerdes, Louise I., ed. What Are the Causes of Prostitution? 2007. (At Issue Ser.). (ENG.). 91p. (gr. 8-12). pap. 24.45 *(978-0-7377-2738-8(1)*, Greenhaven Pr., Inc.) Cengage Gale.

Gilbert, Laura. Everything You Need to Know about Compulsive Sexual Behavior. 2009. (Need to Know Library). 64p. (gr. 5-5). 58.50 *(978-1-60854-059-4(6))* Rosen Publishing Group, Inc., The.

Gross, Craig & Foster, Mike. Questions You Can't Ask Your Mama: 68 1/2 Questions for Craig & Mike. 2003. (C). per. 11.99 *(978-0-9741849-0-6(X))* Fireproof Ministries.

Harris, Robie H. It's So Amazing! A Book about Eggs, Sperm, Birth, Babies, & Families. Emberley, Michael, illus. 2014. (Family Library). (ENG.). 88p. (J). (gr. 2-5). 22.99 *(978-0-7636-6873-0(7))* Candlewick Pr.

—Sexo... Que Es? 2003. (SPA., Illus.). (YA). (gr. 7-8). pap. *(978-84-95040-35-0(2)*, RR7144) Serres, Ediciones, S. L. ESP. Dist: Lectorum Pubns., Inc.

Harris, Robie H. & Cousins, Lucy. Sexo: Que es? Desarrollo, Cambios Corporales, Sexo y Salud Sexual. Saslavsky, Irene, tr. Emberley, Michael, illus. 2005. (SPA.). 96p. (gr. 6-8). pap. 12.99 *(978-84-8488-181-0(4))* Serres, Ediciones, S. L. ESP. Dist: Lectorum Pubns., Inc.

Hickman, Pamela. Animals & Their Mates: How Animals Attract, Fight for & Protect Each Other. Stephens, Pat, illus. 2004. (Animal Behavior Ser.). (ENG.). 40p. (J). (gr. 2-6). 5.95 *(978-1-55337-546-3(7))* Kids Can Pr., Ltd. CAN. Dist: Hachette Bk. Group.

Hill, Z. B. Romantic Attraction. Croft, Cindy, ed. 2014. (Causes & Effects of Emotions Ser.: 13). 64p. (J). (gr. 7-18). 23.95 *(978-1-4222-3077-0(5))* Mason Crest.

Human Sexuality: Human Sexuality (Windows/Macintosh) 36p. (gr. 7-12). cd-rom 126.00 *(978-1-59070-357-1(X))* Goodheart-Willcox Pub.

Johnson, Kathryn T. & Balczon, Mary-Lynne J. The Sexual Dictionary: Terms & Expressions for Teens & Parents. St. John, Charlotte, ed. Date not set. (Life Management Ser.). (Illus.). 176p. (YA). pap. 12.95 *(978-0-89896-400-4(8))* Larksdale.

Jones, Stan & Jones, Brenna. The Story of Me. Spector, Joel, illus. 2007. (God's Design for Sex Ser.: 1). (ENG.). 48p. (Orig.). pap. 10.99 *(978-1-60006-013-7(7))* NavPress Publishing Group.

Lickona, Tom & Lickona, Judy. Sex, Love & You: Making the Right Decision. rev. ed. 2003. (Illus.). 192p. pap. 15.95 *(978-0-87793-987-0(X))* Ave Maria Pr.

Luadzers, Darcy. Virgin Sex for Girls: A No-Regrets Guide to Safe & Healthy Sex. 2006. (ENG.). 320p. (J). (gr. 9-12). per. 13.95 *(978-1-57826-229-8(1)*, Hatherleigh Pr.) Hatherleigh Co., Ltd., The.

—Virgin Sex for Guys: A No-Regrets Guide to Safe & Healthy Sex. 2006. (ENG.). 320p. (J). (gr. 9). per. 13.95 *(978-1-57826-230-4(5)*, Hatherleigh Pr.) Hatherleigh Co., Ltd., The.

Manning, Mick & Granström, Brita. How Did I Begin? (Illus.). 31p. (J). pap. *(978-0-7496-3409-4(X)*, Franklin Watts) Hachette Children's Group.

Marcovitz, Hal. Teens & Sex. Developed in Association with the Gallup Organization Staff, ed. 2013. (Gallup Youth Survey: Major Issues & Trends Ser.: 14). 112p. (J). (gr. 7-18). 24.95 *(978-1-4222-2957-6(2))* Mason Crest.

McKee, Jonathan. Sex Matters. 2015. (ENG.). 128p. (YA). pap. 5.99 *(978-0-7642-2213-9(9))* Bethany Hse. Pubs.

Navarre, Sam. Masculinity, Bullying, & Aggression: A Guy's Guide. 2011. (Young Man's Guide to Contemporary Issues Ser.). (ENG.). 104p. (J). (gr. 9-12). lib. bdg. 34.60 *(978-1-4488-5525-4(X))* Rosen Publishing Group, Inc., The.

Orr, Tamra. Home & Family Relationships. 2010. (Teens: Being Gay, Lesbian, Bisexual, or Transgender Ser.). (Illus.). 80p. (YA). (gr. 7-12). lib. bdg. 33.25 *(978-1-4358-3579-5(4))* Rosen Publishing Group, Inc., The.

Penne, Barbra & Renehan, Patrick. Your Rights As an LGBTQ+ Teen. 2017. (LGBTQ+ Guide to Beating Bullying Ser.). 64p. (J). (gr. 12-11). 34.45 ***(978-1-5081-7439-4(3)***, Rosen Young Adult) Rosen Publishing Group, Inc., The.

Planned Parenthood Federation of America, Inc. Staff. Teensex? It's Okay to Say: No Way! 2003. (YA). pap. 3.00 net. *(978-0-934586-79-5(9))* Planned Parenthood Federation of America, Inc.

Rodi, Robert & Ross, Laura. Living with Religion & Faith, Vol. 10. Jennings, Kevin, ed. 2016. (Living Proud! Growing up LGBTQ Ser.). (Illus.). 64p. (J). (gr. 7). 23.95 *(978-1-4222-3507-2(6))* Mason Crest.

Rose, Lyman Hinckley. Pure & Chased. 2004. ix, 86p. pap. 7.95 *(978-1-55517-774-4(3))* Cedar Fort, Inc./CFI Distribution.

Scherrer, David L. & Klepack, Linda M. Fearless Love: Making Sexual Choices That Honor God. 2004. (Worth Waiting for Ser.). (Illus.). 176p. (YA). (gr. 13-18). 19.99 *(978-0-7814-4076-9(9)*, 0781440769) Cook, David C.

Schiffer, Howard B. First Love: Remembrances. 2004. (YA). 29.95 *(978-0-9723639-2-1(0))* Heartful Loving Pr.

Smiler, Andrew M. Dating & Sex: A Guide for the 21st Century Teen Boy. 2015. 288p. (J). pap. *(978-1-4338-2045-8(5)*, Magination Pr.) American Psychological Assn.

Smith, Louis. Sexual Sins of the Bible: Everything You Want to Know, but Wouldn't Ask! 2004. 200p. pap. 14.99 *(978-0-9744519-1-6(6))* Smith, Kasper.

St. Stephen's Community House Staff. The Little Black Book for Guys: Guys Talk about Sex. 3rd ed. 2008. (ENG., Illus.). 256p. (YA). (gr. 9-12). pap. 9.95 *(978-1-55037-962-4(3)*, 9781550379624) Annick Pr., Ltd. CAN. Dist: Publishers Group West (PGW).

Stenzel, Pam. Sex Has a Price Tag: Discussions about Sexuality, Spirituality, & Self-Respect, 1 vol. 2015. (ENG.). 144p. (YA). pap. 9.99 *(978-0-310-74885-4(2))* Zondervan.

Stenzel, Pam, et al. Sex Has a Price Tag: Discussions about Sexuality, Spirituality, & Self Respect. 2003. (Invert Ser.). (ENG., Illus.). 144p. (YA). pap. 9.99 *(978-0-310-24971-9(6))* Zondervan.

Vitale, Ann. Drug Therapy & Sexual Disorders. 2003. (Psychiatric Disorders: Drugs & Psychology for the Mind & Bod Ser.). (Illus.). 123p. (YA). pap. 14.95 *(978-1-4222-0399-6(9))* Mason Crest.

—Sexual Disorders. McDonnell, Mary Ann & Esherick, Donald, eds. 2013. (State of Mental Illness & Its Therapy Ser.: 19). 128p. (J). (gr. 7-18). 24.95 *(978-1-4222-2836-4(3))* Mason Crest.

Vitale, Ann E. Drug Therapy & Sexual Disorders. 2004. (Encyclopedia of Psychiatric Drugs & Their Disorders Ser.). (Illus.). 128p. (YA). lib. bdg. 24.95 *(978-1-59084-575-2(7))* Mason Crest.

SEX—FICTION

Angelchild, P. Erotic Memoirs Volume 1. 2007. pap. *(978-1-84747-127-7(7))* Chipmunkapublishing.

Arnold, Elana K. Infandous. 2015. (ENG.). 200p. (YA). (gr. 8-12). 18.99 *(978-1-4677-3849-1(2))* Lerner Publishing Group.

Arnold, Elana K. What Girls Are Made Of. 2017. (ENG.). 208p. (YA). (gr. 8-12). 18.99 *(978-1-5124-1024-2(1))*; 9.99 ***(978-1-5124-3437-8(X)***, Carolrhoda Lab™); 38.65 ***(978-1-5124-3438-5(8)***, Carolrhoda Lab™); 38.65 ***(978-1-5124-2694-6(6)***, Carolrhoda Lab™) Lerner Publishing Group.

Banting, Celia. I Only Said Yes So That They'd Like Me. 2006. (Illus.). 224p. (YA). per. 14.99 *(978-0-9786648-1-7(7))* Wighita Pr.

Beth, Robinson. God Made Me: The Safe Touch Coloring Book. Noel, Green, illus. 2007. 20p. (J). pap. 3.99 *(978-0-9799092-0-7(1))* Robinson, Beth.

Bjorkman, Lauren. My Invented Life. 2009. (ENG.). 240p. (YA). (gr. 9-13). 27.99 *(978-0-8050-8950-9(0)*, Holt, Henry & Co. Bks. For Young Readers) Holt, Henry & Co.

The Boy I Love. 2014. (ENG., Illus.). 288p. (YA). (gr. 7). 17.99 *(978-1-4424-8056-8(4)*, Atheneum Bks. for Young Readers) Simon & Schuster Children's Publishing.

Brugman, Alyssa. Alex As Well. 2015. (ENG.). 224p. (YA). (gr. 9). 16.99 *(978-1-62779-014-7(4)*, Holt, Henry & Co. Bks. For Young Readers) Holt, Henry & Co.

Burgess, Melvin, et al. Losing It. Gray, Keith, ed. 2013. (ENG.). 200p. (YA). (gr. 9-12). 17.95 *(978-1-4677-2041-0(0)*, Carolrhoda Lab™) Lerner Publishing Group.

Cabot, Meg. Princess on the Brink. 2007. (Princess Diaries: 8). (ENG.). 272p. (YA). (gr. 8). pap. 9.99 *(978-0-06-072460-3(9)*, HarperTeen) HarperCollins Pubs.

—Ready or Not. 2008. (All-American Girl Ser.: 2). (ENG.). 336p. (YA). (gr. 8). pap. 8.99 *(978-0-06-147996-0(9)*, HarperTeen) HarperCollins Pubs.

Cart, Michael, et al. How Beautiful the Ordinary. 2009. (ENG.). 368p. (YA). (gr. 9-18). 17.99 *(978-0-06-115498-0(9)*, HarperTeen) HarperCollins Pubs.

Dietrich, Cale. The Love Interest. 2017. (ENG.). 384p. (YA). 17.99 *(978-1-250-10713-8(X)*, 9781250107138) Feiwel & Friends.

Downing, Erin. Kiss It. 2010. (ENG.). 288p. (YA). (gr. 9-18). pap. 9.99 *(978-1-4169-9700-9(8)*, Simon Pulse) Simon Pulse.

Flynn, Laurie Elizabeth. Firsts: A Novel. 2016. (ENG.). 336p. (YA). 18.99 *(978-1-250-07596-3(3)*, 9781250075963) St. Martin's Pr.

French, Gillian. Grit. 2017. 304p. (YA). (gr. 9). 17.99 *(978-0-06-264255-4(3)*, HarperTeen) HarperCollins Pubs.

Gingras, Charlotte. Pieces of Me. Ouriou, Susan, tr. from FRE. 2009. (ENG.). 144p. (J). (gr. 7-9). 17.95 *(978-1-55453-242-1(6))* Kids Can Pr., Ltd. CAN. Dist: Hachette Bk. Group.

Gottfred, B. T. The Nerdy & the Dirty. 2016. (ENG.). 304p. (YA). 17.99 *(978-1-62779-850-1(1)*, 9781627798501, Holt, Henry & Co. Bks. For Young Readers) Holt, Henry & Co.

Horowitz, Stacey. Genius with a Penis, Don't Touch! 2012. 24p. 19.95 *(978-1-4575-1326-8(9))* Dog Ear Publishing, LLC.

Hopkins, Ellen. Burned. 2013. (ENG., Illus.). 560p. (YA). (gr. 9). pap. 12.99 *(978-1-4424-9461-9(1)*, McElderry, Margaret K. Bks.) McElderry, Margaret K. Bks.

—Tricks. (ENG.). (YA). (gr. 9). 2017. 656p. pap. 11.99 *(978-1-4814-9824-1(X))* 2009. 640p. 22.99 *(978-1-4169-5007-3(9))* McElderry, Margaret K. Bks. (McElderry, Margaret K. Bks.).

—Tricks. 2011. lib. bdg. 24.50 *(978-0-606-23290-6(7)*, Turtleback) Turtleback Bks.

Karre, Elizabeth. The Fight. 2013. (Surviving Southside Ser.). (ENG.). 128p. (YA). (gr. 6-12). pap. 7.95 *(978-1-4677-0709-1(0))* Lerner Publishing Group.

Kenley, Holli. Another Way: A Novel. 2015. 155p. (YA). pap. *(978-1-61599-259-1(6))* Loving Healing Pr., Inc.

Keplinger, Kody. The DUFF: Designated Ugly Fat Friend. (ENG.). (YA). (gr. 10-17). 2011. 304p. pap., pap. 10.99 *(978-0-316-08424-6(7))* 2015. 320p. pap. 10.00 *(978-0-316-38180-2(2))* Little, Brown Bks. for Young Readers. (Poppy).

Knowles, Jo. Jumping off Swings. 2011. (ENG., Illus.). 240p. (YA). (gr. 9). pap. 7.99 *(978-0-7636-5296-8(2))* Candlewick Pr.

Konigsberg, Bill. Honestly Ben. 2017. (ENG.). 336p. (J). (gr. 9). 17.99 *(978-0-545-85826-7(7))* Scholastic, Inc.

Logsted, Greg. Something Happened. 2008. (ENG.). 208p. (YA). (gr. 7-9). pap. 8.99 *(978-1-4169-5078-3(8)*, Simon Pulse) Simon Pulse.

Lubar, David. Character, Driven: A Novel. 2016. (ENG.). 304p. (YA). 17.99 *(978-0-7653-1633-2(1)*, 9780765316332, Tor Teen) Doherty, Tom Assocs., LLC.

Mackler, Carolyn. Guyaholic. 2009. (ENG., Illus.). 192p. (YA). (gr. 9). pap. 7.99 *(978-0-7636-2801-7(8))* Candlewick Pr.

Martin, C. K. Kelly. The Lighter Side of Life & Death. 2010. (YA). pap. *(978-0-375-84590-1(9))* Random Hse. Children's Bks.

Mayfield, Jamie. Destiny. 2016. (ENG., Illus.). (J). 29.99 ***(978-1-63533-000-7(9))*** 2013. 310p. pap. 17.99 *(978-1-62380-864-8(2))* Dreamspinner Pr. (Harmony Ink Pr.).

Mesrobian, Carrie. Cut Both Ways. 2015. (ENG.). 352p. (YA). (gr. 9). 17.99 *(978-0-06-234988-0(0))* HarperCollins Pubs.

—Perfectly Good White Boy. 2014. (ENG.). 304p. (gr. 8-12). 17.95 *(978-1-4677-3480-6(2)*, Carolrhoda Lab™) Lerner Publishing Group.

—Sex & Violence. 2013. (ENG.). 304p. (YA). (gr. 9-12). 17.95 *(978-1-4677-0597-4(7)*, Carolrhoda Lab™) Lerner Publishing Group.

Miller, Sarah. The Other Girl. 2010. (ENG.). 304p. (YA). (gr. 8). pap. 20.99 *(978-0-312-33416-1(8)*, 9780312334161, St. Martin's Griffin) St. Martin's Pr.

Moore, Stephanie Perry. Back That Thing. 2015. (Illus.). 103p. (YA). 9.99 *(978-1-4677-7892-3(3))* Lerner Publishing Group.

—Give It Up. 2015. (YA). 9.99 *(978-1-4677-7886-2(9))*; (Swoop List Ser.: 1). (ENG., Illus.). 128p. (gr. 6-12). lib. bdg. 27.99 *(978-1-4677-5804-8(3))* Lerner Publishing Group.

—On Your Knees. 2015. (Swoop List Ser.: 2). (ENG., Illus.). 128p. (YA). (gr. 6-12). lib. bdg. 27.99 *(978-1-4677-5805-5(1))* Lerner Publishing Group.

—Sit on Top. 2015. (Swoop List Ser.: 4). (ENG., Illus.). 112p. (YA). (gr. 6-12). pap. 9.99 *(978-1-4677-6052-2(8))* Lerner Publishing Group.

Murphy, Julie. Ramona Blue. (YA). (gr. 8). 2018. (ENG.). 448p. pap. 9.99 ***(978-0-06-241836-4(X))*** 2017. 432p. 17.99 *(978-0-06-241835-7(1))* HarperCollins Pubs.

Naylor, Phyllis Reynolds. Alice on the Outside. 2012. (Alice Ser.: 11). (ENG., Illus.). 208p. (J). (gr. 5-9). pap. 6.99 *(978-1-4424-3495-0(3)*, Atheneum Bks. for Young Readers) Simon & Schuster Children's Publishing.

—Lovingly Alice. 2004. (Alice Bks.). 166p. (J). (gr. 4-6). 13.65 *(978-0-7569-6604-1(3))* Perfection Learning Corp.

Ramsey, Jo. High Heels & Lipstick. 2016. (ENG., Illus.). (J). 24.99 ***(978-1-63533-029-8(7)***, Harmony Ink Pr.) Dreamspinner Pr.

Reed, Amy. Beautiful. 2010. (ENG.). 256p. (YA). (gr. 9). pap. 10.99 *(978-1-4169-7831-2(3)*, Simon Pulse) Simon Pulse.

Reed, Amy Lynn. Beautiful. 2009. (ENG.). 240p. (YA). (gr. 9-18). 16.99 *(978-1-4169-7830-5(5)*, Simon Pulse) Simon Pulse.

Reed, Amy Lynn. The Nowhere Girls. 2017. (YA). pap. ***(978-1-4814-8174-8(6)***, Simon Pulse) Simon Pulse.

Robar, Serena. Giving up the V. 2009. (ENG.). 272p. (YA). (gr. 9-18). pap. 8.99 *(978-1-4169-7558-8(6)*, Simon Pulse) Simon Pulse.

Rosin, Lindsey. Cherry. 2016. (ENG., Illus.). 400p. (YA). (gr. 9). 17.99 *(978-1-4814-5908-2(2)*, Simon Pulse) Simon Pulse.

Ruby, Laura. Good Girls. 2008. (ENG.). 304p. (YA). (gr. 9-12). pap. 8.99 *(978-0-06-088225-9(5))* 2006. 288p. (J). lib. bdg. 17.89 *(978-0-06-088224-2(7))* 2006. (ENG.). 288p. (YA). (gr. 9-12). 16.99 *(978-0-06-088223-5(9))* HarperCollins Pubs. (HarperTeen).

Shaddix, M. K. Aisling's Summer Diary. 2012. 200p. pap. 6.99 *(978-0-9567500-8-2(7))* BeActive Publishing Co.

Snadowsky, Daria. Anatomy of a Boyfriend. 2008. (ENG.). 272p. (YA). (gr. 9). pap. 8.99 *(978-0-440-23944-4(3)*, Ember) Random Hse. Children's Bks.

Strasnick, Lauren. Her & Me & You. (ENG.). 208p. (YA). (gr. 9). 2011. pap. 9.99 *(978-1-4169-8267-8(1))* 2010. 16.99 *(978-1-4169-8266-1(3))* Simon Pulse. (Simon Pulse).

Watt, Erin. Broken Prince. 2016. (Royals Ser.: 2). (ENG.). 370p. (gr. 7-12). pap. 14.99 *(978-1-68230-503-4(1)*, EverAfter Romance) Diversion Publishing Corp.

—Twisted Palace. 2016. (Royals Ser.: 3). (ENG.). 370p. (gr. 7-12). pap. 14.99 *(978-1-68230-506-5(6)*, EverAfter Romance) Diversion Publishing Corp.

Watt, Erin & Frederick, Jen. Paper Princess. 2016. (Royals Ser.: 1). (ENG., Illus.). 370p. pap. 14.99 *(978-1-68230-456-3(6)*, EverAfter Romance) Diversion Publishing Corp.

Zarr, Sara. Story of a Girl. 2008. (ENG.). 224p. (YA). (gr. 7-17). per. 10.99 *(978-0-316-01454-0(0))* Little, Brown Bks. for Young Readers.

SEX CRIMES

see also Child Sexual Abuse; Incest; Rape

Byers, Ann. Sexual Assault & Abuse. 2015. (Confronting Violence Against Women Ser.). (ENG., Illus.). 64p. (J). (gr. 6-7). 32.95 *(978-1-4994-6042-1(2)*, Rosen Young Adult) Rosen Publishing Group, Inc., The.

Farrell, Courtney. Human Trafficking, 1 vol. 2011. (Essential Issues Set 2 Ser.). (ENG., Illus.). 112p. (J). (gr. 6-12). lib. bdg. 35.64 *(978-1-61714-773-9(7)*, Essential Library) ABDO Publishing Co.

Ghafoerkhan, Olivia. Sexual Assault: The Ultimate Teen Guide, Vol. 2016. (It Happened to Me Ser.: 51). (ENG., Illus.). 216p. (J). 45.00 *(978-1-4422-5247-9(2))* Rowman & Littlefield Publishers, Inc.

Gitlin, Marty. Combatting Discrimination Against Women in the Gamer Community. 2016. (Combatting Shaming & Toxic Communities Ser.). 64p. (J). (gr. 7-7). 34.45 *(978-1-5081-7118-8(1))* Rosen Publishing Group, Inc., The.

Haerens, Margaret, ed. Human Trafficking. 2011. (Global Viewpoints Ser.). (Illus.). 224p. (J). pap. 27.95 *(978-0-7377-5659-3(4)*, Greenhaven Pr., Inc.); (YA). (gr. 9-12). 40.45 *(978-0-7377-5658-6(6))* Cengage Gale.

Haugen, David M., ed. Sex. 2013. (Teen Rights & Freedoms Ser.). (ENG., Illus.). 176p. (gr. 10-12). lib. bdg. 37.45 *(978-0-7377-6404-8(X)*, Greenhaven Pr., Inc.) Cengage Gale.

Leese, Vickie. When God Created Little Girls... 2011. 22p. pap. 17.99 *(978-1-61379-521-7(1))* Salem Author Services.

Lohmann, Raychelle Cassada & Raja, Sheela. The Sexual Trauma Workbook for Teen Girls: A Guide to Recovery from Sexual Assault & Abuse. 2016. (ENG.). 200p. (YA). (gr. 6-12). pap. 16.95 *(978-1-62625-399-5(4))* New Harbinger Pubns.

McGee, Kathleen M. & Buddenberg, Laura J. Unmasking Sexual Con Games: Helping Teens Avoid Emotional Grooming & Dating Violence. 3rd ed. 2004. (Leader's Guide with Session Plans Ser.). (ENG., Illus.). 199p. pap. 29.95 *(978-1-889322-54-4(7)*, 25-015) Boys Town Pr.

—Unmasking Sexual Con Games Teen's Guide: A Teen's Guide to Avoiding Emotional Grooming & Dating Violence. 3rd ed. 2004. (Leader's Guide with Session Plans Ser.). (ENG.). 79p. pap. 5.95 *(978-1-889322-55-1(5)*, 25-016) Boys Town Pr.

Penney, Betty. Tell Your Mother. 2004. (Illus.). 32p. (J). pap. 8.95 *(978-0-9631975-4-2(1))* Morgan, E. A.

Roach, Nicole. Private Parts. 2012. 24p. (-18). pap. 14.93 *(978-1-4669-5233-1(4))* Trafford Publishing.

The Truth about, 10 vols., Set. 2010. (Truth about Ser.). (C). (gr. 9). 350.00 *(978-0-8160-8289-6(8))* Facts On File, Inc.

SEX CRIMES—FICTION

Akers, Ellery. Sarah's Waterfall: A Healing Story about Sexual Abuse. Benicio, Angelique, illus. 2009. (J). *(978-1-884444-79-1(2))* Safer Society Pr.

Barth, Amy. Annabelle's Secret. Kinra, Richa, illus. 2009. (J). pap. 12.95 *(978-1-932690-95-8(6))* Loving Healing Pr., Inc.

—Will Was All Boy: A Story about Sexual Abuse. Kinra, Richa, illus. 2009. (J). pap. *(978-1-61599-000-9(3))* Loving Healing Pr., Inc.

Brooks, Kevin. Dawn. (ENG.). (J). (gr. 9). 2010. 272p. pap. 8.99 *(978-0-545-06092-9(3)*, PUSH) 2009. 256p. 17.99 *(978-0-545-06090-5(7)*, Chicken Hse., The) Scholastic, Inc.

Gray, Laurie. Maybe I Will. 2013. 212p. pap. 14.95 *(978-1-935462-72-9(5))* Luminis Bks., Inc.

Hopkins, Ellen. Traffick. (ENG., Illus.). 528p. (YA). (gr. 9). 2017. pap. 10.99 *(978-1-4424-8288-3(5))* 2015. 18.99 *(978-1-4424-8287-6(7))* McElderry, Margaret K. Bks. (McElderry, Margaret K. Bks.).

Jiron, Betsy. Sing for Me. 2013. 170p. 29.99 *(978-0-9897380-4-0(3))* Zaloli, LLC.

Kiely, Brendan. The Gospel of Winter. 2014. (ENG., Illus.). 304p. (YA). (gr. 9). 19.99 *(978-1-4424-8489-4(6)*, McElderry, Margaret K. Bks.) McElderry, Margaret K. Bks.

Kuehn, Stephanie. Delicate Monsters. 2015. (ENG.). 240p. (YA). (gr. 9-12). 19.99 *(978-1-250-06384-7(1)*, 9781250063847, St. Martin's Griffin) St. Martin's Pr.

Polak, Monique. On the Game, 1 vol. 2005. (Lorimer SideStreets Ser.). (ENG.). 184p. (YA). (gr. 9-12). 16.95 *(978-1-55028-877-3(6)*, 9781550288773); 9.95 *(978-1-55028-876-6(8)*, 9781550288766) Lorimer, James & Co., Ltd., Pubs. CAN. Dist: Casemate Pubs. & Bk. Distributors, LLC.

Riggs, Shannon. Not in Room 204: Breaking the Silence of Abuse. Zollars, Jaime, illus. 2017. (ENG.). 32p. (J). (-3). pap. 7.99 ***(978-0-8075-5766-2(8))*** Whitman, Albert & Co.

Sanchez, Alex. Bait. (ENG.). 256p. (YA). (gr. 7). 2010. pap. 12.99 *(978-1-4169-3774-6(9))* 2009. 17.99 *(978-1-4169-3772-2(2))* Simon & Schuster Bks. For Young Readers. (Simon & Schuster Bks. For Young Readers).

Stang, Debra L. Visiting Grandma. 2003. 136p. (YA). pap. 12.95 *(978-1-59113-322-3(X))* Booklocker.com, Inc.

Vaught, Susan. Going Underground. (ENG.). (YA). (gr. 9-12). 2012. 352p. pap. 9.99 *(978-1-59990-919-6(7)*, 9781599909196) 2011. 336p. 16.99 *(978-1-59990-640-9(6)*, 9781599906409) Bloomsbury Publishing USA. (Bloomsbury USA Childrens).

Weeks, Sarah. Jumping the Scratch. 2007. (J). 1.25 *(978-1-4193-8222-2(5))* Recorded Bks., Inc.

Woodson, Jacqueline. I Hadn't Meant to Tell You This. 2010. (ENG.). 160p. (YA). (gr. 7-18). 7.99 *(978-0-14-241704-1(1),* Puffin Books) Penguin Young Readers Group.

—I Hadn't Meant to Tell You This. 2006. 114p. (YA). (gr. 7-12). 13.65 *(978-0-7569-6730-7(9))* Perfection Learning Corp.

SEX INSTRUCTION

Amos, Janine. Is Helen Pregnant. 2003. (Body Matters Ser.: 1). (ENG., Illus.). 32p. (YA). 19.99 *(978-1-84234-107-0(3))* Evans Brothers, Ltd. GBR. Dist: Independent Pubs. Group.

Attwood, Sarah. Making Sense of Sex: A Forthright Guide to Puberty, Sex & Relationships for People with Asperger's Syndrome. Powell, Jonathan, illus. 2008. (ENG.). 320p. (J). (gr. 4-12). pap. 21.95 *(978-1-84310-374-5(5),* 1254) Kingsley, Jessica Pubs. GBR. Dist: Macmillan Distribution Ltd.

Bailey, Jacqui. Sex, Puberty & All That Stuff: A Guide to Growing Up. 2nd rev. ed. 2016. (ENG., Illus.). 124p. (J). (gr. 5-10). pap. 13.99 *(978-1-4380-0857-8(0))* Barron's Educational Series, Inc.

Ballman, Swanee. Where Do Babies Come From? 2003. (Illus.). 32p. (J). per. 6.95 *(978-1-59094-023-5(7),* 1590940237) Jawbone Publishing Corp.

Barlow, C. E. Scary Man. Tharp, Lauren R., illus. 2009. 44p. pap. 18.99 *(978-1-4269-1060-9(6))* Trafford Publishing.

Basso, Michael J. The Underground Guide to Teenage Sexuality. 2nd ed. 2003. (ENG., Illus.). 320p. pap. 16.95 *(978-1-57749-131-6(9))* Taylor Trade Publishing.

Bourgeois, Paulette & Martyn, Kim. Changes in You & Me: A Book about Puberty Mostly for Boys. Phillips, Louise, illus. rev. ed. 2005. (ENG.). 63p. (J). pap. 16.95 *(978-1-55263-668-2(2))* Leaf Storm Pr.

—Changes in You & Me: A Book about Puberty Mostly for Girls. Phillips, Louise, illus. rev. ed. 2005. (ENG.). 64p. (J). pap. 16.95 *(978-1-55263-670-1(4))* Kollath-Stensaas Pubs.

Brynie, Faith Hickman. 101 Questions about Sex & Sexuality: With Answers for the Curious, Cautious, & Confused. Holm, Sharon, illus. 2003. (101 Questions... Ser.). (ENG.). 176p. (gr. 7-12). lib. bdg. 30.60 *(978-0-7613-2310-5(4),* Twenty-First Century Bks.) Lerner Publishing Group.

Burns, Jim. How God Makes Babies. 2009. (Pure Foundations Ser.). (ENG.). 48p. (gr. 1-4). 15.99 *(978-0-7642-0210-0(3))* Bethany Hse. Pubs.

—The Purity Code: God's Plan for Sex & Your Body. 2008. (Pure Foundations Ser.). (ENG., Illus.). 160p. pap. 12.99 *(978-0-7642-0209-4(X))* Bethany Hse. Pubs.

Couwenhoven, Terri. The Boys' Guide to Growing Up: Choices & Changes During Puberty. 2012. (ENG., Illus.). 64p. (J). pap. 16.95 *(978-1-60613-089-6(7))* Woodbine Hse.

—Girls' Guide to Growing Up: Choices & Changes in the Tween Years. 2011. (ENG., Illus.). 62p. pap. 16.95 *(978-1-60613-026-1(9))* Woodbine Hse.

Feinstein, Stephen. Do You Wonder about Sex & Sexuality? 2015. (Got Issues? Ser.). (ENG., Illus.). 128p. (J). (gr. 7-7). 37.27 *(978-0-7660-6989-3(3))* Enslow Pubs., Inc.

Fonda, Jane. Being a Teen: Everything Teen Girls & Boys Should Know about Relationships, Sex, Love, Health, Identity & More. 2014. (ENG., Illus.). 288p. (J). pap. 17.00 *(978-0-8129-7861-2(7),* Random Hse. Trade Paperbacks) Random House Publishing Group.

—Being a Teen: Everything Teen Girls & Boys Should Know about Relationships, Sex, Love, Health, Identity & More. 2014. lib. bdg. 29.40 *(978-0-606-35596-4(0))* Turtleback Bks.

Gitchel, Sam & Foster, Lorri. Let's Talk about S-E-X: A Guide for Kids 9 to 12 & Their Parents. 2nd ed. 2005. (ENG., Illus.). 100p. pap. 9.99 *(978-1-931863-18-6(0))* Book Peddlers.

Greene, Carol. Why Boys & Girls Are Different. 2008. pap. 12.99 *(978-0-7586-1415-5(2))* Concordia Publishing Hse.

—Why Boys & Girls Are Different. Dorankamp, Michelle, illus. 2008. pap. 12.99 *(978-0-7586-1409-4(8))* Concordia Publishing Hse.

Harris, Robie H. It's Not the Stork! A Book about Girls, Boys, Babies, Bodies, Families & Friends. Emberley, Michael, illus. (Family Library). (ENG.). 64p. (J). (gr. -1-3). 2008. pap. 11.99 *(978-0-7636-3331-8(3))* 2006. 16.99 *(978-0-7636-0047-1(4))* Candlewick Pr.

—It's Perfectly Normal. 2014. lib. bdg. 24.50 *(978-0-606-35863-7(3))* Turtleback Bks.

—What's in There? All about Before You Were Born. Emberley, Michael & Westcott, Nadine Bernard, illus. 2013. (Let's Talk about You & Me Ser.). (ENG.). 40p. (J). (-k). 15.99 *(978-0-7636-3630-2(4))* Candlewick Pr.

—Who Has What? All about Girls' Bodies & Boys' Bodies. Westcott, Nadine Bernard, illus. 2011. (Let's Talk about You & Me Ser.). (ENG.). 32p. (J). (gr. -1-2). 15.99 *(978-0-7636-2931-1(6))* Candlewick Pr.

Henderson, Elisabeth & Armstrong, Nancy. 100 Questions You'd Never Ask Your Parents. rev. ed. 2013. (ENG.). 160p. (YA). (gr. 9-13). pap. 14.99 *(978-1-59643-868-2(1),* 9781596438682) Roaring Brook Pr.

Higginbotham, Anastasia, illus. Tell Me about Sex, Grandma. 2017. (Ordinary Terrible Things Ser.). (ENG.). 64p. (J). (gr. -1-3). 17.95 *(978-1-55861-419-2(2))* Feminist Pr. at The City Univ. of New York.

Hirschmann, Kris. Your Sexuality. 2007. (Ripped from the Headlines Ser.). 64p. (YA). (gr. 7-12). 23.95 *(978-1-60217-009-4(6))* Erickson Pr.

Jamiolkowski, Raymond M. A Baby Doesn't Make the Man: Alternative Sources of Power & Manhood for Young Men. 2009. (Teen Pregnancy Prevention Library). 64p. (gr. 5-5). 58.50 *(978-1-60854-244-4(0))* Rosen Publishing Group, Inc., The.

Kahaner, Ellen. Everything You Need to Know about Growing up Female. 2009. (Need to Know Library). 64p. (gr. 5-5). 58.50 *(978-1-60854-070-9(7))* Rosen Publishing Group, Inc., The.

Kelly, Bill. You Ought to Know: A Guy's Guide to Sex. 2005. (Guys' Guides). (Illus.). 48p. (J). (gr. 5-8). lib. bdg. 29.25 *(978-0-8239-3084-5(X),* GUYOSH) Rosen Publishing Group, Inc., The.

Kemp, Kristen. Healthy Sexuality. 2005. (Life Balance Ser.). (ENG., Illus.). 80p. (J). (gr. 5-8). pap. 6.95 *(978-0-531-16689-5(9),* Watts, Franklin) Scholastic Library Publishing.

Lickona, Tom & Lickona, Judy. Sex, Love & You: Making the Right Decision. rev. ed. 2003. (Illus.). 192p. pap. 15.95 *(978-0-87793-987-0(X))* Ave Maria Pr.

Loper, Ami M. The Miracle of Life. Loper, Carol J., illus. 2007. (J). *(978-0-9678798-1-9(7))* Biblical Standards Pubns.

Luadzers, Darcy. Virgin S.e.x: A Girl's No-Regrets Guide to Happy, Healthy Sex... the First Time & Every Time. 2004. 261p. (YA). per. 18.95 *(978-0-9742532-7-5(8))* Palmetto Tree Pr.

Madaras, Lynda & Madaras, Area. My Body, My Self for Boys. 2nd rev. ed. 2007. (What's Happening to My Body? Ser.). (ENG., Illus.). 128p. (gr. 4-6). pap. 12.99 *(978-1-55704-767-0(7),* William Morrow Paperbacks) HarperCollins Pubs.

—My Body, My Self for Girls. 3rd rev. ed. 2007. (What's Happening to My Body? Ser.). (ENG., Illus.). 160p. (gr. 4-6). pap. 12.99 *(978-1-55704-766-3(9),* William Morrow Paperbacks) HarperCollins Pubs.

—¿Que Pasa en Mi Cuerpo? El Libro para Muchachos: La Guía de Mayor Venta Sobre el Desarrollo, Escrita para Adolescentes y Preadolescentes. 2012. (What's Happening to My Body? Ser.). (SPA., Illus.). 256p. (gr. 4-18). pap. 12.99 *(978-1-55704-940-7(8),* William Morrow Paperbacks) HarperCollins Pubs.

—¿Que Pasa en Mi Cuerpo? Libro para Muchachas: La Guía de Mayor Venta Sobre el Desarrollo Escrita para Adolescentes y Preadolescentes. 2011. (What's Happening to My Body? Ser.). (SPA & ENG., Illus.). 288p. (gr. 4-18). pap. 12.95 *(978-1-55704-939-1(4),* William Morrow Paperbacks) HarperCollins Pubs.

Madaras, Lynda, et al. "What's Happening to My Body?" Book for Boys. 3rd rev. ed. 2007. (What's Happening to My Body? Ser.). (ENG., Illus.). 256p. (gr. 5-7). pap. 15.99 *(978-1-55704-765-6(0),* William Morrow Paperbacks) HarperCollins Pubs.

—"What's Happening to My Body?" Book for Girls. 3rd rev. ed. 2007. (What's Happening to My Body? Ser.). (ENG., Illus.). 288p. (gr. 7-9). pap. 14.99 *(978-1-55704-764-9(2),* William Morrow Paperbacks) HarperCollins Pubs.

—The "What's Happening to My Body?" Book for Boys. 3rd rev. ed. 2007. (What's Happening to My Body? Ser.). (ENG., Illus.). 256p. (gr. 7-9). 24.99 *(978-1-55704-769-4(3),* Morrow, William & Co.) HarperCollins Pubs.

Martyn, Kim. All the Way: Sex for the First Time, 1 vol. 2004. (ENG., Illus.). 216p. (YA). (gr. 8-12). pap. *(978-1-894549-26-4(0),* Sumach Pr.) Canadian Scholars.

Nystrom, Carolyn. Before I Was Born. Speidel, Sandra, illus. rev. ed. 2007. (God's Design for Sex Ser.: 2). (ENG.). 40p. pap. 10.99 *(978-1-60006-014-4(5))* NavPress Publishing Group.

Paonessa, Mary. Growth & Development with Friends, 8 vols. 3rd rev. ed. 2003. (Human Growth & Development Ser.). (Illus.). 41p. (J). (gr. 5-18). pap. 9.00 *(978-0-9711721-0-4(2),* 388) Paon Pubns.

—Growth & Development with Friends & School, 8 vols. 3rd ed. 2003. (Human Growth & Development Ser.). (Illus.). (J). (gr. 7-18). 112p. pap., tchr. ed. 15.00 *(978-0-9711721-5-9(3),* 393); 91p. pap. *(978-0-9711721-4-2(5),* 392) Paon Pubns.

Pardes, Bronwen. Doing It Right: Making Smart, Safe, & Satisfying Choices about Sex. (ENG., Illus.). (YA). (gr. 9). 2013. 160p. 18.99 *(978-1-4424-8370-5(9))* 2013. 146p. pap. 12.99 *(978-1-4424-8371-2(7))* 2007. 160p. pap. 14.99 *(978-1-4169-1823-3(X))* Simon Pulse. (Simon Pulse).

parks, peggy j. Teenage Sex & Pregnancy. 2011. (Compact Research Ser.). 96p. (YA). (gr. 7-12). lib. bdg. 27.95 *(978-1-60152-168-2(5))* ReferencePoint Pr., Inc.

Picklesimer, Olivia. Teen Sex. 2010. (At Issue Ser.). (ENG.). 128p. (gr. 10-12). 39.40 *(978-0-7377-5095-9(2));* pap. 27.80 *(978-0-7377-5096-6(0),* Greenhaven Pr., Inc.) Cengage Gale.

Planned Parenthood Federation of America, Inc. Staff. A Young Woman's Guide to Sexuality. 2003. (Illus.). (YA). pap. 3.00 net. *(978-1-930996-17-5(9))* Planned Parenthood Federation of America, Inc.

Roberts, Jillian. Where Do Babies Come From? Our First Talk about Birth, 1 vol. Revell, Cindy, illus. 2015. (Just Enough Ser.). (ENG.). 32p. (J). (gr. k-1). 19.95 *(978-1-4598-0942-0(4))* Orca Bk. Pubs. USA.

Schiffer, Howard B. How to Be the Best Lover - a Guide for Teenage Boys. 2004. (YA). 19.95 *(978-0-9723639-0-7(4))* Heartful Loving Pr.

Silverberg, Cory. Sex Is a Funny Word: A Book about Bodies, Relationships, & YOU. 2015. (ENG., Illus.). 162p. (J). (gr. 2-5). 23.95 *(978-1-60980-606-4(9),* Triangle Square) Seven Stories Pr.

Stephens, Aarti, ed. Teenage Sexuality. 2012. (Opposing Viewpoints Ser.). (ENG., Illus.). 240p. (YA). (gr. 9-12). 42.95 *(978-0-7377-5763-7(9));* 224p. (gr. 10-12). pap. 33.80 *(978-0-7377-5764-4(7),* Greenhaven Pr., Inc.) Cengage Gale.

Vermond, Kira. Growing Up, Inside & Out. 2013. 104p. *(978-1-77147-036-0(4))* Owlkids Bks. Inc.

Williams, Heidi. Teen Pregnancy. 2009. (Issues That Concern You Ser.). (ENG., Illus.). 144p. (J). 36.95 *(978-0-7377-4498-9(7),* 1330228) Cengage Gale.

Wright, Sally Ann. Where Do Babies Come From? Ayres, Honor, illus. 2007. 29p. (J). 9.95 *(978-0-8198-8311-7(5))* Pauline Bks. & Media.

X. Before You Were Born - Our Wish for A Baby - Donor Insemination: Version 2: Donor Insemination. 2004. (ENG., Illus.). 16p. (J). pap. 17.95 *(978-0-9755028-1-5(6))* X, Y, & Me LLC.

—Before You Were Born - Our Wish for A Baby - Donor Sperm/IVF: Version 8: Donor Sperm (IVF) 2004. (ENG., Illus.). 16p. (J). pap. 17.95 *(978-0-9755028-7-7(5))* X, Y, & Me LLC.

—Before You Were Born - Our Wish for A Baby - Embryo Donation: Version 7: Embryo Donation. 2004. (ENG., Illus.). 16p. (J). pap. 17.95 *(978-0-9755028-6-0(7))* X, Y, & Me LLC.

—Before You Were Born - Our Wish for A Baby - Female Partners: Version 9: Female Partners. 2004. (ENG., Illus.). 16p. (J). pap. 17.95 *(978-0-9755028-8-4(3))* X, Y, & Me LLC.

—Before You Were Born - Our Wish for A Baby - Frozen Embryo: Version 6: Frozen Embryo. 2004. (ENG., Illus.). 16p. (J). pap. 17.95 *(978-0-9755028-5-3(9))* X, Y, & Me LLC.

—Before You Were Born - Our Wish for A Baby - Gestational Carrier: Version 5: Gestational Carrier. 2004. (ENG., Illus.). 16p. (J). pap. 17.95 *(978-0-9755028-4-6(0))* X, Y, & Me LLC.

—Before You Were Born - Our Wish for A Baby - IVF: Version 1: in Vitro Fertilization. 2004. (ENG., Illus.). 16p. (J). pap. 17.95 *(978-0-9755028-0-8(8))* X, Y, & Me LLC.

—Before You Were Born - Our Wish for A Baby - Male Partners: Version 10: Male Partners. 2004. (ENG., Illus.). 16p. (J). pap. 17.95 *(978-0-9755028-9-1(1))* X, Y, & Me LLC.

—Before You Were Born - Our Wish for A Baby - Traditional Surrogate: Version 4: Traditional Surrogate. 2004. (ENG., Illus.). 16p. (J). pap. 17.95 *(978-0-9755028-3-9(2))* X, Y, & Me LLC.

Zep. What's Going on down There? All the Stuff Your Body Won't Tell You about Sex. Zimmerman, Dwight Jon, ed. 2005. (Illus.). 96p. pap. 14.95 *(978-1-4165-0458-0(3))* ibooks, Inc.

SEX INSTRUCTION—FICTION

Blackall, Sophie. The Baby Tree. Blackall, Sophie, illus. 2014. (ENG., Illus.). 32p. (J). (gr. k-3). 17.99 *(978-0-399-25718-6(7),* Nancy Paulsen Books) Penguin Young Readers Group.

Ryan, Patrick. In Mike We Trust. 2009. 321p. (J). lib. bdg. 17.89 *(978-0-06-085814-8(1),* HarperTeen) HarperCollins Pubs.

SEX ROLE

Ashour, Monica & Harrald-Pilz, Marilee. God Has a Plan for Boys & for Girls. 2015. (Illus.). 25p. (J). pap. 12.95 *(978-0-8198-3131-6(X))* Pauline Bks. & Media.

Forbes, Jeff Donaldson. Everything You Need to Know about Sexual Identity. 2005. (Need to Know Library). (Illus.). 64p. (YA). (gr. 7-12). lib. bdg. 31.95 *(978-0-8239-3089-0(0),* NTSEID) Rosen Publishing Group, Inc., The.

Hand, Carol. Everything You Need to Know about Sexism. 2017. (J). pap. ***(978-1-5081-7679-4(5))*** Rosen Publishing Group, Inc., The.

Harris, Robie H. It's Not the Stork! A Book about Girls, Boys, Babies, Bodies, Families & Friends. Emberley, Michael, illus. 2006. (Family Library). (ENG.). 64p. (J). (gr. -1-3). 16.99 *(978-0-7636-0047-1(4))* Candlewick Pr.

Haughton, Emma. Equality of the Sexes? 2005. (Viewpoints (Sea to Sea) Ser.). (Illus.). 32p. (YA). (gr. 5-9). lib. bdg. 27.10 *(978-1-932889-58-1(2))* Sea-To-Sea Pubns.

Henneberg, Susan, ed. Gender Politics. 2017. (At Issue Ser.). 128p. (YA). (gr. 10-12). pap. 27.80 ***(978-1-5345-0041-9(3));*** lib. bdg. 39.40 ***(978-1-5345-0014-3(6))*** Greenhaven Publishing LLC. (Greenhaven Publishing).

Kilodavis, Cheryl. My Princess Boy. DeSimone, Suzanne, illus. 2010. (ENG.). 36p. (J). (gr. -1-3). 17.99 *(978-1-4424-2988-8(7),* Aladdin) Simon & Schuster Children's Publishing.

Light, Kate. Gender Identity: The Search for Self. 2017. (Hot Topics Ser.). 104p. (YA). (gr. 7-7). lib. bdg. 39.40 ***(978-1-5345-6023-9(8),*** Lucent Pr.) Greenhaven Publishing LLC.

Lowery, Zoe & Mills, J. Elizabeth. Social Roles & Stereotypes. 2017. (Women in the World Ser.). 112p. (gr. 12-11). 37.10 ***(978-1-5081-7441-7(5),*** Rosen Young Adult) Rosen Publishing Group, Inc., The.

Merino, Noël. Gender. 2010. (Issues on Trial Ser.). (ENG.). 240p. 42.15 *(978-0-7377-4948-9(2),* Greenhaven Pr., Inc.) Cengage Gale.

—Sex Discrimination. 2010. (Issues on Trial Ser.). (Illus.). 240p. 42.15 *(978-0-7377-4740-9(4),* Greenhaven Pr., Inc.) Cengage Gale.

Rajczak, Kristen. 20 Fun Facts about Women in Ancient Greece & Rome. 2015. (Fun Fact File: Women in History Ser.). (ENG., Illus.). 32p. (J). (gr. 2-3). 25.25 *(978-1-4824-2818-6(0))* Stevens, Gareth Publishing LLLP.

Roberts, Jeremy. The Real Deal: A Guy's Guide to Being a Guy. 2005. (Guys' Guides). (Illus.). 48p. (YA). (gr. 5-8). lib. bdg. 29.25 *(978-0-8239-3104-0(8),* GUREDE) Rosen Publishing Group, Inc., The.

Seba, Jaime A. Feeling Wrong in Your Own Body: Understanding What It Means to Be Transgender. 2009. (Gallup's Guide to Modern Gay, Lesbian, & Transgender Lifestyle Ser.). 64p. (YA). (gr. 7-18). lib. bdg. 22.95 *(978-1-4222-1746-7(9))* Mason Crest.

Swisher, Clarice. Women of Victorian England. 2004. (Women in History Ser.). (ENG., Illus.). 112p. (YA). (gr. 7-12). lib. bdg. 33.45 *(978-1-59018-571-1(4),* Lucent Bks.) Cengage Gale.

SEX ROLE—FICTION

Abbott, E. F. Sybil Ludington: Revolutionary War Rider. 2016. (Based on a True Story Ser.). (ENG., Illus.). 192p. (J). 15.99 *(978-1-250-06836-1(3),* 9781250068361) Feiwel & Friends.

Abraham, Susan Gonzales & Abraham, Denise Gonzales. Cecilia's Year. (Latino Fiction for Young Adults Ser.). (ENG., Illus.). (J). 2007. 210p. (gr. 4-6). pap. 11.95 *(978-1-933693-02-6(9))* 2004. 160p. (gr. 7-9). 16.95 *(978-0-938317-87-6(3))* Cinco Puntos Pr.

Al Mansour, Haifaa. The Green Bicycle. 2015. (ENG.). 352p. (J). (gr. 5). 16.99 *(978-0-525-42806-0(2),* Dial Bks) Penguin Young Readers Group.

Anton, Maggie. Secret Scholar. 2008. (ENG.). 160p. (gr. 4-7). pap. 14.00 *(978-0-8276-0869-6(1))* Jewish Pubn. Society.

Atkins, Jeannine. Finding Wonders: A Verse History of Girls & Science. 2017. (ENG., Illus.). 208p. (J). (gr. 5). pap. 7.99 *(978-1-4814-6566-3(X))* Simon & Schuster Children's Publishing.

—Finding Wonders: Three Girls Who Changed Science. 2016. (ENG., Illus.). 208p. (J). (gr. 5). 17.99 *(978-1-4814-6565-6(1),* Atheneum Bks. for Young Readers) Simon & Schuster Children's Publishing.

Avi. The Secret School. 2003. 157p. (J). (gr. 3-7). 13.60 *(978-0-7569-1625-1(9))* Perfection Learning Corp.

—The True Confessions of Charlotte Doyle. 2012. (ENG.). 240p. (J). (gr. 3-7). pap. 6.99 *(978-0-545-47711-6(5),* Scholastic Paperbacks) Scholastic, Inc.

—The True Confessions of Charlotte Doyle. 2012. lib. bdg. 17.20 *(978-0-606-26779-3(4),* Turtleback) Turtleback Bks.

Axel, Brett. Goblinheart: A Fairy Tale. Biddlespacher, Tara, illus. 2012. (J). 15.00 *(978-0-9769771-2-4(5))* Eastwaterfront Pr.

Baer, Jill. Just One of the Princes. 2014. (Sofia the First World of Reading Ser.). (J). lib. bdg. 13.55 *(978-0-606-35263-5(5))* Turtleback Bks.

Baer, Jill & Disney Book Group Staff. World of Reading: Sofia the First Just One of the Princes: Level 1. Disney Storybook Artists Staff, illus. 2014. (World of Reading Ser.). (ENG.). 32p. (J). (gr. -1-k). pap. 3.99 *(978-1-4231-9432-3(2))* Disney Pr.

Baratz-Logsted, Lauren. The Education of Bet. 2011. (ENG.). 192p. (YA). (gr. 7). pap. 11.99 *(978-0-547-55024-4(3))* Houghton Mifflin Harcourt Publishing Co.

Bare, Bart. Girl. 2010. 188p. (YA). pap. 11.95 *(978-0-9825396-4-4(9))* Canterbury Hse. Publishing, Ltd.

Barker, M. P. Mending Horses. 2014. (ENG.). 320p. (J). (gr. 5). 17.95 *(978-0-8234-2948-6(2))* Holiday Hse., Inc.

Barton, Zoe. Always Neverland. 2011. (ENG.). 320p. (J). (gr. 3-7). 16.99 *(978-0-06-196325-4(9))* HarperCollins Pubs.

Blake, Stephanie J. The Marble Queen, 0 vols. 2012. (ENG.). 192p. (YA). (gr. 5-9). 16.99 *(978-0-7614-6227-9(9),* 9780761462279, Amazon Children's Publishing) Amazon Publishing.

Blevins, Wiley. Go, Billy, Go! Being Yourself. Gordon, John, illus. 2015. (ENG.). 24p. (J). (gr. k-2). lib. bdg. 19.99 *(978-1-63440-003-9(8))* Red Chair Pr.

Bower, Tamara. How the Amazon Queen Fought the Prince of Egypt. Bower, Tamara, illus. 2014. (ENG., Illus.). 36p. (J). (gr. 2-6). 16.99 *(978-1-4814-2526-1(9),* Atheneum Bks. for Young Readers) Simon & Schuster Children's Publishing.

Bradman, Tony. Rapunzel Lets Her Hair Down, 1 vol. Warburton, Sarah, illus. (After Happily Ever After Ser.). (ENG.). 56p. (gr. 2-3). 2014. pap. 5.05 *(978-1-4342-7965-1(0))* 2009. lib. bdg. 25.32 *(978-1-4342-1307-5(2))* Stone Arch Bks. (After Happily Ever After).

Brantz, Loryn. Feminist Baby. Brantz, Loryn, illus. 2017. (ENG., Illus.). 22p. (J). (gr. -1 — 1). 12.99 *(978-1-4847-7858-6(8))* Disney Pr.

Browning, Diane. Signed, Abiah Rose. Browning, Diane, illus. 2010. (ENG., Illus.). 32p. (J). (gr. -1-2). 15.99 *(978-1-58246-311-7(5),* Tricycle Pr.) Random Hse. Children's Bks.

Bunting, Eve. Girls A to Z. Bloom, Suzanne, illus. 2013. (ENG.). 32p. (J). (gr. k-2). pap. 6.95 *(978-1-62091-028-3(4))* Boyds Mills Pr.

—The Pirate Captain's Daughter. 2011. (ENG.). 208p. (J). (gr. 6-18). pap. 8.95 *(978-1-58536-525-8(4));* lib. bdg. 15.95 *(978-1-58536-526-5(2))* Sleeping Bear Pr.

Burch, Christian. Hit the Road, Manny: A Manny Files Novel. 2008. (ENG.). 240p. (J). (gr. 3-7). 16.99 *(978-1-4169-2812-6(X),* Atheneum Bks. for Young Readers) Simon & Schuster Children's Publishing.

—The Manny Files. 2008. (Mix Ser.). (ENG.). 304p. (J). (gr. 4-8). pap. 14.99 *(978-1-4169-5534-4(8),* Aladdin) Simon & Schuster Children's Publishing.

Butler, Dori Hillestad. Sliding into Home, 1 vol. Casale, Paul, illus. 2003. (Peachtree Junior Publication Ser.). (ENG.). 192p. (J). (gr. 3-7). 14.95 *(978-1-56145-222-4(X))* Peachtree Pubs.

Capeci, Anne. Missing!, 1 vol. Casale, Paul, illus. 2005. (Cascade Mountain Railroad Mysteries Ser.). (ENG.). 144p. (J). (gr. 2-5). 12.95 *(978-1-56145-334-4(X))* Peachtree Pubs.

Carlson, Caroline. The Buccaneers' Code. (Very Nearly Honorable League of Pirates Ser.: 3). 320p. (J). (gr. 3-7). 2016. pap. 6.99 *(978-0-06-219440-4(2))* 2015. (ENG.). 16.99 *(978-0-06-219439-8(9))* HarperCollins Pubs.

—The Terror of the Southlands. Phillips, Dave, illus. 2014. (ENG.). 336p. (J). pap. *(978-0-06-236178-3(3))* Harper & Row Ltd.

Carlson, Nancy. Louanne Pig in Making the Team. 2005. (Louanne Pig Ser.). (Illus.). 32p. (J). (gr. k-2). lib. bdg. 15.95 *(978-1-57505-914-3(2))* Lerner Publishing Group.

Cheng, Andrea. The Lace Dowry. 2005. (ENG.). 115p. (J). (gr. 6-9). 16.95 *(978-1-932425-20-8(9),* Lemniscaat) Boyds Mills Pr.

Chibbaro, Julie. Deadly. Sovak, Jean-Marc Superville, illus. (ENG.). 304p. (YA). (gr. 7). 2012. pap. 10.99 *(978-0-689-85739-3(X))* 2011. 17.99 *(978-0-689-85738-6(1))* Simon & Schuster Children's Publishing. (Atheneum Bks. for Young Readers).

Cochrane, Mick. The Girl Who Threw Butterflies. 2010. (ENG.). 192p. (J). (gr. 3-7). 6.99 *(978-0-375-84610-6(7),* Yearling) Random Hse. Children's Bks.

Collins, Pat Lowery. The Fattening Hut. 2005. (ENG.). 192p. (YA). (gr. 7). pap. 12.95 *(978-0-618-55209-2(X))* Houghton Mifflin Harcourt Publishing Co.

Corey, Shana. Players in Pigtails. Gibbon, Rebecca, illus. 2006. 28p. (YA). (gr. 8-11). reprint ed. 17.00 *(978-1-4223-5848-1(8))* DIANE Publishing Co.

—Players in Pigtails. Gibbon, Rebecca, illus. 2010. (Rise & Shine Ser.). (ENG.). 40p. (C). (gr. -1-3). per. 17.95 *(978-0-439-18306-2(5))* National Geographic School Publishing, Inc.

—Players in Pigtails. Gibbon, Rebecca, illus. 2003. (ENG.). 40p. (J). (gr. -1-3). 21.99 *(978-0-439-18305-5(7))* Scholastic, Inc.

Cosgrove, Stephen. Button Breaker. 2016. (Treasure Trolls Ser.). (ENG., Illus.). 32p. (J). (gr. k-4). pap. 7.95 *(978-1-941437-79-7(6))* Heritage Builders, LLC.

Courgeon, Rémi. Toothpick. 2017. (ENG., Illus.). 36p. (J). (gr. k-4). 17.95 *(978-1-59270-210-7(4))* Enchanted Lion Bks., LLC.

Coy, John. Top of the Order. 2010. (4 For 4 Ser.: 1). (ENG.). 208p. (J). (gr. 3-7). pap. 8.99 *(978-0-312-61111-8(0),* 9780312611118) Square Fish.

Cremer, Andrea. Rift. 2013. (Nightshade Ser.). (ENG.). 480p. (YA). (gr. 9). pap. 9.99 *(978-0-14-242493-3(5),* Speak) Penguin Young Readers Group.

Day, Karen. No Cream Puffs. 2010. (ENG.). 224p. (J). (gr. 3-7). 6.99 *(978-0-375-83776-0(0),* Yearling) Random Hse. Children's Bks.

Deborah, Ellis. The Breadwinner. 2014. (ENG.). 176p. (J). 13.20 *(978-1-63245-145-3(X))* Lectorum Pubns., Inc.

dePaola, Tomie. Oliver Button Is a Sissy. dePaola, Tomie, illus. 2017. (ENG., Illus.). 48p. (J). (gr. -1-3). 17.99 ***(978-1-4814-7757-4(9),*** Simon & Schuster Bks. For Young Readers) Simon & Schuster Bks. For Young Readers.

Dines, Carol. The Queen's Soprano. 2007. (ENG., Illus.). 336p. (YA). (gr. 9). pap. 18.95 *(978-0-15-206102-9(9))* Houghton Mifflin Harcourt Publishing Co.

Dole, Mayra L. Drum, Chavi, Drum! Tonel, illus. 2013.Tr. of ¡Toca, Chavi, Toca! (ENG & SPA.). 32p. (J). pap. 9.95 *(978-0-89239-302-2(5),* Children's Book Press) Lee & Low Bks., Inc.

S

—Toca, Chavi, Toca! Tonel, illus. 2003.Tr. of Drum, Chavi, Drum! (ENG & SPA.). 32p. (J). 16.95 (978-0-89239-186-8(3)) Lee & Low Bks., Inc.

Donnelly, Jennifer. These Shallow Graves. (ENG.). (YA). (gr. 7). 2016. 512p. pap. 10.99 (978-0-385-73766-1(1), Ember) 2015. 496p. lib. bdg. 22.99 (978-0-385-90679-1(X), Delacorte Pr.) 2015. (Illus.). 496p. 19.99 (978-0-385-73765-4(3), Delacorte Pr.) Random Hse. Children's Bks.

—These Shallow Graves. 2016. (ENG.). 496p. (YA). (gr. 7). 22.10 (978-0-606-39341-6(2)) Turtleback Bks.

Double Reverse, 1 vol. 2014. (Sports Stories Ser.). (ENG.). 128p. (J). (gr. 2-6). pap. 5.95 (978-1-56145-807-3(4)) Peachtree Pubs.

Echols, Jennifer. The Ex Games. 2011. (Romantic Comedies Ser.). (ENG.). 240p. (YA). (gr. 7). pap. 11.99 (978-1-4424-3083-9(4), Simon Pulse) Simon Pulse.

Ellis, Deborah. The Breadwinner. 2013. 164p. pap. (978-1-4596-6483-8(3)) ReadHowYouWant.com, Ltd.

—Mud City. 2013. 156p. pap. (978-1-4596-6445-6(0)) ReadHowYouWant.com, Ltd.

Ellison, Laura. Hard Rock, Hard Times: Coming of Age in Butte Montana, 1911-1917. 2005. 195p. (YA). per. (978-0-9722217-7-1(8)) Horse Creek Pubns.

Engle, Margarita. Drum Dream Girl: How One Girl's Courage Changed Music. López, Rafael, illus. 2015. (ENG.). 48p. (J). (gr. -1-3). 16.99 (978-0-544-10229-3(0), HMH Books For Young Readers) Houghton Mifflin Harcourt Publishing Co.

Ernst, Kathleen. Whistler in the Dark. 2009. (Mysteries Through Time Ser.). 144 - 176p. (YA). (gr. 4-8). 31.95 (978-1-60754-429-6(6)); pap. 15.25 (978-1-60754-432-6(6)) Windmill Bks.

Evans, Loralee. The King's Heir. 2006. 287p. (YA). (gr. 8-12). per. 18.99 (978-1-55517-865-9(0), Bonneville Bks.) Cedar Fort, Inc./CFI Distribution.

Ferrari, Michael. Born to Fly. 2011. (ENG.). 224p. (J). (gr. 3-7). 6.99 (978-0-375-84607-6(7), Yearling) Random Hse. Children's Bks.

Fierstein, Harvey. The Sissy Duckling. Cole, Henry, illus. 2014. (ENG.). 40p. (J). (gr. -1-3). pap. 9.99 (978-1-4424-9817-4(X), Little Simon) Little Simon.

Fisher, Linda C. A Will of Her Own. 2006. (YA). pap. (978-0-88092-641-6(4)); lib. bdg. (978-0-88092-640-9(6)) Royal Fireworks Publishing Co.

FitzGerald, Dawn. Getting in the Game. 2007. (ENG.). 144p. (J). (gr. 4-8). pap. 16.99 (978-0-312-37753-3(3), 9780312377533) Square Fish.

Flint, Shamini. Ten: A Soccer Story. 2017. (ENG.). 176p. (J). (gr. 5-7). 16.99 (978-0-544-85001-9(7), Clarion Bks.) Houghton Mifflin Harcourt Trade & Reference Pubs.

Florence, Debbi Michiko. Jasmine Toguchi, Mochi Queen. 2017. (J). pap. **(978-0-374-30411-9(4))** Farrar, Straus & Giroux.

Friesner, Esther. Spirit's Chosen. 2013. (Princesses of Myth Ser.). (ENG., Illus.). 496p. (YA). (gr. 7). 17.99 (978-0-375-86908-2(5), Random Hse. Bks. for Young Readers) Random Hse. Children's Bks.

Friesner, Esther & Friesner, Esther M. Nobody's Princess. 2008. (Princesses of Myth Ser.). (ENG., Illus.). 336p. (YA). (gr. 7-11). pap. 8.99 (978-0-375-87529-8(8), Ember) Random Hse. Children's Bks.

Friesner, Esther M. Deception's Pawn. 2015. (ENG.). 336p. (YA). (gr. 7). 17.99 (978-0-449-81867-1(5), Random Hse. Bks. for Young Readers) Random Hse. Children's Bks.

—Spirit's Bride. 2014. (Princesses of Myth Ser.). (ENG., Illus.). 512p. (YA). (gr. 7). pap. 10.99 (978-0-375-87316-4(3), Ember) Random Hse. Children's Bks.

—Spirit's Princess. (Princesses of Myth Ser.). (ENG.). (YA). (gr. 7). 2013. 480p. pap. 10.99 (978-0-375-87314-0(7), Bluefire) 2012. 464p. 17.99 (978-0-375-86907-5(7), Random Hse. Bks. for Young Readers) Random Hse. Children's Bks.

—Spirit's Princess. 2012. 449p. (YA). (978-0-375-87315-7(5)) Random Hse., Inc.

Gág, Wanda. Gone Is Gone: Or the Story of a Man Who Wanted to Do Housework. Gág, Wanda, illus. 2003. (Fesler-Lampert Minnesota Heritage Ser.). (Illus.). 64p. 14.95 (978-0-8166-4243-4(5)) Univ. of Minnesota Pr.

Garvin, Jeff. Symptoms of Being Human. 2016. 352p. (YA). (gr. 9). 17.99 (978-0-06-238286-3(1)) HarperCollins Pubs.

Geeslin, Campbell. Elena's Serenade. Juan, Ana, illus. 2004. (ENG.). 40p. (J). (gr. -1-2). 19.99 (978-0-689-84908-4(7), Atheneum Bks. for Young Readers) Simon & Schuster Children's Publishing.

Girard, M-E. Girl Mans Up. 2016. 384p. (YA). (gr. 9). 17.99 (978-0-06-240417-6(2), HarperTeen) HarperCollins Pubs.

Gold, Rachel. Being Emily. 2012. (ENG.). 264p. (gr. 9). pap. 15.95 (978-1-59493-283-0(2)) Bella Bks., Inc.

Goldberg, Whoopi. Perfectly Prima, No. 3. Roos, Maryn, illus. 2010. (ENG.). 160p. (J). (gr. 1-17). pap. 4.99 (978-0-7868-5262-8(3), Jump at the Sun) Hyperion Bks. for Children.

Goodman, Alison. Eon: Dragoneye Reborn. 2010. (ENG.). 576p. (YA). (gr. 7-18). 10.99 (978-0-14-241711-9(4), Firebird) Penguin Young Readers Group.

—Eon: Dragoneye Reborn. 2010. (Eon Ser.: 1). lib. bdg. 22.10 (978-0-606-23647-8(3), Turtleback) Turtleback Bks.

Grambling, Lois G. Nicky Jones & the Roaring Rhinos. Geer, William J., illus. 2004. 32p. (J). 6.95 (978-1-877810-14-5(2)) Rayve Productions, Inc.

Green, Connie Jordan. The War at Home. 2nd ed. 2003. 144p. (J). pap. 15.00 (978-0-916078-75-1(2)) Iris Publishing Group, Inc., The.

Green, D. L. Zeke Meeks vs the Gruesome Girls, 1 vol. Alves, Josh, illus. 2012. (Zeke Meeks Ser.). (ENG.). 128p. (gr. 2-2). pap. 5.95 (978-1-4048-7221-9(3)); lib. bdg. 22.65 (978-1-4048-6805-2(4)) Picture Window Bks. (Zeke Meeks).

Gregory, Kristiana. My Darlin' Clementine. 2009. (ENG.). 192p. (J). (gr. 5-18). 16.95 (978-0-8234-2198-5(8)) Holiday Hse., Inc.

Grosso, Mike. I Am Drums. 2016. (ENG.). 256p. (J). (gr. 5-7). 16.99 (978-0-544-70710-8(9)) Houghton Mifflin Harcourt Publishing Co.

Gutman, Dan. Mickey & Me. 2004. (Baseball Card Adventures Ser.). (ENG., Illus.). 160p. (J). (gr. 5-9). pap. 5.99 (978-0-06-447258-6(2)) HarperCollins Pubs.

—Mickey & Me. 2004. (Baseball Card Adventures Ser.). (J). lib. bdg. 16.00 (978-0-613-99233-6(4), Turtleback) Turtleback Bks.

Haddix, Margaret Peterson. Just Ella. 2015. (Palace Chronicles Ser.: 1). (ENG., Illus.). 208p. (YA). (gr. 7). pap. 10.99 (978-1-4814-2021-1(6), Simon & Schuster Bks. For Young Readers) Simon & Schuster Bks. For Young Readers.

Haines, Lise. Girl in the Arena. (ENG.). 336p. (YA). (gr. 9-13). 2010. pap. 9.99 (978-1-59990-521-1(3), 9781599905211) 2009. 16.99 (978-1-59990-372-9(5), 9781599903729) Bloomsbury Publishing USA. (Bloomsbury USA Childrens).

Hale, Shannon. Palace of Stone. (Princess Academy Ser.: 2). (ENG.). (YA). (gr. 5-8). 2015. 352p. pap. 7.99 (978-1-61963-257-8(8), 9781619632578) 2012. 336p. 17.99 (978-1-59990-873-1(5), 9781599908731) Bloomsbury Publishing USA. (Bloomsbury USA Childrens).

—Palace of Stone. 2015. (Princess Academy Ser.: 2). (YA). lib. bdg. 18.40 (978-0-606-36439-3(0)) Turtleback Bks.

Hannigan, Kate. The Detective's Assistant. 2015. (ENG.). 368p. (J). (gr. 3-7). 17.00 (978-0-316-40351-1(2)) Little Brown & Co.

Hapka, Catherine, pseud & Echols, Jennifer. Winter's Kiss: The Ex Games - The Twelve Dates of Christmas. 2012. (ENG.). 496p. (YA). (gr. 7). pap. 9.99 (978-1-4424-5040-0(1), Simon Pulse) Simon Pulse.

Hardinge, Frances. The Lie Tree. 2016. (ENG.). 384p. (YA). (gr. 8-17). 17.95 (978-1-4197-1895-3(9), Amulet Bks.) Abrams, Inc.

Harlow, Joan Hiatt. Midnight Rider. 2006. (ENG.). 384p. (J). (gr. 4-9). pap. 8.99 (978-0-689-87010-1(8), McElderry, Margaret K. Bks.) McElderry, Margaret K. Bks.

Harper, Charise Mericle & Mericle Harper, Charise. Princess Patty Finds Her Prince. 2014. (ENG., Illus.). 48p. (J). (gr. -1-k). 16.99 (978-1-4231-0804-7(3)) Hyperion Bks. for Children.

Hawes, Louise & Sharratt, Mary. The Vanishing Point. 2007. (ENG.). 240p. (J). (gr. 5-7). pap. 15.95 (978-0-618-74788-7(5)) Houghton Mifflin Harcourt Publishing Co.

Heller, Alyson. Touchdown! Björkman, Steve, illus. 2010. (After-School Sports Club Ser.). (ENG.). 32p. (J). (gr. -1-1). pap. 3.99 (978-1-4169-9413-8(0), Simon Spotlight) Simon Spotlight.

Hemphill, Stephanie. Sisters of Glass. 2013. (ENG.). 160p. (YA). (gr. 7). pap. 7.99 (978-0-307-98141-7(X), Ember) Random Hse. Children's Bks.

Hensley, Joy N. Rites of Passage. 2014. (ENG.). 416p. (YA). (gr. 8). 17.99 (978-0-06-229519-4(5), HarperTeen) HarperCollins Pubs.

Hidden. 2014. (ENG., Illus.). 384p. (YA). (gr. 7). 17.99 (978-1-4424-8300-2(8), Simon & Schuster/Paula Wiseman Bks.) Simon & Schuster/Paula Wiseman Bks.

Hilton, Marilyn. Full Cicada Moon. 2015. (ENG.). 400p. (J). (gr. 3-7). 17.99 (978-0-525-42875-6(5), Dial Bks) Penguin Young Readers Group.

Hoffman, Sarah & Hoffman, Ian. Jacob's New Dress. Case, Chris, illus. 2014. (ENG.). 32p. (J). (gr. -1-3). 16.99 (978-0-8075-6373-1(0)) Whitman, Albert & Co.

Holm, Jennifer L. Our Only May Amelia. unabr. ed. 2004. 253p. (J). (gr. 5-9). pap. 36.00 incl. audio (978-0-8072-8366-0(5), YA191SP, Listening Library) Random Hse. Audio Publishing Group.

—The Trouble with May Amelia. Gustavson, Adam, illus. (ENG.). 224p. (J). (gr. 3-7). 2012. pap. 5.99 (978-1-4169-1374-0(2)) 2011. 15.99 (978-1-4169-1373-3(4)) Simon & Schuster Children's Publishing. (Atheneum Bks. for Young Readers).

Homan, Lynn M. & Reilly, Thomas. Girls Fly!, 1 vol. Shepherd, Rosalie M., tr. Shepherd, Rosalie M., illus. 2003. (ENG.). 32p. (J). (gr. k-3). 16.99 (978-1-58980-154-7(7)) Pelican Publishing Co., Inc.

Hopkinson, Deborah. Knit Your Bit. Guarnaccia, Steven, illus. 2013. (ENG.). 32p. (J). (gr. k-3). 16.99 (978-0-399-25241-9(X), G.P. Putnam's Sons Books for Young Readers) Penguin Young Readers Group.

Howard, Elizabeth Fitzgerald. Virgie Goes to School with Us Boys. Lewis, E. B., illus. 2005. (gr. k-3). 18.00 (978-0-7569-5088-0(0)) Perfection Learning Corp.

Hunt, Meg, illus. Interstellar Cinderella. 2015. (ENG.). 40p. (J). (gr. -1-k). 16.99 (978-1-4521-2532-9(5)) Chronicle Bks. LLC.

Jacobson, Darlene Beck. Wheels of Change. 2014. (ENG., Illus.). 180p. (J). (gr. 2-8). 12.95 (978-1-939547-13-2(X)) Creston Bks.

Jefferson, Joanne K. Lightning & Blackberries, 1 vol. 2008. (ENG.). 192p. (YA). (gr. 7-12). pap. 10.95 (978-1-55109-654-4(4)) Nimbus Publishing, Ltd. CAN. Dist: Orca Bk. Pubs. USA.

Johnson, Angela. Just Like Josh Gibson. Peck, Beth, illus. 2007. (J). 14.65 (978-0-7569-8088-7(7)) Perfection Learning Corp.

—Just Like Josh Gibson. Peck, Beth, illus. (ENG.). 32p. (J). 2004. (gr. -1-2). 17.99 (978-0-689-82628-3(1)) 2007. (gr. k-2). reprint ed. 7.99 (978-1-4169-2728-0(X)) Simon & Schuster Bks. For Young Readers. (Simon & Schuster Bks. For Young Readers).

Jones Yang, Dori. Daughter of Xanadu. 2012. (ENG.). 352p. (YA). (gr. 7). pap. 9.99 (978-0-385-73924-5(9), Ember) Random Hse. Children's Bks.

Kay, Alan N. No Girls Allowed. 2003. (Young Heroes of History Ser.: Vol. 5). (Illus.). 140p. (J). pap. 6.95 (978-1-57249-324-7(0), White Mane Kids) White Mane Publishing Co., Inc.

Kellerhals-Stewart, Heather. Skookum Sal, Birling Gal. Blaine, Janice, illus. unabr. ed. 2003. (ENG.). 32p. (J). pap. 18.95 (978-1-55017-285-0(9)) Harbour Publishing Co., Ltd. CAN. Dist: Midpoint Trade Bks., Inc.

Kelly, Jacqueline. Counting Sheep: Calpurnia Tate, Girl Vet. White, Teagan & Meyer, Jennifer L., illus. 2017. (Calpurnia Tate, Girl Vet Ser.). (ENG.). 112p. (J). 15.99 (978-1-62779-870-9(6), 9781627798709, Holt, Henry & Co. Bks. For Young Readers) Holt, Henry & Co.

—The Curious World of Calpurnia Tate. 2015. (Calpurnia Tate Ser.: 2). (ENG.). 320p. (J). (gr. 4-7). 16.99 (978-0-8050-9744-3(9), 9780805097443, Holt, Henry & Co. Bks. For Young Readers) Holt, Henry & Co.

—The Curious World of Calpurnia Tate. 2017. (Calpurnia Tate Ser.: 2). (J). lib. bdg. 18.40 **(978-0-606-39939-5(9))** Turtleback Bks.

Kemp, Anna. The Worst Princess. Ogilvie, Sara, illus. 2014. (ENG.). 32p. (J). (gr. -1-2). 16.99 (978-0-385-37125-4(X), Random Hse. Bks. for Young Readers) Random Hse. Children's Bks.

Kenneally, Miranda. Catching Jordan. 2011. (Hundred Oaks Ser.: Bk. 1). (ENG.). 288p. (YA). (gr. 7-12). pap. 9.99 (978-1-4022-6227-2(2)) Sourcebooks, Inc.

Kessler, Cristina. The Best Beekeeper of Lalibela: A Tale from Africa. Jenkins, Leonard, illus. 2006. (ENG.). 32p. (J). (gr. -1-3). 16.95 (978-0-8234-1858-9(8)) Holiday Hse., Inc.

Kittinger, Jo S. Cuando Sea Grande. Lucas, Margeaux, illus. 2005. (Rookie Reader Español Ser.). (SPA & ESP.). 23p. (J). (gr. k-2). per. 4.95 (978-0-516-24692-5(5), Children's Pr.) Scholastic Library Publishing.

Klein, Lisa. Love Disguised. 2013. (ENG., Illus.). 320p. (YA). (gr. 7). 17.99 (978-1-59990-968-4(5), 9781599909684, Bloomsbury USA Childrens) Bloomsbury Publishing USA.

Kupchella, Rick. Girls Can! Make it Happen. Brown, Marilyn, illus. 2004. (ENG.). 40p. (J). 16.95 (978-0-9726504-3-4(1)) TRISTAN Publishing, Inc.

Lackey, Mercedes & Edghill, Rosemary. Dead Reckoning. 2012. (ENG.). 336p. (YA). (gr. 7-12). 16.99 (978-1-59990-684-3(8), 9781599906843, Bloomsbury USA Childrens) Bloomsbury Publishing USA.

Lawrence, L. S. Escape by Sea. 2009. 208p. (J). (gr. 3-7). 16.95 (978-0-8234-2217-3(8)) Holiday Hse., Inc.

Lecesne, James. Trevor. (ENG., Illus.). (J). (gr. 5-9). 2013. 112p. pap. 9.95 (978-1-60980-487-9(2)) 2012. 114p. 14.95 (978-1-60980-420-6(1)) Seven Stories Pr. (Triangle Square).

Lee, Stacey. Under a Painted Sky. 2015. (ENG.). 384p. (YA). (gr. 7). 16.99 (978-0-399-16803-1(6), G.P. Putnam's Sons Books for Young Readers) Penguin Young Readers Group.

Lee, Tanith. Piratica: Being a Daring Tale of a Singular Girl's Adventure upon the High Seas. 2006. (ENG.). 304p. (YA). (gr. 7-18). per. 8.99 (978-0-14-240644-1(9), Firebird) Penguin Young Readers Group.

Lee, Y. S. The Agency: A Spy in the House. 2016. (Agency Ser.). (ENG.). 352p. (YA). (gr. 7). pap. 7.99 (978-0-7636-8748-9(0)) Candlewick Pr.

—The Body at the Tower. 2010. (Agency Ser.: 2). (ENG., Illus.). 352p. (YA). (gr. 7-18). 16.99 (978-0-7636-4968-5(6)) Candlewick Pr.

—Rivals in the City. 2015. (Agency Ser.). (ENG.). 304p. (YA). (gr. 7). 16.99 (978-0-7636-5914-1(2)) Candlewick Pr.

—The Traitor in the Tunnel. 2012. (Agency Ser.: 3). (ENG., Illus.). 384p. (YA). (gr. 7). 16.99 (978-0-7636-5316-3(0)) Candlewick Pr.

Luper, Eric. Jeremy Bender vs. the Cupcake Cadets. 2011. (ENG.). 240p. (J). (gr. 3-7). 16.99 (978-0-06-201512-9(5)) HarperCollins Pubs.

Mackall, Dandi Daley. A Girl Named Dan. Graef, Renee, illus. 2008. (ENG.). 32p. (J). (gr. k-6). 16.95 (978-1-58536-351-3(0)) Sleeping Bear Pr.

Maid of Deception. 2014. (Maids of Honor Ser.). (ENG., Illus.). 416p. (YA). (gr. 7). 17.99 (978-1-4424-4141-5(0), Simon & Schuster Bks. For Young Readers) Simon & Schuster Bks. For Young Readers.

Matas, Carol. Rosie in New York City: Gotcha! 2003. (ENG., Illus.). 128p. (J). (gr. 4-7). pap. 9.95 (978-0-689-85714-0(4), Simon & Schuster/Paula Wiseman Bks.) Simon & Schuster/Paula Wiseman Bks.

McDavid-Jones, Elizabeth. Secrets on 26th Street. 2009. (Mysteries Through Time Ser.). 144 - 176p. (YA). (gr. 4-8). 31.95 (978-1-60754-200-1(5)); pap. 15.25 (978-1-60754-201-8(3)) Windmill Bks.

McElroy, Lisa Tucker. Love, Lizzie: Letters to a Military Mom. Paterson, Diane, illus. (ENG.). 32p. (J). (gr. 1-3). 2009. pap. 6.99 (978-0-8075-4778-6(6)) 2005. lib. bdg. 16.99 (978-0-8075-4777-9(8)) Whitman, Albert & Co.

McGowan, Jennifer. Maid of Secrets. (Maids of Honor Ser.). (ENG.). (YA). (gr. 7). 2014. 432p. pap. 9.99 (978-1-4424-4139-2(9)) 2013. 416p. 17.99 (978-1-4424-4138-5(0)) Simon & Schuster Bks. For Young Readers. (Simon & Schuster Bks. For Young Readers).

—Maid of Wonder. 2015. (Maids of Honor Ser.). (ENG., Illus.). 336p. (YA). (gr. 7). 17.99 (978-1-4814-1826-3(2)) Simon & Schuster Children's Publishing.

McMullan, Kate. The Ghost of Sir Herbert Dungeonstone, 1 vol. Basso, Bill, illus. 2006. (Dragon Slayers' Academy Ser.: No. 12). (ENG.). 112p. (gr. 1-7). 24.21 (978-1-59961-124-2(4)) Spotlight.

McNamara, Margaret. The Playground Problem. Gordon, Mike, illus. 2004. (Robin Hill School Ser.). (ENG.). 32p. (J). (gr. -1-1). pap. 3.99 (978-0-689-85876-5(0), Simon Spotlight) Simon Spotlight.

Messner, Kate. Spitfire. 2007. (J). (978-1-59531-018-7(5)) North Country Bks., Inc.

Meyer, L. A. Boston Jacky: Being an Account of the Further Adventures of Jacky Faber, Taking Care of Business. 2015. (Bloody Jack Adventures Ser.: 11). (ENG.). 384p. (YA). (gr. 9). pap. 9.99 (978-0-544-43914-6(7), HMH Books For Young Readers) Houghton Mifflin Harcourt Publishing Co.

—The Mark of the Golden Dragon: Being an Account of the Further Adventures of Jacky Faber, Jewel of the East, Vexation of the West & Pearl of the South China Sea. (Bloody Jack Adventures Ser.: 9). (ENG.). (YA). (gr. 9). 2013. 400p. pap. 9.99 (978-0-544-00328-6(4)) 2011. 384p. 16.99 (978-0-547-51764-3(5)) Houghton Mifflin Harcourt Publishing Co.

—Under the Jolly Roger: Being an Account of the Further Nautical Adventures of Jacky Faber. 2010. (Bloody Jack Adventures Ser.: 3). (ENG., Illus.). 528p. (YA). (gr. 7). pap. 9.99 (978-0-15-205873-9(7)) Houghton Mifflin Harcourt Publishing Co.

—Viva Jacquelina! Being an Account of the Further Adventures of Jacky Faber, over the Hills & Far Away. (Bloody Jack Adventures Ser.: 10). (ENG.). (YA). (gr. 9). 2014. 384p. pap. 9.99 (978-0-544-23439-0(1), HMH Books For Young Readers) 2012. 368p. 16.99 (978-0-547-76350-7(6)) Houghton Mifflin Harcourt Publishing Co.

—The Wake of the Lorelei Lee: Being an Account of the Further Adventures of Jacky Faber, on Her Way to Botany Bay. (Bloody Jack Adventures Ser.: 8). (ENG.). (YA). (gr. 9). 2012. 576p. pap. 9.99 (978-0-547-72194-1(3)) 2010. 560p. 17.00 (978-0-547-32768-6(4)) Houghton Mifflin Harcourt Publishing Co.

—The Wake of the Lorelei Lee: Being an Account of the Further Adventures of Jacky Faber, on Her Way to Botany Bay. 2010. (Bloody Jack Adventures Ser.: Bk. 8). audio compact disk 29.95 (978-1-59316-484-3(X)) Listen & Live Audio, Inc.

Michiko Florence, Debbi. Jasmine Toguchi, Mochi Queen. Vukovic, Elizabet, illus. 2017. (Jasmine Toguchi Ser.). (ENG.). 128p. (J). 15.99 (978-0-374-30410-2(6), 9780374304102, Farrar, Straus & Giroux (BYR)) Farrar, Straus & Giroux.

Miller, Bobbi. The Girls of Gettysburg. 2014. (ENG.). 160p. (J). (gr. 2-7). 16.95 (978-0-8234-3163-2(0)) Holiday Hse., Inc.

Moore, Julianne. Best Friends Forever. Pham, LeUyen, illus. 2011. (Freckleface Strawberry Ser.). (ENG.). 40p. (J). (gr. -1-3). 17.89 (978-1-59990-552-5(3), 9781599905525, Bloomsbury USA Childrens) Bloomsbury Publishing USA.

Mortensen, Lori. The End Zone, 1 vol. Sullivan, Mary, illus. 2009. (My First Graphic Novel Ser.). (ENG.). 32p. (gr. k-2). pap. 6.25 (978-1-4342-1408-9(7), My First Graphic Novel) Stone Arch Bks.

Murphy, Claire Rudolf. Marching with Aunt Susan: Susan B. Anthony & the Fight for Women's Suffrage, 1 vol. Schuett, Stacey, illus. 2011. (ENG.). 36p. (J). (gr. 1-5). 16.95 (978-1-56145-593-5(8), Peachtree Junior) Peachtree Pubs.

Namioka, Lensey. Ties That Bind, Ties That Break: A Novel. 2006. (Reader's Workshop Ser.). (ENG.). 176p. (C). pap. 19.95 (978-0-7362-3149-7(8)) CENGAGE Learning.

Napoli, Donna Jo. Bound. 2006. (ENG., Illus.). 192p. (YA). (gr. 7-12). reprint ed. mass mkt. 7.99 (978-0-689-86178-9(8), Simon Pulse) Simon Pulse.

—Daughter of Venice. 2003. (ENG.). 288p. (YA). (gr. 7). mass mkt. 7.99 (978-0-440-22928-5(6), Laurel Leaf) Random Hse. Children's Bks.

Nix, Garth. Newt's Emerald. 2015. (ENG.). 304p. (YA). (gr. 8-12). 18.99 (978-0-06-236004-5(3)) HarperCollins Pubs.

Nixon, Joan Lowery. Ann's Story, 1747. 2004. (J). (978-0-87935-198-4(5)) Colonial Williamsburg Foundation.

—Maria's Story, 1773. 2004. (J). (978-0-87935-227-1(2)) Colonial Williamsburg Foundation.

Not Every Princess. 2014. (Illus.). (J). (978-1-4338-1647-5(4), Magination Pr.) American Psychological Assn.

O'Brien, Annemarie. Lara's Gift. 2014. (ENG.). 208p. (J). (gr. 5). 7.99 (978-0-307-93175-7(7), Yearling) Random Hse. Children's Bks.

Osborne, Mary Pope. La Hora de Los Juegos Olimpicos. Brovelli, Marcela, tr. Murdocca, Sal, illus. 2007. (Casa del Arbol Ser.: 16).Tr. of Hour of the Olympics Games. (ENG & SPA.). 68p. (J). per. 5.99 (978-1-933032-22-1(7)) Lectorum Pubns., Inc.

—Hour of the Olympics. unabr. ed. 2004. (Magic Tree House Ser.: No. 16). 70p. (J). (gr. k-3). pap. 17.00 incl. audio (978-0-8072-0785-7(3), LFTR 244 SP, Listening Library) Random Hse. Audio Publishing Group.

Osterlund, Anne. Aurelia. 2008. (ENG.). 256p. (YA). (gr. 7-18). 8.99 (978-0-14-240579-6(5), Speak) Penguin Young Readers Group.

Park, Linda Sue. Seesaw Girl. Tseng, Mou-Sien & Tseng, Jean, illus. 2009. (ENG.). 96p. (J). (gr. 2-5). pap. 6.99 (978-0-547-24888-2(1)) Houghton Mifflin Harcourt Publishing Co.

Perkins, Mitali. Rickshaw Girl. Hogan, Jamie, illus. (ENG.). 96p. (J). (gr. 2-5). 2008. pap. 6.95 (978-1-58089-309-1(0)) 2007. 14.95 (978-1-58089-308-4(2)) Charlesbridge Publishing, Inc.

Pierce, Tamora. Lioness Rampant. 2011. (Song of the Lioness Ser.: 4). (ENG., Illus.). 384p. (YA). (gr. 7). pap. 10.99 (978-1-4424-2766-2(3), Atheneum Bks. for Young Readers) Simon & Schuster Children's Publishing.

—The Woman Who Rides Like a Man. (Song of the Lioness Ser.: 3). (ENG., Illus.). 288p. (YA). (gr. 7). 2014. 19.99 (978-1-4814-3962-6(6)) 2011. pap. 10.99 (978-1-4424-2765-5(5)) Simon & Schuster Children's Publishing. (Atheneum Bks. for Young Readers).

Pryor, Bonnie. Captain Hannah Pritchard: The Hunt for Pirate Gold. 2011. (Historical Fiction Adventures (HFA) Ser.). (Illus.). 160p. (J). (gr. 3-18). pap. 10.95 (978-1-59845-283-9(5)); (gr. 4-7). lib. bdg. 29.27 (978-0-7660-3817-2(3)) Enslow Pubs., Inc.

—Hannah Pritchard: Pirate of the Revolution. 2008. (Historical Fiction Adventures (HFA) Ser.). (Illus.). 160p. (J). (gr. 3-7). lib. bdg. 29.27 (978-0-7660-2851-7(8)) Enslow Pubs., Inc.

—Pirate Hannah Pritchard: Captured! 2009. (Historical Fiction Adventures (HFA) Ser.). (Illus.). 160p. (J). (gr. 3-6). lib. bdg. 29.27 (978-0-7660-3310-8(4)) Enslow Pubs., Inc.

Qamar, Amjed. Beneath My Mother's Feet. (ENG.). 208p. (YA). (gr. 7). 2011. pap. 10.99 (978-1-4424-1451-8(0)) 2008. 16.99 (978-1-4169-4728-8(0)) Simon & Schuster Children's Publishing. (Atheneum Bks. for Young Readers).

Quinn, Jordan. Let the Games Begin! McPhillips, Robert, illus. 2015. (Kingdom of Wrenly Ser.: 7). (ENG.). 128p. (J). (gr. k-4). pap. 5.99 (978-1-4814-2379-3(7), Little Simon) Little Simon.

Raczka, Bob. Joy in Mudville. Dibley, Glin, illus. 2014. (ENG.). 32p. (J). (gr. -1-3). 17.95 (978-0-7613-6015-5(8), Carolrhoda Bks.) Lerner Publishing Group.

Redgate, Riley. Noteworthy. 2017. (ENG.). 400p. (YA). (gr. 8-17). 17.95 (978-1-4197-2373-5(1), Amulet Bks.) Abrams, Inc.

Reedy, Trent. Words in the Dust. (ENG.). 272p. (J). 2013. (gr. 5-9). pap. 6.99 (978-0-545-26126-5(0)) 2011. (gr. 4-7). 17.99 (978-0-545-26125-8(2)) Scholastic, Inc. (Levine, Arthur A. Bks.).

Rees, Celia. Sovay. 2010. (ENG.). 432p. (YA). (gr. 7). pap. 9.99 (978-1-59990-483-2(7), 9781599904832, Bloomsbury USA Childrens) Bloomsbury Publishing USA.

—Sovay. 2009. 1.00 (978-1-4074-4516-8(2)) Recorded Bks., Inc.

Reese, Jenn. Mirage. 2014. (Above World Ser.). (ENG.). 368p. (J). (gr. 5). pap. 7.99 (978-0-7636-6929-4(6)) Candlewick Pr.

Reeve, Philip. Fever Crumb. 2011. (Fever Crumb Ser.). (ENG.). 336p. (J). (gr. 7-7). pap. 9.99 (978-0-545-22215-0(X), Scholastic Pr.) Scholastic, Inc.

Reich, Susanna. Penelope Bailey Takes the Stage, 1 vol. 2006. (ENG.). 32p. (J). (gr. 3-7). 16.95 (978-0-7614-5287-4(7)) Marshall Cavendish Corp.

Rinaldi, Ann. The Family Greene. 2011. (ENG.). 256p. (YA). (gr. 7). pap. 14.95 *(978-0-547-57723-4(0))* Houghton Mifflin Harcourt Publishing Co.

Roger, Marie-Sabine. Of Course They Do! Boys & Girls Can Do Anything. Sol, Anne, photos by. 2014. (ENG., Illus.). 40p. (J). (-k). lib. bdg. 9.95 *(978-1-58089-669-6(3))* Charlesbridge Publishing, Inc.

Russell, Ching Yeung. Tofu Quilt. (ENG.). 136p. (J). 2016. (gr. 4-7). pap. 10.95 ***(978-1-62014-354-4(2))*** 2009. (gr. 3-8). 16.95 *(978-1-60060-423-2(4))* Lee & Low Bks., Inc.

Sachar, Louis. Marvin Redpost #3: Is He a Girl? Record, Adam, illus. 2015. (Marvin Redpost Ser.: 3). (ENG.). 96p. (J). (gr. 1-4). lib. bdg. 12.99 *(978-0-553-53542-6(0)*, Random Hse. Bks. for Young Readers) Random Hse. Children's Bks.

Salisbury, Linda G. The Wild Women of Lake Anna: A Bailey Fish Adventure. 2005. (Illus.). 159p. (J). *(978-1-881539-37-7(7))* Tabby Hse. Bks.

Scott, Kate. Spies in Disguise: Boy in Tights. 2016. (ENG., Illus.). 192p. (J). (gr. 1-5). pap. 7.99 *(978-1-63450-689-2(8)*, Sky Pony Pr.) Skyhorse Publishing Co., Inc.

Searching for Silverheels. 2014. (ENG., Illus.). 304p. (J). (gr. 5-9). 16.99 *(978-1-4814-0029-9(0)*, McElderry, Margaret K. Bks.) McElderry, Margaret K. Bks.

Selfors, Suzanne. Ever after High: Hero Training: A Destiny Do-Over Diary. 2015. (ENG., Illus.). 160p. (J). (gr. 3-7). 9.99 *(978-0-316-40139-5(0))* Little, Brown Bks. for Young Readers.

—A Semi-Charming Kind of Life. 2015. (Ever after High Ser.: Bk. 3). 213p. (J). *(978-0-316-40135-7(8))* Little Brown & Co.

—A Semi-Charming Kind of Life. 2015. (Ever after High Ser.: Bk. 3). (ENG., Illus.). 224p. (J). (gr. 3-7). 13.99 *(978-0-316-40136-4(6))* Little, Brown Bks. for Young Readers.

Shickman, Allan Richard. Zan-Gah: A Prehistoric Adventure. 2007. 160p. (J). (gr. 4-7). per. 9.95 *(978-0-9790357-0-8(8))* Earthshaker Bks.

Simmons, Kristen. The Glass Arrow. 2016. (ENG.). 352p. (YA). pap. 9.99 *(978-0-7653-3664-4(2)*, 9780765336644, Tor Teen) Doherty, Tom Assocs., LLC.

Singer, Marilyn. I'm Gonna Climb a Mountain in My Patent Leather Shoes. Avril, Lynne, illus. 2014. (ENG.). 40p. (J). (gr. k-2). 16.95 *(978-1-4197-0336-2(6)*, Abrams Bks. for Young Readers) Abrams, Inc.

Skinner, Constance Lindsay. Becky Landers: Frontier Warrior. 2006. (Living History Library). 198p. (YA). (gr. 10). per. 12.95 *(978-1-932350-06-7(3))* Bethlehem Bks.

Sleiman, Dina L. Chivalrous. 2015. (Valiant Hearts Ser.: 2). (ENG.). 368p. (YA). pap. 16.00 *(978-0-7642-1313-7(X))* Bethany Hse. Pubs.

Smith, Lane. Madam President. Smith, Lane, illus. 2008. (ENG., Illus.). 40p. (J). (gr. -1-k). 16.99 *(978-1-4231-0846-7(9))* Hyperion Pr.

—Madam President. 2011. (J). (gr. 1-4). 29.95 *(978-0-545-10688-7(5))* Weston Woods Studios, Inc.

Snow, Maya. Blade's Edge. 2009. 245p. (J). lib. bdg. 17.89 *(978-0-06-124391-2(4))* HarperCollins Pubs.

—Chasing the Secret. 2010. (Sisters of the Sword Ser.: 2). (ENG.). 272p. (J). (gr. 5). pap. 6.99 *(978-0-06-124392-9(2))* HarperCollins Pubs.

—Sisters of the Sword. 2008. (Sisters of the Sword Ser.). (J). (gr. 5-18). 288p. 16.99 *(978-0-06-124387-5(6))*; 275p. lib. bdg. 17.89 *(978-0-06-124388-2(4))* HarperCollins Pubs.

Spinelli, Jerry. There's a Girl in My Hammerlock. 2008. 199p. (gr. 4-8). 16.00 *(978-0-7569-8465-6(3))* Perfection Learning Corp.

Spinner, Stephanie. Quiver. 2005. (ENG.). 192p. (YA). (gr. 7). reprint ed. per. 5.99 *(978-0-440-23819-5(6)*, Laurel Leaf) Random Hse. Children's Bks.

Stanley, Diane. Bella at Midnight. Ibatoulline, Bagram, illus. 2007. (ENG.). 304p. (J). (gr. 3-7). pap. 7.99 *(978-0-06-077575-9(0))* HarperCollins Pubs.

Staples, Suzanne Fisher. Haveli. 2012. (ENG.). 336p. (YA). (gr. 7). pap. 9.99 *(978-0-307-97789-2(7)*, Ember) Random Hse. Children's Bks.

—Haveli. 2006. 21.50 *(978-0-8446-7291-5(2))* Smith, Peter Pub., Inc.

—The House of Djinn. 2012. (ENG.). 222p. (YA). (gr. 7). pap. 8.99 *(978-0-307-97642-0(4)*, Ember) Random Hse. Children's Bks.

—Shabanu: Daughter of the Wind. 3rd ed. (J). pap. 3.99 *(978-0-13-800053-0(0))* Prentice Hall (Schl. Div.).

—Shabanu: Daughter of the Wind. 2012. (ENG.). 288p. (YA). (gr. 7). pap. 9.99 *(978-0-307-97788-5(9)*, Ember) Random Hse. Children's Bks.

Stewart, Jennifer J. Close Encounters of a Third World Kind. 2004. (ENG.). 128p. (J). (gr. 4-6). tchr. ed. 16.95 *(978-0-8234-1850-3(2))* Holiday Hse., Inc.

—Close Encounters of a Third-World Kind. 2008. (ENG., Illus.). 181p. (J). (gr. 3-7). 6.95 *(978-0-8234-2161-9(9))* Holiday Hse., Inc.

Stites, Clara. Lixia of Gold Mountain: A Story of Early California. 2015. (ENG., Illus.). 100p. (J). pap. 8.95 *(978-1-56474-421-0(3)*, Fithian Pr) Daniel & Daniel, Pubs., Inc.

Stolz, Joelle. The Shadows of Ghadames. Temerson, Catherine, tr. 2006. (ENG.). 128p. (J). (gr. 3-7). 5.99 *(978-0-440-41949-5(2)*, Yearling) Random Hse. Children's Bks.

Stratton-Porter, Gene. A Daughter of the Land. 2008. pap. *(978-1-84830-034-7(4)*, Wildhern Pr.) Echo Library.

—A Daughter of the Land. 2007. 340p. 22.95 *(978-1-934169-46-9(3))*; pap. 11.95 *(978-1-934169-47-6(1))* Norilana Bks.

Sykes, Shelley & Szymanski, Lois. A Whisper of War. 2003. (J). 5.95 *(978-1-57249-327-8(5)*, White Mane Kids) White Mane Publishing Co., Inc.

Thomas, Carroll. The Town on Rambling Creek: A Matty Trescott Novel. 2004. (Illus.). ix, 185p. (J). *(978-1-57525-376-3(3))* Smith & Kraus Pubs., Inc.

Thomas, Carroll, creator. Under the Open Sky: A Matty Trescott Novel. 2005. (Illus.). 184p. (J). per. 12.95 *(978-0-9762091-2-6(8))* Antrim Hse.

Trent, Tiffany. The Unnaturalists. 2013. (ENG., Illus.). 336p. (YA). (gr. 7). pap. 9.99 *(978-1-4424-2207-0(6)*, Simon & Schuster Bks. For Young Readers) Simon & Schuster Bks. For Young Readers.

Waller, Sharon Biggs. A Mad, Wicked Folly. 2014. (ENG.). 448p. (YA). (gr. 7). 17.99 *(978-0-670-01468-2(0)*, Viking Books for Young Readers) Penguin Young Readers Group.

Walter, Mildred Pitts. Justin & the Best Biscuits in the World. Stock, Catherine, illus. 2010. (ENG.). 144p. (J). (gr. 3-7). pap. 5.99 *(978-0-06-195891-5(3)*, Amistad) HarperCollins Pubs.

—Justin & the Best Biscuits in the World. 2011. 8.32 *(978-0-7848-3586-9(1)*, Everbind) Marco Bk. Co.

Weil, Sylvie. Elvina's Mirror. 2009. (ENG.). 150p. (gr. 5-18). pap. 14.00 *(978-0-8276-0885-6(3))* Jewish Pubn. Society.

—My Guardian Angel. Rosner, Gillian, tr. from FRE. 2014. (ENG., Illus.). 208p. (J). pap. 14.95 *(978-0-8276-1211-2(7))* Jewish Pubn. Society.

West, Kasie. On the Fence. 2014. (ENG.). 304p. (YA). (gr. 8). pap. 9.99 *(978-0-06-223567-1(2)*, HarperTeen) HarperCollins Pubs.

Weston Woods Staff, creator. Players in Pigtails. 2004. 29.95 *(978-0-7882-0518-7(8))* Weston Woods Studios, Inc.

Whelan, Gloria. Chu Ju's House. 2004. 240p. (J). (gr. 5-18). lib. bdg. 17.89 *(978-0-06-050725-1(X))* HarperCollins Pubs.

Whitney, Kim Ablon. See You down the Road. 14.85 *(978-0-7569-5710-0(9))* Perfection Learning Corp.

Wiles, Deborah. The Aurora County All-Stars. 2009. (ENG., Illus.). 256p. (J). (gr. 2-5). pap. 7.99 *(978-0-15-206626-0(8))* Houghton Mifflin Harcourt Publishing Co.

Williams, Susan. Wind Rider. 2006. 309p. (J). (gr. 5-9). 16.99 *(978-0-06-087236-6(5))* HarperCollins Pubs.

Wilson, Diane Lee. Firehorse. (ENG.). 336p. (YA). (gr. 7). 2010. pap. 8.99 *(978-1-4424-0331-4(4))* 2006. (Illus.). 17.99 *(978-1-4169-1551-5(6))* McElderry, Margaret K. Bks. (McElderry, Margaret K. Bks.).

Yolen, Jane & Stemple, Heidi E. Y. Not All Princesses Dress in Pink. Lanquetin, Anne-Sophie, illus. 2010. (ENG.). 32p. (J). (gr. -1-3). 17.99 *(978-1-4169-8018-6(0)*, Simon & Schuster Bks. For Young Readers) Simon & Schuster Bks. For Young Readers.

SEXUAL ABSTINENCE

Ascension Press, creator. Theology of the Body for Teens Student Workbook: Discovering God's Plan for Love & Life. 2006. (Illus.). 210p. per. 14.95 *(978-1-932927-86-3(7))* Ascension Pr.

Gitchel, Sam & Foster, Lorri. Let's Talk about S-E-X: A Guide for Kids 9 to 12 & Their Parents. 2nd ed. 2005. (ENG., Illus.). 100p. pap. 9.99 *(978-1-931863-18-6(0))* Book Peddlers.

Rose, Lyman Hinckley. Pure & Chased. 2004. ix, 86p. pap. 7.95 *(978-1-55517-774-4(3))* Cedar Fort, Inc./CFI Distribution.

Sommers, Michael A. & Sommers, Annie Leah. Everything You Need to Know about Virginity. 2005. (Need to Know Library). (Illus.). 64p. (YA). (gr. 7-12). lib. bdg. 31.95 *(978-0-8239-3115-6(3)*, NTVIRG) Rosen Publishing Group, Inc., The.

Stenzel, Pam. Sex Has a Price Tag: Discussions about Sexuality, Spirituality, & Self-Respect, 1 vol. 2015. (ENG.). 144p. (YA). pap. 9.99 *(978-0-310-74885-4(2))* Zondervan.

The True Love Waits Youth Bible. 2004. (Illus.). 1294p. pap. 19.99 *(978-1-55819-621-6(8))* B&H Publishing Group.

SEXUAL EDUCATION

see Sex Instruction

SEXUAL ETHICS

see also Birth Control

Dennis, Rainey. Passport 2 Purity. 2004. 29.99 *(978-1-57229-656-5(9))* FamilyLife.

Feinstein, Stephen. Sexuality & Teens: What You Should Know about Sex, Abstinence, Birth Control, Pregnancy, & STDs. 2009. (Issues in Focus Today Ser.). (Illus.). 104p. (J). (gr. 6-18). lib. bdg. 33.27 *(978-0-7660-3312-2(0))* Enslow Pubs., Inc.

Gilbert, Laura. Everything You Need to Know about Compulsive Sexual Behavior. 2009. (Need to Know Library). 64p. (gr. 5-5). 58.50 *(978-1-60854-059-4(6))* Rosen Publishing Group, Inc., The.

Jamiolkowski, Raymond M. A Baby Doesn't Make the Man: Alternative Sources of Power & Manhood for Young Men. 2009. (Teen Pregnancy Prevention Library). 64p. (gr. 5-5). 58.50 *(978-1-60854-244-4(0))* Rosen Publishing Group, Inc., The.

Lickona, Tom & Lickona, Judy. Sex, Love & You: Making the Right Decision. rev. ed. 2003. (Illus.). 192p. pap. 15.95 *(978-0-87793-987-0(X))* Ave Maria Pr.

Marcovitz, Hal. Teens & Sex. 2008. (Gallup Youth Survey, Major Issues & Trends Ser.). (Illus.). 112,128p. (YA). (gr. 7-9). lib. bdg. 22.95 *(978-1-59084-722-0(9))* Mason Crest.

McKee, Jonathan. Sex Matters. 2015. (ENG.). 128p. (YA). pap. 5.99 *(978-0-7642-2213-9(9))* Bethany Hse. Pubs.

Mooney, Carla. Everything You Need to Know about Sexual Consent. 2017. (Need to Know Library). 64p. (J). (gr. 12-11). 34.45 ***(978-1-5081-7412-7(1))***; pap. 12.95 ***(978-1-5081-7410-3(5))*** Rosen Publishing Group, Inc., The. (Rosen Young Adult).

Nakaya, Andrea C. Teens & Sex. 2015. (J). *(978-1-60152-912-1(0))* ReferencePoint Pr., Inc.

Rose, Lyman Hinckley. Pure & Chased. 2004. ix, 86p. pap. 7.95 *(978-1-55517-774-4(3))* Cedar Fort, Inc./CFI Distribution.

Sommers, Michael A. & Sommers, Annie Leah. Everything You Need to Know about Virginity. 2005. (Need to Know Library). (Illus.). 64p. (YA). (gr. 7-12). lib. bdg. 31.95 *(978-0-8239-3115-6(3)*, NTVIRG) Rosen Publishing Group, Inc., The.

The True Love Waits Youth Bible. 2004. (Illus.). 1294p. pap. 19.99 *(978-1-55819-621-6(8))* B&H Publishing Group.

SEXUAL ETHICS—FICTION

Goobie, Beth. Hello, Groin, 1 vol. 2006. (ENG.). 292p. (YA). (gr. 8-12). 17.95 *(978-1-55143-459-9(8))* Orca Bk. Pubs. USA.

Hamilton, Elizabeth L. Date with Responsibility. 2004. (Character-in-Action Ser.: No. 2). (Illus.). 384p. (YA). per. 19.95 *(978-0-9713749-0-4(2)*, Character-in-Action) Quiet Impact, Inc.

Ruditis, Paul. Rainbow Party. 2005. (ENG.). 256p. (YA). (gr. 9-18). pap. 12.95 *(978-1-4169-0235-5(X)*, Simon Pulse) Simon Pulse.

SEXUAL HARASSMENT

Bouchard, Elizabeth. Everything You Need to Know about Sexual Harassment. 2009. (Need to Know Library). 64p. (gr. 5-5). 58.50 *(978-1-60854-085-3(5))* Rosen Publishing Group, Inc., The.

Gillard, Arthur. Sexual Harassment. Greenhaven Press Editors & Gale Editors, eds. 2014. (Issues That Concern You Ser.). (ENG., Illus.). 144p. (gr. 7-10). lib. bdg. 42.00 *(978-0-7377-6933-3(5)*, Greenhaven Pr., Inc.) Cengage Gale.

Shaw, Victoria. Coping with Sexual Harassment & Gender Bias. 2005. (Coping Ser.). (Illus.). 192p. (YA). (gr. 7-12). lib. bdg. 34.60 *(978-0-8239-3267-2(2)*, COSEHA) Rosen Publishing Group, Inc., The.

Stanley, Debbie. Everything You Need to Know about Student-on-Student Sexual Harassment. 2005. (Need to Know Library). (Illus.). 64p. (YA). (gr. 7-12). lib. bdg. 31.95 *(978-0-8239-3281-8(8)*, NTSTHA) Rosen Publishing Group, Inc., The.

Tamar's Dilemma: An Overview of Sexual Exploitation. 2003. 32p. (YA). per. *(978-0-9746327-0-4(8)*, 1196490) Trammel, Crystal.

SEXUAL HARASSMENT—FICTION

Alpine, Rachele. Canary. 2013. (ENG.). 400p. (YA). (gr. 6). pap. 9.99 *(978-1-60542-587-0(7))* Medallion Pr., Inc.

Banting, Celia. I only said I was telling the Truth. 2006. 240p. (YA). per. 14.99 *(978-0-9786648-4-8(1))* Wighita Pr.

Conford, Ellen. To All My Fans, with Love, From Sylvie. 2013. (ENG.). 200p. (gr. 4). pap. 12.95 *(978-1-939601-01-8(0))* lg Publishing, Inc.

Torres, J. Degrassi The Next Generation Extra Credit Turning Japanese. 2006. (Degrassi the Next Generation Ser.). (ENG., Illus.). 120p. (J). pap. *(978-1-55168-318-8(0))* Fenn, H. B. & Co., Ltd.

West-Smith, Sandy. Who Will Teach Johnny: The Difference Between Good Touches & Bad Touches? 2006. (Illus.). 19p. (J). (gr. -1-2). pap. *(978-1-56167-914-0(3))* American Literary Pr.

Woodson, Marion. Charlotte's Vow. 2006. (ENG.). 144p. (J). (gr. 4). pap., tchr. ed. 8.95 *(978-0-88878-413-1(9))* Dundurn CAN. Dist: Ingram Publisher Services.

SEXUALLY TRANSMITTED DISEASES

Ambrose, Marylou & Deisler, Veronica. Investigating STDs (Sexually Transmitted Diseases) Real Facts for Real Lives. 2010. (Investigating Diseases Ser.). (Illus.). 160p. (YA). (gr. 9-12). 35.94 *(978-0-7660-3342-9(2))* Enslow Pubs., Inc.

—Sexually Transmitted Diseases: Examining STDs. 2014. (Diseases, Disorders, Symptoms Ser.). (Illus.). 96p. (gr. 9-12). (J). 27.94 *(978-1-62293-080-7(0))*; pap. 10.95 *(978-1-62293-081-4(9))* Enslow Pubs., Inc.

Cefrey, Holly. Syphilis & Other Sexually Transmitted Diseases. 2009. (Epidemics Ser.). 64p. (gr. 5-5). 58.50 *(978-1-61512-303-2(2))* Rosen Publishing Group, Inc., The.

Collins, Nicholas & Woods, Samuel G. Frequently Asked Questions about STDs. 2011. (FAQ: Teen Life Ser.). (J). lib. bdg. 31.95 *(978-1-4488-4630-6(7))* Rosen Publishing Group, Inc., The.

Egendorf, Laura K. Sexually Transmitted Diseases. 2007. (At Issue Ser.). (ENG.). 128p. (gr. 10-12). pap. 27.80 *(978-0-7377-1976-5(1)*, Greenhaven Pr., Inc.); (Illus.). 104p. (YA). (gr. 9-12). pap. 34.45 *(978-0-7377-1975-8(3))* Cengage Gale.

Ford, Carol A. & Bowers, Elizabeth Shimer. Living with Sexually Transmitted Diseases. 2009. (Teen's Guides). 184p. (gr. 6-12). 34.95 *(978-0-8160-7672-7(3))* Facts On File, Inc.

Haugen, David M. Sexually Transmitted Diseases. Gale, ed. 2014. (Introducing Issues with Opposing Viewpoints Ser.). (ENG., Illus.). 144p. (gr. 10-12). lib. bdg. 42.00 *(978-0-7377-6928-9(9)*, Greenhaven Pr., Inc.) Cengage Gale.

Hunter, Miranda & Hunter, William. Sexually Transmitted Infections. McDonnell, Mary Ann & Forman, Sara, eds. 2013. (Young Adult's Guide to the Science of Health Ser.: 15). 128p. (J). (gr. 7-18). 24.95 *(978-1-4222-2814-2(2))* Mason Crest.

—Sexually Transmitted Infections. Forman, Sara & McDonnell, Mary Ann, eds. 2013. (Young Adult's Guide to the Science of Health Ser.). (Illus.). 128p. (J). (gr. 7-18). pap. 14.95 *(978-1-4222-3007-7(4))* Mason Crest.

Kolesnikow, Tassia. Sexually Transmitted Diseases. 2003. (Diseases & Disorders Ser.). (Illus.). 112p. (J). (gr. 6-9). 32.45 *(978-1-56006-910-2(4)*, Lucent Bks.) Cengage Gale.

Michaud, Christopher. Gonorrhea. (Library of Sexual Health Ser.). 64p. 2009. (gr. 6-6). 58.50 *(978-1-60853-845-4(1))* 2006. (Illus.). (YA). (gr. 7-12). lib. bdg. 31.95 *(978-1-4042-0908-4(5))* Rosen Publishing Group, Inc., The.

Naff, Clayton Farris, ed. Sexually Transmitted Diseases. 2008. (Perspectives on Diseases & Disorders Ser.). (ENG., Illus.). 144p. (gr. 10-12). lib. bdg. 44.30 *(978-0-7377-4248-0(8)*, LML02109-243160, Greenhaven Pr., Inc.) Cengage Gale.

Planned Parenthood Federation of America, Inc. Staff. The Condom. 2003. (YA). pap. 3.00 net. *(978-0-934586-80-1(2))* Planned Parenthood Federation of America, Inc.

—Sexually Transmitted Infections: The Facts. 2003. (YA). pap. 3.00 net. *(978-0-934586-82-5(9))* Planned Parenthood Federation of America, Inc.

Saulmon, Greg. Genital Herpes. 2009. (Library of Sexual Health Ser.). 64p. (gr. 6-6). 58.50 *(978-1-60853-844-7(3))* Rosen Publishing Group, Inc., The.

Shmaefsky, Brian R. Gonorrhea. 2nd rev. ed. 2010. (Deadly Diseases & Epidemics Ser.). 120p. (C). (gr. 9). 34.95 *(978-1-60413-240-3(X)*, Chelsea Hse.) Facts On File, Inc.

Silverstein, Alvin, et al. The STDs Update. 2006. (Disease Update Ser.). (Illus.). 128p. (J). (gr. 5-9). lib. bdg. 33.27 *(978-0-7660-2484-7(9))* Enslow Pubs., Inc.

Slade, Suzanne. The Phases of the Moon. 2007. (Cycles in Nature Ser.). (Illus.). 24p. (YA). (gr. 3-6). lib. bdg. 22.60 *(978-1-4042-3488-8(8))* Rosen Publishing Group, Inc., The.

Winters, Adam. Syphilis. (Library of Sexual Health Ser.). 64p. 2009. (gr. 6-6). 58.50 *(978-1-60853-849-2(4))* 2006. (Illus.). (YA). (gr. 7-12). lib. bdg. 31.95 *(978-1-4042-0906-0(9))* Rosen Publishing Group, Inc., The.

Wolny, Philip. I Have an STD. Now What?, 1 vol. 2015. (ENG.). 112p. (YA). 35.60 *(978-1-4777-7980-4(9)*, Rosen Young Adult) Rosen Publishing Group, Inc., The.

World Health Organization, Regional Office for the Western Pacific Staff. Responding to Questions about the 100% Condom Use Programme: A Job Aid for Programme Staff. 2nd rev. ed. 2009. (WPRO Publication). (ENG.). 49p. pap. 12.00 *(978-92-9061-425-8(0))* World Health Organization.

WSTDTV: Being Informed Is the First Step to HIV/STD Prevention. 2004. (YA). cd-rom *(978-0-9754754-8-5(7))* Academic Edge, Inc.

Yancey, Diane. STDs. 2011. (USA TODAY Health Reports: Diseases & Disorders Ser.). (ENG., Illus.). 128p. (gr. 6-12). lib. bdg. 34.60 *(978-0-7613-5456-7(5))* Lerner Publishing Group.

SHACKLETON, ERNEST HENRY, SIR, 1874-1922

Bertozzi, Nick. Shackleton: Antarctic Odyssey. Bertozzi, Nick, illus. 2014. (ENG., Illus.). 128p. (YA). (gr. 7-12). pap. 16.99 *(978-1-59643-451-6(1)*, First Second Bks.) Roaring Brook Pr.

Bodden, Valerie. To the South Pole. 2012. (Great Expeditions Ser.). (ENG.). 48p. (J). (gr. 4-7). pap. 12.00 *(978-0-89812-667-9(3)*, Creative Paperbacks) Creative Co., The.

Brasch, Nicolas. Ernest Shackleton's Antarctic Expedition. 2013. (Discovery Education: Sensational True Stories Ser.). (ENG., Illus.). 32p. (J). (gr. 3-6). pap. 10.00 *(978-1-4777-0111-9(7))*; lib. bdg. 25.25 *(978-1-4777-0063-1(3))* Rosen Publishing Group, Inc., The. (PowerKids Pr.).

Buckley, James, Jr. Who Was Ernest Shackleton? Hergenrother, Max, illus. 2013. (Who Was? Ser.). (ENG.). 112p. (J). (gr. 3-7). 5.99 *(978-0-448-47931-6(1)*, Grosset & Dunlap) Penguin Young Readers Group.

Buckley, James. Who Was Ernest Shackleton? 2013. (Who Was... ? Ser.). lib. bdg. 16.00 *(978-0-606-34162-2(5)*, Turtleback) Turtleback Bks.

Davis, Linda. Sir Ernest Shackleton. 2009. (Great Explorers Ser.). (Illus.). 144p. (gr. 6-12). 30.00 *(978-1-60413-421-6(6)*, Chelsea Hse.) Facts On File, Inc.

Ganeri, Anita. Endurance: Shackleton's Incredible Antarctic Expedition. 2016. (ENG., Illus.). 48p. (J). (gr. 4-6). pap. 12.99 *(978-0-7502-9709-7(3)*, Wayland) Hachette Children's Group GBR. Dist: Hachette Bk. Group.

Grill, William, illus. Shackleton's Journey. 2014. (ENG.). 80p. (J). (gr. -1-2). 24.00 *(978-1-909263-10-9(9))* Flying Eye Bks. GBR. Dist: Consortium Bk. Sales & Distribution.

Hoena, Blake A. & Hoena, B. A. Shackleton & the Lost Antarctic Expedition, 1 vol. Hoover, Dave et al, illus. 2006. (Disasters in History Ser.). (ENG.). 32p. (gr. 3-4). 30.65 *(978-0-7368-5482-5(7)*, Graphic Library) Capstone Press of Coughlan Cos.

Johnson, Kristin. The Endurance Expedition, 1 vol. 2011. (Essential Events Set 6 Ser.). (ENG., Illus.). 112p. (J). (gr. 6-12). lib. bdg. 35.64 *(978-1-61714-764-7(8))* ABDO Publishing Co.

Johnson, Rebecca L. Ernest Shackleton: Gripped by the Antarctic. 2003. (Trailblazer Biographies Ser.). (ENG., Illus.). 112p. (gr. 5-9). 31.93 *(978-0-87614-920-1(4))* Lerner Publishing Group.

Kostyal, K. M. Trial by Ice: A Photobiography of Sir Ernest Shackleton. 2006. (Illus.). 64p. pap. 7.99 *(978-0-15-356619-6(1))* Houghton Mifflin Harcourt School Pubs.

McCumiskey, Gavin. Shackleton: A Graphic Account: the Voyage of the James Caird. Butler, David, illus. 2016. (ENG.). 96p. (J). pap. 16.00 *(978-1-84889-281-1(0))* Collins Pr., The IRL. Dist: Dufour Editions, Inc.

Smith, Michael. Shackleton - the Boss: The Remarkable Adventures of Ernest Shackleton. Brady, Annie, illus. 2nd rev. ed. 2010. (ENG.). 128p. (J). pap. 15.95 *(978-1-905172-27-6(3))* Collins Pr., The IRL. Dist: Dufour Editions, Inc.

SHADES AND SHADOWS

see Shadows

SHADOWS

Boothroyd, Jennifer. Playing with Light & Shadows. 2014. (First Step Nonfiction - Light & Sound Ser.). (Illus.). 24p. (gr. k-2). pap. 6.95 *(978-1-4677-4503-1(0))*; (ENG.). lib. bdg. 23.93 *(978-1-4677-3912-2(X)*, Lerner Pubns.) Lerner Publishing Group.

Brasch, Nicolas. Why Do Shadows Change? Level 5 Factbook. 2010. (Cambridge Young Readers Ser.). (ENG., Illus.). 24p. pap. 7.16 *(978-0-521-13731-7(4))* Cambridge Univ. Pr.

Canetti, Yanitzia. De quien es esta Sombra? Adivina Adivinador. 2010. (J). pap. 8.99 *(978-1-59835-129-3(X)*, BrickHouse Education) Cambridge BrickHouse, Inc.

Claybourne, Anna. Light & Dark. 2012. (Illus.). 24p. (gr. k-4). pap. 7.95 *(978-1-926853-57-4(1))* Saunders Bk. Co. CAN. Dist: RiverStream Publishing.

Coan, Sharon. Shadows, 1 vol. (Science Readers: Content & Literacy Ser.). (ENG., Illus.). 24p. (gr. 1-1). 2015. (J). 22.96 *(978-1-4938-1154-0(1))* 2014. pap. 8.99 *(978-1-4807-4567-4(7))* Teacher Created Materials, Inc.

Gregoire, Maryellen. We All Have Shadows. 2011. (Wonder Readers Emergent Level Ser.). (ENG.). (gr. -1-1). 16p. pap. 35.94 *(978-1-4296-8199-5(3))*; 32p. pap. 5.99 *(978-1-4296-7877-3(1))* Capstone Press of Coughlan Cos. (Wonder Readers).

Hall, Pamela. Discover Shadows. Yamada, Jane, illus. 2014. (Science Around Us Ser.). (ENG.). 24p. (J). (gr. -1-2). 25.64 *(978-1-62687-305-6(4)*, 207146) Child's World, Inc., The.

Higgins, Nadia. Super Shadows CD+Book. Martinez Ricci, Andres, illus. 2010. (Science Rocks! Set 2 CD+Book Ser.). 32p. lib. bdg. 54.14 incl. cd-rom *(978-1-60270-996-6(3))* ABDO Publishing Co.

—Super Shadows Site CD+Book. Martinez Ricci, Andres, illus. 2010. (Science Rocks! Set 2 Site CD+Book Ser.). 32p. lib. bdg. 84.14 incl. cd-rom *(978-1-61641-013-1(2))* ABDO Publishing Co.

Jennings, Terry. Light & Dark. 2009. (Science Alive Ser.). (Illus.). 32p. (J). (gr. 4-7). pap. *(978-1-897563-56-4(6))* Saunders Bk. Co.

Jennings, Terry J. Light & Dark. 2009. (J). 28.50 *(978-1-59920-270-9(0))* Black Rabbit Bks.

Johnson, Robin. What Are Shadows & Reflections? 2014. (ENG., Illus.). 24p. (J). *(978-0-7787-0521-5(8))* Crabtree Publishing Co.

S

Lowery, Lawrence F. Dark As a Shadow. Goldsborough, June, illus. 2014. (I Wonder Why Ser.). (ENG.). 36p. (gr. k-3). pap. 11.95 *(978-1-941316-06-1(9))* National Science Teachers Assn.

Nunn, Daniel. Shadows & Reflections, 1 vol. 2012. (Light All Around Us Ser.). (ENG.). 24p. (gr. -1-1). pap. 6.29 *(978-1-4329-6629-4(4))*; lib. bdg. 22.65 *(978-1-4329-6624-9(3))* Heinemann-Raintree. (Acorn).

Read-it! Readers en Español: La Vida de Max. 2010. (Read-it! Readers en Español).Tr. of The Life of Max. (SPA.). 134.70 *(978-1-4048-6533-4(0))* Capstone Digital.

Robertson, Charmaine. Umbrellas & Tents Make Shade. 2016. (Rosen REAL Readers: STEM & STEAM Collection). 12p. (gr. 1-k). pap. 6.33 *(978-1-5081-2443-6(4)*, Rosen Classroom) Rosen Publishing Group, Inc., The.

Royston, Angela. Light & Dark. 2012. (Science Corner Ser.). (Illus.). 24p. (J). (gr. 1-4). lib. bdg. 22.60 *(978-1-4488-5258-1(7))* Rosen Publishing Group, Inc., The.

Spilsbury, Louise & Spilsbury, Richard. Shadows. 2015. (Exploring Light Ser.). (ENG., Illus.). 32p. (gr. 2-4). 30.65 *(978-1-4109-7944-5(X))* Heinemann-Raintree.

Stott-Thornton, Janet. Shadows. Barrett, Virginia, illus. 2007. (Literacy 2000 Satellites: Stage 2 Ser.). 8p. (J). (gr. -1-3). pap. *(978-0-7327-1173-3(8)*, Rigby) Pearson Education Australia.

Tullet, Hervé. The Game of Shadows. 2013. (ENG., Illus.). 14p. 12.95 *(978-0-7148-6532-4(X))* Phaidon Pr., Inc.

SHADOWS—FICTION

Alexander, William. Ghoulish Song. (ENG., Illus.). (J). (gr. 3-7). 2014. 192p. pap. 6.99 *(978-1-4424-2730-3(2))* 2013. 176p. 16.99 *(978-1-4424-2729-7(9))* McElderry, Margaret K. Bks. (McElderry, Margaret K. Bks.).

Allen, Lisa & Sharp, Julis. Time for Bed - The Secret of Shadows: Shadow Theater Inside. Johnson, Vickie, illus. 26p. (J). (gr. -1-2). pap. *(978-1-56021-355-0(8)*, 206) W.J. Fantasy, Inc.

Alvarez, Leticia Herrera. El Pais de las Sombras. Martinez, Enrique & Graullera, Fabiola, illus. 2003. (SPA.). 48p. (J). (gr. 3-5). pap. 7.95 *(978-968-19-0535-4(0))* Santillana USA Publishing Co., Inc.

Asch, Frank. Moonbear's Shadow. Asch, Frank, illus. 2014. (Moonbear Ser.). (ENG., Illus.). 32p. (J). (gr. -1-3). 7.99 *(978-1-4424-9426-8(3)*, Aladdin) Simon & Schuster Children's Publishing.

Auerbach, Joshua. Baby Shadows, 1. Auerbach, Joshua, illus. 2003. (Illus.). 8p. (J). bds. 10.00 *(978-0-9744928-0-3(9))* Baby Shadows.

Barry, Dave & Pearson, Ridley. Peter & the Shadow Thieves. Call, Greg & Brown, Roberta, illus. rev. ed. 2007. (Peter & the Starcatchers Ser.). (ENG.). 592p. (J). (gr. 5-9). pap. 9.99 *(978-1-4231-0855-9(8)*, Disney Editions) Disney Pr.

—Peter & the Shadow Thieves. Call, Greg, illus. 2007. (Starcatchers Ser.: Bk. 2). 556p. (gr. 5-9). 19.00 *(978-0-7569-8060-3(7))* Perfection Learning Corp.

Bartalos, Michael. Shadowville. 2013. (ENG., Illus.). 32p. (J). (gr. -1-2). 16.95 *(978-1-57687-645-9(4)*, powerHouse Bks.) powerHouse Cultural Entertainment, Inc.

Cali, Davide. George & His Shadow. Bloch, Serge, illus. 2017. 40p. (J). (gr. -1-3). 17.99 ***(978-0-06-256830-4(2))*** HarperCollins Pubs.

Calvert, Deanna. Las Sombras. Lester, Mike, illus. 2005. (Rookie Reader Español Ser.). (SPA & ESP.). 23p. (J). (gr. k-2). per. 4.95 *(978-0-516-24697-0(6)*, Children's Pr.) Scholastic Library Publishing.

—Shadows. Lester, Mike, illus. 2004. (Rookie Readers Ser.). 23p. (J). 12.60 *(978-0-7569-4333-2(7))* Perfection Learning Corp.

Castro, Adam-Troy. Gustav Gloom & the Four Terrors. Margiotta, Kristen, illus. 2013. (Gustav Gloom Ser.: 3). (ENG.). 248p. (J). (gr. 3-7). 12.99 *(978-0-448-45835-9(7)*, Grosset & Dunlap) Penguin Young Readers Group.

—Gustav Gloom & the Nightmare Vault, No. 2. Margiotta, Kristen, illus. 2013. (Gustav Gloom Ser.: 2). (ENG.). 248p. (J). (gr. 3-7). 12.99 *(978-0-448-45834-2(9)*, Grosset & Dunlap) Penguin Young Readers Group.

—Gustav Gloom & the Nightmare Vault #2. Margiotta, Kristen, illus. 2014. (Gustav Gloom Ser.: 2). (ENG.). 248p. (J). (gr. 3-7). 7.99 *(978-0-448-48329-0(7)*, Grosset & Dunlap) Penguin Young Readers Group.

—Gustav Gloom & the People Taker. Margiotta, Kristen, illus. 2012. (Gustav Gloom Ser.: 1). (ENG.). 232p. (J). (gr. 3-7). 12.99 *(978-0-448-45833-5(0)*, Grosset & Dunlap) Penguin Young Readers Group.

Castro, Adam-Troy & dePaola, Tomie. Gustav Gloom & the Cryptic Carousel #4. Margiotta, Kristen, illus. 2015. (Gustav Gloom Ser.: 4). (ENG.). 248p. (J). (gr. 3-7). 7.99 *(978-0-448-48719-9(5)*, Grosset & Dunlap) Penguin Young Readers Group.

Cosgrove, Stephen. Snugg N. Flitter: Facing Your Fears. Arroyo, Fian, illus. 2004. (J). *(978-1-58804-377-1(0))* P C I Education.

Cuevas, Michelle. Smoot: A Rebellious Shadow. Smith, Sydney , illus. 2017. (ENG.). 48p. (J). (gr. -1-3). 17.99 ***(978-0-525-42969-2(7)***, Dial Bks) Penguin Young Readers Group.

Cummings, Troy. Attack of the Shadow Smashers. 2013. (Notebook of Doom Ser.: 3). (ENG.). 96p. (J). (gr. 1-3). pap. 4.99 *(978-0-545-55297-4(4))* Scholastic, Inc.

—Attack of the Shadow Smashers. 2013. (Notebook of Doom Ser.: 3). lib. bdg. 14.75 *(978-0-606-32369-7(4)*, Turtleback) Turtleback Bks.

Cyr, Joe. Shadi, the Shadow Who Wanted to Be Free. Owen, Ramon, illus. 2010. 40p. pap. 14.95 *(978-1-936343-08-9(8))* Peppertree Pr., The.

Diamond, Donna. The Shadow. Diamond, Donna, illus. 2010. (ENG., Illus.). 32p. (J). (gr. k-3). 15.99 *(978-0-7636-4878-7(7))* Candlewick Pr.

Flynn, S. E. That Night. 2009. 24p. pap. 11.95 *(978-1-4389-6699-1(7))* AuthorHouse.

Freeman, Don. Gregory's Shadow. Freeman, Don, illus. 2003. (Illus.). pap. 39.95 incl. audio compact disk *(978-1-59112-536-5(7))* Live Oak Media.

Gordon, Amy. The Shadow Collector's Apprentice. 2012. (ENG.). 208p. (J). 16.95 *(978-0-8234-2359-0(X))* Holiday Hse., Inc.

Grant, Holly. The League of Beastly Dreadfuls. 2015. (League of Beastly Dreadfuls Ser.: Bk. 1). (ENG., Illus.). 320p. (J). (gr. 3-7). 16.99 *(978-0-385-37007-3(5)*, Random Hse. Bks. for Young Readers) Random Hse. Children's Bks.

Graves, Jennifer. Ava's Awful Fright! 2009. 28p. pap. 15.99 *(978-1-4415-0482-1(6))* Xlibris Corp.

Gundel, Jean. The Mystery Key at Camp Green Meadow. Robertson, R. H., illus. 2011. (J). pap. 14.95 *(978-1-59571-730-6(7))* Word Association Pubs.

Hatfield, Ruth. The Book of Shadows. 2017. (Book of Storms Trilogy Ser.: 3). (ENG., Illus.). 288p. (J). 16.99 *(978-1-62779-003-1(9)*, 9781627790031, Holt, Henry & Co. Bks. For Young Readers) Holt, Henry & Co.

Hayward, Linda. Monster Bug. Palmisciano, Diane, illus. 2004. 32p. (J). lib. bdg. 20.00 *(978-1-4242-1097-8(6))* Fitzgerald Bks.

—Monster Bug. Palmisciano, Diane, illus. 2004. (Science Solves It Ser.). 32p. (gr. -1-3). 15.00 *(978-0-7569-4313-4(2))* Perfection Learning Corp.

Hegarty, Patricia. Who's There? Beware! 2015. (Amazing Changing Pictures! Ser.). (ENG.). 14p. (J). (gr. -1-3). 12.99 *(978-1-68010-000-6(9))* Tiger Tales.

Hodgkinson, Leigh. Boris & the Wrong Shadow. 2012. (ENG.). 32p. (J). pap. *(978-1-58925-434-3(1))* Tiger Tales.

Hopkins, Douglas. Princess June & the Shadow Pirates, 1 vol. 2007. (ENG., Illus.). 32p. (J). (gr. -1-2). per. 8.95 *(978-1-894294-88-1(2)*, Tuckamore Bks) Creative Bk. Publishing CAN. Dist: Orca Bk. Pubs. USA.

Leathers, Philippa. The Black Rabbit. Leathers, Philippa, illus. (ENG., Illus.). 40p. (J). (gr. -1-2). 2016. 6.99 *(978-0-7636-8879-0(7))* 2013. 14.00 *(978-0-7636-5714-7(X))* Candlewick Pr.

Long, Greg & Edmundson, Chris. Yeti, Turn Out the Light! Kirwan, Wednesday, illus. 2013. (ENG.). 36p. (J). (gr. -1-k). 12.99 *(978-1-4521-1158-2(6))* Chronicle Bks. LLC.

McKinley, Robin. Shadows. 2013. 356p. (YA). *(978-0-399-25625-7(3))* Penguin Publishing Group.

Meomi (Firm) Staff. The Octonauts & the Sea of Shade. 2007. (Octonauts Ser.). (ENG., Illus.). 36p. (J). (gr. k-2). 15.95 *(978-1-59702-010-7(9))* Immedium.

Mitchell, Saundra, et al. Defy the Dark. 2013. (ENG.). 496p. (YA). (gr. 8). 17.99 *(978-0-06-212354-1(8))*; pap. 9.99 *(978-0-06-212353-4(X))* HarperCollins Pubs. (HarperTeen).

Powell, Jillian. Henry & the Hand-Me-Downs. Worsley, Belinda, illus. 2005. 32p. (J). lib. bdg. 9.00 *(978-1-4242-0866-9(6))* Fitzgerald Bks.

Reade, O. K. The Little Girl & Her Shadow. 2015. (Illus.). (J). 12.99 *(978-1-4621-1618-8(3))* Cedar Fort, Inc./CFI Distribution.

Rice, Clay. The Lonely Shadow. 2013. (ENG., Illus.). 64p. (J). (gr. k-4). 19.95 *(978-1-938301-08-7(0))* Familius LLC.

Rogers-Busboom, Kimberly. My Secret Best Friend. Dee, Kati, illus. 2009. 24p. lib. bdg. 16.99 *(978-0-9823145-2-4(3))* Dirks Publishing, LLC.

Stack, David Martin. Good Morning Captain. 2009. 58p. pap. 10.99 *(978-0-557-06575-2(5))* Lulu Pr., Inc.

Valente, Catherynne M. The Girl Who Fell Beneath Fairyland & Led the Revels There. Juan, Ana, illus. 2013. (Fairyland Ser.: 2). (ENG.). 304p. (YA). (gr. 5-9). pap. 7.99 *(978-1-250-03412-0(4)*, 9781250034120) Square Fish.

Young, Timothy. Shadows on My Wall, 1 vol. 2012. (ENG., Illus.). 36p. (J). 16.99 *(978-0-7643-4224-0(X)*, 9780764342240) Schiffer Publishing, Ltd.

Zafón, Carlos Ruiz. The Watcher in the Shadows. (ENG.). (YA). (gr. 7-17). 2014. 288p. pap. 10.99 *(978-0-316-04475-2(X))* 2013. 272p. 18.00 *(978-0-316-04476-9(8))* Little, Brown Bks. for Young Readers.

Zarraonandia, Thomas. Johnny Jingle. Zarraonandia, Thomas, illus. 2nd ed. 2003. (Illus.). 30p. (J). (gr. -1-7). per. 20.00 *(978-0-9741070-0-4(X))* Zarraonandia, Anne.

SHAKERS

Bial, Raymond. The Shaker Village. 2008. (ENG., Illus.). 48p. 24.95 *(978-0-8131-2489-6(1))* Univ. Pr. of Kentucky.

Pérez-Reverte, Arturo. The Queen of the South. 2004. (Illus.). 384p. (J). (gr. 2-5). pap. *(978-0-9655018-2-8(5))* Knot Garden Pr.

Raschka, Chris. Simple Gifts. Raschka, Chris, illus. 2003. (Illus.). pap. 43.95 incl. audio compact disk *(978-1-59112-604-1(5))*; pap. 41.95 incl. audio *(978-0-87499-642-5(2))* Live Oak Media.

Thorne-Thomsen, Kathleen. A Shaker's Dozen: Counting Book. Thorne-Thomsen, Kathleen, illus. Rocheleau, Paul, photos by. 2003. (Illus.). 27p. (J). (gr. k-13). reprint ed. 16.00 *(978-0-7567-9041-7(7))* DIANE Publishing Co.

Turner, Ann Warren. Shaker Hearts. Minor, Wendell, illus. 2006. 35p. (J). (gr. 4-8). pap. 11.00 *(978-1-4223-5856-6(9))* DIANE Publishing Co.

SHAKESPEARE, WILLIAM, 1564-1616

Adams, Jennifer. Romeo & Juliet: A Babylit Counting Primer, 1 vol. Oliver, Alison, illus. 2011. (ENG.). 22p. (J). (gr. k-1). bds. 9.99 *(978-1-4236-2205-5(7))* Gibbs Smith, Publisher.

All's Well That Ends Well. 2010. (Bloom's Shakespeare Through the Ages Ser.). 240p. (C). (gr. 9-18). 50.00 *(978-1-60413-708-8(8)*, Chelsea Hse.) Facts On File, Inc.

Bailey, Gerry & Foster, Karen. Shakespeare's Quill. Radford, Karen & Noyes, Leighton, illus. 2008. (Stories of Great People Ser.). (ENG.). 40p. (J). (gr. 3-7). lib. bdg. *(978-0-7787-3691-2(1))*; pap. *(978-0-7787-3713-1(6))* Crabtree Publishing Co.

Berne, Emma Carlson. William Shakespeare: Playwright & Poet, 1 vol. 2008. (Essential Lives Set 2 Ser.). (ENG., Illus.). 112p. (J). (gr. 6-12). lib. bdg. 35.64 *(978-1-60453-042-1(1))* ABDO Publishing Co.

Bingham, Jane. Shakespeare. 2017. (Explore! Ser.). (ENG., Illus.). 32p. (J). (gr. 4-6). pap. 11.99 *(978-0-7502-9404-1(3)*, Wayland) Hachette Children's Group GBR. Dist: Hachette Bk. Group.

Bloom, Harold & Marson, Janyce, eds. A Midsummer Night's Dream. 2008. (Bloom's Shakespeare Through the Ages Ser.). 260p. (YA). (gr. 9-12). 50.00 *(978-0-7910-9595-9(9))* Facts On File, Inc.

Carew-Miller, Anna. William Shakespeare: Great English Playwright & Poet. (Illus.). 32p. (J). 2013. (People of Importance Ser.: 21). (gr. 4-18). 19.95 *(978-1-4222-2859-3(2))* 2004. (Great Names Ser.). (gr. 3-18). lib. bdg. 19.95 *(978-1-59084-157-0(3))* Mason Crest.

Claybourne, A. & Treays, R. World of Shakespeare. 2004. (Internet-Linked Library of Science). (Illus.). (J). (ENG.). 1p. pap. 9.95 *(978-0-7945-0014-6(5)*, Usborne); 64p. lib. bdg. 17.95 *(978-1-58086-391-9(4))* EDC Publishing.

Claybourne, Anna. Where's Will? Find Shakespeare Hidden in His Plays. Tilly, illus. 2015. (J). *(978-1-61067-407-2(3))* Kane Miller.

Cooke, Tim. William Shakespeare. 2016. (Meet the Greats Ser.). 00048p. (J). pap. 14.05 ***(978-1-4824-5964-7(7))*** Stevens, Gareth Publishing LLLP.

Crystal, David & Crystal, Ben. Oxford Illustrated Shakespeare Dictionary. 2015. (ENG., Illus.). 352p. pap. 17.95 *(978-0-19-273750-2(3))* Oxford Univ. Pr., Inc.

Davidson, Rebecca Piatt. All the World's a Stage. Lobel, Anita, illus. 2003. 32p. (J). 16.89 *(978-0-06-029627-8(5))* HarperCollins Pubs.

Dickins, Rosie. William Shakespeare - Internet Referenced. 2008. (Young Reading Series 3 Gift Books - Famous Lives Ser.). 64p. (J). 8.99 *(978-0-7945-2096-0(0)*, Usborne) EDC Publishing.

Doder, Joshua. Time Traveler's Guide to Shakespeare's London. 2004. (Timetraveller's Guides). (ENG., Illus.). 96p. (J). pap. 8.99 *(978-1-904153-10-8(0))* Watling St., Ltd. GBR. Dist: Independent Pubs. Group.

Dorling Kindersley Publishing Staff. Shakespeare. 2015. (DK Eyewitness Bks.). (ENG., Illus.). 72p. (J). (gr. 3-7). pap. 9.99 *(978-1-4654-3185-1(3)*, DK Children) Dorling Kindersley Publishing, Inc.

Fandel, Jennifer. Voices in Poetry: William Shakespeare. 2015. (Voices in Poetry Ser.). (ENG.). 48p. (J). (gr. 5-8). pap. 12.00 *(978-1-62832-056-5(7)*, Creative Paperbacks) Creative Co., The.

—William Shakespeare. 2014. (J). *(978-1-60818-328-9(9))* 2003. (Illus.). 48p. 19.95 *(978-1-58341-283-1(2))* Creative Co., The. (Creative Education).

Fischel, Emma. William Shakespeare. Remphry, Martin, illus. 2010. (Famous People, Famous Lives Ser.). (KOR.). 46p. (J). *(978-89-491-8826-3(0))* Biryongso Publishing Co.

Fowler, Will S. Shakespeare: His Life & Plays. 2nd ed. 2008. (ENG., Illus.). 72p. pap. 11.99 ***(978-1-4058-8231-6(X))*** Pearson Education.

Gill, Roma & Shakespeare, William. Measure for Measure. 2nd ed. 2013. (Oxford School Shakespeare Ser.). (ENG., Illus.). 176p. pap. 9.95 *(978-0-19-839335-1(0))* Oxford Univ. Pr., Inc.

Hill Nettleton, Pamela. William Shakespeare: The Inspiring Life Story of the Playwright Extraordinaire. 2016. (Inspiring Stories Ser.). (ENG., Illus.). 112p. (gr. 5-7). lib. bdg. 35.99 *(978-0-7565-5163-6(3)*, CPB Grades 4-8) Compass Point Bks.

Hilliam, David. William Shakespeare: England's Greatest Playwright & Poet. (Rulers, Scholars, & Artists of the Renaissance Ser.). 112p. 2009. (gr. 5-8). 66.50 *(978-1-60852-945-2(2)*, Rosen Reference) 2004. (Illus.). lib. bdg. 34.60 *(978-1-4042-0318-1(4))* Rosen Publishing Group, Inc., The.

Johnson, Robin. William Shakespeare. 2016. (ENG., Illus.). 48p. (J). pap. *(978-0-7787-2229-8(5))* Crabtree Publishing Co.

Lamb, Charles & Lamb, Mary. Shakespeare Cuenta. 6th ed. (SPA., Illus.). 136p. (YA). (gr. 5-8). 7.96 *(978-84-239-8860-0(0))* Espasa Calpe, S.A. ESP. Dist: Lectorum Pubns., Inc.

Lamb, Mary. Shakespeare Cuenta. 2003. (Advanced Reading Ser.). (SPA.). 136p. (J). (gr. 5-8). 11.95 *(978-84-239-7082-7(5)*, EC3412) Espasa Calpe, S.A. ESP. Dist: Planeta Publishing Corp., Lectorum Pubns., Inc.

Lebscky, Ibi. William. Cardoni, Paolo, illus. (Coleccion Seran Famosos).Tr. of Little Wm. Shakespeare. (SPA.). 28p. (J). (gr. 2-4). 10.36 *(978-84-233-1663-2(7))* Ediciones Destino ESP. Dist: Lectorum Pubns., Inc.

Maloof, Torrey. Stepping into William Shakespeare's World. 2017. (Time for Kids Nonfiction Readers Ser.). lib. bdg. 20.85 ***(978-0-606-40286-6(1))*** Turtleback Bks.

—Stepping into William Shakespeare's World (Grade 7) 2017. (TIME for KIDS(r) Nonfiction Readers Ser.). (Illus.). 48p. (J). (gr. 7-7). pap. 9.99 ***(978-1-4938-3618-5(8))*** Teacher Created Materials, Inc.

Manning, Mick. William Shakespeare. Granstrom, Brita, illus. 2015. (ENG.). 48p. (J). (gr. -1-2). 19.99 *(978-1-84780-345-0(8)*, Frances Lincoln) Quarto Publishing Group UK GBR. Dist: Hachette Bk. Group.

—William Shakespeare: Scenes from the Life of the World's Greatest Writer. Granström, Brita, illus. 2017. (ENG.). 48p. (J). (gr. 3-7). pap. 11.99 *(978-1-84780-759-5(3)*, Frances Lincoln Children's Bks.) Quarto Publishing Group UK GBR. Dist: Hachette Bk. Group.

Mannis, Celeste Davidson & Davidson, Mannis. Who Was William Shakespeare? O'brien, John, illus. 2006. (Who Was? Ser.). (ENG.). 112p. (J). (gr. 3-7). pap. 5.99 *(978-0-448-43904-4(2)*, Grosset & Dunlap) Penguin Young Readers Group.

Mannis, Celeste Davidson & Kramer, Sydelle. Who Was William Shakespeare? O'brien, John, illus. 2006. (Who Was... ? Ser.). 105p. (gr. 2-6). 15.00 *(978-0-7569-6952-3(2))* Perfection Learning Corp.

Mayhew, James & Ryan, Patrick. Shakespeare's Storybook. 2011. (ENG., Illus.). 120p. (J). (gr. 4-6). pap. 12.99 *(978-1-84686-541-1(7))* Barefoot Bks., Inc.

Middleton, Haydn. True Lives Shakespeare. 2009. (True Lives Ser.). (ENG., Illus.). 32p. (J). pap. 6.99 *(978-0-19-911968-4(6))* Oxford Univ. Pr., Inc.

Mittelstaedt, Walt. A Student's Guide to William Shakespeare. 2005. (Understanding Literature Ser.). (Illus.). 192p. (YA). lib. bdg. 29.27 *(978-0-7660-2284-3(6))* Enslow Pubs., Inc.

Mulherin, Jennifer & Frost, Abigail. Richard III. 2003. (Shakespeare for Everyone Ser.). (ENG., Illus.). 32p. (J). (gr. 4-7). pap. 11.99 *(978-1-84234-049-3(2))* Evans Brothers, Ltd. GBR. Dist: Independent Pubs. Group.

Mussari, Mark. The Sonnets. 2010. (Shakespeare Explained 3 Ser.). (Illus.). 112p. (gr. 7-18). 42.79 *(978-1-60870-018-9(6))* Marshall Cavendish GBR. Dist: Marshall Cavendish Corp.

Nesbit, E. Shakespeare Retold. Caparo, Antonio Javier, illus. 2016. 128p. (J). (gr. 1-5). 19.99 *(978-0-06-240453-4(9))* HarperCollins Pubs.

Page, Philip & Petit, Marilyn. Richard III. 2005. (ENG., Illus.). 64p. pap. *(978-0-340-88811-7(3))* Cambridge Univ. Pr.

Purkiss, Sue. The Life & Times of William Shakespeare: Band 18/Pearl. 2017. (ENG., Illus.). 80p. (J). pap. 9.99 ***(978-0-00-820898-1(0))*** HarperCollins Pubs. Ltd. GBR. Dist: Independent Pubs. Group.

Raum, Elizabeth. Twenty-First Century Shakespeare. 2010. (Culture in Action Ser.). (ENG.). 32p. (gr. 3-6). 30.65 *(978-1-4109-3920-3(0)*, NA-r) Heinemann-Raintree.

Rosen, Michael. Shakespeare: His Work & His World. Ingpen, Robert R., illus. 2006. (ENG.). 96p. (J). (gr. 7-11). pap. 10.99 *(978-0-7636-3201-4(5))* Candlewick Pr.

Ryan, Patrick. Shakespeare's Storybook: Folk Tales That Inspired the Bard. Mayhew, James, illus. (ENG.). (J). 2009. 21.99 *(978-1-84686-271-7(X))* 2006. 80p. (gr. 4-7). pap. 16.99 *(978-1-905236-86-2(7))* Barefoot Bks., Inc.

Saddleback Educational Publishing Staff, ed. A Midsummer Night's Dream. 2011. (Timeless Shakespeare Ser.). (ENG.). 48p. (YA). (gr. 9-12). pupil's gde. ed. 19.95 incl. cd-rom *(978-1-61651-164-7(8))* Saddleback Educational Publishing, Inc.

—Twelfth Night. 2011. (Timeless Shakespeare Ser.). (ENG.). 48p. (YA). (gr. 9-12). pupil's gde. ed. 19.95 incl. cd-rom *(978-1-61651-168-5(0))* Saddleback Educational Publishing, Inc.

Shakespeare, William. Romeo & Juliet: The Inessential Shakespeare. 2003. 52p. (J). (gr. 8-12). pap. 7.00 *(978-0-948662-02-7(6))* Kabet Pr. GBR. Dist: Empire Publishing Service.

—The Tempest. 2008. (Shakespeare Ser.: Level 2). (Illus.). 72p. pap., act. bk. ed. 10.95 *(978-1-55576-327-5(8)*, EDSC-201B) EDCON Publishing Group.

—Twelfth Night: The Inessential Shakespeare. Hort, John & Hort, Leela, eds. 2003. 52p. (YA). (gr. 8-12). pap. 7.00 *(978-0-948662-00-3(X))* Kabet Pr. GBR. Dist: Empire Publishing Service.

Shakespeare, William, et al. Hamlet. (Classics Illustrated Ser.). (Illus.). 52p. (YA). pap. 4.95 *(978-1-57209-004-0(9))* Classics International Entertainment, Inc.

Shuter, Jane. Shakespeare Today, 1 vol. 2014. (Shakespeare Alive Ser.). (ENG.). 64p. (gr. 7-8). lib. bdg. 37.32 *(978-1-4329-9631-4(2))* Heinemann-Raintree.

Shuter, Paul. William Shakespeare: A Man for All Times, 1 vol. 2014. (Shakespeare Alive Ser.). (ENG.). 80p. (gr. 7-8). lib. bdg. 37.32 *(978-1-4329-9629-1(0))* Heinemann-Raintree.

Stanley, Diane & Vennema, Peter. Bard of Avon. Stanley, Diane, illus. 2015. (ENG., Illus.). 48p. (J). (gr. 1-5). pap. 7.99 *(978-0-06-241925-5(0))* HarperCollins Pubs.

Whiting, Jim. William Shakespeare. 2007. (Poets & Playwrights Ser.). (Illus.). 112p. (J). (gr. 3-7). lib. bdg. 37.10 *(978-1-58415-426-6(8))* Mitchell Lane Pubs., Inc.

Williams, Colleen Madonna Flood. My Adventure with Shakespeare. 2009. (ENG.). 44p. (J). 8.99 *(978-1-59092-467-9(3))* Blue Forge Pr.

SHAKESPEARE, WILLIAM, 1564-1616—ADAPTATIONS

Barlow, Steve L. & Skidmore, Steve. The Lost Title of Shakespeare's Ghost Play. 2011. (ENG., Illus.). 128p. (J). pap. 7.99 *(978-0-00-694588-8(0)*, HarperCollins Children's Bks.) HarperCollins Pubs. Ltd. GBR. Dist: HarperCollins Pubs.

Blackman, Malorie. Naughts & Crosses. 2005. (ENG., Illus.). 400p. (YA). (gr. 9-18). 18.99 *(978-1-4169-0016-0(0)*, Simon & Schuster Bks. For Young Readers) Simon & Schuster Bks. For Young Readers.

Fearn, Laura. Usborne Stories from Shakespeare. Temporin, Elena, illus. 2006. 191p. pap. *(978-0-439-88984-1(7))* Scholastic, Inc.

Garfield, Leon. Leon Garfield's Shakespeare Stories. Foreman, Michael, illus. 2015. (ENG.). 576p. (J). (gr. 5). 24.95 *(978-1-59017-931-4(5)*, NYR Children's Collection) New York Review of Bks., Inc., The.

Hinds, Gareth. Romeo & Juliet. Hinds, Gareth, illus. 2013. (ENG., Illus.). 144p. (YA). (gr. 7). 21.99 *(978-0-7636-5948-6(7))*; pap. 12.99 *(978-0-7636-6807-5(9))* Candlewick Pr.

—Romeo & Juliet (Graphic Adaptation) 2013. lib. bdg. 24.50 *(978-0-606-32098-6(9)*, Turtleback) Turtleback Bks.

Lamb, Charles. Tales from Shakespeare, 2 vols. 2013. 425p. reprint ed. lthr. 69.00 *(978-0-7426-2085-8(9))* Classic Bks.

Lamb, Charles & Lamb, Mary. Tales from Shakespeare. Jolivet, Joëlle, illus. 2007. (ENG.). 180p. (gr. 8-17). 21.95 *(978-0-8109-9453-9(4)*, Abrams Image) Abrams, Inc.

—Tales from Shakespeare. 2007. (ENG., Illus.). 352p. (gr. 12-18). 6.95 *(978-0-451-53064-6(0)*, Signet) Penguin Publishing Group.

Nesbit, E. Shakespeare's Stories for Young Readers. 2006. (Dover Children's Classics Ser.). (ENG.). 80p. (YA). (gr. 3-8). per. 4.99 *(978-0-486-44762-9(6))* Dover Pubns., Inc.

Page, Philip & Petit, Marilyn, eds. Romeo & Juliet. Page, Philip, illus. 2005. (Picture This! Shakespeare Ser.). (ENG., Illus.). 64p. per. 8.99 *(978-0-7641-3144-8(3))* Barron's Educational Series, Inc.

Robert, Thando Bint, adapted by. Macbeth: Dual Language Set. 2004. (J). cd-rom *(978-1-84444-473-1(2))*; cd-rom *(978-1-84444-476-2(7))*; cd-rom *(978-1-84444-475-5(9))*; cd-rom *(978-1-84444-474-8(0))*; cd-rom *(978-1-84444-472-4(4))*; cd-rom *(978-1-84444-471-7(6))*; cd-rom *(978-1-84444-470-0(8))*; cd-rom *(978-1-84444-469-4(4))* Mantra Lingua.

Rokison, Abigail. Shakespeare for Young People: Productions, Versions & Adaptations. 2013. (ENG.). 256p. pap. 35.95 *(978-1-4411-2556-9(6)*, 9781441125569) Bloomsbury Academic & Professional.

Rokison, Abigail & Rokison-Woodall, Abigail. Shakespeare for Young People: Productions, Versions & Adaptations. 2013. (ENG.). 256p. 122.00 *(978-1-4411-7228-0(9)*, 9781441172280) Bloomsbury Academic & Professional.

Ross, Lesley & Shakespeare, William. 40 Minute Tempest. 2003. (Plays for Young People Ser.). (ENG.). 96p. pap. 16.95 *(978-1-84002-313-8(9))* Oberon Bks., Ltd. GBR. Dist: Consortium Bk. Sales & Distribution.

Shakespeare, William. As You Like It: Classicscript. Landes, William-Alan, ed. abr. ed. 2003. (Shakespeare Ser.: Vol. 2). 60p. (YA). (gr. 4-12). pap. 7.00 *(978-0-88734-532-6(8))* Players Pr., Inc.

—The Comedy of Errors: Graphic Novel, 1 vol. Espinosa, Rod, illus. 2010. (Graphic Shakespeare Set 2 Ser.). (ENG.). 48p. (J). (gr. 5-9). 29.93 *(978-1-60270-762-7(6))* ABDO Publishing Co.

—Cymbeline: Graphic Novel, 1 vol. Perry, Fred, illus. 2010. (Graphic Shakespeare Set 2 Ser.). (ENG.). 48p. (J). (gr. 5-9). 29.93 *(978-1-60270-763-4(4))* ABDO Publishing Co.

—Henry VIII: Graphic Novel, 1 vol. Allen, Chris, illus. 2010. (Graphic Shakespeare Set 2 Ser.). (ENG.). 48p. (J). (gr. 5-9). 29.93 *(978-1-60270-764-1(2))* ABDO Publishing Co.

—Julius Caesar: Graphic Novel, 1 vol. Perry, Fred, illus. 2010. (Graphic Shakespeare Set 2 Ser.). (ENG.). 48p. (J). (gr. 5-9). 29.93 *(978-1-60270-765-8(0))* ABDO Publishing Co.

—King Lear. 2006. (Classics Ser.). (Illus.). (YA). 48p. per. *(978-1-56254-854-4(9))*; 96p. per. *(978-1-56254-853-7(0))* Saddleback Educational Publishing, Inc.

—Twelfth Night: Classicscript. Landes, William-Alan, ed. abr. ed. 2003. (Shakespeare Ser.: Vol. 3). 68p. (YA). (gr. 4-12). pap. 7.00 *(978-0-88734-530-2(1))* Players Pr., Inc.

Williams, Marcia & Shakespeare, William. Tales from Shakespeare. Williams, Marcia, illus. 2004. (ENG., Illus.). 40p. (J). (gr. 3-7). reprint ed. pap. 7.99 *(978-0-7636-2323-4(7))* Candlewick Pr.

Young, Eleanor Patmore, ed. Shakespeare for Young Actors. 2011. 284p. 48.95 *(978-1-258-08532-2(1))* Literary Licensing, LLC.

SHAKESPEARE, WILLIAM, 1564-1616—ANTONY AND CLEOPATRA

Shakespeare, William. Antony & Cleopatra. Heims, Neil & Bloom, Harold, eds. 2008. (Bloom's Shakespeare Through the Ages Ser.). 290p. (YA). (gr. 9-12). 50.00 *(978-0-7910-9630-7(0))* Facts On File, Inc.

SHAKESPEARE, WILLIAM, 1564-1616—AS YOU LIKE IT

Naden, Corinne J. As You Like It. 2010. (Shakespeare Explained 3 Ser.). (Illus.). 112p. (gr. 7-18). 42.79 *(978-1-60870-015-8(1))* Marshall Cavendish Corp.

Shakespeare, William. As You Like It. Brady, Linzy, ed. 3rd rev. ed. 2015. (Cambridge School Shakespeare Ser.). (ENG., Illus.). 216p. pap. 12.19 *(978-1-107-67512-4(X))* Cambridge Univ. Pr.

—As You Like It: Classicscript. Landes, William-Alan, ed. abr. ed. 2003. (Shakespeare Ser.: Vol. 2). 60p. (YA). (gr. 4-12). pap. 7.00 *(978-0-88734-532-6(8))* Players Pr., Inc.

Shakespeare, William & Gill, Roma. As You Like It. 2009. (Oxford School Shakespeare Ser.). (ENG., Illus.). 160p. pap. 9.95 *(978-0-19-832869-8(9))* Oxford Univ. Pr., Inc.

SHAKESPEARE, WILLIAM, 1564-1616—CRITICISM AND INTERPRETATION

Andersen, Richard. Richard III. 2010. (Shakespeare Explained 3 Ser.). (Illus.). 112p. (J). (gr. 7-18). 42.79 *(978-1-60870-017-2(8))* Marshall Cavendish Corp.

Gleed, Paul. Bloom's How to Write about William Shakespeare. 2007. (Bloom's How to Write about Literature Ser.). 244p. (C). (gr. 9-18). 45.00 *(978-0-7910-9484-6(7)*, Chelsea Hse.) Facts On File, Inc.

Haugen, David M. Sexality in the Comedies of Shakesprear. Gale, ed. 2014. (Social Issues in Literature Ser.). (ENG., Illus.). 224p. (J). (gr. 7-12). lib. bdg. 46.40 *(978-0-7377-6982-1(3)*, Greenhaven Pr., Inc.) Cengage Gale.

Kesselring, Mari. How to Analyze the Works of William Shakespeare, 1 vol. 2012. (Essential Critiques Set 3 Ser.). (ENG.). 112p. (J). (gr. 6-12). lib. bdg. 35.64 *(978-1-61783-460-8(2)*, Essential Library) ABDO Publishing Co.

Mittelstaedt, Walt. Reading & Interpreting the Works of William Shakespeare. 2016. (Lit Crit Guides). 176p. (J). (gr. 6-6). 39.93 *(978-0-7660-7912-0(0))* Enslow Pubs., Inc.

Rokison, Abigail. Shakespeare for Young People: Productions, Versions & Adaptations. 2013. (ENG.). 256p. pap. 35.95 *(978-1-4411-2556-9(6)*, 9781441125569) Bloomsbury Academic & Professional.

Rokison, Abigail & Rokison-Woodall, Abigail. Shakespeare for Young People: Productions, Versions & Adaptations. 2013. (ENG.). 256p. 122.00 *(978-1-4411-7228-0(9)*, 9781441172280) Bloomsbury Academic & Professional.

Warren, Rebecca & Shakespeare, William. Othello. 2nd ed. 2003. (ENG., Illus.). 152p. pap. 20.00 *(978-0-582-78431-4(X))* Pearson Education, Ltd. GBR. Dist: Trans-Atlantic Pubns., Inc.

SHAKESPEARE, WILLIAM, 1564-1616—FICTION

Blackwood, Gary. Shakespeare's Spy. 2005. 281p. (gr. 5-9). 17.00 *(978-0-7569-5216-7(6))* Perfection Learning Corp.

Blackwood, Gary L. Shakespeare's Spy. 2005. (ENG.). 288p. (J). (gr. 3-7). 6.99 *(978-0-14-240311-2(3)*, Puffin Books) Penguin Young Readers Group.

Booth, Molly. Saving Hamlet. 2016. (ENG.). 352p. (YA). (gr. 7-12). 17.99 *(978-1-4847-5274-6(0))* Hyperion Bks. for Children.

Bowe, Julie. So Much Drama. 2016. (Victoria Torres, Unfortunately Average Ser.). (ENG., Illus.). 160p. (gr. 4-4). pap. 5.95 *(978-1-4965-3807-9(2))*; lib. bdg. 26.65 *(978-1-4965-3799-7(8))* Stone Arch Bks.

Broach, Elise. Shakespeare's Secret. 2007. (Illus.). 258p. (gr. 4-9). 17.00 *(978-0-7569-8204-1(9))* Perfection Learning Corp.

—Shakespeare's Secret. 2007. (ENG.). 272p. (YA). (gr. 5-10). per. 7.99 *(978-0-312-37132-6(2)*, 9780312371326) Square Fish.

—Shakespeare's Secret. l.t. ed. 2006. (Thorndike Literacy Bridge Ser.). (Illus.). 263p. (J). (gr. 5-10). 22.95 *(978-0-7862-8735-2(7))* Thorndike Pr.

Castle, M. E. Fakespeare: Something Stinks in Hamlet. Jennewein, Daniel, illus. 2017. (J). pap. ***(978-1-250-10157-0(3))*** St. Martin's Pr.

—Fakespeare: Starcrossed in Romeo & Juliet. Jennewein, Daniel, illus. 2017. (J). pap. ***(978-1-250-10160-0(3))*** St. Martin's Pr.

—Fakespeare: Something Stinks in Hamlet. Jennewein, Daniel, illus. 2017. (Fakespeare Ser.: 1). (ENG.). 272p. (J). 13.99 *(978-1-250-10159-4(X)*, 9781250101594) Imprint IND. Dist: Macmillan.

—Starcrossed in Romeo & Juliet. Jennewein, Daniel, illus. 2017. (Fakespeare Ser.: 2). (ENG.). 304p. (J). 13.99 *(978-1-250-10162-4(X)*, 9781250101624) Imprint IND. Dist: Macmillan.

Cohen, Paula Marantz. Beatrice Bunson's Guide to Romeo & Juliet. 2016. (ENG.). 200p. (J). (gr. 4-9). pap. 11.95 *(978-1-58988-105-1(2))* Dry, Paul Bks., Inc.

Dakos, Kalli & DesMarteau, Alicia. Our Principal Promised to Kiss a Pig. DiRocco, Carl, illus. (ENG.). 32p. (J). 2017. (gr. -1-3). pap. 7.99 ***(978-0-8075-6635-0(7))*** 2004. (gr. 2-5). 16.99 *(978-0-8075-6629-9(2))* Whitman, Albert & Co.

Dionne, Erin. The Total Tragedy of a Girl Named Hamlet. 2011. (ENG.). 304p. (J). (gr. 3-7). 8.99 *(978-0-14-241748-5(3)*, Puffin Books) Penguin Young Readers Group.

Durrant, George D. Shakespeare's Best Work: A Novel of Unexpected Family Ties & Uncommon Faith. 2003. 130p. pap. 10.95 *(978-1-55517-709-6(3)*, 77093) Cedar Fort, Inc./CFI Distribution.

Fisher, Linda C. Runaway Will. 2010. (J). pap. *(978-0-88092-720-8(8))* Royal Fireworks Publishing Co.

—A Will of Her Own. 2006. (YA). pap. *(978-0-88092-641-6(4))*; lib. bdg. *(978-0-88092-640-9(6))* Royal Fireworks Publishing Co.

Gonzalez, Jorge & Shakespeare, William. Romeo & Juliet, 1 vol. Cabrera, Eva, illus. 2011. (Shakespeare Graphics Ser.). (ENG.). 88p. (gr. 2-3). pap. 7.15 *(978-1-4342-3448-3(7))*; lib. bdg. 27.99 *(978-1-4342-2563-4(1))* Stone Arch Bks. (Shakespeare Graphics).

Harper, Suzanne. The Juliet Club. (YA). 2010. (ENG.). 416p. (gr. 8). pap. 9.99 *(978-0-06-136693-2(5)*, Greenwillow Bks.) 2008. 402p. (gr. 7-18). lib. bdg. 18.89 *(978-0-06-136692-5(7)*, HarperTeen) HarperCollins Pubs.

Hartley, James. The Invisible Hand: Shakespeare's Moon, Act I. 2017. (ENG.). 168p. (J). (gr. 6-12). pap. 11.95 *(978-1-78535-498-4(1)*, Lodestone Bks.) Hunt, John Publishing Ltd. GBR. Dist: National Bk. Network.

Hassinger, Peter W. Shakespeare's Daughter. 2004. (ENG., Illus.). 320p. (J). (gr. 5-18). 15.99 *(978-0-06-028467-1(6)*, Geringer, Laura Book) HarperCollins Pubs.

Hicks, Deron R. Secrets of Shakespeare's Grave. Geyer, Mark Edward, illus. 2012. (Shakespeare Mysteries Ser.: 1). (ENG.). 304p. (J). (gr. 2-5). 16.99 *(978-0-547-84034-5(9))* Houghton Mifflin Harcourt Publishing Co.

—Tower of the Five Orders. Geyer, Mark Edward, illus. 2013. (Shakespeare Mysteries Ser.: 2). (ENG.). 320p. (J). (gr. 5-7). 16.99 *(978-0-547-83953-0(7))* Houghton Mifflin Harcourt Publishing Co.

—Tower of the Five Orders: The Shakespeare Mysteries, Book 2. Geyer, Mark Edward, illus. 2014. (Shakespeare Mysteries Ser.). (ENG.). 320p. (J). (gr. 5-7). pap. 7.99 *(978-0-544-33630-8(5)*, HMH Books For Young Readers) Houghton Mifflin Harcourt Publishing Co.

Klein, Lisa. Love Disguised. 2013. (ENG., Illus.). 320p. (YA). (gr. 7). 17.99 *(978-1-59990-968-4(5)*, 9781599909684, Bloomsbury USA Childrens) Bloomsbury Publishing USA.

Lawlor, Laurie. The Two Loves of Will Shakespeare. 2006. (ENG.). 256p. (YA). (gr. 12). 16.95 *(978-0-8234-1901-2(0))* Holiday Hse., Inc.

MacDonald, Bailey. Wicked Will: A Mystery of Young William Shakespeare. 2010. (ENG.). 224p. (J). (gr. 4-7). pap. 5.99 *(978-1-4169-8661-4(8)*, Aladdin) Simon & Schuster Children's Publishing.

—Wicked Will: A Mystery of Young William Shakespeare. 2009. (ENG.). 208p. (J). (gr. 4-7). 16.99 *(978-1-4169-8660-7(X)*, Simon & Schuster/Paula Wiseman Bks.) Simon & Schuster/Paula Wiseman Bks.

Magnuson, Gregory. Crab & Will, a Tale of Shakespeare's Dog. 2012. 36p. pap. 19.95 *(978-1-105-95102-2(2))* Lulu Pr., Inc.

Mayhew, James. Ella Bella Ballerina & the Midsummer Night's Dream. 2015. (Ella Bella Ballerina Ser.). (ENG., Illus.). 32p. (J). (gr. -1-3). 14.99 *(978-0-7641-6797-3(9))* Barron's Educational Series, Inc.

Meyer, Carolyn. Loving Will Shakespeare. 2008. (ENG., Illus.). 272p. (YA). (gr. 7-12). pap. 6.95 *(978-0-15-206221-7(1))* Houghton Mifflin Harcourt Publishing Co.

Mullarkey, Lisa & Mullarkey, John. Shakespeare Saves the Globe, 1 vol. Bernard, Courtney, illus. 2015. (ENG.). 128p. (J). *(978-1-62402-090-2(9))* Magic Wagon.

Ortiz, Michael J. Swan Town: The Secret Journal of Susanna Shakespeare. 2006. (Illus.). 197p. (J). (gr. 5-9). 15.99 *(978-0-06-058126-8(3))* HarperCollins Pubs.

Rees, Celia. The Fool's Girl. 2010. (ENG.). 304p. (YA). (gr. 7-18). 16.99 *(978-1-59990-486-3(1)*, 9781599904863, Bloomsbury USA Childrens) Bloomsbury Publishing USA.

Sutherland, Tui T. This Must Be Love. 256p. (J). 2005. pap. 7.99 *(978-0-06-056477-3(6)*, Harper Trophy) 2004. (gr. 7-18). lib. bdg. 16.89 *(978-0-06-056476-6(8))* HarperCollins Pubs.

Sylvester, Kevin. Neil Flambé & the Bard's Banquet. Sylvester, Kevin, illus. 2015. (Neil Flambe Capers Ser.: 5). (ENG., Illus.). 320p. (J). (gr. 3-7). 12.99 *(978-1-4814-1038-0(5)*, Simon & Schuster Bks. For Young Readers) Simon & Schuster Bks. For Young Readers.

West, Jacqueline. Dreamers Often Lie. 2016. (ENG.). 368p. (YA). (gr. 7). 17.99 *(978-0-8037-3863-8(3)*, Dial Bks) Penguin Young Readers Group.

SHAKESPEARE, WILLIAM, 1564-1616—HAMLET

Christensen, Caitlyn. Hamlet. 2016. (Reading Shakespeare Today Ser.). (ENG.). 112p. (J). (gr. 9-9). 42.79 *(978-1-5026-1034-8(5))* Cavendish Square Publishing.

Johnson, Vernon. Corruption in William Shakespeare's Hamlet. 2010. (Social Issues in Literature Ser.). (Illus.). 224p. (J). 40.95 *(978-0-7377-4809-3(5))*; pap. 28.45 *(978-0-7377-4810-9(9))* Cengage Gale. (Greenhaven Pr., Inc.).

Saddleback Educational Publishing Staff, ed. Hamlet. 2011. (Timeless Shakespeare Ser.). (ENG.). 48p. (YA). (gr. 9-12). pupil's gde. ed. 19.95 incl. cd-rom *(978-1-61651-159-3(1))* Saddleback Educational Publishing, Inc.

Shakespeare, William. Hamlet. Gill, Roma, ed. 2009. (Oxford School Shakespeare Ser.). (ENG., Illus.). 208p. pap. 9.95 *(978-0-19-832870-4(2))* Oxford Univ. Pr., Inc.

Wood, Jeffrey, et al. Hamlet. 2003. (ENG., Illus.). 160p. pap. 20.00 *(978-0-582-78428-4(X))* Pearson Education, Ltd. GBR. Dist: Trans-Atlantic Pubns., Inc.

SHAKESPEARE, WILLIAM, 1564-1616—JULIUS CAESAR

Griffiths, Katie. Julius Caesar. 2016. (Reading Shakespeare Today Ser.). (ENG., Illus.). 112p. (J). (gr. 9-9). 42.79 *(978-1-5026-1043-0(4))* Cavendish Square Publishing.

Literature Connections English: Julius Caesar. 2004. (gr. 6-12). *(978-0-395-77542-4(6)*, 2-80111) Holt McDougal.

Saddleback Educational Publishing Staff, ed. Julius Caesar. 2011. (Timeless Shakespeare Ser.). (ENG.). 48p. (YA). (gr. 9-12). pupil's gde. ed. 19.95 incl. cd-rom *(978-1-61651-160-9(5))* Saddleback Educational Publishing, Inc.

Shakespeare, William. Julius Caesar 2010. 2010. (Oxford School Shakespeare Ser.). (ENG., Illus.). 160p. (YA). pap. 9.95 *(978-0-19-832868-1(0))* Oxford Univ. Pr., Inc.

SHAKESPEARE, WILLIAM, 1564-1616—KING HENRY IV

Sobran, Joseph. Henry IV, Part 1. 2009. (Shakespeare Explained 2 Ser.). 112p. (gr. 7). 42.79 *(978-0-7614-3419-1(4))* Marshall Cavendish Corp.

SHAKESPEARE, WILLIAM, 1564-1616—KING HENRY V

Langston, David, ed. Henry V. 2003. (ENG., Illus.). 80p. pap. 15.00 *(978-0-582-77268-7(0))* Pearson Education, Ltd. GBR. Dist: Trans-Atlantic Pubns., Inc.

SHAKESPEARE, WILLIAM, 1564-1616—KING LEAR

Paley, Caitlyn. King Lear. 2016. (Reading Shakespeare Today Ser.). (ENG., Illus.). 112p. (J). (gr. 9-9). 42.79 *(978-1-5026-1047-8(7))* Cavendish Square Publishing.

Richert, Scott P. King Lear. 2010. (Shakespeare Explained 3 Ser.). (Illus.). 112p. (J). (gr. 7-18). 42.79 *(978-1-60870-016-5(X))* Marshall Cavendish GBR. Dist: Marshall Cavendish Corp.

Saddleback Educational Publishing Staff, ed. King Lear. 2011. (Timeless Shakespeare Ser.). (ENG.). 48p. (YA). (gr. 9-12). pupil's gde. ed. 19.95 incl. cd-rom *(978-1-61651-161-6(3))* Saddleback Educational Publishing, Inc.

Shakespeare, William. King Lear: Classicscript. Landes, William-Alan, ed. 2003. (Shakespeare Ser.: Vol. 8). 71p. (YA). (gr. 6-12). pap. 7.00 *(978-0-88734-537-1(9))* Players Pr., Inc.

Shakespeare, William & SparkNotes Staff. King Lear. Crowther, John, ed. 2003. (No Fear Shakespeare Ser.). (ENG., Illus.). 320p. pap. 6.95 *(978-1-58663-853-5(X)*, Spark Notes) Sterling Publishing Co., Inc.

Warren, Rebecca & Shakespeare, William. King Lear. 2003. (ENG., Illus.). 144p. pap. 20.00 *(978-0-582-78429-1(8))* Pearson Education, Ltd. GBR. Dist: Trans-Atlantic Pubns., Inc.

SHAKESPEARE, WILLIAM, 1564-1616—MACBETH

Burnett, Allan. Macbeth & All That. Anderson, Scoular, illus. 2007. (ENG.). 128p. (gr. 4-7). per. *(978-1-84158-574-1(2))* Birlinn, Ltd.

Cunningham, Patrick. How to Dazzle at Macbeth. 2004. (Illus.). 48p. pap. 30.00 *(978-1-897675-93-9(3))* Brilliant Pubns. GBR. Dist: Parkwest Pubns., Inc.

Griffiths, Katie. Macbeth. 2016. (Reading Shakespeare Today Ser.). (ENG., Illus.). 112p. (J). (gr. 9-9). 42.79 *(978-1-5026-1041-6(8))* Cavendish Square Publishing.

Kohl, Brian. Macbeth Worldview Guide. 2016. (J). pap. ***(978-1-944503-42-0(0))*** Canon Pr.

Saddleback Educational Publishing Staff, ed. Macbeth. 2011. (Timeless Shakespeare Ser.). (ENG.). 48p. (YA). (gr. 9-12). pupil's gde. ed. 19.95 incl. cd-rom *(978-1-61651-162-3(1))* Saddleback Educational Publishing, Inc.

Shakespeare, William. Macbeth. Gill, Roma, ed. 2009. (Oxford School Shakespeare Ser.). (ENG., Illus.). 160p. pap. 9.95 *(978-0-19-832840-3(6))* Oxford Univ. Pr., Inc.

—Macbeth: The Graphic Novel. 2010. (Classic Graphic Novel Collection). 144p. (YA). (gr. 7-12). 34.80 *(978-1-4205-0373-9(1))* Cengage Gale.

—The Tragedy of Macbeth. 2008. (Easy Reading Shakespeare Ser.). (ENG., Illus.). 72p. pap., act. bk. ed. 10.95 *(978-1-55576-331-2(6)*, EDSC401B) EDCON Publishing Group.

—The Tragedy of Macbeth. 2004. (Classic Retelling Ser.). (Illus.). 176p. (gr. 6-12). 13.32 *(978-0-618-03147-4(2)*, 2-00141) Holt McDougal.

Shakespeare, William & SparkNotes Staff. Macbeth. Crowther, John, ed. 2003. (No Fear Shakespeare Ser.). (ENG., Illus.). 240p. pap. 5.95 *(978-1-58663-846-7(7)*, Spark Notes) Sterling Publishing Co., Inc.

SHAKESPEARE, WILLIAM, 1564-1616—MERCHANT OF VENICE

Paley, Caitlyn. Merchant of Venice. 2016. (Reading Shakespeare Today Ser.). (ENG., Illus.). 112p. (J). (gr. 9-9). 42.79 *(978-1-5026-1045-4(0))* Cavendish Square Publishing.

Saddleback Educational Publishing Staff, ed. Merchant of Venice. 2011. (Timeless Shakespeare Ser.). (ENG.). 48p. (YA). (gr. 9-12). pupil's gde. ed. 19.95 incl. cd-rom *(978-1-61651-163-0(X))* Saddleback Educational Publishing, Inc.

Schupack, Sara. The Merchant of Venice. 2009. (Shakespeare Explained 2 Ser.). 112p. (gr. 7). 42.79 *(978-0-7614-3421-4(6))* Marshall Cavendish GBR. Dist: Marshall Cavendish Corp.

Shakespeare, William. Merchant of Venice. 2010. (Oxford School Shakespeare Ser.). (ENG., Illus.). 160p. (YA). pap. 9.95 *(978-0-19-832867-4(2))* Oxford Univ. Pr., Inc.

Shakespeare, William & SparkNotes Staff. The Merchant of Venice. Crowther, John, ed. 2003. (No Fear Shakespeare Ser.). (ENG., Illus.). 256p. pap. 5.95 *(978-1-58663-850-4(5)*, Spark Notes) Sterling Publishing Co., Inc.

SHAKESPEARE, WILLIAM, 1564-1616—MIDSUMMER NIGHT'S DREAM

A Midsummer Night's Dream - William Shakespeare. 2nd rev. ed. 2010. (Bloom's Modern Critical Interpretations Ser.). 198p. (C). (gr. 9-18). 45.00 *(978-1-60413-817-7(3)*, Chelsea Hse.) Facts On File, Inc.

Shakespeare, William. A Midsummer Night's Dream. Bryant, Clive, ed. Nicholson, Kat & Cardy, Jason, illus. 2012. (ENG.). 144p. (gr. 6). lib. bdg. 24.95 *(978-1-907127-44-1(5))* Classical Comics GBR. Dist: Publishers Group West (PGW).

Shakespeare, William & Gill, Roma. A Midsummer Night's Dream. 2009. (Oxford School Shakespeare Ser.). (ENG., Illus.). 128p. pap. 9.95 *(978-0-19-832866-7(4))* Oxford Univ. Pr., Inc.

Walker, Geof. William Shakespeare's 'A Midsummer Night's Dream' - a playscript for younger Students. 2006. 49p. pap. 19.45 *(978-1-4116-4407-6(7))* Lulu Pr., Inc.

SHAKESPEARE, WILLIAM, 1564-1616—MUCH ADO ABOUT NOTHING

Page, Philip & Pettit, Marilyn. Much Ado about Nothing. 2005. (ENG., Illus.). 64p. pap. *(978-0-340-88808-7(3))* Cambridge Univ. Pr.

Shakespeare, William. Much Ado about Nothing. 2010. (Oxford School Shakespeare Ser.). (ENG., Illus.). 160p. (YA). pap. 9.95 *(978-0-19-832872-8(9))* Oxford Univ. Pr., Inc.

SHAKESPEARE, WILLIAM, 1564-1616—OTHELLO

Mussari, Mark. Othello. 2009. (Shakespeare Explained Ser.). (Illus.). 112p. (gr. 7-10). 42.79 *(978-0-7614-3422-1(4))* Marshall Cavendish Corp.

Ryckman, Tatiana & Jones, Edith. Othello. 2016. (Reading Shakespeare Today Ser.). 112p. (J). lib. bdg. 42.79 *(978-1-5026-2333-1(1))* Cavendish Square Publishing.

Saddleback Educational Publishing Staff, ed. Othello. 2011. (Timeless Shakespeare Ser.). (ENG.). 48p. (YA). (gr. 9-12). pupil's gde. ed. 19.95 incl. cd-rom *(978-1-61651-165-4(6))* Saddleback Educational Publishing, Inc.

Shakespeare, William. Othello. abr. ed. 2011. (Go Shakespeare - Set 2 Ser.). (ENG.). (YA). (gr. 9-12). 49.93 ***(978-1-61641-428-3(6)*** , Abdo & Daughters) ABDO Publishing Co.

Shakespeare, William. Othello: Classicscript. Landes, William-Alan, ed. abr. ed. 2003. (Shakespeare Ser.: Vol. 9). 64p. (YA). (gr. 4-12). pap. 7.00 *(978-0-88734-538-8(7))* Players Pr., Inc.

Shakespeare, William & Gill, Roma. Othello. 2009. (Oxford School Shakespeare Ser.). (ENG., Illus.). 208p. pap. 9.95 *(978-0-19-832873-5(7))* Oxford Univ. Pr., Inc.

Smith, Emma. Othello. 2005. (ENG., Illus.). 112p. (C). 80.00 *(978-0-7463-1082-3(X))*; pap. 19.95 *(978-0-7463-0999-5(6))* Northcote Hse. Publishers, Ltd. GBR. Dist: Casemate Academic.

Warren, Rebecca & Shakespeare, William. Othello. 2nd ed. 2003. (ENG., Illus.). 152p. pap. 20.00 *(978-0-582-78431-4(X))* Pearson Education, Ltd. GBR. Dist: Trans-Atlantic Pubns., Inc.

SHAKESPEARE, WILLIAM, 1564-1616—QUOTATIONS

Shakespeare, William. A Treasury of Shakespeare's Verse. Pollinger, Gina, ed. Chichester Clark, Emma, illus. 2006. 96p. (J). (gr. 4-8). reprint ed. pap. 12.00 *(978-1-4223-5444-5(X))* DIANE Publishing Co.

Weiner, Miriam. Shakespeare's Seasons. Whitt, Shannon, illus. 2012. (ENG.). 32p. (J). (gr. -1). 16.99 *(978-1-935703-57-0(9))* Downtown Bookworks.

SHAKESPEARE, WILLIAM, 1564-1616—ROMEO AND JULIET

Gale Editor, ed. Romeo & Juliet: The Graphic Novel. 2011. (Classic Graphic Novel Collection Ser.). (Illus.). 160p. (J). (gr. 7-12). lib. bdg. 34.80 *(978-1-4205-0631-0(5))* Cengage Gale.

Griffiths, Katie. Romeo & Juliet. 2016. (Reading Shakespeare Today Ser.). (ENG.). 112p. (J). (gr. 9-9). 42.79 *(978-1-5026-1036-2(1))* Cavendish Square Publishing.

Lacey, Saskia. The Prehistoric Masters of Literature: Discover Literary History with a Prehistoric Twist! 2016. (Jurassic Classics Ser.). (ENG., Illus.). 40p. (J). (gr. 2-6). 14.95 *(978-1-63322-098-0(2))* Quarto Publishing Group USA.

Saddleback Educational Publishing Staff, ed. Romeo & Juliet. 2011. (Timeless Shakespeare Ser.). (ENG.). 48p. (YA). (gr. 9-12). pupil's gde. ed. 19.95 incl. cd-rom *(978-1-61651-166-1(4))* Saddleback Educational Publishing, Inc.

Shakespeare, William & SparkNotes Staff. Romeo & Juliet. Crowther, John, ed. 2003. (No Fear Shakespeare Ser.). (ENG., Illus.). 304p. pap. 5.95 *(978-1-58663-845-0(9)*, Spark Notes) Sterling Publishing Co., Inc.

SHAKESPEARE, WILLIAM, 1564-1616—STAGE HISTORY

Morley, Jacqueline. You Wouldn't Want to Be a Shakespearean Actor! Some Roles You Might Not Want to Play. Antram, David, illus. 2010. (You Wouldn't Want to Ser.). (ENG.). 32p. (J). (gr. 3-18). pap. 9.95 *(978-0-531-22826-5(6))* Scholastic Library Publishing.

Morley, Jacqueline & Salariya, David. You Wouldn't Want to Be a Shakespearean Actor! Some Roles You Might Not Want to Play. Antram, David, illus. 2010. (You Wouldn't Want to Ser.). (ENG.). 32p. (J). 29.00 *(978-0-531-20471-9(5))* Scholastic Library Publishing.

Shuter, Jane. Shakespeare & the Theater, 1 vol. 2014. (Shakespeare Alive Ser.). (ENG.). 64p. (gr. 7-8). lib. bdg. 37.32 *(978-1-4329-9630-7(4))* Heinemann-Raintree.

—Shakespeare & the Theatre, 1 vol. 2014. (Shakespeare Alive Ser.). (ENG.). 64p. (gr. 7-8). pap. 10.95 *(978-1-4329-9634-5(7))* Heinemann-Raintree.

Shuter, Jane & Shuter, Paul. Shakespeare Alive, 1 vol. 2014. (Shakespeare Alive Ser.). (ENG.). 32p. (gr. 7-8). lib. bdg. 111.96 *(978-1-4329-9632-1(0))* Heinemann-Raintree.

SHAKESPEARE, WILLIAM, 1564-1616—TAMING OF THE SHREW

Naden, Corinne J. The Taming of the Shrew. 2010. (Shakespeare Explained 3 Ser.). (Illus.). 112p. (J). (gr. 7-18). 42.79 *(978-1-60870-019-6(4))* Marshall Cavendish Corp.

Shakespeare, William. The Taming of the Shrew. 2008. (Easy Reading Shakespeare Ser.). (ENG., Illus.). 72p. pap., act. bk. ed. 10.95 *(978-1-55576-348-0(0)*, EDSC-504B) EDCON Publishing Group.

West, Summer & Warner, Hailey. The Taming of the Shrew. 2016. (Reading Shakespeare Today Ser.). 112p. (YA). lib. bdg. 42.79 *(978-1-5026-2343-0(9))* Cavendish Square Publishing.

SHAKESPEARE, WILLIAM, 1564-1616—TEMPEST

Krueger, Susan Heidi. The Tempest. 2009. (Shakespeare Explained Ser.). (Illus.). 112p. (gr. 7-10). lib. bdg. 42.79 *(978-0-7614-3423-8(2))* Marshall Cavendish Corp.

Saddleback Educational Publishing Staff, ed. The Tempest. 2011. (Timeless Shakespeare Ser.). (ENG.). 48p. (YA). (gr. 9-12). pupil's gde. ed. 19.95 incl. cd-rom *(978-1-61651-167-8(2))* Saddleback Educational Publishing, Inc.

Shakespeare, William. The Tempest. 2010. 140p. pap. 20.75 *(978-1-141-55192-7(6))* Creative Media Partners, LLC.

—The Tempest. 2010. (Oxford School Shakespeare Ser.). (ENG., Illus.). 160p. (YA). pap. 9.95 *(978-0-19-832500-0(2))* Oxford Univ. Pr., Inc.

—The Tempest: Adaptation. 2004. (Saddleback Classics Ser.). (Illus.). 96p. (J). per. 6.95 *(978-1-56254-638-0(4)*, SP6384) Saddleback Educational Publishing, Inc.

—The Tempest Study Guide. 2004. (Shakespeare Classics Ser.). (Illus.). 48p. (J). (gr. 4-7). per. 17.95 *(978-1-56254-639-7(2)*, SP6392) Saddleback Educational Publishing, Inc.

Walker, Geof. William Shakespeare's 'the Tempest' - a playscript for younger Students. 2006. 40p. pap. 19.46 *(978-1-4116-7138-6(4))* Lulu Pr., Inc.

West, Summer & Penny, Katherine. The Tempest. 2016. (Reading Shakespeare Today Ser.). 112p. (YA). lib. bdg. 42.79 *(978-1-5026-2339-3(0))* Cavendish Square Publishing.

York Notes Staff & Shakespeare, William. The Tempest. Todd, Loreto, ed. 3rd ed. 2003. (ENG., Illus.). 120p. pap. 20.00 *(978-0-582-78437-6(9))* Pearson Education, Ltd. GBR. Dist: Trans-Atlantic Pubns., Inc.

SHAKESPEARE, WILLIAM, 1564-1616—TWELFTH NIGHT

Schmermund, Elizabeth & Robeson, Dale. Twelfth Night. 2016. (Reading Shakespeare Today Ser.). 112p. (YA). lib. bdg. 42.79 *(978-1-5026-2337-9(4))* Cavendish Square Publishing.

Shakespeare, William. Twelfth Night 2010. 2010. (Oxford School Shakespeare Ser.). (ENG., Illus.). 144p. (YA). pap. 9.95 *(978-0-19-832871-1(0))* Oxford Univ. Pr., Inc.

Sobran, Joseph. Twelfth Night. 2009. (Shakespeare Explained 2 Ser.). 112p. (gr. 7). 42.79 *(978-0-7614-3425-2(9))* Marshall Cavendish Corp.

Walker, Geof. William Shakespeare's 'Twelfth Night' - a playscript for younger Students. 2006. 52p. pap. 19.51 *(978-1-4116-7137-9(6))* Lulu Pr., Inc.

SHAPE

see Size and Shape

SHARES OF STOCK

see Stocks

SHARING

Amos, Janine & Spenceley, Annabel. Let's Share. 2009. (Best Behavior Ser.). (Illus.). 32p. (J). (gr. -1-2). 22.60 *(978-1-60754-508-8(X))*; pap. 10.55 *(978-1-60754-509-5(8))* Windmill Bks.

Barraclough, Sue. Sharing. 2016. (Exploring Citizenship Ser.). (ENG.). 32p. pap. 8.29 *(978-1-4846-4003-6(9)*, Heinemann First Library) Heinemann-Raintree.

Burton, Margie, et al. One for You & One for Me. 2011. (Early Connections Ser.). (J). *(978-1-61672-501-3(X))* Benchmark Education Co.

Carlson, Amie. My Princesses Learn to Share. Heyworth, Heather, illus. 2014. (ENG.). 24p. (J). 6.99 *(978-1-4143-9662-0(7))* Tyndale Hse. Pubs.

Deen, Marilyn. Share & Be Fair, 1 vol. 2011. (Wonder Readers Fluent Level Ser.). (ENG.). (gr. -1-2). 32p. pap. 5.99 *(978-1-4296-7935-0(2))*; 16p. pap. 35.94 *(978-1-4296-8149-0(7))* Capstone Press of Coughlan Cos. (Wonder Readers).

Gordon, Sharon. We Share. 2007. (J). pap. 6.99 *(978-0-7614-3276-0(0))* Marshall Cavendish Corp.

Larsen, Carolyn. Sharing with Others: A Book about Selfishness. O'Connor, Tim, illus. 2017. (Growing God's Kids Ser.). (ENG.). 32p. (J). pap. 4.99 *(978-0-8010-0960-0(X))* Baker Bks.

Marie, Tina. Isabella Learns to Share. 2010. 20p. 12.49 *(978-1-4520-3913-8(5))* AuthorHouse.

Marsico, Katie. Taking Turns! 2012. (21st Century Basic Skills Library: Kids Can Make Manners Count Ser.). (ENG.). 24p. (gr. k-3). 22.79 *(978-1-61080-432-5(5)*, 202042); pap. 12.79 *(978-1-61080-606-0(9)*, 202216) Cherry Lake Publishing.

McClure, Leigh. My School Supplies: Sharing & Reusing. 2017. (Computer Science for the Real World Ser.). 8p. (gr. 5-6). pap. 6.20 ***(978-1-5383-5093-5(9)**, Rosen Classroom)* Rosen Publishing Group, Inc., The.

Meiners, Cheri J. Share & Take Turns. 2003. (Learning to Get Along(r) Ser.). (ENG., Illus.). 40p. (J). (gr. -1-3). pap. 11.99 *(978-1-57542-124-7(0)*, 786) Free Spirit Publishing, Inc.

—Share & Take Turns/Comparte y Turna. 2014. (Learning to Get Along(r) Ser.). (SPA, ENG & MUL., Illus.). 48p. (J). (gr. -1-3). pap. 12.45 *(978-1-57542-474-3(6))* Free Spirit Publishing, Inc.

Nelson, Maria. I Can Share. 2013. (Kids of Character Ser.). 24p. (J). (gr. 1-3). pap. 48.90 *(978-1-4339-9035-9(0))*; (Illus.). 22.60 *(978-1-4339-9033-5(4))*; (ENG., Illus.). pap. 8.15 *(978-1-4339-9034-2(2))* Stevens, Gareth Publishing LLLP.

Nunn, Daniel. I Can Take Turns, 1 vol. 2014. (Me & My Friends Ser.). (ENG.). 24p. (gr. -1-1). pap. 5.99 *(978-1-4846-0248-5(X)*, Acorn) Heinemann-Raintree.

Redford, Marjorie & Rice, Courtney. God's Special Rule. Burroughs, Scott, illus. 2013. (Happy Day Ser.). (ENG.). 16p. (J). pap. 2.49 *(978-1-4143-9300-1(8))* Tyndale Hse. Pubs.

Reynolds, Mattie. Sharing with Others: An Introduction to Financial Literacy. 2013. (Start Smart: Money Ser.). (Illus.). 24p. (J). (gr. k-2). (ENG.). pap. 5.95 *(978-1-937529-40-6(1))*; lib. bdg. 23.93 *(978-1-937529-44-4(4))* Red Chair Pr.

Williams, Sam. Sharing. 2012. (ENG.). 24p. (gr. k-2). pap. 8.95 *(978-1-61810-264-5(8))* Rourke Educational Media.

SHARING—FICTION

Ahmed, Said Salah. The Lion's Share/Qayb Libaax: A Somali Folktale. Dupre, Kelly, illus. 2006. 32p. (J). (gr. -1-3). pap. 7.95 *(978-1-931016-13-1(5))* Minnesota Humanities Ctr.

Albee, Sarah. One for Me, One for You: A Book about Sharing. Craig, Karen, illus. 2006. (Blue's Clues Ser.: 20). (ENG.). 24p. (J). (gr. -1-3). pap. 3.99 *(978-1-4169-1300-9(9)*, Simon Spotlight/Nickelodeon) Simon Spotlight/Nickelodeon.

Alberts, Katharine O. Boo on the Loose. 2006. (J). 14.00 *(978-0-8059-7071-5(1))* Dorrance Publishing Co., Inc.

Alexander, Claire. Millie Shares. 2014. (ENG., Illus.). 32p. (J). (gr. -1-k). pap. 9.99 *(978-1-4052-6409-9(8))* Egmont Bks., Ltd. GBR. Dist: Independent Pubs. Group.

Ardwin, Juanita. Remember When, 1 vol. 2009. 40p. pap. 19.95 *(978-1-4489-2008-2(6))* PublishAmerica, Inc.

Arnone, T. I. The Magic Kazoo. 2009. (Illus.). 50p. pap. 25.00 *(978-0-557-12017-8(9))* Lulu Pr., Inc.

Ashby, Gaylene. STORY TIME A Collection of Three Children's Stories. 2008. 28p. 14.95 *(978-1-4357-1929-3(8))* Lulu Pr., Inc.

Audho, Gaitree. Moral Stories for Kids. 2011. 32p. pap. 12.77 *(978-1-4634-4709-0(4))* AuthorHouse.

Battut, Eric. Little Mouse's Big Secret. 2017. (ENG., Illus.). 22p. (J). (— 1). bds. 6.95 *(978-1-4549-2154-7(4))* Sterling Publishing Co., Inc.

Beck, Andrea. Elliot's Fire Truck, 1 vol. Beck, Andrea, illus. 2010. (ENG., Illus.). 32p. (J). (gr. -1-3). 19.95 *(978-1-55469-143-2(5))* Orca Bk. Pubs. USA.

Bently, Peter & McPhillips, Robert, illus. Say Please, Little Bear. 2013. (J). *(978-1-4351-4727-0(8))* Barnes & Noble, Inc.

Berenstain, Jan & Berenstain, Mike. The Berenstain Bears' Caring & Sharing Treasury, 1 vol. 2016. (Berenstain Bears/Living Lights Ser.). (ENG.). 160p. (J). 10.99 *(978-0-310-75358-2(9))* Zonderkidz.

Berenstain, Stan, et al. The Berenstain Bears Learn to Share, 1 vol. 2010. (Berenstain Bears/Living Lights Ser.). (ENG.). 40p. (J). (gr. -1-2). 6.99 *(978-0-310-71939-7(9))* Zonderkidz.

Bethers, Linda, retold by. Christmas Oranges. 2004. 13p. pap. 3.95 *(978-1-57734-546-6(0)*, 01114387) Covenant Communications, Inc.

Big Idea Entertainment, LLC. VeggieTales SuperComics: Vol 1. Jones, Cory, illus. 2015. (VeggieTales Super Comics Ser.: 1). (ENG.). 104p. (J). (gr. -1-3). pap. 12.99 *(978-1-4336-8534-7(5)*, B&H Kids) B&H Publishing Group.

—VeggieTales SuperComics: Vol 2. Jones, Cory, illus. 2015. (VeggieTales Super Comics Ser.). (ENG.). 104p. (J). (gr. -1-3). pap. 12.99 *(978-1-4336-8535-4(3)*, B&H Kids) B&H Publishing Group.

Blabey, Aaron. Pig the Pug. 2016. (ENG., Illus.). 32p. (J). (gr. -1-k). 14.99 *(978-1-338-11245-0(7)*, Scholastic Pr.) Scholastic, Inc.

Bland, Nick. The Very Brave Bear. 2013. (Illus.). (J). pap. *(978-0-545-65137-0(9))* Scholastic, Inc.

Bland, Nick. The Very Hungry Bear. 2013. (Illus.). (J). pap. ***(978-0-545-52290-8(0))*** Scholastic, Inc.

Bodden, Michelle, adapted by. Obara the Gatekeeper. 2007. (J). 14.95 *(978-0-9753089-1-2(2))* Water Daughter Publishing.

Brandy. WILL & WON't Learn to Share: Big Life Lessons for Little Kids. 2017. (ENG., Illus.). 40p. 10.00 ***(978-981-4771-33-7(3))*** Marshall Cavendish International (Asia) Private Ltd. SGP. Dist: National Bk. Network.

Bright, Rachel. Love Monster & the Last Chocolate. 2015. (ENG., Illus.). 32p. (J). (gr. -1-k). 17.99 *(978-0-374-34690-4(9)*, 9780374346904, Farrar, Straus & Giroux (BYR)) Farrar, Straus & Giroux.

Brooks, Felicity. Take Turns, Max & Millie. 2011. (Toddler Bks). 24p. (J). ring bd. 7.99 *(978-0-7945-3000-6(1)*, Usborne) EDC Publishing.

Bryan-Brown, Kim. The Leaf That Was Left. Curren, Cindy, illus. l.t. ed. 2006. 32p. (J). 16.95 *(978-0-9772564-0-2(5))* Them Potatoes.

Burks, James. Pigs & a Blanket. Burks, James, illus. 2016. (ENG., Illus.). 32p. (J). (gr. -1 — 1). 16.99 *(978-1-4847-2523-8(9))* Hyperion Bks. for Children.

Cannon, Sherrill S. Gimme-Jimmy. 2012. 32p. pap. 13.00 *(978-1-61897-267-5(7)*, Strategic Bk. Publishing) Strategic Book Publishing & Rights Agency (SBPRA).

Carmi, Giora. A Circle of Friends, 1 vol. Carmi, Giora, illus. 2003. (ENG., Illus.). 32p. (J). 15.95 *(978-1-932065-00-8(8))* Star Bright Bks., Inc.

Carmi, Giora, illus. A Circle of Friends, 1 vol. 2006. (ENG.). 32p. (J). (gr. k-9). pap. 5.95 *(978-1-59572-060-3(X))* Star Bright Bks., Inc.

Chamberlin, Mary and Rich. Les Pancakes de Maman Panya. Cairns, Julia, illus. 2016. (FRE.). 40p. (J). (gr. k-5). 8.99 *(978-1-78285-299-5(9))* Barefoot Bks., Inc.

Childs, Barbara. Sammy & the Cow Bird. 2009. 48p. pap. 21.99 *(978-1-4389-8025-6(6))* AuthorHouse.

Cohen, Miriam. Mine! (Spanish/English) A Backpack Baby Story, 1 vol. Fiol, Maria A., tr. 2005. (ENG & SPA., Illus.). 32p. (J). (gr. -1 — 1). bds. 5.95 *(978-1-59572-019-1(7))* Star Bright Bks., Inc.

Cohen, Penny L. Tapuchim & Dvash. Polsky, Beanie, illus. 2012. 36p. 24.95 *(978-1-4626-7769-6(X))*; pap. 24.95 *(978-1-4626-6667-6(1))* PublishAmerica, Inc.

Collins, Carleen. Everyone Loves Chocolate. 2009. 60p. pap. 23.99 *(978-1-4490-3049-0(1))* AuthorHouse.

Cook, Julia. I Want to Be the Only Dog! DuFalla, Anita, illus. 2015. (ENG.). 32p. (J). pap. 10.95 *(978-1-934490-86-0(5))* Boys Town Pr.

—Teamwork Isn't My Thing, & I Don't Like to Share! De Weerd, Kelsey, illus. 2012. (ENG.). 32p. (J). pap. 10.95 *(978-1-934490-35-8(0))* Boys Town Pr.

Cook, Teri Ann. The Adventures of Mrs. Patsy's Farm: A Gift! Is a Gift! Is a Gift!, 1 vol. 2009. 24p. pap. 24.95 *(978-1-60749-549-9(X))* America Star Bks.

Cooper, Helen S. Pumpkin Soup. Cooper, Helen S., illus. 2005. (ENG., Illus.). 32p. (J). (gr. -1-3). per. 7.99 *(978-0-374-46031-0(0)*, 9780374460310) Square Fish.

Cosgrove, Stephen. Big Bubbe Bigg, Jr. Dealing with Bullies. Arroyo, Fian, illus. 2004. (J). *(978-1-58804-352-8(5))* P C I Education.

Costa, Nicoletta. The Little Tree That Would Not Share. Costa, Nicoletta, illus. 2016. (ENG., Illus.). 32p. (J). 16.95 *(978-0-8234-3549-4(0))* Holiday Hse., Inc.

Cotter, Bill. Don't Touch This Book! 2016. (ENG., Illus.). (J). 28p. bds. 6.99 *(978-1-4926-4804-8(3)*, 9781492648048); 32p. 16.99 *(978-1-4926-3224-5(4)*, 9781492632245) Sourcebooks, Inc. (Sourcebooks Jabberwocky).

Crum, Shutta. Mine! Barton, Patrice, illus. 2011. (ENG.). 32p. (J). (gr. -1-2). 16.99 *(978-0-375-86711-8(2)*, Knopf Bks. for Young Readers) Random Hse. Children's Bks.

Dahl, Michael. Playdate for Panda. Vidal, Oriol, illus. 2016. (Hello Genius Ser.). (ENG.). 20p. (gr. 1-2). bds. 7.99 *(978-1-4795-8741-4(9))* Picture Window Bks.

Dean, James. Pete's Big Lunch. 2013. (Pete the Cat I Can Read Ser.). (J). lib. bdg. 13.55 *(978-0-606-27146-2(5)*, Turtleback) Turtleback Bks.

deGroat, Diane. Last One in Is a Rotten Egg! deGroat, Diane, illus. 2011. (Gilbert Ser.). (ENG., Illus.). 32p. (J). (gr. -1-3). pap. 6.99 *(978-0-06-089296-8(X))* HarperCollins Pubs.

Demi. The Shady Tree. Demi, illus. 2016. (ENG., Illus.). 32p. (J). 17.99 *(978-1-62779-769-6(6)*, 9781627797696, Holt, Henry & Co. Bks. For Young Readers) Holt, Henry & Co.

Dewdney, Anna. Llama Llama Time to Share. 2012. (Llama Llama Ser.). (ENG.). 40p. (J). (gr. -1-k). 17.99 *(978-0-670-01233-6(5)*, Viking Books for Young Readers) Penguin Young Readers Group.

Dickson, Irene. Blocks. Dickson, Irene, illus. 2016. (ENG., Illus.). 32p. (J). (-k). 14.99 *(978-0-7636-8656-7(5)*, Nosy Crow) Candlewick Pr.

Divine, Miss Jill. Miles Smiles. 2008. 88p. pap. 15.95 *(978-1-4092-5052-4(0))* Lulu Pr., Inc.

Dixon, Dallas L. Shelby's Collection Day. Williams, Nancy E., ed. Forrest, Grace Metzger, illus. 2013. 24p. (J). pap. 12.98 *(978-1-938526-54-1(6))* Laurus Bks.

Domney, Alexis. Splish, Splat!, 1 vol. Crawford, Alice, illus. 2011. (ENG.). 24p. (J). (gr. 1-3). 15.95 *(978-1-897187-88-3(2))* Second Story Pr. CAN. Dist: Orca Bk. Pubs. USA.

Donaldson, Julia. Sharing a Shell Jigsaw Book. Monks, Lydia, illus. 2008. (ENG.). 14p. (J). (gr. 3-6). 23.95 *(978-0-230-01640-8(5)*, Macmillan) Pan Macmillan GBR. Dist: Trans-Atlantic Pubns., Inc.

Dungy, Tony & Dungy, Lauren. Ruby's New Home. Newton, Vanessa Brantley, illus. 2011. (Tony & Lauren Dungy Ready-To-Reads Ser.). (ENG.). 32p. (J). (gr. k-2). lib. bdg. 15.99 *(978-1-4424-2948-2(8)*, Simon Spotlight) Simon Spotlight.

Dunrea, Olivier. Ollie's Halloween. 2013. (Gossie & Friends Ser.). (ENG., Illus.). 30p. (J). (gr. -1 — 1). bds. 6.99 *(978-0-544-05720-3(1))* Houghton Mifflin Harcourt Publishing Co.

Durnil, Lari. A Tale of Two Sisters. 2009. (J). pap. 11.89 *(978-0-88144-455-1(3)*, Total Publishing & Media) Yorkshire Publishing Group.

Easton, Tom. Pirates Can Share, 01 vols., 1. 2016. (Pirate Pals Ser.). (ENG.). 32p. (J). pap. 10.00 *(978-1-5081-9155-1(7)*, Windmill Bks.) Rosen Publishing Group, Inc., The.

Edwards, W M, illus. Booger Boogie. 2007. (Playdate Kids Musical Ser.). 27p. (J). (gr. -1-3). 14.95 incl. audio compact disk *(978-1-933721-13-2(8))* Playdate Kids Publishing.

Eliopoulos, Chris. Yo Gabba Gabba: Gabba Ball: Gabba Ball. 2010. 16p. bds. 7.99 *(978-1-934964-55-2(7))* Oni Pr., Inc.

Elkins, Christy. The Seedling Heart. 2010. (ENG.). 33p. pap. 12.00 *(978-0-557-23498-1(0))* Lulu Pr., Inc.

Evans, Kristina. The Best Easter Prize. Wallace, John, illus. 2010. (ENG.). 32p. (J). (gr. -1-3). pap. 3.99 *(978-0-545-05112-5(6)*, Cartwheel Bks.) Scholastic, Inc.

Fagan, Cary. Ella May & the Wishing Stone. Cote, Genevieve, illus. 2011. (ENG.). 32p. (J). (gr. -1-1). 17.95 *(978-1-77049-225-7(9)*, Tundra Bks.) Tundra Bks. CAN. Dist: Penguin Random Hse. LLC.

farahay, m. l. The BUTTERFLY, the BEE & the SPIDER. 2009. 32p. pap. 6.94 *(978-0-557-14043-5(9))* Lulu Pr., Inc.

—The BUTTERFLY, the BEE & the SPIDER, Sc3. 2009. 32p. pap. 14.94 *(978-0-557-15287-2(9))* Lulu Pr., Inc.

Fielder, Barbara L. & Broady, Brianna. Missy, the Kitty, Learns about Sharing. (Illus.). 13p. (J). 6.95 *(978-0-9639986-2-0(5))* Fielder Group.

Fotso, Serge. The Little Girl & the Lost Bag. Woods, Michele, illus. 2011. 20p. pap. 24.95 *(978-1-4626-1741-8(7))* America Star Bks.

Frayre, A. R. Shannon Cabbage-Head. 2008. 33p. pap. 14.28 *(978-0-557-00442-3(X))* Lulu Pr., Inc.

Friedman, Becky. Daniel Learns to Share. 2016. (Simon & Schuster Ready-To-Read Level 1 Ser.). lib. bdg. 13.55 ***(978-0-606-39754-4(X))*** Turtleback Bks.

Garland, Sally. Tig & Tog's Dinosaur Discovery. 2015. (ENG., Illus.). 32p. (J). (gr. -1-3). 16.99 *(978-1-4998-0155-2(6))* Little Bee Books Inc.

Garland, Sally Anne. Share. Garland, Sally Anne, illus. 2014. (ENG., Illus.). 32p. (J). (gr. -1-3). 17.95 *(978-1-77147-005-6(4)*, Owlkids) Owlkids Bks. Inc. CAN. Dist: Publishers Group West (PGW).

Gassman, Julie A. Eleanore Won't Share, 1 vol. Mikhail, Jessica, illus. 2010. (Little Boost Ser.). (ENG.). 32p. (gr. k-3). lib. bdg. 23.99 *(978-1-4048-6358-3(3)*, Little Boost) Picture Window Bks.

Gibbs, Lynne. Time to Share: A Story of Sharing. Mitchell, Melanie, illus. 2009. (Let's Grow Together Ser.). 32p. (J). (gr. -1-2). lib. bdg. 22.60 *(978-1-60754-757-0(0))* Windmill Bks.

Gilbert, Harry. Year of Sharing, Level 1. Oxford University Press Staff & Bassett, Jennifer, eds. 3rd ed. 2008. (ENG., Illus.). 64p. 10.00 *(978-0-19-479077-2(0))* Oxford Univ. Pr., Inc.

Goodspeed, Judy. Perky Turkey Finds a Friend. (Illus.). 24p. (J). 2007. per. 11.99 *(978-0-9797574-2-6(8))* 2006. lib. bdg. 24.95 *(978-0-9778651-2-3(6))* Dragonfly Publishing, Inc.

Graham, Judith A. The Didley-Doo's, 1 vol. 2009. 36p. pap. 24.95 *(978-1-60836-035-2(0))* America Star Bks.

Gravett, Emily. Share! Gravett, Emily, illus. 2016. (Bear & Hare Ser.). (ENG., Illus.). 32p. (J). (gr. -1-1). 16.99 *(978-1-4814-6217-4(2)*, Simon & Schuster Bks. For Young Readers) Simon & Schuster Bks. For Young Readers.

Gray, Laurel. The Selfish Shellfish. 2012. 16p. pap. *(978-1-909039-83-4(7))* Legend Pr.

Greve, Meg. Let's Get Pizza. Poole, Helen, illus. 2012. (ENG.). 24p. (gr. k-1). pap. 8.95 *(978-1-61810-306-2(7))* Rourke Educational Media.

Hale, Bruce. Clark the Shark Dares to Share. Francis, Guy, illus. 2013. (Clark the Shark Ser.). (ENG.). 32p. (J). (gr. -1-3). 17.99 *(978-0-06-227905-7(X))* HarperCollins Pubs.

Hallinan, P. K. Let's Play As a Team. 2003. (ENG., Illus.). 28p. (J). 8.75 *(978-0-8249-5452-9(1)*, Ideal Pubns.) Worthy Publishing.

—Let's Share. Hallinan, P. K., illus. 2009. (ENG., Illus.). 24p. (J). (gr. -1-2). 8.99 *(978-0-8249-5610-3(9)*, Ideal Pubns.) Worthy Publishing.

—Let's Share. 2003. (ENG., Illus.). 24p. (J). bds. 8.75 *(978-0-8249-5451-2(3)*, Ideal Pubns.) Worthy Publishing.

Hamilton, Katharine E. Susie at Your Service. 2012. 24p. pap. 17.99 *(978-1-4772-2426-7(2))* AuthorHouse.

Harper, Charise Mericle. The Cookie. 2013. (Bean Dog & Nugget Ser.). lib. bdg. 14.75 *(978-0-606-31945-4(X)*, Turtleback) Turtleback Bks.

Harris, Tumeka. The Goody Bag. Sea Breeze Productions, ed. Miller, Linzi, illus. 2006. 36p. (J). 14.95 *(978-0-9769366-2-6(3))* Dividion Group, LLC, The.

Hauser, Sheri. Frog Frey Fun. 2011. (Illus.). (J). spiral bd. 5.95 *(978-1-60789-218-2(9))* Gloryhound Publishing.

Heap, Sue. Mine! Heap, Sue, illus. 2014. (ENG., Illus.). 32p. (J). (-k). 15.99 *(978-0-7636-6888-4(5))* Candlewick Pr.

Hendricks, Brenda K. What's Better Than That, Seren Dippity? Hendricks, Brenda K., illus. 2013. (Illus.). 32p. pap. 9.99 *(978-0-9826582-4-6(9))* Two Small Fish Pubns.

Henry, Kristina. The Rat Tank, 1 vol. Ambler, Laura & Brown, Amanda, illus. 2011. (ENG.). 40p. (J). 16.99 *(978-0-7643-3842-7(0)*, 9780764338427, Schiffer Publishing Ltd) Schiffer Publishing, Ltd.

Hensdill, Norma Mae. Friends Are Forever. 2009. 36p. pap. 17.99 *(978-1-4389-5053-2(5))* AuthorHouse.

Hibbert, Dee. Share Day, 1 vol. Hibbert, Rhonda, illus. 2009. 31p. pap. 24.95 *(978-1-60813-294-2(3))* America Star Bks.

Himmelman, John. Katie & the Puppy Next Door. Himmelman, John, illus. 2013. (ENG., Illus.). 32p. (J). (gr. -1-1). 16.99 *(978-0-8050-9484-8(9)*, 9780805094848, Holt, Henry & Co. Bks. For Young Readers) Holt, Henry & Co.

Horowitz, Alena Netia. The Tlytiettlym Tree. Horowitz, Alena Netia & De La Fuente, Mary, illus. l.t. ed. 2003. 64p. (J). per. 12.95 *(978-0-923550-42-4(9))* Tetrahedron Publishing LLC.

Hudson, Katy. Too Many Carrots. 2016. (ENG., Illus.). 32p. (gr. -1-1). 14.95 *(978-1-62370-638-8(6))* Capstone Young Readers of Coughlan Cos.

Hudson, Wade. Feelings I Love to Share. 2009. 24p. 5.95 *(978-1-60349-011-5(6)*, Marimba Bks.) Hudson Publishing Group, The.

—Puddin', Jeffrey & Leah. 2008. (Illus.). 16p. (gr. -1). 6.95 *(978-1-60349-006-1(X)*, Marimba Bks.) Hudson Publishing Group, The.

Hulme, Joy N. Mary Clare Likes to Share: A Math Reader. Rockwell, Lizzy, illus. 2006. (Step into Reading Ser.: Vol. 2). (ENG.). 32p. (J). (gr. -1-1). pap. 3.99 *(978-0-375-83421-9(4)*, Random Hse. Bks. for Young Readers) Random Hse. Children's Bks.

Humphrey, Eleanor Cairns. Building Santa's Work Shop from Tales of the Crystal Cave. 2012. 268p. pap. 27.95 *(978-1-4626-7820-4(3))* America Star Bks.

I Can Share. 2004. (J). per. *(978-1-57657-392-1(3))* Paradise Pr., Inc.

Irwin, Gayle. Sage Learns to Share, 1 vol. Araujo, Katie, illus. 2009. 45p. pap. 24.95 *(978-1-60836-409-1(7))* America Star Bks.

Jacobs, Sheila. Jake Earns A Treat: A Life & Money Book. 2011. 24p. 11.99 *(978-1-4567-3001-7(0))* AuthorHouse.

—Jake Saves the Day: A Life & Money Book. 2011. 24p. 11.99 *(978-1-4520-9929-3(4))* AuthorHouse.

Jaekel, Susan M., illus. Stone Soup: A Tale about Sharing. 2006. (J). *(978-1-59939-080-2(9)*, Reader's Digest Young Families, Inc.) Studio Fun International.

Jefferies, Rosie & Naish, Sarah. Callum Kindly & the Very Weird Child: A Story about Sharing Your Home with a Different Child. Evans, Megan, illus. 2017. (Therapeutic Parenting Bks.). (ENG.). 32p. (J). pap. 14.95 ***(978-1-78592-300-5(5)**, 9228)* Kingsley, Jessica Pubs. GBR. Dist: Macmillan Distribution Ltd.

Jin, Chris & Trimmer, Christian. Simon's New Bed. Van der Paardt, Melissa, illus. 2015. (ENG.). 32p. (J). (gr. -1-3). 17.99 *(978-1-4814-3019-7(X))* Simon & Schuster Children's Publishing.

Karapetkova, Holly & Picou, Lin. Ouch! Stitches. Reese, Bob, illus. 2011. (ENG.). 24p. (gr. 1-2). pap. 8.95 *(978-1-61236-023-2(8))* Rourke Educational Media.

Katz, Alan. Me! Me! Mine! Lemaître, Pascal, illus. 2011. (ENG.). 16p. (J). (gr. -1-1). bds. 7.99 *(978-1-4169-8993-6(5)*, Little Simon) Little Simon.

Katz, Karen. I Can Share! 2011. (ENG.). 24p. (J). (gr. -1-k). mass mkt. 4.99 *(978-0-448-45592-1(7)*, Grosset & Dunlap) Penguin Young Readers Group.

Kaufman, Suzanne. Confiscated! Kaufman, Suzanne, illus. 2017. (Illus.). 32p. (J). (gr. -1-3). 17.99 ***(978-0-06-241086-3(5))*** HarperCollins Pubs.

Kaye, Marilyn. Teammates. 2014. (ENG., Illus.). 80p. (J). (gr. 3-7). pap. 13.99 *(978-1-4814-2887-3(X)*, Simon & Schuster/Paula Wiseman Bks.) Simon & Schuster/Paula Wiseman Bks.

Kemnitz, Dianna. A New Hat for Jack. 2012. 38p. 24.95 *(978-1-4626-6816-8(X))* America Star Bks.

Khan, Farheen. Ibrahim Khan & the Mystery of the Roaring Lion. 2010. (Ibrahim Khan Ser.). (ENG., Illus.). 56p. (J). (gr. 2-6). pap. 6.50 *(978-0-86037-467-1(X))* Kube Publishing Ltd. GBR. Dist: Consortium Bk. Sales & Distribution.

Kiernan, Tim. Liams Luck & Finnegans Fortune. 2009. (ENG.). 144p. pap. 10.95 *(978-1-933916-48-4(6)*, Ferne Pr.) Nelson Publishing & Marketing.

Kirk, Daniel. You Are Not My Friend, but I Miss You. 2014. (ENG., Illus.). 32p. (J). (gr. k-2). 16.95 *(978-1-4197-1236-4(5)*, Abrams Bks. for Young Readers) Abrams, Inc.

Kirk, David. Happy Heartwood Day. 2005. (Illus.). (J). *(978-1-4156-3888-0(8)*, Grosset & Dunlap) Penguin Publishing Group.

Kittinger, Jo S. A Lunch with Punch. 2004. (Rookie Reader Español Ser.). (ENG., Illus.). 32p. (J). (gr. k-2). pap. 4.95 *(978-0-516-27785-1(5)*, Children's Pr.) Scholastic Library Publishing.

Klein, Abby. Thanks for Giving. McKinley, John, illus. 2009. (Ready, Freddy! Reader List: No. 4). 32p. (J). pap. *(978-0-545-14176-5(1))* Scholastic, Inc.

Kramer, Jackie Azúa. The Green Umbrella. Sassouni, Maral, illus. 2017. (ENG.). 32p. (J). (gr. -1-3). 17.95 *(978-0-7358-4218-2(3))* North-South Bks., Inc.

Krans, Kim. Whose Moon Is That? 2017. (ENG., Illus.). 48p. (J). (gr. -1-2). 17.99 *(978-1-101-93227-8(9)*, Random Hse. Bks. for Young Readers) Random Hse. Children's Bks.

Kroll, Steven. Jungle Bullies, 0 vols. Nguyen, Vincent, illus. 2006. (ENG.). 34p. (J). (gr. -1-2). 7.99 *(978-0-7614-5620-9(1)*, 9780761456209, Amazon Children's Publishing) Amazon Publishing.

Kurniega, Michelle. The Greedy Bunny. 2008. 28p. pap. 24.95 *(978-1-60672-966-3(7))* America Star Bks.

Lagonegro, Melissa, et al. Sharing & Caring. RH Disney Staff et al, illus. 2014. (Pictureback(R) Ser.). (ENG.). 16p. (J). (gr. -1-2). 4.99 *(978-0-7364-3334-1(1)*, RH/Disney) Random Hse. Children's Bks.

Lakritz, Deborah. Joey & the Giant Box. Byrne, Mike, illus. 2015. (J). (ENG.). 32p. (gr. -1-2). lib. bdg. 17.95 *(978-1-4677-1953-7(6))*; 6.99 *(978-1-4677-6205-2(9))* Lerner Publishing Group. (Kar-Ben Publishing).

Lallemand, Orianne & Strickland, Tessa. The Blue Bird's Palace. Hénaff, Carole, illus. 2016. (J). **(978-1-78285-308-4(1))** Barefoot Bks., Inc.

LaReau, Kara. Ugly Fish. Magoon, Scott, illus. 2006. (ENG.). 40p. (J). (gr. -1-3). 16.99 *(978-0-15-205082-5(5))* Houghton Mifflin Harcourt Publishing Co.

Larsen, Kirsten. It's Sharing Day! Zalme, Ron, illus. 2007. (SPA & ENG.). (J). pap. *(978-0-439-92237-1(2),* Scholastic) Scholastic, Inc.

—It's Sharing Day! Zalme, Ron, illus. 2007. (Dora the Explorer Ser.: 22). (ENG.). 24p. (J). pap. 3.99 *(978-1-4169-1575-1(3),* Simon Spotlight/Nickelodeon) Simon Spotlight/Nickelodeon.

Lawson, Jessica. Sharing & Making Friends. 2010. 20p. pap. 10.00 *(978-1-60911-707-8(7),* Eloquent Bks.) Strategic Book Publishing & Rights Agency (SBPRA).

Layne, Steven L. Share with Brother, 1 vol. Hoyt, Ard, illus. 2010. (ENG.). 32p. (J). (gr. k-3). 16.99 *(978-1-58980-860-7(6))* Pelican Publishing Co., Inc.

Lee, HaeDa. Ida's Present. Kim, InHyeon, illus. 2014. (MySELF Bookshelf Ser.). (ENG.). 32p. (J). (gr. k-2). pap. 11.94 *(978-1-60357-694-9(0))*; lib. bdg. 25.27 *(978-1-59953-659-0(5))* Norwood Hse. Pr.

Lester, Helen. All for Me & None for All. Munsinger, Lynn, illus. 2012. (ENG.). 32p. (J). (gr. -1-3). 16.99 *(978-0-547-68834-3(2))* Houghton Mifflin Harcourt Publishing Co.

Let's Share! (Book of Manners... Ser.). 32p. *(978-1-4054-9482-3(4))* Parragon, Inc.

Liberts, Jennifer. The Cake Monster. VanTuyle, David, illus. 2015. (Step into Reading Ser.). (ENG.). 24p. (J). (gr. -1-1). 4.99 *(978-0-553-52314-0(7),* Random Hse. Bks. for Young Readers) Random Hse. Children's Bks.

Lionni, Leo. It's Mine! 2015. 32p. pap. 7.00 *(978-1-61003-547-7(X))* Center for the Collaborative Classroom.

Lister, Mary. Winter King, Summer Queen. Mayo, Diana, illus. 2007. (ENG.). 32p. (J). (gr. -1-3). pap. 9.99 *(978-1-84686-009-6(1))*; pap. 7.99 *(978-1-84686-080-5(6))* Barefoot Bks., Inc.

Litwin, Eric. Ice Cream & Dinosaurs. Lichtenheld, Tom, illus. 2016. (Groovy Joe Ser.: 1). (ENG.). 40p. (J). (gr. -1-k). 17.99 *(978-0-545-88378-8(4),* Orchard Bks.) Scholastic, Inc.

Lordon, Claire. Lorenzo, the Pizza-Loving Lobster. 2016. (ENG., Illus.). 32p. (J). (gr. -1-3). 16.99 *(978-1-4998-0228-3(5))* Little Bee Books Inc.

Ludmila's Way - Teaching Guide. 2003. (J). 17.95 *(978-1-55942-192-8(4))* Witcher Productions.

Ludmila's Way: Evaluation Guide. 2006. (J). *(978-1-55942-415-8(X))* Witcher Productions.

Luedtke, Courtney. Baby Boo: The Happy Beginning. 2009. (Illus.). 72p. pap. 27.49 *(978-1-4389-2696-4(0))* AuthorHouse.

Mack, Jeff. Mine. 2017. (ENG., Illus.). 40p. (J). 16.99 *(978-1-4521-5234-9(9))* Chronicle Bks. LLC.

Mackall, Dandi Daley. Natalie & the Downside-Up Birthday, 1 vol. Blakeslee, Lys, illus. 2009. (That's Nat! Ser.). (ENG.). 96p. (J). (gr. 1-4). pap. 4.99 *(978-0-310-71569-6(5))* Zonderkidz.

Mardinly, Berdan. Fresh Tarhana Soup: Story in English & in Turkish. 2008. (ENG & TUR., Illus.). 24p. (J). 8.75 *(978-0-9801675-4-2(X))* Robertson Publishing.

Mattern, Joanne. The Tricky Garden. 2005. (J). pap. *(978-1-4108-4191-9(X))* Benchmark Education Co.

Mayer, Mercer. Little Critter(r) I Am Sharing. 2012. (Little Critter Ser.). (ENG., Illus.). 24p. (J). (gr. k — 1). bds. 6.95 *(978-1-4027-9747-7(8))* Sterling Publishing Co., Inc.

Mayhew, James. Boy. Mayhew, James, illus. 2011. (ENG., Illus.). 32p. (J). (gr. -1-k). pap. 8.99 *(978-1-4083-1409-8(6))* Hodder & Stoughton GBR. Dist: Hachette Bk. Group.

Mcevoy, Ariane. Little Monkey Learns to Share. 2012. 28p. pap. 15.99 *(978-1-4691-5830-3(2))* Xlibris Corp.

McKee, David. Elmer & the Hippos. McKee, David, illus. 2010. (Andersen Press Picture Bks). (ENG., Illus.). 32p. (J). (gr. -1-3). 16.95 *(978-0-7613-6442-9(0))* Lerner Publishing Group.

McKissack, Patricia C. The All-I'll-Ever-Want Christmas Doll. Pinkney, Jerry, illus. 2007. (J). *(978-0-375-83615-2(2),* Schwartz & Wade Bks.) Random Hse. Children's Bks.

—The All-I'll-Ever-Want Christmas Doll. Pinkney, Jerry, illus. 2007. (ENG.). 40p. (J). (gr. -1-3). 17.99 *(978-0-375-83759-3(0),* Schwartz & Wade Bks.) Random Hse. Children's Bks.

McNease, Mitzy. Chester's Presents. Cox, Kim, illus. 2006. 28p. (J). 10.95 *(978-0-9779488-0-2(3))* Blancmange Publishing LLC.

Meachen Rau, Dana. Let's Share. 2004. (Compass Point Early Reader Ser.). (J). 18.60 *(978-0-7565-0573-8(9))* Compass Point Bks.

Meddaugh, Susan. Toy Trouble. 2010. (Martha Speaks Ser.). (ENG., Illus.). 24p. (J). (gr. -1-3). pap. 3.99 *(978-0-547-21078-0(7))* Houghton Mifflin Harcourt Publishing Co.

Meinderts, Koos. The Man in the Clouds. Fienieg, Annette, illus. 2012. (ENG.). 38p. (J). (gr. 1). 16.95 *(978-1-935954-13-2(X),* 9781935954132) Lemniscaat USA.

Metzger, Steve. Ice Cream King. Downing, Julie, illus. 2011. (ENG.). 32p. (J). (gr. -1-2). 15.95 *(978-1-58925-096-3(6))*; pap. 7.95 *(978-1-58925-427-5(9))* Tiger Tales.

Mims-Word, Marsha. The Great Vacation. 2011. 36p. pap. 21.99 *(978-1-4568-9675-1(X))* Xlibris Corp.

Moodie, Fiona. Noko's Surprise Party. 2008. (ENG., Illus.). 32p. (J). (gr. k-3). 16.95 *(978-1-84507-587-3(0),* Frances Lincoln) Quarto Publishing Group UK GBR. Dist: Hachette Bk. Group.

Moores, Susanna. It's Not Yours, It's Mine! Moores, Susanna, illus. 2013. (Child's Play Library). (ENG., Illus.). 32p. (J). (gr. -1-2). *(978-1-84643-600-0(1))* Child's Play International Ltd.

Moroney, Tracey, illus. A Snowman for Little Bear. 2016. (J). **(978-0-545-84958-6(6))** Scholastic, Inc.

Muller, Lisa M. Master smokey & mr. Duck. 2006. 15p. (J). 9.99 *(978-1-4276-0027-1(9))* Aardvark Global Publishing.

Muth, Jon J. Stone Soup. 2011. (J). (gr. -1-3). 29.95 *(978-0-545-32741-1(5))* Weston Woods Studios, Inc.

Myracle, Lauren. Bff: A Girlfriend Book You Write Together. 2009. (ENG., Illus.). 256p. (YA). (gr. 7-11). 10.95 *(978-0-8109-8431-8(8),* Amulet Bks.) Abrams, Inc.

Nash, Damien K. H. & Nash, Kathy. Big Box, Little Box: The Forecast Calls for Potential Rain! Miller, Steve, illus. 2012. 80p. pap. 13.99 *(978-0-9846507-1-2(7))* Faith Bks. & MORE.

Nesselrode, Sandra. Princess Kelsie & Her Special Gifts. 2008. 28p. pap. 19.95 *(978-1-4327-1708-7(1))* Outskirts Pr., Inc.

Newman, Jeff. The Greedy Worm. 2014. (J). *(978-1-4424-7195-5(6),* Simon & Schuster Bks. For Young Readers) Simon & Schuster Bks. For Young Readers.

Newman, Nanette. Ben's Book. Birkett, Georgie, illus. 2011. (ENG.). 32p. (J). (gr. -1-k). pap. 9.99 *(978-1-84365-193-2(9),* Pavilion Children's Books) Pavilion Bks. GBR. Dist: Independent Pubs. Group.

Nicholson, Doris. A Day with Grandma. 2006. 9.00 *(978-0-8059-9914-3(0))* Dorrance Publishing Co., Inc.

O'Connor, Jane. Too Many Tutus. 2012. (Fancy Nancy - I Can Read! Ser.). (J). lib. bdg. 13.55 *(978-0-606-27124-0(4),* Turtleback) Turtleback Bks.

Olson, D. A. The Treasure Map. 2011. 36p. pap. 24.95 *(978-1-4626-3655-6(1))* America Star Bks.

One Big Pair of Underwear. 2014. (ENG., Illus.). 40p. (J). (gr. -1-3). 17.99 *(978-1-4424-5336-4(2),* Beach Lane Bks.) Beach Lane Bks.

Opal, Paola, illus. Saffy & Ollie. 2012. (Simply Small Ser.). (ENG.). 24p. (J). (gr. -1 — 1). bds. 7.95 *(978-1-897476-69-7(8))* Simply Read Bks. CAN. Dist: Ingram Publisher Services.

Oram, Hiawyn. My Friend Fred. Reeve, Rosie, illus. 2012. (ENG.). 32p. (J). *(978-1-58925-105-2(9))* Tiger Tales.

Orloff, Karen Kaufman. I Wanna New Room. Catrow, David, III, illus. 2010. (ENG.). 32p. (J). (gr. k-3). 16.99 *(978-0-399-25405-5(6),* G.P. Putnam's Sons Books for Young Readers) Penguin Young Readers Group.

Palazetti, Toulla. Seed Was Planted. Barcita, Pamela, illus. 2010. (ENG.). 32p. (J). (gr. -1-3). pap. 7.95 *(978-1-934960-10-3(1),* Raven Tree Pr.,Csi) Continental Sales, Inc.

Parenteau, Shirley. Bears on Chairs. Walker, David, illus. 2011. (ENG.). 32p. (J). (gr. -1 — 1). bds. 6.99 *(978-0-7636-5092-6(7))* Candlewick Pr.

Parker, David. I Can Share! Dubin, Jill, illus. 2005. (J). *(978-0-439-73587-2(4))* Scholastic, Inc.

—Sharing My Room. Lucas, Margeaux, illus. 2007. (J). *(978-0-545-00386-5(5))* Scholastic, Inc.

Paschkis, Julie. Mooshka, a Quilt Story, 1 vol. Paschkis, Julie, illus. 2012. (ENG., Illus.). 32p. (J). 16.95 *(978-1-56145-620-8(9))* Peachtree Pubs.

Pearson, Mary E. Generous Me. Krejca, Gary, illus. 2011. (Rookie Ready to Learn — All about Me! Ser.). 40p. (J). (gr. -1-k). lib. bdg. 25.00 *(978-0-531-26427-0(0))*; (ENG.). pap. 5.95 *(978-0-531-26652-6(4))* Scholastic Library Publishing. (Children's Pr.).

Pepper, Louise. Got your Back... A Story of Friendship & Caring. 2011. 24p. (gr. -1). pap. 11.50 *(978-1-4567-5527-0(7))* AuthorHouse.

Porter, Jen. I Am Good. Saunders, Katie, illus. 2016. (ENG.). 16p. (J). (-3). bds. 7.99 *(978-1-4926-4167-4(7),* 9781492641674, Sourcebooks Jabberwocky) Sourcebooks, Inc.

Price, Marilyn. Grandma's Cookies. 2011. 32p. pap. 12.95 *(978-1-934527-28-3(9))* Torah Aura Productions.

Principe, Tami. The Green Rabbit: Rabbits Aren't Supposed to Be Green! 2012. 32p. pap. 10.95 *(978-1-4626-7509-8(3))* America Star Bks.

Publications International Ltd. Staff, ed. Finding Nemo - Let's Go to School. 2011. 12p. (J). bds. *(978-1-4508-0510-0(8))* Publications International, Ltd.

—Sesame Street: Potty Time with Elmo (Look & Find) 2010. 20p. (J). pap. 5.98 *(978-1-4508-1471-3(9))* Publications International, Ltd.

Rabei, Carolina. Crunch! Rabei, Carolina, illus. 2016. (Child's Play Library). (ENG., Illus.). 36p. (J). *(978-1-84643-733-5(4))* Child's Play International Ltd.

Ramsey, Dave. The Big Birthday Surprise: Junior Discovers Giving. Ramsey, Marshall, illus. 2003. 26p. (J). 7.95 *(978-0-9726323-2-4(8))* Ramsey Pr.

Randall, Marilyn. A Hard Nut to Crack. 2009. 36p. pap. 18.95 *(978-0-557-15891-1(5))* Lulu Pr., Inc.

Ranganathan, Babu G. The Selfish Apple Tree. 2010. 12p. 7.95 *(978-1-4497-0312-7(7),* WestBow Pr.) Author Solutions, Inc.

Ransome, James E. New Red Bike! 2011. (ENG., Illus.). 32p. (J). (gr. -1-3). 16.95 *(978-0-8234-2226-5(7))* Holiday Hse., Inc.

Rayner, Catherine. The Bear Who Shared. 2011. (ENG.). 32p. (J). (gr. -1-k). 16.99 *(978-0-8037-3576-7(6),* Dial Bks) Penguin Young Readers Group.

Reiss, Mike & Reiss, Mike. The Boy Who Wouldn't Share. Catrow, David, illus. 2008. (ENG.). 32p. (J). (gr. 1-3). 16.99 *(978-0-06-059132-8(3))* HarperCollins Pubs.

Rickerty, Simon. The Crayon: A Colorful Tale about Friendship. Rickerty, Simon, illus. 2014. (ENG., Illus.). 32p. (J). (gr. -1-2). 15.99 *(978-1-4814-0475-4(X),* Aladdin) Simon & Schuster Children's Publishing.

—The Peanut: A Nutty Tale about Sharing. Rickerty, Simon, illus. 2013. (ENG., Illus.). 40p. (J). (gr. -1-2). 15.99 *(978-1-4424-8364-4(4),* Simon & Schuster/Paula Wiseman Bks.) Simon & Schuster/Paula Wiseman Bks.

Robinson, Cindy. Baby Baobab. Robinson, Cindy, illus. 2010. (ENG., Illus.). 32p. (J). (gr. k-2). pap. 9.00 *(978-1-77009-671-4(X))* Jacana Media ZAF. Dist: Independent Pubs. Group.

Rosenthal, Amy Krouse. Plant a Kiss. Reynolds, Peter H., illus. (ENG.). (J). (gr. -1 — 1). 2015. 36p. bds. 7.99 *(978-0-06-241652-0(9),* HarperFestival) 2011. 40p. 14.99 *(978-0-06-198675-8(5))* HarperCollins Pubs.

Ruzzier, Sergio. Bear & Bee. Ruzzier, Sergio, illus. 2013. (Bear & Bee Ser.). (ENG., Illus.). 48p. (J). (gr. -1-k). 14.99 *(978-1-4231-5957-5(8))* Hyperion Pr.

Sanschagrin, Joceline. Caillou: It's Mine! Brignaud, Pierre, illus. 3rd ed. 2013. (Step by Step Ser.). (ENG.). 24p. (J). (gr. -1-k). bds. 5.99 *(978-2-89718-059-1(5))* Caillouet, Gerry.

Santat, Dan & Willems, Mo. The Cookie Fiasco. Santat, Dan & Willems, Mo, illus. 2016. (Elephant & Piggie Like Reading! Ser.). (ENG., Illus.). 64p. (J). (gr. 1-3). 9.99 *(978-1-4847-2636-5(7))* Hyperion Bks. for Children.

Santillo, LuAnn. Gum. Santillo, LuAnn, ed. 2003. (Half-Pint Kids Readers Ser.). (Illus.). 7p. (J). (gr. -1-1). pap. 1.00 *(978-1-59256-087-5(3))* Half-Pint Kids, Inc.

Schmauss, Judy Kentor. Luke's Mule. Costello, Shawn, illus. 2006. (Reader's Clubhouse Level 2 Reader Ser.). (ENG.). 24p. (J). (gr. 1-4). pap. 3.99 *(978-0-7641-3297-1(0))* Barron's Educational Series, Inc.

Schneider, Richard H. The Christmas Pea Coat. Bond, Higgins, illus. 2004. 32p. (J). 14.95 *(978-0-8249-5474-1(2),* Ideal Pubns.) Worthy Publishing.

Schwarz, Evelyn. The Hummingbird Garden. Quinn, Kitty, illus. 2012. (ENG.). 34p. (J). pap. 16.95 *(978-1-4327-9815-4(4))* Outskirts Pr., Inc.

Shea, Therese. Bear Likes to Share. 2006. (Neighborhood Readers Ser.). (ENG.). 8p. (gr. -1-3). pap. 5.15 *(978-1-4042-5696-5(2),* Rosen Classroom) Rosen Publishing Group, Inc., The.

Smith, D. K. Sock 'n Boots - Share. 2010. 32p. pap. 13.60 *(978-0-557-52614-7(0))* Lulu Pr., Inc.

Soleim, Heather. God's Incredible Creatures: The Gift of Sharing. Greisen, Steve, ed. Hedgecock, Sean, illus. 2005. 24p. (J). bds. 14.95 *(978-0-9707422-9-2(0))* Reel Productions, LLC.

Sommer, Carl. Stone Soup. Denman, Michael, illus. 2014. (Sommer-Time Story Classics Ser.). (ENG.). 32p. (J). (gr. k-4). 16.95 *(978-1-57537-078-1(6))* Advance Publishing, Inc.

—Tied up in Knots(Enredados) Budwine, Greg, illus. 2009. (Another Sommer-Time Story Bilingual Ser.). (SPA & ENG.). 48p. (J). lib. bdg. 16.95 *(978-1-57537-169-6(3))* Advance Publishing, Inc.

Sowards, Ben, illus. Christmas Oranges. 2004. 32p. 17.95 *(978-1-59156-098-2(5))* Covenant Communications, Inc.

Stein, Mathilde. Mine! Van Hout, Mies, illus. 2007. (ENG.). 26p. (J). (gr. -1-3). 16.95 *(978-1-59078-506-5(1))* Boyds Mills Pr.

Stoop, Naoko. Red Knit Cap Girl & the Reading Tree. 2014. (ENG., Illus.). 40p. (J). (gr. -1-3). 17.00 *(978-0-316-22886-2(9))* Little, Brown Bks. for Young Readers.

Studio Mouse Staff. Sesame Street Share & Care, It's Only Fair. 2009. (ENG.). 60p. (J). (gr. -1). 12.99 *(978-1-59069-739-9(1))* Studio Mouse LLC.

Suen, Anastasia. Scissors, Paper & Sharing, 1 vol. Ebbeler, Jeffrey, illus. 2007. (Main Street School - Kids with Character Ser.). (ENG.). 32p. (gr. -1-4). 28.50 *(978-1-60270-032-1(X),* Looking Glass Library) ABDO Publishing Co.

SungJa, Cho. Bubbly & Grumpy. SukWon, Sa, illus. rev. ed. 2014. (MySELF Bookshelf Ser.). (ENG.). 32p. (J). (gr. k-2). pap. 11.94 *(978-1-60357-660-4(6))*; lib. bdg. 25.27 *(978-1-59953-651-4(X))* Norwood Hse. Pr.

Szymona, Marlene L. My Sister Beth's Pink Birthday. Battuz, Christine, illus. 2014. (J). *(978-1-4338-1654-3(7))*; pap. *(978-1-4338-1655-0(5))* American Psychological Assn. (Magination Pr.).

Talley, Linda. Ludmila's Way. Chase, Andra, illus. 2003. (J). 17.95 *(978-1-55942-190-4(8))* Witcher Productions.

Tan, Richard. George's Banana. 2015. (Rosen REAL Readers: STEM & STEAM Collection). (ENG.). 8p. pap. 5.46 *(978-1-4994-9530-0(7),* Rosen Classroom) Rosen Publishing Group, Inc., The.

Taylor, Myonna. Show & Tell. Phillips, Hope Ann, illus. 2012. 32p. 24.95 *(978-1-4626-7798-6(3))* America Star Bks.

Tiger Tales, ed. & compiled by. Stories to Share. Tiger Tales, compiled by. 2015. (ENG.). 176p. (J). (gr. -1-3). 12.99 *(978-1-58925-537-1(2))* Tiger Tales.

Tineo, Suzanne Nicoll. Danny the Damsel: Sharing. 2012. 44p. pap. 22.65 *(978-1-4771-1510-7(2))* Xlibris Corp.

Tomlinson, Mark K. Share the Grain. 2010. 12p. pap. 8.49 *(978-1-4490-6059-6(5))* AuthorHouse.

Torres, J. Yo Gabba Gabba: Good Night, Gabbaland: Good Night, Gabbaland. 2010. 16p. bds. 7.99 *(978-1-934964-56-9(5))* Oni Pr., Inc.

Trilling, Richard J. Stories of Stephanie & Friends. 2010. 42p. pap. 15.50 *(978-1-60860-410-4(1),* Eloquent Bks.) Strategic Book Publishing & Rights Agency (SBPRA).

Tym, Kate. Time to Share. 2008. (Manners Ser.). (Illus.). 24p. (J). (gr. -1-1). lib. bdg. 16.95 *(978-1-59566-591-1(9))* QEB Publishing Inc.

van Genechten, Guido. Can't We Share? 2012. (Little Snowman Stan Ser.). (ENG.). 30p. (J). (gr. -1-k). 16.95 *(978-1-60537-121-4(1))* Cobblestone Publishing Co.

Waldman, Debby & Feutl, Rita. Room Enough for Daisy, 1 vol. Revell, Cindy, illus. 2011. (ENG.). 32p. (J). (gr. -1-3). 19.95 *(978-1-55469-255-2(5))* Orca Bk. Pubs. USA.

Walton, Ann. Something to Do. Hinrichsen, Natalie, illus. 2010. (ENG.). 24p. (J). (gr. k-2). pap. 6.00 *(978-1-77009-706-3(6))* Jacana Media ZAF. Dist: Independent Pubs. Group.

Weaver, Susan. My Goofy Girls. 2007. 24p. per. 24.95 *(978-1-4241-8933-5(0))* America Star Bks.

Wilhelm, Hans. I Won't Share! Wilhelm, Hans, illus. 2010. (Scholastic Reader Level 1 Ser.). (ENG., Illus.). 32p. (J). (gr. -1-2). pap. 3.99 *(978-0-439-77353-9(9))* Scholastic, Inc.

Willems, Mo. The Pigeon Finds a Hot Dog! Willems, Mo, illus. 2004. (Pigeon Ser.). (ENG., Illus.). 40p. (J). (gr. -1-k). 16.99 *(978-0-7868-1869-3(7))* Hyperion Pr.

—Should I Share My Ice Cream? Willems, Mo, illus. 2011. (Elephant & Piggie Book Ser.). (ENG., Illus.). 64p. (J). (gr. -1-k). 9.99 *(978-1-4231-4343-7(4))* Hyperion Pr.

Willems, Mo & Campoy, F. Isabel. ¿Debo Compartir Mi Helado? Willems, Mo, illus. 2015. (Elephant & Piggie Book Ser.). (SPA., Illus.). 64p. (J). (gr. -1-k). 9.99 *(978-1-4847-2291-6(4))* Disney Publishing Worldwide.

—¡La Paloma Encuentra un Perro Caliente! Willems, Mo, illus. 2011. (SPA & ENG., Illus.). 40p. (J). (gr. -1-k). pap. 9.99 *(978-1-4231-4051-1(6))* Hyperion Pr.

Williams, Sam. It's My Turn. Dufalla, Anita, illus. 2012. (ENG.). 24p. (gr. k-1). pap. 8.95 *(978-1-61810-296-6(6))* Rourke Educational Media.

Wilson, Geraline. Billy & Willy Learn to Share. 2012. 24p. pap. 24.95 *(978-1-4626-8135-8(2))* America Star Bks.

Wilson, Karma. Bear Says Thanks. Chapman, Jane, illus. 2012. (Bear Bks.). (ENG.). 40p. (J). (gr. -1-3). 17.99 *(978-1-4169-5856-7(8),* McElderry, Margaret K. Bks.) McElderry, Margaret K. Bks.

Winkler, Henry & Oliver, Lin. Dump Trucks & Dogsleds - I'm on My Way, Mom! Watson, Jesse Joshua, illus. 2009. (Hank Zipzer Ser.: 16). (ENG.). 160p. (J). (gr. 3-7). pap. 5.99 *(978-0-448-44380-5(5),* Grosset & Dunlap) Penguin Young Readers Group.

Witte, Anna. El Loro Tico Tango. Witte, Anna, illus. 2011. (SPA., Illus.). 24p. (J). (gr. -1-1). 9.99 *(978-1-84686-670-8(7))* Barefoot Bks., Inc.

Wolff, Ferida & Savitz, Harriet May. The Story Blanket, 1 vol. Odriozola, Elena, illus. 2008. (ENG.). 32p. (J). (gr. -1-3). 16.95 *(978-1-56145-466-2(4),* Peachtree Junior) Peachtree Pubs.

Won, Brian. Hooray for Hat! Big Book. 2016. (ENG., Illus.). 40p. (J). (gr. -1-3). 26.99 *(978-0-544-66831-7(6),* HMH Books For Young Readers) Houghton Mifflin Harcourt Publishing Co.

Woodcock, Fiona. Hiding Heidi. 2016. (ENG., Illus.). 32p. (J). (gr. -1-3). 16.99 *(978-1-4998-0350-1(8))* Little Bee Books Inc.

Woodson, Jacqueline. Pecan Pie Baby. Blackall, Sophie, illus. 2010. (ENG.). 32p. (J). (gr. k-3). 16.99 *(978-0-399-23987-8(1),* G.P. Putnam's Sons Books for Young Readers) Penguin Young Readers Group.

Yaccarino, Dan. Birthday Cake: A Little Moral Story about Sharing. 2016. (Dan Yaccarino's Happyland Ser.). (ENG., Illus.). 22p. (J). (gr. -1 — 1). bds. 5.95 *(978-0-7611-8734-9(0))* Workman Publishing Co., Inc.

Yarlett, Emma. Sidney, Stella, & the Moon. Yarlett, Emma, illus. 2013. (ENG., Illus.). 44p. (J). (gr. k-3). 16.99 *(978-0-7636-6623-1(8),* Templar) Candlewick Pr.

Yates-Velez, C. My Baby Brother & Me. 2011. (Illus.). 24p. pap. *(978-1-4269-6130-4(8))* Trafford Publishing (UK) Ltd.

Yerrid, Gable. Marley's Treasure. Fitzgerald, Jennifer, illus. 2007. 28p. (J). (gr. -1-3). 15.95 *(978-0-9767442-6-9(0))* Yorkville Pr.

Yim, Natasha. Goldy Luck & the Three Pandas. Zong, Grace, illus. (ENG.). 32p. (J). (gr. -1-3). 2015. pap. 7.95 *(978-1-58089-653-5(7))* 2014. lib. bdg. 16.95 *(978-1-58089-652-8(9))* Charlesbridge Publishing, Inc.

Zake, Daiga. Oranges for Everyone. Stojanova, Elena, illus. 2007. 32p. (J). (POL & ENG.). pap. 12.95 *(978-1-60195-104-5(3))*; (ARA.). pap. 12.95 *(978-1-60195-306-3(2))* International Step by Step Assn.

SHARKS

Abramovitz, Melissa. Deadliest Sharks. 2016. (ENG.). 80p. (J). (gr. 5-12). lib. bdg. *(978-1-68282-054-4(8))* ReferencePoint Pr., Inc.

Abramson, Andra Serlin. Kids Meet the Sharks & Other Giant Sea Creatures. 2014. (Kids Meet Ser.: 1). (ENG., Illus.). 96p. (J). 14.95 *(978-1-60433-467-8(3),* Applesauce Pr.) Cider Mill Pr. Bk. Pubs., LLC.

American Museum of Natural History. Sharks. 2017. (Science for Toddlers Ser.). (ENG., Illus.). 26p. (J). (gr. -1). bds. 7.95 **(978-1-4549-2128-8(5))** Sterling Publishing Co., Inc.

Antill, Sara. A Shark's Life. 2012. (Illus.). 24p. (J). 49.50 *(978-1-4488-5111-9(4),* PowerKids Pr.); pap. 8.25 *(978-1-4488-5110-2(6),* PowerKids Pr.); lib. bdg. 22.60 *(978-1-4488-4981-9(0))* Rosen Publishing Group, Inc., The.

Aparicio, Eduardo. Sharks vs. Humans. 2014. (Illus.). 32p. (J). *(978-0-545-72499-6(6))* Scholastic, Inc.

Applesauce Press Staff, et al. Discovering Sharks. 2016. (ENG., Illus.). 96p. (J). 19.95 *(978-1-60433-604-7(8),* Applesauce Pr.) Cider Mill Pr. Bk. Pubs., LLC.

Arlon, Penelope & Burnie, David. Sharks. 2013. (Scholastic Discover More Ser.). (ENG.). 80p. (J). (gr. 2-5). 12.99 *(978-0-545-49561-5(X),* Scholastic Reference) Scholastic, Inc.

Arlon, Penelope & Tuchman, Gail. Scholastic Discover More Reader Level 2: Shark Attack! 2013. (Scholastic Discover More Reader Ser.). (ENG.). 32p. (J). (gr. 1-3). pap. 3.99 *(978-0-545-53377-5(5),* Scholastic Reference) Scholastic, Inc.

Arnold, Tedd. Sharks. Arnold, Tedd, illus. 2013. (Fly Guy Ser.). (ENG., Illus.). 32p. (J). (gr. -1-3). pap. 3.99 *(978-0-545-50771-4(5),* Scholastic Reference) Scholastic, Inc.

—Sharks. 2013. (Fly Guy Presents Ser.). lib. bdg. 13.55 *(978-0-606-31968-3(9),* Turtleback) Turtleback Bks.

Bader, Bonnie. My Little Golden Book about Sharks. 2016. (Little Golden Book Ser.). (ENG., Illus.). 24p. (J). (-k). 4.99 *(978-1-101-93092-2(6),* Golden Bks.) Random Hse. Children's Bks.

Balfour, Barbara. Great White Sharks. 2006. (Amazing Animals Ser.). (Illus.). 24p. (J). (gr. 3-7). pap. 8.95 *(978-1-59036-397-3(3))*; lib. bdg. 24.45 *(978-1-59036-391-1(4))* Weigl Pubs., Inc.

Bantin, John. Shark Bytes - Tales of Diving with the Bizarre & the Beautiful. 2015. (ENG., Illus.). 224p. pap. 30.60 **(978-1-909911-45-1(3))** Fernhurst Bks. GBR. Dist: Casemate Pubs. & Bk. Distributors, LLC.

Barnes, Julia. 101 Facts about Sharks. 2004. (One Hundred One Facts about Predators Ser.). (Illus.). 32p. (gr. 1-4). lib. bdg. 26.00 *(978-0-8368-4039-1(9),* Gareth Stevens Learning Library) Stevens, Gareth Publishing LLLP.

Barnes, Nico. Basking Sharks, 1 vol. 2014. (Sharks Ser.). (ENG.). 24p. (J). (gr. 4-8). lib. bdg. 28.50 *(978-1-62970-064-9(9))* ABDO Publishing Co.

—Great White Sharks, 1 vol. 2014. (Sharks Ser.). (ENG.). 24p. (J). (gr. 4-8). lib. bdg. 28.50 *(978-1-62970-065-6(7))* ABDO Publishing Co.

—Hammerhead Sharks, 1 vol. 2014. (Sharks Ser.). (ENG.). 24p. (J). (gr. 4-8). lib. bdg. 28.50 *(978-1-62970-066-3(5))* ABDO Publishing Co.

—Mako Sharks, 1 vol. 2014. (Sharks Ser.). (ENG.). 24p. (J). (gr. 4-8). lib. bdg. 28.50 *(978-1-62970-067-0(3))* ABDO Publishing Co.

—Whale Sharks, 1 vol. 2014. (Sharks Ser.). (ENG.). 24p. (J). (gr. 4-8). lib. bdg. 28.50 *(978-1-62970-068-7(1))* ABDO Publishing Co.

—Zebra Sharks, 1 vol. 2014. (Sharks Ser.). (ENG.). 24p. (J). (gr. 4-8). lib. bdg. 28.50 *(978-1-62970-069-4(X))* ABDO Publishing Co.

Barnes, Nico, et al. Tiburones Ballena. 2015. (Tiburones Ser.). (SPA., Illus.). 24p. (gr. k-1). pap. 7.95 *(978-1-4966-0513-9(6))* Capstone Classroom.

—Tiburones Blancos. 2015. (Tiburones Ser.). (SPA., Illus.). 24p. (gr. k-1). pap. 7.95 *(978-1-4966-0515-3(2))* Capstone Classroom.

—Tiburones Cebra. 2015. (Tiburones Ser.). (SPA., Illus.). 24p. (gr. k-1). pap. 7.95 *(978-1-4966-0517-7(9))* Capstone Classroom.

S

—Tiburones Mako. 2015. (Tiburones Ser.). (SPA., Illus.). 24p. (gr. k-1). pap. 7.95 *(978-1-4966-0519-1(5))* Capstone Classroom.

—Tiburones Martillo. 2015. (Tiburones Ser.). (SPA., Illus.). 24p. (gr. k-1). pap. 7.95 *(978-1-4966-0521-4(7))* Capstone Classroom.

—Tiburones Peregrinos. 2015. (Tiburones Ser.). (SPA., Illus.). 24p. (gr. k-1). pap. 7.95 *(978-1-4966-0523-8(3))* Capstone Classroom.

Bell, Samantha. Hammerhead Sharks. 2013. (21st Century Skills Library: Exploring Our Oceans Ser.). (ENG., Illus.). 32p. (J). (gr. 3-6). 28.50 *(978-1-62431-408-7(2)*, 202752); pap. 14.21 *(978-1-62431-484-1(8)*, 202754) Cherry Lake Publishing.

—Tiger Sharks. 2013. (21st Century Skills Library: Exploring Our Oceans Ser.). (ENG., Illus.). 32p. (J). (gr. 3-6). 28.50 *(978-1-62431-410-0(4)*, 202760); pap. 14.21 *(978-1-62431-486-5(4)*, 202762) Cherry Lake Publishing.

Benchley, Peter. Shark Life: True Stories about Sharks & the Sea. 2007. (ENG.). 208p. (J). (gr. 3-7). 6.99 *(978-0-440-41954-9(9)*, Yearling) Random Hse. Children's Bks.

Berger, Melvin & Berger, Gilda. Sharks. 2003. (Scholastic Reader Ser.). (Illus.). (J). pap. *(978-0-439-47388-0(8))* Scholastic, Inc.

Bergeron, Alain M., et al. Les Requins. 2008. (FRE., Illus.). 64p. (J). pap. 8.95 *(978-2-89435-369-1(3))* Quintin Pubs./Editions Michel Quintin CAN. Dist: Crabtree Publishing Co.

Berman, Ruth. Sharks. rev. ed. 2009. (Nature Watch Ser.). (ENG.). 48p. (gr. 4-8). 27.93 *(978-0-7613-4243-4(5))* Lerner Publishing Group.

Betz, Adrienne & Time for Kids Editors. Sharks! 2005. (Time for Kids Science Scoops Ser.). (ENG., Illus.). 32p. (J). (gr. 1-3). pap. 3.99 *(978-0-06-057632-5(4))* HarperCollins Pubs.

Bodden, Valerie. Amazing Animals: Sharks. 2011. (Amazing Animals Ser.). (ENG.). 24p. (J). (gr. 1-3). pap. 8.99 *(978-0-89812-744-7(0)*, Creative Paperbacks) Creative Co., The.

—Sharks. 2010. (Amazing Animals Ser.). (Illus.). 24p. (J). (gr. -1-3). 16.95 *(978-1-58341-812-3(1)*, Creative Education) Creative Co., The.

Borgert-Spaniol, Megan. The Sand Tiger Shark. 2012. (Shark Fact Files Ser.). (ENG., Illus.). 24p. (J). (gr. 3-8). lib. bdg. 25.95 *(978-1-60014-806-4(9)*, Pilot Bks.) Bellwether Media.

—The Whale Shark. 2012. (Shark Fact Files Ser.). (ENG., Illus.). 24p. (J). (gr. 3-8). lib. bdg. 25.95 *(978-1-60014-807-1(7)*, Pilot Bks.) Bellwether Media.

Boyd, Ian, et al. Animal Bites: Sharks. 2005. (Illus.). 24p. (J). pap. *(978-0-439-81500-0(2)*, Scholastic) Scholastic, Inc.

Bredeson, Carmen. Great White Sharks up Close. 2006. (Zoom in on Animals! Ser.). (Illus.). 24p. (J). (gr. 1-3). lib. bdg. 22.60 *(978-0-7660-2495-3(4)*, Enslow Elementary) Enslow Pubs., Inc.

Bright, Michael. Spectacular Sharks: An Exciting Investigation into the Most Powerful Predator in the Ocean, Shown in More Than 200 Images. 2016. (ENG., Illus.). 64p. 12.99 *(978-1-86147-496-4(2)*, Armadillo) Anness Publishing GBR. Dist: National Bk. Network.

—3-D Explorer: Sharks. 2015. (3D Explorers Ser.). (ENG., Illus.). 32p. (J). (gr. 1). 19.95 *(978-1-62686-438-2(1)*, Silver Dolphin Bks.) Readerlink Distribution Services, LLC.

Brown, Laaren. Icky Sticky - Super Sharks. 2015. (Scholastic Reader, Level 2 Ser.). (ENG., Illus.). 32p. (J). (gr. 1-3). pap. 4.99 *(978-0-545-87231-7(6)*, Scholastic Nonfiction) Scholastic, Inc.

Brown, Laaren. Super Sharks. 2016. (Illus.). 32p. (J). ***(978-1-5182-0105-9(9))*** Scholastic, Inc.

Brusha, Joe. Top 10 Deadliest Sharks. 2011. (ENG., Illus.). 200p. (J). pap. 9.99 *(978-1-937068-90-5(0)*, 9781937068905) Zenescope Entertainment.

Bulletpoints Sharks. 2005. (Illus.). (J). per. 4.99 *(978-1-933581-07-1(7))* Byeway Bks.

Candelaria, Michael. Sharks! 2003. (World Discovery Science Readers Ser.). (Illus.). 32p. (J). *(978-0-439-56629-2(0))* Scholastic, Inc.

Capstone Press. Shark Zone. 2010. (Shark Zone Ser.). (ENG.). 32p. lib. bdg. 101.28 *(978-1-4296-5913-0(0)*, Blazers) Capstone Press of Coughlan Cos.

Cerullo, Mary M. Journey to Shark Island: A Shark Photographer's Close Encounters, 1 vol. Rotman, Jeffrey L., illus. Rotman, Jeffrey L., photos by. 2014. (Shark Expedition Ser.). (ENG.). 40p. (gr. 5-7). lib. bdg. 31.99 *(978-0-7565-4887-2(X))* Compass Point Bks.

—Searching for Great White Sharks: A Shark Diver's Quest for Mr. Big, 1 vol. Rotman, Jeffrey L., photos by. 2014. (Shark Expedition Ser.). (ENG., Illus.). 40p. (gr. 5-7). lib. bdg. 31.99 *(978-0-7565-4884-1(5))* Compass Point Bks.

—Seeking Giant Sharks: A Shark Diver's Quest for Whale Sharks, Basking Sharks, & Manta Rays, 1 vol. Rotman, Jeffrey L., illus. Rotman, Jeffrey L., photos by. 2014. (Shark Expedition Ser.). (ENG.). 40p. (gr. 5-7). lib. bdg. 31.99 *(978-0-7565-4885-8(3))* Compass Point Bks.

—Shark Expedition, 1 vol. Rotman, Jeffrey L., photos by. 2014. (Shark Expedition Ser.). (ENG., Illus.). 40p. (gr. 5-7). 127.96 *(978-0-7565-4888-9(8)*, CPB Grades 4-8) Compass Point Bks.

—Shark Expedition: A Shark Photographer's Close Encounters. Rotman, Jeffrey L., photos by. 2015. (ENG., Illus.). 144p. (gr. 5-7). pap. 12.95 *(978-1-62370-156-7(2))* Capstone Press of Coughlan Cos.

—Sharks of the Deep: A Shark Photographer's Search for Sharks at the Bottom of the Sea, 1 vol. Rotman, Jeffrey L., illus. Rotman, Jeffrey L., photos by. 2014. (Shark Expedition Ser.). (ENG.). 40p. (gr. 5-7). lib. bdg. 31.99 *(978-0-7565-4886-5(1))* Compass Point Bks.

Chilson, Martin. In Search of Great White Sharks, 01 vols., 1. 2016. (Shark Search Ser.). (ENG., Illus.). 24p. (J). pap. 8.25 *(978-1-5081-4339-0(0)*, PowerKids Pr.) Rosen Publishing Group, Inc., The.

Clark, Willow. Shark! 2010. (Animal Danger Zone Ser.). (ENG.). 24p. (J). (gr. k-3). lib. bdg. 22.60 *(978-1-60754-957-4(3))*; (Illus.). pap. 8.15 *(978-1-60754-964-2(6))* Windmill Bks.

Clarke, Catriona. Sharks: Information for Young Readers - Level 1. Relf, Adam, illus. 2007. (Usborne Beginners Ser.). 32p. (J). (gr. -1-3). 4.99 *(978-0-7945-1581-2(9)*, Usborne) EDC Publishing.

Clarke, Phil. Sharks. 2005. (Usborne Lift the Flap Bks.). (Illus.). 16p. (J). (gr. -1-3). 11.99 *(978-0-7945-1109-8(0)*, Usborne) EDC Publishing.

Clarke, Phillip & Furnival, Keith. Sharks. Scott, Peter David, illus. 2005. (J). *(978-0-439-86358-2(9))* Scholastic, Inc.

Claybourne, Anna. Sharks: Predators of the Sea. 2016. (ENG., Illus.). 80p. (J). (gr. 4-7). pap. 9.95 *(978-1-77085-739-1(7)*, 9781770857391) Firefly Bks., Ltd.

Coldiron, Deborah. Sharks, 1 vol. 2008. (Underwater World Set II Ser.). (ENG.). 32p. (gr. k-4). 27.07 *(978-1-60453-138-1(X)*, Buddy Bks.) ABDO Publishing Co.

Coleman, Miriam. Swimming with Sharks. 2009. (Flippers & Fins Ser.). (Illus.). 24p. (J). (ENG.). pap. 8.25 *(978-1-4358-3239-8(6)*, PowerKids Pr.); (gr. 1-3). lib. bdg. 22.60 *(978-1-4042-8091-5(X))* Rosen Publishing Group, Inc., The.

Coode, Chris & Gibbons, Lynn. Sharks & the World's Scariest Sea Monsters. 2010. (3-D Thrillers Ser.). (ENG.). 32p. (J). (gr. 2-5). pap. 4.99 *(978-0-545-21849-8(7)*, Scholastic Reference) Scholastic, Inc.

Craig, Diane. Whale Shark, 1 vol. 2014. (Giant Animals Ser.). (ENG., Illus.). 24p. (J). (gr. -1-3). 24.21 *(978-1-62403-062-8(9))* ABDO Publishing Co.

Crossingham, John & Kalman, Bobbie. El Ciclo de Vida del Tiburon. 2007. (Ciclos de Vida Ser.). (SPA., Illus.). 32p. (J). (gr. 1-4). pap. *(978-0-7787-8719-8(2))*; (gr. 3-7). lib. bdg. *(978-0-7787-8673-3(0))* Crabtree Publishing Co.

—The Life Cycle of a Shark. 2005. (Life Cycle Ser.). (ENG., Illus.). 32p. (J). (gr. 2-3). pap. *(978-0-7787-0699-1(0))* Crabtree Publishing Co.

Dakota, Heather. Sharks: Menacing or Misunderstood? 2007. (Illus.). 48p. (J). *(978-0-439-92829-8(X))* Scholastic, Inc.

Davies, Nicola. Surprising Sharks: Read & Wonder. Croft, James, illus. 2005. (Read & Wonder Ser.). (ENG.). 32p. (J). (gr. -1-3). reprint ed. pap. 6.99 *(978-0-7636-2742-3(9))* Candlewick Pr.

De la Bédoyère, Camilla. Action Files: Sharks. 2008. 24p. (J). *(978-1-84810-022-0(1))* Miles Kelly Publishing, Ltd.

—My Little Book of Sharks. 2014. (Illus.). 64p. (J). ***(978-1-4351-5529-9(7))*** Barnes & Noble, Inc.

De la Bédoyère, Camilla. The Wild Life of Sharks, 1 vol. 2015. (ENG., Illus.). 24p. (J). lib. bdg. 23.60 *(978-1-4777-5498-6(9)*, Windmill Bks.) Rosen Publishing Group, Inc., The.

Dempski, Seth. In Search of Blue Sharks, 01 vols., 1. 2016. (Shark Search Ser.). (ENG., Illus.). 24p. (J). pap. 8.25 *(978-1-5081-4331-4(5)*, PowerKids Pr.) Rosen Publishing Group, Inc., The.

Discovery & Brockenbrough, Martha. Shark Week. 2016. (ENG., Illus.). 160p. (J). 19.99 *(978-1-250-09777-4(0)*, 9781250097774) Feiwel & Friends.

Discovery Channel. Discovery Channel Sharkopedia: The Complete Guide to Everything Shark. 2013. (ENG., Illus.). 192p. (gr. 3-17). pap. 19.95 *(978-1-60320-964-9(6))* Time Inc. Bks.

Donaldson, Chelsea. Hammerhead Shark: An Up-Close Look at the Body. 2014. (Illus.). 16p. (J). *(978-0-545-75173-5(X))* Scholastic, Inc.

Dorling Kindersley Publishing Staff. DK Findout! Sharks. 2017. (DK Find Out! Ser.). (ENG., Illus.). 64p. (J). (gr. 1-4). pap. 10.99 *(978-1-4654-5751-6(8)*, DK Children) Dorling Kindersley Publishing, Inc.

—Everything You Need to Know about Sharks: And other creatures of the Deep. 2012. (Everything You Need to Know Ser.). (ENG., Illus.). 80p. (J). (gr. 2-5). 15.99 *(978-0-7566-9881-2(2)*, DK Children) Dorling Kindersley Publishing, Inc.

—Pocket Genius: Sharks. 2016. (Pocket Genius Ser.). (ENG., Illus.). 160p. (J). (gr. 3-7). pap. 4.99 *(978-1-4654-4592-6(7)*, DK Children) Dorling Kindersley Publishing, Inc.

—Sharkpedia, 2nd Edition. 2017. (ENG., Illus.). 128p. (J). (gr. 3-7). 12.99 ***(978-1-4654-6312-8(7)***, DK Children) Dorling Kindersley Publishing, Inc.

—Sharks: Open Your Eyes to a World of Discovery. 2014. (Eye Wonder Ser.). (ENG.). 56p. (J). (gr. k-4). 10.99 *(978-1-4654-1831-9(8)*, DK Children) Dorling Kindersley Publishing, Inc.

—Sharks & Other Deadly Ocean Creatures. 2016. (ENG., Illus.). 208p. (J). (gr. 4-7). 16.99 *(978-1-4654-5084-5(X)*, DK Children) Dorling Kindersley Publishing, Inc.

—Sharks & Other Sea Creatures. 2017. (ENG., Illus.). 32p. (J). (-k). 8.99 *(978-1-4654-5658-8(9)*, DK Children) Dorling Kindersley Publishing, Inc.

—Super Shark Encyclopedia. 2015. (ENG., Illus.). 208p. (J). (gr. 3-7). 24.99 *(978-1-4654-3584-2(0)*, DK Children) Dorling Kindersley Publishing, Inc.

—Ultimate Sticker Book: Sharks. 2016. (ENG.). 32p. (J). (gr. k-4). pap. 6.99 *(978-1-4654-4719-7(9)*, DK Children) Dorling Kindersley Publishing, Inc.

Downtown Bookworks Inc. Staff, et al. Shark-Tastic! 2011. (Science with Stuff Ser.: 1). (ENG.). 64p. (J). (gr. 1). lib. bdg. 12.99 *(978-1-935703-29-7(3))* Downtown Bookworks.

Durrie, Karen. Gran Tiburón Blanco. 2013. (SPA.). (J). *(978-1-62127-567-1(1))* Weigl Pubs., Inc.

—I Am a Great White Shark. 2012. (J). *(978-1-61913-223-8(0))*; pap. *(978-1-61913-224-5(9))* Weigl Pubs., Inc.

East Dubowski, Cathy. DK Readers L3: Shark Attack! 2015. (DK Readers Ser.). (ENG., Illus.). 64p. (J). (gr. 2-4). pap. 3.99 *(978-1-4654-3506-4(9)*, DK Children) Dorling Kindersley Publishing, Inc.

Editors of Kingfisher. Amazing Sharks. 2016. (It's All About... Ser.). (ENG., Illus.). 32p. pap. 5.99 *(978-0-7534-7266-8(X)*, 9780753472668, Kingfisher) Roaring Brook Pr.

Equipo Staff. Tiburones. 2004.Tr. of Sharks. (SPA., Illus.). 64p. (J). pap. 8.95 *(978-0-7460-4515-2(8))* EDC Publishing.

Fact Atlas: Sharks. 2009. (FACT ATLAS Ser.). 72p. (J). 15.95 *(978-0-8416-1095-8(9))* Hammond World Atlas Corp.

Field, Nancy H. Discovering Sharks & Rays. Maydak, Michael S., illus. 2003. (Discovering Nature Library). 40p. (J). (gr. 2-6). pap. 7.95 *(978-0-941042-33-8(2))* Dog-Eared Pubns.

Foreman, Niki. Shark Reef. 2014. (DK Readers Ser.). (ENG.). 48p. (J). (gr. 2-4). 14.99 *(978-1-4654-2006-0(1)*, DK Children) Dorling Kindersley Publishing, Inc.

Foreman, Niki & Dorling Kindersley Publishing Staff. Shark Reef. 2014. (DK Readers Ser.). (ENG.). 48p. (J). (gr. 2-4). pap. 3.99 *(978-1-4654-2007-7(X)*, DK Children) Dorling Kindersley Publishing, Inc.

Fowler, Sarah L. Sharks. 2017. (Illus.). 64p. (J). ***(978-1-5364-0133-2(1))*** Dorling Kindersley Publishing, Inc.

Furstinger, Nancy. Great White Shark, 1 vol. 2013. (Great Predators Ser.). (ENG., Illus.). 48p. (J). (gr. 3-6). lib. bdg. 32.79 *(978-1-61783-947-4(7))* ABDO Publishing Co.

—Great White Shark Paperback. 2013. (J). pap. 15.64 *(978-1-62403-012-3(2)*, Core Library) ABDO Publishing Co.

Gagne, Tammy. Sharks: Built for the Hunt. 2015. (Predator Profiles Ser.). (ENG., Illus.). 24p. (gr. 1-2). lib. bdg. 25.32 *(978-1-4914-5037-6(1))* Capstone Press of Coughlan Cos.

Gaines, Richard Marshall. When Sharks Attack! 2006. (When Wild Animals Attack! Ser.). (Illus.). 48p. (J). (gr. 4-10). lib. bdg. 25.27 *(978-0-7660-2664-3(7))* Enslow Pubs., Inc.

Gareth Stevens Publishing Staff, contrib. by. Sharks. 2004. (All about Wild Animals Ser.). (Illus.). 32p. (gr. k-4). lib. bdg. 26.00 *(978-0-8368-4188-6(3)*, Gareth Stevens Learning Library) Stevens, Gareth Publishing LLLP.

Gerstein, Sherry. See-Thru Sharks. 2016. (See-Thru Bks.). (ENG., Illus.). 28p. (gr. 2-4). spiral bd. 12.99 *(978-1-60684-588-2(8)*, Millbrook Pr.) Lerner Publishing Group.

Gibbons, Lynn. Sharks. 2009. (Up Close Ser.). 24p. (gr. 3-3). 47.90 *(978-1-60854-702-9(7)*, PowerKids Pr.) Rosen Publishing Group, Inc., The.

Gibbons, Lynn & Coode, Chris. Sharks. 2007. (Up Close Ser.). (Illus.). 24p. (J). (gr. 3-7). lib. bdg. 25.25 *(978-1-4042-3762-9(3)*, PowerKids Pr.) Rosen Publishing Group, Inc., The.

Gilkerson, Patricia. My Adventure with Sharks. 2009. (ENG.). 44p. (J). 8.99 *(978-1-59092-468-6(1))* Blue Forge Pr.

Gilpin, Daniel. Life-Size Sharks & Other Underwater Creatures. Knowelden, Martin, illus. 2005. (Life-Size Ser.). (ENG.). 28p. (J). (gr. 2-7). 9.95 *(978-1-4027-2537-1(X))* Sterling Publishing Co., Inc.

Gish, Melissa. Sharks. (J). 2017. ***(978-1-60818-821-5(3))*** 2009. (Illus.). 48p. 22.95 *(978-1-58341-742-3(7))* Creative Co., The. (Creative Education).

Goldish, Meish. Shark: The Shredder. 2009. (Afraid of the Water Ser.). (Illus.). 24p. (YA). (gr. 2-5). lib. bdg. 22.61 *(978-1-59716-942-4(0))* Bearport Publishing Co., Inc.

—Tiger Sharks: Blue Blenders. (Disappearing Acts Ser.). 24p. (J). (gr. k-3). 2016. (ENG.). pap. 7.95 *(978-1-944998-37-0(3))* 2010. (Illus.). lib. bdg. 22.61 *(978-1-936087-43-3(X))* Bearport Publishing Co., Inc.

—Whale Shark: The World's Biggest Fish. 2007. (SuperSized! Ser.). (Illus.). 24p. (J). (gr. k-3). lib. bdg. 21.28 *(978-1-59716-397-2(X))* Bearport Publishing Co., Inc.

Gordon, David George & Kitzmüller, Christian. Explore a Shark. Bonadonna, Davide, illus. 2016. (Explore Ser.). (ENG.). 16p. (J). (gr. 2). 21.95 *(978-1-62686-394-1(6)*, Silver Dolphin Bks.) Readerlink Distribution Services, LLC.

Gordon, Sharon. Guess Who Bites: Adivina Quién Muerde. 2007. (Bookworms — Bilingual Editions: Guess Who/Adivina Quien 2 Ser.). (SPA & ENG.). 32p. (gr. k-2). 15.95 *(978-0-7614-2882-4(8))*; 15.95 *(978-0-7614-2865-7(8))* Marshall Cavendish Corp.

Gowen, Fiona, illus. Incredible Sharks & Other Ocean Giants. 2016. (How to Draw Ser.). (ENG.). 32p. (J). (gr. 2-6). pap. 4.99 *(978-1-4380-0853-0(8))* Barron's Educational Series, Inc.

Grack, Rachel. 10 Fascinating Facts about Sharks. 2017. (Rookie Star — Fact Finder Ser.). (ENG., Illus.). 32p. (J). lib. bdg. 25.00 *(978-0-531-22262-1(4)*, Children's Pr.) Scholastic Library Publishing.

Gray, Susan Heinrichs. Mako Sharks. 2013. (21st Century Skills Library: Exploring Our Oceans Ser.). (ENG., Illus.). 32p. (J). (gr. 3-6). 28.50 *(978-1-62431-409-4(0)*, 202756); pap. 14.21 *(978-1-62431-485-8(6)*, 202758) Cherry Lake Publishing.

Great White Sharks, 6 bks. 2005. (Animal Predators Ser.). (Illus.). 40p. (J). (gr. 3-6). pap. 46.95 *(978-0-8225-5488-2(7))* Lerner Publishing Group.

Green, Jen. Great White Shark. 2013. (Science Slam: the Deep End-Animal Life Underwater Ser.). 24p. (J). (gr. -1-3). lib. bdg. 23.93 *(978-1-61772-918-8(3))* Bearport Publishing Co., Inc.

—Make & Move: Shark. 2016. (Make & Move Ser.). (ENG., Illus.). 28p. (J). (gr. k). 19.95 *(978-1-62686-490-0(X)*, Silver Dolphin Bks.) Readerlink Distribution Services, LLC.

—Sharks. 2011. (Amazing Animal Hunters Ser.). (Illus.). 32p. (J). 28.50 *(978-1-60753-046-6(5))* Amicus Publishing.

—Sharks. 2008. (Nature's Children Ser.). (Illus.). 52p. (J). *(978-0-7172-6262-5(6))* Grolier, Ltd.

—Sharks. 2012. (Illus.). 32p. (gr. 3-5). pap. 8.95 *(978-1-926722-50-4(7))* Saunders Bk. Co. CAN. Dist: RiverStream Publishing.

Green, Sara. The Blacktip Reef Shark. 2013. (Shark Fact Files Ser.). (ENG., Illus.). 24p. (J). (gr. 3-8). lib. bdg. 25.95 *(978-1-60014-867-5(0)*, Pilot Bks.) Bellwether Media.

—The Blue Shark. 2012. (Shark Fact Files Ser.). (ENG., Illus.). 24p. (J). (gr. 3-8). lib. bdg. 25.95 *(978-1-60014-802-6(6)*, Pilot Bks.) Bellwether Media.

—The Goblin Shark. 2013. (Shark Fact Files Ser.). (ENG., Illus.). 24p. (J). (gr. 3-8). lib. bdg. 25.95 *(978-1-60014-870-5(0)*, Pilot Bks.) Bellwether Media.

—The Great White Shark. 2012. (Shark Fact Files Ser.). (ENG., Illus.). 24p. (J). (gr. 3-8). lib. bdg. 25.95 *(978-1-60014-803-3(4)*, Pilot Bks.) Bellwether Media.

—The Mako Shark. 2012. (Shark Fact Files Ser.). (ENG., Illus.). 24p. (J). (gr. 3-8). lib. bdg. 25.95 *(978-1-60014-804-0(2)*, Pilot Bks.) Bellwether Media.

—The Oceanic Whitetip Shark. 2012. (Shark Fact Files Ser.). (ENG., Illus.). 24p. (J). (gr. 3-8). lib. bdg. 25.95 *(978-1-60014-805-7(0)*, Pilot Bks.) Bellwether Media.

Gregory, Josh. Great White Sharks. 2013. (ENG.). 48p. (J). 28.00 *(978-0-531-23359-7(6))*; pap. 6.95 *(978-0-531-25157-7(8))* Scholastic Library Publishing.

Griffith, Christine. Perfect Hunter. 2014. (Illus.). 32p. (J). *(978-0-545-72494-4(5))* Scholastic, Inc.

—Shark Attack! 2014. (Illus.). 32p. (J). *(978-0-545-72493-7(7))* Scholastic, Inc.

Grossblatt, Ben. Extreme Animals: Sharks. 2015. (Extreme Animals Ser.). (ENG., Illus.). 48p. (J). (gr. 3). 17.95 *(978-1-62686-382-8(2)*, Silver Dolphin Bks.) Readerlink Distribution Services, LLC.

Guillain, Charlotte. Shocking Sharks, 1 vol. 2013. (Walk on the Wild Side Ser.). (ENG.). 32p. (gr. 1-3). 29.99 *(978-1-4109-5217-2(7))*; pap. 8.95 *(978-1-4109-5224-0(X))* Heinemann-Raintree. (Read Me!).

Gurevich, Margaret. Diving with Sharks! And More True Stories of Extreme Adventures! 2016. (NGK Chapters Ser.). (ENG., Illus.). 112p. (J). (gr. 2-5). pap. 5.99 *(978-1-4263-2461-1(8)*, National Geographic Children's Bks.) National Geographic Society.

—National Geographic Kids Chapters: Diving with Sharks! And More True Stories of Extreme Adventures! 2016. (NGK Chapters Ser.). (ENG., Illus.). 112p. (J). (gr. 2-5). lib. bdg. 15.90 *(978-1-4263-2462-8(6)*, National Geographic Children's Bks.) National Geographic Society.

Hall, Howard. A Frenzy of Sharks: The Surprising Life of a Perfect Predator. Leon, Vicki, ed. 2nd ed. 2006. (Jean-Michel Cousteau Presents Ser.). (ENG., Illus.). 48p. (J). (gr. 3-7). pap. 9.95 *(978-0-9766134-4-2(1))* London Town Pr.

Hamilton, S. L. Sharks. 2010. (Xtreme Predators Ser.). 32p. (gr. 3-9). 27.07 *(978-1-60453-993-6(3)*, A&D Xtreme) ABDO Publishing Co.

Hamilton, Sue. Eaten by a Shark, 1 vol. 2010. (Close Encounters of the Wild Kind Ser.). (ENG.). 32p. (YA). (gr. 4-7). 27.07 *(978-1-60453-931-8(3))* ABDO Publishing Co.

Hammerhead Sharks. 2006. (Ugly Animals Ser.). (Illus.). 24p. (J). (gr. 3-7). lib. bdg. 22.60 *(978-1-4042-3529-8(9)*, PowerKids Pr.) Rosen Publishing Group, Inc., The.

Hammerhead Sharks. 2014. (ENG.). 48p. (J). lib. bdg. 28.00 *(978-0-531-20668-3(8))* Scholastic Library Publishing.

Hayes, Jennifer & Doubilet, David. Face to Face with Sharks. 2009. (Face to Face with Animals Ser.). (ENG., Illus.). 32p. (J). (gr. 1-4). 16.95 *(978-1-4263-0404-0(8))*; lib. bdg. 25.90 *(978-1-4263-0405-7(6))* National Geographic Society. (National Geographic Children's Bks.).

Hibbert, Clare. If You Were a Shark. 2013. (If You Were A... Ser.). 32p. (gr. 2-5). 31.35 *(978-1-59920-962-3(4))* Black Rabbit Bks.

Hirsch, James. The Great White Shark. 2009. (Underwater World of Sharks Ser.). 24p. (gr. 3-3). 42.50 *(978-1-60854-245-1(9)*, PowerKids Pr.) Rosen Publishing Group, Inc., The.

Honders, Christine. How Sharks & Other Animals Sense Electricity. 2015. (Superior Animal Senses Ser.). (ENG., Illus.). 24p. (J). (gr. 3-4). pap. 8.25 *(978-1-4994-0994-9(X)*, PowerKids Pr.) Rosen Publishing Group, Inc., The.

Hopper, Whitney. In Search of Bull Sharks, 01 vols., 1. 2016. (Shark Search Ser.). (ENG., Illus.). 24p. (J). pap. 8.25 *(978-1-5081-4335-2(8)*, PowerKids Pr.) Rosen Publishing Group, Inc., The.

Houran, Lori Haskins. How to Spy on a Shark. Marquez, Francisca, illus. 2015. (ENG.). 24p. (J). (gr. -1-3). 15.99 *(978-0-8075-3402-1(1))* Whitman, Albert & Co.

Huggins-Cooper, Lynn. Savage Sharks. 2006. (Killer Nature! Ser.). (Illus.). 32p. (J). lib. bdg. 28.50 *(978-1-58340-933-6(5))* Black Rabbit Bks.

Hutchison, Patricia. Sharks Are Awesome. 2018. (ENG.). 32p. (gr. 3-6). 31.35 ***(978-1-63235-438-9(1)***, 12-Story Library) Pr. Room Editions LLC.

Jackson, Tom. Ferocious Sharks. 2010. (Dangerous Animals Ser.). (ENG., Illus.). 32p. (J). (gr. 2-6). pap. 10.50 *(978-1-4339-4044-6(2)*, Gareth Stevens Learning Library); (YA). (gr. 3-6). lib. bdg. 26.60 *(978-1-4339-4043-9(4))* Stevens, Gareth Publishing LLLP.

—Inside the Mind of a Killer Shark. 2012. (Animal Instincts Ser.). (ENG., Illus.). 32p. (J). (gr. k-5). pap. 10.00 *(978-1-4488-7072-1(0))*; lib. bdg. 25.25 *(978-1-4488-7031-8(3))* Rosen Publishing Group, Inc., The. (PowerKids Pr.).

—Shark Attack. 2008. (Crabtree Contact Ser.). (ENG., Illus.). 32p. (J). (gr. 3-7). lib. bdg. *(978-0-7787-3765-0(9))* Crabtree Publishing Co.

—Sharks. 2010. (Illus.). (J). *(978-1-74089-957-4(1))* Fog City Pr.

John, Gee. Tiger Sharks. 2011. (Power 100 - Marine Life Ser.). 24p. pap. 39.62 *(978-1-61541-234-1(4))* American Reading Co.

Johnson, Gee & Zorzi, Gina. Tiger Sharks. 2010. (2G Marine Life Ser.). (ENG.). 24p. (J). (gr. k-2). pap. 5.99 *(978-1-61541-167-2(4))* American Reading Co.

Kalman, Bobbie. Tiburones Espectaculares. 2006. (Libro de Bobbie Kalman Ser.). (SPA., Illus.). 32p. (J). pap. *(978-0-7787-8415-9(0))* Crabtree Publishing Co.

Kalman, Bobbie & Aloian, Molly. Spectacular Sharks. 2003. (Living Ocean Ser.). (ENG., Illus.). 32p. (J). (gr. 3-4). pap. *(978-0-7787-1320-3(2))* Crabtree Publishing Co.

—Tiburones Espectaculares. 2006. (Libro de Bobbie Kalman Ser.). (SPA., Illus.). 32p. (J). (gr. 3-7). lib. bdg. *(978-0-7787-8401-2(0))* Crabtree Publishing Co.

Kasso, Martin. Sharks. Jeffirs, Matt, illus. 2008. (ENG.). 24p. (J). (gr. 3-18). 19.95 *(978-1-58117-797-8(6)*, Intervisual/Piggy Toes) Bendon, Inc.

Kavanagh, James. The World of Sharks. 2014. (Jeff Corwin's Explorer Ser.). (ENG., Illus.). 12p. 7.95 *(978-1-58355-816-4(0))* Western National Parks Assn.

Keating, Jess. Shark Lady: The Daring Tale of How Eugenie Clark Dove into History. Alvarez Miguens, Marta, illus. 2017. (ENG.). 40p. (J). (-4). 17.99 *(978-1-4926-4204-6(5)*, Sourcebooks Jabberwocky) Sourcebooks, Inc.

Kenan, Tessa. Look, a Shark! 2016. (Bumba Books (tm) — I See Ocean Animals Ser.). (ENG., Illus.). 24p. (J). (gr. -1-1). lib. bdg. 25.32 *(978-1-5124-1419-6(0))* Lerner Publishing Group.

—¡Mira, un Tiburón! (Look, a Shark!) 2017. (Bumba Books (tm) en Español — Veo Animales Marinos (I See Ocean Animals) Ser.). (SPA., Illus.). 24p. (J). (gr. -1-1). 25.32 *(978-1-5124-2868-1(X))* Lerner Publishing Group.

Kennington, Tammy. Blue Sharks. 2013. (21st Century Skills Library: Exploring Our Oceans Ser.). (ENG., Illus.). 32p. (J). (gr. 3-6). 28.50 *(978-1-62431-404-9(X)*, 202736); pap. 14.21 *(978-1-62431-480-3(5)*, 202738) Cherry Lake Publishing.

—Bull Sharks. 2013. (21st Century Skills Library: Exploring Our Oceans Ser.). (ENG., Illus.). 32p. (J). (gr. 3-6). 28.50 *(978-1-62431-405-6(8)*, 202740); pap. 14.21 *(978-1-62431-481-0(3)*, 202742) Cherry Lake Publishing.

Keppeler, Jill. Sharks Lived with the Dinosaurs! 2016. (Living with the Dinosaurs Ser.). 00024p. (J). pap. 8.15 **(978-1-4824-5675-2(3))** Stevens, Gareth Publishing LLLP.
King, H. Elizabeth. Kemo Shark. Date not set. 14p. (J). pap. 2.95 *(978-0-9647798-0-8(3))* Kidscope, Inc.
Klein, Adam G. Basking Sharks, 1 vol. 2006. (Sharks Set 2 Ser.). (ENG., Illus.). 24p. (gr. k-6). 25.65 *(978-1-59679-285-2(X)*, Checkerboard Library) ABDO Publishing Co.
—Common Sawsharks, 1 vol. 2006. (Sharks Set 2 Ser.). (ENG., Illus.). 24p. (gr. k-6). 25.65 *(978-1-59679-286-9(8)*, Checkerboard Library) ABDO Publishing Co.
—Lantern Sharks, 1 vol. 2006. (Sharks Set 2 Ser.). (ENG., Illus.). 24p. (gr. k-6). 25.65 *(978-1-59679-287-6(6)*, Checkerboard Library) ABDO Publishing Co.
—Mako Sharks, 1 vol. 2006. (Sharks Set 2 Ser.). (ENG., Illus.). 24p. (gr. k-6). 25.65 *(978-1-59679-288-3(4)*, Checkerboard Library) ABDO Publishing Co.
—Seal Sharks, 1 vol. 2006. (Sharks Set 2 Ser.). (ENG., Illus.). 24p. (gr. k-6). 25.65 *(978-1-59679-289-0(2)*, Checkerboard Library) ABDO Publishing Co.
—Thresher Sharks, 1 vol. 2006. (Sharks Set 2 Ser.). (ENG., Illus.). 24p. (gr. k-6). 25.65 *(978-1-59679-290-6(6)*, Checkerboard Library) ABDO Publishing Co.
Kosara, Tori. Big Sharks. 2010. (Illus.). (J). *(978-0-545-30044-5(4))* Scholastic, Inc.
Kratt, Chris & Kratt, Martin. Wild Sea Creatures: Sharks, Whales & Dolphins! 2014. (Step into Reading Ser.). (ENG., Illus.). 32p. (J). (gr. -1-1). lib. bdg. 12.99 *(978-0-553-49902-5(5)*, Random Hse. Bks. for Young Readers) Random Hse. Children's Bks.
—Wild Sea Creatures: Sharks, Whales, & Dolphins! 2014. (Step into Reading Ser.). (ENG., Illus.). 32p. (J). (gr. -1-1). 3.99 *(978-0-553-49901-8(7)*, Random Hse. Bks. for Young Readers) Random Hse. Children's Bks.
Kris Hirschmann. The Whale Shark. 2004. (CREATURES of the SEA Ser.). (ENG., Illus.). 48p. (J). 27.50 *(978-0-7377-2059-4(X)*, Kidhaven) Cengage Gale.
Kurtz, Kevin. Sharks & Dolphins: A Compare & Contrast Book, 1 vol. 2016. (Compare & Contrast Ser.). (ENG., Illus.). 32p. (J). (gr. k-3). 17.95 *(978-1-62855-732-9(X))* Arbordale Publishing.
—Tiburones y Delfines: Un Libro de Comparación y Contraste, 1 vol. 2016. (SPA., Illus.). 32p. (J). (gr. k-3). pap. 9.95 *(978-1-62855-746-6(X))* Arbordale Publishing.
Ladybird. Sharks, Level 3. 2016. (Ladybird Readers Ser.). (ENG.). 64p. (J). (gr. 2-4). pap. 9.99 *(978-0-241-25382-3(9))* Penguin Bks., Ltd. GBR. Dist: Independent Pubs. Group.
Landau, Elaine. Scary Sharks. 2003. (Fearsome, Scary, & Creepy Animals Ser.). (Illus.). 48p. (J). (gr. 1-4). lib. bdg. 25.27 *(978-0-7660-2058-0(4))* Enslow Pubs., Inc.
Lang, Heather. Swimming with Sharks: The Daring Discoveries of Eugenie Clark. Solano, Jordi, illus. 2016. (ENG.). 32p. (J). (gr. -1-3). 16.99 *(978-0-8075-2187-8(6))* Whitman, Albert & Co.
Laughlin, Kara L. Sharks. 2017. (In the Deep Blue Sea Ser.). (ENG.). 24p. (J). (gr. k-3). lib. bdg. 27.07 *(978-1-5038-1692-3(3)*, 211526) Child's World, Inc., The.
Lawrence, Ellen. Bull Shark. 2017. (Apex Predators of the Amazon Rain Forest Ser.). (ENG., Illus.). 24p. (J). (gr. -1-3). 17.95 **(978-1-68402-035-5(2))** Bearport Publishing Co., Inc.
Le Bloas-Julienne, Renee. The Shark: Silent Hunter. Bios Agency, photos by. 2007. (Animal Close-Ups Ser.). (Illus.). 26p. (J). (gr. 1-4). pap. 6.95 *(978-1-57091-631-1(4))* Charlesbridge Publishing, Inc.
Leavitt, Amie Jane. A Daredevil's Guide to Swimming with Sharks, 1 vol. 2013. (Daredevils' Guides). (ENG., Illus.). 48p. (gr. 3-4). lib. bdg. 31.99 *(978-1-4296-9985-3(X))* Capstone Press of Coughlan Cos.
LeBreton, Sue. Whale Shark. 2014. (J). pap. *(978-1-4896-1083-6(9))* Weigl Pubs., Inc.
Lee, Justin. How to Draw Sharks. 2009. (Kid's Guide to Drawing Ser.). 24p. (gr. 3-3). 47.90 *(978-1-61511-040-7(2)*, PowerKids Pr.) Rosen Publishing Group, Inc., The.
Lewis, Brenda Ralph. Sharks. 2006. (Nature's Monsters: Water Creatures Ser.). (Illus.). 32p. (gr. 2-6). lib. bdg. 26.00 *(978-0-8368-6178-5(7)*, Gareth Stevens Learning Library) Stevens, Gareth Publishing LLLP.
Lindeen, Carol K. Sharks [Scholastic]. 2010. (Under the Sea Ser.). 24p. pap. 0.50 *(978-1-4296-5064-9(8)*, Pebble Plus) Capstone Press of Coughlan Cos.
Little & Large Sticker Activity Sharks. 2008. 24p. pap. *(978-1-84810-062-6(0))* Miles Kelly Publishing, Ltd.
Llewellyn, Claire. The Best Book of Sharks. 2005. (Best Book Of Ser.). (ENG., Illus.). 32p. (J). (gr. k-3). pap. 6.99 *(978-0-7534-5875-4(6)*, 9780753458754, Kingfisher) Roaring Brook Pr.
Loh-Hagan, Virginia. Discover Great White Shark. 2015. (21st Century Basic Skills Library: Splash! Ser.). (ENG., Illus.). 24p. (J). (gr. 2-4). 24.21 *(978-1-63362-599-3(2)*, 206576) Cherry Lake Publishing.
—Discover Hammerhead Shark. 2015. (21st Century Basic Skills Library: Splash! Ser.). (ENG., Illus.). 24p. (J). (gr. 2-4). 24.21 *(978-1-63362-599-0(0)*, 206580) Cherry Lake Publishing.
Lynette, Rachel. Bluntnose Sixgill Sharks & Other Strange Sharks, 1 vol. 2011. (Creatures of the Deep Ser.). (ENG., Illus.). 32p. (gr. 3-5). pap. 8.95 *(978-1-4109-4203-6(1)*, NA-r) Heinemann-Raintree.
Magby, Meryl. Hammerhead Sharks. 2012. (Under the Sea Ser.). (ENG., Illus.). 24p. (J). (gr. k-5). pap. 8.25 *(978-1-4488-7477-4(7))*; lib. bdg. 22.60 *(978-1-4488-7398-2(3))* Rosen Publishing Group, Inc., The. (PowerKids Pr.).
Markle, Sandra. Great White Sharks. (Animal Predators Ser.). (ENG.). 40p. (gr. 3-6). 2005. pap. 7.95 *(978-1-57505-747-7(6))* 2004. (Illus.). lib. bdg. 26.60 *(978-1-57505-731-6(X))* Lerner Publishing Group.
—Los Tiburones Blancos; Great White Sharks. 2008. pap. 46.95 *(978-0-8225-7091-2(2))* Lerner Publishing Group.
—Sharks: Biggest! Littlest! Perrine, Doug, photos by. 2011. (Biggest! Littlest! Ser.). (ENG., Illus.). 32p. (J). pap. 10.95 *(978-1-59078-873-8(7))* Boyds Mills Pr.
—Los Tiburones Blancos. 2006. (Animales Depredadores (Animal Predators) Ser.). (SPA., Illus.). 39p. (J). (gr. 3-7). lib. bdg. 25.26 *(978-0-8225-6490-4(4)*, Ediciones Lerner) Lerner Publishing Group.
Markovics, Joyce L. Great White Shark. 2016. (J). lib. bdg. *(978-1-62724-819-8(6))* Bearport Publishing Co., Inc.
Marsh, Nigel. A-Z Sharks & Rays. 2016. (ENG., Illus.). 48p. (J). (gr. 3-4). 14.99 *(978-1-921580-30-7(5))* New Holland Pubs. Pty, Ltd. AUS. Dist: Midpoint Trade Bks., Inc.
Marsico, Katie. Sharks. 2012. (Nature's Children Ser.). (ENG., Illus.). 48p. (J). (gr. 3-5). pap. 6.95 *(978-0-531-21082-6(0))*; lib. bdg. 28.00 *(978-0-531-20907-3(5))* Scholastic Library Publishing. (Children's Pr.).
Mathea, Heidi. Great White Sharks, 1 vol. 2011. (Sharks Set 1 *2011 Ser.). (ENG.). 24p. 25.65 *(978-1-61613-425-9(9)*, Checkerboard Library) ABDO Publishing Co.
—Hammerhead Sharks, 1 vol. 2011. (Sharks Set 1 *2011 Ser.). (ENG., Illus.). 24p. 25.65 *(978-1-61613-426-6(7)*, 1315288, Checkerboard Library) ABDO Publishing Co.
—Nurse Sharks, 1 vol. 2011. (Sharks Set 1 *2011 Ser.). (ENG.). 24p. 25.65 *(978-1-61613-427-3(5)*, Checkerboard Library) ABDO Publishing Co.
—Sand Sharks, 1 vol. 2011. (Sharks Set 1 *2011 Ser.). (ENG.). 24p. 25.65 *(978-1-61613-428-0(3)*, Checkerboard Library) ABDO Publishing Co.
—Tiger Sharks, 1 vol. 2011. (Sharks Set 1 *2011 Ser.). (ENG., Illus.). 24p. 25.65 *(978-1-61613-429-7(1)*, 1315294, Checkerboard Library) ABDO Publishing Co.
—Whale Sharks, 1 vol. 2011. (Sharks Set 1 *2011 Ser.). (ENG.). 24p. 25.65 *(978-1-61613-430-3(5)*, Checkerboard Library) ABDO Publishing Co.
Maydak, Michael S., illus. Wild Stickers - Sharks & Rays. 2003. 4p. (J). 2.50 *(978-0-941042-34-5(0))* Dog-Eared Pubns.
McAneney, Caitie. In Search of Whale Sharks, 01 vols., 1. 2016. (Shark Search Ser.). (ENG., Illus.). 24p. (J). pap. 8.25 *(978-1-5081-4351-2(X)*, PowerKids Pr.) Rosen Publishing Group, Inc., The.
McKay, Sindy. We Both Read-Sharks! Hunt, Judith & Smith, Wendy, illus. 2012. 44p. (J). 9.95 *(978-1-60115-261-9(2))*; pap. 4.99 *(978-1-60115-262-6(0))* Treasure Bay, Inc.
McMillan, Beverly & Musick, John A. Sharks. 2008. (Insiders Ser.). (ENG.). 64p. (J). (gr. 3-7). 17.99 *(978-1-4169-3867-5(2)*, Simon & Schuster Bks. For Young Readers) Simon & Schuster Bks. For Young Readers.
McNeil, Niki, et al. HOCPP 1085 Sharks. 2006. spiral bd. 19.50 *(978-1-60308-085-9(6))* In the Hands of a Child.
Megalodon: Fact or Fiction? 2010. (Creature Scene Investigation: the Science of Cryptozoology Ser.). (Illus.). 104p. (J). (gr. 5-8). 32.95 *(978-0-7910-9777-9(3)*, Chelsea Hse.) Facts On File, Inc.
Meinking, Mary. Shark vs. Penguin, 1 vol. 2011. (Predator vs. Prey Ser.). (ENG.). 32p. (gr. 1-2). pap. 8.29 *(978-1-4109-3946-3(4)*, Read Me!) Heinemann-Raintree.
Meister, Cari. Do You Really Want to Meet a Shark? Fabbri, Daniele, illus. 2015. (Do You Really Want to Meet ... ? Ser.). (ENG.). 24p. (J). (gr. 1-3). 19.95 *(978-1-60753-737-3(0))* Amicus Publishing.
—Sharks. 2013. (ENG.). 24p. (J). lib. bdg. 25.65 *(978-1-62031-035-9(X))* Jump! Inc.
Miller, Jonathan. Sharks. 2004. (Discovery Program Ser.). (SPA., Illus.). 64p. (J). (gr. 2-18). lib. bdg. 16.95 *(978-1-58086-335-3(3))* EDC Publishing.
Mitchell, Susan K. Biggest vs. Smallest Sea Creatures. 2010. (Biggest vs. Smallest Animals Ser.). (Illus.). 24p. (J). 22.60 *(978-0-7660-3580-5(8)*, Enslow Elementary) Enslow Pubs., Inc.
Montgomery, Sy. The Great White Shark Scientist. Ellenbogen, Keith, photos by. 2016. (Scientists in the Field Ser.). (ENG., Illus.). 80p. (J). (gr. 5-7). 18.99 *(978-0-544-35298-8(X)*, HMH Books For Young Readers) Houghton Mifflin Harcourt Publishing Co.
Morey, Allan. Blacktip Reef Sharks. 2016. (Sharks Ser.). (ENG., Illus.). 32p. (J). (gr. 1-4). 20.95 *(978-1-60753-975-9(6))* Amicus Publishing.
—Hammerhead Sharks. 2017. (Sharks Ser.). (ENG., Illus.). 32p. (J). (gr. 1-3). pap. 9.99 *(978-1-68152-091-9(5))* Amicus.
—Hammerhead Sharks. 2016. (Sharks Ser.). (ENG., Illus.). 32p. (J). (gr. 1-4). 20.95 *(978-1-60753-978-0(0))* Amicus Publishing.
—Mako Sharks. 2017. (Sharks Ser.). (ENG., Illus.). 32p. (J). (gr. 1-3). pap. 9.99 *(978-1-68152-092-6(3))* Amicus.
—Mako Sharks. 2016. (Sharks Ser.). (ENG., Illus.). 32p. (J). (gr. 1-4). 20.95 *(978-1-60753-979-7(9))* Amicus Publishing.
—Whale Sharks. 2017. (Sharks Ser.). (ENG., Illus.). 32p. (J). (gr. 1-3). pap. 9.99 *(978-1-68152-094-0(X))* Amicus.
—Whale Sharks. 2016. (Sharks Ser.). (ENG., Illus.). 32p. (J). (gr. 1-4). 20.95 *(978-1-60753-981-0(0))* Amicus Publishing.
Morey, Allan & Waxman, Laura Hamilton. Blacktip Reef Sharks. 2017. (Sharks Ser.). (ENG., Illus.). 32p. (J). (gr. 1-3). pap. 9.99 *(978-1-68152-088-9(5))* Amicus.
Morgan, Sally. Sharks. 2004. (QEB Animal Lives Ser.). (Illus.). 32p. (J). lib. bdg. 18.95 *(978-1-59566-034-3(8))* QEB Publishing Inc.
Morgan, Sally & Teacher Created Resources Staff. Sharks. 2006. (Animal Lives Ser.). (ENG., Illus.). 32p. (gr. 2-9). pap. 7.99 *(978-1-4206-8160-4(5))* Teacher Created Resources, Inc.
Mortensen, Lori. Killer Sharks. 2008. (Monsters Ser.). (ENG., Illus.). 48p. (J). (gr. 4-7). lib. bdg. 35.20 *(978-0-7377-4044-8(2)*, LML02109-240011) Cengage Gale.
Mugford, Simon. Shark. 2004. (Twenty4Sevens Ser.). (Illus.). 48p. (J). pap. *(978-0-439-68102-5(2))* Scholastic, Inc.
Mugford, Simon & Priddy, Roger. Sharks: And Other Dangers of the Deep. l.t. rev. ed. 2005. (Smart Kids Ser.). (ENG., Illus.). 32p. (J). (gr. -1-2). 9.99 *(978-0-312-49533-6(1)*, 9780312495336, Priddy Bks.) St. Martin's Pr.
Murphy, Julie. Whale Sharks. 2013. (21st Century Skills Library: Exploring Our Oceans Ser.). (ENG., Illus.). 32p. (J). (gr. 3-6). 28.50 *(978-1-62431-411-7(2)*, 202764); pap. 14.21 *(978-1-62431-487-2(2)*, 202766) Cherry Lake Publishing.
Murray, Julie. Great White Sharks, 1 vol. 2003. (Buddy Book Ser.). (ENG.). 24p. (gr. k-4). 25.65 *(978-1-57765-706-4(3)*, Buddy Bks.) ABDO Publishing Co.
—Hammerhead Sharks, 1 vol. 2005. (Animal Kingdom Set Ii Ser.). (ENG., Illus.). 24p. (gr. k-4). 25.65 *(978-1-59197-319-5(8)*, Buddy Bks.) ABDO Publishing Co.
—Tiger Sharks, 1 vol. 2005. (Animal Kingdom Set Ii Ser.). (ENG., Illus.). 24p. (gr. k-4). 25.65 *(978-1-59197-336-2(8)*, Buddy Bks.) ABDO Publishing Co.
Musgrave, Ruth. Sharks: All the Shark Facts, Photos, & Fun That You Can Sink Your Teeth Into! 2011. (National Geographic Kids Everything Ser.). (ENG., Illus.). 64p. (J). (gr. 3-7). pap. 12.95 *(978-1-4263-0769-0(1)*, National Geographic Children's Bks.) National Geographic Society.
Musgrave, Ruth A. Shark Rescue: All about Sharks & How to Save Them. 2016. (NG Kids Mission: Animal Rescue Ser.). (ENG., Illus.). 112p. (J). (gr. 5). pap. 12.99 *(978-1-4263-2090-3(6)*, National Geographic Children's Bks.) National Geographic Society.
Nagelhout, Ryan. Diving with Sharks. 2014. (Illus.). 32p. (J). *(978-1-4824-3287-9(0))* Stevens, Gareth Publishing LLLP.
—Sharks. 2013. (Underwater World Ser.). (Illus.). 24p. (J). (gr. k-2). (SPA & ENG.). pap. 8.15 *(978-1-4339-8576-8(4))*; lib. bdg. 22.60 *(978-1-4339-8575-1(6))* Stevens, Gareth Publishing LLLP.
—Sharks: Tiburones. 2013. (Underwater World / el Mundo Submarino Ser.). (SPA & ENG., Illus.). 24p. (J). (gr. k-2). lib. bdg. 22.60 *(978-1-4339-8784-7(8))* Stevens, Gareth Publishing LLLP.
National Geographic Kids Staff. National Geographic Kids Sharks! 2014. (NG Sticker Activity Bks.). (ENG.). 56p. (J). (gr. -1-3). pap., act. bk. ed. 6.99 *(978-1-4263-1774-3(3)*, National Geographic Children's Bks.) National Geographic Society.
Nelson, Kristin L. Hunting Sharks. 2003. (Illus.). 32p. (J). (ENG.). (gr. k-2). pap. 5.95 *(978-0-8225-3648-2(X))*; (gr. 2-6). 22.60 *(978-0-8225-4671-9(X)*, Lerner Pubns.) Lerner Publishing Group.
—Let's Look at Sharks. 2010. pap. 45.32 *(978-0-7613-6982-0(1))*; (ENG., Illus.). 32p. pap. 7.95 *(978-0-7613-6041-4(7))*; (ENG., Illus.). 32p. lib. bdg. 26.60 *(978-0-7613-3894-9(2)*, Lerner Pubns.) Lerner Publishing Group.
Niver, Heather Moore. Bull Sharks after Dark. 2016. (Animals of the Night Ser.). (Illus.). 32p. (J). (gr. 3-3). 25.27 *(978-0-7660-7712-6(8))* Enslow Pubs., Inc.
—20 Fun Facts about Sharks. 2012. (Fun Fact File: Animals! Ser.). (ENG., Illus.). 32p. (J). (gr. 2-5). pap. 10.50 *(978-1-4339-6527-2(5))*; lib. bdg. 25.25 *(978-1-4339-6525-8(9))* Stevens, Gareth Publishing LLLP. (Gareth Stevens Learning Library).
Nobleman, Marc Tyler. Sharks. 2008. (Endangered! Ser.). 48p. (gr. 3-18). lib. bdg. 29.93 *(978-0-7614-2988-3(3)*, Benchmark Bks.) Marshall Cavendish Corp.
Northcutt, Ellen. Extreme Sharks. 2014. (Illus.). 32p. (J). *(978-0-545-72501-9(1))* Scholastic, Inc.
Nuzzolo, Deborah. Bull Shark [Scholastic]. 2010. (Sharks Ser.). (ENG.). 24p. pap. 0.52 *(978-1-4296-5043-4(5)*, Pebble Plus) Capstone Press of Coughlan Cos.
—Bull Sharks. 2017. (All about Sharks Ser.). (ENG.). 24p. (gr. k-1). pap. 6.95 **(978-1-5157-7010-7(9)**, Pebble Plus) Capstone Press of Coughlan Cos.
—Great White Shark [Scholastic]. 2010. (Sharks Ser.). (ENG.). 24p. pap. 0.52 *(978-1-4296-5041-0(9)*, Pebble Plus) Capstone Press of Coughlan Cos.
—Great White Sharks. 2017. (All about Sharks Ser.). (ENG.). 24p. (gr. k-1). pap. 6.95 **(978-1-5157-7008-4(7)**, Pebble Plus) Capstone Press of Coughlan Cos.
—Hammerhead Shark [Scholastic]. 2010. (Sharks Ser.). (ENG.). 24p. pap. 0.52 *(978-1-4296-5042-7(7)*, Pebble Plus) Capstone Press of Coughlan Cos.
—Hammerhead Sharks. 2017. (All about Sharks Ser.). (ENG.). 24p. (gr. k-1). pap. 6.95 **(978-1-5157-7009-1(5)**, Pebble Plus) Capstone Press of Coughlan Cos.
—Mako Sharks. 2017. (All about Sharks Ser.). (ENG.). 24p. (gr. k-1). pap. 6.95 **(978-1-5157-7007-7(9)**, Pebble Plus) Capstone Press of Coughlan Cos.
—Megamouth Shark, 1 vol. 2010. (Shark Zone Ser.). (ENG.). 32p. (gr. 1-2). lib. bdg. 26.65 *(978-1-4296-5417-3(1)*, Blazers) Capstone Press of Coughlan Cos.
—Tiger Shark, 1 vol. 2010. (Shark Zone Ser.). (ENG.). 32p. (gr. 1-2). lib. bdg. 26.65 *(978-1-4296-5415-9(5)*, Blazers) Capstone Press of Coughlan Cos.
—Tiger Shark [Scholastic]. 2010. (Sharks Ser.). (ENG.). 24p. pap. 0.52 *(978-1-4296-5044-1(3)*, Pebble Plus) Capstone Press of Coughlan Cos.
—Tiger Sharks. 2017. (All about Sharks Ser.). (ENG.). 24p. (gr. k-1). pap. 6.95 **(978-1-5157-7006-0(0)**, Pebble Plus) Capstone Press of Coughlan Cos.
—Whale Shark, 1 vol. 2010. (Shark Zone Ser.). (ENG.). 32p. (gr. 1-2). lib. bdg. 26.65 *(978-1-4296-5414-2(7)*, Blazers) Capstone Press of Coughlan Cos.
—Whale Sharks. 2017. (All about Sharks Ser.). (ENG.). 24p. (gr. k-1). lib. bdg. 26.65 **(978-1-5157-6999-6(2)**, Pebble Plus) Capstone Press of Coughlan Cos.
Nuzzolo, Deborah. Zebra Shark, 1 vol. 2010. (Shark Zone Ser.). (ENG.). 32p. (gr. 1-2). lib. bdg. 26.65 *(978-1-4296-5416-6(3)*, Blazers) Capstone Press of Coughlan Cos.
O'DellKathryn. SHARK ATTACK LOW INTERMEDIATE BOOK WITH ONLINE ACCESS. 2014. (ENG.). 28p. (J). pap. 9.50 *(978-1-107-66183-7(8))* Cambridge Univ. Pr.
O'Neill, Michael Patrick, photos by. Shark Encounters. O'Neill, Michael Patrick, . 2008. (Illus.). 48p. (J). (gr. 1-4). 19.95 *(978-0-9728653-4-0(9))* Batfish Bks.
Orme, David. Sea Killers. 2007. (Trailblazers Ser.). (ACE & ENG., Illus.). 36p. pap. *(978-1-84167-592-3(X))* Ransom Publishing Ltd.
Orme, Helen. Sharks. 2011. (Fact to Fiction Grafx Ser.). (ENG., Illus.). 36p. (J). (gr. 4-7). lib. bdg. 17.45 *(978-1-61384-021-4(7))* Perfection Learning Corp.
Osborne, Mary Pope & Boyce, Natalie Pope. Dolphins & Sharks: Dolphins at Daybreak. Murdocca, Sal, illus. 2003. (Magic Tree House - Fact Tracker Ser.: 9). (ENG.). 128p. (J). (gr. 2-5). 6.99 *(978-0-375-82377-0(8)*, Random Hse. Bks. for Young Readers) Random Hse. Children's Bks.
—Sharks & Other Predators. Molinari, Carlo, illus. 2015. (Magic Tree House - Fact Tracker Ser.: 32). (ENG.). 128p. (J). (gr. 2-5). 12.99 *(978-0-385-38642-5(7)*, Random Hse. Bks. for Young Readers) Random Hse. Children's Bks.
Otfinoski, Steven. Hammerheads & More! 2012. (Illus.). 64p. (J). pap. 10.99 *(978-1-62267-002-4(7))* Bright Connections Media.
Owen, Ruth. Great White Shark, 1 vol., 1. 2014. (Real Life Sea Monsters Ser.). (ENG.). 32p. (J). (gr. k-5). 26.25 *(978-1-4777-6249-3(3)*, PowerKids Pr.) Rosen Publishing Group, Inc., The.
—Stealthy Sharks. 2012. (Eye to Eye with Animals Ser.). (ENG., Illus.). 32p. (J). (gr. k-5). 25.25 *(978-1-4488-8072-0(6))*; pap. 10.00 *(978-1-4488-8108-6(0))* Windmill Bks.
Owings, Lisa. Bull Shark Attack. 2012. (Animal Attacks Ser.). (ENG., Illus.). 24p. (J). (gr. 3-7). lib. bdg. 25.95 *(978-1-60014-787-6(9)*, Torque Bks.) Bellwether Media.
—The Great White Shark. 2011. (Nature's Deadliest Ser.). (ENG., Illus.). 24p. (YA). (gr. 3-8). lib. bdg. 25.95 *(978-1-60014-665-7(1)*, Pilot Bks.) Bellwether Media.
Pallotta, Jerry. Hammerhead vs. Bull Shark. Bolster, Robert, illus. 2016. (Who Would Win? Ser.). (ENG.). 32p. (J). (gr. 1-3). pap. 3.99 *(978-0-545-30170-1(X))* Scholastic, Inc.
Parker, Steve. Amazing Sharks. 2016. (Animals Are Wild! Ser.). 40p. (gr. 4-3). pap. 14.05 *(978-1-4824-5018-7(6))* Stevens, Gareth Publishing LLLP.
—Sharks. 2010. (Remarkable Man & Beast Ser.). (Illus.). 48p. (J). (gr. 3-18). lib. bdg. 19.95 *(978-1-4222-1974-4(7))* Mason Crest.
—Sharks. Butler, John, illus. 2010. (I Love Animals Ser.). (ENG.). 24p. (J). (gr. 1-5). 22.60 *(978-1-61533-249-6(9))*; pap. 8.15 *(978-1-61533-254-0(5))* Windmill Bks.
—10 Things You Should Know about Sharks. Gallagher, Belinda & Borton, Paula, eds. Butler, John, illus. 2004. (10 Things You Should Know Ser.). 24p. (J). 6.99 *(978-1-84236-118-4(X))* Miles Kelly Publishing, Ltd. GBR. Dist: Independent Pubs. Group.
Pearl, Norman. Sharks: Ocean Hunters. 2009. (Powerful Predators Ser.). 24p. (gr. 2-3). 42.50 *(978-1-60851-349-9(1))*; (Illus.). (J). (gr. 3-4). lib. bdg. 22.60 *(978-1-4042-4509-9(X))* Rosen Publishing Group, Inc., The. (PowerKids Pr.).
Peterson, Megan Cooley & Rustad, Martha E. H. Sharks, 1 vol. 2013. (Little Scientist Ser.). (ENG., Illus.). 32p. (gr. 1-2). 6.95 *(978-1-4765-3540-1(X))*; 27.99 *(978-1-4765-0246-5(3))*; pap. 6.95 *(978-1-4765-3546-3(9))* Capstone Press of Coughlan Cos.
Pettiford, Rebecca. Great White Sharks. (Great White Sharks Ser.). 24p. (J). (gr. k-3). 2017. pap. 6.99 **(978-1-61891-264-0(X))** 2016. (ENG., Illus.). 25.95 *(978-1-62617-416-0(4))* Bellwether Media. (Blastoff! Readers).
Pfeffer, Wendy & American Museum of Natural History Staff. The World of Sharks. 2011. (Amer Museum of Nat History Easy Readers Ser.: 2). (ENG., Illus.). 32p. (J). (gr. -1-k). pap. 3.95 *(978-1-4027-7783-7(3))* Sterling Publishing Co., Inc.
Phelps, Bonnie. In Search of Mako Sharks, 01 vols., 1. 2016. (Shark Search Ser.). (ENG., Illus.). 24p. (J). pap. 8.25 *(978-1-5081-4343-7(9)*, PowerKids Pr.) Rosen Publishing Group, Inc., The.
Powling, Chris. Sharks. 2009. (Wild Reads Ser.). (ENG., Illus.). 32p. (YA). (gr. k). pap. 4.95 *(978-0-19-911931-8(7))* Oxford Univ. Pr., Inc.
Pringle, Laurence. Sharks! Strange & Wonderful. Henderson, Meryl, illus. 2008. (Strange & Wonderful Ser.). (ENG.). 32p. (J). (gr. 2-4). pap. 9.95 *(978-1-59078-571-3(1))* Boyds Mills Pr.
Rafferty, John P. Meat Eaters: Raptors, Sharks, & Crocodiles. 2011. (Britannica Guide to Predators & Prey Ser.). (Illus.). 208p. (YA). (gr. 9-12). lib. bdg. 51.70 *(978-1-61530-342-7(1))* Rosen Publishing Group, Inc., The.
Randolph, Joanne. The Great White Shark: King of the Ocean. (Sharks: Hunters of the Deep Ser.). 24p. 2009. (gr. 2-3). 42.50 *(978-1-60853-108-0(2))* 2007. (Illus.). (J). (gr. 3-7). lib. bdg. 22.60 *(978-1-4042-3624-0(4)*, 1266081) Rosen Publishing Group, Inc., The. (PowerKids Pr.).
—The Hammerhead Shark: Coastal Killer. (Sharks: Hunters of the Deep Ser.). 24p. 2009. (gr. 2-3). 42.50 *(978-1-60853-109-7(0))* 2007. (Illus.). (J). (gr. 3-7). lib. bdg. 22.60 *(978-1-4042-3625-7(2)*, 1266082) Rosen Publishing Group, Inc., The. (PowerKids Pr.).
—The Mako Shark: Built for Speed. (Sharks: Hunters of the Deep Ser.). 24p. 2009. (gr. 2-3). 42.50 *(978-1-60853-110-3(4)*, PowerKids Pr.) 2007. (Illus.). (J). (gr. 3-7). lib. bdg. 22.60 *(978-1-4042-3627-1(9))* Rosen Publishing Group, Inc., The.
—Sharks: Hunters of the Deep, 4 bks., Set. Incl. Great White Shark: King of the Ocean. lib. bdg. 22.60 *(978-1-4042-3624-0(4)*, 1266081, PowerKids Pr.); Hammerhead Shark: Coastal Killer. lib. bdg. 22.60 *(978-1-4042-3625-7(2)*, 1266082, PowerKids Pr.); Mako Shark: Built for Speed. lib. bdg. 22.60 *(978-1-4042-3627-1(9))*; Whale Shark: Gentle Giant. lib. bdg. 22.60 *(978-1-4042-3626-4(0)*, PowerKids Pr.); (Illus.). 24p. (J). (gr. 3-7). 2007. Set lib. bdg. 85.00 *(978-1-4042-3599-1(X)*, PowerKids Pr.) Rosen Publishing Group, Inc., The.
—The Whale Shark: Gentle Giant. (Sharks: Hunters of the Deep Ser.). 24p. 2009. (gr. 2-3). 42.50 *(978-1-60853-111-0(2))* 2007. (Illus.). (J). (gr. 3-7). lib. bdg. 22.60 *(978-1-4042-3626-4(0))* Rosen Publishing Group, Inc., The. (PowerKids Pr.).
Reher, Matt. The Book of Sharks. 2016. (1G Marine Life Ser.). (ENG., Illus.). 32p. (J). pap. 5.99 **(978-1-63437-671-6(4))** American Reading Co.
Reynolds, Hunter. Hunting with Great White Sharks. 2012. (Animal Attack! Ser.). (Illus.). 24p. (J). (gr. 2-5). 22.60 *(978-1-4339-7075-7(9))*; pap. 8.15 *(978-1-4339-7076-4(7))* Stevens, Gareth Publishing LLLP. (Gareth Stevens Learning Library).
Reynolds, Shaye. In Search of Tiger Sharks, 01 vols., 1. 2016. (Shark Search Ser.). (ENG., Illus.). 24p. (J). pap. 8.25 *(978-1-5081-4347-5(1)*, PowerKids Pr.) Rosen Publishing Group, Inc., The.
Riehecky, Janet. Great White Sharks: On the Hunt. 2016. (Killer Animals Ser.). (ENG.). 32p. (gr. 1-2). pap. 7.95 *(978-1-5157-6265-2(3)*, Blazers) Capstone Press of Coughlan Cos.
—Megalodon, 1 vol. Saunders-Smith, Gail, ed. 2006. (Dinosaurs & Prehistoric Animals Ser.). (ENG., Illus.). 24p. (gr. k-1). 26.65 *(978-0-7368-5354-5(5)*, Pebble Plus) Capstone Press of Coughlan Cos.
Riggs, Kate. Seedlings: Sharks. 2014. (Seedlings Ser.). (ENG.). 24p. (J). (gr. -1-k). pap. 7.99 *(978-0-89812-887-1(0)*, Creative Paperbacks) Creative Co., The.
—Sharks. 2013. (J). 25.65 *(978-1-60818-342-5(4)*, Creative Education) Creative Co., The.

S

Ripley's Believe It or Not Editors & Ripley's Believe It Or Not! Staff. Sharks: And Other Scary Sea Creatures. 2013. (Twist Ser.: 10). (ENG.). 48p. (J). (gr. 1-4). 12.95 (978-1-60991-083-9(4)) Ripley Entertainment, Inc.

Roy, Katherine. Neighborhood Sharks: Hunting with the Great Whites of California's Farallon Islands. Roy, Katherine, illus. 2014. (ENG., Illus.). 48p. (J). (gr. 2-6). 18.99 (978-1-59643-874-3(6), 9781596438743, Macaulay, David Studio) Roaring Brook Pr.

Royston, Angela. Shark. 2013. (Top of the Food Chain Ser.). 32p. (J). (gr. k-5). 25.25 (978-1-61533-737-8(7)); pap. 10.00 (978-1-61533-791-0(1)) Windmill Bks.

—Shark: Killer King of the Ocean. 2013. (Top of the Food Chain Ser.). 32p. (J). (gr. k-5). pap. 60.00 (978-1-61533-792-7(X)) Windmill Bks.

Rustad, Martha E. H. Sharks [Scholastic]. 2009. (Ocean Life Ser.). 24p. (gr. k-1). pap. 2.99 (978-1-4296-3675-9(0), Pebble Bks.) Capstone Press of Coughlan Cos.

Sandler, Michael. Bethany Hamilton: Follow Your Dreams! 2006. (Defining Moments Ser.). (Illus.). 32p. (J). (gr. 2-5). lib. bdg. 25.27 (978-1-59716-270-8(1)) Bearport Publishing Co., Inc.

Schreiber, Anne. Sharks! 2008. (Readers Ser.). (ENG., Illus.). 32p. (J). (gr. k-3). 13.90 (978-1-4263-0288-6(6), National Geographic Children's Bks.) National Geographic Society.

—Sharks. 2008. (Readers Ser.). (ENG., Illus.). 32p. (J). (gr. k-3). pap. 3.99 (978-1-4263-0286-2(X), National Geographic Children's Bks.) National Geographic Society.

Schroeter, Chloe. Sharks. 2014. (Animal Q & A Ser.). (Illus.). 24p. (J). (gr. k-3). lib. bdg. 23.60 (978-1-4777-9198-1(1)) Windmill Bks.

—Why Why Why... Are Sharks so Scary? 2010. (Why Why Why Ser.). 32p. (J). (gr. 1-3). lib. bdg. 18.95 (978-1-4222-1571-5(7)) Mason Crest.

Sengupta, Monalisa. Discover Sharks. 2008. (Discover Animals Ser.). (Illus.). 48p. (J). (gr. 5-9). lib. bdg. 25.27 (978-0-7660-3474-7(7)) Enslow Pubs., Inc.

Sexton, Colleen. Sharks. 2007. (Oceans Alive Ser.). (ENG., Illus.). 24p. (J). (gr. k-3). lib. bdg. 25.95 (978-1-60014-057-0(2)) Bellwether Media.

Shark. 2014. (DK Eyewitness Bks.). (ENG.). 72p. (J). (gr. 3-7). pap. 9.99 (978-1-4654-2615-4(9)); lib. bdg. 19.99 (978-1-4654-2619-2(1)) Dorling Kindersley Publishing, Inc. (DK Children).

Shark: Level 2, 6 vols. (Fluency Strand Ser.). (gr. 4-8). 45.00 (978-1-4045-1210-8(1)) Wright Group/McGraw-Hill.

Shark Discovery [Scholastic]. 2010. (Sharks Ser.). 24p. pap. 2.08 (978-1-4296-5045-8(1), Pebble Plus) Capstone Press of Coughlan Cos.

Shark Zone. 2010. (Shark Zone Ser.). (ENG.). 32p. (gr. 1-2). lib. bdg. 106.60 (978-1-4296-5418-0(X)); lib. bdg. 106.60 (978-1-4296-5419-7(8)) Capstone Press of Coughlan Cos. (Blazers).

Sharks! (Creatures Corner Ser.). 16p. (J). (978-2-7643-0121-0(9)) Phidal Publishing, Inc./Editions Phidal, Inc.

Sharks. (Eyes on Nature Ser.). 32p. (J). (gr. 1). pap. (978-1-882210-55-8(7)) Action Publishing, Inc.

Sharks: An Amazing Discovery Book. 2009. (Amazing Animal Discovery Bks.). (ENG., Illus.). 12p. (J). (gr. -1). 5.95 (978-1-58117-864-7(6), Intervisual/Piggy Toes) Bendon, Inc.

Sharks: Hunters of the Deep, 6 vols. (Book2WebTM Ser.). (gr. 4-8). 36.50 (978-0-322-02973-6(2)) Wright Group/McGraw-Hill.

Sharks: Level M, 6 vols. (Wonder Worldtm Ser.). 16p. 34.95 (978-0-7802-2906-8(1)) Wright Group/McGraw-Hill.

Sharks: Monsters of the Deep. 2008. (Illus.). 32p. (J). (gr. -1-3). 9.99 (978-1-57755-724-1(7)) Flying Frog Publishing, Inc.

Sharks & Rays: Level O, 6 vols. (Explorers Ser.). 32p. (gr. 3-6). 44.95 (978-0-7699-0590-7(0)) Shortland Pubns. (U. S. A.) Inc.

Sharon the Shark 6 Packs. Set D. (Supersonic Phonics Ser.). (gr. k-3). 29.00 (978-0-7635-0553-0(6)) Rigby Education.

Shea, Therese. Hammerhead Sharks. 2009. (Ugly Animals Ser.). 24p. (gr. 2-3). 42.50 (978-1-60854-599-5(7), PowerKids Pr.) Rosen Publishing Group, Inc., The.

—Sharks. 2009. (Big Bad Biters Ser.). 24p. (gr. 2-3). 42.50 (978-1-61511-563-1(3), PowerKids Pr.) Rosen Publishing Group, Inc., The.

Sheikh-Miller, Jonathan. Sharks. 2009. (Discovery Nature Ser.). 64p. (YA). (gr. 3-18). 8.99 (978-0-7945-2241-4(6), Usborne) EDC Publishing.

Shingu, Susumu. Wandering Whale Sharks. 2015. Orig. Title: Whale Shark. (ENG., Illus.). 48p. (J). (gr. k-5). 18.95 (978-1-77147-130-5(1), Owlkids) Owlkids Bks. Inc. CAN. Dist: Publishers Group West (PGW).

Shulman, Mark. Shark Attack: Top 10 Attack Sharks. 2007. (Illus.). 48p. (J). per. 6.99 (978-0-696-23692-1(3)) Meredith Bks.

Silverman, Buffy. Angel Sharks in Action. 2017. (Lightning Bolt Books (tm) — Shark World Ser.). (ENG.). 24p. (J). (gr. 1-3). 25.32 **(978-1-5124-3381-4(0))** Lerner Publishing Group.

—Great White Sharks in Action. 2017. (Lightning Bolt Books (tm) — Shark World Ser.). (ENG.). (J). (gr. 1-3). 24p. 25.32 **(978-1-5124-3377-7(2))**; pap. 6.99 **(978-1-5124-5594-6(6))** Lerner Publishing Group.

—Mako Sharks in Action. 2017. (Lightning Bolt Books (tm) — Shark World Ser.). (ENG.). 24p. (J). (gr. 1-3). 25.32 **(978-1-5124-3378-4(0))** Lerner Publishing Group.

—Tiger Sharks in Action. 2017. (Lightning Bolt Books (tm) — Shark World Ser.). (ENG.). 24p. (J). (gr. 1-3). 25.32 **(978-1-5124-3380-7(2))** Lerner Publishing Group.

Simon, Seymour. Incredible Sharks. 2003. (SeeMore Readers Ser.: SEMR). (ENG., Illus.). 32p. (J). (gr. -1-7). pap. 5.99 (978-1-58717-239-7(9), SeaStar Bks.) Chronicle Bks. LLC.

—Sharks. 2006. (ENG., Illus.). 32p. (J). (gr. k-4). pap. 6.99 (978-0-06-087713-2(8), Collins) HarperCollins Pubs.

—Sharks. 2006. (Illus.). 32p. (gr. k-4). 17.00 (978-0-7569-6751-2(1)) Perfection Learning Corp.

—Sharks. 2005. (Illus.). 24p. (J). (978-0-439-77699-8(6)) Scholastic, Inc.

—Sharks. 2006. (J). 17.20 (978-1-4177-7522-4(X), Turtleback) Turtleback Bks.

SMARTLAB Creative Team. Mega 3D Puzzle Play Sharks. 2010. 3p. mass mkt. 19.99 (978-1-60380-094-5(8)) becker&mayer! books.

Smith, Elizabeth. The Magic School Bus & the Shark Adventure. Bracken, Carolyn, illus. 2007. (Scholastic Reader Ser.). (J). (978-0-545-03464-7(7)) Scholastic, Inc.

Somerville, Louisa. Sharks. 2008. (World of Animals Ser.). 32p. (gr. 2-5). 31.35 (978-1-933834-33-7(1)) Brown Bear Bks.

Sovak, Jan. Shiny Sharks Stickers. 2007. (Dover Little Activity Books Stickers Ser.). (ENG., Illus.). 2p. (J). (gr. 1-4). 1.50 (978-0-486-46228-8(5)) Dover Pubns., Inc.

Spilsbury, Louise. Shark, 1 vol. 2010. (Day in the Life: Sea Animals Ser.). (ENG.). 24p. (gr. k-2). 23.32 (978-1-4329-4003-4(1)); pap. 6.79 (978-1-4329-4010-2(4)) Heinemann-Raintree. (Heinemann Read & Learn).

Stefoff, Rebecca. Whale Sharks. 2014. (Giant Animals Ser.). 48p. (J). (gr. 4-6). lib. bdg. 31.36 (978-1-62712-954-1(5)) Cavendish Square Publishing.

Stephens, David. Sharks: Predators of the Ocean. 2014. (Discovery Education: Animals Ser.). 32p. (J). (gr. 3-6). 26.25 (978-1-4777-6926-3(9)); pap. 10.00 (978-1-4777-6927-0(7)) Rosen Publishing Group, Inc., The. (PowerKids Pr.).

Stewart, Melissa. Shark or Dolphin? How Do You Know? 2011. (Which Animal Is Which? Ser.). (Illus.). 24p. (J). (gr. k-18). pap. 7.95 (978-1-59845-239-6(8), Enslow Elementary); lib. bdg. 22.60 (978-0-7660-3680-2(4)) Enslow Pubs., Inc.

Stone, Tanya Lee. Sharks. 2003. (Wild Wild World Ser.). 24p. (YA). 24.94 (978-1-56711-822-3(4), Blackbirch Pr., Inc.) Cengage Gale.

Taylor, Barbara. Build the Shark. Ruffle, Mark & Bernstein, Galia, illus. 2013. (Build It Ser.). (ENG.). 32p. (J). (gr. k). 19.95 (978-1-60710-414-8(8), Silver Dolphin Bks.) Readerlink Distribution Services, LLC.

Taylor, Leighton. Great White Sharks. 2005. (Early Bird Nature Bks.). (ENG., Illus.). 48p. (gr. 2-5). lib. bdg. 26.60 (978-0-8225-2868-5(1), Lerner Pubns.) Lerner Publishing Group.

Taylor, Trace & Sanchez, Lucia M. Tiburones (Sharks) 2011. (poder de 100 - Animales marinos Ser.). (SPA.). 12p. pap. 39.62 (978-1-61541-279-2(4)) American Reading Co.

Thomas, Elizabeth. Goblin Sharks. 2013. (21st Century Skills Library: Exploring Our Oceans Ser.). (ENG., Illus.). 32p. (J). (gr. 3-6). 28.50 (978-1-62431-406-3(6), 202744); pap. 14.21 (978-1-62431-482-7(1), 202746) Cherry Lake Publishing.

—Great White Sharks. 2013. (21st Century Skills Library: Exploring Our Oceans Ser.). (ENG., Illus.). 32p. (J). (gr. 3-6). 28.50 (978-1-62431-407-0(4), 202748); pap. 14.21 (978-1-62431-483-4(X), 202750) Cherry Lake Publishing.

Thomas, Isabel. Shark vs. Killer Whale. 2017. (Animal Rivals Ser.). (ENG.). 24p. (gr. k-2). lib. bdg. 23.32 **(978-1-4846-4071-5(3)**, Heinemann Read & Learn) Heinemann-Raintree.

Thomson, Sarah L. Amazing Sharks! Wildlife Conservation Society, photos by. 2006. (I Can Read Level 2 Ser.). (ENG., Illus.). 32p. (J). (gr. k-3). pap. 3.99 (978-0-06-054456-0(2)) HarperCollins Pubs.

—Amazing Sharks! 2005. (I Can Read Bks.). (ENG., Illus.). 32p. (J). 15.99 (978-0-06-054458-4(9)) HarperCollins Pubs.

—Amazing Sharks! Wildlife Conservation Society, photos by. 2006. (I Can Read Bks.). (Illus.). 31p. (gr. -1-3). 14.00 (978-0-7569-6957-8(3)) Perfection Learning Corp.

Los tiburones blancos (Great White Sharks) 2006. (J). pap. 7.95 (978-0-8225-6627-4(3), Ediciones Lerner) Lerner Publishing Group.

Los Tiburones y Las Rayas, 6 vols. (Explorers. Exploradores Nonfiction Sets Ser.). (SPA.). 32p. (gr. 3-6). 44.95 (978-0-7699-0626-3(5)) Shortland Pubns. (U. S. A.) Inc.

Top That Publishing Staff, ed. Sharks. 2006. (Illus.). 48p. (978-1-84510-011-7(5)) Top That! Publishing PLC.

Toufexis, George. Ultimate Shark-Athon Facts & Activity Book. 2013. (ENG.). 48p. (J). (gr. 3-8). pap. 4.99 (978-0-486-49185-1(4)) Dover Pubns., Inc.

Toufexis, George & Coloring Books Staff. Sharks! Coloring Book. 2013. (Dover Nature Coloring Book Ser.). (ENG.). 32p. (J). (gr. 2-5). pap. 3.99 (978-0-486-49028-1(9)) Dover Pubns., Inc.

Toufexis, George, et al. Sharks. 2011. (Dover 3-D Coloring Book Ser.). (ENG., Illus.). 32p. (J). (gr. 2-6). 5.99 (978-0-486-48426-6(2)) Dover Pubns., Inc.

Troller, Leah. The Great White Shark. 2016. (1-3Y Marine Life Ser.). (ENG., Illus.). 20p. (J). pap. 5.99 **(978-1-63437-678-5(1))** American Reading Co.

Troupe, Thomas Kingsley. I Want to Be a Great White Shark. Boey, Stephanie, illus. 2015. (I Want to Be... Ser.). (ENG.). 24p. (gr. k-3). lib. bdg. 26.65 (978-1-4795-6859-8(7)) Capstone Press of Coughlan Cos.

Trueit, Trudi Strain. Sharks. 2010. (Benchmark Rebus: Ocean Life Ser.). 24p. (gr. k-1). 15.95 (978-0-7614-4896-9(9)) Marshall Cavendish Corp.

Tunby, Benjamin. Hammerhead Sharks in Action. 2017. (Lightning Bolt Books (tm) — Shark World Ser.). (ENG.). 24p. (J). (gr. 1-3). 25.32 **(978-1-5124-3379-1(9))** Lerner Publishing Group.

—Whale Sharks in Action. 2017. (Lightning Bolt Books (tm) — Shark World Ser.). (ENG.). 24p. (J). (gr. 1-3). 25.32 **(978-1-5124-3382-1(9))** Lerner Publishing Group.

Turnbull, Stephanie. Shark. 2015. (Big Beasts Ser.). (Illus.). 24p. (gr. k-3). 28.50 (978-1-62588-170-0(3)) Black Rabbit Bks.

—Shark. 2015. (ENG., Illus.). 24p. (J). pap. 8.95 (978-1-77092-218-1(0)) RiverStream Publishing.

Ultimate Sticker File Sharks. 2015. (ENG., Illus.). 56p. (J). (gr. -1-7). pap. (978-1-78393-831-5(5)) Make Believe Ideas.

Uttridge, Sarah. Sharks & Sea Creatures Around the World. 2014. (Animals Around the World Ser.). (Illus.). 32p. (gr. 2-5). 31.35 (978-1-62588-196-0(7)) Black Rabbit Bks.

Vadon, Catherine. Meet the Shark. 2007. (ENG., Illus.). 45p. (J). (gr. 4-7). 15.95 (978-1-58728-598-1(3)) Cooper Square Publishing Llc.

Waters, John F. Sharks Have Six Senses. Barner, Bob, illus. 2015. (Let's-Read-And-Find-Out Science 2 Ser.). (ENG.). 40p. (J). (gr. -1-3). 17.99 (978-0-06-028140-3(5)) HarperCollins Pubs.

Waxman, Laura Hamilton. Basking Sharks. 2017. (Sharks Ser.). (ENG., Illus.). 32p. (J). pap. 9.99 (978-1-68152-087-2(7)) Amicus.

—Basking Sharks. 2016. (Sharks Ser.). (ENG., Illus.). 32p. (J). (gr. 1-4). 20.95 (978-1-60753-974-2(8)) Amicus Publishing.

—Bull Sharks. 2017. (Sharks Ser.). (ENG., Illus.). 32p. (J). (gr. 1-3). pap. 9.99 (978-1-68152-089-6(3)) Amicus.

—Bull Sharks. 2016. (Sharks Ser.). (ENG., Illus.). 32p. (J). (gr. 1-4). 20.95 (978-1-60753-976-6(4)) Amicus Publishing.

—Great White Sharks. 2017. (Sharks Ser.). (ENG., Illus.). 32p. (J). (gr. 1-3). pap. 9.99 (978-1-68152-090-2(7)) Amicus.

—Great White Sharks. 2016. (Sharks Ser.). (ENG., Illus.). 32p. (J). (gr. 1-4). 20.95 (978-1-60753-977-3(2)) Amicus Publishing.

—Tiger Sharks. 2016. (Sharks Ser.). (ENG., Illus.). 32p. (J). (gr. 1-4). 20.95 (978-1-60753-980-3(2)) Amicus Publishing.

Waxman, Laura Hamilton & Morey, Allan. Tiger Sharks. 2017. (Sharks Ser.). (ENG., Illus.). 32p. (J). (gr. 1-3). pap. 9.99 (978-1-68152-093-3(1)) Amicus.

Weber, Valerie J. Sharks. 2008. (Animals That Live in the Ocean Ser.). (Illus.). 24p. (gr. -1-3). (J). lib. bdg. 22.60 (978-0-8368-9245-1(3)); pap. 8.15 (978-0-8368-9344-1(1)) Stevens, Gareth Publishing LLLP. (Weekly Reader Leveled Readers).

—Sharks/Tiburones. 2008. (Animals That Live in the Ocean/Animales Que Viven en el Oceano Ser.). (SPA & ENG.). 24p. (gr. -1-3). (J). lib. bdg. 22.60 (978-0-8368-9251-2(8)); pap. 8.15 (978-0-8368-9350-2(6)) Stevens, Gareth Publishing LLLP. (Weekly Reader Leveled Readers).

Weiss, Matthew. Be Nice to Sharks. Botelho, Daniel, photos by. 2016. (ENG., Illus.). 32p. (J). (gr. k-5). 12.95 (978-1-4549-1748-9(2)) Sterling Publishing Co., Inc.

West, David. Mega Shark: Graphic Prehistoric Animals. Poluzzi, Alessandro, illus. 2017. (Graphic Prehistoric Animals Ser.). 32p. (gr. 3-7). lib. bdg. 31.35 (978-1-62588-410-7(9)) Black Rabbit Bks.

Wexo, John Bonnett. Sharks. rev. ed. 2003. (Illus.). 24p. (J). (gr. 1-7). 10.95 (978-1-932396-05-8(5), Zoo Bks.) Wildlife Education, Ltd.

Wildlife Education. Sharks. 2007. (Illus.). 10p. (J). 5.99 (978-1-932396-30-0(6), Critters Up Close) Wildlife Education, Ltd.

William H. Sadlier Staff. Getting to Know Sharks. 2005. (Fluent Library). (gr. 1-3). 29.34 (978-0-8215-8963-2(6)) Sadlier, William H. Inc.

Williams, Lily. If Sharks Disappeared. Williams, Lily, illus. 2017. (ENG., Illus.). 40p. (J). 17.99 (978-1-62672-413-6(X), 9781626724136) Roaring Brook Pr.

Wilsdon, Christina. Sharks. 2009. (Amazing Animals Ser.). 48p. (YA). (gr. 3-6). lib. bdg. 28.00 (978-0-8368-9111-9(2)) Stevens, Gareth Publishing LLLP.

—Sharks. 2007. (J). (978-1-59939-130-4(9), Reader's Digest Young Families, Inc.) Studio Fun International.

Wood, I. Sharks: Learning the SH Sound. 2009. (PowerPhonics Ser.). 24p. (gr. 1-1). 39.90 (978-1-60851-470-0(6), PowerKids Pr.) Rosen Publishing Group, Inc., The.

Worth, Bonnie. Hark! a Shark! All about Sharks. Ruiz, Aristides & Mathieu, Joe, illus. 2013. (Cat in the Hat's Learning Library). (ENG.). 48p. (J). (gr. k-3). 9.99 (978-0-375-87073-6(3), Random Hse. Bks. for Young Readers) Random Hse. Children's Bks.

Yin, Robert, illus. & photos by. Sharks & Rays. Yin, Robert, photos by. 2004. (ENG.). 24p. (J). (gr. 1-2). pap. 7.47 net. (978-0-7685-0357-9(4), Dominie Elementary) Pearson Schl.

Yomtov, Nelson. Terrors from the Deep: True Tales of Surviving Shark Attacks. 2015. (True Stories of Survival Ser.). (ENG., Illus.). 32p. (gr. 3-4). lib. bdg. 30.65 (978-1-4914-6573-8(5)) Capstone Press of Coughlan Cos.

Zenescope Entertainment Staff. Discovery Channel's Great White Sharks. 2014. (ENG., Illus.). 120p. (J). pap. 9.99 (978-1-937068-39-4(0), 9781937068394) Zenescope Entertainment.

—Discovery Channel's Megalodon & Prehistoric Sharks. 2013. (ENG., Illus.). 120p. pap. 9.99 (978-1-937068-38-7(2), 9781937068387) Zenescope Entertainment.

Zoehfeld, Kathleen Weidner. Great White Shark: Ruler of the Sea. Petruccio, Steven James, illus. (Smithsonian Oceanic Collection). (J). 2009. 24.95 incl. audio compact disk (978-1-59249-664-8(4)) 2005. (ENG.). 32p. (gr. -1-2). per. 6.95 (978-1-59249-196-4(0), S4006) Soundprints.

—Great White Shark: Ruler of the Sea. 2005. (ENG., Illus.). 32p. (J). (gr. -1-2). 8.95 (978-1-59249-224-4(X), SC4006) Soundprints.

Zoldak, Joyce. Danger in the Deep: Surviving Shark Attacks. 2010. (Survivors Ser.). 128p. (YA). (gr. 7-12). 24.95 (978-1-4222-0511-2(8)) Mason Crest.

—Danger in the Deep: Survivors of Shark Attacks. 2009. (J). pap. 25.95 (978-1-4222-1475-6(3)) Mason Crest.

Zullo, Allan. Surviving Sharks. 2014. (10 True Tales Ser.). (ENG.). 160p. (J). (gr. 3-7). pap. 5.99 (978-0-545-81838-4(9), Scholastic Nonfiction) Scholastic, Inc.

SHARKS—FICTION

Aldrich, Sandra D. Trouble in the Park. 2012. 28p. 19.95 (978-1-4626-8818-0(7)) America Star Bks.

Altbacker, E. J. The Battle of Riptide, 2 vols. 2011. (Shark Wars Ser.: 2). (ENG.). 256p. (J). (gr. 3-7). 12.99 (978-1-59514-377-8(7), Razorbill) Penguin Young Readers Group.

—Enemy of Oceans. 2013. (Shark Wars Ser.: 5). (ENG., Illus.). 256p. (J). (gr. 3-7). 12.99 (978-1-59514-476-8(5), Razorbill) Penguin Young Readers Group.

—Into the Abyss, 3 vols. 2012. (Shark Wars Ser.: 3). (ENG.). 288p. (J). (gr. 3-7). 12.99 (978-1-59514-382-2(3), Razorbill) Penguin Young Readers Group.

—Kingdom of the Deep. 2012. (Shark Wars Ser.: 4). (ENG.). 240p. (J). (gr. 3-7). 12.99 (978-1-59514-509-3(5), Razorbill) Penguin Young Readers Group.

—The Last Emprex. 2013. (Shark Wars Ser.: 6). (ENG.). 272p. (J). (gr. 3-7). 12.99 (978-1-59514-544-4(3), Razorbill) Penguin Young Readers Group.

—Shark Wars. 2011. (Shark Wars Ser.: 1). (ENG., Illus.). 256p. (J). (gr. 3-7). 12.99 (978-1-59514-376-1(9), Razorbill) Penguin Young Readers Group.

Alten, Steve. Sharkman. 2014. (ENG.). 272p. 22.95 (978-1-63076-019-9(6)) Taylor Trade Publishing.

Arroyo, Yvonne. How the Octopus Got Eight Arms: Two Arms Are Never Enough. 2013. (ENG., Illus.). 45p. (J). pap. 23.95 (978-1-4327-9369-2(1)); pap. 31.95 (978-1-4327-9644-0(5)) Outskirts Pr., Inc.

Awdry, Wilbert V. Thomas & the Shark. Courtney, Richard, illus. 2013. (Step into Reading Ser.). (ENG.). 32p. (J). (gr. -1-1). pap. 3.99 (978-0-307-98200-1(9), Random Hse. Bks. for Young Readers) Random Hse. Children's Bks.

—Thomas & the Shark. 2013. (Thomas & Friends Step into Reading Ser.). lib. bdg. 13.55 (978-0-606-26996-4(7), Turtleback) Turtleback Bks.

Bailey, Lin. Stanley - the Shark Who Lost His Fin. 2012. 38p. pap. (978-1-909395-87-9(0)) Legend Pr.

Ballantyne, R. The Coral Island. 2006. pap. 14.95 (978-1-55742-666-6(X)) Wildside Pr., LLC.

Barton, Chris. Shark vs. Train. Lichtenheld, Tom, illus. (ENG.). (J). (gr. -1 — 1). 2015. 20p. bds. 6.99 (978-0-316-37814-7(3)) 2010. 40p. 18.99 (978-0-316-00762-7(5)) Little, Brown Bks. for Young Readers.

Beserra, Donna. Twirly Shirley In Hurricane Shirley. 2005. 22p. (J). 8.00 (978-0-9729484-4-9(9)) Seventh Street Pr.

Bise, Jr. J. David & Bise, Jr. In Search of a Name a Seahorse Story. 2011. 44p. pap. 15.50 (978-1-60976-288-9(6), Strategic Bk. Publishing) Strategic Book Publishing & Rights Agency (SBPRA).

Cafaro, Phyllis. The Legend of Captain McFinn & Friends. 2012. (ENG.). 24p. (J). 17.99 (978-0-9799283-3-8(8), 9780979928338) Cold River Pubns.

Carlson, Amie. The Shark That Was Afraid of the Deep End. 2016. (Who's Afraid? Ser.). (ENG.). 18p. (J). 15.99 (978-1-4964-1153-2(6)) Tyndale Hse. Pubs.

Clarke, Jane & Fuge, Charles. Gilbert in Deep. 2016. (ENG., Illus.). 32p. (J). (gr. -1-2). 6.95 (978-1-4549-2117-2(X)) Sterling Publishing Co., Inc.

Coombs, Bob. Ted P Bear - A Bitter Tale. 2005. 83p. (YA). pap. 8.69 (978-1-4116-4260-7(0)) Lulu Pr., Inc.

Cottringer, Anne. Mary Is Scary. Gale, Cathy, illus. 2007. (Bloomsbury Paperbacks Ser.). (ENG.). 32p. (J). (gr. k-2). pap. 9.99 (978-0-7475-7927-4(X)) Bloomsbury Publishing Plc GBR. Dist: Independent Pubs. Group.

Cox, Phil Roxbee. Shark in the Park. Tyler, Jenny, ed. Cartwright, Stephen, illus. rev. ed. 2006. (Phonics Readers Ser.). 16p. (J). (gr. -1-k). pap. 6.99 (978-0-7945-1509-6(6), Usborne) EDC Publishing.

Cruz, Stefanie. Delta & Dawn: Mother & Baby Whales' Journey. Toppenberg, Lily, illus. 2007. 32p. (J). lib. bdg. 15.95 (978-0-9791233-2-0(1)) Big Tomato Pr.

Dahl, Michael. Blood Shark! Sinkovec, Igor, illus. 2015. (Igor's Lab of Fear Ser.). (ENG.). 40p. (gr. 1-3). lib. bdg. 23.99 (978-1-4965-0456-2(9)) Stone Arch Bks.

Dembicki, Matt. Xoc: The Journey of a Great White. 2012. (ENG., Illus.). 120p. 19.99 (978-1-934964-85-9(9), 9781934964859) Oni Pr., Inc.

Diesen, Deborah. The Pout-Pout Fish & the Bully-Bully Shark. Hanna, Dan, illus. 2017. (Pout-Pout Fish Adventure Ser.). (ENG.). 32p. (J). 16.99 **(978-0-374-30402-7(5)**, 9780374304027, Farrar, Straus & Giroux (BYR)) Farrar, Straus & Giroux.

Downer, Ann. Shark Baby, 1 vol. Bersani, Shennen, illus. 2013. (SPA & ENG.). 32p. (J). (gr. -1-3). 17.95 (978-1-60718-622-9(5)); pap. 9.95 (978-1-62855-351-2(0)); pap. 9.95 (978-1-60718-634-2(9)) Arbordale Publishing.

—Tiburoncito, 1 vol. Bersani, Shennen, illus. 2013. (SPA.). 32p. (J). (gr. -1-3). 17.95 (978-1-60718-709-7(4)) Arbordale Publishing.

Ellis, Julie. Shark & Crab Big Book Edition. Hawley, Kelvin, illus. 2014. (ENG.). 16p. (gr. 1-1). Beta (978-1-77654-094-5(8), Red Rocket Readers) Flying Start Bks.

Ferry, Beth. Land Shark. Mantle, Ben, illus. 2015. (ENG.). 36p. (J). (gr. -1-k). 16.99 (978-1-4521-2458-2(2)) Chronicle Bks. LLC.

Gaines, Pat. O. O. Octopus: Sheriff of Blue Ribbon Sound. 2008. (Illus.). 24p. (J). lib. bdg. (978-0-9801376-4-4(0)); per. (978-0-9801376-5-1(9)) Dragonfly Publishing, Inc.

Galloway, Ruth. Smiley Shark. Galloway, Ruth, illus. (Illus.). 32p. (J). 2005. 6.95 (978-1-58925-391-9(4)) 2003. tchr. ed. 15.95 (978-1-58925-028-4(1)) Tiger Tales.

Geist, Ken. The Three Little Fish & the Big Bad Shark. Gorton, Julia, illus. 2007. (ENG.). 32p. (J). (gr. -1-3). 7.99 (978-0-439-71962-9(3)) Scholastic, Inc.

—The Three Little Fish & the Big Bad Shark - A Board Book. Gorton, Julia, illus. 2016. (ENG.). 22p. (J). (gr. -1 — 1). bds. 6.99 (978-0-545-94483-0(X), Cartwheel Bks.) Scholastic, Inc.

George, Jean Craighead. Shark Beneath the Reef. (J). pap. 3.50 (978-0-13-800038-7(7)) Prentice Hall (Schl. Div.).

Gill, Timothy. Flip & Fin: Super Sharks to the Rescue! Numberman, Neil, illus. 2016. 32p. (J). (gr. -1-3). 15.99 (978-0-06-224301-0(2), Greenwillow Bks.) HarperCollins Pubs.

—Flip & Fin: We Rule the School! Numberman, Neil, illus. 2014. (ENG.). 32p. (J). (gr. -1-3). 14.99 (978-0-06-224300-3(4), Greenwillow Bks.) HarperCollins Pubs.

Glover, Matt. But It's True. 2012. (Illus.). 32p. pap. 13.50 (978-1-78035-330-2(8), Fastprint Publishing) Upfront Publishing Ltd. GBR. Dist: Printondemand-worldwide.com.

Grant, Richard E. & Bently, Peter. The Wah-Wah Diaries: The Making of a Film. 3 CDs. Cort, Ben, illus. 2008. (ENG.). 32p. (J). (gr. 2-6). 23.95 (978-0-230-01598-2(0), Macmillan) Pan Macmillan GBR. Dist: Trans-Atlantic Pubns., Inc.

Griffin, Wiley Chase. Chase the Shark: Flies Like a Bird. 2010. 28p. pap. 12.50 (978-1-4520-5173-4(9)) AuthorHouse.

Grimm, Kristi. Mommy, Tell Me a Story about a Fish. 2013. (Illus.). 34p. pap. 13.99 (978-0-9899001-3-3(4)) Richer Life, LLC.

Hale, Bruce. Afraid of the Dark. Francis, Guy, illus. 2015. (Clark the Shark Ser.). (ENG.). 32p. (J). (gr. -1-3). 17.99 (978-0-06-237450-9(8)) HarperCollins Pubs.

—Clark the Shark. Francis, Guy, illus. 2013. (Clark the Shark Ser.). (ENG.). 32p. (J). (gr. -1-3). 17.99 (978-0-06-219226-4(4)) HarperCollins Pubs.

—Clark the Shark. 2016. (Clark the Shark: I Can Read Level 1 Ser.). (J). lib. bdg. 13.55 (978-0-606-38774-3(9)) Turtleback Bks.

—Clark the Shark - Tooth Trouble. Francis, Guy, illus. 2014. (I Can Read Level 1 Ser.). (ENG.). 32p. (J). (gr. -1-3). 16.99 (978-0-06-227908-8(4)); pap. 3.99 (978-0-06-227906-4(8)) HarperCollins Pubs.

—Clark the Shark & the Big Book Report. Francis, Guy, illus. 2017. (I Can Read Level 1 Ser.). 32p. (J). (gr. -1-3). pap. 3.99 *(978-0-06-227912-5(2))* HarperCollins Pubs.
—Clark the Shark Dares to Share. Francis, Guy, illus. 2013. (Clark the Shark Ser.). (ENG.). 32p. (J). (gr. -1-3). 17.99 *(978-0-06-227905-7(X))* HarperCollins Pubs.
—Clark the Shark: Lost & Found. Francis, Guy, illus. 2016. (I Can Read Level 1 Ser.). 32p. (J). (gr. -1-3). pap. 3.99 *(978-0-06-227910-1(6))* HarperCollins Pubs.
—Clark the Shark Loves Christmas. Francis, Guy, illus. 2016. (Clark the Shark Ser.). 32p. (J). (gr. -1-3). 17.99 *(978-0-06-237452-3(4))* HarperCollins Pubs.
—Clark the Shark Takes Heart. Francis, Guy, illus. 2014. (Clark the Shark Ser.). (ENG.). 32p. (J). (gr. -1-3). 17.99 *(978-0-06-219227-1(2))* HarperCollins Pubs.
Hanson, Anders. Lone Shark, 1 vol. Haberstroh, Anne, illus. 2007. (Critter Chronicles Ser.). (ENG.). 24p. (J). (gr. k-3). lib. bdg. 24.21 *(978-1-59928-452-1(9),* SandCastle) ABDO Publishing Co.
Harvey, M. A. The Shark Island Mystery: Dare to Take the Test. 2004. (Illus.). 128p. (J). pap. *(978-1-84458-147-4(0),* Pavilion Children's Books) Pavilion Bks.
Herz, Henry, et al. Little Red Cuttlefish, 1 vol. Gotfredson, Kate, illus. 2016. (ENG.). 32p. (J). (gr. k-3). 16.99 *(978-1-4556-2146-0(3))* Pelican Publishing Co., Inc.
High, Linda Oatman. The Shark [1]. 2017. (TERL Boosters Ser.). (ENG.). 48p. (YA). (gr. 9-12). pap. 7.95 ***(978-1-68021-155-9(2))*** Saddleback Educational Publishing, Inc.
Ice Water Press Staff. Secrets of the Deep. 2010. (J). pap. *(978-1-921639-95-1(4))* Ripley Entertainment, Inc.
ImageBooks Staff. Little Shark: Finger Puppet Book. Put, Klaartje van der, illus. 2013. (Little Finger Puppet Board Bks.). (ENG.). 12p. (J). (gr. -1 — 1). bds. 6.99 *(978-1-4521-1251-0(7))* Chronicle Bks. LLC.
Janacone, Matt. Finny the Friendly Shark. Druschel, Bob, illus. 2005. 40p. (J). per. 20.99 *(978-1-58939-655-5(3))* Virtualbookworm.com Publishing, Inc.
Kapai, Tommy. Cuzzies Meet the Motuhoa Shark. Henry, Mike, illus. 2006. (Cuzzies Adventures Ser.). (MAO & ENG.). 32p. (J). (gr. -1-3). pap. 9.00 *(978-1-86969-100-4(8))* Huia Pubs. NZL. Dist: Univ. of Hawaii Pr.
Laird, Donivee M. Ula Li'i & the Magic Shark. Jossem, Carol, illus. 2003. 49p. (J). (gr. k-3). 9.95 *(978-0-940350-23-6(8))* Barnaby Bks., Inc.
Laird, Donivee Martin. The Magic Shark Learns to Cook. Johnson, Carol Ann, illus. 2004. 48p. (J). 9.95 *(978-1-57306-233-6(2))* Bess Pr., Inc.
Landers, Ace. Shark Attack. 2013. (Scholastic Reader Level 1 Ser.). lib. bdg. 13.55 *(978-0-606-32391-8(0),* Turtleback) Turtleback Bks.
Larry, H. I. Zac's Shark Attack. 2014. (Zac Power Test Drive Ser.: 8). (ENG.). 56p. (J). (gr. k-2). 7.99 *(978-1-921502-10-1(X))* Hardie Grant Egmont Pty, Ltd. AUS. Dist: Independent Pubs. Group.
Lloyd, Sam R. Yummy Yummy! Food for My Tummy. Tickle, Jack, illus. 2004. 32p. (J). tchr. ed. 15.95 *(978-1-58925-035-2(4))* Tiger Tales.
Lucas, Nancy T. Peppy's Coral Kingdom. 2008. (ENG.). 24p. pap. 12.99 *(978-1-4196-9046-4(9))* CreateSpace Independent Publishing Platform.
Maddox, Jake. Shark Attack! Tiffany, Sean, illus. 2009. (Jake Maddox Sports Stories Ser.). (ENG.). 72p. (gr. 2-3). 25.32 *(978-1-4342-1210-8(6))* Stone Arch Bks.
Maestro, Betsy & Maestro, Giulio. A Sea Full of Sharks.Tr. of Mer Pleine de Requins. (FRE., Illus.). (J). pap. 7.99 *(978-0-590-74409-6(7))* Scholastic, Inc.
Manley, Curtis. Shawn Loves Sharks. Subisak, Tracy, illus. 2017. (ENG.). 32p. (J). 17.99 *(978-1-62672-134-0(3),* 9781626721340) Roaring Brook Pr.
Manushkin, Fran. Pedro & the Shark. Lyon, Tammie, illus. 2017. (Pedro Ser.). (ENG.). 32p. (gr. k-2). lib. bdg. 21.32 *(978-1-5158-0873-2(4))* Pedro Pubns. GBR. Dist: Capstone Pub.
Marin, Cheech. Captain Cheech. Ramirez, Orlando L., illus. 2008. 32p. (J). (gr. -1-3). lib. bdg. 17.89 *(978-0-06-113208-7(X))* HarperCollins Pubs.
Markel, Michelle. The Shark That Taught Me English/El Tiburon Que Me Enseno Ingles. Kim, Bo Young, illus. 2008. 28p. (J). pap. 8.95 *(978-1-60448-003-0(3))* Lectura Bks.
—The Shark That Taught Me English/El Tiburon Que Me Enseno Ingles. Guerrero, Ernesto, tr. Kim, Bo Young, illus. 2008. (ENG & SPA.). 28p. (J). (gr. 1-2). 15.95 *(978-1-60448-002-3(5))* Lectura Bks.
McDonald, Megan. Stink & the Shark Sleepover. 2015. (Stink Ser.: 9). lib. bdg. 14.75 *(978-0-606-36859-9(0))* Turtleback Bks.
McKenzie, J. Lee. Vampires Don't Believe in Mermaids. 2011. 54p. pap. 16.95 *(978-1-4560-1157-4(X))* America Star Bks.
Meister, Cari. The Brave Puffer Fish, 1 vol. Harpster, Steve, illus. 2011. (Ocean Tales Ser.). (ENG.). 32p. (gr. 2-3). pap. 6.25 *(978-1-4342-3389-9(8))* Stone Arch Bks.
—The Shivery Shark, 1 vol. Harpster, Steve, illus. 2011. (Ocean Tales Ser.). (ENG.). 32p. (gr. 2-3). pap. 6.25 *(978-1-4342-3391-2(X));* lib. bdg. 22.65 *(978-1-4342-3200-7(X))* Stone Arch Bks.
Membrino, Anna. Big Shark, Little Shark. 2017. (Step into Reading Ser.). (ENG., Illus.). 32p. (J). (gr. -1-1). pap. 3.99 *(978-0-399-55728-6(8),* Random Hse. Bks. for Young Readers) Random Hse. Children's Bks.
Metzger, Steve. Big Shark's Valentine Surprise. Hohnstadt, Cedric, illus. 2007. (J). pap. *(978-0-439-92251-7(8))* Scholastic, Inc.
—Five Little Sharks Swimming in the Sea. Bryant, Laura, illus. 2004. (J). *(978-0-439-66139-3(0));* pap. *(978-0-439-59228-4(3))* Scholastic, Inc.
Metzger, Steve & Hohnstadt, Cedric. Big Shark's Halloween Mystery. 2007. (Illus.). (J). pap. *(978-0-545-00237-0(0))* Scholastic, Inc.
Morgan, Michaela. Shy Shark. Gomez, Elena, illus. 2005. (ENG.). 24p. (J). lib. bdg. 23.65 *(978-1-59646-722-4(3))* Dingles & Co.
Morris, Richard & Morris, Winifred. What If the Shark Wears Tennis Shoes? 2007. (ENG.). 36p. (J). (gr. k-3). 11.99 *(978-1-4169-6726-2(5),* Simon & Schuster/Paula Wiseman Bks.) Simon & Schuster/Paula Wiseman Bks.
Northrop, Michael. Surrounded by Sharks. 2014. (ENG.). 224p. (J). (gr. 4-7). 17.99 *(978-0-545-61545-7(3),* Scholastic Pr.) Scholastic, Inc.
Ocean, Davy. The Boy Who Cried Shark. Blecha, Aaron, illus. 2015. (Shark School Ser.: 4). (ENG.). 144p. (J). (gr. 1-4). 16.99 *(978-1-4814-0689-5(2),* Aladdin) Simon & Schuster Children's Publishing.
—Deep-Sea Disaster. Blecha, Aaron, illus. 2014. (Shark School Ser.: 1). (ENG.). 128p. (J). (gr. 1-4). 17.99 *(978-1-4814-0679-6(5),* Aladdin) Simon & Schuster Children's Publishing.
—Deep-Sea Treasury: Deep-Sea Disaster; Lights! Camera! Hammerhead!; Squid-Napped; the Boy Who Cried Shark. Blecha, Aaron, illus. 2015. (Shark School Ser.). (ENG.). 528p. (J). (gr. 1-4). 14.99 *(978-1-4814-5115-4(4),* Aladdin) Simon & Schuster Children's Publishing.
—A Fin-Tastic Finish. Blecha, Aaron, illus. 2015. (Shark School Ser.: 5). (ENG.). 160p. (J). (gr. 1-4). 16.99 *(978-1-4814-0692-5(2),* Aladdin) Simon & Schuster Children's Publishing.
—Lights! Camera! Hammerhead! Blecha, Aaron, illus. 2014. (Shark School Ser.: 2). (ENG.). 128p. (J). (gr. 1-4). 15.99 *(978-1-4814-0682-6(5),* Aladdin) Simon & Schuster Children's Publishing.
—Splash Dance. Blecha, Aaron, illus. 2015. (Shark School Ser.: 6). (ENG.). 128p. (J). (gr. 1-4). pap. 5.99 *(978-1-4814-0694-9(9),* Aladdin) Simon & Schuster Children's Publishing.
—Tooth or Dare. Blecha, Aaron, illus. 2016. (Shark School Ser.: 7). (ENG.). 128p. (J). (gr. 1-4). pap. 5.99 *(978-1-4814-6546-5(5),* Aladdin) Simon & Schuster Children's Publishing.
Olien, Jessica. Shark Detective! Olien, Jessica, illus. 2015. (ENG., Illus.). 32p. (J). (gr. -1-3). 17.99 *(978-0-06-235714-4(X))* HarperCollins Pubs.
Page, Nick & Page, Claire. Read with Me Jonah the Moaner: Sticker Activity Book. Loy, Nikki, illus. 2006. (Read with Me (Make Believe Ideas) Ser.). 12p. (J). (gr. k-2). pap. *(978-1-84610-183-0(2))* Make Believe Ideas.
Page, Nick & Claire. Jonah the Moaner. 2006. (Read with Me (Make Believe Ideas) Ser.). (Illus.). 32p. (J). (gr. k-2). *(978-1-84610-167-0(0))* Make Believe Ideas.
Paterakis, Paul. Henry the Friendly Shark. 2013. 24p. pap. 24.95 *(978-1-62709-447-4(4))* America Star Bks.
Pennington, Stacey & Pennington, J. C. D. Let's Go Aquarium: A Magnetic Storybook. Allen, Marie, illus. 2008. 6p. (J). (gr. -1-1). bds. 10.99 *(978-2-7641-2184-9(9))* Gardner Pubns.
Rash, Ron. The Shark's Tooth. Martin, Cecile L. K., illus. 2015. (Young Palmetto Bks.). (ENG.). 40p. (J). pap. 12.95 *(978-1-61117-527-1(5))* Univ. of South Carolina Pr.
R.D.Haire & Francis, Richard E. When Good Got Better: The Adventures of Fred the Friendly Shark. 2012. 24p. pap. 15.99 *(978-1-4797-3797-0(6))* Xlibris Corp.
Reed, Lynn Rowe. Shark Kiss, Octopus Hug. Cornell, Kevin, illus. 2014. (ENG.). 32p. (J). (gr. -1-3). 14.99 *(978-0-06-220320-5(7))* HarperCollins Pubs.
Rentala, Sita Kanaka Valli. Ocean Flows: In Prose: Zcumby's Judo (on Global Warming) 2010. 44p. (J). pap. 19.99 *(978-1-4490-8780-7(9))* AuthorHouse.
Ripley's Believe It Or Not! Staff. Secrets of the Deep. 2010. (Rbi Ser.: 4). (ENG.). 128p. (J). pap. 4.99 *(978-1-893951-54-9(5))* Ripley Entertainment, Inc.
Rogers, Jewels. The Princess & the Dolphin. 2011. 28p. 12.50 *(978-1-4567-3278-3(1))* AuthorHouse.
—The Princess & the Dolphin. 2010. 28p. pap. 16.99 *(978-1-4269-3966-2(3))* Trafford Publishing.
Rouss, Sylvia & Avalone, C. The Littlest Fish. 2008. 32p. 12.95 *(978-1-934440-53-7(1),* Pitspopany Pr.) Simcha Media Group.
Saddleback Educational Publishing, ed. Treasure, 1 vol. 2013. (Heights Ser.). (ENG.). 52p. (gr. 5-8). 7.95 *(978-1-62250-048-2(2))* Saddleback Educational Publishing, Inc.
Saddleback Educational Publishing Staff, ed. Sail, 1 vol. unabr. ed. 2011. (Heights Ser.). (ENG.). 50p. (gr. 5-8). 7.95 *(978-1-61651-622-2(4))* Saddleback Educational Publishing, Inc.
Sauer, Tammi. Nugget & Fang. 2015. lib. bdg. 17.20 *(978-0-606-36825-4(6))* Turtleback Bks.
—Nugget & Fang: Friends Forever - Or Snack Time? Slack, Michael, illus. 2013. (ENG.). 40p. (J). (gr. -1-3). 16.99 *(978-0-547-85285-0(1))* Houghton Mifflin Harcourt Publishing Co.
—Nugget & Fang: Friends Forever — Or Snack Time? Slack, Michael, illus. 2015. (ENG.). 40p. (J). (gr. -1-3). 6.99 *(978-0-544-48171-8(2),* HMH Books For Young Readers) Houghton Mifflin Harcourt Publishing Co.
Schwarz, Viviane. Shark & Lobster's Amazing Undersea Adventure. Stewart, Joel, illus. 2006. 34p. (J). *(978-1-4156-8140-4(6))* Candlewick Pr.
Shea, Bob. I'm a Shark. Shea, Bob, illus. 2011. (ENG., Illus.). 40p. (J). (gr. -1-1). 16.99 *(978-0-06-199846-1(X))* HarperCollins Pubs.
Simpkins, Debra Burke. The Luna Tuna. 2010. 32p. 12.99 *(978-1-4520-0213-2(4))* AuthorHouse.
Soileau, Hodges, illus. The Great Shark Mystery. 2003. (Boxcar Children Special Ser.). 130p. (gr. 4-7). 15.50 *(978-0-7569-1616-9(X))* Perfection Learning Corp.
Squid-Napped! 2014. (Shark School Ser.: 3). (ENG., Illus.). 144p. (J). (gr. 1-4). pap. 5.99 *(978-1-4814-0684-0(1),* Aladdin) Simon & Schuster Children's Publishing.
Stephens, Ann Marie. Christmas for Bly & Ray. Bolan, Michael P., illus. 2003. 45p. (J). per. 11.95 *(978-0-9729285-0-2(2),* 0-9729285-0-2) Kinkachoo Pr., The.
—A Surprise for Ray. Bolan, Michael P., illus. 2003. 47p. (J). per. 11.95 *(978-0-9729285-1-9(0),* 0-9729285-1-0) Kinkachoo Pr., The.
Tarshis, Lauren. I Survived the Shark Attacks of 1916. 2010. (I Survived Ser.: 2). (ENG.). 112p. (J). (gr. 3-7). pap. 4.99 *(978-0-545-20695-2(2),* Scholastic Paperbacks) Scholastic, Inc.
—I Survived the Shark Attacks of 1916. 2010. (I Survived . Ser.: No. 2). lib. bdg. 14.75 *(978-0-606-23742-0(9),* Turtleback) Turtleback Bks.
Tate, Suzanne. Great Sharky Shark: A Tale of a Big Hunter. Melvin, James, illus. 2004. (Suzanne Tate's Nature Ser.: No. 20). 32p. (J). per. 10.95 *(978-1-878405-46-3(2))* Nags Head Art, Inc.
Verrone, Patric C. W. Sharktooth. 2009. 229p. pap. 14.76 *(978-0-557-09535-3(2))* Lulu Pr., Inc.
Voake, Steve. Hooey Higgins & the Shark. Dodson, Emma, illus. 2012. (ENG.). 112p. (J). (gr. 2-5). 14.99 *(978-0-7636-5782-6(4))* Candlewick Pr.
Wheeler, J. D. Gummery & Lubber. 2008. 56p. pap. 16.95 *(978-1-60563-432-6(8))* America Star Bks.
Williams, Geoffrey T. The Great White Red Alert. Artful Doodlers, illus. Campbell, Tom, photos by. 2008. (Save Our Seas Adventure Bks.). (ENG.). 64p. (J). (gr. 4-7). 8.95 *(978-0-9800444-0-9(5))* Save Our Seas, Ltd.
Wrecks, Billy. Shark Attack! Doescher, Erik, illus. 2017. 24p. (J). ***(978-1-5182-2649-6(3))*** Random Hse., Inc.
—Shark Attack! 2017. (Step into Reading Level 2 Ser.). lib. bdg. 14.75 ***(978-0-606-39852-7(X))*** Turtleback Bks.
Wrecks, Billy. Shark Attack! (DC Super Friends) Random House, illus. 2017. (Step into Reading Ser.). (ENG.). 24p. (J). (gr. -1-1). pap. 4.99 *(978-0-399-55846-7(2),* Random Hse. Bks. for Young Readers) Random Hse. Children's Bks.

SHAVUOT

Marks, Allison & Marks, Wayne. The Art Lesson: A Shavuot Story. Wilkinson, Annie, illus. 2017. (Lag Ba'Omer & Shavuot Ser.). (ENG.). 32p. (gr. -1-2). 23.99 ***(978-1-5124-2720-2(9),*** Kar-Ben Publishing) Lerner Publishing Group.

SHAVUOT—FICTION

Goldin, Barbara Diamond. Mountain of Blintzes, 0 vols. McGrory, Anik, illus. 2010. (ENG.). 32p. (J). (gr. -1-2). pap. 6.99 *(978-0-7614-5790-9(9),* 9780761457909, Amazon Children's Publishing) Amazon Publishing.
Korngold, Jamie. Sadie & the Big Mountain. Fortenberry, Julie, illus. 2012. (Lag B'Omer & Shavuot Ser.). (ENG.). 32p. (J). (gr. -1-1). pap. 7.95 *(978-0-7613-6494-8(3),* Kar-Ben Publishing) Lerner Publishing Group.
MacLeod, Jennifer Tzivia. Yossi & the Monkeys: A Shavuot Story. Waisman, Shirley, illus. 2017. (ENG.). 32p. (gr. -1-3). 17.99 *(978-1-4677-8932-5(1),* Kar-Ben Publishing) Lerner Publishing Group.
Marks, Allison & Marks, Wayne. The Art Lesson: A Shavuot Story. Wilkinson, Annie, illus. 2017. (ENG.). 32p. (gr. -1-2). 17.99 *(978-1-4677-8172-5(X),* Kar-Ben Publishing) Lerner Publishing Group.
Ofanansky, Allison. Cheesecake for Shavuot. Alpern, Eliyahu, photos by. 2013. (Lag B'Omer & Shavuot Ser.). (ENG., Illus.). 32p. (J). (gr. -1-2). 8.95 *(978-1-4677-1411-2(9),* Kar-Ben Publishing) Lerner Publishing Group.
Rouss, Sylvia A. Sammy Spider's First Shavuot. Kahn, Katherine Janus, illus. 2008. (Sammy Spider's First Bks.). (ENG.). 32p. (J). (gr. -1-3). lib. bdg. 15.95 *(978-0-8225-7224-4(9));* per. 7.95 *(978-0-8225-7225-1(7))* Lerner Publishing Group. (Kar-Ben Publishing).

SHAYS' REBELLION, 1786-1787

Roxburgh, Ellis. Shays' Rebellion. 2017. (Rebellions, Revolts, & Uprisings Ser.). 48p. (gr. 5-5). pap. 84.30 ***(978-1-5382-0756-7(7))*** Stevens, Gareth Publishing LLLP.

SHEEP

Alinas, Marv. Sheep. 2016. (In the Barnyard Ser.). (ENG.). 24p. (J). (gr. k-3). 27.07 *(978-1-5038-0830-0(0),* 210674) Child's World, Inc., The.
Barlow, Helen. Easy Read with Grandma Read: Book 1, Stage 3. 2009. (Illus.). 48p. pap. *(978-1-84748-507-6(3))* Athena Pr.
Beck, Isabel L., et al. Trophies Kindergarten: The Big Ram. 2003. (Trophies Ser.). (gr. k-6). 13.80 *(978-0-15-329540-9(6))* Harcourt Schl. Pubs.
Boothroyd, Jennifer. Meet a Baby Sheep. 2016. (Lightning Bolt Books (tm) — Baby Farm Animals Ser.). (ENG., Illus.). 32p. (J). (gr. 1-3). 26.65 *(978-1-5124-0800-3(X))* Lerner Publishing Group.
Borgert-Spaniol, Megan. Bighorn Sheep. 2015. (North American Animals Ser.). (ENG., Illus.). 24p. (J). (gr. k-3). lib. bdg. 25.95 *(978-1-62617-257-9(9),* Blastoff! Readers) Bellwether Media.
Canetti, Yanitzia. Canta y Cuenta Las Ovejas. 2010. (J). *(978-1-59835-224-5(5))* Cambridge BrickHouse, Inc.
—1-2-3 Do, Re, Mi Sheep. 2010. (J). *(978-1-59835-223-8(7))* Cambridge BrickHouse, Inc.
Carraway, Rose. Sheep on the Farm. 2012. (Farm Animals Ser.). (Illus.). 24p. (J). (gr. k-2). 69.20 *(978-1-4339-8057-2(6));* (J). 22.60 *(978-1-4339-7364-2(2));* (J). pap. 8.15 *(978-1-4339-7365-9(0))* Stevens, Gareth Publishing LLLP.
—Sheep on the Farm: Ovejas de Granja. 2012. (Farm Animals / Animales de granja Ser.). (SPA & ENG., Illus.). 24p. (gr. k-2). lib. bdg. 22.60 *(978-1-4339-7404-5(5))* Stevens, Gareth Publishing LLLP.
Carter, Denzel T. Lambs, Lambs, Lambs. 2015. (Rosen REAL Readers: STEM & STEAM Collection). (ENG.). 8p. pap. 5.46 *(978-1-4994-9669-7(9),* Rosen Classroom) Rosen Publishing Group, Inc., The.
Dicker, Katie. Sheep. 2014. (Farm Animals Ser.). (Illus.). 24p. (gr. 2-5). 28.50 *(978-1-62588-024-6(3))* Black Rabbit Bks.
Dieker, Wendy Strobel. Sheep. 2012. (Illus.). 24p. (J). lib. bdg. 25.65 *(978-1-62031-006-9(6))* Jump! Inc.
Dolphin, Colleen. Super Sheep, 1 vol. 2011. (Farm Pets Ser.). (ENG., Illus.). 24p. (J). (gr. k-3). lib. bdg. 24.21 *(978-1-61613-374-0(0))* ABDO Publishing Co.
Doubleday Entertainment USA - Sheep: Down on the Farm. 2006. (J). per. 6.95 *(978-1-59566-227-9(8))* QEB Publishing Inc.
Dunn, Joeming & Denham, Brian. Dolly: The 1st Cloned Sheep, 1 vol. 2011. (Famous Firsts: Animals Making History Ser.). (ENG., Illus.). 32p. (YA). (gr. 3-6). 28.50 *(978-1-61641-640-9(8))* Magic Wagon.
Esseltine, Bruce. At the Sheep Farm. 2016. (Fun on the Farm Ser.). 00024p. (J). pap. 8.15 *(978-1-4824-5532-8(3))* Stevens, Gareth Publishing LLLP.
Feinstein, Stephen. The Bighorn Sheep: Help Save This Endangered Species! 2007. (Saving Endangered Species Ser.). (Illus.). 128p. (J). (gr. 3-7). lib. bdg. 34.60 *(978-1-59845-042-2(5),* MyReportLinks.com Bks.) Enslow Pubs., Inc.
Gagne, Tammy. Bighorn Sheep. 2017. (Animals of North America (paperback) Ser.). (ENG., Illus.). 32p. (J). (gr. 3-5). pap. 9.95 ***(978-1-63517-088-7(5),*** Focus Readers) North Star Editions.
Gandolfo, Glora. Sheep. 2009. (Illus.). 52p. (J). *(978-0-7172-8054-4(3))* Grolier, Ltd.
Gish, Melissa. Bighorn Sheep. 2015. (Illus.). 46p. (J). *(978-1-60818-564-1(8),* Creative Education) Creative Co., The.
—Bighorn Sheep: Living Wild. 2016. (Living Wild Ser.). (ENG.). 48p. (J). (gr. 5-9). pap. 12.00 *(978-1-62832-165-4(2),* Creative Paperbacks) Creative Co., The.
Green, Emily K. Sheep. 2007. (Farm Animals Ser.). (ENG., Illus.). 24p. (J). (gr. k-3). lib. bdg. 25.95 *(978-1-60014-069-3(6))* Bellwether Media.
Hasselius, Michelle M. Sheep. 2016. (Farm Animals Ser.). (ENG.). 24p. (gr. k-1). lib. bdg. 26.65 *(978-1-5157-0927-5(2))* Capstone Press of Coughlan Cos.
Hirsch, Rebecca. Dall Sheep Migration. 2012. (Animal Migrations Ser.). (ENG., Illus.). 32p. (J). (gr. 2-5). lib. bdg. 29.93 *(978-1-60973-619-4(2),* 201196) Child's World, Inc., The.
Hudak, Heather C. Sheep. 2006. (Farm Animals Ser.). (Illus.). 24p. (J). (gr. 3-7). lib. bdg. 24.45 *(978-1-59036-428-4(7));* per. 8.95 *(978-1-59036-435-2(X))* Weigl Pubs., Inc.
Jackson, Tom. Bighorn Sheep. 2008. (Nature's Children Ser.). (Illus.). 52p. (J). *(978-0-7172-6218-2(9))* Grolier, Ltd.
Kawa, Katie. Lambs. 2011. (Cute & Cuddly: Baby Animals Ser.). (Illus.). 24p. (J). (gr. k-2). (J). pap. 8.15 *(978-1-4339-5547-1(4));* (J). lib. bdg. 22.60 *(978-1-4339-5546-4(6));* 69.20 *(978-1-4339-6897-6(5))* Stevens, Gareth Publishing LLLP.
Kopp, Megan. Ovejas. 2013. (Animales en la Granja Ser.). (SPA., Illus.). 24p. (J). (gr. -1-3). lib. bdg. 27.13 *(978-1-62127-591-6(4),* AV2 by Weigl) Weigl Pubs., Inc.
—Sheep. 2012. (J). *(978-1-61913-282-5(6));* *(978-1-61913-278-8(8))* Weigl Pubs., Inc.
Leaf, Christina. Baby Sheep. 2014. (Super Cute! Ser.). (ENG., Illus.). 24p. (J). (gr. k-3). lib. bdg. 25.95 *(978-1-60014-978-8(2),* Blastoff! Readers) Bellwether Media.
Macken, JoAnn Early. Bighorn Sheep. 2nd rev. ed. 2009. (Animals That Live in the Mountains Ser.). 24p. (J). (gr. -1-3). (ENG.). pap. 8.15 *(978-1-4339-2492-7(7));* lib. bdg. 22.60 *(978-1-4339-2409-5(9))* Stevens, Gareth Publishing LLLP. (Weekly Reader Leveled Readers).
—Bighorn Sheep: Carneros de Canada. 2nd rev. ed. 2009. (Animals That Live in the Mountains/Animales de las montañas Ser.). (ENG & SPA.). 24p. (J). (gr. -1-3). pap. 8.15 *(978-1-4339-2499-6(4));* lib. bdg. 22.60 *(978-1-4339-2441-5(2))* Stevens, Gareth Publishing LLLP. (Weekly Reader Leveled Readers).
—Mountain Goats;Cabra Montés. 2nd rev. ed. 2009. (Animals That Live in the Mountains/Animales de las montañas Ser.). 24p. (J). (gr. -1-3). (ENG & SPA.). pap. 8.15 *(978-1-4339-2504-7(4));* (SPA & ENG.). lib. bdg. 22.60 *(978-1-4339-2446-0(3))* Stevens, Gareth Publishing LLLP. (Weekly Reader Leveled Readers).
—Sheep. 2nd rev. ed. 2009. (Animals That Live on the Farm Ser.). (ENG.). 24p. (J). (gr. -1-3). pap. 8.15 *(978-1-4339-2469-9(2));* lib. bdg. 22.60 *(978-1-4339-2400-2(5))* Stevens, Gareth Publishing LLLP. (Weekly Reader Leveled Readers).
—Sheep;Las Ovejas. 2nd rev. ed. 2009. (Animals That Live on the Farm/Animales que viven en la granja Ser.). (ENG & SPA.). 24p. (J). (gr. -1-3). pap. 8.15 *(978-1-4339-2476-7(5));* lib. bdg. 22.60 *(978-1-4339-2432-3(3))* Stevens, Gareth Publishing LLLP. (Weekly Reader Leveled Readers).
Magby, Meryl. Bighorn Sheep. 2012. (American Animals Ser.). (ENG., Illus.). 24p. (J). (gr. k-3). lib. bdg. 22.60 *(978-1-4488-6181-1(0));* pap. 8.25 *(978-1-4488-6321-1(X),* PowerKids Pr.) Rosen Publishing Group, Inc., The.
Marie, Christian. Little Sheep. 2006. (Born to Be Wild Ser.). (Illus.). 24p. (gr. k-3). lib. bdg. 23.00 *(978-0-8368-6169-3(8),* Gareth Stevens Learning Library) Stevens, Gareth Publishing LLLP.
Mercer, Abbie. Sheep on a Farm. 2009. (Barnyard Animals Ser.). (J). 49.50 *(978-1-4042-8062-5(6));* (ENG.). 24p. pap. 8.25 *(978-1-4042-8061-8(8));* (ENG., Illus.). 24p. lib. bdg. 22.60 *(978-1-4042-8050-2(2))* Rosen Publishing Group, Inc., The. (PowerKids Pr.).
Metz, Lorijo. Sheep: Ewes, Rams, & Lambs. 2010. (On the Farm Ser.). (ENG.). 24p. (J). pap. 8.25 *(978-1-4488-1341-4(7));* lib. bdg. 22.60 *(978-1-4488-0690-4(9))* Rosen Publishing Group, Inc., The. (PowerKids Pr.).
Minden, Cecilia. Farm Animals: Sheep. 2009. (21st Century Junior Library: Farm Animals Ser.). (ENG., Illus.). 24p. (gr. 2-4). lib. bdg. 25.64 *(978-1-60279-544-0(4),* 200276) Cherry Lake Publishing.
Murray, Julie. Sheep, 1 vol. (ENG., Illus.). 24p. 2015. 27.07 *(978-1-62970-943-7(3))* 2005. 25.65 *(978-1-59197-335-5(X),* Buddy Bks.) ABDO Publishing Co.
—Sheep to Sweater, 1 vol. 2006. (Beginning to End Set 1 - 8 Titles Ser.). (ENG., Illus.). 24p. (gr. k-4). 25.65 *(978-1-59679-914-1(5),* Buddy Bks.) ABDO Publishing Co.
Nelid, Piper. At the Sheep Farm, 01 vols., 1. 2016. (Rosen REAL Readers: STEM & STEAM Collection). (ENG.). 8p. (J). pap. 5.46 *(978-1-5081-1432-1(3),* Rosen Classroom) Rosen Publishing Group, Inc., The.
Nelson, Robin. From Sheep to Sweater. 2003. (Start to Finish Ser.). (Illus.). 24p. (J). 18.60 *(978-0-8225-0716-1(1),* Lerner Pubns.) Lerner Publishing Group.
—Sheep. 2009. pap. 34.95 *(978-0-7613-4095-9(5));* (ENG.). 24p. 23.93 *(978-0-7613-4062-1(9),* Lerner Pubns.) Lerner Publishing Group.
Owen, Ruth. Meat! Life on a Sheep Farm. 2012. (Food from Farmers Ser.). (ENG., Illus.). 32p. (J). (gr. k-3). pap. 11.75 *(978-1-61533-542-8(0));* lib. bdg. 26.50 *(978-1-61533-533-6(1))* Windmill Bks.
Powell, R. This Little Lamb. Curry, Peter, illus. 2004. (Mini Movers Ser.). (ENG.). 14p. (J). bds. 4.99 *(978-0-7641-5742-4(6))* Barron's Educational Series, Inc.
Ray, Hannah. Sheep. 2008. (Down on the Farm (N.Y.) Ser.). (ENG., Illus.). 24p. (J). (gr. 3-7). pap. *(978-0-7787-4056-8(0))* Crabtree Publishing Co.
—Sheep. 2006. (Down on the Farm Ser.). (Illus.). 24p. (J). (gr. 4-7). lib. bdg. 15.95 *(978-1-59566-182-1(4))* QEB Publishing Inc.
Schalk, Anita. The Lost Sheep. 2015. (Bouncy Bible Buddies Ser.). (ENG.). 10p. (J). bds. 7.99 *(978-1-4964-1090-0(4))* Tyndale Hse. Pubs.

S

Shanks, Cindy. Alfonso Grows up on the Sheep Trail. 2010. 40p. pap. 18.99 (978-1-4520-7980-6(3)) AuthorHouse.

Snelbaker, Carmela. Thank You for Your Service, Sheep! 2013. pap. 17.49 (978-1-4797-4659-0(2)) Xlibris.

Stiefel, Chana. Sheep on the Family Farm. 2013. (Animals on the Family Farm Ser.). 24p. (J). (gr. k-3). pap. 7.95 (978-1-4644-0361-3(9), Enslow Elementary); lib. bdg. 22.60 (978-0-7660-4209-4(X)) Enslow Pubs., Inc.

Stockland, Patricia M. In the Sheep Pasture, 1 vol. Ouren, Todd, illus. 2007. (Barnyard Buddies Ser.). (ENG.). 24p. (gr. -1-2). 27.07 (978-1-60270-026-0(5), Looking Glass Library-Nonfiction) Magic Wagon.

Tebbs, Victoria & Goodings, Christina. The Lost Sheep Story. Mitchell, Melanie, illus. 2009. (See & Say! Ser.). (ENG.). 20p. (J). (gr. k — 1). 6.95 (978-0-7459-6087-6(1)) Lion Hudson PLC GBR. Dist: Independent Pubs. Group.

Ticktock Media, Ltd. Staff. What Do Sheep Do? 2008. (What Do Animals Do? Ser.). (ENG.). 10p. (J). (gr. k — 1). bds. 4.95 (978-1-84696-793-1(7), TickTock Books) Octopus Publishing Group GBR. Dist: Independent Pubs. Group.

Top That Publishing Staff, ed. Wacky Sheep. 2004. (Wacky Animals Ser.). (Illus.). 10p. (J). pap. (978-1-84510-089-6(1)) Top That! Publishing PLC.

Urbigkit, Cat. The Shepherd's Trail. 2008. (ENG., Illus.). 32p. (J). (gr. 2-4). 16.95 (978-1-59078-509-6(6)) Boyds Mills Pr.

Van Frankenhuyzen, Robbyn Smith. Itsy Bitsy & Teeny Weeny. van Frankenhuyzen, Gijsbert, illus. 2009. (Hazel Ridge Farm Stories Ser.). (ENG.). 48p. (J). (gr. 1-4). 16.95 (978-1-58536-417-6(7), 202152) Sleeping Bear Pr.

Wendorff, Anne. Lambs. 2009. (Watch Animals Grow Ser.). (ENG., Illus.). 24p. (J). (gr. k-3). lib. bdg. 25.95 (978-1-60014-241-3(9)) Bellwether Media.

—Lambs. 2009. (Blastoff! Readers Ser.). (ENG., Illus.). 24p. (J). (gr. k-3). 20.00 (978-0-531-21629-3(2), Children's Pr.) Scholastic Library Publishing.

Wilsdon, Christina. Sheep. 2010. (Amazing Animals Ser.). (ENG.). 48p. (J). (gr. 2-6). pap. 10.50 (978-1-4339-4029-3(9)); lib. bdg. 28.00 (978-1-4339-4028-6(0)) Stevens, Gareth Publishing LLLP. (Gareth Stevens Learning Library).

—Sheep. 2006. (J). (978-1-59939-079-6(5), Reader's Digest Young Families, Inc.) Studio Fun International.

Wolfman, Judy. Life on a Sheep Farm. Winston, David Lorenz, illus. Winston, David Lorenz, photos by. 2004. (Life on a Farm Ser.). (ENG.). 48p. (gr. 2-5). lib. bdg. 23.93 (978-1-57505-192-5(3)) Lerner Publishing Group.

Wood, Alix. Babydoll Sheep. 2016. (Mini Animals Ser.). 00032p. (J). (gr. 2-3). pap. 10.00 (978-1-4994-8149-5(7), Windmill Bks.) Rosen Publishing Group, Inc., The.

SHEEP—FICTION

Aesop. The Wolf in Sheep's Clothing: A Tale about Appearances. 2006. (J). (978-1-59939-086-4(8), Reader's Digest Young Families, Inc.) Studio Fun International.

Allard, Harry & Marshall, James. Sheep Out to Eat. 2015. 32p. pap. 7.00 (978-1-61003-508-8(9)) Center for the Collaborative Classroom.

Alphabetical Sleepy Sheep. 2005. (J). bds. 7.95 (978-0-9749305-7-2(1)); (ENG.). bds. 7.95 (978-0-9749305-4-1(7)) Castle Pacific Publishing.

Amery, Heather. Where's Woolly? Tyler, Jenny, ed. Cartwright, Stephen, illus. 2006. (Treasury of Farmyard Tales Ser.). 16p. (J). (gr. -1-18). 15.95 (978-1-58086-531-9(3)) EDC Publishing.

—Woolly the Sheep. Cartwright, Stephen, illus. 2004. (Young Farmyard Tales Board Books Ser.). 10p. (J). bds. 3.95 (978-0-7945-0467-0(1), Usborne) EDC Publishing.

Amundson, Susan D. Three Little Lambs — Somewhere. Geiken, Brenda Joy, illus. 2006. 40p. (J). (978-1-59984-002-4(2)) Bluedoor, llc.

Anderson, Laurie Halse. Left Behind. 2016. (Vet Volunteers Ser.: 17). (ENG.). 128p. (J). (gr. 3-7). 7.99 (978-0-14-241679-2(7), Puffin Books) Penguin Young Readers Group.

Animal I can hear s/s - Sheep. 2005. (J). bds. (978-1-4194-0060-5(6)) Paradise Pr., Inc.

Anónimo. Juguemos en el Bosque. Bergna, Monica, illus. 2004. (SPA.). 28p. (J). (gr. k-18). pap. 6.50 (978-980-257-282-3(9)) Ekare, Ediciones VEN. Dist: Iaconi, Mariuccia Bk. Imports.

Applesauce Press, Applesauce & Cider Mill Press Staff. Baa Baa Black Sheep: A Spinning Sheep Pop-Up Book. 2017. (ENG.). 8p. (J). 14.95 (978-1-60433-688-7(9), Applesauce Pr.) Cider Mill Pr. Bk. Pubs., LLC.

Archer, Dosh. Baaad Sheep. Archer, Dosh, illus. 2016. (Urgency Emergency! Ser.). (ENG., Illus.). 48p. (J). (gr. -1-3). 12.99 (978-0-8075-8349-4(9)) Whitman, Albert & Co.

AZ Books, creator. Lamb Searches for Her Mom. 2012. (Plush Baby Ser.). (ENG., Illus.). 10p. (J). (gr. -1 — 1). 11.95 (978-1-61889-218-8(5)) AZ Bks. LLC.

Baa, Baa Black Sheep. 2003. (J). per. (978-1-57657-799-8(6)) Paradise Pr., Inc.

Bad Boys. 2007. (J). (gr. k-3). 29.95 incl. audio compact disk (978-0-8045-4179-4(5)); 27.95 incl. audio (978-0-8045-6956-9(8)) Spoken Arts, Inc.

Bauer, Michael. The Adventures of Steel Wooly: And my Place on the Farm. 2012. (ENG.). 25p. (J). pap. 12.95 (978-1-4327-8568-0(0)) Outskirts Pr., Inc.

Beaty, Andrea. Hide & Sheep. Mayer, Bill, illus. 2011. (ENG.). 32p. (J). (gr. -1-3). 15.99 (978-1-4169-2544-6(9), McElderry, Margaret K. Bks.) McElderry, Margaret K. Bks.

Bee, Granny. Laffy the Lamb. Werthiemer, Beverly, ed. Sohn, Jeana, illus. 2006. 32p. (J). 16.95 (978-1-932367-00-3(4)) BookBound Publishing.

Beeke, Joel R. & Kleyn, Diana. How God Used a Drought & an Umbrella. Anderson, Jeff, illus. 2006. (Building on the Rock Ser.). (ENG.). 176p. (J). pap. 8.99 (978-1-85792-818-1(0), 9781857928181, CF4Kids) Christian Focus Pubns. GBR. Dist: Bookmasters Distribution.

Beeson, Samantha & Tango Books Staff. Baaah! Abbott, Simon, illus. 2003. (Noisy Pops! Ser.). (ENG.). 10p. (J). (gr. -1-k). 11.99 (978-1-85707-573-1(0)) Tango Bks. GBR. Dist: Independent Pubs. Group.

Bell-Martin, Janelle. Mary Had a Little Lamb, 1 vol. 2011. (Early Childhood Themes Ser.). (ENG.). 16p. (J). (gr. -1-2). pap. 6.99 (978-1-4333-2357-7(5)); pap. 19.99 (978-1-4333-2358-4(3)) Teacher Created Materials, Inc.

Belloni, Giulia. Anything Is Possible. Trevisan, Marco, illus. 2013. (ENG.). 32p. (J). (gr. -1-3). 16.95 (978-1-926973-91-3(7), Owlkids) Owlkids Bks. Inc. CAN. Dist: Publishers Group West (PGW).

Bender, Chris. The Lion & the Lamb. 2011. 24p. 14.93 (978-1-4269-5732-1(7)) Trafford Publishing.

Bently, Peter. The Great Sheep Shenanigans. Matsuoka, Mei, illus. 2012. (Andersen Press Picture Bks). (ENG.). 32p. (J). (gr. -1-3). 16.95 (978-0-7613-8990-3(3)) Lerner Publishing Group.

—Those Magnificent Sheep in Their Flying Machine. Bently, Peter, illus. 2014. (ENG., Illus.). 32p. (J). (gr. -1-3). 16.95 (978-1-4677-4935-0(4)) Lerner Publishing Group.

Beskow, Elsa. Pelle's New Suit, 1 vol. 2007. (ENG., Illus.). 32p. (J). (gr. -1-4). (978-0-86315-584-0(7)) Floris Bks.

Bester, Maryanne. Three Friends & a Taxi. Bester, Shayle, illus. 2007. (Cool Nguni Ser.: 1). (ENG.). 24p. (J). (gr. k-2). 12.00 (978-1-77009-265-5(X)) Jacana Media ZAF. Dist: Independent Pubs. Group.

Bingham, Mark Jay. Woolie & the Bully. 2013. 52p. 30.95 (978-1-4582-0843-9(5)); pap. 23.95 (978-1-4582-0844-6(3)) Author Solutions, Inc. (Abbott Pr.).

Birdsall, Jeanne. My Favorite Pets. Bliss, Harry, illus. 2016. (ENG.). 40p. (J). (gr. -1-2). 16.99 (978-0-385-75570-2(8), Knopf Bks. for Young Readers) Random Hse. Children's Bks.

Blair, Eric. El Pastorcito Mentiroso: Versión de la Fábula de Esopo. Abello, Patricia, tr. from ENG. Silverman, Dianne, illus. 2006. (Read-It! Readers en Español: Fábulas Ser.).Tr. of Boy Who Cried Wolf - A Retelling of Aesop's Fable. (SPA.). 24p. (gr. k-3). 21.32 (978-1-4048-1616-9(X), Easy Readers) Picture Window Bks.

Blyton, Enid. Don't Be Silly Mr Twiddle! (ENG., Illus.). 111p. (J). pap. 7.95 (978-0-7475-3858-5(1)) Bloomsbury Publishing Plc GBR. Dist: Trafalgar Square Publishing.

Bowater, Alan. A Pig Called Pete Meets a Sheep Called Sean. Pascoe, Pete, illus. 2009. (Pig Called Pete Ser.). 32p. (J). (gr. -1-2). 22.60 (978-1-60754-570-5(5)); pap. 10.55 (978-1-60754-571-2(3)) Windmill Bks.

Brennan, Sarah. The Tale of Rodney Ram. Harrison, Harry, illus. 2014. (J). **(978-1-937160-60-9(2))** Eliassen Creative.

Brents, Alan. Sheldon the Sheep. 2011. 24p. pap. 12.79 (978-1-4634-8728-7(2)) AuthorHouse.

Brown, Margaret Wise. The Little Lost Lamb. Date not set. 40p. (J). (gr. -1-3). 14.99 (978-0-06-027290-6(2)); 15.89 (978-0-06-027291-3(0)) HarperCollins Pubs.

Butler, Dori. A Sheep in Wolf's Clothing. 2006. (J). pap. (978-1-4108-6185-6(6)) Benchmark Education Co.

Cabrera, Jane. Baa, Baa, Black Sheep. Cabrera, Jane, illus. 2016. (ENG., Illus.). 24p. (J). (gr. -1-k). bds. 7.99 (978-0-8234-3631-6(4)) Holiday Hse., Inc.

—Baa, Baa, Black Sheep. 2015. (ENG., Illus.). 32p. (J). (gr. -1-k). 16.95 (978-0-8234-3388-9(9)) Holiday Hse., Inc.

Candlewick Press, Candlewick. Shaun the Sheep Movie - Timmy in the City. Aardman Animations Staff, illus. 2015. (Tales from Mossy Bottom Farm Ser.). (ENG.). 12p. (J). (-k). bds. 7.99 (978-0-7636-7875-3(9), Candlewick Entertainment) Candlewick Pr.

Candlewick Press Staff. Shaun the Sheep Movie - Shear Madness. Aardman Animations Staff, illus. 2015. (Tales from Mossy Bottom Farm Ser.). (ENG.). 48p. (J). (gr. k-3). pap. 3.99 (978-0-7636-7737-4(X), Candlewick Entertainment) Candlewick Pr.

Candlewick Press Staff & Aardman Animations Staff, illus. Shaun the Sheep Movie - the Great Escape. 2015. (Tales from Mossy Bottom Farm Ser.). (ENG.). 48p. (J). (gr. k-3). pap. 3.99 (978-0-7636-7738-1(8), Candlewick Entertainment) Candlewick Pr.

Carr, Elias. Ava y el Picnic Raquitico. Garton, Michael, illus. 2016. (SPA.). (J). **(978-1-5064-2095-0(8))** Augsburg Fortress, Pubs.

—Hal y el Nuevo Compañero. Garton, Michael, illus. 2016. (SPA.). (J). **(978-1-5064-2098-1(2))** Augsburg Fortress, Pubs.

—Rufus y Su Cola Enojada. Garton, Michael, illus. 2016. (SPA.). (J). **(978-1-5064-2096-7(6))** Augsburg Fortress, Pubs.

Cartwright, Stephen. Llittle Book of Train Stories. rev. ed. 2011. (Farmyard Tales Readers Ser.). 64p. (J). ring bd. 8.99 (978-0-7945-3070-9(2), Usborne) EDC Publishing.

Cerato, Mattia. Sheep in the Closet. Cerato, Mattia, illus. 2014. (Family Snaps Ser.). (ENG., Illus.). 32p. (J). (gr. k-2). pap. 6.95 (978-1-939656-62-9(1)) Red Chair Pr.

Chalekian, Bobbie. The Legend of the Lamb & the Lion. 2011. 32p. (gr. 2-4). pap. 14.99 (978-1-4567-2713-0(3)) AuthorHouse.

Chance, Robyn. Ewela's Unbaalievable Journey. 2012. 46p. (-18). 23.95 (978-1-936850-87-7(7)) Rhemalda Publishing.

Charles, Kaye Ellen. Macarthur & Martha. 2013. 56p. pap. 20.95 (978-1-4525-8512-3(1), Balboa Pr.) Author Solutions, Inc.

Chin, Oliver. The Year of the Sheep. Chau, Alina, illus. 2014. (Tales from the Chinese Zodiac Ser.: 10). (ENG.). 36p. (J). (gr. -1-3). 15.95 (978-1-59702-104-3(0)) Immedium.

Christian, Focus & Tnt Ministries Staff. God's Zoo. Charnick, Tim, illus. 2005. (King of Clubs Ser.). (ENG.). 96p. (J). per. 17.99 (978-1-84550-069-6(5), 9781845500696) Christian Focus Pubns. GBR. Dist: Bookmasters Distribution.

Churchman, Jennifer & Churchman, John. Brave Little Finn. 2016. (Sweet Pea & Friends Ser.). (ENG., Illus.). 40p. (J). (gr. -1-3). 17.99 (978-0-316-27359-6(7)) Little, Brown Bks. for Young Readers.

Churchman, John & Churchman, Jennifer. The SheepOver. (Sweet Pea & Friends Ser.). (ENG., Illus.). (J). (gr. -1 — 1). 2017. 24p. bds. 7.99 (978-0-316-27355-8(4)) 2015. 36p. 17.99 (978-0-316-27356-5(2)) Little, Brown Bks. for Young Readers.

Colorful Sleepy Sheep. 2005. (J). bds. 7.95 (978-0-9749305-5-8(5)) Castle Pacific Publishing.

Conrad, Liz, illus. Little Lamb. 2009. (My Sparkling Springtime Friends Ser.). (ENG.). 10p. (J). bds. 3.95 (978-1-58117-868-5(9), Intervisual/Piggy Toes) Bendon, Inc.

Cordell, Matthew. Another Brother. Cordell, Matthew, illus. 2012. (ENG., Illus.). 36p. (J). (gr. -1-1). 16.99 (978-0-312-64324-9(1), 9780312643249) Feiwel & Friends.

Cotter, Natasha. The Christmas Blessing. 2012. 24p. 24.95 (978-1-4626-6925-7(5)) America Star Bks.

Cox, Phil Roxbee. Sam Sheep Can't Sleep. Tyler, Jenny, ed. Cartwright, Stephen, illus. rev. ed. 2006. (Usborne Phonics Bks.). 16p. (J). (gr. -1-k). 6.99 (978-0-7945-1508-9(8), Usborne) EDC Publishing.

Cox, Phil Roxbee & Cartwright, S. Sam Sheep Can't Sleep. 2004. (Phonics Board Bks.). (ENG.). 1p. (J). bds. 4.99 (978-0-7945-0060-3(9), Usborne) EDC Publishing.

—Ted's Shed, Toad Makes a Road, Fat Cat on a Mat & Sam Sheep Can't Sleep. 2004. (Easy Words to Read Ser.). (Illus.). 16p. (J). (gr. 1-18). pap. 9.95 (978-0-7945-0245-4(8), Usborne) EDC Publishing.

Crangle, Claudine, illus. Woolfred Does Not Eat Dandelions. 2014. (J). (978-1-4338-1672-7(5)); pap. (978-1-4338-1673-4(3)) American Psychological Assn. (Magination Pr.).

Crayton, Tina Lorice. The Lost Sheep. 2010. 20p. 10.50 (978-1-4490-7707-5(2)) AuthorHouse.

Crayton, Tina Lorice (Anderson). The Wolf in Sheep's Clothing: The Impostor. 2011. 20p. 10.50 (978-1-4567-3011-6(8)) AuthorHouse.

Cvetkovic, Judith. Mandy & Star's Sheep Ranch Getaway, 1 vol. 2010. 108p. pap. 19.95 (978-1-4489-5673-9(0)) America Star Bks.

Dahl, Michael. Story Time for Lamb, 1 vol. Vidal, Oriol, illus. 2011. (Hello Genius Ser.). (ENG.). 20p. (gr. 1-2). bds. 7.99 (978-1-4048-6495-5(4)) Picture Window Bks.

Dalmatian Press Staff. One Little Sheep. 2008. (ENG.). 6p. bds. 4.95 (978-1-58117-719-0(4), Intervisual/Piggy Toes) Bendon, Inc.

Dalton, Sherry A. A New Day - a New Beginning: All about a Day on the Farm. Whitlatch, Jessica A., illus. 2011. 40p. pap. 24.95 (978-1-4560-7462-3(8)) America Star Bks.

Davies, Gill & Freeman, Tina. Lucy Lamb. 2004. (Tales from Yellow Barn Farm Ser.). (Illus.). 24p. (J). 3.99 (978-1-85854-322-2(3)) Brimax Books Ltd. GBR. Dist: Byeway Bks.

Dealey, Erin. Little Bo Peep Can't Get to Sleep. Wakiyama, Hanako, illus. 2010. (ENG.). 40p. (J). (gr. -1-2). 13.99 (978-1-4424-0935-4(5), Atheneum Bks. for Young Readers) Simon & Schuster Children's Publishing.

Debesay, Samson. Cubby, the Lionsheep: Son, you are a lion, live like One! 2011. (Illus.). 24p. pap. 14.89 (978-1-4567-7899-6(4)) AuthorHouse.

DePrisco, Dorothea. One Little Sheep. 2006. (ENG.). 12p. (J). 12.95 (978-1-58117-488-5(8), Intervisual/Piggy Toes) Bendon, Inc.

deRubertis, Barbara. Lana Llama's Little Lamb. Alley, R. W., illus. 2011. (Animal Antics A to Z Ser.). 32p. (J). pap. 45.32 (978-0-7613-7658-3(5)); (ENG.). lib. bdg. 22.60 (978-1-57565-333-4(8)); (gr. -1-3). pap. 7.95 (978-1-57565-324-2(9)) Kane Press, Inc.

deRubertis, Barbara & DeRubertis, Barbara. Lana Llama's Little Lamb. Alley, R. W., illus. 2012. (Animal Antics A to Z Ser.). 32p. (J). (gr. 2 — 1). cd-rom 7.95 (978-1-57565-405-8(9)) Kane Press, Inc.

Devine, Ginger. Hooray for the Circus: A Story of Sam the Lamb. 2008. 36p. pap. 16.99 (978-1-4389-1826-6(7)) AuthorHouse.

Disney Book Group. Doc Mcstuffins Cuddle Me, Lambie. Disney Storybook Art Team, illus. 2015. (ENG.). 40p. (J). (gr. -1-k). 8.99 (978-1-4847-1420-1(2)) Disney Pr.

Don, Lari. The Hungry Wolf: A Story from North America. Williamson, Melanie, illus. 2013. (Animal Stories Ser.). (ENG.). 48p. (J). (gr. 1-4). pap. 8.99 (978-1-84686-872-6(6)) Barefoot Bks., Inc.

Dorner, V. K. The Little Lambs & the Rainbow Zebra. 2011. 36p. 13.95 (978-1-4497-0889-4(7), WestBow Pr.) Author Solutions, Inc.

Doudna, Kelly. Lamb Chops, 1 vol. Chawla, Neena, illus. 2006. (Animal Tales Ser.). 24p. (J). (gr. k-3). (ENG.). lib. bdg. 24.21 (978-1-59679-947-9(1), SandCastle); pap. 48.42 (978-1-59679-948-6(X)) ABDO Publishing Co.

—La Lana de la Oveja, 1 vol. Chawla, Neena, illus. 2007. (Cuentos de Animales Ser.).Tr. of Lamb Chops. (SPA & ENG.). 24p. (J). (gr. k-3). lib. bdg. 24.21 (978-1-59928-661-7(0), SandCastle) ABDO Publishing Co.

Driscoll, Amanda. Wally Does Not Want a Haircut. 2016. (ENG., Illus.). 32p. (J). (gr. -1-2). 16.99 (978-0-553-53579-2(X), Knopf Bks. for Young Readers) Random Hse. Children's Bks.

Durant, Alan. Little Bo-Peep's Missing Sheep. Heming, Leah-Ellen, illus. 2012. (ENG.). 32p. (J). (978-0-7787-8029-8(5)) Crabtree Publishing Co.

Durkee, Noura. The King, the Prince & the Naughty Sheep. Durkee, Noura, illus. 2007. (ENG., Illus.). 24p. (J). (gr. k-5). 16.00 (978-1-879402-58-4(0)) Tahrike Tarsile Quran, Inc.

Dykes, Tami J. Being Too Small Is Big Enough. 2013. 42p. pap. 20.45 (978-1-4497-8483-6(6), WestBow Pr.) Author Solutions, Inc.

Eglin, Lorna. A Boy of Two Worlds. 2014. (Flamingo Fiction 9-13s Ser.). (ENG., Illus.). 208p. (J). (gr. 4-7). per. 8.99 (978-1-84550-126-6(8), 4efaf8ef-841a-4d73-b71e-3ed4bb7cb5a4) Christian Focus Pubns. GBR. Dist: Bookmasters Distribution.

Elliott, David. Baabwaa & Wooliam: A Tale of Literacy, Dental Hygiene, & Friendship. Sweet, Melissa, illus. 2017. (ENG.). 40p. (J). (gr. -1-3). 16.99 **(978-0-7636-6074-1(4))** Candlewick Pr.

Eulate, Ana. Little Cloud Lamb. 2011. (Light (Cuento de Luz) Ser.). (ENG., Illus.). 28p. (J). (gr. 1-4). (978-84-938240-2-0(X)) D P & G Military Pubs.

Falconer, Mary. The Spotted Sheep with the Worthless Wool. 2011. 24p. pap. 10.49 (978-1-4520-9636-0(8)) AuthorHouse.

Farrell, Darren. Doug-Dennis & the Flyaway Fib. 2010. (ENG.). 40p. (J). (gr. k-3). 16.99 (978-0-8037-3437-1(9), Dial Bks) Penguin Young Readers Group.

Fenwick, Margaret. Lonnie the Lost Lamb. 2010. 32p. pap. 13.00 (978-1-60911-038-3(2), Eloquent Bks.) Strategic Book Publishing & Rights Agency (SBPRA).

Following Isabella - Evaluation Guide: Evaluation Guide. 2006. (J). (978-1-55942-406-6(0)) Witcher Productions.

Ford, Bernette. No More Blanket for Lambkin! Williams, Sam, illus. 2010. (Ducky & Piggy Ser.). (ENG.). 26p. (J). (gr. k — 1). bds. 6.95 (978-1-906250-47-8(2)) Boxer Bks., Ltd. GBR. Dist: Sterling Publishing Co., Inc.

Fox, Mem & Horacek, Judy. Where Is the Green Sheep? (¿Dónde Está la Oveja Verde?) Horacek, Judy, illus. 2010. (SPA & ENG., Illus.). 32p. (J). (gr. k — 1). bds. 4.99 (978-0-547-39694-1(5)) Houghton Mifflin Harcourt Publishing Co.

Fraggalosch, Audrey. Trails above the Tree Line: A Story of a Rocky Mountain Meadow. Bond, Higgins, illus. 2005. (Soundprints' Wild Habitats Ser.). (ENG.). (J). (gr. 1-4). 36p. 15.95 (978-1-56899-941-8(0), B7021); 32p. pap. 6.95 (978-1-56899-942-5(9), S7021) Soundprints.

Françoise. Jeanne-Marie Counts Her Sheep. 2003. (Illus.). 32p. (J). mass mkt. 9.99 (978-0-9740599-0-7(0), 1) Omnibus Publishing.

Freitag, Fred. On Hills & Meadows by the River. 2013. 28p. pap. 24.95 (978-1-63000-584-9(3)) America Star Bks.

French, Jackie. Pete the Sheep. Whatley, Bruce, illus. 2008. 30p. (J). bds. (978-0-7322-8794-8(4)) HarperCollins Pubs. Australia.

French, Jackie, et al. Pete the Sheep. 2006. (Illus.). 32p. pap. (978-0-207-19974-5(4)) HarperCollins Pubs. Australia.

Galvin, Laura Gates. Baby Lamb Finds a Friend. (Smithsonian Baby Animals Ser.). (ENG., Illus.). 16p. (gr. -1-k). 2008. 13.95 (978-1-59249-790-4(X)) 2007. 6.95 (978-1-59249-746-1(2)) Soundprints.

Gehl, Laura. And Then Another Sheep Turned Up. Adele, Amy, illus. 2015. (J). 6.99 (978-1-4677-1190-6(X)); (ENG.). 32p. (gr. -1-3). lib. bdg. 17.95 (978-1-4677-1188-3(8)) Lerner Publishing Group. (Kar-Ben Publishing).

Gentry, Beatrice. Piep. Gentry, Beatrice, illus. 2016. (ENG., Illus.). 36p. (J). (978-1-78222-453-2(X)) Paragon Publishing, Rothersthorpe.

Gerstein, Mordicai. The White Ram: A Story of Abraham & Isaac. Gerstein, Mordicai, illus. 2006. (ENG., Illus.). 32p. (J). (gr. -1-3). 16.95 (978-0-8234-1897-8(9)) Holiday Hse., Inc.

Giles, Lisa. The Adventures of Sunny the Bunny: The Easter Egg Hunt. 2010. 20p. 10.49 (978-1-4520-1842-3(1)) AuthorHouse.

Goldhawk, Emma. Little Lamb. Lambert, Jonathan, illus. 2014. (Snuggle Puppet Ser.). (ENG.). 10p. (J). (gr. -1). bds. 14.95 (978-1-62686-014-8(9), Silver Dolphin Bks.) Readerlink Distribution Services, LLC.

Gonzalez Jensen, Margarita. Botas Negras. Sanchez, Enrique O., illus. (SPA.). (J). (gr. 2-4). 3.96 net. (978-0-590-26842-4(2)) Scholastic, Inc.

Graham, Oakley. I'm Just a Little Sheep. Green, Barry, illus. 2014. (ENG.). 12p. (gr. -1). (978-1-78244-591-3(9)) Top That! Publishing PLC.

Griver, Jeanette A. Curio, a Shetland Sheepdog Meets the Crow: A Story of Friendship For Children of All Ages 2004. (Illus.). 44p. (J). pap. 6.95 (978-0-929948-04-1(1)) Compsych Systems, Inc., Pubns. Div.

Gummelt, Donna & Melchiorre, Dondino. Cow Puppies. Wall, Randy Hugh, ed. Varela, Juan D., tr. Varela, Juan D., illus. 2006.Tr. of Cachorros Vaqueros. (SPA.). 32p. (J). 14.95 (978-0-9764798-7-1(7)) Story Store Collection Publishing.

Gunzi, Christiane. On the Farm. 2005. (Feels Real Bks.). (ENG., Illus.). 10p. (J). bds. 6.99 (978-0-7641-5856-8(2)) Barron's Educational Series, Inc.

Gwanas, Bethan. Ramboy. 2009. (ENG.). 112p. (J). pap. 7.95 (978-0-86243-993-4(0)) Y Lolfa GBR. Dist: Dufour Editions, Inc.

Hanlin, Beverly Austin. Little Lamb: A Christmas Story. 2006. (J). pap. 8.00 (978-0-8059-7128-6(9)) Dorrance Publishing Co., Inc.

Harper, Stephan J. The Black Sheep Beach, Mary FitzGerald, illus. l.t. ed. 2005. 32p. (J). lib. bdg. 16.95 (978-0-9741800-1-4(7)) Inspire Press, Inc.

Harrington, Claudia. Book 4: Elmer the Very Sneaky Sheep. 2016. (Hank the Pet Sitter Ser.). (ENG.). (gr. -1-3). lib. bdg. 27.07 **(978-1-62402-190-9(5))** ABDO Publishing Co.

Hartman, Bob. The Sheep in Wolf's Clothing. Raglin, Tim, illus. 2014. (ENG.). 28p. (J). (gr. k-2). 16.99 (978-0-7459-6515-4(6)) Lion Hudson PLC GBR. Dist: Independent Pubs. Group.

Hathorn, Libby & Magerl, Caroline. Over the Moon. 2005. (Illus.). 32p. (978-0-7344-0480-0(8), Lothian Children's Bks.) Hachette Australia.

Helakoski, Leslie. Woolbur. Harper, Lee, illus. 2008. 32p. (J). (gr. -1-3). 17.89 (978-0-06-084727-2(1)); (ENG.). 17.99 (978-0-06-084726-5(3)) HarperCollins Pubs.

—Woolbur. 2008. (J). (gr. -1-2). 29.95 incl. audio (978-0-8045-6971-2(1)) Spoken Arts, Inc.

Hill, Susanna Leonard. Can't Sleep Without Sheep. Wohnoutka, Mike, illus. 2010. (ENG.). 40p. (J). (gr. -1-1). 16.99 (978-0-8027-2066-5(8), 9780802720665, Bloomsbury USA Childrens) Bloomsbury Publishing USA.

Hobbs, Valerie. Sheep. 2009. (ENG.). 144p. (J). (gr. 3-7). pap. 7.99 (978-0-312-56116-1(4), 9780312561161) Square Fish.

—Wolf. 2013. (ENG.). 128p. (J). (gr. 3-7). 15.99 (978-0-374-31575-7(2), 9780374315757, Farrar, Straus & Giroux (BYR)) Farrar, Straus & Giroux.

Horacek, Judy & Fox, Mem. Where Is the Green Sheep? alt. ed. 2009. (ENG., Illus.). 32p. (J). (gr. -1 — 1). bds. 6.99 (978-0-15-206704-5(3)) Houghton Mifflin Harcourt Publishing Co.

Howard, Martin. Shaun the Sheep: Blast to the Past. Janes, Andy, illus. 2017. (Tales from Mossy Bottom Farm Ser.: 6). (ENG.). 112p. (J). (gr. k-3). pap. 4.99 (978-0-7636-9093-9(7), Candlewick Entertainment) Candlewick Pr.

—Shaun the Sheep: Flock to the Seaside. Janes, Andy, illus. 2015. (Tales from Mossy Bottom Farm Ser.). (ENG.). 112p. (J). (gr. k-3). pap. 4.99 (978-0-7636-8058-9(3), Candlewick Entertainment) Candlewick Pr.

—Shaun the Sheep Movie - the Junior Novel. 2015. (Tales from Mossy Bottom Farm Ser.). (ENG.). 152p. (J). (gr. 2-4). pap. 5.99 (978-0-7636-7736-7(1), Candlewick Entertainment) Candlewick Pr.

—Shaun the Sheep: on the Ball. Janes, Andy, illus. 2015. (Tales from Mossy Bottom Farm Ser.). (ENG.). 112p. (J). (gr. k-3). pap. 4.99 (978-0-7636-8059-6(1), Candlewick Entertainment) Candlewick Pr.

—Shaun the Sheep: the Beast of Soggy Moor. Janes, Andy, illus. 2015. (Tales from Mossy Bottom Farm Ser.). (ENG.). (J). (gr. k-3). pap. 4.99 (978-0-7636-7586-8(5), Candlewick Entertainment) Candlewick Pr.

—Shaun the Sheep: the Flock Factor. Janes, Andy, illus. 2014. (Tales from Mossy Bottom Farm Ser.). (ENG.). 96p. (J). (gr. k-3). pap. 4.99 (978-0-7636-7535-6(0), Candlewick Entertainment) Candlewick Pr.

Hub, Ulrich & Ragg-Kirkby, Helena. Becoming the Wolf. Mühle, Jörg, illus. 2012. (ENG.). 64p. (YA). 12.00 *(978-0-8028-5409-4(5))*, Eerdmans Bks For Young Readers) Eerdmans, William B. Publishing Co.

Hughes, Mair Wynn & Jones, Steven. Dwyn Afalau. 2005. (WEL., Illus.). 15p. pap. *(978-0-86243-457-1(2))* Y Lolfa.

Hunt, Susan. Sammy & His Shepherd. Godbey, Corey, illus. 2008. (J). *(978-1-56769-109-2(9))* Reformation Pubs.

Imai, Ayano. The 108th Sheep. Imai, Ayano, illus. 2007. (Illus.). 32p. (gr. -1-2). 15.95 *(978-1-58925-063-5(X))* Tiger Tales.

Jâho. What If Sheep Could Fly? JudyBee, tr. from FRE. 2nd ed. 2011. (Illus.). 28p. pap. *(978-1-78092-006-1(7))* MX Publishing, Ltd.

Jamieson, Victoria. Bea Rocks the Flock. 2009. (J). (gr. -1-3). 17.89 *(978-1-59990-357-6(1))* Bloomsbury Publishing USA.

Jeffs, Dixie. A Baby to Love. 2012. 20p. pap. 24.95 *(978-1-4626-6780-2(5))* America Star Bks.

Jones, V. M. & Tulloch, Scott. Echo & Hush. 2008. (Illus.). 32p. pap. *(978-1-86950-690-2(1))* HarperCollins Pubs. Australia.

Kelly, Mij. One More Sheep. Ayto, Russell, illus. 2006. (ENG.). 32p. (J). (gr. k-3). 16.95 *(978-1-56145-378-8(1))* Peachtree Pubs.

Kitamura, Satoshi. Cuando los Borregos No Pueden Dormir. Kitamura, Satoshi, illus. 2nd ed. 2003. (Picture Books Collection). (SPA., Illus.). 26p. (J). (gr. k-3). pap. 12.95 *(978-84-372-2182-3(X))* Santillana USA Publishing Co., Inc.

—When Sheep Can't Sleep (Cuando los Borregos no Pueden Dormir) (SPA.). (J). (gr. 1-6). 19.95 *(978-84-372-6605-3(X))* Santillana USA Publishing Co., Inc.

Klise, Kate. Grammy Lamby & the Secret Handshake. Klise, Kate & Klise, M. Sarah, illus. 2012. (ENG.). 32p. (J). (gr. -1-3). 17.99 *(978-0-8050-9313-1(3)*, 9780805093131, Holt, Henry & Co. Bks. For Young Readers) Holt, Henry & Co.

Koch, Miriam. Digby Differs. Garlid, Ann, tr. from GER. Koch, Miriam, illus. 2013. (Illus.). 40p. 17.99 *(978-1-4413-1306-5(0))* Peter Pauper Pr. Inc.

Krone, Thelma Smith. Nosey. 2007. (J). 7.95 *(978-1-56167-974-4(7))* American Literary Pr.

Lamont, Priscilla. Nursery Rhyme Crimes: Little Bo Peep. 2012. (Illus.). 24p. (J). pap. *(978-1-84780-354-2(7)*, Frances Lincoln) Quarto Publishing Group UK.

Layne, Steven L. Thomas's Sheep & the Spectacular Science Project, 1 vol. Board, Perry, illus. 2004. (ENG.). 32p. (J). (gr. k-3). 16.99 *(978-1-58980-210-0(1))* Pelican Publishing Co., Inc.

Leavitt, Martine. Blue Mountain. 2014. (ENG.). 176p. (J). (gr. 3-7). 15.99 *(978-0-374-37864-6(9)*, 9780374378646, Farrar, Straus & Giroux (BYR)) Farrar, Straus & Giroux.

The Legend of Teton Tony: King of the Mountain Rams. 2005. (Illus.). 32p. (J). 14.95 *(978-0-9767265-0-0(5))* Fisher Enterprises.

Lenski, Lois. Strawberry Girl. Lenski, Lois, illus. 60th anniv. ed. 2005. (ENG., Illus.). 208p. (J). (gr. 5-18). pap. 6.99 *(978-0-06-440585-0(0))* HarperCollins Pubs.

Leslie, Emma. For Merrie England: A Tale of the Weavers of Norfolk. Taylor, R., illus. 2010. 168p. 20.95 *(978-1-934671-38-2(X))*; pap. 10.95 *(978-1-934671-39-9(8))* Salem Ridge Press LLC.

Lester, Helen. The Sheep in Wolf's Clothing. Munsinger, Lynn, illus. 2014. (Laugh-Along Lessons Ser.). (ENG.). 32p. (J). (gr. -1-3). 8.99 *(978-0-544-23300-3(X))*, HMH Books For Young Readers) Houghton Mifflin Harcourt Publishing Co.

Lewis, Gill. Star on Stormy Mountain. Home, Sarah, illus. 2016. (Puppy Academy Ser.). (ENG.). 128p. (J). 16.99 *(978-1-62779-796-2(3)*, 9781627797962, Holt, Henry & Co. Bks. For Young Readers) Holt, Henry & Co.

Lewis, Kim. Emma's Lamb. 2004. (J). (gr. k-3). spiral bd. *(978-0-616-07563-0(4))* Canadian National Institute for the Blind/Institut National Canadien pour les Aveugles.

The Littlest Lamb: Lap Book. (Pebble Soup Explorations Ser.). 16p. (gr. -1-18). 21.00 *(978-0-7578-1658-1(4))* Rigby Education.

Litton, Jonathan. Planet Pop-Up: Sheep Rules the Roost! Anderson, Nicola, illus. 2015. (Planet Pop-Up Ser.). (ENG.). 12p. (J). (gr. -1). 12.95 *(978-1-62686-354-5(7)*, Silver Dolphin Bks.) Readerlink Distribution Services, LLC.

Lobel, Anita. Playful Pigs from A to Z. 2015. (ENG., Illus.). 40p. (J). (gr. -1-2). lib. bdg. 19.99 *(978-0-553-50833-8(4)*, Knopf Bks. for Young Readers) Random Hse. Children's Bks.

Lodding, Linda Ravin. Little Red Riding Sheep. Atkinson, Cale, illus. 2017. (ENG.). 40p. (J). (gr. -1-3). 17.99 *(978-1-4814-5748-4(9))* Simon & Schuster Children's Publishing.

Lucy Lamb. 2006. (J). per. 3.99 *(978-1-934004-16-6(2))* Byeway Bks.

Lunn, Janet. Amos's Sweater, 1 vol. LaFave, Kim, illus. 2nd ed. 2007. (ENG.). 32p. (J). (gr. -1-k). pap. 7.95 *(978-0-88899-845-3(7))* Groundwood Bks. CAN. Dist: Publishers Group West (PGW).

Lyon, George Ella & Anderson, Stephanie. Weaving the Rainbow. Anderson, Stephanie, illus. 2004. (ENG., Illus.). 40p. (J). (gr. -1-2). 18.99 *(978-0-689-85169-8(3)*, Atheneum/Richard Jackson Bks.) Simon & Schuster Children's Publishing.

Lyon, Tammie Speer, illus. Mary Had a Little Lamb. 2006. 8p. (J). bds. 10.95 *(978-1-57791-210-1(1))* Brighter Minds Children's Publishing.

Mackall, Dandi Daley. Little Shepherd. 2004. 32p. (J). 6.99 *(978-0-7586-0324-1(X))* Concordia Publishing Hse.

—The Lost Lamb & the Good Shepherd. Manuzak, Lisa, illus. 2016. (Flipside Stories Ser.). (ENG.). 48p. (J). 14.99 *(978-1-4964-1121-1(8))* Tyndale Hse. Pubs.

Maguire, Thomas Aquinas. Three Little Dreams, 3 vols. 2010. (ENG., Illus.). 36p. (J). (gr. -1). 16.95 *(978-1-894965-79-8(5))* Simply Read Bks. CAN. Dist: Ingram Publisher Services.

Maier, Inger M. When Fuzzy Was Afraid: Of Losing His Mother. Candon, Jennifer, illus. 2004. 32p. (J). 14.95 *(978-1-59147-168-4(0))*; pap. 9.95 *(978-1-59147-169-1(9))* American Psychological Assn. (Magination Pr.).

—When Fuzzy Was Afraid of Big & Loud Things. Candon, Jennifer, illus. 2005. (Fuzzy the Little Sheep Ser.). (J). (gr. -1-3). 32p. 14.95 *(978-1-59147-322-0(5))*; 30p. per. 9.95 *(978-1-59147-323-7(3))* American Psychological Assn. (Magination Pr.).

—When Lizzie Was Afraid: Of Trying New Things. Candon, Jennifer, illus. 2004. 32p. (J). 14.95 *(978-1-59147-170-7(2))*; pap. 9.95 *(978-1-59147-171-4(0))* American Psychological Assn. (Magination Pr.).

Malandrinos, Cheryl C. Little Shepherd. Ruble, Eugene, illus. 2010. 16p. pap. 9.95 *(978-1-61633-085-9(6))* Guardian Angel Publishing, Inc.

Marcoux, Tom. Crystal Pegasus. 2012. 92p. pap. 18.24 *(978-0-9800511-9-3(3))* Marcoux, Tom Media, LLC.

Marshall, Linda Elovitz. The Passover Lamb. Mai-Wyss, Tatjana, illus. 2013. (ENG.). 32p. (J). (gr. 1-4). 17.99 *(978-0-307-93177-1(3)*, Random Hse. Bks. for Young Readers) Random Hse. Children's Bks.

Mary, Ms. Little Lambie No-No's Great Escape. 2008. 48p. per. 9.95 *(978-1-4327-1917-3(3))* Outskirts Pr., Inc.

Mathews, Leslie. The Sheep Go on Strike. Dumont, Jean-françois, illus. 2014. (ENG.). 34p. (J). 16.00 *(978-0-8028-5470-4(2)*, Eerdmans Bks For Young Readers) Eerdmans, William B. Publishing Co.

Matthews-Dodd, Melissa. Chase Coming Home. 2003. (J). pap. 9.95 *(978-0-7414-1522-6(4))* Infinity Publishing.

McAllister, Margaret. Emily & the Lamb. Vince, Dawn, illus. 2005. (ENG.). 24p. (J). lib. bdg. 23.65 *(978-1-59646-756-9(8))* Dingles & Co.

McQuinn, Anna. Colm's Lambs. Young, Paul, illus. 2014. (ENG.). 32p. (J). pap. 13.95 *(978-1-84717-339-3(X))* O'Brien Pr., Ltd., The IRL. Dist: Dufour Editions, Inc.

Meadows, Daisy. Grace Woollyhop's Musical Mystery (Magic Animal Friends #12) 2016. (Magic Animal Friends Ser.: 12). (ENG., Illus.). 112p. (J). (gr. 2-5). pap. 4.99 *(978-0-545-94079-5(6)*, Scholastic Paperbacks) Scholastic, Inc.

Melling, David. Hugless Douglas & the Big Sleepover. 2013. (ENG., Illus.). 32p. (J). *(978-1-58925-116-8(4))* Tiger Tales.

Merino, Gemma. The Sheep Who Hatched an Egg. Merino, Gemma, illus. 2017. (ENG.). 32p. (J). (gr. -1-3). 16.99 ***(978-0-8075-7338-9(8))*** Whitman, Albert & Co.

Metlen, Ryan W. & Metlen, Ryan. Ewe. 2009. (J). *(978-1-58768-054-0(8)*, HiddenSpring) Paulist Pr.

Meyer, Lisa O. The Sheep & the Chicken. Winward, Makenzie, illus. 2011. 16p. pap. 24.95 *(978-1-4626-0478-4(1))* America Star Bks.

Miura, Taro. Crazy Days. 2009. (ENG., Illus.). 24p. (J). (gr. -1-3). 14.50 *(978-1-85437-850-7(3))* Tate Publishing, Ltd. GBR. Dist: Abrams, Inc.

Monroe, Chris. Sneaky Sheep. Monroe, Chris, illus. 2010. (Carolrhoda Picture Bks.). (ENG., Illus.). 32p. (J). (gr. -1-3). lib. bdg. 16.95 *(978-0-7613-5615-8(0))* Lerner Publishing Group.

More Than a Meal. (Early Intervention Levels Ser.). 28.56 *(978-0-7362-1049-2(0))* CENGAGE Learning.

Moriarty, Kathleen M. Wiil Waal: A Somali Folktale. Adam, Jamal, tr. Amir, Amin Abd al-Fattah Mahmud, illus. 2007. (SOM & ENG.). 32p. (J). (gr. -1-3). 15.95 *(978-1-931016-16-2(X))*; pap. 7.95 *(978-1-931016-17-9(8))* Minnesota Humanities Ctr.

Mustaine Hettinger, Cynthia. Travis, the Shetland Sheep. Ramsey, Jayne, illus. 2004. (Electra's Acres Ser.: Bk. 5). 32p. (J). per. 14.95 *(978-0-9746330-6-0(2))* Anton Berkshire Publishing.

Nation, Kay. Jamie Learns to Love. 2006. pap. 10.00 *(978-1-4257-0534-3(0))* Xlibris Corp.

Noble, Val. Elsie the Sheep & the Kings of the Castle. 2009. (Illus.). 52p. pap. 20.49 *(978-1-4389-5083-9(7))* AuthorHouse.

North, Laura. The Boy Who Cried Sheep! 2016. (ENG., Illus.). 32p. (J). *(978-0-7787-2471-1(9))* Crabtree Publishing Co.

Northfield, Gary. Derek the Sheep. Northfield, Gary, illus. 2009. (ENG., Illus.). 64p. (J). (gr. k-2). 16.95 *(978-0-7475-9424-6(4))* Bloomsbury Publishing Plc GBR. Dist: Independent Pubs. Group.

Numeroff, Laura Joffe. Lots of Lambs. Munsinger, Lynn, illus. 2012. (ENG.). 20p. (J). (gr. k — 1). 9.99 *(978-0-547-40206-2(6))* Houghton Mifflin Harcourt Publishing Co.

Ogorek, Keith. Eli the Stable Boy. 2009. 28p. pap. 13.99 *(978-1-4490-4116-8(7))* AuthorHouse.

Paglia, Rhonda. The Little Lambs & the Very Special Mission. Paglia, Rhonda & Galaska, Taylor, illus. 2013. 44p. pap. 12.95 *(978-0-9899141-6-3(9))* Angels Landing.

Palatini, Margie. Bad Boys. Cole, Henry, illus. 40p. (J). (gr. -1-2). 2003. lib. bdg. 16.89 *(978-0-06-000103-2(8))* 2003. (ENG.). 15.99 *(978-0-06-000102-5(X)*, Tegen, Katherine Bks) 2006. (ENG.). reprint ed. 6.99 *(978-0-06-000104-9(6)*, Tegen, Katherine Bks) HarperCollins Pubs.

Paul, Dwain. The Fox the Hare the Wolf & the Sheep. 2011. 28p. 16.10 *(978-1-4269-5573-0(1))* Trafford Publishing.

Phelps, Karen. The Grass Is Always Greener & Let Sleeping Dogs Lie: Two Original Fables. 2006. (J). pap. *(978-1-4108-7155-8(X))* Benchmark Education Co.

Pileggi, Joe. No Greater Love. 2009. 24p. pap. 10.49 *(978-1-4389-9377-5(3))* AuthorHouse.

Pinson, Joseph. Joey & Big Wooley's Adventures. 2010. 88p. pap. 30.49 *(978-1-4520-4718-8(9))* AuthorHouse.

Pixton, Amy. Mary Had a Little Lamb. 2010. (Indestructibles Ser.). (ENG., Illus.). 12p. (J). (gr. k — 1). pap. 5.95 *(978-0-7611-5860-8(X)*, 15860) Workman Publishing Co., Inc.

Priddy, Roger. Sticker Friends - Lamb. 2017. (Sticker Friends Ser.). (ENG., Illus.). 24p. (J). pap. 4.99 *(978-0-312-52154-7(5)*, 9780312521547, Priddy Bks.) St. Martin's Pr.

Proimos, James. The Complete Adventures of Johnny Mutton. 2014. (ENG., Illus.). 160p. (J). (gr. 1-4). 12.99 *(978-0-544-32404-6(8))*, HMH Books For Young Readers) Houghton Mifflin Harcourt Publishing Co.

Quay, Emma. Good Night, Sleep Tight: A Book about Bedtime. Walker, Anna, illus. 2011. (ENG.). 24p. (J). (gr. -1 — 1). bds. 5.99 *(978-0-8037-3581-1(2)*, Dial Bks) Penguin Young Readers Group.

Rae, Philippa. Count the Sheep to Sleep. Röhr, Stéphanie, illus. 2012. (ENG.). 28p. (J). (gr. -1-k). 12.95 *(978-1-61608-660-2(2)*, 608660, Sky Pony Pr.) Skyhorse Publishing Co., Inc.

Rankin, Laura. My Turn! Rankin, Laura, illus. 2016. (ENG., Illus.). 32p. (J). 16.99 *(978-1-59990-174-9(9)*, 9781599901749, Bloomsbury USA Childrens) Bloomsbury Publishing USA.

Raum, Elizabeth. The Christmas Star. Johnson, Meredith, illus. (ENG.). (J). (gr. -1-k). 2008. 32p. per. 3.99 *(978-0-8249-5567-0(6))* 2005. 28p. bds. 7.95 *(978-0-8249-6620-1(1))* Worthy Publishing. (Ideal Pubns.).

Redmon, Jaylyle. Gracie the Lop-Eared Burro. 2008. 17p. pap. 24.95 *(978-1-60672-626-6(9))* America Star Bks.

Repicci, Albert. The Littlest Angel: A Christmas Story. 2012. 36p. pap. 21.99 *(978-1-4691-9547-6(X))* Xlibris Corp.

Risco, Elle D. Dora Had a Little Lamb. Savitsky, Steve, illus. 2007. (Dora the Explorer Ser.). (J). (gr. -1-2). 11.65 *(978-0-7569-8294-2(4))* Perfection Learning Corp.

Rivers-Moore, Debbie. Lamb Loves Springtime. Fox, Lisa, illus. 2012. (Springtime Shakers Ser.). (ENG.). 8p. (J). bds. 5.99 *(978-0-7641-6487-3(2))* Barron's Educational Series, Inc.

Roche, Jackie, illus. The Derby Ram. 2010. (First Steps in Music Ser.). (ENG.). 32p. (J). (gr. -1-k). 16.95 *(978-1-57999-783-0(X))* G I A Pubns., Inc.

Rock, Michelle L. Nighttime Adventures Counting Sheep. Longmore, Nickolai, illus. 2006. 32p. (J). 3.99 net. *(978-0-9771700-1-2(2))* Mystic Arts, LLC.

Root, Phyllis. Ten Sleepy Sheep. Gaber, Susan, illus. 2009. (ENG.). 12p. (J). (-k). bds. 7.99 *(978-0-7636-4142-9(1))* Candlewick Pr.

Rothstein, Gloria L. Sheep Asleep. Date not set. 224p. (J). (gr. -1-1). pap. 4.99 *(978-0-06-443717-2(5))* HarperCollins Pubs.

Rundstrom, Teressa. Cherry the Sheep Finds Her Sheep Sound. Miller, Bryan & Marshall, H. Keene, illus. 2004. 25p. (J). per. *(978-1-932062-40-3(8))* Hability Solution Services, Inc.

Russell, Christopher & Russell, Christine. The Quest of the Warrior Sheep. 2011. (ENG.). 224p. (gr. 5-8). pap. 6.99 *(978-1-4022-5511-3(X)*, Sourcebooks Jabberwocky) Sourcebooks, Inc.

—Warrior Sheep Go Jurassic. 2014. (Warrior Sheep Ser.). (ENG.). 256p. (J). (gr. 2-4). pap. 7.99 *(978-1-4052-6718-2(6))* Egmont Bks., Ltd. GBR. Dist: Independent Pubs. Group.

Rwakasisi, Rose. How Goats Lost Their Beautiful Tails. 2004. (Illus.). 19p. pap. *(978-9970-02-436-0(1))* Fountain Pubs. Ltd. UGA. Dist: Michigan State Univ. Pr.

Ryan, Candace. Ewe & Aye. Ruble, Stephanie, illus. 2014. (ENG.). 40p. (J). (gr. -1-k). 17.99 *(978-1-4231-7591-9(3))* Hyperion Bks. for Children.

Saillard, Remi, illus. Funny Machines for George the Sheep: A Children's Book Inspired by Leonardo Da Vinci. 2014. (ENG.). 32p. (J). (gr. -1-3). 14.95 *(978-3-7913-7166-5(5))* Prestel Verlag GmbH & Co KG. DEU. Dist: Penguin Random Hse. LLC.

Samuel, Janet, illus. One Sneaky Sheep: A Touch-and-Feel Fluffy Tale. 2007. (ENG.). 20p. (gr. -1). 14.95 *(978-1-58117-560-8(4)*, Intervisual/Piggy Toes) Bendon, Inc.

—One Sneaky Sheep: The Sheep Who Didn't Want to Get Sheared. 2009. (ENG.). 20p. (J). 9.95 *(978-1-58117-841-8(7)*, Intervisual/Piggy Toes) Bendon, Inc.

Sanders, Scott Russell. Warm as Wool. Cogancherry, Helen, illus. 2007. (J). lib. bdg. 18.00 *(978-1-59098-421-5(8))* Wooster Bk. Co., The.

Santillo, LuAnn. Shag. Santillo, LuAnn, ed. 2003. (Half-Pint Readers Ser.). (Illus.). 7p. (J). (gr. -1-1). pap. 1.00 *(978-1-59256-068-4(7))* Half-Pint Kids, Inc.

Sargent, Dave & Sargent, David M., Jr. Petie Pelican: Be Proud of Yourself, 19 vols., Vol. 14. Lenoir, Jane, illus. 2003. (Feather Tales Ser.: 14). 42p. (J). pap. 10.95 *(978-1-56763-746-5(9))* Ozark Publishing.

Savitsky, Steven, illus. Dora Had a Little Lamb. 2007. (Dora the Explorer Ser.: 23). (ENG.). 24p. (J). (gr. -1-2). pap. 3.99 *(978-1-4169-3368-7(9)*, Simon Spotlight/Nickelodeon) Simon Spotlight/Nickelodeon.

Scheffler, Axel, illus. Lizzy the Lamb. 2015. (Buggy Buddies Ser.). (ENG.). 12p. (J). (— 1). bds. 7.99 *(978-0-230-75616-8(6))* Pan Macmillan GBR. Dist: Independent Pubs. Group.

Schwinn, Ruth E. Henry & Dale. Flores, Justin, illus. 2010. (ENG.). 24p. (J). 14.95 *(978-0-578-04719-5(5)*, 9780578047195) PRF Pubs.

Scotton, Rob. Russell & the Lost Treasure. Scotton, Rob, illus. 2006. (ENG., Illus.). 32p. (J). (gr. -1-2). 15.99 *(978-0-06-059851-8(4))* HarperCollins Pubs.

—Russell the Sheep. Scotton, Rob, illus. (ENG., Illus.). 32p. (J). (gr. -1-3). 2015. pap. 5.99 *(978-0-06-239243-5(3)*, HarperFestival) 2011. pap. 6.99 *(978-0-06-059850-1(6))* 2009. bds. 7.99 *(978-0-06-170996-8(4)*, HarperFestival) 2005. 17.99 *(978-0-06-059848-8(4))* HarperCollins Pubs.

—Russell's Christmas Magic. Scotton, Rob, illus. 2007. (Illus.). 32p. (J). (gr. -1-2). lib. bdg. 17.89 *(978-0-06-059855-6(7))* HarperCollins Pubs.

Scraper, Katherine. The Boy Who Cried Wolf: An Aesop's Fable. 2006. (J). pap. *(978-1-4108-6166-5(X))* Benchmark Education Co.

Shanks, Cindy. Emilia Camina la Vereda de Borregos. 2009. 48p. pap. 19.95 *(978-1-4490-2388-1(6))* AuthorHouse.

—Emily Walks the Sheep Trail. 2009. 48p. pap. 19.95 *(978-1-4490-2208-2(1))* AuthorHouse.

Shapely Sleepy Sheep. 2005. (J). bds. 7.95 *(978-0-9749305-6-5(3))* Castle Pacific Publishing.

Shaw, Elizabeth. The Little Black Sheep. Shaw, Elizabeth, illus. 2007. (Pandas Ser.: 06). (ENG., Illus.). 64p. (J). pap. 9.95 *(978-0-86278-463-8(8))* O'Brien Pr., Ltd., The IRL. Dist: Dufour Editions, Inc.

—The Little Black Sheep: Panda 6. Shaw, Elizabeth, illus. 2nd rev. ed. 2017. (ENG., Illus.). 64p. (J). 11.00 ***(978-1-84717-918-0(5))*** O'Brien Pr., Ltd., The IRL. Dist: Dufour Editions, Inc.

Shaw, Elizabeth. An T-Uan Beag Dubh. MacPhaidan, Daire, tr. from ENG. 2004. (Sraith Sos Ser.: 10). (IRI, ENG & GLE., Illus.). 64p. (J). pap. 9.95 *(978-0-86278-867-4(6))* O'Brien Pr., Ltd., The IRL. Dist: Dufour Editions, Inc.

Shaw, Nancy. Me First. Apple, Margot, illus. 2015. 32p. pap. 7.00 *(978-1-61003-505-7(4))* Center for the Collaborative Classroom.

—Sheep Go to Sleep. Apple, Margot, illus. 2015. (ENG.). 32p. (J). (gr. -1-3). 16.99 *(978-0-544-30989-0(8)*, HMH Books For Young Readers) Houghton Mifflin Harcourt Publishing Co.

Shaw, Nancy E. Sheep Blast Off! Apple, Margot, illus. 2011. (ENG.). 32p. (J). (gr. -1-3). pap. 5.99 *(978-0-547-52025-4(5))* Houghton Mifflin Harcourt Publishing Co.

—Sheep Go to Sleep (board Book) Apple, Margot, illus. 2016. (Sheep in a Jeep Ser.). (ENG.). 30p. (J). (gr. -1-3). bds. 7.99 *(978-0-544-64053-5(5)*, HMH Books For Young Readers) Houghton Mifflin Harcourt Publishing Co.

—Sheep in a Jeep. Apple, Margot, illus. (ENG.). (J). (gr. -1-3). 2013. 32p. 26.99 *(978-0-547-99383-6(8))* 2009. 26p. bds. 12.99 *(978-0-547-23775-6(8))* 2006. 32p. audio compact disk 10.99 *(978-0-618-69522-5(2))* Houghton Mifflin Harcourt Publishing Co.

—Sheep in a Shop, 1 vol. Apple, Margot, illus. 2009. (ENG.). 32p. (J). (gr. -1-3). audio compact disk 10.99 *(978-0-547-23767-1(7))* Houghton Mifflin Harcourt Publishing Co.

—Sheep Out to Eat. Apple, Margot, illus. 2005. (ENG.). 28p. (J). (gr. k — 1). bds. 5.95 *(978-0-618-58339-3(4))* Houghton Mifflin Harcourt Publishing Co.

Simon, Mary Manz. Lamb Is Joyful. Harris, Phyllis & Clearwater, Linda, illus. 2006. (First Virtuestm for Toddlers Ser.). 20p. (J). 5.99 *(978-0-7847-1575-8(0)*, 04069) Standard Publishing.

Sloat, Teri. Pablo in the Snow. Bonnet, Rosalinde, illus. 2017. (ENG.). 40p. (J). 16.99 *(978-1-62779-412-1(3)*, 9781627794121, Holt, Henry & Co. Bks. For Young Readers) Holt, Henry & Co.

Smallman, Steve. The Lamb Who Came for Dinner. Dreidemy, Joëlle, illus. 2007. 32p. (J). (gr. -1-2). 15.95 *(978-1-58925-067-3(2))* Tiger Tales.

Smith, Brooke. Mimi & Maty to the Rescue! Book 2: Sadie the Sheep Disappears Without a Peep! Arnold, Ali, illus. 2014. (ENG.). 96p. (J). (gr. 1-5). 14.95 *(978-1-62636-344-1(7)*, Sky Pony Pr.) Skyhorse Publishing Co., Inc.

Smith, Carrie. Little Bo Peep. Abbott, Jason, illus. 2010. (Rising Readers Ser.). (J). 3.49 *(978-1-60719-700-3(6))* Newmark Learning LLC.

Smith, Jodene Lynn & Thompson, Chad. Baa, Baa, Black Sheep, 1 vol. 2010. (Early Childhood Themes Ser.). (ENG., Illus.). 16p. (J). (gr. -1-2). pap. 19.99 *(978-1-4333-1484-1(3))*; pap. 6.99 *(978-1-4333-1483-4(5))* Shell Educational Publishing.

—Beh, Beh, Borreguito Negro, 1 vol. rev. ed. 2010. (Early Childhood Themes Ser.). (SPA., Illus.). 16p. (J). (gr. -1-2). pap. 6.99 *(978-1-4333-2094-1(0))*; pap. 19.99 *(978-1-4333-2095-8(9))* Shell Educational Publishing.

Snow, Ravay L. Hildegarde & the Great Green Shirt Factory. Snow, Ravay L., illus. 2005. (Hildegarde Ser.). (Illus.). 32p. (J). 16.95 *(978-1-932362-10-7(X))* Snowbound Pr., Inc.

Sommerset, Mark. Baa Baa Smart Sheep. Sommerset, Rowan, illus. 2016. (ENG.). 32p. (J). (gr. k-3). 14.00 *(978-0-7636-8066-4(4))* Candlewick Pr.

—I Love Lemonade. Sommerset, Rowan, illus. 2016. (ENG.). 32p. (J). (gr. k-3). 14.00 *(978-0-7636-8067-1(2))* Candlewick Pr.

Stanley, Mandy. Who Tickled Tilly? Stanley, Mandy, illus. 2011. (ENG., Illus.). 32p. (J). (gr. -1-k). pap. 7.99 *(978-1-84365-192-5(0)*, Pavilion) Pavilion Bks. GBR. Dist: Independent Pubs. Group.

Starfall Education. Pete's Sheep. Starfall Education, ed. 2004. (ENG., Illus.). 8p. (J). pap. *(978-1-59577-007-3(0))* Starfall Education.

Stiver, Megan, illus. The Great Bellybutton Cover-Up. 2011. 32p. *(978-0-9810634-7-8(0))* Susan Ross (self publishing).

—Say Please to the Honeybees. 2010. 33p. *(978-0-9810634-3-0(8))* Susan Ross (self publishing).

Stohner, Anu. Brave Charlotte. Wilson, Henrike, illus. 2014. 32p. pap. 8.00 *(978-1-61003-341-1(8))* Center for the Collaborative Classroom.

Sundgaard, Arnold. The Lamb & the Butterfly. Carle, Eric, illus. 2013. (ENG.). 32p. (J). (gr. -1-k). 17.99 *(978-0-545-44326-5(1)*, Orchard Bks.) Scholastic, Inc.

Suzie Sheep & her Friends. 2004. (Play Pals Ser.). (Illus.). 12p. (J). bds. *(978-1-84229-649-3(3))* Top That! Publishing PLC.

Teddy Bear-Sheep. 2003. (J). per. *(978-1-57657-163-7(7))* Paradise Pr., Inc.

Terborg-Hershman, Donna M. Why Sheep Don't Shrink. 2008. 28p. pap. 12.49 *(978-1-4389-3720-5(2))* AuthorHouse.

Theobald, Joseph. Marvin Gets Mad! 2013. pap. *(978-0-545-55294-3(X))* Scholastic, Inc.

—Marvin Wanted More! 2007. (Bloomsbury Paperbacks Ser.). (ENG., Illus.). 32p. (J). (gr. -1-k). 13.99 *(978-0-7475-8873-3(2))* Bloomsbury Publishing Plc GBR. Dist: Independent Pubs. Group.

—Marvin Wanted More! Theobald, Joseph, illus. (ENG., Illus.). 32p. (J). (gr. -1-k). 2005. pap. 12.99 *(978-0-7475-6481-2(7))* 2004. 16.99 *(978-0-7475-5631-2(8))* Bloomsbury Publishing Plc GBR. Dist: Independent Pubs. Group.

Thompson, Kate. I'm Just a Little Sheep. Green, Barry, illus. 2017. (Googley-Eye Bks.). (ENG.). 12p. (J). (gr. -1-k). bds. 7.99 *(978-1-78445-869-0(4))* Top That! Publishing PLC GBR. Dist: Independent Pubs. Group.

Thompson, Lauren. Little Lamb. Butler, John, illus. 2014. (J). *(978-1-4351-5352-3(9)*, Simon & Schuster Bks. For Young Readers) Simon & Schuster Bks. For Young Readers.

—Wee Little Lamb. Butler, John, illus. 2009. (Wee Little Ser.). (ENG.). 32p. (J). (gr. -1-3). 16.99 *(978-1-4169-3469-1(3)*, Simon & Schuster Bks. For Young Readers) Simon & Schuster Bks. For Young Readers.

Twohy, Mike. Wake up, Rupert! Twohy, Mike, illus. 2014. (ENG., Illus.). 32p. (J). (gr. -1-3). 16.99 *(978-1-4424-5998-4(0)*, Simon & Schuster/Paula Wiseman Bks.) Simon & Schuster/Paula Wiseman Bks.

van der Put, Klaartje, et al. Little Lamb. 2006. (Little Finger Puppet Board Bks.: FING). (ENG., Illus.). 12p. (J). (gr. -1-7). bds. 6.99 *(978-0-8118-5235-7(0))* Chronicle Bks. LLC.

Van Patter, Bruce. Farley Found It! 2006. (ENG., Illus.). 32p. (J). (gr. -1-1). 17.95 *(978-1-59078-351-1(4))* Boyds Mills Pr.

Vasquez, Paula. Lili Wool, 1 vol. 2017. (ENG.). 40p. (J). (gr. k-3). 14.99 ***(978-1-4236-4728-7(9))*** Gibbs Smith, Publisher.

Voake, Steve. Daisy Dawson & the Big Freeze. Meserve, Jessica, illus. 2011. (Daisy Dawson Ser.). (ENG.). 96p. (J). (gr. 1-4). pap. 5.99 *(978-0-7636-5627-0(5))* Candlewick Pr.

Warden, Evelyn. Oh, Please, Cricket. 2006. 144p. pap. 24.95 *(978-1-4241-1860-1(3))* America Star Bks.

Watts, Fraces. The Middle Sheep. Watson, Judy, illus. 2010. (ENG.). 80p. (J). (gr. 2-5). pap. 6.00 *(978-0-8028-5368-4(4))* Eerdmans, William B. Publishing Co.

Watts, Frances. Extraordinary Ernie & Marvelous Maud. Watson, Judy, illus. 2010. (ENG.). 80p. (J). (gr. 2-5). pap.

S

6.00 (978-0-8028-5363-9(3), Eerdmans Bks For Young Readers) Eerdmans, William B. Publishing Co.
—Heroes of the Year. Watson, Judy, illus. 2012. (ENG.). 80p. (J). pap. 6.00 (978-0-8028-5412-4(5), Eerdmans Bks For Young Readers) Eerdmans, William B. Publishing Co.
Weeks, Sarah. Counting Ovejas. Diaz, David, illus. 2006. (ENG & SPA.). 40p. (J). (gr. -1-2). 18.99 (978-0-689-86750-7(6), Atheneum Bks. for Young Readers) Simon & Schuster Children's Publishing.
Weeks, Sarah & Weeks. Baa-Choo! Manning, Jane K., illus. 2006. (I Can Read Level 1 Ser.). (ENG.). 32p. (J). (gr. k-3). pap. 3.99 (978-0-06-443740-0(X)) HarperCollins Pubs.
Wegwerth, A. L. Little Bo Peep & Her Bad, Bad Sheep: A Mother Goose Hullabaloo. Flowers, Luke, illus. 2016. (Fiction Picture Bks.). (ENG.). 40p. (gr. -1-2). lib. bdg. 22.65 (978-1-4795-6483-5(4), Fiction Picture Bks.) Picture Window Bks.
Westera, Marleen. Sheep & Goat. Forest-Flier, Nancy, tr. from DUT. Van Ommen, Sylvia, illus. 2006. (ENG.). 99p. (J). 16.95 (978-1-932425-81-9(0), Lemniscaat) Boyds Mills Pr.
Will Mcallister. Sam Rivers & the Night Rustlers. 2009. 88p. pap. 9.95 (978-0-595-46287-2(1)) iUniverse, Inc.
Williams, Kristen. Sheepy Sue & the Bedtime Blues. 2012. 28p. pap. 12.95 (978-1-105-48819-1(5)) Lulu.com GBR. Dist: Lulu Pr., Inc.
Wolfe, Jane. Sleepy Sheep. Benham, Tors, illus. 2013. (ENG.). 8p. (J). (gr. -1-k). bds. 6.99 (978-1-84322-778-6(9), Armadillo) Anness Publishing GBR. Dist: National Bk. Network.
Wonderley, Stanley. My Lamb. 2011. 22.95 (978-0-7414-6357-9(1)) Infinity Publishing.
Wright, Maureen. Barnyard Fun, 0 vols. De Tagyos, Paul Ratz, illus. 2013. (ENG.). 24p. (J). (gr. -1-3). 16.99 (978-1-4778-1643-1(7), 9781477816431, Amazon Children's Publishing) Amazon Publishing.

SHELLFISH
see Mollusks

SHELLS
see also Mollusks
Beaumont, Holly. Why Do Snails & Other Animals Have Shells? 2015. (Animal Body Coverings Ser.). (ENG., Illus.). 24p. (gr. 1-3). 23.32 (978-1-4846-2536-1(6)) Heinemann-Raintree.
Berkes, Marianne Collins. Seashells by the Seashore. Noreika, Robert, illus. 2004. (Sharing Nature with Children Book Ser.). 32p. (J). (gr. -1-5). 16.95 (978-1-58469-035-1(6)); pap. 8.95 (978-1-58469-034-4(8)) Dawn Pubns.
Boothroyd, Jennifer. Shells. 2011. (First Step Nonfiction / Body Coverings Ser.). pap. 33.92 (978-0-7613-8610-0(6)); (ENG.). 24p. pap. 6.95 (978-0-7613-7830-3(8)); (ENG., Illus.). 24p. lib. bdg. 23.93 (978-0-7613-5788-9(2)) Lerner Publishing Group.
Bredeson, Carmen & Cousins, Lindsey. Can You Find These Seashells? 2012. (All about Nature Ser.). 24p. (J). (gr. -1-1). (Illus.). pap. 7.95 (978-1-4644-0068-1(7), Enslow Elementary); 22.60 (978-0-7660-3978-0(1)) Enslow Pubs., Inc.
Douglass, John & Douglass, Jackie Leatherbury. Shells. Peterson, Roger Tory, ed. 2nd ed. 2013. (Peterson Field Guide Color-In Bks.). (ENG., Illus.). 64p. (J). 8.95 (978-0-544-03622-2(0)) Houghton Mifflin Harcourt Publishing Co.
Fiedler, Heidi. Coral: A Close-Up Photographic Look Inside Your World. 2017. (Up Close Ser.). (ENG., Illus.). (J). (gr. k-6). lib. bdg. 27.99 **(978-1-942875-35-2(5)**, Walter Foster Jr) Quarto Publishing Group USA.
Green, Jen. Projects with the Seaside. 2014. (Make & Learn Ser.). (Illus.). 32p. (J). (gr. 3-6). lib. bdg. 27.50 (978-1-4777-7173-0(5), PowerKids Pr.) Rosen Publishing Group, Inc., The.
Hansen, Judith. Seashells in My Pocket: AMC's Family Guide to Exploring the Coast from Maine to Florida. Sabaka, Donna, illus. 3rd ed. 2008. (ENG.). 160p. (gr. 3-7). per. 14.95 (978-1-929173-61-7(X)) Appalachian Mountain Club Bks.
Hopkins, Therese. Shells. 2009. (Home Sweet Home Ser.). 24p. (J). (gr. k-2). pap. 8.25 (978-1-4358-3070-7(9), PowerKids Pr.); 24p. (gr. 1-1). 42.50 (978-1-61513-405-2(0), PowerKids Pr.); (J). (gr. k-2). lib. bdg. 22.60 (978-1-4358-2696-0(5)) Rosen Publishing Group, Inc., The.
Mazurkiewicz, Jessica. Seashell Patterns Coloring Book. 2011. (Dover Nature Coloring Book Ser.). (ENG.). 32p. (J). (gr. 3-5). pap. 3.99 (978-0-486-47559-2(X)) Dover Pubns., Inc.
Moore, David. Expl on Your Own Shell Shapes. 2009. (Explore on Your Own Ser.). (ENG., Illus.). 12p. (J). pap. 7.95 (978-0-7362-5603-2(2)) National Geographic School Publishing, Inc.
Morgan, Emily R. Next Time You See a Seashell. 2012. (Next Time You See Ser.). (ENG., Illus.). 32p. (J). (gr. k-5). pap. 12.95 (978-1-936959-15-0(1)) National Science Teachers Assn.
Pether, Lesley. Shells. 2008. (Discovering & Exploring Science Ser.). (Illus.). 16p. (J). (gr. -1-3). lib. bdg. 12.95 (978-0-7569-8409-0(2)) Perfection Learning Corp.
Richardson, Adele D. Seashells. (Illus.). 32p. pap. 8.95 (978-0-89812-320-3(8)) Creative Co., The.
Salzmann, Mary Elizabeth. Cool Shells: Creating Fun & Fascinating Collections!, 1 vol. 2007. (Cool Collections Ser.). (ENG., Illus.). 32p. (YA). (gr. 2-5). 28.50 (978-1-59679-772-7(X)) ABDO Publishing Co.
—What Has a Shell?, 1 vol. 2007. (Creature Features Ser.). (ENG., Illus.). 24p. (gr. -1-3). 25.65 (978-1-59928-871-0(0), Super SandCastle) ABDO Publishing Co.
Sea Shells of the United States & Canada. 2004. (World Book's Science & Nature Guides Ser.). (Illus.). 80p. (J). (978-0-7166-4218-3(2)) World Bk., Inc.
Skeie, Shari. Sea Shells. 2008. (Oceans Alive Ser.). (ENG., Illus.). 24p. (J). (gr. k-3). lib. bdg. 25.95 (978-1-60014-208-6(7)) Bellwether Media.
Weber, Valerie J. Por qué Algunos Animales Tienen Caparazón. 2008. (Donde viven los animales (Where Animals Live) Ser.). (SPA., Illus.). 24p. (gr. 1-4). lib. bdg. 22.00 (978-0-8368-8811-9(1), Weekly Reader Leveled Readers) Stevens, Gareth Publishing LLLP.
—Why Animals Live in Shells. 2008. (Where Animals Live Ser.). (Illus.). 24p. (gr. 1-4). lib. bdg. 22.00 (978-0-8368-8797-6(2), Weekly Reader Leveled Readers) Stevens, Gareth Publishing LLLP.
Weber, Valerie J. & Weber, Valerie J. Why Animals Live in Shells. 2008. (Where Animals Live Ser.). (SPA.). 24p. (gr. 1-4). pap. 8.15 (978-0-8368-8804-1(9), Weekly Reader Leveled Readers) Stevens, Gareth Publishing LLLP.
Yin, Robert, illus. & photos by. Seashells. Yin, Robert, photos by. 2004. (ENG.). 24p. (J). (gr. 1-2). pap. 6.50 (978-0-7685-0355-5(8), Dominie Elementary) Pearson Schl.
Zoehfeld, Kathleen Weidner. What Lives in a Shell? 2015. (Let's Read & Find Out Science Stage 1 Ser.). (J). lib. bdg. 17.20 (978-0-606-37740-9(9)) Turtleback Bks.

SHEPARD, ALAN B. (ALAN BARTLETT), 1923-1998
Benge, Janet & Benge, Geoff. Christian Heroes Then & Now - Alan Shepard: Higher & Faster. 2007. (Heroes of History Ser.). 229p. (J). (gr. 3-7). per. (978-1-932096-41-5(8)) Emerald Bks.
Orr, Tamra. Alan Shepard: The First American in Space. (Library of Astronaut Biographies Ser.). 112p. (gr. 5-8). 2009. 63.90 (978-1-60853-518-7(5)) 2004. (Illus.). (J). lib. bdg. 34.60 (978-0-8239-4455-2(7)) Rosen Publishing Group, Inc., The. (Rosen Reference).

SHEPHERDS
David, Juliet. The Shepherds, 1 vol. Wood, Hannah, illus. 2009. (Christmas Trio Ser.). 18p. (J). bds. 4.99 (978-0-8254-7406-4(X), Candle Bks.) Lion Hudson PLC GBR. Dist: Kregel Pubns.
Pastores en el Campo (Shepherd's Fields) (SPA.). (J). (978-0-7899-0877-3(8), 496236) Editorial Unilit.
Peregrinos & Extranjeros. El Buen Pastor (The Good Shepherd) (SPA.). (J). 1.59 (978-1-56063-854-4(0), 494016) Editorial Unilit.
Urbigkit, Cat. The Shepherd's Trail. 2008. (ENG., Illus.). 32p. (J). (gr. 2-4). 16.95 (978-1-59078-509-6(6)) Boyds Mills Pr.
—A Young Shepherd. 2006. (Illus.). (J). (978-1-4156-6559-6(1)) Boyds Mills Pr.

SHEPHERDS—FICTION
Adams, Elizabeth. The Boy Who Cried Wolf. 2012. (ENG., Illus.). 24p. (J). pap. (978-0-7787-7902-5(5)) Crabtree Publishing Co.
Banks, Celia. Jacob's Promise: A Story about Faith. Unalp, Janet & Perry, Matt, illus. 2006. 32p. 14.99 (978-0-9764460-6-4(5)) HonorNet.
Blackford. The Eskdale Herd Boy A Scottish Tale for the Instruction & Amusement of Young Persons. 2004. reprint ed. pap. 15.95 (978-1-4191-6125-4(3)) Kessinger Publishing, LLC.
Blanco, César. Hoky the Caring Wolf. 2013. (ENG., Illus.). 32p. (J). (gr. k-2). 15.95 (978-84-15241-92-8(5)) Eastern National.
Cerpok, M. L. The Mobile Monk: A Zen Tale. Wagner, Gavin, illus. 2008. 73p. pap. 19.95 (978-1-60610-138-4(2)) America Star Bks.
Dateno, Maria Grace. Shepherds to the Rescue, 6 vols., Vol. 1. Cunningham, Paul, illus. 2013. 71p. (J). pap. 5.95 (978-0-8198-7251-7(2)) Pauline Bks. & Media.
Fine, Maureen. My Two Shepherds in the Garden: A Lesson in Listening. 2012. 24p. pap. 14.93 (978-1-4669-1991-4(4)) Trafford Publishing.
Flinn, Lisa & Younger, Barbara. The Christmas Garland. Corvino, Lucy, tr. Corvino, Lucy, illus. 2003. 32p. (J). 14.95 (978-0-8249-5460-4(2), Ideal Pubns.) Worthy Publishing.
Fogle, Robin. The Shepherd Boy's Christmas. 2005. (J). pap. 1.79 (978-1-59317-105-6(6)) Warner Pr., Inc.
Hallinan, P. K. That's What a Friend Is! 2003. (ENG.). 24p. (J). bds. 6.95 (978-0-8249-5468-0(8), Ideal Pubns.) Worthy Publishing.
Hennessy, B. G. The Boy Who Cried Wolf. Kulikov, Boris, illus. 2011. (J). (gr. -1-2). 29.95 (978-0-545-09452-8(6)) Weston Woods Studios, Inc.
Henry, Juliann. The Little Shepherd Girl: A Christmas Story. Madsen, Jim, illus. 2007. 32p. (J). (gr. -1-3). 14.99 (978-0-7814-4513-9(2)) Cook, David C.
Herzing, Nancy. The Night the Angels Came. 2012. 46p. pap. 19.99 (978-1-62419-373-6(0)) Salem Author Services.
Hill, Judith J. Champion for Grace. 2012. 128p. pap. 15.00 (978-1-936688-22-7(0)) AKA:yoLa.
Hodgson, Karen J. The King Who Wanted More. Dina, Madalina, illus. 2010. (ENG.). 32p. (J). (gr. -1-4). pap. 9.99 (978-1-907432-03-3(5)) Hogs Back Bks. GBR. Dist: Independent Pubs. Group.
Howell, Trisha Adelena. The Stinky Shepherd. Marshall, Jamie, illus. 2005. 32p. (J). 15.95 (978-1-931210-25-6(X)) Howell Canyon Pr.
Laurel Carter, Anne. The Shepherd's Granddaughter. 2013. 236p. pap. (978-1-4596-6490-6(6)) ReadHowYouWant.com, Ltd.
Mackall, Dandi Daley, adapted by. El Pastorcito: Para ninos de 4-7 Anos.Tr. of Little Shepherd. (SPA.). 32p. 3.99 (978-0-7586-0362-3(2)) Concordia Publishing Hse.
Metlen, Ryan W. & Metlen, Ryan. Ewe. 2009. (J). (978-1-58768-054-0(8), HiddenSpring) Paulist Pr.
Millard, Glenda. Once a Shepherd. Lesnie, Phil, illus. 2014. (ENG.). 32p. (J). (gr. -1-3). 16.99 (978-0-7636-7458-8(3)) Candlewick Pr.
Morning, Carey. The Shepherd Girl of Bethlehem: A Nativity Story. Marks, Alan, illus. 2016. (ENG.). 32p. (J). (gr. -1-k). pap. 8.99 (978-0-7459-6232-0(7)) Lion Hudson PLC GBR. Dist: Independent Pubs. Group.
North, Laura. The Boy Who Cried Sheep! 2016. (ENG., Illus.). 32p. (J). (978-0-7787-2471-1(9)) Crabtree Publishing Co.
Ogorek, Keith. Eli the Stable Boy. 2009. 28p. pap. 13.99 (978-1-4490-4116-8(7)) AuthorHouse.
Rousay II, Richard A. Choose the Right & Walk with Noah. 2008. 82p. pap. 17.50 (978-0-615-19773-9(6)) P.F.P. Pubs.
Schaefer, Jack. Old Ramon. West, Harold E., illus. 2016. (ENG.). 112p. (J). pap. 19.95 (978-0-8263-5764-9(4)) Univ. of New Mexico Pr.
Stockham, Jess, illus. The Boy Who Cried Wolf. 2011. (Flip-Up Fairy Tales Ser.). (ENG.). 24p. (J). (gr. 2-2). (978-1-84643-368-9(1)) Child's Play International Ltd.
Van Dyke, Henry. The Sad Shepherd: A Christmas Story, & the Unruly Sprite. 2007. 48p. per. (978-1-4065-4725-2(5)) Dodo Pr.
Weiss, Ellen & Friedman, Mel. The Stinky Giant. Girasole, Alessia, illus. 2012. (Step into Reading Ser.). (ENG.). 48p. (J). (gr. k-3). pap. 3.99 (978-0-375-86743-9(0), Random Hse. Bks. for Young Readers) Random Hse. Children's Bks.
—The Stinky Giant. Girasole, Alessia, illus. 2012. (Step into Reading Level 3 Ser.). lib. bdg. 13.55 (978-0-606-23858-8(1), Turtleback) Turtleback Bks.

SHERMAN, WILLIAM T. (WILLIAM TECUMSEH), 1820-1891
Hoogenboom, Lynn. William Tecumseh Sherman: The Fight to Preserve the Union. (Library of American Lives & Times Ser.). 112p. 2009. (gr. 5-5). 69.20 (978-1-60853-511-8(8)) 2005. (Illus.). (J). (gr. 4-8). lib. bdg. 34.60 (978-0-8239-6625-7(9)) Rosen Publishing Group, Inc., The.
Koestler-Grack, Rachel A. William Tecumseh Sherman. 2009. (Leaders of the Civil War Era Ser.). (Illus.). 149p. (gr. 6-12). 35.00 (978-1-60413-300-4(7), Chelsea Hse.) Facts On File, Inc.
Whitelaw, Nancy. William Tecumseh Sherman: Defender & Destroyer. rev. exp. ed. 2004. (Illus.). 176p. (J). (gr. 6-12). 26.95 (978-1-931798-31-0(1)) Reynolds, Morgan Inc.

SHERMAN'S MARCH TO THE SEA
Hoogenboom, Lynn. William Tecumseh Sherman: The Fight to Preserve the Union. 2005. (Library of American Lives & Times). (Illus.). 112p. (J). (gr. 4-8). lib. bdg. 34.60 (978-0-8239-6625-7(9)) Rosen Publishing Group, Inc., The.

SHERMAN'S MARCH TO THE SEA—FICTION
Bolden, Tonya. Crossing Ebenezer Creek. 2017. (ENG.). 240p. (YA). 17.99 (978-1-59990-319-4(9), 9781599903194, Bloomsbury USA Childrens) Bloomsbury Publishing USA.

SHIP BUILDING
see Shipbuilding

SHIP MODELS
Green, Cathy, et al. Great Ships on the Great Lakes Teacher's Guide: A Maritime History. 2013. (ENG., Illus.). cd-rom 49.95 (978-0-87020-583-5(8)) Wisconsin Historical Society.
Holloway, Jamie. My Toy Boat. 2015. (Rosen REAL Readers: STEM & STEAM Collection). (ENG.). 8p. pap. 5.46 (978-1-4994-9711-3(3), Rosen Classroom) Rosen Publishing Group, Inc., The.
Sobey, Ed. The Motorboat Book: Build & Launch 20 Jet Boats, Paddle-Wheelers, Electric Submarines & More. 2013. (Science in Motion Ser.). (ENG., Illus.). 224p. (J). (gr. 4). pap. 14.95 (978-1-61374-447-5(1)) Chicago Review Pr., Inc.

SHIPBUILDING
see also Boatbuilding; Ships; Steamboats
Aloian, Sam. How a Ship Is Built. 2016. (Engineering Our World Ser.). (ENG., Illus.). 24p. (J). (gr. 2-3). pap. 8.15 (978-1-4824-3915-1(8)) Stevens, Gareth Publishing LLLP.
Bow, James. Your Guide to Trade in the Middle Ages. 2017. (Destination: Middle Ages Ser.). (ENG., Illus.). 32p. (J). **(978-0-7787-2996-9(6))**; pap. **(978-0-7787-3052-1(2))** Crabtree Publishing Co.
The Complete History of Ships & Boats: From Sails & Oars to Nuclear-Powered Vessels. 2011. (Transportation & Society Ser.). (ENG.). 192p. (YA). (gr. 10-12). 77.50 (978-1-61530-770-8(2)) Rosen Publishing Group, Inc., The.
Curley, Robert, ed. The Complete History of Ships & Boats: From Sails & Oars to Nuclear-Powered Vessels. 2011. (Transportation & Society Ser.). (ENG.). 192p. (YA). (gr. 10-12). lib. bdg. 38.75 (978-1-61530-670-1(6)) Rosen Publishing Group, Inc., The.
Heinrichs, Ann. The Shipbuilder. 2013. 48p. (J). (gr. 4-8). 29.93 (978-0-7614-0005-9(2)); pap. 12.93 (978-1-62712-048-7(3)) Cavendish Square Publishing.
Krebs, Laurie. A Day in the Life of a Colonial Shipwright. 2009. (Library of Living & Working in Colonial Times Ser.). 24p. (gr. 3-3). 42.50 (978-1-60853-738-9(2), PowerKids Pr.) Rosen Publishing Group, Inc., The.
McCollum, Sean, et al. Eyewitness to Titanic. 2015. (ENG., Illus.). 160p. (gr. 3-4). pap. 9.95 (978-1-62370-131-4(7)) Capstone Young Readers of Coughlan Cos.

SHIPPING
Bailey, Gerry. Sea Transportation. 2008. (Simply Science Ser.). (Illus.). 32p. (YA). (gr. 3-6). lib. bdg. 26.00 (978-0-8368-9230-7(5)) Stevens, Gareth Publishing LLLP.
Evans, Lesli. Transport Math. 2008. (Math Alive! Ser.). 32p. (gr. 4-18). lib. bdg. 28.50 (978-0-7614-3211-1(6), Benchmark Bks.) Marshall Cavendish Corp.
Friend, Robyn C. & Cohen, Judith Love. A Cleaner Port; A Brighter Future: The Greening of the Port of Los Angeles. Katz, David Arthur, illus. 2011. 46p. (J). 13.95 (978-1-935999-01-0(X)); pap. 7.00 (978-1-935999-00-3(1)) Cascade Pass, Inc.
Green, Cathy, et al. Great Ships on the Great Lakes: A Maritime History. 2013. (ENG., Illus.). 144p. (J). pap. 18.95 (978-0-87020-582-8(X)) Wisconsin Historical Society.
—Great Ships on the Great Lakes Teacher's Guide: A Maritime History. 2013. (ENG., Illus.). cd-rom 49.95 (978-0-87020-583-5(8)) Wisconsin Historical Society.
Hinton, Kerry. All about Ships. 2016. (Let's Find Out! Ser.). 32p. (J). (gr. 3-2). lib. bdg. 24.45 (978-1-68048-443-4(5)) Rosen Publishing Group, Inc., The.
Meister, Cari. Ships. 2013. (ENG., Illus.). 24p. (J). lib. bdg. 25.65 (978-1-62031-047-2(3)) Jump! Inc.
Miller, Marlene. I Know Where the Freighters Go. Miller, Marlene, illus. 2008. (ENG., Illus.). 32p. pap. 9.95 (978-1-933916-29-3(X)) Nelson Publishing & Marketing.

SHIPPING—FICTION
Kellogg, Elijah. The Ark of Elm Island by Rev Elijah Kellogg. 2006. 300p. per. 23.99 (978-1-4255-2817-1(1)) Michigan Publishing.
Maurer, Tracy Nelson. Storm Codes. Rodriguez, Christina, illus. 2007. 40p. (J). pap. 8.95 (978-0-89317-064-6(X), WW-064X); (gr. 1-7). lib. bdg. 17.95 (978-0-89317-063-9(1), WW-0631) Finney Co., Inc. (Windward Publishing).

SHIPS
see also Boats and Boating; Navigation; Sailing; Steamboats; Submarines (Ships); Warships; Yachts and Yachting
Adamson, Thomas K. Ships. 2017. (Mighty Machines in Action Ser.). (ENG., Illus.). 24p. (J). (gr. k-3). lib. bdg. 25.95 (978-1-62617-608-9(6), Blastoff! Readers) Bellwether Media.
Alter, Judy. Passenger Ships. 2008. (21st Century Skills Innovation Library: Innovation in Transportation Ser.). (ENG., Illus.). 32p. (gr. 4-8). lib. bdg. 28.50 (978-1-60279-236-4(4), 200166) Cherry Lake Publishing.
Amato, William. Cruceros. 2004. (Vehículos de Alta Tecnología (High-Tech Vehicles) Ser.). (SPA & ENG., Illus.). 24p. (J). (gr. 2-4). lib. bdg. 22.60 (978-0-8239-6884-8(7)) Rosen Publishing Group, Inc., The.
—Cruceros (Cruise Ships) 2009. (Vehículos de alta tecnología (High-Tech Vehicles) Ser.). (SPA.). 24p. (gr. 2-3). 42.50 (978-1-60854-718-0(3), Editorial Buenas Letras) Rosen Publishing Group, Inc., The.
—Cruise Ships. 2009. (High-Tech Vehicles Ser.). 24p. (gr. 2-3). 42.50 (978-1-61513-305-5(4), PowerKids Pr.) Rosen Publishing Group, Inc., The.
Anderson, Scoular. Ships, Boats & Things That Float. 2016. (Cambridge Reading Adventures Ser.). (ENG.). 24p. pap. 7.19 (978-1-107-56041-3(1)) Cambridge Univ. Pr.
Arnold, Quinn M. Oasis of the Seas. 2016. (Illus.). 24p. (J). (978-1-60818-715-7(2), Creative Education) Creative Co., The.
AZ Books Staff. Sailing Ships. Tulup, Natasha, ed. 2012. (Workshop Ser.). (ENG.). 10p. (J). (gr. -1-k). bds. 10.95 (978-1-61889-162-4(6)) AZ Bks. LLC.
Bailey, Gerry. Sea Transportation. 2008. (Simply Science Ser.). (Illus.). 32p. (YA). (gr. 3-6). lib. bdg. 26.00 (978-0-8368-9230-7(5)) Stevens, Gareth Publishing LLLP.
Beech, Linda Ward. The Exxon Valdez's Deadly Oil Spill. 2007. (Code Red Ser.). (Illus.). 32p. (YA). (gr. 2-5). lib. bdg. 25.27 (978-1-59716-366-8(X)) Bearport Publishing Co., Inc.
Bender, Lionel. Ships & Boats. 2006. (J). (978-1-59389-268-5(3)) Chrysalis Education.
Benoit, Peter. The Exxon Valdez Oil Spill. 2011. (J). pap. (978-0-531-29028-6(X)) Children's Pr., Ltd.
—The Exxon Valdez Oil Spill. 2011. (True Bks.). 48p. (J). (gr. 3-5). 29.00 (978-0-531-20629-4(7), Children's Pr.) Scholastic Library Publishing.
Best, B. J. Coast Guard Boats. 2017. (J). **(978-1-5026-2556-4(3))** Cavendish Square Publishing.
Biesty, Stephen & Butterfield, Moira. Look Inside Cross-Sections: Ships. (ENG., Illus.). 32p. (J). mass mkt. 8.99 (978-0-590-24342-1(X)) Scholastic, Inc.
Bingham, Jane. The Story of Ships. King, Colin, illus. 2004. (Young Reading Ser.: Vol. 2). 62p. (J). (gr. 2-18). lib. bdg. 13.95 (978-1-58086-700-9(6), Usborne) EDC Publishing.
Biskup, Agnieszka. Captured by Pirates! An Isabel Soto History Adventure, 1 vol. Stewart, Roger, illus. 2012. (Graphic Expeditions Ser.). (ENG.). 32p. (gr. 3-4). lib. bdg. 30.65 (978-1-4296-7545-1(4), Graphic Library) Capstone Press of Coughlan Cos.
Bone, Emily. Ships. King, Colin, illus. 2009. (Beginner's Science Ser.). 32p. (J). 4.99 (978-0-7945-2507-1(5), Usborne) EDC Publishing.
Bowler, Peter J. An Interview with Charles Darwin. 2014. (Meet the Masters Ser.). 112p. (YA). (gr. 9-12). lib. bdg. 42.79 (978-1-62712-909-1(X)) Cavendish Square Publishing.
Bowman, Chris. Monster Ships. 2014. (Monster Machines Ser.). (ENG., Illus.). 24p. (J). (gr. k-3). lib. bdg. 25.95 (978-1-62617-054-4(1), Blastoff! Readers) Bellwether Media.
Build Your Own Pirate Ship. Date not set. (Build Your Own Ser.). (Illus.). 16p. (J). 3.98 (978-0-7525-7658-9(5)) Parragon, Inc.
Carr, Aaron. Cruise Ships. 2014. (J). (978-1-4896-3216-6(6)) Weigl Pubs., Inc.
Carrière, Nicholle. Ships & Boats, 1 vol. 2017. (Super Explorers Ser.). (ENG., Illus.). 64p. (J). pap. 6.99 **(978-1-926700-76-2(7)**, 9781926700762) Blue Bike Bks. CAN. Dist: Lone Pine Publishing USA.
Close, Edward. Wheels, Wings, & Motors, 1 vol., 1. 2014. (Discovery Education: How It Works). (ENG.). 32p. (gr. 3-6). 26.25 (978-1-4777-6313-1(9), PowerKids Pr.) Rosen Publishing Group, Inc., The.
Coffin, Rebecca J., et al, eds. Boats: The Work They Do & the Way They Do It. 2011. 28p. 35.95 (978-1-258-06539-3(8)) Literary Licensing, LLC.
Cottman, Michael & National Geographic Kids Staff. Shackles from the Deep: Tracing the Path of a Sunken Slave Ship, a Bitter Past, & a Rich Legacy. 2017. (ENG.). 128p. (J). (gr. 5-7). 17.99 (978-1-4263-2663-9(7), National Geographic Children's Bks.) National Geographic Society.
Crowther, Robert. Ships: A Pop-Up Book. Crowther, Robert, illus. 2008. (ENG., Illus.). 10p. (J). (gr. 1-4). 17.99 (978-0-7636-3852-8(8)) Candlewick Pr.
Disney Editions, creator. Birnbaum's Disney Cruise Line 2006. (Birnbaum's Disney Cruise Line Ser.). (ENG., Illus.). 224p. (gr. -1-17). per. 13.95 (978-1-4231-0052-2(2), Disney Editions) Disney Pr.
Domiano, Gloria. Ship Shapes: Identify & Describe Shapes. 2013. (Rosen Math Readers Ser.). (ENG.). 16p. (J). (gr. k-1). pap. 42.00 (978-1-4777-1666-3(1)); (Illus.). pap. 7.00 (978-1-4777-1665-6(3)) Rosen Publishing Group, Inc., The. (Rosen Classroom).
Editors of Kingfisher. Spectacular Ships. 2016. (It's All About... Ser.). (ENG.). 32p. pap. 5.99 (978-0-7534-7289-7(9), 9780753472897, Kingfisher) Roaring Brook Pr.
Ellis, Catherine. Ships. (Mega Military Machines Ser.). 24p. 2009. (gr. 1-1). 42.50 (978-1-61514-637-6(7), PowerKids Pr.) 2007. (Illus.). (J). (gr. 3-7). lib. bdg. 22.60 (978-1-4042-3668-4(6)) Rosen Publishing Group, Inc., The.
—Ships/Barcos. 2009. (Mega Military Machines/Megamaquinas militares Ser.). (SPA.). 24p. (gr. 1-1). 42.50 (978-1-61514-642-0(3), Editorial Buenas Letras) Rosen Publishing Group, Inc., The.
—Ships/Barcos. Brusca, Maria Cristina, tr. 2007. (Mega Military Machines / Megamaquinas Militares Ser.). (Illus.). 24p. (J). lib. bdg. 22.60 (978-1-4042-7623-9(8), PowerKids Pr.) Rosen Publishing Group, Inc., The.
Famighetti, Robert, et al. Why Do Ships Float? 2009. (Science in the Real World Ser.). (Illus.). 32p. (gr. 4-6). 28.00 (978-1-60413-466-7(6), Chelsea Clubhouse) Facts On File, Inc.
Farndon, John. Stickmen's Guide to Watercraft. Paul de Quay, John, illus. 2016. (Stickmen's Guides to How Everything Works). (ENG.). 32p. (J). (gr. 3-6). 30.65 (978-1-5124-0699-3(6)); 30.65 (978-1-4677-9594-4(1)) Lerner Publishing Group.
Fein, Eric. The USS Greeneville Submarine Disaster. 2009. (When Disaster Strikes! Ser.). 48p. (gr. 5-8). 53.00 (978-1-60854-783-8(3), Rosen Reference) Rosen Publishing Group, Inc., The.
Flammang, James M. Cargo Ships. 2008. (21st Century Skills Innovation Library: Innovation in Transportation Ser.). (ENG.,

Illus.). 32p. (gr. 4-8). lib. bdg. 28.50 (978-1-60279-233-3(X), 200163) Cherry Lake Publishing.
Gamble, Adam & Jasper, Mark. Good Night Boats. Veno, Joe, illus. 2016. (Good Night Our World Ser.). (ENG.). 20p. (J). (— 1). bds. 9.95 (978-1-60219-500-4(5)) Good Night Bks.
Goldish, Meish. Marine Firefighters. 2014. (Fire Fight! the Bravest Ser.). 32p. (J). (gr. 2-7). lib. bdg. 26.60 (978-1-62724-098-7(5)) Bearport Publishing Co., Inc.
Gould, Jane H. The Flying Dutchman. 2014. (Jr. Graphic Ghost Stories Ser.). 24p. (J). (gr. 3-6). lib. bdg. 26.25 (978-1-4777-7088-7(7), PowerKids Pr.) Rosen Publishing Group, Inc., The.
Graham, Ian. On the Water. 2006. (QEB Machines at Work Ser.). (Illus.). 36p. (J). lib. bdg. 16.95 (978-1-59566-190-6(5)) QEB Publishing Inc.
—Ships. (Mighty Machines Ser.). (Illus.). 2009. 31p. (J). (gr. 4-7). pap. 7.95 (978-1-59920-257-0(3)) 2006. 32p. (YA). (gr. 3-6). lib. bdg. 28.50 (978-1-58340-921-3(1)) Black Rabbit Bks.
Granström, Brita. What Mr Darwin Saw. Manning, Mick, illus. 2014. (ENG.). 48p. (J). (gr. 1-4). pap. 9.95 (978-1-84780-107-4(2), Frances Lincoln) Quarto Publishing Group UK GBR. Dist: Hachette Bk. Group.
Green, Cathy, et al. Great Ships on the Great Lakes: A Maritime History. 2013. (ENG., Illus.). 144p. (J). pap. 18.95 (978-0-87020-582-8(X)) Wisconsin Historical Society.
Gunston, Bill Tudor & Parker, Steve. Fasten Your Seatbelt! Mind-Boggling Machines. 2010. (ENG.). 96p. (J). (gr. 2-4). pap. 9.95 (978-1-84696-205-9(6), TickTock Books) Octopus Publishing Group GBR. Dist: Independent Pubs. Group.
Hamilton, John. Pirate Ships & Weapons, 1 vol. 2007. (Pirates Ser.). (ENG., Illus.). 32p. (gr. 4-8). 27.07 (978-1-59928-763-8(3), Abdo & Daughters) ABDO Publishing Co.
Harris, Nicholas. Let's Explore a Pirate Ship. Lee, Brian, illus. 2010. 36p. (J). 13.99 (978-0-8437-1378-7(X)) Hammond World Atlas Corp.
Harrison, Paul. Superboats. 2015. 32p. (gr. 1-5). lib. bdg. 31.35 (978-1-78404-076-5(2)) Arcturus Publishing GBR. Dist: Black Rabbit Bks.
Hawcock, David & Kentley, Eric. The Pop-Up Book of Ships. 2011. (ENG.). 6p. (J). (gr. k-4). 14.98 (978-0-7893-2408-5(3), Rizzoli Universe Promotional Bks.) Rizzoli International Pubns., Inc.
Hickman, Pamela & Taraschi-Carr, Gola. Righting Canada's Wrongs: the Komagata Maru & Canada's Anti-Indian Immigration Policies in the Twentieth Century. 2014. (Righting Canada's Wrongs Ser.). (ENG., Illus.). 104p. (YA). (gr. 8-12). 34.95 (978-1-4594-0437-3(8), 9781459404373) Lorimer, James & Co., Ltd., Pubs. CAN. Dist: Casemate Pubs. & Bk. Distributors, LLC.
Hinton, Kerry. All about Ships. 2016. (Let's Find Out! Ser.). 32p. (J). (gr. 3-2). lib. bdg. 24.45 (978-1-68048-443-4(5)) Rosen Publishing Group, Inc., The.
Hoena, Blake A. & Hoena, B. A. Shackleton & the Lost Antarctic Expedition, 1 vol. Hoover, Dave et al, illus. 2006. (Disasters in History Ser.). (ENG.). 32p. (gr. 3-4). 30.65 (978-0-7368-5482-5(7), Graphic Library) Capstone Press of Coughlan Cos.
Hopkins, Andrea. Viking Longships. 2009. (Viking Library). 24p. (gr. 3-3). 42.50 (978-1-60854-259-8(9), PowerKids Pr.) Rosen Publishing Group, Inc., The.
Hunt, Jilly & Collins UK Staff. Super Boats. 2016. (ENG.). 32p. (J). (gr. 2-3). pap. 8.95 (978-0-00-816381-5(2)) HarperCollins Pubs. Ltd. GBR. Dist: Independent Pubs. Group.
Ipcizade, Catherine. BIG Boats. 2010. (Big Ser.). (ENG.). 24p. (gr. k-1). lib. bdg. 26.65 (978-1-4296-3993-4(8), Pebble Plus) Capstone Press of Coughlan Cos.
Kacer, Kathy. To Hope & Back: The Journey of the St. Louis, 1 vol. 2011. (Holocaust Remembrance Ser.). (ENG., Illus.). 200p. (J). (gr. 6-8). pap. 14.95 (978-1-897187-96-8(3)) Second Story Pr. CAN. Dist: Orca Bk. Pubs. USA.
Kerr, Daisy. Ships. 2015. (Wonderwise Ser.). (Illus.). 32p. (gr. 2-6). 31.35 (978-1-62588-362-9(5)) Black Rabbit Bks.
Key Porter Books Staff. Gymboree on a Pirate Ship. rev. ed. 2007. (ENG., Illus.). 1p. (J). (978-1-55263-921-4(5)) Magma.
Lacey, Minna. Big Book of Big Ships. Chisholm, Jane, ed. 2012. (Big Bks). 16p. (J). ring bd. 14.99 (978-0-7945-3077-8(X), Usborne) EDC Publishing.
Leacock, Elspeth. Exxon Valdez Oil Spill. 2005. (Environmental Disasters Ser.). (Illus.). 112p. (J). (gr. 6-12). 35.00 (978-0-8160-5754-2(0)) Facts On File, Inc.
Let's Look at Boats. 2009. (Let's Go! Ser.). (Illus.). 18p. (J). (gr. -1-k). bds. 12.75 (978-1-60754-417-3(2)) Windmill Bks.
Levy, Janey. At Sea on a Viking Ship: Solving Problems of Length & Weight Using the Four Math Operations. 2009. (PowerMath Ser.). (ENG., Illus.). 24p. (gr. 3-4). pap. 8.25 (978-0-8239-8922-5(4), PowerKids Pr.) Rosen Publishing Group, Inc., The.
Libretto, Ellen V. The General Slocum Steamboat Fire of 1904. 2004. (Tragic Fires Throughout History Ser.). (Illus.). 48p. (J). (gr. 5-8). lib. bdg. 29.25 (978-0-8239-4486-6(7), Rosen Reference) Rosen Publishing Group, Inc., The.
—The General Slocum Steamboat Fire Of 1904. 2009. (Tragic Fires Throughout History Ser.). 48p. (gr. 5-8). 53.00 (978-1-60854-581-0(4), Rosen Reference) Rosen Publishing Group, Inc., The.
Lindeen, Mary. All about Boats, 1 vol. 2011. (Wonder Readers: Social Studies). (ENG.). (gr. -1-2). 20p. lib. bdg. 22.65 (978-1-4296-8639-6(1)); 16p. pap. 35.94 (978-1-4296-8065-3(2)); 32p. pap. 5.99 (978-1-4296-7906-0(9)) Capstone Press of Coughlan Cos. (Wonder Readers).
—Ships. 2007. (Mighty Machines Ser.). (ENG., Illus.). 24p. (J). (gr. k-3). lib. bdg. 25.95 (978-1-60014-060-0(2)) Bellwether Media.
Lusted, Marcia Amidon. Mighty Military Ships, 1 vol. 2014. (Ready for Military Action Ser.). (ENG.). 48p. (gr. 3-6). lib. bdg. 32.79 (978-1-62403-653-8(8)) ABDO Publishing Co.
Margulies, Philip. The Exxon Valdez Oil Spill: When Disaster Strikes! 2005. (When Disaster Strikes! Ser.). (Illus.). 48p. (YA). (gr. 5-8). lib. bdg. 29.25 (978-0-8239-3675-5(9)) Rosen Publishing Group, Inc., The.
Margulies, Phillip. The Exxon Valdez Oil Spill. 2009. (When Disaster Strikes! Ser.). 48p. (gr. 5-8). 53.00 (978-1-60854-780-7(9), Rosen Reference) Rosen Publishing Group, Inc., The.
Martin, Jacqueline Briggs. The Lamp, the Ice, & the Boat Called Fish: Based on a True Story. Krommes, Beth, illus. 2005. (ENG.). 48p. (J). (gr. -1-3). 7.99 (978-0-618-54895-8(5)) Houghton Mifflin Harcourt Publishing Co.
Mason, Conrad. See Inside Ships. King, Colin, illus. 2011. (See Inside Board Books Ser.). 16p. (J). ring bd. 12.99 (978-0-7945-3005-1(2), Usborne) EDC Publishing.
Maynard, Christopher. I Wonder Why Planes Have Wings: And Other Questions about Transportation. 2012. (I Wonder Why Ser.). (ENG., Illus.). 32p. (J). (gr. k-3). pap. 6.99 (978-0-7534-6703-9(8), 9780753467039, Kingfisher) Roaring Brook Pr.
McNab, Chris. Defending the Seas: The Navy. 2017. (J). **(978-1-4222-3763-2(X))** Mason Crest.
Meister, Cari. Ships. 2013. (ENG., Illus.). 24p. (J). lib. bdg. 25.65 (978-1-62031-047-2(3)) Jump! Inc.
Mitton, Tony & Parker, Ant. Busy Boats. 2005. (Amazing Machines Ser.). (ENG., Illus.). 24p. (J). (gr. -1-k). 4.99 (978-0-7534-5916-4(7), 9780753459164, Kingfisher) Roaring Brook Pr.
Molzahn, Arlene Bourgeois. Ships & Boats. 2003. (Transportation & Communication Ser.). (Illus.). 48p. (J). (gr. 1-4). lib. bdg. 25.27 (978-0-7660-2025-2(8)) Enslow Pubs., Inc.
O'Donnell, Liam. Sink or Swim with Pirate Ships. 2017. (Pirates! Ser.). (ENG.). 32p. (gr. 1-3). lib. bdg. 29.99 **(978-1-4109-8704-4(3)**, Read Me!) Heinemann-Raintree.
Oxlade, Chris. Ships & Boats: Sail; Navigation; Radar; Anchor; Keel. 2015. (ENG., Illus.). 64p. (J). (gr. 3-7). 12.99 (978-1-86147-412-4(1), Armadillo) Anness Publishing GBR. Dist: National Bk. Network.
Oxlade, Chris & Farndon, John. Stickmen's Guide to Watercraft. Pyke, Jerry & Quay, John Paul de, illus. 2016. (Stickmen's Guides to How Everything Works). (ENG.). 32p. (J). (gr. 3-6). lib. bdg. 26.65 (978-1-4677-9362-9(0)) Lerner Publishing Group.
Parker, Steve. On the Sea. 2010. (J). 28.50 (978-1-59920-286-0(7)) Black Rabbit Bks.
Parker, Steven. On Water. 2011. (Future Transport Ser.). (Illus.). 32p. (J). (gr. 4). 28.50 (978-1-60870-780-5(6)) Marshall Cavendish Corp.
Peppas, Lynn. Boats on the Water. 2011. (ENG.). 32p. (J). lib. bdg. (978-0-7787-2727-9(0)); (Vehicles on the Move Ser.: No. 13). pap. (978-0-7787-2734-7(3)) Crabtree Publishing Co.
—Piracy. 2013. (ENG.). 48p. (J). (978-0-7787-1103-2(X)); pap. (978-0-7787-1123-0(4)) Crabtree Publishing Co.
Platt, Richard & Biesty, Stephen. Man-of-War. (Illus.). (J). pap. 21.95 (978-0-590-74610-6(3)) Scholastic, Inc.
Rauf, Don & Vescia, Monique. Choose Your Own Career Adventure on a Cruise Ship. 2016. (Bright Futures Press: Choose Your Own Career Adventure Ser.). (ENG., Illus.). 32p. (J). (gr. 4-6). 29.93 (978-1-63471-910-0(7), 208961) Cherry Lake Publishing.
Renaud, Anne. Into the Mist: The Story of the Empress of Ireland. 2010. (ENG., Illus.). 112p. (YA). (gr. 6). pap. 14.99 (978-1-55488-759-0(3)) Dundurn CAN. Dist: Ingram Publisher Services.
Richter, A. Boats that Float: Learning the OA Sound. 2009. (PowerPhonics Ser.). 24p. (gr. 1-1). 39.90 (978-1-60851-435-9(8), PowerKids Pr.) Rosen Publishing Group, Inc., The.
Ring, Susan. Boats, Boats, Boats. 2005. (Yellow Umbrella Fluent Level Ser.). (ENG., Illus.). 16p. (gr. k-1). pap. 35.70 (978-0-7368-5309-5(X), Yellow Umbrella Bks.) Capstone Press of Coughlan Cos.
Sandler, Martin W. The Impossible Rescue: The True Story of an Amazing Arctic Adventure. 2014. (ENG.). 176p. (J). (gr. 5). pap. 15.99 (978-0-7636-7093-1(6)) Candlewick Pr.
Sandy Creek (Firm) Staff, contrib. by. Liners & Merchant Ships. 2014. (Illus.). 48p. (J). (978-1-4351-5369-1(3)) Barnes & Noble, Inc.
Scarry, Richard. Richard Scarry's Boats. Scarry, Richard, illus. 2015. (ENG., Illus.). 24p. (J). (— 1). bds. 4.99 (978-0-385-39269-3(9), Golden Bks.) Random Hse. Children's Bks.
Scher, Linda. The Texas City Disaster. 2007. (Code Red Ser.). (Illus.). 32p. (YA). (gr. 2-5). lib. bdg. 25.27 (978-1-59716-363-7(5)) Bearport Publishing Co., Inc.
Schuh, Mari. Ships. 2017. (Transportation Ser.). (ENG.). 24p. (gr. k-1). pap. 6.95 **(978-1-5157-7307-8(8)**, Pebble Bks.) Capstone Press of Coughlan Cos.
Ships. (Make it Work Ser.). 42p. (J). (gr. 4-8). pap. (978-1-882210-50-3(6)) Action Publishing, Inc.
Ships: Level N, 6 vols. (Wonder Worldtm Ser.). 48p. 34.95 (978-0-7802-2030-0(7)) Wright Group/McGraw-Hill.
Smith, Steven Michael. New Carissa: The Ship That Refused to Die. 2010. 52p. pap. 22.99 (978-1-4520-6612-7(4)) AuthorHouse.
Stille, Darlene R. Ships, 1 vol. 2004. (Transportation Ser.). (ENG., Illus.). 32p. (gr. 2-3). 21.32 (978-0-7565-0608-7(5), CPB Grades K-3) Compass Point Bks.
Stone, Lynn M. Amphibious Assault Ships. 2005. (Fighting Forces Ser.). (Illus.). 32p. (J). (gr. 4-8). lib. bdg. 28.50 (978-1-59515-460-6(4)) Rourke Educational Media.
Sutherland, Jonathan & Canwell, Diane. Container Ships & Oil Tankers. 2007. (Amazing Ships Ser.). (Illus.). 32p. (gr. 3-6). lib. bdg. 26.00 (978-0-8368-8377-0(2), Gareth Stevens Learning Library) Stevens, Gareth Publishing LLLP.
Tatge, Cathy. Boats. 2007. (My First Look at: Vehicles Ser.). (Illus.). 24p. (J). (gr. -1-3). lib. bdg. 24.25 (978-1-58341-526-9(2), Creative Education) Creative Co., The.
Thomas, Mark. Discoverer Enterprise: La plataforma de perforación más grande del mundo (the Discoverer Enterprise: World's Largest Offshore Drilling Rig) 2009. (Estructuras extraordinarias (Record-Breaking Structures) Ser.). (SPA.). 24p. (gr. 1-2). 42.50 (978-1-61512-310-0(5), Editorial Buenas Letras) Rosen Publishing Group, Inc., The.
—The Discoverer Enterprise: World's Largest Offshore Drilling Rig. 2009. (Record-Breaking Structures Ser.). 24p. (gr. 1-2). 42.50 (978-1-60852-454-9(X), PowerKids Pr.) Rosen Publishing Group, Inc., The.
Tiner, John Hudson. Ships & Boats. (Illus.). 32p. 2004. pap. 8.95 (978-0-89812-390-6(9), Creative Paperbacks) 2003. (J). lib. bdg. 18.95 (978-1-58341-257-2(3), Creative Education) Creative Co., The.
Tomljanovic, Tatiana. Bluenose: Canadian Icons. 2010. (Illus.). 24p. (978-1-77071-576-9(2)); pap. (978-1-77071-583-7(5)) Weigl Educational Pubs. Ltd.
Tripp, Will. Water Adventures. 2005. (Real Deal Ser.). (Illus.). 32p. (J). pap. (978-0-7608-9636-5(4)) Sundance/Newbridge Educational Publishing.
Troupe, Thomas Kingsley. The Pilgrims' Voyage to America: a Fly on the Wall History. Tejido, Jomike, illus. 2017. (Fly on the Wall History Ser.). (ENG.). 32p. (gr. 1-3). lib. bdg. 27.32 (978-1-4795-9786-4(4)) Picture Window Bks.
Tucker, Rosalyn. Pirate Ships. 2015. (Pirates Ahoy! Ser.). (ENG.). 24p. (gr. k-1). lib. bdg. 26.65 (978-1-4914-2113-0(4), Pebble Plus) Capstone Press of Coughlan Cos.
Veitch, Catherine. Big Machines Float!, 1 vol. 2014. (Big Machines Ser.). (ENG.). 24p. (gr. k-1). pap. 3.95 (978-1-4846-0984-2(0)); (Illus.). 23.32 (978-1-4846-0587-5(X)) Heinemann-Raintree. (Heinemann Read & Learn).
Walsh, Alice. Change of Heart, 1 vol. Banks, Erin, illus. 2016. (ENG.). 32p. (J). (gr. -1-4). 19.95 (978-1-77108-371-3(9)) Nimbus Publishing, Ltd. CAN. Dist: Orca Bk. Pubs. USA.
West, David. Ships. 2015. (Mechanic Mike's Machines (continuation) Ser.). (Illus.). 24p. (J). (gr. k-3). 27.10 (978-1-62588-066-6(9)) Black Rabbit Bks.
Wright, Nicola. Ships. 2006. (Illus.). 24p. (YA). (gr. 1-18). lib. bdg. 22.80 (978-1-931983-56-3(9)) Chrysalis Education.
Zimmermann, Karl. Ocean Liners: Crossing & Cruising the Seven Seas. 2008. (ENG., Illus.). 48p. (J). (gr. 4-7). 17.95 (978-1-59078-552-2(5)) Boyds Mills Pr.

SHIPS—FICTION

Arato, Rona. The Ship to Nowhere, 1 vol. 2016. (Holocaust Remembrance Ser.). (ENG.). 144p. (J). (gr. 6-8). pap. 14.95 (978-1-77260-018-6(0)) Second Story Pr. CAN. Dist: Orca Bk. Pubs. USA.
Averill, Esther. Jenny Goes to Sea. Averill, Esther, illus. 2005. (New York Review Children's Collection). (ENG., Illus.). 140p. (J). (gr. k-4). reprint ed. 17.95 (978-1-59017-155-4(1), NYR Children's Collection) New York Review of Bks., Inc., The.
Avi. The True Confessions of Charlotte Doyle. 2012. (ENG.). 240p. (J). (gr. 3-7). pap. 6.99 (978-0-545-47711-6(5), Scholastic Paperbacks) Scholastic, Inc.
—The True Confessions of Charlotte Doyle. 2012. lib. bdg. 17.20 (978-0-606-26779-3(4), Turtleback) Turtleback Bks.
Aviation Staff. Iron Thunder: The Battle Between the Monitor & the Merrimac. 2009. (ENG.). 208p. (J). (gr. 3-7). pap. 7.99 (978-1-4231-0518-3(4)) Hyperion Pr.
Awdry, W. The Lost Ship. Courtney, Richard, illus. 2015. (Step into Reading Ser.). (ENG.). 32p. (J). (gr. -1-1). 3.99 (978-0-553-52171-9(3), Random Hse. Bks. for Young Readers) Random Hse. Children's Bks.
Barton, Bob. Trouble on the Voyage. 2010. (ENG., Illus.). 240p. (J). (gr. 4-7). pap. 10.95 (978-1-926607-10-8(4), Napoleon & Co.) Dundurn CAN. Dist: Ingram Publisher Services.
Base, Graeme. The Legend of the Golden Snail. 2010. (ENG., Illus.). 48p. (J). (gr. k-2). 21.95 (978-0-8109-8965-8(4), Abrams Bks. for Young Readers) Abrams, Inc.
Bell, Loman. Old Glory Faces the Hurricane. Bell, Loman, illus. 2013. (Illus.). 46p. pap. (978-0-9918033-2-3(9)) Wood Islands Prints.
Bentley, Sue. Snowy Wishes. 2013. (Magic Puppy Ser.). lib. bdg. 16.00 (978-0-606-32124-2(1), Turtleback) Turtleback Bks.
Biggs, Brian. Everything Goes - By Sea. Biggs, Brian, illus. 2013. (ENG., Illus.). 56p. (J). (gr. -1-3). 14.99 (978-0-06-195811-3(5)) HarperCollins Pubs.
Boné, Thomas H., illus. The Teacher Who Would Not Retire Retires. 2017. (J). **(978-0-9885295-7-1(2))** Blue Marlin Pubns.
Brown, Corinne. The Stowaway on the Titanic. 2004. 110p. 20.95 (978-0-595-66754-3(6)) iUniverse, Inc.
Bruton, Georgia. Escape. 2012. 210p. pap. 11.95 (978-1-938083-10-5(5)) Silver Knight Publishing, LLC.
Burke, Maria. The Ark of Dun Ruah. 2013. (Ark of Dun Ruah Ser.: 01). (ENG., Illus.). 256p. (J). pap. 23.95 (978-1-85607-794-1(2)) Currach Pr. IRL. Dist: Dufour Editions, Inc.
Butterman, Stephen. Rootbeer Beard. 2012. 74p. pap. 8.95 (978-1-61477-055-8(7)) Bellissima Publishing, LLC.
Carroll, Claudia. Missy Mouse & the Rocket Ship. 2008. 65p. pap. 9.95 (978-0-557-01769-0(6)) Lulu Pr., Inc.
Clark, Joyce. Katie. 2006. 196p. 27.43 (978-1-4122-0067-7(9)) Trafford Publishing.
Coatsworth, Elizabeth Jane. The Fair American. Sewell, Helen, illus. 2005. (Sally (Bethlehem Books) Ser.). 137p. (J). pap. 11.95 (978-1-883937-85-0(X)) Bethlehem Bks.
Collingwood, Harry. The Strange Adventures of Eric Blackburn. 2008. 164p. pap. 13.95 (978-1-60664-210-8(3)) Rodgers, Alan Bks.
Collins, David Paul. Shanghaied. 2011. 320p. 29.95 (978-1-4620-3184-9(6)); pap. 19.95 (978-1-4620-3183-2(8)) iUniverse, Inc.
Costello, David Hyde. Little Pig Saves the Ship. Costello, David Hyde, illus. 2017. (ENG., Illus.). 32p. (J). (gr. -1-2). 14.99 (978-1-58089-715-0(0)) Charlesbridge Publishing, Inc.
Courtauld, Sarah. On a Pirate Ship. Davies, Benji, illus. 2007. (Picture Bks). 24p. (J). (gr. -1-3). 9.99 (978-0-7945-1712-0(9), Usborne) EDC Publishing.
Cummings, Quasheba Giri. The World's First Submarine. 2008. 20p. pap. 15.49 (978-1-4389-1273-8(0)) AuthorHouse.
Danielski, A. The Nick & Austin Chronicles: The Pirate Ship's Magic & a New Home. 2013. 28p. pap. 24.95 (978-1-4626-7709-2(6)) America Star Bks.
Dashner, James. A Mutiny in Time. 2012. (Infinity Ring Ser.: Bk. 1). (ENG.). 192p. (J). (gr. 3-7). 12.99 (978-0-545-38696-8(9)); 16.99 (978-0-545-48321-6(2)) Scholastic, Inc.
David, Christopher. Denholme & the Skeleton Mystery. 2006. 274p. pap. 22.52 (978-1-4120-8014-9(2)) Trafford Publishing.
De la Peña, Matt. The Hunted. 2015. (ENG.). 384p. (YA). (gr. 9). lib. bdg. 20.99 (978-0-375-98992-6(7), Delacorte Pr.) Random Hse. Children's Bks.
—The Living. (ENG.). (YA). (gr. 9). 2015. 336p. pap. 9.99 (978-0-385-74121-7(9), Ember) 2013. 320p. lib. bdg. 20.99 (978-0-375-98991-9(9), Delacorte Pr.) Random Hse. Children's Bks.
Defoe, Daniel. Robinson Crusoe. 2008. (Bring the Classics to Life Ser.). (ENG., Illus.). 72p. (gr. 3-12). pap., act. bk. ed. 10.95 (978-0-931334-30-6(6), EDCTR-301B) EDCON Publishing Group.
Dixon, Franklin W. Ship of Secrets. 2014. (Hardy Boys: Secret Files Ser.: 15). lib. bdg. 14.75 (978-0-606-35781-4(5)) Turtleback Bks.
Fitzgerald, D. M. The True Story of the Big Red Onion. Cudd, Savannah, illus. 2013. 36p. 18.99 (978-0-9890288-7-5(9)); pap. 10.99 (978-0-9890288-5-1(2)) Mindstir Media.
Flanagan, John. Scorpion Mountain. 2014. (Brotherband Chronicles Ser.: 5). (ENG., Illus.). 464p. (J). (gr. 5). 18.99 (978-0-399-16356-2(5), Philomel Bks.) Penguin Publishing Group.
—Scorpion Mountain. 2015. (Brotherband Chronicles Ser.: 5). (ENG.). 480p. (J). (gr. 5). 8.99 (978-0-14-242727-9(6), Puffin Books) Penguin Young Readers Group.
—Scorpion Mountain. 2015. (Brotherband Chronicles Ser.: 5). lib. bdg. 19.65 (978-0-606-37563-4(5)) Turtleback Bks.
—Slaves of Socorro. 2014. (Brotherband Chronicles Ser.: Bk. 4). (ENG., Illus.). 480p. (J). 18.99 (978-0-399-16355-5(7), Philomel Bks.) Penguin Publishing Group.
—Slaves of Socorro. 2015. (Brotherband Chronicles Ser.: 4). (ENG.). 496p. (J). (gr. 5). pap. 8.99 (978-0-14-242726-2(8), Puffin Books) Penguin Young Readers Group.
—Slaves of Socorro. 2015. (Brotherband Chronicles Ser.: 4). lib. bdg. 19.65 (978-0-606-36771-4(3)) Turtleback Bks.
Forward, Toby. The Quayside Cat. Brown, Ruth, illus. 2014. (ENG.). 32p. (J). (gr. -1-3). 16.95 (978-1-4677-3452-3(7)) Lerner Publishing Group.
Fox, Nita. Captain Benjamin Dale. Wallace, Andrea, illus. 2008. 32p. (J). (gr. -1-3). pap. 5.99 (978-0-9816107-0-2(6)) Fox's Den Publishing.
Fredley, Nichole. The Sirius, 1 vol. 2010. 534p. pap. 34.95 (978-1-61582-910-1(5)) America Star Bks.
Friedman, Laurie. Mallory on Board. 2008. pap. 34.95 (978-0-8225-9440-6(4)) Lerner Publishing Group.
Godfrey, Martyn. Mystery in the Frozen Lands, 1 vol. 2nd ed. 2015. (ENG.). 168p. (YA). (gr. 3-8). pap. 12.95 (978-1-4594-0842-5(X), 9781459408425) Lorimer, James & Co., Ltd., Pubs. CAN. Dist: Casemate Pubs. & Bk. Distributors, LLC.
Guest, Jacqueline. Ghost Messages, 1 vol. 2011. (ENG.). 192p. (J). (gr. 4-8). pap. 8.95 (978-1-55050-458-3(4)) Coteau Bks. CAN. Dist: Orca Bk. Pubs. USA.
Gutman, Dan. Flashback Four #2: the Titanic Mission. 2017. (Flashback Four Ser.: 2). 240p. (J). (gr. 3-7). 16.99 (978-0-06-223635-7(0)) HarperCollins Pubs.
Hansen, Andra. The Quest: A Story of a Stow Away, Who Eventually Ends up Owning the Ship. For the Barton Reading & Spelling System. 2003. (J). pap. 7.95 (978-0-9744343-2-2(9), SA-305) Bright Solutions for Dyslexia, LLC.
Havercroft, Elizabeth. A Year on a Pirate Ship. 2009. (Time Goes By Ser.). (ENG.). 24p. (gr. k-3). pap. 6.95 (978-1-58013-799-7(7), First Avenue Editions) Lerner Publishing Group.
Herlong, M. H. The Great Wide Sea. 2010. (ENG.). 288p. (YA). (gr. 7-18). 8.99 (978-0-14-241670-9(3), Puffin Books) Penguin Young Readers Group.
Hofmeister, Alan, et al. The Ship. (Reading for All Learners Ser.). (Illus.). (J). pap. (978-1-56861-133-4(1)) Swift Learning Resources.
Hopkins, William J. The Sandman: His Sea Stories (Yesterday's Classics) Horne, Diantha W., illus. 2009. 188p. pap. 9.95 (978-1-59915-303-2(3)) Yesterday's Classics.
—The Sandman: His Ship Stories (Yesterday's Classics) Horne, Diantha W., illus. 2009. 174p. pap. 9.95 (978-1-59915-302-5(5)) Yesterday's Classics.
Hulme-Cross, Benjamin. Ship of Death. Evergreen, Nelson, illus. 2015. (Dark Hunter Ser.). (ENG.). 64p. (J). (gr. 4-8). pap. 4.99 (978-1-4677-8090-2(1)) Lerner Publishing Group.
Icanberry, Mark. A Pirate's Feast. 2011. (Illus.). 48p. 14.95 (978-1-893327-08-5(6)); pap. 7.95 (978-1-893327-09-2(4)) Ten Speed Pr. (Tricycle Pr.).
Jarman, Julia. Stowaway? Oldroyd, Mark, illus. 2007. (Collins Big Cat Ser.). (ENG.). 48p. (J). (gr. 3-4). pap. 8.99 (978-0-00-723088-4(5)) HarperCollins Pubs. Ltd. GBR. Dist: Independent Pubs. Group.
Johnston, James D. The Adventures of Lucas & Celi: Lucas Stows Away. 2009. 32p. pap. 12.99 (978-1-4343-6372-5(4)) AuthorHouse.
Jones, Rob Lloyd. See Inside Pirate Ships. Muhle, Jorg, illus. 2007. (See Inside Board Bks). 15p. (J). (gr. -1-3). bds. 12.99 (978-0-7945-1601-7(7), Usborne) EDC Publishing.
Keene, Carolyn. Curse of the Arctic Star. 2013. (Nancy Drew Diaries: 1). (ENG.). 208p. (J). (gr. 3-7). pap. 6.99 (978-1-4169-9072-7(0), Aladdin) Simon & Schuster Children's Publishing.
Kellogg, Elijah. The Young Shipbuilders of Elm Island by Rev Elijah Kellogg. 2006. 316p. per. 23.99 (978-1-4255-3063-1(X)) Michigan Publishing.
Kerkow, Larry. Angel Goes to Sea. 2010. 24p. 12.56 (978-1-4269-3490-2(4)) Trafford Publishing.
Kimberly Vogel. Everyone's Price: Book 4 of Rae's Story. 2006. 91p. 20.00 (978-1-4257-1610-3(5)); pap. 10.00 (978-1-4257-1611-0(3)) Xlibris Corp.
Klise, Kate. The Circus Goes to Sea. Klise, M. Sarah, illus. 2014. (Three-Ring Rascals Ser.: Book 3). (ENG.). 160p. (J). 15.95 (978-1-61620-365-8(X), 73365) Algonquin Bks. of Chapel Hill.
Kloepfer, John. The Zombie Chasers - Zombies of the Caribbean. DeGrand, David, illus. 2014. (Zombie Chasers Ser.: 6). (ENG.). 224p. (J). (gr. 3-7). 16.99 (978-0-06-229024-3(X)) HarperCollins Pubs.
Krulik, Nancy. Going Overboard! John and Wendy Staff, illus. 2012. (Katie Kazoo, Switcheroo Ser.: No. 9). (ENG.). 144p. (J). (gr. 2-4). pap. 5.99 (978-0-448-45681-2(8), Grosset & Dunlap) Penguin Young Readers Group.
LaRose, Melinda & Disney Book Group Staff. Bucky Makes a Splash! Disney Storybook Artists Staff, illus. 2013. (ENG.). 16p. (J). (gr. -1-k). pap. 4.99 (978-1-4231-6389-3(3)) Disney Pr.

Lawrence, Iain. The Buccaneers. 2003. (High Seas Trilogy). (Illus.). 244p. (gr. 5-9). 16.50 *(978-0-7569-1454-7(X))* Perfection Learning Corp.

—The Buccaneers. 2003. (ENG., Illus.). 256p. (J). (gr. 3-7). 7.99 *(978-0-440-41671-5(X)*, Yearling) Random Hse. Children's Bks.

Laybourne, Emmy. Sweet. 2015. (ENG.). 288p. (YA). (gr. 8). 17.99 *(978-1-250-05519-4(9))* Feiwel & Friends.

Lee, Brian, illus. A Pirate Ship. 2005. (What's Inside? Ser.). *(978-0-7607-6809-9(9))* backpackbook.

Lefroy, Joy, et al. The Catalpa Escape. 2007. 36p. pap. 13.50 *(978-1-921064-60-9(9))* Fremantle Pr. AUS. Dist: Independent Pubs. Group.

Light, Steve. Boats Go. 2015. (ENG., Illus.). 16p. (J). (gr. -1 — 1). bds. 9.99 *(978-1-4521-2900-6(2))* Chronicle Bks. LLC.

—Swap! Light, Steve, illus. 2016. (ENG., Illus.). 40p. (J). (gr. -1-2). 16.99 *(978-0-7636-7990-3(9))* Candlewick Pr.

Manuel, Lynn. The Summer of the Marco Polo, 1 vol. Charko, Kasia, illus. 2007. (ENG.). 32p. (J). (gr. -1-3). 17.95 *(978-1-55143-330-1(3))* Orca Bk. Pubs. USA.

Mateboer, Hans. Peter the Cruise Ship. 2007. (Illus.). 32p. (J). 16.95 *(978-0-9759487-1-2(7))* Mateboer, Johannes Aart.

—Peter the Cruise Ship - to Alaska. 2007. (Illus.). 32p. (J). 16.95 *(978-0-9759487-2-9(5))* Mateboer, Johannes Aart.

Mattel. Monster High Diaries: Lagoona Blue & the Big Sea Scarecation. 2016. (Monster High Diaries: 3). (ENG.). 160p. (J). (gr. 3-7). 9.99 *(978-0-316-30080-3(2))* Little, Brown Bks. for Young Readers.

McAlister, Hugh. The Flight of the Silver Ship: Around the World Aboard a Giant Dirigible. 2004. reprint ed. pap. 26.95 *(978-1-4179-2616-9(3))* Kessinger Publishing, LLC.

McMullan, Kate. I'm Mighty! McMullan, Jim, illus. 2003. (ENG.). 40p. (J). (gr. -1-3). 17.99 *(978-0-06-009290-0(4))* HarperCollins Pubs.

Metaxas, Eric. The Fool & the Flying Ship, 1 vol. Drescher, Henrick, illus. 2007. (Rabbit Ears: A Classic Tale Ser.). (ENG.). 36p. (gr. -1-3). 25.65 *(978-1-59961-308-6(5))* Spotlight.

Miller, Peggy Reiff. The Seagoing Cowboy. Ewart, Claire, illus. 2016. 39p. (J). *(978-0-87178-212-0(X))* Brethren Pr.

Mireles, Debbie. The Map & the Pirate Ship. 2009. 74p. pap. 19.95 *(978-1-61582-417-5(0))* America Star Bks.

Mitchen, Scott. Will of the Pirates. 2008. 180p. 22.95 *(978-0-595-70652-5(5))* iUniverse, Inc.

Morris, Dudley. Mike the Monk. 2011. 58p. 36.95 *(978-1-258-02967-8(7))* Literary Licensing, LLC.

Mowat, Farley. The Black Joke. 2009. (ENG.). 192p. pap. 9.95 *(978-0-7710-6469-2(1)*, Emblem Editions) McClelland & Stewart CAN. Dist: Random Hse., Inc.

Mulazzi, Paola, et al. Disney Fairies Graphic Novel #4: Tinker Bell to the Rescue. Urbano, Emilio et al, illus. 2010. (Disney Fairies Ser.: 4). (ENG.). 80p. (J). (gr. 1-6). 12.99 *(978-1-59707-230-4(3))*; pap. 7.99 *(978-1-59707-200-7(1)*, 9781597072007) Papercutz.

Naylor, Phyllis Reynolds. Alice on Board. 2012. (Alice Ser.: 24). (ENG., Illus.). 288p. (YA). (gr. 9). 16.99 *(978-1-4424-4588-8(2)*, Atheneum Bks. for Young Readers) Simon & Schuster Children's Publishing.

Neubecker, Robert. Racing the Waves. 2014. (Tales of the Time Dragon Ser.: 2). (ENG.). 32p. (J). (gr. 1-3). 15.99 *(978-0-545-54903-5(5))* Scholastic, Inc.

Newberry, Geoffrey C. The Cape Don Adventure. 2011. 48p. pap. 6.99 *(978-1-61667-262-1(5))* Raider Publishing International.

Nickel, Scott. Blastoff to the Secret Side of the Moon!, 1 vol. Bradley, Jessica, illus. 2013. (Comics Land Ser.). (ENG.). 32p. (gr. k-2). 7.95 *(978-1-4342-4273-0(0))*; lib. bdg. 25.32 *(978-1-4342-4031-6(2))* Stone Arch Bks.

O'Brien, Duncan. Matson the Mouse. Drage, Robyn, illus. 2011. (J). *(978-0-9686734-2-3(2))* Pier 10 Media.

Osborne, Mary Pope. Dark Day in the Deep Sea. 2009. (Magic Tree House Merlin Missions Ser.: 11). lib. bdg. 16.00 *(978-0-606-01778-7(X)*, Turtleback) Turtleback Bks.

Pearson, Ridley. Shell Game. 2013. (Kingdom Keepers Ser.: Bk. 5). (ENG.). 560p. (J). (gr. 5-9). pap. 8.99 *(978-1-4231-7195-9(0))* Hyperion Pr.

—Shell Game. 2013. (Kingdom Keepers Ser.: 5). (J). lib. bdg. 19.65 *(978-0-606-27067-0(1)*, Turtleback) Turtleback Bks.

Pighin, Marcel. Tickles the Bear Goes on a Cruise, 1 bk. Mitchell, Hazel, illus. 2006. 48p. (J). per. 10.49 *(978-0-9776679-7-0(9))* MP2ME Enterprise.

Priddy, Roger. Let's Pretend: My Pirate Ship Sticker Activity Book. 2015. (Let's Pretend Ser.). (ENG.). 72p. (J). (gr. -1-1). pap. 5.99 *(978-0-312-51843-1(9)*, 9780312518431, Priddy Bks.) St. Martin's Pr.

Ransom, Candice. The Life-Saving Adventure of Sam Deal, Shipwreck Rescuer. 2010. pap. 51.02 *(978-0-7613-6918-9(X))* Lerner Publishing Group.

Ransome, Arthur. Swallowdale. 2014. (ENG., Illus.). 464p. (gr. 4-13). 24.95 *(978-1-4683-0956-0(0)*, 460956) Overlook Pr., The.

Reasoner, Charles. Inside Jolly Roger's Pirate Ship. Reasoner, Charles, illus. 2007. (Story Book Ser.), (Illus.). 12p. (J). (gr. k). bds. *(978-1-84666-149-5(8)*, Tide Mill Pr.) Top That! Publishing PLC.

Roddy, Lee. Case of the Dangerous Cruise. 2007. (Ladd Family Adventure Ser.: Vol. 11). (Illus.). 145p. (J). (gr. 3-7). per. 7.99 *(978-0-88062-260-8(1))* Mott Media.

Roots, Arleen. Except Ye Abide in the Ship. 2013. 32p. pap. 12.79 *(978-1-4251-6752-3(7))* Trafford Publishing.

Rothwell, Barbara Yates. The Boy from the Hulks. 2011. 264p. (gr. 4-6). 27.08 *(978-1-4269-9414-2(1))*; pap. 17.08 *(978-1-4269-9415-9(X))* Trafford Publishing.

Roy, Philip. Eco Warrior. 2015. (ENG., Illus.). 232p. pap. 11.95 *(978-1-55380-347-8(7))* Ronsdale Pr. CAN. Dist: SPD-Small Pr. Distribution.

Sanabria, José. As Time Went By. 2016. (ENG., Illus.). 48p. (J). 18.95 *(978-0-7358-4248-9(5))* North-South Bks., Inc.

Scholastic, Inc. Staff & Easton, Marilyn. All Hands on Deck! 2011. (Lego City Ser.). (ENG.). 32p. (J). (gr. -1-k). pap. 3.99 *(978-0-545-33166-1(8))* Scholastic, Inc.

Schrowang, Irene. Sam & Joey's Pirate Ship Adventure. 2013. 16p. pap. 15.99 *(978-1-4817-0333-8(1))* AuthorHouse.

Shearer, Alex. Sea Legs. 2006. (ENG.). 320p. (J). (gr. 5-9). per. 17.99 *(978-0-689-87144-3(9)*, Simon & Schuster/Paula Wiseman Bks.) Simon & Schuster/Paula Wiseman Bks.

The Ship in a Bottle, 6 vols. (Ragged Island Mysteriestm Ser.). 161p. (gr. 5-7). 42.50 *(978-0-322-01648-4(7))* Wright Group/McGraw-Hill.

Shusterman, Neal. Ship Out of Luck. 2014. (ENG.). 320p. (YA). (gr. 7). pap. 7.99 *(978-0-14-242624-1(5)*, Puffin Books) Penguin Young Readers Group.

Sidney, Margaret. Five Little Peppers Abroad. 2008. 212p. per. 14.95 *(978-1-60312-546-8(9))* Aegypan.

Simmons, Jane. Ship's Cat Doris. Simmons, Jane, illus. 2011. (ENG., Illus.). 176p. (J). (gr. k-2). pap. 8.99 *(978-1-4083-0896-7(7))* Hodder & Stoughton GBR. Dist: Hachette Bk. Group.

Smelcer, John. Edge of Nowhere. 2014. (ENG.). 194p. (J). (gr. 6). pap. 9.99 *(978-1-935248-57-6(X))* Leapfrog Pr.

Soto, Gary. Chato Goes Cruisin' Guevara, Susan, illus. 2008. (Chato Ser.). (J). 25.95 incl. audio *(978-1-59519-906-5(3))* Live Oak Media.

—Chato Goes Cruisin' Guevara, Susan, illus. 2007. (Chato Ser.). (J). (gr. -1-3). 14.65 *(978-0-7569-8147-1(6))* Perfection Learning Corp.

Southard, Patricia. Captain Andre's Adventure in the Sky. 2008. 27p. pap. 24.95 *(978-1-4241-8613-6(7))* America Star Bks.

Spradlin, Michael P. Into the Killing Seas. 2015. (ENG.). 224p. (J). (gr. 3-7). 16.99 *(978-0-545-72602-3(6)*, Scholastic Pr.) Scholastic, Inc.

Standish, Burt L. Frank Merriwell's Cruise. Rudman, Jack, ed. 2003. (Frank Merriwell Ser.). (YA). (gr. 9-18). 29.95 *(978-0-8373-9326-1(4))*; pap. 9.95 *(978-0-8373-9026-0(5)*, FM-026) Merriwell, Frank Inc.

Stanley, Robert. Nelly Goes Out to Sea, 1 vol. 2010. 46p. pap. 24.95 *(978-1-4489-8828-0(4))* PublishAmerica, Inc.

Stanmore, Tony. Tide of Chance: A Holiday Adventure. 2010. (Illus.). 60p. pap. 10.49 *(978-1-4520-0650-5(4))* AuthorHouse.

Stewart, Paul & Riddell, Chris. Far-Flung Adventures: Corby Flood. 2012. (Far-Flung Adventures Ser.). (ENG.). 256p. (J). (gr. 3-7). 7.99 *(978-0-385-75097-4(8)*, Yearling) Random Hse. Children's Bks.

—Far-Flung Adventures: Fergus Crane. 2011. (Far-Flung Adventures Ser.). (ENG.). 240p. (J). (gr. 3-7). 7.99 *(978-0-385-75112-4(5)*, Yearling) Random Hse. Children's Bks.

Stuchner, Joan Betty. Bagels on Board, 1 vol. Whamond, Dave, illus. 2015. (Orca Echoes Ser.). (ENG.). 80p. (J). (gr. 2-3). pap. 6.95 *(978-1-4598-0695-5(6))* Orca Bk. Pubs. USA.

Sutton, Laurie S. The Ghost of the Bermuda Triangle, 1 vol. Neely, Scott, illus. 2014. (You Choose Stories: Scooby-Doo Ser.). (ENG.). 112p. (gr. 2-3). 32.65 *(978-1-4342-9126-4(X)*, You Choose Bks.) Capstone Press of Coughlan Cos.

—The Planet Collector, 1 vol. Vecchio, Luciano, illus. 2014. (Superman: Comic Chapter Bks.). (ENG.). 88p. (gr. 3-7). 21.32 *(978-1-4342-9133-2(2))* Stone Arch Bks.

Titelman, Becky. The Wonky Witch & the Witching Well. 2009. 364p. pap. 19.99 *(978-1-4490-2673-8(7))* AuthorHouse.

Turnbull, Samantha. Cruise Control: The Anti-Princess Club 5. Davis, Sarah, illus. 2017. (Anti-Princess Club Ser.: 5). (ENG.). 192p. (J). (gr. 2-4). pap. 9.99 ***(978-1-76029-188-4(9))*** Allen & Unwin AUS. Dist: Independent Pubs. Group.

Tzvieli, Neta. The Private Eyes & the Mysterious Submarine. 2009. 149p. 17.99 *(978-1-59826-286-5(6))* Feldheim Pubs.

Umansky, Kaye. Solomon Snow & the Stolen Jewel. Nash, Scott, illus. 2007. (ENG.). 256p. (J). (gr. 2-5). 12.99 *(978-0-7636-2793-5(3))* Candlewick Pr.

Van Draanen, Wendelin. Sammy Keyes & the Killer Cruise. (Sammy Keyes Ser.). (ENG.). (J). (gr. 5). 2014. 352p. 7.99 *(978-0-307-93062-0(9)*, Yearling) 2013. 336p. 16.99 *(978-0-375-87054-5(7)*, Knopf Bks. for Young Readers) Random Hse. Children's Bks.

Van Dusen, Chris. The Circus Ship. Van Dusen, Chris, illus. (ENG., Illus.). 40p. (J). (gr. -1-3). 2015. 6.99 *(978-0-7636-5592-1(9))* 2009. 16.99 *(978-0-7636-3090-4(X))* Candlewick Pr.

Venable Jr, Al B. Captain Tom, the Sea Adventurer. 2013. 40p. pap. 16.95 *(978-1-63004-037-6(1))* America Star Bks.

Villiers, Alan. Joey Goes to Sea. Dowling, Victor J., illus. 2005. (Maritime Ser.). (ENG.). 70p. (J). (gr. 4-7). pap. 9.95 *(978-0-939511-10-5(X))* Mystic Seaport Museum, Inc.

Weiland, Peter. So Big yet So Small. Coffey, Kevin, illus. 2012. (J). 14.95 *(978-1-937406-16-5(4))* Mascot Bks., Inc.

Wells, Helen. Cherry Ames, Cruise Nurse. 2007. (Cherry Ames Nurse Stories Ser.). 232p. (YA). (gr. 7-12). 14.95 *(978-0-8261-0411-3(8))* Springer Publishing Co., Inc.

Whitney, Kim Ablon. The Other Half of Life. 2010. (ENG.). 256p. (YA). (gr. 7). mass mkt. 7.99 *(978-0-375-84422-5(8)*, Laurel Leaf) Random Hse. Children's Bks.

Wilson, John. Ghosts of James Bay. 2nd ed. 2009. (ENG.). 128p. (J). (gr. 6). pap. 11.99 *(978-1-55002-827-0(8)*, Sandcastle Bks.) Dundurn CAN. Dist: Ingram Publisher Services.

Windham, Ryder. Millennium Falcon. 2010. (Star Wars Ser.). (ENG., Illus.). 24p. (J). (gr. 3-7). bds. 21.99 *(978-0-545-21038-6(0))* Scholastic, Inc.

Wolff, Tracy. Book 4: Arrival. 2016. (Mars Bound Ser.). (ENG.). (J). (gr. 2-8). lib. bdg. 28.50 ***(978-1-62402-200-5(6))*** ABDO Publishing Co.

Yeh, Kat. The Friend Ship. Groenink, Chuck, illus. 2016. (ENG.). 32p. (J). (gr. -1-k). 16.99 *(978-1-4847-0726-5(5))* Disney Pr.

Yomtov, Nelson. Trapped in Antarctica! Nickolas Flux & the Shackleton Expedition. Simmons, Mark, illus. 2015. (Nickolas Flux History Chronicles Ser.). (ENG.). 32p. (gr. 3-4). lib. bdg. 30.65 *(978-1-4914-2069-0(3)*, Graphic Library) Capstone Press of Coughlan Cos.

SHIPS—HISTORY

Beyer, Mark. Barcos del pasado (Boats of the Past) 2009. (transporte ayer y hoy (Transportation Through the Ages) Ser.). (SPA.). 24p. (gr. 1-2). 42.50 *(978-1-61512-253-0(2)*, Editorial Buenas Letras) Rosen Publishing Group, Inc., The.

—Boats of the Past. 2009. (Transportation Through the Ages Ser.). 24p. (gr. 1-1). 42.50 *(978-1-60854-587-2(3)*, PowerKids Pr.) Rosen Publishing Group, Inc., The.

Burns, Phyllis B. Iron Lady at Sea: From Shipyard to Voyage, A Story of the Great Iron-Hulled Sailing Ship, Star of India. 2nd ed. 2003. (Illus.). 112p. (J). pap. 21.95 *(978-0-9620065-0-0(5))* Burns, Phillys.

The Complete History of Ships & Boats: From Sails & Oars to Nuclear-Powered Vessels. 2011. (Transportation & Society Ser.). (ENG.). 192p. (YA). (gr. 10-12). 77.50 *(978-1-61530-770-8(2))* Rosen Publishing Group, Inc., The.

Curley, Robert, ed. The Complete History of Ships & Boats: From Sails & Oars to Nuclear-Powered Vessels. 2011. (Transportation & Society Ser.). (ENG.). 192p. (YA). (gr. 10-12). lib. bdg. 38.75 *(978-1-61530-670-1(6))* Rosen Publishing Group, Inc., The.

Faulkner, Nicholas. A Visual History of Ships & Navigation. 2016. (Visual History of the World Ser.). 00096p. (J). (gr. 8-8). 37.10 *(978-1-4994-6594-5(7))* Rosen Publishing Group, Inc., The.

Ireland, Charles E. Toolbox. Diienno, Trish, illus. 2006. (J). *(978-1-892142-30-6(9))* Cedar Tree Bks.

Janveau, Teri-Lynn & Thompson, Allister. Sailing for Glory: The Story of Captain Angus Walters & the Bluenose. Thompson, Samantha, illus. 2006. (Stories of Canada Ser.: 10). (ENG.). 72p. (J). 18.95 *(978-1-894917-09-4(X)*, Napoleon & Co.) Dundurn CAN. Dist: Ingram Publisher Services.

Kentley, Eric, et al. The Pop-Up Book of Ships. 2009. (ENG., Illus.). 6p. (J). (gr. k-4). 40.00 *(978-0-7893-1862-6(8))* Universe Publishing.

Macdonald, Fiona. You Wouldn't Want to Sail with Christopher Columbus! (Revised Edition) 2014. (You Wouldn't Want to... Ser.). (ENG.). 32p. (J). lib. bdg. 29.00 *(978-0-531-21177-9(0)*, Watts, Franklin) Scholastic Library Publishing.

McCarty, Peter. Jeremy Draws a Monster. McCarty, Peter, illus. 2009. (Jeremy & the Monster Ser.). (ENG., Illus.). 40p. (J). (gr. -1-1). 17.99 *(978-0-8050-6934-1(8)*, 9780805069341, Holt, Henry & Co. Bks. For Young Readers) Holt, Henry & Co.

Morris, Neil. Ships. (Past & Present Ser.). (Illus.). 32p. lib. bdg. 24.25 *(978-1-931983-38-9(0))* Chrysalis Education.

Richardson, Gillian. 10 Ships That Rocked the World. Rosen, Kim, illus. 2015. (World of Tens Ser.). (ENG.). 176p. (J). (gr. 4-7). pap. 14.95 *(978-1-55451-781-7(8)*, 9781554517817) Annick Pr., Ltd. CAN. Dist: Publishers Group West (PGW).

Ships to Forts. Date not set. (Illus.). 32p. (YA). (gr. 6-18). pap. 4.00 *(978-1-890541-16-3(8))* Americana Souvenirs & Gifts.

SHIPS—MODELS

see Ship Models

SHIPS IN ART

Brecke, Nicole & Stockland, Patricia M. Airplanes & Ships You Can Draw. Brecke, Nicole, illus. 2010. (Ready, Set, Draw! Ser.). (ENG., Illus.). 32p. (gr. 2-4). lib. bdg. 25.26 *(978-0-7613-4166-6(8)*, Millbrook Pr.) Lerner Publishing Group.

Curto, Rosa M. Fun & Easy Drawing at Sea. 2013. (Fun & Easy Drawing Ser.). 36p. (J). (gr. k-3). pap. 7.95 *(978-0-7660-6040-1(3)*, Enslow Elementary) Enslow Pubs., Inc.

SHIPWRECKS

see also Salvage; Survival

also names of wrecked ships

Adams, Simon. Titanic. 2014. (DK Eyewitness Bks.). (ENG.). 72p. (J). (gr. 3-7). pap. 9.99 *(978-1-4654-2057-2(6)*, DK Children) Dorling Kindersley Publishing, Inc.

Addario, Yvonne. Treasure Diving with Captain Dom - Special Archival Section: Special Archival Section. 2007. (ENG., Illus.). 56p. (YA). per. 15.99 *(978-0-9743414-1-5(X))* Adventure in Discovery.

Aldridge, Rebecca. The Sinking of the Titanic. 2008. (Great Historic Disasters Ser.). (Illus.). 112p. (gr. 5-8). lib. bdg. 35.00 *(978-0-7910-9643-7(2)*, Chelsea Hse.) Facts On File, Inc.

Benoit, Peter. The Titanic. 2013. (Cornerstones of Freedom™, Third Ser.). (ENG., Illus.). 64p. (J). pap. 8.95 *(978-0-531-21965-2(8))*; lib. bdg. 30.00 *(978-0-531-23607-9(2))* Scholastic Library Publishing.

—The Titanic Disaster. 2011. (J). pap. *(978-0-531-29026-2(3))* Children's Pr., Ltd.

—The Titanic Disaster. 2011. (True Bks.). 48p. (J). (gr. 3-5). 29.00 *(978-0-531-20627-0(0))*; (ENG.). pap. 6.95 *(978-0-531-28996-9(6))* Scholastic Library Publishing. (Children's Pr.).

Bingham, Jane. The Bermuda Triangle, 1 vol. 2013. (Solving Mysteries with Science Ser.). (ENG., Illus.). 48p. (gr. 5-5). pap. 9.95 *(978-1-4109-4991-2(5))* Heinemann-Raintree.

Brook, Henry. True Sea Stories. 2005. (True Adventure Stories Ser.). (Illus.). 154p. (J). (gr. 5). lib. bdg. 12.95 *(978-1-58086-693-4(X))* EDC Publishing.

Brown, Don. All Stations! Distress! April 15, 1912: the Day the Titanic Sank. Brown, Don, illus. 2010. (Actual Times Ser.: 2). (ENG., Illus.). 64p. (J). (gr. 1-5). pap. 8.99 *(978-1-59643-644-2(1)*, 9781596436442) Square Fish.

Burgan, Michael. Titanic: Truth & Rumors. Doty, Eldon, illus. 2010. (Truth & Rumors Ser.). (ENG.). 32p. (gr. 3-4). lib. bdg. 27.99 *(978-1-4296-3951-4(2)*, Edge Bks.) Capstone Press of Coughlan Cos.

Burlingame, Jeff. The Titanic Tragedy. 2011. (Perspectives on 3 Ser.). 112p. (gr. 7). 39.93 *(978-1-60870-450-7(5))* Marshall Cavendish Corp.

Caper, William. Nightmare on the Titanic. 2007. (Code Red Ser.). (Illus.). 32p. (YA). (gr. 2-5). lib. bdg. 25.27 *(978-1-59716-362-0(7))* Bearport Publishing Co., Inc.

Carson, Mary Kay. What Sank the World's Biggest Ship? And Other Questions About... The Titanic. Elliott, Mark, illus. 2012. (Good Question! Ser.). (ENG.). 32p. (J). pap. 5.95 *(978-1-4027-8733-1(2))* Sterling Publishing Co., Inc.

Claybourne, Anna & Daynes, Katie. Titanic. McNee, Ian, illus. 2006. (Usborne Young Reading Ser.). 64p. (J). (gr. 3-7). 8.99 *(978-0-7945-1269-9(0)*, Usborne) EDC Publishing.

Clifford, Barry. Real Pirates: The Untold Story of the Whydah from Slave Ship to Pirate Ship. Manchess, Gregory, illus. Garrett, Kenneth, photos by. 2008. (ENG.). 32p. (J). (gr. 5). 16.95 *(978-1-4263-0279-4(7))*; lib. bdg. 25.90 *(978-1-4263-0280-0(0))* National Geographic Society. (National Geographic Children's Bks.).

Cook, Peter & Salariya, David. Sail on a 19th-Century Whaling Ship! Grisly Tasks You'd Rather Not Do. Antram, David, illus. 2004. (You Wouldn't Want to Ser.). (ENG.). (J). 29.00 *(978-0-531-12356-0(1))* Scholastic Library Publishing.

Cottman, Michael & National Geographic Kids Staff. Shackles from the Deep: Tracing the Path of a Sunken Slave Ship, a Bitter Past, & a Rich Legacy. 2017. (ENG.). 128p. (J). (gr. 5-7). 17.99 *(978-1-4263-2663-9(7)*, National Geographic Children's Bks.) National Geographic Society.

Denenberg, Barry. Titanic Sinks! Experience the Titanic's Doomed Voyage in This Unique Presentation of Fact & Fiction. 2011. (ENG., Illus.). 72p. (J). (gr. 4-7). 19.99 *(978-0-670-01243-5(2)*, Viking Books for Young Readers) Penguin Young Readers Group.

Doeden, Matt. The Sinking of the Titanic, 1 vol. Barnett, Charles, III et al, illus. 2005. (Graphic History Ser.). (ENG.). 32p. (gr. 3-4). 30.65 *(978-0-7368-3834-4(1)*, Graphic Library) Capstone Press of Coughlan Cos.

Dorling Kindersley Publishing Staff. The Story of the Titanic. Noon, Steve, illus. 2012. (ENG.). 48p. (J). (gr. 3-7). 17.99 *(978-0-7566-9171-4(0)*, DK Children) Dorling Kindersley Publishing, Inc.

Dougherty, Terri. The Search for the Titanic: Finding the Ship's Watery Grave, 1 vol. 2014. (Titanic Perspectives Ser.). (ENG.). 48p. (gr. 3-4). 31.99 *(978-1-4914-0418-8(3))* Capstone Press of Coughlan Cos.

Driscoll, Laura. Titanic: The Story Lives On! Kayganich, Bob, illus. 2012. (Penguin Young Readers, Level 4 Ser.). (ENG.). 48p. (J). (gr. 3-4). mass mkt. 3.99 *(978-0-448-45757-4(1)*, Penguin Young Readers) Penguin Young Readers Group.

Dubowski, Mark. DK Readers L3: Titanic: The Disaster That Shocked the World! 2015. (DK Readers Ser.). (ENG., Illus.). 64p. (J). (gr. 2-4). pap. 3.99 *(978-1-4654-2840-0(2)*, DK Children) Dorling Kindersley Publishing, Inc.

Dunn, Joe. The Titanic, 1 vol. 2007. (Graphic History Ser.). (ENG., Illus.). 32p. (gr. 3-6). 28.50 *(978-1-60270-079-6(6)*, Graphic Planet- Nonfiction) ABDO Publishing Co.

Fein, Eric. The USS Greeneville Submarine Disaster. 2009. (When Disaster Strikes! Ser.). 48p. (gr. 5-8). 53.00 *(978-1-60854-783-8(3)*, Rosen Reference) Rosen Publishing Group, Inc., The.

Fullman, Joe. The Story of Titanic for Children. 2016. (ENG., Illus.). 48p. (J). (gr. 3). 17.95 *(978-1-78312-149-6(1))* Carlton Kids GBR. Dist: Sterling Publishing Co., Inc.

Gaetan-Beltran, Daniel. The Titanic. 2015. (Perspectives on Modern World History Ser.). (ENG., Illus.). 224p. (J). (gr. 10-12). 47.80 *(978-0-7377-7310-1(3)*, Greenhaven Pr., Inc.) Cengage Gale.

Ganeri, Anita & West, David. The Sinking of the Titanic & Other Shipwrecks. 2011. (Incredible True Adventures Ser.). (ENG.). 48p. (YA). (gr. 5-8). pap. 11.75 *(978-1-4488-6663-2(4))*; lib. bdg. 29.25 *(978-1-4488-6659-5(6))* Rosen Publishing Group, Inc., The. (Rosen Reference).

Gunderson, Jessica. Your Life as a Cabin Attendant on the Titanic. Dougherty, Rachel, illus. 2012. (Way It Was Ser.). (ENG.). 32p. (gr. 2-3). pap. 8.95 *(978-1-4048-7248-6(5))*; lib. bdg. 26.65 *(978-1-4048-7158-8(6))* Picture Window Bks.

Hamilton, Sue. Air & Sea Mysteries, 1 vol. 2007. (Unsolved Mysteries Ser.). (ENG.). 32p. (gr. 3-7). 27.07 *(978-1-59928-837-6(0)*, Abdo & Daughters) ABDO Publishing Co.

Hawkins, John. Shipwreck Disasters. 2011. (Catastrophe! Ser.). (ENG., Illus.). 48p. (YA). (gr. 5-9). lib. bdg. 29.25 *(978-1-4488-6007-4(5))* Rosen Publishing Group, Inc., The.

Hook. Shipwrecks - Mysteries of the Past. 2004. pap. 48.30 *(978-1-4109-0284-9(6))* Harcourt Schl. Pubs.

Hopkinson, Deborah. Titanic: Voices from the Disaster. (ENG.). 304p. (J). (gr. 3-7). 2014. pap. 7.99 *(978-0-545-11675-6(9)*, Scholastic Paperbacks) 2012. (Illus.). 17.99 *(978-0-545-11674-9(0)*, Scholastic Pr.) Scholastic, Inc.

Houghton, Gillian. The Wreck of the Andrea Gail: Three Days of a Perfect Storm. 2005. (When Disaster Strikes! Ser.). (Illus.). 48p. (J). (gr. 5-8). lib. bdg. 29.25 *(978-0-8239-3677-9(5))* Rosen Publishing Group, Inc., The.

Hunter, Nick. Shipwrecks, 1 vol. 2013. (Treasure Hunters Ser.). (ENG.). 48p. (gr. 5-8). pap. 9.25 *(978-1-4109-4961-5(3))*; lib. bdg. 29.99 *(978-1-4109-4954-7(0))* Heinemann-Raintree.

Jankowski, Susan & Library. True Ocean Rescue Stories. 2010. (True Rescue Stories Ser.). 48p. (J). lib. bdg. 22.60 *(978-0-7660-3665-9(0))* Enslow Pubs., Inc.

Jeffrey, Gary. Spectacular Shipwrecks. 2009. (Graphic Discoveries Ser.). (ENG.). 48p. (YA). (gr. 5-5). 58.50 *(978-1-61512-935-5(9)*, Rosen Reference) Rosen Publishing Group, Inc., The.

—Spectacular Shipwrecks. Saraceni, Claudia, illus. 2008. (Graphic Nonfiction Ser.). (ENG.). 48p. (gr. 3-8). pap. 14.05 *(978-1-4042-9597-1(6))*; (J). (gr. 5-9). lib. bdg. 31.95 *(978-1-4042-1091-2(1))* Rosen Publishing Group, Inc., The.

Jenkins, Martin. Titanic. Sanders, Brian, illus. 2012. (ENG.). 32p. (J). (gr. 3-7). pap. 6.99 *(978-0-7636-6034-5(5))* Candlewick Pr.

—Titanic: Disaster at Sea. 2012. lib. bdg. 17.20 *(978-0-606-23811-3(5)*, Turtleback) Turtleback Bks.

Jenner, Caryn. DK Adventures: Shipwreck: Surviving the Storm. 2015. (DK Adventures Ser.). (ENG., Illus.). 128p. (J). (gr. 3-7). 16.99 *(978-1-4654-3564-4(6)*, DK Children) Dorling Kindersley Publishing, Inc.

Kupperberg, Paul. The Tragedy of the Titanic. 2009. (When Disaster Strikes! Ser.). 48p. (gr. 5-8). 53.00 *(978-1-60854-782-1(5)*, Rosen Reference) Rosen Publishing Group, Inc., The.

—The Tragedy of the Titanic: When Disaster Strikes! 2005. (When Disaster Strikes! Ser.). (Illus.). 48p. (YA). (gr. 5-8). lib. bdg. 29.25 *(978-0-8239-3679-3(1))* Rosen Publishing Group, Inc., The.

Lassieur, Allison. Can You Survive the Titanic? An Interactive Survival Adventure, 1 vol. 2011. (You Choose: Survival Ser.). (ENG.). 112p. (gr. 3-4). pap. 6.95 *(978-1-4296-7351-8(6))*; lib. bdg. 31.99 *(978-1-4296-6586-5(6))* Capstone Press of Coughlan Cos. (You Choose Bks.).

Linnihan, Ellen. Stranded at Sea, 1 vol. unabr. ed. 2012. (Astonishing Headlines Ser.). (ENG.). 92p. (YA). (gr. 9-12). 8.95 *(978-1-61651-926-1(6))* Saddleback Educational Publishing, Inc.

Lusted, Marcia Amidon. The Sinking of the Titanic: A History Perspectives Book. 2013. (Perspectives Library). (ENG., Illus.). 32p. (J). (gr. 4-8). 28.50 *(978-1-62431-421-6(X)*, 202804); pap. 14.21 *(978-1-62431-497-1(X)*, 202806) Cherry Lake Publishing.

MacDonald, Fiona. Shipwrecks. 2010. (Discovery of Life Ser.). 48p. (YA). lib. bdg. 19.95 *(978-1-4222-1527-2(X))* Mason Crest.

Macdonald, Fiona. Shipwrecks. 2015. (100 Facts You Should Know Ser.). (ENG.). 48p. (J). (gr. 4-5). lib. bdg. 31.95 (978-1-4824-2189-7(5)) Stevens, Gareth Publishing LLLP.
Marsh, Nigel. Exploring Shipwrecks. 2016. (ENG., Illus.). 48p. (J). (gr. 3-4). 14.99 (978-1-921580-17-8(8)) New Holland Pubs. Pty, Ltd. AUS. Dist: Midpoint Trade Bks., Inc.
Matsen, Bradford. The Incredible Quest to Find the Titanic. 2003. (Incredible Deep-Sea Adventures Ser.). (Illus.). 48p. (J). lib. bdg. 25.27 (978-0-7660-2191-4(2)) Enslow Pubs., Inc.
—The Incredible Search for the Treasure Ship Atocha. 2003. (Incredible Deep-Sea Adventures Ser.). (Illus.). 48p. (J). lib. bdg. 25.27 (978-0-7660-2193-8(9)) Enslow Pubs., Inc.
McCarthy, Tom. Pirates & Shipwrecks: True Stories. 2016. (Mystery & Mayhem Ser.). (ENG.). 128p. (gr. 3). 19.95 (978-1-61930-471-0(6)) Open City Bks.
McClellan, Ray. The Bermuda Triangle. 2014. (Unexplained Mysteries Ser.). (ENG., Illus.). 24p. (J). (gr. 3-7). lib. bdg. 25.95 (978-1-62617-102-2(5), Epic Bks.) Bellwether Media.
McCollum, Sean. Anatomy of a Shipwreck, 1 vol. (Disasters Ser.). (ENG.). 48p. (gr. 3-4). 2011. pap. 9.95 (978-1-4296-7367-9(2)) 2011. pap. 59.70 (978-1-4296-7368-6(0)) 2010. 31.99 (978-1-4296-4794-6(9)) Capstone Press of Coughlan Cos.
McDonnell, Vincent. Titanic Tragedy. 2007. (ENG.). 160p. (J). (gr. -1-3). per. 12.95 (978-1-905172-41-2(9)) Collins Pr., The IRL. Dist: Dufour Editions, Inc.
McPherson, Stephanie Sammartino. Iceberg, Right Ahead! The Tragedy of the Titanic. (ENG., Illus.). 112p. (gr. 6-12). 2015. 34.65 (978-1-4677-5932-8(5), Lerner Digital) 2011. lib. bdg. 33.26 (978-0-7613-6756-7(X)) Lerner Publishing Group.
Mitchell, Mark. Raising la Belle. Mitchell, Mark, illus. (Professor Wigglestix & the Weather Ser.). (Illus.). 112p. 10.95 (978-1-57168-703-6(3)) Eakin Pr.
Montgomerie, Adrienne. Ghost Ships. 2012. (ENG.). 32p. (J). (978-0-7787-8008-3(2)); pap. (978-0-7787-8013-7(9)) Crabtree Publishing Co.
Mullenbach, Cheryl. Torpedoed! A World War II Story of a Sinking Passenger Ship & Two Children's Survival at Sea. 2017. (ENG.). 176p. (J). (gr. 5). 17.99 **(978-1-61373-824-5(2))** Chicago Review Pr., Inc.
Ohlin, Nancy. The Titanic. Larkum, Adam, illus. 2016. (Blast Back! Ser.). (ENG.). 112p. (J). (gr. 2-5). pap. 5.99 (978-1-4998-0273-3(0)) Little Bee Books Inc.
Otfinoski, Steven. Smooth Sea & a Fighting Chance: The Story of the Sinking of Titanic. 2016. (Tangled History Ser.). (ENG., Illus.). 112p. (gr. 3-4). lib. bdg. 31.99 (978-1-4914-8453-1(5)) Capstone Press of Coughlan Cos.
Owings, Lisa. Ghost Ships. 2015. (Unexplained Mysteries Ser.). (ENG., Illus.). 24p. (J). (gr. 3-7). lib. bdg. 25.95 (978-1-62617-202-9(1), Epic Bks.) Bellwether Media.
Park, Louise. The Sinking of the Titanic. 2013. (Discovery Education: Sensational True Stories Ser.). (ENG., Illus.). 32p. (J). (gr. 3-6). pap. 10.00 (978-1-4777-0099-0(4)); lib. bdg. 25.25 (978-1-4777-0057-0(9)) Rosen Publishing Group, Inc., The. (PowerKids Pr.).
Philbrick, Nathaniel. In the Heart of the Sea (Young Readers Edition) 2015. (ENG., Illus.). 208p. (J). (gr. 3-7). 8.99 (978-1-101-99776-5(1), Puffin Books) Penguin Young Readers Group.
Pipe, Jim. Sail on an Irish Famine Ship! A Trip Across Teh Atlantic You'd Rather Not Make. Antram, David, illus. 2008. (You Wouldn't Want to Ser.). (ENG.). 32p. (J). (gr. 4-7). 29.00 (978-0-531-13913-4(1)) Scholastic Library Publishing.
—You Wouldn't Want to Sail on an Irish Famine Ship! A Trip Across the Atlanic You'd Rather Not Make. Antram, David, illus. 2008. (You Wouldn't Want to...: History of the World Ser.). (ENG.). 32p. (J). (gr. 4-7). pap. 9.95 (978-0-531-14854-9(8), Watts, Franklin) Scholastic Library Publishing.
Porterfield, Jason. Shipwreck: True Stories of Survival. (Survivor Stories Ser.). 48p. (gr. 5-5). 2009. 53.00 (978-1-60853-256-8(9), Rosen Reference) 2006. (Illus.). (YA). lib. bdg. 29.25 (978-1-4042-1000-4(8)) Rosen Publishing Group, Inc., The.
Renaud, Anne. Into the Mist: The Story of the Empress of Ireland. 2010. (ENG., Illus.). 112p. (YA). (gr. 6). pap. 14.99 (978-1-55488-759-0(3)) Dundurn CAN. Dist: Ingram Publisher Services.
Ridley, Frances. Lost at Sea. 2008. (Crabtree Contact Ser.). (ENG., Illus.). 32p. (J). (gr. 3-7). lib. bdg. (978-0-7787-3809-1(4)) Crabtree Publishing Co.
Roland, James. Frightful Ghost Ships. 2017. (Searchlight Books (tm) — Fear Fest Ser.). (ENG.). 32p. (J). (gr. 3-5). pap. 9.99 **(978-1-5124-5605-9(5))**; (Illus.). 30.65 **(978-1-5124-3402-6(7))** Lerner Publishing Group.
Sandler, Martin W. The Whydah: a Pirate Ship Feared, Wrecked, & Found. 2017. (ENG.). 176p. (J). (gr. 5). 19.99 (978-0-7636-8033-6(8)) Candlewick Pr.
Schaefer, Lola M. Tow Trucks in Action. 2012. (Transportation Zone Ser.). (ENG.). 24p. (gr. 1-2). pap. 41.70 (978-1-4296-8396-8(1), First Facts) Capstone Press of Coughlan Cos.
The Science of a Shipwreck. 2014. (21st Century Skills Library: Disaster Science Ser.). (ENG., Illus.). 32p. (J). (gr. 4-8). 28.50 (978-1-63137-627-6(6), 205291) Cherry Lake Publishing.
Shea, Therese. The Sinking of the Titanic. 2015. (Doomed! Ser.). (ENG.). 32p. (J). (gr. 4-5). pap. 10.50 (978-1-4824-2944-2(6)) Stevens, Gareth Publishing LLLP.
Shoulders, Debbie & Shoulders, Michael. T Is for Titanic: A Titanic Alphabet. van Frankenhuyzen, Gijsbert, illus. 2011. (ENG.). 32p. (gr. k-5). 17.95 (978-1-58536-176-2(3)) Sleeping Bear Pr.
Smith, Steven Michael. New Carissa: The Ship That Refused to Die. 2010. 52p. pap. 22.99 (978-1-4520-6612-7(4)) AuthorHouse.
Spence, David & Spence, Susan. A History of Shipwrecks. 2006. (From Past to Present Ser.). (Illus.). 36p. (gr. 3-7). lib. bdg. 26.00 (978-0-8368-6288-1(0), Gareth Stevens Learning Library) Stevens, Gareth Publishing LLLP.
Stewart, David. You Wouldn't Want to Sail on the Titanic! One Voyage You'D Rather Not Make. Antram, David, illus. rev. ed. 2013. (You Wouldn't Want to... Ser.). (ENG.). 40p. (J). pap. 9.95 (978-0-531-24505-7(5), Watts, Franklin) Scholastic Library Publishing.
Stewart, James. Shipwrecks. 2008. (Illus.). 32p. (J). 14.25 (978-1-59920-206-8(9)); (gr. 2-6). lib. bdg. 28.50 (978-1-59920-105-4(4)) Black Rabbit Bks.
Stewart, Melissa. National Geographic Readers: Titanic. 2012. (Readers Ser.). (ENG.). 48p. (J). (gr. 1-4). lib. bdg. 13.90 (978-1-4263-1060-7(9), National Geographic Children's Bks.) National Geographic Society.
Stewart, Melissa & National Geographic Kids Staff. Titanic. 2012. (Readers Ser.). (ENG., Illus.). 48p. (J). (gr. 1-4). pap. 3.99 (978-1-4263-1059-1(5), National Geographic Children's Bks.) National Geographic Society.
Stone, Adam. The Bermuda Triangle. (Illus.). 24p. (J). 2011. (978-0-531-26400-3(9)) 2010. (ENG., (gr. 3-7). lib. bdg. 25.95 (978-1-60014-497-4(7), Torque Bks.) Bellwether Media.
—The Titanic Disaster. 2014. (Disaster Stories Ser.). (ENG.). 24p. (J). (gr. 3-8). 29.95 (978-1-62617-154-1(8), Black Sheep) Bellwether Media.
Temple, Bob. The Titanic: An Interactive History Adventure. 2016. (You Choose: History Ser.). (ENG.). 112p. (gr. 3-4). lib. bdg. 31.99 (978-1-5157-3385-0(8), You Choose Bks.) Capstone Press of Coughlan Cos.
—The Titanic [Scholastic]: An Interactive History Adventure. 2010. (You Choose: History Ser.). 112p. pap. 0.86 (978-1-4296-5119-6(9), You Choose Bks.) Capstone Press of Coughlan Cos.
Thompson, Gare. Civil War Battleship: The Monitor. Day, Larry, illus. 2003. (Penguin Young Readers, Level 4 Ser.). (ENG.). 48p. (J). (gr. 3-4). mass mkt. 3.99 (978-0-448-43245-8(5), Penguin Young Readers) Penguin Young Readers Group.
Tougias, Michael J. & Sherman, Casey. The Finest Hours: The True Story of a Heroic Sea Rescue. 2014. (True Storm Rescues Ser.). (ENG., Illus.). 176p. (YA). (gr. 4-8). 17.99 (978-0-8050-9764-1(3), 9780805097641, Holt, Henry & Co. Bks. For Young Readers) Holt, Henry & Co.
—The Finest Hours: The True Story of a Heroic Sea Rescue. 2015. (ENG., Illus.). 208p. (YA). (gr. 4-8). pap. 7.99 (978-1-250-04423-5(5), 9781250044235) Square Fish.
Walsh, Alice. Change of Heart, 1 vol. Banks, Erin, illus. 2016. (ENG.). 32p. (J). (gr. -1-4). 19.95 (978-1-77108-371-3(9)) Nimbus Publishing, Ltd. CAN. Dist: Orca Bk. Pubs. USA.
Wargin, Kathy-jo. The Edmund Fitzgerald: The Song of the Bell. van Frankenhuyzen, Gijsbert, illus. 2003. (ENG.). 48p. (J). (gr. k-6). 17.95 (978-1-58536-126-7(7)) Sleeping Bear Pr.
Wedge, Hayden. Examining Shipwrecks. 2015. (ENG., Illus.). 48p. (J). lib. bdg. 24.95 net. (978-1-934545-67-6(8)) Oliver Pr., Inc.
Weil, Ann. Sea Disasters, 1 vol. unabr. ed. 2012. (Disasters Ser.). (ENG.). 92p. (YA). (gr. 9-12). 8.95 (978-1-61651-933-9(9)) Saddleback Educational Publishing, Inc.
Welldon, Christine. Children of the Titanic, 1 vol. 2012. (ENG., Illus.). 92p. (J). (gr. 2-4). pap. 14.95 (978-1-55109-892-0(X)) Nimbus Publishing, Ltd. CAN. Dist: Orca Bk. Pubs. USA.
Wick, Walter. Treasure Ship: Picture Puzzles to Search & Solve. Wick, Walter, illus. 2010. (Can You See What I See? Ser.). (ENG., Illus.). 40p. (J). 13.99 (978-0-439-02643-7(1), Cartwheel Bks.) Scholastic, Inc.
Wilkinson, Carole. How to Wreck a Ship. 2007. 96p. (J). pap. (978-1-4207-0737-3(X)) Sundance/Newbridge Educational Publishing.
Wishinsky, Frieda. Remembering the Titanic. 2012. (Scholastic Reader Level 3 Ser.). (ENG.). 32p. (J). (gr. 1-3). pap. 3.99 (978-0-545-35844-6(2), Scholastic Paperbacks) Scholastic, Inc.
Woods, Michael & Woods, Mary B. Disasters at Sea. 2008. (Disasters up Close Ser.). (ENG., Illus.). 64p. (gr. 4-8). lib. bdg. 27.93 (978-0-8225-6773-8(3), Lerner Pubns.) Lerner Publishing Group.
World Book, Inc Staff, contrib. by. The Bermuda Triangle & Other Mysteries of the Deep. 2015. (Illus.). 48p. (J). (978-0-7166-2672-5(1)) World Bk., Inc.
Yasuda, Anita. Sinking of the Titanic, 1 vol. 2013. (History's Greatest Disasters Ser.). (ENG.). 48p. (J). (gr. 3-6). lib. bdg. 32.79 (978-1-61783-960-3(4)) ABDO Publishing Co.
—Sinking of the Titanic Paperback. 2013. (J). 15.64 (978-1-62403-025-3(4), Core Library) ABDO Publishing Co.
Yomtov, Nelson. Adrift & Alone: True Tales of Survival at Sea. 2015. (True Stories of Survival Ser.). (ENG.). 32p. (gr. 3-4). lib. bdg. 30.65 (978-1-4914-6572-1(7)) Capstone Press of Coughlan Cos.
Zullo, Allan. Titanic: Young Survivors. 2015. (Ten True Tales Ser.). (ENG.). 192p. (J). (gr. 3-7). pap. 5.99 (978-0-545-81839-1(7), Scholastic Nonfiction) Scholastic, Inc.

SHIPWRECKS—FICTION

Alger, Horatio. Facing the World. 2006. pap. (978-1-4065-0704-1(0)) Dodo Pr.
Allison, T. A. Noah's Harbour. 2013. 116p. pap. (978-1-78299-579-1(X)) FeedARead.com.
Anton, Amy Way. Ina the Octopus & Her Shipwreck Adventure. Way, MaryFaye, illus. 2008. 28p. pap. 13.99 (978-1-4389-2177-8(2)) AuthorHouse.
Ashley, Bernard. Solitaire. 2012. (Fiction Ser.). 338p. (J). pap. 6.99 (978-0-7945-3031-0(1), Usborne) EDC Publishing.
Autio, Karen. Second Watch, 1 vol. 2005. (ENG., Illus.). 208p. (J). (gr. 3-7). per. 8.95 (978-1-55039-151-0(8)) Sono Nis Pr. CAN. Dist: Orca Bk. Pubs. USA.
Ballantyne, R. The Coral Island. 2006. pap. 14.95 (978-1-55742-666-6(X)) Wildside Pr., LLC.
Ballantyne, R. M. The Young Trawler. 2011. 250p. 27.95 (978-1-4638-9496-2(1)) Rodgers, Alan Bks.
Barnum, P. T. Dick Broadhead: A Story of Perilous Adve. 2006. pap. 30.95 (978-1-4286-1959-3(3)) Kessinger Publishing, LLC.
Bayle, B. J. Perilous Passage. 2007. (ENG.). 184p. (YA). (gr. k-7). pap. 11.99 (978-1-55002-689-4(5), Sandcastle Bks.) Dundurn CAN. Dist: Ingram Publisher Services.
Bingley, Thomas. Tales of Shipwrecks & Other Disasters. 2006. pap. 26.95 (978-1-4286-5637-6(5)) Kessinger Publishing, LLC.
Bodeen, S. A. Found. 2017. (Shipwreck Island Ser.: 4). (ENG.). 160p. (J). 16.99 (978-1-250-02783-2(7), 9781250027832) Feiwel & Friends.
—Lost. 2015. (Shipwreck Island Ser.: 2). (ENG.). 144p. (J). (gr. 5-8). 16.99 (978-1-250-02779-5(9), 9781250027795) Feiwel & Friends.
—Trapped. 2016. (Shipwreck Island Ser.: 3). (ENG.). 160p. (J). 16.99 (978-1-250-02781-8(0), 9781250027818) Feiwel & Friends.
Brezenoff, Steve. Overboard, 1 vol. Murphy, Scott, illus. 2012. (Return to Titanic Ser.). (ENG.). 112p. (gr. 2-3). pap. 6.95 (978-1-4342-3912-9(8)); lib. bdg. 25.32 (978-1-4342-3302-8(2)) Stone Arch Bks. (Return to Titanic).
—Stowaways, 1 vol. Murphy, Scott, illus. 2012. (Return to Titanic Ser.). (ENG.). 112p. (gr. 2-3). pap. 6.95 (978-1-4342-3910-5(1)); lib. bdg. 25.32 (978-1-4342-3300-4(6)) Stone Arch Bks. (Return to Titanic).
—Time Voyage, 1 vol. Murphy, Scott, illus. 2012. (Return to Titanic Ser.). (ENG.). 112p. (gr. 2-3). pap. 6.95 (978-1-4342-3909-9(8)); lib. bdg. 25.32 (978-1-4342-3299-1(9)) Stone Arch Bks. (Return to Titanic).
—An Unsinkable Ship, 1 vol. Murphy, Scott, illus. 2012. (Return to Titanic Ser.). (ENG.). 112p. (gr. 2-3). pap. 6.95 (978-1-4342-3911-2(X)); lib. bdg. 25.32 (978-1-4342-3301-1(4)) Stone Arch Bks. (Return to Titanic).
Bunting, Eve. S. O. S. Titanic. 2012. (ENG.). 256p. (YA). (gr. 7-12). pap. 7.99 (978-0-15-201305-9(9)) Houghton Mifflin Harcourt Publishing Co.
Carbone, Elisa. Heroes of the Surf. Carpenter, Nancy, illus. 2012. (ENG.). 40p. (J). (gr. -1-3). 16.99 (978-0-670-06312-3(6), Viking Books for Young Readers) Penguin Young Readers Group.
Collingwood, Harry. The Castaways. 2008. 172p. 25.95 (978-1-60664-710-3(5)); pap. 13.95 (978-1-60664-209-2(X)) Rodgers, Alan Bks.
Crew, Gary. Pig on the Titanic: A True Story. Whatley, Bruce, illus. 2005. 32p. (J). 15.99 (978-0-06-052305-3(0)) HarperCollins Pubs.
de Brunhoff, Laurent. Babar on Paradise Island. 2014. (ENG., Illus.). 48p. (J). (gr. k-2). 18.95 (978-1-4197-1038-4(9), Abrams Bks. for Young Readers) Abrams, Inc.
Defoe, Daniel. Robinson Crusoe. Cabrera, Eva, illus. 2015. (Graphic Revolve: Common Core Editions Ser.). (ENG.). 72p. (gr. 2-3). lib. bdg. 27.99 (978-1-4965-0371-8(6)) Stone Arch Bks.
—Robinson Crusoe. 2012. 338p. pap. 10.99 (978-1-61382-256-2(1)) Simon & Brown.
—Robinson Crusoe. McKowen, Scott, illus. 2011. (Sterling Unabridged Classics Ser.). (ENG.). 288p. (J). 9.95 (978-1-4027-8406-4(6)) Sterling Publishing Co., Inc.
—Robinson Crusoe. Akib, Jamel, illus. 2006. (Classic Starts(tm) Ser.). (ENG.). 160p. (J). (gr. 2-4). 6.95 (978-1-4027-2664-4(3)) Sterling Publishing Co., Inc.
—Robinson Crusoe: With a Discussion of Resourcefulness. Landgraf, Kenneth, illus. 2003. (Values in Action Illustrated Classics Ser.). 190p. (J). (978-1-59203-035-4(1)) Learning Challenge, Inc.
Defoe, Daniel, et al. Robinson Crusoe: The Complete Story of Robinson Crusoe. (Classics Illustrated Ser.). (Illus.). 52p. (YA). pap. 4.95 (978-1-57209-021-7(9)) Classics International Entertainment, Inc.
Dillsworth-Swift, Tammy. The Bermuda Triangle & the Lost Island. 2009. 182p. pap. 16.53 (978-0-557-14503-4(1)) Lulu Pr., Inc.
DiTerlizzi, Tony, et al. El Arbol Metálico. Abreu, Carlos, tr. 2007. (Escritura desatada Ser.). (SPA., Illus.). 116p. (J). (gr. 4-7). 13.95 (978-84-666-1658-4(6)) Ediciones B ESP. Dist: Spanish Pubs., LLC.
—El Mapa Perdido. 2007. (Escritura desatada Ser.). (SPA., Illus.). 114p. (J). (gr. 4-7). 13.95 (978-84-666-1513-6(X)) Ediciones B ESP. Dist: Spanish Pubs., LLC.
Draper, Penny. Graveyard of the Sea, 1 vol. 2008. (Disaster Strikes! Ser.: 4). (ENG.). 192p. (J). (gr. 4-7). pap. 8.95 (978-1-55050-397-5(9), Coteau Bks. for Kids) Coteau Bks. CAN. Dist: Orca Bk. Pubs. USA.
—Peril at Pier Nine, 1 vol. 2007. (Disaster Strikes! Ser.: 3). (ENG.). 208p. (J). (gr. 4-7). pap. 7.95 (978-1-55050-376-0(6)) Coteau Bks. CAN. Dist: Orca Bk. Pubs. USA.
Duey, Kathleen & Bale, Karen A. Titanic: April 1912. 2014. (Survivors Ser.). (ENG., Illus.). 192p. (J). (gr. 3-7). pap. 7.99 (978-1-4424-9051-2(9), Aladdin) Simon & Schuster Children's Publishing.
—Titanic: April 1912. 2014. (Survivors Ser.). (ENG., Illus.). 192p. (J). (gr. 3-7). 15.99 (978-1-4424-9052-9(7), Simon & Schuster/Paula Wiseman Bks.) Simon & Schuster/Paula Wiseman Bks.
Duplaix, Georges & Golden Books Staff. The Merry Shipwreck. Gergely, Tibor, illus. 2011. (Little Golden Book Ser.). (ENG.). 24p. (J). (gr. -1-2). 4.99 (978-0-375-86800-9(3), Golden Bks.) Random Hse. Children's Bks.
Edwards, Garth. #01 Shipwrecked! Stasyuk, Max, illus. 2011. (Adventures of Titch & Mitch, the Ser.). (J). pap. (978-0-7613-8421-2(9)) Inside Pocket Publishing, Ltd.
Fletcher, Corina. Playbook Pirates. Teckentrup, Britta, illus. 2013. (ENG.). 12p. (J). (gr. -1-2). 24.00 (978-0-7636-6606-4(8), Nosy Crow) Candlewick Pr.
Frazier, Angie. Everlasting. 2010. (ENG.). 336p. (J). (gr. 7-18). 17.99 (978-0-545-11473-8(X), Scholastic Pr.) Scholastic, Inc.
Frolick, Billy. Madagascar. Golden Books, illus. 2017. (Little Golden Book Ser.). (ENG.). 24p. (J). (-k). 4.99 **(978-1-5247-6768-6(9)**, Golden Bks.) Random Hse. Children's Bks.
Garis, Howard Roger. Lulu, Alice & Jammie Wibble Wobble. 2005. 152p. pap. 11.95 (978-1-4218-1564-0(8), 1st World Library - Literary Society) 1st World Publishing, Inc.
—Lulu, Alice & Jimmie Wibblewobble. 2005. 26.95 (978-1-4218-1464-3(1), 1st World Library - Literary Society) 1st World Publishing, Inc.
Hope, Laura Lee. Moving Picture Girls at Sea. 2006. 26.95 (978-1-4218-2979-1(7)); pap. 11.95 (978-1-4218-3079-7(5)) 1st World Publishing, Inc.
—The Moving Picture Girls at Sea: Or A Pictured Shipwreck That Became Real. l.t. ed. 2007. (ENG.). 154p. pap. 21.99 (978-1-4264-9792-6(X)) Creative Media Partners, LLC.
—Moving Picture Girls under the Palms. 2006. 26.95 (978-1-4218-2980-7(0)); pap. 11.95 (978-1-4218-3080-3(9)) 1st World Publishing, Inc.
Hunt, Elizabeth Singer. The Search for the Sunken Treasure Bk. 2: Australia. 2007. (Illus.). 110p. (J). (978-1-4242-4190-3(1), Weinstein Bks.) Perseus Bks. Group.
Johnson, Sandi. Lost Island. Johnson, Britt & Durant, Sybrina, eds. Sturgeon, Bobbi, illus. l.t. ed. 2014. 28p. (J). (gr. k-5). pap. 12.99 (978-1-929063-69-7(5), 168) Moons & Stars Publishing For Children.
Jolley, Dan. Shipwrecked on Mad Island. Huddleston, Courtney, illus. 2009. (Twisted Journeys (r) Ser.: 11). (ENG.). 112p. (J). (gr. 4-7). pap. 7.95 (978-0-8225-8875-7(7), Carolrhoda Bks.);No. 11. 27.93 (978-0-8225-7911-3(1), Graphic Universe™) Lerner Publishing Group.
Kimmel, Eric A. & Trueman, Matthew. Simon & the Bear: A Hanukkah Tale. 2014. (ENG., Illus.). 40p. (J). (gr. -1-k). 16.99 (978-1-4231-4355-0(8)) Hyperion Bks. for Children.
Kingston, William Henry Giles, tr. The Swiss Family Robinson. Wyss, Johann David, illus. 2005. 188p. per. 6.95 (978-1-4209-2269-1(6)) Digireads.com Publishing.
Korman, Gordon. Collision Course, Bk. 2. 2011. (Titanic Ser.: 2). (ENG.). 160p. (J). (gr. 3-7). pap. 6.99 (978-0-545-12332-7(1), Scholastic Paperbacks) Scholastic, Inc.
—Escape. 2008. (Island (Playaway Audio) Ser.). (J). 34.99 (978-1-60514-854-0(7)) Findaway World, LLC.
—Island Trilogy. 2005. 404p. (YA). pap. (978-0-681-15634-0(1)) Scholastic, Inc.
—Unsinkable, Bk. 1. 2011. (Titanic Ser.: 1). (ENG.). 160p. (J). (gr. 3-7). pap. 6.99 (978-0-545-12331-0(3), Scholastic Paperbacks) Scholastic, Inc.
Kositsky, Lynne. Minerva's Voyage. 2009. (ENG., Illus.). 240p. (YA). (gr. 6-18). pap. 10.99 (978-1-55488-439-1(X), Dundurn Pr.) Dundurn CAN. Dist: Ingram Publisher Services.
Law, Felicia & Way, Steve. A Storm at Sea: Sorting, Mapping, & Grids in Action. Spoor, Mike & Mostyn, David, illus. 2010. (Mandrill Mountain Math Mysteries Ser.). 32p. (J). (gr. 2-6). 22.60 (978-1-60754-815-7(1)); pap. 10.55 (978-1-60754-820-1(8)) Windmill Bks.
Maddox, Jake. Shipwreck! Tiffany, Sean, illus. 2009. (Jake Maddox Sports Stories Ser.). (ENG.). 72p. (gr. 2-3). 25.32 (978-1-4342-1207-8(6)) Stone Arch Bks.
Manuel, Lynn. The Summer of the Marco Polo, 1 vol. Charko, Kasia, illus. 2007. (ENG.). 32p. (J). (gr. -1-3). 17.95 (978-1-55143-330-1(3)) Orca Bk. Pubs. USA.
Marsh, Carole. The Mystery of the Graveyard of the Atlantic. 2009. (Real Kids, Real Places Ser.). (Illus.). 144p. (J). lib. bdg. 18.99 (978-0-635-07046-3(4), Marsh, Carole Mysteries) Gallopade International.
—The Mystery on the Great Lakes. 2010. (Real Kids, Real Places Ser.). (Illus.). 158p. (J). 18.99 (978-0-635-07449-2(4), Marsh, Carole Mysteries) Gallopade International.
Marsh, Mike. The Efelant Hunters Part One: Shipwreck! Jain, Priti, illus. 2013. 28p. pap. (978-1-927506-21-9(2)) Yellow Toadstool Pr.
McDavid-Jones, Elizabeth. Ghost Light on Graveyard Shoal. 2009. (Mysteries Through Time Ser.). 144 - 176p. (YA). (gr. 4-8). 31.95 (978-1-60754-443-2(1)); pap. 15.25 (978-1-60754-444-9(X)) Windmill Bks.
McDonald, John. The Tempest: The Graphic Novel. Gale Editor, ed. 2011. (Classic Graphic Novel Collection). (ENG.). 160p. (gr. 7-10). lib. bdg. 39.40 (978-1-4205-0632-7(3)) Cengage Gale.
McKain, Kelly. The Haunted Shipwreck. Johansson, Cecilia, illus. 2004. (Mermaid Rock Ser.). 48p. (J). (978-0-439-62647-7(1)) Scholastic, Inc.
McKenzie, Lyn. Lavinia's Shoes. 2007. (J). pap. 12.95 (978-0-9788628-5-5(6)) Just Write Bks.
McMann, Lisa. Island of Shipwrecks. 2015. (Unwanteds Ser.: 5). (ENG., Illus.). 480p. (J). (gr. 3-7). pap. 8.99 (978-1-4424-9332-2(1), Aladdin) Simon & Schuster Children's Publishing.
McMullan, Kate. Revenge of the Dragon Lady, 1 vol. Basso, Bill, illus. 2007. (Dragon Slayers' Academy Ser.: No. 2). (ENG.). 109p. (gr. -1-3). 24.21 (978-1-59961-378-9(6)) Spotlight.
Millet, Lydia. The Fires Beneath the Sea. 2012. (Dissenters Ser.). (ENG.). 256p. (J). (gr. 3-7). pap. 12.00 (978-1-931520-47-8(X), Big Mouth Hse.) Small Beer Pr.
Osborne, Mary Pope. Tonight on the Titanic. unabr. ed. 2004. (Magic Tree House Ser.: No. 17). 71p. (J). (gr. k-3). pap. 17.00 incl. audio (978-0-8072-0926-4(0), S FTR 249 SP, Listening Library) Random Hse. Audio Publishing Group.
Osborne, Mary Pope & Murdocca, Sal. Esta Noche en el Titanic. Murdocca, Sal, illus. 2008. (Casa del Arbol Ser.: 17).Tr. of Tonight on the Titanic. (SPA., Illus.). (J). (gr. 2-4). pap. 5.99 (978-1-933032-47-4(2)) Lectorum Pubns., Inc.
Phillips, Dee. Titanic. 2014. (Yesterday's Voices Ser.). (YA). lib. bdg. 19.60 (978-0-606-35583-4(9)) Turtleback Bks.
Prager, Ellen. The Shark Whisperer. Caparo, Antonio Javier, illus. 2014. (Tristan Hunt & the Sea Guardians Ser.). (ENG.). 288p. (J). (gr. 3-7). pap. 9.95 (978-1-938063-44-2(9), Mighty Media Junior Readers) Mighty Media Pr.
Prins, Piet. Stefan Derksen's Polar Adventure. 2004. (Illus.). 237p. (J). pap. (978-1-894666-67-1(4)) Inheritance Pubns.
Probst, Jeff & Tebbetts, Chris. Stranded. 2013. (Stranded Ser.: 1). (ENG.). 208p. (J). (gr. 3-7). pap. 6.99 (978-0-14-242424-7(2), Puffin Books) Penguin Young Readers Group.
—Stranded. 2013. (Stranded Ser.: 1). lib. bdg. 17.20 (978-0-606-36788-2(8)) Turtleback Bks.
—Trial by Fire. 2013. (Stranded Ser.: 2). (ENG.). 192p. (J). (gr. 3). pap. 6.99 (978-0-14-242425-4(0), Puffin Books) Penguin Publishing Group.
Probst, Jeff & Tebbetts, Christopher. Desperate Measures. 2016. (Stranded, Shadow Island Ser.: 3). lib. bdg. 17.20 (978-0-606-37562-7(7)) Turtleback Bks.
—The Sabotage. 2015. (Stranded Ser.: 5). (ENG.). 224p. (J). (gr. 3-7). 6.99 (978-0-14-751389-2(8), Puffin Books) Penguin Young Readers Group.
—Trial by Fire. 2013. 174p. (J). (978-0-14-751195-9(X)) Penguin Publishing Group.
R. M. Ballantyne. The Coral Island. 2007. 316p. per. 14.95 (978-1-4218-4004-8(9), 1st World Library - Literary Society) 1st World Publishing, Inc.
Ransom, Candice. The Life-Saving Adventure of Sam Deal, Shipwreck Rescuer. Trover, Zachary, illus. 2010. (History's Kid Heroes Ser.). (ENG.). 32p. (gr. 3-5). pap. 8.95 (978-0-7613-6196-1(0), Graphic Universe™); lib. bdg. 26.60 (978-0-7613-6177-0(4)) Lerner Publishing Group.

S

Ransome, Arthur. Swallowdale. Ransome, Arthur, illus. 2010. (Swallows & Amazons Ser.). (Illus.). 431p. (YA). pap. 14.95 (978-1-56792-421-3(2)) Godine, David R. Pub.

Raver-Lampman, Greg. Adrift: Lost in Life, Marooned at Sea. 2006. 132p. 14.95 (978-1-888842-32-6(6)) Absey & Co.

Reilly, Carmel, et al. Shipwreck. 2008. (Rigby Focus Forward: Level O Ser.). (Illus.). 24p. (J). (gr. 4-7). pap. (978-1-4190-3850-1(8), Rigby) Pearson Education Australia.

Romeu, Emma. Naufragio en las Filipinas. 2003.Tr. of Shipwrecked in the Philippines. (SPA., Illus.). 162p. (J). (gr. 5-8). pap. 9.95 (978-968-19-0555-2(5)) Santillana USA Publishing Co., Inc.

Ruiz Zafón, Carlos. The Prince of Mist. 2011. (ENG.). 256p. (YA). (gr. 7-17). pap., pap. 10.99 (978-0-316-04480-6(6)) Little, Brown Bks. for Young Readers.

Saddleback Educational Publishing Staff, ed. River, 1 vol. unabr. ed. 2011. (Heights Ser.). (ENG.). 49p. (gr. 5-8). pap. 7.95 (978-1-61651-281-1(4)) Saddleback Educational Publishing, Inc.

Shipwrecked!, 6 vols., Pack. (Bookweb Ser.). 32p. (gr. 4-18). 34.00 (978-0-7635-3736-4(5)) Rigby Education.

Slade, Arthur G. The Dark Deeps. 2011. (Hunchback Assignments Ser.: Vol. 2). (ENG.). 320p. (YA). (gr. 7). pap. 9.99 (978-0-375-85404-0(5), Ember) Random Hse. Children's Bks.

Specter, Baron. The Spooky Short Sands Shipwreck: #4, 1 vol. Evans, Dustin, illus. 2010. (Ghostly Graphic Adventures Ser.). (ENG.). 32p. (J). (gr. 3-6). 28.50 (978-1-60270-773-3(1)) ABDO Publishing Co.

Spickett, D. M. The Adventures of Sarah the Seahorse, 1 vol. 2009. 21p. pap. 24.95 (978-1-61546-205-6(8)) America Star Bks.

Stewart, Whitney. Marshall: A Nantucket Sea Rescue. Lyall, Dennis, illus. 2008. (ENG.). 32p. (J). (gr. -1-2). 10.95 (978-1-59249-857-4(4)); 6.95 (978-1-59249-855-0(8)); 2.95 (978-1-59249-856-7(6)) Soundprints.

—Marshall, the Sea Dog. 2010. (ENG.). 56p. (J). (gr. 4-7). 17.95 (978-1-60727-183-3(4)) Soundprints.

Stilton, Geronimo. Cavemice: Surfing for Secrets. 2015. (Geronimo Stilton Cavemice Ser.: 8). (ENG., Illus.). 128p. (J). (gr. 2-5). pap. 7.99 (978-0-545-74617-5(5), Scholastic Paperbacks) Scholastic, Inc.

Stilton, Geronimo & Stilton, Thea. Thea Stilton & the Ghost of the Shipwreck. 2010. (Thea Stilton Ser.: 3). (ENG., Illus.). 176p. (J). (gr. 2-5). mass mkt. 8.99 (978-0-545-15059-0(0), Scholastic Paperbacks) Scholastic, Inc.

—Thea Stilton & the Ghost of the Shipwreck. 2010. (Thea Stilton Ser.: 3). lib. bdg. 19.65 (978-0-606-06843-7(0), Turtleback) Turtleback Bks.

Stilton, Thea. The Journey to Atlantis. 2012. (Thea Stilton Special Edition Ser.). (ENG.). 320p. (J). (gr. 2-5). 14.99 (978-0-545-44020-2(3), Scholastic Paperbacks) Scholastic, Inc.

Swift, Jonathan. Los Viajes de Gulliver. (SPA., Illus.). 144p. (YA). 14.95 (978-84-7281-080-8(1), AF1080) Auriga, Ediciones S.A. ESP. Dist: Continental Bk. Co., Inc.

—Los Viajes de Gulliver. (Coleccion Clasicos de la Juventud). (SPA., Illus.). 204p. (J). 12.95 (978-84-7189-062-7(3), ORT322) Ortells, Alfredo Editorial S.L. ESP. Dist: Continental Bk. Co., Inc.

Tarshis, Lauren. I Survived the Sinking of the Titanic 1912. 2010. (I Survived Ser.: 1). (ENG., Illus.). 112p. (J). (gr. 2-5). 4.99 (978-0-545-20694-5(4), Scholastic Paperbacks) Scholastic, Inc.

—I Survived the Sinking of the Titanic 1912. 2010. (I Survived . Ser.: No. 1). lib. bdg. 14.75 (978-0-606-23741-3(0), Turtleback) Turtleback Bks.

Taylor, Theodore. The Cay. 2003. (ENG.). 160p. (J). (gr. 5-7). mass mkt. 6.99 (978-0-440-22912-4(X), Laurel Leaf) Random Hse. Children's Bks.

—Teetoncey. 2004. (ENG., Illus.). 228p. (J). (gr. 2-5). pap. 13.95 (978-0-15-205294-2(1)) Houghton Mifflin Harcourt Publishing Co.

—Teetoncey & Ben O'Neal. 2004. (ENG., Illus.). 240p. (J). (gr. 2-5). pap. 15.95 (978-0-15-205297-3(6)) Houghton Mifflin Harcourt Publishing Co.

—Timothy of the Cay. 2007. (ENG., Illus.). 176p. (J). (gr. 5-7). pap. 6.99 (978-0-15-206320-7(X)) Houghton Mifflin Harcourt Publishing Co.

Taylor, Theodore & Taylor, Theodore. The Cay. 2003. (gr. 5-8). lib. bdg. 17.20 (978-0-613-72282-7(5), Turtleback) Turtleback Bks.

Tharp, Jason. Monsta Doodle, Bk. 1. 2016. (Super Monsta Friends Ser.: 2). (ENG.). 128p. (J). (gr. 2-5). pap. 12.99 (978-0-545-83964-8(5)) Scholastic, Inc.

Thompson, Paul B. Lost Republic. 2014. 256p. (YA). (gr. 6-12). 19.95 (978-1-62324-000-4(X)) Enslow Pubs., Inc.

Trimper, Marty. Hermione: Shipwrecked! in Ocean City, Maryland. Amy, Holloway, illus. 2004. (J). (978-1-886068-28-5(3)) Fruitbearer Publishing, LLC.

Van Dusen, Chris. The Circus Ship. Van Dusen, Chris, illus. 2015. (ENG., Illus.). 40p. (J). (gr. -1-3). 6.99 (978-0-7636-5592-1(9)) Candlewick Pr.

—The Circus Ship Big Book. 2011. (ENG., Illus.). 40p. (J). (gr. -1-3). pap. 24.99 (978-0-7636-5593-8(7)) Candlewick Pr.

Verne, Jules. Dick Sand. Munro, George, tr. 2008. 296p. pap. 15.95 (978-1-60664-253-5(7)) Rodgers, Alan Bks.

Vicary, Tim. Grace Darling. Oxford University Press Staff & Bassett, Jennifer, eds. 3rd ed. 2008. (ENG., Illus.). 64p. 10.00 (978-0-19-479061-1(4)) Oxford Univ. Pr., Inc.

Wade, Judith. The Mermaid's Gift. 2004. 140p. (J). per. 5.99 (978-0-9728958-1-1(7), 750) Riley Pr.

Walsh, Alice. Heroes of Isle aux Morts. 2004. (J). (gr. k-3). spiral bd. (978-0-616-11139-0(8)); spiral bd. (978-0-616-11138-3(X)) Canadian National Institute for the Blind/Institut National Canadien pour les Aveugles.

Wells, H. G. The Island of Dr Moreau. 2007. (ENG., Illus.). 64p. (C). pap. 11.99 (978-1-4058-4999-9(1)) Pearson Education.

White, Ellen Emerson. Voyage on the Great Titanic. 2010. (Dear America Ser.). (ENG., Illus.). 208p. (J). (gr. 3-7). 12.99 (978-0-545-23834-2(X), Scholastic Pr.) Scholastic, Inc.

Wilkes, Angela & Rawson, Christopher. Robinson Crusoe. 2004. (Young Reading Ser.). (Illus.). 64p. (J). (gr. 2-18). pap. 5.95 (978-0-7945-0410-6(8), Usborne) EDC Publishing.

Wilkinson, Carole. Buried at Sea. 2007. 96p. (YA). pap. (978-1-4207-0738-0(8)) Sundance/Newbridge Educational Publishing.

Wyss, Johann David. The Swiss Family Robinson. 2007. (Aladdin Classics Ser.). (ENG.). 576p. (J). (gr. 3-7). pap. 7.99 (978-1-4169-3490-5(1), Aladdin) Simon & Schuster Children's Publishing.

Yomtov, Nelson. Titanic Disaster! Nickolas Flux & the Sinking of the Great Ship. Simmons, Mark, illus. 2015. (Nickolas Flux History Chronicles Ser.). (ENG.). 32p. (gr. 3-4). lib. bdg. 30.65 (978-1-4914-2070-6(7), Graphic Library) Capstone Press of Coughlan Cos.

Zullo, Allan. Titanic Young Survivors. 2012. 181p. (J). (978-0-545-33315-3(6)) Scholastic, Inc.

SHIRLEY, ANNE (FICTITIOUS CHARACTER)—FICTION

Fields, Jan. Facing a Frenemy, 1 vol. 2014. (Meri's Mirror Ser.). (ENG., Illus.). 80p. (J). (gr. 2-5). lib. bdg. 27.07 (978-1-62402-008-7(9), Calico Chapter Bks) Magic Wagon.

Helldorfer, M. C. Anne of Green Gables. Beier, Ellen, illus. 2003. (ENG.). 40p. (J). (gr. -1-2). pap. 7.99 (978-0-440-41614-2(0), Dragonfly Bks.) Random Hse. Children's Bks.

Kessler, Deirdre & Montgomery, L. M. Anne of Green Gables, 1 vol. Smith, David Preston, illus. 2008. (ENG.). 46p. (J). (gr. k-5). pap. 10.95 (978-1-55109-662-9(5)) Nimbus Publishing, Ltd. CAN. Dist: Orca Bk. Pubs. USA.

Montgomery, L. M. Anne of Avonlea. 2012. (World Classics Ser.). (ENG.). 228p. pap. 19.99 (978-1-909438-94-1(4), Sovereign) Bollinger, Max GBR. Dist: Lightning Source UK, Ltd., Gardners Bks. Ltd.

—Anne of Green Gables. 400p. 2005. 33.95 (978-1-4218-0660-0(6), 1st World Library - Literary Society) 2004. per. 16.95 (978-1-59540-110-6(5)) 1st World Publishing, Inc.

—Anne of Green Gables. 2009. 292p. 27.99 (978-1-60512-375-2(7)); pap. 14.99 (978-1-60512-475-9(3)) Akasha Publishing, LLC. (Akasha Classics).

—Anne of Green Gables. 2008. 316p. 29.99 (978-0-554-23545-5(5)) 2008. 316p. 28.99 (978-0-554-32848-5(8)) 2007. (ENG.). 312p. pap. 24.99 (978-1-4264-4662-7(4)) Creative Media Partners, LLC.

—Anne of Green Gables. 2008. (Anne of Green Gables Ser.). (ENG.). 366p. (J). (gr. 4-7). pap. 9.95 (978-0-9782552-6-8(7)) Davenport Pr. CAN. Dist: Independent Pubs. Group.

—Anne of Green Gables. 2007. per. 6.99 (978-1-4209-2922-5(4)) Digireads.com Publishing.

—Anne of Green Gables. 2007. 284p. per. (978-1-4065-6399-3(4)) Dodo Pr.

—Anne of Green Gables. 2007. 572p. (978-1-84702-773-3(3)) 2006. pap. (978-1-4068-2170-3(5)) Echo Library.

—Anne of Green Gables. 2008. 316p. pap. 16.95 (978-1-60096-565-4(2)); pap. 16.95 (978-1-60096-101-4(0)) Editorium, The.

—Anne of Green Gables. 2009. 242p. pap. 8.58 (978-0-217-43952-7(7)) General Bks. LLC.

—Anne of Green Gables. 2005. (My First Classics Ser.). 112p. (J). (gr. k-3). pap., pap. 4.99 (978-0-06-079147-6(0), HarperFestival) HarperCollins Pubs.

—Anne of Green Gables. 2005. 21.99 (978-1-4142-5125-7(4)) IndyPublish.com.

—Anne of Green Gables. 2008. (ENG.). 376p. (gr. k-12). pap. 14.95 (978-0-7710-9368-5(3), New Can Library) McClelland & Stewart CAN. Dist: Penguin Random Hse. LLC.

—Anne of Green Gables, 1 vol. 2016. (ENG.). 352p. (J). (gr. 2-5). pap. 10.95 (978-1-55109-249-2(2)) Nimbus Publishing, Ltd. CAN. Dist: National Bk. Network.

—Anne of Green Gables. Rubio, Mary Henley & Waterston, Elizabeth, eds. 2007. (Norton Critical Editions Ser.: 0). (ENG., Illus.). 464p. (C). (gr. 9-12). per. 15.02 (978-0-393-92695-8(8), 92695) Norton, W. W. & Co., Inc.

—Anne of Green Gables. 2003. (ENG.). 320p. (gr. 5-7). 5.95 (978-0-451-52882-7(4), Signet) Penguin Publishing Group.

—Anne of Green Gables. 2008. (Puffin Classics Ser.). (ENG., Illus.). 464p. (J). (gr. 3-7). 5.99 (978-0-14-132159-2(8), Puffin Books) Penguin Young Readers Group.

—Anne of Green Gables. 2003. 320p. (J). (gr. 4-7). 12.60 (978-0-7569-1848-4(0)) Perfection Learning Corp.

—Anne of Green Gables. 2009. 224p. pap. 15.45 (978-1-4385-1847-3(1), Book Jungle) Standard Pubns., Inc.

—Anne of Green Gables. 2008. (Modern Library Classics Ser.). (ENG.). 320p. pap. 9.00 (978-0-8129-7903-9(6), Modern Library) Random House Publishing Group.

—Anne of Green Gables. 2012. (World Classics Ser.). (ENG.). 260p. pap. 19.99 (978-1-909438-96-5(0), Sovereign) Bollinger, Max GBR. Dist: Lightning Source UK, Ltd.

—Anne of Green Gables. rev. ed. 2007. 280p. pap. 21.99 (978-1-4264-4611-5(X)) Creative Media Partners, LLC.

—Anne of Green Gables. l.t. ed. 2006. pap. (978-1-4068-3174-0(3)) Echo Library.

—Anne of Green Gables. 2004. reprint ed. pap. 27.95 (978-1-4191-0717-7(8)); pap. 1.99 (978-1-4192-0717-4(2)) Kessinger Publishing, LLC.

—Anne of Green Gables. l.t. ed. 2009. (World Classics Ser.). 288p. pap. 21.95 (978-1-59688-123-5(2)) Large Print Bk. Co., The.

—The Anne of Green Gables Collection: Six Complete & Unabridged Novels in One Volume. 2013. 1140p. (978-1-78139-344-4(3)) Benediction Classics.

—Anne of Green Gables Cookbook. 22.95 (978-0-8488-2657-4(4)) Amereon Ltd.

—Anne of Green Gables Diary. 22.95 (978-0-8488-2654-3(X)) Amereon Ltd.

—Anne of the Green Gables. 2014. (Anne of Green Gables Ser.: 1). (ENG.). 352p. (YA). (gr. 5-12). pap. 9.99 (978-1-4022-8894-4(8)) Sourcebooks, Inc.

—Anne of the Island. 2012. (World Classics Ser.). (ENG.). 212p. pap. 19.99 (978-1-909438-92-7(8), Sovereign) Bollinger, Max GBR. Dist: Lightning Source UK, Ltd.

—Anne of the Island. 2008. (Anne of Green Gables Ser.). (ENG.). 272p. (J). (gr. 4-7). pap. 9.95 (978-0-9782552-8-2(3)) Davenport Pr. CAN. Dist: Independent Pubs. Group.

—Anne of the Island. 2006. (ENG.). pap. (978-1-4068-2171-0(3)); pap. (978-1-4068-3175-7(1)) Echo Library.

—Anne of the Island. 2004. reprint ed. pap. 1.99 (978-1-4192-0718-1(0)); pap. 30.95 (978-1-4179-0885-1(8)) Kessinger Publishing, LLC.

—Anne of the Island. l.t. ed. 2004. 396p. 26.00 (978-1-58287-640-5(1)) North Bks.

—Anne of the Island. 2010. (Puffin Classics Ser.). (ENG.). 368p. (J). (gr. 5-7). pap. 5.99 (978-0-14-132736-5(7), Puffin Books) Penguin Young Readers Group.

—Rilla of Ingleside. 2004. 224p. (YA). pap. 10.95 (978-1-57646-891-3(7)) Quiet Vision Publishing.

Stellings, Caroline. The Contest, 1 vol. 2009. (ENG.). 160p. (J). (gr. 4-7). pap. 9.95 (978-0-9779183-5-5(1), 7th Generation) Book Publishing Co.

Sullivan, Kevin. A New Beginning. 2009. (Anne of Green Gables Ser.). (ENG.). 290p. (J). (gr. 7). pap. 19.95 (978-0-9811418-1-7(1)) Davenport Pr. CAN. Dist: Independent Pubs. Group.

Sullivan, Kevin & Goldman, Leslie. Anne & the Bully. 2010. (Anne of Green Gables for Young Readers Ser.). (ENG.). 64p. (J). (gr. 2-4). pap. 4.95 (978-0-9736803-8-6(5)) Davenport Pr. CAN. Dist: Independent Pubs. Group.

—Anne's Babysitting Blues. 2010. (Anne of Green Gables for Young Readers Ser.). (ENG.). 64p. (J). (gr. 2-4). pap. 4.95 (978-0-9736803-1-7(8)) Davenport Pr. CAN. Dist: Independent Pubs. Group.

—Anne's Red Hair. 2010. (Anne of Green Gables Picture Bks.). (ENG.). 32p. (J). (gr. k-2). pap. 4.95 (978-0-9736803-3-1(4)) Davenport Pr. CAN. Dist: Independent Pubs. Group.

Sullivan, Kevin & Morgan, Elizabeth. Anne's New Home. 2010. (Anne of Green Gables Picture Bks.). (ENG.). 32p. (J). (gr. k-2). pap. 4.95 (978-0-9736803-7-9(7)) Davenport Pr. CAN. Dist: Independent Pubs. Group.

SHOES

Arnoux, Lucie, illus. In Their Shoes: Fairy Tales & Folktales. 2016. (ENG.). 128p. (J). (gr. 4-7). pap. 9.99 (978-1-78269-101-3(4), Pushkin Children's Bks.) Steerforth Pr.

Blaxland, Wendy. Sneakers. 2008. (How Are They Made? Ser.). 32p. (gr. 4-18). lib. bdg. 18.56 (978-0-7614-3810-6(6), Benchmark Bks.) Marshall Cavendish Corp.

Chanko, Pamela & Michael, Joan. What Shoes Would You Choose? 2017. (Rookie Toddler(tm) Ser.). (ENG.). 12p. (J). bds. 6.95 (978-0-531-22980-4(7), Children's Pr.) Scholastic Library Publishing.

Cobb, Vicki. Sneakers. 2008. pap. 52.95 (978-0-8225-9451-2(X)) Lerner Publishing Group.

D'Cruz, Anna-Marie. Make Your Own Shoes & Slippers. 2009. (Do It Yourself Projects! Ser.). (J). (ENG.). 24p. (gr. 3-5). pap. 9.40 (978-1-4358-2921-3(2)); lib. bdg. 25.25 (978-1-4358-2852-0(6)) Rosen Publishing Group, Inc., The. (PowerKids Pr.).

Englehart, Victoria. Whose Shoes? 2012. (Illus.). 34p. (-18). pap. 16.99 (978-1-4525-6056-4(0)) Balboa Pr.

Frisch, Aaron. The Story of Nike. 2003. (Built for Success Ser.). (Illus.). 48p. (J). lib. bdg. 19.95 (978-1-58340-295-5(0)) Black Rabbit Bks.

—The Story of Nike. 2011. (Built for Success Ser.). (ENG.). 48p. (J). (gr. 4-7). pap. 12.00 (978-0-89812-738-6(6), Creative Paperbacks) Creative Co., The.

Jacobson, Ryan. Shoes. 2016. (J). (978-1-4896-4541-8(1)) Weigl Pubs., Inc.

—Shoes Before the Store. McGeehan, Dan, illus. 2012. (Before the Store Ser.). (ENG.). 32p. (J). (gr. 2-5). lib. bdg. 29.93 (978-1-60973-681-1(8), 201256) Child's World, Inc., The.

Jozefowicz, Chris. 10 Fascinating Facts about Sneakers. 2016. (Rookie Star — Fact Finder Ser.). (ENG., Illus.). 32p. (J). lib. bdg. 25.00 (978-0-531-22817-3(7), Children's Pr.) Scholastic Library Publishing.

Kahalewai, Marilyn. Whose Slippers Are Those? Kobayashi, Gavin, illus. 2005. 24p. (J). (gr. -1-3). 10.95 (978-1-57306-238-1(3)) Bess Pr., Inc.

Keyser, Amber. Sneaker Century: A History of Athletic Shoes. 2015. (ENG., Illus.). 64p. (J). (gr. 8-12). lib. bdg. 34.65 (978-1-4677-2640-5(0)) Lerner Publishing Group.

Kulot, Daniela. Un Lio de Cordones. 2006. (Illus.). 32p. (J). (gr. 5-7). 15.99 (978-84-934641-7-2(1)) Lectorum Pubns., Inc.

Liddle, Charlotte. Pimp Your Pumps: 35 Easy Ways to Transform Your Shoes. 2014. (ENG., Illus.). 128p. (J). (gr. 7-11). pap. 14.95 (978-1-78249-106-4(6), CICO Books) Ryland Peters & Small GBR. Dist: WIPRO.

Lindeen, Mary. If the Shoe Fits. 2011. (Wonder Readers Fluent Level Ser.). (ENG.). (gr. -1-2). 16p. pap. 35.94 (978-1-4296-8097-4(0)); 32p. pap. 5.99 (978-1-4296-7928-2(X)) Capstone Press of Coughlan Cos. (Wonder Readers).

MacDonald, Margaret. Boots & Shoes. 2011. (Learn-Abouts: Level 10 Ser.). (Illus.). 16p. (J). pap. 7.95 (978-1-59920-604-2(8)) Black Rabbit Bks.

McNeil, Niki, et al. HOCPP 1094 Red Clogs. 2006. spiral bd. 15.50 (978-1-60308-094-1(5)) In the Hands of a Child.

Meinking, Mary. Stylish Shoes for the Crafty Fashionista, 1 vol. 2011. (Fashion Craft Studio Ser.). (ENG.). 32p. (gr. 3-4). lib. bdg. 27.99 (978-1-4296-6554-4(8), Snap Bks.) Capstone Press of Coughlan Cos.

Merberg, Julie. My Favorite Shoes: A Touch-and-Feel Shoe-Stravaganza! Bove, Neysa & Rucker, Georgia, illus. 2013. (ENG.). 16p. (J). (gr. -1 — 1). bds. 12.99 (978-1-935703-64-8(1)) Downtown Bookworks.

Nelson, Robin. From Leather to Basketball Shoes. 2014. (Start to Finish: Sports Gear Ser.). (Illus.). 24p. (gr. k-3). pap. 6.95 (978-1-4677-4559-8(6)); (ENG., lib. bdg. 23.93 (978-1-4677-3893-4(X), Lerner Pubns.) Lerner Publishing Group.

—From Leather to Football. 2014. (Start to Finish: Sports Gear Ser.). (Illus.). 24p. (gr. k-3). lib. bdg. 23.93 (978-1-4677-3890-3(5), Lerner Pubns.) Lerner Publishing Group.

Peterson, Megan Cooley & Rustad, Martha E. H. Kid Style: Sweet Shoes for You!, 1 vol. 2014. (Make It Mine Ser.). (ENG.). 24p. (gr. k-1). lib. bdg. 26.65 (978-1-4765-3968-3(5), Pebble Plus) Capstone Press of Coughlan Cos.

Ross, Samantha B. "Momby" Wears Combat Boots: Where did she Go? 2011. 28p. pap. 15.99 (978-1-4568-7129-1(3)) Xlibris Corp.

Salzmann, Mary Elizabeth. Shoes, Boots & Cleats, 1 vol. 2012. (Sports Gear Ser.). (ENG., Illus.). 24p. (J). (gr. k-3). lib. bdg. 24.21 (978-1-61714-827-9(X)) ABDO Publishing Co.

Sneaker Factory. (J). pap. 13.15 (978-0-8136-4301-4(5)) Modern Curriculum Pr.

Sneakers. 2006. (Where's the Science Here? Ser.). (J). pap. 8.95 (978-0-8225-9044-6(1)) Lerner Publishing Group.

Steinberg, D. J. King Louie's Shoes. Neubecker, Robert, illus. 2017. (ENG.). 48p. (J). (gr. -1-3). 17.99 **(978-1-4814-2657-2(5)**, Beach Lane Bks.) Beach Lane Bks.

Swinburne, Stephen R. Whose Shoes? A Shoe for Every Job. 2016. (ENG.). 32p. (J). (— 1). bds. 7.99 (978-1-62979-691-8(3)) Boyds Mills Pr.

SHOES—FICTION

Anderson, Charoletta. Mizz Goodie 2 Shoez. 2013. 24p. pap. 17.99 (978-1-4772-9475-8(9)) AuthorHouse.

Andrews, John. Beck's Missing Shoes. 2013. 28p. pap. 9.95 (978-1-4787-2524-4(9)) Outskirts Pr., Inc.

Applegate, Katherine. Never Walk in Shoes That Talk. Biggs, Brian, illus. 2009. (Roscoe Riley Rules Ser.: 6). (ENG.). 96p. (J). (gr. 1-5). 14.99 (978-0-06-114892-7(X)); pap. 4.99 (978-0-06-114891-0(1)) HarperCollins Pubs.

—Never Walk in Shoes That Talk. 2009. (Roscoe Riley Rules Ser.: 06). lib. bdg. 14.75 (978-0-606-05019-7(1), Turtleback) Turtleback Bks.

Arengo, Sue. The Shoemaker & the Elves, Pack. 2nd ed. 2012. (ENG.). 12.81 (978-0-19-423885-4(7)) Oxford Univ. Pr., Inc.

Barrett, Mary Brigid. Shoebox Sam, 1 vol. Morrison, Frank, illus. 2011. (ENG.). 32p. (J). 15.99 (978-0-310-71549-8(0)) Zonderkidz.

Beaumont, Karen. Shoe-la-La! Pham, LeUyen, illus. 2011. (ENG.). 40p. (J). (gr. -1-3). 16.99 (978-0-545-06705-8(7), Scholastic Pr.) Scholastic, Inc.

—Shoe-La-la! Pham, LeUyen, illus. 2013. (ENG.). 32p. (J). (gr. -1 — 1). bds. 6.99 (978-0-545-59478-3(2), Cartwheel Bks.) Scholastic, Inc.

—Shoe-la-La! A Storyplay Book. Leuyen, Pham, illus. 2016. (ENG.). 40p. (J). (gr. -1-k). 5.99 (978-1-338-11555-0(3), Cartwheel Bks.) Scholastic, Inc.

Beck, Crystall. The Adventures of Carter & Vincent. 2012. 28p. pap. 9.95 (978-1-4787-1662-4(2)) Outskirts Pr., Inc.

Bertling, Judy. There's Poo on My Shoe. 2010. 36p. 17.25 (978-1-4269-4300-3(8)) Trafford Publishing.

Boelts, Maribeth. Those Shoes. 2014. 17.00 (978-1-63419-735-9(6)) Perfection Learning Corp.

Boileau, Kim. My New Blue Shoes, 1 vol. 2010. 28p. pap. 24.95 (978-1-4489-8847-1(0)) PublishAmerica, Inc.

Bonar, Troy A. Safety = Caring. 2013. 28p. pap. 9.95 (978-1-4787-0745-5(3)) Outside the Box Publishing, LLC.

Boyd, Sonya. I Have What It Takes. 2011. 28p. pap. 9.95 (978-1-4327-7975-7(3)) Outskirts Pr., Inc.

Brott, Wayne. Shoes! Delosh, Diana Ting, illus. 2013. (ENG.). (J). (gr. -1-3). 14.95 (978-1-62086-239-1(5)) Mascot Bks., Inc.

Bunting, Eve. Whose Shoe? Ruzzier, Sergio, illus. 2015. (ENG.). 32p. (J). (gr. -1-3). 16.99 (978-0-544-30210-5(9)) Houghton Mifflin Harcourt Publishing Co.

Burket, Shelia. Detective Morris Norris & the Case of the Missing Socks. 2011. 20p. pap. 24.95 (978-1-4626-2822-3(2)) America Star Bks.

Carillo, Christina Martin. Mr Plaid. 2011. 24p. pap. 24.95 (978-1-4560-6930-8(6)) America Star Bks.

Cathy Smentkowski. If the Shoe Fits. 2010. 24p. pap. 15.99 (978-1-4535-6417-2(9)) Xlibris Corp.

Church, Peggy Pond. Shoes for the Santo Niño. Carrillo, Charles M., illus. 2013. 64p. 25.95 (978-1-936744-23-7(6), Rio Grande Bks.) LPD Pr.

—Shoes for the Santo Niño: Zapitillos para el Santo Niño: A Bilingual Tale. Carrillo, Charles M., illus. 2009. (SPA & ENG.). 61p. (J). pap. (978-1-890689-64-3(5), Rio Grande Bks.) LPD Pr.

Ciesa, Mary E. Dina Prima the Ballerina. 2013. 36p. pap. 16.99 (978-1-4525-8313-6(7), Balboa Pr.) Author Solutions, Inc.

Cobb, Daryl K. Do Pirates Go to School. 2010. pap. 11.99 (978-0-578-05535-0(X)) 10 To 2 Children's Bks.

Coleman, Tamala J. Donovan's Shoes. 2010. 28p. pap. 9.95 (978-1-4327-5801-1(2)) Outskirts Pr., Inc.

Conti, Alexis. One Blue Shoe. Beth, Shannon, illus. 2013. (ENG.). (J). (gr. -1-3). 14.95 (978-1-937406-11-0(3)) Mascot Bks., Inc.

Conway, Portia. Where My Shoes Have Been, 1 vol. 2010. 22p. 24.95 (978-1-4512-9671-6(1)) PublishAmerica, Inc.

Cooper, William Y. Nakai & the Red Shoes. 2011. 52p. (gr. 4-6). pap. 19.39 (978-1-4269-6048-2(4)) Trafford Publishing.

Cowley, Joy. The Hungry Giant's Shoe. 2009. pap. 8.25 (978-1-60559-223-7(4)) Hameray Publishing Group, Inc.

—The Hungry Giant's Shoe Big Book. 2010. 48.25 (978-1-60559-250-3(1)) Hameray Publishing Group, Inc.

Crawford, Jaleesa. Teeny Tot. 2013. 28p. pap. 24.95 (978-1-62709-372-9(9)) America Star Bks.

Creghan, Brian C. Pauly: The alligator who wore tennis Shoes. 2010. 48p. pap. 24.00 (978-1-4269-3614-2(1)) Trafford Publishing.

Crouch, Cheryl Lynne. Tennis Shoes Trouble. 2006. 48p. 6.50 (978-0-8341-2227-7(8)) Beacon Hill Pr. of Kansas City.

Crow, Melinda Melton. Little Lizard's New Shoes, 1 vol. Rowland, Andrew, illus. 2011. (Little Lizards Ser.). (ENG.). 32p. (gr. -1-1). pap. 6.25 (978-1-4342-3050-8(3)); lib. bdg. 22.65 (978-1-4342-2509-2(7)) Stone Arch Bks.

Dara Cicciarelli. Sam Loses His Sneaker. Hoke, Jason, illus. 2011. 20p. pap. 24.95 (978-1-4560-9178-1(6)) America Star Bks.

Davis, Jacky. Do You Like These Boots? Soman, David, illus. 2014. (Ladybug Girl Ser.). (ENG.). 32p. (J). (gr. k-1). pap. 3.99 (978-0-448-46503-6(5), Penguin Young Readers) Penguin Young Readers Group.

Dean, James, illus. I Love My White Shoes. 2010. (Pete the Cat Ser.). (J). lib. bdg. (978-0-06-107623-7(6)) HarperCollins Pubs.

Dixon, Dallas L. Shelby's Shoes. Williams, Nancy E., ed. Cappoen, Jennifer Tipton, illus. 2013. 24p. (J). pap. 12.98 (978-1-938526-33-6(3)) Laurus Bks.

Dlugos, Josephine. Josie's Red Shoes. 2012. 24p. pap. 15.99 (978-1-4771-4097-0(2)) Xlibris Corp.

Dtpolk. The Shoes & the Laces. Barge III, John, illus. 2011. 32p. pap. 24.95 (978-1-4560-3141-1(4)) America Star Bks.

Dubel, Dorothy. The Magical Shoes of Santa's Elves(c). 2011. 24p. pap. 15.99 (978-1-4568-7883-2(2)) Xlibris Corp.

Dunrea, Olivier. Gossie. 2011. (Gossie & Friends Ser.). (ENG & SPA., Illus.). 32p. (J). (gr. -1-3). bds. 4.99 *(978-0-547-51072-9(1))* Houghton Mifflin Harcourt Publishing Co.
—Gossie (Reader) 2014. (Gossie & Friends Ser.). (ENG., Illus.). 32p. (J). (gr. -1-3). pap. 3.99 *(978-0-544-10573-7(7))* Houghton Mifflin Harcourt Publishing Co.
—Ollie the Stomper (Reader) 2014. (Gossie & Friends Ser.). (ENG., Illus.). 32p. (J). (gr. -1-3). pap. 3.99 *(978-0-544-14676-1(X),* HMH Books For Young Readers) Houghton Mifflin Harcourt Publishing Co.
Dyan, Penelope. New Shoes for Hand Me down Rose. Dyan, Penelope, illus. 2012. (Illus.). 34p. pap. 11.95 *(978-1-61477-041-1(7))* Bellissima Publishing, LLC.
Eddy, Catherine J. Sandbox Sandshoes. Krupnek, Joann J., illus. 2009. 38p. pap. 10.95 *(978-0-9818488-5-3(0))* Ajoyin Publishing, Inc.
Edwards, Garth. The Magic Boots. Stasyuk, Max, illus. 2011. (Adventures of Titch & Mitch Ser.). (J). pap. *(978-0-9567449-8-2(2))* Inside Pocket Publishing, Ltd.
—The #04 Magic Boots. Stasyuk, Max, illus. 2011. (Adventures of Titch & Mitch, the Ser.). (J). pap. *(978-0-7613-8424-3(3))* Inside Pocket Publishing, Ltd.
Edwards, Wallace. Uncle Wally's Old Brown Shoe, 1 vol. 2012. (ENG., Illus.). 32p. (J). (gr. -1-3). 19.95 *(978-1-4598-0154-7(7))* Orca Bk. Pubs. USA.
Erickson, Patricia. The Shiny New Shoes. 2011. 24p. pap. 11.50 *(978-1-4670-2544-7(5))* AuthorHouse.
Farley, Robin. Mia & the Tiny Toe Shoes. Ivanov, Aleksey & Ivanov, Olga, illus. 2012. (My First I Can Read Ser.). (ENG.). 32p. (J). (gr. -1-3). 16.99 *(978-0-06-208683-9(9))*; pap. 3.99 *(978-0-06-208682-2(0))* HarperCollins Pubs.
—Mia Jazzes It Up! 2013. (Mia I Can Read Bks.). (J). lib. bdg. 13.55 *(978-0-606-32164-8(0),* Turtleback) Turtleback Bks.
Finnan, Kristie. Mommy's High Heel Shoes. Achilles, Pat, illus. 2008. 32p. (J). 16.99 *(978-0-9817565-2-3(2))* Mommy Workshop Bks.
Fisher, James C. Oh No! My Shoe! 2013. 24p. pap. 15.99 *(978-1-4797-8210-9(6))* Xlibris Corp.
Fliess, Sue. Shoes for Me!, 0 vols. Laughead, Mike, illus. 2011. (ENG.). 24p. (J). (gr. -1-3). 12.99 *(978-0-7614-5825-8(5),* 9780761458258, Amazon Children's Publishing) Amazon Publishing.
Flinn, Alex. Cloaked. 2011. (YA). 341p. lib. bdg. 17.89 *(978-0-06-087423-0(6))*; (ENG.). 352p. (gr. 8-18). 16.99 *(978-0-06-087422-3(8))* HarperCollins Pubs. (HarperTeen).
Fontes, Justine. Barbie in the Pink Shoes. 2013. (Book & Jewelry Ser.: 1). (ENG.). 24p. (J). (gr. -1-3). 10.99 *(978-0-7944-2785-6(5))* Reader's Digest Assn., Inc., The.
Foster, Evelyn. The Elves & the Trendy Shoes. Venturini, Claudia, illus. 2015. (ENG.). 32p. (J). *(978-0-7787-1932-8(4))* Crabtree Publishing Co.
Franks, Alison. On My Feet! 2013. 24p. pap. 28.03 *(978-1-4797-6958-2(4))* Xlibris Corp.
Gamble, Rev. Vivian T. I Think All the Time.... Ummm. 2012. 28p. pap. 9.95 *(978-1-4787-1359-3(3))* Outskirts Pr., Inc.
—Just to Be Myself. 2012. 28p. pap. 9.95 *(978-1-4787-1358-6(5))* Outskirts Pr., Inc.
Gibson, Beatrice. The Legend of the Sandals. 2008. 28p. pap. 15.99 *(978-1-4363-9169-6(5))* Xlibris Corp.
Gormley, Greg. Dog in Boots. Angaramo, Roberta, illus. 2011. (ENG.). 32p. (J). (gr. -1-1). 17.95 *(978-0-8234-2347-7(6))* Holiday Hse., Inc.
Graham, Cheryl. Stephanie's Shoes. 2010. 28p. pap. 9.95 *(978-1-4327-5944-5(2))* Outskirts Pr., Inc.
Grande, Gabrielle. Fluffy's Book. 2013. 24p. (J). pap. 12.99 *(978-1-4808-0067-0(8))*; (Illus.). 22.99 *(978-1-4808-0068-7(6))* Archway Publishing.
Gregory, Lorraine NAR NEEDED. One, Two, Tie Your Shoes! Carlson, Nancy Gayle, illus. 2010. (J). *(978-0-545-26482-2(0))* Scholastic, Inc.
Guarino, Deborah. If the Shoe Fits. (J). 14.95 *(978-0-8118-3774-3(2))* Chronicle Bks. LLC.
Harlan, My Best Friend. 2011. 28p. pap. 9.95 *(978-1-4327-7164-5(7))* Outskirts Pr., Inc.
Harlow, Honey. Honey's Shoes. 2013. 28p. pap. 9.95 *(978-1-4327-9921-2(5))* Outskirts Pr., Inc.
Harris, Wendell. Elton's Shoes. 2012. 100p. (gr. -1). pap. 13.95 *(978-1-4520-8143-4(3))* AuthorHouse.
Harrison, Paul. The Elves Help Puss in Boots. Sutcliffe, Tim, illus. 2016. (Fairy Tale Mix-Ups Ser.). (ENG.). 24p. (gr. k-2). lib. bdg. 23.32 *(978-1-4109-8303-9(X))* Heinemann-Raintree.
Hayes, Joe. The Lovesick Skunk. Castro L., Antonio, illus. 2010. (ENG.). 32p. (J). (gr. k-7). 16.95 *(978-1-933693-81-1(9))* Cinco Puntos Pr.
Hinbest, Wendy. Frizzy Tizzy Gets New Shoes. 2011. 24p. pap. 11.95 *(978-1-4583-5827-1(5))* Lulu Pr., Inc.
Hoffman, Mary. The Twelve Dancing Princesses. Clara, Miss, illus. 2013. (ENG.). 40p. (J). (gr. 1-5). 17.99 *(978-1-84686-966-2(8))* Barefoot Bks., Inc.
Holmes, Julienne R. The Girl Who Wore Her Shoes on the Wrong Feet. 2012. 24p. pap. 24.95 *(978-1-4626-8726-8(1))* America Star Bks.
Holub, Joan. Don't Get Lost, Odysseus! Patricelli, Leslie, illus. 2016. (Mini Myths Ser.). (ENG.). 24p. (J). (gr. -1 — 1). bds. 6.95 *(978-1-4197-1897-7(5),* Abrams Appleseed) Abrams, Inc.
—Good Job, Athena! Patricelli, Leslie, illus. 2016. (Mini Myths Ser.). (ENG.). 24p. (J). (gr. -1 — 1). bds. 6.95 *(978-1-4197-1898-4(3),* Abrams Appleseed) Abrams, Inc.
Howell, Heather. Emily's Ballet Recital. 2010. 32p. pap. 12.99 *(978-1-4490-8457-8(5))* AuthorHouse.
Ireland, Cameron Robert. The Missing Left Shoe. 2012. 24p. 24.95 *(978-1-4626-6138-1(6))* America Star Bks.
Jannazo, Michelle A. Isabella's Shoes. 2012. 28p. pap. 11.95 *(978-1-4327-9019-6(6))* Outskirts Pr., Inc.
Jones, A. I Can Make a Shoe for You. 2011. 36p. pap. 24.95 *(978-1-4560-9118-7(2))* PublishAmerica, Inc.
Jones, Cheryl. Where Are My Shoes? 2011. 28p. pap. 9.95 *(978-1-4327-7157-7(4))* Outskirts Pr., Inc.
Jones, Lonetha. Big Brother's Missing Shoes. 2010. 28p. pap. 9.95 *(978-1-4327-5926-1(4))* Outskirts Pr., Inc.
Jules, Jacqueline. Freddie Ramos Makes a Splash. Benitez, Miguel, illus. 2013. (Zapato Power Ser.: Book 4). (ENG.). 96p. (J). (gr. 1-5). pap. 4.99 *(978-0-8075-9486-5(5))* Whitman, Albert & Co.
Jules, Jacqueline & Benitez, Miguel. Freddie Ramos Takes Off. 2010. (Zapato Power Ser.: Book 1). (ENG., Illus.). 88p. (J). (gr. 1-5). 14.99 *(978-0-8075-9480-3(6))* Whitman, Albert & Co.
Keast, Jennifer H. Dora the Explorer (Giant First Play-a-Sound) 2010. 10p. (J). bds. 17.98 *(978-1-60553-544-9(3))* Publications International, Ltd.
Kitchen, David. The Adventures of Chesed & Cadence. 2012. 28p. pap. 9.95 *(978-1-4787-1712-6(2))* Outskirts Pr., Inc.
Kliman, Susie. Jonathon's Thongs. Erlich, Esther, illus. 2013. 35p. pap. *(978-0-9875296-1-9(7))* Aly's Bks.
Knapp, Kate. Ruby Red Shoes. 2012. *(978-0-7304-9640-3(6))* HarperCollins Pubs. Australia.
Koontz, Robin Michal. The King's New Clothes. Koontz, Robin Michal, illus. 2011. (ENG., Illus.). 24p. (gr. 2-3). pap. 8.95 *(978-1-61236-028-7(9))* Rourke Educational Media.
Kosara, Tori. Big Kid Shoes. Borlasca, Hector, illus. 2011. (J). *(978-0-545-36967-1(3))* Scholastic, Inc.
Kucharski, Linda. Sneak the Sneaker. 2010. 44p. pap. 15.50 *(978-1-60911-487-9(6),* Eloquent Bks.) Strategic Book Publishing & Rights Agency (SBPRA).
Lemay, Violet. Isabella's Shoe Studio: Read! Doodle! Create! Lemay, Violet, illus. 2013. (Doodle Story Bks.). (ENG., Illus.). 120p. (J). (gr. 2-3). pap. 12.95 *(978-1-938093-18-0(6))* Duo Pr. LLC.
Litwin, Eric. I Love My White Shoes. Dean, James, illus. 2010. (Pete the Cat Ser.). 40p. (J). (gr. -1-3). (ENG.). 17.99 *(978-0-06-190622-0(0))*; lib. bdg. 17.89 *(978-0-06-190623-7(9))* HarperCollins Pubs.
—Rocking in My School Shoes. Dean, James, illus. 2011. (Pete the Cat Ser.). 40p. (J). (gr. -1-3). (ENG.). 17.99 *(978-0-06-191024-1(4))*; lib. bdg. 17.89 *(978-0-06-191025-8(2))* HarperCollins Pubs.
Litwin, Eric, ed. Rocking in My School Shoes. 2011. *(978-0-545-50106-4(7))* Scholastic, Inc.
Litwin, Eric & Dean, James. I Love My White Shoes. 2010. (Pete the Cat Ser.). pap. *(978-0-545-41966-6(2))* Scholastic, Inc.
Lopez, Joe. Solemates. 2013. 28p. pap. 9.95 *(978-1-4787-2494-0(3))* Outskirts Pr., Inc.
Lorang, C. J. Where Are My Shoes. 2011. 28p. pap. 9.95 *(978-1-4327-8290-0(8))* Outskirts Pr., Inc.
Lozano, José. Little Chanclas. 2015. (ENG & SPA., Illus.). 32p. (J). (gr. k-3). 16.95 *(978-1-935955-85-6(3))* Cinco Puntos Pr.
Lucas & His Long Loopy Laces. 2013. (Illus.). 48p. 16.99 *(978-0-9823519-4-9(1))* Tall Tails Publishing Hse.
Macy, Tana. Tap Shoes & Horse Shoes. Gardiner, Nancy, illus. 2011. 50p. pap. 18.00 *(978-1-60976-086-1(7),* Eloquent Bks.) Strategic Book Publishing & Rights Agency (SBPRA).
Mantlo, Mickey A. & Cook, Darren A. Tennis Shoes & Toe Clips, 1 vol. 2010. 204p. pap. 24.95 *(978-1-4512-9683-9(5))* America Star Bks.
Manushkin, Fran. Katie's New Shoes, 1 vol. Lyon, Tammie, illus. 2011. (Katie Woo Ser.). (ENG.). 32p. (gr. k-2). pap. 5.95 *(978-1-4048-6855-7(0))*; lib. bdg. 21.32 *(978-1-4048-6519-8(5))* Picture Window Bks.
Marrero, Rosa M. Nickolas Loves Toby. 2011. 28p. pap. 9.95 *(978-1-4327-7452-3(2))* Outskirts Pr., Inc.
Marrone, Amanda. Master of Mirrors. 2011. (Magic Repair Shop Ser.: 3). (ENG.). 192p. (J). (gr. 3-7). pap. 5.99 *(978-1-4169-9035-2(6),* Aladdin) Simon & Schuster Children's Publishing.
McCarthy, Jenna, et al. Maggie Malone & the Mostly Magical Boots. 2014. (Maggie Malone Ser.: 1). (ENG.). 224p. (J). (gr. 3-6). pap. 6.99 *(978-1-4022-9306-1(2),* 9781402293061, Sourcebooks Jabberwocky) Sourcebooks, Inc.
Meadows, Daisy. Paige the Christmas Play Fairy. 2010. (Rainbow Magic Ser.). (ENG.). 192p. (J). (gr. 2-5). pap. 6.99 *(978-0-545-22177-1(3),* Scholastic Paperbacks) Scholastic, Inc.
Melanson, Caroline. Two Old Shoes. 2011. 24p. pap. 15.99 *(978-1-4628-9238-9(8))* Xlibris Corp.
Meyer, Susan Lynn. New Shoes. Velasquez, Eric, illus. (ENG.). 32p. (J). 2016. 7.99 *(978-0-8234-3573-9(3))* 2015. (gr. 1-4). 16.95 *(978-0-8234-2528-0(2))* Holiday Hse., Inc.
Mihai, Adriana. The Inner of the Diamond Shoes. 2011. 28p. pap. 24.95 *(978-1-4560-0979-3(6))* America Star Bks.
Miller, Denise. Annie's Shoes. 2012. 28p. pap. 9.95 *(978-1-4787-2020-1(4))* Outskirts Pr., Inc.
Miracle, Joan. Tia's Shoes. 2013. 28p. pap. 9.95 *(978-1-4787-2603-6(2))* Outskirts Pr., Inc.
Mitter, Matt & Peyo. I Smurf You! Peyo, illus. 2011. (Smurfs Classic Ser.). (ENG., Illus.). 14p. (J). (gr. -1-k). bds. 10.99 *(978-1-4424-3606-0(9),* Simon Spotlight) Simon Spotlight.
Nelson, Suzanne. Serendipity's Footsteps. 2015. (ENG.). 368p. (YA). (gr. 7). 17.99 *(978-0-385-39212-9(5),* Knopf Bks. for Young Readers) Random Hse. Children's Bks.
Nichols, Cherrie L. Curtiz Says: I Hate My Shoestrings. 2012. 24p. pap. 17.99 *(978-1-4772-7341-8(7))* AuthorHouse.
Onyefulu, Ifeoma. New Shoes for Helen. Onyefulu, Ifeoma, photos by. 2011. (First Experiences Ser.). (ENG., Illus.). 32p. (J). (gr. -1-2). 17.95 *(978-1-84780-128-9(5),* Frances Lincoln) Quarto Publishing Group UK GBR. Dist: Hachette Bk. Group.
Orloff, Karen Kaufman. Nightlight Detective: Big Top Circus Mystery. Smith, Jamie, illus. 2013. 42p. spiral bd. 12.99 *(978-1-4413-1227-3(7))* Peter Pauper Pr. Inc.
Oroge, Sabinah. Oluwatofarati & Friends. 2013. 28p. pap. 9.95 *(978-1-4787-0520-8(5))* Outskirts Pr., Inc.
Osborne, Jill. Riley Mae & the Sole Fire Safari, 1 vol. 2014. (Faithgirlz / the Good News Shoes Ser.). (ENG.). 256p. (J). pap. 7.99 *(978-0-310-74283-8(8))* Zonderkidz.
Owens, C. Denise. Help! I Can't Find My Shoes. 2013. 28p. pap. 9.95 *(978-1-4787-2550-3(8))* Outskirts Pr., Inc.
P., Angie. Sneakers. 2012. 32p. pap. 19.99 *(978-1-4772-4548-4(0))* AuthorHouse.
Parker, Emma. Snafu & the Shoes. 2010. (Illus.). pap. *(978-1-877561-00-9(2))* First Edition Ltd.
Patterson, Eric. The Legend of Skylar Swift, the Fastest Boy on Earth. Chris, Wright, illus. 2010. 122p. pap. 6.95 *(978-1-935105-49-7(3))* Avid Readers Publishing Group.
Pemberton, Bernadette. Marshall's Marvelous Shoes. 2012. 24p. pap. 15.99 *(978-1-4771-4309-4(2))* Xlibris Corp.
Pemberton, Teresa. Trissy's New Shoes. 2013. 32p. pap. 13.95 *(978-1-4497-9337-1(1),* WestBow Pr.) Author Solutions, Inc.
Perry, Daniel. The Case of the Missing Shoes. 2013. 28p. pap. 9.95 *(978-1-4787-2649-4(0))* Outskirts Pr., Inc.
Peters, L. T. Slippery Willie's Stupid, Ugly Shoes, 1 vol. 2010. 20p. 24.95 *(978-1-4512-1511-3(8))* PublishAmerica, Inc.
Picou, Lin. Do I Have To... Reese, Bob, illus. 2011. (ENG.). 24p. (J). (gr. 1-2). pap. 8.95 *(978-1-61236-020-1(3))* Rourke Educational Media.
Primavera, Elise. Louise the Big Cheese & the La-Di-Da Shoes. Goode, Diane, illus. 2010. (ENG.). 40p. (J). (gr. k-3). 16.99 *(978-1-4169-7181-8(5),* Simon & Schuster/Paula Wiseman Bks.) Simon & Schuster/Paula Wiseman Bks.
Pruitt, Lisa A. Savanna & the Magic Boots. 2011. 24p. (gr. 1-2). pap. 11.32 *(978-1-4634-0090-3(X))* AuthorHouse.
Roadhouse, Patricia. Gah Reen Galoshes. 2009. 28p. pap. 16.99 *(978-1-4389-7318-0(7))* AuthorHouse.
Robinson, Jennifer. Isabella's Shoes. 2009. 20p. pap. 10.95 *(978-1-60860-553-8(1),* Strategic Bk. Publishing) Strategic Book Publishing & Rights Agency (SBPRA).
Rodriguez, Marisela. Violet's Shoes. 2012. 28p. pap. 9.95 *(978-1-4327-9616-7(X))* Outskirts Pr., Inc.
Schuette, Leslie Elaine. Kristina's Shoes. 2013. 24p. pap. 24.95 *(978-1-62709-670-6(1))* America Star Bks.
Seibers, Elexis. Jasmine & the Mystery of the Disappearing Shoes. 2011. 28p. pap. 9.95 *(978-1-4327-7626-8(6))* Outskirts Pr., Inc.
Sparrow, Leilani. My New Shoes. Taylor, Dan, illus. 2016. (ENG.). 32p. (J). (gr. -1-k). 16.99 *(978-1-4998-0363-1(X))* Little Bee Books Inc.
Spinelli, Eileen. Love My Shoes! 2011. 18p. (J). (gr. -1-k). bds. 7.99 *(978-0-8249-1853-8(3),* Ideal Pubns.) Worthy Publishing.
Stiles, Dan. Put on Your Shoes! 2013. (ENG., Illus.). 16p. (J). (-k). 9.95 *(978-1-57687-646-6(2),* powerHouse Bks.) powerHouse Cultural Entertainment, Inc.
Stone, Laura. Miss Clarissa & Her Musical Shoes. 2010. 32p. pap. 16.95 *(978-0-557-33226-7(5))* Lulu Pr., Inc.
Themerson, Stefan. The Table That Ran Away to the Woods. Themerson, Franciszka, illus. 2012. (ENG.). 20p. 10.95 *(978-1-84976-057-7(8))* Tate Publishing, Ltd. GBR. Dist: Abrams, Inc.
Toussaint, Simone. Sharing My Shoes. 2010. 28p. pap. 9.95 *(978-1-4327-5701-4(6))* Outskirts Pr., Inc.
Ungerer, Tomi. One, Two, Where's My Shoe? 2014. (ENG., Illus.). 32p. (gr. -1-k). 14.95 *(978-0-7148-6798-4(5))* Phaidon Pr., Inc.
Verde, Susan. My Kicks: A Sneaker Story! Kath, Katie, illus. 2017. (ENG.). 40p. (J). (gr. k-2). 16.95 *(978-1-4197-2309-4(X),* Abrams Bks. for Young Readers) Abrams, Inc.
Wallace, Clinton. H. The Adventures of Roger Eldemire. 2013. 28p. pap. 9.95 *(978-1-4787-2493-3(5))* Outskirts Pr., Inc.
Wardlow, Lynn. Friends with My Brother. 2012. 28p. pap. 9.95 *(978-1-4787-1384-5(4))* Outskirts Pr., Inc.
Wheeler, Lisa. The Christmas Boot. Pinkney, Jerry, illus. 2016. (ENG.). 32p. (J). (gr. -1-3). 17.99 *(978-0-8037-4134-8(0),* Dial Bks) Penguin Young Readers Group.
Wheeler, Ron. Stinky Stevens: The Missing Soggy Soccer Shoe (Book 3) 2012. 114p. pap. 6.95 *(978-0-9829377-6-1(8))* Written World Communications.
Wilder, Beth. Bugs in Shoes, 1 vol. 2012. (ENG., Illus.). 64p. (J). 14.99 *(978-0-7643-3967-7(2),* 9780764339677) Schiffer Publishing, Ltd.
Williams, Dawn. Cyril T. Centipede Looks for New Shoes, 1. Chou, Joey, illus. 2006. 48p. (J). (gr. -1-3). 15.00 *(978-0-9770783-0-1(2))* SunriseHouse Pubs.
Williams, Vanessa A. The Missing Penny. 2013. 28p. pap. 9.95 *(978-1-4787-2429-2(3))* Outskirts Pr., Inc.
Wojtowicz, Jen. The Boy Who Grew Flowers. Adams, Steve, illus. 2012. (ENG.). 32p. (J). (gr. k-5). 8.99 *(978-1-84686-749-1(5))* Barefoot Bks., Inc.

SHOOTING

see also Hunting

Adamson, Thomas K. Duck Hunting, 1 vol. 2010. (Wild Outdoors Ser.). (ENG.). 32p. (J). (gr. 1-2). lib. bdg. 26.65 *(978-1-4296-4809-7(0),* Blazers) Capstone Press of Coughlan Cos.
Browne, Bellmore H. Hunting & Shooting: A Vintage Classic. Beard, Daniel, ed. 2017. (ENG.). 112p. (J). pap. 8.95 *(978-0-486-81327-1(4))* Dover Pubns., Inc.
Cashin, John. Firearms Safety. 2014. (J). 33.95 *(978-1-61900-048-3(2))* Eldorado Ink.
Greenhaven Press Editors. The Columbine School Shootings. 2012. (Perspectives on Modern World History Ser.). (ENG., Illus.). 224p. (J). (gr. 10-12). lib. bdg. 42.45 *(978-0-7377-5768-0(4),* Greenhaven Pr., Inc.) Cengage Gale.
Hemstock, Annie Wendt. Hunting with Rifles. 2014. (Open Season Ser.). 32p. (J). (gr. 4-6). lib. bdg. 26.25 *(978-1-4777-6710-8(X),* PowerKids Pr.) Rosen Publishing Group, Inc., The.
—Hunting with Shotguns. 2014. (Open Season Ser.). (Illus.). 32p. (J). (gr. 4-6). lib. bdg. 26.25 *(978-1-4777-6705-4(3),* PowerKids Pr.) Rosen Publishing Group, Inc., The.
Kevin, Brian. Gun Sports, 1 vol. 2012. (Gun Education & Safety Ser.). (ENG.). 32p. 27.07 *(978-1-61783-317-5(7),* Checkerboard Library) ABDO Publishing Co.
Lambert, Hines. Hunting Ducks. 2013. (Let's Go Hunting Ser.). (ENG., Illus.). 32p. (J). (gr. 4-6). 25.25 *(978-1-4488-9661-5(4))*; pap. 10.00 *(978-1-4488-9780-3(7))* Rosen Publishing Group, Inc., The. (PowerKids Pr.).
Mebane, Jeanie. Pheasant Hunting, 1 vol. 2011. (Wild Outdoors Ser.). (ENG.). 32p. (gr. 1-2). lib. bdg. 26.65 *(978-1-4296-6005-1(8),* Blazers) Capstone Press of Coughlan Cos.
Omoth, Tyler. Duck Hunting for Kids, 1 vol. 2012. (Into the Great Outdoors Ser.). (ENG.). 32p. (gr. 3-4). lib. bdg. 27.99 *(978-1-4296-8616-7(2),* Edge Bks.) Capstone Press of Coughlan Cos.
Omoth, Tyler Dean. Duck Hunting for Kids, 1 vol. 2012. (Into the Great Outdoors Ser.). (ENG.). 32p. (gr. 3-4). pap. 7.95 *(978-1-4296-9268-7(5),* Edge Bks.) Capstone Press of Coughlan Cos.
Pound, Blake. Duck Hunting. 2012. (Outdoor Adventures Ser.). (ENG., Illus.). 24p. (J). (gr. 3-8). lib. bdg. 25.95 *(978-1-60014-797-5(6),* Pilot Bks.) Bellwether Media.
—Pheasant Hunting. 2012. (Outdoor Adventures Ser.). (ENG., Illus.). 24p. (J). (gr. 3-8). lib. bdg. 25.95 *(978-1-60014-801-9(8),* Pilot Bks.) Bellwether Media.
Shooter's Dictionary. 2003. cd-rom 0.00 *(978-0-9747407-1-3(3))* Southwest guns & stuff.
Wolny, Philip. Water Fowl. 2011. (Hunting: Pursuing Wild Game! Ser.). 64p. (YA). (ENG.). pap. 12.95 *(978-1-4488-2273-7(4),* Rosen Reference); (Illus.). (gr. 5-9). lib. bdg. 31.95 *(978-1-4488-1243-1(7))* Rosen Publishing Group, Inc., The.

SHOOTING STARS

see Meteors

SHOP COMMITTEES

see Management—Employee Participation

SHOPLIFTING

Sonnebom, Liz. Frequently Asked Questions about Shoplifting & Theft. 2011. (FAQ: Teen Life Ser.). (ENG.). 64p. (YA). (gr. 7-12). lib. bdg. 31.95 *(978-1-4488-5558-2(6))* Rosen Publishing Group, Inc., The.

SHOPLIFTING—FICTION

Corrigan, Eireann. The Believing Game. 2012. (ENG.). 384p. (J). (gr. 7). 17.99 *(978-0-545-29983-1(7),* Scholastic Pr.) Scholastic, Inc.
Cosgrove, Stephen. The Bugglar Brothers: Consequences of Stealing. Arroyo, Fian, illus. 2007. (J). *(978-1-58804-381-8(9))* P C I Education.
Durst, Sarah Beth. Chasing Power. 2014. (ENG.). 376p. (YA). (gr. 9). 17.99 *(978-0-8027-3755-7(2),* 9780802737557, Bloomsbury USA Childrens) Walker & Co.
Hutchins, Hazel. TJ & the Rockets, 1 vol. 2004. (Orca Young Readers Ser.). (ENG., Illus.). 112p. (J). (gr. 3-6). pap., tchr. ed. 4.99 *(978-1-55143-300-4(1),* 1234543) Orca Bk. Pubs. USA.
Pollack, Jenny. Klepto. 2008. (ENG.). 288p. (YA). (gr. 7-18). 8.99 *(978-0-14-241072-1(1),* Speak) Penguin Young Readers Group.
Tracy, Kristen. Crimes of the Sarahs. 2014. (ENG., Illus.). 384p. (YA). (gr. 9). pap. 9.99 *(978-1-4424-8100-8(5),* Simon Pulse) Simon Pulse.
Weber, Lori. Klepto, 1 vol. 2004. (Lorimer SideStreets Ser.). (ENG.). 160p. (YA). (gr. 9-12). 9.95 *(978-1-55028-836-0(9),* 9781550288360); 16.95 *(978-1-55028-837-7(7),* 9781550288377) Lorimer, James & Co., Ltd., Pubs. CAN. Dist: Casemate Pubs. & Bk. Distributors, LLC.

SHOPPERS' GUIDES

see Consumer Education; Shopping

SHOPPING

see also Consumer Education

At the Toyshop: Individual Title Six-Packs. (gr. -1-2). 23.00 *(978-0-7635-9005-5(3))* Rigby Education.
Big Picture Press, Big Picture. Sticker Style: Shop. Bowers, Jenny, illus. 2015. (ENG.). 12p. (J). (gr. k-3). pap. 12.99 *(978-0-7636-7770-1(1),* Big Picture Press) Candlewick Pr.
Braidich, Shelby. Where to Buy It. 2003. (Rosen REAL Readers Ser.). (ENG.). 8p. (gr. -1-1). pap. 5.15 *(978-0-8239-6337-9(3),* Rosen Classroom) Rosen Publishing Group, Inc., The.
Christmas Shopping: Individual Title Six-Packs. (Literatura 2000 Ser.). (gr. 1-2). 28.00 *(978-0-7635-0088-7(7))* Rigby Education.
Dakers, Diane. Getting Your Money's Worth: Making Smart Financial Choices. 2017. (Financial Literacy for Life Ser.). (ENG.). 48p. (J). ***(978-0-7787-3097-2(2))***; pap. ***(978-0-7787-3106-1(5))*** Crabtree Publishing Co.
Deen, Marilyn. Dollars & Cents, 1 vol. 2011. (Wonder Readers: Mathematics Ser.). (ENG.). (gr. -1-2). 20p. lib. bdg. 22.65 *(978-1-4296-8630-3(8))*; 16p. pap. 35.94 *(978-1-4296-8084-4(9))*; 32p. pap. 5.99 *(978-1-4296-7915-2(8))* Capstone Press of Coughlan Cos. (Wonder Readers).
Donovan, Sandra. Thrift Shopping: Discovering Bargains & Hidden Treasures. 2015. (ENG., Illus.). 64p. (J). (gr. 8-12). lib. bdg. 33.32 *(978-1-4677-5783-6(7),* Twenty-First Century Bks.) Lerner Publishing Group.
—Thrift Shopping: Discovering Bargains & Hidden Treasures. 2015. (J). *(978-1-4677-6310-3(1))* Twenty First Century Bks.
Encyclopaedia Britannica, Inc. Staff, compiled by. Discover English with Ben & Bella: Series 6: Shopping. 2010. 180.00 *(978-1-61535-353-8(4))* Encyclopaedia Britannica, Inc.
Enz, Tammy. Behind the Racks: Exploring the Secrets of a Shopping Mall, 1 vol. 2010. (Hidden Worlds Ser.). (ENG.). 32p. (gr. 1-2). lib. bdg. 26.65 *(978-1-4296-3386-4(7),* Blazers) Capstone Press of Coughlan Cos.
Ganeri, Anita. Super Malls Orange Band. 2016. (Cambridge Reading Adventures Ser.). (ENG.). 16p. pap. 6.56 *(978-1-316-50335-5(6))* Cambridge Univ. Pr.
Gardner, Faye, et al. Shopping in the 1940s. 2011. (When I Was Young Ser.). (ENG., Illus.). 32p. (J). pap. 10.99 *(978-0-237-54389-1(3))* Evans Brothers, Ltd. GBR. Dist: Independent Pubs. Group.
Gillis, Jennifer B. Neighborhood Shopping. 2006. (My Neighborhood Ser.). (Illus.). 24p. (gr. 3-7). 18.50 *(978-0-7569-6930-1(1))* Perfection Learning Corp.
Gillis, Jennifer Blizin. Neighborhood Shopping. 2006. (Readers for Writers Emergent Ser.). (Illus.). 24p. (J). pap. 7.95 *(978-1-59515-559-7(7))* Rourke Educational Media.
Giulieri, Anne. My Shopping, 1 vol. 2012. (Engage Literacy Magenta Ser.). (ENG.). 32p. (gr. k-2). pap. 5.99 *(978-1-4296-8884-0(X),* Engage Literacy) Capstone Press of Coughlan Cos.
Gorman, Jacqueline Laks. The Shopping Mall. 2005. (I Like to Visit Ser.). (Illus.). 24p. (gr. k-3). pap. 8.15 *(978-0-8368-4462-7(9))*; lib. bdg. 22.00 *(978-0-8368-4455-9(6))* Stevens, Gareth Publishing LLLP. (Weekly Reader Leveled Readers).
—The Shopping Mall (El Centro Comercial) 2005. (I Like to Visit/Me Gusta Visitar Ser.). (ENG & SPA., Illus.). 24p. (gr. k-3). lib. bdg. 22.00 *(978-0-8368-4599-0(4),* Weekly Reader Leveled Readers) Stevens, Gareth Publishing LLLP.
Gorman, Jacqueline Laks & Laks Gorman, Jacqueline. The Shopping Mall/El Centro Comercial. 2005. (I Like to Visit/ Me gusta visitar Ser.). (ENG & SPA., Illus.). 24p. (gr. k-3). pap. 8.15 *(978-0-8368-4606-5(0),* Weekly Reader Leveled Readers) Stevens, Gareth Publishing LLLP.
Gosman, Gillian. Earth-Friendly Shopping. 2011. (How to Be Earth Friendly Ser.). (Illus.). 32p. (gr. 3-4). (J). pap. 10.00

(978-1-4488-2771-8(X), PowerKids Pr.); (YA). lib. bdg. 25.25 *(978-1-4488-2591-2(1))* Rosen Publishing Group, Inc., The.
Hill, Mary. Signs at the Store. 2003. (Welcome Bks.). (ENG., Illus.). 24p. (J). (gr. -1-2). pap. 4.95 *(978-0-516-24363-4(2),* Children's Pr.) Scholastic Library Publishing.
Hollander, Barbara. What Are Saving & Spending? 2016. (Let's Find Out! Ser.). (ENG.). 32p. (J). (gr. 3-2). lib. bdg. 24.45 *(978-1-68048-405-2(2))* Rosen Publishing Group, Inc., The.
Houghton, Gillian. Goods & Services. 2009. (Invest Kids Ser.). 24p. (ENG., Illus.). (J). (gr. 2-5). pap. 8.25 *(978-1-4358-3210-7(8),* 1291654); (gr. 2-3). 42.50 *(978-1-61513-617-9(7));* (Illus.). (J). lib. bdg. 22.60 *(978-1-4358-2775-2(9),* 1291654) Rosen Publishing Group, Inc., The. (PowerKids Pr.).
James, Dawn. Store Math. 2015. (Math Around Us Ser.). (ENG.). 24p. (J). (gr. 1-1). pap. 8.22 *(978-1-5026-0165-0(6))* Cavendish Square Publishing.
Johnson, J. Angelique. The Eco-Shopper's Guide to Buying Green, 1 vol. Poling, Kyle, illus. 2010. (Point It Out! Tips for Green Living Ser.). (ENG.). 24p. (gr. 2-3). lib. bdg. 26.65 *(978-1-4048-6029-2(0))* Picture Window Bks.
Keogh, Josie. A Trip to the Grocery Store. 2012. (PowerKids Readers: My Community Ser.). (ENG., Illus.). 24p. (J). (gr. k-2). 22.60 *(978-1-4488-7403-3(3));* pap. 8.25 *(978-1-4488-7482-8(3))* Rosen Publishing Group, Inc., The. (PowerKids Pr.).
Lanz, Helen. Shopping Choices. 2012. (Go Green Ser.). (Illus.). 32p. (gr. 3-6). lib. bdg. 28.50 *(978-1-59771-304-7(X))* Sea-To-Sea Pubns.
Larson, Jennifer S. What Can You Do with Money? Earning, Spending, & Saving. 2010. (Lightning Bolt Books — Exploring Economics Ser.). (ENG., Illus.). 32p. (gr. k-2). pap. 7.95 *(978-0-7613-5666-0(5));* lib. bdg. 26.60 *(978-0-7613-3910-6(8))* Lerner Publishing Group.
Lewis, Clare. Shopping Around the World, 1 vol. 2014. (Around the World Ser.). (ENG., Illus.). 24p. (gr. -1-1). 22.65 *(978-1-4846-0373-4(7),* Acorn) Heinemann-Raintree.
Marsico, Katie. Shopping Trip Math. 2014. (Math Everywhere! Ser.). (Illus.). 32p. (gr. 3-4). (J). lib. bdg. 26.60 *(978-1-4677-1884-4(X),* Lerner Pubns.); pap. 7.95 *(978-1-4677-4515-4(4))* Lerner Publishing Group.
Michele, Tracey. What Can You Buy at the Mall? 2014. (Little Books of Answers: Level F Ser.). (Illus.). 16p. (gr. k-2). pap. 7.95 *(978-1-927136-52-2(0))* Three Crows Media NZL. Dist: RiverStream Publishing.
Minden, Cecilia. Smart Shopping. (21st Century Skills Library: Real World Math Ser.). (ENG., 32p. (gr. 4-7). 2015. Illus.). (J). 29.93 *(978-1-63362-575-4(3),* 206484) 2007. lib. bdg. 28.50 *(978-1-60279-005-6(1),* 200073) Cherry Lake Publishing.
Mitten, Ellen. Consumers & Producers. 2011. (ENG., Illus.). 24p. (gr. k-2). pap. 8.95 *(978-1-61741-992-8(3))* Rourke Educational Media.
Morgan, Elizabeth. My Shopping Trip. 2012. (InfoMax Readers Ser.). (ENG., Illus.). 16 pp.p. (J). (gr. k-1). pap. 7.00 *(978-1-4488-8893-1(X),* Rosen Classroom) Rosen Publishing Group, Inc., The.
Murphy, Stuart J. & Andriani, Renee. Mall Mania. 2006. (Mathstart Ser.). (Illus.). 33p. (gr. 1-4). 16.00 *(978-0-7569-6666-9(3))* Perfection Learning Corp.
Nadeau, Nicole. Caillou - The Shopping Trip. Brignaud, Pierre, illus. 2010. (Big Dipper Ser.). (ENG.). 24p. (J). (gr. -1-k). pap. 3.99 *(978-2-89450-718-6(6))* Caillouet, Gerry.
Reynolds, Mattie. Super-Smart Shopping: An Introduction to Financial Literacy. 2013. (Start Smart: Money Ser.). (Illus.). 24p. (gr. k-2). (J). lib. bdg. 17.95 net. *(978-1-937529-43-7(6));* (ENG., pap. 5.95 *(978-1-937529-39-0(8))* Red Chair Pr.
Rockliff, Mara. Get Real: What Kind of World Are You Buying? 2010. (ENG.). 112p. (YA). (gr. 5-17). pap. 13.95 *(978-0-7624-3745-0(6))* Running Pr. Bk. Pubs.
Roy, Jennifer Rozines & Roy, Gregory. Money at the Store. 2007. (J). pap. 6.99 *(978-0-7614-3385-9(6))* 2006. (Illus.). 32p. (gr. 2-7). lib. bdg. 29.93 *(978-0-7614-2264-8(1),* Benchmark Bks.) Marshall Cavendish Corp.
Santos, Edson. Cool Careers Without College for People Who Love Buying Things. 2017. (Cool Careers Without College Ser.). 112p. (J). (gr. 12-12). 38.45 ***(978-1-5081-7544-5(6),*** Rosen Young Adult) Rosen Publishing Group, Inc., The.
—Cool Careers Without College for People who Love to Buy Things. 2009. (Cool Careers Without College Ser.). 144p. (gr. 6-6). 66.50 *(978-1-61511-971-4(X))* Rosen Publishing Group, Inc., The.
—People Who Love to Buy Things. 2006. (Cool Careers Without College Ser.). (Illus.). 144p. (YA). (gr. 7-12). lib. bdg. 35.95 *(978-1-4042-0751-6(1))* Rosen Publishing Group, Inc., The.
Schwartz, Heather E. Spend Wisely. 2015. (Money Smarts Ser.). (ENG.). 32p. (gr. 2-4). 19.95 *(978-1-60753-795-3(8),* Amicus High Interest) Amicus Publishing.
Senker, Cath. ASOS. 2016. (Big Business Ser.). (ENG., Illus.). 32p. (J). (gr. 4-6). pap. 11.99 *(978-0-7502-8953-5(8),* Wayland) Hachette Children's Group GBR. Dist: Hachette Bk. Group.
Shopping. (Butterfly Bks.). (ARA., Illus.). 15p. (J). 11.95 *(978-0-86685-619-5(6),* LDL360) International Bk. Ctr., Inc.
Steffora, Tracey. Math at the Store, 1 vol. 2013. (Math on the Job Ser.). (ENG., Illus.). 24p. (gr. k-2). pap. 6.29 *(978-1-4329-7160-1(3));* lib. bdg. 22.65 *(978-1-4329-7153-3(0))* Heinemann-Raintree. (Acorn).
Thompson, Helen. Shopping Math. 2013. (Math 24/7 Ser.: 10). 48p. (J). (gr. 5-18). 19.95 *(978-1-4222-2908-8(4))* Mason Crest.
Ticktock Media, Ltd. Staff. Shopping Day. 2009. (Busy Tots Ser.). (ENG.). 10p. (J). (gr. -1-k). bds. 6.95 *(978-1-84696-799-3(6),* TickTock Books) Octopus Publishing Group GBR. Dist: Independent Pubs. Group.

SHOPPING—FICTION

Abbott, Simon, illus. Happy Street: Bookshop. 2016. (Happy Street Ser.). (ENG.). 10p. (J). (gr. -1-k). 9.99 *(978-1-4052-7517-0(0))* Egmont Bks., Ltd. GBR. Dist: Independent Pubs. Group.
Ashley, Bernard. A Present for Paul. Mitchell, David, illus. 2004. 28p. (J). *(978-1-85269-359-6(2)); (978-1-85269-360-2(6))* Mantra Lingua.
Barry, Debra R. Let's Go to the Market. 2012. 28p. pap. 24.95 *(978-1-4626-8533-2(1))* America Star Bks.
Bauer, Joan. Best Foot Forward. 2006. 183p. (gr. 7-12). 18.00 *(978-0-7569-6767-3(8))* Perfection Learning Corp.
Benenfeld, Rikki. Let's Go Shopping. Benenfeld, Rikki, illus. 2005. (Toddler Experience Ser.). (Illus.). 24p. (J). 10.95 *(978-1-929628-20-9(X))* Hachai Publishing.
Bently, Peter. The Great Balloon Hullaballoo. Matsuoka, Mei, illus. 2014. (ENG.). 32p. (J). (gr. -1-3). 16.95 *(978-1-4677-3449-3(7))* Lerner Publishing Group.
Birkett, Georgie, illus. Cook It!/¡A Cocinar! 2009. (Helping Hands English/Spanish Edition Ser.). (ENG & SPA.). 24p. (J). (gr. -1-k). pap. *(978-1-84643-568-3(4))* Child's Play International Ltd.
Bohmer, Kara Dale. Walking Sarah: First Day Out. 2013. 32p. *(978-1-4602-0076-6(4));* pap. *(978-1-4602-0077-3(2))* FriesenPress.
Bond, Michael. Paddington Bear Goes to Market. Alley, R. W., illus. 2014. (Paddington Ser.). (ENG.). 14p. (J). (gr. -1-3). bds. 6.99 *(978-0-06-231722-3(9),* HarperFestival) HarperCollins Pubs.
Bradman, Tony & Quarto Generic Staff. Wait & See. Browne, Eileen, illus. rev. ed. 2012. (ENG.). 32p. (J). (gr. -1-1). pap. 8.99 *(978-1-84780-181-4(1),* Frances Lincoln) Quarto Publishing Group UK GBR. Dist: Hachette Bk. Group.
Brokamp, Elizabeth. Back to School, Picky Little Witch!, 1 vol. Welling, Peter, illus. 2014. (ENG.). 32p. (J). (gr. k-3). 16.99 *(978-1-4556-1887-3(X))* Pelican Publishing Co., Inc.
Christelow, Eileen. Five Little Monkeys Go Shopping. 2012. (Five Little Monkeys Story Ser.). lib. bdg. 17.20 *(978-0-606-23990-5(1),* Turtleback) Turtleback Bks.
Coulton, Mia. Danny & Dad Go Shopping. Coulton, Mia, photos by. 2003. (ENG., Illus.). pap. 5.35 *(978-0-9720295-4-4(0))* Maryruth Bks., Inc.
Curry, Peter. Millie Goes Shopping. 2004. (First Words with Millie Ser.). (Illus.). 12p. (J). bds. 3.99 *(978-1-85854-505-9(6))* Brimax Books Ltd. GBR. Dist: Byeway Bks.
Dames-Johnson, Angela. What's Gerald Done Now? Supermarket Fun. 2009. 24p. pap. 24.95 *(978-1-60749-474-4(4))* America Star Bks.
Derby, Sally. Sunday Shopping, 1 vol. Strickland, Shadra, illus. 2015. (ENG.). 32p. (J). 17.95 *(978-1-60060-438-6(2),* 9781600000000) Lee & Low Bks., Inc.
Dewdney, Anna. Llama Llama Mad at Mama. Dewdney, Anna, illus. 2007. (Llama Llama Ser.). (ENG., Illus.). 40p. (J). (gr. -1-k). 17.99 *(978-0-670-06240-9(5),* Viking Books for Young Readers) Penguin Young Readers Group.
—Llama Llama Mad at Mama. 2009. (Illus.). (J). *(978-0-545-15933-3(4))* Scholastic, Inc.
Donaldson, Julia. Hippo Has a Hat. Sharratt, Nick, illus. 2007. (ENG.). 24p. (J). (gr. k-k). pap. 8.99 *(978-1-4050-2192-0(6))* Macmillan Pubs., Ltd. GBR. Dist: Independent Pubs. Group.
Dulemba, Elizabeth. Soap, Soap, Soap. 2009. (ENG.). 32p. (J). (gr. -1-3). 16.95 *(978-1-934960-64-6(0),* Raven Tree Pr.,Csi) Continental Sales, Inc.
—Soap, Soap, Soap/Jabon, Jabon, Jabon. 2009. (ENG & SPA., Illus.). 32p. (J). (gr. -1-3). 16.95 *(978-1-934960-62-2(4));* pap. 7.95 *(978-1-934960-63-9(2))* Continental Sales, Inc. (Raven Tree Pr.,Csi).
Dulemba, Elizabeth O. Soap, Soap, Soap. Dulemba, Elizabeth O., illus. 2010. (ENG., Illus.). 32p. (J). (gr. -1-3). pap. 7.95 *(978-1-934960-65-3(9),* Raven Tree Pr.,Csi) Continental Sales, Inc.
Dyan, Penelope. A New Bag! Dyan, Penelope, illus. 2012. (Illus.). 34p. pap. 11.95 *(978-1-61477-054-1(9))* Bellissima Publishing, LLC.
Elya, Susan Middleton. Bebé Goes Shopping. Salerno, Steven, illus. 2008. (ENG.). 36p. (J). (gr. -1-3). pap. 7.99 *(978-0-15-206142-5(8))* Houghton Mifflin Harcourt Publishing Co.
Enderle, Dotti & Sansum, Vicki. Grandpa for Sale. Gentry, T. Kyle, illus. 2007. (ENG.). 32p. (J). (gr. k-3). 17.95 *(978-0-9729225-8-6(X))* Flashlight Pr.
Escklsen, Erik E. The Last Mall Rat. 2005. (ENG.). 192p. (YA). (gr. 7). pap. 11.95 *(978-0-618-60896-6(6))* Houghton Mifflin Harcourt Publishing Co.
Evans, K. D. Corey, the Little Purple Shopping Cart. 2008. 28p. per. 24.95 *(978-1-4241-8457-6(6))* America Star Bks.
Florence, Tyler & Frazier, Craig. Tyler Makes Pancakes! Florence, Tyler & Frazier, Craig, illus. 2012. (ENG., Illus.). 40p. (J). (gr. -1-2). 16.99 *(978-0-06-204752-6(3))* HarperCollins Pubs.
Fuerst, Jeffrey B. At the Comma Store. Knuvers, Onno, illus. 2013. (Reader's Theater Word Plays Ser.). (J). (gr. 1-2). *(978-1-4509-8921-3(7))* Benchmark Education Co.
Goodier, Eleanor, et al. The Vermin Family Adventures (Book 1) 2010. 68p. pap. 9.50 *(978-1-4457-5617-2(X))* Lulu Pr., Inc.
Gooding-Alber, Karry. Red Shoelace, 1 vol. 2010. 16p. pap. 24.95 *(978-1-4489-6255-6(2))* America Star Bks.
Goodrich, C. C. Barnabee: Goes Shopping. 2009. (Illus.). 32p. pap. 13.99 *(978-1-4389-9728-5(0))* AuthorHouse.
Hammelef, Danielle S. Shopping with the Nicholas Family. 2006. (Early Explorers Ser.). (J). pap. *(978-1-4108-6117-7(1))* Benchmark Education Co.
Harvey, Matt. Shopping with Dad. Latimer, Miriam, illus. 2008. (ENG.). 32p. (J). (gr. -1-3). 16.99 *(978-1-84686-172-7(1))* Barefoot Bks., Inc.
Henderson, Sara & Zenz, Aaron. Howie Goes Shopping(Fido Va de Compras), 1 vol. Henderson, Sara & Zenz, Aaron, illus. 2009. (I Can Read! / Howie Series / ¡Yo Sé Leer! / Serie: Fido Ser.). (ENG., Illus.). 32p. (J). pap. 3.99 *(978-0-310-71874-1(0))* Zonderkidz.
Hill, Eric. Spot Goes Shopping. Hill, Eric, illus. 2014. (Spot Ser.). (ENG., Illus.). 12p. (J). (gr. -1-k). bds. 5.99 *(978-0-7232-8997-5(2),* Warne) Penguin Young Readers Group.
Hillert, Margaret. Dear Dragon Goes to the Market. Schimmell, David, illus. 2010. (BeginningtoRead Ser.). 32p. (J). (gr. k-2). lib. bdg. 22.60 *(978-1-59953-347-6(2))* Norwood Hse. Pr.
—Querido Dragón Va Al Mercado/Dear Dragon Goes to the Market. Schimmell, David, illus. 2011. (BeginningtoRead Ser.). 32p. (J). (-2). pap. 11.94 *(978-1-60357-553-9(7))* Norwood Hse. Pr.
Husar, Stephane. Cat & Mouse Let's Go Shopping! Mehee, Loic, illus. 2015. (Av2 Fiction Readalong 2016 Ser.). (ENG.). (J). lib. bdg. 34.28 *(978-1-4896-3816-8(4),* AV2 by Weigl) Weigl Pubs., Inc.
Johnstone, Jan. Tom the Grocery Trolley. 2009. (Illus.). 28p. pap. 12.49 *(978-1-4389-3616-1(8))* AuthorHouse.
Kaplan, Michael B. Betty Bunny Wants Everything. Jorisch, Stéphane, illus. 2012. (Betty Bunny Ser.). (ENG.). 32p. (J). (gr. -1-k). 17.99 *(978-0-8037-3408-1(5),* Dial Bks) Penguin Young Readers Group.
Katschke, Judy. Hooray for Shoppywood! 2017. (Shopkins: Shoppies Ser.). (ENG.). 64p. (J). (gr. 1-3). pap. 4.99 ***(978-1-338-12856-7(6))*** Scholastic, Inc.
Klein, Adria F. & National Geographic Learning Staff. Max Goes Shopping. Gallagher-Cole, Memie, illus. 2005. (Read-It! Readers: the Life of Max Ser.). (ENG.). 24p. (gr. -1-2). lib. bdg. 21.32 *(978-1-4048-1177-5(X),* Easy Readers) Picture Window Bks.
LeapFrog Staff, compiled by. Tad Goes Shopping - U. K. 2003. spiral bd. 18.00 *(978-1-58605-950-7(5))* LeapFrog Enterprises, Inc.
Leonard, Marcia. Pantalones Nuevos, No! Handelman, Dorothy, photos by. 2005.Tr. of No New Pants! (Illus.). 32p. (J). (ENG & SPA.). (gr. -1-1). pap. 4.99 *(978-0-8225-3297-2(2));* (SPA., (gr. 1-1). per. 5.95 *(978-0-8225-3296-5(4),* Ediciones Lerner) Lerner Publishing Group.
Lobel, Arnold. On Market Street. Lobel, Anita, illus. 25th anniv. ed. 2006. (ENG.). 40p. (J). (gr. -1-3). pap. 6.99 *(978-0-688-08745-6(0),* Greenwillow Bks.) HarperCollins Pubs.
Manushkin, Fran. Katie Woo, Where Are You?, 1 vol. Lyon, Tammie, illus. 2011. (Katie Woo Ser.). (ENG.). 32p. (gr. k-2). pap. 5.95 *(978-1-4048-6853-3(4));* lib. bdg. 21.32 *(978-1-4048-6517-4(9))* Picture Window Bks.
—Katie's New Shoes, 1 vol. Lyon, Tammie, illus. 2011. (Katie Woo Ser.). (ENG.). 32p. (gr. k-2). pap. 5.95 *(978-1-4048-6855-7(0));* lib. bdg. 21.32 *(978-1-4048-6519-8(5))* Picture Window Bks.
Mass, Wendy. Heaven Looks a Lot Like the Mall. 2008. (ENG.). 256p. (J). (gr. 7-17). pap. 10.00 *(978-0-316-05850-6(5))* Little, Brown Bks. for Young Readers.
Mealue, Monique. Johnny Goes Shopping. 2010. 24p. 12.95 *(978-1-4520-0227-9(4))* AuthorHouse.
Meister, Cari. Buzz Beaker & the Growing Goo, 1 vol. McGuire, Bill, illus. 2011. (Buzz Beaker Bks.). (ENG.). 32p. (gr. 2-3). pap. 6.25 *(978-1-4342-3056-0(2));* lib. bdg. 22.65 *(978-1-4342-2527-6(5))* Stone Arch Bks.
Melvin, Alice. The High Street. 2011. (ENG., Illus.). 52p. (J). (gr. -1-3). 15.95 *(978-1-85437-943-6(7))* Tate Publishing, Ltd. GBR. Dist: Abrams, Inc.
Mills, Nathan & Okon, Jodi. Ava Goes Shopping. 2012. (Rosen Readers Ser.). (ENG., Illus.). 16p. (J). (gr. k-1). pap. 7.00 *(978-1-4488-8658-6(9),* Rosen Classroom) Rosen Publishing Group, Inc., The.
Mom Goes Shopping. 2003. (Mom & Dad Ser.). (J). 7.33 *(978-1-58453-251-4(3))* Pioneer Valley Bks.
Morgan, Beverly. Gregory Likes Saturdays: A Little Story about Being Lost in Wal-Mart. Brady, Jeannette, ed. l.t. ed. 2005. (Illus.). 27p. (J). 4.99 *(978-0-9772109-1-6(X))* Joyful Noise.
Onyefulu, Ifeoma. New Shoes for Helen. Onyefulu, Ifeoma, photos by. 2011. (First Experiences Ser.). (ENG., Illus.). 32p. (J). (gr. -1-2). 17.95 *(978-1-84780-128-9(5),* Frances Lincoln) Quarto Publishing Group UK GBR. Dist: Hachette Bk. Group.
Parker, Emma. The Butterfly on the Subway. 2010. (Illus.). pap. *(978-1-877547-81-2(6))* First Edition Ltd.
Rylant, Cynthia. Brownie & Pearl See the Sights. Biggs, Brian, illus. 2010. (Brownie & Pearl Ser.). (ENG.). 24p. (J). (gr. -1-k). 14.99 *(978-1-4169-8637-9(5),* Beach Lane Bks.) Beach Lane Bks.
—Brownie & Pearl See the Sights. Biggs, Brian, illus. 2013. (Brownie & Pearl Ser.). (ENG.). 24p. (J). (gr. -1-k). 16.99 *(978-1-4424-8744-4(5));* pap. 3.99 *(978-1-4424-8743-7(7))* Simon Spotlight. (Simon Spotlight).
Sadler, Marilyn & Bollen, Roger. Money, Money, Honey Bunny! 2006. (Bright & Early Books(R) Ser.). (ENG., Illus.). 36p. (J). (gr. -1-k). 9.99 *(978-0-375-83370-0(6),* Random Hse. Bks. for Young Readers) Random Hse. Children's Bks.
Sandlin, Pauline. Mannequins. 2011. 32p. pap. 21.99 *(978-1-4568-2707-6(3))* Xlibris Corp.
Santillo, LuAnn. The Pig. Santillo, LuAnn, ed. 2003. (Half-Pint Kids Readers Ser.). (Illus.). 7p. (J). (gr. -1-1). pap. 1.00 *(978-1-59256-064-6(4))* Half-Pint Kids, Inc.
Sebring, Ruthie. Charlie, Itty's Guinea Pig, 1 vol. 2010. 30p. 24.95 *(978-1-4489-4391-3(4))* PublishAmerica, Inc.
Seibold, J. Otto. Lost Sloth. 2013. (ENG., Illus.). 32p. 16.95 *(978-1-938073-35-9(5))* McSweeney's Publishing.
Shaw, Nancy E. Sheep in a Shop, 1 vol. Apple, Margot, illus. 2009. (ENG.). 32p. (J). (gr. -1-3). audio compact disk 10.99 *(978-0-547-23767-1(7))* Houghton Mifflin Harcourt Publishing Co.
Shopping with Dad, 6 vols., Pack. (gr. -1-2). 23.00 *(978-0-7635-8991-2(8))* Rigby Education.
Sitomer, Alan Lawrence. Daddy's Back-To-School Shopping Adventure. Carter, Abby, illus. 2015. (ENG.). 40p. (J). (gr. -1-k). 16.99 *(978-1-4231-8421-8(1))* Hyperion Bks. for Children.
Souvenirs, 6 vols., Pack. (Literatura 2000 Ser.). (gr. 2-3). 33.00 *(978-0-7635-0186-0(7))* Rigby Education.
Stockham, Jess, illus. Shopping! 2011. (Helping Hands Ser.). (ENG.). 24p. (J). *(978-1-84643-412-9(2))* Child's Play International Ltd.
Thiel Annie. The Playdate Kids Dakota Gets Lost. 2007. 32p. 12.95 *(978-1-933721-08-8(1))* Playdate Kids Publishing.
Thiel, Annie & Fanning, Tena. Dakota Gets Lost. Edwards, William M., illus. 2007. (Playdate Kids: Let's Be Friends! Ser.). 27p. (J). (gr. -1-3). per. 6.95 *(978-1-933721-20-0(0))* Playdate Kids Publishing.
Thorp, Gloria J. & Ruotsala, Charity Aili. Anna's Hats: Anna has a hat for every Adventure. 2009. 40p. pap. 19.49 *(978-1-4389-8967-9(9))* AuthorHouse.
Tice, Kimberly & Litvack, Venita. Lou Knows What to Do: Supermarket. Kerry, Andre, illus. 2017. (Lou Knows What to Do Ser.: 1). (ENG.). 32p. (J). (gr. -1-6). pap. 10.95 ***(978-1-944882-14-3(6))*** Boys Town Pr.
Trent, Shanda. Farmers' Market Day. Dippold, Jane, illus. 2013. (ENG.). 32p. (J). (gr. -1-1). 12.95 *(978-1-58925-115-1(6))* Tiger Tales.
Tunkin, David & National Geographic Learning Staff. New Clothes. 2007. (Windows on Literacy Ser.). (ENG., Illus.). 12p. (J). pap. 10.95 *(978-0-7922-8947-0(1))* CENGAGE Learning.
Venable, Colleen A. F. The Ferret's a Foot, 3 vols. Yue, Stephanie, illus. 2011. (Guinea Pig, Pet Shop Private Eye Ser.: 3). (ENG.). 48p. (J). (gr. 2-5). 27.93 *(978-0-7613-6223-5(6))* Lerner Publishing Group.
Verdick, Elizabeth. On-the-Go Time. Heinlen, Marieka, illus. 2011. (Toddler Tools Ser.). (ENG.). 24p. (J). 7.95 *(978-1-57542-379-1(0),* 1331978) Free Spirit Publishing, Inc.
Volker, Kerstin. Emma Goes Shopping. 2003. (Funny Friends Lift-and-Learn Bks.). 14p. (J). 5.99 *(978-1-59384-021-1(7))* Parklane Publishing.
Webb, Sarah. Bridesmaid Blitz. 2012. (Ask Amy Green Ser.: 3). (ENG., Illus.). 320p. (YA). (gr. 7). pap. 6.99 *(978-0-7636-5157-2(5))* Candlewick Pr.
West, Abby. The Adventures of Penny Ann & Alexa Jane. 2013. (ENG., Illus.). 28p. (gr. -1-4). pap. 13.95 *(978-1-936205-33-2(5))* Austin, Stephen F. State Univ. Pr.
Whitley-Kinzett, Sara. Grumpy Ted: The Teds Volume One. Ellams, Victoria, illus. 2009. 16p. pap. 10.65 *(978-1-4251-0051-3(1))* Trafford Publishing.
Williams, Brenda. Lin Yi's Lantern: A Moon Festival Tale. Lacombe, Benjamin, illus. 2009. (ENG.). 32p. (J). (gr. -1-5). 16.99 *(978-1-84686-147-5(0))* Barefoot Bks., Inc.
—Lin Yi's Lantern: A Moon Festival Tale. Tavares, Victor, illus. 2008. 32p. (J). *(978-1-84686-148-2(9))* Barefoot Bks., Inc.
Williams, Shanica. Amy Goes Shopping for School. 2012. 16p. pap. 15.99 *(978-1-4772-1360-5(0))* AuthorHouse.
Wilson, Karma. Mortimer's Christmas Manger. Chapman, Jane, illus. 2007. (ENG.). 40p. (J). (gr. -1-3). 9.99 *(978-1-4169-5049-3(4),* McElderry, Margaret K. Bks.) McElderry, Margaret K. Bks.
Wolfe, Frances. The Little Toy Shop. Wolfe, Frances, illus. 2008. (ENG., Illus.). 32p. (J). (gr. -1-2). 19.95 *(978-0-88776-865-1(2),* Tundra Bks.) Tundra Bks. CAN. Dist: Penguin Random Hse. LLC.
Wynne-Jones, Tim. Secret Agent Man Goes Shopping for Shoes. Won, Brian, illus. 2016. (ENG.). 32p. (J). (gr. -1-3). 16.99 *(978-0-7636-7119-8(3))* Candlewick Pr.
Yanisko, Thomas. What You Eat It's up to You. Hoyes, Kerry, illus. 2012. 36p. pap. 9.99 *(978-1-937260-26-2(7))* Sleepytown Pr.

SHORT STORIES

A Lady. Tales from Ariosto: Retold for Children. 2007. pap. 28.95 *(978-1-4304-5008-5(8))* Kessinger Publishing, LLC.
A&C Black, A&C. The Secret Seven. 2017. (ENG.). 32p. (J). pap. 42.00 ***(978-1-4729-3393-5(1))*** HarperCollins Pubs. Ltd. GBR. Dist: Independent Pubs. Group.
Abbate, Jason. Welcome to Xooxville. 2004. (YA). per. 12.95 *(978-0-9760959-0-3(4))* Rarecity Pr.
Abbott, Jacob. Stories Told to Rollo's Cousin Lucy. 2005. pap. 22.95 *(978-1-4179-5651-7(8))* Kessinger Publishing, LLC.
Abraham, Ametta. Miss Robbie's House. 2009. 64p. pap. 23.49 *(978-1-4490-4571-5(5))* AuthorHouse.
Abraham, Rayna M. Just Imagine: Rayna Abraham's Creative Collection for Kids. 2011. 44p. pap. 16.59 *(978-1-4634-1529-7(X))* AuthorHouse.
Abrefah, Nana K. My Amazing Short Stories & Questions. 2008. 60p. pap. 8.95 *(978-0-595-51861-6(3))* iUniverse, Inc.
Abuhamda, Nasser. Short Stories. 2008. 48p. pap. 14.95 *(978-1-59858-581-0(9))* Dog Ear Publishing, LLC.
—6 Tales of Adventure. 2009. 84p. pap. 14.95 *(978-1-59858-833-0(8))* Dog Ear Publishing, LLC.
Acreman, Hayley. Found You Rabbit! Acreman, Hayley, illus. 2011. (ENG., Illus.). 34p. (J). (gr. k-2). pap. 9.95 *(978-1-905762-87-3(9))* Parthian Bks. GBR. Dist: Independent Pubs. Group.
Adams, Jennifer. Edgar Gets Ready for Bed, 1 vol. Stucki, Ron, illus. 2014. (ENG.). 32p. (J). 16.99 *(978-1-4236-3528-4(0))* Gibbs Smith, Publisher.
Adams, John Joseph, ed. Under the Moons of Mars: New Adventures on Barsoom. 2013. (ENG., Illus.). 368p. (YA). (gr. 7). pap. 9.99 *(978-1-4424-2030-4(8),* Simon & Schuster Bks. For Young Readers) Simon & Schuster Bks. For Young Readers.
—Under the Moons of Mars: New Adventures on Barsoom. Various Artists, illus. 2012. (ENG.). 368p. (YA). (gr. 7). 16.99 *(978-1-4424-2029-8(4),* Simon & Schuster Bks. For Young Readers) Simon & Schuster Bks. For Young Readers.
Adkinson, Gma Mary. Growing up with Princess Lizzy: Little Life Lessons. 2012. (ENG.). 50p. pap. 16.95 *(978-1-4787-1993-9(1))* Outskirts Pr., Inc.
Adler, David A. The Day I Lost My Hampster: And Other True School Stories. 2006. 48p. *(978-0-439-80289-5(X))* Scholastic, Inc.
Aesop. The Aesop for Children. Winter, Milo, illus. 2013. 236p. pap. 9.97 *(978-1-60386-613-2(2))* Rough Draft Printing.
Aesop, illus. Aesop's Fables. 2006. (ENG.). 32p. (J). (gr. -1-3). 16.95 *(978-0-7358-2068-5(6))* North-South Bks., Inc.
Agnew, Kate. Would You Believe It? Parsons, Gary, illus. (ENG.). 128p. (J). pap. 7.50 *(978-1-4052-0520-7(2))* Egmont Bks., Ltd. GBR. Dist: Trafalgar Square Publishing.
Aguado, Bill & Newirth, Richard. Paint Me Like I Am: Teen Poems from WritersCorps. 2003. (ENG., Illus.). 144p. (YA). (gr. 8-18). pap. 8.99 *(978-0-06-447264-7(7),* HarperTeen) HarperCollins Pubs.
Ahmed, Rehana. Walking a Tightrope: New Writing from Asian Britain. unabr. ed. 2005. (ENG.). 272p. (YA). pap. *(978-0-330-41579-8(4),* Macmillan Children's Bks.) Pan Macmillan.
Aiken, Joan. A Necklace of Raindrops & Other Stories. Hawkes, Kevin, illus. 2003. 84p. (J). (gr. 1-5). 13.15 *(978-0-7569-5686-8(2))* Perfection Learning Corp.
—Snow Horse & Other Stories. 2004. *(978-0-7136-7654-9(X),* A&C Black) Bloomsbury Publishing Plc.
Aitken, Amber. Perfect Match, Vol. 4. 2011. (Cupid Company Ser.). (ENG.). 240p. (J). (gr. 4-6). pap. 9.99 *(978-0-00-736263-9(3))* HarperCollins Pubs. Ltd. GBR. Dist: Independent Pubs. Group.
Akers, Martin, et al. Fran Grabs It - Stop! It's a Frog! - the Best Nest: BuildUp Unit 3 Lap Book. Palacios, Sara & Battuz, Christine, illus. 2015. (Build up Core Phonics Ser.). (J). (gr. 1). *(978-1-4900-2602-2(9))* Benchmark Education Co.
Alam, Sarah H. Enchanting Fables. 2008. 48p. pap. 16.95 *(978-1-60441-768-5(4))* America Star Bks.

Albert, Beatrice. Adventure's Unlimited: Great Stories for Great Kids. 2009. 52p. (J). pap. 14.95 (978-1-4327-3224-0(2)) Outskirts Pr., Inc.

Alcott, Louisa May. A Garland for Girls. 2006. pap. (978-1-4065-0587-0(0)) Dodo Pr.

—A Garland for Girls. l.t. ed. 2005. 376p. pap. (978-1-84637-049-6(3)) Echo Library.

—Kitty's Class Day. l.t. ed. 2005. 424p. pap. (978-1-84637-055-7(8)) Echo Library.

—Kitty's Class Day & Other Stories. 2005. 28.95 (978-1-4218-1485-8(4)); 268p. pap. 13.95 (978-1-4218-1585-5(0)) 1st World Publishing, Inc. (1st World Library - Literary Society).

—Kitty's Class Day & Other Stories. 2006. (ENG.). 208p. pap. 20.99 (978-1-4264-0876-2(5)) Creative Media Partners, LLC.

—Kitty's Class Day & Other Stories. 2006. pap. (978-1-4065-0588-7(9)) Dodo Pr.

—Kitty's Class Day, & Other Stories. 2013. 178p. (J). pap. 8.75 (978-1-61720-920-8(1)) Wilder Pubns., Corp.

—Kitty's Class Day & Other Stories. l.t. ed. 2006. 200p. pap. 21.99 (978-1-4264-0857-1(9)) Creative Media Partners, LLC.

—The Louisa Alcott Reader. l.t. ed. 2005. 228p. pap. (978-1-84637-058-8(2)) Echo Library.

—Silver Pitchers & Independence. 2011. 208p. pap. 14.95 (978-1-60664-548-2(X)) Rodgers, Alan Bks.

—Spinning-Wheel Stories. 2011. 202p. 27.95 (978-1-4638-9494-8(5)) Rodgers, Alan Bks.

Alemayehu, Tsehay. Bee-Come! A Collection of Short Stories. 2012. 58p. pap. 20.95 (978-1-4525-4816-6(1)) Balboa Pr.

Alexander, Lloyd. The Foundling: And Other Tales of Prydain. Wyatt, David, illus. 6th rev. ed. 2006. (Chronicles of Prydain Ser.: 6). (ENG.). 112p. (J). (gr. 3-7). pap. 6.99 (978-0-8050-8053-7(8), 9780805080537) Square Fish.

Alfreda. Story Time Stories Without Rhyme. 2003. 21.95 (978-0-913597-90-3(2)) Prosperity & Profits Unlimited, Distribution Services.

Ali, Saleena. Behind My Eyes & Truly in Love Stories of Friendship & Love: Book Two. 2012. 76p. pap. 10.84 (978-1-4669-2217-4(6)) Trafford Publishing.

Allen, Constance & Albee, Sarah. Elmo's Little Golden Book Favorites (Sesame Street) Swanson, Maggie & Ewers, Joe, illus. 2014. (Little Golden Book Favorites Ser.). (ENG.). 80p. (J). (gr. -1-2). 7.99 (978-0-385-37196-4(9), Golden Bks.) Random Hse. Children's Bks.

Allen, Nancy Kelly. Trouble in Troublesome Creek: A Troublesome Creek Kids Story. Crawford, K. Michael, illus. 2010. (ENG.). 32p. (J). (gr. -1-3). 16.95 (978-1-933176-32-1(6)) Red Rock Pr., Inc.

Almond, David. Half a Creature from the Sea: A Life in Stories. Taylor, Eleanor, illus. 2015. (ENG.). 240p. (YA). (gr. 7). 16.99 (978-0-7636-7877-7(5)) Candlewick Pr.

Almond, David, et al. The Great War: Stories Inspired by Items from the First World War. Kay, Jim, illus. 2015. (ENG.). 304p. (J). (gr. 5). 19.99 (978-0-7636-7554-7(7)) Candlewick Pr.

Alonso, Fernando. El Hombrecito Vestido de Gris. Wendell, Ulises, illus. 2003. (SPA.). 94p. (J). (gr. 3-5). pap. 8.95 (978-968-19-0439-5(7)) Santillana USA Publishing Co., Inc.

Altes, Marta. No! 2011. (Child's Play Library). (ENG., Illus.). 32p. (J). (978-1-84643-417-4(3)) Child's Play International Ltd.

Alvarez, Julia. De Como Tia Lola Termino Empezando Otra Vez. 2012. (Tia Lola Stories Ser.). (ENG & SPA.). 192p. (J). (gr. 3-7). 7.99 (978-0-307-93034-7(3), Yearling) Random Hse. Children's Bks.

Amerie. Because You Love to Hate Me: 13 Tales of Villainy. Amerie, ed. 2017. (ENG.). 368p. (YA). 17.99 (978-1-68119-364-9(7), 9781681193649, Bloomsbury USA Childrens) Bloomsbury Publishing USA.

Amery, H. Mini Stories from Around the World. rev. ed. 2013. (Mini Editions Ser.). 128p. (J). ring bd. 7.99 (978-0-7945-3384-7(1), Usborne) EDC Publishing.

—Stories from Around the World. 2004. (Stories for Young Children Ser.). 128p. (J). 7.99 (978-0-7945-0110-5(9), Usborne) EDC Publishing.

Amery, Heather. Little Book of First Stories. 2004. (Mini Storybooks Ser.). (ENG., Illus.). 128p. (J). 7.95 (978-0-7945-0269-0(5), Usborne) EDC Publishing.

Amery, Heather & Cartwright, Stephen. Rusty's Train Ride. rev. ed. 2004. (Treasury of Farmyard Tales Ser.). 16p. (J). pap. 4.95 (978-0-7945-0602-5(X)) EDC Publishing.

Amos, Muriel & Olrun, Prudy. Animals of Nunivak Island. Amos, Muriel & Olrun, Prudy, illus. 2006. (Animal Story Collection Ser.). (Illus.). 16p. (J). (gr. 2-6). pap. 9.00 (978-1-58084-238-9(0)) Lower Kuskokwim Schl. District.

Amy, Brooks. Princess Polly Stories. 2007. (ENG.). 196p. pap. 19.99 (978-1-4346-1976-1(1)) Creative Media Partners, LLC.

Ana, Moh. Kookaburra Tales # 3: Laugh Not at Others. 2013. 16p. pap. 16.81 (978-1-4669-3477-1(8)) Trafford Publishing.

Anaya, Hector. Cuenta Cuenta. Moreno, Sergio, illus. 2nd rev. ed. 2005. (Castillo de la Lectura Verde Ser.). (SPA & ENG.). 184p. (J). (gr. -1-7). pap. 7.95 (978-970-20-0135-5(8)) Castillo, Ediciones, S. A. de C. V. MEX. Dist: Macmillan.

Andersen, Hans Christian. Cuentos de Andersen. 2nd ed. 2003.Tr. of Stories from Han Andersen. (SPA., Illus.). 64p. (978-84-392-8880-0(8), EV6475) Gaviota Ediciones ESP. Dist: Lectorum Pubns., Inc.

—Fairy Tales of Hans Christian Andersen. 2011. 892p. pap. 19.99 (978-1-61382-020-9(8)) Simon & Brown.

—Hans Andersen's Fairy Tales. Lewis, Naomi, tr. from DAN. 2nd ed. 2010. (Puffin Classics Ser.). (ENG., Illus.). 176p. (J). (gr. 5-7). pap. 5.99 (978-0-14-132901-7(7), Puffin Books) Penguin Young Readers Group.

—Hans Christian Andersen Tales. 2014. (Word Cloud Classics Ser.). (ENG., Illus.). 464p. pap. 14.99 (978-1-62686-259-3(1), Thunder Bay Pr.) Readerlink Distribution Services, LLC.

—Hans Christian Andersen's Fairy Tales: An Illustrated Classic. Rackham, Arthur et al, illus. 2017. (Illustrated Classic Ser.). (ENG.). 260p. 12.99 **(978-1-68412-031-4(4))** Readerlink Distribution Services, LLC.

—Stories from Hans Andersen. 2007. (ENG.). 122p. per. 18.99 (978-1-4346-2876-3(0)) Creative Media Partners, LLC.

—Tales of Hans Christian Andersen. Stewart, Joel, illus. 2010. (Candlewick Illustrated Classics Ser.). (ENG.). 208p. (J). (gr. 3-7). pap. 12.99 (978-0-7636-4892-3(2)) Candlewick Pr.

—The Wild Swans & Other Tales. 2012. (Fairy Tales of Hans Christian Andersen Ser.). (ENG.). 152p. pap. 19.99 (978-1-909438-12-5(X), Sovereign) Bollinger, Max GBR. Dist: Lightning Source UK, Ltd.

Anderson, Claire. Talking to the Stars. 2009. 24p. pap. 12.99 (978-1-4389-7268-8(7)) AuthorHouse.

Anderson, Jennifer. Honey Creek Royalty. 2013. 246p. pap. 12.99 (978-1-62237-148-8(8)) Turquoise Morning Pr.

Anderson, M. T. No Such Thing as the Real World. 2009. 8.99 (978-0-06-147060-8(0)) HarperCollins Pubs.

Anderson, Mark A. Ma Ma, I'm Home, 1 vol. 2009. 48p. pap. 16.95 (978-1-4489-9077-1(7)) America Star Bks.

Anderson, Matt & Duming, Tim. Cut the Rope: Strange Delivery. 2012. (ENG., Illus.). 104p. pap. 9.99 (978-1-937676-04-9(8), 9781937676049) Ape Entertainment.

Anderson, Matt & Hutchins, Eric. White Picket Fences: Double Feature One-shot. 2008. (Illus.). 52p. (YA). pap. 6.95 (978-0-9801314-9-9(9)) Ape Entertainment.

Anderson, Matt & Lambert, Chad. Kung Fu Panda Vol. 2: It's Elemental & Other Stories. 2012. (ENG., Illus.). 24p. pap., pap. 6.95 (978-1-936340-56-9(9), 9781936340569) Ape Entertainment.

Anderson, Max Elliot. Terror at Wolf Lake. 2004. (Tweener Press Adventure Ser.). (Illus.). 141p. (J). (gr. 4-7). per. 10.95 (978-0-9729256-6-2(X), Tweener Pr.) Baker Trittin Pr.

Anderson, Phil. The Thomas Family Values. 2012. 84p. pap. 13.95 (978-1-4772-2529-5(3)) AuthorHouse.

Anderson, Robert Gordon. HalfPast Seven Stories Illustrated Editi. 2006. pap. (978-1-4065-0868-0(3)) Dodo Pr.

Anderson, Susannah. Susie. 2010. 60p. pap. 8.50 (978-1-4116-2175-6(1)) Lulu Pr., Inc.

Andrews, Charlie J. Tales of Animals on Farmer Brown's Farm: Children Stories. 2007. 60p. per. 10.95 (978-1-4327-0138-3(X)) Outskirts Pr., Inc.

Andrews, Jan. When Apples Grew Noses & White Horses Flew: Tales of Ti-Jean, 1 vol. Petricic, Dusan, illus. 2011. (ENG.). 72p. (J). (gr. 1-5). 16.95 (978-0-88899-952-8(6)) Groundwood Bks. CAN. Dist: Publishers Group West (PGW).

Andrews, Jane & Hopkins, Louisa Parsons. The Seven Little Sisters Who Live on the Round Ball that Floats in the Air. 2004. reprint ed. pap. 21.95 (978-1-4179-1646-7(X)) Kessinger Publishing, LLC.

Angel, Katharine Ann. Being Forgotten. 2012. (Illus.). 218p. pap. (978-1-908098-45-0(7)) 2QT, Ltd. (Publishing).

Angelchild, P. Erotic Memoirs Volume 1. 2007. pap. (978-1-84747-127-7(7)) Chipmunkapublishing.

Anholt, Catherine & Anholt, Laurence. Catherine & Laurence Anholt's Big Book of Little Children. Anholt, Catherine & Anholt, Laurence, illus. 2003. (ENG., Illus.). 80p. (J). (gr. -1-k). 15.99 (978-0-7636-2210-7(9)) Candlewick Pr.

Anonymous. Anonymous Diary Collection: Lucy in the Sky; Letting Ana Go; The Book of David. 2014. (ENG., Illus.). 880p. (YA). (gr. 9). pap. 29.99 (978-1-4814-1583-5(2), Simon Pulse) Simon Pulse.

Ansell, Liz. The Unforgettable Snow Lady: And Other Memorable Short Stories, Songs & Rhymes. 2012. (Illus.). 40p. (-18). pap. 22.88 (978-1-4772-3533-1(7)) AuthorHouse.

Antologia Staff. El Libro de Oro de los Abuelos. 2004. (SPA.). 128p. (978-980-257-274-8(8)) Ekare, Ediciones.

Anytime Stories. (Anytime Stories Ser.). 48p. (J). Vol 1. (Illus.). bds. (978-2-7643-0177-7(4)) Vol. 2. (978-2-7643-0178-4(2)) Vol. 3. (Illus.). bds. (978-2-7643-0203-3(7)) Phidal Publishing, Inc./Editions Phidal, Inc.

Aperlo, Peter. The Unofficial Magnus Chase & the Gods of Asgard Companion. Editors of Ulysses Press, Editors of, ed. 2015. (ENG., Illus.). 200p. (gr. 2). pap. 12.95 (978-1-61243-482-7(7)) Ulysses Pr.

Apple, Bonnie. The Karisma Tales. 2013. 142p. (gr. 4-6). 28.99 (978-1-4525-7296-3(8)); pap. 11.99 (978-1-4525-7295-6(X)) Author Solutions, Inc. (Balboa Pr.).

Applehead, Zippy. You Are Who You Be. 2012. 28p. pap. 24.95 (978-1-4626-6505-1(5)) America Star Bks.

Appleton, Victor. The Tom Swift Omnibus #1: Tom Swift & his Motor-Cycle, Tom Swift & His Motor-Boat, Tom Swift & His Airship. 2007. 292p. 24.95 (978-1-60459-098-2(X)) Wilder Pubns., Corp.

—The Tom Swift Omnibus #2: Tom Swift & His Submarine Boat, Tom Swift & His Electric Runabout, Tom Swift & His Wireless Message. 2007. 296p. 24.95 (978-1-60459-100-2(5)); per. 12.99 (978-1-60459-099-9(8)) Wilder Pubns., Corp.

Applin, Barbara & Simon, Veronica, eds. Treasure House 1: A Caribbean Anthology. 2006. (ENG., Illus.). 220p. (J). (gr. 3-5). per. 11.95 (978-1-4050-3094-6(1)) Macmillan Caribbean GBR. Dist: Interlink Publishing Group, Inc.

Apps Ltd, Colossi. The Wild Bed Time Stories. 2011. 62p. pap. 12.95 (978-1-4466-1546-1(4)) Lulu Pr., Inc.

árabe, Cuento popular. Ali Baba y Los Cuarenta Ladrones: Ali Baba & the Forty Thieves. 2004. (Troquelados Clasicos Ser.). (SPA.). 16p. (J). pap. 2.95 (978-84-7864-732-3(5)) Combel Editorial, S.A. ESP. Dist: Independent Pubs. Group.

Arengo, Sue. Classic Tales: Thumbelina. Goulding, Celeste, illus. 2006. (ENG.). 24p. 5.50 (978-0-19-422537-3(2)) Oxford Univ. Pr. GBR. Dist: Oxford Univ. Pr., Inc.

Arenstam, Peter. Nicholas, a New Hampshire Tale. Holman, Karen Busch, illus. 2015. (Nicholas Northeastern Ser.: 3). (ENG.). 158p. (J). (gr. k-7). pap. 8.95 (978-1-938170-68-3(7), Mitten Pr.) Ann Arbor Editions LLC.

Arkhurst, Joyce Cooper. The Further Adventures of Spider: West African Folktales. Pinkney, Jerry, illus. 2012. (Passport to Reading Level 4 Ser.). (ENG.). 32p. (J). (gr. -1-3). pap. 4.99 (978-0-316-20345-6(9)) Little, Brown Bks. for Young Readers.

Armstrong, Jennifer. Shattered: Stories of Children & War. 2003. (ENG.). 176p. (YA). (gr. 7). mass mkt. 6.99 (978-0-440-23765-5(3), Laurel Leaf) Random Hse. Children's Bks.

Arnold, Caroline. Wiggle & Waggle. Peterson, Mary, illus. 2009. (ENG.). 48p. (J). (gr. k-3). pap. 5.95 (978-1-58089-307-7(4)) Charlesbridge Publishing, Inc.

Arnold, Lisa Marie. Creative Short Stories for Smart Kids. 2008. 60p. pap. 21.99 (978-1-4343-5515-7(2)) AuthorHouse.

Aronson, Marc & Smith, Charles R., eds. One Death Nine Stories. 2014. (ENG.). 160p. (YA). (gr. 9). 16.99 (978-0-7636-5285-2(7)) Candlewick Pr.

Arthur, Jenny. Little Witch. Arthur, Jenny, illus. 2012. (Spooky Sounds Ser.). (ENG., Illus.). 10p. (J). (gr. k — 1). 7.99 (978-0-230-74487-5(7)) Macmillan Pubs., Ltd. GBR. Dist: Independent Pubs. Group.

Aryal, Aimee. Hello Hairy Dawg. Turnbull, Jesse, illus. 2004. (J). (gr. -1-3). 19.95 (978-1-932888-04-1(7)) Mascot Bks., Inc.

—Hello, Hook 'Em! Craig, Megan, illus. 2004. 24p. (J). (gr. -1-3). lib. bdg. 19.95 (978-1-932888-10-2(1)) Mascot Bks., Inc.

—Hello Joe Bruin! Perez, Gerry, illus. 2004. 24p. (J). 19.95 (978-1-932888-15-7(2)) Mascot Bks., Inc.

—Hello Mr. Wuf! Cooper, Blair, illus. 2004. 24p. (J). 19.95 (978-1-932888-06-5(3)) Mascot Bks., Inc.

—Hello Rameses! Cooper, Blair, illus. 2004. 24p. (J). 19.95 (978-1-932888-17-1(9)) Mascot Bks., Inc.

—Hello Smokey! Higgins, Krystal, illus. 2004. 22p. (J). 19.95 (978-1-932888-09-6(8)) Mascot Bks., Inc.

—Hello Tommy Trojan! Perez, Gerry, illus. 2004. 24p. (J). 19.95 (978-1-932888-08-9(X)) Mascot Bks., Inc.

—Howdy Reveille! Craig, Megan, illus. 2004. 24p. (J). 19.95 (978-1-932888-18-8(7)) Mascot Bks., Inc.

—Let's Go 49ers! 2008. (J). 14.95 (978-1-932888-16-4(0)) Mascot Bks., Inc.

—Let's Go Bears! 2008. (J). 14.95 (978-1-932888-22-5(5)) Mascot Bks., Inc.

Ashby, Gaylene. STORY TIME A Collection of Three Children's Stories. 2008. 28p. 14.95 (978-1-4357-1929-3(8)) Lulu Pr., Inc.

Ashford, Kathy. Spencer's Birthday. 2009. 16p. pap. 24.95 (978-1-60749-778-3(6)) America Star Bks.

Atkinson, Ruth & Atkinson, Brett. Christmas Cutouts. Atkinson, Ruth & Atkinson, Brett, illus. (Illus.). (J). (gr. k-2). pap. (978-1-876367-20-6(2)) Wizard Bks.

Attia, Stephan. Other Christmas Stories. 2009. 42p. pap. 19.68 (978-0-557-11189-3(7)) Lulu Pr., Inc.

Audho, Gaitree. Moral Stories for Kids. 2011. 32p. pap. 12.77 (978-1-4634-4709-0(4)) AuthorHouse.

Aulbach, Kathy. ABC's. 2008. 29p. 15.95 (978-0-615-21180-0(1)) Flower Sprouts.

Ault, Kelly. Let's Sign, Baby! A Fun & Easy Way to Talk with Baby. Landry, Leo, illus. abr. ed. 2010. (ENG.). 40p. (J). (gr. k — 1). bds. 7.99 (978-0-547-31596-6(1)) Houghton Mifflin Harcourt Publishing Co.

Aunt Julie. Paddleduck! #2: Julie, Living in Texas. 2011. 56p. pap. (978-1-4269-6656-9(3)) Trafford Publishing (UK) Ltd.

Avalon-Pai, Phyllis. Children's Stories from Around the World. Arrott, Nancy, illus. 2008. 70p. pap. 9.95 (978-0-9788283-8-7(0)) Acacia Publishing, Inc.

Avanti, Michele. GreeHee the Journey of Five: Tales of Tamoor Book One. 2008. (Illus.). 304p. (J). per. 14.99 (978-0-9779590-4-4(X)) GreeHee Publishing.

Avi. The Most Important Thing: Stories about Sons, Fathers, & Grandfathers. 2016. (ENG.). 224p. (J). (gr. 5). 16.99 (978-0-7636-8111-1(3)) Candlewick Pr.

—Strange Happenings: Five Tales of Transformation. 2008. (ENG., Illus.). 160p. (J). (gr. 2-5). pap. 6.99 (978-0-15-206461-7(3)) Houghton Mifflin Harcourt Publishing Co.

—What Do Fish Have to Do with Anything? 2004. (ENG., Illus.). 208p. (J). (gr. 5-9). reprint ed. 6.99 (978-0-7636-2319-7(9)) Candlewick Pr.

Awdry, W. Thomas the Tank Engine. 2005. (Railway Ser.). (ENG., Illus.). 508p. (J). (gr. -1-2). 35.00 (978-0-375-83409-7(5), Random Hse. Bks. for Young Readers) Random Hse. Children's Bks.

Awdry, Wilbert V. Tales of Discovery. Golden Books Staff, illus. 2011. (Padded Board Book Ser.). (ENG.). 30p. (J). (gr. k — 1). bds. 11.99 (978-0-375-87192-4(6), Golden Bks.) Random Hse. Children's Bks.

Awdry, Wilbert V. & Awdry, Rev. W. Thomas' Colorful Ride (Thomas & Friends) Golden Books Staff, illus. 2011. (Deluxe Chunky Crayon Book Ser.). (ENG.). 128p. (J). (gr. -1-2). pap. 7.99 (978-0-375-87248-8(5), Golden Bks.) Random Hse. Children's Bks.

Ayagalria, Julia, et al. Animals of the River. Ayagalria, Julia et al, illus. 2006. (Animal Story Collection Ser.). 24p. (J). (gr. 2-6). pap. 9.00 (978-1-58084-236-5(4)) Lower Kuskokwim Schl. District.

Azman, Hacer. The Adventures of Kyle. 2011. (ENG.). 96p. (J). (gr. k-1). 14.95 (978-1-59784-231-0(1)) Tughra Bks.

Azore, Barbara. Wanda & the Wild Hair. Graham, Georgia, illus. 2012. (ENG.). 32p. (J). (gr. -1-2). pap. 7.95 (978-1-77049-306-3(9), Tundra Bks.) Tundra Bks. CAN. Dist: Penguin Random Hse. LLC.

Babbitt, Ellen C. Jataka Tales. 2012. 100p. (978-1-78139-120-4(3)) Benediction Classics.

—Jataka Tales I & II. 2008. 80p. pap. 9.95 (978-1-60459-517-8(5)) Wilder Pubns., Corp.

—More Jataka Tales. Young, Ellsworth, illus. 2008. 92p. pap. 7.95 (978-1-59915-310-0(6)) Yesterday's Classics.

Babbitt, Ellen C. & Young, Ellsworth. The Monkey & the Crocodile: And Other Fables from the Jataka Tales of India. 2015. (ENG.). 192p. (gr. 1-6). pap. 8.99 (978-0-486-79614-7(0)) Dover Pubns., Inc.

Babbitt, Natalie. The Devil's Storybooks: 20 Delightfully Wicked Stories. Babbitt, Natalie, illus. 2012. (ENG., Illus.). 224p. (J). (gr. 3-7). pap. 15.99 (978-0-312-64158-0(3), 9780312641580) Square Fish.

Bach, Richard & Gardner, Sally. La Niña Más Pequeña del Mundo. Tapia, Sonia, tr. 2005. (Niños Mágicos Ser.).Tr. of One. (SPA & ENG., Illus.). 128p. (J). (gr. 2-4). pap. 7.95 (978-84-666-1339-2(0)) Ediciones B ESP. Dist: Independent Pubs. Group.

Badger, Pearstina. Jessica's Journeys: Stories about Life's Lessons. 2006. 56p. pap. 16.95 (978-1-4241-1576-1(0)) PublishAmerica, Inc.

Badoe, Adwoa. The Pot of Wisdom. Diakité, Baba Wagué, illus. 2008. (ENG.). 64p. (J). (gr. 1-5). pap. 12.95 (978-0-88899-869-9(4)) Groundwood Bks. CAN. Dist: Publishers Group West (PGW).

Bailen, Mark & Bailen, Leaf. Earf. 2013. 48p. 16.75 (978-0-9910809-0-8(4)) Splendid Benedict.

Bailer, Darice & Domínguez, Madelca. El Flautista de Hamelín. Vila Delclòs, Jordi, illus. 2007. (SPA & ENG.). 28p. (J). (978-0-545-02961-2(9)) Scholastic, Inc.

Bailer, Darice, et al. El León y el Ratón. Subirana, Joan, illus. 2007. (SPA & ENG.). 28p. (J). (978-0-545-02449-5(8)) Scholastic, Inc.

—El Pastorcito Mentiroso. Infante, Francesc, illus. 2007. (SPA & ENG.). 28p. (J). (978-0-545-02960-5(0)) Scholastic, Inc.

Bailey, Carolyn Sherwin. Stories of Great Adventures. Burd, Clara M., illus. 2005. reprint ed. pap. 24.95 (978-1-4179-0215-6(9)) Kessinger Publishing, LLC.

—Tell Me Another Story: The Book of Story Programs. 2007. (ENG.). 248p. pap. 20.99 (978-1-4346-3278-4(4)) Creative Media Partners, LLC.

Bailey, Linda. If You Happen to Have a Dinosaur. Jack, Colin, illus. 2014. (ENG.). 40p. (J). (gr. -1-2). 17.99 (978-1-77049-568-5(1), Tundra Bks.) Tundra Bks. CAN. Dist: Penguin Random Hse. LLC.

Bailey, Sherwin Carolyn. Tell Me Another Story. 2007. 224p. 42.99 (978-1-4280-7529-0(1)); per. 36.99 (978-1-4280-7528-3(3)) IndyPublish.com.

Bak, Jenny. Ten Gifts from Santa Claus: A Counting Book. Harding, Niall, illus. 2011. (ENG.). 22p. (J). (gr. -1-k). 14.99 (978-1-4052-5127-3(1)) Egmont Bks., Ltd. GBR. Dist: Independent Pubs. Group.

Bakare, Rebecca. Short Stories by Rebecc. 2012. 54p. pap. 20.00 (978-1-937911-26-3(8)) Heavenly Realm Publishing.

Bake a Cake & Other Stories: Individual Title Six-Pack. (Story Steps Ser.). (gr. k-2). 42.00 (978-0-7635-9574-6(8)) Rigby Education.

Baker, Alan, illus. Odyssey. 2004. (Kingfisher Epics Ser.). (ENG.). 176p. (YA). (gr. 3-7). pap. 8.99 (978-0-7534-5723-8(7), 9780753457238, Kingfisher) Roaring Brook Pr.

Balcells, Jacqueline. El Archipielago de las Puntuadas. 2003. (SPA.). pap. (978-956-13-1472-6(X), AB0859) Bello, Andres CHL. Dist: Lectorum Pubns., Inc.

Baldwin, James. Fifty Famous People. l.t. ed. 2006. (ENG.). 126p. pap. 19.99 (978-1-4264-1427-5(7)) Creative Media Partners, LLC.

—Fifty Famous Stories Retold. 2007. 188p. 19.99 (978-1-59986-708-3(7)) Filiquarian Publishing, LLC.

—Fifty Famous Stories Retold. 2009. 160p. 32.99 (978-1-59547-545-9(1)) NuVision Pubns., LLC.

—Fifty Famous Stories Retold. 2008. 100p. pap. 9.50 (978-1-60459-518-5(3)) Wilder Pubns., Corp.

Ball, Pauline E. Chubsey Tucker Tales. 2005. (Illus.). 98p. pap. (978-1-84401-211-4(5)) Athena Pr.

Ballantyne, R. M. The Lighthouse. 2006. pap. (978-1-4065-0531-3(5)) Dodo Pr.

Ballantyne, Robert Michael. The Coxswain's Bride: Also Jack Frost & Sons; & A Double Rescue. 2007. (ENG.). 146p. pap. 18.99 (978-1-4346-3664-5(X)); 164p. pap. 21.99 (978-1-4346-3712-3(3)) Creative Media Partners, LLC.

Ballard, George Anne. Read to Me! James, Melody A. & Arelys, Aguilar, illus. 2013. 60p. pap. 10.00 (978-0-9855312-8-7(2)) Bolton Publishing LLC.

Bamford, Desmond Nicholas. Beekemose. 2012. (Illus.). 54p. (gr. 2-4). pap. 13.66 (978-1-4685-7773-0(5)) AuthorHouse.

Bancks, Tristan. Mac Slater Hunts the Cool. 2010. (Mac Slater Hunts the Cool Ser.). (ENG.). 224p. (J). (gr. 3-7). 15.99 (978-1-4169-8574-7(3), Simon & Schuster Bks. For Young Readers) Simon & Schuster Bks. For Young Readers.

Bandala, Luis Rodriguez. El Libro, el Escritor y Otros Cuentos. 2003. (SPA., Illus.). 184p. (YA). (gr. 5-12). 15.95 (978-968-6966-18-3(8)) EDITER'S Publishing Hse. MEX. Dist: EDITER'S Publishing Hse.

Banghart, Tracy E. What the Sea Wants. Blum, Julia C., illus. 2006. 64p. (YA). kivar 16.00 (978-0-9779753-0-3(4)) LizStar Bks.

Bansch, Helga. Odd Bird Out. 2011. (Gecko Press Titles Ser.). (ENG., Illus.). 32p. pap. 17.95 (978-1-877467-08-0(1)) Gecko Pr. NZL. Dist: Lerner Publishing Group.

Barbauld, Anna. Little Stories for Children; Being Easy. 2004. reprint ed. pap. 20.95 (978-0-7661-9037-5(4)) Kessinger Publishing, LLC.

Barber, Rachel, et al. Nine Novels by Younger Americans. 2007. (ENG.). 864p. (J). (gr. 9). pap. 18.00 (978-0-9770844-4-9(2)) 826 Valencia.

Barbini, F. T. Tijaran Tales: White Child. 2011. 214p. pap. (978-0-7552-1349-8(1)) Authors OnLine, Ltd.

Barbour, Ralph Henry. The New Boy at Hilltop & Other Stories. 2006. pap. (978-1-4065-0779-9(2)) Dodo Pr.

Bark, Jasper, et al. DreamWorks Classics Volume 4. Dalton, Alex & Gallant, S. L., illus. 2016. (ENG.). 64p. (J). (gr. 1-4). 6.99 (978-1-78276-249-2(3)) Titan Bks. Ltd. GBR. Dist: Penguin Random Hse. LLC.

Barker, Cicely Mary. The Girls' Book of Flower Fairies. 2008. (Flower Fairies Ser.). (ENG., Illus.). 208p. (J). (gr. -1-2). 20.00 (978-0-7232-6273-2(X), Warne) Penguin Young Readers Group.

Barker, Jane Valentine. Building Up. pap. 7.95 (978-1-878611-07-9(0)) Silver Rim Pr.

Barkley, Roger C. Johnny Grasshopper. 2006. 52p. pap. 16.95 (978-1-4241-0221-1(9)) PublishAmerica, Inc.

Barks, Carl, et al. Walt Disney's Comics & Stories #702. 2009. 64p. pap. 7.99 (978-1-60360-092-7(2)) Gemstone Publishing, Inc.

—Walt Disney's Comics & Stories #704. 2009. 64p. pap. 7.99 (978-1-60360-094-1(9)) Gemstone Publishing, Inc.

Barr, Robert. Dr. Barr's Tales: Stories of Katharine. 2007. 88p. per. 19.95 (978-1-4241-7911-4(4)) America Star Bks.

Barrett, John F. The Stories of Jake. 2008. 64p. pap. 31.99 (978-1-4363-2010-8(0)) Xlibris Corp.

Barrie, J. M. The Complete Adventures of Peter Pan Includes: The Little White Bird, Peter Pan in Kensington Gardens(Illustrated) & Peter. Rackham, Arthur & Bedford, F. D., illus. 2013. 326p. (978-1-78139-361-1(3)) Benediction Classics.

Barron, Liz. Salcombe Seaside Fairies: Louise the Lobster Pot Fairy. 2009. (Illus.). 24p. pap. 11.49 (978-1-4389-8525-1(8)) AuthorHouse.

Barrows, Annie & Blackall, Sophie. Ivy + Bean Take Care of the Babysitter, 1 vol. 2011. (Ivy & Bean Ser.). (ENG., Illus.). 128p. (J). (gr. 1-4). 24.21 (978-1-59961-931-6(8)) Spotlight.

Barto, Linda iLham, illus. Where the Ghost Camel Grins: Muslim Fables for Families of All Faiths. 2009. (ENG.). 119p. (gr. 5). 19.95 (978-1-879402-24-9(6)) Tahrike Tarsile Quran, Inc.
BARWICK, Adam Mark. Three tales of Twaddle. 2009. 73p. pap. 12.50 (978-1-4092-5181-1(0)) Lulu Pr., Inc.
Bass, Saul, illus. Henri's Walk to Paris. 2012. (ENG.). 48p. (J). (gr. k-4). 19.95 (978-0-7893-2263-0(3)) Universe Publishing.
Bassett, Jennifer, ed. Long White Cloud: Stories from New Zealand. 3rd ed. 2008. (ENG., Illus.). 80p. 10.00 (978-0-19-479139-7(4)) Oxford Univ. Pr., Inc.
Bates, Robert L. Lopaka's Legends of Hawaii. 2008. 28p. pap. 19.95 (978-1-4327-3655-2(8)) Outskirts Pr., Inc.
Batt, Tanya Robyn. The Barefoot Book of Faeries. Newey, Gail, illus. 2008. (ENG.). 64p. (J). (gr. -1-3). 15.99 (978-1-84686-163-5(2)) Barefoot Bks., Inc.
Baum, L. Frank. American Fairy Tales. 2007. 112p. per. 9.95 (978-1-60312-100-2(5)); 22.95 (978-1-60312-899-5(9)) Aegypan.
—Collected Short Stories of L. Frank Baum. 2006. (J). 29.95 (978-1-930764-14-9(6)) International Wizard of Oz Club, The.
—Little Wizard Stories of Oz. Neill, John R., illus. 2011. (Dover Children's Classics Ser.). (ENG.). 160p. (J). (gr. 3-5). pap. 14.99 (978-0-486-47644-5(8)) Dover Pubns., Inc.
—Little Wizard Stories of Oz. 2011. 80p. (gr. 3-18). 18.95 (978-1-4638-9617-1(4)) Rodgers, Alan Bks.
—Tales of Mother Goose. 2009. 174p. (J). pap. (978-1-934941-68-3(9)) Red & Black Pubs.
—The Tresury of Oz: The Wonderful Wizard of Oz, the Marvelous Land of Oz, Ozma of Oz, Dorothy & the Wizard in Oz, the Road to Oz, the Emerald City Of. 2007. 548p. per. 19.49 (978-1-60459-029-6(7)) Wilder Pubns., Corp.
—7 Books In: L. Frank Baum's Original Oz Series, Volume 1 of 2. the Wonderful Wizard of Oz, the Marvelous Land of Oz, Ozma of Oz, Dorothy & the W. 2008. 820p. (978-1-905921-02-7(0)) Shoes & Ships & Sealing Wax Ltd.
—7 Books In: L. Frank Baum's Oz Series, volume 1 of 2. the Wonderful Wizard of Oz, the Marvelous Land of Oz, Ozma of Oz, Dorothy & the Wizard In. 2008. 824p. pap. (978-1-905921-01-0(2)) Shoes & Ships & Sealing Wax Ltd.
—8 Books In: L. Frank Baum's Original Oz Series, volume 2 of 2. Little Wizard Stories of Oz, Tik-Tok of Oz, the Scarecrow of Oz, Rinkitink in Oz, T. 2008. 764p. (978-1-905921-03-4(9)) Shoes & Ships & Sealing Wax Ltd.
—8 Books In: L. Frank Baum's Oz Series, volume 2 of 2. Little Wizard Stories of Oz, Tik-Tok of Oz, the Scarecrow of Oz, Rinkitink in Oz, the Lost P. 2008. 812p. pap. (978-1-905921-09-6(8)) Shoes & Ships & Sealing Wax Ltd.
Baum, L. Frank, et al. A Children's Treasury. 2007. 792p. per. 24.95 (978-1-60459-011-1(4)) Wilder Pubns., Corp.
Baxter, Nicola. Bedtime Tales. Press, Jenny, illus. 2013. (ENG.). 80p. (J). (gr. -1-k). pap. 9.99 (978-1-84322-952-0(8)) Anness Publishing GBR. Dist: National Bk. Network.
—Book of Five-Minute Farmyard Tales. Press, Jenny, illus. 2013. (ENG.). 80p. (J). (gr. -1-k). pap. 9.99 (978-1-84322-953-7(6)) Anness Publishing GBR. Dist: National Bk. Network.
—A Book of Five-Minute Kitten Tales: A Treasury of over 35 Bedtime Stories. Press, Jenny, illus. 2013. (ENG.). 80p. (J). (gr. -1-12). pap. 9.99 (978-1-84322-888-2(2)) Anness Publishing GBR. Dist: National Bk. Network.
—A Book of Five-Minute Teddy Bear Tales: A Treasury of over 35 Bedtime Stories. Press, Jenny, illus. 2013. (ENG.). 80p. pap. 9.99 (978-1-84322-889-9(0)) Anness Publishing GBR. Dist: National Bk. Network.
—A Child's Treasury of Classic Stories: Charles Dickens, William Shakespeare, Oscar Wilde. Thorne, Jenny, illus. 2012. (ENG.). 240p. (J). (gr. 2-7). 18.99 (978-1-84322-948-3(X)) Anness Publishing GBR. Dist: National Bk. Network.
—Classic Fairy Tales from Hans Christian Andersen. Shuttleworth, Cathie, illus. 2012. (ENG.). 96p. (J). (gr. 2-7). pap. 9.99 (978-1-84322-875-2(0)) Anness Publishing GBR. Dist: National Bk. Network.
—Classic Fairy Tales from the Brothers Grimm. Shuttleworth, Cathie, illus. 2012. (ENG.). 96p. (J). (gr. 2-7). pap. 9.99 (978-1-84322-874-5(2)) Anness Publishing GBR. Dist: National Bk. Network.
—Classic Folk Tales: 80 Traditional Stories from Around the World. Langton, Roger, illus. 2013. (ENG.). 96p. (J). (gr. 7-12). pap. 9.99 (978-1-84322-855-4(6)) Anness Publishing GBR. Dist: National Bk. Network.
—My Ballet Theatre: Peek Inside the 3-D Windows. Chaffey, Samantha, illus. 2014. (ENG.). 24p. (J). (gr. -1-12). 16.99 (978-1-84322-949-0(8), Armadillo) Anness Publishing GBR. Dist: National Bk. Network.
—My Wonderful Treasury of Five-Minute Stories. Press, Jenny, illus. 2012. (ENG.). 256p. (J). (gr. k-4). 18.99 (978-1-84322-805-9(X)) Anness Publishing GBR. Dist: National Bk. Network.
—Old MacDonald's: Barnyard Tales. Davis, Caroline, illus. 256p. (J). (978-0-7525-8771-4(4)) Parragon Bk. Service Ltd.
—Princess Stories. Smith, Helen, illus. 2013. (ENG.). 80p. (J). (gr. k-4). pap. 9.99 (978-1-84322-954-4(4)) Anness Publishing GBR. Dist: National Bk. Network.
—Tales from the Farmyard: 12 Stories of Grunting Pigs, Quacking Ducks, Clucking Hens, Neighing Horses, Bleating Sheep & Other Animals. Shuttleworth, Cathie, illus. 2013. (ENG.). 80p. (J). (gr. 1-8). pap. 9.99 (978-1-84322-899-8(8)) Anness Publishing GBR. Dist: National Bk. Network.
—Tales from the Toy Box. Press, Jenny, illus. 2012. (ENG.). 80p. (J). (gr. k-4). pap. 9.99 (978-1-84322-951-3(X)) Anness Publishing GBR. Dist: National Bk. Network.
—3-Minute Animal Stories. Everitt-Stewart, Andy, illus. 2013. (ENG.). 80p. (J). (gr. -1-k). pap. 9.99 (978-1-84322-978-0(1), Armadillo) Anness Publishing GBR. Dist: National Bk. Network.
—3-Minute Sleepytime Stories. Siewart, Pauline, illus. 2013. (ENG.). 80p. (J). (gr. -1-3). pap. 9.99 (978-1-84322-977-3(3), Armadillo) Anness Publishing GBR. Dist: National Bk. Network.
Baxter, Nicola, compiled by. The Wonderful World of Fairies: Eight Enchanted Tales from Fairyland. 2013. (ENG., Illus.). 80p. (J). (gr. 3-7). pap. 9.99 (978-1-84322-968-1(4)) Anness Publishing GBR. Dist: National Bk. Network.
Baxter, Nicola, ed. Classic Stories: Charles Dickens, William Shakespeare & Oscar Wilde - A Treasury for Children. Thorne, Jenny, illus. 2015. (ENG.). 240p. 16.99 (978-0-85723-756-9(X), Armadillo) Anness Publishing GBR. Dist: National Bk. Network.
—A Midsummer Night's Dream & Other Classic Tales of the Plays: Six Illustrated Stories from Shakespeare. Thorne, Jenny, illus. 2015. (ENG.). 80p. pap. 9.99 (978-1-86147-466-7(0), Armadillo) Anness Publishing GBR. Dist: National Bk. Network.
Baxter, Nicola & Morton, Ken. A Storybook of Ugly Ogres & Terrible Trolls: Ten Fantastic Tales of Frightful Fun. 2013. (ENG., Illus.). 80p. (J). (gr. -1-12). pap. 9.99 (978-1-84322-938-4(2), Armadillo) Anness Publishing GBR. Dist: National Bk. Network.
Baxter, Nicola & Siewert, Pauline. Sweet Dreams: Soothing Stories for Peaceful Bedtimes. 2012. (ENG., Illus.). 210p. (J). (gr. -1-12). pap. 7.99 (978-1-84322-817-2(3), Armadillo) Anness Publishing GBR. Dist: National Bk. Network.
Bazaldua, Barbara & Bergen, Lara. Rapunzel & the Golden Rule/Jasmine & the Two Tigers (Disney Princess) Studio IBOIX & Disney Storybook Artists Staff, illus. 2011. (Pictureback(R) Ser.). (ENG.). 32p. (J). (gr. -1-2). pap. 4.99 (978-0-7364-2829-3(1), RH/Disney) Random Hse. Children's Bks.
Beaudoin, Beau. Boetry. Beaudoin, Beau, illus. 2007. (Illus.). 40p. (J). per. 15.95 (978-0-9788401-1-2(9)) Red Ink Pr.
Beckett, Bernard. Lester. 160p. (YA). (gr. 8-18). pap. (978-1-877135-21-7(6), Longacre Pr.) Random Hse. New Zealand.
Beeson, J. K. Ali & Friends Adventures. 2010. 56p. pap. 10.49 (978-1-4520-1509-5(0)) AuthorHouse.
Beifus, Ruth. Shlavim Classics 2-in-1 Vol. 1: The Best Reward & the Taste of Truth. 2009. 32p. 14.99 (978-1-59826-329-9(3)) Feldheim Pubs.
—Shlavim Classics 2-in-1 Vol.2: Goodbye to Miri's Mess & Half a Cup of Water. 2009. 32p. 14.99 (978-1-59826-330-5(7)) Feldheim Pubs.
Belanger, Kathleen. Cooldog's New Adventures. 2013. 78p. pap. 16.95 (978-1-63004-207-3(2)) America Star Bks.
Bell, Aaron. Jak's Story. 2010. (ENG., Illus.). 96p. (YA). (gr. 4). pap. 10.99 (978-1-55488-710-1(0)) Dundurn CAN. Dist: Ingram Publisher Services.
Bell, Frank & Bowler, Colin. Panda Power. Seaman, Paul, illus. 2004. 24p. pap. 7.00 (978-1-84161-084-9(4)) Ravette Publishing, Ltd. GBR. Dist: Parkwest Pubns., Inc.
Bell, Krista. No Strings. 2005. (Illus.). 159p. (J). (gr. -1-7). pap. (978-0-7344-0626-2(6), Lothian Children's Bks.) Hachette Australia.
Bell, Lindzi. Sherlock Times Three, 1 vol. 2009. 62p. pap. 19.95 (978-1-61582-028-3(0)) America Star Bks.
Bell, Shirley. Boys on the Make. 2007. 54p. 16.95 (978-1-4241-6575-9(X)) America Star Bks.
Bell, Wade. No Place Fit for a Child. 2009. (Prose Ser.: 80). (ENG.). 144p. 18.00 (978-1-55071-266-7(7)) Guernica Editions, Inc. CAN. Dist: Univ. of Toronto Pr.
Benintendi, Steve. Cyborg Mayhem. 2003. (Powermark Comics Ser.). (Illus.). 32p. (J). pap. 2.95 (978-0-9705669-8-0(0)) PowerMark Productions.
—Face Off. 2003. (Powermark Comics Ser.). (Illus.). 32p. (J). pap. 2.95 (978-0-9705669-4-2(8)) PowerMark Productions.
—Family Matter. 2003. (Powermark Comics Ser.). (Illus.). 32p. (J). pap. 2.95 (978-0-9705669-7-3(2)) PowerMark Productions.
—Fang Shaw Revealed, Vol. 110. 2003. (Powermark Comics Ser.). (Illus.). 32p. (J). pap. 2.95 (978-0-9705669-9-7(9)) PowerMark Productions.
—High & Mighty. 2003. (Powermark Comics Ser.). (Illus.). 32p. (J). pap. 2.95 (978-0-9705669-6-6(4)) PowerMark Productions.
—They All Fall Down. 2003. (Powermark Comics Ser.). (Illus.). 32p. (J). pap. 2.95 (978-0-9705669-5-9(6)) PowerMark Productions.
A Benji's Pup Set, 6 vols. 32p. (gr. 1-3). 37.50 (978-0-322-00338-5(5)); 31.50 incl. 5.25 hd (978-0-7802-8045-8(8)) Wright Group/McGraw-Hill.
Bennet, Jill, et al. Cuentos de Terror, Vol. 2. (SPA.). (YA). 8.95 (978-958-04-3393-4(3)) Norma S.A. COL. Dist: Distribuidora Norma, Inc.
Bennett, Bonnie. My Collection of Short Stories. 2012. 38p. 19.95 (978-1-4626-7691-0(X)) America Star Bks.
Bennett, Jack. Tell Me a Story: A Collection of Short Stories. 2003. 68p. pap. (978-1-894650-25-0(5)) Moose Enterprise.
Bennett, Ruth Elisabeth. Childhood Days: Stories for the Young & Young at Heart, 1 vol. 2009. 91p. pap. 19.95 (978-1-4489-2904-7(0)) America Star Bks.
Bercowetz, Cynthia. Grandpa Herman's Petting Zoo. 2007. (Illus.). 48p. (J). per. 14.95 (978-0-9708430-9-8(7)) Uitti, Daniel.
Berendes, Mary & Aesop. The Maid & the Milk Pail. Harrison, Nancy, illus. 2010. (Aesop's Fables Ser.). (ENG.). 24p. (J). (gr. k-3). 28.50 (978-1-60253-526-8(4), 200030) Child's World, Inc., The.
Berenstain, Jan, et al. The Big Bedtime Book. Berenstain, Jan & Berenstain, Stan, illus. 2008. (Berenstain Bears Ser.). (ENG.). 48p. (J). (gr. -1-3). 12.99 (978-0-06-057434-5(8), HarperFestival) HarperCollins Pubs.
Berenstain, Stan, et al. The Berenstain Bears' Big Bedtime Book. Berenstain, Stan & Berenstain, Jan, illus. 2011. (Berenstain Bears Ser.). (ENG.). 48p. (J). (gr. -1-3). pap. 6.99 (978-0-06-057436-9(4)) HarperCollins Pubs.
—The Berenstain Bears' Big Bedtime Book. Berenstain, Jan & Berenstain, Mike, illus. 2008. (Berenstain Bears Ser.). 48p. (J). (gr. -1-3). 13.89 (978-0-06-057435-2(6)) HarperCollins Pubs.
Beresford, Elisabeth. The Bigfoot Womble. (Illus.). 16p. pap. (978-0-340-74673-8(4)) Hodder & Stoughton.
—The Great Womble Explorer. (Illus.). 16p. (J). (gr. k-6). pap. (978-0-340-74675-2(0)) Hodder & Stoughton.
—The Invisible Womble. Price, Nick, illus. 2012. (Wombles Ser.). (ENG.). 112p. (YA). (gr. 3-5). pap. 12.99 (978-1-4088-0834-4(X), 9781408308344) Bloomsbury Publishing USA.
—The Wombles. Price, Nick, illus. gif. ed. 2012. (Wombles Ser.). (ENG.). 240p. (YA). (gr. 3-5). 31.99 (978-1-4088-2180-0(X), 9781408821800, Bloomsbury USA Childrens) Bloomsbury Publishing USA.
Berger, Carin. All Mixed Up: A Mix-and-Match Book. 2006. (ENG., Illus.). 46p. (J). (gr. -1-7). 8.95 (978-0-8118-4966-1(X)) Chronicle Bks. LLC.
Bergida, Joanna. Wisdom from the Spring: A Collection of Short Storiesbrfrom the Class of 2010brCold Spring Harbor High School. 2007. 124p. per. 10.95 (978-0-595-44281-2(1)) iUniverse, Inc.
Berman, Steve. Speaking Out: LGBTQ Youth Stand Up. 2011. (ENG.). 288p. (J). (gr. 7). pap. 13.95 (978-1-60282-566-6(1)) Bold Strokes Bks.
Berocay, Roy. Babu. (SPA., Illus.). 60p. (J). (gr. 3-5). pap. 8.95 (978-1-58105-634-1(6)) Santillana USA Publishing Co., Inc.
—Pateando Lunas. Soulier, Daniel, illus. 2003. (SPA.). 166p. (J). (gr. 3). pap. 12.95 (978-9974-590-63-2(9)) Santillana S. A. URY. Dist: Santillana USA Publishing Co., Inc.
Best Bubble Blower. (J). (gr. 3-5). 75.00 (978-0-669-13696-8(4)) Houghton Mifflin Harcourt School Pubs.
Beston, Henry. Chimney Farm Bedtime Stories. 2006. (Illus.). 80p. (J). pap. 13.95 (978-0-942396-93-5(6)) Blackberry Maine.
Bettoni, Angela. More Adventures of Edmund & Martha. 2013. 194p. pap. (978-0-9566421-1-0(X)) Angela Bettoni Publishing.
Between the Lions - Set of 5 Early Literacy Kits: Includes; Help!, Huff & Puff, Oh, Yes I Can!, Shooting Star & Zoop! Zoop!, 5 cass., 5 vols. 2005. (Between the Lions Ser.). 120p. (J). VHS 139.95 (978-1-59375-295-8(4), WG38713) WGBH Boston Video.
Beverly, James. Seamus the Sheltie to the Rescue! 2011. 156p. pap. 14.95 (978-1-933449-88-3(8)) Nightengale Pr.
Bevins, Pegi & Doyle, Arthur Conan. Sherlock Holmes. 2003. (Retold Classics Anthologies Ser.). (Illus.). 282p. (J). pap. 9.99 (978-0-7891-5931-1(7)) Perfection Learning Corp.
Bibel, Philip. Tales of the Shtetl. 2004. (Illus.). 215p. per. 14.95 (978-0-9634067-1-2(X)) Metchnikoff, Elie Memorial Library.
Bickel, Karla. Heart Petals on the Hearth: A Collection of Children's Stories. Bickel, Karla, illus. 2004. (Illus.). 64p. (J). (gr. -1-6). 20.00 (978-1-891452-00-0(2)) Heart Arbor Bks.
—Heart Petals on the Hearth: A Collection of Children's Stories. 2004. (Illus.). 64p. (J). (gr. -1-6). pap. 16.00 (978-1-891452-01-7(0)) Heart Arbor Bks.
Biedrzycki, David. Me & My Dragon. Biedrzycki, David, illus. 2011. (ENG., Illus.). 40p. (J). (gr. -1-3). pap. 7.95 (978-1-58089-279-7(5)) Charlesbridge Publishing, Inc.
Bier, David & Bier, Seth. Bedtime with Rollo: The Nightspryte. 2009. (ENG., Illus.). 24p. 14.95 (978-0-9677238-8-4(4)) Conley, Bill.
Bierce, Ambrose. An Occurrence at Owl Creek Bridge. 2010. (J). 19.95 (978-1-58341-922-9(5), Creative Education) Creative Co., The.
Biers-Ariel, Matt. The Seven Species. Goodman, Tama, illus. 2003. 48p. 19.95 (978-0-8074-0852-0(2), 161902) URJ Pr.
Big Book of R Carry-over Stories. 2004. per. 34.99 (978-0-9760490-4-3(X)) Say It Right.
Big Davie. The Lady & Her Cat As Told by Bigdavie: A simple easy reading bedtime story that will leave children with delightful images while drifting off to S. 2009. (Illus.). 28p. pap. 12.49 (978-1-4389-3124-1(7)) AuthorHouse.
Big Idea Entertainment, LLC & B&H Kids Editorial Staff. VeggieTales: Can You Say Peas & Thank You?, a Digital Pop-Up Book (padded) 2017. (VeggieTales Ser.). (ENG.). 20p. (J). (gr. -1-2). bds. 12.99 (978-1-4336-9059-4(4), B&H Kids) B&H Publishing Group.
—VeggieTales: Show You Care & Always Share, a Digital Pop-Up Book (padded) 2017. (VeggieTales Ser.). (ENG.). 20p. (J). (gr. -1-2). bds. 12.99 (978-1-4336-9060-0(8), B&H Kids) B&H Publishing Group.
Bildner, Phil. Busted. 2013. (ENG., Illus.). 256p. (YA). (gr. 9). pap. 16.99 (978-1-4814-2171-3(9), Simon & Schuster Bks. For Young Readers) Simon & Schuster Bks. For Young Readers.
Billingsley, Morgan, et al. The Perfect Summer. 2015. (ENG., Illus.). 132p. (J). pap. 10.00 (978-1-62517-871-8(9), Brown Girls Publishing) INscribe Digital.
Billingsley, ReShonda Tate. Drama Queens. 2010. (Good Girlz Ser.: 8). (ENG., Illus.). 256p. pap. 12.99 (978-1-4391-5687-2(5), Gallery Bks.) Gallery Bks.
Billows, Denis. Down in Bluebell Wood. 2010. 164p. pap. 11.99 (978-1-4490-8822-4(8)) AuthorHouse.
Binder, Betsy. The Wrinkled-at-the Knees Elephant & Other Tuneful Tales. Decenciere, Isabelle, illus. 2008. 28p. (J). pap. 19.95 incl. audio compact disk (978-0-615-26652-7(5)) Velvet Pony Stories.
Binder, Mark. Genies, Giants & a Walrus. 2012. 132p. pap. 14.99 (978-0-9824707-9-4(7)) Light Pubns.
Bingham, Frances. Bedtime Stories for the Inner Child: Reuniting with & Nurturing Your Inner Child. 2009. 68p. pap. 10.49 (978-1-4389-3185-2(9)) AuthorHouse.
Bird Song: The Little Stories of Manoosh & Baloosh. 2003. (J). mass mkt. (978-1-932233-02-5(4)) Aurora Libris Corp.
Bishop, Barbara L. Children Today Around the U S A. Bishop, Barbara L., illus. 2008. (Illus.). 40p. pap. 13.95 (978-1-934246-25-2(5)) Peppertree Pr., The.
Bishop, Michael. In the Wild Wood, 4 vols. Cloke, Rene, illus. 2012. (ENG.). 64p. (J). 4.95 (978-1-84135-785-0(5)) Award Pubns. Ltd. GBR. Dist: Parkwest Pubns., Inc.
Black, & Still Beautiful. 2005. (YA). per. 6.95 (978-0-9630951-3-8(7)) Karnak Co.
Black, Chuck. Lady Carliss & the Waters of Moorue. 2010. (Knights of Arrethtrae Ser.). (ENG.). 208p. (YA). (gr. 5-7). pap. 9.99 (978-1-60142-127-2(3), Multnomah Bks.) Crown Publishing Group.
Black, Holly. The Poison Eaters: And Other Stories. Black, Theo, illus. 2011. (ENG.). 224p. (YA). (gr. 9). pap. 9.99 (978-1-4424-1232-3(1), McElderry, Margaret K. Bks.) McElderry, Margaret K. Bks.
—Zombies vs. Unicorns. 2012. lib. bdg. 22.10 (978-0-606-23686-7(4), Turtleback) Turtleback Bks.
Black, Holly & Castellucci, Cecil, eds. Geektastic: Stories from the Nerd Herd. 2010. (ENG.). 432p. (YA). (gr. 7-17). pap. 12.99 (978-0-316-00810-5(9)) Little, Brown Bks. for Young Readers.
Black, Holly & DiTerlizzi, Tony. The Spiderwick Chronicles Set: The Field Guide - The Seeing Stone - Lucinda's Secret - The Ironwood Tree - The Wrath of Mulgrath. DiTerlizzi, Tony, illus. 2013. (Spiderwick Chronicles Ser.). (ENG., Illus.). (J). (gr. 1-5). 752p. pap. 39.99 (978-1-4424-8798-7(4)); 672p. 79.99 (978-1-4424-8797-0(6)) Simon & Schuster Bks. For Young Readers. (Simon & Schuster Bks. For Young Readers).
Black, Holly & Larbalestier, Justine, eds. Zombies vs. Unicorns. (ENG.). 432p. (YA). (gr. 9). 2012. pap. 11.99 (978-1-4169-8954-7(4)) 2010. 18.99 (978-1-4169-8953-0(6)) McElderry, Margaret K. Bks. (McElderry, Margaret K. Bks.).
Blackburn, Sheila M. Stewie Scraps & the Easy Rider. 2008. 72p. pap. (978-1-903853-85-6(0)) Brilliant Pubns.
—Stewie Scraps & the Space Racer. 2008. 68p. pap. (978-1-903853-84-9(2)) Brilliant Pubns.
—Stewie Scraps & the Super Sleigh. 2008. 72p. pap. (978-1-903853-89-4(3)) Brilliant Pubns.
—Stewie Scraps & the Trolley Cart. 2008. 72p. pap. (978-1-903853-88-7(5)) Brilliant Pubns.
Blackington, Debbie. Mama's Wish/Daughter's Wish. Sommer, Xiaolan, tr. from CHI. 2004. (Illus.). 48p. (J). 17.95 (978-0-9760011-0-2(1)) Pebbleton Pr.
Blackman, Dorothy L. New York Patriots. Gulley, Martha, illus. 2007. (J). (978-1-59531-020-0(7)) North Country Bks., Inc.
Blackstone, Stella. Hip Shapes. Bell, Siobhan, illus. 2012. (ENG.). 24p. (J). (gr. -1-k). 6.99 (978-1-84686-762-0(2)) Barefoot Bks., Inc.
Blake, Jon. House of Fun. Roberts, David, illus. 2005. (ENG.). 128p. (J). (gr. 2-4). pap. 6.95 (978-0-340-88459-1(2)) Hachette Children's Group GBR. Dist: Hachette Bk. Group.
Blanco, Ms. Healing Hearts of Nature: Five Therapeutic Fables for Children. 2009. 52p. pap. 23.00 (978-1-4490-1529-9(8)) AuthorHouse.
Blanquet, Stephane. Toys in the Basement. 2010. (ENG., Illus.). 32p. 14.99 (978-1-60699-402-3(6), 699402) Fantagraphics Bks.
Blitz, Shmuel. Every Story Has a Soul. Katz, Tova, illus. 2006. 47p. (J). 15.99 (978-1-4226-0224-9(9)) Mesorah Pubns., Ltd.
Block, Francesca Lia. Blood Roses. 2008. 144p. (J). (gr. 9-18). 15.99 (978-0-06-076384-8(1), Cotler, Joanna Books) HarperCollins Pubs.
Bloomfield, Susanne George & Reed, Eric Melvin, eds. Adventures in the West: Stories for Young Readers. 2007. (ENG., Illus.). 302p. (gr. 3-7). pap. 19.95 (978-0-8032-5974-4(3), Bison Bks.) Univ. of Nebraska Pr.
Blow, Wind, Blow! & Other Stories: Individual Title Six-Pack. (Story Steps Ser.). (gr. k-2). 42.00 (978-0-7635-9586-9(1)) Rigby Education.
Blue Wolf & Friends Learning Adventure Package, 2 bks. 2004. (Illus.). 100p. lib. bdg. (978-0-9758759-0-2(6)) Progressive Language, Inc.
Blume, Judy. Judy Blume Essentials: Are You There God? It's Me, Margaret; Blubber; Deenie; Iggie's House; It's Not the End of the World; Then Again, Maybe I Won't; Starring Sally J. Freedman As Herself. 2014. (ENG., Illus.). 1616p. (J). (gr. 3-7). pap. 55.99 (978-1-4814-3533-8(7), Atheneum Bks. for Young Readers) Simon & Schuster Children's Publishing.
—The Judy Blume Teen Collection: Are You There God? It's Me, Margaret; Deenie; Forever; Then Again, Maybe I Won't; Tiger Eyes. 2014. (ENG., Illus.). 1056p. (YA). (gr. 9). pap. 49.99 (978-1-4814-3534-5(5), Atheneum Bks. for Young Readers) Simon & Schuster Children's Publishing.
Blyton, Enid. The Adventure of the Secret Necklace. (ENG., Illus.). 84p. (J). pap. 7.99 (978-0-7475-3211-8(7)) Bloomsbury Publishing Plc GBR. Dist: Trafalgar Square Publishing.
—The Boy Who Wanted a Dog. (ENG., Illus.). 91p. (J). pap. 7.99 (978-0-7475-3213-2(3)) Bloomsbury Publishing Plc GBR. Dist: Trafalgar Square Publishing.
—The Children of St. Kidillin. (ENG., Illus.). 110p. (J). pap. 7.99 (978-0-7475-3216-3(8)) Bloomsbury Publishing Plc GBR. Dist: Trafalgar Square Publishing.
—Enid Blyton Circus Stories. (Illus.). (J). 11.95 (978-0-09-914131-0(0)) Random Hse. GBR. Dist: Trafalgar Square Publishing.
—Magic Snow Bird: And Other Stories. Hamilton, Dorothy, illus. 2013. (ENG.). 192p. (J). 9.95 (978-1-84135-420-0(1)) Award Pubns. Ltd. GBR. Dist: Parkwest Pubns., Inc.
—Mr Meddle Stories. 240p. (J). pap. 5.95 (978-0-09-965550-3(0)) Random Hse. GBR. Dist: Trafalgar Square Publishing.
—Mr Pink-Whistle's Party. 2nd ed. (ENG., Illus.). 111p. (J). pap. 7.99 (978-0-7475-3853-0(0)) Bloomsbury Publishing Plc GBR. Dist: Trafalgar Square Publishing.
—Rag, Tag & Bobtail & Other Magical Stories. George, Hannah, illus. 2016. (ENG.). 224p. (J). (gr. 2-5). 9.99 (978-1-5098-1084-0(6)) Pan Macmillan GBR. Dist: Independent Pubs. Group.
—The Secret of Cliff Castle. (ENG., Illus.). 117p. (J). pap. 7.99 (978-0-7475-3214-9(1)) Bloomsbury Publishing Plc GBR. Dist: Trafalgar Square Publishing.
—The Secret of the Lost Necklace: 3 Great Adventure Stories. Biro, Val, illus. 2013. (ENG.). 272p. (J). 16.50 (978-1-84135-587-0(9)) Award Pubns. Ltd. GBR. Dist: Parkwest Pubns., Inc.
—The Strange Umbrella: And Other Stories. Gregory, Sally, illus. 2013. (ENG.). 192p. (J). 9.95 (978-1-84135-461-3(9)) Award Pubns. Ltd. GBR. Dist: Parkwest Pubns., Inc.
Blyton, Enid, et al. The Fairies' Shoemaker & Other Stories. 2013. (ENG., Illus.). 192p. (J). 9.99 (978-1-84135-458-3(9)) Award Pubns. Ltd. GBR. Dist: Parkwest Pubns., Inc.
BMI Staff, compiled by. Fear Street Collection - Set, 98 vols. 2009. (YA). 114.81 (978-1-60884-415-9(3)) BMI Educational Services.
Boatwright-Cook, Jane. The Skeleton Leaf Stories: Behind the Shutters. 2012. 124p. 23.99 (978-1-4772-1346-9(5)); pap. 14.95 (978-1-4772-1347-6(3)) AuthorHouse.
Bock, Caroline. Lie. 2011. (ENG.). 224p. (YA). (gr. 7-18). pap. 18.99 (978-0-312-66832-7(5), 9780312668327, St. Martin's Griffin) St. Martin's Pr.
Bodger, Joan. Tales of Court & Castle. Lang, Mark, illus. 2003. (ENG.). 96p. (J). (gr. 3-7). pap. 9.95 (978-0-88776-614-5(5), Tundra Bks.) Tundra Bks. CAN. Dist: Penguin Random Hse. LLC.
Boelter, Ashaki. Diaries of the Doomed. Boelter, Ashaki, illus. 2004. (Illus.). 88p. (YA). per. 6.95 (978-0-9721067-4-0(X), Writing Wild & Crazy) Shakalot High Entertainment.
—Diaries of the Doomed 2: Fate of the Fatal. 2007. (Illus.). 114p. (J). per. 11.95 (978-0-9796219-0-1(9), Writing Wild & Crazy) Shakalot High Entertainment.

Bogacki, Tomek. Mi Primer Jardin. 2003. (Picture Bks.). (SPA., Illus.). (J). *(978-970-690-649-6(5))* Planeta Mexicana Editorial S. A. de C. V.

Boie, Kirsten. King-Kong, Mi Mascota Secreta. (Torre de Papel Ser.). (SPA.). (J). (gr. 2). 7.95 *(978-958-04-1310-3(X))* Norma S.A. COL. Dist: Distribuidora Norma, Inc.

Bojunga, Lygia. La Cama. (SPA.). (J). *(978-958-04-6492-1(8))* Norma S.A. COL. Dist: Distribuidora Norma, Inc.

Boldt, Claudia. Uugghh! Boldt, Claudia, illus. 2011. (Child's Play Library). (ENG., Illus.). 32p. (J). (gr. 2-2). *(978-1-84643-372-6(X))* Child's Play International Ltd.

Bolt, Ranjit. The Hare & the Tortoise. Potter, Giselle, illus. 2006. (ENG.). 64p. (J). (gr. -1-3). 19.99 *(978-1-905236-54-1(9))* Barefoot Bks., Inc.

Bond, Alan. Tedoul. Swanson, Peter Joseph, illus. 2009. 28p. pap. 8.95 *(978-1-60076-137-9(2))* StoneGarden.net Publishing.

Bondanella Filutze, Ann M. On Gramma's Rocker: Animal Tales & Other Short Stories. 2013. 84p. pap. 27.95 *(978-1-4624-0498-8(7),* Inspiring Voices) Author Solutions, Inc.

Bongiovanni, Debbie. It's All about Magic or Is It?, 1 vol. 2009. 55p. pap. 16.95 *(978-1-61546-875-1(7))* America Star Bks.

—Kindness Pays Off, 1 vol. 2010. 58p. pap. 16.95 *(978-1-4489-6320-1(6))* America Star Bks.

Bono, Elena & Bono, E. El Sombrero de Ramito. Brignole, Giancarla, tr. Bono, Elena, illus. rev. ed. 2006. (Fabulas De Familia Ser.). (SPA & ENG., Illus.). 32p. (J). (gr. k-4). pap. 6.95 *(978-970-20-0261-1(3))* Castillo, Ediciones, S. A. de C. V. MEX. Dist: Macmillan.

Booker, Carolyn. Mr. Green Squash Takes a Journey. 2005. (J). pap. 8.00 *(978-0-8059-6638-1(2))* Dorrance Publishing Co., Inc.

Borchini, Ernest. Three Stories about Jonathan, the Computer, & Little Kitty: Three Short Stories about a Boy & His Magic Cat. 2013. 36p. (gr. -1). pap. 15.49 *(978-1-4669-6636-9(X))* Trafford Publishing.

Borges, Jorge Luis. Breve Ant de Ctos Fantastico. (SPA.). pap. 11.95 *(978-950-07-1350-4(0))* Editorial Sudamericana S.A. ARG. Dist: Distribooks, Inc.

Borges, Jorge Luis, et al. Cuentos Latinoamericanos: Antologia. 2nd ed. 2003. (SPA., Illus.). 134p. (J). (gr. 8-12). 14.95 *(978-968-19-0319-0(6))* Aguilar, Altea, Taurus, Alfaguara, S.A. de C.V MEX. Dist: Santillana USA Publishing Co., Inc.

Bornemann, Elsa. Los Grendelines. Pez, illus. 2003.Tr. of Grendelines. (SPA.). 70p. (J). (gr. 3-5). pap. 11.95 *(978-950-511-244-9(0))* Alfaguara S.A. de Ediciones ARG. Dist: Santillana USA Publishing Co., Inc.

—El Nino Envuelto. Duforu, Sebastian, illus. 2003. (SPA.). 176p. (YA). (gr. 5-8). pap. 13.95 *(978-950-511-623-2(3))* Alfaguara S.A. de Ediciones ARG. Dist: Santillana USA Publishing Co., Inc.

—Socorro! 12 Cuentos para Caerse de Miedo. (SPA., Illus.). 192p. (J). (gr. 5-8). pap. 10.95 *(978-968-19-0549-1(0))* Santillana USA Publishing Co., Inc.

—Socorro Diez y Otros Cuentos.Tr. of Socorro Diez & Other Stories. (SPA.). (YA). (gr. 5-8). pap. 7.95 *(978-958-04-2776-6(3))* Norma S.A. COL. Dist: Distribuidora Norma, Inc.

Boudreau, Bobby A. Inspirational Stories for Spiritual Youth. 2010. 124p. 29.99 *(978-1-4490-8105-8(3));* pap. 18.99 *(978-1-4490-8106-5(1))* AuthorHouse.

Bourne, Sylvia. Animal Tales. 2009. 49p. pap. 31.50 *(978-1-4452-1311-8(7))* Lulu Pr., Inc.

Bowden, Poona. Juno Wonders. 2009. (Illus.). (J). 15.99 *(978-0-9821737-0-1(9))* Elotos Pr., LLC.

—Juno¡¯s Dromen. 2009. (DUT., Illus.). (J). 15.99 *(978-0-9821737-1-8(7))* Elotos Pr., LLC.

Boyer, Allen B. Roberto's Bat. 2003. (Summit Books Ser.). (Illus.). 128p. (gr. 3-6). lib. bdg. 13.95 *(978-0-7569-1642-8(9))* Perfection Learning Corp.

Boyer, Allen B. & Hatala, Dan. Roberto's Bat. 2003. (Illus.). 128p. 6.95 *(978-0-7891-6149-9(4))* Perfection Learning Corp.

Boyle, T. C. The Human Fly & Other Stories. 2005. (ENG.). 192p. (YA). (gr. 7-7). 9.99 *(978-0-14-240363-1(6),* Speak) Penguin Young Readers Group.

Brackett, Leigh & Coppel, Jr., Alfred. Planet Stories - Summer 1949. 2008. 128p. (YA). pap. 14.95 *(978-1-59798-181-1(8))* Adventure Hse.

Bradman, Tony. Dilly & the Birthday Treat. Hellard, Susan & Hellard, Sue, illus. 2011. (Blue Bananas Ser.). (ENG.). 48p. (J). (gr. k-2). pap. 5.99 *(978-1-4052-5303-1(7))* Egmont Bks., Ltd. GBR. Dist: Independent Pubs. Group.

Bradshaw, John. Fun Campfire Ghost Stories. 2009. 114p. pap. 13.98 *(978-0-557-11729-1(1))* Lulu Pr., Inc.

—Fun campfire Stories. 2009. 132p. pap. 13.98 *(978-0-557-17897-1(5))* Lulu Pr., Inc.

—Fun campfire stories Anthology. 2009. 246p. pap. 19.98 *(978-0-557-18835-2(0))* Lulu Pr., Inc.

Brady, Karen. God Is Great: A Collection of 13 Story Book Poems, 1. l.t. ed. 2004. (Illus.). 20p. (J). 12.50 *(978-0-9754169-0-7(1))* Bradybooks.biz.

Brainard, Cecilia M., ed. Growing up Filipino: Stories for Young Adults. 2003. (Illus.). xv, 298p. (YA). per. 18.95 *(978-0-9719458-0-7(2))* PALH.

Brandeis, Madeline. Shaun O'Day of Ireland. 2004. reprint ed. pap. 22.95 *(978-1-4179-2725-8(9))* Kessinger Publishing, LLC.

Braymer, Donna. The Adventures of Rowdy Raccoon. 2006. (J). audio compact disk 5.99 *(978-0-9766823-8-7(9))* Sable Creek Pr. LLC.

Breckon, Brett, illus. Dragon Days. 2004. (ENG.). 82p. 17.95 *(978-1-84323-301-5(0))* Beekman Bks., Inc.

Brennan, Sarah Rees & Clare, Cassandra. The Bane Chronicles. 2015. lib. bdg. 25.75 *(978-0-606-37862-8(6))* Turtleback Bks.

Breshears, Alyce Park. Friends - a Collection of Stories. 2013. 88p. pap. 10.95 *(978-1-60414-682-0(6))* Fideli Publishing, Inc.

Brett, Jan. Annie & the Wild Animals. 2012. (ENG., Illus.). 32p. (J). (gr. -1-3). audio compact disk 10.99 *(978-0-547-85082-5(4))* Houghton Mifflin Harcourt Publishing Co.

Bridwell, Norman. Clifford Collection. Bridwell, Norman, illus. 2012. (ENG., Illus.). 192p. (J). (gr. -1-k). 12.99 *(978-0-545-45013-3(6))* Scholastic, Inc.

Bright, Belle. Crash, Bang, Boom, Zing. Bright, Michael, illus. 2009. 12p. pap. 24.95 *(978-1-60749-383-9(7))* America Star Bks.

Brindis, Laura. Cuentos Universales del Barroco a la Vanguardia. 2003. (SPA., Illus.). 224p. (YA). (gr. 7-18). *(978-968-6966-05-3(6))* EDITER'S Publishing Hse. MEX. Dist: EDITER'S Publishing Hse.

Broberg, Penelope Northrop. Sleuthy Gumshoe: The Remarkable Detective. 2011. 32p. (gr. -1). pap. 14.39 *(978-1-4567-6404-3(7))* AuthorHouse.

Broderick, Paula. The Quest: The First Toby & Sox Adventure. 2011. (ENG., Illus.). 160p. pap. *(978-1-84876-626-6(2))* Troubador Publishing Ltd.

Brodhead, Kimberly Renee. The Seedling: The Osarian Tales. 2008. 232p. pap. 24.95 *(978-1-60703-814-6(5))* America Star Bks.

Brodsky, Slava. Funny Children's Stories (in Russian - Smeshnye detskie Rasskazy) 2007. (RUS.). 144p. pap. 8.76 *(978-0-615-16120-4(0))* Manhattan Academia.

Bromfield, Val. If You Can't Sleep... & Other Stories. 2005. (ENG., Illus.). 48p. pap. *(978-1-84401-416-3(9))* Athena Pr.

Brooke, L. Leslie. The Story of the Three Little Pig & Other Shorts Works. l.t. ed. 2007. 70p. 18.99 *(978-1-4346-1999-0(0))* Creative Media Partners, LLC.

—The Story of the Three Little Pig & Other Shorts Works: The Story of the Three Little Pig & Other Shorts Works. 2007. 70p. 16.99 *(978-1-4346-1975-4(3))* Creative Media Partners, LLC.

Brooks, Amy. Princess Polly Stories. l.t. ed. 2007. 218p. pap. 22.99 *(978-1-4346-2000-2(X))* Creative Media Partners, LLC.

Brooks, Felicity & Litchfield, Jo. Tales from Littletown. 2004. (Usborne Easy Reading Bks.). (ENG., Illus.). 1p. (J). (gr. -1-3). 9.95 *(978-0-7460-3474-3(1))* EDC Publishing.

Brooks, Walter R. Freddy & the Popinjay. Wiese, Kurt, illus. 2011. (ENG.). 256p. (gr. 2-18). 10.99 *(978-1-59020-468-9(9))* Overlook Pr., The.

—Freddy & the Space Ship. Wiese, Kurt, illus. 2011. (ENG.). 266p. (gr. 2-18). 10.99 *(978-1-59020-469-6(7))* Overlook Pr., The.

Brophy, Ann. Novus 3 & Me: Six Short Stories about Friendship. 2010. 44p. pap. 18.49 *(978-1-4490-7132-5(5))* AuthorHouse.

Brothers Grimm. Rapunzel & Other Tales: Includes the Ugly Duckling & the Boy Pirate. 2008. (J). 34.99 *(978-1-60514-832-8(6))* Findaway World, LLC.

Broutin, Christian. In the Jungle. Broutin, Christian, illus. 2013. (ENG., Illus.). 36p. (J). (gr. -1-k). 12.99 *(978-1-85103-417-8(X))* Moonlight Publishing, Ltd. GBR. Dist: Independent Pubs. Group.

Brouwer, Sigmund. Blazer Drive, 1 vol. 2007. (Orca Sports Ser.). (ENG.). 176p. (YA). (gr. 6-10). per. 9.95 *(978-1-55143-717-0(1))* Orca Bk. Pubs. USA.

Brown, Abbie Farwell. Tales of the Red Children. 2006. pap. 20.95 *(978-1-4286-1602-8(0))* Kessinger Publishing, LLC.

Brown, Carron, ed. Beauty & the Beast & Jack & the Beanstalk: Two Tales & Their Histories. 2009. (World of Fairy Tales Ser.). (Illus.). 32p. (J). (gr. -1-2). lib. bdg. 22.60 *(978-1-60754-649-8(3))* Windmill Bks.

—Cinderella & Aladdin: Two Tales & Their Histories. 2009. (World of Fairy Tales Ser.). (Illus.). 32p. (J). (gr. -1-2). pap. 10.55 *(978-1-60754-644-3(2));* lib. bdg. 22.60 *(978-1-60754-643-6(4))* Windmill Bks.

—Hansel & Gretel & the Pied Piper of Hamelin: Two Tales & Their Histories. 2009. (World of Fairy Tales Ser.). (Illus.). 32p. (J). (gr. -1-2). pap. 10.55 *(978-1-60754-647-4(7));* lib. bdg. 22.60 *(978-1-60754-646-7(9))* Windmill Bks.

Brown, Craig. Mule Train Mail. Brown, Craig, illus. 2009. (ENG., Illus.). 32p. (J). (gr. -1-3). pap. 7.95 *(978-1-58089-188-2(8))* Charlesbridge Publishing, Inc.

Brown, Elizabeth. Collection of Children's Tales. 2006. 94p. pap. 16.95 *(978-1-4116-8022-7(7))* Lulu Pr., Inc.

Brown, Marc. Arthur & the Mystery of the Stolen Bike. 2012. (ENG., Illus.). 64p. (J). (gr. 1-4). pap. 4.99 *(978-0-316-13363-0(9))* Little, Brown Bks. for Young Readers.

Brown, Margaret Wise. A Baby's Gift: Goodnight Moon & the Runaway Bunny, 2 vols. Hurd, Clement, illus. 2014. 70p. (J). (gr. -1 — 1). pap. 15.99 *(978-0-694-01638-9(1),* HarperFestival) HarperCollins Pubs.

—Home for a Bunny. Williams, Garth, illus. 2012. (Little Golden Book Ser.). (ENG.). 24p. (J). (gr. k-k). 4.99 *(978-0-307-93009-5(2),* Golden Bks.) Random Hse. Children's Bks.

Brown, Paul. Still Another Time , Times Remembered. 2011. 128p. pap. 38.28 *(978-1-4670-2548-5(8))* AuthorHouse.

Brown, Paul Henry. Grandpa Still Remembers: Life Changing Stories for Kids of All Ages from a Missionary Kid in Africa. Deborah, Brown Armes, illus. 2013. 162p. pap. 14.95 *(978-1-61153-027-8(X))* Light Messages Publishing.

Brown, Roberta Simpson. Scared in School. 2005. (ENG.). 141p. (J). (gr. 6-9). pap. 8.95 *(978-0-87483-496-3(1))* August Hse. Pubs., Inc.

—The Walking Trees & Other Scary Stories. 2006. (ENG.). 140p. (J). (gr. 6-9). pap. 11.95 *(978-0-87483-143-6(1))* August Hse. Pubs., Inc.

Bruce, Ann Elizabeth. Inspire Your Spirit. 2007. 48p. per. *(978-1-897312-54-4(7))* Adlibbed Ltd.

Bruchac, Joseph. Flying with the Eagle, Racing the Great Bear: Tales from Native North America. 2011. (ENG., Illus.). 128p. (J). (gr. 3-9). pap. 12.95 *(978-1-55591-693-0(7))* Fulcrum Publishing.

Bruchac, Joseph, et al. Sports Shorts. 2007. (Illus.). 127p. (J). per. 4.99 *(978-1-58196-058-7(1),* Darby Creek) Lerner Publishing Group.

—Sports Shorts: An Anthology of Short Stories. 2005. (Illus.). 127p. (J). (gr. 4-7). 15.95 *(978-1-58196-040-2(9),* Darby Creek) Lerner Publishing Group.

Bryant, Sara Cone. Stories to Tell Children: Fifty-Four Stories with Some Suggestions for Telling. 2007. (ENG.). 186p. pap. 19.99 *(978-1-4346-0234-3(6));* 206p. pap. 22.99 *(978-1-4346-0308-1(3))* Creative Media Partners, LLC.

Buchan, John. The Magic Walking Stick & Stories from the Arabian Nights. Soper, Vernon, illus. 2007. 336p. per. 19.95 *(978-0-9791702-8-7(1))* Capricorn Hse. Publishing.

Bugs & Other Stories: Individual Title Six-Pack. (Story Steps Ser.). (gr. k-2). 48.00 *(978-0-7635-9616-3(7))* Rigby Education.

Bumpus, Tawanna. Tawanna's Children's Short Story Collections. 2005. (Illus.). 48p. (J). pap. 14.95 *(978-1-59800-007-8(1))* Outskirts Pr., Inc.

Bunting, Eve. Finn McCool & the Great Fish. Pullen, Zachary, illus. 2010. (ENG.). 38p. (J). (gr. k-6). 16.95 *(978-1-58536-366-7(9))* Sleeping Bear Pr.

Burgess, Melvin, et al. Losing It. Gray, Keith, ed. 2013. (ENG.). 200p. (YA). (gr. 9-12). 17.95 *(978-1-4677-2041-0(0),* Carolrhoda Lab™) Lerner Publishing Group.

Burgess, Thornton W. Big Book of Animal Stories. 2011. (Dover Children's Classics Ser.). (ENG., Illus.). 272p. (J). (gr. 3-8). 9.95 *(978-0-486-41980-0(0))* Dover Pubns., Inc.

—Mother West Wind 'Where' Stories. 2009. 108p. 22.95 *(978-1-60664-597-0(8));* 104p. pap. 9.95 *(978-1-60664-326-6(6))* Rodgers, Alan Bks.

—Mother West Wind 'Why' Stories. 108p. (gr. -1-3). 2007. per. 9.95 *(978-1-60312-004-3(1))* 2006. 22.95 *(978-1-59818-467-9(9))* Aegypan.

—Mother West Wind's Children. Kerr, George, illus. 2013. (Dover Children's Classics Ser.). (ENG.). 144p. (J). (gr. 1-5). pap. 3.00 *(978-0-486-49724-2(0))* Dover Pubns., Inc.

—Old Mother West Wind. Kerr, George, illus. annot. ed. 2011. (Dover Children's Classics Ser.). (ENG.). 336p. (J). (gr. 1-5). 20.00 *(978-0-486-48051-0(8))* Dover Pubns., Inc.

—Old Mother West Wind. 2004. reprint ed. pap. 15.95 *(978-1-4191-3812-6(X));* pap. 1.99 *(978-1-4192-3812-3(4))* Kessinger Publishing, LLC.

—Old Mother West Wind. 2011. 110p. 23.95 *(978-1-4638-9554-9(2))* Rodgers, Alan Bks.

—Short Works of Thornton W. Burgess. 2007. (ENG.). 282p. pap. 21.99 *(978-1-4346-1957-0(5));* 340p. pap. 24.99 *(978-1-4346-1981-5(8))* Creative Media Partners, LLC.

—Tales from the Storyteller's House. (J). 19.95 *(978-0-8488-0930-0(0))* Amereon Ltd.

—Thornton Burgess Five-Minute Bedtime Tales: From Old Mother West Wind's Library. Cady, Harrison, illus. 2011. (Dover Children's Classics Ser.). (ENG.). 128p. (J). (gr. 1-5). pap. 14.99 *(978-0-486-47111-2(X))* Dover Pubns., Inc.

Burke, Ruth. Gowandale Adventure: And other stories for Boys. 2007. (Illus.). 96p. 9.00 *(978-1-84625-070-5(6))* DayOne Pubns. GBR. Dist: Send The Light Distribution LLC.

Burkhart, Jessica. Canterwood Crest Stable of Stories: Take the Reins; Chasing Blue; Behind the Bit; Triple Fault. 2014. (Canterwood Crest Ser.). (ENG., Illus.). 1088p. (J). (gr. 4-8). pap. 31.99 *(978-1-4814-1474-6(7),* Aladdin) Simon & Schuster Children's Publishing.

Burleigh, Robert. Night Flight: Amelia Earhart Crosses the Atlantic. Minor, Wendell, illus. 2011. (ENG.). 40p. (J). (gr. -1-3). 17.99 *(978-1-4169-6733-0(8),* Simon & Schuster/Paula Wiseman Bks.) Simon & Schuster/Paula Wiseman Bks.

Burnett, Eric. 21st Century Voices. 2003. 210p. (YA). pap. 17.95 *(978-0-595-29649-1(1))* iUniverse, Inc.

Burnett, Frances Hodgson. Esmeralda, Mère Giraud's Little Daughter, Little Saint Elizabeth & Other Stories: A Collection of Short Stories by Frances Hodgson Burnett. 2012. 378p. *(978-1-78139-164-8(5))* Benediction Classics.

Burnett, Roger J. & Burnett, Wilma J. Short Stories & Tall Tales. 2012. 104p. pap. 9.95 *(978-1-4759-5168-4(X))* iUniverse, Inc.

Burningham, John. John Burningham. Burningham, John, illus. ltd. ed. 2009. (ENG., Illus.). 224p. (gr. k-12). 70.00 *(978-0-7636-4434-5(X))* Candlewick Pr.

Burns, Dal. The Kookaburra & Other Stories. 2007. (ENG.). 76p. per. 16.95 *(978-1-4241-1770-3(4))* PublishAmerica, Inc.

Burrows, Terry. ¡Oh, No! Es Hipo! (SPA.). 78p. (J). (gr. k-2). *(978-968-5308-88-5(8),* Silver Dolphin en Español) Advanced Marketing, S. de R. L. de C. V.

Burt, Steve. Wicked Odd: Still More Stories to Chill the Heart. Hagerman, Jessica, illus. 2006. 144p. (gr. 5-18). pap. 14.95 *(978-0-9741407-2-8(4))* Burt, Steven E.

Burton, Bria & burton, brain. Lance & Ringo Tails: The Wild Adventures of a Dog & a Cat As Told by Their Human. 2013. 134p. pap. 9.99 *(978-1-939181-45-9(3))* Soul Attitude Press.

Burton, Tim. Melancholy Death of Oyster Boy & the Other Stories: Stick Boy's Festive Season. 2008. (ENG., Illus.). 128p. (gr. 7-18). 19.95 *(978-0-06-052649-8(1))* HarperCollins Pubs.

Butler, Ellis Parker. Pigs Is Pigs & Other Favorites. 2004. reprint ed. pap. 20.95 *(978-1-4179-2471-4(3))* Kessinger Publishing, LLC.

Butler, Kynora. Knowing Is Believing in Reading: Facing Your Fears. 2007. 48p. per. 16.95 *(978-1-4241-7559-8(3))* America Star Bks.

Butler, Tom. My Childhood Stories. 2010. 103p. pap. 11.99 *(978-0-557-26571-8(1))* Lulu Pr., Inc.

Butterworth, Nick. The Whisperer. 2004. (Illus.). 31p. (J). *(978-0-00-712017-8(6))* HarperCollins Pubs.

Buyer, Robert & Coute, Ursula T. Family Work & Fun Through the Years: Four Stories about Children & Families Having Fun Working Together. 2013. 64p. (gr. 2-4). pap. 13.99 *(978-1-4624-0614-2(9),* Inspiring Voices) Author Solutions, Inc.

Buzzeo, Toni. No T. Rex in the Library. Yoshikawa, Sachiko, illus. 2010. (ENG.). 32p. (J). (gr. -1-3). 17.99 *(978-1-4169-3927-6(X),* McElderry, Margaret K. Bks.) McElderry, Margaret K. Bks.

Byers, Brian, illus. Noah's Babies Opposites & Offerings. 2005. 22p. (J). bds. 6.95 *(978-0-9746440-6-4(4))* Virtue Bks.

Byrd, Lee Merrill. Lover Boy / Juanito el Carinoso: A Bilingual Counting Book. Delgado, Francisco, illus. 2005. (ENG & SPA.). 32p. (J). (gr. -1-2). 15.95 *(978-0-938317-38-8(5))* Cinco Puntos Pr.

C., Brandi & Flanagan, Logan. City Mom Country Dad. 2009. pap. *(978-1-61584-398-5(1))* Independent Pub.

Cabot, Meg, et al. Prom Nights from Hell. 2010. (ENG.). 336p. (YA). (gr. 9). pap. 9.99 *(978-0-06-197600-1(8),* HarperTeen) HarperCollins Pubs.

Caeden Goes to Daycare. 2004. (Illus.). 32p. (J). 5.95 *(978-0-9759321-1-7(X))* Rascal Treehouse Publishing.

Cagle, Erica. My Little Book of Stories. 2003. 40p. per. *(978-1-59196-418-6(0))* Instant Pub.

Caine, Rachel, pseud, et al. Immortal: Love Stories with Bite. Cast, P. C., ed. 2009. (ENG., Illus.). 280p. (J). (gr. 9-12). pap. 8.95 *(978-1-933771-92-2(5))* BenBella Bks.

The Call of the Wild Guide. 16.47 *(978-0-13-425968-0(8))* Prentice Hall PTR.

Cam, Philip, ed. Thinking Stories 3. (Illus.). 64p. tchr. ed. *(978-0-86806-633-2(8),* Hale & Iremonger) GHR Pr., The.

A Camel Called Bump-Along, 6 vols., Set B. 32p. (gr. 1-3). 31.50 *(978-0-7802-8049-6(0))* Wright Group/McGraw-Hill.

Campbell, Kathy. Down under Advent Calendar of Chrissy Stories: Great Activities for the 2013 Silly Season. 2013. 60p. pap. 23.95 *(978-1-4525-6540-8(6),* Balboa Pr.) Author Solutions, Inc.

Campos, Paula. The Turtle's Shell. Ortega, Macarena, illus. 2008.Tr. of tortuga Golosa. (J). pap. 14.95 *(978-0-9801147-5-1(6))* Jorge Pinto Bks.

Campus Confessions Sample Set: XO Ronette/Frenemies/Choices/Crush. 2013. (ENG.). (YA). (gr. 8-12). pap. 39.80 *(978-1-62250-787-0(8))* Saddleback Educational Publishing, Inc.

Caplan, Frank A. The Donkey Who Lost His Tail. 2010. (Illus.). 20p. 12.49 *(978-1-4520-2778-4(1))* AuthorHouse.

Caple, Kathy. Termite Tales. Caple, Kathy, illus. 2009. (Brand New Readers Ser.). (ENG., Illus.). 48p. (J). (gr. -1-3). pap. 5.99 *(978-0-7636-3901-3(X))* Candlewick Pr.

—Termite Trouble: Brand New Readers. Caple, Kathy, illus. 2005. (Brand New Readers Ser.). (ENG., Illus.). 32p. (J). (gr. -1-3). pap. 5.99 *(978-0-7636-2573-3(6))* Candlewick Pr.

Capstone Press Staff. John Henry - Hammerin' Hero. Evergreen, Nelson, illus. 2010. (Graphic Spin Ser.). (ENG.). 40p. (gr. 1-3). lib. bdg. 25.32 *(978-1-4342-1898-8(8),* Graphic Revolve) Stone Arch Bks.

Captain, Cliff. Fables by the Sea, 2 vols. 2005. 145p. (J). Vol. 1. pap. *(978-0-9766401-0-3(4))* Vol. 2. pap. *(978-0-9766401-1-0(2))* Aenor Trust, The.

Capucilli, Alyssa Satin. Scat, Cat! Meisel, Paul, illus. 2010. (My First I Can Read Ser.). (ENG.). 32p. (J). (gr. -1 — 1). pap. 3.99 *(978-0-06-117756-9(3))* HarperCollins Pubs.

Caracappa, Michael. Storybook: From Age Three to Young Teenager. 2012. 84p. 19.95 *(978-1-4626-6773-4(2))* America Star Bks.

Carbone, Elisa & Lewis, E. B. Night Running. 2012. (ENG., Illus.). 40p. (J). (gr. k-3). pap. 7.99 *(978-0-553-11284-9(8),* Dragonfly Bks.) Random Hse. Children's Bks.

Cardoso, Onelio Jorge. Caballito Blanco. 2003. (SPA.). 78p. *(978-84-85334-48-3(5),* LG0124) Lóguez Ediciones ESP. Dist: Lectorum Pubns., Inc.

Carey-Costa, Denise. A Tale of Three Tails. Sjostrom, Nicole & Iseminger, Jonathon, illus. 2009. 81p. 10.99 *(978-1-4251-8492-6(8))* Trafford Publishing.

Carle, Eric. Animal Stories: 8 Animal Stories, over 35 Sounds. 2014. 36p. (J). bds. 24.98 *(978-1-4508-8529-4(2),* 1450885292) Publications International, Ltd.

—The Eric Carle Mini Library: A Storybook Gift Set. Carle, Eric, illus. 2009. (World of Eric Carle Ser.). (ENG., Illus.). 148p. (J). 14.99 *(978-1-4169-8516-7(6),* Little Simon) Little Simon.

—The Eric Carle Ready-To-Read Collection: Have You Seen My Cat?; the Greedy Python; Pancakes, Pancakes!; Rooster Is off to See the World; a House for Hermit Crab; Walter the Baker. Carle, Eric, illus. 2014. (World of Eric Carle Ser.). (ENG., Illus.). 160p. (J). (gr. -1-2). pap. 15.99 *(978-1-4814-1632-0(4),* Simon Spotlight) Simon Spotlight.

Carlson, Lavelle. Can a Toucan Hoot Too? A Phonemic Awareness Tale, 10 vols. Adams, Lucas, illus. 2003. 32p. (J). (gr. -1-1). per. 16.95 *(978-0-9725803-0-4(1))* Children's Publishing.

Carlson, Lori Marie & Carlson, Lori M. Moccasin Thunder: American Indian Stories for Today. 2005. (ENG.). 176p. (YA). (gr. 8-18). 17.99 *(978-0-06-623957-6(5),* HarperTeen) HarperCollins Pubs.

Carlson, Melody. La Oveja Perdida. 2004.Tr. of Lost Lamb. 8.99 *(978-0-7899-1240-4(6))* Editorial Unilit.

Carman, Patrick. 3:15 Season One Things That Go Bump in the Night. 2011. (3:15 Ser.: 1). (ENG.). 176p. (J). (gr. 5-9). 12.99 *(978-0-545-38475-9(3))* Scholastic, Inc.

Carmen Luisa. The Adventures of Cotin Mirel: Three Short Stories. 2012. 20p. pap. 10.95 *(978-1-4525-5161-6(8))* Balboa Pr.

Carmichael, Bruce. The Little Path by Shadow Mountain. 2003. (J). per. 10.95 *(978-1-58597-198-5(7))* Leathers Publishing.

Carolyn, Larsen. Grandmas 8 Special Stories for Little Boys. 2003. *(978-1-892354-87-7(X))* Educational Publishing Concepts, Inc.

Carpenter, Frances. Tales of a Korean Grandmother: 32 Traditional Tales from Korea. 2017. (ENG., Illus.). 318p. (J). (gr. 4-7). pap. 9.95 *(978-0-8048-4920-3(X))* Tuttle Publishing.

Carrero, Jorge & Cody, William. Buffalo Bill. 2003. (Timeless Classics Ser.). (SPA., Illus.). 92p. (J). (gr. 5-8). pap. 12.95 *(978-84-204-5778-9(7))* Santillana USA Publishing Co., Inc.

Carroll, Lewis, pseud. AILICE'S AVENTURS IN WUNNERLAND. 2011. (GER., Illus.). 140p. pap. *(978-1-904808-64-0(6))* Evertype.

—Alice's Adventures in Wonderland: And Other Stories. Tenniel, John, illus. 2013. (Leather-Bound Classics Ser.). (ENG.). 544p. lthr. 24.99 *(978-1-60710-933-4(6),* Thunder Bay Pr.) Readerlink Distribution Services, LLC.

—LA AVENTURAS DE ALISIA EN LA PAIS DE MERVELIAS. 2012. (GER., Illus.). 136p. pap. *(978-1-904808-88-6(3))* Evertype.

—LES-AVENTURES D'ALICE O PEYIS DES MERVEY. 2012. (GER., Illus.). 150p. pap. *(978-1-904808-87-9(5))* Evertype.

Carroll, Lewis, pseud & Bué, Henri. Les Adventures D'Alice Au Pays des Merveilles. 2010. (FRE., Illus.). 138p. pap. *(978-1-904808-52-7(2))* Evertype.

Carroll, Lewis, pseud & Everson, Michael. Alice's Adventures in Wonderland: Retold in Words of One Syllable. 2010. (Illus.). 108p. pap. *(978-1-904808-44-2(1))* Evertype.

Carroll, Lewis, pseud & Roberts, Selyf. Anturiaethau Alys Yng Ngwlad Hud. 2010.Tr. of Alice in Wonderland. (WEL., Illus.). 126p. pap. *(978-1-904808-46-6(8))* Evertype.

Carroll, Lewis, pseud & Stowell, Brian. Contoyryssyn Ealish Ayns Cheer Ny Yindyssyn. 2010. (Illus.). 144p. pap. *(978-1-904808-48-0(4))* Evertype.

Carryl, Charles E. The Admiral's Caravan: A Tale Inspired by Lewis Carroll's Wonderland. 2011. 110p. pap. *(978-1-904808-66-4(2))* Evertype.

—Davy & the Goblin: Or, What Followed Reading 'Alice's Adventures in Wonderland' 2011. (Illus.). 128p. pap. *(978-1-904808-65-7(4))* Evertype.

Carson, Rae. The Girl of Fire & Thorns Stories. 2014. (Girl of Fire & Thorns Novella Ser.). (ENG.). 272p. (YA). (gr. 8). pap. 9.99 *(978-0-06-233433-6(6)*, Greenwillow Bks.) HarperCollins Pubs.

Cart, Michael. Necessary Noise: Stories about Our Families as They Really Are. Noruzi, Charlotte, illus. 2006. (ENG.). 256p. (YA). (gr. 8-12). reprint ed. pap. 8.99 *(978-0-06-051437-2(X)*, HarperTeen) HarperCollins Pubs.

Cart, Michael, et al. How Beautiful the Ordinary. 2009. (ENG.). 368p. (YA). (gr. 9-18). 17.99 *(978-0-06-115498-0(9)*, HarperTeen) HarperCollins Pubs.

—Taking Aim: Power & Pain, Teens & Guns. 368p. (YA). (gr. 8). 2016. pap. 9.99 *(978-0-06-232736-9(4))* 2015. (ENG.). 17.99 *(978-0-06-232735-2(6))* HarperCollins Pubs. (HarperTeen).

Carter, Alden. Love, Football, & Other Contact Sports. 2008. (ENG.). 261p. (YA). pap. 8.95 *(978-0-8234-2165-7(1))* Holiday Hse., Inc.

Carter, Alden R. Love, Football, & Other Contact Sports. 2006. (ENG.). 192p. (YA). (gr. 7-12). 17.95 *(978-0-8234-1975-3(4))* Holiday Hse., Inc.

Carter, Grant Matthew. The Disaster Caster. Morling, Donovan, illus. 2012. 38p. pap. 16.00 *(978-1-4349-8432-6(X)*, RoseDog Bks.) Dorrance Publishing Co., Inc.

Carter-Johnson, Helen. Golden Memories of Childhood. 2012. 68p. pap. 10.00 *(978-0-9853814-0-0(X))* Professional Publishing Hse. LLC.

Cartwright, Stephen. Llittle Book of Train Stories. rev. ed. 2011. (Farmyard Tales Readers Ser.). 64p. (J). ring bd. 8.99 *(978-0-7945-3070-9(2)*, Usborne) EDC Publishing.

Carvajal, Victor. Como un Salto de Campana. 2003. (Alfaguara Infantil y Juvenil Ser.). (SPA., Illus.). 143p. (J). (gr. 5-8). per. 10.95 *(978-956-270-001-6(1))* Santillana USA Publishing Co., Inc.

—Cuentatrapos. (Barco de Vapor). (SPA.). 120p. (YA). (gr. 5-8). *(978-84-348-1606-0(7)*, SM0595) SM Ediciones.

Carver, Peter, ed. The Blue Jean Collection. 2007. (ENG.). 224p. mass mkt. 9.95 *(978-0-920633-94-6(3))* Thistledown Pr., Ltd. CAN. Dist: Univ. of Toronto Pr.

Carville, Declan. The Fairy Glen. (Illus.). 36p. pap. 7.95 *(978-0-9538222-3-2(0))* Discovery Pubns. GBR. Dist: Irish Bks. & Media, Inc.

Cassidy, Georgina M. The True Make Believe Story: TTMBS Collection. 2011. 64p. pap. 31.99 *(978-1-4628-6236-8(5))* Xlibris Corp.

Cast, Kristin, et al. Kisses from Hell. 2010. (ENG.). 272p. (YA). (gr. 9-18). pap. 9.99 *(978-0-06-195696-6(1)*, HarperTeen) HarperCollins Pubs.

Castor, Harriet. The Incredible Present. Young, Norman, illus. 2004. (Usborne Young Reading: Series Two Ser.). 64p. (J). (gr. k-4). 8.99 *(978-0-7945-1785-4(4)*, Usborne) EDC Publishing.

Cather, Willa. Willa Cather. Balkovek, James, illus. 2004. (Great American Short Stories Ser.). 80p. (gr. 4-7). lib. bdg. 24.00 *(978-0-8368-4251-7(0)*, Gareth Stevens Learning Library) Stevens, Gareth Publishing LLLP.

Catlow, Nikalas & Wesson, Tim. Aliens vs. Mad Scientists under the Ocean. Catlow, Nikalas & Wesson, Tim, illus. 2011. (Mega Mash-Up Ser.). (ENG., Illus.). 96p. (J). (gr. 2-5). pap. 6.99 *(978-0-7636-5874-8(X)*, Nosy Crow) Candlewick Pr.

Cauvin, Raoul. Bluecoats - Greenhorn, Vol. 4. Lambil, Willy, illus. 4th ed. 2011. (Bluecoats Ser.: 4). (ENG.). 48p. (gr. 3-17). pap. 11.95 *(978-1-84918-066-5(0))* CineBook GBR. Dist: National Bk. Network.

Celebrated A Staff. Story Parade: A Collection of Modern Stories for Boys & Girls. 2005. reprint ed. pap. 33.95 *(978-1-4191-1378-9(X))* Kessinger Publishing, LLC.

Cerebellum Corporation, prod. Willow Pond Storybook. 2011. cd-rom 39.95 *(978-1-61867-207-0(X))* Cerebellum Corp.

Cerpok, M. L. The Mobile Monk: A Zen Tale. Wagner, Gavin, illus. 2008. 73p. pap. 19.95 *(978-1-60610-138-4(2))* America Star Bks.

Challenger, Robert James. Grizzly's Home: And Other Northwest Coast Children's Stories, 1 vol. Challenger, Robert James, illus. 2005. (ENG., Illus.). 48p. (J). (gr. k-3). pap. 9.95 *(978-1-894384-94-0(6))* Heritage Hse. CAN. Dist: Orca Bk. Pubs. USA.

—Nature's Circle: And Other Northwest Coast Children's Stories, 1 vol. Challenger, Robert James, illus. 2009. (ENG., Illus.). 48p. (J). (gr. k-3). pap. 9.95 *(978-1-894384-77-3(6))* Heritage Hse. CAN. Dist: Orca Bk. Pubs. USA.

Chambers, Aidan. The Kissing Game: Short Stories. 2013. (ENG.). 224p. (YA). (gr. 9-17). pap. 7.95 *(978-1-4197-0531-1(8)*, Amulet Bks.) Abrams, Inc.

Chananie, Gloria. It's Story Time Grandm. 2009. 82p. pap. 19.95 *(978-1-4489-8091-8(7))* America Star Bks.

Chance, C. The Trepets Book Three Rabbit Race Day. Champion, Vanessa, illus. 2007. 112p. per. *(978-0-9551289-2-9(7)*, Bumble Bks.) Dragonfly Bks. & Arts.

Channing, Blanche Mary. Zodiac Stories. 2006. pap. 30.95 *(978-1-4286-3675-0(7))* Kessinger Publishing, LLC.

Charles, Veronika Martenova. It's Not about the Apple! Parkins, David, illus. 2010. (Easy-To-Read Wonder Tales Ser.). (ENG.). 64p. (J). (gr. k-3). pap. 5.95 *(978-0-88776-955-9(1)*, Tundra Bks.) Tundra Bks. CAN. Dist: Penguin Random Hse. LLC.

—It's Not about the Crumbs! Parkins, David, illus. 2010. (Easy-To-Read Wonder Tales Ser.). (ENG.). 64p. (J). (gr. k-3). pap. 5.95 *(978-0-88776-953-5(5)*, Tundra Bks.) Tundra Bks. CAN. Dist: Penguin Random Hse. LLC.

—It's Not about the Hunter! Parkins, David, illus. 2010. (Easy-To-Read Wonder Tales Ser.). (ENG.). 56p. (J). (gr. k-3). pap. 5.95 *(978-0-88776-948-1(9)*, Tundra Bks.) Tundra Bks. CAN. Dist: Penguin Random Hse. LLC.

—It's Not about the Pumpkin! Parkins, David, illus. 2010. (Easy-To-Read Wonder Tales Ser.). (ENG.). 64p. (J). (gr. k-3). pap. 5.95 *(978-0-88776-949-8(7)*, Tundra Bks.) Tundra Bks. CAN. Dist: Penguin Random Hse. LLC.

—It's Not about the Rose! Parkins, David, illus. 2010. (Easy-To-Read Wonder Tales Ser.). (ENG.). 64p. (J). (gr. k-3). pap. 5.95 *(978-0-88776-954-2(3)*, Tundra Bks.) Tundra Bks. CAN. Dist: Penguin Random Hse. LLC.

Chase, Anita, et al. Tundra Adventures. Chase, Anita et al, illus. 2006. (Adventure Story Collection Ser.). 28p. (J). (gr. 2-6). pap. 10.00 *(978-1-58084-254-9(2))* Lower Kuskokwim Schl. District.

Chen, Ju-Hong, illus. The Jade Stone: A Chinese Folktale, 1 vol. 2005. (ENG.). 32p. (J). (gr. k-3). 16.99 *(978-1-58980-359-6(0))* Pelican Publishing Co., Inc.

Cheyney, Arnold. Legends of Arts. 2007. 128p. pap. 14.95 *(978-1-59647-137-5(9))* Good Year Bks.

A Chicago Winds Set, 6 vols. 32p. (gr. 1-3). 26.50 *(978-0-7802-8047-2(4))* Wright Group/McGraw-Hill.

Chichester Clark, Emma. No Mas Besos! (SPA.). (J). 8.95 *(978-958-04-6884-4(2))* Norma S.A. COL. Dist: Distribuidora Norma, Inc.

Chidebelu-Eze/Dove Publishing, Chibueze / Obi. The Tales of Tortoise: Inspirational Stories of Wisdom. Newborne, David / F., illus. 2005. (ENG.). 76p. (J). 16.00 *(978-0-9766578-0-4(5))* Dove Publishing, Inc.

Chidley, Howard J. FiftyTwo Story Talks to Boys & Girls D. 2007. pap. *(978-1-4065-1446-9(2))* Dodo Pr.

Child, Lauren. I Am Really, Really Concentrating. 2008. (Charlie & Lola Ser.). (ENG.). 24p. (J). (gr. -1-k). mass mkt. 3.99 *(978-0-448-44905-0(6)*, Grosset & Dunlap) Penguin Young Readers Group.

Child, Lydia Maria. The Magician's Show Box & Other Stories. 2007. 124p. pap. 18.99 *(978-1-4346-4663-7(7))*; (ENG.). 144p. pap. 19.99 *(978-1-4346-4664-4(5))* Creative Media Partners, LLC.

—The Magician's Show Box & Other Stories. 2007. (ENG.). 124p. per. *(978-1-4065-1354-7(7))* Dodo Pr.

—The Magician's Show Box & Other Stories. 2007. 88p. per. *(978-1-4068-4552-5(3))* Echo Library.

—The Magician's Show Box & Other Stories. 2004. reprint ed. pap. 1.99 *(978-1-4192-7122-9(9))*; pap. 19.95 *(978-1-4191-7122-2(4))* Kessinger Publishing, LLC.

—The Magician's Show Box, & Other Stories by the Author of Rainbows for Children. 2006. 312p. per. 23.99 *(978-1-4255-2973-4(9))* Michigan Publishing.

Children of Appalachia. Teddy Bear Helps on the Farm. Children of Appalachia, illus. 2007. (Illus.). 64p. (J). per. 14.95 *(978-0-929915-73-9(9))* Headline Bks., Inc.

The Children's Hour. l.t. ed. 2007. 108p. pap. 26.99 *(978-1-4264-8236-6(1))* Creative Media Partners, LLC.

The Children's Portion. 2006. 168p. pap. 19.99 *(978-1-4264-5116-4(4))*; 184p. pap. 21.99 *(978-1-4264-5417-2(1))* Creative Media Partners, LLC.

Children's Press, contrib. by. The Frog in the Pond & Other Animal Stories. 2008. (Rookie Reader Treasury Ser.). (ENG., Illus.). 128p. (J). 11.95 *(978-0-531-21727-6(2)*, Children's Pr.) Scholastic Library Publishing.

—Show-and-Tell Sam & Other School Stories. 2008. (Rookie Reader Treasury Ser.). (ENG., Illus.). 128p. (J). 11.95 *(978-0-531-21726-9(4)*, Children's Pr.) Scholastic Library Publishing.

Childress, Story. The Old Codger, 1 vol. 2009. 23p. pap. 19.95 *(978-1-4489-2511-7(8))* PublishAmerica, Inc.

Chinese, the Singapore. Musical Adventures with Quek Quek: Discover the Sounds of the Chinese Orchestra. Fong, Lee Kow, illus. 2016. (ENG.). 96p. pap. 25.00 incl. cd-rom *(978-981-4677-23-3(X))* Marshall Cavendish International (Asia) Private Ltd. SGP. Dist: National Bk. Network.

Chisiya. Afrikan Lullaby: Folk Tales from Zimbabwe. 2012. (Illus.). 56p. pap. 31.99 *(978-1-4691-7174-6(0))* Xlibris Corp.

Choudhry, Fahima. The Snow Surprise. 2011. 24p. pap. 15.99 *(978-1-4653-4628-5(7))* Xlibris Corp.

Choyce, Lesley. Sudden Impact. 2006. (Orca Currents Ser.). 104p. (gr. 5-9). 19.95 *(978-0-7569-6876-2(3))* Perfection Learning Corp.

Christ at the Coffee Shop. 2004. lib. bdg. *(978-0-9747425-0-2(3)*, 09747425) Tranquility Ranch Publishing.

Christ Legends & Other Stories. 2012. 204p. pap. *(978-1-84902-141-8(4))* Benediction Classics.

Christelow, Eileen. Five Little Monkeys Storybook Treasury. 2009. (Five Little Monkeys Story Ser.). (ENG., Illus.). 192p. (J). (gr. -1-3). 11.99 *(978-0-547-23873-9(8))* Houghton Mifflin Harcourt Publishing Co.

Christensen, Gerda. Troll Peter Discovers the Bog-Woman's Secret & Other Stories. 2010. 40p. pap. 18.27 *(978-1-4251-8822-1(2))* Trafford Publishing.

—Troll Peter Finds A Treasure at the End of the Rainbow & Other Stories: Troll Peter's Adventures, Book 2. 2010. 36p. pap. 18.41 *(978-1-4269-3697-5(4))* Trafford Publishing.

Christian, Lmh. Stories from the Red Glass. 2008. 48p. pap. 14.95 *(978-0-9798154-9-2(5))* Living Waters Publishing Co.

Christie, Jackie. Wacky WaterSlide Wipeout. 2011. 28p. (gr. -1). pap. 16.09 *(978-1-4269-5821-2(8))* Trafford Publishing.

Christmas Is Coming. 2003. (J). 6.99 *(978-1-59384-012-9(8))* Parklane Publishing.

Christophersen, Jane Garlil. Kakadu Calling: Stories for Kids. Christophersen, Christine, illus. 2007. (ENG.). 64p. (J). (gr. 2-7). pap. 9.95 *(978-1-921248-00-9(9))* Magabala Bks. AUS. Dist: Independent Pubs. Group.

Church, Peggy Pond. The Pancake Stories: Cuentos Del Panqueque. Chilton, Noel, tr. Church, Elizabeth Comfort, illus. 2013. (ENG & SPA.). 96p. (J). 12.95 *(978-0-8263-5387-0(8))* Univ. of New Mexico Pr.

Civardi, Anne. Cambiarse de Casa. (SPA.). 16p. (J). 4.50 *(978-84-7655-125-7(8))* Plaza Joven, S.A. ESP. Dist: AIMS International Bks., Inc.

Claflin, Willy. Maynard Moose Tales. 2007. (J). 34.99 *(978-1-59895-864-5(X))* Findaway World, LLC.

Clairmont, Patsy. 5 Cheesy Stories: About Friendship, Bravery, Bullying, & More, 1 vol. Oeltjenbruns, Joni, illus. 2007. (Tails from the Pantry Ser.). (ENG.). 144p. (gr. -1-2). 15.99 *(978-1-4003-1042-5(3))* Nelson, Thomas Inc.

Clare, Cassandra, et al. The Bane Chronicles. Clare, Cassandra, ed. 2014. (Bane Chronicles Ser.). (ENG., Illus.). 528p. (YA). (gr. 9). 22.99 *(978-1-4424-9599-9(5)*, McElderry, Margaret K. Bks.) McElderry, Margaret K. Bks.

Clark, Margery. The Poppy Seed Cakes. 2013. (Everyman's Library Children's Classics Ser.). (ENG.). 160p. 26.95 *(978-0-375-71232-6(1)*, Everyman's Library) Knopf Doubleday Publishing Group.

Clarke, J. Erskine. Chatterbox for 1927. 2005. pap. 30.95 *(978-1-4179-8685-9(9))* Kessinger Publishing, LLC.

—Chatterbox For 1928. 2005. reprint ed. pap. 30.95 *(978-1-4179-8686-6(7))* Kessinger Publishing, LLC.

Clasicos Argentinos. (Clasicos Juveniles Coleccion). (SPA.). (YA). (gr. 5-8). pap. *(978-950-11-1409-6(0)*, SG7924) Sigmar ARG. Dist: Lectorum Pubns., Inc.

Clasicos de Amor. (Clasicos Juveniles Coleccion). (SPA.). (YA). (gr. 5-8). pap. *(978-950-11-1278-8(0)*, SG4719) Sigmar ARG. Dist: Lectorum Pubns., Inc.

Clasicos de Animales. (Coleccion Clasicos Juveniles). (YA). (gr. 5-8). pap. *(978-950-11-1579-6(8)*, SG1714) Sigmar ARG. Dist: Lectorum Pubns., Inc.

Clasicos de Humor. (Coleccion Clasicos Juveniles). (SPA.). (YA). (gr. 5-8). pap. *(978-950-11-1549-9(6)*, SG30754) Sigmar ARG. Dist: Lectorum Pubns., Inc.

Clasicos para Sonar: Bambi, Mago de Oz, Pulgarcita, Sirenita (Libro Rosa) 2003. (SPA.). 84p. 18.95 *(978-84-305-9976-9(2))* Susaeta Ediciones, S.A. ESP. Dist: Giron Bks.

Clasicos para Sonar: Blancanieves, Gato C/Botas, Caperucita (Libro Rojo) 2003. (SPA.). 86p. 18.95 *(978-84-305-9975-2(4))* Susaeta Ediciones, S.A. ESP. Dist: Giron Bks.

Clasicos Para Sonar: Libro de la Selva, Casita Chocolate, Mago Merlin. 2003. (SPA.). 96p. 18.95 *(978-84-305-9974-5(6))* Susaeta Ediciones, S.A. ESP. Dist: Giron Bks.

Clasicos para Sonar: Pinocho, Bella y la Bestia, Alicia (Libro Verde) 2003. (SPA.). 82p. 18.95 *(978-84-305-9977-6(0))* Susaeta Ediciones, S.A. ESP. Dist: Giron Bks.

Class Trip, 6 vols., Set. 2009. (J). (gr. 2-5). lib. bdg. 179.70 *(978-1-58415-812-7(3))* Mitchell Lane Pubs., Inc.

Classic Children's Tales. 2005. (ENG.). 912p. pap. *(978-1-84022-063-6(5))* Wordsworth Editions, Ltd.

Clawson, Kimberly. Fun O' Licious. Bellomy, Gail, illus. 2007. (ENG.). 56p. per. 16.95 *(978-1-4241-5556-9(8))* America Star Bks.

Claybourne, Anna, retold by. Stories from Shakespeare. 2005. (Stories from Shakespeare Ser.). 192p. (J). 24.99 *(978-0-7945-0912-5(6)*, Usborne) EDC Publishing.

Cleary, Beverly. Ramona Empieza el Curso. 2003. (Ramona Quimby Ser.).Tr. of Ramona Quimby, Age 8. (SPA.). 144p. (J). 9.95 *(978-84-239-8891-4(0))* Espasa Calpe, S.A. ESP. Dist: Planeta Publishing Corp.

—Ramona y Su Madre. 2003. (Ramona Quimby Ser.).Tr. of Ramona & Her Mother. (SPA.). 108p. (J). 9.95 *(978-84-239-9040-5(0))* Espasa Calpe, S.A. ESP. Dist: Planeta Publishing Corp.

Clements, Andrew. Andrew Clements' School Stories. 2013. (ENG., Illus.). 1856p. (J). (gr. 3-7). pap. 79.99 *(978-1-4424-9386-5(0)*, Atheneum Bks. for Young Readers) Simon & Schuster Children's Publishing.

—Head of the Class: Frindle - The Landry News - The Janitor's Boy. Selznick, Brian, illus. 2007. (ENG.). 416p. (J). (gr. 3-7). pap. 20.99 *(978-1-4169-4974-9(7)*, Atheneum Bks. for Young Readers) Simon & Schuster Children's Publishing.

Clements, Richmond. Turning Tiger Special Edition. Finbow, Alexander, ed. 2012. (Illus.). 56p. pap. 7.99 *(978-1-926914-87-9(2))* Arcana Studio, Inc.

Clendenin, Arlene M. & Clendenin, Bernard S. The Adventures of the Yellow Beak Bird & the Flying Cats: Yellow Beak Bird & the Flying Cats. 2013. 48p. pap. 11.99 *(978-0-9897662-1-0(7))* Clendenin Fine Art Concepts.

Cloyd, Suzy. Pippi's Silent Message: Adventures of Suzy Q & You Too. Barham, Timothy E., illus. 2012. 24p. 24.95 *(978-1-4512-7832-3(2))* America Star Bks.

Clynes, Kate. Ali Baba. Anstey, David, illus. 2005. (SWA & ENG.). 32p. (J). pap. *(978-1-84444-429-8(5))* Mantra Lingua.

Coates, Theresa. Imaginary Time of Life. 2007. 102p. pap. 10.95 *(978-0-7414-4067-9(9))* Infinity Publishing.

Cofer, Judith Ortiz. Animal Jamboree / La Fiesta de los Animales: Latino Folktales / Leyendas Latinas. Rosales-Yeomans, Natalia, tr. 2012. (SPA & ENG.). (J). pap. 9.95 *(978-1-55885-743-8(5)*, Piñata Books) Arte Publico Pr.

—An Island Like You: Stories of the Barrio. 2011. 9.15 *(978-0-7848-3583-8(7)*, Everbind) Marco Bk. Co.

—An Island Like You: Stories of the Barrio. 2009. 243p. 17.00 *(978-1-60686-446-3(7))* Perfection Learning Corp.

Cohen, Leslie, et al. Jewish Love Stories for Kids: An Anthology of Short Stories. 2005. (Jewish Stories for Kids Ser.). 232p. (J). 16.95 *(978-1-930143-45-6(1)*, 3451); pap. 12.95 *(978-1-930143-46-3(X)*, 346X) Simcha Media Group. (Devora Publishing).

Cohn, Marvin. Tell Me A Story Gramps. 2007. 52p. pap. 16.95 *(978-1-4241-5075-5(2))* America Star Bks.

Colbert, Larry C. Insights from an Out-of-Sight Guy. 2005. 111p. per. 20.00 *(978-0-9766329-0-0(X))* Driving Vision, Inc.

Colburn, Cherie Foster. Bloomin' Tales: Legends of Seven Favorite Texas Wildflowers. Hein, Joy Fisher, illus. 2012. (ENG.). 64p. (J). (gr. 4-4). 24.95 *(978-1-936474-18-9(2)*, 91c14e7a-1c5d-4381-b022-da21965048db) Bright Sky Pr.

Cole, Babette. El Libro de Etiqueta de Lady Lupina. 2003. (Babette Cole Ser.).Tr. of Lady Lupin's Book of Etiquett. (SPA.). (J). 18.95 *(978-84-233-3337-0(X))* Ediciones Destino ESP. Dist: Planeta Publishing Corp.

Cole, Bob. Power Reading: Nail-Biters! 2. Morton, Vivian, illus. 2005. 94p. (J). (gr. 6-18). vinyl bd. 89.95 *(978-1-883186-25-8(0)*, PPNB2) National Reading Styles Institute, Inc.

Cole, Joanna. The Magic School Bus & the Climate Challenge. Degen, Bruce, illus. 2010. (Magic School Bus Ser.). (ENG.). 48p. (J). (gr. 2-5). 16.99 *(978-0-590-10826-3(3)*, Scholastic Pr.) Scholastic, Inc.

Coleman, Ryan S. The Wonderful World of Folli: Milly & Tilly. 2012. 24p. 24.95 *(978-1-4626-6759-8(7))* America Star Bks.

A Collection of Stories Inspired by My Grandchildren. 2005. (YA). per. *(978-1-59872-111-9(9))* Instant Pub.

Collier, Kevin Scott. Hope, the Angelfish. Collier, Kevin Scott, illus. 2008. (Illus.). 24p. pap. 10.95 *(978-1-933090-17-7(0))* Guardian Angel Publishing, Inc.

Collins, Bert McLemore. Excitement at Double B Acres. 2009. 52p. pap. 22.49 *(978-1-4389-8447-6(2))* AuthorHouse.

Collins, Ellen M. My Book: Fun Favorite Stories. 2010. 68p. pap. 26.99 *(978-1-4490-5236-2(3))* AuthorHouse.

Collins, Paul. A Tale of Two Squirrels. 2008. 104p. pap. 9.95 *(978-1-60693-204-9(7)*, Eloquent Bks.) Strategic Book Publishing & Rights Agency (SBPRA).

Comeau, Ceara. Adventures of the Young & Curious. 2008. 136p. pap. 10.94 *(978-0-557-00914-5(6))* Lulu Pr., Inc.

Comella, Maria Angeles & Seix, Merce. Una Tarde con Joan Oro. (SPA., Illus.). (J). (gr. 2-4). *(978-84-261-3075-4(5)*, JV8905) Juventud, Editorial ESP. Dist: Lectorum Pubns., Inc.

The Complete Gideon Trilogy: The Time Travelers; the Time Thief; the Time Quake. 2014. (Gideon Trilogy Ser.). (ENG., Illus.). 1424p. (J). (gr. 5-9). pap. 26.99 *(978-1-4814-2613-8(3)*, Simon & Schuster Bks. For Young Readers) Simon & Schuster Bks. For Young Readers.

Concordia International School Shanghai. Stories from Room 113: International Adventures. 2008. 304p. pap. 18.95 *(978-0-595-53090-8(7))* iUniverse, Inc.

Connell, Richard Edward. The Most Dangerous Game. 2010. (Creative Short Stories Ser.). (Illus.). 48p. (J). (gr. 5-18). 19.95 *(978-1-58341-920-5(9)*, Creative Education) Creative Co., The.

Connolly, Brian A. Allegheny River Christmas & Other Stories. 2007. 56p. per. 20.95 *(978-1-58939-992-1(7))* Virtualbookworm.com Publishing, Inc.

Conrad, Perrin Cothran. The Ballad of the Shirley T & Other Stories. 2011. 80p. pap. 8.95 *(978-1-4620-5671-2(7))* iUniverse, Inc.

Constans, Gabriel. Skin of Lions. 2009. 63p. pap. 13.75 *(978-1-60695-014-2(2))* Callanish Pr.

Conteh, Gerald. I Still Believe in Santa. 2007. 188p. per. 14.95 *(978-1-60264-014-6(9))* Virtualbookworm.com Publishing, Inc.

Cook, Julia. Making Friends Is an Art! Barnes, Bridget A., illus. 2012. (ENG.). 32p. (J). pap. 10.95 *(978-1-934490-30-3(X))* Boys Town Pr.

—Sorry, I Forgot to Ask! My Story about Asking Permission & Making an Apology! De Weerd, Kelsey, illus. 2012. (ENG.). 32p. 16.95 *(978-1-934490-29-7(6))*; pap. 10.95 *(978-1-934490-28-0(8))* Boys Town Pr.

Cooke, Flora J. Nature Myths & Stories for Little Chil. 2006. pap. 19.95 *(978-1-4254-9629-6(6))* Kessinger Publishing, LLC.

Cooling, Wendy. The Puffin Book of Stories for Five-Year-Olds. Cox, Steve, illus. (ENG.). 144p. (J). pap. 9.95 *(978-0-14-037458-2(2))* Penguin Bks., Ltd. GBR. Dist: Trafalgar Square Publishing.

Cooling, Wendy, ed. Ten of the Best: School Stories with a Difference. 2009. (ENG., Illus.). 192p. (J). pap. 7.99 *(978-0-00-713339-0(1)*, HarperCollins Children's Bks.) HarperCollins Pubs. Ltd. GBR. Dist: HarperCollins Pubs.

Cooper, Diana. Tara & Her Talking Kitten Meet a Mermaid. Shannon, Kate, illus. 2012. (Tara & Ash-ting Ser.). (ENG.). 80p. (J). (gr. k-4). *(978-1-84409-580-3(0))* Me to We.

—Tara & the Talking Kitten Meet Angels & Fairies. Shannon, Kate, illus. 2011. (Tara & Ash-ting Ser.). (ENG.). 80p. (J). (gr. k-4). 8.95 *(978-1-84409-551-3(7))* Innovation Pr., The.

Cope, Andrew. Spy Dog & Captured!, 2 bks. in 1. 2014. (Spy Dog Ser.). (ENG., Illus.). 352p. (J). (gr. 2-7). 14.99 *(978-0-14-135097-4(0))* Penguin Bks., Ltd. GBR. Dist: Independent Pubs. Group.

Coppage, Merry Ann. Periwinkle Island. Venema, Lisa J. & Garland, Lynn Rockwell, illus. 2006. 86p. (J). (gr. -1-3). per. 36.99 *(978-1-4259-1931-3(6))* AuthorHouse.

Coppard, A. E. Clorinda Walks in Heaven Stories. 2006. 220p. per. *(978-1-4067-9414-4(7)*, Pomona Pr.) Read Bks.

Cornwell, Brendan W., illus. Aesop in Goudy. 2007. 48p. (J). 20.00 *(978-0-9711321-1-5(9))* Blue Tree LLC.

Cornwell, Nicki. Armel's Revenge. Pal, Erika, illus. 2012. (ENG.). 96p. (J). (gr. 3-6). pap. 8.99 *(978-1-84780-224-8(9)*, Frances Lincoln) Quarto Publishing Group UK GBR. Dist: Hachette Bk. Group.

Coro, Edys. Edys' Collection of Short Tales. 2008. 64p. pap. 19.95 *(978-1-60672-856-7(3))* America Star Bks.

Cortázar, Julio. Todos Los Fuegos el Fuego. (SPA.). (J). 9.00 *(978-958-04-6757-1(9))* Norma S.A. COL. Dist: Distribuidora Norma, Inc.

Cortez, Sarah, ed. You Don't Have a Clue: Latino Mystery Stories for Teens. 2011. 320p. (YA). (gr. 6-18). pap. *(978-1-55885-692-9(7))* Arte Publico Pr.

Cortright, Angel. The Miss Adventure of Animals & Their Short Stories. 2013. 28p. pap. 24.95 *(978-1-62709-063-6(0))* America Star Bks.

Covey, Ken. The Adventures of a Little Boy Named Kenny. 2008. 68p. pap. 10.95 *(978-1-4327-3110-6(6))* Outskirts Pr., Inc.

Covey, Sean. The 7 Habits of Happy Kids. 2008. (Playaway Children Ser.). (J). (gr. -1-3). 39.99 *(978-1-60640-956-5(5))* Findaway World, LLC.

—The 7 Habits of Happy Kids Collection: Just the Way I Am; When I Grow up; a Place for Everything; Sammy & the Pecan Pie; Lily & the Yucky Cookies; Sophie & the Perfect Poem; Goob & His Grandpa. Curtis, Stacy, illus. 2013. (7 Habits of Happy Kids Ser.). (ENG.). 224p. (J). (gr. -1-1). 55.99 *(978-1-4424-9617-0(7)*, Simon & Schuster Bks. For Young Readers) Simon & Schuster Bks. For Young Readers.

Coville, Bruce. Odds Are Good: An Oddly Enough & Odder Than Ever Omnibus. 2006. (ENG., Illus.). 352p. (YA). (gr. 7-12). pap. 16.95 *(978-0-15-205716-9(1))* Houghton Mifflin Harcourt Publishing Co.

Cowell, Cressida. How to Train Your Dragon Special Edition: With Brand New Short Stories! 2014. (ENG., Illus.). 432p. (J). (gr. 3-7). pap. 10.00 *(978-0-316-40747-2(X))* Little, Brown Bks. for Young Readers.

Cowley, Joy. Friends: Snake & Lizard. Bishop, Gavin, illus. 2011. (Gecko Press Titles Ser.). (ENG.). 144p. 16.95 *(978-1-877579-01-1(7))* Gecko Pr. NZL. Dist: Lerner Publishing Group.

—Mrs. Wishy-Washy's Tub. (Story Box Ser.). 8p. 20.95 *(978-0-7802-9365-6(7))* Wright Group/McGraw-Hill.

Cowsert, Sandra. The Continuing Adventures of Tammi & Her Dragon. 2007. 48p. per. 16.95 *(978-1-4241-8313-5(8))* America Star Bks.

Coxon, Rachel. A Collection of Children's Stories. 2005. (J). spiral bd. *(978-0-9761675-3-2(0))* Storybook Acres.

Coy, Steven. Sandwich: Short Stories & Screenplays by Steven Coy. Saia, Karla, ed. Vaughan, Jeremy, illus. 2003.

229p. (YA). per. 10.00 (978-0-9743235-0-3(0)) Better Non Sequitur.
Craig-Gaddis, Lora. Elsie & Pooka Stories of the Sabbats & Seasons. 2008. 126p. pap. 43.18 (978-0-557-01530-6(8)) Lulu Pr., Inc.
Craig, Lindsey. Dancing Feet! Brown, Marc, illus. 2012. (ENG.). 32p. (J). (gr. k-k). bds. 6.99 (978-0-307-93081-1(5), Knopf Bks. for Young Readers) Random Hse. Children's Bks.
Cranch, Christopher Pearse. Three Children's Novels by Christopher Pearse Cranch. Little, Greta D. & Myerson, Joel, eds. 2010. (ENG.). 200p. pap. 25.95 (978-0-8203-3704-3(8), 4325) Univ. of Georgia Pr.
Crane, Walter. The Walter Crane Storybook Collection. 2017. (Calla Editions Ser.). (ENG., Illus.). 128p. 25.00 **(978-1-60660-114-3(8))** Dover Pubns., Inc.
Craven, Georgina. Adventures & Rhymes with Grandmother. 2006. (Illus.). 76p. pap. (978-1-84401-648-8(X)) Athena Pr.
Crenshaw, Mills. The Christmas of 45. 2010. 176p. pap. 11.99 (978-1-59955-455-6(0)) Cedar Fort, Inc./CFI Distribution.
Cribbs, Randy, narrated by. Tales from the Oldest City: Selected Readings Vol 1. 2005. (YA). cd-rom 8.95 (978-0-9725796-3-6(X)) River Pr.
Crockett, Tilly. The Crockett Tales for Children. 2009. (Illus.). 60p. pap. 10.49 (978-1-4389-6154-5(5)) AuthorHouse.
Crompton, Richmal. Just William. Henry, Thomas & Riddell, Chris, illus. 2015. (Just William Ser.: 1). (ENG.). 336p. (J). (gr. 3-7). pap. 10.99 (978-1-4472-8558-8(1)) Pan Macmillan GBR. Dist: Independent Pubs. Group.
Cronin, Doreen. A Barnyard Collection: Click, Clack, Moo & More. Lewin, Betsy, illus. 2010. (Click, Clack Book Ser.). (ENG.). 128p. (J). (gr. -1-3). 19.99 (978-1-4424-1263-7(1), Atheneum Bks. for Young Readers) Simon & Schuster Children's Publishing.
Cross, Linda B. Lines from Linda. l.t. ed. 2003. 104p. (YA). per. 7.00 (978-0-9748591-2-5(5), MSP) Main St Publishing, Inc.
Crossley-Holland, Kevin. Short! A Book of Very Short Stories. 2015. (ENG., Illus.). 96p. 10.95 (978-0-19-278148-2(0)) Oxford Univ. Pr., Inc.
Crowe, Robert L. Children's Stories for ALmost Everyone. l.t. ed. 2006. Orig. Title: Children's Stories for Adults. 92p. (J). per. (978-0-9707173-8-2(5)) Consortium Publishing Co.
Crutcher, Chris. Angry Management. 2009. (ENG.). 256p. (YA). (gr. 9-18). 16.99 (978-0-06-050247-8(9), Greenwillow Bks.) HarperCollins Pubs.
Cudjoe, Dzagbe. Tales My Ghanaian Grandmother Told Me. 2008. 52p. pap. 19.95 (978-1-934925-87-4(X), Strategic Bk. Publishing) Strategic Book Publishing & Rights Agency (SBPRA).
Cuentecitos: El Pajaro Azul.Tr. of Little Stories: The Blue Bird. (SPA.). 12p. (J). 3.98 (978-970-607-902-2(5)) Larousse, Ediciones, S. A. de C. V. MEX. Dist: Giron Bks.
Cuentos Egipcios. (SPA., Illus.). (YA). 11.95 (978-84-7281-068-6(2), AF1068) Auriga, Ediciones S.A. ESP. Dist: Continental Bk. Co., Inc.
Cuentos, Mitos y Leyendas para Ninos de America Latina (Stories, Myths & Legends for Latin American Children) (SPA., Illus.). 72p. (J). 9.95 (978-958-04-0957-1(9), NOR9609) Norma S.A. COL. Dist: Distribuidora Norma, Inc.
El Cuidado del Aire. (Colección Biblioteca Juvenil de Ecología). (SPA., Illus.). (YA). (gr. 5-8). pap. (978-958-04-2406-2(3), 80424062) Norma S.A. COL. Dist: Lectorum Pubns., Inc.
Cumming, Hannah. The Cloud. Cumming, Hannah, illus. 2010. (Child's Play Library). (ENG., Illus.). 32p. (J). (gr. 1-2). pap. (978-1-84643-343-6(6)) Child's Play International Ltd.
—The Lost Stars. Cumming, Hannah, illus. 2011. (Child's Play Library). (ENG., Illus.). 32p. (J). (978-1-84643-416-7(5)) Child's Play International Ltd.
Cummings, Alicia. The Adventures of Jayda. 2010. 44p. pap. 16.99 (978-1-4520-2564-3(9)) AuthorHouse.
Cunningham, Thelma. Lisa's Unforgettable Stories. 2011. 272p. pap. 81.99 (978-1-4568-6746-1(6)) Xlibris Corp.
Curfew, Baron. Around the Houses. 2008. 48p. pap. (978-1-84923-303-3(9)) YouWriteOn.
Currie, Robin. The Baby Bible ABCs, 1 vol. Basaluzzo, Constanza, illus. 2009. (Baby Bible Ser.). (ENG.). 48p. (J). bds. 12.99 (978-1-4347-6542-0(3)) Cook, David C.
—The Baby Bible Animals, 1 vol. Basaluzzo, Constanza, illus. 2009. (Baby Bible Ser.). (ENG.). 48p. (J). bds. 12.99 (978-1-4347-6541-3(5)) Cook, David C.
Currier Brileya, Elizabeth. Grandma B. 's Bedtime Stories. 2006. 68p. (J). pap. 8.39 (978-1-4116-9504-7(6)) Lulu Pr., Inc.
Curtiss, Phebe A. Christmas Stories & Legends. Curtiss, Phebe A., ed. 2011. 118p. 22.95 (978-1-4638-9660-7(3)) Rodgers, Alan Bks.
Curtiss, Phebe A., ed. Christmas Stories & Legends. 2009. 120p. pap. 10.95 (978-1-60664-397-6(5)) Rodgers, Alan Bks.
Cuxart, Bernardette, illus. Cuentame un Cuento, No. 4. (SPA.). 96p. (J). (gr. k-3). (978-84-480-1602-9(5), TM8095) Timun Mas, Editorial S.A. ESP. Dist: Lectorum Pubns., Inc.
Cynthia, Rylant. Every Living Thing. 2014. (ENG.). 96p. (J). (gr. 5-9). 10.24 (978-1-63245-336-5(3)) Lectorum Pubns., Inc.
Cyr, Joe. Magical Trees & Crayons: Great Stories. 2006. (Illus.). pap. 9.95 (978-0-9778525-6-7(3)) Peppertree Pr., The.
—Two Happy Stories. Owen, Ramon, illus. 2007. 36p. per. 12.95 (978-1-934246-73-3(5)) Peppertree Pr., The.
Czarnota, Lorna MacDonald. Medieval Tales: That Kids Can Read & Tell. 2009. (ENG., Illus.). 96p. (J). (gr. 3-7). pap. 14.95 (978-0-87483-588-5(7)) August Hse. Pubs., Inc.
D C Thomson Staff, ed. Animals & You Annual 2004. 2003. (Illus.). 128p. (J). 9.95 (978-0-85116-840-1(X)) Thomson, D.C. & Co., Ltd. GBR. Dist: APG Sales & Distribution Services.
—Bunty Annual for Girls 2004. 2003. (Illus.). 128p. (J). (gr. -1-4). (978-0-85116-825-8(6)) Thomson, D.C. & Co., Ltd. GBR. Dist: APG Sales & Distribution Services.
Dade, Barbara A. Story Time with Grandm. 2008. 88p. pap. 41.99 (978-1-4363-5325-0(4)) Xlibris Corp.
Dadey, Debbie. A Mermaid Tales Sparkling Collection: Trouble at Trident Academy - Battle of the Best Friends - A Whale of a Tale - Danger in the Deep Blue Sea - The Lost Princess. Avakyan, Tatevik, illus. 2013. (Mermaid Tales Ser.). (ENG.). 592p. (J). (gr. 1-4). pap. 29.99 (978-1-4814-0055-8(X), Aladdin) Simon & Schuster Children's Publishing.
Dahl, Michael. The Doll That Waved Goodbye: And Other Scary Tales. Bonet, Xavier, illus. 2015. (Michael Dahl's Really Scary Stories Ser.). (ENG.). 72p. (gr. 2-3). lib. bdg. 25.32 (978-1-4965-0595-8(6)) Stone Arch Bks.
—Frightmares 2: More Scary Stories for the Fearless Reader. Bonet, Xavier, illus. 2016. (Michael Dahl's Really Scary Stories Ser.). (ENG.). 224p. (gr. 2-3). pap. 8.95 (978-1-4965-4136-9(7)) Stone Arch Bks.
—The Phantom on the Phone & Other Scary Tales. Bonet, Xavier, illus. 2015. (Michael Dahl's Really Scary Stories Ser.). (ENG.). 72p. (gr. 2-3). lib. bdg. 25.32 (978-1-4965-0597-2(2)) Stone Arch Bks.
—Zombie Cupcakes: And Other Scary Tales. Bonet, Xavier, illus. 2016. (Michael Dahl's Really Scary Stories Ser.). (ENG.). 72p. (gr. 2-3). lib. bdg. 25.32 (978-1-4965-3774-4(2)) Stone Arch Bks.
Dahl, Roald. Charlie und die Schokoladenfabrik.Tr. of Charlie & the Chocolate Factory. (GER.). pap. 17.95 (978-3-499-21211-6(0)) Rowohlt Taschenbuch Verlag GmbH DEU. Dist: Distribooks, Inc.
—The Complete Adventures of Charlie & Mr. Willy Wonka. Blake, Quentin, illus. 2010. (ENG.). 336p. (J). (gr. 3-7). 10.99 (978-0-14-241740-9(8), Puffin Books) Penguin Young Readers Group.
—Los Cretinos. Blake, Quentin, illus. 2005. (Infantil Ser.).Tr. of Twist. (SPA.). 106p. (gr. 3-5). per. 9.95 (978-968-19-0559-0(8)) Santillana USA Publishing Co., Inc.
—The Missing Golden Ticket & Other Splendiferous Secrets. Blake, Quentin, illus. 2010. (ENG.). 128p. (J). (gr. 3-7). 7.99 (978-0-14-241742-3(4), Puffin Books) Penguin Young Readers Group.
—Roald Dahl's Whipple-Scrumptious Chocolate Box, 3 vols. Blake, Quentin, illus. 2014. (Dahl Ser.). (ENG.). 480p. (J). (gr. 3). 22.97 (978-0-14-751350-2(2), Puffin Books) Penguin Young Readers Group.
—The Umbrella Man & Other Stories. 2004. (ENG.). 288p. (YA). (gr. 7-18). pap. 8.99 (978-0-14-240087-6(4), Speak) Penguin Young Readers Group.
Daines, Ellie. Lolly Luck. 2012. (ENG.). 186p. (J). (gr. 4-7). pap. 8.99 (978-1-84939-396-6(6)) Andersen Pr. GBR. Dist: Independent Pubs. Group.
Dajani, Suad Farsakh. Grandma's Stories: A Collection of Six Children's Stories. 2013. 40p. 25.99 (978-1-4808-0051-9(1)); pap. 16.99 (978-1-4808-0049-6(X)) Archway Publishing.
Daley, James. Great Horse Stories. 2010. (Dover Children's Classics Ser.). (ENG.). 240p. (J). (gr. 3-5). pap. 7.99 (978-0-486-47669-8(3)) Dover Pubns., Inc.
Daley, Michael J. Beach Socks, 1 vol. Corke, Estelle, illus. 2013. (ENG.). 10p. (J). bds. 6.99 (978-1-59572-637-7(3)) Star Bright Bks., Inc.
d'Allancé, Mireille. What a Tantrum. 2005. (SPA., Illus.). 32p. (J). 15.99 (978-84-8470-115-6(8)) Corimbo, Editorial S.L. ESP. Dist: Iaconi, Mariuccia Bk. Imports.
Dalton, Annie. The Cosmic Collection: Three Heavenly Missions in One Book! 2008. (Mel Beeby Agent Angel Ser.). (ENG.). 496p. (J). (gr. 4-7). pap. 19.95 (978-0-00-723308-3(6)) HarperCollins Pubs. Ltd. GBR. Dist: Independent Pubs. Group.
Damron, Dugan. Further Adventures of Old Shorty: Tales of a Midwest Country Boy, 1 vol. 2010. 112p. pap. 19.95 (978-1-4489-5838-2(5)) America Star Bks.
—Old Shorty: Tales of a Midwestern Farm Boy, 1 vol. 2009. 51p. pap. 16.95 (978-1-60813-651-3(5)) America Star Bks.
Daniels, Susan & Vincent, Seth. Student Bylines Vol. 1: Anthology. 2003. 184p. (YA). pap. 13.95 (978-0-595-27133-7(2), Writer's Showcase Pr.) iUniverse, Inc.
Darby, Joel, et al. Milestones. Grant, Lisa, ed. Day, Linda S., illus. l.t. ed. 2004. 32p. (J). 12.95 (978-0-9759579-0-5(2)) Denver Broncos.
Dasent, G. W. East o' the Sun & West o' the Moon. 2005. pap. 28.95 (978-1-4179-0435-8(6)) Kessinger Publishing, LLC.
Datlow, Ellen & Windling, Terri. Teeth: Vampire Tales. 2011. (ENG.). 480p. (YA). (gr. 8-18). 17.99 (978-0-06-193515-2(8)); pap. 9.99 (978-0-06-193514-5(X)) HarperCollins Pubs.
Dave, Grandpa. Children's Stories Iii. 2012. 104p. (gr. 2-4). pap. 11.79 (978-1-4669-1829-0(2)) Trafford Publishing.
David, B. The Littlest Pirate King. 2010. (ENG., Illus.). 48p. 16.99 (978-1-60699-403-0(4), 699403) Fantagraphics Bks.
Davidson, Susanna. Treasury of Animal Stories. 2008. (Stories for Young Children Ser.). 96p. (J). 16.99 (978-0-7945-2095-3(2), Usborne) EDC Publishing.
Davies, Helen Emanuel. Siff a Saff: A Straeon Eraill. Maclean, Andrew, illus. 2005. (WEL.). 64p. pap. (978-0-86381-364-1(X)) Gwasg Carreg Gwalch.
Davies, Robert, adapted by. Lit a Shuck for Texas: Adapted Louis l'Amour Short Stories Series. 2003. (Adapted Louis L'Amour Short Stories Ser.). (Illus.). 56p. (YA). (978-1-57035-983-5(0), 233LIT) Cambium Education, Inc.
—Merrano of the Dry Country: Adapted Louis l'Amour Short Story Series. 2003. (Adapted Louis L'Amour Short Stories Ser.). (Illus.). 60p. (J). (978-1-57035-985-9(7), 233MERRANO) Cambium Education, Inc.
Davis, Anthony C. I Ain't Lying. 2008. 112p. pap. 19.95 (978-1-60474-087-5(6)) America Star Bks.
Davis, Beneta. My Covers. 2008. 24p. pap. 24.95 (978-1-60441-584-1(3)) America Star Bks.
Davis, Jim & Michiels, Cedric. Jon's Night Out. Ellipsanime Staff & Dargaud Media, illus. 2013. (Garfield Show Ser.). (ENG.). 64p. (J). (gr. 1-5). 11.99 (978-1-59707-444-5(6), 9781597074445); pap. 7.99 (978-1-59707-443-8(8), 9781597074438) Papercutz.
Davis, Lowrey. Papa's Storybook. 2008. 116p. 19.99 (978-1-60791-100-5(0)); pap. 11.99 (978-1-60791-099-2(3)) Salem Author Services.
Davis, Richard. The Red Cross Girl & Other Stories. 2004. reprint ed. pap. 1.99 (978-1-4192-7996-6(3)) Kessinger Publishing, LLC.
Day, Ed D. Why Dogs Bark: & Other Tall Tales. Scott, Sarah C., illus. 2006. 50p. (J). per. 12.95 (978-1-933002-20-0(4)) PublishingWorks.
A Day for JJ & Me Set B, 6 vols. 32p. (gr. 1-3). 31.50 (978-0-7802-8050-2(4)) Wright Group/McGraw-Hill.
de Beer, Hans, pseud. The Little Polar Bear Lars & the Husky Pup. 2012. (Little Polar Bear Ser.). (ENG., Illus.). 32p. (J). (gr. -1-2). pap. 7.95 (978-0-7358-4078-2(4)) North-South Bks., Inc.
De Blumenthal, Verra X. K. Folk Tales from the Russian. 2008. 88p. pap. 8.95 (978-1-60664-152-1(2)) Aegypan.
de Fontaine, Jean. Fables. (FRE.). 482p. pap. 9.95 (978-2-266-12775-2(6)) Presses Pocket FRA. Dist: Distribooks, Inc.
De La Ramee, Louise. Bimbi. 2007. 84p. per. (978-1-4068-3736-0(9)) Echo Library.
De La Ramee, Louise & Ouida. Bimbi. 2007. 152p. per. 13.95 (978-1-60312-344-0(X)); 24.95 (978-1-60312-682-3(1)) Aegypan.
de Las Casas, Dianne. The Gigantic Sweet Potato, 1 vol. Gentry, Marita, illus. 2010. (ENG.). 32p. (J). (gr. k-3). 16.99 (978-1-58980-755-6(3)) Pelican Publishing Co., Inc.
de Lint, Charles. Waifs & Strays. 2004. (ENG.). 416p. (YA). (gr. 7-18). 8.99 (978-0-14-240158-3(7), Firebird) Penguin Young Readers Group.
de Pavlova, Chrisi É. Animal Stories from Green Lane Estate: Series Three. 2012. (Illus.). 254p. pap. 22.00 (978-1-78035-292-3(1), Fastprint Publishing) Upfront Publishing Ltd. GBR. Dist: Printondemand-worldwide.com.
Deadman, Ron & Gifford, Griselda. The Goat Monster & Other Stories, 4 vols. 2014. (ENG.). 128p. pap. 46.00 (978-0-17-402427-9(4)) Oxford Univ. Pr., Inc.
Dean - Eb - Tales of Betsy-May. 2007. (978-0-603-56287-7(6)) Egmont Bks., Ltd.
DeAnda, Diane. The Monster in the Mattress & Other Stories: El Monstruo en el Colchón y Otros Cuentos. 2011. (SPA & ENG., Illus.). 90p. (J). (gr. 3-7). pap. 9.95 (978-1-55885-693-6(5), Piñata Books) Arte Publico Pr.
Deborah Strandberg, Rebecca Reynolds and. Trammler Triplet Tales Advente #4 MYSTERIOUS ABBY. 2007. 113p. pap. 8.90 (978-1-4357-0651-4(X)) Lulu Pr., Inc.
Deborah Wanda. Wanda's Wittle Wunders. 2009. 32p. pap. 14.49 (978-1-4389-4862-1(X)) AuthorHouse.
Deegan, J. E. When I Was a Little Guy. 2008. 76p. pap. 19.95 (978-1-60703-120-8(5)) America Star Bks.
Defreitas, Henrietta. Henratty Mortimer: The Meerville Myth. 2012. (Illus.). 84p. pap. 32.03 (978-1-4772-3867-7(0)) AuthorHouse.
Dehm, Debbie. Animal Stories of the Desert. 2009. (Illus.). 41p. (J). pap. 20.95 (978-1-4327-3461-9(X)) Outskirts Pr., Inc.
Deighton, Jo, adapted by. Ali Baba & the Forty Thieves: Traditional Stories:Cinderella: The Elves & the Shoemaker. (Scheherezade Presents Ser.: No. 11). (Illus.). 48p. (J). pap. (978-1-85964-101-9(6), Ithaca Pr.) Garnet Publishing, Ltd.
—Bacbouc the Lazy Tailor: Traditional Stories:Beauty & the Beast: The Red Shoes. (Scheherezade Presents Ser.: No. 12). (Illus.). 48p. (J). pap. (978-1-85964-102-6(4), Ithaca Pr.) Garnet Publishing, Ltd.
—The Fisherman & the Wicked Genie: Traditional Stories:The Shepherdess & the Chimney Sweep: Seven with One Blow. (Scheherezade Presents Ser.: No. 14). (Illus.). 48p. (J). pap. (978-1-85964-104-0(0), Ithaca Pr.) Garnet Publishing, Ltd.
Del Amo, Montserrat. El Nudo. (SPA.). 94p. (YA). (gr. 5-8). (978-84-261-1691-8(4), JV2941) Juventud, Editorial ESP. Dist: Lectorum Pubns., Inc.
Del Negro, Janice M. Passion & Poison: Tales of Shape-Shifters, Ghosts, & Spirited Women, 0 vols. Natale, Vince, illus. 2013. (ENG.). 64p. (J). (gr. 5-7). pap. 9.99 (978-1-4778-1685-1(2), 9781477816851, Amazon Children's Publishing) Amazon Publishing.
del Rio, Ana Maria. La Historia de Manu (Manu's Story) Cardemil, Carmen, illus. 2003. (Coleccion Derechos Del Nino Ser.). (SPA.). 32p. (J). (gr. 3-5). pap. 7.95 (978-84-204-5845-8(7)) Santillana USA Publishing Co., Inc.
Delacre, Lulu. Salsa Stories. Delacre, Lulu, illus. 2012. (ENG., Illus.). 112p. (J). (gr. 2-5). pap. 6.99 (978-0-545-43098-2(4), Scholastic Pr.) Scholastic, Inc.
Delacre, Lulu. Us, in Progress: Short Stories about Young Latinos. Delacre, Lulu, illus. 2017. (Illus.). 256p. (J). (gr. 3-7). 16.99 **(978-0-06-239214-5(X))** HarperCollins Pubs.
DeLand, M. Maitland. The Great Katie Kate Offers Answers about Asthma. 2011. (Illus.). 32p. 14.95 (978-1-60832-074-5(X)) Greenleaf Book Group.
DeLand, M. Maitland. Baby Santa & the Lost Letters. 2011. (Illus.). 36p. (J). 14.95 (978-1-60832-194-0(0)) Greenleaf Book Group.
Delaney, Joseph. A Coven of Witches. Arrasmith, Patrick, illus. (Last Apprentice Short Fiction Ser.: 2). 240p. (YA). (gr. 8). 2011. (ENG.). pap. 9.99 (978-0-06-196040-6(3)) 2010. lib. bdg. 17.89 (978-0-06-196039-0(X)) 2010. (ENG.). 16.99 (978-0-06-196038-3(1)) HarperCollins Pubs. (Greenwillow Bks.).
Demers, Tristan. Comic Collection (Shopkins) 2017. (Shopkins Ser.). (ENG.). 80p. (J). (gr. -1-3). pap. 7.99 **(978-1-338-14857-2(5))** Scholastic, Inc.
Demi. The Pandas & Their Chopsticks: And Other Animal Stories. 2014. (ENG., Illus.). 28p. (J). (gr. k-2). 16.95 (978-1-937786-16-8(1), Wisdom Tales) World Wisdom, Inc.
Denkhaus, Henry. Anna & the Magical Horse - Henry the Hobo - the Pond. 2013. 50p. pap. 8.99 (978-1-4624-0734-7(X), Inspiring Voices) Author Solutions, Inc.
Deogratias Simba. The Mystery Door. 2005. (Illus.). 22p. pap. (978-9987-417-21-6(3)) Mkuki na Nyoka Pubs. TZA. Dist: Michigan State Univ. Pr.
dePaola, Tomie. La Hermanita de Tommy. (Buenas Noches Ser.).Tr. of Baby Sister. (SPA.). (J). (gr. 1-3). pap. 7.95 (978-958-04-4290-5(8)) Norma S.A. COL. Dist: Distribuidora Norma, Inc., Lectorum Pubns., Inc.
DeSantis, Debi. A Bunch of Giggles & Hugs. l.t. ed. 2005. (Illus.). 26p. (J). 12.95 (978-0-9770043-0-0(9)) New Global Publishing.
Deseret Book Company Staff, contrib. by. A Story to Tell: The Classic Book of Virtues for Children. 2nd ed. 2004. 508p. (J). 16.95 (978-1-59038-359-9(1)) Deseret Bk. Co.
Deskins, Charlotte H. Tales from Poplar Hollow. Allen, Dana K., illus. 2004. 104p. pap. (978-0-9753671-1-7(0)) Shamus B. Publishing.
Despeyroux, Denise & Poe, Edgar Allen. Dark Graphic Tales by Edgar Allan Poe. Serratosa, Miquel, illus. 2012. (Dark Graphic Novels Ser.). 96p. (J). (gr. 5-9). 31.94 (978-0-7660-4086-1(0)) Enslow Pubs., Inc.
Diamond Head High Series Pack, Nos. 1-3. 12.95 (978-1-57306-108-7(5)) Bess Pr., Inc.
Diaz, Gloria Cecilia. La Botella Azul. (SPA.). (J). 8.95 (978-958-04-6489-1(8)) Norma S.A. COL. Dist: Distribuidora Norma, Inc.
Diaz Granados, Jose Luiz. Cuentos y Leyendas de Colombia. (Torre de Papel Ser.). (SPA.). (J). (gr. 4-18). 8.95 (978-958-04-5127-3(3)) Norma S.A. COL. Dist: Distribuidora Norma, Inc.
DiCamillo, Kate. The Essential Kate Dicamillo Collection. 2014. (ENG.). (J). (gr. 3-7). pap. 34.95 (978-0-7636-7580-6(6)) Candlewick Pr.
—Francine Poulet Meets the Ghost Raccoon: Tales from Deckawoo Drive, Volume Two. Van Dusen, Chris, illus. 2016. (Tales from Deckawoo Drive Ser.). (ENG.). 112p. (J). (gr. 1-4). pap. 5.99 (978-0-7636-9088-5(0)) Candlewick Pr.
—Where Are You Going, Baby Lincoln? Tales from Deckawoo Drive, Volume Three. Van Dusen, Chris, illus. 2016. (Tales from Deckawoo Drive Ser.: 3). (ENG.). 112p. (J). (gr. 1-4). 14.99 (978-0-7636-7311-6(0)) Candlewick Pr.
Dickens, Charles. Illustrated Stories from Dickens. Ablett, Barry, illus. 2010. (Illustrated Stories Ser.). 352p. (YA). (gr. 3-18). 19.99 (978-0-7945-2628-3(4), Usborne) EDC Publishing.
—Oliver Twist & Other Classic Tales. Thorne, Jenny, illus. 2015. (ENG.). 80p. (J). (gr. -1-12). pap. 9.99 (978-1-86147-408-7(3), Armadillo) Anness Publishing GBR. Dist: National Bk. Network.
Dickens, Charles, et al. Christmas Books & Stories. 2004. (YA). cd-rom, audio compact disk 25.00 (978-0-917466-15-1(2)) Samizdat Express.
Dickins, Rosie, retold by. Illustrated Stories from Shakespeare. 2014. (ENG., Illus.). 414p. (J). 19.99 (978-0-7945-2997-0(6), Usborne) EDC Publishing.
Dickins, Rosie & Sims, Lesley. Aesop's Stories for Little Children. 2015. (Stories for Little Children Gift Bks.). (ENG.). 224p. (J). 19.99 (978-0-7945-2307-7(2), Usborne) EDC Publishing.
Dickinson, Asa Don. Good Cheer Stories Every Child Should Know. 2007. 242p. pap. 20.99 (978-1-4346-3438-2(8)); (ENG.). 268p. pap. 23.99 (978-1-4346-3439-9(6)) Creative Media Partners, LLC.
Dickinson, Asa Don & Dickinson, Helen Winslow, eds. Patriotic Stories Every Child Should Know. 2005. reprint ed. pap. 30.95 (978-1-4179-0694-9(4)) Kessinger Publishing, LLC.
Dickinson, Asa Don & Skinner, Ada M. The Children's Book of Christmas Stories. 2004. reprint ed. pap. 24.95 (978-1-4191-5657-1(8)); pap. 1.99 (978-1-4192-5657-8(2)) Kessinger Publishing, LLC.
Dickinson, Peter. Earth & Air: Tales of Elemental Creatures. 2012. (ENG.). 256p. (J). (gr. 4). pap. 14.95 (978-1-61873-038-1(X), Big Mouth Hse.) Small Beer Pr.
—The Lion Tamer's Daughter & Other Stories. 2015. (ENG.). 230p. (J). (gr. 7-10). pap. 12.99 (978-1-5040-1499-1(5)) Open Road Integrated Media, Inc.
Diffenderfer, David W. The Adventures of Boo & Fred. 2010. 58p. pap. 9.99 (978-1-60911-966-9(5), Eloquent Bks.) Strategic Book Publishing & Rights Agency (SBPRA).
Dillingham Pierson, Clara. Among the Farmyard People. 2008. 112p. pap. 8.15 (978-1-60459-505-5(1)) Wilder Pubns., Corp.
—Among the Forest People. 2008. 92p. pap. 8.15 (978-1-60459-501-7(9)) Wilder Pubns., Corp.
—Among the Meadow People. 2008. 84p. pap. 8.15 (978-1-60459-504-8(3)) Wilder Pubns., Corp.
—Among the Night People. 2008. 96p. pap. 8.15 (978-1-60459-503-1(5)) Wilder Pubns., Corp.
—Among the Pond People. 2008. 96p. pap. 8.15 (978-1-60459-502-4(7)) Wilder Pubns., Corp.
—Clara Dillingham Pierson's Complete among the People Series. 2008. 352p. pap. 19.99 (978-1-60459-528-4(0)) Wilder Pubns., Corp.
Disney Book Club Staff. Pirates of the Caribbean - On Stranger Tides: Six Sea Chanties - An Original Graphic Novel Anthology. 2011. (ENG.). 128p. (YA). (gr. 8-18). pap. 10.99 (978-1-4231-3320-9(X)) Disney Pr.
Disney Book Group. Disney Princess Storybook Collection: Tales to Finish. Disney Storybook Art Team, illus. 2017. (Storybook Collection: Tales to Finish Ser.). (ENG.). 128p. (J). (gr. 1-3). 10.99 (978-1-4847-8957-5(1)) Disney Pr.
—Disney*Pixar Board Book & CD Treasury Box. Disney Storybook Art Team, illus. 2017. (Board Book & CD Treasury Box Ser.). (ENG.). 18p. (J). (gr. -1-k). 12.99 **(978-1-368-00323-0(0))** Disney Pr.
—Disney*Pixar Storybook Collection: Tales to Finish. Disney Storybook Art Team, illus. 2017. (Disney*Pixar Storybook Collection: Tales to Finish Ser.). (ENG.). 128p. (J). (gr. 1-3). 10.99 (978-1-4847-9942-0(9)) Disney Pr.
—Frozen Storybook Collection. 2016. (Storybook Collection). (ENG.). 304p. (J). (gr. -1-k). 16.99 (978-1-4847-5873-1(0)) Disney Pr.
—Star Wars: The Force Awakens. 2016. (ENG.). 128p. (J). (gr. 1-3). 16.99 (978-1-4847-0558-2(0)) Disney Pr.
—Whisker Haven Tales Treasure's Adventures (Storybook Plus Collectible Toy) Five Tiny Tales. Disney Storybook Art Team, illus. 2016. (ENG.). 128p. (J). (gr. 1-3). 14.99 (978-1-4847-4648-6(1)) Disney Pr.
Disney Book Group Staff. Disney Bedtime Favorites. Disney Storybook Artists Staff & Disney Book Group Staff, illus. 2012. (Storybook Collection). (ENG.). 304p. (J). (gr. -1 — 1). 15.99 (978-1-4231-6034-2(7)) Disney Pr.
—Disney Storybook Collection. Disney Storybook Art Team, illus. 2015. (Storybook Collection). (ENG.). 304p. (J). (gr. -1-k). 16.99 (978-1-4847-1348-8(6)) Disney Pr.
—Disney*Pixar Storybook Collection. Disney Storybook Art Team, illus. 2011. (Storybook Collection). (ENG.). 312p. (J). (gr. -1 — 1). 15.99 (978-1-4231-2423-8(5)) Disney Pr.
—Fly-and-Drive Read-Along Storybook. Disney Storybook Artists Staff & Disney Storybook Art Team, illus. 2014. (Read-Along Storybook & CD Ser.). (ENG.). 136p. (J). (gr. 1-3). 12.99 (978-1-4847-0656-5(0)) Disney Pr.
—Meeska Mooska-Tales. Disney Storybook Art Team, illus. 2015. (ENG.). 40p. (J). (gr. -1-k). 10.99 (978-1-4847-2189-6(6)) Disney Pr.
—Princess Adventure Stories. Disney Storybook Artists Staff, illus. 2013. (Storybook Collection). (ENG.). 304p. (J). (gr. -1 — 1). 15.99 (978-1-4231-4691-9(3)) Disney Pr.

—5-Minute Disney*Pixar Stories. 2012. (5-Minute Stories Ser.). (ENG.). 192p. (J). (gr. -1-k). 12.99 *(978-1-4231-6520-0(9))* Disney Pr.

—5-Minute Racing Stories. Disney Storybook Art Team Staff, illus. 2017. (5-Minute Stories Ser.). (ENG.). 192p. (J). (gr. 1-3). 12.99 *(978-1-368-00075-8(4))* Disney Pr.

—5-Minute Spooky Stories. Disney Storybook Artists Staff & Disney Storybook Art Team, illus. 2014. (5-Minute Stories Ser.). (ENG.). 192p. (J). (gr. -1-k). 12.99 *(978-1-4231-8915-2(9))* Disney Pr.

Disney Book Group Staff, et al. Disney Christmas Storybook Collection. Disney Storybook Artists Staff, illus. 2014. (Storybook Collection). (ENG.). 304p. (J). (gr. -1-k). 16.99 *(978-1-4231-8450-8(5))* Disney Pr.

Disney Doc McStuffins. Disney Doc. Disney Doc Mcstuffins Movie Theater Storybook & Movie Projector. 2015. (Movie Theater Ser.: 1). (ENG.). 32p. (J). (gr. -1-1). 19.99 *(978-0-7944-3183-9(6)*, Reader's Digest Children's Bks.) Studio Fun International.

Disney Press Staff & Disney Book Group Staff. 5-Minute Princess Stories. Disney Storybook Artists Staff, illus. 2011. (5-Minute Stories Ser.). (ENG.). 192p. (J). (gr. -1 — 1). 12.99 *(978-1-4231-4657-5(3))* Disney Pr.

Disney Princess Staff, adapted by. Princess Enchanted Palace: Storybook & Play Castle. 2010. (Playbox Ser.). (ENG., Illus.). 32p. (J). (gr. -1-2). bds. 19.99 *(978-0-7944-2035-2(4))* Reader's Digest Assn., Inc., The.

Disney Princess Super Activity Fun Storybook Collection. 2005. (J). *(978-1-59487-168-9(X))* Artist Studios, Ltd.

Disney Staff. Stories to Tell a Three Year Old. 2005. (J). pap. *(978-0-7868-4333-6(0))* Disney Pr.

Disney Storybook Collection. 2005. (J). *(978-1-59487-135-1(3))* Artist Studios, Ltd.

Doherty, Gillian. Stories of Wizards. Edwards, Linda, illus. 2008. (Stories for Young Children Ser.). 95p. (J). (gr. 1). 16.99 *(978-0-7945-1915-5(6)*, Usborne) EDC Publishing.

Donahue, Bill. Grandma Wentworth's Children's Storybooks, Volume One. 2007. 56p. per. 16.95 *(978-1-4241-3269-0(X))* PublishAmerica, Inc.

Donaldson, Julia. Freddie & the Fairy. 7. George, Karen, illus. 4th ed. 2012. (ENG.). 32p. (J). (gr. -1-k). 9.99 *(978-0-330-51118-6(1))* Pan Macmillan GBR. Dist: Independent Pubs. Group.

—Princess Mirror-Belle. Monks, Lydia, illus. 2015. (Princess Mirror-Belle Ser.: 1). (ENG.). 128p. (J). (gr. 2-4). pap. 9.99 *(978-1-4472-8562-5(X))* Pan Macmillan GBR. Dist: Independent Pubs. Group.

—Princess Mirror-Belle & the Magic Shoes. 1. Monks, Lydia, illus. 2013. (Princess Mirror-Belle Ser.). (ENG.). 144p. (J). (gr. k-2). pap. 8.99 *(978-1-4472-2404-4(3))* Pan Macmillan GBR. Dist: Independent Pubs. Group.

—Princess Mirror-Belle & the Party Hoppers. Monks, Lydia, illus. 2015. (Princess Mirror-Belle Ser.). (ENG.). 128p. (J). (gr. 2-4). pap. 8.99 *(978-1-4472-8489-5(5))* Pan Macmillan GBR. Dist: Independent Pubs. Group.

Doo, DooLee. 4D Stories. 2010. 130p. pap. 9.98 *(978-0-557-17618-2(2))* Lulu Pr., Inc.

Doodler, Todd H. Peas on Earth. 2012. (ENG., Illus.). 20p. (J). (gr. k — 1). bds. 6.99 *(978-0-307-93088-0(2)*, Robin Corey Bks.) Random Hse. Children's Bks.

Dostoyevsky, Fyodor. Fiodor Mijailovich Dostoievsky. Acosta, Patricia, illus. 2003. (Cajon de Cuentos Ser.). (SPA.). 223p. (J). (gr. 4-7). *(978-958-30-1027-9(8))* Panamericana Editorial.

Douglas, Kathleen. Johnny, the Unaware Angel. 2007. 108p. per. 19.95 *(978-1-4241-9939-6(5))* PublishAmerica, Inc.

Douglas, Rachel. "You're a Meany!" Drewes, Dan, illus. 2011. 13p. pap. 10.19 *(978-1-4567-8643-4(1))* AuthorHouse.

Dove, Trudy. The Bunnies. 2016. (ENG.). 119p. (J). pap. 13.95 *(978-1-78554-301-2(6)*, c0670ba6-0dfd-4dc5-aa05-8aea2923e1a3) Austin, Stan AUS. Dist: Bookmasters Distribution.

Dovey, Belinda. Alphabet Adventures. 2012. 136p. pap. 71.99 *(978-1-4653-7250-5(4))* Xlibris Corp.

Dowley, T. El Viaje Maravilloso. 2003.Tr. of Amazing Escape. (SPA.). bds. 9.99 *(978-0-7899-1117-9(5))* Editorial Unilit.

Downie, David. Horrible Stories My Dad Told Me. Nanevych, Julia, tr. Seroya, Tea, illus. 2012. 44p. pap. *(978-1-922159-97-7(2))* Blue Peg Publishing.

Doyle, Arthur Conan. Adv of the Devils Foot. 2010. (Illus.). 254p. (J). pap. *(978-4-591-11698-2(0))* Fukuinkan Shoten.

—Sherlock Holmes. 2003. (Retold Ser.). (Illus.). 282p. (J). (gr. 7-18). 15.99 *(978-0-7569-1196-6(6))* Perfection Learning Corp.

Doyle, Christopher. Amazing Tales & Strange Stories of the Bible. 2009. 64p. (J). (gr. -1). 14.99 *(978-0-7586-1785-9(2))* Concordia Publishing Hse.

Doyle, William. Tell Me a Story Please: Read-Aloud Short Stories for Children & the Young at Heart. 2006. 116p. pap. 13.50 *(978-1-84426-387-5(8))* Upfront Publishing Ltd. GBR. Dist: Printondemand-worldwide.com.

Dozier, Kim. The Ear-Less Kingdom. Dozier, Ashlyn McCauley, illus. l.t. ed. 2003. (ENG.). 24p. (J). 7.50 *(978-0-9745839-1-4(X)*, Fun to Read Bks. with Royally Good Morals) MKADesigns.

—The Forgetful Princess. Dozier, Ashlyn McCauley, illus. 2nd l.t. ed. 2003. (ENG.). 24p. (J). 10.00 *(978-0-9745839-0-7(1)*, Fun to Read Bks. with Royally Good Morals) MKADesigns.

Draeger, Manuela. In the Time of the Blue Ball. Evenson, Brian, tr. 2011. 134p. pap. 16.00 *(978-0-9844693-3-8(8))* Dorothy, a publishing project.

Dragonblood, A. The Whispering V: Children of the Others Collection. 2010. 84p. pap. 10.49 *(978-1-4520-3250-4(5))* AuthorHouse.

Dreissigacker Martin, Susan. Princess Stephanie Stories: The Road Trip & the New School. 2009. 32p. pap. 18.79 *(978-1-4389-1836-5(4))* AuthorHouse.

Dreser, Elena. El Secreto del Sauce. Diez, Dalia Alvarado, illus. 2003. (SPA.). 44p. (J). (gr. 3-5). pap. 6.95 *(978-968-19-0617-7(9))* Santillana USA Publishing Co., Inc.

Dube, Jasmine. Tu N'es Plus Seul. Nazaire. Daigle, Sylvie, illus. 2003. (Premier Roman Ser.). (FRE.). 64p. (J). (gr. 2-5). pap. *(978-2-89021-286-2(6))* Diffusion du livre Mirabel (DLM).

Dubois, Claude K. - Norac. QUIERO UN BESO. 2003. (SPA., Illus.). 15p. (J). (gr. -1-k). bds. 9.99 *(978-84-8470-104-0(2))* Corimbo, Editorial S.L. ESP. Dist: Lectorum Pubns., Inc.

—SOY UN CIELO. 2003. (SPA., Illus.). 15p. (J). (gr. -1-k). bds. 9.99 *(978-84-8470-105-7(0))* Corimbo, Editorial S.L. ESP. Dist: Lectorum Pubns., Inc.

Dubois, Marie. The Village Children, an Introduction to the Art of Painting Children & Their Stories. 2009. (FRE & ENG., Illus.). 120p. pap. 36.99 *(978-1-4343-7847-7(0))* AuthorHouse.

Dubrovin, Barbara. Fantasy Fair: Bright Stories of Imagination. Dubrovin, Barbara, illus. 2007. (Illus.). 128p. (J). pap. 17.50 *(978-0-9638339-6-9(0))* Storycraft Publishing.

Dubya, Jay. The Eighteen Story Gingerbread House. 2003. 172p. (J). 23.95 *(978-1-58909-176-4(0))*; pap. 15.95 *(978-1-58909-177-1(9))* Bookstand Publishing.

Duchene-Marshall, Michele A. Charley Finds A Family. Marshall, Alan David, ed. Ousley, Clayton Gerard, photos by. l.t. ed. 2004. Orig. Title: Charley finds a Home. (Illus.). 20p. (J). spiral bd. 10.00 *(978-0-9761675-2-5(2))* Storybook Acres.

Dudley, Sean. Who's Afraid of the Pumpkin Man??? 2009. 47p. pap. 10.01 *(978-0-557-12616-3(9))* Lulu Pr., Inc.

Duerksen, Carol, et al. Short Tales. 2012. (Illus.). 95p. (J). pap. *(978-0-9742716-4-4(0))* WillowSpring Downs.

Duey, K. & Bale, K. A. Salvados! Titanic. 2003. (Survival Ser.).Tr. of Survival! Titanic. (SPA.). (J). pap. 9.95 *(978-0-9715256-4-1(1))* Planeta Publishing Corp.

Dukes, Alicia. Ms. Mabel's Fables. 2010. 94p. pap. 42.20 *(978-0-557-31374-7(0))* Lulu Pr., Inc.

Dultz, Dorothy. Stories for Dreamers. Margolis, Al, illus. 2013. 68p. (J). pap. 9.95 *(978-1-61863-425-2(9))* Bookstand Publishing.

Duncan, Sharyn. The Mouse House & other Stories: You Are the Artist. 2004. 40p. (J). 9.95 *(978-1-933002-04-0(2))* PublishingWorks.

Dunsany, Taylor. The Little Witch Who Lost Her Broom & Other Stories. 2008. 48p. pap. 8.95 *(978-0-595-52506-5(7))* iUniverse, Inc.

Durán, Oscar Manuel. Mama Cuentame un Cuento. Durán, Ivy Adriana, ed. 2013. 146p. pap. 30.00 *(978-0-9886109-1-0(4))* duran, oscar.

Durand, Hallie. Just Desserts. Davenier, Christine, illus. 2010. (ENG.). 208p. (J). (gr. 2-5). 15.99 *(978-1-4169-6387-5(1)*, Atheneum Bks. for Young Readers) Simon & Schuster Children's Publishing.

Dyer-Groves, Beverly E. Spooky Nights on the Island. 2011. 64p. (gr. -1). pap. 11.99 *(978-1-4567-2040-7(6))* AuthorHouse.

Eastman, Peter, et al. The Big Purple Book of Beginner Books. 2012. (Beginner Books(R) Ser.). (ENG., Illus.). 288p. (J). (gr. k-3). 16.99 *(978-0-307-97587-4(8)*, Random Hse. Bks. for Young Readers) Random Hse. Children's Bks.

EDCON Publishing Group Staff. Jack & the Beanstalk - The Stubborn Witch - Rapunzel - Betsy - The Magic Bus. l.t. ed. 2008. (Classic Children's Tales Ser.). 32p. (gr. k-4). pap. 8.95 *(978-1-55576-551-4(3))* EDCON Publishing Group.

—Little Toot - The Story of White Satin - Five Peas in a Pod - Rumpelstiltskin - The Little Magic Pot. l.t. ed. 2008. (Classic Children's Tales Ser.). 32p. (gr. k-4). pap. 8.95 *(978-1-55576-552-1(1))* EDCON Publishing Group.

—Surprise Pies - Snow White & Rose Red - The Emperor's New Clothes - The Three Bears - The Mixed up Family - A Valentine Story. l.t. ed. 2008. (Classic Children's Tales Ser.). 32p. (gr. k-4). pap. 8.95 *(978-1-55576-554-5(8))* EDCON Publishing Group.

Edens, Cooper, compiled by. The Big Book of Little. 2006. (Classic Illustrated Ser.: CLAS). (ENG., Illus.). 124p. (J). (gr. k-17). 19.95 *(978-0-8118-5085-8(4))* Chronicle Bks. LLC.

Edgar Allan Poe Collection of Stories Student Packet. 2004. (YA). 12.99 *(978-1-58130-510-4(9))* Novel Units, Inc.

Edgeworth, Maria. Moral Tales. by Maria Edgeworth Embellished with Original Designs, by Darley. 2006. 532p. per. 29.99 *(978-1-4255-5877-2(1))* Michigan Publishing.

—Parents Assistance or Stories for Child. 2006. 492p. (gr. 4-7). per. *(978-1-4067-9305-5(1)*, Hesperides Pr.) Read Bks.

—The Parent's Assistant; or, Stories for Children. 2007. 468p. (gr. 4-7). per. *(978-1-4065-1649-4(X))* Dodo Pr.

—Rosamond: With Other Tales. by Maria Edgeworth. 2006. 388p. per. 26.99 *(978-1-4255-4076-0(7))* Michigan Publishing.

Edgson, Alison, illus. The Magician's Apprentice. 2011. (Flip-Up Fairy Tales Ser.). (ENG.). 24p. (J). (gr. 2-2). *(978-1-84643-370-2(3))* Child's Play International Ltd.

Edward Eggleston. Queer Stories for Boys & Girls. 2007. 168p. per. 11.95 *(978-1-4218-3949-3(0)*, 1st World Library - Literary Society) 1st World Publishing, Inc.

Edwards, Garth & Statyuk, Max. Heroes of Mercy Hall. 2012. (Thorn Gate Trilogy Ser.). (ENG., Illus.). 112p. (gr. 4-6). pap. *(978-0-9567122-6-4(6))* Inside Pocket Publishing, Ltd.

Edwards, Jean E. Adventure Tales: For Kids Who Want to Become Better Readers. 2012. 102p. pap. 15.99 *(978-1-4771-4117-5(0))* Xlibris Corp.

Effie, Sandy. New Comings of What's Next. 2011. 32p. pap. 16.95 *(978-1-4626-0708-2(X))* America Star Bks.

Egan, Kate & Lane, Mike. The Incredible Twisting Arm, Bk. 2. Wight, Eric, illus. 2014. (Magic Shop Ser.: 2). (ENG.). 160p. (J). (gr. 2-4). pap. 5.99 *(978-1-250-04044-2(2)*, 9781250040442) Feiwel & Friends.

—The Vanishing Coin. Wight, Eric, illus. 2014. (Magic Shop Ser.: 1). (ENG.). 160p. (J). (gr. 2-4). pap. 5.99 *(978-1-250-04043-5(4)*, 9781250040435) Feiwel & Friends.

Egerton, George. Keynotes (Classic Reprint) 2015. (ENG., Illus.). 216p. (J). pap. 13.57 *(978-1-330-45466-4(9))* Forgotten Bks.

Eggleston, Margaret. Fireside Stories for Girls in Their Teen. 2005. pap. 20.95 *(978-1-885529-65-7(1))* Stevens Publishing.

Eggleton, Grace. Children's Stories My Mother Wrote. 2012. 96p. pap. 46.72 *(978-1-4797-3807-6(7))* Xlibris Corp.

Eghdam, Tara. My Little Mici. 2009. (Illus.). 24p. pap. 11.49 *(978-1-4389-8189-5(9))* AuthorHouse.

Ehrlich, Amy, ed. When I Was Your Age Vols. I & II: Original Stories about Growing Up. 2012. (ENG., Illus.). 352p. (J). (gr. 4-7). pap. 14.99 *(978-0-7636-5892-2(8))* Candlewick Pr.

El Wilson, Barbara. Sugarfoot: in the South with Brer' Rabbit: How Handclapping Got Started in the Church Sugarfootstrade; Tattle-Tales Series. Curry, Garrett A., illus. 2010. 24p. 12.99 *(978-1-4520-3145-3(2))* AuthorHouse.

Eley, Kitt. Cindy Lou. 2013. 24p. pap. 24.95 *(978-1-4626-9367-2(9))* America Star Bks.

Eliopoulos, Chris. Okie Dokie Donuts: Open for Business! Open for Business! 2011. (ENG., Illus.). 48p. (J). (gr. 2-5). 9.95 *(978-1-60309-068-1(1)*, 9781603090681) Top Shelf Productions.

Eliotte, Lisa J. The Adventures of Derby Doodle. 2009. 640p. pap. 25.99 *(978-1-4389-3058-9(5))* AuthorHouse.

Elkins, Christy. Sir Stinks-A-Lot. 2010. (ENG.). 43p. pap. 12.00 *(978-0-557-34847-3(1))* Lulu Pr., Inc.

Elliott, Craig. Racer Buddies: Rematch at Richmond. 2005. (Racer Buddies Ser.). (Illus.). 40p. (J). (gr. -1-5). 12.95 *(978-0-9746445-1-6(X)*, 10000) Powerband, LLC.

Elliott, Rebecca. Just Because. Elliott, Rebecca, illus. 2011. (ENG., Illus.). 32p. (J). (gr. -1-2). 14.99 *(978-0-7459-6267-2(X))* Lion Hudson PLC GBR. Dist: Independent Pubs. Group.

Ellis, Sue. Gorgeous Gwendolen Goose & Other Stories. 2015. (ENG.). 49p. (J). (gr. 3-4). mass mkt. 13.95 *(978-1-78455-571-9(1)*, 32f7fc86-9367-414f-b0a7-4ad5f341c9cb) Austin, Stan AUS. Dist: Bookmasters Distribution.

Ellison, Harlan. Troublemakers. 2009. 272p. pap. 13.95 *(978-0-7592-9198-0(5))* Open Road Integrated Media, Inc.

Elschner, Géraldine & Nille, Peggy. The Cat & the Bird: A Children's Book Inspired by Paul Klee. 2012. (ENG., Illus.). 32p. (J). (gr. -1-3). 14.95 *(978-3-7913-7099-6(5))* Prestel Verlag GmbH & Co KG. DEU. Dist: Penguin Random Hse. LLC.

Elwick, Elissa. The Princess & the Sleep Stealer. Elwick, Elissa, illus. 2012. (ENG., Illus.). 32p. (J). (gr. -1-k). pap. 9.99 *(978-0-230-75068-5(0))* Macmillan Pubs., Ltd. GBR. Dist: Independent Pubs. Group.

En la Corte del Rey Blas (In King Blas' Court) (SPA.). 24p. (J). 4.95 *(978-84-246-1629-8(4))* La Galera, S.A. Editorial ESP. Dist: AIMS International Bks., Inc.

Ende, Michael. El Dragon y la Mariposa. De Horna, Luis, illus. 2003.Tr. of Der Lindwurm und der Schmetterling. (SPA.). 48p. (J). (gr. k-3). pap. 8.95 *(978-84-204-3710-1(7))* Santillana USA Publishing Co., Inc.

The Entire World of SH & CH Book of Stories. 2004. per. 34.99 *(978-0-9760490-2-9(3))* Say It Right.

Equipo Staff. Libro de la Selva y Cuatro Cuentos Mas.Tr. of Jungle Book & Four Tales More. (SPA.). 48p. (J). 16.48 *(978-84-305-9297-5(0))* Susaeta Ediciones, S.A. ESP. Dist: AIMS International Bks., Inc.

—Pinocho y Cuatro Cuentos Mas.Tr. of Pinoccui & Four Tales More. (SPA.). 124p. (J). 16.48 *(978-84-305-9296-8(2))* Susaeta Ediciones, S.A. ESP. Dist: AIMS International Bks., Inc.

—365 Cuentos, uno para Cada Dia.Tr. of 365 Tales, One for Everyday. (SPA.). 304p. 29.98 *(978-84-305-2252-1(2))* Susaeta Ediciones, S.A. ESP. Dist: AIMS International Bks., Inc.

Ergun, Erol. The All-Merciful Master. 2009. (Beautiful Names of God Ser.). (ENG.). 128p. (J). (gr. 4-7). 14.95 *(978-1-59784-202-0(8))* Tughra Bks.

Erickson, Arnold. Stories to Be Shared. 2006. 94p. (J). 40.00 *(978-0-9700108-3-4(4))* Creative Well, The.

Erps, Yitzy, illus. Tell Me a Tale: 8 Great Stories. 2005. 64p. (J). *(978-1-4226-0018-4(1))* Mesorah Pubns., Ltd.

Esopo. La Zorra Se Pasa de Lista. (Coleccion Fabulas y Cuentos Populares). (SPA.). 24p. (J). (gr. 2-4). *(978-84-246-1566-6(2)*, GL1066) La Galera, S.A. Editorial ESP. Dist: Lectorum Pubns., Inc.

Espinosa, Marta Catalina Vanni. Testigos 25 D - Y Mas. 2010. 56p. pap. 23.95 *(978-1-61764-285-2(1))* AuthorHouse.

Eureka! Stories of Amazing Discoveries. (Critical Reading Ser.). (YA). (gr. 6-12). pap. *(978-0-8092-1249-1(8))* Jamestown.

The Evangeline Nicholas Collection: 1 Each of 16. (gr. 1-3). tchr. ed., stu. ed. 91.50 *(978-0-322-00761-1(5))* Wright Group/McGraw-Hill.

The Evangeline Nicholas Collection: 1 Each of 6. (gr. 1-3). 199.50 *(978-0-7802-9517-9(X))* Wright Group/McGraw-Hill.

The Evangeline Nicholas Collection Set A: 6 Each of 8. (gr. 1-3). 222.50 *(978-0-7802-8056-4(3))* Wright Group/McGraw-Hill.

The Evangeline Nicholas Collection Set A,B: 6 Each of 16. (gr. 1-3). tchr. ed., stu. ed. 456.50 *(978-0-7802-9516-2(1))* Wright Group/McGraw-Hill.

The Evangeline Nicholas Collection Set B: 6 Each of 8. (gr. 1-3). stu. ed. 235.50 *(978-0-7802-8057-1(1))* Wright Group/McGraw-Hill.

Evans, Alwyn, et al. Monty's Tale. (Illus.). 16p. (J). pap. 7.49 *(978-1-86368-139-1(6))* Fremantle Pr. AUS. Dist: Independent Pubs. Group.

Evans, Florence Adèle. Alice's Adventures in Pictureland: A Tale Inspired by Lewis Carroll's Wonderland. 2011. (Illus.). 152p. pap. *(978-1-904808-63-3(8))* Evertype.

Evans, Michael. Poggle & the Treasure. Evans, Michael, illus. 2011. (Poggle Ser.). (ENG., Illus.). 32p. (J). (gr. k — 1). pap. 8.99 *(978-1-4052-4812-9(2))* Egmont Bks., Ltd. GBR. Dist: Independent Pubs. Group.

Ewing, Juliana Horatia. Brothers of Pity & Other Tales of Beasts & Men. 2007. (ENG.). 152p. pap. 19.99 *(978-1-4264-9205-1(7))*; 168p. pap. 21.99 *(978-1-4264-9262-4(6))* Creative Media Partners, LLC.

—Brothers of Pity & Other Tales of Beasts & Men. 2007. (Illus.). 168p. per. *(978-1-4065-2522-9(7))* Dodo Pr.

—The Brownies & Other Tales. 2007. 140p. per. *(978-1-4065-2523-6(5))* Dodo Pr.

—Mary's Meadow: And Other Tales of Fields & Flowers. 2007. (ENG.). 154p. pap. 19.99 *(978-1-4346-3334-7(9))* Creative Media Partners, LLC.

—Mary's Meadow & Other Tales of Fields & Flowers. 2007. 152p. per. *(978-1-4065-2529-8(4))* Dodo Pr.

—Melchior's Dream & Other Tales. 2007. 176p. per. *(978-1-4065-2530-4(8))* Dodo Pr.

—Miscellanea. 2007. (Illus.). 212p. per. *(978-1-4065-2531-1(6))* Dodo Pr.

A Expressway Jewels Set, 6 vols. 32p. (gr. 1-3). 26.50 *(978-0-7802-8046-5(6))* Wright Group/McGraw-Hill.

Fabian, Ingrid. The Black Arabian Foal. 2011. (Illus.). 53p. pap. 15.95 *(978-1-84624-530-5(3))* Book Guild, Ltd. GBR. Dist: Trans-Atlantic Pubns., Inc.

Fables & Tall Tales (Gr. 3-4) 2003. (J). *(978-1-58232-072-4(1))* ECS Learning Systems, Inc.

Fabregat, Antonio-Manuel. Los Cuentos de Mi Escuela. (SPA.). 128p. (J). (gr. 4-6). *(978-84-216-1185-2(2)*, BU3866) Bruño, Editorial ESP. Dist: Lectorum Pubns., Inc.

Fabulas de Siempre. l.t. ed.Tr. of Traditional Fables. (SPA.). (J). 3.98 *(978-84-7630-901-8(5))* Selector, S.A. de C.V. MEX. Dist: AIMS International Bks., Inc.

Fafoutakis, Anne. Enchanted Talisman & Other Stories for Children of All Ages. 2004. 132p. pap. 13.50 *(978-1-84426-296-0(0))* Upfront Publishing Ltd. GBR. Dist: Printondemand-worldwide.com.

Fagan, Cary. Mr. Zinger's Hat. Petricic, Dusan, illus. 2012. (ENG.). 32p. (J). (gr. -1-1). 17.95 *(978-1-77049-253-0(4)*, Tundra Bks.) Tundra Bks. CAN. Dist: Penguin Random Hse. LLC.

Faine, Edward Allan. More Little Ned Stories. 2003. 112p. (J). pap. 6.95 *(978-0-9716911-2-4(6))* IM Pr.

Falco, Joanna. Diana, the Angel, & the Holy Grail. 2007. 52p. (J). per. 8.95 *(978-0-595-45733-5(9))* iUniverse, Inc.

Falconi, María Inés. Hasta el Domingo. (Torre de Papel Ser.). (SPA.). (YA). (gr. 6-18). 8.95 *(978-958-04-2902-9(2))* Norma S.A. COL. Dist: Distribuidora Norma, Inc.

Falletta, Bernadette & Lewis, Maria. We Love to Read Stories & Songs. 2005. 27p. (J). 14.95 *(978-1-4116-4734-3(3))* Lulu Pr., Inc.

Falwell, Cathryn. Butterflies for Kiri, 1 vol. 2003. (ENG., Illus.). 32p. (J). pap. 9.95 *(978-1-60060-342-6(4))* Lee & Low Bks., Inc.

Family Stories: Jumbo Packs. (gr. k-2). 157.08 *(978-0-7362-0051-6(7))* CENGAGE Learning.

Farina von Buchwald, Martin & Prado Farina, Gabriela. The Joy of Giving. Avendano, Dolores, illus. Testino, Mario et al, photos by. 2005. 89p. (J). 18.00 *(978-0-9777266-0-8(6))* von Buchwald, Martin Farina.

Farjeon, Eleanor. The Little Bookroom. Ardizzone, Edward, illus. 2003. (New York Review Children's Collection). (ENG.). 336p. (J). (gr. 4-7). 19.95 *(978-1-59017-048-9(2)*, NYR Children's Collection) New York Review of Bks., Inc., The.

Farley, Terri. Desert Dancer. 2003. (Phantom Stallion Ser.). (Illus.). 234p. (J). (gr. 5-9). 12.65 *(978-0-7569-3561-0(X))* Perfection Learning Corp.

Farnsworth-Simpson, Patricia Ann. Stories to Thrill & Delight. 2008. 142p. pap. 12.95 *(978-1-4357-3275-9(8))* Lulu Pr., Inc.

Faul, Nicole. The Great Animal Race & Trap the Angry Elephant Finds a Friend. 2009. (Illus.). 44p. pap. 18.49 *(978-1-4389-3320-7(7))* AuthorHouse.

Faundez, Anne, ed. Little Red Riding Hood. 2004. (QEB Start Writing Ser.). (Illus.). 24p. (J). lib. bdg. 15.95 *(978-1-59566-020-6(8))* QEB Publishing Inc.

Fawbert, Malcolm. Tales from Thimble Hall Mrs Stopper's Bottle. 2010. (Illus.). 26p. pap. 12.00 *(978-1-60860-344-2(X)*, Strategic Bk. Publishing) Strategic Book Publishing & Rights Agency (SBPRA).

FeatherHill, Annaha. Little Britches. 2007. 76p. per. 19.95 *(978-1-4241-5303-9(4))* America Star Bks.

Ferrari, G. m. Lake, Sky, Dragonfly. 2009. 44p. pap. 16.99 *(978-1-4490-2895-4(0))* AuthorHouse.

Ferren, Stella. 5 Great Little Read-A-Loud Stories for Grandparents. 2009. 48p. pap. 11.49 *(978-1-4389-2625-4(1))* AuthorHouse.

Ferrier, Paul Eugene. Kavaldo & His Diamond Pills. Gettys, Katherine, illus. 2013. (ENG.). 72p. pap. 12.99 *(978-1-940395-07-4(0))* Yawn's Bks. & More, Inc.

Ferro, Beatriz. Arriba el Telon. (SPA.). (YA). 8.95 *(978-958-04-7263-6(7))* Norma S.A. COL. Dist: Distribuidora Norma, Inc.

Fiction Readers, 30, Set. 2013. (Fiction Readers Ser.). (SPA., Illus.). 20p. (gr. 1-1). spiral bd. 149.70 *(978-1-4938-0207-4(0))* Teacher Created Materials, Inc.

Fiedler, Christamaria. El Verano de los Animales. Kessler, Siglint, illus. 2003. (SPA.). 155p. (J). (gr. 5-8). 9.95 *(978-968-19-0706-8(X))* Aguilar, Altea, Taurus, Alfaguara, S.A. de C.V. MEX. Dist: Santillana USA Publishing Co., Inc.

Field, Eugene. Profitable Tales. 2007. 308p. 29.95 *(978-1-4344-9217-3(6))*; per. 19.95 *(978-1-4344-9123-7(4))* Wildside Pr., LLC.

Fienberg, Anna, et al. Tashi & the Wicked Magician: And Other Stories. Kelly, Geoff, illus. 2017. (Tashi Ser.). (ENG.). 96p. (J). (gr. k-3). pap. 9.99 ***(978-1-76029-050-4(5))*** Allen & Unwin AUS. Dist: Independent Pubs. Group.

Fiesta de Cuentos. (Coleccion Estrella). (SPA., Illus.). 64p. (J). 14.95 *(978-950-11-0016-7(2)*, SGM016) Sigmar ARG. Dist: Continental Bk. Co., Inc.

Fifield, Lisa. Bears Make Rock Soup. Erdrich, Lise, illus. 2013. (ENG.). 32p. (J). pap. 9.95 *(978-0-89239-300-8(9)*, Children's Book Press) Lee & Low Bks., Inc.

Filipek, Nina. Goldilocks & the Three Bears. O'Toole, Jeanette, illus. 2009. (Fairy Tale Firsts Ser.). 12p. (J). (gr. -1-k). bds. 11.40 *(978-1-60754-689-4(2))* Windmill Bks.

Filipi, Carmen. The Marvelous Fountain: And other stories my grandma told Me. Long, Dave, illus. 2007.Tr. of Fuente Maravillosa y otros cuentos que me conto mi Abuela. (ENG & SPA.). 55p. (J). per. 14.95 *(978-0-9797814-0-7(X))* Hispanic Institute of Social Issues.

Finn, Rebecca. Rudy Learns to Fly. 6. 2012. (Sparkly Christmas Ser.). (ENG., Illus.). 12p. (J). (gr. -1-k). bds. 5.99 *(978-0-230-75386-0(8))* Macmillan Pubs., Ltd. GBR. Dist: Independent Pubs. Group.

Fiona Fox Staff & Giles, Sophie. 365 Bedtime Stories. 2013. (ENG., Illus.). 224p. (J). 24.95 *(978-1-84135-614-3(X))* Award Pubns. Ltd. GBR. Dist: Parkwest Pubns., Inc.

First Stories (Gr. K-1) 2003. (J). *(978-1-58232-035-9(7))* ECS Learning Systems, Inc.

Fisher, Daniel, ed. 638 Potential Paper Cuts: 638 Pages of Stories by Sixth-Grade Students of Berkshire Middle School. 2008. (ENG.). 638p. pap. 11.00 *(978-1-4196-9572-8(X))* CreateSpace Independent Publishing Platform.

Fisher, Karin, adapted by. Fish, Fox, & Then Some: Seven Aesop's Fables Retold Using One-syllable Words for the Barton Reading & Spelling System. 2003. (J). pap. 7.95 *(978-0-9744343-1-5(0)*, SA-302) Bright Solutions for Dyslexia, LLC.

Fisher, Lillian M. Feathers in the Wind. 155p. (YA). (gr. 4-8). 9.99 *(978-0-88092-438-2(1))* Royal Fireworks Publishing Co.

Fitzer, Robin. Summer Stories. 2008. 45p. pap. 24.95 *(978-1-60563-742-6(4))* America Star Bks.

Fitzpatrick, Becca. The Complete Hush, Hush Saga: Hush, Hush; Crescendo; Silence; Finale. 2013. (Hush, Hush Saga Ser.). (ENG., Illus.). 1824p. (YA). (gr. 9). pap. 47.99 *(978-1-4814-0084-8(3)*, Simon & Schuster Bks. For Young Readers) Simon & Schuster Bks. For Young Readers.

Flaherty, Mike. Whose Story Is This, Anyway? Vidal, Oriol, illus. 2016. (ENG.). 40p. (J). (gr. -1-1). 14.95 *(978-1-4549-1608-6(7))* Sterling Publishing Co., Inc.

Flanagan, James. Stories Heard Around the Lunchroom. 2010. 96p. pap. 11.49 *(978-1-4490-8443-1(5))* AuthorHouse.

Flanagan, Jim. The School of Scary Stories. 2006. (Illus.). 125p. (J). per. 12.95 *(978-0-9766666-5-3(0))* Arcadian Hse.

Flanagan, John. The Battle for Skandia. 2009. (Ranger's Apprentice Ser.: 4). lib. bdg. 19.65 *(978-0-606-02208-8(2)*, Turtleback) Turtleback Bks.

Fleischman, Paul. Graven Images. Ibatoulline, Bagram, illus. (ENG.). 128p. (YA). 2005. (gr. 5-9). per. 6.99 *(978-0-7636-2984-7(7))* 2006. (gr. 7-9). reprint ed. 16.99 *(978-0-7636-2775-1(5))* Candlewick Pr.

Flett, Julie. Wild Berries. Cook, Earl N., tr. Flett, Julie, illus. 2013. (ENG., Illus.). 32p. (J). (gr. -1-3). pap. 16.95 *(978-1-897476-89-5(2))* Simply Read Bks. CAN. Dist: Ingram Publisher Services.

Flickinger, Joie & Flickinger, Amanda. Clutch the Trucking Cat. 2007. 236p. per. 24.95 *(978-1-4241-9535-0(7))* America Star Bks.

Flint, Shamini. The Collected Diaries of a Sporting Superhero: Five Stories in One! 2017. (Diary of A... Ser.). (ENG.). 500p. (J). (gr. 2-6). pap. 14.99 ***(978-1-76029-345-1(8))*** Allen & Unwin AUS. Dist: Independent Pubs. Group.

Flor Ada, Alma & Campoy, F. Isabel. Una Semilla de Luz. Dávalos, Felipe, illus. 2003. (Coleccion Derechos Del Nino Ser.). (SPA.). 32p. (J). (gr. 3-5). pap. 7.95 *(978-84-204-5818-2(X))* Santillana USA Publishing Co., Inc.

—Yes! We Are Latinos. Diaz, David, illus. 2013. (SPA & ENG.). 96p. (J). (gr. 5). 18.95 *(978-1-58089-383-1(X))* Charlesbridge Publishing, Inc.

Flynn, Ian & Spaziante, Patrick. Let the Games Begin. 2011. (Mega Man Ser.: 1). (ENG., Illus.). 112p. (gr. 4-7). pap. 11.95 *(978-1-879794-85-6(3)*, Archie Comics) Archie Comic Pubns., Inc.

Folk Tales of the West Lake. 2007. 72p. per. 11.95 *(978-1-59654-409-3(0))* Disruptive Publishing.

Foster, Cassandra. Do You Know Us? A Collection of Short Stories. 2006. (Illus.). 48p. (YA). per. 8.00 *(978-0-9778641-1-9(1))* Smith, Mildred C.

—A Good Story: A Collection of Short Short Stories. 2006. (Illus.). 37p. (YA). per. 8.00 *(978-0-9778641-0-2(3))* Smith, Mildred C.

Foster Colburn, Cherie. Bloomin' Tales: Seven Favorite Wildflower Legends. Fisher Hein, Joy, illus. 2012. (ENG.). 64p. (J). pap. 9.95 *(978-1-936474-36-3(0)*, 1987c76b-83d5-44af-9831-cd68dda6cbfd) Bright Sky Pr.

Foth, Horst. Traumreisen. 2011. 120p. 26.50 *(978-1-4477-2150-5(0))* Lulu Pr., Inc.

Four Year Olds. Date not set. 96p. 7.98 *(978-0-7525-8710-3(2))* Parragon, Inc.

Francesca, Sieglinde De. A Donsy of Gnomes. 2009. pap. *(978-1-61623-243-6(9))* Independent Pub.

Frank, Church & Barnas, Aloura. The Epic Adventures of Whiz Grass & Poot Berry. 2011. 164p. (gr. -1). 22.99 *(978-1-4634-4525-6(3))*; pap. 11.99 *(978-1-4634-4524-9(5))* AuthorHouse.

Franklin Watts, contrib. by. Wait Skates! & Other Funny Stories. 2009. (Rookie Reader Treasury Ser.). (ENG., Illus.). 128p. (J). 11.95 *(978-0-531-20849-6(4)*, Children's Pr.) Scholastic Library Publishing.

Fraustino, Lisa Rowe, ed. Don't Cramp My Style: Stories about That Time of the Month. 2012. (ENG.). 304p. (YA). (gr. 7). pap. 14.99 *(978-1-4424-8109-1(9)*, Simon & Schuster Bks. For Young Readers) Simon & Schuster Bks. For Young Readers.

Frederick, Heather Vogel. The Complete Mother-Daughter Book Club Collection: The Mother-Daughter Book Club; Much Ado about Anne; Dear Pen Pal; Pies & Prejudice; Home for the Holidays; Wish You Were Eyre. 2013. (Mother-Daughter Book Club Ser.). (ENG., Illus.). 2320p. (YA). (gr. 4-7). pap. 47.99 *(978-1-4424-9843-3(9)*, Simon & Schuster Bks. For Young Readers) Simon & Schuster Bks. For Young Readers.

Freeberg, Eric, illus. Animal Stories. 2010. (Classic Starts(tm) Ser.). (ENG.). 160p. (J). (gr. 2-4). 6.95 *(978-1-4027-6646-6(7))* Sterling Publishing Co., Inc.

Freedman, Bill. Boy Who Wanted to Marry His Dog. 2011. 50p. (J). pap. 14.99 *(978-1-926780-10-8(8))* Key Publishing Hse., Inc., The CAN. Dist: Bookmasters Distribution.

Freese, Thomas, reader. Fog Swirler & 11 Other Ghost Stories. 2006. (J). Pt. 1. cd-rom 13.95 *(978-0-9789511-0-8(7))*Pt. 2. cd-rom 13.95 *(978-0-9789511-1-5(5))*Pt. 3. cd-rom 13.95 *(978-0-9789511-2-2(3))* Illumination Pubns.

—Shaker Ghost Stories from Pleasant Hill, KY Audio Book/cd. 2006. (J). cd-rom 17.95 *(978-0-9789511-3-9(1))* Illumination Pubns.

French, Moira. The Swingewood Stories. 2009. 36p. pap. 16.99 *(978-1-4490-4777-1(7))* AuthorHouse.

French, Vivian. Down in the Jungle. Young, Selina, illus. 2012. (ENG.). 96p. (J). (gr. -1-k). 7.99 *(978-1-4440-0513-4(8)*, Orion Children's Bks.) Hachette Children's Group GBR. Dist: Hachette Bk. Group.

Friederich, Uve. The World of Bridgett & Emily. Fitzpatrick, Meg & Ravenhill, John A., illus. 2004. 41p. (J). mass mkt. 8.95 *(978-0-9747532-4-9(6))* Taylor-Dth Publishing.

Friend, R. Time Out at Home. 2005. (Down on Friendly Acres Ser.: 2). (J). lib. bdg. *(978-0-9743627-4-8(3))*; pap. 6.95 *(978-0-9743627-1-7(9))* Sunflower Seeds Pr.

Friesen, Ray. Pirate Penguin vs Ninja Chicken Volume 1: Troublems with Frenemies: Troublems with Frenemies. 2011. (Pirate Penguin vs Ninja Chicken Ser.). (ENG., Illus.). 96p. (J). (gr. 2-5). 9.95 *(978-1-60309-071-1(1)*, 9781603090711) Top Shelf Productions.

Fruchter, Yaakov. Best of Olomeinu - Series 2: Stories for All Year 'Round. 2003. 136p. 13.99 *(978-1-57819-398-1(2)*, BO1H); pap. 10.99 *(978-1-57819-399-8(0)*, BO1P) Mesorah Pubns., Ltd.

Fu, Shelley. Hoyi the Archer & other Classic Chinese Tales. Abboreno, Joseph F. & Fu, Sherwin, illus. 2005. 144p. (J). (gr. 4-8). reprint ed. 22.00 *(978-0-7567-9713-3(6))* DIANE Publishing Co.

Fuchs, Menucha. The Picky Eater & Other Stories. 2004. (Children's Learning Ser.: 20). (HEB., Illus.). 48p. (J). per. 4.95 *(978-1-932443-24-0(X)*, TPES) Judaica Pr., Inc., The.

Fuentes, Carlos. Aura. (SPA.). (YA). 8.00 *(978-958-04-6971-1(7))* Norma S.A. COL. Dist: Distribuidora Norma, Inc.

Fuertes, Gloria. Cuentos Para 365 Dias. 2003. (SPA.). 210p. 17.56 *(978-84-305-9282-1(2)*, SU2166) Susaeta Ediciones, S.A. ESP. Dist: Lectorum Pubns., Inc.

Fujikawa, Gyo. Sunny Books - Four-Favorite Tales, 4 bks., Set. Fujikawa, Gyo, illus. (Illus.). (J). (gr. -1). reprint ed. *(978-1-55987-042-9(7)*, Sunny Bks.) J B Communications, Inc.

Fun Short Stories on Values & Morals of Life. 2003. (Illus.). 90p. (YA). per. *(978-0-9742122-0-3(2))* Aunty Ems Boutique.

Furlong, Frank, illus. Pop Pop's Magic Chair. 2010. 24p. pap. 12.95 *(978-1-60844-658-2(1))* Dog Ear Publishing, LLC.

Furman, A. L., ed. Horse Stories: Young Readers. Geer, Charles, illus. 2011. 192p. 42.95 *(978-1-258-09836-0(9))* Literary Licensing, LLC.

—Pioneer Stories: Young Readers. Geer, Charles, illus. 2011. 190p. 42.95 *(978-1-258-09907-7(1))* Literary Licensing, LLC.

—Teenage Frontier Stories. Prezio, Victor, illus. 2011. 256p. 47.95 *(978-1-258-09865-0(2))* Literary Licensing, LLC.

The Furry Friends. 2005. (J). per. *(978-0-9664783-2-7(0))* Jacqueline Beverly Hills.

Fusek Peters, Andrew. The Talkative Tortoise. 2011. (Traditional Tales with a Twist Ser.). (ENG., Illus.). 32p. (J). *(978-1-84643-418-1(1))* Child's Play International Ltd.

Futch, Dorothy R. All about Life: A Collection of Children Stories. 2009. 40p. pap. 21.99 *(978-1-4415-2848-3(2))* Xlibris Corp.

Gaiman, NEil. M Is for Magic. Kristiansen, Teddy, illus. 272p. (J). (gr. 5-9). 2008. (ENG.). pap. 7.99 *(978-0-06-118647-9(3))* 2007. 16.99 *(978-0-06-118642-4(2))* HarperCollins Pubs.

—M Is for Magic. 2007. (Illus.). 151p. (J). (gr. 5-9). 60.00 *(978-1-59606-123-1(5))* Subterranean Pr.

—Unnatural Creatures: Stories Selected by Neil Gaiman. 2013. (ENG., Illus.). 480p. (YA). (gr. 8). 17.99 *(978-0-06-223629-6(6))*; pap. 9.99 *(978-0-06-223630-2(X))* HarperCollins Pubs.

—Unnatural Creatures: Stories Selected by Neil Gaiman. 2013. (YA). lib. bdg. 20.85 *(978-0-606-31804-4(6)*, Turtleback) Turtleback Bks.

Galjanic, Lisa. When Series 6 Volume Set, 6, 6. 2007. (Illus.). 100p. (J). 34.95 *(978-1-933532-06-6(8))* LSG Pubns.

Gall, Chris. Dinotrux. 2012. (Dinotrux Ser.: 1). (ENG., Illus.). 32p. (J). (gr. -1-3). pap. 7.99 *(978-0-316-13392-0(2))* Little, Brown Bks. for Young Readers.

Gallego García, Laura & Gallego García, Laura. El Valle de Los Lobos. 2004. (Ciclo el Valle de Los Lobos the Valley of the Wolves Cycle Ser.). (SPA., Illus.). 222p. (YA). 10.99 *(978-84-348-7361-2(3))* SM Ediciones ESP. Dist: Lectorum Pubns., Inc.

Gallego, Laura, et al. La Leyenda Del Rey Errante. 2004. (SPA.). 224p. (YA). 7.99 *(978-84-348-8818-0(1))* SM Ediciones ESP. Dist: Lectorum Pubns., Inc.

Gallo, Donald. On the Fringe: Stories. Gallo, Donald & Gallo, Donald R., eds. 2003. (ENG., Illus.). 240p. (YA). (gr. 7-7). 6.99 *(978-0-14-250026-2(7)*, Speak) Penguin Young Readers Group.

Gallo, Donald R. First Crossing: Stories about Teen Immigrants. Gallo, Donald R., ed. 2007. (ENG.). 240p. (YA). (gr. 7-12). per. 8.99 *(978-0-7636-3291-5(0))* Candlewick Pr.

—No Easy Answer. 2014. 17.50 *(978-1-63419-721-2(6))* Perfection Learning Corp.

Gallo, Donald R., ed. Owning It: Stories about Teens with Disabilities. (ENG., Illus.). 224p. (YA). (gr. 7). 2010. mass mkt. 6.99 *(978-0-7636-4661-5(X))* 2008. 17.99 *(978-0-7636-3255-7(4))* Candlewick Pr.

Galluzzi, Edward. Twelve upon a Time. Bocik, Adam, illus. 3rd ed. 2009. 298p. (J). pap. *(978-1-926585-69-7(0))* CCB Publishing.

Galvin, Laura Gates & Luther, Jacqueline. Read-A-Picture Collection: First Stories for Family Reading. rev. ed. 2005. (Reading to Grow Ser.). (ENG., Illus.). 40p. (J). (gr. -1-3). 12.99 *(978-1-59069-449-7(X)*, 1A700) Studio Mouse LLC.

Ganz, Yaffa. Four in One: Four Favorites. Klineman, Harvey, illus. 2008. 24.99 *(978-1-59826-183-7(5))* Feldheim Pubs.

Ganzer, Diane & St. Croix, Sammy. Adventures of a Kitten Named Raspberry & Other Tales. 2009. 176p. pap. 9.95 *(978-1-935105-30-5(2))* Avid Readers Publishing Group.

García Márquez, Gabriel. Maria dos Prazeres. (SPA.). 28p. 10.50 *(978-958-04-5572-1(4))* Norma S.A. COL. Dist: Distribuidora Norma, Inc.

Gareth Stevens Publishing, creator. The Doomed & the Dead. 2006. (Ghost Stories Ser.). (Illus.). 128p. (gr. 3-7). lib. bdg. 31.00 *(978-0-8368-6822-7(6)*, Gareth Stevens Learning Library) Stevens, Gareth Publishing LLLP.

Garfein, Stanley Joe. Tales of the Temple Mice. 2006. (Illus.). 92p. (J). 14.95 *(978-0-9787422-0-1(6))* Garfein, Stanley.

Garn, Laura Aimee. Bella Basset Ballerina. Sokolova, Valerie, illus. 2006. 32p. (J). (gr. -1-3). 15.95 *(978-0-9759378-0-8(4))* Pretty Please Pr., Inc.

Gartner, Hans & Poppel, Hans. Osito ILmpio y Osito Sucio. (SPA.). (J). 8.95 *(978-958-04-6257-6(7))* Norma S.A. COL. Dist: Distribuidora Norma, Inc.

Gary R Kirby. Stories of Sunshine & Funtime of Wonder & Thunder of Mystery & Magic for the Young to Grow On. 2009. 404p. pap. 22.95 *(978-1-4401-8640-0(5))* iUniverse, Inc.

Garza, Xavier. The Donkey Lady Fights la Llorona & Other Stories / la Señora Asno Se Enfrenta a la Llorona y Otros Cuentos. Álvarez, Mayra E., tr. 2015. (ENG & SPA., Illus.). 144p. (J). (gr. 3-6). pap. 9.95 *(978-1-55885-816-9(4)*, Piñata Books) Arte Publico Pr.

—Kid Cyclone Fights Devil & Other Stories/Kid Ciclon Se Enfrenta a el Diablo y Otras Historias. Ventura, Gabriela Baeza, tr. from ENG. 2010. (ENG & SPA.). 64p. (J). (gr. 3-7). pap. 10.95 *(978-1-55885-599-1(8)*, Piñata Books) Arte Publico Pr.

Gatty, Alfred. Aunt Judy's Tales. 2007. 132p. per. *(978-1-4065-2814-5(5))* Dodo Pr.

—The Fairy Godmothers & Other Tales. 2007. 120p. per. *(978-1-4065-2815-2(3))* Dodo Pr.

—The Fairy Godmothers & Other Tales. 2007. 104p. (gr. 4-7). per. *(978-1-4068-0918-3(7))* Echo Library.

Gauthier, Bertrand. Les Jumeaux Bulle Series. Dumont, Daniel, illus. 2004. (FRE.). 64p. (J). (gr. 1-4). pap. *(978-2-89021-684-6(5))* Diffusion du livre Mirabel (DLM).

Gauthier, Gilles & Derome, Pierre-Andre. Petit Chausson, Grande Babouche. 2003. (Premier Roman Ser.). 64p. (J). (gr. 2-5). pap. *(978-2-89021-308-1(0))* Diffusion du livre Mirabel (DLM).

Gay, Michele. Leoncio's Adventures. 2013. 20p. pap. 17.99 *(978-1-4817-0427-4(3))* AuthorHouse.

Gbala, Deswin R. Rock University: A Collection of Short Stories & Poems. Gbala, Deswin R., illus. Date not set. (Illus.). 51p. (Orig.). (J). (gr. 3-10). pap. 8.50 *(978-0-9650629-2-3(9))* Coulee Region Pubns., Inc.

Geiger, Nina Friant. The Froblits of Round Pond. 2010. pap. 9.99 *(978-0-578-05331-8(4))* Ingenuity 31 Inc.

Geis, Patricia. Paca Lamar. Geis, Patricia, illus. 2004. (Mi Ciudad Ser.). (SPA & ENG., Illus.). 24p. (J). (gr. -1-k). 6.95 *(978-84-7864-797-2(X))* Combel Editorial, S.A. ESP. Dist: Independent Pubs. Group.

—Pepa Pas. Geis, Patricia, illus. 2004. (Mi Ciudad Ser.). (SPA & ENG., Illus.). 24p. (J). (gr. -1-k). 6.95 *(978-84-7864-796-5(1))* Combel Editorial, S.A. ESP. Dist: Independent Pubs. Group.

George E. Keely, Jr. The Happy Day Fable. 2010. 20p. pap. 10.00 *(978-1-4269-0064-8(3))* Trafford Publishing.

Gerard, Timothy. The City Brigade & Remember the Music. 2012. 112p. (gr. -1). 23.99 *(978-1-4685-2420-8(8))*; pap. 14.95 *(978-1-4685-2421-5(6))* AuthorHouse.

Gerovasiliou, Oreanthy. Yuri the Lion: Three Stories. 2010. (Illus.). 48p. pap. 13.00 *(978-1-60888-069-0(9))* Nimble Bks. LLC.

Gershator, Phillis. Rata-Pata-Scata-Fata: A Caribbean Story, 1 vol. Meade, Holly, illus. 2005. (ENG.). 32p. (J). (gr. -1-3). 5.95 *(978-1-932065-95-4(4))*; 15.95 *(978-1-932065-94-7(6))* Star Bright Bks., Inc.

Giachetti, Julia & Benchmark Education Co. Staff. A Tail for a Tail - Cherokee Trickster Tales. 2014. (Text Connections Ser.). (J). (gr. 5). *(978-1-4900-1375-6(X))* Benchmark Education Co.

Gibbons, Ted & Wilcox, S. Michael. Modern Fables. McCune, Mark, illus. 2010. (J). 14.99 *(978-1-59955-307-8(4))* Cedar Fort, Inc./CFI Distribution.

Gibson, Sherri L. In the Mind of a Child: Children's Stories. 2013. 36p. pap. 24.95 *(978-1-62709-750-5(3))* America Star Bks.

Gifford, P. S. Dr. Offig's Lessons from the Dark Side, Volume 1. 2008. (ENG.). 176p. (YA). pap. 10.95 *(978-0-9801506-2-9(0))* BRP Publishing Group.

Gilliland, Tom. The Adventures of Archie Aardvark. 2012. 60p. pap. 10.00 *(978-1-4691-7957-5(1))* Xlibris Corp.

Gilmore, Rachna. The Flute, 1 vol. Biswas, Pulak, illus. 2012. (ENG.). 32p. (J). (gr. -1-2). 16.95 *(978-1-896580-57-9(2))* Tradewind Bks. CAN. Dist: Orca Bk. Pubs. USA.

Glaser, Shirley. The Alphazeds. Glaser, Milton, illus. 2005. 32p. (J). (gr. k-4). reprint ed. 20.00 *(978-0-7567-9367-8(X))* DIANE Publishing Co.

Gleeson, Joseph M., illus. Just So Stories. 2013. 250p. pap. *(978-1-909302-29-7(5))* Abela Publishing.

Glynn, Gower. Stories Told in the Wigwam. 2006. pap. 24.95 *(978-1-4254-9966-2(X))* Kessinger Publishing, LLC.

Gmeyner, Elizabeth. The Key of the Kingdom: A Book of Stories & Poems for Children. Russell, Joyce, illus. 2004. 100p. (J). pap. 15.00 *(978-0-88010-549-1(6)*, Bell Pond Bks.) SteinerBooks, Inc.

Gogonya, Carol. The African Mermaid & Other Stories. 2011. 40p. pap. 32.70 *(978-1-4568-5416-4(X))* Xlibris Corp.

Golda, Kata. Stories for Bedtime: A Keepsake Pocket & Tales to Cherish. 2011. (ENG.). 7p. (J). (gr. -1 — 1). 14.99 *(978-0-8118-7498-4(2))* Chronicle Bks. LLC.

Golden Books, illus. DC Super Friends Little Golden Book Favorites (DC Super Friends) 2013. (Little Golden Book Favorites Ser.). (ENG.). 80p. (J). (-k). 6.99 *(978-0-449-81621-9(4)*, Golden Bks.) Random Hse. Children's Bks.

—Disney Classics Little Golden Book Library, 5 vols. 2013. (ENG.). 24p. (J). (-k). 24.95 *(978-0-7364-3149-1(7)*, Golden/Disney) Random Hse. Children's Bks.

—Nine Nickelodeon Tales (Nickelodeon) 2016. (Little Golden Book Treasury Ser.). (ENG.). 224p. (J). (-k). 12.99 *(978-0-399-55350-9(9)*, Golden Bks.) Random Hse. Children's Bks.

Golden Books Staff. Animal Tales. 2007. (Little Golden Book Treasury Ser.). (ENG., Illus.). 224p. (J). (gr. -1-2). 12.99 *(978-0-375-84178-1(4)*, Golden Bks.) Random Hse. Children's Bks.

—Eloise Wilkin Stories. Wilkin, Eloise, illus. 2005. (Little Golden Book Treasury Ser.). (ENG.). 224p. (J). (gr. -1-2). 10.95 *(978-0-375-82928-4(8)*, Golden Bks.) Random Hse. Children's Bks.

—Farm Tales. 2007. (Little Golden Book Treasury Ser.). (ENG., Illus.). 224p. (J). (gr. -1-2). 10.99 *(978-0-375-83942-9(9)*, Golden Bks.) Random Hse. Children's Bks.

—Sleepytime Tales. 2006. (Little Golden Book Treasury Ser.). (ENG., Illus.). 224p. (J). (gr. -1-2). 12.99 *(978-0-375-83848-4(1)*, Golden Bks.) Random Hse. Children's Bks.

Golden Books Staff & Benedict, Elizabeth. Classic Characters of Little Golden Books, 5 vols. 2010. (ENG., Illus.). 24p. (J). (gr. -1-k). 24.95 *(978-0-375-85934-2(9)*, Golden Bks.) Random Hse. Children's Bks.

Golden Books Staff & Man-Kong, Mary. Barbie Bedtime Story Collection (Barbie) 2014. (ENG., Illus.). 320p. (J). (gr. -1-2). 15.99 *(978-0-385-38784-2(9)*, Random Hse. Bks. for Young Readers) Random Hse. Children's Bks.

Golding, Jacqueline. Healing Stories: Picture Books for the Big & Small Changes in a Child's Life. 2006. (ENG.). 336p. per. 17.95 *(978-1-59077-097-9(8))* Evans, M. & Co., Inc.

Gonzales Bertrand, Diane. There's a Name for This Feeling / Hay un Nombre para lo Que Siento. Baeza Ventura, Gabriela, tr. 2014. (ENG & SPA.). 72p. (J). pap. 10.95 *(978-1-55885-784-1(2)*, Piñata Books) Arte Publico Pr.

Gonzales, Felipe C. Little Folk Stories & Tales by Don Pablo: Bilingual Stories in Spanish & English = Chistes y Cuentos de Don Pablo: Cuentos Bilingües en Español e Inglés. 2010. (SPA & ENG.). (J). pap. 24.95 *(978-0-86534-772-4(7))* Sunstone Pr.

Goodhart, Pippa. Ginny's Egg. Brouwer, Aafke, illus. 142p. (J). pap. 7.50 *(978-0-7497-4557-8(6))* Egmont Bks., Ltd. GBR. Dist: Trafalgar Square Publishing.

Goodman, Larry. The Cowboy & Other Stories. 2008. 36p. pap. 24.95 *(978-1-60813-546-2(2))* America Star Bks.

Goodrich, C. C. Barnabee: At the Picnic. 2009. (Illus.). 32p. pap. 13.99 *(978-1-4389-8388-2(3))* AuthorHouse.

—Barnabee: Goes Shopping. 2009. (Illus.). 32p. pap. 13.99 *(978-1-4389-9728-5(0))* AuthorHouse.

—Barnabee: Goes to Work. 2009. (Illus.). 32p. pap. 13.99 *(978-1-4389-8461-2(8))* AuthorHouse.

—Barnabee: In the Beehive. 2009. (Illus.). 24p. pap. 12.99 *(978-1-4389-7560-3(0))* AuthorHouse.

—Barnabee: In the Meadow. 2009. (Illus.). 24p. pap. 12.99 *(978-1-4389-8389-9(1))* AuthorHouse.

—Barnabee: Meets New Friends. 2009. (Illus.). 24p. pap. 12.99 *(978-1-4389-8390-5(5))* AuthorHouse.

Goodwin, John. Lion Book of Five-Minute Animal Stories. Bendall-Brunello, John, illus. 2009. (ENG.). 48p. (J). (gr. k-2). 16.99 *(978-0-7459-6084-5(7))* Lion Hudson PLC GBR. Dist: Independent Pubs. Group.

—The Lion Book of Five-Minute Bedtime Stories. Waterhouse, Stephen, illus. 2010. (ENG.). 48p. (J). (gr. k-2). 16.99 *(978-0-7459-6143-9(6))* Lion Hudson PLC GBR. Dist: Independent Pubs. Group.

Gordh, Bill & Pugliano-Martin, Carol. Barbie. Wolcott, Karen, illus. 2006. (Step into Reading Ser.). (ENG.). 192p. (J). (gr. -1-1). pap. 8.99 *(978-0-375-84124-8(5)*, Random Hse. Bks. for Young Readers) Random Hse. Children's Bks.

Gordon, Marie Elaina. My Grand-Mom Told Me..., Book 1. 2006. 48p. pap. 16.95 *(978-1-4241-2655-2(X))* America Star Bks.

—My Grand-Mom Told Me-down by the Sea. 2008. 108p. pap. 19.95 *(978-1-4241-9095-9(9))* America Star Bks.

Gordon, Sylvia. Further Adventures of the Potty Wizard & His Cat, Muddles. 2009. (Illus.). 60p. pap. 10.49 *(978-1-4389-6819-3(1))* AuthorHouse.

Gorey, Edward & Donnelly, James. Three Classic Children's Stories. 2010. (Illus.). 112p. (J). 17.95 *(978-0-7649-5546-4(2))* Pomegranate Communications, Inc.

Gorman, Thomas. The Old Neighborhood. 2003. 77p. pap. 16.95 *(978-1-59286-514-7(3))* PublishAmerica, Inc.

Gorrell, Nancy. Anna Banana. 2006. (ENG., Illus.). 96p. (J). (gr. -1-2). per. 6.99 *(978-1-84550-182-2(9)*, 5a21ceaa-6b5b-4fb6-b215-15915b289e40) Christian Focus Pubns. GBR. Dist: Bookmasters Distribution.

Goscinny, René. Asterix Omnibus 3: Asterix & the Big Fight; Asterix in Britain; Asterix & the Normans. Uderzo, Albert, illus. 2012. (ENG.). 156p. (J). (gr. 4-7). pap. 22.99 *(978-1-4440-0475-5(1)*, Orion) Orion Publishing Group, Ltd. GBR. Dist: Hachette Bk. Group.

—Asterix Omnibus 4: Asterix the Legionary; Asterix & the Chieftain's Shield; Asterix at the Olympic Games. Uderzo, Albert, illus. 2012. (ENG.). 152p. (J). (gr. 4-6). pap. 22.99 *(978-1-4440-0487-8(5)*, Orion) Orion Publishing Group, Ltd. GBR. Dist: Hachette Bk. Group.

—Asterix Omnibus 7: Asterix & the Soothsayer - Asterix in Corsica - And Asterix & Caesar's Gift. Uderzo, Albert, illus. 2013. (ENG.). 156p. (J). (gr. 4-7). 29.99 *(978-1-4440-0835-7(8)*, Orion) Orion Publishing Group, Ltd. GBR. Dist: Hachette Bk. Group.

—Asterix Omnibus 7: Asterix & the Soothsayer, Asterix in Corsica, & Asterix & Caesar's Gift. Uderzo, Albert, illus. 2014. (ENG.). 156p. (J). (gr. 4-6). pap. 22.99 *(978-1-4440-0836-4(6)*, Orion) Orion Publishing Group, Ltd. GBR. Dist: Hachette Bk. Group.

—Asterix Omnibus 9. Uderzo, Albert, illus. 2014. (ENG.). 152p. (J). (gr. 4-6). 29.99 *(978-1-4440-0967-5(2)*, Orion) Orion Publishing Group, Ltd. GBR. Dist: Hachette Bk. Group.

—The Bounty Hunter, Vol. 26. Morris Publishing Company Staff, illus. 2011. (Lucky Luke Ser.: 26). (ENG.). 48p. pap. 11.95 *(978-1-84918-059-7(8))* CineBook GBR. Dist: National Bk. Network.

—Iznogoud - The Infamous, Vol. 7. Tabary, illus. 2011. (Iznogoud Ser.: 7). (ENG.). 48p. (gr. 3-17). pap. 11.95 *(978-1-84918-074-0(1))* CineBook GBR. Dist: National Bk. Network.

—Lucky Luke Versus Joss Jamon. Morris, illus. 27th ed. 2011. (Lucky Luke Ser.: 27). (ENG.). 48p. (gr. 3-17). pap. 11.95 *(978-1-84918-071-9(7))* CineBook GBR. Dist: National Bk. Network.

—Nicholas & the Gang. Bell, Anthea, tr. from FRE. Sempé, Jean-Jacques, illus. 2011. (ENG.). 120p. (gr. 4-7). pap. 9.95 *(978-0-7148-6226-2(6))* Phaidon Pr., Inc.

—Omnibus 5: Asterix & the Cauldron; Asterix in Spain; Asterix & the Roman Agent. Uderzo, Albert, illus. 2013. (ENG.). 156p. (J). (gr. 4-6). pap. 22.99 *(978-1-4440-0490-8(5)*, Orion) Orion Publishing Group, Ltd. GBR. Dist: Hachette Bk. Group.

—Omnibus 8: Asterix & the Great Crossing; Obelix & Co.; & Asterix in Belgium. Uderzo, Albert, illus. 2013. (ENG.). 152p. (J). (gr. 4-6). 29.99 *(978-1-4440-0837-1(4)*, Orion) Orion Publishing Group, Ltd. GBR. Dist: Hachette Bk. Group.

—Rockets to Stardom - Iznogoud, Vol. 8. Tabary, illus. 2011. (Iznogoud Ser.: 8). (ENG.). 48p. pap. 11.95 *(978-1-84918-092-4(X))* CineBook GBR. Dist: National Bk. Network.

—The Stagecoach. Morris Publishing Company Staff, illus. 2011. (Lucky Luke Ser.: 25). (ENG.). 48p. (J). (gr. 3-17). pap. 11.95 *(978-1-84918-052-8(0))* CineBook GBR. Dist: National Bk. Network.

Goscinny, René & Morris Publishing Company Staff. The Dalton Cousins. 2011. (Lucky Luke Ser.: 28). (ENG., Illus.). 48p. (gr. 3-17). pap. 11.95 *(978-1-84918-076-4(8))* CineBook GBR. Dist: National Bk. Network.

Goscinny, René & Sempé, Jean-Jacques. Nicholas in Trouble. Bell, Anthea, tr. from FRE. 2013. (ENG., Illus.). 128p. pap. *(978-0-7148-6686-4(5))* Phaidon Pr., Inc.

—Nicholas on Holiday. Bell, Anthea, tr. from FRE. 2013. (ENG., Illus.). 128p. pap. *(978-0-7148-6223-1(1))* Phaidon Pr., Inc.

Goscinny, René & Uderzo, Albert. Asterix Omnibus 5: Includes Asterix & the Cauldron, Asterix in Spain, & Asterix & the Roman Agent. 2012. (ENG., Illus.). 152p. (J). (gr. 4-6). 29.99

(978-1-4440-0488-5(3), Orion) Orion Publishing Group, Ltd. GBR. Dist: Hachette Bk. Group.
—Bouclier Arverne. 21.95 (978-2-01-210011-4(2)) Hachette Groupe Livre FRA. Dist: Distribooks, Inc.
—Obelix et Compagnie. (FRE.). 21.95 (978-2-01-210023-7(6)) Hachette Groupe Livre FRA. Dist: Distribooks, Inc.
Gottfredson, Floyd, et al. Walt Disney's Comics & Stories #700. 2008. 80p. pap. 9.99 (978-1-60360-057-6(4)) Gemstone Publishing, Inc.
Gould, Terry. The Adventures of Sir Sniffsalot & His Friends. Proulx, Denis, illus. 2007. 48p. (gr. -1-3). pap. 15.99 (978-0-9789057-3-6(3)) Huntington Ludlow Media Group.
Graham, Bob. Tales from the Waterhole. 2004. (Illus.). 64p. (J). (978-0-7445-6593-5(6)) Walker Bks., Ltd.
Grahame, Kenneth. Dream Days. Shepard, Ernest H., illus. 2004. reprint ed. pap. 21.95 (978-1-4179-0979-7(X)) Kessinger Publishing, LLC.
Grandpa Bob. The Dirty Nose Series. 2008. 284p. pap. 16.99 (978-0-557-02079-9(4)) Lulu Pr., Inc.
—The Dirty Nose Series - Olander. 2008. 284p. 33.86 (978-1-4116-9246-6(2)) Lulu Pr., Inc.
Granny's Favorite Tales. 2006. (Illus.). 156p. (J). per. 39.95 (978-1-60002-098-8(4), 3915) Mountain Valley Publishing, LLC.
Grant, Joan Marshall. Redskin Morning & Other Stories. Lavers, Ralph, illus. 2010. (J). pap. (978-1-59731-555-5(9)) Perennis, Sophia.
—Scarlet Fish & Other Stories. Lavers, Ralph, illus. 2010. (J). pap. (978-1-59731-554-8(0)) Perennis, Sophia.
Grant, Susan. Tell Me a Story. Dall, Christopher M., illus. 2013. 56p. pap. (978-1-4602-1356-8(4)) FriesenPress.
Graphic Revolve: Common Core Editions, 1 vol. 2014. (Graphic Revolve: Common Core Editions Ser.). (ENG.). 72p. (gr. 2-3). 559.80 (978-1-4965-0115-8(2), Graphic Revolve) Stone Arch Bks.
Grasso, Lorraine. Short Stories, Tall Tales. 2011. 24p. pap. 15.99 (978-1-4568-5491-1(7)) Xlibris Corp.
Gratton, Tessa, et al. Storybook: A Collection of Stories. 2012. (Carolrhoda YA Ser.). (ENG., Illus.). 304p. (YA). (gr. 7-12). 17.95 (978-0-7613-7527-2(9)) Lerner Publishing Group.
Graves, Damien. The Deadly Catch. 2008. (Midnight Library). (Illus.). 170p. (J). (gr. 4-7). 13.65 (978-0-7569-8824-1(1)) Perfection Learning Corp.
—I Can See You. 2010. (Midnight Library Ser.). 160p. (J). 15.10 (978-1-60686-248-3(0)) Perfection Learning Corp.
Gray, Grandpa. The Land of the Three Elves: Inside the Curve of the River. 2013. (ENG.). 268p. (YA). pap. 14.95 (978-1-4787-0314-3(8)) Outskirts Pr., Inc.
Gray, Keith. Dead Trouble. Scruton, Clive, illus. 90p. (J). pap. 7.50 (978-0-7497-4556-1(8)) Egmont Bks., Ltd. GBR. Dist: Trafalgar Square Publishing.
Grayson, Barry/Scott. Twisted Yarns: Bedtime Stories for Hip Kids. 2007. (Illus.). 40p. (J). pap. (978-0-9774357-1-5(7)) Grayson, Kate.
Great, Alex. Balkan Tales. 2009. 134p. pap. 18.36 (978-1-4452-4363-4(6)) Lulu Pr., Inc.
Great Books Foundation Staff, contrib. by. Junior Great Books. 2011. (J). (978-1-933147-00-0(8)) Great Bks. Foundation.
Greaves, Margaret. The Mice of Nibbling Village. Pinkney, Jane, illus. 2011. (ENG.). 32p. (J). (gr. -1-k). 14.99 (978-1-84365-189-5(0)) National Trust, Aylesbury GBR. Dist: Independent Pubs. Group.
Greaves, Nick. When Bat Was a Bird: And Other Animal Tales from Africa. du Plessis, David, illus. 2005. (ENG.). 144p. per. 15.00 (978-1-86872-998-2(2)) Penguin Random House Grupo Editorial ESP. Dist: Casemate Pubs. & Bk. Distributors, LLC.
Green, John, et al. Let It Snow: Three Holiday Romances. (ENG.). 368p. (YA). (gr. 7). 2014. mass mkt. 7.99 (978-0-14-751501-8(7)) 2008. pap. 10.99 (978-0-14-241214-5(7)) Penguin Young Readers Group. (Speak).
Green, Roger Lancelyn & Green, Richard. Adventures of Robin Hood. Hall, Arthur & Terrazzini, Daniela Jaglenka, illus. 2010. (Puffin Classics Ser.). (ENG.). 320p. (J). (gr. 5-7). 16.99 (978-0-14-133489-9(4), Puffin Books) Penguin Young Readers Group.
Greendyk, William, tr. from ENG. Las Doce Historias de la Tia Margarita. l.t. ed. 2004. Orig. Title: Aunt Margaret's Twelve Stories. (SPA.). 84p. (J). pap. 3.99 (978-1-932789-00-3(6), X001N) Editorial Sendas Antiguas, LLC.
Greene, Janice. Blood & Basketball, 1 vol. unabr. ed. 2010. (Q Reads Ser.). (ENG.). 32p. (YA). (gr. 9-12). pap. 6.95 (978-1-61651-213-2(X)) Saddleback Educational Publishing, Inc.
—Breaking Point, 1 vol. unabr. ed. 2010. (Q Reads Ser.). (ENG.). 32p. (YA). (gr. 9-12). pap. 6.95 (978-1-61651-199-9(0)) Saddleback Educational Publishing, Inc.
—Fat Boy, 1 vol. unabr. ed. 2010. (Q Reads Ser.). (ENG.). 32p. (YA). (gr. 9-12). pap. 6.95 (978-1-61651-201-9(6)) Saddleback Educational Publishing, Inc.
Greene, Kimberly. My Sister's a Pop Star. 2011. (My Sister's a Pop Star Ser.). 277p. (J). pap. 5.99 (978-0-7945-2899-7(6), Usborne) EDC Publishing.
Gregg, Stacy. Riding Star, 3. 2011. (Pony Club Rivals Ser.: 3). (ENG.). 304p. (J). (gr. 4-7). pap. 7.99 (978-0-00-733345-5(5), HarperCollins Children's Bks.) HarperCollins Pubs. Ltd. GBR. Dist: HarperCollins Pubs.
—Showjumpers, 2. 2010. (Pony Club Rivals Ser.: 2). (ENG.). 272p. (J). (gr. 4-7). pap. 7.99 (978-0-00-733344-8(7), HarperCollins Children's Bks.) HarperCollins Pubs. Ltd. GBR. Dist: HarperCollins Pubs.
Gressett, William H., Jr. Nor all your Piety nor Wit.... 2005. (YA). per. 9.99 (978-0-9765467-9-5(5)) Creative Bk. Pubs.
Grethe, James. Weird & Wondrous Tales of Woodland Wyre. 2009. 60p. pap. 11.00 (978-1-4269-1527-7(6)) Trafford Publishing.
Grey, Erika. The Alphabet Bears: Spook-Tales Collection. Grey, Erika, illus. 2010. (Illus.). 127p. (YA). pap. 24.95 (978-0-9790199-3-7(1)) PeDante Pr.
Griffiths, Andy. Killer Koalas from Outer Space: And Lots of Other Very Bad Stuff That Will Make Your Brain Explode! Denton, Terry, illus. 2011. (ENG.). 176p. (J). (gr. 3-7). 12.99 (978-0-312-36789-3(9), 9780312367893) Feiwel & Friends.
Griffiths, Mark. Hanging on Every Word: 48 of the World's Greatest Stories, Retold for Reading Aloud, 1 vol. 2014. (ENG.). 224p. (J). pap. 19.99 (978-0-85721-506-2(X), Monarch Bks.) Lion Hudson PLC GBR. Dist: Kregel Pubns.
Grigorov, Yassen. Los Ángeles de la Guarda. 2003. (Los Especiales de A la Orilla Del Viento Ser.). (SPA.). 28p. (J). 9.99 (978-968-16-7053-5(1)) Fondo de Cultura Economica USA.
Grimes, Charles J. The Boys!, 1 vol. 2010. 186p. pap. 24.95 (978-1-4489-5736-1(2)) America Star Bks.
Grimly, Gris. Little Jordan Ray's Muddy Spud. Grimly, Gris, illus. 2015. (ENG., Illus.). 100p. (J). pap. 19.95 (978-0-9729388-6-0(9)) Baby Tattoo Bks.
Grimm. Bola de cristal. 2005. 24p. incl. cd-rom (978-84-494-2897-5(1)) Oceano Grupo Editoria, S.A.
—Tres pelos diablio. 2005. 24p. incl. audio compact disk (978-84-494-2898-2(X)) Oceano Grupo Editoria, S.A.
Grimm, Brothers. Hans in Luck: Seven Stories by the Brothers Grimm. Hoffmann, Felix, illus. 2017. (ENG.). 256p. (J). (gr. -1-3). 30.00 **(978-0-7358-4281-6(7))** North-South Bks., Inc.
Grimm, Hermanos. El Caperucita Roja.Tr. of My First Library: Little Red Riding Hood. (SPA.). (J). 2.49 (978-968-13-2470-4(6)) Editorial Diana, S.A. MEX. Dist: Continental Bk. Co., Inc.
Grimm, J. & W. The Three Little Pigs. Watts, Edith M B. B., Bernadette, illus. 2012. (ENG.). 32p. (J). 16.95 (978-0-7358-4058-4(X)) North-South Bks., Inc.
Grimm, Jacob & Grimm. Cuentos de Grimm. Rackham, Arthur, illus. (Coleccion Cuentos Universales). (SPA.). 144p. (YA). (gr. 4-18). (978-84-261-1098-5(3), JV30116) Juventud, Editorial ESP. Dist: Lectorum Pubns., Inc.
Grimm, Jacob & Grimm, Wilhelm K. Cuentos de Grimm.Tr. of Stories by Grimm. (SPA.). 144p. (J). (978-84-261-0618-6(8)) Juventud, Editorial.
—Cuentos de Grimm. (Coleccion Estrella).Tr. of Stories by Grimm. (SPA., Illus.). 64p. (J). 14.95 (978-950-11-0015-0(4), SGM015) Sigmar ARG. Dist: Continental Bk. Co., Inc.
Grindley, Sally. Paw Prints in the Snow. Frost, Adam, illus. 2012. (ENG.). 112p. (J). (gr. 3-5). pap. 11.99 (978-1-4088-1945-6(7), 9781408819456, Bloomsbury USA Childrens) Bloomsbury Publishing USA.
Grindley, Sally, compiled by. Classic Animal Stories. 2008. (ENG., Illus.). 160p. (J). (gr. 1-5). 19.95 (978-0-7534-6210-2(9), 9780753462102, Kingfisher) Roaring Brook Pr.
Gripari, Pierre. Le Gentil Petit Diable: Et Autres Contes de la Rue Broca. Rosado, Puig, illus. 2007. (Folio Junior Ser.). 142p. (J). per. (978-2-07-061255-0(4)) National Round Table on the Environment & the Economy (NRTEE)/Table ronde nationale sur l'environnement et l'économie (TRNEE).
—The Good Little Devil & Other Tales. Lewis, Sophie, tr. Puig Rosado, Fernando, illus. 2014. (ENG.). 300p. (J). (gr. 4-7). 20.00 (978-1-78269-008-5(5), Pushkin Press) Steerforth Pr.
—The Witch in the Broom Cupboard & Other Tales. Lewis, Sophie, tr. from FRE. Rosado, Puig, illus. 2015. (ENG.). 144p. (J). (gr. 2-5). pap. 13.95 (978-1-78269-066-5(2), Pushkin Press) Steerforth Pr.
Grizzell, Larry. The Star: A Christmas Song. 2006. (Illus.). 25p. (J). 19.95 (978-0-9759542-2-5(9)) Adventures Galore.
Groenewald, Catherine. The Little Girl Who Didn't Want to Grow Up. 2011. (Best Loved Tales for Africa Ser.). (ENG., Illus.). 32p. (J). (gr. k-2). pap. 10.95 (978-1-77009-819-0(4)) Jacana Media ZAF. Dist: Independent Pubs. Group.
Gross, Jen & Hoch, Jen. A Visit up & down Wall Street. Gross, Margaret, illus. 2005. 32p. (J). 14.95 (978-0-9760875-0-2(2)) Harry & Stephanie Bks.
Grosset & Dunlap. Berry Merry Holiday Treasury. 2014. (Strawberry Shortcake Ser.). (ENG.). 160p. (J). (gr. -1-k). 9.99 (978-0-448-48360-3(2), Grosset & Dunlap) Penguin Young Readers Group.
Gruber, Daveda. Red Barn & other Short Stories. 2010. 45p. pap. 19.50 (978-0-557-41998-2(0)) Lulu Pr., Inc.
—Tales of a Tiny Dog. 2010. 74p. pap. 29.50 (978-0-557-43600-2(1)) Lulu Pr., Inc.
Gruber, Michael. The Legend of the Brog. Gruber, Michael & Graves, Linda, illus. 2005. (J). per. 9.95 (978-0-9770413-0-5(1)) Gruber Enterprises.
Gruskin, Edward I. Roy Rogers: Robin Hood of the Range. Hess, Erwin L., illus. 2011. 420p. 54.95 (978-1-258-04369-8(6)) Literary Licensing, LLC.
Guardino, Dawn M. Nightmare Echoes: Short Scary Stories for Young Teens. 2003. 108p. 22.95 (978-1-4107-8325-7(1)); pap. 11.45 (978-1-4107-8324-0(3)) AuthorHouse.
Guarnaccia, Steven. Goldilocks & the Three Bears: A Tale Moderne. 2010. (ENG., Illus.). 32p. (J). (gr. k-3). 19.95 (978-0-8109-8966-5(2), Abrams Bks. for Young Readers) Abrams, Inc.
Guerrero, Andres. La Noche. Guerrero, Andres, illus. 2003. (SPA., Illus.). 28p. (J). (gr. k-3). 7.95 (978-84-204-4321-8(2)) Santillana USA Publishing Co., Inc.
Guest, Jacqueline & Leavey, Peggy Dymond. Growing up Ivy. 2010. (ENG.). 256p. (YA). (gr. 4-8). pap. 10.99 (978-1-55488-723-1(2)) Dundurn CAN. Dist: Ingram Publisher Services.
Guin, Anatoly. Smart Tales from Brainy the Cat. 2010. 84p. pap. 29.95 (978-1-4327-6147-9(1)) Outskirts Pr., Inc.
Gulliksen, Anne. A Boy from Nøtterøy. 2009. 108p. pap. 13.00 (978-1-59858-939-9(3)) Dog Ear Publishing, LLC.
Gump, Granny. The Giraffe Who Went to School. 2011. 48p. pap. 21.99 (978-1-4568-5805-6(X)) Xlibris Corp.
Gunn, Robin Jones. Christy Miller Collection Vol. 3, Vol. 3. 2006. (Christy Miller Collection: Bks. 7-9). (ENG.). 480p. (J). (gr. 7-12). 16.99 (978-1-59052-586-9(8), Multnomah) Doubleday Religious Publishing Group, The.
—Christy Miller Collection, Vol 4, Vol. 4. 2006. (Christy Miller Collection: Bks. 10-12). (ENG.). 496p. (J). (gr. 7-12). 16.99 (978-1-59052-587-6(6), Multnomah) Doubleday Religious Publishing Group, The.
Guo, Jinsong. Touching Stories by Dr. Guo. 2004. pap. 10.00 (978-0-8059-6606-0(4)) Dorrance Publishing Co., Inc.
Gurney, Stella. Not so Silly Sausage. Million, Liz, illus. 2011. 32p. pap. (978-1-84089-707-4(4)) Zero to Ten, Ltd.
Gustafson, Scott. Classic Bedtime Stories. 2016. (ENG., Illus.). 84p. (J). (gr. k-3). 19.95 (978-1-57965-760-4(5)) Artisan.
Gustafson, Scott, illus. Cuentos y Cantos de Navidad. 2004. (ESP & SPA.). 98p. (YA). 12.98 (978-1-4127-0628-5(9), 7137007) Phoenix International Publications, Inc.
Gutman, Dan. The My Weird School Collection, Bks. 1-4. Paillot, Jim, illus. 2010. (My Weird School Ser.). (J). (gr. 1-5). pap. 16.99 (978-0-06-189489-3(3)) HarperCollins Pubs.
—My Weird School Daze 12-Book Box Set, 12 vols. Paillot, Jim, illus. 2013. (My Weird School Daze Ser.). (ENG.). 500p. (J). (gr. 1-5). pap. 45.00 (978-0-06-228891-2(1)) HarperCollins Pubs.
Guttiere, Benedicte. When Christmas Comes. 2011. (Funny Faces Ser.). (Illus.). 14p. bds. (978-1-84089-710-4(4)) Zero to Ten, Ltd.
Guy, Belinda. A First Aid Manual for Children: In the Form of Three Short Stories. 2012. (Illus.). 28p. pap. 21.35 (978-1-4772-2671-1(0)) AuthorHouse.
Guzaldo, Jessica. Murder & Betrayal DeFalco, Julie & Cowhey, Dennis R., eds. Cowhey, Dennis E., illus. 2003. 72p. (YA). (gr. 7-8). pap. 9.95 (978-0-9642823-2-2(1)) Key Answer Products, Inc.
Hachette Children's Group. The Pardoner's Tale. (Illus.). 48p. (978-0-7502-3670-6(1)) Hodder & Stoughton.
Haight, Travis. 2:30 AM: Wired on Coffee; Six Premium Blended (Not So) Shorts. 2007. 203p. pap. 13.95 (978-1-4303-1004-4(9)) Lulu Pr., Inc.
Hale, Nick. The Edge. 2012. (Striker Ser.: 3). (ENG.). 224p. (J). (gr. 5-7). pap. 7.99 (978-1-4052-5685-8(0)) Egmont Bks., Ltd. GBR. Dist: Independent Pubs. Group.
Hale, Rachael. Hugs & Kisses. 2012. (ENG., Illus.). 20p. (J). (gr. -1 — 1). bds. 6.99 (978-0-316-13063-9(X)) Little, Brown Bks. for Young Readers.
Hall, Desis. Christmas in Jamaica & Other Stories. 2012. 64p. pap. (978-1-908690-06-7(2)) Abba Pr.
Hall, Jennie. The Viking Tales. 2008. 88p. pap. 8.15 (978-1-60459-529-1(9)) Wilder Pubns., Corp.
Hall, S.C. Turns of Fortune & Other Tales. 2007. (ENG.). 116p. per. (978-1-4065-1586-2(8)) Dodo Pr.
Halsey-Cody, J. E. Story Time. 2012. 110p. 29.99 (978-1-4797-1401-8(1)); pap. 19.99 (978-1-4797-1400-1(3)) Xlibris Corp.
Halsted, John David, ed. East of the Sun & West of the Moon & Other Moon Stories. 2012. (Illus.). 54p. pap. (978-1-909302-02-0(3)) Abela Publishing.
Hamilton, Seymour. The Laughing Princess. 2012. (ENG.). 146p. (J). pap. 7.99 (978-1-937291-45-7(6)) Acedrex Publishing.
Hamilton, Tisha. Mickey Mouse Clubhouse. Disney Storybook Artists Staff, illus. 2008. (Carry along Treasury Ser.). (ENG.). 14p. (J). (gr. -1-1). bds. 14.99 (978-0-7944-1481-8(8)) Reader's Digest Assn., Inc., The.
Hamley, Dennis. Beautiful Games. Fenoughty, Charles, illus. 2004. 104p. per. (978-1-904529-13-2(5), Back to Front) Solidus.
—Yule Logs. 2005. 96p. per. (978-1-904529-17-0(8), Back to Front) Solidus.
Hammond, Meredith. The World According to Tiffany: The Airplane Trip. 2011. 28p. (gr. -1). pap. 12.03 (978-1-4567-3150-2(5)) AuthorHouse.
Hampton, Sue. Aliens & Angels: Three Stories for Christmas. 2013. (ENG., Illus.). 96p. (J). pap. (978-1-78228-315-7(3)) Pneuma Springs Publishing.
Handa, Nimret. Good Night Stories. 2004. (Illus.). 20p. (J). (978-81-291-0373-4(7)) Rupa & Co.
Hannan, Peter. The Greatest Snowman in the World! Hannan, Peter, illus. 2010. (ENG., Illus.). 32p. (J). (gr. -1-3). 16.99 (978-0-06-128480-9(7)) HarperCollins Pubs.
Hannigan, Katherine. True (... Sort Of) 2011. (ENG., Illus.). 368p. (J). (gr. 3-7). 16.99 (978-0-06-196873-0(0), Greenwillow Bks.) HarperCollins Pubs.
Hanson, Martina D. & Benchmark Education Co. Staff. Analytical Arguments about Courage. 2014. (Text Connections Ser.). (J). (gr. 6). (978-1-4900-1530-9(2)) Benchmark Education Co.
Harden, Perry Lee. The Percy Hargrove Stories: It's All Elementary. 2012. 160p. pap. 14.95 (978-1-4772-2438-0(6)) AuthorHouse.
harkins, charles. Naptime Adventures of Luksi the Turtle. 2010. 174p. pap. 20.96 (978-0-557-28695-9(6)) Lulu Pr., Inc.
Harman, Michael. El Loro y la Higuera. 2009. (SPA.). 32p. (J). (gr. -1-3). pap. 8.95 (978-0-89800-431-1(4)) Dharma Publishing.
—Parrot & the Fig Tree. 2nd ed. 2009. (Jataka Tales Ser.). (ENG., Illus.). 32p. (J). (gr. -1-3). pap. 8.95 (978-0-89800-430-4(6)) Dharma Publishing.
Harold & I. 2007. (ENG., Illus.). 291p. (J). (gr. 3-8). per. 13.99 (978-0-7684-2432-4(1)) Send The Light Distribution LLC.
Harper, Eleanor. Honey & Harebell. 2010. 64p. pap. 11.95 (978-0-9818092-7-4(8)) Illumina Publishing.
Harris, Christine. Four Tails: An Anthology of Four Tales for Children. 2011. (Illus.). 92p. (gr. -1). pap. 12.10 (978-1-4520-7643-0(X)) AuthorHouse.
Harris, Joel Chandler. Told by Uncle Remus: New Stories of the. 2006. (Illus.). pap. 31.95 (978-1-4254-9964-8(3)) Kessinger Publishing, LLC.
Harris, Kimberly Anne. Only in a Dream Series: Caught in a Web ~ the Trees Are My Friends~What Is All the Buzz About? 2012. 60p. pap. 24.99 (978-1-4772-7005-9(1)) AuthorHouse.
Hartman, Bob. The Lion Storyteller Awesome Book of Stories. Kallai Nagy, Krisztina, illus. 2016. (ENG.). 256p. (J). (gr. k-2). pap. 16.99 (978-0-7459-7636-5(0)) Lion Hudson PLC GBR. Dist: Independent Pubs. Group.
Hartman, Bob & Nagy, Krisztina Kallai. The Lion Storyteller Bedtime Book. 2010. (ENG., Illus.). 128p. (J). (gr. k-2). 19.99 (978-0-7459-6094-4(4)) Lion Hudson PLC GBR. Dist: Independent Pubs. Group.
Hartnett, Edith E. Once upon a Time. 2013. 168p. pap. 22.50 (978-1-882260-22-5(8)) Calm Unity Pr.
Hartt-Sussman, Heather. Here Comes Hortense! Graham, Georgia, illus. 2012. (ENG.). 32p. (J). (gr. -1-1). 17.95 (978-1-77049-221-9(6), Tundra Bks.) Tundra Bks. CAN. Dist: Penguin Random Hse. LLC.
Harvey, A. W. Llewellyn. Christmas Stories: For the Young & Young at Heart. 2012. 114p. (gr. -1). pap. 12.06 (978-1-4669-5800-5(6)) Trafford Publishing.
Harvey, Irene J. William the Fairground Car. 2008. 116p. pap. 30.95 (978-1-60693-210-0(1), Eloquent Bks.) Strategic Book Publishing & Rights Agency (SBPRA).
Hasling, Jack. The Little Rock & Other Stories: And Other Stories. Rogers, Denny, illus. 2003. (ENG.). 32p. (Orig.). (J). (gr. 1-6). pap. 9.95 (978-1-878044-51-8(6), Wild Rose) Mayhaven Publishing, Inc.
—Salamander the Great! 2006. (Illus.). (J). per. 10.00 (978-0-9786988-1-2(9)) Hazel Street Productions.
Hastings, Jacqueline. Jay's Tales. 2013. 70p. pap. (978-1-909878-05-1(7)) Legend Pr.
Hasty, Shaudalon. My Body. 2003. pap. 12.00 (978-0-8059-5968-0(8)) Dorrance Publishing Co., Inc.
Hauff, Wilhelm & Pak, Boris. Little Mook & Dwarf Longnose. 2004. (ENG., Illus.). 124p. 19.95 (978-1-56792-222-6(8)) Godine, David R. Pub.
Hawkins, Colin. Foxy Doesn't Feel Well. (Illus.). 23p. (J). pap. 8.99 (978-0-00-664758-4(8), HarperCollins Children's Bks.) HarperCollins Pubs. Ltd. GBR. Dist: Trafalgar Square Publishing.
Hawley, Jim. Homer & Friends. 2012. 50p. pap. (978-1-77097-709-9(0)) FriesenPress.
Hawthorn, P. Little Book of Bedtime Stories. 2004. (Mini Storybooks Ser.). (ENG., Illus.). 128p. (J). 7.95 (978-0-7945-0268-3(7), Usborne) EDC Publishing.
Hawthorn, Phillip. Usborne Stories for Bedtime. Tyler, Jenny, ed. Cartwright, Stephen, illus. 2007. (Stories for Bedtime Ser.). 190p. (J). (gr. -1-3). 19.99 (978-0-7945-1970-4(9), Usborne) EDC Publishing.
Hawthorne, Nathaniel. Nathaniel Hawthorne. McConnell, James, illus. 2004. (Great American Short Stories Ser.). 80p. (gr. 4-7). lib. bdg. 24.00 (978-0-8368-4252-4(9), Gareth Stevens Learning Library) Stevens, Gareth Publishing LLLP.
Hayashi, Leslie Ann. Fables Beneath the Rainbow. Bishop, Kathleen Wong, illus. 2005. 32p. (J). 14.95 (978-1-56647-741-3(7), 477417) Mutual Publishing LLC.
Hayden, Gwendolen Lampshire. Mary Martha's Really Truly Stories: Book 3. 3rd ed. 2013. 130p. pap. 11.95 (978-1-4796-0105-9(5)) TEACH Services, Inc.
Hayes, Joe. Dance, Nana, Dance (Baila, Nana, Baila) Trenard Sayago, Mauricio, illus. 2010. (ENG & SPA.). 128p. (J). (gr. 3-6). pap. 12.95 (978-1-933693-61-3(4)) Cinco Puntos Pr.
—Juan Verdades - El Hombre Que No Sabia Mentir. Fiedler, Joseph Daniel, illus. 2011.Tr. of Juan Verdades/The Man Who Couldn't Tell a Lie. (SPA & ENG.). 32p. (J). (gr. 3-6). pap. 8.95 (978-1-933693-70-5(3)) Cinco Puntos Pr.
—La Llorona - The Weeping Woman: An Hispanic Legend Told in Spanish & English. Hill, Vicki Trego & Pennypacker, Mona, illus. 2006. (ENG & SPA.). 32p. (J). (gr. 4-6). pap. 7.95 (978-0-938317-39-5(3)) Cinco Puntos Pr.
Hays, Helen Ashe. The Adventures of Prince Lazybones: And Other Stories. 2007. 152p. pap. 19.99 (978-1-4264-8474-2(7)); 168p. pap. 21.99 (978-1-4264-8532-9(8)) Creative Media Partners, LLC.
Hearne, Betsy. The Canine Connection: Stories about Dogs & People. 2007. (ENG.). 128p. (YA). (gr. 7). pap. 8.95 (978-1-4169-6817-7(2), Simon Pulse) Simon Pulse.
Hedderwick, Mairi. Island Stories. Hedderwick, Mairi, illus. 2010. (Katie Morag Ser.: 12). (ENG., Illus.). 32p. (J). (gr. k-2). pap. 19.99 (978-1-84941-088-5(7), Red Fox) Random House Children's Books GBR. Dist: Independent Pubs. Group.
Hedley, Alistair, selected by. Read to Me Daddy. Date not set. (Read to Me Ser.). (Illus.). 192p. (J). 14.98 (978-0-7525-9485-9(0)) Parragon, Inc.
Heer, Andrew De. Three African Short Stories for Young Readers: For Young Readers. 2011. 32p. pap. 21.99 (978-1-4568-7973-0(1)) Xlibris Corp.
Heffernan, Danielle. Puppy Dog Tales. 2010. (Illus.). pap. (978-0-9561590-5-2(2), Blue Cloud Pubns.) Black Leaf Publishing Group, The.
Heger, Bryan. Valor & Virtues from the Mind of a Child, 1 vol. 2009. 124p. pap. 19.95 (978-1-60749-625-0(9)) America Star Bks.
Heichberger, Robert L. Tell Me A Story Grandpa. 2010. 56p. pap. 27.99 (978-1-4520-1584-2(8)) AuthorHouse.
Heide, Florence Parry. Tales for the Perfect Child. Ruzzier, Sergio, illus. 2017. (ENG.). 112p. (J). (gr. 1-5). 16.99 (978-1-4814-6379-9(9)) Simon & Schuster Children's Publishing.
Heide, Florence Parry & Van Clief, Sylvia Worth. Fables You Shouldn't Pay Any Attention To. Ruzzier, Sergio, illus. 2017. (ENG.). 112p. (J). (gr. 1-5). 16.99 (978-1-4814-6382-9(9)) Simon & Schuster Children's Publishing.
Heimdallson, Freydis, et al. Kindertales: Stories Old & New for the Children of the Folk. 2008. 100p. pap. 19.50 (978-1-4357-2563-8(8)) Lulu Pr., Inc.
Heine, Helme. Cuentas de Elefante. 2003. (la Orilla Del Viento Ser.). (SPA.). 40p. (J). pap. 7.50 (978-968-16-6423-7(X), 151) Fondo de Cultura Economica USA.
Heinrichs, Cynthia. Mermaids. Lee, Jumin, illus. 2011. (ENG.). 32p. (J). (gr. -1-3). 16.95 (978-1-897476-37-6(X)) Simply Read Bks. CAN. Dist: Ingram Publisher Services.
Henderson, Barbara. Down in Mr Brown's Garden. 2009. 40p. pap. 14.75 (978-1-60860-703-7(8), Strategic Bk. Publishing) Strategic Book Publishing & Rights Agency (SBPRA).
Henderson, Mary Anne. The Adventures of Linda's Little Frog. 2004. 252p. 29.50 (978-1-4184-1576-1(6)) AuthorHouse.
Henighan, Tom. The Boy from Left Field. 2012. (ENG.). 216p. (J). (gr. 5-5). pap. 12.99 (978-1-4597-0060-4(0)) Dundurn CAN. Dist: Ingram Publisher Services.
Henisz, Jerzy E. SOPHIE in PARIS & other Stories. 2009. 99p. pap. 9.46 (978-0-557-09520-9(4)) Lulu Pr., Inc.
Henisz, Jerzy E. & Henisz, Sophie, illustrator. TEDDY BEAR who went on a Trip around the World & other Stories. 2007. 88p. (J). pap. 30.40 (978-0-615-13851-0(9)) Henisz, Jerzy E.
Henriquez, Cesar, illus. Jonathan's Colorful Campus Tour - University of Connecticut A-Z. 2004. (J). 9.99 (978-1-933069-06-7(6)) Odd Duck Ink, Inc.
—Sebastian's Colorful Campus Tour - University of Miami A-Z. 2004. (J). 9.99 (978-1-933069-05-0(8)) Odd Duck Ink, Inc.
The Henry & Mudge Collector's Set: Henry & Mudge; Henry & Mudge in Puddle Trouble; Henry & Mudge in the Green Time; Henry & Mudge under the Yellow Moon; Henry & Mudge in the Sparkle Days; Henry & Mudge & the Forever Sea. 2014. (Henry & Mudge Ser.). (ENG., Illus.). 280p. (J). (gr. k-2). pap. 15.99 (978-1-4814-2147-8(6), Simon Spotlight) Simon Spotlight.
Henry, Judy. Woodland Stories for Our Grandchildren. 2013. 40p. pap. 19.99 (978-1-4669-7752-5(3)) Trafford Publishing.
Henry, O. One Thousand Dollars & Other Plays, Level 2. Oxford University Press Staff & West, Clare, eds. 2nd ed.

2008. (ENG., Illus.). 64p. 9.38 (978-0-19-423520-4(3)) Oxford Univ. Pr., Inc.
Henry, O. & Gianni, Gary. The Gift of the Magi. (Classics Illustrated Ser.). (Illus.). 52p. (YA). pap. 4.95 (978-1-57209-013-2(8)) Classics International Entertainment, Inc.
Henry Wilson, David. Never Say Moo to a Bull. Scheffler, Axel, illus. 2017. (Jeremy James Ser.: 2). (ENG.). 128p. (J). (gr. k-5). pap. 8.99 (978-1-5098-1878-5(2)) Pan Macmillan GBR. Dist: Independent Pubs. Group.
Henty, George Alfred. G. A. Henty Short Story Collection: Featuring: Sole Survivors, the Frontier Girl, the Ranch in the Valley, & on the Track, Vol. 1. 2004. (YA). pap. (978-1-931587-34-1(5)) Preston-Speed Pubns.
—G. A. Henty Short Story Collecton (Deluxe Heirloom Edition) Featuring: Sole Survivors, the Frontier Girl, the Ranch in the Valley, & on the Track (Deluxe Heirloom Edition), Vol. 1. 2004. (YA). lib. bdg. (978-1-931587-33-4(7)) Preston-Speed Pubns.
Herlihy, Matt & Clarke, Nzingha, selected by. Sweet Fancy Moses: Book 2. 2005. per. (978-0-9767048-0-5(3)) Arts and Minds Studio Inc.
Herman, Carli. Good Graffiti Teen Talk on Tough Issues. 2009. 108p. pap. 10.00 (978-0-578-01524-8(2)) Black Bart Bks.
La Hermanita; El Diente Molesto, 2 bks., Set. (Coleccion Chiquilines - Imagen y Sonido). (SPA.). (J). 15.95 incl. audio (978-950-11-0627-5(6), SGM276) Sigmar ARG. Dist: Continental Bk. Co., Inc.
Hernandez, Gilbert. The Adventures of Venus. 2012. (ENG., Illus.). 104p. (gr. 4-9). 9.99 (978-1-60699-540-2(5), 699540) Fantagraphics Bks.
Herriot, James. James Herriot's Treasury of Inspirational Stories for Children: Warm & Joyful Tales by the Author of All Creatures Great & Small. Brown, Ruth & Barrett, Peter, illus. 2005. (ENG.). 260p. (J). (gr. -1-3). 22.99 (978-0-312-34972-1(6), 9780312349721, St. Martin's Griffin) St. Martin's Pr.
Herzog, Pearl. The Pink Dollhouse. 2008. 112p. 29.99 (978-1-58330-797-7(4)) Feldheim Pubs.
Hester, Denia Lewis. Grandma Lena's Big Ol' Turnip. Urbanovic, Jackie, illus. 2005. (ENG.). 32p. (J). (gr. -1-3). 6.99 (978-0-8075-3023-8(9)) Whitman, Albert & Co.
Hewling, Amy Megan. Wishes. 2010. (ENG.). 29p. (978-1-907629-07-5(6)) ShieldCrest.
Higgins, M. G. Body Switch, 1 vol. 2014. (Red Rhino Ser.). (ENG.). 76p. (J). (gr. 4-6). pap. 7.95 (978-1-62250-944-7(7)) Saddleback Educational Publishing, Inc.
—Flyer, 1 vol. 2014. (Red Rhino Ser.). (ENG.). 68p. (J). (gr. 4-6). pap. 7.95 (978-1-62250-942-3(0)) Saddleback Educational Publishing, Inc.
Hildahl, Melita K. Life Is an Adventure with Ernie. 2008. 156p. per. 15.99 (978-1-60477-139-8(9)) Salem Author Services.
Hill, Annemarie. Meaty Treats. 2012. 16p. pap. 15.41 (978-1-4669-3118-3(3)) Trafford Publishing.
Hill, Clare. Granddad's Circus & Other Stories. 2004. 41p. pap. 19.95 (978-1-4137-3647-2(5)) PublishAmerica, Inc.
Hill, Kathi Harper. The Christmas Closet & Other Works. 2012. (ENG.). 48p. 16.99 (978-1-936815-58-6(3)) Yawn's Bks. & More, Inc.
Hill, Will. Battle Lines: A Department 19 Novel. 2013. (Department Nineteen Ser.: 3). (ENG.). 608p. (J). (gr. 9). 18.99 (978-1-59514-408-9(0), Razorbill) Penguin Young Readers Group.
Hillman, John E. Ancient Stories of the Hodj. 2012. (Illus.). 52p. pap. 27.45 (978-1-4685-8215-4(1)) AuthorHouse.
Hilton, Charlotte. Adventure of the Pen Pot Pals. 2009. 36p. pap. 16.99 (978-1-4389-4434-0(9)) AuthorHouse.
Hinckley, Betts. Mr Bumble. 2011. 24p. pap. 15.99 (978-1-4568-9714-7(4)) Xlibris Corp.
Hines, Jerry E. Silly & Stinky Stories My Grandpa Tells. 2011. (ENG., Illus.). 144p. (J). (gr. 4-7). pap. 8.00 (978-0-9831839-1-4(0)) Amber Skye Publishing LLC.
Hinojosa, Francisco. Ana, Verdad? Gedovius, Juan, illus. 2003. (Coleccion Derechos Del Nino Ser.). (SPA.). 32p. (J). (gr. 3-5). pap. 7.95 (978-84-204-5824-3(4)) Santillana USA Publishing Co., Inc.
—Yanka, Yanka. Hinojosa, Francisco, illus. 2003. (SPA., Illus.). 44p. (J). (gr. k-3). pap. 10.95 (978-968-19-0440-1(0)) Santillana USA Publishing Co., Inc.
Hinrichs, Tambra. Ryley's World, 1 vol. 2010. 28p. pap. 24.95 (978-1-4489-6287-7(0)) PublishAmerica, Inc.
Hobbie, Holly. Gem. 2012. (ENG., Illus.). 32p. (J). (gr. -1-3). 16.99 (978-0-316-20334-0(3)) Little, Brown Bks. for Young Readers.
Hobbs-Wyatt, Debz, ed. Wild N Free Too. 2013. 222p. pap. (978-0-9568939-6-3(1)) Paws n Claws Publishing.
Hobby, Nathan. The Fur. 2004. 220p. (YA). pap. 16.50 (978-1-920731-01-4(6)) Fremantle Pr. AUS. Dist: Independent Pubs. Group.
Hoberman, Mary Ann. Very Short Tall Tales to Read Together. Emberley, Michael, illus. 2014. (ENG.). 32p. (J). (gr. -1-3). 17.00 (978-0-316-18329-1(6)) Little Brown & Co.
—You Read to Me, I'll Read to You: Very Short Stories to Read Together. Emberley, Michael, illus. 2006. (ENG.). 32p. (J). (gr. -1-3). pap. 7.99 (978-0-316-01316-1(1), Tingley, Megan Bks.) Little, Brown Bks. for Young Readers.
Hodgson, Julie. Miniature Horse Tales. 2005. 37p. (J). 15.00 (978-1-4116-4144-0(2)) Lulu Pr., Inc.
Hodgson, Karen J. Hugh's Blue Day. Collins, Ross, illus. 2010. (ENG.). 32p. (J). (gr. -1-k). pap. 9.99 (978-1-907432-00-2(0)) Hogs Back Bks. GBR. Dist: Independent Pubs. Group.
—I Don't Care! Said Claire. Rowe, Harriet, illus. 2010. (ENG.). 32p. (J). (gr. -1-2). pap. 9.99 (978-1-907432-05-7(1)) Hogs Back Bks. GBR. Dist: Independent Pubs. Group.
—The King Who Wanted More. Dina, Madalina, illus. 2010. (ENG.). 32p. (J). (gr. -1-4). pap. 9.99 (978-1-907432-03-3(5)) Hogs Back Bks. GBR. Dist: Independent Pubs. Group.
—The Robot Who Couldn't Cry. Dina, Madalina, illus. 2010. (ENG.). 32p. (J). (gr. -1-2). pap. 9.99 (978-1-907432-01-9(9)) Hogs Back Bks. GBR. Dist: Independent Pubs. Group.
—The Teeny-Weeny Walking Stick. Lambert, Sally Anne, illus. 2010. (ENG.). 32p. (J). (gr. -1-2). pap. 9.99 (978-1-907432-02-6(7)) Hogs Back Bks. GBR. Dist: Independent Pubs. Group.
Hoffmann, Heinrich. Slovenly Kate & Other Stories: From the Struwwelpeter Library. Hosemann, Theodor, illus. 2012. (Dover Children's Classics Ser.). (ENG.). 96p. (J). (gr. 3-5). pap. 12.99 (978-0-486-49032-8(7)) Dover Pubns., Inc.
—Struwwelpeter: Or Pretty Stories & Funny Pictures. Hoffmann, Heinrich, illus. 2010. (ENG., Illus.). 48p. (J). (gr. 2-7). 15.99 (978-1-84365-153-6(X), Pavilion Children's Books) Pavilion Bks. GBR. Dist: Independent Pubs. Group.
Hogan, Robb Dragon. There Was a Time: A Journey into Black & White with Taz. 2003. (Illus.). 43p. 6.00 (978-0-9742178-0-2(8)) TazTales.
Holden, Pam. Stone Soup, 6 pack. Hawley, Kelvin, illus. 2009. (Red Rocket Readers Ser.). (ENG.). 16p. (gr. 2-2). pap. (978-1-877363-84-9(7)) Flying Start Bks.
Holeman, Linda. Toxic Love. 2003. (ENG.). 184p. (J). (gr. 5-9). pap. 8.95 (978-0-88776-647-3(1), Tundra Bks.) Tundra Bks. CAN. Dist: Penguin Random Hse. LLC.
Holland, Karen. The Garden Gang. 2010. (Illus.). 32p. pap. 12.99 (978-1-4490-6532-4(5)) AuthorHouse.
Holling, Holling Clancy. Holling Clancy Holling's Stories from Many Lands. 2014. (ENG., Illus.). 144p. (J). (gr. 3-7). pap. 14.99 (978-0-486-49634-4(1)) Dover Pubns., Inc.
Holly, Julia. Mrs Winkler's Cure. Holly, Julia, illus. 2010. (Illus.). 214p. pap. 19.99 (978-1-883376-45-1(9)) Stellium Pr.
Hood, Karen Jean Matsko. Kids' Kindness Journal: A Daily Journal, bk. 9. Whispering Pine Press International, ed. Artistic Design Service Staff, illus. 2015. (Children's Journal Series). 160p. (J). spiral bd. 15.95 (978-1-59649-416-9(6)) Whispering Pine Pr. International, Inc.
Hooke, R. Schuyler. Thomas & the Treasure. Palone, Terry & Permane, Terry, photos by. 2008. (Thomas & Friends Ser.). (ENG., Illus.). 24p. (J). (gr. -1-2). pap. 3.99 (978-0-375-84287-0(X), Random Hse. Bks. for Young Readers) Random Hse. Children's Bks.
Hooten, K. J. Stories to Amuse the Kids, 1 vol. 2009. 47p. pap. 24.95 (978-1-60749-730-1(1)) PublishAmerica, Inc.
Hooton, Margaret. The Laughing Pot & Other Stories: More Tales for All the Children of the World. 2013. 40p. pap. 16.95 (978-1-4525-8601-4(2), Balboa Pr.) Author Solutions, Inc.
Hope, Kathleen. Jack Eagle the Pirate & Other Mysterious Tales. 2012. (Illus.). 48p. pap. 24.40 (978-1-4678-9611-5(X)) AuthorHouse.
Hope, Laura Lee. The Bobbsey Twins: The First Fifteen Stories, Including Merry Days Indoors & Out, in the Country, at the Seashore, at School, at Snow Lodge, on A. 2013. 1080p. (978-1-78139-372-7(9)) Benediction Classics.
—Short Works of Laura Lee Hope. l.t. ed. 2007. 188p. pap. 21.99 (978-1-4264-2017-7(X)) Creative Media Partners, LLC.
Hopkins, William J. The Sandman: His House Stories (Yesterday's Classics) 2009. 136p. pap. 8.95 (978-1-59915-304-9(1)) Yesterday's Classics.
—The Sandman: His Ship Stories (Yesterday's Classics) Horne, Diantha W., illus. 2009. 174p. pap. 9.95 (978-1-59915-302-5(5)) Yesterday's Classics.
—The Sandman: More Farm Stories (Yesterday's Classics) Williamson, Ada Clendenin, illus. 2009. 150p. pap. 8.95 (978-1-59915-301-8(7)) Yesterday's Classics.
Hopkinson, Deborah. Sky Boys: How They Built the Empire State Building. Ransome, James E., illus. 2012. (ENG.). 48p. (J). (gr. -1-3). pap. 7.99 (978-0-375-86541-1(1), Dragonfly Bks.) Random Hse. Children's Bks.
Hopper, Celia. Violets. 2004. (YA). per. 8.99 (978-0-9754818-7-5(8)) Creative Bk. Pubs.
Horn, Pam, ed. Read-Aloud Classics: 24 Ten-Minute Selections from the World's Best-Loved Children's Books. 2012. (ENG., Illus.). 280p. (J). (gr. -1-17). 14.95 (978-1-57912-920-0(X), Black Dog & Leventhal Pubs. Inc.) Hachette Bks.
Horowitz, Anthony. Bloody Horowitz. 2011. (ENG.). 336p. (J). (gr. 5-18). 6.99 (978-0-14-241874-1(9), Puffin Books) Penguin Young Readers Group.
—The Complete Horowitz Horror. 2008. (ENG.). 448p. (J). (gr. 3-7). 7.99 (978-0-14-241162-9(0), Puffin Books) Penguin Young Readers Group.
Horvath, Polly. Todo Sobre una Wafle. Holguin, Magdalena, tr. Violi, Daniela, illus. 2006. (Coleccion Torre de Papel: Amarilla Ser.). (SPA.). 187p. (J). (gr. 4-7). per. 8.95 (978-958-04-6495-2(2)) Norma S.A. COL. Dist: Distribuidora Norma, Inc.
Houselander, Caryll. Catholic Tales for Boys & Girls. 2003. Orig. Title: Terrible Farmer Timson (New York: Sheed & Ward, 1957). (Illus.). 160p. (J). pap. 11.95 (978-1-928832-74-4(1)) Sophia Institute Pr.
Housman, Laurence. The Field of Clover. 2007. 108p. per. 9.95 (978-1-60312-129-3(3)); 22.95 (978-1-60312-928-2(6)) Aegypan.
Housman, Laurence, ed. Moonshine & Clover. Housman, Clemence, illus. 2013. 236p. (J). pap. (978-1-909302-25-9(2)) Abela Publishing.
Howard, A. G. Untamed (Splintered Series Companion) A Splintered Companion. 2016. (Splintered Ser.). (ENG., Illus.). 304p. (J). (gr. 9-17). pap. 9.95 (978-1-4197-2203-5(4), Amulet Bks.) Abrams, Inc.
Howard, Jim & Welsh-Howard, Paula. Tell Me, Tell Me, What You See. Knight, Vanessa, illus. 2009. 24p. (J). pap. (978-1-926585-65-9(8), CCB Publishing) CCB Publishing.
Howard, Martin. Germs! Stimpson, Colin, illus. 2012. (ENG.). 32p. (J). (gr. k-3). 16.99 (978-1-84365-119-2(X), Pavilion) Pavilion Bks. GBR. Dist: Independent Pubs. Group.
—Wickedest Witch. Stimpson, Colin, illus. 2011. (Witches at War! Ser.: 1). (ENG.). 216p. (J). (gr. 3-7). 12.99 (978-1-84365-131-4(9), Pavilion) Pavilion Bks. GBR. Dist: Independent Pubs. Group.
—The Wild Winter. Stimpson, Colin, illus. 2012. (Witches at War! Ser.: 3). (ENG.). 214p. (J). (gr. 3-7). 12.99 (978-1-84365-180-2(7), Pavilion Children's Books) Pavilion Bks. GBR. Dist: Independent Pubs. Group.
Howe, James. Bunnicula in a Box: Bunnicula; Howliday Inn; the Celery Stalks at Midnight; Nighty-Nightmare; Return to Howliday Inn; Bunnicula Strikes Again; Bunnicula Meets Edgar Allan Crow. Payne, C. F., illus. 2013. (Bunnicula & Friends Ser.). (ENG.). 1136p. (J). (gr. 3-7). pap. 48.99 (978-1-4424-8521-1(3), Atheneum Bks. for Young Readers) Simon & Schuster Children's Publishing.
—The Color of Absence: 12 Stories about Loss & Hope. 2004. 238p. 17.00 (978-0-7569-4097-3(4)) Perfection Learning Corp.
—Harold & Chester Stories. Date not set. (Bunnicula & Friends Ser.). (J). (gr. k-3). (978-0-688-10298-2(0)); lib. bdg. (978-0-688-10299-9(9)) HarperCollins Pubs.
Howe, James, ed. The Color of Absence: 12 Stories about Loss & Hope. 2003. (ENG., Illus.). 256p. (YA). (gr. 7-18). pap. 9.99 (978-0-689-85667-9(9), Atheneum Bks. for Young Readers) Simon & Schuster Children's Publishing.
—13: Thirteen Stories That Capture the Agony & Ecstasy of Being Thirteen. 2006. (ENG., Illus.). 288p. (YA). (gr. 7-12). pap. 7.99 (978-1-4169-2684-9(4), Atheneum Bks. for Young Readers) Simon & Schuster Children's Publishing.
Howe, Kim, illus. American Life Series: Family, Teacher, Friend, 3 books. 2006. 80p. 19.95 (978-1-59971-554-4(6)) Aardvark Global Publishing.
Howells, William Dean. Christmas Every Day & Other Stories. 2008. 68p. pap. 9.99 (978-1-59547-634-0(2)) NuVision Pubns., LLC.
Howker, Janni. El Tejon de la Barca: Y Otras Historias. Tovar Cross, Juan Elias, tr. Janco, Tania, illus. 2003. (la Orilla del Viento Ser.). (SPA.). 160p. (J). per. (978-968-16-6282-0(2)) Fondo de Cultura Economica.
Hoyt, Sarah, et al, eds. Something Magic This Way Comes. 2008. (ENG.). 320p. (gr. 12-18). 7.99 (978-0-7564-0472-7(X), DAW) DAW.
Hronas, Georgia. Tell Us a Story, Grandma: More of Grandma's Orthodox Spiritual Stories. 2005. (ENG., Illus.). 114p. (gr. 3-7). pap. 13.95 (978-1-880971-93-2(3)) Light & Life Publishing Co.
Hubbard, L. Ron, contrib. by. The Crossroads: Literature Guide for Teachers & Librarians, Based on Common Core ELA Standards for Classrooms 6-9. 2013. (Stories from the Golden Age Ser.). (ENG.). 35p. (gr. 6-9). pap., tchr. ed. 14.95 (978-1-59212-810-5(6)) Galaxy Pr., LLC.
Huber, Randy. Of Heroes & Heroines. 2008. 48p. pap. 16.95 (978-1-4241-5421-0(9)) America Star Bks.
Hughes, Shirley. An Evening at Alfie's. Hughes, Shirley, illus. 2009. (Alfie Ser.). (ENG., Illus.). 32p. (J). (gr. k-k). pap. 11.99 (978-1-86230-786-5(5), Red Fox) Random House Children's Books GBR. Dist: Independent Pubs. Group.
Hume, Margaret Anne. Just Mary Reader: Mary Grannan Selected Stories. Evans, Joyce, illus. 2006. (ENG.). 176p. (YA). pap. 24.99 (978-1-55002-598-9(8), Dundurn Pr.) Dundurn CAN. Dist: Ingram Publisher Services.
Hunt, Angela Elwell. Los Tres Árboles: Cento Tradicional. Jonke, Tim, illus. 2010. Orig. Title: The Tale of Three Trees - A Traditional Folktale. (SPA & ENG.). 32p. (J). 5.99 (978-1-4143-3737-1(X)) Tyndale Hse. Pubs.
Hunt, Peter. The Fairy Penguin's Lesson & Other Tales. 2012. 44p. pap. 32.70 (978-1-4797-4712-2(2)) Xlibris Corp.
Hunt, Zoe Paton. Azrael's Magical Moment. 2008. 24p. pap. 18.95 (978-1-60693-070-0(2), Strategic Bk. Publishing) Strategic Book Publishing & Rights Agency (SBPRA).
Hunter, Erin. Tales from the Packs. 2015. (Survivors Ser.). (J). lib. bdg. 17.20 (978-0-606-36959-6(7)) Turtleback Bks.
—The Untold Stories. McLoughlin, Wayne, illus. 2013. (Warriors Ser.). (ENG.). 320p. (J). (gr. 3-7). pap. 6.99 (978-0-06-223292-2(4)) HarperCollins Pubs.
Hunter, Roy. Larry the Bookworm Saves the Day. 2012. 131p. pap. 9.99 (978-1-78035-453-8(3), Fastprint Publishing) Upfront Publishing Ltd. GBR. Dist: Printondemand-worldwide.com.
Hurrell, Dianne. Tom Burrows & Friends: Short Stories, Rhymes & Poems. 2010. (ENG., Illus.). 50p. pap. (978-1-84748-782-7(3)) Athena Pr.
Hurt, John Washington, reader. Rabbit Ears World Tales. 2007. (J). 34.99 (978-0-7393-7549-5(0)) Findaway World, LLC.
Hurwitz, Johanna, ed. I Fooled You: Ten Stories of Tricks, Jokes & Switcheroos. Nihoff, Tim, illus. 2010. (ENG.). 192p. (J). (gr. 4-7). 16.99 (978-0-7636-3789-7(0)) Candlewick Pr.
Hush Foundation Staff. The Hush Treasure Book. 2015. (ENG., Illus.). 48p. (J). (gr. -1-5). 23.99 (978-1-76011-279-0(8)) Allen & Unwin AUS. Dist: Independent Pubs. Group.
Hutchens, David. PageLand: A Story about Love & Sharing & Working Together. Gombert, Bobby, illus. 2004. (gr. 4-8). 14.99 (978-0-8054-2726-4(0)) B&H Publishing Group.
A I am a Gypsy Pot Set, 6 vols. 32p. (gr. 1-3). 31.50 (978-0-322-00336-1(9)); 26.50 (978-0-7802-8041-0(5)) Wright Group/McGraw-Hill.
I Never Want to go There Again. 2007. per. (978-1-59916-217-1(2)) Printing Systems.
I Was a Tree Once. 2008. 272p. pap. 17.95 (978-0-595-52197-5(5)) iUniverse, Inc.
I Write Short Stories by Kids for Kids. 2013. 336p. pap. 9.99 (978-0-9854705-5-5(0)) LongTale Publishing, LLC.
Ibañez, Vincente Blasco & Lorente, Mariano J. Last Lion & Other Stories. 73p. (J). pap. 5.95 (978-0-8283-1444-2(6)) Branden Bks.
Ihebereme, Chidozie . N. Dad Says Write. 2007. per. (978-1-59872-954-2(3)) Instant Pub.
Ikpe, Ernest & Madge. African Stories about the Tortoise. 2011. 32p. pap. 17.00 (978-1-4634-2726-9(3)) AuthorHouse.
Illustrated Fables from Around the World. 2017. (Illustrated Stories Ser.). (ENG.). (J). 19.99 (978-0-7945-3944-3(0), Usborne) EDC Publishing.
Imagine This... Stories Inspired by Agriculture 2012: Stories Inspired by Agriculture 2012. 2013. (ENG., Illus.). 96p. (J). pap. 6.00 (978-0-9850855-1-3(7)) California Foundation for Agriculture in the Classroom.
Impey, Rose. Kerching! 2012. (ENG., Illus.). 192p. (J). (gr. 2-4). pap. 7.99 (978-1-4083-1209-4(3)) Hodder & Stoughton GBR. Dist: Hachette Bk. Group.
Infante, Begona. Takao Yo Soy de Japon (I'm from Japan) (SPA.). 32p. (J). 12.95 (978-84-246-9402-9(3)) La Galera, S.A. Editorial ESP. Dist: AIMS International Bks., Inc.
Ingalls, Melodi J. Everyone Is Differphant. 2008. 20p. pap. 11.99 (978-1-4389-1206-6(4)) AuthorHouse.
International Thriller Writers Association Staff. Fear: 13 Stories of Suspense & Horror. Stine, R. L., ed. 2010. (ENG.). 320p. (YA). (gr. 7-18). 16.99 (978-0-525-42168-9(8), Dutton Books for Young Readers) Penguin Young Readers Group.
Ionesco, Eugène. Stories 1,2,3,4. Delessert, Etienne, illus. 2012. (ENG.). 112p. (J). (gr. k-5). 19.95 (978-1-936365-51-7(0)) McSweeney's Publishing.
Ionescu, Angela C. Cuentos y Leyendas de Rumania. (Torre de Papel Ser.). (SPA.). (J). (gr. 4-18). 8.95 (978-958-04-0781-2(9)) Norma S.A. COL. Dist: Distribuidora Norma, Inc.
Irvine, Patricia McCune. Haunted Pavilion: And Other Short Stories. 2003. 144p. 21.95 (978-0-595-75249-2(7)) iUniverse, Inc.
Irving, Washington. The Legend of Sleepy Hollow & Other Stories. McKowen, Scott, illus. 2013. (Sterling Unabridged Classics Ser.). (ENG.). 96p. (J). (gr. 5). 9.95 (978-1-4549-0871-5(8)) Sterling Publishing Co., Inc.
—The Legend of Sleepy Hollow & Other Stories from the Sketch Book. 2006. (ENG., Illus.). 384p. (gr. 12-18). mass mkt. 6.95 (978-0-451-53012-7(8), Signet) Penguin Publishing Group.
—The Legend of Sleepy Hollow & Rip Van Winkle, 1 vol. McWilliam, Howard, illus. 2011. (Calico Illustrated Classics Ser.). (ENG.). 112p. (YA). (gr. 3-6). 27.07 (978-1-60270-747-4(2)) Magic Wagon.
—Rip Van Winkle. 2010. (Illus.). 40p. (J). 19.95 (978-1-58341-923-6(3), Creative Education) Creative Co., The.
—Rip Van Winkle & Other Stories. 2011. (Puffin Classics Ser.). (ENG.). 208p. (J). (gr. 5-7). 4.99 (978-0-14-133092-1(9), Puffin Books) Penguin Young Readers Group.
—Washington Irving. Hall, Tracy, illus. 2004. (Great American Short Stories Ser.). 80p. (gr. 4-7). lib. bdg. 24.00 (978-0-8368-4253-1(7), Gareth Stevens Learning Library) Stevens, Gareth Publishing LLLP.
Isaacs, John. A Doggone Good Story. 2009. 30p. pap. 16.50 (978-1-60693-471-5(6), Eloquent Bks.) Strategic Book Publishing & Rights Agency (SBPRA).
Isol. Secreto de Familia. 2003. (Los Primerisimos Ser.). (SPA.). 48p. (J). pap. 8.50 (978-968-16-7046-7(9)) Fondo de Cultura Economica USA.
Itterman, Bert. Growing up with Grandpa. 2006. (Illus.). 112p. pap. (978-1-57579-330-6(X)) Pine Hill Pr.
Iturrondo, Angeles Molina. Pepitina. Guevara, Dennis Villanueva, illus. 2004. (Green Ser.). 24p. (J). (978-1-57581-435-3(8)) Ediciones Santillana, Inc.
—Sapo Sapito Sapote. Umpierre, Migdalia, illus. 2004. (Green Ser.). 24p. (J). (978-1-57581-440-7(4)) Ediciones Santillana, Inc.
Iturrondo, Angeles Molina & Iguina, Adriana. The Lost Sock. Ortiz Montanez, Nivea, illus. 2004. (Green Ser.). 24p. (J). (978-1-57581-434-6(X)) Ediciones Santillana, Inc.
Iwamura, Kazuo & Yamashita, Haruo. Seven Little Mice Go to the Beach. 2012. (ENG., Illus.). 32p. (J). (gr. -1-1). 16.95 (978-0-7358-4073-7(3)) North-South Bks., Inc.
Jacen, Kris, ed. Lost & Found. 2013. 430p. pap. 17.99 (978-1-60820-866-1(4)) MLR Pr., LLC.
Jack In The Box Staff. Favorite Children's Stories by Jack in T. 2005. pap. 30.95 (978-1-4179-8943-0(2)) Kessinger Publishing, LLC.
Jackson, Carolyn E. Tales from the Master. 2004. per. 12.95 (978-0-9745866-2-5(5)) Innate Foundation Publishing.
Jackson, Ruth Montgomery. A Bit of Magic with Wee Willie & Double Trouble. 2011. 76p. pap. 27.50 (978-1-4567-0050-8(2)) AuthorHouse.
Jacobs, Evan. Zombies! 2014. (Red Rhino Ser.). (J). lib. bdg. 18.40 (978-0-606-36243-6(6)) Turtleback Bks.
James, Jake. Jake s Short Stories. 2010. 64p. pap. 10.99 (978-1-60957-640-0(3)) Salem Author Services.
Jamieson, Marianne & Benchmark Education Co. Staff. Analytical Arguments about Four Pioneers of Flight. 2014. (Text Connections Ser.). (J). (gr. 6). (978-1-4900-1538-5(8)) Benchmark Education Co.
Jamiol, Paul. Bikers Are Animals: A Children's Book on Motorcycling. Habib, Linda, ed. 2009. 38p. pap. 14.95 (978-1-60844-232-4(2)) Dog Ear Publishing, LLC.
Jansson, Tove. Tales from Moominvalley. Warburton, Thomas, tr. Jansson, Tove, illus. 2010. (Moomins Ser.: 6).Tr. of Osynliga Barnet. (ENG., Illus.). 192p. (J). (gr. 4-7). pap. 7.99 (978-0-312-62542-9(1), 9780312625429) Square Fish.
Jasnoch, Dorothy. Frankie the Bunny: Helping the Birds. Korzeniowski, Samson O., ed. Jasnoch, Dorothy, illus. 2013. (Illus.). 28p. 17.99 (978-1-937752-20-0(8)) Owl About Bks. Pub., Inc.
—Frankie the Bunny: Mystery in the Forest. Korzeniowski, Samson O., ed. Jasnoch, Dorothy, illus. 2013. (Illus.). 32p. 17.99 (978-1-937752-16-3(X)) Owl About Bks. Pub., Inc.
—Frankie the Bunny: The Fall Scramble Begins. Korzeniowski, Samson O., ed. Jasnoch, Dorothy, illus. 2013. (Illus.). 28p. 17.99 (978-1-937752-19-4(4)) Owl About Bks. Pub., Inc.
—Frankie the Bunny: Woodland Warning. Korzeniowski, Samson O., ed. Jasnoch, Dorothy, illus. 2013. (Illus.). 28p. 17.99 (978-1-937752-18-7(6)) Owl About Bks. Pub., Inc.
—Frankie the Bunny: Woodland Warning. Korzeniowski, Samson, ed. Jasnoch, Dorothy, illus. 2012. (Illus.). 28p. pap. 12.99 (978-1-937752-03-3(8)) Owl About Bks. Pub., Inc.
—Frankie the Bunny Helping the Birds. Korzeniowski, Samson, ed. Jasnoch, Dorothy, illus. 2012. (ENG., Illus.). 28p. pap. 12.99 (978-1-937752-05-7(4)) Owl About Bks. Pub., Inc.
—Frankie the Bunny the Fall Scramble Begins. Korzeniowski, Samson, ed. Jasnoch, Dorothy, illus. 2012. (Illus.). 28p. pap. 12.99 (978-1-937752-04-0(6)) Owl About Bks. Pub., Inc.
Jay, Em. Once. 2009. 28p. pap. 12.50 (978-1-4490-2662-2(1)) AuthorHouse.
Jeanmarie, Michele. Curiosity, Curiosity: Lost in an Array. 2008. 74p. pap. 19.95 (978-1-60610-169-8(2)) America Star Bks.
Jeffers, Oliver. Once upon an Alphabet: Short Stories for All the Letters. Jeffers, Oliver, illus. 2014. (ENG., Illus.). 112p. (J). (gr. -1-k). 26.99 (978-0-399-16791-1(9), Philomel Bks.) Penguin Publishing Group.
—Once upon an Alphabet: Short Stories for All the Letters. Jeffers, Oliver, illus. 2017. (ENG., Illus.). 26p. (J). (— 1). bds. 8.99 (978-0-399-54542-9(5), Philomel Bks.) Penguin Young Readers Group.
Jeffrey, Leonard J. Journeys of the Mind-Book. 2012. 140p. pap. 39.88 (978-1-4669-3873-1(0)) Trafford Publishing.
—Journeys of the Mind-Book. 2011. 116p. (J). pap. (978-1-4269-9333-6(1)) Trafford Publishing (UK) Ltd.
Jelloun, Tahar Ben. Papa, Que Es el Racismo? 2003.Tr. of Racism Explained to My Daughter. (SPA.). 92p. (J). (gr. 3-5). pap. 8.95 (978-968-19-1014-3(1)) Santillana USA Publishing Co., Inc.

Jepson, Gill. Out of Time: The Secret of the Swan. 2011. (ENG.). 144p. pap. *(978-1-84876-612-9(2))* Troubador Publishing Ltd.

Jess & Jaylen (Set). 8 vols. 2014. (Jess & Jaylen Ser.). (ENG.). (J). (gr. 1-4). 216.56 *(978-1-60973-168-7(9),* 208272) Child's World, Inc., The.

Jian, Li. The Water Dragon: A Chinese Legend. 2012. (ENG., Illus.). 42p. (J). (gr. -1-3). 16.95 *(978-1-60220-978-7(2))* BetterLink Pr., Inc.

Jippes, Daan, et al. Walt Disney's Comics & Stories #703. 2009. 64p. pap. 7.99 *(978-1-60360-093-4(0))* Gemstone Publishing, Inc.

Jobling, Curtis. Max Helsing & the Thirteenth Curse. 2016. (Max Helsing: Monster Hunter Ser.: Vol. 1). (ENG.). 336p. (J). (gr. 5). 19.65 *(978-0-606-39334-8(X))* Turtleback Bks.

Jocelyn, Marthe, ed. First Times: Stories Selected by Marthe Jocelyn. 2007. (ENG.). 200p. (YA). (gr. 5-8). pap. 9.95 *(978-0-88776-777-7(X),* Tundra Bks.) Tundra Bks. CAN. Dist: Penguin Random Hse. LLC.

Jocelyn, Marthe, selected by. Secrets. 2005. (ENG.). 184p. (J). (gr. 4-7). pap. 8.95 *(978-0-88776-723-4(0),* Tundra Bks.) Tundra Bks. CAN. Dist: Penguin Random Hse. LLC.

Jocelyn, Marthe & Scrimger, Richard. Viminy Crowe's Comic Book. Dávila, Claudia, illus. 2014. (ENG.). 336p. (J). (gr. 4-7). 17.99 *(978-1-77049-479-4(0),* Tundra Bks.) Tundra Bks. CAN. Dist: Penguin Random Hse. LLC.

Johnson, Alice W. & Warner, Allison H. Believe & You're There When Ammon Was a Missionary. Harston, Jerry, illus. 2010. (J). *(978-1-60641-247-3(7))* Deseret Bk. Co.

Johnson, Bud. Chirpy: Chirpy's First Time Flying. 2013. 32p. pap. 13.99 *(978-1-4525-6763-1(8))* Balboa Pr.

Johnson, James. Sugar & Spice. 2007. (Illus.). 48p. per. *(978-1-4065-3490-0(0))* Dodo Pr.

Johnson, James A. The Terror & the Talking Stick: Sundown Stories II. 2011. 56p. pap. 8.95 *(978-1-4502-8156-0(7))* iUniverse, Inc.

Johnson, Jane. Legends of the Shadow World: The Secret Country; the Shadow World; Dragon's Fire. Stower, Adam, illus. 2010. (ENG.). 1120p. (J). (gr. 3-7). pap. 14.99 *(978-1-4169-9082-6(8),* Simon & Schuster Bks. For Young Readers) Simon & Schuster Bks. For Young Readers.

Johnson, Liliane & Dufton, Jo S. Children's Chillers & Thrillers. Bruhn, Joan Z., illus. 136p. (Orig.). (J). pap. 10.00 *(978-0-930069-04-9(8))* Jasmine Pr.

Johnson, Miri & Wachtel, Aleina, eds. 'Twas the Night Before... A Collection of Short Stories by Orchard Middle School Students. 2008. 212p. (YA). pap. 8.77 *(978-0-9663560-3-8(9),* Orchard Pr.) Point Publishing.

Johnson, Rossiter, ed. Stories of Childhood. 2007. 164p. per. *(978-1-4065-3497-9(8))* Dodo Pr.

—Stories of Comedy. 2007. 168p. per. *(978-1-4065-3498-6(6))* Dodo Pr.

Johnson, Sally. Alfabeto Animal.Tr. of Animal Alphabet. (SPA., Illus.). (J). pap. 10.95 *(978-950-04-2009-9(0))* Emecé Editores S.A. ARG. Dist: Planeta Publishing Corp.

Johnson, Tammie D. Tammie's Tales: An ABC Cat Series Featuring Simon, the S Cat. 2004. (J). 14.95 *(978-1-58597-288-3(6))* Leathers Publishing.

Johnston, Annie Fellows. Mildred's Inheritance, Just Her Way & Ann's Own Way. Home, Diantha W., illus. 2007. 48p. per. *(978-1-4065-3515-0(X))* Dodo Pr.

Jones, Carl L. Aaron Burrd, the Paranoid Bird with Acute Acrophobi. Vicki, Jones, ed. 2008. 88p. pap. 16.00 *(978-0-9748266-2-2(6))* Grampa Jones's Publishing Co.

Jones, Carol. Lake of the Lost. 2005. (Illus.). 160p. pap. *(978-0-7344-0646-0(0),* Lothian Children's Bks.) Hachette Australia.

Jones, Diana Wynne. Unexpected Magic: Collected Stories. 2006. 608p. (J). (gr. 3-7). per. 7.99 *(978-0-06-055535-1(1),* Greenwillow Bks.) HarperCollins Pubs.

Jones, Karen. Stories from the Television Show Imagination Way. 2006. 10.00 *(978-0-8059-8195-7(0))* Dorrance Publishing Co., Inc.

Jones, Karen Lee. Giggle with Friends from Imagination Way. 2007. pap. 11.00 *(978-0-8059-8475-0(5))* Dorrance Publishing Co., Inc.

Jones, Marcia Thornton & Dadey, Debbie. Guys & Ghouls. Francis, Guy, illus. 2006. (Ghostville Elementary Ser.: Bk. 13). 81p. *(978-0-439-79402-2(1))* Scholastic, Inc.

Jones, Vernon. Aesop's Fables. Rackham, Arthur, illus. 2007. 160p. (J). pap. 5.00 *(978-0-9788914-4-2(9))* Kahley, Glenn.

Jones, Wendy & Blackwell, Su. The Fairy-Tale Princess: Seven Classic Stories from the Enchanted Forest. 2012. (ENG., Illus.). 96p. (J). 19.95 *(978-0-500-65006-6(3),* 565006) Thames & Hudson.

Jordan, Deloris. Dream Big: Michael Jordan & the Pursuit of Excellence. Root, Barry, illus. 2014. (ENG.). 32p. (J). (gr. -1-3). 7.99 *(978-1-4424-1270-5(4),* Simon & Schuster/Paula Wiseman Bks.) Simon & Schuster/Paula Wiseman Bks.

José, F. Sionil. The Molave & the Orchid & Other Children's Stories. 2004. (Illus.). v, 37p. *(978-971-8845-40-0(2))* Solidaridad Publishing Hse.

Joseph, Lynn. El Color de Mis Palabras. 2004. (SPA., Illus.). (YA). pap. 5.99 *(978-1-930332-75-1(0))* Lectorum Pubns., Inc.

Joseph, Taylor S., compiled by. Your Stories, Volume 1. 2012. (ENG.). 223p. (J). pap. 14.95 *(978-0-9851990-0-5(8))* Four Star Publishing.

Joy Cowley Novels: Novel Set. (Joy Cowley Novels Ser.). 181p. (gr. 3-6). 16.50 *(978-0-7802-8509-5(3))* Wright Group/McGraw-Hill.

Juliao, David Sanchez. El País Mas Hermosod del Mundo. 2012. (Torre de Papel Ser.). (SPA., Illus.). 146p. (gr. 3-5). pap. 10.99 *(978-958-04-0747-8(9))* Norma S.A. COL. Dist: Lectorum Pubns., Inc.

Juravel, Rabbi. A Journey with Rabbi Juravel: The Great Escape & Other Stories, Vol. 3. 2004. (Illus.). 252p. (J). 22.95 *(978-1-931681-63-6(5))* Israel Bookshop Pubns.

Kafer, Kathy & Benchmark Education Co. Staff. Analytical Arguments about Folklore. 2014. (Text Connections Ser.). (J). (gr. 6). *(978-1-4900-1522-4(1))* Benchmark Education Co.

Kalpish Ratna. Nyagrodha. Pandya, Yamini, illus. 2006. 287p. (J). *(978-0-670-04969-1(7),* Puffin) Penguin Publishing Group.

Kandimba, V. T. Folktales from Zimbabwe: Short Stores. 2009. (Illus.). 56p. 24.99 *(978-1-4415-4281-6(7))* Xlibris Corp.

Kandimba, Vt. Folk Tales from Zimbabwe. 2009. 58p. pap. 15.99 *(978-1-4415-4280-9(9))* Xlibris Corp.

Kangira, Jairos. Creatures Great & Small: A Collection of Short Stories. 2005. vi, 114p. *(978-0-86922-786-2(6))* Mambo Pr.

Kanzler, Janine. Things Are Not As They Seem. 2004. 92p. (YA). 14.00 *(978-0-9759363-0-6(1))* Fernhouse Pr.

Kao, Sleepless. Monchan's Bag. 2010. (ENG., Illus.). 36p. (J). (gr. -1-3). 16.95 *(978-1-897476-32-1(9))* Simply Read Bks. CAN. Dist: Ingram Publisher Services.

Karl, Jean E. The Turning Place: Stories of a Future Past. 2016. (ENG.). 224p. (YA). (gr. 5-8). pap. 7.99 *(978-0-486-80459-0(3))* Dover Pubns., Inc.

Karlin, Ann Bell. Eight Bedtime Stories for Jewish Children. Mazo, Chaim, ed. 2012. 64p. pap. 11.95 *(978-1-936778-67-6(X))* Mazo Pubs.

Katz, Karen. Princess Baby. Katz, Karen, illus. 2012. (Princess Baby Ser.). (ENG., Illus.). 30p. (J). (gr. k-k). bds. 7.99 *(978-0-307-93146-7(3),* Schwartz & Wade Bks.) Random Hse. Children's Bks.

Kavanagh, Herminie Templeton. Darby O'Gill & the Crocks of Gold: And Other Irish Tales. Schluenderfritz, Ted, illus. 2003. ix, 155p. (J). pap. 14.95 *(978-1-928832-85-0(7))* Sophia Institute Pr.

Kawahara, Yumiko. Dolls, Vol. 2. Kawahara, Yumiko, illus. 2005. (Dolls Ser.: 2). (ENG., Illus.). 216p. pap. 9.99 *(978-1-59116-670-2(5))* Viz Media.

Kay, Tiny Turtle's Holiday Sleeptime Stories Collection. 2010. 32p. pap. 14.99 *(978-1-4520-0687-1(3))* AuthorHouse.

Kaye, Danny. Danny Kaye's Stories from Far Away Places. Bevans Marks And Barrow, illus. 2011. 30p. 35.95 *(978-1-258-00232-9(9))* Literary Licensing, LLC.

—Danny Kaye's Stories from Many Lands. 2011. 32p. pap. 35.95 *(978-1-258-00179-7(9))* Literary Licensing, LLC.

Keary, Annie & Keary, Eliza. Tales of the Norse Warrior Gods: The Heroes of Asgard. Brock, C. E., illus. 2005. (ENG.). 272p. (gr. 3-7). per. 9.95 *(978-0-486-44053-8(2))* Dover Pubns., Inc.

Keaton, Skeet. The Adventures of Jd Losey. 2005. pap. 9.99 *(978-1-59781-353-2(2))* Salem Author Services.

Keenan, Sheila. Dogs of War. Fox, Nathan, illus. 2013. (ENG.). 176p. (J). (gr. 3-7). pap. 12.99 *(978-0-545-12888-9(9),* Graphix) Scholastic, Inc.

Keep Calm! Individual Title Six-Packs. (Bookweb Ser.). 32p. (gr. 4-18). 34.00 *(978-0-7635-3732-6(2))* Rigby Education.

Kellogg, Catherine Berry. The Moose Who Ate My Fort: Stories from Bella Sage. 2008. 36p. pap. 24.95 *(978-1-60441-696-1(3))* America Star Bks.

Kelly, L. Meme's Christmas Stories. 2005. pap. 16.95 *(978-1-4241-0026-2(7))* America Star Bks.

Kelsey, Avonelle. Grandma Says, 4 bks., Set. Kelsey, Avonelle, illus. (Series of Short Stories). (Illus.). 200p. (J). *(978-0-9640610-1-9(5))* Cheval International.

Kelsey, Juliet Grey. Nettie by the Sea Stories: Set I. 2010. 56p. pap. 23.99 *(978-1-4490-9452-2(X))* AuthorHouse.

Kemp, Dane. Imaginary Tales. 2011. 186p. pap. 24.95 *(978-1-4560-4686-6(1))* America Star Bks.

Kendall, Grace, ed. I See Reality: Twelve Short Stories about Real Life. 2016. (ENG.). 304p. (YA). 17.99 *(978-0-374-30258-0(8),* 9780374302580, Farrar, Straus & Giroux (BYR)) Farrar, Straus & Giroux.

Kendall, Penny. Sleepy Baby. 2011. (Illus.). 14p. bds. *(978-1-84089-609-1(4))* Zero to Ten, Ltd.

—Socks. 2011. (Illus.). 14p. bds. *(978-1-84089-608-4(6))* Zero to Ten, Ltd.

Kenner, Crystal R. The King of All Tickle Bugs & Other Stories. 2011. (Illus.). 124p. (gr. -1). pap. 10.95 *(978-1-4502-9466-9(9))* iUniverse, Inc.

Kenrick, Joanna. Tears of a Friend. 2004. (Shades Ser.). 56p. (J). pap. *(978-0-237-52731-0(6))* Evans Brothers, Ltd.

Kerrin, Jessica Scott & Kerrin, Jessica. Martin Bridge: On the Lookout! Kelly, Joseph, illus. 2005. (Martin Bridge Ser.). (ENG.). 144p. (J). (gr. 2-5). 6.95 *(978-1-55337-773-3(7))* Kids Can Pr., Ltd. CAN. Dist: Hachette Bk. Group.

Kerwin, Betsy. The Adventures of Floret the Woodland Fairy: The Adventures Begin. 2008. 44p. pap. 18.49 *(978-1-4343-9426-2(3))* AuthorHouse.

Kessler, Ramon Wilke. Treasure Trove of Pirate Stories: A Collection of Best Pirate Stories for Young People. Scott, A. O., illus. 2011. 294p. 48.95 *(978-1-258-05706-0(9))* Literary Licensing, LLC.

Keys, Demetria M. The Replacements. 2007. 68p. per. 7.95 *(978-1-4327-0649-4(7))* Outskirts Pr., Inc.

Keyser, Francois. Tiger Loses His Stripes. 2013. (ENG.). 24p. pap. 20.00 *(978-1-4669-9203-0(4))* Trafford Publishing.

Kibuishi, Kazu. The Lost Islands. 2013. (Explorer Ser.). (ENG., Illus.). 128p. (J). (gr. 3-7). 19.95 *(978-1-4197-0881-7(3));* pap. 10.95 *(978-1-4197-0883-1(X))* Abrams, Inc. (Amulet Bks.).

—The Mystery Boxes. 2012. (Explorer Ser.: 2). (YA). lib. bdg. 22.05 *(978-0-606-23820-5(4),* Turtleback) Turtleback Bks.

Kibuishi, Kazu, ed. The Mystery Boxes. 2012. (Explorer Ser.). (ENG., Illus.). 128p. (gr. 4-17). pap. 10.95 *(978-1-4197-0009-5(X));* (YA). 19.95 *(978-1-4197-0010-1(3))* Abrams, Inc. (Amulet Bks.).

Kick, J. D. The Amazing Tale of Archie the Alligator. Just, John, illus. 2nd ed. 2003. (J). per. 12.95 *(978-1-929424-14-6(0),* Owl Creek Farm Bks.) Owl Tree Pr.

Kiesling Garrett, Doris. The Butterfly Book das Schmetterling Buch. 2013. 76p. pap. 25.24 *(978-1-4669-7803-4(1))* Trafford Publishing.

Kiick, Lisa. Bailey & Friends. Stouch, Ryan, illus. 2008. 40p. pap. 14.95 *(978-1-59858-743-2(9))* Dog Ear Publishing, LLC.

Kilgore, Lee. The Mr. Munch Adventures: Six Short Stories, 1 vol. 2010. 73p. pap. 19.95 *(978-1-4489-2876-7(1))* America Star Bks.

Kim, Ja Youn. A Song of Pots. Kim, Seung Ae, tr. 2013. 98p. pap. 11.97 *(978-1-62212-984-3(9),* Strategic Bk. Publishing) Strategic Book Publishing & Rights Agency (SBPRA).

Kimani, Kamande. Why the Hyena Has Short Hind Legs. Therrian, John, illus. 2011. 40p. pap. 24.95 *(978-1-4560-5468-7(6))* America Star Bks.

Kimmel, Eric A. The Lady in the Blue Cloak: Legends from the Texas Missions. Guevara, Susan, illus. 2006. (ENG.). 40p. (J). (gr. 6-10). 16.95 *(978-0-8234-1738-4(7))* Holiday Hse., Inc.

Kimmel, Eric A. & Kang, Setha. The Rolling Stone: And Other Read Aloud Stories. Kuon, Vuthy, illus. 2004. 36p. (J). (gr. k-6). 15.95 *(978-0-9651661-2-6(0))* Providence Publishing.

Kindt, Matt. Super Spy. 2007. (Super Spy Ser.). (ENG., Illus.). 304p. pap. 19.95 *(978-1-891830-96-9(1),* 9781891830969) Top Shelf Productions.

King, Ken. The Sunflower. Kearney, Jennifer, illus. 2008. 24p. (J). pap. 14.99 *(978-1-4343-8463-8(2))* AuthorHouse.

KING, R. O. N. S. A trilogy of magical Tales. 2010. 500p. pap. 26.95 *(978-1-4461-4016-1(4))* Lulu Pr., Inc.

Kinney, Scott. Kozmik. O'Reilly, Sean Patrick, ed. 2013. (Illus.). 78p. (J). pap. 14.95 *(978-1-927424-51-3(8))* Arcana Studio, Inc.

Kipling, Rudyard. A Collection of Rudyard Kipling's Just So Stories. Sís, Peter, illus. 2004. (ENG.). 128p. (J). (gr. k-12). 22.99 *(978-0-7636-2629-7(5))* Candlewick Pr.

—The Complete Children's Short Stories. 2005. (ENG., Illus.). 864p. pap. *(978-1-84022-057-5(0))* Wordsworth Editions, Ltd.

—The Jungle Books. 2004. (Barnes & Noble Classics Ser.). (ENG., Illus.). 432p. pap. 7.95 *(978-1-59308-109-6(X))* Barnes & Noble, Inc.

—The Jungle Books. 2013. (ENG.). 384p. (gr. 12). mass mkt. 5.95 *(978-0-451-41918-7(9),* Signet) Penguin Publishing Group.

—Just So Stories. Kipling, Rudyard, illus. 2017. (ENG., Illus.). 224p. (J). pap. 9.99 ***(978-1-84749-637-9(7),*** 9781847496379, Alma Classics) Bloomsbury Publishing USA.

—Just So Stories. Lewis, Lisa, ed. 2009. (Oxford World's Classics Ser.). (ENG., Illus.). 304p. pap. 6.95 *(978-0-19-953860-7(3))* Oxford Univ. Pr., Inc.

—Just So Stories. Latimer, Alex, illus. 2008. (Puffin Classics Ser.). (ENG.). (J). (gr. 5). lib. bdg. 15.60 ***(978-1-61383-686-6(4))*** Perfection Learning Corp.

—Just So Stories. Bransom, Paul & Gleeson, J. M., illus. 2016. (ENG.). 256p. (J). (gr. 1). 16.99 *(978-1-944686-44-4(4),* Racehorse Publishing) Skyhorse Publishing Co., Inc.

—Just So Stories. Gleeson, J. M. & Bransom, Paul, illus. 2009. 208p. pap. 9.95 *(978-1-59915-172-4(3))* Yesterday's Classics.

—Just So Stories. 2017. (ENG., Illus.). (J). (gr. 4-6). 27.99 ***(978-1-366-55594-6(5))*** Blurb, Inc.

—Just So Stories. 2015. (ENG., Illus.). (J). (gr. 4-6). 25.95 ***(978-1-296-60798-2(4));*** 25.95 ***(978-1-296-58896-0(3))*** Creative Media Partners, LLC.

—Just So Stories. 2016. (ENG., Illus.). (J). (gr. 4). pap. ***(978-1-911224-13-6(1))*** Emma Stern Publishing.

—Just So Stories For Little Children. Date not set. (Illus.). 192p. (YA). (gr. 3-18). reprint ed. 7.95 *(978-1-56852-137-4(5),* Konecky & Konecky) Konecky, William S. Assocs., Inc.

—Just So Stories Set: For Little Children. Salter, Safaya, illus. 2003. (Chrysalis Childrens Classics Ser.). 125p. (YA). pap. *(978-1-84365-036-2(3),* Pavilion Children's Books) Pavilion Bks.

—Rikki-Tikki-Tavi & Toomai of the Elephants. 2008. (Unabridged Classics (in Audio) Ser.). (J). pap. 36.00 incl. audio compact disk *(978-1-58472-431-5(5),* In Audio) Sound Room Pubs., Inc.

—Rudyard Kipling: The Complete Children's Short Stories. 2006. (Illus.). 864p. (J). (gr. 4-8). reprint ed. pap. 22.00 *(978-0-7567-9857-4(4))* DIANE Publishing Co.

Kirby, Matthew. Spider Stories. 2007. (ENG.). 242p. pap. 14.99 *(978-1-4196-6359-8(3))* CreateSpace Independent Publishing Platform.

Kirby, Stan. The Captain Awesome Collection: A MI-TEE Boxed Set: Captain Awesome to the Rescue!; Captain Awesome vs. Nacho Cheese Man; Captain Awesome & the New Kid; Captain Awesome Takes a Dive. O'Connor, George, illus. 2013. (Captain Awesome Ser.). (ENG.). 512p. (J). (gr. k-2). pap. 23.99 *(978-1-4424-8977-6(4),* Little Simon) Little Simon.

Kirkham, Tyler & Kirkham, Rian. My Best Friend's a Booger. O'Reilly, Sean Patrick, ed. 2012. (Illus.). 32p. pap. 6.95 *(978-1-926914-36-7(8))* Arcana Studio, Inc.

Kirkman, Robert. Super Dinosaur, Vol. 1. 2011. (ENG., Illus.). 128p. (J). pap. 9.99 *(978-1-60706-420-6(0),* 9781607064206) Image Comics.

Kjelgaard, Jim. Eleven Novels by Jim Kjelgaard Including: The Spell of the White Sturgeon, the Lost Wagon, Trading Jeff & His Dog, Double. 2013. 1158p. *(978-1-78139-365-9(6))* Benediction Classics.

Klick, Kenn. Little Coyote Tales. 2007. 128p. pap. 12.95 *(978-0-615-16770-1(5))* BlueCougar Studios.

Kloepfer, John. The Zombie Chasers. Wolfhard, Steve, illus. 2011. (Zombie Chasers Ser.: 1). (ENG.). 224p. (J). (gr. 3-7). pap. 6.99 *(978-0-06-185306-7(2))* HarperCollins Pubs.

The Klondike Kid. 2005. (J). pap. *(978-1-60015-070-8(5))* Steps To Literacy, LLC.

Klutz Editors, contrib. by. Wishing Stars. (ENG.). 5.95 *(978-1-57054-560-3(X))* Klutz.

Koch, Claus. The Three Little Wolves & the Big Bad Boar. 2011. 68p. pap. 9.99 *(978-1-4520-5321-9(9))* AuthorHouse.

Kochalka, James. Dragon Puncher Book 2: Dragon Puncher Island: Dragon Puncher Island. 2011. (Dragon Puncher Ser.: 2). (ENG., Illus.). 40p. (J). (gr. 2-5). 9.95 *(978-1-60309-085-8(1),* 9781603090858) Top Shelf Productions.

Kola, Pamela, ed. East African How Stories. 2003. (Illus.). 48p. pap. *(978-9966-46-472-9(7))* Heinemann Kenya, Limited (East African Educational Publishers Ltd E.A.E.P.) KEN. Dist: Michigan State Univ. Pr.

—East African Why Stories. 2003. (Illus.). 48p. pap. *(978-9966-46-448-4(4))* Heinemann Kenya, Limited (East African Educational Publishers Ltd E.A.E.P.) KEN. Dist: Michigan State Univ. Pr.

Kondrchek, Jamie. A Day in the Life (Un Dia en la Vida), 4 vols., Set. Vega, Eida de la, tr. Rasemas, Joe, illus. Incl. My Favorite Time of Day (Mi Hora Preferida del Dia) lib. bdg. 25.70 *(978-1-58415-837-0(9));* On My Way to School (De Camino a la Escuela) Rasemas, Joe. 25.70 *(978-1-58415-840-0(9));* What Day Is It? (Que Dia Es Hoy?) Rasemas, Joe. 25.70 *(978-1-58415-838-7(7));* What Should I Wear Today? (Que Ropa Me Pondre Hoy?) Rasemas, Joe. 25.70 *(978-1-58415-839-4(5));* (Illus.). 32p. (J). (gr. -1-1). 2009. (ENG & SPA.). 2009. Set lib. bdg. 102.80 *(978-1-58415-844-8(1))* Mitchell Lane Pubs., Inc.

Konigsburg, E. L. Altogether, One at a Time. Mayer, Mercer et al, illus. 3rd ed. 2008. (ENG.). 112p. (J). (gr. 3-7). pap. 6.99 *(978-1-4169-5501-6(1),* Atheneum Bks. for Young Readers) Simon & Schuster Children's Publishing.

—The E. L. Konigsburg Newbery Collection: From the Mixed-Up Files of Mrs. Basil E. Frankweiler; Jennifer, Hecate, Macbeth, William Mckinley, & Me, Elizabeth; the View from Saturday. 2013. (ENG., Illus.). 472p. (J). (gr. 3-7). pap. 23.99 *(978-1-4424-9743-6(2),* Atheneum Bks. for Young Readers) Simon & Schuster Children's Publishing.

—Throwing Shadows. 2007. (ENG.). 176p. (J). (gr. 3-7). pap. 7.99 *(978-1-4169-4959-6(3),* Atheneum Bks. for Young Readers) Simon & Schuster Children's Publishing.

Kopple, Deborah. A Spear of Golden Grass: Short Stories by Norwalk High School Honors English Students. 2010. 216p. (J). pap. 15.95 *(978-1-4502-1896-2(2))* iUniverse, Inc.

Kopple, Deborah, ed. Heads in the Ground: Short Stories by Norwalk High School Honor's English Students. 2008. 188p. pap. 13.95 *(978-0-595-50775-7(1))* iUniverse, Inc.

Korhonen, Kari, et al. Walt Disney's Comics & Stories #705. 2009. 64p. pap. 7.99 *(978-1-60360-095-8(7))* Gemstone Publishing, Inc.

Korman, Gordon. The Climb. 2012. (Everest Ser.: 2). lib. bdg. 17.20 *(978-0-606-23934-9(0),* Turtleback) Turtleback Bks.

—The Contest. 2012. (Everest Ser.: 1). lib. bdg. 17.20 *(978-0-606-23933-2(2),* Turtleback) Turtleback Bks.

Kowen, Dorothy. The Gift of Gold. Mathew, Gillian, illus. 2011. (ENG.). 24p. 13.95 *(978-1-77009-796-4(1))* Jacana Media ZAF. Dist: Independent Pubs. Group.

Krahn, Fernando. Quien Ha Visto las Tijeras? 2004.Tr. of Who Has Seen the Scissors? (SPA., Illus.). (J). 20.99 *(978-84-8464-149-0(X))* Kalandraka Editora, S.L. ESP. Dist: Lectorum Pubns., Inc.

Krailing, Tessa. La Cabrita Revoltosa. (Club de las Mascotas Coleccion). (SPA.). 96p. (J). (gr. 3-5). *(978-84-88061-88-1(9))* Serres, Ediciones, S. L. ESP. Dist: Lectorum Pubns., Inc.

Krensky, Stephen. John Henry. Oldroyd, Mark, illus. 2007. (On My Own Folklore Ser.). (ENG.). 48p. (gr. 2-4). per. 6.95 *(978-0-8225-6477-5(7),* First Avenue Editions) Lerner Publishing Group.

—Mike Fink. Reeves, Jeni, illus. 2007. (On My Own Folklore Ser.). (ENG.). 48p. (gr. 2-4). per. 6.95 *(978-0-8225-6478-2(5),* First Avenue Editions) Lerner Publishing Group.

—Pecos Bill. Tong, Paul, illus. 2007. (On My Own Folklore Ser.). (ENG.). 48p. (gr. 2-4). per. 6.95 *(978-0-8225-6475-1(0),* First Avenue Editions) Lerner Publishing Group.

Krensky, Stephen & Sarfatti, Esther. Arturo y la Carrera por la Lectura. 2004.Tr. of Arthur & the Race to Read. (SPA., Illus.). (J). pap. 4.95 *(978-1-930332-60-7(2))* Lectorum Pubns., Inc.

Krohn, Genendel. The Miracle of the Rock & other Stories: Timeless Tales from the Lives of Our Sages. Pelleg, Tirtsa, illus. 2003. 56p. (J). 14.99 *(978-1-58330-650-5(1))* Feldheim Pubs.

Kropp, Paul. El Lunatico y su Hermana Libertad. (SPA.). (YA). 9.95 *(978-958-04-4386-5(6))* Norma S.A. COL. Dist: Distribuidora Norma, Inc.

—Running the Bases: Definitely Not a Book about Baseball. 2005. (ENG.). 160p. (J). (gr. 7). pap. 11.95 *(978-0-385-66147-8(9),* Doubleday Canada) Penguin Random House Canada Young Readers CAN. Dist: Penguin Random Hse. LLC.

Krulik, Nancy. A Collection of Katie: Books 1-4. John and Wendy, illus. 2012. (Katie Kazoo, Switcheroo Ser.). (ENG.). 320p. (J). (gr. 2-4). pap. 7.99 *(978-0-448-46304-9(0),* Grosset & Dunlap) Penguin Young Readers Group.

—Katie Kazoo, Switcheroo: A Collection of Katie. John and Wendy, illus. 2008. (Katie Kazoo, Switcheroo Ser.: Bks. 1-4). (ENG.). 320p. (J). (gr. 2-4). 10.99 *(978-0-448-44910-4(2),* Grosset & Dunlap) Penguin Young Readers Group.

Kruse, Jan, et al. Walt Disney's Spring Fever Volume 3. 2009. 80p. pap. 9.99 *(978-1-60360-097-2(3))* Gemstone Publishing, Inc.

Kryzanowsky, Sari. Grandmother's Tales: Book One. 2008. 36p. pap. 17.99 *(978-1-4389-1630-9(2))* AuthorHouse.

Kuhn, Douglas Wolcik. Animals' Christmas Gift. Clinton, Nicole C., ed. 2011. 24p. pap. 24.95 *(978-1-4560-5244-7(6))* America Star Bks.

Kulkarni, Suresh. The Wise King & Other Stories. 2011. 44p. pap. 21.99 *(978-1-4535-0463-5(X))* Xlibris Corp.

Kunhardt, Dorothy. Now Open the Box. Kunhardt, Dorothy, illus. 2013. (ENG., Illus.). 72p. (J). (gr. -1-2). 16.95 *(978-1-59017-708-2(8),* NYR Children's Collection) New York Review of Bks., Inc., The.

Kunze, Lauren & Onur, Rina. The Ivy. 2010. (Ivy Ser.: 1). (ENG.). 320p. (YA). (gr. 9-18). 16.99 *(978-0-06-196045-1(4),* Greenwillow Bks.) HarperCollins Pubs.

Kuo, Julia. Everyone Eats. Kuo, Julia, illus. 2012. (ENG., Illus.). 22p. (J). (gr. -1). 9.95 *(978-1-897476-74-1(4))* Simply Read Bks. CAN. Dist: Ingram Publisher Services.

Kyber, Manfred. Fables & Fairytales to Delight All Ages: Books One to Three with 'Mantao the Jester King' 2009. (Illus.). 420p. *(978-1-84748-520-5(0))* Athena Pr.

Kyber, Manifred. Fables & Fairytales to Delight All Ages Book Two: Gossamer Kingdoms, 3 vols. 2007. (ENG., Illus.). 140p. per. *(978-1-84401-985-4(3))* Athena Pr.

Kyrja. Rupert's Tales: Making More Magick, 1 vol. Osborn, Tonia Bennington, illus. 2016. (ENG.). 56p. (J). 16.99 *(978-0-7643-5124-2(9),* 9780764351242) Schiffer Publishing, Ltd.

LaBrant, Kenneth R. Uncle Kenny's Crazy Bedtime Stories. 2008. 73p. pap. 19.95 *(978-1-60563-602-3(9))* America Star Bks.

Lacasse, Michael. George & His Special New Friends. 2005. 48p. pap. 16.95 *(978-1-4137-8285-1(X))* PublishAmerica, Inc.

Lagerlöf, Selma. Christ Legends. 2004. pap. 14.95 *(978-0-8095-9388-0(2));* 196p. 29.95 *(978-0-8095-9883-0(3))* Wildside Pr., LLC.

—Christ Legends: & Other Stories. 2010. 200p. pap. 44.50 *(978-1-4092-0934-8(2))* Lulu Pr., Inc.

Lago, Angela. Juan Felizario Contento: El Rey de los Negocios. 2003. (Los Especials de A la Orilla Del Viento

Ser.). (SPA., Illus.). 32p. (J). (gr. 2-13). 14.99 *(978-968-16-7047-4(7))* Fondo de Cultura Economica USA.

Lagonegro, Melissa & Redbank, Tennant. Five Toy Tales. 2012. (Step into Reading Level 1 Ser.). lib. bdg. 18.40 *(978-0-606-23853-3(0)*, Turtleback) Turtleback Bks.

Laks, Shan. The Tale of Brave Ritchie: Be Aware of Strangers; Beat the Bullies & Exercise Changes Health. 2012. 76p. pap. 42.05 *(978-1-4797-2882-4(9))* Xlibris Corp.

Lal, Anupa, tr. Premchand Selected Stories. 2012. (ENG.). 168p. (J). (gr. 3-4). pap. 9.95 *(978-93-5036-122-1(1))* Ratna, Sagar Pvt. Ltd. IND. Dist: Midpoint Trade Bks., Inc.

Lal, Ranjit. Caterpillar Who Went on a Diet & Other Stories. 2004. (Illus.). 188p. (J). pap. *(978-0-14-333593-1(6)*, Puffin) Penguin Publishing Group.

LaMaster, Melissa. Appaloosa Tales with a Christmas Spirit. 2006. 48p. pap. 16.95 *(978-1-4241-3153-2(7))* PublishAmerica, Inc.

Lamichhane, Shiva. Golden Ball in a Piggy Bank. 2012. 84p. pap. 17.95 *(978-1-62709-317-0(6))* America Star Bks.

Lampkins, Antonia. My First Book Collection. 2009. 16p. pap. 24.95 *(978-1-61546-538-5(3))* America Star Bks.

Lampshire Hayden, Gwendolen. Really Truly Stories #5/9. 2006. (Illus.). 130p. (YA). per. 12.95 *(978-1-57258-437-2(8)*, 945-6298) TEACH Services, Inc.

—Really Truly Stories #6/9. 2006. (Illus.). 128p. (YA). per. 11.95 *(978-1-57258-438-9(6)*, 945-6299) TEACH Services, Inc.

—Really Truly Stories #7/9. 2007. (Illus.). 126p. per. 11.95 *(978-1-57258-439-6(4)*, 945-6300) TEACH Services, Inc.

—Really Truly Stories #8/9. 2007. (Illus.). 126p. pap. 11.95 *(978-1-57258-440-2(8))* TEACH Services, Inc.

—Really Truly Stories #9/9. 2007. (Illus.). 125p. pap. 11.95 *(978-1-57258-441-9(6))* TEACH Services, Inc.

Lanagan, Margo. White Time. 2006. 224p. (YA). (gr. 7-18). lib. bdg. 16.89 *(978-0-06-074394-9(8))* HarperCollins Pubs.

—Yellowcake. 2013. (ENG.). 240p. (YA). (gr. 9). 16.99 *(978-0-375-86920-4(4)*, Knopf Bks. for Young Readers) Random Hse. Children's Bks.

—Yellowcake: Stories. 2015. (ENG.). 240p. (YA). (gr. 9). pap. 9.99 *(978-0-375-87335-5(X)*, Ember) Random Hse. Children's Bks.

Lancaster, Shannon E. Becky: The Budding Ballerina. 2008. 36p. pap. 15.99 *(978-1-4343-9860-4(9))* AuthorHouse.

Landen, Cynthia & Phillips, Lorrie. The Elson Readers, Primer. 2005. (ENG.). 120p. (J). (gr. -1-12). pap., tchr. ed. 14.95 *(978-1-890623-24-1(5))* Lost Classic Bks.

Lane Gross, Ila. Uncommon Tales Around the World: Global Understanding/Cultural Literacy. 2004. (Illus.). (YA). pap. 6.95 *(978-0-9713649-6-7(6))* L.E.A.P. (Learning through an Expanded Arts Program, Inc).

Lang, Andrew. Prince Ricardo of Pantouflia. 2006. (Illus.). pap. 24.95 *(978-1-4286-0645-6(9))* Kessinger Publishing, LLC.

—The Strange Story Book. 2006. pap. 31.95 *(978-1-4304-4181-6(X))* Kessinger Publishing, LLC.

—The Yellow Fairy Book. 2007. 396p. per. 15.95 *(978-1-4218-4502-9(4))*; 31.95 *(978-1-4218-4418-3(4))* 1st World Publishing, Inc. (1st World Library - Literary Society).

Lang, Andrew, ed. The Chronicles of Pantouflia: Prince Prigio; Prince Ricardo of Pantouflia. (J). 20.95 *(978-0-89190-088-7(8))* Amereon Ltd.

—The Red Book of Animal Stories 1899. Ford, Henry J., illus. 2004. reprint ed. pap. 34.95 *(978-1-4179-8249-3(7))* Kessinger Publishing, LLC.

Lansky, Bruce, ed. Hidden Courage: 10 Inspiring Stories about Clever & Courageous Girls from Around the World. 2013. (Girls to the Rescue Ser.: 3). (ENG.). 112p. (J). (gr. 3-6). pap. 4.99 *(978-1-4424-9195-3(7))* Meadowbrook Pr.

—Lion on the Prowl: 10 Inspiring Stories about Clever & Courageous Girls from Around the World. 2013. (Girls to the Rescue Ser.: 2). (ENG.). 112p. (J). (gr. 3-6). pap. 4.99 *(978-1-4424-9194-6(9))* Meadowbrook Pr.

—The Royal Joust: 10 Inspiring Stories about Clever & Courageous Girls from Around the World. 2013. (Girls to the Rescue Ser.: 1). (ENG.). 112p. (J). (gr. 3-6). pap. 4.99 *(978-1-4424-9193-9(0))* Meadowbrook Pr.

Larned, W. T. & La Fontaine, Jean de. Reynard the Fox & Other Fables. Rae, John, illus. 2014. (ENG.). 96p. (J). (gr. 3-8). pap. 12.99 *(978-0-486-78197-6(6))* Dover Pubns., Inc.

Larousse Mexico Staff, ed. Historias de Princesas y Hadas. 2008.Tr. of Princess & Fairy Stories. (SPA & ENG., Illus.). 35p. 9.95 *(978-970-22-1449-6(1))* Larousse, Ediciones, S. A. de C. V. MEX. Dist: Houghton Mifflin Harcourt Publishing Co.

Larsen, Angela Sage. Third Time's a Charm, Bk. 3. 2013. (Fifties Chix Ser.: 3). (ENG.). 200p. (YA). pap. 9.95 *(978-1-60746-155-5(2)*, Premiere) FastPrncil, Inc.

Larson, Mary Kay. Tales of Tillie Terwillie: Who Does Tillie Love? 2012. 44p. pap. 21.99 *(978-1-4772-6643-4(7))* AuthorHouse.

Lasky, Kathryn. The Outcast. 2005. (Guardians of Ga'hoole Ser.: 8). (ENG., Illus.). 224p. (J). (gr. 3-7). 6.99 *(978-0-439-73951-1(9)*, Scholastic Paperbacks) Scholastic, Inc.

Lauture, Mireille B. Loulou, Gason Vanyan! / Loulou, the Brave! 2012. 28p. pap. 16.99 *(978-1-4772-6348-8(9))* AuthorHouse.

—Mancy's Haitian Folktale Collection: Father Misery. Minckler, Kathleen L., illus. 2011. 24p. pap. 12.50 *(978-1-4634-3682-7(3))* AuthorHouse.

Lavarello, Jose Maria, illus. Cuentame un Cuento, No. 2. (SPA.). 366p. (J). (gr. k-3). *(978-84-480-1124-6(4)*, TM2346) Timun Mas, Editorial S.A. ESP. Dist: Lectorum Pubns., Inc.

Lawrence, D. H. & Pearson Education Staff. British & American Short Stories. 2nd ed. 2013. (ENG.). 88p. pap. 11.99 *(978-1-4058-8239-2(5))* Pearson Education.

Lawrence, Iain. The Giant-Slayer. 2012. (ENG.). 304p. (J). (gr. 3-7). 6.99 *(978-0-440-23971-0(0)*, Yearling) Random Hse. Children's Bks.

Lawrinson, Julia. Loz & Al. 2004. 148p. (Orig.). (J). pap. 13.50 *(978-1-920731-24-3(5))* Fremantle Pr. AUS. Dist: Independent Pubs. Group.

Lawson, Helen. The Spaceship Saga & Other Stories: Read a Play - Book 1. 2013. (ENG., Illus.). 60p. pap. 12.95 *(978-1-78099-357-7(9)*, Our Street Bks.) Hunt, John Publishing Ltd. GBR. Dist: National Bk. Network.

Lawson, Jessica & Twain, Mark. The Tom Sawyer Collection: The Adventures of Tom Sawyer; the Adventures of Huckleberry Finn; the Actual & Truthful Adventures of Becky Thatcher. Bruno, Iacopo, illus. 2014. (ENG.). 944p. (J). (gr. 3-7). 50.99 *(978-1-4814-0536-2(5)*, Simon & Schuster Bks. For Young Readers) Simon & Schuster Bks. For Young Readers.

Layton, George. The Fib & Other Stories. 2015. (ENG.). 480p. (J). (gr. 4-6). pap. 11.99 *(978-1-4472-8673-8(1))* Pan Macmillan GBR. Dist: Independent Pubs. Group.

—The Trick & Other Stories, 1. 2nd unabr. ed. 2006. (ENG.). 176p. (J). (gr. 1-4). pap. 10.99 *(978-0-330-44161-2(2))* Pan Macmillan GBR. Dist: Independent Pubs. Group.

Lazewnik, Libby. The Burglar & Other Stories. 16.99 *(978-1-56871-307-6(X))* Targum Pr., Inc.

—Jumping In: And Other Stories. 2009. (Illus.). 236p. (J). *(978-1-4226-0942-2(1))* Mesorah Pubns., Ltd.

Le Guin, Ursula K., et al. Diverse Energies, 1 vol. Buckell, Tobias & Monti, Joe, eds. 2012. (ENG.). 368p. (YA). 19.95 *(978-1-60060-887-2(6)*, Tu Bks.) Lee & Low Bks., Inc.

Leal, Luis, compiled by. Cuentos Mexicanos - de los origenes a la Revolucion. 2007. (SPA.). 184p. (J). per. 23.90 *(978-1-934768-04-4(9))* Stockcero, Inc.

Lear, Edward. The Owl & the Pussy-Cat & Other Stories. 2012. (ENG., Illus.). 80p. (J). (gr. 2). 12.99 *(978-0-7123-5876-7(5))* British Library, The GBR. Dist: Independent Pubs. Group.

Learning with Stories. 2017. (Learning with Stories Ser.). 24p. (gr. 4-6). 118.00 ***(978-1-5081-6253-7(0))***; pap. 41.25 ***(978-1-5081-6256-8(5))*** Rosen Publishing Group, Inc., The. (PowerKids Pr.).

Leatham, Alan D. Four Cats, Five Monkeys, Absurd Birds & Other Fanciful Stuff. 2006. 108p. pap. 19.95 *(978-1-4241-0692-9(3))* America Star Bks.

Leavy, Una. The O'Brien Book of Irish Fairy Tales & Legends. Field, Susan, illus. 2012. (ENG.). 96p. (J). pap. 18.95 *(978-1-84717-313-3(6))* O'Brien Pr., Ltd., The IRL. Dist: Dufour Editions, Inc.

Lederer, Susan. I Can Do That. Loehr, Jenny, illus. 2008. 28p. (J). per. 19.95 *(978-0-9789347-0-5(9))* Children's Publishing.

Lee, Anita Lynn. Kenny's Amazing Adventures. 2009. 36p. pap. 16.99 *(978-1-4490-1588-6(3))* AuthorHouse.

Lee, Carolyn A. My World & Me: The & Me Collection. 2010. 28p. 18.00 *(978-1-4269-4054-5(8))* Trafford Publishing.

Lee, Helen. Guide's Greatest Escape from Crime Stories. 2003. (Pathfinder Junior Book Club Ser.). 141p. (J). pap. 10.99 *(978-0-8280-1753-4(0)*, 79-967) Review & Herald Publishing Assn.

Lee, J. Marie. 4Teen Jellybean. 2003. 165p. (J). per. 19.95 *(978-1-59196-327-1(3))* Instant Pub.

Lee, Silver Ann. Amazing Bedtime Stories. 2010. 32p. pap. 19.99 *(978-1-4490-6094-7(3))* AuthorHouse.

Lee, Wan, et al. A Fish Wish - Lunch for Patch - Squid Twins: BuildUp Unit 4 Lap Book. Moor, Beka et al, illus. 2015. (Build up Core Phonics Ser.). (J). (gr. 1). *(978-1-4900-2603-9(7))* Benchmark Education Co.

Lees, Gemma. Smart Stories for Clever Kids. 2013. 44p. pap. *(978-1-84991-862-6(7))* Chipmunkapublishing.

Lefrancois, Viateur. Coureurs des Bois a Clark City. Arseneau, Philippe & Drouin, Julie Saint-Onge, illus. 2003. (Collection des 9 Ans: Vol. 32). (FRE.). 136p. 8.95 *(978-2-922565-69-0(6))* Editions de la Paix CAN. Dist: World of Reading, Ltd.

LeGrand, Hank, 3rd. Paddle Tail. Merrison, Stacy, illus. l.t. ed. 2004. 63p. (J). per. 7.95 *(978-1-59466-020-7(4)*, Growing Years) Port Town Publishing.

Lehti, Kauko. Beautiful Animal Stories for Good Children. 2009. 44p. pap. 18.00 *(978-1-60693-872-0(X)*, Strategic Bk. Publishing) Strategic Book Publishing & Rights Agency (SBPRA).

Leicester, Mal. Early Years Stories for the Foundation Stage: Ideas & Inspiration for Active Learning. 2006. (ENG., Illus.). 128p. per. 50.95 *(978-0-415-37603-7(3)*, RU76033) Routledge.

Lemonde, Connie. Short Stories: For the Young & Young at Heart. 2003. (YA). pap. 10.95 *(978-1-932303-81-0(2)*, Llumina Pr.) Aeon Publishing Inc.

Lenker, David "Papa". The Skin They're In. 2011. 28p. pap. 15.99 *(978-1-4568-7294-6(X))* Xlibris Corp.

Lenzi, Danielle E. My Search for Prince Charming's Normal Brother. 2011. 136p. pap. 25.70 *(978-1-4634-0446-8(8))*; (gr. 10-12). 33.70 *(978-1-4634-0445-1(X))* AuthorHouse.

Leppard, Lois Gladys. The Mandie Collection. (ENG.). (J). Bks. 16-20, Vol. 4. 2009. 608p. pap. 16.99 *(978-0-7642-0663-4(X))* Vol. 2. 2008. (Illus.). 576p. (gr. 3-8). pap. 15.99 *(978-0-7642-0538-5(2))* Bethany Hse. Pubs.

Lester, Helen & Munsinger, Lynn. Laugh-Along Lessons 5-Minute Stories. 2015. (Laugh-Along Lessons Ser.). (ENG., Illus.). 256p. (J). (gr. -1-3). 12.99 *(978-0-544-50392-2(9)*, HMH Books For Young Readers) Houghton Mifflin Harcourt Publishing Co.

Lester, R. A. Clearview Stories, 1 vol. 2009. 238p. pap. 19.95 *(978-1-61582-913-2(X))* PublishAmerica, Inc.

Letria, Andre, illus. A Donkey Reads, 1 vol. 2011. (ENG.). 32p. (J). (gr. k-3). 16.95 *(978-1-59572-255-3(6))*; pap. 6.95 *(978-1-59572-256-0(4))* Star Bright Bks., Inc.

Let's Learn Aesop's Fables. 2017. (Let's Learn Aesop's Fables Ser.). 24p. (gr. 6-7). 123.00 ***(978-1-4994-8272-0(8))***; pap. 41.25 ***(978-1-4994-8409-0(7))*** Rosen Publishing Group, Inc., The. (Windmill Bks.).

Levine, Gussie. The Big Red Umbrella. 2010. 20p. 11.59 *(978-1-4269-4650-9(3))* Trafford Publishing.

Levithan, David. How They Met & Other Stories. 2009. (ENG.). 256p. (YA). (gr. 9). pap. 9.99 *(978-0-375-84323-5(X)*, Knopf Bks. for Young Readers) Random Hse. Children's Bks.

—21 Proms. 2015. lib. bdg. 20.85 *(978-0-606-36327-3(0))* Turtleback Bks.

Lewis, Anne Margaret. Tears of Mother Bear. Fritz, Kathleen Cheney, illus. 2012. (ENG.). 32p. (J). (gr. -1-3). pap. 8.95 *(978-1-934133-62-0(0)*, Mackinac Island Press, Inc.) Charlesbridge Publishing, Inc.

Lewis, J. Patrick. Spot the Plot: A Riddle Book of Book Riddles. Munsinger, Lynn, illus. 2009. (ENG.). 36p. (J). (gr. -1-3). 15.99 *(978-0-8118-4668-4(7))* Chronicle Bks. LLC.

—The Wren & the Sparrow. Nayberg, Yevgenia, illus. 2014. (J). 6.99 *(978-1-4677-6210-6(5)*, Kar-Ben Publishing) Lerner Publishing Group.

Lewman, David. Chuckle & Cringe: SpongeBob's Book of Embarrassing Stories. 2007. (SpongeBob SquarePants Ser.). (ENG., Illus.). 48p. (J). (gr. 2-5). pap. 3.99 *(978-1-4169-4746-2(9)*, Simon Spotlight/Nickelodeon) Simon Spotlight/Nickelodeon.

Leyendas Americanas. (Coleccion Leyendas). (SPA., Illus.). 64p. (J). vinyl bd. 16.95 *(978-950-11-0133-1(9)*, SGM133) Sigmar ARG. Dist: Continental Bk. Co., Inc.

Leyendas Argentinas. (Coleccion Leyendas). (SPA., Illus.). 64p. (J). vinyl bd. 16.95 *(978-950-11-0132-4(0)*, SGM132) Sigmar ARG. Dist: Continental Bk. Co., Inc.

Leyendas Universales. (Coleccion Leyendas). (SPA., Illus.). 64p. (J). vinyl bd. 16.95 *(978-950-11-0002-0(2)*, SGM131) Sigmar ARG. Dist: Continental Bk. Co., Inc.

Lias, Joe. The Wood Rats Dragging Their Long Tales. 2005. 183p. pap. 24.95 *(978-1-4137-5900-6(9))* America Star Bks.

Lichfield, Walter C. Fanciful Bear Stories for Small Kids & Factual Bear Stories for Big Kids. 2003. (Illus.). 84p. per. *(978-1-931456-47-0(X))* Athena Pr.

Liddiard, Merrilee. Fairy Friends: a Colors Primer, 1 vol. 2016. (ENG., Illus.). 22p. (J). bds. 9.99 *(978-1-4236-4531-3(6))* Gibbs Smith, Publisher.

Light, John. The Flower. Evans, Lisa, illus. 2011. (Child's Play Library). (ENG.). 32p. (J). *(978-1-84643-070-1(4))* Child's Play International Ltd.

Lilacs, Lotuses, & Ladybugs Set B, 6 vols. 32p. (gr. 1-3). 31.50 *(978-0-7802-8052-6(0))* Wright Group/McGraw-Hill.

Lim, Charlotte. Attack of the Swordfish & Other Singapore Tales: Text by Charlotte Lim: Illustrations by Alicia Tan Yen Ping: Creative Directing by Ruby Lim-Yang. 2005. (Illus.). 48p. *(978-981-05-3215-4(6))* National Heritage Board.

Linden, Joanne. Ben & Zip: Two Short Friends. Goldsmith, Tom, illus. 2014. (ENG.). 32p. (J). (gr. -1-k). 16.95 *(978-1-936261-28-4(6))* Flashlight Pr.

Lindop, Christine. Jack the Hero. 2010. (ENG., Illus.). 20p. 4.81 *(978-0-19-440085-5(9))* Oxford Univ. Pr., Inc.

Lindsay, Maud. More Mother Stories. Sanborn, F. C. & Railton, Fanny, illus. 2008. 160p. pap. 9.95 *(978-1-59915-168-7(5))* Yesterday's Classics.

Lindskoog, Kathryn & Hunsicker, Ranelda Mack, eds. Faerie Gold: Treasures from the Lands of Enchantment. 2005. (Classics for Young Readers Ser.). 304p. (J). per. 11.99 *(978-0-87552-738-3(8))* P & R Publishing.

Lindstrom, Florence M. Meeting New Friends. 2nd ed. 2007. (Illus.). 185p. pap. 8.95 *(978-1-932971-00-2(9))* Christian Liberty Pr.

Linforth, Veda. More Toy Shop Tales. 2009. 124p. pap. 10.99 *(978-1-4389-0795-6(8))* AuthorHouse.

Link, Kelly. Pretty Monsters. 2010. (ENG., Illus.). 416p. (YA). (gr. 7-18). 9.99 *(978-0-14-241672-3(X)*, Speak) Penguin Young Readers Group.

Link, Kelly & Grant, Gavin J., eds. Monstrous Affections: An Anthology of Beastly Tales. 2014. (ENG., Illus.). 480p. (YA). (gr. 9). 22.99 *(978-0-7636-6473-2(1))* Candlewick Pr.

Linseman, Daniel. Shroobear's First Swim: Book I of the Shroobear Short Stories. 2008. 36p. pap. 15.49 *(978-1-4343-8252-8(4))* AuthorHouse.

Lionni, Leo. Pezzettino. 2012. (ENG., Illus.). 40p. (J). (gr. -1-3). pap. 6.99 *(978-0-307-92999-0(X)*, Dragonfly Bks.) Random Hse. Children's Bks.

Little Golden Book Daddy Stories. 2015. (Little Golden Book Favorites Ser.). (ENG., Illus.). 80p. (J). (gr. -1-1). 6.99 *(978-0-553-49762-5(6)*, Golden Bks.) Random Hse. Children's Bks.

Lloyd, Jennifer. Ella's Umbrellas. Spires, Ashley, illus. 2010. (ENG.). 32p. (J). (gr. -1-3). 16.95 *(978-1-897476-23-9(X))* Simply Read Bks. CAN. Dist: Ingram Publisher Services.

Locker, Thomas, et al. Mountain Dance. Locker, Thomas, illus. 2003. (Avenues Ser.). (ENG., Illus.). 32p. (C). (gr. -1-3). 25.95 *(978-0-15-202622-6(3))* National Geographic School Publishing, Inc.

Lohans, Alison. Picturing Alyssa. 2011. (ENG.). 216p. (J). (gr. 5-6). pap. 12.99 *(978-1-55488-925-9(1))* Dundurn CAN. Dist: Ingram Publisher Services.

Loiske, Jennifer, et al. Tales of an Old Wizard. 2013. 116p. pap. 10.58 *(978-1-291-30601-9(3))* Lulu Pr., Inc.

Lombard, Ernest. Remember the Seagulls: A Modern Fable. 2004. (Illus.). 32p. (J). 3.95 *(978-0-9740473-0-0(9))* Pivotal Force.

Lombardi, Kristine & Disney Storybook Artists Staff. Disney Cars Carry along Treasury. 2010. (Carry along Bks.). (ENG., Illus.). 20p. (J). (gr. -1). bds. 14.99 *(978-0-7944-1947-9(X))* Reader's Digest Assn., Inc., The.

London, Jack. Brown Wolf & Other Stories. 2005. 156p. per. 13.95 *(978-1-59818-706-9(6))* Aegypan.

—Faith of Men. 2006. 116p. per. 9.95 *(978-1-59818-074-9(6))* Aegypan.

—Rumbo Oeste y Otros Cuentos. (Clasicos Juveniles Coleccion).Tr. of Short Stories. (SPA.). (YA). (gr. 5-8). pap. *(978-950-11-1331-0(0)*, SG2441) Sigmar ARG. Dist: Lectorum Pubns., Inc.

Long, Debbie. Short Stories with Imagination: The Imagination Series. 2004. 48p. (J). per. *(978-1-55306-820-4(3)*, Epic Pr.) Essence Publishing.

Long, Robert. Inside the Chrysanthemum: New Japanese Fables. 2007. 156p. pap. 53.30 *(978-1-4303-0543-9(6))* Lulu Pr., Inc.

Longo, Jason, illus. Otto's Colorful Campus Tour - Syracuse University A-Z. 2004. (J). 9.99 *(978-1-933069-04-3(X))* Odd Duck Ink, Inc.

Lopez- Jackson, Lillian. Eight 8 Short Stories for Children. 2011. 104p. pap. 37.66 *(978-1-4634-4672-7(1))* AuthorHouse.

Lopez, Bolivar. Z Finds a Kite. 2010. 32p. pap. 13.49 *(978-1-4490-8650-3(0))* AuthorHouse.

Lopez, Cheyene Montana. Blue Sky Rainbows: A Series of Children's Stories of the World of Dreams & Imaginations, 1 vol. 2009. 82p. pap. 16.95 *(978-1-61582-290-4(9))* PublishAmerica, Inc.

Lopez, Patricia A. Imaginations of Wonders, 1 vol. 2009. 128p. pap. 19.95 *(978-1-60813-276-8(5))* America Star Bks.

Lord, Bruce & Richards, Elisabeth. Humpty Dumpty Was Pushed: And Other Cracked Tales. 2008. 196p. 24.95 *(978-0-595-71559-6(1))*; pap. 14.95 *(978-0-595-47691-6(0))* iUniverse, Inc.

Lord, Grant. Tales of Rex Riley Aged 10 & a Bit, It's A Dog's Life. 2009. 141p. pap. 12.95 *(978-1-4092-4782-1(1))* Lulu Pr., Inc.

Lore, Pittacus. I Am Number Four: The Lost Files: Hidden Enemy, Vol. 3. 2014. (Lorien Legacies: the Lost Files Ser.). (ENG.). 416p. (YA). (gr. 9). pap. 9.99 *(978-0-06-228768-7(0))* HarperCollins Pubs.

Lorenzo, Lucia Ann. Lucky, My Best Friend. 2012. 24p. pap. 17.99 *(978-1-4772-8087-4(1))* AuthorHouse.

Lorimer, Janet. Beasts, 1 vol. unabr. ed. 2010. (Q Reads Ser.). (ENG.). 32p. (YA). (gr. 9-12). pap. 6.95 *(978-1-61651-212-5(1))* Saddleback Educational Publishing, Inc.

—Ben Cody's Treasure, 1 vol. unabr. ed. 2010. (Q Reads Ser.). (ENG.). 32p. (YA). (gr. 9-12). pap. 6.95 *(978-1-61651-189-0(3))* Saddleback Educational Publishing, Inc.

—Danger on Ice, 1 vol. unabr. ed. 2010. (Q Reads Ser.). (ENG.). 32p. (YA). (gr. 9-12). pap. 6.95 *(978-1-61651-179-1(6))* Saddleback Educational Publishing, Inc.

—Death Grip, 1 vol. unabr. ed. 2010. (Q Reads Ser.). (ENG.). 32p. (YA). (gr. 9-12). pap. 6.95 *(978-1-61651-200-2(8))* Saddleback Educational Publishing, Inc.

—Empty Eyes, 1 vol. unabr. ed. 2010. (Q Reads Ser.). (ENG.). 32p. (YA). (gr. 9-12). pap. 6.95 *(978-1-61651-180-7(X))* Saddleback Educational Publishing, Inc.

—Kula'i Street Knights, 1 vol. unabr. ed. 2010. (Q Reads Ser.). (ENG.). 32p. (YA). (gr. 9-12). pap. 6.95 *(978-1-61651-182-1(6))* Saddleback Educational Publishing, Inc.

S

Lotz, Dana R. Kids' Tales. 2008. 85p. pap. 19.95 *(978-1-60672-179-7(8))* America Star Bks.

Loughead, Deb & Shipley, Jocelyn. Cleavage: Breakaway Fiction for Real Girls, 1 vol. 2009. (ENG., Illus.). 192p. (YA). (gr. 7-11). pap. *(978-1-894549-76-9(7)*, Sumach Pr.) Canadian Scholars.

Loux, Matthew. Salt Water Taffy Pt. 2: Caldera's Revenge! 2011. (ENG., Illus.). 80p. pap. 5.99 *(978-1-934964-63-7(8)*, 9781934964637) Oni Pr., Inc.

Love, Katie. Fruit to Live By..., 1 vol. 2009. 62p. pap. 16.95 *(978-1-60836-122-9(5))* PublishAmerica, Inc.

Luba Folk Tales. 2005. (YA). 10.00 *(978-1-59872-207-9(7))* Instant Pub.

Lubar, David. Attack of the Vampire Weenies: And Other Warped & Creepy Tales. 2011. (Weenies Stories Ser.). (ENG.). 224p. (J). (gr. 4-7). 15.99 *(978-0-7653-2345-3(1)*, 9780765323453, Starscape) Doherty, Tom Assocs., LLC.

—The Battle of the Red Hot Pepper Weenies: And Other Warped & Creepy Tales. 2010. (Weenies Stories Ser.). (ENG.). 192p. (J). (gr. 4-7). mass mkt. 5.99 *(978-0-7653-6075-5(6)*, 9780765360755, Starscape) Doherty, Tom Assocs., LLC.

—Beware the Ninja Weenies: And Other Warped & Creepy Tales. (Weenies Stories Ser.). (ENG.). 192p. (J). (gr. 4-7). 2013. mass mkt. 5.99 *(978-0-7653-6879-9(X)*, 9780765368799) 2012. 15.99 *(978-0-7653-3213-4(2)*, 9780765332134) Doherty, Tom Assocs., LLC. (Starscape).

—Curse of the Campfire Weenies: And Other Warped & Creepy Tales. 2008. (Weenies Stories Ser.). (ENG.). 208p. (J). (gr. 4-9). mass mkt. 5.99 *(978-0-7653-5771-7(2)*, 9780765357717, Starscape) Doherty, Tom Assocs., LLC.

—Enter the Zombie. 2011. (Nathan Abercrombie, Accidental Zombie Ser.: 5). (ENG.). 192p. (J). (gr. 3-7). pap. 5.99 *(978-0-7653-2672-0(8)*, 9780765326720, Starscape) Doherty, Tom Assocs., LLC.

—Extremities: Stories of Death, Murder, & Revenge. 2014. (ENG.). 208p. (YA). (gr. 8-12). pap. 9.99 *(978-0-7653-3461-9(5)*, 9780765334619, Tor Teen) Doherty, Tom Assocs., LLC.

—Invasion of the Road Weenies. 2006. (Weenies Stories Ser.). (ENG.). 192p. (J). (gr. 4-7). mass mkt. 5.99 *(978-0-7653-5325-2(3)*, 9780765353252, Starscape) Doherty, Tom Assocs., LLC.

—Lay Ups & Long Shots: Eight Short Stories. 2008. 128p. (YA). (gr. 5-8). 14.95 *(978-1-58196-078-5(6)*, Darby Creek) Lerner Publishing Group.

—Wipeout of the Wireless Weenies: And Other Warped & Creepy Tales. 2014. (Weenies Stories Ser.). (ENG., Illus.). 176p. (J). (gr. 4-7). 15.99 *(978-0-7653-3214-1(0)*, 9780765332141, Starscape) Doherty, Tom Assocs., LLC.

Lucado, Max. A Max Lucado Children's Treasury: A Child's First Collection, 1 vol. 2007. (ENG., Illus.). 144p. (gr. -1-3). 19.99 *(978-1-4003-1048-7(2))* Nelson, Thomas Inc.

Lucan, Dawn. Daily Adventure Memories. 2010. 48p. pap. 16.95 *(978-0-557-53422-7(4))* Lulu Pr., Inc.

Lucas, Edward Verall. Forgotten Tales of Long Ago. 2006. (Illus.). pap. 36.95 *(978-1-4254-9801-6(9))* Kessinger Publishing, LLC.

Lüftner, Kai. Lily Loves. Drews, Judith, illus. 2012. (ENG.). 32p. (J). (gr. -1-3). pap. 16.95 *(978-1-897476-94-9(9))* Simply Read Bks. CAN. Dist: Ingram Publisher Services.

Lukacs, Krisztian. Bud & Barnie: 2 Tales. 2011. 38p. pap. 18.99 *(978-1-4475-9027-9(9))* Lulu Pr., Inc.

Luke, Pauline. Amber Pash on Pink. 2004. (Illus.). 160p. (Orig.). pap. *(978-0-7022-3428-6(1))* Univ. of Queensland Pr.

Luker, Penny. The Green Book. 2013. 68p. pap. *(978-0-9559896-3-6(9))* Bindon Bks.

Luper, Eric. Seth Baumgartner's Love Manifesto. 2010. (ENG.). 304p. (YA). (gr. 8-18). 16.99 *(978-0-06-182753-2(3))* HarperCollins Pubs.

Lupton, Hugh. The Story Tree. Fatus, Sophie, illus. 2009. (ENG.). 64p. (J). 19.99 *(978-1-84686-301-1(5))* Barefoot Bks., Inc.

—Tales of Wisdom & Wonder. Sharkey, Niamh, illus. 2006. (ENG.). 64p. (J). (gr. k-5). 15.99 *(978-1-905236-84-8(0))* Barefoot Bks., Inc.

Lyle-Soffe, Shari. The Misadventures of Rooter & Snuffle. Collier, Kevin Scott, illus. 2008. 20p. pap. 9.95 *(978-1-933090-88-7(X))* Guardian Angel Publishing, Inc.

—On the Go with Rooter & Snuffle. Collier, Kevin Scott, illus. 2008. 20p. pap. 9.95 *(978-1-933090-96-2(0))* Guardian Angel Publishing, Inc.

Lynch, Diane M., ed. Celebrate the Season! Twelve Short Stories for Advent & Christmas. 2010. (J). (gr. 3-6). pap. 7.95 *(978-0-8198-1585-9(3))* Pauline Bks. & Media.

—Family Ties: Thirteen Short Stories. 2010. 112p. (J). (gr. 4-7). pap. 7.95 *(978-0-8198-2688-6(X))* Pauline Bks. & Media.

—Now You're Cooking! Ten Short Stories with Recipes. 2009. (J). (gr. 4-7). pap. 7.95 *(978-0-8198-5167-3(1))* Pauline Bks. & Media.

Lynch, Katherine E. & Radclyffe, eds. OMGQueer. 2012. (ENG.). 264p. (J). (gr. 7). pap. 9.95 *(978-1-60282-682-3(X))* Bold Strokes Bks.
Lyons, Sarah. Fairy stories about sally & Mignonette. 2007. pap. 9.99 *(978-1-60034-860-0(2))* Salem Author Services.
Ma, Zheng & Li, Zheng. Chinese Fables & Folktales (I) She, Liu & Rujin, Ma, illus. 2010. (ENG.). 48p. (J). (gr. -1-3). 16.95 *(978-1-60220-962-6(6))* BetterLink Pr., Inc.
—Chinese Fables & Folktales (II) Wei, Miao & Xianoqing, Pan, illus. 2010. (ENG.). 48p. (J). (gr. -1-3). 16.95 *(978-1-60220-963-3(4))* BetterLink Pr., Inc.
—Stories Behind Chinese Idioms (I) Taixi, Su & Xiaoming, Wang, illus. 2010. (ENG.). 48p. (J). (gr. 3-6). 16.95 *(978-1-60220-965-7(0))* BetterLink Pr., Inc.
—Stories Behind Chinese Idioms (II) Youzhi, He & Xiaofang, Ding, illus. 2010. (ENG.). 48p. (J). (gr. 3-6). 16.95 *(978-1-60220-966-4(9))* BetterLink Pr., Inc.
—Stories Behind Chinese Idioms (III) She, Liu & Xiaoqing, Pan, illus. 2010. (ENG.). 48p. (J). (gr. 3-6). 16.95 *(978-1-60220-967-1(7))* BetterLink Pr., Inc.
Maar, Paul. La Puerta Olvidada. (Torre de Papel Ser.). (SPA.). (J). (gr. 2). 7.95 *(978-958-04-1489-6(0))* Norma S.A. COL. Dist: Distribuidora Norma, Inc.
Mac Iver, Kathi. Ghosts of the Mining District. 2003. (Illus.). 60p. 9.95 *(978-0-9651272-1-9(4))* Columbine Pr.
Macaraeg, Diane. Last Meal. 2008. 132p. pap. *(978-3-639-03548-3(8))* AV Akademikerverlag GmbH & Co. KG.
Macaulay, David. Black & White. 2005. (ENG., Illus.). 32p. (J). (gr. -1-3). 7.99 *(978-0-618-63687-7(0))* Houghton Mifflin Harcourt Publishing Co.
Macauley, Jo. Secrets & Spies, 1 vol. 2014. (Secrets & Spies Ser.). (ENG.). 224p. (gr. 4-7). 106.60 *(978-1-4342-9618-4(0))* Stone Arch Bks.
MacDonald, George. George MacDonald's Fantasy Novels for Children Including: The Princess & the Goblin, the Princess & Curdie & at the Ba. 2013. 444p. *(978-1-78139-368-0(0))* Benediction Classics.
—The Light Princess & Other Fairy Stories. 2007. 102p. pap. 18.99 *(978-1-4346-1408-7(5))* Creative Media Partners, LLC.
—Stephen Archer & Other Tales. 2008. 212p. 26.95 *(978-1-60664-985-5(X))* Aegypan.
MacDonald, Margaret Read. Five-Minute Tales: More Stories to Read & Tell When Time Is Short. 2007. (ENG.). 160p. (J). (gr. -1-3). 24.95 *(978-0-87483-781-0(2))*; per. 14.95 *(978-0-87483-782-7(0))* August Hse. Pubs., Inc.
—Little Rooster's Diamond Button Book & DVD Set, 1 vol. Terry, Will, illus. 2010. (Book & DVD Packages with Nutmeg Media Ser.). (ENG.). 4p. (J). (gr. -1-3). 49.95 *(978-0-8075-9982-2(4))* Whitman, Albert & Co.
MacHado, Ana Maria. Ah, Pajarita Si Yo Pudiera. (Torre de Papel Ser.). (SPA., Illus.). (J). 7.95 *(978-958-04-4526-5(5),* NR31207) Norma S.A. COL. Dist: Distribuidora Norma, Inc., Lectorum Pubns., Inc.
Machado, Ana María. Aunque Parezca Mentira. (SPA., Illus.). 64p. (J). 16.95 *(978-84-207-4412-4(3))* Grupo Anaya, S.A. ESP. Dist: Lectorum Pubns., Inc., Distribooks, Inc.
MacHado, Ana Maria. El Barbero y el Coronel. Coll, Ivar Da, illus.Tr. of Barber & the Colonel. (SPA.). (J). (gr. 2-3). 7.95 *(978-958-04-5035-1(8),* NR1718) Norma S.A. COL. Dist: Distribuidora Norma, Inc., Lectorum Pubns., Inc.
Machetto, Augusto, et al. A Present for Tinker Bell. Urbano, Emilio et al, illus. 2011. (Disney Fairies Ser.: 6). (ENG.). 64p. (J). (gr. 1-6). pap. 7.99 *(978-1-59707-256-4(7),* 9781597072564) Papercutz.
Mack, Karen. The Magical Adventures of Sun Beams. 2009. 42p. 31.99 *(978-1-4415-3636-5(1))* Xlibris Corp.
MacLachlan, Patricia. Your Moon, My Moon: A Grandmother's Words to a Faraway Child. Collier, Bryan, illus. 2011. (ENG.). 32p. (J). (gr. -1-3). 16.99 *(978-1-4169-7950-0(6),* Simon & Schuster Bks. For Young Readers) Simon & Schuster Bks. For Young Readers.
Maclean, Fiona. Death or Victory: Tales of the Clan Maclean. Turnbull, Brian, illus. 2011. 128p. (YA). pap. *(978-2-930583-06-8(1))* White & MacLean Publishing BEL. Dist: Gardners Bks. Ltd.
MacPhail, Cathy. Run, Zan, Run. 2012. (ENG.). 192p. (YA). pap. 12.99 *(978-1-4088-1733-9(0),* 9781408817339, Bloomsbury USA Childrens) Bloomsbury Publishing USA.
Madden, Gloria. Grandmother's Bedtime Stories. 2005. 57p. pap. 16.95 *(978-1-4137-6489-5(4))* America Star Bks.
—Grandmothers Bedtime Stories. 2008. 68p. (gr. -1-7). pap. 10.49 *(978-1-4343-9201-5(5))* AuthorHouse.
—Grandmothers Bedtime Stories: Book 5. 2008. 144p. pap. 11.99 *(978-1-4343-9515-3(4))* AuthorHouse.
Mae, Darcie. Sammy & Robert Discover the Ocean, 1 vol. 2009. 39p. pap. 24.95 *(978-1-61546-827-0(7))* America Star Bks.
Magazine, Stories for Children. Best of Stories for Children Volume 1. 2009. 64p. pap. 26.95 *(978-0-557-02883-2(3))* Lulu Pr., Inc.
Maggiore, Angela T. Short Stories for Children. 2008. 428p. pap. 22.99 *(978-1-4343-3720-7(0))* AuthorHouse.
Magic Wagon Staff & ABDO Publishing Company Staff. Calico Illustrated Classics Set 4, 1 vol. 2012. (Calico Illustrated Classics Ser.: 12). (ENG., Illus.). 112p. 324.84 *(978-1-61641-609-6(2),* Calico Chapter Bks) Magic Wagon.
Magical Bedtime Stories. 2012. (ENG.). 128p. (J). 9.95 *(978-1-84837-866-7(1))* Arcturus Publishing GBR. Dist: Bookmasters Distribution.
Magical Christmas Tales. 2007. 192p. *(978-1-4054-9483-0(2))* Parragon, Inc.
Magona, Sindiwe. The Ugly Duckling. Hinrichsen, Natalie, illus. 2011. (Best Loved Tales for Africa Ser.). (ENG.). 32p. (J). (gr. k-2). pap. 10.95 *(978-1-77009-823-7(2))* Jacana Media ZAF. Dist: Independent Pubs. Group.
Magsamen, Sandra. Bedtime Bunny. 2009. (Board Books with Plush Toy Ser.). (ENG., Illus.). 20p. (J). (gr. -1 — 1). bds. 7.99 *(978-0-316-00390-2(5))* Little, Brown Bks. for Young Readers.
—Peep, Peep, I Love You! 2012. (Padded Cloth Covers with Lift-The-Flaps Ser.). (ENG., Illus.). 10p. (J). (gr. -1-17). bds. 7.99 *(978-0-316-07006-5(8))* Little, Brown Bks. for Young Readers.
Maguire, Gregory. Leaping Beauty: And Other Animal Fairy Tales. Demarest, Chris L., illus. 2006. (ENG.). 224p. (J). (gr. 3-7). reprint ed. pap. 7.99 *(978-0-06-056419-3(9))* HarperCollins Pubs.
Mahy, Margaret. The Great Piratical Rumbustification & the Librarian & the Robbers. Blake, Quentin, illus. 2012. (ENG.). 64p. (J). pap. 6.95 *(978-1-56792-169-4(8))* Godine, David R. Pub.
—Shock Forest: And Other Stories. 2004. *(978-0-7136-7652-5(3),* A&C Black) Bloomsbury Publishing Plc.
Main Street Publishing, compiled by. The Talent among Us: Trail of Tales, Vol. 3. 2004. (ENG.). 142p. (YA). per. 14.00 *(978-0-9741294-2-6(9),* MSP) Main St Publishing, Inc.
Making Words Count. 2007. pap. 8.95 *(978-0-9787472-1-3(6))* Ajoyin Publishing, Inc.
Maltby, Ethel H. My Animal Story Book: A Treasury of Sunshine Stories for Children. Richardson, Frederick, illus. 2004. reprint ed. pap. 15.95 *(978-1-4191-7300-4(6))* Kessinger Publishing, LLC.
Manary, Adria. More Mommy Magic: 506 Ways to Nurture Your Child. 2005. 257p. pap. 14.95 *(978-1-931643-65-8(2))* Seven Locks Pr.
Mannering, Rose. Roses: The Tales Trilogy, Book 1. 2016. (Tales Trilogy Ser.). (ENG.). 328p. (J). (gr. 6). pap. 9.99 *(978-1-63450-188-0(8),* Sky Pony Pr.) Skyhorse Publishing Co., Inc.
Mansfield, Katherine. PARTIES AND PRESENTS THREE SHORT STORIES LEVEL 2 ELEMENTARY/LOWER-INTERMEDIATE WITH CD-ROM/AUDIO CD, 1 vol. 2010. (ENG., Illus.). 62p. pap. 14.25 incl. cd-rom *(978-84-8323-684-0(2))* Cambridge Univ. Pr.
Manson, Beverlie, illus. Rapunzel. 2017. (ENG.). 24p. (J). (gr. -1-12). pap. 7.99 ***(978-1-86147-827-6(5),*** Armadillo) Anness Publishing GBR. Dist: National Bk. Network.
Marcantonio, Patricia Santos, et al. Red Ridin' in the Hood: And Other Cuentos. Alarcão, Renato, illus. 2005. (ENG.). 192p. (J). (gr. 2-5). 17.99 *(978-0-374-36241-6(6),* 9780374362416, Farrar, Straus & Giroux (BYR)) Farrar, Straus & Giroux.
Marder, Larry. Beanworld: Tales of the Beanworld. Schutz, Diana, ed. Marder, Larry, illus. 2012. (ENG., Illus.). 64p. 14.99 *(978-1-59582-897-2(4))* Dark Horse Comics.
Mardinly, Berdan. Fresh Tarhana Soup: Story in English & in Turkish. 2008. (ENG & TUR., Illus.). 24p. (J). 8.75 *(978-0-9801675-4-2(X))* Robertson Publishing.
Mark, Jan. Eyes Wide Open. 2003. (ENG., Illus.). 105p. *(978-0-7136-7648-8(5),* A&C Black) Bloomsbury Publishing Plc.
Marlow, Herb. Sisters, Wild Dogs & Catfish Bait. Caffee, Julie, illus. 2005. 122p. (J). lib. bdg. 24.95 *(978-1-893595-45-3(5))*; per. 16.95 *(978-1-893595-48-4(X))* Four Seasons Bks., Inc.
Marlow, Patricia. What Fairy Tales Are All About: Grandma's Stories. 2007. 94p. pap. 19.95 *(978-1-4241-6580-3(6))* America Star Bks.
Marr, Andrew. Creatures We Dream of Knowing: Stories of Our Life Together. 2011. 208p. 24.95 *(978-1-4502-8071-6(4))*; pap. 14.95 *(978-1-4502-8070-9(6))* iUniverse, Inc.
Marr, Melissa. Faery Tales & Nightmares. 2013. (ENG.). 432p. (YA). (gr. 8). pap. 9.99 *(978-0-06-185273-2(2))* HarperCollins Pubs.
Marr, Melissa, et al. Love Is Hell. 2008. (ENG.). 272p. (YA). (gr. 9-18). pap. 9.99 *(978-0-06-144304-6(2),* HarperTeen) HarperCollins Pubs.
—Shards & Ashes. 2013. (ENG.). 384p. (YA). (gr. 8). 17.99 *(978-0-06-209846-7(2))*; pap. 9.99 *(978-0-06-209845-0(4))* HarperCollins Pubs.
Marr Osb, Andrew. From Beyond to Here: Merendael's Gift & Other Stories. 2012. 320p. (gr. 4-6). 29.95 *(978-1-4759-3460-1(2))*; pap. 19.95 *(978-1-4759-3458-8(0))* iUniverse, Inc.
Marshall, James. The Complete Stories of Two Best Friends. collector's ed. 2008. (ENG., Illus.). 368p. (J). (gr. 2-5). 29.99 *(978-0-618-89195-5(1))* Houghton Mifflin Harcourt Publishing Co.
Marston, Elsa. Figs & Fate: Stories about Growing up in the Arab World Today. 2005. (ENG.). 146p. (J). 22.50 *(978-0-8076-1551-5(X))*; pap. 15.95 *(978-0-8076-1554-6(4))* Braziller, George Inc.
—Santa Claus in Baghdad & Other Stories about Teens in the Arab World. 2008. (ENG.). 216p. (gr. 3-7). pap. 15.95 *(978-0-253-22004-2(1),* 0253220041) Indiana Univ. Pr.
Marta, Karen, ed. Philippe Parreno & Johan Olander: Parade. 2009. (ENG & ENM., Illus.). 36p. pap. 24.00 *(978-3-03764-048-7(0))* JRP Ringier Kunstverlag AG CHE. Dist: D.A.P./Distributed Art Pubs.
Martin, Ann M., et al. Because of Shoe & Other Dog Stories. Ivanov, Aleksey & Ivanov, Olga, illus. 2012. (ENG.). 272p. (J). (gr. 3-7). 15.99 *(978-0-8050-9314-8(1),* 9780805093148, Holt, Henry & Co. Bks. For Young Readers) Holt, Henry & Co.
—Because of Shoe & Other Dog Stories. Ivanov, Olga & Ivanov, Aleksey, illus. 2013. (ENG.). 288p. (J). (gr. 3-7). pap. 7.99 *(978-1-250-02728-3(4),* 9781250027283) Square Fish.
Martin, David. Let's Have a Tree Party! Manders, Jeff & Manders, John, illus. 2012. (ENG.). 32p. (J). (gr. k-k). 15.99 *(978-0-7636-3704-0(1))* Candlewick Pr.
Martin, David Lozell. Piggy & Dad Play Big Book: Brand New Readers. Remkiewicz, Frank, illus. 2009. (Brand New Readers Ser.). (ENG.). 48p. (J). (gr. -1-3). pap. 24.99 *(978-0-7636-4455-0(2))* Candlewick Pr.
Martin, Harvey. The Shaggy Dog Story Book. 2009. 108p. pap. 10.00 *(978-1-59858-932-0(6))* Dog Ear Publishing, LLC.
Martin, Kevin. Arnold Lobel Wrote Great Stories. 2017. (Text Connections Guided Close Reading Ser.). (J). (gr. 1). *(978-1-4900-1800-3(X))* Benchmark Education Co.
Martin, Kristina. Cozzi Dog Can't See. 2012. 40p. pap. 32.70 *(978-1-4771-3053-7(5))* Xlibris Corp.
Martins, E. V. Cookie Nana's Story Book: Featuring " Grumpy Granddad " 2009. (Illus.). 40p. pap. 16.99 *(978-1-4389-2325-3(2))* AuthorHouse.
Martzowka, John M. Quilt of Heroes. 2010. 56p. pap. 23.99 *(978-1-4520-6249-5(8))* AuthorHouse.
Maryann Pasda Diedwardo & Patricia J. Pasda. Pennsylvania Voices Book V: The Legacy of Allison. 2009. 64p. pap. 10.49 *(978-1-4389-4332-9(6))* AuthorHouse.
Masters, Anthony. Ghost Stories to Tell in the Dark. 2012. (ENG.). 92p. pap. 12.99 *(978-1-4482-0501-1(8),* 9781448205011, Bloomsbury Reader) Bloomsbury Publishing Plc GBR. Dist: Macmillan.
Masters, William H. Love & Sex. Cart, Michael, ed. 2003. (ENG.). 240p. (YA). (gr. 8). pap. 13.95 *(978-0-689-85668-6(7),* Simon Pulse) Simon Pulse.
Matheos, George P. Pure Magic. 2011. 156p. (gr. 2-4). 22.95 *(978-1-4620-1619-8(7))*; pap. 12.95 *(978-1-4620-1617-4(0))* iUniverse, Inc.
Matthews, Annette. Mischievous Molly. 2006. (Illus.). x, 48p. pap. 13.00 *(978-1-4120-9693-5(6))* Trafford Publishing.
Matthews, Caitlin, et al. Fireside Stories: Tales for a Winter's Eve. 2007. (ENG., Illus.). 96p. (J). (gr. -1-5). 19.99 *(978-1-84686-065-2(2))* Barefoot Bks., Inc.
Matthews, Penny. The Nellie Stories. 2016. (Our Australian Girl Ser.). (ENG.). 480p. (J). (gr. 3-7). 22.99 *(978-0-670-07915-5(4))* Penguin Books Australia AUS. Dist: Independent Pubs. Group.
Maupassant, Guy de. Contes du jour et de la nuit, Level C. (FRE.). 282p. (YA). (gr. 7-12). 9.99 *(978-0-88436-989-9(7),* 40303) EMC/Paradigm Publishing.
Mawhinney, Art, illus. Dora & Diego to the Rescue! 2010. (Go, Diego, Go! Ser.). (ENG.). 48p. (J). pap. 5.99 *(978-1-4424-0660-5(7),* Simon Spotlight/Nickelodeon) Simon Spotlight/Nickelodeon.
Mawter, J. A. So Grotty! Gordon, Gus, illus. 5th ed. 2004. (So... Ser.: Bk. 5). 160p. (Orig.). (J). *(978-0-207-20007-6(6),* Angus & Robertson) HarperCollins Pubs. Australia.
Maxey, Ann. Country Style Oklahoma. 2005. (Illus.). 71p. (YA). per. 15.95 *(978-0-9771939-1-2(8),* 0001) New World Publishing.
Mayer, Mercer. Fair Play. 2012. (Big Little Critter Ser.: 1). (ENG., Illus.). 98p. (J). 12.95 *(978-1-60746-763-2(1),* Premiere) FastPrncl, Inc.
—Helping Out. 2012. (Big Little Critter Ser.: 2). (ENG., Illus.). 96p. (J). 12.95 *(978-1-60746-071-8(8),* Premiere) FastPrncl, Inc.
—Just a Storybook Collection: Bye-Bye, Mom & Dad; Just a School Project; Just a Snowman; Good for Me & You; Just Big Enough; My Trip to the Hospital. Mayer, Mercer, illus. 2012. (Little Critter Ser.). (ENG., Illus.). 176p. (J). (gr. -1-3). 11.99 *(978-0-06-213452-3(3))* HarperCollins Pubs.
—Little Critter Storybook Collection. Mayer, Mercer, illus. 2005. (Little Critter Ser.). (ENG., Illus.). 176p. (J). (gr. -1-3). 11.99 *(978-0-06-082009-1(8),* HarperFestival) HarperCollins Pubs.
Mayer, Mercer & Mayer, Gina. My Family: A Big Little Critter Book. 2013. (Big Little Critter Ser.: 2). (ENG., Illus.). 98p. (J). 12.95 *(978-1-60746-810-3(7),* Premiere) FastPrncl, Inc.
—On the Go. 2013. (Big Little Critter Ser.: 4). (ENG., Illus.). 96p. (J). 12.95 *(978-1-60746-983-4(9),* Premiere) FastPrncl, Inc.
—Staying Well. 2013. (Big Little Critter Ser.: 5). (ENG.). 96p. (J). 12.95 *(978-1-60746-732-8(1),* Premiere) FastPrncl, Inc.
McAllister, Angela. A Year Full of Stories: 52 Classic Stories from All Around the World. Corr, Christopher, illus. 2016. (ENG.). 128p. (J). (gr. 1-4). 19.99 *(978-1-84780-868-4(9),* Frances Lincoln Children's Bks.) Quarto Publishing Group UK GBR. Dist: Hachette Bk. Group.
Mcauliffe, Timothy & McAuliffe, John Jobin. Snappy the Fox & Other Sleep Time Stories. 2008. 64p. pap. 18.95 *(978-1-4327-1934-0(3))* Outskirts Pr., Inc.
McBride-Smith, Barbara. Greek Myths, Western Style: Toga Tales with an Attitude. 2005. (ENG.). 128p. (J). (gr. 5-17). pap. 8.95 *(978-0-87483-617-2(4))* August Hse. Pubs., Inc.
McCall Smith, Alexander. El Arbol del Chicle Hinchable. (Raton de Biblioteca Coleccion). (SPA.). 128p. (J). (gr. 3). 7.95 *(978-84-88061-86-7(2))* Serres, Ediciones, S. L. ESP. Dist: Lectorum Pubns., Inc.
McCaughrean, Geraldine. Sky Ship & Other Stories. l.t. ed. 2004. *(978-0-7136-7653-2(1),* A&C Black) Bloomsbury Publishing Plc.
McCloskey, Robert. Make Way for McCloskey. 2004. (ENG., Illus.). 144p. (J). (gr. k-3). 26.00 *(978-0-670-05934-8(X),* Viking Books for Young Readers) Penguin Young Readers Group.
McCluskey, J. E. Platypus Tales. 2009. 120p. pap. 14.95 *(978-1-4357-2635-2(9))* Lulu Pr., Inc.
McDaniel, Lurlene. Starry, Starry Night: Three Holiday Stories. 2011. (ENG.). 272p. (YA). (gr. 7). pap. 8.99 *(978-0-385-74045-6(X),* Ember) Random Hse. Children's Bks.
—True Love. 2009. (ENG.). 672p. (YA). (gr. 7). pap. 10.99 *(978-0-375-86148-2(3),* Ember) Random Hse. Children's Bks.
McDonald, Megan. Julie Story Collection. Hunt, Robert, illus. 2007. 472p. pap. 29.95 *(978-1-59369-450-0(4))* American Girl Publishing, Inc.
McDonnell, Patrick. Hug Time. 2012. (ENG., Illus.). 30p. (J). (gr. -1 — 1). bds. 6.99 *(978-0-316-18295-9(8))* Little, Brown Bks. for Young Readers.
Mcduffee, William. Story Time with Grandpa Bill Collection. 2006. 50p. pap. 16.95 *(978-1-4241-4001-5(3))* America Star Bks.
McGill, Debora J. Faith Journeys with Hope & Love: Short Stories of Inspiration. 2011. 114p. pap. 19.99 *(978-1-4415-4203-8(5))* Xlibris Corp.
McGinley, Phyllis, et al. Little Golden Book Farm Favorites. Rojankovsky, Feodor & Gergely, Tibor, illus. 2012. (Little Golden Book Favorites Ser.). (ENG.). 80p. (J). (gr. k-k). 7.99 *(978-0-307-93020-0(3),* Golden Bks.) Random Hse. Children's Bks.
McGovern, Sheila. The Entire World of S & Z Book of Stories: 58 Targeted S & Z Pure Stories to Remediate Frontal & Lateral Lisps. l.t. ed. 2003. (Illus.). 148p. per. 34.99 *(978-0-9723457-5-0(2))* Say It Right.
McGrath, Barbara Barbieri. The Little Red Elf. Bonnet, Rosalinde, illus. 2010. (ENG.). 32p. (J). (gr. -1-2). pap. 7.95 *(978-1-58089-237-7(X))* Charlesbridge Publishing, Inc.
McGreal, Pat, et al. Walt Disney's Comics & Stories #701. 2009. 64p. pap. 7.99 *(978-1-60360-091-0(4))* Gemstone Publishing, Inc.
McHugh, Fiona. The Anne of Green Gables Story Book: Based on the Kevin Sullivan Film of Lucy Maud Montgomery's Classic Novel. 2004. (Illus.). 80p. (J). (gr. 4-8). reprint ed. 20.00 *(978-0-7567-8464-5(6))* DIANE Publishing Co.
McHugh, Maura. Twisted Myths: 20 Classic Stories with a Dark & Dangerous Heart. 2013. (ENG.). 144p. (J). (gr. 6-11). 19.99 *(978-0-7641-6620-4(4))* Barron's Educational Series, Inc.
McIntosh, Gavin. Hausaland Tales from the Nigerian Market Place. 2005. (Illus.). 98p. (J). (gr. 5-9). reprint ed. 22.00 *(978-0-7567-9714-0(4))* DIANE Publishing Co.
McKay, Jane. Tess & the Star Traveller. 2004. (Illus.). 96p. (Orig.). (J). pap. 8.95 *(978-1-920731-43-4(1))* Fremantle Pr. AUS. Dist: Independent Pubs. Group.
McKee, David. Elmer Sobre Zancos. 2003. (SPA., Illus.). 32p. (J). (gr. k-3). 12.95 *(978-84-372-2354-4(7))* Altea, Ediciones, S.A. - Grupo Santillana ESP. Dist: Santillana USA Publishing Co., Inc.
McKinley, Robin & Dickinson, Peter. Fire: Tales of Elemental Spirits. 2010. (ENG.). 304p. (gr. 12). 15.00 *(978-0-441-01919-9(6),* Ace Bks.) Penguin Publishing Group.
—Fire: Tales of Elemental Spirits. 2011. (ENG.). 320p. (YA). (gr. 7-18). 9.99 *(978-0-14-241945-8(1),* Firebird) Penguin Young Readers Group.
McKissack, Patricia C. The Dark-Thirty: Southern Tales of the Supernatural. Pinkney, Brian, illus. 2006. (ENG.). 128p. (J). (gr. 3-7). 18.95 *(978-0-679-81863-2(4),* Knopf Bks. for Young Readers) Random Hse. Children's Bks.
—Porch Lies: Tales of Slicksters, Tricksters, & Other Wily Characters. Carrilho, Andre, illus. 2006. (ENG.). 160p. (J). (gr. 3-7). 19.99 *(978-0-375-83619-0(5),* Schwartz & Wade Bks.) Random Hse. Children's Bks.
McMann, Lisa. Gone. 2010. (Wake Ser.: Bk. 3). (ENG.). 224p. (YA). (gr. 9-18). 17.99 *(978-1-4169-7918-0(2),* Simon Pulse) Simon Pulse.
McNatt, Martha. Grandmother's Face in the Mirror. 2003. (YA). per. 14.00 *(978-0-9741294-0-2(2))* Main St Publishing, Inc.
McQuinn, Anna. Lola Loves Stories. Beardshaw, Rosalind, illus. 2010. (ENG.). 28p. (J). (gr. k-3). pap. 6.95 *(978-1-58089-259-9(0))* Charlesbridge Publishing, Inc.
McSweeney's Books Staff. Noisy Outlaws, Unfriendly Blobs, & Some Other Things... That Aren't As Scary, Maybe, Depending on How You Feel about Lost Lands, Stray Cellphones, Creatures from the Sky, Parents Who Disappear in Peru, a Man Named Lars Farf, & One Other Story We Couldn't Quite Finish, So Maybe You Could Help Us Out. Thompson, Ted & Horowitz, Eli, eds. 2005. (ENG., Illus.). 208p. (YA). (gr. 3-17). 22.00 *(978-1-932416-35-0(8))* McSweeney's Publishing.
Me, Myself, & I & Other Stories: Individual Title Six-Pack. (Story Steps Ser.). (gr. k-2). 48.00 *(978-0-7635-9813-6(5))* Rigby Education.
Meadows, Daisy. Mia the Bridesmaid Fairy. 2010. (Rainbow Magic Ser.). (ENG.). 176p. (J). (gr. 2-5). 6.99 *(978-0-545-20251-0(5),* Scholastic Paperbacks) Scholastic, Inc.
Medearis, Michael & Medearis, Angela Shelf. Daisy & the Doll. Johnson, Larry, illus. 2005. (Vermont Folklife Center Children's Book Ser.). (ENG.). 32p. (J). (gr. -1-3). reprint ed. pap. 7.95 *(978-0-916718-23-7(9))* Vermont Folklife Ctr.
Medemach, T. K. On the High Seas. 2007. 104p. pap. 12.95 *(978-0-615-16040-5(9))* ThunderBolt Pubns.
Mehta, Shyam. Stories for Children. 2009. 68p. pap. 8.47 *(978-1-4092-8990-6(7))* Lulu Pr., Inc.
Melissa, De La Cruz, et al. 21 Proms. Levithan, David & Ehrenhaft, Daniel, eds. 2015. (ENG.). 304p. (J). (gr. 7). pap. 9.99 *(978-0-545-79867-9(1),* PUSH) Scholastic, Inc.
Melodie. The Arabian Nights, 7 vols. Collective Work Staff, illus. 2012. (ENG.). 32p. (J). (gr. 1). 19.95 *(978-2-7338-2150-3(4))* Auzou, Philippe Editions FRA. Dist: Consortium Bk. Sales & Distribution.
Melton, Lexi. Buck Toothed Charlie & Other Stories. 2010. 72p. pap. 34.99 *(978-1-4490-6183-8(4))* AuthorHouse.
Menix, Cinda. Tenbrook Farms. Menix, Cinda & McGuire, Bryan, illus. 2007. 67p. (J). (gr. 4-7). per. 23.99 *(978-1-59879-338-3(1))* Lifevest Publishing, Inc.
Menon, Geeta. Classic Collection: 22 Short Stories. Suman, Surendra, illus. 2005. 143p. (J). *(978-81-7011-970-8(7))* Children's Bk. Trust.
Menotti, Gian Carlo. Amahal y Los Tres Reyes. 2004. (Troquelados Clasicos Ser.). (SPA.). 16p. (J). pap. 2.95 *(978-84-7864-731-6(7))* Combel Editorial, S.A. ESP. Dist: Independent Pubs. Group.
Mercado, Nancy, ed. Baseball Crazy: Ten Stories That Cover All the Bases. 2009. (ENG.). 192p. (J). (gr. 3-7). 6.99 *(978-0-14-241371-5(2),* Puffin Books) Penguin Young Readers Group.
Mercado, Nancy E. & Mercado, Nancy, eds. Every Man for Himself: Ten Short Stories about Being a Guy. 2007. (ENG., Illus.). 176p. (YA). (gr. 7-18). 6.99 *(978-0-14-240813-1(1),* Speak) Penguin Young Readers Group.
Mercer, Christa Blum. German War Child: Growing Up in World War II. 2004. (Illus.). 176p. pap. 14.95 *(978-1-893597-07-5(5))* A. Borough Bks.
Metal, Liana. Storytime. 2008. 33p. pap. 16.50 *(978-1-4092-2451-8(1))* Lulu Pr., Inc.
Metzger, Lois. Be Careful What You Wish For: Ten Stories about Wishes. 2007. 195p. (J). pap. *(978-0-439-93334-6(X))* Scholastic, Inc.
—Can You Keep a Secret? Ten Stories about Secrets. 2007. 156p. (J). *(978-0-439-88022-0(X))* Scholastic, Inc.
Meyer, Carolyn. Rio Grande Stories. 2007. (ENG., Illus.). 272p. (J). (gr. 5-7). pap. 7.99 *(978-0-15-200066-0(6))* Houghton Mifflin Harcourt Publishing Co.
Meyers, Susan & Fox, Mem. Sweet Stories for Baby Gift Set. Frazee, Marla et al, illus. 2015. (ENG.). 128p. (J). (— 1). 16.99 *(978-0-544-53121-5(3),* HMH Books For Young Readers) Houghton Mifflin Harcourt Publishing Co.
Meza, Martin. Martin Mezas Story Time Three Short Stories, Vol. 1. 2007. 64p. pap. 14.21 *(978-1-4116-8486-7(9))* Lulu Pr., Inc.
—Martin Meza's story time Volume 5. 2007. 54p. pap. 25.95 *(978-0-615-16571-4(0))* Meza, Marti.
Mice & Other Stories: Individual Title Six-Pack. (Story Steps Ser.). (gr. k-2). 48.00 *(978-0-7635-9823-5(2))* Rigby Education.
Michael, Ted & Pultz, Josh. Starry-Eyed: 16 Stories That Steal the Spotlight. 2013. (ENG.). 400p. (YA). (gr. 2-17). pap. 9.95 *(978-0-7624-4949-1(7),* Running Pr. Kids) Running Pr. Bk. Pubs.
Michael Vey, the Electric Collection: Michael Vey; Michael Vey 2; Michael Vey 3. 2014. (Michael Vey Ser.). (ENG., Illus.).

1024p. (YA). (gr. 7). pap. 35.99 *(978-1-4814-1411-1(9),* Simon Pulse/Mercury Ink) Simon Pulse/Mercury Ink.
Michael's Faith. 2004. (J). bds. 14.95 *(978-0-9741406-2-9(7),* 0138) Cranberry Quill Publishing Co.
Michel, Pauline. Haunted Childhoods. Spencer, Nigel, tr. from FRE. 2006. (ENG.). 88p. pap. 19.95 *(978-1-894852-21-0(4))* Dundurn CAN. Dist: Ingram Publisher Services.
—Haunted Childhoods. 2006. (ENG & FRE.). 94p. (J). *(978-2-89261-460-2(0))* X Y Z Publishing.
Milbourne, Anna, et al. Myths & Legends. 2007. 192p. (J). 22.99 *(978-0-7945-1451-8(0),* Usborne) EDC Publishing.
Miles Kelly Publishing, creator. Children's Classic Stories: Fairytales, Fables & Folktales. 2007. (Illus.). 512p. (J). pap. *(978-1-84236-384-3(0))* Miles Kelly Publishing, Ltd.
—Stories for Girls. 2007. (Illus.). 512p. (J). pap. *(978-1-84236-586-1(X))* Miles Kelly Publishing, Ltd.
Miller, Bernice J. Bernice's Childrens Stories. 2010. 20p. pap. 10.49 *(978-1-4389-8498-8(7))* AuthorHouse.
Miller, J. Cris. Stories to Read to Children: The Pony & the Unicorn & 3 other Stories, 8 vols., Vol. 1. 2007. (Illus.). 80p. (J). 19.95 *(978-0-9725308-2-8(7))* Miller, J. Cris & Assocs.
Miller, Janet. Fox Tail Farms. 2011. 172p. pap. 19.95 *(978-1-257-85817-0(3))* Lulu Pr., Inc.
Miller, Lois. The Last Three Tall Tales. 2010. 72p. pap. 8.95 *(978-0-557-09181-2(0))* Lulu Pr., Inc.
Miller, Lois J. Three More Tall Tales. 2010. 93p. pap. 8.95 *(978-1-4357-4985-6(5))* Lulu Pr., Inc.
Miller, Michael Paul. Kid Tales. 2008. 103p. pap. 16.95 *(978-1-4357-0183-0(6))* Lulu Pr., Inc.
Milne, A. A. A Gallery of Children. Le Mair, Henriette Willebeek, illus. 2006. 79p. (J). (gr. k-4). reprint ed. 20.00 *(978-1-4223-5106-2(8))* DIANE Publishing Co.
Milroy, Jill & Milroy, Gladys. Eagle, Crow & Emu: Bird Stories. 2017. (ENG.). 88p. (J). (gr. 2-4). 9.95 ***(978-1-925163-71-1(7))*** Fremantle Pr. AUS. Dist: Independent Pubs. Group.
Mincher, Scott. The Blanket. 2009. 48p. pap. 15.99 *(978-1-4415-6632-4(5))* Xlibris Corp.
Mindel, Nissan. Eight Chanukah Tales. Toron, Eli & Graybar, Shmuel, illus. 2007. 78p. (J). 10.95 *(978-0-8266-0039-4(5))* Kehot Pubn. Society.
Mindy, Miss. Artist Sisters Vol. 2: Princess la la & the Little Bee - Teenie Weenie Tales. 2007. (ENG., Illus.). 64p. (YA). (gr. 8-12). pap. 30.00 *(978-0-9778949-7-0(5))* Baby Tattoo Bks.
Minnie & Minnie. The Science Playground: Fun with Science Concepts & Nature. 2009. 48p. pap. 24.99 *(978-1-4389-3466-2(1))* AuthorHouse.
Mirhady, Irandought. Thorn-Bush Boy: Pesare Tigh. Mirhady, Irandought, illus. 2004. Orig. Title: Pesare Tigh. (PEO., Illus.). 63p. (YA). per. *(978-0-9760323-0-4(9))* Mirhady, Farhad.
Miserius, Felicitatus. Terrible Tales: A the Absolutely, Positively, 100 Percent True Stories of Cinderella, Little Red Riding Hood, Those Three Greedy Pigs, Hairy Rapunzel. 2012. 106p. (-18). pap. 9.95 *(978-1-938908-20-0(1),* iUniverse Star) iUniverse, Inc.
Mitchell, Charlie. The Great M & M Caper. 2009. 82p. pap. 15.99 *(978-1-4415-2242-9(5))* Xlibris Corp.
Mitchell, Derrick Lee & Howard, Assuanta. Miyah & Koala's First Day. Mitchell, Derrick Lee, illus. 2012. (Illus.). 30p. 18.00 *(978-1-934947-69-2(5))* Asta Publications, LLC.
Mitchell, Laurence. Fish with Feet: From the Travels of Guppy Flynn, Book # 3. 2009. 32p. pap. 12.99 *(978-1-4389-5300-7(3))* AuthorHouse.
—Parents Don't Always Do the Right Things: Character Tales. 2009. 24p. pap. 12.00 *(978-1-4389-5407-3(7))* AuthorHouse.
Mitchell, Malinda. Spencer the Spring Chicken & Other Stories. Schandy, Rosita & Wooten, Neal, illus. 2007. 88p. pap. 23.95 *(978-0-9800675-0-7(2))* Mirror Publishing.
Mitchell, Stan R. Oskar Wins the Race. 2013. 28p. pap. 24.95 *(978-1-63000-407-1(3))* America Star Bks.
Molina, Maria Isabel. El Senor del Cero. Sole, Francisco, illus. 2003. (SPA.). 153p. (J). (gr. 5-8). pap. 10.95 *(978-968-19-0388-6(9))* Santillana USA Publishing Co., Inc.
Molina Temboury, Pedro. No Encontrarás el Tíbet en un Mapa. 2004. (SPA., Illus.). 160p. (J). *(978-84-667-1418-1(9))* Grupo Anaya, S.A.
Molyneux, Caroline. A 1940 Christmas. 2012. 16p. pap. 15.99 *(978-1-4772-2899-9(3))* AuthorHouse.
momodu, oshiomowe. Tales by Moonlight. 2009. 33p. pap. 5.16 *(978-0-557-03777-3(8))* Lulu Pr., Inc.
Monical, Olivia R. The Forest of Thinks. Monical, Olivia R., illus. 2012. (ENG., Illus.). 28p. (J). pap. 10.95 *(978-1-57733-267-1(9),* Papillon Publishing) Blue Dolphin Publishing, Inc.
Monkman, Olga. Dos Perros y una Abuela. Calderon, Marcela, illus. 2003. (SPA.). 31p. (J). (gr. k-3). pap. 9.95 *(978-950-511-642-3(X))* Santillana USA Publishing Co., Inc.
—Lo Que Cuentan los Inuit. (SPA.). (YA). (gr. 4-18). pap. *(978-950-07-1845-5(6),* SA30064) Editorial Sudamericana S.A. ARG. Dist: Lectorum Pubns., Inc.
—Un Rey sin Corona. Sanchez, Javier G., illus. 2003. (SPA.). 39p. (J). (gr. k-3). pap. 7.95 *(978-950-511-368-2(4))* Santillana USA Publishing Co., Inc.
Montgomery, L. M. Akin to Anne: Tales of Other Orphans. (YA). 22.95 *(978-0-8488-2656-7(6))* Amereon Ltd.
—Along the Shore: Tales by the Sea. (YA). 22.95 *(978-0-8488-2655-0(8))* Amereon Ltd.
—Anne of Green Gables. Fiona Fox Staff, ed. 2012. (ENG., Illus.). 416p. (J). 15.00 *(978-1-84135-842-0(8))* Award Pubns. Ltd. GBR. Dist: Parkwest Pubns., Inc.
—The Anne of Green Gables Collection: Six Complete & Unabridged Novels in One Volume. 2013. 1140p. *(978-1-78139-344-4(3))* Benediction Classics.
Moon, Jonny. The Beach Buoy. 2011. (GUNK Aliens Ser.). (ENG., Illus.). 112p. (J). (gr. 2-4). 7.99 *(978-0-00-732616-7(5))* HarperCollins Pubs. Ltd. GBR. Dist: Independent Pubs. Group.
Moore, Stephanie Perry. Golden Spirit. 2006. (Carmen Browne Ser.: 3). (ENG.). 144p. (YA). (gr. 3-7). per. 6.99 *(978-0-8024-8169-6(8),* Lift Every Voice) Moody Pubs.
Moral, Samantha Caballero Del. 100 Cuentos Clasicos. 2010. 512p. pap. *(978-607-404-198-9(9),* Silver Dolphin en Español) Advanced Marketing, S. de R. L. de C. V.
Morales, Alejandro. Little Nation & Other Stories. 2014. (ENG.). xxvi, 178p. (YA). pap. 17.95 *(978-1-55885-801-5(6))* Arte Publico Pr.
Morgan, Melissa J. Camp Confidential - Complete First Summer. 2009. (Camp Confidential Ser.: Nos. 1-4). (ENG.). 624p. (J). (gr. 3-7). pap. 14.99 *(978-0-448-45188-6(3),* Grosset & Dunlap) Penguin Young Readers Group.
Morgan, Michaela. Never Shake a Rattlesnake, 1. Sharratt, Nick, illus. 2012. (ENG.). 32p. (J). (gr. -1-k). pap. 8.99 *(978-0-330-51229-9(3))* Pan Macmillan GBR. Dist: Independent Pubs. Group.
Morgan, Robert. Bob Tales. Banton, Amy Renee, illus. 2003. 216p. (J). pap. 15.00 *(978-1-888562-06-4(4))* booksonnet.com.
Morgan, Winter. Martian Invasion: Tales of a Terrarian Warrior, Book Four. 2017. (ENG.). 112p. (J). (gr. 1-7). pap. 7.99 *(978-1-5107-2196-8(7),* Sky Pony Pr.) Skyhorse Publishing Co., Inc.
—Snow Fight: Tales of a Terrarian Warrior, Book Two. 2016. (ENG.). 112p. (J). (gr. 1-7). pap. 7.99 *(978-1-5107-1683-4(1),* Sky Pony Pr.) Skyhorse Publishing Co., Inc.
Moro, Robin, et al, illus. Read Aloud Spooky Stories. 2006. 320p. (J). (gr. 4-7). 15.98 *(978-0-7853-6338-5(6),* 7159100) Publications International, Ltd.
Morpurgo, Michael. Christmas Stories. Allsopp, Sophie et al, illus. 2016. (ENG.). 240p. (J). (gr. k-3). pap. 23.99 *(978-1-4052-6911-7(1))* Egmont Bks., Ltd. GBR. Dist: Independent Pubs. Group.
—Conker. Brown, Petra, illus. 2011. (Red Bananas Ser.). (ENG.). 48p. (J). (gr. k-2). pap. 7.99 *(978-1-4052-5639-1(7))* Egmont Bks., Ltd. GBR. Dist: Independent Pubs. Group.
—The Kingfisher Book of Great Boy Stories: A Treasury of Classics from Children's Literature. 2006. (Illus.). 160p. (J). (gr. 4-8). reprint ed. 20.00 *(978-1-4223-5207-6(2))* DIANE Publishing Co.
—The Marble Crusher. 2007. (ENG., Illus.). 96p. (J). (gr. 2-4). pap. 8.99 *(978-1-4052-2924-1(1))* Egmont Bks., Ltd. GBR. Dist: Independent Pubs. Group.
—The White Horse of Zennor & other Stories. 2nd ed. 2012. (ENG.). 160p. (J). (gr. 4-7). pap. 7.99 *(978-1-4052-5675-9(3))* Egmont Bks., Ltd. GBR. Dist: Independent Pubs. Group.
Morpurgo, Michael, selected by. Greatest Animal Stories. 2017. (ENG.). 256p. (J). (gr. 2-7). 16.99 ***(978-1-4380-5003-4(8))*** Barron's Educational Series, Inc.
Morris, April. Eldon the Elephant. 2004. (J). lib. bdg. 25.95 *(978-1-893595-49-1(8))* Four Seasons Bks., Inc.
Morris, Elizabeth. The Quest for the Tellings. Troy, Michael, illus. 2012. 52p. (-18). pap. *(978-1-78222-055-8(0))* Paragon Publishing, Rothersthorpe.
Morris, Neil. African Myths. Sansom, Fiona & Kennedy, Graham, illus. 2009. (Myths from Many Lands Ser.). 48p. (YA). (gr. 4-7). 29.25 *(978-1-60754-215-5(3))* Windmill Bks.
Morris Publishing Company Staff & Goscinny, René. The Daltons' Escape, Vol. 30. 2011. (Lucky Luke Ser.: 30). (ENG., Illus.). 48p. pap. 11.95 *(978-1-84918-091-7(1))* CineBook GBR. Dist: National Bk. Network.
Morrison, Jennifer. Beware of the Bull: Stories for the Young & the Incurably Eccentric. 2004. 90p. (YA). pap. 9.95 *(978-0-595-31054-8(0))* iUniverse, Inc.
Morrison, Toni & Morrison, Slade. Little Cloud & Lady Wind. Qualls, Sean, illus. 2010. (ENG.). 32p. (J). pap. 7.99 *(978-1-4169-8524-2(7),* Simon & Schuster Bks. For Young Readers) Simon & Schuster Bks. For Young Readers.
—Little Cloud & Lady Wind. Qualls, Sean, illus. 2010. (ENG.). 32p. (J). (gr. -1-3). 16.99 *(978-1-4169-8523-5(9),* Simon & Schuster/Paula Wiseman Bks.) Simon & Schuster/Paula Wiseman Bks.
—The Tortoise or the Hare. Cepeda, Joe, illus. 2010. (ENG.). 32p. (J). (gr. -1-3). 17.99 *(978-1-4169-8334-7(1),* Simon & Schuster/Paula Wiseman Bks.) Simon & Schuster/Paula Wiseman Bks.
Morrissette, Cora. Life Stories in the World of Fiction. 2009. 108p. 25.95 *(978-1-4327-3798-6(8))* Outskirts Pr., Inc.
Morse, William A. and & Morse, William A. And Dana Jo. Kurkle Kids: Spirit of America. 2009. 44p. pap. 16.99 *(978-1-4490-1009-6(1))* AuthorHouse.
Moseley, Tabitha. Pearl's Tales a Collection of Children's Stories. 2009. 92p. pap. 17.25 *(978-1-60860-670-2(8),* Strategic Bk. Publishing) Strategic Book Publishing & Rights Agency (SBPRA).
Moser, Erwin. Vicente, el Elefantito. (Buenas Noches Ser.). (SPA.). (J). (gr. k-3). 8.95 *(978-958-04-4903-4(1))* Norma S.A. COL. Dist: Distribuidora Norma, Inc.
Moses, Brian. Animal Pants! Boretzki, Anja, illus. 2012. (ENG.). 24p. (J). (gr. -1-k). pap. 8.99 *(978-0-230-73614-6(9))* Macmillan Pubs., Ltd. GBR. Dist: Independent Pubs. Group.
Moss, J. P. The Kind Fairy Adventures: 3 Loving Fairy Tales from the Land of the Faye. 2010. (Illus.). 52p. pap. 22.99 *(978-1-4520-3868-1(6))* AuthorHouse.
Moss, Yvonne. The Butterfly Princess. 2011. 16p. (gr. -1). pap. 9.49 *(978-1-4567-4044-3(X))* AuthorHouse.
—Seasons Through the Eyes of A Child: The Snow, the Spring, the Summer, the Fall. 2010. 12p. pap. 9.49 *(978-1-4520-3757-8(4))* AuthorHouse.
Motalebi, Majede. Wise Animals 2. 2012. 56p. pap. 24.99 *(978-1-4772-1622-4(7))* AuthorHouse.
Mother Goose Staff & Studio Mouse Staff. Sugar & Spice, 6 Bks. 2005. (ENG., Illus.). 10p. (J). 12.95 *(978-1-59249-471-2(4),* 1D100) Soundprints.
Mourabiti, Hassan & Rosen, Lynn. Once upon a Time in Hunger Land. 2012. 48p. pap. 11.95 *(978-1-4772-0819-9(4))* AuthorHouse.
Mowat, Diane. Pair of Ghostly Hands & Other Stories. 3rd ed. 2008. (ENG., Illus.). 80p. 9.38 *(978-0-19-479125-0(4))* Oxford Univ. Pr., Inc.
Mrs Molesworth & Molesworth, Mary Louisa S. The Thirteen Little Black Pigs & Other Stories. 2011. 66p. 16.95 *(978-1-4638-9845-8(2))* Rodgers, Alan Bks.
Mrs Molesworth, et al. The Thirteen Little Black Pigs & Other Stories. 2011. 66p. pap. 8.95 *(978-1-4638-0052-9(5))* Rodgers, Alan Bks.
Mueller, Sylvia Price. Barnyard Stories. 2003. 40p. pap. 9.00 *(978-0-8059-5939-0(4))* Dorrance Publishing Co., Inc.
Mullican, Norma Waldon & Zivney, Missy Mullican. A Collection of Squirrel Tales: Something to Crow About. 2009. 84p. pap. 10.99 *(978-1-60791-702-1(5))* Salem Author Services.
Mulock, Dinah Maria. The Fairy Book: The Best Popular Stories Selected & Rendered Anew. 2007. (ENG.). 326p. pap. 23.99 *(978-1-4346-4529-6(0));* 358p. pap. 26.99 *(978-1-4346-4530-2(4))* Creative Media Partners, LLC.
Mundy, Charlene & Chapline, Jo. David's Donkey Tales. 2007. 73p. pap. 12.50 *(978-0-615-16825-8(6))* Knee-High Adventures.
Muneefa. My Tales for Children. 2006. 90p. (J). pap. 13.95 *(978-1-58909-339-3(9))* Bookstand Publishing.
Munoz de Coronado, Martha, ed. Subidos de Tono: Cuentos de Amor. 2005. (SPA., Illus.). 253p. (J). pap. 14.95 *(978-9972-40-251-7(7))* Promocion Editorial Inca S.A., PEISA PER. Dist: Iaconi, Mariuccia Bk. Imports.
Munsch, Robert. I Have to Go! Martchenko, Michael, illus. 8th ed. 2010. (ENG.). 24p. (J). (gr. -1-k). bds. 7.99 *(978-1-55451-253-9(0),* 9781554512539) Annick Pr., Ltd. CAN. Dist: Publishers Group West (PGW).
—Mortimer. Martchenko, Michael, illus. 10th ed. 2010. (ENG.). 26p. (J). (gr. -1). bds. 7.99 *(978-1-55451-228-7(X),* 9781554512287) Annick Pr., Ltd. CAN. Dist: Publishers Group West (PGW).
—Mud Puddle. Petricic, Dusan, illus. 4th ed. 2012. (Munsch for Kids Ser.). (ENG.). 32p. (J). (gr. -1-2). 9.95 *(978-1-55451-426-7(6),* 9781554514267) Annick Pr., Ltd. CAN. Dist: Publishers Group West (PGW).
—Munsch Mini-Treasury One. Martchenko, Michael, illus. 5th ed. 2010. (Munsch for Kids Ser.). (ENG.). 144p. (J). (gr. -1-2). 18.95 *(978-1-55451-273-7(5),* 9781554512737) Annick Pr., Ltd. CAN. Dist: Publishers Group West (PGW).
—Munsch Mini-Treasury Two. 4th ed. 2010. (Munsch for Kids Ser.). (ENG., Illus.). 136p. (J). (gr. -1-2). 18.95 *(978-1-55451-274-4(3),* 9781554512744) Annick Pr., Ltd. CAN. Dist: Publishers Group West (PGW).
Munsch, Robert & McGraw, Sheila. Love You Forever. 2012. 18p. 29.95 *(978-1-59530-466-7(5))* Hallmark Card, Inc.
Munson, Weegie. The Tales of Weegie Munson. 2012. 44p. pap. 16.95 *(978-1-62709-684-3(1))* America Star Bks.
Murphy, Elspeth Campbell. God Makes It Right: Three Stories for Children Based on Favorite Bible Verses. Nelson, Jane E., illus. 72p. (J). *(978-1-55513-109-8(3))* Cook, David C.
Murphy, Lisa. Secret Smile. 2008. 52p. pap. 11.95 *(978-1-4092-2767-0(7))* Lulu Pr., Inc.
Murphy, Mary. Let's Go! 2005. (ENG., Illus.). 16p. (J). bds. 14.99 *(978-1-4052-1115-4(6))* Egmont Bks., Ltd. GBR. Dist: Trafalgar Square Publishing.
Murphy, Stuart J. Freda Plans a Picnic. 2010. (I See I Learn Ser.). (ENG., Illus.). 32p. (J). (gr. -1-k). 14.95 *(978-1-58089-456-2(9))* Charlesbridge Publishing, Inc.
—Good Job, Ajay! 2010. (I See I Learn Ser.). (ENG., Illus.). 32p. (J). (gr. -1-k). 14.95 *(978-1-58089-454-8(2))* Charlesbridge Publishing, Inc.
Murray, Brendan. Tev on Home Turf. 2004. 192p. (YA). pap. 13.50 *(978-1-920731-33-5(4))* Fremantle Pr. AUS. Dist: Independent Pubs. Group.
Murray, George. The Tales of Molly Brand & MacNessie. 2008. 70p. pap. 14.95 *(978-1-4092-3724-2(9))* Lulu Pr., Inc.
Murray, Victoria Christopher. Nevergiue. 2009. (Divas Ser.). (ENG., Illus.). 272p. pap. 11.00 *(978-1-4165-6350-1(4),* Gallery Bks.) Gallery Bks.
Muth, Jon J. Zen Shorts. collector's ed. 2008. (ENG., Illus.). 40p. (J). (gr. -1-3). 25.00 *(978-0-545-04087-7(6),* Scholastic) Scholastic, Inc.
Mwanamwalye, Crebby Ilishebo. Story Time. 2013. 52p. pap. 10.03 *(978-1-4669-9028-9(7))* Trafford Publishing.
My First Book of Christmas Stories. 2003. (J). 8.99 *(978-1-59384-014-3(4))* Parklane Publishing.
Myers, Tamar. Angels, Angels Everywhere. 2004. pap. 7.95 *(978-0-9747685-3-3(7))* Bella Rosa Bks.
Myers, Walter Dean. 145th Street: Short Stories. 2012. (ENG.). 192p. (YA). (gr. 7). pap. 9.99 *(978-0-307-97610-9(6),* Ember) Random Hse. Children's Bks.
Mysterious Chills & Thrills: 10 creepy, strange, adventurous short stories for kids to tickle the Imagination. 2004. (J). per. 6.95 *(978-0-9749013-0-5(X))* LH Pubns. & Productions.
Naidoo, Beverley. The Great Tug of War. Grobler, Piet, illus. 2006. (ENG.). 96p. (J). (gr. 2-17). per. 7.95 *(978-1-84507-055-7(0),* Frances Lincoln) Quarto Publishing Group UK GBR. Dist: Hachette Bk. Group.
—Out of Bounds: Seven Stories of Conflict & Hope. 2008. (ENG.). 208p. (J). (gr. 5). pap. 6.99 *(978-0-06-050801-2(9))* HarperCollins Pubs.
Nambiar, Vinesh. Adventures in Human Values - Series 1: Courage, Kindness, Forgiveness, Teamwork, Compassion, Listening, Caring, Self-Confidence, Sharing. 2007. (Illus.). (J). pap. 9.99 *(978-0-9798986-0-0(9))* Human Values 4 Kids Foundation, The.
Nappi, Frank. The Legend of Mickey Tussler. 2012. (ENG.). 304p. (YA). (gr. 6-11). pap. 17.99 *(978-1-61608-658-9(0),* 608658, Sky Pony Pr.) Skyhorse Publishing Co., Inc.
—Sophomore Campaign: A Mickey Tussler Novel. 2012. (ENG.). 280p. (YA). (gr. 6-11). pap. 12.95 *(978-1-61608-663-3(7),* 608663, Sky Pony Pr.) Skyhorse Publishing Co., Inc.
Narváez, Concha López. El Fuego de los Pastores.Tr. of Shepherds' Fire. (SPA.). (YA). (gr. 5). pap. *(978-84-395-0902-8(2))* Espasa Calpe, S.A. ESP. Dist: Lectorum Pubns., Inc.
Nash, Scott. Shrunken Treasures: Literary Classics, Short, Sweet & Silly. Nash, Scott, illus. 2016. (ENG., Illus.). 40p. (J). (gr. k-3). 15.99 *(978-0-7636-6972-0(5))* Candlewick Pr.
Nasir, Safia. Princess Neelam & Other Stories. 2005. 52p. *(978-91-21-51821-2(1)); (978-969-542-109-3(1))* Children Pubns.
Nass, Marcia & Campisi, Stephanie. Mini Mysteries & Kooky Spookies. Innes, Calvin, illus. 2007. 176p. per. 6.99 *(978-0-9795364-2-7(1))* Chowder Bay Bks.
Naughton, Bill. The Goalkeeper's Revenge. 2012. (ENG.). 110p. (YA). pap. 12.99 *(978-1-4482-0443-4(7),* 9781448204434, Bloomsbury Reader) Bloomsbury Publishing Plc GBR. Dist: Macmillan.
Nayeri, Daniel. Straw House, Wood House, Brick House, Blow: Four Novellas by Daniel Nayeri. Weinberg, James, illus. 2011. (ENG.). 432p. (YA). (gr. 9). 19.99 *(978-0-7636-5526-6(0))* Candlewick Pr.
Nesbit, E. Beautiful Stories from Shakespeare. 2009. 116p. pap. 10.50 *(978-1-60459-575-8(2))* Wilder Pubns., Corp.
—The Book of Dragons. 2008. 108p. 23.95 *(978-1-60664-859-9(4));* (gr. 2-13). pap. 9.95 *(978-1-60664-106-4(9))* Aegypan.
—The Book of Dragons. Fell, H. Granville & Millar, H. R., illus. unabr. ed. 2004. (Dover Children's Classics Ser.). (ENG.). 176p. (gr. 3-5). pap. 7.95 *(978-0-486-43648-7(9))* Dover Pubns., Inc.
—The Magic World. 2006. 156p. (gr. -1-7). 24.95 *(978-1-59818-176-0(9))* Aegypan.
—Magic World. 2006. 156p. (gr. -1-7). per. 12.95 *(978-1-59818-966-7(2))* Aegypan.
—The Rainbow & the Rose. l.t. ed. 2006. 124p. pap. *(978-1-84637-280-3(1))* Echo Library.
—The Seven Dragons & Other Stories. 2006. 140p. 24.95 *(978-1-59818-171-5(8))* Aegypan.
—Seven Dragons & Other Stories. 2006. 140p. per. 11.95 *(978-1-59818-964-3(6))* Aegypan.
—7 Books in 1 - "The Railway Children", "Five Children & It", "The Phoenix & the Carpet", "The Story of the Amulet", "The Story of the Treasure-Seekers", "The Would-Be-Goods" & "The Enchanted Castle" 2004. 472p. pap. *(978-0-9548401-0-5(0))* Shoes & Ships & Sealing Wax Ltd.
Nesbit, Edith. Flehes an Hens Horn. Williams, Nicholas, tr. from ENG. Brock, Charles Edmund, illus. 2012. (COR.). 260p. pap. *(978-1-78201-003-6(3))* Evertype.
—Pussy & Doggy Tales. 2011. 106p. 22.95 *(978-1-4638-9856-4(8));* pap. 9.95 *(978-1-4638-0127-4(0))* Rodgers, Alan Bks.
Ness, Berthetta. Originals: Short Stories for Children. 2007. (YA). pap. *(978-1-57579-351-1(2))* Pine Hill Pr.
Neubert, Oliver. Chantel's Quest for the Silver Leaf. 2012. (Chantel's Quest Ser.). (ENG., Illus.). 200p. (J). (gr. 4-7). pap. 9.95 *(978-1-897476-43-7(4))* Simply Read Bks. CAN. Dist: Ingram Publisher Services.
New Burlington Books, creator. The Great Big Book of Bedtime Stories & Rhyme. 2008. (Illus.). 304p. (J). *(978-1-84538-882-9(8))* New Burlington Bks.
Newton, Jill. Don't Wake Mr Bear! Newton, Jill, illus. 2011. (ENG., Illus.). 32p. (J). (gr. -1). pap. 9.99 *(978-1-4052-4966-9(8))* Egmont Bks., Ltd. GBR. Dist: Independent Pubs. Group.
Newton-Kowalsky, Jacqueline. Itsy Bitsy Stories for Itsy Bitsy Tigers. 2012. 32p. pap. *(978-1-77097-138-7(6))* FriesenPress.
Nicholai, Rachel, et al. Bird Adventures. Nicholai, Rachel et al, illus. 2006. (Adventure Story Collection Ser.). 28p. (J). (gr. 2-6). pap. 10.00 *(978-1-58084-246-4(1))* Lower Kuskokwim Schl. District.
Nichols, C. D. Kids Courageous. 2010. 66p. pap. 9.99 *(978-1-60911-809-9(X),* Eloquent Bks.) Strategic Book Publishing & Rights Agency (SBPRA).
Nicholson, Nancy. Devotional Stories for Little Folks Too. 2007. (J). per. *(978-0-9771236-1-2(8))* For Little Folks.
Nick, Papa. Never Ending Stories. 2011. 44p. pap. 24.95 *(978-1-4626-3792-8(2))* America Star Bks.
—Never Ending Stories: Part Three. 2012. 48p. 24.95 *(978-1-4626-6243-2(9))* America Star Bks.
Nickel, Scott. Curse of the Red Scorpion, 1 vol. Harpster, Steve, illus. 2006. (Graphic Sparks Ser.). (ENG.). 40p. (gr. 1-3). per. 5.95 *(978-1-59889-169-0(3),* Graphic Sparks) Stone Arch Bks.
Nicolle, Malachai. Bad Guy Earth, Vol. 1. 2011. (ENG., Illus.). 120p. (J). (gr. 5-12). pap. 14.99 *(978-1-59582-825-5(7))* Dark Horse Comics.
Nikakhtar, Manijeh. Love & Joy. 2010. 65p. pap. 21.95 *(978-1-4327-4394-9(5))* Outskirts Pr., Inc.
Nikola-Lisa, W. La Alegriade Ser Tu Yo. 2004. (SPA., Illus.). (J). (gr. k-3). spiral bd. *(978-0-616-03093-6(2))* Canadian National Institute for the Blind/Institut National Canadien pour les Aveugles.
Nimmo, Jenny. The Beasties. Millward, Gwen, illus. 2012. (ENG.). 32p. (J). (gr. -1-k). pap. 8.99 *(978-1-4052-4335-3(X))* Egmont Bks., Ltd. GBR. Dist: Independent Pubs. Group.
Nimr, Sonia. Ghaddar the Ghoul: And Other Palestinian Stories. Shaw, Hannah, illus. 2008. (ENG.). 96p. (J). (gr. 2-17). per. 7.95 *(978-1-84507-523-1(4),* Frances Lincoln) Quarto Publishing Group UK GBR. Dist: Hachette Bk. Group.
Nino, Jairo Anibal. El Quinto Viaje y Otras Historias del Nuevo Mundo. Isaza, Juanita, illus. 2004. (Literatura Juvenil (Panamericana Editorial) Ser.). (SPA.). 153p. (J). (gr. 4-7). pap. *(978-958-30-0573-2(8),* PV4381) Centro de Informacion y Desarrollo de la Comunicacion y la Literatura MEX. Dist: Lectorum Pubns., Inc.
Nite, Aluta. Folk Tales for Children's Enjoyment Book: Why & How Fables Number Two. 2011. 30p. pap. 16.95 *(978-1-4626-1033-4(1))* America Star Bks.
—Why & How Fables Number Three: Folk Tales for Children's Enjoyment Book 3. 2011. 40p. pap. 16.95 *(978-1-4626-2518-5(5))* America Star Bks.
Nix, Garth. Across the Wall: A Tale of the Abhorsen & Other Stories. 2006. (ENG.). 432p. (YA). (gr. 8-12). pap. 8.99 *(978-0-06-074715-2(3),* HarperTeen) HarperCollins Pubs.
—To Hold the Bridge. 2015. (ENG.). 416p. (YA). (gr. 8). 17.99 *(978-0-06-229252-0(8))* HarperCollins Pubs.
Noel for Jeanne Marie. 2004. (Illus.). 34p. (J). mass mkt. 9.99 *(978-0-9740599-5-2(1))* Omnibus Publishing.
Nolen, Jerdine. Big Jabe. Nelson, Kadir, illus. 2004. (gr. 1). 17.00 *(978-0-7569-3184-1(3))* Perfection Learning Corp.
Norrie, Louise Rosalyn. The Adventures of Flat Cat. 2011. 144p. pap. 19.99 *(978-1-4628-9396-6(1))* Xlibris Corp.
Northcott, Richard. Meet Molly. 2010. (ENG., Illus.). 20p. 4.81 *(978-0-19-440087-9(5))* Oxford Univ. Pr., Inc.
Nöstlinger, Christine. De Por Que a Franz le Dolio el Estomago. (Torre de Papel Ser.). (SPA.). (J). (gr. 2). 7.95 *(978-958-04-1143-7(3))* Norma S.A. COL. Dist: Distribuidora Norma, Inc.
—Juanito Habichuela y Otros Cuentos. (Torre de Papel Ser.). (SPA.). (J). (gr. 4-18). 8.95 *(978-958-04-4533-3(8))* Norma S.A. COL. Dist: Distribuidora Norma, Inc.
—Mas Historias de Franz. (Torre de Papel Ser.). (SPA.). (J). (gr. 2). 7.95 *(978-958-04-1014-0(3))* Norma S.A. COL. Dist: Distribuidora Norma, Inc.
—Nuevas Historias de Franz en la Escuela. (Torre de Papel Ser.). (SPA.). (J). (gr. 2). 7.95 *(978-958-04-1013-3(5))* Norma S.A. COL. Dist: Distribuidora Norma, Inc.
Noyes, Deborah, ed. Gothic! 2006. (ENG.). 256p. (YA). (gr. 9-12). per. 8.99 *(978-0-7636-2737-9(2))* Candlewick Pr.

S

—Sideshow: Ten Original Tales of Freaks, Illusionists, & Other Matters Odd & Magical. 2009. (ENG., Illus.). 240p. (YA). (gr. 9-18). 16.99 *(978-0-7636-3752-1(1))* Candlewick Pr.

Nyamnjoh, Francis B. Stories from Abakwa. 2007. *(978-9956-558-00-1(1))* Langaa Research & Publishing Common Initiative Group CMR. Dist: Michigan State Univ. Pr.

Nye, Naomi Shihab. There Is No Long Distance Now: Very Short Stories. 2011. (ENG.). 208p. (YA). (gr. 8). 17.99 *(978-0-06-201965-3(1)*, Greenwillow Bks.) HarperCollins Pubs.

Nyman, Mary. High School Stories: Short Takes from the Writers' Club. 2010. 64p. pap. 8.95 *(978-1-4502-1585-5(8))* iUniverse, Inc.

Oates, Joyce Carol. Small Avalanches & Other Stories. 2003. 400p. (YA). 17.89 *(978-0-06-001218-2(8)*, HarperTeen) HarperCollins Pubs.

O'Callaghan, G. The Eternals. 2007. 376p. per. *(978-1-84693-055-3(3))* Best Global Publishing Ltd.

—Sorcerers Apprentice. 2007. 244p. per. *(978-1-84693-024-9(3))* Best Global Publishing Ltd.

O'Connell, S. L. Short Stories to Tickle the Imagination. 2009. 48p. pap. 16.50 *(978-1-60693-670-2(0)*, Eloquent Bks.) Strategic Book Publishing & Rights Agency (SBPRA).

O'Connor, Jane. Fancy Nancy's Fabulous Fall Storybook Collection. Glasser, Robin Preiss, illus. 2014. (Fancy Nancy Ser.). (ENG.). 192p. (J). (gr. -1-3). 11.99 *(978-0-06-228884-4(9))* HarperCollins Pubs.

—Nancy Clancy's Ultimate Chapter Book Quartet. Glasser, Robin Preiss, illus. 2015. (Nancy Clancy Ser.). (ENG.). 576p. (J). (gr. 1-5). pap. 17.99 *(978-0-06-242273-6(1))* HarperCollins Pubs.

O'Dea, Rory & Benchmark Education Co. Staff. Books That Changed My Life. 2014. (Text Connections Ser.). (J). (gr. 5). *(978-1-4900-1366-4(0))* Benchmark Education Co.

Odell, Carol. Once upon a Time in the Kitchen. Pignataro, Anna, illus. 2010. (Myths, Legends, Fairy & Folktales Ser.). (ENG.). 48p. (J). (gr. 1-4). 12.95 *(978-1-58536-518-0(1)*, 202208) Sleeping Bear Pr.

O'Dell, Patrick Timothy Wayne. Elvin. 2009. 58p. pap. 16.95 *(978-1-61546-576-7(6))* America Star Bks.

O'Dell, Scott. The Seven Serpents Trilogy. 2009. (ENG.). 560p. (J). (gr. 4-6). pap. 19.99 *(978-1-4022-1836-1(2)*, Sourcebooks Jabberwocky) Sourcebooks, Inc.

Oduwole, Ben. The Flying Tortoise. 2009. 182p. pap. 43.50 *(978-1-60693-611-5(5)*, Eloquent Bks.) Strategic Book Publishing & Rights Agency (SBPRA).

Okeke-Ibezim, Felicia. African Folk Tales: Obiageli & Other Stories. 2006. (YA). per. 9.95 *(978-0-9661598-7-5(X))* Ekwike Bks. & Publishing.

O'Kif, illus. No Somos Irrompibles (12 Cuentos de Chicos Enamorados) 2003. (SPA.). 143p. (J). (gr. 8-12). pap. 9.95 *(978-950-511-243-2(2))* Santillana USA Publishing Co., Inc.

Okubo, Margaret. The Story of Angelo. 2005. (YA). per. 12.95 *(978-0-9763686-2-5(5))* Rapha Publishing.

La Ola Gigante; El Primer Dia de Clases, 2 bks., Set. unabr. ed. (Coleccion Chiquilines - Imagen y Sonido). (SPA., Illus.). (J). 15.95 incl. audio *(978-950-11-0626-8(8)*, SGM268) Sigmar ARG. Dist: Continental Bk. Co., Inc.

Olcott, Frances Jenkins. Good Stories for Great Holidays. l.t. ed. 2006. (ENG.). 324p. pap. 24.99 *(978-1-4264-1125-0(1))* Creative Media Partners, LLC.

—Good Stories for Holidays. 2004. reprint ed. pap. 27.95 *(978-1-4191-2211-8(8))*; pap. 1.99 *(978-1-4192-2211-5(2))* Kessinger Publishing, LLC.

Oldfield, Jenny. I'd Like a Little Word, Leonie! Child, Lauren, illus. 99p. (J). pap. 8.99 *(978-0-340-78501-0(2))* Macmillan Pubs., Ltd. GBR. Dist: Trafalgar Square Publishing.

—Not Now, Nathan! Child, Lauren, illus. 107p. (J). pap. 7.99 *(978-0-340-78502-7(0))* Macmillan Pubs., Ltd. GBR. Dist: Trafalgar Square Publishing.

—When Scott Got Lost No. 2. (Illus.). (J). mass mkt. 8.99 *(978-0-340-85073-2(6))* Macmillan Pubs., Ltd. GBR. Dist: Trafalgar Square Publishing.

O'Leary, Sara. When I Was Small. Morstad, Julie, illus. 2012. (ENG.). 32p. (J). (gr. -1-3). 16.95 *(978-1-897476-38-3(8))* Simply Read Bks. CAN. Dist: Ingram Publisher Services.

O'Leary, Sara & Opal, Paola. Zingy. Morstad, Julie, illus. 2013. (Simply Small Ser.: 10). (ENG.). 24p. (J). (gr. k — 1). bds. 7.95 *(978-1-897476-75-8(2))* Simply Read Bks. CAN. Dist: Ingram Publisher Services.

Oliver, Chad. Far from This Earth & Other Stories. Olson, Priscilla, ed. Dennis, Jane, illus. 2003. (NESFA's Choice Ser.: 25). 480p. 24.00 *(978-1-886778-48-1(5)*, NESFA Pr.) New England Science Fiction Assn., Inc.

—A Star Above It & Other Stories. Olson, Priscilla, ed. Dennis, Jane, illus. 2003. (NESFA's Choice Ser.: 24). 480p. 24.00 *(978-1-886778-45-0(0)*, NESFA Pr.) New England Science Fiction Assn., Inc.

One Woman, One Hustle: Short Stories & Poems Inspired by Sheri J. Booker. 2003. per. 10.00 *(978-0-9727776-0-5(1)*, Book Her Publications) Lyrically Korrect Publishing.

O'Neill, Ian. Jimmy First & Destiny's Watch. 2011. 122p. pap. *(978-0-7552-0675-9(4))* Authors OnLine, Ltd.

Onyefulu, Ifeoma & Quarto Generic Staff. The Girl Who Married a Ghost: And Other Tales from Nigeria. 2010. (ENG., Illus.). 112p. (J). (gr. 3-6). 15.95 *(978-1-84780-176-0(5)*, Frances Lincoln Children's Bks.) Quarto Publishing Group UK GBR. Dist: Hachette Bk. Group.

Opal, Paola, illus. Saffy & Ollie. 2012. (Simply Small Ser.). (ENG.). 24p. (J). (gr. -1 — 1). bds. 7.95 *(978-1-897476-69-7(8))* Simply Read Bks. CAN. Dist: Ingram Publisher Services.

Oppel, Kenneth. The Silverwing Collection: Silverwing; Sunwing; Firewing. 2014. (Silverwing Trilogy Ser.). (ENG., Illus.). 896p. (J). (gr. 3-7). pap. 23.99 *(978-1-4814-2725-8(3)*, Simon & Schuster Bks. For Young Readers) Simon & Schuster Bks. For Young Readers.

Oram, Hiawyn. Counting Leopard's Spots & other Stories. Warnes, Tim, illus. 2005. 96p. (J). (gr. k-4). reprint ed. 17.00 *(978-0-7567-9252-7(5))* DIANE Publishing Co.

Orback, Craig, illus. Paul Bunyan. 2007. (On My Own Folklore Ser.). (ENG.). 48p. (gr. 2-4). per. 6.95 *(978-0-8225-6479-9(3)*, First Avenue Editions) Lerner Publishing Group.

Orczy, Emmuska. Castles in the Air. 2008. 160p. 25.95 *(978-1-60664-927-5(2))*; pap. 14.95 *(978-1-60664-047-0(X))* Aegypan.

—The Gallant Pimpernel - Unabridged - Lord Tony's Wife, the Way of the Scarlet Pimpernel, Sir Percy Leads the Band, the Triumph of the Scarlet Pimpernel. 2012. 804p. *(978-1-78139-227-0(7))* Benediction Classics.

Orford, Margie. The Little Red Hen. Lilje, Karen, illus. 2011. (Best Loved Tales for Africa Ser.). (ENG.). 32p. (J). (gr. k-2). pap. 10.95 *(978-1-77009-821-3(6))* Jacana Media ZAF. Dist: Independent Pubs. Group.

Organ, Beryl E. Tiggy's World. 2010. 26p. pap. 15.99 *(978-1-4500-7915-0(6))* Xlibris Corp.

Orme, David. Plague. 2004. (Shades Ser.). (ENG.). 58p. (J). pap. 7.99 *(978-0-237-52729-7(4))* Evans Brothers, Ltd. GBR. Dist: Independent Pubs. Group.

Ormsby, Nathaniel Hosea. Timeless Tales of Anansi: Ancestral Realm of Africa. 2006. 108p. pap. 19.95 *(978-1-4241-3396-3(3))* PublishAmerica, Inc.

Ostendorf, Jenifer Wirth & Bisbee, Richard J. Worthwhile Family Tales. 2010. 160p. pap. 11.99 *(978-1-4490-7605-4(X))* AuthorHouse.

O'Sullivan, Deirdre. Cousin Caleigh's Cartoons: And Other Stories, 1 vol. 2009. 97p. pap. 19.95 *(978-1-60836-304-9(X))* America Star Bks.

Otenbaker, Audrey Lee. God's Jewel. 2009. 48p. (J). pap. 17.95 *(978-1-4327-3340-7(0))* Outskirts Pr., Inc.

Others, et al. Avatar - The Last Airbender - The Lost Adventures. Gurihiru, illus. 2011. (ENG.). 240p. pap. 14.99 *(978-1-59582-748-7(X))* Dark Horse Comics.

Our Lady of the Winding Sheets: The Cher'azade Series. 2006. (Cher'azade Ser.). (YA). 7.95 *(978-0-9746669-2-1(0))* Franklin, J.E.

Outram, Evelyn. Sav & Josh O Lucky's Christmas Adventure & Magic Street. 2010. 56p. pap. 17.95 *(978-1-60911-876-1(6)*, Eloquent Bks.) Strategic Book Publishing & Rights Agency (SBPRA).

Overell, J. J. The Dancing Flame. Lawrie, Robin, illus. 2003. (ENG.). 128p. (J). per. 17.00 *(978-0-7188-3036-6(9))* Lutherworth Pr., The GBR. Dist: Casemate Academic.

Owings, Jeff. Tiny Todd: Swooped Away. 2009. 20p. pap. 10.49 *(978-1-4490-1214-4(0))* AuthorHouse.

—Tiny Todd: Tiny Todd's First Pet. 2009. 20p. pap. 10.49 *(978-1-4490-1216-8(7))* AuthorHouse.

Oxford University Press Staff & Bassett, Jennifer, eds. Omega Files - Short Stories. 3rd ed. 2008. (ENG., Illus.). 64p. 10.00 *(978-0-19-478913-4(6))* Oxford Univ. Pr., Inc.

Ozaki, Yei. Warriors of Old Japan. 2007. 168p. per. 14.95 *(978-1-59654-553-3(4))* Disruptive Publishing.

& Packer, Knife & McCoshan, Duncan. Captain Fact's Creepy Crawly Adventure. 2004. (Illus.). 96p. (J). pap. *(978-1-4052-0834-5(1))* Egmont Bks., Ltd.

Padma, T. V. The Forbidden Temple: Stories from the Past. Vyas, Bhavana, illus. 2004. 95p. (J). *(978-81-8146-041-7(3))* Tulika Pubs.

Pagan, Joseph. The Collection of Short Stories for Children & Young Adults. 2013. 136p. (gr. 2-4). 22.87 *(978-1-4669-8462-2(7))*; pap. 12.87 *(978-1-4669-8463-9(5))* Trafford Publishing.

Page, Louise. Furballs' Fables. 2008. 100p. pap. 17.50 *(978-1-4092-1068-9(5))* Lulu Pr., Inc.

Pajaroflor. 2003. (SPA.). pap. *(978-956-13-1080-3(5)*, AB8005) Bello, Andres CHL. Dist: Lectorum Pubns., Inc.

Palahicky, Sophia. Kid's Reading Craze - a Collection of 20 Short Stories. 2013. 64p. pap. *(978-1-4602-1576-0(1))* FriesenPress.

Palermo, Miguel Angel. Lo Que Cuentan los Onas. (SPA.). (YA). (gr. 4-18). pap. *(978-950-07-1260-6(1)*, SA30066) Editorial Sudamericana S.A. ARG. Dist: Lectorum Pubns., Inc.

Paloma Sanllehi, David. UNA BUENA COSTUMBRE. 2003. (Caballo Alado Series-Al Galope Ser.). (SPA & ENG., Illus.). 24p. (J). (gr. k-2). pap. 5.95 *(978-84-7864-671-5(X))* Combel Editorial, S.A. ESP. Dist: Independent Pubs. Group.

Panaitescu, Simona. The Unseen Paths of the Forest: 13 Tales about Love & Friendship. Moscal, Manuela, illus. 2012. (ENG.). 263p. pap. 14.95 *(978-1-4327-7908-5(7))* Outskirts Pr., Inc.

Panman, Sandra & Panman, Richard. Short Stories. Panman, Sandra, ed. 5th ed. 2004. (Illus.). 192p. (YA). (gr. 7-12). reprint ed. pap. 23.95 *(978-0-912813-32-5(6))* Active Learning Corp.

Pants & the Bully. 2004. (J). per. 7.99 *(978-0-9755959-1-6(1))* Girl Named Pants, Inc., A.

Pants Feeds the Poor. 2004. (J). per. 7.99 *(978-0-9755959-3-0(8))* Girl Named Pants, Inc., A.

Parish, Peggy & Parish, Herman. An Amelia Bedelia Celebration: Four Stories Tall. Sweat, Lynn & Siebel, Fritz, illus. 2009. (Amelia Bedelia Ser.). (ENG.). 224p. (J). (gr. -1-3). 19.99 *(978-0-06-171030-8(X)*, Greenwillow Bks.) HarperCollins Pubs.

Parker, Emma. Albert & the Dragon. 2010. (Illus.). 20p. pap. *(978-1-877561-50-4(9))* First Edition Ltd.

—Bath Time. 2010. (Illus.). pap. *(978-1-877547-83-6(2))* First Edition Ltd.

—Bill Hides Acorns. 2010. (Illus.). 24p. pap. *(978-1-877561-33-7(9))* First Edition Ltd.

—Billy & the Deep Sea Monster. 2010. (Illus.). 20p. pap. *(978-1-877561-57-3(6))* First Edition Ltd.

—Birthday Surprise. 2010. (Illus.). pap. *(978-1-877547-85-0(9))* First Edition Ltd.

—The Butterfly on the Subway. 2010. (Illus.). pap. *(978-1-877547-81-2(6))* First Edition Ltd.

—Can Your Dog? 2010. (Illus.). pap. *(978-1-877547-96-6(4))* First Edition Ltd.

—Captain Gold. 2010. (Illus.). pap. *(978-1-877561-26-9(6))* First Edition Ltd.

—The Carousel. 2010. (Illus.). 16p. pap. *(978-1-877561-73-3(8))* First Edition Ltd.

—Cat on the High Seas. 2010. (Illus.). 16p. pap. *(978-1-877561-75-7(4))* First Edition Ltd.

—Cecil the Caterpillar. 2010. (Illus.). pap. *(978-1-877547-95-9(6))* First Edition Ltd.

—Delia Dynamite. 2010. (Illus.). 24p. pap. *(978-1-877561-35-1(5))* First Edition Ltd.

—The Frog That Did Not Like Water. 2010. (Illus.). pap. *(978-1-877547-93-5(X))* First Edition Ltd.

—The Fruity Girls. 2010. (Illus.). pap. *(978-1-877561-11-5(8))* First Edition Ltd.

—The Lightning Game. 2010. (Illus.). 24p. pap. *(978-1-877561-55-9(X))* First Edition Ltd.

—The Lucky Pearl. 2010. (Illus.). 20p. pap. *(978-1-877561-18-4(5))* First Edition Ltd.

—Lulu & the Seed. 2010. (Illus.). pap. *(978-1-877547-82-9(4))* First Edition Ltd.

—The Naughty Puppy. 2010. (Illus.). pap. *(978-1-877547-89-8(1))* First Edition Ltd.

—The Not So Scary Scarecrow. 2010. (Illus.). pap. *(978-1-877547-88-1(3))* First Edition Ltd.

—One Leg Ned. 2010. (Illus.). pap. *(978-1-877561-12-2(6))* First Edition Ltd.

—Robot Tim. 2010. (Illus.). 20p. pap. *(978-1-877561-54-2(1))* First Edition Ltd.

Parker, Emma & Renaud, Marguerite. Dragon Bowling. 2010. (Illus.). 24p. pap. *(978-1-877561-82-5(7))* First Edition Ltd.

—Hedgehogs. 2010. (Illus.). 16p. pap. *(978-1-877561-80-1(0))* First Edition Ltd.

—The Honey Bee Race. 2010. (Illus.). 16p. pap. *(978-1-877561-78-8(9))* First Edition Ltd.

Parker, Natalie C. Three Sides of a Heart: Stories about Love Triangles. 2017. 448p. (YA). (gr. 9). 17.99 ***(978-0-06-242447-1(5)***, HarperTeen) HarperCollins Pubs.

Parker, Vic, compiled by. The Blind Men & the Elephant & Other Silly Stories. 2016. (Silly Stories Ser.). (ENG.). 40p. (J). (gr. 2-3). pap. 14.05 *(978-1-4824-4195-6(0))* Stevens, Gareth Publishing LLLP.

—The Fish & the Hare & Other Silly Stories. 2016. (Silly Stories Ser.). (ENG.). 40p. (J). (gr. 2-3). pap. 14.05 *(978-1-4824-4199-4(3))* Stevens, Gareth Publishing LLLP.

—The Hare-Brained Crocodiles & Other Silly Stories. 2016. (Silly Stories Ser.). (ENG.). 40p. (J). (gr. 2-3). pap. 14.05 *(978-1-4824-4202-1(7))* Stevens, Gareth Publishing LLLP.

—The Musicians of Bremen & Other Silly Stories. 2016. (Silly Stories Ser.). (ENG.). 40p. (J). (gr. 2-3). pap. 14.05 *(978-1-4824-4207-6(8))* Stevens, Gareth Publishing LLLP.

—The Open Road & Other Silly Stories. 2016. (Silly Stories Ser.). (ENG.). 40p. (J). (gr. 2-3). pap. 14.05 *(978-1-4824-4211-3(6))* Stevens, Gareth Publishing LLLP.

Parker, Vic, ed. The Demon with the Matted Hair & Other Stories. 2015. (Scary Fairy Tales Ser.). (ENG.). 40p. (J). (gr. 3-4). pap. 14.05 *(978-1-4824-3073-8(8))* Stevens, Gareth Publishing LLLP.

—The Goblin Pony & Other Stories. 2015. (Scary Fairy Tales Ser.). (ENG.). 40p. (J). (gr. 3-4). pap. 14.05 *(978-1-4824-3077-6(0))* Stevens, Gareth Publishing LLLP.

—Jack the Giant Killer & Other Stories. 2015. (Scary Fairy Tales Ser.). (ENG.). 40p. (J). (gr. 3-4). pap. 14.05 *(978-1-4824-3081-3(9))* Stevens, Gareth Publishing LLLP.

—The Little Mermaid & Other Stories. 2015. (Scary Fairy Tales Ser.). (ENG.). 40p. (J). (gr. 3-4). pap. 14.05 *(978-1-4824-3085-1(1))* Stevens, Gareth Publishing LLLP.

—Little Red Riding Hood & Other Stories. 2015. (Scary Fairy Tales Ser.). (ENG.). 40p. (J). (gr. 3-4). pap. 14.05 *(978-1-4824-3089-9(4))* Stevens, Gareth Publishing LLLP.

—The Ogre of Rashomon & Other Stories. 2015. (Scary Fairy Tales Ser.). (ENG.). 40p. (J). (gr. 3-4). pap. 14.05 *(978-1-4824-3093-6(2))* Stevens, Gareth Publishing LLLP.

—The Prince & the Dragon & Other Stories. 2015. (Scary Fairy Tales Ser.). (ENG.). 40p. (J). (gr. 3-4). pap. 14.05 *(978-1-4824-3097-4(5))* Stevens, Gareth Publishing LLLP.

—The Rat Catcher & Other Stories. 2015. (Scary Fairy Tales Ser.). (ENG.). 40p. (J). (gr. 3-4). pap. 14.05 *(978-1-4824-3101-8(7))* Stevens, Gareth Publishing LLLP.

—The Snow Queen & Other Stories. 2015. (Scary Fairy Tales Ser.). (ENG.). 40p. (J). (gr. 3-4). pap. 14.05 *(978-1-4824-3105-6(X))* Stevens, Gareth Publishing LLLP.

—The Wicked Witch of the West & Other Stories. 2015. (Scary Fairy Tales Ser.). (ENG.). 40p. (J). (gr. 3-4). pap. 14.05 *(978-1-4824-3109-4(2))* Stevens, Gareth Publishing LLLP.

Parragon Staff. Mickey Mouse: Adventure Tales & Stories. 2010. (Disney Diecut Classics). 72p. (J). (gr. -1-1). *(978-1-4075-8937-4(7))* Parragon, Inc.

Parry, Rosanne. Second Fiddle. 2012. (ENG.). 240p. (J). (gr. 3-7). 6.99 *(978-0-375-86166-6(1)*, Yearling) Random Hse. Children's Bks.

Pascal, Francine. Ambiente Hostil. Orig. Title: Out of Place. (SPA.). 128p. (J). 6.95 *(978-84-272-3792-6(8))* Molino, Editorial ESP. Dist: AIMS International Bks., Inc.

—Cambios Oportunos.Tr. of Standing Out. (SPA.). 112p. (J). 6.95 *(978-84-272-3795-7(2))* Molino, Editorial ESP. Dist: AIMS International Bks., Inc.

Pasquali, Elena. The Lion Little Book of Bedtime Stories. Smee, Nicola, illus. 2014. (ENG.). 96p. (J). (gr. -1-k). 9.99 *(978-0-7459-6459-1(1))* Lion Hudson PLC GBR. Dist: Independent Pubs. Group.

—Two-Minute Bedtime Stories. Smee, Nicola, illus. 2010. (Two-Minute Stories Ser.). (ENG.). 48p. (J). (gr. -1-k). 12.99 *(978-0-7459-6079-1(0))* Lion Hudson PLC GBR. Dist: Independent Pubs. Group.

Pastor, A. The Pearl Box: Containing One Hundred Beautiful Stories for Young People. 2007. (ENG.). 142p. pap. 18.99 *(978-1-4346-2865-7(5))*; 150p. pap. 19.99 *(978-1-4346-2873-2(6))* Creative Media Partners, LLC.

Paterson, Andrew Barton 'Banjo'. Three Elephant Power & Other Stories. 2004. reprint ed. pap. 15.95 *(978-1-4191-8979-1(4))*; pap. 1.99 *(978-1-4192-8979-8(9))* Kessinger Publishing, LLC.

Paterson, Judy. Scottish Folk Tales for Children. 2017. (Folk Tales for Children Ser.). (ENG., Illus.). 192p. (J). (gr. 2-4). pap. 16.99 *(978-0-7509-6844-7(3))* History Pr. Ltd.,The GBR. Dist: Independent Pubs. Group.

Paterson, Katherine. A Stubborn Sweetness & Other Stories for the Christmas Season. 2013. (ENG.). 200p. 16.00 *(978-0-664-23915-2(3))* Westminster John Knox Pr.

Patten, William. Animal & Nature Stories Vol. 8: The Junior Classics. 2004. reprint ed. pap. 1.99 *(978-1-4192-6805-2(8))* Kessinger Publishing, LLC.

Patterson, Horace. Emie the Ermine. Parker, Jack, illus. 2007. 28p. per. 7.99 *(978-1-58942-374-9(7))* R.H. Boyd Publishing Corp.

Paul Frank Industries. Only in Dreams. 2011. (ENG., Illus.). 24p. (J). (gr. -1 — 1). bds. 6.99 *(978-0-8118-7867-8(8))* Chronicle Bks. LLC.

Paulitz, Kevin. A Letter from the Tooth Fairy. 2011. 28p. pap. 12.95 *(978-1-4490-6671-0(2))* AuthorHouse.

Paulsen, Gary. The Gary Paulsen Collection: Dancing Carl; Dogsong; Hatchet; Woodsong. 2013. (ENG., Illus.). 672p. (J). (gr. 3-7). pap. 31.99 *(978-1-4424-9778-8(5)*, Simon & Schuster Bks. For Young Readers) Simon & Schuster Bks. For Young Readers.

—Paintings from the Cave: Three Novellas. (ENG.). (YA). (gr. 7-7). 2012. 174p. pap. 8.99 *(978-0-553-49466-2(X)*, Ember) 2011. 176p. 15.99 *(978-0-385-74684-7(9)*, Lamb, Wendy Bks.) Random Hse. Children's Bks.

—Shelf Life: Stories by the Book. 2003. (ENG., Illus.). 192p. (J). (gr. 5-9). 17.99 *(978-0-689-84180-4(9)*, Simon & Schuster Bks. For Young Readers) Simon & Schuster Bks. For Young Readers.

Paws & Claws & Other Stories: Individual Title Six-Pack. (Story Steps Ser.). (gr. k-2). 42.00 *(978-0-7635-9580-7(2))* Rigby Education.

Payton-Wright, Kaye. The Secret Wood. 2010. 28p. pap. 21.99 *(978-1-4535-0321-8(8))* Xlibris Corp.

Pearce, Suzannah, ed. Five-Mintue Stories for Boys. 2014. (ENG., Illus.). 96p. (J). *(978-1-74352-049-9(2))* Hinkler Bks. Pty, Ltd.

—Five-Minute Stories for Girls. 2014. (ENG., Illus.). 96p. (J). *(978-1-74352-048-2(4))* Hinkler Bks. Pty, Ltd.

Pearson, Maggie. Short & Shocking! 2014. (ENG., Illus.). 96p. 10.95 *(978-0-19-278191-8(X))* Oxford Univ. Pr., Inc.

Peck, Richard. Past Perfect, Present Tense. 2006. (ENG.). 192p. (J). (gr. 3-7). reprint ed. 6.99 *(978-0-14-240537-6(X)*, Puffin Books) Penguin Young Readers Group.

Peckham, Lori, ed. Guide's Greatest Animal Stories. 2006. 143p. (J). (gr. 5-9). per. 10.99 *(978-0-8280-1944-6(4))* Review & Herald Publishing Assn.

—Guide's Greatest Funny Stories. 2014. (ENG.). 160p. pap. 11.99 *(978-0-8280-2778-6(1))* Review & Herald Publishing Assn.

—Guide's Greatest Mystery Stories. 2007. 155p. per. 11.99 *(978-0-8280-2038-1(8))* Review & Herald Publishing Assn.

Pedersen, Peggy A. Jasmine & the Magic Squirrel. 2008. 12p. pap. 24.95 *(978-1-60474-052-3(3))* America Star Bks.

Pedler, Caroline, illus. My Treasury of Christmas Stories. 2014. 189p. (J). *(978-0-7607-7070-2(0))* Barnes & Noble, Inc.

Pegler, Robin. Having Fun Together: A Collection of Children's Stories. 2010. 514p. pap. 23.95 *(978-1-60693-817-1(7)*, Eloquent Bks.) Strategic Book Publishing & Rights Agency (SBPRA).

Pellicer López, Carlos. Juan y Sus Zapatos. 2003. (Los Especiais de A la Orilla Del Viento Ser.). (SPA.). 20p. (J). 12.95 *(978-968-16-7021-4(3))* Fondo de Cultura Economica USA.

Penick Phillips-Cermak, Mosetta. The Wishing Flower. 2007. 24p. 16.50 *(978-0-615-15573-9(1))* PM Moon Pubs., Ltd.

Penn-Coughin, O. They're Coming for You: Scary Stories that Scream to be Read. 2009. (J). per. *(978-0-9816836-0-7(6))* You Come Too Publishing.

The People on the Corner. 2003. pap. 15.00 *(978-0-9740269-0-9(5))* Cyclops Pr.

Percy, Graham. Tales from Around the World. 2012. (10-Minute Bedtime Stories Ser.). (ENG., Illus.). 96p. (J). (gr. k-2). pap. 8.99 *(978-1-84365-207-6(2)*, Pavilion) Pavilion Bks. GBR. Dist: Independent Pubs. Group.

Perelman, Helen. A Candy Fairies Sweet Collection: Chocolate Dreams; Rainbow Swirl; Caramel Moon; Cool Mint. Waters, Erica-Jane, illus. 2013. (Candy Fairies Ser.). (ENG.). 512p. (J). (gr. 2-5). pap. 23.99 *(978-1-4424-9390-2(9)*, Aladdin) Simon & Schuster Children's Publishing.

Perez, Vivian. Stolen Stories for My Nieces. 2007. (ENG.). 68p. per. 19.95 *(978-1-4241-6679-4(9))* America Star Bks.

Perkins, Lucy Fitch. Short Works of Lucy Fitch Perkins. l.t. ed. 2007. (ENG.). 262p. pap. 23.99 *(978-1-4346-1990-7(7))*; 236p. pap. 20.99 *(978-1-4346-1966-2(4))* Creative Media Partners, LLC.

Perkins, Stephanie. My True Love Gave to Me: Twelve Holiday Stories. (ENG., Illus.). 336p. (YA). 2016. pap. 10.99 *(978-1-250-05931-4(3)*, 9781250059314) 2014. (gr. 8-12). 18.99 *(978-1-250-05930-7(5)*, 9781250059307) St. Martin's Pr. (St. Martin's Griffin).

—Summer Days & Summer Nights: Twelve Love Stories. 2017. (ENG.). 400p. (YA). pap. 10.99 *(978-1-250-07913-8(6)*, 9781250079138, St. Martin's Griffin) St. Martin's Pr.

Perrault, Charles. Cuentos de Antano. (SPA.). 336p. (YA). *(978-84-7525-123-3(4))* Ediciones Generales Anaya SA.

—Cuentos de Perrault.Tr. of Stories by Perrault. (SPA.). 128p. (J). 19.98 *(978-84-305-8325-6(4))* Susaeta Ediciones, S.A. ESP. Dist: Giron Bks.

—Puffin Book of Five Minute Stories. (Illus.). 128p. (J). 24.95 *(978-0-670-87680-8(1))* Penguin Publishing Group.

Perry, Glyn & Parry, Glyn. Invisible Girl. 2003. 160p. (YA). pap. 15.25 *(978-1-920731-48-9(2))* Fremantle Pr. AUS. Dist: Independent Pubs. Group.

Pescetti, Luis Maria. La Tarea Segun Natacha. O'Kif, illus. 2003. (Coleccion Derechos Del Nino Ser.). (SPA.). 32p. (J). (gr. 3-5). pap. 7.95 *(978-84-204-5836-6(8))* Santillana USA Publishing Co., Inc.

Peszle, Brenda, et al. The Cranberry Tales. 2009. 40p. pap. 21.99 *(978-1-4363-5925-2(2))* Xlibris Corp.

Pet Stories Set 2 800888, 3 vols. 2005. (J). pap. *(978-1-59794-063-4(1))* Environments, Inc.

Pet Stories Set 800887, 3 vols. 2005. (J). pap. *(978-1-59794-062-7(3))* Environments, Inc.

Peters, Andrew. Dingo Dog & the Billabong Storm. Wadham, Anna, illus. 2010. (Traditional Tales with a Twist Ser.). (ENG.). 32p. (J). (gr. -1-2). audio compact disk *(978-1-84643-350-4(9))* Child's Play International Ltd.

Petersen, David. Snowy Valentine. Petersen, David, illus. 2011. (ENG., Illus.). 32p. (J). (gr. -1-3). 14.99 *(978-0-06-146378-5(7))* HarperCollins Pubs.

Peterson, Jay D. & Morgan, Collette A., eds. Sky Blue Water: Great Stories for Young Readers. 2016. (ENG.). 240p. (J). 19.95 *(978-0-8166-9876-9(7))* Univ. of Minnesota Pr.

Peterson, Jim. Kitten Tales. 2006. (ENG.). 76p. per. 16.95 *(978-1-4241-4448-8(5))* PublishAmerica, Inc.

Peterson, Scott. The Ultimate Returns. 4th ed. 2009. (Spectrobes Ser.: No. 3). (ENG.). 144p. (J). (gr. 3-7). pap. 4.99 *(978-1-4231-0811-5(6))* Disney Pr.

Petterson, Aline. El Papalote y el Nopal. Pacheco, Gabriel, illus. 2003. (SPA.). 34p. (J). (gr. 3-5). 15.95 (978-968-19-0750-1(7)) Santillana USA Publishing Co., Inc.

Petty, Kate. The Nightspinners. Smith, Mary Claire, illus. 2004. 32p. (J). pap. 8.99 (978-1-84255-105-9(1), Dolphin Paperbacks) Orion Publishing Group, Ltd. GBR. Dist: Trafalgar Square Publishing.

Peyo. The Smurflings. 2013. (Smurfs Graphic Novels Ser.). (ENG., Illus.). 56p. (J). (gr. 2-5). 10.99 (978-1-59707-408-7(X), 9781597074087); pap. 5.99 (978-1-59707-407-0(1), 9781597074070) Papercutz.

Pfeiffer, Kathleen. Spartacus Sprout, Please Watch Out! 2011. 32p. pap. 15.99 (978-1-257-50163-2(1)) Lulu Pr., Inc.

Pfister, Marcus. Ava's Poppy. 2012. (ENG., Illus.). 32p. (J). (gr. -1-3). 16.95 (978-0-7358-4057-7(1)) North-South Bks., Inc.

Philipson, Sandra J. Ollie's Monsters & Other Stories. Campbell, Jenny, illus. 2010. 48p. (J). pap. 10.95 (978-1-929821-09-9(3)) Chagrin River Publishing Co.

Phillips, Dee. Gladiator. 2014. (Yesterday's Voices Ser.). (YA). lib. bdg. 19.60 (978-0-606-35580-3(4)) Turtleback Bks.

Phinn, Gervase. Royston Knapper: Return of the Rogue. Fisher, Chris, illus. 2005. (Child's Play Library - First Chapter Bks.). (ENG.). 126p. (J). (978-0-85953-024-8(8)) Child's Play International Ltd.

Phoenix International Staff, illus. Princess Sofia. 2012. 10p. (J). bds. 14.98 (978-1-4508-6822-8(3), e41cac27-3be3-41b8-8dc5-7fb934c0ea6b) Phoenix International Publications, Inc.

Pierce, Tamora. Tortall & Other Lands: A Collection of Tales. 2012. (Beka Cooper Ser.). (ENG.). 400p. (YA). (gr. 7). pap. 10.99 (978-0-375-86633-3(7), Bluefire) Random Hse. Children's Bks.

La Pierna Lastimada, 2 bks., Set. (Coleccion Chiquilines - Imagen y Sonido). (SPA.). (J). 15.95 incl. audio (978-950-11-0625-1(X), SGM25X) Sigmar ARG. Dist: Continental Bk. Co., Inc.

Pinguilly, Yves. Contes et Legendes de Bretagne. pap. 14.95 (978-2-09-282237-1(3)) Nathan, Fernand FRA. Dist: Distribooks, Inc.

Pinkney, Andrea Davis. Bird in a Box. Qualls, Sean, illus. 2012. (ENG.). 288p. (J). (gr. 3-7). pap. 8.99 (978-0-316-07402-5(0)) Little, Brown Bks. for Young Readers.

Pinkney, Jerry. The Little Red Hen. Pinkney, Jerry, illus. 2006. (ENG., Illus.). 32p. (J). (gr. -1-3). 17.99 (978-0-8037-2935-3(9), Dial Bks) Penguin Young Readers Group.

Pitman, Norman Hinsdale. The Chinese Wonder Book: A Classic Collection of Chinese Tales. Tang, Li Chu, illus. 2011. (ENG.). 96p. (J). (gr. 4-6). 16.95 (978-0-8048-4161-0(6)) Tuttle Publishing.

Plume, Ilse, illus. & adapted by. The Farmer in the Dell. Plume, Ilse, adapted by. 2010. (ENG.). 32p. pap. 8.95 (978-1-56792-390-2(9)) Godine, David R. Pub.

Poe, Edgar Allen. Edgar Allan Poe. McConnell, James, illus. 2004. (Great American Short Stories Ser.). 80p. (gr. 4-7). lib. bdg. 24.00 (978-0-8368-4254-8(5), Gareth Stevens Learning Library) Stevens, Gareth Publishing LLLP.

—Edgar Allan Poe's Tales of Mystery & Madness. Grimly, Gris, illus. 2004. (ENG.). 144p. (J). (gr. 5-9). 19.99 (978-0-689-84837-7(4), Atheneum Bks. for Young Readers) Simon & Schuster Children's Publishing.

—The Stories of Edgar Allan Poe. McKowen, Scott, illus. 2010. (Sterling Unabridged Classics Ser.). (ENG.). 344p. (J). (gr. 5-18). 14.95 (978-1-4027-7325-9(0)) Sterling Publishing Co., Inc.

Pombo, Rafael. Cuentos, Pombo Rafael. Acosta, Patricia, illus. (SPA.). 68p. (J). (gr. 2). pap. (978-958-30-0355-4(7), PV0862) Panamericana Editorial COL. Dist: Lectorum Pubns., Inc.

Ponti, Claude. Mi Valle. 2003. (SPA.). 46p. (978-84-95150-60-8(3)) Corimbo, Editorial S.L.

—La Tempestad. 2003. (SPA.). 32p. (978-84-95150-41-7(7)) Corimbo, Editorial S.L.

Pope, Paul. Sugary Shorts. 2013. (Adventure Time Ser.: 1). (ENG.). 144p. (J). (gr. 4). 34.99 (978-1-60886-333-4(6)) Boom! Studios.

Porte, Barbara Ann. Beauty & the Serpent: Thirteen Tales of Unnatural Animals. Covey, Rosemary Feit, illus. 2008. (ENG.). 128p. (YA). (gr. 7). pap. 7.99 (978-1-4169-7579-3(9), Simon & Schuster/Paula Wiseman Bks.) Simon & Schuster/Paula Wiseman Bks.

Posadas, Carmen. Dorilda. 2nd ed. 2003. (SPA., Illus.). 127p. (J). (gr. 3-5). pap. 13.95 (978-84-204-5800-7(7)) Santillana USA Publishing Co., Inc.

Posner-Sanchez, Andrea. Sofia the First Little Golden Book Favorites (Disney Junior: Sofia the First) Lee, Grace & Disney Storybook Artists, illus. 2015. (Little Golden Book Favorites Ser.). (ENG.). 80p. (J). (-k). 7.99 (978-0-7364-3406-5(2), Golden/Disney) Random Hse. Children's Bks.

Potter, Beatrix. Beatrix Potter Favorite Tales: The Tales of Peter Rabbit & Jemima Puddle-Duck. 2006. (Peter Rabbit Ser.). (ENG., Illus.). 64p. (J). (gr. -1-2). 10.99 (978-0-7232-5879-7(1), Warne) Penguin Young Readers Group.

—The Classic Tale of Peter Rabbit: And Other Cherished Stories. Santore, Charles, illus. 2013. (ENG.). 68p. (J). 19.95 (978-1-60433-376-3(6), Applesauce Pr.) Cider Mill Pr. Bk. Pubs., LLC.

—The Great Big Treasury of Beatrix Potter. 2007. (ENG.). 104p. pap. 18.99 (978-1-4264-3597-3(5)); 114p. pap. 19.99 (978-1-4264-3648-2(3)) Creative Media Partners, LLC.

—The World of Peter Rabbit, 23 vols., Set. 2006. (Peter Rabbit Ser.). (ENG., Illus.). 1388p. (J). (gr. -1-2). 160.00 (978-0-7232-5763-9(9), Warne) Penguin Young Readers Group.

Potter, Beatrix, et al. Classic Children's Tales: 150 Years of Frederick Warne. 2015. (ENG., Illus.). 112p. (J). (gr. -1-2). 25.00 (978-0-241-19871-1(2), Warne) Penguin Young Readers Group.

Potter, Tina M. The Horse Story. 2005. 36p. (J). pap. 9.65 (978-1-4116-5761-8(6)) Lulu Pr., Inc.

Powell, Jillian. Hattie the Dancing Hippo. Dodson, Emma, illus. 2011. 32p. pap. (978-1-84089-709-8(0)) Zero to Ten, Ltd.

Power Reading: Power PAK. 2005. (Illus.). 80p. (J). (gr. 2-4). vinyl bd. 129.95 (978-1-883186-73-9(0), PPMX2-3); (gr. 4-5). vinyl bd. 129.95 (978-1-883186-72-2(2), PPMX4-5) National Reading Styles Institute, Inc.

Power Reading: Power PAK 4C. 2005. (Illus.). 80p. (J). (gr. 4-5). vinyl bd. 129.95 (978-1-883186-70-8(6), PPO4C) National Reading Styles Institute, Inc.

A Prairie Heart. 2007. (Illus.). (J). per. 19.95 (978-0-9793668-0-2(1)) Prairie Heart Publishing.

Pratchett, Terry. Dragons at Crumbling Castle: And Other Tales. Beech, Mark, illus. (ENG.). 352p. (J). 2016. (gr. 5-7). pap. 7.99 (978-0-544-81313-7(8), HMH Books For Young Readers) 2015. (gr. 4-7). 16.99 (978-0-544-46659-3(4)) Houghton Mifflin Harcourt Publishing Co.

Pray, Linda. Characters of the Dark. 2011. 36p. pap. 16.95 (978-1-4626-0329-9(7)) America Star Bks.

Preece, Mary Ellen Goble. The ABC Cousins & Fun from A to Z. 2007. (J). per. 12.00 (978-1-60458-005-1(4)) Instant Pub.

Preece, Phil. Nightmare Park. 2004. (Shades Ser.). 52p. (J). pap. (978-0-237-52730-3(8)) Evans Brothers, Ltd.

Preik, Christel D. Growing up Joyfully. 2012. 36p. pap. 15.49 (978-1-4669-0869-7(6)) Trafford Publishing.

—Sharing the Love. 2013. 36p. pap. 15.49 (978-1-4669-9975-6(6)) Trafford Publishing.

Press, Bothwell. Naughty Madge & Other Old-Fashioned Children's Stories. 2013. 120p. pap. 9.99 (978-0-9855353-0-8(X)) Bothwell Pr.

Prévert, Jacques. Contes pour enfants pas Sage. (FRE.). pap. 16.95 (978-2-07-053885-0(0)) Gallimard, Editions FRA. Dist: Distribooks, Inc.

Price & Wilkinson. The Saga of Aslak. 2004. (ENG., Illus.). 96p. 8.95 (978-0-7136-4076-2(6), A&C Black) Bloomsbury Publishing Plc GBR. Dist: Consortium Bk. Sales & Distribution.

Price, Kevin, ed. Fields of Wheat: And other Romance Stories. 2012. 200p. pap. (978-0-9872559-4-5(0), Crotchet Quaver) Logorythm.

Price, Margaret Evans, illus. & retold by. A Child's Book of Myths. Price, Margaret Evans, retold by. 2011. (Dover Read & Listen Ser.). (ENG.). 96p. (J). (gr. 3-8). pap. 14.99 incl. audio compact disk (978-0-486-48370-2(3)) Dover Pubns., Inc.

Price, Roger & Stern, Leonard. Ad Lib Mad Libs. 2011. (Mad Libs Ser.). (ENG.). 48p. (J). (gr. 3-7). pap. 3.99 (978-0-8431-9883-6(4), Mad Libs) Penguin Young Readers Group.

Price, Roger & Stern, Leonard, creators. Ninjas Mad Libs. 2011. (Mad Libs Ser.). (ENG.). 48p. (J). (gr. 3-7). 4.99 (978-0-8431-9897-3(4), Mad Libs) Penguin Young Readers Group.

Priddy, Roger. Princess Stories. 2009. (Sing-Along Ser.). (ENG.). 32p. (J). (gr. -1 — 1). bds. 12.95 (978-0-312-50649-0(X), 9780312506490, Priddy Bks.) St. Martin's Pr.

Prindle House, creator. Mommy's Pleasures... Children's Treasures!, Volume 1. 2009. (Illus.). 51p. (J). (gr. -1-3). 14.95 (978-0-9759527-9-5(X)) Prindle Hse. Publishing Co.

Pritchett, Lee. The Tale of Greta Gumboot & Other Stories. 2010. (Illus.). 118p. pap. (978-1-84991-155-9(X)) Chipmunkapublishing.

Provensen, Alice. The Master Swordsman & the Magic Doorway: Two Legends from Ancient China. Provensen, Alice, illus. 2014. (ENG., Illus.). 40p. (J). (gr. k-3). 19.99 (978-1-4814-2874-3(8), Simon & Schuster Bks. For Young Readers) Simon & Schuster Bks. For Young Readers.

Publications International Ltd. Staff. Frozen - Anna's Friends. 2013. (Illus.). 10p. (J). (gr. k-3). bds. 10.99 (978-1-4508-6819-8(3), 48412b6e-ab38-47b0-836d-0f0ef6217ed1) Phoenix International Publications, Inc.

—Little Treasuries Best Loved Children's Stories. 2007. 320p. (J). 12.98 (978-1-4127-8306-4(2)) Phoenix International Publications, Inc.

—Mother Goose Treasury. 2007. (ENG., Illus.). 320p. (J). (gr. -1-3). bds. (978-1-4127-6334-9(7), 1412763347) Phoenix International Publications, Inc.

—Mother Goose Treasury. 2007. (Illus.). 316p. 15.98 (978-1-4127-8734-5(3)) Publications International, Ltd.

—My 1St Libraries Disney Baby Animals. 2011. 12p. 12.98 (978-1-4508-1571-0(5)) Phoenix International Publications, Inc.

—My Firstlibrary 12 Board Books Mickey Mouse. 2008. (J). 12.98 (978-1-4127-6851-1(9)) Phoenix International Publications, Inc.

—Sweet Dreams Padded Treasury. 2013. 320p. (J). bds. (978-1-4127-6333-2(9), 1412763339) Phoenix International Publications, Inc.

Publications International Ltd. Staff, creator. Mother Goose. 2007. (Pop-up Treasury Ser.). (Illus.). 16p. (J). (gr. -1-3). 12.98 (978-1-4127-8833-5(1)) Publications International, Ltd.

—Thomas & Friends Musical Pop-up Treasury. 2007. (Thomas & Friends Ser.). (Illus.). 24p. (gr. -1). 15.98 (978-1-4127-9293-6(2)) Publications International, Ltd.

—Treasury of Best Loved Children's Stories. 2007. (Illus.). 320p. 15.98 (978-1-4127-8736-9(X)) Publications International, Ltd.

Publications International Ltd. Staff, ed. Bedtime Stories. 2010. (J). bds. 12.98 (978-0-7853-7921-8(5)) Phoenix International Publications, Inc.

—Cars: Starring Mater. 2010. 40p. (J). bds. 14.98 (978-1-60553-684-2(9)) Publications International, Ltd.

—Disney Princess: 26 Stories of Virtue. 2010. 12p. (J). 25.98 (978-1-60553-692-7(X)) Phoenix International Publications, Inc.

—Lights & Music Treasury 10Led Spa Disney Classics. 2009. 160p. 15.98 (978-1-4127-5454-5(2)) Phoenix International Publications, Inc.

—Musical Pop up Disney Princess. 2008. (SPA.). (J). 15.98 (978-1-4127-8980-6(X)) Publications International, Ltd.

—My 1st Libraries Disney Classics. 2011. 10p. (J). bds. 13.98 (978-1-4508-1029-6(2)) Phoenix International Publications, Inc.

—Once upon a Time. 2009. 24p. (J). bds. 17.98 (978-1-4127-5369-2(4), PIL Kids) Publications International, Ltd.

—Padded Treasury 160 Spa Sesame Street. 2009. 160p. 12.98 (978-1-4127-9548-7(6)) Phoenix International Publications, Inc.

—Play a Sound 10 Stories Winnie the Pooh. 2009. 24p. (J). 17.98 (978-1-4127-5370-8(8), PIL Kids) Publications International, Ltd.

—Puppy Learning. 2007. (J). 4.00 (978-1-4127-6959-4(0)) Publications International, Ltd.

—Really Useful Engines. 2010. 40p. (J). bds. 14.98 (978-1-60553-744-3(6)) Phoenix International Publications, Inc.

—Sesame Street: Good Night Stories. 2010. 40p. (J). bds. 14.98 (978-1-60553-861-7(2)) Phoenix International Publications, Inc.

—Stories to Grow on Spa Disney Classics. 2009. 40p. 9.98 (978-1-4127-1109-8(6)) Phoenix International Publications, Inc.

—Stories to Grow on Spa Mickey Mouse Clubhous. 2009. 40p. 9.98 (978-1-4127-1127-2(4), PIL Kids) Publications International, Ltd.

—Story Reader Me Reader & Disney 8-Book Library. 2013. 1p. (J). bds. 25.98 (978-1-4508-2186-5(3), 5bb65929-302d-4d10-ab25-dd52712ba243) Phoenix International Publications, Inc.

—Whats That Sound? 2009. 24p. (J). bds. 17.98 (978-1-4127-3974-0(8), PIL Kids) Publications International, Ltd.

—Winnie the Pooh. 2005. (J). 14.98 (978-1-4127-3470-7(3)) Publications International, Ltd.

Puncel, Maria. Manana es Domingo y Otras Rimas Infantiles. Recio, Ricardo, illus. 2003. (SPA.). 32p. 4.95 (978-84-372-8021-9(4)) Altea, Ediciones, S.A. - Grupo Santillana ESP. Dist: Santillana USA Publishing Co., Inc.

—El Patio de Mi Casa y Otras Canciones Infantiles. Escrivá, Viví, illus. 2003. (SPA.). 32p. 4.95 (978-84-372-8018-9(4)) Altea, Ediciones, S.A. - Grupo Santillana ESP. Dist: Santillana USA Publishing Co., Inc.

—Yo Subia la Escalera y Otras Rimas Infantiles. Bayley, Nicola, illus. 2003. (SPA.). 24p. 4.95 (978-84-372-8015-8(X)) Altea, Ediciones, S.A. - Grupo Santillana ESP. Dist: Santillana USA Publishing Co., Inc.

Punter, Russell. Stories of Cowboys. Fiorin, Fabiano, illus. 2008. (Usborne Young Reading: Series One Ser.). 48p. (J). 8.99 (978-0-7945-1822-6(2), Usborne) EDC Publishing.

—Stories of Dinosaurs. Decker, Cynthia, illus. 2006. (Usborne Young Reading: Series One Ser.). 48p. (J). (gr. 2). lib. bdg. 13.99 (978-1-58086-940-9(8), Usborne) EDC Publishing.

—Stories of Santa. Webb, Philip, illus. 2006. (Young Reading Series 1 Gift Bks.). 48p. (J). 8.99 (978-0-7945-1476-1(6), Usborne) EDC Publishing.

Punter, Russell, retold by. Illustrated Stories from the Greek Myths. 2014. (ENG., Illus.). 350p. (J). 19.99 (978-0-7945-3237-6(3), Usborne) EDC Publishing.

Pushkin, Alexander, et al. Cuentos Clásicos Juveniles: Antología. Zuluaga, Conrado, ed. 2nd ed. 2003. (Serie Roja Anthologies Ser.). (SPA., Illus.). 124p. (YA). (gr. 8-12). pap. 12.95 (978-968-19-0320-6(X)) Santillana USA Publishing Co., Inc.

Puttock, Simon. Who's the Boss Rhinoceros? Busby, Ailie, illus. 32p. (J). pap. 8.99 (978-0-7497-4354-3(9)) Egmont Bks., Ltd. GBR. Dist: Trafalgar Square Publishing.

Pyle, Howard. The Garden Behind the Moon: A Real Story of the Moon-Angel. 2005. (Dover Children's Classics Ser.). (ENG., Illus.). 128p. (gr. 3-8). pap. 7.95 (978-0-486-44073-6(7)) Dover Pubns., Inc.

Pyrtle Second Graders & Writers' Circle. Poetry & a Fifth Grade Cinderell: An Anthology from Nebraska. 2009. 60p. pap. 8.95 (978-0-595-53233-9(0)) iUniverse, Inc.

Quiller-Couch, Arthur Thomas. The White Wolf & Other Fireside Tales. l.t. ed. 2007. (ENG.). 286p. pap. 23.99 (978-1-4346-5046-7(4)) Creative Media Partners, LLC.

Quiroga, Horacio. Cuentos de la Selva. Vallejo, Esperanza, illus. 2004.Tr. of Jungle Stories. (SPA.). 186p. (YA). (gr. -1-7). pap. (978-958-30-0458-2(8)) Panamericana Editorial.

—Cuentos de la Selva. (Young Classics Ser.).Tr. of Jungle Stories. (SPA.). (J). (gr. 6-8). 5.60 (978-950-11-1268-9(3), SG8741) Sigmar ARG. Dist: Lectorum Pubns., Inc.

—Los Cuentos de Mis Hijos.Tr. of Stories of My Children. (SPA.). 104p. (YA). (gr. 5-8). 7.50 (978-84-204-4585-4(1)) Ediciones Alfaguara ESP. Dist: Lectorum Pubns., Inc.

R. Tatum, W. Brooks. Childrens Short Stories for the Soul. 2012. (ENG.). pap. 9.95 (978-1-4675-3658-5(X)) Independent Pub.

Rach, W. Dennis. The Goofy Principal at Silly School. 2007. (J). per. (978-0-9792579-0-2(5)) Rach, W. Dennis.

Rack, Charlene. The Adventures of Delaware Bear & Young Abraham Lincoln. 2011. 24p. (gr. -1). pap. 12.79 (978-1-4567-5619-2(2)) AuthorHouse.

Rackham, Arthur. A Fairy Book 1923. 2004. reprint ed. pap. 20.95 (978-1-4179-7656-0(X)) Kessinger Publishing, LLC.

Raichert, Lance, illus. Treasury of Values for Children. 2012. 159p. (J). (978-1-4508-3729-3(8)) Phoenix International Publications, Inc.

Ralph, Donna J. Critter Chronicles: Stories of Critters in a Colorado Wildlife Rehabilitator's Life. 2007. 200p. per. 16.95 (978-0-595-47858-3(1)) iUniverse, Inc.

Ramaswamy, Maya, illus. U Sier Lapalang: A Khasi Tale. 2005. (J). (978-81-89020-31-6(5)) Katha.

Ramoutar, Christine L. Tales from the Pine Forest. 2012. 108p. pap. 10.95 (978-1-4620-7030-5(2)) iUniverse, Inc.

Ramsnips, Tunder. The Hardly Boys. 2010. 196p. pap. 15.95 (978-0-557-38767-0(1)) Lulu Pr., Inc.

Randall, Daniel & Randall, Ronne. Tales of King Arthur: Ten Legendary Stories of the Knights of the Round Table. Howells, Graham, illus. 2013. (ENG.). 80p. pap. 9.99 (978-1-84322-922-3(6)) Anness Publishing GBR. Dist: National Bk. Network.

Random House. Adventure Story Collection (Nickelodeon) Random House, illus. 2016. (ENG., Illus.). 320p. (J). (gr. -1-2). 15.99 (978-1-101-93417-3(4), Random Hse. Bks. for Young Readers) Random Hse. Children's Bks.

—Barbie You Can Be 5-Minute Stories (Barbie) 2017. (ENG., Illus.). 160p. (J). (gr. -1-2). 12.99 **(978-1-5247-1505-2(0)**, Random Hse. Bks. for Young Readers) Random Hse. Children's Bks.

Random House. Five Fin-Tastic Stories (Bubble Guppies) Random House, illus. 2015. (Step into Reading Ser.). (ENG., Illus.). 144p. (J). (gr. -1-1). pap. 7.99 (978-0-553-52116-0(0), Random Hse. Bks. for Young Readers) Random Hse. Children's Bks.

Random House Disney Staff. Princess Story Collection. 2007. (Step into Reading Ser.). (ENG., Illus.). 160p. (J). (gr. k-3). pap. 7.99 (978-0-7364-2486-8(5), RH/Disney) Random Hse. Children's Bks.

Random House Disney Staff, illus. Disney Junior: Nine Favorite Tales (Disney Mixed Property) 2014. (Little Golden Book Treasury Ser.). (ENG.). 224p. (J). (-k). 12.99 (978-0-7364-3257-3(4), Golden/Disney) Random Hse. Children's Bks.

—Five Classic Tales (Disney Classics) 2014. (Step into Reading Ser.). (ENG.). 160p. (J). (gr. -1-1). 7.99 (978-0-7364-3180-4(2), RH/Disney) Random Hse. Children's Bks.

—Five Disney/Pixar Tales (Disney/Pixar) 2014. (Step into Reading Ser.). (ENG.). 160p. (J). (gr. -1-1). pap. 7.99 (978-0-7364-3171-2(3), RH/Disney) Random Hse. Children's Bks.

—Five Toy Tales (Disney/Pixar Toy Story) 2012. (Step into Reading Ser.). (ENG.). 160p. (J). (gr. -1-1). pap. 7.99 (978-0-7364-2845-3(3), RH/Disney) Random Hse. Children's Bks.

Random House Editors. Nickelodeon Story Time Collection (Nickelodeon) Random House Editors & Golden Books Staff, illus. 2014. (ENG.). 320p. (J). (gr. -1-2). 15.99 (978-0-385-38777-4(6), Random Hse. Bks. for Young Readers) Random Hse. Children's Bks.

Ranjalkar, Shreyans. My Sunny British Days - Stories for Children by a Child. 2013. (Illus.). 70p. pap. (978-1-78148-596-5(8)) Grosvenor Hse. Publishing Ltd.

Rao, Cheryl. Mixed Score: Ghost & Other Stories. 2004. 122p. 15.00 (978-81-291-0401-4(6)) Rupa & Co. IND. Dist: South Asia Bks.

Rasheed, Winona. Smiles & Frowns Through Animal Town's Storybook. 2008. 55p. pap. 13.70 (978-1-4357-4617-6(1)) Lulu Pr., Inc.

Raspe, Rudolf Erich. The Surprising Adventures of Baron Munchausen. Doré, Gustave, illus. 2012. (Everyman's Library Children's Classics Ser.). (ENG.). 208p. 20.00 (978-0-307-96147-1(8), Everyman's Library) Knopf Doubleday Publishing Group.

Ray, Jane. The Emperor's Nightingale & Other Feathery Tales. 2013. (Story Collector Ser.). (ENG., Illus.). 176p. (J). (gr. k). 19.95 (978-1-907152-90-0(3)) Boxer Bks., Ltd. GBR. Dist: Sterling Publishing Co., Inc.

Ray, Satyajit. Unicorn Expedition & Other Stories: The Exploits of Professor Shonku. 2004. (Illus.). x, 237p. (J). pap. (978-0-14-333584-9(7), Puffin) Penguin Publishing Group.

Read to Me Mommy. Date not set. (Read to Me Ser.). 192p. (J). 14.98 (978-0-7525-9486-6(9)) Parragon, Inc.

Ready Reader Staff. Rush Rush Rush: Digraphs, 6 bks., set, Level B. 2003. (J). (gr. -1-3). 33.50 (978-0-8136-2075-6(9)) Modern Curriculum Pr.

Real, Stuart. The Cone Stories. 2007. 140p. per. 11.95 (978-0-9556755-0-8(2)) Lulu Pr., Inc.

Rebal, Tara. Sarah Sue Smith: A Crooked Wharf Adventure. 2010. 52p. pap. 22.49 (978-1-4520-7165-7(9)) AuthorHouse.

Rebmann, Charles. Christmas Stories from the Jersey Cape. 2003. 94p. pap. 9.95 (978-0-595-29692-7(0)) iUniverse, Inc.

Reed, Talbot Baines. Boycotted & Other Stories. 2007. 276p. pap. 21.99 (978-1-4346-5251-5(3)); (ENG.). 294p. pap. 23.99 (978-1-4346-5252-2(1)) Creative Media Partners, LLC.

Reeve, Elizabeth. Sassy: the short stories of being a service Dog. 2010. 35p. pap. 17.00 (978-0-557-39319-0(1)) Lulu Pr., Inc.

Regan, Anne, ed. Harmonious Hearts. 2016. (ENG., Illus.). (YA). (gr. 9-12). 27.99 **(978-1-63533-024-3(6)**, Harmony Ink Pr.) Dreamspinner Pr.

—Harmonious Hearts 2015. 2016. (ENG., Illus.). (YA). 24.99 **(978-1-63533-025-0(4)**, Harmony Ink Pr.) Dreamspinner Pr.

—Harmonious Hearts 2016: Stories from the Young Author Challenge. 2016. (Harmonious Hearts Ser.). (ENG., Illus.). (YA). pap. 17.99 **(978-1-63477-834-3(0)**, Harmony Ink Pr.) Dreamspinner Pr.

Reggie-Foster, Debbi. It's Cool to Be Me! Mini Stories about. 2006. 48p. pap. 16.95 (978-1-4241-4613-0(5)) PublishAmerica, Inc.

Regis, Tessa. The Hibiscus Conspiracies: Loss of Innocence. 2009. 116p. 20.95 (978-0-595-69133-3(1)); pap. 10.95 (978-0-595-44978-1(6)) iUniverse, Inc.

REID, D. H. Fantasies & Dreams. 2008. 208p. pap. 18.95 (978-0-557-01592-4(8)) Lulu Pr., Inc.

Reid, Rob. Wave Goodbye, 1 vol. Williams, Lorraine, illus. 2013. (ENG.). 24p. (J). pap. 9.95 (978-1-60060-341-9(6)) Lee & Low Bks., Inc.

Relatos Escalofriantes. (SPA.). (YA). (gr. 5-8). pap. (978-956-13-1353-8(7), AB9026) Bello, Andres CHL. Dist: Lectorum Pubns., Inc.

Renee, Lindsey. What Kind of Fairy Is Merry Berry? 2010. (ENG., Illus.). 36p. (J). (gr. -1-1). 12.99 (978-0-8118-7685-8(3)) Chronicle Bks. LLC.

Renshaw, D. M. A Day to Remember. 2008. 100p. per. 23.95 (978-1-4327-0858-0(9)) Outskirts Pr., Inc.

Reviejo, Carlos & Reviejo, Carlos. Dejame Que te Cuente: Cincuenta Cuentos de Animales para Ninos. 2003. (SPA., Illus.). 212p. (978-84-348-7166-3(1), SM31147) SM Ediciones ESP. Dist: Lectorum Pubns., Inc.

Rey, H. A. Curious George Learns the Alphabet, 1 vol. 2009. (Curious George Ser.). (ENG., Illus.). 80p. (J). (gr. -1-3). audio compact disk 10.99 (978-0-618-95966-2(1)) Houghton Mifflin Harcourt Publishing Co.

—Curious George's 5-Minute Stories. 2013. (Curious George Ser.). (ENG., Illus.). 192p. (J). (gr. -1-3). 12.99 (978-0-544-10793-9(4)) Houghton Mifflin Harcourt Publishing Co.

—Storybook Collection. 2010. (Curious George Ser.). (ENG., Illus.). 208p. (J). (gr. -1-3). 10.99 (978-0-547-39631-6(7)) Houghton Mifflin Harcourt Publishing Co.

—Three Tales for a Winter's Night. 2012. (Curious George Ser.). (ENG., Illus.). 72p. (J). (gr. -1-3). pap. 7.99 (978-0-547-83936-3(7)) Houghton Mifflin Harcourt Publishing Co.

—A Treasury of Curious George (Coleccion de Oro Jorge el Curioso) 2011. (Curious George Ser.). (ENG & SPA., Illus.). 208p. (J). (gr. -1-3). 11.99 (978-0-547-52310-1(6)) Houghton Mifflin Harcourt Publishing Co.

Rey, H. A. & Rey, Margret. The H. A. Rey Treasury of Stories. 2015. (Dover Children's Classics Ser.). (ENG., Illus.). 112p. (J). (gr. 2-4). pap. 14.99 *(978-0-486-78468-7(1))* Dover Pubns., Inc.

Rey, Margret & Rey, H. A. Curious George at the Aquarium. 2014. (Curious George 8x8 Ser.). lib. bdg. 14.75 *(978-1-4177-9792-9(4),* Turtleback) Turtleback Bks.

Reyes, Yolanda. Los Anos Terribles. (SPA.). (YA). 9.95 *(978-958-04-5633-9(X))* Norma S.A. COL. Dist: Distribuidora Norma, Inc.

—María de los Dinosaurios. 2011. (Torre de Papel Ser.). (SPA.). 94p. (gr. 2-4). pap. 10.99 *(978-958-04-4277-6(0))* Norma S.A. COL. Dist: Lectorum Pubns., Inc.

RH Disney Staff, illus. Disney/Pixar Little Golden Book Library (Disney/Pixar), 5 vols. 2014. (ENG.). 24p. (J). (-k). 19.95 *(978-0-7364-3163-7(2),* Golden/Disney) Random Hse. Children's Bks.

Ricard, Anouk. Anna & Froga: Wanna Gumball? Dascher, Helge, tr. from FRE. 2012. (Anna & Froga Ser.). (ENG., Illus.). 40p. (J). (gr. k-4). 14.95 *(978-1-77046-070-6(5),* 9781770460706) Drawn & Quarterly Pubns. CAN. Dist: Macmillan.

Rice, David. Crazy Loco. 2008. 135p. 16.00 *(978-0-7569-8951-4(5))* Perfection Learning Corp.

Rice, David & Garcia, Mike D. Heart-Shaped Cookies. 2011. (YA). pap. *(978-1-931010-79-5(X))* Bilingual Pr./Editorial Bilingue.

Rice, David & Rice, David Talbot. Crazy Loco. Clayton, Christian, illus. 2003. (ENG.). 144p. (YA). (gr. 7-11). 6.99 *(978-0-14-250056-9(9),* Speak) Penguin Young Readers Group.

Rice, Dona Herwick. The North Wind & the Sun, 1 vol. 2008. (Building Fluency Through Reader's Theater Ser.). (ENG.). 24p. (J). (gr. 1-3). pap. 6.99 *(978-1-4333-0296-1(9))* Teacher Created Materials, Inc.

Rice, Ernestine. Mr Peacock. 2012. 28p. pap. 19.99 *(978-1-4772-4444-9(1))* AuthorHouse.

Rich, Susan. Half-Minute Horrors. (ENG.). 160p. (J). (gr. 5). 2011. pap. 5.99 *(978-0-06-183381-6(9))* 2009. (Illus.). 14.99 *(978-0-06-183379-3(7))* HarperCollins Pubs.

Richard Bellingham Edd. The Fables of Boris: Invitations to Meaningful Conversations. 2009. 280p. 27.95 *(978-1-4401-6247-3(6));* pap. 17.95 *(978-1-4401-6245-9(X))* iUniverse, Inc.

Richard, Martine. Chapeau, Camomille! Begin, Jean-Guy, illus. 2004. (Des 6 Ans Ser.). (FRE.). 64p. 7.95 *(978-2-922565-96-6(3))* Editions de la Paix CAN. Dist: World of Reading, Ltd.

Richards, J. Danielle Jennson, Life Lessons of a Little Clown. 2006. 72p. per. 8.95 *(978-1-59824-187-7(7))* E-BookTime LLC.

Richards, Justin. Licence to Fish, Vol. 3. 2011. (Agent Alfie Ser.). (ENG., Illus.). 176p. (J). (gr. 2-4). 6.99 *(978-0-00-727359-1(2))* HarperCollins Pubs. Ltd. GBR. Dist: Independent Pubs. Group.

Richards, Laura Elizabeth Howe. Hildegarde's Neighbors. 2007. 92p. per. *(978-1-4068-3864-0(0))* Echo Library.

Richards, Lisa. Family Short Stories Book. 2011. 44p. pap. 24.95 *(978-1-4560-6711-3(7))* America Star Bks.

—Family Stories: A Collection of Short Stories by Lisa Richards, 1 vol. 2010. 52p. pap. 16.95 *(978-1-4512-8988-6(X))* America Star Bks.

Richardson, Arleta. More Stories from Grandma's Attic. rev. ed. 2003. (Grandma's Attic Ser.). (Illus.). 144p. (J). pap. 6.99 *(978-0-7814-3269-6(3),* 0781432693) Cook, David C.

—Still More Stories from Grandma's Attic, 1. rev. ed. 2003. (Grandma's Attic Ser.). (Illus.). 144p. (J). (gr. 8-12). pap., pap. 8.99 *(978-0-7814-3270-2(7),* 0781432707) Cook, David C.

—Treasures from Grandma. rev. ed. 2003. (Grandma's Attic Ser.). (Illus.). 144p. (J). (gr. 8-12). pap. 8.99 *(978-0-7814-3271-9(5),* 0781432715) Cook, David C.

Richmond, Beulah. Anancy & Friends: A Grandmother's Anancy Stories for Her Grandchildren. Brown, Clovis, illus. 2004. (ENG.). 52p. pap. 5.99 *(978-976-8184-48-1(5))* Penguin Publishing Group.

Rider, John Russell. The Adventures of Acorn & Pinecone. 2010. 64p. pap. 25.95 *(978-1-4520-8354-4(1))* AuthorHouse.

Ries, Lori. Aggie & Ben: Three Stories. Dormer, Frank W., illus. 2007. (ENG.). 48p. (J). (gr. -1-3). 5.95 *(978-1-57091-649-6(7))* Charlesbridge Publishing, Inc.

—Aggie the Brave. Dormer, Frank W., illus. (ENG.). 48p. (J). (gr. -1-3). 2012. pap. 5.95 *(978-1-57091-636-6(5))* 2010. 12.95 *(978-1-57091-635-9(7))* Charlesbridge Publishing, Inc.

Riggs-Mayfield, Nellie. A Collection of Short Stories for Children. 2006. (J). per. 19.95 *(978-1-59872-640-4(4))* Instant Pub.

Riggs, Ransom. Tales of the Peculiar. Davidson, Andrew, illus. 2016. (ENG.). 192p. (YA). (gr. 7). 24.99 *(978-0-399-53853-7(4),* Dutton Books for Young Readers) Penguin Young Readers Group.

Rigo, L. Little Owl. 2011. (Look at Me Bks.). (ENG., Illus.). 10p. (J). bds. 8.99 *(978-0-7641-6447-7(3))* Barron's Educational Series, Inc.

Rigo, L., illus. Little Duckling. 2011. (Look at Me Bks.). 10p. (J). bds. 7.99 *(978-0-7641-6425-5(2))* Barron's Educational Series, Inc.

—Little Elephant. 2011. (Look at Me Bks.). 10p. (J). bds. 8.99 *(978-0-7641-6426-2(0))* Barron's Educational Series, Inc.

—Little Lamb. 2011. (Look at Me Bks.). 10p. (J). (gr. -1). bds. 7.99 *(978-0-7641-6427-9(9))* Barron's Educational Series, Inc.

—Little Monkey. 2011. (Look at Me Bks.). 10p. (J). bds. 7.99 *(978-0-7641-6428-6(7))* Barron's Educational Series, Inc.

—Little Panda. 2010. (Look at Me Bks.). (ENG.). 10p. (J). (gr. -1-k). 8.99 *(978-0-7641-6339-5(6))* Barron's Educational Series, Inc.

Rigo, L. & Caviezel, Giovanni, illus. Little Bunny. 2010. (Look at Me Bks.). (ENG.). 10p. (J). (gr. -1-k). bds. 7.99 *(978-0-7641-6322-7(1))* Barron's Educational Series, Inc.

—Little Puppy. 2010. (Look at Me Bks.). (ENG.). 10p. (J). (gr. -1-k). bds. 8.99 *(978-0-7641-6324-1(8))* Barron's Educational Series, Inc.

—Little Tiger. 2010. (Look at Me Bks.). (ENG.). 10p. (J). (gr. -1-k). bds. 8.99 *(978-0-7641-6326-5(4))* Barron's Educational Series, Inc.

Riordan, Rick, et al. Vespers Rising. 2011. (39 Clues Ser.: 11). (ENG.). 240p. (J). (gr. 3-7). 12.99 *(978-0-545-32606-3(0),* Scholastic Pr.) Scholastic, Inc.

Robbins, Maureen. Cuentos de Pesca. 2012. (SPA & ENG.). 24p. (gr. 2-3). pap. 8.95 *(978-1-61810-548-6(5))* Rourke Educational Media.

Roberts, Emrys & Knipping, Rod. Dau Gymro Dewr: A Storïau Gwir Eraill. 2005. (WEL., Illus.). 72p. pap. *(978-0-903131-17-9(X))* Urdd Gobaith Cymru.

Roberts, Nancy. Ghosts of the Wild West. Roberts, Bruce, photos by. 2nd fac. ed. 2008. (Illus.). 110p. (J). (gr. 3-7). 24.95 *(978-1-57003-731-3(0))* Univ. of South Carolina Pr.

—Ghosts of the Wild West: Enlarged Edition Including Five Never-Before-Published Stories. Roberts, Bruce, photos by. 2nd enl. ed. 2008. (ENG., Illus.). 120p. (gr. 3-7). pap. 13.95 *(978-1-57003-732-0(9))* Univ. of South Carolina Pr.

Robinson, Hilary. Over the Moon. Abbott, Jane, illus. 2009. (Tadpoles Ser.). (ENG.). 24p. (J). (gr. k-2). pap. *(978-0-7787-3899-2(X));* lib. bdg. *(978-0-7787-3868-8(X))* Crabtree Publishing Co.

Robinson, Michelle. Yak Yuk. Sim, David, illus. 2012. (ENG.). 12p. (J). (gr. -1-k). 10.99 *(978-1-4088-1703-2(9),* 9781408817032, Bloomsbury USA Childrens) Bloomsbury Publishing USA.

Robinson, Ronnie D. Children Stories. 2nd ed. 2004. 112p. (YA). pap. 11.95 *(978-0-7414-1439-7(2))* Infinity Publishing.

—Children's Stories. 2004. 134p. (YA). pap. 12.95 *(978-0-7414-1438-0(4))* Infinity Publishing.

Robles, Eduardo. La Sombra Vegetal. 2005. (Ediciones Castillo Castillo Del Terror Ser.). (SPA.). 125p. (J). (gr. 4-7). per. 7.95 *(978-970-20-0249-9(4))* Castillo, Ediciones, S. A. de C. V. MEX. Dist: Iaconi, Mariuccia Bk. Imports.

Rochman, Hazel & McCampbell, Darlene Z., eds. Who do you Think you Are? 2005. 176p. (YA). 23.00 *(978-0-8446-7269-4(6),* 3585) Smith, Peter Pub., Inc.

Rock, Lois. The Lion First Book of Nursery Stories. Vagnozzi, Barbara, illus. 2013. (ENG.). 96p. (J). (gr. -1-k). 16.99 *(978-0-7459-6341-9(2))* Lion Hudson PLC GBR. Dist: Independent Pubs. Group.

Rode, Linda & Moodie, Fiona. In the Never-Ever Wood. 2011. (Illus.). 240p. *(978-0-624-04768-1(7))* NB Pubs. Ltd.

Rodriguez, Alfredo. Redfoot. O'Reilly, Sean Patrick, ed. 2011. (Illus.). 43p. pap. 8.95 *(978-1-926914-59-6(7))* Arcana Studio, Inc.

Rodriguez, Elizabeth. Hannah's Ayuna. 2007. per. *(978-1-59916-153-2(2))* Printing Systems.

—Hannah's Fast. 2006. per. *(978-1-59916-144-0(3))* Printing Systems.

Rodriguez, Jason, ed. Colonial Comics: New England, 1620 ¿ 1750. 2014. (Colonial Comics Ser.). (ENG., Illus.). 208p. (gr. 4). pap. 29.95 *(978-1-938486-30-2(7))* Fulcrum Publishing.

Rodríguez, Pedro. Chilling Tales of Horror: Dark Graphic Short Stories. 2012. (Dark Graphic Novels Ser.). (Illus.). 96p. (J). (gr. 5-9). 31.94 *(978-0-7660-4085-4(2))* Enslow Pubs., Inc.

Roelofsen, Marjorie. Where Have All the Puppies Gone? A Sequel to SAM. 2010. 24p. pap. 14.00 *(978-1-4490-6211-8(3))* AuthorHouse.

Rogers, Derek G. Monstrous Myths & Fabulous Fables. 2012. 184p. pap. *(978-1-78176-741-2(6))* FeedARead.com.

Rogers, Roy. Roy Rogers & the Deadly Treasure. 2011. 286p. 48.95 *(978-1-258-03926-4(5))* Literary Licensing, LLC.

Rojas, Emilio. Libro Mágico de los 101 Relatos para Niños: Fábulas, Cuentos y Leyendas. 2003. (SPA., Illus.). 224p. (YA). (gr. 5-18). 15.95 *(978-968-6966-19-0(6))* EDITER'S Publishing Hse. MEX. Dist: EDITER'S Publishing Hse.

Rolón, Rebecca Alisa. Rebecca's Tales. 2007. 48p. pap. 16.95 *(978-1-4241-9198-7(X))* America Star Bks.

Rolt, Molly. The Chocci-Croc & Other Stories. 2006. 64p. pap. *(978-1-84401-890-1(3))* Athena Pr.

Romance, Trisha. A Star for Christmas. 2007. (ENG., Illus.). 40p. (J). (gr. k-12). 22.95 *(978-0-88776-836-1(9),* Tundra Bks.) Tundra Bks. CAN. Dist: Penguin Random Hse. LLC.

Romano, Elaine Ambrose. Gators & Taters: A Week of Bedtime Stories 2003. (Illus.). 64p. (J). pap. 9.95 *(978-0-9728225-0-3(X))* Mill Park Publishing.

Romero Gutiérrez, Astrid. Cuentos de Angeles Para Ninos. 2011. (SPA., Illus.). 160p. (YA). (gr. -1-3). pap. *(978-970-643-065-6(2))* Selector, S.A. de C.V.

Ronnholm, Ursula O. Mi Libro de Palabras, Oraciones y Cuentos. Deliz, Osdila O., ed. Montero, Miguel, illus. (SPA.). 100p. (J). (gr. k-6). pap. 7.00 *(978-0-941911-02-3(0))* Two Way Bilingual, Inc.

Rosario Irish. Ensueño. 2010. 52p. pap. *(978-1-4269-2489-7(5))* Trafford Publishing (UK) Ltd.

Rose, Lela. Truth in Stories for Children 4 Through 6. 2003. pap. 8.00 *(978-0-8059-5923-9(8))* Dorrance Publishing Co., Inc.

Rose, M. E. Kangaroo Christmas. Keenan, Brona, illus. 2007. (ENG.). 140p. (YA). 10.95 *(978-1-896209-89-0(0))* Bayeux Arts, Inc. CAN. Dist: Chicago Distribution Ctr.

Rose, Mary. Little Helpers. 2010. (ENG., Illus.). 20p. 4.81 *(978-0-19-440083-1(2))* Oxford Univ. Pr., Inc.

Rose, Simon. The Time Camera, 1 vol. 2012. (ENG., Illus.). 96p. (J). (gr. 3-6). pap. 9.95 *(978-1-896580-09-8(2))* Tradewind Bks. CAN. Dist: Orca Bk. Pubs. USA.

Rosen, Barry. Do You Know What a Stranger Is? Rosen, Barry & Bell, Greg, illus. 2003. 34p. (J). pap. 7.25 *(978-0-9625593-4-1(2))* B.R. Publishing Co.

Rosenfeld, Dina. A Chanukah Story for Night Number Three. 2009. (Illus.). 32p. (J). 12.95 *(978-1-929628-54-4(4))* Hachai Publishing.

Rosenthal, Amy Krouse. Little Pea; Little Hoot; Little Oink, 3 vols., Set. Corace, Jen, illus. 2009. (ENG.). 80p. (J). (gr. -1 — 1). bds. 19.99 *(978-0-8118-7054-2(5))* Chronicle Bks. LLC.

Rosero, Evelio. Teresita Cantaba. (SPA.). (J). *(978-958-04-6491-4(X))* Norma S.A. COL. Dist: Distribuidora Norma, Inc.

Ross, Stewart. Dear Mum, I Miss You! Clark, Linda, illus. 54p. (J). *(978-0-237-52318-3(3))* Evans Brothers, Ltd.

Ross, Tony. My Favourite Fairy Tales. Ross, Tony, illus. 2012. (ENG., Illus.). 96p. (J). (gr. -1-k). pap. 16.99 *(978-1-84939-211-2(0))* Andersen Pr. GBR. Dist: Independent Pubs. Group.

—Rizos de Oro y los Tres Osos: Little Books. 2003. (Nuevos Horizontes Ser.). (SPA., Illus.). 32p. (J). (gr. 3-5). pap. 5.95 *(978-84-372-1575-4(7))* Santillana USA Publishing Co., Inc.

Ross, Tony, illus. The Nights Before Christmas: 24 Classic Christmas Stories to Read Aloud. 2017. (ENG.). 240p. (J). (gr. 4-6). 25.95 ***(978-1-84939-580-9(2))*** Andersen Pr. GBR. Dist: Independent Pubs. Group.

Rossbacher, John. From Father John's Story Book: Nine Fun Stories for Children & Grandchildren. 2010. 40p. pap. 23.99 *(978-1-4520-7778-9(9))* AuthorHouse.

Rossendale, Helen. Tales from Pinocchio. Philpot, Graham, illus. 2011. (10-Minute Bedtime Stories Ser.). (ENG.). 88p. (J). (gr. k-4). 14.99 *(978-1-84365-147-5(5),* Pavilion) Pavilion Bks. GBR. Dist: Independent Pubs. Group.

Rosseter, Patrick W. Grampa Pat's Little Animal Tales. 2005. 10.00 *(978-0-8059-9797-2(0))* Dorrance Publishing Co., Inc.

Roth, Carol. Where's My Mommy? Julian, Sean, illus. 2012. (ENG.). 32p. (J). 17.95 *(978-0-7358-4032-4(6))* North-South Bks., Inc.

Roth, Jurgen Philip Philip Philip Kevin Kevin P Geneen Philip Philip Philip Marie, Carol. Little Bunny's Sleepless Night. Gorbachev, Valeri, illus. 2013. (ENG.). 40p. (J). (gr. -1-2). 17.95 *(978-0-7358-4123-9(3))* North-South Bks., Inc.

Rothenberger, Charlene. Kara's Kapers with Katy Pillar. Rothenberger, Boyd & Bays, Gail, illus. 2006. 64p. per. 9.99 *(978-0-9776260-6-9(7))* Bearhead Publishing, LLC.

Rounds, Harriet. The Magic Stairway, 1 vol. 2009. 48p. pap. 16.95 *(978-1-60749-707-3(7))* America Star Bks.

Rousay II, Richard A. Choose the Right 'Walk with Alma' 2010. 94p. pap. 17.50 *(978-0-557-13491-5(9))* Lulu Pr., Inc.

—Choose the Right! Walk with Ruth. 2009. 101p. pap. 17.50 *(978-1-4092-5519-2(0))* Lulu Pr., Inc.

Rouse, W. H. D. The Giant Crab & Other Tales from Old Indi. 2011. 90p. 20.95 *(978-1-4638-9898-4(3))* Rodgers, Alan Bks.

Rouse, W. H. D., ed. The Giant Crab & Other Tales from Old Indi. 2011. 90p. pap. 9.95 *(978-1-4638-0139-7(4))* Rodgers, Alan Bks.

Rowe, John. Little Stories for Little People. 2013. 92p. pap. 25.95 *(978-1-62516-542-8(0),* Strategic Bk. Publishing) Strategic Book Publishing & Rights Agency (SBPRA).

Roxbee-Cox, Phil. Find the Teddy. Cartwright, Stephen, illus. 2004. (Rhyming Board Bks.). (ENG.). 1p. (J). (gr. -1-18). bds. 3.95 *(978-0-7460-3825-3(9))* EDC Publishing.

Roxbee Cox, Phil. Phonics Stories for Young Readers, Vol. 2. 2009. (Phonics Readers Ser.). 96p. (J). 14.99 *(978-0-7945-1887-5(7),* Usborne) EDC Publishing.

Roxbee-Cox, Phil. Ted's Shed. 2004. (Easy Words to Read Ser.). (ENG., Illus.). 1p. (J). (gr. 1-18). pap. 6.95 *(978-0-7460-4210-6(8))* EDC Publishing.

Roy, Alene Adele. The Legend of Dragonfly Pond: Book Three. 2010. 60p. pap. 23.99 *(978-1-4490-0834-5(8))* AuthorHouse.

Roy Windham, Windham & Windham, Roy. Uncle Fuddy-Duddy & the Big Bad Bear. 2010. 28p. 16.09 *(978-1-4269-3065-2(8))* Trafford Publishing.

Rsm Ma, Anne Frances Pulling. Tales from the Pumpkin Patch Spooky: Kitten Who Wanted to Fly. 2012. 24p. pap. 12.99 *(978-1-4653-8747-9(1))* Xlibris Corp.

Ruben, Pamela J. Yenta the Chicken & Other Fowl Tales! Ruben, Anthony R., ed. 2004. (Illus.). 19p. (J). 12.95 *(978-0-9764813-0-0(8))* Peppery Pr.

Ruffell, Ann & Orme, David. Treachery by Night. 2004. (Shades Ser.). (ENG.). 62p. (J). pap. *(978-0-237-52728-0(6))* Evans Brothers, Ltd.

Ruffenach, Jessie E., et al. Learn along with Ashkii: First Grade Level 1. Whitethorne, Bahe, Jr., illus. 2003. (NAV & ENG.). 16p. (J). (gr. -1-3). pap. 7.95 *(978-1-893354-41-8(5))* Salina Bookshelf Inc.

The Runaway Engine & Other Stories: Individual Title Six-Pack. (Story Steps Ser.). (gr. k-2). 48.00 *(978-0-7635-9803-7(8))* Rigby Education.

Running Press Staff, ed. A Treasury of Christmas Classics: Includes the Night Before Christmas, the Twelve Days of Christmas, & the Nutcracker. 2014. (ENG., Illus.). 128p. (J). (gr. 3-17). 14.95 *(978-0-7624-5495-2(4),* Running Pr. Kids) Running Pr. Bk. Pubs.

Rupp, Dain Chistopher. The Greatest Saint Stories A-Z: (Book 1 of 2: A-M) 2008. 32p. per. 24.95 *(978-1-60441-067-9(1))* America Star Bks.

Rushford, Betty. Best Buddies: And the Fruit of the Spirit. 2003. 41p. pap. 24.95 *(978-1-59286-746-2(4))* America Star Bks.

Russell, Kitty, compiled by. Fairy Hearts & Charms: Stories of Yesteryear. 2012. (ENG.). 434p. 29.95 *(978-1-937922-03-0(0))* Kittyco Pr.

—Fairy Lovely: Stories of Yesteryear. 2012. (ENG.). 416p. 29.95 *(978-1-937922-04-7(9))* Kittyco Pr.

Russell, Rachel Renée. Dork Diaries, Set. Russell, Rachel Renée, illus. 2013. (Dork Diaries: Nos. 4-6). (ENG., Illus.). 1056p. (J). (gr. 4-8). 41.99 *(978-1-4424-9859-4(5),* Aladdin) Simon & Schuster Children's Publishing.

—Tales from a Not-So-Dorky Drama Queen. 2015. (Dork Diaries: 9). lib. bdg. 25.75 *(978-0-606-37316-6(0))* Turtleback Bks.

Ruurs, Margriet & Gooderham, Andrew. Ms. Bee's magical bookcase. 2004. (Illus.). 32p. (J). pap. 8.95 *(978-1-894601-10-8(6))* Chestnut Publishing Group CAN. Dist: Hushion Hse. Publishing, Ltd.

Ryan, Carrie, ed. Foretold: 14 Tales of Prophecy & Prediction. 2013. (ENG.). 368p. (YA). (gr. 7). pap. 9.99 *(978-0-385-74130-9(8),* Ember) Random Hse. Children's Bks.

S. P. Glynn, Annie S. P. Glynn. Jodie's Adventures with Aunty Ann. 2016. (ENG.). 26p. (J). (gr. 3-4). mass mkt. 10.95 *(978-1-78612-838-6(1),* 66ce91c5-aae4-4fb3-864f-1d2ff1cbc8b5) Austin, Stan AUS. Dist: Bookmasters Distribution.

S, Peter. 12 Minutes: So Short Stories. 2011. 28p. pap. 15.99 *(978-1-4568-8841-1(2))* Xlibris Corp.

Saari, Danial. Tales with Tails: Bed Time Stories. 2012. (KAZ & ENG., Illus.). 68p. pap. 41.99 *(978-1-4771-3252-4(X))* Xlibris Corp.

Sachs, Harley L. A Troll for Christmas & Other Stories. 2009. (ENG., Illus.). 240p. (J). pap. 14.99 *(978-1-934841-80-8(3),* Zumaya Thresholds) Zumaya Pubns. LLC.

Sadi. The Careless King & Other Stories. 2005. (Illus.). 64p. (J). *(978-969-542-068-3(0))* Children Pubns.

Sadu, Itah & Condy, Roy. Christopher Changes His Name. (Tell Me a Story Ser.). (Illus.). 32p. (J). 12.99 *(978-0-590-24670-5(4))* Scholastic, Inc.

Safari Stories. (My Animal Library). (Illus.). 10p. (J). *(978-2-7643-0154-8(5))* Phidal Publishing, Inc./Editions Phidal, Inc.

Saffiedine, Amanda. Goodnight Sweet Baby: A Collection of Short Stories. 2009. 52p. pap. 22.49 *(978-1-4490-0857-4(7))* AuthorHouse.

Saga-Whyte. Why the Naiads Dance: Book One of the Naiad Legends, 8 vols., Vol. 1. Saga-Whyte, illus. 2007. (Illus.). 25p. (J). *(978-90-8885-018-9(6))* Saga-Whyte Pr.

Sakade, Florence. Japanese Children's Favorite Stories. Kurosaki, Yoshisuke, illus. anniv. ed. 2014. (ENG.). 112p. (J). (gr. 3-8). 17.95 *(978-4-8053-1260-5(2))* Tuttle Publishing.

Saldaña, René. Dancing with the Devil & Other Tales from Beyond / Bailando con el Diablo y Otros Cuentos del Más Allá. Baeza Ventura, Gabriela, tr. from ENG. 2012. (SPA & ENG.). (YA). pap. 9.95 *(978-1-55885-744-5(3),* Piñata Books) Arte Publico Pr.

Saldana, Theresa. The Almost Murder & Other Stories. 2008. (ENG.). 144p. (YA). (gr. 6-18). pap. 10.95 *(978-1-55885-507-6(6),* Piñata Books) Arte Publico Pr.

Saleff, Olga. Baba's Bedtime Stories. 2011. 64p. (gr. -1). pap. 25.48 *(978-1-4567-6247-6(8))* AuthorHouse.

Salerno, Tony, et al. Tony Salerno's Good News Express. Thompson, Del et al, illus. 64p. (Orig.). (J). (gr. k-6). pap. *(978-1-881597-00-1(8))* Magination.

Salsi, Lynn Sims. Young Ray Hicks: Learns the Jack Tales. 2005. (ENG., Illus.). 154p. (J). 16.00 *(978-0-9706527-5-1(5));* pap. 8.00 *(978-0-9706527-6-8(3))* Montville Pr.

The Salt Water Bath. 2004. (J). per. *(978-1-57657-472-0(5))* Paradise Pr., Inc.

Sam, Kurutsi Dan'azumi. The Big Photograph of Sir Ahmadu Bello: And Other Short Stories for Children & Young Adults. 2013. 50p. pap. 10.97 *(978-1-62212-440-4(5),* Strategic Bk. Publishing) Strategic Book Publishing & Rights Agency (SBPRA).

Sam, Sam & Other Stories: Individual Title Six-Pack. (Story Steps Ser.). (gr. k-2). 48.00 *(978-0-7635-9610-1(8))* Rigby Education.

Samson, Don. Teenage Aviation Stories. 2005. reprint ed. pap. 26.95 *(978-1-4191-1624-7(X))* Kessinger Publishing, LLC.

San Souci, Robert D. Haunted Houses. Murphy, Kelly & Revoy, Antoine, illus. 2012. (Are You Scared Yet? Ser.). (ENG.). 304p. (J). (gr. 4-7). pap. 10.99 *(978-0-312-55136-0(3),* 9780312551360) Square Fish.

—More Short & Shivery: Thirty Terrifying Tales. Coville, Katherine, illus. 2015. (ENG.). 224p. (J). (gr. 3-7). 6.99 *(978-0-440-41857-3(7),* Yearling) Random Hse. Children's Bks.

San Souci, Robert D. & San Souci, Daniel, illus. Sister Tricksters: Rollicking Tales of Clever Females. 2006. (ENG.). 70p. (J). (gr. 3-7). 19.95 *(978-0-87483-791-9(X))* August Hse. Pubs., Inc.

Sánchez, Gloria. Siete Casas, Siete Brujas y un Huevo. 5th ed. 2005. (SPA., Illus.). 64p. (J). (gr. k-1). 6.95 *(978-84-348-6003-2(1))* SM Ediciones ESP. Dist: Iaconi, Mariuccia Bk. Imports.

Sánchez, Haroldo & McCaughrean, Geraldine. Juegos de la Mente: La\Vida de un Periodista Guatemalteco en 30 Días. 2005. (Mythology Series Collection Mitos Ser.). (SPA., Illus.). 348p. (J). (gr. 2-3). 9.95 *(978-84-348-9385-6(1))* SM Ediciones ESP. Dist: Iaconi, Mariuccia Bk. Imports.

Sand, Marc. Sheltered. 2003. (YA). per. 5.95 *(978-0-9726764-0-3(6))* Sketch Publishing.

Sandage, Charley. I can tell you stories, if you gather round Big Book. 2005. (Illus.). (J). pap. *(978-0-9794044-3-6(6))* Archeological Assessments, Inc.

Sandall, Ellie. Daisy Plays Hide-and-Seek. Sandall, Ellie, illus. 2012. (ENG., Illus.). 32p. (J). (gr. -1-k). pap. 8.99 *(978-1-4052-5457-1(2))* Egmont Bks., Ltd. GBR. Dist: Independent Pubs. Group.

Sandau, Carol E. 10 Puzzling Pieces. 2010. 80p. pap. 8.95 *(978-1-4502-6244-6(9))* iUniverse, Inc.

Sandburg, Carl. Rootabaga Stories. (gr. 3-18). 2011. 126p. 24.95 *(978-1-4638-9902-8(5))* 2009. 128p. pap. 10.95 *(978-1-60664-425-6(4))* Rodgers, Alan Bks.

Sangster, Margaret Elizabeth, ed. Holiday Stories for Young People. 2007. 228p. per. *(978-1-4065-3858-8(2))* Dodo Pr.

Sankey, Alice. Roy Rogers' Surprise for Donnie. Steel, John, illus. 2011. 32p. pap. 35.95 *(978-1-258-03591-4(X))* Literary Licensing, LLC.

Sansone, V. K. A Tweens Book of Shorts. 2009. 32p. pap. 8.98 *(978-0-557-06244-7(6))* Lulu Pr., Inc.

Santan. Good & Evil: The Princess & Devil. 2011. (Illus.). 64p. pap. 25.80 *(978-1-4567-9683-9(6))* AuthorHouse.

Santore, Charles. Aesop's Fables. 2012. (ENG., Illus.). 56p. (J). 14.95 *(978-1-4027-8412-5(0))* Sterling Publishing Co., Inc.

Sargent, Dave & Sargent, Pat. Lizzy Lightning Bug/Lizzy la Luciérnaga, 10 vols., Vol. 17. Robinson, Laura, illus. 2004. (Learn to Read Ser.: 10).Tr. of Lizzy la Luciernaga. (ENG & SPA.). 18p. (J). (gr. k-2). lib. bdg. 20.95 *(978-1-56763-993-3(3))* Ozark Publishing.

Sargent, Dave, et al. The Bundle Keeper: (Pawnee) Be Responsible, 20 vols., Vol. 18. Lenoir, Sue, illus. 2004. (Story Keeper Ser.: No. 18). 42p. (J). lib. bdg. 23.60 *(978-1-56763-937-7(2))* Ozark Publishing.

Sargent, Pat L. Jaguar #8 (PB), 6 vols. 2007. (Barney the Bear Killer Ser.: 8). (YA). pap. 9.95 *(978-1-59381-425-0(9))* Ozark Publishing.

Sastrias, Marta. Cuentos de Todo y de Nada. Martinez y Luis San Vicente, Enrique, illus. 2003. (SPA.). 82p. (J). (gr. 3-5). *(978-968-19-0551-4(2))* Aguilar, Altea, Taurus, Alfaguara, S.A. de C.V.

Satchwell, Sm. Len Stories. 2012. (Illus.). 24p. pap. 19.82 *(978-1-4685-0478-1(9))* AuthorHouse.

A Saturday Sandwiches Set, 6 vols. 32p. (gr. 1-3). 26.50 *(978-0-7802-8043-4(1))* Wright Group/McGraw-Hill.

Saunders. Saunders 2. Date not set. (J). 15.99 *(978-0-380-97785-7(0))* HarperCollins Pubs.

Saunders, Helen B. Sweet Faces Story Book. 2004. Orig. Title: Sweet Faces. (Illus.). 29p. (J). 14.95 *(978-0-9763143-0-1(4))* Happy Heart Kids Publishing.

Saunders, Jami Lynn. Feral: Book I of the Werecat Saga. 2011. 86p. (YA). pap. 4.99 *(978-1-936307-15-9(4),* 711Press) Vendera Publishing.

Sava, Scott Christian. Animal Crackers. 2011. (Illus.). 152p. pap. 11.99 *(978-1-60010-619-4(6))* Idea & Design Works, LLC.
Sawyer, Debra D. Let Me Speak You A Secret. 2004. (YA). reprint ed. per. 16.00 *(978-0-9761207-0-4(4))* DiaShah Pr., LLC.
Saxby, Karen. Storyfun for Flyers Student's Book. 2010. (ENG., Illus.). 96p. pap. 17.50 *(978-0-521-13410-1(2))* Cambridge Univ. Pr.
—Storyfun for Movers Student's Book. 2011. (ENG., Illus.). 95p. pap. 12.75 *(978-0-521-17281-3(0))* Cambridge Univ. Pr.
Scaperrotta, Kirstyn. I Lost My Cracker to the Big Cheese: A Collection of Voices. 2003. 126p. (YA). pap. 10.95 *(978-0-595-26478-0(6),* Writers Club Pr.) iUniverse, Inc.
Scarry, Richard. Biggest, Busiest Storybook Ever. Scarry, Richard, illus. 2009. (Picture Book Ser.). (ENG., Illus.). 184p. (J). (gr. -1-2). 27.99 *(978-0-375-85483-5(5),* Golden Bks.) Random Hse. Children's Bks.
—Richard Scarry's Best Christmas Book Ever! 2010. (ENG., Illus.). 44p. (J). (gr. -1-2). 12.95 *(978-1-4027-7218-4(1))* Sterling Publishing Co., Inc.
—Richard Scarry's the Great Pie Robbery & Other Mysteries. 2008. (ENG., Illus.). 104p. (J). (gr. 1-3). 12.95 *(978-1-4027-5823-2(5))* Sterling Publishing Co., Inc.
—Richard Scarry's Vrooming, Zooming Stories. 2017. (Pictureback(R) Ser.). (ENG., Illus.). 72p. (J). (gr. -1-2). pap. 7.99 *(978-0-399-55592-3(7),* Random Hse. Bks. for Young Readers) Random Hse. Children's Bks.
Scary Stories Treasury Lenticular Cover. 2007. 80p. *(978-1-4054-9871-5(4))* Parragon, Inc.
Scharer, Kathrin. All Aboard with Joanna! 2013. (ENG., Illus.). 34p. 16.99 *(978-88-97737-09-4(9))* Officina Libraria srl ITA. Dist: National Bk. Network.
Schkolnik, Saul. Cuentos Ecologicos. Cardemil, Carmen, illus. 2nd ed. 2003. (la Orilla del Viento Ser.).Tr. of Ecological Tales. (SPA.). 56p. (J). (gr. 3-7). per. *(978-968-16-4757-5(2),* FC6400) Fondo de Cultura Economica MEX. Dist: Lectorum Pubns., Inc.
Schlosser, S. E. Spooky Texas: Tales of Hauntings, Strange Happenings, & Other Local Lore. Hoffman, Paul G., illus. 2008. (Spooky Ser.). (ENG.). 200p. pap. 14.95 *(978-0-7627-4853-2(2))* Globe Pequot Pr., The.
Scholastic, Inc. Staff, contrib. by. Funny Shopville Stories. 2015. (Shopkins Ser.). (ENG.). 32p. (J). (gr. -1-3). pap. 4.99 *(978-0-545-92556-3(8))* Scholastic, Inc.
—Rookie Reader Boxed: Go-With Words Messy Bessey The Secret Code, Set. 2004. (Rookie Reader Ser.). (ENG.). (J). (gr. -1-2). pap. 9.95 *(978-0-516-25002-1(7),* Watts, Franklin) Scholastic Library Publishing.
—A Rookie Reader Boxed Level B, Set. 2004. (Rookie Reader Ser.). (ENG.). (J). (gr. -1-2). pap. 9.95 *(978-0-516-25001-4(9),* Watts, Franklin) Scholastic Library Publishing.
Scholastic Library Publishing. Quite Enough Hot Dogs & Other Silly Stories. 2008. (Rookie Reader Treasury Ser.). (Illus.). 128p. (J). pap. 11.95 *(978-0-531-21728-3(0),* Children's Pr.) Scholastic Library Publishing.
Schonzeit, Miriam. The Sweetest Song & other Stories. 2006. 304p. (YA). 16.95 *(978-1-932443-42-4(8),* SWSH) Judaica Pr., Inc., The.
School, Waverly. Waverly Review: Spring 2003, Issue 1. 2003. 70p. (YA). pap. 8.95 *(978-0-595-27691-2(1))* iUniverse, Inc.
Schraff, Anne. Black Widow Beauty, 1 vol. unabr. ed. 2010. (Q Reads Ser.). (ENG.). 32p. (YA). (gr. 9-12). pap. 6.95 *(978-1-61651-178-4(8))* Saddleback Educational Publishing, Inc.
—Blackout, 1 vol. unabr. ed. 2010. (Q Reads Ser.). (ENG.). 32p. (YA). (gr. 9-12). pap. 6.95 *(978-1-61651-190-6(7))* Saddleback Educational Publishing, Inc.
—Ghost Mountain, 1 vol. 2014. (Red Rhino Ser.). (ENG.). 68p. (J). (gr. 4-6). pap. 7.95 *(978-1-62250-897-6(1))* Saddleback Educational Publishing, Inc.
Schroeder, Lisa. It's Raining Cupcakes. 2010. (ENG., Illus.). 208p. (J). (gr. 3-7). 17.99 *(978-1-4169-9084-0(4),* Aladdin) Simon & Schuster Children's Publishing.
Scieszka, Jon. Garage Tales. Gordon, David et al, illus. 2010. (Jon Scieszka's Trucktown Ser.). (ENG.). 80p. (J). (gr. -1-3). 12.99 *(978-1-4424-1196-8(1),* Simon & Schuster Bks. For Young Readers) Simon & Schuster Bks. For Young Readers.
—Race from A to Z, No. 4. Gordon, David et al, illus. 2014. (Jon Scieszka's Trucktown Ser.). (ENG.). 48p. (J). (gr. -1-3). 17.99 *(978-1-4169-4136-1(3),* Simon & Schuster Bks. For Young Readers) Simon & Schuster Bks. For Young Readers.
Scieszka, Jon, et al. Funny Business. Rex, Adam, illus. 2010. (Guys Read Ser.: 1). (ENG.). 288p. (J). (gr. 3-7). 16.99 *(978-0-06-196374-2(7));* pap. 6.99 *(978-0-06-196373-5(9))* HarperCollins Pubs. (Waldon Pond Pr.).
—Guys Read: Heroes & Villains. 2017. (Guys Read Ser.: 7). 288p. (J). (gr. 3-7). pap. 6.99 *(978-0-06-238560-4(7),* Waldon Pond Pr.) HarperCollins Pubs.
—Guys Read: True Stories. 2014. (Guys Read Ser.: 5). (ENG.). 272p. (J). (gr. 3-7). pap. 7.99 *(978-0-06-196381-0(X),* Waldon Pond Pr.) HarperCollins Pubs.
Scillian, Devin & Young, Judy. Westward Journeys. Ellison, Chris et al, illus. 2013. (American Adventures Ser.). (ENG.). 96p. (J). (gr. 3-6). pap. 6.99 *(978-1-58536-860-0(1),* 202367) Sleeping Bear Pr.
Scollen, Chris. Busy Kids Sticker Storybook Goldilocks. 2008. (Illus.). 12p. (J). (gr. -1-3). pap. *(978-1-84610-641-5(9))* Make Believe Ideas.
—Busy Kids Sticker Storybook Little Mermaid. 2008. (Illus.). 12p. (J). (gr. -1-3). pap. *(978-1-84610-805-1(5))* Make Believe Ideas.
—Busy Kids Sticker Storybook Three Billy Goats. 2008. (Illus.). 12p. (J). (gr. -1-3). pap. *(978-1-84610-803-7(9))* Make Believe Ideas.
—Busy Kids Sticker Storybook Three Little Pigs. 2008. (Illus.). 12p. (J). (gr. -1-3). pap. *(978-1-84610-639-2(7))* Make Believe Ideas.
Scott-Branagan, Brownen. The Pandanuspeople. 2009. 32p. pap. 13.75 *(978-0-60860-006-9(8),* Strategic Bk. Publishing) Strategic Book Publishing & Rights Agency (SBPRA).
Scott, Dee Mary. The Adventures of Charles & Camilla Chinchilla. 2012. (Illus.). 46p. pap. 6.99 *(978-1-78035-389-0(8),* Fastprint Publishing) Upfront Publishing Ltd. GBR. Dist: Printondemand-worldwide.com.
Scott, Goeffrey. Fairy Tales for Adults. 2007. 116p. per. 19.95 *(978-1-4241-6532-2(6))* America Star Bks.
Scott, Robert. Shades of Monte Christo & Other Short Stories. 2004. (YA). per. 19.86 *(978-1-4116-0484-1(9))* Lulu Pr., Inc.
Scretching, Dorothy/Janis. Story Time with Princess Dorothy. Walters, Steve, ed. Brunot, Katerina, illus. 2012. 32p. (J). 20.00 *(978-0-9719767-4-0(0),* Crowned Warrior Publishing) Walters, Steve Ministries.
Seagull. 2004. (J). per. *(978-1-57657-457-7(1))* Paradise Pr., Inc.
Sealls, Arthur. The Three Little Heroes: Book One of Kirk, Chelsea, & Samantha's Adventures. 2007. 84p. per. 8.95 *(978-0-595-44083-2(5))* iUniverse, Inc.
Seamons, Karen. Child of Virtue: SamiTales Relationship Series. 2012. (ENG.). 190p. 49.95 *(978-1-4327-8144-6(8))* Outskirts Pr., Inc.
Seeberger, Beverley, illus. Razzle Dazzler. 2007. (J). per. 15.00 *(978-0-9713589-8-0(2))* Ubavie's Gifts.
Seeger, Laura Vaccaro. Dog & Bear, Level 2: Two Friends, Three Stories. Seeger, Laura Vaccaro, illus. 2012. (My Readers Ser.). (ENG., Illus.). 32p. (J). (gr. k-2). pap. 3.99 *(978-0-312-54799-8(4),* 9780312547998) Square Fish.
Segal, Lore. Tell Me a Mitzi. (Blue-Ribbon Listen-and-Read Ser.). (J). (gr. -1-2). pap. 5.95 incl. audio *(978-0-590-63063-4(6))* Scholastic, Inc.
Selena Who Speaks in Silence Set B, 6 vols. 32p. (gr. 1-3). 26.50 *(978-0-7802-8051-9(2));* 31.50 *(978-0-322-00939-4(1))* Wright Group/McGraw-Hill.
Selfors, Suzanne. Ever after High - Little Pet Stories: A School Story Collection. 2015. (ENG.). 240p. (J). (gr. 3-7). 12.99 *(978-0-316-26481-5(4))* Little, Brown Bks. for Young Readers.
—Smells Like Treasure. 2012. (Smells Like Dog Ser.: 2). (ENG.). 432p. (J). (gr. 3-7). pap. 8.99 *(978-0-316-04402-8(4))* Little, Brown Bks. for Young Readers.
Senior, Suzy. Tales from Christmas Wood Activity Book. Newman Gray, James, illus. 2017. (ENG.). 24p. (J). (gr. k-4). 7.99 **(978-0-7459-7694-5(8))** Lion Hudson PLC GBR. Dist: Independent Pubs. Group.
Sensenig, Janet Martin. María de Guatemala y Otras Historias. 2011. (SPA., Illus.). 233p. (J). *(978-0-7399-7767-5(9))* Rod & Staff Pubs., Inc.
—The Missing Bible: And Other Stories. 2003. (Sunbeam Ser.). (Illus.). 160p. (gr. -1-5). 6.40 *(978-0-7399-0341-4(1),* 2325) Rod & Staff Pubs., Inc.
Sente, Yves. The Sarcophagi of the Sixth Coninent, Pt. 1, Vol. 9. Juillard, André, illus. 2011. (Blake & Mortimer Ser.: 9). (ENG.). 64p. (gr. 5-17). pap. 15.95 *(978-1-84918-067-2(9))* CineBook GBR. Dist: National Bk. Network.
Sente, Yves & Juillard, Andre. The Sarcophagi of the Sixth Continent, Pt. 2. 2011. (Blake & Mortimer Ser.: 10). (ENG., Illus.). 64p. pap. 15.95 *(978-1-84918-077-1(6))* CineBook GBR. Dist: National Bk. Network.
Serafin, Michael. 4 Seasons of Baghdad. 2007. (ENG.). 60p. per. 16.95 *(978-1-4241-2303-2(8))* PublishAmerica, Inc.
Serafin, Mike. 7 Stories from Baghdad. 2005. 50p. pap. 16.95 *(978-1-4137-8808-2(4))* PublishAmerica, Inc.
Serna, Ana. Cuentos y Recetas de la Abuela.Tr. of Tales & Recipes from Grandmother. (SPA.). 144p. (J). 19.98 *(978-84-305-7732-3(7))* Susaeta Ediciones, S.A. ESP. Dist: AIMS International Bks., Inc.
Seton, Ernest Thompson. Wild Animals I Have Known. 2009. 116p. pap. 9.50 *(978-1-60459-623-6(6))* Wilder Pubns., Corp.
Seuss, Dr. The Bippolo Seed & Other Lost Stories. 2011. (Classic Seuss Ser.). (ENG., Illus.). 72p. (J). (gr. k-4). 15.00 *(978-0-375-86435-3(0),* Random Hse. Bks. for Young Readers) Random Hse. Children's Bks.
—Horton & the Kwuggerbug & More Lost Stories. 2014. (ENG., Illus.). 56p. (J). (gr. -1-3). 16.99 *(978-0-385-38298-4(7),* Random Hse. Bks. for Young Readers) Random Hse. Children's Bks.
—Gli Snicci e Altre Storie. pap. 24.95 *(978-88-09-02448-9(6))* Giunti Gruppo Editoriale ITA. Dist: Distribooks, Inc.
—Yoruga la Tortuga y Otros Cuentos. 1. Canetti, Yanitzia, tr. from ENG. 2008.Tr. of Yertle the Turtle & Other Stories. (SPA., Illus.). 76p. (J). (gr. 2-3). 15.99 *(978-1-933032-41-2(3))* Lectorum Pubns., Inc.
Sewell, Anna, et al. The Enchanted Collection: Alice's Adventures in Wonderland; The Secret Garden; Black Beauty; The Wind in the Willows; Little Women, 0 vols. Macdonald, Ross, illus. unabr. ed. 2012. (Heirloom Collection: 0). (ENG.). 1634p. 99.99 *(978-1-61218-415-9(4),* 9781612184159) Amazon Publishing.
Sewell, Byron W. Alix's Adventures in Wonderland: Lewis Carroll's Nightmare. 2011. (Illus.). 130p. pap. *(978-1-904808-72-5(7))* Evertype.
Sewell, Kristin. A Collection of Seven Children's Stories. 2012. 80p. pap. 28.99 *(978-1-4685-3770-3(9))* AuthorHouse.
Shagam, Rodger. Stories from My Gramps. 2013. 76p. pap. 22.97 *(978-1-62516-161-1(1),* Strategic Bk. Publishing) Strategic Book Publishing & Rights Agency (SBPRA).
Shan, Darren, pseud. Vampire Destiny Trilogy: The Lake of Souls; Lord of the Shadows; Sons of Destiny. 2005. (ENG.). 592p. pap., pap., pap. *(978-0-00-717959-6(6))* HarperCollins Pubs. Australia.
Shanddaramon. Pagan Stories for Children: A Fairy's First Year in the Forest of Songs. 2011. (Illus.). 111p. (J). pap. 12.99 *(978-1-257-75438-0(6))* Astor Pr.
Shanghai Animation Studio Staff & Tang, Sanmu. Three Monks. Ying, Wu, tr. from CHI. 2010. (Favorite Children's Ser.). (ENG., Illus.). 32p. (J). (gr. -1-3). pap. 5.95 *(978-1-60220-973-2(1))* BetterLink Pr., Inc.
Shank, Ronald L. Grandpa's Stories: A Compilation of Short Stories Written to Be Read by Grandpa or Grandma to Their Grand Children. 2012. 206p. (gr. 10-12). pap. 16.95 *(978-1-4772-6712-7(3))* AuthorHouse.
Shankman, Ed. The Cods of Cape Cod. O'Neill, Dave, illus. 2009. (Shankman & O'Neill Ser.). (ENG.). 32p. (gr. -1-3). 14.95 *(978-1-933212-78-4(0),* Commonwealth Editions) Applewood Bks.
Shanks Jr. A Father's Stories for His Children: A Christian Reader for Students Grades 5-9. 2006. pap. 9.99 *(978-1-59781-946-6(8))* Salem Author Services.
Sharkey, Niamh, illus. Tales of Wisdom & Wonder. 2005. 64p. (J). *(978-1-84148-231-6(5))* Barefoot Bks., Inc.
Sharmat, Marjorie Weinman. Yo, el Gran Fercho. (Torre de Papel Ser.).Tr. of Nate the Great. (SPA.). (YA). 8.95 *(978-958-04-2599-1(X))* Norma S.A. COL. Dist: Distribuidora Norma, Inc.
Sharpless, Sheila M. Mystery on Bear's Island: A Short Adventure Novel for Girls Aged 8-11. 2012. 74p. 24.99 *(978-1-4691-3576-2(0));* pap. 15.99 *(978-1-4691-3575-5(2))* Xlibris Corp.
Shats, Marina. Nature Knows (Paperback) 2010. 24p. 21.50 *(978-0-557-32587-0(0))* Lulu Pr., Inc.
Shaw, Janet. Kirsten's Short Story Collection. Lewis, Kim & Graef, Renee, illus. 2006. (American Girls Collection). 213p. (J). (gr. 3-8). 12.95 *(978-1-59369-323-7(0))* American Girl Publishing, Inc.
Shaw, Nancy E. Sheep Blast Off! Apple, Margot, illus. 2011. (ENG.). 32p. (J). (gr. -1-3). pap. 5.99 *(978-0-547-52025-4(5))* Houghton Mifflin Harcourt Publishing Co.
Sheffield, Sherry Overton. Children's Choices: What Would YOU Do? 2005. (Illus.). 112p. (J). per. *(978-0-9772513-0-8(6),* 804-337-8915) Thumbs Up Pr.
Shephard, Esther. Paul Bunyan. Kent, Rockwell, illus. 2006. (ENG.). 256p. (J). (gr. 5-7). pap. 15.95 *(978-0-15-205857-9(5))* Houghton Mifflin Harcourt Publishing Co.
Shepherd, J. A., illus. Old Hendrik's Tales - 13 South African Folk Tales. 2013. 198p. pap. *(978-1-909302-15-0(5))* Abela Publishing.
Shepperson, Jacqueline. Martins of the Everglades. 2007. (ENG.). 152p. per. 24.95 *(978-1-4241-5446-3(4))* America Star Bks.
Shepperson, Jacqueline Ruth. The Blue Jay Tales. 2005. 89p. pap. 19.95 *(978-1-4137-3884-1(2))* America Star Bks.
Sherman, Harold Morrow. Flying Heels & Other Hockey Stories. 2011. 264p. 47.95 *(978-1-258-08063-1(X))* Literary Licensing, LLC.
Sherrard, Valerie. Testify. 2011. (ENG.). 144p. (YA). (gr. 8-12). pap. 9.99 *(978-1-55488-927-3(8),* 9781554889273) Dundurn CAN. Dist: Ingram Publisher Services.
Sherwood, C. A. Aj's Easter Surprise. 2008. 56p. pap. 24.29 *(978-1-4343-7583-4(8))* AuthorHouse.
Shetty, Lalitha A. Tales of Toy World. Shetty, Lakshmi, illus. 2010. 48p. pap. 12.00 *(978-1-60911-157-1(5),* Eloquent Bks.) Strategic Book Publishing & Rights Agency (SBPRA).
Shewver, Margaret. Without a Trace & Other Stories. 2005. 91p. (YA). (gr. 6-12). pap. 17.95 *(978-0-936389-59-2(1))* Tudor Pubs., Inc.
Shiga, Jason. Meanwhile: Pick Any Path. 3,856 Story Possibilities. 2010. (ENG., Illus.). 80p. (J). (gr. 3-7). 16.95 *(978-0-8109-8423-3(7),* Amulet Bks.) Abrams, Inc.
Shoemaker, E. W. Mother Nature & the Tales of North Fork. 2009. 220p. pap. 18.75 *(978-1-4389-8604-3(1))* AuthorHouse.
Shoo, Shoo, Shoo! & Other Stories, 6 Packs. (Story Steps Ser.). (gr. k-2). 48.00 *(978-0-7635-9604-0(3))* Rigby Education.
Shoushen, Jin. Bejing Legends. Yang, Gladys, tr. 2007. (Illus.). 124p. per. 11.95 *(978-1-59654-392-8(2))* Disruptive Publishing.
Showstack, Richard. The Gift of the Magic: And Other Enchanting Character-Building Stories for Smart Teenage Girls Who Want to Grow up to Be Strong Women. Eric, Whitfield, illus. 2004. 156p. (YA). per. 14.95 *(978-1-888725-64-3(8),* BeachHouse Bks.) Science & Humanities Pr.
Shuff, Chrissi. The Dancing Tree & other Stories. 2010. (Illus.). 80p. pap. 28.99 *(978-1-4520-0054-1(9))* AuthorHouse.
Shulman, Dee. My Totally Secret Diary - Reality TV Nightmare. 2012. (ENG., Illus.). 144p. (J). (gr. 2-4). pap. 10.99 *(978-1-86230-424-6(6),* Red Fox) Random House Children's Books GBR. Dist: Independent Pubs. Group.
—On Stage in America. 2012. (My Totally Secret Diary Ser.). (ENG., Illus.). 144p. (J). (gr. 2-4). pap. 12.99 *(978-1-86230-423-9(8),* Red Fox) Random House Children's Books GBR. Dist: Independent Pubs. Group.
Shusterman, Neal. The Complete Unwind Dystology: Unwind; Unwholly; Unsouled; Undivided. 2014. (Unwind Dystology Ser.). (ENG., Illus.). 1568p. (YA). (gr. 7). 73.99 *(978-1-4814-2186-7(7),* Simon & Schuster Bks. For Young Readers) Simon & Schuster Bks. For Young Readers.
—Stories from the Unwind World. 2016. (Unwind Dystology Ser.). (ENG.). 336p. (YA). (gr. 7). pap. 11.99 *(978-1-4814-5724-8(1),* Simon & Schuster Bks. For Young Readers) Simon & Schuster Bks. For Young Readers.
—UnBound: Stories from the Unwind World. 2015. (Unwind Dystology Ser.: 5). (ENG., Illus.). 320p. (YA). (gr. 7). 18.99 *(978-1-4814-5723-1(3),* Simon & Schuster Bks. For Young Readers) Simon & Schuster Bks. For Young Readers.
—UnBound: Stories from the Unwind World. 2016. (Unwind Dystology Ser.). lib. bdg. 23.30 **(978-0-606-39748-3(5))** Turtleback Bks.
Shuttleworth, Cathie, illus. Little Tales for Toddlers: 35 Stories about Adorable Teddy Bears, Puppies & Bunnies. 2013. (ENG.). 256p. pap. 14.99 *(978-1-84322-925-4(0))* Anness Publishing GBR. Dist: National Bk. Network.
Sibille, Lucinda. Dragon Swirl: Book II. 2009. 28p. pap. 14.95 *(978-1-4490-1057-7(1))* AuthorHouse.
—Dragon Swirl: Book III. 2009. 32p. pap. 14.95 *(978-1-4490-1072-0(5))* AuthorHouse.
—Dragon Swirl: Book IV. 2009. 32p. pap. 14.95 *(978-1-4490-1075-1(X))* AuthorHouse.
—Dragon Swirl: In the Beginning. 2009. 32p. pap. 14.95 *(978-1-4490-0965-6(4))* AuthorHouse.
Sidney, Margaret. Five Little Peppers Grown Up. 2008. 196p. (gr. -1-3). 26.95 *(978-1-60664-805-6(5))* Aegypan.
Sierra i Fabra, Jordi. La Asombrosa Historia del Viajero de las Estrellas. (SPA.). (YA). 8.95 *(978-958-04-6872-1(9))* Norma S.A. COL. Dist: Distribuidora Norma, Inc.
—El Niño Que Vivía en Las Estrellas. 2003. (SPA., Illus.). 102p. (J). 8.95 *(978-968-19-0557-6(1))* Aguilar, Altea, Taurus, Alfaguara, S.A. de C.V MEX. Dist: Santillana USA Publishing Co., Inc.
Silver, Connie. A Story Book for Beginning Readers. 2007. 124p. 20.95 *(978-0-595-70501-6(4));* per. 10.95 *(978-0-595-46524-8(2))* iUniverse, Inc.
Silver Dolphin en Español Staff. Disney Tesoro de Libros de Calcomanias, Volume 6, Vol. 6. 2005. (Disney Calcomanias Ser.). (SPA., Illus.). 96p. (J). (gr. -1). pap. *(978-970-718-245-5(8))* Advanced Marketing, S. de R. L. de C. V.
Silvestre, R. Quique lo Salvo y Otras Historias. (Raton de Biblioteca Coleccion). (SPA.). 139p. (J). (gr. 3-5). 7.95 *(978-84-88061-70-6(6))* Serres, Ediciones, S. L. ESP. Dist: Lectorum Pubns., Inc.
Simms, Donna A. The Hillsborough Tales. (Children's Book). (Illus.). 76p. (J). (gr. 4-7). *(978-0-942078-22-0(5))* Tanner, Ralph Assocs., Inc.
Simms, Laura. Stories to Nourish the Hearts of Our Children. Krizmanic, Tatjana, illus. 2013. 100p. pap. 19.99 *(978-0-9911692-1-4(2))* Simms, Laura Storyteller.
Simon, Annette. Robot Zombie Frankenstein! Simon, Annette, illus. 2012. (ENG., Illus.). 40p. (J). (gr. -1-3). 16.99 *(978-0-7636-5124-4(9))* Candlewick Pr.
Simon, Francesca. Horrid Henry & the Abominable Snowman, 1 vol. Ross, Tony, illus. 2012. (Horrid Henry Ser.). (ENG.). 112p. (J). (gr. 2-5). lib. bdg. 24.21 *(978-1-59961-186-0(4))* Spotlight.
—Horrid Henry Rocks. Ross, Tony, illus. 2011. (Horrid Henry Ser.: 0). (ENG.). 112p. (J). (gr. 2-5). pap. 7.99 *(978-1-4022-5674-5(4),* 9781402256745, Sourcebooks Jabberwocky) Sourcebooks, Inc.
—Horrid Henry Rocks, 1 vol. Ross, Tony, illus. 2012. (Horrid Henry Ser.). (ENG.). 112p. (J). (gr. 2-5). lib. bdg. 24.21 *(978-1-59961-190-7(2))* Spotlight.
Simonds, William. Ella; or, Turning over a New Leaf by Walter Aimwell [Pseud.]. 2006. 292p. per. 23.99 *(978-1-4255-2794-5(9))* Michigan Publishing.
—Marcus; or, the Boy-Tamer by Walter Aimwell [Pseud.]. 2006. 336p. per. 23.99 *(978-1-4255-3348-9(5))* Michigan Publishing.
Simpson, Pat. A Compilation of Tales to Thrill & Chill. 2008. 103p. pap. 15.95 *(978-1-4357-2976-6(5))* Lulu Pr., Inc.
Sims, Anthony. Princess Zoe. 2012. (Illus.). 44p. pap. 24.40 *(978-1-4772-2365-9(7))* AuthorHouse.
Sims, Lesley. Delightful Illustrated Stories (was Illustrated Stories for Girls) 2015. (Illustrated Stories Ser.). (ENG.). 352p. (J). (gr. k-5). 19.99 *(978-0-7945-3541-4(0),* Usborne) EDC Publishing.
—Illustrated Classics Action & Adventure Stories for Young Readers. 2015. (Illustrated Stories Ser.). (ENG.). 384p. (J). (gr. k-5). 19.99 *(978-0-7945-3565-0(8),* Usborne) EDC Publishing.
—Illustrated Classics Enchanting Stories for Young Readers. 2015. (Illustrated Stories Ser.). (ENG.). 384p. (J). (gr. k-5). 19.99 *(978-0-7945-3532-2(1),* Usborne) EDC Publishing.
—Illustrated Classics for Children. 2015. (Illustrated Stories Ser.). (ENG.). 512p. (J). (gr. k-5). 21.99 *(978-0-7945-3106-5(7),* Usborne) EDC Publishing.
—Magical Stories for Little Children. 2012. (Picture Bks). 128p. (J). ring bd. 18.99 *(978-0-7945-2919-2(4),* Usborne) EDC Publishing.
Sims, Lesley & Stowell, Louie. Illustrated Stories for Boys. McNee, Ian, illus. 2007. (Usborne Illustrated Stories Ser.). 352p. (J). 19.99 *(978-0-7945-1420-4(0),* Usborne) EDC Publishing.
Simwenyi, Robbinson Namasaka. Death, the Only Gift, 1 vol. 2010. 66p. pap. 19.95 *(978-1-4489-4338-8(8))* America Star Bks.
Singer, Isaac Bashevis. Cuentos Judios de la Aldea de Chelm.Tr. of Zlateh the Goat & Other Stories. (SPA.). 62p. (J). 7.96 *(978-84-264-3404-3(5),* LM2595) Editorial Lumen ESP. Dist: Lectorum Pubns., Inc.
Singer, Marilyn, ed. Face Relations: 11 Stories about Seeing Beyond Color. (ENG., Illus.). 240p. (YA). (gr. 7). 2013. pap. 11.99 *(978-1-4424-9616-3(9))* 2004. 18.99 *(978-0-689-85637-2(7))* Simon & Schuster Bks. For Young Readers. (Simon & Schuster Bks. For Young Readers).
Singh, Jay. Once upon a Time in a Forest Far Away. 2009. 394p. pap. 33.12 *(978-1-4251-9122-1(3))* Trafford Publishing.
Singhose, Rose. Granny's Giggles. 2010. 35p. pap. 16.95 *(978-0-557-57269-4(X))* Lulu Pr., Inc.
—Granny's giggles book Three. 2010. 33p. pap. 16.95 *(978-0-557-59768-0(4))* Lulu Pr., Inc.
—Granny's giggles book Two. 2010. 35p. pap. 16.95 *(978-0-557-59182-4(1))* Lulu Pr., Inc.
Sirko, Teodora. Aesop's Fables. 2007. 36p. per. 17.95 *(978-1-84753-698-3(0))* Lulu Pr., Inc.
Slade, Arthur. Villainology: Fabulous Lives of the Big, the Bad, & the Wicked. Mah, Derek, illus. 2007. (ENG.). 96p. (J). (gr. 4-7). per. 9.95 *(978-0-88776-809-5(1),* Tundra Bks.) Tundra Bks. CAN. Dist: Penguin Random Hse. LLC.
Slim, Lillian, et al. Subsistence Adventures. Slim, Lillian et al, illus. 2006. (Adventure Story Collection Ser.). 28p. (J). (gr. 2-6). pap. 10.00 *(978-1-58084-252-5(6))* Lower Kuskokwim Schl. District.
Smith, Bethany. Hiding Sunrise. 2008. 130p. pap. 8.86 *(978-0-557-02630-2(X))* Lulu Pr., Inc.
Smith, Carol & Quest, Suzanne. Dr Daphne & Nurse Moira Stories. 2015. (ENG.). 44p. (J). mass mkt. 13.95 *(978-1-78455-086-8(8),* 62d0eae0-42aa-4e24-9576-96dd0967e0f5) Austin, Stan AUS. Dist: Bookmasters Distribution.
Smith, Cathy Jo. Seamus Mcseamus, an Irish Rover. 2005. (Illus.). 104p. per. 11.95 *(978-0-9766666-0-8(X))* Arcadian Hse.
Smith, Elva S. & Hazeltine, Alice I. Christmas in Legend & Story: A Book for Boys & Girls. 2007. pap. 19.99 *(978-1-4346-2190-0(1));* (ENG.). 200p. pap. 21.99 *(978-1-4346-2250-1(9))* Creative Media Partners, LLC.
Smith, Helen. A Day with Oaky & Other Stories for Small Children. 2017. (ENG., Illus.). 49p. (J). pap. 13.95 **(978-1-78554-601-3(5),** b5fa04ad-d957-4ee0-a0cc-1585aea32de7) Austin, Stan AUS. Dist: Bookmasters Distribution.
Smith, Helene. Dreamstone. Guinard, Geraldine, illus. 2005. 80p. (YA). pap. 13.50 *(978-1-920731-63-2(6))* Fremantle Pr. AUS. Dist: Independent Pubs. Group.
Smith, Jeff & Sniegoski, Tom. Tall Tales. Smith, Jeff, illus. 2010. (Bone Ser.). (ENG., Illus.). 128p. (J). (gr. 4-7). pap. 12.99 *(978-0-545-14096-6(X),* Graphix) Scholastic, Inc.

S

Smith, Marie, et al. N Is for our Nation's Capital: A Washington, DC Alphabet. Gibson, Barbara Leonard, illus. 2005. (Discover America State by State Ser.). (ENG.). 40p. (J). 17.95 (978-1-58536-148-9(8)) Sleeping Bear Pr.

Smith, Molly. Border Breakdown: The Fall of the Berlin Wall. Opie, David, illus. 2010. (ENG.). 32p. (J). (gr. 1-6). 9.95 (978-1-60727-126-0(5)); 19.95 (978-1-60727-125-3(7)); 16.95 (978-1-60727-123-9(0)); pap. 6.95 (978-1-60727-124-6(9)) Soundprints.

Smith, Pamela Colman. Annancy Stories. 2006. (YA). reprint ed. pap. 19.99 (978-0-9769612-2-2(9)) Darker Intentions Pr.

Smith, Stephanie Harms. For Everything There Is a Season in God's Time. 2007. 84p. per. 11.99 (978-1-60477-224-1(7)) Salem Author Services.

Smith, Valerie H. The Spirit Stories: A Series of Short Stories for Children. 2007. 64p. per. 8.95 (978-1-59824-450-2(7)) E-BookTime LLC.

Smoot, Madeline, compiled by. Summer Shorts: A Short Story Collection. 2005. (ENG., Illus.). 360p. (J). (gr. 2-7). pap. 8.95 (978-0-9769417-5-0(9)) Blooming Tree Pr.

Sniegoski, Tom & Smith, Jeff. Tall Tales. Smith, Jeff, illus. 2010. (Bone Ser.). (ENG., Illus.). 128p. (J). (gr. 4-7). 26.99 (978-0-545-14095-9(1), Graphix) Scholastic, Inc.

Snow, Dorothea J. Roy Rogers' Favorite Western Stories. Ushler, John, illus. 2011. 250p. 46.95 (978-1-258-04169-4(3)) Literary Licensing, LLC.

Snowe, Olivia. Twicetold Tales, 1 vol. Lamoreaux, Michelle, illus. 2014. (Twicetold Tales Ser.). (ENG.). 128p. (gr. 3-4). 101.28 (978-1-4342-9469-2(2)) Stone Arch Bks.

So-Un, Kim & Kyoung-Sim, Jeong. Korean Children's Favorite Stories. 2004. (ENG., Illus.). 96p. (J). (gr. k-8). 18.95 (978-0-8048-3591-6(8)) Tuttle Publishing.

Sobol, Donald J. Encyclopedia Brown Keeps the Peace. Shortall, Leonard W., illus. 2008. (Encyclopedia Brown Ser.: 6). (ENG.). 96p. (J). (gr. 3-7). 4.99 (978-0-14-240950-3(2), Puffin Books) Penguin Young Readers Group.

Soffe, Caroline Dawn. Bluebell Wood. 2011. 166p. pap. 24.95 (978-1-4560-5235-5(7)) America Star Bks.

Sohaili, Monira. Stories from Earth & Beyond: Enchanting & Inspirational Stories. 2006. (Illus.). 94p. per. 9.95 (978-1-60002-044-5(5), 2833) Mountain Valley Publishing, LLC.

Sohrabi, Behzad. The Legend of Sigh: A Collection of Fairy Tales. 2012. 76p. pap. 41.99 (978-1-4771-1969-3(8)) Xlibris Corp.

Solomon, Jef. Right in My Own Neighborhood. 2009. 53p. pap. 15.50 (978-0-557-05790-0(6)) Lulu Pr., Inc.

Solorareff, Gregoire. EDU, EL PEQUEÑO LOBO. 2003. (SPA.). 32p. 17.95 (978-84-95150-44-8(1)) Corimbo, Editorial S.L. ESP. Dist: Distribooks, Inc.

—EDU, EL PETIT LLOP -CATALA- 2003. (SPA.). 32p. (978-84-95150-46-2(8)) Corimbo, Editorial S.L.

Somaiah, Ranjan & Somaiah, Rosemarie. Indian Children's Favorite Stories. 2006. (ENG., Illus.). 80p. (J). (gr. k-8). 18.95 (978-0-8048-3687-6(6)) Tuttle Publishing.

Somers, Dayle. Sergeant Steve's Station. 2012. 80p. pap. 42.05 (978-1-4691-8096-0(0)) Xlibris Corp.

Somoskey, Rebecca. Say What? Kool Kids Stories from Appalachia. 2004. (J). 4.00 (978-0-9768514-2-4(3)) Bearwallow Blessings Ministries.

Sones, Sonya. The Sonya Sones Collection: One of Those Hideous Books Where the Mother Dies; What My Mother Doesn't Know; What My Girlfriend Doesn't Know. 2013. (ENG., Illus.). 896p. (J). (gr. 7). pap. 29.99 (978-1-4424-9780-1(7), Simon & Schuster Bks. For Young Readers) Simon & Schuster Bks. For Young Readers.

Soto, G., et al. Multicultural Collection. Byrd, S., illus. 2003. pap. 91.95 incl. audio (978-0-87499-673-9(2)) Live Oak Media.

Soto, Gary. Facts of Life. 2012. (ENG.). 192p. (YA). (gr. 7-7). pap. 7.99 (978-0-547-57734-0(6)) Houghton Mifflin Harcourt Publishing Co.

—Help Wanted: Stories. 2007. (ENG., Illus.). 240p. (YA). (gr. 7-12). pap. 6.95 (978-0-15-205663-6(7)) Houghton Mifflin Harcourt Publishing Co.

—Hey 13! 2011. (ENG.). 256p. (J). 16.95 (978-0-8234-2395-8(6)) Holiday Hse., Inc.

—Local News: Stories. 2003. (ENG., Illus.). 160p. (J). (gr. 2-5). pap. 6.99 (978-0-15-204695-8(X)) Houghton Mifflin Harcourt Publishing Co.

—Petty Crimes. 2006. (ENG., Illus.). 176p. (J). (gr. 5-7). pap. 6.99 (978-0-15-205437-3(5)) Houghton Mifflin Harcourt Publishing Co.

Spanos, Seva, retold by. Thumbelina's Song. 2004. (Treasure Tree Ser.). (Illus.). 32p. (J). (978-0-7166-1601-6(7)) World Bk., Inc.

Speceal, Edetha. The Lost Egg & Other Stories. 2006. (Illus.). 144p. pap. (978-1-84401-644-0(7)) Athena Pr.

Spence, Chris. Chris's Fables. 2017. (ENG.). 60p. (J). pap. 14.95 **(978-1-78629-237-7(8)**, df32f530-2b4a-4031-af50-7496021a2511) Austin, Stan AUS. Dist: Bookmasters Distribution.

A Spicy-Herby Day, 6 vols.; set. 32p. (gr. 1-3). 26.50 (978-0-7802-8044-1(X)) Wright Group/McGraw-Hill.

Spohn, Bruce. Christmas Hope. 2011. 114p. pap. 19.95 (978-1-4560-7541-5(1)) America Star Bks.

Spotswood, Jessica. A Tyranny of Petticoats. 2016. (ENG.). 368p. (YA). (gr. 9). 17.99 (978-0-7636-7848-7(1)) Candlewick Pr.

Springett, Martin. Breakfast on a Dragon's Tail: And Other Book Bites. 2011. (ENG.). 32p. (J). (978-1-55455-200-9(1)) Fitzhenry & Whiteside, Ltd.

Springham, James. Earth-n-Bones: Blue Things. 2006. 54p. pap. 16.95 (978-1-4137-9738-1(5)) America Star Bks.

Spurr, Elizabeth. Happy Sparkling Halloween. Madden, Colleen, illus. 2010. (Sparkling Stories Ser.). (ENG.). 14p. (J). (gr. k-k). bds. 5.95 (978-1-4027-7138-5(X)) Sterling Publishing Co., Inc.

Spyri, Johanna. Moni, the Goat Boy & What Sami Sings with the Birds. 2006. 108p. per. 9.95 (978-1-59818-472-3(5)) Aegypan.

Square Fish Staff. Kisses & Curses. Burniac, Lauren, ed. 2015. (ENG.). 400p. (YA). (gr. 7). pap. 10.99 (978-1-250-06053-2(2), 9781250060532) Square Fish.

Squeaky. 2004. (J). per. (978-1-57657-352-5(4)) Paradise Pr., Inc.

St. Aubyn, Douglas. Caribbean Fables. 2007. 72p. pap. (978-976-8054-72-2(7)) Paria Publishing Co., Ltd.

Stagliano, Michael F. Wesley's Stories: Afterschool Adventures. 2008. 208p. 24.95 (978-0-595-50215-8(6)); pap. 14.95 (978-0-595-50637-8(2)) iUniverse, Inc.

Standiford, Natalie. Countdown, Bk. 3. 2014. (39 Clues: Unstoppable Ser.: 3). (ENG., Illus.). 192p. (J). (gr. 3-7). 12.99 (978-0-545-52145-1(9)) Scholastic, Inc.

Stanek, Robert, pseud. Robert Stanek's Bugville Critters Storybook Treasury. 2008. (ENG., Illus.). 132p. (J). per. 24.95 (978-1-57545-171-8(9)) RP Media.

—Robert Stanek's Bugville Critters Storybook Treasury Volume 2 (the Bugville Critters Storybook Collection, Volume 2), 4 vols., Vol. 2. 2008. (ENG., Illus.). 124p. (J). per. 24.95 (978-1-57545-173-2(5)) RP Media.

—Student's Classroom Handbook for Robert Stanek's Magic Lands. 2005. (ENG.). 116p. (Orig.). pap. 14.00 (978-1-57545-035-3(6), Ruin Mist Pubns.) RP Media.

Stanfield, Michael. Bucky & Becky - the Magic of Wigglepoo Mountain. 2009. 144p. pap. 14.96 (978-0-557-02614-2(8)) Lulu Pr., Inc.

Stanley, John. Melvin Monster: The John Stanley Library, 3 vols. 2011. (John Stanley Library). (ENG., Illus.). 112p. 24.95 (978-1-77046-030-0(6), 9781770460300) Drawn & Quarterly Pubns. CAN. Dist: Macmillan.

Stanwood, Jane. Squeak Jr 's Short Stories: Comments & Information. 2008. 140p. pap. 12.95 (978-1-4327-2819-9(9)) Outskirts Pr., Inc.

Stasse, Lisa M. The Uprising: The Forsaken Trilogy. 2014. (ENG., Illus.). 400p. (YA). (gr. 7). pap. 9.99 (978-1-4424-3269-7(1), Simon & Schuster Bks. For Young Readers) Simon & Schuster Bks. For Young Readers.

Steadman, Pamela M. Hannah Savannah's Favorite Tales. 2005. 78p. (YA). per. 7.95 (978-1-59196-854-2(2)) Instant Pub.

Steedman, Amy. In God's Garden (Yesterday's Classics) 2006. (J). per. 9.95 (978-1-59915-032-1(8)) Yesterday's Classics.

—Our Island Saints (Yesterday's Classics) 2006. (J). per. 9.95 (978-1-59915-031-4(X)) Yesterday's Classics.

Steel, Flora Annie. English Fairy Tales. 2007. (ENG.). 262p. pap. 21.99 (978-1-4346-0692-1(9)); 296p. pap. 23.99 (978-1-4346-0752-2(6)) Creative Media Partners, LLC.

Steele, S. The Tell Me a Story Book. 2007. 116p. per. 13.99 (978-1-4259-7993-5(9)) AuthorHouse.

Steps To Literacy Staff, compiled by. I Can Read: HFC004. 2005. (ENG., Illus.). (J). pap. (978-1-59564-721-4(X)) Steps To Literacy, LLC.

Sternfeld, Nathan. Adventures with Rebbe Mendel. Pomerantz, Riva, tr. Bichman, David, illus. 230p. 21.99 (978-1-58330-550-8(5)) Feldheim Pubs.

Steve Van Der Merwe. Policeman Bobby & Stinky. 2009. (Illus.). 24p. pap. 12.99 (978-1-4389-6935-0(X)) AuthorHouse.

Steven, Kenneth. The Raven's Tale: & other Stories. Wake, Katherine, illus. 2007. (ENG.). 64p. pap. 13.99 (978-0-7152-0846-5(2)) Saint Andrew Pr., Ltd. GBR. Dist: Westminster John Knox Pr.

—Stories for a Fragile Planet: Traditional Tales about Caring for the Earth. Ray, Jane, illus. (ENG.). 48p. (J). (gr. 1-7). 2012. pap. 10.99 (978-0-7459-6386-0(2)) 2011. 16.99 (978-0-7459-6157-6(6)) Lion Hudson PLC GBR. Dist: Independent Pubs. Group.

Stevenson, Charles. The Adventures of the Glo-Worm Family. 2012. (Illus.). 34p. pap. 9.99 (978-1-78035-338-8(3), Fastprint Publishing) Upfront Publishing Ltd. GBR. Dist: Printondemand-worldwide.com.

Stevenson, Robert Louis. The Merry Men. 2004. 304p. pap. 14.95 (978-1-59540-514-2(3), 1st World Library - Literary Society) 1st World Publishing, Inc.

Stine, Faye. The Magic Forest: The Magic of Childhood. 2009. 117p. (J). pap. 10.95 (978-1-4327-3617-0(5)) Outskirts Pr., Inc.

Stine, R. L. La Hora de Las Pesadillas. Batlles Vinn, Camila, tr. 2005. (Escritura desatada Ser.). (SPA.). 192p. (YA). 10.95 (978-84-666-0020-0(5)) Ediciones B ESP. Dist: Independent Pubs. Group.

—Nightmare Hour. movie tie-in ed. 2011. (ENG.). 160p. (J). (gr. 3). pap. 5.99 (978-0-06-210692-6(9)) HarperCollins Pubs.

—Temptation. 2012. (ENG.). 416p. (YA). (gr. 7). pap. 10.99 (978-1-4424-5068-4(1), Simon Pulse) Simon Pulse.

StJohn, Amanda. Medio Pollito (Half-Chick) A Mexican Folktale. Todd, Sue, illus. 2011. (Folktales from Around the World Ser.). (ENG.). 24p. (J). (gr. k-3). 28.50 (978-1-60973-141-0(7), 201144) Child's World, Inc., The.

—The Pied Piper of Hamelin: A German Folktale. Bonder, Dianna, illus. 2011. (Folktales from Around the World Ser.). (ENG.). 24p. (J). (gr. k-3). 28.50 (978-1-60973-142-7(5), 201146) Child's World, Inc., The.

Stockham, Jess, illus. The Boy Who Cried Wolf. 2011. (Flip-Up Fairy Tales Ser.). (ENG.). 24p. (J). (gr. 2-2). (978-1-84643-368-9(1)) Child's Play International Ltd.

—Moving House! 2011. (Helping Hands Ser.). (ENG.). 24p. (J). (978-1-84643-414-3(9)) Child's Play International Ltd.

—Party! 2011. (Helping Hands Ser.). (ENG.). 24p. (J). (978-1-84643-413-6(0)) Child's Play International Ltd.

—Recycling! 2011. (Helping Hands Ser.). (ENG.). 24p. (J). (978-1-84643-415-0(7)) Child's Play International Ltd.

—Shopping! 2011. (Helping Hands Ser.). (ENG.). 24p. (J). (978-1-84643-412-9(2)) Child's Play International Ltd.

Stockham, Jessica, illus. Doctor. 2011. (First Time Ser.). (ENG.). 24p. (J). (gr. 2-2). pap. (978-1-84643-334-4(7)) Child's Play International Ltd.

—Visiting the Dentist. 2011. (First Time Ser.). (ENG.). 24p. (J). (gr. 2-2). pap. (978-1-84643-335-1(5)) Child's Play International Ltd.

—Visiting the Hospital. 2011. (First Time Ser.). (ENG.). 24p. (J). (gr. 2-2). pap. (978-1-84643-336-8(3)) Child's Play International Ltd.

—Visiting the Vet. 2011. (First Time Ser.). (ENG.). 24p. (J). (gr. 2-2). pap. (978-1-84643-337-5(1)) Child's Play International Ltd.

Stockton, Frank Richard. The Bee-Man of Orn & Other Fanciful Tales. 2007. (ENG.). 140p. pap. 18.99 (978-1-4264-5788-3(X)); 154p. pap. 21.99 (978-1-4264-5848-4(7)) Creative Media Partners, LLC.

—John Gayther's Garden & the Stories Told Therein. 2008. 220p. 26.95 (978-1-60664-746-2(6)) Rodgers, Alan Bks.

—The Lady or the Tiger. 2008. (Creative Short Stories Ser.). (Illus.). 32p. (J). lib. bdg. 28.50 (978-1-58341-583-2(1), Creative Education) Creative Co., The.

Stokes, Brenda. Bella's Blessings. DesRosiers, Trisha, illus. 2012. (ENG.). 50p. (J). (gr. -1-3). 17.95 (978-1-897476-61-1(2)) Simply Read Bks. CAN. Dist: Ingram Publisher Services.

Stone Arch Books Staff. John Henry - Hammerin' Hero. Evergreen, Nelson, illus. 2010. (Graphic Spin Ser.). (ENG.). 40p. (gr. 1-3). pap. 5.95 (978-1-4342-2265-7(9), Graphic Revolve) Stone Arch Bks.

Stop! & Other Stories: Individual Title Six-Pack. (Story Steps Ser.). (gr. k-2). 42.00 (978-0-7635-9592-0(6)) Rigby Education.

Stories & Fables from Around the World. 2016. (Stories & Fables from Around the World Ser.). 24p. (gr. 2-1). 73.80 (978-1-4994-8118-1(7)); pap. 24.75 (978-1-4994-8128-0(4)) Rosen Publishing Group, Inc., The. (Windmill Bks.).

Stories from el Barrio. 2nd rev. ed. 2005. 135p. (YA). (gr. 9). per. 19.95 (978-0-915117-11-6(8)) Freedom Voices Pubns.

Storm, Zed. Will Solvit & the Cannibal Cavemen. 2010. (Will Solvit Ser.: Bk. 5). (Illus.). 128p. (J). (gr. 1-7). pap. (978-1-4075-8983-1(0)) Parragon, Inc.

—Will Solvit & the Deadly Gladiator. 2010. (Will Solvit Ser.: Bk. 6). (Illus.). 128p. (J). (gr. 1-7). pap. (978-1-4075-8984-8(9)) Parragon, Inc.

—Will Solvit & the Dreaded Droids. 2010. (Will Solvit Ser.: Bk. 4). (Illus.). 128p. (J). (gr. 1-7). pap. (978-1-4075-8980-0(6)) Parragon, Inc.

—Will Solvit & the Mission of Menace. 2010. (Will Solvit Ser.: Bk. 2). (Illus.). 128p. (J). (gr. 1-7). pap. (978-1-4075-8981-7(4)) Parragon, Inc.

—Will Solvit & the Mummy's Curse. 2010. (Will Solvit Ser.: Bk. 3). (Illus.). 128p. (J). (gr. 1-7). pap. (978-1-4075-8979-4(2)) Parragon, Inc.

—Will Solvit & the T-Rex Terror. 2010. (Will Solvit Ser.: Bk. 1). (Illus.). 128p. (J). (gr. 1-7). pap. (978-1-4075-8982-4(2)) Parragon, Inc.

Stover, Anne Long. Cloudy. Spears, Ashley E., illus. 2005. 20p. (J). (978-0-9762389-0-4(X)) Trent's Prints.

Stowe, Harriet Beecher. Betty's Bright Idea. 2006. pap. (978-1-4068-3093-4(3)) Echo Library.

—The First Christmas of New England & O. 2006. 108p. per. 9.95 (978-1-59818-758-8(9)) Aegypan.

Strasser, Todd. Nighttime: Too Dark to See. Cushman, Doug, illus. 2008. 79p. (J). (978-0-439-80068-6(4)) Scholastic, Inc.

Strauss, Kevin. Loon & Moon: And Other Animal Stories. Scheibe, Nancy, illus. 2005. 48p. (J). (gr. 4-6). per. 12.95 (978-0-9766264-3-5(8)) Raven Productions, Inc.

Strong, Abigail. Troggins Tales. 2010. 60p. pap. 34.95 (978-1-4457-1581-0(3)) Lulu Pr., Inc.

Stuart, Elizabeth Billings. Delightful Stories for Children. 2013. (ENG., Illus.). 142p. (J). (gr. k-6). 16.95 (978-0-911845-70-9(4), Neumann Pr.) TAN Bks.

Students, Liberty Elementary School. Patriot Pages, Liberty Elementary School. 2010. 142p. pap. 12.95 (978-1-936051-95-3(8)) Peppertree Pr., The.

Students of Wallenberg Traditional High School Staff. Exactly: Ten Beavers, Nine Fairies, Eight Dreams, Seven Knights, Six Princesses, Five Dogs, Four Otters, Three Old Men, Two Robots, One Traveling Shoe & Everything Else It Takes to Make a Great Children's Story Book. San Francisco Bay Area Staff, illus. 2007. (ENG.). 256p. (J). (gr. 3-18). 28.00 (978-0-9790073-2-3(1)) 826 Valencia.

Studio Mouse Staff. Puppy Dog Tails. 2005. (Read-Aloud Board Book Ser.). (ENG., Illus.). 12p. (J). (gr. -1-3). bds. 12.95 (978-1-59249-474-3(9), 1D101) Soundprints.

Sturt, M. Canterbury Pilgrims. 2007. pap. (978-1-4068-3599-1(4)) Echo Library.

Stuve-Bodeen, Stephanie & Hale, Christy. Mama Elizabeti. 2005. (ENG., Illus.). 30p. (J). (gr. -1-2). pap. 9.95 (978-1-58430-236-0(4)) Lee & Low Bks., Inc.

Sullivan, Jean. The Blakely Field Stories. 2005. 58p. pap. 16.95 (978-1-4137-8611-8(1)) PublishAmerica, Inc.

Summer & Winter: Individual Title Six-Packs. (Story Steps Ser.). (gr. k-2). 32.00 (978-0-7635-9809-9(7)) Rigby Education.

Summer Sands, 6 vols., Set B. 32p. (gr. 1-3). 31.50 (978-0-7802-8054-0(7)) Wright Group/McGraw-Hill.

Summers, Everette. Grandaddy's Short Stories. 2006. 48p. pap. 16.95 (978-1-4241-2468-8(9)) PublishAmerica, Inc.

Suresh, Shreyas. The Magic Lighthouse & other Stories. 2010. 49p. pap. 23.50 (978-0-557-36448-0(5)) Lulu Pr., Inc.

The Surf Trilogy. 2003. (YA). per. 39.95 (978-0-9640858-5-5(2)) Perelandra Publishing Co.

Surprise! Individual Title Six-Packs. (Story Steps Ser.). (gr. k-2). 32.00 (978-0-7635-9605-7(1)) Rigby Education.

Surprises & Other Stories: Individual Title Six-Pack. (Story Steps Ser.). (gr. k-2). 48.00 (978-0-7635-9818-1(6)) Rigby Education.

Surviving Southside, 6 vols., Set. Incl. Bad Deal. Korman, Susan. lib. bdg. 27.93 (978-0-7613-6152-7(9)); Beaten. Weyn, Suzanne. lib. bdg. 27.93 (978-0-7613-6150-3(2)); Benito Runs. Fontes, Justine. lib. bdg. 27.93 (978-0-7613-6151-0(0)); Plan B. Simon, Chaman. lib. bdg. 27.93 (978-0-7613-6149-7(9)); Recruited. Weyn, Suzanne. lib. bdg. 27.93 (978-0-7613-6153-4(7)); Shattered Star. Simon, Chaman. lib. bdg. 27.93 (978-0-7613-6154-1(5)); 104p. (YA). (gr. 6-12). (Surviving Southside Ser.). (ENG.). 2011. Set lib. bdg. 335.16 (978-0-7613-6148-0(0), Darby Creek) Lerner Publishing Group.

Sutcliff, Rosemary. Heather, Oak, & Olive. Ambrus, Victor, illus. 2015. (Nautilus Ser.). (ENG.). 120p. (J). (gr. 3-6). pap. 11.95 (978-1-58988-106-8(0)) Dry, Paul Bks., Inc.

Sutton, Kay. Nan & Grandad's Book of Short Stories. 2009. (Illus.). 52p. pap. 20.49 (978-1-4490-0575-7(6)) AuthorHouse.

Swain, Gwenyth. Voices for Freedom. Frankenhuyzen, Gijsbert van et al, illus. 2013. (American Adventures Ser.). (ENG.). 72p. (J). (gr. 3-6). 6.99 (978-1-58536-886-0(5), 202900) Sleeping Bear Pr.

Swan, Bill. Man-to-Man, 1 vol. 2009. (Lorimer Sports Stories Ser.). (ENG.). 144p. (J). (gr. 4-8). 16.95 (978-1-55277-443-4(0), 9781552774434) Lorimer, James & Co., Ltd., Pubs. CAN. Dist: Casemate Pubs. & Bk. Distributors, LLC.

Swan, Richard. The Listeners. 2009. (Illus.). 64p. pap. 10.49 (978-1-4389-6224-5(X)) AuthorHouse.

Swanson, Maggie. Best-Loved Aesop's Fables Coloring Book. 2015. (ENG.). 48p. (J). (gr. k-4). pap. 4.99 (978-0-486-79747-2(3)) Dover Pubns., Inc.

Swenson, Dianne. An Ended Friendship: And Other Short Stories. 2006. (Fast Track Ser.). (Illus.). 98p. (YA). (gr. 8-12). lib. bdg. 12.25 (978-0-8124-0632-0(X)) Perfection Learning Corp.

Swift, Jonathan, et al. The Adventure Collection: Treasure Island, the Jungle Book, Gulliver's Travels, White Fang, the Merry Adventures of Robin Hood, 0 vols. Macdonald, Ross, illus. unabr. ed. 2012. (Heirloom Collection: 0). (ENG.). 1588p. 99.99 (978-1-61218-416-6(2), 9781612184166) Amazon Publishing.

Swift, K. Marie. The Adventures of Jake & George: Jake Gets a New Brother. Paul, Kate, illus. 2010. 26p. pap. 11.75 (978-1-60693-863-8(0), Eloquent Bks.) Strategic Book Publishing & Rights Agency (SBPRA).

Swindells, Robert. Doodlebug Alley. (Illus.). 56p. (J). pap. 6.99 (978-0-7497-3860-0(X)) Egmont Bks., Ltd. GBR. Dist: Trafalgar Square Publishing.

Swindells, Robert, et al. Cuentos de Terror. (SPA.). (YA). 8.95 (978-958-04-3392-7(5)) Norma S.A. COL. Dist: Distribuidora Norma, Inc.

Szarka, Balazs. European Folk Tales. 2009. 60p. pap. 22.00 (978-1-60860-432-6(2), Eloquent Bks.) Strategic Book Publishing & Rights Agency (SBPRA).

Tago, Anita. Traditional Stories from Binandere in Oro Province, Papua New Guinea. 2012. 44p. pap. (978-9980-945-71-6(0)) University of Papua New Guinea Press.

Talbert, Marc. Doble o Nada. (Torre de Papel Ser.). (SPA.). (J). (gr. 4-18). 7.95 (978-958-04-2384-3(9)) Norma S.A. COL. Dist: Distribuidora Norma, Inc.

Tamayo, Alex. Horizons Set 1, 5 books. Shea, Steve, ed. 2013. (Illus.). 48p. (YA). pap. 24.00 (978-1-57128-809-7(0)) High Noon Bks.

Tan, Shaun. Lost & Found. Tan, Shaun, illus. 2011. (ENG., Illus.). 128p. (J). (gr. 7-3). 21.99 (978-0-545-22924-1(3), Levine, Arthur A. Bks.) Scholastic, Inc.

—Tales from Outer Suburbia. 2009. (J). pap. (978-0-545-05588-8(1), Levine, Arthur A. Bks.) Scholastic, Inc.

—Tales from Outer Suburbia. Tan, Shaun, illus. 2009. (ENG., Illus.). 96p. (J). (gr. 7-18). 21.99 (978-0-545-05587-1(3), Levine, Arthur A. Bks.) Scholastic, Inc.

Taplin, Sam. Baby's Bedtime Storybook CV. 2011. (Baby Board Bks). 10p. (J). ring bd. 17.99 (978-0-7945-3096-9(6), Usborne) EDC Publishing.

—Night-Night Stories. 2009. (Bedtime Board Books (with Bedtime Rhymes) Ser.). 12p. (J). bds. 12.99 (978-0-7945-2364-0(1), Usborne) EDC Publishing.

—Sleepytime Stories. Chaira, Francesca di, illus. 2011. (Baby Board Books Ser.). 12p. (J). ring bd. 12.99 (978-0-7945-3006-8(0), Usborne) EDC Publishing.

Tappan, Eva March. The Children's Hour: Stories from Seven Old Favorites, 5. l.t. ed. 2006. (ENG.). 338p. pap. 24.99 (978-1-4264-7382-1(6)) Creative Media Partners, LLC.

—The Children's Hour, Volume V: Stories from Seven Old Favorites. 2006. (ENG.). 304p. pap. 23.99 (978-1-4264-7309-8(5)) Creative Media Partners, LLC.

Tarkington, Booth. Beasley's Christmas Party. 2005. 76p. pap. 10.95 (978-1-4218-0407-1(7), 1st World Library - Literary Society) 1st World Publishing, Inc.

—Beasley's Christmas Party. Clements, Ruth Sypherd, illus. 2004. reprint ed. pap. 15.95 (978-1-4179-0186-9(1)) Kessinger Publishing, LLC.

—Beasley's Christmas Party. 2004. reprint ed. pap. 1.99 (978-1-4192-0925-3(6)) Kessinger Publishing, LLC.

Tatulli, Mark. Desmond Pucket Makes Monster Magic. 2013. (Desmond Pucket Ser.: 1). (ENG.). 240p. (J). 13.99 (978-1-4494-3548-6(3)) Andrews McMeel Publishing.

Tauiliili, Pemerika L. The Rat & the Bat: And Other Short Stories. 2009. 88p. pap. 16.99 (978-1-4490-4389-6(5)); pap. 32.49 (978-1-4389-2700-8(2)) AuthorHouse.

Tavaci, Elspeth & Quarto Generic Staff. The Stone of Destiny: Tales from Turkey. Hess, Paul, illus. 2013. (ENG.). 144p. (J). (gr. 3-6). pap. 8.99 (978-1-84780-279-8(6), Frances Lincoln) Quarto Publishing Group UK GBR. Dist: Hachette Bk. Group.

Tavener, Carys. The Adventures of T. C & Friends. 2011. (Illus.). 132p. pap. 38.72 (978-1-4567-7096-9(9)) AuthorHouse.

Taylor, Clifford. Taylor's Tales. 2004. 108p. 20.95 (978-0-595-66558-7(6)) iUniverse, Inc.

Taylor-Gaines, Lonnetta. Fia & the Butterfly: 7 Stories for Character Education. 2005. 13.00 (978-0-8059-9848-1(9)) Dorrance Publishing Co., Inc.

Taylor, Gaylia & Morrison, Frank. George Crum & the Saratoga Chip. 2006. (ENG., Illus.). 32p. (J). pap. 9.95 (978-1-60060-656-4(3)) Lee & Low Bks., Inc.

Taylor, Kenneth N. Family-Time Bible in Pictures. 2007. (ENG., Illus.). 320p. (J). (gr. -1-1). 12.99 (978-1-4143-1577-5(5)) Tyndale Hse. Pubs.

Taylor, Laini. Lips Touch: Three Times. Di Bartolo, Jim, illus. (ENG.). 288p. (J). (gr. 7-7). 2011. pap. 14.99 (978-0-545-05586-4(5)) 2009. 17.99 (978-0-545-05585-7(7)) Scholastic, Inc. (Levine, Arthur A. Bks.).

Taylor, R. W. The Curiosity of Sadie: A Collection of 35 Individual Stories about an Individual Little Girl & Her Puppy. 2011. 172p. (gr. 4-6). pap. 15.66 (978-1-4567-8202-3(9)) AuthorHouse.

Taylor, Vincent. Cornbread Runs for Class President Griffin, Kasana & Griggs, Charles, eds. Latorre, Adolfo, illus. 2004. (Cornbread Ser.: 1). 96p. (J). per. 4.99 (978-0-9704512-4-8(5)) TriEclipse, Inc.

Taylor, William. At the Big Red Rooster. 160p. (YA). (gr. 8-18). pap. (978-1-877135-20-0(8), Longacre Pr.) Random Hse. New Zealand.

Tegen, Katherine Brown. The Story of the Leprechaun. Lambert, Sally Anne, illus. 2011. (J). lib. bdg. 14.89 (978-0-06-143085-5(4)); (ENG.). 40p. (gr. -1-3). 12.99 (978-0-06-143086-2(2)) HarperCollins Pubs.

Templeton Elementary Students. Tales from Templeton III. 2007. 108p. per. 15.95 (978-0-9790446-6-3(9)) Pen & Publish Inc.

Ten Little Ducks & Other Stories: Individual Title Six-Pack. (Story Steps Ser.). (gr. k-2). 48.00 *(978-0-7635-9798-6(8))* Rigby Education.
Terhune, Albert Payson. Buff, a Collie & Other Dog Stories. 2007. 348p. per. 18.95 *(978-1-59462-809-2(2)*, Book Jungle) Standard Pubns., Inc.
Tesler, Ellen. Zeke in Central Park. 2010. 32p. pap. 12.99 *(978-1-4490-7211-7(9))* AuthorHouse.
Tetzlaff, Wendy Jo. A Girl Named Frannie. 2008. 28p. pap. 24.95 *(978-1-60703-055-3(1))* America Star Bks.
Tezuka, Osamu. Phoenix, Vol. 7. 2006. (ENG., Illus.). 208p. pap. 15.99 *(978-1-4215-0517-6(7))* Viz Media.
Themerson, Stefan. The Table That Ran Away to the Woods. Themerson, Franciszka, illus. 2012. (ENG.). 20p. 10.95 *(978-1-84976-057-7(8))* Tate Publishing, Ltd. GBR. Dist: Abrams, Inc.
A These Old Rags Set, 6 vols. 32p. (gr. 1-3). 31.50 *(978-0-7802-8040-3(7))* Wright Group/McGraw-Hill.
Thomas, Amy Maude. Stories in My Eyes. 2011. 20p. pap. 7.99 *(978-1-936750-04-7(X))* Yorkshire Publishing Group.
Thomas, Frances. Polly's Absolutely Worst Birthday Ever. Gardner, Sally, illus. 2012. (ENG.). 96p. (J). (gr. 2-4). pap. 11.99 *(978-1-4088-2516-7(3)*, 9781408825167, Bloomsbury USA Childrens) Bloomsbury Publishing USA.
—Polly's Running Away Book. Gardner, Sally, illus. 2012. (ENG.). 96p. (J). (gr. 2-4). pap. 11.99 *(978-1-4088-2515-0(5)*, 9781408825150, Bloomsbury USA Childrens) Bloomsbury Publishing USA.
Thomas, Gene. Tales from the Tree House. 2011. 112p. (gr. 10-12). 20.95 *(978-1-4620-1864-2(5))*; pap. 10.95 *(978-1-4620-1863-5(7))* iUniverse, Inc.
Thomas, Jatavius. Weird Things Happening at Southside Middle School: And Other Stories. 2010. 52p. pap. 8.95 *(978-1-4502-4049-9(6))* iUniverse, Inc.
Thomas, Marlo, et al, eds. Thanks & Giving: All Year Long. 2005. (ENG., Illus.). 96p. (J). (gr. 1-7). 17.95 *(978-1-4169-1586-7(9)*, Simon & Schuster Bks. For Young Readers) Simon & Schuster Bks. For Young Readers.
Thomas, Terri. Bus 99, 1 vol. unabr. ed. 2010. (Q Reads Ser.). (ENG.). 32p. (YA). (gr. 9-12). pap. 6.95 *(978-1-61651-214-9(8))* Saddleback Educational Publishing, Inc.
Thomas, Terri & Greene, Janice. Dimes to Dollars, 1 vol. unabr. ed. 2010. (Q Reads Ser.). (ENG.). 32p. (YA). (gr. 9-12). pap. 6.95 *(978-1-61651-217-0(2))* Saddleback Educational Publishing, Inc.
Thomas the Tank Engine. 2012. *(978-0-7948-3764-8(6))* Egmont Bks., Ltd.
Thompson, Carol. My Squashy Pumpkin! 2010. (ENG., Illus.). 24p. (J). pap. *(978-1-84643-188-3(3))* Child's Play International Ltd.
Thompson, Colin. The Floods Family Files. Thompson, Colin, illus. 2012. (Floods Ser.: 1). (ENG., Illus.). 32p. (J). (gr. 4-7). pap. 12.99 *(978-1-86471-942-0(7))* Random Hse. Australia AUS. Dist: Independent Pubs. Group.
Thompson, Susan Conklin, et al, eds. Mayan Folktales: Cuentos Folklóricos Mayas, 1 vol. 2007. (World Folklore Ser.). (SPA & ENG., Illus.). 236p. (C). 40.00 *(978-1-59158-138-3(9)*, LU1389, Libraries Unlimited) ABC-CLIO, LLC.
Thompson, Tolya L. Ingrown Tyrone. Brian, Harrold, illus. 2004. (Smarties Ser.: 4). 33p. (J). 16.00 *(978-0-9708296-2-7(0))* Savor Publishing Hse., Inc.
Thury, Fredrick H. Hoshmakaka. van Kampen, Vlasta, illus. 2003.Tr. of Last Straw. (SPA.). (J). (gr. 2-4). 13.56 *(978-84-8418-046-3(8))* Zendrera Zariquiey, Editorial ESP. Dist: Lectorum Pubns., Inc.
Tibbets, Albert B. Youth, Youth, Youth: Stories of Challenge, Confidence & Comradeship. Tibbets, Albert B., ed. 2011. 256p. 47.95 *(978-1-258-05880-7(4))* Literary Licensing, LLC.
Tiddle, Deanna Hessedal. Apartment Horse & Friends. 2003. 62p. (J). pap. 9.95 *(978-0-7414-1724-4(3))* Infinity Publishing.
Tiger Tales, ed. & compiled by. My Favorite Christmas Stories. Tiger Tales, compiled by. 2015. (ENG.). 128p. (J). (gr. -1-3). 12.99 *(978-1-68010-200-0(1))* Tiger Tales.
—Stories to Share. Tiger Tales, compiled by. 2015. (ENG.). 176p. (J). (gr. -1-3). 12.99 *(978-1-58925-537-1(2))* Tiger Tales.
Tingle, Tim & Moore, Doc. More Spooky Texas Tales. Benas, Jeanne A., illus. 2010. (ENG.). 104p. (J). (gr. 4-7). lib. bdg. 18.95 *(978-0-89672-700-7(9))* Texas Tech Univ. Pr.
Tingle, Tim & Moore, James W. Spooky Texas Tales. Miller, Gina, illus. 2005. x, 85p. (J). pap. *(978-0-89672-566-9(9))* Texas Tech Univ. Pr.
Tokyopop and Art Impression Staff & Peymani, Christine. Skelanimals Vol. 1: It's a Wonderful Afterlife. 2011. (Illus.). 36p. 9.99 *(978-1-4278-3255-9(2))* TOKYOPOP, Inc.
Toler, Violet M. Churchmouse Tales: Puppet Plays, 10 vols., Vol. 2. Koefler, Leatha, illus. 2nd rev. ed. 2004. Orig. Title: "Puppet Plays, Adventures of Charlie & His Friends". (J). (gr. -1-6). pap. 10.95 *(978-0-9749749-1-0(9))* Wayside Pubns.
Tolstoi, Leo & Riordan, James. The Lion & the Puppy: And Other Stories for Children. Riordan, James, tr. from RUS. Sievert, Claus, illus. 2012. (ENG.). 76p. (J). (gr. 4-7). 16.95 *(978-1-61608-484-4(7)*, 608484, Sky Pony Pr.) Skyhorse Publishing Co., Inc.
Tomaselli, Mela. The Magic Pot: Folk Tales & Legends of the Giriama of Kenya. 2004. (Illus.). 80p. *(978-9966-21-950-3(1))* Paulines Pubns., Africa.
Tome. Spirou & Fantasio in New York. Janry, illus. 2011. (Spirou & Fantasio Ser.: 2). (ENG.). 48p. (J). (gr. 3-17). pap. 11.95 *(978-1-84918-054-2(7))* CineBook GBR. Dist: National Bk. Network.
A Tonka Tale. 2004. (J). *(978-0-9767179-1-1(3))* ABC Development, Inc.
Too-Tight Shoes, 6 vols. 2004. 32p. (gr. 1-3). 31.50 *(978-0-322-00337-8(7))* Wright Group/McGraw-Hill.
A Too-Tight Shoes Set, 6 vols. 32p. (gr. 1-3). 26.50 *(978-0-7802-8042-7(3))* Wright Group/McGraw-Hill.
La Tormenta de Truenos; Aventura en la Oscuridad, 2 bks., Set. (Coleccion Chiquilines - Imagen y Sonido). (SPA., Illus.). (J). 15.95 incl. audio *(978-950-11-0624-4(1)*, SGM241) Sigmar ARG. Dist: Continental Bk. Co., Inc.
Tormont Publications Inc., des. Perfect Presents, 20 bks. (Illus.). 40p. (J). vinyl bd. *(978-2-7641-1284-7(X))* Tormont Pubns.
Torregrosa, Jose Canas, et al. La Cara de la Inocencia. 2003. (Punto de Encuentro Ser.). (SPA.). 80p. (YA). (gr. 5-12). pap. 11.99 *(978-84-241-8072-0(0))* Everest Editora ESP. Dist: Lectorum Pubns., Inc.
Torres, Eliseo & Sawyer, Timothy L. Stories of Mexico's Independence Days & Other Bilingual Children's Fables. Ramirez, Herman, illus. 2005. (ENG & SPA.). 70p. (J). (gr. 3-7). pap. 15.95 *(978-0-8263-3886-0(0))* Univ. of New Mexico Pr.
Torres, Mario. My Fun Wonderworld: Children's Stories Book, 1 vol. 2009. 74p. pap. 19.95 *(978-1-61582-704-6(8))* America Star Bks.
Tötemeyer, Andree-Jeanne. Under the Story Tree: Readathon Stories. 2005. (Illus.). 93p. *(978-99916-0-509-8(6))* Namibian Children's Bk. Forum.
Travesuras y Aventuras. 2003. (SPA.). pap. *(978-956-13-1045-2(7)*, AB8007) Bello, Andres CHL. Dist: Lectorum Pubns., Inc.
Treadwell, Harriette Taylor & Free, Margaret. The Primer. 2009. (Illus.). 118p. pap. *(978-1-904808-26-8(3))* Evertype.
Treasury of Classic Stories. 2008. (Treasuries Ser.). 192p. *(978-1-4075-1209-9(9))* Parragon, Inc.
El Trencito de los Cuentos. (Coleccion Estrella). (SPA., Illus.). 64p. (YA). 14.95 *(978-950-11-0018-1(9)*, SGM018) Sigmar ARG. Dist: Continental Bk. Co., Inc.
Las Tres Naranjas de la Vida. (Coleccion Fabulas y Cuentos Populares). (SPA.). (J). (gr. 2-4). *(978-84-246-1627-4(8)*, GL1107) La Galera, S.A. Editorial ESP. Dist: Lectorum Pubns., Inc.
Trilling, Richard J. Still More Stories of Stephanie & Friends: Volume 3 in the Stephanie Series. 2011. 72p. pap. 21.00 *(978-1-61204-546-7(4)*, Strategic Bk. Publishing) Strategic Book Publishing & Rights Agency (SBPRA).
Trinidad Joe. Santa's Key West Vacation. 2007. (Illus.). 80p. per. 12.95 *(978-0-9799474-0-7(5))* Seastory Pr.
Tripp, Valerie. Felicity Story Collection. Andreasen, Dan, illus. 2008. (ENG.). 404p. (J). 29.95 *(978-1-59369-452-4(0))* American Girl Publishing, Inc.
—Molly Story Collection. Backes, Nick, illus. 2004. (ENG.). 388p. 29.95 *(978-1-59369-458-6(X))* American Girl Publishing, Inc.
Trotter, Bob. Up the Wooden Hill: Bedtime Stories for Little Ones. Edgar, Barrie, illus. 2011. 98p. pap. 17.99 *(978-1-60976-139-4(1)*, Eloquent Bks.) Strategic Book Publishing & Rights Agency (SBPRA).
Trudell, Devin, illus. 3 Stories. Trudell, Devin, . 2007. (YA). 10.00 *(978-0-9794004-0-7(6))* Art Night Bks.
Truman, Dennay H. The Happy Endings. 2007. 65p. per. 8.95 *(978-1-59824-435-9(3))* E-BookTime LLC.
Tsaliovich, Anatoly. Of Wolves & Lambs & Others. Burke, Daniel, illus. 2005. 73p. (YA). pap. 12.99 *(978-0-9773816-0-9(9))* ATInternational Pubs.
Tucholke, April Genevieve. Slasher Girls & Monster Boys. 2015. (ENG.). 400p. (YA). (gr. 7-12). 17.99 *(978-0-8037-4173-7(1)*, Dial Bks) Penguin Publishing Group.
Tucker, Kathy & Hong, Lily Toy. The Seven Chinese Sisters, Bk. 2. Hong, Lily Toy & Lin, Grace, illus. 2010. (Book & DVD Packages with Nutmeg Media Ser.). (ENG.). 4p. (J). (gr. -1-3). 69.95 *(978-0-8075-9984-6(0))* Whitman, Albert & Co.
Tulik, Alice, et al. Fishing Adventures. Tulik, Alice et al, illus. 2006. (Adventure Story Collection Ser.). 36p. (J). (gr. 2-6). pap. 12.00 *(978-1-58084-248-8(8))* Lower Kuskokwim Schl. District.
Turan, Kemal. The Essence of Wisdom: Parables from Prophet Muhammad. 2011. (ENG.). 192p. (J). (gr. 7-10). pap. 9.95 *(978-1-59784-263-1(X))* Tughra Bks.
Turetsky, Bianca. The Time-Traveling Fashionista on Board the Titanic. 2012. (Time-Traveling Fashionista Ser.: 1). (ENG.). 272p. (J). (gr. 3-7). pap. 12.99 *(978-0-316-10544-6(9)*, Poppy) Little, Brown Bks. for Young Readers.
Turner, Megan Whalen. Instead of Three Wishes: Magical Short Stories. 2006. (ENG.). 160p. (J). (gr. 5-9). per. 6.99 *(978-0-06-084231-4(8)*, Greenwillow Bks.) HarperCollins Pubs.
Turpin, Nick. Molly Is New. Raga, Silvia, illus. 2010. 32p. pap. *(978-1-84089-650-3(7))* Zero to Ten, Ltd.
Twain, Mark, pseud & Clemens, Samuel L. The Prince & the Pauper. 2013. (Works of Mark Twain). 425p. reprint ed. lthr. 79.00 *(978-0-7812-1120-8(4))* Reprint Services Corp.
Tyler, Jenny. Animal Stories for Little Children. 2011. (Picture Books Ser.). 136p. (J). ring bd. 18.99 *(978-0-7945-2632-0(2)*, Usborne) EDC Publishing.
Tyler, Jenny & Doherty, Gillian, eds. Usborne Stories for Little Boys. 2008. (Picture Books Ser.). (Illus.). 135p. (J). (gr. -1-3). 18.99 *(978-0-7945-1973-5(3)*, Usborne) EDC Publishing.
Tyree, Omar R. 12 Brown Boys. 2008. 196p. (J). (gr. 3-7). pap. 9.95 *(978-1-933491-12-7(4))* Just Us Bks., Inc.
Tyson, Leigh Ann. Good Night, Little Dragons. 2012. (Little Golden Book Ser.). (ENG., Illus.). 24p. (J). (gr. k-k). 4.99 *(978-0-307-92957-0(4)*, Golden Bks.) Random Hse. Children's Bks.
Uderzo, Albert & Goscinny, René. Asterix Omnibus 4: Includes Asterix the Legionary #10, Asterix & the Chieftain's Shield #11, & Asterix at the Olympic Games #12. 2011. (ENG., Illus.). 144p. (J). (gr. 4-6). 29.99 *(978-1-4440-0428-1(X)*, Orion) Orion Publishing Group, Ltd. GBR. Dist: Hachette Bk. Group.
Umezawa, Rui. Strange Light Afar: Tales of the Supernatural from Old Japan, 1 vol. Fujita, Mikiko, illus. 2015. (ENG.). 144p. (J). (gr. 6). 18.95 *(978-1-55498-723-8(7))* Groundwood Bks. CAN. Dist: Publishers Group West (PGW).
Uncle Bernie. Michaels Adventures in the Land of Nod Book: Michaels Trip to Orange County. 2008. 32p. pap. 12.99 *(978-1-4389-1097-0(5))* AuthorHouse.
Under the Big Green Umbrella. 2008. (J). spiral bd. *(978-0-9793930-4-4(3))* Dandelion Publishing.
Ure, Jean. Is Anybody There? Seeing Is Believing... Donnelly, Karen, illus. 2004. (ENG.). 192p. (J). (gr. 4-7). pap. 9.95 *(978-0-00-716136-2(0)*, HarperCollins Children's Bks.) HarperCollins Pubs. Ltd. GBR. Dist: HarperCollins Pubs.
Urish, J. D. The Adventures of Rex Bolton Volume 1. 2010. 60p. pap. 9.98 *(978-0-578-03676-2(2))* Jentmedia.
Urrea, Lourdes. Calle Secreto Numero 31. 2005. (Ediciones Castillo Castillo Del Terror Ser.). (SPA.). 119p. (J). (gr. 4-7). per. 7.95 *(978-970-20-0187-4(0))* Castillo, Ediciones, S. A. de C. V. MEX. Dist: Iaconi, Mariuccia Bk. Imports.
—Huellas en la Escalera. rev. ed. 2007. (Ediciones Castillo Castillo Del Terror Ser.). (SPA & ENG.). 120p. (J). (gr. 4-7). pap. 6.95 *(978-970-20-0243-7(5))* Castillo, Ediciones, S. A. de C. V. MEX. Dist: Macmillan.
—El Mago. rev. ed. 2003. (Ediciones Castillo Castillo Del Terror Ser.). (SPA & ENG.). 112p. (J). (gr. 2-6). pap. 6.95 *(978-970-20-0189-8(7))* Castillo, Ediciones, S. A. de C. V. MEX. Dist: Macmillan.
—El Nino de la Ventana. rev. ed. 2005. (Castillo del Terror Ser.). (SPA & ENG.). 312p. (J). (gr. -1-7). pap. 6.95 *(978-970-20-0188-1(9))* Castillo, Ediciones, S. A. de C. V. MEX. Dist: Macmillan.
—Vacaciones Mortales. rev. ed. 2007. (Ediciones Castillo Castillo Del Terror Ser.). (SPA & ENG.). 120p. (J). (gr. 6-9). pap. 6.95 *(978-970-20-0248-2(6))* Castillo, Ediciones, S. A. de C. V. MEX. Dist: Macmillan.
Urrea, Luis. Gruta Encantada. 2005. (Ediciones Castillo Castillo Del Terror Ser.). (SPA.). (J). (gr. 2-6). pap. 7.95 *(978-970-20-0244-4(3))* Castillo, Ediciones, S. A. de C. V. MEX. Dist: Iaconi, Mariuccia Bk. Imports.
Urrea, Luis Alberto & Urrea, Lourdes. Silencio en el Castillo. rev. ed. 2006. (Ediciones Castillo Castillo Del Terror Ser.). (SPA & ENG.). 116p. (J). (gr. 2-6). pap. 6.95 *(978-970-20-0247-5(8))* Castillo, Ediciones, S. A. de C. V. MEX. Dist: Macmillan.
V., Patti. My Na Na Stories. 2005. 18.00 *(978-0-8059-9806-1(3))* Dorrance Publishing Co., Inc.
Vallejo-Nagera, Alejandra. Cuanto me Quieren! Guerrero, Andres, illus. 2003. (SPA.). 23p. (J). (gr. k-1). 8.95 *(978-84-204-4951-7(2))* Santillana USA Publishing Co., Inc.
Van Allsburg, Chris, et al. The Chronicles of Harris Burdick: Fourteen Amazing Authors Tell the Tales. Van Allsburg, Chris, illus. 2011. (ENG., Illus.). 208p. (J). (gr. 5-7). 24.99 *(978-0-547-54810-4(9))* Houghton Mifflin Harcourt Publishing Co.
Van Horn, William, et al. Walt Disney's Comics. Clark, John, ed. 2006. (ENG., Illus.). 64p. Vol. 664. pap. 6.95 *(978-1-888472-17-2(0)*, 9781888472172) Vol. 665. pap. 6.95 *(978-1-888472-18-9(9)*, 9781888472189) Vol. 667. pap. 6.95 *(978-1-888472-20-2(0)*, 9781888472202) Gemstone Publishing, Inc.
Van Laan, Nancy. Teeny Tiny Tingly Tales. Chess, Victoria, illus. 2008. (ENG.). 32p. (J). (gr. -1-2). 8.99 *(978-1-4169-7572-4(1)*, Simon & Schuster/Paula Wiseman Bks.) Simon & Schuster/Paula Wiseman Bks.
Vance, Elsbet, ed. & illus. Mistletoe Madness: A Short Story Collection. Vance, Elsbet, illus. 2004. (ENG.). 384p. (J). (gr. 1-5). pap. 8.95 *(978-0-9718348-2-8(2))* Blooming Tree Pr.
VanCe, Lilo. Once upon a Time & Other Stories. 2012. 52p. *(978-1-4602-0740-6(8))*; pap. *(978-1-4602-0738-3(6))* FriesenPress.
Vande Velde, Vivian. All Hallows' Eve: 13 Stories. 2010. (ENG., Illus.). 240p. (YA). (gr. 7). pap. 8.99 *(978-0-15-206473-0(7))* Houghton Mifflin Harcourt Publishing Co.
—Curses, Inc. & Other Stories. 2007. (ENG., Illus.). 240p. (YA). (gr. 7-12). pap. 12.95 *(978-0-15-206107-4(X))* Houghton Mifflin Harcourt Publishing Co.
—The Rumpelstiltskin Problem. 2013. (ENG.). 128p. (J). (gr. 5-7). pap. 5.99 *(978-0-544-10486-0(2))* Houghton Mifflin Harcourt Publishing Co.
Various. Alvin & the Chipmunks Storybook Collection. 2015. (ENG., Illus.). 192p. (J). (gr. -1-3). 11.99 *(978-0-06-225227-2(5))* HarperCollins Pubs.
Various, illus. Let's Read with Dora! 2010. (Dora the Explorer Ser.). (ENG.). 144p. (J). (gr. -1-1). pap. 7.99 *(978-1-4169-9742-9(3)*, Simon Spotlight/Nickelodeon) Simon Spotlight/Nickelodeon.
—Olivia Ready-To-Read Value Pack #2: Olivia & the Kite Party; Olivia & the Rain Dance; Olivia Becomes a Vet; Olivia Builds a House; Olivia Measures up; Olivia Trains Her Cat. 2013. (Olivia TV Tie-In Ser.). (ENG.). 144p. (J). (gr. -1-k). pap. 15.96 *(978-1-4424-9438-1(7)*, Simon Spotlight) Simon Spotlight.
—Story Time with Princess OLIVIA: Olivia the Princess; Olivia & the Puppy Wedding; Olivia Sells Cookies; Olivia & the Best Teacher Ever; Olivia Meets Olivia; Olivia & Grandma's Visit. 2013. (Olivia TV Tie-In Ser.). (ENG.). 144p. (J). (gr. -1-2). pap. 15.99 *(978-1-4424-9370-4(4)*, Simon Spotlight) Simon Spotlight.
Varonka, Steve. Hard Coal Times: Pennsylvania Anthracite Stories, Vol. 1. 2003. (Illus.). 40p. (J). 4.72 *(978-0-9709630-2-4(5))* Coal Hole Productions.
Vasco, Irene. El Dedo de Estefania y Otros Cuentos. 2003.Tr. of Estefania's Finger & Other Tales. (SPA., Illus.). 47p. (J). (gr. k-3). *(978-958-8061-54-2(7))* Distribuidora y Editora Aguilar, Altea, Taurus en el Sello Alfaguara S.A.
Vaz, Megan X. A Melody of Short Stories. 2011. 28p. pap. 12.03 *(978-1-4634-2651-4(8))* AuthorHouse.
Velvin, Ellen. Rataplan, a Rogue Elephant & Other Stories. 2007. 96p. per. *(978-1-4068-1627-3(2))* Echo Library.
Verma, Monika. My Storyland Animals. 2008. 29p. pap. 24.95 *(978-1-60563-010-6(1))* America Star Bks.
Vermazen, Eve. Dog Tales: Sam, the Tree & the Crystal. 2012. 36p. pap. 32.70 *(978-1-4771-5303-1(9))* Xlibris Corp.
Vermillion, Patricia. Hound Dawg. Pilgrim, Cheryl, illus. 2015. (ENG.). 40p. 21.95 *(978-0-87565-615-1(3))* Texas Christian Univ. Pr.
The Very Best of OLIVIA: A Storybook Treasury. 2013. (Olivia TV Tie-In Ser.). (ENG., Illus.). 248p. (J). (gr. -1-1). 15.99 *(978-1-4424-8597-6(3)*, Simon Spotlight) Simon Spotlight.
Vicente, Alidis. The Missing Chancleta & Other Top-Secret Cases / la Chancleta Perdida y Otros Casos Secretos. 2013. (SPA & ENG., Illus.). 64p. (J). pap. 9.95 *(978-1-55885-779-7(6)*, Piñata Books) Arte Publico Pr.
Vicente, Marta. La Cajita. 2004. (Los Especiales de A la Orilla Del Viento Ser.). (SPA., Illus.). 32p. (J). (gr. -1-7). 12.99 *(978-968-16-7181-5(3))* Fondo de Cultura Economica USA.
Villarreal, Carlos C. The Light Beneath the Shadow: Sharing God's Love with Your Child as You Read Together: A Bedtime Story Intended to Awaken Your Parental Christian Spirit. 2006. 48p. pap. 16.95 *(978-1-4241-1247-0(8))* PublishAmerica, Inc.
Villegas, Eduardo. El Baul de los Cuentos. (SPA.). (J). 7.98 *(978-970-643-159-2(4))* Selector, S.A. de C.V. MEX. Dist: AIMS International Bks., Inc.
Villnerve, Janice C. Mama Cat's Adventures in Child Training Presents No Whining! 2004. (Illus.). 32p. (J). lib. bdg. 14.95 *(978-0-9746013-0-4(6)*, 1230495) Paradigm Publishing.
Villoro, Carmen & Perez, Federico. Amarina y el Viejo Pesadilla y Otros Cuentos. (Torre de Papel Ser.). (SPA.). (J). (gr. 2). 7.95 *(978-958-04-3650-8(9))* Norma S.A. COL. Dist: Distribuidora Norma, Inc.
Vinson, Haley. Horizons Set 2, 5 books. Shea, Steve, ed. 2013. (Illus.). 48p. (YA). pap. 24.00 *(978-1-57128-815-8(5))* High Noon Bks.
Viorst, Judith. Earrings! Malone, Nola Langner, illus. 2010. (ENG.). 32p. (J). (gr. 1-5). 17.99 *(978-1-4424-1281-1(X)*, Atheneum Bks. for Young Readers) Simon & Schuster Children's Publishing.
Virtuous Short Stories of Fun & Prose. 2003. (Illus.). 90p. (YA). per. *(978-0-9742122-2-7(9))* Aunty Ems Boutique.
Vlashka, Vania. The Versaggi Brothers: Indigo Children are Here. 2011. 46p. (J). pap. 26.95 *(978-1-4327-6844-7(1))* Outskirts Pr., Inc.
Vogel, Kimberly. Sticks & Stones. 2013. 388p. pap. 20.00 *(978-1-300-65481-0(3))* Lulu Pr., Inc.
Voigt, Cynthia. Young Fredle. Yates, Louise, illus. 2012. (ENG.). 240p. (J). (gr. 3-7). 6.99 *(978-0-375-85787-4(7)*, Yearling) Random Hse. Children's Bks.
Volke, Gordon. The Big Posh Yacht. Bowler, Colin, illus. 2004. 24p. pap. 7.00 *(978-1-84161-116-7(6))* Ravette Publishing, Ltd. GBR. Dist: Parkwest Pubns., Inc.
—The Nasty Black Stuff. Bowler, Colin, illus. 2004. 24p. pap. 7.00 *(978-1-84161-119-8(0))* Ravette Publishing, Ltd. GBR. Dist: Parkwest Pubns., Inc.
—Old Grumpus & Other Stories. 2004. (Illus.). 91p. 5.00 *(978-1-84161-035-1(6))* Ravette Publishing, Ltd. GBR. Dist: Parkwest Pubns., Inc.
—The Pirate's Gold. Bowler, Colin, illus. 2004. 24p. pap. 7.00 *(978-1-84161-117-4(4))* Ravette Publishing, Ltd. GBR. Dist: Parkwest Pubns., Inc.
—A Spider for Tea & Other Stories. 2004. (Illus.). 90p. 5.00 *(978-1-84161-036-8(4))* Ravette Publishing, Ltd. GBR. Dist: Parkwest Pubns., Inc.
Volkov, Alexander. Tales of Magic Land 1. 2010. 360p. pap. 22.95 *(978-0-557-44825-8(5))* Lulu Pr., Inc.
von Eggers, Jennie, et al, creators. Times Tales. 2003. (J). spiral bd. 13.95 *(978-0-9762024-1-7(7))* Trigger Memory Systems.
Von Wielligh, G. R. Animal Tales, Vol. 1. Bankenaar, Dale, illus. 2012. (ENG.). 93p. pap. 12.00 *(978-1-86919-433-8(0))* Protea Boekhuis ZAF. Dist: Casemate Pubs. & Bk. Distributors, LLC.
—Animal Tales, Vol. 2. Bankenaar, Dale, illus. 2012. (ENG.). 93p. pap. 12.00 *(978-1-86919-504-5(3))* Protea Boekhuis ZAF. Dist: Casemate Pubs. & Bk. Distributors, LLC.
Wadsworth, Wallace. The Modern Story Book. Eger, Caroline Ruth, illus. 2010. (Dover Read & Listen Ser.). (ENG.). 112p. (J). (gr. 1-5). pap. 14.99 incl. audio compact disk *(978-0-486-47844-9(0))* Dover Pubns., Inc.
Wagner, Paul. Jock Jokes: And Other Stories. 2004. 236p. (YA). pap. 15.95 *(978-0-595-30757-9(4))* iUniverse, Inc.
Wake Up! Individual Title Six-Packs. (Story Steps Ser.). (gr. k-2). 29.00 *(978-0-7635-9581-4(0))* Rigby Education.
Walder, Chaim. Kids Speak, Vol. 4. 21.99 *(978-1-58330-442-6(8))* Feldheim Pubs.
Walker, Charmaine. Our Voices Through Writing. 2012. 66p. pap. 24.00 *(978-1-105-40141-1(3))* Lulu Pr., Inc.
Wall, Dorothy. The Complete Adventures of Blinky Bill. 2011. (Illus.). 442p. *(978-1-84902-571-3(1))* Benediction Classics.
Wallace, Karen. The Case of the Howling Armor. 2004. (Illus.). 47p. *(978-0-439-66552-0(3))* Scholastic, Inc.
Wallace, Rich. Sports Camp. 2012. (ENG.). 160p. (J). (gr. 4-7). 6.99 *(978-0-440-23993-2(1)*, Yearling) Random Hse. Children's Bks.
Walls, P. Abby: En busca del Tesoro. 2003. (Abby Ser.).Tr. of Abby: In Search of Treasure. pap. 6.99 *(978-0-7899-0968-8(5))* Editorial Unilit.
Walsh, Ann, ed. Beginnings: Stories of Canada's Past. 2005. (ENG., Illus.). 228p. (J). pap. 12.95 *(978-0-921870-87-6(6))* Ronsdale Pr. CAN. Dist: Literary Pr. Group of Canada.
Walsh, Maria Elena. Chaucha y Palito. Ink, Lancman, illus. 2003. (SPA.). 134p. (J). (gr. 5-8). pap. 11.95 *(978-950-511-615-7(2))* Santillana USA Publishing Co., Inc.
Walter, Jackie. The Ugly Duckling. Home, Sarah, illus. 2016. (Must Know Stories: Level 2 Ser.). (ENG.). 32p. (J). (gr. 1-4). 12.99 *(978-1-4451-4649-2(5)*, Franklin Watts) Hachette Children's Group GBR. Dist: Hachette Bk. Group.
Walther, William. A Collection of Fairy Tales: Volume One. 2007. (YA). per. 12.95 *(978-0-9795087-0-7(3))* Ctr. Stage Puppets.
Walton, Rick. Mini Mysteries 2: 20 More Tricky Tales to Untangle. Scheuer, Lauren, illus. 2006. 87p. (J). *(978-1-4156-6869-6(8)*, American Girl) American Girl Publishing, Inc.
Waltz, Michael. The Hen & I. 2012. (ENG.). pap. 15.00 *(978-1-4675-5236-3(4))* Independent Pub.
Ware, Shirley. Just Kids. 2006. 52p. pap. 16.95 *(978-1-4241-3194-5(4))* America Star Bks.
Warnasuriya, Chandrani. Favorite Folktales of Sri Lank. 2007. 108p. per. 19.95 *(978-1-4241-9965-5(4))* America Star Bks.
—Spooky Tales from the Orient: Tales of Ogres, Demons, Ghosts, Spells, Charms & the Enchanted, 1 vol. 2009. 167p. pap. 24.95 *(978-1-61546-978-9(8))* America Star Bks.
Warne, Frederick & Potter, Beatrix. The Complete Adventures of Peter Rabbit. 2007. (Peter Rabbit Ser.). (ENG., Illus.). 96p. (J). (gr. -1-2). 16.99 *(978-0-7232-5916-9(X)*, Warne) Penguin Young Readers Group.
Warner, Rex. Men & Gods: Myths & Legends of the Ancient Greeks. Gorey, Edward, illus. 2008. (New York Review Books Classics). (ENG.). 288p. 17.95 *(978-1-59017-263-6(9)*, NYRB Classics) New York Review of Bks., Inc., The.
Wassmann, Marilyn B. & Wassman, Paul A., illus. What the Wind Blew In: 6 Stories to Read with Children. 2010. 29p. (J). *(978-1-4535-6303-8(2))* Xlibris Corp.
Waters, Summer. Rising Star. 2011. (Silver Dolphins Ser.). (ENG.). 176p. (J). (gr. 2-4). pap. 7.99 *(978-0-00-734812-1(6))* HarperCollins Pubs. Ltd. GBR. Dist: Independent Pubs. Group.
—Stormy Skies. 2010. (Silver Dolphins Ser.: 8). (ENG.). 176p. (J). (gr. 2-4). pap. 7.99 *(978-0-00-734813-8(4))*, HarperCollins

S

Children's Bks.) HarperCollins Pubs. Ltd. GBR. Dist: HarperCollins Pubs.

Watkins, Fred L. Sue, Mary & Charles, 1 vol. 2009. 127p. pap. 19.95 *(978-1-60749-110-1(9))* America Star Bks.

Watson, Margery. Ruffles & Danny or the Responsibility. 2005. pap. 22.95 *(978-1-4191-0387-2(3))* Kessinger Publishing, LLC.

Watson, Myrtle. Kite Flying in the Village: A Guyanese Girl's Story. 2011. 20p. 10.03 *(978-1-4520-8632-3(X))* AuthorHouse.

Watson, Viola. A Selection of Children's Short Stories. 2007. per. *(978-1-59581-349-7(7),* Brentwood Christian Pr.) Brentwood Communications Group.

Wattley, Jason J. Anthology of Chaconia Creations. 2011. 24p. pap. 15.99 *(978-1-4568-7683-8(X))* Xlibris Corp.

Wax, Wendy A. Musica en Casa: Libro de Cuentos. de Alba, Arlette, tr. 2005. (Disney Princess Ser.). (SPA., Illus.). 38p. (J). (gr. -1-7). incl. audio compact disk *(978-970-718-289-9(X),* Silver Dolphin en Español) Advanced Marketing, S. de R. L. de C. V.

Wealden House Staff. Soul-Fire. 2006. 132p. per. *(978-1-904529-18-7(6),* Back to Front) Solidus.

Webb, Mack Henry, Jr. Webb's Wondrous Tales Book 1. Webb, Celia, illus. 2006. 184p. (YA). per. 14.95 *(978-0-9779576-1-3(6))* Pilinut Pr., Inc.

Weed, Thurlow R. Camel Fables from the Sailors of the Sudan. 2004. 84p. pap. 15.95 *(978-0-7414-2229-3(8))* Infinity Publishing.

Weel, Rosalinda. Dream Clouds: Float Away with Seven Enchanting Children's Stories for Relaxation & Bedtime. 2012. 60p. pap. 23.99 *(978-1-4525-5860-8(4))* Balboa Pr.

Weinbrecht, William. Stories for Amand. 2009. 48p. pap. 15.50 *(978-1-60693-150-9(4),* Eloquent Bks.) Strategic Book Publishing & Rights Agency (SBPRA).

Weir, Liz. Here, There & Everywhere: Stories from Many Lands. 2005. (ENG., Illus.). 80p. (J). pap. 9.95 *(978-0-86278-869-8(2))* O'Brien Pr., Ltd., The IRL. Dist: Dufour Editions, Inc.

Weis, Michael David. Diamond & the Fosters. Avant, Matthew, illus. 2013. 64p. 21.95 *(978-1-59663-635-4(1),* Castle Keep Pr.) Rock, James A. & Co. Pubs.

Wellesley, Rosie. The Very Helpful Hedgehog. Wellesley, Rosie, illus. 2012. (ENG., Illus.). 32p. (J). (gr. -1-k). pap. 11.99 *(978-1-84365-198-7(X),* Pavilion Children's Books) Pavilion Bks. GBR. Dist: Independent Pubs. Group.

Wells, Rosemary. Hungry Bunny Tales. 2012. (Max & Ruby Ser.). lib. bdg. 14.75 *(978-0-606-23658-4(9),* Turtleback) Turtleback Bks.

Weninger, Brigitte. 24 Stories for Advent. Tharlet, Eve, illus. 2015. (ENG.). 120p. (J). 19.95 *(978-0-7358-4229-8(9))* North-South Bks., Inc.

Wenke, Christine. Willa's Secret. 2005. 160p. (Orig.). pap. *(978-0-7344-0675-0(4),* Lothian Children's Bks.) Hachette Australia.

Wernham, Sara. Phonic; Rainforests; Monster Party, 18 vols., Pack. Set. Stephen, Lib & Maddison, Kevin, illus. 2003. (ENG.). (J). pap. 37.50 *(978-1-84414-091-6(1),* Jolly Learning) Jolly Learning, Ltd. GBR. Dist: American International Distribution Corp.

—Snakes; the Tree That Blinked; the Tree Billy Goats Gruff, 18 Bks., Pack. Maddison, Kevin & Stephen, Lib, illus. 2004. (ENG.). (J). pap. 42.00 *(978-1-84414-090-9(3),* Jolly Learning) Jolly Learning, Ltd. GBR. Dist: American International Distribution Corp.

West, Denis. Sam of the Forest Railway. 2012. 66p. pap. 13.50 *(978-1-78035-361-6(8),* Fastprint Publishing) Upfront Publishing Ltd. GBR. Dist: Printondemand-worldwide.com.

West, Hilary. The Secret Kingdom. 2013. 76p. pap. 17.95 *(978-1-62709-626-3(4))* America Star Bks.

West, Shawna Makala. Is There an Alligator at Kaipapau? 2004.Tr. of Aia Ka Alakeka Ma Kaipapau? (ENG & HAW.). (J). lib. bdg. 12.95 *(978-0-9760892-1-6(1),* Ho'ulu Hou Project: Stories Told by Us) Na Kamalei Koolauloa Early Education Program.

Wewer, Iris. My Wild Sister & Me. 2012. (ENG., Illus.). 32p. (J). pap. 7.95 *(978-0-7358-4064-5(4))* North-South Bks., Inc.

Wharton, Edith. Edith Wharton. McConnell, James, illus. 2004. (Great American Short Stories Ser.). 80p. (gr. 4-7). lib. bdg. 24.00 *(978-0-8368-4256-2(1),* Gareth Stevens Learning Library) Stevens, Gareth Publishing LLLP.

What Do I Look Like? (Peek A Boo Pockets Ser.). 12p. (J). bds. *(978-2-7643-0106-7(5))* Phidal Publishing, Inc./Editions Phidal, Inc.

Whelan, Denise. In the Land of Six & Seven. 2010. 48p. 18.99 *(978-1-4520-3399-0(4))* AuthorHouse.

White, Elga Haymon. A Children's Adventure Duo: Thad the Sailor & Little Miss Lavendar. Freudiger, Victoria, ed. Bjornsen, Holly, illus. 2007. 130p. (J). per. 13.95 *(978-0-9785728-2-2(3))* Digi-Tall Media.

White, Paul. Jungle Doctor Looks for Trouble. 2009. (Flamingo Fiction 9-13s Ser.). (ENG., Illus.). 160p. (J). pap. 8.99 *(978-1-84550-499-1(2),* 9302ad19-8b28-4030-be88-ef9afc9f3a6c) Christian Focus Pubns. GBR. Dist: Bookmasters Distribution.

—Jungle Doctor Operates. 2009. (Flamingo Fiction 9-13s Ser.). (ENG., Illus.). 160p. (J). pap. 8.99 *(978-1-84550-500-4(X),* 5b5acc8e-b6fe-4477-b9ac-b1a8ea9426ea) Christian Focus Pubns. GBR. Dist: Bookmasters Distribution.

—Jungle Doctor to the Rescue. 2009. (Flamingo Fiction 9-13s Ser.). (ENG., Illus.). 176p. (J). pap. 8.99 *(978-1-84550-516-5(6),* 052662e3-f01a-4a40-9e4d-88634018ee06) Christian Focus Pubns. GBR. Dist: Bookmasters Distribution.

Who Does That? (Peek A Boo Pockets Ser.). 12p. (J). bds. *(978-2-89393-977-3(5))* Phidal Publishing, Inc./Editions Phidal, Inc.

Wicke, Ed. Wicked Tales. 2006. (ENG., Illus.). 156p. (J). per. 9.99 *(978-0-9677652-7-3(7),* BlacknBlue Pr. UK) Blacknblue Pr.

Wicks, Krista. Mazie Moo & Her Clever Clouds, Wonderful Water & Silly Sunshine. 2012. 24p. pap. 12.45 *(978-1-4497-6901-7(2),* WestBow Pr.) Author Solutions, Inc.

Wigger, Sherry. Scary Stories for Brave Kids, 1 vol. 2009. 73p. pap. 16.95 *(978-1-61582-308-6(5))* PublishAmerica, Inc.

Wiggin, Kate Douglas. The Bird's Christmas Carol. 2011. 88p. (gr. 4-7). 20.95 *(978-1-4638-9984-4(X))* Rodgers, Alan Bks.

—Homespun Tales. 2007. 240p. 26.95 *(978-1-60312-668-7(6));* per. 14.95 *(978-1-60312-410-2(1))* Aegypan.

—The Village Watchtower. 2007. 108p. per. 9.95 *(978-1-60312-209-2(5))* Aegypan.

Wight, Eric. Frankie Pickle & the Pine Run 3000. Wight, Eric, illus. 2010. (Frankie Pickle Ser.). (ENG., Illus.). 96p. (J). (gr. 2-5). 9.99 *(978-1-4169-6485-8(1),* Simon & Schuster Bks. For Young Readers) Simon & Schuster Bks. For Young Readers.

Wilberforce, Samuel. Agathos the Rocky Island & Other Sunday Stories & Parables. 2013. (ENG.). 236p. pap. 30.99 *(978-1-107-67169-0(8))* Cambridge Univ. Pr.

Wilbur's Wild Ride & Other Stories: Individual Title Six-Pack. (Story Steps Ser.). (gr. k-2). 42.00 *(978-0-7635-9598-2(5))* Rigby Education.

Wilde, Oscar. Cuentos de Oscar Wilde. (SPA.). (YA). 8.95 *(978-958-04-2378-2(4))* Norma S.A. COL. Dist: Distribuidora Norma, Inc.

—The Happy Prince. Russell, P. Craig, illus. 5th ed. 2012. (Fairy Tales of Oscar Wilde Ser.: 5). (ENG.). 32p. (J). (gr. 4-7). 16.99 *(978-1-56163-626-6(6))* NBM Publishing Co.

—The Happy Prince & Other Tales. Charles Robinson, illus. 2012. 84p. pap. 3.47 *(978-1-60386-460-2(1),* Watchmaker Publishing) Wexford College Pr.

Wilde, Oscar & Lynch, P. J. Oscar Wilde Stories for Children. 2nd ed. 2006. (ENG., Illus.). 112p. (J). (gr. 2-4). pap. 4.99 *(978-0-340-89436-1(9),* Hodder Children's Books) Hachette Children's Group GBR. Dist: Hachette Bk. Group.

Wilding, Valerie. The Grumpy Queen. Sanfilippo, Simona, illus. 2011. (ENG.). 32p. (J). (gr. -1-k). pap. *(978-1-84089-637-4(X))* Zero to Ten, Ltd.

Wiley, Gordon. Through the Eyes of Imagination. 2004. 108p. 22.95 *(978-1-4140-0758-8(2))* AuthorHouse.

Wilkin, Esther. Baby Listens. Wilkin, Eloise, illus. 2012. (Little Golden Book Ser.). (ENG.). 24p. (J). (gr. k-k). 3.99 *(978-0-307-93012-5(2),* Golden Bks.) Random Hse. Children's Bks.

Wilkinson, Richard. Wilkinson Tales: A Collection of Holiday Short Stories for Young People. 2009. 80p. pap. 26.49 *(978-1-4490-0902-1(6))* AuthorHouse.

Wilkinson, Richard Fergus. Wilkinson Tales: A Collection of Adventure Short Stories for Young People. Murphy, Andrea, illus. 2010. 88p. pap. 27.49 *(978-1-4490-5489-2(7))* AuthorHouse.

Willems, Mo. Time to Sleep, Sheep the Sheep! Willems, Mo, illus. 2010. (Illus.). 32p. (J). (gr. -1-3). (ENG.). 10.99 *(978-0-06-172847-1(0));* lib. bdg. 14.89 *(978-0-06-172848-8(9))* HarperCollins Pubs.

Williams, Ann. The Multifarious Adventures of Fred the Raindrop. 2005. 22p. (J). 8.00 *(978-1-4116-4175-4(2))* Lulu Pr., Inc.

Williams, Earnest L. The Invisible Cell: One Man's Story about Surviving in a Generation Lost in the Social Justice System. 2004. vi, 239p. (YA). per. 12.95 *(978-0-9745244-0-5(9))* William Works, Inc.

Williams, Jan. An Amazing Storytelling Cat. Peecock, Simon & McKissock, Charmaine, illus. 2013. 120p. pap. *(978-0-9568148-6-9(7))* Swift Publishing.

Williams, Marcia. The Elephant's Friend & Other Tales from Ancient India. Williams, Marcia, illus. 2014. (ENG., Illus.). 40p. (J). (gr. 1-4). 6.99 *(978-0-7636-7055-9(3))* Candlewick Pr.

Williams, Marie Sheppard. The Magic Stories. 2012. pap. 12.95 *(978-0-7414-7280-9(5))* Infinity Publishing.

Williams, Sandra. Look with Me. 2012. (Illus.). 40p. pap. 20.99 *(978-1-4772-1318-6(X))* AuthorHouse.

Williston, Teresa Peirce. Hindu Stories. Squire, Maud Hunt, illus. 2011. 110p. 39.95 *(978-1-258-02581-6(7))* Literary Licensing, LLC.

Wilson, Budge. Friendships. 2006. (ENG.). 224p. (J). (gr. 7-18). 11.99 *(978-0-14-301766-0(7),* Puffin Canada) Penguin Random House Canada Young Readers CAN. Dist: Penguin Random Hse. LLC.

—The Leaving, 1 vol. (ENG.). 176p. (J). mass mkt. 6.95 *(978-0-7736-7363-2(6))* Stoddart Kids CAN. Dist: Fitzhenry & Whiteside, Ltd.

Wilson, Essdale. Horses, Tigers & Neighbors. 2007. 160p. per. 24.95 *(978-1-4241-5811-9(7))* America Star Bks.

Wilson, Mary. Kopper "K" Kidds & Corky. 2003. per. *(978-1-59196-169-7(6))* Instant Pub.

Wilson, Pauline. Animal & Other Antics. 2004. (Illus.). 56p. pap. *(978-1-84401-313-5(8))* Athena Pr.

Winchell, Mike & dePaola, Tomie. Been There, Done That: School Dazed. Ceulemans, Eglantine, illus. 2016. (ENG.). 272p. (J). (gr. 5). bds. 17.99 *(978-0-448-48674-1(1),* Grosset & Dunlap) Penguin Young Readers Group.

Windling, Terri & Datlow, Ellen, eds. Troll's-Eye View: A Book of Villainous Tales. 2010. (ENG.). 208p. (J). (gr. 5-18). 7.99 *(978-0-14-241673-0(8),* Firebird) Penguin Young Readers Group.

Wingate, Frank. Herman the Hedgehog: Bedtime Tales from the Woodland. 2009. (Illus.). 84p. pap. 10.49 *(978-1-4389-9134-4(7))* AuthorHouse.

Winkel, Andrew. Raceboy & Super Qwok Adventures. Brault, Christopher, illus. 2012. (ENG.). 356p. (J). pap. 16.00 *(978-0-9837905-1-8(5))* Hierophantasm.

Winners: Poems & Stories, 2003 Spring Writing Contest. 2003. (J). 5.00 *(978-0-9702646-2-6(3));* (YA). 5.00 *(978-0-9702646-3-3(1))* New Sweden Pr.

Winter, Milo, illus. Aesop's Fables for Children. 2008. (Dover Read & Listen Ser.). (ENG.). 112p. (J). (gr. k-2). pap. 14.99 incl. cd-rom *(978-0-486-46770-2(8))* Dover Pubns., Inc.

Winter, Rosalind. The Mice of St Goran. 2010. 70p. pap. *(978-1-84923-461-0(2))* YouWriteOn.

Winters, Ben H. Literally Disturbed No. 1: Tales to Keep You up at Night. Watkins, Adam F., illus. 2013. (ENG.). 64p. (J). (gr. 3-7). 9.99 *(978-0-8431-7194-5(4),* Price Stern Sloan) Penguin Young Readers Group.

Winters, John. Gramps' Children's Stories. 2007. 60p. pap. 6.96 *(978-1-4357-0038-3(4))* Lulu Pr., Inc.

Wise, Linda. Pearl's Gems. 2010. 96p. pap. 28.99 *(978-1-4520-1129-5(X))* AuthorHouse.

Wiseman, Eva. The Last Song. 2012. (ENG., Illus.). 228p. (YA). (gr. 5). 17.95 *(978-0-88776-979-5(9),* Tundra Bks.) Tundra Bks. CAN. Dist: Penguin Random Hse. LLC.

Wittenbach, Jennie. Little Stories for Little Folks. 2011. 36p. pap. 21.99 *(978-1-4628-8818-4(6))* Xlibris Corp.

Wizard Academies I: The Heart of Darkness. 2006. 658p. pap. 24.96 *(978-1-4116-7787-6(0))* Lulu Pr., Inc.

Wolf, Ema. Silencio, Ninos! Y Otros Cuentos. Pez, illus. (Torre de Papel Ser.).Tr. of Quiet, Children! & Other Stories. (SPA.). 116p. (J). (gr. 4-6). 8.95 *(978-958-04-3927-1(3))* Norma S.A. COL. Dist: Distribuidora Norma, Inc.

Wolfe, Carolyn. The Bedtime of the Sky & Other Sleepy-Bye Stories. Mathis, Leslie, illus. 2010. 32p. pap. 11.25 *(978-1-935105-57-2(4))* Avid Readers Publishing Group.

Wolfe, Jaymie Stuart. Family Matters: Thirteen Short Stories. 2011. 126p. (J). pap. *(978-0-8198-2694-7(4))* Pauline Bks. & Media.

Wolos-Fonteno, Mary, et al. Tales with Tails: Animal Stories for Young People. Salaam, Kiini Ibura, ed. Wolos-Fonteno, Mary et al, illus. 2006. 168p. (YA). pap. 15.95 *(978-0-940938-43-4(X),* Pen & Rose Pr.) Harlin Jacque Pubns.

Wood, Carol. Grandma Carol's Book of Stories in Rhyme. 2009. (Illus.). 48p. pap. 19.49 *(978-1-4389-5413-4(1))* AuthorHouse.

Wood, Julie M. Learn to Read with Tug the Pup & Friends!, Set. Braun, Sebastien, illus. 2014. (My Very First I Can Read Ser.). (ENG.). 132p. (J). (gr. -1-3). pap. 12.99 *(978-0-06-226689-7(6))* HarperCollins Pubs.

Wood, Maryrose. The Mysterious Howling. Klassen, Jon, illus. (ENG.). (J). (gr. 3-7). 2011. (Incorrigible Children of Ashton Place Ser.: Bk. 1). 288p. pap. 6.99 *(978-0-06-179110-9(5))*Bk. I. 2010. (Incorrigible Children of Ashton Place Ser.: 1). 272p. 16.99 *(978-0-06-179105-5(9))* HarperCollins Pubs.

Wooden, John. Fiesta. Cornelison, Susan F., illus. 2007. (Coach John Wooden for Kids Ser.). 63p. (J). (gr. k-3). lib. bdg. 11.65 *(978-0-7569-7791-7(6));* pap., per. 4.99 *(978-0-7891-7187-0(2))* Perfection Learning Corp.

Wooden Soldier. 2004. (J). per. *(978-1-57657-383-9(4))* Paradise Pr., Inc.

Woods, Cindy Smith. Once Inside A Storybook... Good Morals in Short Stories to Encourage Correct Behavior in the Little Ones in Your Life. 2006. 59p. pap. 16.95 *(978-1-4241-2905-8(2))* America Star Bks.

Woods, Titania. Fairy Dust. 2011. (ENG., Illus.). 128p. (J). (gr. 2-4). pap. 11.99 *(978-1-4088-2023-0(4),* 9781408820230, Bloomsbury USA Childrens) Bloomsbury Publishing USA.

—Friends Forever. 2011. (ENG., Illus.). 128p. (J). (gr. 2-4). pap. 11.99 *(978-1-4088-2022-3(6),* 9781408820223, Bloomsbury USA Childrens) Bloomsbury Publishing USA.

Woody, Velma B. Branscum. Bandits, Bears & Backaches: A Collection of Short Stories Based on Arkansas History. 2004. (ENG.). 78p. per. 15.00 *(978-0-9708574-2-2(X))* Butler Ctr. for Arkansas Studies.

World Almanac Editors. Great Stories of Courage: The Call of the Wild; the Red Badge of Courage; Treasure Island. 2007. (Bank Street Graphic Novels Ser.). (Illus.). 56p. (gr. 5-8). lib. bdg. 31.00 *(978-0-8368-7926-1(0))* Stevens, Gareth Publishing LLLP.

World Almanac Editors, creator. Great Stories of Courage: The Call of the Wild, the Red Badge of Courage, Treasure Island. 2007. (Bank Street Graphic Novels Ser.). (Illus.). 56p. (gr. 5-8). pap. 14.05 *(978-0-8368-7933-9(3))* Stevens, Gareth Publishing LLLP.

World Almanac Editors, et al. Historical Adventure: A Connecticut Yankee in King Arthur's Court/ Around the World in 80 Days/the Prisoner of Zenda. 2007. (Bank Street Graphic Novels Ser.). (Illus.). 56p. (gr. 5-8). lib. bdg. 31.00 *(978-0-8368-7927-8(9))* Stevens, Gareth Publishing LLLP.

World Peace, Metta & McBride, Heddrick. Metta's Bedtime Stories. Pax, H. H. -, illus. 2013. 36p. pap. 12.95 *(978-0-615-70075-5(6))* McBride, Heddrick.

Wormell, Chris, et al. Dos Ranas. Bourgeois, Elodie, tr. 2004. (SPA., Illus.). 32p. (J). (gr. k-2). 20.99 *(978-84-261-3354-0(1))* Juventud, Editorial ESP. Dist: Lectorum Pubns., Inc.

Worth, Bonnie. Oh, the Places on Earth! A Cat in the Hat's Learning Library Collection, 4 vols. 2012. (ENG., Illus.). 48p. (J). (gr. k-3). 39.96 *(978-0-307-93139-9(0),* Random Hse. Bks. for Young Readers) Random Hse. Children's Bks.

Wray, Zoe, contrib. by. Usborne Illustrated Stories for Girls. 2007. (Usborne Illustrated Stories Ser.). (Illus.). 352p. (J). (gr. -1-3). 19.99 *(978-0-7945-1419-8(7),* Usborne) EDC Publishing.

Wrede, Patricia C. Book of Enchantments. 2005. (ENG., Illus.). 256p. (J). (gr. 5-7). pap. 14.95 *(978-0-15-205508-0(8))* Houghton Mifflin Harcourt Publishing Co.

Wright, Lloyd. Gramp's Variety of Stories. 2007. 200p. 24.95 *(978-0-595-71311-0(4));* per. 14.95 *(978-0-595-47731-9(3))* iUniverse, Inc.

—More Stories for Gramp's Little Friends. 2004. 180p. (J). 23.95 *(978-0-595-66836-6(4))* iUniverse, Inc.

—Stories for Gramp's Little Friends. 2004. 158p. (J). 22.95 *(978-0-595-66287-6(0));* pap. 12.95 *(978-0-595-31266-5(7))* iUniverse, Inc.

Wright, Sharrie. Wee Friends. 2011. (Illus.). 32p. (gr. -1). pap. 14.50 *(978-1-4567-7621-3(5))* AuthorHouse.

Wuest, Marcia. Twelve Things to Do at Age 12. 2009. (ENG.). 26p. pap. 7.25 *(978-0-521-73733-3(8))* Cambridge Univ. Pr.

Yaber, Armando. Mariana Sale el Sol. 2005. (SPA.). (YA). per. 9.99 *(978-0-9765467-1-9(X))* Creative Bk. Pubs.

Yancey, Rick. The Monstrumologist Collection: Monstrumologist; Curse of the Wendigo; Isle of Blood; Final Descent. 2014. (Monstrumologist Ser.). (ENG., Illus.). 1808p. (YA). (gr. 9). pap. 46.99 *(978-1-4814-3012-8(2),* Simon & Schuster Bks. For Young Readers) Simon & Schuster Bks. For Young Readers.

Yang, Gladys. The Frog Rider & Other Folktales from Chin. 2008. 116p. 19.95 *(978-1-59654-569-4(0))* Disruptive Publishing.

Yates, Donnalyn. Let's Memorize States & Capitals Using Pictures & Stories. 2011. 128p. pap. 14.95 *(978-1-257-07566-9(7))* Lulu Pr., Inc.

Yeahpau, Thomas M. X-Indian Chronicles: The Book of Mausape. 2006. (ENG.). 240p. (YA). (gr. 9). 16.99 *(978-0-7636-2706-5(2))* Candlewick Pr.

The Year of Shadows. 2014. (ENG., Illus.). 416p. (J). (gr. 3-7). pap. 7.99 *(978-1-4424-4295-5(6),* Simon & Schuster Bks. For Young Readers) Simon & Schuster Bks. For Young Readers.

Yee, Paul. Tales from Gold Mountain, 1 vol. Ng, Simon, illus. 2011. (ENG.). 64p. (J). (gr. 1-5). pap. 14.95 *(978-1-55498-125-0(5))* Groundwood Bks. CAN. Dist: Publishers Group West (PGW).

Yee, Wong Herbert. Abracadabra! Magic with Mouse & Mole. 2010. (Mouse & Mole Story Ser.). (ENG., Illus.). 48p. (J). (gr. -1-3). pap. 3.99 *(978-0-547-40621-3(5))* Houghton Mifflin Harcourt Publishing Co.

Yellow Bananas, 11 bks. Incl. Amina's Blanket. Dunmore, Helen. Dainton, Paul, illus. lib. bdg. *(978-0-7787-0938-1(8));* Break in the Chain. d'Lacey, Chris. Carey, Joanna, illus. lib. bdg. *(978-0-7787-0931-2(0));* Colly's Barn. Morpurgo, Michael. Andrew, Ian P., illus. lib. bdg. *(978-0-7787-0932-9(9));* Dragon Trouble. Lively, Penelope. Rowland, Andrew, illus. lib. bdg. *(978-0-7787-0941-1(8));* Fine Feathered Friend. Gavin, Jamila. Williams, Dan, illus. lib. bdg. *(978-0-7787-0939-8(6));* Jo-Jo the Melon Donkey. Morpurgo, Michael. Kerins, Tony, illus. lib. bdg. *(978-0-7787-0942-8(6));* Monster from Underground. Cross, Gillian. Priestley, Chris, illus. lib. bdg. *(978-0-7787-0935-0(3));* My Brother Bernadette. Wilson, Jacqueline. Roberts, David, illus. lib. bdg. *(978-0-7787-0940-4(X));* Soccer Star. Hardcastle, Michael. Cox, Ken, illus. lib. bdg. *(978-0-7787-0933-6(7));* Stranger from Somewhere in Time. McBratney, Sam. Chatterton, Martin & Chatterton, Ann, illus. lib. bdg. *(978-0-7787-0937-4(X));* Who's a Clever Girl? Impey, Rose & Ashe, Susan. Amstutz, Andre, illus. lib. bdg. *(978-0-7787-0930-5(2));* 48p. (J). (gr. 3-4). 2002. 2003. *(978-0-7787-0929-9(9))* Crabtree Publishing Co.

Yeoman, John. Quentin Blake's Amazing Animal Stories. Blake, Quentin, illus. (ENG.). (J). (gr. 2-4). 2014. 120p. pap. 14.99 *(978-1-84365-295-3(1),* Pavilion) 2012. 124p. 19.99 *(978-1-84365-195-6(5),* Pavilion Children's Books) Pavilion Bks. GBR. Dist: Independent Pubs. Group.

Yip, Mingmei. Chinese Children's Favorite Stories. 2005. (ENG., Illus.). 96p. (J). (gr. k-8). 18.95 *(978-0-8048-3589-3(6))* Tuttle Publishing.

Yohalem, Eve. Escape under the Forever Sky. 2011. (ENG.). 219p. (YA). (gr. 4-7). pap. 7.99 *(978-0-8118-7874-6(0))* Chronicle Bks. LLC.

Young Folks Treasury, Vol. 2 1t. ed. 2007. (ENG.). 572p. pap. 43.75 *(978-1-4264-8525-1(5))* Creative Media Partners, LLC.

Young Folks Treasury Volume 2. 2007. (ENG.). 508p. pap. 30.99 *(978-1-4264-8467-4(4))* Creative Media Partners, LLC.

Youngquist, D. M. Ghosts of Interstate 80. 2007. (ENG., Illus.). 180p. per. 9.95 *(978-1-57166-459-4(9))* Quixote Pr.

Youngs, Purna Wun. Dreamtime. 2010. 28p. pap. 13.99 *(978-1-4490-8378-6(1))* AuthorHouse.

Yourgrau, Barry. Nasty Book. 2005. (ENG.). 192p. (J). (gr. 5-9). 11.99 *(978-0-06-057978-4(1))* HarperCollins Pubs.

—NASTYbook. 2005. 192p. (J). (gr. k-9). lib. bdg. 13.89 *(978-0-06-057979-1(X))* HarperCollins Pubs.

Yovanoff, Brenna, et al. The Anatomy of Curiosity. 2015. (ENG.). 296p. (YA). (gr. 8-12). 18.99 *(978-1-4677-8812-0(0),* Carolrhoda Lab™) Lerner Publishing Group.

—The Curiosities: A Collection of Stories. 2014. (ENG.). 304p. (YA). (gr. 7-12). pap. *(978-1-4677-1623-9(5),* Carolrhoda Lab™) Lerner Publishing Group.

Yoyo Books Staff. At Home: One Minute Goodnight Stories. 2004. 40p. bds. *(978-90-5843-583-5(0))* YoYo Bks.

—At School: One Minute Goodnight Stories. 2004. 40p. bds. *(978-90-5843-582-8(2))* YoYo Bks.

Yuki, Kaori. Godchild. 2007. (GodChild Ser.: 4). (ENG., Illus.). 200p. pap. 8.99 *(978-1-4215-0478-0(2))* Viz Media.

Zakarin, Debra Mostow. First Fairytales. Fiore, Rob, illus. 2010. 10p. 9.95 *(978-1-60747-746-4(7),* Pickwick Pr.) Phoenix Bks., Inc.

Zeman, Ludmila, illus. & retold by. Sindbad: From the Tales of the Thousand & One Nights. Zeman, Ludmila, retold by. 2011. (ENG.). 32p. (J). (gr. 1-4). pap. 9.95 *(978-1-77049-264-6(X),* Tundra Bks.) Tundra Bks. CAN. Dist: Penguin Random Hse. LLC.

Zemko Tetro, Maria, tr. from UKR. How the Animals Built their House & Other Stories. 2008. (Illus.). 40p. (J). 14.95 *(978-0-9797372-5-1(7))* Winter Light Bks., Inc.

Zimmerschied, P. Grampa Paul's Adventure Stories for Children. 2011. 112p. (gr. -1). 23.99 *(978-1-4634-2885-3(5));* pap. 13.99 *(978-1-4634-2883-9(9))* AuthorHouse.

Zipes, Jack, ed. & tr. Beauties, Beasts & Enchantment: Classic French Fairy Tales. Zipes, Jack, tr. 3rd ed. 2013. 610p. pap. *(978-1-86171-432-9(7))* Crescent Moon Publishing.

Zolotow, Charlotte. Hold My Hand: Five Stories of Love & Family. Thompson, Carol, illus. 2003. (ENG.). 64p. (gr. -1-k). 19.99 *(978-0-7868-0518-1(8))* Hyperion Pr.

Zondervan Staff. Story Early Elementary Curriculum: 31 Lessons, 1 vol. 2011. (Story Ser.). (ENG.). cd-rom 34.99 *(978-0-310-71921-2(6))* Zonderkidz.

—The Story for Kids: Later Elementary Curriculum - 31 Lessons, 1 vol. 2011. (Story Ser.). (ENG.). cd-rom 34.99 *(978-0-310-71922-9(4))* Zonderkidz.

—Story Preschool Curriculum: 31 Lessons, 1 vol. 2011. (Story Ser.). (ENG.). (J). cd-rom 34.99 *(978-0-310-71920-5(8))* Zonderkidz.

Zorro, Sephone. Growing Up: Home & School. Baxter, Rhea, illus. 2017. 144p. pap. 7.99 ***(978-1-941429-55-6(6))*** Handersen Publishing.

Zorro, Sephone. Welcome. 2016. (Illus.). 133p. pap. 5.99 *(978-1-941429-33-4(5))* Handersen Publishing.

Zuill, Veronica M. E. Short Stories for Children Book. 2012. 28p. pap. 21.99 *(978-1-4771-4576-0(1))* Xlibris Corp.

Zullo, Allan. The Haunted Shortstop: True Ghostly Sports Stories. 2007. 128p. (J). pap. *(978-0-439-88618-5(X))* Scholastic, Inc.

Zwerger, Lisbeth & Aesop, illus. Aesop's Fables. 2006. (ENG.). 32p. (J). (gr. -1-3). pap. 6.95 *(978-0-7358-2069-2(4))* North-South Bks., Inc.

3 Minutes Nursery Stories. (Illus.). 160p. (J). 9.98 *(978-0-7853-7821-1(9),* 7177000) Publications International, Ltd.

7 Cuentos para antes de Dormir.Tr. of 7 Bedtime Stories. (SPA.). (J). *(978-84-7773-016-3(4));* Vol. 2.

(978-84-7773-302-7(3)); Vol. 4. (978-84-7773-017-0(2)) Grafalco, S.A.
101 Stories to Tell & Write. (Illus.). (J). (gr. 3-6). pap. (978-1-876367-67-1(9)) Wizard Bks.
365 Fabulas.Tr. of 365 Fables. (SPA.). 208p. (J). (978-84-7773-031-6(8)) Grafalco, S.A.
09' Young Writers Conf. Havana Elem. Words Have Wings. 2009. 32p. pap. 20.00 (978-1-4490-5303-1(3)) AuthorHouse.

SHREWS

Frisch-Schmoll, Joy. Arctic Shrews. 2015. (Ice Age Animals Ser.). (ENG., Illus.). 24p. (gr. k-1). pap. 6.95 (978-1-4914-2317-2(X), Pebble Plus) Capstone Press of Coughlan Cos.

SHRIMPS

Coldiron, Deborah. Shrimp, 1 vol. 2007. (Underwater World Ser.). (ENG.). 32p. (gr. 3-7). 27.07 (978-1-59928-814-7(1), Buddy Bks.) ABDO Publishing Co.
Cunningham, Kevin. Goby Fish & Pistol Shrimp. 2016. (21st Century Junior Library: Better Together Ser.). (ENG., Illus.). 24p. (J). (gr. 2-5). 27.07 (978-1-63471-084-8(3), 208415) Cherry Lake Publishing.
Plattner, Josh. Mantis Shrimp: Master of Punching, 1 vol. 2016. (ENG., Illus.). 24p. (J). (978-1-62403-736-8(4)) ABDO Publishing Co.
Rustad, Martha E. H. Moray Eels & Cleaner Shrimp Work Together. (Animals Working Together Ser.). (ENG.). 24p. (gr. k-1). 2011. pap. 41.70 (978-1-4296-6368-7(5)) 2010. lib. bdg. 26.65 (978-1-4296-5299-5(3)) Capstone Press of Coughlan Cos. (Pebble Plus).
Sexton, Colleen. Shrimp. 2009. (Oceans Alive Ser.). (ENG., Illus.). 24p. (J). (gr. k-3). lib. bdg. 25.95 (978-1-60014-252-9(4)) Bellwether Media.
—Shrimp. 2009. (Blastoff! Readers Ser.). (ENG., Illus.). 24p. (J). (gr. k-3). 20.00 (978-0-531-21716-0(7), Children's Pr.) Scholastic Library Publishing.
Shea, Therese. What Are Crustaceans? 2016. (Let's Find Out! Marine Life Ser.). 00032p. (J). (gr. 2-3). lib. bdg. 24.45 (978-1-5081-0385-1(2)) Rosen Publishing Group, Inc., The.

SHRUBS

see also Landscape Gardening

Aldrich, William & Williamson, Don. Tree & Shrub Gardening for Illinois, 1 vol., Vol. 1. rev. ed. 2004. (ENG., Illus.). 352p. (gr. 4). pap. 18.95 (978-1-55105-404-9(3), 1551054043) Lone Pine Publishing USA.
Buckley, Arabella B. Trees & Shrubs. 2008. (Illus.). 88p. pap. 11.95 (978-1-59915-275-2(4)) Yesterday's Classics.
De Medeiros, Michael. Chaparral. 2006. (J). 9.95 (978-1-59036-439-0(2)) Weigl Pubs., Inc.
Tanem, Bob & Williamson, Don. Tree & Shrub Gardening for Northern California, 1 vol. rev. ed. 2003. (ENG., Illus.). 360p. (gr. 4). pap. 18.95 (978-1-55105-275-5(X), 155105275X) Lone Pine Publishing USA.
Wood, Timothy D. & Beck, Alison. Tree & Shrub Gardening for Michigan, 1 vol. rev. ed. 2003. (ENG., Illus.). 352p. (gr. 4). pap. 18.95 (978-1-55105-347-9(0), 1551053470) Lone Pine Publishing USA.

SIAM

see Thailand

SIBERIA (RUSSIA)

Lengyel, Emil. Siberia. 2004. reprint ed. pap. 36.95 (978-1-4191-0872-3(7)) Kessinger Publishing, LLC.
Sloan, Christopher. Baby Mammoth Mummy: Frozen in Time: A Prehistoric Animal's Journey into the 21st Century. 2011. (ENG., Illus.). 48p. (J). (gr. 3-7). 17.95 (978-1-4263-0865-9(5)); lib. bdg. 26.90 (978-1-4263-0866-6(3)) National Geographic Society. (National Geographic Children's Bks.).

SIBERIA (RUSSIA)—FICTION

Ingram, W. J. Evelyn. Saint Crispin & Other Quaint Conceits. 2005. pap. 24.95 (978-1-4179-6255-6(0)) Kessinger Publishing, LLC.
London, Jonathan. Little Lost Tiger, 0 vols. Spirin, Ilya, illus. 2012. (ENG.). 32p. (J). (gr. k-3). 17.99 (978-0-7614-6130-2(2), 9780761461302, Amazon Children's Publishing) Amazon Publishing.
Mead, Richelle. Blood Promise. 2010. (Vampire Academy Ser.: 4). (ENG.). 528p. (YA). (gr. 7-18). 9.99 (978-1-59514-310-5(6), Razorbill) Penguin Young Readers Group.
—Blood Promise. 2010. (Vampire Academy Ser.: 4). lib. bdg. 20.85 (978-0-606-14565-7(6), Turtleback) Turtleback Bks.
PaleoJoe & Caszatt-Allen, Wendy. Mysterious Mammoths. 2008. (ENG., Illus.). 200p. (J). (gr. 2-5). pap. 7.95 (978-1-934133-43-9(4), Mackinac Island Press, Inc.) Charlesbridge Publishing, Inc.
Popke, Suzanne L. The Adventures of Tolei Mergen. 2013. 36p. pap. 24.95 (978-1-4626-8863-0(2)) America Star Bks.
Sepetys, Ruta. Between Shades of Gray. 2009. 10.36 (978-0-7848-3779-5(1), Everbind) Marco Bk. Co.
—Between Shades of Gray. (ENG., (YA). (gr. 7-18). 2012. Illus.). 384p. pap. 9.99 (978-0-14-242059-1(X), Speak) 2011. 352p. 17.99 (978-0-399-25412-3(9), Philomel Bks.) Penguin Young Readers Group.
—Between Shades of Gray. l.t. ed. 2011. (ENG.). 420p. (YA). 23.99 (978-1-4104-4083-9(4)) Thorndike Pr.
—Between Shades of Gray. 2012. lib. bdg. 20.85 (978-0-606-26089-3(7), Turtleback) Turtleback Bks.
Snell, Roy J. Triple Spies. 2008. 112p. (gr. -1-7). 22.95 (978-1-60664-743-1(1)) Rodgers, Alan Bks.
Spreng, Robert C. The Tahoe Tiger & the Lahontan Lion. 2008. 38p. pap. 14.50 (978-0-557-02370-7(X)) Lulu Pr., Inc.
Young, H. M. (Hal). The huskies & the christmas Fawn. 2007. 56p. pap. 9.95 (978-1-4357-0070-3(8)) Lulu Pr., Inc.

SIBLING RIVALRY—FICTION

Al Shaikh, Latifa. I'm Still Waiting for that Chocolate. 2007. 52p. (YA). per. 8.95 (978-0-595-42982-0(3)) iUniverse, Inc.
Alley, R. W., illus. Bratty Brothers & Selfish Sisters: All about Sibling Rivalry. 2007. (Elf-Help Books for Kids Ser.). 28p. (J). (gr. -1-3). per. 7.95 (978-0-87029-404-4(0)) Abbey Pr.
Baldwin, Quinn. Crossover. 2011. 168p. pap. 15.00 (978-0-557-74844-0(5)) Lulu Pr., Inc.
Blabey, Aaron. The Brothers Quibble. Blabey, Aaron, illus. 2015. (ENG., Illus.). 32p. (J). (gr. k-3). 14.99 **(978-0-14-350706-2(0))** Random Hse. Australia AUS. Dist: Independent Pubs. Group.
Blume, Judy. The Pain & the Great One. Ohi, Debbie Ridpath, illus. 2014. (ENG.). 48p. (J). (gr. 1-5). pap. 5.99 (978-1-4814-1145-5(4), Atheneum Bks. for Young Readers) Simon & Schuster Children's Publishing.
—Soupy Saturdays with the Pain & the Great One. Stevenson, James, illus. 2009. (ENG.). 128p. (J). (gr. 3-7). 5.99 (978-0-440-42092-7(X), Yearling) Random Hse. Children's Bks.
—Superfudge. 2007.Tr. of Superfudge. (ENG.). 208p. (J). (gr. 3-7). 7.99 (978-0-14-240880-3(8), Puffin Books) Penguin Young Readers Group.
Burns, Theresa. Queen Emileen. Burns, Theresa, illus. 2013. (Illus.). 36p. 15.50 (978-1-949224-23-8(6)) Taylor and Seale Publishing, LLC.
Chichester Clark, Emma. Mimi's Book of Opposites. Chichester Clark, Emma, illus. 2004. (Illus.). 24p. (J). 9.95 (978-1-57091-574-1(1)) Charlesbridge Publishing, Inc.
Ciencin, Scott & Cano, Fernando. Power at the Plate, 1 vol. Esparza, Andres et al, illus. 2011. (Sports Illustrated Kids Graphic Novels Ser.). (ENG.). 56p. (gr. 2-3). pap. 7.19 (978-1-4342-3400-1(2)); lib. bdg. 26.65 (978-1-4342-2239-8(X)) Stone Arch Bks.
Coh, Smiljana. The Seven Princesses. 2016. (ENG., Illus.). 40p. (J). (gr. -1-17). 16.95 (978-0-7624-5587-4(X), Running Pr. Kids) Running Pr. Bk. Pubs.
Dempsey, Sheena. Bye-Bye Baby Brother! 2013. (ENG., Illus.). 32p. (J). (gr. -1-2). 15.99 (978-0-7636-6241-7(0)) Candlewick Pr.
Dungy, Tony & Dungy, Lauren. Go, Jade, Go! Newton, Vanessa Brantley, illus. 2013. (Tony & Lauren Dungy Ready-To-Reads Ser.). (ENG.). 32p. (J). (gr. k-2). 16.99 (978-1-4424-5467-5(9)); pap. 3.99 (978-1-4424-5466-8(0)) Simon Spotlight. (Simon Spotlight).
Enderle, Judith Ross & Gordon, Stephanie Jacob. Smile, Principessa! Curmi, Serena, illus. 2012. (ENG.). 40p. (J). (gr. -1-1). 16.99 (978-1-4424-3096-9(6), McElderry, Margaret K. Bks.) McElderry, Margaret K. Bks.
Forsyth, C. A. & Forsyth, Christine. Two on One, 1 vol. 2005. (Lorimer Sports Stories Ser.: 83). (ENG.). 112p. (J). (gr. 4-8). 8.95 (978-1-55028-900-8(4), 9781550289008) Lorimer, James & Co., Ltd., Pubs. CAN. Dist: Casemate Pubs. & Bk. Distributors, LLC.
Forsyth, Christine. Two on One, 1 vol. 2005. (Lorimer Sports Stories Ser.: 83). (ENG.). 112p. (J). (gr. 4-8). 16.95 (978-1-55028-901-5(2), 9781550289015) Lorimer, James & Co., Ltd., Pubs. CAN. Dist: Casemate Pubs. & Bk. Distributors, LLC.
Friedman, Laurie. Mallory vs. Max. Schmitz, Tamara, illus. (Mallory Ser.: 3). (ENG.). 160p. (J). (gr. 2-5). 2006. per. 5.95 (978-1-57505-863-4(4), First Avenue Editions) 2005. 15.95 (978-1-57505-795-8(6)) Lerner Publishing Group.
Gaetz, Dayle Campbell. Spoiled Rotten, 1 vol. 2005. (Orca Currents Ser.). (ENG.). 128p. (J). (gr. 5-9). per. 9.95 (978-1-55143-474-2(1)) Orca Bk. Pubs. USA.
Guest, Elissa Haden. Iris & Walter & Baby Rose. Davenier, Christine, illus. 2012. (Iris & Walter — Green Light Reader Ser.). lib. bdg. 13.55 (978-0-606-26612-3(7), Turtleback) Turtleback Bks.
Gunn, Dusty M. Paul & Peter Possum. 2008. 20p. pap. 24.95 (978-1-60474-503-0(7)) America Star Bks.
Haspiel, Dean. Mo & Jo: Fighting Together Forever. Lynch, Jay, illus. 2013. (ENG.). 40p. (J). (gr. -1-3). pap. 4.99 (978-1-935179-37-5(3)) TOON Books / RAW Junior, LLC.
Henbit & the Roly-Poly. 2007. (J). (978-0-9791982-2-9(4)) Pine Cone Pr.
Henbit & the Roly-Poly - Specially Formatted Edition. l.t. ed. 2007. (J). (978-0-9791982-3-6(2)) Pine Cone Pr.
Henkes, Kevin. Julius, the Baby of the World. Henkes, Kevin, illus. 2003. (Illus.). (J). 28.95 incl. audio compact disk (978-1-59112-518-1(9)); 25.95 incl. audio (978-1-59112-250-0(3)); pap. 33.95 incl. audio (978-1-59112-251-7(1)); pap. 35.95 incl. audio compact disk (978-1-59112-523-5(5)) Live Oak Media.
Hinton, S. E. Tex. 2013. (ENG.). 224p. (YA). (gr. 7). pap. 9.99 (978-0-385-37567-2(0), Delacorte Pr.) Random Hse. Children's Bks.
Hughes, Mair Wynn & Davies, Tracy. Brawd Newydd. 2005. (WEL., Illus.). 15p. pap. (978-0-86243-453-3(X)) Y Lolfa.
Hughes, Mark Peter. I Am the Wallpaper. 2007. (Readers Circle Ser.). (ENG.). 256p. (YA). (gr. 7-11). pap. 8.99 (978-0-440-42046-0(6), Delacorte Bks. for Young Readers) Random Hse. Children's Bks.
Jomo & Mata: Evaluation Guide. 2006. (J). (978-1-55942-411-0(7)) Witcher Productions.
Kantorovitz, Sylvie. The Very Tiny Baby. Kantorovitz, Sylvie, illus. 2014. (ENG., Illus.). 32p. (J). (gr. -1-2). lib. bdg. 14.95 (978-1-58089-445-6(3)) Charlesbridge Publishing, Inc.
—The Very Tiny Baby. 2014. (J). pap. (978-1-58089-446-3(1)) Charlesbridge Publishing, Inc.
Koller, Jackie French & Koller. Horace the Horrible: A Knight Meets His Match, 1 vol. Urbanovic, Jackie, illus. 2003. (ENG.). 32p. (J). 16.95 (978-0-7614-5150-1(1)) Marshall Cavendish Corp.
Lawson, Janet. The Alberts & Me. 2009. (J). (978-0-15-205327-7(1)) Harcourt Trade Pubs.
Layne, Steven L. Share with Brother, 1 vol. Hoyt, Ard, illus. 2010. (ENG.). 32p. (J). (gr. k-3). 16.99 (978-1-58980-860-7(6)) Pelican Publishing Co., Inc.
Li, Deborah, illus. Tricia & the Blue Cap. l.t. ed. 2003. 28p. (J). 7.95 net. (978-0-9706654-5-4(8)) Sprite Pr.
MacCullough, Carolyn. Once a Witch. 2010. (ENG.). 320p. (YA). (gr. 7). pap. 8.99 (978-0-547-41730-1(6)) Houghton Mifflin Harcourt Publishing Co.
MacKey, Cindy. My Sister Sophie. Tebbit, Jake, illus. 2013. 30p. pap. 12.99 (978-0-9892699-9-5(X)) Cyrano Bks.
Marychild, H. D. Skater Sister. 2013. 222p. pap. 9.52 (978-0-9899964-9-5(2)) Small Wonder Publishing.
McAuslan, Fiona & Nicholson, Peter. The Resolving Sibling Rivalry Book. 2010. (Resolving Bks). (ENG., Illus.). 88p. (J). pap. 9.95 (978-1-84730-224-3(6)) Veritas Pubns. IRL. Dist: Dufour Editions, Inc.
McNamee, Kevin. My Brother the Frog. Morris, Alexander, illus. 2011. 24p. 19.95 (978-1-61633-167-2(4)); pap. 10.95 (978-1-61633-159-7(3)) Guardian Angel Publishing, Inc.
Michels-Gualtieri, Akaela S. I Was Born to Be a Sister. Ramsey, Marcy Dunn, illus. 2005. (ENG.). 32p. (J). (gr. 4-7). 9.95 incl. lp (978-1-930775-11-4(3)) Platypus Media, L.L.C.
Noonimals: Presents the New Baby. rev. ed. 2007. (Illus.). 40p. (J). per. 14.99 (978-0-9796832-0-6(3)) Nooni Publishing.
Payton, Belle. May the Best Twin Win. 2015. (It Takes Two Ser.: 7). (ENG., Illus.). 160p. (J). (gr. 3-7). pap. 6.99 (978-1-4814-3134-7(X), Simon Spotlight) Simon Spotlight.
Pennypacker, Sara. Clementine & the Family Meeting. Frazee, Marla, illus. (ENG.). 176p. (J). (gr. 2-5). 2012. pap. 5.99 (978-1-4231-2436-8(7)) 2011. 14.99 (978-1-4231-2356-9(5)) Hyperion Pr.
Petruck, Rebecca. Steering Toward Normal. 2014. (ENG.). 336p. (J). (gr. 3-7). 16.95 (978-1-4197-0732-2(9), Amulet Bks.) Abrams, Inc.
Phillips, Leigh Hope. Birthday Wishes. Fountain, John, illus. 2005. (J). pap. (978-1-933156-10-1(4)); per. (978-1-933156-03-3(1)) GSVQ Publishing. (VisionQuest Kids).
Poole, Philip. The Trouble with Time. 2012. (Illus.). 24p. pap. 19.82 (978-1-4772-3459-4(4)) AuthorHouse.
Reynolds, Peter H. The Best Kid in the World: A SugarLoaf Book. Reynolds, Peter H., illus. 2012. (ENG., Illus.). 48p. (J). (gr. -1-2). pap. 22.99 (978-1-4424-7176-8(6), Atheneum Bks. for Young Readers) Simon & Schuster Children's Publishing.
Rock, Brian. With All My Heart. Banta, Susan, illus. 2012. (ENG.). 24p. (J). (978-1-58925-648-4(4)) Tiger Tales.
Schad, Kristine. Do You Love Me Best? Timmons, Gayle, illus. 2007. 40p. (J). lib. bdg. 23.95 (978-1-58374-156-6(9)) Chicago Spectrum Pr.
Scott, Ann Herbert. En Las Piernas de Mamá. Coalson, Glo, illus. 2007.Tr. of On Mother's Lap. (SPA & ENG.). 14p. (J). (gr. k — 1). bds. 5.95 (978-0-618-75247-8(1)) Houghton Mifflin Harcourt Publishing Co.
Seif, Adam, creator. Tacos, Beans & Rice... the Episodes: From the Beginning. l.t. ed. 2006. (Illus.). 32p. (J). (978-0-9719518-0-8(2)) Doodle Publishing.
Seitz, J. B. Freddy the Flea. 2009. 23p. pap. 24.95 (978-1-60836-759-7(2)) America Star Bks.
Simmons, Cari & Burns, Laura J. Picture Perfect #5: All Together Now. Mingus, Cathi, illus. 2016. (Picture Perfect Ser.: 5). 192p. (J). (gr. 3-7). pap. 6.99 (978-0-06-233676-7(2)) HarperCollins Pubs.
Simmons, Celeste. The Adventures of Booger Malone: Busted in the Backseat. 2007. (J). per. 10.95 (978-0-9777041-2-5(2)) Third Dimension Publishing.
Simons, Joseph. Under a Living Sky, 1 vol. 2005. (Orca Young Readers Ser.). (ENG., Illus.). 112p. (J). (gr. 3-6). per. 5.95 (978-1-55143-355-4(9)) Orca Bk. Pubs. USA.
Skinner, Daphne. Henry Lleva la Cuenta; Henry Keeps Score. 2008. pap. 34.95 (978-1-58013-757-7(1)) Kane Press, Inc.
Speed, Nakesha. Yucky Brother. 2006. pap. 16.95 (978-1-4241-2040-6(3)) PublishAmerica, Inc.
Stine, R. L. Night of the Living Dummy. 2008. (Classic Goosebumps Ser.: 1). (ENG.). 160p. (J). (gr. 3-7). 6.99 (978-0-545-03517-0(1), Scholastic Paperbacks) Scholastic, Inc.
Teitelbaum, Michael, adapted by. Skateboard Adventures. 2012. (Wind-Up Toy Ser.). (ENG., Illus.). 48p. (J). (gr. 1). 12.99 (978-0-7944-2470-1(8)) Reader's Digest Assn., Inc., The.
Torres, J., et al. Blackfire's Back!, 1 vol. 2014. (Teen Titans GO! Ser.). (ENG., Illus.). 32p. (gr. 2-3). 22.60 (978-1-4342-9215-5(0)) Stone Arch Bks.
Uegaki, Chieri. Rosie & Buttercup. Jorisch, Stéphane, illus. 2008. (ENG.). 32p. (J). (gr. -1-2). 18.95 (978-1-55337-997-3(7)) Kids Can Pr., Ltd. CAN. Dist: Hachette Bk. Group.
Vega, Denise. Rock On: A Story of Guitars, Gigs, Girls, & a Brother (Not Necessarily in That Order) 2012. (ENG., Illus.). 304p. (YA). (gr. 7-17). 17.99 (978-0-316-13310-4(8)) Little, Brown Bks. for Young Readers.
—Rock On: A Story of Guitars, Gigs, Girls, & a Brother (not Necessarily in That Order) 2013. (ENG., Illus.). 304p. (YA). (gr. 7-17). pap. 8.99 (978-0-316-13309-8(4)) Little, Brown Bks. for Young Readers.

SICILY (ITALY)—FICTION

Blasi, Kathleen McAlpin. A Name of Honor. Bowman, Leslie W., illus. 2006. (J). (978-1-59336-692-6(2)) Mondo Publishing.
Meyer, Kai. Arcadia Awakens. (Arcadia Ser.: 1). (ENG.). (YA). (gr. 9). 2013. 480p. pap. 9.99 (978-0-06-200607-3(X)) 2012. 464p. 17.99 (978-0-06-200606-6(1)) HarperCollins Pubs.
—Arcadia Falls. 2014. (Arcadia Ser.: 3). (ENG.). 480p. (YA). (gr. 9). 17.99 (978-0-06-200610-3(X)) HarperCollins Pubs.
Napoli, Donna Jo. The Wager. 2010. (ENG.). 272p. (YA). (gr. 7-12). 16.99 (978-0-8050-8781-9(8), 9780805087819, Holt, Henry & Co. Bks. For Young Readers) Holt, Henry & Co.
Vitale, Mary Ann. The Water Lily Fairy. 2011. 28p. (gr. 2-4). pap. 16.95 (978-1-4567-6639-9(2)) AuthorHouse.
Williams, Annie Morris. Marianne's Secret Cousins. Oldham, Cindi, illus. 2005. (Family History Adventures for Young Readers Ser.: 2). 240p. (J). per. 10.00 (978-0-9645272-8-7(6)) Field Stone Pubs.

SICK

see also Diseases; Mentally Ill

Carlson, Hannah. Addiction: The Brain Disease. 2010. (ENG., Illus.). 224p. (gr. 7-18). pap. 14.95 (978-1-884158-35-3(8), 03db31a0-ebf1-4ef8-b49f-db048b863aec) Team Kreskin Productions, LLC.
Edwards, Dianna. Meet Patou. 2006. (J). pap. 29.95 (978-0-9767756-0-7(3)) Patou Bks., LLC.
—When Niki Got Sick, Bk. 2. 2004. (J). (978-0-9767756-2-1(X)) Patou Bks., LLC.
Fetty, Margaret. Seizure-Alert Dogs. 2009. (Dog Heroes Ser.). (Illus.). 32p. (YA). (gr. 2-5). lib. bdg. 25.27 (978-1-59716-865-6(3)) Bearport Publishing Co., Inc.
Geis, Patricia. Let's Get Well! Folch, Sergio, illus. 2009. (Good Habits with Coco & Tula Ser.). 16p. (J). (gr. -1-k). bds. 11.40 (978-1-60754-407-4(5)) Windmill Bks.
Jones, Viola & Wainwright, Tabitha. Living with an Illness in the Family, 01 vols., 1. 2016. (Family Issues & You Ser.). (ENG.). 48p. (J). 30.25 (978-1-4994-3693-8(9), Rosen Central) Rosen Publishing Group, Inc., The.
Murphy, Patricia. Everything You Need to Know about Staying in the Hospital. 2005. (Need to Know Library). (Illus.). 64p. (YA). (gr. 7-12). 31.95 (978-0-8239-3325-9(3)) Rosen Publishing Group, Inc., The.
Rocha, Toni L. Coping When Someone in Your Family Has Cancer. 2009. (Coping Ser.). 192p. (gr. 7-12). 63.90 (978-1-61511-988-2(4)) Rosen Publishing Group, Inc., The.
Wainwright, Tabitha. You & an Illness in Your Family. (Family Matters Ser.). 48p. (gr. 5-8). 2009. 53.00 (978-1-61512-477-0(2), Rosen Reference) 2005. (Illus.). (YA). lib. bdg. 29.25 (978-0-8239-3352-5(0)) Rosen Publishing Group, Inc., The.

SICK—FICTION

Abbott, Roz. A Bump in the Road. Seltzer, Jerry Joe, illus. 2013. 26p. (J). 16.95 (978-1-60131-179-5(6)) Big Tent Bks.
Alda, Arlene. Iris Has a Virus. Desimini, Lisa, illus. 2008. (ENG.). 24p. (J). (gr. -1-1). 18.95 (978-0-88776-844-6(X), Tundra Bks.) Tundra Bks. CAN. Dist: Penguin Random Hse. LLC.
Appelt, Kathi. Mogie: The Heart of the House. Rosenthal, Marc, illus. 2014. (ENG.). 40p. (J). (gr. -1-3). 17.99 (978-1-4424-8054-4(8), Atheneum Bks. for Young Readers) Simon & Schuster Children's Publishing.
Archambault, Marc. Mommy Is Too Tired to Play. 2010. 32p. 18.97 (978-0-557-23350-2(X)) Lulu Pr., Inc.
Archer, Dosh. Baaad Sheep. Archer, Dosh, illus. 2016. (Urgency Emergency! Ser.). (ENG., Illus.). 48p. (J). (gr. -1-3). 12.99 (978-0-8075-8349-4(9)) Whitman, Albert & Co.
Avery, Lara. The Memory Book. 2016. (ENG.). 368p. (YA). (gr. 10-17). 17.99 (978-0-316-28374-8(6), Poppy) Little, Brown Bks. for Young Readers.
—The Memory Book. 2017. (YA). lib. bdg. 20.85 **(978-0-606-39907-4(0))** Turtleback Bks.
Avi. The Barn. 2014. (ENG.). 112p. (J). (gr. 3-7). pap. 6.99 (978-0-545-60744-5(2), Scholastic Paperbacks) Scholastic, Inc.
Banks, Steven. Spongebob Goes to the Doctor. Saunders, Zina, illus. 2005. 22p. (J). lib. bdg. 15.00 (978-1-4242-0976-7(5)) Fitzgerald Bks.
Basoff, Kathleen. Merdove Cove. 2008. 28p. pap. 14.95 (978-1-4389-2095-5(4)) AuthorHouse.
Beasley, Cassie. Circus Mirandus. 2016. (SPA.). 25.99 (978-84-246-5686-7(5)) La Galera, S.A. Editorial ESP. Dist: Lectorum Pubns., Inc.
—Circus Mirandus. (ENG., Illus.). 304p. (J). (gr. 4-7). 2016. pap. 8.99 (978-0-14-751554-4(8), Puffin Books) 2015. 17.99 (978-0-525-42843-5(7), Dial Bks) Penguin Young Readers Group.
—Circus Mirandus. 2016. (ENG.). 304p. (J). (gr. 3-7). 19.65 (978-0-606-39311-9(0)) Turtleback Bks.
Beaufrand, M. J. The Rise & Fall of the Gallivanters. 2015. (ENG., Illus.). 288p. (YA). (gr. 9-17). 16.95 (978-1-4197-1495-5(3), Amulet Bks.) Abrams, Inc.
Becker, Bonny. The Sniffles for Bear. Denton, Kady MacDonald, illus. 2011. (Bear & Mouse Ser.). (ENG.). 32p. (J). (gr. -1-2). 16.99 (978-0-7636-4756-8(X)) Candlewick Pr.
Beilenson, Evelyn. The Zoo Is Closed Today! Kennedy, Anne, illus. 2014. (ENG.). 32p. (J). 16.99 (978-1-4413-1526-7(8), 9781441315267) Peter Pauper Pr. Inc.
Bemelmans, Ludwig. Madeline: Edicion en Espanol. Anasal, Arshes, ed. 2005. (SPA., Illus.). 44p. (J). (gr. k-4). reprint ed. 16.00 (978-0-7567-8842-1(0)) DIANE Publishing Co.
—Madeline 75th Anniversary Edition. 2014. (Madeline Ser.). (ENG.). 56p. (J). (gr. -1-2). 25.00 (978-0-670-78540-7(7), Viking Books for Young Readers) Penguin Young Readers Group.
Berry, Eileen M. Looking for Home. Manning, Maurie J., illus. 2006. 75p. (J). (gr. -1-3). per. (978-1-59166-493-2(4)) BJU Pr.
Blake, Kendare. Antigoddess. (Goddess War Ser.: 1). (ENG.). (YA). (gr. 7-12). 2014. 352p. pap. 9.99 (978-0-7653-3446-6(1), 9780765334466) 2013. 336p. 17.99 (978-0-7653-3443-5(7), 9780765334435) Doherty, Tom Assocs., LLC. (Tor Teen).
—Mortal Gods. 2014. (Goddess War Ser.: 2). (ENG.). 352p. (YA). (gr. 7-12). 17.99 (978-0-7653-3444-2(5), 9780765334442, Tor Teen) Doherty, Tom Assocs., LLC.
Bostic, Megan. Never Eighteen. 2012. (ENG.). 208p. (YA). (gr. 7). pap. 8.99 (978-0-547-55076-3(6)) Houghton Mifflin Harcourt Publishing Co.
Bowen, Cynthia Wiesner. Tamika & Grandpa Jake. 2007. 32p. per. 14.95 (978-1-4327-0642-5(X)) Outskirts Pr., Inc.
Bowles, Coy. When You're Feeling Sick. Elkerton, Andy, illus. 2017. (ENG.). 32p. (J). (gr. -1-2). 12.99 (978-0-399-55286-1(3), Doubleday Bks. for Young Readers) Random Hse. Children's Bks.
Branford, Anna. Violet Mackerel's Remarkable Recovery. Allen, Elanna, illus. 2013. (Violet Mackerel Ser.). (ENG.). 128p. (J). (gr. 1-5). 15.99 (978-1-4424-3588-9(7)); pap. 5.99 (978-1-4424-3589-6(5)) Simon & Schuster Children's Publishing. (Atheneum Bks. for Young Readers).
Brooks, Martha. Queen of Hearts. 2011. (ENG.). 224p. (YA). (gr. 7-12). 17.99 (978-0-374-34229-6(6), 9780374342296, Farrar, Straus & Giroux (BYR)) Farrar, Straus & Giroux.
Carlson, Nancy. Sometimes You Barf. Carlson, Nancy, illus. 2014. (ENG., Illus.). 32p. (J). (gr. k-2). 16.95 (978-1-4677-1412-9(7), Carolrhoda Bks.) Lerner Publishing Group.
Carter, Candace. Sid's Surprise. Kim, Joung Un, illus. 2005. (Green Light Readers Level 1 Ser.). (gr. -1-3). 13.95 (978-0-7569-5242-6(5)) Perfection Learning Corp.
Castro, Anita. Two Hands to Hold. Wroth, Dean, illus. 2013. 32p. (J). pap. 10.49 (978-0-944727-57-7(3)); lib. bdg. 16.95 (978-0-944727-58-4(1)) Jason & Nordic Pubs. (Turtle Bks.).
Castrovilla, Selene. The Girl Next Door. 2010. 240p. (YA). (gr. 9-12). 16.95 (978-1-934813-15-7(X)) Westside Bks.
Cazet, Denys. Grandpa Spanielson's Chicken Pox Stories No. 1: The Octopus. Cazet, Denys, illus. 2005. (I Can Read Bks.). (Illus.). 48p. (J). (gr. -1-3). lib. bdg. 16.89 (978-0-06-051089-3(7)) HarperCollins Pubs.
—The Octopus. Cazet, Denys, illus. 2008. (Grandpa Spanielson's Chicken Pox Stories Ser.). (Illus.). (J). (gr. -1-3). pap. 16.95 incl. audio (978-1-4301-0455-1(4));Set. pap. 29.95 incl. audio (978-1-4301-0457-5(0));Set. pap. 31.95 incl. audio compact disk (978-1-4301-0460-5(0)) Live Oak Media.
Cheng, Andrea. Brushing Mom's Hair. Wong, Nicole, illus. 2009. (ENG.). 64p. (J). (gr. 5-8). 17.95 (978-1-59078-599-7(1), Front Street) Boyds Mills Pr.

S

Christopher, Lucy. Flyaway. 2011. (ENG.). 336p. (J). (gr. 5-9). 16.99 *(978-0-545-31771-9(1)*, Chicken Hse., The) Scholastic, Inc.

Christopher, Matt. Slam Dunk. 2004. (ENG., Illus.). 128p. (J). (gr. 3-7). pap. 5.99 *(978-0-316-60762-9(2))* Little, Brown Bks. for Young Readers.

Cowan, Charlotte. Sadie's Sore Throat. Bratun, Katy, illus. 2007. (Dr. Hippo Ser.). (ENG.). 32p. (J). (gr. 3-7). 17.95 *(978-0-9753516-4-2(8))* Hippocratic Pr., The.

Crutcher, Chris. Deadline. 2009. (ENG.). 336p. (YA). (gr. 9). pap. 9.99 *(978-0-06-085091-3(4)*, Greenwillow Bks.) HarperCollins Pubs.

Damico, Gina. Hellhole. (ENG.). (YA). (gr. 9). 2016. 384p. pap. 9.99 *(978-0-544-54117-7(0))* 2015. 368p. 17.99 *(978-0-544-30710-0(0))* Houghton Mifflin Harcourt Publishing Co. (HMH Books For Young Readers).

Dave & Matt. Yuck's Fart Club. Baines, Nigel, illus. 2013. (Yuck Ser.). (ENG.). 112p. (J). (gr. 2-5). pap. 6.99 *(978-1-4424-8152-7(8)*, Simon & Schuster/Paula Wiseman Bks.) Simon & Schuster/Paula Wiseman Bks.

Davies, Katie. The Great Rabbit Rescue. Shaw, Hannah, illus. 2011. (Great Critter Capers Ser.). (ENG.). 224p. (J). (gr. 3-7). 12.99 *(978-1-4424-2064-9(2)*, Beach Lane Bks.) Beach Lane Bks.

Day, Alexandra. Carl & the Sick Puppy. 2012. (My Readers Ser.). (ENG., Illus.). 32p. (J). (gr. -1-1). 15.99 *(978-1-250-00152-8(8)*, 9781250001528); pap. 4.99 *(978-1-250-00153-5(6)*, 9781250001535) Square Fish.

—Carl & the Sick Puppy. 2012. (My Readers: Level 1 Ser.). (J). lib. bdg. 13.55 *(978-0-606-26121-0(4)*, Turtleback) Turtleback Bks.

De Kockere, Geert & Dom, An. Dragon Fire. Van Hemeldonck, Tineke, illus. 2015. (ENG.). 32p. (J). (gr. -1-k). 16.99 *(978-1-63220-599-5(8)*, Sky Pony Pr.) Skyhorse Publishing Co., Inc.

Dealey, Erin. Goldie Locks Has Chicken Pox. 2004. (Illus.). (J). (gr. k-3). spiral bd. *(978-0-616-14573-9(X))*; spiral bd. *(978-0-616-14572-2(1))* Canadian National Institute for the Blind/Institut National Canadien pour les Aveugles.

—Goldie Locks Has Chicken Pox. Wakiyama, Hanako, illus. 2005. (ENG.). 40p. (J). (gr. -1-2). reprint ed. 8.99 *(978-0-689-87610-3(6)*, Aladdin) Simon & Schuster Children's Publishing.

Dewdney, Anna. Llama Llama Home with Mama. 2011. (Llama Llama Ser.). (ENG.). 32p. (J). (gr. -1-k). 17.99 *(978-0-670-01232-9(7)*, Viking Books for Young Readers) Penguin Young Readers Group.

DiTerlizzi, Tony & DiTerlizzi, Angela. Uh-Oh Sick! DiTerlizzi, Tony, illus. 2010. (Adventure of Meno Ser.: 4). (ENG., Illus.). 52p. (J). (gr. -1-k). 9.99 *(978-1-4169-7153-5(X)*, Simon & Schuster Bks. For Young Readers) Simon & Schuster Bks. For Young Readers.

Duffy, Carol Ann. The Princess's Blankets. Hyde, Catherine Ryan, illus. 2009. (ENG.). 40p. (J). (gr. k-3). 18.99 *(978-0-7636-4547-2(8)*, Templar) Candlewick Pr.

Ehrenhaft, Daniel. 10 Things to Do Before I Die. 2006. (ENG.). 224p. (YA). (gr. 7). per. 7.95 *(978-0-385-73406-6(9)*, Delacorte Bks. for Young Readers) Random Hse. Children's Bks.

Ehrlich, Esther. Nest. 2014. (ENG.). 336p. (J). (gr. 5-7). 16.99 *(978-0-385-38607-4(9)*, Lamb, Wendy Bks.) Random Hse. Children's Bks.

Estes, Don. Willy & Friends traveling through the Seasons: The continuing story of Willy the little fire Jeep. Glass, Eric, illus. 2006. (J). *(978-1-883551-75-9(7)*, Maple Corners Press) Attic Studio Publishing Hse.

Fairy-Tale Flowers: Individual Title, 6 pack. (Story Steps Ser.). (gr. k-2). 23.00 *(978-0-7635-9842-6(9))* Rigby Education.

Farber, Erica. Richard Scarry's Readers (Level 2): One, Two, AH-CHOO! Scarry, Huck, illus. 2014. (Richard Scarry's Great Big Schoolhouse Ser.). (ENG.). 24p. (J). (gr. k-1). 12.95 *(978-1-4549-0380-2(5))* Sterling Publishing Co., Inc.

Fenn, G. Manville. Brownsmith's Boy. 2008. 260p. pap. 15.95 *(978-1-60664-154-5(9))* Aegypan.

Fleming, Denise. Buster Goes to Cowboy Camp. Fleming, Denise, illus. 2008. (ENG., Illus.). 40p. (J). (gr. -1-2). 16.95 *(978-0-8050-7892-3(4)*, 9780805078923, Holt, Henry & Co. Bks. For Young Readers) Holt, Henry & Co.

Fontes, Justine. Jordan's Silly Sick Day. Lee, Jared, tr. Lee, Jared, illus. 2004. (Rookie Readers Ser.). 31p. (J). 19.50 *(978-0-516-25897-3(4)*, Children's Pr.) Scholastic Library Publishing.

Friedman, Laurie. Happy New Year, Mallory! Kalis, Jennifer, illus. (Mallory Ser.: 12). (ENG.). 176p. (J). (gr. 2-5). 2010. pap. 5.95 *(978-0-7613-3947-2(7))* 2009. 15.95 *(978-0-8225-8883-2(8))* Lerner Publishing Group. (Carolrhoda Bks.).

—Happy New Year, Mallory! 12th rev. ed. 2010. pap. 33.92 *(978-0-7613-6996-7(1))* Lerner Publishing Group.

Goldblatt, Mark. Finding the Worm. 2015. (ENG.). 352p. (J). (gr. 4-7). 16.99 *(978-0-385-39108-5(0)*, Random Hse. Bks. for Young Readers) Random Hse. Children's Bks.

—Finding the Worm (Twerp Sequel) 2016. (ENG.). 368p. (J). (gr. 4-7). 7.99 *(978-0-385-39111-5(0)*, Yearling) Random Hse. Children's Bks.

Grant, Michael. Plague. (Gone Ser.: 4). (ENG.). (YA). (gr. 8). 2014. 528p. pap. 9.99 *(978-0-06-144914-7(8))* 2011. 512p. 17.99 *(978-0-06-144912-3(1))* HarperCollins Pubs. (Tegen, Katherine Bks).

Gray, Kes. Daisy & the Trouble with Life. Sharratt, Nick & Parsons, Garry, illus. 2007. (Daisy Ser.: 12). (ENG.). 240p. (J). (gr. 2-4). pap. 11.95 *(978-1-86230-167-2(0)*, Red Fox) Random House Children's Books GBR. Dist: Independent Pubs. Group.

Gray, Libba Moore. Miss Tizzy. Rowland, Jada, illus. 2014. 40p. pap. 8.00 *(978-1-61003-356-5(6))* Center for the Collaborative Classroom.

Greenfield, Eloise. William & the Good Old Days. Date not set. (Illus.). 32p. (J). (gr. k-3). pap. 4.99 *(978-0-06-443453-9(2))* HarperCollins Pubs.

Gregory, Dee. The Accidental Daughter: A Children's Story about Hope. 2008. 96p. pap. 10.49 *(978-1-4389-3338-2(X))* AuthorHouse.

Greves, Julie, et al. Upside down & Backwards: A Sibling's Journey Through Childhood Cancer. 2014. (Illus.). 112p. (J). *(978-1-4338-1637-6(7)*, Magination Pr.) American Psychological Assn.

Guest, Elissa Haden. Iris & Walter - The School Play. Davenier, Christine, illus. 2006. (Iris & Walter Ser.). 44p. (gr. 1-4). 15.95 *(978-0-7569-6679-9(5))* Perfection Learning Corp.

Hannigan, Katherine. Ida B: ... And Her Plans to Maximize Fun, Avoid Disaster, & (Possibly) Save the World. 2004. 256p. (gr. 4-18). lib. bdg. 16.89 *(978-0-06-073025-3(0))*; (ENG.). (J). 17.99 *(978-0-06-073024-6(2)*, Greenwillow Bks.) HarperCollins Pubs.

—Ida B: And Her Plans to Maximize Fun Avoid Disaster, & (Possibly) Save the World. 2011. (ENG.). 272p. (J). (gr. 5-9). reprint ed. pap. 6.99 *(978-0-06-073026-0(9)*, Greenwillow Bks.) HarperCollins Pubs.

Harazin, S. A. Painless. 2015. (ENG.). 304p. (YA). (gr. 8-12). 16.99 *(978-0-8075-6288-8(2))* Whitman, Albert & Co.

Harrison, Christy Gremore. Once upon A Monday. 2010. 40p. pap. 16.99 *(978-1-4490-5854-8(X))* AuthorHouse.

Haydu, Corey Ann. Rules for Stealing Stars. 2015. (ENG.). 336p. (J). (gr. 3-7). 16.99 *(978-0-06-235271-2(7)*, Tegen, Katherine Bks) HarperCollins Pubs.

Hayles, Marsha. Breathing Room. 2013. (ENG., Illus.). 272p. (J). (gr. 5-9). pap. 9.99 *(978-1-250-03411-3(6)*, 9781250034113) Square Fish.

Headley, Maria Dahvana. Magonia. (Magonia Ser.: 1). (YA). (gr. 8). 2016. 336p. pap. 9.99 *(978-0-06-232053-7(X))* 2015. (ENG.). 320p. 17.99 *(978-0-06-232052-0(1)*, HarperTeen) HarperCollins Pubs.

Hershenhorn, Esther. Chicken Soup by Heart. Litzinger, Rosanne, illus. 2010. (ENG.). 40p. (J). (gr. -1-3). 16.99 *(978-1-4424-2197-4(5)*, Simon & Schuster Bks. For Young Readers) Simon & Schuster Bks. For Young Readers.

Hest, Amy. Don't You Feel Well, Sam? Jeram, Anita, illus. 2007. (Sam Bks.). (ENG.). 32p. (J). (gr. -1-k). 4.99 *(978-0-7636-2408-8(X))* Candlewick Pr.

—Guess Who, Baby Duck! Barton, Jill, illus. 2004. (ENG.). 32p. (J). (gr. k-k). 15.99 *(978-0-7636-1981-7(7))* Candlewick Pr.

Hoffmeister, Peter Brown. This Is the Part Where You Laugh. 2016. (ENG.). 336p. (YA). (gr. 9). 17.99 *(978-0-553-53810-6(1)*, Knopf Bks. for Young Readers) Random Hse. Children's Bks.

Holm, Jennifer L. & Holm, Matthew. Deadly Disease of Doom. Holm, Jennifer L. & Holm, Matthew, illus. 2015. (Squish Ser.). (ENG., Illus.). 96p. (J). (gr. 2-5). lib. bdg. 12.99 *(978-0-307-98306-0(4)*, Random Hse. Bks. for Young Readers) Random Hse. Children's Bks.

Hulst, W. G. van de & Hulst, Willem G. van de, illus. The Black Kitten. 2014. (J). *(978-1-928136-07-1(9))* Inheritance Pubns.

—Bruno the Bear. 2014. (J). *(978-1-928136-03-3(6))* Inheritance Pubns.

—The Secret in the Box. 2014. (J). *(978-1-928136-17-0(6))* Inheritance Pubns.

Hurley, Tonya. Homecoming. 2010. (Ghostgirl Ser.: 2). (ENG.). 304p. (YA). (gr. 7-17). pap. 10.00 *(978-0-316-08943-2(5))* Little, Brown Bks. for Young Readers.

Ibarrola, Begonia. Chusco the Stray Dog. Herranz, Yésica, ed. Souto, Jose, illus. 2013. (ENG.). 40p. (J). (gr. k-2). 13.95 *(978-84-95923-99-8(8))* Primera Persona ESP. Dist: Independent Pubs. Group.

Jensen, Patricia. I Am Sick. Hantel, Johanna, illus. (My First Reader Ser.). (ENG.). 32p. (J). (gr. k-1). 2006. per. 3.95 *(978-0-516-24970-4(3))* 2005. lib. bdg. 18.50 *(978-0-516-24878-3(2))* Scholastic Library Publishing. (Children's Pr.).

Jones, Frewin. The Enchanted Quest. 2010. (Faerie Path Ser.: 5). (ENG.). 368p. (YA). (gr. 8-18). 16.99 *(978-0-06-087158-1(X)*, HarperTeen) HarperCollins Pubs.

—The Faerie Path Bk. 4: The Immortal Realm. 2010. (Faerie Path Ser.: 4). (ENG.). 368p. (YA). (gr. 8). pap. 9.99 *(978-0-06-087157-4(1)*, HarperTeen) HarperCollins Pubs.

K/H (Pathways). Kindergarten Stepping Stones: Kindergarten the Bravest Dog Ever - The True Story of Balto Trade Book. rev. ed. 2010. (ENG.). 48p. pap. 9.00 *(978-0-7575-8646-0(5))* Kendall Hunt Publishing Co.

Kang, A. N. Papillon, Book 2 Papillon Goes to the Vet. Kang, A. N., illus. 2017. (Papillon Ser.). (ENG., Illus.). 40p. (J). (gr. -1-k). 16.99 ***(978-1-4847-2881-9(5))*** Hyperion Bks. for Children.

Kann, Victoria. Pinkalicious & the Sick Day. Kann, Victoria, illus. 2015. (I Can Read Level 1 Ser.). (ENG., Illus.). 32p. (J). (gr. -1-3). 16.99 *(978-0-06-224599-1(6))* HarperCollins Pubs.

—The Princess of Pink Slumber Party. Kann, Victoria, illus. 2012. (I Can Read Level 1 Ser.). (ENG., Illus.). 32p. (J). (gr. -1-3). 16.99 *(978-0-06-198963-6(0))* HarperCollins Pubs.

Kantor, Melissa. Maybe One Day. 2014. (ENG.). 400p. (YA). (gr. 8). 17.99 *(978-0-06-227920-0(3)*, HarperTeen) HarperCollins Pubs.

Keeling, Annie E. Andrew Golding A Tale of the Great Plague. 2004. reprint ed. pap. 15.95 *(978-1-4191-0694-1(5))*; pap. 1.99 *(978-1-4192-0694-8(X))* Kessinger Publishing, LLC.

Kellogg, Elijah. The Young Shipbuilders of Elm Island by Rev Elijah Kellogg. 2006. 316p. per. 23.99 *(978-1-4255-3063-1(X))* Michigan Publishing.

Ketteman, Helen. If Beaver Had a Fever, 0 vols. O'Malley, Kevin, illus. 2011. (ENG.). 32p. (J). (gr. -1-3). 16.99 *(978-0-7614-5951-4(0)*, 9780761459514, Amazon Children's Publishing) Amazon Publishing.

Kizer, Amber. Pieces of Me. 2014. (ENG.). 304p. (YA). (gr. 7). 16.99 *(978-0-385-74116-3(2)*, Delacorte Pr.) Random Hse. Children's Bks.

Knights, Harry B. Angel's Star. 2006. (J). lib. bdg. 20.00 *(978-0-9632248-6-0(3))* Synergetic Pubns., Inc.

Koertge, Ronald. Shakespeare Bats Cleanup. 2006. 116p. (gr. 7-12). 16.00 *(978-0-7569-6571-6(3))* Perfection Learning Corp.

Krall, Dan. Sick Simon. Krall, Dan, illus. 2015. (ENG., Illus.). 48p. (J). (gr. -1-3). 17.99 *(978-1-4424-9097-0(7)*, Simon & Schuster Bks. For Young Readers) Simon & Schuster Bks. For Young Readers.

Kraus, Robert. Daddy Long Ears' Halloween. 2014. (ENG., Illus.). 32p. (J). (gr. -1-3). 13.99 *(978-1-4814-3108-8(0)*, Simon & Schuster/Paula Wiseman Bks.) Simon & Schuster/Paula Wiseman Bks.

Krulik, Nancy & dePaola, Tomie. 'Snot Funny! Blecha, Aaron, illus. 2015. (George Brown, Class Clown Ser.: 14). (ENG.). 128p. (J). (gr. 2-4). bds. 4.99 *(978-0-448-48282-8(7)*, Grosset & Dunlap) Penguin Young Readers Group.

Lancett, Peter. Dark Candle. 2007. (Dark Man Ser.). (ENG.). 36p. pap. *(978-1-84167-603-6(9))* Ransom Publishing Ltd.

Lee, Jenny. Elvis & the Underdogs. Light, Kelly, illus. 2013. (Elvis & the Underdogs Ser.: 1). (ENG.). 304p. (J). (gr. 3-7). 16.99 *(978-0-06-223554-1(0))* HarperCollins Pubs.

—Elvis & the Underdogs: Secrets, Secret Service, & Room Service. Light, Kelly, illus. 2014. (Elvis & the Underdogs Ser.: 2). (ENG.). 352p. (J). (gr. 3-7). 16.99 *(978-0-06-223556-5(7))* HarperCollins Pubs.

Lettrick, Robert. The Murk. Disney Storybook Art Team, illus. 2015. (ENG.). 320p. (J). (gr. 5-9). 16.99 *(978-1-4231-8695-3(8))* Hyperion Bks. for Children.

Lotto, Lisa Marie. Oh How We Feel When We Are Sick with the Flu: Oh the Things We See When We Go to the Park. 2008. 28p. pap. 13.99 *(978-1-4343-6009-0(1))* AuthorHouse.

Louie, Therese On & Wang, Suling. Raymond's Perfect Present, 1 vol. 2015. (ENG.). 32p. (J). pap. 9.95 *(978-1-62014-229-5(5))* Lee & Low Bks., Inc.

Lubar, David. Dunk. 2004. (ENG.). 272p. (YA). (gr. 7-18). reprint ed. pap. 7.99 *(978-0-618-43909-6(9))* Houghton Mifflin Harcourt Publishing Co.

Lyons, C. J. Broken. 2014. (ENG.). 320p. (YA). (gr. 7-12). pap. 9.99 *(978-1-4022-9230-9(9))* Sourcebooks, Inc.

Maier, Inger M. Ben's Flying Flowers. Bogade, Maria, illus. 2012. (J). 14.95 *(978-1-4338-1133-3(2))*; pap. 9.95 *(978-1-4338-1132-6(4))* American Psychological Assn. (Magination Pr.).

Manushkin, Fran. Katie Woo Has the Flu, 1 vol. Lyon, Tammie, illus. 2011. (Katie Woo Ser.). (ENG.). 32p. (gr. k-2). pap. 5.95 *(978-1-4048-6854-0(2))*; lib. bdg. 21.32 *(978-1-4048-6518-1(7))* Picture Window Bks.

Matas, Carol. Tales of a Reluctant Psychic: The Freak, Visions, & Far. 2009. (ENG.). 424p. (YA). (gr. 7-18). pap. *(978-1-55470-203-9(8))* Me to We.

Maurer, Shari. Change of Heart. 2010. 290p. (YA). 16.95 *(978-1-934813-36-2(2))* Westside Bks.

Mayer, Mercer. Just a Little Sick. Mayer, Mercer, illus. 2009. (My First I Can Read Ser.). (ENG., Illus.). 32p. (J). (gr. -1-3). 16.99 *(978-0-06-083556-9(7))*; pap. 3.99 *(978-0-06-083555-2(9))* HarperCollins Pubs.

McDonald, Megan. The Doctor Is In! Reynolds, Peter H., illus. 2010. (Judy Moody Ser.: 5). (ENG.). 176p. (J). (gr. 1-4). 15.99 *(978-0-7636-4862-6(0))*; pap. 5.99 *(978-0-7636-4861-9(2))* Candlewick Pr.

—The Doctor Is In! 2010. (Judy Moody Ser.: 5). lib. bdg. 16.00 *(978-0-606-12343-3(1)*, Turtleback) Turtleback Bks.

McGovern, Kate. Rules for 50/50 Chances: If You could Find Out How it All Ends, Would You? 2015. (ENG.). 352p. (YA). (gr. 7). 17.99 *(978-0-374-30158-3(1)*, 9780374301583, Farrar, Straus & Giroux (BYR)) Farrar, Straus & Giroux.

McKissack, Patricia C. & Moss, Onawumi Jean. Precious & the Boo Hag. Brooker, Kyrsten, illus. 2005. (ENG.). 40p. (J). (gr. -1-3). 17.99 *(978-0-689-85194-0(4)*, Atheneum Bks. for Young Readers) Simon & Schuster Children's Publishing.

McPhail, David. Rick Is Sick. 2004. (Green Light Readers Level 1 Ser.). (ENG., Illus.). 24p. (J). (gr. -1-3). pap. 3.95 *(978-0-15-205092-4(2))* Houghton Mifflin Harcourt Publishing Co.

—Rick Is Sick. 2004. (Green Light Readers — Level 1 Ser.). 13.50 *(978-0-613-97286-4(4)*, Turtleback) Turtleback Bks.

—Sick Day. (I Like to Read(r) Ser.). (ENG.). 24p. (J). (gr. -1-3). 2013. pap. 6.99 *(978-0-8234-2910-3(5))* 2012. 14.95 *(978-0-8234-2424-5(3))* Holiday Hse., Inc.

Miller, Jennifer. Run, Rasputin, Run! Trials & Friendships (Book 2) 2006. (ENG., Illus.). 172p. per. 14.85 *(978-1-4120-8494-9(6))* Trafford Publishing.

Mills, Joyce C. Little Tree: A Story for Children with Serious Medical Illness. Sebern, Brian, illus. 2nd ed. 2003. 32p. (J). pap. 9.95 *(978-1-59147-042-7(0))*; 14.95 *(978-1-59147-041-0(2))* American Psychological Assn. (Magination Pr.).

Moncure, Jane Belk. Nanny Goat's Boat: A Book of Rhyming. Girouard, Patrick, illus. 2013. (Magic Castle Readers Ser.). (ENG.). 32p. (J). (gr. -1-2). 25.64 *(978-1-62323-567-3(7)*, 206301) Child's World, Inc., The.

Moore, Helen H. The Secret of Willow Ridge: Gabe's Dad Finds Recovery. Blackford, John, illus. 2010. (ENG.). 128p. (J). (gr. 3-7). pap. 12.95 *(978-0-9818482-0-4(6))* Central Recovery Pr.

Morgan, Matthew, et al. Yuck's Fart Club. Baines, Nigel, illus. 2013. (Yuck Ser.). (ENG.). 112p. (J). (gr. 2-5). 15.99 *(978-1-4424-8153-4(6)*, Simon & Schuster/Paula Wiseman Bks.) Simon & Schuster/Paula Wiseman Bks.

Moses, Shelia P. The Legend of Buddy Bush. 2004. (ENG., Illus.). 224p. (YA). (gr. 7). 19.99 *(978-0-689-85839-0(6)*, McElderry, Margaret K. Bks.) McElderry, Margaret K. Bks.

—The Legend of Buddy Bush. 2005. (Illus.). 211p. (gr. 7-12). 17.00 *(978-0-7569-5459-8(2))* Perfection Learning Corp.

—The Legend of Buddy Bush, 3 vols. unabr. ed. 2005. (YA). (gr. 3-7). 54.75 *(978-1-4193-3575-4(8)*, 42043) Recorded Bks., Inc.

Moss, John. The Girl in a Coma. 2016. (ENG.). 312p. (YA). pap. 10.95 *(978-1-929345-24-3(0))* Poisoned Pen Pr.

Murphy, Jill. Mr. Large in Charge. Murphy, Jill, illus. 2007. (ENG., Illus.). 40p. (J). (gr. -1-3). 16.99 *(978-0-7636-3504-6(9))* Candlewick Pr.

Murphy, Sally. Toppling. James, Rhian Nest, illus. 2012. (ENG.). 128p. (J). (gr. 3-7). 15.99 *(978-0-7636-5921-9(5))* Candlewick Pr.

Nelid, Piper. Sick Visit, 01 vols., 1. 2016. (Rosen REAL Readers: STEM & STEAM Collection). (ENG.). 12p. (J). pap. 6.33 *(978-1-5081-1587-8(7)*, Rosen Classroom) Rosen Publishing Group, Inc., The.

Nolan, Han. When We Were Saints. 2005. (ENG.). 312p. (YA). (gr. 7-12). pap. 15.95 *(978-0-15-205322-2(0))* Houghton Mifflin Harcourt Publishing Co.

Park, Barbara. Shipwrecked, No. 23. Brunkus, Denise, illus. 2005. (Junie B. Jones Ser.: No. 6). (ENG.). 96p. (J). (gr. 1-4). mass mkt. 4.99 *(978-0-375-82805-8(2)*, Random Hse. Bks. for Young Readers) Random Hse. Children's Bks.

Parr, Susan Sherwood. Christopher's Adventures: Chris Visits the Hospital, Vol. 2. Paraschiv, Doina, illus. 2nd alt. ed. 2013. (ENG.). 24p. (J). pap. 8.95 *(978-0-9827998-8-8(8)*, KID-E Bks.) Word Prodns.

Parriera Jr., Jack. What to Do When Your Brother Is Sick. 2012. 34p. pap. 17.97 *(978-1-105-47064-6(4))* Lulu Pr., Inc.

Perrin, Randy, et al. Time Like a River. 2004. 144p. (gr. 5-18). 14.95 *(978-1-57143-061-8(X))* RDR Bks.

Porpora, Donnamarie. Grampa's Wings. 2013. 32p. pap. *(978-1-4602-1366-7(1))* FriesenPress.

Powers, J. L. This Thing Called the Future. 2011. (FRS & ENG.). 208p. (J). (gr. 7-11). 16.95 *(978-1-933693-95-8(9))* Cinco Puntos Pr.

Rakusin, Sudie. Dear Calla Roo... Love, Savannah Blue No. 2: A Letter about Getting Sick & Feeling Better. Rakusin, Sudie, illus. 2003. (Illus.). 32p. (J). (gr. -1-4). 16.95 *(978-0-9664805-3-5(8))* Winged Willow Pr.

Rapp, Adam. 33 Snowfish. Ering, Timothy Basil, illus. 2006. (ENG.). 192p. (YA). (gr. 9-12). per. 7.99 *(978-0-7636-2917-5(0))* Candlewick Pr.

Ray, Jane. The Dollhouse Fairy. Ray, Jane, illus. 2010. (ENG., Illus.). 32p. (J). (gr. -1-2). 16.99 *(978-0-7636-4411-6(0))* Candlewick Pr.

Reuterstrand, Siri. Ellis Goes to the Doctor. Wik, Jenny, illus. 2012. (ENG.). 24p. (J). (gr. -1-k). 12.95 *(978-1-61608-662-6(9)*, 608662, Sky Pony Pr.) Skyhorse Publishing Co., Inc.

Riggs, Sandy. Nick Is Sick. Koeller, Carol, illus. 2006. (Reader's Clubhouse Level 1 Reader Ser.). (ENG.). 24p. (J). (gr. 1-4). pap. 3.99 *(978-0-7641-3284-1(9))* Barron's Educational Series, Inc.

Ritchie, Janet. Remember That I Love You. 2008. (ENG.). 40p. 18.99 *(978-1-4389-3155-5(7))* AuthorHouse.

Rockliff, Mara. Chik Chak Shabbat. Brooker, Kyrsten, illus. 2016. (ENG.). 32p. (J). (gr. -1-2). 7.99 *(978-0-7636-8895-0(9))* Candlewick Pr.

Rose, Naomi C. Tashi & the Tibetan Flower Cure. 2016. (ENG.). 40p. (J). (gr. 1-6). pap. 10.95 ***(978-1-62014-318-6(6))*** Lee & Low Bks., Inc.

Rosenberry, Vera. When Vera Was Sick, 4 bks., Set. Rosenberry, Vera, illus. unabr. ed. 2006. (Picture Book Readalong Ser.). (Illus.). (J). (gr. -1-3). pap. 37.95 incl. audio *(978-1-59519-652-1(8))*; pap. 39.95 incl. audio compact disk *(978-1-59519-653-8(6))* Live Oak Media.

Ross, Tony. I Feel Sick! Ross, Tony, illus. 2015. (ENG., Illus.). 32p. (J). (gr. -1-3). 16.99 *(978-1-4677-5797-3(7))* Andersen Pr. GBR. Dist: Lerner Publishing Group.

Ross, Tony, illus. I Feel Sick! 2015. (J). *(978-1-4677-5798-0(5))* Andersen Pr.

Rouss, Sylvia. Sammy Spider's First Mitzvah. Janus Kahn, Katherine, illus. 2014. (ENG.). 24p. (J). (gr. -1-3). 17.95 *(978-1-4677-1947-6(1)*, Kar-Ben Publishing) Lerner Publishing Group.

Rowley, Deborah. The Miracle of the Wooden Shoes. 2008. 32p. (J). 18.95 *(978-1-59038-990-4(5))* Deseret Bk. Co.

Rylant, Cynthia. Henry & Mudge Get the Cold Shivers. Stevenson, Suçie, illus. (Henry & Mudge Ser.). 9.95 *(978-1-59112-290-6(2))* Live Oak Media.

—Mr. Putter & Tabby Catch the Cold. Howard, Arthur, illus. 2007. (Mr. Putter & Tabby Ser.). pap. 7.93 *(978-1-4189-5220-4(6))* Houghton Mifflin Harcourt Trade & Reference Pubs.

—Mr. Putter & Tabby Catch the Cold. Howard, Arthur, illus. 2003. (Mr. Putter & Tabby Ser.). (gr. 1-4). 16.00 *(978-0-7569-1514-8(7))* Perfection Learning Corp.

Salomon, Bob & Young, Rick. Beyond the Laces. 2015. (ENG., Illus.). (J). pap. 12.95 *(978-1-4951-5694-6(X))* Independent Pub.

Sanschagrin, Joceline. Caillou at the Doctor. Brignaud, Pierre, illus. 3rd ed. 2013. (Step by Step Ser.). (ENG.). 24p. (J). (gr. -1-k). bds. 5.99 *(978-2-89718-058-4(7))* Caillouet, Gerry.

Schmidt, Tiffany. Break Me Like a Promise: Once upon a Crime Family. 2016. (ENG.). 416p. (YA). 17.99 *(978-0-8027-3783-0(8)*, 9780802737830, Bloomsbury USA Childrens) Bloomsbury Publishing USA.

—Hold Me Like a Breath. 2016. (ENG.). 416p. (YA). pap. 9.99 *(978-1-61963-870-9(3)*, 9781619638709, Bloomsbury USA Childrens) Bloomsbury Publishing USA.

Scholastic, Inc. Staff & Bermiss, Aamir Lee. I Hate to Be Sick! Wilson-Max, Ken, illus. 2004. (Just for You Ser.). (ENG.). 32p. (gr. k-3). pap. 3.99 *(978-0-439-56877-7(3)*, Teaching Resources) Scholastic, Inc.

Schubert, Ingrid & Schubert, Dieter. Ophelia. 2009. (ENG.). 32p. (J). (gr. -1-1). 16.95 *(978-1-59078-659-8(9)*, 9781590786598) Lemniscaat USA.

Scott, Laurian. Thisbe's Promise. Sharp, Kelley, illus. 2008. (ENG.). 32p. (J). 16.99 *(978-0-9816642-0-0(2))* ETS Publishing.

Seamon, Hollis. Somebody up There Hates You: A Novel. 2014. (ENG.). 272p. (YA). (gr. 9-12). pap. 9.95 *(978-1-61620-454-9(0)*, 73454) Algonquin Bks. of Chapel Hill.

Shells, B. Malone. Henry Has a Head Cold. 2010. 32p. 17.00 *(978-1-4389-5326-7(7))* AuthorHouse.

Shepherd, Megan. The Secret Horses of Briar Hill. 2016. (ENG., Illus.). 240p. (J). (gr. 5). 16.99 *(978-1-101-93975-8(3)*, Delacorte Bks. for Young Readers) Random Hse. Children's Bks.

Simhaee, Rebeka. Avi's Choice: A Story about Bikur Cholim-Visiting the Sick. Hechter, Janice, illus. 2014. 35p. (J). *(978-0-8266-0043-1(3))* Merkos L'Inyonei Chinuch.

Slate, Joseph. Miss Bindergarten Stays Home from Kindergarten. Wolff, Ashley, illus. 2004. (ENG.). 48p. (J). (gr. -1-k). reprint ed. pap. 6.99 *(978-0-14-230127-2(2)*, Puffin Books) Penguin Young Readers Group.

Sliwerski, Jessica Reid. Cancer Hates Kisses. Song, Mika, illus. 2017. (ENG.). 40p. (J). (-k). 17.99 ***(978-0-7352-2781-1(0)***, Dial Bks) Penguin Young Readers Group.

Sommers, Jackie Lea. Truest. 2015. (ENG.). 384p. (YA). (gr. 8). 17.99 *(978-0-06-234825-8(6)*, Tegen, Katherine Bks) HarperCollins Pubs.

Soto, Gary. Chato Goes Cruisin' Guevara, Susan, illus. 2008. (Chato Ser.). (J). 25.95 incl. audio *(978-1-59519-906-5(3))* Live Oak Media.

—Chato Goes Cruisin' Guevara, Susan, illus. 2007. (Chato Ser.). (J). (gr. -1-3). 14.65 *(978-0-7569-8147-1(6))* Perfection Learning Corp.

Stead, Philip C. A Sick Day for Amos McGee. Stead, Erin E., illus. 2010. (ENG.). 32p. (J). (gr. -1-1). 17.99 *(978-1-59643-402-8(3)*, 9781596434028) Roaring Brook Pr.

—A Sick Day for Amos Mcgee: Book & CD Storytime Set. Stead, Erin E., illus. 2017. (ENG.). 32p. (J). 12.99 *(978-1-4272-8722-9(8)*, 9781427287229) Macmillan Audio.
Stockham, Jessica, illus. Doctor. 2011. (First Time Ser.). (ENG.). 24p. (J). (gr. 2-2). pap. *(978-1-84643-334-4(7))* Child's Play International Ltd.
—Visiting the Hospital. 2011. (First Time Ser.). (ENG.). 24p. (J). (gr. 2-2). pap. *(978-1-84643-336-8(3))* Child's Play International Ltd.
Tague, James E. The Krankel Family. 2008. 32p. pap. 21.99 *(978-1-4363-7170-4(8))* Xlibris Corp.
Taylor-Butler, Christine. Ah-Choo. Koeller, Carol, illus. 2005. (My First Reader Ser.). (ENG.). 32p. (J). (gr. k-1). 18.50 *(978-0-516-25175-2(9)*, Children's Pr.) Scholastic Library Publishing.
Thebo, Mimi. Dreaming the Bear. 2017. (YA). pap. *(978-0-399-55753-8(9))* Earthscan Canada.
Thomas, Shelley Moore. Get Well, Good Knight. Plecas, Jennifer, illus. 2004. (Penguin Young Readers, Level 3 Ser.). (ENG.). 48p. (J). (gr. 1-3). 3.99 *(978-0-14-240050-0(5)*, Penguin Young Readers) Penguin Young Readers Group.
—Get Well, Good Knight. Plecas, Jennifer, illus. 2004. (Easy-to-Read Ser.). 44p. (gr. k-3). 14.00 *(978-0-7569-2923-7(7))* Perfection Learning Corp.
—Get Well, Good Knight. 2004. (Penguin Young Readers Level 3 Ser.). 13.55 *(978-0-613-97291-8(0)*, Turtleback) Turtleback Bks.
Tim Todd. The Town of Ill. 2009. 36p. pap. 18.99 *(978-1-4389-2778-7(9))* AuthorHouse.
Vernick, Audrey & Scanlon, Liz Garton. Bob, Not Bob! Cordell, Matthew, illus. 2017. (ENG.). 40p. (J). (gr. -1-k). 17.99 *(978-1-4847-2302-9(3))* Disney Pr.
Weber, Lori. Tattoo Heaven, 1 vol. 2005. (Lorimer SideStreets Ser.). (ENG.). 168p. (YA). (gr. 9-12). 16.95 *(978-1-55028-903-9(9)*, 9781550289039); 9.95 *(978-1-55028-902-2(0)*, 9781550289022) Lorimer, James & Co., Ltd., Pubs. CAN. Dist: Casemate Pubs. & Bk. Distributors, LLC.
Weston Woods Staff, creator. How Do Dinosaurs Get Well Soon? 2011. 29.95 *(978-0-439-76689-0(3))*; 38.75 *(978-0-439-84622-6(6))*; 18.95 *(978-0-439-84621-9(8))* Weston Woods Studios, Inc.
When I Was Sick: Individual Title, 6 packs. (Literatura 2000 Ser.). (gr. 1-2). 28.00 *(978-0-7635-0018-4(6))* Rigby Education.
White, Ruth. A Month of Sundays. 2013. (ENG.). 192p. (YA). (gr. 5-9). pap. 6.99 *(978-1-250-02730-6(6)*, 9781250027306) Square Fish.
Whitney, A. D. T. Patience Strong's Outings by Mrs a D T Whitney. 2006. 236p. per. 20.99 *(978-1-4255-2007-6(3))* Michigan Publishing.
Wilson, Karma. Bear Feels Sick. Chapman, Jane, illus. 2012. (Bear Bks.). (ENG.). 34p. (J). (gr. -1-2). bds. 7.99 *(978-1-4424-4093-7(7)*, Little Simon) Little Simon.
—Bear Feels Sick. Chapman, Jane, illus. 2007. (Bear Bks.). (ENG.). 40p. (J). (gr. -1-3). 17.99 *(978-0-689-85985-4(6)*, McElderry, Margaret K. Bks.) McElderry, Margaret K. Bks.
Wilson, Rebekah. Grandmother's Hope Chest: Lucie's Snowflakes. l.t. ed. 2004. (Illus.). 80p. (J). 15.00 *(978-1-59565-003-0(2))* Hope Chest Legacy, Inc.
Wunder, Wendy. The Probability of Miracles. 2012. (ENG., Illus.). 336p. (YA). (gr. 9). pap. 9.99 *(978-1-59514-480-5(3)*, Razorbill) Penguin Young Readers Group.
Wylie, Sarah. All These Lives, 1 vol. 2012. (ENG.). 256p. (YA). (gr. 7-12). 24.99 *(978-0-374-30208-5(1)*, 9780374302085, Farrar, Straus & Giroux (BYR)) Farrar, Straus & Giroux.
Yolen, Jane. How Do Dinosaurs Get Well Soon? Teague, Mark, illus. 2003. (How Do Dinosaurs... Ser.). (ENG.). 40p. (J). (gr. -1-3). 16.99 *(978-0-439-24100-7(6)*, Blue Sky Pr., The) Scholastic, Inc.
Yonge, Charlotte M. Little Lucy's Wonderful Globe. 2008. 152p. 36.95 *(978-0-548-97272-4(9))* Kessinger Publishing, LLC.
Young, Judy. Digger & Daisy Go to the Doctor. Sullivan, Dana, illus. 2014. (I AM a READER!: Digger & Daisy Ser.). (ENG.). 32p. (J). (gr. k-2). 9.99 *(978-1-58536-845-7(8)*, 203674); pap. 4.99 *(978-1-58536-846-4(6)*, 203728) Sleeping Bear Pr.
—Digger et Daisy Vont Au Docteur (Digger & Daisy Go to the Doctor) Sullivan, Dana, illus. 2016. (I AM a READER: Digger & Daisy Ser.). (FRE & ENG.). 32p. (J). (gr. k-2). 12.95 *(978-1-62753-949-4(2)*, 204172) Sleeping Bear Pr.
—Digger y Daisy Van Al Médico (Digger & Daisy Go to the Doctor) Sullivan, Dana, illus. 2016. (I AM a READER: Digger & Daisy Ser.). (SPA & ENG.). 32p. (J). (gr. k-2). 9.99 *(978-1-62753-953-1(0)*, 204176) Sleeping Bear Pr.
Youngberg, Norma R. Jungle Thorn. 2010. (Illus.). 132p. reprint ed. per. 11.95 *(978-1-57258-157-9(3)*, 945-6024) TEACH Services, Inc.
Zaugg, Sandra L. A Prayer for Mother. 2005. (Illus.). 95p. (J). *(978-0-8163-2056-1(X))* Pacific Pr. Pubns.

SIDEREAL SYSTEM
see Stars

SIERRA LEONE
Brimson, Samuel. Sierra Leone-United Arab Emirates, 8 vols. 2003. (Nations of the World Ser.: Vol. 7). (Illus.). 64p. (gr. 5-12). lib. bdg. 31.00 *(978-0-8368-5491-6(8)*, Gareth Stevens Secondary Library) Stevens, Gareth Publishing LLLP.
Deprince, Michaela & DePrince, Elaine. Ballerina Dreams: From Orphan to Dancer. Morrison, Frank, illus. 2014. (Step into Reading Ser.). (ENG.). 48p. (J). (gr. 2-4). 3.99 *(978-0-385-75515-3(5)*, Random Hse. Bks. for Young Readers) Random Hse. Children's Bks.
—Taking Flight: From War Orphan to Star Ballerina. 2014. (ENG.). 256p. (YA). (gr. 7). 16.99 *(978-0-385-75511-5(2))*; lib. bdg. 19.99 *(978-0-385-75512-2(0))* Random Hse. Children's Bks. (Knopf Bks. for Young Readers).
Fowler, Will. Counterterrorism in West Africa: The Most Dangerous SAS Assault. 2011. (Most Daring Raids in History Ser.). (Illus.). 64p. (YA). (gr. 7-12). lib. bdg. 31.95 *(978-1-4488-1871-6(0))* Rosen Publishing Group, Inc., The.
Hasday, Judy L. Sierra Leone. 2012. (J). pap. *(978-1-4222-2230-0(6))* Mason Crest.
—Sierra Leone. Rotberg, Robert I., ed. (Evolution of Africa's Major Nations Ser.). (Illus.). 2012. 80p. (J). (gr. 7). 22.95 *(978-1-4222-2202-7(0))* 2009. 79p. (YA). (gr. 3-7). lib. bdg. 21.95 *(978-1-4222-0092-6(2))* Mason Crest.
LeVert, Suzanne. Sierra Leone. 2006. (Cultures of the World Ser.). (Illus.). 144p. (gr. 6-7). lib. bdg. 42.79 *(978-0-7614-2334-8(6)*, Benchmark Bks.) Marshall Cavendish Corp.

SIERRA LEONE—FICTION
Edinger, Monica. Africa Is My Home: A Child of the Amistad. Byrd, Robert, illus. 2015. (ENG.). 64p. (J). (gr. 5). pap. 8.99 *(978-0-7636-7647-6(0))* Candlewick Pr.
Forde, Winston. Airborne Soldiers. 2010. (Illus.). 120p. 29.99 *(978-1-4535-6451-6(9))* Xlibris Corp.

SIERRA NEVADA (CALIF. AND NEV.)
Harkins, Susan Sales & Harkins, William H. The Donner Party. 2008. (What's So Great About... ? Ser.). (Illus.). 32p. (J). (gr. 2-4). lib. bdg. 25.70 *(978-1-58415-669-7(4))* Mitchell Lane Pubs., Inc.
Rajczak, Kristen. The Donner Party. 2015. (Doomed! Ser.). (ENG., Illus.). 32p. (J). (gr. 4-5). pap. 10.50 *(978-1-4824-2928-2(4))* Stevens, Gareth Publishing LLLP.
Smith-Llera, Danielle. Stranded in the Sierra Nevada: The Story of the Donner Party. 2015. (Adventures on the American Frontier Ser.). (ENG., Illus.). 32p. (gr. 3-4). pap. 7.95 *(978-1-4914-4912-7(8))* Capstone Press of Coughlan Cos.
Wadsworth, Ginger. Survival in the Snow. Orback, Craig, illus. 48p. 2011. (J). pap. 6.95 *(978-0-7613-3941-0(8)*, First Avenue Editions) 2009. (ENG.). (gr. 2-4). 25.26 *(978-0-8225-7892-5(1))* Lerner Publishing Group.

SIERRA NEVADA (CALIF. AND NEV.)—FICTION
Engle, Margarita. Mountain Dog. Ivanov, Aleksey & Ivanov, Olga, illus. 2013. (ENG.). 224p. (J). (gr. 3-7). 17.99 *(978-0-8050-9516-6(0)*, 9780805095166, Holt, Henry & Co. Bks. For Young Readers) Holt, Henry & Co.
—Mountain Dog. Ivanov, Aleksey & Ivanov, Olga, illus. 2014. (ENG.). 240p. (J). (gr. 3-7). pap. 7.99 *(978-1-250-04424-2(3)*, 9781250044242) Square Fish.
Pryor, Bonnie. The Iron Dragon: The Courageous Story of Lee Chin. 2010. (Historical Fiction Adventures (HFA) Ser.). (Illus.). 160p. (J). (gr. 3-6). 29.27 *(978-0-7660-3389-4(9))*; (gr. 4-6). pap. 10.95 *(978-1-59845-215-0(0))* Enslow Pubs., Inc.
Roddy, Lee. The City Bear's Adventures. 2008. (D. J. Dillon Adventure Ser.: No. 2). (J). 7.99 *(978-0-88062-266-0(0))* Mott Media.
—Dooger, the Grasshopper Hound. 2008. (D. J. Dillon Adventure Ser.: No. 3). (J). 7.99 *(978-0-88062-267-7(9))* Mott Media.
—The Ghost Dog of Stoney Ridge. 2008. (D. J. Dillon Adventure Ser.: No. 4). (J). 7.99 *(978-0-88062-268-4(7))* Mott Media.
—The Hair-Pulling Bear Dog. 2008. (D. J. Dillon Adventure Ser.: No. 1). (J). 7.99 *(978-0-88062-265-3(2))* Mott Media.
Shahan, Sherry. Death Mountain, 1 vol. (ENG.). 176p. (YA). (gr. 5-9). 2007. pap. 7.95 *(978-1-56145-428-0(1))* 2005. 15.95 *(978-1-56145-353-5(6))* Peachtree Pubs.
Uncle Markie. Piglette & Bobo Join the Manscouts. 2003. (YA). ring bd. 9.95 *(978-1-933129-05-1(0))* Studio 403.

SIGHT
see Vision

SIGN BOARDS
see Signs and Signboards

SIGN LANGUAGE
see also Indian Sign Language
Ace Academics, ed. Sign Language Pt. 1: A Whole Course in a Box!, 3 vols. 2007. (Exambusters Ser.: Part 1 of 3). (Illus.). 192p. (gr. 7-18). 12.95 *(978-1-881374-95-4(5)*, Exambusters) Ace Academics, Inc.
Acredolo, Linda & Goodwyn, Susan. I Can Sign! Playtime. 2007. (Baby Signs (Ideals) Ser.). (ENG., Illus.). 12p. (gr. -1). 9.99 *(978-0-8249-6708-6(9)*, Ideal Pubns.) Worthy Publishing.
Allen, Joy. Baby Signs. 2008. (ENG., Illus.). 16p. (J). (gr. -1 — 1). bds. 6.99 *(978-0-8037-3193-6(0)*, Dial Bks) Penguin Young Readers Group.
Audia, John P. The Creation Story: In Words & Sign Language. Spohn, David, illus. 2007. (ENG.). 16p. (gr. 3-7). 9.95 *(978-0-8146-3174-4(6))* Liturgical Pr.
Awareness & Caring - Sign Language, 10 bks. (J). lib. bdg. 175.50 *(978-1-56674-912-1(3))* Forest Hse. Publishing Co., Inc.
Barfell, Judith A. Learn & Sign Funtime Beginnings. 2004. (Beginnings Ser.: Bk. 1). (Illus.). 40p. (J). per. 14.95 *(978-0-9753717-1-8(1))* Learn & Sign Funtime Bks.
Barfell, Judy. Learn & Sign Funtime: The United States Presidents. 2005. (J). per. 29.90 *(978-0-9753717-4-9(6))* Learn & Sign Funtime Bks.
Beginning Signs: Flip Charts. 2003. (J). spiral bd. 17.95 *(978-1-930820-34-0(8))* Garlic Pr.
Campbell, Diana & Mosher, Nancy, eds. Everyday Signs for the Newborn Baby. Adilman, Katarzyna, illus. 2007. 20p. (J). bds. *(978-0-9791059-0-6(0))* Dakitab, Inc.
Child's Play, creator. Getting Ready. 2006. (Sign About Ser.). (ENG., Illus.). 12p. (J). (gr. -1). bds. *(978-1-84643-029-9(1))* Child's Play International Ltd.
—Going Out. 2006. (Sign About Ser.). (ENG., Illus.). 12p. (J). (gr. -1). bds. *(978-1-84643-032-9(1))* Child's Play International Ltd.
Clay, Kathryn & Vonne, Mira. The Kids' Guide to Sign Language, 1 vol. 2012. (Kids' Guides). (ENG., Illus.). 32p. (gr. 3-4). lib. bdg. 27.99 *(978-1-4296-8426-2(7))* Capstone Press of Coughlan Cos.
—Signing Around Town: Sign Language for Kids, 1 vol. Reid, Mick, illus. 2013. (Time to Sign Ser.). (ENG.). 32p. (gr. 1-2). 27.32 *(978-1-62065-053-0(3)*, Aplus Bks.) Capstone Press of Coughlan Cos.
—Signing at Home: Sign Language for Kids, 1 vol. Chewning, Randy, illus. 2013. (Time to Sign Ser.). (ENG.). 32p. (gr. 1-2). 27.32 *(978-1-62065-051-6(7)*, Aplus Bks.) Capstone Press of Coughlan Cos.
—Signing at School: Sign Language for Kids, 1 vol. Lucas, Margeaux, illus. 2013. (Time to Sign Ser.). (ENG.). 32p. (gr. 1-2). 27.32 *(978-1-62065-052-3(5)*, Aplus Bks.) Capstone Press of Coughlan Cos.
—Signing in My World: Sign Language for Kids, 1 vol. Griffo, Daniel, illus. 2013. (Time to Sign Ser.). (ENG.). 32p. (gr. 1-2). 27.32 *(978-1-62065-054-7(1)*, Aplus Bks.) Capstone Press of Coughlan Cos.
—Time to Sign. 2013. (Time to Sign Ser.). (ENG.). 32p. (gr. 1-2). lib. bdg. 109.28 *(978-1-62065-055-4(X)*, Aplus Bks.) Capstone Press of Coughlan Cos.
—Time to Sign: Sign Language for Kids, 1 vol. Chewning, Randy et al, illus. 2013. (Time to Sign Ser.). (ENG.). 112p. (gr. 1-2). pap. 8.95 *(978-1-62065-687-7(6)*, Aplus Bks.) Capstone Press of Coughlan Cos.
Clothes-Ropa Bilingual Board Book. 2008. (ENG & SPA.). (J). pap. 5.99 *(978-0-9727886-9-4(7))* Osmosis, LLC.
Cooper, Teri. Meet Simple Signman: His quiet talk counting 1 Thru 10. 2011. 24p. 10.95 *(978-1-4497-1137-5(5)*, WestBow Pr.) Author Solutions, Inc.
Dykema, Marjorie. Ella's Joy: Signs of Joy. Helsom, Geoff, illus. 2009. (ENG.). 32p. 16.95 *(978-0-615-31066-4(4))* One Coin Publishing, LLC.
Ehlke, Paul. Clouds: Science Information in American Sign Language: A Paws Science Adventure. 2003. (J). cd-rom 29.95 *(978-0-9752933-2-4(X))* Institute for Disabilities Research & Training, Inc.
Everyday Signs for Bed Time. 2007. (J). bds. *(978-0-9791059-2-0(7))* Dakitab, Inc.
Flodin, Mickey. The Kids' Pocket Signing Guide. 2005. (ENG.). 192p. (gr. 5-9). 14.00 *(978-0-399-53207-8(2)*, TarcherPerigee) Penguin Publishing Group.
—Signing for Kids. rev. ed. 2007. (ENG., Illus.). 160p. (gr. 12-18). 15.00 *(978-0-399-53320-4(6)*, TarcherPerigee) Penguin Publishing Group.
Flora, Sherrill B. Alphabet: Signs, Letters, Sounds. 2010. (ENG.). 26p. (gr. -1-k). 11.99 *(978-1-60268-087-6(6)*, Key Education Publishing Company, LLC) Carson-Dellosa Publishing, LLC.
Gilmartin, Charles. Storybook Sign Language. 2008. 28p. pap. 13.95 *(978-1-4327-2677-5(3))* Outskirts Pr., Inc.
Hack, Brittany. American Sign Language, Counting with Sea Creatures. 2012. 28p. pap. 24.95 *(978-1-4626-8930-9(2))* America Star Bks.
Hall, Susan T. ABC Sign & Color: A Beginner's Book of American Sign Language. 2013. (Dover Coloring Bks.). (ENG.). 32p. (J). (gr. k-5). pap. 3.99 *(978-0-486-49057-1(2))* Dover Pubns., Inc.
Hay, John & Harwich, Mary Belle. Dancing Hands: Signs of Learning. Wapahi, Robert, illus. 2013. 78p. pap. 16.95 *(978-0-9888972-0-5(2))* Scotland Gate, Inc.
Heller, Lora. Sign Language ABC. 2014. (ENG., Illus.). 28p. (J). (— 1). bds. 6.95 *(978-1-4549-1145-6(X))* Sterling Publishing Co., Inc.
—Sign Language for Kids: A Fun & Easy Guide to American Sign Language. 2004. (ENG., Illus.). 96p. (J). (gr. k-7). 14.95 *(978-1-4027-0672-1(3)*, 1233016) Sterling Publishing Co., Inc.
Jensema, Marissa, illus. ASL Songs for Kids - 1: With Songs in American Sign Language. 2003. (J). cd-rom 29.95 *(978-0-9752933-1-7(1))* Institute for Disabilities Research & Training, Inc.
Kelley, Walter P. The "I Love You" Story. McGregor, Tony L., illus. 2004. (J). *(978-0-9729569-4-9(8))* BuTo, Ltd. Co.
Kent, Deborah. What Is It Like to Be Deaf? 2012. (Overcoming Barriers Ser.). (Illus.). 48p. (J). (gr. 3-4). pap. 8.95 *(978-1-4644-0154-1(3)*, Enslow Elementary) Enslow Pubs., Inc.
—What Is Sign Language? 2012. (Overcoming Barriers Ser.). 48p. (J). (gr. 3-4). (Illus.). pap. 8.95 *(978-1-4644-0156-5(X))*; 25.27 *(978-0-7660-3771-7(1))* Enslow Pubs., Inc. (Enslow Elementary).
Kubler, Annie. Itsy, Bitsy Spider. 2005. (Sign & Singalong Ser.). (ENG., Illus.). 12p. (J). (gr. k-k). bds. *(978-1-904550-43-3(6))* Child's Play International Ltd.
Kubler, Annie, illus. Teddy Bear, Teddy Bear. 2005. (Sign & Singalong Ser.). (ENG.). 12p. (J). (gr. k-1). bds. *(978-1-904550-40-2(1))* Child's Play International Ltd.
—Twinkle, Twinkle, Little Star. 2005. (Sign & Singalong Ser.). (ENG.). 12p. (J). (gr. k-k). bds. *(978-1-904550-42-6(8))* Child's Play International Ltd.
Learn & Sign Funtime - Beginnings. 2007. (FRE.). (J). per. 14.95 *(978-0-9753717-9-4(7))* Learn & Sign Funtime Bks.
Learn & Sign Funtime - Beginnings: British Edition. 2005. (J). per. *(978-0-9753717-7-0(0))* Learn & Sign Funtime Bks.
Learn & Sign Funtime - Beginnings: Lakota Edition. 2007. Orig. Title: Learn & Sign Funtime. (SAI.). per. *(978-0-9753717-8-7(9))* Learn & Sign Funtime Bks.
Learn & Sign Funtime - Haitian Edition: Beginnings. 2005. (CRP). (J). per. 14.95 net. *(978-0-9753717-6-3(2))* Learn & Sign Funtime Bks.
Learn & Sign Funtime: Beginnings. 4th ed. 2005. Orig. Title: Learn & Sign Funtime - Beginnings Third Edktion. (J). per. 14.95 *(978-0-9753717-5-6(4))* Learn & Sign Funtime Bks.
Learn & Sign Funtime: Beginnings - Auslan. 3rd ed. 2004. per. 14.95 *(978-0-9753717-3-2(8))* Learn & Sign Funtime Bks.
Lewis, Anthony, illus. Meal Time. 2006. (Sign About Ser.). (ENG.). 12p. (J). (gr. -1). bds. *(978-1-84643-030-5(5))* Child's Play International Ltd.
—Play Time. 2006. (Sign About Ser.). (ENG.). 12p. (J). (gr. -1). bds. *(978-1-84643-031-2(3))* Child's Play International Ltd.
Lindert, Reyna & Anthony, Michelle. My First Signs. 2009. (Signing Smart Ser.). (ENG.). 14p. (J). (gr. k — 1). 7.99 *(978-0-545-10924-6(8)*, Cartwheel Bks.) Scholastic, Inc.
Lowenstein, Felicia. All about Sign Language: Talking with Your Hands. 2004. (Transportation & Communication Ser.). (Illus.). 48p. (J). lib. bdg. 25.27 *(978-0-7660-2028-3(2))* Enslow Pubs., Inc.
Martin, Mabel. Talking with Hands. Witmer, Ruth, illus. 2007. (Little Jewel Book Ser.). 24p. (J). (gr. 2). pap. 2.70 *(978-0-7399-2394-8(3))* Rod & Staff Pubs., Inc.
Neal, Vonda & Herbold, Marvin, compiled by. British Sign Language American Sign Language Translator. 2004. (YA). cd-rom 19.95 *(978-0-9752933-8-6(9))* Institute for Disabilities Research & Training, Inc.
Sandviks HOP, Inc. Staff, ed. Hooked on Baby: Learn to Sign. 2008. 29.99 *(978-1-62499-017-5(7))* HOP, LLC.
Scholastic Book Editors. Sign Language: My First 100 Words. Nelson, Michiyo, illus. 2008. 32p. (gr. -1-3). 17.00 *(978-0-7569-8911-8(6))* Perfection Learning Corp.
Scholastic, Inc. Staff. My First 100 Words. Nelson, Michiyo, illus. 2008. (Sign Language Ser.). (ENG.). 32p. (J). (gr. -1-3). pap. 6.99 *(978-0-545-05657-1(8)*, Cartwheel Bks.) Scholastic, Inc.
—My First Book of Sign Language. Holub, Joan, illus. 2004. (ENG.). 32p. (J). (gr. -1-3). pap. 3.99 *(978-0-439-63582-0(9))* Scholastic, Inc.
Signing Time Flash Cards 5: ABC's. 2006. (J). 10.99 *(978-1-933543-12-3(4))* Two Little Hands Productions LLC.
Signs & Symbols: Lessons & activities for children Ages 5-10. 2005. (J). pap. 14.95 *(978-1-58459-268-6(0))* World Library Pubns.
Thornborough, Kathy. Days & Times. Petelinsek, Kathleen, illus. 2014. (Talking Hands Ser.). (ENG.). 24p. (J). (gr. k-3). 25.64 *(978-1-62687-316-2(X)*, 207156) Child's World, Inc., The.
Time to Sign. Time to Sign with Children Infant/Toddler: Time to Sign with Music Infant/Toddler. 2003. Orig. Title: Time to Sign with Music Infant/Toddler. (Illus.). 42p. per. 19.95 *(978-0-9713666-0-2(8))* Time to Sign, Incorporated.
Two Little Hands, creator. Everyday Signs Board Book. 2007. (Signing Time! (Two Little Hands) Ser.). (Illus.). 30p. (J). (gr. -1-k). bds. *(978-1-933543-02-4(7))* Two Little Hands Productions LLC.
—My First Signs Board Book. 2007. (Signing Time! (Two Little Hands) Ser.). (Illus.). 30p. (J). (gr. -1-k). bds. *(978-1-933543-00-0(0))* Two Little Hands Productions LLC.
—Playtime Signs Board Book. 2007. (Signing Time! (Two Little Hands) Ser.). (Illus.). 30p. (J). (gr. -1-k). bds. *(978-1-933543-01-7(9))* Two Little Hands Productions LLC.
Vinopol, Corinne. Con-SIGN-tration 3: Computer Software Game in American Sign Language. 2003. (J). cd-rom 19.95 *(978-0-9752933-6-2(2))* Institute for Disabilities Research & Training, Inc.
—Con-SIGN-tration 4: Computer Software Game in American Sign Language. 2003. (J). cd-rom *(978-0-9752933-7-9(0))* Institute for Disabilities Research & Training, Inc.
—Spell Well: CD-ROM American Sign Language Spelling Game. 2003. (YA). cd-rom 19.95 *(978-0-9752933-0-0(3))* Institute for Disabilities Research & Training, Inc.
Vinopol, Corinne & Bednarczyk, Angela. American Sign Language Clip & Create: Clip Art Software. 2003. (YA). cd-rom 34.95 *(978-0-9752933-4-8(6))* Institute for Disabilities Research & Training, Inc.
Vinopol, Corinne K. American Sign Language Clip & Create 2. 2nd ed. 2004. cd-rom 34.95 *(978-0-9760818-0-7(6))* Institute for Disabilities Research & Training, Inc.
Warner, Penny. Signing Fun: American Sign Language Vocabulary, Phrases, Games, & Activities. Gray, Paula, illus. 2006. (ENG.). 192p. (gr. 6-7). per. 19.95 *(978-1-56368-292-6(3))* Gallaudet Univ. Pr.
Wyckoff, Edwin Brit & Library. Sign Language Man: Thomas H. Gallaudet & His Incredible Work. 2010. (Genius at Work! Great Inventor Biographies Ser.). (Illus.). 32p. (J). (gr. 2-5). lib. bdg. 23.94 *(978-0-7660-3447-1(X))* Enslow Pubs., Inc.

SIGN LANGUAGE—FICTION
Brightwood, Laura, illus. Debate in Sign Language. Brightwood, Laura, . 2006. (J). *(978-0-9779290-6-1(X))* 3-C Institute for Social Development.
Browne, Anthony. Little Beauty. Browne, Anthony, illus. 2010. (ENG., Illus.). 32p. (J). (gr. -1-2). pap. 6.99 *(978-0-7636-4967-8(8))* Candlewick Pr.
—Little Beauty. 2010. lib. bdg. 17.20 *(978-0-606-14714-9(4)*, Turtleback) Turtleback Bks.
Donaldson, Julia. What the Jackdaw Saw: Book & CD Pack, 2 vols. Sharratt, Nick, illus. 2015. (ENG.). 32p. (J). (gr. -1-k). 14.99 *(978-1-5098-0622-5(9))* Pan Macmillan GBR. Dist: Independent Pubs. Group.
Everyday Signs of Zoo Animals. 2007. (J). bds. *(978-0-9791059-1-3(9))* Dakitab, Inc.
Ferris, Jean. Of Sound Mind. 2004. (ENG.). 224p. (YA). (gr. 7). reprint ed. pap. 10.99 *(978-0-374-45584-2(8)*, 9780374455842, Farrar, Straus & Giroux (BYR)) Farrar, Straus & Giroux.
—Of Sound Mind. 2004. 215p. (YA). (gr. 7). 14.60 *(978-0-7569-2970-1(9))* Perfection Learning Corp.
Fudge, Benjamin. Enrique Speaks with His Hands. Edmonson, Tim, illus. 2008. (ENG.). 32p. (J). (gr. -1-3). 16.95 *(978-0-9800649-3-3(7))* Hilton Publishing Co.
Guest, Jacqueline. Secret Signs, 1 vol. 2006. (Orca Young Readers Ser.). (ENG., Illus.). 144p. (J). (gr. 3-6). per. 7.95 *(978-1-55143-599-2(3))* Orca Bk. Pubs. USA.
Jordan, Sherryl. The Raging Quiet. l.t. ed. 2005. 416p. 22.95 *(978-0-7862-7313-3(5)*, Large Print Pr.) Thorndike Pr.
Kingsley, Linda Kurtz. Bringing up Sophie. Kingsley, Linda Kurtz, illus. 2010. (Illus.). 32p. (J). lib. bdg. 15.95 *(978-0-944727-25-6(5)*, Turtle Bks.) Jason & Nordic Pubs.
—Bringing up Sophie. 2009. (Illus.). 32p. (J). pap. 9.95 *(978-0-944727-24-9(7)*, Turtle Bks.) Jason & Nordic Pubs.
Martin, Kentrell. Shelly Goes to the Zoo. Rodriguez, Marc, illus. 2013. 32p. pap. 8.50 *(978-0-9851845-1-3(5))* Shelly's Adventures LLC.
McCully, Emily Arnold. My Heart Glow: Alice Cogswell, Thomas Gallaudet, & the Birth of American Sign Language. McCully, Emily Arnold, illus. 2008. (ENG., Illus.). 40p. (gr. 1-4). 15.99 *(978-1-4231-0028-7(X))* Hyperion Pr.
Prochovnic, Dawn Babb. Four Seasons! Five Senses! Sign Language for the Seasons & Senses, 1 vol. Bauer, Stephanie, illus. 2012. (ENG.). 32p. 28.50 *(978-1-61641-836-6(2)*, Looking Glass Library) Magic Wagon.
—Hip Hip Hooray! It's Family Day! Sign Language for Family, 1 vol. Bauer, Stephanie, illus. 2012. (ENG.). 32p. 28.50 *(978-1-61641-837-3(0)*, Looking Glass Library) Magic Wagon.
—One Trick for One Treat: Sign Language for Numbers, 1 vol. Bauer, Stephanie, illus. 2012. (ENG.). 32p. 28.50 *(978-1-61641-838-0(9)*, Looking Glass Library) Magic Wagon.
—Opposites Everywhere: Sign Language for Opposites, 1 vol. Bauer, Stephanie, illus. 2012. (ENG.). 32p. 28.50 *(978-1-61641-839-7(7)*, Looking Glass Library) Magic Wagon.
—So Many Feelings: Sign Language for Feelings & Emotions, 1 vol. Bauer, Stephanie, illus. 2012. (ENG.). 32p. (J). 28.50 *(978-1-61641-841-0(9)*, Looking Glass Library) Magic Wagon.
—There's a Story in My Head: Sign Language for Body Parts, 1 vol. Bauer, Stephanie, illus. 2012. (ENG.). 32p. 28.50 *(978-1-61641-842-7(7)*, Looking Glass Library) Magic Wagon.

S

Roth, Judith L. & Rothshank, Brooke, illus. Julia's Words. 2008. (J). (gr. -1-3). pap. 12.99 (978-0-8361-9417-3(9)) Herald Pr.
Sawyer, Louise. Mother's Storybook Signs. 2004. (YA). Vol. 1. spiral bd. 19.95 (978-0-9719842-0-2(4)) Vol. 2. spiral bd. 19.95 (978-0-9719842-8-8(X)) Martin & Brothers.
Schrocke, Kathrin. Freak City. Tammi Reichel, tr. 2014. (Illus.). 224p. (YA). (gr. 9-12). pap. 10.95 (978-1-62324-006-6(9)) Enslow Pubs., Inc.
—Freak City. Reichel, Tammi, tr. from GER. 2014. 224p. (YA). 18.95 (978-1-62324-005-9(0)) Enslow Pubs., Inc.
Shelly's Outdoor Adventure. 2013. (ENG.). 28p. pap. 8.00 (978-0-9851845-0-6(7)) Shelly's Adventures LLC.
Uhlberg, Myron. The Printer, 1 vol. Sørensen, Henri, illus. 2009. (ENG.). 32p. (J). (gr. -1-3). pap. 8.95 (978-1-56145-483-9(4)) Peachtree Pubs.
—The Printer, 1 vol. Sorensen, Henri, tr. Sorensen, Henri, illus. 2003. (ENG.). 32p. (J). (gr. k-3). 16.95 (978-1-56145-221-7(1)) Peachtree Pubs.
Wemple, Sabrina. Gumby & Beanie. 2008. 32p. per. 13.95 (978-1-4327-0780-4(9)) Outskirts Pr., Inc.

SIGNALS AND SIGNALING
see also Flags; Radio
Cefrey, Holly. The Inventions of Martha Coston: Signal Flares That Save Sailors' Lives. 2009. (19th Century American Inventors Ser.). 24p. (gr. 2-3). 42.50 (978-1-60854-953-5(4), PowerKids Pr.) Rosen Publishing Group, Inc., The.
—The Inventions of Martha Coston: Signal Flares That Saved Sailors' Lives. 2003. (19th Century American Inventors Ser.). (Illus.). 24p. (J). lib. bdg. 22.60 (978-0-8239-6444-4(2), PowerKids Pr.) Rosen Publishing Group, Inc., The.
Jocelyn, Marthe. Which Way? Slaughter, Tom, illus. 2010. (ENG.). 24p. (J). (gr. k-k). 15.95 (978-0-88776-970-2(5), Tundra Bks.) Tundra Bks. CAN. Dist: Penguin Random Hse. LLC.
McNab, Chris. Survival in the Wilderness. 2015. (Illus.). 64p. (J). (978-1-4222-3081-7(3)) Mason Crest.
Wilson, Patrick. Surviving with Navigation & Signaling. Carney, John, ed. 2014. (Extreme Survival in the Military Ser.: 12). 64p. (J). (gr. 7-18). lib. bdg. 23.95 (978-1-4222-3093-0(7)) Mason Crest.
Woods, Michael & Woods, Mary B. Ancient Communication Technology: From Hieroglyphics to Scrolls. 2011. (Technology in Ancient Cultures Ser.). (ENG.). 96p. (gr. 6-12). lib. bdg. 31.93 (978-0-7613-6529-7(X)) Lerner Publishing Group.

SIGNERS OF THE DECLARATION OF INDEPENDENCE
see United States—Declaration of Independence

SIGNS (ADVERTISING)
see Signs and Signboards

SIGNS AND SIGNBOARDS
see also Posters
Benchmark Education Co., LLC. Safety Signs Big Book. 2014. (Shared Reading Foundations Ser.). (J). (gr. -1). (978-1-4509-9431-6(8)) Benchmark Education Co.
Byerly, Robbie & Kiley, Kieran. Look at the Signs. rev. ed. 2011. (1-3Y in My World Ser.). (ENG., Illus.). 16p. (J). (gr. k-1). pap. 5.99 (978-1-61541-461-1(4)) American Reading Co.
Gregory, Cam. Who Should Follow Signs? 2014. (Little Books of Answers: Level F Ser.). (Illus.). 16p. (gr. k-2). pap. 7.95 (978-1-927136-53-9(9)) Three Crows Media NZL. Dist: RiverStream Publishing.
Hill, Mary. Signs at the Airport. 2003. (Signs in My World Ser.). (ENG., Illus.). 24p. (J). 19.00 (978-0-516-24272-9(5)); (gr. -1-2). pap. 4.95 (978-0-516-24364-1(0)) Scholastic Library Publishing. (Children's Pr.).
—Signs at the Park. 2003. (Welcome Bks.). (ENG., Illus.). 24p. (J). (gr. -1-2). pap. 4.95 (978-0-516-24365-8(9), Children's Pr.) Scholastic Library Publishing.
—Signs at the Store. 2003. (Welcome Bks.). (ENG., Illus.). 24p. (J). (gr. -1-2). pap. 4.95 (978-0-516-24363-4(2), Children's Pr.) Scholastic Library Publishing.
Leigh, Autumn. Signs on the Road: Learning to Identify the Four Basic Geometric Shapes. 2009. (Math for the Real World: Early Emergent Ser.). (ENG., Illus.). 8p. (gr. k-1). pap. 5.15 (978-0-8239-8857-0(0)) Rosen Publishing Group, Inc., The.
Macken, JoAnn Early. Road Signs. 2010. (My Community Ser.). 24p. (J). 25.65 (978-1-60753-026-8(0)) Amicus Publishing.
Milich, Zoran. City Signs. (ENG., Illus.). 32p. (J). (gr. -1-k). 2013. bds. 12.95 (978-1-55453-980-2(3)) 2005. pap. 6.95 (978-1-55337-748-1(6)) Kids Can Pr., Ltd. CAN. Dist: Hachette Bk. Group.
Rustad, Martha E. H. Reading Is Everywhere, 1 vol. 2013. (Wonderful World of Reading Ser.). (ENG.). 24p. (gr. k-1). lib. bdg. 26.65 (978-1-62065-096-7(7), Pebble Plus) Capstone Press of Coughlan Cos.
Schuh, Mari C. Let's Find Ads on Signs. 2016. (First Step Nonfiction — Learn about Advertising Ser.). (ENG.). 24p. (J). (gr. k-2). 23.99 (978-1-4677-9465-7(1)) Lerner Publishing Group.
Tana, Hoban. I Read Signs. 2014. (ENG.). 32p. (J). (gr. k-3). 11.24 (978-1-63245-283-2(9)) Lectorum Pubns., Inc.

SIGNS AND SIGNBOARDS—FICTION
Armstrong, Jennifer. Once upon a Banana. Small, David, illus. (ENG.). 48p. (J). (gr. -1-3). 2013. 6.99 (978-0-689-85951-9(1)) 2006. 17.99 (978-0-689-84251-1(1)) Simon & Schuster/Paula Wiseman Bks. (Simon & Schuster/Paula Wiseman Bks.).
Bain, Michelle. The Adventures of Thumbs up Johnnie Zipp, Little Digit & the Happy Signs: Zipp, Little Digit & the Happy Signs. Lizana, Lorenzo, illus. 2007. (J). 14.95 (978-0-9795832-0-9(9)) Pixie Stuff LLC.
—Las aventuras de Juanito el Pulgarcito Zipp, Pequeño Dígito, las señales y las Señas: Zipp, Pequeño Digito, las señales y las Señas. Lizana, Lorenzo, illus. 2007.Tr. of Zipp, Digit & the Happy Signs! (SPA.). 28p. (J). (978-0-9795832-3-0(3)) Pixie Stuff LLC.
Bell, Hilari. Crown of Earth. Willis, Drew, illus. 2010. (Shield, Sword, & Crown Ser.: 3). (ENG.). 272p. (J). (gr. 3-7). pap. 5.99 (978-1-4169-0599-8(5), Aladdin) Simon & Schuster Children's Publishing.
—Crown of Earth. Willis, Drew, illus. 2009. (Shield, Sword, & Crown Ser.: 3). (ENG.). 272p. (J). (gr. 3-7). 16.99 (978-1-4169-0598-1(7), Simon & Schuster/Paula Wiseman Bks.) Simon & Schuster/Paula Wiseman Bks.
Blake, Christine & Lopez, Jill. Signs, Signs, Everywhere Signs. 2008. 32p. pap. 15.95 (978-1-4327-2523-5(8)) Outskirts Pr., Inc.
Jordan, Taylor. Movin' on In. Wummer, Amy, illus. 2005. (Social Studies Connects). 32p. (J). (gr. 1-3). pap. 5.95 (978-1-57565-159-0(9)) Kane Press, Inc.
Kehret, Peg. Stolen Children. 2010. (ENG.). 176p. (J). (gr. 3-7). 6.99 (978-0-14-241513-9(8), Puffin Books) Penguin Young Readers Group.
Kondrchek, Jamie & Rasemas, Joe. On My Way to School (De Camino a la Escuela) Vega, Eida de la, tr. Rasemas, Joe, illus. 2009. (Day in the Life Ser.). (SPA & ENG., Illus.). 32p. (J). (gr. -1-1). 25.70 (978-1-58415-840-0(9)) Mitchell Lane Pubs., Inc.
Road Signs. 2005. (J). per. 9.95 (978-1-59352-179-0(0)) Christian Services Publishing.
Say, Allen. The Sign Painter. 2013. (ENG., Illus.). 32p. (J). (gr. -1-3). pap. 6.99 (978-0-544-10514-0(1)) Houghton Mifflin Harcourt Publishing Co.
van Lieshout, Maria. Backseat A-B-See. (ENG., Illus.). (J). (gr. -1-k). 2014. 26p. bds. 7.99 (978-1-4521-3732-2(3)) 2012. 40p. 14.99 (978-1-4521-0664-9(9)) Chronicle Bks. LLC.

SIGNS AND SYMBOLS
see also Ciphers; Cryptography; Heraldry; Signals and Signaling; Symbolism
Avett, Harper. I See the Bald Eagle. 2016. (Symbols of Our Country Ser.). 00024p. (J). (gr. 1-1). 23.60 (978-1-4994-3051-6(5)); pap. 8.25 (978-1-4994-2763-9(8)) Rosen Publishing Group, Inc., The. (PowerKids Pr.).
Benchmark Education Company. Symbols of the United States (Teacher Guide) 2005. (978-1-4108-4638-9(5)) Benchmark Education Co.
Bodach, Vijaya Khisty. Pictografías. 2010. (Hacer Gráficas/Making Graphs Ser.). (MUL, SPA & ENG.). 32p. (gr. 1-2). lib. bdg. 27.32 (978-1-4296-6101-0(1), A+ Bilingue/Bilingual) Capstone Press of Coughlan Cos.
Bow, James. Secret Signs. 2013. (ENG.). 32p. (J). (978-0-7787-1125-4(0)); pap. (978-0-7787-1129-2(3)) Crabtree Publishing Co.
Brannon, Barbara. Discover Symbols of the United States. 2005. (J). pap. (978-1-4108-5144-4(3)) Benchmark Education Co.
Celebrate Freedom: Songs, Symbols, & Sayings of the United States. 2003. (Scott Foresman Social Study Ser.). (Illus.). 32p. (gr. k-2). (978-0-328-03672-1(2)); 48p. (gr. 3-6). (978-0-328-03674-5(9)) Addison-Wesley Educational Pubs., Inc. (Scott Foresman).
Cipriano, Jeri. Symbols of Our Country: Set Of 6. 2011. (Navigators Ser.). (J). pap. 44.00 net. (978-1-4108-5096-6(X)) Benchmark Education Co.
—Symbols of Our Country: Text Pairs. 2008. (Bridges/Navigators Ser.). (J). (gr. 3). 89.00 (978-1-4108-8373-5(6)) Benchmark Education Co.
Crewe, Sabrina. Canadian Coins. 2015. (Canadian Symbols Ser.). (ENG.). 24p. (gr. k-1). lib. bdg. 26.65 (978-1-4914-7093-0(3), Pebble Plus) Capstone Press of Coughlan Cos.
—Canadian Symbols. 2015. (Canadian Symbols Ser.). (ENG.). 24p. (gr. k-1). lib. bdg. 133.25 (978-1-4914-7095-4(X), Pebble Plus) Capstone Press of Coughlan Cos.
Diaz-Cubero, Jose H. Practicas de Ortografia: 5 Grado. (SPA & ENG.). (J). (gr. 5). 9.95 (978-84-357-0125-9(5), CPR92) Ediciones y Distribuciones Codice, S.A. ESP. Dist: Continental Bk. Co., Inc.
Eldridge, Alison & Eldridge, Stephen. The Bald Eagle: An American Symbol. 2012. (All about American Symbols Ser.). 24p. (J). (gr. -1-1). (Illus.). pap. 7.95 (978-1-4644-0047-6(4)); 22.60 (978-0-7660-4058-8(5)) Enslow Pubs., Inc. (Enslow Elementary).
—The Liberty Bell: An American Symbol. 2012. (All about American Symbols Ser.). 24p. (J). (gr. -1-16). 22.60 (978-0-7660-4059-5(3), Enslow Elementary) Enslow Pubs., Inc.
Ferguson, Melissa. American Symbols: What You Need to Know. 2017. (Fact Files Ser.). (ENG.). 24p. (gr. 1-2). lib. bdg. 25.32 **(978-1-5157-8116-5(X)**, First Facts) Capstone Press of Coughlan Cos.
Firestone, Mary, et al. Celebrate America: A Guide to America's Greatest Symbols. Skeens, Matthew, illus. 2010. (American Symbols Ser.). (ENG.). 208p. (gr. 1-2). pap. 15.95 (978-1-4048-6170-1(X)) Picture Window Bks.
Forest, Christopher. Dollar Bill in Translation: What It Really Means. 2016. (Kids' Translations Ser.). (ENG.). 32p. (gr. 3-4). pap. 8.10 (978-1-5157-6249-2(1), Fact Finders) Capstone Press of Coughlan Cos.
Friesen, Helen Lepp. El Tío Sam. 2014. (SPA., Illus.). 24p. (J). (978-1-62127-625-8(2)) Weigl Pubs., Inc.
Goldsworthy, Kaite. Bald Eagle with Code. 2012. (AV2 American Icons Ser.). (ENG., Illus.). 24p. (J). pap. 12.95 (978-1-61913-300-6(8)); lib. bdg. 27.13 (978-1-61913-077-7(7)) Weigl Pubs., Inc. (AV2 by Weigl).
Hicks, Terry Allan. The Bald Eagle. 2006. (Symbols of America Ser.). (Illus.). 40p. (J). (gr. 3-7). lib. bdg. 28.50 (978-0-7614-2133-7(5), Benchmark Bks.) Marshall Cavendish Corp.
—Symbols of America Group 2, 6 bks., Set. Incl. Bald Eagle. (J). lib. bdg. 28.50 (978-0-7614-2133-7(5)); Capitol. lib. bdg. 20.95 (978-0-7614-2132-0(7)); Declaration of Independence. lib. bdg. 20.95 (978-0-7614-2135-1(1)); Ellis Island. lib. bdg. 20.95 (978-0-7614-2134-4(3)); Pledge of Allegiance. lib. bdg. 20.95 (978-0-7614-2136-8(X)); Uncle Sam. lib. bdg. 20.95 (978-0-7614-2137-5(8)); (Illus.). 40p. (gr. 3-7). 2006. 2007. Set lib. bdg. 171.00 (978-0-7614-2130-6(0), Benchmark Bks.) Marshall Cavendish Corp.
James, Trisha. Celebrating Texas: Patriotic Symbols & Landmarks. 2010. (Spotlight on Texas Ser.). (Illus.). 32p. (J). (gr. 3-4). (ENG.). pap. 11.75 (978-1-61532-484-2(4)); lib. bdg. 25.25 (978-1-61532-486-6(0)) Rosen Publishing Group, Inc., The.
Jango-Cohen, Judith. El Aguila Calva. 2005. (Libros para Avanzar (Pull Ahead Bks.)). (SPA., Illus.). 32p. (J). (gr. k-3). per. 5.95 (978-0-8225-3135-7(6), Ediciones Lerner) Lerner Publishing Group.
Johnson, Etta. Symbols of the United States. 2005. (J). pap. (978-1-4108-4590-0(7)) Benchmark Education Co.
Keppeler, Jill. Betsy Ross Didn't Create the American Flag: Exposing Myths about US Symbols. 2016. (Exposed! Myths about Early American History Ser.). 00032p. (J). pap. 10.50 (978-1-4824-5717-9(2)) Stevens, Gareth Publishing LLLP.
Kishel, Ann-Marie. U. S. Symbols. 2007. (First Step Nonfiction - Government Ser.). (ENG., Illus.). 24p. (gr. k-2). lib. bdg. 23.93 (978-0-8225-6394-5(0), Lerner Pubns.) Lerner Publishing Group.
Kubler, Annie. Baa Baa, Black Sheep! 2005. (Sign & Signalong Ser.). (ENG., Illus.). 12p. (J). (gr. -1-k). bds. (978-1-904550-41-9(X)) Child's Play International Ltd.
Kubler, Annie, illus. My First Signs. 2005. (Baby Signing Ser.). (ENG.). 12p. (J). (gr. k-1). bds. (978-1-904550-39-6(8)); bds. (978-1-904550-04-4(5)) Child's Play International Ltd.
Lyons, Shelly. Signs in My Neighborhood. 2013. (My Neighborhood Ser.). (ENG.). 24p. (gr. k-1). pap. 41.70 (978-1-62065-890-1(9)); (Illus.). pap. 7.29 (978-1-62065-889-5(5)); (Illus.). lib. bdg. 26.65 (978-1-62065-098-1(3)) Capstone Press of Coughlan Cos. (Pebble Plus).
Machajewski, Sarah. Our Country's Symbols. 2012. (InfoMax Readers Ser.). (ENG., Illus.). 24p. (J). (gr. 1-2). pap. 8.25 (978-1-4488-8980-8(4), Rosen Classroom) Rosen Publishing Group, Inc., The.
Marcovitz, Hal. The Bald Eagle. 2004. (American Symbols & Their Meanings Ser.). (Illus.). 48p. (J). (gr. 4-18). lib. bdg. 19.95 (978-1-59084-032-0(1)) Mason Crest.
—Bald Eagle: The Story of Our National Bird. Moreno, Barry, ed. 2014. (Patriotic Symbols of America Ser.: 20). 48p. (J). (gr. 4-18). 20.95 (978-1-4222-3120-3(8)) Mason Crest.
Miller, Heather. The 10 Most Outstanding American Symbols. 2008. 14.99 (978-1-55448-508-6(8)) Scholastic Library Publishing.
Mills, Nathan & Machajewski, Sarah. Symbols of the United States. 2012. (Rosen Readers Ser.). (ENG., Illus.). 24p. (J). (gr. 1-2). pap. 8.25 (978-1-4488-8761-3(5), Rosen Classroom) Rosen Publishing Group, Inc., The.
Monroe, Tyler. Bald Eagle. 2013. (U. S. Symbols Ser.). (ENG.). 24p. (gr. k-1). 26.65 (978-1-4765-3089-5(0)); pap. 7.95 (978-1-4765-3538-8(8)) Capstone Press of Coughlan Cos. (Pebble Plus).
Moore, Elizabeth. All Kinds of Signs. 2011. (Wonder Readers Emergent Level Ser.). (ENG.). (gr. -1-1). 8p. pap. 35.94 (978-1-4296-8215-2(9)); 32p. pap. 5.99 (978-1-4296-7837-7(2)) Capstone Press of Coughlan Cos. (Wonder Readers).
Pearl, Norman. The Great Seal of the United States. Skeens, Matthew, illus. 2006. (American Symbols Ser.). (ENG.). 24p. (gr. 1-2). lib. bdg. 26.65 (978-1-4048-2214-6(3)); per. 9.95 (978-1-4048-2220-7(8)) Picture Window Bks.
Primary Sources of American Symbols. (J). (gr. k-6). 119.70 (978-1-4042-3300-3(8)) Rosen Publishing Group, Inc., The.
Raz, Rachel. The Colors of Israel. Raz, Rachel, photos by. 2015. (ENG., Illus.). 24p. (J). (gr. -1-2). 7.99 (978-1-4677-5540-5(0)); lib. bdg. 17.99 (978-1-4677-5539-9(7)) Lerner Publishing Group. (Kar-Ben Publishing).
Robertson, Jean. Pictures of America. 2014. (ENG.). 32p. (gr. 3-6). 32.79 (978-1-62717-736-8(1)) Rourke Educational Media.
Ruble, Eugene. Ancient Symbols, Artwork, Carvings & Alphabets. Burch, Lynda S., ed. 2009. 28p. pap. 10.95 (978-1-935137-90-0(5)) Guardian Angel Publishing, Inc.
Scholastic, Inc. Staff & Keenan, Sheila. O, Say Can You See? America's Symbols, Landmarks, & Important Words. Boyajian, Ann, illus. 2007. (ENG.). 64p. (J). (gr. -1-3). pap. 6.99 (978-0-439-59360-1(3), Scholastic Nonfiction) Scholastic, Inc.
Silate, Jennifer. The Bald Eagle. (Primary Sources of American Symbols Ser.). 24p. 2009. (gr. 3-3). 42.50 (978-1-60851-508-0(7), PowerKids Pr.) 2005. (Illus.). (J). lib. bdg. 22.60 (978-1-4042-2697-5(4)) Rosen Publishing Group, Inc., The.
Thames, Susan. Our American Symbols. 2006. (World Around Me Discovery Library). (Illus.). 24p. (J). (gr. 3-7). lib. bdg. 22.79 (978-1-59515-994-6(0)) Rourke Educational Media.
Traffic Signs Shape Book. 2016. (Illus.). 23p. (J). (978-0-87659-712-5(6)) Gryphon Hse., Inc.
White Fox. The Boy's Book of Signs & Symbols. 2009. (ENG., Illus.). 80p. (J). (gr. 3-7). pap. 10.95 (978-1-59583-349-5(8), 9781595833495, Green Tiger Pr.) Laughing Elephant.
Yasuda, Anita. The 12 Most Amazing American Monuments & Symbols. 2014. (ENG., Illus.). 32p. (J). (978-1-63235-009-1(2)) Pr. Room Editions LLC.

SIKHISM
Barrow, Joy. Sikhism. 2003. (Illus.). lib. bdg. 28.50 (978-1-59389-134-3(2)) Chrysalis Education.
Blake, Philip. We Are Sikhs. 2016. (ENG., Illus.). 32p. (J). (gr. 4-6). pap. 11.99 (978-1-4451-3890-9(5), Franklin Watts) Hachette Children's Group GBR. Dist: Hachette Bk. Group.
Burton, Jennifer. Sikhism. 2017. (J). **(978-1-4222-3821-9(0))** Mason Crest.
Dalton, Dave. Sikhism: Inderjeet's Story. 2013. (Our World of Faith Ser.). (Illus.). 32p. (J). (gr. 3-6). (978-1-84898-617-6(3), TickTock Books) Octopus Publishing Group.
Dicker, Katie & Perihar, Amar Singh. I Belong to the Sikh Faith. 2009. (I Belong Ser.). (Illus.). 24p. (J). (ENG.). pap. 8.25 (978-1-4358-8626-1(7), PowerKids Pr.); (gr. 1-4). lib. bdg. 22.60 (978-1-4358-3036-3(9)) Rosen Publishing Group, Inc., The.
Elby, Tristan & McKain, Neil. World Religions: Hinduism, Buddhism & Sikhism. 2017. (ENG.). 120p. (J). (gr. 6-9). pap. 29.99 **(978-0-00-822769-2(1))** HarperCollins Pubs. Ltd. GBR. Dist: Independent Pubs. Group.
Ganeri, Anita. The Guru Granth Sahib & Sikhism. 2003. 30p. (J). lib. bdg. 24.25 (978-1-58340-245-0(4)) Black Rabbit Bks.
—Sikh Festivals Throughout The Year. 2003. (Year of Festivals Ser.). (Illus.). 30p. lib. bdg. 24.25 (978-1-58340-374-7(4)) Black Rabbit Bks.
—Sikh Stories. Phillips, Rachael, illus. 2003. (Storyteller Ser.). 30p. (J). (978-0-237-52037-3(0)) Evans Brothers, Ltd.
—Sikh Stories. Phillips, Rachael, illus. 2014. (Storyteller Ser.). (ENG.). 32p. (J). (gr. 2-4). pap. 10.99 (978-1-78388-011-9(2)) Tulip Books GBR. Dist: Independent Pubs. Group.
Hawker, Frances & Bhatia, Mohini. Sikhism in India. Campbell, Bruce, photos by. 2009. (ENG., Illus.). 32p. (J). (gr. 3-6). (978-0-7787-5011-6(6)); pap. (978-0-7787-5028-4(0)) Crabtree Publishing Co.
Kaur, Harliv & Kaur, Jasmine, compiled by. My Gurmukhi Khajana: A Gurmat Based Primer. 2007. (ENG & PAN., Illus.). 43p. (J). 13.00 (978-1-60411-000-5(7)) Sikh Research Institute.
Kaur-Singh, Kanwaljit. Sikhism. 2006. (QEB World of Faiths Ser.). (Illus.). 32p. (J). (gr. 3-6). lib. bdg. 27.10 (978-1-59566-211-8(1)) QEB Publishing Inc.
Kaur-Singh, Kanwaljit & Nason, Ruth. Visiting a Gurdwara. 2014. (Start up Religion Ser.). (ENG., Illus.). 32p. (J). (gr. -1-k). pap. 10.99 (978-0-237-54376-1(1)) Evans Brothers, Ltd. GBR. Dist: Independent Pubs. Group.
Marsico, Katie. Sikhism. 2017. (21st Century Skills Library: Global Citizens: World Religions Ser.). (ENG., Illus.). 32p. (J). (gr. 4-7). pap. 14.21 (978-1-63472-291-9(4), 209209) Cherry Lake Publishing.
McKain, Neil. Sikhism. 2017. (ENG.). 40p. (J). (gr. 6-9). pap. 11.99 **(978-0-00-822774-6(8))** HarperCollins Pubs. Ltd. GBR. Dist: Independent Pubs. Group.
Senker, Cath. My Sikh Year. 2007. (Year of Religious Festivals Ser.). (Illus.). 32p. (J). (gr. 1-4). lib. bdg. 25.25 (978-1-4042-3733-9(X)) Rosen Publishing Group, Inc., The.
White, Bender Richardson, et al. Sikhism. 3rd rev. ed. 2009. (World Religions Ser.). (Illus.). 144p. (J). (gr. 6-12). 40.00 (978-1-60413-114-7(4), Chelsea Hse.) Facts On File, Inc.

SIKORSKY, IGOR IVANOVICH, 1889-1972
Wyckoff, Edwin Brit. Helicopter Man: Igor Sikorsky & His Amazing Invention. 2010. (Genius at Work! Great Inventor Biographies Ser.). (Illus.). 32p. (J). 23.94 (978-0-7660-3445-7(3)) Enslow Pubs., Inc.

SILK
see also Silkworms
Gleason, Carrie. The Biography of Silk. 2006. (How Did That Get Here? Ser.). (ENG., Illus.). 32p. (J). (gr. 4-7). pap. (978-0-7787-2523-7(5)); lib. bdg. (978-0-7787-2487-2(5)) Crabtree Publishing Co.
Weil, Ann. The Story Behind Silk, 1 vol. 2011. (True Stories Ser.). (ENG.). 32p. (gr. 3-3). 30.65 (978-1-4329-5442-0(3), NA-h) Heinemann-Raintree.

SILKWORMS
Kite, L. Patricia. Silkworms. 2008. 117p. (Orig.). pap. 14.95 (978-0-7414-4542-1(5)) Infinity Publishing.
Pfeffer, Wendy. Mysterious Spinners. Kim, Julie J., illus. 2005. 48p. (J). (978-1-59336-315-4(X)); pap. (978-1-59336-316-1(8)) Mondo Publishing.

SILVER
see also Money; Silversmithing
Belval, Brian. Silver. 2009. (Understanding the Elements of the Periodic Table Ser.). 48p. (gr. 6-6). 53.00 (978-1-60854-682-4(9), Rosen Reference) Rosen Publishing Group, Inc., The.
Perritano, John. Gold & Silver, Vol. 12. 2015. (North American Natural Resources Ser.). (Illus.). 64p. (J). (gr. 7). 23.95 (978-1-4222-3382-5(0)) Mason Crest.
Petersen, Christine. Silver, 1 vol. 2013. (Earth's Treasures Ser.). (ENG.). 32p. (J). (gr. 3-6). lib. bdg. 27.07 (978-1-61783-874-3(8), Checkerboard Library) ABDO Publishing Co.
Shea, Therese. Silver, Vol. 1. 2014. (Rare & Precious Metals Ser.). (ENG.). 24p. (J). (gr. 2-3). 22.60 (978-1-4824-0509-5(1)) Stevens, Gareth Publishing LLLP.
Sterling, Kristin. Silver & Gold Everywhere. 2010. (Lightning Bolt Books — Colors Everywhere Ser.). (ENG., Illus.). 32p. (gr. k-2). pap. 7.95 (978-0-7613-5662-2(2)); lib. bdg. 26.60 (978-0-7613-4593-0(0), Lerner Pubns.) Lerner Publishing Group.

SILVER MINES AND MINING—FICTION
Wallace, Rich. Double-Crossed at Cactus Flats: An Up2 U Western Adventure, 1 vol. Mitchell, Hazel, illus. 2013. (Up2U Adventures Ser.). (ENG.). 80p. (J). (gr. 2-5). lib. bdg. 27.07 (978-1-61641-966-0(0), Calico Chapter Bks) Magic Wagon.

SILVERSMITHING
see also Metal-Work
Mara, Wil. The Silversmith. 2010. (Colonial People Ser.). 48p. (gr. 3-18). 29.93 (978-0-7614-4804-4(7)) Marshall Cavendish Corp.

SIMPLE (FICTITIOUS CHARACTER)—FICTION
Hughes, Langston. Simple Speaks His Mind. (J). (gr. 5-6). reprint ed. lib. bdg. 22.95 (978-0-88411-061-3(3)) Amereon Ltd.

SIMPSON, O. J., 1947-
Blohm, Craig E. The O. J. Simpson Case. 2008. (Crime Scene Investigations Ser.). (ENG., Illus.). 104p. (YA). (gr. 7-10). lib. bdg. 35.45 (978-1-4205-0038-7(4), LML02109-240025, Lucent Bks.) Cengage Gale.

SINGAPORE
Barber, Nicola. Singapore. 2005. (Great Cities of the World Ser.). (Illus.). 48p. (gr. 5-12). lib. bdg. 31.00 (978-0-8368-5047-5(5), Gareth Stevens Secondary Library) Stevens, Gareth Publishing LLLP.
Bosco, Don. Lion City Adventures: Explore Singapore, Learn Cool Stuff & Solve Mini-Mysteries. 2015. (ENG., Illus.). 80p. pap. 12.99 (978-981-4634-34-2(4)) Marshall Cavendish International (Asia) Private Ltd. SGP. Dist: National Bk. Network.
—Secrets of the Heartlands: Lion City Adventures. 2016. (Sherlock Hong Adventures Ser.: Volume 2). (ENG., Illus.). 96p. pap. 12.99 (978-981-4721-16-5(6)) Marshall Cavendish International (Asia) Private Ltd. SGP. Dist: National Bk. Network.
Kummer, Patricia K. Singapore. 2003. (Enchantment of the World Ser.). (ENG., Illus.). 144p. (YA). (gr. 5-9). 39.00 (978-0-516-22531-9(6)) Scholastic Library Publishing.
Owings, Lisa. Singapore. 2014. (Exploring Countries Ser.). (ENG., Illus.). 32p. (J). (gr. 3-7). lib. bdg. 26.95 (978-1-60014-986-3(3), Blastoff! Readers) Bellwether Media.

SINGAPORE—FICTION
Bidwell, Dafne. Danger Unlimited: Action, Mystery & Adventure. 2007. 244p. pap. 15.50 (978-1-921064-89-0(7)) Fremantle Pr. AUS. Dist: Independent Pubs. Group.
Heidell, Valerie. Mirika's Story. 2006. (YA). per. 10.95 (978-0-9774822-4-5(3)) Crosam Pr.
Irwin, Bindi & Kunz, Chris. Camouflage. 2011. (Bindi's Wildlife Adventures Ser.: 4). (ENG.). 112p. (gr. 3-6). pap. 4.99

(978-1-4022-5523-6(3), Sourcebooks Jabberwocky) Sourcebooks, Inc.

Kok Hoong Derek, Wong. The Little Genius. 2007. 11p. 48.00 (978-1-4303-1605-3(5)) Lulu Pr., Inc.

Lim, Andrew. Tales from the Kopitiam. (Paranormal Singapore Ser.: Vol. 4). (ENG.). 2009. 1p. pap. 9.95 (978-981-08-1081-8(4)) Vol. 3. 3rd ed. 2008. 160p. pap. 9.95 (978-981-08-1080-1(6)) Monsoon Bks. Pte. Ltd. SGP. Dist: Tuttle Publishing, National Bk. Network.

Low, A. J. Sherlock Sam & the Ghostly Moans in Fort Canning: Book Two. 2016. (Sherlock Sam Ser.: 2). (ENG.). 120p. (J). pap. 7.99 (978-1-4494-7788-2(7)) Andrews McMeel Publishing.

—Sherlock Sam & the Missing Heirloom in Katong: Book One. 2016. (Sherlock Sam Ser.: 1). (ENG.). 112p. (J). pap. 7.99 (978-1-4494-7789-9(5)) Andrews McMeel Publishing.

—Sherlock Sam & the Sinister Letters in Bras Basah. 2017. (Sherlock Sam Ser.: 3). (ENG.). 144p. (J). pap. 7.99 (978-1-4494-7975-6(8)) Andrews McMeel Publishing.

Low, J. H. Lost in the Gardens. Low, J. H., illus. 2015. (ENG., Illus.). 48p. 10.00 (978-981-4677-10-3(8)) Marshall Cavendish International (Asia) Private Ltd. SGP. Dist: National Bk. Network.

See, Ee Lin. My Kiasu Teenage Life in Singapore. 2005. (ENG., Illus.). 1p. per. 12.95 (978-981-05-3016-7(1)) Monsoon Bks. Pte. Ltd. SGP. Dist: Tuttle Publishing.

Yunisa. Schoolaholic Princess 2: Romansa Singapura. 2008. 232p. pap. 14.88 (978-1-4357-6044-8(1)) Lulu Pr., Inc.

—Schoolaholic Princess 3: Simfoni Cinta. 2008. 220p. pap. 14.88 (978-1-4357-6045-5(X)) Lulu Pr., Inc.

SINGAPORE—HISTORY

Bankston, John. We Visit Singapore. 2014. (ENG., Illus.). 63p. (J). (gr. 4-8). lib. bdg. 33.95 (978-1-61228-484-2(1)) Mitchell Lane Pubs., Inc.

Bosco, Don. Island of Legends. 2016. (ENG., Illus.). 96p. pap. 12.99 (978-981-4751-36-0(7)) Marshall Cavendish International (Asia) Private Ltd. SGP. Dist: National Bk. Network.

Broadhead, Arp Raph. Mudley Explores Singapore: An Amazing Adventure into the Lion City. 2017. (ENG., Illus.). 64p. pap. 16.50 (978-981-4721-95-0(6)) Marshall Cavendish International (Asia) Private Ltd. SGP. Dist: National Bk. Network.

Layton, Lesley, et al. Singapore. 3rd rev. ed. 2011. (Cultures of the World: 3rd Edition 1 Ser.). (Illus.). 144p. (J). (gr. 6). 47.07 (978-1-60870-787-4(3)) Marshall Cavendish Corp.

Lotlikar, Anita M. Goodnight Singapur. 2012. 28p. pap. 24.95 (978-1-4626-9606-2(6)) America Star Bks.

Mara, Wil. Singapore. 2016. (Enchantment of the World Ser.). (ENG., Illus.). 144p. (J). lib. bdg. 40.00 (978-0-531-23297-2(2), Children's Pr.) Scholastic Library Publishing.

Roydhouse, Sally. Find & Seek Singapore. 2015. (ENG., Illus.). 36p. (gr. -1-7). 24.95 (978-1-939621-11-5(9)) ORO Editions.

SINGERS

Acker, Kerry. Nina Simone. 2003. (Women in the Arts Ser.). (Illus.). 112p. (gr. 6-12). 30.00 (978-0-7910-7456-5(0), Chelsea Hse.) Facts On File, Inc.

Adams, Colleen. Usher. (Stars in the Spotlight Ser.). 32p. (gr. 4-4). 2009. 47.90 (978-1-60853-206-3(2), PowerKids Pr.) 2006. (Illus.). (YA). lib. bdg. 25.25 (978-1-4042-3516-8(7)) Rosen Publishing Group, Inc., The.

Adams, Michelle. Katy Perry. 2011. (Blue Banner Biography Ser.). (Illus.). 32p. (YA). (gr. 4-7). lib. bdg. 25.70 (978-1-61228-051-6(X)) Mitchell Lane Pubs., Inc.

Adams, Michelle Medlock. Jessica Simpson. 2007. (Blue Banner Biography Ser.). (Illus.). 32p. (YA). (gr. 4-7). lib. bdg. 25.70 (978-1-58415-616-1(3)) Mitchell Lane Pubs., Inc.

Alagna, Magdalena. Billie Holiday. (Rock & Roll Hall of Famers Ser.). 112p. (gr. 5-8). 2009. 63.90 (978-1-60852-468-6(X), Rosen Reference) 2006. (Illus.). (YA). lib. bdg. 34.60 (978-0-8239-3640-3(6)) Rosen Publishing Group, Inc., The.

—Elvis Presley. 2009. (Rock & Roll Hall of Famers Ser.). 112p. (gr. 5-8). 63.90 (978-1-60852-474-7(4), Rosen Reference) Rosen Publishing Group, Inc., The.

Aloian, Molly. Lady Gaga. 2011. (ENG.). 32p. (J). pap. (978-0-7787-7614-7(X)); (gr. 3-6). lib. bdg. (978-0-7787-7609-3(3)) Crabtree Publishing Co.

Anderson, Jennifer Joline. Miley Cyrus: Pop Princess, 1 vol. 2014. (Contemporary Lives Set 4 Ser.). (ENG., Illus.). 112p. (J). (gr. 6-12). lib. bdg. 35.64 (978-1-62403-544-9(2), Essential Library) ABDO Publishing Co.

Anderson, Sheila. Miley Cyrus: Music & TV Superstar. 2009. (Hot Celebrity Biographies Ser.). (Illus.). 48p. (J). (gr. 5-9). lib. bdg. 25.27 (978-0-7660-3213-2(2)) Enslow Pubs., Inc.

Angel, Ann. Janis Joplin: Rise up Singing. 2010. (ENG., Illus.). 128p. (YA). (gr. 7-17). 24.95 (978-0-8109-8349-6(4), Amulet Bks.) Abrams, Inc.

Appleby, Alex. I Can Be a Singer. 2014. (When I Grow Up Ser.). 24p. (J). (gr. k-2). 22.60 (978-1-4824-0757-0(4)) Stevens, Gareth Publishing LLLP.

—Puedo Ser una Cantante / I Can Be a Singer. 2014. (Cuando Sea Grande / When I Grow Up Ser.). (SPA.). 24p. (J). (gr. k-2). 22.60 (978-1-4824-0865-2(1)) Stevens, Gareth Publishing LLLP.

Aretha, David. Amy Winehouse: RandB, Jazz, & Soul Musician, 1 vol. 2012. (Lives Cut Short Set 2 Ser.). (ENG.). 112p. (J). (gr. 6-12). 35.64 (978-1-61783-483-7(1)) ABDO Publishing Co.

Aretha Franklin: Singer. 2nd rev. ed. 2010. (Black Americans of Achievement Legacy Edition Ser.). (Illus.). 104p. (gr. 6-12). 35.00 (978-1-60413-712-5(6)) Facts On File, Inc.

Asselin, Kristine Carlson. Jennifer Lopez: Actress & Pop Superstar, 1 vol. 2013. (Contemporary Lives Set 2 Ser.). (ENG.). 112p. (J). (gr. 6-12). lib. bdg. 35.64 (978-1-61783-621-3(4), Essential Library) ABDO Publishing Co.

Azzarelli, Ally. Adele! Singing Sensation. 2013. (Sizzling Celebrities Ser.). 48p. (J). lib. bdg. 25.27 (978-0-7660-4172-1(7)); (gr. 4-9). pap. 8.95 (978-1-4644-0283-8(3)) Enslow Pubs., Inc.

—Justin Bieber: Teen Music Superstar. 2011. (Hot Celebrity Biographies Ser.). (Illus.). 48p. (J). (gr. 5-18). pap. 8.95 (978-1-59845-287-7(8)); lib. bdg. 25.27 (978-0-7660-3873-8(4)) Enslow Pubs., Inc.

—Selena Gomez: Latina TV & Music Star. 2011. (Hot Celebrity Biographies Ser.). (Illus.). 48p. (J). (gr. 5-18). pap. 8.95 (978-1-59845-289-1(4)) Enslow Pubs., Inc.

Bailey, Diane. Miley Cyrus. 2011. (Megastars Ser.). (Illus.). 48p. (YA). (gr. 5-8). lib. bdg. 29.25 (978-1-4358-3573-3(5), Rosen Reference) Rosen Publishing Group, Inc., The.

Baldwin, Garrett. The Justin Bieber Album. 2010. (ENG., Illus.). 64p. (gr. 3-11). pap. 12.95 (978-0-85965-464-7(8)) Plexus Publishing, Ltd. GBR. Dist: Publishers Group West (PGW).

Bankston, John. Alicia Keys. 2004. (Blue Banner Biography Ser.). (Illus.). 32p. (J). lib. bdg. 25.70 (978-1-58415-327-6(X)) Mitchell Lane Pubs., Inc.

—Christina Aguilera. 2004. (Blue Banner Biography Ser.). (Illus.). 32p. (J). lib. bdg. 25.70 (978-1-58415-331-3(8)) Mitchell Lane Pubs., Inc.

—Missy Elliott: Hip-Hop Superstar. l.t. ed. 2004. (Blue Banner Biography Ser.). (Illus.). 32p. (J). (gr. 3-8). lib. bdg. 25.70 (978-1-58415-219-4(2)) Mitchell Lane Pubs., Inc.

—What It's Like to Be Selena Gomez. 2012. (SPA.). (J). lib. bdg. 25.70 (978-1-61228-321-0(7)) Mitchell Lane Pubs., Inc.

Bednar, Chuck. American Idol Profiles Index: Top Finalists from Each Season (82 Contestants) 2009. (Dream Big: American Idol Superstars Ser.). 64p. (YA). (gr. 5-18). pap. 9.95 (978-1-4222-1593-7(8)) Mason Crest.

—Beyoncé. 2010. (Transcending Race in America Ser.). 64p. (YA). (gr. 4-8). lib. bdg. 22.95 (978-1-4222-1607-1(1)) Mason Crest.

—David Archuleta. 2009. (Dream Big: American Idol Superstars Ser.). 64p. (YA). (gr. 5-18). pap. 9.95 (978-1-4222-1597-5(0)); (Illus.). (gr. 4-18). lib. bdg. 22.95 (978-1-4222-1505-0(9)) Mason Crest.

—Kris Allen. 2009. (Dream Big: American Idol Superstars Ser.). 64p. (YA). (gr. 5-18). pap. 9.95 (978-1-4222-1596-8(2)); lib. bdg. 22.95 (978-1-4222-1515-9(6)) Mason Crest.

Benson, Michael. Gloria Estefan. (Biography Ser.). (Illus.). 112p. (gr. 6-12). 2005. lib. bdg. 27.93 (978-0-8225-4982-6(4)) 2003. (YA). pap. 7.95 (978-0-8225-9692-9(X), Carolrhoda Bks.) Lerner Publishing Group.

Bernard, Jan. Justin Bieber. 2012. (Stars of Today Ser.). (ENG.). 32p. (J). (gr. 2-5). 28.50 (978-1-61473-291-4(4), 205043) Child's World, Inc., The.

Betances, Maria. Selena Gomez: Superstar Singer & Actress. 2015. (Exceptional Latinos Ser.). (ENG.). 24p. (J). (gr. 3-4). pap. 9.35 (978-0-7660-6718-9(1)) Enslow Pubs., Inc.

Bezdecheck, Bethany. Missy Elliott. 2009. (Library of Hip-Hop Biographies Ser.). (ENG., Illus.). 48p. (J). (gr. 7-12). pap. 11.75 (978-1-4358-5442-0(X)); 48p. (gr. 5-5). 53.00 (978-1-60853-697-9(1)); (J). lib. bdg. 29.25 (978-1-4358-5056-9(4)) Rosen Publishing Group, Inc., The.

Bieber, Justin. Justin Bieber: First Step 2 Forever - My Story. 2010. (ENG., Illus.). 240p. (J). (gr. 3-7). 21.99 (978-0-06-203974-3(1)) HarperCollins Pubs.

—Justin Bieber: Just Getting Started. 2012. (ENG.). 240p. (J). (gr. 3-7). 21.99 (978-0-06-220208-6(1)) HarperCollins Pubs.

—Justin Bieber: Just Getting Started. (ENG., Illus.). 240p. (978-0-00-744952-1(6)) HarperCollins Pubs. Ltd.

—Justin Bieber - First Step 2 Forever: My Story. 2012. (ENG.). 240p. (J). (gr. 3-7). pap. 12.99 (978-0-06-209158-1(1)) HarperCollins Pubs.

Bingham, Hettie. Adele: The Golden Voice. 2016. (ENG., Illus.). 32p. (J). (gr. 4-6). pap. 11.99 (978-0-7502-8965-8(1), Wayland) Hachette Children's Group GBR. Dist: Hachette Bk. Group.

—Gary Barlow. 2016. (Real-Life Stories Ser.). (ENG., Illus.). 32p. (J). (gr. 4-6). pap. 11.99 (978-0-7502-8955-9(4), Wayland) Hachette Children's Group GBR. Dist: Hachette Bk. Group.

Bloom, Ronny. Justin Bieber. 2011. (SPA.). 192p. (YA). 14.95 (978-84-666-4680-2(9)) Ediciones B ESP. Dist: Spanish Pubs., LLC.

Bodden, Valerie. Justin Bieber: Musical Phenom, 1 vol. 2012. (Contemporary Lives Set 1 Ser.). (ENG.). 112p. (J). (gr. 6-12). lib. bdg. 35.64 (978-1-61783-321-2(5)) ABDO Publishing Co.

—Rihanna. 2013. (Illus.). 24p. (J). (978-1-60818-479-8(X), Creative Education) Creative Co., The.

—Selena Gomez. 2015. (Illus.). 21p. (J). (978-1-60818-498-9(6), Creative Education) Creative Co., The.

Bolte, Mari. Justin Bieber. 2012. (Star Biographies Ser.). (ENG.). 32p. (gr. 3-4). pap. 47.70 (978-1-4296-9457-5(2)); (Illus.). lib. bdg. 27.99 (978-1-4296-8665-5(0)) Capstone Press of Coughlan Cos. (Snap Bks.).

Boone, Mary. Jennette McCurdy. 2010. (Robbie Reader Ser.). (Illus.). 32p. (YA). (gr. 2-5). lib. bdg. 25.70 (978-1-58415-900-1(6)) Mitchell Lane Pubs., Inc.

—Pink. 2009. (Blue Banner Biography Ser.). (Illus.). 32p. (YA). (gr. 4-7). lib. bdg. 25.70 (978-1-58415-767-0(4)) Mitchell Lane Pubs., Inc.

—Vanessa Anne Hudgens. 2008. (Blue Banner Biography Ser.). (Illus.). 32p. (YA). (gr. 4-7). lib. bdg. 25.70 (978-1-58415-672-7(4)) Mitchell Lane Pubs., Inc.

Boone, Mary & Sprinkel, Katy. Bieber Fever. 2011. (ENG., Illus.). 112p. (J). (gr. 7). pap. 12.95 (978-1-60078-634-1(0)) Triumph Bks.

Boyer, Marilyn. For you they Signed. 2010. (YA). lib. bdg. 34.99 (978-0-89051-598-3(0)) Master Bks.

Brian, Janeen. Meet Nellie Melba. Murphy, Claire, illus. 2016. (ENG.). 32p. (J). (gr. k-2). 22.99 (978-0-14-378029-8(8)) Random Hse. Australia AUS. Dist: Independent Pubs. Group.

Briere-Haquet, Alice. Nina. 2017. 40p. (J). (-2). 13.99 **(978-958-30-5461-7(5))** Panamericana Editorial COL. Dist: Lectorum Pubns., Inc.

Briggs, John. Pete Seeger the People's Singer. 2015. (ENG., Illus.). 112p. (J). pap. 6.99 (978-0-9905160-7-1(5)) Atombank Bks.

Broadwater, Andrea. The Life of Marian Anderson: Diva & Humanitarian. 2015. (Legendary African Americans Ser.). 96p. (J). (gr. 6-12). 27.94 (978-0-7660-6285-6(6)); pap. 10.95 (978-0-7660-6286-3(4)) Enslow Pubs., Inc.

Brooks, Riley. Carrie Underwood - American Dream. 2013. (ENG.). 48p. (J). (gr. 3-7). pap. 4.99 (978-0-545-62189-2(5)) Scholastic, Inc.

—Debby Ryan: Her Sweet Life! 2010. (Illus.). 32p. (J). pap. (978-0-545-29637-3(4)) Scholastic, Inc.

—Rachel Crow: from the Heart. 2013. (ENG.). 32p. (J). (gr. 3-7). pap. 3.99 (978-0-545-55000-0(9)) Math Solutions.

—Willow Smith: Pop's Newest Princess. 2011. (Illus.). 46p. (J). pap. (978-0-545-36887-2(1)) Scholastic, Inc.

Brown, Anne K. & Burns, Jan. Gwen Stefani. 2009. (People in the News Ser.). (ENG., Illus.). 128p. (gr. 7-12). lib. bdg. 39.40 (978-1-4205-0126-1(7), LML02109-245440) Cengage Gale.

Brown, Monica. My Name Is Celia: The Life of Celia Cruz. López, Rafael, illus. 2004.Tr. of Me Llamo Celia - La Vida de Celia Cruz. (ENG, SPA & MUL.). 32p. (J). (gr. k-3). 15.95 (978-0-87358-872-0(X)) Cooper Square Publishing Llc.

—My Name is Celia (Me Llamo Celia) The Life of Celia Cruz (La Vida de Celia Cruz) López, Rafael, illus. 2015. (ENG, MUL & SPA.). 32p. (J). (gr. k-3). pap. 7.95 (978-1-58979-998-1(4)) Jaffe Book Solutions.

Brown, Risa. Day by Day with Carrie Underwood. 2014. (ENG., Illus.). 32p. (J). (gr. -1-2). 25.70 (978-1-61228-631-0(3)) Mitchell Lane Pubs., Inc.

Burlingame, Jeff. Avril Lavigne: Celebrity with Heart. 2010. (Celebrities with Heart Ser.). 112p. (J). (gr. 7-12). 33.27 (978-0-7660-3407-5(0)); (Illus.). pap. 10.95 (978-1-59845-204-4(5)) Enslow Pubs., Inc.

—Demi! Latina Star Demi Lovato. 2013. (Sizzling Celebrities Ser.). 48p. (J). (gr. 4-9). pap. 8.95 (978-1-4644-0277-7(9)) Enslow Pubs., Inc.

Burns, Kylie. Carrie Underwood. 2013. (ENG., Illus.). 32p. (J). (978-0-7787-0024-1(0)); pap. (978-0-7787-0043-2(7)) Crabtree Publishing Co.

Buster Books Staff. I Love Niall. 2013. (I Love One Direction Ser.). (ENG., Illus.). 96p. (J). (gr. 3-7). pap. 8.99 (978-1-78055-216-3(5)) O'Mara, Michael Bks., Ltd. GBR. Dist: Independent Pubs. Group.

Cartlidge, Cherese. Beyonce. 2012. (People in the News Ser.). (ENG., Illus.). 128p. (gr. 7-10). lib. bdg. 39.40 (978-1-4205-0752-2(4), Lucent Bks.) Cengage Gale.

Casapulla, Louise. Ashlee Simpson. 2005. (Pop People Ser.). (Illus.). 137p. (J). (978-0-439-76581-7(1)) Scholastic, Inc.

Cefrey, Holly. Justin Timberlake. (Contemporary Musicians & Their Music Ser.). 48p. 2009. (Illus.). (gr. 7-12). pap. 11.75 (978-1-4358-5123-8(4), Rosen Classroom) 2009. (gr. 6-6). 53.00 (978-1-61511-938-7(8)) 2008. (Illus.). (J). lib. bdg. 29.25 (978-1-4042-1815-4(7)) Rosen Publishing Group, Inc., The.

Celia Cruz. 2010. (Great Hispanic Heritage Ser.). (Illus.). 112p. (gr. 6-12). 35.00 (978-1-60413-771-2(1), Chelsea Hse.) Facts On File, Inc.

Chambers, Veronica. Celia Cruz, Queen of Salsa. Maren, Julie, illus. 2008. (J). (gr. -1-3). 25.95 incl. audio (978-1-4301-0281-6(0)); 28.95 incl. audio compact disk (978-1-4301-0284-7(5)); pap. 16.95 incl. audio (978-1-4301-0280-9(2)) Live Oak Media.

—Celia Cruz, Queen of Salsa. Maren, Julie, illus. 2007. (ENG.). 40p. (J). (gr. k-3). pap. 7.99 (978-0-14-240779-0(8), Puffin Books) Penguin Young Readers Group.

—Celia Cruz, Queen of Salsa. Maren, Julie, illus. 2007. (gr. 2-5). 17.00 (978-0-7569-8153-2(0)) Perfection Learning Corp.

Chandler, Michael. The Littlest Cowboy's Christmas, 2 vols. Jacobsen, Terry, illus. 2006. (ENG.). 32p. (J). (gr. k-3). 17.95 (978-1-58980-381-7(7)) Pelican Publishing Co., Inc.

Collins, Tracy Brown & Chuck D. Missy Elliott. 2007. (Hip-Hop Stars Ser.). (Illus.). 100p. (YA). (gr. 7-12). lib. bdg. 30.00 (978-0-7910-9569-0(X)) Facts On File, Inc.

Colson, Mary. Beyoncé: A Life in Music. 2010. (Culture in Action Ser.). (ENG.). 32p. (gr. 3-6). 30.65 (978-1-4109-3914-2(6), NA-r) Heinemann-Raintree.

Cooke, C. W. Fame: Big Time Rush. 2012. (ENG., Illus.). 40p. (YA). pap. 7.99 (978-1-4507-5663-1(8)) Bluewater Productions, Inc.

—Lady Gaga - Fame. 2012. (ENG., Illus.). 40p. (YA). pap. 7.99 (978-1-4507-4920-6(8)) Bluewater Productions, Inc.

Coombs, Karen Mueller. Woody Guthrie: America's Folksinger. 2003. (Illus.). 120p. (J). pap. 8.95 (978-0-8225-3750-2(8)) Lerner Publishing Group.

Corporate Contributor. Selena Gomez. 2012. (ENG.). 32p. (J). (978-0-7787-7617-8(4)); pap. (978-0-7787-7630-7(1)) Crabtree Publishing Co.

Cummings, Judy Dodge. Macklemore & Ryan Lewis: Grammy-Winning Hip-Hop Duo, 1 vol. 2014. (Contemporary Lives Set 4 Ser.). (ENG., Illus.). 112p. (J). (gr. 6-12). lib. bdg. 35.64 (978-1-62403-545-6(0), Essential Library) ABDO Publishing Co.

Currie, Cherie & O'Neill, Tony. Neon Angel: A Memoir of a Runaway. 2010. (ENG.). 368p. 24.99 (978-0-06-196135-9(3)) HarperCollins Pubs.

Currie-McGhee, L. K. Miley Cyrus. 2009. (People in the News Ser.). (ENG., Illus.). 128p. (gr. 7-12). lib. bdg. 39.40 (978-1-4205-0127-8(5), LML02109-245441) Cengage Gale.

Dann, Sarah. Beyoncé. 2013. (ENG., Illus.). 32p. (J). (978-0-7787-0019-7(4)) Crabtree Publishing Co.

—Beyonce. 2013. (ENG., Illus.). 32p. (J). pap. (978-0-7787-0039-5(9)) Crabtree Publishing Co.

Danziger, Meryl. Sing It! A Biography of Pete Seeger. 2016. (ENG., Illus.). 112p. (J). (gr. 3-7). 17.95 (978-1-60980-655-2(7), Triangle Square) Seven Stories Pr.

Davidson, Amy. Darren Criss. 2012. (Rising Stars Ser.). (Illus.). 32p. (gr. 3-6). 25.25 (978-1-4339-7276-8(X)); pap. 10.50 (978-1-4339-7277-5(8)) Stevens, Gareth Publishing LLLP.

—Keke Palmer. 2012. (Rising Stars Ser.). (Illus.). 32p. (J). (gr. 3-6). 25.25 (978-1-4339-7287-4(5)); pap. 10.50 (978-1-4339-7284-3(0)) Stevens, Gareth Publishing LLLP.

Day, Holly. Shakira. 2007. (People in the News Ser.). (ENG., Illus.). 104p. (YA). (gr. 7-12). lib. bdg. 33.95 (978-1-59018-974-0(4)) Cengage Gale.

De Medeiros, James. Justin Timberlake. 2008. (Remarkable People Ser.). (Illus.). 24p. (J). (gr. 4-6). pap. 8.95 (978-1-59036-983-8(1)); lib. bdg. 24.45 (978-1-59036-982-1(3)) Weigl Pubs., Inc.

Diver, Lucas. Austin Mahone: Famous Pop Singer & Songwriter, 1 vol. 2014. (Pop Bios Ser.). (ENG., Illus.). 24p. (J). (gr. 2-4). lib. bdg. 28.50 (978-1-62970-724-2(4)) ABDO Publishing Co.

—Katy Perry: Famous Pop Singer & Songwriter, 1 vol. 2014. (Pop Bios Ser.). (ENG., Illus.). 24p. (J). (gr. 2-4). lib. bdg. 28.50 (978-1-62970-725-9(2)) ABDO Publishing Co.

Doeden, Matt. Adele: Soul Music's Magical Voice. 2013. (USA TODAY Lifeline Biographies Ser.). (ENG., Illus.). 112p. (gr. 6-12). lib. bdg. 34.60 (978-1-4677-0808-1(9)) Lerner Publishing Group.

—Lady Gaga: Pop's Glam Queen. 2012. (USA TODAY Lifeline Biographies Ser.). (ENG., Illus.). 112p. (gr. 6-12). lib. bdg. 34.60 (978-0-7613-8153-2(8)) Lerner Publishing Group.

Donovan, Sandy. Zoe Kravitz: X-Men's Amazing Angel. 2013. (Pop Culture Bios Ser.). (ENG., Illus.). 32p. (gr. 3-6). pap. 7.95 (978-1-4677-0885-2(2)); lib. bdg. 26.60 (978-1-4677-0747-3(3), Lerner Pubns.) Lerner Publishing Group.

Dougherty, Steve. Justin Timberlake. 2009. (Illus.). 112p. (J). (978-0-531-23401-3(0), Franklin Watts) Hachette Children's Group.

Dougherty, Terri. Justin Timberlake. 2008. (People in the News Ser.). (ENG., Illus.). 128p. (gr. 7-10). lib. bdg. 39.40 (978-1-4205-0056-1(2), LML02109-249044, Lucent Bks.) Cengage Gale.

—Raven-Symoné. (Role Model Entertainers Ser.). (Illus.). 64p. (YA). 2010. (gr. 7-12). 22.95 (978-1-4222-0508-2(8)) 2007. pap. 9.95 (978-1-4222-0795-6(1)) Mason Crest.

Duggleby, John. Uh Huh! The Story of Ray Charles. 2005. (Modern Music Masters Ser.). (Illus.). 160p. (gr. 9-12). lib. bdg. 28.95 (978-1-931798-65-5(6)) Reynolds, Morgan Inc.

Dzidrums, Christine. Kelly Clarkson: Behind Her Hazel Eyes. 2013. 104p. pap. 9.99 (978-1-938438-19-6(1)) Creative Media Publishing.

Earl, C. F. Alicia Keys. 2012. (J). pap. (978-1-4222-2547-9(X)); (Illus.). 48p. (gr. 3-4). 19.95 (978-1-4222-2521-9(6)) Mason Crest.

Earl, C. F. & Hill, Z. B. Rihanna. 2012. (Superstars of Hip-Hop Ser.). 48p. (J). (gr. 3-4). pap. 9.95 (978-1-4222-2552-3(6)); (Illus.). 19.95 (978-1-4222-2526-4(7)) Mason Crest.

Eason, Sarah & Levete, Sarah. Kylie Minogue. 2016. (Real-Life Stories Ser.). (ENG., Illus.). 32p. (J). (gr. 4-6). 17.99 (978-0-7502-9046-3(3), Wayland) Hachette Children's Group GBR. Dist: Hachette Bk. Group.

Edge, Laura B. Hilary Duff: Celebrity with Heart. 2010. (Celebrities with Heart Ser.). (Illus.). 128p. (J). pap. 10.95 (978-1-59845-205-1(3)) Enslow Pubs., Inc.

Edge, Laura Bufano. Hilary Duff: Celebrity with Heart. 2010. (Celebrities with Heart Ser.). (Illus.). 128p. (J). (gr. 7-12). 33.27 (978-0-7660-3404-4(6)) Enslow Pubs., Inc.

Edwards, Laurie J. Rihanna. 2009. (People in the News Ser.). (ENG., Illus.). 128p. (YA). (gr. 7-12). lib. bdg. 33.95 (978-1-4205-0129-2(1), LML02109-245443) Cengage Gale.

Ellison, Katie. Who Was Bob Marley? Copeland, Gregory, illus. 2017. (Who Was? Ser.). (ENG.). 112p. (J). (gr. 3-7). 5.99 (978-0-448-48919-3(8), Grosset & Dunlap) Penguin Young Readers Group.

—Who Was Bob Marley? 2017. (Who Was... ? Ser.). lib. bdg. 16.00 **(978-0-606-40115-9(6))** Turtleback Bks.

Figueroa, Acton. Julio Iglesias & Enrique Iglesias. 2009. (Famous Families Ser.). 48p. (gr. 5-5). 53.00 (978-1-61512-508-1(6)) Rosen Publishing Group, Inc., The.

Flores, Christopher Lee. Pharrell Williams: Singer & Songwriter. 2016. (Junior Biographies Ser.). 24p. (J). pap. 9.35 (978-0-7660-8192-5(3)) Enslow Pubs., Inc.

Ford, Carin T. Paul Robeson: I Want to Make Freedom Ring. 2007. (African-American Biography Library). (Illus.). 128p. (J). (gr. 3-7). lib. bdg. 33.27 (978-0-7660-2703-9(1)) Enslow Pubs., Inc.

—Ray Charles: I Was Born with Music Inside Me. 2007. (African-American Biography Library). (Illus.). 128p. (J). (gr. 6-12). lib. bdg. 33.27 (978-0-7660-2701-5(5)) Enslow Pubs., Inc.

Frank, Mary Kate. Carrie Underwood. 2009. (Today's Superstars Ser.). 48p. (J). (gr. 5-8). pap. 14.05 (978-1-4339-2377-7(7)); lib. bdg. 31.95 (978-1-4339-2381-4(5)) Stevens, Gareth Publishing LLLP.

—Rihanna. 2009. (Today's Superstars Ser.). 48p. (J). (gr. 5-8). pap. 14.05 (978-1-4339-2375-3(0)); lib. bdg. 31.95 (978-1-4339-2379-1(3)) Stevens, Gareth Publishing LLLP.

Franke, Aife. Julianne Hough. 2010. (Country Music Stars Ser.). (ENG.). 32p. (J). (gr. 3-8). pap. 10.50 (978-1-4339-3933-4(9)); lib. bdg. 25.25 (978-1-4339-3932-7(0)) Stevens, Gareth Publishing LLLP.

Franke, Livia. Kathleen Battle: American Soprano. 2010. (Inspiring Lives Ser.). (Illus.). 32p. (J). (gr. 5-8). pap. 10.50 (978-1-4339-3635-7(6)); lib. bdg. 25.25 (978-1-4339-3634-0(8), 1309371) Stevens, Gareth Publishing LLLP.

Franks, Katie. Miley Cyrus. 2009. 24p. (gr. 1-6). pap. 9.40 (978-1-4042-4532-7(4), Rosen Classroom); (gr. 2-3). 42.50 (978-1-61513-885-2(4), PowerKids Pr.); (Illus.). (J). (gr. 1-6). lib. bdg. 22.60 (978-1-4042-4467-2(0), PowerKids Pr.) Rosen Publishing Group, Inc., The.

Freedman, Russell. The Voice That Challenged a Nation: Marian Anderson & the Struggle for Equal Rights. (ENG., Illus.). 128p. (J). (gr. 5-7). 2011. pap. 10.99 (978-0-547-48034-3(2)) 2004. tchr. ed. 18.00 (978-0-618-15976-5(2)) Houghton Mifflin Harcourt Publishing Co.

Frisch, Aaron. Justin Bieber. 2013. (Illus.). 24p. (J). 25.65 (978-1-60818-330-2(0), Creative Education) Creative Co., The.

—Katy Perry. 2013. (Illus.). 24p. (J). 25.65 (978-1-60818-331-9(9), Creative Education) Creative Co., The.

—Lady Gaga. 2013. (Illus.). 24p. (J). 25.65 (978-1-60818-332-6(7), Creative Education) Creative Co., The.

Gagne, Tammy. Adele. 2012. (Illus.). 32p. (J). lib. bdg. 25.70 (978-1-61228-314-2(4)) Mitchell Lane Pubs., Inc.

—Day by Day with Justin Bieber. 2011. (Day by Day with... Ser.). (Illus.). 32p. (J). (gr. -1-2). lib. bdg. 25.70 (978-1-58415-984-1(7)) Mitchell Lane Pubs., Inc.

—Debby Ryan. 2012. (Illus.). 32p. (J). lib. bdg. 25.70 (978-1-61228-332-6(2)) Mitchell Lane Pubs., Inc.

—Ed Sheeran. 2017. lib. bdg. 25.70 **(978-1-68020-129-1(8))** Mitchell Lane Pubs., Inc.

—Kesha. 2011. (Blue Banner Biography Ser.). (Illus.). 32p. (YA). (gr. 4-7). lib. bdg. 25.70 (978-1-61228-052-3(8)) Mitchell Lane Pubs., Inc.

Gagne, Tammy. The Weeknd. 2017. lib. bdg. 25.70 **(978-1-68020-124-6(7))** Mitchell Lane Pubs., Inc.

S

Gaines, Ann Graham. Britney Spears. 2004. (Blue Banner Biography Ser.). (Illus.). 32p. (J). lib. bdg. 25.70 *(978-1-58415-329-0(6))* Mitchell Lane Pubs., Inc.

Galaxy of Superstars. 2005. (Galaxy of Superstars Ser.). (gr. 6-12). 375.00 *(978-0-7910-9145-6(7)*, Chelsea Hse.) Facts On File, Inc.

Gale Editor, ed. Jennifer Hudson. 2011. (People in the News Ser.). (Illus.). 128p. (YA). (gr. 7-12). lib. bdg. 33.95 *(978-1-4205-0607-5(2))* Cengage Gale.

—Katy Perry. 2011. (People in the News Ser.). (Illus.). 128p. (J). lib. bdg. 33.95 *(978-1-4205-0609-9(9)*, Lucent Bks.) Cengage Gale.

Ganchy, Sally. Taylor Hicks. (Who's Your Idol? Ser.). 48p. 2009. (gr. 5-5). 53.00 *(978-1-60854-789-0(2)*, Rosen Reference) 2008. (Illus.). (J). (gr. 3-7). lib. bdg. 29.25 *(978-1-4042-1368-5(6))* Rosen Publishing Group, Inc., The.

Gibson, Karen. What It's Like to Be Jennifer Lopez. de la Vega, Eida, tr. from ENG. 2011. (What It's Like to Be... = Que Se Sienta Al Ser... Ser.). (SPA., Illus.). 32p. (J). (gr. -1-2). lib. bdg. 25.70 *(978-1-58415-990-2(1))* Mitchell Lane Pubs., Inc.

Gnojewski, Carol. Madonna: Express Yourself. 2007. (American Rebels Ser.). (Illus.). 160p. (YA). (gr. 4-7). lib. bdg. 35.94 *(978-0-7660-2442-7(3))* Enslow Pubs., Inc.

Gogerly, Liz. Justin Bieber. 2013. (Illus.). 32p. (J). 28.50 *(978-1-59771-415-0(1)*, 1346767) Sea-To-Sea Pubns.

—Taylor Momsen. 2013. (Illus.). 32p. (J). 28.50 *(978-1-59771-418-1(6))* Sea-To-Sea Pubns.

Golio, Gary. Strange Fruit: Billie Holiday & the Power of a Protest Song. Riley-Webb, Charlotte, illus. 2017. (Millbrook Picture Bks.). (ENG.). 40p. (gr. 3-6). 30.65 ***(978-1-5124-2837-7(X)***, Millbrook Pr.) Lerner Publishing Group.

Gomez, Selena. Selena Gomez Style Guide. 2010. 14.99 *(978-1-4231-2976-9(8))* Hyperion Bks. for Children.

Goodall, Lian. Singing Towards the Future: The Story of Portia White. 2nd ed. 2008. (Stories of Canada Ser.: 6). (ENG.). 72p. (J). pap. 18.99 *(978-1-894917-55-1(3)*, Napoleon & Co.) Dundurn CAN. Dist: Ingram Publisher Services.

Gordon, Katherine. Michael Jackson: Ultimate Music Legend. 2010. (Illus.). 48p. (J). pap. 8.95 *(978-0-7613-6002-5(6)*, Lerner Pubns.) Lerner Publishing Group.

Gosman, Gillian. Chris Colfer. 2012. (Kid Stars! Ser.). (ENG., Illus.). 24p. (J). (gr. 1-6). pap. 8.25 *(978-1-4488-6347-1(3))*; lib. bdg. 22.60 *(978-1-4488-6193-4(4))* Rosen Publishing Group, Inc., The. (PowerKids Pr.).

—Justin Bieber. 2012. (Kid Stars! Ser.). (ENG., Illus.). 24p. (J). (gr. 1-6). pap. 8.25 *(978-1-4488-6339-6(2))*; lib. bdg. 22.60 *(978-1-4488-6190-3(X))* Rosen Publishing Group, Inc., The. (PowerKids Pr.).

—Meaghan Jette Martin. 2012. (Kid Stars! Ser.). (ENG., Illus.). 24p. (J). (gr. 1-6). pap. 8.25 *(978-1-4488-6343-3(0))*; lib. bdg. 22.60 *(978-1-4488-6192-7(6))* Rosen Publishing Group, Inc., The. (PowerKids Pr.).

Greenberger, Robert. Christina Aguilera. (Contemporary Musicians & Their Music Ser.). 48p. 2009. (Illus.). (gr. 7-12). pap. 11.75 *(978-1-4358-5124-5(2)*, Rosen Classroom) 2009. (gr. 6-6). 53.00 *(978-1-61511-929-5(9))* 2008. (Illus.). (J). lib. bdg. 29.25 *(978-1-4042-1816-1(5))* Rosen Publishing Group, Inc., The.

Greenfield, Eloise. Paul Robeson. Ford, George, illus. 2009. (ENG.). 40p. (J). (gr. 1-6). pap. 10.95 *(978-1-60060-262-7(2))* Lee & Low Bks., Inc.

Greenfield, Eloise & Ford, George. Paul Robeson. 2009. (ENG., Illus.). 40p. (J). (gr. 1-6). 10.95 *(978-1-60060-256-6(8))* Lee & Low Bks., Inc.

Griffin, Maeve. Ciara. 2012. (Hip-Hop Headliners Ser.). (ENG., Illus.). 32p. (J). (gr. 4-8). pap. 10.50 *(978-1-4339-6602-6(6))*; lib. bdg. 25.25 *(978-1-4339-6600-2(X))* Stevens, Gareth Publishing LLLP.

Griffiths, Katie. Beyoncé. 2017. (J). ***(978-1-5026-2705-6(1))*** Cavendish Square Publishing.

Griffiths, Katie. Rihanna. 2015. (Illus.). 48p. (J). lib. bdg. *(978-1-62713-313-5(5))* Cavendish Square Publishing.

Haldy, Emma E. Marian Anderson. Bane, Jeff, illus. 2016. (My Early Library: My Itty-Bitty Bio Ser.). (ENG.). 24p. (J). (gr. k-1). 28.50 *(978-1-63471-023-7(1)*, 208172) Cherry Lake Publishing.

Hand. Westlife. (Illus.). 128p. (J). *(978-1-85227-995-0(8)*, Virgin Books Limited) Ebury Publishing.

Harris, Ashley Rae. Nicki Minaj: Rapper & Fashion Star, 1 vol. 2013. (Contemporary Lives Set 2 Ser.). (ENG.). 112p. (J). (gr. 6-12). lib. bdg. 35.64 *(978-1-61783-622-0(2)*, Essential Library) ABDO Publishing Co.

Harte, Harlee. I Justin Bieber. 2010. 144p. pap. 4.95 *(978-1-60747-777-8(7)*, Pickwick Pr.) Phoenix Bks., Inc.

Heatley, Michael. Katy Perry. 2015. (Pop Icons Ser.). (Illus.). 64p. (J). (gr. 7). lib. bdg. 23.95 *(978-1-4222-3248-4(4))* Mason Crest.

Heatley, Michael & Gent, Mike. Taylor Swift. 2015. (Pop Icons Ser.). (Illus.). 64p. (J). (gr. 7). lib. bdg. 23.95 *(978-1-4222-3250-7(6))* Mason Crest.

Heos, Bridget. Lady Gaga. 2011. (Megastars Ser.). (Illus.). 48p. (YA). (gr. 5-8). lib. bdg. 29.25 *(978-1-4358-3574-0(3))* Rosen Publishing Group, Inc., The.

—Rihanna. 2011. (Megastars Ser.). (Illus.). 48p. (YA). (gr. 5-8). lib. bdg. 29.25 *(978-1-4358-3576-4(X))* Rosen Publishing Group, Inc., The.

Heppermann, Christine. Whitney Houston: Recording Artist & Actress, 1 vol. 2012. (Lives Cut Short Set 2 Ser.). (ENG.). 112p. (J). (gr. 6-12). lib. bdg. 35.64 *(978-1-61783-544-5(7)*, Essential Library) ABDO Publishing Co.

Herringshaw, DeAnn. Dorothy Dandridge: Singer & Actress, 1 vol. 2011. (Essential Lives Set 6 Ser.). (ENG., Illus.). 112p. (J). (gr. 6-12). lib. bdg. 35.64 *(978-1-61714-779-1(6)*, Essential Library) ABDO Publishing Co.

Higgins, Nadia. Bella Thorne: Shaking up the Small Screen. 2013. (Pop Culture Bios Ser.). (ENG., Illus.). 32p. (gr. 3-6). pap. 7.95 *(978-1-4677-1549-2(2))*; lib. bdg. 26.60 *(978-1-4677-1308-5(2)*, Lerner Pubns.) Lerner Publishing Group.

—Carly Rae Jepsen: Call Her Amazing. 2013. (Pop Culture Bios Ser.). (ENG.). 32p. (gr. 3-6). lib. bdg. 26.60 *(978-1-4677-1306-1(6)*, Lerner Pubns.); (Illus.). pap. 7.95 *(978-1-4677-1547-8(6))* Lerner Publishing Group.

—Justin Bieber: Pop & R & B Idol. 2012. (Pop Culture Bios Ser.). (ENG., Illus.). 32p. (gr. 3-6). pap. 7.95 *(978-1-4677-0295-9(1))*; lib. bdg. 26.60 *(978-1-4677-0294-2(3)*, Lerner Pubns.) Lerner Publishing Group.

—Katy Perry: From Gospel Singer to Pop Star. 2012. (Pop Culture Bios Ser.). (ENG., Illus.). 32p. (gr. 3-6). pap. 7.95 *(978-1-4677-0236-2(6))*; lib. bdg. 26.60 *(978-0-7613-4145-1(5)*, Lerner Pubns.) Lerner Publishing Group.

Hill, Z. B. Beyoncé. 2012. (J). pap. *(978-1-4222-2536-3(4))*; (Illus.). 48p. (gr. 3-4). 19.95 *(978-1-4222-2510-3(0))* Mason Crest.

—Ciara. 2012. (Superstars of Hip-Hop Ser.). (Illus.). 48p. (J). (gr. 3-4). 19.95 *(978-1-4222-2513-4(5))* Mason Crest.

—Usher. 2012. (J). pap. *(978-1-4222-2557-8(7))*; (Illus.). 48p. (gr. 3-4). 19.95 *(978-1-4222-2531-8(3))* Mason Crest.

Hillstrom, Laurie Collier. Kelly Clarkson. 2007. (People in the News Ser.). (ENG., Illus.). 104p. (YA). (gr. 7-12). lib. bdg. 33.95 *(978-1-4205-0013-4(9))* Cengage Gale.

Horn, Geoffrey M. Alicia Keys. 2005. (Today's Superstars). (Illus.). 32p. (gr. 5-8). lib. bdg. 31.95 *(978-0-8368-4233-3(2))* Stevens, Gareth Publishing LLLP.

—Beyonce. 2005. (Today's Superstars). (Illus.). 32p. (gr. 5-8). lib. bdg. 31.95 *(978-0-8368-4230-2(8))* Stevens, Gareth Publishing LLLP.

Howse, Jennifer. Miley Cyrus. 2008. (Remarkable People Ser.). (Illus.). 24p. (J). (gr. 4-6). pap. 8.95 *(978-1-59036-985-2(8))*; lib. bdg. 24.45 *(978-1-59036-984-5(X))* Weigl Pubs., Inc.

—Rihanna: Remarkable People. 2010. 25.70 *(978-1-61690-151-6(9))*; pap. 11.95 *(978-1-61690-152-3(7))* Weigl Pubs., Inc. (AV2 by Weigl).

Hubbard-Brown, Janet. Ray Charles. 2008. (Black Americans of Achievement Ser.). (Illus.). 112p. (gr. 6-12). 35.00 *(978-1-60413-001-0(6)*, Chelsea Hse.) Facts On File, Inc.

Hurst, Heidi. Jennifer Lopez. 2003. (People in the News Ser.). (Illus.). 112p. (J). 32.45 *(978-1-59018-325-0(8)*, Lucent Bks.) Cengage Gale.

Isbell, Hannah. Rihanna: Pop Star. 2017. (Junior Biographies Ser.). 24p. (gr. 3-4). (J). pap. 9.35 ***(978-0-7660-8783-5(2))***; lib. bdg. 22.60 ***(978-0-7660-8674-6(7))*** Enslow Pubs., Inc.

Janic, Susan. Living the Dream: Hannah Montana & Miley Cyrus - The Unofficial Story. 2008. (ENG., Illus.). 144p. (J). (gr. 4-7). pap. *(978-1-55022-848-9(X))* Filmer Ltd.

Jeffery, Marika. Carrie Underwood. (Sharing the American Dream Ser.). 2009. 64p. (YA). (gr. 7-12). 22.95 *(978-1-4222-0599-0(1))* 2008. (J). pap. 9.95 *(978-1-4222-0764-2(1))* Mason Crest.

Jeffrey, Gary. Bob Marley: The Life of a Musical Legend. Riley, Terry, illus. 2007. (Graphic Nonfiction Biographies Ser.). (ENG.). 48p. (YA). (gr. 4-7). lib. bdg. 31.95 *(978-1-4042-0854-4(2))* Rosen Publishing Group, Inc., The.

Johns, Michael-Anne. School Cool. 2009. (Illus.). 48p. (J). *(978-0-545-15901-2(6))* Scholastic, Inc.

Johnson, Robin. Katy Perry. 2011. (ENG.). 32p. (J). pap. *(978-0-7787-7613-0(1))*; (gr. 3-6). lib. bdg. *(978-0-7787-7608-6(5))* Crabtree Publishing Co.

—Rihanna. 2013. (ENG., Illus.). 32p. (J). *(978-0-7787-1051-6(3))*; pap. *(978-0-7787-1055-4(6))* Crabtree Publishing Co.

Jones, Jen. Beyoncé Knowles. 2012. (Star Biographies Ser.). (ENG.). 32p. (gr. 3-4). pap. 47.70 *(978-1-4296-9461-2(0)*, Snap Bks.) Capstone Press of Coughlan Cos.

Jordin Sparks. 2013. (Rising Stars Ser.). 32p. (J). (gr. 3-6). pap. 63.00 *(978-1-4339-8983-4(2))* Stevens, Gareth Publishing LLLP.

Kaminsky, Kristy & Domboski, Brian. Ashlee & Jessica Simpson. 2008. (Pop Culture Ser.). (Illus.). 64p. (YA). (gr. 3-7). lib. bdg. 22.95 *(978-1-4222-0208-1(9))* Mason Crest.

Kampff, Joseph. Beyonce: Singer, Songwriter, & Actress. 2016. (Exceptional African Americans Ser.). (ENG., Illus.). 24p. (J). (gr. 3-3). 22.60 *(978-0-7660-7170-4(7))* Enslow Pubs., Inc.

Kawa, Katie & Cartlidge, Cherese. Taylor Swift: Superstar Singer. 2017. (People in the News Ser.). 104p. (J). (gr. 7-7). lib. bdg. 39.40 ***(978-1-5345-6025-3(4)***, Lucent Pr.) Greenhaven Publishing LLC.

Kelley, True. Who Is Dolly Parton? 2014. (Who Is... ? Ser.). lib. bdg. 16.00 *(978-0-606-34165-3(X)*, Turtleback) Turtleback Bks.

Kennon, Michou. Beyoncé. 2011. (Hip-Hop Headliners Ser.). (Illus.). 32p. (gr. 3-8). pap. 10.50 *(978-1-4339-4789-6(7))*; (J). lib. bdg. 25.25 *(978-1-4339-4788-9(9))* Stevens, Gareth Publishing LLLP.

Kjelle, Marylou Morano. Ashlee Simpson. 2005. (Blue Banner Biography Ser.). (Illus.). 32p. (J). (gr. 4-8). lib. bdg. 25.70 *(978-1-58415-383-2(0))* Mitchell Lane Pubs., Inc.

—Jesse Mccartney. 2006. (Robbie Reader Ser.). (Illus.). 32p. (J). (gr. 2-5). lib. bdg. 25.70 *(978-1-58415-500-3(0))* Mitchell Lane Pubs., Inc.

—Natasha Bedingfield. 2009. (Blue Banner Biography Ser.). (Illus.). 32p. (YA). (gr. 4-7). lib. bdg. 25.70 *(978-1-58415-772-4(0))* Mitchell Lane Pubs., Inc.

Kramer, Barbara. Beyoncé: Singer, Songwriter, & Actress, 1 vol. 2013. (Contemporary Lives Set 2 Ser.). (ENG.). 112p. (J). (gr. 6-12). lib. bdg. 35.64 *(978-1-61783-617-6(6)*, Essential Library) ABDO Publishing Co.

—Gloria Estefan: Never Give Up. 2005. (Awesome Values in Famous Lives Ser.). (Illus.). 48p. (J). (gr. 3-4). lib. bdg. 25.27 *(978-0-7660-2380-2(X)*, Enslow Elementary) Enslow Pubs., Inc.

—Mahalia Jackson: The Voice of Gospel & Civil Rights. 2003. (African-American Biographies Ser.). (Illus.). 128p. (J). lib. bdg. 26.60 *(978-0-7660-2115-0(7))* Enslow Pubs., Inc.

Krohn, Katherine. Biography Gwen Stefani. 2007. (Biography Ser.). (Illus.). 112p. (J). (gr. -1). lib. bdg. *(978-0-8225-7157-5(9))* Twenty First Century Bks.

—Biography Shakira. 2007. (Biography Ser.). (Illus.). 112p. (J). (gr. -1). lib. bdg. 30.60 *(978-0-8225-7159-9(5)*, Twenty-First Century Bks.) Lerner Publishing Group.

Krumenauer, Heidi. Harry Styles of One Direction: Harry Styles. 2014. (ENG.). 32p. (J). 25.70 *(978-1-62469-008-2(4))* Purple Toad Publishing, Inc.

—Lady Gaga. 2010. (Blue Banner Biography Ser.). (Illus.). 32p. (YA). (gr. 4-7). lib. bdg. 25.70 *(978-1-58415-904-9(9))* Mitchell Lane Pubs., Inc.

—Lorde. 2015. (ENG., Illus.). 32p. (J). 26.50 *(978-1-62469-122-5(6))* Purple Toad Publishing, Inc.

—Rihanna. 2008. (Blue Banner Biography Ser.). (Illus.). 32p. (YA). (gr. 4-7). lib. bdg. 25.70 *(978-1-58415-673-4(2))* Mitchell Lane Pubs., Inc.

—Sean Kingston. 2008. (Blue Banner Biography Ser.). (Illus.). 32p. (YA). (gr. 4-7). lib. bdg. 25.70 *(978-1-58415-679-6(1))* Mitchell Lane Pubs., Inc.

La Bella, Laura. Carrie Underwood. (Who's Your Idol? Ser.). 48p. 2009. (gr. 5-5). 53.00 *(978-1-60854-785-2(X)*, Rosen Reference) 2008. (Illus.). (J). (gr. 3-7). lib. bdg. 29.25 *(978-1-4042-1370-8(8))* Rosen Publishing Group, Inc., The.

Lady Gaga. 2011. (People in the News Ser.). 128p. lib. bdg. 33.95 *(978-1-4205-0426-2(6)*, Lucent Bks.) Cengage Gale.

Lady Gaga. 2011. (Megastars Ser.). (ENG.). 48p. (YA). pap. 11.75 *(978-1-4488-2260-7(2))* Rosen Publishing Group, Inc., The.

Lajiness, Katie. Big Buddy Pop Biographies. 2016. (Big Buddy Pop Biographies Ser.: 12). (ENG.). 32p. (J). (gr. 2-5). lib. bdg. 342.00 *(978-1-68078-051-2(4)*, Big Buddy Bks.) ABDO Publishing Co.

—Justin Timberlake, 1 vol. 2016. (Big Buddy Pop Biographies Ser.). (ENG., Illus.). 32p. (J). (gr. 2-5). 28.50 *(978-1-68078-061-1(1))* ABDO Publishing Co.

—Katy Perry, 1 vol. 2016. (Big Buddy Pop Biographies Ser.). (ENG., Illus.). 32p. (J). (gr. 2-5). 28.50 *(978-1-68078-057-4(3))* ABDO Publishing Co.

—Meghan Trainor, 1 vol. 2016. (Big Buddy Pop Biographies Ser.). (ENG., Illus.). 32p. (J). (gr. 2-5). 28.50 *(978-1-68078-062-8(X))* ABDO Publishing Co.

—Nick Jonas, 1 vol. 2016. (Big Buddy Pop Biographies Ser.). (ENG., Illus.). 32p. (J). (gr. 2-5). 28.50 *(978-1-68078-053-6(0))* ABDO Publishing Co.

—Pharrell Williams, 1 vol. 2016. (Big Buddy Pop Biographies Ser.). (ENG., Illus.). 32p. (J). (gr. 2-5). 28.50 *(978-1-68078-063-5(8))* ABDO Publishing Co.

Landau, Elaine. Beyoncé: R & B Superstar. 2012. (Pop Culture Bios Ser.). (ENG., Illus.). 32p. (gr. 3-6). pap. 7.95 *(978-1-4677-0234-8(X))*; lib. bdg. 26.60 *(978-0-7613-4147-5(1)*, Lerner Pubns.) Lerner Publishing Group.

Latham, Donna. Norah Jones. (Sharing the American Dream Ser.). 64p. (YA). (gr. 7-12). 2009. 22.95 *(978-1-4222-0590-7(8))* 2007. pap. 9.95 *(978-1-4222-0751-2(X))* Mason Crest.

Lawlor, Michelle. Kelly Clarkson. (Pop Culture Ser.). (Illus.). 64p. (YA). (gr. 3-7). 2008. lib. bdg. 22.95 *(978-1-4222-0199-2(6))* 2007. pap. 7.95 *(978-1-4222-0353-8(0))* Mason Crest.

—Missy Elliot. 2008. (Hip-Hop Ser.). (Illus.). 64p. (YA). (gr. 7-12). lib. bdg. 22.95 *(978-1-4222-0117-6(1))* Mason Crest.

Leavitt, Amie. Miley Cyrus. 2007. (Robbie Reader Ser.). (Illus.). 32p. (J). (gr. 2-5). lib. bdg. 25.70 *(978-1-58415-590-4(6))* Mitchell Lane Pubs., Inc.

—Raven-Symone. 2007. (Robbie Reader Ser.). (Illus.). 32p. (YA). (gr. 2-5). lib. bdg. 25.70 *(978-1-58415-593-5(0))* Mitchell Lane Pubs., Inc.

Leavitt, Amie Jane. Ciara. 2007. (Blue Banner Biography Ser.). (Illus.). 32p. (YA). (gr. 4-7). lib. bdg. 25.70 *(978-1-58415-610-9(4))* Mitchell Lane Pubs., Inc.

—Day by Day with Miley Cyrus. 2010. (Randy's Corner Ser.). (Illus.). 32p. (J). (gr. -1-2). lib. bdg. 25.70 *(978-1-58415-856-1(5))* Mitchell Lane Pubs., Inc.

—What It's Like to Be Miley Cyrus. Vega, Eida de la, tr. 2009. (What It's Like to Be/Que se Siente al Ser Ser.). (SPA & ENG., Illus.). 32p. (J). (gr. -1-2). lib. bdg. 25.70 *(978-1-58415-841-7(7))* Mitchell Lane Pubs., Inc.

Lee, Sally. Gloria Estefan: Superstar of Song. 2005. (Latino Biography Library). (Illus.). 128p. (J). (gr. 6-12). lib. bdg. 31.93 *(978-0-7660-2490-8(3))* Enslow Pubs., Inc.

Lemmens, Mary Jo. Christina Aguilera. 2009. (Hip-Hop 2 Ser.). 64p. (YA). (gr. 7-12). lib. bdg. 22.95 *(978-1-4222-0285-2(2))*; (Illus.). (gr. 3-7). pap. 7.95 *(978-1-4222-0348-4(4))* Mason Crest.

—Jennifer Lopez. 2009. (Hip Hop (Mason Crest Paperback) Ser.). (Illus.). 64p. (YA). (gr. 4-7). pap. 7.95 *(978-1-4222-0347-7(6))* Mason Crest.

Lemmens, Maryjo. Jennifer Lopez. 2009. (Hip-Hop 2 Ser.). (Illus.). 64p. (YA). (gr. 7-12). lib. bdg. 22.95 *(978-1-4222-0296-8(8))* Mason Crest.

Levete, Sarah. Kylie the Princess of Pop! 2016. (Real-Life Stories Ser.). (ENG., Illus.). 32p. (J). (gr. 4-6). pap. 11.99 *(978-0-7502-9048-7(X)*, Wayland) Hachette Children's Group GBR. Dist: Hachette Bk. Group.

Lovato, Demi. Stay Strong. 2012. (ENG., Illus.). 272p. (YA). 24.99 *(978-1-250-01310-1(0))* Feiwel & Friends.

Lucent Books Staff. Selena Gomez. 2014. (People in the News Ser.). (ENG.). 128p. (gr. 7-10). lib. bdg. 39.40 *(978-1-4205-1213-7(7)*, Lucent Bks.) Cengage Gale.

Lusted, Marcia Amidon. Blake Shelton: Country Singer & TV Personality, 1 vol. 2014. (Contemporary Lives Set 4 Ser.). (ENG., Illus.). 112p. (J). (gr. 6-12). lib. bdg. 35.64 *(978-1-62403-547-0(7)*, Essential Library) ABDO Publishing Co.

—Booboo Stewart: Twilight's Breakout Idol. 2013. (Pop Culture Bios Ser.). (ENG., Illus.). 32p. (gr. 3-6). (J). lib. bdg. 26.60 *(978-1-4677-0746-6(5)*, Lerner Pubns.); pap. 7.95 *(978-1-4677-0880-7(1))* Lerner Publishing Group.

MacCarry, Noel. Who Was Pete Seeger? Marchesi, Stephen, illus. 2017. (Who Was? Ser.). (ENG.). 112p. (J). (gr. 3-7). 5.99 *(978-0-448-48475-4(7)*, Grosset & Dunlap) Penguin Young Readers Group.

Maccarry, Noel. Who Was Pete Seeger? 2017. (Who Was... ? Ser.). lib. bdg. 16.00 ***(978-0-606-40116-6(4))*** Turtleback Bks.

MacDonald, Barry. Everything Real Justin Bieber Fans Should Know & Do. 2012. (ENG.). 192p. (J). (gr. 7). pap. 12.95 *(978-1-60078-770-6(3))* Triumph Bks.

Mahone, Austin. Just How It Happened - My Official Story. 2014. (ENG., Illus.). 224p. (J). (gr. 3-7). 21.00 *(978-0-316-28680-0(X)*, Poppy) Little, Brown Bks. for Young Readers.

Maimone, Max Q. Justin Timberlake. 2011. (Hip-Hop Headliners Ser.). (Illus.). 32p. (J). (gr. 3-8). pap. 10.50 *(978-1-4339-4801-5(X))*; lib. bdg. 25.25 *(978-1-4339-4800-8(1))* Stevens, Gareth Publishing LLLP.

Maloney, Jim. I Love Liam. Maloney, Jim, illus. 2013. (I Love One Direction Ser.). (ENG., Illus.). 96p. (J). (gr. 3-7). pap. 7.99 *(978-1-78055-217-0(3))* O'Mara, Michael Bks., Ltd. GBR. Dist: Independent Pubs. Group.

Maloney, Jim & Buster Books Staff. I Love Harry. Maloney, Jim, illus. 2013. (I Love One Direction Ser.). (ENG., Illus.). 96p. (J). (gr. 3-7). pap. 7.99 *(978-1-78055-213-2(0))* O'Mara, Michael Bks., Ltd. GBR. Dist: Independent Pubs. Group.

Marcovitz, Hal. Elliott Yamin. 2009. (Dream Big: American Idol Superstars Ser.). 64p. (YA). (gr. 5-18). 22.95 *(978-1-4222-1513-5(X))*; pap. 9.95 *(978-1-4222-1599-9(7))* Mason Crest.

—Jordin Sparks. 2009. (Dream Big: American Idol Superstars Ser.). 64p. (YA). (gr. 5-18). pap. 9.95 *(978-1-4222-1602-6(0))*; (Illus.). lib. bdg. 22.95 *(978-1-4222-1511-1(3))* Mason Crest.

—Kellie Pickler. 2009. (Dream Big: American Idol Superstars Ser.). 64p. (YA). (gr. 5-18). pap. 9.95 *(978-1-4222-1603-3(9))*; lib. bdg. 22.95 *(978-1-4222-1510-4(5))* Mason Crest.

Marquez, Heron. Latin Sensations. (Biography Ser.). (Illus.). 112p. (gr. 6-12). 2005. lib. bdg. 27.93 *(978-0-8225-4993-2(X))* 2003. (YA). pap. 7.95 *(978-0-8225-9695-0(4)*, Lerner Pubns.) Lerner Publishing Group.

Marsico, Katie. Lady Gaga: Pop Singer & Songwriter, 1 vol. 2012. (Contemporary Lives Set 1 Ser.). (ENG.). 112p. (J). (gr. 6-12). lib. bdg. 35.64 *(978-1-61783-324-3(X))* ABDO Publishing Co.

Marvis, Barbara. Day by Day with Beyonce. 2010. (Randy's Corner Ser.). (Illus.). 32p. (J). (gr. -1-2). lib. bdg. 25.70 *(978-1-58415-859-2(X))* Mitchell Lane Pubs., Inc.

Marvis, Barbara J. Selena. 2003. (Blue Banner Biography Ser.). (Illus.). 32p. (J). (gr. 3-8). lib. bdg. 25.70 *(978-1-58415-226-2(5))* Mitchell Lane Pubs., Inc.

Mattern, Joanne. Jason Derulo. 2014. (Illus.). 32p. (J). 25.70 *(978-1-61228-643-3(7))* Mitchell Lane Pubs., Inc.

—Jennifer Hudson. 2012. (Illus.). 32p. (gr. 4-8). lib. bdg. 25.70 *(978-1-61228-315-9(2))* Mitchell Lane Pubs., Inc.

—Keke Palmer. 2010. (Robbie Reader Ser.). (Illus.). 32p. (J). (gr. 2-5). lib. bdg. 25.70 *(978-1-58415-896-7(4))* Mitchell Lane Pubs., Inc.

McConnell, Craig, ed. Theo Tams: Inside the Music. 2009. (ENG., Illus.). 48p. pap. 14.95 *(978-1-894917-84-1(7)*, Napoleon & Co.) Dundurn CAN. Dist: Ingram Publisher Services.

McDowell, Pamela. Adele. 2013. (J). *(978-1-62127-389-9(X))* Weigl Pubs., Inc.

—Selena Gomez. 2012. (J). 27.13 *(978-1-61913-588-8(4))*; pap. 13.95 *(978-1-61913-594-9(9))* Weigl Pubs., Inc.

McKissack, Patricia C. & McKissack, Fredrick L. Marian Anderson: Amazing Opera Singer. 2013. (Famous African Americans Ser.). (Illus.). 24p. (J). (gr. k-18). 22.60 *(978-0-7660-4101-1(8))*; pap. 7.95 *(978-1-4644-0202-9(7))* Enslow Pubs., Inc. (Enslow Elementary).

—Paul Robeson: A Voice for Change. 2013. (Famous African Americans Ser.). 24p. (J). (gr. k-3). pap. 7.95 *(978-1-4644-0205-0(1))*; (Illus.). 22.60 *(978-0-7660-4107-3(7))* Enslow Pubs., Inc. (Enslow Elementary).

McNiven, Kelly. Carly Rae Jepsen. 2013. (ENG., Illus.). 32p. (J). *(978-0-7787-0021-0(6))*; pap. *(978-0-7787-0042-5(9))* Crabtree Publishing Co.

McVeigh, Mark. Julio & Enrique Iglesias. 2004. (Famous Families Ser.). (Illus.). 48p. (J). lib. bdg. 29.25 *(978-1-4042-0260-3(9))* Rosen Publishing Group, Inc., The.

Medina, Tony. I & I: Bob Marley. Watson, Jesse Joshua, illus. 2009. (ENG.). 48p. (J). (gr. 3-6). 19.95 *(978-1-60060-257-3(6))* Lee & Low Bks., Inc.

Medina, Tony & Watson, Jesse Joshua. I & I Bob Marley, 1 vol. 2009. (ENG., Illus.). 48p. (J). pap. 10.95 *(978-1-62014-030-7(6))* Lee & Low Bks., Inc.

Meinking, Mary. Demi Lovato. 2012. (Star Biographies Ser.). (ENG.). 32p. (gr. 3-4). pap. 47.70 *(978-1-4296-9455-1(6))*; (Illus.). lib. bdg. 27.99 *(978-1-4296-8770-6(3))* Capstone Press of Coughlan Cos. (Snap Bks.).

Menard, Valerie. Jennifer Lopez. 2003. (Blue Banner Biography Ser.). (Illus.). 32p. (J). (gr. 3-8). lib. bdg. 25.70 *(978-1-58415-225-5(7))* Mitchell Lane Pubs., Inc.

Micklos, John. Jennifer Hudson: A Biography of an American Music Idol. 2014. (African-American Icons Ser.). 104p. (J). lib. bdg. 27.94 *(978-0-7660-4233-9(2))* Enslow Pubs., Inc.

Miley Cyrus. 2011. (Megastars Ser.). (ENG.). 48p. (YA). pap. 11.75 *(978-1-4488-2259-1(9)*, Rosen Reference) Rosen Publishing Group, Inc., The.

Miller, Calvin Craig. Reggae Poet: The Story of Bob Marley. 2007. (Modern Music Masters Ser.). (Illus.). 128p. (YA). (gr. 9-18). lib. bdg. 27.95 *(978-1-59935-071-4(8))* Reynolds, Morgan Inc.

Miller, Elaine Hobson. Nat King Cole: Unforgettable Musician. 2011. (Illus.). 104p. (J). *(978-1-59421-070-9(5))* Seacoast Publishing, Inc.

Miller, Kat. I Love Miley Cyrus. 2010. (Fan Club Ser.). (ENG.). 24p. (J). (gr. 3-6). lib. bdg. 22.60 *(978-1-61533-045-4(3))*; (Illus.). pap. 8.15 *(978-1-61533-046-1(1))* Windmill Bks.

—I Love Taylor Swift. 2010. (Fan Club Ser.). (ENG.). 24p. (J). (gr. 3-6). lib. bdg. 22.60 *(978-1-61533-051-5(8))*; (Illus.). pap. 8.15 *(978-1-61533-052-2(6))* Windmill Bks.

Mitchell, Susan K. Jessica Simpson. 2007. (Today's Superstars). (Illus.). 32p. (gr. 5-8). lib. bdg. 31.95 *(978-0-8368-8201-8(6))* Stevens, Gareth Publishing LLLP.

Mooney, Carla. Vanessa Hudgens. 2007. (Sharing the American Dream Ser.). 64p. (YA). (gr. 7-18). pap. 9.95 *(978-1-4222-0749-9(8))* Mason Crest.

—Vanessa Hudgens/Carla Mooney. 2009. (Sharing the American Dream Ser.). 64p. (YA). (gr. 7-12). 22.95 *(978-1-4222-0583-9(5))* Mason Crest.

Morganelli, Adrianna. Lorde. 2015. (ENG., Illus.). 32p. (J). *(978-0-7787-8080-9(5))* Crabtree Publishing Co.

Morreale, Marie. Ariana Grande. 2014. (ENG.). 48p. (J). lib. bdg. 29.00 *(978-0-531-21197-7(5))* Scholastic Library Publishing.

—Austin Mahone. 2015. (ENG.). 48p. (J). pap. 7.95 *(978-0-531-21430-5(3)*, Children's Pr.) Scholastic Library Publishing.

—Ed Sheeran. 2014. (ENG.). 48p. (J). pap. 7.95 *(978-0-531-21274-5(2))* Scholastic Library Publishing.

—Selena Gomez. 2015. (ENG., Illus.). 48p. pap. 7.95 *(978-0-531-21663-7(2)*, Orchard Bks.) Scholastic, Inc.

—Taylor Swift: Born to Sing! 2017. (Rookie Biographies(tm) Ser.). (ENG., Illus.). 32p. (J). lib. bdg. 25.00

(978-0-531-22292-8(6), Children's Pr.) Scholastic Library Publishing.

Murcia, Rebecca Thatcher. Shakira. 2007. (Blue Banner Biography Ser.). (Illus.). 32p. (YA). (gr. 4-7). lib. bdg. 25.70 (978-1-58415-609-3(0)) Mitchell Lane Pubs., Inc.

Murphy, Maggie. Miley Cyrus: Rock Star. 2010. (Young & Famous Ser.). 24p. (J). (ENG.). (gr. 3-6). 22.60 (978-1-4488-0643-0(7)); (Illus.). pap. 8.85 (978-1-4488-1799-3(4), PowerKids Pr.) Rosen Publishing Group, Inc., The.

Murray, Laura K. Ariana Grande. 2016. (J). (978-1-60818-669-3(5), Creative Education) Creative Co., The.

Nagle, Jeanne. Jennifer Hudson. 2008. (Who's Your Idol? Ser.). (Illus.). 48p. (J). (gr. 3-7). lib. bdg. 29.25 (978-1-4042-1372-2(4)) Rosen Publishing Group, Inc., The.

Neimark, Anne. There Ain't Nobody That Can Sing Like Me: The Life of Woody Guthrie. 2017. (ENG., Illus.). 128p. (J). (gr. 5-9). pap. 13.99 **(978-1-5344-0950-7(5)**, Atheneum Bks. for Young Readers) Simon & Schuster Children's Publishing.

Nelson, Maria. Robert Pattinson. 2011. (Rising Stars Ser.). 32p. (J). (gr. 3-6). pap. 10.50 (978-1-4339-5900-4(3)); lib. bdg. 25.25 (978-1-4339-5898-4(8)) Stevens, Gareth Publishing LLLP.

—Selena Gomez. 2011. (Rising Stars Ser.). 32p. (J). (gr. 3-6). pap. 10.50 (978-1-4339-5904-2(6)); lib. bdg. 25.25 (978-1-4339-5902-8(X)) Stevens, Gareth Publishing LLLP.

Nelson, Robin. Selena Gomez: Pop Star & Actress. 2012. (Pop Culture Bios Ser.). (ENG., Illus.). 32p. (gr. 3-6). pap. 7.95 (978-1-4677-0238-6(2)); lib. bdg. 26.60 (978-0-7613-4142-0(0), Lerner Pubns.) Lerner Publishing Group.

Neri, G. Hello, I'm Johnny Cash. Ford, A. G., illus. 2014. (ENG.). 40p. (J). (gr. 4-7). 16.99 (978-0-7636-6245-5(3)) Candlewick Pr.

Newroad, Adele. Carrie Underwood. 2010. (Country Music Stars Ser.). (Illus.). 32p. (J). (gr. 3-8). pap. 10.50 (978-1-4339-3602-9(X)); lib. bdg. 25.25 (978-1-4339-3601-2(1)) Stevens, Gareth Publishing LLLP.

Nunn, Daniel. Voices, 1 vol. 2011. (Instruments & Music Ser.). (ENG.). 24p. (gr. -1-1). pap. 6.29 (978-1-4329-5068-2(1), Acorn) Heinemann-Raintree.

O'Donnell, Jessica. Leontyne Price: First Lady of Opera. 2010. (Inspiring Lives Ser.). 32p. (J). (gr. 5-8). lib. bdg. 25.25 (978-1-4339-3628-9(3)) Stevens, Gareth Publishing LLLP.

One Direction. Dare to Dream: Life As One Direction. 2011. (ENG., Illus.). 288p. (YA). (gr. 7). 26.95 (978-0-00-744439-7(7)) HarperCollins Pubs. Ltd. GBR. Dist: Independent Pubs. Group.

—One Direction: Dare to Dream; Life as One Direction. 2012. (ENG., Illus.). 288p. pap. (978-0-00-748812-4(2), HarperCollins Children's Bks.) HarperCollins Pubs. Ltd.

—Who We Are: One Direction: Our Autobiography. 2014. (ENG., Illus.). 352p. 21.99 (978-0-00-757731-6(1)) HarperCollins Pubs.

One Direction Staff. One Direction: A Year with One Direction. 2013. 64p. (J). (gr. 3-7). pap. 10.99 (978-0-06-222317-3(8), HarperFestival) HarperCollins Pubs.

—One Direction - Dare to Dream: Life as One Direction. 2012. 288p. (J). (gr. 3-7). pap. 12.99 (978-0-06-221342-6(3)) HarperCollins Pubs.

Orgill, Roxane. Shout, Sister, Shout! Ten Girl Singers Who Shaped a Century. 2007. (ENG.). 160p. (YA). (gr. 7). pap. 12.95 (978-1-4169-6391-2(X), McElderry, Margaret K. Bks.) McElderry, Margaret K. Bks.

—Skit-Scat Raggedy Cat: Ella Fitzgerald. Qualls, Sean, illus. 2012. (Candlewick Biographies Ser.). (ENG.). 48p. (J). (gr. 3-7). 14.99 (978-0-7636-6459-6(6)); pap. 4.99 (978-0-7636-6458-9(8)) Candlewick Pr.

Orr, Tamara. Emily Osment. 2009. (Robbie Reader Ser.). (Illus.). 32p. (YA). (gr. 2-5). lib. bdg. 25.70 (978-1-58415-755-7(0)) Mitchell Lane Pubs., Inc.

Orr, Tamra. Day by Day with Willow Smith. 2011. (Day by Day with... Ser.). (Illus.). 32p. (J). (gr. -1-2). lib. bdg. 25.70 (978-1-58415-983-4(9)) Mitchell Lane Pubs., Inc.

—Jordin Sparks. 2008. (Robbie Reader Ser.). (Illus.). 32p. (YA). (gr. 2-5). lib. bdg. 25.70 (978-1-58415-727-4(5)) Mitchell Lane Pubs., Inc.

Orr, Tamra B. Jamie Foxx. 2006. (Blue Banner Biography Ser.). (Illus.). 32p. (YA). (gr. 4-7). lib. bdg. 25.70 (978-1-58415-503-4(5)) Mitchell Lane Pubs., Inc.

—Jojo. 2007. (Blue Banner Biography Ser.). (Illus.). 32p. (YA). (gr. 4-7). lib. bdg. 25.70 (978-1-58415-615-4(5)) Mitchell Lane Pubs., Inc.

Owings, Lisa. Adele: Grammy-Winning Singer & Songwriter, 1 vol. 2013. (Contemporary Lives Set 2 Ser.). (ENG.). 112p. (J). (gr. 6-12). lib. bdg. 35.64 (978-1-61783-616-9(8), Essential Library) ABDO Publishing Co.

—Katy Perry: Chart-Topping Superstar, 1 vol. 2014. (Contemporary Lives Set 4 Ser.). (ENG.). 112p. (J). (gr. 6-12). lib. bdg. 35.64 (978-1-62403-546-3(9), Essential Library) ABDO Publishing Co.

Parish, James Robert. Gloria Estefan Singer: Singer. 2006. (Ferguson Career Biographies Ser.). (Illus.). 122p. (gr. 6-12). 25.00 (978-0-8160-5833-4(4), Ferguson Publishing Co.) Facts On File, Inc.

Patrick, Chris. Beyoncé & Destiny's Child. 2005. (Illus.). 122p. (J). (978-0-439-80832-3(4)) Scholastic, Inc.

Peppas, Lynn. Demi Lovato. 2013. (ENG., Illus.). 32p. (J). (978-0-7787-1050-9(5)); pap. (978-0-7787-1054-7(8)) Crabtree Publishing Co.

—Justin Bieber. 2011. (ENG.). 32p. (J). pap. (978-0-7787-7612-3(3)); (gr. 3-6). lib. bdg. (978-0-7787-7607-9(7)) Crabtree Publishing Co.

—M. I. A. 2010. (Superstars! Ser.). (ENG., Illus.). 32p. (J). (gr. 3-6). lib. bdg. (978-0-7787-7249-1(7)) Crabtree Publishing Co.

—M.I.A. 2010. (Superstars! Ser.). (ENG., Illus.). 32p. (J). pap. (978-0-7787-7258-3(6)) Crabtree Publishing Co.

—Miley Cyrus. 2010. (Superstars! Ser.). (ENG.). 32p. (J). pap. (978-0-7787-7259-0(4)); (gr. 3-6). lib. bdg. (978-0-7787-7250-7(0)) Crabtree Publishing Co.

—Taylor Swift. 2010. (Superstars! Ser.). (ENG.). 32p. (J). pap. (978-0-7787-7261-3(6)) Crabtree Publishing Co.

—Zac Efron. 2010. (Superstars! Ser.). (ENG., Illus.). 32p. (J). pap. (978-0-7787-7263-7(2)) Crabtree Publishing Co.

Pettinella, Amy. Lady Gaga. 2015. (Illus.). 48p. (J). lib. bdg. (978-1-62713-322-7(4)) Cavendish Square Publishing.

Pink. 2011. (Megastars Ser.). (Illus.). 48p. (YA). pap. 11.75 (978-1-4488-2263-8(7), Rosen Reference) Rosen Publishing Group, Inc., The.

Pinkney, Andrea Davis. Ella Fitzgerald: The Tale of a Vocal Virtuosa. Pinkney, Brian, illus. 2007. (ENG.). 32p. (J). (gr. k-4). pap. 6.99 (978-0-7868-1416-9(0), Jump at the Sun) Hyperion Bks. for Children.

Plantz, Connie. Elvis Presley: Music Legend, Movie Star, the King. 2004. (People to Know Ser.). (Illus.). 128p. (J). lib. bdg. 26.60 (978-0-7660-2103-7(3)) Enslow Pubs., Inc.

Rajczak, Kristen. Demi Lovato. 2011. (Rising Stars Ser.). (Illus.). 32p. (J). (gr. 3-6). pap. 10.50 (978-1-4339-5888-5(0)); lib. bdg. 25.25 (978-1-4339-5886-1(4)) Stevens, Gareth Publishing LLLP.

—Justin Bieber. 2011. (Rising Stars Ser.). (Illus.). 32p. (J). (gr. 3-6). pap. 10.50 (978-1-4339-5896-0(1)); lib. bdg. 25.25 (978-1-4339-5894-6(5)) Stevens, Gareth Publishing LLLP.

Ransom, Candice. Maria von Trapp: Beyond the Sound of Music. 2003. 112p. (J). pap. 8.95 (978-0-8225-3749-6(4)) Lerner Publishing Group.

Rawson, Katherine. Vanessa Hudgens. (Illus.). 24p. (J). 2010. pap. 9.40 (978-1-4358-3408-8(9)) 2009. lib. bdg. 22.60 (978-1-4042-8137-0(1)) Rosen Publishing Group, Inc., The. (PowerKids Pr.).

Reich, Susanna. Stand up & Sing! Pete Seeger, Folk Music, & the Path to Justice. Gustavson, Adam, illus. 2017. (ENG.). 48p. (J). 17.99 (978-0-8027-3812-7(5), 9780802738127, Bloomsbury USA Childrens) Bloomsbury Publishing USA.

Reid, Jamie. Diana Krall. 2004. 224p. pap. 17.95 (978-1-894997-07-2(7)) Kingston Pr. CAN. Dist: SCB Distributors.

Reusser, Kayleen. Day by Day with Taylor Swift. 2010. (Randy's Corner Ser.). (Illus.). 32p. (J). (gr. -1-2). lib. bdg. 25.70 (978-1-58415-857-8(3)) Mitchell Lane Pubs., Inc.

—Leona Lewis. 2009. (Blue Banner Biography Ser.). (Illus.). 32p. (YA). (gr. 4-7). lib. bdg. 25.70 (978-1-58415-775-5(5)) Mitchell Lane Pubs., Inc.

—Selena Gomez. 2009. (Robbie Reader Ser.). (Illus.). 32p. (YA). (gr. 2-5). lib. bdg. 25.70 (978-1-58415-752-6(6)) Mitchell Lane Pubs., Inc.

Rice, Earle. Billie Holiday. 2012. (J). lib. bdg. 29.95 (978-1-61228-267-1(9)) Mitchell Lane Pubs., Inc.

Rihanna. 2011. (Megastars Ser.). (ENG.). 48p. (YA). pap. 11.75 (978-1-4488-2262-1(9)) Rosen Publishing Group, Inc., The.

Rivera, Ursula. Aretha Franklin. (Rock & Roll Hall of Famers Ser.). 112p. (gr. 5-8). 2009. 63.90 (978-1-60852-467-9(1), Rosen Reference) 2006. (Illus.). (YA). lib. bdg. 34.60 (978-0-8239-3639-7(2)) Rosen Publishing Group, Inc., The.

—The Supremes. (Rock & Roll Hall of Famers Ser.). 112p. (gr. 5-8). 2009. 63.90 (978-1-60852-479-2(5), Rosen Reference) 2006. (Illus.). (YA). lib. bdg. 34.60 (978-0-8239-3527-7(2)) Rosen Publishing Group, Inc., The.

Robb, Jackie. Miley Mania! Behind the Scenes with Miley Cyrus. 2008. (Star Scene Ser.). (ENG., Illus.). 48p. (J). (gr. 3-7). pap. 5.99 (978-0-545-08565-6(9)) Scholastic, Inc.

Roberts, Russell. Alicia Keys: Singer-Songwriter, Musician, Actress, & Producer. 2012. (Transcending Race Ser.). 64p. (J). (gr. 5). 22.95 (978-1-4222-2727-5(8)) Mason Crest.

Robertson, Robbie, et al. Legends, Icons & Rebels: Music That Changed the World. (ENG., Illus.). (J). (gr. 4-7). 2016. 128p. pap. 18.99 (978-1-101-91868-5(3)) 2013. 130p. 29.00 (978-1-77049-571-5(1)) Tundra Bks. CAN. (Tundra Bks.). Dist: Penguin Random Hse. LLC.

Robson, David. Miley Cyrus. 2010. (Role Model Entertainers Ser.). (Illus.). 64p. (YA). (gr. 7-12). 22.95 (978-1-4222-0501-3(0)) Mason Crest.

Rose, Ella. Rihanna. 2012. (Hip-Hop Headliners Ser.). (ENG., Illus.). 32p. (J). (gr. 4-8). pap. 10.50 (978-1-4339-6618-7(2)); lib. bdg. 25.25 (978-1-4339-6616-3(6)) Stevens, Gareth Publishing LLLP.

Ryan, Pam Muñoz. When Marian Sang: The True Recital of Marian Anderson. Selznick, Brian, illus. pap. incl. audio compact disk (978-1-59112-949-3(4)); pap. 18.95 incl. audio compact disk (978-1-59112-947-9(8)); pap. incl. audio (978-1-59112-945-5(1)); pap. 16.95 incl. audio (978-1-59112-943-1(5)); 2004. (J). 28.95 incl. audio compact disk (978-1-59112-948-6(6)) Live Oak Media.

Saddleback Educational Publishing. Rihanna, 1 vol. 2013. (Hip-Hop Biographies Ser.). (ENG.). 48p. (YA). (gr. 9-12). 11.95 (978-1-62250-011-6(3)) Saddleback Educational Publishing, Inc.

Saddleback Educational Publishing Staff. Beyonce, 1 vol. 2015. (Hip-Hop Biographies Ser.). (ENG.). 48p. (YA). (gr. 9-12). 11.95 (978-1-62250-927-0(7)) Saddleback Educational Publishing, Inc.

—Beyonce. 2015. (Hip-Hop Biographies (Saddleback Publishing) Ser.). (YA). lib. bdg. 23.25 (978-0-606-36613-7(X)) Turtleback Bks.

—Dr. Dre. 2015. (Hip-Hop Biographies (Saddleback Publishing) Ser.). (YA). lib. bdg. 23.25 (978-0-606-36614-4(8)) Turtleback Bks.

—Pharrell Williams. 2015. (Hip-Hop Biographies (Saddleback Publishing) Ser.). (YA). lib. bdg. 23.25 (978-0-606-36616-8(4)) Turtleback Bks.

—Rihanna. 2013. (Hip-Hop Biographies (Saddleback Publishing) Ser.). (YA). lib. bdg. 23.25 (978-0-606-31489-3(X), Turtleback) Turtleback Bks.

—Sean Combs. 2015. (Hip-Hop Biographies (Saddleback Publishing) Ser.). (YA). lib. bdg. 23.25 (978-0-606-36615-1(6)) Turtleback Bks.

Salazar, Sam. Jordin Sparks. 2013. (Rising Stars Ser.). 32p. (J). (gr. 3-6). pap. 10.50 (978-1-4339-8982-7(4)) Stevens, Gareth Publishing LLLP.

Salazar, Sam & Kennon, Michou. Jordin Sparks. 2013. 32p. (J). (gr. 3-6). 25.25 (978-1-4339-8981-0(6)) Stevens, Gareth Publishing LLLP.

Sapet, Kerrily. Mariah Carey: Singer, Songwriter, Record Producer, Actress. 2009. (Transcending Race in America: Biographies of Biracial Achievers Ser.). 64p. (YA). (gr. 5-18). pap. 9.95 (978-1-4222-1627-9(6)) Mason Crest.

—Mariah Carey: Singer, Songwriter, Record Producer, & Actress. 2012. (Transcending Race Ser.). 64p. (J). (gr. 5). 22.95 (978-1-4222-2730-5(8)) Mason Crest.

Sawyer, Sarah. Avril Lavigne. 48p. 2009. (Illus.). (gr. 7-12). pap. 11.75 (978-1-4358-5128-3(5), Rosen Classroom) 2009. (gr. 6-6). 53.00 (978-1-61511-923-3(X)) 2008. (Illus.). (J). lib. bdg. 29.25 (978-1-4042-1820-8(3)) Rosen Publishing Group, Inc., The.

Scholastic, Inc. Staff. Awkward! Your Stars' Oops, Goofs & Blushes. 2014. (ENG.). 48p. (J). (gr. 1-3). pap. 4.99 (978-0-545-66838-5(7)) Scholastic, Inc.

Scholl, Elizabeth. David Archuleta. 2009. (Robbie Reader Ser.). (Illus.). 32p. (YA). (gr. 2-5). lib. bdg. 25.70 (978-1-58415-758-8(5)) Mitchell Lane Pubs., Inc.

—Shontelle Layne. 2009. (Blue Banner Biography Ser.). (Illus.). 32p. (YA). (gr. 4-7). lib. bdg. 25.70 (978-1-58415-770-0(4)) Mitchell Lane Pubs., Inc.

Schrey, Sophie & Buster Books Staff. I Love Louis. Schrey, Sophie, illus. 2013. (I Love One Direction Ser.). (ENG., Illus.). 96p. (J). (gr. 3-7). pap. 7.99 (978-1-78055-215-6(7)) O'Mara, Michael Bks., Ltd. GBR. Dist: Independent Pubs. Group.

Schroeder, Alan. Baby Flo: Florence Mills Lights up the Stage. Van Wright, Cornelius & Hu, Ying-Hwa, illus. 2012. (ENG.). 40p. (J). 18.95 (978-1-60060-410-2(2)) Lee & Low Bks., Inc.

Schubert, Leda. Listen: How Pete Seeger Got America Singing. Colón, Raúl, illus. 2017. (ENG.). 40p. (J). 17.99 (978-1-62672-250-7(1), 9781626722507) Roaring Brook Pr.

Schuman, Michael A. Beyonc: A Biography of a Legendary Singer. 2014. (African-American Icons Ser.). 104p. (J). lib. bdg. 27.94 (978-0-7660-4230-8(8)) Enslow Pubs., Inc.

—Emma! Amazing Actress Emma Stone. 2013. (Sizzling Celebrities Ser.). 48p. (J). lib. bdg. 25.27 (978-0-7660-4113-4(1)); (gr. 4-9). pap. 8.95 (978-1-4644-0175-6(6)) Enslow Pubs., Inc.

—Rihanna: Music Megastar. 2011. (Hot Celebrity Biographies Ser.). (Illus.). 48p. (J). (gr. 5-18). pap. 8.95 (978-1-59845-285-3(1)); lib. bdg. 25.27 (978-0-7660-3871-4(8)) Enslow Pubs., Inc.

Schwartz, Heather. Ariana Grande: From Actress to Chart-Topping Singer. 2014. (Pop Culture Bios Ser.). (ENG., Illus.). 32p. (gr. 3-6). pap. 7.95 (978-1-4677-4544-4(8)) Lerner Publishing Group.

—Austin Mahone: Vocals Going Viral. 2014. (Pop Culture Bios Ser.). (Illus.). 32p. (gr. 3-6). (J). lib. bdg. 26.60 (978-1-4677-3670-1(8), Lerner Pubns.); (ENG., pap. 7.95 (978-1-4677-4545-1(6)) Lerner Publishing Group.

—Maia Mitchell: Talent from down Under. 2014. (Pop Culture Bios Ser.). (ENG., Illus.). 32p. (gr. 3-6). pap. 7.95 (978-1-4677-4546-8(4)) Lerner Publishing Group.

—Zendaya: Capturing the Stage, Screen, & Modeling Scene. 2014. (Pop Culture Bios Ser.). (ENG., Illus.). 32p. (gr. 3-6). pap. 7.95 (978-1-4677-4548-2(0)) Lerner Publishing Group.

Schwartz, Heather E. Adele: Soulful Singer. 2015. (Pop Culture Bios Ser.). (ENG., Illus.). 32p. (J). (gr. 3-6). pap. 7.95 (978-1-4677-6101-7(X), Lerner Pubns.) Lerner Publishing Group.

—Ariana Grande: From Actress to Chart-Topping Singer. 2014. (Pop Culture Bios Ser.). (ENG.). 32p. (gr. 3-6). lib. bdg. 26.60 (978-1-4677-3669-5(4), Lerner Pubns.) Lerner Publishing Group.

—Cody Simpson: Pop Star from down Under. 2013. (Pop Culture Bios Ser.). (ENG., Illus.). 32p. (gr. 3-6). pap. 7.95 (978-1-4677-1546-1(8)); lib. bdg. 26.60 (978-1-4677-1305-4(8), Lerner Pubns.) Lerner Publishing Group.

—Emma Stone: Star of the Stage, TV, & Film. 2014. (Pop Culture Bios Ser.). (ENG., Illus.). 32p. (gr. 3-6). pap. 7.95 (978-1-4677-2374-9(6)); lib. bdg. 26.60 (978-1-4677-1440-2(2), Lerner Pubns.) Lerner Publishing Group.

—Idina Menzel: Vocal Superpower. 2015. (Pop Culture Bios Ser.). (ENG., Illus.). 32p. (gr. 3-6). pap. 7.95 (978-1-4677-6102-4(8), Lerner Pubns.) Lerner Publishing Group.

—Lorde: Songstress with Style. 2015. (Pop Culture Bios Ser.). (ENG., Illus.). 32p. (J). (gr. 3-6). pap. 7.95 (978-1-4677-6100-0(1)); lib. bdg. 26.60 (978-1-4677-5717-1(9)) Lerner Publishing Group. (Lerner Pubns.).

—Maia Mitchell: Talent from down Under. 2014. (Pop Culture Bios Ser.). (ENG., Illus.). 32p. (J). (gr. 3-6). lib. bdg. 26.60 (978-1-4677-3672-5(4), Lerner Pubns.) Lerner Publishing Group.

—Selena Gomez. 2012. (Star Biographies Ser.). (ENG.). 32p. (gr. 3-4). pap. 47.70 (978-1-4296-9465-0(3)); (Illus.). lib. bdg. 27.99 (978-1-4296-4761-8(2)) Capstone Press of Coughlan Cos. (Snap Bks.).

—Taylor Swift. 2012. (Star Biographies Ser.). (ENG.). 32p. (gr. 3-4). pap. 47.70 (978-1-4296-9469-8(6), Snap Bks.) Capstone Press of Coughlan Cos.

—Zendaya: Capturing the Stage, Screen, & Modeling Scene. 2014. (Pop Culture Bios Ser.). (ENG., Illus.). 32p. (J). (gr. 3-6). lib. bdg. 26.60 (978-1-4677-3673-2(2), Lerner Pubns.) Lerner Publishing Group.

Scott, Celicia. Mariah Carey. 2008. (Hip-Hop Ser.). (Illus.). 64p. (YA). (ENG.). (gr. 4-7). per. 7.95 (978-1-4222-0265-4(8)); (gr. 7-12). lib. bdg. 22.95 (978-1-4222-0114-5(7)) Mason Crest.

Seidman, David. Katharine Mcphee. (Who's Your Idol? Ser.). 48p. 2009. (gr. 5-5). 53.00 (978-1-60854-788-3(4), Rosen Reference) 2008. (Illus.). (J). (gr. 3-7). lib. bdg. 29.25 (978-1-4042-1373-9(2)) Rosen Publishing Group, Inc., The.

Seven, John. Frankie Liked to Sing. Christy, Jana, illus. 2015. (ENG.). 32p. (J). (gr. -1-3). 16.95 (978-1-4197-1644-7(1), Abrams Bks. for Young Readers) Abrams, Inc.

Shaffer, Jody Jensen. Demi Lovato: Taking Another Chance. 2013. (Pop Culture Bios Ser.). (ENG., Illus.). 32p. (gr. 3-6). pap. 7.95 (978-1-4677-1551-5(4)); lib. bdg. 26.60 (978-1-4677-1310-8(4), Lerner Pubns.) Lerner Publishing Group.

—Lea Michele. 2012. (Stars of Today Ser.). (ENG., Illus.). 32p. (J). (gr. 2-5). 28.50 (978-1-61473-294-5(9), 205045) Child's World, Inc., The.

—Victoria Justice: Television's It Girl. 2013. (Pop Culture Bios Ser.). (ENG., Illus.). 32p. (gr. 3-6). pap. 7.95 (978-1-4677-1550-8(6)); lib. bdg. 26.60 (978-1-4677-1309-2(0), Lerner Pubns.) Lerner Publishing Group.

Shapiro, Marc & Ooten, Tara Broeckel. Selena Gomez - Fame. 2012. (ENG., Illus.). 40p. (YA). pap. 7.99 (978-1-4507-6679-1(X)) Bluewater Productions, Inc.

Shea, Abigail. Victoria Justice. 2013. (Rising Stars Ser.). 32p. (J). (gr. 3-6). pap. 10.50 (978-1-4339-8990-2(5)); (ENG., Illus.). lib. bdg. 25.25 (978-1-4339-8989-6(1)) Stevens, Gareth Publishing LLLP.

Shea, Molly. Alicia Keys. 2011. (Hip-Hop Headliners Ser.). (Illus.). 32p. (gr. 3-8). pap. 10.50 (978-1-4339-4785-8(4)); (J). 25.25 (978-1-4339-4784-1(6)) Stevens, Gareth Publishing LLLP.

Shea, Therese. Usher. 2011. (Hip-Hop Headliners Ser.). (Illus.). 32p. (gr. 3-8). pap. 10.50 (978-1-4339-4813-8(3)); (J). 25.25 (978-1-4339-4812-1(5)) Stevens, Gareth Publishing LLLP.

Sherrard, Valerie. Vanessa Hudgens. 2010. (Superstars! Ser.). (ENG., Illus.). 32p. (J). pap. (978-0-7787-7262-0(4)); (gr. 3-6). lib. bdg. (978-0-7787-7253-8(5)) Crabtree Publishing Co.

Silvey, Anita. Let Your Voice Be Heard: The Life & Times of Pete Seeger. 2016. (ENG., Illus.). 112p. (J). (gr. 5-7). 17.99 (978-0-547-33012-9(X)) Houghton Mifflin Harcourt Publishing Co.

Simone, Jacquelyn. Ciara. 2009. (Hip-Hop Ser.). (Illus.). 64p. (YA). pap. 7.95 (978-1-4222-0334-7(4)); (gr. 7-12). lib. bdg. 22.95 (978-1-4222-0286-9(0)) Mason Crest.

Sirota, Lyn. Pink. 2011. (Megastars Ser.). (Illus.). 48p. (YA). (gr. 5-8). 29.25 (978-1-4358-3577-1(8), Rosen Reference) Rosen Publishing Group, Inc., The.

Slavicek, Louise Chipley. Paul Robeson. 2011. (Black Americans of Achievement Legacy Edition Ser.). 120p. (YA). (gr. 6-12). 35.00 (978-1-60413-843-6(2)) Facts On File, Inc.

Sloate, Susan. Ray Charles: Find Another Way! 2006. (Defining Moments Ser.). (Illus.). 32p. (J). (gr. 2-5). lib. bdg. 25.27 (978-1-59716-267-8(1)) Bearport Publishing Co., Inc.

—Ray Charles: Young Musician. Henderson, Meryl, illus. 2007. (Childhood of Famous Americans Ser.). (ENG.). 176p. (J). (gr. 3-7). pap. 6.99 (978-1-4169-1437-2(4), Simon & Schuster/Paula Wiseman Bks.) Simon & Schuster/Paula Wiseman Bks.

Snyder, Gail. Brooke Knows Best. 2010. (Major Reality Shows Ser.). 48p. (YA). (gr. 7-18). lib. bdg. 19.95 (978-1-4222-1680-4(2)) Mason Crest.

—David Cook. 2009. (Dream Big: American Idol Superstars Ser.). (Illus.). 64p. (YA). (gr. 5-18). lib. bdg. 22.95 (978-1-4222-1507-4(5)) Mason Crest.

—Kelly Clarkson. 2009. (Dream Big: American Idol Superstars Ser.). 64p. (YA). (gr. 5-18). pap. 9.95 (978-1-4222-1604-0(7)); lib. bdg. 22.95 (978-1-4222-1506-7(7)) Mason Crest.

Sonneborn, Liz. Fantasia Barrino. (Who's Your Idol? Ser.). 48p. 2009. (gr. 5-5). 53.00 (978-1-60854-787-6(6), Rosen Reference) 2008. (Illus.). (J). (gr. 3-7). lib. bdg. 29.25 (978-1-4042-1369-2(4)) Rosen Publishing Group, Inc., The.

Spencer, Liv. The Miranda Cosgrove & iCarly Spectacular! Unofficial & Unstoppable. 2010. (ENG., Illus.). 142p. (J). (gr. 4-7). pap. (978-1-55022-929-5(X)) Filmer Ltd.

Star Biographies. 2010. (Star Biographies Ser.). 32p. lib. bdg. 213.20 (978-1-4296-5883-6(5), Snap Bks.) Capstone Press of Coughlan Cos.

Stewart, Mark. Music Legends. 2009. (Ultimate 10: Entertainment Ser.). (ENG.). 48p. (J). (gr. 4-8). pap. 10.50 (978-1-4339-2213-8(4)); (YA). (gr. 5-9). lib. bdg. 31.00 (978-0-8368-9165-2(1)) Stevens, Gareth Publishing LLLP.

Summers, Kimberly Dillon. Miley Cyrus: A Biography, 1 vol. 2009. (Greenwood Biographies Ser.). 156p. (C). 39.00 (978-0-313-37847-8(9), GR7847, Greenwood) ABC-CLIO, LLC.

Superstars! Editors. Superstars! One Direction: Inside Their World. Superstars! Editors, ed. 2012. (ENG., Illus.). 128p. (J). (gr. 3-17). pap. 14.95 (978-1-60320-950-2(6), Liberty St.) Time Inc. Bks.

Sutcliffe, Jane. Marian Anderson. 2008. pap. 52.95 (978-0-8225-9394-2(7)) Lerner Publishing Group.

Terp, Gail. Demi Lovato. 2017. (Women Who Rock Ser.). (ENG.). 32p. (gr. 3-7). 31.35 **(978-1-68072-066-2(X))** Black Rabbit Bks.

Thatcher Murcia, Rebecca. What It's Like to Be Shakira. de la Vega, Eida, tr. from SPA. 2010. (What It's Like to Be/Que se Siente al Ser Ser.). (ENG & SPA., Illus.). 32p. (J). (gr. -1-2). lib. bdg. 25.70 (978-1-58415-851-6(4)) Mitchell Lane Pubs., Inc.

The Celebrities Arts Center. Beyonce Knowles, the Marvelous Queen. 2007. 76p. pap. 11.00 (978-0-9774483-9-5(8)) International Development Ctr.

Tieck, Sarah. Adam Levine: Famous Singer & Songwriter, 1 vol. 2013. (Big Buddy Biographies Set 10 Ser.). (ENG.). 32p. (J). (gr. 2-5). lib. bdg. 28.50 (978-1-61783-859-0(4), Big Buddy Bks.) ABDO Publishing Co.

—Adele: Singing Sensation, 1 vol. 2013. (Big Buddy Biographies Set 9 Ser.). (ENG.). 32p. (J). (gr. 2-5). lib. bdg. 28.50 (978-1-61783-747-0(4), Big Buddy Bks.) ABDO Publishing Co.

—Ariana Grande: Famous Actress & Singer, 1 vol. 2014. (Big Buddy Biographies Set 12 Ser.). (ENG.). 32p. (J). (gr. 2-5). 28.50 (978-1-62403-568-5(X)) ABDO Publishing Co.

—Beyonce: Famous Singer/Actress, 1 vol. 2008. (Big Buddy Biographies Ser.). (ENG.). 32p. (J). (gr. 2-5). 28.50 (978-1-60453-117-6(7)) ABDO Publishing Co.

—Big Time Rush: Popular Boy Band, 1 vol. 2013. (Big Buddy Biographies Set 10 Ser.). (ENG.). 32p. (J). (gr. 2-5). lib. bdg. 28.50 (978-1-61783-856-9(X), Big Buddy Bks.) ABDO Publishing Co.

—Carly Rae Jepsen: Pop Star, 1 vol. 2013. (Big Buddy Biographies Set 10 Ser.). (ENG.). 32p. (J). (gr. 2-5). lib. bdg. 28.50 (978-1-61783-858-3(6), Big Buddy Bks.) ABDO Publishing Co.

—Carrie Underwood: American Idol Winner, 1 vol. 2008. (Big Buddy Biographies Ser.). (ENG.). 32p. (J). (gr. 2-5). 28.50 (978-1-60453-125-1(8)) ABDO Publishing Co.

—Chris Colfer: Star of Glee, 1 vol. 2013. (Big Buddy Biographies Set 10 Ser.). (ENG.). 32p. (J). (gr. 2-5). lib. bdg. 28.50 (978-1-61783-857-6(8), Big Buddy Bks.) ABDO Publishing Co.

—Debby Ryan: Disney TV Star, 1 vol. 2014. (Big Buddy Biographies Set 12 Ser.). (ENG.). 32p. (J). (gr. 2-5). 28.50 (978-1-62403-572-2(8)) ABDO Publishing Co.

—Jennifer Lopez: Famous Entertainer, 1 vol. 2012. (Big Buddy Biographies Ser.). (ENG.). 32p. (J). (gr. 2-5). 28.50 (978-1-61783-225-3(1)) ABDO Publishing Co.

S

—Justin Bieber: Pop Music Superstar, 1 vol. 2012. (Big Buddy Biographies Ser.). (ENG.). 32p. (J). (gr. 2-5). 28.50 *(978-1-61783-224-6(3))* ABDO Publishing Co.

—Justin Bieber: Singing Sensation, 1 vol. 2010. (Big Buddy Bks.). (ENG.). 32p. (J). (gr. 2-5). 28.50 *(978-1-61613-974-2(9))* ABDO Publishing Co.

—Justin Timberlake: Famous Entertainer, 1 vol. 2012. (Big Buddy Biographies Ser.). (ENG.). 32p. (J). (gr. 2-5). 28.50 *(978-1-61783-229-1(4))* ABDO Publishing Co.

—Katy Perry: Singing Sensation, 1 vol. 2011. (Big Buddy Biographies Set 7 Ser.). (ENG., Illus.). 32p. (J). (gr. 2-5). 28.50 *(978-1-61783-021-1(6))* ABDO Publishing Co.

—Kelly Clarkson: Original American Idol, 1 vol. 2014. (Big Buddy Biographies Set 11 Ser.). (ENG., Illus.). 32p. (gr. 2-5). 28.50 *(978-1-62403-196-0(X))* ABDO Publishing Co.

—Kyle Massey: Talented Entertainer, 1 vol. 2011. (Big Buddy Biographies Set 7 Ser.). (ENG., Illus.). 32p. (J). (gr. 2-5). 28.50 *(978-1-61783-019-8(4))* ABDO Publishing Co.

—Lady Gaga: Singing Sensation, 1 vol. 2011. (Big Buddy Biographies Set 7 Ser.). (ENG., Illus.). 32p. (J). (gr. 2-5). 28.50 *(978-1-61783-017-4(8))* ABDO Publishing Co.

—Lea Michele: Star of Glee, 1 vol. 2011. (Big Buddy Biographies Set 6 Ser.). (ENG., Illus.). 32p. (J). (gr. 2-5). 28.50 *(978-1-61714-706-7(0))* ABDO Publishing Co.

—Lorde: Singing Sensation, 1 vol. 2014. (Big Buddy Biographies Set 12 Ser.). (ENG.). 32p. (gr. 2-5). 28.50 *(978-1-62403-569-2(8))* ABDO Publishing Co.

—Miley Cyrus: Singer/Actress/ Star of Hannah Montana, 1 vol. 2008. (Big Buddy Biographies Ser.). (ENG.). 32p. (J). (gr. 2-5). 28.50 *(978-1-60453-119-0(3))* ABDO Publishing Co.

—Miley Cyrus CD & Book. 2010. (Big Buddy Biographies CD+Book Ser.). 32p. (gr. 2-5). audio compact disk 57.00 *(978-1-61613-306-1(6)*, Big Buddy Bks.) ABDO Publishing Co.

—Miley Cyrus Site CD & Book. 2010. (Big Buddy Biographies Site CD+Book Ser.). 32p. (gr. 2-5). cd-rom 85.57 *(978-1-61613-278-1(7)*, Big Buddy Bks.) ABDO Publishing Co.

—Miranda Cosgrove: Famous Actress & Singer, 1 vol. 2010. (Big Buddy Biographies Set 4 Ser.). (ENG.). 32p. (J). (gr. 2-5). 28.50 *(978-1-60453-970-7(4))* ABDO Publishing Co.

—Rihanna: Singing Sensation, 1 vol. 2012. (Big Buddy Biographies Ser.). (ENG.). 32p. (J). (gr. 2-5). 28.50 *(978-1-61783-228-4(6))* ABDO Publishing Co.

—Scotty Mccreery: American Idol Winner, 1 vol. 2012. (Big Buddy Biographies Ser.). (ENG.). 32p. (J). (gr. 2-5). 28.50 *(978-1-61783-227-7(8))* ABDO Publishing Co.

—Selena Gomez: Star of Wizards of Waverly Place, 1 vol. 2009. (Big Buddy Biographies Set 2 Ser.). (ENG., Illus.). 32p. (J). (gr. 2-5). 28.50 *(978-1-60453-548-8(2))* ABDO Publishing Co.

—Shakira: International Music Star, 1 vol. 2014. (Big Buddy Biographies Set 12 Ser.). (ENG.). 32p. (gr. 2-5). 28.50 *(978-1-62403-573-9(6))* ABDO Publishing Co.

—Usher: Famous Singer, 1 vol. 2009. (Big Buddy Biographies Set 2 Ser.). (ENG., Illus.). 32p. (J). (gr. 2-5). 28.50 *(978-1-60453-551-8(2))* ABDO Publishing Co.

—Vanessa Hudgens: High School Musical Star, 1 vol. 2008. (Big Buddy Biographies Ser.). (ENG.). 32p. (J). (gr. 2-5). 28.50 *(978-1-60453-121-3(5))* ABDO Publishing Co.

—Victoria Justice: Famous Actress & Singer, 1 vol. 2013. (Big Buddy Biographies Set 9 Ser.). (ENG.). 32p. (J). (gr. 2-5). lib. bdg. 28.50 *(978-1-61783-750-0(4)*, Big Buddy Bks.) ABDO Publishing Co.

Torres, Jennifer. Ashanti. 2005. (Blue Banner Biography Ser.). (Illus.). 32p. (J). lib. bdg. 25.70 *(978-1-58415-378-8(4))* Mitchell Lane Pubs., Inc.

—Selena Gomez: Pop Singer & Actress. 2015. (Influential Latinos Ser.). (ENG., Illus.). 128p. (J). (gr. 7-7). 37.27 *(978-0-7660-6999-2(0))* Enslow Pubs., Inc.

Torres, John. Usher. 2005. (Blue Banner Biography Ser.). (Illus.). 32p. (J). (gr. 4-8). lib. bdg. 25.70 *(978-1-58415-379-5(2))* Mitchell Lane Pubs., Inc.

Torres, John Albert. Clay Aiken. 2004. (Blue Banner Biography Ser.). (Illus.). 32p. (J). (gr. 3-8). lib. bdg. 25.70 *(978-1-58415-316-0(4))* Mitchell Lane Pubs., Inc.

Toyne, Jessica. Justin Bieber. 2015. (Pop Icons Ser.). (Illus.). 64p. (J). (gr. 7). lib. bdg. 23.95 *(978-1-4222-3247-7(6))* Mason Crest.

Tracy, Kathleen. Aly & AJ. 2007. (Robbie Reader Ser.). (Illus.). 32p. (YA). (gr. 2-5). lib. bdg. 25.70 *(978-1-58415-595-9(7))* Mitchell Lane Pubs., Inc.

—Avril Lavigne. 2004. (Uncharted, Unexplored & Unexplained Ser.). (Illus.). 32p. (J). (gr. 3-8). lib. bdg. 25.70 *(978-1-58415-314-6(8))* Mitchell Lane Pubs., Inc.

—Bessie Smith. 2012. (J). lib. bdg. 29.95 *(978-1-61228-271-8(7))* Mitchell Lane Pubs., Inc.

—Beyonce. 2004. (Blue Banner Biography Ser.). (Illus.). 32p. (J). (gr. 3-8). lib. bdg. 25.70 *(978-1-58415-312-2(1))* Mitchell Lane Pubs., Inc.

—Carrie Underwood. 2005. (Blue Banner Biography Ser.). (Illus.). 32p. (J). (gr. 4-8). lib. bdg. 25.70 *(978-1-58415-425-9(X))* Mitchell Lane Pubs., Inc.

—Justin Bieber. 2010. (Robbie Reader Ser.). (Illus.). 32p. (YA). (gr. 2-5). lib. bdg. 25.70 *(978-1-58415-895-0(6))* Mitchell Lane Pubs., Inc.

—Justin Timberlake. 2007. (Blue Banner Biography Ser.). (Illus.). 32p. (YA). (gr. 4-7). lib. bdg. 25.70 *(978-1-58415-611-6(2))* Mitchell Lane Pubs., Inc.

—Kelly Clarkson. 2006. (Blue Banner Biography Ser.). (Illus.). 32p. (YA). (gr. 4-7). lib. bdg. 25.70 *(978-1-58415-518-8(3))* Mitchell Lane Pubs., Inc.

—Mariah Carey. 2006. (Blue Banner Biography Ser.). (Illus.). 32p. (YA). (gr. 4-7). lib. bdg. 25.70 *(978-1-58415-516-4(7))* Mitchell Lane Pubs., Inc.

Triumph Books Staff. Austin Mahone: Startin' Something Spectacular. 2013. (ENG.). 112p. (J). (gr. 4-7). pap. 12.95 *(978-1-60078-915-1(3))* Triumph Bks.

—Believe. 2012. (ENG.). 112p. (YA). (gr. 7). pap. 12.95 *(978-1-60078-792-8(4))* Triumph Bks.

Turck, Mary C. Freedom Song: Young Voices & the Struggle for Civil Rights. 2008. (ENG., Illus.). 160p. (J). (gr. 4). pap. 18.95 *(978-1-55652-773-9(X))* Chicago Review Pr., Inc.

Vaughan, Jenny. Selena Gomez - Teen Stars. 2013. (Illus.). 32p. (J). 28.50 *(978-1-59771-417-4(8))* Sea-To-Sea Pubns.

Victoria Justice. 2013. (Rising Stars Ser.). 32p. (J). (gr. 3-6). pap. 63.00 *(978-1-4339-8991-9(3))* Stevens, Gareth Publishing LLLP.

Waters, Rosa. Ashanti. 2008. (Hip-Hop Ser.). (Illus.). 64p. (YA). (gr. 3-7). lib. bdg. 22.95 *(978-1-4222-0111-4(2))*; per. 7.95 *(978-1-4222-0263-0(1))* Mason Crest.

—Bob Marley & the Wailers. (Pop Rock Ser.). (Illus.). 64p. (YA). 2008. (gr. 7-18). lib. bdg. 22.95 *(978-1-4222-0192-3(9))* 2007. pap. 7.95 *(978-1-4222-0317-0(4))* Mason Crest.

Watson, Renée. Harlem's Little Blackbird. Robinson, Christian, illus. 2012. (ENG.). 40p. (J). (gr. -1-2). 17.99 *(978-0-375-86973-0(5)*, Random Hse. Bks. for Young Readers) Random Hse. Children's Bks.

Watson, Stephanie. Cee lo Green: Rapper, Singer, & Record Producer, 1 vol. 2013. (Contemporary Lives Set 2 Ser.). (ENG.). 112p. (J). (gr. 6-12). lib. bdg. 35.64 *(978-1-61783-619-0(2)*, Essential Library) ABDO Publishing Co.

—Keith Urban: Award-Winning Country Star, 1 vol. 2014. (Contemporary Lives Set 4 Ser.). (ENG., Illus.). 112p. (J). (gr. 6-12). lib. bdg. 35.64 *(978-1-62403-548-7(5)*, Essential Library) ABDO Publishing Co.

Watts, Franklin. Fifth Harmony: The Dream Begins ... Now! 2014. (ENG., Illus.). 48p. (J). (gr. -1-7). 12.99 *(978-1-4451-2690-6(7))* Hodder & Stoughton GBR. Dist: Hachette Bk. Group.

Weatherford, Carole Boston. The Legendary Miss Lena Horne. Zunon, Elizabeth, illus. 2017. (ENG.). 48p. (J). (gr. -1-3). 17.99 *(978-1-4814-6824-4(3))* Simon & Schuster Children's Publishing.

—Leontyne Price: Voice of a Century. Colón, Raúl, illus. 2014. (ENG.). 40p. (J). (gr. k-4). 17.99 *(978-0-375-85606-8(4))*; lib. bdg. 20.99 *(978-0-375-95606-5(9))* Random Hse. Children's Bks. (Knopf Bks. for Young Readers).

Weber, Terri. Alicia Keys. 2004. (J). pap. *(978-1-932724-29-5(X))*; lib. bdg. *(978-1-932724-28-8(1))* Panda Publishing, L.L.C. (Bios for Kids).

Weber, Terri Smith. Dixie Chicks. 2004. (J). lib. bdg. *(978-0-9740180-1-0(5)*, Bios for Kids) Panda Publishing, L.L.C.

—Jennifer Lopez: Living the Dream. 2004. (J). pap. *(978-1-932724-21-9(4))*; lib. bdg. *(978-1-932724-20-2(6))* Panda Publishing, L.L.C. (Bios for Kids).

—Jennifer Lopez: Realizando Los Suenos. 2003. (SPA.). (J). pap. *(978-0-9740180-4-1(X))*; lib. bdg. *(978-0-9740180-3-4(1))* Panda Publishing, L.L.C. (Bios for Kids).

—Shakira: Following Her Heart. 2004. (SPA.). (J). pap. *(978-1-932724-05-9(2))*; lib. bdg. *(978-1-932724-04-2(4))* Panda Publishing, L.L.C. (Bios for Kids).

Webster, Christine. Beyonce Knowles. 2005. (Great African American Women for Kids Ser.). (Illus.). 24p. (J). (gr. 2-3). lib. bdg. 24.45 *(978-1-59036-331-7(0))* Weigl Pubs., Inc.

Wells, Peggy Sue. Fergie. 2007. (Blue Banner Biography Ser.). (Illus.). 32p. (YA). (gr. 4-7). lib. bdg. 25.70 *(978-1-58415-521-8(3))* Mitchell Lane Pubs., Inc.

Weston Woods Staff, creator. Ella Fitzgerald. 2011. 38.75 *(978-0-545-02763-2(2))*; 18.95 *(978-0-545-02761-8(6))* Weston Woods Studios, Inc.

Wheeler, Jill C. Jennifer Lopez. 2003. (Star Tracks Ser.). (Illus.). 64p. (J). (gr. 3-8). lib. bdg. 27.07 *(978-1-57765-770-5(5))* ABDO Publishing Co.

—Kelly Clarkson. 2003. (Young Profiles Ser.). (Illus.). 32p. (J). (gr. k-6). 27.07 *(978-1-57765-994-5(5))* ABDO Publishing Co.

—Madonna. 2003. (Star Tracks Ser.). (Illus.). 64p. (gr. 3-8). 27.07 *(978-1-57765-768-2(3)*, Abdo & Daughters) ABDO Publishing Co.

Whiting, Jim. Mandy Moore. (Pop Culture Ser.). (Illus.). 64p. (YA). (gr. 3-7). 2008. lib. bdg. 22.95 *(978-1-4222-0207-4(0))* 2007. pap. 7.95 *(978-1-4222-0362-0(X))* Mason Crest.

Wilcox, Christine. Justin Bieber. Greenaven Press Staff, ed. 2013. (People in the News Ser.). (ENG., Illus.). 128p. (gr. 7-10). lib. bdg. 39.40 *(978-1-4205-0756-0(7)*, Lucent Bks.) Cengage Gale.

Willett, Edward. Janis Joplin: Take Another Little Piece of My Heart. 2008. (American Rebels Ser.). (Illus.). 152p. (YA). (gr. 3-7). lib. bdg. 35.94 *(978-0-7660-2837-1(2))* Enslow Pubs., Inc.

Williams, Zella. Selena Gomez: Actress & Singer. 2010. (Hispanic Headliners Ser.). (ENG.). 24p. (J). pap. 8.25 *(978-1-4488-1482-4(0))*; lib. bdg. 22.60 *(978-1-4488-1458-9(8))* Rosen Publishing Group, Inc., The. (PowerKids Pr.).

—Selena Gomez: Actress & Singer - Actriz y Cantante. 2010. (Hispanic Headliners / Hispanos en Las Noticias Ser.). (ENG & SPA.). 24p. (J). (gr. 2-5). lib. bdg. 22.60 *(978-1-4488-0715-4(8))* Rosen Publishing Group, Inc., The.

—Shakira: Star Singer. 2010. (Hispanic Headliners Ser.). (ENG.). 24p. (J). pap. 8.25 *(978-1-4488-1480-0(4))*; lib. bdg. 22.60 *(978-1-4488-1457-2(X))* Rosen Publishing Group, Inc., The. (PowerKids Pr.).

—Shakira: Star Singer - Estrella de la Canción. 2010. (Hispanic Headliners / Hispanos en Las Noticias Ser.). (SPA & ENG.). 24p. (J). (gr. 2-5). lib. bdg. 22.60 *(978-1-4488-0714-7(X))* Rosen Publishing Group, Inc., The.

Woog, Adam. Jennifer Lopez. 2008. (Great Hispanic Heritage Ser.). (Illus.). 117p. (gr. 6-12). lib. bdg. 35.00 *(978-0-7910-9724-3(2)*, Chelsea Hse.) Facts On File, Inc.

Worth, Richard. Christina Aguilera: Pop Singer. 2016. (Influential Latinos Ser.). (ENG., Illus.). 128p. (J). (gr. 7-8). lib. bdg. 37.27 *(978-0-7660-7180-3(4))* Enslow Pubs., Inc.

Wright, David K. The Life of Paul Robeson: Actor, Singer, Political Activist. 2014. (Legendary African Americans Ser.). 96p. (J). (gr. 6-12). 27.94 *(978-0-7660-6157-6(4))*; (Illus.). pap. 10.95 *(978-0-7660-6158-3(2))* Enslow Pubs., Inc.

Yasuda, Anita. Justin Bieber. 2011. 24p. (YA). (gr. 2-4). *(978-1-77071-647-6(5))*; pap. *(978-1-77071-651-3(3))* Weigl Educational Pubs. Ltd.

—Justin Bieber. 2011. (J). (gr. 4-6). pap. 12.95 *(978-1-61690-672-6(3)*, AV2 by Weigl); (Illus.). 24p. (YA). (gr. 3-6). 27.13 *(978-1-61690-667-2(7))* Weigl Pubs., Inc.

—Justin Bieber: Ma Vie. Karvonen, Tanjah, tr. from ENG. 2011. (FRE., Illus.). 24p. (YA). (gr. 2-4). *(978-1-77071-432-8(4))* Weigl Educational Pubs. Ltd.

—Lady Gaga. 2012. (J). *(978-1-61913-753-0(4))*; pap. *(978-1-61913-754-7(2))* Weigl Pubs., Inc.

—Miranda Cosgrove. 2011. (J). (gr. 4-6). pap. 12.95 *(978-1-61690-673-3(1)*, AV2 by Weigl); (Illus.). 24p. (YA). (gr. 3-6). 27.13 *(978-1-61690-668-9(5))* Weigl Pubs., Inc.

—Nikki Yanofsky. 2011. 24p. (YA). (gr. 2-4). pap. *(978-1-77071-652-0(1))* Weigl Educational Pubs. Ltd.

—Nikki Yanofsky: Ma Vie. Karvonen, Tanjah, tr. from ENG. 2011. (FRE., Illus.). 24p. (YA). (gr. 2-4). *(978-1-77071-433-5(2))* Weigl Educational Pubs. Ltd.

—Taylor Swift. 2010. (Remarkable People Ser.). (Illus.). 24p. (J). (gr. 4-6). pap. 11.95 *(978-1-61690-158-5(6))*; lib. bdg. 25.70 *(978-1-61690-157-8(8))* Weigl Pubs., Inc.

Zakarin, Debra Mostow. Shawn Mendes Unauthorized Bio. 2016. (ENG., Illus.). 48p. (J). (gr. 1-3). pap. 4.99 *(978-0-545-92665-2(3))* Scholastic, Inc.

SINGERS—FICTION

Adler, Irene. The Soprano's Last Song, 1 vol. Iacopo, Bruno & Bruno, Iacopo, illus. 2014. (Sherlock, Lupin, & Me Ser.). (ENG.). 240p. (gr. 4-8). lib. bdg. 26.65 *(978-1-4342-6522-7(6))* Stone Arch Bks.

Amaury. The Phantom of the Opera: Based on the Novel by Gaston Leroux. Rosner, Gillian, tr. Druvert, Hélène, illus. 2016. (ENG.). 40p. (J). (gr. k-2). 19.95 *(978-1-4197-2086-4(4)*, Abrams Bks. for Young Readers) Abrams, Inc.

Anastasiu, Heather & Brown, Anne Greenwood. Girl Last Seen. 2016. (ENG.). 272p. (YA). (gr. 8-12). pap. 9.99 *(978-0-8075-8141-4(0))* Whitman, Albert & Co.

Barbie. Barbie in Rock 'N Royals. 2015. (Book & Jewelry Ser.: 1). (ENG.). 10p. (J). (gr. -1-1). bds. 9.99 *(978-0-7944-3556-1(4)*, Reader's Digest Children's Bks.) Studio Fun International.

Barrett, Ron. Cats Get Famous. Barrett, Ron, illus. 2015. (ENG., Illus.). 32p. (J). (gr. -1-3). 17.99 *(978-1-4424-9453-4(0)*, Simon & Schuster Bks. For Young Readers) Simon & Schuster Bks. For Young Readers.

Brown, Anne Greenwood & Anastasiu, Heather. Girl Last Seen. 2016. (ENG.). 272p. (YA). (gr. 8-12). 16.99 *(978-0-8075-8140-7(2))* Whitman, Albert & Co.

Bryant, Jen. The Fortune of Carmen Navarro. 2011. (ENG.). 240p. (YA). (gr. 7). pap. 8.99 *(978-0-375-85097-4(X)*, Ember) Random Hse. Children's Bks.

Cass, Kiera. The Selection 4-Book Box Set. 2016. (Selection Ser.). 1456p. (YA). (gr. 8). pap. 39.96 *(978-0-06-242440-2(8)*, HarperTeen) HarperCollins Pubs.

Collard, Claire. Footpaths on the Sea. 2015. (ENG., Illus.). 292p. (J). pap. *(978-1-78222-420-4(3))* Paragon Publishing, Rothersthorpe.

Denman, K. L. Stuff We All Get, 1 vol. 2011. (Orca Currents Ser.). (ENG.). 128p. (J). (gr. 5-9). pap. 9.95 *(978-1-55469-820-2(0))*; lib. bdg. 16.95 *(978-1-55469-821-9(9))* Orca Bk. Pubs. USA.

Dimopoulos, Elaine. Material Girls. (ENG.). 336p. (YA). (gr. 9). 2016. pap. 8.99 *(978-0-544-67173-7(2))* 2015. 17.99 *(978-0-544-38850-5(X))* Houghton Mifflin Harcourt Publishing Co. (HMH Books For Young Readers).

Dolamore, Jaclyn. Magic under Glass. 2011. (Magic under Glass Ser.). (ENG.). 256p. (YA). (gr. 7). pap. 8.99 *(978-1-59990-587-7(6)*, 9781599905877, Bloomsbury USA Childrens) Bloomsbury Publishing USA.

Flinn, Alex. Diva. 2013. (ENG.). 304p. (YA). (gr. 9). pap. 9.99 *(978-0-06-212434-0(X))* HarperCollins Pubs.

Frosting & Friendship. 2014. (ENG., Illus.). 240p. (J). (gr. 3-7). pap. 6.99 *(978-1-4424-7397-3(5)*, Aladdin) Simon & Schuster Children's Publishing.

Graham, Sabrina Depina. Breanna & Amber: Help Each Other Achieve Their Dreams (Christian Version) 2012. 92p. 19.99 *(978-1-4691-6411-3(6))*; pap. 12.99 *(978-1-4691-6410-6(8))* Xlibris Corp.

Greene, Kimberly. Fame Game & Me. 2011. (My Sister's a Pop Star Ser.). 320p. (J). pap. 5.99 *(978-0-7945-2900-0(3)*, Usborne) EDC Publishing.

—My Life on TV. 2011. (My Sister's a Pop Star Ser.). 320p. (J). pap. 5.99 *(978-0-7945-2901-7(1)*, Usborne) EDC Publishing.

Greenwald, Tommy. Katie Friedman Gives up Texting! And Lives to Tell about It. Coovert, J. P., illus. 2015. (ENG.). 240p. (J). (gr. 4-7). 13.99 *(978-1-59643-837-8(1)*, 9781596438378) Roaring Brook Pr.

Harmon, Michael. Brutal. 2011. (ENG.). 240p. (YA). (gr. 9). pap. 8.99 *(978-0-440-23995-6(8)*, Knopf Bks. for Young Readers) Random Hse. Children's Bks.

Hodgin, Molly. Tenney's Journal. 2017. (American Girl: Tenney Grant Ser.). (ENG.). 160p. (J). (gr. 3-7). 11.99 *(978-1-338-13704-0(2))* Scholastic, Inc.

Hopkins, Cathy. The Princess of Pop. 2012. (Truth or Dare Ser.). (ENG.). 224p. (YA). (gr. 7). pap. 10.99 *(978-1-4424-6057-7(1)*, Simon Pulse) Simon Pulse.

Hurley, Jeanette Clinger. The Crystal Prince: Love Is the Only Way. 2010. (Illus.). 77p. pap. 32.95 *(978-0-578-03963-3(X))* Outskirts Pr., Inc.

Jones, Harmony. Girl vs. Boy Band: The Right Track. 2016. (ENG.). 240p. (J). 16.99 *(978-1-61963-947-8(5)*, 9781619639478, Bloomsbury USA Childrens) Bloomsbury Publishing USA.

—The High Note. 2017. (ENG.). 240p. (J). 16.99 *(978-1-61963-949-2(1)*, 9781619639492, Bloomsbury USA Childrens) Bloomsbury Publishing USA.

Jones, Jen. Maren Loves Luke Lewis. Franco, Paula, illus. 2014. (Sleepover Girls Ser.). (ENG.). 128p. (gr. 3-5). lib. bdg. 22.65 *(978-1-4342-9755-6(1))* Stone Arch Bks.

Kadence, Sam. Evolution. 2013. 230p. pap. 14.99 *(978-1-62380-410-7(8)*, Harmony Ink Pr.) Dreamspinner Pr.

—Evolution [Library Edition]. 2013. 230p. pap. 14.99 *(978-1-62380-924-9(X)*, Harmony Ink Pr.) Dreamspinner Pr.

Karpes, H. R. Morris... the Downside-Up Bat. 2013. (ENG., Illus.). 32p. (J). (gr. -1-k). 11.95 *(978-1-62087-987-0(5)*, 620987, Sky Pony Pr.) Skyhorse Publishing Co., Inc.

Ketchum, Liza. The Life Fantastic. 2017. (ENG.). 256p. (YA). 17.99 *(978-1-4405-9876-0(2)*, Simon Pulse) Simon Pulse.

Levy, Marianne. Katie Cox Goes Viral. 2017. (ENG.). 368p. (J). (gr. 5-9). pap. 7.99 *(978-1-4926-4250-3(9)*, 9781492642503, Sourcebooks Jabberwocky) Sourcebooks, Inc.

Lord, Emery. Open Road Summer. 2015. (ENG.). 368p. (YA). (gr. 7). pap. 9.99 *(978-0-8027-3801-1(X)*, 9780802738011, Bloomsbury USA Childrens) Bloomsbury Publishing USA.

MacLachlan, Patricia. Just Dance. 2017. (ENG., Illus.). 128p. (J). (gr. 2). 15.99 ***(978-1-4814-7252-4(6)***, McElderry, Margaret K. Bks.) McElderry, Margaret K. Bks.

Man-Kong, Mary. Listen to Your Heart! 2015. (Pictureback(R) Ser.). (ENG., Illus.). 16p. (J). (gr. -1-2). 4.99 *(978-0-553-52341-6(4)*, Random Hse. Bks. for Young Readers) Random Hse. Children's Bks.

Mancuso, Rudy. How to Be Famous in Six Seconds. 2016. (YA). pap. ***(978-1-5011-2767-0(5)***, Keywords Press) Atria Bks.

Marino, Nan. Hiding Out at the Pancake Palace. 2013. (ENG.). 256p. (J). (gr. 3-7). 16.99 *(978-1-59643-753-1(7)*, 9781596437531) Roaring Brook Pr.

—Hiding Out at the Pancake Palace. 2014. (ENG.). 272p. (J). (gr. 3-7). pap. 7.99 *(978-1-250-04000-8(0)*, 9781250040008) Square Fish.

Marko, Cyndi. Bok! Bok! Boom! 2014. (Kung Pow Chicken Ser.: 2). lib. bdg. 14.75 *(978-0-606-35357-1(7))* Turtleback Bks.

McCarthy, Jenna, et al. Maggie Malone & the Mostly Magical Boots. 2014. (Maggie Malone Ser.: 1). (ENG.). 224p. (J). (gr. 3-6). pap. 6.99 *(978-1-4022-9306-1(2)*, 9781402293061, Sourcebooks Jabberwocky) Sourcebooks, Inc.

McGuire Woods, Molly. Barbie in Rock 'n Royals. 2015. (Barbie Chapters Ser.). (ENG.). 64p. (J). (gr. 1-4). 5.99 *(978-0-553-52435-2(6)*, Random Hse. Bks. for Young Readers) Random Hse. Children's Bks.

Mullarkey, Lisa & Mullarkey, John. Get Ella to the Apollo, 1 vol. Bernard, Courtney, illus. 2015. (ENG.). 128p. (J). *(978-1-62402-087-2(9))* Magic Wagon.

Nall, Gail. Out of Tune. 2016. (Mix Ser.). (ENG., Illus.). 336p. (J). (gr. 4-9). 17.99 *(978-1-4814-5817-7(5)*, Simon & Schuster/Paula Wiseman Bks.) Simon & Schuster/Paula Wiseman Bks.

No Place to Fall. 2014. (ENG.). 368p. (YA). (gr. 9). 17.99 *(978-0-06-227099-3(0))* HarperCollins Pubs.

Novak, Ali. The Heartbreakers. 2015. (Heartbreak Chronicles Ser.: 1). (ENG.). 336p. (YA). (gr. 6-12). pap. 10.99 *(978-1-4926-1256-8(1)*, 9781492612568) Sourcebooks, Inc.

Olsen, Sylvia. Molly's Promise, 1 vol. 2013. (Orca Young Readers Ser.). (ENG.). 136p. (J). (gr. 3-6). pap. 7.95 *(978-1-4598-0277-3(2))* Orca Bk. Pubs. USA.

Ooten, Tara Broeckel. Justin Bieber - Fame. 2011. (ENG., Illus.). 40p. (YA). pap. 7.99 *(978-1-4507-3538-4(X))* Bluewater Productions, Inc.

Philbin, Joanna. The Daughters Take the Stage. 2011. (Daughters Ser.: 3). (ENG.). 304p. (J). (gr. 7-17). pap. 8.99 *(978-0-316-04908-5(5)*, Poppy) Little, Brown Bks. for Young Readers.

Prendergast, Gabrielle. The Frail Days, 1 vol. 2015. (Orca Limelights Ser.). (ENG.). 128p. (J). (gr. 6-9). pap. 9.95 *(978-1-4598-0464-7(3))* Orca Bk. Pubs. USA.

Rippin, Sally. The Scary Solo. Spartels, Stephanie, illus. 2013. (ENG.). 48p. (J). pap. 4.99 *(978-1-61067-122-4(8))* Kane Miller.

Rollins, Ellie. Zip. 2013. (ENG.). 336p. (J). (gr. 3-7). pap. 7.99 *(978-1-59514-571-0(0)*, Razorbill) Penguin Young Readers Group.

Rudnick, Paul. It's All Your Fault. (ENG.). 304p. (J). (gr. 9). 2017. pap. 10.99 *(978-0-545-46429-1(3))* 2016. 19.99 *(978-0-545-46428-4(5)*, Scholastic Pr.) Scholastic, Inc.

Ryan, Tom. Big Time, 1 vol. 2014. (Orca Limelights Ser.). (ENG.). 144p. (J). (gr. 6-9). pap. 9.95 *(978-1-4598-0461-6(9))* Orca Bk. Pubs. USA.

Ryder, Chloe. Princess Ponies 8: a Singing Star. 2015. (Princess Ponies Ser.). (ENG., Illus.). 128p. (J). (gr. 2-4). pap. 5.99 *(978-1-61963-567-8(4)*, 9781619635678, Bloomsbury USA Childrens) Bloomsbury Publishing USA.

Schraff, Anne. Facing It, 1 vol. 2013. (Urban Underground Ser.). (ENG.). 194p. (YA). (gr. 9-12). pap. 9.95 *(978-1-62250-045-1(8))* Saddleback Educational Publishing, Inc.

Schraff, Anne E. Facing It. 2013. (Urban Underground — Harriet Tubman High School Ser.). (YA). lib. bdg. 20.80 *(978-0-606-31583-8(7)*, Turtleback) Turtleback Bks.

Snowe, Olivia. The Glass Voice, 1 vol. Lamoreaux, Michelle, illus. 2014. (Twicetold Tales Ser.). (ENG.). 128p. (gr. 3-4). 25.32 *(978-1-4342-9148-6(0))* Stone Arch Bks.

Stanton, Angie. Rock & a Hard Place. 2013. (Jamieson Brothers Ser.: 1). (ENG.). 304p. (YA). (gr. 9). pap. 9.99 *(978-0-06-227254-6(3)*, HarperTeen) HarperCollins Pubs.

—Snapshot. 2013. (Jamieson Brothers Ser.: 2). (ENG.). 416p. (YA). (gr. 9). pap. 9.99 *(978-0-06-227256-0(X)*, HarperTeen) HarperCollins Pubs.

—Under the Spotlight. 2015. (Jamieson Brothers Ser.: 3). (ENG.). 400p. (YA). (gr. 8). pap. 9.99 *(978-0-06-227260-7(8)*, HarperTeen) HarperCollins Pubs.

Supplee, Suzanne. Somebody Everybody Listens To. 2011. (ENG.). 288p. (YA). (gr. 7-18). 8.99 *(978-0-14-241886-4(2)*, Speak) Penguin Young Readers Group.

Teitelbaum, Michael. The Secret of the Tragic Theater. 2015. (Cold Whispers Ser.). (ENG., Illus.). 32p. (J). (gr. 2-6). lib. bdg. 26.60 *(978-1-62724-809-9(9))* Bearport Publishing Co., Inc.

Warner, Gertrude Chandler, creator. The Mystery of the Missing Pop Idol. 2015. (Boxcar Children Mysteries Ser.: 138). (ENG., Illus.). 128p. (J). (gr. 1-5). 15.99 *(978-0-8075-5605-4(X))* Whitman, Albert & Co.

Waxman, Rachel. The Cricklhowell School for the Muses. 2013. (ENG.). 228p. (YA). pap. 14.95 *(978-1-56474-541-5(4)*, Fithian Pr) Daniel & Daniel, Pubs., Inc.

Winter, Jonah. Jazz Age Josephine: Dancer, Singer- Who's That, Who? Why That's Miss Josephine Baker, to You! Priceman, Marjorie, illus. 2012. (ENG.). 40p. (J). (gr. -1-3). 16.99 *(978-1-4169-6123-9(2)*, Atheneum Bks. for Young Readers) Simon & Schuster Children's Publishing.

SINGING

see also Voice

Appleby, Alex. Puedo Ser una Cantante / I Can Be a Singer. 2014. (Cuando Sea Grande / When I Grow Up Ser.). (SPA.). 24p. (J). (gr. k-2). 22.60 *(978-1-4824-0865-2(1))* Stevens, Gareth Publishing LLLP.

Bartle, Jean Ashworth. Sound Advice: Becoming a Better Children's Choir Conductor. 2012. (ENG., Illus.). 288p. pap. 30.95 *(978-0-19-992270-3(5))* Oxford Univ. Pr., Inc.

Beall, Pamela Conn & Nipp, Susan Hagen. Wee Sing & Move. Guida, Liisa Chauncy & Klein, Nancy, illus. 2009. (Wee Sing Ser.). (ENG.). 64p. (J). (gr. -1-2). 10.99

(978-0-8431-8959-9(2), Price Stern Sloan) Penguin Young Readers Group.
Emerson, Roger. Sing 6-7-8! 50 Ways to Improve Your Elementary or Middle School Choir. 2008. (978-1-4234-5479-3(0)) Leonard, Hal Corp.
Feierabend, John M. The Book of Pitch Exploration: Can Your Voice Do This? 2004. (First Steps in Music Ser.). (ENG.). 33p. (J). pap. 11.95 (978-1-57999-242-2(0)); (Illus.). (gr. -1-2). pap. 12.95 (978-1-57999-265-1(X), G-5276) G I A Pubns., Inc.
Harris, Paul & Brewer, Mike. Improve Sight-Singing! Low/Medium Voice - Elementary level. 2003. (Faber Edition Ser.). (ENG.). 40p. (gr. 1-5). pap. 8.25 (978-0-571-51766-4(8)) Faber & Faber, Ltd. GBR. Dist: Alfred Publishing Co., Inc.
Howard, Elisabeth. ABCs of Vocal Harmony: Music Reading, Ear Training. rev. ed. 2004. (Illus.). 124p. per. 29.95 (978-0-934419-01-7(9)) Vocal Power Inc.
Jacobs, Ruth Krehbiel, ed. Collected Notes on Children's Choirs: Compiled from the Choristers' Guild Letters of September, 1949 to June 1954. 2011. 244p. 46.95 (978-1-258-01814-6(4)) Literary Licensing, LLC.
Johnson, Anne, et al. Shukalaka Shake: Songs for a Young Child's Day, 1 vol. 2011. (Songbooks Ser.). (ENG., Illus.). 64p. (J). pap. 24.95 incl. audio compact disk (978-1-4081-4657-6(6)) HarperCollins Pubs. Ltd. GBR. Dist: Independent Pubs. Group.
Kain, Roger. Xtreme Vocals. 2005. (Illus.). 80p. audio compact disk 11.95 (978-1-84492-034-1(8)) Sanctuary Publishing, Ltd. GBR. Dist: Leonard, Hal Corp.
Landau, Elaine. Is Singing for You? 2010. (Ready to Make Music Ser.). (ENG.). 40p. (gr. 4-6). lib. bdg. 27.93 (978-0-7613-5427-7(1), Lerner Pubns.) Lerner Publishing Group.
Leck, Henry H., et al. Creating Artistry Through Choral Excellence. 2009. (978-1-4234-3711-6(X)) Leonard, Hal Corp.
Moon, Daisy. Simply Singing Assemblies: Key Stage 1. 2017. (ENG.). 80p. (J). pap. 38.95 (978-1-4729-3458-1(X)) HarperCollins Pubs. Ltd. GBR. Dist: Independent Pubs. Group.
Nunn, Daniel. Voices, 1 vol. 2011. (Instruments & Music Ser.). (ENG.). 24p. (gr. -1-1). 22.65 (978-1-4329-5061-3(4), Acorn) Heinemann-Raintree.
Raposo, Joe. Sing. Lichtenheld, Tom, illus. 2013. (ENG.). 40p. (J). (gr. -1-3). 16.99 (978-0-8050-9071-0(1), 9780805090710, Holt, Henry & Co. Bks. For Young Readers) Holt, Henry & Co.
Ross, Mary H. Primary Partners Singing Fun. Guymon-King, Jennette, illus. 2004. (978-1-59156-793-6(9)) Covenant Communications.
Ross, Melanie H. & Guymon-King. Super Little Singers. 2004. pap. 12.95 (978-1-59156-163-7(9)); cd-rom 12.95 (978-1-59156-164-4(7)) Covenant Communications, Inc.
Sieling, Peter. Folk Songs. 2004. (North American Folklore Ser.). (Illus.). 112p. (YA). (gr. 7-18). lib. bdg. 22.95 (978-1-59084-344-4(4)) Mason Crest.
Storey, Rita. The Voice & Singing. 2010. (J). 28.50 (978-1-59920-216-7(6)) Black Rabbit Bks.
Stultz, Marie. Innocent Sounds: Building Choral Tone & Artistry with the Beginning Treble Voice. 2007. pap. 22.95 (978-0-944529-44-7(5)) Morning Star Music Pubs.
—Innocent Sounds, Book II: Building Choral Tone & Artistry in Your Children's Choir. 2008. 240p. per. (978-0-944529-45-4(3)) Morning Star Music Pubs.
Terry, Charles L. Sing Mama's Boy Sing. 2012. (ENG.). (J). pap. (978-1-4675-1270-1(2)) Independent Pub.
Turck, Mary C. Freedom Song: Young Voices & the Struggle for Civil Rights. 2008. (ENG., Illus.). 160p. (J). (gr. 4). pap. 18.95 (978-1-55652-773-9(X)) Chicago Review Pr., Inc.
VanVoorst, Jenny Fretland. El Canto. 2016. (El Estudio del Artista (Artist's Studio)).Tr. of Singing. (SPA.). 24p. (J). (gr. k-2). lib. bdg. 25.65 (978-1-62031-321-3(9), Bullfrog Bks.) Jump! Inc.
—Singing. 2016. (Artist's Studio Ser.). 24p. (J). (gr. k-2). lib. bdg. 25.65 (978-1-62031-285-8(9), Bullfrog Bks.) Jump! Inc.

SINGING—FICTION

Ambatchew, Daniel. Mimi Mystery. 2012. (Illus.). 39p. pap. 10.95 (978-9988-647-83-4(2)) Sub-Saharan Pubs. & Traders GHA. Dist: African Bks. Collective, Ltd.
Andrews, Julie & Hamilton, Emma Walton. The Very Fairy Princess Sparkles in the Snow. Davenier, Christine, illus. 2013. (Very Fairy Princess Ser.). (ENG.). 32p. (J). (gr. -1-1). 18.00 (978-0-316-21963-1(0)) Little Brown & Co.
Arnold, Karen. Leaper Joins the Choir. 2011. 28p. pap. 15.99 (978-1-4568-6535-1(8)) Xlibris Corp.
Baker, Georgette. Cantemos Chiquitos, No. 2. (SPA., Illus.). (J). (gr. k-12). pap. 12.95 incl. audio (978-0-9623930-2-0(9), TAL002) Cantemos-bilingual bks. and music.
Ballantyne, R. M. Red Rooney: Or, the Last of the Crew. 2007. (R. M. Ballantyne Collection). (Illus.). 408p. 22.00 (978-1-934554-08-1(1)) Vision Forum, Inc., The.
Ballantyne, Robert Michael. Red Rooney: The Last of the Crew. 2007. (ENG.). 270p. pap. 21.99 (978-1-4346-3693-5(3)); 302p. pap. 24.99 (978-1-4346-3741-3(7)) Creative Media Partners, LLC.
Barkley, Callie. Ellie's Lovely Idea. Riti, Marsha, illus. 2013. (Critter Club Ser.: 6). (ENG.). 128p. (J). (gr. k-4). 16.99 (978-1-4424-8219-7(2)); pap. 5.99 (978-1-4424-8218-0(4)) Little Simon. (Little Simon).
—Ellie's Lovely Idea. 2013. (Critter Club Ser.: 6). (J). lib. bdg. 16.00 (978-0-606-32321-5(X), Turtleback) Turtleback Bks.
Barton, Suzanne. The Sleepy Songbird. 2016. (ENG., Illus.). 32p. (J). 16.99 (978-0-8027-3648-2(3), 9780802736482, Bloomsbury USA Childrens) Bloomsbury Publishing USA.
Birdsall, Jeanne. The Penderwicks in Spring. 2015. (Penderwicks Ser.). (ENG.). 352p. (J). (gr. 3-7). 16.99 (978-0-375-87077-4(6), Knopf Bks. for Young Readers) Random Hse. Children's Bks.
Bradley, Kimberly Brubaker. For Freedom: The Story of a French Spy. 2005. 181p. 16.00 (978-0-7569-5091-0(0)) Perfection Learning Corp.
—For Freedom: The Story of a French Spy. 2005. (ENG.). 192p. (YA). (gr. 7-9). mass mkt. 5.99 (978-0-440-41831-3(3), Laurel Leaf) Random Hse. Children's Bks.
Brian, Janeen. Cat-Astrophe at the Opera, 1 vol. rev. ed. 2013. (Fiction Readers Ser.). (ENG., Illus.). 28p. (J). (gr. 3-3). pap. 8.99 (978-1-4333-5597-4(3)) Shell Educational Publishing.
—Cat-Astrpohe at the Opera. rev. ed. 2013. (Fiction Readers Ser.). (ENG., Illus.). 28p. (gr. 3-3). pap. 19.96 (978-1-4807-1719-0(3)) Teacher Created Materials, Inc.
Brightwood, Laura, illus. I Am A Frog. Brightwood, Laura, . 2007. (J). DVD (978-1-934409-02-2(2)) 3-C Institute for Social Development.
Brouillard, Anne. The Bathtub Prima Donna. Brouillard, Anne, illus. 2004. (Illus.). 24p. (J). (gr. k-4). reprint ed. 13.00 (978-0-7567-7755-5(0)) DIANE Publishing Co.
Brown, Deborah. Here to Save the Day. 2012. 28p. pap. 24.95 (978-1-4626-0387-9(4)) America Star Bks.
Carmichael, Leslie. Lyranel's Song. (Illus.). 288p. (J). 2007. (ENG.). (gr. 2-7). pap. 8.95 (978-0-9718348-6-6(5)) 2005. 16.95 (978-0-9718348-5-9(7)) Blooming Tree Pr.
Chapman, Jason. Who's That Singing? A Pull-the-Tab Book. Chapman, Jason, illus. 2010. (ENG., Illus.). 12p. (J). (gr. -1-1). bds. 9.99 (978-1-4169-8736-9(3), Little Simon) Little Simon.
Conkling, Neil & Philip, Hilda. A Bird's Way of Singing. Date not set. (J). 12.95 (978-0-8050-4795-0(6), Holt, Henry & Co. Bks. For Young Readers) Holt, Henry & Co.
Cooner, Donna. Skinny. (ENG.). 272p. (J). (gr. 7). 2014. pap. 9.99 (978-0-545-42764-7(9)) 2012. 17.99 (978-0-545-42763-0(0)) Scholastic, Inc.
Cottringer, Anne. Singing It. 2007. (ENG.). 224p. (YA). (gr. 7). pap. 11.95 (978-1-84270-678-7(0)) Andersen Pr. GBR. Dist: Independent Pubs. Group.
Cowley, Joy. Big Bear & Little Bear: Singing. Lam, Amy, illus. 2013. (ENG.). 8p. pap. (978-1-927186-25-1(0), Joy Cowley Club) Flying Start Bks.
Cox, Tiffany. Amy, the Frog Who Loved to Sing. 2006. 9.00 (978-0-8059-8806-2(8)) Dorrance Publishing Co., Inc.
Cronin, Doreen. Dooby Dooby Moo. Lewin, Betsy, illus. 2010. (Click, Clack Book Ser.). (ENG.). 40p. (J). (gr. -1-k). bds. 7.99 (978-1-4424-0890-6(1), Little Simon) Little Simon.
—Dooby Dooby Moo. Lewin, Betsy, illus. 2006. (Click, Clack Book Ser.). (ENG.). 40p. (J). (gr. -1-3). 17.99 (978-0-689-84507-9(3), Atheneum Bks. for Young Readers) Simon & Schuster Children's Publishing.
—Dooby Dooby Moo, 1 vol. Lewin, Betsy, illus. 2008. (Doreen Cronin: Click-Clack & More Ser.). (ENG.). 40p. (gr. -1-3). lib. bdg. 24.21 (978-1-59961-423-6(5)) Spotlight.
—Dooby Dooby Moo. Lewin, Betsy, illus. 2011. (J). (gr. -1-3). 29.95 (978-0-545-04281-9(X)) Weston Woods Studios, Inc.
Crossley-Holland, Kevin. Crossing to Paradise. 2008. (J). pap. (978-0-545-05868-1(6), Levine, Arthur A. Bks.) Scholastic, Inc.
Curry, Jane Louise. The Black Canary. 2005. (ENG., Illus.). 288p. (J). (gr. 5-9). 18.99 (978-0-689-86478-0(7), McElderry, Margaret K. Bks.) McElderry, Margaret K. Bks.
De Gasztold, Carmen B. & Godden, Rumer. The Creatures' Choir. (FRE., Illus.). (J). (gr. 3-8). 29.95 (978-0-8288-9331-2(4), F140841) French & European Pubns., Inc.
Dean, James, illus. I Love My White Shoes. 2010. (Pete the Cat Ser.). (J). lib. bdg. (978-0-06-107623-7(6)) HarperCollins Pubs.
Deedy, Carmen Agra. The Rooster Who Would Not Be Quiet! Yelchin, Eugene, illus. 2017. (ENG.). 48p. (J). (gr. -1-3). 17.99 (978-0-545-72288-9(8), Scholastic Pr.) Scholastic, Inc.
Dixon, Franklin W. Top Ten Ways to Die. 2006. 169p. (J). lib. bdg. 16.92 (978-1-4242-0390-1(2)) Fitzgerald Bks.
Edwards, Antonio. Script the Strong Ant. 2011. 32p. pap. 15.99 (978-1-4634-2201-1(6)) AuthorHouse.
Flaxman, Jessica & Hall, Kirsten. Who Says? Becker, Wayne, illus. 2003. (My First Reader Ser.). (ENG.). 32p. (J). 18.50 (978-0-516-22958-4(3), Children's Pr.) Scholastic Library Publishing.
Flinn, Alex. Diva. 2006. 263p. (YA). (gr. 7-12). 16.99 (978-0-06-056843-6(7)); lib. bdg. 18.89 (978-0-06-056845-0(3)) HarperCollins Pubs. (HarperTeen).
Geller, Beverly. Ellies Shabbat Surprise. 2008. 32p. 13.95 (978-965-229-390-9(3)) Gefen Publishing Hse., Ltd ISR. Dist: Gefen Bks.
Geras, Adèle. Pictures of the Night. 2005. (ENG.). 192p. (YA). (gr. 7-12). pap. 11.95 (978-0-15-205543-1(6)) Houghton Mifflin Harcourt Publishing Co.
Grant, Ruthie. Oh, No! Fancy-Free Amy Gets Bad News. 2012. 24p. pap. 13.99 (978-1-4634-4700-7(0)) AuthorHouse.
Greenfield, Amy Butler. Chantress Alchemy. 2015. (Chantress Ser.). (ENG., Illus.). 368p. (YA). (gr. 7). pap. 10.99 (978-1-4424-5708-9(2), McElderry, Margaret K. Bks.) McElderry, Margaret K. Bks.
Gurtler, Janet. Shyanna's Song. Wood, Katie, illus. 2015. (Mermaid Kingdom Ser.). (ENG.). 96p. (gr. 3-5). lib. bdg. 23.99 (978-1-4342-9693-1(8)) Stone Arch Bks.
Hanson, Anders. Whale Tale, 1 vol. 2007. (Critter Chronicles Ser.). (ENG., Illus.). 24p. (J). (gr. k-3). lib. bdg. 24.21 (978-1-59928-476-7(6), SandCastle) ABDO Publishing Co.
HB Staff. The Little Chicks Sing. 97th ed. 2003. (Signatures Ser.). (gr. 1-18). pap. 16.50 (978-0-15-308159-0(7)) Harcourt Schl. Pubs.
Hendricks, Brenda K. What's Better Than That, Seren Dippity? Hendricks, Brenda K., illus. 2013. (Illus.). 32p. pap. 9.99 (978-0-9826582-4-6(9)) Two Small Fish Pubns.
Holmes, Lynda. Spring Cleaning. 2006. 55p. pap. 16.95 (978-1-4241-4324-5(1)) PublishAmerica, Inc.
Holt, Kimberly Willis. Dear Hank Williams. 2015. (ENG.). 224p. (J). (gr. 4-7). 16.99 (978-0-8050-8022-3(8), 9780805080223, Holt, Henry & Co. Bks. For Young Readers) Holt, Henry & Co.
—Dear Hank Williams. 2016. (J). lib. bdg. 18.40 (978-0-606-38551-0(7)) Turtleback Bks.
Howarth, Kylie. Fish Jam. 2015. (ENG., Illus.). 40p. (J). (gr. -1-2). 16.99 (978-1-4998-0098-2(3)) Little Bee Books Inc.
Howe, James. Horace & Morris Join the Chorus (but What about Dolores?) Walrod, Amy, illus. 2006. (J). pap. 44.95 incl. audio compact disk (978-1-59112-909-7(5)); pap. incl. audio (978-1-59112-449-8(2)) Live Oak Media.
Hudson, Cheryl. Songs I Love to Sing. 2009. 24p. 5.95 (978-1-60349-032-0(9), Marimba Bks.) Hudson Publishing Group, The.
Hyperion Staff. First Signing ABC. Williams, Sam, illus. 2007. (ENG.). 64p. (J). (gr. -1-3). 16.99 (978-1-4231-0248-9(7)) Hyperion Pr.
Inman, Robert. The Christmas Bus. Baskin, Lyle, illus. 2006. 77p. 19.95 (978-0-9760963-6-8(6)) Novello Festival Pr.
Jeong, SoYun. Lulu the Shy Piglet. Orsolini, Laura, illus. rev. ed. 2014. (MySELF Bookshelf Ser.). (ENG.). 32p. (J). (gr. k-2). pap. 11.94 (978-1-60357-654-3(1)); lib. bdg. 25.27 (978-1-59953-645-3(5)) Norwood Hse. Pr.
Joachimowski, Paula L. Swamp Band Lullaby. 2007. (J). per. 12.99 (978-1-59879-211-9(3)) Lifevest Publishing, Inc.
Johnson, Elizabeth. And Then Nicholas Sang: The Story of the Trisagion Hymn. Lobastov, Masha, illus. 2010. 32p. (J). 18.95 (978-1-936270-05-7(6)) Ancient Faith Publishing.
Jules, Jacqueline. Singing Superstar. Smith, Kim, illus. 2016. (Sofia Martinez Ser.). (ENG.). 32p. (gr. k-2). lib. bdg. 21.32 (978-1-4795-8716-2(8), Sofia Martinez) Picture Window Bks.
Keane, Sarah. Cuckoo, Cuckoo: A Folktale from Mexico, 1 vol. 2013. (Fiction Readers Ser.). (ENG., Illus.). 24p. (J). (gr. 2-2). pap. 6.99 (978-1-4333-5526-4(4)) Shell Educational Publishing.
Kemnitz, Dianna. Sing with Jack. 2012. 38p. 24.95 (978-1-4626-5656-1(0)) America Star Bks.
Killian, Brandon. The Seesaw Book. 2011. 20p. 12.90 (978-1-4567-4163-1(2)) AuthorHouse.
Kraegel, Kenneth. The Song of Delphine. Kraegel, Kenneth, illus. 2015. (ENG., Illus.). 40p. (J). (gr. k-3). 15.99 (978-0-7636-7001-6(4)) Candlewick Pr.
Lacámara, Laura. Floating on Mama's Song: Flotando con la Canción de Mamá. Morales, Yuyi, illus. 2010. (SPA & ENG.). 32p. (J). (gr. -1-2). 16.99 (978-0-06-084368-7(3), Tegen, Katherine Bks) HarperCollins Pubs.
Levine, Gail Carson. Fairest. 2006. 326p. (J). (gr. 3-7). lib. bdg. 18.89 (978-0-06-073409-1(4)) HarperCollins Pubs.
—Fairest. l.t. rev. ed. 2007. (Literacy Bridge Young Adult Ser.). 349p. (J). (gr. 3-7). 23.95 (978-0-7862-9270-7(9)) Thorndike Pr.
Levine, Gail Carson & Levine, Gail C. Fairest. 2012. (ENG.). 352p. (J). (gr. 3-7). pap. 6.99 (978-0-06-073410-7(8)) HarperCollins Pubs.
Little Tommy Tucker: 6 Small Books. (gr. k-2). 23.00 (978-0-7635-8502-0(5)) Rigby Education.
Litwin, Eric. I Love My White Shoes. Dean, James, illus. 2010. (Pete the Cat Ser.). 40p. (J). (gr. -1-3). (ENG.). 17.99 (978-0-06-190622-0(0)); lib. bdg. 17.89 (978-0-06-190623-7(9)) HarperCollins Pubs.
—The Nuts: Sing & Dance in Your Polka Dot Pants. Magoon, Scott, illus. 2015. (ENG.). 32p. (J). (gr. -1-3). 18.00 (978-0-316-32250-8(4)) Little Brown & Co.
—Pete the Cat & His Four Groovy Buttons. 2013. (CHI & ENG.). (J). (gr. -1-2). (978-957-570-982-2(9)) Eastern Publishing Co., Ltd., The.
—Pete the Cat & His Four Groovy Buttons. Dean, James, illus. 2012. (Pete the Cat Ser.). 40p. (J). (gr. -1-2). (ENG.). 17.99 (978-0-06-211058-9(6)); lib. bdg. 17.89 (978-0-06-211059-6(4)) HarperCollins Pubs.
—Rocking in My School Shoes. Dean, James, illus. 2011. (Pete the Cat Ser.). 40p. (J). (gr. -1-3). (ENG.). 17.99 (978-0-06-191024-1(4)); lib. bdg. 17.89 (978-0-06-191025-8(2)) HarperCollins Pubs.
Litwin, Eric, ed. Rocking in My School Shoes. 2011. (978-0-545-50106-4(7)) Scholastic, Inc.
Litwin, Eric & Dean, James. I Love My White Shoes. 2010. (Pete the Cat Ser.). pap. (978-0-545-41966-6(2)) Scholastic, Inc.
Loftin, Nikki. Nightingale's Nest. (ENG.). (J). (gr. 3-7). 2015. 272p. pap. 8.99 (978-1-59514-623-6(7)) 2014. 256p. 16.99 (978-1-59514-546-8(X)) Penguin Young Readers Group. (Razorbill).
Lou, Cindy, illus. & text. The King of Ing Wants to Sing. Lou, Cindy, text. 2008. (J). 12.00 (978-1-935332-00-8(7)) Kite Tales Publishing.
Matheson, Anne. I Love to Sing. Cutting, David A., illus. 2014. (ENG.). 32p. (J). (gr. 1-5). 7.99 (978-1-4867-0001-1(2)) Flowerpot Children's Pr. Inc. CAN. Dist: Cardinal Pubs. Group.
Meadows, Daisy. Adele the Voice Fairy. 2013. (Rainbow Magic — the Superstar Fairies Ser.: 2). lib. bdg. 14.75 (978-0-606-31514-2(4), Turtleback) Turtleback Bks.
—Alyssa the Star-Spotter Fairy. 2013. (Rainbow Magic — the Superstar Fairies Ser.: 6). lib. bdg. 14.75 (978-0-606-31518-0(7), Turtleback) Turtleback Bks.
—Frankie the Makeup Fairy. 2013. (Rainbow Magic — the Superstar Fairies Ser.: 5). lib. bdg. 14.75 (978-0-606-31517-3(9), Turtleback) Turtleback Bks.
—Jessie the Lyrics Fairy. 2013. (Rainbow Magic — the Superstar Fairies Ser.: 1). lib. bdg. 14.75 (978-0-606-31513-5(6), Turtleback) Turtleback Bks.
Mills, Claudia. Mason Dixon: Fourth-Grade Disasters. Francis, Guy, illus. 2012. (Mason Dixon Ser.). (ENG.). 176p. (J). (gr. 4-7). 6.99 (978-0-375-87275-4(2), Yearling) Random Hse. Children's Bks.
Mitchell, Margaree King. When Grandmama Sings. Ransome, James E., illus. 2012. (ENG.). 40p. (J). (gr. k-4). 16.99 (978-0-688-17563-4(5), Amistad) HarperCollins Pubs.
Moore, Stephanie Perry. Turn up for Real. 2014. (Sharp Sisters Ser.: 3). (ENG.). 168p. (YA). (gr. 6-12). pap. 7.95 (978-1-4677-4490-4(5), Darby Creek); lib. bdg. 27.93 (978-1-4677-3726-5(7)) Lerner Publishing Group.
Negroni, Jay. Emerald's Flight, 1 vol. 2008. (ENG.). 29p. pap. 24.95 (978-1-60672-863-5(6)) America Star Bks.
Parker, Emma. Karaoke Colin. 2010. (Illus.). 20p. pap. (978-1-877561-34-4(7)) First Edition Ltd.
Paul, Bette. Nurses: Nikki, Barbara & Nick. 2007. 488p. per. (978-1-905665-44-0(X)) Pollinger In Print.
Payne, C. C. Something to Sing About. 2008. (ENG.). 167p. (J). (gr. 4-7). pap. 8.50 (978-0-8028-5344-8(7)) Eerdmans, William B. Publishing Co.
Peschke, Marci. Singing Queen, 1 vol. Mourning, Tuesday, illus. 2012. (Kylie Jean Ser.). (ENG.). 112p. (gr. 2-3). pap. 5.95 (978-1-4048-7211-0(6)); lib. bdg. 22.65 (978-1-4048-6800-7(3)) Picture Window Bks. (Kylie Jean).
Porter, Sarah. Lost Voices. 2011. (Lost Voices Trilogy Ser.: 1). (ENG.). 304p. (YA). (gr. 7-18). 16.99 (978-0-547-48250-7(7)) Houghton Mifflin Harcourt Publishing Co.
Publications International Ltd. Staff, ed. Mickey Mouse Clubhouse: Colors: Sing & Learn. 2010. 12p. (J). bds. 10.98 (978-1-4127-1729-8(9)) Publications International, Ltd.
—Sesame Street: Sing with Elmo, Let's Sing! & Wake up, Elmo! 2011. (J). bds. 14.98 (978-1-4508-0627-5(9)) Phoenix International Publications, Inc.
—9 Button Record Song Dora Superstar. 2011. 18p. 19.98 (978-1-4508-1913-8(3)) Phoenix International Publications, Inc.
Rippin, Sally. The Scary Solo. Spartels, Stephanie, illus. 2012. 43p. (J). (978-1-61067-136-1(8)) Kane Miller.
Romanoff, Zan. A Song to Take the World Apart. 2016. (ENG.). 320p. (YA). (gr. 7). 17.99 (978-1-101-93879-9(X), Knopf Bks. for Young Readers) Random Hse. Children's Bks.
Ryan, John. Pugwash Aloft. Ryan, John, illus. 2008. (ENG., Illus.). 32p. (J). (gr. -1-2). 16.95 (978-1-84507-822-5(5), Frances Lincoln) Quarto Publishing Group UK GBR. Dist: Hachette Bk. Group.
Ryan, Tom. Big Time, 1 vol. 2014. (Orca Limelights Ser.). (ENG.). 144p. (J). (gr. 6-9). pap. 9.95 (978-1-4598-0461-6(9)) Orca Bk. Pubs. USA.
Sandusky, Thomas. The Frogs Stopped Singing. 2011. pap. 8.95 (978-0-7414-6450-7(0)) Infinity Publishing.
Santillo, LuAnn. The King. Santillo, LuAnn, ed. 2003. (Half-Pint Kids Readers Ser.). (Illus.). 7p. (J). (gr. -1-1). pap. 1.00 (978-1-59256-050-9(4)) Half-Pint Kids, Inc.
Sewer, Anecia. Why Transfer Day, Anyway? Samuel, Karen, illus. 2007. 16p. (J). 15.99 (978-0-9752986-0-2(7)) Research Institute Pr., The.
Sharpe, Luke. Billy Sure Kid Entrepreneur Is NOT a Singer! Ross, Graham, illus. 2016. (Billy Sure Kid Entrepreneur Ser.: 9). (ENG.). 160p. (J). (gr. 3-7). pap. 6.99 (978-1-4814-6895-4(2), Simon Spotlight) Simon Spotlight.
Simon, Charnan. Shattered Star. (Surviving Southside Ser.). (ENG.). 104p. (YA). (gr. 6-12). 2015. 34.65 (978-1-4677-6011-9(0), Lerner Digital) 2011. pap. 7.95 (978-0-7613-6168-8(5)) 2011. lib. bdg. 27.93 (978-0-7613-6154-1(5)) Lerner Publishing Group.
Snowe, Olivia. The Glass Voice, 1 vol. Lamoreaux, Michelle, illus. 2014. (Twicetold Tales Ser.). (ENG.). 128p. (gr. 3-4). 25.32 (978-1-4342-9148-6(0)) Stone Arch Bks.
Spyri, Johanna. How Wiseli Was Provided For. 2006. 108p. per. 9.95 (978-1-59818-473-0(3)) Aegypan.
Stalling-Patton, Deborah. Shypoodle: Getting to Know You. 2009. 40p. pap. 17.99 (978-1-4389-3899-8(3)) AuthorHouse.
Steig, William. Roland the Minstrel Pig. 2016. (ENG., Illus.). 32p. (J). (gr. -1-3). 18.99 (978-0-374-30088-3(7), 9780374300883, Farrar, Straus & Giroux (BYR)) Farrar, Straus & Giroux.
Struyk-Bonn, Chris. Nice Girls Endure. 2016. (ENG.). 256p. (gr. 9-12). 16.95 (978-1-63079-047-9(8)) Switch Pr.
Tanemura, Arina. O Sagashite Vol. 6, 7 vols. Tanemura, Arina, illus. 2006. (Full Moon Ser.: 6). (ENG., Illus.). 208p. pap. 8.99 (978-1-4215-0397-4(2)) Viz Media.
Tanner, Lian. Battlesong. Szabla, Liz, ed. 2017. (Icebreaker Trilogy Ser.: 3). (ENG.). 304p. (J). 16.99 (978-1-250-05218-6(1), 9781250052186) Feiwel & Friends.
Thomas Nelson Publishing Staff. The Pirates Who Don't Do Anything - Veggietales Movie: Squawk-Along Songs & Games. 2008. (Adventures in Odyssey Activity Pack Ser.). 48p. (J). pap. 12.99 (978-1-4003-1235-1(3)) Nelson, Thomas Inc.
Thompson, Carol. Sing. Thompson, Carol, illus. 2017. (Amazing Me! Ser.: 4). (ENG., Illus.). 12p. (J). (gr. k-k). bds. (978-1-84643-962-9(0)) Child's Play International Ltd.
Van Dusen, Chris. Hattie & Hudson. Van Dusen, Chris, illus. 2017. (ENG., Illus.). 40p. (J). (gr. -1-3). 16.99 (978-0-7636-6545-6(2)) Candlewick Pr.
Walker, Anna. I Love to Sing. Walker, Anna, illus. 2011. (ENG., Illus.). 32p. (J). (gr. -1-1). 9.99 (978-1-4169-8322-4(8), Simon & Schuster Bks. For Young Readers) Simon & Schuster Bks. For Young Readers.
Walker, Sally M. Freedom Song: The Story of Henry "Box" Brown. Qualls, Sean, illus. 2012. (ENG.). 40p. (J). (gr. -1-3). 17.99 (978-0-06-058310-1(X)) HarperCollins Pubs.
Waxman, Rachel. The Crickhowell School for the Muses. 2013. (ENG.). 228p. (YA). pap. 14.95 (978-1-56474-541-5(4), Fithian Pr) Daniel & Daniel, Pubs., Inc.
Weinheimer, Kim, illus. & as told by. The Bear Song. Weinheimer, Kim, as told by. 2012. 24p. pap. 9.95 (978-1-935752-30-1(8)) Bryce Cullen Publishing.
Wells, Tina. Mackenzie Blue. 2013. (Mackenzie Blue Ser.: 1). (ENG.). 224p. (J). (gr. 3-7). pap. 6.99 (978-0-06-158310-0(3)) HarperCollins Pubs.
—Mackenzie Blue. Segawa, Michael, illus. 2009. (Mackenzie Blue Ser.: 1). (ENG.). 224p. (J). (gr. 3-7). 12.99 (978-0-06-158308-7(1)) HarperCollins Pubs.
West, Tracey. Song of the Poison Dragon: a Branches Book (Dragon Masters #5) Jones, Damien, illus. 2016. (Dragon Masters Ser.: 5). (ENG.). 96p. (J). (gr. 1-3). pap. 4.99 (978-0-545-91387-4(X)) Scholastic, Inc.
Winston, Sherri. The Sweetest Sound. 2017. (ENG.). 272p. (J). (gr. 3-7). 17.99 (978-0-316-30295-1(3)) Little Brown & Co.
Woodward, Caroline. Singing Away the Dark. Morstad, Julie, illus. 2017. (ENG.). 44p. (J). (gr. -1-3). 16.95 (978-1-77229-019-6(X)) Simply Read Bks. CAN. Dist: Ingram Publisher Services.
Wooster, Devin Ann. Sing It Out. 2015. (Step into Reading Ser.). (ENG., Illus.). 24p. (J). (gr. -1-1). 4.99 (978-0-553-52438-3(0), Random Hse. Bks. for Young Readers) Random Hse. Children's Bks.
Wright, Bill & Wright, Bil. When the Black Girl Sings. 2008. (ENG.). 272p. (YA). (gr. 7-12). 16.99 (978-1-4169-3995-5(4), Simon & Schuster Bks. For Young Readers) Simon & Schuster Bks. For Young Readers.
—When the Black Girl Sings. 2009. (ENG.). 272p. (YA). (gr. 7). mass mkt. 6.99 (978-1-4169-4003-6(0), Simon Pulse) Simon Pulse.
Zimmer, Frank. Bird Singing Contest. 2008. 28p. pap. 13.99 (978-1-4343-7971-9(X)) AuthorHouse.
Zion, Gene. Harry & the Lady Next Door. Graham, Margaret Bloy, illus. 2003. (I Can Read Level 1 Ser.). (ENG.). 64p. (J). (gr. k-3). pap. 3.99 (978-0-06-444008-0(7)) HarperCollins Pubs.

S

—Harry & the Lady Next Door. Graham, Margaret Bloy, illus. 2004. (I Can Read Bks.). 64p. (gr. -1-3). 14.00 (978-0-7569-3087-5(1)) Perfection Learning Corp.
—Harry & the Lady Next Door. 2003. (I Can Read! Level 1 Ser.). (J). (gr. k-3). lib. bdg. 13.55 (978-0-8085-2612-4(X), Turtleback) Turtleback Bks.

SINGING GAMES

Albrecht, Sally K. & Althouse, Jay. Rhythm All Around! 10 Songs That Explore Rhythm in Our World. 2007. (ENG.). 72p. pap. 29.95 (978-0-7390-4643-2(8)) Alfred Publishing Co., Inc.
Austin, Michael Allen. London Bridge Is Falling Down. Austin, Michael Allen, illus. 2011. (Favorite Children's Songs Ser.). (ENG., Illus.). 16p. (J). (gr. -1-2). lib. bdg. 25.64 (978-1-60954-292-4(4), 200096) Child's World, Inc., The.
Baxter, Nicola. Head, Shoulders, Knees & Toes & Other Action Rhymes. Buckingham, Gabriella, illus. 2013. (ENG.). 16p. (J). (gr. -1-6). bds. 7.99 (978-1-84322-829-5(7), Armadillo) Anness Publishing GBR. Dist: National Bk. Network.
Beausoleil, Loyan & Wells, Leah. Games That Sing: 25 Activities to Keep Children on Their Toes. 2011. (Illus.). 52p. pap. 16.95 incl. audio compact disk (978-1-4291-2116-3(5)) Heritage Music Pr.
Court, Shirley, et al. Singing Sherlock Vol. 2: The Complete Singing Resorce for Primary Schools. 2004. (ENG.). 88p. pap. 79.00 incl. audio compact disk (978-0-85162-353-5(0), 0851623530) Leonard, Hal Corp.
Ferraro Close, Laura. The Farmer in the Dell. 2011. (Favorite Children's Songs Ser.). (ENG., Illus.). 16p. (J). (gr. -1-2). lib. bdg. 25.64 (978-1-60954-296-2(7), 200100) Child's World, Inc., The.
Freeman, Laura. Here We Go Looby Loo. Freeman, Laura, illus. 2011. (Favorite Children's Songs Ser.). (ENG., Illus.). 16p. (J). (gr. -1-2). lib. bdg. 25.64 (978-1-60954-291-7(6), 200095) Child's World, Inc., The.
Key Porter Books, creator. Music Play: Inspired Ways to Explore Music. rev. ed. 2007. (Gymboree Play & Music Ser.). (ENG., Illus.). 36p. (J). (gr. -1-2). bds. (978-1-55263-964-1(9)) Magma.
Kubler, Annie. Head, Shoulders, Knees & Toes. (Illus.). 10p. (J). 2004. (ENG & SOM.). bds. (978-1-84444-153-2(9)) 2004. (ENG & SPA., bds. (978-1-84444-154-9(7)) 2004. (ENG & TAM., bds. (978-1-84444-155-6(5)) 2004. (ENG & TUR., bds. (978-1-84444-156-3(3)) 2004. (ENG & PAN., bds. (978-1-84444-151-8(2)) 2004. (ENG & GUJ., bds. (978-1-84444-150-1(4)) 2004. (FRE & ENG., bds. (978-1-84444-149-5(0)) 2004. (ENG & PER., bds. (978-1-84444-148-8(2)) 2004. (ENG & CHI., bds. (978-1-84444-147-1(4)) 2004. (ENG & ARA., bds. (978-1-84444-145-7(8)) 2004. (ENG & ALB., bds. (978-1-84444-144-0(X)) 2004. (ENG & POR., bds. (978-1-84444-152-5(0)) 2003. (BEN & ENG., bds. (978-1-84444-146-4(6)) Mantra Lingua.
Kubler, Annie, illus. The Wheels on the Bus Go Round & Round. 2003. (Classic Books with Holes 8x8 Ser.). (ENG.). 16p. (J). (978-0-85953-136-8(8)) Child's Play International Ltd.
Plume, Ilse. The Farmer in the Dell. 2004. (ENG., Illus.). 32p. (J). 17.95 (978-1-56792-270-7(8)) Godine, David R. Pub.
Warhola, James & Scholastic, Inc. Staff. If You're Happy & You Know It. Geist, Ken, ed. Warhola, James, illus. 2007. (ENG., Illus.). 32p. (J). (gr. -1-k). 16.99 (978-0-439-72766-2(9), Orchard Bks.) Scholastic, Inc.

SINGLE-PARENT FAMILIES

Apel, Melanie Ann. Let's Talk about Living with Your Single Dad. 2009. (Let's Talk Library). 24p. (gr. 2-3). 42.50 (978-1-60853-445-6(6), PowerKids Pr.) Rosen Publishing Group, Inc., The.
Greenhaven Press Staff. Single-Parent Families. Greenhaven Press, ed. 2016. (Opposing Viewpoints Ser.). (ENG.). 224p. (J). (gr. 10-12). 48.80 (978-0-7377-7528-0(9), Greenhaven Pr., Inc.) Cengage Gale.
Hadley, Margie. Looking Back in the Mirror. 2013. 36p. pap. 16.95 (978-1-63004-529-6(2)) America Star Bks.
Herbert, Denis & Silver, Joanne. Complément éducatif: Mon Enfance Lilloise Racontée à Ma Fille: Récits D'antan (1950 à 1955) 2010. (978-0-9819417-4-5(5)) Beach Lloyd Pubs., LLC.
Levete, Sarah. The Hidden Story of Family Breakups, 1 vol., 1. 2014. (Undercover Story Ser.). (ENG.). 48p. (J). (gr. 5-8). 30.25 (978-1-4777-2801-7(5), Rosen Reference) Rosen Publishing Group, Inc., The.
—Taking Action Against Family Breakups. 2010. (Taking Action Ser.). (ENG.). 48p. (YA). pap. 11.75 (978-1-61532-311-1(2), Rosen Reference); (gr. 5-9). lib. bdg. 29.25 (978-1-61532-310-4(4)) Rosen Publishing Group, Inc., The.
Levins, Sandra. Was It the Chocolate Pudding? A Story for Little Kids about Divorce. Langdo, Bryan, illus. 2005. 40p. (J). (gr. -1-3). per. 9.95 (978-1-59147-309-1(8), Magination Pr.) American Psychological Assn.
Nielsen, Susin. Word Nerd. 2008. (ENG.). 256p. (J). (gr. 4-7). 18.95 (978-0-88776-875-0(X), Tundra Bks.) Tundra Bks. CAN. Dist: Penguin Random Hse. LLC.
Poole, H. W. Single-Parent Families, Vol. 12. 2016. (Families Today Ser.). (Illus.). 48p. (J). (gr. 5). 20.95 (978-1-4222-3623-9(4)) Mason Crest.
Schuette, Sarah L. Single-Parent Families, 1 vol. 2010. (My Family Ser.). (ENG.). 24p. (gr. k-1). pap. 6.29 (978-1-4296-4838-7(4)); pap. 35.70 (978-1-4296-5160-8(1)); lib. bdg. 21.99 (978-1-4296-3980-4(6)) Capstone Press of Coughlan Cos. (Pebble Bks.).
Simons, Rae. Single Parents. 2010. (Changing Face of Modern Families Ser.). (Illus.). 64p. (YA). (gr. 6-18). 22.95 (978-1-4222-1493-0(1)) Mason Crest.
Tomories, K. G. Someone Special for You to Know. 2010. 28p. pap. 13.99 (978-1-4389-9651-6(9)) AuthorHouse.
Tsioumanis, Marina. Mum & Dad Are Separating: A Practical Resource for Separating Families & Family Therapy Professionals, 2 vols. 2017. (ENG., Illus.). 176p. (C). pap. 51.95 (**978-0-86388-669-0(8)**, Y329910) Routledge.

SINGLE-PARENT FAMILIES—FICTION

Acampora, Paul. Rachel Spinelli Punched Me in the Face. 2013. (ENG.). 192p. (J). (gr. 3-7). pap. 8.99 (978-1-250-01669-0(X), 9781250016690) Square Fish.
Aguirre, Ann. The Queen of Bright & Shiny Things. 2015. (ENG.). 336p. (YA). (gr. 7). 17.99 (978-1-250-04750-2(1), 9781250047502) Feiwel & Friends.
Almond, David. My Name Is Mina. 2011. (ENG.). 304p. (J). (gr. 3-7). 15.99 (978-0-385-74073-9(5), Delacorte Bks. for Young Readers) Random Hse. Children's Bks.
Amato, Mary. Guitar Notes. (ENG., Illus.). 304p. (J). (gr. 7). 2014. pap. 8.99 (978-1-60684-503-5(9)) 2012. 16.99 (978-1-60684-124-2(6)) Lerner Publishing Group. (Carolrhoda Lab™).
—Invisible Lines. Caparo, Antonio, illus. 2011. (ENG.). 336p. (gr. 5). 7.99 (978-1-60684-187-7(4), Carolrhoda Bks.) Lerner Publishing Group.
Arnold, Elana K. Infandous. 2015. (ENG.). 200p. (YA). (gr. 8-12). 18.99 (978-1-4677-3849-1(2)) Lerner Publishing Group.
Atkinson, Elizabeth. I, Emma Freke. (Exceptional Reading & Language Arts Titles for Intermediate Grades Ser.). (ENG.). 240p. (J). (gr. 4-7). 2012. 9.95 (978-0-7613-8500-4(2)) 2010. 16.95 (978-0-7613-5604-2(5)) Lerner Publishing Group. (Carolrhoda Bks.).
Avery, Tom. My Brother's Shadow. 2014. (ENG.). 176p. (J). (gr. 4-7). 16.99 (978-0-385-38487-2(4), Schwartz & Wade Bks.) Random Hse. Children's Bks.
Barnholdt, Lauren. Girl Meets Ghost. 2013. (Girl Meets Ghost Ser.: 1). (ENG.). 240p. (J). (gr. 4-9). pap. 7.99 (978-1-4424-2146-2(0), Aladdin) Simon & Schuster Children's Publishing.
Barrow, Randi. Saving Zasha. 2013. (ENG.). 256p. (J). (gr. 3-7). pap. 6.99 (978-0-545-20633-4(2), Scholastic Paperbacks) Scholastic, Inc.
Bateson, Catherine. The Boyfriend Rules of Good Behavior. 2006. (ENG.). 192p. (YA). (gr. 8-12). 16.95 (978-0-8234-2026-1(4)) Holiday Hse., Inc.
—Magenta Mcphee. 2010. (ENG.). 176p. (J). (gr. 3-7). pap. 16.95 (978-0-8234-2253-1(4)) Holiday Hse., Inc.
Bauer, Joan. Close to Famous. 2012. (ENG.). 272p. (J). (gr. 5-18). 7.99 (978-0-14-242017-1(4), Puffin Books) Penguin Young Readers Group.
Bennett, Jenn. The Anatomical Shape of a Heart. 2015. (ENG.). 304p. (YA). (gr. 7). 17.99 (978-1-250-06645-9(X), 9781250066459) Feiwel & Friends.
Benwell, Sarah. The Last Leaves Falling. 2015. (ENG., Illus.). 368p. (YA). (gr. 9). 17.99 (978-1-4814-3065-4(3)) Simon & Schuster Children's Publishing.
Benyo, Richard. The South Street Gang vs. the Coalcracker Cyclops. 2010. (ENG.). 151p. pap. 8.00 (978-1-58966-208-7(3)) Univ. of Scranton Pr.
Birdsall, Jeanne. The Penderwicks: A Summer Tale of Four Sisters, Two Rabbits, & a Very Interesting Boy. (Penderwicks Ser.). (ENG.). (J). (gr. 3-7). 2007. 288p. 7.99 (978-0-440-42047-7(4), Yearling) 2005. 272p. 16.99 (978-0-375-83143-0(6), Knopf Bks. for Young Readers) Random Hse. Children's Bks.
—The Penderwicks: A Summer Tale of Four Sisters, Two Rabbits & a Very Interesting Boy. 2007. (Penderwicks (Hardback) Ser.). 262p. (gr. 3-7). 18.00 (978-0-7569-7798-6(3)) Perfection Learning Corp.
—The Penderwicks: A Summer Tale of Four Sisters, Two Rabbits, & a Very Interesting Boy. 2007. (Penderwicks Ser.: 1). (Illus.). 262p. (gr. 4-7). lib. bdg. 18.40 (978-1-4177-7275-9(1)) Turtleback Bks.
—The Penderwicks: A Summer Tale of Four Sisters, Two Rabbits & a Very Interesting Boy. 2009. 8.80 (978-0-7848-2826-7(1), Everbind) Marco Bk. Co.
—The Penderwicks: A Summer Tale of Four Sisters, Two Rabbits & a Very Interesting Boy. l.t. ed. 2006. (Penderwick Ser.). 304p. (J). (gr. 3-7). 23.95 (978-0-7862-8897-7(3)) Thorndike Pr.
—The Penderwicks in Spring. 2015. (Penderwicks Ser.). (ENG.). 352p. (J). (gr. 3-7). 16.99 (978-0-375-87077-4(6), Knopf Bks. for Young Readers) Random Hse. Children's Bks.
—The Penderwicks on Gardam Street. 2011. (Playaway Children Ser.). (J). (gr. 3-6). 44.99 (978-1-61707-435-6(7)) Findaway World, LLC.
—The Penderwicks on Gardam Street. (Penderwicks Ser.). (ENG.). (J). (gr. 3-7). 2010. 336p. 7.99 (978-0-440-42203-7(5), Yearling) 2008. 320p. 16.99 (978-0-375-84090-6(7), Knopf Bks. for Young Readers) Random Hse. Children's Bks.
—The Penderwicks on Gardam Street. 2010. (Penderwicks Ser.: 2). lib. bdg. 18.40 (978-0-606-14418-6(8), Turtleback) Turtleback Bks.
Black, Chuck. Rise of the Fallen: Wars of the Realm, Book 2. 2015. (Wars of the Realm Ser.). (ENG.). 320p. (YA). (gr. 7). pap. 11.99 (978-1-60142-504-1(X), Multnomah Bks.) Crown Publishing Group.
Black, Holly & DiTerlizzi, Tony. The Field Guide. DiTerlizzi, Tony, illus. (Spiderwick Chronicles Ser.: 1). (ENG., Illus.). (J). 2013. 128p. (gr. 1-5). 17.99 (978-1-4424-8693-5(7)) 2013. 144p. (gr. 1-5). pap. 7.99 (978-1-4424-8692-8(9)) 2008. 128p. (gr. 2-5). 10.99 (978-1-4169-5017-2(6)) Simon & Schuster Bks. For Young Readers. (Simon & Schuster Bks. For Young Readers).
—The Seeing Stone. DiTerlizzi, Tony, illus. (Spiderwick Chronicles Ser.: 2). (ENG., Illus.). (J). (gr. 1-5). 2013. 128p. 15.99 (978-1-4424-8695-9(3)) 2013. 144p. pap. 7.99 (978-1-4424-8694-2(5))Bk. 2. 2nd ed. 2003. 128p. 11.99 (978-0-689-85937-3(6), 53409541) Simon & Schuster Bks. For Young Readers. (Simon & Schuster Bks. For Young Readers).
—The Spiderwick. DiTerlizzi, Tony, illus. 2009. (Spiderwick Chronicles Ser.). (ENG., Illus.). 608p. (J). (gr. 3-7). 29.99 (978-1-4169-8685-0(5), Simon & Schuster Bks. For Young Readers) Simon & Schuster Bks. For Young Readers.
Bodeen, S. A. The Gardener. 2011. (ENG.). 256p. (YA). (gr. 7-12). pap. 9.99 (978-0-312-65942-4(3), 9780312659424) Square Fish.
Brian, Kate. Endless (a Shadowlands Novel) 2014. (Shadowlands Ser.). (ENG.). 336p. (YA). (gr. 7-12). 17.99 (978-1-4231-6485-2(7)) Hyperion Bks. for Children.
—Hereafter (a Shadowlands Novel) 2014. (Shadowlands Ser.). (ENG.). 336p. (YA). (gr. 9-17). pap. 9.99 (978-1-4231-6526-2(8)) Hyperion Bks. for Children.
—Shadowlands. 2013. (Shadowlands Ser.). (ENG.). 352p. (YA). (gr. 9-17). pap. 9.99 (978-1-4231-6525-5(X)) Hyperion Pr.
Bryant, Jen. Kaleidoscope Eyes. 2010. (ENG.). 272p. (J). (gr. 3-7). 7.99 (978-0-440-42190-0(X), Yearling) Random Hse. Children's Bks.
Bush, Penelope. Alice in Time. 2011. (ENG., Illus.). 208p. (YA). (gr. 7-18). 17.95 (978-0-8234-2329-3(8)) Holiday Hse., Inc.
Caletti, Deb. The Fortunes of Indigo Skye. (ENG.). (YA). (gr. 7). 2009. 320p. pap. 9.99 (978-1-4169-1008-4(5)) 2008. 304p. 15.99 (978-1-4169-1007-7(7)) Simon Pulse. (Simon Pulse).
Cantor, Jillian. The Life of Glass. 2010. (ENG.). 352p. (YA). (gr. 8-18). 16.99 (978-0-06-168651-1(4), HarperTeen) HarperCollins Pubs.
Cerato, Mattia. Mom's New Friend. Cerato, Mattia, illus. 2014. (Family Snaps Ser.). (ENG., Illus.). 32p. (J). (gr. k-2). pap. 6.95 (978-1-939656-61-2(3)) Red Chair Pr.
Chen, Justina. Nothing but the Truth (And a Few White Lies) 2007. (Justina Chen Novel Ser.). (ENG.). 256p. (J). (gr. 7-17). per. 9.99 (978-0-316-01131-0(2)) Little, Brown Bks. for Young Readers.
Clifton, Lutricia. Immortal Max. Sheban, Chris, illus. 2014. (ENG.). 192p. (J). (gr. 3-7). 16.95 (978-0-8234-3041-3(3)) Holiday Hse., Inc.
Cochrane, Mick. Fitz. (ENG.). 192p. (YA). (gr. 7). 2013. pap. 8.99 (978-0-375-84611-3(5), Ember) 2012. 16.99 (978-0-375-85683-9(8), Knopf Bks. for Young Readers) Random Hse. Children's Bks.
Cohn, Edith. Spirit's Key. 2014. (ENG.). 320p. (J). (gr. 4-7). 16.99 (978-0-374-30011-1(9), 9780374300111, Farrar, Straus & Giroux (BYR)) Farrar, Straus & Giroux.
Collins, Amberly & Collins, Brandilyn. Final Touch, 1 vol. 2010. (Rayne Tour Ser.). (ENG.). 224p. (YA). (gr. 8-11). pap. 9.99 (978-0-310-71933-5(X)) Zondervan.
Coolidge, Susan. What Katy Did. 2013. (ENG., Illus.). 200p. (J). 15.00 (978-1-84135-843-7(6)) Award Pubns. Ltd. GBR. Dist: Parkwest Pubs., Inc.
—What Katy Did. 2012. 246p. pap. (978-1-78139-262-1(5)) Benediction Classics.
—What Katy Did. Hellard, Susan, illus. 2016. (ENG.). 246p. (J). pap. 9.99 (**978-1-84749-607-2(5)**, 9781847496072, Alma Classics) Bloomsbury Publishing USA.
—What Katy Did. 2017. (ENG., Illus.). (J). (gr. 4-6). pap. 9.90 (**978-1-366-50696-2(0)**) Blurb, Inc.
—What Katy Did. 2015. (ENG., Illus.). (J). (gr. 2-4). 25.95 (**978-1-297-62709-5(1)**) 2012. 302p. pap. 29.75 (978-1-286-07372-8(3)) 2012. 300p. pap. 29.75 (978-1-286-00091-5(2)) 2011. 290p. (gr. 3-7). pap. 28.75 (978-1-179-65265-8(7)) 2010. (ENG.). 300p. pap. 29.75 (978-1-178-00783-1(9)) 2010. (ENG.). 282p. (gr. 3-7). pap. 28.75 (978-1-177-27477-7(9)) 2010. 302p. pap. 29.75 (978-1-145-74830-9(9)) 2008. 164p. (gr. 4-7). 22.99 (978-0-554-37937-1(6)) 2008. 164p. (gr. 4-7). 25.99 (978-0-554-28634-1(3)) 2007. (ENG.). 144p. pap. 18.99 (978-1-4346-5943-9(7)) 2007. (ENG.). 160p. pap. 21.99 (978-1-4346-5944-6(5)) Creative Media Partners, LLC.
—What Katy Did. 2007. (ENG.). 148p. per. (978-1-4065-1527-5(2)) Dodo Pr.
—What Katy Did. 2006. (Dover Children's Classics Ser.). (ENG., Illus.). 160p. (J). (gr. 3-8). per. 6.95 (978-0-486-44760-5(X)) Dover Pubns., Inc.
—What Katy Did. 2007. (ENG.). 104p. per. (978-1-4068-4855-7(7)) Echo Library.
—What Katy Did. 2010. (Illus.). 92p. (gr. 3-7). pap. 19.99 (978-1-153-74507-9(0)) 2009. 104p. pap. 6.40 (978-0-217-53637-0(9)) General Bks. LLC.
—What Katy Did. 2010. 132p. pap. (978-1-4076-5115-6(3)) HardPr.
—What Katy Did. Ledyard, Addie, illus. 284p. 2010. 35.16 (978-1-163-85079-4(9)) 2010. pap. 23.16 (978-1-163-77965-1(2)) 2007. 43.95 (978-0-548-53870-8(0)) 2007. per. 28.95 (978-0-548-48700-6(6)) Kessinger Publishing, LLC.
—What Katy Did. 2010. (Puffin Classics Ser.). (ENG., Illus.). 240p. (J). (gr. 5-7). pap. 5.99 (978-0-14-132671-9(9), Puffin Books) Penguin Young Readers Group.
—What Katy Did. 2013. (ENG., Illus.). 256p. (J). (gr. 4-7). pap. 12.99 (978-0-09-957312-8(1)) Random Hse. GBR. Dist: Independent Pubs. Group.
—What Katy Did. 2007. (ENG.). 192p. pap. 12.45 (978-1-60424-403-8(8), Book Jungle) Standard Pubns., Inc.
—What Katy Did. 2011. 162p. (gr. 3-7). pap. (978-3-8424-6664-7(1)) Tredition GmbH.
—What Katy Did. 2010. 144p. pap. 4.99 (978-1-61720-100-4(6)) Wilder Pubns., Corp.
Coolidge, Susan & Ledyard, Addie. What Katy Did. 2010. (ENG.). 292p. pap. 28.75 (978-1-172-34659-2(3)) Creative Media Partners, LLC.
Corbett, Sue. Free Baseball. 2008. (ENG.). 160p. (J). (gr. 3-7). 6.99 (978-0-14-241080-6(5), Puffin Books) Penguin Young Readers Group.
Cotugno, Katie. How to Love. 2015. (ENG.). 416p. (YA). (gr. 9). pap. 9.99 (978-0-06-221636-6(8)) HarperCollins Pubs.
Couloumbis, Audrey. Jake. 2011. (ENG.). 176p. (J). (gr. 3-7). pap. 6.99 (978-0-375-85631-0(5), Yearling) Random Hse. Children's Bks.
Courgeon, Rémi. Toothpick. 2017. (ENG., Illus.). 36p. (J). (gr. k-4). 17.95 (978-1-59270-210-7(4)) Enchanted Lion Bks., LLC.
Curtin, Ann. Dreamcatcher. 2015. 201p. (YA). (978-1-61271-246-8(0)) Zumaya Pubns. LLC.
Damico, Gina. Hellhole. (ENG.). (YA). (gr. 9). 2016. 384p. pap. 9.99 (978-0-544-54117-7(0)) 2015. 368p. 17.99 (978-0-544-30710-0(0)) Houghton Mifflin Harcourt Publishing Co. (HMH Books For Young Readers).
Davis, Terrance. Mom & Me. 2012. 24p. (-18). pap. 24.95 (978-1-4626-9502-7(7)) America Star Bks.
Day, Karen. A Million Miles from Boston. 2012. (ENG.). 224p. (J). (gr. 3-7). pap. 6.99 (978-0-375-85974-8(8), Yearling) Random Hse. Children's Bks.
Dee, Barbara. Just Another Day in My Insanely Real Life. 2007. (Mix Ser.). (ENG.). 256p. (J). (gr. 4-8). pap. 7.99 (978-1-4169-4739-4(6), Aladdin) Simon & Schuster Children's Publishing.
Deriso, Christine Hurley. Talia Talk. 2009. 184p. (J). pap. (978-0-375-84496-6(1), Delacorte Pr) Random House Publishing Group.
Deuker, Carl & Perry, Thomas. Runner. 2007. (ENG.). 224p. (YA). (gr. 7-12). pap. 8.99 (978-0-618-73505-1(4)) Houghton Mifflin Harcourt Publishing Co.
DiTerlizzi, Tony & Black, Holly. The Field Guide. DiTerlizzi, Tony, illus. 2003. (Spiderwick Chronicles Ser.: 1). (ENG., Illus.). 128p. (J). (gr. 1-5). 12.99 (978-0-689-85936-6(8), 53409542, Simon & Schuster Bks. For Young Readers) Simon & Schuster Bks. For Young Readers.
Doller, Trish. The Devil You Know. 2015. (ENG.). 256p. (YA). (gr. 9). 17.99 (978-1-61963-416-9(3), 9781619634169, Bloomsbury USA Childrens) Bloomsbury Publishing USA.
Durst, Sarah Beth. Chasing Power. 2014. (ENG.). 376p. (YA). (gr. 9). 17.99 (978-0-8027-3755-7(2), 9780802737557, Bloomsbury USA Childrens) Walker & Co.
Easton, Kelly. To Be Mona. 2008. (ENG.). 224p. (YA). (gr. 7). 16.99 (978-1-4169-0054-2(3), McElderry, Margaret K. Bks.) McElderry, Margaret K. Bks.
Emond, Stephen. Bright Lights, Dark Nights. 2015. (ENG., Illus.). 384p. (YA). (gr. 7). 17.99 (978-1-62672-206-4(4)) Roaring Brook Pr.
Farish, Terry. Either the Beginning or the End of the World. 2015. (ENG.). 200p. (YA). (gr. 8-12). 18.99 (978-1-4677-8813-7(9), Carolrhoda Lab™); 18.99 (978-1-4677-7483-3(9)) Lerner Publishing Group.
Fenn, Jennifer. Flight Risk. 2017. (ENG.). 384p. (YA). 17.99 (978-1-62672-760-1(0), 9781626727601) Roaring Brook Pr.
Ferguson, Alane. The Angel of Death. 2008. (Forensic Mystery Ser.). 258p. 17.00 (978-0-7569-8929-3(9)) Perfection Learning Corp.
Fogelin, Adrian. The Real Question, 1 vol. (ENG.). 256p. (YA). 2009. pap. 7.95 (978-1-56145-501-0(6)) 2006. (gr. 7-18). 15.95 (978-1-56145-383-2(8)) Peachtree Pubs.
—The Sorta Sisters, 1 vol. 2007. (ENG., Illus.). 224p. (J). (gr. 3-7). 15.95 (978-1-56145-424-2(9)) Peachtree Pubs.
—Sorta Sisters, 1 vol. Fogelin, Adrian, illus. 2011. (ENG., Illus.). 288p. pap. 7.95 (978-1-56145-592-8(X), Peachtree Junior) Peachtree Pubs.
Frank, Lucy. Lucky Stars. 2014. (ENG.). 304p. (J). (gr. 5-9). pap. 14.99 (978-1-4814-2901-6(9), Atheneum Bks. for Young Readers) Simon & Schuster Children's Publishing.
Friend, Natasha. For Keeps. 2011. (ENG.). 272p. (YA). (gr. 7-18). 7.99 (978-0-14-241846-8(3), Speak) Penguin Young Readers Group.
Fuqua, Jonathon Scott. The Reappearance of Sam Webber. 2010. (ENG.). 250p. pap. 12.95 (978-1-890862-60-2(6)) Bancroft Pr.
Gallagher, Toni. Twist My Charm - The Popularity Spell. 2015. (Twist My Charm Ser.). (ENG.). 272p. (J). (gr. 3-7). 16.99 (978-0-553-51115-4(7), Random Hse. Bks. for Young Readers) Random Hse. Children's Bks.
Gantos, Jack. Joey Pigza Swallowed the Key. 2009. 8.30 (978-0-7848-3764-1(3)); 8.32 (978-0-7848-1771-1(5)) Marco Bk. Co. (Everbind).
—Joey Pigza Swallowed the Key. unabr. ed. 2004. (Joey Pigza Ser.: Bk. 1). 154p. (J). (gr. 5-9). pap. 29.00 incl. audio (978-0-8072-8166-6(2), YA120SP, Listening Library) Random Hse. Audio Publishing Group.
—Joey Pigza Swallowed the Key. 2007. (Joey Pigza Ser.: 1). (J). 1.25 (978-1-4193-6006-0(X)) Recorded Bks., Inc.
—Joey Pigza Swallowed the Key. 2014. (Joey Pigza Ser.: 1). (ENG.). 176p. (J). (gr. 5-9). pap. 7.99 (978-1-250-06168-3(7), 9781250061683) Square Fish.
—Joey Pigza Swallowed the Key. 2014. (Joey Pigza Ser.: 1). (J). lib. bdg. 18.40 (978-0-606-23019-3(X), Turtleback) Turtleback Bks.
—The Key That Swallowed Joey Pigza. 2014. (Joey Pigza Ser.: 5). (ENG.). 160p. (J). (gr. 5-9). 16.99 (978-0-374-30083-8(6), 9780374300838, Farrar, Straus & Giroux (BYR)) Farrar, Straus & Giroux.
Gervay, Susanne. Being Jack. Wilcox, Cathy, illus. 2015. 167p. (J). (978-1-61067-455-3(3)) Kane Miller.
Gilbert, Melissa. Daisy & Josephine. Kuo, Julia, illus. 2014. (ENG.). 32p. (J). (gr. -1-3). 17.99 (978-1-4424-4578-9(5), Simon & Schuster/Paula Wiseman Bks.) Simon & Schuster/Paula Wiseman Bks.
Goldberg, Whoopi. Terrible Terrel. Roos, Maryn, illus. 2010. (ENG.). 160p. (J). (gr. 1-17). pap. 4.99 (978-0-7868-5263-5(1), Jump at the Sun) Hyperion Bks. for Children.
Goode, John. Going the Distance. (YA). 2016. (ENG., Illus.). (gr. 8-12). 24.99 (**978-1-63533-020-5(3)**, Harmony Ink Pr.) 2015. lib. bdg. (978-1-63216-620-3(8)) Dreamspinner Pr.
Gorman, Carol & Findley, Ron J. The Stumptown Kid, 1 vol. 2005. (ENG.). 224p. (J). (gr. 3-7). 15.95 (978-1-56145-337-5(4)) Peachtree Pubs.
Green, Julia. Hunter's Heart. 2007. 264p. (YA). (gr. 7-12). 16.95 (978-0-7613-9493-8(1), Carolrhoda Bks.) Lerner Publishing Group.
Green, Tim. The Big Time. (Football Genius Ser.: 4). (ENG.). (J). (gr. 3-7). 2011. 304p. pap. 6.99 (978-0-06-168621-4(2)) 2010. 288p. 16.99 (978-0-06-168619-1(0)) HarperCollins Pubs.
Grindele, Jenny. Josh, the Jock of High School. 2005. 48p. pap. 16.95 (978-1-4137-6950-0(0)) America Star Bks.
Grindley, Sally. Bravo, Max! Ross, Tony, illus. 2007. (ENG.). 160p. (J). (gr. 1-4). pap. 8.99 (978-1-4169-3645-9(9), Simon & Schuster/Paula Wiseman Bks.) Simon & Schuster/Paula Wiseman Bks.
Guerra, Stephanie. Torn, 0 vols. 2012. (ENG.). 272p. (YA). (gr. 10-12). 17.99 (978-0-7614-6272-9(4), 9780761462729, Amazon Children's Publishing) Amazon Publishing.
Hahn, Mary Downing. Witch Catcher. (ENG.). 240p. (J). (gr. 5-7). 2011. pap. 7.99 (978-0-547-57714-2(1)) 2006. (Illus.). 16.00 (978-0-618-50457-2(5)) Houghton Mifflin Harcourt Publishing Co.
Hall, Mary Lou. Wirewalker. 2016. (ENG.). 304p. (YA). (gr. 7). 17.99 (978-0-670-01646-4(2), Viking Books for Young Readers) Penguin Young Readers Group.
Halse, Leif. The Boys from Vangen: Vangsgutane. Huntrods, Alexander Knud, tr. Nilssen, Jens R., illus. 2009. (ENG & NNO.). 176p. (J). 19.95 (978-0-9760541-5-3(9)) Astri My Astri Publishing.
Hand, Cynthia. Unearthly. 2011. (Unearthly Ser.: 1). (ENG.). 464p. (YA). (gr. 8). pap. 9.99 (978-0-06-199617-7(3), HarperTeen) HarperCollins Pubs.

Hayes, Christine. The Mothman's Curse. Hindle, James K., illus. 2015. (ENG.). 320p. (J). (gr. 3-7). 15.99 *(978-1-62672-027-5(4),* 9781626720275) Roaring Brook Pr.
—Mothman's Curse. 2016. (J). lib. bdg. 18.40 *(978-0-606-39560-1(1))* Turtleback Bks.
Helmetag Murdock, Kita. Future Flash. 2014. (ENG.). 208p. (J). (gr. 2-7). 12.95 *(978-1-62873-822-3(7),* Sky Pony Pr.) Skyhorse Publishing Co., Inc.
Hemphill, Helen. Runaround. (ENG.). 117p. (J). (gr. 6-9). 2009. pap. 10.95 *(978-1-59078-777-9(3))* 2007. (Illus.). 16.95 *(978-1-932425-83-3(7))* Boyds Mills Pr. (Front Street).
Horvath, Polly. My One Hundred Adventures. 2010. (My One Hundred Adventures Ser.). (ENG., Illus.). 272p. (J). (gr. 3-7). 7.99 *(978-0-375-85526-9(2),* Yearling) Random Hse. Children's Bks.
Howard, J. J. That Time I Joined the Circus. 2013. (ENG.). 272p. (J). (gr. 7). 17.99 *(978-0-545-43381-5(9))* Scholastic, Inc.
Howe, James. Also Known As Elvis. 2015. (Misfits Ser.). (ENG., Illus.). 304p. (J). (gr. 5-9). pap. 7.99 *(978-1-4424-4511-6(4))* Simon & Schuster Children's Publishing.
Hughes, Shirley. The Christmas Eve Ghost. Hughes, Shirley, illus. 2010. (ENG., Illus.). 32p. (J). (gr. -1-3). 15.99 *(978-0-7636-4472-7(2))* Candlewick Pr.
Jayne, Hannah. The Escape. 2015. (ENG., Illus.). 256p. (YA). (gr. 8-12). pap. 9.99 *(978-1-4926-1654-2(0),* 9781492616542) Sourcebooks, Inc.
Jitchotvisut, Donna M. Mittens for Christmas. 2009. 376p. 31.95 *(978-1-4401-0372-8(0))*; pap. 21.95 *(978-1-4401-0370-4(4))* iUniverse, Inc.
Jones, Jen. Lissa & the Fund-Raising Funk, No. 3. 2011. (Team Cheer Ser.). (ENG.). 112p. (gr. 4-4). lib. bdg. 25.32 *(978-1-4342-2996-0(3),* Team Cheer) Stone Arch Bks.
—Lissa & the Fund-Raising Funk: # 3, 1 vol. 2012. (Team Cheer Ser.). (ENG.). 112p. (gr. 4-4). pap. 7.19 *(978-1-4342-4251-8(X),* Team Cheer) Stone Arch Bks.
Jukes, Mavis. The New Kid. (ENG.). 288p. (J). 2012. (gr. 4-7). 7.99 *(978-0-375-85367-8(7),* Yearling) 2011. (gr. 3-7). 14.99 *(978-0-375-85879-6(2),* Knopf Bks. for Young Readers) Random Hse. Children's Bks.
Kamata, Suzanne. Gadget Girl: The Art of Being Invisible. 2013. (ENG., Illus.). 256p. (YA). pap. 14.95 *(978-1-936846-38-2(1))* GemmaMedia.
Kanady, Mary Ellen Murdock. Mommy & Me. 2008. (Illus.). 32p. (J). pap. 8.00 *(978-0-8059-7728-8(7))* Dorrance Publishing Co., Inc.
Karre, Elizabeth. All You Are. 2014. (Gift Ser.). 120p. (YA). (gr. 6-12). (ENG.). pap. 7.95 *(978-1-4677-4477-5(8))*; lib. bdg. 27.93 *(978-1-4677-3510-0(8))* Lerner Publishing Group. (Darby Creek).
Katcher, Brian. Almost Perfect. 2010. (ENG.). 368p. (YA). (gr. 9). pap. 9.99 *(978-0-385-73665-7(7),* Delacorte Bks. for Young Readers) Random Hse. Children's Bks.
Kenyon, Sherrilyn. Infinity, Vol. 1. Ahn, JiYoung, illus. 2013. (Dark-Hunters Ser.: 1). (ENG.). 240p. (gr. 11-17). 13.00 *(978-0-316-19053-4(5),* Yen Pr.) Orbit.
—Infinity. (Chronicles of Nick Ser.: 1). (ENG.). 480p. (YA). (gr. 7-18). 2011. pap. 11.99 *(978-0-312-60304-5(5),* 9780312603045) 2010. 19.99 *(978-0-312-59907-2(2),* 9780312599072) St. Martin's Pr. (St. Martin's Griffin).
Kinsey-Warnock, Natalie. Lumber Camp Library. Bernardin, James, illus. 2003. (ENG.). 96p. (J). (gr. 2-5). pap. 4.99 *(978-0-06-444292-3(6))* HarperCollins Pubs.
Kleinman, Estelle. The Penderwicks: A Study Guide. Friedland, Joyce & Kessler, Rikki, eds. 2008. (Novel-Ties Ser.). (Illus.). 39p. pap. 16.95 *(978-0-7675-1488-0(2))* Learning Links Inc.
Krovatin, Christopher. Venomous. Yates, Kelly, illus. 2011. (ENG.). 336p. (YA). (gr. 8). pap. 8.99 *(978-1-4424-1298-9(4),* Atheneum Bks. for Young Readers) Simon & Schuster Children's Publishing.
Kurzweil, Allen. Leon & the Spitting Image. Bertholf, Bret, illus. (ENG.). 320p. (J). (gr. 3-18). 2005. pap. 7.99 *(978-0-06-053932-0(1),* Greenwillow Bks.) 2003. 16.99 *(978-0-06-053930-6(5))* HarperCollins Pubs.
Kyi, Tanya Lloyd. Anywhere but Here. 2013. (ENG., Illus.). 320p. (YA). (gr. 9). 17.99 *(978-1-4424-8070-4(X))*; pap. 9.99 *(978-1-4424-8069-8(6))* Simon Pulse. (Simon Pulse).
Lacont'e. Overcoming Obstacles. 2012. 28p. 19.95 *(978-1-4626-7076-5(8))* America Star Bks.
Lagercrantz, Rose. Life According to Dani. Eriksson, Eva, illus. 2016. (My Happy Life Ser.: 4). (ENG.). 108p. (gr. k-3). 16.99 *(978-1-77657-070-6(7))* Gecko Pr. NZL. Dist: Lerner Publishing Group.
Lake, Nick. There Will Be Lies. 2015. (ENG.). 464p. (YA). (gr. 9-12). 17.99 *(978-1-61963-440-4(6),* 9781619634404, Bloomsbury USA Childrens) Bloomsbury Publishing USA.
Lange, Erin Jade. Dead Ends. 2013. (ENG.). 336p. (YA). (gr. 9). 17.99 *(978-1-61963-080-2(X),* 9781619630802, Bloomsbury USA Childrens); 288p. pap. 17.99 *(978-1-61963-081-9(8))* Bloomsbury Publishing USA.
Larsen, Jen. Future Perfect. 2015. (ENG.). 320p. (YA). (gr. 8-12). 17.99 *(978-0-06-232123-7(4),* HarperTeen) HarperCollins Pubs.
Lauture, Mireille B. Mancy's Haitian Folktale Collection: Father Misery. Minckler, Kathleen L., illus. 2011. 24p. pap. 12.50 *(978-1-4634-3682-7(3))* AuthorHouse.
Leal, Ann Haywood. Also Known As Harper. 2011. (ENG.). 272p. (J). (gr. 5-7). pap. 10.99 *(978-0-312-65934-9(2),* 9780312659349) Square Fish.
Lean, Sarah. A Dog Called Homeless. 2012. (ENG.). 208p. (J). (gr. 3-7). 16.99 *(978-0-06-212220-9(7),* Tegen, Katherine Bks) HarperCollins Pubs.
Levy, Janice. Totally Uncool. Monroe, Chris, illus. 2003. (Picture Bks.). 32p. (J). (gr. -1-3). reprint ed. 6.95 *(978-1-57505-555-8(4),* Carolrhoda Bks.) Lerner Publishing Group.
Lindelauf, Benny. Nine Open Arms. 2014. (ENG., Illus.). 264p. (J). (gr. 3). 16.95 *(978-1-59270-146-9(9))* Enchanted Lion Bks., LLC.
Lloyd, Natalie. A Snicker of Magic. (ENG.). 320p. (J). (gr. 3-7). 2015. pap. 6.99 *(978-0-545-55273-8(7))* 2014. 16.99 *(978-0-545-55270-7(2))* Scholastic, Inc. (Scholastic Pr.).
—A Snicker of Magic. 2015. lib. bdg. 17.20 *(978-0-606-37089-9(7))* Turtleback Bks.
Lloyd, Natalie, et al. A Snicker of Magic. 2014. (ENG.). mass mkt. *(978-0-545-68447-7(1))* Scholastic, Inc.
Luciani, Brigitte. The Meeting. Burrell, Carol, tr. from FRE. Tharlet, Eve, illus. 2010. (Mr. Badger & Mrs. Fox Ser.: 1). (ENG.). 32p. (J). (gr. k-3). lib. bdg. 25.26 *(978-0-7613-5625-7(8))* Lerner Publishing Group.
—The Meeting. Burrell, Carol, tr. from FRE. Tharlet, Eve, illus. 2010. 1. (ENG.). 32p. (C). (gr. k-3). pap. 10.95 *(978-0-7613-5631-8(2))* National Geographic School Publishing, Inc.
Lundebrek, Amy & Rich, Anna. Under the Night Sky, 1 vol. 2008. (ENG., Illus.). 32p. (gr. 3-6). 16.95 *(978-0-88448-297-0(9),* 884297) Tilbury Hse. Pubs.
Lyga, Barry. Bang. 2017. (ENG.). 304p. (J). (gr. 7-17). 17.99 *(978-0-316-31550-0(8))* Little, Brown Bks. for Young Readers.
—Hero Type. 2009. (ENG.). 312p. (YA). (gr. 7). pap. 8.99 *(978-0-547-24877-6(6))* Houghton Mifflin Harcourt Publishing Co.
Lynch, Chris. Angry Young Man. 2012. (ENG.). 192p. (YA). (gr. 7). pap. 10.99 *(978-1-4424-5419-4(9),* Simon & Schuster Bks. For Young Readers) Simon & Schuster Bks. For Young Readers.
Lyne, Jennifer H. Catch Rider. 2014. (ENG.). 288p. (YA). (gr. 7). pap. 8.99 *(978-0-544-30182-5(X),* HMH Books For Young Readers) Houghton Mifflin Harcourt Publishing Co.
Lyon, George Ella. Sonny's House of Spies. 2007. (ENG.). 304p. (J). (gr. 6-9). pap. 14.95 *(978-1-4169-6815-3(6),* Simon & Schuster/Paula Wiseman Bks.) Simon & Schuster/Paula Wiseman Bks.
Maddox, Jake. Snowboard Struggle. 2016. (Jake Maddox JV Ser.). (ENG., Illus.). 96p. (gr. 3-4). lib. bdg. 25.99 *(978-1-4965-3980-9(X))* Stone Arch Bks.
—Taekwondo Clash. 2016. (Jake Maddox JV Ser.). (ENG.). 96p. (gr. 3-4). lib. bdg. 25.99 *(978-1-4965-3981-6(8))* Stone Arch Bks.
Madonia, Kristen-Paige. Fingerprints of You. 2013. (ENG., Illus.). 272p. (YA). (gr. 9). pap. 9.99 *(978-1-4424-2921-5(6),* Simon & Schuster Bks. For Young Readers) Simon & Schuster Bks. For Young Readers.
—Fingerprints of You. Ribera, Terry, illus. 2012. (ENG.). 272p. (YA). (gr. 9). 16.99 *(978-1-4424-2920-8(8),* Simon & Schuster Bks. For Young Readers) Simon & Schuster Bks. For Young Readers.
Maldonado, Torrey. Secret Saturdays. 2012. (ENG.). 208p. (YA). (gr. 7-18). 7.99 *(978-0-14-241747-8(5),* Puffin Books) Penguin Young Readers Group.
—Secret Saturdays. 2012. lib. bdg. 18.40 *(978-0-606-23645-4(7),* Turtleback) Turtleback Bks.
Mankell, Henning. A Bridge to the Stars. 2009. (Joel Gustafson Stories Ser.: No. 1). (ENG.). 180p. (YA). (gr. 7). pap. 7.99 *(978-0-440-24042-6(5),* Delacorte Bks. for Young Readers) Random Hse. Children's Bks.
—Shadows in the Twilight. 2010. (Joel Gustafson Stories Ser.: No. 2). (ENG.). 208p. (YA). (gr. 7). pap. 7.99 *(978-0-440-24043-3(3),* Delacorte Bks. for Young Readers) Random Hse. Children's Bks.
—When the Snow Fell. 2011. (Joel Gustafson Stories Ser.: No. 3). (ENG.). 256p. (YA). (gr. 7). pap. 8.99 *(978-0-440-24044-0(1),* Delacorte Bks. for Young Readers) Random Hse. Children's Bks.
Mann, Jennifer Ann. Sunny Sweet Is So Dead Meat. 2014. (Sunny Sweet Ser.). (ENG., Illus.). 208p. (YA). (gr. 3-6). 15.99 *(978-1-59990-978-3(2),* 9781599909783, Bloomsbury USA Childrens) Bloomsbury Publishing USA.
—Sunny Sweet Is So Not Sorry. 2013. (Sunny Sweet Ser.). (ENG., Illus.). 208p. (YA). (gr. 3-6). 15.99 *(978-1-59990-977-6(4),* 9781599909776, Bloomsbury USA Childrens) Bloomsbury Publishing USA.
Manzer, Jenny. Save Me, Kurt Cobain. 2016. (ENG.). 272p. (YA). (gr. 7). 17.99 *(978-0-553-52126-9(8),* Delacorte Pr.) Random Hse. Children's Bks.
Mason, David. Davey McGravy. Silverstein, Grant, illus. 2015. (ENG.). 120p. (J). (gr. k). pap. 14.95 *(978-1-58988-099-3(4))* Dry, Paul Bks., Inc.
McClintock, Norah. Watch Me, 1 vol. 2008. (Orca Currents Ser.). (ENG.). (J). (gr. 5-9). 112p. 16.95 *(978-1-55469-040-4(4))*; 128p. pap. 9.95 *(978-1-55469-039-8(0))* Orca Bk. Pubs. USA.
McDaniel, Lurlene. Prey. 2010. (ENG.). 208p. (YA). (gr. 7). mass mkt. 7.99 *(978-0-440-24015-0(8),* Laurel Leaf) Random Hse. Children's Bks.
McNish, Cliff. Breathe: A Ghost Story. (Exceptional Reading & Language Arts Titles for Intermediate Grades Ser.). (ENG.). 264p. (J). (gr. 4-8). 2009. pap. 6.95 *(978-0-7613-4962-4(6),* First Avenue Editions) 2006. lib. bdg. 15.95 *(978-0-8225-6443-0(2),* Carolrhoda Bks.) Lerner Publishing Group.
Mead, Alice. Junebug. 2009. (Junebug Ser.). (ENG.). 128p. (J). (gr. 3-7). pap. 7.99 *(978-0-312-56126-0(1),* 9780312561260) Square Fish.
—Junebug in Trouble. 2003. (ENG., Illus.). 144p. (J). (gr. 3-7). 5.99 *(978-0-440-41937-2(9),* Yearling) Random Hse. Children's Bks.
Michaels, Rune. Nobel Genes. (ENG., (YA). (gr. 7). 2011. Illus.). 208p. pap. 8.99 *(978-1-4424-2401-2(X))* 2010. 192p. 16.99 *(978-1-4169-1259-0(2))* Simon & Schuster Children's Publishing. (Atheneum Bks. for Young Readers).
Mills, Claudia. Being Teddy Roosevelt. Alley, R. W., illus. 2007. (ENG.). 96p. (J). (gr. 2-5). 16.99 *(978-0-374-30657-1(5),* 9780374306571, Farrar, Straus & Giroux (BYR)) Farrar, Straus & Giroux.
—Being Teddy Roosevelt. Alley, R. W., illus. 2012. (ENG.). 112p. (J). (gr. 2-5). pap. 8.99 *(978-0-312-64018-7(8),* 9780312640187) Square Fish.
Mills, Wendy. Positively Beautiful. (ENG.). 368p. (YA). 2016. pap. 9.99 *(978-1-68119-025-9(7),* 9781681190259) 2015. (gr. 9). 17.99 *(978-1-61963-341-4(8),* 9781619633414) Bloomsbury Publishing USA. (Bloomsbury USA Childrens).
Mohr, L. C. Krumbuckets. Musheno, Erica, illus. 2007. (ENG.). 144p. (J). (gr. 2-7). 13.95 *(978-0-9769417-6-7(7))* Blooming Tree Pr.
Monninger, Joseph. Whippoorwill. (ENG.). 288p. (YA). (gr. 7). 2016. pap. 9.99 *(978-0-544-81356-4(1))* 2015. 17.99 *(978-0-544-53123-9(X))* Houghton Mifflin Harcourt Publishing Co. (HMH Books For Young Readers).
—Wish. 2012. (ENG.). 204p. (YA). (gr. 7). pap. 8.99 *(978-0-375-86213-7(7),* Ember) Random Hse. Children's Bks.
Moracho, Cristina. Althea & Oliver. 2014. (ENG.). 384p. (YA). (gr. 9). 17.99 *(978-0-670-78539-1(3),* Viking Books for Young Readers) Penguin Young Readers Group.
Morphew, Chris. The Man in the Shadows. 2017. (Phoenix Files Ser.: 1). (ENG.). 512p. (YA). (gr. 7). pap. 12.99 ***(978-1-76012-425-0(7))*** Hardie Grant Egmont Pty, Ltd. AUS. Dist: Independent Pubs. Group.
Morpurgo, Michael. Private Peaceful. 2006. 18.00 *(978-0-7569-6630-0(2))* Perfection Learning Corp.
—Private Peaceful. 2006. (YA). 1.25 *(978-1-4193-2976-0(6))* Recorded Bks., Inc.
—Private Peaceful. 2006. (After Words Ser.). (ENG., Illus.). 224p. (J). (gr. 7-12). per. 7.99 *(978-0-439-63653-7(1),* Scholastic Paperbacks) Scholastic, Inc.
—Snakes & Ladders. Wilson, Anne, illus. 2006. (Yellow Bananas Ser.). (ENG.). 48p. (J). (gr. -1-3). lib. bdg. *(978-0-7787-0952-7(3))* Crabtree Publishing Co.
Morton-Shaw, Christine. The Hunt for the Seventh. 2009. (ENG.). 288p. (J). (gr. 5). pap. 7.99 *(978-0-06-072824-3(8),* Tegen, Katherine Bks) HarperCollins Pubs.
Naylor, Phyllis Reynolds. Alice in April. 2011. (Alice Ser.: 5). (ENG.). 192p. (J). (gr. 5-9). pap. 6.99 *(978-1-4424-2757-0(4),* Atheneum Bks. for Young Readers) Simon & Schuster Children's Publishing.
—Alice In-Between. 2011. (Alice Ser.: 6). (ENG.). 192p. (J). (gr. 5-9). pap. 6.99 *(978-1-4424-2758-7(2),* Atheneum Bks. for Young Readers) Simon & Schuster Children's Publishing.
—Alice In-Between. 2008. (Alice McKinley Ser.: No. 6). (ENG.). 176p. (J). pap. 5.99 *(978-1-4169-6770-5(2),* Simon & Schuster/Paula Wiseman Bks.) Simon & Schuster/Paula Wiseman Bks.
—Alice in Blunderland. 2005. 200p. (J). (gr. 2-7). 13.65 *(978-0-7569-5075-0(9))* Perfection Learning Corp.
—Alice in Blunderland. 2012. (Alice Ser.). (ENG., Illus.). 240p. (J). (gr. 2-7). pap. 5.99 *(978-1-4424-4643-4(9),* Atheneum Bks. for Young Readers) Simon & Schuster Children's Publishing.
—Alice in Lace. 2009. (Alice McKinley Ser.: No. 8). (ENG.). 160p. (J). pap. 7.99 *(978-1-4169-7543-4(8),* Simon & Schuster/Paula Wiseman Bks.) Simon & Schuster/Paula Wiseman Bks.
—Alice in Rapture, Sort Of. 2011. (Alice Ser.: 2). (ENG.). 208p. (J). (gr. 5-9). pap. 6.99 *(978-1-4424-2362-6(5),* Atheneum Bks. for Young Readers) Simon & Schuster Children's Publishing.
—Alice on the Outside. 2012. (Alice Ser.: 11). (ENG., Illus.). 208p. (J). (gr. 5-9). pap. 6.99 *(978-1-4424-3495-0(3),* Atheneum Bks. for Young Readers) Simon & Schuster Children's Publishing.
—Alice the Brave. (Alice Ser.: 7). (ENG., (J). 2011. Illus.). 176p. (gr. 5-9). pap. 7.99 *(978-1-4424-2851-5(1),* Atheneum Bks. for Young Readers) 2009. 160p. (gr. 4-8). pap. 7.99 *(978-1-4169-7542-7(X),* Aladdin) Simon & Schuster Children's Publishing.
—I Like Him, He Likes Her: Alice Alone; Simply Alice; Patiently Alice. 2010. (Alice Ser.). (ENG.). 640p. (YA). (gr. 7). pap. 12.99 *(978-1-4424-0978-1(9),* Atheneum Bks. for Young Readers) Simon & Schuster Children's Publishing.
—Lovingly Alice. 2004. (Alice Bks.). 166p. (J). (gr. 4-6). 13.65 *(978-0-7569-6604-1(3))* Perfection Learning Corp.
—Lovingly Alice. 2006. (Alice Ser.). (ENG., Illus.). 176p. (J). (gr. 4-7). pap. 5.99 *(978-0-689-84400-3(X),* Atheneum Bks. for Young Readers) Simon & Schuster Children's Publishing.
—Outrageously Alice. 2011. (Alice Ser.: 9). (ENG., Illus.). 176p. (J). (gr. 5-9). pap. 6.99 *(978-1-4424-2853-9(8),* Atheneum Bks. for Young Readers) Simon & Schuster Children's Publishing.
—Reluctantly Alice. 2011. (Alice Ser.: 3). (ENG.). 240p. (J). (gr. 5-9). pap. 6.99 *(978-1-4424-2361-9(7),* Atheneum Bks. for Young Readers) Simon & Schuster Children's Publishing.
—Reluctantly Alice. 2008. (Alice McKinley Ser.: No. 3). (ENG.). 208p. (J). pap. 5.99 *(978-1-4169-5876-5(2),* Simon & Schuster/Paula Wiseman Bks.) Simon & Schuster/Paula Wiseman Bks.
—Starting with Alice. 2004. (Alice Bks.). 181p. (J). (gr. 4-7). 12.65 *(978-0-7569-2940-4(7))* Perfection Learning Corp.
—Starting with Alice. 2012. (Alice Ser.). (ENG., Illus.). 224p. (J). (gr. 2-7). pap. 6.99 *(978-1-4424-4642-7(0),* Atheneum Bks. for Young Readers) Simon & Schuster Children's Publishing.
Nelson, Theresa. Ruby Electric. 2004. 264p. (J). (gr. 5-7). 13.65 *(978-0-7569-3530-6(X))* Perfection Learning Corp.
—Ruby Electric. 2004. (ENG.). 272p. (J). (gr. 5-7). reprint ed. pap. 12.99 *(978-0-689-87146-7(5),* Atheneum Bks. for Young Readers) Simon & Schuster Children's Publishing.
Ness, Patrick. A Monster Calls: Inspired by an Idea from Siobhan Dowd. (ENG.). 240p. (YA). (gr. 7). 2016. pap. 9.99 *(978-0-7636-9215-5(8))* 2015. pap. 12.00 *(978-0-7636-8081-7(8))* Candlewick Pr.
—A Monster Calls: Inspired by an Idea from Siobhan Dowd. Kay, Jim, illus. (ENG.). 224p. (YA). (gr. 7). 2013. pap. 12.00 *(978-0-7636-6065-9(5))* 2011. 16.99 *(978-0-7636-5559-4(7))* Candlewick Pr.
—A Monster Calls: Inspired by an Idea from Siobhan Dowd. 2011. (Playaway Children Ser.). (YA). (gr. 7-12). 54.99 *(978-1-4558-4499-9(3))* Findaway World, LLC.
—A Monster Calls: Inspired by an Idea from Siobhan Dowd. 2013. lib. bdg. 23.30 *(978-0-606-31603-3(5),* Turtleback) Turtleback Bks.
Newman, John. Mimi. 2011. (ENG., Illus.). 192p. (J). (gr. 3-7). 15.99 *(978-0-7636-5415-3(9))* Candlewick Pr.
Nielsen, Susin. Word Nerd. 2010. (ENG.). 264p. (J). (gr. 4-7). pap. 12.95 *(978-0-88776-990-0(X),* Tundra Bks.) Tundra Bks. CAN. Dist: Penguin Random Hse. LLC.
Patrick, Cat. The Originals. (ENG.). (YA). (gr. 7-17). 2014. 320p. pap. 10.00 *(978-0-316-21945-7(2))* 2013. 304p. 18.00 *(978-0-316-21943-3(6))* Little, Brown Bks. for Young Readers.
Pearsall, Shelley. All Shook Up. 2009. (ENG.). 272p. (J). (gr. 3-7). 6.99 *(978-0-440-42139-9(X),* Yearling) Random Hse. Children's Bks.
Perry, Hailey. On the Move. 2010. 188p. pap. 12.00 *(978-1-60844-428-1(7))* Dog Ear Publishing, LLC.
Philbin, Joanna. The Daughters Break the Rules. 2011. (Daughters Ser.: 2). (ENG.). 304p. (J). (gr. 7-17). pap., pap. 10.00 *(978-0-316-04905-4(0),* Poppy) Little, Brown Bks. for Young Readers.
Pimentel, Sandy. The Boy with Two Homes. 2011. 32p. pap. 21.99 *(978-1-4568-3620-7(X))* Xlibris Corp.
Pitchford, Dean. The Big One-Oh. 2009. (ENG.). 208p. (J). (gr. 3-7). 6.99 *(978-0-14-241292-3(9),* Puffin Books) Penguin Young Readers Group.
Polacco, Patricia. Something about Hensley's. Polacco, Patricia, illus. 2006. (ENG., Illus.). 48p. (J). (gr. -1-3). 17.99 *(978-0-399-24538-1(3),* Philomel Bks.) Penguin Young Readers Group.
Quattlebaum, Mary. Jackson Jones & the Curse of the Outlaw Rose. 2008. (ENG.). 112p. (J). (gr. 3-7). 5.99 *(978-0-440-42138-2(1),* Yearling) Random Hse. Children's Bks.
Rapp, Adam. The Children & the Wolves. Ering, Timothy Basil, illus. 2012. (ENG.). 160p. (YA). (gr. 9). 16.99 *(978-0-7636-5337-8(3))* Candlewick Pr.
Reichs, Kathy. Code. 2013. (Virals Ser.: 3). (ENG.). 432p. (J). (gr. 5). pap. 8.99 *(978-1-59514-572-7(9),* Puffin Books) Penguin Young Readers Group.
—Virals. 2014. lthr. 79.00 *(978-1-62715-582-3(1))* Leatherbound Bestsellers.
—Virals. (Virals Ser.: 1). (ENG.). (J). (gr. 5-18). 2011. 480p. 10.99 *(978-1-59514-426-3(9),* Puffin Books) 2010. 464p. 17.99 *(978-1-59514-342-6(4),* Razorbill) Penguin Young Readers Group.
—Virals. 2011. 20.00 *(978-1-61383-226-4(5))* Perfection Learning Corp.
Reichs, Kathy & Reichs, Brendan. Code. 2013. (Virals Ser.: 3). lib. bdg. 19.65 *(978-0-606-32140-2(3),* Turtleback) Turtleback Bks.
—Terminal. 2015. (Virals Ser.: 5). (ENG.). 432p. (J). (gr. 5). 17.99 *(978-1-59514-528-4(1),* G.P. Putnam's Sons Books for Young Readers) Penguin Young Readers Group.
—Virals. 2011. (Virals Ser.: 1). lib. bdg. 20.85 *(978-0-606-23069-8(6),* Turtleback) Turtleback Bks.
Reinhardt, Dana. The Summer I Learned to Fly. 2012. (ENG.). 224p. (YA). (gr. 7). pap. 8.99 *(978-0-385-73955-9(9),* Ember) Random Hse. Children's Bks.
Resau, Laura. The Indigo Notebook. 2010. (ENG.). 336p. (YA). (gr. 7). pap. 9.99 *(978-0-375-84524-6(0),* Ember) Random Hse. Children's Bks.
—The Ruby Notebook. 2012. (ENG.). 384p. (YA). (gr. 7). pap. 9.99 *(978-0-375-84525-3(9),* Ember) Random Hse. Children's Bks.
Rhodes, O. K. & Spencer, Octavia. The Case of the Time-Capsule Bandit. To, Vivienne, illus. 2013. (Randi Rhodes, Ninja Detective Ser.: 1). (ENG.). 224p. (J). (gr. 3-7). 16.99 *(978-1-4424-7681-3(8),* Simon & Schuster Bks. For Young Readers) Simon & Schuster Bks. For Young Readers.
Roberts, Willo Davis. Megan's Island. 2016. (ENG., Illus.). 288p. (J). (gr. 3-7). 17.99 *(978-1-4814-4908-3(7))*; pap. 6.99 *(978-1-4814-4907-6(9))* Simon & Schuster Children's Publishing. (Aladdin).
Rue, Nancy. You Can't Sit with Us - Mean Girl Makeover, 1 vol. 2014. (Mean Girl Makeover Ser.). (ENG.). 224p. (J). pap. 9.99 *(978-1-4003-2371-5(1))* Nelson, Thomas Inc.
Rue, Nancy N. Lucy Out of Bounds, 1 vol. 2016. (Faithgirlz / a Lucy Novel Ser.). (ENG.). 224p. (J). pap. 7.99 *(978-0-310-75505-0(0))* Zonderkidz.
Ryan, Jeanne. Charisma. 2015. (ENG.). 384p. (YA). (gr. 7). 17.99 *(978-0-8037-3966-6(4),* Dial Bks) Penguin Young Readers Group.
Rylant, Cynthia. A Kindness. Date not set. (Sky Bks.). 104p. pap. 54.75 *(978-0-582-08106-2(8))* Addison-Wesley Longman, Ltd. GBR. Dist: Trans-Atlantic Pubns., Inc.
Saldana, Rene. The Whole Sky Full of Stars. 2008. (ENG.). 144p. (YA). (gr. 7-11). mass mkt. 5.99 *(978-0-440-23791-4(2),* Laurel Leaf) Random Hse. Children's Bks.
Savage, Melissa. Lemons. 2017. (ENG.). 320p. (J). (gr. 3-7). 16.99 ***(978-1-5247-0012-6(6))***; lib. bdg. 19.99 ***(978-1-5247-0013-3(4))*** Random Hse. Children's Bks. (Crown Books For Young Readers).
Schindler, Holly. Feral. 2014. (ENG.). 432p. (YA). (gr. 8). 17.99 *(978-0-06-222020-2(9),* HarperTeen) HarperCollins Pubs.
Schotter, Roni. Mama, I'll Give You the World. Gallagher, S. Saelig, illus. 2013. (ENG.). 40p. (J). (gr. -1-3). pap. 7.99 *(978-0-449-81142-9(5),* Dragonfly Bks.) Random Hse. Children's Bks.
Shaw Wolf, Jennifer. Dead Girls Don't Lie. 2013. 336p. pap. 17.99 *(978-0-8027-3450-1(2))* Walker & Co.
Shea, John & Harmon, Michael B. A Kid from Southie. 2011. 240p. (YA). (gr. 9-18). 16.95 *(978-1-934813-53-9(2))* Westside Bks.
Shearer, Alex. Sea Legs. 2006. (ENG.). 320p. (J). (gr. 5-9). per. 17.99 *(978-0-689-87144-3(9),* Simon & Schuster/Paula Wiseman Bks.) Simon & Schuster/Paula Wiseman Bks.
Shofner, Corabel. Almost Paradise. 2017. (ENG.). 304p. (J). 16.99 *(978-0-374-30378-5(9),* 9780374303785, Farrar, Straus & Giroux (BYR)) Farrar, Straus & Giroux.
Shull, Megan. The Swap. 400p. (J). (gr. 5-9). 2016. pap. 7.99 *(978-0-06-231170-2(0))* 2014. (ENG.). 16.99 *(978-0-06-231169-6(7))* HarperCollins Pubs. (Tegen, Katherine Bks).
Sidney, Margaret. Five Little Peppers & How They Grew. 2006. (Dover Children's Classics Ser.). (ENG., Illus.). 224p. (J). (gr. 3-5). per. 6.95 *(978-0-486-45267-8(0))* Dover Pubns., Inc.
—Five Little Peppers & How They Grew. Andreasen, Dan, illus. 2009. (Classic Starts(tm) Ser.). (ENG.). 160p. (J). (gr. 2-4). 6.95 *(978-1-4027-5420-3(5))* Sterling Publishing Co., Inc.
Silvera, Adam. More Happy Than Not. (ENG.). (YA). (gr. 9). 2016. 336p. pap. 10.99 *(978-1-61695-677-6(1))* 2015. 304p. 18.99 *(978-1-61695-560-1(0))* Soho Pr., Inc. (Soho Teen).
Simmons, Ted. Diablo Creek. 2007. (ENG.). 168p. (YA). pap. *(978-0-9776958-7-4(5))* CyPress Pubns.
Sitomer, Alan Lawrence. Caged Warrior. 2014. (ENG., Illus.). 224p. (YA). (gr. 7-12). 16.99 *(978-1-4231-7124-9(1))* Disney Pr.
Sizer, Ralph Robuck. Rashad & Rameen. 2011. 26p. pap. 16.95 *(978-1-4560-6459-4(2))* America Star Bks.

S

Skovron, Jon. Misfit. 2011. (ENG.). 384p. (YA). (gr. 9-17). 16.95 (978-1-4197-0021-7(9), Amulet Bks.) Abrams, Inc.

—Struts & Frets. (ENG.). 304p. (YA). 2011. (gr. 9-17). pap. 7.95 (978-1-4197-0028-6(6)) 2009. (gr. 7-11). 16.95 (978-0-8109-4174-8(0)) Abrams, Inc. (Amulet Bks.).

Snow, Carol. Switch. 2009. (ENG.). 240p. (YA). (gr. 8). pap. 8.99 (978-0-06-145210-9(6), HarperTeen) HarperCollins Pubs.

Sommer, Carl. Dare to Dream! Martínez, Jorge et al, illus. 2007. (Another Sommer-Time Story Ser.). (ENG.). 48p. (J). (gr. -1-3). 16.95 incl. audio compact disk (978-1-57537-523-6(0)) Advance Publishing, Inc.

Stampler, Ann Redisch. Afterparty. 2013. (ENG., Illus.). 416p. (YA). (gr. 9). 17.99 (978-1-4424-2324-4(2), Simon Pulse) Simon Pulse.

Staniszewski, Anna. The Dirt Diary. 2014. (Dirt Diary Ser.: 1). (ENG.). 256p. (J). (gr. 5-9). pap. 6.99 (978-1-4022-8636-0(8), 9781402286360, Sourcebooks Jabberwocky) Sourcebooks, Inc.

—The Gossip File. 2015. (Dirt Diary Ser.: 3). (ENG.). 224p. (J). (gr. 5-9). pap. 6.99 (978-1-4926-0463-1(1), 9781492604631, Sourcebooks Jabberwocky) Sourcebooks, Inc.

—The Prank List. 2014. (Dirt Diary Ser.: 2). (ENG.). 256p. (J). (gr. 5-9). pap. 6.99 (978-1-4022-8639-1(2), 9781402286391, Sourcebooks Jabberwocky) Sourcebooks, Inc.

Stein, Tammar. High Dive. 2011. (ENG.). 208p. (YA). (gr. 7). pap. 7.99 (978-0-440-23903-1(6), Knopf Bks. for Young Readers) Random Hse. Children's Bks.

Susanne, Gervay & Gervay, Susanne. Being Jack. Wilcox, Cathy, illus. 2016. (ENG.). 192p. (J). pap. 5.99 (978-1-61067-379-2(4)) Kane Miller.

Thiel Annie. The Playdate Kids Cosmos' Mom & Dad are Moving Apart 2ED 2007. 2007. 32p. 12.95 (978-1-933721-31-6(6)); pap. 6.95 (978-1-933721-27-9(8)) Playdate Kids Publishing.

Thomas, Leah. Because You'll Never Meet Me. 2015. (ENG.). 352p. (YA). (gr. 9-12). 17.99 (978-1-61963-590-6(9), 9781619635906, Bloomsbury USA Childrens) Bloomsbury Publishing USA.

Thompson, Lauren. A Christmas Gift for Mama. Burke, Jim, illus. 2003. (J). pap. 16.95 (978-0-590-30726-0(6)) Scholastic, Inc.

To Be Perfectly Honest: A Novel Based on an Untrue Story. 2014. (ENG., Illus.). 496p. (YA). (gr. 7). pap. 11.99 (978-0-689-87605-9(X), Simon & Schuster Bks. For Young Readers) Simon & Schuster Bks. For Young Readers.

Toliver, Wendy. Lifted. 2010. (ENG.). 352p. (YA). (gr. 9-18). pap. 9.99 (978-1-4169-9048-2(8), Simon Pulse) Simon Pulse.

Ullman, Barb Bentler. Whistle Bright Magic: A Nutfolk Tale. 2010. 224p. (J). (gr. 3-7). 16.99 (978-0-06-188286-9(0)) HarperCollins Pubs.

Updale, Eleanor. Johnny Swanson. 2012. (ENG.). 384p. (J). (gr. 3-7). 8.99 (978-0-385-75228-2(8), Yearling) Random Hse. Children's Bks.

Valentine, Jenny. Me, the Missing, & the Dead. 2010. 224p. (YA). (gr. 9). pap. 8.99 (978-0-06-085070-8(1), HarperTeen) HarperCollins Pubs.

Verdi, Jessica. What You Left Behind. 2015. (ENG.). 368p. (YA). (gr. 8-12). pap. 9.99 (978-1-4926-0874-5(2)) Sourcebooks, Inc.

Vernick, Audrey. Screaming at the Ump. 2014. (ENG.). 272p. (J). (gr. 5-7). 16.99 (978-0-544-25208-0(X), Clarion Bks.) Houghton Mifflin Harcourt Trade & Reference Pubs.

Vrettos, Adrienne Maria. Sight. 2008. (ENG.). 272p. (YA). (gr. 7). pap. 8.99 (978-1-4169-0658-2(4), McElderry, Margaret K. Bks.) McElderry, Margaret K. Bks.

Warner, Sally. Only Emma. Harper, Jamie, illus. 2006. (Emma Ser.). (ENG.). 144p. (J). (gr. 3-7). 6.99 (978-0-14-240711-0(9), Puffin Books) Penguin Young Readers Group.

Warner, Sally & Harper, Jamie. Only Emma. 2005. (Emma Ser.). (ENG., Illus.). 128p. (J). (gr. 3-7). 14.99 (978-0-670-05979-9(X), Viking Books for Young Readers) Penguin Young Readers Group.

Wells, Rosemary. On the Blue Comet. Ibatoulline, Bagram, illus. (ENG.). 336p. (J). (gr. 5). 2012. pap. 8.99 (978-0-7636-5815-1(4)) 2010. 16.99 (978-0-7636-3722-4(X)) Candlewick Pr.

West, Kasie. The Distance Between Us. 2013. (ENG.). 320p. (YA). (gr. 8). pap. 9.99 (978-0-06-223565-7(6), HarperTeen) HarperCollins Pubs.

—On the Fence. 2014. (ENG.). 304p. (YA). (gr. 8). pap. 9.99 (978-0-06-223567-1(2), HarperTeen) HarperCollins Pubs.

White, Jennifer. Survival Strategies of the Almost Brave. 2015. (ENG.). 320p. (J). (gr. 3-7). 16.99 (978-0-374-30084-5(4), 9780374300845, Farrar, Straus & Giroux (BYR)) Farrar, Straus & Giroux.

Williams, Laura E. Slant. 2008. (ENG.). 160p. (J). (gr. 2-8). pap. 6.95 (978-1-57131-682-0(5)) Milkweed Editions.

Willis, Meredith Sue. Meli's Way. 2015. 178p. (YA). (978-1-932727-15-9(9)) Montemayor Pr.

Wolff, Virginia Euwer. Make Lemonade. unabr. ed. 2004. (Make Lemonade Trilogy: No. 1). 200p. (J). (gr. 7-18). pap. 36.00 incl. audio (978-0-8072-0793-2(4), S YA 348 SP, Listening Library) Random Hse. Audio Publishing Group.

—Make Lemonade. 2006. (ENG.). 208p. (YA). (gr. 5-9). pap. 8.99 (978-0-8050-8070-4(8), 9780805080704) Square Fish.

—True Believer. 2004. (Make Lemonade Trilogy: No. 2). 272p. (J). (gr. 7-18). pap. 38.00 incl. audio (978-0-8072-2283-6(6), Listening Library) Random Hse. Audio Publishing Group.

Woodson, Jacqueline. Pecan Pie Baby. Blackall, Sophie, illus. 2013. (ENG.). 32p. (J). (gr. k-3). 7.99 (978-0-14-751128-7(3), Puffin Books) Penguin Young Readers Group.

Wright, Bil. Putting Makeup on the Fat Boy. (ENG., 240p. (YA). (gr. 7). 2012. Illus.). pap. 9.99 (978-1-4169-4004-3(9)) 2011. 16.99 (978-1-4169-3996-2(2)) Simon & Schuster Bks. For Young Readers. (Simon & Schuster Bks. For Young Readers).

Yolen, Jane. Centaur Rising. 2014. (ENG.). 272p. (J). (gr. 3-7). 16.99 (978-0-8050-9664-4(7), 9780805096644, Holt, Henry & Co. Bks. For Young Readers) Holt, Henry & Co.

Zaugg, Sandra L. Secret of the Yellow Van: A Book about Dealing with Loss. 2008. (J). pap. 8.99 (978-0-8163-2246-6(5)) Pacific Pr. Publishing Assn.

SISTERS

Auld, Mary. Mi Hermana. Coffey, Colleen & Carrillo, Consuelo, trs. from ENG. 2004. (Conoce la Familia Ser.). (SPA., Illus.). 24p. (gr. k-3). lib. bdg. 22.00 (978-0-8368-3930-2(7), Gareth Stevens Learning Library) Stevens, Gareth Publishing LLLP.

—My Sister. 2004. (Meet the Family Ser.). (Illus.). 24p. (gr. k-3). lib. bdg. 22.00 (978-0-8368-3928-9(5), Gareth Stevens Learning Library) Stevens, Gareth Publishing LLLP.

Gamble, Adam & Jasper, Mark. Good Night Little Sister. Kelly, Cooper, illus. 2016. (Good Night Our World Ser.). (ENG.). 20p. (J). (— 1). bds. 9.95 (978-1-60219-506-6(4)) Good Night Bks.

Hannula, Kate. Forever, Jewel. 2011. 32p. pap. 13.95 (978-1-4497-2381-1(0), WestBow Pr.) Author Solutions, Inc.

Jenner, Caryn. My Sister. 2017. (Family World Ser.). (ENG., Illus.). 24p. (J). (gr. 1-3). pap. 9.99 **(978-1-4451-5240-0(1)**, Franklin Watts) Hachette Children's Group GBR. Dist: Hachette Bk. Group.

Litchfield, Jo, illus. Baby Sister Look & Say. 2008. (Look & Say Board Bks). 12p. (J). bds. 7.99 (978-0-7945-2102-8(9), Usborne) EDC Publishing.

Mqp, creator. Sisters Make the Best Friends. 2005. 96p. 9.95 (978-1-84601-014-9(4)) M Q Pubns.

Olsen, Mary-Kate & Olsen, Ashley. The Ultimate Guide to Mary-Kate & Ashley. 2004. (Illus.). 93p. (978-0-00-718136-0(1)) HarperCollins Pubs. Australia.

Powell, Jillian. My New Sister. 2012. (New Beginnings Ser.). (ENG., Illus.). 24p. (J). (gr. k-3). 21.25 (978-1-4488-6634-2(0), PowerKids Pr.) Rosen Publishing Group, Inc., The.

Raatma, Lucia. Sisters Are Part of a Family. 2017. (Our Families Ser.). (ENG.). 24p. (gr. k-1). lib. bdg. 21.99 **(978-1-5157-7460-0(0)**, Pebble Bks.) Capstone Press of Coughlan Cos.

Reef, Catherine. The Brontë Sisters: The Brief Lives of Charlotte, Emily, & Anne. 2012. (ENG., Illus.). 240p. (J). (gr. 5-7). 18.99 (978-0-547-57966-5(7)) Houghton Mifflin Harcourt Publishing Co.

Schaefer, Lola M. Sisters. Saunders-Smith, Gail, ed. rev. ed. 2008. (Families Ser.). (ENG., Illus.). 24p. (gr. k-1). 21.99 (978-1-4296-1228-9(2)); per. 6.29 (978-1-4296-1757-4(8)) Capstone Press of Coughlan Cos. (Pebble Bks.).

Townes-Richards, Carolyn. Nothing Like Christine: Living Through Literature with Aunt Curly's Collection. 2009. 90p. pap. 13.50 (978-1-4251-1129-8(7)) Trafford Publishing.

Whelahan, Marlene Verno. My Best Friend's Sister... A True Story. 2010. 20p. 12.99 (978-1-4389-8729-3(3)) AuthorHouse.

SISTERS—FICTION

Abbott, E. F. Nettie & Nellie Crook: Orphan Train Sisters. 2016. (Based on a True Story Ser.). (ENG., Illus.). 176p. (J). 15.99 (978-1-250-06835-4(5), 9781250068354) Feiwel & Friends.

ABDO Publishing Company Staff. Meri's Mirror. 2014. (Meri's Mirror Ser.: 4). 80p. (J). (gr. 2-5). lib. bdg. 108.28 (978-1-62402-007-0(0), Calico Chapter Bks) Magic Wagon.

Abel, Cheyanne. It's Better by Far, When You Are Who You Are. 2012. 24p. pap. 17.99 (978-1-4685-7492-0(2)) AuthorHouse.

Ackland, Rachel. Princess Penny & Her Dancing Sister! 2017. (ENG.). 22p. (J). (gr. -1-2). pap. 5.99 (978-1-4380-0984-1(4)) Barron's Educational Series, Inc.

Adachi, Mitsuri. Cross Game, Vol. 2. Adachi, Mitsuri, illus. 2011. (ENG., Illus.). 376p. pap. 14.99 (978-1-4215-3766-5(4)) Viz Media.

Adachi, Mitsuru. Cross Game, Vol. 4. Adachi, Mitsuru, illus. 2011. (ENG., Illus.). 376p. pap. 14.99 (978-1-4215-3768-9(0)) Viz Media.

The Adventure's of Prissy & Missy "Sleepwalk Affair" 2nd ed. 2009. (Illus.). (J). 15.95 (978-0-615-28905-2(3)) House of the Guilded Scribe.

Afterglow. 2014. (ENG., Illus.). 336p. (YA). (gr. 9). pap. 11.99 (978-1-4424-5038-7(X), Simon & Schuster Bks. For Young Readers) Simon & Schuster Bks. For Young Readers.

Alcott, Louisa May. Little Women. Corvino, Lucy, illus. 2005. (Classic Starts(tm) Ser.). (ENG.). 160p. (J). (gr. 2-4). 6.95 (978-1-4027-1236-4(7)) Sterling Publishing Co., Inc.

—Little Women. Dunn, Robert, illus. 2013. 46p. (J). (978-1-4351-4813-0(4)) Barnes & Noble, Inc.

—Little Women. 2007. 264p. (YA). 11.95 (978-1-933486-01-7(5)) Core Knowledge Foundation.

—Little Women. 2015. (ENG.). 408p. (J). (gr. 2-4). 14.99 (978-1-4052-7179-0(5)) Egmont Bks., Ltd. GBR. Dist: Independent Pubs. Group.

—Little Women. unabr. ed. 2004. (Chrysalis Childrens Classics Ser.). (Illus.). 190p. (YA). pap. (978-1-84365-049-2(5), Pavilion Children's Books) Pavilion Bks.

—Little Women. 2013. (ENG., Illus.). 426p. (J). (gr. 4-7). pap. 10.99 (978-0-09-957296-1(6)) Random Hse. GBR. Dist: Independent Pubs. Group.

—Little Women. 2013. (Works of Louisa May Alcott). 451p. reprint ed. lthr. 79.00 (978-0-7812-1627-2(3)) Reprint Services Corp.

—Little Women. 2008. (Puffin Classics Ser.). (gr. k-3). lib. bdg. 19.65 (978-0-613-86261-5(9), Turtleback) Turtleback Bks.

—Little Women: Bring the Classics to Life. 2008. (Bring the Classics to Life Ser.). (Illus.). 72p. (gr. 1-12). pap., act. bk. ed. 10.95 (978-1-55576-047-2(3), EDCTR-103B) EDCON Publishing Group.

—Little Women: With a Discussion of Family. Lauter, Richard, illus. 2003. (Values in Action Illustrated Classics Ser.). 191p. (J). (978-1-59203-032-3(7)) Learning Challenge, Inc.

—A Modern Cinderella. l.t. ed. 2005. 224p. pap. (978-1-84637-050-2(7)) Echo Library.

—Modern Cinderella or the Little Old Shoe. 2006. pap. 44.99 (978-1-4219-8892-4(5)) IndyPublish.com.

—Mujercitas.Tr. of Little Women. (SPA., Illus.). 192p. (YA). 11.95 (978-84-7281-101-0(8), AF1101) Auriga, Ediciones S.A. ESP. Dist: Continental Bk. Co., Inc.

—Mujercitas. 2004.Tr. of Little Women. (SPA.). lib. bdg. (978-1-4135-2067-5(7)) El Cid Editor Incorporated.

—Mujercitas. (Coleccion Estrella).Tr. of Little Women. (SPA., Illus.). 64p. (J). 14.95 (978-950-11-0010-5(3), SGM010) Sigmar ARG. Dist: Continental Bk. Co., Inc.

Alcott, Louisa May & Lacey, Mike. Little Women, 1 vol. 2012. (Calico Illustrated Classics Ser.: No. 4). (ENG., Illus.). 112p. (J). (gr. 3-6). 27.07 (978-1-61641-617-1(3)) Magic Wagon.

Alcott, Louisa May & Naxos of America Staff. Little Women. Mims, Ashley, illus. 3rd ed. 2008. (Hear It Read It Classics Ser.: 0). (ENG.). 128p. (J). (gr. 2-4). 9.99 (978-1-4022-1169-0(4), Sourcebooks Jabberwocky) Sourcebooks, Inc.

Alcott, Louisa May, et al. Little Women. 2003. (Norton Critical Editions Ser.: 0). (ENG., Illus.). 665p. (C). pap. 13.00 (978-0-393-97614-4(9), 97614) Norton, W. W. & Co., Inc.

Alegria, Malin. Border Town #2: Quince Clash. 2012. (Border Town Ser.). (ENG.). 192p. (J). (gr. 7). pap. 5.99 (978-0-545-40241-5(7), Scholastic Paperbacks) Scholastic, Inc.

Alender, Katie. As Dead as It Gets. 2013. (Bad Girls Don't Die Ser.). (ENG.). 448p. (J). (gr. 7-17). pap. 9.99 (978-1-4231-3778-8(7)) Hyperion Pr.

—Bad Girls Don't Die. 2010. (ENG.). 352p. (J). (gr. 7-17). pap. 8.99 (978-1-4231-0877-1(9)) Hyperion Pr.

—The Dead Girls of Hysteria Hall. 2015. (ENG.). 336p. (J). (gr. 7). 18.99 (978-0-545-63999-6(9)) Scholastic, Inc.

—From Bad to Cursed. 2012. (ENG.). 448p. (YA). (gr. 7-17). pap. 9.99 (978-1-4231-3777-1(9)) Hyperion Pr.

Alexander, Goldie. Body & Soul. 2003. 236p. pap. (978-0-9578735-9-9(X)) IAD Pr.

Alexander, Heather. The Case of the Tattooed Cat. 2003. (New Adventures of Mary-Kate & Ashley Ser.). (Illus.). 83p. (J). (gr. 1-5). 12.65 (978-0-7569-5351-5(0)) Perfection Learning Corp.

Allen, Elise & Stanford, Halle. Autumn's Secret Gift. Pooler, Paige, illus. 2014. (Enchanted Sisters Ser.). (ENG.). 128p. (J). (gr. 2-4). pap. 5.99 (978-1-61963-254-7(3), 9781619632547, Bloomsbury USA Childrens) Bloomsbury Publishing USA.

—Spring's Sparkle Sleepover. Pooler, Paige, illus. 2015. (Enchanted Sisters Ser.). (ENG.). 128p. (J). (gr. 2-4). 15.99 (978-1-61963-296-7(9), 9781619632967); pap. 5.99 (978-1-61963-269-1(1), 9781619632691) Bloomsbury Publishing USA. (Bloomsbury USA Childrens).

—Summer's Friendship Games. Pooler, Paige, illus. 2015. (Enchanted Sisters Ser.). (ENG.). 128p. (J). (gr. 2-4). 15.99 (978-1-61963-271-4(3), 9781619632714, Bloomsbury USA Childrens) Bloomsbury Publishing USA.

—Winter's Flurry Adventure. Pooler, Paige, illus. 2014. (Enchanted Sisters Ser.). (ENG.). 128p. (YA). (gr. 2-4). pap. 5.99 (978-1-61963-267-7(5), 9781619632677, Bloomsbury USA Childrens) Bloomsbury Publishing USA.

—Winter's Flurry Adventure. Pooler, Paige, illus. 2014. (Enchanted Sisters Ser.: 2). (YA). lib. bdg. 16.00 (978-0-606-36217-7(7)) Turtleback Bks.

Alpine, Rachele. A Void the Size of the World. 2017. (ENG., Illus.). 368p. (YA). (gr. 9). 17.99 **(978-1-4814-8571-5(7)**, Simon Pulse) Simon Pulse.

Alvarez, Julia. How the Garcia Girls Lost Their Accent. 2011. 13.46 (978-0-7848-3532-6(2), Everbind) Marco Bk. Co.

Amato, Carol J. The Lost Treasure of the Golden Sun. 2005. 172p. (J). (978-0-9713756-3-5(1)) Stargazer Publishing Co.

—The Secret of Blackhurst Manor. 2017. (ENG.). 232p. (J). pap. 9.95 (978-1-933277-02-8(5)) Stargazer Publishing Co.

Amirkhan, Michele. Princess Elian's Quest. 2008. 112p. 20.95 (978-0-595-50870-9(7)); pap. 10.95 (978-0-595-51400-7(6)) iUniverse, Inc.

Anderson, E. V. The Many Lives of Lilith Lane, 0 vols. unabr. ed. 2012. (ENG.). 162p. (YA). (gr. 7-9). pap. 9.99 (978-1-61109-792-4(4), 9781611097924, Amazon Children's Publishing) Amazon Publishing.

Anderson, Lynda & Bennett, Melanie. The Micro Meanies. 2008. 180p. pap. (978-0-9783204-7-8(6)) Aaspirations.

Anderson, Paris. The Sisters Kennington. 2004. 140p. (J). per. 16.00 (978-1-58982-195-8(5), Millennial Mind Publishing) American Bk. Publishing Group.

Anderson, Rachael. Los Mejores Amigos. McNicholas, Shelagh, illus. 2003. (SPA.). 120p. (J). (gr. 3-5). 9.95 (978-84-204-4377-5(8)) Ediciones Alfaguara ESP. Dist: Santillana USA Publishing Co., Inc.

Ando, Natsumi. Arisa 1. 2012. (Arisa Ser.). (ENG., Illus.). 208p. pap. 10.99 (978-1-61262-335-1(2)) Kodansha America, Inc.

Andracki, Zenon. Dear Ashley: A Middle Grade Novel. 2006. (ENG.). 84p. per. 19.95 (978-1-4241-6168-3(1)) America Star Bks.

Andrews, Jane. Each & All: The Seven Little Sisters Prove Their Sisterhood (Yesterday's Classics) 2009. 120p. pap. 8.95 (978-1-59915-308-7(4)) Yesterday's Classics.

—Seven Little Sisters Who Live on the Rou. 2006. (Illus.). pap. (978-1-4065-0858-1(6)) Dodo Pr.

—Young Reader's Series: The seven little sisters who live on the round ball that floats in the Air. 2008. 152p. pap. 14.95 (978-1-60444-020-1(1)) IndoEuropeanPublishing.com.

Andrews, Jane & Hopkins, Louisa Parsons. The Seven Little Sisters Who Live on the Round Ball that Floats in the Air. 2004. reprint ed. pap. 21.95 (978-1-4179-1646-7(X)) Kessinger Publishing, LLC.

Andrews-McKinney, Joyce. Jentle & Jewel Fix Things Andrews-McKinney, Joyce, illus. l.t. ed. 2006. (Illus.). 17p. (J). pap. 8.00 (978-0-9728975-4-9(2)) JA-M Pubs., LLC.

Anna, Jennifer. The Best Thing: An Almost True Story of Ladybugs & Sisters. 2007. (Illus.). 64p. (Orig.). (J). pap. 14.99 (978-1-59092-154-8(2)) Blue Forge Pr.

App, Linda Hoogeveen. Emma Pearl, Flower Girl. 2012. 34p. pap. 16.95 (978-1-4497-6619-1(6), WestBow Pr.) Author Solutions, Inc.

Appelt, Kathi & Alison Mcghee. Maybe a Fox. 2017. lib. bdg. 18.40 **(978-0-606-39744-5(2))** Turtleback Bks.

Appelt, Kathi & Mcghee, Alison. Maybe a Fox. 2016. (ENG., Illus.). 272p. (J). (gr. 5-9). 17.99 (978-1-4424-8242-5(7), Atheneum/Caitlyn Dlouhy Books) Simon & Schuster Children's Publishing.

Applegate, Katherine & Grant, Michael. The Islanders Vol. 2: Nina Won't Tell & Ben's in Love. 2015. (Islanders Ser.: 2). (ENG.). 464p. (YA). (gr. 8). pap. 9.99 (978-0-06-234078-8(6), HarperTeen) HarperCollins Pubs.

Archer, Nick & McDonald, Megan. Rule of Three. 2010. (Sisters Club Ser.: 2). (ENG., Illus.). 240p. (J). (gr. 3-7). pap. 5.99 (978-0-7636-4830-5(2)) Candlewick Pr.

—Rule of Three. Consolazio, Pamela A., illus. 2009. (Sisters Club Ser.: 2). (ENG.). 240p. (J). (gr. 3-7). 15.99 (978-0-7636-4153-5(7)) Candlewick Pr.

Arenella, Betsy Bottino. Isabelle's Dream: A Story & Activity Book for a Child's Grief Journey. Henderson, Dana, illus. 2007. 64p. (gr. -1-3). per. 7.95 (978-0-9675532-9-0(6)) Quality of Life Publishing Co.

Aristophane. Zabime Sisters. Madden, Matt, tr. from FRE. Aristophane, illus. 2010. (ENG., Illus.). 96p. (YA). (gr. 7-18). pap. 16.99 (978-1-59643-638-1(7), First Second Bks.) Roaring Brook Pr.

Armstrong, Ashley Sage-Taylor. The Adventures of Starlight & Sunny: Book Four in the Adventures of Starlight & Sunny Series, ?Princesses Don't Need a Job !? How to Be an Indepen. 2013. 52p. pap. (978-1-927863-02-2(3)) Armstrong, Ashley.

—The Adventures of Starlight & Sunny: Building a Dream , How to Focus & Make Your Dreams Come to Life, with Positive Conscious Morals. Picture Boo. 2013. 52p. pap. (978-1-927863-04-6(X)) Armstrong, Ashley.

—The Adventures of Starlight & Sunny: I Am Me ! Who Are You?, How to Find Good Quality Friends & Stand up for One Another, with Positive Morals, Pi. 2013. 52p. pap. (978-1-927863-00-8(7)) Armstrong, Ashley.

Armstrong, Kelley. Empire of Night. 2015. (Age of Legends Trilogy Ser.: 2). 432p. (YA). (gr. 8). 17.99 (978-0-06-207127-9(0)) HarperCollins Pubs.

—Sea of Shadows. (gr. 8). 2015. (Age of Legends Trilogy Ser.: 1). 432p. (YA). pap. 9.99 (978-0-06-207125-5(4)) 2014. (Age of Legends Trilogy: Bk. 1). 416p. (J). 17.99 (978-0-06-207124-8(6)) HarperCollins Pubs.

—Sea of Shadows. 2015. (Age of Legends Ser.: 1). (YA). lib. bdg. 20.85 (978-0-606-36511-6(7)) Turtleback Bks.

Asch, Sheila. Katy's Time. 2007. 184p. pap. 16.95 (978-1-84753-333-3(7)) Lulu Pr., Inc.

Ashby, Gaylene. STORY TIME A Collection of Three Children's Stories. 2008. 28p. 14.95 (978-1-4357-1929-3(8)) Lulu Pr., Inc.

Atwood, Megan. Twin Dangers. 2013. (Dario Quincy Academy of Dance Ser.: 4). (ENG.). 112p. (gr. 6-12). (J). lib. bdg. 27.93 (978-1-4677-0933-0(6)); (YA). pap. 7.95 (978-1-4677-1486-0(0)) Lerner Publishing Group. (Darby Creek).

Austen, Jane. Sense & Sensibility. 2011. (ENG.). 464p. (YA). (gr. 8). pap. 8.99 (978-0-06-201563-1(X), HarperTeen) HarperCollins Pubs.

—Sense & Sensibility. Kronheimer, Ann, illus. 2013. (Jane Austen Ser.). (ENG.). 64p. pap. 6.95 (978-1-906230-11-1(0)) Real Reads Ltd. GBR. Dist: Casemate Pubs. & Bk. Distributors, LLC.

Austen, Jane & Fisher, Eric Scott. Pride & Prejudice, 1 vol. 2012. (Calico Illustrated Classics Ser.: No. 4). (ENG., Illus.). 112p. (J). (gr. 3-6). 27.07 (978-1-61641-619-5(X)) Magic Wagon.

Banks, Lynne Reid. Angela & Diabola. 163p. (J). (gr. 4-6). pap. 4.50 (978-0-8072-1515-9(5), Listening Library) Random Hse. Audio Publishing Group.

Baratz-Logsted, Lauren. Annie's Adventures. Weber, Lisa K., illus. 2008. (Sisters Eight Ser.: 1). (ENG.). 144p. (J). (gr. 1-4). pap. 5.99 (978-0-547-05338-7(X)) Houghton Mifflin Harcourt Publishing Co.

—Durinda's Dangers. Weber, Lisa K., illus. 2008. (Sisters Eight Ser.: 2). (ENG.). 128p. (J). (gr. 1-4). pap. 5.99 (978-0-547-05339-4(8)) Houghton Mifflin Harcourt Publishing Co.

—Georgia's Greatness. 2009. (Sisters Eight Ser.: 3). (ENG., Illus.). 128p. (J). (gr. 1-4). pap. 5.99 (978-0-547-05340-0(1));Bk. 3. 15.00 (978-0-547-16699-5(0)) Houghton Mifflin Harcourt Publishing Co.

—Jackie's Jokes. 2009. (Sisters Eight Ser.: 4). (ENG., Illus.). 128p. (J). (gr. 1-4). pap. 5.99 (978-0-547-05328-8(2)) Houghton Mifflin Harcourt Publishing Co.

—Petal's Problems. 2010. (Sisters Eight Ser.: 6). (ENG., Illus.). 144p. (J). (gr. 1-4). pap. 5.99 (978-0-547-33403-5(6)) Houghton Mifflin Harcourt Publishing Co.

—Rebecca's Rashness, Bk. 7. 2011. (Sisters Eight Ser.: 7). (ENG., Illus.). 144p. (J). (gr. 1-4). pap. 5.99 (978-0-547-55434-1(6)) Houghton Mifflin Harcourt Publishing Co.

—Zinnia's Zaniness. 2011. (Sisters Eight Ser.: 8). (ENG., Illus.). 128p. (J). (gr. 1-4). pap. 5.99 (978-0-547-55439-6(7)) Houghton Mifflin Harcourt Publishing Co.

Baratz-Logsted, Lauren, et al. The Final Battle... for Now Bk. 9. 2012. (Sisters Eight Ser.: 9). (ENG., Illus.). 160p. (J). (gr. 1-4). pap. 6.99 (978-0-547-55441-9(9)) Houghton Mifflin Harcourt Publishing Co.

—Marcia's Madness. Weber, Lisa K., illus. 2010. (Sisters Eight Ser.: 5). (ENG.). 128p. (J). (gr. 1-4). pap. 5.99 (978-0-547-32864-5(8)) Houghton Mifflin Harcourt Publishing Co.

Barden, Stephanie. Cinderella Smith. Goode, Diane, illus. 2011. (Cinderella Smith Ser.: 1). (ENG.). 160p. (J). (gr. 3-7). 16.99 (978-0-06-196423-7(9)) HarperCollins Pubs.

Barker, Kathryn. In the Skin of a Monster. 2016. (ENG.). 304p. (YA). (gr. 10). pap. 12.99 (978-1-76011-171-7(6)) Allen & Unwin AUS. Dist: Independent Pubs. Group.

Barkley, Callie. Amy Meets Her Stepsister. Riti, Marsha, illus. 2013. (Critter Club Ser.: 5). (ENG.). 128p. (J). (gr. k-2). 15.99 (978-1-4424-8216-6(8)); pap. 5.99 (978-1-4424-8215-9(X)) Little Simon. (Little Simon).

—Amy Meets Her Stepsister. 2013. (Critter Club Ser.: 5). lib. bdg. 16.00 (978-0-606-32320-8(1), Turtleback) Turtleback Bks.

—Marion Takes Charge. Riti, Marsha, illus. 2015. (Critter Club Ser.: 12). (ENG.). 128p. (J). (gr. k-4). pap. 5.99 (978-1-4814-2408-0(4), Little Simon) Little Simon.

Barnes, Jennifer Lynn. The Fixer. (ENG.). (YA). 2016. 400p. pap. 9.99 (978-1-61963-598-2(4), 9781619635982) 2015. 384p. (gr. 7). 17.99 (978-1-61963-594-4(1), 9781619635944) Bloomsbury Publishing USA. (Bloomsbury USA Childrens).

Barnholdt, Lauren. Fake Me a Match. 2012. (Mix Ser.). (ENG.). 304p. (J). (gr. 4-8). pap. 6.99 (978-1-4424-2259-9(9), Aladdin) Simon & Schuster Children's Publishing.

Barraclough, Lindsey. Long Lankin. (ENG.). 464p. (YA). (gr. 7). 2014. pap. 9.99 (978-0-7636-6937-9(7)) 2012. (Illus.). 16.99 (978-0-7636-5808-3(1)) Candlewick Pr.

Barrows, Annie. Ivy + Bean Paper Doll Play Set. Blackall, Sophie, illus. 2011. (Ivy & Bean Ser.: IVYB). (ENG.). 11p. (J). (gr. k-5). pap. 14.99 (978-1-4521-0279-5(1)) Chronicle Bks. LLC.

—Ivy + Bean Take Care of the Babysitter. Blackall, Sophie, illus. (Ivy & Bean Ser.: IVYB). (ENG.). 2008. 128p. (J). (gr. 1-5). pap. 5.99 (978-0-8118-6584-5(3)) 2007. pap., tchr. ed. (978-0-8118-8667-3(0)) Chronicle Bks. LLC.

—Magic in the Mix. (ENG.). 288p. (YA). (gr. 3-6). 2015. pap. 7.99 (978-1-61963-798-6(7), 9781619637986) 2014. 16.99 (978-1-61963-482-4(1), 9781619634824) Bloomsbury Publishing USA. (Bloomsbury USA Childrens).

Barrows, Annie & Blackall, Sophie. Ivy + Bean Take Care of the Babysitter, 1 vol. 2011. (Ivy & Bean Ser.). (ENG., Illus.). 128p. (J). (gr. 1-4). 24.21 (978-1-59961-931-6(8)) Spotlight.

Bass, Karen. Summer of Fire, 1 vol. 2009. (ENG.). 295p. (YA). (gr. 9-12). pap. 12.95 (978-1-55050-415-6(0)) Coteau Bks. CAN. Dist: Orca Bk. Pubs. USA.

Bassett-Giehtbrock, Dianne. Sissy & Me. 2011. 16p. pap. 8.99 (978-1-4567-6943-7(X)) AuthorHouse.

Batanda, Jackee Budesta. The Blue Marble. 2005. (Illus.). 44p. pap. (978-9988-550-89-9(8)) Sub-Saharan Pubs. & Traders GHA. Dist: Michigan State Univ. Pr.

Bateman, Rachel. Someone Else's Summer. 2017. (ENG.). 320p. (YA). (gr. 8-17). 17.99 (978-0-7624-6219-3(1), Running Pr.) Running Pr. Bk. Pubs.

Bath, K. P. Flip Side. 2009. (YA). 16.99 (978-0-316-03836-2(9)) Little Brown & Co.

Bauer, Marion Dane. The Red Ghost. Ferguson, Peter, illus. 2009. (Stepping Stone Book Ser.). (ENG.). 96p. (J). (gr. 1-4). 4.99 (978-0-375-84082-1(6), Random Hse. Bks. for Young Readers) Random Hse. Children's Bks.

Bauman, Beth Ann. Rosie & Skate. 2011. (ENG.). 224p. (YA). (gr. 9). pap. 8.99 (978-0-385-73736-4(X), Ember) Random Hse. Children's Bks.

Bayerl, Katie. A Psalm for Lost Girls. 2017. (ENG.). 368p. (YA). (gr. 7). 17.99 (978-0-399-54525-2(5), G.P. Putnam's Sons Books for Young Readers) Penguin Young Readers Group.

Beamish, Diane. Amy's Silent World. 2006. 24p. 10.25 (978-1-4116-5759-5(4)) Lulu Pr., Inc.

Bell, G. F. Angel Wings & S'Mores. 2008. 152p. 29.99 (978-1-4257-7491-2(1)); pap. 19.99 (978-1-4257-7489-9(X)) Xlibris Corp.

Belton-Terrell, Alice F. Kailah & Lyndsey: Sharing Spaces. 2008. 24p. pap. 11.49 (978-1-4389-3726-7(1)) AuthorHouse.

Bemelmans, Ludwig. The Golden Basket. 2016. (ENG., Illus.). 96p. (J). (gr. 1-5). pap. 9.99 (978-0-486-80717-1(7)) Dover Pubns., Inc.

Bendis, Brian Michael. Takio. Oeming, Michael Avon, illus. 2011. (ENG.). 96p. (J). (gr. -1-17). 9.95 (978-0-7851-5326-9(8)) Marvel Worldwide, Inc.

Benevenia, Rose. Dolly & Babe. Benevenia, Rose, illus. l.t. ed. 2004. (Illus.). 9p. (J). (gr. k-2). pap. 9.00 (978-0-9729044-0-7(9)) Cabbage Patch Pr.

Bennett, James W. & Bennett, James. Faith Wish. 2003. (ENG.). 160p. (J). (gr. 7-18). tchr. ed. 16.95 (978-0-8234-1778-0(6)) Holiday Hse., Inc.

Bennett, Sophia. The Look. 2013. (J). (ENG.). 336p. (gr. 7). 17.99 (978-0-545-46438-3(2)); (978-0-545-46439-0(0)) Scholastic, Inc. (Chicken Hse., The).

Bennett, Veronica. Cassandra's Sister: Growing up Jane Austen. 2007. (ENG., Illus.). 240p. (YA). (gr. 7-12). 15.99 (978-0-7636-3464-3(6)) Candlewick Pr.

Bercun, Brenda. I'm Going to Be a Big Sister! Gross, Sue, illus. 2007. (ENG.). 33p. (J). (gr. -1-k). 15.95 (978-0-9767198-6-1(X)) Nurturing Your Children Pr.

Berg, Deva Jean. A Tail of Two Sisters. Berg, Deva Jean, illus. 2013. (Illus.). 26p. pap. 9.95 (978-1-939790-07-1(7)) Lorian Assn., The.

Bergmeier-Johnson. Ya Ya's Boom Booms. 2005. (ENG.). 32p. per. 18.00 (978-1-4184-8826-0(7)) AuthorHouse.

Berten, Jinny Powers & Holt, Norah. Littsie of Cincinnati. 2003. (Illus.). 125p. (J). per. 9.95 (978-0-9724421-0-7(3)) Fountain Square Publishing.

Beskow, Elsa. Aunt Brown's Birthday, 1 vol. 2004. (ENG., Illus.). 32p. (J). 17.95 (978-0-86315-388-4(7)) Floris Bks. GBR. Dist: SteinerBooks, Inc.

Best, Cari. Ava & the Real Lucille, 1 vol. Valentine, Madeline, illus. 2012. (ENG.). 32p. (J). (gr. -1-3). 16.99 (978-0-374-39903-0(4), 9780374399030, Farrar, Straus & Giroux (BYR)) Farrar, Straus & Giroux.

Beynon, Veronica. My Sister Has Autism & That's Okay. 2013. 24p. pap. (978-1-4602-2066-5(8)) FriesenPress.

Bial, Raymond. Shadow Island: A Tale of Lake Superior. 2006. 172p. (J). (gr. 3-7). 18.95 (978-1-883953-37-9(5)); per. 12.95 (978-1-883953-36-2(7)) Great Lakes Literary, LLC. (Blue Horse Books).

Big Little Sister. 2003. per. (978-0-9740182-1-8(X)) HuntForMo Creations.

Billingsley, Franny. Chime. 2011. (Playaway Young Adult Ser.). (YA). 59.99 (978-1-61707-143-0(9)) Findaway World, LLC.

—Chime. 2012. (ENG.). 384p. (YA). (gr. 7-18). 8.99 (978-0-14-242092-8(1), Speak) Penguin Young Readers Group.

Birdsall, Jeanne. The Penderwicks: A Summer Tale of Four Sisters, Two Rabbits, & a Very Interesting Boy. (Penderwicks Ser.). (ENG.). (J). (gr. 3-7). 2007. 288p. 7.99 (978-0-440-42047-7(4), Yearling) 2005. 272p. 16.99 (978-0-375-83143-0(6), Knopf Bks. for Young Readers) Random Hse. Children's Bks.

—The Penderwicks: A Summer Tale of Four Sisters, Two Rabbits & a Very Interesting Boy. 2007. (Penderwicks (Hardback) Ser.). 262p. (gr. 3-7). 18.00 (978-0-7569-7798-6(3)) Perfection Learning Corp.

—The Penderwicks: A Summer Tale of Four Sisters, Two Rabbits, & a Very Interesting Boy. 2007. (Penderwicks Ser.: 1). (Illus.). 262p. (gr. 4-7). lib. bdg. 18.40 (978-1-4177-7275-9(1)) Turtleback Bks.

—The Penderwicks: A Summer Tale of Four Sisters, Two Rabbits & a Very Interesting Boy. 2009. 8.80 (978-0-7848-2826-7(1), Everbind) Marco Bk. Co.

—The Penderwicks: A Summer Tale of Four Sisters, Two Rabbits & a Very Interesting Boy. l.t. ed. 2006. (Penderwick Ser.). 304p. (J). (gr. 3-7). 23.95 (978-0-7862-8897-7(3)) Thorndike Pr.

—The Penderwicks at Point Mouette. 2011. (Playaway Children Ser.). (J). (gr. k). 44.99 (978-1-61707-434-9(9)) Findaway World, LLC.

—The Penderwicks at Point Mouette. (Penderwicks Ser.). (ENG.). (J). (gr. 3-7). 2012. 320p. 7.99 (978-0-375-85135-3(6), Yearling) 2011. 304p. 16.99 (978-0-375-85851-2(2), Knopf Bks. for Young Readers) Random Hse. Children's Bks.

—The Penderwicks on Gardam Street. 2011. (Playaway Children Ser.). (J). (gr. 3-6). 44.99 (978-1-61707-435-6(7)) Findaway World, LLC.

—The Penderwicks on Gardam Street. (Penderwicks Ser.). (ENG.). (J). (gr. 3-7). 2010. 336p. 7.99 (978-0-440-42203-7(5), Yearling) 2008. 320p. 16.99 (978-0-375-84090-6(7), Knopf Bks. for Young Readers) Random Hse. Children's Bks.

—The Penderwicks on Gardam Street. 2010. (Penderwicks Ser.: 2). lib. bdg. 18.40 (978-0-606-14418-6(8), Turtleback) Turtleback Bks.

—The Penderwicks Paperback 4-Book Boxed Set, 4 vols. 2016. (ENG.). 270p. (J). (gr. 3-7). 31.96 (978-1-101-93760-0(2), Yearling) Random Hse. Children's Bks.

Bishop, Jenn. The Distance to Home. (ENG.). 240p. (J). (gr. 3-7). 2017. 6.99 **(978-1-101-93874-4(9)**, Yearling) 2016. 16.99 (978-1-101-93871-3(4), Knopf Bks. for Young Readers) Random Hse. Children's Bks.

Bitner, Amanda Marie. Baby Sister. 2012. 28p. pap. 24.95 (978-1-4626-8684-1(2)) America Star Bks.

Bjorkman, Lauren. My Invented Life. 2009. (ENG.). 240p. (YA). (gr. 9-13). 27.99 (978-0-8050-8950-9(0), Holt, Henry & Co. Bks. For Young Readers) Holt, Henry & Co.

Black, Sonia W. Jumping the Broom. Van Wright, Cornelius & Hu, Ying-Hwa, illus. 2004. 32p. (J). lib. bdg. 15.00 (978-1-4242-0234-8(5)) Fitzgerald Bks.

Black, Yelena. Dance of Shadows. (Dance of Shadows Ser.). (ENG., Illus.). 384p. (YA). (gr. 7). 2014. pap. 9.99 (978-1-61963-185-4(7), 9781619631854) 2013. 17.99 (978-1-59990-940-0(5), 9781599909400) Bloomsbury Publishing USA. (Bloomsbury USA Childrens).

Blackman, S. A. A Smickamookum Drinks Belly. Gubitosi, Lillian, illus. 2003. 32p. (J). (gr. -1-k). 16.95 incl. audio (978-1-929409-02-0(8)) Blade Publishing.

Blake, Kendare. Three Dark Crowns. (YA). (gr. 9). 2018. (Three Dark Crowns Ser.: 1). 432p. pap. 10.99 **(978-0-06-238544-4(5))** 2016. (ENG.). 416p. 17.99 (978-0-06-238543-7(7)) HarperCollins Pubs. (HarperTeen).

—Three Dark Crowns. 2018. lib. bdg. 22.10 **(978-0-606-40404-4(X))** Turtleback Bks.

Blume, Lesley M. M. Cornelia & the Audacious Escapades of the Somerset Sisters. (ENG.). 272p. (J). (gr. 3-7). 2008. 7.99 (978-0-440-42110-8(1), Yearling) 2006. 15.95 (978-0-375-83523-0(7), Knopf Bks. for Young Readers) Random Hse. Children's Bks.

Bobet, Leah. An Inheritance of Ashes. (ENG.). 400p. (YA). (gr. 7). 2016. pap. 9.99 (978-0-544-81322-9(7), HMH Books For Young Readers) 2015. 17.99 (978-0-544-28111-0(X)) Houghton Mifflin Harcourt Publishing Co.

Bohrer, Maddie. Penny's Penny Puzzle. 2010. 24p. pap. 11.49 (978-1-4490-6477-8(9)) AuthorHouse.

Boling, Katharine. January 1905. 2006. (ENG., Illus.). 192p. (J). (gr. 5-7). pap. 6.99 (978-0-15-205121-1(X)) Houghton Mifflin Harcourt Publishing Co.

Bonnett-Rampersaud, Louise. Bubble & Squeak, 1 vol. Banta, Susan, illus. 2006. (ENG.). 24p. (J). (gr. -1-2). 14.99 (978-0-7614-5310-9(5)) Marshall Cavendish Corp.

Boricchio, Frances. A Box of Red Dominos. 2010. 28p. pap. 12.49 (978-1-4520-5946-4(2)) AuthorHouse.

Bosworth, Jennifer. The Killing Jar. 2016. (ENG.). 352p. (YA). 17.99 (978-0-374-34137-4(0), 9780374341374, Farrar, Straus & Giroux (BYR)) Farrar, Straus & Giroux.

Bourgeois, Paulette. Benjamin et Sa Petite Soeur. 2004.Tr. of Franklin's Baby Sister. (FRE., Illus.). (J). (gr. k-3). spiral bd. (978-0-616-14597-5(7)) Canadian National Institute for the Blind/Institut National Canadien pour les Aveugles.

Bowe, Julie. Formula for Friends. 2015. (Victoria Torres, Unfortunately Average Ser.). (ENG.). 160p. (gr. 4-4). pap. 5.95 (978-1-4965-0539-2(5)) Stone Arch Bks.

Boza, Eduardo Robles. Mi Amigo Tiene Hermanita (My Friend Has a Little Sister) (SPA.). (J). 4.95 (978-968-419-844-9(2)) Grijalbo, Editorial MEX. Dist: AIMS International Bks., Inc.

Bozarth, Jan. Kerka's Book. Burden, Andrea, illus. 2010. (Fairy Godmother Academy Ser.: No. 2). (ENG.). 224p. (J). (gr. 3-7). pap. 6.99 (978-0-375-85183-4(6), Yearling) Random Hse. Children's Bks.

—Lilu's Book. 2011. (Fairy Godmother Academy Ser.: No. 4). (ENG., Illus.). 192p. (J). (gr. 3-7). 6.99 (978-0-375-85187-2(9), Yearling) Random Hse. Children's Bks.

Bradford, Arthur. Benny's Brigade. Hanawalt, Lisa, illus. 2012. (ENG.). 48p. 19.95 (978-1-936365-61-6(8)) McSweeney's Publishing.

Brewer, Zac. The Blood Between Us. (YA). (gr. 8). 2017. 304p. pap. 9.99 **(978-0-06-230792-7(4))** 2016. 288p. 17.99 (978-0-06-230791-0(6)) HarperCollins Pubs. (HarperTeen).

Brian, Kate. Endless (a Shadowlands Novel) 2014. (Shadowlands Ser.). (ENG.). 336p. (YA). (gr. 7-12). 17.99 (978-1-4231-6485-2(7)) Hyperion Bks. for Children.

—Hereafter (a Shadowlands Novel) 2014. (Shadowlands Ser.). (ENG.). 336p. (YA). (gr. 9-17). pap. 9.99 (978-1-4231-6526-2(8)) Hyperion Bks. for Children.

—Shadowlands. 2013. (Shadowlands Ser.). (ENG.). 352p. (YA). (gr. 9-17). pap. 9.99 (978-1-4231-6525-5(X)) Hyperion Pr.

Brogle, Jennifer. The Adventures of Jennifer & Sherry: Summertime. 2013. 60p. pap. 25.36 (978-1-4669-7560-6(1)) Trafford Publishing.

Brown, Mia. Goodnight Joy! Abdullah, Tariq, illus. 2010. 20p. 12.49 (978-1-4520-1492-0(2)) AuthorHouse.

Brownlee, Sophia Grace & McClelland, Rosie. Show Time with Sophia Grace & Rosie. McNicholas, Shelagh, illus. 2014. (ENG.). 40p. (J). (gr. -1-k). 17.99 (978-0-545-63135-8(1), Orchard Bks.) Scholastic, Inc.

Bruneau M. D., Denise J. & Bruneau, Denise J. My Baby: Illustrations by MikeMotz. com. 2010. 28p. 13.99 (978-1-4490-8475-2(3)) AuthorHouse.

Bryan, Barbara. Starfish, Seashells, Coral & Gems. 2010. 47p. (J). pap. 27.95 (978-1-4327-6265-0(6)); pap. 21.95 (978-1-4327-6009-0(2)) Outskirts Pr., Inc.

Bryant, Ann. She's No Angel. 2005. (Step-Chain Ser.). 190p. (J). pap. 4.95 (978-1-894222-75-4(X)) Lobster Pr. CAN. Dist: Univ. of Toronto Pr.

Bryson, Karen Mueller. The Incredibly Awesome Adventures of Puggie Liddel, the Graphic Novel. Tisdel, L. L, illus. 2013. 108p. pap. (978-1-927384-09-1(5)) Zeta Comics.

Buckley, Michael. The Council of Mirrors. 2013. (Sisters Grimm Ser.: 9). (J). lib. bdg. 18.40 (978-0-606-31650-7(7), Turtleback) Turtleback Bks.

—The Everafter War. Ferguson, Peter, illus. (Sisters Grimm Ser.: Bk. 7). (ENG.). (J). (gr. 3-7). 2010. 336p. pap. 8.95 (978-0-8109-8429-5(6))Bk. 7. 2009. 320p. 16.95 (978-0-8109-8355-7(9)) Abrams, Inc. (Amulet Bks.).

—The Everafter War. 2010. (Sisters Grimm Ser.: 7). (J). lib. bdg. 19.60 (978-0-606-12500-0(0), Turtleback) Turtleback Bks.

—The Fairy-Tale Detectives. Ferguson, Peter, illus. 2005. (ENG.). 288p. (J). (gr. 3-7). 16.95 (978-0-8109-5925-5(9), Abrams Bks. for Young Readers) Abrams, Inc.

—The Fairy-Tale Detectives. (Sisters Grimm Ser.: 1). (J). 2008. 81.45 (978-1-4361-0398-5(3)) 2007. 214.75 (978-1-4193-6197-5(X)) 2007. 1.25 (978-1-4193-6193-7(7)) 2006. 74.75 (978-1-4193-6196-8(1)) 2006. 86.75 (978-1-4193-8749-4(9)) 2006. 71.75 (978-1-4193-6198-2(8)) 2006. 89.75 (978-1-4193-8747-0(2)) Recorded Bks., Inc.

—The Fairy-Tale Detectives: And the Unusual Suspects. Ferguson, Peter, illus. 2012. 580p. (J). (978-1-4351-4487-3(2), Amulet Bks.) Abrams, Inc.

—The Inside Story. Ferguson, Peter, illus. 2011. (Sisters Grimm Ser.: 8). (ENG.). 288p. (J). (gr. 3-7). pap. 7.95 (978-0-8109-9726-4(6), Amulet Bks.) Abrams, Inc.

—The Inside Story, 6 vols. 2010. (Sisters Grimm Ser.: 8). (J). 89.75 (978-1-4498-1969-9(9)); 72.75 (978-1-4498-1967-5(2)); 1.25 (978-1-4498-1973-6(7)); 219.75 (978-1-4498-1966-8(4)); 87.75 (978-1-4498-1971-2(0)) Recorded Bks., Inc.

—The Inside Story. 2011. (Sisters Grimm Ser.: 8). (J). lib. bdg. 18.40 (978-0-606-23818-2(2), Turtleback) Turtleback Bks.

—The Inside Story Bk. 8, Bk. 8. Ferguson, Peter, illus. 2010. (Sisters Grimm Ser.: Bk. 8). (ENG.). 288p. (J). (gr. 3-7). 16.95 (978-0-8109-8430-1(X), Amulet Bks.) Abrams, Inc.

—Magic & Other Misdemeanors. Ferguson, Peter, illus. (Sisters Grimm Ser.). (ENG.). 304p. (gr. 3-7). 2008. (J). pap. 7.95 (978-0-8109-7263-6(8)) 2007. (YA). 16.95 (978-0-8109-9358-7(9)) Abrams, Inc. (Amulet Bks.).

—Once upon a Crime. Ferguson, Peter, illus. 2007. (ENG.). 288p. (J). (gr. 2-8). 16.95 (978-0-8109-1610-4(X), Amulet Bks.) Abrams, Inc.

—The Problem Child. Ferguson, Peter, illus. 2006. (Sisters Grimm Ser.). (ENG.). 320p. (J). (gr. 3-7). 16.95 (978-0-8109-4914-0(8), Amulet Bks.) Abrams, Inc.

—The Problem Child: The Sisters Grimm. 2007. (Sisters Grimm Ser.: 3). (YA). lib. bdg. 18.40 (978-1-4178-0733-8(4), Turtleback) Turtleback Bks.

—The Sisters Grimm: The Fairy-Tale Detectives. Ferguson, Peter, illus. 10th anniv. ed. 2017. (Sisters Grimm Ser.). (ENG.). 288p. (J). (gr. 3-7). pap. 8.95 (978-1-4197-2005-5(8), Amulet Bks.) Abrams, Inc.

—The Sisters Grimm: The Problem Child. Ferguson, Peter, illus. 10th ed. 2017. (Sisters Grimm Ser.). (ENG.). 288p. (J). (gr. 3-7). pap. 8.95 (978-1-4197-2004-8(X), Amulet Bks.) Abrams, Inc.

—The Sisters Grimm: The Unusual Suspects. Ferguson, Peter, illus. 10th ed. 2017. (Sisters Grimm Ser.). (ENG.). 288p. (J). (gr. 3-7). pap. 8.95 (978-1-4197-2008-6(2), Amulet Bks.) Abrams, Inc.

—Tales from the Hood. Ferguson, Peter, illus. 2008. (Sisters Grimm Ser.). (ENG.). 288p. (J). (gr. 3-7). 16.95 (978-0-8109-9478-2(X), Amulet Bks.) Abrams, Inc.

—The Unusual Suspects. 2006. (Sisters Grimm Ser.: Bk. 2). 1.00 (978-1-4237-8623-8(8)) Recorded Bks., Inc.

—The Unusual Suspects. 2017. (Sisters Grimm Ser.: 2). (J). lib. bdg. 19.60 **(978-0-606-39686-8(1))** Turtleback Bks.

—The Unusual Suspects. 2007. (Sisters Grimm Ser.: 2). (J). lib. bdg. 18.40 (978-1-4178-0732-1(6), Turtleback) Turtleback Bks.

—A Very Grimm Guide. Ferguson, Peter, illus. 2012. (Sisters Grimm Ser.). (ENG.). 128p. (J). (gr. 3-7). 16.95 (978-1-4197-0201-3(7), Amulet Bks.) Abrams, Inc.

Buehrlen, M. G. The Untimely Deaths of Alex Wayfare. 2016. (ENG.). 232p. pap. 15.99 (978-1-68230-058-9(7)) Diversion Publishing Corp.

Bulbring, Edyth. Cornelia Button & the Globe of Gamagion. 2009. (ENG.). 208p. (J). (gr. 4-7). pap. 18.00 (978-1-77009-501-4(2)) Jacana Media ZAF. Dist: Independent Pubs. Group.

Bullen, Alexandra. Wish. 2010. (ENG.). 336p. (J). (gr. 9). pap. 9.99 (978-0-545-13906-9(6)) Scholastic, Inc.

Bunce, Elizabeth C. A Curse Dark as Gold. (ENG.). 400p. (J). (gr. 7). 2010. 9.99 (978-0-439-89577-4(4), Scholastic Paperbacks) 2008. 17.99 (978-0-439-89576-7(6), Levine, Arthur A. Bks.) Scholastic, Inc.

Burbank, Vivian. My Grandma's Playhouse. 2010. 29p. (J). pap. 17.95 (978-1-4327-5112-8(3)) Outskirts Pr., Inc.

Burgis, Stephanie. Kat, Incorrigible. 2012. (Kat, Incorrigible Ser.: 1). (ENG., Illus.). 320p. (J). (gr. 5-9). pap. 7.99 (978-1-4169-9448-0(3), Atheneum Bks. for Young Readers) Simon & Schuster Children's Publishing.

—Renegade Magic. 2012. (Kat, Incorrigible Ser.: 2). (ENG., Illus.). 336p. (J). (gr. 5-9). 16.99 (978-1-4169-9449-7(1), Atheneum Bks. for Young Readers) Simon & Schuster Children's Publishing.

Burgis, Stephanie & Ward, Barnaby. Kat, Incorrigible. 2011. (Kat, Incorrigible Ser.: 1). (ENG., Illus.). 304p. (J). (gr. 5-9). 16.99 (978-1-4169-9447-3(5), Atheneum Bks. for Young Readers) Simon & Schuster Children's Publishing.

Burkhart, Alma J. If You Could See Her Smile. Burns, Sandra, illus. 2013. 24p. pap. 8.99 (978-1-938768-32-3(9)) Gypsy Pubns.

Burns, Jane. My Sister's My Teacher! 2017. (ENG.). 182p. (J). pap. 14.95 **(978-1-78612-482-1(3)**, fe6f0a4c-28f1-46f4-8feb-0bca666a9e82) Austin, Stan AUS. Dist: Bookmasters Distribution.

Busath, Isabelle & Thordsen, Isabella. Little Book of Rules. Burris, Priscilla, illus. 2013. (ENG.). 120p. (J). (gr. 3-7). 12.99 (978-1-4424-9980-5(X), Simon Spotlight) Simon Spotlight.

Busby, Cylin. The Stranger Game. 2016. 288p. (YA). (gr. 8). 17.99 (978-0-06-235460-0(4)) HarperCollins Pubs.

Bush, Rosetta Bowman. My Name Is Violet. 2013. 20p. pap. 24.95 (978-1-63000-515-3(0)) America Star Bks.

Butcher, Nancy, et al. It's Snow Problem, 3 vols. 2003. (ENG., Illus.). 112p. (978-0-00-714466-2(0), HarperCollins Children's Bks.) HarperCollins Pubs. Ltd.

—Two for the Road. 2003. (ENG., Illus.). 112p. (978-0-00-714463-1(6), HarperCollins Children's Bks.) HarperCollins Pubs. Ltd.

Butler, Dori Hillestad. Yes, I Know Monkey Man, 1 vol. 2009. (ENG.). 224p. (YA). (gr. 5-9). 16.95 (978-1-56145-479-2(6)) Peachtree Pubs.

By Kaleena Ma. Glasses for Me? Oh No! Dawn Phillips, illus. 2009. 40p. pap. 18.49 (978-1-4389-5418-9(2)) AuthorHouse.

Byars, Betsy. Golly Sisters Go West. Truesdell, Sue, illus. 2003. (I Can Read Level 3 Ser.). (ENG.). 64p. (J). (gr. k-3). pap. 3.99 (978-0-06-444132-2(6)) HarperCollins Pubs.

—Keeper of the Doves. 2004. (ENG., Illus.). 128p. (J). (gr. 3-7). reprint ed. 7.99 (978-0-14-240063-0(7), Puffin Books) Penguin Young Readers Group.

Byars, Betsy & Byars, B. The Golly Sisters Go West. 2003. (I Can Read! Level 3 Ser.). (J). (gr. k-3). lib. bdg. 13.55 (978-0-8335-4709-5(7), Turtleback) Turtleback Bks.

Caletti, Deb. The Six Rules of Maybe. (ENG.). (YA). (gr. 7). 2011. 352p. pap. 9.99 (978-1-4169-7971-5(9)) 2010. 336p. 16.99 (978-1-4169-7969-2(7)) Simon Pulse. (Simon Pulse).

Callaghan, Cindy. Lost in London. 2013. (Mix Ser.). (ENG., Illus.). 240p. (J). (gr. 4-8). pap. 7.99 (978-1-4424-6653-1(7), Aladdin) Simon & Schuster Children's Publishing.

Calonita, Jen. The Grass Is Always Greener. 2014. (Belles Ser.: 3). (ENG.). 320p. (YA). (gr. 7-17). pap. 10.00 (978-0-316-09109-1(X), Poppy) Little, Brown Bks. for Young Readers.

Cameron, Ann. The Secret Life of Amanda K. Woods. 2014. (ENG.). 208p. (J). (gr. 5-9). pap. 6.99 (978-1-250-04419-8(7), 9781250044198) Square Fish.

Candelario, Margo. Looking to the Clouds for Daddy. Craft, Jerry, illus. 2009. (J). (978-0-9820221-7-7(4)) Hunter, Karen Media.

Cannon, Deborah. The Pirate Vortex: Elizabeth Latimer, Pirate Hunter. 2009. 260p. pap. 20.00 (978-1-4269-0532-2(7)) Trafford Publishing.

Cantor, Jillian. The September Sisters. 2009. (ENG.). 368p. (YA). (gr. 8-18). 16.99 (978-0-06-168648-1(4), HarperTeen) HarperCollins Pubs.

Capozzola, Christine. Angel from Heaven. Nguyen, Cindy, illus. 2014. (ENG.). 28p. pap. 9.95 (978-1-63047-189-7(5)) Morgan James Publishing.

Capucilli, Alyssa Satin. Hannah Is a Big Sister. Stott, Dorothy, illus. 2014. (Hannah & Henry Ser.). (ENG.). 32p. (J). (gr. -1-k). 5.99 (978-0-7641-6750-8(2)) Barron's Educational Series, Inc.

—Katy Duck, Big Sister. Cole, Henry, illus. 2007. (ENG.). 14p. (J). (gr. -1-k). bds. 7.99 (978-1-4169-4209-2(2), Little Simon) Little Simon.

Carey, Lorraine. Cinderella's Stepsister & the Big Bad Wolf. Blanco, Migy, illus. 2015. (ENG.). 32p. (J). (gr. -1-2). 15.99 (978-0-7636-8005-3(2), Nosy Crow) Candlewick Pr.

Caring, Angela. Becoming Bryn. 2013. (ENG.). 297p. (YA). (gr. 7). pap. 11.95 (978-1-935089-66-7(8)) Acacia Publishing, Inc.

Carthage, Lynn. Haunted. 2015. (Arnaud Legacy Ser.: 1). (ENG.). 288p. (YA). (gr. 9). pap. 9.95 (978-1-61773-626-1(0)) Kensington Publishing Corp.

Carvalho, Marcela. Three Sisters, Three Weddings, & One Dress. 2011. 38p. pap. 24.94 (978-0-557-52962-9(X)) Lulu Pr., Inc.

Carvell, Marlene. Sweetgrass Basket. 2005. (ENG.). 256p. (J). (gr. 5-6). 16.99 (978-0-525-47547-7(8), Dutton Books for Young Readers) Penguin Young Readers Group.

Casad, Mary Brooke & Brooke Casad, Mary. Bluebonnet at the East Texas Oil Museum, 1 vol. Vincent, Benjamin, illus. 2005. (Bluebonnet Ser.). (ENG.). 32p. (J). (gr. k-3). 16.99 (978-1-58980-358-9(2)) Pelican Publishing Co., Inc.

The Case of the Secret Box. 2007. 56p. pap. 7.75 (978-0-8341-2288-8(X), 083-412-288X) Beacon Hill Pr. of Kansas City.

Castellucci, Cecil. The Year of the Beasts. Powell, Nate, illus. 2012. (ENG.). 192p. (YA). (gr. 7-12). 16.99 (978-1-59643-686-2(7), 9781596436862) Roaring Brook Pr.

—The Year of the Beasts. Powell, Nate, illus. 2014. (ENG.). 208p. (YA). (gr. 7-12). pap. 9.99 (978-1-250-05076-2(6), 9781250050762) Square Fish.

Castle, Amber. Olivia the Otter Sister. Hall, Mary, illus. 2013. (ENG.). 160p. (J). (gr. 2-4). pap. 7.99 (978-0-85707-253-5(6), Simon & Schuster Children's) Simon & Schuster, Ltd. GBR. Dist: Simon & Schuster, Inc.

Castleman, Virginia. Sara Lost & Found. 2016. (ENG., Illus.). 320p. (J). (gr. 3-7). 16.99 (978-1-4814-3871-1(9), Aladdin) Simon & Schuster Children's Publishing.

Castner, K. D. Daughters of Ruin. 2017. (ENG.). 320p. (YA). (gr. 9). pap. 11.99 (978-1-4814-3666-3(X), McElderry, Margaret K. Bks.) McElderry, Margaret K. Bks.

Catmull, Katherine. Summer & Bird. 2014. (ENG.). 352p. (J). (gr. 5). pap. 8.99 (978-0-14-242505-3(2), Puffin Books) Penguin Young Readers Group.

Cecil, Lauren. Lalaloopsy: Cinder Slippers & the Grand Ball. Hill, Prescott, illus. 2013. (Lalaloopsy Ser.). (ENG.). 24p. (J). (gr. -1-3). pap. 3.99 (978-0-545-47769-7(7)) Scholastic, Inc.

—Lalaloopsy: Here Come the Little Sisters! Hill, Prescott, illus. 2013. (Lalaloopsy Ser.). (ENG.). 5p. (J). (gr. -1-k). bds. 9.99 (978-0-545-44266-4(4)) Scholastic, Inc.

Chaconas, Dori. Dancing with Katya, 1 vol. Bergum, Constance R., illus. 2006. (ENG.). 32p. (J). (gr. k-3). 16.95 (978-1-56145-376-4(5)) Peachtree Pubs.

Chan, Queenie. The Dreaming Collection. 2010. (ENG., Illus.). 576p. pap. 19.99 (978-1-4278-1871-3(1)) TOKYOPOP, Inc.

Chandler, Elizabeth. No Time to Die - The Deep End of Fear No. 2. 2010. (Dark Secrets Ser.: 2). (ENG.). 624p. (YA). (gr. 7). pap. 9.99 (978-1-4169-9462-6(9), Simon Pulse) Simon Pulse.

Chankhamma, Shari. The Sisters' Luck. 2010. (ENG., Illus.). 144p. (YA). pap. 12.95 (978-1-59362-190-2(6), 9781593621902) Slave Labor Bks.

Chapman, Brenda. Where Trouble Leads. 2007. (Jennifer Bannon Mystery Ser.: 3). (ENG., Illus.). 136p. (YA). (gr. 5-18). per. 9.95 (978-1-894917-44-5(8), Napoleon & Co.) Dundurn CAN. Dist: Ingram Publisher Services.

Cherry, Alison. For Real. 2016. (ENG.). 304p. (YA). (gr. 7). pap. 9.99 (978-0-385-74296-2(7), Ember) Random Hse. Children's Bks.

Child, Lauren. Slightly Invisible. Child, Lauren, illus. 2016. (Charlie & Lola Ser.). (ENG., Illus.). 40p. (J). (gr. -1-3). 19.65 (978-0-606-39107-8(X)) Turtleback Bks.

Childs, Tera Lynn. Goddess Boot Camp. 2010. (ENG.). 272p. (YA). (gr. 7-18). pap. 7.99 (978-0-14-241665-5(7), Speak) Penguin Young Readers Group.

—Sweet Legacy. 2013. (Sweet Venom Ser.: 3). (ENG.). 384p. (YA). (gr. 8). 17.99 (978-0-06-200185-6(X), Tegen, Katherine Bks) HarperCollins Pubs.

—Sweet Shadows. (Sweet Venom Ser.: 2). (ENG.). (YA). (gr. 8). 2013. 352p. pap. 9.99 (978-0-06-200184-9(1)) 2012. 336p. 17.99 (978-0-06-200183-2(3)) HarperCollins Pubs. (Tegen, Katherine Bks).

—Sweet Venom. (Sweet Venom Ser.: 1). (ENG.). (YA). (gr. 8). 2012. 384p. pap. 9.99 (978-0-06-200182-5(5)) 2011. 352p. 17.99 (978-0-06-200181-8(7)) HarperCollins Pubs. (Tegen, Katherine Bks).

Church, Caroline Jayne. I Am a Big Sister! 2015. (SPA & ENG.). 24p. (J). (gr. -1 — 1). 6.99 (978-0-545-84718-6(4), Scholastic en Espanol) Scholastic, Inc.

—I Am a Big Sister! Church, Caroline Jayne, illus. 2015. (ENG., Illus.). 24p. (J). (gr. -1 — 1). 6.99 (978-0-545-68898-7(1), Cartwheel Bks.) Scholastic, Inc.

Clare, Mimi St. The Fairbluffs of Pennington Island. 2013. 36p. pap. 12.99 (978-1-935986-49-2(X)) Liberty University Press.

Clark-Elliott, Mary. The Day Ms. Qualbaum Came to Visit. 2013. 44p. pap. 20.72 (978-1-4907-0921-5(5)) Trafford Publishing.

Clarke, Cat. The Lost & the Found. 2016. (ENG.). 368p. (YA). (gr. 9). 17.99 (978-1-101-93204-9(X), Crown Books For Young Readers) Random Hse. Children's Bks.

Cleary, Beverly. Beezus & Ramona. Darling, Louis & Rogers, Jacqueline, illus. 2013. (Ramona Ser.: 1). (ENG.). 208p. (J). (gr. 3-7). pap. 6.99 (978-0-380-70918-2(X)) HarperCollins Pubs.

—Beezus & Ramona. Darling, Louis et al, illus. 2013. (Ramona Ser.: 1). (ENG.). 208p. (J). (gr. 3-7). 16.99 (978-0-688-21076-2(7)) HarperCollins Pubs.

—Beezus & Ramona. Dockray, Tracy & Rogers, Jacqueline, illus. movie tie-in ed. 2010. (Ramona Ser.: 1). (ENG.). 208p. (J). (gr. 3-7). pap. 5.99 (978-0-06-191461-4(4), HarperFestival) HarperCollins Pubs.

—Beezus & Ramona. 2011. 9.01 (978-0-7848-3570-8(5), Everbind) Marco Bk. Co.

—Beezus & Ramona. (Ramona Quimby Ser.). 142p. (J). (gr. 3-5). pap. 4.99 (978-0-8072-1441-1(8), Listening Library) Random Hse. Audio Publishing Group.

—Beezus & Ramona. Darling, Louis, illus. (gr. 3-5). pap. (978-0-545-24980-5(5)) Scholastic, Inc.

—Beezus & Ramona. (Ramona Quimby Ser.: 1). (J). 2013. lib. bdg. 17.20 (978-0-88103-289-5(1)) 2010. lib. bdg. 16.00 (978-0-606-15072-9(2)) Turtleback Bks. (Turtleback).

—The Complete Ramona Collection: Beezus & Ramona; Ramona & Her Father; Ramona & Her Mother; Ramona Quimby; Age 8; Ramona Forever; Ramona the Brave; Ramona the Pest; Ramona's World. Dockray, Tracy & Rogers, Jacqueline, illus. 2013. (Ramona Ser.). (J). (gr. 3-7). pap. 44.99 (978-0-06-196090-1(X)) HarperCollins Pubs.

—The Ramona Collection Vol. 1: Beezus & Ramona, Ramona & Her Father, Ramona the Brave, Ramona the Pest, Vol. 1. Dockray, Tracy & Rogers, Jacqueline, illus. 2013. (Ramona Ser.). (ENG.). (J). (gr. 3-7). pap. 22.99 (978-0-06-124647-0(6)) HarperCollins Pubs.

—The Ramona Collection Vol. 2: Ramona & Her Mother; Ramona Quimby, Age 8; Ramona Forever; Ramona's World. Dockray, Tracy & Rogers, Jacqueline, illus. 2013. (Ramona Ser.). (ENG.). (J). (gr. 3-7). pap. 22.99 (978-0-06-124648-7(4)) HarperCollins Pubs.

—Sister of the Bride. 2007. (ENG., Illus.). 272p. (J). (gr. 5-18). pap. 9.99 (978-0-380-72807-7(9)) HarperCollins Pubs.

Clement-Moore, Rosemary. Texas Gothic. 2012. (ENG.). 416p. (YA). (gr. 9). pap. 10.99 (978-0-385-73694-7(0), Ember) Random Hse. Children's Bks.

Cleverly, Sophie. The Lost Twin. 2016. (Scarlet & Ivy Ser.: 1). (ENG.). 304p. (J). (gr. 5-8). 16.99 (978-1-4926-3339-6(9), 9781492633396, Sourcebooks Jabberwocky) Sourcebooks, Inc.

Cochrane, Ian. Shian & the Corryvreckan. 2013. (Illus.). 96p. pap. (978-1-909465-09-1(7)) Cloister Hse. Pr., The.

Cocks, Heather & Morgan, Jessica. Spoiled. 2012. (ENG.). 384p. (YA). (gr. 10-17). pap. 10.00 (978-0-316-09827-4(2), Poppy) Little, Brown Bks. for Young Readers.

Coh, Smiljana. I Have a Sister. 2012. (ENG.). 24p. (J). (978-1-58925-125-0(3)) Tiger Tales.

—The Seven Princesses. 2016. (ENG., Illus.). 40p. (J). (gr. -1-17). 16.95 (978-0-7624-5587-4(X), Running Pr. Kids) Running Pr. Bk. Pubs.

Cohen, Jeff. Eva & Sadie & the Best Classroom Ever! Allen, Elanna, illus. 2015. (ENG.). 32p. (J). (gr. -1-3). 17.99 (978-0-06-224938-8(X)) HarperCollins Pubs.

—Eva & Sadie & the Worst Haircut EVER! Allen, Elanna, illus. 2014. (ENG.). 32p. (J). (gr. -1-3). 17.99 (978-0-06-224906-7(1)) HarperCollins Pubs.

Cohen, Paula Marantz. Beatrice Bunson's Guide to Romeo & Juliet. 2016. (ENG.). 200p. (J). (gr. 4-9). pap. 11.95 (978-1-58988-105-1(2)) Dry, Paul Bks., Inc.

Cole, Joanna. Soy una Hermana Mayor, 1 vol. Kightley, Rosalinda, illus. 2010.Tr. of I am a Big Sister. (SPA.). 32p. (J). (gr. -1-k). 6.99 (978-0-06-190063-1(X)) HarperCollins Pubs.

Cole, Penelope Anne. Magical Mea. Collier, Kevin, illus. 2013. 24p. 19.95 (978-1-61633-394-2(4)); pap. 10.95 (978-1-61633-395-9(2)) Guardian Angel Publishing, Inc.

Collins, Nancy A. After Dark. 3rd ed. 2009. (Vamps Ser.: 3). (ENG.). 192p. (YA). (gr. 9-18). pap. 8.99 (978-0-06-134919-5(4), HarperTeen) HarperCollins Pubs.

—Night Life. 2009. (Vamps Ser.: 2). (ENG.). 256p. (YA). (gr. 9-18). pap. 8.99 (978-0-06-134918-8(6), HarperTeen) HarperCollins Pubs.

Collins, Rudy. Vanessa Owens & the Bond of Sisterhood. 2011. 106p. pap. 19.95 (978-1-4560-7873-7(9)) America Star Bks.

Coman, Carolyn. The Memory Bank. Shepperson, Rob, illus. 2010. (J). 263p. pap. (978-0-545-21067-6(4)); (ENG.). 288p. (gr. 3-7). 16.99 (978-0-545-21066-9(6)) Scholastic, Inc. (Levine, Arthur A. Bks.).

Condie, Ally. Atlantia. (ENG.). 320p. (gr. 7). 2015. (YA). pap. 10.99 (978-0-14-751065-5(1), Speak) 2014. (J). 18.99 (978-0-525-42644-8(2), Dutton Books for Young Readers) Penguin Young Readers Group.

—Atlantia. 2015. lib. bdg. 22.10 (978-0-606-37576-4(7)) Turtleback Bks.

—Being Sixteen. 2010. (YA). (978-1-60641-233-6(7)) Deseret Bk. Co.

Cone, Carl. There's a Season for All. Cone, Carl, illus. 2008. (ENG., Illus.). pap. 14.95 (978-0-9801555-6-3(8)) Argus Enterprises International, Inc.

Cook, Eileen. Fourth Grade Fairy. 2011. (Fourth Grade Fairy Ser.: 1). (ENG.). 176p. (J). (gr. 3-7). pap. 7.99 (978-1-4169-9811-2(X), Aladdin) Simon & Schuster Children's Publishing.

Cook, Kajsa. Discoveries in the Shriver Family Attic: How a Woman & Her Children Dealt with the Battle of Gettysburg. 2009. (Illus.). 122p. (J). (gr. 4-8). pap. 8.95 (978-1-57249-398-8(4), White Mane Kids) White Mane Publishing Co., Inc.

Coolidge, Susan. What Katy Did at School. 2007. (ENG.). 108p. per. (978-1-4068-4853-3(0)) Echo Library.

—What Katy Did at School. 2006. (ENG.). 180p. per. 8.95 (978-1-59462-472-8(0), 508, Book Jungle) Standard Pubns., Inc.

—What Katy Did at School. 2004. reprint ed. pap. 20.95 (978-1-4191-9354-5(6)); pap. 1.99 (978-1-4192-9354-2(0)) Kessinger Publishing, LLC.

Coonan, Candace N. The Darkest Hour: Tales from Fadreama: Book 1. 2012. 328p. (gr. 4-6). pap. 19.11 (978-1-4669-3565-5(0)) Trafford Publishing.

Cooney, Caroline B. Three Black Swans. 2012. (ENG.). 288p. (YA). (gr. 7). pap. 9.99 (978-0-385-73868-2(4), Ember) Random Hse. Children's Bks.

Cordell, Ryan & Cordell, Evie. Two Girls Want a Puppy. Lam, Maple, illus. 2015. (ENG.). 32p. (J). (gr. -1-3). 17.99 (978-0-06-229261-2(7)) HarperCollins Pubs.

Coster, Charles. Flemish Legends. 2005. pap. 15.50 (978-1-59605-351-9(8), Cosimo Classics) Cosimo, Inc.

Couloumbis, Audrey. Getting near to Baby. unabr. ed. 2004. 211p. (J). (gr. 5-9). pap. 36.00 incl. audio (978-0-8072-8876-4(4), LYA 287 SP, Listening Library) Random Hse. Audio Publishing Group.

—Maude March on the Run! Or Trouble Is Her Middle Name. 2008. (Maude March Ser.). (ENG., Illus.). 320p. (J). (gr. 3-7). pap. 7.99 (978-0-375-83248-2(3), Yearling) Random Hse. Children's Bks.

—The Misadventures of Maude March: Or Trouble Rides a Fast Horse. 2007. (Illus.). 295p. (gr. 3-7). 18.00 (978-0-7569-7770-2(3)) Perfection Learning Corp.

Courtauld, Sarah. Buckle & Squash: the Gigantic Giant Goof-Up. 2016. (Buckle & Squash Ser.). (ENG., Illus.). 192p. (J). 14.99 (978-1-250-05279-7(3), 9781250052797) Feiwel & Friends.

Courtauld, Sarah & Burniac, Lauren. The Perilous Princess Plot. 2015. (Buckle & Squash Ser.). (ENG., Illus.). 192p. (J). (gr. 2-5). 14.99 (978-1-250-05277-3(7), 9781250052773) Feiwel & Friends.

Courtney, Nadine Jolie. Romancing the Throne. 2017. 400p. (YA). (gr. 8). 17.99 (978-0-06-240662-0(0), Tegen, Katherine Bks) HarperCollins Pubs.

Crispin, Paula. I'm Getting a Baby Sister? 2004. 23p. pap. 24.95 (978-1-4137-3380-8(8)) PublishAmerica, Inc.

Cross, Mimi. Shining Sea, 0 vols. 2016. (ENG.). 432p. (YA). (gr. 9-12). pap. 9.99 (978-1-5039-3553-2(1), 9781503935532, Skyscape) Amazon Publishing.

Crossan, Sarah. Apple & Rain. 2015. (ENG.). 352p. (YA). (gr. 7). 17.99 (978-1-61963-690-3(5), 9781619636903, Bloomsbury USA Childrens) Bloomsbury Publishing USA.

—One. 2015. (ENG.). 400p. (YA). (gr. 8). 17.99 (978-0-06-211875-2(7), Greenwillow Bks.) HarperCollins Pubs.

Crowder, Melanie. A Nearer Moon. (ENG., Illus.). (J). (gr. 3-7). 2016. 176p. pap. 7.99 (978-1-4814-4149-0(3), Atheneum Bks. for Young Readers) 2015. 160p. 16.99 (978-1-4814-4148-3(5)) Simon & Schuster Children's Publishing.

—A Nearer Moon. 2016. (ENG.). 176p. (J). (gr. 3-7). 18.40 (978-0-606-39238-9(6)) Turtleback Bks.

Cuasay, Alison Taimanglo. Tasi & Matina: The Story of the First Clown Fish. 2010. 28p. pap. 12.99 (978-1-4520-6672-1(8)) AuthorHouse.

Culbertson, Jan E. The Legend of Dunsmoor Manor. 2006. 88p. pap. 13.95 (978-1-58909-348-5(8)) Bookstand Publishing.

—The Legend of the Lost Tiki. 2006. 95p. (YA). pap. 13.95 (978-1-58909-315-7(1)) Bookstand Publishing.

Culwell, Lori. The Dirt. 2011. (ENG.). 208p. (YA). pap. 11.95 (978-1-935961-36-9(5), Booktrope Editions) Booktrope.

Cupala, Holly. Tell Me a Secret. 2010. (ENG.). 304p. (YA). (gr. 9-18). 16.99 (978-0-06-176666-4(6), HarperTeen) HarperCollins Pubs.

Cushing, Mims. The Sleepover Surprise. Phillips, Alan, illus. 2010. 24p. pap. 12.95 (978-1-936343-01-0(0)) Peppertree Pr., The.

Cypess, Leah. Nightspell. 2011. (ENG.). 336p. (YA). (gr. 8-18). 16.99 (978-0-06-195702-4(X), Greenwillow Bks.) HarperCollins Pubs.

Dadey, Debbie. A Tail of Two Sisters. Avakyan, Tatevik, illus. 2015. (Mermaid Tales Ser.: 10). (ENG.). 128p. (J). (gr. 1-4). 17.99 (978-1-4814-0258-3(7), Aladdin) Simon & Schuster Children's Publishing.

—A Tale of Two Sisters. Avakyan, Tatevik, illus. 2015. (Mermaid Tales Ser.: 10). (ENG.). 128p. (J). (gr. 1-4). pap. 5.99 (978-1-4814-0257-6(9), Aladdin) Simon & Schuster Children's Publishing.

Dalton, Michelle. Fifteenth Summer. 2013. (ENG.). 272p. (YA). (gr. 7). 17.99 (978-1-4424-7267-9(7)); (Illus.). pap. 10.99 (978-1-4424-7266-2(9)) Simon Pulse. (Simon Pulse).

Dalton, R. M. The Sisters' Story: The Legend of Queen Brighton & Sister Jasmine. 2012. 146p. 46.72 (978-1-4771-4886-0(8)); pap. 28.03 (978-1-4771-4885-3(X)) Xlibris Corp.

Daly, Catherine R. Too Many Blooms. 2011. (Petal Pushers Ser.: 1). (ENG.). 192p. (J). (gr. 3-7). pap. 5.99 (978-0-545-21450-6(5), Scholastic Paperbacks) Scholastic, Inc.

Daniels, Babygirl. 16 1/2 on the Block. 2009. (ENG.). 208p. (YA). (gr. 9). 9.95 (978-1-60162-183-2(3), Urban Renaissance) Kensington Publishing Corp.

Daniels, W. J. The Empress Academy: The Secret of Glittershine. 2009. 144p. pap. 16.95 (978-1-4327-2335-4(9)) Outskirts Pr., Inc.

Danna, Natasha. Any Two Can Be Twindollicious. Dye, Jerel, illus. 2013. 32p. (J). 17.95 (978-1-60131-154-2(0), Castlebridge Bks.) Big Tent Bks.

Danticat, Edwidge. Untwine: A Novel. 2015. (ENG.). 320p. (J). (gr. 7). 16.99 (978-0-545-42303-8(1), Scholastic Pr.) Scholastic, Inc.

Darlison, Aleesah. Quinn's Riddles. Brailsford, Jill, illus. 2016. (Unicorn Riders Ser.). (ENG.). 112p. (gr. 3-5). lib. bdg. 22.65 (978-1-4795-6544-3(X)) Picture Window Bks.

—Quinn's Truth Cancelled. Brailsford, Jill, illus. 2017. (Unicorn Riders Ser.). (ENG.). 112p. (gr. 3-5). pap. 5.95 (978-1-4795-6556-6(3)) Picture Window Bks.

Darlison, Aleesha. Quinn's Riddles. Brailsford, Jill, illus. 2017. (Unicorn Riders Ser.). (ENG.). 112p. (gr. 3-5). pap. 5.95 (978-1-4795-6552-8(0)) Picture Window Bks.

Dasilva, D. Mom Has Left & Gone to Vegas. Craig, Dan, illus. 2008. 32p. pap. 19.95 (978-1-59858-603-9(3)) Dog Ear Publishing, LLC.

David, Erica. All Hail the Queen. RH Disney Staff & Robinson, Bill, illus. 2015. (Stepping Stone Book(TM) Ser.: 1). (ENG.). 128p. (J). (gr. 1-4). lib. bdg. 12.99 (978-0-7364-8216-5(4), RH/Disney) Random Hse. Children's Bks.

—Anna & Elsa. RH Disney et al, illus. 2017. (Stepping Stone Book(TM) Ser.: 9). (ENG.). 128p. (J). (gr. 1-4). 9.99 (978-0-7364-3480-5(1), RH/Disney) Random Hse. Children's Bks.

—Anna & Elsa No. 7: The Secret Admirer. Random House Disney Staff et al, illus. 2016. (Stepping Stone Book(TM) Ser.: 7). (ENG.). 128p. (J). (gr. 1-4). 9.99 (978-0-7364-3475-1(5), RH/Disney) Random Hse. Children's Bks.

—Anna & Elsa - A Warm Welcome. RH Disney Staff et al, illus. 2015. (Stepping Stone Book(TM) Ser.: 3). (ENG.). 128p. (J). (gr. 1-4). 9.99 (978-0-7364-3289-4(2), RH/Disney) Random Hse. Children's Bks.

—Anna & Elsa #5: the Polar Bear Piper (Disney Frozen) Robinson, William et al, illus. 2015. (Stepping Stone Book Ser.: 5). (ENG.). 128p. (J). (gr. 1-4). 9.99 (978-0-7364-3436-2(4), RH/Disney) Random Hse. Children's Bks.

—Anna & Elsa #6: the Arendelle Cup (Disney Frozen) RH Disney Staff et al, illus. 2015. (Stepping Stone Book(TM) Ser.: 6). (ENG.). 128p. (J). (gr. 1-4). 9.99 (978-0-7364-3437-9(2), RH/Disney) Random Hse. Children's Bks.

—Anna & Elsa #8. Random House Disney Staff et al, illus. 2016. (Stepping Stone Book(TM) Ser.: 8). (ENG.). 128p. (J). (gr. 1-4). 9.99 (978-0-7364-3476-8(3), RH/Disney) Random Hse. Children's Bks.

—Anna & Elsa: Books 5-8 (Disney Frozen), 4 vols. RH Disney, illus. 2016. (ENG.). 512p. (J). (gr. 1-4). 39.96 (978-0-7364-3631-1(6), RH/Disney) Random Hse. Children's Bks.

—The Great Ice Engine. RH Disney Staff et al, illus. 2015. (Stepping Stone Book(TM) Ser.: 4). (ENG.). 128p. (J). (gr. 1-4). 9.99 (978-0-7364-3431-7(3), RH/Disney) Random Hse. Children's Bks.

—Memory & Magic. RH Disney Staff & Robinson, William E., illus. 2015. (Stepping Stone Book(TM) Ser.: 2). (ENG.). 128p. (J). (gr. 1-4). 9.99 (978-0-7364-3285-6(X), RH/Disney) Random Hse. Children's Bks.

—Return to the Ice Palace. Random House Disney Staff et al, illus. 2016. (Stepping Stone Book Ser.: 8). (ENG.). 128p. (J). (gr. 1-4). lib. bdg. 12.99 (978-0-7364-8211-0(3), RH/Disney) Random Hse. Children's Bks.

—The Secret Admirer. Random House Disney Staff et al, illus. 2016. (Stepping Stone Book(TM) Ser.: 7). (ENG.). 128p. (J). (gr. 1-4). lib. bdg. 12.99 (978-0-7364-8210-3(5), RH/Disney) Random Hse. Children's Bks.

—A Warm Welcome, No. 3. RH Disney Staff et al, illus. 2015. (Stepping Stone Book(TM) Ser.: 3). (ENG.). 128p. (J). (gr. 1-4). lib. bdg. 12.99 (978-0-7364-8247-9(4), RH/Disney) Random Hse. Children's Bks.

David, Erica & Foreman, Matthew Sinclair. Disney Frozen - A Year with Elsa & Anna, & Olaf Too! 2016. (Replica Journal Ser.). (ENG.). 96p. (J). (gr. k-3). 9.99 (978-0-7944-3701-5(X), Reader's Digest Children's Bks.) Studio Fun International.

Davis, Tanita S. Mare's War. 2011. (ENG.). 352p. (YA). (gr. 7). pap. 9.99 (978-0-375-85077-6(5), Knopf Bks. for Young Readers) Random Hse. Children's Bks.

De la Cruz, Melissa. Double Eclipse. 2016. (Summer on East End Ser.). (ENG.). 336p. (YA). (gr. 7). 17.99 (978-0-399-17356-1(0), G.P. Putnam's Sons Books for Young Readers) Penguin Young Readers Group.

de Lint, Charles. Seven Wild Sisters: A Modern Fairy Tale. Vess, Charles, illus. 2014. (ENG.). 272p. (J). (gr. 3-7). 18.00 (978-0-316-05356-3(2)) Little, Brown Bks. for Young Readers.

Deiss, A. The Sullivan Girls & the Mystery of Moonhouse. 2003. 104p. (Orig.). pap. 9.95 (978-0-595-29580-7(0)) iUniverse, Inc.

Delaney, Molly. My Sister. 2013. (ENG., Illus.). 32p. (J). (gr. -1-3). 16.99 (978-1-4814-2130-0(1), Atheneum Bks. for Young Readers) Simon & Schuster Children's Publishing.

Dellaira, Ava. Love Letters to the Dead. 2014. (ENG.). 336p. (YA). (gr. 7). 17.99 (978-0-374-34667-6(4), 9780374346676, Farrar, Straus & Giroux (BYR)) Farrar, Straus & Giroux.

Dematteis, Heidi Gestvang. Sisters Are Forever. 2012. 20p. (-18). pap. 24.95 (978-1-4626-8791-6(1)) America Star Bks.

Demonia, Lori. Leah's Voice. 2013. 28p. 16.95 (978-1-61244-240-2(4)) Halo Publishing International.

—Leah's Voice. Turchan, Monique, illus. 2012. 28p. pap. 12.95 (978-1-61244-089-7(4)) Halo Publishing International.

Denman, K. L. The Shade, 1 vol. 2008. (Orca Currents Ser.). (ENG.). (J). (gr. 5-9). 112p. lib. bdg. 16.95 (978-1-55143-933-4(6)); (Illus.). 128p. pap. 9.95 (978-1-55143-931-0(X)) Orca Bk. Pubs. USA.

Deriso, Christine Hurley. Then I Met My Sister. 2011. (ENG.). 288p. (YA). (gr. 7-18). pap. 9.95 (978-0-7387-2581-9(1), Flux) North Star Editions.

DeVillers, Julia & Roy, Jennifer. Double Feature. 2012. (Mix Ser.). (ENG.). 288p. (J). (gr. 4-8). pap. 7.99 (978-1-4424-3403-5(1), Aladdin) Simon & Schuster Children's Publishing.

—Triple Trouble. 2014. (Mix Ser.). (ENG., Illus.). 240p. (J). (gr. 4-8). pap. 7.99 (978-1-4424-3406-6(6), Aladdin) Simon & Schuster Children's Publishing.

—Triple Trouble. 2013. (ENG.). 240p. (J). (gr. 4-8). 16.99 (978-1-4424-3405-9(8), Simon & Schuster/Paula Wiseman Bks.) Simon & Schuster/Paula Wiseman Bks.

DeVillers, Julia & Roy, Jennifer Rozines. Double Feature. 2012. (ENG.). 272p. (J). (gr. 4-8). 16.99 (978-1-4424-3402-8(3), Aladdin) Simon & Schuster Children's Publishing.

—Take Two. 2010. (Mix Ser.). (ENG.). 304p. (J). (gr. 4-8). pap. 7.99 (978-1-4169-6731-6(1), Aladdin) Simon & Schuster Children's Publishing.

—Take Two. 2010. (ENG.). 240p. (J). (gr. 4-8). 16.99 (978-1-4169-7533-5(0), Simon & Schuster/Paula Wiseman Bks.) Simon & Schuster/Paula Wiseman Bks.

—Times Squared. 2011. (Mix Ser.). (ENG.). (J). (gr. 4-8). 272p. pap. 7.99 (978-1-4169-6732-3(X)); 240p. 16.99 (978-1-4169-7532-8(2)) Simon & Schuster Children's Publishing. (Aladdin).

—Trading Faces. 2008. (ENG.). 304p. (J). (gr. 4-8). 16.99 (978-1-4169-7531-1(4), Simon & Schuster/Paula Wiseman Bks.) Simon & Schuster/Paula Wiseman Bks.

Devlin, Calla. Tell Me Something Real. 2016. (ENG., Illus.). 304p. (YA). (gr. 9). 17.99 (978-1-4814-6115-3(X), Atheneum Bks. for Young Readers) Simon & Schuster Children's Publishing.

Dhami, Narinder. Bindi Babes. 2005. (Bindi Babes Ser.). (ENG.). 192p. (J). (gr. 3-7). reprint ed. 6.99 (978-0-440-42019-4(9), Yearling) Random Hse. Children's Bks.

DiCamillo, Kate. Where Are You Going, Baby Lincoln? Tales from Deckawoo Drive, Volume Three. Van Dusen, Chris, illus. 2017. (Tales from Deckawoo Drive Ser.: 3). (ENG.). 112p. (J). (gr. 1-4). pap. 5.99 **(978-0-7636-9758-7(3))** Candlewick Pr.

Dillon, Elena. Breathe. 2013. 190p. pap. 9.99 (978-0-9886353-2-6(1)) Dillon, Elena.

Dionne, Erin. The Total Tragedy of a Girl Named Hamlet. 2011. (ENG.). 304p. (J). (gr. 3-7). 8.99 (978-0-14-241748-5(3), Puffin Books) Penguin Young Readers Group.

Disney. Frozen Cinestory, Volume 1. 2014. lib. bdg. 26.95 (978-0-606-36645-8(8)) Turtleback Bks.

Disney Book Group. Frozen: The Story of Anna & Elsa. Disney Storybook Art Team, illus. 2016. (ENG.). 112p. (J). (gr. -1-k). 12.99 (978-1-4847-6770-2(5)) Disney Pr.

—Frozen 5-Minute Frozen Stories. Disney Storybook Art Team, illus. 2015. (5-Minute Stories Ser.). (ENG.). 192p. (J). (gr. 1-3). 12.99 (978-1-4847-2330-2(9)) Disney Pr.

Disney Book Group & Rudnick, Elizabeth. A Frozen Heart. Disney Storybook Art Team, illus. 2015. (ENG.). 304p. (J). (gr. 5-9). 14.99 (978-1-4847-3051-5(8)) Disney Pr.

Disney Book Group Staff. Frozen Read-Along Storybook & CD. Disney Storybook Artists Staff, illus. 2013. (Read-Along Storybook & CD Ser.). (ENG.). 32p. (J). (gr. -1-k). pap. 6.99 (978-1-4231-7064-8(4)) Disney Pr.

Disney Editors. Frozen. 2013. lib. bdg. 14.75 (978-0-606-32207-2(8), Turtleback) Turtleback Bks.

—Frozen - Anna's Icy Adventure. 2013. lib. bdg. 14.75 (978-0-606-32206-5(X), Turtleback) Turtleback Bks.

Disney Frozen Melt My Heart. 2014. (Hugs Book Ser.). (ENG.). 10p. (J). (gr. -1-k). bds. 10.99 (978-0-7944-3266-9(2), Reader's Digest Children's Bks.) Studio Fun International.

Dooley, Sarah. Ashes to Asheville. 2017. (ENG.). 256p. (J). (gr. 5). 16.99 (978-0-399-16504-7(5), G.P. Putnam's Sons Books for Young Readers) Penguin Young Readers Group.

Dorling Kindersley Publishing Staff. Disney Frozen: the Enchanted Guide. 2015. (ENG., Illus.). 96p. (J). (gr. 1-4). 14.99 (978-1-4654-4081-5(X), DK Children) Dorling Kindersley Publishing, Inc.

Dower, Laura. Maggie's Magic Chocolate Moon. Lazuli, Lilly, illus. 2016. (Dessert Diaries). (ENG.). 160p. (gr. 4-5). pap. 5.95 (978-1-4965-4141-3(3)) Stone Arch Bks.

Drakeford, Lisa. The Baby. 2016. (ENG.). 256p. (J). (gr. 9). 17.99 (978-0-545-94027-6(3)) Scholastic, Inc.

Driscoll, Laura. Lila the Fair. Sims, Blanche, illus. 2005. (Social Studies Connects). 32p. (J). pap. 5.95 (978-1-57565-148-4(3)) Kane Press, Inc.

—We Are Twins. 2012. (Penguin Young Readers Level 1 Ser.). lib. bdg. 13.55 (978-0-606-26641-3(0), Turtleback) Turtleback Bks.

Duble, Kathleen Benner. The Sacrifice. 2007. (ENG.). 224p. (J). (gr. 5-9). pap. 7.99 (978-0-689-87651-6(3), McElderry, Margaret K. Bks.) McElderry, Margaret K. Bks.

DuJardin, Rosamond. Practically Seventeen: A Tobey Heydon Story. 2003. (YA). per. 12.95 (978-1-930009-68-4(2), 800-691-7779) Image Cascade Publishing.

Dunkle, Clare B. The Hollow Kingdom. 2006. (Hollow Kingdom Trilogy Ser.: 1). (ENG.). 240p. (J). (gr. 6-9). reprint ed. pap. 10.99 (978-0-8050-8108-4(9), 9780805081084, Holt, Henry & Co. Bks. For Young Readers) Holt, Henry & Co.

Dunn, Pintip. Forget Tomorrow. 2015. (Forget Tomorrow Ser.: 1). (ENG.). 400p. (YA). 16.99 (978-1-63375-238-2(0), 9781633752382) Entangled Publishing, LLC.

Durnil, Lari. A Tale of Two Sisters. 2009. (J). pap. 11.89 (978-0-88144-455-1(3), Total Publishing & Media) Yorkshire Publishing Group.

Durst, Sarah Beth. Journey Across the Hidden Islands. 2017. (ENG., Illus.). 352p. (J). (gr. 5-7). 16.99 (978-0-544-70679-8(X), Clarion Bks.) Houghton Mifflin Harcourt Trade & Reference Pubs.

Dyer, Jonah Lisa & Dyer, Stephen. The Season. 2016. (ENG.). 352p. (YA). (gr. 9). 17.99 (978-0-451-47634-0(4), Viking Books for Young Readers) Penguin Young Readers Group.

Dzidrums, Christine. Fair Youth: Emylee of Forest Springs. Lopez, Lyle & Dzidrums, Joseph, illus. 2012. 120p. pap. 9.99 (978-1-938438-05-9(1)) Creative Media Publishing.

Eareckson Tada, Joni & Jensen, Steve. The Mission Adventure. 2005. (Darcy & Friends Ser.). 143p. (gr. 3-6).

pap. 5.99 *(978-1-58134-257-4(8)*, Crossway Bibles) Crossway.
Edmonds, Lin. Patric the Pony & the Shining Star. 2010. 36p. pap. 17.49 *(978-1-4520-7389-7(9))* AuthorHouse.
Egan, Kate. Kate & Nate Are Running Late! Yaccarino, Dan, illus. 2012. (ENG.). 36p. (J). (gr. k-2). 16.99 *(978-1-250-00080-4(7)*, 9781250000804) Feiwel & Friends.
Ele, Delores. Horse Bones: The Adventures of Daisy & Maisy. 2012. 56p. pap. 15.99 *(978-1-4771-4113-7(8))* Xlibris Corp.
Elizabeth's Story 1848. 2014. (Secrets of the Manor Ser.: 3). (ENG., Illus.). 160p. (J). (gr. 3-7). pap. 6.99 *(978-1-4814-1840-9(8)*, Simon Spotlight) Simon Spotlight.
Elliott, Kate, pseud. Court of Fives. 2015. (Court of Fives Ser.: Bk. 1). (ENG., Illus.). 448p. (YA). (gr. 7-17). 18.00 *(978-0-316-36419-5(3))* Little Brown & Co.
—Court of Fives. 2016. (Court of Fives Ser.: 1). (ENG., Illus.). 464p. (YA). (gr. 7-17). pap. 10.99 *(978-0-316-36430-0(4))* Little, Brown Bks. for Young Readers.
—Poisoned Blade. 2016. (Court of Fives Ser.: 2). (ENG., Illus.). 480p. (YA). (gr. 7-17). 17.99 *(978-0-316-34437-1(0))* Little, Brown Bks. for Young Readers.
Ellis, Ann Dee. You May Already Be a Winner. 2017. (ENG.). 352p. (J). (gr. 5-9). 16.99 ***(978-1-101-99385-9(5)***, Dial Bks) Penguin Young Readers Group.
Ellis, Marvie. Keisha's Doors Bk. 1: An Autism Story. l.t. ed. 2005.Tr. of Las Puertas de Keisha. (SPA., Illus.). 32p. (J). per. 16.95 *(978-1-933319-00-1(3))* Speech Kids Texas Pr.
Elliston, Beth. A Baby Book as told by ME! the Big Sister. 2009. 32p. pap. 14.95 *(978-0-557-07646-8(3))* Lulu Pr., Inc.
Esparra, Lydia. Heaven Is All Around You. Esparra, Veronica, illus. 2012. 28p. pap. 12.95 *(978-1-61244-071-2(1))* Halo Publishing International.
Estelle, Carrie. Molly Loves Her Sister. 2011. 20p. pap. 11.00 *(978-1-4567-6425-8(X))* AuthorHouse.
Farley, Brianne. Secret Tree Fort. Farley, Brianne, illus. 2016. (ENG., Illus.). 32p. (J). (gr. -1-3). 16.99 *(978-0-7636-6297-4(6))* Candlewick Pr.
Farley, Robin. Mia & the Big Sister Ballet. Ivanov, Olga & Ivanov, Aleksey, illus. 2012. (My First I Can Read Ser.). (ENG.). 32p. (J). (gr. -1-3). pap. 3.99 *(978-0-06-173307-9(5))* HarperCollins Pubs.
—Mia & the Big Sister Ballet. 2012. (Mia I Can Read Bks.). (J). lib. bdg. 13.55 *(978-0-606-26282-8(2)*, Turtleback) Turtleback Bks.
—Mia & the Tiny Toe Shoes. 2012. (Mia I Can Read Bks.). (J). lib. bdg. 13.55 *(978-0-606-26863-9(4)*, Turtleback) Turtleback Bks.
Farrant, Natasha. The Secret Diary of Lydia Bennet. 2016. (ENG.). 336p. (YA). (gr. 7). 17.99 *(978-0-545-94031-3(1)*, Chicken Hse., The) Scholastic, Inc.
Farshtey, Greg. Way of the Ninja. 2012. (Lego Ninjago Ser.). (ENG.). 32p. (J). (gr. -1-3). pap. 3.99 *(978-0-545-40113-5(5))* Scholastic, Inc.
Fawcett, Heather. Even the Darkest Stars. 2017. (Even the Darkest Stars Ser.: 1). 432p. (YA). (gr. 8). 17.99 ***(978-0-06-246338-8(1))*** HarperCollins Pubs.
Fellure, Kathy Boyd. Mr Snowman Ate Our Picnic Lunch. 2011. 36p. pap. 16.95 *(978-0-557-79684-7(9))* Lulu Pr., Inc.
Fernandez, Alexa. Darn Baby! 2012. 20p. pap. 15.00 *(978-1-105-89540-1(8))* Lulu Pr., Inc.
Figley, Marty Rhodes. The Schoolchildren's Blizzard. Haas, Shelly O., illus. 2004. (On My Own History Ser.). (ENG.). 48p. (gr. 2-4). lib. bdg. 25.26 *(978-1-57505-586-2(4)*, Carolrhoda Bks.) Lerner Publishing Group.
Fisher, Valorie. My Big Sister. Fisher, Valorie, photos by. 2003. (ENG., Illus.). 40p. (J). (gr. -1-3). 17.99 *(978-0-689-85479-8(X)*, Atheneum Bks. for Young Readers) Simon & Schuster Children's Publishing.
Flannigan, Liz. Cara & the Wizard, 2 vols. Docampo, Valeria, illus. 2013. (Magic Stories Ser.). (ENG.). 48p. (J). (gr. 1-4). pap. 8.99 *(978-1-84686-780-4(0))* Barefoot Bks., Inc.
Flood, Nancy Bo. Soldier Sister, Fly Home. Begay, Shonto, illus. 2016. (ENG.). 176p. (YA). (gr. 5). lib. bdg. 16.95 *(978-1-58089-702-0(9))* Charlesbridge Publishing, Inc.
Foggo, Cheryl. I Have Been in Danger, 1 vol. Hotchkiss, Conrad & Graham, Heather, illus. 2005. (In the Same Boat Ser.: No. 3). (ENG.). 184p. (J). (gr. 4-6). pap. 7.95 *(978-1-55050-185-8(2))* Coteau Bks. CAN. Dist: Fitzhenry & Whiteside, Ltd.
Ford, Adam B. The Six Sisters & Their Flying Carpets. Abbott, Kristin, illus. 2012. 34p. (-18). 20.95 *(978-0-9794104-6-8(0))* H Bar Pr.
Foxlee, Karen. The Anatomy of Wings. 2010. (ENG.). 384p. (Orig.). (YA). (gr. 9). pap. 9.99 *(978-0-375-84761-5(8)*, Knopf Bks. for Young Readers) Random Hse. Children's Bks.
Frankel, Jordana. The Isle. 2016. 384p. (YA). (gr. 8). 17.99 *(978-0-06-209537-4(4)*, Tegen, Katherine Bks) HarperCollins Pubs.
—The Ward. (YA). (gr. 8). 2016. 496p. pap. 9.99 *(978-0-06-209535-0(8))* 2013. (ENG.). 480p. 17.99 *(978-0-06-209534-3(X))* HarperCollins Pubs. (Tegen, Katherine Bks).
Franks, Pam. The Magic Gingerbread House. 2015. (ENG.). 32p. (J). 19.95 *(978-1-931721-10-3(6)*, 9781931721103) Bright Sky Pr.
Frazer, Rebecca. An Egg-Cellent Easter! (Barbie) Riley, Kellee, illus. 2012. (Pictureback(R) Ser.). (ENG.). 16p. (J). (gr. -1-2). pap. 3.99 *(978-0-307-93025-5(4)*, Random Hse. Bks. for Young Readers) Random Hse. Children's Bks.
Frazier, Sundee T. The Other Half of My Heart. 2011. (ENG.). 304p. (J). (gr. 3-7). 7.99 *(978-0-440-24006-8(9)*, Yearling) Random Hse. Children's Bks.
Freeman, Martha. The Case of the Bug on the Run. 2014. (First Kids Mystery Ser.: 6). (ENG.). 144p. (J). (gr. 2-7). pap. 6.99 *(978-0-8234-3188-5(6))* Holiday Hse., Inc.
—The Case of the Bug on the Run: First Kids Mystery #6. 2013. (First Kids Mystery Ser.: 6). (ENG.). 144p. (J). (gr. 2-7). 16.95 *(978-0-8234-2872-4(9))* Holiday Hse., Inc.
—The Case of the Diamond Dog Collar. 2nd ed. (First Kids Mystery Ser.: 2). (ENG., 144p. (J). 2012. Illus.). (gr. 3-5). pap. 6.99 *(978-0-8234-2642-3(4))* 2011. 16.95 *(978-0-8234-2337-8(9))* Holiday Hse., Inc.
—The Case of the Missing Dinosaur Egg. Dibley, Glin, illus. 2014. (First Kids Mystery Ser.: 5). (ENG.). 115p. (J). (gr. 3-7). pap. 6.99 *(978-0-8234-3061-1(8))* Holiday Hse., Inc.
—The Case of the Missing Dinosaur Egg. 2013. (First Kids Mystery Ser.: 5). (ENG.). 144p. (J). (gr. 3-7). 16.95 *(978-0-8234-2523-5(1))* Holiday Hse., Inc.
—The Case of the Piggy Bank Thief. 2012. (First Kids Mystery Ser.: 4). (ENG.). 144p. (J). (gr. 1-5). 16.95 *(978-0-8234-2517-4(7))* Holiday Hse., Inc.
—The Case of the Piggy Bank Thief: First Kids Mystery #4. 2013. (First Kids Mystery Ser.: 4). (ENG.). 144p. (J). (gr. 1-5). pap. 6.99 *(978-0-8234-2916-5(4))* Holiday Hse., Inc.
—The Case of the Rock 'N' Roll Dog. 2010. (First Kids Mystery Ser.: 1). (ENG., Illus.). 128p. (J). (gr. 1-5). 16.95 *(978-0-8234-2267-8(4))* Holiday Hse., Inc.
—The Case of the Rock 'n' Roll Dog. 2012. (First Kids Mystery Ser.: 1). (ENG.). 128p. (J). (gr. 3-5). pap. 6.99 *(978-0-8234-2549-5(5))* Holiday Hse., Inc.
—The Case of the Ruby Slippers. (First Kids Mystery Ser.: 3). (ENG.). 128p. (J). 2013. pap. 6.99 *(978-0-8234-2764-2(1))* 2012. 16.95 *(978-0-8234-2409-2(X))* Holiday Hse., Inc.
Freitas, Donna. Gold Medal Summer. (ENG.). 240p. (J). 2014. (gr. 5-9). pap. 6.99 *(978-0-545-32789-3(X))* 2012. (gr. 4-7). 16.99 *(978-0-545-32788-6(1))* Scholastic, Inc. (Levine, Arthur A. Bks.).
Freymann-Weyr, Garret. Stay with Me. 2007. (ENG.). 320p. (YA). (gr. 9-12). pap. 8.99 *(978-0-618-88404-9(1))* Houghton Mifflin Harcourt Publishing Co.
Friedman, Aimee. Two Summers. 2016. (ENG.). 368p. (J). (gr. 7). 17.99 *(978-0-545-51807-9(5))* Scholastic, Inc.
Friedmann, Patty. Taken Away. 2010. (ENG.). 427p. (J). (gr. 6). pap. 18.95 *(978-0-9845318-2-0(3))* Tiny Stachel Pr.
Friend, Natasha. Perfect. 2004. (ENG.). 232p. (J). pap. 7.95 *(978-1-57131-651-6(5))* Milkweed Editions.
Frillman, K. Country Stars: The Road Less Traveled. 2007. 348p. per. 21.95 *(978-1-4303-1234-5(3))* Lulu Pr., Inc.
Froeb, Lori. Disney Frozen: Christmas Magic. 2015. (ENG.). 10p. (J). (gr. -1-1). bds. 8.99 *(978-0-7944-3501-1(7))* Reader's Digest Assn., Inc., The.
—A Sister's Love: Storybook & Necklace. 2016. (ENG.). 32p. (J). (gr. -1-k). 14.99 *(978-0-7944-3574-5(2)*, Reader's Digest Children's Bks.) Studio Fun International.
Fujishima, Kosuke. Oh My Goddess! Volume 36. 2010. (ENG., Illus.). 152p. pap. 10.99 *(978-1-59582-581-0(9))* Dark Horse Comics.
Funk, Constance J. Holy as Thou. 2009. (Illus.). 400p. pap. 22.00 *(978-1-933002-66-8(2))* PublishingWorks.
Gabriel, Nat. Bubble Trouble. Nez, John, illus. 2004. 32p. (J). lib. bdg. 20.00 *(978-1-4242-1085-5(2))* Fitzgerald Bks.
—Bubble Trouble. Nez, John, tr. Nez, John, illus. 2004. (Science Solves It! Ser.). 32p. (J). pap. 5.95 *(978-1-57565-133-0(5))* Kane Press, Inc.
—Bubble Trouble. Nez, John, illus. 2004. (Science Solves It Ser.). 32p. (gr. -1-3). 15.00 *(978-0-7569-4286-1(1))* Perfection Learning Corp.
Galante, Cecilia. The Sweetness of Salt. 2012. (ENG.). 320p. (YA). (gr. 7). pap. 9.99 *(978-1-59990-853-3(0)*, 9781599908533, Bloomsbury USA Childrens) Bloomsbury Publishing USA.
Gallagher, Diana G. Monica & the Bratty Stepsister, 1 vol. Canga, C. B., illus. 2010. (Monica Ser.). (ENG.). 88p. (gr. 2-3). 26.65 *(978-1-4342-1980-0(1))* Stone Arch Bks.
—Monica & the Weekend of Drama, 1 vol. 2011. (Monica Ser.). (ENG.). 88p. (gr. 2-3). lib. bdg. 26.65 *(978-1-4342-2557-3(7))* Stone Arch Bks.
Galvin, Laura Gates & Studio Mouse Editorial. Cinderella: Dreams Do Come True. 2008. (Illus.). 36p. (J). (gr. -1). 7.99 *(978-1-59069-436-7(8))* Studio Mouse LLC.
Gamache, Line. Hello, Me Pretty. Cochrane, KerryAnn, tr. from FRE. 2007. (ENG., Illus.). 64p. per. *(978-1-894994-23-1(X))* Conundrum Pr.
Garber, Stephanie. Caraval. 2017. (SPA.). 432p. pap. 16.95 ***(978-607-07-4044-2(0))*** Editorial Planeta, S. A. ESP. Dist: Two Rivers Distribution.
—Caraval. 2017. (Caraval Ser.). (ENG.). (YA). 416p. 18.99 *(978-1-250-09525-1(5)*, 9781250095251); (gr. 8-12). pap. 11.99 ***(978-1-250-14149-1(4))*** Flatiron Bks.
Garcia McCall, Guadalupe. Summer of the Mariposas. 2016. (ENG.). 352p. (YA). pap. 11.95 *(978-1-62014-010-9(1)*, Tu Bks.) Lee & Low Bks., Inc.
Gardner, Lyn. Out of the Woods. 2011. (ENG., Illus.). 368p. (J). (gr. 3-7). 7.99 *(978-0-385-75226-8(1)*, Yearling) Random Hse. Children's Bks.
Garoche, Camille. Snow Rabbit. 2015. (ENG., Illus.). 56p. (J). (gr. -1-3). 16.95 *(978-1-59270-181-0(7))* Enchanted Lion Bks., LLC.
Gartlan, Daniel. Poor Hannah. 2012. 24p. pap. 24.95 *(978-1-4626-6030-8(4))* America Star Bks.
Gassman, Julie A. Lucille Gets Jealous, 1 vol. Cooke, Charlotte, illus. 2012. (Little Boost Ser.). (ENG.). 32p. (gr. k-3). lib. bdg. 23.99 *(978-1-4048-6797-0(X)*, Little Boost) Picture Window Bks.
Gaydos, Nora. I'M a New Big Sister. Gutierrez, Akemi, illus. 2010. (ENG.). 30p. (J). (gr. -1-17). 6.99 *(978-1-60169-009-8(6))* Innovative Kids.
Gayle, Amber. On the Naive but Honorable Self-Determination of Teenage Girls: My Evil Twin Sister No. 5. 2004. 228p. (YA). pap. 6.00 *(978-0-9712972-8-9(2))* Evil Twin Pubns.
Gee, Randi. Goldfish & Poodle. 2010. 32p. pap. 15.50 *(978-0-557-52979-7(4))* Lulu Pr., Inc.
Gehl, Laura. I'm Not Hatching. Wan, Joyce, illus. 2016. (Peep & Egg Ser.). (ENG.). 40p. (J). 16.99 *(978-0-374-30121-7(2)*, 9780374301217, Farrar, Straus & Giroux (BYR)) Farrar, Straus & Giroux.
—I'm Not Trick-Or-Treating. Wan, Joyce, illus. 2016. (Peep & Egg Ser.). (ENG.). 40p. (J). 16.99 *(978-0-374-30122-4(0)*, 9780374301224, Farrar, Straus & Giroux (BYR)) Farrar, Straus & Giroux.
Gibbs, Lynne. Molly Mouse Is Shy: A Story of Shyness. Mitchell, Melanie, illus. 2009. (Let's Grow Together Ser.). 32p. (J). (gr. -1-2). pap. 10.55 *(978-1-60754-761-7(9))*; lib. bdg. 22.60 *(978-1-60754-756-3(2))* Windmill Bks.
Gill, Shelley. Prickly Rose. Cartwright, Shannon & Love, Judy, illus. 2014. (ENG.). 32p. (J). (gr. -1-3). pap. 7.95 *(978-1-57091-357-0(9))*; lib. bdg. 17.95 *(978-1-57091-356-3(0))* Charlesbridge Publishing, Inc.
Gliori, Debi. Witch Baby & Me after Dark, No. 3. 2010. (ENG., Illus.). 304p. (J). (gr. 2-4). pap. 11.99 *(978-0-552-55678-1(5))* Transworld Publishers Ltd. GBR. Dist: Independent Pubs. Group.
Gliori, Debi & Hurst, Kelly. Witch Baby & Me on Stage. Gliori, Debi, illus. 2011. (ENG., Illus.). 336p. (J). (gr. 2-4). pap. 7.99 *(978-0-552-55679-8(3))* Transworld Publishers Ltd. GBR. Dist: Independent Pubs. Group.
Godbersen, Anna. The Luxe, Rumors, & Envy, Set, Bks. 1-3. 2009. (Luxe Ser.). (YA). (gr. 9). pap. 24.99 *(978-0-06-192118-6(1))* HarperCollins Pubs.
Godwin, Jane. Falling from Grace. 2007. (ENG.). 204p. (J). (gr. 6-12). 16.95 *(978-0-8234-2105-3(8))* Holiday Hse., Inc.
Goldberg, Whoopi. Sugar Plum to the Rescue! Roos, Maryn, illus. 2011. (ENG.). 160p. (J). (gr. 1-5). pap. 4.99 *(978-0-7868-5264-2(X)*, Jump at the Sun) Hyperion Bks. for Children.
Golf, Cali. Umkhuba: The Journal. 2011. 36p. (gr. -1). pap. 19.95 *(978-1-4520-4128-5(8))* AuthorHouse.
Goodell, Mary. The Chicken Pox Puppy: Kate & Jen's Daily Adventures. Goodell, Mary, illus. 2007. (Illus.). 29p. (J). per. 11.99 *(978-1-59879-382-6(9))* Lifevest Publishing, Inc.
Goodman, Leandria D. Firecracker, Firecracker, Boom, Boom, Boom!, 1 vol. 2009. 21p. pap. 24.95 *(978-1-60749-475-1(2))* America Star Bks.
Gow, Kailin. Diary of a Discount Donna: A Fashion Fables Book: A Novel. 2005. 274p. (YA). per. 10.95 *(978-1-59748-858-7(5))* Sparklesoup LLC.
—The Stoker Sisters. 2010. 266p. (YA). pap. *(978-1-59748-947-8(6))* Sparklesoup LLC.
Grady, Karen. It's Not My Fault, She Started It. 2005. (Illus.). (J). *(978-1-59975-127-6(5))* Independent Pub.
Graham, Bob. April & Esme Tooth Fairies. Graham, Bob, illus. (ENG., Illus.). 40p. (J). (gr. k-4). 2013. 6.99 *(978-0-7636-6347-6(6))* 2010. 16.99 *(978-0-7636-4683-7(0))* Candlewick Pr.
Grant, Natalie. The Miracle in Music City, 1 vol. 2016. (Faithgirlz / Glimmer Girls Ser.). (ENG.). 208p. (J). pap. 8.99 *(978-0-310-75250-9(7))* Zonderkidz.
Gray, Mila. Come Back to Me. 2015. (ENG., Illus.). 352p. (YA). (gr. 11). 17.99 *(978-1-4814-3965-7(0)*, Simon Pulse) Simon Pulse.
Green, D. L. Kaitlyn & the Competition. 2016. (Babysitter Chronicles Ser.). (ENG.). 160p. (gr. 4-7). pap. 6.95 *(978-1-4914-8861-4(1))* Stone Arch Bks.
—Sparkling Jewel. Wallis, Emily, illus. 2015. (Silver Pony Ranch Ser.: 1). (ENG.). 96p. (J). (gr. 1-3). pap. 4.99 *(978-0-545-79765-8(9))* Scholastic, Inc.
—Sweet Buttercup. Wallis, Emily, illus. 2016. (Silver Pony Ranch Ser.: 2). (ENG.). 96p. (J). (gr. 1-3). 15.99 *(978-0-545-79770-2(5))* Scholastic, Inc.
Green, Holly G. Don't Slam the Door. Scott, Sarah Chamberlin, illus. 2005. (ENG.). 39p. (J). (gr. 2-7). 19.95 *(978-0-9744803-7-4(1))* PublishingWorks.
Greene, Janice. The Plot, 1 vol. unabr. ed. 2010. (Q Reads Ser.). (ENG.). 32p. (YA). (gr. 9-12). pap. 6.95 *(978-1-61651-204-0(0))* Saddleback Educational Publishing, Inc.
Greene, Kimberly. My Life on TV. 2011. (My Sister's a Pop Star Ser.). 320p. (J). pap. 5.99 *(978-0-7945-2901-7(1)*, Usborne) EDC Publishing.
Greenwood, R. L. A Visit to the Kingdom of Camelot. 2013. 62p. (gr. 2-2). pap. 8.95 *(978-1-4759-8097-4(3))* iUniverse, Inc.
Gregory, Kristiana. My Darlin' Clementine. 2009. (ENG.). 192p. (J). (gr. 5-18). 16.95 *(978-0-8234-2198-5(8))* Holiday Hse., Inc.
Grey, Mini & Gardner, Lyn. Into the Woods. Grey, Mini, illus. 2009. (ENG., Illus.). 448p. (J). (gr. 3-7). 8.99 *(978-0-440-42223-5(X)*, Yearling) Random Hse. Children's Bks.
Griffin, Adele. All You Never Wanted. 2013. (ENG.). 240p. (YA). (gr. 9). pap. 8.99 *(978-0-375-87081-1(4)*, Ember) Random Hse. Children's Bks.
—Where I Want to Be. 2007. (ENG.). 176p. (YA). (gr. 7-18). 7.99 *(978-0-14-240948-0(0)*, Speak) Penguin Young Readers Group.
Grimm, Jacob & Grimm, Wilhelm K. Hut in the Forest, 1 vol. Lawson, Polly, tr. from GER. Stietencron, Bettina, illus. 2007. (Grimm's Fairy Tales Ser.). (ENG.). 28p. (J). *(978-0-86315-615-1(0))* Floris Bks.
Grinti, Mike & Grinti, Rachel. Claws. 2012. (J). *(978-0-545-43314-3(2))*; (ENG.). 256p. (gr. 5-9). 16.99 *(978-0-545-43313-6(4))* Scholastic, Inc. (Chicken Hse., The).
Grogan, Shannon. From Where I Watch You. (ENG.). 304p. (YA). (gr. 9). 2016. pap. 10.99 *(978-1-61695-689-9(5))* 2015. 18.99 *(978-1-61695-554-0(6))* Soho Pr., Inc. (Soho Teen).
Grossman, Bill. My Little Sister Hugged an Ape. Hawkes, Kevin, illus. 2008. (ENG.). 40p. (J). (gr. -1-2). pap. 6.99 *(978-0-385-73660-2(6)*, Dragonfly Bks.) Random Hse. Children's Bks.
Guess, Bob. Hey Mister, How's Your Sister? 2009. 40p. pap. 16.99 *(978-1-4389-7041-7(2))* AuthorHouse.
Guest, Elissa Haden. Iris & Walter: Lost & Found. Davenier, Christine, illus. 2014. (Green Light Readers Level 3 Ser.). (ENG.). 44p. (J). (gr. 1-4). pap. 3.99 *(978-0-544-22789-7(1)*, HMH Books For Young Readers) Houghton Mifflin Harcourt Publishing Co.
—Iris & Walter & Baby Rose. Davenier, Christine, illus. 2012. (Iris & Walter — Green Light Reader Ser.). lib. bdg. 13.55 *(978-0-606-26612-3(7)*, Turtleback) Turtleback Bks.
Gurtler, Janet. I'M Not Her. 2011. (ENG.). 304p. (YA). (gr. 7-12). pap. 12.99 *(978-1-4022-5636-3(1)*, 9781402256363) Sourcebooks, Inc.
Gutman, Anne. Lisa's Baby Sister. Hallensleben, Georg, illus. 2012. (ENG.). 32p. (J). (gr. k-3). pap. 6.99 *(978-0-449-81012-5(7)*, Dragonfly Bks.) Random Hse. Children's Bks.
Hakala, Joann. A Baby Brother! Oh No! Shaw-Peterson, Kimberly, illus. 2006. 32p. (J). (gr. -1). per. 10.95 *(978-1-59298-152-6(6))* Beaver's Pond Pr., Inc.
Half Baked Sistas-in the Beginning. 2004. 242p. (YA). lib. bdg. 12.99 *(978-0-9761819-0-3(8)*, 002) Smart Publishing.
Hall, Angela Marie. Priscilla Pennybrook: Hello World, I Have Arrived!, 1 vol. 2009. 55p. pap. 16.95 *(978-1-61582-899-9(0))* America Star Bks.
Hall, Kirsten. Hide-and-Seek: All about Location. Luedecke, Bev, illus. 2005. (Beastieville Ser.). (ENG.). 32p. (J). (gr. k-1). pap. 3.95 *(978-0-516-25519-4(3)*, Children's Pr.) Scholastic Library Publishing.
Hallinan, P. K. My Sister & I. 2008. (ENG., Illus.). 24p. (J). (gr. -1-k). bds. 7.95 *(978-0-8249-5456-7(4)*, Ideal Pubns.) Worthy Publishing.
—Sisters Forever. Hallinan, P. K., illus. 2014. (Illus.). 22p. (J). bds. 7.99 *(978-0-8249-1921-4(1)*, Ideal Pubns.) Worthy Publishing.
Halstead, Jayce N. The True Legend of White Crow: Adventures of the Fudge Sisters. Twomey-Lange, Marianna, photos by. 2004. (Illus.). 80p. (J). per. 7.95 *(978-0-9749046-3-4(5))* Aarow Pr.
Hamilton, Laura, reader. Sheila Rae, the Brave. 2003. (Illus.). (J). (gr. -1-2). 28.95 incl. audio compact disk *(978-1-59112-550-1(2))* Live Oak Media.
Hamilton, Peter F. The Secret Throne. Eason, Rohan, illus. 2015. (Queen of Dreams Ser.: 1). (ENG.). 288p. (J). (gr. 4-7). pap. 11.99 *(978-1-4472-8865-7(3))* Pan Macmillan GBR. Dist: Independent Pubs. Group.
Han, Jenny. P.S. I Still Love You. 2015. (ENG., Illus.). 352p. (YA). (gr. 7). 17.99 *(978-1-4424-2673-3(X))*; (To All the Boys I've Loved Before Ser.: 2). E-Book *(978-1-4424-2675-7(6))* Simon & Schuster Bks. For Young Readers. (Simon & Schuster Bks. For Young Readers).
—P.S. I Still Love You. 2017. (To All the Boys I've Loved Before Ser.: 2). (ENG.). 352p. (YA). (gr. 7). pap. 10.99 *(978-1-4424-2674-0(8))* Simon & Schuster Children's Publishing.
—To All the Boys I've Loved Before. (ENG., Illus.). (YA). (gr. 7-10). 2016. 384p. pap. 10.99 *(978-1-4424-2671-9(3))* 2014. 368p. 17.99 *(978-1-4424-2670-2(5))* 2017. 1056p. 53.99 *(978-1-4814-9536-3(4))* Simon & Schuster Bks. For Young Readers. (Simon & Schuster Bks. For Young Readers).
—To All the Boys I've Loved Before. 2016. lib. bdg. 22.10 *(978-0-606-38270-0(4))* Turtleback Bks.
Han, Xuemei. Brave Little Mongolian Sisters. Han, Xuemei, illus. 2007. (Illus.). (J). pap. 12.99 *(978-0-9763168-7-9(0))* DigitalKu.
Hannigan, Katherine. Gwendolyn Grace. Hannigan, Katherine, illus. 2015. (ENG., Illus.). 32p. (J). (gr. -1-3). 17.99 *(978-0-06-234519-6(2)*, Greenwillow Bks.) HarperCollins Pubs.
Hansen, Brandy A. Madd Maddox: Sister for Sale. 2012. 16p. pap. 17.99 *(978-1-4685-5969-9(9))* AuthorHouse.
Hardegree, Maureen. Haint She Sweet. 2013. 206p. pap. 12.95 *(978-1-61194-325-2(6)*, Bell Bridge Bks.) BelleBks., Inc.
Hardinge, Frances. The Lost Conspiracy. 2009. 576p. (J). (gr. 5). lib. bdg. 17.89 *(978-0-06-088042-2(2))*; 16.99 *(978-0-06-088041-5(4))* HarperCollins Pubs.
Hardy, Janice. A Blue Fire, Bk. 2. 2010. (Healing Wars Ser.: II). (ENG.). 384p. (J). (gr. 5-18). 16.99 *(978-0-06-174741-0(6))* HarperCollins Pubs.
—The Healing Wars: Book II: Blue Fire. 2011. (Healing Wars Ser.: II). (ENG.). 400p. (J). (gr. 5). pap. 7.99 *(978-0-06-174744-1(0))* HarperCollins Pubs.
—The Shifter. (J). (gr. 5). 2010. (Healing Wars Ser.: I). (ENG.). 400p. pap. 7.99 *(978-0-06-174708-3(4))* 2009. (Healing Wars Ser.). 384p. lib. bdg. 17.89 *(978-0-06-176177-5(X))* HarperCollins Pubs.
Hardy, Sarah Frances. Puzzled by Pink. 2012. (ENG.). 32p. (J). (gr. -1-k). 16.99 *(978-0-670-01320-3(X)*, Viking Books for Young Readers) Penguin Young Readers Group.
Harris, Teresa E. The Perfect Place. 2014. (ENG.). 272p. (J). (gr. 5-7). 17.99 *(978-0-547-25519-4(5))* Houghton Mifflin Harcourt Publishing Co.
Hasbro. Gift of Maud Pie. 2016. (Passport to Reading Level 2 Ser.). (J). lib. bdg. 13.55 *(978-0-606-39194-8(0))* Turtleback Bks.
Hathaway, Jill. Impostor. 2013. (Slide Ser.: 2). (ENG.). 272p. (YA). (gr. 9). 17.99 *(978-0-06-207798-1(8))* HarperCollins Pubs.
—Slide. (Slide Ser.: 1). (ENG.). (YA). (gr. 9). 2013. 272p. pap. 9.99 *(978-0-06-207796-7(1))* 2012. 256p. 17.99 *(978-0-06-207790-5(2))* HarperCollins Pubs.
Haydu, Corey Ann. Making Pretty. 2015. (ENG.). 368p. (YA). (gr. 9). 17.99 *(978-0-06-229408-1(3)*, Tegen, Katherine Bks) HarperCollins Pubs.
—Rules for Stealing Stars. 2015. (ENG.). 336p. (J). (gr. 3-7). 16.99 *(978-0-06-235271-2(7)*, Tegen, Katherine Bks) HarperCollins Pubs.
Hayes, Joe. Don't Say a Word, Mama / No Digas Nada, Mama. 2013. (Illus.). 32p. (gr. -1-3). (ENG & SPA.). 17.95 *(978-1-935955-29-0(2))*; (SPA & ENG.). (J). pap. 8.95 *(978-1-935955-45-0(4))* Cinco Puntos Pr.
HB Staff. My Sister Is My Friend. 97th ed. 2003. (First-Place Reading Ser.). (gr. 1-18). pap., suppl. ed. 16.50 *(978-0-15-308128-6(7))* Harcourt Schl. Pubs.
Hearn, Julie. The Minister's Daughter. 2006. (ENG.). 272p. (YA). (gr. 7-12). pap. 7.99 *(978-0-689-87691-2(2)*, Atheneum Bks. for Young Readers) Simon & Schuster Children's Publishing.
Heckman, Ashley. The Last Three Words. 2013. 104p. pap. *(978-1-77130-651-5(3))* Evernight Publishing.
Heim, Alastair. No Tooting at Tea. Not, Sara, illus. 2017. (ENG.). 40p. (J). (gr. -1-3). 16.99 *(978-0-544-77474-2(4)*, Clarion Bks.) Houghton Mifflin Harcourt Trade & Reference Pubs.
Heine, Theresa & Barefoot Books Staff. Chandra's Magic Light. Gueyfier, Judith, illus. 2013. (J). 16.99 *(978-1-84686-493-3(3))* Barefoot Bks., Inc.
Heller, Maryellen. My Big Sister's First Day of School. Soman, David, illus. 2009. (J). *(978-0-8037-3246-9(5)*, Dial) Penguin Publishing Group.
Hemphill, Helen. Runaround. (ENG.). 117p. (J). (gr. 6-9). 2009. pap. 10.95 *(978-1-59078-777-9(3))* 2007. (Illus.). 16.95 *(978-1-932425-83-3(7))* Boyds Mills Pr. (Front Street).
Hemphill, Stephanie. Sisters of Glass. 2013. (ENG.). 160p. (YA). (gr. 7). pap. 7.99 *(978-0-307-98141-7(X)*, Ember) Random Hse. Children's Bks.
Henbit & the Roly-Poly. 2007. (J). *(978-0-9791982-2-9(4))* Pine Cone Pr.
Henbit & the Roly-Poly - Specially Formatted Edition. l.t. ed. 2007. (J). *(978-0-9791982-3-6(2))* Pine Cone Pr.
Henkes, Kevin. Sheila Rae, the Brave. Henkes, Kevin, illus. (Illus.). 9.95 *(978-1-59112-865-6(X))* Live Oak Media.
Henning, Ann. Cow Patty Patti. 2004. 47p. pap. 24.95 *(978-1-4137-3456-0(1))* PublishAmerica, Inc.

S

Heo, Yumi. Ten Days & Nine Nights: An Adoption Story. Heo, Yumi, illus. 2009. (Rise & Shine Ser.). (ENG., Illus.). 40p. (J). (gr. -1-3). 17.99 *(978-0-375-84718-9(9)*, Schwartz & Wade Bks.) Random Hse. Children's Bks.

Heredia, María Fernanda. Por Si No Te Lo He Dicho. 2003. (SPA., Illus.). 24p. (J). (gr. 3-5). 15.95 *(978-9978-07-467-1(8))* Santillana USA Publishing Co., Inc.

Hershey, Mary. My Big Sister Is So Bossy She Says You Can't Read This Book. 2006. (ENG., Illus.). 176p. (J). (gr. 3-7). per. 6.99 *(978-0-553-48797-8(3)*, Yearling) Random Hse. Children's Bks.

Hesse, Karen. Wish on a Unicorn. 2009. (ENG.). 128p. (J). (gr. 3-7). pap. 16.99 *(978-0-312-37611-6(1)*, 9780312376116) Square Fish.

Hicks, Barbara Jean & Disney Book Group Staff. A Sister More Like Me. Disney Storybook Artists Staff et al, illus. 2013. (ENG.). 32p. (J). (gr. 1-3). 15.99 *(978-1-4231-7014-3(8))* Disney Pr.

Hidden. 2014. (ENG., Illus.). 384p. (YA). (gr. 7). 17.99 *(978-1-4424-8300-2(8)*, Simon & Schuster/Paula Wiseman Bks.) Simon & Schuster/Paula Wiseman Bks.

Higgins, M. G. Falling Out of Place, 1 vol. 2013. (Gravel Road Ser.). (ENG.). 191p. (YA). (gr. 9-12). pap. 9.95 *(978-1-62250-021-5(0))* Saddleback Educational Publishing, Inc.

—Falling Out of Place. 2013. (Gravel Road Ser.). (YA). lib. bdg. 20.80 *(978-0-606-26963-6(0)*, Turtleback) Turtleback Bks.

Higginson, Sheila Sweeny. You're Getting a Baby Sister! Williams, Sam, illus. 2012. (ENG.). 24p. (J). (gr. -1-k). bds. 7.99 *(978-1-4424-2050-2(2)*, Little Simon) Little Simon.

Hill, C. J. Echo in Time. 2014. 387p. (YA). *(978-0-06-212395-4(5))* HarperCollins Pubs.

—Erasing Time. 2012. (Erasing Time Ser.: 1). (ENG.). 368p. (YA). (gr. 8). 17.99 *(978-0-06-212392-3(0)*, Tegen, Katherine Bks) HarperCollins Pubs.

Hites, Kati. Winnie & Waldorf. Hites, Kati, illus. 2015. (ENG., Illus.). 40p. (J). (gr. -1-3). 17.99 *(978-0-06-231161-0(1))* HarperCollins Pubs.

Ho & Ho, Minfong. The Stone Goddess. 2006. (Reader's Workshop Ser.). (ENG., Illus.). 200p. (C). pap. 19.95 *(978-0-7362-3160-2(9))* CENGAGE Learning.

Hoang, Melanie Rowland. The Gift. 2011. 32p. pap. 13.95 *(978-1-4525-3524-1(8))* Get Published.

Hoban, Russell. A Baby Sister for Frances. Hoban, Lillian, illus. 2011. (I Can Read Level 2 Ser.). (ENG.). 48p. (J). (gr. k-3). 16.99 *(978-0-06-083804-1(3))* HarperCollins Pubs.

—Best Friends for Frances. Hoban, Lillian, illus. 2016. (ENG.). 32p. (J). (gr. -1-3). pap. 5.99 *(978-0-06-239244-2(1)*, HarperFestival) HarperCollins Pubs.

Hocking, Amanda. Elegy. (Watersong Novel Ser.: 4). (ENG.). 560p. (YA). (gr. 7). 2014. mass mkt. 9.99 *(978-1-250-05654-2(3)*, 9781250056542, St. Martin's Paperbacks) 2013. 17.99 *(978-1-250-00567-0(1)*, 9781250005670, St. Martin's Griffin) St. Martin's Pr.

—Lullaby. 2013. (Watersong Novel Ser.: 2). (ENG.). 368p. (YA). (gr. 7). mass mkt. 9.99 *(978-1-250-04675-8(0)*, 9781250046758, St. Martin's Paperbacks); pap. 10.99 *(978-1-250-00810-7(7)*, 9781250008107, St. Martin's Griffin) St. Martin's Pr.

—Tidal. (Watersong Novel Ser.: 3). (ENG.). 352p. (YA). (gr. 7). 2014. mass mkt. 9.99 *(978-1-250-05657-3(8)*, 9781250056573, St. Martin's Paperbacks) 2013. 17.99 *(978-1-250-00811-4(5)*, 9781250008114, St. Martin's Griffin) St. Martin's Pr.

—Wake. 2013. (Watersong Novel Ser.: 1). (ENG.). 320p. (YA). (gr. 7). pap. 10.99 *(978-1-250-00564-9(7)*, 9781250005649, St. Martin's Griffin) St. Martin's Pr.

Hodgson, Mona. The Princess Twins & the Puppy, 1 vol. Olson, Julie, illus. 2015. (I Can Read! / Princess Twins Ser.). (ENG.). 32p. (J). pap. 3.99 *(978-0-310-75064-2(4))* Zonderkidz.

—The Princess Twins Play in the Garden, 1 vol. Olson, Julie, illus. 2015. (I Can Read! / Princess Twins Ser.). (ENG.). 32p. (J). pap. 3.99 *(978-0-310-75050-5(4))* Zonderkidz.

Hodgson, Mona Gansberg. The Princess Twins & the Puppy, 1 vol. Hansen, Red, illus. 2011. (I Can Read! / Princess Twins Ser.). (ENG.). 32p. (J). pap. 3.99 *(978-0-310-72709-5(X))* Zonderkidz.

Hoena, Blake. Witch's Brew. Bardin, Dave, illus. 2016. (Monster Heroes Ser.). (ENG.). 32p. (gr. 1-2). lib. bdg. 21.32 *(978-1-4965-3756-0(4))* Stone Arch Bks.

Hofmeister, Alan, et al. Sis in a Mess. (Reading for All Learners Ser.). (Illus.). (J). pap. *(978-1-56861-091-7(2))* Swift Learning Resources.

—Sis in the Well. (Reading for All Learners Ser.). (Illus.). (J). pap. *(978-1-56861-098-6(X))* Swift Learning Resources.

Holder, Nancy & Viguié, Debbie. Crusade. (Crusade Ser.). (ENG.). (YA). (gr. 9). 2011. 496p. pap. 9.99 *(978-1-4169-9803-7(9))* 2010. 480p. 16.99 *(978-1-4169-9802-0(0))* Simon Pulse. (Simon Pulse).

—Vanquished. 2012. (Crusade Ser.). (ENG.). 496p. (YA). (gr. 9). 16.99 *(978-1-4169-9806-8(3))*; pap. 9.99 *(978-1-4169-9807-5(1))* Simon Pulse. (Simon Pulse).

Hollyer, Belinda. Secrets, Lies & My Sister Kate. 2009. (ENG.). 144p. (J). (gr. 3-7). 16.95 *(978-0-8234-2179-4(1))* Holiday Hse., Inc.

Holstein, Ima. A Dragons Daydream. 2011. 24p. pap. 12.99 *(978-1-4634-0430-7(1))* AuthorHouse.

Holt, Kimberly Willis. Navy Brat. Davenier, Christine, illus. 2011. (Piper Reed Ser.: 1). (ENG.). 176p. (J). (gr. 3-6). pap. 6.99 *(978-0-312-62548-1(0)*, 9780312625481) Square Fish.

—Piper Reed, Clubhouse Queen. Davenier, Christine, illus. 2011. (Piper Reed Ser.: 2). (ENG.). 160p. (J). (gr. 3-6). 15.99 *(978-0-8050-9431-2(8)*, 9780805094312, Holt, Henry & Co. Bks. For Young Readers) Holt, Henry & Co.

—Piper Reed, Clubhouse Queen. Davenier, Christine, illus. 2011. (Piper Reed Ser.: 2). (ENG.). 176p. (J). (gr. 3-6). pap. 6.99 *(978-0-312-61676-2(7)*, 9780312616762) Square Fish.

—Piper Reed, Rodeo Star. Davenier, Christine, illus. 2011. (Piper Reed Ser.: 5). (ENG.). 160p. (J). (gr. 3-6). 15.99 *(978-0-8050-9007-9(X)*, 9780805090079, Holt, Henry & Co. Bks. For Young Readers) Holt, Henry & Co.

—Piper Reed, Rodeo Star. Davenier, Christine, illus. 2012. (Piper Reed Ser.: 5). (ENG.). 176p. (J). (gr. 3-6). pap. 6.99 *(978-1-250-00409-3(8)*, 9781250004093) Square Fish.

Holub, Joan & Williams, Suzanne. Cinderella Stays Late. 2014. (Grimmtastic Girls Ser.: 1). (ENG.). 192p. (J). (gr. 3-7). pap. 5.99 *(978-0-545-51983-0(7))* Scholastic, Inc.

—Cinderella Stays Late. 2014. (Grimmtastic Girls Ser.: 1). lib. bdg. 16.00 *(978-0-606-35395-3(X))* Turtleback Bks.

Holyoak, Kathleen & Summers, Sherry. Flowers in Heaven. 2009. 32p. pap. 14.49 *(978-1-4389-4607-8(4))* AuthorHouse.

Homberg, Ruth. Across the Sea (Disney Frozen) Random House Disney Staff, illus. 2016. (Step into Reading Ser.). (ENG.). 24p. (J). (gr. -1-1). 4.99 *(978-0-7364-3398-3(8)*, RH/Disney) Random Hse. Children's Bks.

Hope, Laura Lee. Bunny Brown & His Sister Sue at Aunt Lu's City Home. Lt. ed. 2007. (ENG.). 154p. pap. 21.99 *(978-1-4346-3647-8(X))* Creative Media Partners, LLC.

—Bunny Brown & His Sister Sue at Christmas Tree Cove. 2007. (ENG.). 138p. pap. 18.99 *(978-1-4346-3592-1(9))*; 152p. pap. 21.99 *(978-1-4346-3593-8(7))* Creative Media Partners, LLC.

—Bunny Brown & his Sister Sue Giving a Show. 2007. (ENG.). 140p. per. 18.99 *(978-1-4346-2879-4(5))*; 156p. per. 21.99 *(978-1-4346-2914-2(7))* Creative Media Partners, LLC.

—Bunny Brown & His Sister Sue in the Sunny South. 2007. (ENG.). 138p. pap. 18.99 *(978-1-4346-3608-9(9))*; 152p. pap. 21.99 *(978-1-4346-3609-6(7))* Creative Media Partners, LLC.

—Bunny Brown & His Sister Sue on an Auto Tour. 2007. (ENG.). 138p. pap. 18.99 *(978-1-4346-2850-3(7))*; 152p. pap. 21.99 *(978-1-4346-2885-5(X))* Creative Media Partners, LLC.

—Bunny Brown & His Sister Sue on Grandpa's Farm. 2007. (ENG.). 144p. pap. 18.99 *(978-1-4346-3268-5(7))*; 156p. pap. 21.99 *(978-1-4346-3269-2(5))* Creative Media Partners, LLC.

Hopkins, Ellen. Identical. (ENG.). (YA). (gr. 9-18). 2010. 592p. pap. 12.99 *(978-1-4169-5006-6(0))* 2008. 576p. 17.99 *(978-1-4169-5005-9(2))* McElderry, Margaret K. Bks. (McElderry, Margaret K. Bks.).

—Smoke. (ENG., Illus.). (YA). (gr. 9). 2015. 576p. pap. 12.99 *(978-1-4169-8329-3(5))* 2013. 560p. 19.99 *(978-1-4169-8328-6(7))* McElderry, Margaret K. Bks. (McElderry, Margaret K. Bks.).

Hopkins, Jackie Mims. Three Armadillies Tuff, 1 vol. Brooks, S. G., illus. 2011. (ENG.). 32p. pap. 7.95 *(978-1-56145-598-0(9)*, Peachtree Junior) Peachtree Pubs.

Hopkins, K. C. The Night the Spirits Danced. 2008. 115p. pap. 15.00 *(978-0-615-23929-3(3))* Hopkins, KC.

Horowitz, Nancy Ellis. Nicely Dunn & the Lost Little Sister. 2009. 88p. pap. 30.49 *(978-1-4389-3011-4(9))* AuthorHouse.

Horrocks, Anita. What They Don't Know. braille ed. 2003. (J). (gr. 2). spiral bd. *(978-0-616-15267-6(1))* Canadian National Institute for the Blind/Institut National Canadien pour les Aveugles.

Howard, Elizabeth Fitzgerald. The Train to Lulu's. Casilla, Robert, illus. 2007. (ENG.). 36p. (J). (gr. -1-3). 10.99 *(978-1-4169-6161-1(5)*, Simon & Schuster/Paula Wiseman Bks.) Simon & Schuster/Paula Wiseman Bks.

Howland, Leila. The Brightest Stars of Summer. 2017. (Silver Sisters Ser.: 2). 384p. (J). (gr. 3-7). pap. 6.99 *(978-0-06-231873-2(X))* HarperCollins Pubs.

—The Forget-Me-Not Summer. Kim, Ji-Hyuk, illus. 2015. (Silver Sisters Ser.: 1). (ENG.). 352p. (J). (gr. 3-7). 16.99 *(978-0-06-231869-5(1))* HarperCollins Pubs.

—The Silver Moon of Summer. 2017. (Silver Sisters Ser.: 3). 304p. (J). (gr. 3-7). 16.99 *(978-0-06-231875-6(6))* HarperCollins Pubs.

Howson, Imogen. Linked. 2013. (ENG., Illus.). 368p. (YA). (gr. 7). 16.99 *(978-1-4424-4656-4(0)*, Simon & Schuster Bks. For Young Readers) Simon & Schuster Bks. For Young Readers.

—Unravel. 2014. (ENG., Illus.). 480p. (YA). (gr. 7). 17.99 *(978-1-4424-4658-8(7)*, Simon & Schuster Bks. For Young Readers) Simon & Schuster Bks. For Young Readers.

Howson, Imogen & Smith, Ali. Linked. 2014. (ENG., Illus.). 384p. (YA). (gr. 7). pap. 9.99 *(978-1-4424-4660-1(9)*, Simon & Schuster Bks. For Young Readers) Simon & Schuster Bks. For Young Readers.

Hudson, Katura J. I'm a Big Sister Now. 2009. 32p. pap. 6.95 *(978-1-60349-022-1(1)*, Marimba Bks.) Hudson Publishing Group, The.

Hulst, W. G. van de & Hulst, Willem G. van de, illus. The Woods Beyond the Wall. 2017. (J). *(978-1-928136-08-8(7))* Inheritance Pubns.

Human, Deborah. Pinky Promise. 2009. 40p. (J). pap. 11.99 *(978-0-9818374-0-6(9))* Writing Bench LLC., The.

Hummel, Jim. Imagination: On Planet Hic-Cup. 2013. 36p. pap. 15.49 *(978-1-4669-8903-0(3))* Trafford Publishing.

Hunt, Tiffani "Paradise". Glamorous 5: In the City of Garden Valley. 2012. 24p. pap. 17.99 *(978-1-4772-7922-9(9))* AuthorHouse.

Hunter, Jana. Trick or Treat. 2010. (Sleepover Club Ser.). (ENG., Illus.). 112p. (J). (gr. 2-6). pap. 6.99 *(978-0-00-727254-9(5)*, HarperCollins Children's Bks.) HarperCollins Pubs. Ltd. GBR. Dist: HarperCollins Pubs.

Hurley, Tonya. Homecoming. 2010. (Ghostgirl Ser.: 2). (ENG.). 304p. (YA). (gr. 7-17). pap. 10.00 *(978-0-316-08943-2(5))* Little, Brown Bks. for Young Readers.

Hyde, E. A. Watson. Little Sisters to the Camp Fire Girls. 2004. reprint ed. pap. 15.95 *(978-1-4179-9442-7(8))* Kessinger Publishing, LLC.

I'm a Big Sister! 2008. (I'm a Big Brother/Sister... Ser.). 32p. *(978-1-4075-0858-0(X))* Parragon, Inc.

Iorillo, Kristin. The Wacko Baby. 2011. 28p. pap. 15.99 *(978-1-4628-5792-0(2))* Xlibris Corp.

Isbell, Tom. The Capture. 2016. (Prey Trilogy Ser.: 2). 448p. (YA). (gr. 8). 17.99 *(978-0-06-221605-2(8)*, HarperTeen) HarperCollins Pubs.

—The Prey. 2015. (Prey Trilogy Ser.: 1). (ENG.). 416p. (YA). (gr. 8). 17.99 *(978-0-06-221601-4(5)*, HarperTeen) HarperCollins Pubs.

Ismail, Yasmeen. Christmas for Greta & Gracie. Ismail, Yasmeen, illus. 2016. (ENG., Illus.). 32p. (J). (gr. -1-2). 15.99 *(978-0-7636-8943-8(2)*, Nosy Crow) Candlewick Pr.

Israel, Julie. Juniper Lemon's Happiness Index. 2017. (ENG.). 352p. (YA). (gr. 7). 17.99 ***(978-0-7352-2817-7(5)***, Kathy Dawson Books) Penguin Young Readers Group.

Ius, Dawn. Overdrive. 2016. (ENG., Illus.). 352p. (YA). (gr. 9). 17.99 *(978-1-4814-3944-2(8)*, Simon Pulse) Simon Pulse.

Jacobs, Caroline E. The S. W. F. Club. 2007. (ENG.). 120p. pap. 18.99 *(978-1-4346-2899-2(X))*; 134p. pap. 19.99 *(978-1-4346-2900-5(7))* Creative Media Partners, LLC.

Jacobson, Jennifer Richard. The Complete History of Why I Hate Her. 2010. (ENG.). 192p. (YA). (gr. 7-18). 16.99 *(978-0-689-87800-8(1)*, Atheneum/Richard Jackson Bks.) Simon & Schuster Children's Publishing.

Jaden, Denise. Losing Faith. 2010. (ENG.). 400p. (YA). (gr. 9-18). pap. 9.99 *(978-1-4169-9609-5(5)*, Simon Pulse) Simon Pulse.

—Never Enough. 2012. (ENG.). 400p. (YA). (gr. 9). pap. 9.99 *(978-1-4424-2907-9(0)*, Simon Pulse) Simon Pulse.

Jarzab, Anna. The Opposite of Hallelujah. 2013. (ENG.). 464p. (YA). (gr. 7). pap. 10.99 *(978-0-375-85529-0(7)*, Ember) Random Hse. Children's Bks.

Jasper, Elizabeth. The Golden Cuckoo. 2013. 102p. (J). pap. *(978-1-78299-195-3(6))* FeedARead.com.

Jefferson, Jewell E. I'm Going to Be A Big Sister! 2008. 20p. 12.25 *(978-1-4357-0907-2(1))* Lulu Pr., Inc.

Jenkins, Carla LaVern. The Disappearance of Mrs. Brown: A Jenkins Girl Mystery. 2010. 72p. 23.55 *(978-1-4269-4537-3(X))*; pap. 13.55 *(978-1-4251-6659-5(8))* Trafford Publishing.

Jiya, Tapiwa. The Epic of Goz. 2008. 144p. pap. 11.99 *(978-1-4343-5730-4(9))* AuthorHouse.

Jocelyn, Marthe. Mable Riley: A Reliable Record of Humdrum, Peril, & Romance. 2007. 279p. (gr. 4-7). 17.00 *(978-0-7569-8183-9(2))* Perfection Learning Corp.

—Would You. 2008. (ENG.). 176p. (YA). (gr. 4-7). 19.99 *(978-0-88776-816-3(4)*, Tundra Bks.) Tundra Bks. CAN. Dist: Penguin Random Hse. LLC.

Johnson, Angela. A Cool Moonlight. 2005. (ENG.). 144p. (J). (gr. 3-7). reprint ed. 6.99 *(978-0-14-240284-9(2)*, Puffin Books) Penguin Young Readers Group.

Johnson, Gillian. My Sister Gracie. 2005. (ENG., Illus.). 32p. (J). (gr. -1-k). pap. 7.95 *(978-0-88776-750-0(8)*, Tundra Bks.) Tundra Bks. CAN. Dist: Penguin Random Hse. LLC.

Johnson, Janie, compiled by. Up from the Cotton Fields. 2003. 114p. per. 29.95 net. *(978-0-9718254-8-2(3))* Excel Digital Pr.

Johnson, Maureen. The Key to the Golden Firebird. 2004. (ENG.). 304p. (J). (gr. 7-18). 15.99 *(978-0-06-054138-5(5))* HarperCollins Pubs.

Johnson, Michael E. Barley & Betsy: Journey #1 A cat & dog's great adventure to the Mall. Atchley, Kendra, illus. 2011. 36p. pap. 24.95 *(978-1-4560-4077-2(4))* America Star Bks.

Johnson, Young, et al. Princess Hope & the Hidden Treasure, 1 vol. Aranda, Omar, illus. 2012. (I Can Read! / Princess Parables Ser.). (ENG.). 32p. (J). pap. 3.99 *(978-0-310-73250-1(6))* Zonderkidz.

Johnston, Carol Shaw. Lily & Sophie: Sisters & Best Friends. 2010. 65p. pap. 26.99 *(978-0-557-35894-6(9))* Lulu Pr., Inc.

Johnston, Julie. A Very Fine Line. 2006. (ENG.). 208p. (J). (gr. 5). 18.95 *(978-0-88776-746-3(X)*, Tundra Bks.) Tundra Bks. CAN. Dist: Penguin Random Hse. LLC.

Jones, Patrick. On Guard. 2016. (Bounce Ser.). (ENG.). 104p. (YA). (gr. 6-12). lib. bdg. 26.65 *(978-1-5124-1123-2(X)*, Darby Creek) Lerner Publishing Group.

Jordan, Sophie. Firelight. (Firelight Ser.: 1). (ENG.). (YA). (gr. 8). 2011. 352p. pap. 9.99 *(978-0-06-193509-1(3))* 2010. 336p. 16.99 *(978-0-06-193508-4(5))* HarperCollins Pubs.

Juby, Susan & Wells, Rosemary. The Truth Commission. 2015. (ENG., Illus.). 320p. (YA). (gr. 9). bds. 18.99 *(978-0-451-46877-2(5)*, Viking Books for Young Readers) Penguin Young Readers Group.

Jules, Jacqueline. The Marigold Mess. Smith, Kim, illus. 2015. (Sofia Martinez Ser.). (ENG.). 32p. (gr. k-2). lib. bdg. 21.32 *(978-1-4795-5776-9(5)*, Sofia Martinez) Picture Window Bks.

—The Missing Mouse. Smith, Kim, illus. 2015. (Sofia Martinez Ser.). (ENG.). 32p. (gr. k-2). lib. bdg. 21.32 *(978-1-4795-5774-5(9)*, Sofia Martinez) Picture Window Bks.

—Picture Perfect. Smith, Kim, illus. 2015. (Sofia Martinez Ser.). (ENG.). 32p. (gr. k-2). lib. bdg. 21.32 *(978-1-4795-5773-8(0)*, Sofia Martinez) Picture Window Bks.

Julius, Jessica. A New Reindeer Friend. 2015. lib. bdg. 13.55 *(978-0-606-36680-9(6))* Turtleback Bks.

—A New Reindeer Friend (Disney Frozen) RH Disney Staff, illus. 2015. (Little Golden Book Ser.). (ENG.). 24p. (J). (-k). 4.99 *(978-0-7364-3351-8(1)*, Golden/Disney) Random Hse. Children's Bks.

Juwayriyah, Umm & Ayed, Juwayriyah. Hind's Hands: A Story about Autism. Apple, Emma, illus. 2013. 16p. (J). pap. 6.00 *(978-1-935437-76-5(3)*, As Sabr Pubns.) Imago Pr.

Kadohata, Cynthia. Kira-Kira. (ENG., Illus.). (J). (gr. 5-9). 2004. 256p. 17.99 *(978-0-689-85639-6(3))* 2006. 272p. reprint ed. pap. 7.99 *(978-0-689-85640-2(7))* Simon & Schuster Children's Publishing. (Atheneum Bks. for Young Readers).

—Outside Beauty. (ENG.). (YA). (gr. 7). 2009. 288p. pap. 8.99 *(978-1-4169-9818-1(7))* 2008. (Illus.). 272p. 16.99 *(978-0-689-86575-6(9))* Simon & Schuster Children's Publishing. (Atheneum Bks. for Young Readers).

Kain, Jamie. The Good Sister. 2015. (ENG.). 304p. (YA). (gr. 9-12). pap. 9.99 *(978-1-250-04774-8(9)*, 9781250047748, St. Martin's Griffin) St. Martin's Pr.

Kato, Shakila Maria Inviolata & Kato, Sharifa Maria Inviolata. The Adventures by the Magic Bicycle. 2012. 134p. 24.95 *(978-1-4137-5716-3(2))* America Star Bks.

Katschke, Judy, et al. Bye-Bye Boyfriend, 3 vols. 2003. (ENG., Illus.). 112p. *(978-0-00-714467-9(9)*, HarperCollins Children's Bks.) HarperCollins Pubs. Ltd.

Katz, Bebe Weinberg. Princess Claudia & the Freckles. 2007. 48p. per. 16.95 *(978-1-4241-6446-2(X))* America Star Bks.

Katz, Karen. Best-Ever Big Sister. 2006. (ENG., Illus.). 14p. (J). (gr. -1-k). 6.99 *(978-0-448-43915-0(8)*, Grosset & Dunlap) Penguin Young Readers Group.

Kauffman, Christopher G. Faith's Star. Jenkins, Jacqueline, illus. 2011. 32p. pap. 24.95 *(978-1-4560-9584-0(6))* America Star Bks.

Kaupp, Rosemarie. The Amberella Tales: Amberella in the City. 2012. 120p. (gr. 4-6). 22.33 *(978-1-4669-0594-8(8))*; pap. 12.33 *(978-1-4669-0595-5(6))* Trafford Publishing.

Kawashita, Mizuki. Ichigo 100% Sweet Little Sister, Vol. 7. (JPN., Illus.). 180p. (YA). pap. *(978-4-08-873518-4(8))* Shuei-Sha.

Kay, Susan. Abby & Gabby Tales. 2009. 16p. pap. 9.99 *(978-1-4389-6467-6(6))* AuthorHouse.

Kehret, Peg. Runaway Twin. 2011. (ENG.). 208p. (J). (gr. 5-18). 6.99 *(978-0-14-241849-9(8)*, Puffin Books) Penguin Young Readers Group.

Kelley, Jane. The Girl Behind the Glass. 2012. (ENG.). 192p. (J). (gr. 4-7). pap. 6.99 *(978-0-375-86219-9(6)*, Yearling) Random Hse. Children's Bks.

Kelly, Erin Entrada. Hello, Universe. Roxas, Isabel, illus. 2017. 320p. (J). (gr. 3-7). 16.99 *(978-0-06-241415-1(1)*, Greenwillow Bks.) HarperCollins Pubs.

—The Land of Forgotten Girls. (J). (gr. 3-7). 2017. 320p. pap. 6.99 *(978-0-06-223865-8(5))* 2016. 304p. 16.99 *(978-0-06-223864-1(7))* HarperCollins Pubs. (Greenwillow Bks.).

Kelly, J. M. Speed of Life. 2016. (ENG.). 352p. (YA). (gr. 9). 17.99 *(978-0-544-74782-1(6)*, HMH Books For Young Readers) Houghton Mifflin Harcourt Publishing Co.

Kerry, Mary. Saving the Scrolls. 2003. 159p. (J). (gr. 4-7). 16.95 *(978-1-888842-30-2(X))* Absey & Co.

Khan, Rukhsana. Big Red Lollipop. Blackall, Sophie, illus. 2010. (ENG.). 40p. (J). (gr. -1-3). 16.99 *(978-0-670-06287-4(1)*, Viking Books for Young Readers) Penguin Young Readers Group.

Kiernan, Kristy. Catching Genius. 2007. (ENG.). 384p. (gr. 12-18). 15.00 *(978-0-425-21435-0(4)*, Berkley) Penguin Publishing Group.

Kilgus, Walter C. Bess Takes a Ride. 2008. 36p. pap. 17.49 *(978-1-4257-8807-0(6))* Xlibris Corp.

Kim, Cecil. The Three Pig Sisters. Park, Keun, illus. 2014. (MySELF Bookshelf Ser.). (ENG.). 32p. (J). (gr. k-2). pap. 11.94 *(978-1-60357-689-5(4))*; lib. bdg. 25.27 *(978-1-59953-654-5(4))* Norwood Hse. Pr.

Klein, Abby. April Fool's Surprise. McKinley, John, illus. 2012. (Double Trouble Ser.: Vol. 2). (ENG.). 96p. (J). (gr. -1-3). pap. 5.99 *(978-0-545-29495-9(9)*, Scholastic Paperbacks) Scholastic, Inc.

Kleinman, Estelle. The Penderwicks: A Study Guide. Friedland, Joyce & Kessler, Rikki, eds. 2008. (Novel-Ties Ser.). (Illus.). 39p. pap. 16.95 *(978-0-7675-1488-0(2))* Learning Links Inc.

Knight, Karsten. Afterglow. 2013. (ENG., Illus.). 336p. (YA). (gr. 9). 17.99 *(978-1-4424-5037-0(1)*, Simon & Schuster Bks. For Young Readers) Simon & Schuster Bks. For Young Readers.

—Embers & Echoes. (ENG.). (YA). (gr. 9). 2013. Illus.). 496p. pap. 9.99 *(978-1-4424-5035-6(5))* 2012. 480p. 16.99 *(978-1-4424-5030-1(4))* Simon & Schuster Bks. For Young Readers. (Simon & Schuster Bks. For Young Readers).

—Wildefire. 2011. (ENG.). 400p. (YA). (gr. 9-18). 16.99 *(978-1-4424-2117-2(7)*, Simon & Schuster Bks. For Young Readers) Simon & Schuster Bks. For Young Readers.

Knudsen, Michelle. El Caso de Vivian la Vampira. Wummer, Amy, illus. 2008. (Science Solves It! en Espanol Ser.). (SPA.). 32p. (J). (gr. -1-3). pap. 5.95 *(978-1-57565-277-1(3))* Kane Press, Inc.

—El Caso de Vivian la Vampira (the Case of Vampire Vivian) Wummer, Amy, illus. 2009. (Science Solves It! (r) en Espanol Ser.). (SPA.). (gr. 1-3). pap. 33.92 *(978-0-7613-4800-9(X))* Lerner Publishing Group.

Knudson, Michelle. The Case of Vampire Vivian. Wummer, Amy, illus. 2003. (Science Solves It! Ser.). 32p. (J). pap. 5.95 *(978-1-57565-127-9(0))* Kane Press, Inc.

Koontz, Robin. Zelda la Cenicienta. 2012. (SPA & ENG.). 24p. (gr. 2-3). pap. 8.95 *(978-1-61810-544-8(2))* Rourke Educational Media.

Korba, Joanna. Cindy Eller Plays Ball: A Modern-Day Cinderella Tale. 2006. (J). pap. *(978-1-4108-6164-1(3))* Benchmark Education Co.

Korngold, Jamie S. Mazel Tov! It's a Boy: Mazel Tov! It's a Girl. Finkelstein, Jeff, illus. Finkelstein, Jeff, photos by. 2015. (J). (ENG.). 32p. (gr. -1-1). lib. bdg. 17.95 *(978-1-4677-1957-5(9))*; 6.99 *(978-1-4677-6206-9(7))* Lerner Publishing Group. (Kar-Ben Publishing).

—Sadie's Sukkah Breakfast. Fortenberry, Julie, illus. 2011. (Sukkot & Simchat Torah Ser.). (ENG.). 24p. (J). (gr. -1-1). pap. 7.95 *(978-0-7613-5648-6(7))*; lib. bdg. 16.95 *(978-0-7613-5647-9(9))* Lerner Publishing Group. (Kar-Ben Publishing).

Kraus, Joanna H. A Night of Tamales & Roses. Caravela, Elena, illus. 2007. (ENG.). 32p. (J). (gr. -1-3). 15.95 *(978-0-9726614-4-7(1))* Shenanigan Bks.

Krauss, Trisha. Charlotte's Very Own Dress. 2016. (ENG., Illus.). 40p. (J). (gr. -1-2). 16.99 *(978-0-553-52095-8(4)*, Random Hse. Bks. for Young Readers) Random Hse. Children's Bks.

Kuipers, Alice. Lost for Words. 2010. 224p. (YA). (gr. 8-18). 16.99 *(978-0-06-142922-4(8)*, HarperTeen) HarperCollins Pubs.

Kurilovitch, Mike. Silly Sisters. 2012. 32p. pap. 18.48 *(978-1-4772-6011-1(0))* AuthorHouse.

Kurtagich, Dawn. And the Trees Crept In. (ENG.). (gr. 10-17). 2017. 368p. (J). pap. 9.99 ***(978-0-316-29871-1(9))*** 2016. 352p. (YA). 17.99 *(978-0-316-29870-4(0))* Little, Brown Bks. for Young Readers.

Kvasnosky, Laura McGee. The Big Picture. Kvasnosky, Laura McGee, illus. 2010. (Zelda & Ivy Ser.). (ENG., Illus.). 48p. (J). (gr. k-4). 14.99 *(978-0-7636-4180-1(4))* Candlewick Pr.

—Keeping Secrets. Kvasnosky, Laura McGee, illus. 2009. (Zelda & Ivy Ser.). (ENG., Illus.). 48p. (J). (gr. k-4). 15.99 *(978-0-7636-4179-5(0))* Candlewick Pr.

—The Runaways. Kvasnosky, Laura McGee, illus. 2006. (Zelda & Ivy Ser.). (ENG., Illus.). 48p. (J). (gr. k-4). 14.99 *(978-0-7636-2689-1(9))* Candlewick Pr.

—The Runaways. 2007. (Zelda & Ivy Ser.). (Illus.). 42p. (J). (gr. -1-3). 12.65 *(978-0-7569-8140-2(9))* Perfection Learning Corp.

—Zelda & Ivy - Keeping Secrets. Kvasnosky, Laura McGee, illus. 2013. (Candlewick Sparks Ser.). (ENG., Illus.). 48p. (J). (gr. k-4). pap. 3.99 *(978-0-7636-6636-1(X))* Candlewick Pr.

—Zelda & Ivy - The Big Picture. Kvasnosky, Laura McGee, illus. 2013. (Candlewick Sparks Ser.). (ENG., Illus.). 48p. (J). (gr. k-4). pap. 3.99 *(978-0-7636-6637-8(8))* Candlewick Pr.

—Zelda & Ivy - The Runaways. Kvasnosky, Laura McGee, illus. 2013. (Candlewick Sparks Ser.). (ENG., Illus.). 48p. (J). (gr. k-4). pap. 3.99 *(978-0-7636-6635-4(1))* Candlewick Pr.

—Zelda & Ivy & the Boy Next Door. Kvasnosky, Laura McGee, illus. (Candlewick Sparks Ser.). (ENG., Illus.). 40p. (J). (gr. k-4). 2014. pap. 3.99 *(978-0-7636-7182-2(7))* 2008. 15.99 *(978-0-7636-4004-0(2))* Candlewick Pr.
—Zelda & Ivy One Christmas. Kvasnosky, Laura McGee, illus. 2013. (Candlewick Sparks Ser.). (ENG., Illus.). 40p. (J). (gr. k-4). pap. 3.99 *(978-0-7636-6865-5(6))* Candlewick Pr.
Lagonegro, Melissa. Frozen - A Tale of Two Sisters. 2013. (Disney Princess Step into Reading Ser.). lib. bdg. 13.55 *(978-0-606-32205-8(1)*, Turtleback) Turtleback Bks.
Lake, Donna C. The Big Sister. 2011. 24p. pap. 15.99 *(978-1-4628-5250-5(5))* Xlibris Corp.
Lambert, Mary E. Family Game Night & Other Catastrophes. 2017. (ENG.). 256p. (J). (gr. 3-7). 16.99 *(978-0-545-93198-4(3)*, Scholastic Pr.) Scholastic, Inc.
Lambert, Megan Dowd & Daniels, Peter. Real Sisters Pretend, 1 vol. Carmb, Sara Lynn & Tadgell, Nicole, illus. 2016. (ENG.). 32p. (J). (gr. k-5). 17.95 *(978-0-88448-441-7(6)*, 884441) Tilbury Hse. Pubs.
Lane, Dakota. Orpheus Obsession. 2005. (Illus.). 288p. (J). lib. bdg. 17.89 *(978-0-06-074174-7(0)*, HarperTeen) HarperCollins Pubs.
—The Orpheus Obsession. 2008. (ENG., Illus.). 288p. (YA). (gr. 9). pap. 8.99 *(978-0-06-074175-4(9)*, HarperTeen) HarperCollins Pubs.
Langer, Dana. Siren Sisters. 2017. (ENG., Illus.). 256p. (J). (gr. 4-8). 16.99 *(978-1-4814-6686-8(0)*, Simon & Schuster/Paula Wiseman Bks.) Simon & Schuster/Paula Wiseman Bks.
LaReau, Kara. Unintentional Adventures of the Bland Sisters. Hill, Jen, illus. 2017. (ENG.). 176p. (J). (gr. 3-7). 14.95 *(978-1-4197-2136-6(4)*, Amulet Bks.) Abrams, Inc.
Larsen, Kirsten. Tara Pays Up! Billin-Frye, Paige, illus. 2006. (Social Studies Connects). 32p. (J). (gr. 1-3). pap. 5.95 *(978-1-57565-187-3(4))* Kane Press, Inc.
Las dos Hermanas: Lap Book. (Pebble Soup Exploraciones Ser.). (SPA.). 16p. (gr. -1-18). 21.00 *(978-0-7578-1692-5(4))* Rigby Education.
Las dos Hermanas: Small Book. (Pebble Soup Exploraciones Ser.). (SPA.). 16p. (gr. -1-18). 5.00 *(978-0-7578-1732-8(7))* Rigby Education.
Laure, Estelle. This Raging Light. 2015. (ENG.). 288p. (YA). (gr. 9). 17.99 *(978-0-544-53429-2(8)*, HMH Books For Young Readers) Houghton Mifflin Harcourt Publishing Co.
Lauter, Richard, illus. Little Women. (Young Collector's Illustrated Classics Ser.). 192p. (J). 9.95 *(978-1-56156-371-5(4))* Kidsbooks, LLC.
Lazebnik, Claire. Epic Fail. 2011. (ENG.). 304p. (YA). (gr. 8-18). pap. 9.99 *(978-0-06-192126-1(2)*, HarperTeen) HarperCollins Pubs.
—Things I Should Have Known. 2017. (ENG.). 320p. (YA). (gr. 7). 17.99 *(978-0-544-82969-5(7)*, HMH Books For Young Readers) Houghton Mifflin Harcourt Publishing Co.
Leaver, Trisha. The Secrets We Keep. 2015. (ENG.). 304p. (YA). (gr. 7). 17.99 *(978-0-374-30046-3(1)*, Farrar, Straus & Giroux (BYR)) Farrar, Straus & Giroux.
Leavitt, Lindsey. Going Vintage. 2013. (ENG.). 320p. (YA). (gr. 7-12). 16.99 *(978-1-59990-787-1(9)*, 9781599907871, Bloomsbury USA Childrens) Bloomsbury Publishing USA.
Leprechaun, Seamus T. The o'Shea Chronicles. 2013. 312p. pap. *(978-1-78407-190-5(0))* FeedARead.com.
Levine, Gail Carson. The Two Princesses of Bamarre. (J). 2012. (ENG.). 272p. (gr. 3-7). pap. 6.99 *(978-0-06-440966-7(X))* 2004. (Illus.). 304p. (gr. 7-18). reprint ed. pap. 6.99 *(978-0-06-057580-9(8))* HarperCollins Pubs.
Levinson, Robin K. Miriam's Journey: Discovering a New World. 2006. (Illus.). 64p. (J). per. 12.00 *(978-0-9773673-0-6(4))* Gali Girls, Inc.
Levy, Janice. Flip-Flop & the Absolutely Awful New Baby, 1 vol. Madden, Colleen M., illus. 2011. (Flip-Flop Adventure Ser.). (ENG.). 32p. (J). (gr. k-3). 28.50 *(978-1-61641-651-5(3))* Magic Wagon.
Lichtwardt, Rita, illus. Barbie - A Perfect Christmas. 2011. (Book & Jewelry Ser.). (ENG.). 24p. (J). (gr. -1-1). 10.99 *(978-0-7944-2319-3(1)*, Reader's Digest Children's Bks.) Studio Fun International.
Lieurance, Suzanne. The Locket: Surviving the Triangle Shirtwaist Fire. 2008. (Historical Fiction Adventures (HFA) Ser.). (Illus.). 160p. (J). (gr. 3-7). lib. bdg. 29.27 *(978-0-7660-2928-6(X))* Enslow Pubs., Inc.
Lilly-Lolly Little-Legs: Individual Title, 6 packs. (Literatura 2000 Ser.). (gr. 1-2). 28.00 *(978-0-7635-0095-5(X))* Rigby Education.
Lin, Grace. Ling & Ting: Not Exactly the Same! (Passport to Reading Level 3 Ser.). (ENG.). 48p. (J). (gr. 1-4). 2011. pap. 3.99 *(978-0-316-02453-2(8))* 2010. (Illus.). 14.99 *(978-0-316-02452-5(X))* Little, Brown Bks. for Young Readers.
—Ling & Ting: Together in All Weather. 2015. (ENG., Illus.). 48p. (J). (gr. 1-4). 16.00 *(978-0-316-33549-2(5))* Little Brown & Co.
—Ling & Ting Share a Birthday. (ENG.). 48p. (J). (gr. 1-4). 2014. pap. 4.99 *(978-0-316-18404-5(7))* 2013. (Illus.). 15.00 *(978-0-316-18405-2(5))* Little, Brown Bks. for Young Readers.
—Ling & Ting Share a Birthday. 2014. (Passport to Reading Level 3 Ser.). (J). lib. bdg. 14.75 *(978-0-606-35932-0(X))* Turtleback Bks.
—Ling & Ting: Together in All Weather. 2016. (ENG.). 48p. (J). (gr. 1-4). pap. 4.99 *(978-0-316-33548-5(7))* Little, Brown Bks. for Young Readers.
—Ling & Ting: Twice As Silly. 2014. (ENG., Illus.). 48p. (J). (gr. 1-4). 16.00 *(978-0-316-18402-1(0))* Little, Brown Bks. for Young Readers.
Lindman. Flicka, Ricka, Dicka & the Little Dog. Lindman, illus. 2013. (Flicka, Ricka, Dicka Ser.). (ENG., Illus.). 32p. (J). (gr. k-3). 9.99 *(978-0-8075-2509-8(X))* Whitman, Albert & Co.
—Flicka, Ricka, Dicka & the Strawberries. Lindman, illus. 2013. (Flicka, Ricka, Dicka Ser.). (ENG., Illus.). 32p. (J). (gr. k-3). 9.99 *(978-0-8075-2512-8(X))* Whitman, Albert & Co.
—Flicka, Ricka, Dicka & the Three Kittens. Lindman, illus. 2013. (Flicka, Ricka, Dicka Ser.). (ENG., Illus.). 32p. (J). (gr. k-3). 9.99 *(978-0-8075-2515-9(4))* Whitman, Albert & Co.
—Flicka, Ricka, Dicka & Their New Skates: Updated Edition with Paperdolls. Lindman, illus. 2011. (Flicka, Ricka, Dicka Ser.). (ENG., Illus.). 32p. (J). (gr. k-3). 9.99 *(978-0-8075-2496-1(4))* Whitman, Albert & Co.
—Flicka, Ricka, Dicka Bake a Cake. Lindman, illus. 2013. (Flicka, Ricka, Dicka Ser.). (ENG., Illus.). 32p. (J). (gr. k-3). 9.99 *(978-0-8075-2506-7(5))* Whitman, Albert & Co.
Lindman, Maj. Flicka, Ricka, Dicka & the New Dotted Dresses. Lindman, Maj, illus. 2012. (Flicka, Ricka, Dicka Ser.). (ENG., Illus.). 32p. (J). (gr. k-3). 9.99 *(978-0-8075-2484-8(0))* Whitman, Albert & Co.
—Flicka, Ricka, Dicka & Their New Skates. Lindman, Maj, illus. 2011. (ENG., Illus.). 32p. (J). (gr. k-3). 9.99 *(978-0-8075-2491-6(3))* Whitman, Albert & Co.
—Flicka, Ricka, Dicka Go to Market. Lindman, Maj, illus. 2012. (ENG., Illus.). 32p. (J). (gr. -1-3). 9.99 *(978-0-8075-2478-7(6))*; (gr. k-3). 9.99 *(978-0-8075-2479-4(4))* Whitman, Albert & Co.
Liniers. The Big Wet Balloon (El Globo Grande y Mojado) Liniers, illus. 2013. (ENG & SPA., Illus.). 32p. (J). (gr. -1-3). 12.95 *(978-1-935179-40-5(3))* TOON Books / RAW Junior, LLC.
—The Big Wet Balloon (El Globo Grande y Mojado) Liniers, illus. 2013. (ENG & SPA., Illus.). 32p. (J). (gr. -1-3). pap. 4.99 *(978-1-935179-39-9(X))* TOON Books / RAW Junior, LLC.
Liniers, Ricardo. The Big Wet Balloon. Liniers, Ricardo, illus. 2013. (ENG., Illus.). 32p. (J). (gr. -1-3). 12.95 *(978-1-935179-32-0(2))* TOON Books / RAW Junior, LLC.
Lipinski, Maureen. Cleopatra Ascending. 2013. (Shadow's Edge Novel Ser.: 2). (ENG.). 240p. (YA). pap. 9.99 *(978-0-7387-3193-3(5)*, Flux) North Star Editions.
Lispi, Robert. Buddy Hawk: Story of Buddy Hawk. 2005. (J). pap. 8.00 *(978-0-8059-6602-2(1))* Dorrance Publishing Co., Inc.
Little, Ashley. The New Normal, 1 vol. 2013. (ENG.). 232p. (YA). (gr. 8-12). pap. 12.95 *(978-1-4598-0074-8(5))* Orca Bk. Pubs. USA.
Little Reader Digital Storybook: Cinderella. 2005. (J). cd-rom 8.99 *(978-0-9767657-7-6(2))* Mullings Media.
Littman, Sarah Darer. Backlash. 2015. (ENG.). 336p. (J). (gr. 7). 17.99 *(978-0-545-65126-4(3)*, Scholastic Pr.) Scholastic, Inc.
Liv‡n, Paco. WHAT A SNOUT! 2007. (ENG., Illus.). 48p. (J). 18.95 *(978-84-96788-87-9(3))* OQO, Editora ESP. Dist: Baker & Taylor Bks.
Lloyd-Jones, Sally. How to Be a Baby: By Me, the Big Sister. Heap, Sue, illus. 2007. (How to Ser.). (ENG.). 40p. (J). (gr. -1-3). 16.99 *(978-0-375-83843-9(0)*, Schwartz & Wade Bks.) Random Hse. Children's Bks.
—How to Be a Baby... by Me, the Big Sister. Heap, Sue, illus. 2011. (How to Ser.). (ENG.). 40p. (J). (gr. -1-3). pap. 7.99 *(978-0-375-87388-1(0)*, Dragonfly Bks.) Random Hse. Children's Bks.
The Lonely. 2014. (ENG.). 288p. (YA). pap. 9.99 *(978-0-7387-4133-8(7)*, Flux) North Star Editions.
López, Diana. Choke. 2012. (ENG.). 240p. (J). (gr. 7). 17.99 *(978-0-545-41822-5(4))* Scholastic, Inc.
Lopuszynski, Barbara. Angel & Brie. 2013. (ENG.). 246p. (YA). pap. 14.95 *(978-1-4787-0886-5(7))* Outskirts Pr., Inc.
Love, Jessica. In Real Life: A Novel. 2016. (ENG.). 240p. (YA). 18.99 *(978-1-250-06471-4(6)*, 9781250064714, St. Martin's Griffin) St. Martin's Pr.
Lovelady, W. f. The Adventures of Johnny Saturday: Back to the Drawing Board. 2012. 76p. pap. 12.95 *(978-1-4685-5286-7(4))* AuthorHouse.
Lowrey, Becky. Chirps. 2004. 45p. pap. 24.95 *(978-1-4137-2984-9(3))* PublishAmerica, Inc.
Lucas, Luke. Falls the Shadow. 2014. (ENG., Illus.). 352p. (YA). (gr. 7). 18.99 *(978-1-4424-9753-5(X)*, Simon & Schuster Bks. For Young Readers) Simon & Schuster Bks. For Young Readers.
MacColl, Michaela & Nichols, Rosemary. Rory's Promise. 2014. (Hidden Histories Ser.). (ENG.). 288p. (J). (gr. 4-7). 16.95 *(978-1-62091-623-0(1)*, Calkins Creek) Boyds Mills Pr.
MacDonald, Betty Bard. Nancy & Plum. GrandPré, Mary, illus. 2011. (ENG.). 240p. (J). (gr. 3-7). 7.99 *(978-0-375-85986-1(1)*, Yearling) Random Hse. Children's Bks.
MacGregor, Doug. The Incredible Tongue Twister That Swallowed My Sister: Another Santa Story by Doug MacGregor. MacGregor, Doug, illus. ltd. ed. 2006. (Illus.). 40p. (J). per. *(978-0-9654843-5-0(1))* MacGregor, Doug.
MacHoka, Rebecca. The Dog Sisters: One Missing Sister. 2010. 36p. pap. 15.49 *(978-1-4490-8306-9(4))* AuthorHouse.
MacIntyre, R. P. Revved. 2006. (ENG.). 220p. pap. 12.95 *(978-1-894345-46-0(0))* Thistledown Pr., Ltd. CAN. Dist: Univ. of Toronto Pr.
Mackall, Dandi Daley. Please Reply! 2004. 128p. (J). pap. 5.99 *(978-1-4003-0328-1(1))* Nelson, Thomas Inc.
MacKey, Cindy. My Sister Sophie. Tebbit, Jake, illus. 2013. 30p. pap. 12.99 *(978-0-9892699-9-5(X))* Cyrano Bks.
Maddox, Jake & Berne, Emma Carlson. Rebound Time, 1 vol. Wood, Katie, illus. 2013. (Jake Maddox Girl Sports Stories Ser.). (ENG.). 72p. (gr. 2-3). pap. 5.95 *(978-1-4342-4202-0(1))*; lib. bdg. 25.32 *(978-1-4342-4013-2(4))* Stone Arch Bks.
Madison, Alan. Velma Gratch & the Way Cool Butterfly. Hawkes, Kevin, illus. 2007. (ENG.). 40p. (J). (gr. -1-3). 17.99 *(978-0-375-83597-1(0)*, Schwartz & Wade Bks.) Random Hse. Children's Bks.
—Velma Gratch & the Way Cool Butterfly. Hawkes, Kevin, illus. 2012. (ENG.). 40p. (J). (gr. -1-3). pap. 7.99 *(978-0-307-97804-2(4)*, Dragonfly Bks.) Random Hse. Children's Bks.
Madison, Jefferson & Madison, Juliet. Sight: The Delta Girls - Book One. 2015. (Delta Girls Ser.: 1). (ENG.). 218p. pap. 14.99 *(978-1-62681-551-3(8))* Diversion Publishing Corp.
Madonna, pseud. Big-Sister Blues, No. 5. Fulvimari, Jeffrey, illus. 2008. (English Roses Ser.: 5). (ENG.). 128p. (J). (gr. 3-7). 10.99 *(978-0-14-241093-6(4)*, Puffin Books) Penguin Young Readers Group.
Magnin, Joyce. Cake: Love, Chickens, & a Taste of Peculiar, 1 vol. Ivanov, Alexsey & Ivanov, Olga, illus. 2013. (ENG.). 224p. (J). 14.99 *(978-0-310-73333-1(2))* Zonderkidz.
Magor, Dianne M. Ed. Lauren's Wish. 2012. 32p. (-18). pap. 21.99 *(978-1-4691-3986-9(3))* Xlibris Corp.
Mahoney, Tammy. Eddie the Eagle Learns to Fly. 2012. 24p. pap. 19.99 *(978-1-4772-1747-4(9))* AuthorHouse.
Maizel, Rebecca. Between Us & the Moon. 2015. (ENG.). 384p. (YA). (gr. 9). 17.99 *(978-0-06-232761-1(5))* HarperCollins Pubs.
Make Believe Ideas. Katie the Candy Cane Fairy Storybook. 2013. (ENG.). 32p. (J). 15.99 *(978-1-78235-526-7(X))* Make Believe Ideas GBR. Dist: Nelson, Thomas Inc.
Maloney, Brenna. Philomena's New Glasses. 2017. (ENG., Illus.). 40p. (J). (gr. -1-1). 16.99 ***(978-0-425-28814-6(5)***, Viking Books for Young Readers) Penguin Young Readers Group.
Malouf, Juman. The Trilogy of Two. 2015. (ENG.). 416p. (J). (gr. 5-7). 17.99 *(978-0-399-17114-7(2)*, G.P. Putnam's Sons Books for Young Readers) Penguin Young Readers Group.
Man-Kong, Mary. A Boo-Tiful Halloween! Riley, Kellee, illus. 2013. (Pictureback(R) Ser.). (ENG.). 16p. (J). (gr. -1-2). 4.99 *(978-0-449-81860-2(8)*, Random Hse. Bks. for Young Readers) Random Hse. Children's Bks.
Man-Kong, Mary & Tillworth, Mary. A Perfect Christmas (Barbie) Golden Books Staff, illus. 2011. (Pictureback(R) Ser.). (ENG.). 16p. (J). (gr. -1-2). pap. 3.99 *(978-0-375-87363-8(5)*, Random Hse. Bks. for Young Readers) Random Hse. Children's Bks.
Mann, Jennifer Ann. Sunny Sweet Can So Get Lost. 2015. (Sunny Sweet Ser.). (ENG., Illus.). 208p. (YA). (gr. 3-6). 15.99 *(978-1-61963-505-0(4)*, 9781619635050, Bloomsbury USA Childrens) Bloomsbury Publishing USA.
—Sunny Sweet Is So Dead Meat. (Sunny Sweet Ser.). (ENG., Illus.). 208p. (YA). (gr. 3-6). 2015. pap. 6.99 *(978-1-61963-563-0(1)*, 9781619635630) 2014. 15.99 *(978-1-59990-978-3(2)*, 9781599909783) Bloomsbury Publishing USA. (Bloomsbury USA Childrens).
—Sunny Sweet Is So Not Scary. 2015. (Sunny Sweet Ser.). (ENG.). 192p. (YA). (gr. 3-6). 15.99 *(978-1-61963-507-4(0)*, 9781619635074, Bloomsbury USA Childrens) Bloomsbury Publishing USA.
—Sunny Sweet Is So Not Sorry. 2013. (Sunny Sweet Ser.). (ENG., Illus.). 208p. (YA). (gr. 3-6). 15.99 *(978-1-59990-977-6(4)*, 9781599909776, Bloomsbury USA Childrens) Bloomsbury Publishing USA.
Mantchev, Lisa. Sister Day! Sánchez, Sonia, illus. 2017. (ENG.). 32p. (J). (gr. -1-3). 17.99 *(978-1-4814-3795-0(X)*, Simon & Schuster Bks. For Young Readers) Simon & Schuster Bks. For Young Readers.
Manushkin, Fran. Big Sisters Are the Best, 1 vol. Richards, Kirsten, illus. 2012. (Fiction Picture Bks.). (ENG.). 24p. (gr. -1 — 1). 6.95 *(978-1-4048-7225-7(6))*; lib. bdg. 22.65 *(978-1-4048-7138-0(1))* Picture Window Bks. (Fiction Picture Bks.).
Marconi, Martina. Birthday Wishes, 1 vol. 2010. 20p. pap. 24.95 *(978-1-4489-6067-5(3))* PublishAmerica, Inc.
Margulies, Julianna & Margulies, Paul. Three Magic Balloons. Shaffer, Grant, illus. 2016. (ENG.). 40p. (J). (gr. -1-2). 17.99 *(978-1-101-93523-1(5)*, Random Hse. Bks. for Young Readers) Random Hse. Children's Bks.
Marillier, Juliet. Cybele's Secret. 2011. (ENG.). 444p. (YA). (gr. 7). pap. 9.99 *(978-0-553-49486-0(4)*, Knopf Bks. for Young Readers) Random Hse. Children's Bks.
—Wildwood Dancing. 2008. (ENG.). 432p. (YA). (gr. 7). pap. 10.99 *(978-0-375-84474-4(0)*, Knopf Bks. for Young Readers) Random Hse. Children's Bks.
Marina, Budhos. Ask Me No Questions. 2014. (ENG.). 176p. (YA). (gr. 7-12). 14.24 *(978-1-63245-300-6(2))* Lectorum Pubns., Inc.
Marlow, Herb. Sisters, Wild Dogs & Catfish Bait. Caffee, Julie, illus. 2005. 122p. (J). lib. bdg. 24.95 *(978-1-893595-45-3(5))*; per. 16.95 *(978-1-893595-48-4(X))* Four Seasons Bks., Inc.
Marshall, Carly. The Babysitter & Little Miss Bossy. 2013. 26p. 24.95 *(978-1-63000-618-1(1))*; 28p. pap. 24.95 *(978-1-63000-541-2(X))* America Star Bks.
Marsoli, Lisa Ann & Disney Book Group Staff. The Halloween Ball. Disney Storybook Art Team, illus. 2013. (ENG.). 24p. (J). (gr. -1-k). pap. 5.99 *(978-1-4231-7144-7(6))* Disney Pr.
Martin, Ann M. Best Friends. 2008. (Illus.). 195p. (J). pap. *(978-0-545-05062-3(6))* Scholastic, Inc.
—Needle & Thread. 2007. (Main Street Ser.). (Illus.). 205p. (J). (gr. 4-7). 14.65 *(978-0-7569-8328-4(2))* Perfection Learning Corp.
—Needle & Thread. Andreasen, Dan, illus. 2007. 205p. (J). pap. *(978-0-545-03660-3(7))* Scholastic, Inc.
—The Secret Book Club. 2008. (Main Street Ser.). (Illus.). 212p. (J). (gr. 4-7). 14.65 *(978-0-7569-8823-4(3))* Perfection Learning Corp.
—Ten Good & Bad Things about My Life (So Far) 2013. (ENG.). 288p. (J). (gr. 4-7). pap. 7.99 *(978-1-250-03413-7(2)*, 9781250034137) Square Fish.
—Ten Rules for Living with My Sister. 2011. (ENG.). 240p. (J). (gr. 4-7). 16.99 *(978-0-312-36766-4(X)*, 9780312367664) Feiwel & Friends.
—Ten Rules for Living with My Sister. 2012. (ENG.). 256p. (J). (gr. 4-7). pap. 7.99 *(978-1-250-01021-6(7)*, 9781250010216) Square Fish.
—Tis the Season. 2007. (Main Street Ser.). (Illus.). 195p. (J). (gr. 4-7). 14.65 *(978-0-7569-8327-7(4))* Perfection Learning Corp.
—Welcome to Camden Falls. 2007. (Main Street Ser.). (Illus.). 174p. (J). (gr. 4-7). 14.65 *(978-0-7569-8326-0(6))* Perfection Learning Corp.
—Welcome to Camden Falls. 2007. (Main Street Ser.: 1). (ENG., Illus.). 192p. (J). (gr. 3-7). 6.99 *(978-0-439-86879-2(3)*, Scholastic Paperbacks) Scholastic, Inc.
Martin, Ann M. & Martin Ann, M. Claudia & Mean Janine. Telgemeier, Raina, illus. 2016. (Baby-Sitters Club Graphix Ser.: 4). (ENG.). 176p. (J). (gr. 3-7). lib. bdg. 22.10 *(978-0-606-38056-0(6))* Turtleback Bks.
Martinez, Jessica. The Space Between Us. (ENG., (YA). (gr. 9). 2013. Illus.). 416p. pap. 9.99 *(978-1-4424-2056-4(1))* 2012. 400p. 16.99 *(978-1-4424-2055-7(3))* Simon Pulse. (Simon Pulse).
Marychild, H. D. Skater Sister. 2013. 222p. pap. 9.52 *(978-0-9899964-9-5(2))* Small Wonder Publishing.
Mason-Black, Jennifer. Devil & the Bluebird. 2016. (ENG.). 336p. (J). (gr. 8-17). 17.95 *(978-1-4197-2000-0(7)*, Amulet Bks.) Abrams, Inc.
Matthews, Elli. Surprising Katie on Halloween. Written by Elli Matthews; Illustrated by, illus. 2011. 24p. pap. 24.95 *(978-1-4560-7486-9(5))* America Star Bks.
Matthews, L. S. Lexi. 2008. 200p. (J). pap. *(978-0-385-73575-9(8)*, Delacorte Pr) Random House Publishing Group.
Matute, Ana María. El Polizón del Ulises. (SPA.). 126p. (YA). (gr. 5-18). 10.36 *(978-84-264-3022-9(8)*, LM0588) Editorial Lumen ESP. Dist: Lectorum Pubns., Inc.
Mayfield, Marilee Joy. The Tiny Adventures of Big Sister & Little Sister: A Hearts-Beared Book. 2004. 48p. (J). lib. bdg. 19.95 *(978-0-9659222-2-7(7))* Leaping Antelope Productions.
Mazer, Anne. Violet Makes a Splash. Brown, Bill, illus. 2007. (Sister Magic Ser.: 2). (ENG.). 96p. (J). (gr. 2-5). 4.99 *(978-0-439-87247-8(2))* Scholastic, Inc.
Mazer, Norma Fox. The Missing Girl. 2010. (ENG.). 304p. (YA). (gr. 8). pap. 8.99 *(978-0-06-447365-1(1)*, HarperTeen) HarperCollins Pubs.
—Ten Ways to Make My Sister Disappear. 2007. (ENG.). 128p. (J). (gr. 4-7). 16.99 *(978-0-439-83983-9(1)*, Levine, Arthur A. Bks.) Scholastic, Inc.
—Ten Ways to Make My Sister Disappear. l.t. ed. 2008. (Thorndike Literacy Bridge Ser.). 207p. (J). (gr. 4-7). 22.95 *(978-1-4104-0510-4(9))* Thorndike Pr.
McCafferty, Megan. Bumped. (Bumped Ser.: 1). (ENG.). (YA). (gr. 9). 2012. 352p. pap. 9.99 *(978-0-06-196275-2(9))* 2011. 336p. 16.99 *(978-0-06-196274-5(0))* HarperCollins Pubs.
—Thumped. 2013. (Bumped Ser.: 2). (ENG.). 304p. (YA). (gr. 8). pap. 8.99 *(978-0-06-196277-6(5))* HarperCollins Pubs.
—The (Totally Not) Guaranteed Guide to Popularity, Prettiness & Perfection. 2014. (Jessica Darling's It List Ser.: 1). (ENG.). 240p. (J). (gr. 3-7). pap. 8.99 *(978-0-316-24498-5(8)*, Poppy) Little, Brown Bks. for Young Readers.
McCahan, Erin. Love & Other Foreign Words. 2014. (ENG.). 336p. (YA). (gr. 7). 17.99 *(978-0-8037-4051-8(4)*, Dial Bks) Penguin Young Readers Group.
McCall, Guadalupe Garcia. Summer of the Mariposas. 2012. (ENG.). 352p. (YA). 19.95 *(978-1-60060-900-8(7)*, Tu Bks.) Lee & Low Bks., Inc.
McCarthy, Maureen. The Convent. 2015. (ENG.). 440p. (YA). (gr. 9-12). pap. 12.99 *(978-1-74331-834-8(0))* Allen & Unwin AUS. Dist: Independent Pubs. Group.
McCartney, Tania. Peas in a Pod. Snerling, Tina, illus. (ENG.). 32p. (J). (gr. -1-2). 2016. pap. 9.99 *(978-1-925335-28-6(3)*, EK Bks.) 2015. 17.95 *(978-1-921966-71-2(8))* Exisle Publishing Pty Ltd. AUS. Dist: Hachette Bk. Group.
McCombie, Karen. Candy Girl. 2012. (Stoke Books Titles Ser.). 64p. (J). (gr. 5-8). pap. 7.95 *(978-1-78112-012-5(9))*; lib. bdg. 22.60 *(978-1-78112-011-8(0))* Stoke Bks.
McCormack, Caren McNelly. The Fiesta Dress: A Quinceanera Tale, 0 vols. Aviles, Martha, illus. 2012. (ENG.). 42p. (J). (gr. k-4). pap. 7.99 *(978-0-7614-6236-1(8)*, 9780761462361, Amazon Children's Publishing) Amazon Publishing.
McCoy, Mary. Dead to Me. 2015. (ENG.). 304p. (YA). (gr. 7-12). 17.99 *(978-1-4231-8712-7(1))* Hyperion Bks. for Children.
McDaniel, Lurlene. Briana's Gift. 2008. (ENG.). 176p. (YA). (gr. 7-12). mass mkt. 6.50 *(978-0-440-23869-0(2)*, Laurel Leaf) Random Hse. Children's Bks.
—The End of Forever. 2013. (ENG.). 320p. (YA). (gr. 7). pap. 8.99 *(978-0-385-74380-8(7)*, Ember) Random Hse. Children's Bks.
—Somebody's Baby. 2017. (ENG.). 320p. (YA). (gr. 7). 17.99 *(978-0-385-74423-2(4)*, Delacorte Pr.) Random Hse. Children's Bks.
McDonald, Abby. Jane Austen Goes to Hollywood. (ENG.). 336p. (YA). (gr. 9). 2015. pap. 8.99 *(978-0-7636-7669-8(1))* 2013. 17.99 *(978-0-7636-5508-2(2))* Candlewick Pr.
McDonald, Megan. Cloudy with a Chance of Boys. (Sisters Club Ser.: 3). (ENG., Illus.). 272p. (J). (gr. 3-7). 2012. pap. 5.99 *(978-0-7636-5577-8(5))* 2011. 15.99 *(978-0-7636-4615-8(6))* Candlewick Pr.
—The Sisters Club. 2008. (Sisters Club Ser.: 1). (ENG., Illus.). 208p. (J). (gr. 3-7). pap. 5.99 *(978-0-7636-3251-9(1))* Candlewick Pr.
—The Sisters Club. 2008. (Sisters Club Ser.: 1). lib. bdg. 16.00 *(978-1-4178-1785-6(2)*, Turtleback) Turtleback Bks.
Mcelfresh, Lynn. Strong Deaf. 2012. 130p. 18.95 *(978-1-60898-126-7(6))*; pap. 9.95 *(978-1-60898-127-4(4))* namelos llc.
Mcghee, Alison. All Rivers Flow to the Sea. 2005. (ENG.). 176p. (YA). (gr. 9-12). 15.99 *(978-0-7636-2591-7(4))* Candlewick Pr.
—The Sweetest Witch Around. Bliss, Harry, illus. 2014. (ENG.). 32p. (J). (gr. -1-3). 15.99 *(978-1-4424-7833-6(0)*, Simon & Schuster/Paula Wiseman Bks.) Simon & Schuster/Paula Wiseman Bks.
McGowan, Patricia. House of Friends. 2012. 242p. 46.95 *(978-1-258-23494-2(7))*; pap. 31.95 *(978-1-258-24543-6(4))* Literary Licensing, LLC.
McGuire Woods, Molly. Barbie & Her Sisters in a Puppy Chase. 2016. (Barbie Chapters Ser.). (ENG., Illus.). 64p. (J). (gr. 1-4). 5.99 *(978-0-399-55136-9(0)*, Random Hse. Bks. for Young Readers) Random Hse. Children's Bks.
—Puppy Chase. 2016. (Barbie Chapters Ser.). (ENG.). 64p. (J). (gr. 1-4). lib. bdg. 12.99 *(978-0-399-55137-6(9)*, Random Hse. Bks. for Young Readers) Random Hse. Children's Bks.
McKay, Hilary. The Exiles at Home. 2007. (ENG.). 208p. (J). (gr. 3-7). pap. 12.95 *(978-1-4169-6729-3(X)*, McElderry, Margaret K. Bks.) McElderry, Margaret K. Bks.
—The Exiles in Love. 2007. (ENG.). 176p. (J). (gr. 3-7). pap. 9.95 *(978-1-4169-6797-2(4)*, McElderry, Margaret K. Bks.) McElderry, Margaret K. Bks.
Mckee, Jessica. Piddle Diddle Stuck in the Middle. 2010. 24p. (J). pap. *(978-0-9867017-0-2(X))* Little Black Dog Publishing.
McKinnon, Hannah Roberts. The Properties of Water. 2010. (ENG.). 176p. (YA). (gr. 5-9). 27.99 *(978-0-374-36145-7(2)*, 9780374361457, Farrar, Straus & Giroux (BYR)) Farrar, Straus & Giroux.
McKissack, Patricia C. The All-I'll-Ever-Want Christmas Doll. Pinkney, Jerry, illus. 2007. (J). *(978-0-375-83615-2(2)*, Schwartz & Wade Bks.) Random Hse. Children's Bks.
—The All-I'll-Ever-Want Christmas Doll. Pinkney, Jerry, illus. 2007. (ENG.). 40p. (J). (gr. -1-3). 17.99 *(978-0-375-83759-3(0)*, Schwartz & Wade Bks.) Random Hse. Children's Bks.
McKnight, Gillian. To Catch a Prince. 2010. (ENG.). 240p. (YA). (gr. 7). pap. 11.99 *(978-1-4424-2718-1(3)*, Simon Pulse) Simon Pulse.

S

McLaughlin, Dawn L. Two Tickets to Heaven, Please! 2009. 48p. pap. 16.25 *(978-1-60693-061-8(3)*, Eloquent Bks.) Strategic Book Publishing & Rights Agency (SBPRA).

McNamara, Margaret. Clara & the Magical Charms. Denos, Julia, illus. 2013. (Fairy Bell Sisters Ser.: 4). (ENG.). 128p. (J). (gr. 1-5). 15.99 *(978-0-06-222811-6(0))*; pap. 4.99 *(978-0-06-222810-9(2))* HarperCollins Pubs.

—The Fairy Bell Sisters No. 3: Golden at the Fancy-Dress Party. Denos, Julia, illus. 2013. (Fairy Bell Sisters Ser.: 3). (ENG.). 144p. (J). (gr. 1-5). pap. 4.99 *(978-0-06-222807-9(2))* HarperCollins Pubs.

—The Fairy Bell Sisters - Christmas Fairy Magic. 2014. (Fairy Bell Sisters Ser.: 6). (ENG.). 144p. (J). (gr. 1-5). pap. 4.99 *(978-0-06-226723-8(X))* HarperCollins Pubs.

—The Fairy Bell Sisters #3: Golden at the Fancy-Dress Party. Denos, Julia, illus. 2013. (Fairy Bell Sisters Ser.: 3). (ENG.). 144p. (J). (gr. 1-5). 15.99 *(978-0-06-222808-6(0))* HarperCollins Pubs.

—Golden at the Fancy-Dress Party. 2013. (Fairy Bell Sisters Ser.: 3). (J). lib. bdg. 14.75 *(978-0-606-32154-9(3)*, Turtleback) Turtleback Bks.

—Rosy & the Secret Friend. Denos, Julia, illus. 2013. (Fairy Bell Sisters Ser.: 2). (ENG.). 128p. (J). (gr. 1-5). 15.99 *(978-0-06-222805-5(6))*; pap. 4.99 *(978-0-06-222804-8(8))* HarperCollins Pubs.

—Rosy & the Secret Friend. 2013. (Fairy Bell Sisters Ser.: 2). (J). lib. bdg. 14.75 *(978-0-606-31797-9(X)*, Turtleback) Turtleback Bks.

—Sylva & the Fairy Ball. Denos, Julia, illus. 2013. (Fairy Bell Sisters Ser.: 1). (ENG.). 128p. (J). (gr. 1-5). 15.99 *(978-0-06-222802-4(1))*; pap. 4.99 *(978-0-06-222801-7(3))* HarperCollins Pubs.

—Sylva & the Fairy Ball. 2013. (Fairy Bell Sisters Ser.: 1). (J). lib. bdg. 14.75 *(978-0-606-31796-2(1)*, Turtleback) Turtleback Bks.

McNeal, Laura. The Incident on the Bridge. 2016. (ENG.). 336p. (YA). (gr. 7). 17.99 *(978-0-375-87079-8(2)*, Knopf Bks. for Young Readers) Random Hse. Children's Bks.

McPhail, David. Sisters. 2010. (ENG., Illus.). 28p. (J). (gr. -1 — 1). bds. 6.99 *(978-0-547-48087-9(3))* Houghton Mifflin Harcourt Publishing Co.

McPhail, J. A. Dawn of Day. Battis, Gwen, illus. 2012. 200p. pap. 10.99 *(978-0-9851196-1-4(6))* Rowe Publishing and Design.

McVoy, Terra Elan. Being Friends with Boys. 2013. (ENG., Illus.). 384p. (YA). (gr. 9). pap. 10.99 *(978-1-4424-2160-8(6)*, Simon Pulse) Simon Pulse.

—The Summer of Firsts & Lasts. (ENG.). (YA). (gr. 9). 2012. 448p. pap. 9.99 *(978-1-4424-0214-0(8))* 2011. 432p. 16.99 *(978-1-4424-0213-3(X))* Simon Pulse. (Simon Pulse).

Mcwherter, Barbara. Oliver & His Mountain Climbing Adventures. McWherter, Shelley, illus. 2012. 34p. 24.95 *(978-1-4626-7601-9(4))* America Star Bks.

Meadows, Daisy. Heather the Violet Fairy. Ripper, Georgie, illus. 2006. (Rainbow Magic Ser.: 7). (ENG.). 80p. (J). (gr. -1-3). 4.99 *(978-0-439-74686-1(8)*, Scholastic Paperbacks) Scholastic, Inc.

Meister, Cari. The Clever Dolphin, 1 vol. Harpster, Steve, illus. 2012. (Ocean Tales Ser.). (ENG.). 32p. (gr. 2-4). pap. 6.25 *(978-1-4342-4229-7(3))* Stone Arch Bks.

Mendle, Jane. My Ultimate Sister Disaster: A Novel. 2010. (ENG.). 208p. (YA). (gr. 7-18). pap. 18.99 *(978-0-312-36904-0(2)*, 9780312369040, St. Martin's Griffin) St. Martin's Pr.

Mercer, Sienna. Date with Destiny. 2014. (My Sister the Vampire Ser.: 10). (ENG.). 224p. (J). (gr. 4-6). 6.99 *(978-1-4052-5985-9(X))* Egmont Bks., Ltd. GBR. Dist: Independent Pubs. Group.

—Fangs for the Memories. 2017. (My Sister the Vampire Ser.: 18). (ENG.). 208p. (J). (gr. 4-6). pap. 8.99 *(978-1-4052-7844-7(7))* Egmont Bks., Ltd. GBR. Dist: Independent Pubs. Group.

—Fangtastic! 2007. (My Sister the Vampire Ser.: 2). (ENG.). 208p. (J). (gr. 3-7). per. 6.99 *(978-0-06-087115-4(6))* HarperCollins Pubs.

—Fashion Frightmare! 2014. (My Sister the Vampire Ser.: 16). (ENG.). 240p. (J). (gr. 4-6). pap. 6.99 *(978-1-4052-6573-7(6))* Egmont Bks., Ltd. GBR. Dist: Independent Pubs. Group.

—Flipping Out ! 2014. (My Sister the Vampire Ser.: 14). (ENG.). 256p. (J). (gr. 4-6). pap. 6.99 *(978-1-4052-6571-3(X))* Egmont Bks., Ltd. GBR. Dist: Independent Pubs. Group.

—Love Bites. 2014. (My Sister the Vampire Ser.: 6). (ENG.). 256p. (J). (gr. 4-6). pap. 6.99 *(978-1-4052-5698-8(2))* Egmont Bks., Ltd. GBR. Dist: Independent Pubs. Group.

—Lucky Break. 2014. (My Sister the Vampire Ser.: 7). (ENG.). 256p. (J). (gr. 4-6). 6.99 *(978-1-4052-5699-5(0))* Egmont Bks., Ltd. GBR. Dist: Independent Pubs. Group.

—My Sister the Vampire - Twin Spins! 2014. (My Sister the Vampire Ser.: 9). (ENG.). 224p. (J). (gr. 4-6). pap. 6.99 *(978-1-4052-5984-2(1))* Egmont Bks., Ltd. GBR. Dist: Independent Pubs. Group.

—Secrets & Spies. 2014. (My Sister the Vampire Ser.: 15). (ENG.). 224p. (J). (gr. 4-6). pap. 8.99 *(978-1-4052-6572-0(8))* Egmont Bks., Ltd. GBR. Dist: Independent Pubs. Group.

—Star Style. 2014. (My Sister the Vampire Ser.: 8). (ENG.). 256p. (J). (gr. 4-6). pap. 6.99 *(978-1-4052-5700-8(8))* Egmont Bks., Ltd. GBR. Dist: Independent Pubs. Group.

Mercer, Sienna & Miller, Sienna. Double Disaster! 2014. (My Sister the Vampire Ser.: 13). (ENG.). 256p. (J). (gr. 4-6). pap. 6.99 *(978-1-4052-6570-6(1))* Egmont Bks., Ltd. GBR. Dist: Independent Pubs. Group.

—Flying Solo. 2014. (My Sister the Vampire Ser.: 11). (ENG.). 224p. (J). (gr. 4-6). pap. 6.99 *(978-1-4052-5987-3(6))* Egmont Bks., Ltd. GBR. Dist: Independent Pubs. Group.

—Stake Out! 2014. (My Sister the Vampire Ser.: 12). (ENG.). 240p. (J). (gr. 4-6). pap. 6.99 *(978-1-4052-5988-0(4))* Egmont Bks., Ltd. GBR. Dist: Independent Pubs. Group.

Meredith, Christina. Kiss Crush Collide. (ENG.). 320p. (YA). (gr. 9). 2012. pap. 9.99 *(978-0-06-206225-3(5))* 2011. 16.99 *(978-0-06-206224-6(7))* HarperCollins Pubs. (Greenwillow Bks.).

Messer, Celeste M. The Ghost of Piper's Landing. Hoeffner, Deb, illus. 2004. 82-92p. 4.95 *(978-0-9702171-7-2(X))* AshleyAlan Enterprises.

Metcalf, Paula. A Guide to Sisters. Barton, Suzanne, illus. 2015. (ENG.). 32p. (J). (gr. -1-2). 17.99 *(978-0-553-49899-8(1)*, Random Hse. Bks. for Young Readers) Random Hse. Children's Bks.

Meyer, Carolyn. Anastasia & Her Sisters. 2015. (ENG., Illus.). 320p. (YA). (gr. 7). 17.99 *(978-1-4814-0326-9(5)*, Simon & Schuster Bks. For Young Readers) Simon & Schuster Bks. For Young Readers.

Meyer, Shawna Rae. When the Baby-Sitter Comes. 2011. 28p. pap. 14.95 *(978-1-4567-3808-2(9))* AuthorHouse.

Michels-Gualtieri, Akaela S. I Was Born to Be a Sister. Ramsey, Marcy Dunn, illus. 2005. (ENG.). 32p. (J). (gr. 4-7). 9.95 incl. lp *(978-1-930775-11-4(3))* Platypus Media, L.L.C.

Mikaelsen, Ben. Tree Girl. 2005. (ENG.). 240p. (YA). (gr. 8). pap. 9.99 *(978-0-06-009006-7(5)*, HarperTeen) HarperCollins Pubs.

Miller, Sarah. The Lost Crown. (ENG., Illus.). 448p. (gr. 7). 2012. (YA). pap. 9.99 *(978-1-4169-8341-5(4))* 2011. (J). 17.99 *(978-1-4169-8340-8(6))* Simon & Schuster Children's Publishing. (Atheneum Bks. for Young Readers).

Mills, Tessa L. The Adventures of Avery & Cali. 2007. 60p. per. 16.95 *(978-1-4241-7982-4(3))* America Star Bks.

Mindy, Miss. Artist Sisters Vol. 2: Princess la la & the Little Bee - Teenie Weenie Tales. 2007. (ENG., Illus.). 64p. (YA). (gr. 8-12). pap. 30.00 *(978-0-9778949-7-0(5))* Baby Tattoo Bks.

Mitchard, Jacquelyn. Look Both Ways. 2010. (Midnight Twins Ser.: No. 2). (ENG.). 304p. (YA). (gr. 7-18). 8.99 *(978-1-59514-281-8(9)*, Razorbill) Penguin Young Readers Group.

Mitchell, Carolann. The Song of the Snow. 2011. 68p. (gr. 4-6). pap. 8.95 *(978-0-595-46609-2(5))* iUniverse, Inc.

Mittal, Anjali. The Convent Rules. 2009. (Illus.). 80p. pap. 10.49 *(978-1-4389-8575-6(4))* AuthorHouse.

Miyazaki, Hayao. My Neighbor Totoro Picture Book (New Edition) 2013. (ENG., Illus.). 112p. (J). 19.99 *(978-1-4215-6122-6(0))* Viz Media.

Mlynowski, Sarah. Spells & Sleeping Bags. 2008. (Magic in Manhattan Ser.: No. 3). (ENG.). 320p. (YA). (gr. 7-12). pap. 8.99 *(978-0-385-73388-5(7)*, Delacorte Pr.) Random Hse. Children's Bks.

Montana, Brenda. Jamie & Lacy & the Adventures of the White Chihuahuas Book. 2011. 48p. pap. 15.99 *(978-1-4653-6752-5(7))* Xlibris Corp.

Moore, Mykela. Meet the Super Sisters. Garrett, Myers, illus. 2013. (J). 9.99 *(978-0-9852746-9-6(7))* Hope of Vision Publishing.

Moore, Stephanie. Better Than Picture Perfect. 2014. (Sharp Sisters Ser.: 2). (ENG.). 160p. (YA). (gr. 6-12). pap. 7.95 *(978-1-4677-4486-7(7)*, Darby Creek) Lerner Publishing Group.

—Make Something of It. 2014. (Sharp Sisters Ser.: 1). (ENG.). 152p. (YA). (gr. 6-12). pap. 7.95 *(978-1-4677-4488-1(3)*, Darby Creek) Lerner Publishing Group.

Moore, Stephanie Perry. Icing on the Cake. 2014. (Sharp Sisters Ser.: 5). (ENG.). 160p. (YA). (gr. 6-12). pap. 7.95 *(978-1-4677-4487-4(5)*, Darby Creek); lib. bdg. 27.93 *(978-1-4677-3728-9(3))* Lerner Publishing Group.

—Truth & Nothing But. 2014. (Sharp Sisters Ser.: 4). (ENG.). 160p. (YA). (gr. 6-12). pap. 7.95 *(978-1-4677-4489-8(1)*, Darby Creek); lib. bdg. 27.93 *(978-1-4677-3727-2(5))* Lerner Publishing Group.

—Turn up for Real. 2014. (Sharp Sisters Ser.: 3). (ENG.). 168p. (YA). (gr. 6-12). pap. 7.95 *(978-1-4677-4490-4(5)*, Darby Creek); lib. bdg. 27.93 *(978-1-4677-3726-5(7))* Lerner Publishing Group.

Morah, Chizoba. The Anderson Twins. 2007. 76p. per. 19.95 *(978-1-60441-015-0(9))* America Star Bks.

Morgan, C. M. Silver Doorway #6: The Alchemist's Girl. 2008. 108p. pap. 6.99 *(978-0-9771005-2-1(9))* Sabledrake Enterprises.

Morgan, Page. The Beautiful & the Cursed. (Dispossessed Ser.). (ENG.). 352p. (YA). (gr. 7). 2014. pap. 9.99 *(978-0-385-74312-9(2)*, Ember) 2013. 18.99 *(978-0-385-74311-2(4)*, Delacorte Pr.) Random Hse. Children's Bks.

Morris, David. My Twins First Christmas. 2008. (Illus.). 24p. (J). pap. 14.95 *(978-0-9799885-0-9(0))* New Year Publishing.

Morris, Lynn. Don't eat your Broccoli! Mettler, Joe, illus. 2007. 32p. (J). per. 6.95 *(978-0-9755548-2-1(4))* Log Cabin Bks.

Morris, Paris. My Twins First Halloween. 2008. (J). pap. 12.95 *(978-0-9760095-9-7(5))* New Year Publishing.

Morris, Paris & Florzak, Douglas. My Twins First Birthday. 2010. (ENG., Illus.). 24p. (J). pap. 12.95 *(978-0-9760095-8-0(7))* New Year Publishing.

Moss, Marissa. Amelia's 6th-Grade Notebook. Moss, Marissa, illus. 2005. (Amelia Ser.). (ENG., Illus.). 80p. (J). (gr. 4-7). 12.99 *(978-0-689-87040-8(X)*, Simon & Schuster/Paula Wiseman Bks.) Simon & Schuster/Paula Wiseman Bks.

—Amelia's Are-We-There-Yet Longest Ever Car Trip. Moss, Marissa, illus. (Amelia Ser.). (ENG., Illus.). 40p. (J). (gr. 2-5). 2012. pap. 6.99 *(978-1-4169-1287-3(8))* 2006. 10.99 *(978-1-4169-0906-4(0))* Simon & Schuster/Paula Wiseman Bks. (Simon & Schuster/Paula Wiseman Bks.).

—Amelia's Longest, Biggest, Most-Fights-Ever Family Reunion. Moss, Marissa, illus. 2006. (Amelia Ser.). (ENG., Illus.). 80p. (J). (gr. 4-7). 12.99 *(978-0-689-87447-5(2)*, Simon & Schuster/Paula Wiseman Bks.) Simon & Schuster/Paula Wiseman Bks.

—Amelia's Most Unforgettable Embarrassing Moments. Moss, Marissa, illus. 2005. (Amelia Ser.). (ENG., Illus.). 80p. (J). (gr. 4-7). 12.99 *(978-0-689-87041-5(8)*, Simon & Schuster/Paula Wiseman Bks.) Simon & Schuster/Paula Wiseman Bks.

—Amelia's Notebook. Moss, Marissa, illus. 2006. (Amelia Ser.). (ENG., Illus.). (J). 5.99 *(978-1-4169-1286-6(X))*; 40p. (gr. 2-5). 12.99 *(978-1-4169-0905-7(2))* Simon & Schuster/Paula Wiseman Bks. (Simon & Schuster/Paula Wiseman Bks.).

—Amelia's Summer Survival Guide: Amelia's Longest, Biggest, Most-Fights-Ever Family Reunion; Amelia's Itchy-Twitchy, Lovey-Dovey Summer at Camp Mosquito. Moss, Marissa, illus. 2011. (Amelia Ser.). (ENG., Illus.). 160p. (J). (gr. 5-8). 12.99 *(978-1-4424-2331-2(5)*, Simon & Schuster/Paula Wiseman Bks.) Simon & Schuster/Paula Wiseman Bks.

Moulton, Erin E. Flutter: The Story of Four Sisters & an Incredible Journey. 2012. (ENG.). 224p. (J). (gr. 3-7). pap. 6.99 *(978-0-14-242133-8(2)*, Puffin Books) Penguin Young Readers Group.

—Tracing Stars. 2013. (ENG.). 256p. (J). (gr. 3-7). pap. 6.99 *(978-0-14-242653-1(9)*, Puffin Books) Penguin Young Readers Group.

Mowry, Tia & Mowry, Tamera. Double Vision. 2015. (Twintuition Ser.: 1). (ENG.). 208p. (J). (gr. 3-7). 16.99 *(978-0-06-237286-4(6))* HarperCollins Pubs.

—Twintuition: Double Dare. 2017. (Twintuition Ser.: 3). 208p. (J). (gr. 3-7). 16.99 *(978-0-06-237292-5(0))* HarperCollins Pubs.

Mukherjee, Sonya. Gemini. 2016. (ENG., Illus.). 336p. (YA). (gr. 9). 17.99 *(978-1-4814-5677-7(6)*, Simon & Schuster Bks. For Young Readers) Simon & Schuster Bks. For Young Readers.

Muller, Rachel Dunstan. The Solstice Cup, 1 vol. 2009. (ENG.). 176p. (J). (gr. 4-7). pap. 9.95 *(978-1-55469-017-6(X))* Orca Bk. Pubs. USA.

Murdoch, Emily. If You Find Me. (ENG.). (YA). (gr. 7). 2014. 288p. pap. 10.99 *(978-1-250-03327-7(6)*, 9781250033277) 2013. 256p. 17.99 *(978-1-250-02152-6(9)*, 9781250021526) St. Martin's Pr. (St. Martin's Griffin).

Murguia, Bethanie Deeney. Zoe's Jungle. 2014. (ENG.). 40p. (J). (gr. -1-k). 16.99 *(978-0-545-55869-3(7)*, Levine, Arthur A. Bks.) Scholastic, Inc.

—Zoe's Room (No Sisters Allowed) Murguia, Bethanie Deeney, illus. 2013. (ENG., Illus.). 40p. (J). (gr. -1-k). 16.99 *(978-0-545-45781-1(5)*, Levine, Arthur A. Bks.) Scholastic, Inc.

Murphy, Barbara & Murphy, Barbara Beasley. Life! How I Love You! Baca, Elena, illus. 2004. (ENG.). 136p. (J). 9.95 *(978-0-89013-468-9(5))* Museum of New Mexico Pr.

Murphy, Patricia J. Horse Club. 2013. (DK Adventures Ser.). (ENG.). 128p. (J). (gr. 3-7). 16.99 *(978-1-4654-1811-1(3))*; pap. 5.99 *(978-1-4654-1723-7(0))* Dorling Kindersley Publishing, Inc. (DK Children).

Musgrove, Marianne. Forget-Me-Not Fairy Treasury. MacCarthy, Patricia, illus. 2013. (ENG.). 192p. (J). (gr. -1-3). *(978-1-74308-536-3(2))* Hinkler Bks. Pty, Ltd.

My Sister Jess: Set C Individual Title Six-Packs. (Supersonic Phonics Ser.). (gr. k-3). 29.00 *(978-0-7635-0546-2(3))* Rigby Education.

Myracle, Lauren. Peace, Love, & Baby Ducks. (ENG.). (YA). (gr. 7-18). 2010. 304p. 8.99 *(978-0-14-241527-6(8)*, Speak) 2009. 272p. 16.99 *(978-0-525-47743-3(8)*, Dutton Books for Young Readers) Penguin Young Readers Group.

Nahall Nikoo Fells. Drowning in the Mainstream: Confessions of a Sister. 2010. 284p. 27.95 *(978-1-4502-0552-8(6))* iUniverse, Inc.

Nash, Ronza R. The Chocolate Wonders: The Adventures of Lila & Lester. 2011. 36p. pap. 16.86 *(978-1-4634-1619-5(9))* AuthorHouse.

Naylor, Phyllis Reynolds. The Boys Return. 2003. (Boys Against Girls Ser.: No. 7). 132p. (gr. 4-7). 16.00 *(978-0-7569-1381-6(0))* Perfection Learning Corp.

—The Girls Take Over. 2004. (Boy/Girl Battle Ser.: No. 8). (ENG.). 160p. (J). (gr. 3-7). 6.99 *(978-0-440-41678-4(7)*, Yearling) Random Hse. Children's Bks.

—Who Won the War? 2008. (Boy/Girl Battle Ser.). (ENG.). 160p. (J). (gr. 3-7). 5.99 *(978-0-440-41991-4(3)*, Yearling) Random Hse. Children's Bks.

Nazarian, Leslie. Orelda & Corelda's Ocean Voyage. 2007. 52p. (J). 15.94 *(978-1-4116-2373-6(8))* Lulu Pr., Inc.

Neasi, Barbara J. Just Like Me. Hantel, Johanna, illus. 2011. (Rookie Ready to Learn — All about Me! Ser.). 40p. (J). (gr. -1-k). lib. bdg. 25.00 *(978-0-531-26371-6(1)*, Children's Pr.); (ENG.). pap. 5.95 *(978-0-531-26676-2(1))* Scholastic Library Publishing.

Nefflen, Marjorie E. My Big Sister Knows... 2012. 32p. pap. 10.95 *(978-1-4626-8879-1(9))*; 30p. 24.95 *(978-1-62709-509-9(8))* America Star Bks.

Nelson, Jandy. The Sky Is Everywhere. (ENG.). (YA). (gr. 9-18). 2011. 320p. 9.99 *(978-0-14-241780-5(7)*, Speak) 2010. 288p. 17.99 *(978-0-8037-3495-1(6)*, Dial Bks) Penguin Young Readers Group.

—The Sky Is Everywhere. 2011. (ENG., Illus.). 275p. (gr. 9-12). 19.00 *(978-1-61383-223-3(0))* Perfection Learning Corp.

Nicholls, Sally. Season of Secrets. 2011. (J). 225p. pap. *(978-0-545-21826-9(8))*; (ENG.). 240p. (gr. 3-7). 16.99 *(978-0-545-21825-2(X))* Scholastic, Inc. (Levine, Arthur A. Bks.).

Nichols, Lori. Maple. Nichols, Lori, illus. 2014. (ENG., Illus.). 32p. (J). (gr. -1-k). 16.99 *(978-0-399-16085-1(X)*, Nancy Paulsen Books) Penguin Young Readers Group.

—Maple & Willow Together. Nichols, Lori, illus. 2014. (ENG., Illus.). 32p. (J). (gr. -1-k). 16.99 *(978-0-399-16283-1(6)*, Nancy Paulsen Books) Penguin Young Readers Group.

—Maple & Willow's Christmas Tree. Nichols, Lori, illus. 2016. (ENG., Illus.). 32p. (J). (-k). 16.99 *(978-0-399-16756-0(0)*, Nancy Paulsen Books) Penguin Young Readers Group.

Nickelodeon. Shimmer & Shine - Sleepover Wishes. 2016. (ENG.). 10p. (J). (gr. -1-2). bds. 9.99 *(978-0-7944-3827-2(X))* Studio Fun International.

Night, P. J. The House Next Door. 2013. (You're Invited to a Creepover Ser.: 16). (ENG., Illus.). 160p. (J). (gr. 3-7). pap. 6.99 *(978-1-4424-8233-3(8)*, Simon Spotlight) Simon Spotlight.

—Together Forever. 2012. (You're Invited to a Creepover Ser.: 8). (ENG.). 160p. (J). (gr. 3-7). pap. 5.99 *(978-1-4424-5159-9(9)*, Simon Spotlight) Simon Spotlight.

Nix, Garth. Frogkisser! 2017. (ENG.). 384p. (J). (gr. 7). 18.99 *(978-1-338-05208-4(X)*, Scholastic Pr.) Scholastic, Inc.

Noël, Alyson. Dreamland. 2011. (Riley Bloom Book Ser.: 3). (ENG.). 224p. (J). (gr. 4-7). pap. 7.99 *(978-0-312-56375-2(2)*, 9780312563752) Square Fish.

Noland, Charles. The Adventures of Drew & Ellie: The Magical Dress. Baker, Sherri, illus. 2006. (J). *(978-0-9789297-1-8(3))*; 2nd rev. ed. 84p. per. 7.95 *(978-0-9789297-0-1(5))* TMD Enterprises.

Nolen, Jerdine. Pitching in for Eubie. Lewis, E. B., illus. 2007. (ENG.). 32p. (J). (gr. k-3). 16.99 *(978-0-688-14917-8(0)*, Amistad) HarperCollins Pubs.

Noonan, Rosalind, et al. The Love Factor. 2003. (ENG., Illus.). 128p. *(978-0-00-714454-9(7)*, HarperCollins Children's Bks.) HarperCollins Pubs. Ltd.

Nöstlinger, Christine. Por Favor, Vuelve a Casa (Please, Come Back Home) (SPA.). 176p. (YA). (gr. 7-9). 9.95 *(978-958-04-2379-9(2)*, 10266266) Norma S.A. COL. Dist: Distribuidora Norma, Inc.

Novak, Ali. The Heartbreakers. 2015. (Heartbreak Chronicles Ser.: 1). (ENG.). 336p. (YA). (gr. 6-12). pap. 10.99 *(978-1-4926-1256-8(1)*, 9781492612568) Sourcebooks, Inc.

Numeroff, Laura Joffe. The Chicken Sisters. Collicott, Sharleen, illus. abr. ed. 2003. (J). (gr. -1-2). 28.95 incl. audio compact disk *(978-1-59112-533-4(2))* Live Oak Media.

—What Sisters Do Best. Munsinger, Lynn, illus. 2012. (ENG.). 20p. (J). (gr. -1 — 1). bds. 6.99 *(978-1-4521-1074-5(3))* Chronicle Bks. LLC.

Nusom, Jacqueline. My Little Sister & Me. 2006. 12p. (J). 8.47 *(978-1-4116-7352-6(2))* Lulu Pr., Inc.

Nyikos, Stacy. Dragon Wishes. 2008. (ENG.). 256p. (J). (gr. 2-7). 16.95 *(978-1-933831-11-4(1))* Blooming Tree Pr.

Oaks, Tina. Sister Trap, No. 2. 2003. (Stepsisters Ser.). (ENG.). (J). pap. 2.50 *(978-0-590-40903-2(4))* Scholastic, Inc.

O'Brien, Caragh M. Prized. 2011. (Birthmarked Trilogy Ser.: 2). (ENG., Illus.). 368p. (YA). (gr. 7). 16.99 *(978-1-59643-570-4(4)*, 9781596435704) Roaring Brook Pr.

—Prized. 2012. (Birthmarked Trilogy Ser.: 2). (ENG.). 400p. (YA). (gr. 7). pap. 12.99 *(978-1-250-01031-5(4)*, 9781250010315) Square Fish.

—Promised. 2012. (Birthmarked Trilogy Ser.: 3). (ENG.). 304p. (YA). (gr. 7). 17.99 *(978-1-59643-571-1(2)*, 9781596435711) Roaring Brook Pr.

—Promised. 2013. (Birthmarked Trilogy Ser.: 3). (ENG.). 336p. (YA). (gr. 7-12). pap. 9.99 *(978-1-250-03428-1(0)*, 9781250034281) Square Fish.

O'Brien, Thomas E. The Magic of Finbar. 2011. 68p. pap. 19.95 *(978-1-4560-4235-6(1))* America Star Bks.

O'Connor, Jane. Fancy Nancy & the Fabulous Fashion Boutique. Glasser, Robin Preiss, illus. 2010. (Fancy Nancy Ser.). 32p. (J). (gr. -1-3). (ENG.). 17.99 *(978-0-06-123592-4(X))*; lib. bdg. 18.89 *(978-0-06-123593-1(8))* HarperCollins Pubs.

—Fancy Nancy: Jojo & Daddy Bake a Cake. Glasser, Robin Preiss, illus. 2017. (My First I Can Read Ser.). 32p. (J). (gr. -1-3). pap. 3.99 ***(978-0-06-237801-9(5))*** HarperCollins Pubs.

—Lulu & the Witch Baby. Sinclair, Bella, illus. 2014. (I Can Read Level 2 Ser.). (ENG.). 48p. (J). (gr. -1-3). pap. 3.99 *(978-0-06-230516-9(6))* HarperCollins Pubs.

—Saturday Night Sleepover. Glasser, Robin Preiss, illus. 2016. (Fancy Nancy Ser.). 32p. (J). (gr. -1-3). 17.99 *(978-0-06-226985-0(2))* HarperCollins Pubs.

—Stellar Stargazer! Glasser, Robin Preiss, illus. 2011. (Fancy Nancy Ser.). (ENG.). 32p. (J). (gr. -1-2). 12.99 *(978-0-06-191523-9(8))* HarperCollins Pubs.

Odierno, Lisa. Kitten & Her Sister. 2009. (ENG.). 16p. (J). 6.95 *(978-1-60727-000-3(5))* Soundprints.

Olaizola, José Luis. Mi Hermana Gabriela. (SPA., Illus.). 120p. (YA). (gr. 5-8). *(978-84-207-3065-3(3)*, GS4005) Grupo Anaya, S.A. ESP. Dist: Lectorum Pubns., Inc.

Olena Rudge. The Adventures of Sophie & Katia in the Enchanted Forest. 2013. 220p. pap. *(978-3-85438-685-8(0))* united p.c. Verlag.

Olivas, Silvia. Disney Elena of Avalor: a Sister's Promise: Storybook & Necklace. 2016. (ENG.). 32p. (J). (gr. -1 — 1). 14.99 *(978-0-7944-3842-5(3)*, Reader's Digest Children's Bks.) Studio Fun International.

Oliver, Lauren. Vanishing Girls. (gr. 9). 2016. 384p. (YA). pap. 9.99 *(978-0-06-222411-8(5))* 2015. (ENG.). 368p. (J). 18.99 *(978-0-06-222410-1(7))* HarperCollins Pubs.

—Vanishing Girls. 2016. (YA). lib. bdg. 20.85 *(978-0-606-38171-0(6))* Turtleback Bks.

Oliver, Lin. Almost Identical. 2012. (Almost Identical Ser.: 1). (ENG.). 224p. (J). (gr. 3-7). pap. 7.99 *(978-0-448-45191-6(3)*, Grosset & Dunlap) Penguin Young Readers Group.

—Twice as Nice. 2014. (Almost Identical Ser.: 4). (ENG.). 224p. (J). (gr. 3-7). 6.99 *(978-0-448-46447-3(0)*, Grosset & Dunlap) Penguin Young Readers Group.

—Two-Faced, No. 2. 2012. (Almost Identical Ser.: 2). (ENG.). 224p. (J). (gr. 3-7). pap. 7.99 *(978-0-448-45192-3(1)*, Grosset & Dunlap) Penguin Young Readers Group.

Olsen, Mary-Kate & Olsen, Ashley. Dare to Scare. 2005. (ENG., Illus.). 112p. *(978-0-00-715887-4(4))* HarperCollins Pubs. Australia.

—Love, Set, Match. 2005. (ENG., Illus.). 112p. *(978-0-00-715885-0(8))* HarperCollins Pubs. Australia.

—Santa Girls, 3 vols. 2005. (ENG., Illus.). 112p. *(978-0-00-715888-1(2))* HarperCollins Pubs. Australia.

—Two of a Kind Diaries: Winner Take All. 2003. (ENG., Illus.). 112p. *(978-0-00-714471-6(7)*, HarperCollins Children's Bks.) HarperCollins Pubs. Ltd.

Olson, Norah. Twisted Fate. (YA). (gr. 8). 2016. 288p. pap. 9.99 *(978-0-06-227206-5(3)*, Tegen, Katherine Bks) 2015. (ENG.). 272p. 17.99 *(978-0-06-227204-1(7))* HarperCollins Pubs.

Omara, Charlotte. My Scary First Day of School. 2012. 26p. 24.95 *(978-1-4626-7652-1(9))* America Star Bks.

Omololu, C. J. The Third Twin. 2015. (ENG.). 336p. (YA). (gr. 7). 20.99 *(978-0-375-99171-4(9)*, Delacorte Pr.) Random Hse. Children's Bks.

Orante, Ann-Jeanette P. Best Sisters for Life... 2007. (ENG., Illus.). 36p. (J). per. 11.95 *(978-1-59800-972-9(9))* Outskirts Pr., Inc.

Orgel, Doris. Sarah's Room. Sendak, Maurice, illus. 2005. 47p. (J). (gr. k-4). reprint ed. 15.00 *(978-0-7567-9683-9(0))* DIANE Publishing Co.

Orr, Wendy. The Princess & Her Panther. Stringer, Lauren, illus. 2010. (ENG.). 40p. (J). (gr. -1-3). 16.99 *(978-1-4169-9780-1(6)*, Beach Lane Bks.) Beach Lane Bks.

O'Ryan, Ray. Operation Twin Trouble. Kraft, Jason, illus. 2015. (Galaxy Zack Ser.: 12). (ENG.). 128p. (J). (gr. k-4). pap. 5.99 *(978-1-4814-4399-9(2)*, Little Simon) Little Simon.

Osbourne, Ozzy, pseud & Zink, Michelle. Guardian of the Gate. 2011. (Prophecy of the Sisters Trilogy Ser.: 2). (ENG.). 368p. (YA). (gr. 7-17). pap. 8.99 *(978-0-316-02740-3(5))* Little, Brown Bks. for Young Readers.

Otten, Charlotte F. Home in a Wilderness Fort: Copper Harbor 1844. 2006. (Illus.). 232p. (J). (gr. 2-7). per. 14.95 *(978-0-9766104-5-8(0))* Arbutus Pr.

Oud, Pauline. Big Sister Sarah. Oud, Pauline, illus. 2013. (ENG., Illus.). 32p. (J). (gr. -1-k). 15.95 *(978-1-60537-151-1(3))* Cobblestone Publishing Co.

Pagratis, Maggie. My Sister the Bee. 2004. 29p. (J). per. 16.68 *(978-1-4116-1098-9(9))* Lulu Pr., Inc.
Palmer, Iva-Marie. The Summers, 0 vols. 2014. (ENG.). 272p. (J). (gr. 10-12). pap. 9.99 *(978-1-4778-2730-7(7),* 9781477827307, Skyscape) Amazon Publishing.
Palmer, Robin. Girl vs. Superstar, Bk. 1. 2010. (Yours Truly, Lucy B. Parker Ser.: 1). (ENG.). 224p. (J). (gr. 5-18). 6.99 *(978-0-14-241500-9(6),* Puffin Books) Penguin Young Readers Group.
—Sealed with a Kiss, 2 vols., No. 2. 2010. (Yours Truly, Lucy B. Parker Ser.: 2). (ENG.). 224p. (J). (gr. 5-18). 6.99 *(978-0-14-241501-6(4),* Puffin Books) Penguin Young Readers Group.
—Take My Advice!, 4 vols. 2012. (Yours Truly, Lucy B. Parker Ser.: 4). (ENG.). 224p. (J). (gr. 5-18). 6.99 *(978-0-14-241503-0(0),* Puffin Books) Penguin Young Readers Group.
—Vote for Me!, 3 vols. 2011. (Yours Truly, Lucy B. Parker Ser.: 3). (ENG.). 224p. (J). (gr. 5-18). 6.99 *(978-0-14-241502-3(2),* Puffin Books) Penguin Young Readers Group.
Palmieri, Kathryn & Palmieri, Patricia. GYPSY McPHEE: The New Kid in Town. 2011. (Illus.). 40p. (J). pap. 12.95 *(978-1-58909-750-6(5))* Bookstand Publishing.
Pandanas, Ms L. A. The Slinky Luminescence: Two Plus Who? 2013. 84p. pap. *(978-0-9870702-9-6(0))* Reed, Laura.
Pandora. Ankh: Conquering the Seven Deadly Sins. 2013. 100p. pap. 10.95 *(978-1-62212-908-9(3),* Strategic Bk. Publishing) Strategic Book Publishing & Rights Agency (SBPRA).
Pantages, Joanna. Fairytale Fitness: The Goobyland Race. 2009. 20p. pap. 11.95 *(978-1-4389-5480-6(8))* AuthorHouse.
Papademetriou, Lisa. Confectionately Yours #2: Taking the Cake! 2012. (Confectionately Yours Ser.: 2). (ENG.). 240p. (J). (gr. 3-7). pap. 5.99 *(978-0-545-22229-7(X),* Scholastic Paperbacks) Scholastic, Inc.
The Paper Pup. 2004. 39p. pap. 24.95 *(978-1-4137-3012-8(4))* PublishAmerica, Inc.
Parker, Emma & Renaud, Marguerite. Who Took My Things? 2010. (Illus.). 20p. pap. *(978-1-877561-76-4(2))* First Edition Ltd.
Parragon Publishing Staff. I'm a Big Sister. (Big Brother/Sister Ser.). 32p. *(978-1-4054-5024-9(X))* Parragon, Inc.
Parunia, Des. The Quest for the Magic Funnel. 2012. (Illus.). 196p. (gr. 4-6). pap. 18.24 *(978-1-4772-3508-9(6))* AuthorHouse.
Paschkis, Julie. Mooshka, a Quilt Story, 1 vol. Paschkis, Julie, illus. 2012. (ENG., Illus.). 32p. (J). 16.95 *(978-1-56145-620-8(9))* Peachtree Pubs.
Paterson, Katherine. Jacob Have I Loved. 2003. (Trophy Bk.). (ENG.). 272p. (YA). (gr. 8-18). pap. 6.99 *(978-0-06-440368-9(8))* HarperCollins Pubs.
Patrick, Cat. The Originals. (ENG.). (YA). (gr. 7-17). 2014. 320p. pap. 10.00 *(978-0-316-21945-7(2))* 2013. 304p. 18.00 *(978-0-316-21943-3(6))* Little, Brown Bks. for Young Readers.
Patron, Susan. Maybe Yes, Maybe No, Maybe Maybe. Halpin, Abigail, illus. 2009. (ENG.). 128p. (J). (gr. 3-5). pap. 5.99 *(978-1-4169-6176-5(3),* Atheneum Bks. for Young Readers) Simon & Schuster Children's Publishing.
Patterson, James. Crazy House. 2017. (Crazy House Ser.: 1). (ENG.). 368p. (YA). (gr. 9-17). 17.99 ***(978-0-316-43131-6(1),*** Jimmy Patterson) Little Brown & Co.
Patterson, Valerie O. The Other Side of Blue. 2011. (ENG.). 240p. (YA). (gr. 7). pap. 13.99 *(978-0-547-55215-6(7))* Houghton Mifflin Harcourt Publishing Co.
Pattison, Darcy. The Scary Slopes, 1 vol. Harpster, Steve, illus. 2011. (My First Graphic Novel Ser.). (ENG.). 32p. (gr. k-2). lib. bdg. 24.65 *(978-1-4342-2534-4(8),* My First Graphic Novel) Stone Arch Bks.
Paul, Dominique. The Possibility of Fireflies. 2007. (ENG.). 224p. (YA). (gr. 8-12). pap. 8.99 *(978-1-4169-1311-5(4),* Simon & Schuster Bks. For Young Readers) Simon & Schuster Bks. For Young Readers.
Paulits, John. Philip & the Case of the Mistaken Identity & Philip & the Baby. 2007. (ENG.). 150p. (YA). pap. 10.95 *(978-1-59705-897-1(1))* Wings ePress, Inc.
Payton, Belle. Two Cool for School. 2014. (It Takes Two Ser.: 2). (ENG., Illus.). 160p. (J). (gr. 3-7). 16.99 *(978-1-4814-0645-1(0),* Simon Spotlight) Simon Spotlight.
—A Whole New Ball Game. 2014. (It Takes Two Ser.: 1). (ENG., Illus.). 160p. (J). (gr. 3-7). pap. 6.99 *(978-1-4814-0641-3(8),* Simon Spotlight) Simon Spotlight.
Pearce, Jackson. Fathomless. 2013. (Fairy Tale Retelling Ser.). (ENG.). 320p. (YA). (gr. 10-17). pap. 8.99 *(978-0-316-20777-5(2))* Little, Brown Bks. for Young Readers.
—Sisters Red. 2011. (Fairy Tale Retelling Ser.). (ENG.). 352p. (YA). (gr. 10-17). pap. 10.99 *(978-0-316-06867-3(5))* Little, Brown Bks. for Young Readers.
Pearson, Mary E. Generous Me. Krejca, Gary, illus. 2011. (Rookie Ready to Learn — All about Me! Ser.). 40p. (J). (gr. -1-k). lib. bdg. 25.00 *(978-0-531-26427-0(0));* (ENG.). pap. 5.95 *(978-0-531-26652-6(4))* Scholastic Library Publishing. (Children's Pr.).
Peloquin, Lili. The Innocents. 2013. (Innocents Ser.: 1). (ENG.). 288p. (YA). (gr. 7). pap. 9.99 *(978-1-59514-502-4(8),* Razorbill) Penguin Young Readers Group.
Perez, Marlene. Dead Is Just a Rumor. 2010. (Dead Is Ser.: 4). (ENG., Illus.). 224p. (YA). (gr. 7-18). pap. 7.99 *(978-0-547-34592-5(5))* Houghton Mifflin Harcourt Publishing Co.
—Dead Is Just a Rumor. 2010. (Dead Is Ser.: 4). lib. bdg. 18.40 *(978-0-606-14958-7(9),* Turtleback) Turtleback Bks.
—Dead Is Not an Option. 2011. (Dead Is Ser.: 5). (ENG.). 256p. (YA). (gr. 7-18). pap. 7.99 *(978-0-547-34593-2(3))* Houghton Mifflin Harcourt Publishing Co.
—Dead Is So Last Year. 2009. (Dead Is Ser.: 3). (ENG., Illus.). 208p. (J). (gr. 7-18). pap. 7.99 *(978-0-15-206216-3(5))* Houghton Mifflin Harcourt Publishing Co.
Perez, Melissa E. Adventures of Camron, Tiffany & Lydi. 2011. 24p. pap. 24.95 *(978-1-4626-3724-9(8))* America Star Bks.
Perkins, Mitali. Secret Keeper. 2010. (ENG.). 240p. (YA). (gr. 7). pap. 8.99 *(978-0-440-23955-0(9),* Ember) Random Hse. Children's Bks.
Perkyns, Dorothy. Bridget's Black '47. 2009. (ENG.). 160p. (J). (gr. 5-18). pap. 12.99 *(978-1-55488-400-1(4))* Dundurn CAN. Dist: Ingram Publisher Services.
Peters, Julie Anne. Rage: A Love Story. 2010. (ENG.). 306p. (YA). (gr. 9). pap. 9.99 *(978-0-375-84411-9(2),* Knopf Bks. for Young Readers) Random Hse. Children's Bks.
Peterson, Jeanne Whitehouse. Don't Forget Winona. Root, Kimberly Bulcken, illus. 2004. 32p. (J). (gr. -1-3). lib. bdg. 15.89 *(978-0-06-027198-5(1))* HarperCollins Pubs.
Petrone, Epp. Anna's Teeth. Maiste, Piia, illus. 2013. 94p. pap. *(978-9949-511-27-3(5))* Petrone Print.
Pham, LeUyen. Big Sister, Little Sister. Pham, LeUyen, illus. 2005. (ENG., Illus.). 40p. (J). (gr. -1-k). 15.99 *(978-0-7868-5182-9(1))* Hyperion Pr.
Phillips, Helen. Here Where the Sunbeams Are Green. (ENG.). 304p. (J). (gr. 5). 2013. 7.99 *(978-0-307-93145-0(5),* Yearling) 2012. E-Book *(978-0-307-97487-7(1),* Delacorte Bks. for Young Readers) Random Hse. Children's Bks.
Pichon, Liz. Excellent Excuses (and Other Good Stuff) 2016. (Brilliant World of Tom Gates Ser.: 2). lib. bdg. 18.40 *(978-0-606-37941-0(X))* Turtleback Bks.
—Tom Gates: Excellent Excuses (And Other Good Stuff) Pichon, Liz, illus. 2015. (Tom Gates Ser.: 2). (ENG., Illus.). 352p. (J). (gr. 3-7). 12.99 *(978-0-7636-7474-8(5))* Candlewick Pr.
Pilon, Laura. Just Like My Little Sister. 2013. 24p. pap. 17.99 *(978-1-4817-0562-2(8))* AuthorHouse.
Pilumeli, Tanya. The Dragonfly Keeper. 2008. 264p. (J). per. 12.95 *(978-0-9801396-0-0(0))* FAVA Pr.
Pixley, Marcella. Freak. 2013. (ENG.). 160p. (YA). (gr. 7-10). pap. 10.99 *(978-1-250-02742-9(X),* 9781250027429) Square Fish.
—Without Tess. 2014. (ENG.). 304p. (YA). (gr. 7-12). pap. 9.99 *(978-1-250-04435-8(9),* 9781250044358) Square Fish.
Plum, Amy. Die for Me. (Die for Me Ser.: 1). (ENG.). (YA). (gr. 9). 2012. 368p. pap. 8.99 *(978-0-06-200402-4(6))* 2011. 352p. 17.99 *(978-0-06-200401-7(8))* HarperCollins Pubs. (HarperTeen).
Pollock, Tom. The Glass Republic. 2016. (Skyscraper Throne Ser.: 2). (ENG.). 448p. (YA). (gr. 7-9). pap. 14.99 *(978-1-68144-348-5(1),* Jo Fletcher Books) Quercus NA.
Poploff, Michelle. Where Triplets Go, Trouble Follows. Jamieson, Victoria, illus. 2015. (ENG.). 96p. (J). (gr. 2-6). 16.95 *(978-0-8234-3289-9(0))* Holiday Hse., Inc.
Popovic, Lana. Wicked Like a Wildfire. 2017. 416p. (YA). (gr. 9). 17.99 *(978-0-06-243683-2(X),* Tegen, Katherine Bks) HarperCollins Pubs.
Posner-Sanchez, Andrea. A Frozen Christmas (Disney Frozen) Random House Disney Staff, illus. 2015. (Glitter Board Book Ser.). (ENG.). 12p. (J). (gr. -1 — 1). bds. 8.99 *(978-0-7364-3479-9(8),* RH/Disney) Random Hse. Children's Bks.
Potter, Giselle. Tell Me What to Dream About. 2015. (ENG., Illus.). 40p. (J). (gr. -1-2). 17.99 *(978-0-385-37423-1(2),* Schwartz & Wade Bks.) Random Hse. Children's Bks.
Powell, Joyce. The Greatest Marriage Ever. Schacher, Tracey, illus. 2011. 26p. pap. 11.95 *(978-1-4575-0215-6(1))* Dog Ear Publishing, LLC.
Powell, Pamela. La Patrulla de las Tortugas. 2003. (SPA., Illus.). 190p. (YA). (gr. 5-8). *(978-84-236-3791-1(3),* ED1183) Edebé ESP. Dist: Lectorum Pubns., Inc.
Preble, Joy. Finding Paris. 2015. (ENG.). 272p. (YA). (gr. 9). 17.99 *(978-0-06-232130-5(7))* HarperCollins Pubs.
Pryor, Bonnie. Jenny's New Baby Sister. 2013. (ENG.). 24p. (J). (gr. -1-3). 11.99 *(978-1-4424-8875-5(1),* Atheneum Bks. for Young Readers) Simon & Schuster Children's Publishing.
Psanis, Maria. I Love My Sister but Sometimes I Don't. 2013. 70p. pap. 14.99 *(978-1-4817-0846-3(5))* AuthorHouse.
Pyles, Mary Kay. Rise & Shine Rosie. 2013. 134p. pap. 11.95 *(978-0-9887836-9-0(X))* Taylor and Seale Publishing, LLC.
Pyrnelle, Louise Clarke. Diddie Dumps & Tot: Or, Plantation Child-life. 2007. 138p. pap. 18.99 *(978-1-4346-0721-8(6));* (ENG.). 150p. pap. 19.99 *(978-1-4346-0781-2(X))* Creative Media Partners, LLC.
Quartey, Esme. Life with My Sister ChanSadiefay Thompso. 2006. 64p. per. 8.95 *(978-0-595-39224-7(5))* iUniverse, Inc.
Racaniello, P. Emilia & Emma Say Please. 2011. 20p. pap. 9.99 *(978-1-257-65455-0(1))* Lulu Pr., Inc.
—Emilia & Emma Say Sorry. 2012. 20p. pap. 9.99 *(978-1-257-63118-6(7))* Lulu Pr., Inc.
—Emilia & Emma Say Thank You. 2012. 20p. pap. 9.99 *(978-1-257-63119-3(5))* Lulu Pr., Inc.
Raether, Erin F. When Auntie Angie Left for Iraq & Remi Came to Stay. 2008. 15p. pap. 24.95 *(978-1-4241-8735-5(4))* America Star Bks.
Raghbeer, Anjali. Rescue by Design: Madhubani Art. Modak, Tejas, illus. 2012. (Art Tales from India Ser.). (ENG.). 24p. 14.95 *(978-81-8328-194-2(X))* Wisdom Tree IND. Dist: SCB Distributors.
Raheb, Donna. The Adventures of Henrietta Ham. 2007. 32p. per. 14.95 *(978-1-4327-0142-0(8))* Outskirts Pr., Inc.
Rahim, Rahimah. The Trunk. 2012. 64p. pap. *(978-1-78176-715-3(7))* FeedARead.com.
Ramos, Ramona J. A Summer with Kaitlyn & Lexi. 2011. 48p. pap. 16.95 *(978-1-4626-1890-3(1))* America Star Bks.
Random House. Barbie 5-Minute Stories: the Sister Collection (Barbie) 2016. (ENG., Illus.). 160p. (J). (gr. -1-2). 12.99 *(978-0-399-55209-0(X),* Random Hse. Bks. for Young Readers) Random Hse. Children's Bks.
—Best Sisters Ever!(Barbie) 2016. (Pictureback(R) Ser.). (ENG., Illus.). 24p. (J). (gr. -1-2). pap. 6.99 *(978-1-101-93796-9(3),* Random Hse. Bks. for Young Readers) Random Hse. Children's Bks.
—Make It Sparkle! (Shimmer & Shine) Random House, illus. 2016. (Glitter Board Book Ser.). (ENG., Illus.). 12p. (J). (— 1). bds. 8.99 *(978-1-5247-0159-8(9),* Random Hse. Bks. for Young Readers) Random Hse. Children's Bks.
—Meet Shimmer & Shine! (Shimmer & Shine) Cardona, Jose Maria, illus. 2016. (Step into Reading Ser.). (ENG.). 24p. (J). (gr. -1-1). 4.99 *(978-0-553-52203-7(5),* Random Hse. Bks. for Young Readers) Random Hse. Children's Bks.
—Somebunny Loves You (Barbie) 2016. (Pictureback(R) Ser.). (ENG., Illus.). 16p. (J). (gr. -1-2). 4.99 *(978-1-101-93195-0(7),* Random Hse. Bks. for Young Readers) Random Hse. Children's Bks.
Random House Disney Staff. Frozen Story Collection (Disney Frozen) Random House Disney Staff, illus. 2015. (Step into Reading Ser.). (ENG., Illus.). 160p. (J). (gr. -1-2). pap. 7.99 *(978-0-7364-3435-5(6),* RH/Disney) Random Hse. Children's Bks.
—A New Reindeer Friend. Random House Disney Staff, illus. 2014. (Big Golden Book Ser.). (ENG., Illus.). 32p. (J). (gr. -1-2). 9.99 *(978-0-7364-3295-5(7),* Golden/Disney) Random Hse. Children's Bks.
Random House Staff. An Egg-Stra Special Easter! (Barbie) Duarte, Pamela, illus. 2014. (Color Plus Card Stock Ser.). (ENG.). 48p. (J). (gr. -1-2). pap. 3.99 *(978-0-385-37319-7(8),* Random Hse. Bks. for Young Readers) Random Hse. Children's Bks.
Raven, Margot Theis. America's White Table. Ellison, Chris & Benny, Mike, illus. 2005. (ENG.). 48p. (J). (gr. k-6). 16.95 *(978-1-58536-216-5(6))* Sleeping Bear Pr.
Raye, Marianna & Raye, Daniel. Olis & the Big Outside. 2011. (Illus.). 32p. pap. 14.09 *(978-1-4567-7157-7(4))* AuthorHouse.
Reavis, Vicky 'A' Blevins. The Night Before Christmas. 2013. 72p. pap. 17.95 *(978-1-4241-2838-9(2))* America Star Bks.
Redbank, Tennant. The Beach Bandit. 2016. (Barbie Chapters Ser.). (ENG., Illus.). 64p. (J). (gr. 1-4). lib. bdg. 12.99 *(978-0-375-97413-7(X),* Random Hse. Bks. for Young Readers) Random Hse. Children's Bks.
—The Haunted Boardwalk. 2016. (Barbie Chapters Ser.). (ENG., Illus.). 64p. (J). (gr. 1-4). lib. bdg. 12.99 *(978-0-375-97412-0(1),* Random Hse. Bks. for Young Readers) Random Hse. Children's Bks.
Redman, Kati. Kate & the Fairy. 2010. 32p. pap. 7.50 *(978-0-557-60891-1(0))* Lulu Pr., Inc.
Redmond, Zelie. The Adventures of Sister Regina Marie: Sister Finds a Friend. Redmond, Zelie, . 2005. (J). per. 6.95 *(978-0-9774345-0-3(8))* Joy of my Youth Pubns., The.
Rees, Gwyneth. My Super Sister, 1. Monks, Lydia & Okstad, Ella, illus. unabr. ed. 2013. (ENG.). 176p. (J). (gr. 4). pap. 6.99 *(978-0-330-46114-6(1))* Pan Macmillan GBR. Dist: Independent Pubs. Group.
Reeves, Dia. Slice of Cherry. 2011. (ENG.). (YA). (gr. 9). 528p. pap. 9.99 *(978-1-4169-8621-8(9));* 512p. 16.99 *(978-1-4169-8620-1(0))* Simon Pulse. (Simon Pulse).
Reinhardt, Dana. We Are the Goldens. 2015. (ENG.). 208p. (YA). (gr. 9). pap. 9.99 *(978-0-385-74258-0(4),* Ember) Random Hse. Children's Bks.
Reisfeld, Randi & Gilmour, H. B. What the Dog Said. 2012. (ENG.). 256p. (YA). (gr. 4-14). 16.99 *(978-1-59990-702-4(X),* 9781599907024, Bloomsbury USA Childrens) Bloomsbury Publishing USA.
Renninson, Lou. Frontalknutschen. pap. 17.95 *(978-3-570-30008-4(0))* Bertelsman, Verlagsgruppe C. GmbH DEU. Dist: Distribooks, Inc.
Restivo, Andrea E. Arabella & the Perilous Pantheon. 2010. 28p. pap. 12.99 *(978-1-60693-790-7(1),* Strategic Bk. Publishing) Strategic Book Publishing & Rights Agency (SBPRA).
Rice, Luanne. The Secret Language of Sisters. (ENG.). 352p. (J). (gr. 7). 2017. pap. 10.99 *(978-1-338-09554-8(4))* 2016. 18.99 *(978-0-545-83955-6(6))* Scholastic, Inc.
Rippin, Sally. The Big Sister: Billie B. Brown. Fukuoka, Aki, illus. 2014. (ENG.). 48p. (J). pap. 4.99 *(978-1-61067-184-2(8))* Kane Miller.
Rivers, Karen. Finding Ruby Starling. 2014. (ENG.). 304p. (J). (gr. 4-7). 17.99 *(978-0-545-53479-6(8),* Levine, Arthur A. Bks.) Scholastic, Inc.
Rizzo, Cynthia. Julie & the Unicorn 2. 2004. 55p. pap. 16.95 *(978-1-4137-4841-3(4))* America Star Bks.
Roberts, D. W. Pep Squad Mysteries Book 1: Cavern in the Hills. 2009. 71p. pap. 8.95 *(978-0-557-05513-5(X))* Lulu Pr., Inc.
—Pep Squad Mysteries Book 2:the Haunting of Townsand Hall. 2009. 77p. pap. 8.95 *(978-0-557-05289-9(0))* Lulu Pr., Inc.
Roberts, Dw. Pep Squad Mysteries Book: Cavern in the Hills. 2008. (Illus.). 68p. pap. 9.96 *(978-0-557-02446-9(3))* Lulu Pr., Inc.
Roberts, Willo Davis. The One Left Behind. 2007. (ENG., Illus.). 144p. (J). (gr. 3-7). pap. 7.99 *(978-0-689-85083-7(2),* Aladdin) Simon & Schuster Children's Publishing.
Robinson, A. M. Vampire Crush. 2010. (ENG.). 416p. (YA). (gr. 8-18). pap. 8.99 *(978-0-06-198971-1(1),* HarperTeen) HarperCollins Pubs.
Robinson, Jimmie. Evil & Malice - Save the World! 2009. (ENG., Illus.). 128p. (J). pap. 14.99 *(978-1-60706-091-8(4),* 9781607060918) Image Comics.
Robinson, Kathleen Marie. Snowflake Sandwiches. 2007. 15p. pap. 24.95 *(978-1-4241-8620-4(X))* America Star Bks.
Robinson, Kelley. Naming: Book One of the Magic of Io Series. Curtiss, Melody, illus. 2013. 138p. pap. 8.95 *(978-0-9745865-1-9(X),* SarahRose Children's Bks.) SarahRose Publishing.
Robinson, Kerby Mae. Give 'N Go. 2010. 84p. pap. 8.95 *(978-1-4502-5075-7(0))* iUniverse, Inc.
Rock, Peter. Klickitat. 2016. (ENG.). 240p. (YA). (gr. 8-17). 17.95 *(978-1-4197-1894-6(0),* Amulet Bks.) Abrams, Inc.
Rogers, Amy Keating. The Journal of the Two Sisters: The Official Chronicles of Celestia & Luna. 2014. (ENG., Illus.). 192p. (J). (gr. 3-17). 14.99 *(978-0-316-28224-6(3))* Little, Brown Bks. for Young Readers.
Roorda, Julie. Wings of a Bee, 1 vol. 2008. (ENG., Illus.). 224p. (YA). (gr. 7-11). pap. *(978-1-894549-68-4(6),* Sumach Pr.) Canadian Scholars.
Rosenbaum, Andria Warmflash. Big Sister, Little Monster. Fotheringham, Edwin, illus. 2017. (ENG.). 40p. (J). (gr. -1-3). 17.99 ***(978-0-545-83192-5(X),*** Scholastic Pr.) Scholastic, Inc.
Rosenthal, Amy Krouse. Little Miss, Big Sis. Reynolds, Peter H., illus. 2015. (ENG.). 40p. (J). (gr. -1-3). 17.99 *(978-0-06-230203-8(5))* HarperCollins Pubs.
Ross, Chudney. Lone Bean. 2012. (ENG.). 208p. (J). (gr. 3-7). 16.99 *(978-0-06-166011-5(6),* Amistad) HarperCollins Pubs.
Rotellar, Carlos. Little Red Monster: Tales of Monica. 2009. 24p. pap. 11.49 *(978-1-4490-2812-1(8))* AuthorHouse.
Rothberg, Abraham. Pinocchio's Sister: A Feminist Fable. 2005. 159p. pap. 11.95 *(978-1-4116-4347-5(X))* Lulu Pr., Inc.
Rozevskis, Diana. Crystal Waters & on to North America. 2013. 280p. pap. *(978-1-78299-851-8(9))* FeedARead.com.
Rubiano, Brittany. Frozen Anna Loves Elsa. Lee, Brittney, illus. 2015. (ENG.). 14p. (J). (gr. -1-k). bds. 9.99 *(978-1-4847-2470-5(4))* Disney Pr.
Rubino, Tony. Who Ate the Brownies. 2013. 28p. pap. 24.95 *(978-1-63004-481-7(4))* America Star Bks.
Ryals, Lexi. Liv & Maddie: Sisters Forever. 2015. (Liv & Maddie Junior Novel Ser.). (ENG., Illus.). 112p. (J). (gr. 3-7). pap. 5.99 *(978-1-4847-1079-1(7))* Disney Pr.
Ryan, Amy Kathleen. Zen & Xander Undone. 2011. (ENG.). 228p. (YA). (gr. 9). pap. 13.99 *(978-0-547-55030-5(8))* Houghton Mifflin Harcourt Publishing Co.
S., Lisa Hamilton Ed. The Tale of the Talking Trees: The Tale of the Talking Trees a Story of Suspense & Surprise. 2012. 32p. pap. 21.99 *(978-1-4691-7846-2(X))* Xlibris Corp.
Sacks, Nathan & Paty, Miss. May's Wild Walk. MissPaty, illus. 2017. (Whiskers Sisters Ser.: 1). (ENG.). 40p. (J). (gr. k-3). 26.65 ***(978-1-5124-2527-7(3),*** Graphic Universe™) Lerner Publishing Group.
Safren, Hannah. Dive: The Life & Fight of Reba Tutt. 2013. (ENG.). 154p. pap. 15.00 *(978-1-938912-28-3(4))* Write Bloody Publishing.
Salemi, Dianne K. We Hear the Dead. 2010. (ENG.). 448p. (YA). (gr. 7-12). pap. 14.99 *(978-1-4022-3092-9(3),* Sourcebooks Jabberwocky) Sourcebooks, Inc.
Salisbury, Linda G. No Sisters Sisters Club: A Bailey Fish Adventure. Grotke, Christopher A., illus. 2005. 188p. (J). per. 8.95 *(978-1-881539-40-7(7))* Tabby Hse. Bks.
Santillo, LuAnn. Jane. Santillo, LuAnn, ed. 2003. (Half-Pint Kids Readers Ser.). (Illus.). 7p. (J). (gr. -1-1). pap. 1.00 *(978-1-59256-099-8(7))* Half-Pint Kids, Inc.
Santopolo, Jill. All That Glitters. 2014. (Sparkle Spa Ser.: 1). (ENG., Illus.). 128p. (J). (gr. 2-5). pap. 5.99 *(978-1-4424-7380-5(0),* Aladdin) Simon & Schuster Children's Publishing.
—Bad News Nails. 2015. (Sparkle Spa Ser.: 5). (ENG., Illus.). 128p. (J). (gr. 2-5). pap. 5.99 *(978-1-4814-2384-7(3),* Aladdin) Simon & Schuster Children's Publishing.
—Bling It On! 2015. (Sparkle Spa Ser.: 7). (ENG., Illus.). 112p. (J). (gr. 2-5). pap. 5.99 *(978-1-4814-2390-8(8),* Aladdin) Simon & Schuster Children's Publishing.
—Fashion Disaster. Mingus, Cathi, illus. 2016. (Sparkle Spa Ser.: 9). (ENG.). 96p. (J). (gr. 2-5). pap. 5.99 *(978-1-4814-6391-1(8),* Aladdin) Simon & Schuster Children's Publishing.
—Fashion Disaster. Mingus, Cathi, illus. 2016. (Sparkle Spa Ser.: 9). (ENG.). 96p. (J). (gr. 2-5). 16.99 *(978-1-4814-6392-8(6),* Simon & Schuster/Paula Wiseman Bks.) Simon & Schuster/Paula Wiseman Bks.
—Glam Opening! Mingus, Cathi, illus. 2017. (Sparkle Spa Ser.: 10). (ENG.). 112p. (J). (gr. 2-5). pap. 5.99 ***(978-1-4814-6395-9(0),*** Aladdin) Simon & Schuster Children's Publishing.
—A Picture-Perfect Mess. 2015. (Sparkle Spa Ser.: 6). (ENG., Illus.). 112p. (J). (gr. 2-5). pap. 5.99 *(978-1-4814-2387-8(8),* Aladdin) Simon & Schuster Children's Publishing.
—Purple Nails & Puppy Tails. 2014. (Sparkle Spa Ser.: 2). (ENG., Illus.). 128p. (J). (gr. 2-5). pap. 5.99 *(978-1-4424-7383-6(5),* Aladdin) Simon & Schuster Children's Publishing.
—Sparkle Spa 4-Books-In-1! All That Glitters; Purple Nails & Puppy Tails; Makeover Magic; True Colors. 2016. (Sparkle Spa Ser.). (ENG., Illus.). 496p. (J). (gr. 2-5). 14.99 *(978-1-4814-7594-5(0),* Aladdin) Simon & Schuster Children's Publishing.
—True Colors. 2014. (Sparkle Spa Ser.: 4). (ENG., Illus.). 128p. (J). (gr. 2-5). pap. 5.99 *(978-1-4424-7389-8(4),* Aladdin) Simon & Schuster Children's Publishing.
—True Colors. 2014. (Sparkle Spa Ser.: 4). (ENG., Illus.). 128p. (J). (gr. 2-5). 16.99 *(978-1-4424-7390-4(8),* Simon & Schuster/Paula Wiseman Bks.) Simon & Schuster/Paula Wiseman Bks.
—Wedding Bell Blues. 2016. (Sparkle Spa Ser.: 8). (ENG., Illus.). 112p. (J). (gr. 2-5). pap. 5.99 *(978-1-4814-2393-9(2),* Aladdin) Simon & Schuster Children's Publishing.
Savage, Kim. Beautiful Broken Girls. 2017. (ENG.). 336p. (YA). 17.99 *(978-0-374-30059-3(3),* 9780374300593, Farrar, Straus & Giroux (BYR)) Farrar, Straus & Giroux.
Saxon, Victoria. Anna & Elsa's Secret Playtime (Disney Frozen) RH Disney, illus. 2016. (Big Golden Book Ser.). (ENG.). 32p. (J). (-k). 9.99 *(978-0-7364-3493-5(3),* Golden/Disney) Random Hse. Children's Bks.
—Frozen (Disney Frozen) Lee, Grace & Cagol, Andrea, illus. 2015. (Little Golden Book Ser.). (ENG.). 24p. (J). (-k). 4.99 *(978-0-7364-3471-3(2),* Golden/Disney) Random Hse. Children's Bks.
Scattergood, Augusta. Glory Be. (ENG.). 208p. (J). (gr. 3-7). 2014. pap. 6.99 *(978-0-545-33181-4(1))* 2012. 16.99 *(978-0-545-33180-7(3))* Scholastic, Inc. (Scholastic Pr.).
Schaefer, Laura. Littler Women: A Modern Retelling. 2017. (ENG., Illus.). 224p. (J). (gr. 3-7). 16.99 ***(978-1-4814-8761-0(2),*** Simon & Schuster/Paula Wiseman Bks.) Simon & Schuster/Paula Wiseman Bks.
Scholastic, Inc. Staff & Black, Sonia. Jumping the Broom. Hu, Ying-Hwa & Van Wright, Cornelius, illus. 2004. (Just for You Ser.). (ENG.). 32p. pap. 3.99 *(978-0-439-56878-4(1),* Teaching Resources) Scholastic, Inc.
Schott, Joanna. Bellows in Hell. 2013. 416p. pap. 18.95 *(978-1-59299-804-3(6))* Inkwater Pr.
Schrefer, Eliot. The Deadly Sister. 2010. (ENG.). 320p. (J). (gr. 7-18). 17.99 *(978-0-545-16574-7(1),* Scholastic Pr.) Scholastic, Inc.
Schroeder, Lisa. Sealed with a Secret. 2016. (ENG.). 224p. (J). (gr. 3-7). 16.99 *(978-0-545-90734-7(9),* Scholastic Pr.) Scholastic, Inc.
Schumacher, Julie. Black Box. 2010. (ENG.). 176p. (YA). (gr. 7-18). pap. 7.99 *(978-0-440-24064-8(6),* Delacorte Bks. for Young Readers) Random Hse. Children's Bks.
Schwabach, Karen. The Hope Chest. 2010. (ENG.). 288p. (J). (gr. 3-7). 7.99 *(978-0-375-84096-8(6),* Yearling) Random Hse. Children's Bks.
Schwartz, Amy. Dee Dee & Me. Schwartz, Amy, illus. 2014. (ENG., Illus.). 32p. (J). (gr. -1-3). pap. 6.99 *(978-0-8234-3178-6(9))* Holiday Hse., Inc.
—Dee Dee & Me. 2013. (ENG., Illus.). 32p. (J). (gr. -1-3). 16.95 *(978-0-8234-2524-2(X))* Holiday Hse., Inc.
—Polka Dots for Poppy. 2016. (ENG., Illus.). 32p. (J). 16.95 *(978-0-8234-3431-2(1))* Holiday Hse., Inc.
Schwartz, Corey Rosen. Twinderella, a Fractioned Fairy Tale. Marcero, Deborah, illus. 2017. (ENG.). 32p. (J). (gr. -1-3). 17.99 ***(978-0-399-17633-3(0),*** G.P. Putnam's Sons Books for Young Readers) Penguin Young Readers Group.

Schwemm, Diane. The Year I Turned Sixteen: Rose, Daisy, Laurel, Lily. 2010. (ENG.). 720p. (YA). (gr. 7). pap. 12.99 *(978-1-4169-8597-6(2),* Simon Pulse) Simon Pulse.

Scott, Elizabeth. Between Here & Forever. (ENG.). (YA). (gr. 9). 2012. 272p. pap. 9.99 *(978-1-4169-9485-5(8))* 2011. 256p. 16.99 *(978-1-4169-9484-8(X))* Simon Pulse. (Simon Pulse).

Scott, Gwen. Blackberry Junction. Baker, David, illus. 2011. 28p. pap. 24.95 *(978-1-4560-0951-9(6))* America Star Bks.

Scotton, Rob. Splat the Cat & the Big Secret. Farley, Rick & Eberz, Robert, illus. 2016. (J). ***(978-1-4844-8600-9(5))*** Publishers Quality Library Service.

Seewald, Jacqueline. Clair's Curse. 2004. 228p. (YA). per. 22.00 *(978-1-58982-191-0(2),* Bedside Bks.) American Bk. Publishing Group.

Sgarlato, Dawn. Big Sister. 2012. 24p. pap. 17.99 *(978-1-4685-9426-3(5))* AuthorHouse.

Shakespeare, Nancy. Benjamin the Bear Gets a Sister. Clouette, Katie, illus. 2013. (Benjamin the Bear Ser.). (ENG.). (J). (gr. -1-3). 14.95 *(978-1-62086-316-9(2))* Mascot Bks., Inc.

Shanker, Tarun & Zekas, Kelly. These Vicious Masks. 2016. (These Vicious Masks Ser.). (ENG.). 320p. (YA). pap. 9.99 *(978-1-250-07389-1(8),* 9781250073891) Feiwel & Friends.

Shaw, J. D. The Secrets of Loon Lake. 2010. (ENG.). 338p. (J). (gr. 5). pap. 16.95 *(978-0-9845318-0-6(7))* Tiny Stachel Pr.

Shaw, Natalie. A Guide to Being a Big Sister. 2014. (Olivia 8x8 Ser.). lib. bdg. 16.00 *(978-0-606-35761-6(0))* Turtleback Bks.

Shay, Kenley. Prommy Meets Her Match: An Unofficial Story for Shopkins Collectors. 2015. (Unofficial Shopkins Collectors Ser.). (ENG.). 112p. (J). (gr. 1-7). pap. 7.99 *(978-1-5107-0374-2(8),* Sky Pony Pr.) Skyhorse Publishing Co., Inc.

Shear, Dani. The Foodie Club. Weinstein, Holly, illus. 2013. (ENG.). 50p. (J). 16.99 *(978-1-61053-027-9(6))* Blackbird Bks.

Shepard, Sara. Cross My Heart, Hope to Die. 2013. (Lying Game Ser.: 5). (ENG.). 336p. (YA). (gr. 9). 17.99 *(978-0-06-212819-5(1),* HarperTeen) HarperCollins Pubs.

—Hide & Seek. (YA). 2013. (Lying Game Ser.: 4). (ENG.). 320p. (gr. 9). pap. 10.99 *(978-0-06-186977-8(5))* 2012. (Lying Game Ser.: 4). (ENG.). 304p. (gr. 9). 17.99 *(978-0-06-186976-1(7))* 2012. (Lying Game Ser.: Bk. 4). 289p. 9.99 *(978-0-06-219369-8(4))* HarperCollins Pubs. (HarperTeen).

—The Lying Game. (Lying Game Ser.: 1). (ENG.). (YA). (gr. 9-18). 2011. 336p. pap. 10.99 *(978-0-06-186971-6(6))* 2010. 320p. 16.99 *(978-0-06-186970-9(8))* 2011. 336p. 16.99 *(978-0-06-211416-7(6))* HarperCollins Pubs. (HarperTeen).

—The Lying Game. 2011. (Lying Game (Quality) Ser.: Vol. 1). (ENG.). (YA). (gr. 9). lib. bdg. 20.60 ***(978-1-61383-667-5(8))*** Perfection Learning Corp.

—Never Have I Ever. (Lying Game Ser.: 2). (ENG.). (YA). (gr. 9). 2012. 336p. pap. 9.99 *(978-0-06-186973-0(2))* 2011. 320p. 16.99 *(978-0-06-186972-3(4))* HarperCollins Pubs. (HarperTeen).

—Seven Minutes in Heaven. 2014. (Lying Game Ser.: 6). (ENG.). 400p. (YA). (gr. 9). pap. 10.99 *(978-0-06-212823-2(X),* HarperTeen) HarperCollins Pubs.

—Two Truths & a Lie. (Lying Game Ser.: 3). (ENG.). (YA). (gr. 9). 2013. 320p. pap. 9.99 *(978-0-06-186975-4(9))* 2012. 304p. 17.99 *(978-0-06-186974-7(0))* HarperCollins Pubs. (HarperTeen).

Sherri L. Berner. Healthy Fun with Benjamin & Jasmine: ABCs of the Human Body. Michael A. Cicchetti, illus. 2009. 32p. pap. 12.99 *(978-1-4343-8297-9(4))* AuthorHouse.

Shevah, Emma. Dream on, Amber. Crawford-White, Helen, illus. 2015. (ENG.). 272p. (J). (gr. 3-7). 12.99 *(978-1-4926-2250-5(8),* 9781492622505, Sourcebooks Jabberwocky) Sourcebooks, Inc.

Shields, Brooke. Welcome to Your World, Baby. Doerrfeld, Cori, illus. 2008. 32p. (J). (gr. -1-3). lib. bdg. 17.89 *(978-0-06-125312-6(X))* HarperCollins Pubs.

Shore, Diane Z. How to Drive Your Sister Crazy. Rankin, Laura, illus. 2012. (I Can Read Level 2 Ser.). (ENG.). 48p. (J). (gr. k-3). pap. 3.99 *(978-0-06-052764-8(1))* HarperCollins Pubs.

Shu, Sammy. There's a Season for All. Cone, Carl, illus. 2006. 54p. (J). (gr. -1-3). 16.95 *(978-0-9778211-0-5(2),* Raynestorm Bks.) Silver Rose Publishing.

Sidwell, Beth. Zack the Zombie. 2012. 24p. pap. 15.99 *(978-1-4797-0962-5(X))* Xlibris Corp.

Siebel, Kathryn. The Trouble with Twins. 2016. (ENG., Illus.). 256p. (J). (gr. 3-7). 16.99 *(978-1-101-93273-5(2),* Knopf Bks. for Young Readers) Random Hse. Children's Bks.

Simoneau, Shelly. The Cows Came Running & the Horses Did Too! 2011. 28p. pap. 14.99 *(978-1-4567-3107-6(6))* AuthorHouse.

Slaughter, Kristi. Emma & Allie. Hanks, Carol, illus. 2009. 28p. pap. 12.49 *(978-1-4389-9812-1(0))* AuthorHouse.

Smelcer, John. The Great Death. 2009. (ENG.). 176p. (YA). (gr. 5-9). 17.99 *(978-0-8050-8100-8(3),* 9780805081008, Holt, Henry & Co. Bks. For Young Readers) Holt, Henry & Co.

Smith, Debora Ann Baker. The Magnificent Fairy Party. 2010. (Illus.). 30p. pap. 13.00 *(978-1-60911-404-6(3),* Eloquent Bks.) Strategic Book Publishing & Rights Agency (SBPRA).

Smith, Evelyn. Seven Sisters at Queen Anne's. Coller, H., illus. 2013. 162p. pap. *(978-1-909423-07-7(6))* Bks. to Treasure.

Smith, John D. H. The Whale Whisperers, 1 vol. Smith, Anne, illus. 2009. 17p. pap. 24.95 *(978-1-60749-211-5(3))* America Star Bks.

Smith, Roland. Kitty Hawk. 2012. (I, Q Ser.: Bk. 3). (ENG., Illus.). 240p. (J). (gr. 5). pap. 8.95 *(978-1-58536-604-0(8))*; lib. bdg. 15.95 *(978-1-58536-605-7(6))* Sleeping Bear Pr.

Smith, Sherwood. The Emerald Wand of Oz. Stout, William, illus. 2007. 262p. (J). 17.00 *(978-1-4223-6710-0(X))* DIANE Publishing Co.

Snow, Maya. Blade's Edge. 2009. 245p. (J). lib. bdg. 17.89 *(978-0-06-124391-2(4))* HarperCollins Pubs.

—Chasing the Secret. 2010. (Sisters of the Sword Ser.: 2). (ENG.). 272p. (J). (gr. 5). pap. 6.99 *(978-0-06-124392-9(2))* HarperCollins Pubs.

—Sisters of the Sword. 2008. (Sisters of the Sword Ser.). (J). (gr. 5-18). 288p. 16.99 *(978-0-06-124387-5(6))*; 275p. lib. bdg. 17.89 *(978-0-06-124388-2(4))* HarperCollins Pubs.

Soderberg, Erin. The Quirks & the Quirkalicious Birthday. Light, Kelly, illus. 2015. (Quirks Ser.). (ENG.). 208p. (YA). (gr. 3-6). 13.99 *(978-1-61963-370-4(1),* 9781619633704, Bloomsbury USA Childrens) Bloomsbury Publishing USA.

Soontornvat, Christina. The Changelings. (Changelings Ser.: 1). (ENG.). (J). (gr. 5-8). 2017. 304p. pap. 7.99 ***(978-1-4926-4795-9(0))*** 2016. 288p. 16.99 *(978-1-4926-3260-3(0),* 9781492632603) Sourcebooks, Inc. (Sourcebooks Jabberwocky).

Spangler, Paula Jeanne. Abigail's Christmas ~ Christmas Morn Reveals A Newborn. 2004. 17p. (J). pap. 14.08 *(978-1-4116-1045-3(8))* Lulu Pr., Inc.

Sparkes, Ali. Spider Stampede. Collins, Ross, illus. 2013. (S. W. I. T. C. H. Ser.: 1). (ENG.). 104p. (J). (gr. 2-5). pap. 7.95 *(978-1-4677-0710-7(4))* Lerner Publishing Group.

The Sparkle Spa Shimmering Collection: All That Glitters - Purple Nails & Puppy Tails - Makeover Magic - True Colors. 2014. (Sparkle Spa Ser.). (ENG., Illus.). 512p. (J). (gr. 2-5). pap. 23.99 *(978-1-4814-1658-0(8),* Aladdin) Simon & Schuster Children's Publishing.

Spirn, Michele Sobel. The Bridges in Edinburgh. 2004. (Going to Ser.). 144p. (J). pap. 6.95 *(978-1-893577-11-4(2))* Fruitbearer Publishing, LLC.

Spotswood, Jessica. Born Wicked. 2013. (Cahill Witch Chronicles Ser.: 1). (ENG.). 352p. (YA). (gr. 7). pap. 10.99 *(978-0-14-242187-1(1),* Speak) Penguin Young Readers Group.

—Born Wicked. 2013. lib. bdg. 22.10 *(978-0-606-26729-8(8),* Turtleback) Turtleback Bks.

—Sisters' Fate. 2015. (Cahill Witch Chronicles Ser.: 3). (ENG.). 384p. (YA). (gr. 7). pap. 9.99 *(978-0-14-751442-4(8),* Speak) Penguin Young Readers Group.

Stadelmann, Amy Marie. The Not-So Itty-Bitty Spiders. 2015. (Olive & Beatrix Ser.: 1). (ENG., Illus.). 80p. (J). (gr. k-2). pap. 4.99 *(978-0-545-81480-5(4))* Scholastic, Inc.

—The Super-Smelly Moldy Blob. Stadelmann, Amy Marie, illus. 2016. (Olive & Beatrix Ser.: 2). (ENG., Illus.). 80p. (J). (gr. k-2). 15.99 *(978-0-545-81485-0(5))* Scholastic, Inc.

Standiford, Natalie. Confessions of the Sullivan Sisters. (ENG.). 320p. (J). 2012. (gr. 9). pap. 9.99 *(978-0-545-10711-2(3),* Scholastic Paperbacks) 2010. (gr. 8-18). 17.99 *(978-0-545-10710-5(5),* Scholastic Pr.) Scholastic, Inc.

Stella, Lennon & Stella, Maisy. In the Waves. Björkman, Steve, illus. 2015. (ENG.). 40p. (J). (gr. -1-3). 17.99 *(978-0-06-235939-1(8))* HarperCollins Pubs.

Stern, Jacqueline. Mystery of the Whispering Walls. 2004. (J). 148p. pap. *(978-1-57168-844-6(7))*; (Hollow Tree Mystery Ser.: Bk. 6). (Illus.). v, 142p. *(978-1-57168-850-7(1),* Eakin Pr.) Eakin Pr.

Steven, Ruth Lauren & Lauren, Ruth. Prisoner of Ice & Snow. 2017. (ENG.). 288p. (J). 16.99 *(978-1-68119-131-7(8),* 9781681191317, Bloomsbury USA Childrens) Bloomsbury Publishing USA.

Stevenson, Robin. Record Breaker, 1 vol. 2013. (ENG.). 152p. (J). (gr. 4-7). pap. 9.95 *(978-1-55469-959-9(2))* Orca Bk. Pubs. USA.

Stewart, Nancy. One Pelican at a Time: A Story of the Gulf Oil Spill. Bell, Samantha, illus. 2011. 26p. (J). 19.95 *(978-1-61633-138-2(0))*; pap. 11.95 *(978-1-61633-139-9(9))* Guardian Angel Publishing, Inc.

Stilton, Geronimo. Shipwreck on the Pirate Islands. 2005. (Geronimo Stilton Ser.: 18). (ENG., Illus.). 128p. (J). (gr. 2-5). 7.99 *(978-0-439-69141-3(9),* Scholastic Paperbacks) Scholastic, Inc.

Stilton, Geronimo & Stilton, Thea. Thea Stilton & the Blue Scarab Hunt. 2012. (Thea Stilton Ser.: 11). (ENG.). 176p. (J). (gr. 2-5). pap. 8.99 *(978-0-545-34104-2(3),* Scholastic Paperbacks) Scholastic, Inc.

—Thea Stilton & the Dragon's Code. 2009. (Thea Stilton Ser.: 1). (ENG.). 176p. (J). (gr. 2-5). pap. 8.99 *(978-0-545-10367-1(3),* Scholastic Paperbacks) Scholastic, Inc.

—Thea Stilton & the Ice Treasure. 2011. (Thea Stilton Ser.: 9). (ENG., Illus.). 176p. (J). (gr. 2-5). pap. 8.99 *(978-0-545-33134-0(X),* Scholastic Paperbacks) Scholastic, Inc.

—Thea Stilton & the Mountain of Fire. 2009. (Thea Stilton Ser.: 2). (ENG.). 176p. (J). (gr. 2-5). pap. 8.99 *(978-0-545-15060-6(4),* Scholastic Paperbacks) Scholastic, Inc.

—Thea Stilton & the Mystery on the Orient Express. 2012. (Thea Stilton Ser.: 13). (ENG.). 176p. (J). (gr. 2-5). pap. 8.99 *(978-0-545-34105-9(1),* Scholastic Paperbacks) Scholastic, Inc.

—Thea Stilton & the Prince's Emerald. 2012. (Thea Stilton Ser.: 12). (ENG.). 176p. (J). (gr. 2-5). pap. 8.99 *(978-0-545-34108-0(6),* Scholastic Paperbacks) Scholastic, Inc.

Stilton, Thea. Big Trouble in the Big Apple. 2011. (Thea Stilton Ser.: 8). (ENG., Illus.). 176p. (J). (gr. 2-5). pap. 8.99 *(978-0-545-22775-9(5),* Scholastic Paperbacks) Scholastic, Inc.

—The Spanish Dance Mission. 2013. (Thea Stilton Ser.: 16). (ENG., Illus.). 176p. (J). (gr. 2-5). pap. 8.99 *(978-0-545-55626-2(0),* Scholastic Paperbacks) Scholastic, Inc.

—Thea Stilton & the Frozen Fiasco. 2017. (Thea Stilton Ser.: 25). lib. bdg. 19.65 ***(978-0-606-40181-4(4))*** Turtleback Bks.

—Thea Stilton & the Hollywood Hoax. 2016. (Thea Stilton Ser.: 23). lib. bdg. 18.40 *(978-0-606-38799-6(4))* Turtleback Bks.

—Thea Stilton & the Journey to the Lion's Den. 2013. (Thea Stilton Ser.: 17). (ENG.). 176p. (J). (gr. 2-5). pap. 8.99 *(978-0-545-55627-9(9),* Scholastic Paperbacks) Scholastic, Inc.

—Thea Stilton & the Journey to the Lion's Den. 2013. (Thea Stilton Ser.: 17). lib. bdg. 19.65 *(978-0-606-32382-6(1),* Turtleback) Turtleback Bks.

—Thea Stilton & the Legend of the Fire Flowers. 2013. (Thea Stilton Ser.: 15). lib. bdg. 19.65 *(978-0-606-32000-9(8),* Turtleback) Turtleback Bks.

—Thea Stilton & the Missing Myth. 2014. (Thea Stilton Ser.: 20). lib. bdg. 19.65 *(978-0-606-36058-6(1))* Turtleback Bks.

—Thea Stilton & the Mystery on the Orient Express. 2012. (Thea Stilton Ser.: 13). lib. bdg. 19.65 *(978-0-606-26757-1(3),* Turtleback) Turtleback Bks.

Stine, Megan, et al. Girl Talk. 2003. (ENG., Illus.). 128p. *(978-0-00-714453-2(9),* HarperCollins Children's Bks.) HarperCollins Pubs. Ltd.

—Sealed with a Kiss. 2003. (ENG., Illus.). 112p. *(978-0-00-714461-7(X),* HarperCollins Children's Bks.) HarperCollins Pubs. Ltd.

—Surprise Surprise! 2003. (ENG., Illus.). 112p. *(978-0-00-714462-4(8),* HarperCollins Children's Bks.) HarperCollins Pubs. Ltd.

—War of the Wardrobes. 2003. (ENG., Illus.). 112p. *(978-0-00-714468-6(7),* HarperCollins Children's Bks.) HarperCollins Pubs. Ltd.

Stine, R. L. Bitten: Dangerous Girls & the Taste of Night. 2010. (ENG.). 496p. (YA). (gr. 9). pap. 9.99 *(978-0-06-200739-1(4),* HarperTeen) HarperCollins Pubs.

—Dangerous Girls. 2003. 256p. (J). 111.92 *(978-0-06-056909-9(3))*; 111.92 *(978-0-06-056910-5(7))*; (ENG., Illus.). (gr. 7-18). 13.99 *(978-0-06-053080-8(4))* HarperCollins Pubs.

—First Evil. 2011. (Fear Street Cheerleaders Ser.: 1). (ENG.). 176p. (YA). (gr. 9). pap. 9.99 *(978-1-4424-3086-0(9),* Simon Pulse) Simon Pulse.

Stokes, Paula. Vicarious. 2016. (Vicarious Ser.). (ENG.). 336p. (YA). 17.99 *(978-0-7653-8094-4(3),* 9780765380944, Tor Teen) Doherty, Tom Assocs., LLC.

Stone, Phoebe. Paris for Two. 2016. (ENG.). 272p. (J). (gr. 3-7). 16.99 *(978-0-545-44362-3(8),* Levine, Arthur A. Bks.) Scholastic, Inc.

Stork, Francisco X. Irises. 2012. (YA). pap. *(978-0-545-15136-8(8))*; (ENG.). 304p. (J). (gr. 9). 17.99 *(978-0-545-15135-1(X))* Scholastic, Inc. (Levine, Arthur A. Bks.).

Suguitan, Jazel A. We're Moving?! Shari Tucker's Wacky World #1. 2010. 124p. 20.95 *(978-1-4502-6874-5(9))*; pap. 10.95 *(978-1-4502-6871-4(4))* iUniverse, Inc.

Sullivan, Laura L. Delusion. 2014. (ENG.). 352p. (YA). (gr. 7). pap. 18.99 *(978-0-544-10478-5(1))* Houghton Mifflin Harcourt Publishing Co.

Suma, Nova Ren. Imaginary Girls. 2012. (ENG.). 352p. (YA). (gr. 9-18). pap. 8.99 *(978-0-14-242143-7(X),* Speak) Penguin Young Readers Group.

Sumner, Bea. Sisters Three: Scary's Not a Part of Me. 2007. (J). pap. *(978-0-9787375-0-4(4))* Sisters Three Publishing Inc.

Szymona, Marlene L. My Sister Beth's Pink Birthday. Battuz, Christine, illus. 2014. (J). *(978-1-4338-1654-3(7))*; pap. *(978-1-4338-1655-0(5))* American Psychological Assn. (Magination Pr.).

Talhah, Abu & Books, Greenbird. My Sister Saarah. Fowler, Claire, illus. 2013. 30p. pap. *(978-0-9576379-6-2(9))* Greenbird Bks.

Tansil-Mitchell, Angela. Kimmie C Sunshine: When Mommy & Daddy Loses Their Jobs. 2011. 24p. pap. 13.79 *(978-1-4567-5666-6(4))* AuthorHouse.

Taranta, Mary. Shimmer & Burn. 2017. (YA). pap. ***(978-1-4814-7200-5(3)***, McElderry, Margaret K. Bks.) McElderry, Margaret K. Bks.

Tate, Nikki. Fallout, 1 vol. 2011. (Orca Soundings Ser.). (ENG.). (YA). (gr. 8-12). 168p. pap. 9.95 *(978-1-55469-272-9(5))*; 128p. lib. bdg. 16.95 *(978-1-55469-976-6(2))* Orca Bk. Pubs. USA.

Taylor, G. P. The First Escape. 2008. (Dopple Ganger Chronicles Ser.: 1). (ENG., Illus.). 288p. (J). (gr. 3-7). 19.99 *(978-1-4143-1947-6(9),* SaltRiver) Tyndale Hse. Pubs.

—The Great Mogul Diamond. 2011. (Dopple Ganger Chronicles Ser.: 3). (ENG.). 304p. (J). (gr. 3-7). 19.99 *(978-1-4143-1949-0(5),* SaltRiver) Tyndale Hse. Pubs.

—The Secret of Indigo Moon. 2009. (Dopple Ganger Chronicles Ser.: 2). (ENG., Illus.). 304p. (J). (gr. 3-7). 19.99 *(978-1-4143-1948-3(7),* SaltRiver) Tyndale Hse. Pubs.

Taylor, Jessica. A Map for Wrecked Girls. 2017. (ENG.). 368p. (YA). (gr. 9). 17.99 ***(978-0-7352-2811-5(6)***, Dial Bks) Penguin Young Readers Group.

Taylor, Sydney. All-Of-a-Kind Family Uptown. 2014. (ENG.). 200p. (J). (gr. 3). pap. 12.95 *(978-1-939601-17-9(7))* Ig Publishing, Inc.

Telgemeier, Raina. Ghosts. Telgemeier, Raina, illus. 2016. (ENG., Illus.). 256p. (J). (gr. 3-7). 24.99 *(978-0-545-54061-2(5),* Graphix) Scholastic, Inc.

Temairik, Jaime. Alice & Lucy Will Work for Bunk Beds. Temairik, Jaime, illus. 2016. (ENG., Illus.). 40p. (J). (gr. -1-k). 16.99 *(978-1-4847-0816-3(4))* Disney Publishing Worldwide.

Terry, Teri. The Book of Lies. 2017. (ENG.). 384p. (YA). (gr. 7). 17.99 ***(978-0-544-90048-6(0)***, Clarion Bks.) Houghton Mifflin Harcourt Trade & Reference Pubs.

Thame, Val. Witches in Deed. l.t. ed. 2007. 100p. per. *(978-1-905665-25-9(3))* Pollinger In Print.

Thomas, Kara. The Darkest Corners. (ENG.). (YA). (gr. 9). 2017. 352p. pap. 9.99 ***(978-0-553-52148-1(9)***, Ember) 2016. 336p. 17.99 *(978-0-553-52145-0(4),* Delacorte Pr.) Random Hse. Children's Bks.

Thompson, Don. Bunny World: Kindness Is the Key to Happiness. 2009. 28p. pap. 14.99 *(978-1-4389-5475-2(1))* AuthorHouse.

Thompson, Lauren. Little Quack's ABC's. Anderson, Derek, illus. 2010. (Super Chubbies Ser.). (ENG.). 26p. (J). (gr. -1 — 1). bds. 5.99 *(978-1-4169-6091-1(0),* Little Simon) Little Simon.

Thor, Annika. A Faraway Island. Schenck, Linda, tr. 2011. (ENG.). 256p. (J). (gr. 3-7). 6.99 *(978-0-375-84495-9(3),* Yearling) Random Hse. Children's Bks.

Thornton, M. H. Kylee & Lexie: Mystery of the Gholdees. 2010. 64p. pap. 10.99 *(978-1-4269-3713-2(X))* Trafford Publishing.

Tiernan, Cate. A Chalice of Wind - A Circle of Ashes - A Feather of Stone - A Necklace of Water. 2011. (Balefire Ser.). (ENG.). 976p. (YA). (gr. 7-18). 9.99 *(978-1-59514-411-9(0),* Razorbill) Penguin Young Readers Group.

Tillworth, Mary. Leah's Dream Dollhouse (Shimmer & Shine) Yum, Heekyoung, illus. 2016. (Pictureback(R) Ser.). (ENG.). 16p. (J). (gr. -1-2). 4.99 *(978-1-101-93249-0(X),* Random Hse. Bks. for Young Readers) Random Hse. Children's Bks.

—The Sweetest Cupcake (Shimmer & Shine) Cartobaleno, illus. 2016. (Pictureback(R) Ser.). (ENG.). 16p. (J). (gr. -1-2). 4.99 *(978-0-553-52201-3(9),* Random Hse. Bks. for Young Readers) Random Hse. Children's Bks.

Tims, Laura. Please Don't Tell. 2016. 336p. (YA). (gr. 8). 17.99 *(978-0-06-231732-2(6),* HarperTeen) HarperCollins Pubs.

Torras, Meri. Mi Hermana Aixa. Valverde, Mikel, illus. (SPA.). 120p. (J). (gr. 3-5). *(978-84-246-5915-8(5),* GL6491) La Galera, S.A. Editorial ESP. Dist: Lectorum Pubns., Inc.

Trionfo, Nikki. Shatter. 2017. (YA). pap. 18.99 ***(978-1-4621-2013-0(X)***, Horizon Pubs.) Cedar Fort, Inc./CFI Distribution.

Tripp, Valerie. Nellie's Promise. England, Tamara, ed. Andreasen, Dan, illus. 2004. (ENG.). 96p. (gr. 2-18). pap. 6.95 *(978-1-58485-890-4(7))* American Girl Publishing, Inc.

Troulis, Jennifer. Penelope & Priscilla: And the Enchanted House of Whispers. 2nd ed. 2004. (Illus.). 229p. per. 13.95 *(978-0-9768602-0-4(1))* Twin Monkeys Pr.

Troupe, Thomas Kingsley. Darling Doll. Faber, Rudy, illus. 2016. (Hauntiques Ser.). (ENG.). 128p. (gr. 4-6). lib. bdg. 25.32 *(978-1-4965-3548-1(0))* Stone Arch Bks.

—Ghostly Goalie. Faber, Rudy, illus. 2016. (Hauntiques Ser.). (ENG.). 128p. (gr. 4-6). lib. bdg. 25.32 *(978-1-4965-3544-3(8))* Stone Arch Bks.

Trueit, Trudi. The Sister Solution. Valencia, Adrian, illus. 2015. (Mix Ser.). (ENG.). 240p. (J). (gr. 4-8). pap. 7.99 *(978-1-4814-3239-9(7),* Aladdin) Simon & Schuster Children's Publishing.

Tucker, Kathy. The Seven Chinese Sisters. Lin, Grace, illus. 2003. (ENG.). 32p. (J). (gr. k-3). per. 6.99 *(978-0-8075-7310-5(8))* Whitman, Albert & Co.

Tucker, Kathy & Hong, Lily Toy. The Seven Chinese Sisters, Bk. 2. Hong, Lily Toy & Lin, Grace, illus. 2010. (Book & DVD Packages with Nutmeg Media Ser.). (ENG.). 4p. (J). (gr. -1-3). 69.95 *(978-0-8075-9984-6(0))* Whitman, Albert & Co.

Tupper Ling, Nancy. My Sister, Alicia May. Bersani, Shennen, illus. 2009. (ENG.). 32p. (J). (gr. k-2). 16.95 *(978-0-9792035-9-6(7))* Pleasant St. Pr.

Turner, Diane. Tangle-Leina? I'll Tangle-Leina Them. Mason, Roberta Black, illus. 2008. 48p. pap. 24.95 *(978-1-60563-586-6(3))* America Star Bks.

Turner, Suzy. The Ghost of Josiah Grimshaw: A Morgan Sisters Novel. 2013. 286p. pap. *(978-989-97348-6-9(1))* Turner, Suzanne.

Two Peas in a Pod: 7. 2013. 68p. pap. 12.95 *(978-1-4772-7082-0(5))* AuthorHouse.

The Two Sisters: Lap Book. (Pebble Soup Explorations Ser.). (SPA.). 16p. (gr. -1-18). 21.00 *(978-0-7578-1668-0(1))* Rigby Education.

The Two Sisters: Small Book. (Pebble Soup Explorations Ser.). (SPA.). 16p. (gr. -1-18). 5.00 *(978-0-7578-1708-3(4))* Rigby Education.

Two Sisters Circle. The Lady of the Lane. 2013. 116p. pap. 19.95 *(978-1-63004-330-8(3))* America Star Bks.

Tym, Kate. Time to Share. 2008. (Manners Ser.). (Illus.). 24p. (J). (gr. -1-1). lib. bdg. 16.95 *(978-1-59566-591-1(9))* QEB Publishing Inc.

Uegaki, Chieri. Rosie & Buttercup. Jorisch, Stéphane, illus. 2008. (ENG.). 32p. (J). (gr. -1-2). 18.95 *(978-1-55337-997-3(7))* Kids Can Pr., Ltd. CAN. Dist: Hachette Bk. Group.

Ultman, Suzy, illus. Masha & Her Sisters. 2017. (ENG.). 10p. (J). bds. 9.99 *(978-1-4521-5159-5(8))* Chronicle Bks. LLC.

Ure, Jean. Boys Beware. 2011. (ENG., Illus.). 192p. (J). (gr. 4-7). pap. 7.99 *(978-0-00-716138-6(7))* HarperCollins Pubs. Ltd. GBR. Dist: HarperCollins Pubs.

—Love & Kisses. 2009. (ENG.). 192p. (J). (gr. 4-7). pap. 9.99 *(978-0-00-728172-5(2),* HarperCollins Children's Bks.) HarperCollins Pubs. Ltd. GBR. Dist: HarperCollins Pubs.

Vail, Rachel. Brilliant. 2011. (Avery Sisters Trilogy Ser.: 3). (ENG., Illus.). 256p. (YA). (gr. 8). pap. 8.99 *(978-0-06-089051-3(7))* HarperCollins Pubs.

Vande Velde, Vivian. Deadly Pink. 2013. (ENG.). 288p. (J). (gr. 5-7). pap. 6.99 *(978-0-544-02278-2(5))* Houghton Mifflin Harcourt Publishing Co.

Varveris, Ariana Eleni. The Adventures of Magic Island: Book I- Welcome to Magic Island. 2012. 122p. (gr. 2-2). pap. 9.95 *(978-1-4620-5751-1(9))* iUniverse, Inc.

Veit, Kimberly Michelle. To Be Thirteen. 2006. 57p. pap. 16.95 *(978-1-4241-1392-7(X))* PublishAmerica, Inc.

Viorst, Judith. Super-Completely & Totally the Messiest! Glasser, Robin Preiss, illus. 2006. (ENG.). 32p. (J). (gr. -1-2). 16.99 *(978-1-4169-4200-9(9),* Atheneum Bks. for Young Readers) Simon & Schuster Children's Publishing.

Vitello, Suzy. The Moment Before. 2014. (ENG.). 216p. pap. 12.99 *(978-1-62681-167-6(9))* Diversion Publishing Corp.

Voudrie, Krista. Sisters of Destiny. 2011. 96p. pap. 19.95 *(978-1-4560-5636-0(0))* America Star Bks.

Wait for Me. 2007. 169p. (gr. 4-7). 18.00 *(978-0-7569-7959-1(5))* Perfection Learning Corp.

Wakefield, Vikki. In-Between Days. 2016. (ENG., Illus.). 352p. (YA). (gr. 9). 17.99 *(978-1-4424-8656-0(2),* Simon & Schuster Bks. For Young Readers) Simon & Schuster Bks. For Young Readers.

Waldman, Alan/A. Erica from America & the Start of the Gang of Four. Scobie, Andrea, illus. 2013. 44p. pap. *(978-0-9840514-2-7(2))* Roxby Media Ltd.

Walker, Nan. Stressbusters. Wummer, Amy, illus. 2006. (Social Studies Connects). 32p. (J). (gr. 1-3). pap. 5.95 *(978-1-57565-185-9(8))* Kane Press, Inc.

Wallace-Brodeur, Ruth. Stories from the Big Chair. 2010. (ENG.). 48p. (J). (gr. -1-3). 6.99 *(978-1-4424-1439-6(1),* McElderry, Margaret K. Bks.) McElderry, Margaret K. Bks.

Wallace, Kali. The Memory Trees. 2017. 432p. (YA). (gr. 9). 17.99 ***(978-0-06-236623-8(8)***, Tegen, Katherine Bks) HarperCollins Pubs.

Wallace, Lizzie. My Sister's Turning into a Monster. 2011. (Illus.). 20p. 10.96 *(978-1-4520-9930-9(8))* AuthorHouse.

Walters, Nicole Y. Charis: A Journey to Pandora's Jar. Conard, Vincent, illus. 2013. 214p. 32.95 *(978-1-62015-318-5(1),* Booktrope Editions) Booktrope.

Ward, Dan. Meet the Boomer Sisters. 2006. 131p. pap. 13.95 *(978-1-4116-6927-7(4))* Lulu Pr., Inc.

Ward, Marcia. The Girl Who Found Her Voice. 2013. (ENG.). 276p. pap. 14.99 *(978-1-939927-28-6(5))* Telemachus Pr., LLC.

Warman, Jessica. Beautiful Lies. 2014. (ENG.). 432p. (YA). (gr. 9). pap. 9.99 *(978-0-8027-3543-0(6),* 9780802735430, Bloomsbury USA Childrens) Bloomsbury Publishing USA.

—The Last Good Day of the Year. (ENG.). 288p. (YA). 2016. pap. 9.99 *(978-0-8027-3663-5(7),* 9780802736635) 2015. (gr. 9). 17.99 *(978-0-8027-3662-8(9),* 9780802736628) Bloomsbury Publishing USA. (Bloomsbury USA Childrens).

Waters, Fiona, retold by. Faithful Sister. (ENG., Illus.). 94p. (J). pap. 10.99 *(978-0-7475-4704-4(1))* Bloomsbury Publishing Plc GBR. Dist: Trafalgar Square Publishing.
Watkins, Steve. Juvie. (ENG.). 320p. (YA). (gr. 9). 2017. pap. 7.99 *(978-0-7636-8756-4(1))* 2013. 17.99 *(978-0-7636-5509-9(0))* Candlewick Pr.
Watson, Renée. This Side of Home. 2015. (ENG.). 336p. (YA). (gr. 7). 17.99 *(978-1-59990-668-3(6),* 9781599906683, Bloomsbury USA Childrens) Bloomsbury Publishing USA.
WATTS, Bernadette. Mother Holly. 2016. (ENG., Illus.). 32p. 17.95 *(978-0-7358-4267-0(1))* North-South Bks., Inc.
Weaver, Susan. My Goofy Girls. 2007. 24p. per. 24.95 *(978-1-4241-8933-5(0))* America Star Bks.
Weber, Lori. Klepto, 1 vol. 2004. (Lorimer SideStreets Ser.). (ENG.). 160p. (YA). (gr. 9-12). 9.95 *(978-1-55028-836-0(9),* 9781550288360); 16.95 *(978-1-55028-837-7(7),* 9781550288377) Lorimer, James & Co., Ltd., Pubs. CAN. Dist: Casemate Pubs. & Bk. Distributors, LLC.
Webster, Christy. A Perfect Christmas. Random House Staff, illus. 2011. (Step into Reading Ser.: 1). (ENG.). 32p. (J). (gr. -1-1). pap. 3.99 *(978-0-375-86932-7(8),* Random Hse. Bks. for Young Readers) Random Hse. Children's Bks.
Weidner, Teri. Always Twins. Weidner, Teri, illus. 2015. (ENG., Illus.). 32p. (J). (gr. -1-k). 16.95 *(978-0-8234-3159-5(2))* Holiday Hse., Inc.
Weingarten, Lynn. Wherever Nina Lies. 2010. (ENG.). 320p. (J). (gr. 7-12). 8.99 *(978-0-545-06633-4(6))* Scholastic, Inc.
Welch, Lester. Last Summer. 2004. 12.95 *(978-1-930252-96-7(X))* PageFree Publishing, Inc.
Wells, Rosemary. Use Your Words, Sophie! 2015. (ENG., Illus.). 24p. (J). (gr. -1 — 1). 16.99 *(978-0-670-01663-1(2),* Viking Books for Young Readers) Penguin Young Readers Group.
Wesley, Valerie Wilson. How to Almost Ruin Your School Play. 2005. (Illus.). 105p. (J). lib. bdg. 15.00 *(978-1-4242-0645-2(6))* Fitzgerald Bks.
West, Carly Anne. The Murmurings. (ENG., 384p. (YA). (gr. 9). 2014. Illus.). pap. 11.99 *(978-1-4424-4180-4(1))* 2013. 16.99 *(978-1-4424-4179-8(8))* Simon Pulse. (Simon Pulse).
Weston, Carol. Ava & Pip. (Ava & Pip Ser.: 1). (ENG.). 224p. (J). (gr. 5-7). 2015. pap. 6.99 *(978-1-4926-0183-8(7))* 2014. 15.99 *(978-1-4022-8870-8(0),* 9781402288708) Sourcebooks, Inc. (Sourcebooks Jabberwocky).
Weyn, Suzanne. Dr. Frankenstein's Daughters. 2013. (ENG.). 256p. (J). (gr. 7). 17.99 *(978-0-545-42533-9(6),* Scholastic Pr.) Scholastic, Inc.
—The Night Dance: A Retelling of the Twelve Dancing Princesses. 2008. (Once upon a Time Ser.). (ENG.). 224p. (YA). (gr. 7). mass mkt. 6.99 *(978-1-4169-6132-1(1),* Simon Pulse) Simon Pulse.
—The Titanic Locket. 2014. (Haunted Museum Ser.: 1). (ENG.). 208p. (J). (gr. 3-7). pap. 6.99 *(978-0-545-58842-3(1),* Scholastic Paperbacks) Scholastic, Inc.
White, Jennifer. Survival Strategies of the Almost Brave. 2015. (ENG.). 320p. (J). (gr. 3-7). 16.99 *(978-0-374-30084-5(4),* 9780374300845, Farrar, Straus & Giroux (BYR)) Farrar, Straus & Giroux.
White, Kiersten. Mind Games. 2013. (Mind Games Ser.: 1). (ENG.). (YA). (gr. 8). 304p. pap. 9.99 *(978-0-06-213532-2(5));* 256p. 17.99 *(978-0-06-213531-5(7))* HarperCollins Pubs. (HarperTeen).
—Perfect Lies. 2014. (Mind Games Ser.: 2). (ENG.). 240p. (YA). (gr. 8). 17.99 *(978-0-06-213584-1(8),* HarperTeen) HarperCollins Pubs.
White, Kiersten & Di Bartolo, Jim. In the Shadows. Di Bartolo, Jim, illus. 2014. (ENG., Illus.). 384p. (J). (gr. 7). 21.99 *(978-0-545-56144-0(2),* Scholastic Pr.) Scholastic, Inc.
Whitten, A. J. The Cellar. 2011. (ENG.). 288p. (YA). (gr. 7-18). pap. 16.99 *(978-0-547-23253-9(5))* Houghton Mifflin Harcourt Publishing Co.
Whybrow, Ian. Through the Cat-Flap. 2017. (ENG.). 64p. (J). (gr. 1-6). pap. 7.99 ***(978-1-4449-3577-6(1))*** Hachette Children's Group GBR. Dist: Hachette Bk. Group.
Wiebe, Trina. Lizards Don't Wear Lip Gloss. Sarrazin, Marisol, illus. 2004. (Abby & Tess Pet-Sitters Ser.). 91p. 15.95 *(978-0-7569-3425-5(7))* Perfection Learning Corp.
Wilder, Laura Ingalls. Pioneer Sisters. Kim, Ji-Hyuk, illus. 2017. (Little House Chapter Book Ser.: 2). 112p. (J). (gr. 1-5). pap. 4.99 *(978-0-06-237710-4(8))* HarperCollins Pubs.
Wilder, Vickie. The Umbrella. 2013. 24p. pap. 11.97 *(978-1-62212-534-0(7),* Strategic Bk. Publishing) Strategic Book Publishing & Rights Agency (SBPRA).
Wiley, Melissa. Beyond the Heather Hills. Graef, Renee, illus. 2003. (Little House Ser.). 189p. (J). (gr. 3-7). 14.65 *(978-0-7569-3467-5(2))* Perfection Learning Corp.
Wilhite, Becca. Bright Blue Miracle. 2009. 176p. (J). pap. 8.99 *(978-1-60641-031-8(8),* Shadow Mountain) Shadow Mountain Publishing.
Willard, Eliza, et al. Love Is in the Air. 2004. (ENG.). 128p. *(978-0-00-718094-3(2))* HarperCollins Pubs. Australia.
Williams, Carol Lynch. Glimpse. 2010. (ENG.). 496p. (YA). (gr. 9-18). 16.99 *(978-1-4169-9730-6(X),* Simon & Schuster/Paula Wiseman Bks.) Simon & Schuster/Paula Wiseman Bks.
Williams, Carol Lynch & Gregg, L. B. Glimpse. Gregg, Anna, photos by. 2012. (ENG., Illus.). 512p. (YA). (gr. 9). pap. 12.99 *(978-1-4169-9731-3(8),* Simon & Schuster/Paula Wiseman Bks.) Simon & Schuster/Paula Wiseman Bks.
Williams-Garcia, Rita. Gone Crazy in Alabama. (J). (gr. 3-7). 2016. 320p. pap. 6.99 *(978-0-06-221589-5(2),* Amistad) 2015. (ENG., Illus.). 304p. 16.99 *(978-0-06-221587-1(6))* HarperCollins Pubs.
—One Crazy Summer. 2009. (KOR.). 272p. (J). pap. *(978-89-7199-494-8(0))* Dolbegae Publishing Co.
—One Crazy Summer. (J). (gr. 4-7). 2011. (ENG.). 240p. pap. 7.99 *(978-0-06-076090-8(7))* 2010. (ENG.). 224p. 16.99 *(978-0-06-076088-5(5))* 2010. 224p. lib. bdg. 16.89 *(978-0-06-076089-2(3))* HarperCollins Pubs. (Amistad).
—One Crazy Summer. (J). 2011. 1.25 *(978-1-4498-2201-9(0))* 2010. 69.75 *(978-1-4498-2197-5(9))* 2010. 67.75 *(978-1-4498-2199-9(5))* Recorded Bks., Inc.
—One Crazy Summer. 2011. (J). lib. bdg. 17.20 *(978-0-606-23555-6(8),* Turtleback) Turtleback Bks.
—P. S. Be Eleven. 2015. (ENG.). 304p. (J). (gr. 3-7). pap. 7.99 *(978-0-06-193864-1(5),* Amistad) HarperCollins Pubs.
Williams, Venus & Williams, Serena. SisterTales 2. 2010. (gr. 5-9). *(978-0-618-44915-6(9))* Houghton Mifflin Harcourt Trade & Reference Pubs.
Willis, S. J. The Wishwasher. 2011. 128p. (gr. 4-6). pap. 13.32 *(978-1-4567-8751-6(9))* AuthorHouse.
Willis, Wren. Why Is My Name September? 2005. 155p. pap. 11.39 *(978-1-4116-6534-7(1))* Lulu Pr., Inc.
Winn, Sheridan. The Sprite Sisters: Magic at Drysdale's School (Vol 7) Winn, Christopher, illus. 2013. 256p. pap. *(978-0-9574231-2-1(8))* Winn, Sheridan.
Wishinsky, Frieda. You're Mean, Lily Jean! Denton, Kady MacDonald, illus. 2011. (ENG.). 32p. (J). (gr. -1-3). 16.99 *(978-0-8075-9476-6(8))* Whitman, Albert & Co.
Witek, Jo. Hello in There! A Big Sister's Book of Waiting. Roussey, Christine, illus. 2013. (Growing Hearts Ser.). (ENG.). 28p. (J). (gr. -1 — 1). 16.95 *(978-1-4197-0371-3(4),* Abrams Appleseed) Abrams, Inc.
Wojton, Roxane. My Mommy & Me & Baby Makes Three. 2012. (Illus.). 38p. pap. 19.99 *(978-1-105-06616-0(9))* Lulu Pr., Inc.
Wong, Karine. Don't Sit on Her! 2013. 44p. pap. 21.99 *(978-1-4797-6912-4(6))* Xlibris Corp.
Woods, Brenda. The Red Rose Box. Woods, Brenda, illus. 2003. (ENG., Illus.). 144p. (J). (gr. 3-7). 5.99 *(978-0-14-250151-1(4),* Puffin Books) Penguin Young Readers Group.
Wooster, Devin Ann. Barbie & Her Sisters in the Great Puppy Adventure. 2015. (Barbie Chapters Ser.). (ENG.). 64p. (J). (gr. 1-4). pap. 5.99 *(978-0-553-53764-2(4),* Random Hse. Bks. for Young Readers) Random Hse. Children's Bks.
Wright, Betty Ren. The Dollhouse Murders. 2008. (ENG.). 149p. (J). (gr. 4-7). pap. 7.99 *(978-0-8234-2172-5(4))* Holiday Hse., Inc.
Wulf, Linda Press. The Night of the Burning. 2007. (ENG.). 224p. pap. *(978-0-7475-9051-4(6))* Bloomsbury Publishing Plc.
Wylie, Sarah. All These Lives, 1 vol. 2012. (ENG.). 256p. (YA). (gr. 7-12). 24.99 *(978-0-374-30208-5(1),* 9780374302085, Farrar, Straus & Giroux (BYR)) Farrar, Straus & Giroux.
Yeh, Kat. The Truth about Twinkie Pie. 2015. (J). *(978-0-316-23671-3(3))* Little Brown & Co.
Yost, Beth. The Mysterious Sock Caper. 2007. 20p. per. 10.95 *(978-1-4327-1242-6(X))* Outskirts Pr., Inc.
Young, Judy. A Book for Black-Eyed Susan. Ettlinger, Doris, illus. 2011. (Tales of Young Americans Ser.). (ENG.). 32p. (J). (gr. k-6). lib. bdg. 16.95 *(978-1-58536-463-3(0))* Sleeping Bear Pr.
Yum, Hyewon. The Twins' Blanket. Yum, Hyewon, illus. 2011. (ENG., Illus.). 40p. (J). (gr. -1-1). 17.99 *(978-0-374-37972-8(6),* 9780374379728, Farrar, Straus & Giroux (BYR)) Farrar, Straus & Giroux.
—The Twins' Little Sister. Yum, Hyewon, illus. 2014. (ENG., Illus.). 40p. (J). (gr. -1-1). 17.99 *(978-0-374-37973-5(4),* 9780374379735, Farrar, Straus & Giroux (BYR)) Farrar, Straus & Giroux.
Yusuf, Hanna S. & Day, Cansarra. Katie Mcchoir. 2010. 80p. pap. 10.49 *(978-1-4490-7378-7(6))* AuthorHouse.
Zahler, Diane. Sleeping Beauty's Daughters. 2013. 216p. (J). lib. bdg. *(978-0-06-200497-0(2))* Harper & Row Ltd.
—The Thirteenth Princess. 2011. (ENG.). 272p. (J). (gr. 3-7). pap. 6.99 *(978-0-06-182500-2(X))* HarperCollins Pubs.
Zapf, Marlena. Underpants Dance. Avril, Lynne, illus. 2014. (ENG.). 40p. (J). (gr. -1-k). 16.99 *(978-0-8037-3539-2(1),* Dial Bks) Penguin Young Readers Group.
Zemach, Margot & Zemach, Kaethe, illus. Eating up Gladys. 2005. (J). *(978-0-439-66491-2(8),* Levine, Arthur A. Bks.) Scholastic, Inc.
Zenk, Molly. Hyperion Keats. 2013. 134p. pap. 5.49 *(978-0-9895262-5-8(9))* Highland Pr.
Zhang, Kat. Echoes of Us: The Hybrid Chronicles, Book 3. 2015. (Hybrid Chronicles Ser.: 3). (ENG.). 368p. (YA). (gr. 8). pap. 9.99 *(978-0-06-211494-5(8))* HarperCollins Pubs.
—Once We Were: The Hybrid Chronicles, Book 2. 2014. (Hybrid Chronicles Ser.: 2). (ENG.). 384p. (YA). (gr. 8). pap. 9.99 *(978-0-06-211491-4(3))* HarperCollins Pubs.
—What's Left of Me. 2013. (Hybrid Chronicles Ser.: 1). (ENG.). 368p. (YA). (gr. 8). pap. 9.99 *(978-0-06-211488-4(3))* HarperCollins Pubs.
Ziegler, Jennifer. Revenge of the Angels. 2015. (ENG.). 256p. (J). (gr. 3-7). 16.99 *(978-0-545-83899-3(1),* Scholastic Pr.) Scholastic, Inc.
—Revenge of the Flower Girls. 2014. (ENG.). 240p. (J). (gr. 3-7). 16.99 *(978-0-545-56141-9(8),* Scholastic Pr.) Scholastic, Inc.
—Sass & Serendipity. 2012. (ENG.). 384p. (YA). (gr. 7). pap. 9.99 *(978-0-375-85964-9(0),* Ember) Random Hse. Children's Bks.
Zimmerman, Mary Joyce. Just Four. 2005. (Illus.). 32p. (gr. -1-5). 2.70 *(978-0-7399-2340-5(4),* 2779) Rod & Staff Pubs., Inc.
Zink, Michelle. Circle of Fire. 2012. (Prophecy of the Sisters Trilogy Ser.: 3). (ENG.). 368p. (YA). (gr. 7-17). pap. 22.99 *(978-0-316-03446-3(0))* Little, Brown Bks. for Young Readers.
—Prophecy of the Sisters. 2010. (Prophecy of the Sisters Trilogy Ser.: 1). (ENG.). 368p. (YA). (gr. 7-17). pap. 8.99 *(978-0-316-02741-0(3))* Little, Brown Bks. for Young Readers.

SISTERS (IN RELIGIOUS ORDERS, CONGREGATIONS, ETC.)

see Nuns

SITTING BULL, 1831-1890

Abnett, Dan. Sitting Bull & the Battle of the Little Bighorn. (Jr. Graphic Biographies Ser.). (ENG.). 24p. 2009. (J). (gr. 2-3). 47.90 *(978-1-61513-822-7(6),* PowerKids Pr.) 2007. (Illus.). (J). (gr. 2-5). lib. bdg. 25.25 *(978-1-4042-3394-2(6))* 2007. (Illus.). (gr. 3-8). pap. 10.60 *(978-1-4042-2147-5(6),* PowerKids Pr.) Rosen Publishing Group, Inc., The.
—Toro Sentado y la Batalla de Little Bighorn. 2009. (Historietas Juveniles: Biografías (Jr. Graphic Biographies) Ser.). (SPA., Illus.). 24p. (J). (gr. 2-5). 25.25 *(978-1-4358-8562-2(7));* (gr. 3-8). pap. 10.60 *(978-1-4358-3318-0(X))* Rosen Publishing Group, Inc., The.
Bailey, Gerry & Foster, Karen. Sitting Bull's Tomahawk. Radford, Karen & Noyes, Leighton, illus. 2008. (Stories of Great People Ser.). (ENG.). 40p. (J). (gr. 3-8). pap. *(978-0-7787-3714-8(4));* lib. bdg. *(978-0-7787-3692-9(X))* Crabtree Publishing Co.
Collard, Sneed B., III. Sitting Bull: Tatanka-Iyotake. 2009. (American Heroes Ser.). 48p. (gr. 3-18). 29.93 *(978-0-7614-4059-8(3))* Marshall Cavendish Corp.
Collier, James Lincoln. The Sitting Bull You Never Knew. 2004. (You Never Knew Ser.). (ENG.). 80p. (J). (gr. 4-6). pap. 6.95 *(978-0-516-25836-2(2),* Children's Pr.) Scholastic Library Publishing.
Davis, Kenneth C. Don't Know Much about Sitting Bull Sitting Bull, Vol. 2. 2003. (Don't Know Much About Ser.). (Illus.). 144p. (J). (gr. 3-7). 16.89 *(978-0-06-028818-1(3))* HarperCollins Pubs.
DeFord, Diane. Chief Sitting Bull. 2009. pap. 13.25 *(978-1-60559-070-7(3))* Hameray Publishing Group, Inc.
Evento, Susan. Sitting Bull. 2005. (Rookie Biographies Ser.). (ENG., Illus.). 32p. (J). (gr. 1-2). pap. 4.95 *(978-0-516-25829-4(X),* Children's Pr.) Scholastic Library Publishing.
Hayhurst, Chris. Sitting Bull: Sioux War Chief. 2009. (Primary Sources of Famous People in American History Ser.). 32p. (gr. 2-3). 47.90 *(978-1-60851-724-4(1))* Rosen Publishing Group, Inc., The.
—Sitting Bull / Toro Sentado: Sioux War Chief / Jefe Sioux. 2009. (Famous People in American History/Grandes personajes en la historia de los Estados Unidos Ser.). (SPA.). 32p. (gr. 2-3). 47.90 *(978-1-61512-555-5(8),* Editorial Buenas Letras) Rosen Publishing Group, Inc., The.
—Toro Sentado: Jefe sioux (Sitting Bull: Sioux War Chief) 2009. (Grandes personajes en la historia de los Estados Unidos (Famous People in American History) Ser.). (SPA.). 32p. (gr. 2-3). 47.90 *(978-1-61512-809-9(3),* Editorial Buenas Letras) Rosen Publishing Group, Inc., The.
Jeffrey, Gary. Sitting Bull: The Life of a Lakota Chief. 2009. (Graphic Nonfiction Biographies Ser.). (ENG.). 48p. (YA). (gr. 4-5). 58.50 *(978-1-61513-027-6(6),* Rosen Reference) Rosen Publishing Group, Inc., The.
Jeffrey, Gary & Petty, Kate. Sitting Bull: The Life of a Lakota Sioux Chief. 2005. (Graphic Nonfiction Biographies Ser.). (ENG., Illus.). 48p. (YA). (gr. 4-7). lib. bdg. 31.95 *(978-1-4042-0247-4(1))* Rosen Publishing Group, Inc., The.
Laplante, Walter. Sitting Bull. 2015. (Native American Heroes Ser.). (ENG., Illus.). 24p. (J). (gr. 1-2). 22.60 *(978-1-4824-2702-8(8))* Stevens, Gareth Publishing LLLP.
Mapua, Jeff. Sitting Bull, 01 vols., 1. 2016. (Britannica Beginner Bios Ser.). (ENG., Illus.). 32p. (J). pap. 12.90 *(978-1-5081-0062-1(4),* Britannica Educational Publishing) Rosen Publishing Group, Inc., The.
Marsh, Carole. Sitting Bull. 2003. 12p. (gr. k-4). 2.95 *(978-0-635-02378-0(4))* Gallopade International.
McDonnell, Julia. Sitting Bull in His Own Words. 2014. (Eyewitness to History Ser.). 32p. (J). (gr. 4-6). pap. 63.00 *(978-1-4824-1223-9(3))* Stevens, Gareth Publishing LLLP.
McLeese, Don. Sitting Bull. 2003. (Native American Legends Ser.). (Illus.). 32p. (J). lib. bdg. 28.50 *(978-1-58952-730-0(5))* Rourke Educational Media.
Minor, Wendell. Sitting Bull Remembers. Date not set. 32p. (J). (gr. -1-3). 15.99 *(978-0-06-029153-2(2));* pap. 5.99 *(978-0-06-443725-7(6));* lib. bdg. 16.89 *(978-0-06-029154-9(0))* HarperCollins Pubs.
Nelson, S. D. Sitting Bull: Lakota Warrior & Defender of His People. 2015. (ENG., Illus.). 64p. (J). (gr. 3-7). 19.95 *(978-1-4197-0731-5(0),* Abrams Bks. for Young Readers) Abrams, Inc.
Roxburgh, Ellis. Sitting Bull vs. George Armstrong Custer: The Battle of the Little Bighorn. 2016. (History's Greatest Rivals Ser.). (ENG., Illus.). 48p. (J). (gr. 6-8). pap. 14.05 *(978-1-4824-4235-9(3))* Stevens, Gareth Publishing LLLP.
Rucker, Jeffrey A. La historia de Toro Sentado (the Story of Sitting Bull) 2009. (Reading Room Collection: Spanish Ser.). (SPA.). 24p. (gr. 3-4). 42.50 *(978-1-60854-178-2(9),* Editorial Buenas Letras) Rosen Publishing Group, Inc., The.
—The Story of Sitting Bull. (Reading Room Collection 2 Ser.). 24p. (gr. 3-4). 2009. 42.50 *(978-1-60851-998-9(8),* PowerKids Pr.) 2003. (ENG.). 43.95 *(978-0-8239-8731-3(0))* Rosen Publishing Group, Inc., The.
Sanford, William R. Hunkpapa Lakota Chief Sitting Bull. 2013. (Native American Chiefs & Warriors Ser.). 48p. (J). (gr. 5-18). lib. bdg. 22.60 *(978-0-7660-4097-7(6))* Enslow Pubs., Inc.
Shaffer, Jody Jensen. Sitting Bull: Eagles Cannot Be Crows. 2017. (Primary Source Readers Ser.). 32p. (J). (gr. 4-5). pap. 8.99 *(978-1-4938-3800-4(8))* Teacher Created Materials, Inc.
Silate, Jennifer. Seeing the Future: The Final Vision of Sitting Bull. 2009. (Great Moments in American History Ser.). 32p. (gr. 3-3). 47.90 *(978-1-61513-150-1(7))* Rosen Publishing Group, Inc., The.
Sitting Bull. 2010. (Legends of the Wild West Ser.). (Illus.). 128p. (gr. 6-12). 35.00 *(978-1-60413-527-5(1),* Chelsea Hse.) Facts On File, Inc.
Spinner, Stephanie. Who Was Sitting Bull? Eldridge, Jim & Harrison, Nancy, illus. 2014. (Who Was? Ser.). (ENG.). 112p. (J). (gr. 3-7). 5.99 *(978-0-448-47965-1(6),* Grosset & Dunlap) Penguin Young Readers Group.
—Who Was Sitting Bull? 2014. (Who Was... ? Ser.). lib. bdg. 16.00 *(978-0-606-36179-8(0))* Turtleback Bks.
Weil, Ann. Sitting Bull, 1 vol. 2012. (American Biographies Ser.). (ENG.). 48p. (gr. 4-6). pap. 9.95 *(978-1-4329-6460-3(7));* lib. bdg. 32.65 *(978-1-4329-6449-8(6))* Heinemann-Raintree. (NA-h).

SIX DAY WAR, 1967

see Israel-Arab War, 1967

SIZE AND SHAPE

ABDO Publishing Company Staff. Shapes Everywhere. 2013. (Shapes Everywhere Ser.: 6). 24p. (gr. k-4). lib. bdg. 153.90 *(978-1-61783-410-3(6),* Super SandCastle) ABDO Publishing Co.
ABDO Publishing Company Staff & Hanson, Anders. 3-D Shapes, 1 vol. 2008. (3-D Shapes Ser.: 6). (ENG.). 24p. (J). (gr. k-3). lib. bdg. 145.26 *(978-1-59928-885-7(0),* SandCastle) ABDO Publishing Co.
Aboff, Marcie. If You Were a Polygon, 1 vol. Dillard, Sarah, illus. 2009. (Math Fun Ser.). (ENG.). 24p. (gr. 2-4). pap. 7.95 *(978-1-4048-5692-9(7))* Picture Window Bks.
Ackland, Nick. Opposites. Bradley, Jennie, illus. 2016. (Baby Sparkler Ser.). (ENG.). 10p. (J). (gr. -1 — 1). bds. 5.99 *(978-0-7641-6858-1(4))* Barron's Educational Series, Inc.
Adams, Colleen. Carlos's Cubby. 2006. (Neighborhood Readers Ser.). (ENG.). 12p. (gr. -1-3). pap. 5.90 *(978-1-4042-5756-6(X),* Rosen Classroom) Rosen Publishing Group, Inc., The.
Adler, David A. Triangles. Miller, Edward, illus. 2015. (ENG.). 32p. (J). (gr. 1-5). 7.99 *(978-0-8234-3305-6(6))* Holiday Hse., Inc.
Aigner-Clark, Julie. Asomate y Ve Las Figuras. Zaidi, Nadeem, illus. 2004. (Baby Einstein Ser.). (SPA.). 16p. (J). bds. *(978-970-718-151-9(6),* Silver Dolphin en Español) Advanced Marketing, S. de R. L. de C. V.
Alaina, Maria. Shapes. 2011. (Wonder Readers Early Level Ser.). (ENG.). (gr. -1-1). 16p. pap. 35.94 *(978-1-4296-8145-2(4));* 32p. pap. 5.99 *(978-1-4296-7810-0(0))* Capstone Press of Coughlan Cos. (Wonder Readers).
—Shapes in the City, 1 vol. 2011. (Wonder Readers Early Level Ser.). (ENG.). (gr. -1-1). 32p. pap. 5.99 *(978-1-4296-7811-7(9));* 16p. pap. 35.94 *(978-1-4296-8147-6(0))* Capstone Press of Coughlan Cos. (Wonder Readers).
Albers, Josef. Squares & Other Shapes: With Josef Albers. 2016. (ENG., Illus.). 30p. (gr. -1 — 1). bds. 9.95 *(978-0-7148-7256-8(3))* Phaidon Pr., Inc.
Albers, Joseph. Squares & Other Shapes: With Josef Albers. 2016. (ENG., Illus.). 30p. bds. 9.95 *(978-0-7148-7255-1(5))* Phaidon Pr., Inc.
Alexander, Emmett. Formas / Sort It by Shape. de la Vega, Eida, tr. 2015. (Vamos a Agrupar Por... / Sort It Out! Ser.). (ENG & SPA., Illus.). 24p. (J). (gr. k-1). lib. bdg. 22.60 *(978-1-4824-3217-6(X),* 1390345) Stevens, Gareth Publishing LLLP.
Alvarez, Lourdes M. My First Book Shapes. Brooks, David, illus. 2005. (My First Book Ser.). 9p. (J). (gr. -1-1). bds. 3.95 *(978-1-933050-11-9(X))* Sweetwater Pr.
Amery, Heather. What's Happening on the Farm? Cartwright, Stephen, illus. rev. ed. 2006. (What's Happening? Ser.). 32p. (J). (gr. -1-3). 5.99 *(978-0-7945-1288-0(7),* Usborne) EDC Publishing.
Anderson, Graylin. Seeing the Shapes + Drawing the Shapes = Drawing the Object. 2008. (ENG.). 32p. pap. 11.99 *(978-1-4196-9609-1(2))* CreateSpace Independent Publishing Platform.
Anderson, James. Around Home. rev. ed. 2011. (Mathematics Readers Ser.). (ENG.). 32p. (J). (gr. k-k). pap. 8.99 *(978-1-4333-3439-9(9))* Teacher Created Materials, Inc.
—Around Town. rev. ed. 2011. (Mathematics Readers Ser.). (ENG.). 32p. (J). (gr. k-k). pap. 8.99 *(978-1-4333-3438-2(0))* Teacher Created Materials, Inc.
Anderson, Jill. Finding Shapes with Sebastian Pig & Friends at the Museum. Amy Huntington, illus. 2013. (Math Fun with Sebastian Pig & Friends! Ser.). 32p. (J). (gr. k-3). pap. 7.95 *(978-0-7660-5981-8(2),* Enslow Elementary) Enslow Pubs., Inc.
—Finding Shapes with Sebastian Pig & Friends at the Museum. Huntington, Amy, illus. 2009. (Math Fun with Sebastian Pig & Friends! Ser.). 32p. (J). (gr. k-3). lib. bdg. 23.94 *(978-0-7660-3363-4(5))* Enslow Pubs., Inc.
Anderson, Lynne. Rocket Ship Shapes. 2011. (Early Connections Ser.). (J). *(978-1-61672-596-9(6))* Benchmark Education Co.
Armadillo Press. Dog & Friends! A Box of Exciting Picture Books, 6 vols. 2017. (ENG., Illus.). 54p. (J). (gr. -1-12). bds. 14.99 *(978-1-86147-640-1(X),* Armadillo) Anness Publishing GBR. Dist: National Bk. Network.
Arps, Melissa. Shapes. 2006. (Illus.). (J). *(978-0-7364-2383-0(4))* Random Hse., Inc.
Ashley, Michele. Who Has Ears Like These? 2014. (Little Books of Answers: Level C Ser.). (Illus.). 16p. (gr. k-2). pap. 7.95 *(978-1-927136-27-0(X))* Three Crows Media NZL. Dist: RiverStream Publishing.
Avery, Sebastian. The School Garden: Reason with Shapes & Their Attributes. 2014. (Rosen Common Core Math Readers Ser.). (ENG.). 24p. (J). (gr. 3-4). pap. 8.25 *(978-1-4777-4875-6(X),* Rosen Classroom) Rosen Publishing Group, Inc., The.
Avett, Harper. Go Fly a Kite! Reason with Shapes & Their Attributes. 2014. (Rosen Common Core Math Readers Ser.). (ENG., Illus.). 24p. (J). (gr. 3-4). pap. 8.25 *(978-1-4777-4881-7(4),* Rosen Classroom) Rosen Publishing Group, Inc., The.
AZ Books, creator. What Shape? 2012. (Smarty Ser.). (ENG., Illus.). 10p. (J). (gr. -1 — 1). 9.95 *(978-1-61889-247-8(9))* AZ Bks. LLC.
AZ Books Staff. Colors & Shapes. Petrovskaya, Olga, ed. 2012. (Matching Game Ser.). (ENG.). 18p. (J). (gr. -1-k). spiral bd. 4.95 *(978-1-61889-201-0(0))* AZ Bks. LLC.
—Find a Pair. Petrovskaya, Olga, ed. 2012. (Matching Game Ser.). (ENG.). 18p. (J). (gr. -1-k). spiral bd. 4.95 *(978-1-61889-009-2(3))* AZ Bks. LLC.
—Shapes. Slusar, Julia, ed. 2012. (Pull It Out Ser.). (ENG.). 10p. (J). (— 1). 7.95 *(978-1-61889-194-5(4))* AZ Bks. LLC.
Baker, Ella. Big & Small. 2012. (InfoMax Readers Ser.). (ENG., Illus.). 16 pp.p. (J). (gr. k-1). pap. 7.00 *(978-1-4488-8875-7(1),* Rosen Classroom) Rosen Publishing Group, Inc., The.
Barradas, Michele. Rainbow of Shapes: Learn shapes & Colors. 2008. 20p. pap. 15.95 *(978-1-4389-0177-0(1))* AuthorHouse.
Bartowski, Amy. Shapes at the Store: Identify & Describe Shapes. 2013. (InfoMax Math Readers Ser.). (ENG.). 16p. (J). (gr. k-1). pap. 42.00 *(978-1-4777-1974-9(1));* (Illus.). pap. 7.00 *(978-1-4777-1973-2(3))* Rosen Publishing Group, Inc., The. (Rosen Classroom).
Begin Smart Books Staff, contrib. by. What Shapes Do You See? 2010. (Illus.). 14p. (J). bds. *(978-1-60906-005-3(9))* Begin Smart LLC.
Benchmark Education Company, compiled by. Insects Measure up! & ¡Vamos a Medir Insectos! 2005. (J). 62.00 net. *(978-1-4108-4496-5(X))* Benchmark Education Co.
Benchmark Education Company, LLC Staff, compiled by. Patterns & Shapes. 2006. (J). 265.00 *(978-1-4108-7049-0(9))* Benchmark Education Co.
—Patterns & Shapes: Theme Set. 2006. (J). 274.00 *(978-1-4108-7075-9(8));* 147.00 *(978-1-4108-7092-6(8))* Benchmark Education Co.

S

Benduhn, Tea. What Is Shape? 2009. (Get Art Smart Ser.). (ENG., Illus.). 24p. (J). (gr. k-3). pap. *(978-0-7787-5139-7(2))*; lib. bdg. *(978-0-7787-5125-0(2))* Crabtree Publishing Co.

Berger, Melvin & Berger, Gilda. Supersize Animals. 2015. (Scholastic Reader Level 2 Ser.). lib. bdg. 13.55 *(978-0-606-37756-0(5))* Turtleback Bks.

Bicknell, Joanna. My First BK of Animals. 2010. 16p. (J). bds. 8.99 *(978-1-84879-361-3(8))* Make Believe Ideas GBR. Dist: Nelson, Thomas Inc.

Bienik, Stella. Sculpting with Clay: Reason with Shapes & Their Attributes. 2014. (Math Masters: Geometry Ser.). 24p. (J). (gr. 2-3). 23.60 *(978-1-4777-6444-2(5))*; (ENG.). pap. 8.25 *(978-1-4777-4906-7(3))* Rosen Publishing Group, Inc., The. (Rosen Classroom).

BIG [Capstone Sole Source]. 2010. (Big Ser.). 24p. lib. bdg. 215.91 *(978-1-4296-5846-1(0)*, Pebble Plus) Capstone Press of Coughlan Cos.

Big KeyBoard IR. 2017. (My First KeyBDs Ser.). (ENG.). (J). spiral bd. 24.99 ***(978-0-7945-3933-7(5)***, Usborne) EDC Publishing.

Blaisdell, Molly. If You Were a Circle, 1 vol. Carabelli, Francesca, illus. 2009. (Math Fun Ser.). (ENG.). 24p. (gr. 2-4). lib. bdg. 27.99 *(978-1-4048-5514-4(9))* Picture Window Bks.

—If You Were a Quadrilateral, 1 vol. Carabelli, Francesca, illus. 2009. (Math Fun Ser.). (ENG.). 24p. (gr. 2-4). pap. 7.95 *(978-1-4048-5690-5(0))* Picture Window Bks.

Bluemel Oldfield, Dawn. Patterns at the Seashore. 2014. (Math Blast!: Seeing Patterns All Around Ser.). (ENG.). 32p. (J). (gr. -1-3). lib. bdg. 26.60 *(978-1-62724-335-3(6))* Bearport Publishing Co., Inc.

Blyton, Enid, et al. My First Colours & Shapes. 2013. (ENG., Illus.). 20p. (J). bds. 11.50 *(978-1-84135-760-7(X))* Award Pubns. Ltd. GBR. Dist: Parkwest Pubns., Inc.

Bogart, Jo Ellen. Big & Small, Room for All. Newland, Gillian, illus. (ENG.). (J). (— 1). 2017. 30p. bds. 7.99 ***(978-0-14-319893-2(9))*** 2009. 32p. 18.95 *(978-0-88776-891-0(1))* Tundra Bks. CAN. (Tundra Bks.). Dist: Penguin Random Hse. LLC.

Boothroyd, Jennifer. Combining Shapes. 2007. (First Step Nonfiction - Early Math Ser.). (ENG.). 8p. (gr. -1-1). pap. 4.95 *(978-0-8225-6831-5(4))* Lerner Publishing Group.

—Cone. 2008. pap. 22.95 *(978-0-8225-9364-5(5))* Lerner Publishing Group.

—Patterns. 2007. (First Step Nonfiction - Early Math Ser.). (ENG.). 8p. (gr. -1-1). pap. 4.95 *(978-0-8225-6829-2(2))* Lerner Publishing Group.

Borth, Teddy. Shapes Are Fun! 2016. (Shapes Are Fun! Ser.: 6). (ENG.). 24p. (J). (gr. k-2). lib. bdg. 162.42 *(978-1-68080-141-5(4))* ABDO Publishing Co.

Braidich, Victoria. Animals on the Farm: Learning to Compare Size. 2009. (Math for the REAL World Ser.). 12p. (gr. 1-2). pap. 5.90 *(978-0-8239-8847-1(3)*, Rosen Classroom) Rosen Publishing Group, Inc., The.

—Shapes at Home: Learning to Recognize Basic Geometric Shapes. 2009. (Math for the REAL World Ser.). 12p. (gr. 1-2). pap. 5.90 *(978-0-8239-8863-1(5)*, Rosen Classroom) Rosen Publishing Group, Inc., The.

Brocket, Jane. Circles, Stars, & Squares: Looking for Shapes. Brocket, Jane, photos by. 2012. (Jane Brocket's Clever Concepts Ser.). (ENG., Illus.). 32p. (gr. -1-2). lib. bdg. 26.60 *(978-0-7613-4611-1(2)*, Millbrook Pr.) Lerner Publishing Group.

Brocket, Jane, photos by. Spotty, Stripy, Swirly: What Are Patterns? 2012. (Jane Brocket's Clever Concepts Ser.). (ENG., Illus.). 32p. (gr. -1-2). lib. bdg. 26.60 *(978-0-7613-4613-5(9))* Lerner Publishing Group.

Brook-Piper, Holly. Animal Shapes: A Touch-and-Feel Book. 2015. (ENG., Illus.). 12p. (J). (gr. -1 — 1). bds. 6.99 *(978-1-4998-0039-5(8))* Little Bee Books Inc.

Brooks, Felicity. First Shapes. Litchfield, Jo, illus. MMStudios, photos by. 2007. (Usborne Look & Say Ser.). 12p. (J). (gr. -1-k). bds. 14.99 *(978-0-7945-1450-1(2)*, Usborne) EDC Publishing.

—Usborne Shapes Jigsaw Book. 2008. (Usborne Jigsaw Bks.). (Illus.). 12p. (J). (gr. -1-3). bds. 9.99 *(978-0-7945-2046-5(4)*, Usborne) EDC Publishing.

Brown, Lisa, illus. Baby Fix My Car. 2006. (ENG.). 12p. bds. 6.95 *(978-1-932416-56-5(0))* McSweeney's Publishing.

Brown, Margery W. Afro-Bets Book of Shapes. Blair, Culverson & Simpson, Howard, illus. 2nd ed. 2004. (Afro-Bets Ser.). 24p. (J). (gr. -1-1). pap. 3.95 *(978-0-940975-58-3(0)*, Sankofa Bks.) Just Us Bks., Inc.

Bruna, Dick. Round, Square, Triangle. 2012. (ENG., Illus.). 28p. 7.95 *(978-1-84976-077-5(2))* Tate Publishing, Ltd. GBR. Dist: Abrams, Inc.

Buchanan, Theodore. Fractals. 2017. (J). pap. 9.97 ***(978-1-4938-3626-0(9))*** Teacher Created Materials, Inc.

Bullard, Lisa. Big & Small [Scholastic]: An Animal Opposites Book. 2009. (Animal Opposites Ser.). 32p. (gr. 1-2). pap. 1.00 *(978-1-4296-4230-9(0)*, Aplus Bks.) Capstone Press of Coughlan Cos.

Burton, Margie, et al. Bigger Than? Smaller Than? 2011. (Early Connections Ser.). (J). *(978-1-61672-249-4(5))* Benchmark Education Co.

—The Guessing Jar. 2011. (Early Connections Ser.). (J). *(978-1-61672-541-9(9))* Benchmark Education Co.

—Looking for Shapes. 2011. (Early Connections Ser.). (J). *(978-1-61672-498-6(6))* Benchmark Education Co.

—What Comes Next? & ¿Qué Sigue? 6 English, 6 Spanish Adaptations. 2011. (J). spiral bd. 75.00 net. *(978-1-4108-5628-9(3))* Benchmark Education Co.

Butler, Roberta. Making Shapes. Moon, Jo, illus. 2006. (Making... Ser.). 14p. (J). (gr. -1-3). bds. 7.95 *(978-1-57791-250-7(0))* Brighter Minds Children's Publishing.

Caillou: Colors & Shapes. 2003. 32p. pap., wbk. ed. 14.95 incl. cd-rom *(978-1-57791-029-9(X))* Brighter Minds Children's Publishing.

Canavan, Thomas. Shapes & Symmetry: 50 Math Super Puzzles. 2011. (Math Standards Workout Ser.). (ENG., Illus.). 48p. (YA). (gr. 5-8). pap. 11.75 *(978-1-4488-6683-0(9)*, Rosen Reference); lib. bdg. 29.25 *(978-1-4488-6676-2(6))* Rosen Publishing Group, Inc., The.

Canetti, Yanitzia. Colorful Shapes/Figuras de Colores: A World of Color. 2010. (SPA & ENG.). 24p. (J). pap. 6.99 *(978-1-59835-278-8(4)*, BrickHouse Education) Cambridge BrickHouse, Inc.

Capote, Lori. Monster Knows Shapes, 1 vol. Wass, Chip, illus. 2013. (Monster Knows Math Ser.). (ENG.). 24p. (gr. 3-4). lib. bdg. 24.65 *(978-1-4048-7948-5(X))* Picture Window Bks.

Carle, Eric. My Very First Book of Shapes. Carle, Eric, illus. 2005. (ENG., Illus.). 20p. (J). (gr. -1 — 1). bds. 5.99 *(978-0-399-24387-5(9)*, Philomel Bks.) Penguin Young Readers Group.

Carr, Aaron. Formas. 2013. (SPA.). (J). *(978-1-62127-613-5(9))* Weigl Pubs., Inc.

—Grandes y Pequeño. 2012. (SPA.). (J). *(978-1-61913-205-4(2))* Weigl Pubs., Inc.

—Shapes. 2012. (Science Kids Ser.). (ENG., Illus.). 24p. (J). (gr. -1-1). pap. 12.95 *(978-1-61913-307-5(5))*; lib. bdg. 27.13 *(978-1-61913-084-5(X))* Weigl Pubs., Inc. (AV2 by Weigl).

Carroll, Danielle. Tiling with Shapes. 2005. (Yellow Umbrella Fluent Level Ser.). (ENG., Illus.). 16p. (gr. k-1). pap. 35.70 *(978-0-7368-5323-1(5)*, Yellow Umbrella Bks.) Capstone Press of Coughlan Cos.

Carrow, Ian. Jackson's Surprise Party. 2013. (InfoMax Math Readers Ser.). (ENG.). 24p. (J). (gr. 1-2). pap. 8.25 *(978-1-4777-2204-6(1)*, Rosen Classroom) Rosen Publishing Group, Inc., The.

—Jackson's Surprise Party: Shapes & Their Attributes. 2013. (InfoMax Math Readers Ser.). (ENG.). 24p. (J). (gr. 1-2). pap. 49.50 *(978-1-4777-2205-3(X)*, Rosen Classroom) Rosen Publishing Group, Inc., The.

Carson-Dellosa Publishing Staff. Colors & Shapes. 2006. (ENG., Illus.). 54p. (gr. -1-1). 2.99 *(978-0-7696-4689-3(1)*, Brighter Child) Carson-Dellosa Publishing, LLC.

—Shapes, Grades PK - K. 2010. (Home Workbooks Ser.). (ENG.). 64p. (gr. -1-k). pap. 4.49 *(978-1-60418-764-9(6))* Carson-Dellosa Publishing, LLC.

Carter, David A. The Happy Shiny Blue Circle: A Touch-And-Feel Book of Shapes. 2014. (ENG., Illus.). 16p. (J). (gr. -1-k). 14.99 *(978-1-85707-861-9(6))* Tango Bks. GBR. Dist: Independent Pubs. Group.

Cartogna, Eileen. Jobs Around Town: Learning to Sort & Classify. (Math for the Real World: Early Emergent Ser.). (ENG., Illus.). 8p. (gr. k-1). 2009. pap. 5.15 *(978-0-8239-8910-2(0))* 2004. 29.95 *(978-0-8239-7629-4(7))* Rosen Publishing Group, Inc., The.

Cartonia, Lucia. What Shape Is It? 2009. (Real Life Readers Ser.). 8p. (gr. k-1). pap. 5.15 *(978-1-4042-7985-8(7)*, Rosen Classroom) Rosen Publishing Group, Inc., The.

Chapman, Joan. Heavy & Light: Learning to Compare Weights of Objects. 2009. (Math for the Real World: Early Emergent Ser.). (ENG., Illus.). 8p. (gr. k-1). pap. 5.15 *(978-0-8239-8844-0(9))* Rosen Publishing Group, Inc., The.

Childrens Press Staff & Scholastic, Inc. Staff, contrib. by. Do You See Shapes? 2010. (Rookie Toddler: First Concepts Ser.). (ENG.). 12p. (J). bds. 6.95 *(978-0-531-25234-5(5))* Scholastic Library Publishing.

Chronicle Books Staff & Museum of Modern Art (New York, N.Y.) Staff. String-Along Books. 2010. (ENG., Illus.). 10p. (J). (gr. -1-17). 18.99 *(978-0-8118-7342-0(0))* Chronicle Bks. LLC.

Clark Sawyer, J. Patterns in the City. 2015. (J). lib. bdg. *(978-1-62724-336-0(4))* Bearport Publishing Co., Inc.

—Patterns in the Park. 2015. (J). lib. bdg. *(978-1-62724-339-1(9))* Bearport Publishing Co., Inc.

Clarke, Isabel. Sticker & Color-In Playbook: With over 50 Reusable Stickers: Teddy Bear Sizes. Tulip, Jenny, illus. 2016. (ENG.). 16p. (J). (gr. -1-12). pap. 4.99 *(978-1-86147-736-1(8)*, Armadillo) Anness Publishing GBR. Dist: National Bk. Network.

Cleary, Brian P. Windows, Rings, & Grapes: A Look at Different Shapes. Gable, Brian, illus. 2009. (Math Is CATegorical (r) Ser.). (ENG.). 32p. (gr. k-3). 16.95 *(978-0-8225-7879-6(4))* Lerner Publishing Group.

—Windows, Rings, & Grapes - A Look at Different Shapes. Gable, Brian, illus. 2011. (Math Is CATegorical Ser.). pap. 39.62 *(978-0-7613-8360-4(3))*; (ENG.). 32p. pap. 6.95 *(978-1-58013-846-8(2))* Lerner Publishing Group. (Millbrook Pr.).

Cocagne, Marie-Pascale. The Big Book of Shapes. Stevens-Marzo, Bridget, illus. 2009. (ENG.). 60p. (J). (gr. -1-3). 15.95 *(978-1-85437-851-4(1))* Tate Publishing, Ltd. GBR. Dist: Abrams, Inc.

Cohen, Marina. 3-D Shapes. 2010. (My Path to Math Ser.). (ENG.). 24p. (J). (gr. k-3). *(978-0-7787-6779-4(5))*; pap. *(978-0-7787-6788-6(4))* Crabtree Publishing Co.

Coirault, Christine, illus. My First Book of Learning. 2009. (J). *(978-1-74089-930-7(X))* Fog City Pr.

Collins Easy Learning Staff & HarperCollins UK Staff. Shapes, Colours & Patterns, Bk. 1. 2008. (Collins Easy Learning Age 3-5 Ser.). (ENG.). 88p. (J). pap. 4.99 *(978-0-00-730092-1(1))* HarperCollins Pubs. Ltd. GBR. Dist: Independent Pubs. Group.

Colors & Shapes. rev. ed. 2007. (ENG., Illus.). 28p. (J). (gr. -1-1). 16.99 *(978-1-59069-505-0(4)*, 1C1000) Studio Mouse LLC.

Connelly, Neil O. Shapes. Thornburgh, Rebecca, illus. 10p. (J). (gr. -1). bds. 3.95 *(978-1-58989-002-2(7))* Thurman Hse., LLC.

Cornell, Kari. Goldilocks & the Three Pancakes: A Story of Shapes, Numbers, & Friendship. Sevig, Kirsten, illus. 2016. 32p. (J). pap. *(978-0-87659-706-4(1))* Gryphon Hse., Inc.

Corrigan, Kathleen. My First Shapes, 1 vol. 2015. (Maple Leaf Learners Ser.). (ENG.). 20p. bds. 7.99 *(978-1-62370-221-2(6))* Capstone Young Readers of Coughlan Cos.

Coss, Lauren. Let's Sort by Size. 2014. (21st Century Basic Skills Library: Sorting Ser.). (ENG., Illus.). 24p. (J). (gr. k-3). 22.79 *(978-1-63137-635-1(7)*, 205323) Cherry Lake Publishing.

—Let's Sort Shapes. 2014. (21st Century Basic Skills Library: Sorting Ser.). (ENG.). 24p. (J). (gr. k-3). 22.79 *(978-1-63137-632-0(2)*, 205311) Cherry Lake Publishing.

Cox, Tracey M. Shaping up the Year. Bell, Samantha, illus. 2009. 24p. pap. 10.95 *(978-1-935137-73-3(5))* Guardian Angel Publishing, Inc.

Cuxart, Bernadette. Modeling Clay with 3 Basic Shapes: Model More Than 40 Animals with Drops, Balls, & Worms. 2016. (ENG.). 96p. (J). (gr. -1-3). pap. 11.99 *(978-1-4380-0908-7(9))* Barron's Educational Series, Inc.

Dale, Jay. I Am Big, 1 vol. Gulliver, Amanda, illus. 2012. (Engage Literacy Magenta Ser.). (ENG.). 32p. (gr. k-2). pap. 5.99 *(978-1-4296-8874-1(2)*, Engage Literacy) Capstone Press of Coughlan Cos.

Danielson, Christopher. Which One Doesn't Belong? 2016. (ENG., Illus.). 36p. (gr. k-12). stu. ed. 16.67 *(978-1-62531-080-4(3))* Stenhouse Pubs.

de Alba, Laura, tr. Caritas Felices. 2007. (Disney Winnie the Pooh (SilverDolphin) Ser.). (Illus.). 8p. (J). (gr. -1). bds. *(978-970-718-391-9(8)*, Silver Dolphin en Español) Advanced Marketing, S. de R. L. de C. V.

de Klerk, Roger, illus. Foxy Learns Colors. 2009. (Foxy Learns Ser.). 16p. (J). pap. 4.95 *(978-1-59496-181-6(6))* Teora USA LLC.

—Foxy Learns Shapes. 2009. (Foxy Learns Ser.). 16p. (J). pap. 4.95 *(978-1-59496-179-3(4))* Teora USA LLC.

—Foxy Learns to Add. 2009. (Foxy Learns Ser.). 16p. (J). pap. 4.95 *(978-1-59496-178-6(6))* Teora USA LLC.

Deen, Marilyn. Taking Shape, 1 vol. 2011. (Wonder Readers: Mathematics Ser.). (ENG.). (gr. -1-2). 20p. lib. bdg. 22.65 *(978-1-4296-8631-0(6))*; 16p. pap. 35.94 *(978-1-4296-8165-0(9))*; 32p. pap. 5.99 *(978-1-4296-7936-7(0))* Capstone Press of Coughlan Cos. (Wonder Readers).

—Tiling Shapes. 2011. (Wonder Readers Fluent Level Ser.). (ENG.). 16p. (gr. -1-2). pap. 35.94 *(978-1-4296-8188-9(8)*, Wonder Readers) Capstone Press of Coughlan Cos.

Del Moral, S., tr. Formas. 2006. (Disney Learning (Silver Dolphin en Espanol) Ser.). (Illus.). 22p. (J). (gr. -1). *(978-970-718-429-9(9)*, Silver Dolphin en Español) Advanced Marketing, S. de R. L. de C. V.

Del Moral, Susana. El Juego de las Formas. Zaidi, Nadeem, illus. 2005. (Baby Einstein: Libros de Carton Ser.). (SPA.). 6p. (J). (gr. -1). bds. *(978-970-718-303-2(9)*, Silver Dolphin en Español) Advanced Marketing, S. de R. L. de C. V.

del Risco, Eida, tr. What's in My Toybox? (Spanish/English) Un libro de formas/A Book of Shapes, 1 vol. 2009. (ENG & SPA., Illus.). 32p. (J). bds. 6.25 *(978-1-59572-179-2(7))* Star Bright Bks., Inc.

Demitri, Alyssa. I See Shapes. 2012. (InfoMax Readers Ser.). (ENG., Illus.). 16 pp.p. (J). (gr. k-1). pap. 7.00 *(978-1-4488-8637-1(6)*, Rosen Classroom) Rosen Publishing Group, Inc., The.

Deneux, Xavier. Shapes. 2014. (ENG., Illus.). 20p. (J). (gr. -1 — 1). bds. 14.99 *(978-1-4521-1727-0(6))* Chronicle Bks. LLC.

Diaz, James & Diaz, Francesca. Making Shapes: A Pop-Up Book. 2013. (ENG., Illus.). 10p. 19.95 *(978-1-85707-827-5(6))* Tango Bks. GBR. Dist: Independent Pubs. Group.

Dicmas, Courtney. Shapes. Dicmas, Courtney, illus. 2017. (Wild! Concepts Ser.: 4). (ENG., Illus.). 14p. (J). bds. ***(978-1-84643-994-0(9))*** Child's Play International Ltd.

Dilkes, D. H. I See Circles. 2010. (All about Shapes Ser.). (Illus.). 24p. (J). pap. 7.95 *(978-1-59845-150-4(2)*, Enslow Elementary) Enslow Pubs., Inc.

—I See Ovals. 2010. (All about Shapes Ser.). (Illus.). 24p. (J). lib. bdg. 22.60 *(978-0-7660-3800-4(9)*, Enslow Elementary) Enslow Pubs., Inc.

—I See Rectangles. 2010. (All about Shapes Ser.). (Illus.). 24p. (J). pap. 7.95 *(978-1-59845-152-8(9))*; lib. bdg. 22.60 *(978-0-7660-3801-1(7))* Enslow Pubs., Inc. (Enslow Elementary).

—I See Squares. 2010. (All about Shapes Ser.). (Illus.). 24p. (J). pap. 7.95 *(978-1-59845-153-5(7))*; lib. bdg. 22.60 *(978-0-7660-3802-8(5))* Enslow Pubs., Inc. (Enslow Elementary).

—I See Stars. 2010. (All about Shapes Ser.). (Illus.). 24p. (J). pap. 7.95 *(978-1-59845-154-2(5))*; lib. bdg. 22.60 *(978-0-7660-3803-5(3))* Enslow Pubs., Inc. (Enslow Elementary).

—I See Triangles. 2010. (All about Shapes Ser.). (Illus.). 24p. (J). pap. 7.95 *(978-1-59845-155-9(3))*; lib. bdg. 22.60 *(978-0-7660-3804-2(1))* Enslow Pubs., Inc. (Enslow Elementary).

Dingles, Molly. Crescent Kitchen. Brodie, Neale, illus. 2006. (Community of Shapes Ser.). (J). *(978-1-59646-049-2(0))* Dingles & Co.

—Crescent Kitchen: Cocina de Medialuna. Brodie, Neale, illus. 2006. (ENG & SPA.). (J). 21.65 *(978-1-59646-050-8(4))* Dingles & Co.

—Diamond Downhill. Dobson, Len, illus. 2005. (Community of Shapes Ser.). 32p. (J). pap. 10.95 *(978-1-59646-240-3(X))*; lib. bdg. 21.65 *(978-1-59646-043-0(1))*; per. 10.95 *(978-1-59646-241-0(8))* Dingles & Co.

—Diamond Downhill/Cuesta abajo en forma de Rombo. Dobson, Len, illus. 2005. (Community of Shapes Ser.).Tr. of Cuesta abajo en forma de Rombo. (ENG & SPA.). 32p. (J). pap. 10.95 *(978-1-59646-242-7(6))*; lib. bdg. 20.65 *(978-1-59646-044-7(X))*; per. 10.95 *(978-1-59646-243-4(4))* Dingles & Co.

—Oval Opera. Brodie, Neale, illus. 2006. (Community of Shapes Ser.). 29p. (J). *(978-1-59646-047-8(4))* Dingles & Co.

—Oval Opera: Ópera de óvalos. Brodie, Neale, illus. 2006. (SPA & ENG.). (J). *(978-1-59646-048-5(2))* Dingles & Co.

—Rectangle Ranch. Dobson, Len, illus. 2005. (Community of Shapes Ser.). 32p. (J). pap. 10.95 *(978-1-59646-244-1(2))*; lib. bdg. 21.65 *(978-1-59646-035-5(0))*; per. 10.95 *(978-1-59646-245-8(0))* Dingles & Co.

—Rectangle Ranch/Rancho Rectangular. Dobson, Len, illus. 2005. (Community of Shapes Ser.).Tr. of Rancho Rectangular. (ENG & SPA.). 32p. (J). pap. 10.95 *(978-1-59646-246-5(9))*; lib. bdg. 20.65 *(978-1-59646-036-2(9))*; per. 10.95 *(978-1-59646-247-2(7))* Dingles & Co.

—Seaside Circles. Brodie, Neale, illus. 2006. (Community of Shapes Ser.). 32p. (J). pap. 10.95 *(978-1-59646-256-4(6))*; lib. bdg. 21.65 *(978-1-59646-033-1(4))*; per. 10.95 *(978-1-59646-257-1(4))* Dingles & Co.

—Seaside Circles/Círculos a la orilla del Mar. Brodie, Neale, illus. 2006. (Community of Shapes Ser.).Tr. of Círculos a la orilla del Mar. (ENG & SPA.). 32p. (J). pap. 10.95 *(978-1-59646-258-8(2))*; lib. bdg. 21.65 *(978-1-59646-034-8(2))* Dingles & Co.

—Seaside Circles/Círculos a la orilla del Mar. Brodie, Neal, illus. 2006. (Community of Shapes Ser.).Tr. of Círculos a la orilla del Mar. (ENG & SPA.). 32p. (J). per. 10.95 *(978-1-59646-259-5(0))* Dingles & Co.

—Star Ship. Brodie, Neale, illus. 2006. (Community of Shapes Ser.). 29p. (J). *(978-1-59646-039-3(3))* Dingles & Co.

—Star Ship: Barco de Estrellas. Brodie, Neale, illus. 2006. (SPA & ENG.). (J). *(978-1-59646-040-9(7))* Dingles & Co.

—Sweet Hearts. Brodie, Neale, illus. 2006. (Community of Shapes Ser.). (J). *(978-1-59646-037-9(7))* Dingles & Co.

—Sweet Hearts: Dulce Corazón. Brodie, Neale, illus. 2006. (SPA & ENG.). (J). *(978-1-59646-038-6(5))* Dingles & Co.

—Town Squares. Brodie, Neale, illus. 2006. (Community of Shapes Ser.). 32p. (J). pap. 10.95 *(978-1-59646-264-9(7))*; lib. bdg. 21.65 *(978-1-59646-041-6(5))*; per. 10.95 *(978-1-59646-265-6(5))* Dingles & Co.

—Town Squares/Cuadrados en la Plaza. Brodie, Neale, illus. 2006. (Community of Shapes Ser.).Tr. of Cuadrados en la Plaza. (ENG & SPA.). 32p. (J). pap. 10.95 *(978-1-59646-266-3(3))*; lib. bdg. 21.65 *(978-1-59646-042-3(3))*; per. 10.95 *(978-1-59646-267-0(1))* Dingles & Co.

—Triangle Trail: Sendero de Triángulos. 2005. (ENG & SPA., Illus.). 32p. (J). lib. bdg. 21.65 *(978-1-59646-046-1(6))* Dingles & Co.

Disney Book Group. Disney Baby Shapes All Around. Disney Storybook Art Team, illus. 2017. (ENG.). 18p. (J). (gr. -1 — 1). bds. 8.99 *(978-1-368-00079-6(7))* Disney Pr.

Disney Staff, contrib. by. Write, Slide & Learn Disney Mickey Mouse Clubhouse: Colors & Shapes. 2011. (Disney Write, Slide & Learn Ser.). 12p. (J). 9.99 *(978-1-74183-850-3(9))* Hinkler Bks. Pty. Ltd. AUS. Dist: Ideals Pubns.

Does It Belong? 2003. (Preschool Ser.). (ENG.). (J). cd-rom 19.99 *(978-1-58947-903-6(3))* School Zone Publishing Co.

Domiano, Gloria. Ship Shapes: Identify & Describe Shapes. 2013. (Rosen Math Readers Ser.). (ENG.). 16p. (J). (gr. k-1). pap. 42.00 *(978-1-4777-1666-3(1))*; (Illus.). pap. 7.00 *(978-1-4777-1665-6(3))* Rosen Publishing Group, Inc., The. (Rosen Classroom).

Dorling Kindersley Publishing Staff. My First Shapes. 2017. (My First Bks.). (ENG., Illus.). 36p. (J). (— 1). bds. 5.99 ***(978-1-4654-6082-0(9)***, DK Children) Dorling Kindersley Publishing, Inc.

—Shapes. (DK Braille Ser.). (ENG., (J). 2016. Illus.). 18p. (-k). bds. 14.99 *(978-1-4654-3612-2(X))* 2013. 12p. (gr. -1-k). bds. 6.99 *(978-1-4654-0920-1(3))* Dorling Kindersley Publishing, Inc. (DK Children).

—Shapes. 2008. (Gymboree Play & Music Ser.). (ENG., Illus.). 24p. (J). (gr. -1). bds. *(978-1-55470-040-0(X))* Me to We.

—Skills for Starting School Shapes & Sizes. 2017. (Skills for Starting School Ser.). (ENG.). 40p. (J). (-k). pap. 6.99 *(978-1-4654-6013-4(6)*, DK Children) Dorling Kindersley Publishing, Inc.

Draze, Dianne. Attribute Block - Thinking Activities - Sequences. 2005. (ENG.). 32p. pap. 9.95 *(978-1-59363-053-9(0))* Prufrock Pr.

Dudley, Linda S. Aunt Linda's Shape Book. Neal, Jill Faith, illus. 2007. (ENG.). 32p. per. 24.95 *(978-1-4241-8618-1(8))* America Star Bks.

Eagan, Mary. Alexee's Animals from A-Z, 1 vol. King, Cheryl, illus. 2010. 30p. 24.95 *(978-1-4489-3967-1(4))* PublishAmerica, Inc.

Earle, Erin. Surprise Party! 2013. (Core Math Skills: Measurement & Geometry Ser.). 24p. (J). (gr. 1-2). 22.60 *(978-1-4777-2230-5(0))*; (ENG.). pap. 8.25 *(978-1-4777-2103-2(7))* Rosen Publishing Group, Inc., The. (Rosen Classroom).

—Surprise Party! Shapes & Their Attributes. 2013. (Rosen Math Readers Ser.). (ENG.). 24p. (J). (gr. 1-2). pap. 49.50 *(978-1-4777-2104-9(5)*, Rosen Classroom) Rosen Publishing Group, Inc., The.

Eck, Kristin. Shapes in My House. 2004. (Look-And-Learn Books). (Illus.). (J). lib. bdg. 8.95 *(978-1-4042-2699-9(0)*, PowerKids Pr.) Rosen Publishing Group, Inc., The.

Ellis, Belinda. Baby See-A-Shape Things That Go! 2005. (Baby See a Shape Ser.). (Illus.). 10p. (gr. -1 — 1). bds. *(978-1-84610-022-2(4))* Make Believe Ideas.

Emberley, Ed. The Wing on a Flea. 2015. (ENG., Illus.). 48p. 17.95 *(978-1-62326-058-3(2))* AMMO Bks., LLC.

Evanson, Ashley. Paris: A Book of Shapes. Evanson, Ashley, illus. 2015. (Hello, World Ser.). (ENG., Illus.). 14p. (J). (— 1). bds. 6.99 *(978-0-448-48915-5(5)*, Grosset & Dunlap) Penguin Young Readers Group.

Falk, Liane. Spots. 2009. 24p. pap. 13.50 *(978-1-4389-8724-8(2))* AuthorHouse.

Feldman, Jean. Highway Letters, Numbers & Shapes: PreK-1. 2010. 80p. pap. 22.99 *(978-1-61601-036-2(3))* Creative Teaching Pr., Inc.

Felix, Rebecca. Patterns at School. 2015. (21st Century Basic Skills Library: Patterns All Around Ser.). (ENG., Illus.). 24p. (J). (gr. k-3). pap. 12.79 *(978-1-63188-934-9(6)*, 205997) Cherry Lake Publishing.

Fish, Simon. Silly Shapes. 2012. (ENG.). (J). pap. *(978-1-4675-0898-8(5))* Independent Pub.

Flash Kids Editors, ed. Colors & Shapes: Grade Pre-K-K (Flash Skills) 2010. (Flash Skills Ser.). (ENG.). 64p. (J). pap. 3.95 *(978-1-4114-3470-7(6)*, Spark Publishing Group) Sterling Publishing Co., Inc.

Flatt, Lizann. Shaping up Summer. Barron, Ashley, illus. 2014. (Math in Nature Ser.: 4). (ENG.). 32p. (J). (gr. k-4). 14.95 *(978-1-926973-87-6(9)*, Owlkids) Owlkids Bks. Inc. CAN. Dist: Publishers Group West (PGW).

Flowerpot Press Staff, contrib. by. Sockheadz: Shapes. 2013. (ENG., Illus.). 20p. (J). (gr. -1-k). 6.99 *(978-1-77093-596-9(7))* Flowerpot Children's Pr. Inc. CAN. Dist: Cardinal Pubs. Group.

Formas. (Coleccion Mi Primer Libro). (SPA., Illus.). (J). 13.95 *(978-84-207-3781-2(X)*, ANY877) Grupo Anaya, S.A. ESP. Dist: Continental Bk. Co., Inc.

Formas. (Coleccion Libritos Acordeon). (SPA., Illus.). 10p. (J). pap. 5.50 *(978-950-11-0793-7(0)*, SGM930) Sigmar ARG. Dist: Continental Bk. Co., Inc.

Formas (Shapes) (SPA.). (J). 6.95 *(978-968-419-056-6(5))* Grijalbo, Editorial MEX. Dist: AIMS International Bks., Inc.

Formas y Colores. (Coleccion Picaros Peluchines). (SPA.). (J). 5.50 *(978-950-11-0400-4(1)*, SGM400) Sigmar ARG. Dist: Continental Bk. Co., Inc.

Forte, Imogene. Ready to Learn Shapes & Colors. 2003. (Illus.). 64p. per. 7.95 *(978-0-86530-593-9(5))* Incentive Pubns., Inc.
Fretland VanVoorst, Jenny. Las Formas en la Ciudad. 2015.Tr. of Shapes in the City. (SPA., Illus.). 24p. (J). lib. bdg. *(978-1-62031-246-9(8)*, Bullfrog Bks.) Jump! Inc.
—Las Formas en la Escuela. 2015.Tr. of Shapes at School. (SPA., Illus.). 24p. (J). lib. bdg. *(978-1-62031-248-3(4)*, Bullfrog Bks.) Jump! Inc.
—Las Formas en la Playa. 2015.Tr. of Shapes by the Sea. (SPA., Illus.). 24p. (J). lib. bdg. *(978-1-62031-249-0(2)*, Bullfrog Bks.) Jump! Inc.
—Shapes at School. 2015. (Illus.). 24p. (J). lib. bdg. *(978-1-62031-203-2(4)*, Bullfrog Bks.) Jump! Inc.
—Shapes by the Sea. 2015. (Illus.). 24p. (J). lib. bdg. *(978-1-62031-202-5(6)*, Bullfrog Bks.) Jump! Inc.
—Shapes in the City. 2015. (Illus.). 24p. (J). lib. bdg. *(978-1-62031-200-1(X)*, Bullfrog Bks.) Jump! Inc.
—Shapes on the Farm. 2015. 24p. (J). lib. bdg. *(978-1-62031-201-8(8)*, Bullfrog Bks.) Jump! Inc.
Fried, Miriam. My Jelly Bean Book. 2005. (Illus.). (J). *(978-1-57400-049-8(7))* Data Trace Publishing, Co.
Furstinger, Nancy. Cones. 2014. (3-D Shapes Ser.). (ENG.). 24p. (J). (gr. 1-4). 27.07 *(978-1-62323-981-7(8)*, 206760) Child's World, Inc., The.
—Cubes. 2014. (3-D Shapes Ser.). (ENG.). 24p. (J). (gr. 1-4). 27.07 *(978-1-62323-982-4(6)*, 206761) Child's World, Inc., The.
—Cylinders. 2014. (3-D Shapes Ser.). (ENG.). 24p. (J). (gr. 1-4). 27.07 *(978-1-62323-983-1(4)*, 206762) Child's World, Inc., The.
—Prisms. 2014. (3-D Shapes Ser.). (ENG.). 24p. (J). (gr. 1-4). 27.07 *(978-1-62323-984-8(2)*, 206763) Child's World, Inc., The.
—Pyramids. 2014. (3-D Shapes Ser.). (ENG.). 24p. (J). (gr. 1-4). 27.07 *(978-1-62323-985-5(0)*, 206764) Child's World, Inc., The.
—Spheres. 2014. (3-D Shapes Ser.). (ENG.). 24p. (J). (gr. 1-4). 27.07 *(978-1-62323-986-2(9)*, 206765) Child's World, Inc., The.
Gaarder-Juntti, Oona. Shapes at Home, 1 vol. 2013. (Shapes Everywhere Ser.). (ENG.). 24p. (gr. k-4). lib. bdg. 25.65 *(978-1-61783-411-0(4)*, Super SandCastle) ABDO Publishing Co.
—Shapes at School, 1 vol. 2013. (Shapes Everywhere Ser.). (ENG.). 24p. (gr. k-4). lib. bdg. 25.65 *(978-1-61783-412-7(2)*, Super SandCastle) ABDO Publishing Co.
—Shapes in Food, 1 vol. 2013. (Shapes Everywhere Ser.). (ENG.). 24p. (gr. k-4). lib. bdg. 25.65 *(978-1-61783-413-4(0)*, Super SandCastle) ABDO Publishing Co.
—Shapes in Nature, 1 vol. 2013. (Shapes Everywhere Ser.). (ENG.). 24p. (gr. k-4). lib. bdg. 25.65 *(978-1-61783-414-1(9)*, Super SandCastle) ABDO Publishing Co.
—Shapes in Sports, 1 vol. 2013. (Shapes Everywhere Ser.). (ENG.). 24p. (gr. k-4). lib. bdg. 25.65 *(978-1-61783-415-8(7)*, Super SandCastle) ABDO Publishing Co.
—Shapes on a Farm, 1 vol. 2013. (Shapes Everywhere Ser.). (ENG.). 24p. (gr. k-4). lib. bdg. 25.65 *(978-1-61783-416-5(5)*, Super SandCastle) ABDO Publishing Co.
Galvin, Laura Gates. Peep's Shapes. 2006. (Peep & the Big Wide World Ser.). (ENG., Illus.). 24p. (J). (gr. -1-k). 15.99 *(978-1-59249-521-4(4)*, 1C304) Soundprints.
George, Chris. I Want Pizza. 2017. (Early Concepts Ser.). 24p. (gr. 4-6). pap. 8.25 ***(978-1-5081-6213-1(1)***, PowerKids Pr.) Rosen Publishing Group, Inc., The.
Gerstein, Sherry. Imagination Vacation: A Color-Foil Shapes Book. Bennett, Andy, illus. 2006. 14p. (J). (gr. -1-3). bds. 6.95 *(978-1-57791-261-3(6))* Brighter Minds Children's Publishing.
Ghigna, Charles. Shapes Are Everywhere! Jatkowska, Ag, illus. 2013. 24p. (J). pap. *(978-1-4795-1929-3(4))*; (ENG.). (gr. -1-2). lib. bdg. 21.99 *(978-1-4048-8309-3(6))* Picture Window Bks.
Giles, Angela & Picthall, Chez. Colours & Shapes. Calver, Paul, illus. 2015. (ENG.). 6p. (J). 9.99 *(978-1-909763-42-5(X))* Award Pubns. Ltd. GBR. Dist: Parkwest Pubns., Inc.
Ginsburg, Herbert P., et al. Favorite Shapes. 2003. (Illus.). 9.95 *(978-0-7690-3043-2(2))* Seymour, Dale Pubns.
Giulieri, Anne. Here Is a Robot, 1 vol. Kreinberg, Sylvia, photos by. 2012. (Engage Literacy Magenta Ser.). (ENG., Illus.). 32p. (gr. k-2). pap. 5.99 *(978-1-4296-8848-2(3)*, Engage Literacy) Capstone Press of Coughlan Cos.
—Look at the Picture, 1 vol. Kreinberg, Sylvia, photos by. 2012. (Engage Literacy Magenta Ser.). (ENG., Illus.). 32p. (gr. k-2). pap. 5.99 *(978-1-4296-8858-1(0)*, Engage Literacy) Capstone Press of Coughlan Cos.
Glaser, Byron & Higashi, Sandra. Zolocolor! Doodling Between Black & White. Glaser, Byron & Higashi, Sandra, illus. 2011. (ENG., Illus.). 96p. (J). 7.99 *(978-1-4424-2261-2(0)*, Little Simon) Little Simon.
Gobo, creator. Little Learners Ready to Read & Write. 2007. (Magnix Little Learners Ser.). (Illus.). 40p. (J). (gr. -1-3). 14.95 *(978-1-932915-44-0(3))* Sandvik Innovations, LLC.
Goodman, David & Miller, Zoe. Shape. 2009. (ENG., Illus.). 64p. (gr. -1-3). 22.50 *(978-1-85437-779-1(5))* Tate Publishing, Ltd. GBR. Dist: Abrams, Inc.
Gordon, Sharon. Big/Small/Grande/Pequeno. 2006. (Bookworms Ser.). (ENG & SPA., Illus.). 24p. (gr. k-1). lib. bdg. 15.95 *(978-0-7614-2445-1(8))* Marshall Cavendish Corp.
Gould, Jane. In the Garden. rev. ed. 2011. (Mathematics Readers Ser.). (ENG.). 32p. (J). (gr. k-k). pap. 8.99 *(978-1-4333-3431-3(3))* Teacher Created Materials, Inc.
Graire, Virginie, illus. Shapes. 2016. (ENG.). 12p. (J). (gr. -1 — 1). bds. 6.99 *(978-1-4998-0294-8(3))* Little Bee Books Inc.
Greathouse, Lisa. Farm Animals: Classifying & Sorting. rev. ed. 2011. (Mathematics Readers Ser.). (ENG.). 32p. (J). (gr. k-k). pap. 8.99 *(978-1-4333-3442-9(9))* Teacher Created Materials, Inc.
—Games Are Fun. rev. ed. 2011. (Mathematics Readers Ser.). (ENG.). 32p. (J). (gr. k-k). pap. 8.99 *(978-1-4333-3437-5(2))* Teacher Created Materials, Inc.
—Recess Time: Patterns. rev. ed. 2011. (Mathematics Readers Ser.). (ENG.). 32p. (J). (gr. k-k). pap. 8.99 *(978-1-4333-3436-8(4))* Teacher Created Materials, Inc.
—Wild Animals, Level K. rev. ed. 2011. (Mathematics Readers Ser.). (ENG.). 32p. (J). (gr. k-k). pap. 8.99 *(978-1-4333-3443-6(7))* Teacher Created Materials, Inc.
Gunderson, Jessica & Weakland, Mark. Wacky Comparisons. Bolton, Bill & Sinkovec, Igor, illus. 2013. (Wacky Comparisons Ser.). (ENG.). 32p. (gr. -1-2). 14.95 *(978-1-62370-037-9(X))* Capstone Young Readers of Coughlan Cos.
—Wacky Comparisons. 2013. (Wacky Comparisons Ser.). (ENG.). 24p. (gr. -1-2). pap. 31.80 *(978-1-4795-1970-5(7))*; lib. bdg. 111.96 *(978-1-4048-8145-7(X))* Picture Window Bks.
Gunzi, Christiane. Las Formas. 2004. (My Very First Look At Ser.). (SPA & ENG., Illus.). 24p. (J). (gr. -1-k). pap. 5.95 *(978-1-58728-431-1(6))* Cooper Square Publishing Llc.
Gunzl, Christiane. Shapes. 2014. (ENG., Illus.). 20p. pap. 8.95 *(978-1-907604-25-6(1))* Award Pubns. Ltd. GBR. Dist: Parkwest Pubns., Inc.
Haas, Kristin. The Shape Family Babies, 1 vol. Bersani, Shennen, illus. 2014. (ENG.). 32p. (J). (gr. -1-3). 17.95 *(978-1-62855-211-9(5))* Arbordale Publishing.
Haas, Kristin, et al. Los Bebés de la Familia Geométrica, 1 vol. Bersani, Shennen, illus. 2014.Tr. of Shape Family Babies. (SPA.). 32p. (J). (gr. -1-3). pap. 9.95 *(978-1-62855-229-4(8))* Arbordale Publishing.
Hall, Pamela. Rectangles, 1 vol. Holm, Sharon, illus. 2007. (Shapes Ser.). (ENG.). 24p. (gr. -1-2). 27.07 *(978-1-60270-046-8(X)*, Looking Glass Library- Nonfiction) Magic Wagon.
—Squares, 1 vol. Holm, Sharon, illus. 2007. (Shapes Ser.). (ENG.). 24p. (gr. -1-2). 27.07 *(978-1-60270-047-5(8)*, Looking Glass Library- Nonfiction) Magic Wagon.
Hamilton, Laura. Cones, 1 vol. Mitter, Kathryn, illus. 2012. (Everyday 3-D Shapes Ser.). (ENG.). 24p. (J). (gr. -1-2). lib. bdg. 27.07 *(978-1-61641-872-4(9)*, Looking Glass Library) Magic Wagon.
—Cubes, 1 vol. Mitter, Kathryn, illus. 2012. (Everyday 3-D Shapes Ser.). (ENG.). 24p. (J). (gr. -1-2). lib. bdg. 27.07 *(978-1-61641-873-1(7)*, Looking Glass Library) Magic Wagon.
—Cylinders, 1 vol. Mitter, Kathryn, illus. 2012. (Everyday 3-D Shapes Ser.). (ENG.). 24p. (J). (gr. -1-2). lib. bdg. 27.07 *(978-1-61641-874-8(5)*, Looking Glass Library) Magic Wagon.
—Prisms, 1 vol. Mitter, Kathryn, illus. 2012. (Everyday 3-D Shapes Ser.). (ENG.). 24p. (J). (gr. -1-2). lib. bdg. 27.07 *(978-1-61641-875-5(3)*, Looking Glass Library) Magic Wagon.
—Pyramids, 1 vol. Mitter, Kathryn, illus. 2012. (Everyday 3-D Shapes Ser.). (ENG.). 24p. (J). (gr. -1-2). lib. bdg. 27.07 *(978-1-61641-876-2(1)*, Looking Glass Library) Magic Wagon.
—Spheres, 1 vol. Mitter, Kathryn, illus. 2012. (Everyday 3-D Shapes Ser.). (ENG.). 24p. (J). (gr. -1-2). lib. bdg. 27.07 *(978-1-61641-877-9(X)*, Looking Glass Library) Magic Wagon.
Harbo, Christopher L. Shapes. Banks, Timothy, illus. 2013. (Wizard of Oz Ser.). (ENG.). 24p. (gr. 1-2). 27.99 *(978-1-4765-3767-2(4))* Capstone Press of Coughlan Cos.
Harcourt, creator. I Know Shapes: Math Concept Reader. 2007. (Illus.). (J). pap. 31.53 *(978-0-15-379896-2(3))* Houghton Mifflin Harcourt School Pubs.
Harmon, Minnie P. Golden's Shapes & Colors. 2011. 36p. pap. 21.99 *(978-1-4628-6253-5(5))* Xlibris Corp.
Harrison, Lorraine. Flat Shapes, Solid Shapes: Identify & Describe Shapes. 2013. (Rosen Math Readers Ser.). (ENG.). 16p. (J). (gr. k-1). pap. 42.00 *(978-1-4777-1615-1(7))*; (Illus.). pap. 7.00 *(978-1-4777-1614-4(9))* Rosen Publishing Group, Inc., The. (Rosen Classroom).
Harvey, Jayne. Busy Bugs: A Book about Patterns. Adnet, Bernard, illus. 2003. (Penguin Young Readers, Level 2 Ser.: Level 1). (ENG.). 32p. (J). (gr. 1-2). pap. 3.99 *(978-0-448-43159-8(9)*, Penguin Young Readers) Penguin Young Readers Group.
Heinze, Monica Bacon. A Day with Shapes. Dow, S. B., illus. 2004. (J). *(978-0-9761710-0-3(7))* Paisley Publishing.
Helenek, Sophie. My First Book SHAPES: GOLD Mom's Choice Awards Recipient. 2014. (My First Book Ser.). (ENG., Illus.). 16p. (J). (gr. -1 — 1). bds. 5.99 *(978-0-9894505-1-5(1))* Nursery Bks.
Herbst, Kailee. Who's Short? Who's Tall? Learning to Compare Heights. 2009. (Math for the Real World: Early Emergent Ser.). (ENG., Illus.). 8p. (gr. k-1). pap. 5.15 *(978-0-8239-8856-3(2))* Rosen Publishing Group, Inc., The.
Hewitt, Angie. Colors & Shapes: Touch-And-Trace Early Learning Fun! 2017. (Little Groovers Ser.). (ENG., Illus.). 12p. (J). (— 1). bds. 7.99 *(978-1-5107-0837-2(5)*, Sky Pony Pr.) Skyhorse Publishing Co., Inc.
Hicks, Barbara Jean. I Like Colors. Prap, Lila, illus. 2006. 24p. (J). (gr. -1-3). 9.95 *(978-1-58925-057-4(5))* Tiger Tales.
Holden, Arianne. It's Fun to Learn about Shapes: A Busy Picture Book Full of Fabulous Facts & Things to Do! 2016. (ENG., Illus.). 32p. 9.99 *(978-1-86147-709-5(0)*, Armadillo) Anness Publishing GBR. Dist: National Bk. Network.
Holden, Pam. Show Me a Shape, 6 pack. Cooper, Jenny, illus. 2009. (Red Rocket Readers Ser.). (ENG.). 16p. (gr. -1-1). pap. *(978-1-877363-27-6(8)*, Red Rocket Readers) Flying Start Bks.
—Show Me a Shape - BIG BOOK. Cooper, Jenny, illus. 2016. (ENG.). 16p. (-1). Beta *(978-1-77654-160-7(X)*, Red Rocket Readers) Flying Start Bks.
Horne, Jane. Busy Baby Sparklies 4 Volume Boxed Set: Baby's First Box of Books. 2007. (Illus.). 12p. (gr. -1-k). bds., bds. *(978-1-84610-565-4(X))* Make Believe Ideas.
Houghton Mifflin Harcourt Publishing Company Staff & Nouvian, Judith. Shapes. 2015. (Picture This Ser.). (ENG., Illus.). 40p. (J). (gr. -1-3). bds. 7.99 *(978-0-544-51830-8(6)*, HMH Books For Young Readers) Houghton Mifflin Harcourt Publishing Co.
Howells, Tania. Starring Shapes! Howells, Tania, illus. 2015. (ENG., Illus.). 24p. (J). (gr. -1-2). 15.95 *(978-1-55453-743-3(6))* Kids Can Pr., Ltd. CAN. Dist: Hachette Bk. Group.
Hubbard, Ben. Top 10 Biggest. 2010. (Crabtree Contact Ser.). (ENG., Illus.). 32p. (J). (gr. 3-6). lib. bdg. *(978-0-7787-7487-7(2)*, 1308100) Crabtree Publishing Co.
—Top 10 Longest. 2010. (ENG., Illus.). 32p. (J). pap. *(978-0-7787-7510-2(0))*; lib. bdg. *(978-0-7787-7489-1(9))* Crabtree Publishing Co.
—Top 10 Smallest. 2010. (ENG., Illus.). 32p. (J). lib. bdg. *(978-0-7787-7491-4(0))* Crabtree Publishing Co.
Hughes, Mónica. Shapes: Band 01A/Pink A. 2006. (Collins Big Cat Ser.). (ENG., Illus.). 16p. (J). (gr. -1-k). pap. 5.99 *(978-0-00-718649-5(5))* HarperCollins Pubs. Ltd. GBR. Dist: Independent Pubs. Group.
Hughes, Tom. Tall & Short. 2016. (All about Opposites Ser.). (Illus.). 24p. (J). pap. 9.35 *(978-0-7660-8078-2(1))* Enslow Pubs., Inc.
—Tight & Loose. 2016. (All about Opposites Ser.). (Illus.). 24p. (J). pap. 9.35 *(978-0-7660-8116-1(8))* Enslow Pubs., Inc.
—Wide & Narrow. 2016. (All about Opposites Ser.). (Illus.). 24p. (J). pap. 9.35 *(978-0-7660-8117-8(6))* Enslow Pubs., Inc.
Hunt, Darleen L. Samantha Visits Grandpa Geo: Shapes. Komarck, Michael, illus. 2003. (Sherman's Math Corner Ser.). (J). (gr. -1-3). *(978-1-929591-01-5(2))* Reading Rock, Inc.
Hunt, Janie. Shapes. Chrystall, Claire, illus. 2003. (Busy Finger Ser.). 10p. (J). bds. 10.95 *(978-1-57145-938-1(3)*, Silver Dolphin Bks.) Readerlink Distribution Services, LLC.
Hvass & Hannibal. Pattern-Tastic Treasure Hunt: Spot the Odd One Out with Nature. 2016. (ENG.). 14p. (J). (gr. -1-k). bds. 12.99 *(978-1-84780-779-3(8)*, Wide Eyed Editions) Quarto Publishing Group UK GBR. Dist: Hachette Bk. Group.
I Know My Shapes. 2005. (J). pap., stu. ed. 19.95 *(978-1-58970-699-6(4))* Lakeshore Learning Materials.
I Know My Shapes! Big Book Series. 2005. (J). pap. 49.95 *(978-1-58970-698-9(6))* Lakeshore Learning Materials.
Ikids Staff. Shapes. Larranaga, Ana Martin, illus. 2009. (ENG.). 12p. (J). (gr. -1 — 1). bds. 5.99 *(978-1-58476-937-8(8))* Innovative Kids.
—Soft Shapes: Dinosaurs (Baby's First Book + Puzzle) Ski, Jenn, illus. 2010. (ENG.). 8p. (J). (gr. -1 — 1). 10.99 *(978-1-60169-043-2(6))* Innovative Kids.
—Soft Shapes: Trucks (Baby's First Book + Puzzle) Ski, Jenn, illus. 2010. (ENG.). 8p. (J). (gr. -1 — 1). 10.99 *(978-1-60169-044-9(4))* Innovative Kids.
Imperato, Teresa. Trick or Treat! A Halloween Shapes Book. Winston, Jeannie, illus. 2005. 12p. (J). 7.95 *(978-1-58117-325-3(3)*, Intervisual/Piggy Toes) Bendon, Inc.
Innovative Kids Staff. Shapes - Soft Shapes. 2010. (ENG.). 8p. (J). (gr. -1 — 1). 10.99 *(978-1-58476-961-3(0))* Innovative Kids.
Innovative Kids Staff, creator. Soft Shapes - Animals. 2010. (ENG.). 8p. (J). (gr. -1 — 1). 10.99 *(978-1-58476-964-4(5))* Innovative Kids.
—Soft Shapes - Colors. 2010. (ENG.). 8p. (J). (gr. -1 — 1). 10.99 *(978-1-58476-963-7(7))* Innovative Kids.
—Soft Shapes - Counting. 2010. (ENG.). 8p. (J). (gr. -1 — 1). 10.99 *(978-1-58476-962-0(9))* Innovative Kids.
Jaramillo, Gloria. Busy Kids' Colors, Shapes & Sizes. Poirier, Nadine, illus. 2008. (Busy Kids Ser.). 36p. (J). (gr. -1-k). bds. 12.99 *(978-2-7641-1677-7(2))* Gardner Pubns.
Jeffries, Joyce. Long & Short. 2013. (Dinosaur School Ser.). (Illus.). 24p. (gr. -1-1). 22.60 *(978-1-4339-8095-4(9))*; pap. 8.15 *(978-1-4339-8096-1(7))* Stevens, Gareth Publishing LLLP.
—Shapes at School: Identify & Describe Shapes. 2013. (Rosen Math Readers Ser.). (ENG.). 16p. (J). (gr. k-1). pap. 42.00 *(978-1-4777-1588-8(6))*; (Illus.). pap. 7.00 *(978-1-4777-1587-1(8))* Rosen Publishing Group, Inc., The. (Rosen Classroom).
Jocelyn, Marthe. One Some Many. Slaughter, Tom, illus. 2006. (ENG.). 16p. (J). (gr. k-k). bds. 7.95 *(978-0-88776-789-0(3)*, Tundra Bks.) Tundra Bks. CAN. Dist: Penguin Random Hse. LLC.
—Over Under. Slaughter, Tom, illus. 2005. (ENG.). 24p. (J). (gr. k-k). 15.95 *(978-0-88776-708-1(7)*, Tundra Bks.) Tundra Bks. CAN. Dist: Penguin Random Hse. LLC.
Johnson, Jinny & Woods, Michael. How Big Is a Whale? (Illus.). (J). pap. 18.99 *(978-0-590-24629-3(1))* Scholastic, Inc.
Johnson, Rebecca L. Sizing up Shapes. 2007. (Reading Expeditions Ser.). (ENG., Illus.). 24p. (J). pap. 14.95 *(978-0-7922-4589-6(X))* CENGAGE Learning.
Johnstone, Michael. Sticker & Color-In Playbook: Teddy Bear Shapes. Tulip, Jenny, illus. 2016. (ENG.). 16p. (J). (gr. -1-12). pap. 4.99 *(978-1-86147-734-7(1)*, Armadillo) Anness Publishing GBR. Dist: National Bk. Network.
Jones, Bryony. Very Tasty Vegetables. 2011. (ENG., Illus.). 14p. (J). (gr. -1-k). bds. *(978-1-84089-615-2(9))* Zero to Ten, Ltd.
Jones, Otis. Geonopolis, the Shapely City of Geometry. 2003. (ENG., Illus.). 21p. (J). *(978-0-9744123-0-6(9))* Jeb Cool Kids Entertainment, Inc.
Jones, Tammy. Look at the Shapes. 2009. (Sight Word Readers Set A Ser.). (J). 3.49 net. *(978-1-60719-152-0(0))* Newmark Learning LLC.
—What Has Stripes? 2009. (Sight Word Readers Set A Ser.). (J). 3.49 net. *(978-1-60719-151-3(2))* Newmark Learning LLC.
Jordan, Christopher. Hockey Shapes. 2010. (My First NHL Bks.). (ENG., Illus.). 30p. (J). (gr. -1). bds. *(978-1-55168-370-6(9))* Me to We.
—Hockey Shapes. 2011. (My First NHL Book Ser.). (ENG., Illus.). 30p. (J). (-k). bds. 8.99 *(978-1-77049-321-6(2))* Tundra Bks. CAN. Dist: Random Hse., LLC.
—NASCAR Shapes. 2012. (My First NASCAR Racing Ser.). (ENG., Illus.). 28p. (J). (-k). bds. 7.95 *(978-1-77049-431-2(6)*, Fenn-Tundra) Tundra Bks. CAN. Dist: Penguin Random Hse. LLC.
Joyce, Jeffrey. Pablo's Paper Crafts. 2013. (Core Math Skills: Measurement & Geometry Ser.). (Illus.). 24p. (J). (gr. 1-2). 22.60 *(978-1-4777-2232-9(7)*, 1359255, Rosen Classroom) Rosen Publishing Group, Inc., The.
—Pablo's Paper Crafts: Shapes & Their Attributes. 2013. (Rosen Math Readers Ser.). (ENG., Illus.). 24p. (J). (gr. 1-2). pap. 49.50 *(978-1-4777-2050-9(2)*, 1359255); pap. 8.25 *(978-1-4777-2049-3(9)*, 1359255) Rosen Publishing Group, Inc., The. (Rosen Classroom).
Kalman, Bobbie. ¿Es Grande O Pequeño? 2008. (SPA.). 24p. (J). pap. *(978-0-7787-8733-4(8))* Crabtree Publishing Co.
—How Does It Look? 2007. (Looking at Nature Ser.). (ENG., Illus.). 24p. (J). (gr. -1-2). pap. *(978-0-7787-3335-5(1))*; lib. bdg. *(978-0-7787-3315-7(7))* Crabtree Publishing Co.
—Is It Big or Small? 2007. (Looking at Nature Ser.). (ENG., Illus.). 24p. (J). (gr. -1-2). pap. *(978-0-7787-3336-2(X))* Crabtree Publishing Co.
—My Big & Small Pets. 2010. (My World Ser.). (ENG., Illus.). 16p. (J). (gr. k-2). *(978-0-7787-9426-4(1))*; pap. *(978-0-7787-9470-7(9))* Crabtree Publishing Co.
—My Toys Have Shapes. 2010. (ENG., Illus.). 16p. (J). (gr. k-2). *(978-0-7787-9413-4(X))*; pap. *(978-0-7787-9457-8(1))* Crabtree Publishing Co.
—¿Qué Aspecto Tiene? 2008. (SPA.). 24p. (J). pap. *(978-0-7787-8732-7(X))* Crabtree Publishing Co.
—¿Qué forma Tiene? 2008. (SPA & ENG., Illus.). 24p. (J). lib. bdg. *(978-0-7787-8728-0(1))* Crabtree Publishing Co.
—¿Qué Forma Tiene? 2008. (SPA & ENG., Illus.). 24p. (J). pap. *(978-0-7787-8737-2(0))* Crabtree Publishing Co.
—¿Qué Sigue? 2008. (SPA.). 24p. (J). pap. *(978-0-7787-8736-5(2))* Crabtree Publishing Co.
—What Shape Is It? 2007. (Looking at Nature Ser.). (ENG., Illus.). 24p. (J). (gr. -1-2). pap. *(978-0-7787-3340-9(8))* Crabtree Publishing Co.
Katirgis, Jane. Big & Little. 2011. (All about Opposites Ser.). (Illus.). 24p. (J). (gr. -1-18). pap. 7.95 *(978-1-59845-263-1(0)*, Enslow Elementary); (gr. k-3). lib. bdg. 22.60 *(978-0-7660-3911-7(0))* Enslow Pubs., Inc.
—Tall & Short. 2011. (All about Opposites Ser.). (Illus.). 24p. (J). (gr. -1-18). pap. 7.95 *(978-1-59845-261-7(4)*, Enslow Elementary) Enslow Pubs., Inc.
Katz, David. DC Super Heroes Colors, Shapes & More! 2012. (DC Super Heroes Ser.). (ENG.). 20p. (J). (gr. -1 — 1). bds. 9.99 *(978-1-935703-73-0(0))* Downtown Bookworks.
Katz, Karen. Baby's Shapes. Katz, Karen, illus. 2010. (ENG., Illus.). 14p. (J). (gr. -1 — 1). bds. 7.99 *(978-1-4169-9824-2(1)*, Little Simon) Little Simon.
Kenah, Katharine. Big Beasts. 2006. (Extreme Readers: Level 1 Ser.). (Illus.). 32p. (gr. -1-3). 13.95 *(978-0-7569-6839-7(9))* Perfection Learning Corp.
Kenison, Misti, illus. Egypt - The Tiny Traveler: A Book of Shapes. 2015. (ENG.). 24p. (J). (— 1). bds. 5.95 *(978-1-62914-607-2(2)*, Sky Pony Pr.) Skyhorse Publishing Co., Inc.
King, Zelda. Try it with Triangles: Learning to Put Triangles Together to Form Other Shapes. 2004. (Math Big Bookstm Ser.). (ENG.). 16p. (gr. 2-3). 37.95 *(978-0-8239-7641-6(6))* Rosen Publishing Group, Inc., The.
Kompelein, Tracy. Lets Compare, If You Dare!, 1 vol. 2007. (Math Made Fun Ser.). (ENG., Illus.). 24p. (J). (gr. k-3). lib. bdg. 24.21 *(978-1-59928-537-5(1)*, SandCastle) ABDO Publishing Co.
Kompelien, Tracy. I See a Pattern, What Can I Learn?, 1 vol. 2007. (Math Made Fun Ser.). (ENG., Illus.). 24p. (J). (gr. k-3). lib. bdg. 24.21 *(978-1-59928-533-7(9)*, SandCastle) ABDO Publishing Co.
—2-D Shapes Are Behind the Drapes!, 1 vol. 2007. (Math Made Fun Ser.). (ENG., Illus.). 24p. (J). (gr. k-3). lib. bdg. 24.21 *(978-1-59928-507-8(X)*, SandCastle) ABDO Publishing Co.
—3-D Shapes Are Like Green Grapes!, 1 vol. 2007. (Math Made Fun Ser.). (ENG., Illus.). 24p. (J). (gr. k-3). lib. bdg. 24.21 *(978-1-59928-509-2(6)*, SandCastle) ABDO Publishing Co.
Kumon Staff. Let's Cut Paper!, 4 vols. 2005. (Kumon First Steps Workbooks Ser.). (Illus.). 40p. (J). (gr. -1). pap. 5.95 *(978-1-933241-14-2(4))* Kumon Publishing North America, Inc.
Lady Bird Johnson Wildflower Center Staff, Lady Bird Johnson, compiled by. Exploring the Native Plant World Pre-K-K: Patterns & Shapes. 2004. 44p. (J). pap. 14.95 *(978-1-57168-680-0(0)*, Eakin Pr.) Eakin Pr.
Lafette, Jordan. Kites: Shapes in the Air: Reason with Shapes & Their Attributes, 1 vol. 2015. (InfoMax Common Core Math Readers Ser.). (ENG.). 24p. (J). pap. 8.25 *(978-1-4777-4582-3(3)*, Rosen Classroom) Rosen Publishing Group, Inc., The.
Lamb, Stacey. Shapes Sticker Book. Lamb, Stacey, illus. 2009. (Sticker Bks). (Illus.). 16p. (J). pap. 6.99 *(978-0-7945-2501-9(6)*, Usborne) EDC Publishing.
Lawrence, Elizabeth. I See Circles. 2015. (Shapes! Ser.). (ENG.). 24p. (J). (gr. 1-1). pap. 8.22 *(978-1-5026-0263-3(6))* Cavendish Square Publishing.
—I See Ovals. 2015. (Shapes! Ser.). (ENG.). 24p. (J). (gr. 1-1). 24.21 *(978-1-5026-0264-0(4))* Cavendish Square Publishing.
—I See Rectangles. 2015. (Shapes! Ser.). (ENG.). 24p. (J). (gr. 1-1). pap. 8.22 *(978-1-5026-0259-6(8))* Cavendish Square Publishing.
Learning Company Books Staff, ed. Reader Rabbit Fun with Paint: Shapes. 2004. (Illus.). 32p. (J). pap. *(978-0-7630-7739-6(9))* Magma.
Leech, Bonnie Coulter. Circles & Spheres. 2006. (Exploring Shapes Ser.). (Illus.). 24p. (J). (gr. 3-7). lib. bdg. 22.60 *(978-1-4042-3494-9(2)*, PowerKids Pr.) Rosen Publishing Group, Inc., The.
—Triangles. (Exploring Shapes Ser.). 24p. 2009. (gr. 2-3). 42.50 *(978-1-61512-376-6(8))* 2006. (Illus.). (J). (gr. 3-7). lib. bdg. 22.60 *(978-1-4042-3495-6(0))* Rosen Publishing Group, Inc., The. (PowerKids Pr.).
Leigh, Autumn. Signs on the Road: Learning to Identify the Four Basic Geometric Shapes. 2009. (Math for the Real World: Early Emergent Ser.). (ENG., Illus.). 8p. (gr. k-1). pap. 5.15 *(978-0-8239-8857-0(0))* Rosen Publishing Group, Inc., The.
Leonard, Barry, ed. Squishy Shapes: Dinosaurs. 2005. (Illus.). 10p. (J). (gr. -1-2). reprint ed. 13.00 *(978-0-7567-8529-1(4))* DIANE Publishing Co.
LernerClassroom Editors. First Step Nonfiction-Shapes Set Ii Teaching Guide. 2009. pap. 7.95 *(978-0-8225-6885-8(3))* Lerner Publishing Group.
Let's Draw with Shapes: Set 2.Tr. of Vamos a dibujar con figuras Set 2. (Illus.). (J). (ENG & SPA.). (gr. -1-1). 103.50 *(978-1-4042-7560-7(6)*, Editorial Buenas Letras); (gr. k-1). 103.50 *(978-1-4042-2947-1(7)*, Powerstart Pr.) Rosen Publishing Group, Inc., The.

Lewis, J. Patrick. Big Is Big & Little, Little: A Book of Contrasts. Barner, Bob, illus. 2007. (ENG.). 32p. (J). (gr. -1-3). 16.95 (978-0-8234-1909-8(6)) Holiday Hse., Inc.

El Libro de Contar de los Chocolates M & M's Brand. 2004. 32p. (J). pap. 6.95 (978-1-57091-370-9(6)) Charlesbridge Publishing, Inc.

Linda, Winder. Glitter: My First Book of Shapes Numbers Colors & the Alphabet Gods Way. 2003. (978-1-892354-85-3(3)) Educational Publishing Concepts, Inc.

Line & Circle. 2004. (Illus.). 24p. (J). (CHI & ENG.). (978-1-84444-004-7(4)); (ENG & POR., (978-1-84444-014-6(1)) Mantra Lingua.

Lionni, Leo. Pezzettino. Lionni, Leo, illus. 2006. (Illus.). 40p. (J). (gr. -1-3). lib. bdg. 17.99 (978-0-394-93156-2(4), Pantheon) Knopf Doubleday Publishing Group.

little bee books, little bee & Blake, Carly. Baby's First Shapes. Max and Sid Staff, illus. 2015. (Baby's First Ser.). (ENG.). 12p. (J). (gr. -1 — 1). bds. 4.99 (978-1-4998-0053-1(3)) Little Bee Books Inc.

Llewellyn, Claire. It's Fun to Learn about Sizes: A Busy Picture Book Full of Fabulous Facts & Things to Do! 2016. (ENG., Illus.). 32p. (J). (gr. -1-12). 9.99 (978-1-86147-761-3(9), Armadillo) Anness Publishing GBR. Dist: National Bk. Network.

Long, Dorian. What Are Polygons? Reason with Shapes & Their Attributes. 2014. (Math Masters: Geometry Ser.). 24p. (J). (gr. 2-3). 23.60 (978-1-4777-6409-1(7), Rosen Classroom) Rosen Publishing Group, Inc., The.

Lorbiecki, Marybeth. Triangles, 1 vol. Holm, Sharon, illus. 2007. (Shapes Ser.). (ENG.). 24p. (gr. -1-2). 27.07 (978-1-60270-048-2(6), Looking Glass Library- Nonfiction) Magic Wagon.

Lorenz Books Staff, creator. Patterns, 12 vols. 2006. (Learn-A-Word Picture Bks.). (ENG., Illus.). 12p. (J). (gr. -1-k). bds. 6.99 (978-0-7548-1460-3(2)) Anness Publishing GBR. Dist: National Bk. Network.

Loughrey, Anita. Cirles. 2011. (ENG., Illus.). 24p. (J). pap. 8.95 (978-1-77092-003-3(X)) Saunders Bk. Co. CAN. Dist: RiverStream Publishing.

—Rectangles. 2011. (ENG., Illus.). 24p. (J). pap. 8.95 (978-1-77092-004-0(8)) Saunders Bk. Co. CAN. Dist: RiverStream Publishing.

—Squares. 2011. (ENG., Illus.). 24p. (J). 8.95 (978-1-77092-005-7(6)) Saunders Bk. Co. CAN. Dist: RiverStream Publishing.

—Triangles. 2011. (ENG., Illus.). 24p. (J). pap. 8.95 (978-1-77092-006-4(4)) Saunders Bk. Co. CAN. Dist: RiverStream Publishing.

Lowery, Lawrence F. Look & See. 2nd ed. 2004. (J). per. (978-0-9762724-9-6(0)) Educational Research & Applications, LLC.

Lucarelli, Marco. Finding Shapes at the Fair: Identify & Describe Shapes. 2013. (InfoMax Math Readers Ser.). (ENG.). 16p. (J). (gr. k-1). pap. 42.00 (978-1-4777-1956-5(3)); (Illus.). pap. 7.00 (978-1-4777-1955-8(5)) Rosen Publishing Group, Inc., The. (Rosen Classroom).

Lucas, Bruce. Drawing Shapes: Shapes & Their Attributes. 2013. (InfoMax Math Readers Ser.). (ENG.). 24p. (J). (gr. 1-2). pap. 49.50 (978-1-4777-2149-0(5)); pap. 8.25 (978-1-4777-2148-3(7)) Rosen Publishing Group, Inc., The. (Rosen Classroom).

Lunis, Natalie. Pet-Sized Dinos. 2008. (Dino Times Trivia Ser.). (Illus.). 24p. (J). (gr. k-3). lib. bdg. 21.28 (978-1-59716-710-9(X)) Bearport Publishing Co., Inc.

MacDonald, Suse. Dino Shapes. MacDonald, Suse, illus. 2014. (ENG., Illus.). 20p. (J). (gr. -1-2). bds. 7.99 (978-1-4814-0093-0(2), Little Simon) Little Simon.

Mack, Steve. Mazes. Flash Kids Editors, ed. 2012. (Flash Kids Preschool Activity Bks.). (ENG., Illus.). 80p. (J). pap. 5.95 (978-1-4114-5809-3(5), Spark Publishing Group) Sterling Publishing Co., Inc.

Maderna, Victoria. Look & Find Shapes to Color. 2011. (Dover Children's Activity Bks.). (ENG.). 48p. (J). (gr. -1-2). pap. 4.99 (978-0-486-47991-0(9)) Dover Pubns., Inc.

Maile, Ruby. Shapes. 2008. (Discovering & Exploring Science Ser.). (Illus.). 16p. (J). (gr. -1-3). lib. bdg. 12.95 (978-0-7569-8255-3(3)) Perfection Learning Corp.

Maisano, Lucy. Who Thought Learning Could be Fun: The Fun Book. 2011. 84p. pap. 13.99 (978-1-4567-3678-1(7)) AuthorHouse.

Make Believe Ideas, creator. Busy Baby Shapes: First Concepts. 2007. (Busy Baby Ser.). (Illus.). 12p. (gr. -1-k). per., bds. (978-1-84610-470-1(X)) Make Believe Ideas.

Mamada, Mineko. Which Is Round? Which Is Bigger? Mamada, Mineko, illus. 2013. (ENG., Illus.). 24p. (J). (gr. -1-1). 16.95 (978-1-55453-973-4(0)) Kids Can Pr., Ltd. CAN. Dist: Hachette Bk. Group.

Markovics, Joyce. Play with Shapes! 2012. (ENG.). 24p. (gr. -1-1). pap. 8.95 (978-1-61810-211-9(7)) Rourke Educational Media.

Markovics, Joyce L. Patterns in the Desert. 2014. (Math Blast!: Seeing Patterns All Around Ser.). (ENG.). 32p. (J). (gr. -1-3). lib. bdg. 26.60 (978-1-62724-337-7(2)) Bearport Publishing Co., Inc.

—Patterns in the Jungle. 2014. (Math Blast!: Seeing Patterns All Around Ser.). (ENG.). 32p. (J). (gr. -1-3). lib. bdg. 26.60 (978-1-62724-338-4(0)) Bearport Publishing Co., Inc.

Marks, Jennifer L. Clasificar por Tamaño. 2012. (Vamos a Ordenar / Sorting Ser.). (MUL & SPA., Illus.). 32p. (gr. 1-2). lib. bdg. 27.32 (978-1-4296-8253-4(1), A+ Bilingue/Bilingual) Capstone Press of Coughlan Cos.

Marqina, Mignon. Shapes & Me: A Flip & Learn Book. l.t. ed. 2006. (Illus.). 32p. (J). lib. bdg. (978-1-934190-05-0(5)) Ocean Front Bk. Publishing, Inc.

Maruda, Trotsky. Line & Circle. 2004. (J). (ENG & RUS.). (978-1-84444-015-3(X)); (FRE & ENG., Illus.). 24p. (978-1-84444-007-8(9)); (ENG & POL., Illus.). 24p. (978-1-84444-013-9(3)); (ENG & GER., Illus.). 24p. (978-1-84444-008-5(7)); (Illus.). 24p. (978-1-84444-010-8(9)); (ENG & KUR., Illus.). 24p. (978-1-84444-011-5(7)) Mantra Lingua.

—Line & Circle. Maruda, Trotsky, illus. 2004. (Illus.). 32p. (J). (URD & ENG.). pap. (978-1-84444-020-7(6)); (ENG & TUR., pap. (978-1-84444-019-1(2)); (SOM & ENG., pap. (978-1-84444-017-7(6)); (SER & ENG., pap. (978-1-84444-016-0(8)); (PAN & ENG., pap. (978-1-84444-012-2(5)); (ARA & ENG., pap. (978-1-84444-002-3(8)); (ENG & PER., pap. (978-1-84444-006-1(0)); (CZE & ENG., pap. (978-1-84444-005-4(2)); (BEN & ENG., pap. (978-1-84444-003-0(6)); (ALB & ENG., pap. (978-1-84444-000-9(1)); (VIE & ENG., pap. (978-1-84444-021-4(4)) Mantra Lingua.

Marudu, Trotsky. Line & Circle. 2004. (GUJ & ENG., Illus.). 32p. (J). pap. (978-1-84444-009-2(5)) Mantra Lingua.

McAneney, Caitlin. Quadrilaterals in Art: Reason with Shapes & Their Attributes. 2014. (Rosen Common Core Math Readers Ser.). (ENG.). 24p. (J). (gr. 3-4). pap. 8.25 (978-1-4777-4878-7(4), PowerKids Pr.) Rosen Publishing Group, Inc., The.

McCallister, Wendy. Shapes: 4 Friends Lost. 2004. (Illus.). 32p. (J). (gr. -1-18). 14.99 (978-1-59094-004-4(0), Top Shelf) Jawbone Publishing Corp.

McMahon, Brett & Mcmahon, Brett. Baby Read Patterns: For Fun & Play. 2009. (ENG., Illus.). 1p. (J). bds. 4.95 (978-1-921073-57-1(8)) New Holland Pubs. Pty, Ltd. AUS. Dist: Tuttle Publishing.

Meachen Rau, Dana. Bookworms: The Shape of the World, 6 bks., Set. Incl. Circles. lib. bdg. 15.95 (978-0-7614-2280-8(3)); Many-Sided Shapes. lib. bdg. 15.95 (978-0-7614-2279-2(X)); Ovals. lib. bdg. 15.95 (978-0-7614-2281-5(1)); Rectangles: The Shape of the World. lib. bdg. 15.95 (978-0-7614-2282-2(X)); Squares. lib. bdg. 15.95 (978-0-7614-2284-6(6)); Triangles. lib. bdg. 15.95 (978-0-7614-2286-0(2)); (Illus.). 24p. (gr. k-1). (Bookworms: the Shape of the World Ser.). 2006. Set lib. bdg. 95.70 (978-0-7614-2278-5(1), Benchmark Bks.) Marshall Cavendish Corp.

—Many-Sided Shapes. 2006. (Bookworms Ser.). (Illus.). 24p. (gr. k-1). lib. bdg. 15.95 (978-0-7614-2279-2(X), Benchmark Bks.) Marshall Cavendish Corp.

Meet the Shapes. 2005. (J). 7.99 (978-0-9770215-1-2(3)) Preschool Prep Co.

Meet the Shapes Lift the Flap Book. 2005. (J). bds. 9.99 (978-0-9770215-0-5(5)) Preschool Prep Co.

Menon, Radhika. Line & Circle. Marudu, Trotsky, illus. 2004. (ENG & SPA.). 24p. (J). (978-1-84444-018-4(4)) Mantra Lingua.

Meyers, Nancy. Doodles Shapes. Meyers, Nancy, illus. 2012. (Doodles Ser.). (ENG., Illus.). 64p. (J). (gr. k-5). pap. 7.95 (978-1-61608-668-8(8), 608668, Sky Pony Pr.) Skyhorse Publishing Co., Inc.

Micklethwait, Lucy. I Spy Shapes in Art. 2004. (ENG., Illus.). 40p. (J). (gr. -1-3). 19.99 (978-0-06-073193-9(1), Greenwillow Bks.) HarperCollins Pubs.

Miesen, Christina & Novick, Mary. Colours & Shapes: With Flip the Flap Pages. 2013. (Mini Marvels Ser.). (ENG., Illus.). 10p. (J). (gr. -1-k). 9.99 (978-1-921049-62-0(6)) Little Hare Bks. AUS. Dist: Independent Pubs. Group.

Miles Kelly Staff. Sizes: Let's Learn. Nilsen, Anna, ed. 2003. (Let's Learn Ser.). (Illus.). 20p. (J). 7.95 (978-1-84236-140-5(6)) Miles Kelly Publishing, Ltd. GBR. Dist: Independent Pubs. Group.

Miles Kelly Staff & Nilsen, Anna. Shapes: Let's Learn. 2003. (Let's Learn Ser.). (Illus.). 20p. (J). 7.95 (978-1-84236-016-3(7)) Miles Kelly Publishing, Ltd. GBR. Dist: Independent Pubs. Group.

Mills, Nathan & Flynn, Wesley. Big or Small? 2012. (Rosen Readers Ser.). (ENG., Illus.). 16p. (J). (gr. k-1). pap. 7.00 (978-1-4488-8640-1(6), Rosen Classroom) Rosen Publishing Group, Inc., The.

Mills, Nathan & Star, Pat. Describe It: Size, Shape, & Color. 2012. (Rosen Readers Ser.). (ENG., Illus.). 16p. (J). (gr. k-1). pap. 7.00 (978-1-4488-8755-2(0), Rosen Classroom) Rosen Publishing Group, Inc., The.

Mills, Nathan & Worthy, Shanya. Shapes. 2012. (Rosen Readers Ser.). (ENG., Illus.). 16p. (J). (gr. k-1). pap. 7.00 (978-1-4488-8634-0(1), Rosen Classroom) Rosen Publishing Group, Inc., The.

Minden, Cecilia. Shapes Everywhere. 2010. (21st Century Basic Skills Library: Measurements Ser.). (ENG.). 24p. (gr. k-3). lib. bdg. 22.79 (978-1-60279-850-2(8), 200566) Cherry Lake Publishing.

Mitchell, Susan K. Biggest vs. Smallest Amazing Mammals. 2010. (Biggest vs. Smallest Animals Ser.). (Illus.). 24p. (J). 22.60 (978-0-7660-3582-9(4), Enslow Elementary) Enslow Pubs., Inc.

—Biggest vs. Smallest Creepy, Crawly Creatures. 2010. (Biggest vs. Smallest Animals Ser.). (Illus.). 24p. (J). 22.60 (978-0-7660-3581-2(6), Enslow Elementary) Enslow Pubs., Inc.

—Biggest vs. Smallest Incredible Insects. 2010. (Biggest vs. Smallest Animals Ser.). (Illus.). 24p. (J). 22.60 (978-0-7660-3583-6(2), Enslow Elementary) Enslow Pubs., Inc.

—Biggest vs. Smallest Sea Creatures. 2010. (Biggest vs. Smallest Animals Ser.). (Illus.). 24p. (J). 22.60 (978-0-7660-3580-5(8), Enslow Elementary) Enslow Pubs., Inc.

—Biggest vs. Smallest Slimy, Scaly Creatures. 2010. (Biggest vs. Smallest Animals Ser.). (Illus.). 24p. (J). 22.60 (978-0-7660-3579-9(4), Enslow Elementary) Enslow Pubs., Inc.

—Biggest vs. Smallest Things with Wings. 2010. (Biggest vs. Smallest Animals Ser.). (Illus.). 24p. (J). 22.60 (978-0-7660-3578-2(6), Enslow Elementary) Enslow Pubs., Inc.

Mitten, Luana K. Three Dimensional Shapes: Cones. 2008. (Concepts Ser.). (Illus.). 24p. (J). (gr. -1-k). lib. bdg. 22.79 (978-1-60472-415-8(3)) Rourke Educational Media.

Montague-Smith, Ann. Sizes & Shapes. 2004. (QEB Start Math Ser.). (Illus.). 24p. (J). Vol. 1. lib. bdg. 15.95 (978-1-59566-026-8(7)) Vol. 2. lib. bdg. 15.95 (978-1-59566-030-5(5)) QEB Publishing Inc.

Moore, Cassandra. Shape/Color Master. 2007. (Illus.). 75p. (J). spiral bd. 12.95 (978-1-886297-30-2(4)) Omega Publishing Hse.

Moore, Gareth. Think Outside the Box. 2015. (Brain Benders Ser.). (ENG., Illus.). 32p. (J). (gr. 3-6). pap. 7.99 (978-1-4677-7205-1(4), Lerner Pubns.) Lerner Publishing Group.

Murphy, Stuart J. A House for Birdie. Miller, Edward, illus. 2004. (MathStart 1 Ser.). (ENG.). 40p. (J). (gr. -1). pap. 5.99 (978-0-06-052353-4(0)) HarperCollins Pubs.

Murray, Julie. Biggest Animals, 1 vol. 2010. (That's Wild!: A Look at Animals Ser.). (ENG.). 32p. (J). (gr. 2-5). 28.50 (978-1-60453-976-9(3)) ABDO Publishing Co.

—Smallest Animals, 1 vol. 2010. (That's Wild!: A Look at Animals Ser.). (ENG.). 32p. (J). (gr. 2-5). 28.50 (978-1-60453-980-6(1)) ABDO Publishing Co.

My Big Box of Colors, Shapes, & Numbers: Contains Twenty Beautifully Illustrated Board Books. (Illus.). (J). bds. (978-1-904613-80-0(2)) O'Mara, Michael Bks., Ltd.

My First Book of Shapes. 2003. (J). 41.70 (978-0-590-66408-0(5)) Scholastic, Inc.

Nancy Giorgio-Kupiec. Nanje's Imagination or Is It ? 2009. 20p. pap. 10.49 (978-1-4389-7068-4(4)) AuthorHouse.

Napier, Angi. Bible Baby: Shapes. 2012. 28p. 24.95 (978-1-4626-5633-2(1)) America Star Bks.

National Geographic Kids Staff. Shapes! 2012. (Look & Learn Ser.). (ENG., Illus.). 24p. (J). (gr. k-k). bds. 6.99 (978-1-4263-1042-3(0), National Geographic Children's Bks.) National Geographic Society.

National Geographic Society (U.S.) Staff, contrib. by. Shapes! 2013. (Illus.). (J). (978-0-545-62212-7(3)) Scholastic, Inc.

Nations, Susan. I Know Big & Small. 2006. (I'm Ready for Math Ser.). (Illus.). 16p. (gr. -1-2). lib. bdg. 19.00 (978-0-8368-6474-8(3), Weekly Reader Leveled Readers) Stevens, Gareth Publishing LLLP.

Nations, Susan & Weekly Reader Editorial Staff. I Know Big & Small/Grande y Pequeño. 2006. (I'm Ready for Math/YA Puedo Aprender Matematicas Ser.). (ENG & SPA., Illus.). 16p. (gr. -1-2). lib. bdg. 19.00 (978-0-8368-6484-7(0), Weekly Reader Leveled Readers) Stevens, Gareth Publishing LLLP.

Norma Staff, ed. Formas. 2005. 14p. (978-958-04-8070-9(2)) Norma S.A.

Nunn, Daniel. Animals Big & Small, 1 vol. 2012. (Math Every Day Ser.). (ENG., Illus.). 24p. (gr. -1-k). pap. 9.95 (978-1-4329-5738-4(4)); lib. bdg. 25.99 (978-1-4329-5733-9(3)) Heinemann-Raintree.

—Patterns Outside, 1 vol. 2012. (Math Every Day Ser.). (ENG.). 24p. (gr. -1-k). pap. 9.95 (978-1-4329-5736-0(8)); lib. bdg. 25.99 (978-1-4329-5731-5(7)) Heinemann-Raintree.

—Shapes Around Us, 1 vol. 2012. (Math Every Day Ser.). (ENG.). 24p. (gr. -1-k). pap. 9.95 (978-1-4329-5737-7(6)); lib. bdg. 25.99 (978-1-4329-5732-2(5)) Heinemann-Raintree.

Nussbaum, Ben. Tracing Shapes. rev. ed. 2005. (Trace & Learn Ser.). (ENG., Illus.). 28p. (J). (gr. -1-3). 16.49 (978-1-59069-445-9(7), 1A600) Studio Mouse LLC.

O'Brien, Jeanne. Finding Shapes in Nature: Parks, Forests & Backyards. 2010. 28p. pap. 15.99 (978-1-4500-5772-1(1)) Xlibris Corp.

Omary, Rachel, illus. Shapes & Colors in Dari. 2004. 5p. (J). spiral bd. 14.95 (978-0-9740535-7-8(0)) Knight Publishing.

—Shapes & Colors in Farsi. l.t. ed. 2004. 5p. (J). spiral bd. 14.95 (978-0-9740535-6-1(2)) Knight Publishing.

—Shapes & Colors in Pashto. l.t. ed. 2004. 5p. (J). spiral bd. 14.95 (978-0-9740535-8-5(9)) Knight Publishing.

Owen, Ruth. Top 10 Tallest. 2010. (Crabtree Contact Ser.). (ENG., Illus.). 32p. (J). (gr. 3-6). pap. (978-0-7787-7513-3(5)); lib. bdg. (978-0-7787-7492-1(9)) Crabtree Publishing Co.

Pagni, Gianpaolo. Gianpaolo Pagni: Double Face. 2010. (ENG., Illus.). 40p. pap. 27.00 (978-88-7570-218-2(7)) Corraini ITA. Dist: D.A.P./Distributed Art Pubs.

Penn, M. W. It's a Shape!, 1 vol. 2011. (Pebble Math Ser.). (ENG.). 24p. (gr. k-1). pap. 6.29 (978-1-4296-7068-5(1)); pap. 35.70 (978-1-4296-7073-9(8)); lib. bdg. 21.99 (978-1-4296-6040-2(6)) Capstone Press of Coughlan Cos. (Pebble Bks.).

—2 Lines. Firos, Daphne, illus. 2011. (ENG.). 32p. (J). pap. 11.95 (978-0-9840425-0-0(4)) MathWord Pr., LLC.

Penton Overseas, Inc. Staff. Colors, Shapes & Sizes. abr. ed. 2003. (J). (gr. -1-3). 12.99 incl. audio, cd-rom (978-1-894677-24-0(2)) Kidzup Productions.

Perez, Nomar. It's Circle Time! Shapes. 2009. (Rookie Preschool Ser.). (ENG.). 24p. (J). (gr. -1). 23.00 (978-0-531-24401-2(6)) Scholastic Library Publishing.

Perritano, John. Start the Game: Geometry in Sports. 2013. (IMath Ser.). (Illus.). 32p. (J). (gr. 3-4). lib. bdg. 22.60 (978-1-59953-563-0(7)) Norwood Hse. Pr.

Peterson, Ingela, illus. Ellie & Pinky's Pop-Up Shapes. 2003. (First Concepts Ser.). 10p. (J). 7.95 (978-1-58117-184-6(6), Intervisual/Piggy Toes) Bendon, Inc.

Phidal Publishing Staff, ed. Shapes. (Turn & Learn Ser.). 12p. (J). (978-2-7643-0078-7(6)) Phidal Publishing, Inc./Editions Phidal, Inc.

Phillips, Dee. Big Zoo. 2009. (Flip Flap Fun Bks.). (ENG.). 5p. (J). (gr. -1-k). bds. 5.95 (978-1-84696-086-4(X), TickTock Books) Octopus Publishing Group GBR. Dist: Independent Pubs. Group.

Phillips, Sarah & Tattam, Mark. Shapes. 2005. (Baby See a Shape Ser.). (Illus.). 12p. (gr. -1-k). bds. (978-1-905051-90-8(5)) Make Believe Ideas.

Picthall, Chez, creator. Flip Flaps Shapes. 2014. (ENG., Illus.). 32p. bds. 10.00 (978-1-906572-80-8(1)) Award Pubns. Ltd. GBR. Dist: Parkwest Pubns., Inc.

Picthall, Chez, des. Hearts & Stars. 2015. (ENG., Illus.). 10p. (J). 9.99 (978-1-909763-05-0(5)) Award Pubns. Ltd. GBR. Dist: Parkwest Pubns., Inc.

Piddock, Claire. Slides, Flips, & Turns. 2010. (ENG., Illus.). 24p. (J). (978-0-7787-5251-6(8)); pap. (978-0-7787-5298-1(4)) Crabtree Publishing Co.

Pistoia, Sara. Shapes. 2013. (Simply Math Ser.). (ENG.). 24p. (J). (gr. -1-2). 27.07 (978-1-62323-534-5(0), 206340) Child's World, Inc., The.

Pluckrose, Henry. What Shape Is It? 2006. (Let's Explore, Maths Set Ser.). (Illus.). 32p. (J). (gr. -1-3). lib. bdg. 27.10 (978-1-59771-039-8(3)) Sea-To-Sea Pubns.

—What Size Is It? 2006. (Let's Explore, Maths Set Ser.). (Illus.). 32p. (J). (gr. -1-3). lib. bdg. 27.10 (978-1-59771-040-4(7)) Sea-To-Sea Pubns.

Poitier, Anton, illus. Shapes. 2015. (Twisters Ser.). (ENG.). 10p. (J). (gr. -1 — 1). bds. 7.99 (978-0-7641-6810-9(X)) Barron's Educational Series, Inc.

Price, Justine. The Class Mural: Reason with Shapes & Their Attributes. 2014. (Math Masters: Geometry Ser.). 24p. (J). (gr. 2-3). 23.60 (978-1-4777-6443-5(7)); (ENG.). pap. 8.25 (978-1-4777-4903-6(9)) Rosen Publishing Group, Inc., The. (Rosen Classroom).

Priddy, Roger. Alphaprints: Dinoshapes. 2016. (Alphaprints Ser.). (ENG.). 14p. (J). bds. 9.99 (978-0-312-52056-4(5), 9780312520564, Priddy Bks.) St. Martin's Pr.

—Big & Small. 2015. (Little Friends Ser.). (ENG., Illus.). 12p. (J). (gr. -1 — 1). bds. 8.99 (978-0-312-51778-6(5), 9780312517786, Priddy Bks.) St. Martin's Pr.

—Big Board Books Colors, ABC, Numbers. 2008. (First 100 Ser.). (ENG.). 14p. (J). (gr. -1 — 1). bds. 8.95 (978-0-312-50219-5(2), 9780312502195, Priddy Bks.) St. Martin's Pr.

—Hello Baby, Set. 2013. (Hello Baby Ser.). (ENG.). (J). (gr. -1 — 1). 19.99 (978-0-312-51641-3(X), 9780312516413, Priddy Bks.) St. Martin's Pr.

—Numbers Colors Shapes. 2011. (First 100 Ser.). (ENG., Illus.). 26p. (J). (gr. -1 — 1). bds. 5.99 (978-0-312-51081-7(0), 9780312510817, Priddy Bks.) St. Martin's Pr.

—Sticker Early Learning: Shapes. 2016. (ENG., Illus.). 24p. (J). pap. 4.99 (978-0-312-52015-1(8), 9780312520151, Priddy Bks.) St. Martin's Pr.

—Words: A High Contrast Board Book. 2013. (Hello Baby Ser.). (ENG., Illus.). 16p. (J). (gr. -1 — 1). bds. 4.99 (978-0-312-51598-0(7), 9780312515980, Priddy Bks.) St. Martin's Pr.

Princess Adjepong. My First Shapes & Numbers Colouring Book. 2013. 52p. pap. 27.45 (978-1-4817-9519-7(8)) AuthorHouse.

Professor Q's Chinese-English Language Books: Xíng Zhuàng - Shapes. 2006. (J). (978-0-9743359-4-0(0)) Murdock Publishing Co.

Publications International Ltd. Staff, ed. Baby's Shapes. 2010. 18p. (J). bds. 7.98 (978-1-60553-963-8(5)); (Illus.). bds. 7.98 (978-1-60553-965-2(1)) Phoenix International Publications, Inc.

—My Shapes Book. 2011. 32p. (J). bds. (978-1-4508-1023-4(3)) Publications International, Ltd.

Pugliano-Martin, Carol. Building with Shapes. 2004. (Shared Connections Ser.). (J). pap., instr.'s gde. ed. 27.00 (978-1-4108-1613-9(3)) Benchmark Education Co.

—Building with Shapes: Small Book. 2004. (Shared Connections Ser.). (J). pap. (978-1-4108-1637-5(0)) Benchmark Education Co.

QEB Start Math Book Stores Edition: Sizes & Shapes - Book 1. 2006. (J). per. (978-1-59566-273-6(1)) QEB Publishing Inc.

QEB Start Math Book Stores Edition: Sizes & Shapes Book 2. 2006. (J). per. (978-1-59566-277-4(4)) QEB Publishing Inc.

Ranchetti, Sebastiano. Shapes in Animals. 2008. (Learn with Animals;Aprende con los animales Ser.). 24p. (gr. -1-2). (SPA & ENG.). pap. 8.15 (978-0-8368-9045-7(0)); (Illus.). pap. 8.15 (978-0-8368-8829-4(4)); (Illus.). lib. bdg. 22.00 (978-0-8368-8824-9(3)) Stevens, Gareth Publishing LLLP. (Weekly Reader Leveled Readers).

—Shapes in Animals/Figuras en los Animales. 2008. (Learn with Animals/Aprende con los Animales Ser.). (SPA & ENG., Illus.). 24p. (gr. -1-2). lib. bdg. 22.00 (978-0-8368-9040-2(X), Weekly Reader Leveled Readers) Stevens, Gareth Publishing LLLP.

Randolph, Joanne. Let's Draw a Bird with Shapes. 2009. (Let's Draw with Shapes Ser.). 24p. (gr. k-k). 42.50 (978-1-61514-203-3(7), PowerKids Pr.) Rosen Publishing Group, Inc., The.

—Let's Draw a Bird with Shapes. Muschinske, Emily, illus. 2005. (Let's Draw with Shapes Ser.). 24p. (J). (gr. k-1). lib. bdg. 22.60 (978-1-4042-2792-7(X), PowerKids Pr.) Rosen Publishing Group, Inc., The.

—Let's Draw a Bird with Shapes: Vamos a Dibujar un Ave Usando Figuras. Muschinske, Emily, illus. 2005. (Let's Draw with Shapes / Vamos a Dibujar con Figuras Ser.). (J). 22.60 (978-1-4042-7555-3(X), PowerKids Pr.) Rosen Publishing Group, Inc., The.

—Let's Draw a Bird with Shapes/Vamos a dibujar un ave usando Figuras. 2009. (Let's Draw with Shapes / Vamos a dibujar con figuras Ser.). (ENG & SPA.). 24p. (gr. k-1). 42.50 (978-1-61514-214-9(2), Editorial Buenas Letras) Rosen Publishing Group, Inc., The.

Ranson, Erin. Magnetic Playtime Shapes. Parry, Jo, illus. 2007. (Magnetic Playtime Shapes Ser.). 10p. (J). (gr. -1-3). (978-1-84666-363-5(6), Tide Mill Pr.) Top That! Publishing PLC.

Rau, Dana Meachen & Meachen, Dana. A Star in My Orange: Looking for Nature's Shapes. 2006. (ENG., Illus.). 32p. (J). (gr. k-2). pap. 6.95 (978-0-8225-5992-4(7), First Avenue Editions) Lerner Publishing Group.

Rebman, Nick. What Is Biggest? A Book about Sizes. 2016. (Concept Fun Ser.). (ENG.). 16p. (J). (gr. -1-2). 25.64 (978-1-5038-0766-2(5), 210614) Child's World, Inc., The.

—Which Is the Circle? A Book about Shapes. 2016. (Concept Fun Ser.). (ENG.). 16p. (J). (gr. -1-2). 25.64 (978-1-5038-0765-5(7), 210613) Child's World, Inc., The.

Reisberg, Joanne. Zachary Zormer - Shape Transformer. Hohn, David & Clark, David, illus. 2006. (Math Adventures Ser.). (ENG.). 32p. (J). (gr. 2-5). per. 7.95 (978-1-57091-876-6(7)) Charlesbridge Publishing, Inc.

Rice, Dona. Use Your Math Mind: Describe It. 2015. (TIME for KIDS(r) Nonfiction Readers Ser.). (ENG., Illus.). 12p. (gr. k-k). 4.99 (978-1-4938-2142-6(3)) Teacher Created Materials, Inc.

Rice, Dona Herweck. Big & Little, 1 vol. 2nd rev. ed. 2013. (Nonfiction Readers Ser.). (ENG., Illus.). 12p. (J). (gr. 1-1). pap. 15.96 (978-1-4807-1004-7(0)) Shell Educational Publishing.

—Big & Little, 1 vol. 2nd rev. ed. 2011. (Nonfiction Readers Ser.). (ENG.). 12p. (J). (gr. 1-1). pap. 4.99 (978-1-4333-3565-5(4)) Teacher Created Materials, Inc.

—Figuras, 1 vol. 2nd rev. ed. 2011. (Nonfiction Readers Ser.). (SPA.). 12p. (J). (gr. 1-1). pap. 4.99 (978-1-4333-4406-0(8)) Teacher Created Materials, Inc.

—Grande y Pequeño, 1 vol. 2nd rev. ed. 2011. (Nonfiction Readers Ser.). (SPA.). 12p. (J). (gr. 1-1). pap. 4.99 (978-1-4333-4404-6(1)) Teacher Created Materials, Inc.

—Shapes, 1 vol. 2nd rev. ed. 2014. (TIME for KIDS(r) Nonfiction Readers Ser.). (ENG., Illus.). 12p. (J). (gr. 1-1).

pap. 15.96 (978-1-4807-1006-1(7)) Shell Educational Publishing.

—Shapes, 1 vol. 2nd rev. ed. 2011. (Nonfiction Readers Ser.). (ENG.). 12p. (J). (gr. 1-1). pap. 4.99 (978-1-4333-3567-9(0)) Teacher Created Materials, Inc.

Rigby Education Staff. Discovery World Yel Sizes. (Discovery World Ser.). (Illus.). 12p. (gr. k-1). 23.00 (978-0-7635-2695-5(9)) Rigby Education.

—Little & Big. (Illus.). 8p. (J). bds. 3.95 (978-0-7635-6467-4(2), 764672C99) Rigby Education.

Rigol, Francesc, illus. Dan & Din Learn Shapes. 2009. (Learning with Dan & Din Ser.). 12p. (J). (gr. -1-k). bds. 11.40 (978-1-60754-400-5(8)) Windmill Bks.

Riley, Matt. Making Shapes: Analyze, Compare, Create, & Compose Shapes. 2013. (Rosen Math Readers Ser.). (ENG.). 16p. (J). (gr. k-1). pap. 42.00 (978-1-4777-1657-1(2)); (Illus.). pap. 7.00 (978-1-4777-1656-4(4)) Rosen Publishing Group, Inc., The. (Rosen Classroom).

Ripley's Believe It or Not Editors. Expect the Unexpected: Larger than Life. 2010. (Ripley's Remarkable & Unexpected Ser.). 36p. (J). (gr. 3-18). lib. bdg. 19.95 (978-1-4222-2023-8(0)) Mason Crest.

Rivera, Sheila. Is It Big or Little? 2005. (First Step Nonfiction - Properties of Matter Ser.). (ENG.). 8p. (gr. -1-1). pap. 4.95 (978-0-8225-5406-6(2), Lerner Pubns.) Lerner Publishing Group.

Rosenthal-Gazit, Roni. On Shapes & More. 2007. (J). per. 7.99 (978-0-9792800-0-9(1)) StoryTime World Publishing Hse.

Ross, Catherine Sheldrick. Shapes in Math, Science & Nature: Squares, Triangles & Circles. Slavin, Bill, illus. 2014. (ENG.). 192p. (J). (gr. 4-9). 24.95 (978-1-77138-124-6(8)) Kids Can Pr., Ltd. CAN. Dist: Hachette Bk. Group.

Ross, Tony. Figuras. 2006. (Little Princess Ser.).Tr. of Shapes. (SPA.). (J). (gr. -1-k). bds. 7.95 (978-968-19-1486-8(4), AT33280) Lectorum Pubns., Inc.

Roy, Jennifer Rozines & Roy, Gregory. Shapes in Transportation. (Math All Around Ser.). (Illus.). 31p. (J). 2007. (gr. 4-7). pap. 6.99 (978-0-7614-3387-3(2)) 2006. (gr. 3-7). lib. bdg. 29.93 (978-0-7614-2265-5(X)) Marshall Cavendish Corp. (Benchmark Bks.).

San Antonio Museum of Art Staff & Budnick, Madeleine. Hello, Círculos! Shapes in English y Espanol. 2013. (ArteKids Ser.). (ENG., Illus.). 16p. (J). (gr. k-k). bds. 7.95 (978-1-59534-140-2(4)) Trinity Univ. Pr.

Santillana & Dorling Kindersley Publishing Staff. Figuras. (Ensename Ser.). (SPA., Illus.). 16p. (J). (gr. -1-k). bds. 6.95 (978-1-58986-327-9(5)) Santillana USA Publishing Co., Inc.

—Tamanos. (Ensename Ser.). (SPA., Illus.). 16p. (J). (gr. -1-k). bds. 6.95 (978-1-58986-328-6(3)) Santillana USA Publishing Co., Inc.

Sargent, Brian. Grandfather's Shape Story. 2006. (Rookie Read-About Math Ser.). (ENG., Illus.). 32p. (J). (gr. -1-3). 20.50 (978-0-516-29919-8(0), Children's Pr.) Scholastic Library Publishing.

Savary, Fabien. Caillou: Que Falta? Tipeo, illus. 2004. (Caillou Ser.).Tr. of What's Missing? (SPA & ENG.). 12p. (J). (gr. -1-17). bds. 4.95 (978-1-58728-349-9(2)) Cooper Square Publishing Llc.

Saviola, Ava. Dinosaur Shapes. 2012. (Dinosaur School Ser.). (Illus.). 24p. (J). (gr. -1-1). pap. 8.15 (978-1-4339-7148-8(8)); lib. bdg. 22.60 (978-1-4339-7147-1(X)) Stevens, Gareth Publishing LLLP.

Scholastic, Inc. Staff. Carry & Learn Shapes. Ward, Sarah, illus. 2015. (ENG.). 12p. (J). (— 1). bds. 7.99 (978-0-545-79791-7(8), Cartwheel Bks.) Scholastic, Inc.

Scholastic, Inc. Staff, contrib. by. Big & Little: Things That Go. 2013. (ENG.). 12p. (J). bds. 6.95 (978-0-531-27253-4(2)) Scholastic Library Publishing.

—I Am Bigger Than... 2014. (Rookie Toddler(r) Ser.). (ENG., Illus.). 12p. (J). bds. 6.95 (978-0-531-20492-4(8)) Scholastic Library Publishing.

—Shapes. 2013. (Rookie Toddler(r) Ser.). (ENG., Illus.). 12p. (J). bds. 6.95 (978-0-531-21579-1(2), Children's Pr.) Scholastic Library Publishing.

—Shapes at Home. 2015. (Rookie Toddler(r) Ser.). (ENG.). 12p. (J). bds. 6.95 (978-0-531-20573-0(8)) Scholastic Library Publishing.

—Shapes in the Sky. 2016. (Rookie Toddlers Ser.). (ENG.). 12p. (J). bds. 6.95 (978-0-531-22457-1(0), Children's Pr.) Scholastic Library Publishing.

—Shapes That Go. 2014. (Rookie Toddler(r) Ser.). (ENG.). 12p. (J). bds. 6.95 (978-0-531-20915-8(6)) Scholastic Library Publishing.

Scholastic, Inc. Staff, ed. Secret Shapes. (Changing Picture Bks.). (Illus.). (J). pap. 9.99 (978-0-590-24644-6(5)) Scholastic, Inc.

Scholastic Teaching Resources Staff. Kindergarten Basic Skills: Visual Perception, Classifying & More. 2012. (Kindergarten Basic Skills Ser.). (ENG.). 48p. pap. 6.99 (978-0-545-42963-4(3)) Teacher's Friend Pubns., Inc.

—Preschool Basic Skills: Colors, Shapes & More. 2012. (Preschool Basic Skills Ser.). (ENG.). 48p. pap. 6.99 (978-0-545-42969-6(2)) Teacher's Friend Pubns., Inc.

—Preschool Basic Skills: Visual Perception & Drawing. 2012. (Preschool Basic Skills Ser.). (ENG.). 48p. pap. 6.99 (978-0-545-42967-2(6)) Teacher's Friend Pubns., Inc.

School Zone Publishing. Same or Different. 2003. (Preschool Ser.). (ENG.). (J). cd-rom 19.99 (978-1-58947-902-9(5)) School Zone Publishing Co.

School Zone Publishing Company Staff. Colors & Shapes. 2005. (ENG.). 64p. (J). (gr. -1-k). pap., wbk. ed. 3.99 (978-1-58947-357-7(4)) School Zone Publishing Co.

School Zone Staff. Bilingual Colors, Shapes & More. 2004. (ENG.). (J). 2.99 (978-1-58947-988-3(2)) School Zone Publishing Co.

Schuette, Sarah L. Círculos: Círculos a Nuestro Alrededor. 2010. (Figuras Geométricas/Shapes Ser.).Tr. of Circles - Seeing Circles All Around Us. (MUL & SPA.). 32p. (gr. 1-2). lib. bdg. 27.32 (978-1-4296-4587-4(3), A+ Bilingue/Bilingual) Capstone Press of Coughlan Cos.

—Cuadrados: Cuadrados a Nuestro Alrededor. 2010. (Figuras Geométricas/Shapes Ser.).Tr. of Squares - Seeing Squares All Around Us. (MUL, SPA & ENG.). 32p. (gr. 1-2). lib. bdg. 27.32 (978-1-4296-4588-1(1), A+ Bilingue/Bilingual) Capstone Press of Coughlan Cos.

—Figuras Geométricas/Shapes. 2012. (Figuras Geométricas/Shapes Ser.). (MUL.). 32p. (gr. 1-2). pap. 31.80 (978-1-4296-8536-8(0)); pap. 190.80 (978-1-4296-8537-5(9)) Capstone Press of Coughlan Cos. (A+ Bilingue/Bilingual).

—So Many Shapes! A Spot-It, Learn-It Challenge, 1 vol. 2014. (Spot It, Learn It! Ser.). (ENG.). 32p. (gr. 1-2). lib. bdg. 27.32 (978-1-4765-4010-8(1), Aplus Bks.) Capstone Press of Coughlan Cos.

Schuh, Mari. The World's Biggest Mammals. 2015. (Illus.). 24p. (J). lib. bdg. 25.65 (978-1-62031-204-9(2)) Jump! Inc.

Schuh, Mari C. The Crayola Shapes Book. 2017. (Crayola (r) Concepts Ser.). (ENG.). 24p. (J). (gr. -1-3). 26.65 **(978-1-5124-3284-8(9))** Lerner Publishing Group.

Schumacher, Bev. Patterns. 2007. 20p. (J). lib. bdg. 9.95 (978-0-9768706-3-0(0)) Learning Props.

—Shape Land. 2004. (ENG.). 20p. (J). lib. bdg. 9.95 (978-0-9741549-8-5(9)) Learning Props.

—Shapeland / Figuralandia. 2004.Tr. of Figuralandia. (SPA.). 20p. lib. bdg. 9.95 (978-0-9741549-2-3(X)) Learning Props.

—What Color Is It? / de Que Color Es? 2004. (SPA & CHI., Illus.). 20p. (J). lib. bdg. 9.95 (978-0-9741549-0-9(3)) Learning Props.

Sesame Street Staff, creator. Sesame Street: Early Learning Boxed Set. 2011. 72p. (J). bds. 12.99 (978-1-60745-237-9(5)) Flying Frog Pubs.

Shapes. (Sparkly Board Bks.). (Illus.). (J). bds. (978-1-84239-256-0(5)) Alligator Bks. Ltd.

Shapes. 2003. (Illus.). 12p. 5.95 (978-0-7548-0378-2(3), Lorenz Bks.) Anness Publishing GBR. Dist: National Bk. Network.

Shapes. 2004. 12p. (J). bds. 3.99 (978-1-85997-814-6(2)) Byeway Bks.

Shapes. 2003. (J). per. (978-1-57657-917-6(4)); per. (978-1-57657-915-2(8)) Paradise Pr., Inc.

Shapes. Date not set. (Illus.). 16p. (J). 2.98 (978-0-7525-9454-5(0)) Parragon, Inc.

Shapes. 2003. (Preschool Ser.). (ENG.). (J). cd-rom 19.99 (978-1-58947-904-3(1)) School Zone Publishing Co.

Shapes! 2015. (Shapes! Ser.). (ENG.). 24p. (J). (gr. 1-1). 49.32 (978-1-5026-0331-9(4)); 145.26 (978-1-5026-0314-2(4)) Cavendish Square Publishing.

Shapes, Vol. 4. (Early Intervention Levels Ser.). 3.85 (978-1-56334-972-0(8)) CENGAGE Learning.

Shapes All Around. 2010. (Shapes Around Town Ser.). 32p. lib. bdg. 155.94 (978-1-4048-6221-0(8)) Picture Window Bks.

Shapes anc colors shaped layer Book. 2006. (J). bds. 4.99 (978-1-934004-08-1(1)) Byeway Bks.

Shapes in My World: Big Book: Level F. (Visions Ser.). 8p. 20.95 (978-0-322-00629-4(5)) Wright Group/McGraw-Hill.

Sharman, Lydia. The Amazing Book of Shapes. (Illus.). 40p. (J). pap. 18.95 (978-0-590-24306-3(3)) Scholastic, Inc.

Shepard, Daniel. Solid Shapes. 2005. (Yellow Umbrella Fluent Level Ser.). (ENG.). 16p. (gr. k-1). pap. 35.70 (978-0-7368-5319-4(7), Yellow Umbrella Bks.) Capstone Press of Coughlan Cos.

Shepherd, Jodie. The Crayola Comparing Sizes. 2017. (Crayola (r) Concepts Ser.). (ENG.). 24p. (J). (gr. -1-3). 26.65 **(978-1-5124-3289-3(X))** Lerner Publishing Group.

Shulman, Mark. My Square Breakfast. Miline, Bill, photos by. 2006. (Illus.). 10p. (J). (gr. k-4). reprint ed. 6.00 (978-1-4223-5710-1(4)) DIANE Publishing Co.

Sidman, Joyce. Round. Yoo, Taeeun, illus. 2017. (ENG.). 32p. (J). (gr. -1-3). 17.99 (978-0-544-38761-4(9), HMH Books For Young Readers) Houghton Mifflin Harcourt Publishing Co.

Siminovich, Lorena. I Like Toys. Siminovich, Lorena, illus. 2011. (Petit Collage Ser.). (ENG., Illus.). 10p. (J). (— 1). bds. 6.99 (978-0-7636-5074-2(9), Templar) Candlewick Pr.

Siwanowicz, Igor. Animals up Close: Zoom in on the World's Most Incredible Creatures. 2014. (Illus.). 96p. (J). (978-1-4351-5620-3(X)) Barnes & Noble, Inc.

Sizes: Individual Title Six-Packs. (Discovery World Ser.). 12p. (gr. k-1). 28.00 (978-0-7635-8447-4(9)) Rigby Education.

Sizes & Shapes. 2005. (J). Bk. 1. per. 8.95 (978-1-59566-155-5(7))Bk. 2. per. 8.95 (978-1-59566-159-3(X)) QEB Publishing Inc.

Slaughter, Tom. One, Two, Three. 2003. (ENG., Illus.). 24p. (J). (gr. k-k). 12.95 (978-0-88776-664-0(1), Tundra Bks.) Tundra Bks. CAN. Dist: Penguin Random Hse. LLC.

Smith, Carrie. Finding Shapes: Lap Book. 2009. (My First Reader's Theater Set B Ser.). (J). 28.00 (978-1-4108-8542-5(9)) Benchmark Education Co.

Smith, Mary Lou. I See Squares. 2015. (Shapes! Ser.). (ENG.). 24p. (J). (gr. 1-1). 24.21 (978-1-5026-0260-2(1)) Cavendish Square Publishing.

Smith, Mary-Lou. I See Stars. 2015. (Shapes! Ser.). (ENG.). 24p. (J). (gr. 1-1). 24.21 (978-1-5026-0271-8(7)) Cavendish Square Publishing.

Smith, Mary Lou. I See Triangles. 2015. (J). pap. (978-1-62713-511-5(1)) Musa Publishing.

Smith, Sian. Big & Small, 1 vol. 2014. (Opposites Ser.). (ENG.). 24p. (gr. -1-1). pap. 5.99 (978-1-4846-0332-1(X), Acorn) Heinemann-Raintree.

Snozek, Lee Anne. Terrific Triangles. 2010. (Dover Design Coloring Bks.). (ENG., Illus.). 32p. (gr. 3-8). pap. 3.99 (978-0-486-47678-0(2)) Dover Pubns., Inc.

Sosa, Maritza, concept. Formas - Shapes. 2006. (ENG & SPA.). (J). bds. 5.99 (978-1-934113-02-8(6)) Little Cubans, LLC.

Stadler, Charlotte. Building a Castle. 2011. (Early Connections Ser.). (J). (978-1-61672-628-7(8)) Benchmark Education Co.

Stanley, Joseph. Is It Flat or Is It Solid? Identify & Describe Shapes. 2013. (InfoMax Math Readers Ser.). (ENG.). 16p. (J). (gr. k-1). pap. 42.00 (978-1-4777-2001-1(4)); (Illus.). pap. 7.00 (978-1-4777-2000-4(6)) Rosen Publishing Group, Inc., The. (Rosen Classroom).

Steck-Vaughn Staff. Early Math: Shapes, 10 Pack. 2005. pap. 29.95 (978-1-4190-0344-8(5)) Steck-Vaughn.

—Early Math Set 1: Shapes. 2005. pap. 2.99 (978-1-4190-0320-2(8)) Steck-Vaughn.

—Head for Home: Colors & Shapes. 2004. (Illus.). pap. (978-0-7398-8554-3(5)) Steck-Vaughn.

—Super Sizes! 2003. pap. 4.10 (978-0-7398-7658-9(9)) Steck-Vaughn.

Steffora, Tracey. Shapes in the Kitchen, 1 vol. 2011. (Math Around Us Ser.). (ENG.). 24p. (gr. -1-1). 22.65 (978-1-4329-4922-8(5)); pap. 6.29 (978-1-4329-4930-3(6)) Heinemann-Raintree. (Acorn).

Stella, Heather. Get Ready for Pre-K: Numbers, Shapes & Colors - 249 Fun Exercises for Mastering Basic Skills. 2013. (Get Ready for School Ser.). (ENG.). 128p. (J). (gr. -1-17). pap. 7.95 (978-1-57912-936-1(6), 81936, Black Dog & Leventhal Pubs. Inc.) Hachette Bks.

Sterling Publishing Co., Inc. Begin Smart(tm) Play Shapes/Formas de Jugar. 2016. (Begin Smart(tm) Ser.). (ENG & SPA., Illus.). 16p. (J). (— 1). bds. 8.95 (978-1-4549-1758-8(X)) Sterling Publishing Co., Inc.

Sterling Publishing Co., Inc. & Verlag, Arena. Kids' First Mandalas. 2005. (ENG., Illus.). 64p. (J). (gr. -1-2). pap. 4.95 (978-1-4027-1801-4(2)) Sterling Publishing Co., Inc.

Stich, Tim. Paper Crafts: Shapes & Their Attributes. 2013. (InfoMax Math Readers Ser.). (ENG.). 24p. (J). (gr. 1-2). pap. 8.25 (978-1-4777-2142-1(8)); pap. 49.50 (978-1-4777-2143-8(6)) Rosen Publishing Group, Inc., The. (Rosen Classroom).

Studio Mouse. Princess Colors & Shapes Pack. 2003. (ENG., Illus.). 36p. (J). (gr. -1-3). 12.99 (978-1-59069-366-7(3), 1A501) Studio Mouse LLC.

Studio Mouse, creator. Princess Shapes. 2004. (Early Learning Ser.). (ENG., Illus.). 36p. (J). (gr. -1-3). 12.99 (978-1-59069-369-8(8), 1A103) Studio Mouse LLC.

Sugimoto, Nao. 100 Shapes. 2010. (ENG., Illus.). 45p. (gr. k). spiral bd. 12.95 (978-1-934734-45-2(4)) Seven Footer Pr.

Tagel, Peggy, illus. On the Go. 2003. (Squishy Shapes Ser.). 10p. (J). 12.95 (978-1-57145-739-4(9), Silver Dolphin Bks.) Readerlink Distribution Services, LLC.

Takeuchi, Mayuko. Circle, Triangle, Elephant! A Book of Shapes & Surprises. 2017. (ENG., Illus.). 22p. (gr. -1 — 1). bds. 9.95 **(978-0-7148-7411-1(6))** Phaidon Pr., Inc.

Teacher's Friend Publications Staff, creator. Color & Shape Puzzles. 2006. (Scholastic Hands-on Learning Ser.). (ENG., Illus.). 12.99 (978-0-439-82388-3(9), Teaching Resources) Scholastic, Inc.

Teckentrup, Britta. Find the Circle. 2016. (Find the Shape Ser.). (ENG., Illus.). 24p. (J). (— 1). bds. 6.95 (978-1-4549-1759-5(8)) Sterling Publishing Co., Inc.

—Find the Line. 2016. (Find the Shape Ser.). (ENG., Illus.). 24p. (J). (— 1). bds. 6.95 (978-1-4549-1760-1(1)) Sterling Publishing Co., Inc.

—Find the Square. 2016. (Find the Shape Ser.). (ENG., Illus.). 24p. (J). (— 1). bds. 6.95 (978-1-4549-1761-8(X)) Sterling Publishing Co., Inc.

—Find the Triangle. 2016. (Find the Shape Ser.). (ENG., Illus.). 24p. (J). (— 1). bds. 6.95 (978-1-4549-1762-5(8)) Sterling Publishing Co., Inc.

Teis, Kyra. Look!, 1 vol. 2005. (ENG., Illus.). 16p. (J). (gr. -1). bds. 6.95 (978-1-59572-022-1(7)) Star Bright Bks., Inc.

Thong, Roseanne Greenfield. Round Is a Tortilla: A Book of Shapes. 2015. (J). lib. bdg. 18.40 (978-0-606-37442-2(6)) Turtleback Bks.

Thornborough, Kathy. Colors & Shapes. Petelinsek, Kathleen, illus. 2014. (Talking Hands Ser.). (ENG.). 24p. (J). (gr. k-3). 25.64 (978-1-62687-315-5(1), 207155) Child's World, Inc., The.

Thornton, Geoffrey. What's Wrong? Visual Adventures in Critical Thinking. 2007. 32p. per. 19.95 (978-1-59858-296-3(8)) Dog Ear Publishing, LLC.

Ticktock Media, Ltd. Staff. Favorite Foods: Colors & Shapes. 2008. (Tab Bks.). (ENG.). 10p. (J). (gr. -1-k). bds. 4.95 (978-1-84696-821-1(6), TickTock Books) Octopus Publishing Group GBR. Dist: Independent Pubs. Group.

—Friendly Dinosaurs. 2009. (Dinosaur Shape Bks.). (ENG.). 10p. (J). (gr. -1-k). bds. 5.95 (978-1-84696-833-4(X), TickTock Books) Octopus Publishing Group GBR. Dist: Independent Pubs. Group.

—Hungry Dinosaurs. 2009. (Dinosaur Shape Bks.). (ENG.). 10p. (J). (gr. -1-k). bds. 5.95 (978-1-84696-834-1(8), TickTock Books) Octopus Publishing Group GBR. Dist: Independent Pubs. Group.

Top That! Kids, creator. Magnetic Play + Learn Shapes. 2005. (Magnetic Play & Learn Ser.). (Illus.). 12p. (J). (gr. -1-3). bds. (978-1-84510-048-3(4)) Top That! Publishing PLC.

Traffic Signs Shape Book. 2016. (Illus.). 23p. (J). (978-0-87659-712-5(6)) Gryphon Hse., Inc.

Tullet, Hervé. The Game of Mix & Match. Edicare, ed. 2011. (ENG., Illus.). 14p. (gr. -1 — 1). 9.95 (978-0-7148-6073-2(5)) Phaidon Pr., Inc.

—The Game of Shapes. 2015. (ENG., Illus.). 14p. (gr. -1 — 1). 12.95 (978-0-7148-6975-9(9)) Phaidon Pr., Inc.

Tuxworth, Nicola. Patterns: Learn-a-Word Book. 2016. (ENG., Illus.). 20p. bds. 6.99 (978-1-86147-462-9(8), Armadillo) Anness Publishing GBR. Dist: National Bk. Network.

Twine, Alice. My Favorite Book of Shapes. 2008. (Board Bks.). (Illus.). 14p. (J). (gr. -1-k). bds. 11.95 (978-1-4042-4255-5(4)) Rosen Publishing Group, Inc., The.

Vogel, Julia. Crescents, 1 vol. Holm, Sharon, illus. 2007. (Shapes Ser.). (ENG.). 24p. (gr. -1-2). 27.07 (978-1-60270-044-4(3), Looking Glass Library- Nonfiction) Magic Wagon.

—Ovals, 1 vol. Holm, Sharon, illus. 2007. (Shapes Ser.). (ENG.). 24p. (gr. -1-2). 27.07 (978-1-60270-045-1(1), Looking Glass Library- Nonfiction) Magic Wagon.

Walter Foster Creative Team. Shapes: Learn Shapes with Reusable Chalkboard Pages! 2017. (ENG., Illus.). 14p. (J). (gr. -1-1). bds. 12.95 **(978-1-63322-256-4(X)**, Walter Foster Jr) Quarto Publishing Group USA.

Walter, Jackie. What Shape Is It? 2016. (My First Maths Ser.). (ENG., Illus.). 24p. (J). (gr. -1-1). 12.99 (978-1-4451-4926-4(5), Franklin Watts) Hachette Children's Group GBR. Dist: Hachette Bk. Group.

Watt, Mélanie. Shapes. Watt, Mélanie, illus. 2005. (Learning with Animals Ser.). (ENG., Illus.). 24p. (J). (gr. -1 — 1). bds. 5.95 (978-1-55337-833-4(4)) Kids Can Pr., Ltd. CAN. Dist: Hachette Bk. Group.

Weakland, Mark. Hockey Shapes, 1 vol. (SI Kids Rookie Bks.). (ENG., (gr. 1-2). 2014. Illus.). 20p. bds. 7.95 (978-1-4765-3578-4(7)) 2013. 32p. 27.32 (978-1-4765-0225-0(0)) Capstone Press of Coughlan Cos.

Weekly Reader Editorial Staff. I Know Big & Small: Grande y Pequeño. 2006. (I'm Ready for Math/ Ya puedo aprender matematicas Ser.). (ENG & SPA., Illus.). 16p. (gr. -1-2). pap. 5.30 (978-0-8368-6489-2(1), Weekly Reader Leveled Readers) Stevens, Gareth Publishing LLLP.

—I Know Shapes: Las Figuras. 2006. (I'm Ready for Math/ Ya puedo aprender matematicas Ser.). (ENG & SPA., Illus.). 16p. (gr. -1-2). pap. 5.30 (978-0-8368-6492-2(1), Weekly Reader Leveled Readers) Stevens, Gareth Publishing LLLP.

—I Know Shapes (Las Figuras) 2006. (I'm Ready for Math/YA Puedo Aprender Matematicas Ser.). (ENG & SPA., Illus.). 16p. (gr. -1-2). lib. bdg. 19.00 (978-0-8368-6487-8(5), Weekly Reader Leveled Readers) Stevens, Gareth Publishing LLLP.

Weekly Reader Editorial Staff, contrib. by. I Know Big & Small. 2006. (I'm Ready for Math Ser.). (Illus.). 16p. (gr. -1-2). pap. 5.30 (978-0-8368-6479-3(4), Weekly Reader Leveled Readers) Stevens, Gareth Publishing LLLP.

Wells, Robert E. Is a Blue Whale the Biggest Thing There Is? 2012. (J). 34.28 (978-1-61913-116-3(1)) Weigl Pubs., Inc.

—What's Smaller Than a Pygmy Shrew? 2012. (J). (978-1-61913-158-3(7)) Weigl Pubs., Inc.

Welzen, Jon. I Know Shapes. 2016. (What I Know Ser.). 00024p. (J). pap. 8.15 (978-1-4824-5478-9(5)) Stevens, Gareth Publishing LLLP.

Winn, Michael. The Shape People. 2008. 28p. pap. 24.95 (978-1-60474-544-3(4)) America Star Bks.

Winslow, Jeremy. Hours of Coloring Fun with Shapes & Patterns. 2011. 182p. 30.99 (978-1-4568-8227-3(9)); pap. 20.99 (978-1-4568-8226-6(0)) Xlibris Corp.

Wise the Turtle Counts to Tenb & Shapes. 2003. 3.99 (978-0-915960-05-7(2)) Ebon Research Systems Publishing, LLC.

Wojick, Luke. I Can Draw Shapes. 2013. (Core Math Skills: Measurement & Geometry Ser.). (Illus.). 24p. (J). (gr. 1-2). 22.60 (978-1-4777-2231-2(9)); (ENG., pap. 8.25 (978-1-4777-2055-4(3)) Rosen Publishing Group, Inc., The. (Rosen Classroom).

—I Can Draw Shapes: Shapes & Their Attributes. 2013. (Rosen Math Readers Ser.). (ENG., Illus.). 24p. (J). (gr. 1-2). pap. 49.50 (978-1-4777-2056-1(1), Rosen Classroom) Rosen Publishing Group, Inc., The.

Wooster, Devin Ann. Big Dinosaur, Little Dinosaur. 2016. (Step into Reading Level 1 Ser.). lib. bdg. 14.75 (978-0-606-38479-7(0)) Turtleback Bks.

World Book, Inc Staff, contrib. by. Fun with Shapes. 2011. (J). (978-0-7166-0229-3(6)) World Bk., Inc.

The World of Eric Carle My Shapes Activity Kit. 2007. (J). 16.99 (978-0-9794445-3-1(5)) Loew-Cornell, Inc.

Yates, Gene. The Snake Shapes Book. 2004. (Illus.). 14p. (J). (978-1-58865-155-6(X)) Kidsbooks, LLC.

Yates, Gene, illus. The Snake Shapes Book. 2006. (J). (978-1-58865-365-9(X)) Kidsbooks, LLC.

Yegoryan, Kristina & Yegoryan, Rubik. I Know Digits & Shapes. 2009. 108p. pap. 33.49 (978-1-4389-5444-8(1)) AuthorHouse.

Yorke, Jane & Dorling Kindersley Publishing Staff. Colors & Shapes Touch & Feel Picture Cards. Thomson, Maria & Hester, Elizabeth, eds. 2005. (My 1st T&F Picture Cards Ser.). (ENG., Illus.). 16p. (J). (gr. -1 — 1). 9.99 (978-0-7566-1516-1(X), DK Children) Dorling Kindersley Publishing, Inc.

Your Baby Can Learn! Shapes, Vol. 1. 2007. (J). 7.95 (978-1-931026-13-0(0)) Infant Learning Co., The.

Zaidi, Nadeem, illus. Formas: Libro con Ventanas. 2007. (Baby Einstein Ser.). 5p. (J). (gr. -1). (978-970-718-468-8(X), Silver Dolphin en Español) Advanced Marketing, S. de R. L. de C. V.

Zuckerman, Rory. Shapely Sleepy Sheep. Roos, Maryn, illus. 2004. (J). bds. 12.95 (978-0-9749305-2-7(0)) Castle Pacific Publishing.

—Shapely Sleepy Sheep. Roos, Maryn, illus. 2007. (Sleepy Sheep Ser.). (J). (gr. -1). bds. 7.95 incl. audio compact disk (978-0-9796393-4-0(4)) Little Lion Pr.

SIZE AND SHAPE—FICTION

Adler, David A. Don't Throw It to Mo! Ricks, Sam, illus. 2015. (Mo Jackson Ser.: bk.1). (ENG.). 32p. (J). (gr. 1-2). 14.99 (978-0-670-01631-0(4), Penguin Young Readers) Penguin Young Readers Group.

—Don't Throw It to Mo! 2016. (Penguin Young Readers Level 2 Ser.). lib. bdg. 13.55 (978-0-606-38852-8(4)) Turtleback Bks.

—Get a Hit, Mo! Ricks, Sam, illus. (Mo Jackson Ser.: bk.2). (ENG.). 32p. (J). (gr. 1-2). 2017. pap. 3.99 (978-0-448-48010-7(7)) 2016. 14.99 (978-0-670-01632-7(2)) Penguin Young Readers Group. (Penguin Young Readers).

Albee, Sarah. Kidoozle Kids & the Great Shape Rescue! 2004. (Illus.). 12p. bds. 9.95 (978-1-932915-02-0(8)) Sandvik Publishing.

Baby's Box of Toys. 2008. (Baby Gold Stars Fabric Ser.). 6p. bds. (978-1-4075-2520-4(4)) Parragon, Inc.

Baldwin, Kevin. Beetle Dan & the Big Purple Slide: A Beetle Dan Story. 2006. (Beetle Dan Story Ser.). (ENG., Illus.). 32p. (J). (gr. -1-2). 14.99 (978-1-59185-921-5(2), Creation Hse.) Charisma Media.

Banks, Kate. Max's Math. Kulikov, Boris, illus. 2015. (Max's Words Ser.: 4). (ENG.). 40p. (J). (gr. -1-3). 17.99 (978-0-374-34875-5(8), 9780374348755, Farrar, Straus & Giroux (BYR)) Farrar, Straus & Giroux.

Barchers, Suzanne I. How Big Is Kip?, 1 vol. 2011. (Targeted Phonics Ser.). (ENG., Illus.). 16p. (J). (gr. k-2). pap. 5.99 (978-1-4333-2410-9(5)) Teacher Created Materials, Inc.

Barnett, Mac. Triangle. Klassen, Jon, illus. 2017. (ENG.). 48p. (J). (gr. k-4). 15.99 (978-0-7636-9603-0(X)) Candlewick Pr.

Bauer, Joan. Stand Tall. 2005. (ENG.). 192p. (YA). (gr. 7-5). pap. 8.99 (978-0-14-240427-0(6), Speak) Penguin Young Readers Group.

Bedford, David. Big Bears Can! Hansen, Gaby, illus. 2007. (Storytime Board Bks.). 16p. (J). (gr. -1-k). bds. 6.95 (978-1-58925-826-6(6)) Tiger Tales.

Bedford, David & Worthington, Leonie. Big. 2006. (Illus.). 16p. pap. (978-1-921049-22-4(7)) Little Hare Bks. AUS. Dist: HarperCollins Pubs. Australia.

Benjamin, A. H. I'm Taller Than You! O'Kif, illus. 2008. (Tadpoles Ser.). (ENG.). 24p. (J). (gr. -1-3). lib. bdg. (978-0-7787-3854-1(X)) Crabtree Publishing Co.

Bentley, Jonathan, illus. Little Big. 2015. (ENG.). 32p. (J). 16.00 (978-0-8028-5462-9(1), Eerdmans Bks For Young Readers) Eerdmans, William B. Publishing Co.

Berrios, Frank & RH Disney Staff. Shapes, Colors, Counting & More! (Disney/Pixar Cars) RH Disney Staff, illus. 2013. (Friendship Box Ser.). (ENG., Illus.). 48p. (J). (gr. -1-2). bds.

S

10.99 (978-0-7364-3105-7(5), RH/Disney) Random Hse. Children's Bks.

Bertier, Anne, creator. Wednesday. 2014. (ENG., Illus.). 48p. (J). (gr. -1-2). 17.95 (978-1-59270-152-0(3)) Enchanted Lion Bks., LLC.

Bessen, Luc. Arthur & the Minimoys. Sowchek, Ellen, tr. from FRE. 2005. (ENG.). 240p. (J). 15.99 (978-0-06-059623-1(6)) HarperCollins Pubs.

Besson, Luc. Arthur & the Forbidden City. Sowchek, Ellen, tr. 2006. (ENG., Illus.). 192p. (J). (gr. 3-7). pap., pap. 5.99 (978-0-06-059628-6(7), Harper Trophy) HarperCollins Pubs.

—Arthur & the Forbidden City. 2005. (ENG., Illus.). 192p. (J). 15.99 (978-0-06-059626-2(0)) HarperCollins Pubs.

—Arthur & the Minimoys. 2005. (Illus.). 240p. (J). lib. bdg. 16.89 (978-0-06-059624-8(4)) HarperCollins Pubs.

Bingham, Kelly. Circle, Square, Moose. Zelinsky, Paul O., illus. 2014. (ENG.). 48p. (J). (gr. -1-3). 17.99 (978-0-06-229003-8(7), Greenwillow Bks.) HarperCollins Pubs.

Bird, Benjamin. Scooby-Doo's Shape Mystery. 2015. (Scooby-Doo! Little Mysteries Ser.). (ENG., Illus.). 20p. (gr. -1 — 1). bds. 7.99 (978-1-62370-178-9(3)) Capstone Press of Coughlan Cos.

Birkhead, Jennifer. Peeping Through the Low, Green Grass. 2011. 28p. pap. 12.03 (978-1-4490-5490-8(0)) AuthorHouse.

Blackstone, Stella. Ship Shapes. Bell, Siobhan, illus. (J). 2008. (ENG.). 24p. (gr. -1-k). bds. 7.99 (978-1-84686-157-4(8)) 2006. (978-1-4156-6474-2(9)) Barefoot Bks., Inc.

—Ship Shapes. 2012. lib. bdg. 17.20 (978-0-606-23826-7(3), Turtleback) Turtleback Bks.

Blackstone, Stella & Meza-Riedewald, Leticia. Oso en un Cuadrado. Harter, Debbie, illus. 2009. (SPA & ENG.). 24p. (J). (gr. -1-k). pap. 6.99 (978-1-84686-387-5(2)) Barefoot Bks., Inc.

Blevins, Wiley. Big Box of Shapes. Kreloff, Elliott, illus. 2016. (Basic Concepts Ser.). (ENG.). 24p. (J). (gr. -1-1). lib. bdg. 14.99 (978-1-63440-082-4(8)) Red Chair Pr.

Boldt, Mike. Colors Versus Shapes. Boldt, Mike, illus. 2014. (ENG., Illus.). 40p. (J). (gr. -1-3). 16.99 (978-0-06-210303-1(2)) HarperCollins Pubs.

Borando, Silvia. Shapes at Play: A Minibombo Book. Borando, Silvia, illus. 2016. (Minibombo Ser.). (ENG., Illus.). 48p. (J). (-k). 14.00 (978-0-7636-9038-0(4)) Candlewick Pr.

—Shapes, Reshape! A Minibombo Book. Borando, Silvia, illus. 2016. (Minibombo Ser.). (ENG., Illus.). 48p. (J). (-k). 14.00 (978-0-7636-9039-7(2)) Candlewick Pr.

Bova, Della L. The Adventures of Pono: A Puppy Dog's Tale. 2011. 24p. pap. 11.49 (978-1-4490-7354-1(9)) AuthorHouse.

Bowen, Fred. Full Court Fever, 1 vol. 2009. (All-Star Sports Story Ser.). (ENG., Illus.). 112p. (J). pap. 5.95 (978-1-56145-508-9(3)) Peachtree Pubs.

Boxes, 6 Pack. (Literatura 2000 Ser.). (gr. 1-2). 28.00 (978-0-7635-0122-8(0)) Rigby Education.

Boyd, Lizi. Big Bear Little Chair. 2015. (ENG., Illus.). 36p. (J). (gr. -1-k). 16.99 (978-1-4521-4447-4(8)) Chronicle Bks. LLC.

Braun, Sebastien. Toot & Pop! Braun, Sebastien, illus. 2012. (Illus.). 32p. (J). (gr. -1-2). 12.99 (978-0-06-207750-9(3)) HarperCollins Pubs.

Brexel, Bernadette. Gloria's Triangles. 2015. (Rosen REAL Readers: STEM & STEAM Collection). (ENG.). 8p. pap. 5.46 (978-1-4994-9535-5(8), Rosen Classroom) Rosen Publishing Group, Inc., The.

Bridwell, Norman. Clifford Makes the Team. Bridwell, Norman, illus. 2011. (Scholastic Reader Level 1 Ser.). (ENG., Illus.). 32p. (J). (gr. -1-2). pap. 3.99 (978-0-545-23141-1(8)) Scholastic, Inc.

—Clifford's Puppy Days. 2010. (Clifford 8x8 Ser.). (ENG., Illus.). 32p. (J). (gr. -1-3). pap. 3.99 (978-0-545-21583-1(8), Cartwheel Bks.) Scholastic, Inc.

Brière-Haquet, Alice. ONE Very Big Bear. Philipponneau, Olivier & Enjary, Raphaële, illus. 2016. (ENG.). 32p. (J). (gr. -1-k). 14.95 (978-1-4197-2117-5(8), Abrams Appleseed) Abrams, Inc.

Briere-Haquet, Alice. Peter & the Moon, 1 vol. Chauffrey, Celia, illus. 2012. (Big Picture Book Ser.). (ENG.). 48p. (J). (gr. k). 16.95 (978-2-7338-1940-1(2)) Auzou, Philippe Editions FRA. Dist: Consortium Bk. Sales & Distribution.

Bright, Paul. The Hole Story. Ingman, Bruce, illus. 2017. (Andersen Press Picture Bks.). (ENG.). 32p. (gr. -1-3). 35.99 **(978-1-5124-3972-4(X))** Lerner Publishing Group.

Can I Come Too?, 1 vol. 2014. (ENG., Illus.). 32p. (J). (gr. -1-3). pap. 16.95 (978-1-56145-796-0(5)) Peachtree Pubs.

Carle, Eric. My First Busy Book. Carle, Eric, illus. 2015. (World of Eric Carle Ser.). (ENG., Illus.). 12p. (J). bds. 14.99 (978-1-4814-5791-0(8), Little Simon) Little Simon.

Carlson, Nancy. ¡Piensa en Grande! 2005. (Libros Ilustrados (Picture Bks.)). (SPA., Illus.). 32p. (J). (gr. k-2). lib. bdg. 15.95 (978-0-8225-3192-0(5), Ediciones Lerner) Lerner Publishing Group.

—Think Big! 2005. (Illus.). 28p. (J). (gr. -1-3). 15.95 (978-1-57505-622-7(4), Carolrhoda Bks.) Lerner Publishing Group.

Caviezel, Giovanni. Cowboy. Mesturini, C., illus. 2009. (Little People Shape Bks.). (ENG.). 12p. (J). (gr. -1-2). bds. 10.99 (978-0-7641-6191-9(1)) Barron's Educational Series, Inc.

Chaconas, Dori. Short & Tall No. 2, 2 vols. McCue, Lisa, illus. 2010. (Cork & Fuzz Ser.: 2). (ENG.). 32p. (J). (gr. 1-3). mass mkt. 3.99 (978-0-14-241594-8(4), Penguin Young Readers) Penguin Young Readers Group.

Chernesky, Felicia Sanzari. Pick a Circle, Gather Squares: A Fall Harvest of Shapes. Swan, Susan, illus. 2013. (ENG.). 32p. (J). (gr. -1-3). 16.99 (978-0-8075-6538-4(5)) Whitman, Albert & Co.

Child, Lauren. I Want to Be Much More Bigger Like You. 2008. (Charlie & Lola Ser.). (ENG.). 24p. (J). (gr. -1-k). mass mkt. 3.99 (978-0-448-44867-1(X), Grosset & Dunlap) Penguin Young Readers Group.

Choi, SeoYun. Let's Be Friends. Furukawa, Masumi, illus. rev. ed. 2014. (MySELF Bookshelf Ser.). (ENG.). 32p. (J). (gr. k-2). pap. 11.94 (978-1-60357-658-1(4)); lib. bdg. 25.27 (978-1-59953-649-1(8)) Norwood Hse. Pr.

Clay III, J. Percy. Sampson's Pumpkin Playhouse. 2012. 30p. 24.95 (978-1-4626-7226-4(4)) America Star Bks.

Cole, Henry. Big Bug. Cole, Henry, illus. 2014. (ENG., Illus.). 32p. (J). (gr. -1-2). 14.99 (978-1-4424-9897-6(8), Little Simon) Little Simon.

Costello, David Hyde. Little Pig Joins the Band. Costello, David Hyde, illus. 2014. (ENG., Illus.). 32p. (J). (gr. -1-3). pap. 7.95 (978-1-58089-265-0(5)) Charlesbridge Publishing, Inc.

Coulton, Mia. Danny's Favorite Shapes. Coulton, Mia, photos by. 2004. (ENG., Illus.). pap. (978-0-9746475-4-8(3)) Maryruth Bks., Inc.

Coville, Bruce. Jeremy Thatcher, Dragon Hatcher: A Magic Shop Book. Lippincott, Gary A., illus. 20th ed. 2007. (Magic Shop Book Ser.: 2). (ENG.). 176p. (J). (gr. 5-7). pap. 7.99 (978-0-15-206252-1(1)) Houghton Mifflin Harcourt Publishing Co.

Crews, Donald. Los Diez Puntos Negros, 1 vol. Crews, Donald, illus. 2009. (SPA & ENG., Illus.). 32p. (J). (gr. -1-k). 16.99 (978-0-06-177138-5(4)) HarperCollins Pubs.

—Ten Black Dots Board Book. Crews, Donald, illus. 2010. (ENG., Illus.). 32p. (J). (gr. -1-3). bds. 7.99 (978-0-06-185779-9(3), Greenwillow Bks.) HarperCollins Pubs.

Crocker, Carter & Swift, Jonathan. The Last of the Gullivers. 2012. (ENG.). 224p. (J). (gr. 4-7). 16.99 (978-0-399-24231-1(7), Philomel Bks.) Penguin Young Readers Group.

Curato, Mike. Little Elliot, Big City. Curato, Mike, illus. 2014. (Little Elliot Ser.). (ENG., Illus.). 40p. (J). (gr. -1-3). 16.99 (978-0-8050-9825-9(9), 9780805098259, Holt, Henry & Co. Bks. For Young Readers) Holt, Henry & Co.

Dahl, Roald. Esio Trot. 2009. 8.32 (978-0-7848-2293-7(X), Everbind) Marco Bk. Co.

—Esio Trot. Blake, Quentin, illus. 2009. (ENG.). 96p. (J). (gr. 3-7). 7.99 (978-0-14-241382-1(8), Puffin Books) Penguin Young Readers Group.

—Esio Trot. 2004. (CHI.). (J). pap. 11.70 (978-957-574-477-9(2)) Youth Cultural Publishing Co. CHN. Dist: Chinasprout, Inc.

Dale, Katie. Thumbelina Thinks Big! 2016. (ENG., Illus.). 32p. (J). (978-0-7787-2473-5(5)) Crabtree Publishing Co.

D'Aulaire, Ingri & D'Aulaire, Edgar Parin. Too Big. 2008. (New York Review Children's Collection). (ENG., Illus.). 40p. (J). (gr. k-k). 14.95 (978-1-59017-291-9(4), NYR Children's Collection) New York Review of Bks., Inc., The.

David, Lawrence. The Terror of the Pink Dodo Balloons. Gott, Barry, illus. 2003. (Horace Splattly Ser.). 153p. (J). (gr. 4-7). 12.65 (978-0-7569-2816-2(8)) Perfection Learning Corp.

DeStefano, Anthony. Little Star. Elliott, Mark, illus. 2013. (ENG.). 36p. (J). 14.99 (978-0-7369-5859-2(2)) Harvest Hse. Pubs.

Diaz, Nelbaliz. Laura y Su Caja de Sorpresas. 2007. (SPA.). 48p. 14.95 (978-0-8477-0452-1(1)) Univ. of Puerto Rico Pr.

Donahue, Laurie. Mr. Blue a Job for You. Bryan, Hintz, illus. 2010. 32p. (J). 15.95 (978-0-9799116-2-0(1)) LifeSong Pubs.

Donnio, Sylviane. I'd Really Like to Eat a Child. 2012. (ENG., Illus.). 32p. (J). (gr. -1-2). pap. 7.99 (978-0-307-93008-8(4), Dragonfly Bks.) Random Hse. Children's Bks.

—I'd Really Like to Eat a Child. 2012. lib. bdg. 18.40 (978-0-606-23845-8(X), Turtleback) Turtleback Bks.

Dougherty, Brandi. The Littlest Elf. Richards, Kirsten, illus. 2012. (ENG.). 24p. (J). (gr. -1-k). pap. 4.99 (978-0-545-43654-0(0)) Scholastic, Inc.

—The Littlest Elf. Richards, Kristen, illus. 2012. (J). pap. (978-0-545-48978-2(4), WestBow Pr.) Scholastic, Inc.

—The Littlest Pilgrim. Richards, Kirsten, illus. 2008. (ENG.). 32p. (J). (gr. -1-k). pap. 3.99 (978-0-545-05372-3(2), Cartwheel Bks.) Scholastic, Inc.

Dr. Seuss Enterprises Staff & Roberts, Al. The Nose Book. Mathieu, Joe, illus. 2003. (Bright & Early Board Books(TM) Ser.). (ENG.). 24p. (J). (— 1). bds. 4.99 (978-0-375-82493-7(6), Random Hse. Bks. for Young Readers) Random Hse. Children's Bks.

Dull, Dennis Stanley. Baby Basics & Beyond: ABC's, 123's & Shapes. Dull, Dennis Stanley, illus. 2nd ed. 2004. (Illus.). (J). (978-0-9717475-4-8(7)) Laurel Valley Graphics, Inc.

Duvall, Sheila Marie. I See Fun. 2009. 16p. pap. 8.75 (978-1-4389-4963-5(4)) AuthorHouse.

Emberley, Rebecca & Emberley, Ed. The Lion & the Mice. 2011. (I Like to Read(r) Ser.). (ENG., Illus.). 24p. (J). (gr. -1-2). 14.95 (978-0-8234-2357-6(3)) Holiday Hse., Inc.

Emberley, Rebecca & Emberley, Edward R. The Lion & the Mice. Emberley, Rebecca & Emberley, Edward R., illus. 2012. (I Like to Read(r) Ser.). (ENG., Illus.). 24p. (J). (gr. -1-2). pap. 6.99 (978-0-8234-2641-6(6)) Holiday Hse., Inc.

Emma Treehouse Ltd. My Friends. Davis, Caroline, illus. 2007. (Easy Flaps Ser.). 10p. (J). (gr. -1). bds. 6.95 (978-1-58925-823-5(1)) Tiger Tales.

Enderle, Dotti. Clawed! An Up2U Horror Adventure, 1 vol. To, Vivienne, illus. 2013. (Up2U Adventures Ser.). (ENG.). 80p. (J). (gr. 2-5). lib. bdg. 27.07 (978-1-61641-965-3(2), Calico Chapter Bks) Magic Wagon.

Engle, Margarita. Tiny Rabbit's Big Wish. Walker, David, illus. 2014. (ENG.). 32p. (J). (gr. -1-3). 16.99 (978-0-547-85286-7(X), HMH Books For Young Readers) Houghton Mifflin Harcourt Publishing Co.

Evert, Lori. The Tiny Wish. Breiehagen, Per, illus. 2015. (ENG.). 48p. (J). (gr. -1-2). lib. bdg. 20.99 (978-0-375-97336-9(2), Random Hse. Bks. for Young Readers) Random Hse. Children's Bks.

Fawcett, Sally. What Could It Be? Exploring the Imaginative World of Shapes. 2016. (ENG., Illus.). 32p. (J). (gr. -1-2). 17.99 (978-1-925335-02-6(X), EK Bks.) Exisle Publishing Pty Ltd. AUS. Dist: Hachette Bk. Group.

Findlay, Lisa & Swift, Jonathan. Gulliver in Lilliput. Caparó, Antonio Javier, illus. 2010. (Step into Reading Ser.). (ENG.). 48p. (J). (gr. k-3). pap. 3.99 (978-0-375-86585-5(3), Random Hse. Bks. for Young Readers) Random Hse. Children's Bks.

Fisher, Doris. Happy Birthday to Whooo? A Baby Animal Riddle Book, 1 vol. Downey, Lisa, illus. 2006. (ENG.). 32p. (J). (gr. -1-3). 15.95 (978-0-9768823-1-2(0)); pap. 8.95 (978-1-934359-06-8(8)) Arbordale Publishing.

Fleming, Denise. Go, Shapes, Go! Fleming, Denise, illus. 2014. (ENG., Illus.). 40p. (J). (gr. -1-3). 17.99 (978-1-4424-8240-1(0), Beach Lane Bks.) Beach Lane Bks.

Flory, Neil. The Short Giraffe. 2015. (Illus.). 24p. (J). (978-1-4896-3885-4(7)) Weigl Pubs., Inc.

Fontes, Justine. Black Meets White. Waring, Geoff, illus. 2005. (ENG.). 24p. (J). (— 1). 12.99 (978-0-7636-1933-6(7)) Candlewick Pr.

Foxley, Janet. Muncle Trogg. 2012. (J). (978-0-545-37801-7(X)) Scholastic, Inc.

—Muncle Trogg. O'Kif, illus. 2012. (ENG.). 224p. (J). (gr. 2-5). 14.99 (978-0-545-37800-0(1), Chicken Hse., The) Scholastic, Inc.

Freytag, Lorna. My Humongous Hamster Goes to School. Freytag, Lorna, illus. 2015. (My Humongous Hamster Ser.). (ENG., Illus.). 32p. (J). (gr. -1-3). 16.99 (978-1-62779-140-3(X), 9781627791403, Holt, Henry & Co. Bks. For Young Readers) Holt, Henry & Co.

Friedman, Mel, et al. Un Castillo para Gatitos. Adams, Lynn, illus. 2008. (SPA.). (J). (978-1-57565-275-7(7)) Kane Press, Inc.

Gall, Chris, illus. NanoBots. 2016. (ENG.). 40p. (J). (gr. -1-3). 16.99 (978-0-316-37552-8(7)) Little Brown & Co.

Galvin, Laura. Pooh & Friends Colors & Shapes. 2008. (ENG.). 24p. (J). (gr. -1). 4.99 (978-1-59069-736-8(7)) Studio Mouse LLC.

Galvin, Laura Gates. Mickey Mouse Clubhouse Fun with Numbers & Shapes. 2008. (ENG.). 20p. (J). (gr. -1-3). 9.99 (978-1-59069-655-2(7)) Studio Mouse LLC.

Garland, Michael. Hooray José!, 1 vol. Garland, Michael, illus. 2007. (ENG., Illus.). 32p. (J). (gr. -1-3). 16.99 (978-0-7614-5345-1(8)) Marshall Cavendish Corp.

Garner, Albert. The Adventures of Dimi. 2013. (ENG.). 48p. (J). 24.95 (978-1-4787-1677-8(0)) Outskirts Pr., Inc.

Gerver, Jane E. Christmas Shapes. Davis, Nancy & Davis, Kathryn Lynn, illus. 2010. (ENG.). 14p. (J). (gr. -1 — 1). bds. 6.99 (978-1-4169-9759-7(8), Little Simon) Little Simon.

Gillespie, Jane. Diving for Shapes in Hawaii: An Identification Book for Keiki. Bosgra, Johann, illus. 2004. (ENG.). 20p. (J). bds. 8.95 (978-1-933067-04-9(7)) Beachhouse Publishing, LLC.

Goldberg, Ella, ed. Simple Shapes. 2013. (Matching Pictures Ser.). (ENG.). 20p. (J). (gr. -1-k). bds. 5.95 (978-1-61889-311-6(4)) AZ Bks. LLC.

Golden Books. Mighty Adventures (Team Umizoomi) Fruchter, Jason, illus. 2012. (Super Color with Stickers Ser.). (ENG.). 96p. (J). (gr. -1-2). pap. 3.99 (978-0-307-93085-9(8), Golden Bks.) Random Hse. Children's Bks.

Gomi, Taro. Hide & Seek. 2013. (ENG., Illus.). 22p. (J). (gr. -1 — 1). bds. 6.99 (978-1-4521-0840-7(4)) Chronicle Bks. LLC.

Gourlay, Candy. Tall Story. 2012. (ENG.). 304p. (J). (gr. 5). 6.99 (978-0-385-75233-6(4), Yearling) Random Hse. Children's Bks.

Graham, Elspeth. Sandwich that Jack Made. Mould, Chris, illus. 2004. (ENG.). 24p. (J). lib. bdg. 23.65 (978-1-59646-698-2(7)) Dingles & Co.

Granhold, Adriana. Mattie Knowsmath & the Great Shape Hunt. 2012. 32p. pap. 24.95 (978-1-4626-7202-8(7)) America Star Bks.

Graves, Keith. Chicken Big. 2010. (ENG., Illus.). 40p. (J). (gr. -1-3). 16.99 (978-0-8118-7237-9(8)) Chronicle Bks. LLC.

Gravett, Emily. Blue Chameleon. Gravett, Emily, illus. 2011. (ENG., Illus.). 32p. (J). (gr. -1-1). 16.99 (978-1-4424-1958-2(X), Simon & Schuster Bks. For Young Readers) Simon & Schuster Bks. For Young Readers.

Greban, Tanguy. Sarah So Small. Greban, Quentin, illus. 2004. 32p. (J). 16.95 (978-0-689-03594-4(2), Milk & Cookies) ibooks, Inc.

Green, Judy. The Little Blue Octopus. 2009. 28p. pap. 21.99 (978-1-4415-3393-7(1)) Xlibris Corp.

Greenburg, J. C. In Uncle Al, No. 16. Gerardi, Jan, illus. 2007. (Andrew Lost Ser.: 16). (ENG.). 96p. (J). (gr. 1-4). 3.99 (978-0-375-83565-0(2), Random Hse. Bks. for Young Readers) Random Hse. Children's Bks.

—With the Frogs. Gerardi, Jan, illus. 2008. (Andrew Lost Ser.: 18). (ENG.). 96p. (J). (gr. 1-4). 3.99 (978-0-375-84668-7(9), Random Hse. Bks. for Young Readers) Random Hse. Children's Bks.

Guettier, Nancy. Jude's Moon. Walsh, Tina, illus. 2014. (ENG.). 32p. (gr. -1-4). pap. 9.95 (978-1-61448-964-1(5)) Morgan James Publishing.

Hall, Kirsten. Tug-of-War: All about Balance. Luedecke, Bev, illus. 2004. (Beastieville Ser.). 31p. (J). 19.50 (978-0-516-22899-0(4), Children's Pr.) Scholastic Library Publishing.

Hall, Michael. Perfect Square. Hall, Michael, illus. 2011. (ENG., Illus.). 40p. (J). (gr. -1-k). 16.99 (978-0-06-191513-0(0), Greenwillow Bks.) HarperCollins Pubs.

Hansen, Dustin. Microsaurs: Adventure Awaits. Hansen, Dustin, illus. 2017. (Microsaurs Ser.: 1). (ENG., Illus.). 224p. (J). 13.99 (978-1-250-09021-8(0), 9781250090218) Feiwel & Friends.

Hanson, Warren. Grandpa Has a Great Big Face. Elliott, Mark, illus. 2006. 32p. (J). (gr. -1-3). 17.89 (978-0-06-078776-9(7), Geringer, Laura Book) HarperCollins Pubs.

Hanton, Sophie. Shapes on the Farm. 2009. (Mag-NUT-Tics! Ser.). (Illus.). (J). bds. 9.99 (978-1-934650-74-5(9)) Just For Kids Pr., LLC.

Harper, Charise Mericle. Wedgieman & the Big Bunny Trouble. Shea, Bob, illus. 2014. (Step into Reading Ser.). (ENG.). 48p. (J). (gr. k-3). 3.99 (978-0-307-93073-6(4), Random Hse. Bks. for Young Readers) Random Hse. Children's Bks.

Hartmann, Annabelle. As Big As a Mountain. 2003. (Illus.). 32p. (YA). (978-1-84365-001-0(0), Pavilion Children's Books) Pavilion Bks.

Have You Seen Joe?, Pk. 6. (gr. -1-2). 23.00 (978-0-7635-8800-7(8)) Rigby Education.

Hawkes, Kevin. The Wicked Big Toddlah. 2010. (ENG.). 40p. (J). (gr. -1-2). pap. 7.99 (978-0-440-41788-0(0), Dragonfly Bks.) Random Hse. Children's Bks.

—The Wicked Big Toddlah Goes to New York. 2011. (ENG., Illus.). 40p. (J). (gr. -1-2). 16.99 (978-0-375-86188-8(2), Knopf Bks. for Young Readers) Random Hse. Children's Bks.

Hays, Anna Jane. So Big! Moroney, Christopher, illus. 2003. (Sesame Beginnings Ser.). (ENG.). 14p. (J). (gr. k — 1). bds. 7.99 (978-0-375-81537-9(6), Random Hse. Bks. for Young Readers) Random Hse. Children's Bks.

Henry, Steve. Here Is Big Bunny. 2017. (I Like to Read(r) Ser.). (ENG.). 32p. (J). (gr. -1-3). 6.99 (978-0-8234-3774-0(4)) Holiday Hse., Inc.

—Here Is Big Bunny. Henry, Steve, illus. 2016. (ENG., Illus.). 32p. (J). (gr. -1-3). 15.95 (978-0-8234-3458-9(3)) Holiday Hse., Inc.

Henson, Tara. The Littlest Blue Jay. 2011. 24p. pap. 15.99 (978-1-4568-7956-3(1)) Xlibris Corp.

Herman, R. A. The Littlest Christmas Tree. Rogers, Jacqueline, illus. 2007. (ENG.). 32p. (J). (gr. -1-3). pap. 3.99 (978-0-439-54007-0(0)) Scholastic, Inc.

—Pal Saves the Day. Ogden, Betina, illus. 2004. (Pal the Pony Ser.). 32p. (J). pap. (978-0-439-64985-8(4)); pap. (978-0-439-57746-5(2)) Scholastic, Inc.

Hillert, Margaret. Dear Dragon's Fun with Shapes. Schimmell, David, illus. 2015. (BeginningtoRead Ser.). 32p. (J). (-2). lib. bdg. 22.60 (978-1-59953-544-9(0)) Norwood Hse. Pr.

—Dear Dragon's Fun with Shapes. del Risco, Eida, tr. Schimmell, David, illus. 2015. (BeginningtoRead Ser.). 32p. (J). (-2). pap. 11.94 (978-1-60357-447-1(6)) Norwood Hse. Pr.

—I Like Things. (J). 4.95 (978-0-87895-683-8(2)) Modern Curriculum Pr.

—I Like Things. Hopkins, Jeff, illus. 2016. (BeginningtoRead Ser.). (ENG.). 32p. (J). (gr. 1-2). 22.60 (978-1-59953-817-4(2)) Norwood Hse. Pr.

—¿Qué Tengo en el Bolsillo, Querido Dragón? Fernandez, Queta, tr. from ENG. Schimmell, David, illus. 2014. (BeginningtoRead Ser.).Tr. of What's in My Pocket, Dear Dragon? (ENG & SPA.). 32p. (J). (-2). lib. bdg. 22.60 (978-1-59953-611-8(0)) Norwood Hse. Pr.

—What's in My Pocket, Dear Dragon? Schimmell, David, illus. 2014. (BeginningtoRead Ser.). (ENG.). 32p. (J). (-2). pap. 11.94 (978-1-60357-415-0(8)); lib. bdg. 22.60 (978-1-59953-579-1(3)) Norwood Hse. Pr.

Hodgkinson, Jo. The Talent Show. Hodgkinson, Jo, illus. 2011. (ENG., Illus.). 32p. (J). (gr. -1-3). 16.95 (978-0-7613-7487-9(6)) Lerner Publishing Group.

Holub, Joan. Itty Bitty Kitty. Burks, James, illus. 2015. (ENG.). 32p. (J). (gr. -1-3). 17.99 (978-0-06-232219-7(2)) HarperCollins Pubs.

—Itty Bitty Kitty & the Rainy Play Day. Burks, James, illus. 2016. 32p. (J). (gr. -1-3). 17.99 (978-0-06-232220-3(6)) HarperCollins Pubs.

Hopgood, Tim. Walter's Wonderful Web. 2016. (ENG., Illus.). 32p. (J). 16.99 (978-0-374-30352-5(5), 9780374303525, Farrar, Straus & Giroux (BYR)) Farrar, Straus & Giroux.

Hopper, Ada. Invasion of the Insects. Ricks, Sam, illus. 2017. (DATA Set Ser.: 6). (ENG.). 128p. (J). (gr. -1-4). 16.99 (978-1-4814-7117-6(1), Little Simon) Little Simon.

Houran, Lori Haskins. Make a Wish, Albert: 3-D Shapes. Melmon, Deborah, illus. 2015. (ENG.). 32p. (J). (gr. -1-1). lib. bdg. 22.60 (978-1-57565-797-4(X)) Kane Press, Inc.

Howe, James. Brontorina. Cecil, Randy, illus. 2013. (ENG.). 32p. (J). (gr. -1-3). 6.99 (978-0-7636-5323-1(3)) Candlewick Pr.

—Brontorina. 2013. lib. bdg. 17.20 (978-0-606-31600-2(0), Turtleback) Turtleback Bks.

Hutchins, Pat. Titch. 2014. 32p. pap. 7.00 (978-1-61003-367-1(1)) Center for the Collaborative Classroom.

If Big Can... I Can. (Picture Books... Ser.). 28p. (978-1-4054-9536-3(7)) Parragon, Inc.

Inches, Alison. I'm Not Little! Thomas, Glenn, illus. 2017. (ENG.). 32p. (J). (gr. -1-3). 16.99 (978-1-4998-0377-8(X)) Little Bee Books Inc.

Jensen, Joel, et al. Tiny Hamster Is a Giant Monster. 2015. (ENG., Illus.). 32p. (J). (gr. -1-3). 17.99 (978-1-4814-5110-9(3), Simon & Schuster Bks. For Young Readers) Simon & Schuster Bks. For Young Readers.

John, Louise. Small. Elkerton, Andy, illus. 2013. (Start Reading Ser.). (ENG.). 24p. (gr. k-1). pap. 41.94 (978-1-4765-3231-8(1)); pap. 7.95 (978-1-4765-3202-8(8)) Capstone Press of Coughlan Cos.

Jolley, Dan. Attack of the Mutant Meteors. Witt, David, illus. 2010. (Twisted Journeys (r) Ser.: 14). (ENG.). 112p. (J). (gr. 4-7). pap. 7.95 (978-0-8225-9255-6(X), Graphic Universe™); lib. bdg. 27.93 (978-0-8225-9249-5(5)) Lerner Publishing Group.

Joyce, William. George Shrinks. Joyce, William, illus. 2017. (World of William Joyce Ser.). (ENG., Illus.). 40p. (J). (gr. -1-3). 17.99 **(978-1-4814-8953-9(4)**, Atheneum/Caitlyn Dlouhy Books) Simon & Schuster Children's Publishing.

Katz, Susan B. All Year Round. Ojala, Eiko, illus. 2016. (ENG.). 32p. (J). (gr. -1-1). 17.99 (978-0-545-74100-2(9), Orchard Bks.) Scholastic, Inc.

Keane, Claire. Little Big Girl. 2016. (ENG., Illus.). 32p. (J). (-k). 17.99 (978-0-8037-3912-3(5), Dial Bks) Penguin Young Readers Group.

Klimo, Kate. Twinky the Dinky Dog. Fleming, Michael, illus. 2013. (Step into Reading Ser.). (ENG.). 48p. (J). (gr. k-3). pap. 3.99 (978-0-307-97667-3(X), Random Hse. Bks. for Young Readers) Random Hse. Children's Bks.

Kling, Kevin. Big Little Brother. Monroe, Chris, illus. 2011. (ENG.). 48p. (J). (gr. -1-2). 17.95 (978-0-87351-844-4(6), Borealis Bk.) Minnesota Historical Society Pr.

Kolar, Bob. Big Kicks. Kolar, Bob, illus. 2008. (ENG., Illus.). 40p. (J). (gr. -1-1). 16.99 (978-0-7636-3390-5(9)) Candlewick Pr.

Krajenbrink Hulin, Yvonne. My Magic Box of Shapes. 2013. 28p. pap. 11.99 (978-0-9794133-7-7(0)) TV Acres Bks.

Krauss, Ruth. Big & Little. Szilagyi, Mary, illus. 2003. (J). pap. 12.95 (978-0-590-40698-7(1)) Scholastic, Inc.

Lane, Alison Hoffman. Uncle Arnel & the Awful, Angry Alligator. 2009. (Uncle Arnel Ser.). (Illus.). 32p. (J). 15.95 (978-1-58980-645-0(X)) Pelican Publishing Co., Inc.

Latimer, Miriam. Shrinking Sam. Latimer, Miriam, illus. 2007. (ENG., Illus.). 32p. (J). (gr. -1-3). 16.99 (978-1-84686-038-6(5)) Barefoot Bks., Inc.

Law, Felicia. Shapes. Knight, Paula, illus. 2015. (Patchwork Ser.). (ENG.). 24p. (J). (gr. k-3). pap. 11.94 (978-1-60357-804-2(8)); lib. bdg. 22.60 (978-1-59953-714-6(1)) Norwood Hse. Pr.

—Size. Knight, Paula, illus. 2015. (Patchwork Ser.). (ENG.). 24p. (J). (gr. k-3). pap. 11.94 (978-1-60357-803-5(X)); lib. bdg. 22.60 (978-1-59953-713-9(3)) Norwood Hse. Pr.

Law, Felicia & Way, Steve. Crocodile Teeth: Geometric Shapes in Action. Spoor, Mike & Mostyn, David, illus. 2010. (Mandrill Mountain Math Mysteries Ser.). 32p. (J). (gr. 2-6). 22.60 (978-1-60754-816-4(X)); pap. 10.55 (978-1-60754-821-8(6)) Windmill Bks.

Lee, Lori K. Bonnie the Honeybee & the Case of the Butterfly Blues. 2011. (ENG., Illus.). 30p. (J). 12.95

(978-0-9828689-6-6(0), BQB Publishing) Boutique of Quality Books Publishing Co., Inc.

Leigh, Autumn. Spots & Stripes. 2003. (Rosen REAL Readers Ser.). (ENG.). 8p. (gr. -1-1). pap. 5.15 *(978-0-8239-6335-5(7)*, Rosen Classroom) Rosen Publishing Group, Inc., The.

Lepp, Bil. The King of Little Things, 1 vol. Wenzel, David T., illus. 2013. (ENG.). 32p. (J). (gr. -1-3). 16.95 *(978-1-56145-708-3(6))* Peachtree Pubs.

Lichtenheld, Tom. Cloudette. Lichtenheld, Tom, illus. 2011. (ENG., Illus.). 40p. (J). (gr. -1-2). 17.99 *(978-0-8050-8776-5(1)*, 9780805087765, Holt, Henry & Co. Bks. For Young Readers) Holt, Henry & Co.

Light, Steven. Have You Seen My Monster? Light, Steve, illus. 2015. (ENG.). 48p. (J). (-k). 16.99 *(978-0-7636-7513-4(X))* Candlewick Pr.

Litwin, Eric. The Nuts: Keep Rolling! Magoon, Scott, illus. 2017. (ENG.). 32p. (J). (gr. -1-3). 17.99 *(978-0-316-32251-5(2))* Little, Brown Bks. for Young Readers.

Loughran, Kelley. A Crab Called Mouse. 2006. (Illus.). (J). (gr. -1-3). pap. 9.50 *(978-0-9787995-2-6(6))* High-Pitched Hum Inc.

Love, Pamela. Dos pies suben, dos pies Bajan: Two Feet up, Two Feet Down. Chapman, Lynne, illus. 2005. (Rookie Reader Español Ser.). 32p. (gr. k-2). 19.50 *(978-0-516-25252-0(6)*, Children's Pr.) Scholastic Library Publishing.

MacDonald, Suse. Shape by Shape. MacDonald, Suse, illus. 2009. (ENG., Illus.). 24p. (J). (gr. -1-3). 16.99 *(978-1-4169-7147-4(5)*, Little Simon) Little Simon.

Magsamen, Sandra. I Love Shapes! 2014. (I Love Learning Ser.). (ENG., Illus.). 14p. (J). (gr. -1 — 1). bds. 7.99 *(978-0-316-13357-9(4))* Little, Brown Bks. for Young Readers.

Make Believe Ideas. Flower Friends Poppy's Shapes. 2013. (ENG.). 10p. (J). bds. 6.99 *(978-1-78235-603-5(7))* Make Believe Ideas GBR. Dist: Nelson, Thomas Inc.

Malone, Marianne. The Secret of the Key: a Sixty-Eight Rooms Adventure. 2015. (Sixty-Eight Rooms Adventures Ser.). (ENG., Illus.). 256p. (J). (gr. 3-7). 6.99 *(978-0-307-97724-3(2)*, Yearling) Random Hse. Children's Bks.

—The Sixty-Eight Rooms. Triplett, Gina & Call, Greg, illus. 2011. (Sixty-Eight Rooms Adventures Ser.). (ENG.). 288p. (J). (gr. 3-7). pap. 6.99 *(978-0-375-85711-9(7)*, Yearling) Random Hse. Children's Bks.

—Stealing Magic. Call, Greg, illus. (Sixty-Eight Rooms Adventures Ser.). (ENG.). (J). (gr. 3-7). 2013. 272p. pap. 6.99 *(978-0-375-86790-3(2)*, Yearling) 2012. 256p. 16.99 *(978-0-375-86819-1(4)*, Random Hse. Bks. for Young Readers) Random Hse. Children's Bks.

Mann, Elizabeth. Little Man: A Novel. 2014. (ENG., Illus.). 208p. (J). (gr. 5-7). 18.95 *(978-1-931414-49-4(1)*, 9781931414494) Mikaya Pr.

Mara, Nichole. All Aboard! Let's Ride a Train. Kolb, Andrew, illus. 2017. (ENG.). 10p. (J). (gr. -1 — 1). bds. 9.95 ***(978-1-4197-2567-8(X)***, Abrams Appleseed) Abrams, Inc.

Marshall, Natalie. My Turn to Learn Shapes. 2013. (My Turn to Learn Ser.). (ENG., Illus.). 12p. (J). (gr. -1 — 1). bds. 6.99 *(978-0-316-25166-2(6))* Little, Brown Bks. for Young Readers.

Martin, Emily Winfield. The Littlest Family's Big Day. 2016. (ENG., Illus.). 36p. (J). (gr. -1-2). 17.99 *(978-0-553-51101-7(7))*; lib. bdg. 20.99 *(978-0-375-97431-1(8))* Random Hse. Children's Bks. (Random Hse. Bks. for Young Readers).

Marvel Books Staff & Strathearn, Chris. Marvel's Ant-Man. 2015. (ENG., Illus.). 24p. (J). (gr. -1-3). pap. 3.99 *(978-0-316-25668-1(4))* Little, Brown Bks. for Young Readers.

Mary-Todd, Jonathan. The Giant. 2014. (Bareknuckle Ser.). 104p. (YA). (gr. 6-12). lib. bdg. 27.93 *(978-1-4677-1457-0(7)*, Darby Creek) Lerner Publishing Group.

May, Eleanor. Albert's Bigger Than Big Idea. Melmon, Deborah, illus. 2013. (Mouse Math Ser.). (ENG.). 32p. (gr. -1-1). pap. 7.95 *(978-1-57565-522-2(5))* Kane Press, Inc.

—Mice on Ice. Melmon, Deborah, illus. 2013. (Mouse Math Ser.). 32p. (J). (gr. -1-1). 22.60 *(978-1-57565-527-7(6))*; (ENG.). pap. 7.95 *(978-1-57565-528-4(4))* Kane Press, Inc.

Mayer, Mercer. Just Big Enough. Mayer, Mercer, illus. 2013. (Little Critter Ser.). (ENG., Illus.). 24p. (J). (gr. -1-2). pap. 3.99 *(978-0-06-147805-5(9)*, HarperFestival) HarperCollins Pubs.

—Just Big Enough. 2013. (Little Critter Ser.). (J). lib. bdg. 13.55 *(978-0-606-31809-9(7)*, Turtleback) Turtleback Bks.

—When I Get Bigger. 2014. 24p. pap. 4.00 *(978-1-61003-373-2(6))* Center for the Collaborative Classroom.

McClure, Brian D. The Raindrop. 2006. (Illus.). 36p. (J). 14.95 *(978-1-933426-01-3(2))* Universal Flag Publishing.

McCully, Emily Arnold. Sam & the Big Kids. McCully, Emily Arnold, illus. (I Like to Read(r) Ser.). (ENG., Illus.). 24p. (J). (gr. -1-3). 2014. 6.99 *(978-0-8234-3060-4(X))* 2013. 14.95 *(978-0-8234-2427-6(8))* Holiday Hse., Inc.

McDonald, Jill. Shapes: A Play-with-Me BK. McDonald, Jill, illus. 2007. (ENG., Illus.). 10p. bds. 6.95 *(978-1-58117-604-9(X)*, Intervisual/Piggy Toes) Bendon, Inc.

McDonald, Megan. The Incredible Shrinking Kid. Reynolds, Peter H., illus. 2013. (Stink Ser.: 1). (ENG.). (J). (gr. 1-4). 112p. 12.99 *(978-0-7636-6388-9(3))*; 128p. pap. 4.99 *(978-0-7636-6426-8(X))* Candlewick Pr.

—Stink. 2013. (Stink Ser.: 1). lib. bdg. 14.75 *(978-0-606-31587-6(X)*, Turtleback) Turtleback Bks.

—Stink: The Incredible Shrinking Kid. Reynolds, Peter H., illus. 2010. (Stink Ser.: No. 1). 112p. (J). (gr. k-4). 24.21 *(978-1-59961-686-5(6))* Spotlight.

—Stink, el Increíble Niño Menguante. 2008. (SPA.). 272p. (J). (gr. 3-5). pap. 7.95 *(978-1-60396-193-6(3))* Ediciones Alfaguara ESP. Dist: Two Rivers Distribution.

McGrath, Barbara Barbieri. Teddy Bear Counting. Nihoff, Tim, illus. 2010. (McGrath Math Ser.). (ENG.). 32p. (J). (gr. -1-2). pap. 7.95 *(978-1-58089-216-2(7))* Charlesbridge Publishing, Inc.

McNamara, Margaret. How Many Seeds in a Pumpkin? Karas, G. Brian, illus. 2007. (Mr. Tiffin's Classroom Ser.). (ENG.). 40p. (J). (gr. -1-2). 17.99 *(978-0-375-84014-2(1)*, Schwartz & Wade Bks.) Random Hse. Children's Bks.

Mead, David. Noah's Babies Shapes & Sharing. Byers, Brian, illus. 2005. 22p. (J). bds. 6.95 *(978-0-9746440-5-9(6))* Virtue Bks.

Membrino, Anna. Big Shark, Little Shark. 2017. (Step into Reading Ser.). (ENG., Illus.). 32p. (J). (gr. -1-1). pap. 3.99 *(978-0-399-55728-6(8)*, Random Hse. Bks. for Young Readers) Random Hse. Children's Bks.

Miura, Taro. The Big Princess. Miura, Taro, illus. 2015. (ENG., Illus.). 40p. (J). (-k). 14.99 *(978-0-7636-7459-5(1))* Candlewick Pr.

Moncure, Jane Belk. Apes Find Shapes: A Book about Recognizing Shapes. Ronney, Ronnie, illus. 2013. (Magic Castle Readers Ser.). (ENG.). 32p. (J). (gr. -1-2). 25.64 *(978-1-62323-577-2(4)*, 206312) Child's World, Inc., The.

—The Biggest Snowball of All: A Book about Sizes. Rooney, Ronnie, illus. 2013. (Magic Castle Readers Ser.). (ENG.). 32p. (J). (gr. -1-2). 25.64 *(978-1-62323-578-9(2)*, 206315) Child's World, Inc., The.

Montgomery, Ross. Perijee & Me. 2016. (ENG.). 224p. (J). (gr. 3-7). 16.99 *(978-0-399-55397-4(5)*, Lamb, Wendy Bks.) Random Hse. Children's Bks.

Mueller, Doris. Small One's Adventure. Fulton, Parker, illus. 2004. 32p. (J). (gr. k-5). 16.95 *(978-0-9710278-1-7(1))* All About Kids Publishing.

Mullican, Judy & Crowell, Knox. Caillou Finds Shapes. Gillen, Lisa P., illus. I.t. ed. 2005. (HRL Board Book Ser.). (J). (gr. -1-k). bds. 10.95 *(978-1-57332-312-3(8)*, HighReach Learning, Incorporated) Carson-Dellosa Publishing, LLC.

Muncaster, Harriet. The Biggest Smallest Christmas Present. Muncaster, Harriet, illus. 2016. (ENG., Illus.). 32p. (J). (-k). 16.99 *(978-0-399-16432-3(4)*, G.P. Putnam's Sons Books for Young Readers) Penguin Young Readers Group.

Munsch, Robert. Marilou Casse-Cou. 2004.Tr. of Up, Up, Down. (FRE., Illus.). (J). (gr. k-3). spiral bd. *(978-0-616-11144-4(4))* Canadian National Institute for the Blind/Institut National Canadien pour les Aveugles.

My Daddy Is a Giant. 2004. (J). (ENG & KUR.). *(978-1-84444-514-1(3))*; (ENG & PAN.). *(978-1-84444-515-8(1))*; (ENG & POL.). *(978-1-84444-516-5(X))*; (ENG & POR.). *(978-1-84444-517-2(8))*; (ENG & SOM.). *(978-1-84444-519-6(4))*; (ENG & SPA.). *(978-1-84444-520-2(8))*; (ENG & TAG.). *(978-1-84444-508-0(9))*; (ENG & TAM.). *(978-1-84444-521-9(6))*; (ENG & TUR.). *(978-1-84444-522-6(4))*; (ENG & URD.). *(978-1-84444-523-3(2))*; (ENG & GUJ.). *(978-1-84444-509-7(7))*; (ENG & HIN.). *(978-1-84444-510-3(0))*; (ENG & ITA.). *(978-1-84444-511-0(9))*; (ENG & JPN.). *(978-1-84444-512-7(7))*; (ALB & ENG.). *(978-1-84444-499-1(6))*; (ARA & ENG.). *(978-1-84444-501-1(1))*; (CHI & ENG.). *(978-1-84444-504-2(6))*; (CRO & ENG.). *(978-1-84444-505-9(4))*; (ENG & PER.). *(978-1-84444-506-6(2))*; (ENG & FRE.). *(978-1-84444-507-3(0))* Mantra Lingua.

Nakagawa, Chihiro. Who Made This Cake? Koyose, Junji, illus. 2008. (ENG.). 32p. (J). (gr. -1-2). 16.95 *(978-1-59078-595-9(9)*, Front Street) Boyds Mills Pr.

Nash, Margaret. Sammy's Secret. Axworthy, Anni, illus. 2008. (Tadpoles Ser.). (ENG.). 24p. (J). (gr. -1-3). pap. *(978-0-7787-3894-7(9))*; lib. bdg. *(978-0-7787-3863-3(9))* Crabtree Publishing Co.

Nolan, Dennis. Hunters of the Great Forest. Nolan, Dennis, illus. 2014. (ENG., Illus.). 40p. (J). (gr. -1-2). 17.99 *(978-1-59643-896-5(7)*, 9781596438965) Roaring Brook Pr.

Nolen, Jerdine. Hewitt Anderson's Great Big Life. Nelson, Kadir, illus. (ENG.). 40p. (J). (gr. k-3). 2013. 7.99 *(978-1-4424-6035-5(0))* 2005. 18.99 *(978-0-689-86866-5(9))* Simon & Schuster/Paula Wiseman Bks. (Simon & Schuster/Paula Wiseman Bks.).

Norac, Carl. My Daddy Is a Giant. 2005. (J). (ENG & RUS.). 16.95 *(978-1-84444-518-9(6))*; (ENG & KOR.). 16.95 *(978-1-84444-513-4(5))*; (CHI & ENG.). 16.95 *(978-1-84444-503-5(8))*; (BEN & ENG.). 16.95 *(978-1-84444-502-8(X))*; (ENG & VIE.). 16.95 *(978-1-84444-524-0(0))* Mantra Lingua GBR. Dist: Chinasprout, Inc.

O'Connell, Rebecca. Baby Party. Poole, Susie, illus. 2015. (ENG.). 24p. (J). (gr. -1-3). 15.99 *(978-0-8075-0512-0(9))* Whitman, Albert & Co.

Ofelia, Dumas Lachtman. Big Enough Bastante Grande. Enrique, Sanchez, illus. 2008. 32p. (J). pap. 7.95 *(978-1-55885-239-6(5))* Arte Publico Pr.

O'Leary, Sara. When You Were Small. Morstad, Julie, illus. 2006. (ENG.). 32p. (J). (gr. -1-3). 16.95 *(978-1-894965-36-1(1))* Simply Read Bks. CAN. Dist: Ingram Publisher Services.

Oliver, Lin. Attack of the Growling Eyeballs. Gilpin, Stephen, illus. 2009. (Who Shrunk Daniel Funk? Ser.: 1). (ENG.). 160p. (J). (gr. 3-7). pap. 6.99 *(978-1-4169-0958-3(3)*, Simon & Schuster Bks. For Young Readers) Simon & Schuster Bks. For Young Readers.

—Escape of the Mini-Mummy. Gilpin, Stephen, illus. 2009. (Who Shrunk Daniel Funk? Ser.: 2). (ENG.). 160p. (J). (gr. 3-7). pap. 8.99 *(978-1-4169-0960-6(5)*, Simon & Schuster Bks. For Young Readers) Simon & Schuster Bks. For Young Readers.

—Revenge of the Itty-Bitty Brothers. Gilpin, Stephen, illus. (Who Shrunk Daniel Funk? Ser.: 3). (ENG.). 176p. (J). (gr. 3-7). 2010. pap. 6.99 *(978-1-4169-0962-0(1))* 2009. 14.99 *(978-1-4169-0961-3(3))* Simon & Schuster Bks. For Young Readers. (Simon & Schuster Bks. For Young Readers).

—Secret of the Super-Small Superstar. Gilpin, Stephen, illus. 2010. (Who Shrunk Daniel Funk? Ser.: 4). (ENG.). 160p. (J). (gr. 3-7). 14.99 *(978-1-4169-0963-7(X)*, Simon & Schuster Bks. For Young Readers) Simon & Schuster Bks. For Young Readers.

Olsen, Jan Z. Mat Man on the Go. Delaney, Molly, illus. 2010. (ENG.). stu. ed. 13.75 *(978-1-934825-39-6(5))* Handwriting Without Tears.

Owens, Robert. The Littlest Warrior. 2008. 32p. pap. 24.95 *(978-1-4241-9156-7(4))* America Star Bks.

Paton Walsh, Jill. A Parcel of Patterns. 137p. (YA). (gr. 7-18). pap. 3.95 *(978-0-8072-1485-5(X)*, Listening Library) Random Hse. Audio Publishing Group.

Patricelli, Leslie. Silencio Ruido. Rozarena, P., tr. Patricelli, Leslie, illus. 2003. (SPA., Illus.). 25p. (J). (gr. -1-k). bds. 7.95 *(978-970-29-0987-3(2))* Santillana USA Publishing Co., Inc.

Paul, Chris. Long Shot: Never Too Small to Dream Big. Morrison, Frank, illus. 2009. (ENG.). 32p. (J). (gr. -1-3). 17.99 *(978-1-4169-5079-0(6)*, Simon & Schuster Bks. For Young Readers) Simon & Schuster Bks. For Young Readers.

Perry, Gina. Small. 2017. (ENG.). 40p. (J). (gr. -1-3). 17.99 ***(978-1-4998-0401-0(6))*** Little Bee Books Inc.

Petty, Dev. I Don't Want to Be a Frog. Boldt, Mike, illus. 2016. (ENG.). 32p. (J). (gr. -1-2). 16.99 *(978-1-101-93920-8(6)*, Doubleday Bks. for Young Readers) Random Hse. Children's Bks.

Pfister, Marcus. Penguin Pete. 2013. (Penguin Pete Ser.). (ENG., Illus.). 32p. (J). (gr. -1-3). 14.95 *(978-0-7358-4118-5(7))* North-South Bks., Inc.

Pig & Small, 1 vol. 2014. (ENG., Illus.). 32p. (J). (gr. -1-3). 15.95 *(978-1-56145-797-7(3))* Peachtree Pubs.

Pitino, Donna Marie. Too-Tall Tina. Woodruff, Liza, illus. 2005. (Math Matters Ser.). (ENG.). 32p. (J). (gr. -1-3). pap. 5.95 *(978-1-57565-150-7(5))* Kane Press, Inc.

Plourde, Lynn. Maxi's Secrets: (or What You Can Learn from a Dog) (ENG.). 272p. (J). (gr. 5). 2017. 8.99 ***(978-0-399-54568-9(9)***, Puffin Books) 2016. 16.99 *(978-0-399-54567-2(0)*, Nancy Paulsen Books) Penguin Young Readers Group.

Pollack, Pam & Belviso, Meg. Gallinas de Aqui para Alla; Chickens on the Move. 2008. pap. 34.95 *(978-1-58013-784-3(9))* Kane Press, Inc.

Potter, Beatrix. Peter Rabbit Rainbow Shapes & Colors. Potter, Beatrix, illus. 2006. (Peter Rabbit Seedlings Ser.). (ENG., Illus.). 10p. (J). (gr. k-18). bds. 5.99 *(978-0-7232-5722-6(1)*, Puffin) Penguin Publishing Group.

Powell, Richard. What's in the Box? Martin Larrañaga, Ana, illus. 2004. (Ana's Mini Movers Ser.). 12p. (J). 5.95 *(978-1-58925-742-9(1))* Tiger Tales.

Pratchett, Terry. The Carpet People. (ENG., Illus.). 304p. (J). (gr. 2-5). 2015. pap. 6.99 *(978-0-544-43954-2(6)*, HMH Books For Young Readers) 2013. 17.99 *(978-0-544-21247-3(9))* Houghton Mifflin Harcourt Publishing Co.

Prochovnic, Dawn Babb. Shape Detective: Sign Language for Shapes, 1 vol. Bauer, Stephanie, illus. 2012. (ENG.). 32p. 28.50 *(978-1-61641-840-3(0)*, Looking Glass Library) Magic Wagon.

Publications International Ltd. Staff, ed. Shapes Wipe off Learning Board. 2011. 1p. (J). bds. *(978-1-4508-1432-4(8))* Publications International, Ltd.

Rand, Betseygail & Rand, Colleen. Big Bunny. Rand, Colleen, illus. 2011. (ENG., Illus.). 32p. (J). (gr. -1-2). 14.99 *(978-1-58246-376-6(X)*, Tricycle Pr.) Random Hse. Children's Bks.

Random House. Shape Patrol! (Paw Patrol) MJ Illustrations, illus. 2016. (ENG.). 24p. (J). (— 1). bds. 6.99 *(978-1-101-93695-5(9)*, Random Hse. Bks. for Young Readers) Random Hse. Children's Bks.

Rayner, Catherine. Ernest, the Moose Who Doesn't Fit. Rayner, Catherine, illus. 2010. (ENG., Illus.). 32p. (J). (gr. -1-1). 18.99 *(978-0-374-32217-5(1)*, 9780374322175, Farrar, Straus & Giroux (BYR)) Farrar, Straus & Giroux.

Reasoner, Charles. Pumpkin Shapes. 2015. (Charles Reasoner Halloween Bks.). (ENG., Illus.). 12p. (gr. -1 — 1). bds. 5.99 *(978-1-4795-8499-4(1))* Picture Window Bks.

—Shapes at the Beach. Pitt, Sarah, illus. 2009. (3D Board Bks.). 12p. (J). (gr. -1-k). bds. 9.99 *(978-1-934650-36-3(6))* Just For Kids Pr., LLC.

—Shapes for Lunch! 2009. (Bite Bks.). (Illus.). (J). bds. 7.99 *(978-1-934650-16-5(1))* Just For Kids Pr., LLC.

Reid, Camilla. Lulu Loves Shapes. Busby, Ailie, illus. 2015. (ENG.). 12p. (J). (gr. -1-1). bds. 8.99 *(978-1-4088-4958-3(5)*, 9781408849583, Bloomsbury USA Childrens) Bloomsbury Publishing USA.

Richmond, Lori. Pax & Blue. Richmond, Lori, illus. 2017. (ENG., Illus.). 32p. (J). (gr. -1-3). 17.99 *(978-1-4814-5132-1(4)*, Simon & Schuster/Paula Wiseman Bks.) Simon & Schuster/Paula Wiseman Bks.

Rizvi, Sobia. Zebra Stripes. 2011. 24p. pap. 15.99 *(978-1-4653-4618-6(X))* Xlibris Corp.

Rockliff, Mara. Al lado de una Hormiga: Next to an Ant. Constantin, Pascale, illus. 2005. (Rookie Reader Español Ser.). (ENG & SPA.). 24p. (J). (gr. k-2). 19.50 *(978-0-516-25251-3(8)*, Children's Pr.) Scholastic Library Publishing.

—Next to an Ant. Constantin, Pascale, illus. 2011. (Rookie Ready to Learn - Numbers & Shapes Ser.). 32p. (J). (gr. -1-k). lib. bdg. 23.00 *(978-0-531-26447-8(5)*, Children's Pr.) Scholastic Library Publishing.

Roddie, Shen. You're Too Small! Lavis, Steve, illus. 2004. 32p. (J). 6.95 *(978-1-58925-385-8(X))*; tchr. ed. 15.95 *(978-1-58925-038-3(9))* Tiger Tales.

Root, Andrew. Hamsters Don't Fight Fires! Olien, Jessica, illus. 2017. 40p. (J). (gr. -1-3). 17.99 ***(978-0-06-245294-8(0))*** HarperCollins Pubs.

Rorvik, Bjorn F. The Little Paintbrush. Hansen, Thore, illus. 2014. (ENG.). 32p. (J). (gr. -1-k). 12.95 *(978-1-62087-996-2(4)*, 620996, Sky Pony Pr.) Skyhorse Publishing Co., Inc.

Rumph-Geddis, Ashlye V. Tori Finds Shapes All Around. 2007. (Illus.). 12p. (J). 9.45 *(978-0-9792934-0-5(5))* Ashlye V. Enterprises, LLC.

Sagerman, Evan. Giraffe Rescue Company. Chou, Joey, illus. 2016. (J). *(978-1-4424-1366-5(2))* Simon & Schuster Children's Publishing.

Saltzberg, Barney. Redbird: Friends Come in Different Sizes. 2015. (ENG., Illus.). 22p. (J). bds. 5.95 *(978-0-7611-8190-3(3))* Workman Publishing Co., Inc.

Salzano, Tammi. One Sunny Day. 2013. pap. *(978-0-545-53655-4(3))* Scholastic, Inc.

Sazaklis, John. The Biggest Little Hero, 1 vol. Baltazar, Art, illus. 2012. (DC Super-Pets Ser.). (ENG.). 56p. (gr. 2-2). pap. 4.95 *(978-1-4048-7664-4(2))*; lib. bdg. 23.99 *(978-1-4048-6490-0(3))* Picture Window Bks. (DC Super-Pets).

Schafer, Milton. I'm Big! Lew-Vriethoff, Joanne, illus. 2006. (J). *(978-1-4156-8150-3(3)*, Dial) Penguin Publishing Group.

Schoonmaker, Elizabeth. Square Cat. Schoonmaker, Elizabeth, illus. 2011. (ENG., Illus.). 32p. (J). (gr. -1-3). 16.99 *(978-1-4424-0619-3(4)*, Aladdin) Simon & Schuster Children's Publishing.

Schreiber, Joe. Lenny Cyrus, School Virus. Smith, Matt, illus. 2014. (ENG.). 288p. (J). (gr. 5-7). pap. 6.99 *(978-0-544-33628-5(3)*, HMH Books For Young Readers) Houghton Mifflin Harcourt Publishing Co.

Shapur, Fredun. Round & Round & Square. 2016. (ENG., Illus.). 48p. (J). (gr. -1-k). 19.95 *(978-1-84976-363-9(1))* Tate Publishing, Ltd. GBR. Dist: Abrams, Inc.

Sheena, Roberts & Roberts, Sheena. We All Go Traveling By. Siobhan, Bell, illus. 2003. (ENG.). 24p. (J). pap. 6.99 *(978-1-84148-595-9(0))* Barefoot Bks., Inc.

Sherry, Kevin. I'm the Biggest Thing in the Ocean. 2007. (ENG., Illus.). 32p. (J). (gr. -1-3). 17.99 *(978-0-8037-3192-9(2)*, Dial Bks) Penguin Young Readers Group.

—I'm the Biggest Thing in the Ocean! 2010. (ENG.). 28p. (J). (gr. k — 1). bds. 6.99 *(978-0-8037-3529-3(4)*, Dial Bks) Penguin Young Readers Group.

Shulevitz, Uri. Troto & the Trucks. 2015. (ENG., Illus.). 32p. (J). (gr. -1-1). 17.99 *(978-0-374-30080-7(1)*, 9780374300807, Farrar, Straus & Giroux (BYR)) Farrar, Straus & Giroux.

Shulman, Mark. Big Cat. Chambers, Sally, illus. 2004. 8p. (J). bds. 6.95 *(978-1-58925-737-5(5))* Tiger Tales.

Silver Dolphin Staff, creator. Disney Caritas Felices: Dumbo. 2007. (Illus.). 8p. (J). (gr. -1). bds. *(978-970-718-394-0(2)*, Silver Dolphin en Español) Advanced Marketing, S. de R. L. de C. V.

S

Simon, Charnan. Pumpkin Fever. Bryan-Hunt, Jan, illus. 2011. (Rookie Ready to Learn Ser.). 40p. (J). (ENG.). pap. 5.95 *(978-0-531-26803-2(9))*; (gr. -1-k). lib. bdg. 23.00 *(978-0-531-25643-5(X))* Scholastic Library Publishing. (Children's Pr.).

Simon, Coco. Alexis: The Icing on the Cupcake. 2014. (Cupcake Diaries: 20). lib. bdg. 17.20 *(978-0-606-35786-9(6))* Turtleback Bks.

—Alexis the Icing on the Cupcake. 2014. (Cupcake Diaries: 20). (ENG., Illus.). 160p. (J). (gr. 3-7). pap. 6.99 *(978-1-4814-0468-6(7)*, Simon Spotlight) Simon Spotlight.

Simson, Dana. Shapes. 2003. (Dana Simson Chunky Books Ser.). 10p. (J). bds. 2.95 *(978-1-74047-257-9(8))* Book Co. Publishing Pty, Ltd., The AUS. Dist: Penton Overseas, Inc.

Sloan, Holly Goldberg. Short. 2017. (ENG.). 304p. (J). (gr. 3-7). 16.99 *(978-0-399-18621-9(2)*, Dial Bks) Penguin Young Readers Group.

Snyder, Zilpha Keatley. The Treasures of Weatherby. 2008. (ENG.). 240p. (J). (gr. 3-7). pap. 7.99 *(978-1-4169-1399-3(8)*, Atheneum Bks. for Young Readers) Simon & Schuster Children's Publishing.

Sperring, Mark. The Shape of My Heart. Paterson, Alys, illus. 2012. (ENG.). 32p. (J). lib. bdg. 15.89 *(978-1-59990-963-9(4)*, 9781599909639); (gr. -1-k). 16.99 *(978-1-59990-962-2(6)*, 9781599909622) Bloomsbury Publishing USA. (Bloomsbury USA Childrens).

Stein, Peter. Toys Galore. Staake, Bob, illus. 2013. (ENG.). 32p. (J). (gr. -1-3). 15.99 *(978-0-7636-6254-7(2))* Candlewick Pr.

Stine, R. L. Night of the Giant Everything. 2011. (Goosebumps Hall of Horrors Ser.: 2). (ENG.). 160p. (J). (gr. 3-7). pap. 6.99 *(978-0-545-28935-1(1)*, Scholastic Paperbacks) Scholastic, Inc.

Stinson, Kathy. Big or Little? Bell, Jennifer & Goffe, Toni, illus. 2nd ed. 2014. (ENG.). 24p. (J). (gr. -1 — 1). bds. 6.95 *(978-1-55451-610-0(2)*, 9781554516100) Annick Pr., Ltd. CAN. Dist: Publishers Group West (PGW).

—Big or Little? Goffe, Toni, illus. 2nd rev. ed. 2009. (ENG.). 32p. (J). (gr. -1-1). 19.95 *(978-1-55451-169-3(0)*, 9781554511693) Annick Pr., Ltd. CAN. Dist: Publishers Group West (PGW).

—Big or Little? Goffe, Toni & Bell, Jennifer A., illus. 2nd rev. ed. 2009. (ENG.). 32p. (J). (gr. -1-1). pap. 6.95 *(978-1-55451-168-6(2)*, 9781554511686) Annick Pr., Ltd. CAN. Dist: Publishers Group West (PGW).

Streich, Michel. Grumpy Little King. Streich, Michel, illus. 2012. (ENG., Illus.). 32p. (J). (gr. k-3). 19.99 *(978-1-74237-572-4(3))* Allen & Unwin AUS. Dist: Independent Pubs. Group.

Studio Mouse Staff. Sesame Street Colors & Shapes. 2008. (ENG.). 36p. (J). (gr. -1). 12.99 *(978-1-59069-741-2(3))* Studio Mouse LLC.

Sundberg, Norma J. An Odd Fable. Leiper, Esther M., illus. 2007. 32p. (J). pap. 13.95 *(978-0-9776958-5-0(9))* CyPress Pubns.

Tagel, Peggy, illus. Animal Safari. 2003. (Squishy Shapes Ser.). 10p. (J). 12.95 *(978-1-57145-741-7(0)*, Silver Dolphin Bks.) Readerlink Distribution Services, LLC.

—Dinosaurs. 2003. (Squishy Shapes Ser.). 10p. (J). 12.95 *(978-1-57145-740-0(2)*, Silver Dolphin Bks.) Readerlink Distribution Services, LLC.

ten Cate, Marijke. Who Has the Biggest Bottom. 2013. (ENG., Illus.). 32p. (J). (gr. -1). 17.95 *(978-1-935954-25-5(3)*, 9781935954255) Lemniscaat USA.

Thompson, Lauren. Little Chick. Butler, John, illus. 2014. (ENG.). 30p. (J). (gr. -1-k). bds. 5.99 *(978-1-4424-9311-7(9)*, Little Simon) Little Simon.

—Little Chick. Butler, John, illus. 2014. (J). *(978-1-4351-5351-6(0)*, Simon & Schuster Bks. For Young Readers) Simon & Schuster Bks. For Young Readers.

—Wee Little Chick. Butler, John, illus. 2008. (Wee Little Ser.). (ENG.). 32p. (J). (gr. -1-1). 15.99 *(978-1-4169-3468-4(5)*, Simon & Schuster Bks. For Young Readers) Simon & Schuster Bks. For Young Readers.

Thong, Roseanne Greenfield. Round Is a Mooncake: A Book of Shapes. 2014. (Multicultural Shapes & Colors Ser.). (Illus.). 40p. (J). lib. bdg. 28.50 *(978-1-60753-564-5(5))* Amicus Publishing.

—Round Is a Tortilla. Parra, John, illus. 2015. (ENG.). 40p. (J). (gr. -1-k). 7.99 *(978-1-4521-4568-6(7))* Chronicle Bks. LLC.

—Round Is a Tortilla: A Book of Shapes. 2014. (Multicultural Shapes & Colors Ser.). (Illus.). 40p. (J). lib. bdg. 28.50 *(978-1-60753-566-9(1))* Amicus Publishing.

Top That! Playtime Shapes (large Version) Parry, Jo, illus. 2007. 10p. (J). (gr. -1). *(978-1-84666-555-4(8)*, Tide Mill Pr.) Top That! Publishing PLC.

Townsend, Stephanie Z. Not Too Small at All: A Mouse Tale. Looney, Bill, illus. 2008. 30p. (J). (gr. -1). 13.99 *(978-0-89051-524-2(7))* Master Bks.

Tuxworth, Nicola. Shapes. 2015. (ENG., Illus.). 20p. bds. 6.99 *(978-1-86147-648-7(5),* Armadillo) Anness Publishing GBR. Dist: National Bk. Network.

Van Fleet, Matthew. Tails. 2017. (ENG., Illus.). 20p. (J). (— 1). 14.99 ***(978-1-328-88685-9(9)***, HMH Books For Young Readers) Houghton Mifflin Harcourt Publishing Co.

Vere, Ed. Everyone's Little. 2003. (ENG., Illus.). 12p. (J). bds. 6.95 *(978-0-333-78039-8(6))* Macmillan Pubs., Ltd. GBR. Dist: Trafalgar Square Publishing.

Viswanath, Shobha. When the Earth Lost Its Shapes. Kastl, Christine, illus. 2013. (ENG.). 36p. (J). (gr. -1). pap. 9.95 *(978-81-8190-192-7(4))* Karadi Tales Co. Pvt, Ltd. IND. Dist: Consortium Bk. Sales & Distribution.

Wallace, Rich. Fast Company. 3rd ed. 2005. (Winning Season Ser.: Bk. 3). (ENG.). 128p. (J). (gr. 3-7). 5.99 *(978-0-14-240468-3(3),* Puffin Books) Penguin Young Readers Group.

Weiland, Peter. So Big yet So Small. Coffey, Kevin, illus. 2012. (J). 14.95 *(978-1-937406-16-5(4))* Mascot Bks., Inc.

Weinberg, Steven. You Must Be This Tall. Weinberg, Steven, illus. 2016. (ENG., Illus.). 40p. (J). (gr. -1-3). 17.99 *(978-1-4814-2981-8(7),* McElderry, Margaret K. Bks.) McElderry, Margaret K. Bks.

Weston Woods Staff, creator. The Caterpillar & the Polliwog. 2011. 18.95 *(978-0-439-73152-2(6));* 38.75 *(978-0-439-73154-6(2))* Weston Woods Studios, Inc.

Wiede, Matt, illus. Star, Circle, Baylor: A Little Bear Shapes Book, 5460 vols. 2013. (Big Bear Bks.). (ENG.). 18p. (gr. 17). bds. 9.95 *(978-1-60258-979-7(8))* Baylor Univ. Pr.

Willis, Jeanne. Cottonball Colin. Ross, Tony, illus. 2008. 26p. (J). (gr. -1-4). 16.00 *(978-0-8028-5331-8(5),* Eerdmans Bks For Young Readers) Eerdmans, William B. Publishing Co.

Wilson, Barbara E. Small Enough Tall Enough. Gospodinov, George, illus. 2012. 46p. pap. 14.95 *(978-0-9838964-0-1(2))* Simply Silly Stories.

Wilson, Zachary. A Circle in the Sky. Adinolfi, JoAnn, illus. (Rookie Ready to Learn Ser.). (J). 2011. (ENG.). 40p. pap. 5.95 *(978-0-531-26746-2(6))* 2011. 40p. (gr. -1-k). lib. bdg. 23.00 *(978-0-531-26446-1(7))* 2006. (ENG.). 32p. (gr. k-2). lib. bdg. 19.50 *(978-0-531-12570-0(X))* Scholastic Library Publishing. (Children's Pr.).

—Un Circulo en el Cielo. Adinolfi, JoAnn, illus. 2011. (Rookie Ready to Learn Español Ser.). (SPA.). 40p. (J). pap. 5.95 *(978-0-531-26791-2(1),* Children's Pr.) Scholastic Library Publishing.

Wilson, Zachary & Adinolfi, JoAnn. Un Circulo en el Cielo. Adinolfi, JoAnn, illus. 2011. (Rookie Ready to Learn Español Ser.). (SPA., Illus.). 40p. (J). lib. bdg. 23.00 *(978-0-531-26123-1(9),* Children's Pr.) Scholastic Library Publishing.

Winters, Kay. The Teeny Tiny Ghost & the Monster, Vol. 3. Munsinger, Lynn, illus. 2004. (ENG.). 32p. (J). (gr. -1-3). 14.99 *(978-0-06-028884-6(1))* HarperCollins Pubs.

Wynne-Jones, Tim. I'll Make You Small. (J). pap. 4.95 *(978-0-88899-105-8(3));* pap. 15.95 *(978-0-88899-045-7(6))* Groundwood Bks. CAN. Dist: Publishers Group West (PGW).

Yates, Gene. What Can Simon Be? 2005. (Illus.). (J). *(978-1-58865-284-3(X))* Kidsbooks, LLC.

Yates, Gene & Frank, Thomas. What Can Simon Be? Yates, Gene, illus. 2006. (Illus.). (J). *(978-1-58865-366-6(8))* Kidsbooks, LLC.

YoYo. Forms, Colors, & Opposites. 2005. 40p. bds. *(978-90-5843-888-1(0))* YoYo Bks.

SKATEBOARDING

Adamson, Thomas K. Big Air Skateboarding. 2015. (Extreme Sports Ser.). (ENG., Illus.). 24p. (J). (gr. 3-7). lib. bdg. 25.95 *(978-1-62617-272-2(2),* Epic Bks.) Bellwether Media.

—Skateboarding Street Style. 2015. (Extreme Sports Ser.). (ENG., Illus.). 24p. (J). (gr. 3-7). lib. bdg. 25.95 *(978-1-62617-277-7(3),* Epic Bks.) Bellwether Media.

Arcy, Sean & Marshall, Phillip. Freestyle Skateboarding Tricks: Flat Ground, Rails, Transitions. 2010. (ENG., Illus.). 128p. pap. 14.95 *(978-1-55407-666-6(8),* 9781554076666) Firefly Bks., Ltd.

Beal, Becky. Skateboarding: The Ultimate Guide, 1 vol. 2013. (Greenwood Guides to Extreme Sports Ser.). (Illus.). 150p. (C). 37.00 *(978-0-313-38112-6(7),* A2257C, Greenwood) ABC-CLIO, LLC.

Becker, Helaine. Skateboarding Science. 2008. (Sports Science Ser.). (ENG., Illus.). 32p. (J). (gr. 4-6). pap. *(978-0-7787-4553-2(8));* lib. bdg. *(978-0-7787-4536-5(8))* Crabtree Publishing Co.

Blaine, Victor. Mi Monopatín / My Skateboard, 1 vol. 2015. (¡Mírame, Ahí Voy! / Watch Me Go! Ser.). (ENG & SPA., Illus.). 24p. (J). 23.60 *(978-1-4994-0278-0(3),* 1384311, PowerKids Pr.) Rosen Publishing Group, Inc., The.

—Mis Patines de Ruedas / My Skates, 1 vol. 2015. (¡Mírame, Ahí Voy! / Watch Me Go! Ser.). (ENG & SPA.). 24p. (J). 23.60 *(978-1-4994-0280-3(5),* PowerKids Pr.) Rosen Publishing Group, Inc., The.

—My Ripstik, 1 vol. 2015. (ENG., Illus.). 24p. (J). lib. bdg. 23.60 *(978-1-4994-0251-3(1),* PowerKids Pr.) Rosen Publishing Group, Inc., The.

—My Skateboard, 1 vol. 2015. (ENG., Illus.). 24p. (J). lib. bdg. 23.60 *(978-1-4994-0252-0(X),* PowerKids Pr.) Rosen Publishing Group, Inc., The.

Blomquist, Christopher. Skateboarding in the X Games. 2009. (Kid's Guide to the X Games Ser.). 24p. (gr. 3-3). 42.50 *(978-1-61511-210-4(3),* PowerKids Pr.) Rosen Publishing Group, Inc., The.

Bloomquist, Christopher. Skateboarding in the X Games. 2003. (Kid's Guide to the X Games Ser.). (Illus.). 24p. (J). lib. bdg. 22.60 *(978-0-8239-6300-3(4),* PowerKids Pr.) Rosen Publishing Group, Inc., The.

Bowman, Chris. Vert Skateboarding. 2016. (Extreme Sports Ser.). (ENG., Illus.). 24p. (J). (gr. 3-7). lib. bdg. 25.95 *(978-1-62617-354-5(0),* Epic Bks.) Bellwether Media.

Bradley, Michael. Tony Hawk. 2004. (Illus.). 48p. (J). 31.36 *(978-0-7614-1759-0(1),* Benchmark Bks.) Marshall Cavendish Corp.

Braun, Eric. Tony Hawk. (Amazing Athletes Ser.). (Illus.). 32p. 2004. (J). (gr. 3-4). lib. bdg. 23.93 *(978-0-8225-1367-4(6))* 2003. (ENG., (gr. 2-5). pap. 7.95 *(978-0-8225-3686-4(2))* Lerner Publishing Group.

Bussiere, Desireé. Skateboarding by the Numbers, 1 vol. 2013. (Sports by the Numbers Ser.). (ENG.). 24p. (J). (gr. k-3). lib. bdg. 24.21 *(978-1-61783-845-3(4),* SandCastle) ABDO Publishing Co.

Cain, Patrick G. Skateboarding Street. 2013. (Extreme Summer Sports Zone Ser.). (ENG., Illus.). 32p. (gr. 4-8). pap. 8.95 *(978-1-4677-1084-8(9));* lib. bdg. 26.60 *(978-1-4677-0749-7(X),* Lerner Pubns.) Lerner Publishing Group.

—Skateboarding Vert. 2013. (Extreme Summer Sports Zone Ser.). (ENG., Illus.). 32p. (gr. 4-8). pap. 8.95 *(978-1-4677-1085-5(7));* lib. bdg. 26.60 *(978-1-4677-0748-0(1),* Lerner Pubns.) Lerner Publishing Group.

Carr, Aaron. Skateboard. 2013. (ENG & SPA.). (J). *(978-1-62127-631-9(7))* Weigl Pubs., Inc.

—Skateboarding. (Illus.). 24p. (J). 2013. *(978-1-61913-512-3(4),* 1345813) 2012. (ENG., pap. 12.95 *(978-1-61913-518-5(3),* AV2 by Weigl) Weigl Pubs., Inc.

Casil, Amy Sterling. Tony Hawk: Skateboard Mogul. 2009. (Super Skateboarding Ser.). (Illus.). 48p. (J). (gr. 5-8). pap. 11.75 *(978-1-4358-5391-1(1));* (YA). (gr. 4-7). lib. bdg. 29.25 *(978-1-4358-5047-7(5))* Rosen Publishing Group, Inc., The.

Castellano, Peter. Longboard Skateboarding. 2015. (Daredevil Sports Ser.). (ENG., Illus.). 32p. (J). (gr. 1-1). pap. 10.50 *(978-1-4824-2972-5(1));* lib. bdg. 25.25 *(978-1-4824-2978-7(0))* Stevens, Gareth Publishing LLLP.

Cefrey, Holly. Competitive Skateboarding. 2009. (Super Skateboarding Ser.). 48p. (gr. 5-8). 53.00 *(978-1-60853-207-0(0),* Rosen Reference); (Illus.). (YA). (gr. 4-7). lib. bdg. 29.25 *(978-1-4358-5050-7(5))* Rosen Publishing Group, Inc., The.

Cobb, Allan B. Skating the X-Games. 2009. (Super Skateboarding Ser.). (Illus.). 48p. (J). (gr. 5-8). pap. 11.75 *(978-1-4358-5392-8(X));* (YA). (gr. 4-7). lib. bdg. 29.25 *(978-1-4358-5048-4(3))* Rosen Publishing Group, Inc., The.

—Skating the X Games. 2009. (Super Skateboarding Ser.). 48p. (gr. 5-8). 53.00 *(978-1-60853-213-1(5),* Rosen Reference) Rosen Publishing Group, Inc., The.

Craats, Rennay. Skateboarding. (J). 2013. 27.13 *(978-1-62127-319-6(9))* 2013. pap. 12.95 *(978-1-62127-324-0(5))* 2009. 24p. (gr. 3-5). pap. 8.95 *(978-1-60596-121-7(3))* 2009. (Illus.). 24p. (gr. 3-5). lib. bdg. 24.45 *(978-1-60596-120-0(5))* Weigl Pubs., Inc.

Crabtree Editors & Winters, Jaime. Shred It Skateboarding. 2012. (Sports Starters Ser.). (ENG., Illus.). 32p. (J). (gr. 1-4). lib. bdg. *(978-0-7787-3151-1(0))* Crabtree Publishing Co.

Crossingham, John. Extreme Skateboarding. 2003. (Extreme Sports - No Limits Ser.). (ENG., Illus.). 32p. (J). (gr. 3). pap. *(978-0-7787-1714-0(3))* Crabtree Publishing Co.

—Patinetas en Acción. 2005. (Deportes en Acción Ser.). (SPA., Illus.). 32p. (J). lib. bdg. *(978-0-7787-8574-3(2))* Crabtree Publishing Co.

Donovan, Sandy. Cool Skateboarding Facts, 1 vol. (Cool Sports Facts Ser.). (ENG., 24p. (gr. k-1). 2011. Illus.). pap. 7.29 *(978-1-4296-6203-1(4))* 2011. pap. 41.70 *(978-1-4296-6374-8(X))* 2010. lib. bdg. 26.65 *(978-1-4296-5303-9(5))* Capstone Press of Coughlan Cos. (Pebble Plus).

Enz, Tammy. Engineering a Totally Rad Skateboard with Max Axiom, Super Scientist, 1 vol. Pop Art Studios, illus. 2013. (Graphic Science & Engineering in Action Ser.). (ENG.). 32p. (gr. 3-4). pap. 8.10 *(978-1-62065-703-4(1),* Graphic Library) Capstone Press of Coughlan Cos.

—Engineering a Totally Rad Skateboard with Max Axiom, Super Scientist, 1 vol. Pop Art Studios Staff, illus. 2013. (Graphic Science & Engineering in Action Ser.). (ENG.). 32p. (gr. 3-4). lib. bdg. 30.65 *(978-1-4296-9935-8(3),* Graphic Library) Capstone Press of Coughlan Cos.

Fandel, Jennifer. Skateboarding. 2007. (Active Sports Ser.). (Illus.). 24p. (J). (gr. -1-3). lib. bdg. 24.25 *(978-1-58341-469-9(X),* Creative Education) Creative Co., The.

Fitzpatrick, Jim. Skateboarding. 2008. (21st Century Skills Innovation Library: Innovation in Sports Ser.). (ENG., Illus.). 32p. (gr. 4-8). lib. bdg. 28.50 *(978-1-60279-259-3(3),* 200033) Cherry Lake Publishing.

Fredrikson, Magnus. Skateboarding Coloring Book. 2011. (ENG., Illus.). 64p. mass mkt. 9.95 *(978-91-85639-45-8(1))* Dokument forlag, Fotograf Malcolm Jacobsson SWE. Dist: SCB Distributors.

Gifford, Clive & Dorling Kindersley Publishing Staff. Skateboarding. 2006. (ENG., Illus.). 64p. (J). (gr. 5-12). pap. 9.99 *(978-0-7566-2074-5(0),* DK Children) Dorling Kindersley Publishing, Inc.

Greathouse, Lisa. Bicicletas y Tablas, 1 vol. rev. ed. 2010. (Science Readers: a Closer Look Ser.). (SPA., Illus.). 32p. (J). (gr. 2-3). pap. 8.99 *(978-1-4333-2146-7(7))* Shell Educational Publishing.

Greene, Edgar. Tony Hawk. 2003. (Sports Heroes & Legends Ser.). (Illus.). 103p. (J). *(978-0-7607-3216-8(7))* Barnes & Noble, Inc.

Hamilton, John. Skateboarding. 2014. (Action Sports Ser.). (ENG., Illus.). 32p. (gr. 8-15). lib. bdg. 27.07 *(978-1-62403-443-5(8),* A&D Xtreme) ABDO Publishing Co.

Hocing, Justin. Skateboard Design & Construction: How Your Board Gets Built. 2009. (Power Skateboarding Ser.). 24p. (gr. 3-4). 42.50 *(978-1-60851-339-0(4),* PowerKids Pr.) Rosen Publishing Group, Inc., The.

Hocking, Justin. Dream Builders: The World's Best Skate Park Creators. 2009. (Skateboarder's Guide to Skate Parks, Half-Pipes, Bowls, & Obstacles Ser.). 48p. (gr. 5-8). 53.00 *(978-1-60854-229-1(7),* Rosen Reference) Rosen Publishing Group, Inc., The.

—Off the Wall: A Skateboarder's Guide to Riding Bowls & Pools. (Skateboarder's Guide to Skate Parks, Half-Pipes, Bowls, & Obstacles Ser.). 48p. 2009. (gr. 5-8). 53.00 *(978-1-60854-230-7(0),* Rosen Reference) 2004. (Illus.). (J). lib. bdg. 29.25 *(978-1-4042-0339-6(7))* Rosen Publishing Group, Inc., The.

—Rippin' Ramps: A Skateboarder's Guide to Riding Half-Pipes. 2009. (Skateboarder's Guide to Skate Parks, Half-Pipes, Bowls, & Obstacles Ser.). 48p. (gr. 5-8). 53.00 *(978-1-60854-231-4(9),* Rosen Reference) Rosen Publishing Group, Inc., The.

—Rippin' Ramps: A Skateboarder's Guide to Riding Halfpipes. 2004. (World of Skateboard Parks Ser.). (Illus.). 48p. (J). lib. bdg. 26.50 *(978-1-4042-0340-2(0))* Rosen Publishing Group, Inc., The.

—Skate Parks. 2006. (Power Skateboarding Ser.). (Illus.). 24p. (J). (gr. 3-7). lib. bdg. 22.60 *(978-1-4042-3047-7(5),* PowerKids Pr.) Rosen Publishing Group, Inc., The.

—Skateboarding Competitions. 2006. (Power Skateboarding Ser.). (Illus.). 24p. lib. bdg. 22.60 *(978-1-4042-3052-1(1),* PowerKids Pr.) Rosen Publishing Group, Inc., The.

—Skateboarding Design & Construction: How Your Board Gets Built. 2006. (Power Skateboarding Ser.). (Illus.). 24p. (J). (gr. 3-7). lib. bdg. 22.60 *(978-1-4042-3048-4(3),* PowerKids Pr.) Rosen Publishing Group, Inc., The.

—Skateboarding Half-Pipes, Ramps, & Obstacles. 2006. (Power Skateboarding Ser.). (Illus.). 24p. lib. bdg. 22.60 *(978-1-4042-3051-4(3),* PowerKids Pr.) Rosen Publishing Group, Inc., The.

—Skateboarding Half-pipes, Ramps, & Obstacles. 2009. (Power Skateboarding Ser.). 24p. (gr. 3-4). 42.50 *(978-1-60851-341-3(6),* PowerKids Pr.) Rosen Publishing Group, Inc., The.

—Taking Action: How to Get Your City to Build a Public Skatepark. 2004. (Skateboarder's Guide to Skate Parks, Half-Pipes, Bowls, & Obstacles Ser.). (Illus.). 48p. (J). lib. bdg. 29.25 *(978-1-4042-0341-9(9))* Rosen Publishing Group, Inc., The.

—The World's Greatest Skate Parks. 2009. (Super Skateboarding Ser.). 48p. (Illus.). (J). (gr. 5-8). pap. 11.75 *(978-1-4358-5390-4(3));* (YA). (gr. 4-7). lib. bdg. 29.25 *(978-1-4358-5046-0(7))* Rosen Publishing Group, Inc., The.

Hocking, Justin & Michalski, Peter. Riding Bowls & Pools. 2016. (Skateboarding Tips & Tricks Ser.). 48p. (J). (gr. 5-5). pap. 11.75 *(978-1-4777-8866-0(2),* Rosen Reference) Rosen Publishing Group, Inc., The.

—Riding Half-Pipes. 2016. (Skateboarding Tips & Tricks Ser.). 48p. (J). (gr. 5-5). pap. 11.75 *(978-1-4777-8878-3(6),* Rosen Reference) Rosen Publishing Group, Inc., The.

Holden, Pam. Let's Go Riding. 2015. (ENG., Illus.). 16p. (-1). pap. *(978-1-77654-114-0(6),* Red Rocket Readers) Flying Start Bks.

Horsley, Andrew. How to Improve at Skateboarding. 2009. (How to Improve at... Ser.). (ENG., Illus.). 48p. (J). (gr. 4-8). lib. bdg. *(978-0-7787-3575-5(3))* Crabtree Publishing Co.

Horsley, Andy. Skateboarding. 2008. (ENG., Illus.). 32p. (J). (gr. 5-9). lib. bdg. *(978-0-7787-3771-1(3))* Crabtree Publishing Co.

—Skateboarding. 2012. (To the Limit Ser.). (ENG., Illus.). 32p. (J). (gr. 5-8). pap. 10.00 *(978-1-4488-7068-4(2));* lib. bdg. 25.25 *(978-1-4488-7029-5(1))* Rosen Publishing Group, Inc., The. (PowerKids Pr.).

Junor, Amy. Skate! Level 4. 2008. (DK Readers Ser.). (ENG., Illus.). 48p. (J). (gr. 3-7). pap. 3.99 *(978-0-7566-3829-0(1),* DK Children) Dorling Kindersley Publishing, Inc.

Kamberg, Mary-Lane. Longboarding. 2016. (Skateboarding Tips & Tricks Ser.). 48p. (J). (gr. 5-5). pap. 11.75 *(978-1-4777-8863-9(8),* Rosen Reference) Rosen Publishing Group, Inc., The.

Kelley, K. C. Skateboard Stars. 2007. (Reading Rocks! Ser.). (ENG., Illus.). 32p. (J). (gr. 2-5). 28.50 *(978-1-59296-861-9(9),* 200750) Child's World, Inc., The.

—Skateboarding. 2003. (Extreme Sports Ser.). (Illus.). 24p. (gr. 2-5). lib. bdg. 23.00 *(978-0-8368-3724-7(X),* Gareth Stevens Learning Library) Stevens, Gareth Publishing LLLP.

Kennedy, Mike. Tony Hawk. 2009. (People We Should Know Ser.). 48p. (J). (gr. 3-5). pap. 10.50 *(978-1-4339-2191-9(X));* lib. bdg. 31.00 *(978-1-4339-1952-7(4))* Stevens, Gareth Publishing LLLP. (Gareth Stevens Learning Library).

Kjelle, Marylou Morano. Extreme Skateboarding with Paul Rodriquez JR. 2006. (Extreme Sports Ser.). (Illus.). 32p. (J). (gr. 1-4). lib. bdg. 25.70 *(978-1-58415-489-1(6))* Mitchell Lane Pubs., Inc.

Knutson, Jeff. The Business of Skateboarding: From Board to Boardroom. 2009. (Super Skateboarding Ser.). (Illus.). 48p. (J). (gr. 5-8). pap. 11.75 *(978-1-4358-5394-2(6));* (YA). (gr. 5-8). pap. 11.75 *(978-1-4358-5395-9(4),* Rosen Reference); (YA). (gr. 4-7). lib. bdg. 29.25 *(978-1-4358-5051-4(3))* Rosen Publishing Group, Inc., The.

Knutson, Jeffrey. The Business of Skateboarding: From Board to Boardroom. 2009. (Super Skateboarding Ser.). 48p. (gr. 5-8). 53.00 *(978-1-60853-216-2(X),* Rosen Reference) Rosen Publishing Group, Inc., The.

Labrecque, Ellen. Cool Board Tricks, 1 vol. 2013. (Try This at Home! Ser.). (ENG., Illus.). 32p. (gr. 1-2). pap. 8.29 *(978-1-4109-5009-3(3));* lib. bdg. 29.99 *(978-1-4109-5002-4(6))* Heinemann-Raintree. (Read Me!).

Lakin, Patricia. Skateboards. 2017. (Made by Hand Ser.: 1). (ENG., Illus.). 32p. (J). (gr. 3-7). 17.99 *(978-1-4814-4833-8(1),* Simon & Schuster/Paula Wiseman Bks.) Simon & Schuster/Paula Wiseman Bks.

Loh-Hagan, Virginia. Extreme Ice Cross Downhill. 2016. (Illus.). 32p. (J). *(978-1-63470-486-1(X))* Cherry Lake Publishing.

—Extreme Skateboarding. 2015. (Illus.). 32p. (J). *(978-1-63470-015-3(5))* Cherry Lake Publishing.

Lovitt, Chip. Skate Parks: On a Roll! 2003. (ENG., Illus.). 32p. (J). (gr. 6-8). pap. 7.97 net. *(978-0-7652-3274-8(X),* Celebration Pr.) Pearson Schl.

Lucent Books, ed. Skateboarding. 2014. (Science Behind Sports Ser.). (ENG.). 112p. (gr. 7-10). lib. bdg. 37.45 *(978-1-4205-1211-3(0),* Lucent Bks.) Cengage Gale.

MacDonald, Margaret. Scooters & Skates. 2011. (Learn-Abouts Ser.). (Illus.). 16p. (J). pap. 7.95 *(978-1-59920-650-9(1))* Black Rabbit Bks.

Mahaney, Ian. Tony Hawk: Skateboarding Champ. 2005. (Extreme Sports Biographies Ser.). (Illus.). 24p. (J). 22.60 *(978-1-4042-2747-7(4),* PowerKids Pr.) Rosen Publishing Group, Inc., The.

Mahaney, Ian F. Tony Hawk: Skateboarding Champion. 2009. (Extreme Sports Biographies Ser.). 24p. (gr. 3-4). 42.50 *(978-1-61512-472-5(1),* PowerKids Pr.) Rosen Publishing Group, Inc., The.

Marsh, James. Super.Activ Skateboarding. (Illus.). 128p. (YA). pap. 8.99 *(978-0-340-79160-8(8))* Hodder & Stoughton GBR. Dist: Trafalgar Square Publishing.

McClellan, Ray. Skateboarding. 2010. (My First Sports Ser.). (ENG., Illus.). 24p. (J). (gr. 2-5). lib. bdg. 25.95 *(978-1-60014-462-2(4),* Blastoff! Readers) Bellwether Media.

Michalski, Peter & Hocking, Justin. Riding Street Courses. 2016. (Skateboarding Tips & Tricks Ser.). 48p. (J). (gr. 5-5). pap. 11.75 *(978-1-4777-8874-5(3),* Rosen Reference) Rosen Publishing Group, Inc., The.

Miller, Raymond H. Tony Hawk. 2004. (Stars of Sport Ser.). (ENG., Illus.). 48p. (J). 27.50 *(978-0-7377-1568-2(5),* Greenhaven Pr., Inc.) Cengage Gale.

Murdico, Suzanne J. Street Luge & Dirtboarding. (World of Skateboarding Ser.). 48p. (gr. 5-8). 2009. 53.00 *(978-1-60854-316-8(1),* Rosen Reference) 2005. (Illus.). (YA). lib. bdg. 29.25 *(978-0-8239-3647-2(3))* Rosen Publishing Group, Inc., The.

Murdico, Suzanne J. & Michalski, Peter. Street Luge & Dirtboarding. 2016. (Skateboarding Tips & Tricks Ser.). 48p. (J). (gr. 5-5). pap. 11.75 *(978-1-4777-8870-7(0),* Rosen Reference) Rosen Publishing Group, Inc., The.

Nixon, James. Skateboarding Champion. 2016. (How to Be a Champion Ser.). (ENG., Illus.). 32p. (J). (gr. 4-6). 17.99 *(978-1-4451-3620-2(1),* Franklin Watts) Hachette Children's Group GBR. Dist: Hachette Bk. Group.

Noll, Rhyn. Skateboarding: Past — Present — Future, 1 vol. 2003. (ENG., Illus.). 192p. (gr. 10-13). pap. 29.95 *(978-0-7643-1845-0(4),* 9780764318450) Schiffer Publishing, Ltd.

Otfinoski, Steven. Extreme Skateboarding. 2013. (Sports on the Edge 2 Ser.). 48p. (J). (gr. 4-8). pap. 12.93 *(978-1-62712-131-6(5));* (Illus.). 29.93 *(978-1-60870-221-3(9))* Cavendish Square Publishing.

Perez, Marlene. Skateboarding. 2004. (Shared Connections Ser.). (J). pap. *(978-1-4108-1636-8(2));* pap., instr.'s gde. ed. 27.00 *(978-1-4108-1612-2(5))* Benchmark Education Co.

Polydoros, Lori. Awesome Skateboard Tricks & Stunts, 1 vol. 2010. (Big Air Ser.). (ENG.). 32p. (gr. 1-2). lib. bdg. 26.65 *(978-1-4296-5409-8(0),* Blazers) Capstone Press of Coughlan Cos.

—Big Air, 4 vols., Set. Incl. Awesome Skateboard Tricks & Stunts. lib. bdg. 26.65 *(978-1-4296-5409-8(0));* Awesome Snowboard Tricks & Stunts. lib. bdg. 26.65 *(978-1-4296-5412-8(0));* (gr. 1-2). (Big Air Ser.). (ENG.). 32p. 2010. Set lib. bdg. 79.95 *(978-1-4296-5413-5(9),* Blazers) Capstone Press of Coughlan Cos.

Powell, Ben. Skateboarding. 2003. (Extreme Sports Ser.). (ENG., Illus.). 32p. (gr. 3-6). lib. bdg. 22.60 *(978-0-8225-1241-7(6))* Lerner Publishing Group.

Rajczak, Kristen. Skateboarding. 2015. (Sports to the Extreme Ser.). (ENG., Illus.). 48p. (J). (gr. 5-6). 30.25 *(978-1-4994-3569-6(X),* Rosen Central) Rosen Publishing Group, Inc., The.

Rosenberg, Aaron & Michalski, Peter. Advanced Skateboarding. 2016. (Skateboarding Tips & Tricks Ser.). 48p. (J). (gr. 5-5). pap. 11.75 *(978-1-4777-8859-2(X),* Rosen Reference) Rosen Publishing Group, Inc., The.

Sandler, Michael. Gnarly Skateboarders. 2009. (X-Moves Ser.). (Illus.). 24p. (J). (gr. 2-5). lib. bdg. 22.61 *(978-1-59716-950-9(1))* Bearport Publishing Co., Inc.

Segovia, Patty. Skate Girls. 2006. (Reading Rocks! Ser.). (ENG., Illus.). 32p. (J). (gr. 2-5). 28.50 *(978-1-59296-748-3(5),* 200734) Child's World, Inc., The.

—Skate Girls. 2016. (Illus.). 32p. (J). *(978-1-4896-4783-2(X))* Weigl Pubs., Inc.

Segovia, Patty & Meredith Books Staff. On the Edge Skateboarding/on the Edge Snowboarding: Tips & Tricks from Six of the Coolest Skateboarders/Tips & Tricks from Six of the Coolest Snowboarders. 2008. (On the Edge Ser.). (Illus.). 48p. (YA). (gr. 8-12). per. 6.99 *(978-0-696-23980-9(9))* Meredith Bks.

Sheen, Barbara. Tony Hawk. 2007. (People in the News Ser.). (ENG., Illus.). 104p. (YA). (gr. 7-12). lib. bdg. 33.95 *(978-1-4205-0016-5(3))* Cengage Gale.

Skateboarding Tips & Tricks. 2016. (Skateboarding Tips & Tricks Ser.). 48p. (gr. 5-5). 190.50 *(978-1-4994-3840-6(0));* pap. 70.50 *(978-1-4777-8984-1(7))* Rosen Publishing Group, Inc., The. (Rosen Central).

Smith, Terri Smith. Tony Hawk: Flying High. 2003. (J). pap. *(978-1-932724-01-1(X),* Bios for Kids) Panda Publishing, L.L.C.

Sohn, Emily. Skateboarding: How It Works. 2010. (Science of Sports (Sports Illustrated for Kids) Ser.). (ENG.). 48p. (gr. 3-4). pap. 59.70 *(978-1-4296-5110-3(5))* Capstone Press of Coughlan Cos.

Sterling Casil, Amy. Tony Hawk: Skateboard Mogul. 2009. (Super Skateboarding Ser.). 48p. (gr. 5-8). 53.00 *(978-1-60853-219-3(4),* Rosen Reference) Rosen Publishing Group, Inc., The.

Stewart, Mark. One Wild Ride: The Life of Skateboarding Superstar Tony Hawk. 2003. (Illus.). 64p. (gr. 6-18). pap. 9.95 *(978-0-7613-1689-3(2),* Twenty-First Century Bks.) Lerner Publishing Group.

Streissguth, Thomas. Skateboard Vert. 2008. (Action Sports Ser.). (ENG., Illus.). 24p. (J). (gr. 3-7). lib. bdg. 25.95 *(978-1-60014-141-6(2))* Bellwether Media.

—Skateboarding Street Style. 2008. (Action Sports Ser.). (ENG., Illus.). 24p. (J). (gr. 3-7). lib. bdg. 25.95 *(978-1-60014-142-3(0))* Bellwether Media.

Super Skateboarding, 6 vols., Set. Incl. Business of Skateboarding: From Board to Boardroom. Knutson, Jeff. (Illus.). lib. bdg. 29.25 *(978-1-4358-5051-4(3));* Competitive Skateboarding. Cefrey, Holly. (Illus.). lib. bdg. 29.25 *(978-1-4358-5050-7(5));* Skateboarding Today & Tomorrow. Hasan, Heather. (Illus.). lib. bdg. 29.25 *(978-1-4358-5049-1(1));* Skating the X-Games. Cobb, Allan B. (Illus.). lib. bdg. 29.25 *(978-1-4358-5048-4(3));* Tony Hawk: Skateboard Mogul. Casil, Amy Sterling. (Illus.). lib. bdg. 29.25 *(978-1-4358-5047-7(5));* World's Greatest Skate Parks. Hocking, Justin. lib. bdg. 29.25 *(978-1-4358-5046-0(7));* 48p. (YA). (gr. 4-7). 2009. Set lib. bdg. 159.00 *(978-1-4358-5216-7(8))* Rosen Publishing Group, Inc., The.

Teller, Jackson. Skateboarding. 2012. (Adrenaline Rush Ser.). (Illus.). 32p. (gr. 4-7). lib. bdg. 31.35 *(978-1-59920-685-1(4))* Black Rabbit Bks.

Tieck, Sarah. Skateboarding, 1 vol. 2013. (Move Your Body Ser.). (ENG.). 32p. (J). (gr. 2-5). 27.07 *(978-1-61783-563-6(3))* ABDO Publishing Co.

Weber, Terri Smith. Tony Hawk: Flying High. 2003. (J). lib. bdg. *(978-1-932724-00-4(1),* Bios for Kids) Panda Publishing, L.L.C.

Weigl Publishers Staff & Craats, Rennay. For the Love of Skateboarding. Nault, Jennifer & Turner, Kara, eds. 2003. (For the Love of Sports Ser.). (Illus.). 24p. (J). pap. 8.95 *(978-1-59036-070-5(2))* Weigl Pubs., Inc.

Willet, Edward. Skateboarding: Techniques & Tricks. 2009. (Rad Sports: Techniques & Tricks Ser.). 48p. (gr. 5-8). 53.00 *(978-1-60851-937-8(6)*, Rosen Reference) Rosen Publishing Group, Inc., The.
Willett, Edward. Skateboarding: Techniques & Tricks. 2005. (Rad Sports: Techniques & Tricks Ser.). (Illus.). 48p. (YA). (gr. 5-8). lib. bdg. 29.25 *(978-0-8239-3848-3(4))* Rosen Publishing Group, Inc., The.
Wingate, Brian. Tony Hawk: Skateboarding Champion. (World of Skateboarding Ser.). 48p. (gr. 5-8). 2009. 53.00 *(978-1-60854-320-5(X)*, Rosen Reference) 2005. (Illus.). (YA). lib. bdg. 29.25 *(978-0-8239-3651-9(1))* Rosen Publishing Group, Inc., The.
Winters, Jaime. Shred It Skateboarding. 2012. (ENG., Illus.). 32p. (J). pap. *(978-0-7787-3162-7(6))* Crabtree Publishing Co.
Wiseman, Blaine. Skateboarding. 2015. (J). *(978-1-5105-0004-4(9))* SmartBook Media, Inc.
—Skateboarding: X Games. 2008. (Extreme Ser.). (Illus.). 32p. (J). (gr. 4-6). pap. 9.95 *(978-1-59036-913-5(0))*; lib. bdg. 26.00 *(978-1-59036-912-8(2))* Weigl Pubs., Inc.
The World of Skateboarding. 2005. (Illus.). 48p. (gr. 5-8). lib. bdg. 159.00 *(978-0-8239-3891-9(3))* Rosen Publishing Group, Inc., The.

SKATEBOARDING—FICTION

Barwin, Steven. Sk8er, 1 vol. 2007. (Lorimer Sports Stories Ser.). (ENG., 128p. (J). (gr. 4-8). Illus.). 16.95 *(978-1-55028-985-5(3)*, 9781550289855); 8.95 *(978-1-55028-983-1(7)*, 9781550289831) Lorimer, James & Co., Ltd., Pubs. CAN. Dist: Casemate Pubs. & Bk. Distributors, LLC.
Berend, Janet Eoff. True Vert. 2016. (ENG.). 128p. (J). (gr. 5-10). pap. 12.95 *(978-1-62124-024-2(X))* Breakaway Bks.
—Vertical. 2012. (ENG.). 160p. (J). (gr. 5-10). pap. 12.95 *(978-1-891369-98-8(9))* Breakaway Bks.
Birle, Pete. Locals Only. 2013. (Av2 Audio Chapter Bks.). (ENG.). 121p. (J). 27.13 *(978-1-62127-985-3(5)*, AV2 by Weigl) Weigl Pubs., Inc.
Carlson, Nancy. Arnie & the Skateboard Gang. Carlson, Nancy, illus. 2012. (Nancy Carlson Picture Bks). (Illus.). 32p. (J). (gr. k-2). (ENG.). 9.95 *(978-0-7613-8948-4(2))*; 56.72 *(978-0-7613-9303-0(X))* Lerner Publishing Group. (Carolrhoda Bks.).
Chapman, Megan Joy. Lion Heart & Alessio Book 2: Mission, Peace, Patience, Kindness. 2014. (ENG.). 192p. (J). (gr. 3-7). pap. 11.99 *(978-1-62136-755-0(X)*, Creation Hse.) Charisma Media.
Choyce, Lesley. Skate Freak, 1 vol. 2008. (Orca Currents Ser.). (ENG.). (J). (gr. 5-9). 112p. 16.95 *(978-1-55469-043-5(9))*; 128p. pap. 9.95 *(978-1-55469-042-8(0))* Orca Bk. Pubs. USA.
—Smoke & Mirrors. 2004. (ENG.). 200p. (YA). (gr. 7). pap. 8.99 *(978-1-55002-534-7(1))* Dundurn CAN. Dist: Ingram Publisher Services.
Christopher, Matt. The Extreme Team: Skateboard Moves. Leonard, David, illus. 2013. (Passport to Reading Level 3 Ser.: 1). (ENG.). 32p. (J). (gr. 1-4). 3.99 *(978-0-316-25230-0(1))* Little, Brown Bks. for Young Readers.
—Into the Danger Zone. Koelsch, Michael, illus. 6th ed. 2004. (ENG.). 64p. (J). (gr. 1-4). pap. 13.99 *(978-0-316-76267-0(9)*, Tingley, Megan Bks.) Little, Brown Bks. for Young Readers.
—Skateboard Tough. 2007. (New Matt Christopher Sports Library). 167p. (J). (gr. 4-6). lib. bdg. 26.60 *(978-1-59953-115-1(1))* Norwood Hse. Pr.
Cowan, Brad V. Skinner's Banks, 1 vol. 2013. (Seven Stair Crew Ser.). (ENG., Illus.). 160p. (J). (gr. 4-7). 19.95 *(978-1-4594-0521-9(8)*, 9781459405219); pap. 12.95 *(978-1-4594-0522-6(6)*, 9781459405226) Lorimer, James & Co., Ltd., Pubs. CAN. Dist: Casemate Pubs. & Bk. Distributors, LLC.
—Street Kings, 1 vol. 2013. (Seven Stair Crew Ser.). (ENG.). 136p. (J). (gr. 4-7). 12.95 *(978-1-4594-0450-2(5)*, 9781459404502); 18.95 *(978-1-4594-0451-9(3)*, 9781459404519) Lorimer, James & Co., Ltd., Pubs. CAN. Dist: Casemate Pubs. & Bk. Distributors, LLC.
Doeden, Matt. Shaun White. 2006. (Amazing Athletes Ser.). (Illus.). 32p. (J). (gr. 2-5). pap. 6.95 *(978-0-8225-6841-4(1)*, First Avenue Editions) Lerner Publishing Group.
Earle, Phil. The Bubble Wrap Boy. 2015. (ENG., Illus.). 288p. (J). (gr. 5). 16.99 *(978-0-553-51315-8(X))*; 19.99 *(978-0-553-51316-5(8))* Random Hse. Children's Bks. (Delacorte Bks. for Young Readers).
Emberley, Rebecca & Emberley, Ed. Mice on Ice. 2013. (I Like to Read(r) Ser.). (ENG.). 24p. (J). (gr. -1-3). pap. 6.99 *(978-0-8234-2908-0(3))* Holiday Hse., Inc.
Faber, Toni Tuso. The Poodle Tales: Book Five. Rudd, Benton, illus. 2013. 24p. 16.99 *(978-0-9892711-0-3(2))*; pap. 10.99 *(978-0-9892711-1-0(0))* Mindstir Media.
Fein, Eric & Fuentes, Benny. Skateboard Breakdown, 1 vol. Sandoval, Gerardo, illus. 2010. (Sports Illustrated Kids Graphic Novels Ser.). (ENG.). 56p. (gr. 2-3). 26.65 *(978-1-4342-2011-0(7))*; pap. 7.19 *(978-1-4342-2785-0(5))* Stone Arch Bks.
Free Wheelin' Coloring/Activity Book (English) 2005. (Illus.). (J). 2.99 *(978-0-9770455-7-0(9))* Mighty Kids Media.
Harmon, Michael B. Under the Bridge. 2013. (ENG.). 272p. (YA). (gr. 9). pap. 8.99 *(978-0-375-85930-4(6)*, Ember) Random Hse. Children's Bks.
Hoena, Blake. Daring, 1 vol. Cano, Fernando, illus. 2014. (Tony Hawk: Live2Skate Ser.). (ENG.). 72p. (gr. 4-5). lib. bdg. 25.32 *(978-1-4342-9139-4(1))* Stone Arch Bks.
—Skateboard Scare. Regan, Dana, illus. 2014. (Jess & Jaylen Ser.). (ENG.). 48p. (J). (gr. 1-4). 27.07 *(978-1-63143-441-9(1)*, 208265) Child's World, Inc., The.
Hoena, Blake A. Raw. Cano, Fernando, illus. 2013. (Tony Hawk: Live2Skate Ser.). (ENG.). 72p. (gr. 3-4). pap. 35.70 *(978-1-4342-6268-4(5)*, Tony Hawk's 900 Revolution) Stone Arch Bks.
—Raw, 1 vol. Cano, Fernando, illus. 2013. (Tony Hawk: Live2Skate Ser.). (ENG.). 72p. (gr. 4-5). pap. 5.95 *(978-1-4342-6188-5(3))*; lib. bdg. 25.32 *(978-1-4342-4086-6(X))* Stone Arch Bks.
—Rival, 1 vol. Cano, Fernando, illus. 2014. (Tony Hawk: Live2Skate Ser.). (ENG.). 72p. (gr. 4-5). pap. 5.95 *(978-1-4342-6562-3(5)*, Tony Hawk's 900 Revolution) Stone Arch Bks.
—Zombified: Volume Nine, 1 vol. Majado, Caio, illus. 2013. (Tony Hawk's 900 Revolution Ser.). (ENG.). 128p. (gr. 3-4). pap. 7.19 *(978-1-4342-4898-5(4)*, Tony Hawk's 900 Revolution) Stone Arch Bks.
Hoena, Blake A. & Terrell, Brandon. Tony Hawk's 900 Revolution. 2013. (Tony Hawk's 900 Revolution Ser.). (ENG.). 128p. (gr. 3-4). 106.60 *(978-1-4342-4109-2(2)*, Tony Hawk's 900 Revolution) Stone Arch Bks.
Hoena, Blake A. & Tortosa, Wilson. Amplified, Vol. 5. Ito, Leonardo, illus. 2012. (Tony Hawk's 900 Revolution Ser.). (ENG.). 128p. (gr. 3-4). pap. 7.19 *(978-1-4342-3887-0(3))*; lib. bdg. 26.65 *(978-1-4342-3311-0(1))* Stone Arch Bks. (Tony Hawk's 900 Revolution).
—Zombified, Vol. 9. Majado, Caio, illus. 2013. (Tony Hawk's 900 Revolution Ser.). (ENG.). 128p. (gr. 3-4). lib. bdg. 26.65 *(978-1-4342-3840-5(7))* Stone Arch Bks.
Hornby, Nick. Slam. (ENG.). 320p. (gr. 12). 2009. 16.00 *(978-1-59448-471-1(6))* 2008. 15.00 *(978-1-59448-345-5(0))* Penguin Publishing Group. (Riverhead Bks. (Hardcover)).
Hurd, Thacher. Bad Frogs. Hurd, Thacher, illus. 2009. (ENG., Illus.). 40p. (J). (gr. -1-2). 15.99 *(978-0-7636-3253-3(8))* Candlewick Pr.
Jenkins, Emily. The Little Bit Scary People. Boiger, Alexandra, illus. 2008. (ENG.). 32p. (gr. -1-1). 16.99 *(978-1-4231-0075-1(1))* Hyperion Pr.
Kovalkova-McKenna, Svetlana & McKenna, Alexandra. The Fairy Book. 2009. 52p. pap. 7.58 *(978-0-557-06160-0(1))* Lulu Pr., Inc.
Krebs, Patricia, illus. On Your Mark, Get Set, Go! 2009. 32p. (J). 16.95 *(978-0-9796380-1-5(1))* Three Wishes Publishing Co.
Lemke, Donald B. Drop In, 1 vol., Vol. 1. Majado, Caio et al, illus. 2011. (Tony Hawk's 900 Revolution Ser.). (ENG.). 128p. (gr. 3-4). pap. 7.19 *(978-1-4342-3451-3(7))*; lib. bdg. 26.65 *(978-1-4342-3214-4(X))* Stone Arch Bks. (Tony Hawk's 900 Revolution).
Little Dinosaur's Skateboard. 2005. (Georgie Giraffe Set 1 Ser.). (J). 7.33 *(978-1-932570-42-7(X))* Pioneer Valley Bks.
Maddox, Jake. Board Battle, 1 vol. Aburtov, Jesus Aburto, illus. 2013. (Jake Maddox Sports Stories Ser.). (ENG.). 72p. (gr. 2-3). pap. 5.95 *(978-1-4342-6208-0(1))* Stone Arch Bks.
—Board Battle. 2013. (Jake Maddox Sports Stories Ser.). (ENG.). 72p. (gr. 2-3). pap. 35.70 *(978-1-4342-6235-6(9))* Stone Arch Bks.
—Board Battle, 1 vol. Aburtov, Jesus Aburto, illus. 2013. (Jake Maddox Sports Stories Ser.). (ENG.). 72p. (gr. 2-3). lib. bdg. 25.32 *(978-1-4342-5975-2(7))* Stone Arch Bks.
—Board Rebel. Tiffany, Sean, illus. 2007. (Jake Maddox Sports Stories Ser.). (ENG.). 72p. (gr. 2-3). pap. 5.95 *(978-1-59889-414-1(5))*; lib. bdg. 25.32 *(978-1-59889-319-9(X))* Stone Arch Bks.
—El Rebelde de la Patineta, 1 vol. Heck, Claudia, tr. from ENG. Tiffany, Sean, illus. 2012. (Jake Maddox en Español Ser.). (SPA.). 72p. (gr. 2-3). 25.32 *(978-1-4342-3816-0(4))* Stone Arch Bks.
—Skate Park Challenge, 1 vol. Tiffany, Sean, illus. 2006. (Jake Maddox Sports Stories Ser.). (ENG.). 72p. (gr. 2-3). 25.32 *(978-1-59889-064-8(6))* Stone Arch Bks.
—Skateboard Idol. 2016. (Jake Maddox JV Ser.). (ENG.). 96p. (gr. 3-4). lib. bdg. 25.99 *(978-1-4965-2631-1(7))* Stone Arch Bks.
—Skateboard Save, 1 vol. Tiffany, Sean, illus. 2008. (Jake Maddox Sports Stories Ser.). (ENG.). 72p. (gr. 2-3). pap. 5.95 *(978-1-4342-0871-2(0))* Stone Arch Bks.
—Skateboard Struggle, 1 vol. Tiffany, Sean, illus. 2011. (Jake Maddox Sports Stories Ser.). (ENG.). 72p. (gr. 2-3). lib. bdg. 25.32 *(978-1-4342-2987-8(4))* Stone Arch Bks.
—Skatepark Challenge. Tiffany, Sean, illus. 2010. (Jake Maddox Sports Story Ser.). 72p. pap. 0.60 *(978-1-4342-3207-6(7)*, Impact Bks.) Stone Arch Bks.
Manning, Matthew K. Strong, 1 vol. Cano, Fernando, illus. 2013. (Tony Hawk: Live2Skate Ser.). (ENG.). 72p. (gr. 4-5). pap. 5.95 *(978-1-4342-6187-8(5))*; lib. bdg. 25.32 *(978-1-4342-4085-9(1))* Stone Arch Bks.
Manning, Matthew K. & Majado, Caio. Lockdown, Vol. 8. Ito, Leonardo, illus. 2012. (Tony Hawk's 900 Revolution Ser.). (ENG.). 128p. (gr. 3-4). pap. 7.19 *(978-1-4342-3890-0(3))*; lib. bdg. 26.65 *(978-1-4342-3314-1(6))* Stone Arch Bks. (Tony Hawk's 900 Revolution).
Nelson, Blake. Paranoid Park. 2008. (ENG.). 192p. (YA). (gr. 7-18). 6.99 *(978-0-14-241156-8(6)*, Puffin Books) Penguin Young Readers Group.
O'Donnell, Liam. Ramp Rats: A Graphic Guide Adventure, 1 vol. Deas, Mike, illus. 2008. (Graphic Guides). (ENG.). 64p. (J). (gr. 3-7). pap. 9.95 *(978-1-55143-880-1(1))* Orca Bk. Pubs. USA.
Pavey, Stephen. Free RollinApos. 2005. pap. 24.95 *(978-1-4137-0890-5(0))* PublishAmerica, Inc.
Phillips, Dee. Grind, 1 vol. unabr. ed. 2011. (Right Now! Ser.). (ENG., Illus.). 45p. (YA). (gr. 9-12). pap. 8.95 *(978-1-61651-250-7(4))* Saddleback Educational Publishing, Inc.
Sherman, M. Zachary. Impulse, Vol. 2. Majado, Caio et al, illus. 2011. (Tony Hawk's 900 Revolution Ser.). (ENG.). 128p. (gr. 3-4). pap. 7.19 *(978-1-4342-3452-0(5))*; lib. bdg. 26.65 *(978-1-4342-3203-8(4))* Stone Arch Bks. (Tony Hawk's 900 Revolution).
Sommer, Isabell & Reinhardt, Swen. CHIP CHIPS JAM - 4: Der Schatz in der Elbe. 2010. 86p. pap. *(978-3-8391-0219-0(7))* Books on Demand GmbH.
Steele, Michael A. At Large. 2013. (Tony Hawk: Live2Skate Ser.). (ENG.). 72p. (gr. 3-4). pap. 35.70 *(978-1-4342-6267-7(7)*, Tony Hawk's 900 Revolution) Stone Arch Bks.
—At Large, 1 vol. Cano, Fernando, illus. 2013. (Tony Hawk: Live2Skate Ser.). (ENG.). 72p. (gr. 4-5). lib. bdg. 25.32 *(978-1-4342-4087-3(8))* Stone Arch Bks.
—On Cue, 1 vol. Cano, Fernando, illus. 2014. (Tony Hawk: Live2Skate Ser.). (ENG.). 72p. (gr. 4-5). pap. 5.95 *(978-1-4342-6559-3(5)*, Tony Hawk's 900 Revolution) Stone Arch Bks.
—Revive, 1 vol. Cano, Fernando, illus. 2014. (Tony Hawk: Live2Skate Ser.). (ENG.). 72p. (gr. 4-5). pap. 5.95 *(978-1-4342-6560-9(9)*, Tony Hawk's 900 Revolution) Stone Arch Bks.
Steele, Michael Anthony. At Large, 1 vol. Cano, Fernando, illus. 2013. (Tony Hawk: Live2Skate Ser.). (ENG.). 72p. (gr. 4-5). pap. 5.95 *(978-1-4342-6189-2(1))* Stone Arch Bks.
—Fresh, 1 vol. Cano, Fernando, illus. 2014. (Tony Hawk: Live2Skate Ser.). (ENG.). 72p. (gr. 4-5). lib. bdg. 25.32 *(978-1-4342-9140-0(5))* Stone Arch Bks.
Stevens, Eric & Fuentes, Benny. Skateboard Sonar, 1 vol. Sandoval, Gerardo, illus. 2010. (Sports Illustrated Kids Graphic Novels Ser.). (ENG.). 56p. (gr. 2-3). pap. 7.19 *(978-1-4342-2295-4(0))*; 26.65 *(978-1-4342-1910-7(0))* Stone Arch Bks.
Stoudemire, Amar'e. Home Court. 2012. (STAT: Standing Tall & Talented Ser.: 1). lib. bdg. 16.00 *(978-0-606-26169-2(9)*, Turtleback) Turtleback Bks.
Strange, Jason. Text 4 Revenge, 1 vol. Parks, Phil & Dal Lago, Alberto, illus. 2011. (Jason Strange Ser.). (ENG.). 72p. (gr. 2-3). pap. 6.25 *(978-1-4342-3432-2(0))*; lib. bdg. 25.32 *(978-1-4342-3233-5(6))* Stone Arch Bks.
Suen, Anastasia. Skate Trick: A Robot & Rico Story, 1 vol. Laughead, Mike, illus. 2009. (Robot & Rico Ser.). (ENG.). 32p. (gr. 1-2). pap. 6.25 *(978-1-4342-1750-9(7))* Stone Arch Bks.
—Trucos en la Patineta. Heck, Claudia M., tr. from ENG. Laughead, Mike, illus. 2012. (Robot y Rico/Robot & Rico Ser.).Tr. of Skate Trick. (MUL & SPA.). 32p. (gr. 1-2). pap. 5.05 *(978-1-4342-3917-4(9))*; lib. bdg. 21.32 *(978-1-4342-3778-1(8))* Stone Arch Bks. (Bilingual Stone Arch Readers).
Terrell, Brandon. Above, 1 vol. Cano, Fernando, illus. 2013. (Tony Hawk: Live2Skate Ser.). (ENG.). 72p. (gr. 4-5). pap. 5.95 *(978-1-4342-6186-1(7))*; (gr. 3-4). pap. 35.70 *(978-1-4342-6266-0(9)*, Tony Hawk's 900 Revolution); (gr. 4-5). lib. bdg. 25.32 *(978-1-4342-4084-2(3))* Stone Arch Bks.
—Flipside, Vol. 11. Majado, Caio, illus. 2013. (Tony Hawk's 900 Revolution Ser.). (ENG.). 128p. (gr. 3-4). lib. bdg. 26.65 *(978-1-4342-3842-9(3))* Stone Arch Bks.
—Flipside: Volume Eleven, 1 vol. Majado, Caio, illus. 2013. (Tony Hawk's 900 Revolution Ser.). (ENG.). 128p. (gr. 3-4). pap. 7.19 *(978-1-4342-4895-4(X)*, Tony Hawk's 900 Revolution) Stone Arch Bks.
—Horizon, 1 vol. Dal Bello, Thiago & Tortosa, Wilson, illus. 2013. (Tony Hawk's 900 Revolution Ser.). (ENG.). 128p. (gr. 3-4). pap. 7.19 *(978-1-4342-6218-9(9))*; lib. bdg. 26.65 *(978-1-4342-6032-1(1))* Stone Arch Bks.
—Recharged, Vol. 12. Tortosa, Wilson, illus. 2013. (Tony Hawk's 900 Revolution Ser.). (ENG.). 128p. (gr. 3-4). lib. bdg. 26.65 *(978-1-4342-3843-6(1))* Stone Arch Bks.
—Recharged: Volume Twelve, 1 vol. Tortosa, Wilson, illus. 2013. (Tony Hawk's 900 Revolution Ser.). (ENG.). 128p. (gr. 3-4). pap. 7.19 *(978-1-4342-4896-1(8)*, Tony Hawk's 900 Revolution) Stone Arch Bks.
—Solo, 1 vol. 2014. (Tony Hawk: Live2Skate Ser.). (ENG., Illus.). 72p. (gr. 4-5). pap. 5.95 *(978-1-4342-6561-6(7)*, Tony Hawk's 900 Revolution) Stone Arch Bks.
—Unearthed, Vol. 10. Tortosa, Wilson, illus. 2013. (Tony Hawk's 900 Revolution Ser.). (ENG.). 128p. (gr. 3-4). lib. bdg. 26.65 *(978-1-4342-3841-2(5))* Stone Arch Bks.
—Unearthed: Volume Ten, 1 vol. Tortosa, Wilson, illus. 2013. (Tony Hawk's 900 Revolution Ser.). (ENG.). 128p. (gr. 3-4). pap. 7.19 *(978-1-4342-4897-8(6)*, Tony Hawk's 900 Revolution) Stone Arch Bks.
Terrell, Brandon & Majado, Caio. Tunnel Vision, Vol. 6. Ito, Leonardo, illus. 2012. (Tony Hawk's 900 Revolution Ser.). (ENG.). 128p. (gr. 3-4). pap. 7.19 *(978-1-4342-3888-7(1))*; lib. bdg. 26.65 *(978-1-4342-3312-7(X))* Stone Arch Bks. (Tony Hawk's 900 Revolution).
Terrell, Brandon & Tortosa, Wilson. Exiled, Vol. 7. Ito, Leonardo, illus. 2012. (Tony Hawk's 900 Revolution Ser.). (ENG.). 128p. (gr. 3-4). pap. 7.19 *(978-1-4342-3889-4(X))*; lib. bdg. 26.65 *(978-1-4342-3313-4(8))* Stone Arch Bks. (Tony Hawk's 900 Revolution).
Thompson, Vinny. Vinny & Bud. 2009. 64p. pap. 11.99 *(978-1-4490-2551-9(X))* AuthorHouse.
Tony Hawk: Live2Skate, 1 vol. 2014. (Tony Hawk: Live2Skate Ser.). (ENG.). 72p. (gr. 4-5). 75.96 *(978-1-4342-9519-4(2)*, Tony Hawk's 900 Revolution) Stone Arch Bks.
Walters, Eric. A Fond la Planche!, 1 vol. 2010. (FRE.). 136p. (YA). (gr. 8-12). pap. 9.95 *(978-1-55469-373-3(X))* Orca Bk. Pubs. USA.
Warner, Sally. EllRay Jakes & the Beanstalk. Biggs, Brian, illus. 2013. (EllRay Jakes Ser.: 5). (ENG.). (J). (gr. 1-3). 128p. 14.99 *(978-0-670-78499-8(0)*, Viking Books for Young Readers); 144p. pap. 5.99 *(978-0-14-242359-2(9)*, Puffin Books) Penguin Young Readers Group.
—EllRay Jakes & the Beanstalk. 2013. (EllRay Jakes Ser.: 5). lib. bdg. 16.00 *(978-0-606-32137-2(3)*, Turtleback) Turtleback Bks.
Yasuda, Anita. I've Got the No-Skateboard Blues, 1 vol. Santillan, Jorge H., illus. 2012. (Sports Illustrated Kids Victory School Superstars Ser.). (ENG.). 56p. (gr. 1-3). pap. 5.95 *(978-1-4342-3866-5(0))*; lib. bdg. 26.65 *(978-1-4342-2244-2(6))* Stone Arch Bks.

SKATING

Barnas, Jo-Ann. Great Moments in Olympic Skating, 1 vol. 2014. (Great Moments in Olympic Sports Ser.). (ENG.). 64p. (gr. 10-14). lib. bdg. 32.79 *(978-1-62403-396-4(2)*, SportsZone) ABDO Publishing Co.
Bix, Jasper. Let's Go Ice-Skating! 2016. (Winter Fun Ser.). (ENG.). 24p. (J). (gr. k-k). lib. bdg. 22.60 *(978-1-4824-3757-7(0))*; (Illus.). pap. 8.15 *(978-1-4824-3755-3(4))* Stevens, Gareth Publishing LLLP.
—Let's Go Sledding! 2016. (Winter Fun Ser.). (ENG.). 24p. (J). (gr. k-k). lib. bdg. 22.60 *(978-1-4824-3761-4(9))* Stevens, Gareth Publishing LLLP.
Blaine, Victor. My Skates, 1 vol. 2015. (ENG., Illus.). 24p. (J). lib. bdg. 23.60 *(978-1-4994-0254-4(6)*, PowerKids Pr.) Rosen Publishing Group, Inc., The.
Browning, Kurt. A Is for Axel: An Ice Skating Alphabet. Rose, Melanie, illus. rev. ed. 2005. (Sports Ser.). (ENG.). 40p. (J). (gr. -1-5). 17.95 *(978-1-58536-280-6(8))* Sleeping Bear Pr.
—A Is for Axel: An Ice Skating Alphabet. Rose, Melanie, illus. 2015. (Av2 Fiction Readalong 2016 Ser.). (ENG.). (J). (gr. 1-4). lib. bdg. 34.28 *(978-1-4896-3732-1(X)*, AV2 by Weigl) Weigl Pubs., Inc.
Challen, Paul. Spin It Figure Skating. 2010. (ENG., Illus.). 32p. (J). pap. *(978-0-7787-3178-8(2))*; lib. bdg. *(978-0-7787-3146-7(4))* Crabtree Publishing Co.
Cohen, Sasha. Sasha Cohen: Autobiography of a Champion Figure Skater. Goedeken, Kathy, illus. 2005. (ENG.). 192p. (J). (gr. 3-18). pap. 9.99 *(978-0-06-072489-4(7))* HarperCollins Pubs.
Dzidrums, Christine. Yuna Kim: Ice Queen. Rendon, Leah, ed. Dzidrums, Joseph et al, photos by. 2011. (Skate Stars Ser.: Vol. 2). (Illus.). 72p. (YA). pap. 10.99 *(978-0-9826435-9-4(4))* Creative Media Publishing.
Dzidrums, Christine & Rendon, Leah. Joannie Rochette: Canadian Ice Princess. Allison, Elizabeth, ed. Adeff, Jay & Mittan, J. Barry, photos by. 2nd exp. rev. ed. 2010. (Skate Stars Ser.: Vol. 1). (Illus.). 100p. (YA). pap. 12.99 *(978-0-9826435-0-1(0))* Creative Media Publishing.
Farbs, C. Olympic Ice Skating. (Great Moments in Olympic History Ser.). 48p. 2009. (gr. 5-6). 53.00 *(978-1-61513-161-7(2)*, Rosen Reference) 2007. (Illus.). (J). (gr. 3-7). lib. bdg. 26.50 *(978-1-4042-0969-5(7))* Rosen Publishing Group, Inc., The.
First Sticker Book Ice Skating. 2017. (First Sticker Bks.). (ENG.). (J). pap. 6.99 ***(978-0-7945-3875-0(4)**, Usborne)* EDC Publishing.
Freese, Joan. Play-by-Play Figure Skating. King, Andy, illus. King, Andy, photos by. 2004. (Play-by-Play Ser.). 80p. (J). (gr. 4-8). lib. bdg. 23.93 *(978-0-8225-3934-6(9))* Lerner Publishing Group.
Gaetz, Dayle. Catriona le May Doan: La Plus Rapide des Patineuses. 2004. (FRE., Illus.). (J). *(978-2-7650-0745-6(4))* Les Editions de la Cheneliere, Inc.
Goodridge, Catherine. Michelle Kwan & Michelle Kwan (Spanish) 6 English, 6 Spanish Adaptations. 2011. (ENG & SPA.). (J). 79.00 net. *(978-1-4108-5659-3(3))* Benchmark Education Co.
—Michelle Kwan (Spanish) 2011. (SPA.). (J). pap. 40.00 net. *(978-1-4108-2428-8(4)*, A24284) Benchmark Education Co.
Gustaitis, Joseph. Figure Skating. 2009. (Winter Olympic Sports Ser.). (ENG., Illus.). 32p. (J). (gr. 3-6). lib. bdg. *(978-0-7787-4022-3(6))* Crabtree Publishing Co.
—Speed Skating. 2009. (Winter Olympic Sports Ser.). (ENG., Illus.). 32p. (J). (gr. 3-6). lib. bdg. *(978-0-7787-4027-8(7))* Crabtree Publishing Co.
Hamilton, John. Inline Skating. 2014. (Action Sports Ser.). (ENG., Illus.). 32p. (J). (gr. 8-15). lib. bdg. 27.07 *(978-1-62403-441-1(1)*, Abdo & Daughters) ABDO Publishing Co.
Heller, Alyson. Let's Go Skating! Björkman, Steve, illus. 2009. (After-School Sports Club Ser.). (ENG.). 32p. (J). (gr. -1-1). pap. 3.99 *(978-1-4169-9411-4(4)*, Simon Spotlight) Simon Spotlight.
Hill, Anne E. Sasha Cohen. 2008. (ENG.). (gr. 5-12). pap. 56.72 *(978-0-8225-9400-0(5))* Lerner Publishing Group.
Hughes, Morgan. Ice Skating. 2005. (Junior Sports Ser.). (Illus.). 32p. (gr. 2-4). 19.95 *(978-1-59515-192-6(3))* Rourke Educational Media.
Kirkpatrick, Rob. Tara Lipinski: Super Ice-Skater. 2009. (Great Record Breakers in Sports Ser.). 24p. (gr. 3-3). 42.50 *(978-1-61513-191-4(4)*, PowerKids Pr.) Rosen Publishing Group, Inc., The.
Labrecque, Ellen. The Science of a Triple Axel. 2015. (21st Century Skills Library: Full-Speed Sports Ser.). (ENG., Illus.). 32p. (J). (gr. 4-7). 29.93 *(978-1-63362-587-7(7)*, 206532) Cherry Lake Publishing.
MacKay, Jenny. Figure Skating. 2012. (Science Behind Sports Ser.). (ENG.). 128p. 39.40 *(978-1-4205-0784-3(2)*, Lucent Bks.) Cengage Gale.
Macy, Sue. Roller Derby Rivals. Collins, Matt, illus. 2014. (ENG.). 32p. (J). (gr. k-5). 16.95 *(978-0-8234-2923-3(7))* Holiday Hse., Inc.
Marsico, Katie. Speed Skating. 2008. (21st Century Skills Library: Real World Math Ser.). (ENG.). 32p. (gr. 4-8). lib. bdg. 28.50 *(978-1-60279-250-0(X)*, 200128) Cherry Lake Publishing.
McDougall, Chros. Girls Play to Win Figure Skating. 2010. (Girls Play to Win Ser.). 64p. (J). (gr. 3-6). lib. bdg. 27.93 *(978-1-59953-389-6(8))* Norwood Hse. Pr.
Michalski, Pete & Moncrief, Kathryn M. Figure Skating: Girls Rocking It, 01 vols., 1. 2016. (Title IX Rocks! Ser.). (ENG.). 64p. (J). 32.95 *(978-1-5081-7033-4(9)*, Rosen Young Adult) Rosen Publishing Group, Inc., The.
Miller, Raymond H. Michelle Kwan. 2003. (Stars of Sports Ser.). (ENG., Illus.). 48p. (J). 27.50 *(978-0-7377-1540-8(5)*, Greenhaven Pr., Inc.) Cengage Gale.
Pettiford, Rebecca. Zamboni Ice Resurfacers. 2017. (Mighty Machines in Action Ser.). (ENG., Illus.). 24p. (J). (gr. k-3). lib. bdg. 25.95 ***(978-1-62617-634-8(5)**, Blastoff! Readers)* Bellwether Media.
Publications International Ltd. Staff, ed. Teenage Ninja Turtles: Skateboard Heroes! 2014. 12p. (J). bds. 12.98 *(978-1-4508-8453-2(9)*, 5b3a6351-f0d0-4a36-b0d1-c89677f0352a) Phoenix International Publications, Inc.
Ruscoe, Michael. Skating to Spelling Success. 2009. (Grammar All-Stars: Writing Tools Ser.). 32p. (J). (gr. 2-5). pap. 10.50 *(978-1-4339-2137-7(5))*; lib. bdg. 26.00 *(978-1-4339-1944-2(3))* Stevens, Gareth Publishing LLLP. (Gareth Stevens Learning Library).
Sandler, Michael. Ice Skating: The Incredible Michelle Kwan. 2006. (Upsets & Comebacks Ser.). (Illus.). 32p. (J). (gr. 3-6). lib. bdg. 25.27 *(978-1-59716-252-4(3))* Bearport Publishing Co., Inc.
Schulte, Mary E. Synchronized Skating. 2017. (Figure Skating Ser.). (ENG.). 32p. (gr. 3-4). lib. bdg. 27.99 ***(978-1-5157-8186-8(0)**, Snap Bks.)* Capstone Press of Coughlan Cos.
Schwartz, Heather E. Freestyle Skating. 2017. (Figure Skating Ser.). (ENG.). 32p. (gr. 3-4). lib. bdg. 27.99 ***(978-1-5157-8188-2(7)**, Snap Bks.)* Capstone Press of Coughlan Cos.
—Pairs Skating. 2017. (Figure Skating Ser.). (ENG.). 32p. (gr. 3-4). lib. bdg. 27.99 ***(978-1-5157-8187-5(9)**, Snap Bks.)* Capstone Press of Coughlan Cos.
Skating: Big Book: Level E. Group 2. (Story Box Ser.). 16p. 20.95 *(978-0-7802-9369-4(X))* Wright Group/McGraw-Hill.
Streeter, Michael. Ice Skating. 2005. (Sports Injuries Ser.). (Illus.). 64p. (YA). lib. bdg. 19.95 *(978-1-59084-635-3(4))* Mason Crest.
Suen, Anastasia. La Historia Del Patinaje Artistico. 2004. (Historia de Los Deportes (Sports History) Ser.). (SPA &

S

ENG., Illus.). 24p. (J). (gr. 3-6). lib. bdg. 22.60 *(978-0-8239-6872-5(3),* Editorial Buenas Letras) Rosen Publishing Group, Inc., The.

—La historia del patinaje artístico (the Story of Figure Skating) 2009. (Historia de los deportes (Sports History) Ser.). (SPA.). 24p. (gr. 2-2). 42.50 *(978-1-61513-314-7(3),* Editorial Buenas Letras) Rosen Publishing Group, Inc., The.

Throp, Claire. Figure Skating, 1 vol. 2013. (Winter Sports Ser.). (ENG.). 48p. (gr. 3-6). pap. 6.95 *(978-1-4109-5456-5(0))* Heinemann-Raintree.

Uschan, Michael V. Apolo Ohno. 2011. (People in the News Ser.). (ENG.). 128p. (gr. 7-10). lib. bdg. 39.40 *(978-1-4205-0603-7(X),* Lucent Bks.) Cengage Gale.

Waxman, Laura Hamilton. Figure Skating. 2017. (Winter Olympic Sports Ser.). (ENG.). 32p. (J). (gr. 2-5). pap. 9.99 *(978-1-68152-179-4(2))* Amicus.

—Figure Skating. 2017. (Winter Olympic Sports Ser.). (ENG.). 32p. (gr. 1-4). 20.95 *(978-1-68151-148-1(7))* Amicus Publishing.

Waxman, Laura Hamilton. Speed Skating: By Laura Hamilton Waxman. 2017. (Winter Olympic Sports Ser.). (ENG.). 32p. (J). (gr. 2-5). pap. 9.99 ***(978-1-68152-184-8(9))*** Amicus.

—Speed Skating: By Laura Hamilton Waxman. 2017. (Winter Olympic Sports Ser.). (ENG.). 32p. (gr. 1-4). 20.95 ***(978-1-68151-153-5(3))*** Amicus Publishing.

Weyn, Suzanne, adapted by. Ice Princess. 2005. (Illus.). 124p. (J). pap. *(978-0-439-74552-9(7))* Scholastic, Inc.

Where Is Kate's Skate? KinderReaders Individual Title Six-Packs. (Kinderstarters Ser.). 8p. (gr. -1-1). 21.00 *(978-0-7635-8644-7(7))* Rigby Education.

Wood, Alix. You Can Be an Ice-Skater, Vol. 1. 2014. (Let's Get Moving! Ser.). (ENG.). 32p. (J). (gr. 3-4). 26.60 *(978-1-4824-0283-4(1))* Stevens, Gareth Publishing LLLP.

SKATING—FICTION

Allen, Kenny. A Great Day to Skate. 2006. (Neighborhood Readers Ser.). (ENG.). 8p. (gr. 1-3). pap. 5.15 *(978-1-4042-6819-7(7),* Rosen Classroom) Rosen Publishing Group, Inc., The.

Alma, Ann. Skateway to Freedom. 2nd ed. 2008. (ENG.). 136p. (YA). (gr. 5-8). pap. 11.99 *(978-1-55002-719-8(0))* Dundurn CAN. Dist: Ingram Publisher Services.

Bailey, Linda. The Best Figure Skater in the Whole Wide World. 2004. (Illus.). (J). (gr. k-3). spiral bd. *(978-0-616-11094-2(4));* spiral bd. *(978-0-616-11093-5(6))* Canadian National Institute for the Blind/Institut National Canadien pour les Aveugles.

Barragan, Sophia & Barragan, Ivy. Susana Banana the Fantastic Figure Skater. 2008. 32p. pap. 12.99 *(978-1-4389-0169-5(0))* AuthorHouse.

Bentley, Sue. Sparkling Skates. 2014. (Magic Puppy Ser.: 13). lib. bdg. 14.75 *(978-0-606-35685-5(1))* Turtleback Bks.

Biggs, Brian. Henry Goes Skating. Biggs, Brian & Abbott, Simon, illus. 2012. (My First I Can Read Ser.). (ENG.). 32p. (J). (gr. -1-3). 16.99 *(978-0-06-195821-2(2));* pap. 3.99 *(978-0-06-195820-5(4))* HarperCollins Pubs.

—Henry Goes Skating. Abbott, Simon, illus. 2012. (My First I Can Read Ser.). (J). lib. bdg. 13.55 *(978-0-606-26852-3(9),* Turtleback) Turtleback Bks.

Bradley, Sandra. Henry Holton Takes the Ice. Palacios, Sara, illus. 2015. (ENG.). 40p. (J). (gr. k-3). 16.99 *(978-0-8037-3856-0(0),* Dial Bks) Penguin Young Readers Group.

Brown, Jeff. Flat Stanley - On Ice. Pamintuan, Macky, illus. 2015. (I Can Read Level 2 Ser.). (ENG.). 32p. (J). (gr. -1-3). pap. 3.99 *(978-0-06-218981-3(6))* HarperCollins Pubs.

Carlson, Nancy. Snowden. Carlson, Nancy, illus. 2012. (Nancy Carlson Picture Bks). (Illus.). 32p. (J). (gr. k-2). 56.72 *(978-0-7613-9307-8(2));* (ENG., 9.95 *(978-0-7613-8952-1(0))* Lerner Publishing Group. (Carolrhoda Bks.).

Christopher, Matt. Inline Skater. 2005. (Sports Classics IV Ser.). 153p. (J). lib. bdg. 15.00 *(978-1-59054-759-5(4))* Fitzgerald Bks.

—Snowboard Maverick. 2005. (Sports Classics IV Ser.). 156p. (J). lib. bdg. 15.00 *(978-1-59054-769-4(1))* Fitzgerald Bks.

Clark, Catherine. Frozen Rodeo. 2003. (ENG.). 304p. (J). (gr. 8-18). 15.99 *(978-0-06-009070-8(7))* HarperCollins Pubs.

Disney Frozen Let It Go! 2014. (ENG.). 12p. (J). (gr. -1-k). bds. 10.99 *(978-0-7944-3267-6(0),* Reader's Digest Children's Bks.) Studio Fun International.

Dodge, Mary Mapes. Hans Brinker, or the Silver Skates. 2007. 308p. (gr. 3-7). 32.95 *(978-1-4344-9309-5(1));* per. 19.95 *(978-1-4344-9308-8(3))* Wildside Pr., LLC.

—Hans Brinker or the Silver Skates A Story of Life in Holland. Doggett, Allen B., illus. 2004. reprint ed. pap. 34.95 *(978-1-4179-4127-8(8))* Kessinger Publishing, LLC.

—Hans Brinker; or, the Silver Skates (Dod. 2006. pap. *(978-1-4065-0961-8(2))* Dodo Pr.

Emberley, Rebecca & Emberley, Edward R. Mice on Ice. Emberley, Rebecca & Emberley, Edward R., illus. 2012. (I Like to Read(r) Ser.). (ENG., Illus.). 24p. (J). (gr. -1-3). 14.95 *(978-0-8234-2576-1(2))* Holiday Hse., Inc.

Fisch, Sarah. Skating with Friends. Durk, Jim, illus. 2007. (Little Red Reader Ser.). (J). pap. *(978-0-439-90898-6(1))* Scholastic, Inc.

Flynn, Pat. Alex Jackson: Closing Out. 2003. 168p. (J). pap. *(978-0-7022-3353-1(6))* Univ. of Queensland Pr.

Freitas, Donna. Gold Medal Winter. 2014. (ENG.). 320p. (J). (gr. 4-7). 16.99 *(978-0-545-64377-1(5))* Scholastic, Inc.

Garis, Howard Roger. Daddy Takes Us Skating. 2004. reprint ed. pap. 15.95 *(978-1-4191-1489-2(1));* pap. 1.99 *(978-1-4192-1489-9(6))* Kessinger Publishing, LLC.

Gassman, Julie A. Skating Is Hard When You're Homesick, 1 vol. Santillan, Jorge H., illus. 2011. (Sports Illustrated Kids Victory School Superstars Ser.). (ENG.). 56p. (gr. 1-3). pap. 5.95 *(978-1-4342-3398-1(7));* lib. bdg. 26.65 *(978-1-4342-2237-4(3))* Stone Arch Bks.

Gibson, Sylvia Scott. Ricky the Skating Worm & Friends, 1 vol. Gibson, Gregory V., illus. 2009. 21p. pap. 24.95 *(978-1-60836-473-2(9))* America Star Bks.

Harvey, John. My New Skates. 2006. (Neighborhood Readers Ser.). (ENG.). 16p. (gr. 1-3). pap. 6.50 *(978-1-4042-7172-2(4),* Rosen Classroom) Rosen Publishing Group, Inc., The.

Hawley, Mabel C. Four Little Blossoms Through the Holidays. 2005. pap. 22.95 *(978-1-4179-9003-0(1))* Kessinger Publishing, LLC.

Hope, Lee Laura. The Outdoor Girls in a Winter Camp or Glorious Days on Skates & Ice Boats. 2007. 156p. 41.99 *(978-1-4280-7498-9(8));* per. 35.99 *(978-1-4280-7509-2(7))* IndyPublish.com.

Huang, Yu-Hsuan. Let's Play... Ice Skating. 2014. (Let's Play Ser.). (ENG.). 10p. (J). (gr. -1 — 1). 15.99 *(978-1-4472-7644-9(2))* Pan Macmillan GBR. Dist: Independent Pubs. Group.

Hutchins, Hazel. Skate, Robyn, Skate. Cathcart, Yvonne, illus. 2004. 57p. (J). lib. bdg. 12.00 *(978-1-4242-1244-6(8))* Fitzgerald Bks.

—Skate, Robyn, Skate, 1 vol. Cathcart, Yvonne, illus. 2004. (Formac First Novels Ser.: 30). (ENG.). 64p. (J). (gr. 1-5). 4.95 *(978-0-88780-626-1(0),* 9780887806261) Formac Publishing Co., Ltd. CAN. Dist: Casemate Pubs. & Bk. Distributors, LLC.

Hutchins, Hazel J. & Hutchins, Hazel. Skate, Robyn, Skate. Cathcart, Yvonne, illus. 2004. (Formac First Novels Ser.: 30). (ENG.). 64p. (J). (gr. 1-5). 14.95 *(978-0-88780-627-8(9),* 9780887806278) Formac Publishing Co., Ltd. CAN. Dist: Casemate Pubs. & Bk. Distributors, LLC.

Idle, Molly. Flora & the Penguin. 2014. (ENG., Illus.). 40p. (J). (gr. -1-k). 16.99 *(978-1-4521-2891-7(X))* Chronicle Bks. LLC.

Jewel, Judy. Sole Shoes: Nate the Skate in Search of His Mate. 2005. 19.95 *(978-0-9767066-0-1(1))* Dunamis Development.

Johnson, Shane L., illus. Olivia & the Ice Show: A Lift-The-Flap Story. 2013. (Olivia TV Tie-In Ser.). (ENG.). 16p. (J). (gr. -1-2). pap. 6.99 *(978-1-4424-2083-0(9),* Simon Spotlight) Simon Spotlight.

Keller, Holly. Pearl's New Skates. Keller, Holly, illus. 2005. (Illus.). 24p. (J). lib. bdg. 17.89 *(978-0-06-056281-6(1))* HarperCollins Pubs.

Kovalski, Maryann. Omar on Ice. 2004. (J). (gr. k-3). spiral bd. *(978-0-616-01691-6(3));* spiral bd. *(978-0-616-01690-9(5))* Canadian National Institute for the Blind/Institut National Canadien pour les Aveugles.

Krulik, Nancy E. 'Snot Funny! 2015. (George Brown, Class Clown Ser.: 14). lib. bdg. 14.75 *(978-0-606-36584-0(2))* Turtleback Bks.

LEVEL 1 WONDER WHEELS PREPACK [News Group]. 2013. (Wonder Wheels Ser.). (ENG.). pap. 94.80 *(978-1-4342-9031-1(X))* Stone Arch Bks.

Lewis, Beverly. Girls Only! 2008. (Girls Only (Go!) Ser.: Vols. 5-8). (ENG.). (J). (gr. 4-7). 510p. pap. 20.00 *(978-0-7642-0462-3(9));*Vols. 1-4. 512p. pap. 16.00 *(978-0-7642-0461-6(0))* Bethany Hse. Pubs.

Lindman. Flicka, Ricka, Dicka & Their New Skates: Updated Edition with Paperdolls. Lindman, illus. 2011. (Flicka, Ricka, Dicka Ser.). (ENG., Illus.). 32p. (J). (gr. k-3). 9.99 *(978-0-8075-2496-1(4))* Whitman, Albert & Co.

Maddox, Jake. Skater's Secret, 1 vol. Mourning, Tuesday, illus. 2009. (Jake Maddox Girl Sports Stories Ser.). (ENG.). 72p. (gr. 2-3). 25.32 *(978-1-4342-1212-2(2))* Stone Arch Bks.

Manning, Matthew K. Strong. 2013. (Tony Hawk: Live2Skate Ser.). (ENG.). 72p. (gr. 3-4). pap. 35.70 *(978-1-4342-6269-1(3),* Tony Hawk's 900 Revolution) Stone Arch Bks.

Marychild, H. D. Skater Sister. 2013. 222p. pap. 9.52 *(978-0-9899964-9-5(2))* Small Wonder Publishing.

May, Eleanor. Mice on Ice. Melmon, Deborah, illus. 2013. (Mouse Math Ser.). 32p. (J). (gr. -1-1). 22.60 *(978-1-57565-527-7(6));* (ENG.). pap. 7.95 *(978-1-57565-528-4(4))* Kane Press, Inc.

McBride, Susan Carr. Katrina & the Magic Skates. 2011. 32p. pap. 21.99 *(978-1-4500-0730-6(9))* Xlibris Corp.

McClatchy, Lisa. Eloise Skates! Lyon, Tammie, illus. 2008. (Eloise Ser.). (ENG.). 32p. (J). (gr. -1-1). pap. 3.99 *(978-1-4169-6406-3(1),* Simon Spotlight) Simon Spotlight.

Morrill, Lauren. Being Sloane Jacobs. 2015. (ENG.). 352p. (YA). (gr. 7). pap. 9.99 *(978-0-385-74180-4(4),* Ember) Random Hse. Children's Bks.

Mun-Ensor, Michelle. The Faithful Christmas. 2011. 28p. pap. 24.95 *(978-1-4560-7077-9(0))* America Star Bks.

Nall, Gail. Breaking the Ice. 2015. (ENG., Illus.). 320p. (J). (gr. 3-7). 16.99 *(978-1-4814-1911-6(0),* Aladdin) Simon & Schuster Children's Publishing.

Ockler, Sarah. Bittersweet. 2012. (ENG.). (YA). (gr. 9). 400p. pap. 9.99 *(978-1-4424-3036-5(2));* 384p. 16.99 *(978-1-4424-3035-8(4))* Simon Pulse. (Simon Pulse).

O'Neill, Jacquie, illus. Figure Skating. 2010. (Sticker Stories Ser.). (ENG.). 16p. (J). (gr. -1-k). pap. 5.99 *(978-0-448-45343-9(6),* Grosset & Dunlap) Penguin Publishing Group.

Paulsen, Gary. Dancing Carl. 2007. (ENG.). 112p. (J). (gr. 5-9). pap. 8.99 *(978-1-4169-3938-2(5),* Simon & Schuster Bks. For Young Readers) Simon & Schuster Bks. For Young Readers.

Perkins, Stephanie. Lola & the Boy Next Door. (ENG.). (YA). (gr. 9). 2013. 368p. pap. 10.99 *(978-0-14-242201-4(0),* Speak) 2011. 352p. 16.99 *(978-0-525-42328-7(1),* Dutton Books for Young Readers) Penguin Young Readers Group.

Polak, Monique. Scarred, 1 vol. 2007. (Lorimer SideStreets Ser.). (ENG.). 168p. (YA). (gr. 9-12). 16.95 *(978-1-55028-965-7(9),* 9781550289657); 9.95 *(978-1-55028-964-0(0),* 9781550289640) Lorimer, James & Co., Ltd., Pubs. CAN. Dist: Casemate Pubs. & Bk. Distributors, LLC.

Sandrey, Alexander & Sellers, Carolyn. Cold Weather Bro's Arctic Adventure. 2012. 36p. 17.95 *(978-1-4575-1701-3(9))* Dog Ear Publishing, LLC.

Shaw, Mary. Brady Brady & the Super Skater, 11 vols. Temple, Chuck, illus. I.t. ed. 2005. 32p. (J). per. *(978-1-897169-06-3(X))* Brady Brady, Inc.

Sparks, Megan. Boot Camp Blues, 1 vol. 2014. (Roller Girls Ser.). (ENG.). 256p. (gr. 8-10). 12.95 *(978-1-62370-057-7(4))* Capstone Young Readers of Coughlan Cos.

—In a Jam, 1 vol. 2014. (Roller Girls Ser.). (ENG.). 256p. (gr. 8-10). 12.95 *(978-1-62370-058-4(2))* Capstone Young Readers of Coughlan Cos.

Staunton, Ted. Morgan on Ice, 1 vol. Slavin, Bill, illus. 2013. (Formac First Novels Ser.). (ENG.). 56p. (J). (gr. 2-3). 14.95 *(978-1-4595-0289-5(2),* 9781459502895); pap. 5.95 *(978-1-4595-0290-1(6),* 9781459502901) Formac Publishing Co., Ltd. CAN. Dist: Casemate Pubs. & Bk. Distributors, LLC.

Stilton, Thea. Thea Stilton & the Lost Letters. 2015. (Thea Stilton Ser.: 21). (Illus.). 159p. (J). lib. bdg. 18.40 *(978-0-606-37061-5(7))* Turtleback Bks.

Streatfeild, Noel. Skating Shoes. 2009. (Shoe Bks.). (ENG.). 224p. (Orig.). (J). (gr. 3-7). 6.99 *(978-0-440-47731-0(X),* Yearling) Random Hse. Children's Bks.

Tony Hawk: Live 2 Skate. 2013. (Tony Hawk: Live2Skate Ser.). (ENG.). 72p. (gr. 4-5). 101.28 *(978-1-4342-6574-6(9),* Tony Hawk's 900 Revolution) Stone Arch Bks.

Tony Hawk: Live2Skate. 2013. (Tony Hawk: Live2Skate Ser.). (ENG.). 72p. (gr. 3-4). pap. 142.80 *(978-1-4342-6304-9(5));* (gr. 4-5). pap. 23.80 *(978-1-4342-6225-7(1))* Stone Arch Bks. (Tony Hawk's 900 Revolution).

Turcotte, Michael. Colours Made in Heaven, 1 vol. Turcotte, Derek, illus. 2009. 13p. pap. 24.95 *(978-1-60836-316-2(3))* America Star Bks.

Van Stockum, Hilda. A Day on Skates: The Story of a Dutch Picnic. Van Stockum, Hilda, illus. 2007. (Illus.). 40p. (J). (gr. 1). 19.95 *(978-1-932350-18-0(7))* Bethlehem Bks.

Vaughan, Garth. Tommy's New Block Skates, 1 vol. Smith, David Preston, illus. 2007. (ENG.). 32p. (J). (gr. -1-3). pap. 12.95 *(978-1-55109-620-9(X))* Nimbus Publishing, Ltd. CAN. Dist: Orca Bk. Pubs. USA.

Warren, George A. The Banner Boy Scouts on a Tour. 2005. pap. 30.95 *(978-1-885529-38-1(4))* Stevens Publishing.

Wisler, Joelle. Ariana Gold. 2016. (What's Your Dream? Ser.). (ENG., Illus.). 96p. (gr. 3-4). lib. bdg. 25.32 *(978-1-4965-3442-2(5))* Capstone Press of Coughlan Cos.

Wright, Johanna. Bunnies on Ice. Wright, Johanna, illus. 2013. (ENG., Illus.). 32p. (J). (gr. -1-1). 16.99 *(978-1-59643-404-2(X),* 9781596434042) Roaring Brook Pr.

Yamaguchi, Kristi. Dream Big, Little Pig! Bowers, Tim, illus. 2011. (ENG.). 32p. (J). (gr. -1-3). 16.99 *(978-1-4022-5275-4(7),* Sourcebooks Jabberwocky) Sourcebooks, Inc.

—It's a Big World, Little Pig! Bowers, Tim, illus. 2012. (ENG.). 32p. (J). (gr. k-3). 16.99 *(978-1-4022-6644-7(8),* Sourcebooks Jabberwocky) Sourcebooks, Inc.

Yep, Laurence. Bravo, Mia! England, Tamara, ed. Papp, Robert, illus. 2008. (ENG.). 136p. (J). (gr. 3). pap. 6.95 *(978-1-59369-410-4(5))* American Girl Publishing, Inc.

—Mia, Bk. 1. England, Tamara, ed. Papp, Robert, illus. 2008. (ENG.). 136p. (gr. 3-18). pap. 6.95 *(978-1-59369-409-8(1))* American Girl Publishing, Inc.

SKELETON

Arnau, Eduard. Nuestra Arquitectura Osea. (Mundo Invisible Ser.). (SPA., Illus.). (YA). (gr. 5-8). pap. 8.00 *(978-958-04-3227-2(9))* Norma S.A. COL. Dist: Distribuidora Norma, Inc., Lectorum Pubns., Inc.

—Nuestra Arquitectura Osea. (SPA.). 88p. (J). 10.00 *(978-84-342-1739-3(2))* Parramon Ediciones S.A. ESP. Dist: Distribuidora Norma, Inc.

Arnold, Caroline. El Sistema Óseo. Translations.com Staff, tr. 2006. (Libros Sobre el Cuerpo Humano para Madrugadores Ser.).Tr. of Skeletal System. (ENG & SPA., Illus.). 48p. (gr. 2-4). lib. bdg. 26.60 *(978-0-8225-6257-3(X))* Lerner Publishing Group.

—El sistema oseo (the Skeletal System) 2007. (Libros Sobre el Cuerpo Humano para Madrugadores Ser.). (Illus.). 48p. (J). (gr. -1-3). per. 8.95 *(978-0-8225-6648-9(6))* Lerner Publishing Group.

—The Skeletal System. 2005. (Early Bird Body Systems Ser.). (Illus.). 48p. (J). (gr. 2-4). lib. bdg. 25.26 *(978-0-8225-5140-9(3))* Lerner Publishing Group.

—Skeletal System. 2005. (Early Bird Body Systems Ser.). (ENG., Illus.). 48p. (gr. 2-5). pap. 7.95 *(978-0-8225-2523-3(2),* Lerner Pubns.) Lerner Publishing Group.

—Your Skeletal System. 2012. (Searchlight Books — How Does Your Body Work? Ser.). (ENG., Illus.). 40p. (gr. 3-5). pap. 8.95 *(978-1-58013-964-9(7));* lib. bdg. 27.93 *(978-0-7613-7452-7(3),* Lerner Pubns.) Lerner Publishing Group.

Autumn Publishing Staff, illus. My Skeleton. 2004. (Wall Charts Ser.). (J). pap. 4.99 *(978-1-85997-268-7(3))* Byeway Bks.

Beevor, Lucy. Understanding Our Skeleton. 2017. (Brains, Body, Bones! Ser.). (ENG., Illus.). 32p. (gr. 3-5). lib. bdg. 30.65 *(978-1-4109-8578-1(4),* Raintree Perspectives) Heinemann-Raintree.

Benchmark Education Company. Your Skeleton (Teacher Guide) 2005. *(978-1-4108-4643-3(1))* Benchmark Education Co.

Bounford, Trevor. The Skeleton. 2005. (Glow in the Dark Ser.). 24p. (J). *(978-1-902626-74-1(5))* Red Bird Publishing.

Brannon, Barbara. Discover Your Skeleton. 2005. (J). pap. *(978-1-4108-5135-2(4))* Benchmark Education Co.

Brett, Flora. Your Skeletal System Works! 2015. (Your Body Systems Ser.). (ENG.). 24p. (gr. 1-2). lib. bdg. 25.32 *(978-1-4914-2068-3(5))* Capstone Press of Coughlan Cos.

Build a Skeleton. 2004. (J). per. 7.99 *(978-1-932855-16-6(5))* becker&mayer! books.

Clark, Katie. A Tour of Your Muscular & Skeletal Systems. Jones, Chris B., illus. 2012. (First Graphics: Body Systems Ser.). (ENG.). 24p. (gr. 1-2). pap. 35.70 *(978-1-4296-9327-1(4))* Capstone Press of Coughlan Cos.

Cumbaa, Stephen. The Bones Book & Skeleton. 2nd ed. 2006. (ENG., Illus.). 64p. (J). (gr. k-6). 19.95 *(978-0-7611-4218-8(5),* 14218) Workman Publishing Co., Inc.

Dornauer, Teresa. The Skeletal System. 2003. (Illus.). 24p. (J). lib. bdg. 21.35 *(978-1-58340-311-2(6))* Black Rabbit Bks.

Edmunds, Kate, illus. Dry Bones. 2007. (Classic Books with Holes Board Book Ser.). (ENG.). (J). 14p. (gr. -1-1). bds. *(978-1-84643-112-8(3));* 16p. (gr. 1-1). pap. *(978-1-84643-108-1(5))* Child's Play International Ltd.

Gilbert, Laura. The Skeletal System. 2009. (Insider's Guide to the Body Ser.). 48p. (gr. 5-8). 53.00 *(978-1-61513-586-8(3),* Rosen Reference) Rosen Publishing Group, Inc., The.

Gold, Susan Dudley. The Musculoskeletal System & the Skin. 2003. (Human Body Library). (Illus.). 48p. (J). (gr. 4-10). lib. bdg. 25.27 *(978-0-7660-2023-8(1))* Enslow Pubs., Inc.

Green, Emily & Manolis, Kay. The Skeletal System. 2009. (Body Systems Ser.). (ENG., Illus.). 24p. (J). (gr. 2-5). lib. bdg. 25.95 *(978-1-60014-247-5(8))* Bellwether Media.

Gross, Ruth Belov & Björkman, Steve. A Book about Your Skeleton. (Hello Reader! Ser.). (FRE., Illus.). 42p. (J). pap. 5.99 *(978-0-590-16005-6(2))* Scholastic, Inc.

Halvorson, Karin. Inside the Bones, 1 vol. 2016. (Super Simple Body Set 2 Ser.). (ENG., Illus.). 32p. (J). (gr. k-4). 27.07 *(978-1-62403-939-3(1))* ABDO Publishing Co.

Haywood, Karen. Skeletal System. 2008. (Amazing Human Body Ser.). 80p. (gr. 5-18). lib. bdg. 34.21 *(978-0-7614-3056-8(3),* Benchmark Bks.) Marshall Cavendish Corp.

Hewitt, Sally. My Bones. 2012. (My Body Ser.). (ENG., Illus.). 24p. (gr. k-4). pap. 7.95 *(978-1-926853-95-6(4))* Saunders Bk. Co. CAN. Dist: RiverStream Publishing.

Houghton, Gillian. Bones: The Skeletal System. 2009. (Body Works Ser.). 24p. (gr. 2-3). 42.50 *(978-1-61511-642-3(7),* PowerKids Pr.) Rosen Publishing Group, Inc., The.

—The Skeletal System. 2007. (How Your Body Works). (ENG., Illus.). 24p. (gr. 3-5). pap. 7.05 *(978-1-4042-2182-6(4),* PowerKids Pr.) Rosen Publishing Group, Inc., The.

Levine, Sara C. Bone by Bone: Comparing Animal Skeletons. Spookytooth, T. S., illus. 2013. (ENG.). 32p. (J). (gr. k-4). lib. bdg. 26.60 *(978-0-7613-8464-9(2),* Millbrook Pr.) Lerner Publishing Group.

Loria, Laura. The Bones in Your Body, 1 vol. 2015. (ENG.). 32p. (J). 23.45 *(978-1-62275-624-7(X),* Britannica Educational Publishing) Rosen Publishing Group, Inc., The.

Lundgren, Julie K. Skeletons & Exoskeletons. 2012. (ENG.). 24p. (gr. 3-4). pap. 8.95 *(978-1-61810-221-8(4))* Rourke Educational Media.

Maestro, Betsy. What Is a Skeleton? Date not set. 40p. (J). (gr. -1-1). 15.99 *(978-0-06-029006-1(4));* pap. 4.99 *(978-0-06-445215-1(8));* lib. bdg. 16.89 *(978-0-06-029007-8(2))* HarperCollins Pubs.

Manolis, Kay. The Skeletal System. 2009. (Blastoff! Readers Ser.). (ENG., Illus.). 24p. (J). (gr. k-3). 20.00 *(978-0-531-21706-1(X),* Children's Pr.) Scholastic Library Publishing.

Mason, Paul. Your Strong Skeleton & Amazing Muscular System. 2015. (Your Brilliant Body! Ser.). (ENG., Illus.). 32p. (J). (gr. 3-7). lib. bdg. *(978-0-7787-2208-3(2))* Crabtree Publishing Co.

Naughton, Diane. Bones: And the Stories They Tell. 2014. (ENG.). 28p. (J). pap. 9.50 *(978-1-107-67054-9(3))* Cambridge Univ. Pr.

Nettleton, Pamela Hill. Bend & Stretch: Learning about Your Bones & Muscles. Shipe, Becky, illus. 2004. (Amazing Body Ser.). (ENG.). 24p. (gr. k-3). per. 8.95 *(978-1-4048-0507-1(9))* Picture Window Bks.

Our Skeleton, 6 vols. (Sunshinetm Science Ser.). 24p. (gr. 1-2). 31.50 *(978-0-7802-0299-3(6))* Wright Group/McGraw-Hill.

Parsons, Michelle Hyde. Your Skeleton. 2005. (J). pap. *(978-1-4108-4595-5(8))* Benchmark Education Co.

Petrie, Kristin. The Skeletal System, 1 vol. 2007. (Human Body Ser.). (ENG., Illus.). 32p. (gr. 4-7). 27.07 *(978-1-59679-714-7(2),* Checkerboard Library) ABDO Publishing Co.

Rau, Dana Meachen. My Bones & Muscles. 2007. (J). pap. 6.99 *(978-0-7614-3351-4(1))* Marshall Cavendish Corp.

Ribke, Simone T. I Have a Skeleton. 2016. (Rookie Read-About Health Ser.). (ENG., Illus.). 32p. (J). pap. 5.95 *(978-0-531-22579-0(8),* Children's Pr.) Scholastic Library Publishing.

Rose, Simon. Skeletal System. 2014. (J). *(978-1-4896-1182-6(7))* Weigl Pubs., Inc.

Rotner, Shelley. Body Bones. White, David, illus. Rotner, Shelley, photos by. 2014. (ENG.). 32p. (J). (gr. k-5). 16.95 *(978-0-8234-3162-5(2))* Holiday Hse., Inc.

—Body Bones. 2014. pap. *(978-0-8234-3249-3(1))* Holiday Hse., Inc.

Rushworth, Gary. Body Systems: Set of 6: Skeletal & Muscular. 2011. (Navigators Ser.). (J). pap. *(978-1-4108-5085-0(4))* Benchmark Education Co.

Skeleton Sticker Book. 2003. (Illus.). 16p. (J). 2.98 *(978-1-84273-121-5(1),* Exclusive Editions) Parragon, Inc.

Snedden, Robert. Understanding Muscles & the Skeleton. 2010. (Understanding the Human Body Ser.). (Illus.). 48p. (YA). (gr. 5-8). (ENG.). pap. 11.75 *(978-1-4358-9692-5(0));* lib. bdg. 29.25 *(978-1-4358-9686-4(6))* Rosen Publishing Group, Inc., The. (Rosen Reference).

Spilsbury, Louise & Spilsbury, Richard. The Science of the Skeleton & Muscles. 2017. (Flowchart Smart Ser.). 48p. (gr. 4-5). pap. 84.30 ***(978-1-5382-0686-7(2))*** Stevens, Gareth Publishing LLLP.

Super Skeleton. 2008. (Build it now Ser.). 16p. pap. *(978-1-4075-2246-3(9))* Parragon, Inc.

Taylor, Lauren & Taylor, Sean. My Strong Bones. 2012. (Inside Me Ser.). (ENG.). 24p. (J). (gr. -1-k). 15.99 *(978-1-60992-311-2(1))* QEB Publishing Inc.

Thames, Susan. Our Skeleton. 2007. (ENG., Illus.). 24p. (gr. k-1). 28.50 *(978-1-60472-113-3(8))* Rourke Educational Media.

Williams, Ben. Look Inside: Your Skeleton & Muscles, 1 vol. 2nd rev. ed. 2013. (Nonfiction Readers Ser.). (ENG., Illus.). 28p. (J). (gr. 2-2). pap. 23.96 *(978-1-4807-1056-6(3))* Shell Educational Publishing.

—Your Skeleton & Muscles, 1 vol. 2nd rev. ed. 2011. (Nonfiction Readers Ser.). (ENG.). 28p. (J). (gr. 2-2). pap. 6.99 *(978-1-4333-3635-5(9))* Teacher Created Materials, Inc.

World Book, Inc Staff, contrib. by. The Skeletal System/The Muscular System. 2006. (World Book's Human Body Works). (Illus.). 48p. (J). *(978-0-7166-4426-2(6))* World Bk., Inc.

SKETCHING

see Drawing

SKIING

see Skis and Skiing

SKIN

Andrus, Aubre. Gloss, Floss, & Wash: DIY Crafts & Recipes for a Fresh Face & Teeth. 2017. (DIY Day Spa Ser.). (ENG., Illus.). 48p. (gr. 4-5). lib. bdg. 31.32 *(978-1-5157-3447-5(1))* Capstone Press of Coughlan Cos.

Baines, Becky. Your Skin Holds You In. 2008. (ZigZag Ser.). (ENG., Illus.). 32p. (J). (gr. k-3). 19.90 *(978-1-4263-0312-8(2),* National Geographic Children's Bks.) National Geographic Society.

Baines, Becky & National Geographic Kids Staff. Your Skin Holds You In. 2010. (ZigZag Ser.). (ENG., Illus.). 32p. (J). (gr. k-3). pap. 5.95 *(978-1-4263-0624-2(5),* National Geographic Children's Bks.) National Geographic Society.

—ZigZag: Your Skin Holds You In: A Book about Your Skin. 2008. (ZigZag Ser.). (ENG., Illus.). 32p. (J). (gr. k-3). 14.95 (978-1-4263-0311-1(4), National Geographic Children's Bks.) National Geographic Society.

Berger, Melvin & Berger, Gilda. Your Skin. 2005. (Illus.). pap. (978-0-439-77372-0(5)) Scholastic, Inc.

Boothroyd, Jennifer. Skin. 2011. (First Step Nonfiction / Body Coverings Ser.). pap. 33.92 (978-0-7613-8611-7(4)); (ENG.). 24p. pap. 6.95 (978-0-7613-7831-0(6)); (ENG., Illus.). 24p. lib. bdg. 23.93 (978-0-7613-5789-6(0)) Lerner Publishing Group.

Bozzo, Linda. Amazing Animal Skin. (Creature Features Ser.). 24p. 2009. (gr. 2-3). 42.50 (978-1-61512-067-3(X)) 2008. (Illus.). (J). (gr. 3-7). lib. bdg. 22.60 (978-1-4042-4168-8(X)) Rosen Publishing Group, Inc., The. (PowerKids Pr.).

Brown, Jonatha A. Animal Skin & Fur. 2006. (Why Animals Look Different Ser.). (Illus.). 24p. (gr. 1-4). pap. 8.15 (978-0-8368-6867-8(6)); lib. bdg. 22.00 (978-0-8368-6862-3(5)) Stevens, Gareth Publishing LLLP. (Weekly Reader Leveled Readers).

—La Piel y el Pelo de los Animales. 2006. (En que se diferencian los animales (Why Animals Look Different) Ser.). (SPA., Illus.). 24p. (J). (gr. 1-4). lib. bdg. 22.00 (978-0-8368-7415-0(3), Weekly Reader Leveled Readers) Stevens, Gareth Publishing LLLP.

Buckmaster, Marjorie L. Skin Cancer. 2007. (Health Alert Ser.). (Illus.). 60p. (J). (gr. 3-7). lib. bdg. 31.36 (978-0-7614-2703-2(1), Benchmark Bks.) Marshall Cavendish Corp.

Cardenas, Ernesto A. Textures. 2009. 23.95 (978-1-60698-047-7(5)); pap. 4.95 (978-1-60698-045-3(9)) Milo Educational Bks. & Resources.

Caster, Shannon. Skin. 2010. (Body Works Ser.). (Illus.). 24p. (J). pap. 8.25 (978-1-4358-9822-6(2), PowerKids Pr.); (YA). (gr. 2-5). lib. bdg. 22.60 (978-1-4358-9367-2(0)) Rosen Publishing Group, Inc., The.

Ceasar, Jennifer. Everything You Need to Know about Acne. 2009. (Need to Know Library). 64p. (gr. 5-5). 58.50 (978-1-60854-051-8(0)) Rosen Publishing Group, Inc., The.

Ceaser, Jennifer. Everything You Need to Know about Acne. rev. ed. 2005. (Need to Know Library). (Illus.). 64p. (YA). (gr. 4-6). lib. bdg. 31.95 (978-0-8239-3769-1(0)) Rosen Publishing Group, Inc., The.

Chang, Heidi. The Skin on Your Body, 1 vol. 2015. (ENG.). 32p. (J). 23.45 (978-1-62275-644-5(4), Britannica Educational Publishing) Rosen Publishing Group, Inc., The.

Cobb, Vicki. Your Body Battles A Skinned Knee. 2009. pap. 40.95 (978-0-7613-4620-3(1)) Lerner Publishing Group.

Donovan, Sandy. Stay Clear! What You Should Know about Skin Care. Desrocher, Jack, illus. 2008. (Health Zone Ser.). (ENG.). 64p. (gr. 4-7). lib. bdg. 30.60 (978-0-8225-7550-4(7)) Lerner Publishing Group.

Faulk, Michelle. The Case of the Flesh-Eating Bacteria: Annie Biotica Solves Skin Disease Crimes. 2013. (Body System Disease Investigations Ser.). 48p. (J). (gr. 5-12). lib. bdg. 25.27 (978-0-7660-3945-2(5)) Enslow Pubs., Inc.

Gold, Susan Dudley. Learning about the Musculoskeletal System & the Skin. 2013. (Learning about the Human Body Systems Ser.). 48p. (J). (gr. 5-12). pap. 8.95 (978-1-4644-0239-5(6)); 25.27 (978-0-7660-4159-2(X)) Enslow Pubs., Inc.

—The Musculoskeletal System & the Skin. 2003. (Human Body Library). (Illus.). 48p. (J). (gr. 4-10). lib. bdg. 25.27 (978-0-7660-2023-8(1)) Enslow Pubs., Inc.

Gordon, Sharon. My Skin. 2004. (Bookworms Ser.). (ENG & SPA., Illus.). 31p. (J). 22.79 (978-0-7614-1778-1(8), Benchmark Bks.) Marshall Cavendish Corp.

Guillain, Charlotte. Nuestra Piel, 1 vol. 2010. (Nuestros Cuerpos Ser.). (SPA.). 24p. (gr. -1-1). 22.65 (978-1-4329-4302-8(2)); pap. 6.29 (978-1-4329-4311-0(1)) Heinemann-Raintree. (Bellota).

—Our Skin, 1 vol. 2010. (Our Bodies Ser.). (ENG.). 24p. (gr. -1-1). pap. 6.29 (978-1-4329-3606-8(9), Acorn) Heinemann-Raintree.

Halvorson, Karin. Inside the Skin, Hair, & Nails, 1 vol. 2016. (Super Simple Body Set 2 Ser.). (ENG., Illus.). 32p. (J). (gr. k-4). 27.07 (978-1-62403-942-3(1)) ABDO Publishing Co.

Harrison, Emma. From Head to Toe: The Girls' Life Guide to Taking Care of You. Montagna, Frank, illus. 2004. 124p. (J). (978-0-439-44983-0(9)) Scholastic, Inc.

Jaworski, Sabrina K. & Chehoski, Robert. Skin Care. 2011. (Girls' Health Ser.). (YA). (gr. 5-9). lib. bdg. 29.25 (978-1-4488-4574-3(2)) Rosen Publishing Group, Inc., The.

Jordan, Apple & Rau, Dana Meachen. My Skin. 2nd ed. 2013. 24p. (gr. 1-3). 21.36 (978-1-60870-436-1(X)) Cavendish Square Publishing.

Kenney, Karen Latchana. Skin Care & Makeup Tips & Tricks. Heschke, Elena, illus. 2015. (ENG.). 32p. (J). (gr. 4-8). lib. bdg. 26.65 (978-1-4677-5219-0(3), Lerner Pubns.) Lerner Publishing Group.

Kirk, Bill. The Skin We're In: The Sum of Our Parts Series. Ruble, Eugene, illus. 2012. 24p. pap. 10.95 (978-1-61633-296-9(4)) Guardian Angel Publishing, Inc.

Kissinger, Katie. All the Colors We Are/Todos Los Colores de Nuestra Piel: The Story of How We Get Our Skin Color/la Historia de Por Que Tenemos Diferentes Colores de Piel. 2014. (ENG., Illus.). 32p. (J). (gr. -1-5). 16.95 (978-1-60554-079-5(X)) Redleaf Pr.

Klingel, Cynthia & Noyed, Robert B. Skin. 2010. (Let's Read about Our Bodies Ser.). (Illus.). 24p. (gr. k-3). pap. 8.15 (978-1-4339-3375-2(6)); (J). lib. bdg. 22.00 (978-1-4339-3374-5(8)) Stevens, Gareth Publishing LLLP.

—Skin / la Piel. 2010. (Let's Read about Our Bodies / Hablemos del cuerpo humano Ser.). (SPA., Illus.). 24p. (gr. k-3). pap. 8.15 (978-1-4339-3751-4(4)) Stevens, Gareth Publishing LLLP.

—Skin/la Piel. 2010. (Let's Read about Our Bodies / Hablemos del cuerpo humano Ser.). (SPA., Illus.). 24p. (J). (gr. k-3). lib. bdg. 22.00 (978-1-4339-3750-7(6)) Stevens, Gareth Publishing LLLP.

Klosterman, Lorrie. Skin. 2008. (Amazing Human Body Ser.). 80p. (gr. 5-18). lib. bdg. 34.21 (978-0-7614-3057-5(1), Benchmark Bks.) Marshall Cavendish Corp.

Labella, Susan. Chameleons & Other Animals with Amazing Skin. 2005. (Scholastic News Nonfiction Readers Ser.). (ENG., Illus.). 24p. (J). (gr. 1-2). lib. bdg. 22.00 (978-0-516-24925-4(8)) Scholastic Library Publishing.

Light, Douglas B. Cells, Tissues, & Skin. 2009. (Human Body: How It Works Ser.). (Illus.). 160p. (C). (gr. 9-18). 35.00 (978-1-60413-370-7(8), Chelsea Hse.) Facts On File, Inc.

Markle, Sandra. Bad Burns. 2010. (Powerful Medicine Ser.). (ENG.). 48p. (gr. 5-8). lib. bdg. 27.93 (978-0-8225-8702-6(5)) Lerner Publishing Group.

Marsico, Katie. I Get Sunburned. 2015. (Tell Me Why Library). (ENG., Illus.). 24p. (J). (gr. 2-5). pap. 12.79 (978-1-63362-034-6(4), 205893) Cherry Lake Publishing.

Meachen Rau, Dana. My Skin/la Piel. 2006. (Bookworms Ser.). (ENG & SPA., Illus.). 32p. (gr. 1-2). lib. bdg. 15.95 (978-0-7614-2484-0(9)) Marshall Cavendish Corp.

—La Piel: Que Hay Dentro de Mi? 2006. (Bookworms Ser.). (SPA & ENG., Illus.). 32p. (gr. 1-2). lib. bdg. 15.95 (978-0-7614-2406-2(7)) Marshall Cavendish Corp.

Miller, Sara Swan. All Kinds of Skin. 2007. (All Kinds Of Ser.). (Illus.). 48p. (gr. 3-3). lib. bdg. 29.93 (978-0-7614-2713-1(9)) Marshall Cavendish Corp.

My Skin: Big Book: Level E. (Wonder Worldtm Ser.). 16p. 26.50 (978-0-7802-3475-8(8)) Wright Group/McGraw-Hill.

My Skin: Level E, 6 vols. (Wonder Worldtm Ser.). 16p. 29.95 (978-0-7802-1229-9(0)) Wright Group/McGraw-Hill.

The Nervous System/The Senses/The Skin. 2006. (World Book's Human Body Works). (Illus.). 48p. (J). (978-0-7166-4430-9(4)) World Bk., Inc.

Ollhoff, Jim. The Skin. 2012. (J). (978-1-61783-257-4(X)) ABDO Publishing Co.

Parker, Steve. Why Does This Bug Bite Itch? Skin & Healing, 1 vol. 2011. (Inside My Body Ser.). (ENG.). 32p. (gr. 3-5). 30.65 (978-1-4109-4018-6(7), NA-r) Heinemann-Raintree.

Parker, Vic. I Know Someone with Eczema, 1 vol. 2011. (Understanding Health Issues Ser.). (ENG.). 32p. (gr. 1-3). 27.32 (978-1-4329-4559-6(9), Heinemann First Library) Heinemann-Raintree.

Rau, Dana Meachen. My Skin. 2013. (Bookworms Fluent — My Body Ser.). 24p. (gr. 1-3). pap. 8.22 (978-1-62712-036-4(X)) Cavendish Square Publishing.

René, Ellen. Investigating Why Animals Shed Their Skin. 2009. (Science Detectives Ser.). 24p. (gr. 2-3). 42.50 (978-1-60853-015-1(9), PowerKids Pr.); (Illus.). (J). lib. bdg. 22.60 (978-1-4042-4486-3(7)) Rosen Publishing Group, Inc., The.

Rice, Dona. Always Growing. 2015. (TIME for KIDS(r) Nonfiction Readers Ser.). (ENG., Illus.). 12p. (gr. k-k). 4.99 (978-1-4938-2060-3(5)) Teacher Created Materials, Inc.

Rissman, Rebecca. Makeup & Skin Hacks: Your Skin Situations Solved! 2017. (Beauty Hacks Ser.). (ENG.). 48p. (gr. 4-5). lib. bdg. 31.32 **(978-1-5157-6828-9(7))** Capstone Press of Coughlan Cos.

Rissman, Rebecca & Smith, Sian. Staying Safe in the Sun, 1 vol. 2012. (Take Care of Yourself! Ser.). (ENG.). 24p. (gr. -1-1). 22.65 (978-1-4329-6712-3(6)); pap. 6.29 (978-1-4329-6719-2(3)) Heinemann-Raintree. (Acorn).

ShackletonCaroline. SKIN UPPER INTERMEDIATE BOOK WITH ONLINE ACCESS. 2014. (ENG.). 28p. (J). pap. 9.50 (978-1-107-64189-1(6)) Cambridge Univ. Pr.

Sheen, Barbara. Acne. 2007. (Diseases & Disorders Ser.). (ENG., Illus.). 96p. (J). 32.45 (978-1-59018-345-8(2), Lucent Bks.) Cengage Gale.

Silverstein, Virginia. Handy Health Guide to Burns & Blisters. 2013. (Handy Health Guides). 48p. (J). (gr. 5-12). pap. 8.95 (978-1-4644-0487-0(9)) Enslow Pubs., Inc.

Stewart, Melissa. Here We Grow: The Secrets of Hair & Nails. 2010. (Gross & Goofy Body 2 Ser.). 48p. (gr. 3). 29.93 (978-0-7614-4172-4(7)) Marshall Cavendish Corp.

—The Skin You're In: The Secrets of Skin. 2010. (Gross & Goofy Body 2 Ser.). 48p. (gr. 3). 29.93 (978-0-7614-4169-4(7)) Marshall Cavendish Corp.

Turnbull, Stephanie. Beauty Blitz. 2016. (Sleepover Secrets Ser.). 24p. (gr. 2-6). 28.50 (978-1-62588-376-6(5), Smart Apple Media) Black Rabbit Bks.

VanVoorst, Jenny Fretland. Take a Closer Look at Your Skin. 2013. (Take a Closer Look Ser.). (ENG.). 24p. (J). (gr. 2-5). 28.50 (978-1-62323-554-3(5), 206356) Child's World, Inc., The.

Waldron, Melanie. Your Skin & Bones: Understand Them with Numbers, 1 vol. 2014. (Your Body by Numbers Ser.). (ENG.). 48p. (gr. 3-5). lib. bdg. 32.65 (978-1-4109-5981-2(3)) Heinemann-Raintree.

Wheeler-Toppen, Jodi Lyn. Our Skin Can Touch. 2017. (Our Amazing Senses Ser.). (ENG.). 24p. (gr. k-1). lib. bdg. 21.99 **(978-1-5157-6715-2(9))** Capstone Press of Coughlan Cos.

SKIN, COLOR OF

see Human Skin Color

SKIN—DISEASES

Abramovitz, Melissa. Lupus. 2007. (Diseases & Disorders Ser.). (ENG., Illus.). 96p. (YA). (gr. 7-12). lib. bdg. 34.95 (978-1-59018-999-3(X)) Cengage Gale.

Cobb, Vicki. Your Body Battles a Skinned Knee. Harris, Andrew, illus. Kunkel, Dennis, photos by. 2009. (Body Battles Ser.). (ENG.). 32p. (gr. 2-5). lib. bdg. 25.26 (978-0-8225-6814-8(4)) Lerner Publishing Group.

Donovan, Sandy. Stay Clear! What You Should Know about Skin Care. 2009. pap. 52.95 (978-0-7613-4686-9(4)) Lerner Publishing Group.

Egan, Tracie. Skin Cancer: Current & Emerging Trends in Detection & Treatment. 2009. (Cancer & Modern Science Ser.). 64p. (gr. 5-5). 58.50 (978-1-61511-788-8(1)) Rosen Publishing Group, Inc., The.

Faulk, Michelle. The Case of the Flesh-Eating Bacteria: Annie Biotica Solves Skin Disease Crimes. 2013. (Body System Disease Investigations Ser.). 48p. (J). (gr. 5-12). pap. 8.95 (978-1-4644-0224-1(8)) Enslow Pubs., Inc.

Fromer, Liza & Gerstein, Francine. My Itchy Body. Weissmann, Joe, illus. 2012. (Body Works). (ENG.). 24p. (J). (gr. 1-4). 12.95 (978-1-77049-311-7(5), Tundra Bks.) Tundra Bks. CAN. Dist: Penguin Random Hse. LLC.

Goldsmith, Connie. Skin Cancer. 2010. (USA TODAY Health Reports: Diseases & Disorders Ser.). (ENG.). 128p. (gr. 6-12). 34.60 (978-0-7613-5469-7(7)) Lerner Publishing Group.

Haugen, Hayley Mitchell. Lupus. 2010. (Perspectives on Diseases & Disorders Ser.). (Illus.). 144p. (YA). 38.95 (978-0-7377-4789-8(7), Greenhaven Pr., Inc.) Cengage Gale.

Landau, Elaine. Burns. 2010. (Head-to Toe Health 3 Ser.). 32p. (gr. 2). 28.50 (978-0-7614-4832-7(2)) Marshall Cavendish GBR. Dist: Marshall Cavendish Corp.

—Rashes. 2010. (Head-to Toe Health 3 Ser.). 32p. (gr. 2). 28.50 (978-0-7614-4835-8(7)) Marshall Cavendish Corp.

—Warts. 2010. (Head-to Toe Health 3 Ser.). 32p. (gr. 2). 28.50 (978-0-7614-4836-5(5)) Marshall Cavendish Corp.

Lew, Kristi & Lewandowski, Laura C. Itch & Ooze: Gross Stuff on Your Skin. Slack, Michael H., illus. 2009. (Gross Body Science Ser.). (ENG.). 48p. (gr. 3-5). lib. bdg. 29.27 (978-0-8225-8963-1(X)) Lerner Publishing Group.

Rhines, Karin. Lupus. 2012. (USA TODAY Health Reports: Diseases & Disorders Ser.). (ENG., Illus.). 112p. (gr. 6-12). lib. bdg. 34.60 (978-0-8225-8582-4(0)) Lerner Publishing Group.

Royston, Angela. Head Lice. 2009. (How's Your Health? Ser.). (J). (gr. 1-4). 28.50 (978-1-59920-218-1(2)) Black Rabbit Bks.

San-Joyz, Naweko. Acne Messages: Crack the Code of Your Zits & Say Goodbye to Acne. 2004. (Illus.). 224p. (YA). per. 14.99 (978-0-9749122-0-2(4)) Noixia's Reading Circle.

Sanchez, Anita. Itch! Everything You Didn't Want to Know about What Makes You Scratch. Ford, Gilbert, illus. 2017. (ENG.). 80p. (J). (978-0-544-81101-0(1)) Harcourt.

Sheen, Barbara. Acne. 2007. (Diseases & Disorders Ser.). (ENG., Illus.). 96p. (J). 32.45 (978-1-59018-345-8(2), Lucent Bks.) Cengage Gale.

Silverstein, Virginia & Nunn, Laura Silverstein. Handy Health Guide to Burns & Blisters. 2013. (Handy Health Guides). 48p. (J). lib. bdg. 25.27 (978-0-7660-4272-8(3)) Enslow Pubs., Inc.

Simons, Rae. Healthy Skin. McDonnell, Mary Ann & Forman, Sara, eds. 2013. (Young Adult's Guide to the Science of Health Ser.: 15). 128p. (J). (gr. 7-18). 24.95 (978-1-4222-2812-8(6)) Mason Crest.

SKIN DIVING

Here are entered works on free diving with the use of mask, fins, and snorkel. Works on free diving with the use of a self-contained underwater breathing apparatus are entered under Scuba Diving.

see also Underwater Exploration

Dessen, Maci. Let's Go Snorkeling! Use Place Value Understanding. 2014. (Rosen Common Core Math Readers Ser.). (ENG.). 24p. (J). (gr. 3-4). pap. 8.25 (978-1-4777-4938-8(1), Rosen Classroom) Rosen Publishing Group, Inc., The.

Ertle-Rickard, Stephen. Deep Sea Dive. 2008. (321 Go! Ser.). (ENG., Illus.). 36p. pap. (978-1-84167-782-8(5)) Ransom Publishing Ltd.

Ralphs, Matt. Space Jump. 2014. (Collins Big Cat Progress Ser.). (ENG., Illus.). 32p. (J). (gr. 5-6). pap. 7.99 (978-0-00-751938-5(9)) HarperCollins Pubs. Ltd. GBR. Dist: Independent Pubs. Group.

SKIN DIVING—FICTION

Alexander, Sarah. The Art of Not Breathing. 2017. (ENG.). 288p. (YA). (gr. 9). pap. 9.99 (978-0-544-93687-4(6), HMH Books For Young Readers) Houghton Mifflin Harcourt Publishing Co.

Gillingham, Sara. In My Nest. Siminovich, Lorena, illus. 2009. (ENG.). 12p. (J). (gr. -1 — 1). bds. 8.99 (978-0-8118-6555-5(X)) Chronicle Bks. LLC.

Lemke, Amy J. Snorkeling with Sea-Bots, 1 vol. Bradley, Jessica, illus. 2013. (Comics Land Ser.). (ENG.). 32p. (gr. k-2). 7.95 (978-1-4342-4271-6(4)); lib. bdg. 25.32 (978-1-4342-4030-9(4)) Stone Arch Bks.

Somper, Justin. Dead Deep. 2009. pap. 1.00 (978-1-4074-4559-5(6)) Recorded Bks., Inc.

SKINS

see Hides and Skins

SKIS AND SKIING

Abramovitz, Melissa. Skiing. Lucent Books, ed. 2014. (Science Behind Sports Ser.). (ENG., Illus.). 128p. (gr. 7-10). lib. bdg. 39.40 (978-1-4205-1155-0(6), Lucent Bks.) Cengage Gale.

Bailer, Darice. Ski Slopestyle. 2013. (Extreme Winter Sports Zone Ser.). (ENG., Illus.). 32p. (gr. 4-8). lib. bdg. 26.60 (978-1-4677-0756-5(2), Lerner Pubns.) Lerner Publishing Group.

—Ski Superpipe. 2013. (Extreme Winter Sports Zone Ser.). (ENG., Illus.). 32p. (gr. 4-8). lib. bdg. 26.60 (978-1-4677-0757-2(0), Lerner Pubns.) Lerner Publishing Group.

Bailey, Diane. Heliskiing. 2015. (ENG.). 48p. (gr. 3-6). 35.64 (978-1-63430-441-2(1)) Rourke Educational Media.

Bailey, Ellen. Katya's Gold: What Will Her Dreams Cost? 2008. (ENG.). 123p. (J). (gr. 4-9). pap. 10.99 (978-0-8280-2335-1(2)) Review & Herald Publishing Assn.

Bowman, Chris. Ski Patroller. 2014. (Dangerous Jobs Ser.). (ENG., Illus.). 24p. (J). (gr. 3-7). lib. bdg. 25.95 (978-1-62617-113-8(0), Torque Bks.) Bellwether Media.

Braun, Eric. Lindsey Vonn. 2017. (Sports All-Stars Ser.). (ENG.). 32p. (J). (gr. 2-5). 12.99 **(978-1-5124-3786-7(7)**, Lerner Pubns.); 39.99 **(978-1-5124-3785-0(9)**, Lerner Pubns.); (Illus.). 26.65 (978-1-5124-2580-2(X)); (Illus.). 39.99 **(978-1-5124-2825-4(6)**, Lerner Pubns.) Lerner Publishing Group.

Burns, Kylie. Biathlon, Cross Country, Ski Jumping, & Nordic Combined. 2009. (Winter Olympic Sports Ser.). (ENG., Illus.). 32p. (J). (gr. 3-6). lib. bdg. (978-0-7787-4021-6(8)); (gr. 4-6). pap. (978-0-7787-4040-7(4)) Crabtree Publishing Co.

Carr, Aaron. Esqui. 2013. (Deportes de Moda Ser.). (SPA., Illus.). 24p. (J). (gr. k-2). lib. bdg. 27.13 (978-1-62127-633-3(3), AV2 by Weigl) Weigl Pubs., Inc.

—Skiing. (Illus.). (J). 2013. 32p. (978-1-61913-514-7(0)) 2012. (ENG., 24p. pap. 12.95 (978-1-61913-520-8(5), AV2 by Weigl) Weigl Pubs., Inc.

Catel, Patrick. Skiing, 1 vol. 2013. (Winter Sports Ser.). (ENG., Illus.). 48p. (gr. 3-6). pap. 6.95 (978-1-4109-5458-9(7)); 32.65 (978-1-4109-5452-7(8)) Heinemann-Raintree.

Champion, Neil. Wild Snow: Skiing & Snowboarding. 2013. (Illus.). 32p. (J). lib. bdg. (978-1-59920-808-4(3)) Black Rabbit Bks.

Crossingham, John & Kalman, Bobbie. Skiing in Action. 2004. (Sports in Action Ser.). (ENG., Illus.). 32p. (J). pap. (978-0-7787-0357-0(6)); lib. bdg. (978-0-7787-0337-2(1)) Crabtree Publishing Co.

Dann, Sarah. Lindsey Vonn. 2013. (ENG., Illus.). 32p. (J). (978-0-7787-0025-8(9)); pap. (978-0-7787-0067-8(4)) Crabtree Publishing Co.

Gifford, Clive. Skiing. 2016. (Get Outdoors Ser.). (ENG., Illus.). 32p. (J). (gr. 4-6). pap. 11.99 (978-0-7502-8894-1(9), Wayland) Hachette Children's Group GBR. Dist: Hachette Bk. Group.

—Skiing. 2011. (Get Outdoors Ser.). (Illus.). 32p. (J). (gr. 4-6). lib. bdg. 25.25 (978-1-4488-3298-9(5), PowerKids Pr.) Rosen Publishing Group, Inc., The.

Kelley, K. C. Freestyle Skiing. 2011. (Extreme Sports Ser.). (ENG., Illus.). 32p. (J). (gr. 2-5). lib. bdg. 28.50 (978-1-60973-210-3(3), 201124) Child's World, Inc., The.

Kenney, Karen L. Skiing & Snowboarding. 2010. (Girls Play to Win Ser.). 64p. (J). (gr. 3-6). lib. bdg. 27.93 (978-1-59953-391-9(X)) Norwood Hse. Pr.

Laughlin, Kara L. Cross-Country Skiing. 2016. (Beginning Sports Ser.). (ENG.). 24p. (J). (gr. k-3). 27.07 (978-1-5038-0772-3(X), 210600) Child's World, Inc., The.

—Downhill Skiing. 2016. (Beginning Sports Ser.). (ENG.). 24p. (J). (gr. k-3). 27.07 (978-1-5038-0774-7(6), 210602) Child's World, Inc., The.

Loh-Hagan, Virginia. Extreme Downhill Ski Racing. 2016. (Nailed It! Ser.). (ENG., Illus.). 32p. (J). (gr. 4-8). 29.93 (978-1-63471-092-3(4), 208479, 45th Parallel Press) Cherry Lake Publishing.

—Extreme Snow Skiing. 2015. (Illus.). 32p. (J). (978-1-63470-017-7(1)) Cherry Lake Publishing.

MacAulay, Kelley & Kalman, Bobbie. Extreme Skiing. 2006. (Extreme Sports No Limits! Ser.). (ENG., Illus.). 32p. (J). (gr. 3-7). pap. (978-0-7787-1728-7(3), 1253447); lib. bdg. (978-0-7787-1682-2(1), 1253447) Crabtree Publishing Co.

Mattern, Joanne. Bernie Mac. 2006. (Blue Banner Biography Ser.). (Illus.). 32p. (J). (gr. 3-7). lib. bdg. 25.70 (978-1-58415-488-4(8)) Mitchell Lane Pubs., Inc.

Nagelhout, Ryan. Lindsey Vonn. 2016. (Sports MVPs Ser.). 24p. (J). (gr. 2-1). 22.60 (978-1-4824-4641-8(3)) Stevens, Gareth Publishing LLLP.

Phillips, H. Edwards. On a Jet Ski. 2014. (Life in the Fast Lane Ser.). (Illus.). 48p. (J). (gr. 4-6). 31.36 (978-1-62713-046-2(2)) Cavendish Square Publishing.

Schindler, John E. Extreme Skiing. 2005. (Extreme Sports Ser.). (Illus.). 24p. (gr. 2-5). pap. 8.15 (978-0-8368-4546-4(3)); lib. bdg. 23.00 (978-0-8368-4539-6(0)) Stevens, Gareth Publishing LLLP. (Gareth Stevens Learning Library).

SchreyerKarmel. TRAGEDY ON THE SLOPES UPPER INTERMEDIATE BOOK WITH ONLINE ACCESS. 2014. (ENG., Illus.). 28p. pap. 9.50 (978-1-107-62159-6(3)) Cambridge Univ. Pr.

Teitelbaum, Michael. Skiing. 2007. (21st Century Skills Library: Healthy for Life Ser.). (ENG., Illus.). 32p. (gr. 4-8). lib. bdg. 28.50 (978-1-60279-015-5(9), 200034) Cherry Lake Publishing.

Tieck, Sarah. Lindsey Vonn: Olympic Champion, 1 vol. 2010. (Big Buddy Bks.). (ENG., Illus.). 32p. (J). (gr. 2-5). 28.50 (978-1-61613-978-0(1)) ABDO Publishing Co.

Tomljanovic, Tatiana. Skiing. 2015. (J). (978-1-5105-0006-8(5)) SmartBook Media, Inc.

—Skiing: X Games. 2008. (Extreme Ser.). (Illus.). 32p. (J). (gr. 4-6). pap. 9.95 (978-1-59036-919-7(X)); lib. bdg. 26.00 (978-1-59036-918-0(1)) Weigl Pubs., Inc.

Trusdell, Brian. Great Moments in Olympic Skiing, 1 vol. 2014. (Great Moments in Olympic Sports Ser.). (ENG.). 64p. (gr. 10-14). lib. bdg. 32.79 (978-1-62403-397-1(0), SportsZone) ABDO Publishing Co.

Turnbull, Stephanie. Skiing & Snowboarding. 2016. (Adventure Sports Ser.). 24p. (gr. 2-6). 28.50 (978-1-62588-387-2(0), Smart Apple Media) Black Rabbit Bks.

Waxman, Laura Hamilton. Skiing. 2017. (Winter Olympic Sports Ser.). (ENG.). 32p. (J). (gr. 1-4). 20.95 **(978-1-68151-151-1(7)**, Amicus High Interest) Amicus Publishing.

—Winter Olympic Sports: Skiing. 2017. (Winter Olympic Sports Ser.). (ENG.). 32p. (J). (gr. 2-5). pap. 9.99 **(978-1-68152-182-4(2))** Amicus.

Yomtov, Nel. The Science of a Carve Turn. 2015. (21st Century Skills Library: Full-Speed Sports Ser.). (ENG., Illus.). 32p. (J). (gr. 4-7). 29.93 (978-1-63362-580-8(X), 206504) Cherry Lake Publishing.

Zweig, Eric. Crazy Canucks: The Uphill Battle of Canada's Downhill Ski Team, 1 vol. 2008. (Lorimer Recordbooks Ser.). (ENG., Illus.). 144p. (gr. 8-12). 9.95 (978-1-55277-019-1(2), 9781552770191); 16.95 (978-1-55277-020-7(6)) Lorimer, James & Co., Ltd., Pubs. CAN. Dist: Casemate Pubs. & Bk. Distributors, LLC.

SKIS AND SKIING—FICTION

Balaban, Mariah. Scooby-Doo & the Scary Snowman, 1 vol. Duendes Del Sur Staff, illus. 2012. (Scooby-Doo! Set 2 Ser.: No. 2). (ENG.). 24p. (J). (gr. k-3). lib. bdg. 24.21 (978-1-59961-869-2(9)) Spotlight.

Bates, Sonya. Wildcat Run, 1 vol. Charko, Kasia, illus. 2011. (Orca Echoes Ser.). (ENG.). 64p. (J). (gr. 2-3). pap. 6.95 (978-1-55469-830-1(8)) Orca Bk. Pubs. USA.

Blackburn, Sheila M. Stewie Scraps & the Super Sleigh. 2008. 72p. pap. (978-1-903853-89-4(3)) Brilliant Pubns.

Bryant, Louella. Two Tracks in the Snow. Fargo, Todd, illus. l.t. ed. 2004. (Turtle Bks.). 32p. (J). lib. bdg. 15.95 (978-0-944727-46-1(8)); per. 9.95 (978-0-944727-45-4(X)) Jason & Nordic Pubs. (Turtle Bks.).

Butcher, Nancy, et al. It's Snow Problem, 3 vols. 2003. (ENG., Illus.). 112p. (978-0-00-714466-2(0), HarperCollins Children's Bks.) HarperCollins Pubs. Ltd.

Crossingham, John & Kalman, Bobbie. Le Ski Alpin. Briere, Marie-Josee, tr. from ENG. 2007. (Sans Limites Ser.). (FRE., Illus.). 32p. (J). pap. 9.95 (978-2-89579-167-6(8)) Bayard Canada Livres CAN. Dist: Crabtree Publishing Co.

Daly, Catherine. The Ghost of Christmas Past. 2012. 162p. (J). (978-0-545-48422-0(7)) Scholastic, Inc.

Dower, Laura. Give Me a Break. 2004. 166p. (J). lib. bdg. 16.92 (978-1-4242-0649-0(9)) Fitzgerald Bks.

Feldkamp, Jim And Cate. The Adventures of Tommy & Clara on Mount Catherine. 2008. 32p. pap. 14.49 (978-1-4389-1366-7(4)) AuthorHouse.

Fields, T. S. Missing in the Mountains. 2008. (ENG.). 108p. (J). (gr. 4-7). pap. 6.95 (978-0-87358-950-5(5)) Cooper Square Publishing Llc.

Fincher, Cecilia. Chandra's Adventure. 2012. 28p. pap. 19.99 (978-1-4772-0137-4(8)) AuthorHouse.
Friedman, Laurie. A Twist of Fate. Shaloshvili, Natasha, illus. (Mostly Miserable Life of April Sinclair Ser.: Vol. 7). (ENG.). 168p. (gr. 5-9). 2017. (J). pap. 5.95 **(978-1-5124-5866-4(X))** 2016. 17.95 (978-1-4677-8590-7(3)) 2016. 35.99 (978-1-5124-0899-7(9)) Lerner Publishing Group. (Darby Creek).
Gehrke, William & Gehrke, Dolores. Sonia's Choice. 2011. 28p. pap. 15.99 (978-1-4634-0825-1(0)) AuthorHouse.
Gerber, Linda. The Finnish Line. 2007. (S. A. S. S. Ser.). (ENG.). 224p. (YA). (gr. 7-18). 7.99 (978-0-14-240916-9(2), Speak) Penguin Young Readers Group.
Giacomoni, Carol A. I can ski despite these Ducky feet on Me. 2010. 24p. 14.95 (978-1-4269-3187-1(5)) Trafford Publishing.
Gibbs, Stuart. Spy Ski School. 2016. (Spy School Ser.). (ENG., Illus.). 368p. (J). (gr. 3-7). 16.99 (978-1-4814-4562-7(6), Simon & Schuster Bks. For Young Readers) Simon & Schuster Bks. For Young Readers.
Gregory, Matt. To Announce at a Later Date. 2005. (Illus.). 36p. (J). 20.00 (978-0-9766442-0-0(7)) Gregory, Charles Matthew.
Harvey, Jacqueline. Alice-Miranda in the Alps. 2016. (Alice-Miranda Ser.: 12). (ENG.). 336p. (J). (gr. 3-7). pap. 9.99 (978-0-85798-274-2(5)) Random Hse. Australia AUS. Dist: Independent Pubs. Group.
High Escape (Ski Racing) 64p. (YA). (gr. 6-12). pap. 10.95 (978-0-8224-6478-5(0)) Globe Fearon Educational Publishing.
Imagine This, James Robert: Individual Title, 6 packs. (Action Packs Ser.). 120p. (gr. 3-5). 44.00 (978-0-7635-8418-4(5)) Rigby Education.
Jacks, C. S. The Adventures of Pisten Billy: Pisten Billy Makes the Grade! 2010. 32p. pap. 12.99 (978-1-4520-6624-0(8)) AuthorHouse.
Jay, Basil. The Adventures of Twig. 2011. (Illus.). 120p. pap. 32.90 (978-1-4567-8631-1(8)) AuthorHouse.
Jones, Melanie Davis. I Can Ski! 2004. (Rookie Reader Skill Set Ser.). (ENG., Illus.). 32p. (J). (gr. k-2). pap. 4.95 (978-0-516-27901-5(7), Children's Pr.) Scholastic Library Publishing.
—I Can Ski! Boles, Terry, illus. 2003. (Rookie Readers Ser.). 32p. (J). 19.50 (978-0-516-22878-5(1), Children's Pr.) Scholastic Library Publishing.
Keene, Carolyn. Ski School Sneak. Pamintuan, Macky, illus. 11th ed. 2007. (Nancy Drew & the Clue Crew Ser.: 11). (ENG.). 96p. (J). (gr. 1-4). pap. 5.99 (978-1-4169-4936-7(4), Aladdin) Simon & Schuster Children's Publishing.
Krulik, Nancy. It's Snow Joke. John and Wendy Staff, illus. 2006. (Katie Kazoo, Switcheroo Ser.: 22). (ENG.). 80p. (J). (gr. 2-4). pap. 3.99 (978-0-448-44396-6(1), Grosset & Dunlap) Penguin Young Readers Group.
Leblanc, Louise. Leo's Skiing Surprise. Prud'homme, Jules, illus. 2007. (Formac First Novels Ser.). (ENG.). 64p. (J). (gr. 2-5). 14.95 (978-0-88780-738-1(0), 9780887807381) Formac Publishing Co., Ltd. CAN. Dist: Casemate Pubs. & Bk. Distributors, LLC.
Lemke, Donald B. The Invincible Boy-Bot. 2012. (Zinc Alloy Ser.). (ENG.). 128p. (gr. 1-3). pap. 8.95 (978-1-4342-4597-7(7)) Stone Arch Bks.
Lewis, Beverly. Girls Only! 2008. (Girls Only (Go!) Ser.: Vols. 5-8). (ENG.). (J). (gr. 4-7). 510p. pap. 20.00 (978-0-7642-0462-3(9));Vols. 1-4. 512p. pap. 16.00 (978-0-7642-0461-6(0)) Bethany Hse. Pubs.
Linkowski, Tami Leli. Lynn Was a Cow Who Could Ski. 2008. 20p. pap. 24.95 (978-1-4241-9626-5(4)) America Star Bks.
Lorenz Guest, Donna. The Enchanted Ride. 2009. 32p. pap. 14.99 (978-1-4389-8116-1(3)) AuthorHouse.
Mead, Richelle. Frostbite. 2008. (Vampire Academy Ser.: Bk. 2). (ENG.). 335p. (YA). (gr. 7-18). pap. 10.99 (978-1-59514-175-0(8), Razorbill) Penguin Publishing Group.
—Frostbite. 2012. (Vampire Academy (Graphic Novels) Ser.: 2). lib. bdg. 24.50 (978-0-606-23631-7(7), Turtleback) Turtleback Bks.
Meister, Cari. Buzz Beaker & the Speed Secret. McGuire, Bill, illus. 2010. (Buzz Beaker Bks.). (ENG.). 32p. (gr. 2-3). pap. 6.25 (978-1-4342-2798-0(7)); 22.65 (978-1-4342-2061-5(3)) Stone Arch Bks.
Morrison, Janet Love. Radar the Rescue Dog. 2013. 40p. pap. (978-1-4602-2575-2(9)) FriesenPress.
Moscovich, Rotem, et al. Curious George Snowy Day. 2007. (Curious George Ser.). (ENG., Illus.). 24p. (J). (gr. -1-3). 3.99 (978-0-618-80043-8(3)) Houghton Mifflin Harcourt Publishing Co.
Nickel, Scott. Skiing Has Its Ups & Downs, 1 vol. Santillan, Jorge H., illus. 2011. (Sports Illustrated Kids Victory School Superstars Ser.). (ENG.). 56p. (gr. 1-3). pap. 5.95 (978-1-4342-3395-0(2)); lib. bdg. 26.65 (978-1-4342-2234-3(9)) Stone Arch Bks.
Nielsen, Gwyn English. Torey the Turkey Goes Skiing. 2003. (Illus.). 24p. (Orig.). (gr. -1-4). pap. 5.99 (978-0-9660726-0-0(X)) C.G.S. Pr.
Oceanak, Karla. Hotdogger. Spanjer, Kendra, illus. 2013. (Aldo Zelnick Comic Novel Ser.: 8). (ENG.). 160p. (J). (gr. 3-7). 12.95 (978-1-934649-37-4(6)) Bailiwick Pr.
Osorio, Rick. The Great Adventure of Sally Rock & el Lobo. 2007. (ENG.). 96p. per. 19.95 (978-1-4241-5869-0(9)) America Star Bks.
O'Sullivan, Joanne. Between Two Skies. 2017. (ENG.). 272p. (YA). (gr. 7). 16.99 (978-0-7636-9034-2(1)) Candlewick Pr.
Parker, Emma. The Snowman Olympics. 2010. (Illus.). 20p. pap. (978-1-877561-36-8(3)) First Edition Ltd.
Parker, John. Chaos Mountain. 2007. 96p. (YA). pap. (978-1-4207-0734-2(5)) Sundance/Newbridge Educational Publishing.
Pogo the Clown. The Great Blue Sky: Harley's Great Adventures. Miller, Richard D., illus. 2005. (J). 12.95 (978-0-9755253-6-4(0)) Chiliric Pubns.
Ray, J. Hamilton. Squirrels on Skis. Lemaître, Pascal, illus. 2013. (Beginner Books Ser.). (ENG.). 64p. (J). (gr. k-3). 9.99 (978-0-449-81081-1(X), Random Hse. Bks. for Young Readers) Random Hse. Children's Bks.
Ribeiro, Nelson, et al. Betty & Veronica in Trendsetter. 2007. (Betty & Veronica Ser.). (ENG., Illus.). 80p. (J). (gr. 3-6). 24.21 (978-1-59961-268-3(2)) Spotlight.
Rueda, Claudia. Bunny Slopes. 2016. (ENG., Illus.). 60p. (J). (gr. -1-k). 15.99 (978-1-4521-4197-8(5)) Chronicle Bks. LLC.
Seuling, Barbara. Robert & the Great Escape. Brewer, Paul, illus. 2003. (Robert Bks.). (ENG.). 120p. (J). 15.95 (978-0-8126-2700-8(8)) Cricket Bks.
Skiing: KinderConcepts Individual Title Six-Packs. (Kinderstarters Ser.). 8p. (gr. -1-1). 21.00 (978-0-7635-8718-5(4)) Rigby Education.
Smith, Alex T. Claude on the Slopes, 1 vol. Smith, Alex T., illus. 2016. (Claude Ser.). (ENG., Illus.). 96p. (J). (gr. 1-3). pap. 7.95 (978-1-56145-923-0(2)) Peachtree Pubs.
Van Dusen, Chris. Learning to Ski with Mr. Magee. 2010. (ENG., Illus.). 36p. (J). (gr. -1-3). 15.99 (978-0-8118-7495-3(8)) Chronicle Bks. LLC.
Weinmann, Julianne. The Mis-Adventures of Frissue the Tissue. 2005. 48p. (J). pap. 15.69 (978-1-4116-5310-8(6)) Lulu Pr., Inc.
Wells, Helen. Cherry Ames, Ski Nurse Mystery. 2007. (Cherry Ames Nurse Stories Ser.). 224p. (J). (gr. 3-7). 14.95 (978-0-8261-0437-3(1)) Springer Publishing Co., Inc.
Wilshire, Florence A. They're all from the Skies. 2005. 82p. pap. 24.95 (978-1-4116-3892-1(1)) Lulu Pr., Inc.

SKULL

see Brain

SKUNKS

Bekkering, Annalise. Skunks. 2007. (Backyard Animals Ser.). (Illus.). 24p. (J). (gr. -1-3). lib. bdg. 24.45 (978-1-59036-685-1(9)) Weigl Pubs., Inc.
—Skunks. Hudak, Heather C., ed. 2007. (Backyard Animals Ser.). (Illus.). 24p. (J). (gr. -1-3). pap. 8.95 (978-1-59036-686-8(7)) Weigl Pubs., Inc.
Bodden, Valerie. Skunks. 2016. (Amazing Animals Ser.). (Illus.). 24p. (J). (ENG.). (gr. 1-3). pap. 8.99 (978-1-62832-220-0(9), Creative Paperbacks); 28.50 (978-1-60818-614-3(8), Creative Education) Creative Co., The.
Bogue, Gary. There's a Skunk in My Backyard: The Big Stink. Todd, Chuck, illus. 2017. (J). **(978-1-59714-399-8(5))** Heyday.
Borgert-Spaniol, Megan. Baby Skunks. 2017. (Super Cute! Ser.). (ENG., Illus.). 24p. (J). (gr. k-3). lib. bdg. 25.95 (978-1-62617-547-1(0), Blastoff! Readers) Bellwether Media.
Bowman, Chris. Striped Skunks. 2016. (North American Animals Ser.). (ENG., Illus.). 24p. (J). (gr. k-3). lib. bdg. 25.95 (978-1-62617-338-5(9), Blastoff! Readers) Bellwether Media.
Campbell, Sam. Sweet Sue's Adventures. Fox, Charles Philip, photos by. 2010. (Illus.). 119p. reprint ed. pap. 10.95 (978-1-57258-210-1(3)) TEACH Services, Inc.
Dieker, Wendy Strobel. Skunks. 2017. (Spot Backyard Animals Ser.). (ENG.). 16p. (J). (gr. k-3). 17.95 **(978-1-68151-096-5(0))** Amicus Publishing.
—El Zorrillo (Skunks) 2017. (Spot Backyard Animals Ser.). (ENG & SPA.). 16p. (J). (gr. k-3). 17.95 **(978-1-68151-276-1(9)**, Amicus Readers) Amicus Publishing.
Doudna, Kelly. It's a Baby Skunk!, 1 vol. 2008. (Baby Mammals Ser.). (ENG., Illus.). 24p. (J). (gr. k-3). lib. bdg. 24.21 (978-1-60453-032-2(4)) ABDO Publishing Co.
Gish, Melissa. Living Wild: Skunks. 2014. (Living Wild Ser.). (ENG., Illus.). 48p. (J). (gr. 4-7). pap. 12.00 (978-0-89812-843-7(9), Creative Paperbacks) Creative Co., The.
—Skunks. 2013. (Illus.). 46p. (J). 35.65 (978-1-60818-290-9(8), Creative Education) Creative Co., The.
Gonzales, Doreen. Skunks in the Dark. 2009. 24p. (YA). pap. 8.25 (978-1-4358-3255-8(8)); (Illus.). (J). (gr. 1-3). 22.60 (978-1-4042-8099-1(5)) Rosen Publishing Group, Inc., The.
Gray, Susan H. Skunks Smell Bad. 2015. (Tell Me Why Library). (ENG., Illus.). 24p. (J). (gr. 2-5). 27.07 (978-1-63188-999-8(0), 205908) Cherry Lake Publishing.
Green, Emily. Skunks. 2010. (Backyard Wildlife Ser.). (ENG., Illus.). 24p. (J). (gr. k-3). lib. bdg. 25.95 (978-1-60014-445-5(4), Blastoff! Readers) Bellwether Media.
Heckt, Jackie. Skunks. 2016. (Creatures of the Forest Habitat Ser.). 00024p. (J). (gr. 3-3). pap. 8.25 (978-1-4994-2716-5(6), PowerKids Pr.) Rosen Publishing Group, Inc., The.
Hildebrand, Cody. How the Skunk Earned His Stripes: A Pet Parent's Guide to Having a Skunk in the Family. 2004. (YA). 14.95 (978-0-9753729-0-6(4)) Hildebrand, Betty.
Jobes, Cecily. Watch Out for Skunks!, 01 vols., 1. 2016. (Wild Backyard Animals Ser.). (ENG., Illus.). 24p. (J). pap. 8.25 (978-1-5081-4267-6(X), PowerKids Pr.) Rosen Publishing Group, Inc., The.
Krueger, Carol. Smelly Skunks. 2004. (Rigby Sails Early Ser.). (ENG., Illus.). 16p. (gr. 1-2). pap. 6.95 (978-0-7578-9955-3(2)) Houghton Mifflin Harcourt Publishing Co.
Markle, Sandra. Los Zorrillos (Skunks) 2009. (SPA.). pap. 46.95 (978-0-7613-4722-4(4)) Lerner Publishing Group.
—Skunks. (Animal Prey Ser.). 2008. (Illus.). 39p. (J). (gr. 3-7). per. 7.95 (978-0-8225-6440-9(8), First Avenue Editions) 2008. pap. 46.95 (978-0-8225-9324-9(6)) 2007. (ENG., Illus.). 40p. (gr. 3-6). lib. bdg. 25.26 (978-0-8225-6437-9(8)) Lerner Publishing Group.
—Los Zorrillos. Translations.com Staff, tr. from ENG. 2008. (Animales Presa (Animal Prey) Ser.). (SPA.). 40p. (gr. 3-6). 25.26 (978-0-7613-3899-4(3)) Lerner Publishing Group.
—Los Zorrillos (Skunks) 2008. 40p. (J). pap. 7.95 (978-0-7613-3903-8(5), Ediciones Lerner) Lerner Publishing Group.
Mattern, Joanne. Skunks Are Night Animals. 2007. (Night Animals Ser.). (Illus.). 24p. (gr. k-3). lib. bdg. 22.00 (978-0-8368-7850-9(7), Weekly Reader Leveled Readers) Stevens, Gareth Publishing LLLP.
—Skunks Are Night Animals (Los Zorrillos Son Animales Nocturnos) 2007. (Night Animals/ Animales Nocturnos Ser.). (SPA & ENG., Illus.). 24p. (gr. k-3). pap. 8.15 (978-0-8368-8054-0(4)); lib. bdg. 22.00 (978-0-8368-8047-2(1)) Stevens, Gareth Publishing LLLP. (Weekly Reader Leveled Readers).
McGill, Jordan. Skunks. 2011. (J). 27.13 (978-1-61690-934-5(X)); (978-1-61690-580-4(8)) Weigl Pubs., Inc.
—Zorrillos. 2012. (SPA.). (J). (978-1-61913-196-5(X)) Weigl Pubs., Inc.
Moore Niver, Heather. Skunks after Dark. 2016. (Animals of the Night Ser.). (ENG.). 32p. (J). (gr. 3-3). pap. 10.52 (978-0-7660-7358-6(0)); (Illus.). lib. bdg. 25.27 (978-0-7660-7360-9(2)) Enslow Pubs., Inc.
Nelson, Kristin L. Spraying Skunks. 2003. (Pull Ahead Bks.). (Illus.). 32p. (J). 22.60 (978-0-8225-4670-2(1), Lerner Pubns.) Lerner Publishing Group.
Nichols, Catherine. Smelly Skunks. 2008. (Gross-Out Defenses Ser.). (Illus.). 24p. (J). (gr. k-3). lib. bdg. 21.28 (978-1-59716-716-1(9), 1284316) Bearport Publishing Co., Inc.
Otfinoski, Steven. Skunks. 2008. (Animals Animals Ser.). 48p. (gr. 3-18). lib. bdg. 29.93 (978-0-7614-2929-6(8), Benchmark Bks.) Marshall Cavendish Corp.
Owen, Ruth. Skunk Kits. 2011. (Wild Baby Animals Ser.). 24p. (J). (gr. k-3). lib. bdg. 19.96 (978-1-61772-161-8(1)); lib. bdg., E-Book 39.93 (978-1-61772-243-1(X)) Bearport Publishing Co., Inc.
Roza, Greg. Phew! The Skunk & Other Stinky Animals. 2011. (Armed & Dangerous Ser.). (Illus.). 24p. (J). pap. 8.25 (978-1-4488-2682-7(9), PowerKids Pr.); (YA). (gr. 1-4). lib. bdg. 22.60 (978-1-4488-2549-3(0)) Rosen Publishing Group, Inc., The.
Schuh, Mari. Skunks. 2017. (Black & White Animals Ser.). (ENG., Illus.). 24p. (gr. k-1). lib. bdg. 21.99 (978-1-5157-3622-6(9), Pebble Bks.) Capstone Press of Coughlan Cos.
—Skunks. 2015. (My First Animal Library). 24p. (J). (gr. k-2). lib. bdg. 25.65 (978-1-62031-291-9(3), Bullfrog Bks.) Jump! Inc.
Shoemaker, Kate. Skunk Stench. 2015. (Nature's Grossest Ser.). (ENG., Illus.). 24p. (J). (gr. 1-2). 22.60 (978-1-4824-1851-4(7)) Stevens, Gareth Publishing LLLP.

SKUNKS—FICTION

Amato, Mary. Sniff a Skunk! Jenkins, Ward, illus. 2015. (Good Crooks Ser.: 3). (ENG.). 128p. (gr. 2-4). (J). 14.99 (978-1-5124-0169-1(2));Bk. 3. 14.99 (978-1-60684-598-1(5)) Lerner Publishing Group. (Darby Creek).
Barnett, Mac. The Skunk. McDonnell, Patrick, illus. 2015. (ENG.). 40p. (J). (gr. -1-3). 17.99 (978-1-59643-966-5(1), 9781596439665) Roaring Brook Pr.
Beckstedt, Cynthia M. The Great Smoky Mountain Skunk Adventure, 1 vol. 2009. 28p. pap. 24.95 (978-1-60836-034-5(2)) America Star Bks.
Burgess, Thornton W. The Adventures of Jimmy Skunk. 112p. 2008. per. 9.95 (978-1-60312-416-4(0)) 2007. 22.95 (978-1-60312-594-9(9)) Aegypan.
—The Adventures of Jimmy Skunk. (J). 18.95 (978-0-8488-0384-1(1)) Amereon Ltd.
—The Adventures of Jimmy Skunk. 2016. (ENG., Illus.). (J). 22.95 **(978-1-358-39350-1(8))** Creative Media Partners, LLC.
—The Adventures of Jimmy Skunk. 2011. 110p. 23.95 (978-1-4638-9560-0(7)) Rodgers, Alan Bks.
Calvani, Mayra. Humberto, the Bookworm Hamster. Grady, Kit, illus. 2009. 20p. pap. 10.95 (978-1-935137-92-4(1)) Guardian Angel Publishing, Inc.
Choyce, Lesley. Skunks for Breakfast, 1 vol. Jones, Brenda, illus. 2007. (ENG.). 32p. (J). (gr. -1-2). pap. 8.95 (978-1-55109-586-8(6)) Nimbus Publishing, Ltd. CAN. Dist: Orca Bk. Pubs. USA.
Covey, Sean. Lily & the Yucky Cookies. Curtis, Stacy, illus. 2013. (7 Habits of Happy Kids Ser.: 5). (ENG.). 32p. (J). (gr. -1-1). 7.99 (978-1-4424-7649-3(4), Simon & Schuster Bks. For Young Readers) Simon & Schuster Bks. For Young Readers.
Crenshaw, Glenda. Friends of the Enchanted Forest: How they Save Christmas. 2011. 28p. pap. 15.47 (978-1-4520-0512-6(5)) AuthorHouse.
Deak, Gloria. The Kissing Skunks. Nathan, Cheryl, illus. 2006. 40p. (J). (gr. -1). 16.95 (978-1-932065-46-6(6)) Star Bright Bks., Inc.
DeLuise, Dom & Carter, Derek. Pouch Potato. 2007. 33p. pap. 9.95 (978-0-9717952-0-4(7)) Bacchus Bks.
Derubertis, Barbara. Sammy Skunk's Super Sniffer. Alley, R. W., illus. 2011. (Animal Antics A to Z Set III Ser.). pap. 45.32 (978-0-7613-8428-1(6)) Kane Press, Inc.
deRubertis, Barbara. Sammy Skunk's Super Sniffer. Alley, R. W., illus. 2011. (Animal Antics A to Z Ser.). pap. 7.95 (978-1-57565-344-0(3)); lib. bdg. 22.60 (978-1-57565-352-5(4)) Kane Press, Inc.
deRubertis, Barbara & DeRubertis, Barbara. Sammy Skunk's Super Sniffer. Alley, R. W., illus. 2012. (Animal Antics A to Z Ser.). 32p. (J). (gr. 2 — 1). cd-rom 7.95 (978-1-57565-412-6(1)) Kane Press, Inc.
Dyan, Penelope. There's a Skunk in My Trunk. Dyan, Penelope, illus. 2012. (Illus.). 34p. pap. 11.95 (978-1-61477-045-9(X)) Bellissima Publishing, LLC.
Erickson, John R. The Case of the Perfect Dog. Holmes, Gerald L., illus. 2012. 127p. (J). (978-1-59188-259-6(1)) Maverick Bks.
—The Case of the Perfect Dog. Holmes, Gerald L., illus. 2012. (Hank the Cowdog (Quality) Ser.). (ENG.). 127p. (J). (gr. 3-6). pap. 5.99 (978-1-59188-159-9(5)) Maverick Bks., Inc.
—The Case of the Secret Weapon. Holmes, Gerald L., illus. 2011. (Hank the Cowdog Ser.). (ENG.). 125p. (J). (gr. 3-6). pap. 5.99 (978-1-59188-155-1(2)) Maverick Bks., Inc.
Fabrizio, Anthony. The Last Forest, 1 vol. 2009. 64p. pap. 19.95 (978-1-61546-861-4(7)) America Star Bks.
Hamilton, Elizabeth L. Stinky Skunk's Self-Control. 2004. (Character Critters Ser.: No. 4). (Illus.). 32p. (J). (gr. -1-3). per. 5.95 (978-0-9713749-6-6(1), Character-in-Action) Quiet Impact, Inc.
Hayes, Joe. The Lovesick Skunk. Castro L., Antonio, illus. (ENG.). 32p. (J). 2016. 7.95 (978-1-941026-04-5(4)) 2010. 16.95 (978-1-933693-81-1(9)) Cinco Puntos Pr.
Hillenbrand, Will. All for a Dime! A Bear & Mole Story. (ENG.). 32p. (J). (gr. -1-1). 2016. 7.99 (978-0-8234-3684-2(5)) 2015. (Illus.). 16.95 (978-0-8234-2946-2(6)) Holiday Hse., Inc.
Jenkins, Emily. Skunkdog. Pratt, Pierre, illus. 2008. (ENG.). 32p. (J). (gr. -1-3). 16.95 (978-0-374-37009-1(5), 9780374370091, Farrar, Straus & Giroux (BYR)) Farrar, Straus & Giroux.
Kelly, Jacqueline. Skunked! White, Teagan & Meyer, Jennifer L., illus. 2016. (Calpurnia Tate, Girl Vet Ser.). (ENG.). 112p. (J). 15.99 (978-1-62779-868-6(4), 9781627798686, Holt, Henry & Co. Bks. For Young Readers) Holt, Henry & Co.
Mack, Jeff. Who Needs a Bath? Mack, Jeff, illus. 2015. (ENG., Illus.). 40p. (J). (gr. -1-3). 17.99 (978-0-06-222028-8(4)) HarperCollins Pubs.
—Who Wants a Hug? Mack, Jeff, illus. 2015. (ENG., Illus.). 40p. (J). (gr. -1-3). 17.99 (978-0-06-222026-4(8)) HarperCollins Pubs.
Martin, Anne E. Midnight Kitties. 2007. (Illus.). 35p. (J). per. 13.99 (978-1-59879-245-4(8)) Lifevest Publishing, Inc.
Masterson, Josephine. A Smelly Surprise. 2015. (Rosen REAL Readers: STEM & STEAM Collection). (ENG.). 8p. pap. 5.46 (978-1-4994-9485-3(8), Rosen Classroom) Rosen Publishing Group, Inc., The.
Nanette. Buddy & Muddy: The Twin Brown Skunks. 2004. (J). 12.95 (978-0-9741269-5-1(0)) St. Bernard Publishing, LLC.
Pate, Ginger. Would You Invite a Skunk to Your Wedding? Blanski, Maribeth, illus. 2009. 32p. (J). 16.95 (978-1-880851-73-9(3)) Greene Bark Pr., Inc.
Penn, Audrey. A Kiss Goodbye. Gibson, Barbara Leonard, illus. 2007. (Kissing Hand Ser.). (ENG.). 32p. (J). (gr. -1-3). 16.95 (978-1-933718-04-0(8)) Tanglewood Pr.
Penn, Audrey & Cosgrove, Stephen. Sassafras. Harper, Ruth E. & James, Robin, illus. 2006. (ENG.). 32p. (J). (gr. -1-3). 16.95 (978-1-933718-03-3(X)) Tanglewood Pr.
Pochocki, Ethel. The Blessing of the Beasts. Moser, Barry, illus. 2014. (ENG.). 40p. (J). pap. 15.99 (978-1-61261-582-0(1)) Paraclete Pr., Inc.
Pochocki, Ethel & Helms, Hal M. The Blessing of the Beasts. Moser, Barry, illus. 2007. (ENG.). 40p. (gr. -1-3). 18.95 (978-1-55725-502-0(4)) Paraclete Pr., Inc.
Sargent, Dave. Finding Sammy #1 (PB), 10 vols. 2007. (Little Stinker Ser.: 1). (J). pap. 10.95 (978-1-59381-274-4(4)) Ozark Publishing.
—I Named Him Sammy #7, 10 vols. 2007. (Little Stinker Ser.: 7). (J). lib. bdg. 23.60 (978-1-59381-291-1(4)) Ozark Publishing.
—I Named Him Sammy #7 (PB), 10 vols. 2007. (Little Stinker Ser.: 7). (J). pap. 10.95 (978-1-59381-292-8(2)) Ozark Publishing.
Sargent, Dave & Sargent, Pat. Sammy Skunk: I'm a Little Stinker, 56 vols., Vol. 9. Huff, Jeane, illus. 2nd rev. ed. 2003. (Animal Pride Ser.: 9). 42p. (J). lib. bdg. 20.95 (978-1-56763-775-5(2)) Ozark Publishing.
Schmid, Paul. A Pet for Petunia. 2011. (J). lib. bdg. 14.89 (978-0-06-196332-2(1)) HarperCollins Pubs.
—A Pet for Petunia. Schmid, Paul, illus. 2011. (ENG., Illus.). 40p. (J). (gr. -1-2). 12.99 (978-0-06-196331-5(3)) HarperCollins Pubs.
Shaskan, Trisha Speed. Punk Skunks. Shaskan, Stephen, illus. 2016. 40p. (J). (gr. -1-3). 17.99 (978-0-06-236396-1(4)) HarperCollins Pubs.
Stauffacher, Sue. Animal Rescue Team: Special Delivery! Lamont, Priscilla, illus. 2011. (Animal Rescue Team Ser.). (ENG.). 176p. (J). (gr. 3-7). 6.99 (978-0-375-85132-2(1), Yearling) Random Hse. Children's Bks.
—Special Delivery! Lamont, Priscilla, illus. 2010. (Animal Rescue Team Ser.: No. 2). (ENG.). 176p. (J). (gr. 3-7). 12.99 (978-0-375-85848-2(2), Knopf Bks. for Young Readers) Random Hse. Children's Bks.
Thomas, Jan. The Easter Bunny's Assistant. Thomas, Jan, illus. 2012. (ENG., Illus.). 40p. (J). (gr. -1-3). 12.99 (978-0-06-169286-4(7)) HarperCollins Pubs.
Weiss, Dylan. Sebastian's Tale: A Skunk Tales Trilogy Book. 2016. (J). (978-1-943267-16-3(2)) Red Engine Pr.
Wilhelm, Hans. Noodles & the Bully. 2012. (Illus.). (J). (978-0-545-34499-9(9)) Scholastic, Inc.
Yardi, Robin. The Midnight War of Mateo Martinez. 2016. (ENG.). 184p. (J). (gr. 3-6). 17.99 (978-1-4677-8306-4(4), Carolrhoda Bks.) Lerner Publishing Group.

SKY DIVING

see Skydiving

SKYDIVING

Bailey, Diane. Skydiving. 2015. (ENG.). 48p. (gr. 3-6). 35.64 (978-1-63430-443-6(8)) Rourke Educational Media.
Boothroyd, Jennifer. How Do Parachutes Work? 2013. (Lightning Bolt Books (tm) — How Flight Works). (ENG., Illus.). 32p. (gr. k-2). lib. bdg. 26.60 (978-0-7613-8968-2(7), Lerner Pubns.) Lerner Publishing Group.
Ertle-Rickard, Stephen. Sky Dive. 2008. (321 Go! Ser.). (ENG., Illus.). 36p. pap. (978-1-84167-785-9(X)) Ransom Publishing Ltd.
Gigliotti, Jim. Skydiving. 2011. (Extreme Sports Ser.). (ENG., Illus.). 32p. (J). (gr. 2-5). lib. bdg. 28.50 (978-1-60973-211-0(1), 201132) Child's World, Inc., The.
Goldish, Meish. Skydiving Dogs. 2014. (Dog Heroes Ser.). 32p. (J). (gr. 2-7). lib. bdg. 25.27 (978-1-62724-087-1(X)) Bearport Publishing Co., Inc.
Gordon, Nick. Smoke Jumper. 2012. (Dangerous Jobs Ser.). (ENG., Illus.). 24p. (J). (gr. 3-7). lib. bdg. 25.95 (978-1-60014-781-4(X), Torque Bks.) Bellwether Media.
Kelley, K. C. BASE Jumping. 2011. (Extreme Sports Ser.). (ENG., Illus.). 32p. (J). (gr. 2-5). lib. bdg. 28.50 (978-1-60973-205-9(7), 201121) Child's World, Inc., The.
Kennedy, Robert C. Would You Dare Go Skydiving? 2016. (Would You Dare? Ser.). 00032p. (J). pap. 10.50 (978-1-4824-5818-3(7)) Stevens, Gareth Publishing LLLP.
Labrecque, Ellen. Sky Surfing. 2012. (Extreme Sports Ser.). (ENG., Illus.). 32p. (J). (gr. 2-5). lib. bdg. 28.50 (978-1-60973-212-7(X), 201133) Child's World, Inc., The.
Loh-Hagan, Virginia. Extreme Sky Diving. 2015. (Illus.). 32p. (978-1-63470-021-4(X)) Cherry Lake Publishing.
McFee, Shane. Skydiving. (Living on the Edge Ser.). 24p. (gr. 2-3). 2009. 42.50 (978-1-61514-299-6(1), PowerKids Pr.) 2008. (Illus.). (J). lib. bdg. 22.60 (978-1-4042-4215-9(5)) Rosen Publishing Group, Inc., The.
Montana, Jack. Parachute Regiment. 2010. (Special Forces Ser.). 64p. (YA). (gr. 7-18). lib. bdg. 22.95 (978-1-4222-1845-7(7)) Mason Crest.
Mooney, Carla. Skydiving. 2015. (Sports to the Extreme Ser.). (ENG., Illus.). 48p. (J). (gr. 5-6). 30.25 (978-1-4994-3577-1(0), Rosen Central) Rosen Publishing Group, Inc., The.
Niver, Heather Moore. Skydiving. 2014. (Illus.). 32p. (J). (978-1-4339-9916-1(1)) Stevens, Gareth Publishing LLLP.
Norman, Tony. Skydiving. 2006. (Action Sports Ser.). (Illus.). 32p. (gr. 3-6). lib. bdg. 26.00 (978-0-8368-6369-7(0), Gareth Stevens Learning Library) Stevens, Gareth Publishing LLLP.

Orr, Tamara B. Extreme Skysurfing. 2013. (Sports on the Edge 2 Ser.). 48p. (J). (gr. 4-8). pap. 12.93 *(978-1-62712-136-1(6))* Cavendish Square Publishing.

Schindler, John E. Skydiving. 2005. (Extreme Sports Ser.). (Illus.). 24p. (gr. 2-5). pap. 8.15 *(978-0-8368-4550-1(1))*; lib. bdg. 23.00 *(978-0-8368-4543-3(9))* Stevens, Gareth Publishing LLLP. (Gareth Stevens Learning Library).

Young, Jeff C. Pulling the Rip Cord: Skydiving, 1 vol. 2011. (Adrenaline Adventure Ser.). (ENG., Illus.). 32p. (YA). (gr. 3-6). 27.07 *(978-1-61613-550-8(6))* ABDO Publishing Co.

SKYDIVING—FICTION

Alexander, Sarah. The Art of Not Breathing. 2016. (ENG.). 288p. (YA). (gr. 9). 17.99 *(978-0-544-63388-9(1))*, HMH Books For Young Readers) Houghton Mifflin Harcourt Publishing Co.

Clark, Tracy. Mirage. (ENG.). 272p. (gr. 9). 2017. (YA). pap. 9.99 *(978-0-544-93727-7(9))* 2016. (J). 17.99 *(978-0-544-51790-5(3))* Houghton Mifflin Harcourt Publishing Co. (HMH Books For Young Readers).

Marsh, Laura. Take a Leap! 2009. (Toot & Puddle Ser.). (ENG., Illus.). 24p. (J). (gr. -1-2). pap. 3.99 *(978-1-4263-0416-3(1))*; lib. bdg. 11.90 *(978-1-4263-0417-0(X))* National Geographic Society. (National Geographic Children's Bks.).

Stadler, John. Three Cheers for Hippo!, 1 vol. 2006. (ENG., Illus.). 32p. (J). (gr. -1-3). reprint ed. pap. 5.95 *(978-1-59572-046-7(4))* Star Bright Bks., Inc.

Starfall Education. Sky Ride. Starfall Education, ed. 2004. (ENG., Illus.). 8p. (J). pap. *(978-1-59577-008-0(9))* Starfall Education.

SKYSCRAPERS

Barker, Geoff. Incredible Skyscrapers. 2010. (Superstructures Ser.). 32p. (YA). (gr. 4-7). 28.50 *(978-1-60753-133-3(X))* Amicus Publishing.

Barker, Geoff P. Incredible Skyscrapers. 2012. (What's in My Food Ser.). (Illus.). 32p. (gr. 1-4). lib. bdg. 27.10 *(978-1-59920-419-2(3))* Black Rabbit Bks.

Burns, Kylie. A Skyscraper Reaches Up. 2017. 24p. (J). ***(978-0-7787-2904-4(4))*** Crabtree Publishing Co.

Cornille, Didier. Who Built That? Skyscrapers: An Introduction to Skyscrapers & Their Architects. 2014. (Who Built That? Ser.). (ENG., Illus.). 84p. (J). (gr. 2-7). 16.95 *(978-1-61689-270-8(6))* Princeton Architectural Pr.

Curlee, Lynn. Skyscraper. Curlee, Lynn, illus. 2007. (ENG., Illus.). 48p. (J). (gr. 3-7). 19.99 *(978-0-689-84489-8(1))*, Atheneum Bks. for Young Readers) Simon & Schuster Children's Publishing.

Currie, Stephen. The Tallest Building. 2003. (Extreme Places Ser.). (ENG., Illus.). 48p. (J). (gr. 3-5). 27.50 *(978-0-7377-1374-9(7))*, Kidhaven) Cengage Gale.

Diemer, Lauren. Sears Tower. 2009. (Structural Wonders Ser.). (Illus.). 32p. (J). (gr. 4-6). 9.95 *(978-1-60596-139-2(6))*; lib. bdg. 26.00 *(978-1-60596-138-5(8))* Weigl Pubs., Inc.

Duke, Shirley. Skyscrapers & Towers. 2015. (ENG.). 48p. (gr. 3-6). 35.64 *(978-1-63430-416-0(0))* Rourke Educational Media.

Finger, Brad. 13 Skyscrapers Children Should Know, 1 vol. 2016. (ENG., Illus.). 48p. (J). (gr. 3-7). 14.95 *(978-3-7913-7251-8(3))* Prestel Verlag GmbH & Co KG. DEU. Dist: Penguin Random Hse. LLC.

Franchino, Vicky. How Did They Build That? Skyscraper. 2009. (Community Connections: How Did They Build That? Ser.). (ENG.). 24p. (gr. 2-5). lib. bdg. 25.64 *(978-1-60279-485-6(5))*, 200258) Cherry Lake Publishing.

Gibbons, Gail. Up Goes the Skyscraper! 2017. (ENG.). 32p. (J). (gr. -1-3). pap. 13.99 ***(978-1-5344-2233-9(1)***, Aladdin) Simon & Schuster Children's Publishing.

Goldish, Meish. Spectacular Skyscrapers. 2011. (So Big Compared to What? Ser.). 24p. (YA). (gr. 1-4). lib. bdg. 22.61 *(978-1-61772-303-2(7))* Bearport Publishing Co., Inc.

Hardyman, Robyn. Skyscrapers. 2016. (Engineering Eurekas Ser.). 00032p. (J). (gr. 3-4). pap. 10.00 *(978-1-4994-3105-6(8))*, PowerKids Pr.) Rosen Publishing Group, Inc., The.

Hayes, Amy. Building Bridges & Roads: Civil Engineers, 01 vols., 1. 2016. (Engineers Rule Ser.). (ENG., Illus.). 32p. (J). pap. 11.75 *(978-1-5081-4532-5(6))*, PowerKids Pr.) Rosen Publishing Group, Inc., The.

Holland, Gini. The Empire State Building: How It Was Built & How It Is Used. 2004. (Illus.). 48p. (J). (gr. 4-8). reprint ed. 15.00 *(978-0-7567-7718-0(6))* DIANE Publishing Co.

Hurley, Michael. The World's Most Amazing Skyscrapers, 1 vol. 2011. (Landmark Top Tens Ser.). (ENG., Illus.). 32p. (gr. 3-5). pap. 8.29 *(978-1-4109-4253-1(8))*; 30.65 *(978-1-4109-4242-5(2))* Heinemann-Raintree. (Raintree Perspectives).

Joseph, Leonard. Rascacielos: Por dentro y por fuera (Skyscrapers: Inside & Out) 2009. (Tecnología: Mapas para el Futuro Ser.). (SPA.). 48p. (gr. 4-4). 53.00 *(978-1-60853-288-9(7))*, Editorial Buenas Letras) Rosen Publishing Group, Inc., The.

—Skyscrapers: Inside & Out. 2009. (Technology: Blueprints of the Future Ser.). 48p. (gr. 4-4). 53.00 *(978-1-60853-284-1(4))* Rosen Publishing Group, Inc., The.

Kallen, Stuart. Burj Khalifa: The Tallest Tower in the World. 2014. (Great Idea Ser.). (ENG.). 48p. (J). (gr. 4-6). pap. 13.26 *(978-1-60357-578-2(2))* Norwood Hse. Pr.

Kallen, Stuart A. Burj Khalifa: The Tallest Tower in the World. 2014. (Great Idea Ser.). (ENG.). 48p. (J). (gr. 4-6). lib. bdg. 26.60 *(978-1-59953-598-2(X))* Norwood Hse. Pr.

Koll, Hilary, et al. Using Math to Build a Skyscraper. 2006. (Mathworks!). (Illus.). 32p. (gr. 2-6). pap. 10.50 *(978-0-8368-6771-8(8))*; lib. bdg. 26.00 *(978-0-8368-6764-0(5))* Stevens, Gareth Publishing LLLP. (Gareth Stevens Learning Library).

Latham, Donna. Skyscrapers: Investigate Feats of Engineering with 25 Projects. Christensen, Andrew, illus. 2013. (Build It Yourself Ser.). (ENG.). 128p. (J). (gr. 3-7). 21.95 *(978-1-61930-189-4(X))*; pap. 16.95 *(978-1-61930-193-1(8))* Open City Bks.

Lee, Michelle. Burj Khalifa. 2015. (How Did They Build That? Ser.). (ENG., Illus.). 32p. (gr. 3-8). 27.99 *(978-1-62920-557-1(5))* Scobre Pr. Corp.

Loh-Hagan, Virginia. Skyscrapers. 2017. (21st Century Junior Library: Extraordinary Engineering Ser.). (ENG., Illus.). 24p. (J). (gr. 2-5). lib. bdg. 27.07 *(978-1-63472-165-3(9))*, 209232) Cherry Lake Publishing.

Malam, John. Be a Skyscraper Builder! A Hazardous Job You'd Rather Not Take. 2009. (You Wouldn't Want to Ser.). (ENG., Illus.). 32p. (J). (gr. 3-18). 29.00 *(978-0-531-20824-3(9))*, Watts, Franklin) Scholastic Library Publishing.

—You Wouldn't Want to Be a Skyscraper Builder! 2009. (You Wouldn't Want To Ser.). lib. bdg. 20.80 *(978-0-606-04274-1(1))*, Turtleback) Turtleback Bks.

—You Wouldn't Want to Be a Skyscraper Builder! A Hazardous Job You'd Rather Not Take. 2009. (You Wouldn't Want to... Ser.). (ENG., Illus.). 32p. (J). (gr. 3-18). pap. 9.95 *(978-0-531-21048-2(0))*, Children's Pr.) Scholastic Library Publishing.

Marsico, Katie. Skyscrapers. 2016. (True Book(tm) — Engineering Wonders Ser.). (ENG., Illus.). 48p. (J). pap. 6.95 *(978-0-531-22273-7(X))*, Children's Pr.) Scholastic Library Publishing.

Meachen Rau, Dana. Bookworms: The Inside Story, 6 bks., Set. Incl. Castle. 32p. (gr. k-2). lib. bdg. 15.95 *(978-0-7614-2272-3(2))*; Igloo. 32p. (gr. k-2). lib. bdg. 15.95 *(978-0-7614-2273-0(0))*; Log Cabin. 31p. (J). (gr. -1-3). lib. bdg. 22.79 *(978-0-7614-2274-7(9))*; Pyramid. 32p. (gr. k-2). lib. bdg. 15.95 *(978-0-7614-2275-4(7))*; Skyscraper. 32p. (gr. k-2). lib. bdg. 15.95 *(978-0-7614-2276-1(5))*; Tepee. 31p. (J). (gr. -1-3). lib. bdg. 22.79 *(978-0-7614-2277-8(3))*; (Illus.). 2006. 2006. Set lib. bdg. 136.71 *(978-0-7614-2271-6(4))*, Benchmark Bks.) Marshall Cavendish Corp.

—Skyscraper. 2006. (Bookworms Ser.). (Illus.). 32p. (gr. k-2). lib. bdg. 15.95 *(978-0-7614-2276-1(5))*, Benchmark Bks.) Marshall Cavendish Corp.

Monsman, Stacy. Engineering Marvels: Stand-Out Skyscrapers: Area (Grade 3) 2017. (Mathematics Readers Ser.). (Illus.). 32p. (gr. 3-3). pap. 8.99 ***(978-1-4807-5810-0(8))*** Teacher Created Materials, Inc.

Murray, Julie. Sears Tower, 1 vol. 2005. (Buddy Book Ser.). (ENG., Illus.). 24p. (gr. k-4). 25.65 *(978-1-59197-508-3(5))*, Buddy Bks.) ABDO Publishing Co.

O'Connor, Jim. What Were the Twin Towers? Hammond, Ted & McVeigh, Kevin, illus. 2016. (What Was? Ser.). (ENG.). 112p. (J). (gr. 3-7). lib. bdg. 15.99 *(978-0-399-54231-2(0))*, Grosset & Dunlap) Penguin Young Readers Group.

Parker, Vic. How Tall Is Tall? Comparing Structures, 1 vol. 2010. (Measuring & Comparing Ser.). (ENG.). 32p. (gr. 1-3). 27.32 *(978-1-4329-3955-7(6))*, Heinemann First Library) Heinemann-Raintree.

Perish, Patrick. Skyscraper Builder. 2015. (Dangerous Jobs Ser.). (ENG., Illus.). 24p. (J). (gr. 3-7). lib. bdg. 25.95 *(978-1-62617-197-8(1))*, Torque Bks.) Bellwether Media.

Pettiford, Rebecca. Skyscrapers. 2015. (Illus.). 24p. (J). lib. bdg. 25.65 *(978-1-62031-210-0(7))* Jump! Inc.

Phillips, Cynthia & Priwer, Shana. Skyscrapers & High Rises. 2009. (ENG., Illus.). 115p. (C). (gr. 6-18). lib. bdg. 158.00 *(978-0-7656-8121-8(8))*, Y183566) Routledge.

Rau, Dana Meachen. Skyscraper. 2007. (J). pap. 6.99 *(978-0-7614-3303-3(1))* Marshall Cavendish Corp.

Romero, Libby. Skyscrapers. 2017. (Readers Ser.). (ENG., Illus.). 48p. (J). (gr. 1-4). pap. 3.99 *(978-1-4263-2681-3(5))*, National Geographic Children's Bks.) National Geographic Society.

Scremin, Lauren. The 10 Most Amazing Skyscrapers. 2007. (J). 14.99 *(978-1-55448-480-5(4))* Scholastic Library Publishing.

Shea, Therese. How a Skyscraper Is Built. 2016. (Engineering Our World Ser.). (ENG.). 24p. (J). (gr. 2-3). pap. 8.15 *(978-1-4824-3935-9(2))* Stevens, Gareth Publishing LLLP.

Spielman, Madison. Build It: Skyscrapers, 1 vol. 2nd rev. ed. 2014. (TIME for KIDS(r) Nonfiction Readers Ser.). (ENG., Illus.). 28p. (J). (gr. 2-2). pap. 23.96 *(978-1-4807-1047-4(4))* Shell Educational Publishing.

—Build It: Skyscrapers, 1 vol. 2nd rev. ed. 2011. (Nonfiction Readers Ser.). (ENG.). 28p. (J). (gr. 2-2). pap. 6.99 *(978-1-4333-3620-1(0))* Teacher Created Materials, Inc.

Stefoff, Rebecca. Building Skyscrapers. 2015. (Great Engineering Ser.). (ENG.). 32p. (J). (gr. 3-4). 28.50 *(978-1-5026-0607-5(0))* Cavendish Square Publishing.

Stern, Steven L. Building Green-Scrapers. 2009. (Going Green Ser.). (Illus.). 32p. (YA). (gr. 3-6). lib. bdg. 25.27 *(978-1-59716-962-2(5))* Bearport Publishing Co., Inc.

Thomas, Mark. The Petronas Twin Towers: World's Tallest Buildings. 2009. (Record-Breaking Structures Ser.). 24p. (gr. 1-2). 42.50 *(978-1-60852-457-0(4))*, PowerKids Pr.) Rosen Publishing Group, Inc., The.

—Las Torres Gemelas Petronas: Los Edificios Más Altos del Mundo (The Petronas Twin Towers: World'S Tallest Building) 2009. (Estructuras extraordinarias (Record-Breaking Structures) Ser.). (SPA.). 24p. (gr. 1-2). 42.50 *(978-1-61512-314-8(8))*, Editorial Buenas Letras) Rosen Publishing Group, Inc., The.

Wolny, Philip. High Risk Construction Work: Life Building Skyscrapers, Bridges, & Tunnels. 2008. (Extreme Careers Ser.). (Illus.). 64p. (YA). (gr. 5-9). lib. bdg. 31.95 *(978-1-4042-1789-8(4))* Rosen Publishing Group, Inc., The.

—High-Risk Construction Work: Life Building Skyscrapers, Bridges, & Tunnels. 2009. (Extreme Careers Ser.). 64p. (gr. 5-5). 58.50 *(978-1-61512-397-1(0))*, Rosen Reference) Rosen Publishing Group, Inc., The.

SKYSCRAPERS—FICTION

Hopkinson, Deborah. Sky Boys: How They Built the Empire State Building. Ransome, James E., illus. 2012. lib. bdg. 18.40 *(978-0-606-23847-2(6))*, Turtleback) Turtleback Bks.

Skyscrapers & Farms. 2005. (J). per. 5.00 *(978-1-59872-020-4(1))* Instant Pub.

SKYWALKER, ANAKIN (FICTITIOUS CHARACTER)—FICTION

see Vader, Darth (Fictitious Character)—Fiction

SKYWALKER, LUKE (FICTITIOUS CHARACTER)—FICTION

ABDO Publishing Company Staff & Wood, Brian. Star Wars: In the Shadow of Yavin. D'Anda, Carlos, illus. 2014. (Star Wars: in the Shadow of Yavin Ser.: 6). (ENG.). 24p. (J). (gr. 9-14). lib. bdg. 145.26 *(978-1-61479-285-7(2))*, Graphic Planet) Magic Wagon.

Angleberger, Tom. Star Wars - Return of the Jedi: Beware the Power of the Dark Side! McCaig, Iain, illus. 2015. (ENG.). 432p. (J). (gr. 3-7). 17.99 *(978-1-4847-0913-9(6))*, Disney Lucasfilm Press) Disney Publishing Worldwide.

Bracken, Alexandra. Star Wars - A New Hope: The Princess, the Scoundrel, & the Farm Boy. McCaig, Iain, illus. 2015. (ENG.). 336p. (J). (gr. 3-7). 17.99 *(978-1-4847-0912-2(8))*, 1384321, Disney Lucasfilm Press) Disney Publishing Worldwide.

Disney Book Group. Trapped in the Death Star! 2016. (Star Wars: World of Reading Ser.). (J). lib. bdg. 14.75 ***(978-0-606-39174-0(6))*** Turtleback Bks.

Disney Book Group Staff & DiTerlizzi, Tony. The Adventures of Luke Skywalker, Jedi Knight. McQuarrie, Ralph, illus. 2014. (ENG.). 64p. (J). (gr. 1-3). 19.99 *(978-1-4847-0668-8(4))* Disney Pr.

Dorling Kindersley Publishing Staff & Beecroft, Simon. Luke Skywalker's Amazing Story. 2008. (DK Readers Ser.). (ENG.). 32p. (J). (gr. k-2). pap. 3.99 *(978-0-7566-4518-2(2))*, DK Children) Dorling Kindersley Publishing, Inc.

Dorling Kindersley Publishing Staff & Hibbert, Clare. Tatooine Adventures, Level 1. 2011. (DK Readers Ser.). (ENG.). 48p. (J). (gr. k-4). 3.99 *(978-0-7566-7128-0(0))*, DK Children) Dorling Kindersley Publishing, Inc.

Landers, Ace. The Empire Strikes Out. 2013. (Lego Star Wars Ser.). (ENG., Illus.). 48p. (J). (gr. 2-5). pap. 4.99 *(978-0-545-55224-0(9))* Math Solutions.

—Empire Strikes Out. 2013. (LEGO Star Wars Chapter Bks.). lib. bdg. 14.75 *(978-0-606-31554-8(3))*, Turtleback) Turtleback Bks.

Lucas Film Book Group. Trouble on Tatooine. 2017. (Star Wars: World of Reading Ser.). (J). lib. bdg. 14.75 ***(978-0-606-39963-0(1))*** Turtleback Bks.

LucasFilm Press Staff & Fry, Jason. The Weapon of a Jedi: A Luke Skywalker Adventure. Noto, Phil, illus. 2015. (ENG.). 192p. (J). (gr. 5-9). 12.99 *(978-1-4847-2496-5(8))*, Disney Lucasfilm Press) Disney Publishing Worldwide.

Smith, Geof. Star Wars: Return of the Jedi (Star Wars) Cohee, Ron, illus. 2015. (Little Golden Book Ser.). (ENG.). 24p. (J). (-k). 4.99 *(978-0-7364-3548-2(4))*, Golden Bks.) Random Hse. Children's Bks.

Wang, Holman & Wang, Jack. Star Wars Epic Yarns: A New Hope. 2015. (ENG., Illus.). 24p. (J). (gr. -1 — 1). 9.95 *(978-1-4521-3393-5(X))* Chronicle Bks. LLC.

—Star Wars Epic Yarns: Return of the Jedi. 2015. (ENG., Illus.). 24p. (J). (gr. -1 — 1). 9.95 *(978-1-4521-3500-7(2))* Chronicle Bks. LLC.

—Star Wars Epic Yarns: The Empire Strikes Back. 2015. (ENG., Illus.). 24p. (J). (gr. -1 — 1). 9.95 *(978-1-4521-3499-4(5))* Chronicle Bks. LLC.

Watson, Jude. The Desperate Mission. 2005. (Star Wars Ser.: No. 1). 168p. (J). lib. bdg. 20.00 *(978-1-4242-0774-9(6))* Fitzgerald Bks.

Windham, Ryder. A New Hope: The Life of Luke Skywalker. 2009. 208p. (J). *(978-0-545-16177-0(0))* Scholastic, Inc.

SLAVE TRADE

Alexander, Richard. The Transatlantic Slave Trade: The Forced Migration of Africans to America (1607-1830), 01 vols., 1. 2016. (Spotlight on Immigration & Migration Ser.). (ENG.). 24p. (J). pap. 10.00 *(978-1-5081-4100-6(2))*, PowerKids Pr.) Rosen Publishing Group, Inc., The.

Amistad 2nd Edition 2009: Freedom Is not given, it Is a Birthright. 2009. (My Ancestors — My Heroes Ser.: Vol. 9). (ENG., Illus.). 86p. (J). (gr. 3-4). incl. cd-rom *(978-1-893091-08-5(2))*, My Ancestors, My Heroes) Parker-Wallace Publishing Co., LLC.

Aretha, David. The Middle Passage. 2014. xvi, 585p. (J). *(978-1-59935-408-8(X))* Reynolds, Morgan Inc.

Azarian, Melissa Eisen. The Amistad Mutiny: From the Court Case to the Movie. 2009. (Famous Court Cases That Became Movies Ser.). (Illus.). 128p. (J). (gr. 6-18). lib. bdg. 33.27 *(978-0-7660-3054-1(7))* Enslow Pubs., Inc.

Baumann, Susan K. The Middle Passage & the Revolt on the Amistad. 2013. (Jr. Graphic African American History Ser.). (ENG., Illus.). 24p. (J). (gr. 3-6). pap. 10.60 *(978-1-4777-1447-8(2))*; lib. bdg. 25.25 *(978-1-4777-1311-2(5))* Rosen Publishing Group, Inc., The. (PowerKids Pr.).

Clifford, Barry. Real Pirates: The Untold Story of the Whydah from Slave Ship to Pirate Ship. Manchess, Gregory, illus. Garrett, Kenneth, photos by. 2008. (ENG.). 32p. (J). (gr. 5). 16.95 *(978-1-4263-0279-4(7))*; lib. bdg. 25.90 *(978-1-4263-0280-0(0))* National Geographic Society. (National Geographic Children's Bks.).

Cottman, Michael & National Geographic Kids Staff. Shackles from the Deep: Tracing the Path of a Sunken Slave Ship, a Bitter Past, & a Rich Legacy. 2017. (ENG.). 128p. (J). (gr. 5-7). 17.99 *(978-1-4263-2663-9(7))*, National Geographic Children's Bks.) National Geographic Society.

Granfield, Linda. Out of Slavery: The Journey to Amazing Grace. Wilson, Janet, illus. 2009. (ENG.). 40p. (J). (gr. k-12). 15.95 *(978-0-88776-915-3(2))*, Tundra Bks.) Tundra Bks. CAN. Dist: Penguin Random Hse. LLC.

Grayson, Robert. The Amistad, 1 vol. 2011. (Essential Events Set 6 Ser.). (ENG., Illus.). 112p. (J). (gr. 6-12). lib. bdg. 35.64 *(978-1-61714-761-6(3))* ABDO Publishing Co.

Haskins, James & Benson, Kathleen. Africa: A Look Back. 2006. (Drama of African-American History Ser.). (Illus.). 80p. (J). (gr. 6-7). lib. bdg. 35.64 *(978-0-7614-2148-1(3))*, Benchmark Bks.) Marshall Cavendish Corp.

Hatt, Christine. The African-American Slave Trade. 2003. (Questioning History Ser.). (J). lib. bdg. 28.50 *(978-1-58340-265-8(9))* Black Rabbit Bks.

Keller, Kristin Thoennes. The Slave Trade in Early America. 2016. (Colonial America Ser.). (ENG.). 48p. (gr. 3-4). pap. 8.19 *(978-1-5157-5192-2(9))*, Let Freedom Ring) Capstone Press of Coughlan Cos.

Littlejohn, Randy. A Timeline of the Slave Trade in America. 2009. (Timelines of American History Ser.). 32p. (gr. 4-4). 47.90 *(978-1-60854-390-8(0))*, Rosen Reference) Rosen Publishing Group, Inc., The.

Mann, Charles. 1493 for Young People: From Columbus's Voyage to Globalization. 2016. (For Young People Ser.). (ENG., Illus.). 416p. (J). (gr. 7). pap. 18.95 *(978-1-60980-663-7(8))*, Triangle Square) Seven Stories Pr.

McKissack, Patricia C. Amistad: The Story of a Slave Ship. Stanley, Sanna, illus. 2005. (Penguin Young Readers, Level 4 Ser.). (ENG.). 48p. (J). (gr. 3-4). mass mkt. 3.99 *(978-0-448-43900-6(X))*, Penguin Young Readers) Penguin Young Readers Group.

The Middle Passage & the Revolt on the Amistad. 2013. (Jr. Graphic African American History Ser.). 24p. (J). (gr. 3-6). pap. 63.60 *(978-1-4777-1448-5(0))*, PowerKids Pr.) Rosen Publishing Group, Inc., The.

Nardo, Don. The Atlantic Slave Trade. 2007. (Lucent Library of Black History Ser.). (ENG., Illus.). 128p. (gr. 8-12). lib. bdg. 39.40 *(978-1-4205-0007-3(4))*, Lucent Bks.) Cengage Gale.

Sharp, S. Pearl. The Slave Trade & the Middle Passage. 2006. (Drama of African-American History Ser.). (Illus.). 80p. (gr. 6-7). lib. bdg. 35.64 *(978-0-7614-2176-4(9))*, Benchmark Bks.) Marshall Cavendish Corp.

Theophile, Conneau & Canot, Theodore. Captain Canot; or Twenty Years of an African Slaver. Theophile, Conneau, ed. 2016. (ENG., Illus.). 448p. (YA). (gr. 8-12). act. bk. ed. incl. cd-rom *(978-1-892824-83-7(3))* AFCHRON.

Toler, Pamela D. Transatlantic Slave Networks. 2017. (J). ***(978-1-5026-2696-7(9))*** Cavendish Square Publishing.

Worth, Richard. Africans in America. 2004. (Immigration to the United States Ser.). (Illus.). 96p. (gr. 4-9). 35.00 *(978-0-8160-5691-0(9))* Facts On File, Inc.

—The Slave Trade in America: Cruel Commerce. 2004. (Slavery in American History Ser.). (Illus.). 128p. (J). lib. bdg. 27.94 *(978-0-7660-2151-8(3))* Enslow Pubs., Inc.

SLAVERY

Africans in America: America's Journey Through Slavery. 2004. (gr. 7-18). tchr. ed. 19.95 incl. VHS, cd-rom *(978-1-57807-195-1(X))*, WG665) WGBH Boston Video.

Altman, Linda Jacobs. The Story of Slavery & Abolition in United States History. 2015. (In United States History Ser.). 96p. (J). (gr. 5-12). 27.94 *(978-0-7660-6330-3(5))* Enslow Pubs., Inc.

Aronson, Marc & Budhos, Marina Tamar. Sugar Changed the World: A Story of Magic, Spice, Slavery, Freedom, & Science. 2010. (ENG., Illus.). 176p. (YA). (gr. 7-18). 21.99 *(978-0-618-57492-6(1))* Houghton Mifflin Harcourt Publishing Co.

Ashley, Bernard, et al. Angel Boy. 2009. (ENG.). 96p. (J). (gr. 3-7). pap. 7.95 *(978-1-84507-809-6(8))*, Frances Lincoln) Quarto Publishing Group UK GBR. Dist: Hachette Bk. Group.

Azarian, Melissa Eisen. The Amistad Mutiny: From the Court Case to the Movie. 2009. (Famous Court Cases That Became Movies Ser.). (Illus.). 128p. (J). (gr. 6-18). lib. bdg. 33.27 *(978-0-7660-3054-1(7))* Enslow Pubs., Inc.

Blair, Margaret Whitman. Liberty or Death: The Surprising Story of Runaway Slaves Who Sided with the British During the American Revolution. 2010. (ENG., Illus.). 64p. (J). (gr. 5-8). 18.95 *(978-1-4263-0590-0(7))*, National Geographic Children's Bks.) National Geographic Society.

Brownell, Richard. The Civil War: The Fall of the Confederacy & the End of Slavery. 2005. (History's Great Defeats Ser.). (ENG., Illus.). 109p. (YA). (gr. 7-10). lib. bdg. 30.85 *(978-1-59018-429-5(7))*, Lucent Bks.) Cengage Gale.

Buell, Tonya. Slavery in America: A Primary Source History of the Intolerable Practice of Slavery. 2009. (Primary Sources in American History Ser.). 64p. (gr. 5-8). 58.50 *(978-1-60851-491-5(9))* Rosen Publishing Group, Inc., The.

Burchard, Peter. Frederick Douglass: For the Great Family of Man. 2007. (ENG., Illus.). 240p. (YA). (gr. 7). pap. 13.95 *(978-1-4169-6752-1(4))*, Atheneum Bks. for Young Readers) Simon & Schuster Children's Publishing.

Cheng, Andrea. Etched in Clay: The Life of Dave, Enslaved Potter & Poet. Cheng, Andrea, illus. 2013. (ENG., Illus.). 146p. (J). 17.95 *(978-1-60060-451-5(X))* Lee & Low Bks., Inc.

A Child's Anti-Slavery Book. 2004. reprint ed. pap. 1.99 *(978-1-4192-0040-3(2))*; pap. 15.95 *(978-1-4191-0040-6(8))* Kessinger Publishing, LLC.

A Child's Anti-Slavery Book. 2008. 72p. pap. 7.95 *(978-1-60597-847-5(7))*, Book Jungle) Standard Pubns., Inc.

Cline-Ransome, Lesa. Words Set Me Free: The Story of Young Frederick Douglass. Ransome, James E., illus. 2012. (ENG.). 32p. (J). (gr. k-4). 17.99 *(978-1-4169-5903-8(3))*, Simon & Schuster/Paula Wiseman Bks.) Simon & Schuster/Paula Wiseman Bks.

Courtauld, Sarah. The Story of Slavery. 2008. (Usborne Young Reading: Series Three Ser.). (Illus.). 60p. (J). 8.99 *(978-0-7945-1895-0(8))*, Usborne) EDC Publishing.

Currie, Stephen. A Peculiar Institution: Slavery in the Plantation South. 2005. (Lucent Library of Black History). (ENG., Illus.). 112p. (YA). (gr. 7-10). lib. bdg. 33.45 *(978-1-59018-704-3(0))*, Lucent Bks.) Cengage Gale.

Edwards, Judith. Abolitionists & Slave Resistance: Breaking the Chains of Slavery. 2004. (Slavery in American History Ser.). (Illus.). 128p. (J). lib. bdg. 27.94 *(978-0-7660-2155-6(6))* Enslow Pubs., Inc.

Farrell, Courtney. Children's Rights, 1 vol. 2010. (Essential Issues Set 1 Ser.). (ENG.). 112p. (J). (gr. 6-12). lib. bdg. 35.64 *(978-1-60453-952-3(6))*, Essential Library) ABDO Publishing Co.

Fradin, Dennis Brindell. The Underground Railroad. 2008. (Turning Points in U. S. History Ser.). 48p. (gr. 3-18). lib. bdg. 31.36 *(978-0-7614-3014-8(8))*, Benchmark Bks.) Marshall Cavendish Corp.

Fradin, Dennis Brindell & Fradin, Judith Bloom. 5,000 Miles to Freedom: Ellen & William Craft's Flight from Slavery. 2006. (National Geographic Ser.). (ENG., Illus.). 96p. (J). (gr. 5-9). 19.95 *(978-0-7922-7885-6(2))*; lib. bdg. 29.90 *(978-0-7922-7886-3(0))* National Geographic Society. (National Geographic Children's Bks.).

Ganeri, Anita. Harriet Tubman: The Life of an African-American Abolitionist. Shone, Rob, illus. 2005. (Graphic Biographies Ser.). (ENG.). 48p. (gr. 5-8). pap. 14.05 *(978-1-4042-5172-4(3))* Rosen Publishing Group, Inc., The.

Gann, Marjorie & Willen, Janet. Five Thousand Years of Slavery. (ENG., Illus.). (YA). (gr. 5). 2015. 168p. pap. 15.99 *(978-1-101-91792-3(X))* 2011. 176p. 27.95 *(978-0-88776-914-6(4))* Tundra Bks. CAN. (Tundra Bks.). Dist: Penguin Random Hse. LLC.

Greenhaven Press Staff. Slavery & Human Trafficking. 2016. (Opposing Viewpoints Ser.). (ENG.). 224p. (gr. 10-12). 48.80 *(978-0-7377-7530-3(0))*, Greenhaven Pr., Inc.) Cengage Gale.

Gregory, Josh. Frederick Douglass. 2015. (ENG., Illus.). 48p. (J). lib. bdg. *(978-0-531-21597-5(0))*, Orchard Bks.) Scholastic, Inc.

S

Hoffman, Kurt. Young Heroes, a Learner's Guide to Changing the World: Abolish Slavery Edition. 2012. *(978-0-9865555-8-8(X))*; pap. *(978-0-9865555-6-5(8))* Brighter Bks. Publishing Hse.

House, Catherine. Voices Against Slavery: Ten Christians Who Spoke Out for Freedom. 2006. (ENG.). 160p. (J). per. 7.99 *(978-1-84550-145-7(4),* f5c1a561-d66b-406d-8c3f-a677f6747c6b) Christian Focus Pubns. GBR. Dist: Bookmasters Distribution.

Huey, Lois Miner. Forgotten Bones: Uncovering a Slave Cemetery. 2015. (ENG., Illus.). 56p. (gr. 4-8). 30.65 *(978-1-4677-6300-4(4),* Millbrook Pr.) Lerner Publishing Group.

King, Wilma. Children of the Emancipation. 2005. (Picture the American Past Ser.). (Illus.). 48p. (gr. 2-5). 22.60 *(978-1-57505-396-7(9))* Lerner Publishing Group.

Kramer, Barbara. Frederick Douglass. 2017. (Readers Bios Ser.). (ENG., Illus.). 32p. (J). (gr. k-3). pap. 3.99 *(978-1-4263-2756-8(0),* National Geographic Children's Bks.) National Geographic Society.

Landau, Elaine. The Underground Railroad: Would You Help Them Escape? 2014. (What Would You Do? Ser.). (Illus.). 48p. (J). (gr. 3-4). 25.27 *(978-0-7660-4225-4(1))* Enslow Pubs., Inc.

Levin, Judy. A Timeline of the Abolitionist Movement. 2009. (Timelines of American History Ser.). 32p. (gr. 4-4). 47.90 *(978-1-60854-381-6(1),* Rosen Reference) Rosen Publishing Group, Inc., The.

Linde, Barbara M. Slavery in North America. 2017. (American History Ser.). 104p. (YA). (gr. 7-7). lib. bdg. 39.40 ***(978-1-5345-6060-4(2),*** Lucent Pr.) Greenhaven Publishing LLC.

Llanas, Sheila Griffin. The Underground Railroad: A History Perspectives Book. 2013. (Perspectives Library). (ENG., Illus.). 32p. (J). (gr. 4-8). pap. 14.21 *(978-1-62431-499-5(6),* 202814) Cherry Lake Publishing.

Macdonald, Fiona. You Wouldn't Want to Be a Slave in Ancient Greece! A Life You'd Rather Not Have. Antram, David, illus. rev. ed. 2013. (ENG.). (J). 32p. 29.00 *(978-0-531-27102-5(1))*; 40p. pap. 9.95 *(978-0-531-23853-0(9))* Scholastic Library Publishing. (Watts, Franklin).

Maloof, Torrey. True Life: Frederick Douglass. 2017. (J). pap. 9.97 ***(978-1-4938-3634-5(X))*** Teacher Created Materials, Inc.

Marcovitz, Hal. The History of Slavery. 2014. (Understanding World History Ser.). (ENG., Illus.). 96p. (J). lib. bdg. *(978-1-60152-742-4(X))* ReferencePoint Pr., Inc.

McKissack, Patricia C. & McKissack, Fredrick L. Carter G. Woodson: Black History Pioneer. 2013. (Famous African Americans Ser.). 24p. (J). (gr. k-3). pap. 7.95 *(978-1-4644-0195-4(0),* Enslow Elementary) Enslow Pubs., Inc.

—Frederick Douglass: Fighter Against Slavery. 2013. (Famous African Americans Ser.). 24p. (J). (gr. k-3). pap. 7.95 *(978-1-4644-0196-1(9),* Enslow Elementary) Enslow Pubs., Inc.

Moore, Cathy. Ellen Craft's Escape from Slavery. 2010. pap. 56.72 *(978-0-7613-6925-7(2))* Lerner Publishing Group.

Morley, Jacqueline. Be a Sumerian Slave! A Life of Hard Labor You'd Rather Avoid. Antram, David, illus. 2007. (You Wouldn't Want to... Ser.). (ENG.). 32p. (J). (gr. 4-7). 29.00 *(978-0-531-18728-9(4),* Watts, Franklin); pap. 9.95 *(978-0-531-18921-4(X))* Scholastic Library Publishing.

Myers, Walter Dean. Frederick Douglass: The Lion Who Wrote History. Cooper, Floyd, illus. 2017. 40p. (J). (gr. -1-3). 17.99 *(978-0-06-027709-3(2))* HarperCollins Pubs.

Nardo, Don. Slavery Through the Ages. Greenhaven Press Editors, ed. 2014. (World History Ser.). (ENG., Illus.). 128p. (gr. 7-10). lib. bdg. 39.90 *(978-1-4205-0860-4(1),* Lucent Bks.) Cengage Gale.

Nelson, Kadir. Heart & Soul: The Story of America & African Americans. Nelson, Kadir, illus. 2013. (ENG., Illus.). 112p. (J). (gr. 1-5). pap. 8.99 *(978-0-06-173079-5(3))* HarperCollins Pubs.

—Heart & Soul: The Story of America & African Americans. 2013. (J). lib. bdg. 19.65 *(978-0-606-35050-1(0),* Turtleback) Turtleback Bks.

Raatma, Lucia. The Underground Railroad. 2011. (Cornerstones of Freedom, Third Ser.). (Illus.). 64p. (J). (ENG.). pap. 8.95 *(978-0-531-26568-0(4))*; lib. bdg. 30.00 *(978-0-531-25043-3(1))* Scholastic Library Publishing. (Children's Pr.).

Rausch, Monica. Harriet Tubman. 2007. (Great Americans Ser.). (Illus.). 24p. (gr. 1-4). lib. bdg. 22.00 *(978-0-8368-7686-4(5),* Weekly Reader Leveled Readers) Stevens, Gareth Publishing LLLP.

Rikson, Paule. Daily Life on a Southern Plantation 1853. 2004. (Illus.). 48p. (J). (gr. 4-8). reprint ed. 17.00 *(978-0-7567-7709-8(7))* DIANE Publishing Co.

Roop, Peter & Roop, Connie. Who Conducted the Underground Railroad? And Other Questions about the Path to Freedom. 2008. (Illus.). 44p. (J). pap. *(978-0-439-02524-9(9))* Scholastic, Inc.

Schraff, Anne E. John Brown: We Came to Free the Slaves. 2010. (Americans—the Spirit of a Nation Ser.). (Illus.). 128p. (J). lib. bdg. 33.27 *(978-0-7660-3355-9(4))* Enslow Pubs., Inc.

Senker, Cath. Who Traveled the Underground Railroad?, 1 vol. 2014. (Primary Source Detectives Ser.). (ENG., Illus.). 64p. (gr. 7-8). lib. bdg. 35.99 *(978-1-4329-9603-1(7))* Heinemann-Raintree.

Sepahban, Lois. 12 Questions about Slave Narratives. 2017. (Examining Primary Sources Ser.). (ENG., Illus.). 32p. (J). (gr. 3-6). 21.95 *(978-1-63235-287-3(7))* Pr. Room Editions LLC.

Shaffer, Jody Jensen. What's Your Story, Frederick Douglass? 2016. (Cub Reporter Meets Famous Americans Ser.). (ENG., Illus.). 32p. (J). (gr. k-3). pap. 8.99 *(978-1-4677-9647-7(6),* Lerner Pubns.) Lerner Publishing Group.

Sharp, S. Pearl. The Slave Trade & the Middle Passage. 2006. (Drama of African-American History Ser.). (Illus.). 80p. (gr. 6-7). lib. bdg. 35.64 *(978-0-7614-2176-4(9),* Benchmark Bks.) Marshall Cavendish Corp.

Shea, Nicole. Frederick Douglass in His Own Words, Vol. 1. 2014. (Eyewitness to History Ser.). 32p. (J). (gr. 4-6). pap. 10.50 *(978-1-4824-3288-6(9))* Stevens, Gareth Publishing LLLP.

Shone, Rob & Ganeri, Anita. Harriet Tubman: The Life of an African-American Abolitionist. 2005. (Graphic Nonfiction Biographies Ser.). (ENG., Illus.). 48p. (J). (gr. 4-7). lib. bdg. 31.95 *(978-1-4042-0245-0(5))* Rosen Publishing Group, Inc., The.

Slavery in the Nineteenth Century. (YA). (gr. 5-8). spiral bd., tchr.'s planning gde. ed. 13.00 *(978-0-382-40935-6(3))* Cobblestone Publishing Co.

Sparling, Rebecca. Amendment XIII: Abolishing Slavery. Biscontini, Tracey Vasil, ed. 2008. (Constitutional Amendments Ser.). (ENG., Illus.). 160p. (gr. 10-12). lib. bdg. 43.20 *(978-0-7377-4122-3(8),* LML02109-243011, Greenhaven Pr., Inc.) Cengage Gale.

Stein, R. Conrad. Escaping Slavery on the Underground Railroad. 2008. (From Many Cultures, One History Ser.). (Illus.). 128p. (J). (gr. 5-18). lib. bdg. 33.27 *(978-0-7660-2799-2(6))* Enslow Pubs., Inc.

Vander Hook, Sue. Frederick Douglass: Fugitive Slave & Abolitionist, 1 vol. 2010. (Essential Lives Set 5 Ser.). (ENG., Illus.). 112p. (J). (gr. 6-12). lib. bdg. 35.64 *(978-1-61613-513-3(1))* ABDO Publishing Co.

Watkins, Richard. Slavery: Bondage throughout History. Watkins, Richard, photos by. 2006. (Illus.). 136p. (J). (gr. 4-8). reprint ed. 18.00 *(978-1-4223-5333-2(8))* DIANE Publishing Co.

Whitman Blair, Margaret. Liberty or Death: The Surprising Story of Runaway Slaves Who Sided with the British During the American Revolution (Large Print 16pt) l.t. ed. 2013. 122p. pap. *(978-1-4596-6716-7(6))* ReadHowYouWant.com, Ltd.

Willen, Janet & Gann, Marjorie. Speak a Word for Freedom: Women Against Slavery. 2015. (ENG., Illus.). 208p. (J). (gr. 7). 21.99 *(978-1-77049-651-4(3),* Tundra Bks.) Tundra Bks. CAN. Dist: Penguin Random Hse. LLC.

Wilson, Camilla. Frederick Douglass: A Voice for Freedom in the 1800s. 2003. (Scholastic Biography Ser.). (Illus.). 90p. (J). pap. *(978-0-439-38082-9(0))* Scholastic, Inc.

Wolny, Philip. The Underground Railroad: A Primary Source History of the Journey to Freedom. 2009. (Primary Sources in American History Ser.). 64p. (gr. 5-8). 58.50 *(978-1-60851-505-9(2))* Rosen Publishing Group, Inc., The.

SLAVERY—FICTION

Allen, Becky. Bound by Blood & Sand. 2016. (ENG.). 320p. (YA). (gr. 9). 17.99 *(978-1-101-93214-8(7),* Delacorte Pr.) Random Hse. Children's Bks.

Allen, Crystal. The Laura Line. 2013. (ENG.). 336p. (J). (gr. 3-7). 16.99 *(978-0-06-199274-2(7))* HarperCollins Pubs.

Amateau, Gigi. Come August, Come Freedom: The Bellows, the Gallows, & the Black General Gabriel. (ENG.). (YA). (gr. 7). 2014. 256p. pap. 6.99 *(978-0-7636-6870-9(2))* 2012. (Illus.). 240p. 16.99 *(978-0-7636-4792-6(6))* Candlewick Pr.

Amnesty International Staff, ed. Free? Stories about Human Rights. 2010. (ENG., Illus.). 224p. (J). (gr. 5-18). pap. 9.99 *(978-0-7636-4926-5(0))* Candlewick Pr.

Anderson, Laurie Halse. Ashes. l.t. ed. 2017. (Seeds of America Ser.: 3). (ENG.). 430p. 23.99 ***(978-1-4104-9607-2(4))*** Cengage Gale.

—Ashes. (Seeds of America Trilogy Ser.: Bk. 3). (ENG., Illus.). (J). (gr. 5). 2017. 320p. pap. 8.99 *(978-1-4169-6147-5(X))* 2016. 304p. 16.99 *(978-1-4169-6146-8(1),* Atheneum/Caitlyn Dlouhy Books) Simon & Schuster Children's Publishing.

—Chains. l.t. ed. 2017. (Seeds of America Ser.). (ENG.). 442p. 22.99 ***(978-1-4104-9917-2(0))*** Cengage Gale.

—Chains. 2014. (Seeds of America Trilogy). (ENG.). 336p. (J). 12.24 *(978-1-63245-094-4(1))* Lectorum Pubns., Inc.

—Chains. 2009. 9.00 *(978-0-7848-3678-1(7),* Everbind) Marco Bk. Co.

—Chains. (Seeds of America Trilogy Ser.). (ENG., Illus.). (J). (gr. 5-9). 2010. 336p. pap. 8.99 *(978-1-4169-0586-8(3))* 2008. 320p. 18.99 *(978-1-4169-0585-1(5))* Simon & Schuster Children's Publishing. (Atheneum Bks. for Young Readers).

—Chains. l.t. ed. 2009. (ENG.). 390p. (YA). 23.95 *(978-1-4104-1425-0(6))* Thorndike Pr.

—Chains. 2010. (Seeds of America Trilogy Ser.: 1). lib. bdg. 19.65 *(978-0-606-14520-6(6),* Turtleback) Turtleback Bks.

—Forge. l.t. ed. 2017. (Seeds of America Ser.). (ENG.). 418p. 22.99 ***(978-1-4104-9918-9(9))*** Cengage Gale.

—Forge. 2012. 18.00 *(978-1-61383-316-2(4))* Perfection Learning Corp.

—Forge. (Seeds of America Trilogy Ser.). (ENG., Illus.). (J). (gr. 5-9). 2012. 320p. pap. 8.99 *(978-1-4169-6145-1(3))* 2010. 304p. 18.99 *(978-1-4169-6144-4(5))* Simon & Schuster Children's Publishing. (Atheneum Bks. for Young Readers).

—Forge. 2012. (Seeds of America Trilogy Ser.: 2). lib. bdg. 18.40 *(978-0-606-23680-5(5),* Turtleback) Turtleback Bks.

Anderson, M. T. The Kingdom on the Waves. (Astonishing Life of Octavian Nothing, Traitor to the Nation Ser.: Vol. 2). (ENG., Illus.). 592p. 2011. pap. 14.00 *(978-0-7636-5377-4(2))* 2009. (YA). (gr. 9). pap. 12.99 *(978-0-7636-4626-4(1))* Candlewick Pr.

—The Pox Party. (Astonishing Life of Octavian Nothing, Traitor to the Nation Ser.: Vol. 1). (ENG., Illus.). 2006. 368p. (YA). (gr. 9-12). 17.99 *(978-0-7636-2402-6(0))* Vol. I. 2011. 384p. pap. 14.00 *(978-0-7636-5376-7(4))* Candlewick Pr.

Armand, Glenda. Love Twelve Miles Long. Bootman, Colin, illus. (ENG.). 32p. (J). 2015. pap. 9.95 *(978-1-62014-254-7(6))* 2013. 17.95 *(978-1-60060-245-0(2))* Lee & Low Bks., Inc.

Avi. Something Upstairs. 2010. (ENG.). 144p. (J). (gr. 3-7). 5.99 *(978-0-545-21491-9(2),* Scholastic Pr.) Scholastic, Inc.

—Something Upstairs. 2010. lib. bdg. 16.00 *(978-0-606-14682-1(2),* Turtleback) Turtleback Bks.

Bachorz, Pam. Drought. 2011. (ENG.). 400p. (gr. 7-18). 17.99 *(978-1-60684-016-0(9))* Lerner Publishing Group.

Ballard, Allen. Where Im Bound. 2006. pap. 18.95 *(978-0-595-39856-0(1),* Backinprint.com) iUniverse, Inc.

Bauer Mueller, Pamela. Neptune's Honor: A Story of Loyalty & Love. 2005. (ENG., Illus.). 195p. (YA). (gr. 6). pap. 11.99 *(978-0-9685097-5-3(4))* Piñata Publishing CAN. Dist: Midpoint Trade Bks., Inc.

Booth, Bradley. Plagues in the Palace. 2006. 159p. (J). 10.99 *(978-0-8163-2143-8(4))* Pacific Pr. Publishing Assn.

Bouwman, H. M. A Crack in the Sea. 2017. (ENG., Illus.). 368p. (J). (gr. 5). 16.99 *(978-0-399-54519-1(0),* G.P. Putnam's Sons Books for Young Readers) Penguin Young Readers Group.

Bradbury, Jennifer. River Runs Deep. 2015. (ENG., Illus.). 336p. (J). (gr. 4-8). 17.99 *(978-1-4424-6824-5(6),* Atheneum Bks. for Young Readers) Simon & Schuster Children's Publishing.

Bradley, Kimberly Brubaker. Jefferson's Sons: A Founding Father's Secret Children. 2013. (ENG.). 400p. (J). (gr. 3-7). pap. 7.99 *(978-0-14-242184-0(7),* Puffin Books) Penguin Young Readers Group.

Brill, Marlene Targ. Allen Jay & the Undergound Railroad, 4 bks., Set. Porter, Janice Lee, illus. 2007. (Readalongs for Beginning Readers Ser.). (J). (gr. 1-3). pap. 37.95 incl. audio *(978-1-59519-947-8(0))* Live Oak Media.

—The Underground Railroad Adventure of Allen Jay, Antislavery Activist. Hammond, Ted & Carbajal, Richard Pimentel, illus. 2011. (History's Kid Heroes Set III Ser.). pap. 51.02 *(978-0-7613-8622-3(X))*; (ENG.). 32p. (gr. 3-5). pap. 8.95 *(978-0-7613-7806-8(5))* Lerner Publishing Group. (Graphic Universe™).

Brook, Harry, retold by. Kidnapped. 2004. (Paperback Classics Ser.). 144p. (J). lib. bdg. 12.95 *(978-1-58086-640-8(9),* Usborne) EDC Publishing.

Brown, Marc. D. W. the Big Boss. 2005. (ENG., Illus.). 24p. (J). (gr. -1-1). per. 3.99 *(978-0-316-73395-3(4))* Little, Brown Bks. for Young Readers.

Broyles, Anne. Priscilla & the Hollyhocks. Alter, Anna, illus. 2008. (ENG.). 32p. (J). (gr. 1-4). 15.95 *(978-1-57091-675-5(6))* Charlesbridge Publishing, Inc.

Bryan, Ashley. Freedom over Me: Eleven Slaves, Their Lives & Dreams Brought to Life. Bryan, Ashley, illus. 2016. (ENG., Illus.). 56p. (J). (gr. 4-6). 17.99 *(978-1-4814-5690-6(3),* Atheneum/Caitlyn Dlouhy Books) Simon & Schuster Children's Publishing.

Bugtime Adventures - Blessing in Disguise. 2005. (J). 3.95 *(978-1-933262-26-0(5))* Lightning Bug Flix.

Burg, Ann E. Unbound. 2016. (ENG.). 352p. (J). (gr. 4-6). 16.99 *(978-0-545-93427-5(3),* Scholastic Pr.) Scholastic, Inc.

C. Larene Hall. Martha's Freedom Train. 2009. 100p. pap. 10.49 *(978-1-4389-7977-9(0))* AuthorHouse.

Capstone Press Staff. Follow the Drinking Gourd: An Underground Railroad Story, 1 vol. Squier, Robert, illus. 2012. (Night Sky Stories Ser.). (ENG.). 24p. (gr. 2-3). lib. bdg. 26.65 *(978-1-4048-7375-9(9))* Picture Window Bks.

Carbone, Elisa. Stealing Freedom. 2003. (EMC Masterpiece Series Access Editions). (Illus.). xix, 284p. (J). 12.99 *(978-0-8219-2507-2(5))* EMC/Paradigm Publishing.

Carbone, Elisa & Lewis, E. B. Night Running. 2012. (ENG., Illus.). 40p. (J). (gr. k-3). pap. 7.99 *(978-0-553-11284-9(8),* Dragonfly Bks.) Random Hse. Children's Bks.

Carter, Noni. Good Fortune. (ENG.). 496p. (YA). (gr. 7). 2011. pap. 9.99 *(978-1-4169-8481-8(X))* 2010. 16.99 *(978-1-4169-8480-1(1))* Simon & Schuster Bks. For Young Readers. (Simon & Schuster Bks. For Young Readers).

Chimombo, S. The Bird Boy's Song. 2004. 96p. pap. *(978-99908-48-07-6(6))* Wasi Pubns. ZWE. Dist: Michigan State Univ. Pr.

Chiu, Harry. Erwe Lopt Unfolded. 2007. 268p. per. 17.95 *(978-0-595-44707-7(4))* iUniverse, Inc.

Cline-Ransome, Lesa. Light in the Darkness: A Story about How Slaves Learned in Secret. Ransome, James E., illus. 2013. (ENG.). 40p. (J). (gr. k-3). 16.99 *(978-1-4231-3495-4(8),* Jump at the Sun) Hyperion Bks. for Children.

Coatsworth, Elizabeth. The White Horse. Sewell, Helen, illus. 2006. (Sally (Bethlehem Books) Ser.). 169p. (J). (gr. 5-7). per. 11.95 *(978-1-883937-86-7(8))* Bethlehem Bks.

Cohen, Deborah Bodin. Nachshon, Who Was Afraid to Swim: A Passover Story. Jago, illus. 2008. (Passover Ser.). (ENG.). 32p. (J). (gr. -1-3). 17.95 *(978-0-8225-8764-4(5),* Kar-Ben Publishing) Lerner Publishing Group.

Cooper, Floyd. Juneteenth for Mazie. Cooper, Floyd, illus. 2015. (Fiction Picture Bks.). (ENG., Illus.). 40p. (J). (gr. 1-2). lib. bdg. 25.32 *(978-1-4795-5819-3(2),* Fiction Picture Bks.) Picture Window Bks.

Curry, Kenneth. The Legend of the Dancing Trees: An African American Folk Tale. 2007. 111p. (J). per. 14.95 *(978-0-9798364-0-4(9))* Curry Brothers Publishing Group.

Curry, Kenneth, et al. The Legend of the Dancing Tees Teachers Resource: The Legend of the Dancing Trees. 2007.Tr. of Teachers Resource. per. 19.95 *(978-0-9798364-1-1(7))* Curry Brothers Publishing Group.

Curtis, Christopher Paul. Elijah of Buxton. (ENG.). (J). (gr. 3-7). 2009. 368p. 7.99 *(978-0-439-02345-0(9),* Scholastic Paperbacks) 2007. 352p. 16.99 *(978-0-439-02344-3(0),* Scholastic Pr.) Scholastic, Inc.

Curtis, Christopher Paul & Paul, Curtis Christopher. Elias de Buxton. 2008. (SPA.). 368p. (gr. 6-12). pap. 12.99 *(978-84-441-4101-5(1))* Everest Editora ESP. Dist: Lectorum Pubns., Inc.

Dauphin, Lili. I Will Fly Again: The Restavek. 2007. 284p. 29.95 *(978-0-9748329-9-5(5))*; per. 18.95 *(978-0-9748329-8-2(7))* MiraQuest.

Demetrios, Heather. Exquisite Captive. 2014. (Dark Caravan Cycle Ser.: 1). (ENG., Illus.). 480p. (YA). (gr. 8). 17.99 *(978-0-06-231856-5(X))* HarperCollins Pubs.

Downey, Glen. Gladiators. 2007. (Illus.). 48p. (J). lib. bdg. 23.08 *(978-1-4242-1627-7(3))* Fitzgerald Bks.

Draper, Sharon M. Copper Sun. 2014. (ENG.). 336p. (YA). 14.24 *(978-1-63245-110-1(7))* Lectorum Pubns., Inc.

—Copper Sun. 2011. 11.04 *(978-0-7848-3373-5(7),* Everbind) Marco Bk. Co.

—Copper Sun. (ENG.). (YA). 2008. 336p. (gr. 9-12). pap. 10.99 *(978-1-4169-5348-7(5))* 2006. 320p. (gr. 8-18). 19.99 *(978-0-689-82181-3(6))* Simon & Schuster Children's Publishing. (Atheneum Bks. for Young Readers).

—Copper Sun. l.t. ed. 2006. 358p. (YA). (gr. 8-18). 22.95 *(978-0-7862-8948-6(1))* Thorndike Pr.

—Copper Sun. 2008. lib. bdg. 22.10 *(978-1-4177-9702-8(9),* Turtleback) Turtleback Bks.

Durango, Julia. The Walls of Cartagena. Pohrt, Tom, illus. 2008. (ENG.). 160p. (J). (gr. 3-7). 15.99 *(978-1-4169-4102-6(9),* Simon & Schuster Bks. For Young Readers) Simon & Schuster Bks. For Young Readers.

Dyer, Mary E. Secret Whispers. 2008. 99p. pap. 19.95 *(978-1-60610-261-9(3))* America Star Bks.

Edinger, Monica. Africa Is My Home: A Child of the Amistad. Byrd, Robert, illus. 2013. (ENG.). 64p. (J). (gr. 5). 17.99 *(978-0-7636-5038-4(2))* Candlewick Pr.

Elliott, L. M. Annie, Between the States. 2006. (ENG.). 544p. (YA). (gr. 8-12). per. 9.99 *(978-0-06-001213-7(7),* Tegen, Katherine Bks) 2004. (Illus.). 496p. (J). (gr. 7-18). 16.99 *(978-0-06-001211-3(0))* HarperCollins Pubs.

Engle, Margarita. Lion Island: Cuba's Warrior of Words. 2017. (ENG.). 192p. (J). (gr. 5). pap. 7.99 *(978-1-4814-6113-9(3))* Simon & Schuster Children's Publishing.

—Lion Island: Cuba's Warrior of Words. 2016. (ENG., Illus.). 176p. (J). (gr. 5). 16.99 *(978-1-4814-6112-2(5),* Atheneum Bks. for Young Readers) Simon & Schuster Children's Publishing.

Esenwa, Anthony. Jaja, King of Opobo. 2009. (Illus.). 24p. pap. 11.49 *(978-1-4389-5886-6(2))* AuthorHouse.

Evans, Freddi Williams. Hush Harbor: Praying in Secret. Banks, Erin, illus. 2008. (ENG.). 32p. (J). (gr. k-3). 16.95 *(978-0-8225-7965-6(0),* Carolrhoda Bks.) Lerner Publishing Group.

Ewing, Amy. The Black Key. 2017. (Lone City Trilogy Ser.: 3). 304p. (YA). (gr. 9). pap. 9.99 ***(978-0-06-223585-5(0),*** HarperTeen) 2016. (Lone City Trilogy Ser.: 3). 304p. (YA). (gr. 9). 17.99 *(978-0-06-223584-8(2),* HarperTeen) 2016. 295p. (J). ***(978-0-06-256581-5(8))*** HarperCollins Pubs.

—The Jewel. (Lone City Trilogy Ser.: 1). (ENG.). (YA). (gr. 9). 2015. 400p. pap. 9.99 *(978-0-06-223578-7(8))* 2014. 368p. 17.99 *(978-0-06-223579-4(6))* HarperCollins Pubs. (HarperTeen).

—The White Rose. 2016. (Lone City Trilogy Ser.: 2). 336p. (YA). (gr. 9). pap. 9.99 *(978-0-06-223582-4(6),* HarperTeen) 2015. (Lone City Trilogy Ser.: 2). (ENG.). 320p. (YA). (gr. 9). 17.99 *(978-0-06-223581-7(8),* HarperTeen) 2015. 320p. pap. 17.99 *(978-0-06-241475-5(5))* HarperCollins Pubs.

Finotti, M. C. The Treasure of Amelia Island. 2008. (Florida Historical Fiction for Youth Ser.). (ENG., Illus.). 97p. (J). (gr. 3-7). 14.95 *(978-1-56164-416-2(1))* Pineapple Pr., Inc.

Finotti, M. C. & National Geographic Learning Staff. The Treasure of Amelia Island. 2012. (ENG.). 108p. (C). pap. 14.95 *(978-1-56164-536-7(2))* National Geographic School Publishing, Inc.

Fleischman, Sid. The Whipping Boy. Sís, Peter, illus. 2003. (HarperClassics Ser.). (ENG.). 96p. (J). (gr. 3-8). pap. 6.99 *(978-0-06-052122-6(8),* Greenwillow Bks.) HarperCollins Pubs.

Fleischner, Jennifer. Nobody's Boy. 2006. (ENG., Illus.). 112p. (gr. 4). per. 12.95 *(978-1-883982-58-4(8))* Missouri Historical Society Pr.

Fox, Paula. The Slave Dancer. unabr. ed. 2004. 152p. (J). (gr. 5-9). pap. 38.00 incl. audio *(978-0-8072-0458-0(7),* Listening Library) Random Hse. Audio Publishing Group.

Frank, Pat. Little Warriors. 2008. 88p. pap. 18.95 *(978-1-60594-158-5(1),* Llumina Pr.) Aeon Publishing Inc.

Friesner, Esther. Spirit's Chosen. 2013. (Princesses of Myth Ser.). (ENG., Illus.). 496p. (YA). (gr. 7). 17.99 *(978-0-375-86908-2(5),* Random Hse. Bks. for Young Readers) Random Hse. Children's Bks.

Friesner, Esther M. Spirit's Bride. 2014. (Princesses of Myth Ser.). (ENG., Illus.). 512p. (YA). (gr. 7). pap. 10.99 *(978-0-375-87316-4(3),* Ember) Random Hse. Children's Bks.

Gaillard, Frye. Go South to Freedom. 2016. (ENG., Illus.). 72p. (J). 17.95 *(978-1-58838-316-7(4),* NewSouth Bks.) NewSouth, Inc.

Gaines, Ernest J. The Autobiography of Miss Jane Pittman: And Related Readings. 2006. (McDougal Littell Literature Connections Ser.). (ENG.). 384p. (gr. 6-8). 16.90 *(978-0-395-86993-2(5),* 2-70829) Great Source Education Group, Inc.

Gary, Paulsen. Nightjohn. 2014. (ENG.). 112p. (YA). 11.24 *(978-1-63245-096-8(8))* Lectorum Pubns., Inc.

Gayle, Sharon Shavers. Emma's Escape: A Story of America's Underground Railroad. Velasquez, Eric, illus. 3rd ed. 2003. (Soundprints' Read-and-Discover Ser.). (ENG.). 48p. (J). (gr. -1-3). pap. 3.95 *(978-1-59249-021-9(2),* S2009) Soundprints.

Gee, Maurice. Gool, 1 vol. 2012. (Salt Trilogy Ser.: 2). (ENG.). 240p. (YA). (gr. 7-12). pap. 12.95 *(978-1-4598-0196-7(2))* Orca Bk. Pubs. USA.

—Salt, 1 vol. 2011. (Salt Trilogy Ser.: 1). (ENG., Illus.). 272p. (J). (gr. 7-12). pap. 12.95 *(978-1-55469-369-6(1))* Orca Bk. Pubs. USA.

Gilfert, Shirley Tankersley. The Other Side of Jordan: A Story of the Underground Railroad. 2007. 140p. 21.95 *(978-0-595-70289-3(9))*; per. 11.95 *(978-0-595-46274-2(X))* iUniverse, Inc.

Golding, Julia. Cat among the Pigeons. 2010. (Cat Royal Adventure Ser.: 2). (ENG.). 400p. (J). (gr. 5-9). pap. 22.99 *(978-0-312-60215-4(4),* 9780312602154) Square Fish.

—The Silver Sea, 0 vols. 2013. (ENG.). 352p. (YA). (gr. 7-11). pap. 9.99 *(978-1-4778-1598-4(8),* 9781477815984, Amazon Children's Publishing) Amazon Publishing.

Gordon, Bonnie J. Escape from Goshen. 2012. (ENG.). (J). pap. 10.00 *(978-1-4675-1915-1(4))* Independent Pub.

Grimes, Nikki. Chasing Freedom: The Life Journeys of Harriet Tubman & Susan B. Anthony, Inspired by Historical Facts. Wood, Michele, illus. 2015. (ENG.). 56p. (J). (gr. 2-5). 18.99 *(978-0-439-79338-4(6),* Orchard Bks.) Scholastic, Inc.

Guzman, Lila & Guzman, Rick. Lorenzo's Secret Mission. 2005. 153p. (gr. 4-7). 19.95 *(978-0-7569-5599-1(8))* Perfection Learning Corp.

Hahn, Mary Downing. Promises to the Dead. 2009. (ENG.). 208p. (J). (gr. 5-7). pap. 7.99 *(978-0-547-25838-6(0))* Houghton Mifflin Harcourt Publishing Co.

Haislip, Phyllis Hall. Between the Lines: A Revolutionary War Slave's Journey to Freedom. 2012. (ENG., Illus.). 190p. (J). pap. 8.95 *(978-1-57249-409-1(3),* White Mane Kids) White Mane Publishing Co., Inc.

—Lottie's Courage: A Contraband Slave's Story. 2003. (Illus.). 120p. (J). pap. 7.95 *(978-1-57249-311-7(9),* White Mane Kids) White Mane Publishing Co., Inc.

Hamilton, Virginia. The People Could Fly: The Picture Book. Dillon, Leo & Dillon, Diane, illus. movie tie-in ed. 2004. (ENG.). 32p. (J). (gr. k-12). 16.95 *(978-0-375-82405-0(7),*

Knopf Bks. for Young Readers) Random Hse. Children's Bks.
Hart, Alison. Bell's Star. Sanderson, Ruth, illus. 2009. (Horse Diaries: No. 2). (ENG.). 144p. (J). (gr. 3-7). pap. 7.99 *(978-0-375-85204-6(2),* Random Hse. Bks. for Young Readers) Random Hse. Children's Bks.
—Gabriel's Horses, 1 vol. 2007. (Racing to Freedom Trilogy). (ENG.). 160p. (J). (gr. 3-7). 14.95 *(978-1-56145-398-6(6))* Peachtree Pubs.
Hawke, Rosanne. Spirit of a Mountain Wolf. 2014. (Illus.). 216p. (YA). (gr. 9-12). pap. 10.95 *(978-1-62324-034-9(4))* Enslow Pubs., Inc.
Haynes, Betsy. Cowslip. 2008. (J). (gr. 4-7). 22.50 *(978-0-8446-6244-2(5))* Smith, Peter Pub., Inc.
Hearn, Julie. Hazel. 2009. (ENG.). 400p. (YA). (gr. 7-18). 17.99 *(978-1-4169-2504-0(X),* Atheneum Bks. for Young Readers) Simon & Schuster Children's Publishing.
Helget, Nicole. Wonder at the Edge of the World. 2015. (ENG., Illus.). 384p. (J). (gr. 3-7). 17.00 *(978-0-316-24510-4(0))* Little, Brown Bks. for Young Readers.
Helwani, Najiyah Diana. Sophia's Journal: Time Warp 1857. 2008. (YA). per. *(978-0-9793577-2-5(1))* Muslim Writers Publishing.
Herwick Rice, Dona & Isecke, Harriet. The Sojourner Truth Story, 1 vol. 2009. (Building Fluency Through Reader's Theater Ser.). (ENG.). 32p. (J). (gr. 3-5). pap. 7.99 *(978-1-4333-0544-3(5))* Teacher Created Materials, Inc.
Hicks, Clifford B. Alvin Fernald's Incredible Buried Treasure. Bradfield, Roger, illus. 2009. (J). 17.95 *(978-1-930900-43-1(0))* Purple Hse. Pr.
Higgins, Joanna. Waiting for the Queen: A Novel of Early America. 2013. (ENG.). 256p. (J). (gr. 4-10). 16.95 *(978-1-57131-700-1(7))* Milkweed Editions.
Hopkinson, Deborah. From Slave to Soldier: Based on a True Civil War Story. Floca, Brian, illus. (Ready-To-Reads Ser.). (ENG.). 48p. (J). (gr. 1-3). 2007. pap. 3.99 *(978-0-689-83966-5(9))* 2005. 16.99 *(978-0-689-83965-8(0))* Simon Spotlight. (Simon Spotlight).
—Our Kansas Home. Farley, Patrick, illus. 2003. (Prairie Skies Ser.). 69p. (J). 11.65 *(978-0-7569-3448-4(6))* Perfection Learning Corp.
—Under the Quilt of Night. Ransome, James E., illus. 2005. (gr. k-5). 18.00 *(978-0-7569-5077-4(5))* Perfection Learning Corp.
Hubbs, M. E. The Secret of Wattensaw Bayou. Lyndon, Tracy S., illus. 2013. 170p. pap. 12.95 *(978-1-934610-76-3(3))* Bluewater Pubns.
Hulme, Lucy V. Passages, 1 bk. Redpath, Dale, illus. 2005. 40p. (J). 7.95 *(978-0-9769854-0-2(3),* 001) Combs-Hulme Publishing.
Hurmence, Belinda. A Girl Called Boy. 2006. (ENG.). 176p. (J). (gr. 5-7). pap. 12.95 *(978-0-618-68925-5(7))* Houghton Mifflin Harcourt Publishing Co.
Hush: An Irish Princess' Tale. 2014. (ENG., Illus.). 336p. (YA). (gr. 7). pap. 11.99 *(978-1-4424-9496-1(4),* Simon & Schuster/Paula Wiseman Bks.) Simon & Schuster/Paula Wiseman Bks.
Jacques, Brian. Voyage of Slaves: A Tale from the Castaways of the Flying Dutchman. 2007. (ENG.). 320p. (gr. 12-18). 7.99 *(978-0-441-01528-3(X),* Ace Bks.) Penguin Publishing Group.
Jameson, Bernadette. The Boy Who Played His Way to Freedom. 2012. 80p. pap. 12.95 *(978-1-4710-6968-0(0))* Lulu Pr., Inc.
Johnson, Lois Walfrid. The Raider's Promise. 2006. (Viking Quest Ser.: 5). (ENG., Illus.). 304p. (J). (gr. 3-7). per. 8.99 *(978-0-8024-3116-5(X))* Moody Pubs.
Jones, Joyce Elaine. For Such a Journey. 2005. (J). 5.99 *(978-0-9766559-0-9(X))* Treorca Pr.
Jones, Vernon. Aesop's Fables. Rackham, Arthur, illus. 2007. 160p. (J). pap. 5.00 *(978-0-9788914-4-2(9))* Kahley, Glenn.
Kendall, Jane F. Tennessee Rose. Sheckels, Astrid, illus. 2012. (Horse Diaries). (ENG.). 160p. (J). (gr. 3-7). pap. 7.99 *(978-0-375-87006-4(7),* Random Hse. Bks. for Young Readers) Random Hse. Children's Bks.
Kenney, Rebecca. Where I Belong. 2008. (J). 8.99 *(978-1-59166-873-2(5))* BJU Pr.
Kirkpatrick, Katherine. Escape Across the Wide Sea. 2004. (ENG., Illus.). 224p. (J). (gr. 4-6). tchr. ed. 17.95 *(978-0-8234-1854-1(5))* Holiday Hse., Inc.
Kliever, S. I. A Slave's Quest. 2011. 284p. pap. *(978-1-77069-178-0(2))* Word Alive Pr.
Lawrence, Caroline. The Dolphins of Laurentum. 2005. (Roman Mysteries Ser.). (Illus.). 161p. (J). (gr. 6-9). 13.65 *(978-0-7569-6538-9(1))* Perfection Learning Corp.
—The Pirates of Pompeii. 2004. (Roman Mysteries Ser.). (Illus.). 159p. (J). (gr. 3-7). 13.65 *(978-0-7569-5938-8(1))* Perfection Learning Corp.
Lee, Stacey. Under a Painted Sky. 2015. (ENG.). 384p. (YA). (gr. 7). 16.99 *(978-0-399-16803-1(6),* G.P. Putnam's Sons Books for Young Readers) Penguin Young Readers Group.
—Under a Painted Sky. 2016. lib. bdg. 22.10 *(978-0-606-38391-2(3))* Turtleback Bks.
Leslie, Emma. From Bondage to Freedom: A Tale of the Times of Mohammed. Symmons, Sheeres, illus. 2007. 308p. 24.95 *(978-1-934671-10-8(X))* Salem Ridge Press LLC.
—Glaucia the Greek Slave: A Tale of Athens in the First Century. Felter & Butterworth & Heath, illus. 2007. 308p. per. 14.95 *(978-1-934671-01-6(0))* Salem Ridge Press LLC.
—Gytha's Message: A Tale of Saxon England. Staniland, C., illus. 2007. 256p. 22.95 *(978-1-934671-11-5(8))* Salem Ridge Press LLC.
LeSourd, Nancy. Escape on the Underground Railroad, 1 vol. 2008. (Liberty Letters Ser.). (ENG.). 224p. (J). pap. 7.99 *(978-0-310-71391-3(9))* Zonderkidz.
—Secrets of Civil War Spies, 1 vol. 2008. (Liberty Letters Ser.). (ENG.). 224p. (J). pap. 7.99 *(978-0-310-71390-6(0))* Zonderkidz.
Lester, Julius. Day of Tears. 2007. (ENG., Illus.). 192p. (J). (gr. 5-9). pap. 7.99 *(978-1-4231-0409-4(9),* Jump at the Sun) Hyperion Bks. for Children.
Letters from a Slave Girl. 2011. 8.32 *(978-0-7848-3635-4(3),* Everbind) Marco Bk. Co.
Levine, Ellen. Henry's Freedom Box: A True Story from the Underground Railroad. Nelson, Kadir, illus. 2007. (ENG.). 40p. (J). (gr. -1-3). 17.99 *(978-0-439-77733-9(X),* Scholastic Pr.) Scholastic, Inc.
—Henry's Freedom Box: A True Story from the Underground Railroad. Nelson, Kadir, illus. 2011. (J). (gr. 2-5). 29.95 *(978-0-545-13455-2(2))* Weston Woods Studios, Inc.
Lovejoy, Sharon. Running Out of Night. 2014. (ENG., Illus.). 304p. (J). (gr. 4-7). lib. bdg. 19.99 *(978-0-375-99147-9(6),* Delacorte Bks. for Young Readers) Random Hse. Children's Bks.
Lyons, Kelly Starling. Ellen's Broom. Minter, Daniel, illus. 2012. (ENG.). 32p. (J). (gr. k-3). 16.99 *(978-0-399-25003-3(4),* G.P. Putnam's Sons Books for Young Readers) Penguin Young Readers Group.
—Hope's Gift. Tate, Don, illus. 2012. (ENG.). 32p. (J). (gr. 1-3). 16.99 *(978-0-399-16001-1(9),* G.P. Putnam's Sons Books for Young Readers) Penguin Young Readers Group.
Lyons, Mary E. Letters from a Slave Boy: The Story of Joseph Jacobs. 2009. (ENG.). 208p. (YA). (gr. 7). mass mkt. 7.99 *(978-0-689-87868-8(0),* Simon Pulse) Simon Pulse.
—Letters from a Slave Girl: The Story of Harriet Jacobs. 2008. (Illus.). 175p. (gr. 7-12). 16.00 *(978-0-7569-8474-8(2))* Perfection Learning Corp.
—Letters from a Slave Girl: The Story of Harriet Jacobs. 2007. (ENG., Illus.). 192p. (YA). (gr. 7). mass mkt. 6.99 *(978-1-4169-3637-4(8),* Simon Pulse) Simon Pulse.
—The Poison Place. 2007. (ENG.). 160p. (YA). (gr. 7). pap. 9.95 *(978-1-4169-6842-9(3),* Simon & Schuster/Paula Wiseman Bks.) Simon & Schuster/Paula Wiseman Bks.
MacColl, Michaela & Nichols, Rosemary. Freedom's Price. 2015. (Hidden Histories Ser.). (ENG., Illus.). 288p. (J). (gr. 3-7). 17.95 *(978-1-62091-624-7(X),* Calkins Creek) Boyds Mills Pr.
MacHado, Ana Maria. Del Otro Lado Hay Secretos. (SPA.). pap. 11.95 *(978-950-07-2221-6(6))* Editorial Sudamericana S.A. ARG. Dist: Distribooks, Inc.
MacHado, Ana Maria & Machado, Ana Maria. From Another World, 1 vol. Baeta, Luisa, tr. from POR. Brandao, Lucia, illus. 2005. (ENG.). 128p. (J). (gr. 3-7). pap. 9.95 *(978-0-88899-641-1(1))* Groundwood Bks. CAN. Dist: Publishers Group West (PGW).
Mack, Stan & Champlin, Susan. Fight for Freedom. 2012. (Cartoon Chronicles of America Ser.). (ENG., Illus.). 128p. (J). (gr. 5-7). pap. 10.99 *(978-1-59990-835-9(2),* 9781599908359, Bloomsbury USA Childrens) Bloomsbury Publishing USA.
Malaspina, Ann. The People Could Fly: An African-American Folktale. Otero, Sole, illus. 2013. (Folktales from Around the World Ser.). (ENG.). 24p. (J). (gr. k-3). 28.50 *(978-1-62323-617-5(7),* 206385) Child's World, Inc., The.
Marlow, Susan K. Andrea Carter & the San Francisco Smugglers: A Novel, 1 vol. 2008. (Circle C Adventures Ser.). 144p. (J). pap. 7.99 *(978-0-8254-3446-4(7))* Kregel Pubns.
Marshall, G. Skies of Dawn. 2007. 160p. per. 12.95 *(978-0-595-42946-2(7))* iUniverse, Inc.
Masters, Susan Rowan. Night Journey to Vicksburg. Killcoyne, Hope L., ed. Smith, Duane A., illus. 2003. (Adventures in America Ser.). 74p. (gr. 4). 14.95 *(978-1-893110-30-4(3))* Silver Moon Pr.
McCormick, Patricia. Sold. 2008. (ENG.). 272p. (J). (gr. 7-17). pap. 8.99 *(978-0-7868-5172-0(4))* Hyperion Pr.
—Sold. 2011. 10.36 *(978-0-7848-3420-6(2),* Everbind) Marco Bk. Co.
—Sold. 2008. 263p. (J). (gr. 7-12). 19.65 *(978-1-4178-1810-5(7),* Turtleback) Turtleback Bks.
McCully, Emily Arnold. The Escape of Oney Judge: Martha Washington's Slave Finds Freedom. McCully, Emily Arnold, illus. 2007. (ENG., Illus.). 32p. (J). (gr. 1-4). 17.99 *(978-0-374-32225-0(2),* 9780374322250, Farrar, Straus & Giroux (BYR)) Farrar, Straus & Giroux.
McDougal-Littell Publishing Staff. Literature Connections English: I, Juan de Pareja. 2004. (McDougal Littell Literature Connections Ser.). (ENG.). 224p. (gr. 7-7). 16.90 *(978-0-395-77531-8(0),* 2-80100) Great Source Education Group, Inc.
McKissack, Patricia C. Never Forgotten. Dillon, Leo & Dillon, Diane, illus. 2011. (ENG.). 48p. (J). (gr. k-12). 18.99 *(978-0-375-84384-6(1),* Schwartz & Wade Bks.) Random Hse. Children's Bks.
—A Picture of Freedom: The Diary of Clotee, a Slave Girl, Belmont Plantation, Virginia, 1859. 2011. (Dear America Ser.). (ENG.). 240p. (J). (gr. 3-7). 14.99 *(978-0-545-24253-0(3),* Scholastic Pr.) Scholastic, Inc.
McMann, Lisa. The Trap Door. 2015. (Infinity Ring Ser.: 3). (ENG.). 192p. (J). (gr. 3-7). pap. 6.99 *(978-0-545-90109-3(X))* Scholastic, Inc.
—The Trap Door. 2015. (Infinity Ring Ser.: 3). lib. bdg. 17.20 *(978-0-606-37788-1(3))* Turtleback Bks.
McMullan, Margaret. How I Found the Strong: A Civil War Story. 2006. (ENG.). 144p. (YA). (gr. 7-12). reprint ed. mass mkt. 5.99 *(978-0-553-49492-1(9),* Laurel Leaf) Random Hse. Children's Bks.
Meloy, Alice McFeely. As the Crow Flies: Preface to Gettysburg: the Enemy Is Here! 2012. 106p. (J). pap. 8.95 *(978-1-57249-411-4(5),* White Mane Kids) White Mane Publishing Co., Inc.
Meltzer, Milton. Underground Man. 2006. (ENG.). 288p. (J). (gr. 5-7). pap. 8.99 *(978-0-15-205524-0(X))* Houghton Mifflin Harcourt Publishing Co.
Moody Publishing Staff & Lawton, Wendy G. Freedom's Pen: A Story Based on the Life of Freed Slave & Author Phillis Wheatley 2009. (Daughters of the Faith Ser.). (ENG.). 144p. (gr. 3-7). pap. 7.99 *(978-0-8024-7639-5(2))* Moody Pubs.
Morris, J. & J. Little Black Pearl. 2010. 80p. pap. *(978-1-905553-51-8(X))* BookPublishingWorld.
Morrow, Barbara Olenyik. A Good Night for Freedom. Jenkins, Leonard, illus. 2003. (ENG.). 32p. (J). (gr. k-3). tchr. ed. 17.95 *(978-0-8234-1709-4(3))* Holiday Hse., Inc.
Moses, Shelia P. The Baptism. (ENG., 144p. 2008. Illus.). (J). (gr. 5-9). pap. 5.99 *(978-1-4169-5833-8(9))* 2007. (YA). (gr. 7-12). 15.99 *(978-1-4169-0671-1(1))* McElderry, Margaret K. Bks. (McElderry, Margaret K. Bks.).
Moses, Tammy. The Prophecy. 2006. 288p. per. 19.99 *(978-1-58169-194-8(7))* Genesis Communications, Inc.
Mosley, Walter. 47. 2006. (ENG., Illus.). 240p. (J). (gr. 7-17). reprint ed. per. 10.99 *(978-0-316-01635-3(7))* Little, Brown Bks. for Young Readers.
Moulder, Holly. Eyes of the Calusa. 2007. 111p. (J). pap. 8.95 *(978-0-9790405-0-4(7))* White Pelican Pr.
Murray, Maturin. The Circassian Slave. 2009. 116p. 23.95 *(978-1-60664-664-9(8));* pap. 9.95 *(978-1-60664-292-4(8))* Rodgers, Alan Bks.
Mussi, Sarah. The Door of No Return. (ENG.). 400p. (YA). (gr. 7). 2009. pap. 10.99 *(978-1-4169-6825-2(3))* 2008. 17.99 *(978-1-4169-1550-8(6))* McElderry, Margaret K. Bks. (McElderry, Margaret K. Bks.).
Myers, Walter Dean. The Glory Field. 2008. (ENG.). 400p. (J). (gr. 7). pap. 9.99 *(978-0-545-05575-8(X),* Scholastic Paperbacks) Scholastic, Inc.
Nelson, Marilyn. Pemba's Song. 2008. (ENG.). 112p. (J). (gr. 7-18). 16.99 *(978-0-545-02076-3(X),* Scholastic Pr.) Scholastic, Inc.
Nelson, Vaunda Micheaux. Almost to Freedom. Bootman, Colin, illus. 2003. (Carolrhoda Picture Books Ser.). (ENG.). 40p. (J). (gr. k-3). 16.95 *(978-1-57505-342-4(X))* Lerner Publishing Group.
Nibali, Ellen Cook. Secret of St. Nicholas. 2010. 32p. 16.95 *(978-0-9818154-1-1(3))* Fairland Bks.
Nielsen, Jennifer A. Mark of the Thief. 2015. (Mark of the Thief Ser.: 1). (ENG.). 352p. (J). (gr. 4-7). 17.99 *(978-0-545-56154-9(X),* Scholastic Pr.) Scholastic, Inc.
—Wrath of the Storm. 2017. (Mark of the Thief Ser.: 3). (ENG.). 352p. (J). (gr. 4-7). 16.99 *(978-0-545-56207-2(4),* Scholastic Pr.) Scholastic, Inc.
Nixon, Joan Lowery. Caesar's Story, 1759. 2004. (J). *(978-0-87935-199-1(3))* Colonial Williamsburg Foundation.
—Will's Story, 1771. 2004. (J). *(978-0-87935-226-4(4))* Colonial Williamsburg Foundation.
Noël, Alyson. Shimmer. 2011. pap. *(978-0-545-39923-4(8))* Scholastic, Inc.
—Shimmer. 2011. (Riley Bloom Book Ser.: 2). (ENG.). 208p. (J). (gr. 4-7). pap. 9.99 *(978-0-312-64825-1(1),* 9780312648251) Square Fish.
—Shimmer. 2011. (Riley Bloom Ser.: 2). (J). lib. bdg. 20.85 *(978-0-606-21683-8(9),* Turtleback) Turtleback Bks.
Nolen, Jerdine. Big Jabe. Nelson, Kadir, illus. 2003. (ENG.). 32p. (J). (gr. k-5). pap. 7.99 *(978-0-06-054061-6(3),* Amistad) HarperCollins Pubs.
—Big Jabe. Nelson, Kadir, illus. 2004. (gr. 1). 17.00 *(978-0-7569-3184-1(3))* Perfection Learning Corp.
—Calico Girl. 2017. (ENG., Illus.). 192p. (J). (gr. 3-7). 16.99 *(978-1-4814-5981-5(3),* Simon & Schuster/Paula Wiseman Bks.) Simon & Schuster/Paula Wiseman Bks.
—Eliza's Freedom Road: An Underground Railroad Diary. Strickland, Shadra, illus. 2011. (ENG.). 160p. (J). (gr. 3-7). 16.99 *(978-1-4169-5814-7(2),* Simon & Schuster/Paula Wiseman Bks.) Simon & Schuster/Paula Wiseman Bks.
O'Callaghan, G. Slave Prince. 2007. 172p. per. *(978-1-84693-031-7(6))* Best Global Publishing Ltd.
O'Maley, Elizabeth. By Freedom's Light. 2009. 188p. (J). 15.95 *(978-0-87195-273-8(4));* pap. 7.95 *(978-0-87195-274-5(2))* Indiana Historical Society.
Optic, Oliver, pseud. Watch & Wait; or, the Young Fugitives a Story for Young People by Oliver Optic [Pseud.]. 2006. 284p. per. 23.99 *(978-1-4255-2683-2(7))* Michigan Publishing.
Oron, Judie. Cry of the Giraffe. 2010. (ENG., Illus.). 208p. (YA). (gr. 9-12). 21.95 *(978-1-55451-272-0(7),* 9781554512720); pap. 12.95 *(978-1-55451-271-3(9),* 9781554512713) Annick Pr., Ltd. CAN. Dist: Publishers Group West (PGW).
Orzechowski, Shawneen. Midnight Journey: Running for Freedom on the Underground Railroad. 2006. 112p. (J). (gr. 3-7). per. 8.95 *(978-1-57249-379-7(8),* White Mane Kids) White Mane Publishing Co., Inc.
Pace, Lorenzo. Jalani & the Lock, 1 vol. 2015. (ENG.). 48p. (J). 30.25 *(978-1-4777-9277-3(5),* Windmill Bks.) Rosen Publishing Group, Inc., The.
Paterson, Katherine. Jip: His Story. 2005. (Puffin Modern Classics Ser.). (ENG.). 192p. (J). (gr. 3-7). pap. 6.99 *(978-0-14-240411-9(X),* Puffin Books) Penguin Young Readers Group.
Paulsen, Gary. The Legend of Bass Reeves: Being the True & Fictional Account of the Most Valiant Marshal in the West. 2008. (ENG., Illus.). 160p. (YA). (gr. 7-9). mass mkt. 6.99 *(978-0-553-49429-7(5),* Laurel Leaf) Random Hse. Children's Bks.
—Nightjohn: El Esclavo Que Me Enseno a Leer. 2003. (SPA., Illus.). 72p. (YA). (gr. 5-8). *(978-84-8453-003-9(5),* PT2562) Ediciones del Bronce ESP. Dist: Lectorum Pubns., Inc.
Pearsall, Shelley. Trouble Don't Last. 2003. (ENG.). 256p. (J). (gr. 3-7). reprint ed. 6.99 *(978-0-440-41811-5(9),* Yearling) Random Hse. Children's Bks.
Peet, Mal. The Penalty. 2016. (ENG.). 272p. (J). (gr. 7). pap. 8.99 *(978-0-7636-8747-2(2))* Candlewick Pr.
Phillips, Dee. Runaway. 2014. (Yesterday's Voices Ser.). (YA). lib. bdg. 19.60 *(978-0-606-35594-1(7))* Turtleback Bks.
Pinkney, Andrea Davis. Sojourner Truth's Step-Stomp Stride. Pinkney, Brian, illus. 2009. (ENG.). 32p. (J). (gr. k-4). 16.99 *(978-0-7868-0767-3(9),* Jump at the Sun) Hyperion Bks. for Children.
Platt, Richard. Roman Diary: The Journal of Iliona, a Young Slave. Parkins, David, illus. 2014. (ENG.). 128p. (J). (gr. 4-7). pap. 6.99 *(978-0-7636-7053-5(7))* Candlewick Pr.
Polacco, Patricia. January's Sparrow. Polacco, Patricia, illus. 2009. (ENG., Illus.). 96p. (J). (gr. 3-7). 23.99 *(978-0-399-25077-4(8),* Philomel Bks.) Penguin Young Readers Group.
Polisar, Barry Louis. Stolen Man: The Story of the Amistad Rebellion. 2007. (ENG.). 32p. (J). (gr. 4-7). per. 7.95 *(978-0-938663-50-8(X))* Rainbow Morning Music Alternatives.
Porter, Janice Lee, illus. Allen Jay & the Underground Railroad, 4 bks., Set. 2006. (Readalongs for Beginning Readers Ser.). (J). (gr. 2-5). pap. 39.95 incl. audio compact disk *(978-1-59519-951-5(9))* Live Oak Media.
Purcell, Kim. Trafficked. 2013. (ENG.). 400p. (YA). (gr. 7). pap. 9.99 *(978-0-14-242416-2(1),* Speak) Penguin Young Readers Group.
Pyrnelle, Louise Clarke. Diddie Dumps & Tot: Or, Plantation Child-life. 2007. 138p. pap. 18.99 *(978-1-4346-0721-8(6));* (ENG.). 150p. pap. 19.99 *(978-1-4346-0781-2(X))* Creative Media Partners, LLC.
Raasch, Sara. Frost Like Night. (Snow Like Ashes Ser.: 3). (YA). (gr. 9). 2017. 512p. pap. 9.99 ***(978-0-06-228699-4(4))*** 2016. (Illus.). 496p. 17.99 *(978-0-06-228698-7(6))* HarperCollins Pubs.
—Ice Like Fire. (YA). 2016. (Snow Like Ashes Ser.: 2). 512p. (gr. 9). pap. 9.99 *(978-0-06-228696-3(X))* 2015. (Snow Like Ashes Ser.: Bk. 2). (ENG., Illus.). 496p. (gr. 9-12). 17.99 *(978-0-06-228695-6(1))* 2015. (Illus.). 496p. pap. ***(978-0-06-242793-9(8))*** HarperCollins Pubs.
—Snow Like Ashes. (Snow Like Ashes Ser.: 1). (ENG., Illus.). (YA). (gr. 9). 2015. 448p. pap. 9.99 *(978-0-06-228693-2(5))* 2014. 432p. 17.99 *(978-0-06-228692-5(7))* HarperCollins Pubs.
Raven, Margot Theis. Night Boat to Freedom. Lewis, E. B., illus. 2008. (ENG.). 40p. (J). (gr. 1-4). pap. 8.99 *(978-0-312-55018-9(9),* 9780312550189) Square Fish.
Reed, Jennifer. Hadi's Journey. 2003. 110p. pap. 10.95 *(978-0-595-29375-9(1))* iUniverse, Inc.
Reed, Stephanie. The Light Across the River, 1 vol. 2008. (Illus.). 216p. (J). (gr. 4-7). pap. 10.99 *(978-0-8254-3574-4(9))* Kregel Pubns.
Rees, Celia. Pirates! The True & Remarkable Adventures of Minerva Sharpe & Nancy Kington, Female Pirates. 2005. (Illus.). 379p. (YA). (gr. 9-12). 16.60 *(978-0-7569-6304-0(4))* Perfection Learning Corp.
Riley, Lehman, et al. The Adventures of Papa Lemon's Little Wanderers Bk. 2: The Dangerous Escape from Slavery. 2005. 52p. pap. 5.99 *(978-0-9760523-1-9(8))* Matter of Africa America Time.
Rinaldi, Ann. Come Juneteenth. 2009. (ENG., Illus.). 256p. (YA). (gr. 7). pap. 7.99 *(978-0-15-206392-4(7))* Houghton Mifflin Harcourt Publishing Co.
—The Ever-After Bird. 2010. (ENG.). 240p. (J). (gr. 5-7). pap. 8.99 *(978-0-547-25854-6(2))* Houghton Mifflin Harcourt Publishing Co.
—Hang a Thousand Trees with Ribbons: The Story of Phillis Wheatley. 2005. (Great Episodes Ser.). 336p. (gr. 5-9). 18.00 *(978-0-7569-5018-7(X))* Perfection Learning Corp.
—The Letter Writer. 2010. (ENG., Illus.). 224p. (YA). (gr. 7). pap. 8.99 *(978-0-547-32785-3(4))* Houghton Mifflin Harcourt Publishing Co.
—Taking Liberty: The Story of Oney Judge, George Washington's Runaway Slave. Dudash, C. Michael, illus. 2004. (ENG.). 272p. (YA). (gr. 7). mass mkt. 7.99 *(978-0-689-85188-9(X),* Simon Pulse) Simon Pulse.
—An Unlikely Friendship: A Novel of Mary Todd Lincoln & Elizabeth Keckley. 2008. (ENG., Illus.). 256p. (J). (gr. 5-7). pap. 7.99 *(978-0-15-206398-6(6))* Houghton Mifflin Harcourt Publishing Co.
Robbins, Dean. Two Friends: Susan B. Anthony & Frederick Douglass: Susan B. Anthony & Frederick Douglass. Qualls, Sean & Alko, Selina, illus. 2016. (ENG.). 32p. (J). (gr. -1-3). 17.99 *(978-0-545-39996-8(3),* Orchard Bks.) Scholastic, Inc.
Roop, Peter. Lead Us to Freedom, Harriet Tubman! 2006. (Illus.). 58p. (J). pap. *(978-0-439-79255-4(X))* Scholastic, Inc.
Rosen, Michael J. A School for Pompey Walker. 2012. (ENG.). (J). pap. *(978-1-4675-1412-5(8))* Independent Pub.
Ruby, Lois. The Secret of Laurel Oaks. 2009. (ENG.). 288p. (YA). (gr. 6-9). 5.99 *(978-0-7653-5229-3(X),* 9780765352293, Starscape) Doherty, Tom Assocs., LLC.
Russell, Krista. Chasing the Nightbird, 1 vol. 2011. (ENG.). 192p. (YA). (gr. 5-9). 15.95 *(978-1-56145-597-3(0),* Peachtree Junior) Peachtree Pubs.
—The Other Side of Free, 1 vol. 2013. (ENG.). 256p. (J). (gr. 5-9). 16.95 *(978-1-56145-710-6(8))* Peachtree Pubs.
Sánchez-Korrol, Virginia. Feminist & Abolitionist: The Story of Emilia Casanova. 2013. (ENG.). 248p. (YA). pap. 12.95 *(978-1-55885-765-0(6),* Piñata Books) Arte Publico Pr.
Schraff, Anne. The Burning of the Valley. 2008. (Passages to History Ser.). 115p. (J). (gr. 4-6). lib. bdg. 13.95 *(978-0-7569-8400-7(9))* Perfection Learning Corp.
—Freedom Knows No Color. 2008. (Passages to History Ser.). 118p. (J). lib. bdg. 13.95 *(978-0-7569-8392-5(4));* (YA). (gr. 7-12). pap. 8.50 *(978-0-7891-7567-0(3))* Perfection Learning Corp.
Schwabach, Karen. The Storm Before Atlanta. 2011. (ENG.). 320p. (J). (gr. 3-7). pap. 6.99 *(978-0-375-85867-3(9),* Yearling) Random Hse. Children's Bks.
Shan, Darren, pseud. The Thin Executioner. 2011. (ENG.). 512p. (YA). (gr. 10-17). pap. 10.99 *(978-0-316-07864-1(6))* Little, Brown Bks. for Young Readers.
Shazak. Out of Egypt. 2007. 104p. 24.99 *(978-1-930925-11-3(5))* Feldheim Pubs.
Shecter, Vicky Alvear. Curses & Smoke: A Novel of Pompeii. 2014. (ENG.). 336p. (J). (gr. 7). 17.99 *(978-0-545-50993-0(9),* Levine, Arthur A. Bks.) Scholastic, Inc.
Simmons, Kristen. The Glass Arrow. (ENG.). (YA). 2016. 352p. pap. 9.99 *(978-0-7653-3664-4(2),* 9780765336644) 2015. 336p. (gr. 8-12). 17.99 *(978-0-7653-3661-3(8),* 9780765336613) Doherty, Tom Assocs., LLC. (Tor Teen).
Smolik, Jane Petrlik. Currents. 2015. (ENG., Illus.). 336p. (YA). (gr. 4-7). lib. bdg. 16.95 *(978-1-58089-648-1(0))* Charlesbridge Publishing, Inc.
Snyder, Laurel. The Longest Night: A Passover Story. Chien, Catia, illus. 2013. (ENG.). 40p. (J). (gr. -1-3). 17.99 *(978-0-375-86942-6(5),* Schwartz & Wade Bks.) Random Hse. Children's Bks.
Soentpiet, Chris K., et al. Molly Bannaky. 2009. (ENG., Illus.). 32p. (J). (gr. -1-3). pap. 6.99 *(978-0-547-07676-8(2))* Houghton Mifflin Harcourt Publishing Co.
Squier, Robert, illus. Follow the Drinking Gourd: An Underground Railroad Story, 1 vol. 2012. (Night Sky Stories Ser.). (ENG.). 24p. (gr. 2-3). pap. 8.95 *(978-1-4048-7714-6(2))* Picture Window Bks.
Steenwyk, Elizabeth Van. Blacksmith's Song. Rich, Anna, illus. 2018. (ENG.). 32p. (J). (gr. 1-5). 17.95 *(978-1-56145-580-5(6))* Peachtree Pubs.
Stewart, A. W. Rooktime. 2010. 284p. pap. 15.49 *(978-1-4520-1460-9(4))* AuthorHouse.
Stiles, Martha Bennett. Sailing to Freedom. 2012. (ENG.). 256p. (J). (gr. 3-7). 16.99 *(978-0-8050-9238-7(2),* 9780805092387, Holt, Henry & Co. Bks. For Young Readers) Holt, Henry & Co.
—Sailing to Freedom. 2014. (ENG.). 256p. (J). (gr. 3-7). pap. 6.99 *(978-1-250-03991-0(6),* 9781250039910) Square Fish.
Stockton, Frank Richard. Ting-a-Ling Tales. 2008. 88p. pap. 8.95 *(978-1-60664-056-2(9))* Aegypan.
Stowe, Harriet Beecher. Uncle Tom's Cabin Vol. 1: Or, Life among the Lowly. Solimene, Laura, ed. 2008. (Bring the Classics to Life Ser.). (Illus.). 72p. (gr. 1-12). pap., act. bk. ed.

S

10.95 (978-1-55576-323-7(5), EDCTR-108B) EDCON Publishing Group.
—Uncle Toms Cabin Young Folks Edition Ill. 2006. pap. (978-1-4065-1077-5(7)) Dodo Pr.
Strohmeier, Lenice & Strohmeier. Mingo, 1 vol. Farnsworth, Bill, illus. 2003. (ENG.). 32p. (J). 16.95 (978-0-7614-5111-2(0)) Marshall Cavendish Corp.
Stroud, Bettye. The Patchwork Path: A Quilt Map to Freedom. Bennett, Erin Susanne, illus. 2007. (ENG.). 32p. (J). (gr. k-3). pap. 7.99 (978-0-7636-3519-0(7)) Candlewick Pr.
Sullivan, Tara. The Bitter Side of Sweet. 2016. (ENG.). 320p. (J). (gr. 7). 17.99 (978-0-399-17307-3(2), G.P. Putnam's Sons Books for Young Readers) Penguin Young Readers Group.
Sutcliff, Rosemary. The Mark of the Horse Lord. 2006. (ENG.). 289p. (YA). (gr. 12). per. 10.95 (978-1-932425-62-8(4), Lemniscaat) Boyds Mills Pr.
—The Mark of the Horse Lord. 2015. (Rediscovered Classics Ser.). (ENG.). 296p. (YA). (gr. 7). pap. 12.95 (978-1-61373-154-3(X)) Chicago Review Pr., Inc.
Swain, Gwenyth. Voices for Freedom. Frankenhuyzen, Gijsbert van et al, illus. 2013. (American Adventures Ser.). (ENG.). 72p. (J). (gr. 3-6). 6.99 (978-1-58536-886-0(5), 202900) Sleeping Bear Pr.
The Sword, the Ring, & the Parchment. 2006. (J). per. 7.99 (978-0-9785523-0-5(X)) Cross & Crown Publishing.
Tingle, Tim. Crossing Bok Chitto: A Choctaw Tale of Friendship & Freedom. Bridges, Jeanne Rorex, illus. (ENG.). 40p. (J). 2008. (gr. 2-7). pap. 8.95 (978-1-933693-20-0(7)) 2006. (gr. 1-8). 17.95 (978-0-938317-77-7(6)) Cinco Puntos Pr.
Towell, Ann. Grease Town. 2010. (ENG.). 240p. (YA). (gr. 5-9). 17.95 (978-0-88776-983-2(7), Tundra Bks.) Tundra Bks. CAN. Dist: Penguin Random Hse. LLC.
Turner, Diane D. My Name Is Oney Judge. Massey, Cal, illus. 2010. (J). pap. (978-0-88378-321-4(5)) Third World Press.
—My Name Is Oney Judge. Massey, Cal, illus. 2010. (ENG.). 40p. (J). 19.95 (978-0-88378-304-7(5)) Third World Press.
Turner, Glennette Tilley. Running for Our Lives. 2004. (J). pap. 7.95 (978-0-938990-06-2(3)) Newman Educational Publishing Co.
Turner, Megan Whalen. Thick As Thieves. 2017. (Queen's Thief Ser.: 5). (ENG.). 352p. (YA). (gr. 8). 17.99 (978-0-06-256824-3(8), Greenwillow Bks.) HarperCollins Pubs.
Twain, Mark, pseud. The Adventures of Huckleberry Finn. Andreasen, Dan, illus. 2006. (Classic Starts(tm) Ser.). (ENG.). 160p. (J). (gr. 2-4). 6.95 (978-1-4027-2499-2(3)) Sterling Publishing Co., Inc.
—The Adventures of Huckleberry Finn. (Coleccion Clasicos de la Juventud). (SPA., Illus.). 192p. (J). 12.95 (978-84-7189-027-6(5), ORT313) Ortells, Alfredo Editorial S.L. ESP. Dist: Continental Bk. Co., Inc.
—The Adventures of Huckleberry Finn. 2008. (Puffin Classics Ser.). 386p. (gr. 3-7). lib. bdg. 16.00 (978-0-613-63913-2(8), Turtleback) Turtleback Bks.
—The Adventures of Huckleberry Finn: With a Discussion of Friendship. Lauter, Richard, tr. Lauter, Richard, illus. 2003. (Values in Action Illustrated Classics Ser.). (J). (978-1-59203-042-2(4)) Learning Challenge, Inc.
—The Adventures of Tom Sawyer. Ingpen, Robert R., illus. 2010. (Sterling Illustrated Classics Ser.). (ENG.). 240p. (J). (gr. 5-18). 19.95 (978-1-4027-6762-3(5)) Sterling Publishing Co., Inc.
Vande Velde, Vivian. There's a Dead Person Following My Sister Around. 2008. (ENG., Illus.). 160p. (J). (gr. 5-7). pap. 11.95 (978-0-15-206467-9(2)) Houghton Mifflin Harcourt Publishing Co.
Verne, Jules. Dick Sand. Munro, George, tr. 2008. 296p. 29.95 (978-1-60664-752-3(0)) Rodgers, Alan Bks.
—Dick Sands: The Boy Captain. ELLEN E. FREWER, tr. 2007. (ENG.). 298p. pap. 21.99 (978-1-4264-3403-7(0)) Creative Media Partners, LLC.
—Dick Sands: The Boy Captain. Frewer, Ellen E., tr. l.t. ed. 2007. (ENG.). 328p. pap. 24.99 (978-1-4264-3453-2(7)) Creative Media Partners, LLC.
Voigt, Cynthia. The Tale of Birle. 2015. (Tales of the Kingdom Ser.: 2). (ENG., Illus.). 416p. (YA). (gr. 7). 19.99 (978-1-4424-8356-9(3), Atheneum Bks. for Young Readers) Simon & Schuster Children's Publishing.
Wait, Lea. Seaward Born. 2004. (ENG., Illus.). 160p. (J). (gr. 3-7). pap. 8.99 (978-0-689-84860-5(9), McElderry, Margaret K. Bks.) McElderry, Margaret K. Bks.
Walker, Sally M. Freedom Song: The Story of Henry "Box" Brown. Qualls, Sean, illus. 2012. (ENG.). 40p. (J). (gr. -1-3). 17.99 (978-0-06-058310-1(X)) HarperCollins Pubs.
Walter, Jon. My Name Is Not Friday. 2017. (ENG.). 400p. (J). (gr. 7). pap. 9.99 **(978-1-338-16064-2(8))** Scholastic, Inc.
Walter, Jon. My Name's Not Friday. 2016. (ENG.). 384p. (YA). (gr. 7). 18.99 (978-0-545-85522-8(5)) Scholastic, Inc.
Walter, Mildred Pitts. Alec's Primer. Johnson, Larry, illus. 2005. (ENG.). 32p. (J). (gr. -1-3). 15.95 (978-0-916718-20-6(4)) Vermont Folklife Ctr.
Wang, Jack, et al. Mark Twain's the Adventures of Huckleberry Finn. 2016. (ENG., Illus.). 24p. (J). (gr. -1 — 1). bds. 9.95 (978-1-4521-5249-3(7)) Chronicle Bks. LLC.
Ward, David. Beneath the Mask, Bk. 2. 2008. (ENG.). 272p. (YA). (gr. 5-9). 16.95 (978-0-8109-7074-8(0), Amulet Bks.) Abrams, Inc.
Warner, Susan & Wetherell, Elizabeth. Daisy in the Field. 2011. 272p. 29.95 (978-1-4638-9964-6(5)); pap. 16.95 (978-1-4638-0163-2(7)) Rodgers, Alan Bks.
Warren, Bertie. Sammie's Journey to Freedom. 2006. (ENG.). 52p. per. 16.95 (978-1-4241-5142-4(2)) America Star Bks.
Weatherford, Carole Boston. Freedom in Congo Square. Christie, R. Gregory, illus. 2016. (ENG.). 40p. (J). (gr. -1-3). 17.99 (978-1-4998-0103-3(3)) Little Bee Books Inc.
Weston Woods Staff, creator. Henry's Freedom Box. 2011. 38.75 (978-0-545-31403-9(8)); 18.95 (978-0-545-31402-2(X)) Weston Woods Studios, Inc.
Westrick, A. B. Brotherhood. 2014. (ENG.). 384p. (J). (gr. 5). pap. 8.99 (978-0-14-242237-3(1), Puffin Books) Penguin Young Readers Group.
Westrick, Anne. Brotherhood. 2013. (ENG., Illus.). 368p. (J). (gr. 5). 17.99 (978-0-670-01439-2(7), Viking Books for Young Readers) Penguin Young Readers Group.
Whelan, Gloria. The Listeners. Benny, Mike, illus. 2009. (Tales of Young Americans Ser.). (ENG.). 32p. (J). (gr. k-6). 17.95 (978-1-58536-419-0(3)) Sleeping Bear Pr.
Wilson, Diane Lee. Black Storm Comin' 2006. (ENG.). 240p. (J). (gr. 5-9). pap. 7.99 (978-0-689-87138-2(4), McElderry, Margaret K. Bks.) McElderry, Margaret K. Bks.
—Black Storm Comin' 2006. (Illus.). 291p. (gr. 5-9). 17.00 (978-0-7569-6908-0(5)) Perfection Learning Corp.
Winter, Jeanette. Follow the Drinking Gourd. Winter, Jeanette, illus. 2008. (ENG., Illus.). 48p. (J). (gr. -1-2). 17.99 (978-0-394-89694-6(7), Knopf Bks. for Young Readers) Random Hse. Children's Bks.
Wisler, G. Clifton. Caleb's Choice. 2004. 154p. (gr. 5-9). 16.00 (978-0-7569-4090-4(7)) Perfection Learning Corp.
Woods, Brenda. My Name Is Sally Little Song. 2007. (ENG.). 192p. (J). (gr. 3-7). 7.99 (978-0-14-240943-5(X), Puffin Books) Penguin Young Readers Group.
—My Name Is Sally Little Song. 2007. (Illus.). 182p. (gr. 2-7). 17.00 (978-0-7569-8156-3(5)) Perfection Learning Corp.
Woodson, Jacqueline. Show Way. Talbott, Hudson, illus. 2005. (ENG.). 48p. (J). (gr. -1-3). 17.99 (978-0-399-23749-2(6), G.P. Putnam's Sons Books for Young Readers) Penguin Young Readers Group.
Wyeth, Sharon Dennis. Message in the Sky Bk. 3: Corey's Underground Railroad Diary. 2003. (My America Ser.). (ENG.). 112p. (J). 10.95 (978-0-439-37057-8(4), Scholastic Pr.) Scholastic, Inc.

SLAVERY—UNITED STATES

see also Abolitionists; Slave Trade; Southern States—History; Underground Railroad

Abnett, Dan. Harriet Tubman & the Underground Railroad. 2007. (Jr. Graphic Biographies Ser.). (ENG., Illus.). 24p. (J). (gr. 2-5). lib. bdg. 25.25 (978-1-4042-3393-5(8)); (gr. 3-8). pap. 10.60 (978-1-4042-2146-8(8), PowerKids Pr.) Rosen Publishing Group, Inc., The.
—Harriet Tubman y el Ferrocarril Clandestino. 2009. (Historietas Juveniles: Biografias (Jr. Graphic Biographies) Ser.). (SPA., Illus.). 24p. (J). (gr. 2-5). 25.25 (978-1-4358-8563-9(5)); (gr. 3-8). pap. 10.60 (978-1-4358-3320-3(1)) Rosen Publishing Group, Inc., The.
Adler, David A. Enemies of Slavery. Smith, Donald A., illus. 2004. (ENG.). 32p. (J). (gr. k-3). lib. bdg., tchr. ed. 16.95 (978-0-8234-1596-0(1)) Holiday Hse., Inc.
—Harriet Tubman & the Underground Railroad. 2012. (ENG.). 144p. (J). 18.95 (978-0-8234-2365-1(4)) Holiday Hse., Inc.
Allen, Thomas B. Harriet Tubman, Secret Agent: How Daring Slaves & Free Blacks Spied for the Union During the Civil War. 2008. (ENG., Illus.). 192p. (J). (gr. 5). 5.95 (978-1-4263-0401-9(3), National Geographic Children's Bks.) National Geographic Society.
Altman, Linda Jacobs. The Politics of Slavery: Fiery National Debates Fueled by the Slave Economy. 2004. (Slavery in American History Ser.). (Illus.). 128p. (J). lib. bdg. 27.94 (978-0-7660-2150-1(5)) Enslow Pubs., Inc.
—The Story of Slavery & Abolition in United States History. 2015. (In United States History Ser.). 96p. (J). (gr. 5-12). pap. 10.95 (978-0-7660-6331-0(3)) Enslow Pubs., Inc.
Anderson, Dale. The Causes of the Civil War. 2004. (World Almanac Library of the Civil War). (Illus.). 48p. (gr. 5-12). pap. 14.05 (978-0-8368-5590-6(6)); lib. bdg. 31.00 (978-0-8368-5581-4(7)) Stevens, Gareth Publishing LLLP. (Gareth Stevens Secondary Library).
Anthony, David H. Freedom: Life after Slavery, 1 vol. 2011. (Primary Source Readers Ser.). (ENG.). 32p. (J). (gr. 5-5). pap. 8.99 (978-1-4333-1521-3(1)) Teacher Created Materials, Inc.
Apte, Sunita & Hess, Debra. Amistad: Fight for Freedom. 2007. (Read on! Special Edition: Level RA Ser.). (Illus.). 23p. pap. 18.51 (978-1-4190-3507-4(X)) Steck-Vaughn.
Arato, Rona. Working for Freedom: The Story of Josiah Henson. 2009. (Stories of Canada Ser.: 13). (ENG., Illus.). 88p. (J). (gr. 4-18). 18.95 (978-1-894917-50-6(2), Napoleon & Co.) Dundurn CAN. Dist: Ingram Publisher Services.
Aretha, David. Sabotage, Sedition, & Sundry Acts of Rebellion. 2014. (J). (978-1-59935-406-4(3)) Reynolds, Morgan Inc.
Arnéz, Lynda. My Journey on the Underground Railroad. 2016. (My Place in History Ser.). (ENG., Illus.). 24p. (J). (gr. 2-3). 22.60 (978-1-4824-3997-7(2)); pap. 8.15 (978-1-4824-4010-2(5)) Stevens, Gareth Publishing LLLP.
Ashby, Ruth. The Underground Railroad. 2016. (Civil War Chronicles Ser.: Vol. 1). (ENG., Illus.). (J). (gr. 4-6). 23.95 **(978-1-59687-515-9(1)**, ipicturebooks) ibooks, Inc.
Barton, Jen. What's Your Story, Harriet Tubman? 2015. (Cub Reporter Meets Famous Americans Ser.). (ENG., Illus.). 32p. (J). (gr. k-3). pap. 8.99 (978-1-4677-8533-4(4), Lerner Pubns.) Lerner Publishing Group.
Beckett, Leslie. Abolitionists & Human Rights: Fighting for Emancipation. 2016. (Spotlight on American History Ser.). 24p. (J). (gr. 6-4). 26.25 (978-1-5081-4937-8(2), PowerKids Pr.) Rosen Publishing Group, Inc., The.
Berne, Emma Carlson. Face of Freedom: How the Photos of Frederick Douglass Celebrated Racial Equality. 2017. (Captured History Ser.). (ENG.). 64p. (gr. 5-7). lib. bdg. 34.65 **(978-0-7565-5617-4(1)**, CPB Grades 4-8) Compass Point Bks.
Bjornlund, Lydia D. Women in Colonial America. 2003. (Women in History Ser.). (ENG., Illus.). 112p. (J). 33.45 (978-1-59018-470-7(X), Lucent Bks.) Cengage Gale.
Blair, Margaret Whitman. Liberty or Death: The Surprising Story of Runaway Slaves Who Sided with the British During the American Revolution. 2010. (ENG., Illus.). 64p. (J). (gr. 5-8). 27.90 (978-1-4263-0591-7(5), National Geographic Children's Bks.) National Geographic Society.
Blue, Rose & Naden, Corinne J. Dred Scott: Person or Property? 2004. (Supreme Court Milestones Ser.). (Illus.). 128p. (J). 37.07 (978-0-7614-1841-2(5), Benchmark Bks.) Marshall Cavendish Corp.
Bodden, Valerie. How to Analyze the Works of Frederick Douglass, 1 vol. 2013. (Essential Critiques Set 4 Ser.). (ENG.). 112p. (J). (gr. 6-12). lib. bdg. 35.64 (978-1-61783-644-2(3), Essential Library) ABDO Publishing Co.
Bolte, Mari. Flight to Freedom! Nickolas Flux & the Underground Railroad, 1 vol. Foster, Brad W. & Simmons, Mark, illus. 2014. (Nickolas Flux History Chronicles Ser.). (ENG.). 32p. (gr. 3-4). lib. bdg. 30.65 (978-1-4914-0254-2(7), Graphic Library) Capstone Press of Coughlan Cos.
Brill, Marlene Targ. Allen Jay Y el Ferrocarril Subterraneo; Allen Jay & the Underground Railroad. 2008. pap. 40.95 (978-0-8225-9679-0(2)) Lerner Publishing Group.
Brown, Susan Taylor. Robert Smalls Sails to Freedom. Marshall, Felicia, illus. 2006. (On My Own History Ser.). 48p. (J). (gr. 3-7). pap. 6.95 (978-0-8225-6051-7(8), First Avenue Editions) Lerner Publishing Group.
Buell, Tonya. Slavery in America. 2004. (Primary Sources in American History Ser.). (Illus.). 64p. (gr. 5-8). lib. bdg. 31.95 (978-0-8239-4513-9(8), Rosen Reference) Rosen Publishing Group, Inc., The.
Burgan, Michael. African Americans in the Thirteen Colonies. 2013. (Cornerstones of Freedom™, Third Ser.). (ENG., Illus.). 64p. (J). pap. 8.95 (978-0-531-21958-4(5)); lib. bdg. 30.00 (978-0-531-23600-0(5)) Scholastic Library Publishing.
—The Underground Railroad. Schwarz, Philip, ed. 2006. (Slavery in the Americas Ser.). (Illus.). 112p. (gr. 5-8). 35.00 (978-0-8160-6137-2(8)) Facts On File, Inc.
Campbell, Clara. Slavery in America. 2015. (African American Experience: from Slavery to the Presidency Ser.). (ENG., Illus.). 80p. (J). (gr. 7-8). 32.90 (978-1-68048-036-8(7), Britannica Educational Publishing) Rosen Publishing Group, Inc., The.
Campbell, Clara, ed. Slavery in America. 2015. (African American Experience: from Slavery to the Presidency Ser.). (ENG.). 80p. (YA). (gr. 7-8). 65.80 (978-1-68048-037-5(5), Britannica Educational Publishing) Rosen Publishing Group, Inc., The.
Carosella, Melissa. The Fight for Freedom: Ending Slavery in America, 1 vol. 2011. (Primary Source Readers Ser.). (ENG.). 32p. (J). (gr. 5-5). pap. 8.99 (978-1-4333-1519-0(X)) Teacher Created Materials, Inc.
Carson, Mary Kay. Which Way to Freedom? And Other Questions about the Underground Railroad. 2015. (Good Question! Ser.). (ENG., Illus.). 40p. (J). (gr. 2). 12.95 (978-1-4549-0784-8(3)) Sterling Publishing Co., Inc.
Cartlidge, Cherese. Reparations for Slavery. 2007. (Lucent Library of Black History Ser.). (ENG., Illus.). 128p. (gr. 3-7). lib. bdg. 39.40 (978-1-59018-868-2(3), Lucent Bks.) Cengage Gale.
Cary, Lorene. Free! Great Escapes from Slavery on the Underground Railroad. 2011. (J). pap. 15.00 (978-0-9819560-3-9(3)); 2nd ed. (ENG., Illus.). 86p. pap. 20.95 (978-0-9819560-2-2(5)) New City Community Pr.
Child, Lydia Maria. The Duty of Disobedience to the Fugitive Slave Act. 2007. (ENG.). 48p. per. (978-1-4065-1352-3(0)) Dodo Pr.
Clark, Willow. The True Story of the Emancipation Proclamation. 2013. (What Really Happened? Ser.). (ENG., Illus.). 24p. (J). (gr. 3-6). 22.60 (978-1-4488-9695-0(9)); pap. 8.25 (978-1-4488-9848-0(X)) Rosen Publishing Group, Inc., The. (PowerKids Pr.).
Clinton, Catherine. When Harriet Met Sojourner. Evans, Shane W., illus. 2007. (ENG.). 32p. (J). (gr. k-2). 16.99 (978-0-06-050425-0(0), Tegen, Katherine Bks) HarperCollins Pubs.
Cloud Tapper, Suzanne & Tapper, Suzanne Cloud. Views on Slavery: In the Words of Enslaved Africans, Merchants, Owners, & Abolitionists. 2016. (Slavery & Slave Resistance Ser.). (Illus.). 128p. (J). (gr. 6-6). 37.27 (978-0-7660-7553-5(2)) Enslow Pubs., Inc.
Collard, Sneed B., III. Phillis Wheatley: She Loved Words. 2009. (American Heroes Ser.). 48p. (gr. 3-18). 29.93 (978-0-7614-4057-4(7)) Marshall Cavendish Corp.
Conkling, Winifred. Passenger on the Pearl: The True Story of Emily Edmonson's Flight from Slavery. (ENG., 176p. (YA). (gr. 7-10). 2016. Illus.). pap. 10.95 (978-1-61620-550-8(4)) 2015. 17.95 (978-1-61620-196-8(7), 73196) Algonquin Bks. of Chapel Hill.
Cooke, Tim. Causes of the War. 2012. (American Civil War: the Right Answer Ser.). (Illus.). 48p. (J). (gr. 6-8). pap. 14.05 (978-1-4339-7536-3(X)); lib. bdg. 31.95 (978-1-4339-7535-6(1)) Stevens, Gareth Publishing LLLP.
—Causes of the War: 1860-1861. 2012. (Civil War Highlights Ser.). (Illus.). 48p. (gr. 5-12). lib. bdg. 37.10 (978-1-59920-813-8(X)) Black Rabbit Bks.
Corrick, James A. The Civil War & Emancipation. 2007. (Lucent Library of Black History Ser.). (ENG., Illus.). 128p. (gr. 3-7). lib. bdg. 39.40 (978-1-4205-0008-0(2), Lucent Bks.) Cengage Gale.
Creative Media Applications. Slavery in the Americas Set. 2006. (Slavery in the Americas Ser.). 672p. (gr. 5-8). 210.00 (978-0-8160-6133-4(5)) Facts On File, Inc.
Currie, Stephen. Escapes from Slavery. 2003. (Great Escapes Ser.). (ENG., Illus.). 112p. (J). 30.85 (978-1-59018-276-5(6), Lucent Bks.) Cengage Gale.
—The Quest for Freedom: The Abolitionist Movement. 2005. (Lucent Library of Black History). (ENG., Illus.). 112p. (YA). (gr. 7-10). lib. bdg. 33.45 (978-1-59018-703-6(2), Lucent Bks.) Cengage Gale.
Davis, Kenneth C. In the Shadow of Liberty: The Hidden History of Slavery, Four Presidents, & Five Black Lives. 2016. (ENG., Illus.). 304p. (J). 17.99 (978-1-62779-311-7(9), 9781627793117, Holt, Henry & Co. Bks. For Young Readers) Holt, Henry & Co.
De Medeiros, James. Slavery. 2013. (J). (978-1-62127-195-6(1)) 2013. (J). pap. (978-1-62127-201-4(X)) 2008. (Illus.). 48p. (YA). (gr. 5-8). pap. 10.95 (978-1-59036-875-6(4)) 2008. (Illus.). 48p. (YA). (gr. 5-8). lib. bdg. 29.05 (978-1-59036-874-9(6)) Weigl Pubs., Inc.
DeFord, Deborah H. Life under Slavery. Schwarz, Philip, ed. 2006. (Slavery in the Americas Ser.). (Illus.). 112p. (gr. 5-8). 35.00 (978-0-8160-6135-8(1)) Facts On File, Inc.
DeFord, Diane. Harriet Tubman. 2009. pap. 13.25 (978-1-60559-061-5(4)) Hameray Publishing Group, Inc.
Deiters, Erika & Deiters, Jim. The African Community in America. 2003. (J). lib. bdg. (978-1-58417-032-7(8)) Lake Street Pubs.
Doak, Robin S. Harriet Tubman. 2015. (ENG., Illus.). 48p. (J). pap. 6.95 (978-0-531-21757-3(4)); lib. bdg. (978-0-531-21595-1(4)) Scholastic, Inc. (Orchard Bks.).
—Phillis Wheatley: The Inspiring Life Story of the American Poet. 2016. (Inspiring Stories Ser.). (ENG., Illus.). 112p. (J). (gr. 5-7). lib. bdg. 35.99 (978-0-7565-5166-7(8), CPB Grades 4-8) Compass Point Bks.
Doak, Robin Santos. Slave Rebellions. Schwarz, Philip, ed. 2006. (Slavery in the Americas Ser.). (Illus.). 112p. (gr. 5-8). 35.00 (978-0-8160-6136-5(X)) Facts On File, Inc.
Dunn, Joe. The Underground Railroad, 1 vol. 2007. (Graphic History Ser.). (ENG., Illus.). 32p. (gr. 3-7). 28.50 (978-1-60270-080-2(X), Graphic Planet- Nonfiction) ABDO Publishing Co.
Edison, Erin. Harriet Tubman, 1 vol. 2013. (Great Women in History Ser.). (ENG.). 24p. (gr. k-1). pap. 6.29 (978-1-62065-859-8(3)); pap. 35.70 (978-1-62065-860-4(7)) Capstone Press of Coughlan Cos. (Pebble Bks.).
Edwards, Judith. Abolitionists & Slave Resistance: Breaking the Chains of Slavery. 2004. (Slavery in American History Ser.). (Illus.). 128p. (J). lib. bdg. 27.94 (978-0-7660-2155-6(6)) Enslow Pubs., Inc.
The Emancipation Proclamation & the End of Slavery in America. 2014. (Celebration of the Civil Rights Movement Ser.). (Illus.). 80p. (J). (gr. 7-12). 34.25 (978-1-4777-7749-7(0)) Rosen Publishing Group, Inc., The.
Erickson, Paul. Daily Life on a Southern Plantation. Gabbey, Terry, illus. Slingsby, Miki, photos by. 2006. 48p. (J). (gr. 2-5). reprint ed. pap. 8.00 (978-1-4223-5727-9(9)) DIANE Publishing Co.
Eskridge, Ann E. Slave Uprisings & Runaways: Fighting for Freedom & the Underground Railroad. 2004. (Slavery in American History Ser.). (Illus.). 128p. (J). lib. bdg. 27.94 (978-0-7660-2154-9(8)) Enslow Pubs., Inc.
Evans, Shane W. Underground: Finding the Light to Freedom. Evans, Shane W., illus. 2011. (ENG., Illus.). 32p. (J). (gr. -1-3). 16.99 (978-1-59643-538-4(0), 9781596435384) Roaring Brook Pr.
Figley, Marty Rhodes. Washington Is Burning. Orback, Craig, illus. 2007. (On My Own History Ser.). (ENG.). 48p. (gr. 2-4). per. 6.95 (978-0-8225-6050-0(X), First Avenue Editions) Lerner Publishing Group.
Findley, Violet. Easy Reader Biographies: Harriet Tubman: Follow the North Star. 2007. (ENG.). 16p. pap. 2.99 (978-0-439-92330-9(1), Teaching Resources) Scholastic, Inc.
Finegan, Jeffrey E., Sr. Colonel Washington & Me: George Washington, His Slave William Lee & Their Incredible Journey Together. Nikolopoulos, Stephanie, ed. 2012. (ENG., Illus.). 32p. (J). 16.95 (978-0-9852819-0-8(1)) Seigle Bks.
Ford, Carin T. The Emancipation Proclamation, Lincoln, & Slavery Through Primary Sources. 2013. (Civil War Through Primary Sources Ser.). 48p. (J). (gr. 4-10). pap. 8.95 (978-1-4644-0187-9(X)); lib. bdg. 25.27 (978-0-7660-4129-5(8)) Enslow Pubs., Inc.
—Lincoln, Slavery, & the Emancipation Proclamation. 2004. (Civil War Library). (Illus.). 48p. (J). lib. bdg. 25.27 (978-0-7660-2252-2(8)) Enslow Pubs., Inc.
—Slavery & the Underground Railroad: Bound for Freedom. 2004. (Civil War Library). (Illus.). 48p. (J). lib. bdg. 25.27 (978-0-7660-2251-5(X)) Enslow Pubs., Inc.
—The Underground Railroad & Slavery Through Primary Sources. 2013. (Civil War Through Primary Sources Ser.). 48p. (J). (gr. 4-10). pap. 8.95 (978-1-4644-0185-5(3)); lib. bdg. 25.27 (978-0-7660-4127-1(1)) Enslow Pubs., Inc.
A Forgotten History: The Slave Trade & Slavery in New England, 2. 2005. (Illus.). 104p. (YA). pap. (978-1-891306-86-0(3)) Choices Program, Watson Institute, Brown Univ.
Fradin, Dennis B. The Underground Railroad. 2011. (Great Escapes Ser.). 80p. (gr. 6). 34.21 (978-1-60870-476-7(9)) Marshall Cavendish Corp.
Fradin, Dennis Brindell. The Emancipation Proclamation. 2007. (Turning Points in U. S. History Ser.). (J). lib. bdg. 31.36 (978-0-7614-2038-5(X), Benchmark Bks.) Marshall Cavendish Corp.
Gold, Susan Dudley. The Missouri Compromise. 2010. (Landmark Legislation Ser.). 128p. (YA). (gr. 7-12). 39.93 (978-1-60870-041-7(0)) Marshall Cavendish Corp.
—United States V. Amistad: Slave Ship Mutiny. 2006. (Supreme Court Milestones Ser.). (Illus.). 128p. (gr. 7-7). lib. bdg. 42.79 (978-0-7614-2143-6(2), Benchmark Bks.) Marshall Cavendish Corp.
Grady, Cynthia. Like a Bird: The Art of the American Slave Song. Wood, Michele, illus. 2016. (ENG.). 40p. (gr. 3-6). 38.65 (978-1-5124-0889-8(1), Millbrook Pr.) Lerner Publishing Group.
Gunderson, Cory Gideon. Dred Scott Decision, 1 vol. 2004. (American Moments Ser.). (ENG.). 48p. (gr. 4-8). 27.07 (978-1-59197-283-9(3), Abdo & Daughters) ABDO Publishing Co.
Hall, Shyima. Hidden Girl: The True Story of a Modern-Day Child Slave. 2014. (ENG., Illus.). 240p. (YA). (gr. 9). 18.99 (978-1-4424-8168-8(4), Simon & Schuster Bks. For Young Readers) Simon & Schuster Bks. For Young Readers.
Hansen, Joyce & McGowan, Gary. Freedom Roads: Searching for the Underground Railroad. Ransome, James E., illus. 2003. (ENG.). 166p. (J). (gr. 5-9). 18.95 (978-0-8126-2673-5(7)) Cricket Bks.
Haskins, James & Benson, Kathleen. Africa: A Look Back. 2006. (Drama of African-American History Ser.). (Illus.). 80p. (J). (gr. 6-7). lib. bdg. 35.64 (978-0-7614-2148-1(3), Benchmark Bks.) Marshall Cavendish Corp.
Hatt, Christine. The African-American Slave Trade. 2003. (Questioning History Ser.). (J). lib. bdg. 28.50 (978-1-58340-265-8(9)) Black Rabbit Bks.
Herda, D. J. The Dred Scott Case: Slavery & Citizenship. rev. ed. 2010. (Landmark Supreme Court Cases, Gold Edition Ser.). (Illus.). 104p. (J). (gr. 6-18). 33.27 (978-0-7660-3427-3(5)) Enslow Pubs., Inc.
—Slavery & Citizenship: The Dred Scott Case. 2016. (US Supreme Court Landmark Cases Ser.). 128p. (J). 37.27 (978-0-7660-8426-1(4)) Enslow Pubs., Inc.
Hicks, Kyra E. Martha Ann's Quilt for Queen Victoria. Fodi, Lee Edward, illus. 2006. 28p. (J). (gr. -1-3). 16.95 (978-1-933285-59-7(1)) Brown Books Publishing Group.
Hill, Laban Carrick. Dave the Potter: Artist, Poet, Slave. Collier, Bryan, illus. 2010. (ENG.). 40p. (J). (gr. -1-3). 18.99 (978-0-316-10731-0(X)) Little, Brown Bks. for Young Readers.
Hill, Laban Carrik. Dave the Potter: Artist, Poet, Slave. 2011. (J). (978-1-4618-1706-2(4)) Recorded Bks., Inc.

Holzer, Harold. Lincoln: How Abraham Lincoln Ended Slavery in America - A Companion Book for Young Readers to the Steven Spielberg Film. 2012. (ENG.). 240p. 16.99 *(978-0-06-226509-8(1))* HarperCollins Pubs.

—Lincoln: How Abraham Lincoln Ended Slavery in America: A Companion Book for Young Readers to the Steven Spielberg Film. 2013. (ENG.). 240p. pap. 7.99 *(978-0-06-226511-1(3)*, Newmarket for It Bks.) HarperCollins Pubs.

Hopper, Whitney. Slavery in the United States: "The Abominable Trade" 2016. (Spotlight on American History Ser.). (Illus.). 24p. (J). (gr. 6-4). 26.25 *(978-1-5081-4940-8(2)*, PowerKids Pr.) Rosen Publishing Group, Inc., The.

Howell, Brian. U. S. Growth & Change in the 19th Century, 1801 to 1861. 2011. (Explorer Library: Language Arts Explorer Ser.). (ENG.). 32p. (gr. 4-8). lib. bdg. 28.50 *(978-1-61080-202-4(0)*, 201180) Cherry Lake Publishing.

—U.S. Growth & Change in the 19th Century. 2011. (Explorer Library: Language Arts Explorer Ser.). (ENG.). 32p. (gr. 4-8). pap. 14.21 *(978-1-61080-290-1(X)*, 201213) Cherry Lake Publishing.

Howse, Jennifer. Reconstruction. 2013. (J). *(978-1-62127-194-9(3))*; pap. *(978-1-62127-200-7(1))* Weigl Pubs., Inc.

Hudson, Wade. The Underground Railroad. 2005. (Cornerstones of Freedom Ser.). (ENG., Illus.). 48p. (J). (gr. 4-6). 26.00 *(978-0-516-23630-8(X)*, Children's Pr.) Scholastic Library Publishing.

Huey, Lois Miner. Forgotten Bones: Uncovering a Slave Cemetery. 2015. (ENG., Illus.). 56p. (J). (gr. 4-8). lib. bdg. 30.65 *(978-1-4677-3393-9(8)*, Millbrook Pr.) Lerner Publishing Group.

Imbriaco, Alison. Causes of the Civil War: A MyReportLinks.com Book. 2004. (American Civil War Ser.). (Illus.). 48p. (J). lib. bdg. 25.26 *(978-0-7660-5186-7(2)*, MyReportLinks.com Bks.) Enslow Pubs., Inc.

Jarrow, Jesse. Phillis Wheatley: African American Poet / Poeta Afroamericana. 2009. (Famous People in American History/Grandes personajes en la historia de los Estados Unidos Ser.). (ENG & SPA.). 32p. (gr. 2-3). 47.90 *(978-1-61512-554-8(X)*, Editorial Buenas Letras) Rosen Publishing Group, Inc., The.

—Phillis Wheatley: Poeta afroamericana (Phillis Wheatley: African American Poet) 2009. (Grandes personajes en la historia de los Estados Unidos (Famous People in American History) Ser.). (SPA.). 32p. (gr. 2-3). 47.90 *(978-1-61512-807-5(7)*, Editorial Buenas Letras) Rosen Publishing Group, Inc., The.

Johnson, Claudia Durst. Slavery & Racism in the Narrative Life of Freddrick Douglass. 2014. (Social Issues in Literature Ser.). (ENG., Illus.). 224p. (gr. 7-12). lib. bdg. 46.40 *(978-0-7377-6986-9(6)*, Greenhaven Pr., Inc.) Cengage Gale.

Jones, Lynda. Mrs. Lincoln's Dressmaker: The Unlikely Friendship of Elizabeth Keckley & Mary Todd Lincoln. 2009. (ENG., Illus.). 80p. (J). (gr. 5). lib. bdg. 27.90 *(978-1-4263-0378-4(5))*; 18.95 *(978-1-4263-0377-7(7))* National Geographic Society. (National Geographic Children's Bks.).

Jordan, Anne Devereaux. Slavery & Resistance. 2006. (Drama of African-American History Ser.). (Illus.). 80p. (gr. 6-7). lib. bdg. 35.64 *(978-0-7614-2178-8(5)*, Benchmark Bks.) Marshall Cavendish Corp.

Kamma, Anne. If You Lived When There Was Slavery in America. Johnson, Pamela, illus. 2004. (If You Lived Ser.). 63p. (J). 14.65 *(978-0-7569-3016-5(2))* Perfection Learning Corp.

—If You Lived When There Was Slavery in America. Johnson, Pamela, illus. 2004. (If You... Ser.). (ENG.). 64p. (J). (gr. 2-5). pap. 6.99 *(978-0-439-56706-0(8))* Scholastic, Inc.

Kent, Jacqueline C. Phillis Wheatley. 2003. (Women of the Revolution Ser.). (J). pap. *(978-1-58417-089-1(1))*; lib. bdg. *(978-1-58417-026-6(3))* Lake Street Pubs.

Kimmel, Allison Crotzer. A Primary Source History of Slavery in the United States. 2015. (Primary Source History Ser.). (ENG.). 32p. (gr. 3-4). lib. bdg. 27.32 *(978-1-4914-1839-0(7))* Capstone Press of Coughlan Cos.

Knudsen, Shannon. When Were the First Slaves Set Free During the Civil War? And Other Questions about the Emancipation Proclamation. 2010. (Six Questions of American History Ser.). (ENG., Illus.). 48p. (gr. 4-6). lib. bdg. 30.60 *(978-1-58013-670-9(2))* Lerner Publishing Group.

—When Were the First Slaves Set Free During the Civil War? And Other Questions about the Emancipation Proclamation. 2010. (Six Questions of American History Ser.). (ENG.). 48p. (gr. 4-6). pap. 9.95 *(978-0-7613-6121-3(9))* Lerner Publishing Group.

Krensky, Stephen. The Emancipaton Proclamation. 2011. (Documents of Democracy Ser.). 96p. (gr. 8). 34.21 *(978-0-7614-4915-7(9))* Marshall Cavendish Corp.

Landau, Elaine. The Emancipation Proclamation: Would You Do What Lincoln Did? (What Would You Do? Ser.). (Illus.). 48p. (J). 2010. pap. 8.95 *(978-1-59845-194-8(4))* 2008. (gr. 3-7). lib. bdg. 25.27 *(978-0-7660-2899-9(2))* Enslow Pubs., Inc. (Enslow Elementary).

—Fleeing to Freedom on the Underground Railroad: The Courageous Slaves, Agents, & Conductors. 2006. (People's History Ser.). (ENG., Illus.). 88p. (gr. 5-12). lib. bdg. 33.26 *(978-0-8225-3490-7(8))* Lerner Publishing Group.

Lanier, Wendy. What Was the Missouri Compromise? And Other Questions about the Struggle over Slavery. 2012. (Six Questions of American History Ser.). (ENG.). 48p. (gr. 4-6). pap. 9.95 *(978-0-7613-8565-3(7))*; (Illus.). lib. bdg. 30.60 *(978-0-7613-5331-7(3))* Lerner Publishing Group.

Lanier, Wendy & Nelson, Robin. What Was the Missouri Compromise? And Other Questions about the Struggle over Slavery. 2012. (Start to Finish, Second Series: Nature's Cycles Ser.). (ENG.). 48p. (gr. k-3). pap. 39.62 *(978-0-7613-9293-4(9))* Lerner Publishing Group.

Lantier, Patricia. Harriet Tubman: Conductor on the Underground Railroad. 2009. (Voices for Freedom Ser.). (ENG., Illus.). 64p. (J). (gr. 5-8). pap. *(978-0-7787-4838-0(3))*; lib. bdg. *(978-0-7787-4822-9(7))* Crabtree Publishing Co.

Leavitt, Amie Jane. Harriet Tubman. 2007. (What's So Great About...? Ser.). (Illus.). 32p. (J). (gr. 2-4). lib. bdg. 25.70 *(978-1-58415-577-5(9))* Mitchell Lane Pubs., Inc.

Lester, Julius. To Be a Slave. Feelings, Tom, illus. 2005. (Puffin Modern Classics Ser.). (ENG.). 176p. (J). (gr. 3-7). 7.99 *(978-0-14-240386-0(5)*, Puffin Books) Penguin Young Readers Group.

Levy, Debbie. Slaves on a Southern Plantation. 2004. (Daily Life Ser.). (ENG., Illus.). 48p. (J). 27.50 *(978-0-7377-1827-0(7)*, Greenhaven Pr., Inc.) Cengage Gale.

Levy, Janey. Juneteenth: Celebrating the End of Slavery. 2009. (Reading Room Collection 2 Ser.). 24p. (gr. 3-4). 42.50 *(978-1-60851-976-7(7)*, PowerKids Pr.) Rosen Publishing Group, Inc., The.

Linde, Barbara M. Slavery in Early America. 2011. (Story of America Ser.). (Illus.). 32p. (J). (gr. 4-6). lib. bdg. 26.60 *(978-1-4339-4776-6(5)*, Gareth Stevens Learning Library) Stevens, Gareth Publishing LLLP.

Littlejohn, Randy. A Timeline of the Slave Trade in America. 2009. (Timelines of American History Ser.). 32p. (gr. 4-4). 47.90 *(978-1-60854-390-8(0)*, Rosen Reference) Rosen Publishing Group, Inc., The.

Llanas, Sheila Griffin. The Underground Railroad: A History Perspectives Book. 2013. (Perspectives Library). (ENG., Illus.). 32p. (J). (gr. 4-8). 28.50 *(978-1-62431-423-0(6)*, 202812) Cherry Lake Publishing.

Malaspina, Ann. Harriet Tubman. 2009. (Leaders of the Civil War Era Ser.). (Illus.). 120p. (gr. 6-12). 35.00 *(978-1-60413-303-5(1)*, Chelsea Hse.) Facts On File, Inc.

Marlowe, Sam. Learning about Dedication from the Life of Frederick Douglass. 2009. (Character Building Book Ser.). 24p. (gr. 2-3). 42.50 *(978-1-60854-970-2(4)*, PowerKids Pr.) Rosen Publishing Group, Inc., The.

McArthur, Debra. The Kansas-Nebraska Act & Bleeding Kansas in American History. 2003. (In American History Ser.). (Illus.). 128p. (J). lib. bdg. 27.94 *(978-0-7660-1988-1(8))* Enslow Pubs., Inc.

McClafferty, Carla Killough. Buried Lives: Slaves of George Washington's Mount Vernon. 2017. (J). ***(978-0-8234-3697-2(7))*** Holiday Hse., Inc.

McConaghy, Lorraine & Bentley, Judy. Free Boy: A True Story of Slave & Master. 2013. (V Ethel Willis White Bks.). (ENG., Illus.). 112p. pap. 18.95 *(978-0-295-99271-6(9))* Univ. of Washington Pr.

McDonough, Yona Zeldis. Who Was Harriet Tubman? Harrison, Nancy, illus. 2003. (Who Was...? Ser.). 106p. (gr. 4-7). 15.00 *(978-0-7569-1590-2(2))* Perfection Learning Corp.

McDougal-Littell Publishing Staff, contrib. by. A Nation Dividing 1800-1860. 2004. (Stories in History Ser.). (Illus.). 176p. (gr. 6-12). 13.32 *(978-0-618-14222-4(3)*, 2-00242) Holt McDougal.

McGill, Alice. Way up & over Everything. Daly, Jude, illus. 2008. (ENG.). 32p. (J). (gr. 2-5). 16.00 *(978-0-618-38796-0(X))* Houghton Mifflin Harcourt Publishing Co.

McKissack, Fredrick, Jr. & McKissack, Patricia C. Hard Labor: The First African-Americans 1619. Fiedler, Joseph Daniel, illus. 2004. (Milestone Ser.). (ENG.). 64p. (J). (gr. 2-5). pap. 6.99 *(978-0-689-86149-9(4)*, Simon & Schuster/Paula Wiseman Bks.) Simon & Schuster/Paula Wiseman Bks.

McKissack, Patricia C. & McKissack, Fredrick L. Frederick Douglass: Fighter Against Slavery. 2013. (Famous African Americans Ser.). (Illus.). 24p. (J). (gr. k-18). 22.60 *(978-0-7660-4098-4(4)*, Enslow Elementary) Enslow Pubs., Inc.

McLendon, Jacquelyn. Phillis Wheatley: A Revolutionary Poet. 2009. (Library of American Lives & Times Ser.). 112p. (gr. 5-5). 69.20 *(978-1-60853-499-9(5))* Rosen Publishing Group, Inc., The.

McNeese, Tim. Dred Scott V. Sandford: The Pursuit of Freedom. 2006. (Great Supreme Court Decisions Ser.). (Illus.). 120p. (YA). (gr. 5-9). lib. bdg. 32.95 *(978-0-7910-9236-1(4))* Facts On File, Inc.

—The Rise & Fall of American Slavery: Freedom Denied, Freedom Gained. 2004. (Slavery in American History Ser.). (Illus.). 128p. (J). lib. bdg. 27.94 *(978-0-7660-2156-3(4))* Enslow Pubs., Inc.

Meadows, James. Slavery: The Struggle for Freedom. 2009. (Journey to Freedom Ser.). (ENG., Illus.). 32p. (J). (gr. 4-7). 29.93 *(978-1-60253-134-5(X)*, 200400) Child's World, Inc., The.

Metz, Lorijo. El Movimiento Abolicionista / the Abolitionist Movement, 1 vol., 1. Beullens-Maoui, Nathalie, ed. 2014. (¡Celebremos la Libertad! / Let's Celebrate Freedom! Ser.). (SPA & BYN.). 24p. (J). (gr. 3-6). 23.60 *(978-1-4777-3249-6(7)*, PowerKids Pr.) Rosen Publishing Group, Inc., The.

Miller, Barbara Kiely. Frederick Douglass. 2007. (Grandes Personajes (Great Americans) Ser.). 24p. (gr. 1-4). (SPA.). pap. 8.15 *(978-0-8368-8335-0(7))*; pap. 8.15 *(978-0-8368-8322-0(5))*; lib. bdg. 22.00 *(978-0-8368-8315-2(2))*; (SPA., Illus.). lib. bdg. 22.00 *(978-0-8368-8328-2(4))* Stevens, Gareth Publishing LLLP. (Weekly Reader Leveled Readers).

Moore, Cathy. Ellen Craft's Escape from Slavery. Braught, Mark, illus. 2010. (History Speaks: Picture Books Plus Reader's Theater Ser.). (ENG.). 48p. (gr. 2-4). pap. 9.95 *(978-0-7613-6672-0(5))*; lib. bdg. 27.93 *(978-0-7613-5875-6(7)*, Millbrook Pr.) Lerner Publishing Group.

Moriarty, J. T. Phillis Wheatley: African American Poet. 2009. (Primary Sources of Famous People in American History Ser.). 32p. (gr. 2-3). 47.90 *(978-1-60851-717-6(9))* Rosen Publishing Group, Inc., The.

National Geographic Learning, National Geographic Learning & Rossi, Ann. Reading Expeditions - The Anti-Slavery Movement. 2007. (Rise & Shine Ser.). (ENG.). 40p. pap. 19.95 *(978-0-7922-8622-6(7))* National Geographic School Publishing, Inc.

National Park Service Staff, ed. Discovering the Underground Railroad: Junior Ranger Activity Book. 2012. (ENG., Illus.). 20p. (gr. -1-6). pap. 6.00 *(978-0-16-090018-1(2))* National Park Service Div. of Pubns.

Nelson, Robin. Juneteenth. 2009. (First Step Nonfiction - American Holidays Ser.). (ENG.). 24p. (gr. k-2). 23.93 *(978-0-7613-4934-1(0))* Lerner Publishing Group.

Nelson, Vaunda Micheaux & Nelson, Drew. Juneteenth. Schroder, Mark, illus. 2006. (On My Own Holidays Ser.). (ENG.). 48p. (gr. 2-4). per. 6.95 *(978-0-8225-5974-0(9)*, First Avenue Editions) Lerner Publishing Group.

Norwich, Grace. I Am #6: Harriet Tubman. 2013. (I Am Ser.: 6). (ENG.). 128p. (J). (gr. 2-5). pap. 5.99 *(978-0-545-48436-7(7)*, Scholastic Paperbacks) Scholastic, Inc.

—I Am Harriet Tubman. Simon, Ute, illus. 2013. 127p. (J). *(978-0-545-61344-6(2))* Scholastic, Inc.

O'Connell, Kim A. Slavery, Emancipation, & the Civil War: A MyReportLinks. com Book. 2004. (American Civil War Ser.). (Illus.). 48p. (J). lib. bdg. 26.60 *(978-0-7660-5190-4(0)*, MyReportLinks.com Bks.) Enslow Pubs., Inc.

Ollhoff, Jim. The Civil War: Slavery, 1 vol. 2012. (Civil War Ser.). (ENG.). 32p. (YA). (gr. 5-9). 27.07 *(978-1-61783-276-5(6))* ABDO Publishing Co.

—Years of Slavery, 1 vol. 2011. (African American History Ser.). (ENG., Illus.). 32p. (YA). (gr. 5-9). lib. bdg. 27.07 *(978-1-61714-714-2(1))* ABDO Publishing Co.

Osborne, Linda Barrett. Traveling the Freedom Road: From Slavery & the Civil War Through Reconstruction. 2009. (ENG., Illus.). 128p. (J). (gr. 3-7). 25.95 *(978-0-8109-8338-0(9)*, Abrams Bks. for Young Readers) Abrams, Inc.

Otfinoski, Steven. From Fugitive to Freedom: The Story of the Underground Railroad. 2017. (Tangled History Ser.). (ENG., Illus.). 112p. (gr. 3-4). lib. bdg. 31.99 *(978-1-5157-3604-2(0))* Capstone Press of Coughlan Cos.

Owens, Tom. Traveling on the Freedom Machines of the Transportation Age. 2003. (Reading Essentials in Social Studies). (Illus.). 40p. pap. 8.00 *(978-0-7891-5873-4(6))* Perfection Learning Corp.

Paley, Caitlyn. Slave Narratives & the Writings of Freedmen. 2015. (Primary Sources of the Abolitionist Movement Ser.). (ENG., Illus.). 64p. (J). (gr. 6-6). 34.21 *(978-1-5026-0524-5(4))* Cavendish Square Publishing.

Patterson, Marie. Slavery in America, 1 vol. 2005. (Primary Source Readers Ser.). (ENG.). 24p. (J). (gr. 5-5). pap. 8.99 *(978-0-7439-8911-4(2))* Shell Educational Publishing.

Peppas, Lynn. Juneteenth. 2010. (Celebrations in My World Ser.). (ENG.). 32p. (J). (gr. k-3). *(978-0-7787-4928-8(2))*; pap. *(978-0-7787-4935-6(5))* Crabtree Publishing Co.

Perrin, Pat & Coleman, Wim. The Mystery of the Vanishing Slaves. 2004. (Cover-To-Cover Books). (Illus.). 64p. (J). (gr. 4-7). lib. bdg. 17.95 *(978-0-7569-1041-9(2))* Perfection Learning Corp.

Perritano, John. Free at Last! How the Freeing of the Slaves Changed American History. 2008. (Graphic America Ser.). (ENG., Illus.). 32p. (J). (gr. 3-6). pap. *(978-0-7787-4212-8(1))*; lib. bdg. *(978-0-7787-4185-5(0))* Crabtree Publishing Co.

Porterfield, Jason. Frederick Douglass: Abolitionist & Fighter for Equality. 2017. (J). pap. ***(978-1-68048-802-9(3)***, Britannica Educational Publishing) Rosen Publishing Group, Inc., The.

Press, David P. Abraham Lincoln: The Great Emancipator. 2013. (ENG., Illus.). 64p. (J). *(978-0-7787-1061-5(0))*; pap. *(978-0-7787-1064-6(5))* Crabtree Publishing Co.

Pringle, Laurence. American Slave, American Hero: York of the Lewis & Clark Expedition. Van Wright, Cornelius & Hu, Ying-Hwa, illus. 2006. (ENG.). 40p. (J). (gr. 3-3). 19.95 *(978-1-59078-282-8(8))* Boyds Mills Pr.

Rappaport, Doreen. No More! Stories & Songs of Slave Resistance. Evans, Shane W., illus. 2005. (ENG.). 64p. (J). (gr. 4-7). reprint ed. pap. 9.99 *(978-0-7636-2876-5(X))* Candlewick Pr.

Ratliff, Thomas. You Wouldn't Want to Be a Civil War Soldier! A War You'D Rather Not Fight. 2013. (You Wouldn't Want To... Ser.). lib. bdg. 20.80 *(978-0-606-31627-9(2)*, Turtleback) Turtleback Bks.

Rausch, Monica L. Harriet Tubman. 2007. (Grandes personajes (Great Americans) Ser.). (ENG & SPA., Illus.). 24p. (gr. 1-4). lib. bdg. 22.00 *(978-0-8368-7985-8(6)*, Weekly Reader Leveled Readers) Stevens, Gareth Publishing LLLP.

Reece, Richard. Bleeding Kansas, 1 vol. 2012. (Essential Events Set 8 Ser.). (ENG.). 112p. (J). (gr. 6-12). lib. bdg. 35.64 *(978-1-61783-307-6(X))* ABDO Publishing Co.

Rosen, Daniel. Dred Scott & the Supreme Court: Set Of 6. 2011. (Navigators Ser.). (J). pap. 48.00 net. *(978-1-4108-6258-7(5))* Benchmark Education Co.

Roxburgh, Ellis. Nat Turner's Slave Rebellion. 2017. (Rebellions, Revolts, & Uprisings Ser.). 48p. (gr. 5-5). pap. 84.30 ***(978-1-5382-0753-6(2))*** Stevens, Gareth Publishing LLLP.

Ruffin, Frances E. Sally Hemings. 2009. (American Legends Ser.). 24p. (gr. 3-3). 42.50 *(978-1-61511-386-6(X)*, PowerKids Pr.) Rosen Publishing Group, Inc., The.

Sawyer, Kem Knapp. Harriet Tubman - A Photographic Story of a Life. 2010. (DK Biography Ser.). (ENG.). 128p. (J). (gr. 5-12). 6.99 *(978-0-7566-5806-9(3)*, DK Children) Dorling Kindersley Publishing, Inc.

Schmid, Katie Kelley. Nat Turner & Slave Life on a Southern Plantation. 2013. (Jr. Graphic African American History Ser.). 24p. (J). (gr. 3-6). pap. 63.60 *(978-1-4777-1454-6(5))*; (ENG., Illus.). pap. 10.60 *(978-1-4777-1453-9(7))*; (ENG., Illus.). lib. bdg. 25.25 *(978-1-4777-1314-3(X))* Rosen Publishing Group, Inc., The. (PowerKids Pr.).

Senker, Cath. Who Traveled the Underground Railroad?, 1 vol. 2014. (Primary Source Detectives Ser.). (ENG., Illus.). 64p. (gr. 7-8). lib. bdg. 35.99 *(978-1-4329-9603-1(7))* Heinemann-Raintree.

Shea, Therese. The African Burial Ground. 2016. (Hidden History Ser.). 00032p. (J). pap. 10.50 *(978-1-4824-5787-2(3))* Stevens, Gareth Publishing LLLP.

Sherman, Patrice. Ben & the Emancipation Proclamation. Cooper, Floyd, illus. 2009. (ENG.). 32p. (J). (gr. 3-7). 17.00 *(978-0-8028-5319-6(6)*, Eerdmans Bks For Young Readers) Eerdmans, William B. Publishing Co.

Simon, Barbara Brooks. Escape to Freedom: The Underground Railroad Adventures of Callie & William. 2004. (I Am American Ser.). (ENG., Illus.). 40p. (J). (gr. 3-7). pap. 6.99 *(978-0-7922-6551-1(3)*, National Geographic Children's Bks.) National Geographic Society.

—The Underground Railroad: Voices from America's Past. 2007. (Nonfiction Reading & Writing Workshops Ser.). (ENG., Illus.). 40p. (J). pap. 19.95 *(978-0-7922-4549-0(0))* National Geographic School Publishing, Inc.

Sirimarco, Elizabeth. The Time of Slavery. 2006. (American Voices Ser.). (Illus.). 114p. (J). (gr. 3-7). lib. bdg. 38.50 *(978-0-7614-2169-6(6)*, Benchmark Bks.) Marshall Cavendish Corp.

Skog, Jason. The Dred Scott Decision. 2006. (We the People: Civil War Era Ser.). (ENG., Illus.). 48p. (gr. 5-6). 7.95 *(978-0-7565-2038-0(X)*, We the People) Compass Point Bks.

Slavery: Analyzing Visual Primary Sources. 2006. cd-rom 59.95 net. *(978-1-56004-262-4(1))* Social Studies Schl. Service.

Slavery & Slave Resistance. 2016. (Slavery & Slave Resistance Ser.). 128p. (gr. 6-6). lib. bdg. 223.62 *(978-0-7660-7504-7(4))* Enslow Pubs., Inc.

Slavicek, Louise Chipley. Harriet Tubman & the Underground Railroad. 2006. (Lucent Library of Black History). (ENG., Illus.). 104p. (J). (gr. 3-7). lib. bdg. 34.80 *(978-1-59018-927-6(2)*, Lucent Bks.) Cengage Gale.

Smith, Charles R., Jr. Brick by Brick. Cooper, Floyd, illus. 2012. (ENG.). 32p. (J). (gr. -1-3). 17.99 *(978-0-06-192082-0(7)*, Amistad) HarperCollins Pubs.

—Brick by Brick. Cooper, Floyd, illus. 2015. (ENG.). 32p. (J). (gr. -1-3). pap. 6.99 *(978-0-06-192084-4(3)*, Amistad) HarperCollins Pubs.

—Brick by Brick. 2015. (J). lib. bdg. 17.20 *(978-0-606-37371-5(3))* Turtleback Bks.

Smith, Maximilian. The History of Juneteenth. 2016. (History of Our Holidays Ser.). (ENG.). 24p. (J). (gr. 1-2). pap. 8.15 *(978-1-4824-3894-9(1))* Stevens, Gareth Publishing LLLP.

Stearns, Dan. Harriet Tubman & the Underground Railroad. 2006. (In the Footsteps of American Heroes Ser.). (Illus.). 64p. (gr. 5-12). pap. 14.05 *(978-0-8368-6433-5(6))*; lib. bdg. 34.00 *(978-0-8368-6428-1(X))* Stevens, Gareth Publishing LLLP. (Gareth Stevens Secondary Library).

Stein, R. Conrad. Harriet Tubman: On My Underground Railroad I Never Ran My Train off the Track. 2010. (Americans—the Spirit of a Nation Ser.). (Illus.). 128p. (J). lib. bdg. 33.27 *(978-0-7660-3481-5(X))* Enslow Pubs., Inc.

Sterling, Dorothy. Forever Free: The Story of the Emancipation Proclamation. Crichlow, Ernest, illus. 2012. 216p. 44.95 *(978-1-258-25034-8(9))*; pap. 29.95 *(978-1-258-25547-3(2))* Literary Licensing, LLC.

Sullivan, Laura L. The Colonial Slave Family. 2015. (Colonial People Ser.). (ENG., Illus.). 48p. (J). (gr. 4-4). 31.36 *(978-1-5026-0486-6(8))* Cavendish Square Publishing.

Sutherland, Jonathan. Slavery & the Abolition Movement. 2017. (Civil War Ser.: Vol. 5). (ENG.). (YA). (gr. 7-12). 24.95 ***(978-1-4222-3883-7(0))*** Mason Crest.

Swain, Gwenyth. Dred & Harriet Scott: A Family's Struggle for Freedom. 2004. (ENG., Illus.). 112p. (J). 22.95 *(978-0-87351-482-8(3))*; pap. 14.95 *(978-0-87351-483-5(1))* Minnesota Historical Society Pr. (Borealis Bk.).

Tapper, Suzanne Cloud. Voices from Slavery's Past: Yearning to Be Heard. 2004. (Slavery in American History Ser.). (Illus.). 128p. (J). lib. bdg. 27.94 *(978-0-7660-2157-0(2))* Enslow Pubs., Inc.

Taylor, Charlotte. Phillis Wheatley: Colonial African-American Poet. 2016. (Exceptional African Americans Ser.). (ENG., Illus.). 24p. (J). (gr. 3-3). 22.60 *(978-0-7660-7326-5(2))* Enslow Pubs., Inc.

Taylor, Charlotte & Feinstein, Stephen. Harriet Tubman: Hero of the Underground Railroad. 2015. (Exceptional African Americans Ser.). (ENG., Illus.). 24p. (J). (gr. 3-4). 22.60 *(978-0-7660-7128-5(6))* Enslow Pubs., Inc.

Taylor, Yuval, ed. Growing up in Slavery: Stories of Young Slaves as Told by Themselves. Judge, Kathleen, illus. 2007. (ENG.). 256p. (J). (gr. 9). pap. 11.95 *(978-1-55652-635-0(0))* Chicago Review Pr., Inc.

Thomas, Paul. Olaudah Equiano: From Slavery to Freedom. Ambrus, Victor, illus. 2007. (Collins Big Cat Ser.). (ENG.). 48p. (J). (gr. 3-4). pap. 8.99 *(978-0-00-723096-9(6))* HarperCollins Pubs. Ltd. GBR. Dist: Independent Pubs. Group.

Thomas, William David. William Lloyd Garrison: A Radical Voice Against Slavery. 2009. (Voices for Freedom Ser.). (ENG.). 64p. (J). (gr. 5-8). pap. *(978-0-7787-4841-0(3))*; lib. bdg. *(978-0-7787-4825-0(1))* Crabtree Publishing Co.

Trumbauer, Lisa. Abraham Lincoln & the Civil War. 2016. (Life in the Time Of Ser.). (ENG.). 32p. pap. 8.29 *(978-1-4846-3822-4(0)*, Heinemann First Library) Heinemann-Raintree.

Turner, Glennette Tilley. Fort Mosé: And the Story of the Man Who Built the First Free Black Settlement in Colonial America. 2010. (ENG., Illus.). 48p. (J). (gr. 3-7). 18.95 *(978-0-8109-4056-7(6)*, Abrams Bks. for Young Readers) Abrams, Inc.

The Underground Railroad: The Journey to Freedom. 2010. (Milestones in American History Ser.). (Illus.). 152p. (gr. 6-12). 35.00 *(978-1-60413-694-4(4)*, Chelsea Hse.) Facts On File, Inc.

Underwood, Deborah. Nat Love. 2008. (History Maker Biographies Ser.). (ENG., Illus.). 48p. (gr. 3-6). lib. bdg. 27.93 *(978-0-8225-7171-1(4)*, Lerner Pubns.) Lerner Publishing Group.

Uschan, Michael V. The Civil Rights Movement. 2010. (American History Ser.). (ENG.). 128p. 34.80 *(978-1-4205-0261-9(1)*, Lucent Bks.) Cengage Gale.

Waldman, Neil. Voyages: Reminiscences of Young Abe Lincoln. 2009. (ENG., Illus.). 32p. (J). (gr. 5-9). 16.95 *(978-1-59078-471-6(5)*, Calkins Creek) Boyds Mills Pr.

Waxman, Laura Hamilton. How Did Slaves Find a Route to Freedom? And Other Questions about the Underground Railroad. 2011. (Six Questions of American History Ser.). (ENG.). 48p. (gr. 4-6). pap. 56.72 *(978-0-7613-7641-5(0))*; pap. 9.95 *(978-0-7613-7129-8(X))*; lib. bdg. 30.60 *(978-0-7613-5229-7(5))* Lerner Publishing Group.

Weatherford, Carole Boston. The Beatitudes: From Slavery to Civil Rights. Ladwig, Tim, illus. 2009. (ENG.). 36p. (J). (gr. 3-7). 17.00 *(978-0-8028-5352-3(8)*, Eerdmans Bks For Young Readers) Eerdmans, William B. Publishing Co.

Wells-Cole, Catherine. Slavery & the Forging of Early America. 2014. (J). *(978-1-59935-410-1(1))* Reynolds, Morgan Inc.

Winter, Jonah. My Name Is James Madison Hemings. Widener, Terry, illus. 2016. (ENG.). 40p. (J). (gr. k-4). 17.99 *(978-0-385-38342-4(8)*, Schwartz & Wade Bks.) Random Hse. Children's Bks.

Woelfle, Gretchen. Mumbet's Declaration of Independence. Delinois, Alix, illus. 2014. (ENG.). 32p. (J). (gr. 1-4). 17.95 (978-0-7613-6589-1(3), Carolrhoda Bks.) Lerner Publishing Group.

Wolny, Philip. The Underground Railroad: A Primary Source History of the Journey to Freedom. 2004. (Primary Sources in American History Ser.). (Illus.). 64p. (J). (gr. 5-8). lib. bdg. 31.95 (978-0-8239-4008-0(X), Rosen Reference) Rosen Publishing Group, Inc., The.

Worth, Richard. Africans in America. 2004. (Immigration to the United States Ser.). (Illus.). 96p. (gr. 4-9). 35.00 (978-0-8160-5691-0(9)) Facts On File, Inc.

—Slave Life on the Plantation: Prisons Beneath the Sun. 2004. (Slavery in American History Ser.). (Illus.). 128p. (J). lib. bdg. 27.94 (978-0-7660-2152-5(1)) Enslow Pubs., Inc.

5,000 Miles to Freedom: Ellen & William Craft's Flight from Slavery. l.t. ed. 2013. 202p. pap. (978-1-4596-6713-6(1)) ReadHowYouWant.com, Ltd.

SLAVERY—UNITED STATES—POETRY

Alexander, Richard. The Transatlantic Slave Trade: The Forced Migration of Africans to America (1607-1830), 01 vols., 1. 2016. (Spotlight on Immigration & Migration Ser.). (ENG.). 24p. (J). pap. 10.00 (978-1-5081-4100-6(2), PowerKids Pr.) Rosen Publishing Group, Inc., The.

Engle, Margarita. The Poet Slave of Cuba: A Biography of Juan Francisco Manzano. Qualls, Sean, illus. 2011. (ENG & SPA.). 208p. (YA). (gr. 7-12). pap. 10.99 (978-0-312-65928-8(8), 9780312659288) Square Fish.

Hinton, KaaVonia. To Preserve the Union: Causes & Effects of the Missouri Compromise, 1 vol. 2013. (Cause & Effect Ser.). (ENG.). 32p. (gr. 3-4). 27.32 (978-1-4765-0238-0(2)); pap. 8.95 (978-1-4765-3404-6(7)) Capstone Press of Coughlan Cos. (Fact Finders).

McLeese, Don. Phillis Wheatley. 2004. (Heroes of the American Revolution Ser.). (Illus.). 32p. (J). (gr. -1 — 1). pap. 5.95 (978-1-59515-320-3(9)) Rourke Educational Media.

Rissman, Rebecca. Slavery in the United States, 1 vol. 2014. (African-American History Ser.). (ENG.). 48p. (gr. 8-12). 32.79 (978-1-62403-148-9(X)) ABDO Publishing Co.

Schraff, Anne E. The Life of Frederick Douglass: Speaking Out Against Slavery. 2014. (Legendary African Americans Ser.). 96p. (J). (gr. 6-12). 27.94 (978-0-7660-6132-3(9)) Enslow Pubs., Inc.

SLAVS—UNITED STATES

Fradin, Dennis Brindell. The Underground Railroad. 2008. (Turning Points in U. S. History Ser.). 48p. (gr. 3-18). lib. bdg. 31.36 (978-0-7614-3014-8(8), Benchmark Bks.) Marshall Cavendish Corp.

SLEEP

see also Dreams

Alda, Arlene. The Book of ZZZs. 2009. (ENG., Illus.). 16p. (J). (gr. k-k). bds. 7.95 (978-0-88776-906-1(3), Tundra Bks.) Tundra Bks. CAN. Dist: Penguin Random Hse. LLC.

Barraclough, Sue. Sleep & Rest. 2012. (Healthy Habits Ser.). (Illus.). 24p. (gr. 1-3). lib. bdg. 24.25 (978-1-59771-309-2(0)) Sea-To-Sea Pubns.

Beck, Isabel L., et al. Trophies Kindergarten: I Nap. 2003. (Trophies Ser.). (gr. k-6). 13.80 (978-0-15-329528-7(7)) Harcourt Schl. Pubs.

Berger, Melvin & Berger, Gilda. Go to Sleep. 2007. (Illus.). 32p. (J). pap. (978-0-439-02450-1(1)) Scholastic, Inc.

Berry, Joy. I Love Bedtime. Regan, Dana, illus. 2010. (Teach Me About Ser.). (ENG.). 20p. (J). (gr. k — 1). pap. 5.99 (978-1-60577-004-8(3)) Berry, Joy Enterprises.

—Teach Me about Bedtime. 2009. (ENG.). 40p. (J). (gr. k — 1). bds. 7.95 (978-1-60577-010-9(8)) Berry, Joy Enterprises.

Bonnett-Rampersaud, Louise. How Do You Sleep?, 0 vols. Kest, Kristin, illus. 2013. (ENG.). 32p. (J). (gr. -1-1). pap. 9.99 (978-1-4778-1669-1(0), 9781477816691, Amazon Children's Publishing) Amazon Publishing.

Boudreau, Helene. I Dare You Not to Yawn. Bloch, Serge, illus. 2013. (ENG.). 32p. (J). (gr. -1-3). 15.99 (978-0-7636-5070-4(6)) Candlewick Pr.

Brignaud, Pierre, illus. Caillou: Good Night! Sleep Well: Nighttime. 2017. (Caillou's Essentials Ser.). (ENG.). 24p. (J). (gr. -1-k). bds. 7.99 (978-2-89718-357-8(8)) Caillouet, Gerry.

Cleland, Jo. Getting Your Zzzzs. 2012. (ENG.). 24p. (gr. k-2). pap. 8.95 (978-1-61810-218-8(4)) Rourke Educational Media.

Colligan, L. H. Sleep Disorders. 2008. (Health Alert Ser.). 64p. (YA). (gr. 4-7). lib. bdg. 32.79 (978-0-7614-2913-5(1)) Marshall Cavendish Corp.

Currie-McGhee, L. K. What Are Sleep Disorders? 2015. (ENG., Illus.). 80p. (J). lib. bdg. (978-1-60152-930-5(9)) ReferencePoint Pr., Inc.

Dodd, Emma. Sweet Dreams, Baby: A Book to Melt Your Heart. 2017. (Sprinkle with Kisses Ser.). (ENG., Illus.). 10p. (J). (gr. -1 — 1). bds. 6.99 (978-0-7641-6885-7(1)) Barron's Educational Series, Inc.

Esherick, Joan. Drug Therapy & Sleep Disorders. 2003. (Psychiatric Disorders: Drugs & Psychology for the Mind & Bod Ser.). (Illus.). 126p. (YA). (gr. 7). pap. 14.95 (978-1-4222-0400-9(6)) Mason Crest.

—Sleep Deprivation & Its Consequences. Bridgemohan, Carolyn & Forman, Sara, eds. 2013. (Young Adult's Guide to the Science of Health Ser.). (Illus.). 128p. (J). (gr. 7-18). pap. 14.95 (978-1-4222-3003-9(1)) Mason Crest.

Esherick, Joan, frwd. Drug Therapy & Sleep Disorders. 2004. (Encyclopedia of Psychiatric Drugs & Their Disorders Ser.). (Illus.). 128p. (YA). lib. bdg. 24.95 (978-1-59084-576-9(5)) Mason Crest.

Feldman, Eve B. Animals Don't Wear Pajamas: A Book about Sleeping. 2004. (Illus.). 32p. (J). pap. 16.95 (978-0-9764957-0-3(8)) Saturn International.

Gaestel, Tiffany & Benchmark Education Co. Staff. The Science of Sleep & Dreams. 2014. (Text Connections Ser.). (J). (gr. 5). (978-1-4900-1381-7(4)) Benchmark Education Co.

Gaston, P. J. How Do You Know When It's Time to Go to Bed? Gaston, Carter J., illus. 2008. (ENG.). 28p. (J). 10.00 (978-0-9675574-2-7(9)) "How Do You Know".

Gelb, John. Power Nap Kit. 2003. (YA). 34.95 (978-0-9742002-0-0(4)) At Peace Media, LLC.

Gleisner, Jenna Lee. My Body Needs Rest. 2015. (Healthy Me Ser.). (Illus.). 24p. (J). 27.10 (978-1-60753-588-1(2)) Amicus Publishing.

Harris, Brooke. Are You Sleeping? Oliver, Mark, illus. 2010. (Rising Readers Ser.). (J). 3.49 (978-1-60719-685-3(9)) Newmark Learning LLC.

La Hora de Dormir, 6 Packs. (Chiquilibros Ser.). (SPA.). (gr. k-1). 23.00 (978-0-7635-8597-6(1)) Rigby Education.

Janisch, Heinz & Bansch, Helga. Good Night Giants. 2011. (Illus.). 32p. (J). (gr. -1-3). 14.95 (978-1-4338-0950-7(8)); pap. 9.95 (978-1-4338-0951-4(6)) American Psychological Assn. (Magination Pr.).

Johnson, Marion. Caillou, What's That Noise. CINAR Corporation Staff, illus. 2004. (Clubhouse Usa Ser.). (ENG.). 24p. (J). pap. 3.95 (978-2-89450-489-5(6)) Ellipsis Pr.

Kocienda, Genevieve. Do Not Disturb: the Importance of Sleep High Beginning Book with Online Access. 2014. (ENG., Illus.). 24p. pap. 9.50 (978-1-107-64682-7(0)) Cambridge Univ. Pr.

Kuskowski, Alex. Cool Sleeping: Healthy & Fun Ways to Sleep Tight, 1 vol. 2012. (Cool Health & Fitness Ser.). (ENG.). 32p. (J). (gr. 3-6). lib. bdg. 27.07 (978-1-61783-429-5(7), Checkerboard Library) ABDO Publishing Co.

Maerov, Jeff. Boca Buddies. Can't We Just Say Goodnight? 2012. 40p. pap. 11.99 (978-0-578-11402-6(X)) Maerov, Jeffrey.

Mahjouri. The Science of Sleep. Mahjouri, illus. 2014. (ENG., Illus.). pap. 9.99 (978-1-941006-04-7(3)) SoGo Creation.

Maile, Ruby. When Do You Sleep? 2014. (Little Books of Answers: Level e Ser.). (Illus.). 16p. (gr. k-2). pap. 7.95 (978-1-927136-40-9(7)) Three Crows Media NZL. Dist: RiverStream Publishing.

Marcus, Mary Brophy. Sleep Disorders. 2009. (Psychological Disorders Ser.). (Illus.). 128p. (YA). (gr. 7-12). 37.50 (978-1-60413-085-0(7)) Facts On File, Inc.

Marsico, Katie. Get a Good Night's Sleep! 2015. (21st Century Junior Library: Your Healthy Body Ser.). (ENG., Illus.). 24p. (J). (gr. 2-5). 27.07 (978-1-63188-988-2(5), 205864) Cherry Lake Publishing.

McAneney, Caitie. Freaky Stories While You Sleep. 2016. (Freaky True Science Ser.). (Illus.). 32p. (J). (gr. 5-4). pap. 10.50 (978-1-4824-4851-1(3)) Stevens, Gareth Publishing LLLP.

Moriarty, Susie. Mmmmmm My Blankie. 2012. 20p. pap. 13.77 (978-1-4269-6573-9(7)) Trafford Publishing.

Nelson, Robin. Getting Rest. 2006. (Pull Ahead Books: Health Ser.). (ENG., Illus.). 32p. (gr. k-3). lib. bdg. 22.60 (978-0-8225-3487-7(8)) Lerner Publishing Group.

Olive, M. Foster. Sleep AIDS. Triggle, David J., ed. 2005. (Drugs: the Straight Facts Ser.). (Illus.). 112p. (C). (gr. 9-12). 30.00 (978-0-7910-8200-3(8), Chelsea Hse.) Facts On File, Inc.

Owen, Ruth. What Happens When I Sleep? 2013. (My Body: Inside & Out! Ser.). 24p. (J). (gr. -1-3). lib. bdg. 23.93 (978-1-909673-30-4(7)) Ruby Tuesday Books Limited GBR. Dist: Bearport Publishing Co., Inc.

Pipe, Jim. You Wouldn't Want to Live Without Sleep! Bergin, Mark, illus. 2016. (You Wouldn't Want to Live Without... Ser.). (ENG.). 32p. (J). lib. bdg. 29.00 (978-0-531-21492-3(3)) Scholastic Library Publishing.

Poole, H. W. Sleep Disorders, Vol. 13. Walters, Anne S., ed. 2015. (Mental Illnesses & Disorders: Awareness & Understanding Ser.). (Illus.). 48p. (J). (gr. 5). 20.95 (978-1-4222-3376-4(6)) Mason Crest.

Rissman, Rebecca & Smith, Sian. Getting Rest, 1 vol. 2012. (Take Care of Yourself! Ser.). (ENG.). 24p. (gr. -1-1). pap. 6.29 (978-1-4329-6720-8(7), Acorn) Heinemann-Raintree.

Royston, Angela. Why Do I Sleep? 2012. (My Body Ser.). (ENG., Illus.). 24p. (gr. k-4). pap. 7.95 (978-1-77092-001-9(3)) Saunders Bk. Co. CAN. Dist: RiverStream Publishing.

Salzmann, Mary Elizabeth. Sleep All Night! Healthy Sleeping Habits, 1 vol. 2014. (Healthy Habits Ser.). (ENG.). 24p. (J). (gr. -1-3). 24.21 (978-1-62403-531-9(0)) ABDO Publishing Co.

Silverstein, Virginia. Handy Health Guide to Better Sleep. 2013. (Handy Health Guides). 48p. (J). (gr. 5-12). pap. 8.95 (978-1-4644-0499-3(2)) Enslow Pubs., Inc.

Silverstein, Virginia & Nunn, Laura Silverstein. Handy Health Guide to Better Sleep. 2013. (Handy Health Guides). 48p. (J). lib. bdg. 25.27 (978-0-7660-4278-0(2)) Enslow Pubs., Inc.

Sjonger, Rebecca. You Need Rest to Be at Your Best! 2015. (ENG., Illus.). 24p. (J). (978-0-7787-1881-9(6)) Crabtree Publishing Co.

Sleeping: Individual Title Six-Packs. (Literatura 2000 Ser.). (gr. 1-2). 28.00 (978-0-7635-0113-6(1)) Rigby Education.

Studio Mouse & Studio Mouse. My First Sleepover. rev. ed. 2007. (Carry Tune Ser.). (ENG., Illus.). 24p. (J). 4.99 (978-1-59069-607-1(7)) Studio Mouse LLC.

Vallejo-Nagera, Alejandra. No Tengo Sueno! Guerrero, Andres, illus. (SPA.). 31p. (J). (gr. k-1). 8.95 (978-1-58986-546-4(4)) Santillana USA Publishing Co., Inc.

Verdick, Elizabeth & Lisovskis, Marjorie. Rest. 2014. (Happy Healthy Baby(r) Ser.). (ENG., Illus.). 22p. (J). bds. 6.99 (978-1-57542-427-9(4)) Free Spirit Publishing, Inc.

Zolotow, Charlotte. Sleepy Book. Date not set. (ENG.). 40p. (J). (gr. -1-3). pap. 5.99 (978-0-06-443737-0(X)) HarperCollins Pubs.

SLEEP—FICTION

Ackerley, Sarah. Patrick the Somnambulist. Ackerley, Sarah, illus. 2008. (ENG., Illus.). 32p. (J). (gr. -1 — 1). 14.95 (978-1-933831-07-7(3)) Blooming Tree Pr.

Albee, Sarah. Time for Bed, Elmo! (Sesame Street) Swanson, Maggie, illus. 2014. (Little Golden Book Ser.). (ENG.). 24p. (J). (-k). 4.99 (978-0-385-37138-4(1), Golden Bks.) Random Hse. Children's Bks.

Ambrosio, Michael. It Takes a Lot of Love. Awes, Jennifer, illus. 2007. 32p. (J). 14.95 (978-0-9716085-4-2(7)) LionX Publishing.

Amen, Daniel. Time for Bed, Sleepyhead: The Falling Asleep Book, 1 vol. Yerrill, Gail, illus. 2016. (ENG.). 32p. (J). 16.99 (978-0-310-75822-8(X)) Zonderkidz.

Arnold, Marsha Diane. Baby Animals Take a Nap. Tildes, Phyllis Limbacher, illus. 2017. (ENG.). 10p. (J). (— 1). bds. 6.99 (978-1-58089-539-2(5)) Charlesbridge Publishing, Inc.

Ashby, Gaylene. STORY TIME A Collection of Three Children's Stories. 2008. 28p. 14.95 (978-1-4357-1929-3(8)) Lulu Pr., Inc.

Baker, Ken. Cow Can't Sleep, 0 vols. Gray, Steve, illus. 2012. (ENG.). 24p. (J). (gr. -1-3). 12.99 (978-0-7614-6198-2(1), 9780761461982, Amazon Children's Publishing) Amazon Publishing.

Banks, Kate. Close Your Eyes. Hallensleben, Georg, illus. 2015. (ENG.). 36p. (J). (gr. -1-1). bds. 7.99 (978-0-374-30101-9(8), 9780374301019, Farrar, Straus & Giroux (BYR)) Farrar, Straus & Giroux.

Barchers, Suzanne I. Dad Wants a Nap, 1 vol. 2011. (Targeted Phonics Ser.). (ENG., Illus.). 16p. (J). (gr. k-2). pap. 5.99 (978-1-4333-2407-9(5)) Teacher Created Materials, Inc.

—Pete Has Fast Feet, 1 vol. 2011. (Targeted Phonics Ser.). (ENG., Illus.). 16p. (J). (gr. k-2). pap. 5.99 (978-1-4333-2915-9(8)) Teacher Created Materials, Inc.

Bean, Jonathan. At Night. Bean, Jonathan, illus. 2007. (ENG., Illus.). 32p. (J). (gr. -1-3). 17.99 (978-0-374-30446-1(7), 9780374304461, Farrar, Straus & Giroux (BYR)) Farrar, Straus & Giroux.

Beaumont, Karen. No Sleep for the Sheep! Urbanovic, Jackie, illus. 2011. (ENG.). 32p. (J). (gr. -1-3). 17.99 (978-0-15-204969-0(X)) Houghton Mifflin Harcourt Publishing Co.

Before I Go to Sleep. 2008. 32p. (978-1-4075-1843-5(7)) Parragon, Inc.

Benchmark Education Co., LLC. Mr. Jitters & the Sleep Machine Big Book. 2014. (Shared Reading Foundations Ser.). (J). (gr. -1). (978-1-4509-9435-4(0)) Benchmark Education Co.

—One Frosty Night at the Farm Big Book. 2014. (Shared Reading Foundations Ser.). (J). (gr. -1). (978-1-4509-9443-9(1)) Benchmark Education Co.

Berger, Samantha. Snoozefest. Litten, Kristyna, illus. 2015. (ENG.). 34p. (J). (gr. -1-k). 16.99 (978-0-8037-4046-4(8), Dial Bks) Penguin Young Readers Group.

Bergren, Lisa Tawn. God Gave Us Sleep. Bryant, Laura J., illus. 2015. (ENG.). 40p. (J). (gr. -1-2). 10.99 (978-1-60142-663-5(1), WaterBrook Pr.) Crown Publishing Group.

Berry, Ron & Sharp, Chris. It's Bedtime. Sharp, Chris & Currant, Gary, illus. 2003. (It's Time to Ser.). (ENG.). 14p. (J). (gr. -1-k). bds. 6.95 (978-1-891100-61-1(0)) Smart Kidz Media, Inc.

Blackmore, Jeanne C. How Does Sleep Come? Sayles, Elizabeth, illus. 2012. (ENG.). 32p. (J). (-3). 16.99 (978-1-4022-7105-2(0), Sourcebooks Jabberwocky) Sourcebooks, Inc.

Blair, Eric. Sleeping Beauty: A Retelling of the Grimm's Fairy Tale, 1 vol. Ouren, Todd, illus. 2011. (My First Classic Story Ser.). (ENG.). 32p. (gr. k-3). pap. 7.10 (978-1-4048-7360-5(0), My First Classic Story) Picture Window Bks.

Blecha, Aaron. Goodnight, Grizzle Grump! Blecha, Aaron, illus. 2015. (ENG., Illus.). 32p. (J). (gr. -1-3). 17.99 (978-0-06-229746-4(5)) HarperCollins Pubs.

Blomgren, Jennifer. Where Do I Sleep? A Pacific Northwest Lullaby. Gabriel, Andrea, illus. (ENG.). 20p. (J). (— 1). 2015. bds. 9.99 (978-1-63217-019-4(1)) 2008. pap. 10.99 (978-1-57061-593-1(4)) Sasquatch Bks. (Little Bigfoot).

Bonnell, Kris. Where Can Louis Sleep? 2007. (J). pap. 5.95 (978-1-933727-57-8(8)) Reading Reading Bks., LLC.

Bonnett-Rampersaud, Louise. How Do You Sleep?, 1 vol. Kest, Kristin, illus. 2008. (ENG.). 34p. (J). (gr. -1). 6.99 (978-0-7614-5449-6(7)) Marshall Cavendish Corp.

Boynton, Sandra. The Going to Bed Book. Boynton, Sandra, illus. (ENG., Illus.). (J). 2006. 14p. bds. 12.95 (978-1-4169-2794-5(8)) 30th anniv. ed. 2012. 18p. (gr. -1-3). bds. 7.99 (978-1-4424-5409-5(1)) Little Simon. (Little Simon).

Boza, Eduardo Robles. Mi Amiga No Qiere Dormir.Tr. of My Friend Doesn't Want to Sleep. (SPA.). (J). 4.95 (978-970-05-0130-7(2)) Grijalbo, Editorial MEX. Dist: AIMS International Bks., Inc.

Brannock, Martha Lee. Teddy Bear Too-Too. 2007. 28p. per. 18.65 (978-1-4257-4143-3(6)) Xlibris Corp.

Braun, Sebastien. Back to Bed, Ed! Braun, Sebastien, illus. 2010. (Illus.). 32p. (J). (gr. -1-1). 15.95 (978-1-56145-518-8(0)) Peachtree Pubs.

Bray, Libba. Lair of Dreams. 2015. (Diviners Ser.: 2). (ENG.). 624p. (YA). (gr. 10-17). 19.00 (978-0-316-12604-5(7)); (gr. 7-17). E-Book (978-0-316-36488-1(6)) Little, Brown Bks. for Young Readers.

Brewer, Elly. Jerry & the Jannans. 2006. (ENG.). 320p. (J). (gr. 4-7). pap. 11.99 (978-0-7475-8213-7(0)) Bloomsbury Publishing Plc GBR. Dist: Independent Pubs. Group.

Brunell, Heather. Bedtime Monster. Adamson, Bonnie, illus. 2010. (ENG.). 32p. (J). (gr. -1-12). lib. bdg. 16.95 (978-1-934960-03-5(9), Raven Tree Pr.,Csi) Continental Sales, Inc.

—Bedtime Monster/A Dormir, Monstruito! Del Risco, Eida & de la Vega, Eida, trs. 2010. (ENG & SPA., Illus.). 32p. (J). (gr. -1-3). pap. 7.95 (978-1-932748-81-9(4), Raven Tree Pr.,Csi) Continental Sales, Inc.

—Bedtime Monster/A Dormir, Monstruito! de la Vega, Eida, tr. Adamson, Bonnie, illus. 2010. (ENG & SPA.). 32p. (J). (gr. -1-3). lib. bdg. 16.95 (978-1-932748-80-2(6), Raven Tree Pr.,Csi) Continental Sales, Inc.

Bunting, Eve. No Nap. Meddaugh, Susan, illus. 2014. (ENG.). 32p. (J). (— 1). audio compact disk 10.99 (978-0-544-33917-0(7), HMH Books For Young Readers) Houghton Mifflin Harcourt Publishing Co.

Burlingham, Abi. All Grown Up. Everitt-Stewart, Andy, illus. 2009. (Stories to Grow with Ser.). 24p. (J). (gr. -1-2). 22.60 (978-1-60754-469-2(5)); pap. 8.15 (978-1-60754-470-8(9)) Windmill Bks.

Cabral, Jeane. Good Night Little Moo. Howarth, Daniel, illus. 2007. (Night Light Book Ser.). 10p. (gr. -1-k). (978-1-84666-128-0(5), Tide Mill Pr.) Top That! Publishing PLC.

Camacho, Celi C. Bedtime for Meaghan. 2008. 33p. pap. 24.95 (978-1-60563-527-9(8)) America Star Bks.

Chacon, Dulce. LA VOZ DORMIDA. 2005. (SPA., Illus.). 384p. pap. 22.95 (978-84-204-6438-1(4), AF13909, Alfaguara) Santillana USA Publishing Co., Inc.

Chadha, Radhika & Kuriyan, Priya. I'm So Sleepy. 2004. (Illus.). 24p. (J). (978-81-8146-033-2(2)) Tulika Pubs.

Chapman, Jason. Who's That Snoring? A Pull-the-Tab Bedtime Book. Chapman, Jason, illus. 2010. (ENG., Illus.). 12p. (J). (gr. -1-1). bds. 9.99 (978-1-4169-8937-0(4), Little Simon) Little Simon.

Cheever, Karen J. The Tuck-In: (a Child's Event) 2012. 24p. (-18). pap. 17.99 (978-1-4772-7546-7(0)) AuthorHouse.

Choldenko, Gennifer. Putting the Monkeys to Bed. Davis, Jack E., illus. 2015. (ENG.). 32p. (J). (gr. -1-k). 16.99 (978-0-399-24623-4(1), G.P. Putnam's Sons Books for Young Readers) Penguin Young Readers Group.

Chriscoe, Sharon. Race Car Dreams. Mottram, Dave, illus. 2016. (ENG.). 32p. (J). (gr. -1 — 1). 16.95 (978-0-7624-5964-3(6), Running Pr. Kids) Running Pr. Bk. Pubs.

Christine Battuz, Christine, illus. Goodnight, Sleepy Animals: A Nightlight Book. 2016. (Nightlight Ser.). (ENG.). 14p. (J). (gr. -1-k). 12.99 (978-2-89718-338-7(1)) CrackBoom! Bks. CAN. Dist: Publishers Group West (PGW).

Claflin, Willy. The Little Moose Who Couldn't Go to Sleep. Stimson, James, illus. 2014. (ENG.). 36p. audio compact disk 18.95 (978-1-939160-67-6(7)) August Hse. Pubs., Inc.

Cook, Sally. Good Night Pillow Fight. Date not set. (Illus.). (J). pap. 5.99 (978-0-06-205932-1(7)) HarperCollins Pubs.

Cornell, Kevin. Go to Sleep, Monster! Cornell, Kevin, illus. 2016. (Illus.). 32p. (J). (gr. -1-3). 17.99 (978-0-06-234915-6(5)) HarperCollins Pubs.

Cosgrove, Stephen. Good Night, Wheedle. James, Robin, illus. 2016. (ENG.). 20p. (J). (— 1). bds. 9.99 (978-1-63217-075-0(2), Little Bigfoot) Sasquatch Bks.

—Wheedle on the Needle. James, Robin, illus. 2009. (ENG.). 32p. (J). (gr. -1-2). 17.99 (978-1-57061-628-0(0), Little Bigfoot) Sasquatch Bks.

Cowlard, Irene. Moriarty's Dream. 2007. (Illus.). 52p. per. (978-1-84748-062-0(4)) Athena Pr.

Cox, Phil Roxbee. Sam Sheep Can't Sleep. Tyler, Jenny, ed. Cartwright, Stephen, illus. rev. ed. 2006. (Usborne Phonics Bks.). 16p. (J). (gr. -1-k). 6.99 (978-0-7945-1508-9(8), Usborne) EDC Publishing.

Cronin, Doreen. Click, Clack, Peep! Lewin, Betsy, illus. 2015. (Click, Clack Book Ser.). (ENG.). 40p. (J). (gr. -1-3). 17.99 (978-1-4814-2411-0(4)) Simon & Schuster Children's Publishing.

Cushing, Mims. The Sleepover Surprise. Phillips, Alan, illus. 2010. 24p. pap. 12.95 (978-1-936343-01-0(0)) Peppertree Pr., The.

Dahl, Michael. Nap Time for Kitty, 1 vol. Vidal, Oriol, illus. 2011. (Hello Genius Ser.). (ENG.). 20p. (gr. 1-2). bds. 7.99 (978-1-4048-5216-7(6)) Picture Window Bks.

Daniels, Kristine. Floyd & the Mysterious Night Time Noise. 2011. (Illus.). 34p. pap. 18.00 (978-1-4575-0141-8(4)) Dog Ear Publishing, LLC.

Daniels, Linda. A Friend Called Glen. 2011. 28p. pap. 16.09 (978-1-4269-4848-0(4)) Trafford Publishing.

de Monfreid, Dorothée. Shhh! I'm Sleeping. de Monfreid, Dorothée, illus. 2016. (ENG., Illus.). 24p. (gr. -1-1). 12.99 (978-1-927271-95-7(9)) Gecko Pr. NZL. Dist: Lerner Publishing Group.

de Moüy, Iris. Naptime, 1 vol. Tanaka, Shelley, tr. from FRE. 2014. (ENG., Illus.). 28p. (J). (-k). 16.95 (978-1-55498-487-9(4)) Groundwood Bks. CAN. Dist: Publishers Group West (PGW).

Dealey, Erin. Little Bo Peep Can't Get to Sleep. Wakiyama, Hanako, illus. 2010. (ENG.). 40p. (J). (gr. -1-2). 13.99 (978-1-4424-0935-4(5), Atheneum Bks. for Young Readers) Simon & Schuster Children's Publishing.

Dennis, Jen. Snoozy Sam. 2013. 42p. pap. (978-1-922204-78-3(1)) Vivid Publishing.

Derubertis, Barbara. Zachary Zebra's Zippity Zooming. Alley, R. W., illus. 2011. (Animal Antics A to Z Set III Ser.). pap. 45.32 (978-0-7613-8435-9(9)) Kane Press, Inc.

deRubertis, Barbara. Zachary Zebra's Zippity Zooming. Alley, R. W., illus. 2011. (Animal Antics A to Z Ser.). 32p. (J). pap. 7.95 (978-1-57565-351-8(6)); lib. bdg. 22.60 (978-1-57565-359-4(1)) Kane Press, Inc.

deRubertis, Barbara & DeRubertis, Barbara. Zachary Zebra's Zippity Zooming. Alley, R. W., illus. 2012. (Animal Antics A to Z Ser.). 32p. (J). (gr. 2 — 1). cd-rom 7.95 (978-1-57565-419-5(9)) Kane Press, Inc.

Disney Baby Staff & Disney Book Group Staff. Cozy Baby. Disney Storybook Artists Staff, illus. 2010. (ENG.). 6p. (J). (gr. -1 — 1). 7.99 (978-1-4231-2827-4(3)) Disney Pr.

Donaldson, Julia. Wake up Do, Lydia Lou!, 2. George, Karen, illus. 2nd ed. 2015. (ENG.). 24p. (J). (gr. -1-k). pap. 10.99 (978-1-4472-0957-7(5)) Pan Macmillan GBR. Dist: Independent Pubs. Group.

Elwick, Elissa. The Princess & the Sleep Stealer. Elwick, Elissa, illus. 2012. (ENG., Illus.). 32p. (J). (gr. -1-k). pap. 9.99 (978-0-230-75068-5(0)) Macmillan Pubs., Ltd. GBR. Dist: Independent Pubs. Group.

Eulate, Ana. Little Cloud Lamb. 2011. (Light (Cuento de Luz) Ser.). (ENG., Illus.). 28p. (J). (gr. 1-4). (978-84-938240-2-0(X)) D P & G Military Pubs.

Fahy, Thomas. Sleepless. 2010. (ENG.). 224p. (YA). (gr. 7). pap. 8.99 (978-1-4169-5902-1(5), Simon & Schuster Bks. For Young Readers) Simon & Schuster Bks. For Young Readers.

Fahy, Thomas Richard & Fahy, Thomas. Sleepless. 2009. (ENG.). 224p. (YA). (gr. 7-18). 15.99 (978-1-4169-5901-4(7), Simon & Schuster Bks. For Young Readers) Simon & Schuster Bks. For Young Readers.

Fehrenbach, Heather. Go to Sleep Dinosaurs. 2011. 36p. pap. 15.99 (978-1-4567-6302-2(4)) AuthorHouse.

Finney, Shad. Princess Nap. 2008. 28p. pap. 15.99 (978-1-4363-2119-8(0)) Xlibris Corp.

Flam, Chanie. Good Night. (Goldie Gold Board Book Ser.: Vol. 6). (Illus.). (J). (gr. -1-1). bds. 4.95 (978-1-58330-030-5(9)) Feldheim Pubs.

Fletcher, Ralph J. The Sandman. Cowdrey, Richard, illus. rev. ed. 2008. (ENG.). 32p. (J). (gr. -1-1). 17.99 (978-0-8050-7726-1(X), 9780805077261, Holt, Henry & Co. Bks. For Young Readers) Holt, Henry & Co.

Fleuriel, Allison. Are You Done Sleeping? 2006. (J). pap. 16.00 (978-0-8059-7115-6(7)) Dorrance Publishing Co., Inc.

Forssén Ehrlin, Carl-Johan. The Little Elephant Who Wants to Fall Asleep: A New Way of Getting Children to Sleep. Hanson, Sydney, illus. 2016. (ENG.). 40p. (J). (gr. -1-2). 16.99 (978-0-399-55423-0(8), Crown Books For Young Readers) Random Hse. Children's Bks.

Fourie, Amanda. Daddy Bird's Lousy Night. 2013. 20p. pap. 15.29 (978-1-4669-9145-3(3)) Trafford Publishing.
Fox, Mem & Horacek, Judy. Where Is the Green Sheep? 2004. (ENG., Illus.). 32p. (J). (gr. -1-3). 16.99 (978-0-15-204907-2(X)) Houghton Mifflin Harcourt Publishing Co.
Fraley, Patty. Fear at Night: To Matthew. 2011. 24p. (gr. -1). pap. 12.79 (978-1-4567-5555-3(2)) AuthorHouse.
Frampton, David. The Whole Night Through. Frampton, David, illus. Date not set. (Illus.). 32p. (J). (gr. -1-1). pap. 5.99 (978-0-06-443652-6(7)) HarperCollins Pubs.
—The Whole Night Through: A Lullaby. Frampton, David, illus. 2004. (Illus.). 30p. (J). (gr. k-4). reprint ed. (978-0-7567-7723-4(2)) DIANE Publishing Co.
Ganges, Montse. Cooper, King of Cushion Island. Urberuaga, Emilio, illus. 2009. (Cooper Ser.). 24p. (J). (gr. -1-3). pap. 8.15 (978-1-60754-243-8(9)) Windmill Bks.
—King of Cushion Island. Urberuaga, Emilio, illus. 2009. (Cooper Ser.). 24p. (J). (gr. -1-3). lib. bdg. 22.60 (978-1-60754-242-1(0)) Windmill Bks.
Gates, Mysti. Noises in the Night. 2009. 52p. pap. 22.99 (978-1-4389-4359-6(8)) AuthorHouse.
Geis, Patricia. Let's Go to Sleep! Folch, Sergio, illus. 2009. (Good Habits with Coco & Tula Ser.). 16p. (J). (gr. -1-k). bds. 11.40 (978-1-60754-408-1(3)) Windmill Bks.
Gershator, Phillis. Time for a Nap. Walker, David, illus. 2017. (Snuggle Time Stories Ser.). (ENG.). 32p. (J). (gr. -1-k). 9.95 (978-1-4549-1981-0(7)) Sterling Publishing Co., Inc.
Giles, Mike, illus. Sleep & Dream of Happy Things. 2009. (Yo Gabba Gabba! Ser.). (ENG.). 26p. (J). (gr. -1 — 1). bds. 5.99 (978-1-4169-7823-7(2), Simon Spotlight) Simon Spotlight.
Glass, Timothy. Sleepytown Beagles Penny's 4th of July. Mikle, Toby, illus. 2006. 24p. (J). per. 15.95 (978-1-888461-10-7(1)); 16.95 (978-1-888461-11-4(X)) Islewest Publishing.
Golden Books Staff. Sleepy Bunny. 2003. (Cloth Book Ser.). (ENG., Illus.). 8p. (J). (gr. -1 — 1). 14.99 (978-0-375-82531-6(2), Golden Bks.) Random Hse. Children's Bks.
Golden, Christopher. When Rose Wakes. 2010. (ENG.). 320p. pap. 19.99 (978-1-4391-4823-5(6), MTV Bks.) MTV Books.
Graux, Amélie, et al. I Love to Sleep. Graux, Amélie, illus. deluxe ed. 2012. (ENG, SPA & FRE., Illus.). 12p. (J). (gr. k — 1). bds. 9.99 (978-0-547-84843-3(9)) Houghton Mifflin Harcourt Publishing Co.
Graves, Sue. Night, Night. 2009. (ENG., Illus.). 24p. (J). pap. (978-0-7787-3898-5(1)); lib. bdg. (978-0-7787-3867-1(1)) Crabtree Publishing Co.
Greenway, Bethany. Waikiki Lullaby. America, illus. 2009. (ENG.). 20p. (J). (gr. -1-1). bds. 7.95 (978-1-933067-30-8(6)) Beachhouse Publishing, LLC.
Gribel, Christiane & Orlando. No Voy a Dormir/I Am Not Going to Sleep. Gribel, Christiane & Orlando, illus. 2009. (ENG & SPA., Illus.). 40p. (J). (gr. -1-1). pap. 7.99 (978-1-933032-51-1(0)) Lectorum Pubns., Inc.
Grover, Neha Lamba. Shaurya's Adventures. 2010. 43p. pap. 17.40 (978-0-557-12636-1(3)) Lulu Pr., Inc.
Guiffre, William. The Wrong Side of the Bed. Baron, Cheri Ann, illus. 2008. 32p. (J). (gr. -1-3). pap. 9.95 (978-1-931650-34-2(9)) Bks. for Children Publishing.
Gutierrez, Rochelle. Dear Monster. 2010. 16p. pap. 8.95 (978-1-4490-7281-0(X)) AuthorHouse.
Guy, Ginger Foglesong & Guy, Ginger F. Siesta. Moreno, Rene King, illus. 2005. (ENG & SPA.). 32p. (J). (gr. -1-k). 17.99 (978-0-06-056061-4(4), Greenwillow Bks.) HarperCollins Pubs.
—Siesta Board Book. Moreno, Rene King, illus. 2009. (SPA & ENG.). 34p. (J). (gr. -1 — 1). bds. 7.99 (978-0-06-168884-3(3), Greenwillow Bks.) HarperCollins Pubs.
Halpern, Jake & Kujawinski, Peter. Dormia. 2010. (ENG.). 528p. (J). (gr. 5-7). pap. 7.99 (978-0-547-32887-4(7)) Houghton Mifflin Harcourt Publishing Co.
Hamilton, Covette J. Begethie Wenferd Meets King Tut. 2012. 32p. pap. (978-1-77097-189-9(0)) FriesenPress.
Hamm, Diane Johnston. Rock-a-Bye Farm. Natchev, Alexi, illus. 2008. (ENG.). 32p. (J). (gr. -1 — 1). bds. 7.99 (978-1-4169-3621-3(1), Little Simon) Little Simon.
Hanson, Warren. Sea of Sleep. LaMarche, Jim, illus. 2010. (ENG.). 32p. (J). (gr. -1-3). 16.99 (978-0-439-69735-4(2), Scholastic Pr.) Scholastic, Inc.
Harder, Christopher. It's Tough to Nap on a Turtle. Harder, Rolf, illus. 2008. (ENG.). 11p. (J). (gr. -1). bds. 5.95 (978-0-9726614-9-2(2)) Shenanigan Bks.
Harshman, Marc. All the Way to Morning. Dávalos, Felipe, illus. 2006. (J). per. 7.95 (978-1-891852-49-7(3)) Quarrier Pr.
Heine, Helme. Wunderbare Reise Durch Die Na. 12.95 (978-3-7876-9528-7(1)) Middelhauve Verlags GmbH DEU. Dist: Distribooks, Inc.
Henry, Jed. Good Night, Mouse! Henry, Jed, illus. 2013. (ENG., Illus.). 32p. (J). (gr. -1-3). 16.99 (978-0-547-98156-7(2)) Houghton Mifflin Harcourt Publishing Co.
Hest, Amy. Charley's First Night. Oxenbury, Helen, illus. 2012. (ENG.). 32p. (J). (gr. -1-2). 15.99 (978-0-7636-4055-2(7)) Candlewick Pr.
Higgins, Gladys. Goodnight, Charlie. 2005. 18.00 (978-0-8059-8116-2(0)) Dorrance Publishing Co., Inc.
Hill, Susanna Leonard. Can't Sleep Without Sheep. Wohnoutka, Mike, illus. 2010. (ENG.). 40p. (J). (gr. -1-1). 16.99 (978-0-8027-2066-5(8), 9780802720665, Bloomsbury USA Childrens) Bloomsbury Publishing USA.
Hillard, Shirley. Who's Not Asleep? 2004. (Illus.). 24p. (J). 15.95 (978-1-933014-31-9(8)) Mamoo Hse.
Hillenbrand, Will. Spring Is Here. Hillenbrand, Will, illus. 2012. (ENG., Illus.). 32p. (J). pap. 7.99 (978-0-8234-2431-3(6)) Holiday Hse., Inc.
Hinman, Bobbie. The Knot Fairy. Bridgeman, Kristi, illus. 2010. (ENG.). 32p. (J). (gr. -1-1). 16.95 (978-0-9786791-0-1(5)) Best Fairy Bks.
Hiris, Monica. Sleepy Polar Bear. Harston, Jerry, illus. l.t. ed. 2006. (ENG.). 24p. (gr. k-2). pap. 8.95 (978-1-57874-072-7(X), Kaeden Bks.) Kaeden Corp.
Holub, Joan. Bed, Bats, & Beyond. Gallagher-Cole, Mernie, illus. 2010. (Darby Creek Exceptional Titles Ser.). (ENG.). 64p. (J). (gr. 1-3). pap. 6.95 (978-0-7613-6451-1(X)) Lerner Publishing Group.
Howatt, Sandra J. Sleepyheads. Wan, Joyce, illus. 2014. (ENG.). 32p. (J). (gr. -1-3). 17.99 (978-1-4424-2266-7(1), Beach Lane Bks.) Beach Lane Bks.
Hulme, John & Wexler, Michael. The Glitch in Sleep. 2007. (Seems Ser.). (ENG., Illus.). 288p. (YA). (gr. 5-18). 16.95 (978-1-59990-129-9(3), 9781599901299, Bloomsbury USA Childrens) Bloomsbury Publishing USA.
Ira Sleeps Over. 2005. (J). (978-1-59564-973-7(5)) Steps To Literacy, LLC.
Iriyama, Satoshi. Good Night, Chirp. 2015. (Chirp the Chick Ser.). (ENG., Illus.). 36p. (J). (— 1). 8.99 (978-0-544-35994-9(1), HMH Books For Young Readers) Houghton Mifflin Harcourt Publishing Co.
Irving, Washington & Busch, Jeffrey. Rip Van Winkle. (Classics Illustrated Ser.). (Illus.). 52p. (YA). pap. 4.95 (978-1-57209-009-5(X)) Classics International Entertainment, Inc.
Jam, Teddy. Night Cars, 1 vol. Beddows, Eric, illus. 2006. (ENG.). 32p. (J). (gr. k — 1). bds. 11.95 (978-0-88899-748-7(5)) Groundwood Bks. CAN. Dist: Publishers Group West (PGW).
James, Lincoln. Sal Sleeps In. 2006. (Neighborhood Readers Ser.). (ENG.). 8p. (gr. -1-3). pap. 5.15 (978-1-4042-5780-1(2), Rosen Classroom) Rosen Publishing Group, Inc., The.
Jarvis. Lazy Dave. Jarvis, illus. 2015. (ENG., Illus.). 32p. (J). (gr. -1-3). 17.99 (978-0-06-235598-0(8)) HarperCollins Pubs.
Jefferson, Coretta Carte. Cranky Christopher. 2013. 20p. pap. 24.95 (978-1-4626-9671-0(6)) America Star Bks.
Jennings, Patrick. Hissy Fitz. Allen, Michael, illus. 2015. (ENG.). 128p. (J). (gr. 2-4). 14.99 (978-1-5124-0137-0(4), Carolrhoda Bks.) Lerner Publishing Group.
—Hissy Fitz. Austin, Michael Allen, illus. 2015. (ENG.). 128p. (gr. 2-4). 14.99 (978-1-60684-596-7(9), Carolrhoda Bks.) Lerner Publishing Group.
Jepsen, D. R. Fred's Exciting Night. 2008. 20p. pap. 24.95 (978-1-60813-547-9(0)) America Star Bks.
Johnson, Linda & Hodges, Quae. 21st Century Parables: A Child's Book. 2006. 48p. pap. 14.95 (978-1-60145-071-5(0)) Booklocker.com, Inc.
Johnstone, G. L. Sleep Tight Nancy... 2012. (Illus.). 12p. pap. 18.30 (978-1-4772-1517-3(4)) AuthorHouse.
Kalman, Maira. Hey Willy, See the Pyramids. 2017. (ENG., Illus.). 48p. (J). (gr. k-3). 18.95 **(978-1-68137-168-9(5)**, NYR Children's Collection) New York Review of Bks., Inc., The.
Kapoor, Natalya. My Favorite Time of Day. 2013. 12p. pap. 12.99 (978-1-4772-8344-8(7)) AuthorHouse.
Kay, Devora. The Sleep Sheep Story. 2012. (ENG.). pap. (978-1-4675-4640-9(2)) Independent Pub.
Kelly, Mij. One More Sheep. Ayto, Russell, illus. 2006. (ENG.). 32p. (J). (gr. k-3). 16.95 (978-1-56145-378-8(1)) Peachtree Pubs.
Keselman, Gabriela. Marc Just Couldn't Sleep. Villamuza, Noemi, illus. 2007. (ENG.). 32p. (J). (gr. -1-k). pap. 5.99 (978-1-929132-91-1(3)) Kane Miller.
Kitamura, Satoshi. When Sheep Can't Sleep (Cuando los Borregos no Pueden Dormir) (SPA.). (J). (gr. 1-6). 19.95 (978-84-372-6605-3(X)) Santillana USA Publishing Co., Inc.
Kite, Justin. Even Tigers Need to Sleep. 2012. 24p. pap. 28.03 (978-1-4691-8880-5(5)) Xlibris Corp.
Kleinberg, Naomi. Naptime/Cuddlies (Sesame Street) Moroney, Christopher, illus. 2017. (ENG.). 24p. (J). (— 1). bds. 8.99 **(978-1-5247-1636-3(7)**, Random Hse. Bks. for Young Readers) Random Hse. Children's Bks.
Koniver, Laura. Together We Sleep. 2012. 54p. pap. 16.99 (978-1-937848-01-9(9)) Do Life Right, Inc.
Kopczynski, Megan. Anastasia Rose Sleeps in Her Own Room, 1 vol. Stasiuk, Max, illus. 2010. 26p. pap. 24.95 (978-1-4489-4923-6(8)) PublishAmerica, Inc.
Krauss, Ruth. Goodnight Goodnight Sleepyhead. Dyer, Jane, illus. 32p. (J). (gr. -1-3). 2007. (ENG.). bds. 7.99 (978-0-694-01501-6(6), HarperFestival) 2004. lib. bdg. 16.89 (978-0-06-028895-2(7)) HarperCollins Pubs.
Krosoczka, Jarrett J. Naptastrophe! 2017. (ENG.). 40p. (J). (gr. -1-2). 17.99 **(978-0-385-75483-5(3))**; lib. bdg. 20.99 **(978-0-385-75484-2(1))** Random Hse. Children's Bks. (Knopf Bks. for Young Readers).
Kuskin, Karla. The Lullaway of Rockabye. Date not set. 32p. (J). (gr. -1-18). 14.89 (978-0-06-027716-1(5)) HarperCollins Pubs.
Kwaymullina, Ezekiel;Morgan. We All Sleep. Morgan, Sally, illus. 2017. (ENG.). 24p. (J). (gr. -1-1). 12.99 **(978-1-925163-18-6(0))** Fremantle Pr. AUS. Dist: Independent Pubs. Group.
Lake Press Ltd. Fun at Home. 2016. (Little Grabbers Ser.). (ENG., Illus.). 6p. (J). (gr. -1 — 1). bds. 5.99 (978-0-7641-6835-2(5)) Barron's Educational Series, Inc.
Langford, Jane. Hero. Vince, Dawn, illus. 2005. (ENG.). 24p. (J). lib. bdg. 23.65 (978-1-59646-720-0(7)) Dingles & Co.
Lester, Helen & Munsinger, Lynn. Boris & the Worrisome Wakies. Lester, Helen & Munsinger, Lynn, illus. 2017. (ENG., Illus.). 32p. (J). (gr. -1-3). 16.99 (978-0-544-64094-8(2), HMH Books For Young Readers) Houghton Mifflin Harcourt Publishing Co.
Lewis, Anne Margaret. Sleeping Bear: The Legend. Grant, Sarah, illus. 2007. (ENG.). 40p. (J). (gr. -1-2). 16.95 (978-1-934133-15-6(9), Mackinac Island Press, Inc.) Charlesbridge Publishing, Inc.
Llewellyn, Claire. Good Night, Baby!, 1 vol. Lovsin, Polona, illus. 2013. (Start Reading Ser.). (ENG.). 24p. (gr. k-1). pap. 7.95 (978-1-4765-3184-7(6)); pap. 41.94 (978-1-4765-3216-5(8)) Capstone Press of Coughlan Cos.
Lodding, Linda Ravin. Wakey, Wakey, Elephant! Robertson, Michael, illus. 2017. (ENG.). 32p. (J). (gr. -1). 16.95 **(978-1-4549-1999-5(X))** Sterling Publishing Co., Inc.
Logue, Mary. Sleep Like a Tiger. Zagarenski, Pamela, illus. 2012. (ENG.). 40p. (J). (gr. -1-3). 17.99 (978-0-547-64102-7(8)) Houghton Mifflin Harcourt Publishing Co.
Long, Ethan. One Drowsy Dragon. 2010. (Illus.). (J). (978-0-545-23412-2(3), Orchard Bks.) Scholastic, Inc.
—Pig Has a Plan. Long, Ethan, illus. 2012. (I Like to Read(r) Ser.). (ENG., Illus.). 24p. (J). (gr. -1-3). 14.95 (978-0-8234-2428-3(6)) Holiday Hse., Inc.
Lujan Ed.D., Nan. The Snoozles. Montgomery, Samantha, illus. 2012. 20p. pap. 24.95 (978-1-4626-8831-9(4)) America Star Bks.
Lum, Misha Anne. Sleepy Time, Baby Mine, 1 vol. 2010. 18p. 24.95 (978-1-60749-202-3(4)) PublishAmerica, Inc.
Luning, Barbara. The Quilted Zoo. 2008. 28p. pap. 15.99 (978-1-4363-1778-8(9)) Xlibris Corp.
Lyon, Tammie Speer, illus. Now I Lay Me down to Sleep. 2006. 8p. (J). bds. 10.95 (978-1-57791-211-8(X)) Brighter Minds Children's Publishing.
Mackall, Deborah. What Happens When I'm Asleep? Mackall, Debbie, illus. 2008. (ENG.). 32p. (J). (gr. -1-k). 15.95 (978-0-9762273-1-1(2)) Dimensions in Media, Inc.
Madel, Dan. Cracker the Cat, Almost Caught. 2008. 24p. pap. 24.95 (978-1-4241-9252-6(8)) America Star Bks.
Magic Moon Dreams. 2003. (J). 11.95 (978-0-89610-767-0(1)) Island Heritage Publishing.
Mahr, Frank J. I Can Sleep Alone. Milstrey, Dawn Bourdeau, illus. 2013. 34p. pap. 6.99 (978-1-4575-1895-9(3)) Dog Ear Publishing, LLC.
Marchini, Tracy. Chicken Wants a Nap. Felix, Monique, illus. 2017. (ENG.). 24p. (J). (gr. 1-3). 17.99 **(978-1-56846-308-7(1)**, Creative Editions) Creative Co., The.
Markes, Julie. Shhhhh! Everybody's Sleeping. Parkins, David, illus. 32p. (J). (gr. -1-1). 2005. lib. bdg. 16.89 (978-0-06-053791-3(4)) 2004. (ENG.). 16.99 (978-0-06-053790-6(6)) HarperCollins Pubs.
Marks, Allison & Marks, Wayne. Og's Ark. Peluso, Martina, illus. 2016. (ENG.). 32p. (J). (gr. -1-3). 17.99 (978-1-4677-6149-9(4), Kar-Ben Publishing) Lerner Publishing Group.
Marsh, Richard Phillip. Mattress People Go to Bear Park. 2009. 44p. pap. 10.95 (978-1-935125-39-6(7)) Robertson Publishing.
Marx, Patricia. Now I Will Never Go to Sleep. Date not set. (Illus.). (J). 15.89 (978-0-06-027482-5(4)); 14.99 (978-0-06-027483-2(2)) HarperCollins Pubs.
Massie, Diane Redfield. The Baby Beebee Bird. Kellogg, Steven, illus. 2003. (ENG.). 32p. (J). (gr. -1-1). pap. 6.99 (978-0-06-051784-7(0)) HarperCollins Pubs.
McCourt, Lisa. Goodnight, Stinky Face. Moore, Cyd, illus. 2016. (ENG.). 32p. (J). (— 1). bds. 6.99 (978-0-545-90592-3(3), Cartwheel Bks.) Scholastic, Inc.
McOmber, Rachel B., ed. McOmber Phonics Storybooks: Snores & More. rev. ed. (Illus.). (J). (978-0-944991-59-6(9)) Swift Learning Resources.
Meadows, Michelle. Hibernation Station. Cyrus, Kurt, illus. 2010. (ENG.). 40p. (J). (gr. -1-3). 17.99 (978-1-4169-3788-3(9), Simon & Schuster Bks. For Young Readers) Simon & Schuster Bks. For Young Readers.
Mellgren, Jöns. Elsa & the Night. 2014. (ENG., Illus.). 32p. (J). (gr. -1-3). 19.95 (978-3-89955-716-9(6)) Die Gestalten Verlag DEU. Dist: Penguin Random Hse. LLC.
Merkel, Tara & Monahan, Ryan. The Thunderstorm. 2007. 20p. per. 11.00 (978-1-4343-0585-5(6)) AuthorHouse.
Michaels, Kat. Gentle Is the Night. 2008. (J). 15.95 (978-0-9745052-7-5(7)) Tree Of Life Publishing.
Milligan, Domino. The Sandman. Spiller, Michael, illus. 2008. 16p. pap. 24.95 (978-1-60703-728-6(9)) America Star Bks.
Moracho, Cristina. Althea & Oliver. 2014. (ENG.). 384p. (YA). (gr. 9). 17.99 (978-0-670-78539-1(3), Viking Books for Young Readers) Penguin Young Readers Group.
Morales, Yuyi. Little Night / Nochecita. 2016. (ENG & SPA.). (J). lib. bdg. 18.40 (978-0-606-38443-8(X)) Turtleback Bks.
Morris, Kerry Nicole. The Baby Who Just... WON't Sleep! Parker's Story. 2004. 35p. pap. 24.95 (978-1-4137-3724-0(2)) PublishAmerica, Inc.
Morrissey, Dean. Ship of Dreams. 2016. (ENG., Illus.). 40p. (J). (gr. -1-2). 17.95 (978-1-63226-051-2(4), Prospecta Pr.) Easton Studio Pr., LLC.
Mortimer, Anne. Bunny's Easter Egg. Mortimer, Anne, illus. 2010. (ENG., Illus.). 32p. (J). (gr. -1-2). 12.99 (978-0-06-136664-2(1), Tegen, Katherine Bks) HarperCollins Pubs.
Moulton, Eugena. The Age of Merrik: The Anointing. 2007. 200p. 24.95 (978-0-595-67899-0(8)); per. 14.95 (978-0-595-41367-6(6)) iUniverse, Inc.
Muldrow, Diane. How Do Giraffes Take Naps? Walker, David, illus. 2016. (Little Golden Book Ser.). (ENG.). 24p. (J). (gr. -1-k). 4.99 (978-0-553-51333-2(8), Golden Bks.) Random Hse. Children's Bks.
Munoz, Isabel. It's Mine (Es Mío) Mazali, Gustavo, illus. 2006. (Eric & Julieta Ser.). (ENG & SPA.). 24p. (J). (gr. -1-3). pap. 3.99 (978-0-439-78370-5(4)) Scholastic, Inc.
Murguia, Bethanie Deeney. Buglette, the Messy Sleeper. Murguia, Bethanie Deeney, illus. 2011. (ENG., Illus.). 32p. (J). (gr. -1-2). 15.99 (978-1-58246-375-9(1), Tricycle Pr.) Random Hse. Children's Bks.
Murray, Marjorie Dennis. Don't Wake up the Bear!, 0 vols. Wittmann, Patricia, illus. unabr. ed. 2006. (ENG.). 34p. (J). (gr. -1-2). per. 9.99 (978-0-7614-5330-7(X), 9780761453307, Amazon Children's Publishing) Amazon Publishing.
Na, Il Sung. A Book of Sleep. 2011. (ENG.). 24p. (J). (gr. k — 1). bds. 6.99 (978-0-375-86618-0(3), Knopf Bks. for Young Readers) Random Hse. Children's Bks.
Nastanlieva, Vanya. Mo & Beau. 2015. (ENG., Illus.). 36p. (J). (gr. -1-3). 15.95 (978-1-927018-63-7(3)) Simply Read Bks. CAN. Dist: Ingram Publisher Services.
Neubeck, Jon. The Quest. 2009. 47p. pap. 23.10 (978-0-557-07108-1(9)) Lulu Pr., Inc.
North, Laura. The Princess & the Frozen Peas. 2014. (ENG., Illus.). 32p. (J). (978-0-7787-0446-1(7)); pap. (978-0-7787-0481-2(5)) Crabtree Publishing Co.
Noullet, Georgette. Bed Hog, 0 vols. Slonim, David, illus. 2011. (ENG.). 24p. (J). (gr. -1-3). 12.99 (978-0-7614-5823-4(9), 9780761458234, Amazon Children's Publishing) Amazon Publishing.
O'Connor, Jane. Every Day Is Earth Day. 2010. (Fancy Nancy - I Can Read! Ser.). (J). lib. bdg. 13.55 (978-0-606-12294-8(X), Turtleback) Turtleback Bks.
—Fancy Nancy & the Late, Late, Late Night. Glasser, Robin Preiss, illus. 2010. (Fancy Nancy Ser.). (ENG.). 24p. (J). (gr. -1-3). pap. 3.99 (978-0-06-170377-5(X), HarperFestival) HarperCollins Pubs.
—Fancy Nancy & the Late, Late, Late Night. 2010. (Fancy Nancy Picture Bks.). (J). lib. bdg. 13.55 (978-0-606-12312-9(1), Turtleback) Turtleback Bks.
Offill, Jenny. While You Were Napping. Blitt, Barry, illus. 2014. (ENG.). 40p. (J). (gr. -1-3). 16.99 (978-0-375-86572-5(1), Schwartz & Wade Bks.) Random Hse. Children's Bks.
Oppenheim, Joanne. Wake up, Baby! Lynn, Sweat, illus. 2015. (ENG.). 34p. (J). pap. 11.95 (978-1-899694-56-3(0), ipicturebooks) ibooks, Inc.
Owen, Dan. Ellen. 2006. 32p. (J). pap. 11.99 (978-1-4116-9069-1(9)) Lulu Pr., Inc.
Paiva, Teresa & Pinto, Helena Rebelo. Mein Freund, der Schlaf. 2011. (FRE.). 60p. (gr. 1-2). pap. 14.95 (978-1-4567-8991-6(0)) AuthorHouse.
—My Friend, Sleep. 2011. (Illus.). 68p. pap. 35.25 (978-1-4567-8990-9(2)); 60p. (gr. 1-2). pap. 14.95 (978-1-4567-8952-7(X)) AuthorHouse.
Palfreman-Bunker, Claire. Can Kittens Take a Catnap? Relf, Adam, illus. 2007. (J). pap. (978-0-545-02595-9(8)) Scholastic, Inc.
Paniagua, Kelly. Bedtime for Sarah Sullivan. Warrick, Jessica, illus. 2012. 36p. (J). 13.95 (978-1-60131-119-1(2)); pap. 10.95 (978-1-60131-120-7(6)) Big Tent Bks. (Castlebridge Bks.).
Pappas, Diane H. & Covey, Richard D. Why I Need My Sleep. Estrada, Ric, illus. 2007. (J). pap. (978-0-545-01427-4(1)) Scholastic, Inc.
Partridge, Helen L. Blinky: The Bear Who Wouldn't Hibernate. 2008. 32p. per. 24.95 (978-1-4241-9261-8(7)) America Star Bks.
Penelope Panda's Shooting Star. 2008. (Illus.). 32p. (J). (gr. k-3). pap. 14.99 (978-0-9717290-3-2(4)) Adrema Pr.
Pierce, Barbara A. The Game That Sam Plays. 2011. 24p. pap. 15.99 (978-1-4568-4143-0(2)) Xlibris Corp.
Pilkey, Dav. The Paperboy. 2015. 32p. pap. 7.00 (978-1-61003-556-9(9)) Center for the Collaborative Classroom.
Price, Mathew. Gatito. Goldman, Judy, tr. Kemp, Moira, illus. 2010. (SPA & ENG.). 10p. bds. 5.99 (978-1-935021-99-5(0)) Price, Mathew Ltd.
Price, Rebecca. Toby & the Flood, 1 vol. 2008. (ENG., Illus.). 32p. (J). pap. (978-0-86315-635-9(5)) Floris Bks.
Price, Tom, illus. Champion Sleeper. 2008. 32p. (J). pap. 9.95 (978-0-9748226-1-7(2)) Murphy's Bone Publishing.
Publications International Ltd. Staff, ed. Sleepy Baby. 2011. 8p. (J). bds. 7.98 (978-1-4508-1241-2(4)) Publications International, Ltd.
Quintart, Natalie. Mama Bear. Blanchart, Stephanie, illus. 2005. (Tiger Tales Ser.). 32p. (J). (gr. -1-2). 6.95 (978-1-58925-394-0(9)) Tiger Tales.
Raab, Brigitte. Mama, I Can't Sleep. Olten, Manuela, illus. 2012. (ENG.). 32p. (J). (gr. -1-k). 16.95 (978-1-61608-965-8(2), 608965, Sky Pony Pr.) Skyhorse Publishing Co., Inc.
Radzinski, Kandy. Where to Sleep. 2010. (ENG.). 22p. (J). 9.95 (978-1-58536-535-7(1)) Sleeping Bear Pr.
—Where to Sleep. Radzinski, Kandy, illus. 2009. (ENG., Illus.). 32p. (J). (gr. k-6). 15.95 (978-1-58536-436-7(3)) Sleeping Bear Pr.
Remsburg, Rebecca. Night, Night, Knight, 1 vol. 2009. 19p. pap. 24.95 (978-1-60836-942-3(0)) America Star Bks.
Renee, Sherry. Bye Bye Bed-Dy: Andrew Gets a Big Boy Bed. 2012. 20p. pap. 17.99 (978-1-4685-7498-2(1)) AuthorHouse.
Reyes, Yolanda. Una Cama para Tres. Coll, Ivar Da, illus. 2004. (SPA.). 36p. (J). (gr. k-3). 14.95 (978-958-704-055-5(4)) Santillana USA Publishing Co., Inc.
Riddell, Chris. Mr Underbed. Riddell, Chris, illus. (ENG., Illus.). 32p. (J). (gr. -1-k). 2012. pap. 10.99 (978-1-84270-942-9(9)) 2010. 19.99 (978-1-84270-821-7(X)) Andersen Pr. GBR. Dist: Independent Pubs. Group.
Roash, Riki. Mom, I Can Sleep in My Bed Tonight! 2013. 24p. pap. 24.95 (978-1-4626-8255-3(3)) America Star Bks.
Rock, Michelle L. Nighttime Adventures Counting Sheep. Longmore, Nickolai, illus. 2006. 32p. (J). 3.99 net. (978-0-9771700-1-2(2)) Mystic Arts, LLC.
Root, Phyllis. Ten Sleepy Sheep. Gaber, Susan, illus. 2009. (ENG.). 12p. (J). (-k). bds. 7.99 (978-0-7636-4142-9(1)) Candlewick Pr.
Rosen, Michael. Snore! Langley, Jonathan, illus. 2003. (ENG.). 32p. (J). (gr. -1-k). pap. 10.99 (978-0-00-716031-0(3), HarperCollins Children's Bks.) HarperCollins Pubs. Ltd. GBR. Dist: HarperCollins Pubs.
Rosenberg, Natascha & Kempter, Christa. When Mama Can't Sleep. 2011. (ENG., Illus.). 24p. (J). (gr. -1 — 1). 6.95 (978-0-7358-4015-7(6)) North-South Bks., Inc.
Roth, Judith. Goodnight, Dragons [padded Board Book]. Lemaître, Pascal, illus. 2015. (ENG.). 32p. (J). (gr. -1-k). bds. 8.99 (978-1-4847-2190-2(X)) Hyperion Bks. for Children.
Rothstein, Nancy H. & Gilpin, Stephen. My Daddy Snores. 2006. (Illus.). (J). pap. (978-0-439-87142-6(5)) Scholastic, Inc.
Runion, Laura K. Sleepy Faces in Sleeping Places. 2012. 28p. pap. 16.10 (978-1-4669-4020-8(4)) Trafford Publishing.
Saltzberg, Barney. Chengdu Could Not, Would Not, Fall Asleep. Saltzberg, Barney, illus. (Chengdu Ser.). (ENG., Illus.). (J). (gr. -1-k). 2017. 32p. bds. 6.99 **(978-1-4847-7565-3(1))** 2014. 48p. 16.99 (978-1-4231-6721-1(X)) Hyperion Bks. for Children.
Samarrippas, Gloria. In Search for Lucky's Lost Toys. 2006. 17.00 (978-0-8059-7329-7(X)) Dorrance Publishing Co., Inc.
Sapp, Karen. Who Is Sleeping? 2009. (Rookie Preschool-NEW Ser.). (ENG.). 24p. (J). pap. 6.95 (978-0-531-24586-6(1)); (gr. -1). lib. bdg. 23.00 (978-0-531-24411-1(3)) Scholastic Library Publishing. (Children's Pr.).
Schmidt, Hans-Christian. Are You Sleeping Little One. Lindgren, Laura, tr. from GER. Nemet, Andrea, illus. 2012. (ENG.). 18p. (J). (gr. k-k). bds. 6.95 (978-0-7892-1120-0(3), Abbeville Kids) Abbeville Pr., Inc.
Schneider, Dianna. Rocky Ford Stories: Sleepytime at Rocky Ford. 2012. 42p. pap. 17.45 (978-1-4525-5310-8(6)) Balboa Pr.
Scotton, Rob. Russell the Sheep. Scotton, Rob, illus. (ENG., Illus.). (J). (gr. -1-3). 2015. 32p. pap. 5.99 (978-0-06-239243-5(3), HarperFestival) 2011. 32p. pap. 6.99 (978-0-06-059850-1(6)) 2009. 32p. bds. 7.99 (978-0-06-170996-8(4), HarperFestival) 2007. 16p. 9.99 (978-0-06-128434-2(3)) 2005. 32p. 17.99 (978-0-06-059848-8(4)) HarperCollins Pubs.
Segel, Jason & Miller, Kirsten. The Sleepwalker Tonic. Kwasny, Karl, illus. 2015. (Nightmares! Ser.). (ENG.). 368p. (J). (gr. 3-7). 16.99 (978-0-385-74427-0(7)); lib. bdg. 19.99

(978-0-375-99158-5(1)) Random Hse. Children's Bks. (Delacorte Bks. for Young Readers).

Seuss, Dr. Dr. Seuss's Sleep Softly Book. 2012. (Dr. Seuss Nursery Collection). (ENG., Illus.). 12p. (J). (gr. k — 1). 11.99 (978-0-375-87003-3(2), Random Hse. Bks. for Young Readers) Random Hse. Children's Bks.

Shapely Sleepy Sheep. 2005. (J). bds. 7.95 (978-0-9749305-6-5(3)) Castle Pacific Publishing.

Sharmat, Mitchell. Berkley, the Terrible Sleeper. Kurilla, Renée, illus. 2015. (Ready-To-Reads Ser.). (ENG.). 32p. (J). (gr. k-2). pap. 3.99 (978-1-4814-3832-2(8), Simon Spotlight) Simon Spotlight.

Shields, Gillian & Reed, Nathan. Angel Baby. 2006. (ENG., Illus.). 24p. (J). (gr. -1-k). pap. 9.99 (978-0-00-718006-6(3), HarperCollins Children's Bks.) HarperCollins Pubs. Ltd. GBR. Dist: Independent Pubs. Group.

Shyba, Jessica. Naptime with Theo & Beau. 2015. (ENG., Illus.). 40p. (J). (gr. -1-k). 16.99 (978-1-250-05906-2(2), 9781250059062) Feiwel & Friends.

Singlehurst, Naomi. Grandpa, What's That Sound in the Middle of the Night? Ellen Koski, Rachel, ed. Jamieson, Victoria, illus. 2008. (ENG.). 32p. (J). (gr. k-2). 14.95 (978-1-930650-24-4(8)) mTrellis Publishing, Inc.

Singleton, Debbie. The King Who Wouldn't Sleep. Swain, Holly, illus. 2012. (Andersen Press Picture Bks). (ENG.). 32p. (J). (gr. -1-3). 16.95 (978-0-7613-8997-2(0)) Lerner Publishing Group.

Sleep Tight Spaceboy. 2003. (Spaceboy Set 1 Ser.). (J). 7.33 (978-1-932570-02-1(0)) Pioneer Valley Bks.

Slegers, Liesbet. Sleeping. 2010. (Clavis Toddler: Daily Life Ser.). (ENG.). 12p. (J). (gr. k — 1). bds. 5.95 (978-1-60537-068-2(1)) Cobblestone Publishing Co.

Smith, Carrie. Little Bo Peep. Abbott, Jason, illus. 2010. (Rising Readers Ser.). (J). 3.49 (978-1-60719-700-3(6)) Newmark Learning LLC.

Star, Nancy. Mystery of the Snow Day Bigfoot. Bernardin, James, illus. 2005. (Calendar Club Mysteries Ser.: Vol. 3). 77p. (J). pap. 3.95 (978-0-439-67262-7(7)) Scholastic, Inc.

Stewart, Dianne. Who's Afraid of the Dark? Rankin, Joan, illus. 2012. (ENG.). 32p. (J). (gr. k-2). pap. 6.95 (978-1-4314-0118-5(8)) Jacana Media ZAF. Dist: Independent Pubs. Group.

Surovec, Yasmine. A Bed for Kitty. Surovec, Yasmine, illus. 2014. (ENG., Illus.). 40p. (J). (gr. -1-1). 16.99 (978-1-59643-863-7(0), 9781596438637) Roaring Brook Pr.

Sweeney, Monica & Yelvington, Lauren. Can You Snore Like a Dinosaur? A Help-Your-Child-To-Sleep Book. Watkins, Laura, illus. 2017. (ENG.). 32p. (J). 15.99 (978-1-250-11868-4(9), 9781250118684) St. Martin's Pr.

—Can You Yawn Like a Fawn? Watkins, Laura, illus. 2016. (ENG.). 32p. (J). 15.99 (978-1-250-10416-8(5), 9781250104168) St. Martin's Pr.

Teckentrup, Britta. Don't Wake up the Tiger. Teckentrup, Britta, illus. 2016. (ENG., Illus.). 30p. (J). (-k). 15.99 (978-0-7636-8996-4(3), Nosy Crow) Candlewick Pr.

—Sleep Tight, Little Bear. 2014. (ENG., Illus.). 40p. (J). 17.95 (978-0-7358-4180-2(2)) North-South Bks., Inc.

Ted in a Red Bed Kid Kit. 2004. (Kid Kits Ser.). (Illus.). 10p. (J). bds. 9.95 (978-1-58086-404-6(X)) EDC Publishing.

Theobald, Joseph. When Arthur Wouldn't Sleep. Theobald, Joseph, illus. 2006. (Collins Big Cat Ser.). (ENG., Illus.). 24p. (J). (gr. 2-2). pap. 6.99 (978-0-00-718688-4(6)) HarperCollins Pubs. Ltd. GBR. Dist: Independent Pubs. Group.

Thereza, Rowe & Rowe, Thereza. Mister Pip. 2016. (ENG., Illus.). 32p. (J). (gr. -1-k). 16.95 (978-1-84976-382-0(8)) Tate Publishing, Ltd. GBR. Dist: Abrams, Inc.

Thompson, Lauren & Anderson, Derek. Little Quack's Bedtime. 2009. (Classic Board Bks.). (ENG., Illus.). 34p. (J). (gr. -1-k). bds. 7.99 (978-1-4169-6873-3(3), Little Simon) Little Simon.

Tillman, Nancy & Metaxas, Eric. It's Time to Sleep, My Love. Tillman, Nancy, illus. 2008. (ENG., Illus.). 32p. (J). (gr. -1 — 1). 16.95 (978-0-312-38371-8(1), 9780312383718) Feiwel & Friends.

Topper, Wendy. Where's the Pacifier? 2008. 8p. pap. 24.95 (978-1-60563-823-2(4)) America Star Bks.

Torrel, Wendy. GUARDIAN of DREAMS (1st Edition) Klingbeil, Kendall, illus. l.t. ed. 2004. 32p. (J). 14.95 (978-0-9746890-0-5(9)); pap. 10.95 (978-0-9746890-1-2(7)) White Tulip Publishing.

Toshiley. The Sponge & the River of Sleepiness. 2009. 24p. pap. 13.50 (978-1-60860-562-0(0), Eloquent Bks.) Strategic Book Publishing & Rights Agency (SBPRA).

Trasler, Janee. Bedtime for Chickies. Trasler, Janee, illus. 2014. (Chickies Ser.). (ENG., Illus.). 24p. (J). (gr. -1 — 1). bds. 8.99 (978-0-06-227468-7(6), HarperFestival) HarperCollins Pubs.

Tremblay, Carole. Floop in the Dark. Beshwaty, Steve, illus. 2009. (Floop Ser.). 24p. (J). (gr. -1-k). 22.60 (978-1-60754-341-1(9)); pap. 8.15 (978-1-60754-342-8(7)) Windmill Bks.

Valério, Geraldo, illus. Go to Sleep, Gecko! A Balinese Folktale. 2015. (ENG.). 32p. (J). (gr. -1-3). pap. 8.95 (978-1-939160-92-8(8)) August Hse. Pubs., Inc.

van Genechten, Guido. The Big Sleep Book. 2008. (Clavis Toddler: Daily Life Ser.). (ENG & DUT.). 20p. (J). (gr. k — 1). bds. 12.95 (978-1-60537-012-5(6)) Cobblestone Publishing Co.

Van Patter, Bruce. Farley Found It! 2006. (ENG., Illus.). 32p. (J). (gr. -1-1). 17.95 (978-1-59078-351-1(4)) Boyds Mills Pr.

Vere, Ed. A Dormir, Monstruos! 2012. (SPA.). 32p. (J). (gr. -1-1). pap. 21.99 (978-84-261-3890-3(X)) Juventud, Editorial ESP. Dist: Lectorum Pubns., Inc.

—Everyone's Sleepy. 2003. (ENG., Illus.). 12p. (J). 8.99 (978-0-333-78038-1(8)) Macmillan Pubs., Ltd. GBR. Dist: Trafalgar Square Publishing.

Volker, Kerstin. Suzie Goes to Sleep. 2003. (Funny Friends Lift-and-Learn Bks.). (Illus.). 14p. (J). 5.99 (978-1-59384-024-2(1)) Parklane Publishing.

Waber, Bernard. Ira Sleeps Over, 1 vol. 2008. (Read along Book & CD Ser.). (ENG., Illus.). 48p. (J). (gr. -1-3). audio compact disk 10.99 (978-0-618-85282-6(4)) Houghton Mifflin Harcourt Publishing Co.

Walker, Nan. The Midnight Kid. Gott, Barry, illus. 2007. (Science Solves It! Ser.). 32p. (J). (gr. -1-3). pap. 5.95 (978-1-57565-238-2(2)) Kane Press, Inc.

Watt, F. Felices Suenos! 2004. (Mundo del Pequenin Ser.).Tr. of Baby's Bedtime. (SPA., Illus.). 16p. (YA). (gr. -1-18). pap. 4.95 (978-0-7460-3869-7(0)) EDC Publishing.

Watt, Mélanie. Scaredy Squirrel at Night. Watt, Mélanie, illus. 2009. (ENG., Illus.). 32p. (J). (gr. -1-3). 16.95 (978-1-55453-288-9(4)) Kids Can Pr., Ltd. CAN. Dist: Hachette Bk. Group.

Weinstone, David. All My Friends Are Fast Asleep. Le Huche, Magali, illus. 2017. (ENG.). 40p. (J). 17.99 **(978-0-374-30535-2(8)**, 9780374305352, Farrar, Straus & Giroux (BYR)) Farrar, Straus & Giroux.

Weir, Jaime L. Out of Bed. 2008. 20p. pap. 24.95 (978-1-60474-363-0(8)) America Star Bks.

Wells, Rosemary. Max's Bedtime. 2003. (Max & Ruby Ser.). (ENG.). 12p. (J). (gr. 1 — 1). bds. 6.99 (978-0-670-88710-1(2), Viking Books for Young Readers) Penguin Young Readers Group.

Weston Woods Staff, creator. The Napping House. 2011. 29.95 (978-0-439-72863-8(0)) Weston Woods Studios, Inc.

Wheeler, Lisa. Even Monsters Need to Sleep. Van Dusen, Chris, illus. 2017. 32p. (J). (gr. -1-3). 17.99 (978-0-06-236640-5(8)) HarperCollins Pubs.

Willems, Mo. I Will Take a Nap! Willems, Mo, illus. 2015. (Elephant & Piggie Ser.). (ENG., Illus.). 64p. (J). (gr. 1-3). 9.99 (978-1-4847-1630-4(2)) Hyperion Bks. for Children.

Williams, Annik. Mr. Mole's Day Off: With Goodnight Little Birdie. 2010. 20p. 15.78 (978-1-4520-3756-1(6)) AuthorHouse.

Williams, Becky. Good Night Little Piggy. Howarth, Daniel, illus. 2007. (Night Light Book Ser.). 10p. (gr. -1-k). bds. (978-1-84666-129-7(3), Tide Mill Pr.) Top That! Publishing PLC.

Wilson, Karma. Bear Stays up for Christmas. Chapman, Jane, illus. 2011. (Bear Bks.). (ENG.). 34p. (J). (gr. -1 — 1). bds. 7.99 (978-1-4424-2790-7(6), Little Simon) Little Simon.

Wolf, Karina. The Insomniacs. Hilts, Brothers, illus. 2012. (ENG.). 32p. (J). (gr. -1-k). 16.99 (978-0-399-25665-3(2), G.P. Putnam's Sons Books for Young Readers) Penguin Young Readers Group.

Wolfe, Myra & Monescillo, Maria. Charlotte Jane Battles Bedtime. Monescillo, Maria, illus. 2011. (ENG., Illus.). 32p. (J). (gr. -1-3). 16.99 (978-0-15-206150-0(9)) Houghton Mifflin Harcourt Publishing Co.

Wood, Audrey. The Full Moon at the Napping House. Wood, Don, illus. 2015. (ENG.). 32p. (J). (gr. -1-3). 17.99 (978-0-544-30832-9(8), HMH Books For Young Readers) Houghton Mifflin Harcourt Publishing Co.

—The Napping House. Wood. Audrey & Wood, Don, illus. 25th ed. 2009. (ENG.). 32p. (J). (gr. -1-3). 18.99 (978-0-15-256708-8(9)) Houghton Mifflin Harcourt Publishing Co.

—Napping House / La Casa Adormecida. Wood, Don, illus. 2012. (ENG & SPA.). 32p. (J). (gr. -1 — 1). bds. 6.99 (978-0-547-71920-7(5)) Houghton Mifflin Harcourt Publishing Co.

Written By Tori Velle; Illustrated By Al. Tia Tot Rules! Aguila, Alicia del, illus. 2011. 44p. pap. 24.95 (978-1-4241-7833-9(9)) America Star Bks.

Yisrael, A'mon. Mr. Jerry's Nap. 2005. (Illus.). 9p. (J). 8.99 (978-0-9772424-0-5(4)) Yisrael, Sean Publishing Co.

Yovanoff, Brenna. Places No One Knows. 2016. (ENG.). 384p. (YA). (gr. 9). 17.99 (978-0-553-52263-1(9), Delacorte Pr.) Random Hse. Children's Bks.

Yuly, Toni. Cat Nap. 2016. (ENG., Illus.). 40p. (J). 16.99 (978-1-250-05458-6(3), 9781250054586) Feiwel & Friends.

Zaibak, Bushra. I am Not Afraid. 2007. (Illus.). 37p. (J). mass mkt. (978-0-9787849-7-3(9)) Lucent Interpretations, LLC.

SLEEPING BEAUTY (FICTITIOUS CHARACTER)—FICTION

Amery, H. & Cartwright, S. Sleeping Beauty. 2004. (First Stories Ser.). 16p. (J). pap. 4.95 (978-0-7945-0604-9(6)) EDC Publishing.

AZ Books Staff. Sleeping Beauty. Zyl, Olga, ed. 2012. (Classic Fairy Tales Ser.). (ENG.). 10p. (J). (gr. -1-k). bds. 9.95 (978-1-61889-006-1(9)) AZ Bks. LLC.

Baker, Sara, illus. Ready to Read Sleeping Beauty. 2007. (Ready to Read Ser.). 31p. (J). (gr. k-2). (978-1-84610-441-1(6)) Make Believe Ideas.

Barella, Laura, illus. Sleeping Beauty. 2009. (Flip-Up Fairy Tales Ser.). (ENG.). 24p. (J). (gr. -1-2). pap. (978-1-84643-252-1(9)) Child's Play International Ltd.

Belle, Trixie & Caruso-Scott, Melissa. Sleeping Beauty: Les Petits Fairytales. Lake, Oliver, illus. 2013. (Petits Fairytales Ser.). (ENG.). 26p. (J). (gr. -1 — 1). bds. 7.99 (978-0-8050-9791-7(0), 9780805097917, Holt, Henry & Co. Bks. For Young Readers) Holt, Henry & Co.

Braswell, Liz. Once upon a Dream. 2017. (Twisted Tale Ser.). (YA). lib. bdg. 20.85 **(978-0-606-39935-7(6))** Turtleback Bks.

Braswell, Liz. Once upon a Dream: A Twisted Tale. 2016. (Twisted Tale Ser.). (ENG.). 448p. (J). (gr. 7-17). 17.99 (978-1-4847-0725-8(7)) Disney Pr.

Brown, Carron, ed. Sleeping Beauty & Snow White & the Seven Dwarfs: Two Tales & Their Histories. 2009. (World of Fairy Tales Ser.). (Illus.). 32p. (J). (gr. -1-2). pap. 10.55 (978-1-60754-635-1(3)); lib. bdg. 22.60 (978-1-60754-634-4(5)) Windmill Bks.

Carney, Larry, adapted by. Sleeping Beauty. 2009. (ENG., Illus.). 24p. (J). 6.95 (978-1-60072-116-8(8)) PC Treasures, Inc.

Cartwright, Stephen, illus. Sleeping Beauty. 2006. (First Stories Sticker Bks.). 16p. (J). (gr. -1-3). pap. 6.99 (978-0-7945-1313-9(1), Usborne) EDC Publishing.

Disney Staff. The Sleeping Beauty. (FRE.). 96p. (J). (gr. k-5). pap. 9.95 (978-0-7859-8854-0(8)) French & European Pubns., Inc.

Dulac, Edmund, illus. The Sleeping Beauty & Other Fairy Tales. 2011. (Calla Editions Ser.). (ENG.). 208p. 35.00 (978-1-60660-019-1(2)) Dover Pubns., Inc.

Dwyer, Mindy. Alaska's Sleeping Beauty. Dwyer, Mindy, illus. 2014. (Paws IV Ser.). (ENG., Illus.). 32p. (J). (gr. k-3). pap. 10.99 (978-1-57061-872-7(0), Little Bigfoot) Sasquatch Bks.

Evans, C. S. Sleeping Beauty. Rackham, Arthur, illus. 2012. (ENG.). 104p. (J). 12.95 (978-1-59583-457-7(5), Green Tiger Pr.) Laughing Elephant.

Fairy Tales- Sleeping Beauty. 2005. (J). bds. (978-1-4194-0042-1(8)) Paradise Pr., Inc.

Fear, Sharon, retold by. Sleeping Beauty. 2004. (Treasure Tree Ser.). (Illus.). 32p. (J). (978-0-7166-1605-4(X)) World Bk., Inc.

Gaiman, NEil. The Sleeper & the Spindle. Riddell, Chris, illus. 2015. (ENG.). 64p. (YA). (gr. 8). 19.99 (978-0-06-239824-6(5)) HarperCollins Pubs.

Gardner, Sally. Sleeping Beauty. 2011. (ENG., Illus.). 64p. (J). (gr. -1-k). 7.99 (978-1-4440-0242-3(2), Orion Children's Bks.) Hachette Children's Group GBR. Dist: Hachette Bk. Group.

Gibb, Sarah. Sleeping Beauty: Based on the Original Story by the Brothers Grimm. Gibb, Sarah, illus. 2015. (ENG., Illus.). 32p. (J). (gr. -1-3). 16.99 (978-0-8075-7351-8(5)) Whitman, Albert & Co.

Heapy, Teresa. Very Little Sleeping Beauty. Heap, Sue, illus. 2016. (Very Little Ser.). (ENG.). 32p. (J). (gr. -1-3). 16.99 (978-0-544-28279-7(5), HMH Books For Young Readers) Houghton Mifflin Harcourt Publishing Co.

Holub, Joan & Williams, Suzanne. Sleeping Beauty Dreams Big. 2015. (Grimmtastic Girls Ser.: 5). (ENG.). 192p. (J). (gr. 3-7). pap. 5.99 (978-0-545-78393-4(3), Scholastic Paperbacks) Scholastic, Inc.

Jenny Press Staff, illus. Sleeping Beauty. 2016. (ENG.). 24p. pap. 7.99 (978-1-86147-816-0(X), Armadillo) Anness Publishing GBR. Dist: National Bk. Network.

Leonard, Barry, ed. Sleeping Beauty. 2003. (Illus.). 12p. (J). (gr. k-4). reprint ed. 17.00 (978-0-7567-6865-2(9)) DIANE Publishing Co.

Lewis, Jan, illus. First Fairy Tales: Sleeping Beauty. 2013. (ENG.). 24p. (J). (gr. -1-k). bds. 6.99 (978-1-86147-338-7(9), Armadillo) Anness Publishing GBR. Dist: National Bk. Network.

Man-Kong, Mary. Sleeping Beauty. 2014. (Disney Princess Step into Reading Ser.). lib. bdg. 13.55 (978-0-606-36001-2(8)) Turtleback Bks.

—Sleeping Beauty Step into Reading (Disney Princess) RH Disney Staff, illus. 2014. (Step into Reading Ser.). (ENG.). 32p. (J). (gr. -1-1). 3.99 (978-0-7364-3226-9(4), RH/Disney) Random Hse. Children's Bks.

Mass, Wendy. Sleeping Beauty: The One Who Took the Really Long Nap. 2012. (Twice upon a Time Ser.: 2). lib. bdg. 17.20 (978-0-606-26530-0(9), Turtleback) Turtleback Bks.

Mayhew, James. The Sleeping Beauty. 2008. (Ella Bella Ballerina Ser.). (ENG., Illus.). 32p. (J). (gr. -1-3). 14.99 (978-0-7641-6118-6(0)) Barron's Educational Series, Inc.

McGowan, Maureen. Sleeping Beauty: Vampire Slayer. 2010. 320p. pap. 8.95 (978-1-60747-779-2(3), Pickwick Pr.) Phoenix Bks., Inc.

Mlynowski, Sarah. Dream On. 2013. (Whatever After Ser.: 4). (ENG.). 176p. (J). (gr. 3-7). 14.99 (978-0-545-41571-2(3), Scholastic Pr.) Scholastic, Inc.

Oliver, Jana. Briar Rose, 1. unabr. ed. 2015. (ENG.). 480p. (YA). (gr. 8). pap. 9.99 (978-1-4472-4109-6(6)) Pan Macmillan GBR. Dist: Independent Pubs. Group.

Ottolenghi, Carol. La Bella Durmiente. 2009. (Keepsake Stories Ser.).Tr. of Sleeping Beauty. (SPA & ENG.). 32p. (gr. -1-2). pap. 3.99 (978-0-7696-5862-9(8), Brighter Child) Carson-Dellosa Publishing, LLC.

—Sleeping Beauty. 2009. (Keepsake Stories Ser.): (ENG.). 32p. (gr. -1-3). pap. 3.99 (978-0-7696-5866-7(0), Brighter Child) Carson-Dellosa Publishing, LLC.

Roberts, Lynn & Roberts, David. Sleeping Beauty. 2017. (ENG., Illus.). 32p. (J). (gr. -1-1). 17.99 (978-1-84365-291-5(9), Pavilion) Pavilion Bks. GBR. Dist: Independent Pubs. Group.

Rossi, Francesca, illus. The Sleeping Beauty. 2015. (Fairy Tale Adventures Ser.). (ENG.). 64p. (J). (gr. 2-6). 7.95 (978-1-4549-1512-6(9)) Sterling Publishing Co., Inc.

Scollen, Chris. Busy Kids Sticker Storybook Sleeping Beauty. 2008. (Illus.). 12p. (J). (gr. -1-3). pap. (978-1-84610-807-5(1)) Make Believe Ideas.

Sleeping Beauty. (Read-Along Ser.). (J). 7.99 incl. audio (978-1-55723-010-2(2)) Walt Disney Records.

Susaeta, Equipo. La Bella Durmiente -Sleeping Beauty. Susaeta Publishing, Inc., Staff, ed. 2011. (Cuentos Bilingües Ser.). (SPA & ENG.). 34p. (J). (gr. k-2). 6.95 (978-84-305-2453-2(3)) Susaeta Ediciones, S.A. ESP. Dist: Independent Pubs. Group.

Taplin, Sam. Sleeping Beauty. 2008. (First Fairytales Look & Say Ser.). 12p. (J). (gr. -1). bds. 9.99 (978-0-7945-2200-1(9), Usborne) EDC Publishing.

Teitelbaum, Michael & Golden Books Staff. Sleeping Beauty. DiCicco, Sue & Dias, Ron, illus. 2004. (Little Golden Book Ser.). (ENG.). 24p. (J). (gr. -1-k). 4.99 (978-0-7364-2198-0(X), Golden/Disney) Random Hse. Children's Bks.

Umansky, Kaye. Sleeping Beauty. Crossland, Caroline, illus. 2003. (Plays & Play Collections). (ENG.). 48p. (J). pap. 15.00 (978-0-7136-5371-7(X), A&C Black) Bloomsbury Publishing Plc GBR. Dist: Players Pr., Inc.

Young, Lesley. A Storyteller Book Sleeping Beauty. Press, Jenny, illus. 2013. (ENG.). 48p. (J). (gr. -1-12). pap. 7.99 (978-1-84322-910-0(2), Armadillo) Anness Publishing GBR. Dist: National Bk. Network.

Zahler, Diane. Sleeping Beauty's Daughters. 2013. (ENG.). 224p. (J). (gr. 3-7). 16.99 (978-0-06-200496-3(4)) HarperCollins Pubs.

SLEEPOVERS

Goldsack, Gaby. The Ultimate Sleepover Pack. Reeves, Sue, illus. 24p. (J). 79.60 (978-0-7641-7662-3(5)) Barron's Educational Series, Inc.

Guillain, Charlotte. My First Sleepover, 1 vol. 2011. (Growing Up Ser.). (ENG.). 24p. (gr. k-2). 23.32 (978-1-4329-4802-3(4), Heinemann Read & Learn) Heinemann-Raintree.

Hurley, Jo. Slumber-Ific! Great Sleepover Ideas for You & Your Friends. Morley, Taia, illus. 2007. 63p. (J). (978-0-439-02015-2(8)) Scholastic, Inc.

Kenney, Karen Latchana. Cool Slumber Parties: Perfect Party Planning for Kids, 1 vol. 2012. (Cool Parties Ser.). (ENG., Illus.). 32p. (J). (gr. 3-6). 28.50 (978-1-61714-976-4(4)) ABDO Publishing Co.

Nicholson, Sue. Sleepover. 2003. (Wicked Wallets Ser.). (Illus.). 96p. (YA). pap. (978-1-84347-061-8(6), Pavilion Children's Books) Pavilion Bks.

Olsen, Mary-Kate & Olsen, Ashley. Mary-Kate & Ashley Yearbook. 2005. (Illus.). 96p. (978-0-00-720729-9(8)) HarperCollins Pubs. Australia.

—Sleepover Party Mini Box. 2005. 32p. (978-0-00-719585-5(0)) HarperCollins Pubs. Australia.

Peters, Rosalind. Midnight Feast Magic: Sleepover Fun & Food. Pankhurst, Kate, illus. Boursnell, Clive, photos by. 2009. (ENG.). 64p. (J). (gr. 3-6). pap. 15.95 (978-1-84507-783-9(0), Frances Lincoln) Quarto Publishing Group UK GBR. Dist: Hachette Bk. Group.

Rober, Harold. Having a Sleepover. 2017. (Bumba Books (tm) — Fun Firsts Ser.). (ENG.). 24p. (J). (gr. -1-1). 12.99 **(978-1-5124-3684-6(4))**; 38.65 **(978-1-5124-3683-9(6))**; 38.65 **(978-1-5124-2751-6(9))** Lerner Publishing Group. (Lerner Pubns.).

Rober, Harold T. Having a Sleepover. 2017. (Bumba Books (tm) — Fun Firsts Ser.). (ENG., Illus.). 24p. (J). (gr. -1-1). 25.32 (978-1-5124-2555-0(9)) Lerner Publishing Group.

Ross, Kathy. Girlfriends' Get-Together Craft Book. Bosch, Nicole in den, illus. 2007. (Girl Crafts Ser.). (ENG.). 48p. (gr. 2-5). pap. 7.95 (978-0-7613-9465-5(6), First Avenue Editions) Lerner Publishing Group.

—Girlfriends' Get-Together Craft Book. In Den Bosch, Nicole, illus. 2007. (Girl Crafts Ser.). (ENG.). 48p. (gr. 2-5). lib. bdg. 26.60 (978-0-7613-3408-8(4), Millbrook Pr.) Lerner Publishing Group.

Ventura, Marne. A Girl's Guide to the Perfect Sleepover. 2017. (Go-To Guides). (ENG., Illus.). 32p. (gr. 3-4). lib. bdg. 27.99 (978-1-5157-3663-9(6), Snap Bks.) Capstone Press of Coughlan Cos.

Watson, Stephanie. Plan a Sleepover Party. 2014. (Party Time! Ser.). (ENG., Illus.). 32p. (gr. 4-8). lib. bdg. 26.60 (978-1-4677-3832-3(8), Lerner Pubns.) Lerner Publishing Group.

SLEEPOVERS—FICTION

Allen, Elise & Stanford, Halle. Spring's Sparkle Sleepover. Pooler, Paige, illus. 2015. (Enchanted Sisters Ser.). (ENG.). 128p. (J). (gr. 2-4). 15.99 (978-1-61963-296-7(9), 9781619632967); pap. 5.99 (978-1-61963-269-1(1), 9781619632691) Bloomsbury Publishing USA. (Bloomsbury USA Childrens).

—Spring's Sparkle Sleepover. Pooler, Paige, illus. 2015. (Enchanted Sisters Ser.: 3). (J). lib. bdg. 16.00 (978-0-606-36218-4(5)) Turtleback Bks.

Barker, Henry. Vino del Espacio. Gott, Barry, illus. 2008. (Science Solves It! en Espanol Ser.). (SPA.). 32p. (J). (gr. -1-3). pap. 5.95 (978-1-57565-265-8(X)) Kane Press, Inc.

—Vino Del Espacio (It Came from Outer Space) Gott, Barry, illus. 2009. (Science Solves It! (r) en Espanol Ser.). (SPA.). (gr. 1-3). pap. 33.92 (978-1-58013-771-3(7)) Lerner Publishing Group.

Barkley, Callie. Liz at Marigold Lake. Riti, Marsha, illus. 2014. (Critter Club Ser.: 7). (ENG.). 128p. (J). (gr. k-4). pap. 5.99 (978-1-4424-9525-8(1), Little Simon) Little Simon.

—Liz at Marigold Lake. 2014. (Critter Club Ser.: 7). lib. bdg. 16.00 (978-0-606-35445-5(X)) Turtleback Bks.

—Liz's Night at the Museum. Bishop, Tracy, illus. 2016. (Critter Club Ser.: 15). (ENG.). 128p. (J). (gr. k-4). pap. 5.99 (978-1-4814-7164-0(3), Little Simon) Little Simon.

Beck, Scott. Monster Sleepover! 2009. (ENG., Illus.). 32p. (J). (gr. k-2). 15.95 (978-0-8109-4059-8(0), Abrams Bks. for Young Readers) Abrams, Inc.

Becker, Bonny. A Bedtime for Bear. Denton, Kady MacDonald, illus. 2010. (J). (Bear & Mouse Ser.: 3). (ENG.). 48p. (gr. -1-2). 16.99 (978-0-7636-4101-6(4)); (978-0-7636-5364-4(0)) Candlewick Pr.

Bell, Cece. Rabbit & Robot. 2014. (Candlewick Sparks Ser.). lib. bdg. 13.55 (978-0-606-35169-0(8)) Turtleback Bks.

—Rabbit & Robot: The Sleepover. Bell, Cece, illus. 2012. (ENG., Illus.). 56p. (J). (gr. k-4). 14.99 (978-0-7636-5475-7(2)) Candlewick Pr.

—Rabbit & Robot - The Sleepover. Bell, Cece, illus. 2014. (Candlewick Sparks Ser.). (ENG., Illus.). 56p. (J). (gr. k-4). pap. 3.99 (978-0-7636-6875-4(3)) Candlewick Pr.

Benenfeld, Rikki. I Go Visiting. 2007. (Toddler Experience Ser.). (Illus.). 32p. (J). (gr. -1-k). 10.95 (978-1-929628-33-9(1)) Hachai Publishing.

Berenstain, Jan & Berenstain, Mike. The Berenstain Bears' Sleepover. Berenstain, Jan & Berenstain, Mike, illus. 2008. (I Can Read Level 1 Ser.). (ENG., Illus.). 32p. (J). (gr. k-3). 16.99 (978-0-06-168974-1(2)) HarperCollins Pubs.

Bergen, Lara Rice & Bergen, Lara. Dora's Sleepover. Miller, Victoria, illus. 2006. (Dora the Explorer Ser.: 12). (ENG.). 24p. (J). (gr. -1-1). pap. 3.99 (978-1-4169-1508-9(7), Simon Spotlight/Nickelodeon) Simon Spotlight/Nickelodeon.

Butler, Dori Hillestad. The Case of the Library Monster. Tugeau, Jeremy & Crisp, Dan, illus. 2012. (Buddy Files Ser.: 5). (ENG.). 128p. (J). (gr. 1-5). pap. 5.99 (978-0-8075-0936-4(1)) Whitman, Albert & Co.

—The Case of the School Ghost. 2013. (Buddy Files Ser.: 6). lib. bdg. 16.00 (978-0-606-31843-3(7), Turtleback) Turtleback Bks.

—The Case of the School Ghost. Tugeau, Jeremy, illus. (Buddy Files Ser.: 6). (ENG.). (J). (gr. 1-5). 2012. 128p. 14.99 (978-0-8075-0915-9(9))Bk. 6. 2013. 144p. pap. 5.99 (978-0-8075-0937-1(X)) Whitman, Albert & Co.

Capucilli, Alyssa Satin. Biscuit's First Sleepover. Schories, Pat & Berlin, Rose Mary, illus. 2008. (Biscuit Ser.). (ENG.). 24p. (J). (gr. -1-1). pap. 3.99 (978-0-06-112842-4(2), HarperFestival) HarperCollins Pubs.

Carnesi, Mônica. Sleepover with Beatrice & Bear. Carnesi, Mônica, illus. 2014. (ENG., Illus.). 32p. (J). (gr. -1-k). 15.99 (978-0-399-25667-7(9), Nancy Paulsen Books) Penguin Young Readers Group.

Carroll, Jody. Mitsy Morgan: Six Monkeys Past Midnight. 2010. 44p. pap. 18.75 (978-1-4520-0796-0(9)) AuthorHouse.

Castor, Harriet. Dance Off. 2009. (Sleepover Club Ser.). (ENG.). 144p. (J). (gr. 2-6). pap. 6.99 (978-0-00-726492-6(5)) HarperCollins Pubs. Ltd. GBR. Dist: Independent Pubs. Group.

—Hit the Beach! 2010. (Sleepover Club Ser.). (ENG.). 128p. (J). (gr. 2-6). pap. 6.99 (978-0-00-727256-3(1), HarperCollins Children's Bks.) HarperCollins Pubs. Ltd. GBR. Dist: HarperCollins Pubs.

Churchman, John & Churchman, Jennifer. The SheepOver. (Sweet Pea & Friends Ser.). (ENG., Illus.). (J). (gr. -1 — 1). 2017. 24p. bds. 7.99 (978-0-316-27355-8(4)) 2015. 36p. 17.99 (978-0-316-27356-5(2)) Little, Brown Bks. for Young Readers.

Cousins, Lucy. Maisy Goes on a Sleepover. Cousins, Lucy, illus. 2016. (Maisy Ser.). (ENG., Illus.). 32p. (J). (gr. -1-2). 6.99 *(978-0-7636-8947-6(5))* Candlewick Pr.
—Maisy Goes on a Sleepover. Cousins, Lucy, illus. 2016. (Maisy First Experiences Ser.). (ENG., Illus.). 32p. (gr. -1-2). 17.20 *(978-0-606-39089-7(8))* Turtleback Bks.
Coven, Wanda. Heidi Heckelbeck Might Be Afraid of the Dark. Burris, Priscilla, illus. 2015. (Heidi Heckelbeck Ser.: 15). (ENG.). 128p. (J). (gr. k-4). pap. 5.99 *(978-1-4814-4627-3(4),* Little Simon) Little Simon.
Cummings, Fiona. TV Stars! 2011. (Sleepover Club Ser.). (ENG.). 144p. (J). (gr. 2-6). pap. 7.99 *(978-0-00-726493-3(3))* HarperCollins Pubs. Ltd. GBR. Dist: HarperCollins Pubs.
Dean, James. Pete the Cat's Train Trip. 2015. (Pete the Cat I Can Read Ser.). (J). lib. bdg. 13.55 *(978-0-606-36967-1(8))* Turtleback Bks.
Dean, James & Dean, Kimberly. Pete the Cat & the Bedtime Blues. Dean, James, illus. 2015. (Pete the Cat Ser.). (Illus.). 40p. (J). (gr. -1-3). (ENG.). 17.99 *(978-0-06-230430-8(5));* lib. bdg. 18.89 *(978-0-06-230431-5(3))* HarperCollins Pubs.
Denton, P. J. Girls Against Boys. Denos, Julia, illus. 2013. (Sleepover Squad Ser.: 7). (ENG.). 96p. (J). (gr. 1-4). pap. 4.99 *(978-1-4169-5933-5(5),* Simon & Schuster/Paula Wiseman Bks.) Simon & Schuster/Paula Wiseman Bks.
Dewdney, Anna & Wells, Rosemary. Llama Llama Gram & Grandpa. 2015. (Llama Llama Ser.). (ENG., Illus.). 40p. (J). (-k). bds. 17.99 *(978-0-670-01396-8(X),* Viking Books for Young Readers) Penguin Young Readers Group.
Edwards, Helen L. Clara's Imagination. Doggett, Al, illus. 2005. 19.95 *(978-0-9765414-0-0(8))* Bad Publishing.
Edwards, Pamela Duncan. Dinosaur Sleepover. Allwright, Deborah, illus. 2013. (J). *(978-1-4351-4923-6(8))* Barnes & Noble, Inc.
Epstein, Robin. Choose or Lose: How to Pick a Winner. 2005. (Groovy Girls Sleepover Club Ser.: Vol. 5). 60p. (J). *(978-0-439-65793-8(8))* Scholastic, Inc.
—Pranks a Lot: The Girls vs. the Boys. 2005. (Groovy Girls Sleepover Club Ser.: Vol. 2). (Illus.). 58p. (J). pap. *(978-0-439-65790-7(3))* Scholastic, Inc.
Fox, Jennifer. Teen Titans Go! - Boys Versus Girls. 2015. (Passport to Reading Level 2 Ser.). (ENG., Illus.). 32p. (J). (gr. -1-3). pap. 4.99 *(978-0-316-37727-0(9))* Little, Brown Bks. for Young Readers.
Friedman, Laurie. Mallory's Super Sleepover. Kalis, Jennifer, illus. (Mallory Ser.: 16). (ENG.). 160p. (J). (gr. 2-5). 2012. pap. 5.95 *(978-1-4677-0209-6(9))*No. 16. 2011. 15.95 *(978-0-8225-8887-0(0))* Lerner Publishing Group. (Darby Creek).
Fruchter, Jason, illus. Daniel's First Sleepover. 2015. (Daniel Tiger's Neighborhood Ser.). (ENG.). 24p. (J). (gr. -1-2). pap. 3.99 *(978-1-4814-2893-4(4),* Simon Spotlight) Simon Spotlight.
Galante, Cecilia. Be Brave, Willa Bean! Valiant, Kristi, illus. 2011. (Little Wings Ser.: 2). (ENG.). 112p. (J). (gr. 1-4). 4.99 *(978-0-375-86948-8(4),* Random Hse. Bks. for Young Readers) Random Hse. Children's Bks.
Gianferrari, Maria. Slumber under the Stars. Heder, Thyra, illus. 2016. (Penny & Jelly Ser.). (ENG.). 32p. (J). (gr. -1-3). 16.99 *(978-0-544-28005-2(9),* HMH Books For Young Readers) Houghton Mifflin Harcourt Publishing Co.
Giglio, Judy. The Tapping Tale. Cepeda, Joe, illus. 2003. (Green Light Readers Level 1 Ser.). (ENG.). 24p. (J). (gr. -1-3). pap. 3.95 *(978-0-15-204852-5(9))* Houghton Mifflin Harcourt Publishing Co.
Greve, Meg. A Tricky Sleepover. 2015. (ENG.). 48p. (gr. k-3). 27.07 *(978-1-63430-368-2(7))* Rourke Educational Media.
Grosset and Dunlap Staff & Child, Lauren. I Slightly Want to Go Home. 2011. (Charlie & Lola Ser.). (ENG.). 24p. (J). (gr. k-3). mass mkt. 3.99 *(978-0-448-45461-0(0),* Grosset & Dunlap) Penguin Young Readers Group.
Guest, Elissa Haden. Iris & Walter, the Sleepover. Davenier, Christine, illus. 2006. (Iris & Walter Ser.). 44p. (gr. 1-4). 15.95 *(978-0-7569-6681-2(7))* Perfection Learning Corp.
—Iris & Walter: the Sleepover. Davenier, Christine, illus. alt. ed. 2012. (Green Light Readers Level 3 Ser.). (ENG.). 44p. (J). (gr. 1-4). pap. 3.99 *(978-0-547-74556-5(7))* Houghton Mifflin Harcourt Publishing Co.
—The Sleepover. 2012. (Iris & Walter — Green Light Reader Ser.). lib. bdg. 13.55 *(978-0-606-24266-0(X),* Turtleback) Turtleback Bks.
Haave, Meghan. Christopher's Night at Grandma & Grandpa's. 2012. 32p. (J). 9.95 *(978-1-59530-458-2(4))* Hallmark Card, Inc.
Hale, Bruce. Afraid of the Dark. Francis, Guy, illus. 2015. (Clark the Shark Ser.). (ENG.). 32p. (J). (gr. -1-3). 17.99 *(978-0-06-237450-9(8))* HarperCollins Pubs.
—Clark the Shark. 2016. (Clark the Shark: I Can Read Level 1 Ser.). (J). lib. bdg. 13.55 *(978-0-606-38774-3(9))* Turtleback Bks.
Harper, Charise Mericle. Just Grace & the Super Sleepover. 2014. (Just Grace Ser.: 11). (ENG., Illus.). 208p. (J). (gr. 1-4). 15.99 *(978-0-544-04584-2(X))* Houghton Mifflin Harcourt Publishing Co.
HarperCollins Publishers Ltd. Staff. A My Little Pony. 2003. 115.84 *(978-0-06-056197-0(1))* HarperCollins Pubs.
Hartley, Susan. Jake's Sleepover. 2011. (Early Connections Ser.). (J). *(978-1-61672-583-9(4))* Benchmark Education Co.
—Jake's Sleepover: Set Of 6. 2011. (Early Connections Ser.). (J). pap. 37.00 net. *(978-1-4108-1090-8(9))* Benchmark Education Co.
Hopkins, Cathy. Besties: Mates, Dates, & Sleepover Secrets; Mates, Dates, & Sole Survivors; Mates, Dates, & Mad Mistakes. 2009. (Mates, Dates Ser.). (ENG.). 576p. (YA). (gr. 7). pap. 8.99 *(978-1-4169-7837-4(2),* Simon Pulse) Simon Pulse.
—Mates, Dates, & Sleepover Secrets. 2010. (Mates, Dates Ser.). (ENG.). 208p. (YA). (gr. 7). pap. 10.99 *(978-1-4424-1421-1(9),* Simon Pulse) Simon Pulse.
Hunter, Jana. Trick or Treat. 2010. (Sleepover Club Ser.). (ENG., Illus.). 112p. (J). (gr. 2-6). pap. 6.99 *(978-0-00-727254-9(5),* HarperCollins Children's Bks.) HarperCollins Pubs. Ltd. GBR. Dist: HarperCollins Pubs.
Impey, Rose. Best Friends! 2008. (Sleepover Club Ser.). (ENG., Illus.). 128p. (J). (gr. 2-6). pap. 6.99 *(978-0-00-726494-0(1),* HarperCollins Children's Bks.) HarperCollins Pubs. Ltd. GBR. Dist: HarperCollins Pubs.
Jakubowski, Michele. Sleepover. 2017. (Ashley Small & Ashlee Tall Ser.). (ENG., Illus.). 64p. (gr. 1-3). pap. 4.95 *(978-1-5158-0015-6(6))* Capstone Press of Coughlan Cos.
—Sleepover. 2016. (Ashley Small & Ashlee Tall Ser.). (ENG., Illus.). 64p. (gr. 1-3). lib. bdg. 20.65 *(978-1-5158-0011-8(3))* Picture Window Bks.
Jones, Jen. Ashley Goes Viral. Franco, Paula, illus. 2015. (Sleepover Girls Ser.). (ENG.). 128p. (gr. 3-5). pap. 6.95 *(978-1-62370-306-6(9))* Stone Arch Bks.
—Delaney vs. the Bully. Franco, Paula, illus. 2015. (Sleepover Girls Ser.). (ENG.). 128p. (gr. 3-5). lib. bdg. 22.65 *(978-1-4965-0541-5(7))* Stone Arch Bks.
—Maren's New Family. Franco, Paula, illus. 2015. (Sleepover Girls Ser.). (ENG.). 128p. (gr. 3-5). lib. bdg. 22.65 *(978-1-4965-0540-8(9))* Stone Arch Bks.
—Sleepover Girls. Franco, Paula, illus. 2014. (Sleepover Girls Ser.). (ENG.). 128p. (gr. 3-5). 90.60 *(978-1-4965-0316-9(3))* Stone Arch Bks.
—Willow's: Spring Break Adventure. Franco, Paula, illus. 2015. (Sleepover Girls Ser.). (ENG.). 128p. (gr. 3-5). pap. 6.95 *(978-1-62370-305-9(0))* Stone Arch Bks.
Joyner, Andrew. Boris Sees the Light. 2013. (Boris Ser.: 4). (ENG.). 80p. (J). (gr. k-2). pap. 4.99 *(978-0-545-48454-1(5))* Scholastic, Inc.
Kann, Victoria. The Princess of Pink Slumber Party. Kann, Victoria, illus. 2012. (I Can Read Level 1 Ser.). (ENG., Illus.). 32p. (J). (gr. -1-3). 16.99 *(978-0-06-198963-6(0))* HarperCollins Pubs.
—The Princess of Pink Slumber Party. 2012. (Pinkalicious I Can Read Ser.). (J). lib. bdg. 13.55 *(978-0-606-23581-5(7),* Turtleback) Turtleback Bks.
Katz, Karen. Princess Baby on the Go. Katz, Karen, illus. 2010. (Princess Baby Ser.). (ENG., Illus.). 14p. (J). (— 1). 7.99 *(978-0-375-85664-8(1),* Schwartz & Wade Bks.) Random Hse. Children's Bks.
Keene, Carolyn. The Nancy Drew & the Clue Crew Collection: Sleepover Sleuths; Scream for Ice Cream; Pony Problems; the Cinderella Ballet Mystery; Case of the Sneaky Snowman. Pamintuan, Macky, illus. 2014. (Nancy Drew & the Clue Crew Ser.). (ENG.). 480p. (J). (gr. 1-4). pap. 29.99 *(978-1-4814-1472-2(0),* Aladdin) Simon & Schuster Children's Publishing.
—Sleepover Sleuths. Pamintuan, Macky, illus. 2006. (Nancy Drew & the Clue Crew Ser.: 1). (ENG.). 96p. (J). (gr. 1-4). pap. 5.99 *(978-1-4169-1255-2(X),* Aladdin) Simon & Schuster Children's Publishing.
—Sleepover Sleuths, 1 vol. Pamintuan, Macky, illus. 2007. (Nancy Drew & the Clue Crew Ser.). (ENG.). 81p. (gr. 1-4). 24.21 *(978-1-59961-348-2(4))* Spotlight.
Kellie, Kerrie. The Sleep over Adventure. 2011. 20p. pap. 24.95 *(978-1-4560-6884-4(9))* America Star Bks.
Klein, Adria F. Max Se Queda a Dormir, 1 vol. Robledo, Sol, tr. from ENG. Gallagher-Cole, Mernie, illus. 2007. (Read-It! Readers en Español: la Vida de Max Ser.). (SPA.). 24p. (gr. -1-3). lib. bdg. 21.32 *(978-1-4048-3797-3(3),* Easy Readers) Picture Window Bks.
London, Jonathan. Froggy's Sleepover. Remkiewicz, Frank, illus. 2007. (Froggy Ser.). (ENG.). 32p. (J). (gr. -1-k). pap. 6.99 *(978-0-14-240750-9(X),* Puffin Books) Penguin Young Readers Group.
Long, Kathy. Christopher SAT Straight up in Bed. Cantor, Patricia, illus. 2013. (ENG.). 40p. (J). 16.00 *(978-0-8028-5359-2(5),* Eerdmans Bks For Young Readers) Eerdmans, William B. Publishing Co.
Lozano, Neal. Can God See Me in the Dark? Hatke, Ben, illus. 2007. (ENG.). 32p. (J). 16.95 *(978-1-883551-45-2(5),* Maple Corners Press) Attic Studio Publishing Hse.
MacDonald, Anne Louise. The Memory Stone, 1 vol. Ouellet, Joanne, illus. 2003. (ENG.). 24p. (J). (gr. -1-2). 7.95 *(978-1-55109-442-7(8))* Nimbus Publishing, Ltd. CAN. Dist: Orca Bk. Pubs. USA.
Maed, Mary Ann Graziani. Filled to Capacity. 2008. 56p. pap. 24.50 *(978-0-615-16077-1(8))* Wishing Star Children's Bks.
Malone, Jen. The Sleepover. (Mix Ser.). (ENG., Illus.). (J). (gr. 4-8). 2017. 256p. pap. 7.99 ***(978-1-4814-5260-1(6))*** 2016. 240p. 16.99 *(978-1-4814-5261-8(4))* Simon & Schuster Children's Publishing. (Aladdin).
Man-Kong, Mary. Sleepover Fun! 2014. (Pictureback(R) Ser.). (ENG., Illus.). 16p. (J). (gr. -1-2). 4.99 *(978-0-385-38478-0(5),* Random Hse. Bks. for Young Readers) Random Hse. Children's Bks.
Mann, Jennifer Ann. Sunny Sweet Is So Not Scary. 2015. (Sunny Sweet Ser.). (ENG.). 192p. (YA). (gr. 3-6). 15.99 *(978-1-61963-507-4(0),* 9781619635074, Bloomsbury USA Childrens) Bloomsbury Publishing USA.
Manning, Jane. Millie Fierce Sleeps Out. Manning, Jane, illus. 2014. (Millie Fierce Ser.). (ENG., Illus.). 32p. (J). (gr. -1-2). 16.99 *(978-0-399-16093-6(0),* Philomel Bks.) Penguin Young Readers Group.
Manushkin, Fran. Katie's Spooky Sleepover. Lyon, Tammie, illus. 2016. (Katie Woo Ser.). (ENG.). 32p. (gr. k-2). lib. bdg. 21.32 *(978-1-4795-9640-9(X))* Picture Window Bks.
—A Nervous Night, 1 vol. Lyon, Tammie, illus. 2010. (Katie Woo Ser.). (ENG.). 32p. (gr. k-2). pap. 5.95 *(978-1-4048-6060-5(6));* lib. bdg. 21.32 *(978-1-4048-5725-4(7))* Picture Window Bks.
Mattel. Ever after High - Sleepover Spellebration Party Planner. 2014. (Ever after High Ser.). (ENG., Illus.). 48p. (J). (gr. 3-7). 9.99 *(978-0-316-28359-5(2))* Little, Brown Bks. for Young Readers.
McDonald, Megan. Stink & the Shark Sleepover. Reynolds, Peter H., illus. (Stink Ser.: 9). (ENG.). 176p. (J). (gr. 1-4). 2014. 12.99 *(978-0-7636-6474-9(X))*Bk. 9. 2015. pap. 4.99 *(978-0-7636-7678-0(0))* Candlewick Pr.
—Stink & the Shark Sleepover. 2015. (Stink Ser.: 9). lib. bdg. 14.75 *(978-0-606-36859-9(0))* Turtleback Bks.
McDonnell, Patrick. Thank You & Good Night. 2015. (ENG., Illus.). 40p. (J). (gr. -1-3). 15.99 *(978-0-316-33801-1(X))* Little Brown & Co.
McPhail, David. The Blue Door. Ellis, Sarah, ed. O'Connor, John, illus. 2003. (ENG.). 32p. pap. *(978-1-55041-802-6(5))* Fitzhenry & Whiteside, Ltd.
Mcveigh, Mark. Hello Kitty's Superterrific Sleepover! (Hello Kitty) Hino, Sachiho, illus. 2017. (Hello Kitty Ser.). (ENG.). 32p. (J). (gr. k-2). pap. 3.99 *(978-1-338-11363-1(1))* Scholastic, Inc.
Meddaugh, Susan. Campfire Stories. 2013. (Martha Speaks Ser.). (ENG., Illus.). 96p. (J). (gr. 1-4). pap. 5.99 *(978-0-547-97021-9(8))* Houghton Mifflin Harcourt Publishing Co.
—Martha Speaks: Campfire Stories (Chapter Book) 2013. (Martha Speaks Ser.). (ENG., Illus.). 96p. (J). (gr. 1-4). 14.99 *(978-0-547-97024-0(2))* Houghton Mifflin Harcourt Publishing Co.
Melling, David. Hugless Douglas & the Big Sleepover. 2013. (ENG., Illus.). 32p. (J). *(978-1-58925-116-8(4))* Tiger Tales.
Morrissey, Dean & Krensky, Stephen. The Monster Trap. Morrissey, Dean, illus. 2004. (Illus.). 40p. (J). lib. bdg. 17.89 *(978-0-06-052499-9(5))* HarperCollins Pubs.
Mullins, Julie. The Sleepover. Foye, Lloyd, illus. 2005. (Girlz Rock! Ser.). (J). pap. *(978-1-59336-707-7(4))* Mondo Publishing.
Nickelodeon. Shimmer & Shine - Sleepover Wishes. 2016. (ENG.). 10p. (J). (gr. -1-2). bds. 9.99 *(978-0-7944-3827-2(X))* Studio Fun International.
Night, P. J. Best Friends Forever. 2012. (You're Invited to a Creepover Ser.: 6). (ENG.). 160p. (J). (gr. 3-7). pap. 6.99 *(978-1-4424-4150-7(X),* Simon Spotlight) Simon Spotlight.
—Best Friends Forever. 2012. (Creepover Ser.: 6). lib. bdg. 17.20 *(978-0-606-26336-8(5),* Turtleback) Turtleback Bks.
—Is She for Real? 2012. (You're Invited to a Creepover Ser.: 7). (ENG.). 160p. (J). (gr. 3-7). pap. 6.99 *(978-1-4424-5056-1(8),* Simon Spotlight) Simon Spotlight.
—Is She for Real? 2012. (Creepover Ser.: 7). lib. bdg. 17.20 *(978-0-606-26340-5(3),* Turtleback) Turtleback Bks.
—Ready for a Scare?, 1 vol. 2013. (You're Invited to a Creepover Ser.). (ENG.). 160p. (J). (gr. 3-6). lib. bdg. 24.21 *(978-1-61479-062-4(0),* Essential Library) ABDO Publishing Co.
—Ready for a Scare? 2011. (You're Invited to a Creepover Ser.: 3). (ENG.). 160p. (J). (gr. 3-7). pap. 6.99 *(978-1-4424-2903-1(8),* Simon Spotlight) Simon Spotlight.
—Ready for a Scare? 2011. (Creepover Ser.: 3). lib. bdg. 17.20 *(978-0-606-23747-5(X),* Turtleback) Turtleback Bks.
—The Show Must Go On! 2011. (You're Invited to a Creepover Ser.: 4). (ENG.). 160p. (J). (gr. 3-7). pap. 6.99 *(978-1-4424-2905-5(4),* Simon Spotlight) Simon Spotlight.
—The Show Must Go On! 2011. (Creepover Ser.: 4). lib. bdg. 16.00 *(978-0-606-23748-2(8),* Turtleback) Turtleback Bks.
—There's Something Out There, 1 vol. 2013. (You're Invited to a Creepover Ser.). (ENG.). 160p. (J). (gr. 3-6). lib. bdg. 24.21 *(978-1-61479-064-8(7),* Essential Library) ABDO Publishing Co.
—There's Something Out There. 2011. (You're Invited to a Creepover Ser.: 5). (ENG.). 160p. (J). (gr. 3-7). pap. 6.99 *(978-1-4424-4148-4(8),* Simon Spotlight) Simon Spotlight.
O'Connor, Jane. Saturday Night Sleepover. Glasser, Robin Preiss, illus. 2016. (Fancy Nancy Ser.). 32p. (J). (gr. -1-3). 17.99 *(978-0-06-226985-0(2))* HarperCollins Pubs.
Oram, Hiawyn. My Unwilling Witch Goes to Ballet School. Warburton, Sarah, illus. 2009. (Rumblewick's Diary Ser.: 1). (ENG.). 112p. (J). (gr. 1-4). 7.99 *(978-0-316-03472-2(X))* Little, Brown Bks. for Young Readers.
Orme, Helen. Sleepover. 2008. (Siti's Sisters Ser.). (ENG., Illus.). 36p. pap. *(978-1-84167-741-5(8))* Ransom Publishing Ltd.
Pace, Anne Marie. Vampirina Ballerina Hosts a Sleepover. Pham, LeUyen, illus. 2013. (Vampirina Ser.). (ENG.). 40p. (J). (gr. -1-k). 16.99 *(978-1-4231-7570-4(0))* Hyperion Pr.
Parish, Herman. Amelia Bedelia Sleeps Over. Avril, Lynne, illus. 2012. (I Can Read Level 1 Ser.). (ENG.). 32p. (J). (gr. -1-3). 16.99 *(978-0-06-209524-4(2));* pap. 3.99 *(978-0-06-209523-7(4))* HarperCollins Pubs. (Greenwillow Bks.).
—Amelia Bedelia Sleeps Over. 2012. (Amelia Bedelia: I Can Read! Ser.). (J). lib. bdg. 13.55 *(978-0-606-26849-3(9),* Turtleback) Turtleback Bks.
Penn, Audrey. Chester Raccoon & the Almost Perfect Sleepover. Gibson, Barbara Leonard, illus. 2017. (Kissing Hand Ser.). (ENG.). 32p. (J). (gr. -1-3). 16.95 *(978-1-939100-11-5(9))* Tanglewood Pr.
Perl, Erica S. Aces Wild. (ENG.). 224p. (J). (gr. 3-7). 2015. 7.99 *(978-0-307-93173-3(0),* Yearling) 2013. 15.99 *(978-0-307-93172-6(2),* Knopf Bks. for Young Readers) Random Hse. Children's Bks.
Peschke, Marci. Party Queen, 1 vol. Mourning, Tuesday, illus. 2013. (Kylie Jean Ser.). (ENG.). 112p. (gr. 2-3). lib. bdg. 22.65 *(978-1-4048-7582-1(4),* Kylie Jean) Picture Window Bks.
Pinkwater, Daniel. Sleepover Larry, 0 vols. 2013. (ENG.). 34p. (J). (gr. -1-3). pap. 9.99 *(978-1-4778-4765-7(0),* 9781477847657, Amazon Children's Publishing) Amazon Publishing.
Pinkwater, Daniel M. Sleepover Larry. 2007. (Illus.). 32p. 16.99 *(978-0-7614-5335-2(0))* Marshall Cavendish Corp.
Punter, Russell. Llamas in Pajamas. 2015. (Phonics Readers (no Flaps) Ser.). (ENG.). 24p. (J). pap. 6.99 *(978-0-7945-2739-6(6),* Usborne) EDC Publishing.
Quin-Harkin, Janet. Sleepover Madness. 2014. (Tgif Ser.: 1). (ENG., Illus.). 128p. (J). (gr. 3-7). pap. 13.99 *(978-1-4814-2879-8(9),* Simon & Schuster/Paula Wiseman Bks.) Simon & Schuster/Paula Wiseman Bks.
Regan, Dian. The Snow Blew Inn. Cushman, Doug, illus. 2011. (ENG.). 32p. (J). 16.95 *(978-0-8234-2351-4(4))* Holiday Hse., Inc.
Reuterstrand, Siri. Ellis Is Scared of the Dark. Wik, Jenny, illus. 2012. (ENG.). 24p. (J). (gr. -1-k). 12.95 *(978-1-61608-667-1(X),* 608667, Sky Pony Pr.) Skyhorse Publishing Co., Inc.
Rey, H. A. Curious George & the Sleepover. 2017. (Curious George Ser.). (ENG., Illus.). 24p. (J). (gr. -1-3). 14.99 *(978-0-544-76346-3(7),* HMH Books For Young Readers) Houghton Mifflin Harcourt Publishing Co.
Rippin, Sally. The Worst Sleepover: Hey Jack! Spartels, Stephanie, illus. 2014. (ENG.). 48p. (J). pap. 4.99 *(978-1-61067-185-9(6))* Kane Miller.
Ruelle, Karen Gray. Easy As Apple Pie: A Harry & Emily Adventure. 2003. (Holiday House Readers Ser.). (ENG., Illus.). 32p. (J). (gr. k-3). 4.95 *(978-0-8234-1800-8(6))* Holiday Hse., Inc.
Russo, Marisabina. Sophie Sleeps Over. Russo, Marisabina, illus. 2014. (ENG., Illus.). 32p. (J). (gr. -1-2). 16.99 *(978-1-59643-933-7(5),* 9781596439337) Roaring Brook Pr.
Rylant, Cynthia. Annie & Snowball & the Grandmother Night. Stevenson, Suçie, illus. (Annie & Snowball Ser.: 12). (ENG.). 40p. (J). (gr. k-2). 2013. pap. 3.99 *(978-1-4169-7204-4(8))* 2012. 16.99 *(978-1-4169-7203-7(X))* Simon Spotlight. (Simon Spotlight).
—Annie & Snowball & the Grandmother Night. 2013. (Annie & Snowball Ready-To-Read Ser.). lib. bdg. 13.55 *(978-0-606-35183-6(3))* Turtleback Bks.
—Henry & Mudge & the Big Sleepover. Stevenson, Suçie, illus. 2007. (Henry & Mudge Ser.). 40p. (gr. k-2). lib. bdg. 14.00 *(978-0-7569-8117-4(4))* Perfection Learning Corp.
—Henry & Mudge & the Big Sleepover. Stevenson, Suçie & Stevenson, Suçie, illus. 2006. (Henry & Mudge Ser.: 28). (ENG.). 40p. (J). (gr. k-2). 16.99 *(978-0-689-81171-5(3),* Simon Spotlight) Simon Spotlight.
—Henry & Mudge & the Big Sleepover, Bk. 28. Stevenson, Suçie, illus. 2007. (Henry & Mudge Ser.: 28). (ENG.). 40p. (J). (gr. k-2). pap. 3.99 *(978-0-689-83451-6(9),* Simon Spotlight) Simon Spotlight.
—Henry & Mudge & the Big Sleepover. Stevenson, Suçie, illus. 2007. (Henry & Mudge Ready-To-Read Ser.: 28). 40p. (gr. -1-3). lib. bdg. 13.55 *(978-1-4177-8140-9(8),* Turtleback) Turtleback Bks.
Santomero, Angela C. Daniel's First Sleepover. 2015. (Daniel Tiger's Neighborhood 8X8 Ser.). lib. bdg. 13.55 *(978-0-606-36315-0(7))* Turtleback Bks.
Scholastic Editors. La Primera Fiesta de Pijamas de Peppa (Peppa's First Sleepover) 2016. (Peppa Pig 8X8 Ser.). (ENG & SPA., Illus.). 24p. (J). (gr. -1-k). 13.55 *(978-0-606-39159-7(2))* Turtleback Bks.
Scholastic, Inc. Staff. Peppa's First Sleepover. Eone, François René, illus. 2014. (Peppa Pig Ser.). (ENG.). 24p. (J). (gr. -1-k). pap. 3.99 *(978-0-545-69093-5(5))* Scholastic, Inc.
Scholastic, Inc. Staff & Ladybird Books Staff. Peppa's First Sleepover. 2014. (Peppa Pig 8X8 Ser.). lib. bdg. 13.55 *(978-0-606-36374-7(2))* Turtleback Bks.
Sesame Street Staff & Studio Mouse Staff. Learning Fun. 2008. (ENG.). 60p. (J). 4.99 *(978-1-59069-671-2(9))* Studio Mouse LLC.
Sheinmel, Courtney. Scaredy Cat. Bell, Jennifer A., illus. 2016. (Stella Batts Ser.). (ENG.). 160p. (J). (gr. 1-3). 9.99 *(978-1-58536-919-5(5),* 204026) Sleeping Bear Pr.
Siamon, Sharon. Haunted Hotel Sleepover, Bk. 3. (Illus.). 152p. (J). pap. 8.99 *(978-0-340-67278-5(1))* Hodder & Stoughton GBR. Dist: Trafalgar Square Publishing.
—Lost Attic, Bk. 6. (Illus.). 137p. (J). pap. 8.99 *(978-0-340-70905-4(7))* Hodder & Stoughton GBR. Dist: Trafalgar Square Publishing.
—Sleepover: Secret Room. (Illus.). 137p. (J). pap. *(978-0-340-67276-1(5))* Hodder & Stoughton.
Sleepover Girls, 4 vols. 2015. (Sleepover Girls Ser.). (ENG.). 128p. (gr. 3-5). 90.60 *(978-1-4965-2022-7(X));* 181.20 *(978-1-4965-2023-4(8))* Stone Arch Bks.
Spinner, Stephanie. It Came from Outer Space. Gott, Barry, illus. 2003. (Science Solves It! Ser.). 32p. (J). pap. 5.95 *(978-1-57565-122-4(X))* Kane Press, Inc.
Stanek, Robert, pseud. The Bugville Critters Have a Sleepover. 2008. (ENG.). 28p. (J). per. 9.99 *(978-1-57545-146-6(8))* RP Media.
—Have a Sleepover. 2008. (ENG., Illus.). 28p. (J). pap. 5.29 *(978-1-57545-189-3(1))* RP Media.
Stierle, Cynthia. Diego in the Dark: Being Brave at Night. Maher, Alex, illus. 2008. (Go, Diego, Go! Ser.). (ENG.). 16p. (J). (gr. -1-2). pap. 6.99 *(978-1-4169-5935-9(1),* Simon Spotlight/Nickelodeon) Simon Spotlight/Nickelodeon.
Thaler, Mike. New Year's Eve Sleepover from the Black Lagoon, 1 vol. 2014. (Black Lagoon Adventures Set 3 Ser.). (ENG.). 64p. (J). (gr. 3-6). lib. bdg. 24.21 *(978-1-61479-204-8(6))* Spotlight.
Tillworth, Mary. Wish upon a Sleepover (Shimmer & Shine) Hee, Liana, illus. 2016. (Little Golden Book Ser.). (ENG.). 24p. (J). (gr. -1-2). 4.99 *(978-1-101-93672-6(X),* Golden Bks.) Random Hse. Children's Bks.
Ventura, Marne. Edgy Estella Aces the Sleepover Party. Trinidad, Leo, illus. 2016. (Worry Warriors Ser.). (ENG.). 96p. (gr. 2-4). lib. bdg. 25.99 *(978-1-4965-3610-5(X))* Stone Arch Bks.
Viselman, Kenn. The Surprise. 2003. 32p. pap. 3.99 *(978-0-06-054839-1(8),* Harper Entertainment) HarperCollins Pubs.
Waber, Bernard. Quique Duerme Fuera de Casa. Mlawer, Teresa, tr. 2003. (SPA., Illus.). (J). (gr. k-2). pap. *(978-968-6579-15-4(X),* SI6510) Sistemas Tecnicos de Edicion, S.A. de C.V. MEX. Dist: Lectorum Pubns., Inc.
Wallace, Nancy K. The Haunted Sleepover, 1 vol. Chronister, Amanda, illus. 2013. (Abby & the Book Bunch Ser.). (ENG.). 80p. (J). (gr. 2-5). 27.07 *(978-1-61641-913-4(X))* Magic Wagon.
White, Kathryn. Ruby's Sleepover. Latimer, Miriam, illus. 2012. (ENG.). 32p. (J). 16.99 *(978-1-84686-593-0(X))* Barefoot Bks., Inc.
Willems, Mo. Time to Sleep, Sheep the Sheep! Willems, Mo, illus. 2010. (Illus.). 32p. (J). (gr. -1-3). (ENG.). 10.99 *(978-0-06-172847-1(0));* lib. bdg. 14.89 *(978-0-06-172848-8(9))* HarperCollins Pubs.
Winthrop, Elizabeth. Squashed in the Middle. Cummins, Pat, illus. 2008. (J). (gr. k-4). 25.95 incl. audio *(978-1-4301-0440-7(6));* 28.95 incl. audio compact disk *(978-1-4301-0443-8(0))* Live Oak Media.

SLEIGHT OF HAND

see Magic

SLESSOR, MARY MITCHELL, 1848-1915

Jay, Ruth Johnson. Mary Slessor: Missionary to Calabar. 2006. (Illus.). 143p. (J). *(978-1-56265-077-3(7))* Accelarated Christian Education, Inc.
Kelly, Terri B. Mary Slessor: Missionary Mother. 2014. (Illus.). 164p. (J). *(978-1-60682-630-0(1))* BJU Pr.

SLOTHS

Bader, Bonnie. Slow, Slow Sloths. 2016. (Penguin Young Readers, Level 2 Ser.). (ENG., Illus.). 32p. (J). (gr. 1-2). pap. 3.99 *(978-0-399-54116-2(0),* Penguin Young Readers) Penguin Young Readers Group.
Bell, Samantha. Sloths Are Awesome. 2018. (ENG.). 32p. (gr. 3-6). 31.35 ***(978-1-63235-439-6(X),*** 12-Story Library) Pr. Room Editions LLC.

S

Borgert-Spaniol, Megan. Sloths. 2015. (Animal Safari Ser.). (ENG., Illus.). 24p. (J). (gr. k-3). lib. bdg. 25.95 (978-1-62617-214-2(5), Blastoff! Readers) Bellwether Media.

Clark, Willow. Three-Toed Sloths. 2012. (Up a Tree Ser.). (ENG., Illus.). 24p. (J). (gr. k-3). lib. bdg. 22.60 (978-1-4488-6186-6(1)); pap. 8.25 (978-1-4488-6331-0(7), PowerKids Pr.) Rosen Publishing Group, Inc., The.

Cooke, Lucy. A Little Book of Sloth. Cooke, Lucy, photos by. 2013. (ENG., Illus.). 64p. (J). (gr. k). 17.99 (978-1-4424-4557-4(2), McElderry, Margaret K. Bks.) McElderry, Margaret K. Bks.

Frisch, Joy. Ground Sloths. 2015. (Ice Age Animals Ser.). (ENG.). 24p. (gr. k-1). pap. 6.95 (978-1-4914-2319-6(6), Pebble Plus) Capstone Press of Coughlan Cos.

Gish, Melissa. Sloths. (Living Wild Ser.). (Illus.). (J). 2017. (ENG.). 48p. (gr. 4-7). pap. 12.00 (978-1-62832-305-4(1), Creative Paperbacks) 2016. 46p. (978-1-60818-709-6(8), Creative Education) Creative Co., The.

Goecke, Michael P. Giant Ground Sloth, 1 vol. 2003. (Prehistoric Animals Ser.). (ENG.). 24p. (gr. k-4). 25.65 (978-1-57765-968-6(6), Buddy Bks.) ABDO Publishing Co.

Gregory, Josh. Sloths. 2015. (ENG., Illus.). 48p. (J). lib. bdg. (978-0-531-21391-9(9), Orchard Bks.) Scholastic, Inc.

Guidone, Julie. Sloths. 2009. (Animals That Live in the Rain Forest Ser.). 24p. (J). (gr. -1-3). pap. 8.15 (978-1-4339-0108-9(0)); lib. bdg. 22.60 (978-1-4339-0026-6(2)) Stevens, Gareth Publishing LLLP. (Weekly Reader Leveled Readers).

—Sloths; Perezosos. 2009. (Animals That Live in the Rain Forest/Animales de la selva Ser.). (SPA & ENG.). 24p. (J). (gr. -1-3). pap. 8.15 (978-1-4339-0115-7(3)); lib. bdg. 22.60 (978-1-4339-0065-5(3)) Stevens, Gareth Publishing LLLP. (Weekly Reader Leveled Readers).

Lunis, Natalie. Three-Toed Sloths: Green Mammals. 2010. (Disappearing Acts Ser.). (Illus.). 24p. (J). (gr. k-3). lib. bdg. 22.61 (978-1-936087-42-6(1)) Bearport Publishing Co., Inc.

Lynette, Rachel. Three-Toed Sloths. 2013. (Jungle Babies of the Amazon Rain Forest Ser.). 24p. (J). (gr. -1-3). lib. bdg. 21.32 (978-1-61772-756-6(3)) Bearport Publishing Co., Inc.

McDonnell, Julia . Being a Sloth. 2013. (Can You Imagine Ser.). 32p. (gr. 2-5). pap. 10.50 (978-1-4824-3274-9(9)) Rosen Publishing Group, Inc., The.

McDonnell, Julia. Being a Sloth, Vol. 1. 2014. (Can You Imagine? Ser.). (ENG., Illus.). 32p. (J). (gr. 2-3). 25.25 (978-1-4824-0099-1(5)) Stevens, Gareth Publishing LLLP.

Miller, Sara Swan. Sloths. (Paws & Claws Ser.). 24p. 2009. (gr. 2-3). 42.50 (978-1-60851-154-9(5)) 2008. (Illus.). (J). (gr. 3-7). lib. bdg. 22.60 (978-1-4042-4166-4(3)) Rosen Publishing Group, Inc., The. (PowerKids Pr.).

Paige, Joy. The Sloth: World's Slowest Mammal. 2009. (Record-Breaking Animals Ser.). 24p. (gr. 1-1). 42.50 (978-1-60852-443-3(4), PowerKids Pr.) Rosen Publishing Group, Inc., The.

—The Sloth / el Perezoso: The World's Slowest Mammal / el mamífero más lento del Mundo. 2009. (Record-Breaking Animals / Campeones del mundo animal Ser.). (ENG & SPA.). 24p. (gr. 1-1). 42.50 (978-1-60852-449-5(3), Editorial Buenas Letras) Rosen Publishing Group, Inc., The.

—The Sloth: The World's Slowest Mammal: El Perezoso: El Mamifero Mas Lento Del Mundo. 2004. (Record-Breaking Animals / Campeones Del Mundo Animal Ser.). (SPA & ENG., Illus.). 24p. (J). (gr. 3-6). lib. bdg. 22.60 (978-0-8239-6893-0(6), Editorial Buenas Letras) Rosen Publishing Group, Inc., The.

Piehl, Janet. Let's Look at Sloths. 2010. pap. 45.32 (978-0-7613-6979-0(1)); (ENG., Illus.). 32p. pap. 7.95 (978-0-7613-6042-1(5)); (ENG., Illus.). 32p. lib. bdg. 26.60 (978-0-8225-7900-7(6), Lerner Pubns.) Lerner Publishing Group.

Rafferty, John P., ed. Rats, Bats, & Xenarthrans. 2011. (Britannica Guide to Predators & Prey Ser.). (Illus.). 256p. (YA). 103.40 (978-1-61530-456-1(8)) Rosen Publishing Group, Inc., The.

Ryndak, Rob. Sloths. 2015. (Jungle Animals Ser.). (ENG., Illus.). 24p. (J). (gr. k-k). 22.60 (978-1-4824-1760-9(X)) Stevens, Gareth Publishing LLLP.

Schuetz, Kari. Baby Sloths. 2013. (Super Cute! Ser.). (ENG., Illus.). 24p. (J). (gr. k-3). lib. bdg. 25.95 (978-1-60014-933-7(2), Blastoff! Readers) Bellwether Media.

Schuh, Mari. Sloths. 2014. (Illus.). 24p. (J). lib. bdg. 25.65 (978-1-62031-112-7(7), Bullfrog Bks.) Jump! Inc.

Schuh, Mari C. Sloths, 1 vol. 2012. (South American Animals Ser.). (ENG., Illus.). 24p. (gr. k-1). lib. bdg. 26.65 (978-1-4296-8680-8(4), Pebble Plus) Capstone Press of Coughlan Cos.

Stewart, Melissa. Sloths. 2005. (Nature Watch Ser.). (Illus.). 48p. (J). (gr. 3-7). lib. bdg. 25.26 (978-1-57505-577-0(5), Carolrhoda Bks.) Lerner Publishing Group.

Thornhill, Jan. Kyle Goes Alone. Barron, Ashley, illus. 2015. (ENG.). 32p. (J). (gr. -1-3). 17.95 (978-1-77147-075-9(5), Owlkids) Owlkids Bks. Inc. CAN. Dist: Publishers Group West (PGW).

Waldendorf, Kurt. How Slow Is a Sloth? 2017. (Comparison Fun Ser.). (ENG.). 24p. (J). (gr. -1-2). lib. bdg. 27.07 (978-1-5038-1679-4(6), 211514) Child's World, Inc., The.

West, David. Giant Sloth: Graphic Prehistoric Animals. Poluzzi, Alessandro, illus. 2017. (Graphic Prehistoric Animals Ser.). 32p. (gr. 3-7). lib. bdg. 31.35 (978-1-62588-409-1(5)) Black Rabbit Bks.

Windsor, Jo. An Upside down Life: Early Level Satellite Individual Title Six-Packs. (Sails Literacy Ser.). 16p. (gr. 1-2). 27.00 (978-0-7578-2937-6(6)) Rigby Education.

SLOTHS—FICTION

Berger, Samantha. Snoozefest. Litten, Kristyna, illus. 2015. (ENG.). 34p. (J). (gr. -1-k). 16.99 (978-0-8037-4046-4(8), Dial Bks) Penguin Young Readers Group.

Carle, Eric. "Slowly, Slowly, Slowly," Said the Sloth. Carle, Eric, illus. 2007. (ENG., Illus.). 32p. (J). (gr. -1-2). pap. 7.99 (978-0-14-240847-6(6), Puffin Books) Penguin Young Readers Group.

—"Slowly, Slowly, Slowly," Said the Sloth. Carle, Eric, illus. 2007. (Illus.). (gr. -1-3). 18.00 (978-0-7569-8002-3(X)) Perfection Learning Corp.

—"Slowly, Slowly, Slowly," Said the Sloth. 2007. 18.40 (978-1-4177-7475-3(4), Turtleback) Turtleback Bks.

Clarke, Jane. Plodney Creeper, Supersloth. 2006. (Blue Bananas Ser.). (ENG., Illus.). 48p. (J). (gr. -1-3). lib. bdg. (978-0-7787-0850-6(0)) Crabtree Publishing Co.

Emerson, Carl. Speed up, Sammy the Tree Sloth!, 1 vol. Trover, Zachary, illus. 2007. (Animal Underdogs Ser.). (ENG.). 32p. (gr. -1-3). 28.50 (978-1-60270-019-2(2), Looking Glass Library) ABDO Publishing Co.

Lee, Bonnie. Go Go Sadie. Taylor, Erin, illus. 2011. 46p. 24.00 (978-1-4349-8679-5(9), RoseDog Bks.) Dorrance Publishing Co., Inc.

Masterson, Hoss. Soccer Sloth. Alves, Josh, illus. 2017. (Animal All-Stars Ser.). (ENG.). 56p. (gr. 1-3). lib. bdg. 25.32 (978-1-4965-4306-6(8)) Stone Arch Bks.

Murray, Andrew. The Very Sleepy Sloth. Tickle, Jack, tr. Tickle, Jack, illus. 2003. 32p. (J). tchr. ed. 15.95 (978-1-58925-033-8(8)) Tiger Tales.

Preston-Gannon, Frann. Sloth Slept On. 2015. (ENG., Illus.). 32p. (J). (gr. -1 — 1). 14.95 (978-1-4549-1611-6(7)) Sterling Publishing Co., Inc.

Seibold, J. Otto. Lost Sloth. 2013. (ENG., Illus.). 32p. 16.95 (978-1-938073-35-9(5)) McSweeney's Publishing.

Venable, Colleen Af. Mervin the Sloth Is about to Do the Best Thing in the World. Chan, Ruth, illus. 2016. 40p. (J). (gr. -1-3). 17.99 (978-0-06-233847-1(1), Greenwillow Bks.) HarperCollins Pubs.

SLUMBER SONGS

see Lullabies

SLUMS

see Housing

SMALL ARMS

see Firearms

SMALL BUSINESS

Bernstein, Daryl. Better Than a Lemonade Stand! Small Business Ideas for Kids. Husberg, Rob, illus. 2012. (ENG.). 224p. (J). (gr. 4-9). 19.99 (978-1-58270-360-2(4)); pap. 12.99 (978-1-58270-330-5(2)) Aladdin/Beyond Words.

Bochner, Arthur, et al. The New Totally Awesome Business Book for Kids. 3rd rev. ed. 2007. (New Totally Awesome Ser.: 2). (ENG., Illus.). 192p. (gr. 7-9). per. 11.99 (978-1-55704-757-1(X), William Morrow Paperbacks) HarperCollins Pubs.

Earl, C. F. Building a Business in the Virtual World. Madrian, Brigitte, ed. 2013. (Young Adult Library of Small Business & Finance Ser.: 10). 64p. (J). (gr. 7-18). 22.95 (978-1-4222-2913-2(0)); (Illus.). pap. 12.95 (978-1-4222-2980-4(7)) Mason Crest.

—Business Funding & Finances. Madrian, Brigitte, ed. 2013. (Young Adult Library of Small Business & Finance Ser.: 10). 64p. (J). (gr. 7-18). 22.95 (978-1-4222-2915-6(7)) Mason Crest.

—Marketing Your Business. Madrian, Brigitte, ed. 2013. (Young Adult Library of Small Business & Finance Ser.: 10). 64p. (J). (gr. 7-18). 22.95 (978-1-4222-2919-4(X)) Mason Crest.

—What Does It Mean to Be an Entrepreneur? Madrian, Brigitte, ed. 2013. (Young Adult Library of Small Business & Finance Ser.: 10). 64p. (J). (gr. 7-18). 22.95 (978-1-4222-2922-4(X)) Mason Crest.

Fischer, James. Keeping Your Business Organized: Time Management & Workflow. Madrian, Brigitte, ed. 2013. (Young Adult Library of Small Business & Finance Ser.: 10). 64p. (J). (gr. 7-18). 22.95 (978-1-4222-2917-0(3)); (Illus.). pap. 12.95 (978-1-4222-2982-8(3)) Mason Crest.

—Starting a Business: Creating a Plan. 2013. (J). (978-1-4222-2912-5(2)) Mason Crest.

—Starting a Business: Creating a Plan. Madrian, Brigitte, ed. 2013. (Young Adult Library of Small Business & Finance Ser.). 64p. (J). (gr. 7-18). pap. 12.95 (978-1-4222-2984-2(X)); 22.95 (978-1-4222-2920-0(3)) Mason Crest.

Hyde, Natalie. What Is Entrepreneurship? 2016. (Your Start-Up Starts Now! a Guide to Entrepreneurship Ser.). (ENG., Illus.). 48p. (J). (gr. 5-8). (978-0-7787-2758-3(0)); pap. (978-0-7787-2766-8(1)) Crabtree Publishing Co.

Kahan, Alex. Entrepreneurship: Create Your Own Business. Crosier, Mike, illus. 2014. (Build It Yourself Ser.). (ENG.). 128p. (J). (gr. 3-7). pap. 17.95 (978-1-61930-265-5(9)) Open City Bks.

Larsen, Becca. Buying & Selling. 2013. (Rosen Readers Ser.). (ENG.). 24p. (J). (gr. 2-3). pap. 8.25 (978-1-4777-2260-2(2)); pap. 49.50 (978-1-4777-2261-9(0)) Rosen Publishing Group, Inc., The. (Rosen Classroom).

Mariotti, Steve. Entrepreneurship: How to Start & Operate a Small Business. 2005. (YA). pap., stu. ed. 15.00 (978-1-890859-19-0(2)); (gr. 9-12). tchr. ed. 46.95 (978-1-890859-21-3(4)); (gr. 9-12). pap. 79.95 (978-1-890859-20-6(6)); (gr. 9-12). trans. 15.00 (978-1-890859-23-7(0)) National Foundation for Teaching Entrepreneurship, The.

—How to Start & Operate a Small Business: Exam View Text Bank - CD. 2005. (YA). (gr. 9-12). pap. incl. cd-rom (978-1-890859-24-4(9)) National Foundation for Teaching Entrepreneurship, The.

Meinking, Mary. Start Your Crafting Business. 2017. (Build Your Business Ser.). (ENG.). 32p. (gr. 3-4). lib. bdg. 27.99 **(978-1-5157-6690-2(X))** Capstone Press of Coughlan Cos.

Minden, Cecilia. Starting Your Own Business. (21st Century Skills Library: Real World Math Ser.). (ENG., 32p. (gr. 4-7). 2015. Illus.). (J). 29.93 (978-1-63362-576-1(1), 206488) 2009. lib. bdg. 28.50 (978-1-60279-313-2(1), 200209) Cherry Lake Publishing.

Mooney, Carla. Starting a Business: Have Fun & Make Money. 2010. (Creative Adventure Guides). 48p. (J). (gr. 3-6). 26.60 (978-1-59953-386-5(3)) Norwood Hse. Pr.

Offord, Alexander. What Is Environmental Entrepreneurship? 2016. (Your Start-Up Starts Now! a Guide to Entrepreneurship Ser.). (ENG., Illus.). 48p. (J). (gr. 5-8). (978-0-7787-2756-9(4)); pap. (978-0-7787-2764-4(5)) Crabtree Publishing Co.

Ruffin, Frances E. Let's Have a Bake Sale: Calculating Profit & Unit Cost. 2009. (PowerMath Ser.). (ENG., Illus.). 224p. (gr. 3-4). pap. 8.25 (978-0-8239-8893-8(7), PowerKids Pr.) Rosen Publishing Group, Inc., The.

Snyder, Gail. Teen Guide to Starting a Business. 2016. (ENG.). 64p. (J). (gr. 5-12). lib. bdg. (978-1-68282-088-9(2)) ReferencePoint Pr., Inc.

Thompson, Helen. Business & the Government: Law & Taxes. Madrian, Brigitte, ed. 2013. (Young Adult Library of Small Business & Finance Ser.: 10). 64p. (J). (gr. 7-18). 22.95 (978-1-4222-2916-3(5)) Mason Crest.

—Managing Employees. Madrian, Brigitte, ed. 2013. (Young Adult Library of Small Business & Finance Ser.: 10). 64p. (J). (gr. 7-18). 22.95 (978-1-4222-2918-7(1)) Mason Crest.

SMALLS, ROBERT, 1839-1915

Brown, Susan Taylor. Robert Smalls Sails to Freedom. Marshall, Felicia, illus. 2006. (On My Own History Ser.). 48p. (J). (gr. 3-7). pap. 6.95 (978-0-8225-6051-7(8), First Avenue Editions); (ENG.). (gr. 2-4). lib. bdg. 25.26 (978-1-57505-872-6(3)) Lerner Publishing Group.

Halfmann, Janet. Seven Miles to Freedom: The Robert Smalls Story. Smith, Duane, illus. 2008. 40p. (J). (gr. 1-6). 17.95 (978-1-60060-232-0(0)) Lee & Low Bks., Inc.

Halfmann, Janet & Smith, Duane. Seven Miles to Freedom: The Robert Smalls Story, 1 vol. 2008. (ENG., Illus.). 40p. (J). pap. 10.95 (978-1-60060-986-2(4)) Lee & Low Bks., Inc.

SMELL

Aloian, Molly. What Is Smell? 2013. (ENG., Illus.). 24p. (J). (978-0-7787-0971-8(X)); pap. (978-0-7787-0999-2(X)) Crabtree Publishing Co.

Appleby, Alex. What I Smell. 2014. (My Five Senses Ser.). 24p. (J). (gr. k-2). 22.60 (978-1-4824-0813-3(9)); pap. 8.15 (978-1-4824-0814-0(7)) Stevens, Gareth Publishing LLLP.

Barnham, Kay. Smell. 2005. (Our Senses Ser.). (Illus.). 24p. (gr. k-3). lib. bdg. 23.00 (978-0-8368-4408-5(4), Gareth Stevens Learning Library) Stevens, Gareth Publishing LLLP.

Barraclough, Sue. What Can I Smell? 2005. (J). (978-1-4034-7079-9(0)); (ENG.). 32p. pap. (978-1-4034-7085-0(5)) Steck-Vaughn.

Beaumont, Susanna & Baby Senses Staff. Smell. 2005. (Baby Senses Ser.). (Illus.). 12p. (gr. -1-k). bds. (978-1-905051-49-6(2)) Make Believe Ideas.

Beck, Esther. Cool Odor Decoders: Fun Science Projects about Smells, 1 vol. 2008. (Cool Science Ser.). (ENG.). 32p. (YA). (gr. 2-5). 28.50 (978-1-59928-909-0(1)) ABDO Publishing Co.

Bellamy, Adam. What's That Smell? 2017. (All about My Senses Ser.). 24p. (J). (gr. k-1). lib. bdg. 22.60 **(978-0-7660-8607-4(0))** Enslow Pubs., Inc.

Boothroyd, Jennifer. What Is Smell? 2009. (Lightning Bolt Books (tm) — Your Amazing Senses Ser.). (ENG.). 32p. (gr. k-2). 26.60 (978-0-7613-4253-3(2), Lerner Pubns.); pap. 7.95 (978-0-7613-5016-3(0)) Lerner Publishing Group.

Carr, Aaron. El Olfato. 2013. (Mis Sentidos Ser.). (SPA., Illus.). 24p. (J). (gr. 3-7). lib. bdg. 27.13 (978-1-62127-579-4(5), AV2 by Weigl) Weigl Pubs., Inc.

Casado, Dami & Casado, Alicia. El Olfato. 2005. (Sentidos y Algo Más). (SPA & ESP.). 16p. 8.99 (978-84-272-6413-7(5)) Molino, Editorial ESP. Dist: Santillana USA Publishing Co., Inc.

Castaldo, Nancy F. Sniffer Dogs: How Dogs (and Their Noses) Save the World. 2014. (ENG., Illus.). 160p. (J). (gr. 5-7). 16.99 (978-0-544-08893-1(X), HMH Books For Young Readers) Houghton Mifflin Harcourt Publishing Co.

Chapman, Jared & Smeldit, H. W. Farts in the Wild: A Spotter's Guide. 2012. (ENG., Illus.). 24p. (J). (gr. -1-17). 15.99 (978-1-4521-0631-1(2)) Chronicle Bks. LLC.

Cleland, JoAnn. I Smell, Sing & Read. 2010. (Our Five Senses Sing & Read Ser.). (Illus.). 24p. (J). (gr. -1-k). 22.79 (978-1-61590-287-3(2)) Rourke Educational Media.

Durrie, Karen. Smell. 2012. (J). (978-1-61913-311-2(3)); pap. (978-1-61913-316-7(4)) Weigl Pubs., Inc.

Enslow, Brian. My Nose. 2010. (All about My Body Ser.). (Illus.). 24p. (J). 22.60 (978-0-7660-3814-1(9)); pap. 7.95 (978-1-59845-170-2(7)) Enslow Pubs., Inc. (Enslow Elementary).

Equipo Staff. El Olfato. (Coleccion Mundo Maravilloso). (SPA., Illus.). 38p. (J). (gr. 2-4). (978-84-348-4778-1(7), OL2004) SM Ediciones.

Furgang, Kathy. My Nose. 2009. (My Body Ser.). 24p. (gr. 3-3). 42.50 (978-1-61514-691-8(1), PowerKids Pr.) Rosen Publishing Group, Inc., The.

Ganeri, Anita. Smell. 2013. (Senses Ser.). (Illus.). 24p. (gr. k-3). 28.50 (978-1-59920-853-4(9)) Black Rabbit Bks.

George, Patrick. I Smell... 2013. (ENG., Illus.). 36p. (J). (gr. -1-k). 12.99 (978-1-908473-05-9(3)) PatrickGeorge GBR. Dist: Independent Pubs. Group.

Hall, Kirsten. Animal Smell. 2005. (Animals & Their Senses Ser.). (Illus.). 24p. (J). (gr. k-3). pap. 8.15 (978-0-8368-4810-6(1)); lib. bdg. 22.00 (978-0-8368-4804-5(7)) Stevens, Gareth Publishing LLLP. (Weekly Reader Leveled Readers).

—Animal Smell (El Olfato en los Animales) 2005. (Animals & Their Senses/ Los sentidos de los animales Ser.). (ENG & SPA., Illus.). 24p. (J). (gr. k-3). lib. bdg. 22.00 (978-0-8368-4816-8(0), Weekly Reader Leveled Readers) Stevens, Gareth Publishing LLLP.

Hanel, Rachael. Smell. 2003. 24p. (J). lib. bdg. 21.35 (978-1-58340-306-8(X)) Black Rabbit Bks.

Hengel, Katherine. Noses Are for Picking: The Sense of Smell, 1 vol. 2012. (All about Your Senses Ser.). (ENG.). 24p. (J). (gr. k-3). lib. bdg. 24.21 (978-1-61783-200-0(6), SandCastle) ABDO Publishing Co.

Hewitt, Sally. Smell It! 2008. (Let's Start Science Ser.). (ENG., Illus.). 24p. (J). (gr. 3-7). pap. (978-0-7787-4060-5(9)) Crabtree Publishing Co.

Issa, Joanna. What Can I Smell?, 1 vol. 2014. (These Are My Senses Ser.). (ENG., Illus.). 24p. (gr. -1-1). pap. 5.99 (978-1-4846-0434-2(2), Acorn) Heinemann-Raintree.

Koontz, Robin Michal. Sniffs & Stinks: How Animals Use Odor to Survive. 2011. (Amazing Animal Skills Ser.). (Illus.). 48p. (J). (gr. 4). 29.93 (978-0-7614-4908-9(6)) Marshall Cavendish GBR. Dist: Marshall Cavendish Corp.

Korb, Rena B. & Weinhaus, Anthony J. My Nose, 1 vol. Simard, Remy, illus. 2010. (My Body Ser.). (ENG.). 32p. (J). (gr. k-3). 28.50 (978-1-60270-808-2(8)) Magic Wagon.

Kubler, Annie, illus. What Can I Smell? 2011. (Small Senses Ser.). (ENG.). 12p. (J). bds. (978-1-84643-376-4(2)) Child's Play International Ltd.

Kurtz, John. The World Around Us! Smelling. 2011. (Dover Coloring Bks.). (ENG.). 32p. (J). (gr. k-3). pap. 4.99 (978-0-486-48036-7(4)) Dover Pubns., Inc.

Lay, Kathryn. Smelling Their Prey: Animals with an Amazing Sense of Smell, 1 vol. Wald, Christina, illus. 2012. (Sensing Their Prey Ser.). (ENG.). 32p. (J). (gr. -1-4). lib. bdg. 28.50 (978-1-61641-868-7(0), Looking Glass Library) Magic Wagon.

Llewellyn, Claire. Smelling & Tasting. 2005. (I Know That! Ser.). (Illus.). 24p. (J). (gr. 1-3). lib. bdg. 22.80 (978-1-932889-49-9(3)) Sea-To-Sea Pubns.

Lowery, Lawrence F. Fragrant As a Flower: I Wonder Why. 2017. (I Wonder Why Ser.). (ENG., Illus.). 36p. (J). (gr. k-2). pap. 11.95 (978-1-68140-353-3(6)) National Science Teachers Assn.

Match Game Staff. Smelly Scented Memory Game. 2005. pap. 19.95 (978-0-9762524-3-6(0)) Gimme Gimme Toys & Games, Inc.

Meachen Rau, Dana. Sniff, Sniff [Scholastic]: A Book about Smell. Peterson, Rick, illus. 2010. (Amazing Body: the Five Senses Ser.). 24p. pap. 0.56 (978-1-4048-6542-6(X), Nonfiction Picture Bks.) Picture Window Bks.

Milet Publishing Staff. My Bilingual Book - Smell. 2014. (My Bilingual Book Ser.). (ENG & CHI., Illus.). 28p. (J). (gr. -1-k). 9.95 (978-1-84059-806-3(9)) Milet Publishing.

—My Bilingual Book-Smell. 2014. (My Bilingual Book Ser.). (ENG & KOR., Illus.). 28p. (J). (gr. -1-k). 9.95 (978-1-84059-811-7(5)); 9.95 (978-1-84059-816-2(6)) Milet Publishing.

—My Bilingual Book-Smell (English-Arabic) 2014. (My Bilingual Book Ser.). (ENG & ARA., Illus.). 28p. (J). (gr. -1-k). 9.95 (978-1-84059-804-9(2)) Milet Publishing.

—My Bilingual Book-Smell (English-Bengali) 2014. (My Bilingual Book Ser.). (ENG & BEN., Illus.). 28p. (J). (gr. -1-k). 9.95 (978-1-84059-805-6(0)) Milet Publishing.

—My Bilingual Book-Smell (English-Farsi) 2014. (My Bilingual Book Ser.). (ENG & PER., Illus.). 28p. (J). (gr. -1-k). 9.95 (978-1-84059-807-0(7)) Milet Publishing.

—My Bilingual Book-Smell (English-Italian) 2014. (My Bilingual Book Ser.). (ENG & ITA., Illus.). 28p. (J). (gr. -1-k). 9.95 (978-1-84059-810-0(7)) Milet Publishing.

—My Bilingual Book-Smell (English-Polish) 2014. (My Bilingual Book Ser.). (ENG, POL & POR., Illus.). 28p. (J). (gr. -1-k). 9.95 (978-1-84059-812-4(3)) Milet Publishing.

—My Bilingual Book-Smell (English-Russian) 2014. (My Bilingual Book Ser.). (ENG & RUS., Illus.). 28p. (J). (gr. -1-k). 9.95 (978-1-84059-814-8(X)) Milet Publishing.

—My Bilingual Book-Smell (English-Somali) 2014. (My Bilingual Book Ser.). (ENG & SOM., Illus.). 28p. (J). (gr. -1-k). 9.95 (978-1-84059-815-5(8)) Milet Publishing.

—My Bilingual Book-Smell (English-Turkish) 2014. (My Bilingual Book Ser.). (ENG & TUR., Illus.). 28p. (J). (gr. -1-k). 9.95 (978-1-84059-817-9(4)) Milet Publishing.

—My Bilingual Book-Smell (English-Urdu) 2014. (My Bilingual Book Ser.). (ENG & URD., Illus.). 28p. (J). (gr. -1-k). 9.95 (978-1-84059-818-6(2)) Milet Publishing.

—My Bilingual Book-Smell (English-Vietnamese) 2014. (My Bilingual Book Ser.). (ENG & VIE., Illus.). 28p. (J). (gr. -1-k). 9.95 (978-1-84059-819-3(0)) Milet Publishing.

—Smell / Das Riechen. 2014. (My Bilingual Book Ser.). (ENG & GER., Illus.). 28p. (J). (gr. -1-k). 9.95 (978-1-84059-809-4(3)) Milet Publishing.

—Smell (English-French) 2014. (My Bilingual Book Ser.). (ENG & FRE., Illus.). 28p. (J). (gr. -1-k). 9.95 (978-1-84059-808-7(5)) Milet Publishing.

—Smell O olfato. 2014. (My Bilingual Book Ser.). (ENG & POR., Illus.). 28p. (J). (gr. -1-k). 9.95 (978-1-84059-813-1(1)) Milet Publishing.

Miller, Connie Colwell. The Stinkiest Animals. 2011. (Extreme Animals Ser.). (ENG.). 24p. (gr. k-1). pap. 41.70 (978-1-4296-6380-9(4), Pebble Plus) Capstone Press of Coughlan Cos.

Mlawer, Teresa, tr. What Do I Smell? / ¿Qué Huelo? Kubler, Annie, illus. 2015. (Small Senses Bilingual Ser.: 5). (ENG & SPA.). 12p. (J). bds. (978-1-84643-723-6(7)) Child's Play International Ltd.

Morgan, Sally. How Smell Works. 2010. (Our Senses Ser.). 24p. (J). (gr. k-2). pap. 8.25 (978-1-61532-561-0(1), PowerKids Pr.); (Illus.). (gr. -1-2). lib. bdg. 22.60 (978-1-61532-554-2(9)) Rosen Publishing Group, Inc., The.

Murray, Julie. I Can Smell, 1 vol. 2016. (ENG., Illus.). 24p. (J). (978-1-62970-927-7(1), 1391208) ABDO Publishing Co.

Nelson, Robin. El Olfato. Translations.com Staff, tr. from ENG. 2006. (Mi Primer Paso Al Mundo Real - Los Sentidos (First Step Nonfiction - Senses) Ser.). (SPA., Illus.). 24p. (gr. k-2). lib. bdg. 23.93 (978-0-8225-6223-8(5), Ediciones Lerner) Lerner Publishing Group.

—El Olfato (Smelling) 2006. (Mi Primer Paso al Mundo Real Ser.). (Illus.). 23p. (J). (gr. -1-3). per. 5.95 (978-0-8225-6546-8(3), Ediciones Lerner) Lerner Publishing Group.

Patent, Dorothy Hinshaw. Super Sniffers: Dog Detectives on the Job. 2014. (ENG., Illus.). 48p. (J). (gr. 2-4). 17.99 (978-0-8027-3618-5(1), 9780802736185, Bloomsbury USA Childrens) Bloomsbury Publishing USA.

Pryor, Kimberley Jane. Smelling. 2003. (Senses Ser.). (Illus.). 32p. (gr. 2-4). 23.00 (978-0-7910-7556-2(7), Chelsea Hse.) Facts On File, Inc.

Qamaruddin, Rizwana. Allah Gave Me a Nose to Smell. Stratford, Stevan, illus. 2015. (ENG.). 32p. (J). 8.95 (978-0-86037-333-9(9)) Kube Publishing Ltd. GBR. Dist: Consortium Bk. Sales & Distribution.

Randolph, Joanne. Whose Nose Is This? 2009. (Animal Clues Ser.). 24p. (gr. 1-1). 42.50 (978-1-61511-433-7(5), PowerKids Pr.) Rosen Publishing Group, Inc., The.

—Whose Nose Is This? / ¿de quién es esta Nariz? 2009. (Animal Clues / ¿Adivina de Quién Es? Ser.). (ENG & SPA.). 24p. (gr. 1-1). 42.50 (978-1-61511-439-9(4), Editorial Buenas Letras) Rosen Publishing Group, Inc., The.

Reade, Clara. El Olfato / Smell, 1 vol., 1. De La Vega, Eida, ed. 2014. (Tus Cinco Sentidos y Tu Sexto Sentido / Your Five Senses & Your Sixth Sense Ser.). (SPA & BYN.). 24p. (J). (gr. k-2). 23.60 (978-1-4777-3277-9(2), PowerKids Pr.) Rosen Publishing Group, Inc., The.

—Smell, 1 vol., 1. 2014. (Your Five Senses & Your Sixth Sense Ser.). (ENG.). 24p. (J). (gr. k-2). 23.60 (978-1-4777-2857-4(0), PowerKids Pr.) Rosen Publishing Group, Inc., The.

Rustad, Martha E. H. Smelling. 2014. (Illus.). 24p. (J). lib. bdg. 25.65 (978-1-62031-117-2(8), Bullfrog Bks.) Jump! Inc.

Rybolt, Thomas R. & Rybolt, Leah M. Smelly Science Fair Projects. 2015. (Prize-Winning Science Fair Projects Ser.).

(ENG.). 128p. (J). (gr. 7-7). lib. bdg. 37.27 *(978-0-7660-7022-6(0))* Enslow Pubs., Inc.
Sarkisian, K. You Need Your Nose: Learning the N Sound. 2009. (PowerPhonics Ser.). 24p. (gr. 1-1). 39.90 *(978-1-60851-482-3(X),* PowerKids Pr.) Rosen Publishing Group, Inc., The.
Schuh, Mari. The Sense of Smell. 2007. (Senses Ser.). (ENG., Illus.). 24p. (J). (gr. 2-5). lib. bdg. 25.95 *(978-1-60014-072-3(6))* Bellwether Media.
Stewart, Melissa. Nifty Noses up Close. 2012. (Animal Bodies up Close Ser.). 24p. (J). (gr. k-3). 22.60 *(978-0-7660-3892-9(0),* Enslow Elementary) Enslow Pubs., Inc.
Tekiela, Stan. Snouts & Sniffers, 1 vol. 2013. (Adventure Boardbook Ser.). (ENG.). 22p. (J). (gr. -1-k). bds. 6.95 *(978-1-59193-426-4(5))* Adventure Pubns.
Towne, Isobel & Viegas, Jennifer. The Mouth & Nose in 3D. 2015. (Human Body In 3D Ser.). (ENG., Illus.). 64p. (J). (gr. 5-6). 32.95 *(978-1-4994-3609-9(2),* Rosen Central) Rosen Publishing Group, Inc., The.
Tyler, Jenny & Hawthorn, P. Who's Making That Smell? rev. ed. 2004. (Illus.). 16p. (J). (gr. 1-18). pap. 7.95 *(978-0-7945-0523-3(6))* EDC Publishing.
VanVoorst, Jenny Fretland. Take a Closer Look at Your Nose. 2013. (Take a Closer Look Ser.). (ENG.). 24p. (J). (gr. 2-5). 28.50 *(978-1-62323-546-8(4),* 206355) Child's World, Inc., The.
Vogel, Julie & Vogel, Julia. Your Sensational Sense of Smell. Squier, Robert, illus. 2011. (Sensational Senses Ser.). (ENG.). 32p. (J). (gr. k-3). lib. bdg. 27.07 *(978-1-60954-288-7(6),* 200817) Child's World, Inc., The.
Wearing, Judy. Smell. 2009. (World of Wonder Ser.). (Illus.). 24p. (J). (gr. 2-4). pap. 8.95 *(978-1-60596-061-6(6));* lib. bdg. 24.45 *(978-1-60596-060-9(8))* Weigl Pubs., Inc.
Weiss, Ellen. The Sense of Smell. (True Book(tm), a — Health & the Human Body Ser.). (ENG., 48p. (J). 2008. Illus.). (gr. 2-5). 31.00 *(978-0-531-16872-1(7))* 2009. pap. 6.95 *(978-0-531-21834-1(1),* Children's Pr.) Scholastic Library Publishing.
Wheeler-Toppen, Jodi Lyn. Our Noses Can Smell. 2017. (Our Amazing Senses Ser.). (ENG.). 24p. (J). (gr. k-1). lib. bdg. 21.99 ***(978-1-5157-6711-4(6),*** Pebble Bks.) Capstone Press of Coughlan Cos.

SMELL—FICTION

Beaty, Andrea. Fluffy Bunnies 2: The Schnoz of Doom. Santat, Dan, illus. (Fluffy Bunnies Ser.). (ENG.). (J). (gr. 3-7). 2016. 208p. pap. 7.95 *(978-1-4197-1942-4(4))* 2015. 192p. 12.95 *(978-1-4197-1051-3(6))* Abrams, Inc. (Amulet Bks.).
Chartrand, Lili. The Smelly Story of Hazel the Weasel. Eid, Jean-Paul, illus. 2009. (Rainy Day Readers Ser.). 32p. (J). (gr. -1-3). 22.60 *(978-1-60754-379-4(6));* pap. 10.55 *(978-1-60754-380-0(X))* Windmill Bks.
Cook, Sherry & Johnson, Terri. Nosey Nina, 26 vols. Kuhn, Jesse, illus. l.t. ed. 2006. (Quirkles — Exploring Phonics through Science Ser.: 14). 32p. (J). 7.99 *(978-1-933815-13-8(2),* Quirkles, The) Creative 3, LLC.
Derubertis, Barbara. Sammy Skunk's Super Sniffer. Alley, R. W., illus. 2011. (Animal Antics A to Z Set III Ser.). pap. 45.32 *(978-0-7613-8428-1(6))* Kane Press, Inc.
deRubertis, Barbara. Sammy Skunk's Super Sniffer. Alley, R. W., illus. 2011. (Animal Antics A to Z Ser.). pap. 7.95 *(978-1-57565-344-0(3));* lib. bdg. 22.60 *(978-1-57565-352-5(4))* Kane Press, Inc.
deRubertis, Barbara & DeRubertis, Barbara. Sammy Skunk's Super Sniffer. Alley, R. W., illus. 2012. (Animal Antics A to Z Ser.). 32p. (J). (gr. 2 — 1). cd-rom 7.95 *(978-1-57565-412-6(1))* Kane Press, Inc.
Devany, Betsy. Lucy's Lovey. Denise, Christopher, illus. 2016. (ENG.). 40p. (J). 17.99 *(978-1-62779-147-2(7),* 9781627791472, Holt, Henry & Co. Bks. For Young Readers) Holt, Henry & Co.
Gabbitas, Jay. A Smell in the Air. 2011. (Illus.). 20p. (gr. 2-4). pap. 12.12 *(978-1-4520-3220-7(3))* AuthorHouse.
Gates, Laura. A Very Good Smell. 2006. (ENG., Illus.). 28p. (J). (gr. -1-3). pap. 2.99 *(978-1-59249-552-8(4))* Soundprints.
Hyde, Margaret. Mo Smells Christmas: A Scentsational Journey. Giacomini, Amanda, illus. 4th ed. 2010. (Mo's Nose Ser.). (ENG.). 24p. (J). (gr. k-k). 17.95 *(978-0-9816255-6-0(8))* Mo's Nose, LLC.
—Mo Smells Green: A Scentsational Journey. Giacomini, Amanda, illus. 2009. (Mo's Nose Ser.). (ENG.). 16p. (J). (gr. k-k). 17.95 *(978-0-9816255-2-2(5))* Mo's Nose, LLC.
—Mo Smells Pink: A Scentsational Journey. Giacomini, Amanda, illus. 5th ed. 2011. (Mo's Nose Ser.). (ENG.). 24p. (J). (gr. k-k). 17.95 *(978-0-9816255-5-3(X))* Mo's Nose, LLC.
—Mo Smells the Ballpark. Chaudhary, Aman, illus. 2014. (ENG.). 24p. (J). (gr. -1-k). 14.95 *(978-1-62873-668-7(2),* Sky Pony Pr.) Skyhorse Publishing Co., Inc.
—Mo Smells the Holidays: A Scentsational Journey. Giacomini, Amanda, illus. 2009. (Mo's Nose Ser.). (ENG.). 24p. (J). (gr. k-k). 17.95 *(978-0-9816255-3-9(3))* Mo's Nose, LLC.
Isadora, Rachel. I Hear a Pickle: And Smell, See, Touch, & Taste It, Too! Isadora, Rachel, illus. 2016. (ENG., Illus.). 32p. (J). (-k). 16.99 *(978-0-399-16049-3(3),* Nancy Paulsen Books) Penguin Young Readers Group.
Lubar, David. The Big Stink. 2010. (Nathan Abercrombie, Accidental Zombie Ser.: 4). (ENG.). 176p. (J). (gr. 3-7). pap. 7.99 *(978-0-7653-2510-5(1),* 9780765325105, Starscape) Doherty, Tom Assocs., LLC.
McDonald, Megan. Stink & the World's Worst Super-Stinky Sneakers, Bk. 3. Reynolds, Peter H., illus. 2013. (Stink Ser.: 3). (ENG.). 144p. (J). (gr. 1-4). pap. 4.99 *(978-0-7636-6424-4(3));*Bk. 3. 12.99 *(978-0-7636-6390-2(5))* Candlewick Pr.
—Stink & the World's Worst Super-Stinky Sneakers. Reynolds, Peter H., illus. 2010. (Stink Ser.: No. 3). 144p. (J). (gr. k-4). 24.21 *(978-1-59961-685-8(8))* Spotlight.
—Stink & the World's Worst Super-Stinky Sneakers. 2013. (Stink Ser.: 3). lib. bdg. 14.75 *(978-0-606-31589-0(6),* Turtleback) Turtleback Bks.
—Stink It Up! A Guide to the Gross, the Bad, & the Smelly. Reynolds, Peter H., illus. 2013. (Stink Ser.). (ENG.). 128p. (J). (gr. 1-4). pap. 5.99 *(978-0-7636-5942-4(8))* Candlewick Pr.
—Stink: the Absolutely Astronomical Collection: Books 4-6. Reynolds, Peter H., illus. 2013. (Stink Ser.). (ENG.). 256p. (J). (gr. k-3). pap. 14.97 *(978-0-7636-6830-3(3))* Candlewick Pr.
—Stink y los Tenis Más Apestosos del Mundo. 2008. (SPA.). 208p. (J). (gr. 3-5). pap. 7.95 *(978-1-60396-195-0(X),* Alfaguara) Santillana USA Publishing Co., Inc.
Meddaugh, Susan. Martha Speaks: Martha Stinks! (Reader) 2013. (Martha Speaks Ser.). (ENG., Illus.). 24p. (J). (gr. -1-3). 12.99 *(978-0-544-09662-2(2))* Houghton Mifflin Harcourt Publishing Co.
—Martha Stinks! 2013. (Martha Speaks Ser.). (ENG., Illus.). 24p. (J). (gr. -1-3). pap. 3.99 *(978-0-544-10012-1(3))* Houghton Mifflin Harcourt Publishing Co.
Meisel, Peter. Stinky Spike & the Royal Rescue. Meisel, Paul, illus. 2017. (ENG.). 80p. (J). 9.99 *(978-1-61963-883-9(5),* 9781619638839, Bloomsbury USA Childrens) Bloomsbury Publishing USA.
—Stinky Spike the Pirate Dog. Meisel, Paul, illus. 2017. (ENG.). 80p. (J). 9.99 *(978-1-61963-778-8(2),* 9781619637788, Bloomsbury USA Childrens) Bloomsbury Publishing USA.
Munsch, Robert. Smelly Socks. 2005. 15.00 *(978-0-7569-5139-9(9))* Perfection Learning Corp.
Nash, Sarah. Smelly Blanket. Everitt-Stewart, Andy, illus. 2009. (Stories to Grow with Ser.). 24p. (J). (gr. -1-2). 22.60 *(978-1-60754-466-1(0));* pap. 8.15 *(978-1-60754-467-8(9))* Windmill Bks.
Sias, Ryan. Sniff! Sniff! 2015. (ENG., Illus.). 32p. (J). (gr. -1-2). 14.95 *(978-1-4197-1490-0(2))* Abrams, Inc.
Slater, David Michael. Ned's Nose Is Running, 1 vol. Brooks, S. G., illus. 2009. (David Michael Slater Set 2 Ser.). (ENG.). 32p. (gr. -1-4). 28.50 *(978-1-60270-658-3(1),* Looking Glass Library) ABDO Publishing Co.
Taylor, Alastair. Mr. Blewitt's Nose. 2005. (J). (gr. k-3). 16.00 *(978-0-618-58111-5(1))* Houghton Mifflin Harcourt Trade & Reference Pubs.
Tyler, Jenny & Hawthorn, Phillip. Who's Making That Smell? Cartwright, Stephen, illus. 2007. (Luxury Flap Bks). 16p. (J). (gr. -1-3). 9.99 *(978-0-7945-1696-3(3),* Usborne) EDC Publishing.
Urey, Gary. Super Schnoz & the Booger Blaster Breakdown. Frawley, Keith, illus. 2015. (Super Schnoz Ser.: 3). (ENG.). 192p. (J). (gr. 3-7). 14.99 *(978-0-8075-7562-8(3))* Whitman, Albert & Co.
—Super Schnoz & the Gates of Smell. Long, Ethan, illus. (Super Schnoz Ser.: 1). (ENG.). 160p. (J). (gr. 3-7). 2015. pap. 6.99 *(978-0-8075-7560-4(7))* 2013. 14.99 *(978-0-8075-7555-0(0))* Whitman, Albert & Co.
—Super Schnoz & the Invasion of the Snore Snatchers. Frawley, Keith, illus. 2014. (Super Schnoz Ser.: 2). (ENG.). 160p. (J). (gr. 3-7). 14.99 *(978-0-8075-7557-4(7))* Whitman, Albert & Co.
Young, Judy. Digger & Daisy Go on a Picnic. Sullivan, Dana, illus. 2014. (I Am a Reader: Digger & Daisy Ser.). (ENG.). 32p. (J). (gr. k-1). 9.99 *(978-1-58536-843-3(1),* 203006) Sleeping Bear Pr.
—Digger y Daisy Van de Picnic (Digger & Daisy Go on a Picnic) Sullivan, Dana, illus. 2016. (I AM a READER: Digger & Daisy Ser.). (SPA & ENG.). 32p. (J). (gr. k-2). 9.99 *(978-1-62753-952-4(2),* 204175) Sleeping Bear Pr.

SMITH, BESSIE, 1898-1937

Tracy, Kathleen. Bessie Smith. 2012. (J). lib. bdg. 29.95 *(978-1-61228-271-8(7))* Mitchell Lane Pubs., Inc.

SMITH, JEDEDIAH STRONG, 1799-1831

Maynard, Charles W. Jedediah Smith: Mountain Man of the American West. (Famous Explorers of the American West Ser.). 24p. 2009. (gr. 3-4). 42.50 *(978-1-61512-501-2(9))* 2003. (Illus.). (J). lib. bdg. 22.60 *(978-0-8239-6287-7(3))* Rosen Publishing Group, Inc., The. (PowerKids Pr.).

SMITH, JOHN, 1580-1631

Adams, Colleen. Pocahontas. 2009. (Reading Room Collection 1 Ser.). 16p. (gr. 2-3). 37.50 *(978-1-60851-949-1(X),* PowerKids Pr.) Rosen Publishing Group, Inc., The.
—Pocahontas: The Life of an Indian Princess. 2006. (Rosen Publishing Group's Reading Room Collection). (Illus.). 16p. (J). (gr. 3-7). lib. bdg. 17.25 *(978-1-4042-3348-5(2),* PowerKids Pr.) Rosen Publishing Group, Inc., The.
—The True Story of Pocahontas. 2009. (What Really Happened? Ser.). 24p. (gr. 2-3). 42.50 *(978-1-60854-765-4(5),* PowerKids Pr.); (Illus.). (J). (gr. 3-6). lib. bdg. 22.60 *(978-1-4042-4475-7(1))* Rosen Publishing Group, Inc., The.
Benge, Janet & Benge, Geoff. Heroes of History - John Smith: A Foothold in the New World. 2006. (Heroes of History Ser.). (ENG., Illus.). 224p. (YA). (gr. 3-7). pap. 9.99 *(978-1-932096-36-1(1))* Emerald Bks.
Bruchac, Joseph. Pocahontas. 2005. (ENG., Illus.). 192p. (YA). (gr. 7-12). pap. 6.99 *(978-0-15-205465-6(0))* Houghton Mifflin Harcourt Publishing Co.
—Pocahontas. 2005. (Illus.). 173p. (gr. 7). 15.95 *(978-0-7569-5604-2(8))* Perfection Learning Corp.
Edison, Erin. Pocahontas, 1 vol. 2013. (Great Women in History Ser.). (ENG.). 24p. (gr. k-1). pap. 6.29 *(978-1-62065-861-1(5));* pap. 35.70 *(978-1-62065-862-8(3));* lib. bdg. 21.99 *(978-1-62065-074-5(6))* Capstone Press of Coughlan Cos. (Pebble Bks.).
Harkins, Susan Sales & Harkins, William H. Pochantas. 2008. (What's So Great About... ? Ser.). (Illus.). 32p. (J). (gr. 2-4). lib. bdg. 25.70 *(978-1-58415-682-6(1))* Mitchell Lane Pubs., Inc.
Jones, Rebecca C. Captain John Smith's Big & Beautiful Bay, 1 vol. Shute, Linda, illus. 2011. (ENG.). 32p. (J). 14.99 *(978-0-7643-3869-4(2),* 9780764338694, Schiffer Publishing Ltd) Schiffer Publishing, Ltd.
Loker, Aleck. Fearless Captain: The Adventures of John Smith. 2006. (Founders of the Republic Ser.). (Illus.). 176p. (J). (gr. 6-12). lib. bdg. 26.95 *(978-1-931798-83-9(4))* Reynolds, Morgan Inc.
McNeese, Tim. John Smith. 2010. (Leaders of the Colonial Era Ser.). 128p. (gr. 5-8). 35.00 *(978-1-60413-742-2(8),* Chelsea Hse.) Facts On File, Inc.
Nagle, Jeanne. Pocahontas: Facilitating Exchange Between the Powhatan & the Jamestown Settlers. 2017. (Women Who Changed History Ser.). 48p. (gr. 10-12). pap. 14.05 ***(978-1-68048-653-7(5),*** Britannica Educational Publishing) Rosen Publishing Group, Inc., The.
Petrie, Kristin. John Smith, 1 vol. 2007. (Explorers Set 2 Ser.). (ENG., Illus.). 32p. (gr. 4-7). 27.07 *(978-1-59679-751-2(7),* Checkerboard Library) ABDO Publishing Co.
Schanzer, Rosalyn. John Smith Escapes Again! 2006. (ENG., Illus.). 64p. (J). (gr. 4-7). 16.95 *(978-0-7922-5930-5(0));* lib. bdg. 25.90 *(978-0-7922-5931-2(9))* National Geographic Society. (National Geographic Children's Bks.).
Sita, Lisa. Pocahontas: The Powhatan Culture & the Jamestown Colony. 2009. (Library of American Lives & Times Ser.). 112p. (gr. 5-5). 69.20 *(978-1-60853-500-2(2))* Rosen Publishing Group, Inc., The.

SMITH, JOHN, 1580-1631—FICTION

Ransom, Candice. Sam Collier & the Founding of Jamestown. Archambault, Matthew, illus. 2006. (On My Own History Ser.). 48p. (J). (gr. 1-2). 25.26 *(978-1-57505-874-0(X),* Millbrook Pr.) Lerner Publishing Group.
Smith, Andrea P. Pocahontas & John Smith. 2012. (Illus.). 24p. (J). 63.60 *(978-1-4488-5219-2(6));* pap. 10.60 *(978-1-4488-5218-5(8));* lib. bdg. 25.25 *(978-1-4488-5190-4(4))* Rosen Publishing Group, Inc., The. (PowerKids Pr.).

SMITH, JOSEPH, JR., 1805-1844

Bagley, Val Chadwick. Joseph's First Vision. 2005. (Illus.). (J). *(978-1-59156-996-1(6))* Covenant Communications.
Lasater, Amy. This Is the Hill. Gerber, Patric, illus. 2005. (J). *(978-1-59156-720-2(3))* Covenant Communications.
Passey, Marion. My Tiny Book of Joseph Smith. 2004. (Illus.). (J). 5.95 *(978-1-59038-243-1(9))* Deseret Bk. Co.
Perry, David Earl, retold by. Joseph Smith, a Sacred Story. 2005. (Illus.). 149p. (J). per. *(978-0-941518-51-2(5))* Perry Enterprises.
Turley, Richard & Littke, Lael. Stories from the Life of Joseph Smith. 2008. 192p. pap. 16.95 *(978-1-60641-080-6(6))* Deseret Bk. Co.
Turley, Richard E. & Littke, Lael. Stories from the Life of Joseph Smith. 2003. (Illus.). viii, 184p. (J). *(978-1-57008-915-2(9))* Deseret Bk. Co.

SMITHSONIAN INSTITUTION

Smith, Roland & Smith, Marie. S Is for Smithsonian: America's Museum Alphabet. Frankenhuyzen, Gijsbert van, illus. 2010. (Sleeping Bear Alphabets Ser.). (ENG.). 32p. (J). (gr. 1-5). 17.95 *(978-1-58536-314-8(6))* Sleeping Bear Pr.

SMITHSONIAN INSTITUTION—FICTION

Messner, Kate. Capture the Flag. (ENG.). 240p. (J). (gr. 3-7). 2013. pap. 6.99 *(978-0-545-41974-1(3),* Scholastic Paperbacks) 2012. 16.99 *(978-0-545-39539-7(9),* Scholastic Pr.) Scholastic, Inc.

SMOKING

see also Tobacco Habit

Bass, Elissa. E-Cigarettes: The Risks of Addictive Nicotine & Toxic Chemicals. 2015. (Dangerous Drugs Ser.). (ENG.). 64p. (J). (gr. 6-6). lib. bdg. 34.21 *(978-1-5026-0564-1(3))* Cavendish Square Publishing.
Chastain, Zachary. Tobacco: Through the Smoke Screen. Henningfield, Jack E., ed. 2012. (Illicit & Misused Drugs Ser.). 128p. (J). (gr. 7). 24.95 *(978-1-4222-2442-7(2));* pap. 14.95 *(978-1-4222-2461-8(9))* Mason Crest.
Connelly, Elizabeth Russell. Nicotine= 2006. (Busted! Ser.). (Illus.). 112p. (J). (gr. 6-15). lib. bdg. 33.27 *(978-0-7660-2473-1(3))* Enslow Pubs., Inc.
Crozrock. Dr Crozrock Says Don't Smoke! 2010. 12p. pap. 8.49 *(978-1-4490-8163-8(0))* AuthorHouse.
Egendorf, Laura K. & Des Chenes, Elizabeth, eds. Smoking. 2007. (Issues That Concern You Ser.). (ENG., Illus.). 134p. (YA). (gr. 7-12). lib. bdg. 36.95 *(978-0-7377-2420-2(X),* LML02109-196221) Cengage Gale.
Esherick, Joan. No More Butts: Kicking the Tobacco Habit. 2008. (J). pap. 26.95 *(978-1-4222-1330-8(7))* Mason Crest.
—Smoking-Related Health Issues. McDonnell, Mary Ann & Forman, Sara, eds. 2013. (Young Adult's Guide to the Science of Health Ser.: 15). 128p. (J). (gr. 7-18). 24.95 *(978-1-4222-2816-6(9))* Mason Crest.
Espejo, Roman. Teen Smoking. Greenhaven Press Editors, ed. 2014. (At Issue Ser.). (ENG.). 128p. (gr. 10-12). pap. 27.80 *(978-0-7377-6867-1(3));* lib. bdg. 39.40 *(978-0-7377-6866-4(5))* Cengage Gale. (Greenhaven Pr., Inc.).
—Tobacco & Smoking. Greenhaven Press Editors, ed. 2014. (Teen Rights & Freedoms Ser.). (ENG., Illus.). 176p. (gr. 10-12). lib. bdg. 42.00 *(978-0-7377-6405-5(8),* Greenhaven Pr., Inc.) Cengage Gale.
—Tobacco & Smoking. 2015. (Opposing Viewpoints Ser.). (ENG., Illus.). 224p. (J). (gr. 10-12). 48.80 *(978-0-7377-7294-4(8),* Greenhaven Pr., Inc.) Cengage Gale.
Evans, Lesli. But All My Friends Smoke: Cigarettes & Peer Pressure. 2009. (Illus.). 112p. (J). pap. 26.95 *(978-1-4222-1327-8(7),* 1291217) Mason Crest.
Green, Carl R. Nicotine & Tobacco: A Myreportlinks. com Book. 2005. (Drugs Ser.). (Illus.). 48p. (J). (gr. 4-10). lib. bdg. 26.60 *(978-0-7660-5283-3(4),* MyReportLinks.com Bks.) Enslow Pubs., Inc.
Holt, Rinehart and Winston Staff. Decisions for Health Blue, Chptr. 14: Tobacco. 4th ed. 2004. (YA). pap. 11.20 *(978-0-03-068048-9(4))* Holt McDougal.
Hudson, David L. Smoking Bans. 2nd rev. ed. 2008. (Point/Counterpoint Ser.). (Illus.). 128p. (C). (gr. 9). 35.00 *(978-0-7910-9795-3(1),* Chelsea Hse.) Facts On File, Inc.
Hunnicutt, Susan C. Tobacco & Smoking. 2008. (Opposing Viewpoints Ser.). (ENG., Illus.). 222p. (YA). (gr. 10-12). 27.50 *(978-0-7377-4243-5(7),* LML01709-243155); pap. 39.70 *(978-0-7377-4242-8(9),* LML01709-243120) Cengage Gale. (Greenhaven Pr., Inc.).
Hunter, David. But Smoking Makes Me Happy: The Link Between Nicotine & Depression. 2009. (Tobacco: the Deadly Drug Ser.). (Illus.). 112p. (YA). (gr. 7-12). 26.95 *(978-1-4222-0244-9(5));* (J). pap. 26.95 *(978-1-4222-1335-3(8))* Mason Crest.
Jaime, Everett. Baby Don't Smoke. Brown, Eliot R., illus. 2012. (ENG.). 40p. (J). pap. 9.95 *(978-1-935826-20-0(4))* Kalindi Pr.
Jones, David C. One Person to Another: Smoking, Chewing Tobacco & Young Peopole. l.t. ed. 2003. 20p. (YA). 4.00 *(978-1-878400-17-8(7))* Dolphin Publishing.
Keyishan, Elizabeth. Todo lo que necesitas saber sobre el cigarillo (Everything You Need to Know about Smoking) 2009. (Todo lo que necesitas (the Need to Know Library) Ser.). (SPA.). 64p. (gr. 6-6). 58.50 *(978-1-60854-407-3(9),* Editorial Buenas Letras) Rosen Publishing Group, Inc., The.
Keyishian, Elizabeth. Everything You Need to Know about Smoking. 2009. (Need to Know Library). 64p. (gr. 5-5). 58.50 *(978-1-60854-086-0(3))* Rosen Publishing Group, Inc., The.
—Smoking. rev. ed. 2005. (Need to Know Library). (Illus.). 64p. (J). (gr. 7-12). lib. bdg. 31.95 *(978-0-8239-4092-9(6))* Rosen Publishing Group, Inc., The.
Landau, Elaine. Cigarettes. 2003. (Watts Library). (ENG.). 64p. (J). (gr. 5-7). pap. 8.95 *(978-0-531-16666-6(X),* Watts, Franklin) Scholastic Library Publishing.
LeVert, Suzanne. The Facts about Nicotine. 2006. (Drugs Ser.). (Illus.). 112p. (YA). (gr. 9-12). lib. bdg. 42.79 *(978-0-7614-2244-0(7))* Marshall Cavendish Corp.
Malaspina, Ann. False Images, Deadly Promises: Smoking & the Media. 2007. (Tobacco: the Deadly Drug Ser.). (Illus.). 112p. (YA). pap. 12.95 *(978-1-4222-0812-0(5))* Mason Crest.
marcovitz, hal. Should Smoking Be Banned? 2012. (Illus.). 96p. (J). lib. bdg. *(978-1-60152-462-1(5))* ReferencePoint Pr., Inc.
Mason, Paul. Know the Facts about Drinking & Smoking. 2009. (J). 70.50 *(978-1-4358-5463-5(2),* Rosen Reference); (ENG.). 48p. (YA). pap. 11.75 *(978-1-4358-5462-8(4),* Rosen Reference); (ENG., Illus.). 48p. (YA). (gr. 5-9). lib. bdg. 29.25 *(978-1-4358-5339-3(3))* Rosen Publishing Group, Inc., The.
Meinking, Mary. Cash Crop to Cash Cow: The History of Tobacco & Smoking in America. 2007. (Tobacco: the Deadly Drug Ser.). (Illus.). 112p. (YA). pap. 12.95 *(978-1-4222-0811-3(7))* Mason Crest.
Paris, Stephanie. Hablemos Claro: Fumar. 2017. (TIME for Kids en Español - Level 4 Ser.). (SPA.). 48p. (gr. 4-4). lib. bdg. 31.99 *(978-1-5157-5139-7(2))* Time for Kids Inc AUS. Dist: Capstone Pub.
—Straight Talk: Smoking, 1 vol. 2nd rev. ed. 2013. (Nonfiction Readers Ser.). (ENG., Illus.). 48p. (J). (gr. 4-4). pap. 29.96 *(978-1-4807-1110-5(1))* Shell Educational Publishing.
—Straight Talk: Smoking, 1 vol. 2nd rev. ed. 2012. (TIME for KIDS(r) Nonfiction Readers Ser.). (ENG., Illus.). 48p. (J). (gr. 4-4). pap. 9.99 *(978-1-4333-4858-7(6))* Teacher Created Materials, Inc.
Parks, Peggy J. The Dangers of E-Cigarettes. 2016. (ENG.). 80p. (J). (gr. 5-12). *(978-1-68282-014-8(9))* ReferencePoint Pr., Inc.
—Smoking. rev. ed. 2014. (Matters of Opinion Ser.). (ENG.). 64p. (J). (gr. 4-6). pap. 14.60 *(978-1-60357-582-9(0));* lib. bdg. 27.93 *(978-1-59953-602-6(1))* Norwood Hse. Pr.
Price, Sean. Nicotine. 2008. (Junior Drug Awareness Ser.). (Illus.). 120p. (gr. 5-8). 30.00 *(978-0-7910-9696-3(3),* Chelsea Hse.) Facts On File, Inc.
Reimer, Jackie. No Thanks, but I'd Love to Dance! Choosing to Live Smoke Free. Reimer, Jackie, illus. 2010. (ENG., Illus.). 32p. (J). (gr. 2-4). 14.95 *(978-1-60443-027-1(3))* American Cancer Society, Inc.
Sharp, Katie John. Smokeless Tobacco: Not a Safe Alternative. 2009. (Illus.). 112p. (J). pap. 26.95 *(978-1-4222-1332-2(3),* 1291227) Mason Crest.
Smoking. (Introducing Issues with Opposing Viewpoints Ser.). 2011. (ENG.). 144p. 36.95 *(978-0-7377-5101-7(0))* 2008. (Illus.). 176-240p. (gr. 10-12). 36.20 *(978-0-7377-3293-1(8))* 2008. (Illus.). 176-240p. (gr. 10-12). pap. 24.95 *(978-0-7377-3294-8(6))* Cengage Gale. (Greenhaven Pr., Inc.).
Smoking. 2nd rev. ed. 2009. (Truth about Ser.). (Illus.). 240p. (C). (gr. 9-18). 35.00 *(978-0-8160-7632-1(4))* Facts On File, Inc.
Stewart, Gail B. Ripped from the Headlines: Smoking. 2007. (Ripped from the Headlines Ser.). (J). (gr. 7-12). 23.95 *(978-1-60217-017-9(7))* Erickson Pr.
Stollers, Veronica & Keyishian, Elizabeth. Frequently Asked Questions about Smoking. 2011. (FAQ: Teen Life Ser.). (J). lib. bdg. 31.95 *(978-1-4488-4631-3(5))* Rosen Publishing Group, Inc., The.
Synder, Gail. Teens & Smoking. 2015. (Illus.). 80p. (J). *(978-1-60152-918-3(X))* ReferencePoint Pr., Inc.
Thomas, Amy N. Burning Money: The Cost of Smoking. (Tobacco: the Deadly Drug Ser.). (Illus.). 112p. 2009. (YA). (gr. 7-12). 26.95 *(978-1-4222-0242-5(9))* 2009. (J). pap. 26.95 *(978-1-4222-1326-1(9))* 2007. (YA). (gr. 3-7). pap. 12.95 *(978-1-4222-0808-3(7))* Mason Crest.
Walker, Ida. Addiction in America: Society, Psychology & Heredity. 2012. (Illus.). 128p. (J). *(978-1-4222-2443-4(0));* *(978-1-4222-2424-3(4))* Mason Crest.
Wilcox, Christine. Thinking Critically: E-Cigarettes & Vaping. 2016. (Thinking Critically Ser.). (ENG., Illus.). 80p. (J). (gr. 5-12). 38.60 *(978-1-60152-956-5(2))* ReferencePoint Pr., Inc.

SMOKING—FICTION

Baker, Susan F. Don't Smoke, Daddy. 2008. 27p. 30.95 *(978-1-4357-2127-2(6))* Lulu Pr., Inc.
Gosselin, Kim. Smoking Stinks!! Buttner, Thom, illus. 2nd ed. 2009. (Substance Free Kids Ser.). 30p. (J). (gr. -1-3). pap. 16.95 *(978-1-891383-20-5(5))* JayJo Bks., LLC.
Hankins, M. Lil' Mikie Tells It Like It Is. 2007. 20p. per. 24.95 *(978-1-4137-0168-5(X))* America Star Bks.
MacGregor, Doug, creator. Ochre the Smoker: A fantastic Fable. 2007. (Illus.). 48p. (J). per. 14.95 *(978-0-9654843-2-9(7))* MacGregor, Doug.
Maria Muirhead. Smoking = Problems: Flora-Lee's Journal. 2010. 56p. pap. 8.95 *(978-1-4502-0645-7(X))* iUniverse, Inc.
McDaniel, Carren. Fresh Air Friends: The Dangers of Secondhand Smoke. 2012. (ENG.). 33p. (J). pap. 14.95 *(978-1-4327-9818-5(9))* Outskirts Pr., Inc.
Proctor, Darrell. The Cigarette Monster. 2006. (J). pap. 8.00 *(978-0-8059-6790-6(7))* Dorrance Publishing Co., Inc.
Thuma, Chris. Cigarette Sue. 2008. 24p. per. 12.95 *(978-1-59858-561-2(4))* Dog Ear Publishing, LLC.
The Tobacco Temptation. (J). 39.50 *(978-1-56230-082-1(2))* Syndistar, Inc.

SMUGGLING

Nichols, Katherine. Deep Water. 2017. (Simon True Ser.). (ENG., Illus.). 288p. (YA). (gr. 9). pap. 10.99 ***(978-1-4814-8106-9(1),*** Simon Pulse) Simon Pulse.

SMUGGLING—FICTION

Aldridge, Janet. The Meadow-Brook Girls by the Sea, or Th. 2006. pap. *(978-1-4065-0693-8(1))* Dodo Pr.

S

Anderson, Sandra. Rockcliffe. 2007. 156p. per. 8.95 *(978-1-59800-893-7(5))* Outskirts Pr., Inc.

Baker, Mary. Christmas Annie. 2009. 70p. pap. 7.96 *(978-0-557-17289-4(6))* Lulu Pr., Inc.

Balliett, Blue. Hold Fast. 2015. (ENG.). 288p. (J). (gr. 3-7). pap. 6.99 *(978-0-545-29989-3(6),* Scholastic Paperbacks) Scholastic, Inc.

Barnett, Mac. Danger Goes Berserk. Myers, Matthew, illus. (Brixton Brothers Ser.: 4). (ENG.). 256p. (J). (gr. 3-7). 2013. pap. 7.99 *(978-1-4424-3978-8(5))* 2012. 17.99 *(978-1-4424-3977-1(7))* Simon & Schuster Bks. For Young Readers. (Simon & Schuster Bks. For Young Readers).

Benjamin, Ruth. The Mysterious Lighthouse of Chelton. 2006. (ENG.). 160p. (J). 14.95 *(978-1-932443-57-8(6))* Judaica Pr., Inc., The.

Bollback, Anthony G. Smugglers in Hong Kong. 2012. 156p. pap. 8.99 *(978-0-9849359-0-1(8))* Finding the Cause, LLC.

Chamberlain, Penny. Chasing the Mooon, 1 vol. 2007. (ENG.). 252p. (J). (gr. 3-8). per. 8.95 *(978-1-55039-157-2(7))* Sono Nis Pr. CAN. Dist: Orca Bk. Pubs. USA.

Decary, Marie. Adam et le Raton Dessinateur. Beshwathy, Steve, illus. 2004. (Premier Roman Ser.). (FRE.). 64p. (J). (gr. 1-4). pap. *(978-2-89021-643-3(8))* Diffusion du livre Mirabel (DLM).

—Adam's Tropical Adventure. Beshwaty, Steve, illus. 2005. 54p. (J). lib. bdg. 12.00 *(978-1-4242-1202-6(2))* Fitzgerald Bks.

Deuker, Carl & Perry, Thomas. Runner. 2007. (ENG.). 224p. (YA). (gr. 7-12). pap. 8.99 *(978-0-618-73505-1(4))* Houghton Mifflin Harcourt Publishing Co.

Falkner, John Meade. Moonfleet. 2013. (Oxford Children's Classics Ser.). (ENG.). 304p. 9.95 *(978-0-19-273478-5(4))* Oxford Univ. Pr., Inc.

—Moonfleet: A Classic Tale of Smuggling. Marks, Alan, illus. 2007. (Young Reading Series 3 Gift Bks). 63p. (J). (gr. 4-7). 8.99 *(978-0-7945-1906-3(7),* Usborne) EDC Publishing.

Furtney, Charles S. Tryconnel: An Antebellum Adventure along the C & O Canal. 2004. (Illus.). iii, 156p. (J). pap. *(978-0-9711835-3-7(8))* Local History Co., The.

Grant, Myrna. Ivan & the Secret in the Suitcase. 2006. (Flamingo Fiction 9-13s Ser.). (ENG., Illus.). 144p. (J). (gr. 4-7). per. 6.99 *(978-1-84550-136-5(5),* 90ba43f9-c4f3-4eac-aa9d-e552a2ffb74d) Christian Focus Pubns. GBR. Dist: Bookmasters Distribution.

Harvey, M. A. The Scorpion Secret: Dare to Take the Test. 2004. (Illus.). 128p. (J). pap. *(978-1-84458-050-7(4),* Pavilion Children's Books) Pavilion Bks.

Holmes, Victoria. Rider in the Dark: An Epic Horse Story. 2004. (Illus.). 320p. (J). (gr. 5-18). (ENG.). 15.99 *(978-0-06-052025-0(6));* lib. bdg. 16.89 *(978-0-06-052026-7(4))* HarperCollins Pubs.

Inspector Grub & the Fizzer-X Spy: Individual Title Six-Packs. (Bookweb Ser.). 32p. (gr. 5-18). 34.00 *(978-0-7635-3786-9(1))* Rigby Education.

Jorgensen, Norman. Smuggler's Curse The. 2017. (ENG.). 356p. (J). (gr. 4-7). 8.95 ***(978-1-925164-19-0(5))*** Fremantle Pr. AUS. Dist: Independent Pubs. Group.

Korman, Gordon. Escape. 2008. (Island (Playaway Audio) Ser.). (J). 34.99 *(978-1-60514-854-0(7))* Findaway World, LLC.

McClintock, Norah. Nothing to Lose. 2012. (Robyn Hunter Mysteries Ser.: 3). (ENG.). 200p. (YA). (gr. 6-12). pap. 8.95 *(978-0-7613-8531-8(2),* Darby Creek); lib. bdg. 27.93 *(978-0-7613-8313-0(1))* Lerner Publishing Group.

Milford, Kate. Ghosts of Greenglass House. 2017. (ENG., Illus.). 464p. (J). (gr. 5-7). 17.99 ***(978-0-544-99146-0(X),*** Clarion Bks.) Houghton Mifflin Harcourt Trade & Reference Pubs.

Morgan, Nicola. The Highwayman's Curse. 2009. (J). *(978-0-7636-4066-8(2))* Candlewick Pr.

Mowat, Farley. The Black Joke. 2009. (ENG.). 192p. pap. 9.95 *(978-0-7710-6469-2(1),* Emblem Editions) McClelland & Stewart CAN. Dist: Random Hse., Inc.

Prins, Piet. The Haunted Castle. 2006. (Illus.). 139p. (J). pap. *(978-1-894666-44-2(5))* Inheritance Pubns.

Renn, Diana. Blue Voyage. 2015. (ENG.). 464p. (YA). (gr. 7). 18.99 *(978-0-670-01559-7(8),* Viking Books for Young Readers) Penguin Young Readers Group.

Service, Pamela F. Camp Alien. 2010. pap. 33.92 *(978-0-7613-6955-4(4))* Lerner Publishing Group.

—Camp Alien. Gorman, Mike, illus. (Alien Agent Ser.: 2). (ENG.). 160p. (J). (gr. 4-6). 2010. pap. 5.95 *(978-0-7613-5247-1(3))* 2009. 16.95 *(978-0-8225-8656-2(8),* Carolrhoda Bks.) Lerner Publishing Group.

Sherman, M. Zachary & Iligan, Marlon. Heart of the Enemy, 1 vol. Cage, Josef, illus. 2012. (Bloodlines Ser.). (ENG.). 88p. (gr. 4-8). lib. bdg. 26.65 *(978-1-4342-3767-5(2))* Stone Arch Bks.

Stem, Jacqueline. The Ghosts of Goliad. 2003. iii, 165p. (J). 17.95 *(978-1-57168-785-2(8),* Eakin Pr.) Eakin Pr.

Striker, Fran. Lone Ranger Traps Smugglers. (J). 21.95 *(978-0-8488-1183-9(6))* Amereon Ltd.

Taranta, Mary. Shimmer & Burn. 2017. (YA). pap. ***(978-1-4814-7200-5(3),*** McElderry, Margaret K. Bks.) McElderry, Margaret K. Bks.

Wells, Helen. Cherry Ames Jungle Nurse. 2007. (Cherry Ames Nurse Stories Ser.). 224p. (J). (gr. 3-7). 14.95 *(978-0-8261-0433-5(9))* Springer Publishing Co., Inc.

—Cherry Ames, Ski Nurse Mystery. 2007. (Cherry Ames Nurse Stories Ser.). 224p. (J). (gr. 3-7). 14.95 *(978-0-8261-0437-3(1))* Springer Publishing Co., Inc.

SMURFS (FICTITIOUS CHARACTERS)—FICTION

Delporte, Peyo, et al. The Smurfs & the Howlbird. 2011. (Smurfs Graphic Novels Ser.). (ENG., Illus.). 56p. (J). (gr. 2-5). 10.99 *(978-1-59707-261-8(3),* 9781597072618) Papercutz.

Delporte, Yvan. The Purple Smurfs. Peyo, illus. 2010. (Smurfs Graphic Novels Ser.). (ENG.). 56p. (J). (gr. 2-5). pap. 6.99 *(978-1-59707-206-9(0),* 9781597072069) Papercutz.

—The Smurfs & the Magic Flute. Peyo, illus. 2010. (Smurfs Graphic Novels Ser.). (ENG.). 64p. (J). (gr. 2-5). pap. 5.99 *(978-1-59707-208-3(7),* 9781597072083) Papercutz.

Delporte, Yvan & Peyo. The Purple Smurf, No. 1. 2010. (Smurfs Graphic Novels Ser.). (ENG., Illus.). 56p. (J). (gr. 2-5). 12.99 *(978-1-59707-207-6(9),* 9781597072076) Papercutz.

—The Smurf King. 2010. (Smurfs Graphic Novels Ser.). (ENG., Illus.). 64p. (J). (gr. 2-5). 10.99 *(978-1-59707-225-0(7),* 9781597072250) Papercutz.

—The Smurfs & the Magic Flute. 2010. (Smurfs Graphic Novels Ser.). (ENG., Illus.). 64p. (J). (gr. 2-5). 10.99 *(978-1-59707-209-0(5),* 9781597072090) Papercutz.

Gallo, Tina. Behold the Power of Gargamel! Riley, Kellee, illus. 2011. (Smurfs Movie Ser.). (ENG.). 24p. (J). (gr. -1-3). pap. 6.99 *(978-1-4424-2395-4(1),* Simon Spotlight) Simon Spotlight.

Gos & Peyo. The Astrosmurf. 2011. (Smurfs Graphic Novels Ser.). (ENG., Illus.). 56p. (J). (gr. 2-5). 10.99 *(978-1-59707-251-9(6),* 9781597072519) Papercutz.

Gos, Charles & Peyo. The Astrosmurf. 2011. (Smurfs Graphic Novels Ser.). (ENG., Illus.). 56p. (J). (gr. 2-5). pap. 5.99 *(978-1-59707-250-2(8),* 9781597072502) Papercutz.

Peyo. The Aerosmurf. 2013. (Smurfs Graphic Novels Ser.). (ENG., Illus.). 56p. (J). (gr. 2-5). 10.99 *(978-1-59707-427-8(6),* 9781597074278); pap. 5.99 *(978-1-59707-426-1(8),* 9781597074261) Papercutz.

—All about Brainy Smurf! 2013. (Smurfs Classic Ser.). (ENG.). 12p. (J). (gr. -1-k). bds. 5.99 *(978-1-4424-7264-8(2),* Simon Spotlight) Simon Spotlight.

—Astro Smurf Blasts Off! Peyo, illus. 2013. (Smurfs Classic Ser.). (ENG., Illus.). 24p. (J). (gr. -1-2). pap. 3.99 *(978-1-4424-8514-3(0),* Simon Spotlight) Simon Spotlight.

—The Baby Smurf. 2013. (Smurfs Graphic Novels Ser.). (ENG., Illus.). 56p. (J). (gr. 1-5). pap. 5.99 *(978-1-59707-381-3(4),* 9781597073813) Papercutz.

—Find the 100 Smurfs! Peyo, illus. 2012. (Smurfs Classic Ser.). (ENG., Illus.). 12p. (J). (gr. -1-2). bds. 9.99 *(978-1-4424-5350-0(8),* Simon Spotlight) Simon Spotlight.

—The Giant Smurf. Peyo, illus. 2013. (Smurfs Classic Ser.). (ENG., Illus.). 24p. (J). (gr. -1-2). pap. 3.99 *(978-1-4424-6178-9(0),* Simon Spotlight) Simon Spotlight.

—It's a Smurfy World! Peyo, illus. 2013. (Smurfs Classic Ser.). (ENG., Illus.). 16p. (J). (gr. -1-k). bds. 7.99 *(978-1-4424-6709-5(6),* Simon Spotlight) Simon Spotlight.

—Lazy Smurf Takes a Nap. 2012. (Smurfs Classic Ser.). (ENG.). 24p. (J). (gr. -1-3). pap. 3.99 *(978-1-4424-4647-2(1),* Simon Spotlight) Simon Spotlight.

—Marry Me, Smurfette! 2012. (Smurfs Classic Ser.). (ENG.). 16p. (J). (gr. -1-3). pap. 5.99 *(978-1-4424-5911-3(5),* Simon Spotlight) Simon Spotlight.

—Meet Smurfette. Peyo, illus. 2011. (Smurfs Classic Ser.). (ENG., Illus.). 24p. (J). (gr. -1-2). pap. 3.99 *(978-1-4424-2290-2(4),* Simon Spotlight) Simon Spotlight.

—Off to School! Peyo, illus. 2011. (Smurfs Classic Ser.). (ENG., Illus.). 32p. (J). (gr. k-2). pap. 3.99 *(978-1-4424-2138-7(X));* lib. bdg. 15.99 *(978-1-4424-3062-4(1))* Simon Spotlight. (Simon Spotlight).

—Papa Smurf's Favorite Things. Peyo, illus. 2013. (Smurfs Classic Ser.). (ENG., Illus.). 12p. (J). (gr. -1-k). bds. 5.99 *(978-1-4424-6167-3(5),* Simon Spotlight) Simon Spotlight.

—Rain, Rain, Smurf Away. Peyo, illus. 2012. (Smurfs Classic Ser.). (ENG., Illus.). 24p. (J). (gr. -1-3). pap. 3.99 *(978-1-4424-3600-8(X),* Simon Spotlight) Simon Spotlight.

—The Return of the Smurfette. 2012. (Smurfs Graphic Novels Ser.). (ENG., Illus.). 56p. (J). (gr. 2-5). pap. 5.99 *(978-1-59707-292-2(3),* 9781597072922) Papercutz.

—Sky-High Smurf. Peyo, illus. 2014. (Smurfs Classic Ser.). (ENG., Illus.). 16p. (J). (gr. -1-3). 5.99 *(978-1-4424-9740-5(8),* Simon Spotlight) Simon Spotlight.

—Smurf Cake. Peyo, illus. 2013. (Smurfs Classic Ser.). (ENG., Illus.). 32p. (J). (gr. k-2). 16.99 *(978-1-4424-8493-1(4));* pap. 3.99 *(978-1-4424-8492-4(6))* Simon Spotlight. (Simon Spotlight).

—The Smurf Championship Games. Peyo, illus. 2012. (Smurfs Classic Ser.). (ENG., Illus.). 32p. (J). (gr. k-2). pap. 3.99 *(978-1-4424-4993-0(4),* Simon Spotlight) Simon Spotlight.

—The Smurf Championship Games. 2012. (Simon & Schuster Ready-To-Read Level 2 Ser.). lib. bdg. 13.55 *(978-0-606-26363-4(2),* Turtleback) Turtleback Bks.

—Smurfette & the Beast: A Smurftastic Pop-Up Book. Peyo, illus. 2013. (Smurfs Classic Ser.). (ENG., Illus.). 12p. (J). (gr. -1-3). 17.99 *(978-1-4424-8317-0(2),* Simon Spotlight) Simon Spotlight.

—Smurfiness to Go! A Smurfin' Big Adventure, Meet Smurfette!, Lazy Smurf Takes a Nap, the Thankful Smurf, Rain, Rain Smurf Away, the 100th Smurf. Peyo, illus. 2012. (Smurfs Classic Ser.). (ENG., Illus.). 144p. (J). (gr. -1-2). pap. 15.99 *(978-1-4424-6520-6(4),* Simon Spotlight) Simon Spotlight.

—The Smurflings. 2013. (Smurfs Graphic Novels Ser.). (ENG., Illus.). 56p. (J). (gr. 2-5). 10.99 *(978-1-59707-408-7(X),* 9781597074087); pap. 5.99 *(978-1-59707-407-0(1),* 9781597074070) Papercutz.

—The Smurfs #14: the Baby Smurf. 2013. (Smurfs Graphic Novels Ser.). (ENG., Illus.). 56p. (J). (gr. 1-5). 10.99 *(978-1-59707-382-0(2),* 9781597073820) Papercutz.

—The Smurfs & the Magic Egg. Peyo, illus. 2014. (Smurfs Classic Ser.). (ENG., Illus.). 32p. (J). (gr. k-2). pap. 3.99 *(978-1-4424-9570-8(7),* Simon Spotlight) Simon Spotlight.

—The Smurfs Anthology #2. 2013. (Smurfs Anthology Ser.). (ENG., Illus.). 192p. (J). (gr. 6-5). 19.99 *(978-1-59707-445-2(4),* 9781597074452) Papercutz.

—The Smurfs Apprentice. 2013. (Smurfs Classic Ser.). (ENG.). 24p. (J). (gr. -1-2). pap. 3.99 *(978-1-4424-7263-1(4),* Simon Spotlight) Simon Spotlight.

—The Smurfs Christmas. 2013. (Smurfs Graphic Novels Ser.). (ENG., Illus.). 56p. (J). (gr. 2-5). 10.99 *(978-1-59707-452-0(7),* 9781597074520); pap. 5.99 *(978-1-59707-451-3(9),* 9781597074513) Papercutz.

—The Smurfs Graphic Novels Boxed Set: Vol. #10-12. 2013. (Smurfs Graphic Novels Ser.). (ENG., Illus.). 168p. (J). (gr. 2-5). 17.99 *(978-1-59707-386-8(5),* 9781597073868) Papercutz.

—Smurfs Mini Library: Rise & Shine; Happy Smurfdays; Fun & Games; Making Music; Whatever the Weather. Peyo, illus. 2014. (Smurfs Classic Ser.). (ENG., Illus.). 70p. (J). (gr. -1-2). bds. 6.99 *(978-1-4424-9543-2(X),* Simon Spotlight) Simon Spotlight.

—The Thankful Smurf. 2012. (Smurfs Classic Ser.). (ENG., Illus.). 24p. (J). (gr. -1-3). pap. 3.99 *(978-1-4424-5292-3(7),* Simon Spotlight) Simon Spotlight.

—Welcome, Baby Smurf! Peyo, illus. 2014. (Smurfs Classic Ser.). (ENG., Illus.). 24p. (J). (gr. -1-2). pap. 3.99 *(978-1-4424-9542-5(1),* Simon Spotlight) Simon Spotlight.

—Who's That Smurf? Peyo, illus. 2013. (Smurfs Classic Ser.). (ENG., Illus.). 18p. (J). (gr. -1-1). bds. 5.99 *(978-1-4424-7235-8(9),* Simon Spotlight) Simon Spotlight.

—Why Do You Cry, Baby Smurf? Peyo, illus. 2013. (Smurfs Classic Ser.). (ENG., Illus.). 32p. (J). (gr. k-2). 15.99 *(978-1-4424-6193-2(4));* pap. 3.99 *(978-1-4424-6191-8(8))* Simon Spotlight. (Simon Spotlight).

Peyo & Delporte, Yvan. The Smurf Olympics. 2012. (Smurfs Graphic Novels Ser.). (ENG., Illus.). 56p. (J). (gr. 2-5). 10.99 *(978-1-59707-302-8(4),* 9781597073028); pap. 7.99 *(978-1-59707-301-1(6),* 9781597073011) Papercutz.

—Smurf Soup. 2012. (Smurfs Graphic Novels Ser.). (ENG., Illus.). 56p. (J). (gr. 1-6). pap. 5.99 *(978-1-59707-358-5(X),* 9781597073585) Papercutz.

—Smurf vs. Smurf. 2012. (Smurfs Graphic Novels Ser.). (ENG., Illus.). 56p. (J). (gr. 2-5). 10.99 *(978-1-59707-321-9(0),* 9781597073219); pap. 5.99 *(978-1-59707-320-2(2),* 9781597073202) Papercutz.

—The Smurfette. 2011. (Smurfs Graphic Novels Ser.). (ENG., Illus.). 64p. (J). (gr. 2-5). pap. 5.99 *(978-1-59707-236-6(2),* 9781597072366) No. 4. 10.99 *(978-1-59707-237-3(0),* 9781597072373) Papercutz.

—The Smurfs, 3 Vols., Set. 2011. (Smurfs Graphic Novels Ser.). (ENG., Illus.). 184p. (J). (gr. 2-5). 17.99 *(978-1-59707-273-1(7),* 9781597072731) Papercutz.

—The Smurfs #10: the Return of the Smurfette. 2012. (Smurfs Graphic Novels Ser.). (ENG., Illus.). 56p. (J). (gr. 2-5). 10.99 *(978-1-59707-293-9(1),* 9781597072939) Papercutz.

—The Smurfs #13: Smurf Soup. 2012. (Smurfs Graphic Novels Ser.). (ENG., Illus.). 56p. (J). (gr. 1-6). 10.99 *(978-1-59707-359-2(8),* 9781597073592) Papercutz.

—The Smurfs #9: Gargamel & the Smurfs. 2011. (Smurfs Graphic Novels Ser.). (ENG., Illus.). 56p. (J). (gr. 2-5). 10.99 *(978-1-59707-290-8(7),* 9781597072908); pap. 5.99 *(978-1-59707-289-2(3),* 9781597072892) Papercutz.

—The Smurfs & the Egg. 2011. (Smurfs Graphic Novels Ser.). (ENG., Illus.). 64p. (J). (gr. 2-5). 10.99 *(978-1-59707-247-2(8),* 9781597072472); pap. 5.99 *(978-1-59707-246-5(X),* 9781597072465) Papercutz.

—The Smurfs Graphic Novels Boxed Set: Vol. #7-9. Gos, illus. 2012. (Smurfs Graphic Novels Ser.). (ENG.). 168p. (J). (gr. 2-5). 17.99 *(978-1-59707-340-0(7),* 9781597073400) Papercutz.

Peyo, et al. The Smurfs, Set, Vols. 4-6. 2012. (Smurfs Graphic Novels Ser.). (ENG., Illus.). 184p. (J). (gr. 2-5). 17.99 *(978-1-59707-306-6(7),* 9781597073066) Papercutz.

—The Smurfs #8: the Smurf Apprentice. 2011. (Smurfs Graphic Novels Ser.). (ENG., Illus.). 56p. (J). (gr. 2-5). 10.99 *(978-1-59707-280-9(X),* 9781597072809); pap. 5.99 *(978-1-59707-279-3(6),* 9781597072793) Papercutz.

—The Smurfs & the Howlibird. 2011. (Smurfs Graphic Novels Ser.). (ENG., Illus.). 56p. (J). (gr. 2-5). pap. 5.99 *(978-1-59707-260-1(5),* 9781597072601) Papercutz.

Publications International Ltd. Staff, ed. The Smurfs Large Play a Sound. 2011. 24p. (J). 14.98 *(978-1-60553-403-9(X))* Phoenix International Publications, Inc.

Shaw, Natalie & Barton, Elizabeth Dennis. The Smurfin' Guide to the Smurfs. 2011. (Smurfs Classic Ser.). (ENG., Illus.). 96p. (J). (gr. 1-5). pap. 5.99 *(978-1-4424-2291-9(2),* Simon Spotlight) Simon Spotlight.

SNAILS

Alessi, Jolene. Zombie Snails. 2015. (Zombie Animals: Parasites Take Control! Ser.). (ENG., Illus.). 24p. (J). (gr. 2-3). pap. 8.15 *(978-1-4824-2848-3(2))* Stevens, Gareth Publishing LLLP.

Allen, Judy. Are You a Snail? Humphries, Tudor, illus. 2003. (Backyard Bks.). (ENG.). 31p. (J). (gr. k-3). pap. 6.99 *(978-0-7534-5604-0(4),* 9780753456040, Kingfisher) Roaring Brook Pr.

Appleton-Smith, Laura & Blackaby, Susan. Keeping Track of Snail Facts. 2014. (Book to Remember Ser.). (ENG., Illus.). 26p. (J). pap. 8.95 *(978-1-60541-148-4(5),* Books To Remember) Flyleaf Publishing.

Bader, Bonnie. Snail-Snaily-Snails. 2017. (Penguin Young Readers, Level 2 Ser.). (ENG., Illus.). 32p. (J). (gr. 1-2). 14.99 *(978-0-451-53440-8(9),* Penguin Young Readers) Penguin Young Readers Group.

Baxter, Bethany. Conches. 2013. (Awesome Armored Animals Ser.). 24p. (J). (gr. k-5). 22.60 *(978-1-4777-0796-8(4));* pap. 49.50 *(978-1-4777-0965-8(7));* pap. 8.25 *(978-1-4777-0964-1(9))* Rosen Publishing Group, Inc., The. (PowerKids Pr.).

Cain, Marie Mowery. Slow Slugs & Snails. 2013. (Big Books, Red Ser.). (ENG & SPA., Illus.). 16p. pap. 33.00 *(978-1-59246-221-6(9))* Big Books, by George!

Campbell, Sarah C. Wolfsnail: A Backyard Predator. Campbell, Sarah C. & Campbell, Richard P., photos by. 2008. (ENG., Illus.). 32p. (J). (gr. -1-2). 16.95 *(978-1-59078-554-6(1))* Boyds Mills Pr.

Caviezel, Giovanni, illus. Little Snail. 2014. (Mini-Creatures Ser.). (ENG.). 8p. (J). (gr. -1 — 1). bds. 4.99 *(978-0-7641-6715-7(4))* Barron's Educational Series, Inc.

Clark, Willow & Rockwood, Leigh. Snails Are Gross! 2010. (Creepy Crawlies Ser.). (Illus.). 24p. (J). (gr. k-2). lib. bdg. 22.60 *(978-1-4488-0699-7(2));* pap. 8.25 *(978-1-4488-1359-9(X),* PowerKids Pr.) Rosen Publishing Group, Inc., The.

Fredericks, Anthony D. In One Tidepool: Crabs, Snails, & Salty Tails. DiRubbio, Jennifer, illus. 2004. (Sharing Nature with Children Book Ser.). 32p. (J). (gr. -1-2). 16.95 *(978-1-58469-039-9(9));* pap. 7.95 *(978-1-58469-038-2(0))* Dawn Pubns.

Gates, Margo. Snails. 2013. (Backyard Wildlife Ser.). (ENG., Illus.). 24p. (J). (gr. k-3). lib. bdg. 25.95 *(978-1-60014-920-7(0),* Blastoff! Readers) Bellwether Media.

Gray, Susan H. Giant African Snail. 2008. (21st Century Skills Library: Animal Invaders Ser.). (ENG., Illus.). 32p. (gr. 4-8). lib. bdg. 28.50 *(978-1-60279-241-8(0),* 200115) Cherry Lake Publishing.

How Snails Live: 6 Each of 1 Student Book, 6 vols. (Sunshinetm Science Ser.). 24p. (gr. 1-2). 41.95 *(978-0-7802-2702-6(6))* Wright Group/McGraw-Hill.

How Snails Live: Big Book. (Sunshinetm Science Ser.). 24p. (gr. 1-2). 37.50 *(978-0-7802-2785-9(9))* Wright Group/McGraw-Hill.

How Snails Protect Themselves: 6 Each of 1 Student Book, 6 vols. (Sunshinetm Science Ser.). 24p. (gr. 1-2). 41.95 *(978-0-7802-2704-0(2))* Wright Group/McGraw-Hill.

How Snails Protect Themselves: Big Book. (Sunshinetm Science Ser.). 24p. (gr. 1-2). 37.50 *(978-0-7802-2786-6(7))* Wright Group/McGraw-Hill.

Jacobs, Liza. Snails. 2003. (Wild Wild World Ser.). (Illus.). 24p. (J). 22.45 *(978-1-4103-0034-8(X),* Blackbirch Pr., Inc.) Cengage Gale.

Jones, Tammy. At the Shore. 2009. (Sight Word Readers Set A Ser.). (J). 3.49 net. *(978-1-60719-137-7(7))* Newmark Learning LLC.

Legg, Gerald. Minibeasts. 2008. (Hot Topics Ser.). (Illus.). 32p. (J). (gr. 3-7). *(978-1-84239-936-1(5))* Alligator Bks. Ltd.

Levine, Michelle & Waxman, Laura. Let's Look at Snails. 2009. (Lightning Bolt Books — Animal Close-Ups Ser.). (ENG., Illus.). 32p. (gr. k-2). lib. bdg. 26.60 *(978-0-8225-7899-4(9),* Lerner Pubns.) Lerner Publishing Group.

The Life Cycle of a Snail. (Sunshinetm Science Ser.). 24p. (gr. 1-2). 37.50 *(978-0-7802-2784-2(0))* Wright Group/McGraw-Hill.

The Life Cycle of a Snail: 6 Each of 1 Student Book, 6 vols. (Sunshinetm Science Ser.). 24p. (gr. 1-2). 41.95 *(978-0-7802-2700-2(X))* Wright Group/McGraw-Hill.

Ross, Michael Elsohn. Snailology. Erickson, Darren, illus. Grogan, Brian, photos by. 2003. (Backyard Buddies Ser.). 48p. (YA). (gr. 3-5). 6.95 *(978-1-57505-437-7(X),* Carolrhoda Bks.) Lerner Publishing Group.

The Snail Trail. 2004. 10p. (J). bds. 5.99 *(978-1-85997-875-7(4))* Byeway Bks.

Snails Sets: 1 Each of 3 Big Books. (Sunshinetm Science Ser.). (gr. 1-2). 111.50 *(978-0-7802-2822-1(7))* Wright Group/McGraw-Hill.

Snails Sets: 1 Each of 3 Student Books. (Sunshinetm Science Ser.). (gr. 1-2). 20.95 *(978-0-7802-2823-8(5))* Wright Group/McGraw-Hill.

Trueit, Trudi Strain. Slugs, Snails, & Worms. 2013. 32p. (J). (gr. 6-9). 28.50 *(978-1-60870-247-3(2))* Cavendish Square Publishing.

—Slugs, Snails & Worms. 2013. (Backyard Safari 2 Ser.). 32p. (J). (gr. 6-9). pap. 10.58 *(978-1-62712-030-2(0))* Cavendish Square Publishing.

Waxman, Laura Hamilton. Let's Look at Snails. 2009. (Lightning Bolt Books — Animal Close-Ups Ser.). (ENG., Illus.). 32p. (gr. k-2). pap. 7.95 *(978-1-58013-865-9(9),* Lerner Pubns.) Lerner Publishing Group.

—Slimy Snails. 2016. (First Step Nonfiction — Backyard Critters Ser.). (ENG., Illus.). 24p. (J). (gr. k-2). 23.99 *(978-1-5124-0879-9(4));* 35.99 *(978-1-5124-1003-7(9),* Lerner Pubns.) Lerner Publishing Group.

White, Nancy. Creeping Land Snails. 2009. (No Backbone! Ser.). (Illus.). 24p. (J). (gr. k-3). lib. bdg. 21.28 *(978-1-59716-753-6(3))* Bearport Publishing Co., Inc.

Woodward, John. Snail. 2010. (Garden Minibeasts up Close Ser.). 32p. (gr. 2-4). 30.00 *(978-1-60413-900-6(5),* Chelsea Clubhouse) Facts On File, Inc.

SNAILS—FICTION

Adkins, Laura. Ordinary Oscar. Hearn, Sam, illus. 2010. (ENG.). 32p. (J). (gr. -1-2). 15.95 *(978-1-58925-085-7(0));* (gr. k-2). pap. 7.95 *(978-1-58925-418-3(X))* Tiger Tales.

Ana, Moh. Kookaburra Tales # 3: Laugh Not at Others. 2013. 16p. pap. 16.81 *(978-1-4669-3477-1(8))* Trafford Publishing.

Andersen, Hans Christian. IceMaiden & Other Tales. 2006. pap. *(978-1-4068-0421-8(5))* Echo Library.

Aspesi, Carol. The Tale of the Snail. 2008. 25p. pap. 24.95 *(978-1-60672-794-2(X))* America Star Bks.

Avi. A Beginning, a Muddle, & an End: The Right Way to Write Writing. Tusa, Tricia, illus. 2008. (ENG.). 176p. (J). (gr. 2-5). 14.95 *(978-0-15-205555-4(X))* Houghton Mifflin Harcourt Publishing Co.

—The End of the Beginning: Being the Adventures of a Small Snail (and an Even Smaller Ant) Tusa, Tricia, illus. 2008. (ENG.). 144p. (J). (gr. 2-5). pap. 6.95 *(978-0-15-205532-5(0))* Houghton Mifflin Harcourt Publishing Co.

Base, Graeme. The Legend of the Golden Snail. 2010. (ENG., Illus.). 48p. (J). (gr. k-2). 21.95 *(978-0-8109-8965-8(4),* Abrams Bks. for Young Readers) Abrams, Inc.

Brewin, Barbara. Sidney Snail's Wonderful World of Adventure. 2009. (Illus.). 32p. pap. 14.49 *(978-1-4389-4100-4(5))* AuthorHouse.

Bridges, Sonya. A Snail's Pace. 2011. 28p. pap. 11.32 *(978-1-4634-2752-8(2))* AuthorHouse.

Brown, Ruth. Snail Trail. Brown, Ruth, illus. 2013. (ENG., Illus.). 24p. (J). (gr. -1-k). 12.99 *(978-1-84939-252-5(8))* Andersen Pr. GBR. Dist: Independent Pubs. Group.

Carlton, Glenis. Four Snails & an Umbrella. 2016. (ENG.). 22p. (J). 23.95 *(978-1-78612-332-9(0),* f4b5e8cc-5376-41df-9771-3c2f8cfc4526) Austin, Stan AUS. Dist: Bookmasters Distribution.

Cazet, Denys. Snail & Slug. Cazet, Denys, illus. 2016. (ENG., Illus.). 32p. (J). (gr. -1-3). 17.99 *(978-1-4814-4506-1(5),* Atheneum/Richard Jackson Bks.) Simon & Schuster Children's Publishing.

Chojnowski, Bryan. Muffin Time: Origins. 2005. 98p. pap. 25.01 *(978-1-4116-4440-3(9))* Lulu Pr., Inc.

Crowl, Janice. Kili & the Singing Snails. Orme, Harinani, illus. 2011. (J). 16.95 *(978-1-58178-104-5(0))* Bishop Museum Pr.

d'Lacey, Chris. The Snail Patrol. Reeve, Philip, illus. 2005. 123p. (J). (gr. 2-5). per. 5.95 *(978-1-903015-30-8(8))* Barn Owl Bks, London GBR. Dist: Independent Pubs. Group.

Donaldson, Julia. The Snail & the Whale. Scheffler, Axel, illus. (ENG.). 32p. (J). (gr. -1-2). 2004. 18.99 *(978-0-8037-2922-3(7),* Dial Bks) 2006. reprint ed. pap. 6.99 *(978-0-14-240580-2(9),* Puffin Books) Penguin Young Readers Group.

Ferry, Ann. Gusty the Cloud & Streakie the Snail. Swope, Brenda, illus. 2011. 28p. pap. 24.95 *(978-1-4560-0928-1(1))* America Star Bks.

Flowers, Natasha. Sammy the Snail. 2006. 10.00 *(978-0-8059-9158-1(1))* Dorrance Publishing Co., Inc.

Foley, Greg. Willoughby & the Moon. Foley, Greg, illus. 2010. (ENG., Illus.). 40p. (J). (gr. -1-2). 18.99 *(978-0-06-154753-9(0))* HarperCollins Pubs.

Freedman, Deborah. The Story of Fish & Snail. 3rd ed. 2013. (ENG., Illus.). 40p. (J). (gr. -1-k). 16.99 *(978-0-670-78489-9(3)*, Viking Books for Young Readers) Penguin Young Readers Group.

George, Lindsay Barrett. The Secret. George, Lindsay Barrett, illus. 2005. (Illus.). 32p. (J). 16.89 *(978-0-06-029600-1(3))* HarperCollins Pubs.

Gram, Golden. Gail the Snail: A Holiday Tale. 2008. 20p. pap. 11.95 *(978-1-59858-848-4(6))* Dog Ear Publishing, LLC.

—Gail the Snail: Goes on Vacation. 2008. 20p. pap. 11.95 *(978-1-59858-860-6(5))* Dog Ear Publishing, LLC.

—Gail the Snail: How I Met Gail. 2007. 16p. per. 10.95 *(978-1-59858-430-1(8))* Dog Ear Publishing, LLC.

—Gail the Snail: Night Owl. 2008. 20p. pap. 11.95 *(978-1-59858-859-0(1))* Dog Ear Publishing, LLC.

—Gail the Snail: Snailing Around. 2007. 20p. per. 11.95 *(978-1-59858-435-6(9))* Dog Ear Publishing, LLC.

Hanna, Virginie. Shelby the Flying Snail, 1 vol. Piu, Amandine, illus. 2012. (My Little Picture Book Ser.). (ENG.). 32p. (J). (gr. -1). pap. 6.95 *(978-2-7338-1946-3(1))* Auzou, Philippe Editions FRA. Dist: Consortium Bk. Sales & Distribution.

Harvey, Damian. Snail's Legs. Paul, Korky, illus. 2015. (ENG.). 32p. (J). (gr. -1-2). pap. 8.99 *(978-1-84780-712-0(7)*, Frances Lincoln) Quarto Publishing Group UK GBR. Dist: Hachette Bk. Group.

—Snail's Legs. Paul, Korky, illus. 2006. (ENG.). 32p. (J). (gr. -1-4). *(978-1-84507-112-7(3))* ReiseArt Buchhandlung GmbH.

Hazen, Lynn E. The Amazing Trail of Seymour Snail. Cushman, Doug, illus. 2009. (ENG.). 64p. (J). (gr. 1-4). 16.99 *(978-0-8050-8698-0(6)*, 9780805086980, Holt, Henry & Co. Bks. For Young Readers) Holt, Henry & Co.

Henry, Kristina, et al. The Fish Tank, 1 vol. 2011. (ENG., Illus.). 48p. (J). 16.99 *(978-0-7643-3706-2(8)*, 9780764337062, Schiffer Publishing Ltd) Schiffer Publishing, Ltd.

Holladay, Shirley. Gail the Snail. 2009. 28p. pap. 14.99 *(978-1-4389-8744-6(7))* AuthorHouse.

Howe, Tina Field. Snailsworth, a slow lttle Story. Howe, Tina Field, illus. 2007. (Illus.). 24p. (J). per. 12.95 *(978-0-9768585-3-9(3))* Howe, Tina Field.

Howells, Angela. The Tails of Victoria Way. 2009. (Illus.). 32p. pap. 12.99 *(978-1-4490-4432-9(8))* AuthorHouse.

Hughes, Christina Margaret Ann. Lucy & Her Unusual Pet. 2008. (Illus.). 64p. per. *(978-1-84748-238-9(4))* Athena Pr.

Hyde, Margaret. Dreddielocks & the Three Slugs, 1 vol. Parker, Curtis, illus. 2003. (ENG.). 36p. (J). (gr. k-3). 17.99 *(978-1-58980-231-5(4))* Pelican Publishing Co., Inc.

Hyde, Margaret E. DreddieLocks & the Three Slugs. Parker, Curtis, illus. 2003. 36p. (J). lib. bdg. 16.95 *(978-1-888108-07-1(X))* Budding Artists, Inc.

Karre, Nancy. On Herman's Pond. 2005. 8.00 *(978-1-933281-00-1(6)*, 2267) Battle Creek Area Mathematics & Science Ctr.

King-Chai, Sharon. Snail Mail. 2017. (ENG., Illus.). 32p. (J). (gr. -1-k). 17.99 *(978-1-4449-2254-7(8))* Hachette Children's Group GBR. Dist: Hachette Bk. Group.

Kugler, Tina. Snail & Worm Again. 2017. (ENG., Illus.). 32p. (J). (gr. 1-4). 16.99 *(978-0-544-79249-4(1)*, HMH Books For Young Readers) Houghton Mifflin Harcourt Publishing Co.

Kügler, Tina & Kügler, Carson, illus. Snail & Worm: Meet My Friend. 2016. (ENG.). 32p. (J). (gr. 1-4). 16.99 *(978-0-544-49412-1(1)*, HMH Books For Young Readers) Houghton Mifflin Harcourt Publishing Co.

Laing, Marilyn. Why the Turtle & the Snail Carried their Houses on Their Back. 2011. 24p. pap. 13.50 *(978-1-4567-3154-0(8))* AuthorHouse.

Lecher, Doris. A New House for Charlie. 2014. (ENG., Illus.). 28p. (J). (gr. -1-k). 16.95 *(978-1-62873-814-8(6)*, Sky Pony Pr.) Skyhorse Publishing Co., Inc.

Lee, Laura. Snail Race at Penny's Place. 2009. 24p. pap. 11.99 *(978-1-4389-9958-6(5))* AuthorHouse.

Lhomme, Sandrine & Piu, Amandine. Sammy the Snail's Amazing Day, 1 vol. Lhomme, Sandrine, illus. 2012. (My Baby Stories Ser.). (ENG., Illus.). 24p. (J). (gr. -1). bds. 9.95 *(978-2-7338-1981-4(X))* Auzou, Philippe Editions FRA. Dist: Consortium Bk. Sales & Distribution.

Loth, Sebastian. Clementine. 2011. (ENG., Illus.). 32p. (J). (gr. -1-3). 14.95 *(978-0-7358-4009-6(1))* North-South Bks., Inc.

Lstarte. Sam the Slug. 2012. 30p. (J). pap. 10.99 *(978-0-9830686-4-8(X))* Capital Apple Pr.

Lustig, Lindsey Beth. Snail's Trail. 2008. 21p. pap. 24.95 *(978-1-60610-310-4(5))* America Star Bks.

May, Eleanor. Albert's Amazing Snail. Melmon, Deborah, illus. 2012. (Mouse Math Ser.). (ENG.). 32p. (J). (gr. -1-1). 22.60 *(978-1-57565-448-5(2))*; pap. 7.95 *(978-1-57565-442-3(3))* Kane Press, Inc.

McKirdy, Mark. The Garden Party. 2004. 19p. (J). pap. 13.95 *(978-1-4116-1847-3(5))* Lulu Pr., Inc.

Miranda, Conchita. Yago's Heartbeat. 2011. (Light (Cuento de Luz) Ser.). (ENG., Illus.). 42p. (J). (gr. 1-4). *(978-84-938240-3-7(8))* D P & G Military Pubs.

Moh Ana. Kookaburra Tales # 4: Lighten My Path, Brighten My Heart. 2013. 16p. pap. 16.81 *(978-1-4669-9129-3(1))* Trafford Publishing.

Murphy, Mary. Slow Snail. 2013. (ENG., Illus.). 16p. (J). (— 1). bds. 6.99 *(978-0-7636-6023-9(X))* Candlewick Pr.

Murray, Alison. Fairy Felicity's Moonlight Adventure. Murray, Alison, illus. 2016. (ENG., Illus.). 24p. (J). (gr. -1-2). 15.99 *(978-0-7636-8945-2(9)*, Nosy Crow) Candlewick Pr.

Nath, D. Smith. She, the Tale of a Sail. 30p. (J). (gr. k-2). pap. 5.95 *(978-1-886134-03-4(0))* Miraculous Fingerprints Pubs.

New Home for Snail. 2003. (Daisy Board Books Ser.). 10p. (J). bds. 9.95 *(978-0-7525-8299-3(2))* Parragon, Inc.

Nicholson, Devon, et al. Fundi the Snail. 2008. 48p. pap. 26.50 *(978-1-4357-1551-6(9))* Lulu Pr., Inc.

Niddrie, June. Sweetpea & His Friends. 2010. 36p. pap. 17.30 *(978-0-557-31853-7(X))* Lulu Pr., Inc.

Ostrow, Kim. The Great Snail Race. Bond, Clint & Clark, Andy, illus. 2005. (SpongeBob SquarePants Ser.: No. 6). 22p. (J). lib. bdg. 15.00 *(978-1-59054-830-1(2))* Fitzgerald Bks.

Parker, Emma. Sam the Traveling Snail. 2010. (Illus.). pap. *(978-1-877561-19-1(3))* First Edition Ltd.

Paul, Ann Whitford. Snail's Good Night. Litzinger, Rosanne, illus. 2008. (Holiday House Readers: Level 1 Ser.). (ENG.). 32p. (J). (gr. -1-3). 14.95 *(978-0-8234-1912-8(6))* Holiday Hse., Inc.

Pearson, Susan. Slugger, 0 vols. Slonim, David, illus. 2013. (ENG.). 32p. (J). (gr. -1-2). 14.99 *(978-1-4778-1641-7(0)*, 9781477816417, Amazon Children's Publishing) Amazon Publishing.

—Slugs in Love, 0 vols. O'Malley, Kevin, illus. 2012. (ENG.). 34p. (J). (gr. -1-3). pap. 7.99 *(978-0-7614-6248-4(1)*, 9780761462484, Amazon Children's Publishing) Amazon Publishing.

Peterson, Mary. Snail Has Lunch. Peterson, Mary, illus. 2016. (Pix Ser.). (ENG., Illus.). 64p. (J). (gr. 1-4). 12.99 *(978-1-4814-5302-8(5)*, Aladdin) Simon & Schuster Children's Publishing.

Porter, Marylyn Kight. Speedy the Snail & His New Family. 2006. 10.00 *(978-0-8059-9134-5(4))* Dorrance Publishing Co., Inc.

Punter, Russell & MacKinnon, Mairi. Snail Brings the Mail. Blunt, Fred, illus. 2014. (Usborne Phonics Readers Ser.). (ENG.). (J). pap. 6.99 *(978-0-7945-3369-4(8)*, Usborne) EDC Publishing.

Rempt, Fiona. Snail's Birthday Wish. Smit, Noelle, illus. 2007. (ENG.). 32p. (J). (gr. -1-1). 14.95 *(978-1-905417-52-0(7))* Boxer Bks., Ltd. GBR. Dist: Sterling Publishing Co., Inc.

Rigby Education Staff. Animals Say... (Sails Literacy Ser.). (Illus.). 16p. (gr. 2-3). 27.00 *(978-0-7635-9943-0(3)*, 699433C99) Rigby Education.

Rinne, Teresa & Dillon, Preston. Snail Tails: Let's Play Ball! 2009. 40p. pap. 16.99 *(978-1-4389-7076-9(5))* AuthorHouse.

Russell, Philip. A Sunny Day for Snails. 2011. 24p. pap. 15.99 *(978-1-4628-2950-7(3))* Xlibris Corp.

Santillo, LuAnn. Bee. Santillo, LuAnn, ed. 2003. (Half-Pint Kids Readers Ser.). (Illus.). 7p. (J). (gr. -1-1). pap. *(978-1-59256-108-7(X))* Half-Pint Kids, Inc.

—Snail. Santillo, LuAnn, ed. 2003. (Half-Pint Kids Readers Ser.). (Illus.). 7p. (J). (gr. -1-1). pap. 1.00 *(978-1-59256-106-3(3))* Half-Pint Kids, Inc.

Santos, Dennis. Earl the Pearl. 2007. 28p. per. 10.95 *(978-1-59526-833-4(2)*, Llumina Kids) Aeon Publishing Inc.

Shaw, Natalie. Get Your Shell On. 2013. (Simon & Schuster Ready-To-Read Level 1 Ser.). lib. bdg. 13.55 *(978-0-606-32058-0(X)*, Turtleback) Turtleback Bks.

The Shy Snail. 2003. (J). per. *(978-1-57657-937-4(9))* Paradise Pr., Inc.

Slater, Dashka. Escargot. Hanson, Sydney, illus. 2017. (ENG.). 40p. (J). 16.99 *(978-0-374-30281-8(2)*, 9780374302818, Farrar, Straus & Giroux (BYR)) Farrar, Straus & Giroux.

Snail Trail. 2008. (Baby Gold Stars Trail Board Ser.). 6p. bds. *(978-1-4075-1797-1(X))* Parragon, Inc.

Stadler, John. Snail Saves the Day, 1 vol. 2006. (ENG., Illus.). 32p. (J). (gr. -1-3). reprint ed. pap. 5.95 *(978-1-59572-045-0(6))* Star Bright Bks., Inc.

Stokholm, Susan Mary. Between a Shadow & the Moon. 2010. 252p. pap. 14.49 *(978-1-4520-1752-5(2))* AuthorHouse.

Strack, Beth. Sammy the Snail's Bright Ideas. 2013. 32p. pap. 9.99 *(978-0-9898991-0-9(1))* Strack, Beth.

Strickland, A. W. The Adventures of Ralph & Elmer This Potato Is for You. 2012. 38p. pap. 14.95 *(978-0-9820649-9-3(3))* Andromeda Pr., Inc.

Tafoya, Jody. Sammy: A Day in the Life of a Snail. 2012. 24p. pap. 24.95 *(978-1-62709-389-7(3))* America Star Bks.

Ticktock Media, Ltd. Staff. In the Garden with the Hungry Little Snail. 2009. (Touch & Feel Fun Ser.). (ENG.). 10p. (J). (gr. k — 1). bds. 5.95 *(978-1-84696-810-5(0)*, TickTock Books) Octopus Publishing Group GBR. Dist: Independent Pubs. Group.

Ungerer, Tomi. Snail, Where Are You? 2015. (ENG., Illus.). 32p. (gr. -1-k). 14.95 *(978-0-7148-6799-1(3))* Phaidon Pr., Inc.

Volta, A. Patulous, the Different Caterpillar. 2008. (Illus.). 28p. (J). 17.99 *(978-0-9711040-0-6(X))* Working Parents, LLC.

Waring, Geoff. Oscar & the Snail: A Book about Things That We Use. Waring, Geoff, illus. (Start with Science Ser.). (ENG., Illus.). 32p. (J). (gr. -1-3). 2011. pap. 6.99 *(978-0-7636-5303-3(9))* 2009. 14.99 *(978-0-7636-4039-2(5))* Candlewick Pr.

Wenger, Shaunda. Caterpillar Can't Wait! 2006. (Early Explorers Ser.). (J). pap. *(978-1-4108-6101-6(5))* Benchmark Education Co.

Woodford, Pamela. Sortof the Snail. 2013. (Brighter Little Minds Ser.). (ENG., Illus.). 24p. (J). pap. 9.99 *(978-1-871305-83-8(7))* Orpen Pr. IRL. Dist: M.H. Gill & Co. U. C.

SNAKES

Alinsky, Shelby. National Geographic Readers: Slither, Snake! 2015. (Readers Ser.). (ENG., Illus.). 24p. (J). (-k). pap. 3.99 *(978-1-4263-1955-6(X)*, National Geographic Children's Bks.) National Geographic Society.

—Slither, Snake! (1 Hardcover/1 CD) 2017. (National Geographic Kids Ser.). (ENG.). (J). 29.95 ***(978-1-4301-2657-7(4))*** Live Oak Media.

—Slither, Snake! (1 Paperback/1 CD) 2017. (National Geographic Kids Ser.). (ENG.). (J). pap. 19.95 ***(978-1-4301-2656-0(6))*** Live Oak Media.

—Slither, Snake! (4 Paperbacks/1 CD) 2017. (National Geographic Kids Ser.). (ENG.). (J). pap. 31.95 ***(978-1-4301-2658-4(2))*** Live Oak Media.

Allyn, Daisy. Python. 2011. (Killer Snakes Ser.). (Illus.). 24p. (J). (gr. 1-3). lib. bdg. 22.60 *(978-1-4339-4559-5(2))* Stevens, Gareth Publishing LLLP.

—Python / Pitón. 2011. (Killer Snakes / Serpientes asesinas Ser.). (SPA., Illus.). 24p. (J). (gr. 1-3). 22.60 *(978-1-4339-4563-2(0))* Stevens, Gareth Publishing LLLP.

Amazing Snakes. 2014. (Amazing Snakes Ser.). 24p. (J). (gr. 3-6). 113.00 *(978-1-4777-6512-8(3))*; pap. 41.25 *(978-1-4777-7211-9(1))* Rosen Publishing Group, Inc., The. (PowerKids Pr.).

Arnold, Tedd. Snakes. Arnold, Tedd, illus. 2016. (Fly Guy Presents Ser.). (ENG., Illus.). 32p. (J). (gr. k-2). pap. 3.99 *(978-0-545-85188-6(2))* Scholastic, Inc.

Arnold, Tedd, illus. Fly Guy Presents: Snakes. 2016. (J). *(978-1-5182-0352-7(3))* Scholastic, Inc.

Austen, Amy. Pythons. 2016. (Snakes on the Hunt Ser.). (Illus.). 24p. (J). (gr. 3-3). pap. 8.25 *(978-1-4994-2198-9(2)*, PowerKids Pr.) Rosen Publishing Group, Inc., The.

Avery, Sebastian. Anacondas. 2016. (Snakes on the Hunt Ser.). 24p. (J). (gr. 3-3). pap. 8.25 *(978-1-4994-2190-3(7)*, PowerKids Pr.) Rosen Publishing Group, Inc., The.

Barnes, Julia. 101 Facts about Snakes. 2004. (One Hundred One Facts about Predators Ser.). (Illus.). 32p. (gr. 1-4). lib. bdg. 26.00 *(978-0-8368-4040-7(2)*, Gareth Stevens Learning Library) Stevens, Gareth Publishing LLLP.

Barr, Brady. Scrapes with Snakes! True Stories of Adventures with Animals. 2015. (NGK Chapters Ser.). (ENG.). 112p. (J). (gr. 2-5). pap. 5.99 *(978-1-4263-1914-3(2)*, National Geographic Children's Bks.) National Geographic Society.

Barr, Brady & Zoehfeld, Kathleen Weidner. National Geographic Kids Chapters: Scrapes with Snakes: And More True Stories of Adventures with Animals. 2015. (NGK Chapters Ser.). (ENG.). 112p. (J). (gr. 2-5). lib. bdg. 14.90 *(978-1-4263-1916-7(9)*, National Geographic Children's Bks.) National Geographic Society.

Barraclough, Susan. Snakes & Reptiles: The Scariest Cold-Blooded Creatures on Earth. 2008. (Illus.). 192p. (J). *(978-1-4351-0774-8(8))* Barnes & Noble, Inc.

Batten, Mary. Rattler. 2016. (Penguin Core Concepts Ser.). (ENG., Illus.). 32p. (J). (gr. -1-1). pap. 3.99 *(978-0-448-48841-7(8)*, Grosset & Dunlap) Penguin Young Readers Group.

Bell, Samantha. Anaconda. 2015. (21st Century Skills Library: Exploring Our Rainforests Ser.). (ENG., Illus.). 32p. (J). (gr. 3-6). 29.93 *(978-1-63188-973-8(7)*, 205804) Cherry Lake Publishing.

—Copperheads, 1 vol. 2014. (Amazing Reptiles Ser.). (ENG.). 48p. (gr. 8-12). lib. bdg. 32.79 *(978-1-62403-371-1(7))* ABDO Publishing Co.

Berger, Melvin & Berger, Gilda. A Snake Grows Up. 2008. (Illus.). 32p. (J). *(978-0-439-02526-3(5))* Scholastic, Inc.

Bishop, Nic. Snakes. Bishop, Nic, illus. 2012. (Nic Bishop Ser.). (ENG., Illus.). 48p. (J). (gr. -1-3). 17.99 *(978-0-545-20638-9(3)*, Scholastic Nonfiction) Scholastic, Inc.

—Snakes (Scholastic Reader, Level 2: Nic Bishop Reader #5) 2016. (Scholastic Reader, Level 2 Ser.). (ENG.). 32p. (J). (gr. k-2). pap. 3.99 *(978-0-545-60571-7(7))* Scholastic, Inc.

Blake, Kevin. Guam's Brown Tree Snakes: Hanging Out. 2015. (They Don't Belong: Tracking Invasive Species Ser.). (ENG., Illus.). 32p. (J). (gr. 2-7). lib. bdg. 26.60 *(978-1-62724-830-3(7))* Bearport Publishing Co., Inc.

Blazeman, Christopher. Snakes up Close, 1 vol. 2nd rev. ed. 2014. (TIME for KIDS(r) Nonfiction Readers Ser.). (ENG., Illus.). 28p. (J). (gr. 2-2). pap. 23.96 *(978-1-4807-1045-0(8))* Shell Educational Publishing.

—Snakes up Close, 1 vol. 2nd rev. ed. 2011. (Nonfiction Readers Ser.). (ENG.). 28p. (J). (gr. 2-2). pap. 6.99 *(978-1-4333-3618-8(9))* Teacher Created Materials, Inc.

Blobaum, Cindy. Awesome Snake Science! 40 Activities for Learning about Snakes. 2012. (Young Naturalists Ser.). (ENG., Illus.). 144p. (J). (gr. 4-6). pap. 14.95 *(978-1-56976-807-5(2))* Chicago Review Pr., Inc.

Boa Constrictor: Killer King of the Jungle. 2013. (Top of the Food Chain Ser.). 32p. (J). (gr. k-5). pap. 60.00 *(978-1-61533-800-9(4)*, PowerKids Pr.) Rosen Publishing Group, Inc., The.

Bodden, Valerie. Amazing Animals: Snakes. 2011. (Amazing Animals Ser.). (ENG.). 24p. (J). (gr. 1-3). pap. 8.99 *(978-0-89812-751-5(3)*, Creative Paperbacks) Creative Co., The.

—Grow with Me: Snake. 2015. (Grow with Me Ser.). (ENG.). 32p. (J). (gr. 3-5). pap. 9.99 *(978-0-89812-992-2(3)*, Creative Paperbacks) Creative Co., The.

—Snake. 2014. (Illus.). 32p. (J). *(978-1-60818-406-4(4)*, Creative Education) Creative Co., The.

—Snakes. (J). 2011. (ENG.). 24p. (gr. 1-17). pap. 5.99 *(978-1-926722-28-3(0)*, Creative Paperbacks) 2010. 24p. (gr. -1-3). 16.95 *(978-1-58341-813-0(X)*, Creative Education) 2009. (gr. 1-5). 24.25 *(978-1-58341-724-9(9)*, Creative Education) Creative Co., The.

Books Are Fun 8 Title Animal Lives Set: Snakes. 2006. (J). *(978-1-59566-306-1(1))* QEB Publishing Inc.

Bowman, Chris. Gaboon Vipers. 2014. (Amazing Snakes! Ser.). (ENG.). 24p. (J). (gr. 3-7). 25.95 *(978-1-62617-123-7(8)*, Epic Bks.) Bellwether Media.

—Inland Taipans. 2014. (Amazing Snakes! Ser.). (ENG.). 24p. (J). (gr. 3-7). 25.95 *(978-1-62617-124-4(6)*, Epic Bks.) Bellwether Media.

—Rainbow Boas. 2014. (Amazing Snakes! Ser.). (ENG.). 24p. (J). (gr. 3-7). 25.95 *(978-1-62617-125-1(4)*, Epic Bks.) Bellwether Media.

—Western Diamondback Rattlesnakes. 2014. (Amazing Snakes! Ser.). (ENG.). 24p. (J). (gr. 3-7). 25.95 *(978-1-62617-126-8(2)*, Epic Bks.) Bellwether Media.

Braidich, Victoria. Copperhead. 2011. (Killer Snakes Ser.). 24p. (J). (gr. 1-3). pap. 8.15 *(978-1-4339-5629-4(2))*; lib. bdg. 22.60 *(978-1-4339-5627-0(6))* Stevens, Gareth Publishing LLLP.

—Copperhead / Serpiente Cabeza de Cobre. 2011. (Killer Snakes / Serpientes asesinas Ser.). (SPA & ENG., Illus.). 24p. (J). (gr. 1-3). 22.60 *(978-1-4339-5631-7(4))* Stevens, Gareth Publishing LLLP.

Bredeson, Carmen. Fun Facts about Snakes! 2007. (I Like Reptiles & Amphibians! Ser.). (Illus.). 24p. (J). (gr. 1-3). lib. bdg. 22.60 *(978-0-7660-2787-9(2)*, Enslow Elementary) Enslow Pubs., Inc.

Brown, Laaren. Scary Snakes. 2015. (Scholastic Discover More Ser.). (ENG.). 32p. (J). (gr. 1-3). pap. 4.99 *(978-0-545-80649-7(6)*, Scholastic Nonfiction) Scholastic, Inc.

Burke, Johanna. Anaconda. 2011. (Killer Snakes Ser.). (Illus.). 24p. (J). (gr. 1-3). 22.60 *(978-1-4339-4523-6(1))*; pap. 8.15 *(978-1-4339-4524-3(X))* Stevens, Gareth Publishing LLLP.

—Anaconda / Anaconda. 2011. (Killer Snakes / Serpientes asesinas Ser.). (ENG & SPA., Illus.). 24p. (J). (gr. 1-3). 22.60 *(978-1-4339-4527-4(4))* Stevens, Gareth Publishing LLLP.

Byars, Betsy. The Moon & I. 2014. 112p. pap. 6.00 *(978-1-61003-379-4(5))* Center for the Collaborative Classroom.

Calhoun, Kelly. Deslizadores Furtivos. 2016. (Adivina (Guess What) Ser.). (SPA., Illus.). 24p. (J). (gr. k-2). 28.50 *(978-1-63471-452-5(0)*, 208871); pap. 12.79 *(978-1-63471-468-6(7)*, 208872) Cherry Lake Publishing.

—Slinky Sliders: Rattlesnake. 2015. (Guess What Ser.). (ENG., Illus.). 24p. (J). (gr. k-2). pap. 12.79 *(978-1-63362-721-5(7)*, 206697) Cherry Lake Publishing.

Campbell, Jonathan A. & Lamar, William W. The Venomous Reptiles of the Western Hemisphere, 2 vols. 2004. (Comstock Books in Herpetology). (ENG., Illus.). 976p. 180.00 *(978-0-8014-4141-7(2)*, 80140100664830) Cornell Univ. Pr.

Carraway, Rose. Slithering Snakes. 2012. (Pet Corner Ser.). (ENG., Illus.). 24p. (J). (gr. k-2). pap. 8.15 *(978-1-4339-6303-2(5))*; lib. bdg. 22.60 *(978-1-4339-6301-8(9))* Stevens, Gareth Publishing LLLP.

—Slithering Snakes: Serpientes Resbaladizas. 2012. (Pet Corner / RincóN de Las Mascotas Ser.). (SPA & ENG.). 24p. (J). (gr. k-3). lib. bdg. 22.60 *(978-1-4339-6645-3(X))* Stevens, Gareth Publishing LLLP.

Cheng, Christopher. Python. Jackson, Mark, illus. 2016. (Read & Wonder Ser.). (ENG.). 32p. (J). (gr. k-3). 6.99 *(978-0-7636-8773-1(1))* Candlewick Pr.

Christiansen, Per. Constrictor Snakes. 2008. (Nature's Monsters Ser.). (Illus.). 32p. (YA). (gr. 3-6). lib. bdg. 26.00 *(978-0-8368-9220-8(8))* Stevens, Gareth Publishing LLLP.

Ciletti, Barbara. Burmese Pythons. 2017. (Invasive Species Takeover Ser.). (ENG., Illus.). 32p. (J). (gr. 3-7). 31.35 ***(978-1-68072-017-4(1)***, Bolt) Black Rabbit Bks.

Clark Sawyer, J. Las Serpientes de Cascabel de Bandas. 2014. (¿a dónde Van en Invierno? Ser.). (SPA.). 24p. (J). (gr. -1-3). lib. bdg. 23.93 *(978-1-62724-460-2(3))* Bearport Publishing Co., Inc.

—Timber Rattlesnakes. 2015. (Illus.). 24p. (J). lib. bdg. *(978-1-62724-318-6(6))* Bearport Publishing Co., Inc.

Clark, Willow. Burmese Pythons. 2012. (Animals of Asia Ser.). (ENG., Illus.). 24p. (J). (gr. 1-5). 22.60 *(978-1-4488-7418-7(1))*; pap. 8.25 *(978-1-4488-7491-0(2))* Rosen Publishing Group, Inc., The. (PowerKids Pr.).

—Green Tree Pythons. 2012. (Up a Tree Ser.). (ENG., Illus.). 24p. (J). (gr. k-3). lib. bdg. 22.60 *(978-1-4488-6187-3(X))*; pap. 8.25 *(978-1-4488-6333-4(3)*, PowerKids Pr.) Rosen Publishing Group, Inc., The.

—Rattlesnake! 2010. (Animal Danger Zone Ser.). (ENG.). 24p. (J). (gr. k-3). lib. bdg. 22.60 *(978-1-60754-958-1(1))*; (Illus.). pap. 8.15 *(978-1-60754-970-3(0))* Windmill Bks.

Cleave, Andrew. Snakes & Reptiles - Pb: A Portrait of the Animal World. 2013. (Portrait of the Animal World Ser.). (Illus.). 80p. pap. 9.95 *(978-1-59764-318-4(1))* New Line Bks.

Coates, Jennifer. Snakes. (J). 2009. (Illus.). 112p. 14.95 *(978-1-932904-41-3(7))* 2008. *(978-1-932904-33-8(6))* Eldorado Ink.

Colson, Rob. Snake. 2017. (Pet to Get Ser.). (ENG., Illus.). 32p. (J). (gr. 4-6). pap. 12.99 ***(978-0-7502-8933-7(3)***, Wayland) Hachette Children's Group GBR. Dist: Hachette Bk. Group.

Corwin, Jeff. Snake-Tacular. Pascoe, Elaine, ed. 2003. (Jeff Corwin Experience Ser.). (J). 9.95 *(978-1-4103-0206-9(7))*; 23.70 *(978-1-4103-0205-2(9))* Cengage Gale. (Blackbirch Pr., Inc.).

Craats, Rennay. Caring for Your Snake. (Caring for Your Pet Ser.). (Illus.). 32p. (J). 2005. (gr. 4-7). per. 9.95 *(978-1-59036-216-7(0))* 2004. lib. bdg. 26.00 *(978-1-59036-196-2(2))* Weigl Pubs., Inc.

—Snake. 2010. pap. 9.95 *(978-1-61690-083-0(0))*; 32p. (J). (gr. 3-5). lib. bdg. 27.13 *(978-1-61690-082-3(2))* Weigl Pubs., Inc.

Crossingham, John & Kalman, Bobbie. The Life Cycle of a Snake. 2003. (Life Cycle Ser.). (ENG., Illus.). 32p. (J). (gr. 3-4). pap. *(978-0-7787-0690-8(7))*; lib. bdg. *(978-0-7787-0660-1(5))* Crabtree Publishing Co.

—Les Serpents. 2006. (Petit Monde Vivant Ser.). (FRE., Illus.). 32p. (J). (gr. k-6). pap. 9.95 *(978-2-89579-100-3(7))* Bayard Canada Livres CAN. Dist: Crabtree Publishing Co.

Las Culebras, 6 vols., Vol. 2. (Explorers. Exploradores Nonfiction Sets Ser.). (SPA.). 32p. (gr. 3-6). 44.95 *(978-0-7699-0639-3(7))* Shortland Pubns. (U. S. A.) Inc.

Davies, Nicola. I (Don't) Like Snakes. Lozano, Luciano, illus. 2015. (ENG.). 32p. (J). (gr. k-4). 15.99 *(978-0-7636-7831-9(7))* Candlewick Pr.

De la Bédoyère, Camilla. Snakelet to Snake. 2011. (LifeCycles Ser.). (ENG.). 24p. (J). (gr. -1-k). lib. bdg. 15.99 *(978-1-60992-046-3(5))* QEB Publishing Inc.

De Medeiros, James. Anacondas. 2008. (Amazing Animals Ser.). (Illus.). 24p. (J). (gr. 2-4). pap. 8.95 *(978-1-59036-961-6(0))*; lib. bdg. 24.45 *(978-1-59036-960-9(2))* Weigl Pubs., Inc.

Dennard, Deborah. Snakes. Dewey, Jennifer Owings, illus. 2003. (Our Wild World Ser.). (ENG.). 48p. (J). (gr. 2-5). pap. 7.95 *(978-1-55971-855-4(2))* Cooper Square Publishing Llc.

Dibble, Traci. Cobras. 2011. (Predator Animals Ser.). 16p. pap. 39.62 *(978-1-61541-368-3(5))* American Reading Co.

—Cobras. Dibble, Traci, illus. 2010. (1-3Y Wild Animals Ser.). (ENG., Illus.). 16p. (J). (gr. k-2). pap. 5.99 *(978-1-61541-367-6(7))* American Reading Co.

Dibble, Traci & Sánchez, Lucía M. Cobras. 2011. (2Y Animales Depredador Ser.). (SPA.). 16p. (J). (gr. k-2). pap. 6.99 *(978-1-61541-369-0(3))* American Reading Co.

Donovan, Sandy. A Snake in Its Burrow. 2003. (Where Do Animals Live? Ser.). (J). pap. *(978-1-58417-193-5(6))*; lib. bdg. *(978-1-58417-192-8(8))* Lake Street Pubs.

Dorisi-Winget, Dianna. Pythons. 2011. (Wild about Snakes Ser.). (ENG.). 32p. (gr. 3-4). pap. 47.70 *(978-1-4296-7288-7(9))*; lib. bdg. 27.99 *(978-1-4296-6014-3(7))* Capstone Press of Coughlan Cos. (Edge Bks.).

Dorling Kindersley Publishing Staff. DK Readers L0: Snakes Slither & Hiss: Snakes Slither & Hiss. 2015. (DK Readers Ser.). (ENG., Illus.). 32p. (J). (gr. -1-1). pap. 3.99 *(978-1-4654-3504-0(2)*, DK Children) Dorling Kindersley Publishing, Inc.

—Everything You Need to Know about Snakes. 2013. (Everything You Need to Know Ser.). (ENG.). 80p. (J). (gr. 2-5). 15.99 *(978-1-4654-0246-2(2)*, DK Children) Dorling Kindersley Publishing, Inc.

Doudna, Kelly. Bashful Ball Pythons, 1 vol. Nobens, C. A., illus. 2013. (Unusual Pets Ser.). (ENG.). 24p. (J). (gr. -1-3). 24.21 *(978-1-61783-397-7(5))* ABDO Publishing Co.

Duhaime, Darla. Snakes. 2017. (Reptiles! Ser.). (ENG., Illus.). (J). (gr. k-1). 28.51 ***(978-1-68342-156-6(6))*** Rourke Educational Media.

S

Dunn, Mary. Garter Snakes, 1 vol. 2013. (Snakes Ser.). (ENG.). 24p. (gr. k-1). lib. bdg. 26.65 *(978-1-4765-2072-8(0),* Pebble Plus) Capstone Press of Coughlan Cos.

Dunn, Mary R. Copperheads, 1 vol. 2013. (Snakes Ser.). (ENG., Illus.). 24p. (gr. k-1). lib. bdg. 26.65 *(978-1-4765-2071-1(2),* Pebble Plus) Capstone Press of Coughlan Cos.

—Rattlesnakes, 1 vol. 2013. (Snakes Ser.). (ENG.). 24p. (gr. k-1). lib. bdg. 26.65 *(978-1-4765-2085-8(2),* Pebble Plus) Capstone Press of Coughlan Cos.

Elston, Heidi. Snakes: Level 1. 2014. (Magic Readers Ser.). (ENG.). 24p. (J). (gr. 5-9). lib. bdg. 24.21 *(978-1-62402-069-8(0))* Magic Wagon.

—Snakes Eat & Grow: Level 2. 2014. (Magic Readers Ser.). (ENG.). 24p. (J). (gr. 5-9). lib. bdg. 24.21 *(978-1-62402-070-4(4))* Magic Wagon.

—Snakes in the Desert: Level 3. 2014. (Magic Readers Ser.). (ENG.). 24p. (J). (gr. 5-9). lib. bdg. 24.21 *(978-1-62402-071-1(2))* Magic Wagon.

Feldman, Heather. Copperheads. (Really Wild Life of Animals Ser.). 24p. 2009. (gr. 3-4). 42.50 *(978-1-60854-185-0(1))* 2004. (Illus.). (J). lib. bdg. 22.60 *(978-0-8239-6721-6(2))* Rosen Publishing Group, Inc., The. (PowerKids Pr.).

—Coral Snakes. (Really Wild Life of Animals Ser.). 24p. 2009. (gr. 3-4). 42.50 *(978-1-60854-186-7(X))* 2004. (Illus.). (J). lib. bdg. 22.60 *(978-0-8239-6719-3(0))* Rosen Publishing Group, Inc., The. (PowerKids Pr.).

—King Snakes. (Really Wild Life of Animals Ser.). 24p. 2009. (gr. 3-4). 42.50 *(978-1-60854-195-9(9))* 2004. (Illus.). (J). lib. bdg. 22.60 *(978-0-8239-6723-0(9))* Rosen Publishing Group, Inc., The. (PowerKids Pr.).

—Milk Snakes. (Really Wild Life of Animals Ser.). 24p. 2009. (gr. 3-4). 42.50 *(978-1-60854-200-0(9))* 2004. (J). lib. bdg. 22.60 *(978-0-8239-6720-9(4))* Rosen Publishing Group, Inc., The. (PowerKids Pr.).

Feldman, Thea & American Museum of Natural History Staff. Snakes up Close! 2012. (Amer Museum of Nat History Easy Readers Ser.: 1). (ENG., Illus.). 32p. (J). (gr. k-1). pap. 3.95 *(978-1-4027-7788-2(4))* Sterling Publishing Co., Inc.

Fiedler, Julie. Boas. (Scary Snakes Ser.). 24p. (gr. 2-3). 2009. 42.50 *(978-1-60852-986-5(X),* PowerKids Pr.) 2007. (Illus.). (J). lib. bdg. 22.60 *(978-1-4042-3836-7(0))* Rosen Publishing Group, Inc., The.

—Cobras. (Scary Snakes Ser.). 24p. 2009. (gr. 2-3). 42.50 *(978-1-60852-987-2(8))* 2007. (Illus.). (J). (gr. -1-3). lib. bdg. 22.60 *(978-1-4042-3837-4(9))* Rosen Publishing Group, Inc., The. (PowerKids Pr.).

—Mambas. (Scary Snakes Ser.). 24p. (gr. 2-3). 2009. 42.50 *(978-1-60852-988-9(6),* PowerKids Pr.) 2007. (Illus.). (YA). lib. bdg. 22.60 *(978-1-4042-3838-1(7))* Rosen Publishing Group, Inc., The.

—Pythons. (Scary Snakes Ser.). 24p. (gr. 2-3). 2009. 42.50 *(978-1-60852-989-6(4),* PowerKids Pr.) 2007. (Illus.). (J). lib. bdg. 22.60 *(978-1-4042-3835-0(2))* Rosen Publishing Group, Inc., The.

—Rattlesnakes. (Scary Snakes Ser.). 24p. (gr. 2-3). 2009. 42.50 *(978-1-60852-990-2(8),* PowerKids Pr.) 2007. (Illus.). (YA). lib. bdg. 22.60 *(978-1-4042-3834-3(4))* Rosen Publishing Group, Inc., The.

—Vipers. (Scary Snakes Ser.). 24p. (gr. 2-3). 2009. 42.50 *(978-1-60852-991-9(6),* PowerKids Pr.) 2007. (Illus.). (YA). lib. bdg. 22.60 *(978-1-4042-3833-6(6))* Rosen Publishing Group, Inc., The.

Figorito, Juliet. Banded Sea Snake. 2011. (Killer Snakes Ser.). 24p. (J). (gr. 1-3). pap. 8.15 *(978-1-4339-5623-2(3));* lib. bdg. 22.60 *(978-1-4339-5621-8(7))* Stevens, Gareth Publishing LLLP.

—Banded Sea Snake: Serpiente Marina Rayada. 2011. (Killer Snakes / Serpientes asesinas Ser.). (SPA & ENG., Illus.). 24p. (J). (gr. 1-3). lib. bdg. 22.60 *(978-1-4339-5625-6(X))* Stevens, Gareth Publishing LLLP.

Franchino, Vicky. Black Mambas. 2015. (ENG., Illus.). 48p. (J). lib. bdg. *(978-0-531-21392-6(7),* Orchard Bks.) Scholastic, Inc.

Frazel, Ellen. Bull Snakes. 2011. (Snakes Alive Ser.). (ENG., Illus.). 24p. (J). (gr. k-3). lib. bdg. 25.95 *(978-1-60014-613-8(9),* Blastoff! Readers) Bellwether Media.

—Kraits. 2011. (Snakes Alive Ser.). (ENG., Illus.). 24p. (J). (gr. k-3). lib. bdg. 25.95 *(978-1-60014-614-5(7),* Blastoff! Readers) Bellwether Media.

—Tiger Snakes. 2011. (Snakes Alive Ser.). (ENG., Illus.). 24p. (J). (gr. k-3). lib. bdg. 25.95 *(978-1-60014-615-2(5),* Blastoff! Readers) Bellwether Media.

Gagne, Tammy. Rattlesnakes, 1 vol. 2014. (Amazing Reptiles Ser.). (ENG.). 48p. (gr. 8-12). lib. bdg. 32.79 *(978-1-62403-374-2(1))* ABDO Publishing Co.

—Snakes: Built for the Hunt. 2015. (Predator Profiles Ser.). (ENG., Illus.). 24p. (gr. 1-2). lib. bdg. 25.32 *(978-1-4914-5039-0(8))* Capstone Press of Coughlan Cos.

Gallagher, Debbie. Snakes. 2009. (Zoo Animals 2 Ser.). 32p. (gr. 2). lib. bdg. 18.56 *(978-0-7614-4749-8(0))* Marshall Cavendish Corp.

Gambino, Karlie. Cottonmouth. 2011. (Killer Snakes Ser.). 24p. (J). (gr. 1-3). pap. 8.15 *(978-1-4339-5640-9(3));* lib. bdg. 22.60 *(978-1-4339-5638-6(1))* Stevens, Gareth Publishing LLLP.

—Cottonmouth: Serpiente Boca de Algodón. 2011. (Killer Snakes / Serpientes asesinas Ser.). (SPA & ENG., Illus.). 24p. (J). (gr. 1-3). lib. bdg. 22.60 *(978-1-4339-5642-3(X))* Stevens, Gareth Publishing LLLP.

Ganeri, Anita. Anaconda, 1 vol. 2010. (Day in the Life: Rain Forest Animals Ser.). (ENG.). 24p. (J). (gr. k-2). 23.32 *(978-1-4329-4112-3(7));* pap. 6.79 *(978-1-4329-4123-9(2))* Heinemann-Raintree. (Heinemann Read & Learn).

Gangemi, Angelo. Black Mamba. 2011. (Killer Snakes Ser.). (Illus.). 24p. (J). (gr. 1-3). pap. 8.15 *(978-1-4339-4530-4(4));* lib. bdg. 22.60 *(978-1-4339-4529-8(0))* Stevens, Gareth Publishing LLLP.

—Black Mamba / Mamba Negra. 2011. (Killer Snakes / Serpientes asesinas Ser.). (ENG & SPA., Illus.). 24p. (J). (gr. 1-3). 22.60 *(978-1-4339-4533-5(9))* Stevens, Gareth Publishing LLLP.

George, Gale. Sea Snakes. 2016. (Snakes on the Hunt Ser.). 24p. (J). (gr. 3-3). pap. 8.25 *(978-1-4994-2206-1(7),* PowerKids Pr.) Rosen Publishing Group, Inc., The.

Giant Anaconda & Other Cryptids: Fact or Fiction? 2010. (Creature Scene Investigation: the Science of Cryptozoology Ser.). (Illus.). 112p. (gr. 5-8). 32.95 *(978-0-7910-9782-3(X),* Chelsea Hse.) Facts On File, Inc.

Gibbons, Gail. Snakes. Gibbons, Gail, illus. 2010. (ENG., Illus.). 32p. (J). (gr. -1-3). pap. 7.99 *(978-0-8234-2300-2(X))* Holiday Hse., Inc.

—Snakes. 2007. (ENG., Illus.). 32p. (J). (gr. -1-3). 16.95 *(978-0-8234-2122-0(8))* Holiday Hse., Inc.

Gillenwater, Chadwick. Anacondas, 1 vol. 2012. (South American Animals Ser.). (ENG., Illus.). 24p. (gr. k-1). lib. bdg. 26.65 *(978-1-4296-7585-7(3),* Pebble Plus) Capstone Press of Coughlan Cos.

Gish, Melissa. Snakes. 2017. (J). ***(978-1-60818-822-2(1),*** Creative Education) Creative Co., The.

Goldish, Meish. Reticulated Python: The World's Longest Snake. 2010. (More SuperSized! Ser.). (Illus.). 24p. (J). (gr. k-3). lib. bdg. 22.61 *(978-1-936087-30-3(8))* Bearport Publishing Co., Inc.

Gordon, Sharon. Guess Who Hisses: Adivina Quién Silba. 2007. (Bookworms — Bilingual Editions: Guess Who/Adivina Quien 2 Ser.). (SPA & ENG.). 32p. (gr. k-2). 15.95 *(978-0-7614-2883-1(6));* 15.95 *(978-0-7614-2866-4(6))* Marshall Cavendish Corp.

Graham, Audry. Boa Constrictor. 2011. (Killer Snakes Ser.). (Illus.). 24p. (J). (gr. 1-3). 22.60 *(978-1-4339-4535-9(5));* pap. 8.15 *(978-1-4339-4536-6(3))* Stevens, Gareth Publishing LLLP.

—Boa Constrictor / Boa Constrictora. 2011. (Killer Snakes / Serpientes asesinas Ser.). (ENG & SPA., Illus.). 24p. (J). (gr. 1-3). 22.60 *(978-1-4339-4539-7(8))* Stevens, Gareth Publishing LLLP.

—King Cobra. 2011. (Killer Snakes Ser.). (Illus.). 24p. (J). (gr. 1-3). lib. bdg. 22.60 *(978-1-4339-4553-3(3))* Stevens, Gareth Publishing LLLP.

Graham, Chris. So Many Snakes. (Real Readers - Upper Emergent Ser.). (ENG., Illus.). 12p. (gr. 1-2). 2008. pap. 5.90 *(978-0-8239-8197-7(5))* 2006. 33.50 *(978-1-4042-6214-0(8))* Rosen Publishing Group, Inc., The.

Gray, Leon. King Cobra: The World's Longest Venomous Snake. 2013. (Even More SuperSized! Ser.). 24p. (J). (gr. k-3). lib. bdg. 23.93 *(978-1-61772-732-0(6))* Bearport Publishing Co., Inc.

Gray, Susan Heinrichs. Snakes Shed Their Skin. 2015. (Tell Me Why Library). (ENG., Illus.). 24p. (J). (gr. 2-5). 27.07 *(978-1-63362-616-4(4),* 206648) Cherry Lake Publishing.

Green, Emily. Snakes. 2010. (Backyard Wildlife Ser.). (ENG., Illus.). 24p. (J). (gr. k-3). lib. bdg. 25.95 *(978-1-60014-446-2(2),* Blastoff! Readers) Bellwether Media.

Green, Jen. Snakes. 2011. (Amazing Animal Hunters Ser.). (Illus.). 32p. (J). 28.50 *(978-1-60753-047-3(3))* Amicus Publishing.

—Snakes. 2012. (Illus.). 32p. (gr. 3-5). pap. 8.95 *(978-1-926722-51-1(5))* Saunders Bk. Co. CAN. Dist: RiverStream Publishing.

Gregory, Helen. All about Snakes & Lizards. 2011. (Wonder Readers Early Level Ser.). (ENG.). (gr. -1-1). 16p. pap. 35.94 *(978-1-4296-8068-4(7));* 32p. pap. 5.99 *(978-1-4296-7796-7(1))* Capstone Press of Coughlan Cos. (Wonder Readers).

Gregory, Josh. Anacondas. 2016. (Nature's Children Ser.). (ENG., Illus.). 48p. (J). pap. 6.95 *(978-0-531-22517-2(8),* Children's Pr.) Scholastic Library Publishing.

—Rattlesnakes. 2015. (ENG.). 48p. (J). pap. 6.95 *(978-0-531-21186-1(X),* Orchard Bks.) Scholastic Library Publishing.

Guidone, Julie. Snakes. 2009. (Animals That Live in the Rain Forest Ser.). 24p. (gr. -1-3). (J). lib. bdg. 22.60 *(978-1-4339-0027-3(0));* pap. 8.15 *(978-1-4339-0109-6(9))* Stevens, Gareth Publishing LLLP. (Weekly Reader Leveled Readers).

—Snakes (Serpientes) 2009. (Animals That Live in the Rain Forest/Animales de la selva Ser.). (SPA & ENG.). 24p. (gr. -1-3). pap. 8.15 *(978-1-4339-0116-4(1),* Weekly Reader Leveled Readers) Stevens, Gareth Publishing LLLP.

—Snakes/Serpientes. 2009. (Animals That Live in the Rain Forest/Animales de la selva Ser.). (SPA & ENG.). 24p. (gr. -1-3). lib. bdg. 22.60 *(978-1-4339-0066-2(1),* Weekly Reader Leveled Readers) Stevens, Gareth Publishing LLLP.

Gunderson, Megan M. Anacondas, 1 vol. 2011. (Snakes Set 1 *2011 Ser.). (ENG.). 24p. 25.65 *(978-1-61613-432-7(1),* Checkerboard Library) ABDO Publishing Co.

—Boa Constrictors, 1 vol. 2011. (Snakes Set 1 *2011 Ser.). (ENG.). 24p. (J). (gr. 2-5). 25.65 *(978-1-61613-433-4(X))* ABDO Publishing Co.

—Copperheads, 1 vol. 2011. (Snakes Set 1 *2011 Ser.). (ENG.). 24p. 25.65 *(978-1-61613-434-1(8),* Checkerboard Library) ABDO Publishing Co.

—Diamondback Rattlesnakes, 1 vol. 2011. (Snakes Set 1 *2011 Ser.). (ENG.). 24p. (J). (gr. 2-5). 25.65 *(978-1-61613-435-8(6))* ABDO Publishing Co.

—King Cobras, 1 vol. 2011. (Snakes Set 1 *2011 Ser.). (ENG.). 24p. 25.65 *(978-1-61613-436-5(4),* Checkerboard Library) ABDO Publishing Co.

—Pythons, 1 vol. 2011. (Snakes Set 1 *2011 Ser.). (ENG.). 24p. 25.65 *(978-1-61613-437-2(2),* Checkerboard Library) ABDO Publishing Co.

Hamilton, S. L. Snakes. 2010. (Xtreme Predators Ser.). 32p. (gr. 3-9). 27.07 *(978-1-60453-994-3(1),* A&D Xtreme) ABDO Publishing Co.

Hamilton, Sue. Bitten by a Rattlesnake, 1 vol. 2010. (Close Encounters of the Wild Kind Ser.). (ENG.). 32p. (YA). (gr. 4-7). 27.07 *(978-1-60453-930-1(5))* ABDO Publishing Co.

Hansen, Grace. Snakes, 1 vol. 2014. (Reptiles Ser.). (ENG.). 24p. (J). (gr. 4-8). lib. bdg. 28.50 *(978-1-62970-061-8(4))* ABDO Publishing Co.

Hansen, Grace, et al. Serpientes. 2015. (Reptiles Ser.). (SPA., Illus.). 24p. (gr. k-1). pap. 7.95 *(978-1-4966-0507-8(1))* Capstone Classroom.

Hansen, Paul. When Snakes Attack! 2006. (When Wild Animals Attack! Ser.). (Illus.). 48p. (J). (gr. 4-10). lib. bdg. 25.27 *(978-0-7660-2667-4(1))* Enslow Pubs., Inc.

Harris, Tim. Nonvenomous Snakes. 2010. (Slimy, Scaly, Deadly Reptiles & Amphibians Ser.). (Illus.). 32p. (J). (gr. 2-6). pap. 10.50 *(978-1-4339-3433-9(7));* lib. bdg. 26.00 *(978-1-4339-3432-2(9))* Stevens, Gareth Publishing LLLP. (Gareth Stevens Learning Library).

—Snakes. 2008. (Nature's Children Ser.). (Illus.). 52p. (J). *(978-0-7172-6244-1(8))* Grolier, Ltd.

—Venomous Snakes. 2010. (Slimy, Scaly, Deadly Reptiles & Amphibians Ser.). (Illus.). 32p. (J). (gr. 2-6). pap. 10.50 *(978-1-4339-3430-8(2));* lib. bdg. 26.00 *(978-1-4339-3429-2(9))* Stevens, Gareth Publishing LLLP. (Gareth Stevens Learning Library).

Harrison, Paul. Snakes. (Up Close Ser.). 24p. (gr. 3-3). 2009. 47.90 *(978-1-60854-703-6(5))* 2007. (Illus.). (J). lib. bdg. 25.25 *(978-1-4042-3764-3(X))* Rosen Publishing Group, Inc., The. (PowerKids Pr.).

Hart, Joyce. Snakes. 2008. (Great Pets Ser.). 48p. (gr. 3-18). lib. bdg. 29.93 *(978-0-7614-2996-8(4),* Benchmark Bks.) Marshall Cavendish Corp.

Heos, Bridget. Do You Really Want a Snake? Longhi, Katya, illus. 2015. (Do You Really Want a Pet? Ser.). (ENG.). 24p. (J). (gr. 1-3). 19.95 *(978-1-60753-751-9(6))* Amicus Publishing.

Hernandez-Divers, Sonia. Snakes, 1 vol. 2nd ed. 2010. (Keeping Unusual Pets Ser.). (ENG., Illus.). 48p. (gr. 3-6). 32.65 *(978-1-4329-3851-2(7),* NA-h) Heinemann-Raintree.

Herrington, Lisa M. It's a Good Thing There Are Snakes. 2014. (Rookie Read-About(r) Science — It's a Good Thing... Ser.). (ENG.). 32p. (J). pap. 5.95 *(978-0-531-22833-3(9));* lib. bdg. 25.00 *(978-0-531-22361-1(2))* Scholastic Library Publishing.

Hibbert, Clare. If You Were a Snake. 2013. (If You Were A... Ser.). 32p. (gr. 2-5). 31.35 *(978-1-59920-963-0(2))* Black Rabbit Bks.

Higgins, Melissa. Anacondas, 1 vol. 2013. (Snakes Ser.). (ENG.). 24p. (gr. k-1). lib. bdg. 26.65 *(978-1-4765-2066-7(6),* Pebble Plus) Capstone Press of Coughlan Cos.

—Boa Constrictors, 1 vol. 2013. (Snakes Ser.). (ENG.). 24p. (gr. k-1). lib. bdg. 26.65 *(978-1-4765-2067-4(4),* Pebble Plus) Capstone Press of Coughlan Cos.

—Cobras, 1 vol. 2013. (Snakes Ser.). (ENG., Illus.). 24p. (gr. k-1). lib. bdg. 26.65 *(978-1-4765-2070-4(4),* Pebble Plus) Capstone Press of Coughlan Cos.

Higgins, Melissa & Dunn, Mary R. Snakes. 2013. (Snakes Ser.). (ENG.). 24p. (gr. k-1). lib. bdg. 159.90 *(978-1-4765-3713-9(5),* Pebble Plus) Capstone Press of Coughlan Cos.

Hinton, Kerry. Pythons. 2009. (Really Wild Life of Animals Ser.). 24p. (gr. 3-4). 42.50 *(978-1-60854-207-9(6),* PowerKids Pr.) Rosen Publishing Group, Inc., The.

Hirsch, Rebecca E. King Cobras: Hooded Venomous Reptiles. 2015. (ENG., Illus.). 32p. (J). (gr. 2-4). 26.65 *(978-1-4677-7983-8(0))* Lerner Publishing Group.

Hirschmann, Kris. Deadliest Snakes. 2016. (ENG.). 80p. (J). (gr. 5-12). *(978-1-68282-056-8(4))* ReferencePoint Pr., Inc.

Hoff, Mary. Snakes. 2006. (Wild World of Animals Ser.). (Illus.). 31p. (J). (gr. 3-5). 18.95 *(978-1-58341-436-1(3),* Creative Education) Creative Co., The.

Hoffmeister, Noelle. Amazing Animals: Venomous Snakes: Fractions & Decimals (Grade 4) 2017. (Mathematics Readers Ser.). (Illus.). 32p. (J). (gr. 4-4). pap. 8.99 ***(978-1-4258-5557-4(1))*** Teacher Created Materials, Inc.

Holmes, Parker. Amazing Snakes of the Northeast. 2014. (Amazing Snakes Ser.). (Illus.). 24p. (J). (gr. 3-6). 23.60 *(978-1-4777-6487-9(9),* PowerKids Pr.) Rosen Publishing Group, Inc., The.

—Amazing Snakes of the Northwest. 2014. (Amazing Snakes Ser.). (Illus.). 24p. (J). (gr. 3-6). 23.60 *(978-1-4777-6507-4(7),* PowerKids Pr.) Rosen Publishing Group, Inc., The.

—Amazing Snakes of the Southeast. 2014. (Amazing Snakes Ser.). (Illus.). 24p. (J). (gr. 3-6). 23.60 *(978-1-4777-6496-1(8),* PowerKids Pr.) Rosen Publishing Group, Inc., The.

—Amazing Snakes of the Southwest & West Coast. 2014. (Amazing Snakes Ser.). (Illus.). 24p. (J). (gr. 3-6). pap. 8.25 *(978-1-4777-6503-6(4),* PowerKids Pr.) Rosen Publishing Group, Inc., The.

Holmes, Parker. Pythons on the Hunt. 2017. (Searchlight Books (tm) — Predators Ser.). (ENG.). (J). (gr. 3-5). pap. 9.99 ***(978-1-5124-5612-7(8));*** (Illus.). lib. bdg. 30.65 ***(978-1-5124-3396-8(9))*** Lerner Publishing Group.

Holub, Joan. Why Do Snakes Hiss? And Other Questions about Snakes, Lizards, & Turtles. DiVito, Anna, illus. 2004. (Penguin Young Readers, Level 3 Ser.). (ENG.). 48p. (J). (gr. 1-3). mass mkt. 3.99 *(978-0-14-240105-7(6),* Penguin Young Readers) Penguin Young Readers Group.

Honders, Jamie. Coral Snake. 2011. (Killer Snakes Ser.). 24p. (J). (gr. 1-3). pap. 8.15 *(978-1-4339-5634-8(9));* lib. bdg. 22.60 *(978-1-4339-5632-4(2))* Stevens, Gareth Publishing LLLP.

Howard, Melanie A. Black Mambas, 1 vol. 2011. (Wild about Snakes Ser.). (ENG.). 32p. (gr. 3-4). pap. 8.29 *(978-1-4296-7281-8(1));* pap. 47.70 *(978-1-4296-7282-5(X));* lib. bdg. 27.99 *(978-1-4296-6012-9(0))* Capstone Press of Coughlan Cos. (Edge Bks.).

—Boa Constrictors, 1 vol. 2011. (Wild about Snakes Ser.). (ENG.). 32p. (gr. 3-4). pap. 8.29 *(978-1-4296-7283-2(8));* pap. 47.70 *(978-1-4296-7284-9(6));* lib. bdg. 27.99 *(978-1-4296-6011-2(2))* Capstone Press of Coughlan Cos. (Edge Bks.).

—Copperheads. 2012. (Wild about Snakes Ser.). (ENG.). 32p. (gr. 3-4). pap. 47.70 *(978-1-4296-8513-9(1),* Edge Bks.) Capstone Press of Coughlan Cos.

—Corn Snakes, 1 vol. 2012. (Wild about Snakes Ser.). (ENG.). 32p. (gr. 3-4). pap. 8.29 *(978-1-4296-8018-9(0));* pap. 47.70 *(978-1-4296-8514-6(X));* lib. bdg. 27.99 *(978-1-4296-7664-9(7))* Capstone Press of Coughlan Cos. (Edge Bks.).

—Wild about Snakes. 2012. (Wild about Snakes Ser.). (ENG.). 32p. (gr. 3-4). pap. 477.00 *(978-1-4296-8516-0(6));* pap. 41.45 *(978-1-4296-8515-3(8));* lib. bdg. 251.91 *(978-1-4296-8213-8(2))* Capstone Press of Coughlan Cos. (Edge Bks.).

Howard, Melanie A., et al. Wild about Snakes, 4 vols., Set. 2011. (Wild about Snakes Ser.). (ENG.). 32p. (gr. 3-4). lib. bdg. 111.96 *(978-1-4296-6537-7(8),* Edge Bks.) Capstone Press of Coughlan Cos.

Huggins-Cooper, Lynn. Slithering Snakes. 2006. (Killer Nature! Ser.). (Illus.). 32p. (J). (gr. 4-7). lib. bdg. 28.50 *(978-1-58340-934-3(3),* 1262609) Black Rabbit Bks.

Jackson, Tom. Deadly Snakes. 2010. (Dangerous Animals Ser.). (ENG., Illus.). 32p. (J). (gr. 2-6). pap. 10.50 *(978-1-4339-4041-5(8),* Gareth Stevens Learning Library); (YA). (gr. 3-6). lib. bdg. 26.60 *(978-1-4339-4040-8(X))* Stevens, Gareth Publishing LLLP.

—Inside the Mind of a Deadly Cobra. 2012. (Animal Instincts Ser.). (ENG., Illus.). 32p. (J). (gr. k-5). pap. 10.00 *(978-1-4488-7076-9(3));* lib. bdg. 25.25 *(978-1-4488-7033-2(X))* Rosen Publishing Group, Inc., The. (PowerKids Pr.).

—Snake Bite. 2008. (ENG., Illus.). 32p. (J). (gr. 5-9). pap. *(978-0-7787-3794-0(2))* Crabtree Publishing Co.

James, Lincoln. Death Adder. 2011. (Killer Snakes Ser.). (Illus.). 24p. (J). (gr. 1-3). 22.60 *(978-1-4339-4541-0(X));* pap. 8.15 *(978-1-4339-4542-7(8))* Stevens, Gareth Publishing LLLP.

—Death Adder / Víboras de la Muerte. 2011. (Killer Snakes / Serpientes asesinas Ser.). (ENG & SPA., Illus.). 24p. (J). (gr. 1-3). 22.60 *(978-1-4339-4545-8(2))* Stevens, Gareth Publishing LLLP.

Johnson, Sylvia A. Cobras. 2007. (Nature Watch Ser.). (ENG., Illus.). 48p. (gr. 4-8). lib. bdg. 27.93 *(978-1-57505-871-9(5),* Lerner Pubns.) Lerner Publishing Group.

Jones, Cede. King Cobra / Cobra Real. 2011. (Killer Snakes / Serpientes asesinas Ser.). (ENG & SPA., Illus.). 24p. (J). (gr. 1-3). 22.60 *(978-1-4339-4557-1(6))* Stevens, Gareth Publishing LLLP.

Jordan, Apple. Guess Who Bites. 2nd rev. ed. 2011. (Bookworms 2nd Edition: Guess Who Ser.). (Illus.). 24p. (J). (gr. k-2). 21.36 *(978-1-60870-428-6(9))* Marshall Cavendish GBR. Dist: Marshall Cavendish Corp.

Jordan, Meredith & Abramson, Andra Serlin. Kids Meet the Snakes. 2013. (Kids Meet Ser.: 1). (ENG., Illus.). 96p. (J). spiral bd. 12.95 *(978-1-60433-303-9(0),* Applesauce Pr.) Cider Mill Pr. Bk. Pubs., LLC.

Kavanagh, James. The World of Snakes. 2014. (Jeff Corwin's Explorer Ser.). (ENG., Illus.). 12p. 7.95 *(978-1-58355-850-8(0))* Western National Parks Assn.

Kenan, Tessa. Es una Boa Constrictora! 2017. (Bumba Books (tm) en Español — Animales de la Selva Tropical (Rain Forest Animals) Ser.). (SPA., Illus.). 24p. (J). (gr. -1-1). 25.32 ***(978-1-5124-4126-0(0))*** Lerner Publishing Group.

Klein, Adam G. Black Mambas, 1 vol. 2006. (Snakes Set 2 Ser.). (ENG., Illus.). 24p. (gr. k-6). 25.65 *(978-1-59679-278-4(7),* Checkerboard Library) ABDO Publishing Co.

—Common Adders, 1 vol. 2006. (Snakes Set 2 Ser.). (ENG., Illus.). 24p. (gr. k-6). 25.65 *(978-1-59679-279-1(5),* Checkerboard Library) ABDO Publishing Co.

—Coral Snakes, 1 vol. 2006. (Snakes Set 2 Ser.). (ENG., Illus.). 24p. (gr. k-6). 25.65 *(978-1-59679-280-7(9),* Checkerboard Library) ABDO Publishing Co.

—Pit Vipers, 1 vol. 2006. (Snakes Set 2 Ser.). (ENG., Illus.). 24p. (gr. k-6). 25.65 *(978-1-59679-282-1(5),* Checkerboard Library) ABDO Publishing Co.

—Water Moccasins, 1 vol. 2006. (Snakes Set 2 Ser.). (ENG.). 24p. (gr. k-6). 25.65 *(978-1-59679-283-8(3),* Checkerboard Library) ABDO Publishing Co.

—Yellow-Bellied Sea Snakes, 1 vol. 2006. (Snakes Set 2 Ser.). (ENG., Illus.). 24p. (gr. k-6). 25.65 *(978-1-59679-281-4(7),* Checkerboard Library) ABDO Publishing Co.

Klepeis, Alicia. The Boomslang Snake. 2017. (J). ***(978-1-5026-2581-6(4))*** Cavendish Square Publishing.

—Snakes Are Awesome. 2018. (ENG.). 32p. (gr. 3-6). 31.35 ***(978-1-63235-440-2(3),*** 12-Story Library) Pr. Room Editions LLC.

Kopp, Megan. Anacondas. (Wild about Snakes Ser.). (ENG.). 32p. (gr. 3-4). 2011. pap. 47.70 *(978-1-4296-6423-3(1))* 2010. lib. bdg. 27.99 *(978-1-4296-5432-6(5))* Capstone Press of Coughlan Cos. (Edge Bks.).

—Cobras. (Wild about Snakes Ser.). (ENG.). 32p. (gr. 3-4). 2011. pap. 47.70 *(978-1-4296-6424-0(X))* 2010. lib. bdg. 27.99 *(978-1-4296-5430-2(9))* Capstone Press of Coughlan Cos. (Edge Bks.).

Landau, Elaine. Big Snakes: Hunters of the Night. 2007. (Animals after Dark Ser.). (Illus.). 32p. (J). (gr. 2-4). lib. bdg. 23.94 *(978-0-7660-2769-5(4),* Enslow Elementary) Enslow Pubs., Inc.

—Sinister Snakes. 2003. (Fearsome, Scary, & Creepy Animals Ser.). (Illus.). 48p. (J). (gr. 1-4). lib. bdg. 25.27 *(978-0-7660-2057-3(6))* Enslow Pubs., Inc.

Lanser, Amanda. Boa Constrictor, 1 vol. 2013. (Great Predators Ser.). (ENG., Illus.). 48p. (J). (gr. 3-6). lib. bdg. 32.79 *(978-1-61783-945-0(0))* ABDO Publishing Co.

—Boa Constrictor Paperback. 2013. (Great Predators Ser.). (ENG., Illus.). 48p. (J). (gr. 3-6). pap. 15.64 *(978-1-62403-010-9(6),* Core Library) ABDO Publishing Co.

Lawrence, Ellen. Cottonmouth. 2016. (Swamp Things: Animal Life in a Wetland Ser.). (ENG.). 24p. (J). (gr. -1-3). 17.95 *(978-1-944102-52-4(3))* Bearport Publishing Co., Inc.

—Green Anaconda. 2017. (Apex Predators of the Amazon Rain Forest Ser.). (ENG., Illus.). 24p. (J). (gr. -1-3). 17.95 ***(978-1-68402-031-7(X))*** Bearport Publishing Co., Inc.

Lawrence, Ellen. A Snake's Life. 2012. (Animal Diaries: Life Cycles Ser.). 24p. (J). (gr. -1-3). lib. bdg. 23.93 *(978-1-61772-416-9(5))* Bearport Publishing Co., Inc.

Leigh, Autumn. Diamondback Rattlesnake. 2011. (Killer Snakes Ser.). (Illus.). 24p. (J). (gr. 1-3). pap. 8.15 *(978-1-4339-4548-9(7));* lib. bdg. 22.60 *(978-1-4339-4547-2(9))* Stevens, Gareth Publishing LLLP.

—Diamondback Rattlesnake / Cascabel Diamantada. 2011. (Killer Snakes / Serpientes asesinas Ser.). (ENG & SPA., Illus.). 24p. (J). (gr. 1-3). 22.60 *(978-1-4339-4551-9(7))* Stevens, Gareth Publishing LLLP.

Lewis, Brenda Ralph. Poisonous Snakes. 2006. (Nature's Monsters Ser.). (Illus.). 32p. (gr. 2-6). lib. bdg. 26.00 *(978-0-8368-6174-7(4),* Gareth Stevens Learning Library) Stevens, Gareth Publishing LLLP.

Linde, Barbara M. Snakes Are Not Pets! 2013. (When Pets Attack! Ser.). 32p. (J). (gr. 3-6). 26.60 *(978-1-4339-9298-8(1));* pap. 63.00 *(978-1-4339-9300-8(7))* Stevens, Gareth Publishing LLLP.

Llewellyn, Claire. Snakes. 2009. (Wild Reads Ser.). (ENG., Illus.). 32p. (YA). (gr. k). pap. 4.95 *(978-0-19-911932-5(5))* Oxford Univ. Pr., Inc.

Lukeman, Noah. Do Snakes Wear Socks? 2015. (ENG., Illus.). 24p. (J). pap. 5.99 *(978-1-63291-413-2(1))* Morgan Rice Bks.

Lynch, Michelle & Taylor, Trace. Cobras. Taylor, Trace, illus. 2011. (2G Predator Animals Ser.). (ENG., Illus.). 24p. (J). (gr. k-2). pap. 5.99 *(978-1-61541-504-5(1))* American Reading Co.

Lynette, Rachel. Anacondas. 2013. (Monsters of the Animal Kingdom Ser.). (ENG., Illus.). 24p. (J). (gr. k-5). pap. 8.25 *(978-1-4488-9719-3(X))*; lib. bdg. 22.60 *(978-1-4488-9631-8(2))* Rosen Publishing Group, Inc., The. (PowerKids Pr.).

Macken, JoAnn Early. Rattlesnakes. 2nd rev. ed. 2009. (Animals That Live in the Desert Ser.). (ENG.). 24p. (J). (gr. -1-3). pap. 8.15 *(978-1-4339-2451-4(X))*; lib. bdg. 22.60 *(978-1-4339-2150-6(2))* Stevens, Gareth Publishing LLLP. (Weekly Reader Leveled Readers).

—Rattlesnakes;Serpientes de Cascabel. 2nd rev. ed. 2009. (Animals That Live in the Desert/Animales del desierto Ser.). (SPA & ENG.). 24p. (J). (gr. -1-3). pap. 8.15 *(978-1-4339-2459-0(5))*; lib. bdg. 22.60 *(978-1-4339-2133-9(2))* Stevens, Gareth Publishing LLLP. (Weekly Reader Leveled Readers).

—Snakes/Las Serpientes. 2004. (Animals I See at the Zoo/ Animales que veo en el zoologico Ser.). (SPA., Illus.). 24p. (gr. k-3). lib. bdg. 22.00 *(978-0-8368-4385-9(1)*, Weekly Reader Leveled Readers) Stevens, Gareth Publishing LLLP.

MacLaine, James. Snakes. Parker, Paul & Moor, Becka, illus. 2014. (Usborne Beginners Ser.). (ENG.). 32p. (J). (gr. 1-4). 4.99 *(978-0-7945-2686-3(1)*, Usborne) EDC Publishing.

Macleod, Steve. Anacondas. 2011. (J). *(978-1-61690-755-6(X))*; *(978-1-61690-762-4(2))* Weigl Pubs., Inc.

Markle, Sandra. Rattlesnakes. 2009. (Animal Predators Ser.). (ENG.). 40p. (gr. 3-6). 26.60 *(978-1-58013-539-9(0))* Lerner Publishing Group.

—Snakes: Biggest! Littlest! McDonald, Joe, photos by. 2011. (Biggest! Littlest! Ser.). (ENG., Illus.). 32p. (J). pap. 10.95 *(978-1-59078-874-5(5))* Boyds Mills Pr.

Marsico, Katie. King Cobras. 2013. (Nature's Children Ser.). (ENG.). 48p. (J). 28.00 *(978-0-531-20978-3(4))*; pap. 6.95 *(978-0-531-24304-6(4))* Scholastic Library Publishing. (Children's Pr.).

Mason, Adrienne. Snakes. Ogle, Nancy Gray & Ogle, Nancy, illus. 2005. (Kids Can Press Wildlife Ser.). (ENG.). 32p. (J). (gr. k-5). 6.95 *(978-1-55337-628-6(5))* Kids Can Pr., Ltd. CAN. Dist: Hachette Bk. Group.

Mattern, Joanne. King Cobras. 2010. (Asian Animals Ser.). (ENG.). 24p. (gr. k-1). pap. 41.70 *(978-1-4296-5096-0(6)*, Pebble Plus) Capstone Press of Coughlan Cos.

McDonald, Mary Ann. Boas. 2015. (Animals of the Rain Forest Ser.). (ENG.). 24p. (J). (gr. 2-6). 27.07 *(978-1-63143-701-4(1)*, 208515) Child's World, Inc., The.

McDonnell, Mary Rose. Sorting with Snakes. 2013. (Animal Math Ser.). 24p. (J). (gr. 1-3). 22.60 *(978-1-4339-9328-2(7))* Stevens, Gareth Publishing LLLP.

McFadden, Jesse. Watch Out for Rattlesnakes!, 01 vols., 1. 2016. (Wild Backyard Animals Ser.). (ENG., Illus.). 24p. (J). pap. 8.25 *(978-1-5081-4263-8(7)*, PowerKids Pr.) Rosen Publishing Group, Inc., The.

Meadows, Graham & Vial, Claire. Introducing Snakes. 2004. (ENG., Illus.). 24p. (J). (gr. 2-3). pap. 7.47 net. *(978-0-7685-1637-1(4)*, Dominie Elementary) Pearson Schl.

Meister, Cari. Pythons. 2015. (Illus.). 24p. (J). lib. bdg. *(978-1-62031-198-1(4)*, Bullfrog Bks.) Jump! Inc.

Menon, Sujatha. Discover Snakes. 2008. (Discover Animals Ser.). (Illus.). 48p. (J). (gr. 5-9). lib. bdg. 25.27 *(978-0-7660-3471-6(2))* Enslow Pubs., Inc.

Merritt, Robin. The Life Cycle of a Snake. 2011. (Life Cycles Ser.). (ENG., Illus.). 32p. (J). (gr. k-3). lib. bdg. 29.93 *(978-1-60973-192-2(1)*, 201178) Child's World, Inc., The.

Mitchell, Melanie S. Snakes. (First Step Nonfiction Ser.). (Illus.). (gr. k-2). 2005. 24p. lib. bdg. 17.27 *(978-0-8225-4606-1(X))* 2003. 23p. (J). pap. 5.95 *(978-0-8225-4607-8(8)*, Lerner Pubns.) Lerner Publishing Group.

Montgomery, Heather L. Garter Snakes. (Wild about Snakes Ser.). (ENG.). 32p. (gr. 3-4). 2011. pap. 47.70 *(978-1-4296-6425-7(8))* 2010. lib. bdg. 27.99 *(978-1-4296-5433-3(3))* Capstone Press of Coughlan Cos. (Edge Bks.).

—Kingsnakes, 1 vol. 2011. (Wild about Snakes Ser.). (ENG.). 32p. (gr. 3-4). pap. 8.29 *(978-1-4296-7285-6(4))*; pap. 47.70 *(978-1-4296-7286-3(2))*; lib. bdg. 27.99 *(978-1-4296-6013-6(9))* Capstone Press of Coughlan Cos. (Edge Bks.).

—Rattlesnakes, 1 vol. (Wild about Snakes Ser.). (ENG., 32p. (gr. 3-4). 2011. Illus.). pap. 8.29 *(978-1-4296-6258-1(1))* 2011. pap. 47.70 *(978-1-4296-6426-4(6))* 2010. lib. bdg. 27.99 *(978-1-4296-5434-0(1))* Capstone Press of Coughlan Cos. (Edge Bks.).

Morgan, Sally. Lizards & Snakes. 2012. (Pets Plus Ser.). 32p. (gr. 3-6). lib. bdg. 31.35 *(978-1-59920-704-9(4))* Black Rabbit Bks.

Mulks, Mitchell. Zonata: The California Mountain Kingsnake. Merker, Gerold, photos by. 2004. (Illus.). 64p. pap. 15.95 *(978-0-9760770-0-8(0))* LM Digital.

Munro, Roxie. Slithery Snakes, 0 vols. 2013. (ENG.). 40p. (J). (gr. 1-5). 17.99 *(978-1-4778-1658-5(5)*, 9781477816585, Amazon Children's Publishing) Amazon Publishing.

Murray, Julie. Copperheads, 1 vol. 2005. (Animal Kingdom Set Ii Ser.). (ENG., Illus.). 24p. (gr. k-4). 25.65 *(978-1-59197-309-6(0)*, Buddy Bks.) ABDO Publishing Co.

—King Cobras, 1 vol. 2003. (Buddy Book Ser.). (ENG.). 24p. (gr. k-4). 25.65 *(978-1-57765-731-6(4)*, Buddy Bks.) ABDO Publishing Co.

—Pythons, 1 vol. 2003. (Animal Kingdom Ser.). (ENG.). 24p. (gr. k-4). 25.65 *(978-1-57765-730-9(6)*, Buddy Bks.) ABDO Publishing Co.

—Rattlesnakes, 1 vol. 2005. (Animal Kingdom Set Ii Ser.). (ENG., Illus.). 24p. (gr. k-4). 25.65 *(978-1-59197-333-1(3)*, Buddy Bks.) ABDO Publishing Co.

National Geographic Editors. Creepy Crawly Collection. 2012. lib. bdg. 18.40 *(978-0-606-26822-6(7)*, Turtleback) Turtleback Bks.

Nichols, Catherine. Emerald Boas: Rain Forest Undercover. 2010. (Disappearing Acts Ser.). (Illus.). 24p. (J). (gr. k-3). lib. bdg. 22.61 *(978-1-936087-41-9(3))* Bearport Publishing Co., Inc.

Oachs, Emily Rose. Burmese Pythons. 2014. (Amazing Snakes! Ser.). (ENG., Illus.). 24p. (J). (gr. 3-7). lib. bdg. 25.95 *(978-1-62617-089-6(4)*, Epic Bks.) Bellwether Media.

—Green Anacondas. 2014. (Amazing Snakes! Ser.). (ENG., Illus.). 24p. (J). (gr. 3-7). lib. bdg. 25.95 *(978-1-62617-093-3(2)*, Epic Bks.) Bellwether Media.

—Spitting Cobras. 2014. (Amazing Snakes! Ser.). (ENG., Illus.). 24p. (J). (gr. 3-7). lib. bdg. 25.95 *(978-1-62617-095-7(9)*, Epic Bks.) Bellwether Media.

O'Donnell, Jessica. Egyptian Cobra. 2011. (Killer Snakes Ser.). (Illus.). 24p. (J). (gr. 1-3). pap. 8.15 *(978-1-4339-5645-4(4))*; lib. bdg. 22.60 *(978-1-4339-5643-0(8))* Stevens, Gareth Publishing LLLP.

—Egyptian Cobra / Cobra Egipcia. 2011. (Killer Snakes / Serpientes asesinas Ser.). (SPA & ENG., Illus.). 24p. (J). (gr. 1-3). 22.60 *(978-1-4339-5647-8(0))* Stevens, Gareth Publishing LLLP.

O'Donnell, Kerri. Snakes of the World: Learning to Use Inches & Feet to Measure an Object. 2009. (Math for the REAL World Ser.). 16p. (gr. 2-3). pap. 7.05 *(978-0-8239-8874-7(0)*, Rosen Classroom) Rosen Publishing Group, Inc., The.

O'Hare, Ted. Boas. 2005. (Amazing Snakes Discovery Library Ser.). (Illus.). 24p. (gr. 1-4). 14.95 *(978-1-59515-143-8(5))* Rourke Educational Media.

Ohare, Ted. Boas. Rourke Publishing Staff, ed. 2009. 24p. (J). pap. 3.99 *(978-0-8249-5147-4(6)*, Ideal Pubns.) Worthy Publishing.

O'Hare, Ted. Cobras. 2005. (Amazing Snakes Discovery Library Ser.). (Illus.). 24p. (J). (gr. 1-4). 14.95 *(978-1-59515-144-5(3))* Rourke Educational Media.

Ohare, Ted. Cobras. Rourke Publishing Staff, ed. 2009. 24p. (J). pap. 3.99 *(978-0-8249-5148-1(4)*, Ideal Pubns.) Worthy Publishing.

O'Hare, Ted. Copperheads. 2005. (Amazing Snakes Discovery Library Ser.). (Illus.). 24p. (gr. 1-4). 14.95 *(978-1-59515-145-2(1))* Rourke Educational Media.

—Coral Snakes. 2005. (Amazing Snakes Discovery Library). (Illus.). 24p. (gr. 1-4). 14.95 *(978-1-59515-142-1(7))* Rourke Educational Media.

—Mambas. 2005. (Amazing Snakes Discovery Library Ser.). (Illus.). 24p. (gr. 1-4). 14.95 *(978-1-59515-147-6(8))* Rourke Educational Media.

—Pythons. 2005. (Amazing Snakes Discovery Library Ser.). (Illus.). 24p. (gr. 1-4). 14.95 *(978-1-59515-148-3(6))* Rourke Educational Media.

Ohare, Ted. Rattlesnakes. Rourke Publishing Staff, ed. 2009. 24p. (J). pap. 3.99 *(978-0-8249-5146-7(8)*, Ideal Pubns.) Worthy Publishing.

Orr, Tamra B. Reticulated Python. 2015. (21st Century Skills Library: Exploring Our Rainforests Ser.). (ENG., Illus.). 32p. (J). (gr. 3-6). 29.93 *(978-1-63188-979-0(6)*, 205828) Cherry Lake Publishing.

Osborne, Mary Pope & Boyce, Natalie Pope. Snakes & Other Reptiles: A Nonfiction Companion to a Crazy Day with Cobras. Murdocca, Sal, illus. 2011. (Magic Tree House - Fact Tracker Ser.: 23). (ENG.). 128p. (J). (gr. 2-5). 6.99 *(978-0-375-86011-9(8)*, Random Hse. Bks. for Young Readers) Random Hse. Children's Bks.

O'Shaughnessy, Ruth. Snakes after Dark. 2015. (Animals of the Night Ser.). (ENG.). 32p. (J). (gr. 3-4). pap. 10.52 *(978-0-7660-6766-0(1))*; (Illus.). 25.27 *(978-0-7660-6768-4(8))* Enslow Pubs., Inc.

Owings, Lisa. The Black Mamba. 2013. (Nature's Deadliest Ser.). (ENG., Illus.). 24p. (J). (gr. 3-8). lib. bdg. 25.95 *(978-1-60014-877-4(8)*, Pilot Bks.) Bellwether Media.

—The King Cobra. 2012. (Nature's Deadliest Ser.). (ENG., Illus.). 24p. (J). (gr. 3-8). lib. bdg. 25.95 *(978-1-60014-743-2(7)*, Pilot Bks.) Bellwether Media.

—Snake Attack. 2012. (Animal Attacks Ser.). (ENG., Illus.). 24p. (J). (gr. 3-7). lib. bdg. 25.95 *(978-1-60014-791-3(7)*, Torque Bks.) Bellwether Media.

Pallotta, Jerry. Komodo Dragon vs. King Cobra. Bolster, Robert, illus. 2016. (Who Would Win? Ser.). (ENG.). 32p. (J). (gr. 1-3). pap. 3.99 *(978-0-545-30171-8(9))* Scholastic, Inc.

Peterson, Megan Cooley & Rustad, Martha E. H. King Cobras Are Awesome! 2015. (Awesome Asian Animals Ser.). (ENG., Illus.). 32p. (gr. 1-2). lib. bdg. 27.32 *(978-1-4914-3906-7(8))* Capstone Press of Coughlan Cos.

Petrie, Kristin. Garter Snakes, 1 vol. 2014. (Backyard Animals Ser.). (ENG.). 32p. (gr. 3-6). 27.07 *(978-1-62403-660-6(0))* ABDO Publishing Co.

Phillips, Dee. Green Tree Python. 2013. (Science Slam: Treed-Animal Life in the Trees Ser.). 24p. (J). (gr. -1-3). lib. bdg. 23.93 *(978-1-61772-909-6(4))* Bearport Publishing Co., Inc.

Polydoros, Lori. Anacondas: On the Hunt. 2016. (Killer Animals Ser.). (ENG.). 32p. (gr. 1-2). pap. 7.95 *(978-1-5157-6257-7(2)*, Blazers) Capstone Press of Coughlan Cos.

Pressberg, Dava. Vipers. 2016. (Snakes on the Hunt Ser.). (Illus.). 24p. (J). (gr. 3-3). pap. 8.25 *(978-1-4994-2210-8(5)*, PowerKids Pr.) Rosen Publishing Group, Inc., The.

Pringle, Laurence. Snakes! Strange & Wonderful. Henderson, Meryl, illus. 2009. (Strange & Wonderful Ser.). (ENG.). 32p. (J). (gr. 2-4). pap. 9.95 *(978-1-59078-744-1(7))* Boyds Mills Pr.

Raatma, Lucia. How Do We Live Together? Snakes. 2010. (Community Connections: How Do We Live Together? Ser.). (ENG.). 24p. (gr. 2-5). lib. bdg. 25.64 *(978-1-60279-620-1(3)*, 200331) Cherry Lake Publishing.

—Pythons. 2012. (Nature's Children Ser.). (ENG., Illus.). 48p. (J). pap. 6.95 *(978-0-531-25482-0(8))*; lib. bdg. 28.00 *(978-0-531-26837-7(3))* Scholastic Library Publishing.

Rajczak, Kristen. How Snakes & Other Animals Taste the Air. 2015. (Superior Animal Senses Ser.). (ENG., Illus.). 24p. (J). (gr. 3-4). pap. 8.25 *(978-1-4994-0995-6(8)*, PowerKids Pr.) Rosen Publishing Group, Inc., The.

Rake, Jody Sullivan. Pythons. 2010. (African Animals Ser.). (ENG.). 24p. (gr. k-1). pap. 41.70 *(978-1-4296-5084-7(2)*, Pebble Plus) Capstone Press of Coughlan Cos.

Rake, Matthew. Scaly, Slippery Creatures. Mendez, Simon, illus. 2015. (Real-Life Monsters Ser.). (ENG.). 32p. (J). (gr. 3-6). pap. 7.99 *(978-1-4677-7645-5(9)*, Lerner Pubns.) Lerner Publishing Group.

Randolph, Joanne. Snakes. (Classroom Pets Ser.). 24p. 2009. (gr. 2-3). 42.50 *(978-1-61511-859-5(4))* 2007. (Illus.). (J). (gr. 3-7). lib. bdg. 22.60 *(978-1-4042-3679-0(1))* Rosen Publishing Group, Inc., The. (PowerKids Pr.).

Rathburn, Betsy. Diamondback Rattlesnakes. 2017. (North American Animals Ser.). (ENG., Illus.). 24p. (J). (gr. k-3). lib. bdg. 25.95 ***(978-1-62617-637-9(X)***, Blastoff! Readers) Bellwether Media.

The Really Wild Life of Snakes: Set 5. (Illus.). (J). (gr. k-5). 112.50 *(978-0-8239-7671-3(8))* Rosen Publishing Group, Inc., The.

Reynolds, Shaye. Rattlesnakes. 2016. (Snakes on the Hunt Ser.). (Illus.). 24p. (J). (gr. 3-3). pap. 8.25 *(978-1-4994-2202-3(4)*, PowerKids Pr.) Rosen Publishing Group, Inc., The.

Riehecky, Janet. Cobras: On the Hunt. 2016. (Killer Animals Ser.). (ENG.). 32p. (gr. 1-2). pap. 7.95 *(978-1-5157-6262-1(9)*, Blazers) Capstone Press of Coughlan Cos.

Riggs, Kate. Seedlings: Snakes. 2014. (Seedlings Ser.). (ENG.). 24p. (J). (gr. -1-k). pap. 7.99 *(978-0-89812-888-8(9)*, Creative Paperbacks) Creative Co., The.

—Snakes. 2013. (J). 25.65 *(978-1-60818-343-2(2)*, Creative Education) Creative Co., The.

Ripley's Believe It Or Not! Staff, compiled by. Ripley Twists: Snakes & Reptiles. 2015. (Twist Ser.: 13). (ENG., Illus.). 48p. (J). 12.95 *(978-1-60991-141-6(5))* Ripley Entertainment, Inc.

Robbins, Maureen & Steinkraus, Kyla. Fish Stories. Reese, Bob, illus. 2011. (ENG.). 24p. (gr. 2-3). pap. 8.95 *(978-1-61236-035-5(1))* Rourke Educational Media.

Rothaus, Don P. Pythons. 2015. (Animals of the Rain Forest Ser.). (ENG.). 24p. (J). (gr. 2-5). 27.07 *(978-1-63143-751-9(8)*, 208580) Child's World, Inc., The.

Royston, Angela & Dussling, Jennifer. Slinky, Scaly Snakes. 2011. (DK Readers Ser.). (ENG.). 32p. (J). (gr. 1-3). 3.99 *(978-0-7566-7587-5(1)*, DK Children) Dorling Kindersley Publishing, Inc.

Roza, Greg. Poison! The Spitting Cobra & Other Venomous Animals. 2011. (Armed & Dangerous Ser.). (Illus.). 24p. (J). pap. 8.25 *(978-1-4488-2684-1(5)*, PowerKids Pr.); (YA). (gr. 1-4). lib. bdg. 22.60 *(978-1-4488-2550-9(4))* Rosen Publishing Group, Inc., The.

Rudenko, Dennis. Cobras. 2016. (Snakes on the Hunt Ser.). 24p. (J). (gr. 3-3). pap. 8.25 *(978-1-4994-2194-1(X)*, PowerKids Pr.) Rosen Publishing Group, Inc., The.

Rudy, Lisa Jo. Snakes! 2005. 32p. (J). lib. bdg. 13.85 *(978-1-4242-0861-6(0))* Fitzgerald Bks.

Rustad, Martha E. H. Snakes, 1 vol. 2014. (Little Scientist Ser.). (ENG., Illus.). 32p. (gr. 1-2). 6.95 *(978-1-4765-5271-2(1))* Capstone Press of Coughlan Cos.

Scheunemann, Pam. Snakes Hiss!, 1 vol. 2011. (Animal Sounds Set 2 Ser.). (ENG., Illus.). 24p. (J). (gr. k-3). lib. bdg. 24.21 *(978-1-61613-575-1(1)*, SandCastle) ABDO Publishing Co.

Schwartz, David M. Green Snake. Kuhn, Dwight, photos by. (Life Cycles Ser.). (Illus.). 16p. (J). (gr. 1-3). pap. 2.99 *(978-1-57471-557-6(7)*, 3067) Creative Teaching Pr., Inc.

Scott, L. K. Snakes. Mangiat, Jeff, illus. 2008. (ENG.). 24p. (J). (gr. 3-18). 19.95 *(978-1-58117-799-2(2)*, Intervisual/Piggy Toes) Bendon, Inc.

Sexton, Colleen. Anacondas. 2010. (Snakes Alive Ser.). (ENG., Illus.). 24p. (J). (gr. k-3). lib. bdg. 25.95 *(978-1-60014-313-7(X)*, Blastoff! Readers) Bellwether Media.

—Boa Constrictors. 2010. (Snakes Alive Ser.). (ENG., Illus.). 24p. (J). (gr. k-3). lib. bdg. 25.95 *(978-1-60014-314-4(8)*, Blastoff! Readers) Bellwether Media.

—Cobras. 2010. (Snakes Alive Ser.). (ENG., Illus.). 24p. (J). (gr. k-3). lib. bdg. 25.95 *(978-1-60014-315-1(6)*, Blastoff! Readers) Bellwether Media.

—Copperheads. 2010. (Snakes Alive Ser.). (ENG., Illus.). 24p. (J). (gr. k-3). lib. bdg. 25.95 *(978-1-60014-453-0(5)*, Blastoff! Readers) Bellwether Media.

—Coral Snakes. 2010. (Snakes Alive Ser.). (ENG., Illus.). 24p. (J). (gr. k-3). lib. bdg. 25.95 *(978-1-60014-316-8(4)*, Blastoff! Readers) Bellwether Media.

—Cottonmouths. 2010. (Snakes Alive Ser.). (ENG., Illus.). 24p. (J). (gr. k-3). lib. bdg. 25.95 *(978-1-60014-454-7(3)*, Blastoff! Readers) Bellwether Media.

—Mambas. 2010. (Snakes Alive Ser.). (ENG., Illus.). 24p. (J). (gr. k-3). lib. bdg. 25.95 *(978-1-60014-317-5(2)*, Blastoff! Readers) Bellwether Media.

—Pythons. 2010. (Snakes Alive Ser.). (ENG., Illus.). 24p. (J). (gr. k-3). lib. bdg. 25.95 *(978-1-60014-318-2(0)*, Blastoff! Readers) Bellwether Media.

—Rat Snakes. 2010. (Snakes Alive Ser.). (ENG., Illus.). 24p. (J). (gr. k-3). lib. bdg. 25.95 *(978-1-60014-455-4(1)*, Blastoff! Readers) Bellwether Media.

—Rattlesnakes. 2010. (Snakes Alive Ser.). (ENG., Illus.). 24p. (J). (gr. k-3). lib. bdg. 25.95 *(978-1-60014-319-9(9)*, Blastoff! Readers) Bellwether Media.

—Sea Snakes. 2010. (Snakes Alive Ser.). (ENG., Illus.). 24p. (J). (gr. k-3). lib. bdg. 25.95 *(978-1-60014-320-5(2)*, Blastoff! Readers) Bellwether Media.

—Sidewinders. 2010. (Snakes Alive Ser.). (ENG., Illus.). 24p. (J). (gr. k-3). lib. bdg. 25.95 *(978-1-60014-456-1(X)*, Blastoff! Readers) Bellwether Media.

Shea, Therese. Snakes. (Big Bad Biters Ser.). 24p. 2009. (gr. 2-3). 42.50 *(978-1-61511-564-8(1)*, PowerKids Pr.) 2006. (Illus.). (J). (gr. 3-7). lib. bdg. 22.60 *(978-1-4042-3520-5(5))* Rosen Publishing Group, Inc., The.

Sheikh-Miller, Jonathan. Snakes. 2004. (Discovery Program Ser.). (SPA., Illus.). 64p. (J). (gr. 2-18). pap. 8.95 *(978-0-7945-0004-7(8)*, Usborne); lib. bdg. 16.95 *(978-1-58086-344-5(2))* EDC Publishing.

Shelkh-Miller, Jonathan. Snakes II. 2010. (Discovery Nature Ser.). 64p. (J). 8.99 *(978-0-7945-2240-7(8)*, Usborne) EDC Publishing.

Silverman, Buffy. Gliding Garter Snakes. 2006. (Pull Ahead Bks.). (Illus.). 32p. (J). (gr. 3-7). lib. bdg. 22.60 *(978-0-8225-6043-2(7)*, Lerner Pubns.); (ENG., per. 6.95 *(978-0-8225-6509-3(9)*, First Avenue Editions) Lerner Publishing Group.

Silverstein, Alvin, et al. Boas & Pythons: Cool Pets! Kelley, Gerald, illus. 2012. (Far-Out & Unusual Pets Ser.). 48p. (J). (gr. 3-4). pap. 8.95 *(978-1-4644-0129-9(2))*; 25.27 *(978-0-7660-3878-3(5))* Enslow Pubs., Inc. (Enslow Elementary).

Simon, Seymour. Giant Snakes. 2006. (SeeMore Readers Ser.: SEMR). (ENG., Illus.). 32p. (J). (gr. 1-3). pap. 5.99 *(978-0-8118-5411-5(6))* Chronicle Bks. LLC.

—Poisonous Snakes. Downey, William, illus. 2012. (Dover Children's Science Bks.). (ENG.). 80p. (J). (gr. 3-5). pap. 5.99 *(978-0-486-48470-9(X))* Dover Pubns., Inc.

Simon, Seymour & Simon. Snakes. 2007. (ENG., Illus.). 32p. (J). (gr. k-4). pap. 6.99 *(978-0-06-114095-2(3)*, Collins) HarperCollins Pubs.

Singer, Marilyn. Venom. 2007. (Junior Library Guild Selection Ser.). (Illus.). 96p. (J). (gr. 4-7). 19.95 *(978-1-58196-043-3(3)*, Darby Creek) Lerner Publishing Group.

Smith, Molly. Green Anaconda: The World's Heaviest Snake. (SuperSized! Ser.). 24p. (J). (gr. k-3). 2016. (ENG.). pap. 7.95 ***(978-1-944998-38-7(1))*** 2007. (Illus.). lib. bdg. 21.28 *(978-1-59716-391-0(0)*, 1265936) Bearport Publishing Co., Inc.

The Snake: Individual Title Six-Packs. (Sails Literacy Ser.). 16p. (gr. k-18). 27.00 *(978-0-7635-4429-4(9))* Rigby Education.

Snake Animals in Wild Series. 2003. (J). pap. 2.50 *(978-0-590-44625-9(8))* Scholastic, Inc.

Snakes! (Creatures Corner Ser.). 16p. (J). *(978-2-7643-0124-1(3))* Phidal Publishing, Inc./Editions Phidal, Inc.

Snakes. (Eyes on Nature Ser.). 32p. (J). (gr. 1). pap. *(978-1-882210-58-9(1))* Action Publishing, Inc.

Snakes. 96p. *(978-1-4075-0193-2(3))* Parragon, Inc.

Snakes. 2007. (Nonfiction Collection). (J). 8.00 *(978-1-60343-010-4(5))* Pioneer Valley Bks.

Snakes: Level N, 6 vols. (Wonder Worldtm Ser.). 48p. 34.95 *(978-0-7802-4601-0(2))* Wright Group/McGraw-Hill.

Snakes: Level P, 6 vols., Vol. 2. (Explorers Ser.). 32p. (gr. 3-6). 44.95 *(978-0-7699-0603-4(6))* Shortland Pubns. (U. S. A.) Inc.

Snakes Discovery Library, 5 bks. (J). (gr. 1-4). Set I. lib. bdg. 111.60 *(978-0-86592-954-8(8))*Set II. lib. bdg. 111.60 *(978-0-86592-243-3(8))* Rourke Enterprises, Inc.

Snakes on the Hunt. 2016. (Snakes on the Hunt Ser.). 24p. (gr. 3-3). 141.60 *(978-1-4994-1918-4(X))*; pap. 49.50 *(978-1-4994-2458-4(2))* Rosen Publishing Group, Inc., The. (PowerKids Pr.).

Somervill, Barbara. Brown Treesnake. 2008. (21st Century Skills Library: Animal Invaders Ser.). (ENG., Illus.). 32p. (gr. 4-8). lib. bdg. 28.50 *(978-1-60279-239-5(9)*, 200114) Cherry Lake Publishing.

—Python. 2010. (21st Century Skills Library: Animal Invaders Ser.). (ENG.). 32p. (gr. 4-8). lib. bdg. 28.50 *(978-1-60279-629-4(7)*, 200335) Cherry Lake Publishing.

Somerville, Louisa. Snakes. 2008. (World of Animals Ser.). 32p. (gr. 2-5). 31.35 *(978-1-933834-32-0(3))* Brown Bear Bks.

Spilsbury, Louise. Boa Constrictor. 2013. (Top of the Food Chain Ser.). 32p. (J). (gr. k-5). 25.25 *(978-1-61533-741-5(5))*; pap. 10.00 *(978-1-61533-799-6(7))* Rosen Publishing Group, Inc., The. (PowerKids Pr.).

Steffora, Tracey. Shapes with Snakes, 1 vol. 2013. (Animal Math Ser.). (ENG.). 24p. (gr. -1-1). 22.65 *(978-1-4329-7562-3(5)*, NA-h) Heinemann-Raintree.

Stewart, Melissa. Snakes! 2009. (Readers Ser.). (ENG., Illus.). 32p. (J). (gr. k-3). 3.99 *(978-1-4263-0428-6(5))*; lib. bdg. 13.90 *(978-1-4263-0429-3(3))* National Geographic Society. (National Geographic Children's Bks.).

Stone, Tanya Lee. Snakes. 2003. (Wild Wild World Ser.). 24p. (YA). 24.94 *(978-1-56711-823-0(2)*, Blackbirch Pr., Inc.) Cengage Gale.

Sweazey, Davy. Ball Pythons. 2014. (Amazing Snakes! Ser.). (ENG., Illus.). 24p. (J). (gr. 3-7). lib. bdg. 25.95 *(978-1-62617-088-9(6)*, Epic Bks.) Bellwether Media.

—Bush Vipers. 2014. (Amazing Snakes! Ser.). (ENG., Illus.). 24p. (J). (gr. 3-7). lib. bdg. 25.95 *(978-1-62617-090-2(8)*, Epic Bks.) Bellwether Media.

—Death Adders. 2014. (Amazing Snakes! Ser.). (ENG., Illus.). 24p. (J). (gr. 3-7). lib. bdg. 25.95 *(978-1-62617-091-9(6)*, Epic Bks.) Bellwether Media.

—King Cobras. 2014. (Amazing Snakes! Ser.). (ENG., Illus.). 24p. (J). (gr. 3-7). lib. bdg. 25.95 *(978-1-62617-094-0(0)*, Epic Bks.) Bellwether Media.

Taylor, Barbara. Exploring Nature - Amazing Snakes: An Exciting Insight into the Weird & Wonderful World of Snakes & How They Live, with 190 Pictures. 2013. (ENG., Illus.). 64p. (J). (gr. 3-7). 12.99 *(978-1-84322-736-6(3))* Anness Publishing GBR. Dist: National Bk. Network.

—Snakes. 2010. (Remarkable Man & Beast Ser.). (Illus.). 48p. (J). (gr. 3-18). lib. bdg. 19.95 *(978-1-4222-1975-1(5))* Mason Crest.

Taylor, Trace & Lynch, Michelle. Cobras. 2011. (ARC Press / Power 100 - Predator Animals Ser.). pap. 45.32 *(978-1-61541-505-2(X))* American Reading Co.

Thatcher, Henry. Pythons & Garter Snakes, 1 vol., 1. 2014. (Big Animals, Small Animals Ser.). (ENG.). 32p. (J). (gr. k-5). 26.25 *(978-1-4777-6110-6(1)*, PowerKids Pr.) Rosen Publishing Group, Inc., The.

Thomas, Isabel. Slinky's Guide to Caring for Your Snake, 1 vol. Peterson, Rick, illus. 2014. (Pets' Guides). (ENG.). 32p. (gr. 1-3). pap. 8.29 *(978-1-4846-0270-6(6))*; 27.32 *(978-1-4846-0263-8(3))* Heinemann-Raintree. (Heinemann First Library).

Thomson, Sarah L. Amazing Snakes! Wildlife Conservation Society, photos by. 2006. (I Can Read Level 2 Ser.). (ENG., Illus.). 32p. (J). (gr. k-3). pap. 3.99 *(978-0-06-054464-5(3))* HarperCollins Pubs.

Troller, Leah. Look at the Snakes. 2016. (1-3Y Animals Ser.). (ENG., Illus.). 16p. (J). pap. 5.99 ***(978-1-63437-595-5(5))*** American Reading Co.

Turnbull, Stephanie. Snake. 2015. (Big Beasts Ser.). (Illus.). 24p. (gr. k-3). 28.50 *(978-1-62588-171-7(1))* Black Rabbit Bks.

—Snake. 2015. (ENG., Illus.). 24p. (J). pap. 8.95 *(978-1-77092-219-8(9))* RiverStream Publishing.

Wallach, Van. Una Cobra Al Descubierto. 2007. (Al Descubierto Ser.). (Illus.). 16p. (J). (gr. 3-7). *(978-970-718-497-8(3)*, Silver Dolphin en Español) Advanced Marketing, S. de R. L. de C. V.

Walske, Christine Zuchora. Pythons, 1 vol. 2014. (Amazing Reptiles Ser.). (ENG.). 48p. (gr. 8-12). lib. bdg. 32.79 *(978-1-62403-373-5(3))* ABDO Publishing Co.

Weakland, Mark. Scooby-Doo! an Addition Mystery: The Case of the Angry Adder, 1 vol. Gross, Scott, illus. 2014. (Solve It with Scooby-Doo!: Math Ser.). (ENG.). 24p. (gr. k-2). lib. bdg. 27.99 *(978-1-4914-1539-9(8))* Capstone Press of Coughlan Cos.

S

Wechsler, Doug. Garter Snakes. 2009. (Really Wild Life of Animals Ser.). 24p. (gr. 3-4). 42.50 (978-1-60854-192-8(4), PowerKids Pr.) Rosen Publishing Group, Inc., The.

—Rattlesnakes. 2009. (Really Wild Life of Animals Ser.). 24p. (gr. 3-4). 42.50 (978-1-60854-208-6(4), PowerKids Pr.) Rosen Publishing Group, Inc., The.

—Really Wild Life of Snakes, Vol. I. (Illus.). 80.70 (978-0-8239-7078-0(7)) Rosen Publishing Group, Inc., The.

Wexo, John Bonnett. Serpientes. Rountree, Monica, tr. 2003. (Zoobooks Ser.). Orig. Title: Snakes. (SPA., Illus.). 24p. (J). (gr. 1-7). lib. bdg. 15.95 (978-1-888153-83-5(0)) Wildlife Education, Ltd.

—Snakes. rev. ed. 2003. (Illus.). 24p. 10.95 (978-1-888153-96-5(2), Zoo Bks.) Wildlife Education, Ltd.

White, Nancy. Black Mambas: Sudden Death! 2009. (Fangs Ser.). (Illus.). 24p. (YA). (gr. 1-4). lib. bdg. 22.61 (978-1-59716-766-6(5)) Bearport Publishing Co., Inc.

—Coral Snakes: Beware the Colors! 2009. (Fangs Ser.). (Illus.). 24p. (YA). (gr. 1-4). lib. bdg. 22.61 (978-1-59716-763-5(0)) Bearport Publishing Co., Inc.

—Death Adders: Super Deadly! 2009. (Fangs Ser.). (Illus.). 24p. (J). (gr. 1-4). lib. bdg. 22.61 (978-1-59716-764-2(9)) Bearport Publishing Co., Inc.

—Diamondback Rattlers: America's Most Venomous Snakes! (Fangs Ser.). 24p. (gr. 1-6). 2016. (ENG.). (J). pap. 7.95 **(978-1-944998-65-3(9))** 2009. (Illus.). (YA). lib. bdg. 22.61 (978-1-59716-765-9(7)) Bearport Publishing Co., Inc.

—Fer-de-Lance: Master Killer! 2009. (Fangs Ser.). (Illus.). 24p. (YA). (gr. 1-4). lib. bdg. 22.61 (978-1-59716-769-7(X)) Bearport Publishing Co., Inc.

—King Cobras: The Biggest Venomous Snakes of All! 2009. (Fangs Ser.). (Illus.). 24p. (J). (gr. 1-4). lib. bdg. 22.61 (978-1-59716-767-3(3)) Bearport Publishing Co., Inc.

Whiting, Jim. Care for a Pet Snake. 2007. (How to Convince Your Parents You Can ... Ser.). (Illus.). 32p. (YA). (gr. 1-4). lib. bdg. 25.70 (978-1-58415-604-8(X)) Mitchell Lane Pubs., Inc.

Wild about Snakes. (Wild about Snakes Ser.). (ENG.). 32p. (gr. 3-4). 2011. pap. 381.60 (978-1-4296-7290-0(0)) 2011. pap. 190.80 (978-1-4296-6427-1(4)) 2010. lib. bdg. 111.96 (978-1-4296-5435-7(X)) Capstone Press of Coughlan Cos. (Edge Bks.).

Wild about Snakes, 8 vols., Set. Incl. Anacondas. Kopp, Megan. 2010. lib. bdg. 27.99 (978-1-4296-5432-6(5)); Black Mambas. Howard, Melanie A. 2011. lib. bdg. 27.99 (978-1-4296-6012-9(0)); Boa Constrictors. Howard, Melanie A. 2011. lib. bdg. 27.99 (978-1-4296-6011-2(2)); Cobras. Kopp, Megan. 2010. lib. bdg. 27.99 (978-1-4296-5430-2(9)); Garter Snakes. Montgomery, Heather L. 2010. lib. bdg. 27.99 (978-1-4296-5433-3(3)); Kingsnakes. Montgomery, Heather L. 2011. lib. bdg. 27.99 (978-1-4296-6013-6(9)); Pythons. Dorisi-Winget, Dianna. 2011. lib. bdg. 27.99 (978-1-4296-6014-3(7)); Rattlesnakes. Montgomery, Heather L. 2010. lib. bdg. 27.99 (978-1-4296-5434-0(1)); (gr. 3-4). (Wild about Snakes Ser.). (ENG.). 32p. 2011. Set lib. bdg. 223.92 (978-1-4296-6538-4(6), Edge Bks.) Capstone Press of Coughlan Cos.

Wilhelm, Doug. Snake Invasion. 2016. (Illus.). (J). pap. 6.99 (978-1-937133-52-8(4)) Chooseco LLC.

Willebrandt, Avery. Spitting Cobra / Cobra Escupidora. 2011. (Killer Snakes / Serpientes asesinas Ser.). (SPA., Illus.). 24p. (J). (gr. 1-3). 22.60 (978-1-4339-5653-9(5)) Stevens, Gareth Publishing LLLP.

—Spitting Cobras. 2011. (Killer Snakes Ser.). (Illus.). 24p. (J). (gr. 1-3). pap. 8.15 (978-1-4339-5651-5(9)); lib. bdg. 22.60 (978-1-4339-5649-2(7)) Stevens, Gareth Publishing LLLP.

Wilsdon, Christina. Snakes. (Amazing Animals Ser.). 48p. 2009. (gr. 2-6). pap. 10.50 (978-1-4339-2019-6(0), Gareth Stevens Learning Library) 2008. (YA). (gr. 3-6). lib. bdg. 28.00 (978-0-8368-9102-7(3)) Stevens, Gareth Publishing LLLP.

—Snakes. 2007. (J). (978-1-59939-137-3(6), Reader's Digest Young Families, Inc.) Studio Fun International.

Wimmer, Teresa. Snakes. 2009. (Living Wild Ser.). (Illus.). 48p. (J). 22.95 (978-1-58341-743-0(5), Creative Education) Creative Co., The.

Wood, Selina. Snakes. 2009. (Extreme Pets Ser.). (YA). (gr. 4-7). 28.50 (978-1-59920-233-4(6)) Black Rabbit Bks.

Worthy, Shanya. Taipan. 2011. (Killer Snakes Ser.). (Illus.). 24p. (J). (gr. 1-3). pap. 8.15 (978-1-4339-4566-3(5)); lib. bdg. 22.60 (978-1-4339-4565-6(7)) Stevens, Gareth Publishing LLLP.

—Taipan / Taipán. 2011. (Killer Snakes / Serpientes asesinas Ser.). (ENG & SPA., Illus.). 24p. (J). (gr. 1-3). 22.60 (978-1-4339-4569-4(X)) Stevens, Gareth Publishing LLLP.

Yates, Gene, illus. The Snake Shapes Book. 2006. (J). (978-1-58865-365-9(X)) Kidsbooks, LLC.

Young, Phil. The Best Book on Northern Brown Snakes. 2010. 49p. pap. 23.98 (978-0-557-43753-5(9)) Lulu Pr., Inc.

SNAKES—FICTION

Adler, David A. The Scary Snake Mystery. Natti, Susanna, illus. 2005. (Cam Jansen Ser.: 17). (ENG.). 64p. (J). (gr. 2-5). 4.99 (978-0-14-240288-7(5), Puffin Books) Penguin Young Readers Group.

Aldinoff, Elsie V. The Garden. 2005. (ENG.). 416p. (J). (gr. 9). pap. 6.99 (978-0-06-055607-5(2), HarperTeen) HarperCollins Pubs.

Ata, Te. Baby Rattlesnake. Reisberg, Mira, illus. 2013. (ENG.). 32p. (J). (gr. -1). pap. 10.95 (978-0-89239-216-2(9)) Lee & Low Bks., Inc.

—Baby Rattlesnake. Alarcón, Francisco X., tr. Reisberg, Mira, illus. 2013. (SPA & ENG.). 32p. (J). pap. 9.95 (978-0-89239-188-2(X)) Lee & Low Bks., Inc.

Ata, Te, et al. Baby Rattlesnake. Reisberg, Mira, illus. 2013. (ENG.). 32p. (J). (gr. -1-18). pap. 9.95 (978-0-89239-049-6(2)) Lee & Low Bks., Inc.

Atwater-Rhodes, Amelia. Falcondance. 2007. (Kiesha'ra Ser.: Bk. 3). (ENG.). 208p. (YA). (gr. 7-12). per. 7.99 (978-0-440-23885-0(4), Delacorte Pr.) Random Hse. Children's Bks.

—Snakecharm. 2007. (Kiesha'ra Ser.: Bk. 2). (ENG.). 176p. (YA). (gr. 7-12). per. 7.99 (978-0-385-73493-6(X), Delacorte Pr.) Random Hse. Children's Bks.

—Wolfcry. 2008. (Kiesha'ra Ser.: Bk. 4). (ENG.). 208p. (YA). (gr. 9-12). pap. 7.99 (978-0-440-23886-7(2), Delacorte Pr.) Random Hse. Children's Bks.

Bagley, Conor. Ziggy McFinster's Nantucket Adventure. Bernard Westcott, Nadine, illus. 2008. (ENG.). 40p. (J). (gr. -1-3). 16.95 (978-1-56625-315-4(2)) Bonus Bks., Inc.

Bapiraju Gandham. The Wizard of Ants. 2010. 88p. pap. 33.48 (978-1-4269-1940-4(9)) Trafford Publishing.

Barchers, Suzanne. The Shipwrecked Sailor: A Tale from Egypt. Hehenberger, Shelly, illus. 2015. (Tales of Honor Ser.). (ENG.). 32p. (gr. 1-3). lib. bdg. 26.60 (978-1-939656-86-5(9)) Red Chair Pr.

Beeson, Jan. Mysterious World of the Puffins the Treasure Hunt Book 1. 2013. 74p. pap. 19.99 (978-0-9890482-0-0(9)) Beeson, Jan.

Bellingham, Brenda. Lilly & the Snakes. MacDonald, Clarke, illus. 2007. (Formac First Novels Ser.: 37). (ENG & GER.). 64p. (J). (gr. 2-5). 14.95 (978-0-88780-727-5(5), 9780887807275); 4.95 (978-0-88780-723-7(2), 9780887807237) Formac Publishing Co., Ltd. CAN. Dist: Casemate Pubs. & Bk. Distributors, LLC.

Bernstrom, Daniel. One Day in the Eucalyptus, Eucalyptus Tree. Wenzel, Brendan, illus. 2016. 32p. (J). (gr. -1-3). 17.99 (978-0-06-235485-3(X), Tegen, Katherine Bks) HarperCollins Pubs.

Brennan, Sarah. The Tale of Sybil Snake. Harrison, Harry, illus. 2012. (ENG.). 32p. (J). (978-1-937160-53-1(X)) Auspicious Times.

Bruneau, Clotilde, et al. The Planet of the Snake. Nautilus Studio Staff, illus. 2015. (ENG.). 48p. (J). (gr. 4-8). pap. 7.95 (978-1-4677-6027-0(7), Graphic Universe™) Lerner Publishing Group.

Buckley, Richard. The Foolish Tortoise. Carle, Eric, illus. 2013. (World of Eric Carle Ser.). (ENG.). 24p. (J). (gr. -1-3). pap. 9.99 (978-1-4424-6638-8(3), Little Simon) Little Simon.

—The Greedy Python. Carle, Eric, illus. 2012. (World of Eric Carle Ser.). (ENG.). 24p. (J). (gr. -1-1). 16.99 (978-1-4424-4577-2(7)); pap. 3.99 (978-1-4424-4576-5(9)) Simon Spotlight. (Simon Spotlight).

—The Greedy Python. Carle, Eric, illus. 2009. (World of Eric Carle Ser.). (ENG.). 24p. (J). (gr. -1-k). bds. 7.99 (978-1-4169-8290-6(6), Little Simon) Little Simon.

—The Greedy Python. 2012. (Eric Carle Ready-To-Read Ser.). lib. bdg. 13.55 (978-0-606-26357-3(8), Turtleback) Turtleback Bks.

—The Greedy Python: Lap Edition. Carle, Eric, illus. 2013. (World of Eric Carle Ser.). (ENG.). 24p. (J). (gr. -1-k). bds. 12.99 (978-1-4424-8991-2(X), Little Simon) Little Simon.

Burton, Thomas. Bluey & Dingo's Outback Adventure. 2011. 40p. 15.66 (978-1-4567-7006-8(3)) AuthorHouse.

Byrd, Betty. They Call Me Pharaoh. 2008. 20p. pap. 24.95 (978-1-60563-008-3(X)) America Star Bks.

Cannon, Janell. Verdi. pap. 24.95 (978-85-325-1343-4(3)) Rocco, Editora, Ltda BRA. Dist: Distribooks, Inc.

Cannon, Janell & Cannon. Verdi. 2003. (SPA., Illus.). 48p. (J). (gr. 1-3). (978-84-261-3042-6(9), JV7591) Juventud, Editorial ESP. Dist: Lectorum Pubns., Inc.

Carter, Candace. Sid's Surprise. Kim, Joung Un, illus. 2005. (Green Light Readers Level 1 Ser.). (ENG.). 32p. (J). (gr. -1-3). pap. 3.95 (978-0-15-205182-2(1)) Houghton Mifflin Harcourt Publishing Co.

—Sid's Surprise. Kim, Joung Un, illus. 2005. (Green Light Readers Level 1 Ser.). (gr. -1-3). 13.95 (978-0-7569-5242-6(5)) Perfection Learning Corp.

Cheng, Christopher. Python. Jackson, Mark, illus. 2013. (ENG.). 32p. (J). (gr. k-3). 15.99 (978-0-7636-6396-4(4)) Candlewick Pr.

Chin, Oliver, ed. The Year of the Snake: Tales from the Chinese Zodiac. Wood, Jennifer, illus. 2012. (Tales from the Chinese Zodiac Ser.: 8). (ENG.). 36p. (J). (gr. -1-3). 15.95 (978-1-59702-038-1(9)) Immedium.

Clark, Clara Gillow. Willie & the Rattlesnake King. 2003. (ENG., Illus.). 168p. (YA). (gr. 4-6). pap. 7.95 (978-1-56397-763-3(X)) Boyds Mills Pr.

Clark, Jeanne B. The Second Encounter: With the Snake Named Bully. 2012. 40p. pap. 24.99 (978-1-4772-1568-5(9)) AuthorHouse.

Clarke, Ella. The Snake's Diary by Little Yellow, 1 vol. 2013. (Fiction Readers Ser.). (ENG., Illus.). 24p. (J). (gr. 2-2). pap. 6.99 (978-1-4333-5531-8(0)) Shell Educational Publishing.

Condi-Babich, Kris. 4Cam. us. 2004. 71p. pap. 19.95 (978-1-4137-2241-3(5)) America Star Bks.

Cook, Beatrice. A Journey with the Spider & Snake to Arizona. Campis, Adrian, Jr., illus. 2007. (J). 14.95 (978-0-9795867-0-5(4)) Travel America Bks.

Cook, Sherry & Johnson, Terri. Susie Sound, 26. Kuhn, Jesse, illus. I.t. ed. 2006. 32p. (J). 7.99 (978-1-933815-18-3(3), Quirkles, The) Creative 3, LLC.

Cote, Jenny. The Ark, the Reed & the Fire Cloud: The Amazing Tales of Max & Liz Book One, 2 bks, Bk 1. 2008. (Amazing Tales of Max & Liz Ser.: 1). (ENG., Illus.). 432p. (J). (gr. 5-11). pap. 16.99 (978-0-89957-198-0(0), Living Ink Bks.) AMG Pubs.

Cotton, Peter B. When Jungle Jim Comes to Visit Fred the Snake. Lemaire, Bonnie, illus. 2013. 48p. 24.95 (978-0-9883370-4-6(5)) Fig & The Vine, LLC, The.

Coudakpo, Agrey Emile A. The Malignant & a Malignant One & Half: The Story of the Baby Frog & the Vicious Viper. 2013. 44p. pap. 20.72 (978-1-4669-8247-5(0)) Trafford Publishing.

Cowley, Joy. Friends: Snake & Lizard. Bishop, Gavin, illus. 2011. (Gecko Press Titles Ser.). (ENG.). 144p. 16.95 (978-1-877579-01-1(7)) Gecko Pr. NZL. Dist: Lerner Publishing Group.

Dale, Jay. Where Is Carl the Corn Snake?, 1 vol. Alder, Charlie, illus. 2012. (Engage Literacy Green Ser.). (ENG.). 32p. (gr. k-2). pap. 5.99 (978-1-4296-8994-6(3), Engage Literacy) Capstone Press of Coughlan Cos.

Darlene, Cannon. Dollygal, Peacock, & the Serpent. Mathis, Leslie, illus. 2011. 108p. pap. 19.95 (978-1-61286-001-5(X)) Avid Readers Publishing Group.

Davey, Keith Peter. Squeaks Narrow Squeaks. Frost, Justine, illus. 2009. 32p. pap. 14.62 (978-1-4120-4402-8(2)) Trafford Publishing.

de Lint, Charles. The Cats of Tanglewood Forest. 2014. (J). lib. bdg. 22.10 (978-0-606-36532-1(X)) Turtleback Bks.

Degman-Reed, Ruth. Blake the Snake Had a Bellyache. 2011. 24p. (gr. -1). pap. 12.79 (978-1-4520-9652-0(X)) AuthorHouse.

Dixon, Franklin W. The Great Escape. Burroughs, Scott, illus. 2015. (Hardy Boys: the Secret Files Ser.: 17). (ENG.). 112p. (J). (gr. 1-4). pap. 4.99 (978-1-4814-2267-3(7), Aladdin) Simon & Schuster Children's Publishing.

Doudna, Kelly. Snake Charmer, 1 vol. 2007. (Critter Chronicles Ser.). (ENG., Illus.). 24p. (J). (gr. k-3). lib. bdg. 24.21 (978-1-59928-470-5(7), SandCastle) ABDO Publishing Co.

Downie, David. David & Jacko. Tatsi, Andreanna, tr. Seroya, Tea, illus. 2012. 52p. pap. (978-1-922159-15-1(8)); pap. (978-1-922159-24-3(7)) Blue Peg Publishing.

—David & Jacko. Ivanova, Kalina, tr. Seroya, Tea, illus. 2012. 52p. pap. (978-1-922159-01-4(8)) Blue Peg Publishing.

—David & Jacko. Seroya, Tea, illus. 2012. 52p. pap. (978-1-922159-99-1(9)) Blue Peg Publishing.

Downing, Johnette. Why the Oyster Has the Pearl, 1 vol. Hill, Bethanne, illus. 2011. (ENG.). 32p. (J). (gr. k-3). 16.99 (978-1-4556-1460-8(2)) Pelican Publishing Co., Inc.

Dubos, Delphine. The Planet of Wind. Burrell, Carol klio, tr. Élyum Studio Staff, illus. 2012. (Little Prince Ser.: 1). (ENG.). 56p. (J). (gr. 4-8). pap. 7.95 (978-0-8225-9422-2(6), Graphic Universe™) Lerner Publishing Group.

Duckers, John. The Amazing Adventures of the Silly Six. 2013. (Illus.). 188p. pap. (978-1-78148-626-9(3)) Grosvenor Hse. Publishing Ltd.

Dunlap, Jim. Sam Snake Says. Holland, Kathy, illus. 2008. 35p. pap. 24.95 (978-1-60672-709-6(5)) America Star Bks.

Eagle, Golden. It's Good to Shed Your Skin (Snake Medicine) l.t. ed. 2004. (Illus.). 20p. (J). per. 12.99 (978-1-932338-38-6(1)) Lifevest Publishing, Inc.

Estes-Hill, Katrina. My Imagination. Kwong, Alvina, illus. 2007. 32p. (J). (gr. -1-2). 15.95 (978-0-9745715-6-0(3)) KRBY Creations, LLC.

Ferrara, Gin. I'm Not Afraid of Snakes. 2009. 39p. pap. 22.95 (978-0-557-15979-6(2)) Lulu Pr., Inc.

Fewer, Patrick W. Sammy the Snow Snake: A Halloween Haunting Yukon Style. 2009. 24p. pap. 11.49 (978-1-4490-2075-0(5)) AuthorHouse.

—Sammy the Snow Snake: Christmas Rain. 2008. (ENG.). 28p. 12.49 (978-1-4389-4283-4(4)) AuthorHouse.

Fitzpatrick-Hale-Herself, Donna Marie. Snake & Mouse: Ryan's birthday Tea. 2011. (Illus.). 44p. pap. 17.04 (978-1-4567-8590-1(7)) AuthorHouse.

Fletcher, Perry. Why Snakes Don't Have Legs. 2008. 44p. pap. 24.95 (978-1-60474-973-1(3)) America Star Bks.

Foltyn, Sue. Mayzeemioletu. 2009. 12p. pap. 9.95 (978-1-4490-2244-0(8)) AuthorHouse.

Forde, Catherine. Slippy. 2012. (Stoke Books Titles Ser.). 72p. (J). (gr. 5-8). pap. 45.32 (978-0-7613-9223-1(8)); pap. 7.95 (978-1-78112-032-3(3)); lib. bdg. 22.60 (978-1-78112-031-6(5)) Stoke Bks.

Fowler, Lisa. Snakes & Stones. 2016. (ENG.). 240p. (J). (gr. 2-7). 15.99 (978-1-5107-1031-3(0), Sky Pony Pr.) Skyhorse Publishing Co., Inc.

Funk, Lynda. The Snake, the Humming Bird & Me. 2013. 44p. pap. 19.99 (978-1-4685-3329-3(0)) AuthorHouse.

Giff, Patricia Reilly. Watch Out! Man-Eating Snake. 79p. (J). (gr. 1-2). pap. 3.99 (978-0-8072-1281-3(4), Listening Library) Random Hse. Audio Publishing Group.

Goss, Jamie. The Snake Without a Hiss, 1 vol. 2010. 36p. pap. 24.95 (978-1-4489-4446-0(5)) PublishAmerica, Inc.

Graham, Bobby G. Jake the Snake. 2010. 24p. pap. 16.95 (978-1-4497-0568-8(5), WestBow Pr.) Author Solutions, Inc.

Green, Poppy. Forget-Me-Not Lake. Bell, Jennifer A., illus. 2015. (Adventures of Sophie Mouse Ser.: 3). (ENG.). 128p. (J). (gr. k-4). 16.99 (978-1-4814-3000-5(9), Little Simon) Little Simon.

—A New Friend. Bell, Jennifer A., illus. 2015. (Adventures of Sophie Mouse Ser.: 1). (ENG.). 128p. (J). (gr. k-4). pap. 5.99 (978-1-4814-2832-3(2), Little Simon) Little Simon.

Greenburg, Dan. Secrets of Dripping Fang, Book Eight: When Bad Snakes Attack Good Children. Fischer, Scott M., illus. 2007. (Secrets of Dripping Fang Ser.: Bk. 8). (ENG.). 144p. (J). (gr. 2-5). 11.99 (978-0-15-206056-5(1)) Houghton Mifflin Harcourt Publishing Co.

Greene, Joshua M. Kaliya, Serpent King. Wire, Patrick, illus. rev. ed. 2012. (ENG.). 24p. (gr. -1). 14.99 (978-1-60887-148-3(7)) Mandala Publishing.

Grover, Kuloa A. Charlie the Snake. 2012. 32p. pap. 19.99 (978-1-4685-5568-4(5)) AuthorHouse.

Guillain, Charlotte. Rumplesnakeskin, 1 vol. Beacon, Dawn, illus. 2014. (Animal Fairy Tales Ser.). (ENG.). 24p. (gr. 1-2). lib. bdg. 23.99 (978-1-4109-6111-2(7), NA-r) Heinemann-Raintree.

Gutman, Dan. My Weird School: Class Pet Mess! Paillot, Jim, illus. 2017. (I Can Read Level 2 Ser.). 32p. (J). (gr. -1-3). pap. 3.99 (978-0-06-236746-4(3)) HarperCollins Pubs.

Halfmann, Janet. Garter Snake at Willow Creek Lane. Wertheim, Anne, illus. 2011. (ENG.). 32p. (J). (gr. k-4). 19.95 (978-1-60727-206-9(7)); pap. 8.95 (978-1-60727-208-3(3)) Soundprints.

Hamilton, Libby & Haworth, Katie. Through the Town. Shuttlewood, Craig, illus. 2015. (ENG.). 10p. (J). (gr. -1 — 1). bds. 6.99 (978-1-4998-0076-0(2)) Little Bee Books Inc.

Haussinger, D. & Hassinger, Peter W. Susanna the Snake. Date not set. (ENG.). 320p. (YA). (gr. 7-18). pap. 5.99 (978-0-06-447212-8(4)) HarperCollins Pubs.

Hayes, Joe. The Gum-Chewing Rattler. Castro L., Antonio, illus. 2008. (ENG.). 32p. (J). (gr. k-6). pap. 7.95 (978-1-933693-19-4(3)) Cinco Puntos Pr.

—The Gum-Chewing Rattler. 2006. (ENG., Illus.). 32p. (J). (gr. k-6). 16.95 (978-0-938317-99-9(7)) Cinco Puntos Pr.

—My Pet Rattlesnake. 2014. (ENG., Illus.). 32p. (J). 16.95 (978-1-935955-61-0(6)); pap. 7.95 (978-1-935955-62-7(4)) Cinco Puntos Pr.

Heilbroner, Joan. A Pet Named Sneaker. Lemaître, Pascal, illus. 2013. (Beginner Books Ser.). (ENG.). 48p. (J). (gr. k-3). 8.99 (978-0-307-97580-5(0), Random Hse. Bks. for Young Readers) Random Hse. Children's Bks.

Hiiasen, Carl. Hoot. 2014. 17.00 (978-1-63419-707-6(0)) Perfection Learning Corp.

Hill, Michelle M. Stanley. 2012. 12p. pap. 15.99 (978-1-4772-2923-1(X)) AuthorHouse.

Himes, John. Everyone Is Special. 2012. 24p. pap. 24.95 (978-1-4626-7462-6(3)) America Star Bks.

Hobson, Joseph. The Snake River Adventures: Floating the Snake. 2012. 88p. pap. 10.95 (978-1-938223-04-4(7)) Salem Author Services.

Hoenecke, Karen. Snake Hunts for Lunch. Drzewiecki, Paul, illus. l.t. ed. 2005. (ENG.). 12p. (gr. k-2). pap. 7.95 (978-1-57874-006-2(1), Kaeden Bks.) Kaeden Corp.

Hsia, Pei Chen. The Little Dumpling. 2012. 82p. pap. 19.95 (978-1-4626-8041-2(0)) America Star Bks.

Huxley, Aldous. The Crows of Pearblossom. Blackall, Sophie, illus. 2011. (ENG.). 40p. (J). (gr. k-2). 17.95 (978-0-8109-9730-1(4), Abrams Bks. for Young Readers) Abrams, Inc.

—The Crows of Pearblossom. (J). 15.95 (978-0-89190-167-9(1)) Amereon Ltd.

Jackson, Barry E. Danny Diamondback. Jackson, Barry E., illus. 2008. (Illus.). 40p. (J). (gr. k-2). lib. bdg. 17.89 (978-0-06-113185-1(7)) HarperCollins Pubs.

Jake the Snake: Set D Individual Title, 6 Packs. (Supersonic Phonics Ser.). (gr. k-3). 29.00 (978-0-7635-0550-9(1)) Rigby Education.

Jamesson, Christine. The Adventures of Samantha the Black Racer Snake. 2005. (ENG.). 28p. per. 18.00 (978-1-4208-1873-4(2)) AuthorHouse.

Jarman, Julia. Class Two at the Zoo. Chapman, Lynne, illus. 2007. (Carolrhoda Picture Bks.). (ENG.). 32p. (J). (gr. k-2). 16.95 (978-0-8225-7132-2(3), Carolrhoda Bks.) Lerner Publishing Group.

Jennings, Patrick. We Can't All Be Rattlesnakes. (J). 2011. (ENG.). 144p. (gr. 3-7). pap. 5.99 (978-0-06-082117-3(5)) 2009. 121p. lib. bdg. 16.89 (978-0-06-082116-6(7)) HarperCollins Pubs.

Jones, C. B. The Cats' Meow. Green, Chris, illus. 2017. (Bog Hollow Boys Ser.). (ENG.). 72p. (gr. 4-5). lib. bdg. 25.32 (978-1-4965-4057-7(3)) Stone Arch Bks.

—Kiss of the Snake. Green, Chris, illus. 2017. (Bog Hollow Boys Ser.). (ENG.). 72p. (gr. 4-5). lib. bdg. 25.32 (978-1-4965-4056-0(5)) Stone Arch Bks.

Joosse, Barbara M. Wally Wants to Hug. Ashdown, Rebecca, illus. 2017. (ENG.). 32p. (J). (gr. -1-3). 16.99 (978-1-4998-0404-1(0)) Little Bee Books Inc.

Josephine Breglia. The Adventures of Poke Sa' Baar. 2012. 28p. pap. 24.95 (978-1-4626-8820-3(9)) America Star Bks.

Jostand, Jeffrey Jay. Sedrick the Snake. Llamas, Kristin, illus. 2008. 32p. pap. 24.95 (978-1-4241-9944-0(1)) America Star Bks.

Kaneko, Amanda Bullard. Darza the Little Dragon. Hildebrandt, Lowell, illus. 2010. 28p. 13.99 (978-1-4520-4198-8(9)) AuthorHouse.

Karapetkova, Holly. Las Serpientes en el Tercer Grado. 2012.Tr. of Snakes in Third Grade. (SPA & ENG.). 24p. (gr. 2-3). pap. 8.95 (978-1-61810-545-5(0)) Rourke Educational Media.

Kidd, Jessica A. Zachary Zoom. 2009. 28p. pap. 12.25 (978-1-60860-502-6(7), Eloquent Bks.) Strategic Book Publishing & Rights Agency (SBPRA).

Kimmel, Eric A. Hiss-S-S-S! 2012. (ENG.). 208p. (J). 17.95 (978-0-8234-2415-3(4)) Holiday Hse., Inc.

—Why the Snake Crawls on Its Belly. Davis, Allen, illus. 2005. 32p. (J). (gr. 1-4). 14.95 (978-1-930143-20-3(6), Devora Publishing) Simcha Media Group.

Kipling, Rudyard & Pinkney, Jerry. Rikki-Tikki-Tavi. 2004. (Illus.). (gr. -1-3). 17.00 (978-0-7569-3250-3(5)) Perfection Learning Corp.

Klemer, Amy Wade. The Scary Snake Monster. 2003. (Illus.). 16p. (J). pap. 8.00 (978-0-9729216-1-9(3)) ABCDMoon Publishing.

Krepela, Rebecca. Vernon, Drake & Chomp. 2013. 20p. pap. 24.95 (978-1-62709-841-0(0)) America Star Bks.

Krulik, Nancy. Free the Worms! John and Wendy Staff, illus. 2008. (Katie Kazoo, Switcheroo Ser.: 28). (ENG.). 80p. (J). (gr. 2-4). pap. 3.99 (978-0-448-44675-2(8), Grosset & Dunlap) Penguin Young Readers Group.

—Free the Worms! John & Wendy, illus. 2008. (Katie Kazoo, Switcheroo Ser.). 78p. (J). 11.65 (978-0-7569-8807-4(1)) Perfection Learning Corp.

LaFevers, R. L. The Basilisk's Lair. Murphy, Kelly, illus. 2nd ed. 2010. (Nathaniel Fludd, Beastologist Ser.: 2). (ENG.). 160p. (J). (gr. 1-4). 15.00 (978-0-547-23867-8(3)) Houghton Mifflin Harcourt Publishing Co.

Lane, Leonie. Fork Tongue Freimon. 2006. 164p. per. (978-1-84667-009-1(8)) Derwent Pr., The.

Lawrence, Cherry. David & the Blue Racer. 2006. 53p. pap. 16.95 (978-1-4241-3339-0(4)) PublishAmerica, Inc.

Little, Lorna. The Mark of the Wagarl. Lyndon, Janice, illus. 2004. 28p. (J). (978-1-875641-97-0(1)) Magabala Bks.

Lorenzen, Margartet. Slinky Slithertail & the Talent Show. Sawyer, Jocelyn, illus. 2004. 96p. (J). per. 12.50 (978-0-9708053-9-3(X)) Authors & Artists Publishers of New York, Inc.

Lumry, Amanda & Hurwitz, Laura. Operation Orangutan. 2007. (Adventures of Riley (Unnumbered) Ser.). (Illus.). 36p. (J). (gr. -1-3). 18.95 (978-0-9748411-7-5(X)) Eaglemont Pr.

Maelor, Gwawr, et al. Neli Neidr. 2005. (WEL., Illus.). 12p. pap. (978-1-85644-839-0(8)) CAA.

Marchetti, Dave. Nestle's Big Adventure. 2012. 28p. pap. 21.99 (978-1-4691-4672-0(X)) Xlibris Corp.

Marino, Nan. Neil Armstrong Is My Uncle & Other Lies Muscle Man McGinty Told Me. 2009. (ENG.). 160p. (J). (gr. 3-7). 16.95 (978-1-59643-499-8(6), 9781596434998) Roaring Brook Pr.

Marsh, Carole. The Mystery at Rattlesnake Ridge. 2014. (Wildlife Mysteries Ser.). (ENG., Illus.). 158p. (J). (gr. 2-9). pap. 7.99 (978-0-635-11188-3(8), Marsh, Carole Bks.) Gallopade International.

McBrayer, Cassidy. You Can, Toucan! You Can. 2008. 20p. pap. 15.95 (978-1-4327-1132-0(6)) Outskirts Pr., Inc.

McKee, David. Elmer & Snake. McKee, David, illus. 2013. (ENG., Illus.). 32p. (J). (gr. -1-3). 16.95 (978-1-4677-2033-5(X)) Lerner Publishing Group.

Meister, Cari. Clues in the Attic, 1 vol. Simard, Remy, illus. 2010. (My First Graphic Novel Ser.). (ENG.). 32p. (gr. k-2). pap. 6.25 (978-1-4342-2283-1(7), My First Graphic Novel) Stone Arch Bks.

Miller, Scott. Prairie Whispers. 2006. 99p. pap. 16.95 (978-1-4241-4790-8(5)) PublishAmerica, Inc.

Minz-Kammer, Koda. Pinpot Tiger & the Lost Monkey. 2008. 54p. pap. 20.00 (978-0-557-01646-4(0)) Lulu Pr., Inc.

Montgomery Gibson, Jane. Jake the Fake Snake. Montgomery Gibson, Jane, illus. 2005. (Illus.). (J). bds. 8.99 (978-1-4183-0026-5(8)) Christ Inspired, Inc.

Morpurgo, Michael. Snakes & Ladders. Wilson, Anne, illus. 2006. (Yellow Bananas Ser.). (ENG.). 48p. (J). (gr. -1-3). lib. bdg. *(978-0-7787-0952-7(3))* Crabtree Publishing Co.
Mullarkey, Lisa. Carly, 1 vol. Franco, Paula, illus. 2016. (Pony Girls Ser.). (ENG.). 112p. (J). (gr. 1-4). 27.07 *(978-1-62402-127-5(1))* Magic Wagon.
Murakami, Yasanuri & Kimura, ken, illus. 999 Frogs & a Little Brother. 2015. (ENG.). 40p. (J). 17.95 *(978-0-7358-4202-1(7))* North-South Bks., Inc.
Nelson, Sean. Bungles Does the Bunny Op. 2012. 36p. pap. 16.95 *(978-1-4575-1106-6(1))* Dog Ear Publishing, LLC.
Newton-Kowalsky, Jacqueline. Itsy Bitsy Stories for Itsy Bitsy Tigers. 2012. 32p. pap. *(978-1-77097-138-7(6))* FriesenPress.
Noble, Trinka Hakes. Jimmy's Boa & the Bungee Jump Slam Dunk. Kellogg, Steven, illus. 2005. 28p. (gr. -1-3). 16.00 *(978-0-7569-5765-0(6))* Perfection Learning Corp.
Noruziaan, Bahman. The Lonely Snake: Stories of Inspector Rabbit. 2013. 20p. pap. 13.77 *(978-1-4669-8678-7(6))* Trafford Publishing.
O'Brien, May L. Wunambi the Water Snake. Wyatt, Sue, illus. 2nd ed. 2005. (ENG.). 32p. (J). (gr. k-5). pap. 17.95 *(978-0-85575-500-3(8))* Aboriginal Studies Pr. AUS. Dist: Independent Pubs. Group.
Parker, Emma. Square Sidney. 2010. 16p. pap. *(978-1-877561-31-3(2))* First Edition Ltd.
Partee, Andrea. Jed, the Boy, the Snake & the Window. 2007. 160p. 30.99 *(978-1-4257-6401-2(0))*; per. 20.99 *(978-1-4257-6399-2(5))* Xlibris Corp.
Patton, Jack. The Snake Fight. 2016. (Battle Bugs Ser.: 8). (ENG.). 128p. (J). (gr. 2-5). pap. 4.99 *(978-0-545-94512-7(7)*, Scholastic Paperbacks) Scholastic, Inc.
Paul, Ann Whitford. Count on Culebra. Long, Ethan, illus. 2010. (ENG.). 40p. (J). (gr. -1-3). pap. 6.95 *(978-0-8234-2310-1(7))* Holiday Hse., Inc.
—Count on Culebra: Go from 1 to 10 in Spanish. Long, Ethan, illus. 2008. (ENG.). 40p. (J). (gr. -1-3). 16.95 *(978-0-8234-2124-4(4))* Holiday Hse., Inc.
Perry, Marie/Fritz. Cecil's New Year's Eve Tail. Perry, Marie/Fritz, illus. 2007. (Illus.). 32p. (J). lib. bdg. *(978-0-9755675-2-4(7))* Buttonweed Pr., L.L.C.
Provencher, Rose-Marie. Slithery Jake. Carter, Abby, illus. 2004. (ENG.). 32p. (J). 15.99 *(978-0-06-623820-3(X))* HarperCollins Pubs.
Rhiger, Tenna. The Story about How the Spotted Wobblepig Got Its Spots. 2012. 40p. pap. *(978-1-84903-152-3(5))* Schiel & Denver Publishing Ltd.
Ricchi, Brenda. The Grandchildren's Bible Journey-the Big Fall. 2010. 32p. pap. 15.51 *(978-0-557-38645-1(4))* Lulu Pr., Inc.
Riordan, Rick. The Kane Chronicles Box Set. Rocco, John, illus. 2013. (Kane Chronicles Ser.). (ENG.). 1472p. (J). (gr. 3-7). pap. 26.99 *(978-1-4231-9962-5(6))* Hyperion Bks. for Children.
Ripes, Laura. The Spaghetti-Slurping Sewer Serpent, 0 vols. Zenz, Aaron, illus. 2012. (ENG.). 32p. (J). (gr. k-3). 16.99 *(978-0-7614-6101-2(9)*, 9780761461012, Amazon Children's Publishing) Amazon Publishing.
Rogers, Kelly. Buyer Beware, 1 vol. Peterschmidt, Betsy, illus. 2016. (ENG.). 48p. (J). lib. bdg. 28.50 *(978-1-62402-167-1(0))* Magic Wagon.
Rose, Chloe Gayle & Rose, Tammy Marie. The Snake That Eats Cake. 2012. 28p. pap. 24.95 *(978-1-4626-9882-0(4))* America Star Bks.
Sande, Hans. Snake in the Grass. Vetleseter, Tonje, tr. from NOR. Moursund, Gry, illus. 2008. 40p. (J). (gr. -1-1). 16.95 *(978-0-9815761-0-7(9))* Mackenzie Smiles, LLC.
Sargent, Dave & Sargent, Pat. Young Redi: Friendship!, Vol. 3. Woodward, Elaine, illus. 2003. (Young Animal Pride Ser.: 3). 24p. (J). pap. 10.95 *(978-1-56763-868-4(6))*; lib. bdg. 20.95 *(978-1-56763-867-7(8))* Ozark Publishing.
Schleuning, Todd & Schleuning, Cheryl. The Misphits: Story of Snake. Vene, Alessandro, illus. 2013. (ENG.). (J). (gr. -1-3). 15.95 *(978-1-62086-302-2(2))* Mascot Bks., Inc.
Scholastic, Inc. Staff & West, Tracey. Snake Attack! 2012. (LEGO Ninjago Chapter Bks.: 5). lib. bdg. 14.75 *(978-0-606-26770-0(0)*, Turtleback) Turtleback Bks.
Schraff, Anne. Something Dreadful down Below, 1 vol. unabr. ed. 2010. (Q Reads Ser.). (ENG.). 32p. (YA). (gr. 9-12). pap. 6.95 *(978-1-61651-205-7(9))* Saddleback Educational Publishing, Inc.
Schwartz, Jean. The Snake with a Bellyache. Fisher, Todd, illus. 2007. 20p. per. 10.95 *(978-1-934246-41-2(7))* Peppertree Pr., The.
Seuling, Barbara. Robert & the Great Escape. Brewer, Paul, illus. 2003. (Robert Bks.). (ENG.). 120p. (J). 15.95 *(978-0-8126-2700-8(8))* Cricket Bks.
Sharp, Kevin. The Amazing Adventures of Ted Shuttle: Book One. 2012. (Illus.). 24p. pap. 19.82 *(978-1-4772-4286-5(4))* AuthorHouse.
Shepherd, Donna J. Sully's Topsy Tale. Collier, Kevin Scott, illus. 2010. 20p. pap. 10.95 *(978-1-61633-047-7(3))* Guardian Angel Publishing, Inc.
Shi, Charleston. The Quest of the Phoenix: Book 3, Rage of the Serpents. 2010. 188p. pap. 14.95 *(978-1-60844-403-8(1))* Dog Ear Publishing, LLC.
Siegel, Randy. My Snake Blake. Bloch, Serge, illus. 2012. (ENG.). 32p. (J). (gr. -1-1). 16.99 *(978-1-59643-584-1(4)*, 9781596435841) Roaring Brook Pr.
Slider-Baker, Belinda. Lost Stripes, Please Return. 2008. 32p. pap. 24.95 *(978-1-60813-075-7(4))* America Star Bks.
Smiley, Mark. A Journey Far Away. 2006. 164p. pap. 13.95 *(978-1-59526-494-7(9))* Aeon Publishing Inc.
Snake's Reward: Individual Title Six-Packs. (Story Steps Ser.). (gr. k-2). 32.00 *(978-0-7635-9821-1(6))* Rigby Education.
Snicket, Lemony, pseud. Le Laboratoire aux Serpents. 24.95 *(978-2-09-211034-8(9))* Nathan, Fernand FRA. Dist: Distribooks, Inc.
Snyder, Susan E. Shivers & Shakes. 2006. (Illus.). 31p. (J). (gr. k-2). 9.95 *(978-0-9767163-5-8(6))* Kotzig Publishing, Inc.
Sparkes, Ali. Anaconda Adventure. Collins, Ross, illus. 2014. (S. W. I. T. C. H. Ser.: 13). (ENG.). 104p. (J). (gr. 2-5). lib. bdg. 27.93 *(978-1-4677-2116-5(6)*, Darby Creek) Lerner Publishing Group.
Spohn, Kate. Turtle & Snake's Day at the Beach. Spohn, Kate, illus. 2004. (Penguin Young Readers, Level 2 Ser.). (ENG., Illus.). 32p. (J). (gr. 1-2). mass mkt. 3.99 *(978-0-14-240157-6(9)*, Penguin Young Readers) Penguin Young Readers Group.
—Turtle & Snake's Day at the Beach. Spohn, Kate, illus. 2004. (Puffin Easy-to-Read Ser.). (Illus.). 32p. (gr. k-3). 14.00 *(978-0-7569-2826-1(5))* Perfection Learning Corp.
—Turtle & Snake's Spooky Halloween. Spohn, Kate, illus. 2003. (Easy-to-Read Ser.). (Illus.). 32p. (J). (gr. -1-3). 11.65 *(978-0-7569-1949-8(5))* Perfection Learning Corp.
Standish, Joyce, ed. The Adventures of Ryan Lincoln. Cooper, Nicole, illus. 2012. 46p. (J). pap. 10.00 *(978-0-9716244-5-0(3))* TLS Publishing.
Stengel, Joyce A. St. Patrick & the Three Brave Mice, 1 vol. Leonhard, Herb, illus. 2009. (ENG.). 32p. (J). (gr. k-3). 16.99 *(978-1-58980-663-4(8))* Pelican Publishing Co., Inc.
Stepp, Shirley. Santa Lost His Cell Phone. 2012. 24p. 24.95 *(978-1-4626-5479-6(7))* America Star Bks.
Stycznski, Gary. The Animals of Greenback Valley: The Magic Card. 2009. 32p. pap. 24.95 *(978-1-59858-930-6(X))* Dog Ear Publishing, LLC.
Style Guide, Style, illus. The Furry & the Furious. 2014. (Kung Fu Panda TV Ser.). (ENG.). 96p. (J). (gr. 2-5). pap. 4.99 *(978-1-4814-1703-7(7)*, Simon Spotlight) Simon Spotlight.
Suen, Anastasia. A Great Idea? An Up2U Character Education Adventure, 1 vol. Dippold, Jane, illus. 2015. (ENG.). 80p. (J). *(978-1-62402-093-3(3))* Magic Wagon.
Taylor, Melissa Utz. Sneaky Snake. 2011. 24p. (gr. 1-2). pap. 14.99 *(978-1-4567-5518-8(8))* AuthorHouse.
Top That, ed. Revolving Nursery Rhymes. 2008. 12p. *(978-1-84666-573-8(6)*, Tide Mill Pr.) Top That! Publishing PLC.
—Sammy the Snake. 2008. (Story Book Ser.). 18p. (J). (gr. -1). *(978-1-84666-541-7(8)*, Tide Mill Pr.) Top That! Publishing PLC.
Trevethan, Glenn A. The Adventures of Sammi Snake: Sammi's Coat. 2012. 24p. pap. 13.97 *(978-1-61897-926-1(4)*, Strategic Bk. Publishing) Strategic Book Publishing & Rights Agency (SBPRA).
Turner, Nicci. Milky's Story, 1 vol. 2010. 18p. pap. 24.95 *(978-1-4489-6808-4(9))* PublishAmerica, Inc.
Twinem, Neecy. Baby Snake's Shapes. 2004. (New Board Book Ser.).Tr. of Las formas de Bebe Serpiente. (ENG., Illus.). 12p. (J). (gr. -1-k). 5.95 *(978-0-87358-850-8(9))*; 6.95 *(978-0-87358-866-9(5))* Cooper Square Publishing Llc.
Velle, Tori. Jake the Snake. 2009. 40p. pap. 16.99 *(978-1-4490-4431-2(X))* AuthorHouse.
Virginia H. Lasher. The Secret of Crooked Creek. 2006. 58p. 20.00 *(978-1-59926-625-1(3))*; pap. 10.00 *(978-1-4134-9728-1(4))* Xlibris Corp.
Walker, Cheryl. Black Snake, King Snake. 2003. 7p. (J). pap. 1.50 *(978-0-9726326-2-1(X))* TechArts International LLC.
Walsh, Vivian. June & August. McCauley, Adam, illus. 2009. (ENG.). 32p. (J). (gr. k-2). 16.95 *(978-0-8109-8410-3(5)*, Abrams Bks. for Young Readers) Abrams, Inc.
Warner, Michael N. Tales to Make You Scream for Your Momma. Warner, Robert, illus. 2015. 208p. (J). pap. 11.95 *(978-0-9963756-1-0(9))* All About Kids Publishing.
Weigl Publishers, creator. The Snake & His Tail: How Can You Support Your Team? 2013. (AV2 Animated Storytime Ser.: Vol. 19). (ENG., Illus.). 32p. (J). (gr. -1-3). lib. bdg. 29.99 *(978-1-62127-923-5(5)*, AV2 by Weigl) Weigl Pubs., Inc.
Welsh, Mary Reddick. Sammy, the Little Green Snake Who Wanted to Fly. Welsh, Mary Reddick, illus. 2011. (Illus.). 26p. pap. 11.95 *(978-1-936411-09-2(1))* YBK Pubs., Inc.
West, Tracey. Rise of the Snakes. 2012. (Lego Ninjago Ser.). (ENG.). 32p. (J). (gr. -1-3). pap. 3.99 *(978-0-545-43592-5(7))* Scholastic, Inc.
—Rise of the Snakes. 2012. (Ninjago Readers Ser.: 4). lib. bdg. 13.55 *(978-0-606-26556-0(2)*, Turtleback) Turtleback Bks.
—Snake Attack!, Bk. 5. 2012. (Lego Ninjago Ser.). (ENG.). 80p. (J). (gr. 2-5). pap. 4.99 *(978-0-545-46518-2(4))* Scholastic, Inc.
Weston, Anne. My Brother Needs a Boa, 1 vol. Nathan, Cheryl, illus. 2005. (ENG.). 32p. (J). (gr. -1-3). 15.95 *(978-1-932065-96-1(2))* Star Bright Bks., Inc.
Weston Woods Staff, creator. Crictor. 2011. 38.75 *(978-0-545-23361-3(5))*; 18.95 *(978-0-545-23360-6(7))* Weston Woods Studios, Inc.
—Rikki-Tikki-Tavi. 2011. 18.95 *(978-0-439-72977-2(7))*; 38.75 *(978-0-439-72979-6(3))* Weston Woods Studios, Inc.
Wheeler, J. D. Gummery & Lubber. 2008. 56p. pap. 16.95 *(978-1-60563-432-6(8))* America Star Bks.
Whitmore, Gary. Prince Luna & the Space Dreamers. 2011. (ENG.). 204p. pap. 8.50 *(978-1-4565-8438-2(3))* CreateSpace Independent Publishing Platform.
Wildsmith, Brian. Jungle Party, 1 vol. Wildsmith, Brian, illus. 2006. (ENG., Illus.). 32p. (J). pap. 6.95 *(978-1-59572-053-5(7))* Star Bright Bks., Inc.
—Jungle Party, 1 vol. 2006. (ENG., Illus.). 32p. (J). (gr. -1-3). 17.95 *(978-1-59572-052-8(9))* Star Bright Bks., Inc.
Willems, Mo. Can I Play Too? 2012. (Elephant & Piggie Bks.). (CHI & JPN.). (J). (gr. -1-3). pap. ***(978-986-189-329-7(6))*** Grimm Cultural Ent., Co., Ltd.
—Can I Play Too? Willems, Mo, illus. 2010. (Elephant & Piggie Book Ser.). (ENG., Illus.). 64p. (J). (gr. -1-k). 9.99 *(978-1-4231-1991-3(6))* Hyperion Pr.
Williamson, Sarah, illus. Where Are You? 2017. (ENG.). 32p. (J). (— 1). 16.99 *(978-1-5247-0063-8(0)*, Knopf Bks. for Young Readers) Random Hse. Children's Bks.
Willis, Jeanne. Be Gentle, Python! Birchall, Mark, illus. 2005. (Picture Bks.). 28p. (J). (gr. k-2). 7.95 *(978-1-57505-508-4(2))* Lerner Publishing Group.
—Boa's Bad Birthday. Ross, Tony, illus. 2014. (ENG.). 32p. (J). (gr. -1-3). 16.95 *(978-1-4677-3450-9(0))* Lerner Publishing Group.
Wilson-Timmons, Karen & Dubois, Marie Thérèse. Agha the Eight-Mile Monster. rev. ed. 2012. (ENG., Illus.). 32p. (J). (gr. -1). 16.99 *(978-1-60887-124-7(X))* Mandala Publishing.
Winkler, Henry & Oliver, Lin. Fake Snakes & Weird Wizards. Garrett, Scott, illus. 2015. (Here's Hank Ser.: No. 4). (ENG.). 128p. (J). (gr. 1-3). 5.99 *(978-0-448-48252-1(5)*, Grosset & Dunlap) Penguin Young Readers Group.
Wright, Johanna. The Orchestra Pit. Wright, Johanna, illus. 2014. (ENG., Illus.). 32p. (J). (gr. -1-1). 16.99 *(978-1-59643-769-2(3)*, 9781596437692) Roaring Brook Pr.
Yates, Gene. What Can Simon Be? 2005. (Illus.). (J). *(978-1-58865-284-3(X))* Kidsbooks, LLC.
Yates, Gene & Frank, Thomas. What Can Simon Be? Yates, Gene, illus. 2006. (Illus.). (J). *(978-1-58865-366-6(8))* Kidsbooks, LLC.
Yoon, Salina. Opposnakes: A Lift-the-Flap Book about Opposites. Yoon, Salina, illus. 2009. (ENG., Illus.). 16p. (J). (gr. -1-1). 12.99 *(978-1-4169-7875-6(5)*, Little Simon) Little Simon.

SNOOPY (FICTITIOUS CHARACTER)—FICTION

Abramson, Andra. Snoopy's Happy Day: A Peanuts Puppet Book. Whitlock, Matt, illus. 2015. (ENG.). 16p. (J). (gr. -1). bds. 9.99 *(978-1-60433-545-3(9)*, Applesauce Pr.) Cider Mill Pr. Bk. Pubs., LLC.
Lundell, Margo. Where's Woodstock? (Peanuts) Schulz, Charles & Ellis, Kim, illus. 2015. (Little Golden Book Ser.). (ENG.). 24p. (J). (gr. -1-1). 4.99 *(978-1-101-93517-0(0)*, Golden Bks.) Random Hse. Children's Bks.
Publications International Ltd. Staff, ed. Look & Find: Snoopy. 2013. 24p. (J). (gr. 1-3). 7.99 *(978-1-4127-1722-9(1)*, 6273d751-5dbd-41ad-a19f-1ef74baf570f) Phoenix International Publications, Inc.
Schulz, Charles. Alles Peanuts. Herbst, Gabriele & Rolle, Ekkehard, trs. from ENG. (Snoopy & die Peanuts Ser.: Vol. 26). (GER., Illus.). 96p. (J). pap. *(978-3-8105-1871-2(9))* Kruger, Wolfgang Verlag, GmbH DEU. Dist: International Bk. Import Service, Inc.
—Allzeit Bereit. Herbst, Gabriele & Rolle, Ekkehard, trs. from ENG. (Snoopy & die Peanuts Ser.: Vol. 35). (GER., Illus.). 96p. (J). pap. *(978-3-8105-1891-0(3))* Kruger, Wolfgang Verlag, GmbH DEU. Dist: International Bk. Import Service, Inc.
— An der Langen Leine. Herbst, Gabriele & Rolle, Ekkehard, trs. from ENG. (Snoopy & die Peanuts Ser.: Vol. 30). (GER., Illus.). 96p. (J). pap. *(978-3-8105-1880-4(8))* Kruger, Wolfgang Verlag, GmbH DEU. Dist: International Bk. Import Service, Inc.
—Auf den Hund Gekommen. Herbst, Gabriele & Rolle, Ekkehard, trs. from ENG. (Snoopy & die Peanuts Ser.: Vol. 34). (GER., Illus.). 96p. (J). pap. *(978-3-8105-1888-0(3))* Kruger, Wolfgang Verlag, GmbH DEU. Dist: International Bk. Import Service, Inc.
—A Charlie Brown Christmas, 1 vol. 2013. (Peanuts Picture Bks.). (ENG., Illus.). 48p. (J). (gr. -1-4). lib. bdg. 24.21 *(978-1-61479-029-7(9))* ABDO Publishing Co.
—A Charlie Brown Christmas. Running Press Staff, ed. 2010. (ENG., Illus.). 10p. (J). (gr. -1-3). 22.95 *(978-0-7624-4004-7(X))* Running Pr. Bk. Pubs.
—Cowabunga! 2013. (Peanuts Kids Ser.: 1). (ENG., Illus.). 224p. (J). 9.99 *(978-1-4494-5079-3(2))* Andrews McMeel Publishing.
—Den Wind im Ruecken. Herbst, Gabriele & Rolle, Ekkehard, trs. from ENG. (Snoopy & die Peanuts Ser.: Vol. 6). (GER., Illus.). 96p. (J). pap. *(978-3-8105-1819-4(0))* Kruger, Wolfgang Verlag, GmbH DEU. Dist: International Bk. Import Service, Inc.
—Einfach Genial. Herbst, Gabriele & Rolle, Ekkehard, trs. from ENG. (Snoopy & die Peanuts Ser.: Vol. 31). (GER., Illus.). 96p. (J). pap. *(978-3-8105-1881-1(6))* Kruger, Wolfgang Verlag, GmbH DEU. Dist: International Bk. Import Service, Inc.
—Einfach Unschlagbar. Herbst, Gabriele & Rolle, Ekkehard, trs. from ENG. (Snoopy & die Peanuts Ser.: Vol. 1). (GER., Illus.). 96p. (J). pap. *(978-3-8105-1811-8(5))* Kruger, Wolfgang Verlag, GmbH DEU. Dist: International Bk. Import Service, Inc.
—Grundlos Gluecklich. Herbst, Gabriele & Rolle, Ekkehard, trs. from ENG. (Snoopy & die Peanuts Ser.: Vol. 37). (GER., Illus.). 96p. (J). pap. *(978-3-8105-1893-4(X))* Kruger, Wolfgang Verlag, GmbH DEU. Dist: International Bk. Import Service, Inc.
—Gut Aufgelegt. Herbst, Gabriele & Rolle, Ekkehard, trs. from ENG. (Snoopy & die Peanuts Ser.: Vol. 12). (GER., Illus.). 96p. (J). pap. *(978-3-8105-1828-6(X))* Kruger, Wolfgang Verlag, GmbH DEU. Dist: International Bk. Import Service, Inc.
—Herzlich Unverschaemt. Herbst, Gabriele & Rolle, Ekkehard, trs. from ENG. (Snoopy & die Peanuts Ser.: Vol. 9). (GER., Illus.). 128p. (J). pap. *(978-3-8105-1823-1(9))* Kruger, Wolfgang Verlag, GmbH DEU. Dist: International Bk. Import Service, Inc.
—Himmel & Hoelle. Herbst, Gabriele & Rolle, Ekkehard, trs. from ENG. (Snoopy & die Peanuts Ser.: Vol. 23). (GER., Illus.). 96p. (J). pap. *(978-3-8105-1867-5(0))* Kruger, Wolfgang Verlag, GmbH DEU. Dist: International Bk. Import Service, Inc.
—Hoch die Tassen. Herbst, Gabriele & Rolle, Ekkehard, trs. from ENG. (Snoopy & die Peanuts Ser.: Vol. 36). (GER., Illus.). 96p. (J). pap. *(978-3-8105-1892-7(1))* Kruger, Wolfgang Verlag, GmbH DEU. Dist: International Bk. Import Service, Inc.
—Immer Dabei. Herbst, Gabriele & Rolle, Ekkehard, trs. from ENG. (Snoopy & die Peanuts Ser.: Vol. 27). (GER., Illus.). 96p. (J). pap. *(978-3-8105-1872-9(7))* Kruger, Wolfgang Verlag, GmbH DEU. Dist: International Bk. Import Service, Inc.
—Kaum zu Bremsen. Rolle, Ekkehard, tr. from ENG. (Snoopy & die Peanuts Ser.: Vol. 11). (GER., Illus.). 128p. (J). pap. *(978-3-8105-1827-9(1))* Kruger, Wolfgang Verlag, GmbH DEU. Dist: International Bk. Import Service, Inc.
—The Many Faces of Snoopy. 2006. (ENG., Illus.). 352p. per. 22.00 *(978-0-345-47983-9(1)*, Ballantine Bks.) Random House Publishing Group.
—Peanuts Movie Novelization. 2015. (Peanuts Movie Ser.). (ENG., Illus.). 144p. (J). (gr. 3-7). 17.99 *(978-1-4814-6044-6(7))*; pap. 6.99 *(978-1-4814-4136-0(1))* Simon Spotlight. (Simon Spotlight).
—Pfoten Hoch! Herbst, Gabriele & Rolle, Ekkehard, trs. from ENG. (Snoopy & die Peanuts Ser.: Vol. 33). (GER., Illus.). 96p. (J). pap. *(978-3-8105-1887-3(5))* Kruger, Wolfgang Verlag, GmbH DEU. Dist: International Bk. Import Service, Inc.
—Schwer in Fahrt. Herbst, Gabriele & Rolle, Ekkehard, trs. from ENG. (Snoopy & die Peanuts Ser.: Vol. 7). (GER., Illus.). 128p. (J). pap. *(978-3-8105-1820-0(4))* Kruger, Wolfgang Verlag, GmbH DEU. Dist: International Bk. Import Service, Inc.
—Snoopy's Thanksgiving. 2014. (Peanuts Seasonal Ser.: 0). (ENG., Illus.). 64p. 9.99 *(978-1-60699-778-9(5)*, 699778) Fantagraphics Bks.
—The Ultimate Box, Set. 2007. (Peanuts(r) Ser.). (ENG., Illus.). 648p. 39.95 *(978-1-933662-71-8(9))* Cider Mill Pr. Bk. Pubs., LLC.
—Voll auf die Schnauze. Herbst, Gabriele & Rolle, Ekkehard, trs. from ENG. (Snoopy & die Peanuts Ser.: Vol. 32). (GER., Illus.). 96p. (J). pap. *(978-3-8105-1886-6(7))* Kruger, Wolfgang Verlag, GmbH DEU. Dist: International Bk. Import Service, Inc.
—Voll im Griff. Herbst, Gabriele & Rolle, Ekkehard, trs. from ENG. (Snoopy & die Peanuts Ser.: Vol. 13). (GER., Illus.). 128p. (J). pap. *(978-3-8105-1829-3(8))* Kruger, Wolfgang Verlag, GmbH DEU. Dist: International Bk. Import Service, Inc.
—Where Is Woodstock?, 1 vol. 2013. (Peanuts Picture Bks.). (ENG.). 24p. (J). (gr. -1-4). lib. bdg. 24.21 *(978-1-61479-033-4(7))* ABDO Publishing Co.
Schulz, Charles & Houghton, Shane. Peanuts, Vol. 2. Braddock, Paige, illus. 2013. (Peanuts Ser.). (ENG.). 112p. (J). (gr. 1). pap. 13.99 *(978-1-60886-299-3(2))* Boom! Studios.
Schulz, Charles & Pastis, Stephan. Happiness Is a Warm Blanket, Charlie Brown! Scott, Bob, illus. 2011. (Peanuts Ser.). (ENG.). 96p. (gr. 3). pap. 9.99 *(978-1-60886-681-6(5))*; (J). 19.99 *(978-1-60886-682-3(3))* Boom! Studios.
Schulz, Charles & Schulz, Charles M. It's the Great Pumpkin, Charlie Brown: with Sound & Music. 2012. (ENG., Illus.). 48p. (J). (gr. -1-3). 19.95 *(978-0-7624-4606-3(4)*, Running Pr. Kids) Running Pr. Bk. Pubs.
Schulz, Charles M. Be Kind: Peanuts Wisdom to Carry You Through. 2013. (ENG., Illus.). 72p. (J). (gr. -1-17). 7.95 *(978-0-7624-4862-3(8)*, Running Pr. Kids) Running Pr. Bk. Pubs.
—Be Thankful: Peanuts Wisdom to Carry You Through. 2013. (ENG., Illus.). 72p. (J). (gr. -1-17). 7.95 *(978-0-7624-5045-9(2)*, Running Pr. Kids) Running Pr. Bk. Pubs.
—It's the Easter Beagle, Charlie Brown, 1 vol. 2013. (Peanuts Picture Bks.). (ENG.). 48p. (J). (gr. -1-4). lib. bdg. 24.21 *(978-1-61479-031-0(0))* ABDO Publishing Co.
—It's the Easter Beagle, Charlie Brown. Scott, Vicki, illus. 2016. (Peanuts Ser.). (ENG.). 32p. (J). (gr. -1). 7.99 *(978-1-4814-6159-7(1)*, Simon Spotlight) Simon Spotlight.
—Peanuts: Be Friends. 2013. (ENG., Illus.). 72p. (J). (gr. -1-17). 7.95 *(978-0-7624-5044-2(4)*, Running Pr. Kids) Running Pr. Bk. Pubs.
Schulz, Charles M., creator. Be Yourself! 2013. (ENG., Illus.). 40p. (J). (gr. -1-17). 12.95 *(978-0-7624-4718-3(4)*, Running Pr. Kids) Running Pr. Bk. Pubs.
—Peanuts: Be Brave: Peanuts Wisdom to Carry You Through. 2013. (ENG., Illus.). 72p. (J). (gr. -1-17). 7.95 *(978-0-7624-4861-6(X)*, Running Pr. Kids) Running Pr. Bk. Pubs.
Verr, Harry Coe. Let's Fly a Kite, Charlie Brown! (Peanuts) Ellis, Kim & Schulz, Charles, illus. 2015. (Little Golden Book Ser.). (ENG.). 24p. (J). (gr. -1-1). 4.99 *(978-1-101-93519-4(7)*, Golden Bks.) Random Hse. Children's Bks.

SNORKELING

see Skin Diving

SNOW

Appleby, Alex. It's Snowing! 2013. (What's the Weather? Ser.). 24p. (J). (gr. k-2). 22.60 *(978-1-4339-9400-5(3))*; pap. 48.90 *(978-1-4339-9402-9(X))*; pap. 8.15 *(978-1-4339-9401-2(1))* Stevens, Gareth Publishing LLLP.
—It's Snowing! / Est Nevando! 2013. (What's the Weather? / Qu Tiempo Hace? Ser.). (SPA & ENG., Illus.). 24p. (J). (gr. k-2). 22.60 *(978-1-4339-9458-6(5))* Stevens, Gareth Publishing LLLP.
Bauer, Marion Dane. Snow. Wallace, John, illus. 2003. (Weather Ready-To-Reads Ser.). (ENG.). 32p. (J). (gr. -1-1). pap. 3.99 *(978-0-689-85437-8(4)*, Simon Spotlight) Simon Spotlight.
Berger, Melvin & Berger, Gilda. Snowflakes Are Falling. 2010. (Illus.). 16p. (J). *(978-0-545-16082-7(0))* Scholastic, Inc.
Bix, Jasper. Building a Snowman. 2016. (Winter Fun Ser.). (ENG., Illus.). 24p. (J). (gr. k-k). pap. 8.15 *(978-1-4824-3747-8(3))* Stevens, Gareth Publishing LLLP.
Bobek, Joanne R. A Day at Pond Snow. 2011. 16p. 8.47 *(978-1-4567-1706-3(5))* AuthorHouse.
Bodden, Valerie. Our Wonderful Weather: Snow. 2014. (Our Wonderful Weather Ser.). (ENG., Illus.). 24p. (J). (gr. 4-7). pap. 9.99 *(978-0-89812-921-2(4)*, Creative Paperbacks) Creative Co., The.
—Snow. 2012. (J). 25.65 *(978-1-60818-148-3(0)*, Creative Education) Creative Co., The.
Boyett, Suzi. Let's Read about Snow. 2007. (Let's Read about Weather Ser.). (Illus.). 12p. (gr. -1-2). lib. bdg. 15.00 *(978-0-8368-7806-6(X)*, Weekly Reader Leveled Readers) Stevens, Gareth Publishing LLLP.
—Nieva. 2007. (Que Tiempo Hace? (Let's Read about Weather) Ser.). (SPA., Illus.). 12p. (J). (gr. -1-2). pap. 4.10 *(978-0-8368-8119-6(2))*; lib. bdg. 15.00 *(978-0-8368-8114-1(1))* Stevens, Gareth Publishing LLLP. (Weekly Reader Leveled Readers).
Bundey, Nikki. Snow & People. 2005. (Science of Weather Ser.). (Illus.). 32p. (gr. 4-6). lib. bdg. 21.27 *(978-1-57505-496-4(5))* Lerner Publishing Group.
—Snow & the Earth. 2005. (Science of Weather Ser.). (Illus.). 32p. (gr. 4-6). lib. bdg. 21.27 *(978-1-57505-471-1(X))* Lerner Publishing Group.
Butterworth, Nick. Tiger in the Snow! 2008. (ENG., Illus.). 32p. (J). (gr. k — 1). pap. 7.95 *(978-0-00-711969-1(0))* HarperCollins Pubs. Ltd. GBR. Dist: Independent Pubs. Group.
Cassino, Mark, photos by. The Story of Snow: The Science of Winter's Wonder. 2017. (ENG., Illus.). 36p. (J). (gr. k-3). pap. 7.99 ***(978-1-4521-6436-6(3))*** Chronicle Bks. LLC.
Cox Cannons, Helen. Snow, 1 vol. 2014. (Weather Wise Ser.). (ENG., Illus.). 24p. (gr. -1-1). pap. 5.99 *(978-1-4846-0556-1(X)*, Acorn) Heinemann-Raintree.
D'Aubuisson, Elisabeth. Snowy Days. 2007. (What's the Weather? Ser.). (Illus.). 24p. (J). (gr. 3-7). lib. bdg. 22.60 *(978-1-4042-3684-4(8)*, PowerKids Pr.) Rosen Publishing Group, Inc., The.

S

d'Aubuisson, Elisabeth. Snowy Days. 2009. (What's the Weather? Ser.). 24p. (gr. 2-3). 42.50 *(978-1-60854-776-0(0)*, PowerKids Pr.) Rosen Publishing Group, Inc., The.

deMarin, Layne. Too Much Snow! 2011. (Wonder Readers Fluent Level Ser.). (ENG.). (gr. -1-2). 16p. pap. 35.94 *(978-1-4296-8192-6(6))*; 32p. pap. 5.99 *(978-1-4296-7944-2(1))* Capstone Press of Coughlan Cos. (Wonder Readers).

—Too Much Snow, 1 vol. 2011. (Wonder Readers: Science Ser.). (ENG.). 20p. (gr. -1-2). lib. bdg. 22.65 *(978-1-4296-8637-2(5)*, Wonder Readers) Capstone Press of Coughlan Cos.

Doubleday Entertainment USA - Weather Watch: Snow. 2006. (J). per. 7.95 *(978-1-59566-232-3(4))* QEB Publishing Inc.

Doudna, Kelly. It Is Snowing, 1 vol. 2003. (Weather Ser.). (ENG., Illus.). 24p. (J). (gr. k-3). lib. bdg. 24.21 *(978-1-57765-775-0(6)*, SandCastle) ABDO Publishing Co.

Drake, Jane & Love, Ann. Snow Amazing: Cool Facts & Warm Tales. Thurman, Mark, illus. 2004. (ENG.). 80p. (J). (gr. 4-7). 19.95 *(978-0-88776-670-1(6)*, Tundra Bks.) Tundra Bks. CAN. Dist: Penguin Random Hse. LLC.

Dymock, Melissa. Sliding in the Snow: Winter Activities for Kids, 1 vol. Lee, Frances Cook, illus. 2015. (ENG.). 64p. (J). pap. 9.99 *(978-1-4236-3893-3(X))* Gibbs Smith, Publisher.

Edison, Erin. Snow, 1 vol. 2011. (Weather Basics Ser.). (ENG.). 24p. (gr. k-1). pap. 7.29 *(978-1-4296-7080-7(0))*; pap. 41.70 *(978-1-4296-7086-9(X))*; lib. bdg. 26.65 *(978-1-4296-6059-4(7))* Capstone Press of Coughlan Cos. (Pebble Plus).

Felix, Rebecca. How's the Weather in Winter? 2014. (21st Century Basic Skills Library: Let's Look at Winter Ser.). (ENG.). 24p. (J). (gr. k-3). 22.79 *(978-1-63137-605-4(5)*, 205203) Cherry Lake Publishing.

—We See Snowflakes in Winter. 2014. (21st Century Basic Skills Library: Let's Look at Winter Ser.). (ENG., Illus.). 24p. (J). (gr. k-3). 22.79 *(978-1-63137-612-2(8)*, 205231) Cherry Lake Publishing.

Filella, Nacho, et al. La Nieve. 2005. (El Juego de Leer Ser.). (SPA.). 6p. 9.95 *(978-84-272-6681-0(2))* Molino, Editorial ESP. Dist: Distribooks, Inc.

The First Snowfall. 2014. (ENG., Illus.). 24p. (J). (gr. -1-3). 14.99 *(978-1-4814-1135-6(7)*, Aladdin) Simon & Schuster Children's Publishing.

Gamble, Adam & Jasper, Mark. Good Night Snow. 2016. (Good Night Our World Ser.). (ENG., Illus.). 20p. (J). (— 1). bds. 9.95 *(978-1-60219-412-0(2))* Good Night Bks.

Ganeri, Anita. Snow. 2004. (Weather Around You Ser.). (Illus.). 24p. (gr. 1-4). lib. bdg. 22.00 *(978-0-8368-4300-2(2)*, Weekly Reader Leveled Readers) Stevens, Gareth Publishing LLLP.

Gibbons, Gail. It's Snowing! Gibbons, Gail, illus. 2012. (ENG., Illus.). 32p. (J). (gr. -1-2). pap. 7.99 *(978-0-8234-2545-7(2))* Holiday Hse., Inc.

Greene, Carol. Snow Joe. Sharp, Paul, illus. 2011. (Rookie Ready to Learn Ser.). 40p. (J). (ENG.). pap. 5.95 *(978-0-531-26804-9(7))*; (gr. -1-k). lib. bdg. 23.00 *(978-0-531-25644-2(8))* Scholastic Library Publishing. (Children's Pr.).

Hansen, Grace. La Nieve. 2016. (Clima Ser.). (SPA.). 24p. (J). (gr. 1-6). pap. 7.95 *(978-1-4966-0694-5(9))* Capstone Classroom.

—Snow, 1 vol. 2016. (ENG., Illus.). 24p. (J). *(978-1-62970-933-8(6))* ABDO Publishing Co.

Hardyman, Robyn. Snow & Blizzards. 2010. (Weatherwise Ser.). 32p. (ENG.). (J). pap. 10.60 *(978-1-61532-276-3(0)*, PowerKids Pr.); (Illus.). (YA). (gr. 3-6). lib. bdg. 26.50 *(978-1-61532-264-0(7))* Rosen Publishing Group, Inc., The.

Head, Honor. Snow. Taylor, Lauren, ed. 2012. (Whatever the Weather Ser.). (ENG.). 24p. (J). (gr. -1-k). 15.99 *(978-1-60992-308-2(1))* QEB Publishing Inc.

Helget, Nicole. Snow. 2006. (My First Look at Weather Ser.). (Illus.). 24p. (J). (gr. -1-3). lib. bdg. 15.95 *(978-1-58341-451-4(7)*, Creative Education) Creative Co., The.

Herriges, Ann. Snow. 2011. (Blastoff! Readers Ser.). 24p. (J). pap. 5.95 *(978-0-531-27623-5(6)*, Children's Pr.) Scholastic Library Publishing.

Higgins, Nadia. It's Snowing!, 1 vol. Ward, Damian, illus. 2010. (Weather Watchers Ser.). (ENG.). 32p. (J). (gr. k-3). 28.50 *(978-1-60270-734-4(0))* Magic Wagon.

Kaner, Etta. Who Likes the Snow? Lafrance, Marie, illus. 2006. (Exploring the Elements Ser.). (ENG.). 32p. (J). (gr. -1-2). 14.95 *(978-1-55337-842-6(3))* Kids Can Pr., Ltd. CAN. Dist: Hachette Bk. Group.

Lay, Kathryn. Sno-Vember!, 1 vol., Vol. 3. Wolff, Jason, illus. 2011. (Wendy's Weather Warriors Ser.). (ENG.). 80p. (gr. 2-5). 27.07 *(978-1-60270-756-6(1)*, Calico Chapter Bks) Magic Wagon.

Libbrecht, Kenneth. The Secret Life of a Snowflake: An up-Close Look at the Art & Science of Snowflakes. Sorenson, Vanessa, illus. 2010. (ENG.). 48p. (J). (gr. 1-17). 17.00 *(978-0-7603-3676-2(8)*, 0760336768, Voyageur Pr) Quarto Publishing Group USA.

Lindeen, Mary. Winter! 2015. (BeginningtoRead Ser.). (ENG., Illus.). 32p. (J). (gr. k-2). lib. bdg. 22.60 *(978-1-59953-682-8(X))* Norwood Hse. Pr.

Manolis, Kay. Blizzards. 2008. (Extreme Weather Ser.). (ENG., Illus.). 24p. (J). (gr. 2-5). lib. bdg. 25.95 *(978-1-60014-183-6(8))* Bellwether Media.

Martin, Jacqueline Briggs. Snowflake Bentley. 2004. (Illus.). (J). (gr. -1-3). spiral bd. *(978-0-616-01714-2(6))* Canadian National Institute for the Blind/Institut National Canadien pour les Aveugles.

Masterson, Josephine. We Can Build a Snowman. 2015. (Rosen REAL Readers: STEM & STEAM Collection). (ENG.). 8p. pap. 5.46 *(978-1-4994-9736-6(9)*, Rosen Classroom) Rosen Publishing Group, Inc., The.

McAuliffe, Bill. Snow. 2017. (J). ***(978-1-60818-826-0(4)***, Creative Education) 2010. 48p. (YA). (gr. 4-7). lib. bdg. 23.95 *(978-1-58341-929-8(2))* Creative Co., The.

McNeil, Niki, et al. HOCPP 1136 Let it Snow. 2006. spiral bd. 14.00 *(978-1-60308-136-8(4))* In the Hands of a Child.

Nelson, John. Polar Ice Caps in Danger: Expedition to Antarctica. 2008. (Jr. Graphic Environmental Dangers Ser.). (ENG.). 24p. (J). 47.90 *(978-1-61532-097-4(0))*; (Illus.). (gr. 3-6). lib. bdg. 25.25 *(978-1-4042-4227-2(9))* Rosen Publishing Group, Inc., The. (PowerKids Pr.).

Nelson, John & Obregón, José María. Casquetes Polares en Riesgo: Expedición a la Antártida. 2009. (Historietas Juveniles: Peligros Del Medioambiente (Jr. Graphic Environmental Dangers) Ser.). (SPA., Illus.). 24p. (gr. 3-6). (YA). lib. bdg. 25.25 *(978-1-4358-8474-8(4))*; pap. 10.60 *(978-1-4358-8475-5(2))* Rosen Publishing Group, Inc., The.

Nelson, Robin. Un Dia Nevado. Translations.com Staff, tr. from ENG. 2006. (Mi Primer Paso Al Mundo Real - el Estado Del Tiempo (First Step Nonfiction - Weather) Ser.). (SPA., Illus.). 24p. (gr. k-2). lib. bdg. 23.93 *(978-0-8225-6212-2(X)*, Ediciones Lerner) Lerner Publishing Group.

—Un Día nevado (A Snowy Day) 2006. (Mi Primer Paso al Mundo Real Ser.). (Illus.). 23p. (J). (gr. -1-3). per. 5.95 *(978-0-8225-6551-2(X)*, Ediciones Lerner) Lerner Publishing Group.

—Snowy. (First Step Nonfiction - Kinds of Weather Ser.). (ENG., 8p. (gr. -1-1). 2015. Illus.). 11.99 *(978-1-5124-1038-9(1))* 2005. pap. 4.95 *(978-0-8225-5366-3(X)*, Lerner Pubns.) Lerner Publishing Group.

Orr, Tamra B. It Snows. 2015. (Tell Me Why Library). (ENG.). 24p. (J). (gr. 2-5). 27.07 *(978-1-63188-998-1(2)*, 205904) Cherry Lake Publishing.

Peters, Elisa. It's Snow! 2009. (Everyday Wonders Ser.). 24p. (gr. 1-1). 42.50 *(978-1-61512-326-1(1)*, PowerKids Pr.); (Illus.). (J). lib. bdg. 22.60 *(978-1-4042-4462-7(X))* Rosen Publishing Group, Inc., The.

—It's Snow! La Nieve! 2009. (Everyday Wonders / Maravillas de Todos Los días Ser.). (SPA & ENG.). 24p. (J). lib. bdg. 22.60 *(978-1-4358-2527-7(6)*, PowerKids Pr.) Rosen Publishing Group, Inc., The.

—It's Snow! / ¡la Nieve! 2009. (Everyday Wonders / Maravillas de todos los días Ser.). (ENG & SPA.). 24p. (gr. 1-1). 42.50 *(978-1-61512-332-2(6)*, Editorial Buenas Letras) Rosen Publishing Group, Inc., The.

Pettiford, Rebecca. Snowplows. 2017. (Mighty Machines in Action Ser.). (ENG., Illus.). 24p. (J). (gr. k-3). lib. bdg. 25.95 ***(978-1-62617-633-1(7)***, Blastoff! Readers) Bellwether Media.

Purslow, Frances. Precipitation. 2015. (Illus.). 24p. (J). *(978-1-5105-0054-9(5))*; pap. *(978-1-5105-0286-4(6))* SmartBook Media, Inc.

Rain, Snow, & Hail: Individual Title Six-Packs. (Discovery World Ser.). 16p. (gr. 1-2). 28.00 *(978-0-7635-8466-5(5))* Rigby Education.

Rao, Joe. The Cool Story Behind Snow. Downey, Dagney, illus. 2015. (Science of Fun Stuff Ser.). (ENG.). 48p. (J). (gr. 1-3). pap. 3.99 *(978-1-4814-4413-2(1)*, Simon Spotlight) Simon Spotlight.

Rau, Dana Meachen. Building Snow Forts. 2012. (How-To Library). (ENG., Illus.). 32p. (J). (gr. 3-6). 28.50 *(978-1-61080-469-1(4)*, 202079); pap. 14.21 *(978-1-61080-643-5(3)*, 202253) Cherry Lake Publishing.

Ring, Susan. Snow, 6 vols., Set. 2005. (Yellow Umbrella Fluent Level Ser.). (ENG., Illus.). 16p. (gr. k-1). pap. 35.70 *(978-0-7368-5297-5(2)*, Yellow Umbrella Bks.) Capstone Press of Coughlan Cos.

Rustad, Martha E. H. Snowflakes (Copos de Nieve) 2012. (Todo Sobre el Invierno/All about Winter Ser.). (ENG, SPA & MUL.). 24p. (gr. k-1). lib. bdg. 26.65 *(978-1-4296-8242-8(6))* Capstone Press of Coughlan Cos.

—Today Is a Snowy Day. 2017. (What Is the Weather Today? Ser.). (ENG., Illus.). 24p. (gr. k-1). lib. bdg. 21.99 *(978-1-5157-4919-6(3))*; pap. 6.29 *(978-1-4966-0942-7(5))* Capstone Press of Coughlan Cos. (Pebble Bks.).

—100 Snowflakes: A Winter Counting Book. 2017. (1, 2, 3 Count with Me Ser.). (ENG., Illus.). 24p. (J). (gr. k-2). pap. 8.99 *(978-1-68152-109-1(1))* Amicus.

—100 Snowflakes: A Winter Counting Book. 2016. (1, 2, 3 Count with Me Ser.). (ENG., Illus.). 24p. (J). (gr. k-3). 20.95 *(978-1-60753-918-6(7))* Amicus Publishing.

Ruth, Angie. My Adventure in the Snow. 2006. 44p. (J). 8.99 *(978-1-59092-435-8(5))* Blue Forge Pr.

Sayre, April Pulley. Best in Snow. Sayre, April Pulley, photos by. 2016. (ENG., Illus.). 40p. (J). (gr. -1-3). 17.99 *(978-1-4814-5916-7(3)*, Beach Lane Bks.) Beach Lane Bks.

Sevigny, Eric, illus. Caillou Makes a Snowman. 2014. (Clubhouse Ser.). (ENG.). 24p. (J). (gr. -1 — 1). pap. 3.99 *(978-2-89718-143-7(5))* Caillouet, Gerry.

Shaw, Gina & dePaola, Tomie. Curious about Snow. 2016. (Smithsonian Ser.). (ENG., Illus.). 32p. (J). (gr. 1-3). bds. 3.99 *(978-0-448-49018-2(8)*, Grosset & Dunlap) Penguin Young Readers Group.

Sherman, Josepha. Flakes & Flurries: A Book about Snow. Yesh, Jeff, illus. 2003. (Amazing Science: Weather Ser.). (ENG.). 24p. (gr. -1-3). 26.65 *(978-1-4048-0098-4(0))* Picture Window Bks.

Silverman, Maida. Snow Search Dogs. 2005. (Dog Heroes Ser.). 32p. (J). lib. bdg. 25.27 *(978-1-59716-017-9(2))* Bearport Publishing Co., Inc.

Slegers, Liesbet. Winter Snow. 2012. (Clavis Toddler: the World Ser.). (ENG.). 12p. (J). (gr. k — 1). bds. 5.95 *(978-1-60537-123-8(8))* Cobblestone Publishing Co.

Snow, Virginia Brimhall. Winter Walk, 1 vol. 2014. (ENG., Illus.). 32p. (J). 16.99 *(978-1-4236-3747-9(X))* Gibbs Smith, Publisher.

Sommers, Michael A. Antarctic Melting: The Disappearing Antarctic Ice Cap. 2009. (Extreme Environmental Threats Ser.). 64p. (gr. 6-6). 58.50 *(978-1-61512-423-7(3))* Rosen Publishing Group, Inc., The.

Sterling, Kristin. It's Snowy Today. 2009. (Lightning Bolt Books — What's the Weather Like? Ser.). (ENG., Illus.). 32p. (gr. k-2). 26.60 *(978-0-7613-4258-8(3)*, Lerner Pubns.); pap. 7.95 *(978-0-7613-5021-7(7))* Lerner Publishing Group.

Stewart, Melissa. Under the Snow, 1 vol. Bergum, Constance Rummel, illus. 2009. (ENG.). 32p. (J). (gr. -1-3). 16.95 *(978-1-56145-493-8(1))* Peachtree Pubs.

Sturm, Matthew & Sturm, M. Apun: The Arctic Snow. 2nd ed. 2009. (ENG., Illus.). 44p. (J). pap. 12.95 *(978-1-60223-069-9(2))* Univ. of Alaska Pr.

Taylor, Clif. Snowflake. Whitmire, Anna, illus. 2010. (J). *(978-1-886769-97-7(4))* Gold Leaf Pr.

Trueit, Trudi Strain. Snowy Days. 2009. (Benchmark Rebus: Weather Watch Ser.). 24p. (gr. k-1). 15.95 *(978-0-7614-4015-4(1))* Marshall Cavendish Corp.

Urmston, Kathleen & Evans, Karen. Snowflakes. Kaeden Corp. Staff, ed. Graves, Dennis, illus. 2006. (ENG.). 12p. (gr. k-1). pap. 7.95 *(978-1-879835-01-6(0)*, Kaeden Bks.) Kaeden Corp.

Waldman, Neil. The Snowflake: A Water Cycle Story. Waldman, Neil, illus. 2003. (ENG., Illus.). 32p. (J). (gr. k-3). 17.95 *(978-0-7613-2347-1(3)*, Millbrook Pr.) Lerner Publishing Group.

Weston Woods Staff, creator. Snowflake Bentley. 2011. 18.95 *(978-0-545-31414-5(3))*; 38.75 *(978-0-545-31415-2(1))* Weston Woods Studios, Inc.

Williams, Judith. How Come It's Snowing? 2015. (How Does Weather Happen? Ser.). 24p. (J). (gr. k-3). pap. 7.95 *(978-0-7660-6386-0(0))*; lib. bdg. 22.60 *(978-0-7660-6385-3(2))* Enslow Pubs., Inc. (Enslow Elementary).

—Why Is It Snowing? 2005. (I Like Weather! Ser.). (Illus.). 24p. (J). lib. bdg. 22.60 *(978-0-7660-2319-2(2)*, Enslow Elementary) Enslow Pubs., Inc.

Yomtov, Nelson. Polar Ice Caps in Danger: Expedition to Antarctica. 2009. (Jr. Graphic Environmental Dangers Ser.). (ENG., Illus.). 24p. (gr. 3-8). pap. 10.60 *(978-1-4042-4594-5(4)*, PowerKids Pr.) Rosen Publishing Group, Inc., The.

Zuehlke, Jeffrey. Snowplows. 2006. (Pull Ahead Books-Mighty Movers Ser.). (ENG., Illus.). 32p. (gr. k-3). pap. 7.95 *(978-0-8225-5897-2(1)*, First Avenue Editions); lib. bdg. 22.60 *(978-0-8225-6009-8(7)*, Lerner Pubns.) Lerner Publishing Group.

SNOW—FICTION

Adams, Colleen. Jugando en la nieve (Playing in the Snow) 2007. (Lecturas del barrio (Neighborhood Readers) Ser.). (SPA.). 8p. 29.95 *(978-1-4042-7064-0(7)*, Rosen Classroom) Rosen Publishing Group, Inc., The.

—Playing in the Snow. (Neighborhood Readers Ser.). (ENG.). 8p. 2007. 29.95 *(978-1-4042-7059-6(0))* 2006. (gr. -1-3). pap. 5.15 *(978-1-4042-5657-6(1))* Rosen Publishing Group, Inc., The. (Rosen Classroom).

Aikins, Dave, illus. Dora Saves the Snow Princess. 2008. (Dora the Explorer Ser.: 27). (ENG.). 24p. (J). (gr. -1-2). pap. 3.99 *(978-1-4169-5866-6(5)*, Simon Spotlight/Nickelodeon) Simon Spotlight/Nickelodeon.

Ailes, Mark Cusco. The Snow Dargles: Book Two: the Chronicles of Weekland. 2010. 244p. pap. 16.95 *(978-1-4327-5223-1(5))* Outskirts Pr., Inc.

Albrecht, Sally K., et al. Snow Way Out! A Vacation in Winter's Wonderland: A Mini-Musical for Unison & 2-Part Voices. 2009. (ENG.). 68p. pap. 34.99 *(978-0-7390-5835-0(5))* Alfred Publishing Co., Inc.

Alexander, Annette M. Snow Magic & the Sad Little Christmas Tree. 2011. (Illus.). 32p. 14.66 *(978-1-4567-7182-9(5))* AuthorHouse.

Allen, J. J. Hello Kitty's Fun Friend Day! 2003. (Illus.). 32p. (J). pap. *(978-0-439-44917-5(0))* Scholastic, Inc.

Alley, R. W. Annabelle at the South Pole. 2016. (ENG., Illus.). 32p. (J). (gr. -1-3). 14.99 *(978-0-547-90704-8(4)*, Clarion Bks.) Houghton Mifflin Harcourt Trade & Reference Pubs.

Anderson, H.C. La Reine des Neiges. (FRE.). pap. 16.95 *(978-2-07-051630-8(X))* Gallimard, Editions FRA. Dist: Distribooks, Inc.

Arena, Jen. One Hundred Snowmen, 0 vols. Gilpin, Stephen, illus. 2013. (ENG.). 24p. (J). (gr. k-3). 14.99 *(978-1-4778-4703-9(0)*, 9781477847039, Amazon Children's Publishing) Amazon Publishing.

Arnold, Marsha Diane. Waiting for Snow. Liwska, Renata, illus. 2016. (ENG.). 32p. (J). (gr. -1-3). 14.99 *(978-0-544-41687-1(2)*, HMH Books For Young Readers) Houghton Mifflin Harcourt Publishing Co.

August, Elaine. It Only Snows in Brooklyn. 2012. 30p. 24.95 *(978-1-4626-9438-9(1))*; 32p. pap. 24.95 *(978-1-4626-7588-3(3))* America Star Bks.

Baccalario, Pierdomenico, et al. The Story of Snowflake & Inkdrop. 2015. (ENG., Illus.). 56p. (J). (gr. -1-3). 22.95 *(978-1-59270-186-5(8))* Enchanted Lion Bks., LLC.

Balaban, Mariah. Scooby-Doo & the Scary Snowman, 1 vol. Duendes Del Sur Staff, illus. 2012. (Scooby-Doo! Set 2 Ser.: No. 2). (ENG.). 24p. (J). (gr. k-3). lib. bdg. 24.21 *(978-1-59961-869-2(9))* Spotlight.

Barner. Snow. (J). 16.95 *(978-0-8118-4171-9(5))* Chronicle Bks. LLC.

Bauer, Dane. Snow. Wallace, John, illus. 2005. 32p. (J). lib. bdg. 15.00 *(978-1-59054-934-6(1))* Fitzgerald Bks.

Bean, Jonathan. Big Snow. Bean, Jonathan, illus. 2013. (ENG., Illus.). 32p. (J). (gr. -1-1). 16.99 *(978-0-374-30696-0(6)*, 9780374306960, Farrar, Straus & Giroux (BYR)) Farrar, Straus & Giroux.

Beeke, Joel R. & Kleyn, Diana. How God Used a Snowdrift. Anderson, Jeff, illus. 2013. (Building on the Rock Ser.). (ENG.). 176p. (J). pap. 8.99 *(978-1-85792-817-4(2)*, 9781857928174, CF4Kids) Christian Focus Pubns. GBR. Dist: Bookmasters Distribution.

Bentley, Sue. Winter Wonderland. 2013. (Magic Ponies Ser.: 5). lib. bdg. 16.00 *(978-0-606-32118-1(7)*, Turtleback) Turtleback Bks.

Berenstain, Mike. The Berenstain Bears & the Christmas Angel, 1 vol. 2016. (Berenstain Bears/Living Lights Ser.). (ENG.). 24p. (J). pap. 3.99 *(978-0-310-74924-0(7))* Zonderkidz.

Berger, Carin. A Perfect Day. Berger, Carin, illus. 2012. (ENG., Illus.). 40p. (J). (gr. -1-3). 16.99 *(978-0-06-201580-8(X)*, Greenwillow Bks.) HarperCollins Pubs.

Bianchi, John. Snowed in at Pokeweed Public School. (Illus.). 24p. (J). (gr. 1-5). *(978-1-894323-34-5(3))* Pokeweed Pr.

Biggs, Brian. Henry Goes Skating. Abbott, Simon, illus. 2012. (My First I Can Read Ser.). (J). lib. bdg. 13.55 *(978-0-606-26852-3(9)*, Turtleback) Turtleback Bks.

Bildner, Phil. Turkey Bowl. Payne, C. F., illus. 2008. (ENG.). 32p. (J). (gr. k-3). 15.99 *(978-0-689-87896-1(6)*, Simon & Schuster Bks. For Young Readers) Simon & Schuster Bks. For Young Readers.

Bishop, Celeste. It's Snowing. 2016. (What's the Weather Like? Ser.). 24p. (gr. 1-1). pap. 8.25 *(978-1-4994-2355-6(1)*, PowerKids Pr.) Rosen Publishing Group, Inc., The.

Blackstone, Stella. Cleo in the Snow. Mockford, Caroline, illus. 2013. (ENG.). 24p. (J). 6.99 *(978-1-78285-055-7(4))*; 6.99 *(978-1-78285-054-0(6))* Barefoot Bks., Inc.

Blanca Nieves - (Estrella de Mar) 2003. (SPA., Illus.). 16p. 2.95 *(978-968-855-185-1(6))* Suromex, Ediciones, S.A. MEX. Dist: Giron Bks.

Blizzard: Colorado 1886. 2014. (Survivors Ser.). (ENG., Illus.). 160p. (J). (gr. 3-7). pap. 6.99 *(978-1-4814-0969-8(7)*, Aladdin) Simon & Schuster Children's Publishing.

Bonnell, Kris. The White, White Snow. 2007. (J). pap. 5.95 *(978-1-933727-44-8(6))* Reading Reading Bks., LLC.

Brege, K. B. Abominable Snowman A Frozen Nightmare! 2009. (Mick Morris Myth Solver Ser.: No. 5). (Illus.). 156p. (J). pap. 6.99 *(978-0-9774119-4-8(X))* Team B Creative LLC.

Briggs, Raymond. The Snowman & the Snowdog. 2015. (Step into Reading Ser.). (ENG., Illus.). 32p. (J). (gr. -1-1). 12.99 *(978-0-385-38735-4(0)*, Random Hse. Bks. for Young Readers) Random Hse. Children's Bks.

Brooke, S. The Snow Diamond: the Fourth Journey, 1 vol. 2010. 180p. pap. 24.95 *(978-1-4512-1383-6(2))* America Star Bks.

Brothers Grimm. Snow White & Rose Red: A Grimms' Fairy Tale. Marshall, Denise, illus. 2008. 28p. (J). 17.95 *(978-0-88010-591-0(7)*, Bell Pond Bks.) SteinerBooks, Inc.

Brown, Gina Bates. Zen & Bodhi's Snowy Day. Hinder, Sarah Jane, illus. 2014. (ENG.). 24p. (J). 15.95 *(978-1-61429-165-7(9))* Wisdom Pubns.

Brown, Jeff. The Intrepid Canadian Expedition. 2009. (Flat Stanley's Worldwide Adventures Ser.: 4). (J). lib. bdg. 14.75 *(978-0-606-10068-7(7)*, Turtleback) Turtleback Bks.

Brown, Marc. Arthur & the Big Snow. Brown, Marc, illus. 2005. (ENG., Illus.). 24p. (J). (gr. -1-1). per. 3.99 *(978-0-316-05770-7(3))* Little, Brown Bks. for Young Readers.

Bruel, Nick. Bad Kitty Does Not Like Snow. 2016. (Bad Kitty Ser.). (ENG., Illus.). 24p. (J). pap. 4.99 *(978-1-62672-581-2(0)*, 9781626725812) Roaring Brook Pr.

—Bad Kitty Does Not Like Snow. 2016. (Bad Kitty Picture Bks.). (ENG.). 24p. (J). (gr. -1-k). 14.75 *(978-0-606-39296-9(3))* Turtleback Bks.

Bryant, Megan E. My Snow Globe: a Sparkly Peek-Through Story. Iwai, Melissa, illus. 2016. (ENG.). 10p. (J). bds. 7.99 *(978-0-545-92176-3(7)*, Cartwheel Bks.) Scholastic, Inc.

Buehner, Caralyn. Snowmen All Year. Buehner, Mark, illus. 2010. (ENG.). 32p. (J). (gr. -1-2). 16.99 *(978-0-8037-3383-1(6)*, Dial Bks) Penguin Young Readers Group.

—Snowmen at Night. Buehner, Mark, illus. 2004. (ENG.). 26p. (J). (gr. -1-k). bds. 6.99 *(978-0-8037-3041-0(1)*, Dial Bks) Penguin Young Readers Group.

Burton, Virginia Lee. Katy & the Big Snow, 1 vol. 2009. (ENG., Illus.). 40p. (J). (gr. -1-3). audio compact disk 10.99 *(978-0-547-25264-3(1))* Houghton Mifflin Harcourt Publishing Co.

Butler, M. Christina. The First Snow. Endersby, Frank, illus. 2012. (J). *(978-1-4351-4320-3(5))* Barnes & Noble, Inc.

—One Snowy Rescue. Macnaughton, Tina, illus. 2015. (ENG.). 32p. (J). (gr. -1-3). 16.99 *(978-1-58925-196-0(2))* Tiger Tales.

Butterworth, Nick. One Snowy Night. Butterworth, Nick, illus. 2008. (Tales from Percy's Park Ser.). (ENG., Illus.). 32p. (J). (gr. k-2). pap. 12.95 incl. audio compact disk *(978-0-00-726024-9(5))* HarperCollins Pubs.

—One Snowy Night. Butterworth, Nick, illus. (ENG., Illus.). 32p. (J). 2007. 24.00 *(978-0-00-725942-7(5))* 2011. pap. 11.00 *(978-0-00-714693-2(0)*, HarperCollins Children's Bks.) HarperCollins Pubs. Ltd. GBR. Dist: Independent Pubs. Group, HarperCollins Pubs.

Candlewick Press, Candlewick. Peppa Pig & the Day at Snowy Mountain. 2014. (Peppa Pig Ser.). (ENG.). 32p. (J). (-k). 12.99 *(978-0-7636-7455-7(9)*, Candlewick Entertainment) Candlewick Pr.

Capozzi, Suzy. Frosty the Snowman Big Golden Book (Frosty the Snowman) Laguna, Fabio & Cagol, Andrea, illus. 2014. (Big Golden Book Ser.). (ENG.). 48p. (J). (gr. -1-2). 9.99 *(978-0-385-38877-1(2)*, Golden Bks.) Random Hse. Children's Bks.

Carbone, Courtney. Snow Day! 2014. (Step into Reading Level 2 Ser.). lib. bdg. 13.55 *(978-0-606-36009-8(3))* Turtleback Bks.

—Snow Day! (Frosty the Snowman) Random House, illus. 2014. (Step into Reading Ser.). (ENG.). 32p. (J). (gr. -1-1). 3.99 *(978-0-385-38726-2(1)*, Random Hse. Bks. for Young Readers) Random Hse. Children's Bks.

Carey, Catherine Elaine. The Colorful & Playful Animal Friends, 1 vol. 2009. 73p. pap. 16.95 *(978-1-60749-480-5(9))* PublishAmerica, Inc.

Carle, Eric. Dream Snow. Carle, Eric, illus. 2015. (ENG., Illus.). 22p. (J). (gr. -1 — 1). bds. 9.99 *(978-0-399-17314-1(5)*, Philomel Bks.) Penguin Young Readers Group.

Carlson, Claudia & Koffsky, Ann D. Avi the Ambulance & the Snowy Day. Decker, C. B., illus. 2017. (J). *(978-1-68115-528-9(1))* Behrman Hse., Inc.

Carlson, Nancy. Harriet & Walt. rev. ed. 2004. (Carolrhoda Picture Books Ser.). (ENG., Illus.). 32p. (J). (gr. k-2). 15.95 *(978-1-57505-672-2(0))*; pap. 6.95 *(978-1-57505-723-1(9))* Lerner Publishing Group.

—Take Time to Relax! Carlson, Nancy, illus. 2012. (Nancy Carlson Picture Bks). (Illus.). 32p. (J). (gr. k-2). 56.72 *(978-0-7613-9304-7(8))*; (ENG., 9.95 *(978-0-7613-8949-1(0))* Lerner Publishing Group. (Carolrhoda Bks.).

Carlstrom, Nancy White. Mama, Will It Snow Tonight? Tong, Paul, illus. 2009. (ENG.). 32p. (J). (gr. k-3). 16.95 *(978-1-59078-562-1(2))* Boyds Mills Pr.

Carter, David A. A Snowy Day in Bugland! Carter, David A., illus. 2012. (David Carter's Bugs Ser.). (ENG., Illus.). 24p. (J). (gr. -1-1). 15.99 *(978-1-4424-3895-8(9))*; pap. 3.99 *(978-1-4424-3894-1(0))* Simon Spotlight. (Simon Spotlight).

—Winter. 2015. (Seasons Pop-Up Ser.). (ENG., Illus.). 12p. (J). (gr. -1-k). 14.95 *(978-1-4197-1823-6(1)*, Abrams Appleseed) Abrams, Inc.

Casanova, Mary. One-Dog Sleigh. Hoyt, Ard, illus. 2013. (ENG.). 32p. (J). (gr. k-3). 16.99 *(978-0-374-35639-2(4)*, 9780374356392, Farrar, Straus & Giroux (BYR)) Farrar, Straus & Giroux.

Caviezel, Giovanni. Little Snowman. Mesturini, C., illus. 2014. (Mini People Shape Bks.). (ENG.). 10p. (J). (gr. -1-2). bds. 4.99 *(978-0-7641-6737-9(5))* Barron's Educational Series, Inc.

Chelsea, David. Snow Angel. Chelsea, David, illus. 2016. (ENG., Illus.). 112p. (J). (gr. 3-7). pap. 9.99 *(978-1-61655-940-3(3))* Dark Horse Comics.

Chessa, Francesca. Holly's Red Boots. Chessa, Francesca, illus. 2008. (ENG., Illus.). 32p. (J). (gr. -1-1). 16.95 (978-0-8234-2158-9(9)) Holiday Hse., Inc.

Child, Jeremy. Santa. Leach, Emma, illus. 2010. (Snow Shakers Ser.). (ENG.). 8p. (J). (gr. -1-k). bds. 4.99 (978-0-7641-6384-5(1)) Barron's Educational Series, Inc.

Christopher, Matt. Snowboard Maverick. 2007. (New Matt Christopher Sports Library). 152p. (J). (gr. 4-6). lib. bdg. 26.60 (978-1-59953-116-8(X)) Norwood Hse. Pr.

—Snowboard Showdown. l.t. ed. 2007. (New Matt Christopher Sports Library). 160p. (J). (gr. 4-6). lib. bdg. 26.60 (978-1-59953-109-0(7)) Norwood Hse. Pr.

Claude on the Slopes, 1 vol. 2014. (Claude Ser.). (ENG., Illus.). 96p. (J). (gr. 1-3). 12.95 (978-1-56145-805-9(8)) Peachtree Pubs.

Colandro, Lucille. There Was a Cold Lady Who Swallowed Some Snow! Lee, Jared, illus. (J). 2006. (ENG.). (gr. -1-3). 18.95 (978-0-439-89841-6(2)) 2003. (ENG.). 32p. (gr. -1-3). pap. 6.99 (978-0-439-56703-9(3), Cartwheel Bks.) 2003. 32p. (gr. k-3). pap. 5.95 (978-0-439-47109-1(5), Cartwheel Bks.) 2006. (ENG.). (gr. -1-3). 9.95 (978-0-439-89556-9(1)) Scholastic, Inc.

Coleman, Roger. The Pope & the Snowman: A Christmas Tale. 2009. (Illus.). 108p. 23.99 (978-1-4490-1128-4(4)); pap. 12.49 (978-1-4490-1127-7(6)) AuthorHouse.

Collingridge, Richard. When It Snows. Collingridge, Richard, illus. 2013. (ENG., Illus.). 32p. (J). (gr. -1-1). 16.99 (978-1-250-02831-0(0), 9781250028310) Feiwel & Friends.

Cordell, Matthew. Wolf in the Snow. 2017. (ENG., Illus.). 48p. (J). 17.99 (978-1-250-07636-6(6), 9781250076366) Feiwel & Friends.

Costa, Deborah Da. Snow in Jerusalem. Hu, Ying-Hwa & Wright, Cornelius Van, illus. 2008. (ENG.). 32p. (J). (gr. 1-3). 6.99 (978-0-8075-7525-3(9)) Whitman, Albert & Co.

Cotten, Cynthia. Snow Ponies. Cockcroft, Jason, illus. 2013. (ENG.). 32p. (J). (gr. -1-1). 6.99 (978-1-250-03429-8(9), 9781250034298) Square Fish.

Courtin, Thierry. T choupi fait un bonhomme De. 13.95 (978-2-09-202037-1(4)) Nathan, Fernand FRA. Dist: Distribooks, Inc.

Courtney, Richard, illus. Thomas Gets a Snowplow. 2004. (Pictureback Ser.). (ENG.). 24p. (J). (gr. -1-2). 3.99 (978-0-375-82783-9(8), Random Hse. Bks. for Young Readers) Random Hse. Children's Bks.

Cox, Judy. Snow Day for Mouse. Ebbeler, Jeffrey, illus. (ENG.). 32p. (J). (gr. -1). 2013. pap. 7.99 (978-0-8234-2913-4(X)) 2012. 16.95 (978-0-8234-2408-5(1)) Holiday Hse., Inc.

Crow, Melinda Melton. Snow Trouble, 1 vol. Rooney, Ronnie, illus. 2009. (Truck Buddies Ser.). (ENG.). 32p. (gr. -1-1). pap. 6.25 (978-1-4342-1755-4(8)) Stone Arch Bks.

Cummings, Troy. Flurry of the Snombies. 2015. (Notebook of Doom Ser.: 7). (ENG., Illus.). 96p. (J). (gr. 1-3). 15.99 (978-0-545-79551-7(6)); pap. 4.99 (978-0-545-79550-0(8)) Scholastic, Inc.

—Flurry of the Snombies. 2015. (Notebook of Doom Ser.: 7). lib. bdg. 14.75 (978-0-606-36340-2(8)) Turtleback Bks.

Cuyler, Margery. The Christmas Snowman. Westerman, Johanna, illus. 2011. (ENG.). 32p. (J). (gr. k-2). 12.95 (978-1-61608-483-7(9), 608483, Sky Pony Pr.) Skyhorse Publishing Co., Inc.

Dal Santo, Sandy. I See a Zoo up in the Sky. 2009. 28p. pap. 12.89 (978-1-4389-4871-3(9)) AuthorHouse.

Daniel, Noel, ed. A Treasury of Wintertime Tales. 2014. (ENG.). 324p. 39.99 (978-3-8365-4400-9(8)) TASCHEN DEU. Dist: Ingram Publisher Services.

David, Erica. Anna & Elsa. RH Disney et al, illus. 2017. (Stepping Stone Book(TM) Ser.: 9). (ENG.). 128p. (J). (gr. 1-4). 9.99 (978-0-7364-3480-5(1), RH/Disney) Random Hse. Children's Bks.

David, Erica & Foreman, Matthew Sinclair. Disney Frozen - A Year with Elsa & Anna, & Olaf Too! 2016. (Replica Journal Ser.). (ENG.). 96p. (J). (gr. k-3). 9.99 (978-0-7944-3701-5(X), Reader's Digest Children's Bks.) Studio Fun International.

Davis, Jacky & Soman, David. Ladybug Girl & the Big Snow. Soman, David, illus. 2013. (Ladybug Girl Ser.). (ENG., Illus.). 40p. (J). (gr. -1-k). 17.99 (978-0-8037-3583-5(9), Dial Bks) Penguin Young Readers Group.

Day, Alexandra. Carl's Snowy Afternoon. Day, Alexandra, illus. 2009. (Carl Ser.). (ENG., Illus.). 32p. (J). (gr. -1-1). 13.99 (978-0-374-31086-8(6), 9780374310868, Farrar, Straus & Giroux (BYR)) Farrar, Straus & Giroux.

De La Cour, Gary, illus. & creator. Counting in the Snow. De La Cour, Gary, creator. gif. ed. 2005. 10p. (J). bds. 9.99 (978-1-57791-186-9(5)) Brighter Minds Children's Publishing.

Dean, James. Pete the Cat: Snow Daze. Dean, James, illus. 2016. (My First I Can Read Ser.). (Illus.). 32p. (J). (gr. -1-3). 16.99 (978-0-06-240425-1(3)) HarperCollins Pubs.

—Snow Daze. Dean, James, illus. 2016. (Pete the Cat I Can Read Ser.). (ENG., Illus.). 32p. (J). (gr. -1-3). lib. bdg. 13.55 (978-0-606-39264-8(5)) Turtleback Bks.

deGroat, Diane. Jingle Bells, Homework Smells. deGroat, Diane, illus. 2008. (Illus.). (J). (gr. -1-3). pap. 16.95 incl. audio (978-1-4301-0419-3(8)) Live Oak Media.

Delsol, Wendy. Frost. (ENG., Illus.). (YA). (gr. 7). 2012. 384p. pap. 8.99 (978-0-7636-6249-3(6)) 2011. 376p. 15.99 (978-0-7636-5386-6(1)) Candlewick Pr.

dePaola, Tomie. Andy & Sandy & the First Snow. dePaola, Tomie, illus. 2016. (Andy & Sandy Book Ser.). (ENG., Illus.). 32p. (J). (gr. -1-3). 8.99 (978-1-4814-4159-9(0), Simon & Schuster Bks. For Young Readers) Simon & Schuster Bks. For Young Readers.

DePrisco, Dorothea. Snowbear's Winter Day: A Winter Wonder Book. Fehlau, Dagmar, illus. 2005. 18p. (J). (gr. -1). 9.95 (978-1-58117-133-4(1), Intervisual/Piggy Toes) Bendon, Inc.

Disney Book Group. Do You Want a Hug? Disney Storybook Art Team, illus. 2016. (ENG.). 64p. (J). (gr. 1-3). 10.99 (978-1-4847-8775-5(7)) Disney Pr.

—Frozen, Level 1. 2016. (World of Reading Ser.). (ENG.). 96p. (J). (gr. -1-k). pap. 7.99 (978-1-4847-9032-8(4)) Disney Pr.

Disney Book Group Staff. Frozen Read-Along Storybook & CD. Disney Storybook Artists Staff, illus. 2013. (Read-Along Storybook & CD Ser.). (ENG.). 32p. (J). (gr. -1-k). pap. 6.99 (978-1-4231-7064-8(4)) Disney Pr.

Disney Editors. Frozen. 2013. lib. bdg. 14.75 (978-0-606-32207-2(8), Turtleback) Turtleback Bks.

—Frozen - Anna's Icy Adventure. 2013. lib. bdg. 14.75 (978-0-606-32206-5(X), Turtleback) Turtleback Bks.

Disney Frozen Melt My Heart. 2014. (Hugs Book Ser.). (ENG.). 10p. (J). (gr. -1-k). bds. 10.99 (978-0-7944-3266-9(2), Reader's Digest Children's Bks.) Studio Fun International.

DiVito, Anna. Annie Oakley Saves the Day. DiVito, Anna, illus. 2005. (Illus.). 32p. (J). lib. bdg. 15.00 (978-1-59054-939-1(2)) Fitzgerald Bks.

Dooley, Norah. Everybody Serves Soup. Thornton, Peter, illus. 2004. (Carolrhoda Picture Books Ser.). (ENG.). 40p. (J). (gr. -1-3). per. 6.95 (978-1-57505-791-0(3)) Lerner Publishing Group.

—Everybody Serves Soup. Thornton, Peter J., illus. 2004. (Picture Bks.). 40p. (J). (gr. -1-3). 15.95 (978-1-57505-422-3(1)) Lerner Publishing Group.

Dorling Kindersley Publishing Staff. Disney Frozen: the Enchanted Guide. 2015. (ENG., Illus.). 96p. (J). (gr. 1-4). 14.99 (978-1-4654-4081-5(X), DK Children) Dorling Kindersley Publishing, Inc.

Downey, Glen. Ice Journey. Brucker, Glenn, illus. 2007. 48p. (J). lib. bdg. 23.08 (978-1-4242-1618-5(4)) Fitzgerald Bks.

Downey, Tika. The Biggest Snowball. 2006. (Neighborhood Readers Ser.). (ENG.). 16p. (gr. 1-3). pap. 6.50 (978-1-4042-7200-2(3), Rosen Classroom) Rosen Publishing Group, Inc., The.

—Tracks in the Snow. 2006. (Neighborhood Readers Ser.). (ENG.). 16p. (gr. 1-3). pap. 6.50 (978-1-4042-7180-7(5), Rosen Classroom) Rosen Publishing Group, Inc., The.

Drake, Paula. How to Make a Snow Day: The Official Rules & Regulations. 2011. 28p. (gr. -1). pap. 15.00 (978-1-4567-1830-5(4)) AuthorHouse.

Drummond, Ree. Charlie the Ranch Dog: Charlie's New Friend. deGroat, Diane, illus. 2014. (I Can Read Level 1 Ser.). (ENG.). 32p. (J). (gr. -1-3). 16.99 (978-0-06-221915-2(4)); pap. 3.99 (978-0-06-221914-5(6)) HarperCollins Pubs.

—Charlie's Snow Day. 2013. (I Can Read! Level 1 Ser.). (J). lib. bdg. 13.55 (978-0-606-32161-7(6), Turtleback) Turtleback Bks.

Dunrea, Olivier. It's Snowing! Dunrea, Olivier, illus. 2009. (ENG., Illus.). 32p. (J). (gr. -1-1). pap. 6.99 (978-0-312-60216-1(2), 9780312602161) Square Fish.

Dunshee, Gloria Fjare. Will & the Magic Snowman. 2010. 32p. pap. 11.95 (978-0-9828231-1-8(8)) WillGo Pr.

Echols, Jennifer. The Ex Games. 2011. (Romantic Comedies Ser.). (ENG.). 240p. (YA). (gr. 7). pap. 11.99 (978-1-4424-3083-9(4), Simon Pulse) Simon Pulse.

Edwards, Richard. We Love the Snow. Wallace, John, illus. 2015. (ENG.). 32p. (J). (gr. -1-3). 7.99 (978-1-85733-719-8(0)) Lerner Publishing Group.

Ehlert, Lois. Snowballs. 2004. (Illus.). (gr. -1-3). 17.00 (978-0-7569-4243-4(8)) Perfection Learning Corp.

Emerson, Alice B. Ruth Fielding at Snow Camp: Or, Lost in the Backwoods. 2007. (ENG.). 134p. pap. 18.99 (978-1-4264-5024-2(9)); 144p. pap. 19.99 (978-1-4264-5325-0(6)) Creative Media Partners, LLC.

Emmett, Jonathan. Foxes in the Snow, 11. Harry, Rebecca, illus. 3rd ed. 2012. (ENG.). 32p. (J). (gr. -1-k). pap. 9.99 (978-0-230-71229-4(0)) Pan Macmillan GBR. Dist: Independent Pubs. Group.

Ernst, Lisa Campbell. Snow Surprise. 2008. (Green Light Readers Level 2 Ser.). (ENG., Illus.). 24p. (J). (gr. k-2). pap. 3.95 (978-0-15-206559-1(8)) Houghton Mifflin Harcourt Publishing Co.

Etherington Dilks, Barbara. The Snowman. 2015. (ENG.). 50p. (J). (gr. 2-3). mass mkt. 14.95 (978-1-78612-050-2(X), 81054dbd-4c58-4cbd-98dc-c4631d79a99c) Austin, Stan AUS. Dist: Bookmasters Distribution.

Farber, Erica. Richard Scarry's Readers (Level 1): Snow Dance. Scarry, Huck, illus. 2014. (Richard Scarry's Great Big Schoolhouse Ser.). (ENG.). 24p. (J). (gr. -1 — 1). pap. 3.95 (978-1-4027-9896-2(2)); 12.95 (978-1-4027-9895-5(4)) Sterling Publishing Co., Inc.

Farley, Robin. The Snow Day Ballet. Ivanov, Olga & Ivanov, Aleksey, illus. 2014. (Mia Ser.). (ENG.). 24p. (J). (gr. -1-k). pap. 4.99 (978-0-06-210015-3(7), HarperFestival) HarperCollins Pubs.

Fisher, Carolyn. The Snow Show. 2008. (ENG., Illus.). 48p. (J). (gr. k-5). 17.00 (978-0-15-206019-0(7)) Houghton Mifflin Harcourt Publishing Co.

Flodin, Louise E. Sherman the Frog Meets the Snow Princess. l.t. ed. 2006. (Illus.). 24p. (J). (gr. -1-3). 15.95 (978-0-9745052-5-1(0), 1) Tree Of Life Publishing.

Ford, Bernette G. First Snow. Braun, Sebastien, illus. 2005. 32p. (J). (978-0-9547373-3-7(4)) Boxer Bks., Ltd.

Ford, Bernette G. & Ford, Bernette. First Snow. Braun, Sebastien, illus. 2005. (ENG.). 32p. (J). (gr. -1-3). 16.95 (978-0-8234-1937-1(1)) Holiday Hse., Inc.

Foster, Ron, illus. I Like Snow! 2006. 28p. (J). (gr. -1-3). (978-1-929039-37-1(9)) Ambassador Bks., Inc.

French, Vivian. The Snow Dragon. Fisher, Chris, illus. 2003. (ENG.). 32p. (J). pap. 11.99 (978-0-552-54595-2(3)) Transworld Publishers Ltd. GBR. Dist: Trafalgar Square Publishing.

Friend, Larry. Icy the Iceberg. Makis, Sidney, illus. 2008. 28p. pap. 13.95 (978-1-4327-3777-1(5)) Outskirts Pr., Inc.

Froeb, Lori. Disney Frozen: Christmas Magic. 2015. (ENG.). 10p. (J). (gr. -1-1). bds. 8.99 (978-0-7944-3501-1(7)) Reader's Digest Assn., Inc., The.

Fun in the Snow. 2003. (Bella & Rosie Set 1 Ser.). (J). 7.67 (978-1-932570-13-7(6)) Pioneer Valley Bks.

Gaffney, Sean. Larryboy & the Sinister Snow Day, 1 vol. 2003. (Big Idea Books / LarryBoy Ser.). (ENG., Illus.). 96p. (J). pap. 4.99 (978-0-310-70561-1(4)) Zonderkidz.

Garland, Michael. Super Snow Day Seek & Find. 2010. (ENG.). 32p. (J). (gr. -1-2). 16.99 (978-0-525-42245-7(5), Dutton Books for Young Readers) Penguin Young Readers Group.

Garoche, Camille. Snow Rabbit. 2015. (ENG., Illus.). 56p. (J). (gr. -1-3). 16.95 (978-1-59270-181-0(7)) Enchanted Lion Bks., LLC.

Gay, Marie-Louise. Stella, Queen of the Snow. 2004. (J). (gr. -1-1). spiral bd. (978-0-616-08493-9(5)) Canadian National Institute for the Blind/Institut National Canadien pour les Aveugles.

—Stella, Reine des Neiges. 2004. Tr. of Stella, Queen of the Snow. (FRE., Illus.). (J). (gr. k-3). spiral bd. (978-0-616-14596-8(9)) Canadian National Institute for the Blind/Institut National Canadien pour les Aveugles.

Gay, Marie-Louise, illus. Stella, Queen of the Snow. braille ed. 2004. (J). (gr. -1-1). spiral bd. (978-0-616-08492-2(7)) Canadian National Institute for the Blind/Institut National Canadien pour les Aveugles.

George, Jean Craighead. Snowboard Twist. Minor, Wendell, illus. 2004. (Outdoor Adventures Ser.). (ENG.). 32p. (J). 15.99 (978-0-06-050595-0(8)) HarperCollins Pubs.

Ghigna, Charles. Snow Wonder. Woolf, Julia, illus. 2008. (Step into Reading Ser.: Vol. 2). (ENG.). 24p. (J). (gr. -1-1). 3.99 (978-0-375-85586-3(6), Random Hse. Bks. for Young Readers) Random Hse. Children's Bks.

Giff, Patricia Reilly. Fiercely & Friends: the Sneaky Snow Fox. Palmisciano, Diane, illus. 2012. (Fiercely & Friends Ser.). (ENG.). 40p. (J). (gr. k-2). 16.99 (978-0-545-43378-5(9), Orchard Bks.) Scholastic, Inc.

Gilbert in the Snow. 2005. (Gilbert the Pig Chapter Ser.). (J). 7.67 (978-1-58453-297-2(1)) Pioneer Valley Bks.

Gilman, Grace. Dixie & the Best Day Ever. Rogers, Jacqueline, illus. 2014. (I Can Read Level 1 Ser.). (ENG.). 32p. (J). (gr. -1-3). pap. 3.99 (978-0-06-208659-4(6)) HarperCollins Pubs.

Gilman, Phoebe. Jillian Jiggs & the Great Big Snow. 2004. (Illus.). (J). (gr. k-3). spiral bd. (978-0-616-14582-1(9)); spiral bd. (978-0-616-14583-8(7)) Canadian National Institute for the Blind/Institut National Canadien pour les Aveugles.

Glass, Calliope. Do You Want to Build a Snowman? Mosqueda, Olga, illus. 2015. (ENG.). 48p. (J). (gr. -1-k). 12.99 (978-1-4847-1467-6(9)) Disney Pr.

Goggins, Jean. The Adventures of Boo & Koty: Snow. 2009. 36p. pap. 21.99 (978-1-4415-4670-8(7)) Xlibris Corp.

Golden Books. Snow Wonder! (Frosty the Snowman) Golden Books, illus. 2013. (Deluxe Paint Box Book Ser.). (ENG., Illus.). 128p. (J). (gr. -1-2). pap. 7.99 (978-0-385-37179-7(9), Golden Bks.) Random Hse. Children's Bks.

Gorbachev, Valeri. Me Too! 2013. (I Like to Read(r) Ser.). (ENG., Illus.). 24p. (J). (gr. -1-3). 14.95 (978-0-8234-2744-4(7)) Holiday Hse., Inc.

—Pizza-Pie Snowman. 2016. (ENG., Illus.). 32p. (J). 16.95 (978-0-8234-3654-5(3)) Holiday Hse., Inc.

Gore, Leonid. Danny's First Snow. Gore, Leonid, illus. 2007. (ENG., Illus.). 40p. (J). (gr. -1-2). 16.99 (978-1-4169-1330-6(0), Atheneum Bks. for Young Readers) Simon & Schuster Children's Publishing.

Grandma Sue. Bubba the Bear. 2010. 12p. pap. 8.49 (978-1-4490-1813-9(0)) AuthorHouse.

Gravett, Emily. Bear & Hare Snow! Gravett, Emily, illus. 2015. (Bear & Hare Ser.). (ENG., Illus.). 32p. (J). (gr. -1-3). 16.99 (978-1-4814-4514-6(6), Simon & Schuster Bks. For Young Readers) Simon & Schuster Bks. For Young Readers.

Grimm, Jacob & Grimm, Wilhelm K. Snow White. Garcia, Camille Rose, illus. 2012. (ENG.). 80p. 14.99 (978-0-06-206446-2(0), Collins Design) HarperCollins Pubs.

Grizzell, Larry. What Would You Like to Do Today? Fun in the Snow. 2006. (Illus.). 30p. (J). 16.95 (978-0-9759542-1-8(0)) Adventures Galore.

Grogan, John. Snow Dog Marley. Cowdrey, Richard, illus. 2010. (I Can Read Level 2 Ser.). (ENG.). 32p. (J). (gr. k-3). 16.99 (978-0-06-185393-7(3)); pap. 3.99 (978-0-06-185392-0(5)) HarperCollins Pubs.

Hader, Berta and Elmer. The Big Snow & Other Stories: A Treasury of Caldecott Award Winning Tales. 2015. (ENG., Illus.). 160p. (J). (gr. 1-4). pap. 14.99 (978-0-486-78163-1(1)) Dover Pubns., Inc.

Hall, Kirsten. The Big Sled Race. Burnett, Lindy, illus. 2003. (Hello Reader! Ser.). (J). pap. 3.99 (978-0-439-32104-4(2)) Scholastic, Inc.

Hamilton, Pamela Greenhalgh. Snow Day. 2011. 34p. (J). pap. 18.95 (978-1-4327-5743-4(1)) Outskirts Pr., Inc.

Hanson, Bonnie Compton. Lost on Monster Mountain. 2004. (Ponytail Girls Ser.). (Illus.). 208p. (J). pap. 7.99 (978-1-58411-031-6(7), Legacy Pr.) Rainbow Pubs. & Legacy Pr.

Harper, Lee. Snow! Snow! Snow! Harper, Lee, illus. 2009. (ENG., Illus.). 40p. (J). (gr. -1-3). 14.99 (978-1-4169-8454-2(2), Simon & Schuster/Paula Wiseman Bks.) Simon & Schuster/Paula Wiseman Bks.

Harris, Shelly J. A Snowman's Love, 1 vol. 2009. 19p. pap. 24.95 (978-1-60836-708-5(8)) America Star Bks.

Harrison, Joanna & Briggs, Raymond. The Snowman & the Snowdog. 2014. (ENG., Illus.). 40p. (J). (gr. -1-2). 17.99 (978-0-385-38714-9(8), Random Hse. Bks. for Young Readers) Random Hse. Children's Bks.

Harrison, Paula. The Snow Jewel. 2013. (Rescue Princesses Ser.: 5). lib. bdg. 14.75 (978-0-606-32372-7(4), Turtleback) Turtleback Bks.

Heigh, Stephen. The Snowman in the Moon. Burton, Kevin, ed. Heigh, Stephen, illus. 2005. (Illus.). 28p. (J). (gr. -1-3). 16.95 (978-0-9745715-5-3(5)) KRBY Creations, LLC.

Heinz, Brian J. A Coming of Winter in the Adirondacks. Healy, Maggie, illus. 2011. 32p. (J). 19.95 (978-1-59531-038-5(X)) North Country Bks., Inc.

Helquist, Brett. Bedtime for Bear. Helquist, Brett, illus. 2010. (ENG., Illus.). 32p. (J). (gr. -1-2). 16.99 (978-0-06-050205-8(3)) HarperCollins Pubs.

Hendry, Diana. The Very Snowy Christmas. Chapman, Jane, illus. (J). 2013. (ENG.). 16p. (gr. -1). bds. 8.95 (978-1-58925-617-0(4)) 2007. 32p. pap. 6.95 (978-1-58925-406-0(6)) 2005. 32p. (gr. -1-2). 15.95 (978-1-58925-051-2(6)) Tiger Tales.

Hest, Amy. The Reader, 0 vols. Castillo, Lauren, illus. 2012. (ENG.). 32p. (J). (gr. -1-1). 16.99 (978-0-7614-6184-5(1), 9780761461845, Amazon Children's Publishing) Amazon Publishing.

Higginson, Sheila Sweeny. Chilly Catches a Cold. 2013. (Doc Mcstuffins 8X8 Ser.). (J). lib. bdg. 13.55 (978-0-606-35109-6(4), Turtleback) Turtleback Bks.

Higginson, Sheila Sweeny, et al. Chilly Catches a Cold. 2013. (Illus.). 24p. (J). (978-1-4844-1108-7(0)) Disney Pr.

Hileman, Jane & Pitt, Marilyn. Snow Dog. Bianchi, John, illus. 2011. (Power 50 - Potato Chip Bks). 12p. pap. 33.92 (978-1-61541-298-3(0)) American Reading Co.

Hillert, Margaret. I Did It, Dear Dragon. Schimmell, David, illus. 2009. (BeginningtoRead Ser.). 32p. (J). (gr. k-2). lib. bdg. 22.60 (978-1-59953-295-0(6)) Norwood Hse. Pr.

—The Snow Baby. Krushak-Green, Laura, illus. 2016. (BeginningtoRead Ser.). (ENG.). 32p. (J). (gr. -1-2). pap. 11.94 (978-1-60357-945-2(1)); (gr. 1-2). 22.60 (978-1-59953-804-4(0)) Norwood Hse. Pr.

Hills, Tad. It's Time for Christmas! Hills, Tad, illus. 2010. (Duck & Goose Ser.). (ENG., Illus.). 22p. (J). (gr. k — 1). bds. 7.99 (978-0-375-86484-1(9), Schwartz & Wade Bks.) Random Hse. Children's Bks.

Hoffman, Don. A Very Special Snowflake. Dakins, Todd, illus. 2nd ed. 2016. (ENG.). 28p. (J). (gr. -1-k). pap. 3.99 (978-1-943154-01-2(5)) Peek-A-Boo Publishing.

Holub, Joan. Snow Day! A Winter Tale. Terry, Will, illus. 2008. (Ant Hill Ser.). (ENG.). 24p. (J). (gr. -1-k). pap. 3.99 (978-1-4169-5135-3(0), Simon Spotlight) Simon Spotlight.

Houghton Mifflin Harcourt Publishing Company Staff & Rey, H. A. Start Your Engines 5-Minute Stories. 2014. (5-Minute Stories Ser.). (ENG., Illus.). 224p. (J). (gr. -1-3). 12.99 (978-0-544-15881-8(4), HMH Books For Young Readers) Houghton Mifflin Harcourt Publishing Co.

Howard, Kate. Snowball Trouble. Gilpin, Stephen, illus. 2015. (ANG.). 40p. (J). pap. (978-0-545-75839-0(4)) Scholastic, Inc.

Howell, Gail L. Sarah & the Blue Sled: Sarah's World (Series) 2010. 32p. pap. 12.99 (978-1-4389-7597-9(X)) AuthorHouse.

Howell, Gill. Snow King. Cann, Helen, illus. 2005. (ENG.). 24p. (J). lib. bdg. 23.65 (978-1-59646-742-2(8)) Dingles & Co.

Hubbell, Patricia. Snow Happy! Nakata, Hiroe, illus. 2010. (ENG.). 32p. (J). (gr. -1-2). 15.99 (978-1-58246-329-2(8), Tricycle Pr.) Random Hse. Children's Bks.

Hulst, W. G. van de & Hulst, Willem G. van de, illus. Footprints in the Snow. 2014. (J). (978-1-928136-13-2(3)) Inheritance Pubns.

Huneck, Stephen. Sally's Snow Adventure. Huneck, Stephen, illus. 2006. (ENG., Illus.). 32p. (J). (gr. -1-3). 15.95 (978-0-8109-7061-8(9)) Abrams, Inc.

Hutchins, Hazel J. Ben's Snow Song: A Winter Picnic. 2004. (Illus.). (J). (gr. k-3). spiral bd. (978-0-616-01677-0(8)) Canadian National Institute for the Blind/Institut National Canadien pour les Aveugles.

S

ImageBooks Staff. Snow Baby Finger Puppet Book. 2011. (Little Finger Puppet Board Bks.). (ENG.). 12p. (J). (gr. -1 — 1). bds. 6.99 (978-1-4521-0220-7(1)) Chronicle Bks. LLC.

ImageBooks Staff, et al. Little Snowman. 2008. (Little Finger Puppet Board Bks.). (ENG., Illus.). 12p. (J). (gr. -1 — 1). bds. 6.99 (978-0-8118-6356-8(5)) Chronicle Bks. LLC.

Isadora, Rachel. Mr. Moon. Date not set. (J). 15.99 (978-0-06-029821-0(9)); lib. bdg. 16.89 (978-0-06-029822-7(7)) HarperCollins Pubs.

Jack, Keats Ezra. The Snowy Day. 2014. (ENG.). 40p. (J). (gr. 3-7). 12.24 (978-1-63245-154-5(9)) Lectorum Pubns., Inc.

Jackson, Laura Gower. The Snowman & the Magic Eyeglasses. 2010. 24p. 11.99 (978-1-4520-3544-4(X)) AuthorHouse.

Jakubowski, Michele. Snowy Blast. Waters, Erica-Jane, illus. 2014. (Perfectly Poppy Ser.). (ENG.). 32p. (gr. k-2). lib. bdg. 22.65 (978-1-4795-2283-5(X)) Picture Window Bks.

Jeannine & Egan, Jennifer. Jack the Brave Conquers the Snow. 2012. 44p. pap. 21.99 (978-1-4797-1713-2(4)) Xlibris Corp.

Jenkins, Barbie. The Legend of the Christmas Kiss. 2010. (ENG.). 32p. pap. 11.99 (978-1-4391-9623-6(0), Howard Bks.) Howard Books.

Jenkins, Emily. Toys Meet Snow. Zelinsky, Paul O., illus. 2015. (ENG.). 40p. (J). (gr. -1-2). 17.99 (978-0-385-37330-2(9), Schwartz & Wade Bks.) Random Hse. Children's Bks.

Johnson, Andi. Hailey Snowstorm. 2004. (Illus.). 16p. 9.00 (978-1-84161-113-6(1)) Ravette Publishing, Ltd. GBR. Dist: Parkwest Pubns., Inc.

Johnson, Christine. Deep in Alaska. Johnson, Gary R., illus. 2013. 42p. pap. 12.95 (978-1-60223-215-0(6)) Univ. of Alaska Pr.

Johnson, Crockett. Time for Spring. Johnson, Crockett, illus. 2016. (Illus.). 40p. (J). (gr. -1-3). 14.99 (978-0-06-243033-5(5)) HarperCollins Pubs.

Johnson, Shane L., illus. OLIVIA & the Snow Day. 2010. (Olivia TV Tie-In Ser.). (ENG.). 24p. (J). (gr. -1-1). 15.99 (978-1-4423-3638-4(2), Simon Spotlight) Simon Spotlight.

Jules, Jacqueline. Freddie Ramos Stomps the Snow. Benitez, Miguel, illus. 2014. (Zapato Power Ser.: Book 5). (ENG.). 96p. (J). (gr. 1-5). 14.99 (978-0-8075-9487-2(3)) Whitman, Albert & Co.

K/H (Pathways). Kindergarten Stepping Stones: Kindergarten the Bravest Dog Ever - The True Story of Balto Trade Book. rev. ed. 2010. (ENG.). 48p. pap. 9.00 (978-0-7575-8646-0(5)) Kendall Hunt Publishing Co.

Kann, Victoria. Pinkalicious & the Snow Globe. Kann, Victoria, illus. 2015. (Pinkalicious Ser.). (ENG., Illus.). 24p. (J). (gr. -1-3). pap. 4.99 (978-0-06-224588-5(0), HarperFestival) HarperCollins Pubs.

—Pinkalicious & the Snow Globe. 2015. (Pinkalicious Ser.). (J). lib. bdg. 14.75 (978-0-606-37641-9(0)) Turtleback Bks.

Kauflin, Chris. Smiletown's Big Snow Day. 2006. (J). per. 14.95 (978-0-9785132-0-7(7), Smiletown Bks.) Smile-a-Lot, LLP.

Keats, Ezra Jack. The Snowy Day. (ENG.). (J). 2012. 32p. (gr. -1 — 1). bds. 12.99 (978-0-670-01325-8(0)) 50th anniv. ed. 2011. 48p. (gr. k-3). 19.99 (978-0-670-01270-1(X)) Penguin Young Readers Group. (Viking Books for Young Readers).

Kessler, Kathryn. Marvin Discovers Snow. 2010. 36p. (J). pap. 15.77 (978-1-4520-0590-4(7)) AuthorHouse.

Keyes, Diane. Spirit of the Snowpeople. Stevens, Helen, illus. 2008. (ENG.). 32p. (J). (gr. -1-3). 15.95 (978-0-89272-710-0(1)) Down East Bks.

Kim, JeongHo. Oh That Snow! Ok, SeoJeong, illus. 2014. (MySELF Bookshelf Ser.). (ENG.). 32p. (J). (gr. k-2). pap. 11.94 (978-1-60357-697-0(5)) Norwood Hse. Pr.

Kirby, Stan. Captain Awesome Has the Best Snow Day Ever? O'Connor, George, illus. 2016. (Captain Awesome Ser.: 18). (ENG.). 128p. (J). (gr. k-4). 16.99 (978-1-4814-7816-8(8), Little Simon) Little Simon.

Kneen, Maggie. The Christmas Surprise. Kneen, Maggie, illus. 2006. (Illus.). 18p. (J). (gr. k-4). reprint ed. 16.00 (978-0-7567-9837-6(X)) DIANE Publishing Co.

Koehler, Lora. The Little Snowplow. Parker, Jake, illus. 2015. (ENG.). 32p. (J). (gr. -1-2). 15.99 (978-0-7636-7074-0(X)) Candlewick Pr.

Korda, Lerryn. Millions of Snow. Korda, Lerryn, illus. 2010. (Playtime with Little Nye Ser.). (ENG., Illus.). 32p. (J). (— 1). 8.99 (978-0-7636-4651-6(2)) Candlewick Pr.

Kountz, Charity. Jason, Lizzy & the Snowman Village. Klock, Kimberly, illus. 2013. 132p. 24.99 (978-0-9859601-1-7(6)) Texas Pride Publishing.

Krackow, Eric T. Have an Abominably Good Day, 1 vol. 2010. (ENG., Illus.). 64p. (J). 16.99 (978-0-7643-3496-2(4), 9780764334962) Schiffer Publishing, Ltd.

Krackow, Eric T. & Krackow, Krackow. Bill the Snowman, 1 vol. 2009. (ENG., Illus.). 64p. (J). 16.99 (978-0-7643-3219-7(8), 9780764332197) Schiffer Publishing, Ltd.

Kreder Sr., Edward G. & Kreder, Mary Ellen DeLuca. Sparkle's Journey. Vanden Berg, Myra, illus. 2013. 32p. pap. 5.99 (978-0-9913232-0-3(3)) Kreder, Mary Ellen DeLuca.

Labatt, Mary. Sam's Snowy Day. Sarrazin, Marisol, illus. 2005. (Kids Can Read Ser.). (ENG.). 32p. (J). (gr. k-1). pap. 3.95 (978-1-55337-790-0(7)) Kids Can Pr., Ltd. CAN. Dist: Hachette Bk. Group.

LaBree Stute, Lela. The Sunnyset Pugs. 2010. 34p. pap. 19.99 (978-0-557-41751-3(1)) Lulu Pr., Inc.

Lagonegro, Melissa. Frozen - A Tale of Two Sisters. 2013. (Disney Princess Step into Reading Ser.). lib. bdg. 13.55 (978-0-606-32205-8(1), Turtleback) Turtleback Bks.

Lakin, Patricia. Max & Mo Make a Snowman. Floca, Brian, illus. 2007. (Max & Mo Ser.). (ENG.). 32p. (J). (gr. -1-1). pap. 3.99 (978-1-4169-2537-8(6), Simon Spotlight) Simon Spotlight.

Lamerton, Todd. A Tale from Flurryville: The Berg's Big Surprise. 2003. 28p. 7.61 (978-0-7575-0655-0(0)) Kendall Hunt Publishing Co.

Laminack, Lester L. Snow Day!, 1 vol. Gustavson, Adam, illus. 2007. (ENG.). 32p. (J). (gr. k-2). 16.95 (978-1-56145-418-1(4)) Peachtree Pubs.

Laughing Elephant Staff, ed. The Truth about Snow People. 2005. (ENG., Illus.). 32p. (J). (gr. -1-3). 9.95 (978-1-59583-052-4(9), 9781595830524) Laughing Elephant.

Lawler, Janet. Snowzilla, 0 vols. Haley, Amanda, illus. 2012. (ENG.). 32p. (J). (gr. -1-3). 16.99 (978-0-7614-6188-3(4), 9780761461883, Amazon Children's Publishing) Amazon Publishing.

Lê, Christine & Lê, Michel, illus. The Hawai'i Snowman. 2008. (J). 14.95 (978-1-56647-879-3(0)) Mutual Publishing LLC.

Lecis, Alessandro & Shirtliffe, Leanne. I Am Not Little Red Riding Hood. Wolfsgruber, Linda, illus. 2013. (ENG.). 32p. (J). (gr. -1-1). 16.95 (978-1-62087-985-6(9), 620985, Sky Pony Pr.) Skyhorse Publishing Co., Inc.

Lewis, Anthony, illus. Little Snow Explorers. 2007. (Little Explorers Ser.). (ENG.). 14p. (J). (gr. -1-k). bds. (978-1-84643-037-4(2)) Child's Play International Ltd.

Lewis, J. Patrick. The Snowflake Sisters. Desimini, Lisa, illus. 2012. (ENG.). 32p. (J). (gr. -1-3). pap. 16.99 (978-1-4424-6719-4(3), Atheneum Bks. for Young Readers) Simon & Schuster Children's Publishing.

Linkowski, Tami Leli. Lynn Was a Cow Who Could Ski. 2008. 20p. pap. 24.95 (978-1-4241-9626-5(4)) America Star Bks.

Little Bee Books Staff. Snowflake. Graire, Virginie, illus. 2015. (ENG.). 12p. (J). (gr. -1 — 1). 6.99 (978-1-4998-0148-4(3)) Little Bee Books Inc.

London, Jonathan. Froggy Gets Dressed, 1 vol. Remkiewicz, Frank, illus. 2007. (Froggy Ser.). (ENG.). 15p. (J). (gr. -1-k). 9.99 (978-0-14-240870-4(0), Puffin Books) Penguin Young Readers Group.

Louise, Märtha. Why Kings & Queens Don't Wear Crowns. Sevig-Fajardo, Mari Elise, tr. from NOR. Nyhus, Svein, illus. 2005. Orig. Title: Hvorfor de kongelige ikke har krone på Hodet. 32p. (J). 17.95 (978-1-57534-037-1(2), CSC 100) Skandisk, Inc.

Lukkarinen, Ritva. Amy. Vainio, Pirkko, illus. 2009. (ENG.). 30p. (J). (gr. -1-k). 16.95 (978-1-60537-058-3(4)) Cobblestone Publishing Co.

MacLachlan, Patricia. Snowflakes Fall. Kellogg, Steven, illus. 2013. (ENG.). 32p. (J). (gr. -1-2). 17.99 (978-0-385-37693-8(6), Random Hse. Bks. for Young Readers) Random Hse. Children's Bks.

Macnaughton, Tina. One Snowy Rescue. 2015. (ENG.). pap. (978-0-545-92909-7(1)) Scholastic, Inc.

Majestic's Search. 2004. (J). (978-0-615-12544-2(1)) Jadenaila Publishing.

Man-Kong, Mary. Frosty the Snowman Pictureback (Frosty the Snowman) Random House, illus. 2014. (Pictureback(R) Ser.). (ENG.). 24p. (J). (gr. -1-2). 3.99 (978-0-385-38724-8(5), Random Hse. Bks. for Young Readers) Random Hse. Children's Bks.

—Happy, Jolly Fun! (Frosty the Snowman) Golden Books, illus. 2014. (Color Plus Chunky Crayons Ser.). (ENG.). 48p. (J). (gr. -1-2). pap. 3.99 (978-0-385-38723-1(7), Golden Bks.) Random Hse. Children's Bks.

—Snow Much Fun! (Barbie) 2015. (Pictureback(R) Ser.). (ENG., Illus.). 16p. (J). (gr. -1-2). 5.99 (978-0-553-52338-6(4), Random Hse. Bks. for Young Readers) Random Hse. Children's Bks.

Mancusi, Mari. Golden Girl. 2015. (Mix Ser.). (ENG., Illus.). 336p. (J). (gr. 4-8). pap. 7.99 (978-1-4814-3762-2(3), Aladdin) Simon & Schuster Children's Publishing.

Markey, Kevin. Wall Ball. 2011. (Super Sluggers Ser.). (ENG.). 208p. (J). (gr. 3-7). pap. 5.99 (978-0-06-115223-8(4)) HarperCollins Pubs.

Marsoli, Lisa Ann & Bridwell, Norman. The Snow Dog. Haefele, Steve, illus. 2004. (Big Red Reader Ser.). (J). pap. (978-0-439-58559-0(7)) Scholastic, Inc.

Mason, Jane B. & Stephens, Sarah Hines. Snowfall Surprise. 2009. (Candy Apple Ser.: 21). (ENG.). 144p. (J). (gr. 3-7). 5.99 (978-0-545-10067-0(4), Scholastic Paperbacks) Scholastic, Inc.

May, Eleanor. Let's Go, Snow! Pillo, Cary, illus. 2017. (Math Matters (r) Ser.). (ENG.). 32p. (J). (gr. k-3). pap. 5.95 (978-1-57565-807-0(0)) Kane Press, Inc.

May, Eleanor. Let's Go, Snow! Temperature Measurement. Pillo, Cary, illus. 2017. (Math Matters (r) Ser.). (ENG.). 32p. (gr. k-3). 23.99 **(978-1-57565-808-7(9))** Kane Press, Inc.

Mayer, Mercer. Little Critter: Just a Snowman. Mayer, Mercer, illus. 2004. (Little Critter Ser.). (ENG., Illus.). 24p. (J). (gr. -1-2). pap. 3.99 (978-0-06-053947-4(X), HarperFestival) HarperCollins Pubs.

Mazer, Harry. Snow Bound. 144p. (YA). (gr. 7-18). pap. 4.99 (978-0-8072-1367-4(5), Listening Library) Random Hse. Audio Publishing Group.

McBratney, Sam. Let's Play in the Snow. Jeram, Anita, illus. 2012. (Guess How Much I Love You Ser.). (ENG.). 24p. (J). (gr. k — 1). bds. 4.99 (978-0-7636-6121-2(X)) Candlewick Pr.

McCarty, Peter. First Snow. McCarty, Peter, illus. 2015. (ENG., Illus.). 40p. (J). (gr. -1-3). 16.99 (978-0-06-218996-7(4)) HarperCollins Pubs.

McClatchy, Lisa. Eloise & the Snowman, 1 vol. Lyon, Tammie, illus. 2016. (ENG.). 32p. (J). **(978-1-61479-402-8(2))** Spotlight.

McClatchy, Lisa & Thompson, Kay. Eloise & the Snowman. Lyon, Tammie Speer, illus. 2006. (Eloise Ser.). (ENG.). 32p. (J). (gr. -1-1). pap. 3.99 (978-0-689-87451-2(0), Simon Spotlight) Simon Spotlight.

McCully, Emily Arnold. First Snow. McCully, Emily Arnold, illus. 2003. (ENG., Illus.). 32p. (J). (gr. -1-3). 17.99 (978-0-06-623852-4(8)) HarperCollins Pubs.

McDaniels, Preston. A Perfect Snowman. McDaniels, Preston, illus. 2007. (ENG., Illus.). 40p. (J). (gr. -1-3). 18.99 (978-1-4169-1026-8(3), Simon & Schuster Bks. For Young Readers) Simon & Schuster Bks. For Young Readers.

McDonald, Kirsten. Tío Time, 1 vol. Meza, Erika, illus. 2016. (ENG.). 32p. (J). (978-1-62402-143-5(3)) Magic Wagon.

Mcghee, Alison. Making a Friend. Rosenthal, Marc, illus. 2011. (ENG.). 40p. (J). (gr. -1-3). 16.99 (978-1-4169-8998-1(6), Atheneum Bks. for Young Readers) Simon & Schuster Children's Publishing.

McKee, David. Elmer in the Snow. McKee, David, illus. 2004. (Elmer Bks.). (Illus.). 32p. (J). 9.99 (978-0-06-075240-8(8)) HarperCollins Pubs.

McPhail, David. Peter Loves Penguin. 2014. (David Mcphail's Love Ser.). (ENG., Illus.). 22p. (J). (gr. -1 — 1). bds. 8.95 (978-1-4197-1337-8(X), Abrams Appleseed) Abrams, Inc.

Meadows, Daisy. Alyssa the Snow Queen Fairy. 2016. (Rainbow Magic Special Edition Ser.). (ENG.). 176p. (J). (gr. 2-5). pap. 6.99 (978-0-545-85201-2(3), Scholastic Paperbacks) Scholastic, Inc.

Meister, Cari. Snorp on the Slopes, 1 vol. Messner, Dennis, illus. 2010. (Monster Friends Ser.). (ENG.). 32p. (gr. 2-3). pap. 6.25 (978-1-4342-2306-7(X)); lib. bdg. 22.65 (978-1-4342-1873-5(2)) Stone Arch Bks.

Meschenmoser, Sebastian. Waiting for Winter. Meschenmoser, Sebastian, illus. 2015. (ENG., Illus.). 58p. (J). (gr. k-3). 10.99 (978-1-61067-435-5(9)) Kane Miller.

Messner, Kate. Over & under the Snow. Neal, Christopher Silas, illus. 2014. (ENG.). 44p. (J). (gr. k-3). 7.99 (978-1-4521-3646-2(7)) Chronicle Bks. LLC.

Metzger, Steve. The Little Snowflake. Wellington, Monica, illus. 2003. (J). (978-0-439-55656-9(2)) Scholastic, Inc.

Milbourne, Anna. The Snowy Day. Temporin, Elena, illus. 2007. (J). (978-0-439-88988-9(X)) Scholastic, Inc.

Mills, Charles. Storm on Shadow Mountain. 2003. 127p. (J). 7.99 (978-0-8163-1993-0(6)) Pacific Pr. Publishing Assn.

Milway, Alex. Operation Robot Storm: The Mythical 9th Division. Milway, Alex, illus. 2013. (ENG., Illus.). 224p. (J). pap. 5.99 (978-1-61067-074-6(4)) Kane Miller.

Milz, Cynthia A. Waiting for the Last Leaf to Fall. 2008. 20p. per. 24.95 (978-1-4241-8965-6(9)) America Star Bks.

Mitchell, Robin. Snowy & Chinook. Steedman, Judith, illus. 2005. (ENG.). 22p. (J). (gr. -1-3). 15.95 (978-0-9688768-9-3(7)) Simply Read Bks. CAN. Dist: Ingram Publisher Services.

Mitchell, Sherry. Snowy Days. 2012. 20p. pap. 17.99 (978-1-4685-8086-0(8)) AuthorHouse.

Moncure, Jane Belk. The Biggest Snowball of All: A Book about Sizes. Rooney, Ronnie, illus. 2013. (Magic Castle Readers Ser.). (ENG.). 32p. (J). (gr. -1-2). 25.64 (978-1-62323-578-9(2), 206315) Child's World, Inc., The.

Moscovich, Rotem, et al. Curious George Snowy Day. 2007. (Curious George Ser.). (ENG., Illus.). 24p. (J). (gr. -1-3). 3.99 (978-0-618-80043-8(3)) Houghton Mifflin Harcourt Publishing Co.

Moulton, Mark Kimball. A Snowman Named Just Bob. Crouch, Karen Hillard, illus. 2003. (ENG.). 36p. (J). 14.95 (978-0-8249-5860-2(8), 53876801, Ideal Pubns.) Worthy Publishing.

Mozelle, Shirley. Zack's Alligator & the First Snow. Watts, James, illus. 2011. (I Can Read Level 2 Ser.). (ENG.). 32p. (J). (gr. k-3). pap. 3.99 (978-0-06-147372-2(3)) HarperCollins Pubs.

Muldrow, Diane. Frosty the Snowman. Golden Books, illus. 2013. (Big Golden Board Book Ser.). (ENG.). 22p. (J). (-k). bds. 10.99 (978-0-385-37870-3(X), Golden Bks.) Random Hse. Children's Bks.

Nakagawa, Masafumi. Dr. Mouse's Mission. Perry, Mia Lynn, tr. Yamawaki, Yuriko, illus. 2007. (R. I. C. Story Chest Ser.). 27p. (J). (gr. -1-1). 14.95 incl. audio compact disk (978-1-74126-051-9(5)) R.I.C. Pubns. AUS. Dist: SCB Distributors.

Neubecker, Robert. Winter Is for Snow. Neubecker, Robert, illus. 2013. (ENG., Illus.). 32p. (J). (gr. -1-k). 16.99 (978-1-4231-7831-6(9)) Hyperion Pr.

Night, P. J. Ready for a Scare?, 1 vol. 2013. (You're Invited to a Creepover Ser.). (ENG.). 160p. (J). (gr. 3-6). lib. bdg. 24.21 (978-1-61479-062-4(0), Essential Library) ABDO Publishing Co.

—Ready for a Scare? 2011. (You're Invited to a Creepover Ser.: 3). (ENG.). 160p. (J). (gr. 3-7). pap. 6.99 (978-1-4424-2903-1(8), Simon Spotlight) Simon Spotlight.

—Ready for a Scare? 2011. (Creepover Ser.: 3). lib. bdg. 17.20 (978-0-606-23747-5(X), Turtleback) Turtleback Bks.

Nolan, Allia Zobel. God's Winter Wonderland. Mitchell, Melanie, illus. 2006. 10p. (J). bds. 8.99 (978-0-8254-5526-1(X)) Kregel Pubns.

Norman, Kimberly. If It's Snowy & You Know It, Clap Your Paws! Woodruff, Liza, illus. 2013. (ENG.). 26p. (J). (gr. -1). 14.95 (978-1-4549-0384-0(8)) Sterling Publishing Co., Inc.

O'Connell, Matthew J. The Adventures of Rick Cliff: The Almost Great Penguin Race. 2004. 80p. (J). pap. 6.95 (978-1-932560-66-4(1), Llumina Pr.) Aeon Publishing Inc.

O'Connor, Jane. Fancy Nancy - There's No Day Like a Snow Day. 2012. (Fancy Nancy Picture Bks.). (J). lib. bdg. 14.75 (978-0-606-26857-8(X), Turtleback) Turtleback Bks.

—The Snow Globe Family. Schindler, S. D., illus. 2008. (ENG.). 40p. (J). (gr. 1-3). pap. 6.99 (978-0-14-241242-8(2), Puffin Books) Penguin Young Readers Group.

—There's No Day Like a Snow Day. Glasser, Robin Preiss, illus. 2012. (Fancy Nancy Ser.). (ENG.). 24p. (J). (gr. -1-3). pap. 4.99 (978-0-06-208629-7(4), HarperFestival) HarperCollins Pubs.

O'Malley, Kevin. Straight to the Pole. 2004. (Illus.). 32p. (J). (gr. -1-3). 16.85 (978-0-8027-8868-9(8)) Walker & Co.

O'Neill, Jacquie, illus. Figure Skating. 2010. (Sticker Stories Ser.). (ENG.). 16p. (J). (gr. -1-k). pap. 5.99 (978-0-448-45343-9(6), Grosset & Dunlap) Penguin Publishing Group.

O'Reilly, Sean. The Abominable Snow Kid, 1 vol. 2012. (Mighty Mighty Monsters Ser.). (ENG.). 48p. (gr. 2-3). lib. bdg. 23.99 (978-1-4342-3892-4(X)) Stone Arch Bks.

—Abominable Snow Kid. 2013. (Mighty Mighty Monsters Ser.). (ENG., Illus.). 48p. (gr. 2-3). pap. 6.10 (978-1-4342-4227-3(7)) Stone Arch Bks.

Ori, Anthony. Snow Makes a Snowman. 2008. 24p. pap. 24.95 (978-1-60703-308-0(9)) America Star Bks.

O'Ryan, Ray. A Green Christmas! Jack, Colin, illus. 2013. (Galaxy Zack Ser.: 6). (ENG.). 128p. (J). (gr. k-2). 16.99 (978-1-4424-8225-8(7)); pap. 4.99 (978-1-4424-8224-1(9)) Little Simon. (Little Simon).

—A Green Christmas! 2013. (Galaxy Zack Ser.: 6). lib. bdg. 14.75 (978-0-606-35185-0(X)) Turtleback Bks.

Paradis, Susan. Snow Princess. 2005. (ENG., Illus.). 32p. (J). (gr. -1-3). 16.95 (978-1-932425-31-4(4), Lemniscaat) Boyds Mills Pr.

Parenteau, Shirley. Bears in the Snow. Walker, David, illus. 2016. (ENG.). 32p. (J). (-k). 15.99 (978-0-7636-8148-7(2)) Candlewick Pr.

Parisi, Anthony. Baby Harp Seal's Snowy Day. 2010. (ENG.). 16p. (J). (gr. -1). 6.95 (978-1-60727-136-9(2)) Soundprints.

Park, Bomi. First Snow. 2016. (ENG., Illus.). 40p. (J). (gr. -1 — 1). 16.99 (978-1-4521-5472-5(4)) Chronicle Bks. LLC.

Parker, Emma. The Magic Snow Globe. 2010. (Illus.). pap. (978-1-877561-30-6(4)) First Edition Ltd.

Parker, Sydney. Scoop That Snow! Shannon, David et al, illus. 2009. (Jon Scieszka's Trucktown Ser.). (ENG.). 12p. (J). (gr. -1-k). 7.99 (978-1-4169-4182-8(7), Little Simon) Little Simon.

Parker, Vic, ed. The Snow Queen & Other Stories. 2015. (Scary Fairy Tales Ser.). (ENG.). 40p. (J). (gr. 3-4). pap. 14.05 (978-1-4824-3105-6(X)) Stevens, Gareth Publishing LLLP.

Parvensky Barwell, Catherine A. Tommi's First Snowfall, 4 vols. 2006. (Illus.). 32p. (J). (978-0-9774409-1-7(5), TL002) ILT Publishing.

Payne, Liane. The Snowy Day. 2007. (ENG., Illus.). 32p. (J). (978-1-55168-317-1(2)) Fenn, H. B. & Co., Ltd.

Perkins, Lynne Rae. Snow Music. Perkins, Lynne Rae, illus. 2003. (Illus.). 40p. (J). lib. bdg. 16.89 (978-0-06-623958-3(3)) HarperCollins Pubs.

Perkins, Lynne Rae & Perkins, Lynne R. Snow Music. Perkins, Lynne Rae, illus. 2003. (ENG., Illus.). 40p. (J). (gr. -1-3). 16.99 (978-0-06-623956-9(7), Greenwillow Bks.) HarperCollins Pubs.

Perkins, Nicole D. I Wish for Snow. Ogene, Chuma C., illus. 2005. (J). per. 19.95 (978-0-9755566-0-3(6)) Azreal Publishing Co.

Pfister, Marcus. Snow Puppy. 2011. (ENG., Illus.). 32p. (J). (gr. -1-2). 17.95 (978-0-7358-4031-7(8)) North-South Bks., Inc.

Pil, et al. Frosty the Snowman. McGee, Warner, illus. 2011. (J). (978-1-4508-2604-4(0)) Publications International, Ltd.

Pinder, Eric. How to Build a Snow Bear. Graegin, Stephanie, illus. 2016. (ENG.). 40p. (J). 16.99 (978-0-374-30020-3(8), 9780374300203, Farrar, Straus & Giroux (BYR)) Farrar, Straus & Giroux.

Pingk, Rubin. Samurai Santa: A Very Ninja Christmas. Pingk, Rubin, illus. 2015. (ENG., Illus.). 40p. (J). (gr. -1-3). 17.99 (978-1-4814-3057-9(2), Simon & Schuster Bks. For Young Readers) Simon & Schuster Bks. For Young Readers.

Pitt, Marilyn & Sanchez, Lucia M. La Nevada: Snow Dog. Bianchi, John, illus. 2011. (poder de 50 - Libros papas fritas Ser.). (SPA.). 12p. pap. 33.92 (978-1-61541-439-0(8)) American Reading Co.

Plourde, Lynn. The Blizzard Wizard. Aardema, John, illus. 2010. (ENG.). 32p. (J). (gr. -1-3). 16.95 (978-0-89272-789-6(6)) Down East Bks.

Potvin, James E. The Adventures of Forest the Ferret: Forest's First Snowfall & Forest's Cottage. 2007. 32p. per. 13.95 (978-1-4327-0556-5(3)) Outskirts Pr., Inc.

Publications International Ltd. Staff, ed. Disney(r) Frozen Sing-Along Songs! Features Do You Want to Build a Snowman? 2014. 12p. (J). bds. (978-1-4508-9139-4(X), 145089139X) Publications International, Ltd.

Pugiano-Martin, Carol & Bridwell, Norman. The Snow Champion. Haefele, Steve, illus. 2006. (Big Red Reader Ser.). (J). (978-0-439-80845-3(6)) Scholastic, Inc.

Quin-Harkin, Janet. Forever Friday. 2014. (Tgif Ser.: 4). (ENG., Illus.). 128p. (J). (gr. 3-7). pap. 13.99 (978-1-4814-2882-8(9), Simon & Schuster/Paula Wiseman Bks.) Simon & Schuster/Paula Wiseman Bks.

Ragland, Jean. I Want to Be A Snowman. 2011. 24p. (gr. 1-2). 11.95 (978-1-4567-1140-5(7)) AuthorHouse.

Random House. Here Comes Frosty! (Frosty the Snowman) Random House, illus. 2015. (Board Book Ser.). (ENG., Illus.). 24p. (J). (-k). bds. 4.99 (978-0-553-52124-5(1), Random Hse. Bks. for Young Readers) Random Hse. Children's Bks.

Random House Disney Staff. Frozen Story Collection (Disney Frozen) Random House Disney Staff, illus. 2015. (Step into Reading Ser.). (ENG., Illus.). 160p. (J). (gr. -1-2). pap. 7.99 (978-0-7364-3435-5(6), RH/Disney) Random Hse. Children's Bks.

Ravera, Giuseppe. Snowflake. 2014. (ENG., Illus.). 10p. (J). (gr. -1 — 1). bds. 6.99 (978-0-7641-6719-5(7)) Barron's Educational Series, Inc.

Reasoner, Charles. Let It Snow. Jones, Anna, illus. 2013. (Charles Reasoner Holiday Bks.). (ENG.). 10p. (gr. -1 — 1). bds. 9.99 (978-1-4048-8147-1(6)) Picture Window Bks.

RH Disney Staff. Sparkle Magic! (Disney Frozen) RH Disney Staff, illus. 2015. (Pictureback Ser.). (ENG., Illus.). 16p. (J). (gr. -1-2). 5.99 (978-0-7364-3366-2(X), RH/Disney) Random Hse. Children's Bks.

RH Disney Staff & Julius, Jessica. Anna's Birthday Surprise. RH Disney Staff, illus. 2015. (Pictureback(R) Ser.). (ENG., Illus.). 24p. (J). (gr. -1-2). 4.99 (978-0-7364-3439-3(9), RH/Disney) Random Hse. Children's Bks.

Richards, Stephen J. The Twins First Snow. 2010. 28p. pap. 13.99 (978-1-4490-8853-8(8)) AuthorHouse.

Robbins, James L. Aristotle & Burgoo & the Ditto-Flake-Flu. 2012. 44p. pap. 21.99 (978-1-4771-3551-8(0)) Xlibris Corp.

Robinson, Kathleen Marie. Snowflake Sandwiches. 2007. 15p. pap. 24.95 (978-1-4241-8620-4(X)) America Star Bks.

Rocco, John. Blizzard. Rocco, John, illus. 2014. (ENG., Illus.). 40p. (J). (gr. -1-k). 17.99 (978-1-4231-7865-1(3)) Disney Pr.

Rockhill, Dennis. Polar Slumber. Rockhill, Dennis, illus. 2007. (ENG., Illus.). 32p. (J). (gr. -1-3). 16.95 (978-0-9741992-8-3(1), Raven Tree Pr.,Csi) Continental Sales, Inc.

Rockwell, Anne. The First Snowfall. Rockwell, Lizzy, illus. 2016. (ENG.). 24p. (J). (gr. -1-3). 6.99 (978-1-4814-1136-3(5), Aladdin) Simon & Schuster Children's Publishing.

Rohmann, Eric. A Kitten Tale. 2012. (ENG.). 32p. (J). (gr. -1-2). pap. 7.99 (978-0-307-97774-8(9), Dragonfly Bks.) Random Hse. Children's Bks.

Rollins, Walter & Nelson, Steve. Frosty the Snowman. Williams, Sam, illus. 2013. (ENG.). 16p. (J). (gr. -1-k). bds. 9.99 (978-0-545-45005-8(5), Cartwheel Bks.) Scholastic, Inc.

Roode, Daniel. Little Bea & the Snowy Day. Roode, Daniel, illus. 2011. (ENG., Illus.). 32p. (J). (gr. -1-k). 12.99 (978-0-06-199395-4(6), Greenwillow Bks.) HarperCollins Pubs.

Root, Phyllis. Snowy Sunday. Craig, Helen, illus. 2015. (ENG.). 24p. (J). (-k). 14.99 (978-0-7636-3627-2(4)) Candlewick Pr.

Ruelle, Karen Gray. The Crunchy, Munchy Christmas Tree. Ruelle, Karen Gray, illus. 2003. (Holiday House Readers Ser.). (ENG., Illus.). 32p. (J). (gr. k-3). tchr. ed. 14.95 (978-0-8234-1787-2(5)) Holiday Hse., Inc.

—Crunchy, Munchy Christmas Tree. 2003. (ENG., Illus.). 32p. (J). (gr. k-3). pap. 4.95 (978-0-8234-1799-5(9)) Holiday Hse., Inc.

—Snow Valentines. 2003. (Holiday House Reader Level 2 Ser.). (ENG., Illus.). 48p. (J). (gr. k-3). 4.95 (978-0-8234-1782-7(4)) Holiday Hse., Inc.

Rylant, Cynthia. Annie & Snowball & the Wedding Day. 2015. (Annie & Snowball Ready-To-Read Ser.). lib. bdg. 13.55 (978-0-606-36310-5(6)) Turtleback Bks.

—Snow. Stringer, Lauren, illus. 2008. (ENG.). 40p. (J). (gr. -1-3). 17.99 (978-0-15-205303-1(4)) Houghton Mifflin Harcourt Publishing Co.

Sabuda, Robert. Winter in White: A Mini Pop-Up Treat. Sabuda, Robert, illus. 2007. (ENG., Illus.). 18p. (J). (gr. -1-3). 17.99 (978-0-689-85365-4(3), Little Simon) Little Simon.

Saddleback Educational Publishing Staff, ed. Blizzard, 1 vol. unabr. ed. 2011. (Heights Ser.). (ENG.). 49p. (gr. 5-8). 7.95 (978-1-61651-623-9(2)) Saddleback Educational Publishing, Inc.

Sagar, Marie. Magical Snowman. 2009. 36p. pap. 16.99 (978-1-4490-2194-8(8)) AuthorHouse.

Sakai, Komako. The Snow Day. 2009. (J). pap. (978-0-545-01322-2(4), Levine, Arthur A. Bks.) Scholastic, Inc.

Salzano, Tammi. One Snowy Day. Wood, Hannah, illus. 2010. (ENG.). 24p. (J). (gr. -1-k). bds. 8.95 (978-1-58925-857-0(6)) Tiger Tales.

Sander, Sonia, adapted by. Dragon's Snowy Day. 2005. (Scholastic Reader Ser.). (Illus.). 32p. (J). pap. (978-0-439-80163-8(X)) Scholastic, Inc.

Sateren, Shelley Swanson. Max & Zoe at School, 1 vol. Sullivan, Mary, illus. 2013. (Max & Zoe Ser.). (ENG.). 32p. (gr. k-2). pap. 5.19 (978-1-4048-8059-7(3), Max & Zoe) Picture Window Bks.

Sauers, Joey. How to Make a Snowman. 2012. 24p. pap. 15.99 (978-1-4691-7780-9(3)) Xlibris Corp.

Saxon, Victoria. Anna & Elsa's Secret Playtime (Disney Frozen) RH Disney, illus. 2016. (Big Golden Book Ser.). (ENG.). 32p. (J). (-k). 9.99 (978-0-7364-3493-5(3), Golden/Disney) Random Hse. Children's Bks.

Schaffer, Jacqueline. Porsha & the Great Snowmen Adventure. 2009. 36p. pap. 15.99 (978-1-4490-5421-2(8)) AuthorHouse.

Scheffler, Axel & Nosy Crow Staff. Pip & Posy: the Snowy Day. Scheffler, Axel, illus. 2013. (Pip & Posy Ser.). (ENG., Illus.). 32p. (J). (-k). 12.99 (978-0-7636-6607-1(6), Nosy Crow) Candlewick Pr.

Schertle, Alice. All You Need for a Snowman. Lavallee, Barbara, illus. 2007. (ENG.). 32p. (J). (gr. -1-3). pap. 6.99 (978-0-15-206115-9(0)) Houghton Mifflin Harcourt Publishing Co.

Scholastic, Inc. Staff & Hudson, Cheryl Willis. What Do You Know? Snow! Walker, Sylvia, illus. 2004. (Just for You Ser.). (ENG.). 32p. pap. 3.99 (978-0-439-56851-7(X), Teaching Resources) Scholastic, Inc.

Scieszka, Jon. Snow Trucking! Gordon, David et al, illus. 2008. (Jon Scieszka's Trucktown Ser.). (ENG.). 24p. (J). (gr. -1-1). pap. 3.99 (978-1-4169-4140-8(1), Simon Spotlight) Simon Spotlight.

Scotton, Rob. Blow, Snow, Blow. 2013. (Splat the Cat: I Can Read Ser.). (J). lib. bdg. 13.55 (978-0-606-32160-0(8), Turtleback) Turtleback Bks.

Scraper, Katherine. Max's Job. 2006. (Early Explorers Ser.). (J). pap. (978-1-4108-6035-4(3)) Benchmark Education Co.

Shaw, Gina. Waiting for Snow. Barton, Patrice, illus. 2010. 48p. (J). pap. (978-0-545-24385-8(8)) Scholastic, Inc.

Shea, Christine. Las Aventuras de Max, el Camión Volteador: El Mejor Día de Nieve! = the Adventures of Max the Dump Truck: The Greatest Snow Day Ever! Chase, Michelle B. & Chase, Tanor R., illus. 2007. (ENG & SPA.). (J). (978-1-933002-01-9(8)) PublishingWorks.

Shopping for Snowflakes. (J). pap. 13.75 (978-0-8136-3403-6(2)) Modern Curriculum Pr.

Shulevitz, Uri. Snow. 2004. (J). (gr. k-3). spiral bd. (978-0-616-01781-4(2)) Canadian National Institute for the Blind/Institut National Canadien pour les Aveugles.

—Snow, 1 vol. Shulevitz, Uri, illus. 2012. (ENG., Illus.). 34p. (J). (gr. -1-2). bds. 7.99 (978-0-374-37093-0(1), 9780374370930, Farrar, Straus & Giroux (BYR)) Farrar, Straus & Giroux.

—Snow. Shulevitz, Uri, illus. 2004. (ENG., Illus.). 32p. (J). (gr. -1-2). reprint ed. pap. 7.99 (978-0-374-46862-0(1), 9780374468620) Square Fish.

—Snow Storytime Set. Shulevitz, Uri, illus. unabr. ed. 2013. (ENG., Illus.). (J). 12.99 *(978-1-4272-4370-6(0)*, 9781427243706) Macmillan Audio.

Shulimson, Sarene. Lights Out Shabbat. Ebbeler, Jeff, illus. 2012. (Shabbat Ser.). (ENG.). 32p. (J). (gr. -1-2). pap. 7.95 *(978-0-7613-7565-4(1)*, Kar-Ben Publishing) Lerner Publishing Group.

—Lights Out Shabbat. Ebbeler, Jeffrey, illus. 2012. (Shabbat Ser.). (ENG.). 32p. (J). (gr. -1-2). lib. bdg. 17.95 *(978-0-7613-7564-7(3)*, Kar-Ben Publishing) Lerner Publishing Group.

Sidman, Joyce. Before Morning. Krommes, Beth, illus. 2016. (ENG.). 48p. (J). (gr. -1-3). 17.99 *(978-0-547-97917-5(7)*, HMH Books For Young Readers) Houghton Mifflin Harcourt Publishing Co.

Simon, Francesca. Horrid Henry & the Abominable Snowman. Ross, Tony, illus. 2010. (Horrid Henry Ser.: 0). (ENG.). 112p. (J). (gr. 2-5). pap. 6.99 *(978-1-4022-4256-4(5)*, 9781402242564, Sourcebooks Jabberwocky) Sourcebooks, Inc.

—Horrid Henry & the Abominable Snowman, 1 vol. Ross, Tony, illus. 2012. (Horrid Henry Ser.). (ENG.). 112p. (J). (gr. 2-5). lib. bdg. 24.21 *(978-1-59961-186-0(4))* Spotlight.

Simon, Jenne. Snow Day!, Level 2. Hill, Prescott, illus. 2013. (Lalaloopsy Ser.). (ENG.). 32p. (J). (gr. -1-3). pap. 3.99 *(978-0-545-58123-3(0))* Scholastic, Inc.

Slater, Jean M. Wonderful Snow! Slater, Jean M., illus. 2003. (Illus.). 9p. (J). bds. 16.00 *(978-0-9743149-1-4(9))* Slater Software, Inc.

Sloat, Teri. Pablo in the Snow. Bonnet, Rosalinde, illus. 2017. (ENG.). 40p. (J). 16.99 *(978-1-62779-412-1(3)*, 9781627794121, Holt, Henry & Co. Bks. For Young Readers) Holt, Henry & Co.

Slusser, Janet S. Smokey & the Big Snow. 2003. (Illus.). 32p. (J). per. 15.95 *(978-0-9745171-0-0(0))* RiverCreek Bks., Inc.

Snow X-mas. 2004. (J). per. *(978-1-57657-384-6(2))* Paradise Pr., Inc.

Snyder, Donna. Rose & Rosey. 2008. 16p. pap. 24.95 *(978-1-60441-618-3(1))* America Star Bks.

Solomon, Harry. The Day Silver Snowed. Solomon, Harry, illus. 2009. (Illus.). 112p. 80.00 *(978-0-9630376-1-9(7))* Figure 8 Pr.

Stead, Philip C. Samson in the Snow. 2016. (ENG., Illus.). 40p. (J). 17.99 *(978-1-62672-182-1(3)*, 9781626721821) Roaring Brook Pr.

Steers, Billy. Tractor Mac Saves Christmas. 2015. (Tractor Mac Ser.). (ENG., Illus.). 32p. (J). (gr. -1-2). 8.99 *(978-0-374-30112-5(3)*, 9780374301125, Farrar, Straus & Giroux (BYR)) Farrar, Straus & Giroux.

Steig, William. Brave Irene. Steig, William, illus. 2011. (ENG., Illus.). 32p. (J). (gr. -1-3). pap. 7.99 *(978-0-312-56422-3(8)*, 9780312564223) Square Fish.

Stoeke, Janet Morgan. Snow Hens. 2016. (Loopy Coop Hens Ser.). (ENG., Illus.). 32p. (J). (gr. 1-2). pap. 3.99 *(978-0-448-48843-1(4)*, Penguin Young Readers) Penguin Young Readers Group.

Stoick, Jean & Sams, Carl R., II, photos by. First Snow in the Woods. 2007. (ENG., Illus.). 49p. (J). (gr. -1-3). 19.95 *(978-0-9770108-6-8(4))* Sams, II, Carl R. Photography, Inc.

Stoick, Jean & Sams II, Carl R., photos by. Stranger in the Woods: Snowflake Edition. 2010. (ENG., Illus.). 48p. 21.95 *(978-0-9827625-0-9(X))* Sams, II, Carl R. Photography, Inc.

Stones, Yvonne. Olivia's Magical Moment. 2010. 36p. pap. 16.99 *(978-1-4490-8045-7(6))* AuthorHouse.

Suen, Anastasia. Snow Games: A Robot & Rico Story. Laughead, Mike, illus. 2010. (Robot & Rico Ser.). (ENG.). 32p. (gr. 1-2). pap. 6.25 *(978-1-4342-2302-9(7))*; lib. bdg. 22.65 *(978-1-4342-1869-8(4))* Stone Arch Bks.

Sullivan, Kate. On Linden Square. Sullivan, Kate, illus. 2013. (ENG., Illus.). 40p. 15.99 *(978-1-58536-832-7(6))* Sleeping Bear Pr.

Taylor, Mark. Henry the Explorer. Booth, Graham, illus. 2011. (J). 18.95 *(978-1-930900-48-6(1))* Purple Hse. Pr.

TBD, Disney Frozen - Do You Want to Build an Olaf? Storybook & Snowman Kit. 2015. (ENG.). 24p. (J). (gr. -1-3). 24.99 *(978-0-7944-3502-8(5))* Studio Fun International.

Thaler, Mike. The Snow Day from the Black Lagoon. Lee, Jared, illus. 2008. 63p. (J). pap. *(978-0-545-01766-4(1))* Scholastic, Inc.

The Series, Superdaddies. Superdaddies; the Series, Presents: Daddy, I Broke My Snowball! 2009. 32p. pap. 14.49 *(978-1-4490-2632-5(X))* AuthorHouse.

Thomas, Peggy. Snow Dance, 1 vol. Facklam, Paul, illus. 2008. (ENG.). 32p. (J). (gr. 1-3). 16.99 *(978-1-58980-478-4(3))* Pelican Publishing Co., Inc.

Thompson, Carol. Snow! 2014. (Whatever the Weather Ser.). (ENG., Illus.). 12p. (J). (gr. k-k). bds. *(978-1-84643-681-9(8))* Child's Play International Ltd.

Thompson, Lauren. Mouse's First Snow. Erdogan, Buket, illus. 2011. (Classic Board Bks.). (ENG.). 34p. (J). (gr. -1 — 1). bds. 7.99 *(978-1-4424-2651-1(9)*, Little Simon) Little Simon.

—Mouse's First Snow. Erdogan, Buket, illus. 2005. (ENG.). 32p. (J). (gr. -1-3). 15.99 *(978-0-689-85836-9(1)*, Simon & Schuster Bks. For Young Readers) Simon & Schuster Bks. For Young Readers.

Thomson, Sarah L. Imagine a Night. Gonsalves, Rob, illus. 2003. (Imagine A... Ser.). (ENG.). 40p. (J). (gr. -1-3). 19.99 *(978-0-689-85218-3(5)*, Atheneum Bks. for Young Readers) Simon & Schuster Children's Publishing.

Tinyrannosaurus & the Bigfootosaurus. 2015. (ENG., Illus.). 24p. (J). (gr. -1-3). 7.99 *(978-1-85733-734-1(4))* Lerner Publishing Group.

Tyrell, Melissa. Hurray for Snow! Patrick, Tom, illus. enl. ed. 2005. (ENG.). 10p. (J). (gr. -1-3). 4.95 *(978-1-58117-118-1(8)*, Intervisual/Piggy Toes) Bendon, Inc.

Tyrrell, Colm. Snow Day. 2015. (Illus.). 32p. (J). *(978-1-5182-0102-8(4))* Disney Publishing Worldwide.

Uhlberg, Myron. Flying over Brooklyn, 1 vol. Fitzgerald, Gerald, illus. 2003. (ENG.). 32p. (J). (gr. k-3). pap. 7.95 *(978-1-56145-294-1(7))* Peachtree Pubs.

Usher, Sam. Snow. Usher, Sam, illus. 2015. (ENG., Illus.). 40p. (J). (gr. -1-2). 16.99 *(978-0-7636-7958-3(5)*, Templar) Candlewick Pr.

van Genechten, Guido. Little Snowman Stan. 2011. (ENG., Illus.). 32p. (J). (gr. -1-k). 16.95 *(978-1-60537-108-5(4))* Cobblestone Publishing Co.

Villanueva, Pedro. Chronicle of a New Kid. 2017. (Text Connections Guided Close Reading Ser.). (J). (gr. 1). *(978-1-4900-1825-6(5))* Benchmark Education Co.

von Olfers, Sibylle. Story of the Snow Children, 1 vol. 2005. (ENG., Illus.). 24p. (J). *(978-0-86315-499-7(9))* Floris Bks.

Wahman, Joe. Snowboy 1, 2, 3. Wahman, Wendy, illus. 2012. (ENG.). 32p. (J). (gr. -1-1). 14.99 *(978-0-8050-8732-1(X)*, 9780805087321, Holt, Henry & Co. Bks. For Young Readers) Holt, Henry & Co.

Wallace, Sharolyn. The Adventures of Bruce, Ben & Gerry: The Surprise. 2013. 24p. pap. 17.99 *(978-1-4772-9489-5(9))* AuthorHouse.

Ward, Lindsay. When Blue Met Egg. 2012. (ENG.). 32p. (J). (gr. -1-k). 16.99 *(978-0-8037-3718-1(1)*, Dial Bks) Penguin Young Readers Group.

Watt, Fiona. That's Not My Snowman. Wells, Rachel, illus. 2006. (Usborne Touchy-Feely Board Bks.). 10p. (J). (gr. -1). bds. 9.99 *(978-0-7945-1414-3(6)*, Usborne) EDC Publishing.

—That's Not My Snowman. rev. ed. 2011. (Touchy-Feely Board Bks). 10p. (J). ring bd. 8.99 *(978-0-7945-3120-1(2)*, Usborne) EDC Publishing.

Weinshall Liberman, Judith. Ice Cream Snow. 2012. (Illus.). 34p. 18.99 *(978-1-4575-1578-1(4))* Dog Ear Publishing, LLC.

Wells, Erica. Diamonds in the Snow: A Story about the Magic of Snow. 2010. 24p. pap. 16.99 *(978-1-4490-4969-0(9))* AuthorHouse.

Weston Woods Staff, creator. The Snowy Day. 2004. 29.95 *(978-1-55592-853-7(6))* Weston Woods Studios, Inc.

Wetterer, Margaret K. & Wetterer, Charles M. The Snow Walker. Young, Mary O'Keefe, illus. unabr. ed. (Historical Fiction Ser.). (J). (gr. 1-6). 24.95 incl. audio *(978-0-87499-394-3(6))* Live Oak Media.

White, S.D. Sing along with the Santa Claus That Never Saw a Child. 2008. 20p. pap. 12.89 *(978-1-4389-0305-7(7))* AuthorHouse.

Williams, Rozanne Lanczak. Tess Builds a Snowman. Maio, Barbara & Faulkner, Stacey, eds. Harris, Jenny B., illus. 2006. (J). per. 6.99 *(978-1-59198-337-8(1))* Creative Teaching Pr., Inc.

Williams, Teresa Ann. Friends of Wildwood, 1 vol. 2009. 48p. pap. 16.95 *(978-1-4489-9419-9(5))* America Star Bks.

Wilson, CeCe. Snow Much Fun! 2015. (Rosen REAL Readers: STEM & STEAM Collection). (ENG.). 8p. pap. 5.46 *(978-1-4994-9551-5(X)*, Rosen Classroom) Rosen Publishing Group, Inc., The.

Wing, Natasha. The Night Before the Snow Day. Wummer, Amy, illus. 2016. (Night Before Ser.). (ENG.). 32p. (J). (-k). pap. 4.99 *(978-0-399-53942-8(5)*, Grosset & Dunlap) Penguin Young Readers Group.

—The Night Before the Snow Day. Wummer, Amy, illus. 2016. (Night Before Ser.). (ENG.). 32p. (J). (gr. -1-1). 14.75 *(978-0-606-39315-7(3))* Turtleback Bks.

Wood, David. The Toy Cupboard. Fowler, Richard, illus. 2005. 14p. (J). (gr. -1-3). 14.95 *(978-1-58117-103-7(X)*, Intervisual/Piggy Toes) Bendon, Inc.

Wood, Francis. The SnowPeople. Larsen, Dan, illus. 2003. 96p. (YA). per. 14.95 *(978-0-9746372-0-4(3))* Tip-Of-The-Moon Publishing Co.

Wozniak, Paul. Stranded in a Snowstorm! Webber, Mike, illus. 2014. (ENG.). 82p. pap. 11.95 *(978-1-63047-173-6(9))* Morgan James Publishing.

Xiong, Kim, illus. Paper Horse. 2008. (ENG & CHI.). 37p. (J). 18.95 *(978-1-60603-003-5(5))* Better Chinese LLC.

Yee, Wong Herbert. Mouse & Mole, a Winter Wonderland. Yee, Wong Herbert, illus. 2011. (Mouse & Mole Story Ser.). (ENG., Illus.). 48p. (J). (gr. 1-4). pap. 3.99 *(978-0-547-57697-8(8))* Houghton Mifflin Harcourt Publishing Co.

—Tracks in the Snow. Yee, Wong Herbert, illus. 2007. (ENG., Illus.). 32p. (J). (gr. -1-1). per. 7.99 *(978-0-312-37134-0(9)*, 9780312371340) Square Fish.

Yelchin, Eugene & Kuryla, Mary. Heart of a Snowman. Yelchin, Eugene & Kuryla, Mary, illus. 2009. (ENG., Illus.). 40p. (J). (gr. -1-3). 16.99 *(978-0-06-125926-5(8))* HarperCollins Pubs.

Yerxa, Leo. Last Leaf First Snowflake to Fall. Yerxa, Leo, illus. (Illus.). (J). 16.95 *(978-0-88899-183-6(5))* Groundwood Bks. CAN. Dist: Publishers Group West (PGW).

Yildirim, Rabia. Wind, Rain & Snow. 2013. (ENG., Illus.). 53p. (J). (gr. k-1). pap. 9.95 *(978-1-59784-284-6(2))* Tughra Bks.

Young, Francis Kerr. The Paperweight. Steele, Andrew & Clement, Devyn, illus. 2008. 39p. pap. 24.95 *(978-1-60610-034-9(3))* America Star Bks.

Young, Ned. Zoomer's Summer Snowstorm. Young, Ned, illus. 2011. (ENG., Illus.). 32p. (J). (gr. -1-2). 16.99 *(978-0-06-170092-7(4))* HarperCollins Pubs.

Ziegler, Argentina Palacios, tr. Dora y la Princesa de la Nieve (Dora Saves the Snow Princess) Aikins, Dave, illus. 2008. (Dora la Exploradora Ser.). (SPA.). 24p. (J). (gr. -1-2). pap. 3.99 *(978-1-4169-5870-3(3)*, Libros Para Ninos) Libros Para Ninos.

SNOWBOARDING

Adamson, Thomas K. Big Air Snowboarding. 2016. (Extreme Sports Ser.). (ENG., Illus.). 24p. (J). (gr. 3-7). lib. bdg. 25.95 *(978-1-62617-351-4(6)*, Epic Bks.) Bellwether Media.

—Snowboarding Slopestyle. 2016. (Extreme Sports Ser.). (ENG., Illus.). 24p. (J). (gr. 3-7). lib. bdg. 25.95 *(978-1-62617-353-8(2)*, Epic Bks.) Bellwether Media.

Bailer, Darice. Snowboard Cross. 2013. (Extreme Winter Sports Zone Ser.). (ENG., Illus.). 32p. (gr. 4-8). lib. bdg. 26.60 *(978-1-4677-0755-8(4)*, Lerner Pubns.) Lerner Publishing Group.

—Snowboard Superpipe. 2013. (Extreme Winter Sports Zone Ser.). (ENG., Illus.). 32p. (gr. 4-8). lib. bdg. 26.60 *(978-1-4677-0754-1(6)*, Lerner Pubns.) Lerner Publishing Group.

Barr, Matt & Moran, Chris. Snowboarding. 2003. (Extreme Sports Ser.). (ENG., Illus.). 32p. (gr. 3-6). lib. bdg. 22.60 *(978-0-8225-1242-4(4))* Lerner Publishing Group.

Benjamin, Daniel. Extreme Snowboarding. 2011. (Sports on the Edge Ser.). 48p. (gr. 6). 29.93 *(978-1-60870-229-9(4))* Marshall Cavendish GBR. Dist: Marshall Cavendish Corp.

Brouwer, Sigmund. Snowboarding . . . to the Extreme: Rippin' 2004. (Illus.). 60p. (YA). pap. 3.99 *(978-1-55305-011-7(8))* Cygnet Publishing Group, Inc./Coolreading.com CAN. Dist: Orca Bk. Pubs. USA.

Carr, Aaron. Snowboard. 2013. (ENG & SPA.). (J). *(978-1-62127-635-7(X))* Weigl Pubs., Inc.

—Snowboarding. (Illus.). (J). 2013. 32p. *(978-1-61913-513-0(2))* 2012. (ENG.). 24p. pap. 12.95 *(978-1-61913-519-2(1)*, AV2 by Weigl) Weigl Pubs., Inc.

Champion, Neil. Wild Snow: Skiing & Snowboarding. 2013. (Illus.). 32p. (J). lib. bdg. *(978-1-59920-808-4(3))* Black Rabbit Bks.

Craats, Rennay. Snowboarding. 2007. (Outdoor Adventures (Weigl Hardcover) Ser.). (Illus.). 24p. (J). (gr. 4-7). lib. bdg. 24.45 *(978-1-59036-687-5(5))*; per. 8.95 *(978-1-59036-688-2(3))* Weigl Pubs., Inc.

Crabtree Editors & Winters, Jaime. Carve It Snowboarding. 2012. (Sports Starters Ser.). (ENG., Illus.). 32p. (J). (gr. 1-4). lib. bdg. *(978-0-7787-3148-1(0))* Crabtree Publishing Co.

Doeden, Matt. Shaun White. (Amazing Athletes Ser.). 32p. (gr. 2-5). 2006. (Illus.). (J). lib. bdg. 23.93 *(978-0-8225-6840-7(3)*, Lerner Pubns.) 2012. (ENG.). pap. 7.95 *(978-0-7613-9067-1(7))* Lerner Publishing Group.

—Shaun White (Revised Edition) 2012. (Amazing Athletes Ser.). 32p. (J). (gr. 2-5). pap. 45.32 *(978-0-7613-9139-5(8))* Lerner Publishing Group.

Endres, Hollie. Snowboarding. 2007. (Action Sports Ser.). (ENG., Illus.). 24p. (J). (gr. 3-7). lib. bdg. 25.95 *(978-1-60014-128-7(5))* Bellwether Media.

Fandel, Jennifer. Snowboarding. 2007. (Active Sports Ser.). (Illus.). 24p. (J). (gr. -1-3). lib. bdg. 24.25 *(978-1-58341-470-5(3)*, Creative Education) Creative Co., The.

Figorito, Marcus. Friction & Gravity: Snowboarding Science. 2009. (Real Life Readers Ser.). (ENG., Illus.). 32p. (J). (gr. 5-6). pap. 10.00 *(978-1-4358-0185-1(7))*; 32p. (gr. 5-5). 47.90 *(978-1-60853-053-3(1))*; (J). (gr. 4-6). lib. bdg. 25.25 *(978-1-4358-2995-4(6))* Rosen Publishing Group, Inc., The. (PowerKids Pr.).

Fitzpatrick, Jim. Snowboarding. 2008. (21st Century Skills Innovation Library: Innovation in Sports Ser.). (ENG., Illus.). 32p. (gr. 4-8). lib. bdg. 28.50 *(978-1-60279-260-9(7)*, 200035); lib. bdg. 28.50 *(978-1-60279-018-6(3)*, 200202) Cherry Lake Publishing.

Gustaitis, Joseph. Snowboard. 2009. (Winter Olympic Sports Ser.). (ENG., Illus.). 32p. (J). (gr. 3-6). lib. bdg. *(978-0-7787-4026-1(9))* Crabtree Publishing Co.

Hamilton, John. Snowboarding. 2014. (Action Sports Ser.). (ENG.). 32p. (gr. 8-15). lib. bdg. 27.07 *(978-1-62403-444-2(6)*, A&D Xtreme) ABDO Publishing Co.

Hantula, Richard. Science at Work in Snowboarding. 2011. (Benchmark Rockets: Sports Science Ser.). (Illus.). 32p. (J). (gr. 4). 28.50 *(978-1-60870-590-0(0))* Marshall Cavendish Corp.

Herman, Gail. Snowboarding Similes & Metaphors. 2009. (Grammar All-Stars: Writing Tools Ser.). 32p. (J). (gr. 2-5). (ENG.). pap. 10.50 *(978-1-4339-2138-4(3))*; lib. bdg. 26.00 *(978-1-4339-1945-9(1))* Stevens, Gareth Publishing LLLP. (Gareth Stevens Learning Library).

Hile, Lori. The Science of Snowboarding, 1 vol. 2014. (Science of Speed Ser.). (ENG.). 48p. (gr. 3-4). lib. bdg. 31.99 *(978-1-4765-3911-9(1))* Capstone Press of Coughlan Cos.

Howell, Brian. Great Moments in Olympic Snowboarding, 1 vol. 2014. (Great Moments in Olympic Sports Ser.). (ENG.). 64p. (gr. 10-14). lib. bdg. 32.79 *(978-1-62403-398-8(9)*, SportsZone) ABDO Publishing Co.

Iguchi, Bryan. Jovenes Aficionados al Snowboard (The Young Snowboarder) (SPA.). 38p. (YA). (gr. 2-18). 18.36 *(978-84-272-4970-7(5))* Molino, Editorial ESP. Dist: Lectorum Pubns., Inc.

Kalman, Bobbie & MacAulay, Kelley. Extreme Snowboarding. 2003. (Extreme Sports - No Limits Ser.). (ENG., Illus.). 32p. (J). pap. *(978-0-7787-1718-8(6))*; lib. bdg. *(978-0-7787-1672-3(4))* Crabtree Publishing Co.

Kennedy, Mike. Shaun White. 2009. (Today's Superstars Ser.). (ENG.). 48p. (J). (gr. 5-8). pap. 14.05 *(978-1-4339-2161-2(8))*; lib. bdg. 31.95 *(978-1-4339-1968-8(0))* Stevens, Gareth Publishing LLLP.

Kenney, Karen L. Skiing & Snowboarding. 2010. (Girls Play to Win Ser.). 64p. (J). (gr. 3-6). lib. bdg. 27.93 *(978-1-59953-391-9(X))* Norwood Hse. Pr.

Laughlin, Kara L. Snowboarding. 2016. (Beginning Sports Ser.). (ENG.). 24p. (J). (gr. k-3). 27.07 *(978-1-5038-0779-2(7)*, 210607) Child's World, Inc., The.

Loh-Hagan, Virginia. Extreme Snowboarding. 2015. (Illus.). 32p. (J). *(978-1-63470-018-4(X))* Cherry Lake Publishing.

Lurie, Jon. Play-by-Play Snowboarding. 2004. (Play-by-Play Ser.). (Illus.). 80p. (J). (gr. 4-8). lib. bdg. 23.93 *(978-0-8225-3937-7(3))* Lerner Publishing Group.

—Play-by-Play Snowboarding. Clarke, Jimmy, photos by. 2003. (Play-by-Play Ser.). (Illus.). 80p. (J). (gr. 5-18). pap. 7.95 *(978-0-8225-9881-7(7))* Lerner Publishing Group.

Mason, Paul. Snowboarding, 1 vol. 2013. (Winter Sports Ser.). (ENG., Illus.). 48p. (gr. 3-6). pap. 6.95 *(978-1-4109-5459-6(5))*; 32.65 *(978-1-4109-5453-4(6))* Heinemann-Raintree.

—Snowboarding. 2012. (To the Limit Ser.). (ENG., Illus.). 32p. (J). (gr. 5-8). pap. 10.00 *(978-1-4488-7131-5(X))*; lib. bdg. 25.25 *(978-1-4488-7130-8(1))* Rosen Publishing Group, Inc., The. (PowerKids Pr.).

McClellan, Ray. Snowboarding. 2010. (My First Sports Ser.). (ENG., Illus.). 24p. (J). (gr. 2-5). lib. bdg. 25.95 *(978-1-60014-463-9(2)*, Blastoff! Readers) Bellwether Media.

Murdico, Suzanne J. Snowboarding. 2005. (Rad Sports: Techniques & Tricks Ser.). (Illus.). 48p. (YA). (gr. 5-8). lib. bdg. 29.25 *(978-0-8239-3849-0(2))* Rosen Publishing Group, Inc., The.

—Snowboarding: Techniques & Tricks. 2009. (Rad Sports: Techniques & Tricks Ser.). 48p. (gr. 5-8). 53.00 *(978-1-60851-938-5(4)*, Rosen Reference) Rosen Publishing Group, Inc., The.

O'Neal, Claire. Extreme Snowboarding with Lindsey Jacobellis. 2007. (Extreme Sports Ser.). (Illus.). 32p. (J). (gr. 1-4). lib. bdg. 25.70 *(978-1-58415-598-0(1))* Mitchell Lane Pubs., Inc.

Polydoros, Lori. Awesome Snowboard Tricks & Stunts, 1 vol. 2010. (Big Air Ser.). (ENG.). 32p. (gr. 1-2). lib. bdg. 26.65 *(978-1-4296-5412-8(0)*, Blazers) Capstone Press of Coughlan Cos.

—Snowboarding Greats, 1 vol. 2012. (Best of the Best Ser.). (ENG., Illus.). 32p. (gr. 1-2). lib. bdg. 26.65 *(978-1-4296-8434-7(8))* Capstone Press of Coughlan Cos.

Raum, Elizabeth. Chloe Kim. 2017. (Pro Sports Biographies Ser.). (ENG.). 24p. (J). (gr. 1-4). 20.95 ***(978-1-68151-134-4(7)**, Amicus High Interest)* Amicus Publishing.

—Pro Sports Biographies: Chloe Kim. 2017. (Pro Sports Biographies Ser.). (ENG.). 24p. (J). (gr. 1-3). pap. 8.99 ***(978-1-68152-165-7(2))*** Amicus.

Sandler, Michael. Cool Snowboarders. 2009. (X-Moves Ser.). (Illus.). 24p. (YA). (gr. 2-5). lib. bdg. 22.61 *(978-1-59716-949-3(8))* Bearport Publishing Co., Inc.

Schweitzer, Karen. Shaun White. 2010. (Modern Role Models Ser.). (Illus.). 64p. (YA). (gr. 7-12). lib. bdg. 22.95 *(978-1-4222-0493-1(6))* Mason Crest.

Segovia, Patty & Meredith Books Staff. On the Edge Skateboarding/on the Edge Snowboarding: Tips & Tricks from Six of the Coolest Skateboarders/Tips & Tricks from Six of the Coolest Snowboarders. 2008. (On the Edge Ser.). (Illus.). 48p. (YA). (gr. 8-12). per. 6.99 *(978-0-696-23980-9(9))* Meredith Bks.

Slade, Suzanne. Let's Go Snowboarding. (Adventures Outdoors Ser.). 32p. 2009. (gr. 4-5). 47.90 *(978-1-61511-272-2(3))* 2007. (Illus.). (J). (gr. 3-7). lib. bdg. 25.25 *(978-1-4042-3648-6(1))* Rosen Publishing Group, Inc., The. (PowerKids Pr.).

Snowboarding. 2007. (Nonfiction Collection). (J). 8.00 *(978-1-932570-99-1(3))* Pioneer Valley Bks.

Thorpe, Yvonne. Snowboarding. 2012. (Adrenaline Rush Ser.). (Illus.). 32p. (gr. 4-7). lib. bdg. 31.35 *(978-1-59920-686-8(2))* Black Rabbit Bks.

Turnbull, Stephanie. Skiing & Snowboarding. 2016. (Adventure Sports Ser.). 24p. (gr. 2-6). 28.50 *(978-1-62588-387-2(0)*, Smart Apple Media) Black Rabbit Bks.

Waxman, Laura Hamilton. Snowboarding. 2017. (Winter Olympic Sports Ser.). (ENG.). 32p. (J). (gr. 1-4). 20.95 ***(978-1-68151-152-8(5)**, Amicus High Interest)* Amicus Publishing.

—Winter Olympic Sports: Snowboarding. 2017. (Winter Olympic Sports Ser.). (ENG.). 32p. (J). (gr. 2-5). pap. 9.99 ***(978-1-68152-183-1(0))*** Amicus.

Weinstein, Anna. Kevin Jones: Snowboarding Superstar. 2009. (Extreme Sports Biographies Ser.). 64p. (gr. 3-4). 58.50 *(978-1-61512-466-4(7)*, Rosen Reference) Rosen Publishing Group, Inc., The.

—Kevin Jones, Snowboarding Superstar. 2005. (Extreme Sports Biographies Ser.). (Illus.). 64p. (J). (gr. 5-8). lib. bdg. 31.95 *(978-1-4042-0068-5(1))* Rosen Publishing Group, Inc., The.

Winters, Jaime. Carve It Snowboarding. 2012. (ENG., Illus.). 32p. (J). pap. *(978-0-7787-3159-7(6))* Crabtree Publishing Co.

Wiseman, Blaine. Shaun White. 2010. (Remarkable People Ser.). (Illus.). 24p. (J). (gr. 4-6). pap. 11.95 *(978-1-60596-998-5(2))*; lib. bdg. 25.70 *(978-1-60596-997-8(4))* Weigl Pubs., Inc.

—Snowboarding. 2015. (J). *(978-1-5105-0008-2(1))* SmartBook Media, Inc.

—Snowboarding: X Games. 2008. (Extreme Ser.). (Illus.). 32p. (J). (gr. 4-6). pap. 9.95 *(978-1-59036-921-0(1))*; lib. bdg. 26.00 *(978-1-59036-920-3(3))* Weigl Pubs., Inc.

Woods, Bob. Snowboarding. 2003. (Extreme Sports Ser.). (Illus.). 24p. (gr. 2-5). lib. bdg. 23.00 *(978-0-8368-3725-4(8)*, Gareth Stevens Learning Library) Stevens, Gareth Publishing LLLP.

Young, Jeff. Shaun White. 2008. (Xtreme Athletes Ser.). (Illus.). 112p. (YA). (gr. 7-12). lib. bdg. 27.95 *(978-1-59935-081-3(5))* Reynolds, Morgan Inc.

SNOWMOBILES

Bailer, Darice. Snowmobile Snocross. 2013. (Extreme Winter Sports Zone Ser.). (ENG., Illus.). 32p. (gr. 4-8). lib. bdg. 26.60 *(978-1-4677-0758-9(9)*, Lerner Pubns.) Lerner Publishing Group.

Carpenter, Jake. Snowmobile Best Trick. 2013. (Extreme Winter Sports Zone Ser.). (ENG., Illus.). 32p. (gr. 4-8). lib. bdg. 26.60 *(978-1-4677-0759-6(7)*, Lerner Pubns.) Lerner Publishing Group.

Katirgis, Jane & Woods, Bob. Racing Snowmobiles. 2017. (J). ***(978-0-7660-9272-3(0))*** Enslow Pubs., Inc.

Older, Jules. Snowmobile: Bombardier's Dream Machine. Lauritano, Michael, illus. 2012. (ENG.). 64p. (J). (gr. 3-7). 14.95 *(978-1-58089-334-3(1))*; pap. 6.95 *(978-1-58089-335-0(X))* Charlesbridge Publishing, Inc.

Scheff, Matt. Snowmobiles, 1 vol. 2014. (Speed Machines Ser.). (ENG., Illus.). 32p. (gr. 3-6). lib. bdg. 27.07 *(978-1-62403-613-2(9)*, SportsZone) ABDO Publishing Co.

Sommers, Michael A. Snowmobiling: Have Fun, Be Smart. (Explore the Outdoors Ser.). 64p. 2009. (gr. 5-5). 58.50 *(978-1-61512-344-5(X))* 2005. (Illus.). (YA). (gr. 7-12). lib. bdg. 31.95 *(978-0-8239-3761-5(5))* Rosen Publishing Group, Inc., The.

Tieck, Sarah. Snowmobiles, 1 vol. 2009. (Amazing Vehicles Ser.). (ENG., Illus.). 32p. (gr. 2-5). 28.50 *(978-1-60453-543-1(1)*, Big Buddy Bks.) ABDO Publishing Co.

Von Finn, Denny. Snowmobiles. 2009. (Torque Ser.). (ENG.). 24p. (J). (gr. 3-7). 20.00 *(978-0-531-21739-9(6)*, Children's Pr.) Scholastic Library Publishing.

Wiseman, Blaine. Snowmobiling. 2009. (Extreme Ser.). (Illus.). 32p. (J). (gr. 4-6). pap. 9.95 *(978-1-60596-135-4(3))*; lib. bdg. 26.00 *(978-1-60596-134-7(5))* Weigl Pubs., Inc.

Zahensky, Kenneth & Sommers, Michael A. Snowmobiling, 01 vols., 1. 2016. (Outdoor Life Ser.). (ENG., Illus.). 64p. (J). 32.95 *(978-1-4994-6229-6(8)*, Rosen Young Adult) Rosen Publishing Group, Inc., The.

SOAP

Best, B. J. Fat to Soap. 2016. (How It Is Made Ser.). 24p. (J). pap. 8.22 *(978-1-5026-2122-1(3))* Cavendish Square Publishing.

Ditchfield, Christin. The Story Behind Soap, 1 vol. 2011. (True Stories Ser.). (ENG.). 32p. (gr. 3-3). 30.65 *(978-1-4329-5435-2(0)*, NA-h) Heinemann-Raintree.

Pyper, Brittanie. Adorkable Bubble Bath Crafts: 50 Easy, Geeky Clean Crafts to Make Kids' Bath Time Awesome. 2017. (ENG., Illus.). 192p. pap. 19.99 *(978-1-62414-375-5(X)*, 9781624143755) Page Street Publishing Co.

Scholastic & Klutz Editors. Make Your Own Soap. 2017. (ENG.). 32p. (J). (gr. k-7). 21.99 *(978-1-338-10645-9(7))* Klutz.

Tocci, Salvatore. Experiments with Soap. 2003. (True Bks.). (ENG.). 48p. (gr. 3-5). pap. 6.95 *(978-0-516-27466-9(X),* Children's Pr.) Scholastic Library Publishing.

Wagner, Lisa. Cool Melt & Pour Soap, 1 vol. 2005. (Cool Crafts Ser.). (ENG., Illus.). 32p. (gr. k-6). 28.50 *(978-1-59197-741-4(X),* Checkerboard Library) ABDO Publishing Co.

Woolf, Alex. You Wouldn't Want to Live Without Soap! Bergin, Mark, illus. 2015. (You Wouldn't Want to Live Without... Ser.). (ENG.). 32p. (J). lib. bdg. 29.00 *(978-0-531-21927-0(5),* Watts, Franklin) Scholastic Library Publishing.

—You Wouldn't Want to Live Without Soap! 2015. (You Wouldn't Want to Live Without Ser.). lib. bdg. 20.80 *(978-0-606-37473-6(6))* Turtleback Bks.

SOAP BOX DERBIES—FICTION

Holm, Jennifer L. & Holm, Matthew. Burns Rubber. 2010. (Babymouse Ser.: 12). lib. bdg. 17.20 *(978-0-606-07025-6(7),* Turtleback) Turtleback Bks.

SOAP CARVING

see Soap Sculpture

SOAP SCULPTURE

Asher, Melissa. Toys, Blocks & Cars, Oh My, 1 vol. 2009. 56p. pap. 16.95 *(978-1-4489-1959-8(2))* America Star Bks.

SOARING (AERONAUTICS)

see Gliding and Soaring

SOCCER

Adamson, Heather. ¡Vamos a Jugar al Fútbol! 2012. (Deportes y Actividades/Sports & Activities Ser.). (MUL & SPA.). 24p. (gr. k-1). lib. bdg. 26.65 *(978-1-4296-8245-9(0))* Capstone Press of Coughlan Cos.

Alaníz, Eduardo Martínez. Hugo Sanchez. 2012. (Superstars of Soccer SPANISH Ser.). (SPA.). 32p. (J). (gr. 4). 19.95 *(978-1-4222-2615-5(8))* Mason Crest.

—Hugo Sanchez. 2012. (Superstars of Soccer ENGLISH Ser.). (Illus.). 32p. (J). (gr. 4). 19.95 *(978-1-4222-2668-1(9))* Mason Crest.

Alexander, Heather. U. S. Women's Soccer: Go for Gold! 2016. (Penguin Young Readers, Level 4 Ser.). (ENG., Illus.). 32p. (J). (gr. 3-4). pap. 3.99 *(978-0-399-54223-7(X),* Penguin Young Readers) Penguin Young Readers Group.

Anness Publishing Staff. The Step-by-Step Training Manual of Soccer Skills & Techniques. 2011. (ENG., Illus.). 192p. (J). (gr. -1-12). pap. 9.99 *(978-1-84322-771-7(1))* Anness Publishing GBR. Dist: National Bk. Network.

Apps, Roy. Cristiano Ronaldo. 2017. (EDGE: Sporting Heroes Ser.). (ENG., Illus.). 48p. (J). (gr. 2-7). 12.99 ***(978-1-4451-5318-6(1),*** Franklin Watts) Hachette Children's Group GBR. Dist: Hachette Bk. Group.

—Jamie Vardy. 2017. (EDGE: Sporting Heroes Ser.). (ENG., Illus.). 48p. (J). (gr. 2-7). 12.99 ***(978-1-4451-5322-3(X),*** Franklin Watts) Hachette Children's Group GBR. Dist: Hachette Bk. Group.

Apps, Roy. Leo Messi. King, Chris, illus. 2017. (EDGE - Dream to Win Ser.). (ENG.). 48p. (J). (gr. 2-4). pap. 9.99 *(978-1-4451-4145-9(0),* Franklin Watts) Hachette Children's Group GBR. Dist: Hachette Bk. Group.

Arnold. Fifa Latin America. 2005. (J). pap. 2.50 *(978-0-00-638306-2(8))* HarperCollins Pubs.

Arnold, Quinn M. & Whiting, Jim. AC Milan. 2017. (Soccer Stars Ser.). (ENG.). 24p. (J). (gr. 1-3). pap. 9.99 *(978-1-62832-352-8(3),* Creative Paperbacks) Creative Co., The.

Arturo Miranda Bravo, Jorge. Andres Guardado. 2012. (Superstars of Soccer ENGLISH Ser.). 32p. (J). (gr. 4). 19.95 *(978-1-4222-2666-7(2));* (SPA., Illus.). 19.95 *(978-1-4222-2613-1(1))* Mason Crest.

Bage, Grant & Collins UK Staff. The Story of Football. 2016. (ENG.). 56p. (J). (gr. 5-6). pap. 9.95 *(978-0-00-816398-3(7))* HarperCollins Pubs. Ltd. GBR. Dist: Independent Pubs. Group.

Bailey, Diane. Great Moments in World Cup History. 2010. (World Soccer Books Ser.). (Illus.). 64p. (YA). (gr. 5-8). lib. bdg. 31.95 *(978-1-4358-9139-5(2),* Rosen Reference) Rosen Publishing Group, Inc., The.

Bankston, John. Abby Wambach. 2013. (ENG.). 32p. (gr. 4-8). lib. bdg. 25.70 *(978-1-61228-465-1(5))* Mitchell Lane Pubs., Inc.

Barker, Geoff, et al. Soccer Star: Find Out How Your Favorite Soccer Players Made It! 2012. (Celeb Ser.). (Illus.). 32p. (gr. 4-6). lib. bdg. 28.50 *(978-1-59771-334-4(1))* Sea-To-Sea Pubns.

Barth, Katrin & Zempel, Ullrich, trs. from GER. Learning Soccer. 2004. (Illus.). 136p. pap. 14.95 *(978-1-84126-130-0(0))* Meyer & Meyer Sport, Ltd. GBR. Dist: Lewis International, Inc.

—Training Soccer. 2004. (Illus.). 152p. pap. 14.95 *(978-1-84126-131-7(9))* Meyer & Meyer Sport, Ltd. GBR. Dist: Lewis International, Inc.

Bazemore, Suzanne. Soccer: How It Works. 2010. (Science of Sports (Sports Illustrated for Kids) Ser.). (ENG.). 48p. (gr. 3-4). pap. 59.70 *(978-1-4296-5111-0(3))* Capstone Press of Coughlan Cos.

Berne, Emma Carlson. What a Kick: How a Clutch World Cup Win Propelled Women's Soccer. 2016. (Captured History Sports Ser.). (ENG., Illus.). 64p. (gr. 5-7). lib. bdg. 34.65 *(978-0-7565-5293-0(1),* CPB Grades 4-8) Compass Point Bks.

Besley, Adrian. Zlatan Ibrahimovic: The Ultimate Fan Book. (ENG., Illus.). 64p. (J). 2017. (gr. 4). pap. 9.95 *(978-1-78097-934-2(7))* 2016. (gr. 3). 14.99 *(978-1-78097-767-6(0))* Carlton Bks., Ltd. GBR. Dist: Sterling Publishing Co., Inc., Independent Pubs. Group.

Bielby, Paul. Simply the Best: 500 Football Tips for Youngsters. 2011. (ENG.). 260p. pap. 12.95 *(978-1-84358-350-9(X))* Blake, John Publishing, Ltd. GBR. Dist: Independent Pubs. Group.

Bishop, Amanda. Soccer Superstars: The Best of the Best. 2013. (ENG., Illus.). 32p. (J). *(978-0-7787-0243-6(X));* pap. *(978-0-7787-0252-8(9))* Crabtree Publishing Co.

—Winning Big: World & Euro Cup Soccer. 2013. (ENG., Illus.). 32p. (J). *(978-0-7787-0245-0(6));* pap. *(978-0-7787-0253-5(7))* Crabtree Publishing Co.

Bliss, Dominic. My First Soccer Book: Learn How to Play Like a Champion with This Fun Guide to Soccer: Tackling, Shooting, Tricks,tactics. 2015. (ENG., Illus.). 112p. (J). (gr. 7-11). pap. 14.95 *(978-1-78249-255-9(0),* CICO Books) Ryland Peters & Small GBR. Dist: Simon & Schuster, Inc.

Borth, Teddy. Soccer: Great Moments, Records, & Facts, 1 vol. 2014. (Great Sports Ser.). (ENG., Illus.). 24p. (J). (gr. 2-4). lib. bdg. 28.50 *(978-1-62970-692-4(2))* ABDO Publishing Co.

Bratton, Deboral B. & Bratton, Ashley D. Record-a-Sport Soccer Sport Organizer. Bratton, Deboral B. & Bratton, Ashley D., eds. 2003. (Illus.). (gr. 1-18). 18.95 *(978-1-931746-04-5(4))* Sport Your Stuff Corp.

Brown, Jonatha A. Soccer. 2004. (My Favorite Sport Ser.). (Illus.). 24p. (gr. 1-4). lib. bdg. 22.00 *(978-0-8368-4341-5(X),* Weekly Reader Leveled Readers) Stevens, Gareth Publishing LLLP.

Brown, Monica. Pelé, King of Soccer (Pelé, el Rey del Fútbol) Gayesky, Fernando, tr. Gutierrez, Rudy, illus. 2008. (SPA & ENG.). 40p. (J). (gr. -1-3). 17.99 *(978-0-06-122779-0(X),* Rayo) HarperCollins Pubs.

—Pele, King of Soccer/Pele, el Rey Del Futbol. Gutierrez, Rudy, illus. 2017. 40p. (J). (gr. -1-3). pap. 6.99 *(978-0-06-122780-6(3),* Rayo) HarperCollins Pubs.

Buckley, Jim. Soccer. 2008. (21st Century Skills Innovation Library: Innovation in Sports Ser.). (ENG., Illus.). 32p. (gr. 4-8). lib. bdg. 28.50 *(978-1-60279-261-6(5),* 200123) Cherry Lake Publishing.

Burlingame, Jeff. Soccer Star Andrés Iniesta. 2014. (Goal! Latin Stars of Soccer Ser.). 48p. (J). (gr. 4-9). pap. 8.95 *(978-1-62285-226-0(5))* Enslow Pubs., Inc.

—Soccer Star AndrS Iniesta. 2014. (Goal! Latin Stars of Soccer Ser.). 48p. 14.95 *(978-1-62285-225-3(7))* Enslow Pubs., Inc.

—Soccer Star Kak. 2014. (Goal! Latin Stars of Soccer Ser.). 48p. 14.95 *(978-1-62285-230-7(3))* Enslow Pubs., Inc.

—Soccer Star Kaká. 2014. (Goal! Latin Stars of Soccer Ser.). 48p. (J). (gr. 4-9). pap. 8.95 *(978-1-62285-231-4(1))* Enslow Pubs., Inc.

Burshtein, Karen. Lionel Messi: Soccer's Top Scorer. 2015. (Living Legends of Sports Ser.). (ENG.). 48p. (J). (gr. 5-6). pap. 14.05 *(978-1-68048-130-3(4));* (Illus.). 25.85 *(978-1-68048-129-7(0))* Rosen Publishing Group, Inc., The. (Britannica Educational Publishing).

Callow, Nick. Neymar: The Ultimate Fan Book. 2017. (ENG., Illus.). 64p. (J). (gr. 4). 11.95 ***(978-1-78097-954-0(1))*** Carlton Bks., Ltd. GBR. Dist: Sterling Publishing Co., Inc.

Capucilli, Alyssa Satin. My First Soccer Game. Jensen, Leyah, photos by. 2016. (My First Ser.). (ENG., Illus.). 32p. (J). (gr. -1-k). pap. 3.99 *(978-1-4814-6185-6(0),* Simon Spotlight) Simon Spotlight.

—My First Soccer Game: A Book with Foldout Pages. Jensen, Leyah, photos by. 2011. (My First Ser.). (ENG., Illus.). 14p. (J). (gr. -1-k). 9.99 *(978-1-4424-2747-1(7),* Little Simon) Little Simon.

Castillo, Rodolfo Iguaran. Freddy Rincon. 2012. (Superstars of Soccer ENGLISH Ser.). (ENG., Illus.). 32p. (J). (gr. 4-7). lib. bdg. 19.95 *(978-1-4222-2662-9(X))* Mason Crest.

Chacoff, Juan Domingo. Carlos Valderrama. 2012. (Superstars of Soccer ENGLISH Ser.). (ENG., Illus.). 32p. (J). (gr. 4-7). lib. bdg. 19.95 *(978-1-4222-2661-2(1))* Mason Crest.

Christopher, Matt. Great Americans in Sports: Mia Hamm. 2015. (ENG., Illus.). 192p. (J). (gr. 3-7). pap. 5.99 *(978-0-316-26101-2(7))* Little, Brown Bks. for Young Readers.

Christopher, Matt & Peters, Stephanie True. World Cup. 2010. (ENG., Illus.). 128p. (J). (gr. 3-7). pap. 5.99 *(978-0-316-04484-4(9))* Little Brown & Co.

Cline-Ransome, Lesa. Young Pele: Soccer's First Star. Ransome, James E., illus. 2011. (ENG.). 40p. (J). (gr. -1-3). pap. 7.99 *(978-0-375-87156-6(X),* Dragonfly Bks.) Random Hse. Children's Bks.

Contro, Arturo. Cristiano Ronaldo. 2009. (World Soccer Stars / Estrellas del fútbol mundial Ser.). (ENG & SPA.). 24p. (gr. 2-2). 42.50 *(978-1-60854-839-2(2),* Editorial Buenas Letras) Rosen Publishing Group, Inc., The.

—Cristiano Ronaldo. Benson, Megan, tr. 2008. (World Soccer Stars / Estrellas del Ftbol Mundial Ser.). (Illus.). 24p. (J). (gr. 4-7). lib. bdg. 21.25 *(978-1-4042-7669-7(6),* Editorial Buenas Letras) Rosen Publishing Group, Inc., The.

—Gianluigi Buffon. 2009. (World Soccer Stars / Estrellas del fútbol mundial Ser.). (ENG & SPA.). 24p. (gr. 2-2). 42.50 *(978-1-60854-844-6(9),* Editorial Buenas Letras) Rosen Publishing Group, Inc., The.

—Gianluigi Buffon. Benson, Megan, tr. from SPA. 2008. (World Soccer Stars / Estrellas Del Fútbol Mundial Ser.). (SPA., Illus.). 24p. (J). (gr. 2-5). lib. bdg. 22.60 *(978-1-4042-7668-0(8))* Rosen Publishing Group, Inc., The.

—Landon Donovan. 2009. (World Soccer Stars / Estrellas del fútbol mundial Ser.). (ENG & SPA.). 24p. (gr. 2-2). 42.50 *(978-1-60854-847-7(3),* Editorial Buenas Letras) Rosen Publishing Group, Inc., The.

—Landon Donovan. Benson, Megan, tr. 2008. (World Soccer Stars / Estrellas Del Fútbol Mundial Ser.). (SPA., Illus.). 24p. (J). (gr. 2-5). lib. bdg. 22.60 *(978-1-4042-7666-6(1))* Rosen Publishing Group, Inc., The.

—Rafael Marquez. 2009. (World Soccer Stars / Estrellas del fútbol mundial Ser.). (ENG & SPA.). 24p. (gr. 2-2). 42.50 *(978-1-60854-849-1(X),* Editorial Buenas Letras) Rosen Publishing Group, Inc., The.

—Rafael Marquez. Benson, Megan, tr. from SPA. 2008. (World Soccer Stars / Estrellas Del Fútbol Mundial Ser.). (SPA., Illus.). 24p. (J). (gr. 2-5). lib. bdg. 22.60 *(978-1-4042-7667-3(X))* Rosen Publishing Group, Inc., The.

Cook, Malcolm. 101 Youth Soccer Drills for 12 to 16 Year Olds. 2003. (Illus.). 128p. (YA). pap. 14.95 *(978-1-890946-23-4(0))* Reedswain, Inc.

Cox, Michael. Fitter, Faster, Funnier Football! Everything You Ever Wanted to Know about Football... 2014. (ENG., Illus.). 112p. (J). (gr. 2-4). pap. 9.99 *(978-1-4081-9467-6(8),* 9781408194676, Bloomsbury USA Childrens) Bloomsbury Publishing USA.

Crats, Rennay & Rediger, Pat. For the Love of Soccer. Kissock, Heather, ed. 2003. (For the Love of Sports Ser.). (Illus.). 24p. (J). pap. 8.95 *(978-1-59036-069-9(9))* Weigl Pubs., Inc.

Crisfield, Deborah & Murphy, Patrick. Winning Soccer for Girls. 3rd rev. ed. 2009. (Winning Sports for Girls Ser.). (Illus.). 224p. (gr. 6-12). pap. 14.95 *(978-0-8160-7715-1(0),* Chelsea Hse.) Facts On File, Inc.

Crisfield, Deborah, et al. Winning Soccer for Girls. 3rd rev. ed. 2009. (Winning Sports for Girls Ser.). (Illus.). 184p. (gr. 6-12). 39.50 *(978-0-8160-7714-4(2),* Chelsea Hse.) Facts On File, Inc.

Crowther, Robert. Soccer: Facts & Stats & the World Cup & Superstars: A Pop-up Book. Crowther, Robert, illus. 2004. (Illus.). 14p. (J). (gr. 2-8). reprint ed. 18.00 *(978-0-7567-7368-7(7))* DIANE Publishing Co.

Czeskleba, Abby. Cool Soccer Facts. Saunders-Smith, Gail, illus. 2011. (Cool Sports Facts Ser.). (ENG.). 24p. (gr. k-1). pap. 41.70 *(978-1-4296-7397-6(4),* Pebble Plus) Capstone Press of Coughlan Cos.

—Cool Soccer Facts (Datos Geniales Sobre Fútbol) Strictly Spanish Translation Services Staff, tr. from SPA. 2012. (Datos Geniales Sobre Deportes/Cool Sports Facts Ser.). (ENG & MUL., Illus.). 24p. (gr. k-1). lib. bdg. 26.65 *(978-1-4296-9216-8(2))* Capstone Press of Coughlan Cos.

Dann, Sarah. Play Like a Pro: Soccer Skills & Drills. 2013. (ENG., Illus.). 32p. (J). *(978-0-7787-0241-2(3));* pap. *(978-0-7787-0250-4(2))* Crabtree Publishing Co.

D'Arcy, Sean. Freestyle Soccer Street Moves: Tricks, Stepovers, Passes. 2009. (ENG., Illus.). 128p. pap. 14.95 *(978-1-55407-583-6(1),* 9781554075836) Firefly Bks., Ltd.

Derr, Aaron. Soccer: An Introduction to Being a Good Sport. Angle, Scott, illus. 2017. (Start Smart (tm) — Sports Ser.). (ENG.). 32p. (J). (gr. k-3). lib. bdg. 26.65 *(978-1-63440-132-6(8));* 39.99 ***(978-1-63440-144-9(1))*** Red Chair Pr.

Doeden, Matt. Cristiano Ronaldo. 2017. (Sports All-Stars Ser.). (ENG.). 32p. (J). (gr. 2-5). 12.99 ***(978-1-5124-3783-6(2),*** Lerner Pubns.); 39.99 ***(978-1-5124-2826-1(4),*** Lerner Pubns.); 39.99 ***(978-1-5124-3782-9(4),*** Lerner Pubns.); (Illus.). 26.65 *(978-1-5124-2582-6(6))* Lerner Publishing Group.

Doeden, Matt. The World's Greatest Soccer Players. 2010. (World's Greatest Sports Stars (Sports Illustrated for Kids) Ser.). (ENG.). 32p. (gr. 2-3). pap. 53.70 *(978-1-4296-5105-9(9))* Capstone Press of Coughlan Cos.

Dolphin, Colleen. Soccer by the Numbers, 1 vol. 2010. (Team Sports by the Numbers Ser.). (ENG.). 24p. (J). (gr. k-3). lib. bdg. 24.21 *(978-1-60453-771-0(X),* SandCastle) ABDO Publishing Co.

Donaldson, Chelsea. Christine Sinclair, 1 vol. 2014. (Canadian Biographies Ser.). (ENG.). 24p. (gr. k-1). 26.65 *(978-1-4914-1959-5(8),* Pebble Plus) Capstone Press of Coughlan Cos.

Dorling Kindersley Publishing Staff. DK Readers L3: Soccer School: Soccer School. 2015. (DK Readers Ser.). (ENG., Illus.). 64p. (J). (gr. 2-4). 14.99 *(978-1-4654-3582-8(4),* DK Children) Dorling Kindersley Publishing, Inc.

Douglas, Peter. Soccer: Breaking Away on the Pitch. 2017. (Preparing for Game Day Ser.: Vol. 10). (ENG.). (YA). (gr. 7-12). 24.95 ***(978-1-4222-3919-3(5))*** Mason Crest.

Downing, Erin. For Soccer-Crazy Girls Only. 2014. (ENG., Illus.). 160p. (J). (gr. 2-5). 15.99 *(978-1-250-04709-0(9),* 9781250047090) Feiwel & Friends.

Doyle, Brian. Cristiano Ronaldo: World-Beater. 2017. (J). ***(978-1-5026-2834-3(1))*** Cavendish Square Publishing.

duopress labs, et al. 1000 Totally Epic, True & Wacky Soccer Stories. 2017. (ENG., Illus.). 156p. (J). (gr. 3-7). pap. 12.95 *(978-1-938093-81-4(X),* Duo Pr. Llc (US)) Duo Pr. LLC.

Duopress Labs Staff. Messi, Superstar: His Records, His Life, His Epic Awesomeness. 2016. (ENG., Illus.). 140p. (J). (gr. 3-7). pap. 14.99 *(978-1-938093-57-9(7))* Duo Pr. LLC.

Durrie, Karen. Al Fútbol. 2012. (J). *(978-1-61913-203-0(6))* Weigl Pubs., Inc.

—Soccer. 2011. (J). 27.13 *(978-1-61690-942-0(0));* *(978-1-61690-588-0(3))* Weigl Pubs., Inc.

Edom, Helen & Osborne, Mike. Starting Soccer. Young, Norman, illus. 2006. (First Skills Ser.). 32p. (J). (gr. k-3). lib. bdg. 12.99 *(978-1-58086-907-2(6),* Usborne) EDC Publishing.

Ejaz, Khadija. Lionel Messi. 2013. (ENG.). 32p. (gr. 4-8). lib. bdg. 25.70 *(978-1-61228-467-5(1))* Mitchell Lane Pubs., Inc.

Elliott, Ned & Somerville, Charles C. F Is for Football. Somerville, Charles C., illus. 2014. (ENG., Illus.). 32p. (J). (gr. -1-3). pap. 9.99 *(978-1-907432-16-3(7))* Hogs Back Bks. GBR. Dist: Independent Pubs. Group.

Elzaurdia, Paco. Cuauhtemoc Blanco. 2012. (Superstars of Soccer SPANISH Ser.). (Illus.). 32p. (J). (gr. 4). (SPA.). 19.95 *(978-1-4222-2614-8(X));* 19.95 *(978-1-4222-2667-4(0))* Mason Crest.

—Rafael Marquez. 32p. (J). 2013. (Illus.). *(978-1-4222-2594-3(1))* 2012. (SPA.). (gr. 4). 19.95 *(978-1-4222-2598-1(4))* 2012. (Illus.). (gr. 4). 19.95 *(978-1-4222-2651-3(4))* Mason Crest.

England World Cup Junior Companion: Everything You Need to Know about the 2006 World Cup. 2006. (ENG., Illus.). 48p. (J). pap. 8.99 *(978-0-00-721698-7(X),* HarperCollins Children's Bks.) HarperCollins Pubs. Ltd. GBR. Dist: Independent Pubs. Group.

Falk, Laine. Let's Talk Riding. 2008. (Scholastic News Nonfiction Readers Ser.). (ENG.). 24p. (J). (gr. 1-2). pap. 6.95 *(978-0-531-20426-9(X))* Scholastic Library Publishing.

Faulkner, Nicholas & Sherman, Josepha. Soccer: Girls Rocking It, 01 vols., 1. 2016. (Title IX Rocks! Ser.). (ENG., Illus.). 64p. (J). 32.95 *(978-1-5081-7039-6(8),* Rosen Young Adult) Rosen Publishing Group, Inc., The.

Feldman, Heather. Mia Hamm: Soccer Superstar. 2009. (Sports Superstars Ser.). 24p. (gr. 1-1). 42.50 *(978-1-60853-180-6(5),* PowerKids Pr.) Rosen Publishing Group, Inc., The.

—Mia Hamm: Soccer/Soccer Superstar/Superestrella del Fútbol. 2009. (Superstars of Sports/Superestrellas del deporte Ser.). (ENG & SPA.). 24p. (gr. 1-2). 42.50 *(978-1-60853-240-7(2),* Editorial Buenas Letras) Rosen Publishing Group, Inc., The.

—Mia Hamm: Superestrella del Fútbol Soccer (Soccer Superstar. 2009. (Superestrellas del Deporte (Superstars of Sports) Ser.). (SPA.). 24p. (gr. 1-2). 42.50 *(978-1-60853-228-5(3),* Editorial Buenas Letras) Rosen Publishing Group, Inc., The.

—Mia Hamm, Soccer Superstar/Superestrella del Futbol Soccer. De Leon, Mauricio Velzaquez, tr. 2008. (Reading Power Ser.). (ENG., Illus.). 24p. (gr. 1-6). pap. 8.85 *(978-1-4042-7543-0(6))* Rosen Publishing Group, Inc., The.

Fischer, David. Cristiano Ronaldo. 2017. (J). ***(978-0-7660-9205-1(4))*** Enslow Pubs., Inc.

Fishman, Jon M. Alex Morgan. 2016. (Amazing Athletes Ser.). (ENG., Illus.). 32p. (J). (gr. 2-5). 26.65 *(978-1-4677-9386-5(8))* Lerner Publishing Group.

—Carli Lloyd. 2016. (Amazing Athletes Ser.). (ENG., Illus.). 32p. (J). (gr. 2-5). 26.65 *(978-1-5124-0866-9(2),* Lerner Pubns.) Lerner Publishing Group.

—Lionel Messi. 2017. (Sports All-Stars Ser.). (ENG.). 32p. (J). (gr. 2-5). 26.65 ***(978-1-5124-3454-5(X))*** Lerner Publishing Group.

Fishman, Jon M. Tim Howard. 2015. (Amazing Athletes Ser.). (ENG., Illus.). 32p. (J). (gr. 2-5). lib. bdg. 25.26 *(978-1-4677-5746-1(2),* Lerner Pubns.) Lerner Publishing Group.

Flynn, Brendan. ¡Hora de Fútbol! 2017. (Bumba Books (tm) en Español — ¡Hora de Deportes! (Sports Time!) Ser.). (SPA.). 24p. (J). (gr. -1-1). 25.32 *(978-1-5124-2874-2(4))* Lerner Publishing Group.

—Soccer Time! 2016. (Bumba Books (tm) — Sports Time! Ser.). (ENG., Illus.). 24p. (J). (gr. -1-1). 25.32 *(978-1-5124-1434-9(4))* Lerner Publishing Group.

Forest, Christopher. Play Soccer Like a Pro: Key Skills & Tips. 2010. (Play Like the Pros (Sports Illustrated for Kids) Ser.). (ENG.). 32p. (gr. 3-4). pap. 7.19 *(978-1-4296-5647-4(6));* pap. 41.70 *(978-1-4296-5956-7(4));* lib. bdg. 26.65 *(978-1-4296-4827-1(9))* Capstone Press of Coughlan Cos.

Friedman, Laura, et al. Let's Talk Soccer. 2008. (Scholastic News Nonfiction Readers Ser.). (ENG., Illus.). 24p. (J). (gr. k-1). lib. bdg. 22.00 *(978-0-531-13830-4(5),* Children's Pr.) Scholastic Library Publishing.

Gagne, Tammy. Day by Day with Mia Hamm. 2012. (J). lib. bdg. 25.70 *(978-1-61228-327-2(6))* Mitchell Lane Pubs., Inc.

—Hope Solo. 2014. (Illus.). 32p. (J). 25.70 *(978-1-61228-642-6(9))* Mitchell Lane Pubs., Inc.

Gatto, Kimberly. Lionel Messi: A Soccer Star Who Cares. 2013. (Sports Stars Who Care Ser.). 48p. (J). 25.27 *(978-0-7660-4299-5(5));* (gr. 3-4). pap. 8.95 *(978-1-4644-0543-3(3),* Enslow Elementary) Enslow Pubs., Inc.

Gibbons, Alan. Being Rooney. 2014. (Read On Ser.). (ENG., Illus.). 160p. (J). (gr. 5). 9.99 *(978-0-00-748894-0(7))* HarperCollins Pubs. Ltd. GBR. Dist: Independent Pubs. Group.

Gifford, Clive. The Business of Soccer. 2010. (Spotlight on Soccer Ser.). (Illus.). 32p. (J). (gr. 3-6). lib. bdg. 25.25 *(978-1-61532-610-5(3),* PowerKids Pr.) Rosen Publishing Group, Inc., The.

—Champions League Fact File. 2016. (ENG., Illus.). 96p. (J). (gr. 3-7). pap. 14.99 *(978-1-78312-131-1(9))* Carlton Bks., Ltd. GBR. Dist: Independent Pubs. Group.

—Football. (Sports Skills Ser.). (ENG., Illus.). 32p. (J). (gr. 4-6). 2017. pap. 12.99 ***(978-1-4451-4094-0(2))*** 2016. pap. 11.99 *(978-1-4451-4964-6(8))* Hachette Children's Group GBR. (Franklin Watts). Dist: Hachette Bk. Group.

—Greatest Fans. 2017. (Planet Football Ser.). (ENG., Illus.). 32p. (J). (gr. 4-6). 17.99 *(978-0-7502-9573-4(2),* Wayland) Hachette Children's Group GBR. Dist: Hachette Bk. Group.

—Greatest Managers. 2017. (Planet Football Ser.). (ENG., Illus.). 32p. (J). (gr. 4-6). 17.99 *(978-0-7502-9572-7(4),* Wayland) Hachette Children's Group GBR. Dist: Hachette Bk. Group.

—Greatest Players. 2017. (Planet Football Ser.). (ENG., Illus.). 32p. (J). (gr. 4-6). pap. 12.99 *(978-1-5263-0127-7(X),* Wayland) Hachette Children's Group GBR. Dist: Hachette Bk. Group.

—The Inside Story of Soccer. 2011. (Sports World Ser.). (YA). (gr. 5-9). lib. bdg. 29.25 *(978-1-4488-4847-8(4))* Rosen Publishing Group, Inc., The.

—The Inside Story of World Cup Soccer. 2011. (Sports World Ser.). (YA). (gr. 5-9). lib. bdg. 29.25 *(978-1-4488-4849-2(0))* Rosen Publishing Group, Inc., The.

—Kingfisher Book of Soccer Skills. 2012. (ENG., Illus.). 64p. (J). (gr. 3-12). 15.99 *(978-0-7534-6873-9(5),* 9780753468739, Kingfisher) Roaring Brook Pr.

—The Kingfisher Soccer Encyclopedia. (ENG.). 144p. (J). 2016. 19.99 *(978-0-7534-7308-5(9),* 9780753473085) 3rd rev. ed. 2014. (Illus.). (gr. 5-9). 19.99 *(978-0-7534-7167-8(1),* 9780753471678) Roaring Brook Pr. (Kingfisher).

—My First Soccer Book: A Brilliant Introduction to the Beautiful Game. 2012. (ENG., Illus.). 48p. (J). (gr. k-5). 12.99 *(978-0-7534-6783-1(6),* 9780753467831, Kingfisher) Roaring Brook Pr.

—So You Think You Know David Beckham? 2003. 128p. (J). pap. 9.99 *(978-0-340-87765-4(0))* Hodder & Stoughton GBR. Dist: Trafalgar Square Publishing.

—Soccer. 2009. (Tell Me about Sports Ser.). 32p. (gr. 3-5). 28.50 *(978-0-7614-4460-2(2))* Marshall Cavendish Corp.

—Soccer. 2008. (Personal Best Ser.). (Illus.). 32p. (YA). (gr. 3-6). lib. bdg. 26.50 *(978-1-4042-4441-2(7))* Rosen Publishing Group, Inc., The.

—Soccer: The Ultimate Guide to the Beautiful Game. 2004. (ENG., Illus.). 96p. (J). (gr. 3-7). pap. 9.99 *(978-0-7534-5752-8(0),* 9780753457528, Kingfisher) Roaring Brook Pr.

—The Soccer Book. 2016. (ENG., Illus.). 64p. (J). (gr. 4-7). pap. 12.95 *(978-1-77085-729-2(X),* 9781770857292) Firefly Bks., Ltd.

—Soccer Legends. 2009. (ENG., Illus.). 32p. (J). (gr. 4-7). lib. bdg. *(978-0-7787-3777-3(2))* Crabtree Publishing Co.

—Soccer Players & Skills. 2010. (Spotlight on Soccer Ser.). (Illus.). 32p. (J). (gr. 3-6). lib. bdg. 25.25 *(978-1-61532-611-2(1),* PowerKids Pr.) Rosen Publishing Group, Inc., The.

—Soccer Rules & Regulations. 2010. (Spotlight on Soccer Ser.). (Illus.). 32p. (J). (gr. 3-6). lib. bdg. 25.25 *(978-1-61532-608-2(1),* PowerKids Pr.) Rosen Publishing Group, Inc., The.

—Teamwork in Soccer. 2010. (Spotlight on Soccer Ser.). (Illus.). 32p. (J). (gr. 3-6). lib. bdg. 25.25 *(978-1-61532-609-9(X),* PowerKids Pr.) Rosen Publishing Group, Inc., The.

Gifford, Clive & Phillips, Dee. Soccer World Cup. 2009. (ENG., Illus.). 32p. (J). (gr. 4-7). lib. bdg. *(978-0-7787-3778-0(0))* Crabtree Publishing Co.

Gitlin, Martin. Soccer Star Robinho. 2014. (Goal! Latin Stars of Soccer Ser.). 48p. 14.95 *(978-1-62285-216-1(8))* Enslow Pubs., Inc.

Glaser, Jason. David Beckham. (Sports Idols Ser.). 24p. (gr. 2-3). 2009. 42.50 *(978-1-60853-141-7(4)*, PowerKids Pr.) 2008. (Illus.). (J). lib. bdg. 22.60 *(978-1-4042-4182-4(5))* Rosen Publishing Group, Inc., The.

Glave, Tom. Incredible Soccer Records. 2016. (Incredible Sports Records Ser.). (ENG.). 24p. (J). (gr. 2-5). 28.50 *(978-1-5038-0891-1(2)*, 210680) Child's World, Inc., The.

Goldsworthy, Steve. Soccer. 2011. (J). (gr. 4-6). pap. 13.95 *(978-1-61690-704-4(5)*, AV2 by Weigl); (Illus.). 32p. (YA). (gr. 2-5). 28.55 *(978-1-61690-699-3(5))* Weigl Pubs., Inc.

Goodstein, Madeline P. Goal! Science Projects with Soccer. 2009. (Score! Sports Science Projects Ser.). (Illus.). 104p. (J). (gr. 5-9). lib. bdg. 33.27 *(978-0-7660-3106-7(3))* Enslow Pubs., Inc.

Grady, Daniel John. Diego Forlan. 2012. (Superstars of Soccer ENGLISH Ser.). (ENG., Illus.). 32p. (J). (gr. 4-7). lib. bdg. 19.95 *(978-1-4222-2665-0(4))* Mason Crest.

—Mario Yepes. 2012. (Superstars of Soccer ENGLISH Ser.). (ENG., Illus.). 32p. (J). (gr. 4-7). lib. bdg. 19.95 *(978-1-4222-2664-3(6))* Mason Crest.

Greathouse, Lisa. Count Me In! Soccer Tournament, 1 vol. 2nd rev. ed. 2014. (TIME for KIDS(r) Nonfiction Readers Ser.). (ENG., Illus.). 28p. (J). (gr. 2-2). pap. 23.96 *(978-1-4807-1059-7(8))* Shell Educational Publishing.

—Count Me In! Soccer Tournament, 1 vol. 2nd rev. ed. 2011. (TIME for KIDS(r) Nonfiction Readers Ser.). (ENG.). 28p. (J). (gr. 2-2). pap. 6.99 *(978-1-4333-3638-6(3))* Teacher Created Materials, Inc.

Group/McGraw-Hill, Wright. SoCer: Level I, 6 vols. (Take Twostm Ser.). 16p. 29.95 *(978-0-322-08970-9(0))* Wright Group/McGraw-Hill.

Guillain, Charlotte. Fútbol, 1 vol. 2010. (Deporte y Mi Cuerpo Ser.). (SPA.). 24p. (gr. k-2). 23.32 *(978-1-4329-4345-5(6))*; pap. 6.79 *(978-1-4329-4351-6(0))* Heinemann-Raintree.

Hachette Children's Group. Football. 2017. (Mad About Ser.). (ENG., Illus.). 32p. (J). (gr. 4-6). pap. 11.99 *(978-0-7502-9457-7(4)*, Wayland) Hachette Children's Group GBR. Dist: Hachette Bk. Group.

Hamm, Mia, et al. Mia Hamm. 2015. (Quotes from the Greatest Athletes Ser.). (ENG., Illus.). 24p. (J). lib. bdg. 12.95 *(978-1-4896-3365-1(0))*; lib. bdg. 28.55 *(978-1-4896-3364-4(2))* Weigl Pubs., Inc. (AV2 by Weigl).

Hammelef, Danielle S. First Source to Soccer: Rules, Equipment, & Key Playing Tips. 2017. (First Sports Source Ser.). (ENG.). 24p. (gr. 1-2). lib. bdg. 25.32 ***(978-1-5157-6946-0(1)***, First Facts) Capstone Press of Coughlan Cos.

Hammelef, Danielle S. Top Soccer Tips. 2017. (Top Sports Tips Ser.). (ENG., Illus.). 32p. (gr. 3-4). lib. bdg. 27.99 *(978-1-5157-4722-2(0)*, Snap Bks.) Capstone Press of Coughlan Cos.

Hantula, Richard. Science at Work in Soccer. 2011. (Benchmark Rockets: Sports Science Ser.). (Illus.). 32p. (J). (gr. 4). 28.50 *(978-1-60870-591-7(9))* Marshall Cavendish Corp.

HarperCollins Children's Books, creator. England the Facts Sticker Book: All the Facts, All the Stats, All the Stickers! 2006. (ENG., Illus.). 32p. (J). pap. 8.99 *(978-0-00-721695-6(5)*, HarperCollins Children's Bks.) HarperCollins Pubs. Ltd. GBR. Dist: Independent Pubs. Group.

HarperCollins UK Staff. England World Cup Dream Team: Live Your Own World Cup Dream! 2006. (ENG., Illus.). 6p. (J). pap. 8.99 *(978-0-00-721696-3(3)*, HarperCollins Children's Bks.) HarperCollins Pubs. Ltd. GBR. Dist: Independent Pubs. Group.

Haw, Jennie. Score! The Story of Soccer. 2013. (ENG., Illus.). 32p. (J). *(978-0-7787-0242-9(1))*; pap. *(978-0-7787-0251-1(0))* Crabtree Publishing Co.

Herzog, Brad. K Is for Kick: A Soccer Alphabet. Rose, Melanie, illus. rev. ed. (Sports Ser.). (ENG.). 40p. (J). (gr. -1-3). 2006. pap. 7.95 *(978-1-58536-339-1(1))* 2003. 16.95 *(978-1-58536-130-4(5))* Sleeping Bear Pr.

—K Is for Kick: A Soccer Alphabet. Rose, Melanie, illus. 2015. (Av2 Fiction Readalong 2016 Ser.). (ENG.). (J). (gr. 1-4). lib. bdg. 34.28 *(978-1-4896-3756-7(7)*, AV2 by Weigl) Weigl Pubs., Inc.

—Little Soccer. Bowles, Doug, illus. 2011. (Little Sports Ser.). (ENG.). 22p. 9.95 *(978-1-58536-197-7(6))* Sleeping Bear Pr.

Hoena, Blake. National Geographic Kids Everything Soccer: Score Tons of Photos, Facts, & Fun. 2014. (ENG.). 64p. (J). (gr. 3-7). pap. 12.99 *(978-1-4263-1713-2(1)*, National Geographic Children's Bks.) National Geographic Society.

—Soccer. 2015. (J). lib. bdg. 25.65 *(978-1-62031-181-3(X)*, Bullfrog Bks.) Jump! Inc.

Hollar, Sherman. Soccer & Its Greatest Players. 2011. (Illus.). 96p. (J). lib. bdg. 31.70 *(978-1-61530-516-2(5))* Rosen Publishing Group, Inc., The.

Hornby, Hugh. Soccer. 2010. (DK Eyewitness Bks.). (ENG.). 72p. (J). (gr. 3-7). 19.99 *(978-0-7566-6295-0(8)*, DK Children) Dorling Kindersley Publishing, Inc.

Hornby, Hugh & Dorling Kindersley Publishing Staff. Soccer. 2010. (DK Eyewitness Bks.). (ENG.). 72p. (J). (gr. 3-7). 16.99 *(978-0-7566-6294-3(X)*, DK Children) Dorling Kindersley Publishing, Inc.

Howard, Tim. The Keeper: The Unguarded Story of Tim Howard. 2014. (ENG., Illus.). 288p. (J). (gr. 3-7). 16.99 *(978-0-06-238755-4(3))* HarperCollins Pubs.

—The Keeper - The Unguarded Story of Tim Howard. 2015. (ENG.). 288p. (J). (gr. 3-7). pap. 6.99 *(978-0-06-238758-5(8))* HarperCollins Pubs.

Huberts, Al. Learn All about Soccer: Color & Activity. Bailey, Frank, illus. 2013. (Rule 1, Sports Color & Activity Bks.). (ENG.). 176p. (J). (gr. -1-3). pap. 9.99 *(978-1-77049-506-7(1)*, Fenn-Tundra) Tundra Bks. CAN. Dist: Penguin Random Hse. LLC.

Hughes, Morgan. Soccer. 2005. (Junior Sports Ser.). (Illus.). 32p. (gr. 2-4). 19.95 *(978-1-59515-187-2(7))* Rourke Educational Media.

Hurley, Michael. A-Z of the World Cup, 1 vol. 2014. (World Cup Fever Ser.). (ENG., Illus.). 48p. (gr. 4-5). pap. 9.95 *(978-1-4109-5517-3(6))* Heinemann-Raintree.

—Soccer, 1 vol. 2013. (Fantastic Sports Facts Ser.). (ENG.). 32p. (gr. 1-3). pap. 8.29 *(978-1-4109-5110-6(3))*; lib. bdg. 29.99 *(978-1-4109-5103-8(0))* Heinemann-Raintree. (Read Me!).

—The World Cup, 5 vols., Set. Incl. World Cup 2010. 29.99 *(978-1-4329-3449-1(X))*; World of Soccer. (Illus.). 29.99 *(978-1-4329-3452-1(X))*; (gr. 3-5). (World Cup Ser.). (ENG.). 32p. 2010. Set lib. bdg. 119.96 o.p. *(978-1-4329-3453-8(8)*, NA-h) Heinemann-Raintree.

—World Cup 2010, 1 vol. 2010. (World Cup Ser.). (ENG.). 32p. (gr. 3-5). 29.99 *(978-1-4329-3449-1(X)*, NA-h) Heinemann-Raintree.

—World Cup 2014, 1 vol. 2014. (World Cup Fever Ser.). (ENG.). 48p. (gr. 4-5). pap. 9.95 *(978-1-4109-5518-0(4))* Heinemann-Raintree.

—World Cup Fever, 1 vol. 2014. (World Cup Fever Ser.). (ENG.). 48p. (gr. 4-5). pap. 35.96 *(978-1-4109-5519-7(2))* Heinemann-Raintree.

—World Cup Heroes, 1 vol. 2014. (World Cup Fever Ser.). (ENG.). 48p. (gr. 4-5). pap. 9.95 *(978-1-4109-5516-6(8))* Heinemann-Raintree.

—World Cup Nations, 1 vol. 2014. (World Cup Fever Ser.). (ENG., Illus.). 48p. (gr. 4-5). pap. 9.95 *(978-1-4109-5515-9(X))* Heinemann-Raintree.

Hyde, Natalie. Soccer Science. 2008. (Sports Science Ser.). (ENG., Illus.). 32p. (J). (gr. 4-6). pap. *(978-0-7787-4554-9(6))* Crabtree Publishing Co.

Jankowski, Emily. Soccer's Greatest Records, 1 vol. 2015. (Greatest Records in Sports Ser.). (ENG.). 32p. (J). pap. 10.00 *(978-1-4994-0001-4(2))*; (Illus.). lib. bdg. 26.25 *(978-1-4994-0000-7(4))* Rosen Publishing Group, Inc., The. (PowerKids Pr.).

Jökulsson, Illugi. Alex Morgan. 2015. (World Soccer Legends Ser.). (ENG., Illus.). 64p. (J). (gr. 1). 13.95 *(978-0-7892-1216-0(1)*, Abbeville Kids) Abbeville Pr., Inc.

—FC Barcelona: More Than a Club. 2014. (World Soccer Legends Ser.). (ENG., Illus.). 64p. (J). (gr. 1). 12.95 *(978-0-7892-1158-3(0)*, Abbeville Kids) Abbeville Pr., Inc.

—James Rodriguez. 2015. (World Soccer Legends Ser.). (ENG.). 64p. (J). (gr. 1). 13.95 *(978-0-7892-1237-5(4)*, Abbeville Kids) Abbeville Pr., Inc.

—Manchester United: The Biggest & the Best. 2014. (World Soccer Legends Ser.). (ENG., Illus.). 64p. (J). (gr. 1). 12.95 *(978-0-7892-1162-0(9)*, Abbeville Kids) Abbeville Pr., Inc.

—Messi. 2nd ed. 2015. (ENG., Illus.). 64p. (J). (gr. 1). 13.95 *(978-0-7892-1225-2(0)*, Abbeville Kids) Abbeville Pr., Inc.

Jokulsson, Illugi. Messi, Neymar, & Suarez: The Magnificent Three of Barcelona. 2016. (World Soccer Legends Ser.). (ENG.). 62p. (J). (gr. 1). 13.95 *(978-0-7892-1284-9(6)*, Abbeville Kids) Abbeville Pr., Inc.

—Neymar. 2015. (World Soccer Legends Ser.). (ENG., Illus.). 64p. (J). (gr. 1). 13.95 *(978-0-7892-1227-6(7)*, Abbeville Kids) Abbeville Pr., Inc.

Jökulsson, Illugi. Real Madrid: The Most Successful Club in the World. 2014. (World Soccer Legends Ser.). (ENG., Illus.). 64p. (J). (gr. 1). 12.95 *(978-0-7892-1160-6(2)*, Abbeville Kids) Abbeville Pr., Inc.

Jokulsson, Illugi. Ronaldo. Jokulsson, Illugi, ed. 2015. (ENG., Illus.). 64p. (J). (gr. 1). 13.95 *(978-0-7892-1226-9(9)*, Abbeville Kids) Abbeville Pr., Inc.

Jökulsson, Illugi. Stars of Women's Soccer. 2015. (World Soccer Legends Ser.). (ENG., Illus.). 64p. (J). (gr. 1). 13.95 *(978-0-7892-1238-2(2)*, Abbeville Kids) Abbeville Pr., Inc.

—Stars of World Soccer. 2015. (World Soccer Legends Ser.). (ENG., Illus.). 64p. (J). (gr. 1). 13.95 *(978-0-7892-1239-9(0)*, Abbeville Kids) Abbeville Pr., Inc.

—U. S. Men's Team: New Stars on the Field. 2014. (World Soccer Legends Ser.). (ENG., Illus.). 64p. (J). (gr. 1). 12.95 *(978-0-7892-1180-4(7)*, Abbeville Kids) Abbeville Pr., Inc.

—U. S. Women's Team. 2015. (World Soccer Legends Ser.). (ENG., Illus.). 64p. (J). (gr. 1). 13.95 *(978-0-7892-1215-3(3)*, Abbeville Kids) Abbeville Pr., Inc.

—Zlatan. 2014. (ENG., Illus.). 64p. (J). (gr. 1). 12.95 *(978-0-7892-1169-9(6)*, Abbeville Kids) Abbeville Pr., Inc.

Jones, Jeremy V. The Keeper: The Tim Howard Story. 2010. (ZonderKidz Biography Ser.). (ENG.). 128p. (J). (gr. 4-7). pap. 6.99 *(978-0-310-72004-1(6))* Zonderkidz.

—Toward the Goal: The Kaká Story, 1 vol. 2010. (ZonderKidz Biography Ser.). (ENG.). 128p. (J). (gr. 4-7). pap. 6.99 *(978-0-310-72003-4(6))* Zonderkidz.

—Toward the Goal: The Kaka Story, 1 vol. rev. ed. 2014. (ZonderKidz Biography Ser.). (ENG.). 160p. (J). pap. 7.99 *(978-0-310-73840-4(7))* Zonderkidz.

Kajumulo, Alex. Soccer Monster: Mwalimu Wa Soca. 2012. (ENG.). pap. 8.95 *(978-1-4675-1671-6(6))* Independent Pub.

Kalman, Bobbie & Crossingham, John. Fútbol para Patear. 2008.Tr. of Kick It Soccer. (SPA.). 32p. (J). pap. *(978-0-7787-8647-4(1))* Crabtree Publishing Co.

—Kick It Soccer. 2007. (Sports Starters Ser.). (ENG., Illus.). 32p. (J). (gr. 3-7). lib. bdg. *(978-0-7787-3138-2(3))*; (gr. -1-3). pap. *(978-0-7787-3170-2(7))* Crabtree Publishing Co.

Kassouf, Jeff. Girls Play to Win Soccer. 2011. (Girls Play to Win Ser.). 64p. (J). (gr. 3-6). lib. bdg. 27.93 *(978-1-59953-464-0(9))* Norwood Hse. Pr.

Kennedy, Mike & Stewart, Mark. Soccer in Africa. 2011. (Smart about Soccer Ser.). 24p. (J). (gr. k-3). lib. bdg. 22.60 *(978-1-59953-441-1(X))* Norwood Hse. Pr.

—Soccer in Asia. 2011. (Smart about Soccer Ser.). 24p. (J). (gr. k-3). lib. bdg. 22.60 *(978-1-59953-448-0(7))* Norwood Hse. Pr.

—Soccer in Central America. 2011. (Smart about Soccer Ser.). 24p. (J). (gr. k-3). lib. bdg. 22.60 *(978-1-59953-443-5(6))* Norwood Hse. Pr.

—Soccer in Eastern Europe. 2011. (Smart about Soccer Ser.). 24p. (J). (gr. k-3). lib. bdg. 22.60 *(978-1-59953-445-9(2))* Norwood Hse. Pr.

—Soccer in South America. 2011. (Smart about Soccer Ser.). 24p. (J). (gr. k-3). lib. bdg. 22.60 *(978-1-59953-446-6(0))* Norwood Hse. Pr.

—Soccer in the British Isles. 2011. (Smart about Soccer Ser.). 24p. (J). (gr. k-3). lib. bdg. 22.60 *(978-1-59953-442-8(8))* Norwood Hse. Pr.

—Soccer in Western Europe. 2011. (Smart about Soccer Ser.). 24p. (J). (gr. k-3). lib. bdg. 22.60 *(978-1-59953-447-3(9))* Norwood Hse. Pr.

Kirkpatrick, Rob. Alexi Lalas: Sensación del Fútbol Soccer (Soccer Sensation) 2009. (Grandes Idolos (Hot Shots) Ser.). 24p. (gr. 1-1). 42.50 *(978-1-61512-733-7(X)*, Editorial Buenas Letras) Rosen Publishing Group, Inc., The.

—Alexi Lalas: Soccer Sensation / Sensación del Fútbol Soccer. 2009. (Hot Shots/Grandes idolos Ser.). (SPA.). 24p. (gr. 1-1). 42.50 *(978-1-61513-411-3(5)*, Editorial Buenas Letras) Rosen Publishing Group, Inc., The.

—Cobi Jones: Estrella del Fútbol Soccer (Soccer Star) 2009. (Grandes Idolos (Hot Shots) Ser.). (SPA.). 24p. (gr. 1-1). 42.50 *(978-1-61512-734-4(8)*, Editorial Buenas Letras) Rosen Publishing Group, Inc., The.

—Cobi Jones: Soccer Star / Estrella del Fútbol Soccer. 2009. (Hot Shots/Grandes idolos Ser.). (ENG & SPA.). 24p. (gr. 1-1). 42.50 *(978-1-61513-412-0(3)*, Editorial Buenas Letras) Rosen Publishing Group, Inc., The.

—Mia Hamm: Soccer Star. 2009. (Great Record Breakers in Sports Ser.). 24p. (gr. 3-3). 42.50 *(978-1-61513-189-1(2)*, PowerKids Pr.) Rosen Publishing Group, Inc., The.

Kortemeier, Todd. Superstars of World Soccer. 2016. (Pro Sports Superstars Ser.). (ENG., Illus.). 24p. (J). (gr. 1-4). 20.95 *(978-1-60753-942-1(X))* Amicus Publishing.

Laínez, René Colato. Juguemos Al Futbol y Al Football!/Let's Play Futbol & Football! 2014. (ENG & SPA., Illus.). 31p. (J). (gr. -1-2). 16.00 *(978-0-88272-328-0(6)*, Alfaguara) Santillana USA Publishing Co., Inc.

Laughlin, Kara L. Soccer. 2016. (Beginning Sports Ser.). (ENG.). 24p. (J). (gr. k-3). 27.07 *(978-1-5038-0780-8(0)*, 210608) Child's World, Inc., The.

Lindeen, Mary. Let's Play Soccer. 2015. (BeginningtoRead Ser.). (ENG., Illus.). 32p. (J). (gr. k-2). pap. 11.94 *(978-1-60357-743-4(2))*; lib. bdg. 22.60 *(978-1-59953-683-5(8))* Norwood Hse. Pr.

Logothetis, Paul. Cristiano Ronaldo: International Soccer Star, 1 vol. 2016. (ENG., Illus.). 32p. (J). *(978-1-62403-841-9(7)*, SportsZone) ABDO Publishing Co.

—Lionel Messi: Soccer Sensation, 1 vol. 2016. (ENG., Illus.). 32p. (J). *(978-1-62403-839-6(5)*, SportsZone) ABDO Publishing Co.

Lozano, Gustavo Vazquez, et al. Luis Suarez. 2012. (Superstars of Soccer SPANISH Ser.). (SPA., Illus.). 32p. (J). (gr. 4-7). lib. bdg. 19.95 *(978-1-4222-2603-2(4))* Mason Crest.

Luke, Andrew. Soccer, Vol. 13. 2016. (Inside the World of Sports Ser.: Vol. 13). (ENG., Illus.). 80p. (J). (gr. 7-12). 24.95 *(978-1-4222-3465-5(7))* Mason Crest.

MacDonald, Margaret. Rules on the Soccer Field. 2011. (Learn-Abouts Ser.). (Illus.). 16p. (J). pap. 7.95 *(978-1-59920-616-5(1))* Black Rabbit Bks.

Macmillan Children's Books Staff. Match! Incredible Stats & Facts. 2016. (ENG., Illus.). 224p. (J). (gr. 2-9). pap. 9.99 *(978-1-5098-2500-4(2))* Pan Macmillan GBR. Dist: Independent Pubs. Group.

Mahaney, Ian F. The Math of Soccer. 2011. (J). 49.50 *(978-1-4488-2701-5(9)*, PowerKids Pr.); pap. 8.25 *(978-1-4488-2700-8(0)*, PowerKids Pr.); (gr. 2-5). lib. bdg. 22.60 *(978-1-4488-2557-8(1))* Rosen Publishing Group, Inc., The.

Mahoney, Emily Jankowski. The Science of Soccer. 2015. (Sports Science Ser.). (ENG., Illus.). 32p. (J). (gr. 4-5). pap. 10.00 *(978-1-4994-1071-6(9)*, PowerKids Pr.) Rosen Publishing Group, Inc., The.

Mara, Wil. Soccer. 2012. (Rookie Read-about Ser.). (ENG., Illus.). 32p. (J). pap. 5.95 *(978-0-531-20927-1(X))*; (gr. -1-1). lib. bdg. 23.00 *(978-0-531-20858-8(3))* Scholastic Library Publishing. (Children's Pr.).

Martínez Alaniz, Eduardo. Hugo Sanchez. 2013. (Illus.). 32p. (J). *(978-1-4222-2647-6(6))* Mason Crest.

Mason, Paul & Eason, Sarah. Street Soccer. 2011. (On the Radar: Sports Ser.). (ENG., Illus.). 32p. (gr. 4-8). lib. bdg. 26.60 *(978-0-7613-7760-3(3))* Lerner Publishing Group.

Mattern, Joanne. Brian Mcbride. 2005. (No Hands Allowed Ser.). (Illus.). 32p. (J). (gr. 2-4). lib. bdg. 25.70 *(978-1-58415-389-4(X))* Mitchell Lane Pubs., Inc.

—I Know Soccer. 2013. (21st Century Basic Skills Library: I Know Sports Ser.). (ENG., Illus.). 24p. (J). (gr. k-3). 22.79 *(978-1-62431-402-5(3)*, 202728); pap. 12.79 *(978-1-62431-478-0(3)*, 202730) Cherry Lake Publishing.

May, Pete. Players. 2014. (Illus.). 32p. (J). *(978-1-62588-133-5(9))* Black Rabbit Bks.

—Teams. 2014. (Illus.). 32p. (J). *(978-1-62588-134-2(7))* Black Rabbit Bks.

McDougall, Chros. Best Soccer Players of All Time, 1 vol. 2014. (Sports' Best Ever Ser.). (ENG., Illus.). 64p. (J). (gr. 3-6). lib. bdg. 32.79 *(978-1-62403-621-7(X)*, SportsZone) ABDO Publishing Co.

—Soccer, 1 vol. 2012. (ENG.). 64p. 32.79 *(978-1-61783-146-1(8)*, SportsZone) ABDO Publishing Co.

McFee, Shane. Let's Play Soccer. (Let's Get Active Ser.). 24p. 2009. (gr. 2-3). 42.50 *(978-1-61514-255-2(X))* 2008. (Illus.). (J). (gr. 3-7). lib. bdg. 22.60 *(978-1-4042-4191-6(4))* Rosen Publishing Group, Inc., The. (PowerKids Pr.).

McGrath, Barbara Barbieri & Alderman, Peter. Soccer Counts! Estrada, Pau, illus. 2003. (ENG.). 32p. (J). (gr. -1-3). pap. 7.95 *(978-1-57091-554-3(7))* Charlesbridge Publishing, Inc.

—Soccer Counts! (El Futbol Cuenta!) Estrada, Pau, illus. 2011. (SPA & ENG.). 32p. (J). (gr. -1-3). pap. 7.95 *(978-1-57091-794-3(9))* Charlesbridge Publishing, Inc.

McIntosh, J. S. Soccer. 2010. (Getting the Edge Ser.). 96p. (YA). lib. bdg. 24.95 *(978-1-4222-1739-9(6))* Mason Crest.

Miller, Calvin Craig. David Beckham. 2008. (Xtreme Athletes Ser.). (Illus.). 100p. (J). (gr. 5-13). lib. bdg. 27.95 *(978-1-59935-082-0(3))* Reynolds, Morgan Inc.

Minden, Cecilia. Soccer. 2008. (21st Century Skills Library: Real World Math Ser.). (ENG., Illus.). 32p. (gr. 4-8). lib. bdg. 28.50 *(978-1-60279-244-9(5)*, 200195) Cherry Lake Publishing.

Mitchell Lane Publishers Inc. Staff. A Robbie Reader-No Hands Allowed, 13 vols. 2007. (No Hands Allowed Ser.). (Illus.). (J). lib. bdg. 334.10 *(978-1-58415-602-4(3))* Mitchell Lane Pubs., Inc.

Monnig, Alex. Girls' Soccer, 1 vol. 2013. (Girls' SportsZone Ser.). (ENG., Illus.). 48p. (J). (gr. 3-6). lib. bdg. 32.79 *(978-1-61783-989-4(2)*, SportsZone) ABDO Publishing Co.

—World Cup, 1 vol. 2013. (Sports' Great Championships Ser.). (ENG.). 64p. (J). (gr. 4-6). lib. bdg. 32.79 *(978-1-61783-675-6(3)*, SportsZone) ABDO Publishing Co.

Morgan, Alex. Breakaway. 2015. (ENG., Illus.). 320p. (YA). (gr. 7). 17.99 *(978-1-4814-5107-9(3)*, Simon & Schuster Bks. For Young Readers) Simon & Schuster Bks. For Young Readers.

Morreale, Marie. Lionel Messi. 2016. (Real Bios Ser.). (ENG.). 48p. (J). lib. bdg. 29.00 *(978-0-531-22379-6(5)*, Children's Pr.) Scholastic Library Publishing.

Murcia, Rebecca Thatcher. Ronaldinho. 2007. (No Hands Allowed Ser.). (Illus.). 32p. (J). (gr. 2-4). lib. bdg. 25.70 *(978-1-58415-600-0(7))* Mitchell Lane Pubs., Inc.

—What It's Like to Be Kaka. de la Vega, Eida, tr. 2011. (What It's Like to Be... = Que Se Sienta Al Ser... Ser.). (ENG & SPA., Illus.). 32p. (J). (gr. -1-2). lib. bdg. 25.70 *(978-1-58415-989-6(8))* Mitchell Lane Pubs., Inc.

Murphy, Patricia J. First Day at Soccer, Level 1. 2008. (DK Readers Ser.). (ENG., Illus.). 32p. (J). (gr. k-2). pap. 3.99 *(978-0-7566-3458-2(X)*, DK Children) Dorling Kindersley Publishing, Inc.

Murray, Laura K. Alex Morgan. 2016. (Illus.). 21p. (J). *(978-1-60818-667-9(9)*, Creative Education) Creative Co., The.

—Cristiano Ronaldo. 2016. (Illus.). 21p. (J). *(978-1-60818-670-9(9)*, Creative Education) Creative Co., The.

Murray, Stuart A. P. Score with Soccer Math. 2013. (Score with Sports Math Ser.). 48p. (J). lib. bdg. 25.27 *(978-0-7660-4175-2(1))*; (gr. 3-4). pap. 8.95 *(978-1-4644-0289-0(2))* Enslow Pubs., Inc. (Enslow Elementary).

S

Nagelhout, Ryan. Abby Wambach. 2016. (Sports MVPs Ser.). (Illus.). 24p. (J). (gr. 2-1). 22.60 *(978-1-4824-4639-5(1))* Stevens, Gareth Publishing LLLP.

—I Love Soccer. 2014. (My Favorite Sports Ser.). (Illus.). 24p. (J). (gr. k-2). 22.60 *(978-1-4824-0734-1(5))* Stevens, Gareth Publishing LLLP.

—Me Encanta el Fútbol / I Love Soccer. 2014. (My Favorite Sports Ser.). (SPA.). 24p. (J). (gr. k-2). 22.60 *(978-1-4824-0855-3(4))* Stevens, Gareth Publishing LLLP.

—Soccer: Who Does What? 2017. (Sports: What's Your Position? Ser.). 32p. (gr. 3-4). pap. 10.50 ***(978-1-5382-0413-9(4))*** Stevens, Gareth Publishing LLLP.

—Talk Like a Soccer Player. 2016. (Let's Talk Sports! Ser.). 00032p. (J). pap. 10.50 ***(978-1-4824-5712-4(1))*** Stevens, Gareth Publishing LLLP.

Nagelhout, Ryan. 20 Fun Facts about Soccer. 2016. (Fun Fact File: Sports! Ser.). (ENG., Illus.). 32p. (J). (gr. 2-3). lib. bdg. 25.25 *(978-1-4824-3982-3(4))* Stevens, Gareth Publishing LLLP.

Nelson, Robin. From Plastic to Soccer Ball. 2014. (Start to Finish: Sports Gear Ser.). (Illus.). 24p. (gr. k-3). pap. 6.95 *(978-1-4677-4562-8(6))*; (ENG.). lib. bdg. 23.93 *(978-1-4677-3889-7(1)*, Lerner Pubns.) Lerner Publishing Group.

—Soccer Is Fun! 2013. (First Step Nonfiction - Sports Are Fun! Ser.). (ENG., Illus.). 24p. (gr. k-2). pap. 6.95 *(978-1-4677-1538-6(7))*; lib. bdg. 23.93 *(978-1-4677-1105-0(5)*, Lerner Pubns.) Lerner Publishing Group.

Nixon, James. Defending & Goaltending. 2011. (Soccer File Ser.). 32p. (gr. 4-7). lib. bdg. 31.35 *(978-1-59920-527-4(0))* Black Rabbit Bks.

—Football. 2017. (First Sport Ser.). (ENG., Illus.). 24p. (J). (gr. k-2). pap. 9.99 *(978-1-4451-4906-6(0)*, Franklin Watts) Hachette Children's Group GBR. Dist: Hachette Bk. Group.

—Passing & Dribbling. 2011. (Soccer File Ser.). 32p. (gr. 4-7). lib. bdg. 31.35 *(978-1-59920-528-1(9))* Black Rabbit Bks.

—Rules of the Game. Humphrey, Bobby, photos by. 2011. (Soccer File Ser.). (Illus.). 32p. (gr. 4-7). lib. bdg. 31.35 *(978-1-59920-529-8(7))* Black Rabbit Bks.

No Hands Allowed: Stories for Kids Who Love Soccer, 7 bks., Set. Incl. Brandi Chastain. Adams, Michelle Medlock. (gr. 1-4). lib. bdg. 25.70 *(978-1-58415-390-0(3))*; Brian Mcbride. Mattern, Joanne. (gr. 2-4). lib. bdg. 25.70 *(978-1-58415-389-4(X))*; DaMarcus Beasley: Soccer Star Sensation. Smalley, Carol Parenzan. (gr. 1-4). lib. bdg. 25.70 *(978-1-58415-387-0(3))*; David Beckham. Murcia, Rebecca Thatcher. (gr. 1-4). lib. bdg. 25.70 *(978-1-58415-384-9(9))*; Freddy Adu. Murcia, Rebecca Thatcher. (gr. 1-4). lib. bdg. 25.70 *(978-1-58415-385-6(7))*; Josh Wolff: Three-Team Player. Kjelle, Marylou Morano. (gr. 2-4). lib. bdg. 25.70 *(978-1-58415-388-7(1))*; Landon Donovan. Murcia, Rebecca Thatcher. (gr. 1-4). lib. bdg. 25.70 *(978-1-58415-386-3(5))*; 32p. (J). 2005. (Robbie Reader Ser.). (Illus.). 2005. Set lib. bdg. 118.65 *(978-1-58415-413-6(6))* Mitchell Lane Pubs., Inc.

Obregon, Jose M. David Beckham. Benson, Megan, tr. 2008. (World Soccer Stars / Estrellas Del Fútbol Mundial Ser.). (SPA., Illus.). 24p. (J). (gr. 2-5). lib. bdg. 22.60 *(978-1-4042-7665-9(3))* Rosen Publishing Group, Inc., The.

Obregón, José María. Argentina. 2009. (Great National Soccer Teams / Grandes selecciones del fútbol mundial Ser.). (SPA & ENG.). 24p. pap. 8.25 *(978-1-4358-2495-9(4)*, PowerKids Pr.) Rosen Publishing Group, Inc., The.

—Argentina. Benson, Megan, tr. from SPA. 2009. (Great National Soccer Teams / Grandes Selecciones Del Fútbol Mundial Ser.). (SPA & ENG., Illus.). 24p. (J). (gr. 2-5). lib. bdg. 22.60 *(978-1-4042-8088-5(X)*, PowerKids Pr.) Rosen Publishing Group, Inc., The.

—Brazil: Brasil. 2009. (Great National Soccer Teams / Grandes selecciones del fútbol mundial Ser.). (SPA & ENG.). 24p. pap. 8.25 *(978-1-4358-2489-8(X))*; (Illus.). lib. bdg. 22.60 *(978-1-4042-8085-4(5))* Rosen Publishing Group, Inc., The. (PowerKids Pr.).

—Cuauhtémoc Blanco. 2009. (World Soccer Stars / Estrellas del fútbol mundial Ser.). 24p. (ENG & SPA.). (gr. 2-2). 42.50 *(978-1-60854-840-8(6))*; (SPA, ENG & MUL., Illus.). (J). lib. bdg. 22.60 *(978-1-4358-2731-8(7))* Rosen Publishing Group, Inc., The. (Editorial Buenas Letras).

Obregon, Jose Maria. David Beckham. 2009. (World Soccer Stars / Estrellas del fútbol mundial Ser.). (ENG & SPA.). 24p. (gr. 2-2). 42.50 *(978-1-60854-841-5(4)*, Editorial Buenas Letras) Rosen Publishing Group, Inc., The.

Obregón, José María. Didier Drogba. 2009. (World Soccer Stars / Estrellas Del Fútbol Mundial Ser.). (SPA & ENG.). 24p. (J). lib. bdg. 22.60 *(978-1-4358-2967-1(0)*, Editorial Buenas Letras) Rosen Publishing Group, Inc., The.

—England: Inglaterra. 2009. (Great National Soccer Teams / Grandes selecciones del fútbol mundial Ser.). (SPA & ENG.). 24p. pap. 8.25 *(978-1-4358-3235-0(3)*, PowerKids Pr.) Rosen Publishing Group, Inc., The.

—England: Inglaterra. Benson, Megan, tr. 2009. (Great National Soccer Teams / Grandes Selecciones Del Fútbol Mundial Ser.). (SPA & ENG., Illus.). 24p. (J). (gr. 2-5). lib. bdg. 22.60 *(978-1-4042-8089-2(8)*, PowerKids Pr.) Rosen Publishing Group, Inc., The.

—Freddy Adu. 2009. (World Soccer Stars / Estrellas Del Fútbol Mundial Ser.). (SPA, ENG & MUL., Illus.). 24p. (J). lib. bdg. 22.60 *(978-1-4358-2730-1(9)*, Editorial Buenas Letras) Rosen Publishing Group, Inc., The.

—Germany: Alemania. 2009. (Great National Soccer Teams / Grandes selecciones del fútbol mundial Ser.). (SPA & ENG.). 24p. pap. 8.25 *(978-1-4358-2493-5(8))* Rosen Publishing Group, Inc., The.

—Germany: Alemania. Benson, Megan, tr. 2009. (Great National Soccer Teams / Grandes Selecciones Del Fútbol Mundial Ser.). (SPA & ENG., Illus.). 24p. (J). (gr. 2-5). lib. bdg. 22.60 *(978-1-4042-8087-8(1))* Rosen Publishing Group, Inc., The.

—Italy: Italia. 2009. (Great National Soccer Teams / Grandes selecciones del fútbol mundial Ser.). (SPA & ENG.). 24p. pap. 8.25 *(978-1-4358-2491-1(1)*, PowerKids Pr.) Rosen Publishing Group, Inc., The.

—Italy: Italia. Benson, Megan, tr. 2009. (Great National Soccer Teams / Grandes Selecciones Del Fútbol Mundial Ser.). (SPA & ENG., Illus.). 24p. (J). (gr. 2-5). lib. bdg. 22.60 *(978-1-4042-8086-1(3)*, PowerKids Pr.) Rosen Publishing Group, Inc., The.

—Juan Pablo Ángel. 2009. (World Soccer Stars / Estrellas del fútbol mundial Ser.). (ENG & SPA.). 24p. (gr. 2-2). 42.50 *(978-1-60854-845-3(7))*; (SPA & ENG.). (J). lib. bdg. 22.60 *(978-1-4358-2732-5(5))* Rosen Publishing Group, Inc., The. (Editorial Buenas Letras).

—Kaká. 2009. (World Soccer Stars / Estrellas del fútbol mundial Ser.). (ENG & SPA.). 24p. (gr. 2-2). 42.50 *(978-1-60854-846-0(5))*; (SPA & ENG.). (J). lib. bdg. 22.60 *(978-1-4358-2733-2(3))* Rosen Publishing Group, Inc., The. (Editorial Buenas Letras).

—Lionel Messi. 2009. (World Soccer Stars / Estrellas del fútbol mundial Ser.). (ENG & SPA.). 24p. (gr. 2-2). 42.50 *(978-1-60854-848-4(1))*; (SPA & ENG.). (J). lib. bdg. 22.60 *(978-1-4358-2729-5(5))* Rosen Publishing Group, Inc., The. (Editorial Buenas Letras).

—Mexico/México. Benson, Megan, tr. 2009. (Great National Soccer Teams / Grandes Selecciones Del Fútbol Mundial Ser.). (SPA & ENG., Illus.). 24p. (J). (gr. 2-5). lib. bdg. 22.60 *(978-1-4358-2497-3(0)*, PowerKids Pr.) Rosen Publishing Group, Inc., The.

—Mexico/México. 2009. (SPA & ENG.). (J). 49.50 *(978-1-4358-3234-3(5))*; pap. 8.25 *(978-1-4358-2498-0(9))* Rosen Publishing Group, Inc., The. (PowerKids Pr.).

Obregon, Jose Maria. Ronaldhino. 2009. (World Soccer Stars / Estrellas del fútbol mundial Ser.). (ENG & SPA.). 24p. (gr. 2-2). 42.50 *(978-1-60854-850-7(3)*, Editorial Buenas Letras) Rosen Publishing Group, Inc., The.

—Ronaldinho. Benson, Megan, tr. 2008. (World Soccer Stars / Estrellas Del Fútbol Mundial Ser.). (SPA., Illus.). 24p. (J). (gr. 2-5). lib. bdg. 22.60 *(978-1-4042-7664-2(5))* Rosen Publishing Group, Inc., The.

Oldfield, Matt & Oldfield, Tom. Alexis Sanchez: the Wonder Boy. 2016. (ENG.). 160p. (J). (gr. 4-7). pap. 8.99 *(978-1-78606-013-6(2))* Blake, John Publishing, Ltd. GBR. Dist: Independent Pubs. Group.

—Eden Hazard: the Boy in Blue. 2016. (ENG.). 160p. (J). (gr. 4-7). pap. 8.99 *(978-1-78606-014-3(0))* Blake, John Publishing, Ltd. GBR. Dist: Independent Pubs. Group.

—Luis Suarez: el Pistolero. 2016. (ENG., Illus.). 160p. (J). (gr. 4-7). pap. 8.99 *(978-1-78606-012-9(4))* Blake, John Publishing, Ltd. GBR. Dist: Independent Pubs. Group.

Oldfield, Tom & Oldfield, Matt. Gareth Bale: The Boy Who Became a Galáctico. 2016. (ENG.). 160p. (J). (gr. 4-7). pap. 8.99 *(978-1-78418-645-6(7))* Blake, John Publishing, Ltd. GBR. Dist: Independent Pubs. Group.

—Raheem Sterling: Red Lightning. 2016. (ENG.). 160p. (J). (gr. 4-7). pap. 8.99 *(978-1-78418-646-3(5))* Blake, John Publishing, Ltd. GBR. Dist: Independent Pubs. Group.

—Sergio Agüero. 2017. (ENG.). 160p. (J). (gr. 4-7). pap. 9.99 ***(978-1-78606-218-5(6))*** Blake, John Publishing, Ltd. GBR. Dist: Independent Pubs. Group.

—Steven Gerrard. 2017. (ENG.). 160p. (J). (gr. 4-7). pap. 9.99 ***(978-1-78606-219-2(4))*** Blake, John Publishing, Ltd. GBR. Dist: Independent Pubs. Group.

—Wayne Rooney: Captain of England. 2016. (ENG.). 160p. (J). (gr. 4-7). pap. 8.99 *(978-1-78418-647-0(3))* Blake, John Publishing, Ltd. GBR. Dist: Independent Pubs. Group.

Oldfield, Tom & Oldfield, Matt. Zlatan Ibrahimovic. 2017. (ENG.). 160p. (J). (gr. 4-7). pap. 9.99 ***(978-1-78606-217-8(8))*** Blake, John Publishing, Ltd. GBR. Dist: Independent Pubs. Group.

Orme, David. Football. 2007. (Trailblazers Ser.). (ENG., Illus.). 36p. (J). (gr. -1-3). pap. *(978-1-84167-425-4(7))* Ransom Publishing Ltd.

Orr, Tamra B. Abby Wambach. 2007. (No Hands Allowed Ser.). (Illus.). 32p. (J). (gr. 2-4). lib. bdg. 25.70 *(978-1-58415-601-7(5))* Mitchell Lane Pubs., Inc.

Osborne, Mary Pope & Boyce, Natalie Pope. Soccer. 2014. (Magic Tree House Fact Tracker Ser.: 29). lib. bdg. 17.20 *(978-0-606-36016-6(6))* Turtleback Bks.

—Soccer: Soccer on Sunday. Murdocca, Sal, illus. 2014. (Magic Tree House - Fact Tracker Ser.: 29). (ENG.). 128p. (J). (gr. 2-5). 6.99 *(978-0-385-38629-6(X)*, Random Hse. Bks. for Young Readers) Random Hse. Children's Bks.

Otten, Jack. Futbol. 2004. (Entrenamiento Deportivo (Sports Training) Ser.). (SPA & ENG., Illus.). 24p. (J). lib. bdg. 22.60 *(978-0-8239-6850-3(2)*, Editorial Buenas Letras) Rosen Publishing Group, Inc., The.

—Fútbol (Soccer) 2009. (Entrenamiento deportivo (Sports Training) Ser.). (SPA.). 24p. (gr. 1-2). 42.50 *(978-1-61512-269-1(9)*, Editorial Buenas Letras) Rosen Publishing Group, Inc., The.

—*Soccer. 2009. (Sports Training Ser.). 24p. (gr. 1-2). 42.50 (978-1-60853-188-2(0)*, PowerKids Pr.) Rosen Publishing Group, Inc., The.

Page, Jason. Basketball, Soccer, & Other Ball Games. 2008. (Olympic Sports Ser.). (ENG., Illus.). 32p. (J). (gr. 4-7). pap. *(978-0-7787-4029-2(3))*; lib. bdg. *(978-0-7787-4012-4(9))* Crabtree Publishing Co.

—El Futbol. 2004. (Club Deportivo Ser.).Tr. of Soccer. (SPA., Illus.). 32p. (J). (gr. 3-6). 9.95 *(978-1-58728-398-7(0)*, Two-Can Publishing) T&N Children's Publishing.

Parrish, Charles & Naught, John. Soccer Around the World: A Cultural Guide to the World's Favorite Sport, 1 vol. 2014. (Illus.). 400p. (C). 89.00 *(978-1-61069-302-8(7)*, A3997C) ABC-CLIO, LLC.

Pendleton, Ken. David Beckham. 2007. (Sports Heroes & Legends Ser.). (Illus.). 106p. (YA). (gr. 7-12). lib. bdg. 30.60 *(978-0-8225-7161-2(7))* Twenty First Century Bks.

Pendleton, Ken & Savage, Jeff. David Beckham. 2008. (Sports Heroes & Legends Ser.). (ENG.). (gr. 5-12). pap. 56.72 *(978-1-57505-993-8(2))* Lerner Publishing Group.

Perez, Mike. Lionel Messi: The Ultimate Fan Book. (ENG., Illus.). 64p. (J). 2017. (gr. 4). pap. 9.95 *(978-1-78097-921-2(5))* 2016. (gr. 3). 14.99 *(978-1-78097-768-3(9))* 2014. (gr. 3-9). 14.99 *(978-1-78097-443-9(4))* Carlton Bks., Ltd. GBR. Dist: Sterling Publishing Co., Inc., Independent Pubs. Group.

Peterson, Megan Cooley. Wacky Soccer Trivia: Fun Facts for Every Fan. 2016. (Wacky Sports Trivia Ser.). (ENG., Illus.). 32p. (gr. 3-4). lib. bdg. 27.99 *(978-1-5157-1996-0(0))* Capstone Press of Coughlan Cos.

Porter, Esther. Abby Wambach. 2016. (Women in Sports Ser.). (ENG., Illus.). 24p. (gr. k-1). lib. bdg. 26.65 *(978-1-4914-7974-2(4)*, Pebble Plus) Capstone Press of Coughlan Cos.

Poulton, J. Alexander. World's Best Soccer Player: Today's Hottest Superstars, 1 vol. rev. ed. 2006. (ENG., Illus.). 144p. per. 9.95 *(978-0-9737681-9-0(3)*, 0973768193, OverTime Bks.) Editions de la Montagne Verte, Inc. CAN. Dist: Lone Pine Publishing USA.

Powell, Elizabeth. Math at the Game. 2016. (Math Is Everywhere! Ser.). 00024p. (J). pap. 8.15 *(978-1-4824-5482-6(3))* Stevens, Gareth Publishing LLLP.

Raum, Elizabeth. Carli Lloyd. 2017. (Pro Sports Biographies Ser.). (ENG.). 24p. (gr. 1-4). 20.95 ***(978-1-68151-132-0(0))*** Amicus Publishing.

—Pro Sports Biographies: Carli Lloyd. 2017. (Pro Sports Biographies Ser.). (ENG.). 24p. (J). (gr. 1-3). pap. 8.99 ***(978-1-68152-163-3(6))*** Amicus.

Rausch, David. Major League Soccer. 2014. (Major League Sports Ser.). (ENG.). 24p. (J). (gr. 3-7). 25.95 *(978-1-62617-134-3(3)*, Epic Bks.) Bellwether Media.

Rediger, Pat. Soccer. 2009. (In the Zone Ser.). 24p. (J). (gr. 3-5). pap. 8.95 *(978-1-60596-125-5(6))*; (Illus.). lib. bdg. 24.45 *(978-1-60596-124-8(8))* Weigl Pubs., Inc.

Riner, Dax. Pelé. 2010. (Sports Heroes & Legends Ser.). (ENG.). 120p. (gr. 5-12). lib. bdg. 30.60 *(978-0-7613-5368-3(2))* Lerner Publishing Group.

Robinson, Sacha. My Soccer Journal. 2015. (ENG., Illus.). 46p. (J). pap. *(978-1-78222-419-8(X))* Paragon Publishing, Rothersthorpe.

Robinson, Tom. David Beckham: Soccer's Superstar. 2008. (People to Know Today Ser.). (Illus.). 112p. (J). (gr. 3-7). lib. bdg. 33.27 *(978-0-7660-3110-4(1))* Enslow Pubs., Inc.

Roselius, J. Chris. David Beckham: Gifted & Giving Soccer Star. 2010. (Sports Stars Who Give Back Ser.). (Illus.). 128p. (J). (gr. 5-9). lib. bdg. 33.27 *(978-0-7660-3587-4(5))* Enslow Pubs., Inc.

—Soccer Skills: How to Play Like a Pro. 2008. (How to Play Like a Pro Ser.). (Illus.). 48p. (J). (gr. 3-6). lib. bdg. 25.27 *(978-0-7660-3206-4(X))* Enslow Pubs., Inc.

Ross, Dev. We Both Read-Soccer! Wenzel, David, illus. 2010. 44p. (J). 9.95 *(978-1-60115-239-8(6))*; pap. 4.99 *(978-1-60115-240-4(X))* Treasure Bay, Inc.

Roth, B. A. David Beckham: Born to Play. 2007. (All Aboard Reading Station Stop 3 Collection). (Illus.). 48p. (gr. 1-3). 14.00 *(978-0-7569-8918-7(3))* Perfection Learning Corp.

Roytman, Arkady. The Soccer Coloring Book. 2016. (Dover Coloring Bks.). (ENG.). 32p. (J). (gr. 2-5). pap. 3.99 *(978-0-486-80481-1(X))* Dover Pubns., Inc.

Roza, Greg. David Beckham: Soccer Superstar. 2006. (Tony Stead Nonfiction Independent Reading Collection). (ENG.). 24p. (gr. 3-6). pap. 8.85 *(978-1-4042-5539-5(7))* Rosen Publishing Group, Inc., The.

Roza, Greg & Burdick, Mason. Soccer. 2012. (On the Team Ser.). (ENG., Illus.). 24p. (J). (gr. 2-5). pap. 8.15 *(978-1-4339-6454-1(6))*; lib. bdg. 22.60 *(978-1-4339-6452-7(X))* Stevens, Gareth Publishing LLLP. (Gareth Stevens Learning Library).

Rumaner, Marc. Let's Play Soccer! Incl. 2 1/2 " Soccer Ball. (Illus.). 12p. (J). (gr. -1-1). bds. *(978-1-56021-373-4(6)*, 220) W.J. Fantasy, Inc.

Sad, Elizabeth Levy & Eliaszevich, Esteban. Gonzalo Higuain. 2012. (Superstars of Soccer ENGLISH Ser.). (ENG., Illus.). 32p. (J). (gr. 4-7). lib. bdg. 19.95 *(978-1-4222-2649-0(2))* Mason Crest.

—Luis Amaranto Perea. 2012. (Superstars of Soccer ENGLISH Ser.). (ENG., Illus.). 32p. (J). (gr. 4-7). lib. bdg. 19.95 *(978-1-4222-2654-4(9))* Mason Crest.

—Radamel Falcao. 2012. (Superstars of Soccer ENGLISH Ser.). (ENG., Illus.). 32p. (J). (gr. 4-7). lib. bdg. 19.95 *(978-1-4222-2653-7(0))* Mason Crest.

Sandler, Michael. Soccer: The Amazing U. S. World Cup Team. 2006. (Upsets & Comebacks Ser.). (Illus.). 32p. (J). (gr. 3-6). lib. bdg. 25.27 *(978-1-59716-169-5(1))* Bearport Publishing Co., Inc.

Savage, Jeff. David Beckham. 2008. (Amazing Athletes Ser.). (Illus.). 32p. (J). (gr. -1). per. 6.95 *(978-0-8225-8975-4(3)*, First Avenue Editions); (Illus.). 32p. (YA). (gr. 2-5). lib. bdg. 23.93 *(978-0-8225-8834-4(X))*; pap. 40.95 *(978-0-8225-9491-8(9))* Lerner Publishing Group.

—Freddy Adu. 2006. (Amazing Athletes Ser.). (Illus.). 32p. (gr. 2-5). (J). pap. 6.95 *(978-0-8225-3595-9(5)*, First Avenue Editions); (ENG., lib. bdg. 25.26 *(978-0-8225-3430-3(4))* Lerner Publishing Group.

—Soccer Super Stats. 2017. (Pro Sports Stats Ser.). (ENG., Illus.). 32p. (J). (gr. 3-6). 27.99 ***(978-1-5124-3409-5(4))*** Lerner Publishing Group.

Savage, Jeff. Top 25 Soccer Skills, Tips, & Tricks. 2011. (Top 25 Sports Skills, Tips, & Tricks Ser.). (Illus.). 48p. (J). (gr. 2-5). lib. bdg. 25.27 *(978-0-7660-3860-8(2))*; (gr. 4-18). pap. 8.95 *(978-1-59845-359-1(9))* Enslow Pubs., Inc.

Schrier, Allyson Valentine. A Girl's Guide to Soccer, 1 vol. 2012. (Get in the Game Ser.). (ENG.). 32p. (gr. 3-4). lib. bdg. 27.99 *(978-1-4296-7671-7(X)*, Snap Bks.) Capstone Press of Coughlan Cos.

Schuh, Mari C. Cristiano Ronaldo. 2016. (Famous Athletes Ser.). (ENG., Illus.). 24p. (gr. k-1). lib. bdg. 26.65 *(978-1-4914-8508-8(6))* Capstone Press of Coughlan Cos.

Schuh, Mari C. Soccer. 2017. (Spot Sports Ser.). (ENG.). 16p. (gr. k-3). 17.95 ***(978-1-68151-089-7(8))*** Amicus Publishing.

Shea, Therese. Soccer Stars. Shea, Therese, illus. 2007. (Sports Stars Ser.). (ENG., Illus.). 48p. (J). (gr. 4-7). pap. 6.95 *(978-0-531-18705-0(5))* Scholastic Library Publishing.

Sheaffer, C. H. Soccer Heart: A Story & Guide for the Friendly Contender. 2010. (Illus.). 168p. *(978-0-9840922-0-8(X))* SilverBrown Bks.

Soccer: Level 30. 2003. 31.95 *(978-0-673-57967-6(0))* Celebration Pr.

Soccer Smarts. 2017. (Soccer Smarts Ser.). 32p. (gr. 8-8). 105.00 ***(978-1-4994-3403-3(0))***; pap. 40.00 ***(978-1-4994-3498-9(7))*** Rosen Publishing Group, Inc., The. (PowerKids Pr.).

Solo, Hope. Hope Solo: My Story. 2012. (ENG.). 256p. (J). (gr. 3-7). 16.99 *(978-0-06-222065-3(9)*, Collins) HarperCollins Pubs.

—Hope Solo - My Story. 2013. (ENG.). 256p. (J). (gr. 3-7). pap. 5.99 *(978-0-06-222066-0(7))* HarperCollins Pubs.

Sommers, Annie Leah. Great National Soccer Teams. 2010. (World Soccer Books Ser.). (Illus.). 64p. (YA). (gr. 5-8). lib. bdg. 31.95 *(978-1-4358-9138-8(4)*, Rosen Reference) Rosen Publishing Group, Inc., The.

Sosa, Carlos. Lionel Messi. 2012. (Superstars of Soccer ENGLISH Ser.). (ENG., Illus.). 32p. (J). (gr. 4-7). lib. bdg. 19.95 *(978-1-4222-2659-9(X))* Mason Crest.

Spragg, Iain. Cristiano Ronaldo: The Ultimate Fan Book. 2017. (ENG., Illus.). 64p. (J). (gr. 4). pap. 9.95 *(978-1-78097-920-5(7))* Carlton Bks., Ltd. GBR. Dist: Sterling Publishing Co., Inc.

St. John, Warren. Outcasts United: The Story of a Refugee Soccer Team That Changed a Town. 2013. (ENG.). 240p. (YA). (gr. 7). pap. 9.99 *(978-0-385-74195-8(2)*, Ember) Random Hse. Children's Bks.

Sterling Children's, Sterling. My First Soccer Book. 2015. (First Sports Ser.). (ENG., Illus.). 22p. (J). (— 1). bds. 6.95 *(978-1-4549-1489-1(0))* Sterling Publishing Co., Inc.

Stewart, Mark. A. C. Milan. 2017. (First Touch Soccer Ser.). (ENG.). 24p. (J). (gr. k-3). 23.93 ***(978-1-59953-855-6(5))*** Norwood Hse. Pr.

—Arsenal F. C. 2017. (First Touch Soccer Ser.). (ENG.). 24p. (J). (gr. k-3). 23.93 ***(978-1-59953-856-3(3))*** Norwood Hse. Pr.

—C. A. River Plate. 2017. (First Touch Soccer Ser.). (ENG.). 24p. (J). (gr. k-3). 23.93 ***(978-1-59953-867-9(9))*** Norwood Hse. Pr.

—Chelsea F. C. 2017. (First Touch Soccer Ser.). (ENG.). 24p. (J). (gr. k-3). 23.93 ***(978-1-59953-858-7(X))*** Norwood Hse. Pr.

—F. C. Barcelona. 2017. (First Touch Soccer Ser.). (ENG.). 24p. (J). (gr. k-3). 23.93 ***(978-1-59953-859-4(8))*** Norwood Hse. Pr.

—F. C. Bayern Munich. 2017. (First Touch Soccer Ser.). (ENG.). 24p. (J). (gr. k-3). 23.93 ***(978-1-59953-857-0(1))*** Norwood Hse. Pr.

—Houston Dynamo. 2017. (First Touch Soccer Ser.). (ENG.). 24p. (J). (gr. k-3). 23.93 ***(978-1-59953-863-1(6))*** Norwood Hse. Pr.

—Los Angeles Galaxy. 2017. (First Touch Soccer Ser.). (ENG.). 24p. (J). (gr. k-3). 23.93 ***(978-1-59953-864-8(4))*** Norwood Hse. Pr.

—Manchester United. 2017. (First Touch Soccer Ser.). (ENG.). 24p. (J). (gr. k-3). 23.93 ***(978-1-59953-860-0(1))*** Norwood Hse. Pr.

—New York Red Bulls. 2017. (First Touch Soccer Ser.). (ENG.). 24p. (J). (gr. k-3). 23.93 ***(978-1-59953-865-5(2))*** Norwood Hse. Pr.

—Paris Saint-Germain. 2017. (First Touch Soccer Ser.). (ENG.). 24p. (J). (gr. k-3). 23.93 ***(978-1-59953-861-7(X))*** Norwood Hse. Pr.

—Portland Timbers. 2017. (First Touch Soccer Ser.). (ENG.). 24p. (J). (gr. k-3). 23.93 ***(978-1-59953-866-2(0))*** Norwood Hse. Pr.

—Real Madrid C. F. 2017. (First Touch Soccer Ser.). (ENG.). 24p. (J). (gr. k-3). 23.93 ***(978-1-59953-862-4(8))*** Norwood Hse. Pr.

—São Paulo F. C. 2017. (First Touch Soccer Ser.). (ENG.). 24p. (J). (gr. k-3). 23.93 ***(978-1-59953-868-6(7))*** Norwood Hse. Pr.

—Seattle Sounders F. C. 2017. (First Touch Soccer Ser.). (ENG.). 24p. (J). (gr. k-3). 23.93 ***(978-1-59953-869-3(5))*** Norwood Hse. Pr.

—Toronto F. C. 2017. (First Touch Soccer Ser.). (ENG.). 24p. (J). (gr. k-3). 23.93 ***(978-1-59953-870-9(9))*** Norwood Hse. Pr.

Stewart, Mark. The World Cup. Kennedy, Mike, ed. 2003. (Watts History of Sports Ser.). (ENG., Illus.). 96p. (J). 34.50 *(978-0-531-11957-0(2))* Scholastic Library Publishing.

Stone, Lynn M. Goalies. 2007. (Playmakers (High Interest) Ser.). (Illus.). 24p. (YA). (gr. 3-6). lib. bdg. 27.07 *(978-1-60044-593-4(4))* Rourke Educational Media.

—Strikers. 2007. (Playmakers (High Interest) Ser.). (Illus.). 24p. (YA). (gr. 3-6). lib. bdg. 27.07 *(978-1-60044-598-9(5))* Rourke Educational Media.

Suen, Anastasia. La historia del fútbol (the Story of Soccer) 2009. (Historia de los deportes (Sports History) Ser.). (SPA.). 24p. (gr. 2-2). 42.50 *(978-1-61513-311-6(9)*, Editorial Buenas Letras) Rosen Publishing Group, Inc., The.

—The Story of Soccer. 2009. (Sports History Ser.). 24p. (gr. 2-2). 42.50 *(978-1-60853-139-4(2)*, PowerKids Pr.) Rosen Publishing Group, Inc., The.

Sullivan, George. All about Soccer. 2005. (Illus.). 122p. (J). (gr. 4-8). reprint ed. pap. 10.00 *(978-0-7567-9750-8(0))* DIANE Publishing Co.

Sutherland, Adam. Manchester United. 2017. (Big Business Ser.). (ENG., Illus.). 32p. (J). (gr. 4-6). pap. 11.99 *(978-0-7502-8945-0(7)*, Wayland) Hachette Children's Group GBR. Dist: Hachette Bk. Group.

—Soccer Stars. 2012. (Celebrity Secrets Ser.). (ENG., Illus.). 24p. (J). (gr. 5-8). pap. 8.25 *(978-1-4488-7086-8(0))*; lib. bdg. 22.60 *(978-1-4488-7038-7(0))* Rosen Publishing Group, Inc., The. (PowerKids Pr.).

Sutherland, Jon & Chalk, Gary. Avon United - Diamond. 2005. (Football Fantasy S. Ser.). (ENG., Illus.). 304p. 9.50 *(978-1-84046-622-5(7))* Icon Bks., Ltd. GBR. Dist: Publishers Group Canada.

—Clyde Rovers. 2005. (Football Fantasy S. Ser.). (ENG., Illus.). 272p. 9.50 *(978-1-84046-621-8(9))* Icon Bks., Ltd. GBR. Dist: Publishers Group Canada.

—Tyne Athletic - 4-3-3. 2004. (Football Fantasy S. Ser.). (ENG., Illus.). 272p. pap. 9.50 *(978-1-84046-596-9(4)*, Wizard Books) Icon Bks., Ltd. GBR. Dist: Publishers Group Canada.

Swope, Bob. Teach'n Beginning Offensive Soccer Drills, Plays, Strategies, & Games Free Flow Handbook. 2013. 96p. pap. 19.95 *(978-0-9911151-2-9(0))* Jacobob Pr., LLC.

Taylor, Sean. Goal! Vilela, Caio, photos by. 2014. (ENG., Illus.). 40p. (J). (gr. -1-3). 17.99 *(978-1-62779-123-6(X)*, 9781627791236, Holt, Henry & Co. Bks. For Young Readers) Holt, Henry & Co.

Taylor, Trace. Soccer. Taylor, Trace, illus. 2009. (2G Sports Ser.). (ENG., Illus.). 16p. (J). (gr. k-2). pap. 5.99 *(978-1-59301-878-8(9))* American Reading Co.

Teixeira, Thiago Jorge. Neymar. 2012. (Superstars of Soccer ENGLISH Ser.). (ENG., Illus.). 32p. (J). (gr. 4-7). lib. bdg. 19.95 *(978-1-4222-2648-3(4))* Mason Crest.

Thatcher Murcia, Rebecca. What Its Like to Be Marta Vieira. de la Vega, Eida, tr. 2010. (What It's Like to Be/Que se Siente al Ser Ser.). (ENG & SPA., Illus.). 32p. (J). (gr. -1-2). lib. bdg. 25.70 *(978-1-58415-852-3(2))* Mitchell Lane Pubs., Inc.

Thomas, Keltie. How Soccer Works. MacEachern, Stephen & Owlkids Books Inc. Staff, illus. 2007. (How Sports Work Ser.). (ENG.). 64p. (J). (gr. 4-7). pap. 10.95 *(978-1-897349-01-4(7)*, Maple Tree Pr.) Owlkids Bks. Inc. CAN. Dist: Publishers Group West (PGW).

Thomas, Mark. The Maracana: World's Largest Soccer Stadium. 2009. (Record-Breaking Structures Ser.). 24p. (gr. 1-2). 42.50 *(978-1-60852-456-3(6)*, PowerKids Pr.) Rosen Publishing Group, Inc., The.

Tieck, Sarah. David Beckham: Soccer Superstar, 1 vol. 2008. (Big Buddy Biographies Ser.). (ENG.). 32p. (J). (gr. 2-5). 28.50 *(978-1-60453-116-9(9))* ABDO Publishing Co.

Torres, John. Cristiano Ronaldo: Champion Soccer Star. 2017. (Sports Star Champions Ser.). 48p. (J). (gr. 5-6). lib. bdg. 27.93 ***(978-0-7660-8688-3(7))*** Enslow Pubs., Inc.

—Neymar: Champion Soccer Star. 2017. (Sports Star Champions Ser.). 48p. (gr. 5-6). pap. 11.70 ***(978-0-7660-8757-6(3))***; lib. bdg. 27.93 ***(978-0-7660-8694-4(1))*** Enslow Pubs., Inc.

Torres, John Albert. Lionel Messi. 2016. (Influential Latinos Ser.). (ENG.). 128p. (J). (gr. 7-8). 37.27 *(978-0-7660-7260-2(6))* Enslow Pubs., Inc.

—Soccer Star Cristiano Ronaldo. 2014. (Goal! Latin Stars of Soccer Ser.). 48p. 14.95 *(978-1-62285-222-2(2))* Enslow Pubs., Inc.

—Soccer Star Lionel Messi. 2014. (Goal! Latin Stars of Soccer Ser.). 48p. 14.95 *(978-1-62285-221-5(4))* Enslow Pubs., Inc.

—Soccer Star Ronaldinho. 2014. (Goal! Latin Stars of Soccer Ser.). 48p. 14.95 *(978-1-62285-223-9(0))* Enslow Pubs., Inc.

Trollinger, Patsi B. Thrill in The 'Ville. Thompson, Elizabeth, illus. 2012. 128p. (J). pap. 6.99 *(978-0-9836106-1-8(4))* Benjamin Pr.

Trusdell, Brian. Soccer Record Breakers, 1 vol. 2016. (ENG., Illus.). 48p. (J). ***(978-1-62403-850-1(6)***, SportsZone) ABDO Publishing Co.

Turner, Tracy. Soccer Stars. 2015. (Head-To-Head Ser.). (ENG., Illus.). 24p. (gr. 3-8). 28.50 *(978-1-62588-154-0(1))* Black Rabbit Bks.

Uschan, Michael V. David Beckham. 2008. (People in the News Ser.). (ENG., Illus.). 128p. (gr. 3-7). lib. bdg. 39.40 *(978-1-4205-0054-7(6)*, Lucent Bks.) Cengage Gale.

Valay, Ana Patricia. Giovani Dos Santos. 2012. (Superstars of Soccer SPANISH Ser.). 32p. (J). (gr. 4). (SPA.). 19.95 *(978-1-4222-2597-4(6))*; (ENG., Illus.). lib. bdg. 19.95 *(978-1-4222-2650-6(6))* Mason Crest.

Valay, Ana Patricia & Sandoval, Ana Valay. Arnoldo Iguaran. 2012. (Superstars of Soccer ENGLISH Ser.). (ENG., Illus.). 32p. (J). (gr. 4-7). lib. bdg. 19.95 *(978-1-4222-2663-6(8))* Mason Crest.

Vazquez, Gustavo & Vargas, Fredrico. Chicharito Hernndez. 2012. (Superstars of Soccer ENGLISH Ser.). 32p. (J). (gr. 4). 19.95 *(978-1-4222-2660-5(3))* Mason Crest.

Vazquez-Lozano, Gustavo. Ivan Cordoba. 2012. (Superstars of Soccer ENGLISH Ser.). (ENG., Illus.). 32p. (J). (gr. 4-7). lib. bdg. 19.95 *(978-1-4222-2652-0(2))* Mason Crest.

Vazquez-Lozano, Gustavo & Benard, Federico Vargas. Luis Suarez. 2012. (Superstars of Soccer ENGLISH Ser.). (ENG., Illus.). 32p. (J). (gr. 4-7). lib. bdg. 19.95 *(978-1-4222-2656-8(5))* Mason Crest.

Velázquez de León, Mauricio. Top Soccer Tournaments Around the World. 2010. (World Soccer Books Ser.). (Illus.). 64p. (YA). (gr. 5-8). lib. bdg. 31.95 *(978-1-4358-9140-1(6)*, Rosen Reference) Rosen Publishing Group, Inc., The.

—20 Soccer Legends. 2010. (World Soccer Books Ser.). (Illus.). 64p. (YA). (gr. 5-8). lib. bdg. 31.95 *(978-1-4358-9136-4(8)*, Rosen Reference) Rosen Publishing Group, Inc., The.

Vilela, Caio. Goal! Taylor, Sean, tr. from POR. 2015. (ENG., Illus.). 40p. (J). pap. 10.99 *(978-1-84780-597-3(3)*, Frances Lincoln) Quarto Publishing Group UK GBR. Dist: Littlehampton Bk Services, Ltd.

Waddell, Martin. Football Spy. Keylock, Andy & Veres, Laszlo, illus. 2007. (Collins Big Cat Ser.). (ENG.). 80p. (J). (gr. 2-3). pap. 8.99 *(978-0-00-723086-0(9))* HarperCollins Pubs. Ltd. GBR. Dist: Independent Pubs. Group.

Walker, Niki & Dann, Sarah. Fútbol en Acción. 2005. (Deportes en Accion Ser.). (SPA., Illus.). 32p. (J). (gr. 6-9). pap. *(978-0-7787-8616-0(1))* Crabtree Publishing Co.

—Le Soccer. Briere, Marie-Josee, tr. from ENG. rev. ed. 2007. (Sans Limites Ser.). (FRE., Illus.). 32p. (J). (gr. 1-7). pap. 9.95 *(978-2-89579-124-9(4))* Bayard Canada Livres CAN. Dist: Crabtree Publishing Co.

Wambach, Abby. Forward: Young Reader's Edition. 224p. (J). (gr. 3-7). 2017. pap. 6.99 *(978-0-06-245793-6(4))* 2016. 16.99 *(978-0-06-245792-9(6))* HarperCollins Pubs.

Wandersman, Aldo. Ronaldinho. 2012. (Superstars of Soccer SPANISH Ser.). (Illus.). 32p. (J). (gr. 4). (SPA.). 19.95

(978-1-4222-2604-9(2)); (ENG., lib. bdg. 19.95 (978-1-4222-2657-5(3)) Mason Crest.
—Ronaldo. 2012. (Superstars of Soccer ENGLISH Ser.). (ENG., Illus.). 32p. (J). (gr. 4-7). lib. bdg. 19.95 (978-1-4222-2658-2(1)) Mason Crest.
Ward, Adam. Motson's National Obsession: The Greatest Football Trivia Book Ever. 2004. (Illus.). 200p. (978-1-86074-601-7(2)) Sanctuary Publishing, Ltd.
Watson, Galadriel. David Beckham. 2007. (Remarkable People Ser.). (Illus.). 24p. (J). (gr. 3-7). pap. 8.95 (978-1-59036-642-4(5)) Weigl Pubs., Inc.
Watson, Galadriel Findlay. David Beckham. 2007. (Remarkable People Ser.). (Illus.). 24p. (J). (gr. 3-7). lib. bdg. 24.45 (978-1-59036-641-7(7)) Weigl Pubs., Inc.
Watson, Stephanie. The Science Behind Soccer, Volleyball, Cycling, & Other Popular Sports. 2016. (Science of the Summer Olympics Ser.). (ENG., Illus.). 32p. (gr. 3-4). lib. bdg. 27.99 (978-1-4914-8160-8(9), Edge Bks.) Capstone Press of Coughlan Cos.
Wendorff, Anne. Soccer. 2009. (My First Sports Ser.). (ENG., Illus.). 24p. (J). (gr. 2-5). lib. bdg. 25.95 (978-1-60014-329-8(6), Blastoff! Readers) Bellwether Media.
Whitfield, David. World Cup. (J). 2012. (978-1-61913-062-3(9)) 2012. pap. (978-1-61913-624-3(4)) 2007. (Illus.). 32p. (gr. 4-7). lib. bdg. 26.00 (978-1-59036-695-0(6)) 2007. (Illus.). 32p. (gr. 4-7). per. 9.95 (978-1-59036-696-7(4)) Weigl Pubs., Inc.
Whitfield, David. The World Cup. 2017. (Illus.). 32p. **(978-1-5105-0858-3(9))** Lightbox, The.
Whiting, Jim. AC Milan. 2016. (J). (978-1-56660-846-6(5), Creative Education) Creative Co., The.
—AC Milan: Soccer Champions. 2016. (Soccer Champions Ser.). (ENG.). 48p. (J). (gr. 5-9). pap. 12.00 (978-1-62832-195-1(4), Creative Paperbacks) Creative Co., The.
—Bayern Munich. (Illus.). (J). 2016. 24p. (978-1-60818-800-0(0)) 2015. 48p. (978-1-60818-587-0(7)) Creative Co., The. (Creative Education).
—Bayern Munich: Soccer Champions. 2016. (Soccer Champions Ser.). (ENG.). 48p. (J). (gr. 5-9). pap. 12.00 (978-1-62832-192-0(X), Creative Paperbacks) Creative Co., The.
—David Beckham. 2012. (Role Model Athletes Ser.). 64p. (J). (gr. 7). 22.95 (978-1-4222-2708-4(1)) Mason Crest.
—FC Barcelona. (Illus.). (J). 2016. 24p. (978-1-60818-801-7(9)) 2015. 48p. (978-1-60818-586-3(9)) Creative Co., The. (Creative Education).
—FC Barcelona: Soccer Champions. 2016. (Soccer Champions Ser.). (ENG.). 48p. (J). (gr. 5-9). pap. 12.00 (978-1-62832-191-3(1), Creative Paperbacks) Creative Co., The.
—Liverpool FC. 2015. (Illus.). 48p. (J). (978-1-60818-588-7(5), Creative Education) Creative Co., The.
—Manchester United. (Illus.). (J). 2016. 24p. (978-1-60818-803-1(5)) 2015. 48p. (978-1-60818-589-4(3)) Creative Co., The. (Creative Education).
—Manchester United: Soccer Champions. 2016. (Soccer Champions Ser.). (ENG.). 48p. (J). (gr. 5-9). pap. 12.00 (978-1-62832-194-4(6), Creative Paperbacks) Creative Co., The.
—Real Madrid. 2015. (Illus.). 48p. (J). (978-1-60818-591-7(5), Creative Education) Creative Co., The.
Williams, Cinthia Louise. The Flippin' Soccer Guide. 2003. (Illus.). 40p. (YA). 14.95 (978-0-9742500-0-7(7)) Flippin' Bks. LLC.
Wingate, Brian. Soccer: Rules, Tips, Strategy, & Safety. (Sports from Coast to Coast Ser.). 48p. 2009. (gr. 6-6). 53.00 (978-1-60853-129-5(5), Rosen Reference) 2006. (Illus.). (J). (gr. 5-8). lib. bdg. 29.25 (978-1-4042-0995-4(6)) Rosen Publishing Group, Inc., The.
Wiseman, Blaine. Soccer. 2010. (Record Breakers Ser.). (Illus.). 24p. (YA). (gr. 3-6). lib. bdg. 27.13 (978-1-61690-106-6(3)); (J). (gr. 4-6). pap. 12.95 (978-1-61690-107-3(1)) Weigl Pubs., Inc.
Woods, Mark & Owen, Ruth. Goal! 2010. (Top Score Maths Ser.). (Illus.). 32p. pap. (978-0-237-54279-5(X)) Evans Brothers, Ltd.
—Goal! Soccer Facts & Stats. 2011. (Top Score Math Ser.). (Illus.). 32p. (J). (gr. 3-6). lib. bdg. 26.60 (978-1-4339-5015-5(4)) Stevens, Gareth Publishing LLLP.
Woods, P. Improve Your Soccer Skills. 2004. (Superskills Ser.). (Illus.). 48p. (YA). (gr. 6-10). lib. bdg. 13.95 (978-0-88110-296-3(2)) EDC Publishing.
Woods, Sadie. It's Time for the Soccer Game. 2017. (Let's Tell Time Ser.). 24p. (gr. 4-6). 23.60 **(978-1-5081-5727-4(8)**, PowerKids Pr.) Rosen Publishing Group, Inc., The.
World Soccer Books, 5 vols., Set. Incl. Great Moments in World Cup History. Bailey, Diane. lib. bdg. 31.95 (978-1-4358-9139-5(2), Rosen Reference); Great National Soccer Teams. Sommers, Annie Leah. lib. bdg. 31.95 (978-1-4358-9138-8(4), Rosen Reference); Top Soccer Tournaments Around the World. Velázquez de León, Mauricio. lib. bdg. 31.95 (978-1-4358-9140-1(6), Rosen Reference); 20 Soccer Legends. Velázquez de León, Mauricio. lib. bdg. 31.95 (978-1-4358-9136-4(8), Rosen Reference); 20 Soccer Superstars. Velázquez de León, Mauricio. lib. bdg. 31.95 (978-1-4358-9137-1(6)); (YA). (gr. 5-8). (Illus.). 64p. 2010. Set lib. bdg. 146.25 (978-1-4358-9141-8(4), Rosen Reference) Rosen Publishing Group, Inc., The.
Yomtov, Nelson. Being Your Best at Soccer. 2016. (True Book(tm), a — Sports & Entertainment Ser.). (ENG., Illus.). 48p. (J). lib. bdg. 31.00 (978-0-531-23261-3(1), Children's Pr.) Scholastic Library Publishing.

SOCCER—FICTION

Alexander, Kwame. Booked. 2016. (ENG.). 320p. (J). (gr. 5-7). 16.99 (978-0-544-57098-6(7), HMH Books For Young Readers) Houghton Mifflin Harcourt Publishing Co.
—Booked. 2016. lib. bdg. 29.40 (978-0-606-37992-2(4)) Turtleback Bks.
Andreae, Giles. Wacky World Cup! Gerrell, Spike, illus. 2014. (ENG.). 128p. (J). (gr. 2-4). pap. 7.99 (978-1-4083-3058-6(X)) Hodder & Stoughton GBR. Dist: Hachette Bk. Group.
Andrews, Phil. Own Goals. 320p. (J). pap. 16.95 (978-0-340-74821-3(4)) Hodder & Stoughton GBR. Dist: Trafalgar Square Publishing.
Arena, Felice & Kettle, Phil. Park Soccer. Gordon, Gus, illus. 2004. (J). (978-1-59336-366-6(4)) Mondo Publishing.
Aronson, Sarah. Beyond Lucky. 2011. (ENG.). 256p. (J). (gr. 3-7). 16.99 (978-0-8037-3520-0(0), Dial Bks) Penguin Young Readers Group.
Ashman, Linda. Hey, Coach! Smith, Kim, illus. 2016. (ENG.). 32p. (J). (gr. -1). 14.95 (978-1-4549-1607-9(9)) Sterling Publishing Co., Inc.
Ayarbe, Heidi. Compulsion. 2011. (ENG.). 304p. (YA). (gr. 9-18). 17.99 (978-0-06-199386-2(7)) HarperCollins Pubs.
Barshaw, Ruth McNally. The Ellie McDoodle Diaries: Most Valuable Player. Barshaw, Ruth McNally, illus. 2013. (Ellie Mcdoodle Diaries). (ENG., Illus.). 192p. (YA). (gr. 3-6). 12.99 (978-1-61963-176-2(8), 9781619631762, Bloomsbury USA Childrens) Bloomsbury Publishing USA.
Bedford, David. Soccer Camp. Brumpton, Keith, illus. 3rd ed. 2004. 80p. (978-1-877003-45-5(X)) Little Hare Bks. AUS. Dist: HarperCollins Pubs. Australia.
—The Soccer Machine. Brumpton, Keith, illus. 2003. 80p. (978-1-877003-26-4(3)) Little Hare Bks. AUS. Dist: HarperCollins Pubs. Australia.
—The Team Bind-up. 2007. (Illus.). 227p. (978-1-921272-04-2(X)) Little Hare Bks. AUS. Dist: HarperCollins Pubs. Australia.
—Top of the League. Brumpton, Keith, illus. 2nd ed. 2003. 80p. (978-1-877003-30-1(1)) Little Hare Bks. AUS. Dist: HarperCollins Pubs. Australia.
Benson, Donna. Spotlight on the Cupcakes: The Cupcakes Club #3. 2008. (ENG.). 115p. (J). pap. 7.95 (978-0-9799159-2-5(9)) Pink Lemonade, LLC.
Berenstain, Jan, et al. The Berenstain Bears Play a Good Game, 1 vol. 2009. (Berenstain Bears/Living Lights Ser.). (ENG., Illus.). 32p. (J). (gr. -1-2). pap. 3.99 (978-0-310-71252-7(1)) Zonderkidz.
Berenstain, Mike. We Love Soccer! 2016. (Berenstain Bears: I Can Read! Ser.). (J). lib. bdg. 13.55 (978-0-606-38123-9(6)) Turtleback Bks.
Berg, Dorlisa H. Fat Freddy Gets Fit. 2012. 158p. pap. 19.99 (978-1-4797-6309-2(8)) Xlibris Corp.
Berne, Emma Carlson. Under Pressure. 2013. (Counterattack Ser.). (ENG.). 104p. (YA). (gr. 6-12). pap. 7.95 (978-1-4677-0718-3(X)); lib. bdg. 27.93 (978-1-4677-0303-1(6)) Lerner Publishing Group.
Berrios, Frank. Soccer with Mom. Golden, Jess, illus. 2016. (Little Golden Book Ser.). (ENG.). 24p. (J). (-k). 4.99 (978-0-553-53854-0(3), Golden Bks.) Random Hse. Children's Bks.
Berry, Andrea. Goalie: The Dynamite Diaries. 2003. 144p. (YA). pap. 11.95 (978-0-595-27678-3(4)) iUniverse, Inc.
Bester, Maryanne. The Missing Ball. Bester, Shayle, illus. 2010. (Cool Nguni Ser.: 4). (ENG.). 32p. (J). (gr. k-2). 12.00 (978-1-77009-704-9(X)) Jacana Media ZAF. Dist: Independent Pubs. Group.
Bildner, Phil. The Soccer Fence: A Story of Friendship, Hope, & Apartheid in South Africa. Watson, Jesse Joshua, illus. 2014. (ENG.). 40p. (J). (gr. 1-3). 16.99 (978-0-399-24790-3(4), G.P. Putnam's Sons Books for Young Readers) Penguin Young Readers Group.
Blackburn, Sheila M. Football Crazy: Sam's Football Stories - Set a, Book 1. 2015. (ENG., Illus.). 34p. pap. (978-1-903853-01-6(X)) Brilliant Pubns.
Blacklaws, Troy. Bafana Bafana: A Story of Soccer, Magic & Mandela. Stooke, Andrew, illus. 2010. (ENG.). 64p. pap. 24.00 (978-1-77009-718-6(X)) Jacana Media ZAF. Dist: Independent Pubs. Group.
Bloor, Edward. Tangerine. (ENG.). 320p. (J). (gr. 5-7). 2007. 18.00 (978-0-15-201246-5(X)) 2006. (Illus.). pap. 8.99 (978-0-15-205780-0(3)) Houghton Mifflin Harcourt Publishing Co.
—Tangerine Spanish Edition. de la Vega, Pablo, tr. 2014. (ENG.). 384p. (J). (gr. 5-7). 16.99 (978-0-544-33611-7(9), HMH Books For Young Readers) Houghton Mifflin Harcourt Publishing Co.
Boelts, Maribeth. El Futbol Me Hace Feliz (Happy Like Soccer) Castillo, Lauren, illus. 2016. (ENG & SPA.). 32p. (J). (gr. k-4). 17.20 (978-0-606-39111-5(8)) Turtleback Bks.
—Happy Like Soccer. Castillo, Lauren, illus. 2014. (ENG.). 32p. (J). (gr. k-4). pap. 6.99 (978-0-7636-7049-8(9)) Candlewick Pr.
Bosco, Don & Boo, Benedict. Time to Play. 2017. (ENG.). 88p. pap. 8.99 **(978-981-4771-41-2(4))** Marshall Cavendish International (Asia) Private Ltd. SGP. Dist: National Bk. Network.
Bossiey, Michele Martin. Kicker, 1 vol. 2007. (Orca Sports Ser.). (ENG.). 160p. (YA). (gr. 6-10). per. 9.95 (978-1-55143-706-4(6)) Orca Bk. Pubs. USA.
Bowen, Fred. Go for the Goal!, 1 vol. 2012. (Fred Bowen Sports Stories Ser.). (ENG.). 128p. (J). pap. 5.95 (978-1-56145-632-1(2)) Peachtree Pubs.
—Out of Bounds, 1 vol. 2016. (Stanley Ser.). 132p. (J). (ENG.). (gr. -1-2). pap. 14.95 (978-1-56145-894-3(5)); (SPA & ENG.). (gr. 1-5). 17.95 (978-1-56145-845-5(7)) Peachtree Pubs.
—Soccer Team Upset, 1 vol. 2009. (Fred Bowen Sports Story Ser.). (ENG.). 128p. (J). (gr. 2-7). pap. 6.95 (978-1-56145-495-2(8)) Peachtree Pubs.
Brenda Seabrooke. Jerry on the Line. 2010. 132p. pap. 10.95 (978-1-4401-8766-7(5)) iUniverse, Inc.
Brouwer, Sigmund. Maverick Mania, 1 vol. 2008. (Orca Sports Ser.). (ENG.). 176p. (YA). (gr. 6-10). pap. 9.95 (978-1-55469-047-3(1)) Orca Bk. Pubs. USA.
Brown, Monica. Lola Levine & the Ballet Scheme. 2016. (Lola Levine Ser.: 3). (ENG., Illus.). 112p. (J). (gr. 1-5). 14.99 (978-0-316-25844-9(X)) Little, Brown Bks. for Young Readers.
Brug, Sandra Gilbert. Soccer Beat. Moseng, Elisabeth, illus. 2012. (ENG.). 32p. (J). (gr. -1-1). 16.99 (978-1-4424-8610-2(4), McElderry, Margaret K. Bks.) McElderry, Margaret K. Bks.
Bryant, Anne. The Fantasy Soccer Wall. 2015. (Race Further with Reading Ser.). (ENG., Illus.). 48p. (J). (978-0-7787-2061-4(6)) Crabtree Publishing Co.
Burton, Margie, et al. New Soccer Nets. 2011. (Early Connections Ser.). (J). (978-1-61672-529-7(X)) Benchmark Education Co.
Calkhoven, Laurie. A Winning Goal. Studios, Arcana, illus. 2011. (ENG.). 120p. (YA). (gr. 3-18). pap. 8.95 (978-1-59369-836-2(4)) American Girl Publishing, Inc.
Carey, Becky. Wilma Goes to the Hospital. 2007. (Illus.). (J). 9.95 (978-0-9791331-0-7(6)) Carey, Rebecca.
Carman, Patrick. The Walnut Cup. James, Steve, illus. 2009. (Elliot's Park Ser.: Bk. 3). 80p. (J). (gr. 1-5). 8.99 (978-0-545-01932-3(X), Orchard Bks.) Scholastic, Inc.
Carmona, Adela. The Boy Who Could See. Chapman, Robert E., illus. 2008. 32p. pap. 24.95 (978-1-60672-697-6(8)) PublishAmerica, Inc.
Carr, Patrick W. The Legend's Granddaughter: Not Quite Super, Book 1. Dabbs, Douglas, illus. 2007. 281p. (J). pap. (978-0-9793168-0-7(4)) NQSBks.
Chambers, Sally, et al. Waldo'n Ennill y Dydd. 2005. (WEL., Illus.). 32p. pap. (978-1-85596-658-1(1)) Dref Wen.
Childs, Rob. Keeper's Ball. Sheppard, Kate, illus. 2005. (Corgi Pups Ser.). (ENG.). 64p. (J). pap. 7.50 (978-0-552-55030-7(2)) Transworld Publishers Ltd. GBR. Dist: Independent Pubs. Group.
Choat, Beth. Soccerland, 0 vols. Beck, Robert, illus. 2012. (International Sports Academy Ser.: 0). (ENG.). 242p. (YA). (gr. 7-9). pap. 8.99 (978-0-7614-6249-1(X), 9780761462491, Amazon Children's Publishing) Amazon Publishing.
Choyce, Lesley. Sudden Impact, 1 vol. 2005. (Orca Currents Ser.). (ENG.). 128p. (J). (gr. 5-9). per. 9.95 (978-1-55143-476-6(8)) Orca Bk. Pubs. USA.
—Sudden Impact. 2006. (Orca Currents Ser.). 104p. (gr. 5-9). 19.95 (978-0-7569-6876-2(3)) Perfection Learning Corp.
Chrisotpher, Matt. Top Wing. 2005. (Sports Classics III Ser.). 154p. (J). lib. bdg. 15.00 (978-1-59054-776-2(4)) Fitzgerald Bks.
Christopher, Matt. Comeback Challenge. 2008. (New Matt Christopher Sports Library). 160p. (J). (gr. 4-6). lib. bdg. 26.60 (978-1-59953-211-0(5)) Norwood Hse. Pr.
—Heads Up. Vasconcellos, Daniel, illus. 2003. (Soccer Cats Ser.: Bk. 6). 54p. (J). (gr. 1-4). 12.65 (978-0-7569-3904-5(6)) Perfection Learning Corp.
—Heads Up! Vasconcellos, Daniel, illus. 6th ed. 2003. (ENG.). 64p. (J). (gr. 1-4). pap. 13.99 (978-0-316-16497-9(6)) Little, Brown Bks. for Young Readers.
—Kick It! Vasconcellos, Daniel, illus. 2003. (ENG.). 64p. (J). (gr. 1-4). pap. 13.99 (978-0-316-73808-8(5)) Little, Brown Bks. for Young Readers.
—Soccer Halfback. l.t. ed. 2007. (New Matt Christopher Sports Library). 160p. (J). (gr. 4-6). lib. bdg. 26.60 (978-1-59953-110-6(0)) Norwood Hse. Pr.
—Soccer Scoop. 2007. (New Matt Christopher Sports Library). 133p. (J). (gr. 4-6). lib. bdg. 26.60 (978-1-59953-117-5(8)) Norwood Hse. Pr.
—Switch Play! Vasconcellos, Daniel, illus. 9th ed. 2003. (ENG.). 64p. (J). (gr. 1-4). pap. 13.99 (978-0-316-73807-1(7)) Little, Brown Bks. for Young Readers.
—You Lucky Dog. Vasconcellos, Daniel, illus. 8th ed. 2003. (ENG.). 64p. (J). (gr. 1-4). pap. 13.99 (978-0-316-73805-7(0)) Little, Brown Bks. for Young Readers.
—You Lucky Dog. Vasconcellos, Daniel, illus. 2003. (Soccer Cats Ser.: Bk. 8). 49p. (J). (gr. 2-4). 12.65 (978-0-7569-3907-6(0)) Perfection Learning Corp.
Clinch, Kelly. The Soccer Princess. 2008. (Illus.). (J). 10.95 (978-0-9800835-1-4(6)) Clinch Media.
Connor, Lexi. The Runaway Spell. 2011. (B Magical Ser.: 3). (ENG.). 144p. (J). (gr. 3-7). pap. 5.99 (978-0-545-26552-2(5), Scholastic Paperbacks) Scholastic, Inc.
Cooper, Ilene. Lucy on the Ball. Merrell, David, illus. 2011. (Lucy Ser.). (ENG.). 112p. (J). (gr. 1-4). 4.99 (978-0-375-85559-7(9), Random Hse. Bks. for Young Readers) Random Hse. Children's Bks.
Couric, Katie & Couric, Katherine. The Blue Ribbon Day. Priceman, Marjorie, illus. 2004. (ENG.). 32p. (J). (gr. k-4). lib. bdg. 17.95 (978-0-385-51292-3(9), Doubleday) Knopf Doubleday Publishing Group.
Courtney, Richard, illus. Reds Against Blues! 2016. 22p. (J). **(978-1-4806-9772-0(9))** Random Hse., Inc.
Cousins, Lucy. Maisy Plays Soccer. Cousins, Lucy, illus. 2014. (Maisy Ser.). (ENG., Illus.). 32p. (J). (gr. -1-2). pap. 6.99 (978-0-7636-7238-6(6)) Candlewick Pr.
—Maisy Plays Soccer. 2014. (Maisy First Experiences Ser.). lib. bdg. 17.20 (978-0-606-35155-3(8)) Turtleback Bks.
Coy, John. Eyes on the Goal, Bk. 2. 2012. (4 For 4 Ser.: 2). (ENG.). 192p. (J). (gr. 3-7). pap. 7.99 (978-0-312-65922-6(9), 9780312659226) Square Fish.
Crespo, Ana. The Sock Thief. 2016. (Av2 Fiction Readalong 2017 Ser.). (ENG.). (J). (gr. -1-2). 34.28 **(978-1-4896-5329-1(5)**, AV2 by Weigl) Weigl Pubs., Inc.
—The Sock Thief. Gonzales, Nana, illus. 2015. (ENG.). 32p. (J). (gr. -1-3). 16.99 (978-0-8075-7538-3(0)) Whitman, Albert & Co.
Croall, Marie P. My Boyfriend Is a Monster - Under His Spell. Park, Hyeondo, illus. 2011. (My Boyfriend Is a Monster Ser.: 4). (ENG.). 128p. (YA). (gr. 7-12). pap. 9.95 (978-0-7613-7076-5(5), Graphic Universe™) Lerner Publishing Group.
—Under His Spell, 4 vols., No. 4. Park, Hyeondo, illus. 2011. (My Boyfriend Is a Monster Ser.: 4). (ENG.). 128p. (YA). (gr. 7-12). 29.27 (978-0-7613-5602-8(9)) Lerner Publishing Group.
Cunningham, Elaine. Ethan, a Soccer Player for Jesus. Valliant, Kristi, illus. 2010. 32p. (J). (978-0-8341-2486-8(6)) Beacon Hill Pr. of Kansas City.
Dakota, Heather. Emma's Very Busy Week. Panaccione, Nancy, illus. 2009. 31p. (J). (978-0-545-17227-1(6)) Scholastic, Inc.
Davies, Eigan Philip. Cic O'r Smotyn. 2005. (WEL., Illus.). 56p. pap. (978-1-902416-18-2(X)) Cymdeithas Lyfrau Ceredigion.
DiDomenico, Allison. You Can Do It, Fiona! 2010. 28p. pap. 12.95 (978-1-4490-9913-8(0)) AuthorHouse.
Diersch, Sandra. Play On, 1 vol. 2004. (Lorimer Sports Stories Ser.). (ENG.). 118p. (J). (gr. 4-8). 16.95 (978-1-55028-857-5(1), 9781550288575) Lorimer, James & Co., Ltd., Pubs. CAN. Dist: Casemate Pubs. & Bk. Distributors, LLC.
Douglass Thom, Kara. Soccer Girl Cassie's Story: Teamwork Is the Goal. Seatter, Pamela, illus. 2014. (Go! Go! Sports Girls Ser.). (ENG.). 32p. (J). (gr. k-2). pap. 4.99 (978-1-940731-00-1(3)) Dream Big Toy Co.
Doyle, Malachy & Parsons, Garry. The Football Ghosts. 2007. (Red Bananas Ser.). (ENG., Illus.). 48p. (J). (gr. k-2). pap. 5.99 (978-1-4052-2749-0(4)) Egmont Bks., Ltd. GBR. Dist: Independent Pubs. Group.
—Spooky Soccer. 2nd ed. 2016. (Reading Ladder Ser.). (ENG., Illus.). 48p. (J). (gr. k-2). 7.99 (978-1-4052-8245-1(2)) Egmont Bks., Ltd. GBR. Dist: Independent Pubs. Group.
Dungy, Tony & Dungy, Lauren. Justin & the Bully. Newton, Vanessa Brantley, illus. 2012. (Tony & Lauren Dungy Ready-To-Reads Ser.). (ENG.). 32p. (J). (gr. k-2). pap. 3.99 (978-1-4424-5718-8(X), Simon Spotlight) Simon Spotlight.
Dyer, Jonah Lisa & Dyer, Stephen. The Season. 2016. (ENG.). 352p. (YA). (gr. 9). 17.99 (978-0-451-47634-0(4), Viking Books for Young Readers) Penguin Young Readers Group.
Efaw, Amy. After. 2010. (ENG.). 368p. (YA). (gr. 7-18). 8.99 (978-0-14-241590-0(1), Speak) Penguin Young Readers Group.
Emerson, Carl. Monster Boy's Soccer Game, 1 vol. Levin, Lon, illus. 2008. (Monster Boy Ser.). (ENG.). 32p. (gr. -1-4). 28.50 (978-1-60270-239-4(X), Looking Glass Library) ABDO Publishing Co.
Everett, Reese. Wolfpack Gang Is Outta Sight! 2015. (ENG.). 48p. (gr. k-3). 27.07 (978-1-63430-375-0(X)) Rourke Educational Media.
FitzGerald, Dawn. Soccer Chick Rules. 2007. (ENG.). 160p. (J). (gr. 5-9). per. 9.99 (978-0-312-37662-8(6), 9780312376628) Square Fish.
Flint, Shamini. Ten: A Soccer Story. 2017. (ENG.). 176p. (J). (gr. 5-7). 16.99 (978-0-544-85001-9(7), Clarion Bks.) Houghton Mifflin Harcourt Trade & Reference Pubs.
Foreman, Michael. Wonder Goal! Foreman, Michael, illus. 2010. (ENG., Illus.). 32p. (J). (gr. k-2). pap. 12.99 (978-1-84270-934-4(8)) Andersen Pr. GBR. Dist: Independent Pubs. Group.
Fox, R. J. Stuart & His Incredibly Obnoxious Magical Book: Soccer, 1 vol. 2009. 86p. pap. 19.95 (978-1-4489-9833-3(6)) America Star Bks.
Furgang, Kathy. Shrimp Joins the Team & Chaparro se une al Equipo: 6 English, 6 Spanish Adaptations. 2011. (ENG & SPA.). (J). 75.00 net. (978-1-4108-5651-7(8)) Benchmark Education Co.
Gallo, Tina. OLIVIA Plays Soccer. Osterhold, Jared, illus. 2013. (Olivia TV Tie-In Ser.). (ENG.). 24p. (J). (gr. -1-1). pap. 3.99 (978-1-4424-7248-8(0), Simon Spotlight) Simon Spotlight.
—Olivia Plays Soccer. 2013. (Olivia Ready-To-Read Level 1 Ser.). lib. bdg. 13.55 (978-0-606-32060-3(1), Turtleback) Turtleback Bks.
Garlando, Luigi. Un Gran Equipo: Gol 1. 2012. (Vintage Espanol Ser.). (SPA.). 160p. (J). (gr. 2-5). pap. 8.95 (978-0-345-80422-8(8), Vintage Espanol) Knopf Doubleday Publishing Group.
—¡Nos Vamos a Brasil! ¡Gol! 2013. (Vintage Espanol Ser.). (SPA.). 144p. (J). (gr. 2-5). pap. 9.95 (978-0-345-80423-5(6), Vintage Espanol) Knopf Doubleday Publishing Group.
—La Union Hace la Fuerza: ¡Gol! 2013. (Vintage Espanol Ser.). (SPA.). 174p. (J). (gr. 2-4). pap. 9.95 (978-0-345-80533-1(X), Vintage Espanol) Knopf Doubleday Publishing Group.
Giff, Patricia Reilly. Soccer Song. Sims, Blanche, illus. 2008. (Green Light Readers Level 2 Ser.). (ENG.). 24p. (J). (gr. k-2). pap. 3.95 (978-0-15-206565-2(2)) Houghton Mifflin Harcourt Publishing Co.
Gorrell, Nancy. Corey's Story. 2007. (ENG., Illus.). 96p. (J). (gr. 2-5). per. 6.99 (978-1-84550-258-4(2), f3ae651d-4c6d-4b03-9761-9d54cb71a3e3) Christian Focus Pubns. GBR. Dist: Bookmasters Distribution.
Green, D. L. Zeke Meeks vs the Stinky Soccer Team. Alves, Josh, illus. 2015. (Zeke Meeks Ser.). (ENG.). 128p. (gr. 2-2). 22.65 (978-1-4795-5768-4(4), Zeke Meeks) Picture Window Bks.
Green, Tim. Deep Zone. 2012. (Football Genius Ser.: 5). (ENG.). 304p. (J). (gr. 3-7). pap. 6.99 (978-0-06-201245-6(2)) HarperCollins Pubs.
Greve, Meg. Kickin' It. 2015. (ENG.). 48p. (gr. k-3). 27.07 (978-1-63430-370-5(9)) Rourke Educational Media.
Guest, Jacqueline. Soccer Star!, 1 vol. 2003. (Lorimer Sports Stories Ser.: 61). (ENG.). 104p. (J). (gr. 4-8). 16.95 (978-1-55028-789-9(3), 9781550287899) Lorimer, James & Co., Ltd., Pubs. CAN. Dist: Casemate Pubs. & Bk. Distributors, LLC.
Guillain, Adam & Steiner, Elke. Bella's Brazilian Football. Steiner, Elke, illus. 2007. (Bella Balistica Ser.). (ENG., Illus.). 32p. (J). (gr. k-2). pap. 8.95 (978-1-84059-488-1(8)) Milet Publishing.
Hale, Nick. The Edge. 2012. (Striker Ser.: 3). (ENG.). 224p. (J). (gr. 5-7). pap. 7.99 (978-1-4052-5685-8(0)) Egmont Bks., Ltd. GBR. Dist: Independent Pubs. Group.
Hamley, Dennis. Beautiful Games. Fenoughty, Charles, illus. 2004. 104p. per. (978-1-904529-13-2(5), Back to Front) Solidus.
Hamm, Mia. Winners Never Quit! Thompson, Carol, illus. 2006. (ENG.). 32p. (J). (gr. -1-2). pap. 6.99 (978-0-06-074052-8(3)) HarperCollins Pubs.
Hardcastle, Michael. Hit It!, 1 vol. Moulder, Bob, illus. 2006. (Graphic Quest Ser.). (ENG.). 88p. (gr. 3-3). per. 6.95 (978-1-59889-164-5(2), Graphic Quest) Stone Arch Bks.
Harrison, Paul. Billy on the Ball. Raga, Silvia, illus. 2010. 32p. pap. (978-1-84089-634-3(5)) Zero to Ten, Ltd.
Haselhurst, Maureen. The Emperor's New Uniform. Kennedy, Kelly, illus. 2015. (ENG.). 32p. (J). (978-0-7787-1933-5(2)) Crabtree Publishing Co.
Hazuka, Tom. Last Chance for First. 2008. 296p. (YA). (gr. 9-18). pap. 8.95 (978-0-9798824-0-1(0)) Brown Barn Bks.
Hegarty, Pat. If I Were a... Soccer Star. Pope, Liz & Pope, Kate, illus. 2008. (If I Were A Ser.). 10p. (J). (gr. -1-k). bds. 6.95 (978-1-58925-835-8(5)) Tiger Tales.
Heller, Alyson. Soccer Day. Björkman, Steve, illus. 2009. (After-School Sports Club Ser.). (ENG.). 32p. (J). (gr. -1-1). pap. 3.99 (978-1-4169-9410-7(6), Simon Spotlight) Simon Spotlight.
Hellman, Charles. Adventures in SportsLand - the Soccer Bully (with accompanying CD) Tiritilli, Robert, illus. 2008. (Adventures in SportsLand: the Bully Ser.). 32p. (gr. -1-3). pap. 19.95 (978-0-935938-26-5(5)) Stogo, Malcolm Assocs.
Herrera, Juan Felipe & Cuevas, Ernesto, illus. Featherless. 2013.Tr. of Desplumado. (SPA & ENG.). 32p. (J). pap. 8.95 (978-0-89239-303-9(3)) Lee & Low Bks., Inc.

S

Higgins, Chris. The Secrets Club: No Match for Dani. 3rd ed. 2016. (Secrets Club Ser.: 3). (ENG.). 176p. (J). (gr. 2-4). pap. 9.99 *(978-0-14-133524-7(6))* Penguin Bks., Ltd. GBR. Dist: Independent Pubs. Group.

Higgins, M. G. Blow Out. 2013. (Counterattack Ser.). (ENG.). 112p. (YA). (gr. 6-12). pap. 7.95 *(978-1-4677-0717-6(1))*; lib. bdg. 27.93 *(978-1-4677-0302-4(8))* Lerner Publishing Group.

—Offside. 2013. (Counterattack Ser.). (ENG.). 112p. (YA). (gr. 6-12). pap. 7.95 *(978-1-4677-0720-6(1))*; lib. bdg. 27.93 *(978-1-4677-0305-5(2))* Lerner Publishing Group.

Hillert, Margaret. It's a Good Game, Dear Dragon. Schimmell, David, illus. 2009. (BeginningtoRead Ser.). 32p. (J). (gr. k-2). lib. bdg. 22.60 *(978-1-59953-293-6(X))* Norwood Hse. Pr.

—It's a Good Game, Dear Dragon (Es un Buen Juego, Querido Dragon) Del Risco, Eida, tr. from ENG. Schimmell, David, illus. 2010. (BeginningtoRead Ser.). (SPA & ENG.). 32p. (J). (gr. k-2). lib. bdg. 22.60 *(978-1-59953-362-9(6))* Norwood Hse. Pr.

Hinks, Roy H. Cybo Soccer & Heavens Above. 2011. 116p. pap. 13.32 *(978-1-4567-7327-4(5))* AuthorHouse.

Hoblin, Paul & Hueller, Patrick. Archenemy. 2013. (Counterattack Ser.). (ENG.). 112p. (YA). (gr. 6-12). pap. 7.95 *(978-1-4677-0721-3(X))*; lib. bdg. 27.93 *(978-1-4677-0306-2(0))* Lerner Publishing Group.

—The Beast. 2013. (Counterattack Ser.). (ENG.). 112p. (YA). (gr. 6-12). pap. 7.95 *(978-1-4677-0716-9(3))*; lib. bdg. 27.93 *(978-1-4677-0301-7(X))* Lerner Publishing Group.

Hoena, Blake A. & Fuentes, Benny. Spotlight Striker, 1 vol. Sandoval, Gerardo, illus. 2010. (Sports Illustrated Kids Graphic Novels Ser.). (ENG.). 56p. (gr. 2-3). 26.65 *(978-1-4342-2128-5(8))*; pap. 7.19 *(978-1-4342-2787-4(1))* Stone Arch Bks.

Holm, Jennifer L. & Holm, Matthew. Captain Disaster. Holm, Jennifer L. & Holm, Matthew, illus. 2012. (Squish Ser.: No. 4). (ENG., Illus.). 96p. (J). (gr. 2-5). pap. 6.99 *(978-0-375-84392-1(2))*; lib. bdg. 12.99 *(978-0-375-93786-6(2))* Random Hse. Children's Bks. (Random Hse. Bks. for Young Readers).

—Captain Disaster. 2012. (Squish Ser.: 4). lib. bdg. 17.20 *(978-0-606-26812-7(X)*, Turtleback) Turtleback Bks.

Humann, Amanda. Out of Sync. 2013. (Counterattack Ser.). (ENG.). 104p. (YA). (gr. 6-12). pap. 7.95 *(978-1-4677-0719-0(8))*; lib. bdg. 27.93 *(978-1-4677-0304-8(4))* Lerner Publishing Group.

Jakubowski, Michele. Soccer Star. Waters, Erica-Jane, illus. 2015. (Perfectly Poppy Ser.). (ENG.). 32p. (gr. k-2). 22.65 *(978-1-4795-5800-1(1))* Picture Window Bks.

Javaherbin, Mina. Goal! Ford, A. G., illus. 2012. (ENG.). 40p. (J). (gr. 1-4). pap. 6.99 *(978-0-7636-5822-9(7))* Candlewick Pr.

—Soccer Star. Alarcao, Renato, illus. 2014. (ENG.). 40p. (J). (gr. k-3). 16.99 *(978-0-7636-6056-7(6))* Candlewick Pr.

Johansson, J. R. Insomnia. 2013. (Night Walkers Ser.: 1). (ENG.). 360p. (YA). pap. 9.99 *(978-0-7387-3593-1(0)*, Flux) North Star Editions.

Joven, C. C. Soccer Score. Lopez, Alex, illus. 2017. (Sports Illustrated Kids Starting Line Readers Ser.). (ENG.). 32p. (gr. -1-1). pap. 3.95 *(978-1-4965-4258-8(4))*; lib. bdg. 22.65 *(978-1-4965-4251-9(7))* Capstone Press of Coughlan Cos.

Kalu, Pete. Zombie XI: The Boy Who Got Sick of Warming the Bench. 2017. (ENG.). 202p. (J). (gr. 6). pap. 11.99 *(978-1-908446-48-0(X))* HopeRoad Publishing Ltd GBR. Dist: Consortium Bk. Sales & Distribution.

Kann, Victoria. Soccer Star. Kann, Victoria, illus. 2012. (I Can Read Level 1 Ser.). (ENG., Illus.). 32p. (J). (gr. -1-3). 16.99 *(978-0-06-198865-0(7))* HarperCollins Pubs.

—Soccer Star. 2012. (Pinkalicious I Can Read Ser.). (J). lib. bdg. 13.55 *(978-0-606-26280-4(6)*, Turtleback) Turtleback Bks.

Kaplan, Michael B. Betty Bunny Wants a Goal. Jorisch, Stéphane, illus. 2014. (Betty Bunny Ser.). (ENG.). 32p. (J). (gr. -1-k). 16.99 *(978-0-8037-3859-1(5)*, Dial Bks) Penguin Young Readers Group.

Kelly, David A. The Soccer Surprise. Brundage, Scott, illus. 2016. (Most Valuable Players Ser.: 2). (ENG.). 128p. (J). (gr. 1-4). 4.99 *(978-0-553-51322-6(2)*, Random Hse. Bks. for Young Readers) Random Hse. Children's Bks.

Kenneally, Miranda. Defending Taylor. 2016. (Hundred Oaks Ser.: Bk. 7). (ENG.). 304p. (YA). (gr. 8-12). pap. 10.99 *(978-1-4926-3008-1(X)*, 9781492630081) Sourcebooks, Inc.

Keplinger, Kody. Shut Out. 2012. (ENG.). 288p. (YA). (gr. 10-17). pap. 10.99 *(978-0-316-17555-5(2)*, Poppy) Little, Brown Bks. for Young Readers.

Kew, Trevor. Trading Goals, 1 vol. 2009. (Lorimer Sports Stories Ser.). (ENG.). 144p. (J). (gr. 4-8). 16.95 *(978-1-55277-425-0(2)*, 9781552774250) Lorimer, James & Co., Ltd., Pubs. CAN. Dist: Casemate Pubs. & Bk. Distributors, LLC.

The Kicks Collection: Saving the Team; Sabotage Season; Win or Lose. 2014. (Kicks Ser.). (ENG., Illus.). 544p. (J). (gr. 3-7). pap. 20.99 *(978-1-4814-2478-3(5)*, Simon & Schuster Bks. For Young Readers) Simon & Schuster Bks. For Young Readers.

Kim, YoeongAh. Shooting Stars Soccer Team. Lee, Hyeongjin, illus. rev. ed. 2014. (MySELF Bookshelf Ser.). (ENG.). 32p. (J). (gr. k-2). pap. 11.94 *(978-1-60357-657-4(6))* Norwood Hse. Pr.

—The Shooting Stars Soccer Team. Lee, Hyeongjin, illus. rev. ed. 2014. (MySELF Bookshelf Ser.). (ENG.). 32p. (J). (gr. k-2). lib. bdg. 25.27 *(978-1-59953-648-4(X))* Norwood Hse. Pr.

Kirby, Stan. Captain Awesome, Soccer Star. O'Connor, George, illus. 2012. (Captain Awesome Ser.: 5). (ENG.). 128p. (J). (gr. k-4). 16.99 *(978-1-4424-4332-7(4))*; pap. 5.99 *(978-1-4424-4331-0(6))* Little Simon. (Little Simon).

—Captain Awesome, Soccer Star. 2012. (Captain Awesome Ser.: 5). lib. bdg. 16.00 *(978-0-606-26545-4(7)*, Turtleback) Turtleback Bks.

Klass, David. Home of the Braves. 2004. 355p. (YA). (gr. 7-12). 17.65 *(978-0-7569-2805-6(2))* Perfection Learning Corp.

Knowlton, Laurie. N 2 Deep. 2004. 128p. (J). pap. 5.99 *(978-1-4003-0327-4(3))* Nelson, Thomas Inc.

Kolar, Bob. Big Kicks. Kolar, Bob, illus. 2008. (ENG., Illus.). 40p. (J). (gr. -1-1). 16.99 *(978-0-7636-3390-5(9))* Candlewick Pr.

Kowen, Dorothy. Thando Rocker. Sherrell, Craig, illus. 2012. (ENG.). 24p. (J). (gr. k-2). pap. 7.95 *(978-1-4314-0087-4(4))* Jacana Media ZAF. Dist: Independent Pubs. Group.

Krech, Bob & Krecht, R.J. Love Puppies & Corner Kicks. 2011. (ENG.). 224p. (J). (gr. 5-18). 7.99 *(978-0-14-241783-6(1)*, Puffin Books) Penguin Young Readers Group.

Kreie, Chris. Who Wants to Play Just for Kicks?, 1 vol. Santillan, Jorge H., illus. 2011. (Sports Illustrated Kids Victory School Superstars Ser.). (ENG.). 56p. (gr. 1-3). pap. 5.95 *(978-1-4342-3079-9(1))*; lib. bdg. 26.65 *(978-1-4342-2229-9(2))* Stone Arch Bks.

Krivitzky, Nathan & Nathan, Krivitzky. Always Late Nate. O'Connell, Dave, illus. 2009. (ENG.). 32p. (J). pap. 10.95 *(978-1-933916-41-5(9))* Nelson Publishing & Marketing.

Krulik, Nancy & Burwasser, Amanda Elizabeth. Soccer Shocker! Moran, Mike, illus. 2016. (Project Droid Ser.). (ENG.). 104p. (J). (gr. 1-4). pap. 4.99 *(978-1-5107-1029-0(9)*, Sky Pony Pr.) Skyhorse Publishing Co., Inc.

—Soccer Shocker: Project Droid #2. Moran, Mike, illus. 2016. (Project Droid Ser.). (ENG.). 104p. (J). (gr. 1-4). 13.99 *(978-1-5107-1019-1(1)*, Sky Pony Pr.) Skyhorse Publishing Co., Inc.

Lampard, Frank. Frankie vs. the Cowboy's Crew. 2014. (Frankie's Magic Soccer Ball Ser.: 4). (ENG., Illus.). 112p. (J). (gr. 2-5). pap. 4.99 *(978-0-545-66618-3(X))*; pap. 4.99 *(978-0-545-66616-9(3))* Scholastic, Inc. (Scholastic Paperbacks).

—Frankie vs. the Knight's Nasties. 2016. (Frankie's Magic Soccer Ball Ser.: 5). (ENG., Illus.). 112p. (J). (gr. 2-5). pap. 4.99 *(978-1-338-08907-3(2))* Scholastic, Inc.

—Frankie vs. the Pirate Pillagers. 2014. (Frankie's Magic Soccer Ball Ser.: 1). (ENG., Illus.). 96p. (J). (gr. 2-5). pap. 4.99 *(978-0-545-66612-1(0)*, Scholastic Paperbacks) Scholastic, Inc.

—Frankie vs. the Rowdy Romans. 2014. (Frankie's Magic Soccer Ball Ser.: 2). (ENG., Illus.). 112p. (J). (gr. 2-5). pap. 4.99 *(978-0-545-66614-5(7)*, Scholastic Paperbacks) Scholastic, Inc.

Lavoie, Jennifer. Andy Squared. 2012. (ENG.). 264p. (J). (gr. 7). pap. 11.95 *(978-1-60282-743-1(5))* Bold Strokes Bks.

Levine, Caroline. David's Secret Soccer Goals. 2004. (ENG.). 40p. (J). pap. 13.95 *(978-1-84310-772-9(4)*, 3659) Kingsley, Jessica Pubs. GBR. Dist: Macmillan Distribution Ltd.

Lewman, David. SpongeBob, Soccer Star! Reed, Stephen, illus. 2010. (SpongeBob SquarePants Ser.). (ENG.). 24p. (J). (gr. -1-3). pap. 3.99 *(978-1-4169-9445-9(9)*, Simon Spotlight/Nickelodeon) Simon Spotlight/Nickelodeon.

Lineker, Gary. More of Gary Lineker's Favourite Football Stories. 2003. (ENG.). 224p. (J). 19.99 *(978-0-333-73782-8(2))* Macmillan Pubs., Ltd. GBR. Dist: Trafalgar Square Publishing.

Loughlin, Patrick. Football High - Young Gun. 2016. (Football High Ser.: 1). (ENG.). 192p. (J). (gr. 3-7). pap. 12.99 *(978-1-925324-50-1(8))* Random Hse. Australia AUS. Dist: Independent Pubs. Group.

Lupica, Mike. Shoot-Out. (Comeback Kids Ser.). (ENG.). 176p. (J). (gr. 3-7). 2011. 6.99 *(978-0-14-241844-4(7)*, Puffin Books) 2010. 10.99 *(978-0-399-24718-7(1)*, Philomel Bks.) Penguin Young Readers Group.

—Shoot-Out, 1 vol. 2012. (Comeback Kids Ser.). (ENG.). 176p. (J). (gr. 4-8). lib. bdg. 27.07 *(978-1-59961-178-5(3))* Spotlight.

Maddox, Jake. Definición por Penales. Heck, Claudia M., tr. from ENG. Tiffany, Sean, illus. 2012. (Jake Maddox en Español Ser.). (SPA.). 72p. (gr. 2-3). 25.32 *(978-1-4342-3814-6(8))* Stone Arch Bks.

—Second-Chance Soccer, 1 vol. Ray, Mike, illus. 2014. (Jake Maddox JV Ser.). (ENG.). 96p. (gr. 3-4). 25.99 *(978-1-4342-9154-7(5))* Stone Arch Bks.

—Soccer Shake-Up. Aburto, Jesus, illus. 2015. (Jake Maddox Sports Stories Ser.). (ENG.). 72p. (gr. 2-3). lib. bdg. 25.32 *(978-1-4965-0495-1(X))* Stone Arch Bks.

—Soccer Shootout, 1 vol. Tiffany, Sean, illus. 2007. (Jake Maddox Sports Stories Ser.). (ENG.). 72p. (gr. 2-3). 25.32 *(978-1-59889-844-6(2))*; per. 5.95 *(978-1-59889-896-5(5))* Stone Arch Bks.

—Soccer Show-Off, 1 vol. Wood, Katie, illus. 2014. (Jake Maddox Girl Sports Stories Ser.). (ENG.). 72p. (gr. 2-3). 25.32 *(978-1-4342-4144-3(0))* Stone Arch Bks.

—Soccer Spirit. Mourning, Tuesday, illus. 2008. (Jake Maddox Girl Sports Stories Ser.). (ENG.). 72p. (gr. 2-3). 25.32 *(978-1-4342-0780-7(3))* Stone Arch Bks.

—Soccer Stand-Off. 2016. (Jake Maddox JV Ser.). (ENG.). 96p. (gr. 3-4). lib. bdg. 25.99 *(978-1-4965-3983-0(4))* Stone Arch Bks.

—Soccer Step-Up. 2016. (Jake Maddox JV Girls Ser.). (ENG.). 96p. (gr. 3-4). lib. bdg. 25.99 *(978-1-4965-3675-4(4))* Stone Arch Bks.

—Soccer Switch. Aburtov, Jesus Aburto, illus. 2017. (Jake Maddox Graphic Novels Ser.). (ENG.). 72p. (gr. 2-5). lib. bdg. 26.65 *(978-1-4965-3699-0(1))* Stone Arch Bks.

—Striker Assist, 1 vol. Tiffany, Sean, illus. 2012. (Jake Maddox Sports Stories Ser.). (ENG.). 72p. (gr. 2-3). 25.32 *(978-1-4342-4011-8(8))* Stone Arch Bks.

Maddox, Jake & Berne, Emma Carlson. Soccer Surprise, 1 vol. Wood, Katie, illus. 2012. (Jake Maddox Girl Sports Stories Ser.). (ENG.). 72p. (gr. 2-3). pap. 5.95 *(978-1-4342-3906-8(3))*; lib. bdg. 25.32 *(978-1-4342-3291-5(3))* Stone Arch Bks.

Manushkin, Fran. Pedro's Big Goal. Lyon, Tammie, illus. 2016. (Pedro Ser.). (ENG.). 32p. (gr. k-2). lib. bdg. 21.32 *(978-1-5158-0086-6(5))* Pedro Pubns. GBR. Dist: Capstone Pub.

Margolin, Phillip & Rome, Ami Margolin. Vanishing Acts. 2012. (ENG.). 176p. (J). (gr. 3-7). pap. 8.99 *(978-0-06-188558-7(4))* HarperCollins Pubs.

Marsh, Carole. The Secret Soccer Ball. 2006. 64p. (gr. 2-4). 14.95 *(978-0-635-06219-2(4))*; pap. 3.99 *(978-0-635-06213-0(5))* Gallopade International.

Masannak, Joachim. The Wild Soccer Bunch, Book 2, Diego the Tornado: Diego the Tornado. Part, Michael, ed. Schier, Helga, tr. Birck, Jan, illus. 2011. (ENG.). 148p. (J). (gr. 4-7). 12.95 *(978-0-9844257-1-6(3))* Sole Bks.

Masterson, Hoss. Soccer Sloth. Alves, Josh, illus. 2017. (Animal All-Stars Ser.). (ENG.). 56p. (gr. 1-3). lib. bdg. 25.32 *(978-1-4965-4306-6(8))* Stone Arch Bks.

Maurer, Shari. Change of Heart. 2010. 290p. (YA). 16.95 *(978-1-934813-36-2(2))* Westside Bks.

May, Eleanor. The Great Shape-up. 2008. pap. 34.95 *(978-1-58013-763-8(6))* Kane Press, Inc.

—The Great Shape-up. Gott, Barry, illus. 2007. (Science Solves It! Ser.). 32p. (J). (gr. -1-3). pap. 5.95 *(978-1-57565-248-1(X))* Kane Press, Inc.

McGowan, Anthony. The Bare Bum Gang Battles the Dogsnatchers. 2010. (ENG., Illus.). 144p. (J). (gr. 2-4). pap. 11.99 *(978-1-86230-387-4(8)*, Red Fox) Random House Children's Books GBR. Dist: Independent Pubs. Group.

McKnight, Marty. Jim Nasium Is a Soccer Goofball. Jones, Chris B., illus. 2015. (Jim Nasium Ser.). (ENG.). 88p. (gr. 2-3). pap. 5.95 *(978-1-4965-0525-5(5))* Stone Arch Bks.

McNamara, Margaret. The Playground Problem. Gordon, Mike, illus. 2004. (Robin Hill School Ser.). (ENG.). 32p. (J). (gr. -1-1). pap. 3.99 *(978-0-689-85876-5(0)*, Simon Spotlight) Simon Spotlight.

Meadows, Daisy. Stacey the Soccer Fairy. 2010. (Sports Fairies Ser.: 2). (ENG.). 80p. (J). (gr. 2-5). 4.99 *(978-0-545-20253-4(1)*, Scholastic Paperbacks) Scholastic, Inc.

Meister, Cari. Goalkeeper Goof, 1 vol. Doerrfeld, Cori, illus. 2009. (My First Graphic Novel Ser.). (ENG.). 32p. (gr. k-2). pap. 6.25 *(978-1-4342-1409-6(5))*; lib. bdg. 24.65 *(978-1-4342-1292-4(0))* Stone Arch Bks. (My First Graphic Novel).

Milway, Katie Smith. The Banana-Leaf Ball: How Play Can Change the World. Evans, Shane W., illus. 2017. (CitizenKid Ser.). (ENG.). 32p. (J). (gr. 3-7). 18.95 *(978-1-77138-331-8(3))* Kids Can Pr., Ltd. CAN. Dist: Hachette Bk. Group.

Mirabella, Erin. Shawn Sheep the Soccer Star. Davis, Sarah, illus. 2008. (Barnsville Sports Squad Ser.). (ENG.). 32p. (J). (gr. k-3). 15.95 *(978-1-934030-16-5(3))* VeloPress.

Mitchard, Jacquelyn & Lewis, Michael S. Eagle Eyes. 2009. (ENG.). 128p. (gr. 4-7). pap. 9.99 *(978-0-9790072-2-4(4))* MAHVL Publishing.

Montalbano, Andrea. Breakaway. 2011. (ENG.). 208p. (J). (gr. 3-7). 6.99 *(978-0-14-241903-8(6)*, Puffin Books) Penguin Young Readers Group.

—Lily Out of Bounds. 2012. (ENG.). 132p. (J). pap. 8.99 *(978-0-9858956-1-7(6))* In This Together Media.

—Out of Bounds. 2017. (ENG.). (J). (gr. 3-7). (Soccer Sisters Ser.: 1). 176p. pap. 7.99 *(978-1-4926-4481-1(1)*, 9781492644811, Sourcebooks Jabberwocky); (Illus.). 18.99 ***(978-1-4926-6233-4(X))*** Sourcebooks, Inc.

—Out of Bounds. 2017. (Soccer Sisters Ser.: 1). lib. bdg. 18.40 ***(978-0-606-40353-5(1))*** Turtleback Bks.

Morgan, Alex. Hat Trick. 2015. (Kicks Ser.). (ENG., Illus.). 128p. (J). (gr. 3-7). 16.99 *(978-1-4814-5096-6(4)*, Simon & Schuster Bks. For Young Readers) Simon & Schuster Bks. For Young Readers.

—Sabotage Season. (Kicks Ser.). (ENG., Illus.). (J). (gr. 3-7). 2014. 192p. pap. 6.99 *(978-1-4424-8576-1(0))* 2013. 176p. 15.99 *(978-1-4424-8574-7(4))* Simon & Schuster Bks. For Young Readers. (Simon & Schuster Bks. For Young Readers).

—Saving the Team. 2014. (Kicks Ser.). (ENG., Illus.). 192p. (J). (gr. 3-7). pap. 6.99 *(978-1-4424-8571-6(X)*, Simon & Schuster Bks. For Young Readers) Simon & Schuster Bks. For Young Readers.

—Saving the Team. Franco, Paula, illus. 2013. (Kicks Ser.). (ENG.). 176p. (J). (gr. 3-7). 17.99 *(978-1-4424-8570-9(1)*, Simon & Schuster Bks. For Young Readers) Simon & Schuster Bks. For Young Readers.

—Settle the Score. 2016. (Kicks Ser.). (ENG., Illus.). 128p. (J). (gr. 3-7). 16.99 *(978-1-4814-5104-8(9)*, Simon & Schuster Bks. For Young Readers) Simon & Schuster Bks. For Young Readers.

—Shaken Up. 2015. (Kicks Ser.). (ENG., Illus.). 128p. (J). (gr. 3-7). 16.99 *(978-1-4814-5100-0(6)*, Simon & Schuster Bks. For Young Readers) Simon & Schuster Bks. For Young Readers.

—Under Pressure. 2017. (J). pap. ***(978-1-4814-8151-9(7)***, Simon & Schuster Bks. For Young Readers) Simon & Schuster Bks. For Young Readers.

Morgan, Alex. Win or Lose. 2014. (Kicks Ser.). (ENG., Illus.). 160p. (J). (gr. 3-7). 15.99 *(978-1-4424-8580-8(9)*, Simon & Schuster Bks. For Young Readers) Simon & Schuster Bks. For Young Readers.

Morningstar, Jeremy. Penalty Kick. 2005. 56p. pap. 9.00 *(978-1-4116-6572-9(4))* Lulu Pr., Inc.

Morpurgo, Michael. Billy the Kid. Foreman, Michael, illus. 2013. (ENG.). 80p. (J). (gr. 2-4). pap. 11.99 *(978-1-84365-260-1(9)*, Pavilion) Pavilion Bks. GBR. Dist: Independent Pubs. Group.

Murray, Stuart A. P. Matty in the Goal. 2012. (Champion Sports Story Ser.). 104p. (J). (gr. 3-18). pap. 10.95 *(978-1-4644-0003-2(2))*; 27.94 *(978-0-7660-3877-6(7))* Enslow Pubs., Inc.

—Todd Goes for the Goal. 2012. (Champion Sports Story Ser.). 104p. (J). (gr. 3-18). pap. 10.95 *(978-1-4644-0000-1(8))*; lib. bdg. 27.94 *(978-0-7660-3887-5(4))* Enslow Pubs., Inc.

Myers, Bill. My Life as a Stupendously Stomped Soccer Star, 1 vol. 2006. (Incredible Worlds of Wally Mcdoogle Ser.: 26). (ENG.). 128p. (gr. 3-7). per. 6.99 *(978-1-4003-0635-0(3))* Nelson, Thomas Inc.

Myers, Bob. Trinity Goes to Soccer Camp. Bunker, Tom, illus. 2012. 36p. 24.95 *(978-1-4560-2906-7(1))* America Star Bks.

Myers, Walter Dean & Workman, Ross. Kick. (ENG.). (YA). (gr. 9). 2012. 224p. pap. 9.99 *(978-0-06-200491-8(3))* 2011. 208p. 16.99 *(978-0-06-200489-5(1))* HarperCollins Pubs. (HarperTeen).

Nesbø, Jo. The Magical Fruit. 2014. (Doctor Proctor's Fart Powder Ser.). (ENG., Illus.). 320p. (J). (gr. 3-7). pap. 7.99 *(978-1-4424-9343-8(7)*, Aladdin) Simon & Schuster Children's Publishing.

—The Magical Fruit. Chace, Tara F., tr. from NOR. Lowery, Mike, illus. 2013. (Doctor Proctor's Fart Powder Ser.). (ENG.). 320p. (J). (gr. 3-7). 17.99 *(978-1-4424-9342-1(9)*, Aladdin) Simon & Schuster Children's Publishing.

Newman, Tracy. Uncle Eli's Wedding. Isik, Semur, illus. 2015. (ENG.). 32p. (J). (gr. -1-3). 16.99 *(978-0-8075-8293-0(X))* Whitman, Albert & Co.

Nunes, Ernest. Oh! How I Wish I Could Play Soccer with Ernie & the Dreamers. 2013. 70p. pap. 12.99 *(978-1-62509-705-7(0))* Salem Author Services.

O'Brien, Joe. Legends' Lair. 2016. (ENG., Illus.). 192p. (J). pap. 13.00 *(978-1-84717-826-8(X))* O'Brien Pr., Ltd., The IRL. Dist: Dufour Editions, Inc.

O'Connor, Heather. Betting Game, 1 vol. 2015. (Orca Sports Ser.). (ENG.). 216p. (YA). (gr. 6-10). pap. 9.95 *(978-1-4598-0930-7(0))* Orca Bk. Pubs. USA.

O'Connor, Jane. Fancy Nancy: Nancy Clancy, Soccer Mania. Glasser, Robin Preiss, illus. (Nancy Clancy Ser.: 6). (J). (gr. 1-5). 2016. 144p. pap. 4.99 *(978-0-06-226966-9(6))* 2015. (ENG.). 128p. 9.99 *(978-0-06-226967-6(4))* HarperCollins Pubs.

O'connor, Jane. Nancy Clancy, Soccer Mania. Glasser, Robin Preiss, illus. 2016. (Nancy Clancy Ser.: 6). (ENG.). 144p. (J). (gr. 1-5). 14.75 *(978-0-606-39270-9(X))* Turtleback Bks.

O'Donnell, Liam. Soccer Sabotage: A Graphic Guide Adventure, 1 vol. Deas, Mike, illus. 2009. (Graphic Guides). (ENG.). 64p. (J). (gr. 3-7). pap. 9.95 *(978-1-55143-884-9(4))* Orca Bk. Pubs. USA.

O'Hara, Susan. Tim's First Soccer Game. Barrett, Rebecca, illus. 2012. 38p. pap. 14.97 *(978-1-61897-199-9(9)*, Strategic Bk. Publishing) Strategic Book Publishing & Rights Agency (SBPRA).

Oldfield, Tom & Oldfield, Matt. Ryan Giggs: Wing Wizard. 2017. (Heroes Ser.). (ENG.). 160p. (J). (gr. 4-8). pap. 9.99 ***(978-1-78606-378-6(6))*** Blake, John Publishing, Ltd. GBR. Dist: Independent Pubs. Group.

Olin, Rita & Olin, Spencer. Trouble in Soccertown: A Lazer Mcnulty Adventure. 2009. 108p. 20.95 *(978-1-4401-5374-7(4))*; pap. 10.95 *(978-1-4401-5376-1(0))* iUniverse, Inc.

O'Nan, Gerald D. The Adventures of Andy Ant: Lawn Mower on the Loose. McGary, Norman, illus. 2014. (ENG.). 28p. (gr. -1-4). pap. 9.95 *(978-1-61448-673-2(5))* Morgan James Publishing.

Orr, Tamra. No Hands Allowed, Plus Robbie & Ryan Play Indoor Soccer, 11 vols., Set. 2006. (Robbie Reader, Weekend Soccer Ser.). (J). (gr. 1-4). lib. bdg. *(978-1-58415-490-7(X))* Mitchell Lane Pubs., Inc.

Osborne, Mary Pope. Soccer on Sunday. Murdocca, Sal, illus. (Magic Tree House Merlin Missions Ser.: No. 24). (ENG.). (J). (gr. 2-5). 2016. 144p. 5.99 *(978-0-307-98056-4(1))* 2014. 128p. 12.99 *(978-0-307-98053-3(7))* Random Hse. Children's Bks. (Random Hse. Bks. for Young Readers).

Osterhold, Jared, illus. OLIVIA Plays Soccer. 2013. (Olivia TV Tie-In Ser.). (ENG.). 24p. (J). (gr. -1-1). 16.99 *(978-1-4424-7249-5(9)*, Simon Spotlight) Simon Spotlight.

Padian, Maria. Out of Nowhere. (ENG.). 352p. (YA). (gr. 7). 2015. pap. 9.99 *(978-0-375-86562-6(4)*, Ember) 2013. 16.99 *(978-0-375-86580-0(2)*, Knopf Bks. for Young Readers) Random Hse. Children's Bks.

Palmer, Tom. Boys United. 2009. (Football Academy Ser.). (ENG., Illus.). 176p. (J). (gr. 2-4). pap. 10.99 *(978-0-14-132467-8(8))* Penguin Bks., Ltd. GBR. Dist: Independent Pubs. Group.

—Reading the Game, Bk. 4. 4th ed. 2009. (Football Academy Ser.). (ENG., Illus.). 160p. (J). (gr. 2-4). pap. 10.99 *(978-0-14-132470-8(8))* Penguin Bks., Ltd. GBR. Dist: Independent Pubs. Group.

—The Real Thing, Bk. 3. 3rd ed. 2009. (Football Academy Ser.). (ENG., Illus.). 176p. (J). (gr. 2-4). pap. 10.99 *(978-0-14-132469-2(4))* Penguin Bks., Ltd. GBR. Dist: Independent Pubs. Group.

—Striking Out. 2nd ed. 2009. (Football Academy Ser.). (ENG., Illus.). 160p. (J). (gr. 2-4). pap. 10.99 *(978-0-14-132468-5(6))* Penguin Bks., Ltd. GBR. Dist: Independent Pubs. Group.

Palonen, Jukka & Conrad, Tim. The Game Plan: A Kids' Musical about God's Master Plan for Each of Us. 2009. (ENG.). 96p. pap. 7.99 *(978-0-8341-7742-0(0)*, 9780834177420) Lillenas Publishing Co.

Parsons, Garry. Spooky Soccer. Doyle, Malachy, illus. 2010. (Red Bananas Ser.). (ENG.). 48p. (J). (gr. k-2). pap. 5.99 *(978-1-4052-4924-9(2))* Egmont Bks., Ltd. GBR. Dist: Independent Pubs. Group.

Pedraza, M. Eugenia Rueda. Nico's Voyage. 2013. 32p. pap. *(978-1-4602-2360-4(8))* FriesenPress.

Pedro, Coach & Rita, Susan Adam. The Magic Soccer Ball: Trapping & My 1st Game. 2008. 44p. pap. 18.49 *(978-1-4343-6593-4(X))* AuthorHouse.

Pee-Wee Soccer. 2003. (J). per. *(978-1-57657-941-1(7))* Paradise Pr., Inc.

Peet, Mal. Alf Saves the Day. Hammond, Andy, illus. 2004. (ENG.). 24p. (J). lib. bdg. 23.65 *(978-1-59646-692-0(8))* Dingles & Co.

—Keeper. (ENG.). 240p. (YA). (gr. 5). 2016. pap. 8.99 *(978-0-7636-8746-5(4))* 2005. 15.99 *(978-0-7636-2749-2(6))* Candlewick Pr.

Peirce, Lincoln. Big Nate — Here Goes Nothing. 2012. (Big Nate Graphic Novels Ser.: 6). (J). lib. bdg. 20.85 *(978-0-606-26526-3(0)*, Turtleback) Turtleback Bks.

Perry, Ellyse;Clark. Double Time. 2017. (Ellyse Perry Ser.: 4). (ENG.). 160p. (J). (gr. 4-7). 12.99 *(978-0-14-378130-1(8))* Random Hse. Australia AUS. Dist: Independent Pubs. Group.

—Winning Touch. 2017. (Ellyse Perry Ser.: 3). (ENG.). 160p. (J). (gr. 4-7). 12.99 *(978-0-14-378128-8(6))* Random Hse. Australia AUS. Dist: Independent Pubs. Group.

Peschke, Marci. Soccer Queen. Mourning, Tuesday, illus. 2015. (Kylie Jean Ser.). (ENG.). 112p. (gr. 2-3). 22.65 *(978-1-4795-5882-7(6)*, Kylie Jean) Picture Window Bks.

Peters, Stephanie & Christopher, Matt. Soccer Hero. rev. ed. 2007. (ENG.). 96p. (J). (gr. 3-7). per. 5.99 *(978-0-316-11345-8(X))* Little, Brown Bks. for Young Readers.

Phillips, Dee. Goal, 1 vol. unabr. ed. 2011. (Right Now! Ser.). (ENG., Illus.). 45p. (YA). (gr. 9-12). pap. 8.95 *(978-1-61651-249-1(0))* Saddleback Educational Publishing, Inc.

Pinkney, Brian. On the Ball. Pinkney, Brian, illus. 2015. (ENG., Illus.). 40p. (J). (gr. -1-k). 17.99 *(978-1-4847-2329-6(5))* Disney Pr.

Popescu, Petru. Birth of the Pack. rev. ed. 2007. (ENG.). 352p. (YA). (gr. 8-12). pap. 20.99 *(978-0-7653-1641-7(2)*, 9780765316417, Tor Teen) Doherty, Tom Assocs., LLC.

Potter, Noel Gyro. The Spoiled Sport, 1 vol. Cannon, Joseph, illus. 2010. (Adventures of Marshall & Art Set 2 Ser.). (ENG.). 32p. (gr. -1-4). 28.50 *(978-1-60270-737-5(5),* Looking Glass Library) ABDO Publishing Co.

Price, Mathew. Me Encanta el Futbol. (SPA.). pap. 11.95 *(978-950-07-2081-6(7))* Editorial Sudamericana S.A. ARG. Dist: Distribooks, Inc.

Priebe, Val. It's Hard to Dribble with Your Feet, 1 vol. Santillan, Jorge H., illus. 2010. (Sports Illustrated Kids Victory School Superstars Ser.). (ENG.). 56p. (gr. 1-3). 26.65 *(978-1-4342-2016-5(8));* pap. 5.95 *(978-1-4342-2782-9(0))* Stone Arch Bks.

Random House. Reds Against Blues! (Thomas & Friends) Courtney, Richard, illus. 2016. (Step into Reading Ser.). (ENG.). 24p. (J). (gr. -1-1). 4.99 *(978-1-101-93284-1(8),* Random Hse. Bks. for Young Readers) Random Hse. Children's Bks.

Random House Editors. Reds Against Blues! 2016. (Thomas & Friends Step into Reading Ser.). lib. bdg. 14.75 *(978-0-606-38474-2(X))* Turtleback Bks.

Rayner, Robert. Falling Star, 1 vol. 2007. (Lorimer Sports Stories Ser.). (ENG.). 136p. (J). (gr. 4-8). 16.95 *(978-1-55028-971-8(3),* 9781550289718) Lorimer, James & Co., Ltd., Pubs. CAN. Dist: Casemate Pubs. & Bk. Distributors, LLC.

—Suspended, 1 vol. 2004. (Lorimer Sports Stories Ser.). (ENG.). 112p. (J). (gr. 4-8). 16.95 *(978-1-55028-861-2(X),* 9781550288612) Lorimer, James & Co., Ltd., Pubs. CAN. Dist: Casemate Pubs. & Bk. Distributors, LLC.

Rayner, Shoo. Ginger Ninja 5: World Cup Winners. (Illus.). 63p. (J). (gr. k-6). pap. 8.99 *(978-0-340-69379-7(7))* Hodder & Stoughton GBR. Dist: Trafalgar Square Publishing.

Regan, Peter. Riverside: Spring Fever. 2007. (ENG.). 112p. (J). pap. 10.95 *(978-1-901737-56-1(X))* Anvil Bks., Ltd. IRL. Dist: Dufour Editions, Inc.

—Riverside: The Curse. Myler, Terry, illus. 2004. (Riverside Ser.). (ENG.). 127p. (J). pap. 11.95 *(978-1-901737-46-2(2))* Anvil Bks., Ltd. IRL. Dist: Dufour Editions, Inc.

—Riverside: The Spy. 2007. (ENG.). 112p. (J). pap. 10.95 *(978-1-901737-53-0(5))* Anvil Bks., Ltd. IRL. Dist: Dufour Editions, Inc.

Renner, C. J., et al. Soccer Longshot, 1 vol. Maese, Fares & Aburto, Jesus, illus. 2011. (Sports Illustrated Kids Graphic Novels Ser.). (ENG.). 56p. (gr. 2-3). pap. 7.19 *(978-1-4342-3402-5(9))* Stone Arch Bks.

—Soccer Longshot, 1 vol. Maese, Fares, illus. 2011. (Sports Illustrated Kids Graphic Novels Ser.). (ENG.). 56p. (gr. 2-3). lib. bdg. 26.65 *(978-1-4342-2241-1(1))* Stone Arch Bks.

Rey, H. A. Curious George Plays Soccer. 2017. (Curious George Ser.). (ENG., Illus.). 24p. (J). (gr. -1-3). 14.99 *(978-0-544-91246-5(2),* HMH Books For Young Readers) Houghton Mifflin Harcourt Publishing Co.

Rigby, Robert. Goal! The Dream Begins. 2006. (ENG., Illus.). 240p. (YA). (gr. 7-9). pap. 7.99 *(978-0-15-205798-5(6))* Houghton Mifflin Harcourt Publishing Co.

—Goal - Glory Days. 2010. (ENG., Illus.). 252p. (YA). (gr. 7-18). pap. 7.99 *(978-0-15-205921-7(0))* Houghton Mifflin Harcourt Publishing Co.

—Goal II: Living the Dream. 2007. (ENG., Illus.). 224p. (YA). (gr. 7-7). pap. 14.95 *(978-0-15-205881-4(8))* Houghton Mifflin Harcourt Publishing Co.

Riley, Zach. Surprise Kick. Ricci, Andrés, illus. 2012. (Zach Riley Ser.). 80p. (J). (gr. 3-6). lib. bdg. 27.07 *(978-1-61783-536-0(6))* Magic Wagon.

Rippin, Sally. The Soccer Star. Fukuoka, Aki, illus. (J). 2013. (ENG.). 48p. pap. 4.99 *(978-1-61067-096-8(5))* 2012. 44p. *(978-1-61067-133-0(3))* Kane Miller.

—The Winning Goal. Spartels, Stephanie, illus. (J). 2013. (ENG.). 48p. pap. 4.99 *(978-1-61067-123-1(6))* 2012. 43p. *(978-1-61067-137-8(6))* Kane Miller.

Ross, David & Cattell, Bob. Bad Boys. 2010. (Strikers Ser.: 3). (ENG., Illus.). 123p. (J). (gr. 4-7). pap. 7.99 *(978-1-84732-538-9(6))* Carlton Bks., Ltd. GBR. Dist: Independent Pubs. Group.

—Big Deal. 2010. (Strikers Ser.: 2). (ENG., Illus.). 128p. (J). (gr. 5-7). pap. 7.99 *(978-1-84732-491-7(6))* Carlton Bks., Ltd. GBR. Dist: Independent Pubs. Group.

—Young Blood. 2010. (Strikers Ser.: 1). (ENG., Illus.). 128p. (J). (gr. 4-7). pap. 7.99 *(978-1-84732-490-0(8))* Carlton Bks., Ltd. GBR. Dist: Independent Pubs. Group.

Ross, Jeff. Above All Else, 1 vol. 2014. (Orca Sports Ser.). (ENG.). 176p. (YA). (gr. 6-10). pap. 9.95 *(978-1-4598-0388-6(4))* Orca Bk. Pubs. USA.

Rue, Nancy N. Lucy Out of Bounds, 1 vol. 2016. (Faithgirlz / a Lucy Novel Ser.). (ENG.). 224p. (J). pap. 7.99 *(978-0-310-75505-0(0))* Zonderkidz.

Sanchez, Ricardo. Spotlight Soccer, 1 vol. Waryanto, Ian, illus. 2014. (Sports Illustrated Kids Graphic Novels Ser.). (ENG.). 72p. (gr. 2-5). 26.65 *(978-1-4342-4165-8(3))* Stone Arch Bks.

Sateren, Shelley Swanson. Max & Zoe at Soccer Practice, 1 vol. Sullivan, Mary, illus. 2012. (Max & Zoe Ser.). (ENG.). 32p. (gr. k-2). lib. bdg. 21.32 *(978-1-4048-6213-5(7),* Max & Zoe) Picture Window Bks.

Scholastic. Peppa Plays Soccer (Peppa Pig: 8x8) Eone, illus. 2016. (Peppa Pig Ser.). (ENG.). 24p. (J). (gr. -1-k). pap. 4.99 *(978-1-338-03279-6(8))* Scholastic, Inc.

Scholastic Editors. Peppa Plays Soccer. 2016. (Peppa Pig 8X8 Ser.). lib. bdg. 14.75 *(978-0-606-38825-2(7))* Turtleback Bks.

Scudamore, Beverly. Foul Play, 1 vol. 2005. (Lorimer Sports Stories Ser.). (ENG.). 112p. (J). (gr. 4-8). 16.95 *(978-1-55028-875-9(X),* 9781550288759) Lorimer, James & Co., Ltd., Pubs. CAN. Dist: Casemate Pubs. & Bk. Distributors, LLC.

Shahan, Sherry. That's Not How You Play Soccer, Daddy!, 1 vol. Mai-Wyss, Tatjana, illus. 2007. (ENG.). 32p. (J). (gr. -1-3). 15.95 *(978-1-56145-416-7(8),* Peachtree Junior) Peachtree Pubs.

Shaw, Natalie. A Special Day with Dad. 2014. (Olivia 8x8 Ser.). lib. bdg. 14.75 *(978-0-606-35460-8(3))* Turtleback Bks.

Simmons, Cari & Douglas, Lola. You First. 2015. (Picture Perfect Ser.: 2). (ENG.). 256p. (J). (gr. 3-7). pap. 6.99 *(978-0-06-231058-3(5))* HarperCollins Pubs.

Simon, Francesca. Horrid Henry & the Soccer Fiend. Ross, Tony, illus. 2009. (Horrid Henry Ser.: 0). (ENG.). 112p. (J). (gr. 2-5). pap. 6.99 *(978-1-4022-1778-4(1),* Sourcebooks Jabberwocky) Sourcebooks, Inc.

—Horrid Henry & the Soccer Fiend, 1 vol. Ross, Tony, illus. 2012. (Horrid Henry Ser.). (ENG.). 112p. (J). (gr. 2-5). lib. bdg. 24.21 *(978-1-59961-189-1(9))* Spotlight.

—Horrid Henry & the Soccer Fiend. 2009. (Horrid Henry Ser.). lib. bdg. 17.20 *(978-0-606-06798-0(1),* Turtleback) Turtleback Bks.

Sís, Peter. Madlenka. Sís, Peter, illus. 2010. (ENG., Illus.). 48p. (J). (gr. -1-3). pap. 8.99 *(978-0-312-65912-7(1),* 9780312659127) Square Fish.

Skead, Robert. Elves Can't Kick. 2005. 84p. per. 7.99 *(978-1-929478-66-8(6))* Cross Training Publishing.

Sloan, Holly Goldberg. Keeper. 2005. (Dream Ser.). 146p. (gr. 3-8). pap. 9.95 *(978-0-9708992-3-1(8))* Scobre Pr. Corp.

Smiley, Sophie. Team Trouble. Foreman, Michael, illus. 2007. (ENG.). 64p. (J). (gr. 2-4). pap. 9.95 *(978-1-84270-684-8(5))* Andersen Pr. GBR. Dist: Independent Pubs. Group.

Smith, Annette. Saturday Morning Soccer. Holt, Richard, illus. 2009. 16p. pap. 10.67 *(978-1-4190-5503-4(8))* Rigby Education.

Spring, Debbie. Breathing Soccer, 1 vol. 2008. (ENG.). 208p. (J). (gr. 4-8). pap. 10.95 *(978-1-897235-42-3(9))* Thistledown Pr., Ltd. CAN. Dist: Univ. of Toronto Pr.

Stamper, Judith Bauer & Stamper, Judith. Go, Fractions! Demarest, Chris L., illus. 2003. (Penguin Young Readers, Level 3 Ser.). (ENG.). 48p. (J). (gr. 1-3). mass mkt. 3.99 *(978-0-448-43113-0(0),* Penguin Young Readers) Penguin Young Readers Group.

Staunton, Ted. Great Play, Morgan. Slavin, Bill, illus. 2008. (First Novel Ser.). (ENG.). 64p. (J). (gr. 2-6). *(978-0-88780-772-5(0))* Formac Publishing Co., Ltd. CAN. Dist: Casemate Pubs. & Bk. Distributors, LLC.

Stein, Joshua. Chasing the King. 2005. (Dream Ser.). 150p. (gr. 3-8). pap. 9.95 *(978-0-9708992-4-8(6))* Scobre Pr. Corp.

Stiles, Amanda. The Runaway Soccer Ball. Torrey, Rich, illus. 2010. 16p. (J). pap. *(978-0-545-24819-8(1))* Scholastic, Inc.

Stultz, Janice. Harry Turnaround. 2012. 24p. pap. 15.99 *(978-1-4691-7141-8(4))* Xlibris Corp.

Stuve-Bodeen, Stephanie. Babu's Song. Boyd, Aaron, illus. 2003. (ENG.). 32p. (J). 16.95 *(978-1-58430-058-8(2))* Lee & Low Bks., Inc.

Styles, Walker. The Soccer Ball Monster Mystery. Whitehouse, Ben, illus. 2016. (Rider Woofson Ser.: 6). (ENG.). 128p. (J). (gr. k-4). pap. 5.99 *(978-1-4814-7110-7(4),* Little Simon) Little Simon.

Swanson, Julie A. Going for the Record. 2004. 223p. (YA). pap. 8.00 *(978-0-8028-5273-1(4))* Eerdmans, William B. Publishing Co.

Tamar, Erika. Venus & the Comets. 2004. (Junior Library Guild Selection Ser.). 96p. (J). (gr. 2-18). 14.95 *(978-1-58196-007-5(7));* pap. 4.99 *(978-1-58196-018-1(2))* Lerner Publishing Group. (Darby Creek).

Taylor, Dereen. Paulo & the Football Thieves: Peek Inside the Pop-Up Windows! Hutchinson, Tim, illus. 2014. (ENG.). 12p. 16.99 *(978-1-86147-409-4(1),* Armadillo) Anness Publishing GBR. Dist: National Bk. Network.

Teamwork Works. 2005. 39p. (J). 3.99 *(978-0-9763213-3-0(5))* OHC Group LLC.

Thielbar, Melinda. The Hundred-Dollar Robber. Pantoja, Tintin, illus. 2010. (Manga Math Mysteries Ser.: 2). (ENG.). 48p. (gr. 3-5). pap. 6.95 *(978-0-7613-5243-3(0),* Graphic Universe™) Lerner Publishing Group.

—The Hundred-Dollar Robber. 2nd rev. ed. 2010. pap. 39.62 *(978-0-7613-6943-1(0))* Lerner Publishing Group.

—The Hundred-Dollar Robber: A Mystery with Money. Pantoja, Maria Kristina, illus. 2009. (Manga Math Mysteries Ser.: 2). (ENG.). 48p. (gr. 3-5). 29.27 *(978-0-7613-3854-3(3))* Lerner Publishing Group.

Thorpe, Kiki. In the Game. 2016. (Never Girls Ser.: 12). lib. bdg. 16.00 *(978-0-606-38468-1(5))* Turtleback Bks.

Torrey, Richard L. Beans Baker's Best Shot. Torrey, Richard L., illus. 2006. (Step into Reading Ser.: Vol. 3). (ENG., Illus.). 48p. (J). (gr. k-3). per. 3.99 *(978-0-375-82839-3(7),* Random Hse. Bks. for Young Readers) Random Hse. Children's Bks.

Toye, Clive. Toby & the Greatest Game. 2012. 136p. (gr. 4-6). pap. 11.95 *(978-1-4697-9516-4(7))* iUniverse, Inc.

Voigt, David & Voigt, Grady. Socky, the Soft-Hearted Soccer Ball. Wagner, Steve, illus. 2011. pap. 12.00 *(978-0-9833310-6-3(5))* Aperture Pr., LLC.

Wallace, Rich. The Ball Hogs, No. 1. Holder, Jimmy, illus. 2011. (Kickers Ser.: Bk. 1). (ENG.). 128p. (J). (gr. 1-4). 5.99 *(978-0-375-85092-9(9),* Yearling) Random Hse. Children's Bks.

—Benched. Holder, Jimmy, illus. 2011. (Kickers Ser.). (ENG.). 128p. (J). (gr. 1-4). 5.99 *(978-0-375-85094-3(5),* Yearling) Random Hse. Children's Bks.

—Between the Sticks, 1 vol. Heitz, Tim, illus. 2016. (Game Face Ser.). (ENG.). 112p. (J). (gr. 3-7). 27.07 *(978-1-62402-132-9(8))* Magic Wagon.

—Fake Out. Holder, Jimmy, illus. 2011. (Kickers Ser.: Bk. 2). (ENG.). 128p. (J). (gr. 1-4). 6.99 *(978-0-375-85093-6(7),* Yearling) Random Hse. Children's Bks.

—Game-Day Jitters. Holder, Jimmy, illus. 2012. (Kickers Ser.). (ENG.). 128p. (J). (gr. 2-5). 5.99 *(978-0-375-85095-0(3),* Yearling) Random Hse. Children's Bks.

—Shots on Goal. 2005. (ENG.). 160p. (YA). (gr. 7-11). per. 5.99 *(978-0-679-88671-6(0),* Laurel Leaf) Random Hse. Children's Bks.

Warner, Gertrude Chandler. The Mystery of the Soccer Snitch. VanArsdale, Anthony, illus. 2014. (Boxcar Children Mysteries Ser.: 136). (ENG.). 128p. (J). (gr. 1-5). pap. 5.99 *(978-0-8075-0896-1(9))* Whitman, Albert & Co.

Weninger, Brigitte. Davy, Soccer Star! Tharlet, Eve, illus. 2010. (ENG.). 40p. (J). (gr. -1-3). pap. 7.95 *(978-0-7358-2287-0(5))* North-South Bks., Inc.

Westcott, Jim. The Gift. 2014. (Red Rhino Ser.). (J). lib. bdg. 18.40 *(978-0-606-36201-6(0))* Turtleback Bks.

Weyn, Suzanne, et al. Gracie. 2007. (Newmarket Medallion Editions for Young Readers: Ser.). (ENG., Illus.). 160p. (gr. 4-6). per. 6.95 *(978-1-55704-779-3(0),* William Morrow Paperbacks) HarperCollins Pubs.

Wheeler, Lisa. Dino-Soccer. Gott, Barry, illus. 2009. (Carolrhoda Picture Bks.). (ENG.). 32p. (J). (gr. k-3). 16.95 *(978-0-8225-9028-6(X))* Lerner Publishing Group.

Williams, Mark. The Little Welsh Football Fan. 2016. (ENG., Illus.). 32p. (J). pap. 7.00 ***(978-1-78461-364-8(9))*** Y Lolfa GBR. Dist: Dufour Editions, Inc.

Williams, Michael. Now Is the Time for Running. 2013. (ENG.). 240p. (YA). (gr. 7-17). pap. 10.99 *(978-0-316-07788-0(7))* Little, Brown Bks. for Young Readers.

Wilson, Bob. Stanley Bagshaw & the Short-Sighted Football Trainer. 2006. (Stanley Bagshaw Ser.). (Illus.). 32p. (J). (gr. k-2). pap. 6.95 *(978-1-903015-26-1(X))* Barn Owl Bks, London GBR. Dist: Independent Pubs. Group.

Yelchin, Eugene. Arcady's Goal. Yelchin, Eugene, illus. 2014. (ENG., Illus.). 240p. (J). (gr. 4-7). 15.99 *(978-0-8050-9844-0(5),* 9780805098440, Holt, Henry & Co. Bks. For Young Readers) Holt, Henry & Co.

—Arcady's Goal. Yelchin, Eugene, illus. 2015. (ENG., Illus.). 256p. (J). (gr. 4-7). pap. 7.99 *(978-1-250-06814-9(2),* 9781250068149) Square Fish.

—Arcady's Goal. 2015. (J). lib. bdg. 18.40 *(978-0-606-37584-9(8))* Turtleback Bks.

Young, Julian. The Daniel Model: Understanding the Pathway to Promotion & Power in the Kingdom of God. 2017. (ENG.). pap. 13.99 ***(978-0-9990279-9-8(9))*** Crown Media Publishing.

—The Peter Model: Understanding the Key That Unlock Maximum Kingdom Impact. 2017. (ENG.). pap. 14.99 ***(978-0-9990279-8-1(0))*** Crown Media Publishing.

Zepeda, Gwendolyn. I Kick the Ball: Pateo el Balón. Ventura, Gabriela Baeza, tr. Torrecilla, Pablo, illus. 2011. (SPA & ENG.). 32p. (J). (gr. -1-3). 16.95 *(978-1-55885-688-2(9),* Piñata Books) Arte Publico Pr.

SOCIAL ADJUSTMENT

Amos, Janine. Don't Do That! How Not to Act. 2009. (Best Behavior Ser.). (Illus.). 32p. (J). (gr. -1-2). pap. 10.55 *(978-1-60754-052-6(5))* Windmill Bks.

Rocha, Toni L. Coping When Someone in Your Family Has Cancer. 2009. (Coping Ser.). 192p. (gr. 7-12). 63.90 *(978-1-61511-988-2(4))* Rosen Publishing Group, Inc., The.

SOCIAL CHANGE

Amidon Lusted, Marcia. Civic Unrest: Investigate the Struggle for Social Change. Chandhok, Lena, illus. 2015. (Inquire & Investigate Ser.). (ENG.). 128p. (gr. 6-10). 22.95 *(978-1-61930-241-9(1))* Open City Bks.

Arégui, Matthias & Ramstein, Anne-Margot. Before After. Arégui, Matthias & Ramstein, Anne-Margot, illus. 2014. (ENG., Illus.). 176p. (J). (gr. -1-3). 19.99 *(978-0-7636-7621-6(7))* Candlewick Pr.

Braun, Sandra. Women Inventors Who Changed the World. 2011. (Great Women of Achievement Ser.). (ENG., Illus.). 112p. (YA). (gr. 5-8). lib. bdg. 34.60 *(978-1-4488-5996-2(4),* Rosen Reference) Rosen Publishing Group, Inc., The.

Clinton, Chelsea. It's Your World: Get Informed, Get Inspired & Get Going! 2017. (ENG., Illus.). 432p. (J). (gr. 5). pap. 9.99 *(978-0-399-54532-0(8),* Puffin Books) Penguin Young Readers Group.

Cohen, Marina. Changing Cultural Landscapes: How Are People & Their Communities Affected by Migration & Settlement? 2010. (Investigating Human Migration & Settlement Ser.). (ENG., Illus.). 48p. (J). (gr. 5-8). *(978-0-7787-5178-6(3));* pap. *(978-0-7787-5193-9(7))* Crabtree Publishing Co.

Craats, Rennay. Trends. 2008. (USA Past Present Future Ser.). (Illus.). 48p. (J). (gr. 4-6). pap. 10.95 *(978-1-59036-977-7(7));* lib. bdg. 29.05 *(978-1-59036-976-0(9))* Weigl Pubs., Inc.

Etheredge, Laura. Saudi Arabia & Yemen. 2011. (Middle East: Region in Transition Ser.). (Illus.). 176p. (YA). (gr. 9-12). lib. bdg. 40.00 *(978-1-61530-335-9(9))* Rosen Publishing Group, Inc., The.

—Syria, Lebanon, & Jordan. 2011. (Middle East: Region in Transition Ser.). (Illus.). 248p. (YA). (gr. 9-12). lib. bdg. 40.00 *(978-1-61530-329-8(4))* Rosen Publishing Group, Inc., The.

Etheredge, Laura S., ed. Egypt. 2011. (Middle East: Region in Transition Ser.). (Illus.). 208p. (YA). (gr. 9-12). 40.00 *(978-1-61530-325-0(1))* Rosen Publishing Group, Inc., The.

Faulkner, Nicholas, ed. Top 101 Reformers, Revolutionaries, Activists, & Change Agents. 2016. (People You Should Know Ser.). 184p. (J). (gr. 8-8). lib. bdg. 36.25 *(978-1-68048-509-7(1))* Rosen Publishing Group, Inc., The.

Ganeri, Anita. The Top Ten Leaders That Changed the World. 2009. (J). 60.00 *(978-1-4358-9166-1(X),* PowerKids Pr.); (ENG., Illus.). 32p. (J). pap. 10.00 *(978-1-4358-9165-4(1),* PowerKids Pr.); (Illus.). 32p. (YA). (gr. 3-6). 26.50 *(978-1-4358-9164-7(3))* Rosen Publishing Group, Inc., The.

Heinz, Brian J. Nathan of Yesteryear & Michael of Today. Friar, Joanne, illus. 2006. (Exceptional Social Studies Titles for Intermediate Grades). (ENG.). 32p. (J). (gr. 3-6). lib. bdg. 22.60 *(978-0-7613-2893-3(9),* Millbrook Pr.) Lerner Publishing Group.

La Bella, Laura. World Financial Meltdown. 2010. (Doomsday Scenarios: Separating Fact from Fiction Ser.). 64p. (YA). (gr. 5-8). E-Book 58.50 *(978-1-4488-1209-7(7))* Rosen Publishing Group, Inc., The.

Lindeen, Mary. Then & Now, 1 vol. (Wonder Readers: Social Studies). (ENG.). (gr. -1-2). 2012. 20p. lib. bdg. 22.65 *(978-1-4296-9616-6(8))* 2011. 32p. pap. 5.99 *(978-1-4296-7972-5(7))* 2011. 16p. pap. 35.94 *(978-1-4296-8177-3(2))* Capstone Press of Coughlan Cos. (Wonder Readers).

Love, Ann & Drake, Jane. Yes You Can! Your Guide to Becoming an Activist. 2010. (ENG.). 144p. (YA). (gr. 5-18). pap. 12.95 *(978-0-88776-942-9(X),* Tundra Bks.) Tundra Bks. CAN. Dist: Penguin Random Hse. LLC.

McNeese, Tim. The Progressive Movement: Advocating Social Change. 2007. (Reform Movements in American History Ser.). (Illus.). 144p. (YA). (gr. 7-12). lib. bdg. 32.50 *(978-0-7910-9501-0(0))* Facts On File, Inc.

Peal, Robert. Modern Britain - The Age of Reform. 2017. (Knowing History Ser.). (ENG.). 16p. (J). (gr. 5-9). 3.99 ***(978-0-00-819542-7(0))*** HarperCollins Pubs. Ltd. GBR. Dist: Independent Pubs. Group.

Petrikowski, Nicki Peter. Working for Tolerance & Social Change Through Service Learning, 1 vol. 2015. (ENG.). 80p. (J). 34.60 *(978-1-4777-7967-5(1),* Rosen Young Adult) Rosen Publishing Group, Inc., The.

Pinkney, Andrea Davis. Hand in Hand: Ten Black Men Who Changed America. Pinkney, Brian, illus. 2012. (ENG.). 243p. (YA). (gr. 4-7). 19.99 *(978-1-4231-4257-7(8))* Hyperion Pr.

Progressivism. 2010. (Key Concepts in American History Ser.). (Illus.). 128p. (gr. 6-12). 45.00 *(978-1-60413-223-6(X),* Chelsea Hse.) Facts On File, Inc.

Rosen, Michael J. & Kaboom! Staff. Let's Build a Playground. Kelson, Ellen & Cecil, Jennifer, illus. 2013. (ENG.). 32p. (J). (gr. 1-4). 15.99 *(978-0-7636-5532-7(5))* Candlewick Pr.

Stone, Tanya Lee. Girl Rising: Changing the World One Girl at a Time. 2017. (ENG.). 208p. (YA). (gr. 9). 22.99 *(978-0-553-51146-8(7),* Lamb, Wendy Bks.) Random Hse. Children's Bks.

We are What We Do Staff. 31 Ways to Change the World. 2010. (ENG., Illus.). 80p. (J). (gr. 3-7). pap. 8.99 *(978-0-7636-4506-9(0))* Candlewick Pr.

SOCIAL CLASSES

see also Aristocracy (Social Class); Working Class

Geragotelis, Brittany. What the Spell. 2014. (Life's a Witch Ser.). (ENG., Illus.). 352p. (YA). (gr. 9). pap. 9.99 *(978-1-4424-6707-1(X),* Simon & Schuster Bks. For Young Readers) Simon & Schuster Bks. For Young Readers.

Hartley Steiner. This Is Gabriel Making Sense of School: A Book about Sensory Processing Disorder. 2010. 28p. pap. 13.95 *(978-1-4269-2777-5(0))* Trafford Publishing.

Haugen, David M. The Middle Class. 2010. (Opposing Viewpoints Ser.). (Illus.). 240p. (J). 42.95 *(978-0-7377-4777-5(3));* pap. 29.45 *(978-0-7377-4778-2(1))* Cengage Gale. (Greenhaven Pr., Inc.).

Henneberg, Susan. The Wealth Gap. 2017. (Opposing Viewpoints Ser.). 224p. (J). (gr. 10-12). lib. bdg. 48.80 ***(978-1-5345-0024-2(3),*** Greenhaven Publishing) Greenhaven Publishing LLC.

Henneberg, Susan, ed. The Wealth Gap. 2017. (Opposing Viewpoints Ser.). 224p. (J). (gr. 10-12). pap. 33.80 ***(978-1-5345-0034-1(0),*** Greenhaven Publishing) Greenhaven Publishing LLC.

Hinds, Kathryn. Everyday Life in the Roman Empire. 2009. 320p. (YA). (gr. 6-18). 42.79 *(978-0-7614-4484-8(X))* Marshall Cavendish Corp.

—The Patricians. 2004. (Life in the Roman Empire Ser.). (Illus.). 80p. (gr. 6). 34.21 *(978-0-7614-1654-8(4),* Benchmark Bks.) Marshall Cavendish Corp.

Jacobs, Denise. Patricians in the Roman Empire. 2016. (Life in the Roman Empire Ser.). 80p. (J). 35.64 *(978-1-5026-2257-0(2))* Cavendish Square Publishing.

Robertson, Jean. My Community. 2010. (ENG., Illus.). 24p. (gr. k-2). pap. 8.95 *(978-1-61590-565-2(0))* Rourke Educational Media.

SOCIAL CONDITIONS

see Social History

SOCIAL CONFLICT

Gallagher, Jim & Kavanaugh, Dorothy. A Guys' Guide to Conflict. 2008. (Flip-It-Over Guides to Teen Emotions Ser.). (Illus.). 128p. (J). (gr. 3-7). lib. bdg. 33.27 *(978-0-7660-2852-4(6))* Enslow Pubs., Inc.

Gibson, Brylee. Scams. 2007. (Connectors Ser.). (gr. 2-5). pap. *(978-1-877453-01-4(3))* Global Education Systems Ltd.

Hiber, Amanda. Should Governments Negotiate with Terrorists? 2008. (At Issue Ser.). (ENG., Illus.). 128p. (gr. 10-12). pap. 27.80 *(978-0-7377-3933-6(9),* Greenhaven Pr., Inc.); 80-128p. (YA). (gr. 9-12). pap. 34.45 *(978-0-7377-3932-9(0))* Cengage Gale.

Holt, Rinehart and Winston Staff. Decisions for Health Blue, Chptr. 12: Conflict Management. 4th ed. 2004. pap. 11.20 *(978-0-03-068046-5(8))* Holt McDougal.

Judson, Karen. Resolving Conflicts: How to Get along When You Don't Get Along. 2005. (Issues in Focus Today Ser.). (Illus.). 112p. (J). (gr. 6-12). lib. bdg. 33.27 *(978-0-7660-2359-8(1))* Enslow Pubs., Inc.

McCollum, Sean & Banas, Sharon L. Managing Conflict Resolution. 2009. (Character Education Ser.). (Illus.). 112p. (gr. 6-12). 35.00 *(978-1-60413-122-2(5),* Chelsea Hse.) Facts On File, Inc.

Naidoo, Beverley. Making It Home: Real-Life Stories from Children Forced to Flee. 2005. (Illus.). 117p. (gr. 3-7). 17.00 *(978-0-7569-5823-7(7))* Perfection Learning Corp.

Obadina, Elizabeth. Ethnic Groups in Africa. Ojakorotu, Victor & Rotberg, Robert I., eds. 2013. (Africa: Progress & Problems Ser.: 13). (Illus.). 112p. (J). (gr. 7-18). 24.95 *(978-1-4222-2939-2(4))* Mason Crest.

Rue, Nancy N. Everything You Need to Know about Peer Mediation. 2009. (Need to Know Library). 64p. (gr. 5-5). 58.50 *(978-1-60854-080-8(4))* Rosen Publishing Group, Inc., The.

Slavens, Elaine. Arguing: Word by Word, 1 vol. Murray, Steven, illus. 2010. (Lorimer Deal with It Ser.). (ENG.). 32p. (J). (gr. 4-6). 24.95 *(978-1-55277-498-4(8),* 9781552774984) Lorimer, James & Co., Ltd., Pubs. CAN. Dist: Casemate Pubs. & Bk. Distributors, LLC.

—Fighting: Without Coming to Blows, 1 vol. Murray, Steven, illus. 2nd ed. 2010. (Lorimer Deal with It Ser.). (ENG.). 32p. (J). (gr. 4-6). 24.95 *(978-1-55277-501-1(1),* 9781552775011) Lorimer, James & Co., Ltd., Pubs. CAN. Dist: Casemate Pubs. & Bk. Distributors, LLC.

Slavens, Elaine & James Lorimer and Company Ltd. Staff. Fighting: Without Coming to Blows, 1 vol. Murray, Steven, illus. 2nd ed. 2010. (Lorimer Deal with It Ser.). (ENG.). 32p. (J). (gr. 4-8). pap. 12.95 *(978-1-55277-517-2(8),* 9781552775172) Lorimer, James & Co., Ltd., Pubs. CAN. Dist: Orca Bk. Pubs. USA.

Thomas, Pat. Is It Right to Fight? A First Look at Anger. Harker, Lesley, illus. 2003. (First Look At... Ser.). (ENG.). 32p. (J). pap. 7.99 *(978-0-7641-2458-7(7))* Barron's Educational Series, Inc.

SOCIAL CUSTOMS

see Manners and Customs

SOCIAL DEMOCRACY

see Socialism

SOCIAL DISTINCTIONS

see Social Classes

SOCIAL EQUALITY

see Equality

SOCIAL HISTORY

see also Economic History; Social Problems

Amery, Heather. Then & Now. Firmin, Peter, illus. 2008. (Then & Now Ser.). 24p. (J). (gr. -1-3). pap. 4.99 *(978-0-7945-2211-7(4),* Usborne) EDC Publishing.

Barraclough, Sue & Hachette Children's Books Staff. Be an Eco Hero at Home. 2013. (Be an Eco Hero Ser.). (Illus.).

S

24p. (J). (gr. 2-4). lib. bdg. 25.65 (978-1-59771-379-5(1)) Sea-To-Sea Pubns.

Barraclough, Sue & Hachette Children's Group. Be an Eco Hero Outdoors. 2013. (Be an Eco Hero Ser.). (Illus.). 24p. (J). (gr. 2-4). lib. bdg. 25.65 (978-1-59771-382-5(1)) Sea-To-Sea Pubns.

Barraclough, Sue, et al. Be an Eco Hero on the Move. 2013. (Be an Eco Hero Ser.). (Illus.). 24p. (J). (gr. 2-4). lib. bdg. 25.65 (978-1-59771-380-1(5)) Sea-To-Sea Pubns.

Butterfield, Moira. Lady of the Manor. 2009. (Medieval Lives Ser.). 32.80 (978-1-59920-169-6(0)) Black Rabbit Bks.

Davies, Gill. The One Wind. 2008. 32p. (J). pap. 7.99 (978-1-905470-22-8(3)) SeaSquirt Pubns. GBR. Dist: Basic Distribution, Inc.

Down, Susan. Theodore Weld: Architect of Abolitionism. 2013. (ENG., Illus.). 64p. (J). (978-0-7787-1062-2(9)); pap. (978-0-7787-1065-3(3)) Crabtree Publishing Co.

Global Hotspots, 6 bks., Set. Incl. Afghanistan. Downing, David & Cavendish, Marshall. lib. bdg. 18.56 (978-0-7614-3177-0(2)); Indian Subcontinent. Mason, Paul & Cavendish, Marshall. lib. bdg. 18.56 (978-0-7614-3178-7(0)); Iran. Downing, David & Marshall Cavendish Corporation Staff. lib. bdg. 18.56 (978-0-7614-3179-4(9)); Iraq. Mason, Paul & Marshall Cavendish Corporation Staff. lib. bdg. 18.56 (978-0-7614-3180-0(2)); Israel & Palestine. Mason, Paul & Marshall Cavendish Staff. lib. bdg. 18.56 (978-0-7614-3181-7(0)); Sudan. Barker, Geoff & Marshall Cavendish Corporation Staff. lib. bdg. 18.56 (978-0-7614-3182-4(9)); 32p. (gr. 5-18). (Global Hotspots Ser.). 2008. Set lib. bdg. 111.36 (978-0-7614-3175-6(6), Benchmark Bks.) Marshall Cavendish Corp.

Grayson, Robert. Ed Begley, Jr. Living Green. 2009. (Voices for Green Choices Ser.). (ENG., Illus.). 48p. (J). (gr. 5-9). lib. bdg. (978-0-7787-4667-6(4)) Crabtree Publishing Co.

Hughes, Shirley. A Brush with the Past, 1900-1950: The Years That Changed Our Lives. 2005. (ENG., Illus.). 112p. (gr. 5-18). 45.00 (978-0-370-32839-3(6)) Random Hse. GBR. Dist: Independent Pubs. Group.

McCarthy, Pat. Friends of the Earth: A History of American Environmentalism with 21 Activities. 2013. (For Kids Ser.). (ENG., Illus.). 144p. (J). (gr. 4). pap. 16.95 (978-1-56976-718-4(1)) Chicago Review Pr., Inc.

McFall, Sally, ed. Pro/Con 2, 6 vols. 2003. (Illus.). 1392p. (YA). 339.00 (978-0-7172-5753-9(3)) Scholastic Library Publishing.

—Pro/Con 3, 12 vols. 2004. (Illus.). (YA). 339.00 (978-0-7172-5927-4(7), Grolier) Scholastic Library Publishing.

Parker, Victoria. Helping the Environment, 1 vol. 2012. (I Can Make a Difference Ser.). (ENG., Illus.). 32p. (gr. 1-3). pap. 8.29 (978-1-4329-5951-7(4), Heinemann First Library) Heinemann-Raintree.

Perritano, John. Education, Poverty, & Inequality. 2017. (Illus.). 64p. (J). (978-1-4222-3634-5(X)) Mason Crest.

Sonneborn, Liz. The Environmental Movement: Protecting Our Natural Resources. 2007. (Reform Movements in American History Ser.). (Illus.). 128p. (YA). (gr. 7-12). lib. bdg. 32.50 (978-0-7910-9537-9(1)) Facts On File, Inc.

Watson, Stephanie. Gay Rights Movement, 1 vol. 2013. (Essential Library of Social Change Ser.). (ENG.). 112p. (J). (gr. 6-12). lib. bdg. 35.64 (978-1-61783-887-3(X), Essential Library) ABDO Publishing Co.

Wormwood: Solution toTerrorism, Poverty, & Despair. 2004. (978-0-9755927-0-0(X)) Masha, Segun Inc.

Young, Mary. Nos Gusta Vivir Verde: We Like to Live Green. Parker, Zachary, illus. 2010. (SPA & ENG.). 32p. (J). pap. 10.95 (978-1-935387-01-5(4)) Hohm Pr.

SOCIAL HYGIENE

see Health; Public Health

SOCIAL LIFE AND CUSTOMS

see Manners and Customs

SOCIAL POLICY

see also Multiculturalism

Love, Ann & Drake, Jane. Yes You Can! Your Guide to Becoming an Activist. 2010. (ENG.). 144p. (YA). (gr. 5-18). pap. 12.95 (978-0-88776-942-9(X), Tundra Bks.) Tundra Bks. CAN. Dist: Penguin Random Hse. LLC.

Marzilli, Alan. Affirmative Action. 2004. (Point/Counterpoint Ser.). (Illus.). 110p. (C). (gr. 9-13). 35.00 (978-0-7910-7918-8(X), Chelsea Hse.) Facts On File, Inc.

Open for Debate, 6 bks., Group 2. Incl. Animal Testing. Judson, Karen. 128p. (gr. 7-7). lib. bdg. 42.79 (978-0-7614-1882-5(2), Benchmark Bks.); Censorship. Gottfried, Ted. 128p. (YA). (gr. 7-12). lib. bdg. 42.79 (978-0-7614-1883-2(0)); Civil Liberties. Spangenburg, Ray & Moser, Kit. 128p. (YA). (gr. 7-12). lib. bdg. 42.79 (978-0-7614-1886-3(5)); Environmental Issues. Fridell, Ron. 128p. (gr. 7). lib. bdg. 42.79 (978-0-7614-1885-6(7), Benchmark Bks.); Taxes. Kowalski, Kathiann M. 139p. (YA). (gr. 9-12). lib. bdg. (978-0-7614-1887-0(3), Benchmark Bks.); (Illus.). 2005. (978-0-7614-1881-8(4), Benchmark Bks.) Marshall Cavendish Corp.

Staley, Erin. Improving Community Health & Safety Through Service Learning, 1 vol. 2015. (ENG.). 80p. (YA). 34.60 (978-1-4777-7955-2(8), Rosen Young Adult) Rosen Publishing Group, Inc., The.

SOCIAL PROBLEMS

see also Child Labor; Crime; Discrimination; Divorce; Emigration and Immigration; Ethnic Relations; Housing; Juvenile Delinquency; Migrant Labor; Public Health; Race Relations

ABDO Publishing Company Staff. Essential Issues, 1 vol., Set. 2011. (Essential Issues Set 3 Ser.: 8). (ENG., Illus.). 112p. (J). (gr. 6-12). lib. bdg. 285.12 (978-1-61783-130-0(1), Essential Library) ABDO Publishing Co.

—Essential Viewpoints Set 2 (Set Of 8) 2008. (Essential Viewpoints Set 2 Ser.: 8). (ENG., Illus.). 112p. (J). (gr. 6-12). lib. bdg. 285.12 (978-1-60453-052-0(9), Essential Library) ABDO Publishing Co.

Bausum, Ann. Muckrakers: How Ida Tarbell, Upton Sinclair, & Lincoln Steffens Helped Expose Scandal, Inspire Reform, & Invent Investigative Journalism. 2007. (ENG., Illus.). 112p. (J). (gr. 5-18). 32.90 (978-1-4263-0138-4(3)); 21.95 (978-1-4263-0137-7(5)) National Geographic Society. (National Geographic Children's Bks.).

Bryfonski, Dedria. Class Conflict in a Tale of Two Cities. Greenhaven Press Editors, ed. 2013. (Social Issues in Literature Ser.). (ENG., Illus.). 224p. (gr. 10-12). pap. 32.00 (978-0-7377-6975-3(0), Greenhaven Pr., Inc.) Cengage Gale.

—Class Conflict in Charles Dicken's a Tale of Two Cities. Greenhaven Press Editors, ed. 2013. (Social Issues in Literature Ser.). (ENG., Illus.). 224p. (gr. 10-12). lib. bdg. 46.40 (978-0-7377-6974-6(2), Greenhaven Pr., Inc.) Cengage Gale.

—Death in Old Man & Sea. Greenhaven Press Editors, ed. 2014. (Social Issues in Literature Ser.). (ENG., Illus.). 224p. (gr. 10-12). lib. bdg. 46.40 (978-0-7377-6978-4(5)); (gr. 7-12). pap. 32.00 (978-0-7377-6979-1(3)) Cengage Gale. (Greenhaven Pr., Inc.).

Edwards, Nicola. Bullying. (Illus.). 32p. 18.95 (978-1-932333-07-7(X)) Chrysalis Education.

Espejo, Roman. Urban America. 2011. (Opposing Viewpoints Ser.). 240p. (J). lib. bdg. 42.95 (978-0-7377-5249-6(1), Greenhaven Pr., Inc.) Cengage Gale.

—What Is Humanity's Greatest Challenge? 2010. (At Issue Ser.). (Illus.). 128p. (J). 34.45 (978-0-7377-4314-2(X)); pap. 24.45 (978-0-7377-4313-5(1)) Cengage Gale.

Gallagher, Aileen. The Muckrakers: American Journalism During the Age of Reform. 2009. (Progressive Movement 1900-1920: Efforts to Reform America's New Industrial Society Ser.). 32p. (gr. 3-4). 47.90 (978-1-60854-173-7(8)) Rosen Publishing Group, Inc., The.

Global Issues, 9 bks., Set. Incl. Closing the Borders. Davies, Wendy. 1995. lib. bdg. 19.98 (978-1-56847-335-2(4), AS335-4); Exploitation of Children. Ennew, Judith. 1996. lib. bdg. 19.98 (978-0-8172-4546-7(4)); Gender Issues. Stearman, Kaye & Vander Gaag, Nikki. 1996. lib. bdg. 19.98 (978-0-8172-4545-0(6)); Genetic Engineering. Bryan, Jenny. 1997. lib. bdg. 19.98 (978-0-8172-4860-4(9)); Racism. Garg, Samidha & Hardy, Jan. 1997. lib. bdg. 19.98 (978-0-8172-4548-1(0)); Refugees. Warner, Rachel. 1997. lib. bdg. 19.98 (978-0-8172-4547-4(2)); Rich-Poor Divide. Garlake, Teresa. 1995. lib. bdg. 19.98 (978-1-56847-336-9(2), AS336-2); United Nations - Peacekeeper? Johnson, Edward. 1995. lib. bdg. 19.98 (978-1-56847-267-6(6), AS267-6); (Illus.). 64p. (YA). (gr. 5-10). Set lib. bdg. 179.82 (978-0-7398-1534-2(2)) Heinemann-Raintree.

Hamilton, Jill. Activism. 2009. (Issues That Concern You Ser.). (ENG., Illus.). 144p. (gr. 10-12). 42.00 (978-0-7377-4493-4(6)) Cengage Gale.

Harmony Island: ATropical Adventure in Conflict Resolutuion. 2005. (YA). cd-rom (978-0-9754754-4-7(4)) Academic Edge, Inc.

Haugen, David M. Welfare. 2008. (Opposing Viewpoints Ser.). (ENG., Illus.). 218p. (YA). (gr. 10-12). 27.50 (978-0-7377-4017-2(5), LML02109-239975); pap. 39.70 (978-0-7377-4016-5(7), LML02109-239982) Cengage Gale. (Greenhaven Pr., Inc.).

Hazen, Walter A. Everyday Life: Reform in America. 2004. (Illus.). iv, 100p. pap. 12.95 (978-0-673-58898-2(X)) Good Year Bks.

Kallen, Stuart A. Does Equality Exist in America? 2006. (At Issue Ser.). (ENG., Illus.). 106p. (YA). (gr. 9-12). pap. 34.45 (978-0-7377-3433-1(7)) Cengage Gale.

Kent, Deborah. Dorothy Day: Friend to the Forgotten. 2004. (Illus.). 187p. (J). pap. 12.00 (978-0-8028-5265-6(3)) Eerdmans, William B. Publishing Co.

Let's Work It Out, 6 bks., Set. Incl. How to Deal with Anger. Fiedler, Julie. (J). (gr. 2-5). lib. bdg. 22.60 (978-1-4042-3671-4(6)); How to Deal with Bullies. Kravetz, Jonathan. (J). (gr. 2-5). lib. bdg. 22.60 (978-1-4042-3670-7(8)); How to Deal with Fighting. Kravetz, Jonathan. (J). (gr. 2-5). lib. bdg. 22.60 (978-1-4042-3672-1(4)); How to Deal with Insults. Fiedler, Julie. (J). (gr. 2-5). lib. bdg. 22.60 (978-1-4042-3673-8(2)); How to Deal with Jealousy. Kravetz, Jonathan. (YA). (gr. 2-5). lib. bdg. 22.60 (978-1-4042-3674-5(0)); How to Deal with Teasing. Fieldler, Julie. (J). (gr. 3-7). lib. bdg. 22.60 (978-1-4042-3675-2(9), PowerKids Pr.); (Illus.). 24p. 2007. 2007. Set lib. bdg. 127.50 (978-1-4042-3607-3(4), PowerKids Pr.) Rosen Publishing Group, Inc., The.

McFall, Sally, ed. Pro/Con 2, 6 vols. 2003. (Illus.). 1392p. (YA). 339.00 (978-0-7172-5753-9(3)) Scholastic Library Publishing.

—Pro/Con 3, 12 vols. 2004. (Illus.). (YA). 339.00 (978-0-7172-5927-4(7), Grolier) Scholastic Library Publishing.

Open for Debate - Group 5, 4 bks., Set. Incl. National Health Care. Kowalski, Kathiann M. lib. bdg. 42.79 (978-0-7614-2943-2(3)); Political Campaigns. Naden, Corinne J. lib. bdg. 42.79 (978-0-7614-2944-9(1)); Religious Fundamentalism. Fridell, Ron. lib. bdg. 42.79 (978-0-7614-2945-6(X)); Right to Die. Stefoff, Rebecca. lib. bdg. 42.79 (978-0-7614-2948-7(4)); 128p. (gr. 7-18). (Open for Debate 5 Ser.). 2008. Set lib. bdg. 171.16 (978-0-7614-2940-1(9), Benchmark Bks.) Marshall Cavendish Corp.

Peters, Elisa. Malala Yousafzai: Pakistani Activist for Female Education. 2017. (J). **(978-1-5081-7749-4(X))** Rosen Publishing Group, Inc., The.

Progressivism. 2010. (Key Concepts in American History Ser.). (Illus.). 128p. (gr. 6-12). 45.00 (978-1-60413-223-6(X), Chelsea Hse.) Facts On File, Inc.

Sakany, Lois. Progressive Leaders: The Platforms & Policies of America's Reform Politicians. (Progressive Movement 1900-1920: Efforts to Reform America's New Industrial Society Ser.). 32p. 2009. (gr. 3-4). 47.90 (978-1-60854-168-3(1)) 2004. (Illus.). (YA). (gr. 5-9). lib. bdg. 22.50 (978-1-4042-0193-4(9)) Rosen Publishing Group, Inc., The.

Scherer, Lauri S. Death & Dying. Greenhaven Press Editors, ed. 2014. (Issues That Concern You Ser.). (ENG., Illus.). 144p. (gr. 7-10). lib. bdg. 42.00 (978-0-7377-6937-1(8), Greenhaven Pr., Inc.) Cengage Gale.

Steele, Philip. Activists. 2011. (20th Century Lives Ser.). (Illus.). 32p. (YA). (gr. 3-6). 26.50 (978-1-4488-3292-7(6)) Rosen Publishing Group, Inc., The.

Swarts, Katherine. Welfare. 2008. (Social Issues Firsthand Ser.). (ENG., Illus.). 192p. (gr. 10-12). lib. bdg. 38.30 (978-0-7377-4079-0(5), LML02109-242669, Greenhaven Pr., Inc.) Cengage Gale.

Vogel, Elizabeth. The Conflict Resolution Library: Set 4: Facing Changes, 6 bks. Incl. Dealing with Being the Middle Child in Your Family. (gr. 3). lib. bdg. 22.60 (978-0-8239-5408-7(0), PowerKids Pr.); Dealing with Being the Oldest Child in Your Family. (gr. 3). lib. bdg. 22.60 (978-0-8239-5409-4(9), PowerKids Pr.); Dealing with Being the Youngest Child in Your Family. (gr. 3). lib. bdg. 19.95 (978-0-8239-5407-0(2), PowerKids Pr.); Dealing with Choices. (gr. k-3). lib. bdg. 22.60 (978-0-8239-5410-0(2)); Dealing with Rules at Home. (gr. 3). lib. bdg. 22.60 (978-0-8239-5411-7(0), PowerKids Pr.); Dealing with Showoffs. (gr. 3). lib. bdg. 22.60 (978-0-8239-5412-4(9), PowerKids Pr.); 24p. (J). 2000. (Illus.). Set lib. bdg. 95.58 (978-0-8239-7007-0(8), PowerKids Pr.) Rosen Publishing Group, Inc., The.

SOCIAL PROBLEMS—FICTION

Alexander, Adam. The Flurple Woozle. 2013. 26p. 16.99 (978-0-9910324-7-1(0)) Mindstir Media.

Alexiou, Michelle. A Bully for Berl: Playground Escapades. 2012. (ENG.). 45p. (J). pap. 26.95 (978-1-4327-8370-9(X)); pap. 22.95 (978-1-4327-8364-8(5)) Outskirts Pr., Inc.

The Ask & the Answer: With Bonus Short Story. 2014. (Chaos Walking Ser.). (ENG., Illus.). (YA). (gr. 9). pap. 10.99 (978-0-7636-7617-9(9)) Candlewick Pr.

Azore, Barbara. Wanda's Freckles. Graham, Georgia, illus. 2009. (ENG.). 24p. (J). (gr. -1-2). 19.95 (978-0-88776-862-0(8), Tundra Bks.) Tundra Bks. CAN. Dist: Penguin Random Hse. LLC.

Berenstain, Stan, et al. The Berenstain Bears & the Bad Influence. Berenstain, Stan et al, illus. 2008. (Berenstain Bears Ser.). 32p. (J). (gr. -1-2). 8.99 (978-0-06-057404-8(6)); (ENG.). pap. 3.99 (978-0-06-057388-1(0)) HarperCollins Pubs. (HarperFestival).

Blume, Judy. Then Again, Maybe I Won't. (J). 125p. pap. 3.99 (978-0-8072-1445-9(0)); 2004. 164p. (gr. 5-9). pap. 29.00 incl. audio (978-0-8072-0796-3(9), LYA 354 SP) Random Hse. Audio Publishing Group. (Listening Library).

Christopher, Matt. Power Pitcher. 2008. (ENG.). 112p. (J). (gr. 3-7). pap. 5.99 (978-0-316-05207-8(8)) Little, Brown Bks. for Young Readers.

Coleman, Sadie. The Biggest Heart Ever. Coleman, Sadie, illus. 2013. (Illus.). 24p. 14.99 (978-0-9881969-0-2(5)) Vorpal Words, LLC.

Dana, Kimberly. Lucy & Cecee's How to Survive (and Thrive) in Middle School. 2012. 278p. (gr. 4-6). 27.95 (978-1-4620-3967-8(7)); pap. 17.95 (978-1-4620-3966-1(9)) iUniverse, Inc.

Davies, Stephen. Outlaw. 2011. (ENG.). 304p. (YA). (gr. 7). 16.99 (978-0-547-39017-8(3)) Houghton Mifflin Harcourt Publishing Co.

Defrange, Tom. A Tinker Tale: Celebrating Differences. 2011. 36p. pap. 24.95 (978-1-4560-5081-8(8)) America Star Bks.

Dickens, Charles. Hard Times. 2009. (Real Reads Ser.). (Illus.). 64p. (J). (gr. 4-8). lib. bdg. 29.25 (978-1-60754-385-5(0)) Windmill Bks.

Divine, L. Cold as Ice. 2010. (ENG., Illus.). 256p. (YA). (gr. 9-18). 15.00 (978-0-7582-3113-0(X), K-Teen/Dafina) Kensington Publishing Corp.

Ellis, Ann Dee. This Is What I Did. 2009. (ENG.). 176p. (J). (gr. 7-17). pap. 7.99 (978-0-316-01362-8(5)) Little, Brown Bks. for Young Readers.

Feder, Aliza & Sofer, Rochel. We Need to Talk. 2008. 250p. 18.95 (978-1-934440-30-8(2), Devora Publishing) Simcha Media Group.

Fisk, Katie. Flying with the Angels. 2008. 62p. pap. 19.95 (978-1-60563-608-5(8)) America Star Bks.

Fleming, Candace. Lowji Discovers America. 2008. (ENG.). 160p. (J). (gr. 2-6). pap. 7.99 (978-1-4169-5832-1(0), Aladdin) Simon & Schuster Children's Publishing.

Forler, Nan. Bird Child. Thisdale, Francois, illus. 2009. (ENG.). 32p. (J). (gr. k-3). 19.95 (978-0-88776-894-1(6), Tundra Bks.) Tundra Bks. CAN. Dist: Penguin Random Hse. LLC.

Galante, Cecilia. Hershey Herself. 2008. (Mix Ser.). (ENG.). 336p. (J). (gr. 4-8). pap. 15.99 (978-1-4169-5463-7(5), Simon & Schuster/Paula Wiseman Bks.) Simon & Schuster/Paula Wiseman Bks.

Garrett, Troy. Kramer's World. 204p. 2010. pap. 12.50 (978-1-60693-155-4(5)) 2008. 23.50 (978-1-60693-518-7(6)) Strategic Book Publishing & Rights Agency (SBPRA). (Eloquent Bks.).

Godbersen, Anna. Envy. 2009. (Luxe Ser.: 3). (ENG.). 432p. (YA). (gr. 9). pap. 9.99 (978-0-06-134574-6(1)) HarperCollins Pubs.

Gómez Cerda, Alfredo. Barro de Medellín/ Mud of Medellin. Lopez, Xan, illus. 2010. (SPA.). 146p. (YA). (gr. 5-8). (978-84-263-6849-2(2)) Vives, Luis Editorial (Edelvives).

Handy Manny Pop-up Tool Book. 2009. 6p. 12.99 (978-1-4231-2114-5(7)) Disney Pr.

Hichens, Joanne. Stained. 2008. (Cutting Edge Ser.). (ENG.). 200p. pap. (978-1-84167-715-6(9)) Ransom Publishing Ltd.

Hinton, S. E. Esto Ya Es Otra Historia. (SPA.). (J). 6.95 (978-84-204-4121-4(X)) Santillana USA Publishing Co., Inc.

—Rumble Fish. 2006. 21.50 (978-0-8446-7283-0(1)) Smith, Peter Pub., Inc.

—Rumble Fish. 2013. lib. bdg. 18.40 (978-0-606-35120-1(5)) Turtleback Bks.

Hoban, Russell. Best Friends for Frances. Hoban, Lillian, illus. 2009. (I Can Read Book 2 Ser.). 48p. (J). (gr. -1-3). 16.99 (978-0-06-083801-0(9)) HarperCollins Pubs.

Holcomb, T. Toot-Toot & Her Troubles: Name Calling. 2008. 12p. pap. 24.95 (978-1-60563-472-2(7)) America Star Bks.

Immenschuh, Marilyn Y. Samantha & the Kids of Room 220. 2007. 148p. per. 11.95 (978-0-595-46842-3(X)) iUniverse, Inc.

Irwin, Judy. What's It to You? 2013. 106p. pap. (978-0-9877088-7-8(2)) Irwin, Judy.

James, Debra & James, Jessica. The Social Pyramid. 2010. 57p. pap. 7.50 (978-0-557-40789-7(3)) Lulu Pr., Inc.

Jens, Charlene. Ookie Gets a New Best Friend. 2008. 39p. pap. 24.95 (978-1-60474-475-0(8)) America Star Bks.

Jones Med, Marquita J. Marvette Made Fun of Me. 2012. (ENG.). 34p. (J). pap. 23.95 (978-1-4327-8551-2(6)) Outskirts Pr., Inc.

Jonsberg, Barry. Dreamrider. 2009. (ENG.). 256p. (YA). (gr. 9). pap. 8.99 (978-0-375-84458-4(9), Knopf Bks. for Young Readers) Random Hse. Children's Bks.

The Knife of Never Letting Go: With Bonus Short Story. 2014. (Chaos Walking Ser.). (ENG., Illus.). 512p. (YA). (gr. 9). pap. 10.99 (978-0-7636-7618-6(7)) Candlewick Pr.

Madonna, pseud. Being Binah, No. 6. Fulvimari, Jeffrey, illus. 2008. (English Roses Ser.: 6). (ENG.). 128p. (J). (gr. 3-7). 9.99 (978-0-14-241095-0(0), Puffin Books) Penguin Young Readers Group.

Martínez, Rafael. El Deseo de Aurelio. Martinez, Enrique, illus. 2006. (la Orilla del Viento Ser.). (SPA.). 48p. (J). (gr. 8-10). pap. (978-968-16-7988-0(1)) Fondo de Cultura Economica.

McKee, David. Conquerors. 2005. (ENG., Illus.). 32p. (J). (gr. k-2). pap. 12.99 (978-1-84270-468-4(0)) Andersen Pr. GBR. Dist: Independent Pubs. Group.

McMann, Lisa. Island of Shipwrecks. 2015. (Unwanteds Ser.: 5). (ENG., Illus.). 480p. (J). (gr. 3-7). pap. 8.99 (978-1-4424-9332-2(1), Aladdin) Simon & Schuster Children's Publishing.

—Island of Silence. 2013. (Unwanteds Ser.: 2). (ENG., Illus.). 432p. (J). (gr. 3-7). pap. 8.99 (978-1-4424-0772-5(7), Aladdin) Simon & Schuster Children's Publishing.

—Island of Silence. 2013. (Unwanteds Ser.: 2). lib. bdg. 18.40 (978-0-606-32044-3(X), Turtleback) Turtleback Bks.

Milan, D. S. A Year of Starless Nights. 2013. 154p. pap. 14.95 (978-1-62432-012-5(0)) Loose Leaves Publishing.

Miller, Jonathan. Kim's Introductions. 2009. 48p. pap. 21.99 (978-1-4389-0856-4(3)) AuthorHouse.

Monsters of Men. 2014. (Chaos Walking Ser.). (ENG., Illus.). (YA). (gr. 9). pap. 10.99 (978-0-7636-7619-3(5)) Candlewick Pr.

Morgan, Melissa J. Sunset. 2009. (Summer Confidential Ser.: 2). (ENG.). 240p. (J). (gr. 5-18). pap. 7.99 (978-0-448-44989-0(7), Grosset & Dunlap) Penguin Young Readers Group.

Ness, Patrick. Monsters of Men, Bk. 3. 2010. (Chaos Walking Ser.: 3). (ENG., Illus.). 608p. (YA). (gr. 9-18). 18.99 (978-0-7636-4751-3(9)) Candlewick Pr.

Olaogbebikan, Michael Olumide. Playmate. 2013. (Illus.). 20p. pap. 19.82 (978-1-4772-4659-7(2)) AuthorHouse.

Reisfeld, Randi. Rehab. 2008. (ENG.). 256p. (YA). (gr. 9-18). pap. 8.99 (978-1-4169-6121-5(6), Simon Pulse) Simon Pulse.

Root, Phyllis. Toot Toot Zoom! Cordell, Matthew, illus. 2009. (ENG.). 40p. (J). (gr. -1-2). 15.99 (978-0-7636-3452-0(2)) Candlewick Pr.

Students of the Los Angeles School of Global Studies Staff. The Elotes Man Will Soon Be Gone. 2008. (ENG.). 176p. (J). pap. 15.00 (978-0-9790073-3-0(X)) 826 Valencia.

Sullivan, Therese M. & Bitner, Pamela. A Gift from Valentine. 2007. 24p. (J). per. 12.95 (978-1-58939-981-5(1)) Virtualbookworm.com Publishing, Inc.

Sydor, Colleen. Timmerman Was Here. Debon, Nicolas, illus. 2009. (ENG.). 32p. (J). (gr. -1-1). 19.95 (978-0-88776-890-3(3), Tundra Bks.) Tundra Bks. CAN. Dist: Penguin Random Hse. LLC.

Tavner, Gill & Dickens, Charles. Hard Times. Donnelly, Karen, illus. 2009. (Real Reads Ser.). 64p. (J). (gr. 4-8). pap. 13.55 (978-1-60754-386-2(9)) Windmill Bks.

Thomas, Joyce Carol. Linda Brown, You Are Not Alone: The Brown v. Board of Education Decision. 2003. (ENG., Illus.). 128p. (J). 16.49 (978-0-7868-2640-7(1)) Hyperion Pr.

Topakian, Patricia E. The Mystery of the Old Brown Suitcase. 2007. (ENG.). 26p. pap. 15.99 (978-1-4196-2819-1(4)) CreateSpace Independent Publishing Platform.

Valentine, Billy. Trust Love: A Tale of Angels. 2008. 176p. (J). pap. 13.95 (978-0-595-44989-7(1)) iUniverse, Inc.

Wagner, Jane. J. T. 125p. (J). (gr. 3-5). pap. 3.00 (978-0-8072-1403-9(5), Listening Library) Random Hse. Audio Publishing Group.

Walters, Eric. Au Pas, Camarade, 1 vol. 2011. (FRE., Illus.). 144p. (J). (gr. 5-9). pap. 9.95 (978-1-4598-0003-8(6)) Orca Bk. Pubs. USA.

West, Steve, reader. Island of Legends. 2014. (Unwanteds Ser.: 4). (ENG., Illus.). 496p. (J). (gr. 3-7). 18.99 (978-1-4424-9328-5(3), Aladdin) Simon & Schuster Children's Publishing.

SOCIAL PSYCHOLOGY

see also Attitude (Psychology); Interpersonal Relations; Psychology, Applied; Social Adjustment; Violence

Amos, Janine & Spenceley, Annabel. Let's Make Friends. 2009. (Best Behavior Ser.). (Illus.). 32p. (J). (gr. -1-2). 22.60 (978-1-60754-500-2(4)); pap. 10.55 (978-1-60754-499-9(7)) Windmill Bks.

Antill, Sara. Social Intelligence. 2013. (Character Strength Ser.). 24p. (J). (gr. 3-6). pap. 49.50 (978-1-4488-9819-0(6)); pap. 8.25 (978-1-4488-9818-3(8)); lib. bdg. 22.60 (978-1-4488-9680-6(0)) Rosen Publishing Group, Inc., The. (PowerKids Pr.).

Cómo Organizar una Manifestación. 2014. (Sé un líder de la Comunidad (Be a Community Leader) Ser.). (SPA.). 32p. (J). (gr. 4-6). lib. bdg. 26.25 (978-1-4777-6913-3(7), PowerKids Pr.) Rosen Publishing Group, Inc., The.

Dwyer, Helen, ed. The Individual & Society. 2011. (CC: Psychology Ser.). (Illus.). 112p. (gr. 6-12). lib. bdg. 42.80 (978-1-936333-19-6(8)) Brown Bear Bks.

Gordon, Sharon. Somos un Equipo. 2006. (Bookworms Ser.). (SPA & ENG., Illus.). 24p. (gr. k-1). lib. bdg. 15.95 (978-0-7614-2357-7(5), Benchmark Bks.) Marshall Cavendish Corp.

—We Are a Team/Somos un Equipo. 2006. (Bookworms Ser.). (ENG & SPA., Illus.). 24p. (gr. k-1). lib. bdg. 15.95 (978-0-7614-2436-9(9)) Marshall Cavendish Corp.

HolmesKaren. SLOW MOTION: TAKING YOUR TIME HIGH BEGINNING BOOK WITH ONLINE ACCESS. 2014. (ENG., Illus.). 24p. (J). pap. 7.50 (978-1-107-69129-2(X)) Cambridge Univ. Pr.

How to Organize a Rally. 2014. (Be a Community Leader Ser.). (Illus.). 32p. (J). (gr. 4-6). lib. bdg. 26.25 (978-1-4777-6693-4(6), PowerKids Pr.) Rosen Publishing Group, Inc., The.

January, Brendan. Information Insecurity: Privacy under Siege. 2015. (ENG.). 96p. (J). (gr. 7-12). lib. bdg. 34.65 (978-1-4677-2517-0(X), Twenty-First Century Bks.) Lerner Publishing Group.

Lowery, Zoe & Mills, J. Elizabeth. Social Roles & Stereotypes. 2017. (Women in the World Ser.). 112p. (gr. 12-11). 37.10 **(978-1-5081-7441-7(5)**, Rosen Young Adult) Rosen Publishing Group, Inc., The.

Lynette, Rachel. How to Deal with Feeling Left Out. 2009. (Let's Work It Out Ser.). 24p. (gr. 2-3). 42.50 *(978-1-61514-260-6(6),* PowerKids Pr.); (Illus.). (J). lib. bdg. 22.60 *(978-1-4042-4520-4(0))* Rosen Publishing Group, Inc., The.

Mills, J. Elizabeth. Expectations for Women: Confronting Stereotypes. 2010. (Young Woman's Guide to Contemporary Issues Ser.). 112p. (YA). (gr. 9-12). lib. bdg., E-Book 63.90 *(978-1-61532-907-6(2))* Rosen Publishing Group, Inc., The.

Rodriguez, Gaby. The Pregnancy Project: A Memoir. 2013. (ENG., Illus.). 240p. (YA). (gr. 9). pap. 10.99 *(978-1-4424-4623-6(4),* Simon & Schuster Bks. For Young Readers) Simon & Schuster Bks. For Young Readers.

Souder, Patti. On the Edge of Disaster: Youth in the Juvenile Court System, 15 vols. 2004. (Youth with Special Needs Ser.). (Illus.). 128p. (J). lib. bdg. *(978-1-59084-727-5(X))* Mason Crest.

SOCIAL REFORM

see Social Problems

SOCIAL SCIENCES

see also Economics; Political Science; Social Change; Sociology

Accelerated Curriculum for Social Studies Grade 11 Exit TAKS Student Edition. 2005. (Region IV ESC Resources for Social Studies Ser.). spiral bd. *(978-1-932797-29-9(7))* Region IV Education Service Ctr.

Ahearn, Janet Reed. A Bird's-Eye View. 2003. (Shutterbug Books: Social Studies). (Illus.). 16p. (J). (gr. -1-3). pap. 4.10 *(978-0-7398-7649-7(X))* Steck-Vaughn.

—Lady Liberty. 2003. (Shutterbug Books: Social Studies). (Illus.). 16p. pap. 4.10 *(978-0-7398-7646-6(5))* Steck-Vaughn.

Al rescate de Ballenas: Libros Aventuras (Adventure Books) 2003. (MacMillan/McGraw-Hill. Estudios Sociales Ser.). (ENG & SPA.). (gr. 4-18). *(978-0-02-150115-1(7))* Macmillan/McGraw-Hill Schl. Div.

Alaina, Maria. Wonder Readers Next Steps: Social Studies. 2013. (Wonder Readers Next Steps: Social Studies). (ENG.). 20p. (gr. -1-1). lib. bdg. 67.95 *(978-1-4765-0046-1(0),* Wonder Readers) Capstone Press of Coughlan Cos.

The Allyn & Bacon Atlas for Elementary Social Studies. 2005. (J). *(978-1-930194-19-9(6))* Maps.com.

Analyzing the Issues: Set 1. 2016. (Analyzing the Issues Ser.). 208p. (gr. 8-8). lib. bdg. 287.58 *(978-0-7660-7503-0(6))* Enslow Pubs., Inc.

Analyzing the Issues: Set 2. 2016. (Analyzing the Issues Ser.). 208p. (YA). lib. bdg. 287.58 *(978-0-7660-8374-5(8))* Enslow Pubs., Inc.

Andersen, Jill. The Great Debate. 2016. (Rosen REAL Readers: Social Studies Nonfiction / Fiction: Family, Community, & the World Ser.). 12p. (gr. 1-k). pap. 6.33 *(978-1-5081-2553-2(8),* Rosen Classroom) Rosen Publishing Group, Inc., The.

Andersen, W. H. Hooray for the Red, White, & Blue: A Content Area Reader-Social Studies. 2005. (Emergent/Early (Prek-2) Social Studies Package Ser.). 16p. (gr. k-2). 25.20 *(978-0-8215-7819-3(7))* Sadlier, William H. Inc.

Antarctica. (Early Intervention Levels Ser.). 31.86 *(978-0-7362-0664-8(7))* CENGAGE Learning.

Aprenda Preparacion y Practica: Assessment. 2003. (MacMillan/McGraw-Hill. Estudios Sociales Ser.). (ENG & SPA.). (gr. 1-18). *(978-0-02-149775-1(3));* (gr. 4-18). *(978-0-02-149778-2(8))* Macmillan/McGraw-Hill Schl. Div.

Aprenda preparacion y practica, Guia del Maestro: Assessment. 2003. (MacMillan/McGraw-Hill. Estudios Sociales Ser.). (ENG & SPA.). (gr. 2-18). *(978-0-02-150016-1(9))* Macmillan/McGraw-Hill Schl. Div.

Aprenda preparacion y practica, Libro del Estudiante: Assessment. 2003. (MacMillan/McGraw-Hill. Estudios Sociales Ser.). (ENG & SPA.). (gr. 2-18). *(978-0-02-149776-8(1))* Macmillan/McGraw-Hill Schl. Div.

Aprenda preparacion y practica, Pupil Edition: Assessment. 2003. (MacMillan/McGraw-Hill. Estudios Sociales Ser.). (ENG & SPA.). (gr. 3-18). *(978-0-02-149777-5(X));* (gr. 5-18). *(978-0-02-149779-9(6))* Macmillan/McGraw-Hill Schl. Div.

Archer, Anita, et al. REWARDS Plus: Application to Social Studies: Reading Excellence: Word Attack & Rate Development Strategies: Student Book. 2003. (Illus.). 154p. (gr. 6-8). pap. 11.49 *(978-1-57035-803-6(6),* 136SOCSE) Cambium Education, Inc.

Archibald, Donna, et al. NETS*S Curriculum Series: Social Studies Units for Grades 9-12. McKenzie, Walter, ed. 2004. (Nets-S Curriculum Ser.). (Illus.). 195p. pap. 38.95 *(978-1-56484-212-1(6))* International Society for Technology in Education.

Ashbe, Jeanne. Es hora de Recoger: Traduccion Anna Coll-Vinent. 2004. (SPA.). 16p. *(978-84-8470-163-7(8))* Corimbo, Editorial S.L.

—La hora del Bano. 2004. (SPA.). 16p. *(978-84-8470-165-1(4))* Corimbo, Editorial S.L.

—Oh!, esta Oscuro. 2004. (SPA.). 16p. *(978-84-8470-164-4(6))* Corimbo, Editorial S.L.

At Play in the USA, 6 vols. (Book2WebTM Ser.). (gr. 4-8). 36.50 *(978-0-322-02983-5(X))* Wright Group/McGraw-Hill.

Auch, Allison. Electrifying Personalities: Set Of 6. 2011. (Navigators Ser.). (J). pap. 48.00 net. *(978-1-4108-0440-2(2))* Benchmark Education Co.

Axiom Press, ed. CultureGrams Kids Edition. 2003. spiral bd. 69.99 *(978-1-931694-63-6(X));* ring bd. 69.99 incl. cd-rom *(978-1-931694-64-3(8))* ProQuest LLC.

—CultureGrams States Edition. 2003. spiral bd. 59.99 incl. cd-rom *(978-1-931694-65-0(6));* ring bd. 59.99 incl. cd-rom *(978-1-931694-66-7(4))* ProQuest LLC.

Bauer, David. People Change the Land, 6 vols., Set. 2003. (Yellow Umbrella Early Level Ser.). (ENG.). 16p. (gr. k-1). pap. 35.70 *(978-0-7368-3006-5(5),* Yellow Umbrella Bks.) Capstone Press of Coughlan Cos.

Bednarz, Robert, et al. About My Community. 3rd ed. 2003. (Harcourt School Publishers Horizons Ser.). (ENG.). 376p. (gr. 2-2). pupil's gde. ed. 60.75 *(978-0-15-320179-0(7))* Harcourt Schl. Pubs.

Benchmark Education Company, LLC Staff, compiled by. Being a Good Citizen: Theme Set. 2006. (J). 136.00 *(978-1-4108-7065-0(0))* Benchmark Education Co.

—Civic Ideals & Practices. 2005. spiral bd. 60.00 *(978-1-4108-5428-5(0));* spiral bd. 65.00 *(978-1-4108-4504-7(4));* spiral bd. 90.00 *(978-1-4108-3937-4(0));* spiral bd. 110.00 *(978-1-4108-5427-8(2))* Benchmark Education Co.

—Community Counts & Community Change. 2005. spiral bd. 225.00 *(978-1-4108-5803-0(0))* Benchmark Education Co.

—Community Counts & Local GOVT. 2005. spiral bd. 225.00 *(978-1-4108-5802-3(2))* Benchmark Education Co.

—Individual Development & Identity. 2005. spiral bd. 1100.00 *(978-1-4108-3746-2(7));* spiral bd. 400.00 *(978-1-4108-3938-1(9));* spiral bd. 245.00 *(978-1-4108-3939-8(7));* spiral bd. 715.00 *(978-1-4108-5840-5(5));* spiral bd. 1050.00 *(978-1-4108-5424-7(8));* spiral bd. 685.00 *(978-1-4108-4505-4(2));* spiral bd. 35.00 *(978-1-4108-3981-7(8));* spiral bd. 585.00 *(978-1-4108-3963-3(X));* spiral bd. 360.00 *(978-1-4108-3964-0(8));* spiral bd. 75.00 *(978-1-4108-3973-2(7))* Benchmark Education Co.

—Individuals, Groups & Institutions. 2005. spiral bd. 25.00 *(978-1-4108-4500-9(1))* Benchmark Education Co.

—Individuals, Groups, & Institutions. 2005. spiral bd. 55.00 *(978-1-4108-3969-5(9));* spiral bd. 80.00 *(978-1-4108-5431-5(0))* Benchmark Education Co.

—Neighborhoods & Communities. 2006. (J). 235.00 *(978-1-4108-7040-7(5))* Benchmark Education Co.

—Neighborhoods & Communities: Theme Set. 2006. (J). 258.00 *(978-1-4108-7085-8(5))* Benchmark Education Co.

—People, Places & Environments. 2005. spiral bd. 150.00 *(978-1-4108-5837-5(5));* spiral bd. 575.00 *(978-1-4108-3748-6(3));* spiral bd. 55.00 *(978-1-4108-3968-8(0));* spiral bd. 235.00 *(978-1-4108-5836-8(7))* Benchmark Education Co.

—People, Places, & Environments. 2005. spiral bd. 245.00 *(978-1-4108-3944-2(3));* spiral bd. 185.00 *(978-1-4108-3945-9(1));* spiral bd. 315.00 *(978-1-4108-5421-6(3));* spiral bd. 450.00 *(978-1-4108-5420-9(5));* spiral bd. 315.00 *(978-1-4108-4503-0(6));* spiral bd. 50.00 *(978-1-4108-3975-6(3));* spiral bd. 110.00 *(978-1-4108-3967-1(2));* spiral bd. 145.00 *(978-1-4108-3955-8(9));* spiral bd. 75.00 *(978-1-4108-3956-5(7))* Benchmark Education Co.

—Regions of the U. S. 2006. spiral bd. 330.00 *(978-1-4108-7006-3(5))* 2005. (J). spiral bd. 265.00 *(978-1-4108-5769-9(7))* Benchmark Education Co.

—Regions of the U. S. Theme Set. 2006. (J). 259.00 *(978-1-4108-7111-4(8))* Benchmark Education Co.

—Social Studies Theme: People, Places & Environments. 2005. spiral bd. 220.00 *(978-1-4108-5328-8(4))* Benchmark Education Co.

—Social Studies Theme: Time, Continuity & Change. 2005. spiral bd. 560.00 *(978-1-4108-5322-6(5))* Benchmark Education Co.

—Spanish Social Studies Standard Set. 2005. spiral bd. 3225.00 *(978-1-4108-5845-0(6))* Benchmark Education Co.

—Time, Continuity, & Change. 2005. spiral bd. 55.00 *(978-1-4108-3971-8(0));* spiral bd. 715.00 *(978-1-4108-5835-1(9));* spiral bd. 265.00 *(978-1-4108-5834-4(0));* spiral bd. 365.00 *(978-1-4108-4502-3(8));* spiral bd. 110.00 *(978-1-4108-3978-7(8));* spiral bd. 190.00 *(978-1-4108-3977-0(X));* spiral bd. 55.00 *(978-1-4108-3970-1(2));* spiral bd. 75.00 *(978-1-4108-3953-4(2));* spiral bd. 640.00 *(978-1-4108-3952-7(4));* spiral bd. 120.00 *(978-1-4108-3943-5(5));* spiral bd. 340.00 *(978-1-4108-3942-8(7));* spiral bd. 1250.00 *(978-1-4108-3745-5(9))* Benchmark Education Co.

—Time, Continuity & Change. 2005. spiral bd. 550.00 *(978-1-4108-5417-9(5));* spiral bd. 1050.00 *(978-1-4108-5418-6(3))* Benchmark Education Co.

—World Communities: Theme Set. 2006. (J). 121.00 *(978-1-4108-7098-8(7))* Benchmark Education Co.

Billings. How: People, Places, & Ideas. 2003. (Steck-Vaughn History of Our World Ser.). (ENG., Illus.). 296p. (gr. 6-12). pap. 48.80 *(978-0-7398-7948-1(0))* Houghton Mifflin Harcourt Publishing Co.

—The Modern World, Vol. 2. 2003. (Steck-Vaughn History of Our World Ser.). (ENG., Illus.). 296p. (gr. 6-12). pap. 48.80 *(978-0-7398-7949-8(9))* Houghton Mifflin Harcourt Publishing Co.

BJU Staff. Geography Activity Student Gr9. 2004. 14.50 *(978-1-57924-300-5(2))* BJU Pr.

—World Studies Activity St Grd7. 2004. pap. 14.50 *(978-1-57924-302-9(9))* BJU Pr.

Blane, Francisco. What Will You Be? Lap Book. 2009. (My First Reader's Theater Set B Ser.). (J). 28.00 *(978-1-60634-993-9(7))* Benchmark Education Co.

Boehm, Richard G., et al. Activity Books: Communities. 2003. (Harcourt Brace Social Studies). (gr. k-7). act. bk. ed. 7.70 *(978-0-15-310306-3(X))* Harcourt Schl. Pubs.

—Activity Books: Making a Difference. 2003. (Harcourt Brace Social Studies). (gr. k-7). act. bk. ed. 5.80 *(978-0-15-310305-6(1))* Harcourt Schl. Pubs.

—Assessment Programs: A Child's Place. 2003. (Harcourt Brace Social Studies). (gr. k-7). 44.60 *(978-0-15-310297-4(7))* Harcourt Schl. Pubs.

—Assessment Programs: Making a Difference. 2003. (Harcourt Brace Social Studies). (gr. k-7). 44.60 *(978-0-15-310298-1(5))* Harcourt Schl. Pubs.

—Big Book Libraries. 2003. (Harcourt Brace Social Studies). (gr. 1-18). 317.70 *(978-0-15-310448-0(1));* (gr. 2-18). 317.70 *(978-0-15-310455-8(4))* Harcourt Schl. Pubs.

—Game Time! A Child's Place. 2003. (Harcourt Brace Social Studies). (gr. k-7). 7.30 *(978-0-15-312349-8(4))* Harcourt Schl. Pubs.

—Game Time! Making a Difference. 2003. (Harcourt Brace Social Studies). (gr. k-7). 7.30 *(978-0-15-312351-1(6))* Harcourt Schl. Pubs.

—Great Beginnings. 2003. (Harcourt Brace Estudios Sociales Ser.). (SPA.). (gr. k-7). pap. 107.90 *(978-0-15-306559-0(1));* (gr. k-7). pap., act. bk. ed. 12.90 *(978-0-15-306554-5(0));* 97th ed. (gr. k-7). pap., tchr. ed. 184.50 *(978-0-15-309127-8(4));* 97th ed. (gr. k-7). pap., suppl. ed. 233.60 *(978-0-15-309148-3(7));* 97th ed. (gr. k-7). pap., act. bk. ed. 11.40 *(978-0-15-309128-5(2));* 97th ed. (gr. k-7). pap., act. bk. ed. 12.90 *(978-0-15-309143-8(6));* 97th ed. (gr. 3-7). pap., tchr. ed., act. bk. ed. 18.70 *(978-0-15-309129-2(0));* 97th ed. (gr. 3-7). pap., tchr. ed., act. bk. ed. 21.30 *(978-0-15-307926-9(6));* 97th ed. (gr. 3-7). pap., tchr. ed., act. bk. ed. 21.30 *(978-0-15-309144-5(4));* Vol. 1. (gr. k-7). tchr. ed. 141.30 *(978-0-15-306548-4(6));* Vol. 1. 97th ed. (gr. k-7). pap., tchr. ed. 143.90 *(978-0-15-309141-4(X));* Vol. 2. (gr. k-7). tchr. ed. 141.30 *(978-0-15-306549-1(4));* Vol. 2. 97th ed. (gr. k-7). pap., tchr. ed. 143.90 *(978-0-15-309142-1(8))* Harcourt Schl. Pubs.

—El Mundo y Sus Gentes: Hemisferio Occidental, Europa y Rusia. 2005. (Illus.). 570p. (J). (gr. 4-7). 60.00 *(978-0-07-868380-0(7))* Glencoe/McGraw-Hill.

—My World & Me: A Kindergarten Program. 2003. (Harcourt Brace Social Studies). (gr. k-7). act. bk. ed. 5.30 *(978-0-15-310303-2(5))* Harcourt Schl. Pubs.

—Reading Support & Test Preparation: Communities. 2003. (Harcourt Brace Social Studies). (gr. k-7). 27.00 *(978-0-15-312379-5(6))* Harcourt Schl. Pubs.

—Reading Support & Test Preparation: Making a Difference. 2003. (Harcourt Brace Social Studies). (gr. k-7). 27.00 *(978-0-15-312376-4(1))* Harcourt Schl. Pubs.

—Relatos de la Historia: La Historia de Estados Unidos. 2003. (Harcourt Brace Estudios Sociales Ser.). (SPA.). (gr. k-7). pupil's gde. ed. 88.40 *(978-0-15-306543-9(5))* Harcourt Schl. Pubs.

—Social Studies Libraries: Making a Difference. 2003. (Harcourt Brace Social Studies). (gr. k-7). 95.70 *(978-0-15-310443-5(0))* Harcourt Schl. Pubs.

—Vocabulary Picture Cards. 2003. (Harcourt Brace Social Studies). (SPA.). (gr. 1-18). 61.90 *(978-0-15-310295-0(0));* (gr. 2-18). 69.30 *(978-0-15-310296-7(9))* Harcourt Schl. Pubs.

—Write-on Charts. 2003. (Harcourt Brace Social Studies). (SPA.). (gr. 3-18). 216.40 *(978-0-15-310292-9(6))* Harcourt Schl. Pubs.

Bolivar, Simon. Champion of Freedom. 2007. (Read on! Special Edition: Level BA Ser.). (Illus.). 23p. pap. 18.51 *(978-1-4190-3527-2(4))* Steck-Vaughn.

Borgenicht, David & Heimberg, Justin. Extreme. 2008. (Worst Case Scenario Ser.: WORS). (ENG., Illus.). 128p. (J). (gr. 4-7). pap., instr.'s hndbk. ed. 9.99 *(978-0-8118-6568-5(1))* Chronicle Bks. LLC.

Brocker, Susan. Voices from the Civil War: Set Of 6. 2011. (Navigators Ser.). (J). pap. 48.00 net. *(978-1-4108-0434-1(8))* Benchmark Education Co.

Burke, Juliet. Let's Play! 2012. (InfoMax Readers Ser.). (ENG., Illus.). 16 pp.p. (J). (gr. k-1). pap. 7.00 *(978-1-4488-8899-3(9),* Rosen Classroom) Rosen Publishing Group, Inc., The.

El campamento de Lewis y Clark: Libros Aventuras (Adventure Books) 2003. (MacMillan/McGraw-Hill. Estudios Sociales Ser.). (ENG & SPA.). (gr. 4-18). *(978-0-02-150121-2(1))* Macmillan/McGraw-Hill Schl. Div.

Cane, Ella. My World. 2013. (My World Ser.). (ENG.). 24p. (gr. k-1). pap. 35.70 *(978-1-4765-3683-5(X));* lib. bdg. 131.94 *(978-1-4765-3682-8(1))* Capstone Press of Coughlan Cos. (Pebble Bks.).

—Neighborhoods in My World, 1 vol. 2013. (My World Ser.). (ENG.). 24p. (gr. k-1). 21.99 *(978-1-4765-3119-9(6));* pap. 6.95 *(978-1-4765-3461-9(6))* Capstone Press of Coughlan Cos. (Pebble Bks.).

Cannon, Shannon. The Letter Qq Set: Past & Present, 6. 2004. (Letter Bks.). (ENG.). 8p. (gr. k-1). pap. 29.70 *(978-0-7368-4116-0(4),* Letter Bks.) Capstone Press of Coughlan Cos.

Catala, Ellen. What Does a Firefighter Do?, 6 vols., Set. 2003. (Yellow Umbrella Early Level Ser.). (ENG.). 16p. (gr. k-1). pap. 35.70 *(978-0-7368-2988-5(1),* Yellow Umbrella Bks.) Capstone Press of Coughlan Cos.

La ceramica de los indigenas Pueblo: Libros Aventuras (Adventure Books) 2003. (MacMillan/McGraw-Hill. Estudios Sociales Ser.). (ENG & SPA.). (gr. 5-18). *(978-0-02-150124-3(6))* Macmillan/McGraw-Hill Schl. Div.

Cheyney, Arnold. History Challenge Level 1: 190 Brainteasers about the United States. 2005. (Challenge Ser.). (Illus.). 192p. (J). (gr. 3-5). per. 9.95 *(978-1-59647-065-1(8),* EAS002) Good Year Bks.

—History Challenge Level 2: 190 Brainteasers about the World. 2005. (Challenge Ser.). 192p. (J). (gr. 4-7). per. 9.95 *(978-1-59647-066-8(6),* EAS002) Good Year Bks.

A Child's Day Series, 5 bks., Set. 79.75 *(978-0-7614-1406-3(1),* Benchmark Bks.) Marshall Cavendish Corp.

Cipriano, Jeri S. At the Park, 6 vols., Set. 2003. (Yellow Umbrella Early Level Ser.). (ENG.). 16p. (gr. k-1). pap. 35.70 *(978-0-7368-2984-7(9),* Yellow Umbrella Bks.) Capstone Press of Coughlan Cos.

—Celebrations, 6, Set. 2003. (Yellow Umbrella Early Level Ser.). (ENG.). 16p. (gr. k-1). pap. 35.70 *(978-0-7368-3002-7(2),* Yellow Umbrella Bks.) Capstone Press of Coughlan Cos.

—Harvest Time, 6 vols., Set. 2003. (Yellow Umbrella Early Level Ser.). (ENG.). 16p. (gr. k-1). pap. 35.70 *(978-0-7368-3003-4(0),* Yellow Umbrella Bks.) Capstone Press of Coughlan Cos.

Coetzee, Eirka, et al. Social Science Matters Grade 8 Learner's Book Afrikaans Translation. 2nd ed. 2006. 192p. pap., stu. ed. 14.00 *(978-0-521-67890-2(0))* Cambridge Univ. Pr.

Coletti, Sharon. The Power of One: A Guide to Service-Learning & Social Science Research. 2005. (YA). ring bd. 99.95 *(978-1-933558-07-3(5))* InspirEd Educators.

Coll-Seck, Jayden. Our School Motto, 01 vols., 1. 2016. (Rosen REAL Readers: Social Studies Nonfiction / Fiction: Family, Community, & the World Ser.). (ENG.). 12p. (J). pap. 6.33 *(978-1-5081-1749-0(7),* Rosen Classroom) Rosen Publishing Group, Inc., The.

—Sally Does Not Like Broccoli, 01 vols., 1. 2016. (Rosen REAL Readers: Social Studies Nonfiction / Fiction: Family, Community, & the World Ser.). (ENG.). 8p. (J). pap. 5.46 *(978-1-5081-1656-1(3),* Rosen Classroom) Rosen Publishing Group, Inc., The.

—This Is My Class, 01 vols., 1. 2016. (Rosen REAL Readers: Social Studies Nonfiction / Fiction: Family, Community, & the World Ser.). (ENG.). 8p. (J). pap. 5.46 *(978-1-5081-1674-5(1),* Rosen Classroom) Rosen Publishing Group, Inc., The.

—We Are All Different, 01 vols., 1. 2016. (Rosen REAL Readers: Social Studies Nonfiction / Fiction: Family, Community, & the World Ser.). (ENG.). 8p. (J). pap. 5.46 *(978-1-5081-1707-0(1),* Rosen Classroom) Rosen Publishing Group, Inc., The.

—We Buy Food at the Store, 01 vols., 1. 2016. (Rosen REAL Readers: Social Studies Nonfiction / Fiction: Family, Community, & the World Ser.). (ENG.). 12p. (J). pap. 6.33 *(978-1-5081-1725-4(X),* Rosen Classroom) Rosen Publishing Group, Inc., The.

—We Celebrate Kwanzaa, 01 vols., 1. 2016. (Rosen REAL Readers: Social Studies Nonfiction / Fiction: Family, Community, & the World Ser.). (ENG.). 12p. (J). pap. 6.33 *(978-1-5081-1797-1(7),* Rosen Classroom) Rosen Publishing Group, Inc., The.

Collins UK. Secondary Social Studies for the Caribbean, Bk. 1. 2016. (ENG.). 256p. (J). pap. 23.99 ***(978-0-00-811588-3(5))*** HarperCollins Pubs. Ltd. GBR. Dist: Independent Pubs. Group.

Colonial America Classroom Library. (gr. 2-5). lib. bdg. 49.95 *(978-0-7368-4488-8(0))* Red Brick Learning.

Community Helpers Classroom Library. (gr. 2-5). lib. bdg. 116.95 *(978-0-7368-7074-0(1))* Red Brick Learning.

Community Helpers Complete Unit. (gr. 2-5). 664.95 *(978-0-7368-7075-7(X))* Red Brick Learning.

The Continents Collection. 2005. (J). pap. *(978-1-60015-012-8(8))* Steps To Literacy, LLC.

The Cotton Tale. abr. ed. 2004. (Thrilling Tales in Time Ser.: Vol. 41). (J). 19.95 *(978-1-58123-372-8(8))* Larson Learning, Inc.

Cuaderno de Evaluacion: Student & Teacher Support Resources. 2003. (MacMillan/McGraw-Hill. Estudios Sociales Ser.). (ENG & SPA.). (gr. 1-18). *(978-0-02-149458-3(4));* (gr. 2-18). *(978-0-02-149459-0(2));* (gr. 3-18). *(978-0-02-149461-3(4));* (gr. 4-18). *(978-0-02-149971-7(3));* (gr. 5-18). *(978-0-02-149463-7(0))* Macmillan/McGraw-Hill Schl. Div.

Cuaderno de practica y Actividades: Student & Teacher Support Resources. 2003. (MacMillan/McGraw-Hill. Estudios Sociales Ser.). (ENG & SPA.). (gr. 1-18). *(978-0-02-149453-8(3));* (gr. 1-18). *(978-0-02-150009-3(6));* (gr. 2-18). *(978-0-02-150010-9(X));* (gr. 2-18). *(978-0-02-149454-5(1));* (gr. 3-18). *(978-0-02-149455-2(X));* (gr. 3-18). *(978-0-02-150011-6(8));* (gr. 4-18). *(978-0-02-149970-0(5));* (gr. 5-18). *(978-0-02-150014-7(2));* (gr. 5-18). *(978-0-02-149457-6(6))* Macmillan/McGraw-Hill Schl. Div.

CultureGrams 2005 World Edition. 2004. (YA). per. 129.99 *(978-1-931694-87-2(7));* ring bd. 139.99 *(978-1-931694-88-9(5))* ProQuest LLC.

Cushing, Christopher. Let's Celebrate! 2012. (InfoMax Readers Ser.). (ENG., Illus.). 16 pp.p. (J). (gr. k-1). pap. 7.00 *(978-1-4488-8962-4(6),* Rosen Classroom) Rosen Publishing Group, Inc., The.

Daily Activity Bank: Scott Foresman Social Studies: All Together. 2003. (gr. 1-18). *(978-0-328-03919-7(5),* Scott Foresman) Addison-Wesley Educational Pubs., Inc.

Daily Activity Bank: Scott Foresman Social Studies: Communities. 2003. (gr. 3-18). *(978-0-328-03921-0(7),* Scott Foresman) Addison-Wesley Educational Pubs., Inc.

Daily Activity Bank: Scott Foresman Social Studies: People & Places. 2003. (gr. 2-18). *(978-0-328-03920-3(9),* Scott Foresman) Addison-Wesley Educational Pubs., Inc.

Daily Activity Bank: Scott Foresman Social Studies: Regions. 2003. (gr. 4-18). *(978-0-328-03922-7(5),* Scott Foresman) Addison-Wesley Educational Pubs., Inc.

Daily Activity Bank: Scott Foresman Social Studies: The United States. 2003. (gr. 5-18). *(978-0-328-03926-5(8),* Scott Foresman) Addison-Wesley Educational Pubs., Inc.

Daily Activity Bank: Scott Foresman Social Studies: The World. 2003. (gr. 6-18). *(978-0-328-03927-2(6),* Scott Foresman) Addison-Wesley Educational Pubs., Inc.

Daronco, Mickey & Ohanesian, Diane. Am I Sad? Set Of 6. 2nd rev. ed. 2011. (BuildUp Ser.). (J). pap. 27.00 net. *(978-1-4108-0740-3(1))* Benchmark Education Co.

Dell, Pamela. Honey for Sale. 2016. (Spring Forward Ser.). (J). (gr. 1). *(978-1-4900-2230-7(9))* Benchmark Education Co.

Desert Day: Level B, 6 vols. 8p. 24.95 *(978-0-7802-8916-1(1))* Wright Group/McGraw-Hill.

Diario de la Frontera: Libros Aventuras (Adventure Books) 2003. (MacMillan/McGraw-Hill. Estudios Sociales Ser.). (ENG & SPA.). (gr. 4-18). *(978-0-02-150118-2(1))* Macmillan/McGraw-Hill Schl. Div.

El diario de una nina Inmigrante: Libros Aventuras (Adventure Books) 2003. (MacMillan/McGraw-Hill. Estudios Sociales Ser.). (ENG & SPA.). (gr. 5-18). *(978-0-02-150126-7(2))* Macmillan/McGraw-Hill Schl. Div.

Dictionary, Oxford, ed. Oxford Illustrated Social Studies Dictionary. 2013. (ENG., Illus.). iii, 217p. pap. 24.94 *(978-0-19-407132-1(4))* Oxford Univ. Pr., Inc.

DiPiazza, Francesca Davis. Friend Me! 600 Years of Social Networking in America. 2015. (ENG., Illus.). 112p. (gr. 5-12). 34.65 *(978-1-4677-5931-1(7),* Lerner Digital) Lerner Publishing Group.

Discos compactos: Libro del Estudiante: Technology. 2003. (MacMillan/McGraw-Hill. Estudios Sociales Ser.). (ENG & SPA.). (gr. 2-18). *(978-0-02-150052-9(5));* (gr. 3-18). *(978-0-02-150053-6(3));* (gr. 4-18). *(978-0-02-150055-0(X));* (gr. 5-18). *(978-0-02-150056-7(8))* Macmillan/McGraw-Hill Schl. Div.

Discovering Cultures Series - Group 1, 6 bks., Set. 158.86 *(978-0-7614-1181-9(X),* Benchmark Bks.) Marshall Cavendish Corp.

Dunn, Justine. Hey! There's Social Studies in My Literature! Grades 1-2. Radtke, Becky, illus. 2007. (Rigby Best Teachers Press Ser.). 96p. per. 13.99 *(978-1-4190-3400-8(6))* Houghton Mifflin Harcourt Supplemental Pubs.

DynaNotes Grade 8 Social Studies Review Guide Transparency Set. 2006. (YA). trans. *(978-1-933854-35-9(9))* DynaStudy, Inc.

DynaNotes Grade 8 Social Studies TAKS Review Guide. 2006. pap. *(978-1-933854-31-1(6))* DynaStudy, Inc.

Endres, Hollie J. The Letter Gg Set: The World Around You, 6. 2004. (Letter Bks.). (ENG.). 8p. (gr. k-1). pap. 29.70

S

(978-0-7368-4106-1(7), Letter Bks.) Capstone Press of Coughlan Cos.

—The Letter Vv Set: Sink or Float?, 6 vols. 2004. (Letter Bks.). (ENG.). 8p. (gr. k-1). pap. 29.70 (978-0-7368-4121-4(0), Letter Bks.) Capstone Press of Coughlan Cos.

Engdahl, Sylvia. Welfare. 2010. (Issues on Trial Ser.). (ENG.). 240p. 42.15 (978-0-7377-5110-9(X), Greenhaven Pr., Inc.) Cengage Gale.

Eri busca de un Hogar: Libros Aventuras (Adventure Books) 2003. (MacMillan/McGraw-Hill. Estudios Sociales Ser.). (ENG & SPA.). (gr. 5-18). (978-0-02-150123-6(8)) Macmillan/McGraw-Hill Schl. Div.

Estudios sociales Scott Foresman. 2003. (Scott Foresman Social Study Ser.). (SPA.). (gr. k-18). stu. ed. (978-0-328-05613-2(8)); (gr. 1-18). stu. ed. (978-0-328-05499-2(2)); (gr. 2-18). stu. ed. (978-0-328-05500-5(X)) Addison-Wesley Educational Pubs., Inc. (Scott Foresman).

Estudios sociales Scott Foresman: Additional Resources. 2003. (Scott Foresman Social Study Ser.). (SPA.). (gr. k-2). (978-0-328-03696-7(X)); (gr. k-2). tchr. ed. (978-0-328-04213-5(7)); (gr. 1-18). (978-0-328-03861-9(X)); (gr. 1-18). (978-0-328-05737-5(1)); (gr. 1-18). (978-0-328-04202-9(1)); (gr. 1-18). (978-0-328-03867-1(9)); (gr. 1-18). (978-0-328-05504-3(2)); (gr. 2-18). (978-0-328-05505-0(0)); (gr. 2-18). (978-0-328-03868-8(7)); (gr. 2-18). (978-0-328-04203-6(X)); (gr. 2-18). (978-0-328-05738-2(X)); (gr. 3-18). (978-0-328-03869-5(5)); (gr. 3-18). (978-0-328-05506-7(9)); (gr. 3-5). (978-0-328-03698-1(6)); (gr. 3-5). tchr. ed. (978-0-328-04214-2(5)); (gr. 4-18). (978-0-328-05777-1(0)); (gr. 4-18). (978-0-328-05784-9(3)); (gr. 4-18). (978-0-328-05779-5(7)); (gr. 4-18). (978-0-328-05776-4(2)); (gr. 4-18). (978-0-328-05780-1(0)); (gr. 5-18). (978-0-328-03871-8(7)); (gr. 5-18). (978-0-328-05508-1(5)); (gr. 5-18). (978-0-328-03865-7(2)) Addison-Wesley Educational Pubs., Inc. (Scott Foresman).

Estudios sociales Scott Foresman: Practice/Assessment. 2003. (Scott Foresman Social Study Ser.). (SPA.). (gr. 1-18). (978-0-328-03463-5(0)); (gr. 1-18). (978-0-328-03855-8(5)); (gr. 3-18). (978-0-328-03465-9(7)); (gr. 4-18). (978-0-328-05687-3(1)); (gr. 5-18). (978-0-328-03467-3(3)); (gr. 5-18). (978-0-328-03859-6(8)) Addison-Wesley Educational Pubs., Inc. (Scott Foresman).

Estudios Sociales Scott Foresman: Practice/Assessment. 2003. (SPA.). (gr. 2-18). (978-0-328-03464-2(9), Scott Foresman) Addison-Wesley Educational Pubs., Inc.

Estudios sociales Scott Foresman: Technology. 2003. (Scott Foresman Social Study Ser.). (SPA.). (gr. 1-18). (978-0-328-09220-8(7)); (gr. 1-18). (978-0-328-05726-9(6)); (gr. 1-18). cd-rom (978-0-328-05932-4(3)); (gr. 1-18). cd-rom (978-0-328-05744-3(4)); (gr. 2-18). (978-0-328-09221-5(5)); (gr. 2-18). (978-0-328-05727-6(4)); (gr. 2-18). cd-rom (978-0-328-05745-0(2)); (gr. 2-18). cd-rom (978-0-328-05933-1(1)); (gr. 3-18). (978-0-328-05728-3(2)); (gr. 3-18). (978-0-328-09222-2(3)); (gr. 3-18). cd-rom (978-0-328-05934-8(X)); (gr. 3-18). cd-rom (978-0-328-05746-7(0)); (gr. 4-18). (978-0-328-05800-6(9)); (gr. 4-18). (978-0-328-09223-9(1)); (gr. 4-18). cd-rom (978-0-328-05936-2(6)); (gr. 4-18). cd-rom (978-0-328-05786-3(X)); (gr. 5-18). (978-0-328-05730-6(4)); (gr. 5-18). (978-0-328-09224-6(X)); (gr. 5-18). cd-rom (978-0-328-05937-9(4)); (gr. 5-18). cd-rom (978-0-328-05748-1(7)) Addison-Wesley Educational Pubs., Inc. (Scott Foresman).

¡Estudios Sociales y más! Un enfoque practico: Estudios Sociales Scott Foresman. 2003. (SPA.). (gr. k-18). (978-0-328-05503-6(4), Scott Foresman) Addison-Wesley Educational Pubs., Inc.

The Events to Independence. 2004. (Thrilling Tales in Time Ser.: Vol. 3). (J). (978-1-58123-369-8(8)) Larson Learning, Inc.

Every Student Learns: Scott Foresman Social Studies. 2003. (gr. k-18). tchr. ed. (978-0-328-03608-0(0), Scott Foresman) Addison-Wesley Educational Pubs., Inc.

Every Student Learns: Scott Foresman Social Studies: All Together. 2003. (SPA.). (gr. 1-18). tchr. ed. (978-0-328-03609-7(9), Scott Foresman) Addison-Wesley Educational Pubs., Inc.

Every Student Learns: Scott Foresman Social Studies: Communities. 2003. (SPA.). (gr. 3-18). tchr. ed. (978-0-328-03611-0(0), Scott Foresman) Addison-Wesley Educational Pubs., Inc.

Every Student Learns: Scott Foresman Social Studies: People & Places. 2003. (SPA.). (gr. 2-18). tchr. ed. (978-0-328-03610-3(2), Scott Foresman) Addison-Wesley Educational Pubs., Inc.

Every Student Learns: Scott Foresman Social Studies: Regions. 2003. (SPA.). (gr. 4-18). tchr. ed. (978-0-328-03612-7(9), Scott Foresman) Addison-Wesley Educational Pubs., Inc.

Every Student Learns: Scott Foresman Social Studies: The United States. 2003. (SPA.). (gr. 5-18). tchr. ed. (978-0-328-03613-4(7), Scott Foresman) Addison-Wesley Educational Pubs., Inc.

Every Student Learns: Scott Foresman Social Studies: The World. 2003. (gr. 6-18). tchr. ed. (978-0-328-03614-1(5), Scott Foresman) Addison-Wesley Educational Pubs., Inc.

Explora el Mundo. 288p. (J). (gr. 3-8). (978-0-7166-7096-4(8)) World Bk., Inc.

Faherty, Sara. Welfare Reform. 2004. (Point/Counterpoint Ser.). (Illus.). 112p. (C). (gr. 9-14). 35.00 (978-0-7910-8093-1(5), Chelsea Hse.) Facts On File, Inc.

Ferraro, Bonita. Be a Good Citizen: A Content Area Reader-Social Studies. 2005. (Sadlier-Oxford Content Area Readers Ser.). 12p. (gr. k-2). 25.20 (978-0-8215-7820-9(0)) Sadlier, William H. Inc.

Firth, Rachel. Los Caballeros - Internet Linked. Gaudenzi, Giacinto, illus. 2004. (Titles in Spanish Ser.). (SPA.). 48p. (J). pap. 8.95 (978-0-7460-5083-5(6), Usborne) EDC Publishing.

Fisher, Douglas & McGraw-Hill Book Company Staff. The World & Its People: Eastern Hemisphere, Active Reading Note-Taking Guide. 2004. (WORLD & ITS PEOPLE EASTERN Ser.). (ENG., Illus.). 323p. (gr. 6-9). stu. ed., per. 12.80 (978-0-07-868058-8(1), 0078680581) McGraw-Hill Education.

Fisher, Douglas & McGraw-Hill Staff. The World & Its People. 2004. (GEOGRAPHY: WORLD & ITS PEOPLE Ser.). (ENG., Illus.). 404p. (gr. 6-9). stu. ed., per., wbk. ed. 12.80 (978-0-07-868140-0(5), 0078681405) McGraw-Hill Education.

Flash Kids Editors, Flash Kids, ed. Summer Study, Grade 1. 2016. (Summer Study Ser.). (ENG., Illus.). 160p. (J). (gr. 1-1). pap. 9.95 (978-1-4114-7857-2(6), Spark Publishing Group) Sterling Publishing Co., Inc.

For a Better Life. 2003. (Illus.). pap. 5.60 (978-0-7398-7508-7(6)) Steck-Vaughn.

Foresman, Scott. Estudios sociales Scott Foresman. 2003. (SPA & ENG.). (gr. 4-4). stu. ed. 74.47 net. (978-0-328-05001-7(6), Scott Foresman) Pearson Schl.

—Estudios sociales Scott Foresman: Practice/Assessment. 2003. (SPA & ENG.). (gr. 4-4). pap. 16.47 net. (978-0-328-05781-8(9), Scott Foresman) Pearson Schl.

—Estudios sociales Scott Foresman: Technology. 2003. (SPA & ENG.). (gr. k-6). cd-rom 64.97 net. (978-0-328-05749-8(5), Scott Foresman) Pearson Schl.

—Scott Foresman Social Studies: Technology. 2003. (SPA & ENG.). (gr. 4-4). cd-rom 120.47 net. (978-0-328-05667-5(7)); (ENG.). (gr. 1-1). cd-rom 72.97 net. (978-0-328-05878-5(5)); (ENG.). (gr. 2-2). cd-rom 72.97 net. (978-0-328-05879-2(3)); (ENG.). (gr. 3-3). cd-rom 70.47 net. (978-0-328-05880-8(7)); (SPA & ENG.). (gr. 4-4). cd-rom 120.47 net. (978-0-328-05668-2(5)); (ENG.). (gr. 4-4). cd-rom 72.97 net. (978-0-328-06259-1(6)); (ENG.). (gr. 5-5). cd-rom 72.97 net. (978-0-328-05882-2(3)); (ENG.). (gr. 6-6). cd-rom 120.47 net. (978-0-328-05669-9(3)) Pearson Schl. (Scott Foresman).

Foster, Ruth. Nonfiction Reading Comprehension - Social Studies, Grades 1-2. 2006. (ENG.). 144p. pap. 16.99 (978-1-4206-8027-0(7)) Teacher Created Resources, Inc.

—Nonfiction Reading Comprehension - Social Studies, Grades 2-3. 2006. (ENG.). 144p. pap. 16.99 (978-1-4206-8023-2(4)) Teacher Created Resources, Inc.

—Social Studies, Grade 3. 2006. (Nonfiction Reading Comprehension Ser.). (ENG., Illus.). 144p. per. 16.99 (978-1-4206-8024-9(2)) Teacher Created Resources, Inc.

Francis, Amy. Road Rage. Greenhaven Press Editors, ed. 2014. (At Issue Ser.). (ENG.). 128p. (gr. 10-12). lib. bdg. 39.40 (978-0-7377-6197-9(0), Greenhaven Pr., Inc.) Cengage Gale.

Frontline Coverage of Current Events, 6 Bks., Set. 2005. (J). 159.00 (978-1-4042-0378-5(8)) Rosen Publishing Group, Inc., The.

Garza, Carmen Lomas, illus. Cuadros de Familia. 15th anniv. ed. 2005.Tr. of Family Pictures. (ENG & SPA.). 32p. (J). (gr. -1-17). 16.95 (978-0-89239-206-3(1)) Lee & Low Bks., Inc.

Gateway Biographies, 12 vols., Set. Incl. Al Gore: Fighting for a Greener Planet. Stefoff, Rebecca. 2008. 26.60 (978-1-57505-948-8(7)); Alberto Gonzales: Attorney General. McElroy, Lisa Tucker. (Illus.). (J). 2006. lib. bdg. 23.93 (978-0-8225-3418-1(5)); Barack Obama: President for a New Era. Brill, Marlene Targ. 2009. 26.60 (978-1-57505-950-1(9)); Condoleezza Rice. Wade, Mary Dodson. (Illus.). 2005. lib. bdg. 26.60 (978-0-7613-9550-8(4)); Green Day: Keeping Their Edge. Doeden, Matt. (Illus.). 2006. lib. bdg. 26.60 (978-0-8225-6390-7(8), Lerner Pubns.); John G. Roberts, Jr: Chief Justice. McElroy, Lisa Tucker. (Illus.). 2006. lib. bdg. 26.60 (978-0-8225-6389-1(4), Lerner Pubns.); Michael Jackson: Ultimate Music Legend. Krohn, Katherine E. (Illus.). 2010. lib. bdg. 26.60 (978-0-7613-5762-9(9), Lerner Pubns.); Michelle Obama: From Chicago's South Side to the White House. Brill, Marlene Targ. (Illus.). 2009. 26.60 (978-0-7613-5033-0(0)); Nancy Pelosi: First Woman Speaker of the House. McElroy, Lisa Tucker. (Illus.). 2007. lib. bdg. 26.60 (978-0-8225-8685-2(1), Lerner Pubns.); Sonia Sotomayor: First Hispanic U. S. Supreme Court Justice. McElroy, Lisa Tucker. 2010. lib. bdg. 26.60 (978-0-7613-5861-9(7)); Ted Kennedy: A Remarkable Life in the Senate. McElroy, Lisa Tucker. 2009. 26.60 (978-0-7613-4457-5(8)); Tyra Banks: From Supermodel to Role Model. Hill, Anne E. 2009. 26.60 (978-1-57505-949-5(5)); 48p. (gr. 4-8). 2010. Set lib. bdg. 319.20 (978-0-8225-8069-0(1)) Lerner Publishing Group.

Gay, Kathlyn. Activism: The Ultimate Teen Guide. 2016. (It Happened to Me Ser.: 47). (ENG., Illus.). 234p. (J). 45.00 (978-1-4422-4293-7(0)) Rowman & Littlefield Publishers, Inc.

—Cultural Diversity: Conflicts & Challenges. 2003. (It Happened to Me Ser.: 6). (ENG., Illus.). 144p. pap. 45.00 (978-0-8108-4805-4(8)) Scarecrow Pr., Inc.

Gensmer, Laura. Where We Live. 2011. (Social Studies). (ENG.). 16p. (gr. -1-1). 25.95 (978-1-4296-8668-6(5), Wonder Readers) Capstone Press of Coughlan Cos.

Georgia Striving Readers Social Studies K-5. 2012. (CAP-Marketing Ser.). (ENG.). (gr. k-5). pap. 2161.30 (978-1-62065-958-8(1)) Capstone Press of Coughlan Cos.

Gerber, Paul. Is It Alive? 2012. (InfoMax Readers Ser.). (ENG., Illus.). 16 pp.p. (J). (gr. k-1). pap. 7.00 (978-1-4488-8965-5(0), Rosen Classroom) Rosen Publishing Group, Inc., The.

Gerdes, Louise, ed. Are Government Bailouts Effective? 2012. (At Issue Ser.). (ENG.). 128p. (gr. 10-12). pap. 24.45 (978-0-7377-6180-1(6)); lib. bdg. 39.40 (978-0-7377-6179-5(2)) Cengage Gale. (Greenhaven Pr., Inc.).

Gerdes, Louise I. Should the US Close Its Borders? Greenhaven Press Editors & Gale, A. G., eds. 2014. (At Issue Ser.). (ENG.). 128p. (gr. 10-12). pap. 27.80 (978-0-7377-6861-9(4), Greenhaven Pr., Inc.) Cengage Gale.

—Should the US Close Its Borders? Greenhaven Press Editors & Gale Editors, eds. 2014. (At Issue Ser.). (ENG.). 128p. (gr. 10-12). lib. bdg. 39.40 (978-0-7377-6860-2(6), Greenhaven Pr., Inc.) Cengage Gale.

—Super Pacs. Greenhaven Press Editors & Gale Editors, eds. 2014. (At Issue Ser.). (ENG.). 128p. (gr. 10-12). pap. 27.80 (978-0-7377-6865-7(7), Greenhaven Pr., Inc.) Cengage Gale.

—Super Pacs. Greenhaven Press Editors, ed. 2014. (At Issue Ser.). (ENG.). 128p. (gr. 10-12). lib. bdg. 39.40 (978-0-7377-6864-0(9), Greenhaven Pr., Inc.) Cengage Gale.

Geschichte. (Duden-Schuelerduden Ser.). (GER., Illus.). 540p. (YA). (978-3-411-05413-8(1)) Bibliographisches Institut & F. A. Brockhaus AG DEU. Dist: International Bk. Import Service, Inc.

Geschichte I. (Duden Abiturhilfen Ser.). (GER.). 86p. (YA). (gr. 12-13). (978-3-411-02640-1(5)) Bibliographisches Institut & F. A. Brockhaus AG DEU. Dist: International Bk. Import Service, Inc.

Get a Clue: An Introduction to Primary Sources. 2005. (J). pap. (978-1-932663-09-9(6)) History Compass, LLC.

Gifford, Clive. Racism. (Illus.). 64p. (YA). (gr. 5-18). lib. bdg. 29.95 (978-1-931983-83-9(6)) Chrysalis Education.

Goodwin, Evelyn. Meet the Children from the Fifty States in Poetry. 2007. 106p. pap. 37.50 (978-0-615-16145-7(6)) Goodwin, Evelyn.

Got Issues? 2015. (Got Issues? Ser.). (ENG.). 128p. (J). (gr. 7-7). 260.89 (978-0-7660-6697-7(5)) Enslow Pubs., Inc.

Greenhaven Press Editors & Gale Editors, eds. Privacy. 2014. (Global Viewpoints Ser.). (ENG., Illus.). 224p. (gr. 7-12). pap. 31.70 (978-0-7377-6913-5(0), Greenhaven Pr., Inc.) Cengage Gale.

Gregoire, Maryellen. Storytime. 2011. (Social Studies). (ENG.). 16p. (gr. -1-1). 25.95 (978-1-4296-8670-9(7), Wonder Readers) Capstone Press of Coughlan Cos.

Gritzner, Charles F., contrib. by. Global Connections, 10 vols., Set. 2010. (Global Connections Ser.). (gr. 5-8). 350.00 (978-1-60413-960-0(9), Chelsea Hse.) Facts On File, Inc.

Group/McGraw-Hill, Wright. Amazing Asia, 6 vols. (Book2WebTM Ser.). (gr. 4-8). 36.50 (978-0-322-04437-1(5)) Wright Group/McGraw-Hill.

—Ancient Egypt: The Realm of Pharaohs, 6 vols. (Book2WebTM Ser.). (gr. 4-8). 36.50 (978-0-322-04451-7(0)) Wright Group/McGraw-Hill.

—Las Aranas, 6 vols., Vol. 2. (First Explorers. Primeros Exploradores Nonfiction Sets Ser.). (SPA.). (gr. 1-2). 34.95 (978-0-7699-1489-3(6)) Shortland Pubns. (U. S. A.) Inc.

—Cold Facts about Ice Ages, 6 vols. (Book2WebTM Ser.). (gr. 4-8). 36.50 (978-0-322-04434-0(0)) Wright Group/McGraw-Hill.

—Como nos Transportamos, 6 vols. (First Explorers. Primeros Exploradores Nonfiction Sets Ser.). (SPA.). (gr. 1-2). 29.95 (978-0-7699-1470-1(5)) Shortland Pubns. (U. S. A.) Inc.

—D-Man & Beans: Classroom Library Set. (D-Man Beans Ser.). (J). (gr. 4-6). 150.95 (978-0-322-09210-5(8)) Wright Group/McGraw-Hill.

—D-Man & Beans: Complete Set. (D-Man Beans Ser.). (gr. 4-6). 479.95 (978-0-322-09211-2(6)) Wright Group/McGraw-Hill.

—D-Man's Escape, 6 vols. (D-Man Beans Ser.). 47p. (gr. 4-6). 42.50 (978-0-322-06267-2(5)) Wright Group/McGraw-Hill.

—Donde Vive la Gente, 6 vols., Vol. 2. (First Explorers. Primeros Exploradores Nonfiction Sets Ser.). (SPA.). (gr. 1-2). 29.95 (978-0-7699-1486-2(1)) Shortland Pubns. (U. S. A.) Inc.

—Fuerzas de la Naturaleza, 6 vols., Vol. 2. (First Explorers. Primeros Exploradores Nonfiction Sets Ser.). (SPA.). (gr. 1-2). 34.95 (978-0-7699-1482-4(9)) Shortland Pubns. (U. S. A.) Inc.

—Going Places: Level I, 6 vols. (First Explorers Ser.). 24p. (gr. 1-2). 29.95 (978-0-7699-1446-6(2)) Shortland Pubns. (U. S. A.) Inc.

—Lagunas y Rios, 6 vols. (First Explorers. Primeros Exploradores Nonfiction Sets Ser.). (SPA.). (gr. 1-2). 29.95 (978-0-7699-1475-6(6)) Shortland Pubns. (U. S. A.) Inc.

—Making Sense of Sound & Music, 6 vols. (Book2WebTM Ser.). (gr. 4-8). 36.50 (978-0-322-04430-2(8)) Wright Group/McGraw-Hill.

—Mountain Majesty, 6 vols. (Book2WebTM Ser.). (gr. 4-8). 36.50 (978-0-322-04440-1(5)) Wright Group/McGraw-Hill.

—Para Que Construye el Hombre, 6 vols., Vol. 2. (First Explorers. Primeros Exploradores Nonfiction Sets Ser.). (SPA.). (gr. 1-2). 34.95 (978-0-7699-1480-0(2)) Shortland Pubns. (U. S. A.) Inc.

—People on the Path Toward Human Rights, 6 vols. (Book2WebTM Ser.). (gr. 4-8). 36.50 (978-0-322-04466-1(9)) Wright Group/McGraw-Hill.

—Por Que se Mueven Las Cosas, 6 vols., Vol. 2. (First Explorers. Primeros Exploradores Nonfiction Sets Ser.). (SPA.). (gr. 1-2). 34.95 (978-0-7699-1490-9(X)) Shortland Pubns. (U. S. A.) Inc.

—El Sonido, 6 vols., Vol. 2. (First Explorers. Primeros Exploradores Nonfiction Sets Ser.). (SPA.). (gr. 1-2). 34.95 (978-0-7699-1488-6(8)) Shortland Pubns. (U. S. A.) Inc.

—Take-Twos Social Studies Vol. 2: Fluency - Complete Kit. (gr. 3-4). 483.50 (978-0-322-09177-1(2)) Wright Group/McGraw-Hill.

—Take-Twos Social Studies Vol. 2: Fluency - Student Book Set - 1 Each of 12 Titles. (gr. 3-4). 81.95 (978-0-322-09305-8(8)) Wright Group/McGraw-Hill.

—Why Things Move: Level K, 6 vols., Vol. 2. (First Explorers Ser.). 24p. (gr. 1-2). 34.95 (978-0-7699-1466-4(7)) Shortland Pubns. (U. S. A.) Inc.

—Wonder World Complete Sets: Social Studies Set - 1 Each of 73 Titles. (Wonder Worldtm Ser.). (gr. k-6). 398.95 (978-0-322-06713-4(8)) Wright Group/McGraw-Hill.

—Wonder World Early & Upper Emergent Sets: Social Studies Set - 1 Each of 43 Titles. (Wonder Worldtm Ser.). (gr. k-6). 204.95 (978-0-322-06719-6(7)) Wright Group/McGraw-Hill.

—Wonder World Early Fluency & Fluency: Social Studies Set - 1 Each of 30 Titles. (Wonder Worldtm Ser.). (gr. k-6). 194.50 (978-0-322-06716-5(2)) Wright Group/McGraw-Hill.

—World Leaders Through the Ages, 6 vols. (Book2WebTM Ser.). (gr. 4-8). 36.50 (978-0-322-04471-5(5)) Wright Group/McGraw-Hill.

Gustando. (Coleccion Mil Preguntas). (SPA., Illus.). 24p. (J). pap. 5.50 (978-950-11-0660-2(8), SGM627) Sigmar ARG. Dist: Continental Bk. Co., Inc.

Haerens, Margaret. Mexico's Drug War. Greenhaven Press Editors, ed. 2013. (At Issue Ser.). (ENG.). 128p. (gr. 10-12). pap. 27.80 (978-0-7377-6845-9(2)); lib. bdg. 39.40 (978-0-7377-6844-2(4)) Cengage Gale. (Greenhaven Pr., Inc.).

Hands: Level B, 6 vols. 8p. 24.95 (978-0-7802-8915-4(3)) Wright Group/McGraw-Hill.

Hansen, Merrily P. Homes Around the World: A Content Area Reader-Social Studies. 2005. (Emergent/Early (Prek-2) Social Studies Package Ser.). 12p. (gr. k-2). 25.20 (978-0-8215-7817-9(0)) Sadlier, William H. Inc.

Harcourt School Publishers Staff. All about People, Unit 4. 3rd ed. 2003. (Horizons Ser.). (Illus.). pap. 166.70 (978-0-15-340223-4(7)) Harcourt Schl. Pubs.

—All the People, No. 4. 2nd ed. 2003. (Illus.). (gr. 1). pap. 139.70 (978-0-15-337559-0(0)) Harcourt Schl. Pubs.

—At Home with the Family, Unit 2. 3rd ed. 2003. (Harcourt Brace Social Studies). pap. 76.00 (978-0-15-341059-8(0)) Harcourt Schl. Pubs.

—Beginnings 2005. 3rd ed. 2003. (Harcourt Horizons Ser.). (ENG.). 744p. (gr. 4-5). stu. ed. 86.80 (978-0-15-339620-5(2)) Harcourt Schl. Pubs.

—Being a Citizen, Unit 5. 3rd ed. 2003. (Harcourt Brace Social Studies). pap. 76.00 (978-0-15-341070-3(1)) Harcourt Schl. Pubs.

—Catch a Dream Level 1-2. 3rd ed. 2003. (Harcourt School Publishers Trophies Ser.). (ENG., Illus.). 176p. (gr. 1-1). pupil's gde. ed. 38.10 (978-0-15-322470-6(3)) Harcourt Schl. Pubs.

—Distant Voyages. 3rd ed. 2003. (Harcourt School Publishers Trophies Ser.). (ENG., Illus.). 768p. (gr. 5-5). pupil's gde. ed. 82.55 (978-0-15-322479-9(7)) Harcourt Schl. Pubs.

—Going to School Big Book No. 1. 2nd ed. 2003. (Illus.). (gr. 1). pap. 139.70 (978-0-15-337556-9(6)) Harcourt Schl. Pubs.

—Here & There 2003 Level 1-3. 3rd ed. 2003. (Harcourt School Publishers Trophies Ser.). (ENG., Illus.). 192p. (gr. 1-1). stu. ed. 42.10 (978-0-15-322471-3(1)) Harcourt Schl. Pubs.

—Horizons. 3rd ed. 2003. (Harcourt School Publishers Horizons Ser.). (ENG., Illus.). 810p. (gr. 6-6). pupil's gde. ed. 93.40 (978-0-15-320183-7(5)) Harcourt Schl. Pubs.

—Horizons: "All About Me" Unit. 3rd ed. 2003. (Harcourt Horizons Ser.). (Illus.). (gr. k-7). pap. 254.10 (978-0-15-320943-7(7)) Harcourt Schl. Pubs.

—Horizons: Assessment Program. 3rd ed. 2003. (Harcourt Horizons Ser.). (ENG.). 48p. (gr. 1-1). pap. 72.15 (978-0-15-340284-5(9)); pap. 72.15 (978-0-15-340285-2(7)) Harcourt Schl. Pubs.

—Horizons Bk. 2: World Regions. 3rd ed. 2003. (Illus.). pap. 9.30 (978-0-15-333944-8(6)) Harcourt Schl. Pubs.

—Horizons ESL Summary. 4th ed. 2004. (gr. 3). pap. 10.80 (978-0-15-343720-5(0)) Harcourt Schl. Pubs.

—Horizons, Grade 2: Time for Kids Readers. 3rd ed. 2003. (Harcourt Horizons Ser.). pap., tchr. ed. 51.20 (978-0-15-334647-7(7)) Harcourt Schl. Pubs.

—Horizons with Ancient Civilizations. 4th ed. 2004. (gr. 3). 53.20 (978-0-15-344221-6(2)) Harcourt Schl. Pubs.

—Horizontes: Unit Big Book Collection. 3rd ed. 2003. (Harcourt Horizontes Ser.). (SPA., Illus.). (gr. k-6). 1112.80 (978-0-15-325844-2(6)); 1112.80 (978-0-15-325845-9(4)) Harcourt Schl. Pubs.

—Horizontes, Grade 1. 2nd ed. 2003. (Harcourt Horizontes Ser.). (SPA.). (gr. k-6). Vol. 1. tchr. ed. 114.40 (978-0-15-328413-7(7)) Vol. 2. tchr. ed. 114.40 (978-0-15-328414-4(5)) Harcourt Schl. Pubs.

—Horizontes, Grade 2, Vol. 1. 2nd ed. 2003. (Harcourt Horizontes Ser.). (SPA.). (gr. k-6). tchr. ed. 121.50 (978-0-15-328415-1(3)) Harcourt Schl. Pubs.

—Horizontes, Grade 3. 2nd ed. 2003. (Harcourt Horizontes Ser.). (SPA.). (gr. k-6). Vol. 1. tchr. ed. 121.50 (978-0-15-328509-7(5)) Vol. 2. tchr. ed. 121.50 (978-0-15-328510-3(9)) Harcourt Schl. Pubs.

—In & Around the Land, Unit 4. 3rd ed. 2003. (Harcourt Brace Social Studies). pap. 76.00 (978-0-15-341061-1(2)) Harcourt Schl. Pubs.

—Land Around, No. 3. 2nd ed. 2003. (Illus.). (gr. 1). pap. 139.70 (978-0-15-337558-3(2)) Harcourt Schl. Pubs.

—Learn about People, Unit 4. 3rd ed. 2003. (Horizons Ser.). (Illus.). pap. 166.70 (978-0-15-340230-2(X)) Harcourt Schl. Pubs.

—Learn about the People No. 4. 2nd ed. 2003. (Illus.). pap. 139.70 (978-0-15-337569-9(8)) Harcourt Schl. Pubs.

—Lets Visit Museum, Above Level Reader Grade K: Harcourt School Publishers Social Studies. 2005. pap. 5.60 (978-0-15-351872-0(3)) Harcourt Schl. Pubs.

—Living in a Community, Unit 1. 3rd ed. 2003. (Horizons Ser.). (Illus.). (gr. 2). pap. 166.70 (978-0-15-340227-2(X)) Harcourt Schl. Pubs.

—Looking Back Big Book No. 5. 2nd ed. 2003. (Illus.). pap. 139.70 (978-0-15-337560-6(4)) Harcourt Schl. Pubs.

—My Heros, Unit 5. 3rd ed. 2003. (Harcourt Brace Social Studies). pap. 76.00 (978-0-15-341062-8(0)) Harcourt Schl. Pubs.

—Our Government, Unit 2. 3rd ed. 2003. (Horizons Ser.). (Illus.). pap. 166.70 (978-0-15-340228-9(8)) Harcourt Schl. Pubs.

—Past & Present, Unit 5. 3rd ed. 2003. (Horizons Ser.). (Illus.). (gr. 2). pap. 166.70 (978-0-15-340231-9(8)) Harcourt Schl. Pubs.

—Past & Present Big Book No. 5. 2nd ed. 2003. (Illus.). pap. 139.70 (978-0-15-337570-5(1)) Harcourt Schl. Pubs.

—People at Work, Unit 6. 3rd ed. 2003. (Horizons Ser.). (Illus.). pap. 166.70 (978-0-15-340232-6(6)) Harcourt Schl. Pubs.

—People in History, Unit 4. 3rd ed. 2003. (Harcourt Brace Social Studies). pap. 76.00 (978-0-15-341069-7(8)) Harcourt Schl. Pubs.

—People in Time, Unit 6. 3rd ed. 2003. (Harcourt Brace Social Studies). pap. 76.00 (978-0-15-341071-0(X)) Harcourt Schl. Pubs.

—School Days, Unit 1. 3rd ed. 2003. (Harcourt Brace Social Studies). (gr. 1). pap. 76.00 (978-0-15-341058-1(2)) Harcourt Schl. Pubs.

—Social Studies: States & Regions: Library Book Collection. 2003. (Harcourt Brace Social Studies). (Illus.). (gr. k-7). 76.00 (978-0-15-308392-1(1)) Harcourt Schl. Pubs.

—Social Studies Library. 2003. (Harcourt Brace Estudios Sociales Ser.). (SPA., Illus.). (gr. k-18). 37.60 (978-0-15-310599-9(2)) Harcourt Schl. Pubs.

—TIME for Kids. 3rd ed. 2003. (Horizontes (Social Studies) Ser.). Bk. 1. (SPA.). (gr. 3). pap. 7.00 (978-0-15-333782-6(6))Bk. 2. (SPA.). pap. 7.00 (978-0-15-333784-0(2))Bk. 3. (SPA.). pap. 7.00 (978-0-15-333786-4(9))Bk. 4. (SPA.). pap. 7.00 (978-0-15-333788-8(5))Bk. 5. (SPA.). pap. 7.00 (978-0-15-333790-1(7))Bk. 6. (SPA.). pap. 7.00 (978-0-15-333792-5(3))Bk. 7. pap. 7.00

(978-0-15-333794-9(X))Bk. 8. (SPA.). pap. 7.00
(978-0-15-333796-3(6))Bk. 9. (SPA.). pap. 7.00
(978-0-15-333798-7(2))Bk. 13. (SPA.). pap. 7.00
(978-0-15-333806-9(7))Bk. 14. (SPA.). pap. 7.00
(978-0-15-333808-3(3))Bk. 15. (SPA.). pap. 7.00
(978-0-15-333810-6(5))Bk. 16. (SPA.). pap. 7.00
(978-0-15-333812-0(1))Bk. 17. (SPA.). pap. 7.00
(978-0-15-333814-4(8))Bk. 18. (SPA.). pap. 7.00
(978-0-15-333816-8(4)) Harcourt Schl. Pubs.

—TIME for Kids: World Regions. 3rd ed. 2003. (Horizontes (Social Studies) Ser.). (SPA., Illus.). Bk. 1. pap. 9.30
(978-0-15-333942-4(X))Bk. 3. pap. 9.30
(978-0-15-333946-2(2))Bk. 4. pap. 9.30
(978-0-15-333948-6(9))Bk. 5. pap. 9.30
(978-0-15-333950-9(0))Bk. 6. pap. 9.30
(978-0-15-333952-3(7))Bk. 7. pap. 9.30
(978-0-15-333954-7(3))Bk. 8. pap. 9.30
(978-0-15-333956-1(X))Bk. 9. pap. 9.30
(978-0-15-333958-5(6))Bk. 10. pap. 9.30
(978-0-15-333960-8(8))Bk. 11. pap. 9.30
(978-0-15-333962-2(4))Bk. 12. pap. 9.30
(978-0-15-333964-6(0))Bk. 13. pap. 9.30
(978-0-15-333966-0(7))Bk. 14. pap. 9.30
(978-0-15-333968-4(3))Bk. 16. pap. 9.30
(978-0-15-333972-1(1))Bk. 17. pap. 9.30
(978-0-15-333974-5(8))Bk. 18. pap. 9.30
(978-0-15-333976-9(4))Bk. 19. pap. 9.30
(978-0-15-333978-3(0))Bk. 20. pap. 9.30
(978-0-15-333980-6(2))Bk. 21. pap. 9.30
(978-0-15-333982-0(9))Bk.15. pap. 9.30
(978-0-15-333970-7(5)) Harcourt Schl. Pubs.

—TIME for Kids Bk. 11: World Region, 5 Packs. 3rd ed. 2003. (Horizontes (Social Studies) Ser.). (SPA.). (gr. 3-18). pap. 46.20 (978-0-15-333963-9(2)) Harcourt Schl. Pubs.

—TIME for Kids 5 Pack. 3rd ed. 2003. (Horizontes (Social Studies) Ser.). (SPA.). (gr. 3-18). Bk. 2. pap. 34.90 (978-0-15-333785-7(0))Bk. 3. pap. 34.90 (978-0-15-333787-1(7)) Harcourt Schl. Pubs.

—Timeless Treasure. 3rd ed. 2003. (Harcourt School Publishers Trophies Ser.). (ENG., Illus.). 752p. (gr. 6-6). pupil's gde. ed. 87.50 (978-0-15-322480-5(0)) Harcourt Schl. Pubs.

—United States History Beginnings, Vol. 1. 3rd ed. 2003. (Harcourt Horizons Ser.). (ENG.). 756p. (gr. 4-5). tchr. ed., spiral bd. 191.95 (978-0-15-339634-2(2)) Harcourt Schl. Pubs.

—United States History Civil War to Present. 3rd ed. 2003. (Harcourt Horizons Ser.). (ENG.). 576p. (gr. 5-6). tchr. ed., spiral bd. 192.00 (978-0-15-339637-3(7)) Harcourt Schl. Pubs.

—US History: The Civil War to the Present, Vol. 1. 3rd ed. 2003. (Harcourt Horizons Ser.). (ENG.). 696p. (gr. 5-6). tchr. ed., spiral bd. 192.00 (978-0-15-339636-6(9)) Harcourt Schl. Pubs.

—US History, Grade 5 Vol. 2: Beginnings. 3rd ed. 2003. (Harcourt Horizons Ser.). (ENG.). 648p. (gr. 4-5). tchr. ed., spiral bd. 191.95 (978-0-15-339635-9(0)) Harcourt Schl. Pubs.

—We Belong in Groups, Unit 1. 3rd ed. 2003. (Harcourt Brace Social Studies). (gr. 2). pap. 76.00 (978-0-15-341066-6(3)) Harcourt Schl. Pubs.

—We Work Together, Unit 3. 3rd ed. 2003. (Harcourt Brace Social Studies). pap. 76.00 (978-0-15-341068-0(X)) Harcourt Schl. Pubs.

—World History: States & Regions. 3rd ed. 2003. (Harcourt Horizons Ser.). (ENG.). (gr. 3-4). 600p. tchr. ed., spiral bd. 153.45 (978-0-15-339630-4(X)); (Illus.). 584p. 79.75 (978-0-15-339618-2(0)) Harcourt Schl. Pubs.

—World History, Grade 4 Vol. 2: States & Regions. 3rd ed. 2003. (Harcourt Horizons Ser.). (ENG.). 588p. (gr. 3-4). tchr. ed., spiral bd. 153.45 (978-0-15-339631-1(8)) Harcourt Schl. Pubs.

Health Social Studies. Incl. The World Past to Present. pap., tchr. ed. 61.59: The World Past to Present. pap., tchr. ed. The World Past to Present. suppl. ed. (978-0-669-11425-6(1)); The World Past to Present. pap., wbk. ed. (978-0-669-11405-8(7)); The World Past to Present. tchr. ed., wbk. ed. (978-0-669-11410-2(3)); The World Past to Present. suppl. ed. (978-0-669-11431-7(6)); The World Past to Present. suppl. ed. (978-0-669-11727-1(7)); The World Past to Present. suppl. ed. 11.28 (J). (gr. 6-7). (978-0-669-11391-4(3)) Houghton Mifflin Harcourt School Pubs.

Helgren. People, Places & Changes: Online Edition Plus. 3rd ed. 2003. 17.26 (978-0-03-037418-0(9)) Holt McDougal.

Helgren, David M. People, Places & Change: Enhanced Online Edition. 3rd ed. 2003. 70.53 (978-0-03-072533-3(X)) Holt McDougal.

Hinds, Kathryn. The Palace. 2008. (Life in the Medieval Muslim World Ser.). 96p. (gr. 6-18). lib. bdg. 34.21 (978-0-7614-3086-9(1), Benchmark Bks.) Marshall Cavendish Corp.

Hinton, Kerry. 10 Great Makerspace Projects Using Social Studies. 2017. (Using Makerspaces for School Projects Ser.). 64p. (gr. 11-11). 34.45 **(978-1-4994-3850-5(8)**, Rosen Central) Rosen Publishing Group, Inc., The.

Hirsch, E. D., Jr., ed. History & Geography: Level 4. 2003. stu. ed. 44.50 (978-0-7690-5025-6(5)) Pearson Learning.

—History & Geography: Level 5. 2003. stu. ed. 49.95 (978-0-7690-5026-3(3)) Pearson Learning.

The History of the Humanities & Social Sciences. 2016. (History of the Humanities & Social Sciences Ser.). 208p. (gr. 7-7). 138.30 (978-1-5081-7166-9(1), Rosen Young Adult) Rosen Publishing Group, Inc., The.

Holba, Annette. Handbook for the Humanities Doctoral Student. 2005. 113p. pap. 19.95 (978-1-4137-9929-3(9)) PublishAmerica, Inc.

Holidays & Celebrations Set. (gr. k-2). 346.95 (978-0-7368-9406-7(3)) Red Brick Learning.

Holt, Rinehart and Winston Staff. People, Places & Change: Texas Online Edition. 2003. cd-rom 71.00 (978-0-03-073348-2(0)) Holt McDougal.

Holzschuher, Cythnia. Our Country Thematic Unit. 2005. (Emergent/Early (Prek-2) Social Studies Package Ser.). 12p. (gr. -1-1). 25.20 (978-0-8215-7832-2(4)) Sadlier, William H. Inc.

El Honesto Abe: Libros Aventuras (Adventure Books) 2003. (MacMillan/McGraw-Hill. Estudios Sociales Ser.). (ENG & SPA.). (gr. 1-18). (978-0-02-150111-3(4)) Macmillan/McGraw-Hill Schl. Div.

Hotchkins, Dewayne. Our Man-Made Resources. 2016. (Rosen REAL Readers: Social Studies Nonfiction / Fiction: Family, Community, & the World Ser.). 12p. (gr. 1-k). pap. 6.33 (978-1-5081-2347-7(0), Rosen Classroom) Rosen Publishing Group, Inc., The.

Hunter, Dru. Why Do We Behave Like That? 2015. 48p. (J). (978-1-60818-597-9(4), Creative Education) Creative Co., The.

—Why Do We Behave Like That? Think Like a Scientist. 2016. (Think Like a Scientist Ser.). (ENG.). 48p. (J). (gr. 5-9). pap. 12.00 (978-1-62832-202-6(0), Creative Paperbacks) Creative Co., The.

Hutton, Stacie. Jr. Social Studies Investigator. 2005. (J). pap. 14.95 (978-1-931334-64-8(1)) Pieces of Learning.

Ignite! Learning, compiled by. Social Studies COW Subscription. 2005. (J). (978-0-9791935-1-4(6)) Ignite! Learning.

—Social Studies Texas COW Subscription. 2005. (J). (978-0-9791935-2-1(4)) Ignite! Learning.

—SuperCOW - Science & Social Studies Subscription: Science & Social Studies US. 2005. (J). (978-0-9791935-3-8(2)) Ignite! Learning.

—SuperCOW - Science & Social Studies TX Subscription: Science & Social Studies TX. 2005. (J). (978-0-9791935-4-5(0)) Ignite! Learning.

La influencia espanola en Texas: Libros Aventuras (Adventure Books) 2003. (MacMillan/McGraw-Hill. Estudios Sociales Ser.). (ENG & SPA.). (gr. 4-18). (978-0-02-150116-8(5)) Macmillan/McGraw-Hill Schl. Div.

International Day 6 Packs. Individual Title. (gr. -1-2). 23.00 (978-0-7635-8801-4(6)) Rigby Education.

International Encyclopedia of Social Sciences, 9 vols., Set. 2nd rev. ed. 2007. (ENG., Illus.). 5602p. (C). 1652.00 (978-0-02-865965-7(1)) Cengage Gale.

Iopeners: Big Book Collection, 20 vols. 2005. (J). (gr. k-18). 525.95 (978-0-7652-4972-2(3)); (gr. 1-18). 587.50 (978-0-7652-4976-0(6)) Modern Curriculum Pr.

Iopeners: Classroom Library. 2005. (J). (gr. k-18). 440.50 (978-0-7652-4969-2(3)); (gr. 1-18). 518.50 (978-0-7652-4973-9(1)); (gr. 2-18). 518.50 (978-0-7652-4977-7(4)); (gr. 3-18). 616.50 (978-0-7652-4980-7(4)); (gr. 4-18). 616.50 (978-0-7652-4983-8(9)); (gr. 5-18). 694.50 (978-0-7652-4986-9(3)); (gr. 6-18). 694.50 (978-0-7652-4989-0(8)) Modern Curriculum Pr.

Iopeners: Social Studies Library, 10 vols. 2005. (J). (gr. k-18). 220.95 (978-0-7652-4971-5(5)) Modern Curriculum Pr.

Jackson, Abby. Homes, 6 vols., Set. 2003. (Yellow Umbrella Early Level Ser.). (ENG.). 16p. (gr. k-1). pap. 35.70 (978-0-7368-3004-1(9), Yellow Umbrella Bks.) Capstone Press of Coughlan Cos.

—Making Money, 6 vols., Set. 2003. (Yellow Umbrella Early Level Ser.). (ENG.). 16p. (gr. k-1). pap. 35.70 (978-0-7368-3005-8(7), Yellow Umbrella Bks.) Capstone Press of Coughlan Cos.

James, Eric. Up & Down. 2012. (InfoMax Readers Ser.). (ENG., Illus.). 16 pp.p. (J). (gr. k-1). pap. 7.00 (978-1-4488-8878-8(6), Rosen Classroom) Rosen Publishing Group, Inc., The.

James, Wayan. Grandma Tells a Story. 2016. (Rosen REAL Readers: Social Studies Nonfiction / Fiction: Family, Community, & the World Ser.). 8p. (gr. 1-k). pap. 5.46 (978-1-5081-2491-7(4), Rosen Classroom) Rosen Publishing Group, Inc., The.

Jarrett, Mark. Mastering New York's Elementary Social Studies Standards: Grade 5. 2007. (J). (gr. 5). pap. 11.95 (978-0-9795493-3-5(7)) Jarrett Publishing Co.

The Journey West. 2004. (Thrilling Tales in Time Ser.: 5). (J). 19.95 (978-1-58123-373-5(6)) Larson Learning, Inc.

Kachur, Matthew. Our Current World: Set Of 6. 2011. (Navigators Ser.). (J). pap. 44.00 net. (978-1-4108-0415-0(1)) Benchmark Education Co.

Kohart, Georgia. A Heritage of the Heart Teaching Companion. 2003. (Illus.). ring bd. 24.95 (978-0-9706348-1-8(1)) Heritage Heart Farm.

Kramer, Candice. Ben Franklin's Visit: A When Machine Play. 2004. (Reader's Theater Ser.). (J). pap. (978-1-4108-0799-1(1)) Benchmark Education Co.

—Cesar Chavez Comes to Visit. 2004. (Reader's Theater Ser.). (J). pap. (978-1-4108-0795-3(9)) Benchmark Education Co.

Language Arts Explorer, 26 vols., Set. Incl. Save the Planet: Compost It. Barker, David. 32p. 2010. lib. bdg. 28.50 (978-1-60279-656-0(4), 200349); Save the Planet: Growing Your Own Garden. Hirsch, Rebecca. 32p. 2010. lib. bdg. 28.50 (978-1-60279-657-7(2), 200350); Save the Planet: Helping Endangered Animals. Hirsch, Rebecca. 32p. 2010. lib. bdg. 28.50 (978-1-60279-658-4(0), 200351); Save the Planet: Keeping Water Clean. Farrell, Courtney. 32p. 2010. lib. bdg. 28.50 (978-1-60279-659-1(9), 200352); Save the Planet: Local Farms & Sustainable Foods. Vogel, Julia. 32p. 2010. lib. bdg. 28.50 (978-1-60279-660-7(2), 200353); Save the Planet: Protecting Our Natural Resources. Hirsch, Rebecca. 32p. 2010. lib. bdg. 28.50 (978-1-60279-661-4(0), 200354); Save the Planet: Reduce, Reuse, & Recycle. Minden, Cecilia. 32p. 2010. lib. bdg. 28.50 (978-1-60279-662-1(9), 200355); Save the Planet: Using Alternative Energies. Farrell, Courtney. 32p. 2010. lib. bdg. 28.50 (978-1-60279-663-8(7), 200356); Set. Language Arts Explorer: History Digs. Cherry Lake Publishing Staff. (J). 2011. lib. bdg. 285.00 (978-1-61080-243-7(8)); Set. Language Arts Explorer: Science Lab. Cherry Lake Publishing Staff. (J). 2011. lib. bdg. 228.00 (978-1-61080-245-1(4)); (gr. 4-8). 2011. Set lib. bdg. 741.00 (978-1-61080-239-0(X)) Cherry Lake Publishing.

Language Arts Explorer: History Digs, 10 vols., Set. Incl. America's Colonization & Settlement. Lusted, Marcia Amidon. lib. bdg. 28.50 (978-1-61080-194-2(6), 201164); Birth of the United States. Brennan, Linda Crotta. lib. bdg. 28.50 (978-1-61080-197-3(0), 201170); Contemporary United States. Cunningham, Kevin. (Illus.). lib. bdg. 28.50 (978-1-61080-195-9(4), 201166); Development of U.S. Industry. Meinking, Mary. lib. bdg. 28.50 (978-1-61080-198-0(9), 201172); Great Depression & World War II. Peterson, Sheryl. lib. bdg. 28.50 (978-1-61080-199-7(7), 201174); Postwar United States. Combs, Maggie. lib. bdg. 28.50 (978-1-61080-196-6(2), 201168); Three Worlds Meet. Cosson, M. J. lib. bdg. 28.50 (978-1-61080-193-5(8), 201162); U. S. Growth & Change in the 19th Century, 1801 to 1861. Howell, Brian. lib. bdg. 28.50 (978-1-61080-202-4(0), 201180); United States Enters the 20th Century. Herringshaw, DeAnn. lib. bdg. 28.50 (978-1-61080-200-0(4), 201176); US Civil War & Reconstruction. Howell, Brian. lib. bdg. 28.50 (978-1-61080-201-7(2), 201178); 32p. (gr. 4-8). 2011. Set lib. bdg. 285.00 (978-1-61080-243-7(8)) Cherry Lake Publishing.

Lankford, Ronnie D. Green Cities. 2011. (At Issue Ser.). (ENG.). 128p. (gr. 12-12). pap. 27.80 (978-0-7377-5152-9(5)); lib. bdg. 39.40 (978-0-7377-5151-2(7)) Cengage Gale. (Greenhaven Pr., Inc.).

Lansford, Tom. Dictatorships. Greenhaven Press Staff, ed. 2013. (Opposing Viewpoints Ser.). (ENG., Illus.). 224p. (gr. 10-12). pap. 33.80 (978-0-7377-6315-7(9)); lib. bdg. 48.80 (978-0-7377-6314-0(0)) Cengage Gale. (Greenhaven Pr., Inc.).

Lee, April. How We Get Around Town. 2012. (InfoMax Readers Ser.). (ENG., Illus.). 16 pp.p. (J). (gr. k-1). pap. 7.00 (978-1-4488-8941-9(3), Rosen Classroom) Rosen Publishing Group, Inc., The.

Let's See Library_Farms Complete Set. (Let's See Library-Farms Ser.). (gr. 1-3). 119.58 (978-0-7565-0729-9(4)) Compass Point Bks.

Lewis, Kelly. Making Choices. 2016. (Spring Forward Ser.). (J). (gr. 2). (978-1-4900-9440-3(7)) Benchmark Education Co.

Libertad: Libros Aventuras (Adventure Books) 2003. (MacMillan/McGraw-Hill. Estudios Sociales Ser.). (ENG & SPA.). (gr. 4-18). (978-0-02-150119-9(X)) Macmillan/McGraw-Hill Schl. Div.

Libro del Estudiante: Gente y Lugares. 2003. (MacMillan/McGraw-Hill. Estudios Sociales Ser.). (ENG & SPA.). (gr. 1-18). (978-0-02-149960-1(8)) Macmillan/McGraw-Hill Schl. Div.

Libro del Estudiante: Nuestra Nacion. 2003. (MacMillan/McGraw-Hill. Estudios Sociales Ser.). (ENG & SPA.). (gr. 5-18). (978-0-02-149964-9(0)) Macmillan/McGraw-Hill Schl. Div.

Libro del Estudiante: Nuestras Comunidades. 2003. (MacMillan/McGraw-Hill. Estudios Sociales Ser.). (ENG & SPA.). (gr. 3-18). (978-0-02-149962-5(4)) Macmillan/McGraw-Hill Schl. Div.

Libro del Estudiante: Regiones de Nuestro Pais. 2003. (MacMillan/McGraw-Hill. Estudios Sociales Ser.). (ENG & SPA.). (gr. 4-18). (978-0-02-149963-2(2)) Macmillan/McGraw-Hill Schl. Div.

Libro del Estudiante: Vivimos Juntos. 2003. (MacMillan/McGraw-Hill. Estudios Sociales Ser.). (ENG & SPA.). (gr. 2-18). (978-0-02-149961-8(6)) Macmillan/McGraw-Hill Schl. Div.

Libros Aventuras Classroom Set: Libros Aventuras (Adventure Books) 2003. (MacMillan/McGraw-Hill. Estudios Sociales Ser.). (ENG & SPA.). (gr. 1-18). (978-0-02-150096-3(7)); (gr. 3-18). (978-0-02-150098-7(3)); (gr. 4-18). (978-0-02-150059-8(2)); (gr. 5-18). (978-0-02-150100-7(9)) Macmillan/McGraw-Hill Schl. Div.

Libros Aventuras Deluxe Classroom Set: Libros Aventuras (Adventure Books) 2003. (MacMillan/McGraw-Hill. Estudios Sociales Ser.). (ENG & SPA.). (gr. 1-18). (978-0-02-150101-4(7)); (gr. 3-18). (978-0-02-150103-8(3)); (gr. 4-18). (978-0-02-150060-4(6)); (gr. 5-18). (978-0-02-150105-2(X)) Macmillan/McGraw-Hill Schl. Div.

Lindeen, Mary. How Things Change, 6 vols., Set. 2004. (Letter Bks.). (ENG.). 8p. (gr. k-1). pap. 29.70 (978-0-7368-4114-6(8), Letter Bks.) Capstone Press of Coughlan Cos.

—Wonder Readers: Social Studies. (Wonder Readers: Social Studies). (ENG.). 20p. (gr. k-1). 2012. lib. bdg. 90.60 (978-1-4296-9622-7(2)) 2012. lib. bdg. 181.20 (978-1-4296-9623-4(0)) 2011. lib. bdg. 90.60 (978-1-4296-8643-3(X)) Capstone Press of Coughlan Cos. (Wonder Readers).

Longhi, Sarah & Van Zile, Susan. Social Studies Graphic Organizers & Mini-Lessons. 2006. (Best Practices in Action Ser.). (ENG., Illus.). 48p. per. 10.99 (978-0-439-54894-6(2), Teaching Resources) Scholastic, Inc.

Lunt, Nigel. Working Together Social Studies for Grade 8. 2014. (ENG.). 88p. spiral bd., instr.'s training gde. ed. 33.00 (978-0-7487-9975-6(3)) Oxford Univ. Pr., Inc.

Macmillan/Mcgraw. Alternative Learning Strategies: Staff Development Videotapes. (Staff Development Ser.). (gr. k-8). (978-0-02-176701-2(8)) Macmillan/McGraw-Hill Schl. Div.

—Cooperative Learning: Staff Development Videotapes. (Staff Development Ser.). (gr. k-8). (978-0-02-178702-9(6)) Macmillan/McGraw-Hill Schl. Div.

Making Headlines. 2016. (Making Headlines Ser.). 160p. (J). lib. bdg. 239.58 (978-0-7660-8399-8(3)) Enslow Pubs., Inc.

Making Patterns: Level C. 8p. 20.95 (978-0-322-00361-3(X)) Wright Group/McGraw-Hill.

Martin, Elena. Working Together, 6 vols., Set. 2003. (Yellow Umbrella Early Level Ser.). (ENG.). 16p. (gr. k-1). pap. 35.70 (978-0-7368-2987-8(3), Yellow Umbrella Bks.) Capstone Press of Coughlan Cos.

McCune, Susan. Our School Nurse, 01 vols., 1. 2016. (Rosen REAL Readers: Social Studies Nonfiction / Fiction: Family, Community, & the World Ser.). (ENG.). 8p. (J). pap. 5.46 (978-1-5081-1683-7(0), Rosen Classroom) Rosen Publishing Group, Inc., The.

—Tanika Walks Her Dog Every Day, 01 vols., 1. 2016. (Rosen REAL Readers: Social Studies Nonfiction / Fiction: Family, Community, & the World Ser.). (ENG.). 8p. (J). pap. 5.46 (978-1-5081-1668-4(7), Rosen Classroom) Rosen Publishing Group, Inc., The.

McDowell, Frank. Critical World Issues: Equal Opportunities, Vol. 16. 2016. (Critical World Issues Ser.: Vol. 16). (ENG., Illus.). 112p. (J). (gr. 7-12). 25.95 (978-1-4222-3652-9(8)) Mason Crest.

McGraw-Hill Education Editors. The World & Its People: Eastern Hemisphere. 2004. (WORLD & ITS PEOPLE EASTERN Ser.). (ENG.). (gr. 6-9). stu. ed., wbk. ed. 12.80 (978-0-07-868055-7(7), 0078680557) McGraw-Hill Education.

—The World & Its People: Western Hemisphere, Europe & Russia. 2004. (WORLD & ITS PEOPLE WESTERN Ser.). (ENG., Illus.). (gr. 6-9). 256p. stu. ed., per. 12.80 (978-0-07-868033-5(6), 0078680336); 34p. pap., stu. ed., wbk. ed. 7.40 (978-0-07-868026-7(3), 0078680263) McGraw-Hill Education.

—The World & Its People, Western Hemisphere, Europe, & Russia, StudentWorks Plus CD-ROM. 2005. (WORLD & ITS PEOPLE WESTERN Ser.). (ENG.). (gr. 6-9). 125.32 (978-0-07-866322-2(9), 0078663229) McGraw-Hill Education.

McGraw-Hill Education Staff. The World & Its People. 2004. (GEOGRAPHY: WORLD & ITS PEOPLE Ser.). (ENG., Illus.). 346p. (gr. 6-9). per., wbk. ed., pupil's gde. ed. 12.80 (978-0-07-865513-5(7), 0078655137) McGraw-Hill Education.

—The World & Its People: Western Hemisphere, Europe & Russia: Spanish Reading Essentials. 2004. (WORLD & ITS PEOPLE WESTERN Ser.). (SPA., Illus.). 216p. (gr. 6-9). stu. ed., per., wbk. ed. 12.80 (978-0-07-868050-2(6), 0078680506) McGraw-Hill Education.

—The World & Its People, Reading Essentials & Study Guide Student Workbook: Western Hemisphere, Europe & Russia. 2004. (WORLD & ITS PEOPLE WESTERN Ser.). (ENG., Illus.). 209p. (gr. 6-9). stu. ed., per., wbk. ed. 12.80 (978-0-07-868030-4(1), 0078680301) McGraw-Hill Education.

—The World & Its People, StudentWorks Plus CD-ROM. 2005. (GEOGRAPHY: WORLD & ITS PEOPLE Ser.). (ENG.). (gr. 6-9). 153.64 (978-0-07-866345-1(8), 0078663458) McGraw-Hill Education.

McGraw-Hill-Glencoe Staff, creator. The World & Its People: Spanish Reading Essentials & Study Guide: Student Workbook. 2004. (GEOGRAPHY: WORLD & ITS PEOPLE Ser.). (SPA., Illus.). 346p. (gr. 6-9). stu. ed., per., wbk. ed. 12.80 (978-0-07-865518-0(8), 0078655188) McGraw-Hill Education.

McGraw-Hill Staff. Journey Across Time: Early Ages. 2004. (MS World History Ser.). (ENG.). (gr. 6-9). pap., stu. ed., wbk. ed. 14.00 (978-0-07-868197-4(9), 0078681979) McGraw-Hill Education.

McGraw-Hill Staff, creator. The World & Its People - Eastern Hemisphere. 2004. (WORLD & ITS PEOPLE EASTERN Ser.). (ENG., Illus.). 46p. (gr. 6-9). pap., wbk. ed. 7.40 (978-0-07-868120-2(0), 0078681200) McGraw-Hill Education.

Measure It: Big Book: Level D. 8p. 20.95 (978-0-322-00362-0(8)) Wright Group/McGraw-Hill.

El mejor Precio: Libros Aventuras (Adventure Books) 2003. (MacMillan/McGraw-Hill. Estudios Sociales Ser.). (ENG & SPA.). (gr. 3-18). (978-0-02-150113-7(0)) Macmillan/McGraw-Hill Schl. Div.

Meredith, Susan Markowitz. Connecting the World. 2016. (Spring Forward Ser.). (J). (gr. 2). (978-1-4900-9476-2(8)) Benchmark Education Co.

Merino, Noël. The European Union. 2008. (Opposing Viewpoints Ser.). (ENG., Illus.). (gr. 10-12). 224p. lib. bdg. 48.80 (978-0-7377-3998-5(3), LML02109-239954); 197p. (YA). 29.45 (978-0-7377-3999-2(1), LML02109-239962) Cengage Gale. (Greenhaven Pr., Inc.).

—Privacy. Greenhaven Press Editors, ed. 2014. (Global Viewpoints Ser.). (ENG., Illus.). 224p. (gr. 10-12). lib. bdg. 46.20 (978-0-7377-6912-8(2), Greenhaven Pr., Inc.) Cengage Gale.

Meyers Schlaglichter des 20 Jahrhunderts. (978-3-411-07411-2(6)) Bibliographisches Institut & F. A. Brockhaus AG DEU. Dist: i. b. d., Ltd.

Meyers Taschenlexikon in einem Band. (978-3-411-10134-4(2)) Bibliographisches Institut & F. A. Brockhaus AG DEU. Dist: i. b. d., Ltd.

Micklos, John, Jr. What Went Wrong? 2015. (What Went Wrong? Ser.). (ENG.). 32p. (gr. 3-4). lib. bdg. 54.64 (978-1-4914-2482-7(6), Fact Finders) Capstone Press of Coughlan Cos.

Milenio 1: Serie de Estudies Sociales para la Escuela Elemental. (SPA.). 25.00 (978-958-04-5593-6(7)) Norma S.A. COL. Dist: Distribuidora Norma, Inc.

Milenio 2: Serie de Estudies Sociales para la Escuela Elemental. (SPA.). 25.00 (978-958-04-5594-3(5)) Norma S.A. COL. Dist: Distribuidora Norma, Inc.

Milenio 3: Serie de Estudies Sociales para la Escuela Elemental. (SPA.). 30.00 (978-958-04-5595-0(3)) Norma S.A. COL. Dist: Distribuidora Norma, Inc.

Milenio 4: Serie de Estudies Sociales para la Escuela Elemental. (SPA.). 40.00 (978-958-04-5596-7(1)) Norma S.A. COL. Dist: Distribuidora Norma, Inc.

Milenio 5: Serie de Estudies Sociales para la Escuela Elemental. (SPA.). 45.00 (978-958-04-5597-4(X)) Norma S.A. COL. Dist: Distribuidora Norma, Inc.

Milenio 6: Serie de Estudies Sociales para la Escuela Elemental. (SPA.). 45.00 (978-958-04-5598-1(8)) Norma S.A. COL. Dist: Distribuidora Norma, Inc.

Milenio K: Serie de Estudies Sociales para la Escuela Elemental. (SPA.). 25.00 (978-958-04-5592-9(9)) Norma S.A. COL. Dist: Distribuidora Norma, Inc.

Miles, Liz. Timeline History, 1 vol., Set. Incl. Sports: From Ancient Olympics to the Super Bowl. (ENG.). 32p. (gr. 3-5). 2010. pap. 8.95 (978-1-4329-3813-0(4), NA-h); (Timeline History Ser.). (ENG.). 32p. 2010. Set pap. 16.94 o.p. (978-1-4329-3817-8(7), NA-h) Heinemann-Raintree.

Miller, Debra A. Civil Liberties. 2009. (Hot Topics Ser.). (ENG., Illus.). 128p. (gr. 7-10). 39.40 (978-1-4205-0080-6(5), Lucent Bks.) Cengage Gale.

—Social Security. Greenhaven Press Editors, ed. 2013. (Current Controversies Ser.). (ENG., Illus.). 224p. (gr. 10-12). pap. 32.00 (978-0-7377-6246-4(2)); lib. bdg. 46.40 (978-0-7377-6245-7(4)) Cengage Gale. (Greenhaven Pr., Inc.).

Mills, Nathan. Living or Nonliving? 2012. (Rosen Readers Ser.). (ENG., Illus.). 16p. (J). (gr. k-1). pap. 7.00 (978-1-4488-8746-0(1), Rosen Classroom) Rosen Publishing Group, Inc., The.

Mills, Nathan & Allyn, Daisy. Around My Neighborhood. 2012. (Rosen Readers Ser.). (ENG., Illus.). 16p. (J). (gr. k-1). pap.

S

7.00 *(978-1-4488-8646-3(5)*, Rosen Classroom) Rosen Publishing Group, Inc., The.

Mills, Nathan & Baker, Rick. More or Less? 2012. (Rosen Readers Ser.). (ENG., Illus.). 16p. (J). (gr. k-1). pap. 7.00 *(978-1-4488-8649-4(X)*, Rosen Classroom) Rosen Publishing Group, Inc., The.

Mills, Nathan & Biehn, Mike. Things I Need, Things I Want. 2012. (Rosen Readers Ser.). (ENG., Illus.). 16p. (J). (gr. k-1). pap. 7.00 *(978-1-4488-8728-6(3)*, Rosen Classroom) Rosen Publishing Group, Inc., The.

Mills, Nathan & Christopher, Nick. Time for a Field Trip. 2012. (Rosen Readers Ser.). (ENG., Illus.). 16p. (J). (gr. k-1). pap. 7.00 *(978-1-4488-8752-1(6)*, Rosen Classroom) Rosen Publishing Group, Inc., The.

Mills, Nathan & Davidson, Amy. My Busy Week. 2012. (Rosen Readers Ser.). (ENG., Illus.). 16p. (J). (gr. k-1). pap. 7.00 *(978-1-4488-8689-0(9)*, Rosen Classroom) Rosen Publishing Group, Inc., The.

Mills, Nathan & Ericson, Emma. Up or Down? 2012. (Rosen Readers Ser.). (ENG., Illus.). 16p. (J). (gr. k-1). pap. 7.00 *(978-1-4488-8643-2(0)*, Rosen Classroom) Rosen Publishing Group, Inc., The.

Mills, Nathan & Fudoli, Melissa. I Have One More. 2012. (Rosen Readers Ser.). (ENG., Illus.). 16p. (J). (gr. k-1). pap. 7.00 *(978-1-4488-8655-5(4)*, Rosen Classroom) Rosen Publishing Group, Inc., The.

Mills, Nathan & Goodwin, Josh. How Do I Get There? 2012. (Rosen Readers Ser.). (ENG., Illus.). 24p. (J). (gr. 1-2). pap. 8.25 *(978-1-4488-8779-8(8)*, Rosen Classroom) Rosen Publishing Group, Inc., The.

Mills, Nathan & Miller, Andy. Is It Cloth, Clay, or Paper? 2012. (Rosen Readers Ser.). (ENG., Illus.). 16p. (J). (gr. k-1). pap. 7.00 *(978-1-4488-8707-1(0)*, Rosen Classroom) Rosen Publishing Group, Inc., The.

Mills, Nathan & White, Ella. Months of the Year. 2012. (Rosen Readers Ser.). (ENG., Illus.). 24p. (J). (gr. 1-2). pap. 8.25 *(978-1-4488-8785-9(2)*, Rosen Classroom) Rosen Publishing Group, Inc., The.

Mix It Up: Big Book: Level E. 8p. 20.95 *(978-0-322-00363-7(6))* Wright Group/McGraw-Hill.

MoCasins: Level A, 6 vols. 8p. 24.95 *(978-0-7802-9109-6(3))* Wright Group/McGraw-Hill.

Monsters in Myth, 8 vols., Set. Incl. Cerberus. Tracy, Kathleen. lib. bdg. 29.95 *(978-1-58415-924-7(3))*; Chimaera. LaRoche, Amy. lib. bdg. 29.95 *(978-1-58415-925-4(1))*; Cyclopes. Roberts, Russell. lib. bdg. 29.95 *(978-1-58415-926-1(X))*; Medusa. Tracy, Kathleen. lib. bdg. 29.95 *(978-1-58415-928-5(6))*; Minotaur. Roberts, Russell. lib. bdg. 29.95 *(978-1-58415-929-2(4))*; Monsters of Hercules. Orr, Tamra. lib. bdg. 29.95 *(978-1-58415-927-8(8))*; Sirens. Orr, Tamra. lib. bdg. 29.95 *(978-1-58415-930-8(8))*; Sphinx. DiPrimio, Pete. lib. bdg. 29.95 *(978-1-58415-931-5(6))*; (Illus.). 48p. (J). (gr. 4-7). 2010. 239.60 *(978-1-58415-932-2(4))* Mitchell Lane Pubs., Inc.

Moore, Elizabeth & Gregory, Helen. Where Do People Work? 2011. (Wonder Readers Emergent Level Ser.). (ENG.). 16p. (gr. -1-1). pap. 35.94 *(978-1-4296-8206-0(X)*, Wonder Readers) Capstone Press of Coughlan Cos.

Moran, Margaret. Cowhands & Cattle Trails: Set Of 6. 2011. (Navigators Ser.). (J). pap. 48.00 net. *(978-1-4108-0426-6(7))* Benchmark Education Co.

Museums: Collections to Share, 6 vols. (Book2WebTM Ser.). (gr. 4-8). 36.50 *(978-0-322-02986-6(4))* Wright Group/McGraw-Hill.

My Favorite Things. (Totally Girls Ser.). 16p. (J). *(978-2-7643-0189-0(8))* Phidal Publishing, Inc./Editions Phidal, Inc.

My World: E-Journals. (Technology: Social Studies). (SPA.). (gr. k-1). *(978-0-02-147228-4(9))* Macmillan/McGraw-Hill Schl. Div.

Mystery Hunters. 2016. (Mystery Hunters Ser.). 00048p. (J). lib. bdg. 191.70 ***(978-1-4824-5857-2(8))*** Stevens, Gareth Publishing LLLP.

Nations of the World Series, 4 vols., Set. 2003. pap. 137.12 *(978-0-7398-7002-0(5))* Steck-Vaughn.

Nelid, Piper. Bill Is My Forever Dad, 01 vols., 1. 2016. (Rosen REAL Readers: Social Studies Nonfiction / Fiction: Family, Community, & the World Ser.). (ENG.). 8p. (J). pap. 5.46 *(978-1-5081-1629-5(6)*, Rosen Classroom) Rosen Publishing Group, Inc., The.

—Our School Is New, 01 vols., 1. 2016. (Rosen REAL Readers: Social Studies Nonfiction / Fiction: Family, Community, & the World Ser.). (ENG.). 8p. (J). pap. 5.46 *(978-1-5081-1680-6(6)*, Rosen Classroom) Rosen Publishing Group, Inc., The.

—Our School Mission, 01 vols., 1. 2016. (Rosen REAL Readers: Social Studies Nonfiction / Fiction: Family, Community, & the World Ser.). (ENG.). 12p. (J). pap. 6.33 *(978-1-5081-1788-9(8)*, Rosen Classroom) Rosen Publishing Group, Inc., The.

—Saving for College, 01 vols., 1. 2016. (Rosen REAL Readers: Social Studies Nonfiction / Fiction: Family, Community, & the World Ser.). (ENG.). 12p. (J). pap. 6.33 *(978-1-5081-1770-4(5)*, Rosen Classroom) Rosen Publishing Group, Inc., The.

—We Respect Our Classmates, 01 vols., 1. 2016. (Rosen REAL Readers: Social Studies Nonfiction / Fiction: Family, Community, & the World Ser.). (ENG.). 12p. (J). pap. 6.33 *(978-1-5081-1824-4(8)*, Rosen Classroom) Rosen Publishing Group, Inc., The.

—Ximena Is from Colombia, 01 vols., 1. 2016. (Rosen REAL Readers: Social Studies Nonfiction / Fiction: Family, Community, & the World Ser.). (ENG.). 12p. (J). pap. 6.33 *(978-1-5081-1806-0(X)*, Rosen Classroom) Rosen Publishing Group, Inc., The.

Nelson, Maria. I Am a Good Neighbor. 2013. (Kids of Character Ser.). 24p. (J). (gr. 1-3). 22.60 *(978-1-4339-9021-2(0))*; pap. 48.90 *(978-1-4339-9023-6(7))*; (ENG., Illus.). pap. 8.15 *(978-1-4339-9022-9(9))* Stevens, Gareth Publishing LLLP.

The New World. 2004. (Thrilling Tales in Time Ser.: Vol. 2). (J). 19.95 *(978-1-58123-371-1(X))* Larson Learning, Inc.

Nuestra primera Bandera: Libros Aventuras (Adventure Books) 2003. (MacMillan/McGraw-Hill. Estudios Sociales Ser.). (ENG & SPA.). (gr. 1-18). *(978-0-02-150110-6(6))* Macmillan/McGraw-Hill Schl. Div.

La Oficina de Libertos: Libros Aventuras (Adventure Books) 2003. (MacMillan/McGraw-Hill. Estudios Sociales Ser.). (ENG & SPA.). (gr. 4-18). *(978-0-02-150117-5(3))* Macmillan/McGraw-Hill Schl. Div.

Ohio 8th Gr Social Studies. 2007. 52p. pap. 8.95 *(978-0-9769459-6-3(7))* Hollandays Publishing Corp.

O'Keefe, Cynthia A. Exploring the Real World: Middle School Edition. Date not set. 200p. (Orig.). (J). pap. 85.00 *(978-0-913956-89-2(9))* E B S C O Industries, Inc.

—Exploring the Real World: Primary School Edition. Date not set. 200p. (Orig.). (J). (gr. 4-6). pap. 65.00 *(978-0-913956-88-5(0))* E B S C O Industries, Inc.

—Exploring the Real World: Secondary Edition. Date not set. 366p. (Orig.). (YA). (gr. 7-12). pap. 283.00 *(978-0-913956-87-8(2))* E B S C O Industries, Inc.

O'Kelley, Jeff. Mapping the Way. 2006. (Early Explorers Ser.). (J). pap. *(978-1-4108-6106-1(6))* Benchmark Education Co.

Paderewski, Elliot. Global Citizens Protect the World Community. 2016. (Rosen REAL Readers: Social Studies Nonfiction / Fiction: Family, Community, & the World Ser.). 12p. (gr. 1-k). pap. 6.33 *(978-1-5081-2353-8(5)*, Rosen Classroom) Rosen Publishing Group, Inc., The.

Parnell, Declan. The Globe in Our Classroom, 01 vols., 1. 2016. (Rosen REAL Readers: Social Studies Nonfiction / Fiction: Family, Community, & the World Ser.). (ENG.). 8p. (J). pap. 5.46 *(978-1-5081-1635-6(0)*, Rosen Classroom) Rosen Publishing Group, Inc., The.

—My Aunt's Wedding, 01 vols., 1. 2016. (Rosen REAL Readers: Social Studies Nonfiction / Fiction: Family, Community, & the World Ser.). (ENG.). 12p. (J). pap. 6.33 *(978-1-5081-1758-2(6)*, Rosen Classroom) Rosen Publishing Group, Inc., The.

—Street Signs in My Neighborhood, 01 vols., 1. 2016. (Rosen REAL Readers: Social Studies Nonfiction / Fiction: Family, Community, & the World Ser.). (ENG.). 12p. (J). pap. 6.33 *(978-1-5081-1719-3(5)*, Rosen Classroom) Rosen Publishing Group, Inc., The.

—We Have Rules in School, 01 vols., 1. 2016. (Rosen REAL Readers: Social Studies Nonfiction / Fiction: Family, Community, & the World Ser.). (ENG.). 8p. (J). pap. 5.46 *(978-1-5081-1671-4(7)*, Rosen Classroom) Rosen Publishing Group, Inc., The.

Pebble Books: One World, Many Cultures. 2005. (YA). (gr. k-3). 712.80 *(978-0-7368-4217-4(9)*, Pebble Bks.) Capstone Press of Coughlan Cos.

People to Know, 55 bks., Set. (Illus.). (YA). (gr. 6-12). lib. bdg. 1152.25 *(978-0-89490-450-9(7))* Enslow Pubs., Inc.

El Pescador: Libros Aventuras (Adventure Books) 2003. (MacMillan/McGraw-Hill. Estudios Sociales Ser.). (ENG & SPA.). (gr. 3-18). *(978-0-02-150112-0(2))* Macmillan/McGraw-Hill Schl. Div.

Peters, Jennifer. Critical Perspectives on Social Justice. 2017. (J). ***(978-0-7660-9165-8(1))*** Enslow Pubs., Inc.

Pike, Kathy, et al. 25 Totally Terrific Social Studies Activities: Step-by-Step Directions for Motivating Projects That Students Can Do Independently. 2009. (ENG.). 64p. (gr. 3-6). pap. 11.99 *(978-0-439-49830-2(9)*, Teaching Resources) Scholastic, Inc.

Pinkney, Andrea Davis. Peace Warriors. 2013. (Profiles Ser.: 6). (ENG.). 144p. (J). (gr. 5-9). pap. 6.99 *(978-0-545-51857-4(1)*, Scholastic Paperbacks) Scholastic, Inc.

Pohl, Kathleen. Descubramos Países del Mundo (Looking at Countries), 6 vols., Set. Incl. Alemania. lib. bdg. 26.00 *(978-0-8368-8781-5(6))*; Descubramos Argentina. lib. bdg. 26.00 *(978-0-8368-8779-2(4))*; Descubramos el Congo. lib. bdg. 26.00 *(978-0-8368-8780-8(8))*; Descubramos Iran. lib. bdg. 26.00 *(978-0-8368-8782-2(4))*; Descubramos Irlanda. lib. bdg. 26.00 *(978-0-8368-8783-9(2))*; Descubramos Israel. lib. bdg. 26.00 *(978-0-8368-8784-6(0))*; (Illus.). (gr. 1-5)., Gareth Stevens Learning Library (Descubramos países del mundo (Looking at Countries) Ser.). (SPA.). 32p. 2008. 151.62 o.p. *(978-0-8368-8778-5(6))* Stevens, Gareth Publishing LLLP.

—Looking at Countries, 6 vols., Set. Incl. Looking at Argentina. lib. bdg. 26.00 *(978-0-8368-8765-5(4))*; Looking at Germany. lib. bdg. 26.00 *(978-0-8368-8767-9(0))*; Looking at Iran. lib. bdg. 26.00 *(978-0-8368-8768-6(9))*; Looking at Ireland. lib. bdg. 26.00 *(978-0-8368-8769-3(7))*; Looking at Israel. lib. bdg. 26.00 *(978-0-8368-8770-9(0))*; Looking at the Congo. lib. bdg. 26.00 *(978-0-8368-8766-2(2))*; (Illus.). (gr. 1-5)., Gareth Stevens Learning Library (Looking at Countries Ser.). 32p. 2008. 151.62 o.p. *(978-0-8368-8764-8(6))* Stevens, Gareth Publishing LLLP.

Portalupi, Laura. Spies! Set: Real People, Real Stories, 6 vols. 2003. (High Five Reading - Green Ser.). (ENG.). 48p. (gr. 3-4). pap. 54.00 *(978-0-7368-2840-6(0)*, High Five Reading (RBL)) Capstone Press of Coughlan Cos.

Prentiss, Timothy. What Is a Good Citizen? 2006. (Early Explorers Ser.). (J). pap. *(978-1-4108-6110-8(4))* Benchmark Education Co.

Proyecto Raices: un sueno hecho Realidad: Libros Aventuras (Adventure Books) 2003. (MacMillan/McGraw-Hill. Estudios Sociales Ser.). (ENG & SPA.). (gr. 5-18). *(978-0-02-150127-4(0))* Macmillan/McGraw-Hill Schl. Div.

Que hay de Nuevo? Libros Aventuras (Adventure Books) 2003. (MacMillan/McGraw-Hill. Estudios Sociales Ser.). (ENG & SPA.). (gr. 1-18). *(978-0-02-150109-0(2))* Macmillan/McGraw-Hill Schl. Div.

Raintree. Itip 2004 Grade 4 Soc Stud Sta. 2004. pap. *(978-1-4109-1575-7(1))*; pap. *(978-1-4109-1577-1(8))* Harcourt Schl. Pubs.

—Itip 2004 Grades 2-4 Soc Stud. 2004. pap. *(978-1-4109-1578-8(6))*; pap. *(978-1-4109-1573-3(5))* Harcourt Schl. Pubs.

—Itip 2004 Grades 3-4 Soc Stud. 2004. pap. *(978-1-4109-1576-4(X))*; pap. *(978-1-4109-1574-0(3))* Harcourt Schl. Pubs.

—Itip 2004 Grades K-1 Soc Stud. 2004. pap. *(978-1-4109-1572-6(7))* Harcourt Schl. Pubs.

—Itip 2004 Grades K-2 Science S. 2004. pap. *(978-1-4109-1568-9(9))* Harcourt Schl. Pubs.

La rata Cambalachera: Libros Aventuras (Adventure Books) 2003. (MacMillan/McGraw-Hill. Estudios Sociales Ser.). (ENG & SPA.). (gr. 4-18). *(978-0-02-150114-4(9))* Macmillan/McGraw-Hill Schl. Div.

Read Alouds & Primary Sources: Scott Foresman Social Studies. 2003. (gr. k-18). *(978-0-328-03775-9(3)*, Scott Foresman) Addison-Wesley Educational Pubs., Inc.

Read Alouds & Primary Sources: Scott Foresman Social Studies: All Together. 2003. (gr. 1-18). *(978-0-328-03776-6(1)*, Scott Foresman) Addison-Wesley Educational Pubs., Inc.

Read Alouds & Primary Sources: Scott Foresman Social Studies: Communities. 2003. (gr. 3-18). *(978-0-328-03778-0(8)*, Scott Foresman) Addison-Wesley Educational Pubs., Inc.

Read Alouds & Primary Sources: Scott Foresman Social Studies: People & Places. 2003. (gr. 2-18). *(978-0-328-03777-3(X)*, Scott Foresman) Addison-Wesley Educational Pubs., Inc.

Read Alouds & Primary Sources: Scott Foresman Social Studies:Regions. 2003. (gr. 4-18). *(978-0-328-03779-7(6)*, Scott Foresman) Addison-Wesley Educational Pubs., Inc.

Read Alouds & Primary Sources: Scott Foresman Social Studies: The United States. 2003. (gr. 5-18). *(978-0-328-03780-3(X)*, Scott Foresman) Addison-Wesley Educational Pubs., Inc.

Read Alouds & Primary Sources: Scott Foresman Social Studies: The World. 2003. (gr. 6-18). *(978-0-328-03781-0(8)*, Scott Foresman) Addison-Wesley Educational Pubs., Inc.

Reed, Janet. Everyone Eats Bread!, 6 vols., Set. 2003. (Yellow Umbrella Early Level Ser.). (ENG.). 16p. (gr. k-1). pap. 35.70 *(978-0-7368-2986-1(5)*, Yellow Umbrella Bks.) Capstone Press of Coughlan Cos.

—¡Todos Comen Pan!, 6 vols., Set. 2003. (Yellow Umbrella Spanish Emergent Level Ser.).Tr. of Everyone Eats Bread! Social Studies. (SPA.). 16p. (gr. k-1). pap. 35.70 *(978-0-7368-3022-5(7))* Capstone Press of Coughlan Cos.

Region 4 Education Service Center. Reading to Learn in Social Studies for Grades 6-8. 2006. spiral bd. *(978-1-933049-56-4(1))* Region IV Education Service Ctr.

—Reading to Learn in Social Studies for Grades 9-12. 2006. spiral bd. *(978-1-933049-57-1(X))* Region IV Education Service Ctr.

Regions Near & Far. (J). (gr. 4). suppl. ed. *(978-0-669-11381-5(6))* Houghton Mifflin Harcourt School Pubs.

Regions Near & Far. Incl. suppl. ed. *(978-0-669-11381-5(6))*; Regions Near & Far. tchr. ed. *(978-0-669-11397-6(2))*; Regions Near & Far. suppl. ed. *(978-0-669-11423-2(5))*; Regions Near & Far. pap., wbk. ed. *(978-0-669-11402-7(2))*; Regions Near & Far. tchr. ed., wbk. ed. *(978-0-669-11408-9(1))*; Regions Near & Far. suppl. ed. *(978-0-669-11428-7(6))*; Regions Near & Far. suppl. ed. *(978-0-669-11724-0(2))*; Regions Near & Far. suppl. ed. (J). (gr. 4-6). pap. *(978-0-669-11389-1(1))* Houghton Mifflin Harcourt School Pubs.

Remy, Richard C., et al. Civics Today: Citizenship, Economics, & You. 2nd ed. 2004. (Civics Today: Citzshp Econ You Ser.). (ENG., Illus.). 710p. (gr. 7-10). lib. bdg., stu. ed. 115.68 *(978-0-07-860970-1(4)*, 0078609704) McGraw-Hill Higher Education.

Resumenes de las Lecciones: Student & Teacher Support Resources. 2003. (MacMillan/McGraw-Hill. Estudios Sociales Ser.). (ENG & SPA.). (gr. 3-18). *(978-0-02-149901-4(2))*; (gr. 5-18). *(978-0-02-149903-8(9))* Macmillan/McGraw-Hill Schl. Div.

Resumes de las Lecciones: Student & Teacher Support Resources. 2003. (MacMillan/McGraw-Hill. Estudios Sociales Ser.). (ENG & SPA.). (gr. 4-18). *(978-0-02-150075-8(4))* Macmillan/McGraw-Hill Schl. Div.

Rhodes, Immacula A. & Julio, Susan. Social Studies: 10 Ready-to-Go Games That Help Children Learn Key Social Studies Concepts & Vocabulary - Independently. 2009. (File-Folder Games in Color Ser.). (ENG.). 144p. pap. 19.99 *(978-0-439-51763-8(X)*, Teaching Resources) Scholastic, Inc.

Ring, Susan. From Here to There, 6 vols., Set. 2003. (Yellow Umbrella Early Level Ser.). (ENG.). 16p. (gr. k-1). pap. 35.70 *(978-0-7368-2985-4(7)*, Yellow Umbrella Bks.) Capstone Press of Coughlan Cos.

Robertson, Charmaine. The Landmarks of My Town. 2016. (Rosen REAL Readers: Social Studies Nonfiction / Fiction: Family, Community, & the World Ser.). 8p. (gr. 1-k). pap. 5.46 *(978-1-5081-2269-2(5)*, Rosen Classroom) Rosen Publishing Group, Inc., The.

Ross, Stewart. Point of Impact Series, 12 bks., Set. (Illus.). (J). (gr. 5-7). lib. bdg. 290.64 *(978-1-58810-187-7(8))* Heinemann-Raintree.

Rotsky, Leslie A. At Work in the Neighborhood: A Content Area Reader-Social Stuides. 2005. (Emergent/Early (Prek-2) Social Studies Package Ser.). 16p. (gr. k-2). 25.20 *(978-0-8215-7818-6(9))* Sadlier, William H. Inc.

Schaefer, Lola M. Somos Iguales: Set Of 6. 2011. (Primeras Conexiones Ser.).Tr. of We Are All Alike. (SPA.). (J). pap. 40.00 net. *(978-1-4108-0324-5(4))* Benchmark Education Co.

Schaub, Michelle. Where Are We? 2006. (Early Explorers Ser.). (J). pap. *(978-1-4108-6108-5(2))* Benchmark Education Co.

Schorr, Titus. Ben Is Good at Spelling, 01 vols., 1. 2016. (Rosen REAL Readers: Social Studies Nonfiction / Fiction: Family, Community, & the World Ser.). (ENG.). 8p. (J). pap. 5.46 *(978-1-5081-1662-2(8)*, Rosen Classroom) Rosen Publishing Group, Inc., The.

—Our Town Is 100 Years Old, 01 vols., 1. 2016. (Rosen REAL Readers: Social Studies Nonfiction / Fiction: Family, Community, & the World Ser.). (ENG.). 8p. (J). pap. 5.46 *(978-1-5081-1695-0(4)*, Rosen Classroom) Rosen Publishing Group, Inc., The.

—Places in Our Classroom, 01 vols., 1. 2016. (Rosen REAL Readers: Social Studies Nonfiction / Fiction: Family, Community, & the World Ser.). (ENG.). 8p. (J). pap. 5.46 *(978-1-5081-1644-8(X)*, Rosen Classroom) Rosen Publishing Group, Inc., The.

—Symbols of America, 01 vols., 1. 2016. (Rosen REAL Readers: Social Studies Nonfiction / Fiction: Family, Community, & the World Ser.). (ENG.). 12p. (J). pap. 6.33 *(978-1-5081-1767-4(5)*, Rosen Classroom) Rosen Publishing Group, Inc., The.

Schwartz, Linda. Social Studies & Science Quiz Whiz 3-5, Vol. 432. VanBlaricum, Pam, ed. Armstrong, Beverly, illus. 2004. 128p. (J). (gr. 3-5). pap. 10.99 *(978-0-88160-375-0(9)*, LW-432) Creative Teaching Pr., Inc.

Scott Foresman Social Studies: Additional Resources. 2003. (Multi-Leveled Library). (gr. k-18). *(978-0-328-06262-1(6))*; (gr. k-18). *(978-0-328-03918-0(7))*; (gr. k-2). tchr. ed. *(978-0-328-04180-0(7))*; (gr. 1-18). *(978-0-328-06263-8(4))*; (gr. 2-18). *(978-0-328-06264-5(2))*; (gr. 3-18). *(978-0-328-03601-1(3))*; (gr. 3-18). *(978-0-328-06265-2(0))*; (gr. 3-6). tchr. ed. *(978-0-328-04181-7(5))*; (gr. 4-18). *(978-0-328-03602-8(1))*; (gr. 4-18). *(978-0-328-06266-9(9))*; (gr. 5-18). *(978-0-328-06267-6(7))*; (gr. 6-18). *(978-0-328-03604-2(8))*; (gr. 6-18). *(978-0-328-06268-3(5))* Addison-Wesley Educational Pubs., Inc. (Scott Foresman).

Scott Foresman Social Studies: Kindergarten Package. 2003. stu. ed. *(978-0-328-04348-4(6)*, Scott Foresman) Addison-Wesley Educational Pubs., Inc.

Scott Foresman Social Studies: Practice/Assessment. 2003. (gr. k-18). *(978-0-328-03090-3(2))*; (gr. 1-18). *(978-0-328-03091-0(0))*; (gr. 2-18). *(978-0-328-03092-7(9))*; (gr. 3-18). *(978-0-328-03093-4(7))* Addison-Wesley Educational Pubs., Inc. (Scott Foresman).

Scott Foresman Social Studies: Pupil Edition. 2003. (Scott Foresman Social Study Ser.). (gr. 5-18). *(978-0-328-01763-8(9)*, Scott Foresman) Addison-Wesley Educational Pubs., Inc.

Scott Foresman Social Studies: Technology. 2003. (Multimedia Library). (gr. k-18). *(978-0-328-05696-5(0))*; (SPA.). (gr. k-18). cd-rom *(978-0-328-05663-7(4))*; (gr. k-18). cd-rom *(978-0-328-03875-6(X))*; (gr. 1-18). *(978-0-328-05697-2(9))*; (SPA.). (gr. 1-18). cd-rom *(978-0-328-05664-4(2))*; (gr. 1-18). cd-rom *(978-0-328-03876-3(8))*; (gr. 2-18). *(978-0-328-05698-9(7))*; (SPA.). (gr. 2-18). cd-rom *(978-0-328-05665-1(0))*; (gr. 2-18). cd-rom *(978-0-328-03877-0(6))*; (gr. 3-18). *(978-0-328-05699-6(5))*; (gr. 3-18). cd-rom *(978-0-328-03878-7(4))*; (SPA.). (gr. 3-18). cd-rom *(978-0-328-05666-8(9))*; (gr. 4-18). *(978-0-328-05700-9(2))*; (gr. 4-18). cd-rom *(978-0-328-03879-4(2))*; (gr. 5-18). *(978-0-328-05701-6(0))*; (gr. 5-18). cd-rom *(978-0-328-03880-0(6))*; (gr. 6-18). *(978-0-328-05702-3(9))*; (gr. 6-18). cd-rom *(978-0-328-03881-7(4))* Addison-Wesley Educational Pubs., Inc. (Scott Foresman).

Scott Foresman Social Studies: Building A Nation: Practice/Assessment. 2003. (gr. 5-18). *(978-0-328-03100-9(3)*, Scott Foresman) Addison-Wesley Educational Pubs., Inc.

Scott Foresman Social Studies: Regions: Practice/Assessment. 2003. (gr. 4-18). *(978-0-328-03094-1(5)*, Scott Foresman) Addison-Wesley Educational Pubs., Inc.

Scott Foresman Social Studies: The United States: Practice/Assessment. 2003. (gr. 5-18). *(978-0-328-03095-8(3)*, Scott Foresman) Addison-Wesley Educational Pubs., Inc.

Scott Foresman Social Studies: The World: Practice/Assessment. 2003. (gr. 6-18). *(978-0-328-03096-5(1)*, Scott Foresman) Addison-Wesley Educational Pubs., Inc.

Secondary Social Studies for the Caribbean, Bk. 1. 2016. (ENG.). 96p. (YA). pap., wbk. ed. 9.95 ***(978-0-00-811592-0(3))*** HarperCollins Pubs. Ltd. GBR. Dist: Independent Pubs. Group.

Shades of Gray. (J). pap., stu. ed. *(978-0-13-620188-5(1))* Prentice Hall (Schl. Div.).

Shafer, Jean. Learning from Charts & Graphs: Lessons in History, Civics, Geography, & Economics 2003. (Illus.). 48p. (J). 15.95 *(978-0-938682-76-9(8))* River Road Pubns., Inc.

Shava, Ryder. Baik Speaks Korean, 01 vols., 1. 2016. (Rosen REAL Readers: Social Studies Nonfiction / Fiction: Family, Community, & the World Ser.). (ENG.). 12p. (J). pap. 6.33 *(978-1-5081-1818-3(3)*, Rosen Classroom) Rosen Publishing Group, Inc., The.

—Blonde Hair, Red Hair, 01 vols., 1. 2016. (Rosen REAL Readers: Social Studies Nonfiction / Fiction: Family, Community, & the World Ser.). (ENG.). 8p. (J). pap. 5.46 *(978-1-5081-2021-6(8)*, Rosen Classroom) Rosen Publishing Group, Inc., The.

—Our School's Special Song, 01 vols., 1. 2016. (Rosen REAL Readers: Social Studies Nonfiction / Fiction: Family, Community, & the World Ser.). (ENG.). 12p. (J). pap. 6.33 *(978-1-5081-1746-9(2)*, Rosen Classroom) Rosen Publishing Group, Inc., The.

—This Is My School, 01 vols., 1. 2016. (Rosen REAL Readers: Social Studies Nonfiction / Fiction: Family, Community, & the World Ser.). (ENG.). 8p. (J). pap. 5.46 *(978-1-5081-1677-6(6)*, Rosen Classroom) Rosen Publishing Group, Inc., The.

Shepard, Daniel. All Kinds of Farms, 6 vols., Set. 2003. (Yellow Umbrella Early Level Ser.). (ENG.). 16p. (gr. k-1). pap. 35.70 *(978-0-7368-2989-2(X)*, Yellow Umbrella Bks.) Capstone Press of Coughlan Cos.

—What Did People Use Long Ago? 2003. (Shutterbug Books: Social Studies). (Illus.). 16p. (J). (gr. -1-3). pap. 4.10 *(978-0-7398-7643-5(0))* Steck-Vaughn.

Simpson, Louie. My Mom Votes! 2012. (InfoMax Readers Ser.). (ENG., Illus.). 24p. (J). (gr. 1-2). pap. 8.25 *(978-1-4488-9055-2(1)*, Rosen Classroom) Rosen Publishing Group, Inc., The.

Sims, Kathy C., illus. & text. Louisiana Potpourri from A to Z. Sims, Kathy C., text. 2004.Tr. of Potpourri Louisianais d' A à Z. (FRE.). 64p. (YA). lib. bdg. 24.95 *(978-0-9753435-0-0(5))* Louisiana Ladybug Pr.

SIRS Enduring Issues 2006, 8 vols., Set. 2005. (Illus.). (YA). ring bd. 849.00 *(978-0-89777-554-0(6))* SIRS Publishing, Inc.

Snakes are Not Slimy, 6 vols. (Book2WebTM Ser.). (gr. 4-8). 36.50 *(978-0-322-02976-7(7))* Wright Group/McGraw-Hill.

Social Studies Explorer, 21 vols., Set. Incl. Bangladesh. Orr, Tamra. 48p. 2010. lib. bdg. 31.36 *(978-1-60279-829-8(X)*, 200524); Brazil. Franchino, Vicky. 48p. 2010. lib. bdg. 31.36 *(978-1-60279-827-4(3)*, 200520); China. Raatma, Lucia. 48p. 2010. lib. bdg. 31.36 *(978-1-60279-823-6(0)*, 200512); India. Raatma, Lucia. 48p. 2010. lib. bdg. 31.36 *(978-1-60279-824-3(9)*, 200514); Indonesia. Orr, Tamra. 48p. 2010. lib. bdg. 31.36 *(978-1-60279-826-7(5)*, 200518); Japan. Somervill, Barbara. 48p. 2010. lib. bdg. 31.36 *(978-1-60279-832-8(X)*, 200530); Mexico. Somervill,

Barbara. 48p. 2010. lib. bdg. 31.36 *(978-1-60279-833-5(8),* 200532); Nigeria. Rau, Dana Meachen. 48p. 2010. lib. bdg. 31.36 *(978-1-60279-830-4(3),* 200526); Pakistan. Labrecque, Ellen. 48p. 2010. lib. bdg. 31.36 *(978-1-60279-828-1(1),* 200522); Philippines. Franchino, Vicky. 48p. 2010. lib. bdg. 31.36 *(978-1-60279-834-2(6),* 200534); Russia. Marsico, Katie. 48p. 2010. lib. bdg. 31.36 *(978-1-60279-831-1(1),* 200528); United States. Marsico, Katie. 48p. 2010. lib. bdg. 31.36 *(978-1-60279-825-0(7),* 200516); Set. Social Studies Explorer: It's Cool to Learn about Countries. Cherry Lake Publishing Staff. (J). 2011. lib. bdg. 125.44 *(978-1-61080-148-5(2));* Set. Social Studies Explorer: It's Cool to Learn about the United States. Cherry Lake Publishing Staff. (J). 2011. lib. bdg. 156.80 *(978-1-61080-191-1(1));* (gr. 4-8). 2011. Set lib. bdg. 658.56 *(978-1-61080-253-6(5))* Cherry Lake Publishing.

Social Studies Explorer: It's Cool to Learn about Countries, 4 vols., Set. Incl. Egypt. Marsico, Katie. lib. bdg. 31.36 *(978-1-61080-100-3(8),* 201094); Ethiopia. Somervill, Barbara. lib. bdg. 31.36 *(978-1-61080-099-0(0),* 201092); Germany. Franchino, Vicky. lib. bdg. 31.36 *(978-1-61080-098-3(2),* 201090); Vietnam. Rau, Dana Meachen. lib. bdg. 31.36 *(978-1-61080-097-6(4),* 201088); 48p. (gr. 4-8). (Social Studies Explorer Ser.). 2011. Set lib. bdg. 125.44 *(978-1-61080-148-5(2))* Cherry Lake Publishing.

Social Studies Program, Early Level. 2003. (Yellow Umbrella Early Level Ser.). (ENG.). 16p. (gr. k-1). pap. 428.40 *(978-0-7368-3060-7(X),* Yellow Umbrella Bks.) Capstone Press of Coughlan Cos.

The Social Studies Reading Room Collection. (J). (gr. k-5). 79.50 *(978-1-4042-3381-2(4))* Rosen Publishing Group, Inc., The.

Social Studies Set, 8 vols. (Content Collections). (gr. k-2). 265.66 *(978-0-7362-2270-9(7))* CENGAGE Learning.

Social Studies: The World: Scott Foresman Social Studies. 2003. (gr. 6-18). stu. ed. *(978-0-328-01766-9(3),* Scott Foresman) Addison-Wesley Educational Pubs., Inc.

Staniford, Linda. Wants vs Needs. 2015. (Wants vs Needs Ser.). (ENG.). 24p. (gr. k-2). lib. bdg. 93.28 *(978-1-4846-0946-0(8),* Heinemann Read & Learn) Heinemann-Raintree.

Steck-Vaughn Staff. Arctic People. 2003. pap. 4.10 *(978-0-7398-7650-3(3))* Steck-Vaughn.

—Life on the Tallest Tree. 2003. pap. 4.10 *(978-0-7398-7636-7(8))* Steck-Vaughn.

—Matter All Around Us. 2003. pap. 4.10 *(978-0-7398-7639-8(2))* Steck-Vaughn.

—People & Places Nearby Level B. 2005. (Steck-Vaughn Social Studies). (ENG.). 112p. (gr. 2-2). pap. 29.50 *(978-0-7398-9219-0(3))* Houghton Mifflin Harcourt Publishing Co.

—Social Studies Level C: Living in Communities. 2005. (Steck-Vaughn Social Studies). (ENG.). 144p. (gr. 3-3). pap., stu. ed. 33.70 *(978-0-7398-9220-6(7))* Houghton Mifflin Harcourt Publishing Co.

—Social Studies Level C: Living in Communities. 2005. pap. 112.30 *(978-0-7398-9226-8(6));* pap., tchr. ed. 15.10 *(978-0-7398-9232-9(0))* Steck-Vaughn.

—Social Studies Level D: Regions of the Country. 2005. (Steck-Vaughn Social Studies). (ENG.). 160p. (gr. 4-4). pap. 33.70 *(978-0-7398-9221-3(5))* Houghton Mifflin Harcourt Publishing Co.

—Social Studies Level A: Homes & Families. 2005. (Steck-Vaughn Social Studies). (ENG.). 112p. (gr. 1-1). pap. 29.50 *(978-0-7398-9218-3(5))* Houghton Mifflin Harcourt Publishing Co.

—Social Studies Level A: Homes & Families. 2005. pap. 112.30 *(978-0-7398-9224-4(X));* pap., tchr. ed. 15.10 *(978-0-7398-9230-5(4))* Steck-Vaughn.

—Social Studies Level B: People & Places. 2005. (Steck-Vaughn Social Studies). (ENG.). 48p. (gr. 2-2). pap., tchr. ed. 26.60 *(978-0-7398-9231-2(2))* Houghton Mifflin Harcourt Publishing Co.

—Social Studies Level B: People & Places. 2005. pap. 112.30 *(978-0-7398-9225-1(8))* Steck-Vaughn.

—Social Studies Level E: History of the Country. 2005. pap. 137.30 *(978-0-7398-9228-2(2));* pap., tchr. ed. 15.10 *(978-0-7398-9234-3(7))* Steck-Vaughn.

—Social Studies Level F: World Cultures. 2005. (Steck-Vaughn Social Studies). (ENG.). 208p. (gr. 6-6). pap. 37.65 *(978-0-7398-9223-7(1))* Houghton Mifflin Harcourt Publishing Co.

—Social Studies Level F: World Cultures. 2005. pap. 96.70 *(978-0-7398-9229-9(0));* pap., tchr. ed. 15.10 *(978-0-7398-9235-0(5))* Steck-Vaughn.

—What's the Question? 2003. pap. 4.10 *(978-0-7398-7663-3(5))* Steck-Vaughn.

Stradling, Jan. People & Places: Level I, 6 vols., Vol. 2. (First Explorers Ser.). 24p. (gr. 1-2). 29.95 *(978-0-7699-1462-6(4))* Shortland Pubns. (U. S. A.) Inc.

—Under Attack: Level I, 6 vols. (First Explorers Ser.). 24p. (gr. 1-2). 29.95 *(978-0-7699-1453-4(5))* Shortland Pubns. (U. S. A.) Inc.

—You are Special: Level I, 6 vols. (First Explorers Ser.). 24p. (gr. 1-2). 29.95 *(978-0-7699-1454-1(3))* Shortland Pubns. (U. S. A.) Inc.

Sullivan, Erin Ash. Communities Helping Communities: Set Of 6. 2010. (Navigators Ser.). (J). pap. 44.00 net. *(978-1-4108-6246-4(1))* Benchmark Education Co.

Sundance/Newbridge LLC Staff. One World, Many Cultures. 2004. (Reading PowerWorks Ser.). (gr. 1-3). 37.50 *(978-0-7608-8952-7(X));* pap. 6.10 *(978-0-7608-8953-4(8))* Sundance/Newbridge Educational Publishing.

Superlibro Recursos: Superlibros. 2003. (MacMillan/McGraw-Hill. Estudios Sociales Ser.). (ENG & SPA.). (gr. 1-18). *(978-0-02-149977-9(2))* Macmillan/McGraw-Hill Schl. Div.

Superlibro Recursos: Vivimos Juntos: Superlibros. 2003. (MacMillan/McGraw-Hill. Estudios Sociales Ser.). (ENG & SPA.). (gr. 2-18). *(978-0-02-149978-6(0))* Macmillan/McGraw-Hill Schl. Div.

Syverson, Carolyn. Community Helpers. 2011. (Social Studies). (ENG.). 16p. (gr. -1-1). 25.95 *(978-1-4296-8538-2(7),* Wonder Readers) Capstone Press of Coughlan Cos.

TAKS Social Studies Preparation Grade 11 Exit - Student Workbook. 2003. (Region IV ESC Resources for Social Studies Ser.). stu. ed., per. *(978-1-932524-67-3(3))* Region IV Education Service Ctr.

TAKS Social Studies Preparation Grade 8. 2004. (Region IV ESC Resources for Social Studies Ser.). stu. ed., per., wbk. ed. *(978-1-932524-65-9(7))* Region IV Education Service Ctr.

Talmadge Salle, Katherine. Daily Life Around the World: Set Of 6. 2011. (Navigators Ser.). (J). pap. 44.00 net. *(978-1-4108-6245-7(3))* Benchmark Education Co.

Test Generator: Technology. 2003. (MacMillan/McGraw-Hill. Estudios Sociales Ser.). (ENG & SPA.). (gr. 5-18). incl. audio compact disk *(978-0-02-150074-1(6))* Macmillan/McGraw-Hill Schl. Div.

Thompson, Tamara. Expanding the Human Lifespan. Greenhaven Press Editors, ed. 2013. (At Issue Ser.). (ENG.). 128p. (gr. 10-12). pap. 27.80 *(978-0-7377-6837-4(1),* Greenhaven Pr., Inc.) Cengage Gale.

Transgender Life. 2016. (Transgender Life Ser.). 00064p. (J). (gr. 6-6). 172.25 *(978-1-5081-7353-3(2),* Rosen Young Adult) Rosen Publishing Group, Inc., The.

Trowell, Cynthia. Out of the Mist: A Survival Guide for Young Adults. 2004. (Illus.). 104p. (YA). per. 16.95 *(978-1-59094-045-7(8),* Top Shelf) Jawbone Publishing Corp.

True Book of the Continents Collection. 2005. (J). pap. *(978-1-60015-013-5(6))* Steps To Literacy, LLC.

Under Water: Big Book: Level C. 8p. 20.95 *(978-0-322-00625-6(2))* Wright Group/McGraw-Hill.

Underground: Big Book: Level D. 8p. 20.95 *(978-0-322-00345-3(8))* Wright Group/McGraw-Hill.

Unidad 1 Superlibro: Familias: Superlibros. 2003. (MacMillan/McGraw-Hill. Estudios Sociales Ser.). (ENG & SPA.). (gr. 1-18). *(978-0-02-149434-7(7))* Macmillan/McGraw-Hill Schl. Div.

Unidad 3 Superlibro: Civismo: Superlibros. 2003. (MacMillan/McGraw-Hill. Estudios Sociales Ser.). (ENG & SPA.). (gr. 1-18). *(978-0-02-149436-1(3))* Macmillan/McGraw-Hill Schl. Div.

Unidad 3 Superlibro: Historia: Vivimos Juntos: Superlibros (Big Books) 2003. (MacMillan/McGraw-Hill. Estudios Sociales Ser.). (ENG & SPA.). (gr. 2-18). *(978-0-02-149443-9(6))* Macmillan/McGraw-Hill Schl. Div.

Unidad 5 Superlibro: Gobierno: Vivimos Juntos: Superlibros (Big Books) 2003. (MacMillan/McGraw-Hill. Estudios Sociales Ser.). (ENG & SPA.). (gr. 2-18). *(978-0-02-149445-3(2))* Macmillan/McGraw-Hill Schl. Div.

Unidad 5 Superlibro: Historia: Superlibros. 2003. (MacMillan/McGraw-Hill. Estudios Sociales Ser.). (ENG & SPA.). (gr. 1-18). *(978-0-02-149438-5(X))* Macmillan/McGraw-Hill Schl. Div.

VanVoorst, Jennifer. The Letter Zz: How Things Move. 2004. (Letter Bks.). (ENG.). 8p. (gr. k-1). pap. 29.70 *(978-0-7368-4125-2(3),* Letter Bks.) Capstone Press of Coughlan Cos.

—Things That Are Cold, 6 vols., Set. 2004. (Letter Bks.). (ENG.). 8p. (gr. k-1). pap. 29.70 *(978-0-7368-4108-5(3),* Letter Bks.) Capstone Press of Coughlan Cos.

—Working, 6 vols., Set. 2003. (Yellow Umbrella Early Level Ser.). (ENG.). 16p. (gr. k-1). pap. 35.70 *(978-0-7368-3007-2(3),* Yellow Umbrella Bks.) Capstone Press of Coughlan Cos.

Verderosa, Laura. My Favorite Places. 2010. (Sight Word Readers Ser.). (J). 3.49 *(978-1-60719-611-2(5))* Newmark Learning LLC.

Viaje a la selva Tropical: Libros Aventuras (Adventure Books) 2003. (MacMillan/McGraw-Hill. Estudios Sociales Ser.). (ENG & SPA.). (gr. 5-18). *(978-0-02-150128-1(9))* Macmillan/McGraw-Hill Schl. Div.

Viaje por la Historia: Libros Aventuras (Adventure Books) 2003. (MacMillan/McGraw-Hill. Estudios Sociales Ser.). (ENG & SPA.). (gr. 4-18). *(978-0-02-150120-5(3))* Macmillan/McGraw-Hill Schl. Div.

The Viking Saga. 2004. (Thrilling Tales in Time Ser.: Vol. 1). (J). *(978-1-58123-370-4(1))* Larson Learning, Inc.

Warm up to Social Studies for Grade 11. 2005. spiral bd. *(978-1-933049-17-5(0))* Region IV Education Service Ctr.

Waters, Carrie. A Look Back in Time: A Content Area Reader-Social Studies. 2005. (Emergent/Early (Prek-2) Social Studies Package Ser.). 20p. (gr. k-2). 25.20 *(978-0-8215-7816-2(2))* Sadlier, William H. Inc.

Weber, Rebecca. Lost Cities: Set Of 6. 2011. (Navigators Ser.). (J). pap. 48.00 net. *(978-1-4108-0419-8(4))* Benchmark Education Co.

What Kind of Dog Am I? Level C. 8p. 20.95 *(978-0-322-00371-2(7))* Wright Group/McGraw-Hill.

What's Black & White & Moos? Level F. 16p. 31.50 *(978-0-7802-9741-8(5))* Wright Group/McGraw-Hill.

Who Says? Big Book: Level F. 16p. 31.50 *(978-0-322-00377-4(6))* Wright Group/McGraw-Hill.

Whose Shoes? Level F. 16p. 31.50 *(978-0-322-00351-4(2))* Wright Group/McGraw-Hill.

Why? Big Book: Level F. 16p. 31.50 *(978-0-322-00352-1(0))* Wright Group/McGraw-Hill.

A Wicked History, 4 vols., Set. Incl. Attila the Hun: Leader of the Barbarian Hordes. Price, Sean Stewart & Price, Sean. 31.00 *(978-0-531-21801-3(5));* Catherine the Great: Empress of Russia. Vincent, Zu. 31.00 *(978-0-531-21802-0(3));* King George III: America's Enemy. Brooks, Philip. 31.00 *(978-0-531-21803-7(1));* Sir Francis Drake: Slave Trader & Pirate. Nick, Charles. 31.00 *(978-0-531-21800-6(7));* (Illus.). 128p. (J). (gr. 6-12). 2009. 2009. Set lib. bdg. 120.00 *(978-0-531-26140-8(9),* Watts, Franklin) Scholastic Library Publishing.

Wiener, Gary. War in Ernest Hemingway's for Whom the Bell Tolls. 2013. (Social Issues in Literature Ser.). (ENG., Illus.). 224p. (gr. 10-12). lib. bdg. 46.40 *(978-0-7377-6393-5(0),* Greenhaven Pr., Inc.) Cengage Gale.

Wiener, Gary, ed. War in Ernest Hemingway's for Whom the Bell Tolls. 2013. (Social Issues in Literature Ser.). (ENG., Illus.). 224p. (gr. 10-12). pap. 28.45 *(978-0-7377-6394-2(9),* Greenhaven Pr., Inc.) Cengage Gale.

William H. Sadlier Staff. Family Fun. 2005. (Social Studies). (gr. -1-2). 25.20 *(978-0-8215-7835-3(9))* Sadlier, William H. Inc.

—My Favorite Things. 2005. (Emergent/Early (Prek-2) Social Studies Package Ser.). 12p. (gr. -1-1). 25.20 *(978-0-8215-7831-5(6))* Sadlier, William H. Inc.

Williams, Brian. Way We Live: Biggest & Best. 2004. (Biggest & Best Ser.). (Illus.). 40p. (J). pap. 7.95 *(978-1-84236-064-4(7))* Miles Kelly Publishing, Ltd. GBR. Dist: Independent Pubs. Group.

Wilson, Mike. The Election Process. 2008. (Introducing Issues with Opposing Viewpoints Ser.). (ENG., Illus.). 112-144p. (YA). (gr. 7-10). 36.95 *(978-0-7377-3975-6(4),* Greenhaven Pr., Inc.) Cengage Gale.

Wood: Big Book: Level D. 8p. 20.95 *(978-0-7802-9743-2(1))* Wright Group/McGraw-Hill.

World Cultures Classroom Library. (gr. k-2). lib. bdg. 109.95 *(978-0-7368-9454-8(3))* Red Brick Learning.

World Cultures Complete Unit. (gr. k-2). 624.95 *(978-0-7368-9455-5(1))* Red Brick Learning.

World in Crisis. 2014. (World in Crisis Ser.). 48p. (YA). (gr. 5-8). 181.50 *(978-1-4777-7852-4(7),* Rosen Reference) Rosen Publishing Group, Inc., The.

World Today: Heath Social Studies. Incl. The World Today. tchr. ed. *(978-0-669-11400-3(6));* The World Today. suppl. ed. *(978-0-669-11426-3(X));* The World Today. pap., wbk. ed. *(978-0-669-11406-5(5));* The World Today. pap., wbk. ed. *(978-0-669-11412-6(X));* The World Today. suppl. ed. *(978-0-669-11432-4(4));* The World Today. suppl. ed. *(978-0-669-11728-8(5));* The World Today. suppl. ed. (J). (gr. 6-7). *(978-0-669-11392-1(1))* Houghton Mifflin Harcourt School Pubs.

Yellowstone: Libros Aventuras (Adventure Books) 2003. (MacMillan/McGraw-Hill. Estudios Sociales Ser.). (ENG & SPA.). (gr. 4-18). *(978-0-02-150122-9(X))* Macmillan/McGraw-Hill Schl. Div.

Young, Ian. Amazing Journeys: Following in History's Footsteps, 6 vols. 2003. (High Five Reading - Green Ser.). (ENG.). 48p. (gr. 3-4). pap. 54.00 *(978-0-7368-2841-3(9),* High Five Reading (RBL)) Capstone Press of Coughlan Cos.

Zoom in on Communities. 2016. (Zoom in on Communities Ser.). 24p. (gr. 2-2). pap. 56.10 *(978-0-7660-7976-2(7));* lib. bdg. 135.60 *(978-0-7660-7493-4(5))* Enslow Pubs., Inc.

SOCIAL SCIENCES—STUDY AND TEACHING

Boehm, Richard G., et al. Carteles de la Unidad: La Historia de Nuestro Mundo: Relatos de la Historia. 97th ed. 2003. (Harcourt Brace Estudios Sociales Ser.). (SPA.). (gr. k-7). pap. 84.30 *(978-0-15-309146-9(0))* Harcourt Schl. Pubs.

—Desk Maps: Intermediate (3-7) Package Of 10. 2003. (Harcourt Brace Social Studies). (SPA.). (gr. 3-7). 27.00 *(978-0-15-310432-9(5))* Harcourt Schl. Pubs.

—Desk Maps: Primary (K-2) Package Of 10. 2003. (Harcourt Brace Social Studies). (SPA.). (gr. k-2). 27.00 *(978-0-15-310431-2(7))* Harcourt Schl. Pubs.

—Relatos de la Historia: Assessment Program. 97th ed. 2003. (Harcourt Brace Estudios Sociales Ser.). (SPA.). (gr. k-7). pap. 93.50 *(978-0-15-309130-8(4));* pap. 115.10 *(978-0-15-309145-2(2))* Harcourt Schl. Pubs.

—Relatos de la Historia: Estados y Regiones. 97th ed. 2003. (Harcourt Brace Estudios Sociales Ser.). (SPA.). (gr. k-7). pupil's gde. ed. 81.70 *(978-0-15-309126-1(6))* Harcourt Schl. Pubs.

—Relatos de la Historia: La Historia de Estados Mundo. 97th ed. 2003. (Harcourt Brace Estudios Sociales Ser.). (SPA.). (gr. k-7). pupil's gde. ed. 88.40 *(978-0-15-309140-7(1))* Harcourt Schl. Pubs.

—Transparencias: La Historia de Nuestro Mundo: Relatos de la Historia. 97th ed. 2003. (Harcourt Brace Estudios Sociales Ser.). (SPA.). (gr. k-7). pap. 138.70 *(978-0-15-309147-6(9))* Harcourt Schl. Pubs.

—Write-on Charts. 2003. (Harcourt Brace Estudios Sociales Ser.). (SPA.). (gr. 1-18). 248.40 *(978-0-15-313132-5(2));* (gr. 2-18). 248.40 *(978-0-15-313133-2(0))* Harcourt Schl. Pubs.

Hama, Larry. The Battle of First Bull Run: The War Begins! 2007. (Graphic Battles: Civil War Ser.). (ENG., Illus.). 48p. (gr. 5-6). pap. 14.05 *(978-1-4042-6476-2(0),* Rosen Classroom) Rosen Publishing Group, Inc., The.

—The Battle of Shiloh: Surprise Attack! 2007. (Graphic Battles: Civil War Ser.). (ENG., Illus.). 48p. (gr. 5-8). pap. 14.05 *(978-1-4042-6478-6(7),* Rosen Classroom) Rosen Publishing Group, Inc., The.

Harcourt School Publishers Staff. Horizontes. 3rd ed. 2003. (Harcourt Horizontes Ser.). (SPA., Illus.). (gr. k-6). 7.00 *(978-0-15-324549-7(2));* act. bk. ed. 8.40 *(978-0-15-324551-0(4));* act. bk. ed. 10.20 *(978-0-15-324552-7(2));* act. bk. ed. 8.40 *(978-0-15-324550-3(6));* pupil's gde. ed. 54.10 *(978-0-15-324533-6(6));* pupil's gde. ed. 47.30 *(978-0-15-324531-2(X))* Harcourt Schl. Pubs.

—Horizontes: Big Book. 3rd ed. 2003. (Harcourt Horizontes Ser.). (SPA., Illus.). (gr. k-6). tchr. ed. 268.00 *(978-0-15-324832-0(7))* Harcourt Schl. Pubs.

—Horizontes: States & Regions. 3rd ed. 2003. (Harcourt Horizontes Ser.). (SPA., Illus.). (gr. k-6). act. bk. ed. 10.50 *(978-0-15-324553-4(0));* pupil's gde. ed. 64.60 *(978-0-15-324534-3(4))* Harcourt Schl. Pubs.

—Horizontes: World Regions. 3rd ed. 2003. (Harcourt Horizontes Ser.). (SPA., Illus.). (gr. k-6). act. bk. ed. 11.80 *(978-0-15-324556-5(5))* Harcourt Schl. Pubs.

—Horizontes, Grade 2, Vol. 2. 2nd ed. 2003. (Harcourt Horizontes Ser.). (SPA.). (gr. k-6). tchr. ed. 121.50 *(978-0-15-328508-0(7))* Harcourt Schl. Pubs.

—Horizontes, Grade 4: States & Regions. 3rd ed. 2003. (Harcourt Horizontes Ser.). (SPA.). (gr. k-6). Vol. 1. tchr. ed. 133.80 *(978-0-15-321975-7(0))* Vol. 2. tchr. ed. 133.80 *(978-0-15-321976-4(9))* Harcourt Schl. Pubs.

—World Regions. 3rd ed. 2003. (Horizontes (Social Studies) Ser.). (SPA., Illus.). (gr. k-6). pupil's gde. ed. 75.50 *(978-0-15-324537-4(9))* Harcourt Schl. Pubs.

Kowalski, Kathiann M. It's Your World! A Crash Course in Social Studies, 1 vol. 2014. (Crash Course Ser.). (ENG.). 64p. (gr. 4-5). pap. 8.95 *(978-1-4914-0783-7(2))* Capstone Press of Coughlan Cos.

Provenzo, Eugene F., Jr., et al. 100 Experiential Learning Activities for Social Studies, Literature, & the Arts, Grades 5-12. 2008. (ENG., Illus.). 176p. 76.95 *(978-1-4129-3999-7(2),* B39992C) Corwin Pr.

Stevens, Stefan. Understanding Civilizations. 2013. (InfoMax Readers Ser.). (ENG.). 24p. (J). (gr. 3-4). pap. 49.50 *(978-1-4777-2620-4(9));* pap. 8.25 *(978-1-4777-2619-8(5))* Rosen Publishing Group, Inc., The. (Rosen Classroom).

Walch Publishing Staff. Humanities. 2007. (Daily Warm-Ups Ser.). 197p. (gr. 5-6). tchr. ed., spiral bd. 24.99 *(978-0-8251-6449-1(4))* Walch Education.

Wilkie, Sara. Super Smart Information Strategies: Social Studies Projects That Shine. 2011. (Explorer Library: Information Explorer Ser.). (ENG.). 32p. (gr. 4-8). lib. bdg. 28.50 *(978-1-61080-123-2(7),* 201132) Cherry Lake Publishing.

Yespolov, Johnson & Kalna-Dubinyuk, Arynova. Extension in Kazakhstan & the Experience of the Us: Lessons from a Working National Model. 2012. 154p. 29.99 *(978-1-4771-4694-1(6))* Xlibris Corp.

SOCIAL SCIENTISTS

Hunter, Dru. Why Do We Behave Like That? Think Like a Scientist. 2016. (Think Like a Scientist Ser.). (ENG.). 48p. (J). (gr. 5-9). pap. 12.00 *(978-1-62832-202-6(0),* Creative Paperbacks) Creative Co., The.

Levy, Janey. Careers in Criminal Profiling. 2008. (Careers in Forensics Ser.). (Illus.). 64p. (J). (gr. 3-7). lib. bdg. 31.95 *(978-1-4042-1342-5(2))* Rosen Publishing Group, Inc., The.

SOCIAL SECURITY

Ruschmann, Paul & Nasiatska, Maryanne. Social Security. 2011. (Point/Counterpoint Ser.). (Illus.). 136p. (C). (gr. 9). 35.00 *(978-1-60413-775-0(4),* Chelsea Hse.) Facts On File, Inc.

Worth, Richard. Social Security ACT. 2010. (Landmark Legislation Ser.). 128p. (YA). (gr. 7-12). 39.93 *(978-1-60870-043-1(7))* Marshall Cavendish Corp.

SOCIAL SERVICE

see also Social Settlements

Bily, Cynthia A. Welfare. 2009. (Introducing Issues with Opposing Viewpoints Ser.). (ENG., Illus.). 144p. (gr. 10-12). 42.00 *(978-0-7377-4485-9(5),* Greenhaven Pr., Inc.) Cengage Gale.

Bryfonski, Dedria. Street Teens. 2011. (Opposing Viewpoints Ser.). (ENG., Illus.). 224p. (gr. 10-12). 48.80 *(978-0-7377-5761-3(2));* pap. 33.80 *(978-0-7377-5762-0(0),* Greenhaven Pr., Inc.) Cengage Gale.

Byers, Ann. Working with Veterans & Military Families Through Service Learning, 1 vol. 2015. (ENG.). 80p. (YA). 34.60 *(978-1-4777-7963-7(9),* Rosen Young Adult) Rosen Publishing Group, Inc., The.

Cahill, Bryon. Freedom from Want. 2013. (Four Freedoms Ser.). (Illus.). 32p. (gr. 3-5). pap. 8.95 *(978-1-937529-85-7(1))* Red Chair Pr.

Catalano, Angela. Community Resources: The Land & the People in Communities. (Communities at Work Ser.). 24p. 2009. (gr. 2-2). 42.50 *(978-1-61511-891-5(8),* PowerKids Pr.) 2005. (Illus.). (J). (gr. 1-4). lib. bdg. 22.60 *(978-1-4042-2781-1(4))* 2005. (ENG., Illus.). (gr. 2-3). pap. 8.25 *(978-1-4042-5016-1(6),* PowerKids Pr.) Rosen Publishing Group, Inc., The.

Center for Learning Staff. Doing My Part: Curriculum Unit. 2003. (Cross-Curriculum Ser.). 42p. (YA). tchr. ed., spiral bd. 19.95 *(978-1-56077-740-3(0))* Center for Learning, The.

—Doing My Part Student Edition: Curriculum Unit. 2003. (Cross-Curriculum Ser.). 96p. (YA). stu. ed., per. 8.95 *(978-1-56077-741-0(9))* Center for Learning, The.

Cerone, Lulu. PhilanthroParties! A Party-Planning Guide for Kids Who Want to Give Back. 2017. (ENG., Illus.). 208p. (J). (gr. 5-9). 17.99 ***(978-1-58270-587-3(9))*** Aladdin/Beyond Words.

Christian, Mary Blount. Working with Immigrants & Migrant Populations Through Service Learning, 1 vol. 2015. (ENG.). 80p. (YA). 34.60 *(978-1-4777-7969-9(8),* Rosen Young Adult) Rosen Publishing Group, Inc., The.

Cohn, Jessica. Hand to Heart: Improving Communities, 1 vol. 2nd rev. ed. 2012. (Nonfiction Readers Ser.). (ENG.). 48p. (J). (gr. 4-4). pap. 9.99 *(978-1-4333-4866-2(7))* Teacher Created Materials, Inc.

Community Workers. 2014. (Community Workers Ser.). 24p. (J). (gr. k-2). 145.26 *(978-1-62713-140-7(X))* Cavendish Square Publishing.

Davies, Elaine, et al. Dysgu Gofalu / Learning to Care. 2005. *(978-0-9543372-0-9(4))* Cofal Cymru.

Deedrick, Tami & Ready, Dee. Our Community Helpers, 1 vol. 2014. (Our Community Helpers Ser.). (ENG.). 24p. (gr. k-1). lib. bdg. 87.96 *(978-1-4765-7069-3(8),* Pebble Bks.) Capstone Press of Coughlan Cos.

Emmer, Rae. Community Service. 2009. (School Activities Ser.). 24p. (gr. 1-1). 42.50 *(978-1-60852-997-1(5),* PowerKids Pr.) Rosen Publishing Group, Inc., The.

—Community Service: Servicio Comunitario. 2004. (School Activities / Actividades Escolares Ser.). (SPA & ENG., Illus.). 24p. (J). (gr. 1-4). lib. bdg. 22.60 *(978-0-8239-6900-5(2))* Rosen Publishing Group, Inc., The.

—Community Service / Servicio Comunitario. 2009. (School Activities / Actividades escolares Ser.). (ENG & SPA.). 24p. (gr. 1-2). 42.50 *(978-1-60853-003-8(5),* Editorial Buenas Letras) Rosen Publishing Group, Inc., The.

Flath, Camden. Social Workers: Finding Solutions for Tomorrow's Society. 2010. (New Careers for the 21st Century Ser.). (Illus.). 64p. (YA). (gr. 7-18). lib. bdg. 22.95 *(978-1-4222-1821-1(X))* Mason Crest.

Flikkema, Elizabeth. Make the World a Better Place! My Sharing Time, Talent & Treasure Activity Book. Olsen, Christian, illus. 2006. 47p. 19.95 *(978-0-9774155-0-2(3))* Learning to Give.

Gibbons, Susan. Love Grows: El Amor Crece. 2012. 32p. (-18). pap. 19.99 *(978-1-4772-6732-5(8))* AuthorHouse.

Graham, Amy. Choosing a Community Service Career: A How-to Guide. 2011. (Life—a How-To Guide Ser.). (Illus.). 128p. (J). lib. bdg. 33.27 *(978-1-59845-147-4(2));* (gr. 6-18). pap. 10.95 *(978-1-59845-312-6(2))* Enslow Pubs., Inc.

Greenhaven Press Editors, ed. Welfare. 2011. (Opposing Viewpoints Ser.). (Illus.). 240p. (J). pap. 29.45 *(978-0-7377-5431-5(1),* Greenhaven Pr., Inc.); (YA). (gr. 9-12). 42.95 *(978-0-7377-5430-8(3))* Cengage Gale.

Haugen, David M. Welfare. 2008. (Opposing Viewpoints Ser.). (ENG., Illus.). 218p. (YA). (gr. 10-12). 27.50 *(978-0-7377-4017-2(5),* LML02109-239975); pap. 39.70 *(978-0-7377-4016-5(7),* LML02109-239982) Cengage Gale. (Greenhaven Pr., Inc.).

S

Honders, Jamie. Our Community Helpers. 2012. (InfoMax Readers Ser.). (ENG., Illus.). 16 pp.p. (J). (gr. k-1). pap. 7.00 *(978-1-4488-8917-4(0),* Rosen Classroom) Rosen Publishing Group, Inc., The.

Horne, Arthur M., et al, eds. Best Practices in Prevention. 2012. (Prevention Practice Kit Ser.). (ENG.). 72p. pap. 21.00 *(978-1-4522-5797-6(3),* B57976P) SAGE Pubns., Inc.

Houle, Michelle E. Lindsey Williams: Gardening for Impoverished Families. 2007. (Young Heroes Ser.). (ENG., Illus.). 48p. (J). (gr. 3-7). lib. bdg. 28.75 *(978-0-7377-3867-4(7),* Kidhaven) Cengage Gale.

Kishel, Ann-Marie. Jane Addams: A Life of Cooperation. 2007. (Pull Ahead Books-Biographies Ser.). (ENG.). 32p. (gr. k-3). pap. 7.95 *(978-0-8225-6436-2(X))* Lerner Publishing Group.

Kramer, Barbara. Jimmy Carter: A Life of Service. 2005. (Awesome Values in Famous Lives Ser.). (Illus.). 48p. (J). (gr. 3-7). lib. bdg. 25.27 *(978-0-7660-2379-6(6),* Enslow Elementary) Enslow Pubs., Inc.

Kreisman, Rachelle. Being a Good Citizen: A Kids' Guide to Community Involvement. Haggerty, Tim, illus. 2015. (Start Smart: Community Ser.). (ENG.). 32p. (gr. 1-3). 26.65 *(978-1-937529-50-5(9))* Red Chair Pr.

—People Who Help: A Kids' Guide to Community Heroes. Haggerty, Tim, illus. 2015. (Start Smart: Community Ser.). (ENG.). 32p. (gr. 1-3). 26.65 *(978-1-937529-35-2(5))* Red Chair Pr.

Leavitt, Amie Jane. Helping People with Disabilities & Special Needs Through Service Learning, 1 vol. 2015. (ENG., Illus.). 80p. (J). 34.60 *(978-1-4777-7965-1(5),* Rosen Young Adult) Rosen Publishing Group, Inc., The.

Lewis, Barbara A. The Kid's Guide to Service Projects: Over 500 Service Ideas for Young People Who Want to Make a Difference. 2nd rev. ed. 2009. (ENG., Illus.). 160p. (J). (gr. 3-18). pap. 14.99 *(978-1-57542-338-8(3))* Free Spirit Publishing, Inc.

The Library of Social Activism. 2005. (Illus.). (gr. 7-12). lib. bdg. 212.00 *(978-0-8239-9330-7(2))* Rosen Publishing Group, Inc., The.

Lüsted, Marcia Amidon. Supporting the Elderly Through Service Learning, 1 vol. 2015. (ENG.). 80p. (YA). 34.60 *(978-1-4777-7957-6(4),* Rosen Young Adult) Rosen Publishing Group, Inc., The.

Lynette, Rachel. What to Do When Your Family Is on Welfare. 2010. (Let's Work It Out Ser.). 24p. (J). (ENG.). pap. 8.25 *(978-1-4358-9762-5(5),* PowerKids Pr.); (Illus.). (gr. 2-5). lib. bdg. 22.60 *(978-1-4358-9337-5(9))* Rosen Publishing Group, Inc., The.

Marsico, Katie. Doctors Without Borders. 2014. (Community Connections: How Do They Help? Ser.). (ENG.). 24p. (J). (gr. 2-5). 25.64 *(978-1-63188-027-8(6),* 205515) Cherry Lake Publishing.

—The Red Cross. 2014. (Community Connections: How Do They Help? Ser.). (ENG.). 24p. (J). (gr. 2-5). 25.64 *(978-1-63188-028-5(4),* 205519) Cherry Lake Publishing.

—Ymca. 2016. (Community Connections: How Do They Help? Ser.). (ENG., Illus.). 24p. (J). (gr. 2-5). 27.07 *(978-1-63471-056-5(8),* 208304) Cherry Lake Publishing.

O'Neal, Claire. Volunteering in School: A Guide to Giving Back. 2010. (How to Help Ser.). (Illus.). 48p. (J). (gr. 4-8). lib. bdg. 29.95 *(978-1-58415-920-9(0))* Mitchell Lane Pubs., Inc.

Parker, Vic. Inspiring Others, 1 vol. 2012. (Kids Making a Difference Ser.). (ENG.). 48p. (gr. 3-5). lib. bdg. 32.65 *(978-1-4329-6502-0(6),* NA-h) Heinemann-Raintree.

Parker, Victoria. Helping in the Community, 1 vol. 2012. (I Can Make a Difference Ser.). (ENG., Illus.). 32p. (gr. 1-3). pap. 8.29 *(978-1-4329-5950-0(6));* lib. bdg. 27.32 *(978-1-4329-5945-6(X))* Heinemann-Raintree. (Heinemann First Library).

Petrikowski, Nicki Peter. Working for Tolerance & Social Change Through Service Learning, 1 vol. 2015. (ENG.). 80p. (J). 34.60 *(978-1-4777-7967-5(1),* Rosen Young Adult) Rosen Publishing Group, Inc., The.

Prentiss, Timothy. A Volunteer Helps. 2006. (Early Explorers Ser.). (J). pap. *(978-1-4108-6112-2(0))* Benchmark Education Co.

Rauf, Don. Protecting the Environment Through Service Learning, 1 vol. 2015. (ENG., Illus.). 80p. (J). 34.60 *(978-1-4777-7961-3(2),* Rosen Young Adult) Rosen Publishing Group, Inc., The.

Raum, Elizabeth. Helping Others, 1 vol. 2012. (Kids Making a Difference Ser.). (ENG.). 48p. (gr. 3-5). pap. 9.95 *(978-1-4329-6506-8(9));* lib. bdg. 32.65 *(978-1-4329-6501-3(8))* Heinemann-Raintree. (NA-h).

Ready, Dee. Our Community Helpers. 2013. (Our Community Helpers Ser.). (ENG.). 24p. (gr. k-1). pap. 35.70 *(978-1-62065-853-6(4));* pap. 214.20 *(978-1-62065-854-3(2));* lib. bdg. 131.94 *(978-1-62065-085-1(1))* Capstone Press of Coughlan Cos. (Pebble Bks.).

Riddle, John & Simons, Rae. Veterinarian. 2013. 96p. (J). *(978-1-4222-2750-3(2))* Mason Crest.

Russell, Bernadette. Be the Change, Make It Happen. Russell, Bernadette, illus. 2017. (ENG., Illus.). 96p. (J). pap. 14.99 *(978-1-61067-404-1(9))* Kane Miller.

Sanna, Ellyn. Childcare Worker. Riggs, Ernestine G. & Gholar, Cheryl, eds. 2013. (Careers with Character Ser.: 18). 96p. (J). (gr. 7-18). 22.95 *(978-1-4222-2752-7(9))* Mason Crest.

Scraper, Katherine, et al. Around Town: Things You Can Do in Your Community. 2011. (J). pap. *(978-1-4509-5327-6(1))* Benchmark Education Co.

Staley, Erin. Improving Community Health & Safety Through Service Learning, 1 vol. 2015. (ENG.). 80p. (YA). 34.60 *(978-1-4777-7955-2(8),* Rosen Young Adult) Rosen Publishing Group, Inc., The.

Swarts, Katherine. Welfare. 2008. (Social Issues Firsthand Ser.). (ENG., Illus.). 192p. (gr. 10-12). lib. bdg. 38.30 *(978-0-7377-4079-0(5),* LML02109-242669, Greenhaven Pr., Inc.) Cengage Gale.

The Giving Tree. Expressions of Charity. 2012. 146p. pap. 26.95 *(978-0-7414-7754-5(8))* Infinity Publishing.

Warner, Emily B. Dottie Lamm: A Friend to Families. 2007. (Now You Know Bio Ser.: 8). (J). pap. 8.95 *(978-0-86541-085-5(2))* Filter Pr., LLC.

Wiener, Gary, ed. The Environment in Rachel Carson's Silent Spring. 2011. (Social Issues in Literature Ser.). (Illus.). 224p. pap. 28.45 *(978-0-7377-5816-0(3),* Greenhaven Pr., Inc.) Cengage Gale.

SOCIAL SERVICE—FICTION

FableVision. Spf 40. Reynolds, Peter H., illus. 2013. (Zebrafish Ser.). (ENG.). 128p. (J). (gr. 5-9). 19.99 *(978-1-4169-9708-5(3),* Atheneum Bks. for Young Readers) Simon & Schuster Children's Publishing.

FableVision Staff. Spf 40. Reynolds, Peter H., illus. 2013. (Zebrafish Ser.). (ENG.). 128p. (J). (gr. 5-9). pap. 9.99 *(978-1-4169-9709-2(1),* Atheneum Bks. for Young Readers) Simon & Schuster Children's Publishing.

Lupica, Mike. Heat. 2007. (ENG.). 256p. (J). (gr. 5-18). 7.99 *(978-0-14-240757-8(7),* Puffin Books) Penguin Young Readers Group.

—Heat. 2007. 220p. (gr. 5-9). 18.00 *(978-0-7569-8131-0(X))* Perfection Learning Corp.

—Heat. 2007. 18.40 *(978-1-4177-7264-3(6),* Turtleback) Turtleback Bks.

Randall, Angel. Snow Angels. 2011. (Illus.). 32p. (J). 17.99 *(978-1-60641-046-2(6),* Shadow Mountain) Shadow Mountain Publishing.

Schillow, Ned W. and Schillow. Titanic Hearts. 2007. 100p. per. 10.00 *(978-1-4257-3842-6(7))* Xlibris Corp.

SOCIAL SERVICE—VOCATIONAL GUIDANCE

Brinkerhoff, Shirley. Social Worker. Gholar, Cheryl & Riggs, Ernestine G., eds. 2013. (Careers with Character Ser.: 18). 96p. (J). (gr. 7-18). 22.95 *(978-1-4222-2766-4(9))* Mason Crest.

Ferguson Publishing Staff, contrib. by. Social Work. 3rd rev. ed. 2010. (Careers in Focus Ser.). (Illus.). 200p. (gr. 6-12). 32.95 *(978-0-8160-8028-1(3),* Ferguson Publishing Co.) Facts On File, Inc.

Flath, Camden. Social Workers: Finding Solutions for Tomorrow's Society. 2010. (New Careers for the 21st Century Ser.). (Illus.). 64p. (YA). (gr. 7-18). pap. 9.95 *(978-1-4222-2042-9(7))* Mason Crest.

Snyder, Gail. Careers If You Like Helping People. 2017. (ENG.). 80p. (YA). (gr. 5-12). 39.93 ***(978-1-68282-136-7(6))*** ReferencePoint Pr., Inc.

SOCIAL SETTLEMENTS

see also Playgrounds

also names of settlements, e.g. Hull House (Chicago., Ill.)

Friedman, Michael. Settlement Houses: Improving the Social Welfare of America's Immigrants. 2009. (Progressive Movement 1900-1920: Efforts to Reform America's New Industrial Society Ser.). 32p. (gr. 3-4). 47.90 *(978-1-60854-170-6(3))* Rosen Publishing Group, Inc., The.

Friedman, Michael & Friedman, Brett. Settlement Houses: Improving the Social Welfare of America's Immigrants. (Progressive Movement, 1900-1920 — Efforts to Reform America's New Industrial Society Ser.). (Illus.). 32p. 2006. (ENG.). (gr. 4-8). pap. 10.00 *(978-1-4042-0859-9(3))* 2004. (YA). (gr. 5-9). lib. bdg. 22.50 *(978-1-4042-0194-1(7))* Rosen Publishing Group, Inc., The.

Owens, Tom. Immigrants & Neighbors. 2003. (Illus.). 40p. pap. 8.00 *(978-0-7891-5850-5(7))* Perfection Learning Corp.

Perez, Jessica. Hello Kitty Helps Out! 2003. (Illus.). 48p. (J). pap. *(978-0-439-44628-0(7))* Scholastic, Inc.

SOCIAL SETTLEMENTS—FICTION

Ayres, Katherine. Under Copp's Hill. 2009. (Mysteries Through Time Ser.). 176p. (YA). (gr. 4-8). 31.95 *(978-1-60754-185-1(8));* pap. 15.25 *(978-1-60754-186-8(6))* Windmill Bks.

Faigen, Anne G. New World Waiting. 2006. iii, 188p. (J). pap. *(978-0-9744715-5-6(0))* Local History Co., The.

SOCIAL STUDIES

see Geography; Social Sciences

SOCIAL WELFARE

see Social Problems; Social Service

SOCIAL WORK

see Social Service

SOCIALISM

see also Capitalism; Communism; Labor Unions; National Socialism

Berne, Emma Carlson. Paris & Nicky Hilton. 2007. (Popular Culture: A View from the Paparazzi Ser.). (Illus.). 64p. (YA). (gr. 3-7). pap. 7.95 *(978-1-4222-0358-3(1))* Mason Crest.

Hunter, Nick. What Is Socialism?, Vol. 1. 2014. (Understanding Political Systems Ser.). 48p. (gr. 6-8). (ENG.). (J). pap. 14.05 *(978-1-4824-0322-0(6));* (YA). lib. bdg. 31.95 *(978-1-4824-0321-3(8))* Stevens, Gareth Publishing LLLP.

Jarnow, Jesse. Socialism: A Primary Source Analysis. (Primary Sources of Political Systems Ser.). 64p. 2009. (gr. 5-8). 58.50 *(978-1-60851-839-5(6))* 2003. (Illus.). (J). lib. bdg. 31.95 *(978-0-8239-4521-4(9))* Rosen Publishing Group, Inc., The.

Murphy, John, ed. Socialism & Communism. 2014. (Political & Economic Systems Ser.). 312p. (YA). (gr. 9-12). 90.00 *(978-1-62275-336-9(4));* 45.00 *(978-1-62275-335-2(6))* Rosen Publishing Group, Inc., The.

SOCIALISM—UNITED STATES

Skahill, Carolyn M. The Socialist Party: Eugene V. Debs & the Radical Politics of the American Working Class. (Progressive Movement 1900-1920: Efforts to Reform America's New Industrial Society Ser.). 32p. 2009. (gr. 3-4). 47.90 *(978-1-60854-174-4(6))* 2006. (Illus.). (YA). (gr. 5-9). lib. bdg. 22.50 *(978-1-4042-0198-9(X))* Rosen Publishing Group, Inc., The.

SOCIETY OF FRIENDS

Haines, Marie. Lion-Hearted Quakers. Putman, Stanley, illus. 2011. 152p. 41.95 *(978-1-258-03120-6(5))* Literary Licensing, LLC.

Woog, Adam. What Makes Me a Quaker? 2004. (What Makes Me A — ? Ser.). (ENG., Illus.). 48p. (J). (gr. 3-7). lib. bdg. 27.50 *(978-0-7377-3082-1(X),* Greenhaven Pr., Inc.) Cengage Gale.

SOCIETY OF FRIENDS—FICTION

Kerr, M. E., pseud. Slap Your Sides. 2003. 198p. (YA). 13.65 *(978-0-7569-4240-3(3))* Perfection Learning Corp.

Rinaldi, Ann. Finishing Becca: A Story about Peggy Shippen & Benedict Arnold. 2004. (Great Episodes Ser.). (ENG.). 384p. (YA). (gr. 7-8). pap. 17.95 *(978-0-15-205079-5(5))* Houghton Mifflin Harcourt Publishing Co.

Roop, Peter & Roop, Connie. The Top-Secret Adventure of John Darragh, Revolutionary War Spy. Trover, Zachary, illus. 2010. (History's Kid Heroes Ser.). (ENG.). 32p. (gr. 3-5). pap. 8.95 *(978-0-7613-6193-0(6),* Graphic Universe™) Lerner Publishing Group.

Vernon, Louise A. Key to the Prison. Eitzen, Allan, illus. 2nd ed. 2007. (Louise A. Vernon Ser.). (ENG.). 144p. (YA). (gr. 4-9). pap. 8.99 *(978-0-8361-1813-1(8))* Herald Pr.

SOCIOLOGY

see also Aristocracy (Social Class); Cities and Towns; Civilization; Communism; Emigration and Immigration; Equality; Ethnic Relations; Population; Psychology; Race Relations; Social Change; Social Classes; Social History; Social Problems; Socialism

ABDO Publishing Company Staff. Essential Issues Set 4. 2014. (Essential Issues Set 4 Ser.: 8). (ENG.). 112p. (J). (gr. 6-12). lib. bdg. 285.12 *(978-1-62403-415-2(2),* Essential Library) ABDO Publishing Co.

Alexander, Stephanie J. Sociology: The Study of Human Social Behavior, 01 vols., 1. 2016. (Britannica Guide to the Social Sciences Ser.). (ENG.). 128p. (J). lib. bdg. 35.25 *(978-1-62275-555-4(3),* Britannica Educational Publishing) Rosen Publishing Group, Inc., The.

Analyzing the Issues: Set 3. 2017. (Analyzing the Issues Ser.). 208p. (gr. 8-8). lib. bdg. 287.58 ***(978-0-7660-8569-5(4))*** Enslow Pubs., Inc.

Aucoin, Lee. Mi Comunidad, 1 vol. rev. ed. 2010. (Early Childhood Themes Ser.).Tr. of My Community. (SPA., Illus.). 16p. (J). (gr. -1-2). pap. 19.99 *(978-1-4333-1949-5(7));* pap. 6.99 *(978-1-4333-1948-8(9))* Shell Educational Publishing.

Austen, Mary. I Learn from My Friends. 2016. (Things I Learn Ser.). (Illus.). 24p. (J). (gr. 1-1). pap. 8.25 *(978-1-4994-2345-7(4),* PowerKids Pr.) Rosen Publishing Group, Inc., The.

Berendes, Mary. People/Las Personas. Petelinsek, Kathleen, illus. 2007. (WordBooks/Libros de Palabras Ser.). (SPA & ENG.). 24p. (J). (gr. k-3). 25.64 *(978-1-59296-800-8(7),* 201097) Child's World, Inc., The.

Blundell, Jonathan. Sociology. 2014. (Cambridge International IGCSE Ser.). (ENG.). 288p. pap. 43.13 *(978-1-107-64513-4(1))* Cambridge Univ. Pr.

Blundell, Jonathan, et al. Sociology AS: The Complete Companion AQA. 2003. (ENG., Illus.). 168p. pap. 35.00 *(978-0-7487-7212-4(X))* Nelson Thornes Ltd. GBR. Dist: Trans-Atlantic Pubns., Inc.

Coldwell, Lamar. A Folktale from the Dominican Republic. 2016. (Rosen REAL Readers: Social Studies Nonfiction / Fiction: Family, Community, & the World Ser.). 12p. (gr. 1-k). pap. 6.33 *(978-1-5081-2341-5(1),* Rosen Classroom) Rosen Publishing Group, Inc., The.

Connolly, Sean. Oxfam. 2009. (J). 32.80 *(978-1-59920-305-8(7))* Black Rabbit Bks.

Cook, Diane. Mohandas K. Gandi: Spiritual Leader. 2004. (Great Names Ser.). (Illus.). 32p. (J). (gr. 3-18). lib. bdg. 19.95 *(978-1-59084-143-3(3))* Mason Crest.

Cronin, Ali & Sayer, Melissa. Making a Difference: The Changing the World Handbook. 2009. (Really Useful Handbooks Ser.). (ENG., Illus.). 48p. (J). (gr. 5-11). lib. bdg. *(978-0-7787-4390-3(X))* Crabtree Publishing Co.

Cultures of the World (Third Edition, Group 6) (r). 2014. (Cultures of the World (r) Ser.). 144p. (YA). (gr. 5-10). 282.42 *(978-0-7614-4990-4(6))* Cavendish Square Publishing.

Diamond, Susan. Social Rules for Kids-the Top 100 Social Rules Kids Need to Succeed. 2011. (ENG.). 132p. (J). pap. 19.95 *(978-1-934575-84-0(4))* Autism Asperger Publishing Co.

Diane O'Connell. People Person: The Story of Sociologist Marta Tienda. 2006. (ENG., Illus.). 128p. (gr. 7-9). per. 19.95 *(978-0-309-09557-0(3),* Joseph Henry Pr.) National Academies Pr.

Dingles, Molly. Oval Opera. Brodie, Neale, illus. 2006. (Community of Shapes Ser.). 29p. (J). *(978-1-59646-047-8(4))* Dingles & Co.

—Star Ship. Brodie, Neale, illus. 2006. (Community of Shapes Ser.). 29p. (J). *(978-1-59646-039-3(3))* Dingles & Co.

—Sweet Hearts. Brodie, Neale, illus. 2006. (Community of Shapes Ser.). (J). *(978-1-59646-037-9(7))* Dingles & Co.

Duffy, Beth. Sociology for Youth. 2006. 216p. spiral bd. *(978-0-9778602-0-3(5))* Newport Valley Pr.

Engdahl, Sylvia. Driving. Greenhaven Press Staff, ed. 2014. (Teen Rights & Freedoms Ser.). (ENG., Illus.). 176p. (gr. 10-12). lib. bdg. 42.00 *(978-0-7377-6997-5(1),* Greenhaven Pr., Inc.) Cengage Gale.

First Graphics - My Community, 7 vols. 2010. (First Graphics: My Community Ser.). (ENG.). 24p. (gr. 1-2). lib. bdg. 71.97 *(978-1-4296-5373-2(6))* Capstone Press of Coughlan Cos.

First Graphics: My Community. 2011. (First Graphics: My Community Ser.). (ENG.). 24p. (gr. 1-2). pap. 249.90 *(978-1-4296-6405-9(3))* Capstone Press of Coughlan Cos.

Furgang, Kathy. Ending Hunger & Homelessness Through Service Learning, 1 vol. 2015. (ENG.). 80p. (YA). 34.60 *(978-1-4777-7959-0(0),* Rosen Young Adult) Rosen Publishing Group, Inc., The.

Gardner, Alicia. We Are Different, We Are the Same. 2012. (InfoMax Readers Ser.). (ENG., Illus.). 16 pp.p. (J). (gr. k-1). pap. 7.00 *(978-1-4488-8950-1(2),* Rosen Classroom) Rosen Publishing Group, Inc., The.

Gerdes, Louise, ed. What Are the Causes of Prostitution? 2007. (At Issue Ser.). (ENG.). 128p. (gr. 10-12). 39.40 *(978-0-7377-2737-1(3),* Greenhaven Pr., Inc.) Cengage Gale.

Glencoe McGraw-Hill Staff. Sociology & You. 2007. (NTC: SOCIOLOGY & YOU Ser.). (ENG.). (gr. 9-12). cd-rom 140.36 *(978-0-07-878105-6(1),* 0078781051) McGraw-Hill Higher Education.

Greenhaven Press Staff, ed. Adele. 2013. (People in the News Ser.). (ENG., Illus.). 128p. (J). (gr. 7-10). lib. bdg. 33.95 *(978-1-4205-0882-6(2),* Lucent Bks.) Cengage Gale.

Hawker, Louise & Bryfonski, Dedria. Industrialism in John Steinbeck's: The Grapes of Wrath. 2008. (Social Issues in Literature Ser.). (ENG., Illus.). 224p. (gr. 10-12). 46.40 *(978-0-7377-4034-9(5),* LML02109-239998, Greenhaven Pr., Inc.) Cengage Gale.

—Industrialism in John Steinbeck's the Grapes of Wrath. 2008. (Social Issues in Literature Ser.). (ENG., Illus.). 224p. (gr. 10-12). pap. 32.00 *(978-0-7377-4035-6(3),* LML02109-249003, Greenhaven Pr., Inc.) Cengage Gale.

Hello From 2030: The Science of the Future & You. 2014. (ENG., Illus.). 224p. (J). (gr. 3-7). 15.99 *(978-1-58270-474-6(0))* Aladdin/Beyond Words.

In the News, 6 vols., Set 4. Incl. Egg Donation: The Reasons & the Risks. Lew, Kristi. lib. bdg. 31.95 *(978-1-4358-5276-1(1));* Hunger: Food Insecurity in America. Wilson, Michael R. lib. bdg. 31.95 *(978-1-4358-5278-5(8));* Organ Donation: Risks, Rewards, & Research. Brezina, Corona. lib. bdg. 31.95 *(978-1-4358-5275-4(3));* (Illus.). 64p. (YA). (gr. 7-12). 2009. 2009. Set lib. bdg. 175.50 *(978-1-4358-3310-4(4))* Rosen Publishing Group, Inc., The.

Kaner, Etta. Earth-Friendly Buildings, Bridges & More: The Eco-Journal of Corry Lapont. MacEachern, Stephen, illus. 2012. (ENG.). 64p. (J). (gr. 3-7). 18.95 *(978-1-55453-570-5(0))* Kids Can Pr., Ltd. CAN. Dist: Hachette Bk. Group.

Kaplan, Arie. Social Intelligence. 2013. (7 Character Strengths of Highly Successful Students Ser.). 64p. (J). (gr. 5-8). 31.95 *(978-1-4488-9552-6(9));* pap. 12.95 *(978-1-4488-9565-6(0));* pap. 77.70 *(978-1-4488-9566-3(9))* Rosen Publishing Group, Inc., The.

Kiesbye, Stefan. Cliques. 2009. (Social Issues Firsthand Ser.). (ENG.). 192p. (gr. 10-12). 33.75 *(978-0-7377-4029-5(9),* Greenhaven Pr., Inc.) Cengage Gale.

Kyi, Tanya Lloyd. 50 Body Questions: A Book That Spills Its Guts. Kinnaird, Ross, illus. 2014. (50 Questions Ser.). (ENG.). 108p. (J). (gr. 4-6). 22.95 *(978-1-55451-613-1(7),* 9781554516131); 2nd ed. pap. 14.95 *(978-1-55451-612-4(9),* 9781554516124) Annick Pr., Ltd. CAN. Dist: Publishers Group West (PGW).

Laidlaw, Jill A. Cities. 2012. (What's in My Food Ser.). 32p. (gr. 1-4). lib. bdg. 27.10 *(978-1-59920-421-5(5))* Black Rabbit Bks.

Langston-George, Rebecca. For the Right to Learn. Bock, Janna, illus. 2015. (Encounter: Narrative Nonfiction Picture Bks.). (ENG.). 40p. (gr. 3-4). 15.95 *(978-1-62370-426-1(X))* Encounter Bks.

Lewis, Clare. History in Living Memory. 2015. (History in Living Memory Ser.). (ENG.). 24p. (gr. k-2). lib. bdg. 93.28 *(978-1-4846-0927-9(1),* Heinemann Read & Learn) Heinemann-Raintree.

McFall, Sally, ed. Pro/Con 2, 6 vols. 2003. (Illus.). 1392p. (YA). 339.00 *(978-0-7172-5753-9(3))* Scholastic Library Publishing.

—Pro/Con 3, 12 vols. 2004. (Illus.). (YA). 339.00 *(978-0-7172-5927-4(7),* Grolier) Scholastic Library Publishing.

Miller, Jay. American Indian Families. 2006. (True Bks). (Illus.). 47p. (gr. 3-5). 16.95 *(978-0-7569-7130-4(6))* Perfection Learning Corp.

Moehn, Heather. Everything You Need to Know about Cliques. 2009. (Need to Know Library). 64p. (gr. 5-5). 58.50 *(978-1-60854-058-7(8))* Rosen Publishing Group, Inc., The.

Morrow, Carol. Forgiveness Is Smart for the Heart. Alley, R. W., illus. 2003. (Elf-Help Books for Kids). 32p. (J). per. 6.95 *(978-0-87029-370-2(2))* Abbey Pr.

Mototsune, Kat. Cliques: Using What You Have Inside, 1 vol. Shannon, Ben, illus. (Lorimer Deal with It Ser.). (ENG.). 32p. (J). (gr. 4-12). 2011. pap. 12.95 *(978-1-55277-544-8(5),* 9781552775448) 2010. lib. bdg. 24.95 *(978-1-55277-545-5(3),* 9781552775455) Lorimer, James & Co., Ltd., Pubs. CAN. Dist: Orca Bk. Pubs. USA, Casemate Pubs. & Bk. Distributors, LLC.

O'Connell, Diane. People Person: The Story of Sociologist Marta Tienda. 2005. (Women's Adventures in Science Ser.). (ENG., Illus.). 120p. (YA). (gr. 5-9). lib. bdg. 31.50 *(978-0-531-16781-6(X))* Scholastic Library Publishing.

Parnell, Declan. Daniel Is Haitian American, 01 vols., 1. 2016. (Rosen REAL Readers: Social Studies Nonfiction / Fiction: Family, Community, & the World Ser.). (ENG.). 12p. (J). pap. 6.33 *(978-1-5081-1794-0(2),* Rosen Classroom) Rosen Publishing Group, Inc., The.

Payne, Lauren Murphy. We Can Get Along: A Child's Book of Choices. Iwai, Melissa, illus. 2nd rev. ed. 2015. (ENG.). 40p. (Orig.). (J). (gr. -1-2). pap. 9.99 *(978-1-63198-027-5(0))* Free Spirit Publishing, Inc.

Ratliff, Thomas. You Wouldn't Want to Be a Civil War Soldier! A War You'D Rather Not Fight. 2013. (You Wouldn't Want To... Ser.). lib. bdg. 20.80 *(978-0-606-31627-9(2),* Turtleback) Turtleback Bks.

Reed, Cristie. Problem Solving. 2012. (ENG., Illus.). 24p. (gr. k-2). pap. 8.95 *(978-1-61810-266-9(4))* Rourke Educational Media.

Return of the Native. (ARA., Illus.). 48p. (J). 12.00 *(978-0-86685-625-6(0))* International Bk. Ctr., Inc.

Rice, Dona Herweck. Puedo Hacer Cualquier Cosa, 1 vol. rev. ed. 2010. (Early Childhood Themes Ser.).Tr. of I Can Be Anything. (SPA., Illus.). 16p. (J). (gr. -1-2). pap. 19.99 *(978-1-4333-1951-8(9));* pap. 6.99 *(978-1-4333-1950-1(0))* Shell Educational Publishing.

Ring, Susan. Helping Hands. 2005. (Yellow Umbrella Fluent Level Ser.). (ENG.). 16p. (gr. k-1). pap. 35.70 *(978-0-7368-5306-4(5),* Yellow Umbrella Bks.) Capstone Press of Coughlan Cos.

Rothenberg, Annye. Why Do I Have To? Wenzel, David T., illus. 2009. 40p. (J). pap. 9.95 *(978-0-9790420-1-0(1))* Perfecting Parenting Pr.

Schuette, Sarah L. Communities, 1 vol. rev. ed. 2009. (People Ser.). (ENG.). 24p. (gr. k-1). pap. 6.29 *(978-1-4296-3461-8(8),* Pebble Bks.) Capstone Press of Coughlan Cos.

Shepard, Jon M., et al. Sociology & You. 2006. (NTC: SOCIOLOGY & YOU Ser.). (ENG., Illus.). 601p. (gr. 9-12). stu. ed. 122.88 *(978-0-07-874519-5(5),* 0078745195) McGraw-Hill Higher Education.

Somervill, Barbara A., et al. True Stories. 2016. (True Stories Ser.). (ENG.). 32p. lib. bdg. 306.50 *(978-1-4846-3624-4(4),* NA-h) Heinemann-Raintree.

Suen, Anastasia. Medicos Sin Fronteras. 2004. (Organizaciones de Ayuda (Helping Organizations) Ser.). (SPA & ENG., Illus.). 24p. (J). (gr. 3-6). lib. bdg. 22.60 *(978-0-8239-6860-2(X),* Editorial Buenas Letras) Rosen Publishing Group, Inc., The.

Thompson, Chad. Viera Madre Hubbard, 1 vol. rev. ed. 2010. (Early Childhood Themes Ser.).Tr. of Old Mother Hubbard. (SPA., Illus.). 16p. (J). (gr. -1-2). pap. 19.99 *(978-1-4333-1953-2(5));* pap. 6.99 *(978-1-4333-1952-5(7))* Shell Educational Publishing.

Turning Points in History, 4 vols., Set. Incl. Britannica Guide to Explorers & Explorations That Changed the Modern World.

Pletcher, Kenneth. 352p. lib. bdg. 45.00 *(978-1-61530-028-0(7))*; Britannica Guide to Inventions That Changed the Modern World. Curley, Robert, ed. 392p. lib. bdg. 45.00 *(978-1-61530-020-4(1))*; (YA). (gr. 9-12). (Turning Points in History Ser.). (Illus.). 392p. 2009. Set lib. bdg. 180.00 *(978-1-61530-034-1(1))* Rosen Publishing Group, Inc., The.

Warren, Rick H. Quinn at School: Relating, Connecting & Responding at School. 2011. (ENG., Illus.). 121p. (J). pap. 18.95 *(978-1-934575-87-1(9))* Autism Asperger Publishing Co.

Weitzman, Elizabeth. Let's Talk about Staying in a Shelter. 2004. (Let's Talk Library). (Illus.). 24p. (J). lib. bdg. 22.60 *(978-0-8239-6812-1(X)*, PowerKids Pr.) Rosen Publishing Group, Inc., The.

Willis, Laurie. Extremism. (Opposing Viewpoints Ser.). (ENG., Illus.). 2011. 240p. pap. 29.45 *(978-0-7377-4965-6(2))* 2010. 224p. (gr. 12-12). 48.80 *(978-0-7377-4964-9(4))* Cengage Gale. (Greenhaven Pr., Inc.).

SOCIOLOGY, RURAL

see also Country Life; Peasants

Miller, Jake. Who's Who in a Rural Community. 2009. (Communities at Work Ser.). 24p. (gr. 2-2). 42.50 *(978-1-61511-899-1(3)*, PowerKids Pr.) Rosen Publishing Group, Inc., The.

Sterling, Kristin. Living in Rural Communities. 2008. pap. 34.95 *(978-0-8225-9478-9(1))*; (ENG., Illus.). 24p. lib. bdg. 23.93 *(978-0-8225-8599-2(5)*, Lerner Pubns.) Lerner Publishing Group.

SOCIOLOGY, URBAN

see also Cities and Towns; Urban Renewal

Braun, Eric. The Guys' Guide to Making City Life More Awesome, 1 vol. 2014. (Guys' Guides). (ENG.). 32p. (gr. 3-4). lib. bdg. 27.99 *(978-1-4765-3923-2(5)*, Edge Bks.) Capstone Press of Coughlan Cos.

Cane, Ella. Communities in My World, 1 vol. 2013. (My World Ser.). (ENG.). 24p. (gr. k-1). pap. 6.95 *(978-1-4765-3462-6(4)*, Pebble Bks.) Capstone Press of Coughlan Cos.

Colligan, L. H. The City. 2014. (J). pap. *(978-1-62712-883-4(2))* Cavendish Square Publishing.

Downer, Ann. Wild Animal Neighbors: Sharing Our Urban World. 2013. (ENG., Illus.). 64p. (gr. 5-12). 33.27 *(978-0-7613-9021-3(9)*, Twenty-First Century Bks.) Lerner Publishing Group.

Harasymiw, Therese. Life in a Colonial City. 2009. (Real Life Readers Ser.). 32p. (gr. 4-5). pap. 10.00 *(978-1-4358-0165-3(2)*, Rosen Classroom) Rosen Publishing Group, Inc., The.

Held, George. Neighbors: The Yard Critters Too. Kim, Joung Un, illus. 2013. (ENG.). 32p. 20.00 *(978-0-916754-26-6(X))* Filsinger & Co., Ltd.

Hopkinson, Deborah. Shutting Out the Sky: Life in the Tenements of New York, 1880-1924. 2003. (ENG., Illus.). 144p. (J). (gr. 3-7). 19.99 *(978-0-439-37590-0(8)*, Orchard Bks.) Scholastic, Inc.

Laidlaw, Jill. Cities. 2010. (Sustaining Our Environment Ser.). 48p. (J). lib. bdg. 35.65 *(978-1-60753-135-7(6))* Amicus Publishing.

Lang, Glenna & Wunsch, Marjory. Genius of Common Sense: Jane Jacobs & the Story of the Death & Life of Great American Cities. 2012. pap. 15.95 *(978-1-56792-456-5(5))* Godine, David R. Pub.

Lang, Glenna W. & Wunsch, Marjory. Genius of Common Sense: Jane Jacobs & the Story of the Death & Life of Great American Cities. 2009. (ENG., Illus.). 128p. (YA). (gr. 5-18). 17.95 *(978-1-56792-384-1(4))* Godine, David R. Pub.

Leardi, Jeanette. Making Cities Green. 2009. (Going Green Ser.). (Illus.). 32p. (YA). (gr. 3-6). lib. bdg. 25.27 *(978-1-59716-961-5(7))* Bearport Publishing Co., Inc.

McAllan, Kate. Urban Habitats. 2013. (Discovery Education: Habitats Ser.). 32p. (J). (gr. 3-6). 25.25 *(978-1-4777-1327-3(1))*; pap. 10.00 *(978-1-4777-1489-8(8))* Rosen Publishing Group, Inc., The. (PowerKids Pr.).

McDonald, Caryl. Rural Life, Urban Life. 2013. (InfoMax Readers Ser.). (ENG.). 24p. (J). (gr. 2-3). pap. 8.25 *(978-1-4777-2346-3(3))*; pap. 49.50 *(978-1-4777-2347-0(1))* Rosen Publishing Group, Inc., The. (Rosen Classroom).

Meissner, David. My Neighborhood. 2011. (Early Connections Ser.). (J). *(978-1-61672-666-9(0))* Benchmark Education Co.

Rau, Dana Meachen & National Geographic Learning Staff. In the City. 2010. (Rise & Shine Ser.). (ENG.). (C). pap. 18.95 *(978-0-7614-3306-4(6))* National Geographic School Publishing, Inc.

Urban Habitats. 2013. (Discovery Education: Habitats Ser.). 32p. (J). (gr. 3-6). pap. 60.00 *(978-1-4777-1490-4(1)*, PowerKids Pr.) Rosen Publishing Group, Inc., The.

Wirkner, Linda. Learning about Urban Growth in America with Graphic Organizers. 2009. (Graphic Organizers in Social Studies). 24p. (gr. 3-4). 42.50 *(978-1-61513-087-0(X)*, PowerKids Pr.) Rosen Publishing Group, Inc., The.

SOCRATES

Bowen, Richard. Socrates: Greek Philosopher. (Illus.). 32p. (J). 2013. (People of Importance Ser.: 21). (gr. 4-18). 19.95 *(978-1-4222-2857-9(6))* 2004. (Great Names Ser.). (gr. 3-18). lib. bdg. 19.95 *(978-1-59084-150-1(6))* Mason Crest.

Dhillon, Natasha C. & Lim, Jun. Socrates: The Father of Ethics & Inquiry. 2015. (Greatest Greek Philosophers Ser.). (ENG.). 112p. (J). (gr. 7-8). 35.60 *(978-1-4994-6134-3(8)*, Rosen Young Adult) Rosen Publishing Group, Inc., The.

Zamosky, Lisa. Socrates: Greek Philosopher, 1 vol. 2007. (Primary Source Readers Ser.). (ENG.). 32p. (J). (gr. 4-4). pap. 8.99 *(978-0-7439-0435-3(4))* Shell Educational Publishing.

Zannos, Susan. The Life & Times of Socrates. 2004. (Biography from Ancient Civilizations Ser.). (Illus.). 48p. (J). (gr. 4-8). lib. bdg. 29.95 *(978-1-58415-282-8(6))* Mitchell Lane Pubs., Inc.

SOFTBALL

Baker, Jayne & Hofstetter, Adam. An Insider's Guide to Softball. 2014. (Sports Tips, Techniques, & Strategies Ser.). (Illus.). 48p. (J). (gr. 5-8). pap. 11.75 *(978-1-4777-8588-1(4)*, Rosen Reference) Rosen Publishing Group, Inc., The.

Bonnet, Robert L. & Keen, Dan. Home Run! Science Projects with Baseball & Softball. 2009. (Score! Sports Science Projects Ser.). (Illus.). 104p. (J). (gr. 5-9). lib. bdg. 33.27 *(978-0-7660-3365-8(1))* Enslow Pubs., Inc.

Bratton, Deborah B. & Bratton, Ashley D. Record-a-Sport Baseball & Softball Organizer. Bratton, Deborah B. & Bratton, Ashley D., eds. Bratton, Deborah B. & Bratton, Ashley D., illus. 2003. (Illus.). (gr. 1-18). 18.95 *(978-1-931746-03-8(6))* Sport Your Stuff Corp.

Douglas, Peter. Baseball & Softball: Success on the Diamond. 2017. (Preparing for Game Day Ser.: Vol. 10). (ENG.). (YA). (gr. 7-12). 24.95 ***(978-1-4222-3913-1(6))*** Mason Crest.

Fauchald, Nick. Batter Up! You Can Play Softball, 1 vol. Rooney, Ronnie, illus. 2005. (Game Day Ser.). (ENG.). 24p. (gr. k-3). lib. bdg. 26.65 *(978-1-4048-1152-2(4))* Picture Window Bks.

Gitlin, Marty. Girls Play to Win Softball. 2011. (Girls Play to Win Ser.). 64p. (J). (gr. 3-6). lib. bdg. 27.93 *(978-1-59953-465-7(7))* Norwood Hse. Pr.

Gola, Mark. Winning Softball for Girls, Second Edition. 2nd rev. ed. 2009. (Winning Sports for Girls Ser.). (gr. 6-12). 224p. pap. 14.95 *(978-0-8160-7717-5(7)*, Checkmark Bks.); (Illus.). 240p. 39.50 *(978-0-8160-7716-8(9)*, Chelsea Hse.) Facts On File, Inc.

Hofstetter, Adam B. Softball: Rules, Tips, Strategy, & Safety. (Sports from Coast to Coast Ser.). 48p. 2009. (gr. 6-6). 53.00 *(978-1-60853-130-1(9)*, Rosen Reference) 2006. (Illus.). (J). (gr. 5-8). lib. bdg. 29.25 *(978-1-4042-0996-1(4))* Rosen Publishing Group, Inc., The.

Howell, Brian. Girls' Softball, 1 vol. 2013. (Girls' SportsZone Ser.). (ENG., Illus.). 48p. (J). (gr. 3-6). lib. bdg. 32.79 *(978-1-61783-990-0(6)*, SportsZone) ABDO Publishing Co.

McIntyre, Abigael & Wesley, Ann. Fastpitch Softball: Girls Rocking It, 01 vols., 1. 2016. (Title IX Rocks! Ser.). (ENG.). 64p. (J). 32.95 *(978-1-4994-6241-8(7)*, Rosen Young Adult) Rosen Publishing Group, Inc., The.

Nitz, Kristin Wolden. Softball. King, Andy, photos by. 2005. (Play-by-Play Ser.). (Illus.). 80p. (gr. 4-8). pap., lib. bdg. 23.93 *(978-0-8225-9875-6(2))* Lerner Publishing Group.

Rissman, Rebecca. Top Softball Tips. 2017. (Top Sports Tips Ser.). (ENG., Illus.). 32p. (gr. 3-4). lib. bdg. 27.99 *(978-1-5157-4721-5(2)*, Snap Bks.) Capstone Press of Coughlan Cos.

Rogers, Amy B. Girls Play Softball. 2016. (Girls Join the Team Ser.). 24p. (J). (gr. 3-3). pap. 8.25 *(978-1-5081-4964-4(X)*, PowerKids Pr.) Rosen Publishing Group, Inc., The.

Sanna, Gabriel. Baseball & Softball. 2010. (Getting the Edge Ser.). 96p. (YA). lib. bdg. 24.95 *(978-1-4222-1730-6(2))* Mason Crest.

Woodyard, Janelle Valido. A Girl's Guide to Softball, 1 vol. 2012. (Get in the Game Ser.). (ENG.). 32p. (gr. 3-4). lib. bdg. 27.99 *(978-1-4296-7672-4(8)*, Snap Bks.) Capstone Press of Coughlan Cos.

SOFTBALL—FICTION

Bowe, Julie. Curve Ball. 2017. (Victoria Torres, Unfortunately Average Ser.). (ENG.). 160p. (gr. 4-4). pap. 5.95 *(978-1-4965-3820-8(X))*; lib. bdg. 26.65 *(978-1-4965-3818-5(8))* Stone Arch Bks.

Cook, Jacqueline. On to Nationals. 2008. 296p. per. 12.95 *(978-1-4327-1681-3(6))* Outskirts Pr., Inc.

Funk, Constance J. Holy as Thou. 2009. (Illus.). 400p. pap. 22.00 *(978-1-933002-66-8(2))* PublishingWorks.

Gassman, Julie A. I Am on Strike Against Softball, 1 vol. Santillan, Jorge H., illus. 2012. (Sports Illustrated Kids Victory School Superstars Ser.). (ENG.). 56p. (gr. 1-3). pap. 5.95 *(978-1-4342-3870-2(9))*; lib. bdg. 26.65 *(978-1-4342-2247-3(0))* Stone Arch Bks.

The Grumpy Millionaire: Individual Title Six-Packs. (Bookweb Ser.). 32p. (gr. 5-18). 34.00 *(978-0-7635-3777-7(2))* Rigby Education.

Johnson, Maureen. The Key to the Golden Firebird. 2004. (ENG.). 304p. (J). (gr. 7-18). 15.99 *(978-0-06-054138-5(5))* HarperCollins Pubs.

Key, Anne. Stealing Bases. 2016. (ENG., Illus.). (YA). 24.99 ***(978-1-63533-075-5(0)***, Harmony Ink Pr.) Dreamspinner Pr.

Mackel, Kathy. MadCat. 2005. (Illus.). 192p. (J). 15.99 *(978-0-06-054869-8(X))* HarperCollins Pubs.

Mackey, Weezie Kerr. Throwing Like a Girl, 0 vols. 2010. (ENG.). 272p. (YA). (gr. 7-9). pap. 9.99 *(978-0-7614-5606-3(6)*, 9780761456063, Amazon Children's Publishing) Amazon Publishing.

Maddox, Jake. Softball Surprise, 1 vol. Wood, Katie, illus. 2014. (Jake Maddox Girl Sports Stories Ser.). (ENG.). 72p. (gr. 2-3). 25.32 *(978-1-4342-4141-2(6))* Stone Arch Bks.

—Stolen Bases. Mourning, Tuesday, illus. 2008. (Jake Maddox Girl Sports Stories Ser.). (ENG.). 72p. (gr. 2-3). 25.32 *(978-1-4342-0779-1(X))* Stone Arch Bks.

McCorkle, Denise. On Angels Wings - Softball. 2008. 32p. pap. 17.95 *(978-1-4327-3102-1(5))* Outskirts Pr., Inc.

RealBuzz Studios Staff. Hits & Misses. 2007. 128p. (YA). No. 1. pap. 4.97 *(978-1-59789-569-5(5))*No. 2. pap. 4.97 *(978-1-59789-570-5(9))*No. 3. pap. 4.97 *(978-1-59789-571-2(7))*No. 4. pap. 4.97 *(978-1-59789-572-9(5))* Barbour Publishing, Inc. (Barbour Bks.).

Ritter, John H. Under the Baseball Moon. 2008. (ENG., Illus.). 320p. (J). (gr. 5-18). 9.99 *(978-0-14-241090-5(X)*, Puffin Books) Penguin Young Readers Group.

—Under the Baseball Moon. 2008. (Illus.). 283p. (gr. 8-12). 17.00 *(978-0-7569-8934-7(5))* Perfection Learning Corp.

Robyn Washburn. Singled Out in Center Field: Diamonds Are A Girl's Best Friend - Book One. Lisa Byers, illus. 2009. 80p. pap. 12.00 *(978-1-4389-6245-0(2))* AuthorHouse.

Van Draanen, Wendelin. Sammy Keyes & the Search for Snake Eyes. 2008. (Sammy Keyes Ser.: Bk. 7). (J). 64.99 *(978-1-60640-645-8(0))* Findaway World, LLC.

—Sammy Keyes & the Search for Snake Eyes. Van Draanen, Wendelin, illus. 2003. (Sammy Keyes Ser.: Bk. 7). (Illus.). pap. 54.95 incl. audio compact disk *(978-1-59112-281-4(3))*; pap. 36.95 incl. audio *(978-1-59112-273-9(2))* Live Oak Media.

—Sammy Keyes & the Search for Snake Eyes. 2003. (Sammy Keyes Ser.: Bk. 7). (Illus.). 277p. (gr. 5-9). 17.00 *(978-0-7569-1445-5(0))* Perfection Learning Corp.

—Sammy Keyes & the Search for Snake Eyes. 2003. (Sammy Keyes Ser.: 7). (ENG.). 320p. (J). (gr. 5-7). 7.99 *(978-0-440-41900-6(X)*, Yearling) Random Hse. Children's Bks.

—Sammy Keyes & the Sisters of Mercy. 2008. (Sammy Keyes Ser.: Bk. 3). (J). 59.99 *(978-1-60640-646-5(9))* Findaway World, LLC.

Wilson, Wendy. Just Desserts. 2007. 53p. pap. 16.95 *(978-1-4241-9285-4(4))* America Star Bks.

Winkler, Henry & Oliver, Lin. A Tale of Two Tails. Watson, Jesse Joshua, illus. 2008. (Hank Zipzer Ser.: 15). (ENG.). 160p. (J). (gr. 3-7). pap. 5.99 *(978-0-448-44378-2(3)*, Grosset & Dunlap) Penguin Young Readers Group.

—The Zippity Zinger. 2004. (Hank Zipzer Ser.: No. 4). 160p. (J). (gr. 2-6). pap. 29.00 incl. audio *(978-1-4000-9009-9(1)*, Listening Library) Random Hse. Audio Publishing Group.

—The Zippity Zinger. 2006. (Hank Zipzer Ser.: No. 4). 154p. (J). (gr. 3-9). lib. bdg. 24.21 *(978-1-59961-103-7(1))* Spotlight.

Wolff, Virginia Euwer. Bat 6. 256p. (J). (gr. 4-6). pap. 4.99 *(978-0-8072-8223-6(5))*; 2004. (gr. 5-9). pap. 36.00 incl. audio *(978-0-8072-8222-9(7)*, YYA144SP) Random Hse. Audio Publishing Group. (Listening Library).

SOIL CONSERVATION

see also Erosion

Cunningham, Kevin. Soil. 2009. (Diminishing Resources Ser.). 111p. (J). 28.95 *(978-1-59935-114-8(5))* Reynolds, Morgan Inc.

Food and Agriculture Organization of the United Nations Staff & Youth and United Nations Global Alliance Staff. Soils Challenge Badge. 2014. (ENG.). 117p. pap. 20.00 *(978-92-5-108433-5(5))* Food & Agriculture Organization of the United Nations ITA. Dist: Rowman & Littlefield Publishers, Inc.

Stefoff, Rebecca. Soil for Agriculture. 2016. (Science of Soil Ser.). 48p. (J). 31.36 *(978-1-5026-2225-9(4))* Cavendish Square Publishing.

SOIL EROSION

see Erosion

SOIL FERTILITY

see Soils

SOILS

see also Clay; Irrigation; Reclamation of Land

also headings beginning with the word Soil

Aloian, Molly. Different Kinds of Soil. 2010. (Everybody Digs Soil Ser.). (ENG., Illus.). 32p. (J). (gr. 3-6). pap. *(978-0-7787-5413-8(8))*; lib. bdg. *(978-0-7787-5400-8(6))* Crabtree Publishing Co.

Barker, David M. Science Lab: Soil. 2011. (Explorer Library: Language Arts Explorer Ser.). (ENG.). 32p. (gr. 4-8). pap. 14.21 *(978-1-61080-296-3(9)*, 201218); lib. bdg. 28.50 *(978-1-61080-207-9(1)*, 201190) Cherry Lake Publishing.

Bourgeois, Paulette. The Dirt on Dirt. Newbigging, Martha, illus. 2008. (ENG.). 48p. (J). (gr. 3-7). pap. 7.95 *(978-1-55453-102-8(0))* Kids Can Pr., Ltd. CAN. Dist: Hachette Bk. Group.

Bowman, Chris. Soil. 2014. (Earth Science Rocks! Ser.). (ENG., Illus.). 24p. (J). (gr. k-3). lib. bdg. 25.95 *(978-1-60014-982-5(0)*, Blastoff! Readers) Bellwether Media.

Cardenas, Ernesto A. Soils. 2009. pap. 4.95 *(978-1-60698-088-0(2))* Milo Educational Bks. & Resources.

Coldwell, Lamar. All about Soil. 2016. (Rosen REAL Readers: STEM & STEAM Collection). 8p. (gr. 1-k). pap. 5.46 *(978-1-5081-2413-9(2)*, Rosen Classroom) Rosen Publishing Group, Inc., The.

Conners, Cathy. Let's Look at Soil. 2013. (Rosen Readers Ser.). (ENG.). 24p. (J). (gr. 2-3). pap. 8.25 *(978-1-4777-2342-5(0)*, Rosen Classroom) Rosen Publishing Group, Inc., The.

Connors, Cathy. Let's Look at Soil. 2013. (Rosen Readers Ser.). (ENG.). 24p. (J). (gr. 2-3). pap. 49.50 *(978-1-4777-2768-3(X)*, Rosen Classroom) Rosen Publishing Group, Inc., The.

Cunningham, Kevin. Soil. 2009. (Diminishing Resources Ser.). 111p. (J). 28.95 *(978-1-59935-114-8(5))* Reynolds, Morgan Inc.

Ditchfield, Christin. Soil. 2010. (ENG., Illus.). 48p. (C). (gr. 3-5). pap. 10.95 *(978-0-516-29368-4(0))* National Geographic School Publishing, Inc.

Food and Agriculture Organization of the United Nations Staff & Youth and United Nations Global Alliance Staff. Soils Challenge Badge. 2014. (ENG.). 117p. pap. 20.00 *(978-92-5-108433-5(5))* Food & Agriculture Organization of the United Nations ITA. Dist: Rowman & Littlefield Publishers, Inc.

Franchino, Vicky. Experiment with Soil. 2010. (Explorer Junior Library: Science Explorer Junior Ser.). (ENG.). 32p. (gr. 3-6). lib. bdg. 28.50 *(978-1-60279-837-3(0)*, 200540) Cherry Lake Publishing.

—Super Cool Science Experiments: Soil. 2009. (Explorer Library: Science Explorer Ser.). (ENG., Illus.). 32p. (gr. 4-8). lib. bdg. 28.50 *(978-1-60279-526-6(6)*, 200297) Cherry Lake Publishing.

Freed, Kira. The Secrets of Soil. 2017. (Text Connections Guided Close Reading Ser.). (J). (gr. 2). *(978-1-4900-1835-5(2))* Benchmark Education Co.

Gardner, Robert. Science Fair Projects about Water & Soil. 2016. (Hands-On Science Ser.). 48p. (J). pap. 11.70 *(978-0-7660-8211-3(3))* Enslow Pubs., Inc.

—Soil: Green Science Projects for a Sustainable Planet. 2011. (Team Green Science Projects Ser.). (Illus.). 128p. (J). (gr. 5-9). lib. bdg. 33.27 *(978-0-7660-3647-5(2))* Enslow Pubs., Inc.

—Super Science Projects about Earth's Soil & Water. LaBaff, Tom, illus. 2007. (Rockin' Earth Science Experiments Ser.). 48p. (J). (gr. 3-4). lib. bdg. 25.27 *(978-0-7660-2735-0(X)*, Enslow Elementary) Enslow Pubs., Inc.

Graham, Ian. You Wouldn't Want to Live Without Dirt! Bergin, Mark, illus. 2016. (You Wouldn't Want to Live Without... Ser.). (ENG.). 32p. (J). lib. bdg. 29.00 *(978-0-531-21488-6(5)*, Children's Pr.) Scholastic Library Publishing.

Greek, Joe. What Is Soil?, 01 vols., 1. 2016. (Junior Geologist Ser.). (ENG., Illus.). 32p. (J). pap. 12.90 *(978-1-5081-0051-5(9)*, Britannica Educational Publishing) Rosen Publishing Group, Inc., The.

Green, Jen. Rocks & Soil. 2008. (Our Earth Ser.). (Illus.). 24p. (YA). (gr. 1-4). lib. bdg. 21.25 *(978-1-4042-4271-5(6))* Rosen Publishing Group, Inc., The.

Gurney, Beth. Sand & Soil. 2004. (Rocks, Minerals, & Resources Ser.). (ENG., Illus.). 32p. (J). pap. *(978-0-7787-1449-1(7))* Crabtree Publishing Co.

Hagler, Gina. Soils. 2016. (J). *(978-1-4896-5289-8(2))* Weigl Pubs., Inc.

—Step-by-Step Experiments with Soils. Ostrom, Bob, illus. 2012. (Step-By-Step Experiments Ser.). (ENG.). 32p. (J). (gr. 1-4). lib. bdg. 29.93 *(978-1-60973-592-0(7)*, 201238) Child's World, Inc., The.

Hall, Pamela. Discover Dirt. Yamada, Jane, illus. 2014. (Science Around Us Ser.). (ENG.). 24p. (J). (gr. -1-2). 25.64 *(978-1-62687-301-8(1)*, 207142) Child's World, Inc., The.

Hansen, Grace. Soils, 1 vol. 2016. (ENG., Illus.). 24p. (J). *(978-1-62970-910-9(7)*, 1391190) ABDO Publishing Co.

—Tierra. 2016. (¡Súper Geología! Ser.). (SPA.). 24p. (J). (gr. 1-6). pap. 7.95 *(978-1-4966-0683-9(3))* Capstone Classroom.

Hayes, Amy. We Need Worms. 2015. (Creatures We Can't Live Without Ser.). (ENG., Illus.). 24p. (J). (gr. 3-4). pap. 8.25 *(978-1-4994-0986-4(9)*, PowerKids Pr.) Rosen Publishing Group, Inc., The.

Hirsch, Rebecca. Soil, 1 vol. 2014. (Rocks & Minerals Ser.). (ENG.). 48p. (gr. 8-12). lib. bdg. 32.79 *(978-1-62403-391-9(1))* ABDO Publishing Co.

Hodge, Judith. Riches from Earth & Las riquezas de la Tierra: 6 English, 6 Spanish Adaptations. 2011. (ENG & SPA.). (J). 97.00 net. *(978-1-4108-5716-3(6))* Benchmark Education Co.

Hoffman, Steven M. Rocks & Soil. 2011. (Rock It! Ser.). (Illus.). 24p. (J). pap. 8.25 *(978-1-4488-2706-0(X))*; lib. bdg. 22.60 *(978-1-4488-2560-8(1))* Rosen Publishing Group, Inc., The. (PowerKids Pr.).

Holt, Rinehart and Winston Staff. Holt Science & Technology Chapter 10: Earth Science: Weathering of Soil. 5th ed. 2004. (Illus.). pap. 12.86 *(978-0-03-030311-1(7))* Holt McDougal.

Hyde, Natalie. Micro Life in Soil. 2010. (Everybody Digs Soil Ser.). (ENG., Illus.). 32p. (J). (gr. 3-6). pap. *(978-0-7787-5415-2(4))*; lib. bdg. *(978-0-7787-5402-2(2))* Crabtree Publishing Co.

Ivancic, Linda. Soil for Tools & Art. 2016. (Science of Soil Ser.). 48p. (J). 31.36 *(978-1-5026-2166-5(5))* Cavendish Square Publishing.

James, Emily. The Simple Science of Dirt. 2017. (Simply Science Ser.). (ENG.). 32p. (gr. 1-2). lib. bdg. 27.32 ***(978-1-5157-7085-5(0)***, Aplus Bks.) Capstone Press of Coughlan Cos.

Jennings, Terry. Rocas y Suelos (Rocks & Soils) (SPA.). 32p. (J). 6.95 *(978-84-348-1912-2(0))* SM Ediciones ESP. Dist: AIMS International Bks., Inc.

Korb, Rena. Digging on Dirt, 1 vol. Reibeling, Brandon, illus. 2007. (Science Rocks Ser.). (ENG.). 32p. (gr. -1-4). 28.50 *(978-1-60270-038-3(9)*, Looking Glass Library- Nonfiction) Magic Wagon.

Kwarta, James. The Science of Soil. 2009. (Real Life Readers Ser.). 16p. (gr. 2-3). pap. 7.05 *(978-1-4358-0033-5(8)*, Rosen Classroom) Rosen Publishing Group, Inc., The.

Lawrence, Ellen. Dirt. 2013. (Science Slam: FUN-Damental Experiments Ser.). 24p. (J). (gr. -1-3). lib. bdg. 23.93 *(978-1-61772-737-5(7))* Bearport Publishing Co., Inc.

—Dirt or Soil: What's the Difference? 2015. (Down & Dirty Ser.). (ENG., Illus.). 24p. (J). (gr. -1-3). lib. bdg. 23.93 *(978-1-62724-833-4(1))* Bearport Publishing Co., Inc.

—How Do Animals Help Make Soil? 2015. (Down & Dirty Ser.). (ENG., Illus.). 24p. (J). (gr. -1-3). lib. bdg. 23.93 *(978-1-62724-835-8(8))* Bearport Publishing Co., Inc.

—Is Soil All the Same? 2015. (Down & Dirty Ser.). (ENG., Illus.). 24p. (J). (gr. -1-3). lib. bdg. 23.93 *(978-1-62724-836-5(6))* Bearport Publishing Co., Inc.

—What Is Soil Made Of? 2015. (Down & Dirty Ser.). (ENG., Illus.). 24p. (J). (gr. -1-3). lib. bdg. 23.93 *(978-1-62724-834-1(X))* Bearport Publishing Co., Inc.

—Why Do Most Plants Need Soil? 2015. (Down & Dirty Ser.). (ENG., Illus.). 24p. (J). (gr. -1-3). lib. bdg. 23.93 *(978-1-62724-837-2(4))* Bearport Publishing Co., Inc.

Lindbo, David L., et al, texts. Soil! Get the Inside Scoop. 2008. (J). 20.00 *(978-0-89118-848-3(7))* ASA-CSSA-SSSA.

MacAulay, Kelley. Why Do We Need Soil? 2014. (ENG., Illus.). 24p. (J). lib. bdg. *(978-0-7787-0493-5(9))* Crabtree Publishing Co.

Mack, Dave L. In the Soil. 2015. (Garden Squad! Ser.). (ENG., Illus.). 24p. (J). (gr. 3-4). pap. 8.25 *(978-1-4994-0975-8(3)*, PowerKids Pr.) Rosen Publishing Group, Inc., The.

Meredith, Susan. Las Rocas, los Minerales y el Suelo. 2012. (SPA & ENG.). 48p. (gr. 4-8). pap. 10.95 *(978-1-61810-470-0(5))* Rourke Educational Media.

—Rocks, Minerals, & Soil. 2009. (Let's Explore Science Ser.). (Illus.). 48p. (gr. 4-8). (J). lib. bdg. 32.79 *(978-1-60694-411-0(8))*; (ENG., pap. 10.95 *(978-1-60694-529-2(7))* Rourke Educational Media.

Messner, Kate. Up in the Garden & down in the Dirt. Neal, Christopher Silas, illus. 2017. (ENG.). 56p. (J). pap. 7.99 *(978-1-4521-6136-5(4))* Chronicle Bks. LLC.

—Up in the Garden & down in the Dirt. 2015. (ENG., Illus.). 52p. (J). (gr. k-3). 16.99 *(978-1-4521-1936-6(8))* Chronicle Bks. LLC.

Montgomery, Heather L. How Is Soil Made? 2010. (Everybody Digs Soil Ser.). (ENG., Illus.). 32p. (J). (gr. 3-6). pap. *(978-0-7787-5414-5(6))* Crabtree Publishing Co.

Nelson, Robin. Soil. 2005. (First Step Nonfiction Ser.). (J). (Illus.). 23p. (gr. 3-7). lib. bdg. 18.60 *(978-0-8225-2612-4(3)*, Lerner Pubns.); pap. 5.95 *(978-0-8225-5376-2(7))* Lerner Publishing Group.

Newson, Lesley & Wadsworth, Pamela. Rhagor Am Greigiau, Pridd a Thywydd. 2005. (WEL., Illus.). 24p. pap. *(978-1-85596-238-5(1))* Dref Wen.

Owen, Ruth. Science & Craft Projects with Rocks & Soil. 2013. (Get Crafty Outdoors Ser.). (ENG., Illus.). 32p. (J). (gr. k-3). 26.50 *(978-1-4777-0246-8(6))*; pap. 11.75 *(978-1-4777-0255-0(5))* Rosen Publishing Group, Inc., The. (PowerKids Pr.).

Oxlade, Chris. Soil. 2016. (Rock On! Ser.). (ENG., Illus.). 32p. (gr. 2-4). lib. bdg. 30.65 *(978-1-4109-8138-7(X)*, Raintree Perspectives) Heinemann-Raintree.

Parker, Steve. Microlife That Lives in Soil, 1 vol. 2005. (Amazing World of Microlife Ser.). (ENG., Illus.). 32p. (gr. 3-3). pap. 7.99 *(978-1-4109-1851-2(3)*, Raintree Perspectives) Heinemann-Raintree.

Petersen, Christine. Super Soils, 1 vol. 2010. (Rock on!: a Look at Geology Ser.). (ENG.). 32p. (J). (gr. 3-6). 27.07 (978-1-60453-747-5(7)) ABDO Publishing Co.

Peterson, Cris. Seed, Soil, Sun: Earth's Recipe for Food. Lundquist, David R., photos by. (ENG., Illus.). 32p. (J). (gr. k-4). 2012. pap. 7.95 (978-1-59078-947-6(4)) 2010. 17.95 (978-1-59078-713-7(7)) Boyds Mills Pr.

Rake, Jody Sullivan. Roots, Bulbs, & Bacteria: Growths of the Underground. 2015. (Underground Safari Ser.). (ENG., Illus.). 24p. (gr. 1-2). lib. bdg. 25.32 (978-1-4914-5062-8(2)) Capstone Press of Coughlan Cos.

—Soil, Silt, & Sand: Layers of the Underground. 2015. (Underground Safari Ser.). (ENG., Illus.). 24p. (gr. 1-2). lib. bdg. 25.32 (978-1-4914-5063-5(0)) Capstone Press of Coughlan Cos.

Redlin, Janice L., ed. Land Abuse & Soil Erosion. 2006. (Understanding Global Issues Ser.). (Illus.). 56p. (J). (gr. 3-7). lib. bdg. 28.50 (978-1-59036-237-2(3)) Weigl Pubs., Inc.

Reilly, Kathleen M. Explore Soil! With 25 Great Projects. Stone, Bryan, illus. 2015. (Explore Your World Ser.). (ENG.). 96p. (J). (gr. 1-5). pap. 14.95 (978-1-61930-295-2(0)) Open City Bks.

Reynolds, Shaye. Volcanoes. 2016. (Spotlight on Earth Science Ser.). 00024p. (J). (gr. 4-6). pap. 10.00 (978-1-4994-2537-6(6), PowerKids Pr.) Rosen Publishing Group, Inc., The.

Riley, Peter. Rocks & Soil. 2016. (Moving up with Science Ser.). 00032p. (J). (gr. 3-4). pap. 10.00 (978-1-4994-3153-7(8), PowerKids Pr.) Rosen Publishing Group, Inc., The.

Rissman, Rebecca. Rocks & Soil. 2013. (Real Size Science Ser.). (ENG., Illus.). 24p. (gr. -1-1). 22.65 (978-1-4329-7882-2(9)); pap. 6.95 (978-1-4329-7889-1(6)) Heinemann-Raintree. (Acorn).

Rosinsky, Natalie M. El Suelo: Tierra y Arena, 1 vol. Robledo, Sol, tr. Boyd, Sheree, illus. 2007. (Ciencia Asombrosa Ser.). (SPA.). 24p. (gr. k-4). lib. bdg. 26.65 (978-1-4048-3211-4(4)) Picture Window Bks.

Royston, Angela. Soil: Let's Look at a Garden. 2005. (J). (978-1-4109-1821-5(1)); (ENG.). 24p. pap. (978-1-4109-1830-7(0)) Steck-Vaughn.

Schuh, Mari. Soil Basics, 1 vol. 2011. (Science Builders Ser.). (ENG.). 24p. (gr. k-1). pap. 7.29 (978-1-4296-7110-1(6), Pebble Plus) Capstone Press of Coughlan Cos.

Schuh, Mari C. Soil Basics. 2011. (Science Builders Ser.). (ENG.). 24p. (gr. k-1). pap. 41.70 (978-1-4296-7116-3(5)); lib. bdg. 26.65 (978-1-4296-6071-6(6)) Capstone Press of Coughlan Cos. (Pebble Plus).

The Science of Soil. 2016. (Science of Soil Ser.). 48p. (J). lib. bdg. 188.16 (978-1-5026-2437-6(0)) Cavendish Square Publishing.

Sharp, Katie. Soil. 2009. (21st Century Skills Library: Real World Science Ser.). (ENG.). 32p. (gr. 4-8). lib. bdg. 28.50 (978-1-60279-464-1(2), 200234) Cherry Lake Publishing.

Sherman, Jill. Fertile Land & Soil. 2017. (J). pap. **(978-0-7660-9139-9(2))** Enslow Pubs., Inc.

Sian Revision Soil Studies. 2004. (J). (978-1-59242-071-1(0)) Delta Education, LLC.

Sohn, Emily & Bair, Diane. Pebbles, Sand, & Silt. 2011. (IScience Readers Ser.). 24p. (J). (gr. k-2). lib. bdg. 21.27 (978-1-59953-409-1(6)) Norwood Hse. Pr.

Soil. 2007. 48p. (gr. 3-8). 26.20 (978-0-7377-3638-0(0), Kidhaven) Cengage Gale.

Spilsbury, Louise. El Suelo. 2011. (Las Rocas Ser.). (SPA.). 32p. (gr. 3-5). pap. 8.29 (978-1-4329-5663-9(9)); lib. bdg. 33.32 (978-1-4329-5655-4(8)) Heinemann-Raintree. (Heinemann InfoSearch).

Spilsbury, Louise & Spilsbury, Richard. Soil, 1 vol. 2011. (Let's Rock Ser.). (ENG.). 32p. (gr. 3-6). 33.32 (978-1-4329-4685-2(4)); pap. 8.29 (978-1-4329-4693-7(5)) Heinemann-Raintree. (Heinemann InfoSearch).

Stefoff, Rebecca. Soil for Building Materials. 2016. (Science of Soil Ser.). 48p. (J). 31.36 (978-1-5026-2164-1(9)) Cavendish Square Publishing.

Sullivan, Laura L. Soil for Fossils & History. 2016. (Science of Soil Ser.). 48p. (J). 31.36 (978-1-5026-2203-7(3)) Cavendish Square Publishing.

Sundance/Newbridge LLC Staff. Rocks & Soil. 2007. (Early Science Ser.). (gr. k-3). 18.95 (978-1-4007-6441-9(6)); pap. 6.10 (978-1-4007-6437-2(8)) Sundance/Newbridge Educational Publishing.

Taylor-Butler, Christine. Experiments with Soil, 1 vol. 2011. (My Science Investigations Ser.). (ENG.). 32p. (gr. 1-3). pap. 8.29 (978-1-4329-5369-0(9), Heinemann First Library) Heinemann-Raintree.

Tillen, James. A Close Look at Soil. 2013. (InfoMax Readers Ser.). (ENG.). 24p. (J). (gr. 2-3). pap. 8.25 (978-1-4777-2767-6(1)); pap. 49.50 (978-1-4777-2327-2(7)) Rosen Publishing Group, Inc., The. (Rosen Classroom).

Tomecek, Steve. Dirt. Woodman, Nancy, illus. (Jump into Science Ser.). (ENG.). 32p. (J). (gr. -1-3). 2016. pap. 7.99 (978-1-4263-2362-1(X)) 2007. pap. 6.95 (978-1-4263-0089-9(1)) National Geographic Society. (National Geographic Children's Bks.).

—Dirt. 2014. 16.95 (978-1-63419-657-4(0)) Perfection Learning Corp.

Wade, Mary Dodson. Tiny Life on the Ground. 2005. (Rookie Read-About Science Ser.). (ENG., Illus.). 32p. (J). (gr. 1-2). 20.50 (978-0-516-25298-8(4), Children's Pr.) Scholastic Library Publishing.

Wadsworth, Pamela. Creigiau, Pridd a Thywydd. 2005. (WEL., Illus.). 24p. pap. (978-1-85596-237-8(3)) Dref Wen.

Wadsworth, Pamela & Tate, Sylvia. Golwg Gyntaf Ar Greigiau, Pridd a Thywydd. 2005. (WEL., Illus.). 24p. pap. (978-1-85596-253-8(5)) Dref Wen.

Walker, Kate. Soil. 2011. (Investigating Earth Ser.). 32p. (gr. 2). 28.50 (978-1-60870-561-0(7)) Marshall Cavendish Corp.

Walker, Sally M. Soil. (Illus.). 48p. (J). 2007. pap. 8.95 (978-0-8225-6622-9(2)) 2006. (gr. 3-7). lib. bdg. 25.26 (978-0-8225-5948-1(X), Lerner Pubns.) Lerner Publishing Group.

—Studying Soil. 2013. (Searchlight Books (tm) — Do You Dig Earth Science? Ser.). (ENG., Illus.). 40p. (gr. 3-5). pap. 8.95 (978-1-4677-0794-7(5)); lib. bdg. 27.93 (978-1-4677-0023-8(1), Lerner Pubns.) Lerner Publishing Group.

Waring, Kerry Jones. Soil for Minerals & Medicine. 2016. (Science of Soil Ser.). 48p. (J). 31.36 (978-1-5026-2162-7(2)) Cavendish Square Publishing.

Watts, Pam. Soil. 2016. (Geology Rocks! Ser.). (ENG.). 24p. (J). (gr. 3-6). 28.50 (978-1-5038-0806-5(8), 210641) Child's World, Inc., The.

Wermund, Jerry. Soil: More Than Just Dirt. 2009. (Illus.). 48p. 18.95 (978-0-9726255-3-1(4)) Rockon Publishing.

SOLAR ENERGY

Bailey, Diane. Harnessing Energy: Solar Power. 2015. (Harnessing Energy Ser.). (ENG.). 48p. (J). (gr. 5-8). pap. 12.00 (978-0-89812-998-4(2), Creative Paperbacks) Creative Co., The.

—Solar Power. 2014. lib. bdg. 35.65 (978-1-60818-412-5(9), Creative Education) Creative Co., The.

Bearce, Stephanie. How to Harness Solar Power for Your Home. 2009. (Tell Your Parents Ser.). (Illus.). 48p. (J). (gr. 4-7). lib. bdg. 29.95 (978-1-58415-761-8(5)) Mitchell Lane Pubs., Inc.

Benduhn, Tea. Energía Solar. 2008. (Energía para el presente (Energy for Today) Ser.). (SPA.). 24p. (gr. 2-6). (J). lib. bdg. 22.00 (978-0-8368-9269-7(0)); pap. 8.15 (978-0-8368-9368-7(9)) Stevens, Gareth Publishing LLLP. (Weekly Reader Leveled Readers).

—Solar Power. 2008. (Energy for Today Ser.). 24p. (gr. 2-6). (J). lib. bdg. 22.00 (978-0-8368-9263-5(1)); pap. 8.15 (978-0-8368-9362-5(X)) Stevens, Gareth Publishing LLLP. (Weekly Reader Leveled Readers).

Bow, James. Energy from the Sun: Solar Power. 2015. (Next Generation Energy Ser.). (ENG., Illus.). 32p. (J). (978-0-7787-1982-3(0)) Crabtree Publishing Co.

Bright, Michael. From Sunshine to Light Bulb. 2016. (Illus.). 32p. (J). (978-0-7787-2707-1(6)) Crabtree Publishing Co.

Coldwell, Lamar. My Uncle's Factory Produces Solar Panels. 2016. (Rosen REAL Readers: Social Studies Nonfiction / Fiction: Family, Community, & the World Ser.). 12p. (gr. 1-k). pap. 6.33 (978-1-5081-2359-0(4), Rosen Classroom) Rosen Publishing Group, Inc., The.

Dickmann, Nancy. Harnessing Solar Energy. 2016. (Future of Power Ser.). 00032p. (J). (gr. 4-5). pap. 10.00 (978-1-4994-3214-5(3), PowerKids Pr.) Rosen Publishing Group, Inc., The.

Doeden, Matt. Finding Out about Solar Energy. 2014. (Searchlight Books — What Are Energy Sources? Ser.). (Illus.). 40p. (gr. 3-4). (J). lib. bdg. 27.93 (978-1-4677-3657-2(0), Lerner Pubns.); pap. 8.95 (978-1-4677-4557-4(X)) Lerner Publishing Group.

friend, robyn C. & cohen, Judith Love. A Clean Planet: The Solar Power Story. katz, david A., illus. 2009. 48p. (J). pap. 7.00 (978-1-880599-86-0(4)) Cascade Pass, Inc.

friend, robyn C. & Cohen, Judith Love. A Clean Planet: The Solar Power Story. Katz, David A., illus. 2009. 48p. (J). 13.95 (978-1-880599-87-7(2)) Cascade Pass, Inc.

Garbe, Suzanne. The Science Behind Wonders of the Sun: Sun Dogs, Lunar Eclipses, & Green Flash. 2016. (Science Behind Natural Phenomena Ser.). (ENG., Illus.). 32p. (gr. 3-4). lib. bdg. 27.99 (978-1-5157-0778-3(4), Edge Bks.) Capstone Press of Coughlan Cos.

Gould, Alan. Hot Water & Warm Homes from Sunlight. Gould, Alan et al, illus. Sneider, Cary I., photos by. rev. ed. 2005. (Great Explorations in Math & Science Ser.). 80p. 13.50 (978-1-931542-04-3(X), GEMS) Univ. of California, Berkeley, Lawrence Hall of Science.

Grady, Colin. Solar Energy. 2016. (Saving the Planet Through Green Energy Ser.). 24p. (J). pap. 9.35 (978-0-7660-8292-2(X)) Enslow Pubs., Inc.

Hansen, Amy. Solar Energy: Running on Sunshine. 2010. (Powering Our World Ser.). (ENG.). 24p. (J). pap. 8.25 (978-1-4358-9740-3(4)) Rosen Publishing Group, Inc., The.

Hansen, Amy S. Solar Energy: Running on Sunshine. 2010. (Powering Our World Ser.). 24p. (J). (gr. 2-5). E-Book 42.50 (978-1-4488-0197-8(4)); (Illus.). lib. bdg. 22.60 (978-1-4358-9326-9(3)) Rosen Publishing Group, Inc., The.

Hantula, Richard, et al. How Do Solar Panels Work? 2009. (Science in the Real World Ser.). (Illus.). 32p. (gr. 4-6). 28.00 (978-1-60413-472-8(0), Chelsea Clubhouse) Facts On File, Inc.

—Solar Power. 2010. (Energy Today Ser.). 48p. (J). (gr. 3-6). 30.00 (978-1-60413-779-8(7)) Facts On File, Inc.

Hardyman, Robyn. How a Solar-Powered Home Works. 2013. (EcoWorks Ser.). 32p. (J). (gr. 3-5). pap. 10.50 (978-1-4339-9549-1(2), Gareth Stevens Learning Library); pap. 63.00 (978-1-4339-9550-7(6)); (ENG., Illus.). lib. bdg. 26.60 (978-1-4339-9548-4(4)) Stevens, Gareth Publishing LLLP.

Harper, Reggie. Using the Sun's Energy: If... Then. 2017. (Computer Science for the Real World Ser.). 16p. (gr. 7-8). pap. 7.95 **(978-1-5383-5249-6(4)**, Rosen Classroom) Rosen Publishing Group, Inc., The.

Huggett, Audrey. Solar Energy Projects. 2016. (21st Century Skills Innovation Library: Makers As Innovators Ser.). (ENG., Illus.). 32p. (J). (gr. 4-8). lib. bdg. 29.93 (978-1-63471-417-4(2), 208447) Cherry Lake Publishing.

Jones, Susan. Solar Power of the Future: New Ways of Turning Sunlight into Energy. (Library of Future Energy Ser.). 64p. 2009. (gr. 5-5). 58.50 (978-1-60853-629-0(7)) 2005. (Illus.). (YA). (gr. 7-12). lib. bdg. 31.95 (978-0-8239-3663-2(5)) Rosen Publishing Group, Inc., The.

Kallen, Stuart A. Real-World Stem: Develop Economical Solar Power. 2017. (Real-World Stem Ser.). (ENG.). 80p. (YA). (gr. 5-12). **(978-1-68282-239-5(7))** ReferencePoint Pr., Inc.

Kenney, Karen Latchana. Energy Investigations. 2017. (Key Questions in Physical Science Ser.). (ENG.). 32p. (J). (gr. 3-6). 27.99 **(978-1-5124-4003-4(5))** Lerner Publishing Group.

The Library of Future Energy. 2005. (Illus.). (gr. 7-12). lib. bdg. 212.00 (978-0-8239-3901-5(4)) Rosen Publishing Group, Inc., The.

Mahaney, Ian. Solar Energy. 2007. 28p. pap. 21.25 (978-1-4358-3825-3(4), PowerKids Pr.) Rosen Publishing Group, Inc., The.

Mahaney, Ian F. Solar Energy. 2007. (Journeys Ser.). (ENG., Illus.). 24p. (gr. 3-8). pap. 7.05 (978-1-4042-2188-8(3), PowerKids Pr.) Rosen Publishing Group, Inc., The.

Morris, Neil. Solar Power. 2007. (Energy Sources Ser.). (Illus.). 32p. (YA). (gr. 4-7). lib. bdg. 28.50 (978-1-58340-908-4(4)) Black Rabbit Bks.

—Solar Power: Now & in the Future. 2010. (J). 34.25 (978-1-59920-342-3(1)) Black Rabbit Bks.

Muschal, Frank. Energy from Wind, Sun, & Tides. 2007. (21st Century Skills Library: Power Up! Ser.). (ENG.). 32p. (gr. 4-8). pap. 14.21 (978-1-60279-096-4(5), 200657); (Illus.). lib. bdg. 28.50 (978-1-60279-046-9(9), 200052) Cherry Lake Publishing.

Naff, Clay Farris. Solar Power. 2006. (Fueling the Future Ser.). (ENG., Illus.). 244p. (YA). (gr. 9-18). lib. bdg. 39.35 (978-0-7377-3565-9(1), Greenhaven Pr., Inc.) Cengage Gale.

Ollhoff, Jim. Solar Power, 1 vol. 2010. (Future Energy Ser.). (ENG., Illus.). 32p. (YA). (gr. 4-7). 27.07 (978-1-60453-938-7(0)) ABDO Publishing Co.

Owen, Ruth. Energy from the Sun: Solar Power. 2013. (Power: Yesterday, Today, Tomorrow Ser.). (ENG., Illus.). 32p. (J). (gr. 3-6). 25.25 (978-1-4777-0270-3(9)); pap. 11.75 (978-1-4777-0279-6(2)) Rosen Publishing Group, Inc., The. (PowerKids Pr.).

Oxlade, Chris. Solar Power, 1 vol. 2011. (Tales of Invention Ser.). (ENG.). 32p. (gr. 3-5). pap. 8.95 (978-1-4329-5459-8(8), NA-h) Heinemann-Raintree.

Parker, Steve. Solar Power. 2004. (Science Files Ser.). (Illus.). 32p. (gr. 2-6). lib. bdg. 26.00 (978-0-8368-4032-2(1), Gareth Stevens Learning Library) Stevens, Gareth Publishing LLLP.

Pipe, Jim. Solar Power. 2011. (J). 28.50 (978-1-59604-215-5(X)) Black Rabbit Bks.

Porter, Esther. Sun Power: A Book about Renewable Energy. 2013. (Earth Matters Ser.). (ENG.). 32p. (gr. 1-2). pap. 47.70 (978-1-62065-740-9(6), Aplus Bks.); pap. 8.10 (978-1-62065-739-3(2)); lib. bdg. 27.32 (978-1-62065-046-2(0)) Capstone Press of Coughlan Cos.

Reynoldson, Fiona. Understanding Solar Power. 2010. (World of Energy Ser.). (ENG.). 48p. (J). (gr. 6-8). lib. bdg. 31.95 (978-1-4339-4127-6(9), Gareth Stevens Learning Library) Stevens, Gareth Publishing LLLP.

Richards, Julie. Solar Energy. 2009. (J). 19.95 (978-0-7614-4427-5(0)) Marshall Cavendish GBR. Dist: Marshall Cavendish Corp.

Rooney, Anne. Solar Power. 2007. (Energy for the Future & Global Warming Ser.). 32p. (gr. 5-8). pap. 11.70 (978-0-8368-8412-8(4)); (Illus.). lib. bdg. 27.00 (978-0-8368-8403-6(5)) Stevens, Gareth Publishing LLLP.

Rowe, Brooke. Playing with Solar Heat. Bane, Jeff, illus. 2016. (My Early Library: My Science Fun Ser.). (ENG.). 24p. (J). (gr. k-1). 28.50 (978-1-63471-031-2(2), 208204) Cherry Lake Publishing.

Science stories foss spanish solar energy ea Cr05. 2005. (J). (978-1-59242-595-2(X)) Delta Education, LLC.

Solar-Wind-Riding Electric Sail: Meet NASA Inventor Bruce Wiegmann & His Team's. 2017. (J). **(978-0-7166-6162-7(4))** World Bk., Inc.

Solway, Andrew. From Sunlight to Blockbuster Movies: An Energy Journey Through the World of Light. 2015. (Energy Journeys Ser.). (ENG.). 48p. (gr. 3-6). 33.32 (978-1-4846-0882-1(8), Heinemann InfoSearch) Heinemann-Raintree.

Spilsbury, Richard & Spilsbury, Louise. Solar Power. 2012. (Let's Discuss Energy Resources Ser.). (Illus.). 32p. (YA). (gr. 4-7). lib. bdg. 26.50 (978-1-4488-5262-8(5)) Rosen Publishing Group, Inc., The.

Spiro, Ruth & Chan, Irene. Baby Loves Thermodynamics! 2017. (ENG., Illus.). 20p. (J). (— 1). bds. 8.99 **(978-1-58089-768-6(1))** Charlesbridge Publishing, Inc.

Sullivan, Laura L. The Pros & Cons of Solar Power. 2014. (Economics of Energy Ser.). (Illus.). 80p. (J). (gr. 7-10). lib. bdg. 35.64 (978-1-62712-924-4(3)) Cavendish Square Publishing.

Sundance/Newbridge LLC Staff. Energy from the Sun. 2004. (Reading PowerWorks Ser.). (gr. 1-3). 37.50 (978-0-7608-9711-9(5)); pap. 6.10 (978-0-7608-9712-6(3)) Sundance/Newbridge Educational Publishing.

Taylor-Butler, Christine. Experiment with Solar Energy. 2010. (Explorer Junior Library: Science Explorer Junior Ser.). (ENG.). 32p. (gr. 3-6). lib. bdg. 28.50 (978-1-60279-840-3(0), 200546) Cherry Lake Publishing.

—Super Cool Science Experiments: Solar Energy. 2009. (Explorer Library: Science Explorer Ser.). (ENG., Illus.). 32p. (gr. 4-8). lib. bdg. 28.50 (978-1-60279-527-3(4), 200295) Cherry Lake Publishing.

Thomas, Isabel. The Pros & Cons of Solar Power. 2007. (Energy Debate Ser.). (Illus.). 48p. (YA). (gr. 5-9). lib. bdg. 29.25 (978-1-4042-3741-4(0)) Rosen Publishing Group, Inc., The.

Vogel, Julia. Solar Power. 2013. (J). (978-1-61080-973-3(4)); (ENG.). 32p. (gr. 4-8). 28.50 (978-1-61080-898-9(3), 202571); (ENG.). 32p. (gr. 4-8). pap. 14.21 (978-1-61080-923-8(8), 202573) Cherry Lake Publishing.

Walker, Niki. Harnessing Power from the Sun. 2006. (Energy Revolution Ser.). (ENG., Illus.). 32p. (J). (gr. 3-7). pap. (978-0-7787-2926-6(5)) Crabtree Publishing Co.

SOLAR HEATING

see Solar Energy; Sun

SOLAR PHYSICS

see Sun

SOLAR POWER

see Solar Energy

SOLAR RADIATION

see also Solar Energy

Sterling, Kristin. It's Sunny Today. 2009. (Lightning Bolt Books — What's the Weather Like? Ser.). (ENG., Illus.). 32p. (gr. k-2). 26.60 (978-0-7613-4259-5(1), Lerner Pubns.); pap. 7.95 (978-0-7613-5022-4(5)) Lerner Publishing Group.

Stewart, Tobi Stanton. Solar Storms. 2003. (Rosen REAL Readers Ser.). 24p. (ENG.). (gr. 3-4). pap. 7.05 (978-0-8239-6398-0(5), Rosen Classroom); (Illus.). (J). lib. bdg. 22.60 (978-0-8239-3709-7(7)) Rosen Publishing Group, Inc., The.

SOLAR SYSTEM

Adamson, Thomas K. Sun, Moon, & Stars Pack [Scholastic]. 2011. (Exploring the Galaxy Ser.). 24p. pap. 1.50 (978-1-4296-6292-5(1), Pebble Plus) Capstone Press of Coughlan Cos.

Aguilar, David A. Seven Wonders of the Solar System. 2017. (Smithsonian Ser.). (ENG., Illus.). 80p. (J). (gr. 5). 18.99 (978-0-451-47685-2(9), Viking Books for Young Readers) Penguin Young Readers Group.

—13 Planets: The Latest View of the Solar System. 2011. (ENG., Illus.). 64p. (J). (gr. 3-7). 16.95 (978-1-4263-0770-6(5)); lib. bdg. 25.90 (978-1-4263-0771-3(3)) National Geographic Society. (National Geographic Children's Bks.).

Anderson, Michael. The Nature of Planets, Dwarf Planets, & Space Objects. 2011. (Illus.). 96p. (J). lib. bdg. 31.70 (978-1-61530-517-9(3)) Rosen Publishing Group, Inc., The.

Arlon, Penelope & Gordon-Harris, Tory. Planets. 2012. (J). lib. bdg. (978-0-531-22957-6(2)) Scholastic, Inc.

Arlon, Penelope & Gordon-Harris, Tory. Planets: A LEGO Adventure in the Real World. 2016. (Illus.). 64p. (J). **(978-1-4844-8522-4(X))** Scholastic, Inc.

Ashby, Ruth. How the Solar System Was Formed. 2003. (New Solar System Ser.). (J). lib. bdg. 28.50 (978-1-58340-285-6(3)) Black Rabbit Bks.

Asimov, Isaac & Hantula, Richard. Our Planetary System. 2005. (Isaac Asimov's 21st Century Library of the Universe). (Illus.). 32p. (gr. 2-6). lib. bdg. 26.00 (978-0-8368-3969-2(2), Gareth Stevens Learning Library) Stevens, Gareth Publishing LLLP.

Asselin, Kristine Carlson. Our Sun. 2011. (Solar System & Beyond Ser.). (ENG.). 32p. (gr. 3-4). pap. 47.70 (978-1-4296-6409-7(6), Fact Finders) Capstone Press of Coughlan Cos.

Asteroids. 2015. (J). (978-1-60818-480-4(3), Creative Education) Creative Co., The.

Astronomy Now!, 9 vols., Set. Incl. Look at Earth. Dunn, Mary R. (J). (gr. 3-7). lib. bdg. 21.25 (978-1-4042-3827-5(1), PowerKids Pr.); Look at Jupiter. Slade, Suzanne. (J). (gr. 2-5). lib. bdg. 22.60 (978-1-4042-3829-9(8)); Look at Mars. Dunn, Mary R. (YA). (gr. 2-5). lib. bdg. 21.25 (978-1-4042-3828-2(X)); Look at Mercury. Dunn, Mary R. (YA). (gr. 2-5). lib. bdg. 22.60 (978-1-4042-3825-1(5)); Look at Neptune. Slade, Suzanne. (YA). (gr. 2-5). lib. bdg. 22.60 (978-1-4042-3832-9(8)); Look at Pluto & Other Dwarf Planets. Kaspar, Anna. (YA). (gr. 2-5). lib. bdg. 22.60 (978-1-4042-3824-4(7)); Look at Saturn. Slade, Suzanne. (J). (gr. 2-5). lib. bdg. 22.60 (978-1-4042-3830-5(1)); Look at Uranus. Slade, Suzanne. (J). (gr. 2-5). lib. bdg. 22.60 (978-1-4042-3831-2(X)); Look at Venus. Dunn, Mary R. (YA). (gr. 2-5). lib. bdg. 22.60 (978-1-4042-3826-8(3)); (Illus.). 24p. 2007. 2007. Set lib. bdg. 191.25 (978-1-4042-3863-3(8)) Rosen Publishing Group, Inc., The.

Autumn Publishing Staff, illus. Solar System. 2004. (Wall Charts Ser.). (J). pap. 4.99 (978-1-85997-257-1(8)) Byeway Bks.

Baines, Becky. Explore My World Planets. 2016. (Explore My World Ser.). (ENG., Illus.). 32p. (J). (gr. -1-2). pap. 4.99 (978-1-4263-2322-5(0), National Geographic Children's Bks.) National Geographic Society.

Baines, Becky & National Geographic Kids Staff. Every Planet Has a Place. 2010. (ZigZag Ser.). (ENG., Illus.). 32p. (J). (gr. k-3). pap. 5.95 (978-1-4263-0662-4(8), National Geographic Children's Bks.) National Geographic Society.

Ball, Nate. The Solar System. Hargis, Wes, illus. 2017. (Let's Investigate with Nate Ser.: 2). 40p. (J). (gr. -1-3). pap. 6.99 (978-0-06-235742-7(5)) HarperCollins Pubs.

Basher, Simon & Green, Dan. Astronomy: Out of This World! Basher, Simon, illus. 2009. (Basher Science Ser.). (ENG., Illus.). 128p. (J). (gr. 5-9). pap. 8.99 (978-0-7534-6290-4(7), 9780753462904, Kingfisher) Roaring Brook Pr.

Bell, Trudy E. Comets, Meteors, Asteroids, & the Outer Reaches. 2003. (New Solar System Ser.). (J). lib. bdg. 28.50 (978-1-58340-289-4(6)) Black Rabbit Bks.

Benchmark Education Company, LLC Staff, compiled by. Earth & Space. 2005. spiral bd. 110.00 (978-1-4108-3873-5(0)) Benchmark Education Co.

—Earth & Space: Theme Set. 2006. (J). 237.00 (978-1-4108-7106-0(1)); 239.00 (978-1-4108-7120-6(7)) Benchmark Education Co.

—Our Solar System: Theme Set. 2006. (J). 105.00 (978-1-4108-7062-9(6)) Benchmark Education Co.

Berger, Melvin & Berger, Gilda. El Sistema Solar: The Solar System. 2006. (ENG & SPA., Illus.). (J). (978-0-439-82865-9(1)) Scholastic, Inc.

—Think Factory: Solar System. 2005. (Illus.). 47p. (J). (978-0-439-51155-1(0)) Scholastic, Inc.

Berkes, Marianne Collins. Going Around the Sun: Some Planetary Fun, 1 vol. Mason, Janeen, illus. 2008. (ENG.). 32p. (J). (gr. -1-4). 16.95 (978-1-58469-099-3(2)); pap. 8.95 (978-1-58469-100-6(X)) Dawn Pubns.

Beullens-Maoui, Nathalie, ed. Our Solar System: Armenian, 01 vols., 1. 2016. (Our Wonderful World Ser.). (ENG & SPA.). 8p. (J). pap. 9.35 (978-1-5081-1211-2(8), Rosen Classroom) Rosen Publishing Group, Inc., The.

—Our Solar System: Cantonese, 01 vols., 1. 2016. (Our Wonderful World Ser.). (ENG & SPA.). 8p. (J). pap. 9.35 (978-1-5081-1223-5(1), Rosen Classroom) Rosen Publishing Group, Inc., The.

—Our Solar System: Filipino, 01 vols., 1. 2016. (Our Wonderful World Ser.). (ENG & SPA.). 8p. (J). pap. 9.35 (978-1-5081-1217-4(7), Rosen Classroom) Rosen Publishing Group, Inc., The.

—Our Solar System: Hmong Green, 01 vols., 1. 2016. (Our Wonderful World Ser.). (ENG & SPA.). 8p. (J). pap. 9.35 (978-1-5081-1229-7(0), Rosen Classroom) Rosen Publishing Group, Inc., The.

—Our Solar System: Hmong White, 01 vols., 1. 2016. (Our Wonderful World Ser.). (ENG & SPA.). 8p. (J). pap. 9.35 (978-1-5081-1235-8(5), Rosen Classroom) Rosen Publishing Group, Inc., The.

—Our Solar System: Korean, 01 vols., 1. 2016. (Our Wonderful World Ser.). (ENG & SPA.). 8p. (J). pap. 9.35 (978-1-5081-1241-9(X), Rosen Classroom) Rosen Publishing Group, Inc., The.

—Our Solar System: Russian, 01 vols., 1. 2016. (Our Wonderful World Ser.). (ENG & SPA.). 8p. (J). pap. 9.35 (978-1-5081-1247-1(9), Rosen Classroom) Rosen Publishing Group, Inc., The.

—Our Solar System: Spanish, 01 vols., 1. 2016. (Our Wonderful World Ser.). (ENG & SPA.). 8p. (J). pap. 9.35 (978-1-5081-1253-2(3), Rosen Classroom) Rosen Publishing Group, Inc., The.

—Our Solar System: Vietnamese, 01 vols., 1. 2016. (Our Wonderful World Ser.). (ENG & SPA.). 8p. (J). pap. 9.35 *(978-1-5081-1259-4(2),* Rosen Classroom) Rosen Publishing Group, Inc., The.

Block, Dakota. Exploring the Solar System. 2012. (Exploring Earth & Space Ser.). (ENG., Illus.). 24p. (J). (gr. 1-3). 22.60 *(978-1-4488-8572-5(8),* PowerKids Pr.) Rosen Publishing Group, Inc., The.

Bloom, J. P. Mars, 1 vol. 2014. (Planets Ser.). (ENG., Illus.). 24p. (J). (gr. 2-4). lib. bdg. 28.50 *(978-1-62970-717-4(1))* ABDO Publishing Co.

Bone, Emily. The Solar System Internet Referenced. Pastor, Terry & Haggerty, Tim, illus. 2010. (Beginner's Science Ser.). 32p. (J). (gr. 1). 4.99 *(978-0-7945-2812-6(0),* Usborne) EDC Publishing.

Bow, James. Space Mysteries Revealed. 2010. (ENG., Illus.). 32p. (J). pap. *(978-0-7787-7431-0(7));* (gr. 4-7). lib. bdg. *(978-0-7787-7416-7(3))* Crabtree Publishing Co.

Bowman, Donna H. What Is the Moon Made Of? And Other Questions Kids Have about Space, 1 vol. Lubach, Peter, illus. (Kids' Questions Ser.). (ENG.). 24p. (gr. 1-2). 2011. pap. 7.49 *(978-1-4048-6726-0(0))* 2009. lib. bdg. 26.65 *(978-1-4048-5529-8(7))* Picture Window Bks.

Brake, Mark & Lonely Planet Publications Staff. How to Be a Space Explorer: Your Out-of-This-World Adventure, 1 vol. 2014. (Lonely Planet Kids Ser.). (ENG., Illus.). 160p. (J). 17.99 *(978-1-74360-434-2(3),* 4798) Lonely Planet Pubns.

Bredeson, Carmen. What Is the Solar System? 2008. (I Like Space! Ser.). (Illus.). 32p. (J). (gr. 3-7). lib. bdg. 23.94 *(978-0-7660-2944-6(1),* Enslow Elementary) Enslow Pubs., Inc.

Bredeson, Carmen & Dyson, Marianne. Exploring the Solar System. 2015. (Launch into Space! Ser.). (ENG.). 32p. (J). (gr. 3-4). pap. 10.52 *(978-0-7660-6825-4(0))* Enslow Pubs., Inc.

Bredeson, Carmen, et al. Exploring the Solar System. 2015. (Launch into Space! Ser.). (ENG., Illus.). 32p. (J). (gr. 3-4). 25.27 *(978-0-7660-6827-8(7))* Enslow Pubs., Inc.

Britannica, Learning Library. Exploring Space. 2003. (Illus.). 64p. 14.95 *(978-1-59339-031-0(9))* Encyclopaedia Britannica, Inc.

Cain, Marie Mowery. What's Out There. 2013. (Big Books, Red Ser.). (ENG & SPA., Illus.). 16p. pap. 33.00 *(978-1-59246-220-9(0))* Big Books, by George!

Carlton Books, ed. ISolar System. 2014. (IExplore Ser.). (ENG., Illus.). 32p. (J). (gr. 3). 12.95 *(978-1-78312-080-2(0))* Carlton Bks., Ltd. GBR. Dist: Sterling Publishing Co., Inc.

Carroll, Jillian. Zoom Around a Moon. 2003. (J). pap. *(978-1-58417-241-3(X));* lib. bdg. *(978-1-58417-240-6(1))* Lake Street Pubs.

Carson, Mary Kay. Far-Out Guide to Asteroids & Comets. 2010. (Far-Out Guide to the Solar System Ser.). (Illus.). 48p. (J). pap. 8.95 *(978-1-59845-191-7(X),* Enslow Elementary) Enslow Pubs., Inc.

—Far-Out Guide to Earth. 2010. (Far-Out Guide to the Solar System Ser.). (Illus.). 48p. (J). pap. 8.95 *(978-1-59845-183-2(9),* Enslow Elementary); (gr. 2-5). 25.27 *(978-0-7660-3182-1(9))* Enslow Pubs., Inc.

—Far-Out Guide to Jupiter. 2010. (Far-Out Guide to the Solar System Ser.). (Illus.). 48p. (J). pap. 8.95 *(978-1-59845-186-3(3),* Enslow Elementary) Enslow Pubs., Inc.

—Far-Out Guide to Mars. 2010. (Far-Out Guide to the Solar System Ser.). (Illus.). 48p. (J). pap. 8.95 *(978-1-59845-185-6(5),* Enslow Elementary) Enslow Pubs., Inc.

—Far-Out Guide to Mercury. 2010. (Far-Out Guide to the Solar System Ser.). (Illus.). 48p. (J). pap. 8.95 *(978-1-59845-181-8(2),* Enslow Elementary) Enslow Pubs., Inc.

—Far-Out Guide to Neptune. 2010. (Far-Out Guide to the Solar System Ser.). (Illus.). 48p. (J). pap. 8.95 *(978-1-59845-189-4(8),* Enslow Elementary); (gr. 2-5). 25.27 *(978-0-7660-3186-9(1))* Enslow Pubs., Inc.

—Far-Out Guide to Saturn. 2010. (Far-Out Guide to the Solar System Ser.). (Illus.). 48p. (J). pap. 8.95 *(978-1-59845-187-0(1),* Enslow Elementary); (gr. 2-5). 25.27 *(978-0-7660-3178-4(0))* Enslow Pubs., Inc.

—Far-Out Guide to the Icy Dwarf Planets. 2010. (Far-Out Guide to the Solar System Ser.). 48p. (J). (gr. 2-5). 25.27 *(978-0-7660-3187-6(X));* (Illus.). pap. 8.95 *(978-1-59845-190-0(1),* Enslow Elementary) Enslow Pubs., Inc.

—Far-Out Guide to the Moon. 2010. (Far-Out Guide to the Solar System Ser.). (Illus.). 48p. (J). pap. 8.95 *(978-1-59845-184-9(7),* Enslow Elementary) Enslow Pubs., Inc.

—Far-Out Guide to the Sun. 2010. (Far-Out Guide to the Solar System Ser.). (Illus.). 48p. (J). pap. 8.95 *(978-1-59845-180-1(4),* Enslow Elementary); (gr. 2-5). 25.27 *(978-0-7660-3179-1(9))* Enslow Pubs., Inc.

—Far-Out Guide to Uranus. 2010. (Far-Out Guide to the Solar System Ser.). (Illus.). 48p. (J). pap. 8.95 *(978-1-59845-188-7(X),* Enslow Elementary); (gr. 2-5). 25.27 *(978-0-7660-3185-2(3))* Enslow Pubs., Inc.

—Far-Out Guide to Venus. 2010. (Far-Out Guide to the Solar System Ser.). 48p. (J). (gr. 2-5). 25.27 *(978-0-7660-3181-4(0));* (Illus.). pap. 8.95 *(978-1-59845-182-5(0),* Enslow Elementary) Enslow Pubs., Inc.

—How Many Planets Circle the Sun? And Other Questions about Our Solar System. Miller, Ron, illus. 2014. (Good Question! Ser.). (ENG.). 40p. (J). (gr. 1). 12.95 *(978-1-4549-0668-1(5))* Sterling Publishing Co., Inc.

Carson, Mary Kay & Carson, Mary K. Extreme Planets Q & A. 2008. (Illus.). 48p. (J). (gr. k-4). 17.99 *(978-0-06-089975-2(1))* HarperCollins Pubs.

Carson, Mary Kay & Library Association Staff. Far-Out Guide to Asteroids & Comets. 2010. (Far-Out Guide to the Solar System Ser.). 48p. (J). (gr. 2-5). 25.27 *(978-0-7660-3188-3(8))* Enslow Pubs., Inc.

—Far-Out Guide to Jupiter. 2010. (Far-Out Guide to the Solar System Ser.). (Illus.). 48p. (J). (gr. 2-5). 25.27 *(978-0-7660-3184-5(5))* Enslow Pubs., Inc.

—Far-Out Guide to Mars. 2010. (Far-Out Guide to the Solar System Ser.). 48p. (J). (gr. 2-5). 25.27 *(978-0-7660-3183-8(7))* Enslow Pubs., Inc.

—Far-Out Guide to Mercury. 2010. (Far-Out Guide to the Solar System Ser.). 48p. (J). (gr. 2-5). 25.27 *(978-0-7660-3180-7(2))* Enslow Pubs., Inc.

—Far-Out Guide to the Moon. 2010. (Far-Out Guide to the Solar System Ser.). 48p. (J). (gr. 2-5). 25.27 *(978-0-7660-3189-0(6))* Enslow Pubs., Inc.

Chiger, Arielle & Houk Maley, Adrienne. 20 Fun Facts about Asteroids & Comets. 2014. (Fun Fact File: Space! Ser.). 32p. (J). (gr. 2-5). pap. 10.50 *(978-1-4824-0792-1(2))* Stevens, Gareth Publishing LLLP.

Close, Edward. Earth's Place in Space, 1 vol., 1. 2014. (Discovery Education: Earth & Space Science Ser.). (ENG.). 32p. (gr. 3-6). 26.25 *(978-1-4777-6174-8(8),* PowerKids Pr.) Rosen Publishing Group, Inc., The.

Cole, Joanna. Lost in the Solar System. Degen, Bruce, illus. 2010. (Magic School Bus Ser.). (ENG.). (J). (gr. -1-3). 18.95 *(978-0-545-22337-9(7))* Scholastic, Inc.

—Our Solar System. 2014. (Magic School Bus Presents Ser.). lib. bdg. 17.20 *(978-0-606-35816-3(1))* Turtleback Bks.

Cole, Joanna & Jackson, Tom. Our Solar System. Degen, Bruce & Bracken, Carolyn, illus. 2014. (Magic School Bus Presents Ser.). (ENG.). 32p. (J). (gr. 1-3). pap. 6.99 *(978-0-545-68365-4(3),* Scholastic Paperbacks) Scholastic, Inc.

Cole, Joanna, et al. Magic School Bus 3-D: Journey Through the Solar System. Degen, Bruce, illus. 2014. (ENG.). 32p. (J). (gr. -1-3). pap. 7.99 *(978-0-545-67352-5(6),* Scholastic Paperbacks) Scholastic, Inc.

Collins. Solar System. rev. ed. 2016. (Collins Fascinating Facts Ser.). (ENG., Illus.). 72p. (J). (gr. 1-3). pap. 10.99 *(978-0-00-816922-0(5))* HarperCollins Pubs. Ltd. GBR. Dist: Independent Pubs. Group.

Crabtree Publishing, compiled by. Exploring Our Solar System Set. 2008. (J). (gr. 4-7). pap. *(978-0-7787-3744-5(6))* Crabtree Publishing Co.

Dalmatian Press Staff. My Race into Space! 2008. (ENG.). 9p. bds. 4.95 *(978-1-58117-717-6(8),* Intervisual/Piggy Toes) Bendon, Inc.

Davis, Kenneth C. Don't Know Much about the Solar System. Martin, Pedro, illus. 2004. (Don't Know Much About Ser.). (ENG.). 48p. (J). (gr. 1-4). pap. 6.99 *(978-0-06-446230-3(7))* HarperCollins Pubs.

Demuth, Patricia Brennan. The Sun: Our Amazing Star. 2016. (Penguin Core Concepts Ser.). (ENG., Illus.). 32p. (J). (gr. -1-1). pap. 3.99 *(978-0-448-48828-8(0),* Grosset & Dunlap) Penguin Young Readers Group.

DeYoe, Aaron. Moons, 1 vol. 2015. (ENG., Illus.). 24p. (J). *(978-1-62403-743-6(7))* ABDO Publishing Co.

—Planets, 1 vol. 2015. (ENG., Illus.). 24p. (J). *(978-1-62403-744-3(5))* ABDO Publishing Co.

Dickmann, Nancy. Exploring Beyond the Solar System. 2015. (Spectacular Space Science Ser.). (ENG., Illus.). 48p. (J). (gr. 5-6). 30.25 *(978-1-4994-3641-9(6),* Rosen Central) Rosen Publishing Group, Inc., The.

Dillard, Mark. Journey Through the Asteroid Belt, 1 vol. 2014. (Spotlight on Space Science Ser.). (ENG., Illus.). 32p. (J). (gr. 5-5). pap. 11.75 *(978-1-4994-0367-1(4),* 1384622, PowerKids Pr.) Rosen Publishing Group, Inc., The.

Dils, Tracey E. Around the Moon 1,2,3: A Space Counting Book. 2015. (1, 2, 3... Count with Me Ser.). (ENG., Illus.). 24p. (J). (gr. k-2). 19.95 *(978-1-60753-714-4(1))* Amicus Publishing.

DiSiena, Laura Lyn & Eliot, Hannah. Saturn Could Sail: And Other Fun Facts. Oswald, Pete & Spurgeon, Aaron, illus. 2014. (Did You Know? Ser.). (ENG.). 32p. (J). (gr. -1-3). 17.99 *(978-1-4814-1429-6(1));* pap. 6.99 *(978-1-4814-1428-9(3))* Little Simon. (Little Simon).

Dobeck, Maryann. Circling the Sun. 2004. (Reading PowerWorks Ser.). (Illus.). 16p. (gr. 1-3). pap. 6.10 *(978-0-7608-8917-6(1))* Sundance/Newbridge Educational Publishing.

Dompierre, Judith E. No More Than Four of a Kind. 2012. 36p. pap. 24.95 *(978-1-4626-9329-0(6))* America Star Bks.

Dorling Kindersley Publishing Staff. Eyewitness Explorer: Night Sky Detective: Night Sky Detective. 2015. (ENG., Illus.). 72p. (J). (gr. 3-7). pap. 9.99 *(978-1-4654-3501-9(8),* DK Children) Dorling Kindersley Publishing, Inc.

—First Space Encyclopedia. 2016. (ENG., Illus.). 136p. (J). (gr. 1-4). 16.99 *(978-1-4654-4343-4(6),* DK Children) Dorling Kindersley Publishing, Inc.

—My Best Pop-Up Space Book. 2015. (ENG., Illus.). 18p. (J). (-k). bds. 14.99 *(978-1-4654-3914-7(5),* DK Children) Dorling Kindersley Publishing, Inc.

—Solar System. 2016. (DK Find Out! Ser.). (ENG., Illus.). 64p. (J). (gr. 1-4). pap. 10.99 *(978-1-4654-5428-7(4),* DK Children) Dorling Kindersley Publishing, Inc.

—Space! 2015. (ENG., Illus.). 208p. (J). (gr. 5-12). 24.99 *(978-1-4654-3806-5(8),* DK Children) Dorling Kindersley Publishing, Inc.

—The Solar System & Beyond. 2012. (ENG.). 64p. (J). (gr. 2-5). 14.99 *(978-0-7566-8994-0(5),* DK Children) Dorling Kindersley Publishing, Inc.

—Universo. 2016. (SPA., Illus.). 208p. (J). (gr. 5-12). 24.99 *(978-1-4654-6088-2(8),* DK Children) Dorling Kindersley Publishing, Inc.

Dusek, Jiri & Pisala, Jan. Space Atlas. Tuma, Tomas, illus. 2014. (ENG.). 34p. (J). (gr. 1-3). 16.95 *(978-1-4549-1237-8(5))* Sterling Publishing Co., Inc.

Dyer, Alan. Space. 2007. (Insiders Ser.). (ENG., Illus.). 64p. (J). (gr. 3-7). 17.99 *(978-1-4169-3860-6(5),* Simon & Schuster Bks. For Young Readers) Simon & Schuster Bks. For Young Readers.

Early Bird Astronomy, 15 vols., Set. Incl. Dwarf Planet Pluto. Vogt, Gregory. 2009. lib. bdg. 26.60 *(978-0-7613-4157-4(9));* Earth. Zuehlke, Jeffrey. 2009. lib. bdg. 26.60 *(978-0-7613-4149-9(8));* Jupiter. Hansen, Rosanna. 2009. lib. bdg. 26.60 *(978-0-7613-4153-6(6));* Mars. Storad, Conrad J. 2009. lib. bdg. 26.60 *(978-0-7613-4152-9(8));* Mercury. Vogt, Gregory. 2009. lib. bdg. 26.60 *(978-0-7613-4150-5(1));* Meteors & Comets. Vogt, Gregory. 2010. lib. bdg. 26.60 *(978-0-7613-3876-5(4));* Milky Way. Vogt, Gregory. 2010. lib. bdg. 26.60 *(978-0-7613-3875-8(6));* Moon. Waxman, Laura Hamilton. 2010. lib. bdg. 26.60 *(978-0-7613-3872-7(1));* Neptune. Fleisher, Paul. 2009. lib. bdg. 26.60 *(978-0-7613-4155-0(2));* Saturn. Waxman, Laura Hamilton. 2009. lib. bdg. 26.60 *(978-0-7613-4154-3(4));* Solar System. Waxman, Laura Hamilton. 2010. lib. bdg. 26.60 *(978-0-7613-3874-1(8));* Stars. Vogt, Gregory. 2010. lib. bdg. 26.60 *(978-0-7613-3873-4(X));* Sun. Waxman, Laura Hamilton. 2010. lib. bdg. 26.60 *(978-0-7613-3871-0(3));* Uranus. Vogt, Gregory. 2009. lib. bdg. 26.60 *(978-0-7613-4156-7(0));* Venus. Fleisher, Paul. 2009. lib. bdg. 26.60 *(978-0-7613-4151-2(X));* 48p. (gr. 2-5). 2009. Set lib. bdg. 399.00 *(978-0-7613-3870-3(5),* Lerner Pubns.) Lerner Publishing Group.

Editors of Kingfisher. Super Solar System. 2016. (It's All About... Ser.). (ENG., Illus.). 32p. (J). pap. 5.99 *(978-0-7534-7267-5(8),* 9780753472675, Kingfisher) Roaring Brook Pr.

Elkins-Tanton, Linda T. Uranus, Neptune, Pluto, & the Outer Solar System. 2nd rev. ed. 2010. (Solar System Ser.). (Illus.). 272p. (C). (gr. 9). 39.50 *(978-0-8160-7701-4(0))* Facts On File, Inc.

Exploring the Galaxy Pack [Scholastic]. 2010. (Exploring the Galaxy Ser.). 24p. pap. 4.41 *(978-1-4296-5818-8(5),* Pebble Plus) Capstone Press of Coughlan Cos.

Finton, Nancy. Explore the Solar System! 2010. (Illus.). 29p. (J). *(978-0-545-28884-2(3))* Scholastic, Inc.

Fleisher, Paul. Neptune. 2009. (Early Bird Astronomy Ser.). (ENG., Illus.). 48p. (gr. 2-5). pap. 8.95 *(978-0-7613-4984-6(7),* Lerner Pubns.) Lerner Publishing Group.

—Venus. 2009. (Early Bird Astronomy Ser.). (ENG.). 48p. (gr. 2-5). lib. bdg. 26.60 *(978-0-7613-4151-2(X))* Lerner Publishing Group.

Ford, Adam. Stars: A Family Guide to the Night Sky. 2016. (Discover Together Guides). (ENG., Illus.). 48p. 16.95 *(978-1-61180-283-2(0),* Roost Books) Shambhala Pubns., Inc.

Fraknoi, Andrew & Schatz, Dennis. When the Sun Goes Dark. 2017. (ENG.). 36p. (J). (gr. 4-7). pap. 14.95 *(978-1-68140-011-2(1))* National Science Teachers Assn.

Fun Fact File: Space! 2014. (Fun Fact File: Space! Ser.). 32p. (J). (gr. 2-5). pap. 63.00 *(978-1-4824-1603-9(4))* Stevens, Gareth Publishing LLLP.

Gendell, Megan & Sweitzer, James. Spinning 'round the Sun: Everything You Wanted to Know about the Solar System & Everything in It. 2008. (Illus.). 32p. (J). pap. *(978-0-545-04459-2(6))* Scholastic, Inc.

Gifford, Clive. Out of This World: All the Cool Stuff about Space You Want to Knkow. 2012. (ENG.). 144p. (YA). (gr. 4-6). 9.99 *(978-1-60652-519-7(0))* Reader's Digest Assn., Inc., The.

—Out of This World: All the Cool Stuff about Space You Want to Know. Pinder, Andrew, illus. 2012. (J). *(978-1-60652-571-5(9))* Reader's Digest Assn., Inc., The.

—The Solar System, Meteors, & Comets. 2015. (Watch This Space! Ser.). (ENG., Illus.). 32p. (J). (gr. 3-7). lib. bdg. *(978-0-7787-2023-2(3))* Crabtree Publishing Co.

Goldsmith, Mike. The Kingfisher Space Encyclopedia. 2017. (Kingfisher Encyclopedias Ser.). (ENG.). 160p. (J). pap. 13.99 *(978-0-7534-7353-5(4),* 9780753473535, Kingfisher) Roaring Brook Pr.

—Space. 2010. (Ripley Twists Ser.). 48p. (J). (gr. 3-18). lib. bdg. 19.95 *(978-1-4222-1833-4(3))* Mason Crest.

—Space Adventure. Abbott, Simon, illus. 2011. (Flip Flap Science Ser.). (ENG.). 10p. (J). (gr. -1-k). 9.95 *(978-1-84898-364-9(6),* TickTock Books) Octopus Publishing Group GBR. Dist: Independent Pubs. Group.

Goldstein, Margaret. The Sun. 2009. pap. 6.95 *(978-0-8225-4760-0(0))* Lerner Publishing Group.

Goldstein, Margaret J. The Solar System. 2003. (Our Universe Ser.). (ENG., Illus.). 32p. (gr. 2-4). lib. bdg. 22.60 *(978-0-8225-4657-3(4))* Lerner Publishing Group.

—The Sun. 2003. (Our Universe Ser.). (ENG., Illus.). 32p. (gr. 2-4). lib. bdg. 22.60 *(978-0-8225-4647-4(7))* Lerner Publishing Group.

Graham, Ian. What Do We Know about the Solar System?, 1 vol. 2011. (Earth, Space, & Beyond Ser.). (ENG.). 48p. (gr. 3-3). pap. 9.49 *(978-1-4109-4185-5(X),* Raintree Freestyle Express); (gr. 6-6). pap. 9.49 *(978-1-4109-4167-1(1),* Raintree Freestyle); (gr. 6-6). 34.65 *(978-1-4109-4161-9(2),* Raintree Freestyle) Heinemann-Raintree.

Green, Jen. The Sun & Our Solar System. 2017. (Great Scientific Theories Ser.). (ENG.). 32p. (J). (gr. 4-6). lib. bdg. 30.65 ***(978-1-4109-8730-3(2),*** Raintree Perspectives) Heinemann-Raintree.

Group/McGraw-Hill, Wright. Earth & Physical Science: Our Solar System, 6 vols. (Book2WebTM Ser.). (gr. 4-8). 36.50 *(978-0-322-04427-2(8))* Wright Group/McGraw-Hill.

Hamilton, S. L. Solar System. 2011. (Xtreme Space Ser.). (Illus.). 32p. (gr. 3-9). 27.07 *(978-1-61714-740-1(0),* A&D Xtreme) ABDO Publishing Co.

Hansen, Rosanna. Jupiter. 2009. (Early Bird Astronomy Ser.). (ENG., Illus.). 48p. (gr. 2-5). pap. 8.95 *(978-0-7613-4979-2(0),* Lerner Pubns.) Lerner Publishing Group.

Harman, Alice. Planets, 01 vols., 1. 2016. (Fact Finders: Space Ser.). (ENG., Illus.). 24p. (J). pap. 8.25 *(978-1-5081-9133-9(6),* 1397743, Windmill Bks.) Rosen Publishing Group, Inc., The.

Heather Zschock. Solar System Scratch & Sketch. 2006. (Activity Book Ser.). 64p. (J). spiral bd. 12.99 *(978-1-59359-917-1(X))* Peter Pauper Pr. Inc.

Higgins, Nadia. The Solar System Through Infographics. Waananen, Lisa, illus. 2013. (Super Science Infographics Ser.). (ENG.). 32p. (gr. 3-5). pap. 8.95 *(978-1-4677-1594-2(8));* lib. bdg. 26.60 *(978-1-4677-1289-7(2),* Lerner Pubns.) Lerner Publishing Group.

—Solar Systems: Planets, Stars, & Orbits. 2014. (ENG.). 24p. (gr. k-3). 28.50 *(978-1-62717-730-6(2))* Rourke Educational Media.

Highlights for Children Editorial Staff, creator. Twinkle, Twinkle, Little Star. 2016. (Highlights(tm) Song & Puzzle Bks.). (ENG.). 48p. (J). (gr. -1-k). pap. 4.99 *(978-1-62979-713-7(8),* Highlights) Boyds Mills Pr.

Hill, Carolyn L. Journey Through Eclipses, 1 vol. 2014. (Spotlight on Space Science Ser.). (ENG.). 32p. (J). (gr. 5-5). pap. 11.75 *(978-1-4994-0377-0(1),* PowerKids Pr.) Rosen Publishing Group, Inc., The.

Hoffmann, Sara. The Little Book of Space. 2005. (Little Bks.). (ENG., Illus.). 24p. (J). (gr. -1-2). 9.95 *(978-1-58728-485-4(5))* Cooper Square Publishing Llc.

Holt, Rinehart and Winston Staff. Holt Science & Technology Chapter 20: Earth Science: Formation of the Solar System. 5th ed. 2004. (Illus.). pap. 12.86 *(978-0-03-030341-8(9))* Holt McDougal.

—Holt Science Spectrum Chptr. 19: The Solar System. 4th ed. Date not set. pap. 11.20 *(978-0-03-068058-8(1))* Holt McDougal.

Howard, Fran. The Kuiper Belt, 1 vol. 2008. (Universe Ser.). (ENG.). 32p. (gr. k-4). 27.07 *(978-1-59928-927-4(X),* Buddy Bks.) ABDO Publishing Co.

—The Milky Way, 1 vol. 2008. (Universe Ser.). (ENG.). 32p. (gr. k-4). 27.07 *(978-1-59928-928-1(8),* Buddy Bks.) ABDO Publishing Co.

—The Solar System, 1 vol. 2008. (Universe Ser.). (ENG.). 32p. (gr. k-4). 27.07 *(978-1-59928-930-4(X),* Buddy Bks.) ABDO Publishing Co.

Jackson, Ellen. Worlds Around Us: A Space Voyage. Miller, Ron, illus. 2006. (Exceptional Science Title for Intermediate Grades). 37p. (J). (gr. 3-7). lib. bdg. 23.93 *(978-0-7613-3405-7(X),* Millbrook Pr.) Lerner Publishing Group.

Jacobson, Linda. Our Super Solar System. 2012. (InfoMax Readers Ser.). (ENG., Illus.). 24p. (J). (gr. 1-2). pap. 8.25 *(978-1-4488-9070-5(5),* Rosen Classroom) Rosen Publishing Group, Inc., The.

James, Brian. Eight Spinning Planets. Benfanti, Russell, illus. 2010. (ENG.). 16p. (J). (gr. k — 1). 12.99 *(978-0-545-23517-4(0),* Cartwheel Bks.) Scholastic, Inc.

Jemison, Mae & Rau, Dana Meachen. Journey Through Our Solar System. 2013. (True Book™—Dr. Mae Jemison & 100 Year Starship™ Ser.). (ENG., Illus.). 48p. (J). pap. 6.95 *(978-0-531-24061-8(4));* lib. bdg. 29.00 *(978-0-531-25501-8(8))* Scholastic Library Publishing.

Jenkins, Martin. Exploring Space: from Galileo to the Mars Rover & Beyond. Biesty, Stephen, illus. 2017. (ENG.). 64p. (J). (gr. 3-7). 17.99 *(978-0-7636-8931-5(9))* Candlewick Pr.

Kazlow, Samuel, ed. Astronomy: Understanding Celestial Bodies. 2014. (Study of Science Ser.). 160p. (YA). (gr. 7-12). 35.25 *(978-1-62275-406-9(9))* Rosen Publishing Group, Inc., The.

Kessler, Colleen. A Project Guide to the Solar System. 2010. (Earth Science Projects for Kids Ser.). (Illus.). 48p. (J). (gr. 4-7). lib. bdg. 29.95 *(978-1-58415-867-7(0))* Mitchell Lane Pubs., Inc.

Kortenkamp, Steve. Asteroids, Comets, & Meteoroids, 1 vol. 2011. (Solar System & Beyond Ser.). (ENG.). 32p. (gr. 3-4). pap. 8.10 *(978-1-4296-7223-8(4));* pap. 47.70 *(978-1-4296-7224-5(2))* Capstone Press of Coughlan Cos. (Fact Finders).

—The Dwarf Planets. 2011. (Solar System & Beyond Ser.). (ENG.). 32p. (gr. 3-4). pap. 47.70 *(978-1-4296-6406-6(1),* Fact Finders) Capstone Press of Coughlan Cos.

—The Planets of Our Solar System. (Solar System & Beyond Ser.). (ENG.). 32p. (gr. 3-4). 2011. pap. 47.70 *(978-1-4296-6410-3(X))* 2010. lib. bdg. 27.32 *(978-1-4296-5396-1(5))* Capstone Press of Coughlan Cos. (Fact Finders).

Koupelis, Theo. In Quest of the Solar System. rev. ed. 2010. (ENG.). 399p. (J). pap. 149.95 *(978-0-7637-6629-0(1))* Jones & Bartlett Learning, LLC.

Kruesi, Liz. Discover Space Exploration. 2016. (Searchlight Books (tm) — What's Cool about Science? Ser.). (ENG., Illus.). 40p. (J). (gr. 3-5). 30.65 *(978-1-5124-0811-9(5))* Lerner Publishing Group.

Ladybird. Our Solar System. 2016. (Read It Yourself with Ladybird Ser.). (ENG.). 48p. (J). (gr. 2-4). 5.99 *(978-0-241-23743-4(2))* Penguin Bks., Ltd. GBR. Dist: Independent Pubs. Group.

—Our Solar System, Level 4. 2016. (Read It Yourself with Ladybird Ser.). (ENG.). 48p. (J). (gr. 2-4). pap. 9.99 *(978-0-241-23741-0(6))* Penguin Bks., Ltd. GBR. Dist: Independent Pubs. Group.

Law, Felicia. Trouble in Space. 2015. (Science to the Rescue Ser.). (ENG., Illus.). 32p. (J). (gr. 3-6). *(978-0-7787-1676-1(7))* Crabtree Publishing Co.

Lawrence, Ellen. Comets, Meteors, & Asteroids: Voyagers of the Solar System. 2013. (Zoom into Space Ser.). 24p. (J). (gr. -1-3). lib. bdg. 23.93 *(978-1-909673-22-9(6))* Ruby Tuesday Books Limited GBR. Dist: Bearport Publishing Co., Inc.

—Earth: Our Home in the Solar System. 2013. (Zoom into Space Ser.). 24p. (J). (gr. -1-3). lib. bdg. 23.93 *(978-1-909673-06-9(4))* Ruby Tuesday Books Limited GBR. Dist: Bearport Publishing Co., Inc.

—Jupiter: The Giant of the Solar System. 2013. (Zoom into Space Ser.). 24p. (J). (gr. -1-3). lib. bdg. 23.93 *(978-1-909673-12-0(9))* Ruby Tuesday Books Limited GBR. Dist: Bearport Publishing Co., Inc.

—Mars: The Dusty Planet. 2013. (Zoom into Space Ser.). 24p. (J). (gr. -1-3). lib. bdg. 23.93 *(978-1-909673-10-6(2))* Ruby Tuesday Books Limited GBR. Dist: Bearport Publishing Co., Inc.

—Mercury: The High-Speed Planet. 2013. (Zoom into Space Ser.). 24p. (J). (gr. -1-3). lib. bdg. 23.93 *(978-1-909673-02-1(1))* Ruby Tuesday Books Limited GBR. Dist: Bearport Publishing Co., Inc.

—Neptune: The Stormiest Planet. 2013. (Zoom into Space Ser.). 24p. (J). (gr. -1-3). lib. bdg. 23.93 *(978-1-909673-18-2(8))* Ruby Tuesday Books Limited GBR. Dist: Bearport Publishing Co., Inc.

—Pluto & the Dwarf Planets. 2013. (Zoom into Space Ser.). 24p. (J). (gr. -1-3). lib. bdg. 23.93 *(978-1-909673-20-5(X))* Ruby Tuesday Books Limited GBR. Dist: Bearport Publishing Co., Inc.

—Saturn: The Ringed Wonder. 2013. (Zoom into Space Ser.). 24p. (J). (gr. -1-3). lib. bdg. 23.93 *(978-1-909673-14-4(5))* Ruby Tuesday Books Limited GBR. Dist: Bearport Publishing Co., Inc.

—The Sun: The Star of Our Solar System. 2013. (Zoom into Space Ser.). (Illus.). 24p. (J). (gr. -1-3). lib. bdg. 23.93 *(978-1-909673-00-7(5))* Ruby Tuesday Books Limited GBR. Dist: Bearport Publishing Co., Inc.

—Uranus: The Sideways-Spinning Planet. 2013. (Zoom into Space Ser.). 24p. (J). (gr. -1-3). lib. bdg. 23.93 *(978-1-909673-16-8(1))* Ruby Tuesday Books Limited GBR. Dist: Bearport Publishing Co., Inc.

—Venus: The Hot & Toxic Planet. 2013. (Zoom into Space Ser.). 24p. (J). (gr. -1-3). lib. bdg. 23.93 *(978-1-909673-04-5(8))* Ruby Tuesday Books Limited GBR. Dist: Bearport Publishing Co., Inc.

Lawrence, Richard. Our Universe. 2004. (Illus.). vi, 134p. (gr. 1-6). pap. 18.00 *(978-0-9725365-4-7(X))* Boarding House Publishing.

Leigh, Autumn. A Trip Through Our Solar System. (Reading Room Collection 1 Ser.). 16p. 2009. (gr. 2-3). 37.50 *(978-1-60851-940-8(6)*, PowerKids Pr.) 2006. (ENG.). (gr. 2-3). 37.95 *(978-1-4042-6219-5(9))* 2006. (Illus.). (J). (gr. 3-7). lib. bdg. 17.25 *(978-1-4042-3345-4(8)*, PowerKids Pr.) Rosen Publishing Group, Inc., The.

L'Hommedieu, Arthur John. Children of the Sun. L'Hommedieu, Arthur John, illus. (GER., Illus.). (J). (gr. k-11). 10.99 *(978-0-85953-939-5(3))* Child's Play International Ltd. GBR. Dist: Child's Play-International.

Linde, Barbara. Math in Our Solar System: Applying Problem-Solving Strategies. 2009. (PowerMath: Proficiency Plus Ser.). 32p. (gr. 4-5). 47.90 *(978-1-60851-413-7(7)*, PowerKids Pr.) Rosen Publishing Group, Inc., The.

Linde, Barbara M. Math in Our Solar System: Applying Problem-Solving Strategies. (PowerMath Ser.). 32p. 2009. (ENG.). (gr. 5-6). pap. 10.00 *(978-1-4042-5135-9(9))* 2005. (Illus.). (J). (gr. 3-6). lib. bdg. 25.25 *(978-1-4042-2936-5(1)*, PowerKids Pr.) Rosen Publishing Group, Inc., The.

little bee books, little bee. Listopia: Space. 2016. (ENG., Illus.). 208p. (J). (gr. 2-4). pap. 9.99 *(978-1-4998-0280-1(3))* Little Bee Books Inc.

Lopez, Delano. Amazing Solar System Projects: You Can Build Yourself. 2008. (Build It Yourself Ser.). (ENG., Illus.). 128p. (J). (gr. 3-7). per. 14.95 *(978-0-9792268-1-6(3))* Octavio Publishing.

Lopez, Delano & Braley, Shawn. Amazing Solar System Projects. 2008. (Build It Yourself Ser.). (ENG., Illus.). 128p. (J). (gr. 3-7). 21.95 *(978-1-934670-00-2(6))* Octavio Publishing.

Loria, Laura. What Is a Constellation? 2014. (Let's Find Out! Ser.). 32p. (J). (gr. 3-6). 23.45 *(978-1-62275-476-2(X))* Rosen Publishing Group, Inc., The.

The Magic School Bus: Lost in the Solar System. 2011. (J). audio compact disk 9.99 *(978-0-545-22880-0(8))* Scholastic, Inc.

Margles, Samantha. Earth's Solar System. 2014. (Illus.). 32p. (J). pap. *(978-0-545-58517-0(1))* Scholastic, Inc.

Martin, Justin McCory. Planets. 2010. (Illus.). 16p. (J). pap. *(978-0-545-13738-6(1))* Scholastic, Inc.

Mason Crest. Far Planets & Beyond, Vol. 7. 2016. (Solar System Ser.: Vol. 7). (ENG., Illus.). 48p. (J). (gr. 5-8). 20.95 *(978-1-4222-3550-8(5))* Mason Crest.

—Our Home Planet, Vol. 7. 2016. (Solar System Ser.: Vol. 7). (ENG., Illus.). 48p. (J). (gr. 5-8). 20.95 *(978-1-4222-3549-2(1))* Mason Crest.

Mattern, Joanne. Our Earth. 2011. (Solar System & Beyond Ser.). (ENG.). 32p. (gr. 3-4). pap. 47.70 *(978-1-4296-6407-3(X)*, Fact Finders) Capstone Press of Coughlan Cos.

—Our Moon. 2011. (Solar System & Beyond Ser.). (ENG.). 32p. (gr. 3-4). pap. 47.70 *(978-1-4296-6408-0(8)*, Fact Finders) Capstone Press of Coughlan Cos.

Maunsell, Simonne. Fluffy Clouds. 2013. 20p. pap. 10.95 *(978-1-4525-7180-5(5)*, Balboa Pr.) Author Solutions, Inc.

McDonald, Jill. Hello, World! Solar System. 2016. (ENG., Illus.). 26p. (J). (— 1). bds. 7.99 *(978-0-553-52103-0(9)*, Doubleday Bks. for Young Readers) Random Hse. Children's Bks.

McGranaghan, John. Conoce Los Planetas, 1 vol. Klein, Laurie Allen, illus. 2011. (SPA.). 32p. (J). (gr. k-5). pap. 9.95 *(978-1-62855-411-3(8))* Arbordale Publishing.

—Meet the Planets, 1 vol. Klein, Laurie Allen, illus. 2011. (ENG.). 32p. (J). (gr. k-5). 16.95 *(978-1-60718-123-1(1))*; pap. 9.95 *(978-1-60718-869-8(4))* Arbordale Publishing.

McMahon, Michael. Why Do Stars Twinkle? 2010. (Solving Science Mysteries Ser.). (Illus.). 24p. (J). pap. 8.25 *(978-1-61531-921-3(2)*, PowerKids Pr.); (YA). (gr. 3-6). lib. bdg. 22.60 *(978-1-61531-895-7(X))* Rosen Publishing Group, Inc., The.

Meachen Rau, Dana & Picture Window Books Staff. Giran en el Espacio: Un Libro Sobre Los Planetas. Robledo, Sol, tr. from ENG. Shea, Denise, illus. 2007. (Ciencia Asombrosa: Exploremos el Espacio Ser.). (SPA.). 24p. (gr. k-4). 26.65 *(978-1-4048-3231-2(9))* Picture Window Bks.

Miller, Ron. Seven Wonders Beyond the Solar System. 2011. (Seven Wonders Ser.). (ENG., Illus.). 80p. (gr. 5-8). 33.26 *(978-0-7613-5454-3(9))* Lerner Publishing Group.

—Stars & Galaxies. 2006. (Worlds Beyond Ser.). (Illus.). 96p. (J). (gr. 5-9). 27.93 *(978-0-7613-3466-8(1)*, Twenty-First Century Bks.) Lerner Publishing Group.

Mills, Nathan & Block, Dakota. Exploring the Solar System. 2012. (Rosen Readers Ser.). (ENG., Illus.). 24p. (J). (gr. 1-2). pap. 8.25 *(978-1-4488-8857-3(3)*, Rosen Classroom) Rosen Publishing Group, Inc., The.

Mitton, Jacqueline. The Planet Gods: Myths & Facts about the Solar System. Balit, Christina, illus. 2008. (ENG.). 32p. (J). (gr. 1-4). 7.95 *(978-1-4263-0448-4(X))*; 25.90 *(978-1-4263-0449-1(8))* National Geographic Society. (National Geographic Children's Bks.).

Monier, Eric M., ed. How Life on Earth Is Affected by Earth's Unique Placement & Orientation in Our Solar System: An Anthology of Current Thought. 2009. (Contemporary Discourse in the Field of Astronomy Ser.). 240p. (gr. 10-10). 63.90 *(978-1-61511-903-5(5))* Rosen Publishing Group, Inc., The.

Moore, Patrick & Lawrence, Pete. Exploring the Mysteries of Astronomy. 2016. (STEM Guide to the Universe Ser.). (ENG.). 192p. (YA). (gr. 9-9). lib. bdg. 46.10 *(978-1-4994-6411-5(8))* Rosen Publishing Group, Inc., The.

Nagelhout, Ryan. What Is a Moon? 2014. (Let's Find Out! Ser.). 32p. (J). (gr. 3-6). 23.45 *(978-1-62275-466-3(2))* Rosen Publishing Group, Inc., The.

Nardo, Don. Asteroids & Comets. 2009. (Extreme Threats Ser.). 112p. (YA). lib. bdg. 28.95 *(978-1-59935-121-6(8))* Reynolds, Morgan Inc.

Nelson, John. Collision Course: Asteroids & Earth. 2008. (Jr. Graphic Environmental Dangers Ser.). (ENG.). 24p. (J). 47.90 *(978-1-61532-098-1(9)*, PowerKids Pr.) Rosen Publishing Group, Inc., The.

—Trayectoria de Choque: Los Asteroides y la Tierra. 2009. (Historietas Juveniles: Peligros Del Medioambiente (Jr. Graphic Environmental Dangers) Ser.). (SPA., Illus.). 24p. (gr. 3-6). (YA). lib. bdg. 25.25 *(978-1-4358-8477-9(9))*; pap. 10.60 *(978-1-4358-8478-6(7))* Rosen Publishing Group, Inc., The.

The New Solar System Set, 12-Volumes. 2008. (New Solar System Ser.). (gr. 4-6). 276.00 *(978-1-60413-244-1(2)*, Chelsea Clubhouse) Facts On File, Inc.

Nicolson, Cynthia Pratt & Bourgeois, Paulette. The Jumbo Book of Space. Nicolson, Cynthia Pratt & Slavin, Bill, illus. 2007. (Jumbo Bks.). (ENG.). 208p. (J). 17.95 *(978-1-55453-020-5(2))* Kids Can Pr., Ltd. CAN. Dist: Hachette Bk. Group.

O'Donnell, Kerri. Moons of Our Solar System. 2009. (Real Life Readers Ser.). (ENG., Illus.). 32p. (J). (gr. 5-6). pap. 10.00 *(978-1-4358-0181-3(4))*; 32p. (gr. 5-5). 47.90 *(978-1-60853-055-7(8))*; (J). lib. bdg. 25.25 *(978-1-4358-2996-1(4))* Rosen Publishing Group, Inc., The. (PowerKids Pr.).

—Space Circles: Learning about Radius & Diameter. (PowerMath Ser.). (ENG., 32p. (gr. 4-5). 2009. Illus.). pap. 10.00 *(978-0-8239-8878-5(3)*, PowerKids Pr.) 2004. 47.50 *(978-0-8239-7651-5(3))* Rosen Publishing Group, Inc., The.

Olien, Rebecca. Exploring the Planets in Our Solar System. (Objects in the Sky Ser.). 24p. (gr. 3-3). 2009. 42.50 *(978-1-60851-141-9(3))* 2007. (Illus.). (J). lib. bdg. 22.60 *(978-1-4042-3467-3(5))* Rosen Publishing Group, Inc., The. (PowerKids Pr.).

Orme, David. Comets. 2009. (Fact to Fiction Ser.). (Illus.). 36p. (J). pap. 6.95 *(978-0-7891-7899-2(0))* Perfection Learning Corp.

Orme, Helen. Solar System. 2010. (Science Everywhere! Ser.). 24p. 24.25 *(978-1-84898-292-5(5))* Black Rabbit Bks.

Our Solar System. (Jump Ser.). 36p. (J). (gr. 2-7). pap. *(978-1-882210-23-7(9))* Action Publishing, Inc.

Our Solar System: An easy, practical book to understand the planets in our Solar System. Written especially for kids to learn about science & Nature. 2006. 108p. per. *(978-956-291-336-2(8))* Editorial Benei Noaj.

Our Solar System: Level Q, 6 vols. (Wonder Worldtm Ser.). 48p. 39.95 *(978-0-7802-2952-5(5))* Wright Group/McGraw-Hill.

Outer Space. 2014. (Ken Jennings' Junior Genius Guides). (ENG., Illus.). 160p. (J). (gr. 3-5). pap. 7.99 *(978-1-4814-0170-8(X)*, Little Simon) Little Simon.

Owen, Ruth. Asteroids & the Asteroid Belt. 2012. (Explore Outer Space Ser.). (ENG., Illus.). 32p. (J). (gr. 3-6). 25.25 *(978-1-4488-8073-7(4))*; pap. 10.00 *(978-1-4488-8115-4(3))* Windmill Bks.

Oxlade, Chris. Space Watch: The Sun. 2010. (Eye on Space Ser.). 24p. (J). pap. 8.25 *(978-1-61532-550-4(6)*, PowerKids Pr.); (ENG.). lib. bdg. 22.60 *(978-1-61532-543-6(3))* Rosen Publishing Group, Inc., The.

Pamplona, Alberto Hernández. A Visual Guide to the Universe. 2017. (Visual Exploration of Science Ser.). 96p. (J). (gr. 12-13). 37.10 ***(978-1-5081-7585-8(3)***, Rosen Young Adult) Rosen Publishing Group, Inc., The.

Paris, Stephanie. Siglo Xxi: Misterios Del Espacio Sideral. 2016. (TIME for Kids en Español - Level 5 Ser.). (SPA.). 64p. (gr. 5-5). lib. bdg. 31.99 *(978-1-5157-2937-2(0))* Time for Kids Inc AUS. Dist: Capstone Pub.

Parker, Steve. Beyond the Solar System: From Red Giants to Black Holes. 2007. (Earth & Space Ser.). (Illus.). 48p. (YA). (gr. 5-9). lib. bdg. 29.25 *(978-1-4042-3739-1(9))* Rosen Publishing Group, Inc., The.

Peddicord, Jane Ann. Night Wonders. 2005. (ENG., Illus.). 32p. (J). (gr. 1-4). pap. 7.95 *(978-1-57091-878-0(3))* Charlesbridge Publishing, Inc.

Peters, Elisa. The Planets. 2012. (PowerKids Readers: the Universe Ser.). (ENG., Illus.). 24p. (J). (gr. k-2). pap. 8.25 *(978-1-4488-7468-2(8))*; lib. bdg. 22.60 *(978-1-4488-7389-0(4))* Rosen Publishing Group, Inc., The. (PowerKids Pr.).

—The Planets: Los Planetas. 2012. (PowerKids Readers: the Universe / el universo Ser.). (SPA & ENG., Illus.). 24p. (J). (gr. k-2). lib. bdg. 22.60 *(978-1-4488-7825-3(X)*, PowerKids Pr.) Rosen Publishing Group, Inc., The.

Phelan, Glen. Earth in Space. 2007. (Language, Literacy, & Vocabulary - Reading Expeditions Ser.). (ENG., Illus.). 36p. (J). pap. 18.95 *(978-0-7922-5428-7(7))* CENGAGE Learning.

Pop-Out Play Pak: Solar System. Orig. Title: Child's Play. (Illus.). 24p. (J). (gr. -1-4). reprint ed. *(978-1-881469-77-3(8))* Safari, Ltd.

Portman, Michael. Are There Other Earths? 2013. (Space Mysteries Ser.). (Illus.). 32p. (gr. 2-5). 25.25 *(978-1-4339-8257-6(9))*; pap. 10.50 *(978-1-4339-8258-3(7))* Stevens, Gareth Publishing LLLP. (Gareth Stevens Learning Library).

—Could an Asteroid Harm Earth? 2013. (Space Mysteries Ser.). (Illus.). 32p. (J). (gr. 2-5). pap. 10.50 *(978-1-4339-8268-2(4))*; lib. bdg. 25.25 *(978-1-4339-8267-5(6))* Stevens, Gareth Publishing LLLP.

Poynter, Margaret. Doomsday Rocks from Space. 2011. (Bizarre Science Ser.). (Illus.). 48p. (J). (gr. 5-18). pap. 8.95 *(978-1-59845-221-1(5))*; lib. bdg. 25.27 *(978-0-7660-3673-4(1))* Enslow Pubs., Inc.

Prinja, Raman. In Focus: Space. 2017. (In Focus Ser.). (ENG.). 64p. (J). 17.99 *(978-0-7534-7349-8(6)*, 9780753473498, Kingfisher) Roaring Brook Pr.

Prokos, Anna. Star Light, Star Bright: Exploring Our Solar System. Clegg, Dave, illus. 2017. (Imagine That! Ser.). (ENG.). 32p. (J). (gr. 2-4). lib. bdg. 26.65 *(978-1-63440-152-4(2))*; 39.99 ***(978-1-63440-164-7(6))*** Red Chair Pr.

Publications International Ltd. Staff, ed. Solar System Puzzle. 2010. (J). 13.98 *(978-1-60553-351-3(3))* Publications International, Ltd.

Pulliam, Christine & Daniels, Patricia. Space Encyclopedia: A Tour of Our Solar System & Beyond. Aguilar, David A., illus. 2013. 191p. (J). *(978-1-4263-1629-6(1))* National Geographic Society.

Rabe, Tish. Planet Name Game. 2015. (Step into Reading Level 2 Ser.). lib. bdg. 13.55 *(978-0-606-37271-8(7))* Turtleback Bks.

Reid, Stephanie. Space, 1 vol. 2012. (Early Childhood Themes Ser.). (ENG.). 16p. (J). (gr. -1-2). pap. 6.99 *(978-1-4333-3467-2(4))*; pap. 19.99 *(978-1-4333-3468-9(2))* Teacher Created Materials, Inc.

Reyes, Sonja. How Do Planets Move? What Will Happen? 2017. (Computer Science for the Real World Ser.). 16p. (gr. 7-8). pap. 7.95 ***(978-1-5383-5234-2(6)***, Rosen Classroom) Rosen Publishing Group, Inc., The.

Rhatigan, Joe. Space: Planets, Moons, Stars, & More! Girard, Thomas, illus. 2016. (Step into Reading Ser.). (ENG.). 48p. (J). (gr. k-3). 3.99 *(978-0-553-52316-4(3)*, Random Hse. Bks. for Young Readers) Random Hse. Children's Bks.

Richards, Jon & Simkins, Ed. Record-Breaking Earth & Space Facts. 2015. (Infographic Top 10s Ser.). (ENG., Illus.). 32p. (J). (gr. 4-6). 26.65 *(978-1-4677-8595-2(4)*, Lerner Pubns.) Lerner Publishing Group.

Ride, Sally & O'Shaughnessy, Tam E. Voyager: An Adventure to the Edge of the Solar System. 2nd rev. ed. 2005. (J). per. 20.00 *(978-0-9753920-5-8(0))* Sally Ride Science.

Riggs, Kate. Across the Universe: Asteroids. 2015. (Across the Universe Ser.). (ENG.). 24p. (J). (gr. 1-3). pap. 9.99 *(978-1-62832-080-0(X)*, Creative Paperbacks) Creative Co., The.

—Across the Universe: Moons. 2015. (Across the Universe Ser.). (ENG.). 24p. (J). (gr. 1-3). pap. 9.99 *(978-1-62832-083-1(4)*, Creative Paperbacks) Creative Co., The.

—Across the Universe: Planets. 2015. (Across the Universe Ser.). (ENG.). 24p. (J). (gr. 1-3). pap. 9.99 *(978-1-62832-084-8(2)*, Creative Paperbacks) Creative Co., The.

—Moons. 2015. (J). *(978-1-60818-483-5(8)*, Creative Education) Creative Co., The.

—Planets. 2015. (J). *(978-1-60818-484-2(6)*, Creative Education) Creative Co., The.

Riley, Peter. Earth, Moon & Sun. 2007. (Essential Science/Watts Ser.). (Illus.). 32p. (YA). (gr. 3-6). lib. bdg. 28.50 *(978-1-59920-025-5(2))* Black Rabbit Bks.

Ring, Susan & Roumanis, Alexis. Dwarf Planets. 2016. (Illus.). 24p. (J). *(978-1-5105-0968-9(2))* SmartBook Media, Inc.

—Earth. 2016. (Illus.). 24p. (J). *(978-1-5105-0971-9(2))* SmartBook Media, Inc.

—Jupiter. 2016. (Illus.). 24p. (J). *(978-1-5105-0974-0(7))* SmartBook Media, Inc.

—Neptune. 2016. (Illus.). 24p. (J). *(978-1-5105-0986-3(0))* SmartBook Media, Inc.

—Saturn. 2016. (Illus.). 24p. (J). *(978-1-5105-0989-4(5))* SmartBook Media, Inc.

—Venus. 2016. (Illus.). 24p. (J). *(978-1-5105-0995-5(X))* SmartBook Media, Inc.

Roca, Núria, et al. The Sky. 2014. (Solar System Ser.). (ENG., Illus.). 36p. (J). (gr. -1-2). pap. 7.99 *(978-1-4380-0477-8(X))* Barron's Educational Series, Inc.

Roop, Connie, et al. Our Solar System. 2016. (Science for Toddlers Ser.: 1). (ENG., Illus.). 26p. (J). (gr. -1 — 1). bds. 7.95 *(978-1-4549-1418-1(1)*, 1404673) Sterling Publishing Co., Inc.

Rosen Publishing Group, creator. Mysteries of the Milky Way. 2008. (Scientific American Cutting-Edge Science Ser.). (Illus.). 136p. (YA). (gr. 9-12). lib. bdg. 34.60 *(978-1-4042-1404-0(6))* Rosen Publishing Group, Inc., The.

Roumanis, Alexis. Dwarf Planets. 2016. (J). ***(978-1-5105-2043-1(0))*** SmartBook Media, Inc.

Roumanis, Alexis. The Sun. 2016. (Illus.). 24p. (J). *(978-1-5105-0983-2(6))* SmartBook Media, Inc.

Rowe, Dana. Pavo Explores the Solar System. 2013. 40p. pap. 14.95 *(978-1-937829-67-4(7)*, Total Publishing & Media) Yorkshire Publishing Group.

Roza, Greg. Comets & Asteroids: Space Rocks. 2010. (Our Solar System Ser.). 24p. (J). (gr. k-3). (ENG.). pap. 8.15 *(978-1-4339-3816-0(2))*; (Illus.). lib. bdg. 22.60 *(978-1-4339-3815-3(4))* Stevens, Gareth Publishing LLLP.

—Neptune: The Stormy Planet. 2010. (Our Solar System Ser.). 24p. (J). (gr. k-3). (ENG.). pap. 8.15 *(978-1-4339-3834-4(0))*; (Illus.). lib. bdg. 22.60 *(978-1-4339-3833-7(2))* Stevens, Gareth Publishing LLLP.

Russell, Harriet. Drawing in Space. 2017. (ENG.). 64p. (J). (gr. 1-3). pap. 18.95 *(978-1-61689-497-9(0))* Princeton Architectural Pr.

Rustad, Martha E. Space. 2016. (Space Ser.). (ENG.). 24p. (gr. k-1). 87.96 *(978-1-4914-8337-4(7)*, Pebble Bks.) Capstone Press of Coughlan Cos.

Rustad, Martha E. H. Does the Sun Sleep? Noticing Sun, Moon, & Star Patterns. Conger, Holli, illus. 2015. (ENG.). 24p. (J). (gr. k-2). 25.32 *(978-1-4677-8560-0(1)*, Millbrook Pr.) Lerner Publishing Group.

—Planets. 2016. (Space Ser.). (ENG., Illus.). 24p. (gr. k-1). lib. bdg. 21.99 *(978-1-4914-8322-0(9)*, Pebble Bks.) Capstone Press of Coughlan Cos.

—Space, 1 vol. 2013. (Little Scientist Ser.). (ENG., Illus.). 32p. (gr. 1-2). 6.95 *(978-1-4765-3545-6(0))*; 27.99 *(978-1-4765-0251-9(X))*; pap. 6.95 *(978-1-4765-3551-7(5))* Capstone Press of Coughlan Cos.

Semadini, Tomassino. Lukie the Astro-Dog. 2008. 52p. pap. 10.49 *(978-1-4389-0359-0(6))* AuthorHouse.

Sexton, Colleen. The Solar System. 2010. (Exploring Space Ser.). (ENG., Illus.). 24p. (J). (gr. k-3). lib. bdg. 25.95 *(978-1-60014-411-0(X)*, Blastoff! Readers) Bellwether Media.

Sherman, Josepha. Asteroids, Meteors, & Comets. 2009. (Space!). 64p. (gr. 5-18). lib. bdg. 32.79 *(978-0-7614-4252-3(9))* Marshall Cavendish Corp.

Sian revision Earth-sun. 2004. (J). *(978-1-59242-020-9(6))* Delta Education, LLC.

Silverstein, Alvin, et al. The Universe. rev. ed. 2009. (Science Concepts, Second Ser.). (ENG.). 112p. (gr. 6-8). 31.93 *(978-0-7613-3937-3(X))* Lerner Publishing Group.

Simon, Seymour. Our Solar System. (J). (gr. 1-5). 2014. (ENG.). 48p. 17.99 *(978-0-06-233379-7(8))* 2014. (ENG.). 48p. pap. 6.99 *(978-0-06-114010-5(4))* 2007. 72p. lib. bdg. 20.89 *(978-0-06-114009-9(0)*, Collins) 2007. (ENG., Illus.). 72p. 19.99 *(978-0-06-114008-2(2)*, Collins) HarperCollins Pubs.

El Sistema Solar. (Coleccion Ventana Transparente). (SPA.). *(978-950-11-1135-4(0)*, SG5232) Sigmar ARG. Dist: Lectorum Pubns., Inc.

Smith, Alexander Gordon. The Solar System. 2010. (ENG., Illus.). 128p. (J). (gr. -1-12). pap. 17.99 *(978-1-84476-893-6(7))* Anness Publishing GBR. Dist: National Bk. Network.

—The Solar System: A Breathtaking Tour of the Universe & How It Works with More Than 300 Incredible Photographs & Illustrations. 2014. (ENG., Illus.). 128p. (J). (gr. k-3). 14.99 *(978-1-86147-327-1(3)*, Armadillo) Anness Publishing GBR. Dist: National Bk. Network.

Smyer, Lori. Journey Through Galaxies, 1 vol. 2014. (Spotlight on Space Science Ser.). (ENG.). 32p. (J). (gr. 5-5). pap. 11.75 *(978-1-4994-0369-5(0)*, PowerKids Pr.) Rosen Publishing Group, Inc., The.

Sohn, Emily & Harter, Adam. Sun, Moon, & Stars: A Cosmic Case. 2011. (IScience Readers Ser.). 32p. (J). (gr. 3-4). lib. bdg. 22.60 *(978-1-59953-421-3(5))* Norwood Hse. Pr.

The Solar System. (First Facts about Ser.). 24p. (J). (gr. 3-7). pap. *(978-1-882210-16-9(6))* Action Publishing, Inc.

The Solar System. 2004. (Illus.). 32p. (J). (gr. 2-4). pap. 6.95 *(978-0-8225-4769-3(4))* Lerner Publishing Group.

The Solar System & Beyond. (Solar System & Beyond Ser.). (ENG.). 32p. (gr. 3-4). 2011. pap. 477.00 *(978-1-4296-7232-0(3))* 2011. pap. 79.50 *(978-1-4296-7231-3(5))* 2011. lib. bdg. 191.24 *(978-1-4296-6496-7(7))* 2011. pap. 286.20 *(978-1-4296-6412-7(6))* 2010. pap. 47.70 *(978-1-4296-6244-4(1))* 2010. lib. bdg. 163.92 *(978-1-4296-5399-2(X))* Capstone Press of Coughlan Cos. (Fact Finders).

Solner Heimer, Patricia. Li'l Earth. Solner Heimer, Patricia, illus. 2010. (Illus.). 32p. (J). (gr. k-4). 15.99 *(978-0-9844453-0-1(7))* Maple Road Publishing, Inc.

Space Quest: Exploring Our Solar System: Individual Title Six-Packs. (Discovery World Ser.). 24p. (gr. 1-2). 33.00 *(978-0-7635-8481-8(9))* Rigby Education.

Sparrow, Giles. Destination Asteroids, Comets, & Meteors. 2009. (Destination Solar System Ser.). (Illus.). 32p. (J). 25.25 *(978-1-4358-3449-1(6))*; pap. 10.00 *(978-1-4358-3469-9(0))* Rosen Publishing Group, Inc., The. (PowerKids Pr.).

Sparrow, Giles. Our Solar System. 2017. (J). ***(978-0-7660-9267-9(4))*** Enslow Pubs., Inc.

Sparrow, Giles & John, Judith. The Solar System. 2016. (Discoveries in Space Science Ser.). (ENG.). 80p. (YA). (gr. 9-9). lib. bdg. 35.64 *(978-1-5026-1018-8(3))* Cavendish Square Publishing.

Stefoff, Rebecca. Earth or Sun: Which One Is in the Center? 2013. (J). *(978-0-7614-8147-8(8))* Marshall Cavendish.

Storad, Conrad J. Mars. 2009. (Early Bird Astronomy Ser.). (ENG., Illus.). 48p. (gr. 2-5). pap. 8.95 *(978-0-7613-4980-8(4)*, Lerner Pubns.) Lerner Publishing Group.

Stott, Carole. Mission: Space: Explore the Galaxy. 2016. (Illus.). 128p. (J). *(978-1-4654-5376-1(8))* Dorling Kindersley Publishing, Inc.

Sundance/Newbridge LLC Staff. Circling the Sun. 2004. (Reading PowerWorks Ser.). (gr. 1-3). 37.50 *(978-0-7608-8916-9(3))* Sundance/Newbridge Educational Publishing.

Teacher Created Resources Staff. Space Guides: Discovering the Solar System. 2008. (ENG., Illus.). 32p. pap. 7.99 *(978-1-4206-8267-0(9))* Teacher Created Resources, Inc.

Time for Kids Editors. Time for Kids - Planets! 2005. (Time for Kids Ser.). (ENG., Illus.). 32p. (J). 14.99 *(978-0-06-078203-0(X))* HarperCollins Pubs.

Trammel, Howard K. The Solar System. 2009. (True Book Ser.). (ENG.). 48p. (J). (gr. 2-5). 29.00 *(978-0-531-16898-1(0))* Scholastic Library Publishing.

A True Book & Trade - Dr. Mae Jemison & 100 Year Starship & Trade. 2013. (True Book™—Dr. Mae Jemison & 100 Year Starship™ Ser.). (J). 116.00 *(978-0-531-25339-7(2)*, Children's Pr.) Scholastic Library Publishing.

Turiel, Isaac. How Do We Know the Size of the Solar System? 2009. (Great Scientific Questions & the Scientists Who Answered Them Ser.). 112p. (gr. 7-12). 63.90 *(978-1-61513-206-5(6))* Rosen Publishing Group, Inc., The.

Vogt, Gregory. The Dwarf Planet Pluto. 2009. (Early Bird Astronomy Ser.). (ENG.). 48p. (gr. 2-5). lib. bdg. 26.60 *(978-0-7613-4157-4(9))* Lerner Publishing Group.

—Pluto: A Dwarf Planet. 2009. (Early Bird Astronomy Ser.). (ENG., Illus.). 48p. (gr. 2-5). pap. 8.95 *(978-0-7613-4988-4(X)*, Lerner Pubns.) Lerner Publishing Group.

—Solar System. 2012. (Scholastic Reader Level 2 Ser.). (ENG.). 32p. (J). (gr. -1-3). pap. 3.99 *(978-0-545-38267-0(X)*, Scholastic Paperbacks) Scholastic, Inc.

Waldeck, Aaron. Space Rocks: A Look at Asteriods & Comets. 2003. (Rosen Real Readers Big Bookstm Ser.). (ENG.). 24p. (gr. 3-4). 43.95 *(978-0-8239-8729-0(9))* Rosen Publishing Group, Inc., The.

—Space Rocks: A Look at Asteroids & Comets. 2009. (Reading Room Collection 2 Ser.). 24p. (gr. 3-4). 42.50 *(978-1-60851-990-3(2)*, PowerKids Pr.) Rosen Publishing Group, Inc., The.

Walsh, Kenneth. The Solar System, 1 vol. 2nd rev. ed. 2013. (Nonfiction Readers Ser.). (ENG., Illus.). 28p. (J). (gr. 2-2). pap. 23.96 *(978-1-4807-1054-2(7))* Shell Educational Publishing.

—The Solar System, 1 vol. 2nd rev. ed. 2011. (TIME for KIDS(r) Nonfiction Readers Ser.). (ENG.). 28p. (J). (gr. 2-2). pap. 6.99 *(978-1-4333-3633-1(2))* Teacher Created Materials, Inc.

Waxman, Laura Hamilton. Saturn. 2009. (Early Bird Astronomy Ser.). (ENG., Illus.). 48p. (gr. 2-5). pap. 8.95 *(978-0-7613-4985-3(5)*, Lerner Pubns.) Lerner Publishing Group.

—The Solar System. 2010. (Early Bird Astronomy Ser.). 48p. (ENG.). (gr. 2-5). lib. bdg. 26.60 *(978-0-7613-3874-1(8))*; (Illus.). (J). 8.95 *(978-0-7613-4990-7(1)*, 1306464, Lerner Pubns.) Lerner Publishing Group.

Wells, Robert E. What's So Special about Planet Earth? 2012. (J). *(978-1-61913-154-5(4))* Weigl Pubs., Inc.

Whitt, Kelly Kizer. Solar System Forecast, 1 vol. Klein, Laurie Allen, illus. 2012. (SPA.). 32p. (J). (gr. -1-4). pap. 9.95 *(978-1-62855-425-0(8))* Arbordale Publishing.

Whitt, Kelly Kizer. El Pronóstico Del Sistema Solar, 1 vol. Klein, Laurie Allen, illus. 2012. (SPA & ENG.). 32p. (J). (gr. -1-4). 17.95 *(978-1-60718-678-6(0))* Arbordale Publishing.

—Solar System Forecast, 1 vol. Klein, Laurie Allen, illus. 2012. 32p. (J). (gr. -1-4). (ENG & SPA.). 17.95 *(978-1-60718-523-9(7))*; (SPA & ENG.). pap. 9.95 *(978-1-60718-532-1(6))* Arbordale Publishing.

Wilkins, Mary-Jane. Asteroids, Comets, & Meteors. 2017. (Fast Track: Our Solar System Ser.). 24p. (gr. k-3). 28.50 ***(978-1-78121-368-1(2))*** Brown Bear Bks.

—Earth. 2017. (Fast Track: Our Solar System Ser.). 24p. (gr. k-3). 28.50 ***(978-1-78121-364-3(X))*** Brown Bear Bks.

—The Inner Planets. 2017. (Fast Track: Our Solar System Ser.). (Illus.). 24p. (gr. k-3). 28.50 ***(978-1-78121-366-7(6))*** Brown Bear Bks.

—The Moon. 2017. (Fast Track: Our Solar System Ser.). 24p. (gr. k-3). 28.50 ***(978-1-78121-365-0(8))*** Brown Bear Bks.

—The Outer Planets. 2017. (Fast Track: Our Solar System Ser.). (Illus.). 24p. (gr. k-3). 28.50 ***(978-1-78121-367-4(4))*** Brown Bear Bks.

—The Sun. 2017. (Fast Track: Our Solar System Ser.). (Illus.). 24p. (gr. k-3). 28.50 ***(978-1-78121-363-6(1))*** Brown Bear Bks.

Willett, Edward. Space Q&a. 2014. (Science Discovery Ser.). (ENG., Illus.). 48p. (J). (gr. 4-7). lib. bdg. 28.55 *(978-1-4896-0692-1(0)*, AV2 by Weigl) Weigl Pubs., Inc.

Williams, Brian & Egan, Vicky. The Solar System. Dogi, Flammetta, illus. 2007. (Back to Basics Ser.). 32p. (J). lib. bdg. *(978-88-6098-049-6(6))* McRae Bks. Srl.

Woolf, Alex. An Asteroid Strike. 2013. (World After Ser.). (ENG., Illus.). 56p. (gr. 7-8). 34.65 *(978-1-4329-7618-7(4))*; pap. 9.95 *(978-1-4329-7623-1(0))* Heinemann-Raintree.

World Book, contrib. by. Galaxies & the Universe. 2nd ed. 2006. (World Book's Solar System & Space Exploration Library). (Illus.). 64p. (J). *(978-0-7166-9513-4(8))* World Bk., Inc.

World Book, Inc Staff, contrib. by. Earth & Earth's Moon. 2010. (J). *(978-0-7166-9540-0(5))* World Bk., Inc.

—Galaxies & the Universe. 2010. (J). *(978-0-7166-9542-4(1))* World Bk., Inc.

—Mars. 2010. (J). *(978-0-7166-9536-3(7))* World Bk., Inc.

—Mercury & Venus. 2010. (J). *(978-0-7166-9534-9(0))* World Bk., Inc.

—Neptune, Comets, & Dwarf Planets. 2010. (J). *(978-0-7166-9538-7(3))* World Bk., Inc.

—Saturn & Uranus. 2010. (J). *(978-0-7166-9535-6(9))* World Bk., Inc.

—The Sun & Other Stars. 2010. (J). *(978-0-7166-9539-4(1))* World Bk., Inc.

—Telescopes & Space Probes. 2010. (J). *(978-0-7166-9541-7(3))* World Bk., Inc.

Yasuda, Anita & Stone, Bryan. Explore the Solar System! 25 Great Projects, Activities, Experiments. Stone, Bryan, illus. 2009. (Explore Your World Ser.). (ENG., Illus.). 96p. (J). (gr. k-4). pap. 12.95 *(978-1-934670-36-1(7))* Octavio Publishing.

Yomtov, Nel. Sailing the Solar System: The Next 100 Years of Space Exploration. Pota, Giovanni & Brown, Alan, illus. 2016. (Our World: the Next 100 Years Ser.). (ENG.). 32p. (gr. 3-4). lib. bdg. 30.65 *(978-1-4914-8265-0(6)*, Graphic Library) Capstone Press of Coughlan Cos.

Young-Brown, Fiona. The Universe to Scale: Similarities & Differences in Objects in Our Solar System. 2016. (Space Systems Ser.). 112p. (YA). 42.79 *(978-1-5026-2289-1(0))* Cavendish Square Publishing.

Zobel, Derek. Asteroids. 2010. (Exploring Space Ser.). (ENG., Illus.). 24p. (J). (gr. k-3). lib. bdg. 25.95 *(978-1-60014-196-6(X)*, Blastoff! Readers) Bellwether Media.

Zuchora-Walske, Christine. Your Mission to Mercury, 1 vol. 2011. (Planets Ser.). (ENG., Illus.). 32p. (J). (gr. k-3). 28.50 *(978-1-61641-680-5(7))* Magic Wagon.

21st Century Junior Library: Solar System, 8 vols., Set. Incl. Earth. Simon, Charnan. lib. bdg. 25.64 *(978-1-61080-081-5(8)*, 201072); Jupiter. Kazunas, Ariel. lib. bdg. 25.64 *(978-1-61080-086-0(9)*, 201082); Mars. Simon, Charnan. lib. bdg. 25.64 *(978-1-61080-082-2(6)*, 201074); Mercury. Kazunas, Ariel. lib. bdg. 25.64 *(978-1-61080-088-4(5)*, 201086); Neptune. Kazunas, Ariel. lib. bdg. 25.64 *(978-1-61080-083-9(4)*, 201076); Saturn. Kazunas, Ariel. lib. bdg. 25.64 *(978-1-61080-087-7(7)*, 201084); Uranus. Kazunas, Ariel. lib. bdg. 25.64 *(978-1-61080-084-6(2)*, 201078); Venus. Kazunas, Ariel. lib. bdg. 25.64 *(978-1-61080-085-3(0)*, 201080); 24p. (gr. 2-5). 2011. Set lib. bdg. 205.12 *(978-1-61080-147-8(4))* Cherry Lake Publishing.

SOLDIERS

Here are entered works dealing with members of the armed forces in general, including the Navy, Marine Corps, etc. as well as the Army.

see also Armies; Generals; Military Art and Science; Scouts and Scouting

also names of countries with the subdivision Army—Military Life, e.g. United States—Army—Military life; etc.

Aluri, Rao. Backcountry Fury: A Sixteen-Year-Old Patriot in the Revolutionary War. 2010. (J). pap. 19.95 *(978-1-59712-409-6(5))* Catawba Publishing Co.

Anderson, Dale. Soldiers & Sailors in the American Revolution. 2005. (World Almanac Library of the American Revolution Ser.). 48p. (gr. 5-12). pap. 14.05 *(978-0-8368-5938-6(3))*; lib. bdg. 31.00 *(978-0-8368-5929-4(4))* Stevens, Gareth Publishing LLLP. (Gareth Stevens Secondary Library).

AZ Books Staff. Great Warriors. Aksinovich, Natalia & Yaroshevich, Angelica, eds. 2012. (Sounds Around Us Ser.). (ENG.). 16p. (J). (gr. 1-3). bds. 17.95 *(978-1-61889-033-7(6))* AZ Bks. LLC.

Barile, Mary. Alphonso Wetmore: Soldier, Adventurer, & Writer. 2015. (ENG., Illus.). 48p. (J). 24.00 *(978-1-61248-147-0(7))* Truman State Univ. Pr.

Beller, Susan Provost. Yankee Doodle & the Redcoats: Soldiering in the Revolutionary War. Day, Larry, illus. 2003. (Single Titles Ser.). (ENG.). 96p. (gr. 5-8). lib. bdg. 26.60 *(978-0-7613-2612-0(X)*, Twenty-First Century Bks.) Lerner Publishing Group.

Bingham, Jane. Courageous Children, 1 vol. 2011. (War Stories Ser.). (ENG.). 32p. (gr. 3-6). 30.65 *(978-1-4329-4836-8(9)*, NA-h) Heinemann-Raintree.

Brooker, Marion Fargey. Hold the Oxo! A Teenage Soldier Writes Home. 2011. (Canadians at War Ser.: 6). (ENG., Illus.). 144p. (YA). pap. 14.99 *(978-1-55488-870-2(0))* Dundurn CAN. Dist: Ingram Publisher Services.

Burgan, Michael. You Choose - Warriors Set. Incl. Life as a Gladiator: An Interactive History Adventure. (ENG.). 112p. (gr. 3-4). 2010. 31.99 *(978-1-4296-4784-7(1)*, You Choose Bks.); (You Choose: Warriors Ser.). (ENG.). 112p. 2010. 31.99 o.p. *(978-1-4296-4788-5(4)*, You Choose Bks.) Capstone Press of Coughlan Cos.

Burns, Kylie. Sparta! 2013. (ENG.). 48p. (J). *(978-0-7787-1099-8(8))*; pap. *(978-0-7787-1105-6(6))* Crabtree Publishing Co.

Byers, Ann. Working with Veterans & Military Families Through Service Learning, 1 vol. 2015. (ENG.). 80p. (YA). 34.60 *(978-1-4777-7963-7(9)*, Rosen Young Adult) Rosen Publishing Group, Inc., The.

Calvert, Patricia. Kit Carson: He Led the Way. 2006. (Great Explorations Ser.). (Illus.). 80p. (gr. 6-7). lib. bdg. 22.95 *(978-0-7614-2223-5(4)*, Benchmark Bks.) Marshall Cavendish Corp.

Capstone Press. You Choose: Warriors. 2010. (You Choose: Warriors Ser.). (ENG.). 32p. 153.25 *(978-1-4296-5897-3(5)*, You Choose Bks.) Capstone Press of Coughlan Cos.

Catel, Patrick. Soldiers of the Revolutionary War, 1 vol. (Why We Fought: the Revolutionary War Ser.). (ENG.). 48p. (gr. 3-6). 2011. pap. 9.95 *(978-1-4329-3903-8(3))* 2010. 33.32 *(978-1-4329-3898-7(3))* Heinemann-Raintree. (Heinemann InfoSearch).

Chambers, Catherine. Silent Soldiers. Bustamante, Maryin & Juta, Jason, illus. 2016. (Warriors! Ser.). (ENG.). 32p. (J). (gr. 3-6). lib. bdg. 26.65 *(978-1-4677-9356-8(6))* Lerner Publishing Group.

Cheatham, Mark. The Life of a Colonial Soldier. 2013. (Jr. Graphic Colonial America Ser.). (ENG., Illus.). 24p. (J). (gr. 3-6). pap. 10.60 *(978-1-4777-1439-3(1))*; lib. bdg. 25.25 *(978-1-4777-1310-5(7))* Rosen Publishing Group, Inc., The. (PowerKids Pr.).

Coleman, Miriam. Women in the Military. 2015. (Women Groundbreakers Ser.). (ENG.). 32p. (J). (gr. 4-5). pap. 10.00 *(978-1-4994-1052-5(2)*, PowerKids Pr.) Rosen Publishing Group, Inc., The.

Cooke, Tim. World War I on the Front Lines, 1 vol. 2014. (Life on the Front Lines Ser.). (ENG., Illus.). 32p. (gr. 3-4). 27.99 *(978-1-4914-0843-8(X)*, Edge Bks.) Capstone Press of Coughlan Cos.

Crew, Hilary S. Women Engaged in War in Literature for Youth: A Guide to Resources for Children & Young Adults, Vol. 2007. (Literature for Youth Ser.: 11). (ENG.). 324p. per. 75.00 *(978-0-8108-4929-7(1))* Scarecrow Pr., Inc.

Dinzeo, Paul. Spartans. 2012. (History's Greatest Warriors Ser.). (ENG., Illus.). 24p. (J). (gr. 3-7). lib. bdg. 25.95 *(978-1-60014-749-4(6)*, Torque Bks.) Bellwether Media.

Dorling Kindersley Publishing Staff & Adams, Simon. Soldier. 2009. (DK Eyewitness Bks.). (ENG.). 72p. (J). (gr. 3-7). 16.99 *(978-0-7566-4539-7(5)*, DK Children) Dorling Kindersley Publishing, Inc.

Doyle, Bill H. Behind Enemy Lines. 2009. 135p. (J). pap. *(978-0-545-14705-7(0))* Scholastic, Inc.

Ellis, Deborah. Off to War: Voices of Soldiers' Children. 2008. (ENG., Illus.). 144p. (J). (gr. 2-18). 15.95 *(978-0-88899-894-1(5))* Groundwood Bks. CAN. Dist: Publishers Group West (PGW).

Ellis, Edward Sylvester. The Life of Kit Carson: The Life of Kit Carson. 2007. (ENG.). 180p. pap. 19.99 *(978-1-4264-5784-5(7))* Creative Media Partners, LLC.

Ferguson. Careers in Focus: Armed Forces. 2008. (Careers in Focus Ser.). 204p. (gr. 6-12). 32.95 *(978-0-8160-7288-0(4)*, Ferguson Publishing Co.) Facts On File, Inc.

Frontline Families. 2015. (Frontline Families Ser.). (ENG.). 48p. (J). (gr. 5-6). pap., pap. 505.80 *(978-1-4824-3471-2(7))* Stevens, Gareth Publishing LLLP.

Greenwood, Mark. The Donkey of Gallipoli: A True Story of Courage in World War I. Lessac, Frané, illus. 2008. (ENG.). 32p. (J). (gr. 1-4). 16.99 *(978-0-7636-3913-6(3))* Candlewick Pr.

Gunderson, Jessica. Conquistadors. 2012. (Fearsome Fighters Ser.). 48p. (gr. 5-12). 23.95 *(978-1-60818-183-4(9)*, Creative Education) Creative Co., The.

Hanson, Anders & Mann, Elissa. Biggest, Baddest Book of Warriors, 1 vol. 2012. (Biggest, Baddest Books for Boys Ser.). (ENG.). 24p. (gr. k-4). 25.65 *(978-1-61783-409-7(2))* ABDO Publishing Co.

Harding, Lauri. Do Veterans Receive Adequate Health Care? 2008. (At Issue Ser.). (ENG., Illus.). 91p. (gr. 10-12). pap. 24.45 *(978-0-7377-3917-6(7)*, Greenhaven Pr., Inc.); 80-128p. (YA). (gr. 9-12). 34.45 *(978-0-7377-3916-9(9))* Cengage Gale.

Hawes, Alison. A Roman Soldier's Handbook. 2010. (Crabtree Connections Ser.). (ENG.). 24p. (J). (gr. 3-6). *(978-0-7787-9952-8(2))*; pap. *(978-0-7787-9974-0(3))* Crabtree Publishing Co.

Hepplewhite, Peter. Roman Soldiers. 2013. (Greatest Warriors Ser.). 32p. (gr. 3-7). 28.50 *(978-1-78212-402-3(0))* Arcturus Publishing GBR. Dist: Black Rabbit Bks.

History's Greatest Warriors. 2011. (History's Greatest Warriors Ser.). (ENG.). 48p. (gr. 3-4). lib. bdg. 63.98 *(978-1-4296-6604-6(8))* Capstone Press of Coughlan Cos.

Humphreys, Jessica Dee & Chikwanine, Michel. Child Soldier: When Boys & Girls Are Used in War. Dávila, Claudia, illus. 2015. (CitizenKid Ser.). (ENG.). 48p. (J). (gr. 5-9). 17.95 *(978-1-77138-126-0(4))* Kids Can Pr., Ltd. CAN. Dist: Hachette Bk. Group.

Innes, Stephanie & Endrulat, Harry. A Bear in War, 1 vol. Deines, Brian, illus. 2013. (ENG.). 40p. (J). (gr. k-4). 19.95 *(978-1-927485-12-5(6))* Pajama Pr. CAN. Dist: Ingram Publisher Services.

Jones, Carrie. Sarah Emma Edmonds Was a Great Pretender: The True Story of a Civil War Spy. Oldroyd, Mark, illus. 2011. (Carolrhoda Picture Bks.). (ENG.). 32p. (J). (gr. 2-5). 17.95 *(978-0-7613-5399-7(2))* Lerner Publishing Group.

Kerley, Barbara & National Geographic Kids Staff. Brave Like Me. 2016. (ENG., Illus.). 48p. (J). (gr. -1-3). 17.99 *(978-1-4263-2360-7(3)*, National Geographic Children's Bks.) National Geographic Society.

Kohl, Peter. My Dad Is in the Army, 01 vols., 1. 2016. (Military Families Ser.). (ENG., Illus.). 24p. (J). pap. 8.25 *(978-1-5081-4434-2(6)*, PowerKids Pr.) Rosen Publishing Group, Inc., The.

Krasner, Barbara. Returning Soldiers & PTSD. 2017. (J). pap. ***(978-1-5345-0087-7(1))*** Greenhaven Publishing LLC.

Lassieur, Allison. At Battle in the Civil War: An Interactive Battlefield Adventure. 2015. (You Choose: Battlefields Ser.). (ENG.). 112p. (gr. 3-4). lib. bdg. 31.99 *(978-1-4914-2149-9(5)*, You Choose Bks.) Capstone Press of Coughlan Cos.

Levete, Sarah. Special Forces. 2016. (Defend & Protect Ser.). (ENG.). 48p. (J). (gr. 4-5). pap. 14.05 *(978-1-4824-4115-4(2))* Stevens, Gareth Publishing LLLP.

—Undercover Operations. 2016. (Defend & Protect Ser.). (ENG.). 48p. (J). (gr. 4-5). pap. 14.05 *(978-1-4824-4127-7(6))* Stevens, Gareth Publishing LLLP.

Liebman, Dan. I Want to Be a Soldier. 2012. (I Want to Be Ser.). (ENG., Illus.). 24p. (J). (gr. -1-2). pap. 3.99 *(978-1-77085-036-1(8)*, 9781770850361) Firefly Bks., Ltd.

Liebman, Daniel & Liebman, Dan. I Want to Be a Soldier. 2012. (I Want to Be Ser.). (ENG., Illus.). 24p. (J). (gr. -1-2). 14.95 *(978-1-77085-035-4(X)*, 9781770850354) Firefly Bks., Ltd.

The Life of a Colonial Soldier. 2013. (Jr. Graphic Colonial America Ser.). 24p. (J). (gr. 3-6). pap. 63.60 *(978-1-4777-1440-9(5)*, PowerKids Pr.) Rosen Publishing Group, Inc., The.

Linde, Barbara M. Heroes of the US Army. 2012. (Heroes of the US Military Ser.). (Illus.). 32p. (J). (gr. 3-6). pap. 10.50 *(978-1-4339-7237-9(9))*; lib. bdg. 26.60 *(978-1-4339-7236-2(0))* Stevens, Gareth Publishing LLLP.

Llanas, Sheila Griffin. Women of the U. S. Army: Pushing Limits, 1 vol. 2010. (Women in the U. S. Armed Forces Ser.). (ENG.). 32p. (gr. 3-4). lib. bdg. 27.99 *(978-1-4296-5447-0(3)*, Snap Bks.) Capstone Press of Coughlan Cos.

Loveless, Antony & Nixon, James. Infantry Soldiers. 2012. (ENG.). 32p. (J). *(978-0-7787-5100-7(7))*; (The World's Most Dangerous Jobs Ser.: No. 7). pap. *(978-0-7787-5114-4(7))* Crabtree Publishing Co.

Macdonald, Fiona. Do You Want to Be a Roman Soldier? 2015. (Do You Want to Be... Ser.). (Illus.). 32p. (gr. 3-6). 28.50 *(978-1-909645-38-7(9))* Book Hse. GBR. Dist: Black Rabbit Bks.

MacDonald, Fiona. How to Be a Roman Soldier. Hewetson, Nicholas J., illus. 2008. (How to Be Ser.). (ENG.). 32p. (J). (gr. 3-7). pap. 5.95 *(978-1-4263-0169-8(4))*, National Geographic Children's Bks.) National Geographic Society.

Macdonald, Fiona. Top 10 Worst Ruthless Warriors. Antram, David, illus. 2012. (Top 10 Worst Ser.). (ENG.). 32p. (J). (gr. 3-6). pap. 10.50 *(978-1-4339-6686-6(7))*; lib. bdg. 26.60 *(978-1-4339-6685-9(9))* Stevens, Gareth Publishing LLLP. (Gareth Stevens Learning Library).

Malam, John. Warriors. 2013. (Illus.). 48p. (J). *(978-1-4351-5100-0(3))* Barnes & Noble, Inc.

—Warriors. 2010. (Remarkable Man & Beast Ser.). (Illus.). 48p. (J). (gr. 3-18). lib. bdg. 19.95 *(978-1-4222-1979-9(8))* Mason Crest.

Mancini, Candice. Child Soldiers. 2010. (Global Viewpoints Ser.). (Illus.). 224p. (J). 40.45 *(978-0-7377-4839-0(7))*; pap. 27.95 *(978-0-7377-4840-6(0))* Cengage Gale. (Greenhaven Pr., Inc.).

Margulies, Phillip. A Timeline of the Continental Army. 2009. (Timelines of American History Ser.). 32p. (gr. 4-4). 47.90 *(978-1-60854-383-0(8)*, Rosen Reference) Rosen Publishing Group, Inc., The.

Marston, Elsa. The Compassionate Warrior: Abd el-Kader of Algeria. 2013. (ENG., Illus.). 184p. (J). (gr. 8-12). pap. 16.95 *(978-1-937786-10-6(2)*, Wisdom Tales) World Wisdom, Inc.

Matthews, Rupert. Assyrian Soldier! An Ancient Army You'd Rather Not Join. Antram, David, illus. 2007. (You Wouldn't Want to... Ser.). (ENG.). 32p. (J). (gr. 2-5). 29.00 *(978-0-531-18727-2(6))* Scholastic Library Publishing.

—Spartans. 2015. (History's Fearless Fighters Ser.). (ENG., Illus.). 48p. (J). (gr. 5-6). pap. 14.05 *(978-1-4824-3181-0(5))* Stevens, Gareth Publishing LLLP.

McDonnell, Peter. A Soldier in Disguise. Tormey, Carlotta, illus. 2005. 16p. (J). pap. *(978-0-7367-2909-3(7))* Zaner-Bloser, Inc.

McLeese, Don. Spartans. 2009. 32p. pap. 7.99 *(978-0-8249-1446-2(5)*, Ideal Pubns.) Worthy Publishing.

Micklos, John. How the Revolutionary War Was Won. 2008. (Revolutionary War Library). (Illus.). 48p. (J). (gr. 3-4). lib. bdg. 25.27 *(978-0-7660-3016-9(4)*, Enslow Elementary) Enslow Pubs., Inc.

—Why We Won the American Revolution—Through Primary Sources. 2013. (American Revolution Through Primary Sources Ser.). 48p. (J). (gr. 4-10). pap. 8.95 *(978-1-4644-0192-3(6))* Enslow Pubs., Inc.

Miller, Adam, et al. Courage under Fire: Tales of Bravery, 1 vol. 2014. (Courage under Fire Ser.). (ENG.). 32p. (gr. 3-4). 111.96 *(978-1-4765-9939-7(4)*, Edge Bks.) Capstone Press of Coughlan Cos.

Miller, Mara. The Iraq War: A Controversial War in Perspective. 2010. (Issues in Focus Today Ser.). 128p. (J). (gr. 7-12). 33.27 *(978-0-7660-3488-4(7))* Enslow Pubs., Inc.

Murrell, Deborah Jane & Dennis, Peter. Greek Warrior. 2012. (Illus.). 32p. (gr. 3-5). pap. 8.95 *(978-1-926853-53-6(9))* Saunders Bk. Co. CAN. Dist: RiverStream Publishing.

Nelson, Sheila & Zoldak, Joyce. In Defense of Our Country: Survivors of Military Conflict. 2009. (J). pap. 24.95 *(978-1-4222-1465-7(6))* Mason Crest.

Nelson, Sheila, et al. In Defense of Our Country: Survivors of Military Conflict. 2010. (Survivors Ser.). 128p. (YA). (gr. 7-12). 24.95 *(978-1-4222-0452-8(9))* Mason Crest.

Otfinoski, Steven. Spartans, 1 vol. 2013. (ENG.). 48p. (J). (Great Warriors Ser.). (gr. 3-6). lib. bdg. 32.79 *(978-1-61783-728-9(8))*; (Great Warriors EBook Ser.:). (Illus.). pap. 15.64 *(978-1-61783-778-4(4)*, Core Library) ABDO Publishing Co.

Park, Louise & Love, Timothy. The Spartan Hoplites. 2009. (Ancient & Medieval People Ser.). 32p. (gr. 5). 28.50 *(978-0-7614-4449-7(1))* Marshall Cavendish GBR. Dist: Marshall Cavendish Corp.

Poole, H. W. Military Families, Vol. 12. 2016. (Families Today Ser.). (Illus.). 48p. (J). (gr. 5). 20.95 *(978-1-4222-3620-8(X))* Mason Crest.

Pullen, John J. Something Abides: The Story of Joshua Chamberlain. 2003. (Illus.). 67p. (J). per. 7.95 *(978-0-9704408-1-5(2))* 20th Maine, Inc.

Quasha, Jennifer. Robert Rogers: Rogers' Rangers, & the French & Indian War. 2009. (Library of American Lives & Times Ser.). 112p. (gr. 5-5). 69.20 *(978-1-60853-503-3(7))* Rosen Publishing Group, Inc., The.

Rabjohn, R. H. & Wilson, John. A Soldier's Sketchbook: The Illustrated First World War Diary of R.H. Rabjohn. 2017. (ENG., Illus.). 112p. (J). (gr. 5). 16.99 *(978-1-77049-854-9(0)*, Tundra Bks.) Tundra Bks. CAN. Dist: Penguin Random Hse. LLC.

Ratliff, Thomas. Do You Want to Be a Revolutionary War Soldier? 2015. (Do You Want to Be... Ser.). (Illus.). 32p. (gr. 3-6). 28.50 *(978-1-909645-37-0(0))* Book Hse. GBR. Dist: Black Rabbit Bks.

Rauch, Georg. Unlikely Warrior: A Jewish Soldier in Hitler's Army. 2015. (ENG., Illus.). 352p. (YA). (gr. 7). 17.99 *(978-0-374-30142-2(5)*, Farrar, Straus & Giroux (BYR)) Farrar, Straus & Giroux.

Rhimer, Linda. Is He Really Coming Home! 2010. 20p. 13.77 *(978-1-4269-3109-3(3))* Trafford Publishing.

Richards, Tracy. My Navy Dad. 2010. 20p. pap. 14.95 *(978-1-4490-3217-3(6))* AuthorHouse.

Robertson, David. The Scout: Tommy Prince. Henderson, Scott B., illus. 2014. (Tales from Big Spirit Ser.: 6). (ENG.). 32p. (J). (gr. 4-6). pap. *(978-1-55379-478-3(8)*, 78912685-2d85-4153-9f88-b7d8feb31ffe, HighWater Pr.) Portage & Main Pr.

Roche, Tim. Soldiers of the Civil War, 1 vol. (Why We Fought: the Civil War Ser.). (ENG.). 48p. (gr. 3-6). 2011. pap. 9.95 *(978-1-4329-3920-5(3))* 2010. 33.32 *(978-1-4329-3914-4(9))* Heinemann-Raintree. (Heinemann InfoSearch).

Russell, Marcia. A Visit to a Marine Base, 1 vol. 2nd rev. ed. 2011. (Nonfiction Readers Ser.). (ENG.). 24p. (J). (gr. 2-2). pap. 6.99 *(978-1-4333-3609-6(X))* Teacher Created Materials, Inc.

Russo, Kristen J. Surprising Facts about Being an Army Soldier. 2017. (What You Didn't Know about the U. S. Military Life Ser.). (ENG.). 32p. (gr. 3-4). lib. bdg. 27.99 ***(978-1-5157-7429-7(5)***, Edge Bks.) Capstone Press of Coughlan Cos.

Samuels, Charlie. Soldiers. 2012. (World War II Sourcebook Ser.). (Illus.). 48p. (gr. 5-12). lib. bdg. 37.10 *(978-1-936333-24-0(4))* Brown Bear Bks.

—Soldiers. 2017. (World War II Sourcebook Ser.). (ENG., Illus.). 48p. (J). (gr. 4-6). pap. 11.99 *(978-0-7502-8884-2(1)*, Wayland) Hachette Children's Group GBR. Dist: Hachette Bk. Group.

Sawyer, Kem Knapp. Grace Akallo & the Pursuit of Justice for Child Soldiers. 2015. (J). *(978-1-59935-456-9(X))* Reynolds, Morgan Inc.

Schorr, Titus. My Dad Is in the Army Overseas, 01 vols., 1. 2016. (Rosen REAL Readers: Social Studies Nonfiction / Fiction: Family, Community, & the World Ser.). (ENG.). 12p. (J). pap. 6.33 *(978-1-5081-1821-3(3)*, Rosen Classroom) Rosen Publishing Group, Inc., The.

Sepahban, Lois. Spartan Warriors. 2015. (Ancient Warriors Ser.). (ENG.). 32p. (J). (gr. 2-5). 28.50 *(978-1-63143-760-1(7)*, 208592) Child's World, Inc., The.

Shames, Stephen. Transforming Lives: Turning Uganda's Forgotten Children into Leaders. Shames, Stephen, photos by. 2009. (Illus.). 40p. (YA). pap. 12.95 *(978-1-59572-213-3(0))* Star Bright Bks., Inc.

Sims, Lesley. The Roman Soldier's Handbook: Everything a Beginner Soldier Needs to Know. McNee, Ian, illus. 2006. (English Heritage Ser.). 80p. (J). (gr. 4-7). 12.99 *(978-0-7945-0837-1(5)*, Usborne) EDC Publishing.

A Soldier Comes Home. 2011. (ENG., Illus.). 32p. (J). pap. 9.99 *(978-0-578-06838-1(9))* Yari Publishing.

Soriano, Joan & Malizia, Diana, eds. A Visual History of Soldiers & Armies Around the World. 2016. (Visual History of the World Ser.). 00096p. (YA). (gr. 8-8). 37.10 *(978-1-4994-6592-1(0)*, Rosen Young Adult) Rosen Publishing Group, Inc., The.

Stark, William N. Mighty Military Robots. 2016. (Military Machines on Duty Ser.). (ENG.). 24p. (gr. 1-2). lib. bdg. 25.32 *(978-1-4914-8847-8(6)*, First Facts) Capstone Press of Coughlan Cos.

Sterngass, Jon. Great Careers with a High School Diploma: Armed Forces. 2008. (Great Careers with a High School Diploma Ser.). 121p. (C). (gr. 9). 32.95 *(978-0-8160-7042-8(3)*, Ferguson Publishing Co.) Facts On File, Inc.

Stewart, Alex. Gladiators. 2013. (Greatest Warriors Ser.). 32p. (gr. 3-7). 28.50 *(978-1-78212-398-9(9))* Arcturus Publishing GBR. Dist: Black Rabbit Bks.

—Greek Soldiers. 2013. (Greatest Warriors Ser.). 32p. (gr. 3-7). 28.50 *(978-1-78212-399-6(7))* Arcturus Publishing GBR. Dist: Black Rabbit Bks.

Stotts, Stuart. Lucius Fairchild: Civil War Hero. 2011. (Badger Biographies Ser.). (ENG., Illus.). 112p. (J). pap. 12.95 *(978-0-87020-460-9(2))* Wisconsin Historical Society.

Thiel, Kristin. Joan of Arc. 2017. (J). ***(978-1-5026-2791-9(4))*** Cavendish Square Publishing.

Tripp, Natalie. We Care! Making Care Packages: Understand the Relationship Between Multiplication & Division. 2014. (Rosen Common Core Math Readers Ser.). (ENG., Illus.). 24p. (J). (gr. 3-4). pap. 8.25 *(978-1-4777-4955-5(1)*, PowerKids Pr.) Rosen Publishing Group, Inc., The.

Turner, Tracey. Hard as Nails Warriors. Lenman, Jamie, illus. 2015. (ENG.). 64p. (J). pap. *(978-0-7787-1517-7(5))* Crabtree Publishing Co.

UNESCO. Women Soldiers of Dahomey. 2016. (ENG., Illus.). 112p. (J). (gr. 3-7). 13.95 *(978-0-00-814936-9(4))* HarperCollins Pubs. Ltd. GBR. Dist: Independent Pubs. Group.

The U.S. Army in World War II. 2014. (ENG.). 48p. (J). lib. bdg. 29.00 *(978-0-531-20496-2(0))* Scholastic Library Publishing.

Williams, Brian. Heroes of the Battlefield. 2015. (Heroes of World War II Ser.). (ENG., Illus.). 48p. (gr. 4-6). 32.65 *(978-1-4109-8048-9(0))* Heinemann-Raintree.

Williams, Jack S. & Davis, Thomas L. Soldiers & Their Families of the California Mission Frontier. 2004. (People of the California Missions Ser.). (Illus.). 64p. (J). lib. bdg. 26.50 *(978-0-8239-6285-3(7))* Rosen Publishing Group, Inc., The.

Yomtov, Nelson. True Stories of World War I, 1 vol. Proctor, Jon, illus. 2012. (Stories of War Ser.). (ENG.). 32p. (gr. 3-4). pap. 8.10 *(978-1-4296-9344-8(4))*; lib. bdg. 30.65

S

(978-1-4296-8625-9(1)) Capstone Press of Coughlan Cos. (Graphic Library).

You Choose: Warriors, 1 vol. 2010. (You Choose: Warriors Ser.). (ENG.). 112p. (gr. 3-4). pap. 13.90 (978-1-4296-5729-7(4)); pap. 83.40 (978-1-4296-5732-7(4)); pap. 13.90 (978-1-4296-5731-0(6)); pap. 13.90 (978-1-4296-5730-3(8)) Capstone Press of Coughlan Cos. (You Choose Bks.).

Zullo, Allan. Vietnam War Heroes. 2015. (Ten True Tales Ser.). (ENG.). 192p. (J). (gr. 3-7). pap. 5.99 (978-0-545-83750-7(2)) Scholastic, Inc.

—War Heroes: Voices from Iraq. 2014. (10 True Tales Ser.). (ENG.). 160p. (J). (gr. 3-7). pap. 5.99 (978-0-545-81840-7(0), Scholastic Nonfiction) Scholastic, Inc.

—World War I Heroes. (Ten True Tales Ser.). (J). 2015. (ENG.). 176p. (gr. 3-7). pap. 5.99 (978-0-545-83751-4(0)) 2014. 162p. pap. **(978-0-545-67533-8(2))** Scholastic, Inc.

SOLDIERS—FICTION

Abbott, E. F. John Lincoln Clem: Civil War Drummer Boy. 2016. (Based on a True Story Ser.). (ENG., Illus.). 192p. (J). 15.99 (978-1-250-06837-8(1), 9781250068378) Feiwel & Friends.

Addison, George R. Iii. When Mom Came Home. 2012. 32p. pap. 21.99 (978-1-4691-6406-9(X)) Xlibris Corp.

Almond, David. Raven Summer. 2011. (ENG.). 208p. (YA). (gr. 7). pap. 7.99 (978-0-385-73807-1(2), Ember) Random Hse. Children's Bks.

Altsheler, Joseph A. The Forest of Swords: A Story of Paris & the Marne. 2006. (World War I Ser.: Vol. 3). 284p. (J). reprint ed. 28.95 (978-1-4218-1772-9(1)); pap. 13.95 (978-1-4218-1872-6(8)) 1st World Publishing, Inc. (1st World Library - Literary Society).

—The Forest of Swords: A Story of Paris & the Marne. 2004. (World War I Ser.: Vol. 3). (J). reprint ed. 32.95 (978-0-8488-3005-2(9)) Amereon Ltd.

—The Forest of Swords: A Story of Paris & the Marne. l.t. ed. (World War I Ser.: Vol. 3). (J). 2007. (ENG.). 252p. pap. 23.99 (978-1-4264-8960-0(9)) 2008. 256p. reprint ed. 25.99 (978-0-554-34719-6(9)) 2008. 256p. reprint ed. 28.99 (978-0-554-25416-6(6)) 2007. (ENG.). 226p. reprint ed. pap. 20.99 (978-1-4264-8902-0(1)) Creative Media Partners, LLC.

—The Forest of Swords: A Story of Paris & the Marne. 2006. (World War I Ser.: Vol. 3). (J). reprint ed. pap. (978-1-4065-0809-3(8)) Dodo Pr.

—The Forest of Swords: A Story of Paris & the Marne. 2006. (World War I Ser.: Vol. 3). (J). reprint ed. pap. (978-1-4068-0742-4(7)) Echo Library.

—The Forest of Swords: A Story of Paris & the Marne. 2010. (World War I Ser.: Vol. 3). 216p. (J). reprint ed. pap. (978-1-4076-1521-9(1)) HardPr.

—The Forest of Swords: A Story of Paris & the Marne. 2011. (World War I Ser.: Vol. 3). 252p. (J). (gr. 4-7). reprint ed. pap. (978-3-8424-7930-2(1)) Tredition GmbH.

Amodeo, Darlene. Samantha & the Soldier: A Letter of Love. 2012. 40p. pap. 20.99 (978-1-4772-9263-1(2)) AuthorHouse.

Anderson, Laurie Halse. Forge. 2012. 18.00 (978-1-61383-316-2(4)) Perfection Learning Corp.

—Forge. (Seeds of America Trilogy Ser.). (ENG., Illus.). (J). (gr. 5-9). 2012. 320p. pap. 8.99 (978-1-4169-6145-1(3)) 2010. 304p. 18.99 (978-1-4169-6144-4(5)) Simon & Schuster Children's Publishing. (Atheneum Bks. for Young Readers).

—Forge. 2012. (Seeds of America Trilogy Ser.: 2). lib. bdg. 18.40 (978-0-606-23680-5(5), Turtleback) Turtleback Bks.

Ayers, Michelle. Michael. 2011. 134p. pap. 9.99 (978-0-557-78630-5(4)) Lulu Pr., Inc.

Ayozie, Ben-EL. Ants Everywhere. 2011. 20p. 11.49 (978-1-4520-3431-7(1)) AuthorHouse.

Bacigalupi, Paolo. The Drowned Cities. 2013. (ENG.). 464p. (J). (gr. 10-17). pap. 10.99 (978-0-316-05622-9(7)) 2012. 448p. (YA). 17.99 (978-0-316-20037-0(9)) Little, Brown Bks. for Young Readers.

—The Drowned Cities. 2012. 352p. (978-1-59606-506-2(0)) Subterranean Pr.

—The Drowned Cities. 2013. (J). lib. bdg. 22.10 (978-0-606-31749-8(X), Turtleback) Turtleback Bks.

Barry, Rick. Gunner's Run: A World War II Novel. 2007. 215p. (YA). (gr. 8-12). per. 8.99 (978-1-59166-761-2(5)) BJU Pr.

Bates, Gordon. The Khaki Boys over the Top: Doing & Daring for Uncle Sam. 2006. (ENG.). 140p. pap. 18.99 (978-1-4264-6542-0(4)) Creative Media Partners, LLC.

Beaty, Erin. The Traitor's Kiss. 2017. (Traitor's Trilogy Ser.: 1). (ENG.). 352p. (YA). 18.99 (978-1-250-11794-6(1), 9781250117946) Imprint IND. Dist: Macmillan.

Boat, Patty. A Disappointing Homecoming: (A Soldier's Story), 1 vol. 2009. 158p. pap. 24.95 (978-1-61546-997-0(4)) PublishAmerica, Inc.

Bond, Douglas. Guns of Providence. 2010. (J). pap. (978-1-59638-156-8(6)) P & R Publishing.

Borden, Louise & Borden, Louise W. Across the Blue Pacific: A World War II Story. Parker, Robert Andrew, illus. 2006. (ENG.). 48p. (J). (gr. -1-3). 17.00 (978-0-618-33922-8(1)) Houghton Mifflin Harcourt Publishing Co.

Borden, Louise W. Across the Blue Pacific: A World War II Story. Parker, Robert Andrew, illus. 2015. (ENG.). 48p. (J). (gr. -1-3). 7.99 (978-0-544-55552-5(X), HMH Books For Young Readers) Houghton Mifflin Harcourt Publishing Co.

Bowen, Carl. Shadow Squadron, 1 vol. (Shadow Squadron Ser.). (ENG.). 112p. (gr. 4-8). 2014. 159.90 (978-1-4342-8768-7(8)) 2014. pap. 11.90 (978-1-4342-8963-6(X)) 2013. 106.60 (978-1-4342-4813-8(5)) Stone Arch Bks.

Bowen, Carl & Fuentes, Benny. Critical Strike. Tortosa, Wilson, illus. 2014. (Shadow Squadron Ser.). (ENG.). 224p. (gr. 4-8). pap. 8.95 (978-1-62370-109-3(0)) Capstone Young Readers of Coughlan Cos.

—Rogue Agent. Tortosa, Wilson, illus. 2015. (Shadow Squadron Ser.). (ENG.). 224p. (gr. 4-8). pap. 8.95 (978-1-62370-296-0(8)) Capstone Young Readers of Coughlan Cos.

—Sand Spider, 1 vol. Tortosa, Wilson, illus. 2014. (Shadow Squadron Ser.). (ENG.). 112p. (gr. 4-8). 26.65 (978-1-4342-9169-1(3)) Stone Arch Bks.

—Steel Hammer. Tortosa, Wilson, illus. 2015. (Shadow Squadron Ser.). (ENG.). 112p. (gr. 4-8). lib. bdg. 26.65 (978-1-4965-0385-5(6)) Stone Arch Bks.

Brenes, Carlos A. Private Billy. 2011. 32p. pap. 16.95 (978-1-4560-9096-8(8)) America Star Bks.

Brown, Bruce, et al. Brit - Awol, 3 vols., Vol. 2. Kirkman, Robert, ed. 2008. (ENG., Illus.). 160p. (YA). pap. 14.99 (978-1-58240-864-4(5), 9781582408644) Image Comics.

Brown, Skila. Caminar. 2014. (ENG.). 208p. (J). (gr. 5). 15.99 (978-0-7636-6516-6(9)) Candlewick Pr.

Campbell, Suzy. My Daddy Is a Soldier, 1 vol. 2009. 19p. pap. 24.95 (978-1-61546-724-2(6)) America Star Bks.

—My Daddy Is a Soldier, 1 vol. 2010. 20p. 24.95 (978-1-4512-1163-4(5)) PublishAmerica, Inc.

Carroll, James Christopher. Papa's Backpack. Carroll, James Christopher, illus. 2015. (ENG., Illus.). 32p. (J). (gr. 1-3). pap. 15.99 (978-1-58536-613-2(7), 203942) Sleeping Bear Pr.

Cauvin, Raoul. Bluecoats - Greenhorn, Vol. 4. Lambil, Willy, illus. 4th ed. 2011. (Bluecoats Ser.: 4). (ENG.). 48p. (gr. 3-17). pap. 11.95 (978-1-84918-066-5(0)) CineBook GBR. Dist: National Bk. Network.

—The Blues in the Mud. Lambil, Willy, illus. 2014. (Bluecoats Ser.: 7). (ENG.). 48p. pap. 11.95 (978-1-84918-183-9(7)) CineBook GBR. Dist: National Bk. Network.

—Bronco Benny. Lambil, Willy, illus. 2013. (Bluecoats Ser.: 6). (ENG.). 48p. pap. 11.95 (978-1-84918-146-4(2)) CineBook GBR. Dist: National Bk. Network.

—The Navy Blues. Lambil, Willy, illus. 2009. (Bluecoats Ser.: 2). (ENG.). 46p. (J). (gr. 4-7). pap. 11.95 (978-1-905460-82-3(1)) CineBook GBR. Dist: National Bk. Network.

—Robertsonville Prison, Volume 1. Lambil, Willy, illus. 2009. (Bluecoats Ser.: 1). (ENG.). 46p. (J). (gr. -1-17). pap. 11.95 (978-1-905460-71-7(6)) CineBook GBR. Dist: National Bk. Network.

—Rumberley. Lambil, Willy, illus. 2012. (Bluecoats Ser.: 5). (ENG.). 48p. (J). (gr. 3-8). pap. 11.95 (978-1-84918-108-2(X)) CineBook GBR. Dist: National Bk. Network.

Cheaney, J. B. I Don't Know How the Story Ends. 2015. (ENG.). 288p. (J). (gr. 4-7). 16.99 (978-1-4926-0944-5(7), 9781492609445, Sourcebooks Jabberwocky) Sourcebooks, Inc.

Cohen, Miriam. My Big Brother, 1 vol. Himler, Ronald, illus. 2005. (ENG.). 32p. (J). 15.95 (978-1-59572-007-8(3)); pap. 6.95 (978-1-59572-158-7(4)) Star Bright Bks., Inc.

—My Big Brother (Spanish/English), 1 vol. Himler, Ronald, illus. 2008. (ABK, SPA & ENG.). 32p. (J). (gr. -1-3). pap. 5.95 (978-1-59572-037-5(5)) Star Bright Bks., Inc.

Collins, Suzanne. Year of the Jungle. Proimos, James, illus. 2013. (ENG.). 40p. (J). (gr. -1-7). 17.99 (978-0-545-42516-2(6), Scholastic Pr.) Scholastic, Inc.

Connell, Kate. Yankee Blue or Rebel Grey? The Civil War Adventures of Sam Shaw. 2003. (I Am American Ser.). (ENG., Illus.). 40p. (J). (gr. 3-7). pap. 6.99 (978-0-7922-5179-8(2), National Geographic Children's Bks.) National Geographic Society.

Coy, John. Eyes on the Goal, Bk. 2. 2012. (4 For 4 Ser.: 2). (ENG.). 192p. (J). (gr. 3-7). pap. 7.99 (978-0-312-65922-6(9), 9780312659226) Square Fish.

Crump, Fred, Jr. The Brave Toy Soldier. 2007. (Illus.). 32p. (J). 12.95 (978-1-934056-20-2(0)) UMI (Urban Ministries, Inc.).

Crump Jr., Fred. The Brave Toy Soldier. 2007. (Illus.). 32p. (J). (gr. -1). pap. 9.95 (978-1-932715-82-8(7)) UMI (Urban Ministries, Inc.).

Dahl, Michael. The Girl Who Breathed Fire. Piatti, Federico, illus. 2010. (Dragonblood Ser.). (ENG.). 40p. (gr. 1-3). lib. bdg. 23.99 (978-1-4342-1925-1(9), Zone Bks.) Stone Arch Bks.

De Graaf, Anne. Son of a Gun. 2012. (ENG.). 125p. (YA). pap. 8.00 (978-0-8028-5406-3(0), Eerdmans Bks For Young Readers) Eerdmans, William B. Publishing Co.

DePalma, Johnny & Crabapple, Molly. Once upon a Christmas Tree - A Holiday Fairy Tale. 2007. 88p. pap. 10.50 (978-0-615-15448-0(4)) Umbrelly Bks.

Dixon, Franklin W. & Walker, Jeff. The Secret of the Soldier's Gold. 2003. (Hardy Boys Ser.: 182). (ENG., Illus.). 160p. (J). (gr. 3-7). pap. 5.99 (978-0-689-85885-7(X), Aladdin) Simon & Schuster Children's Publishing.

Doreen Norberg. The Soldier's Dog. 2010. 24p. pap. 15.99 (978-1-4535-0898-5(8)) Xlibris Corp.

Dowell, Frances O'Roark. Shooting the Moon. 2008. (ENG., Illus.). 176p. (J). (gr. 5-9). 16.99 (978-1-4169-2690-0(9), Atheneum Bks. for Young Readers) Simon & Schuster Children's Publishing.

Duble, Kathleen Benner. Phantoms in the Snow. 2011. (ENG.). 240p. (J). (gr. 7-7). 17.99 (978-0-545-19770-0(8), Scholastic Pr.) Scholastic, Inc.

Duey, Kathleen. Pony Express: Time Soldiers Book #7. 2009. (Time Soldiers Ser.). (ENG., Illus.). (J). (gr. k-2). 48p. 15.95 (978-1-929945-68-9(X)); 96p. pap. 5.95 (978-1-929945-69-6(8)) Big Guy Bks., Inc.

Ehrmantraut, Brenda. Hope Weavers. Magnuson, Diana, illus. 2009. (J). (978-0-9729833-8-9(4)) Bubble Gum Pr.

—Night Catch. Wehrman, Vicki, illus. 2014. (J). pap. (978-1-934617-28-1(8)) Elva Resa Publishing, LLC.

Ellis, Deborah. The Cat at the Wall, 1 vol. (ENG., Illus.). (J). 2015. 152p. pap. 9.95 (978-1-55498-707-8(5)) 2014. 144p. (gr. 3-7). 16.95 (978-1-55498-491-6(2)) Groundwood Bks. CAN. Dist: Publishers Group West (PGW).

Etheridge, Judy. Olivia's Wish. 2009. 32p. pap. 21.99 (978-1-4415-3915-1(8)) Xlibris Corp.

Everett-Green, Evelyn. A Heroine of France. 2006. (ENG.). 188p. pap. 19.99 (978-1-4264-7060-8(6)) 2007. 206p. pap. 22.99 (978-1-4264-7136-0(X)) Creative Media Partners, LLC.

Flanagan, John. The Battle of Hackham Heath. 2016. (Ranger's Apprentice: the Early Years Ser.: 2). (ENG., Illus.). 352p. (J). (gr. 5). 18.99 (978-0-399-16362-3(X), Philomel Bks.) Penguin Young Readers Group.

Forde, Winston. Airborne Soldiers. 2010. (Illus.). 120p. 29.99 (978-1-4535-6451-6(9)) Xlibris Corp.

Fortner, Tama. God Is Always Good: Comfort for Kids Facing Grief, Fear, or Change, 1 vol. Vasylenko, Veronica, illus. 2014. (ENG.). 32p. (J). 12.99 (978-0-7180-1145-1(7)) Nelson, Thomas Inc.

Frost, Helen. Crossing Stones. 2009. (ENG., Illus.). 192p. (YA). (gr. 7-18). 18.99 (978-0-374-31653-2(8), 9780374316532, Farrar, Straus & Giroux (BYR)) Farrar, Straus & Giroux.

Furtney, Charles S. Tryconnel: An Antebellum Adventure along the C & O Canal. 2004. (Illus.). iii, 156p. (J). pap. (978-0-9711835-3-7(8)) Local History Co., The.

Fussell, Sandy. Shaolin Tiger. James, Rhian Nest, illus. 2011. (Samurai Kids Ser.: 3). (ENG.). 272p. (J). (gr. 4-7). pap. 6.99 (978-0-7636-5702-4(6)) Candlewick Pr.

Garland, Sherry. The Buffalo Soldier, 1 vol. Himler, Ronald, illus. 2006. (ENG.). 32p. (J). (gr. k-3). 16.99 (978-1-58980-391-6(4)) Pelican Publishing Co., Inc.

George, Jessica Day. Princess of the Midnight Ball. 2010. (Twelve Dancing Princesses Ser.). (ENG.). 304p. (YA). (gr. 7-9). pap. 9.99 (978-1-59990-455-9(1), 9781599904559, Bloomsbury USA Childrens) Bloomsbury Publishing USA.

Gilberstadt, Debra Pack. Unmarked Grave: Remembering an American Patriot. 2005. (YA). lib. bdg. 29.95 (978-0-9763033-0-5(2)) Eslinger Hse. Publishing.

Grant, Michael. Front Lines. (Front Lines Ser.: 1). (YA). (gr. 9). 2017. 592p. pap. 9.99 (978-0-06-234216-4(9)) 2016. 576p. 18.99 (978-0-06-234215-7(0)) HarperCollins Pubs. (Tegen, Katherine Bks).

—Silver Stars. 2017. (Front Lines Ser.: 2). (Illus.). 576p. (YA). (gr. 9). 18.99 (978-0-06-234218-8(5), Tegen, Katherine Bks) HarperCollins Pubs.

Gray, Anthony. The Confederate Adventure of Jed Bodine & Ruefus: The Old Tulip Train Raid. 2012. (ENG.). (J). pap. 4.99 (978-1-4675-2270-0(8)) Independent Pub.

Gray, Claudia. Defy the Stars. 2017. (Defy the Stars Ser.: 1). (ENG.). 512p. (YA). (gr. 10-17). 17.99 (978-0-316-39403-1(3)) Little, Brown Bks. for Young Readers.

Gray, Mila. Come Back to Me. 2015. (ENG., Illus.). 352p. (YA). (gr. 11). 17.99 (978-1-4814-3965-7(0), Simon Pulse) Simon Pulse.

Haar, Jaap Ter & Mearns, Martha. Boris. Poortvliet, Rien, illus. 2009. (J). pap. (978-0-921100-72-0(8)) Inheritance Pubns.

Haarsma, P. J. Awakening on Orbis 4. 2010. (Softwire Ser.: 4). (ENG., Illus.). 368p. (YA). (gr. 7-18). 16.99 (978-0-7636-2712-6(7)) Candlewick Pr.

Hardin, Melinda. Hero Dad, 0 vols. Langdo, Bryan, illus. 2010. (ENG.). 24p. (J). (gr. -1-3). 12.99 (978-0-7614-5713-8(5), 9780761457138, Two Lions) Amazon Publishing.

Hart, Alison. Darling, Mercy Dog of World War I, 1 vol. Montgomery, Michael G., illus. 2013. (Dog Chronicles Ser.). (ENG.). 160p. (J). (gr. 2-5). 12.95 (978-1-56145-705-2(1)) Peachtree Pubs.

—Gabriel's Journey, 1 vol. (Racing to Freedom Ser.). (ENG.). 160p. (J). 2011. pap. 4.99 (978-1-56145-530-0(X)) 2008. (Illus.). (gr. 3-7). 14.95 (978-1-56145-442-6(7)) Peachtree Pubs.

Hartnett, Sonya. The Silver Donkey. Powers, Don, illus. 2014. (ENG.). 272p. (J). (gr. 5). 16.99 (978-0-7636-7211-9(4)) Candlewick Pr.

—The Silver Donkey. Spudvilas, Anne, illus. 2004. viii, 193p. (J). (978-0-670-04240-1(4), Viking Adult) Penguin Publishing Group.

Hendrix, John, illus. Shooting at the Stars: The Christmas Truce of 1914. 2014. (ENG.). 40p. (J). (gr. 3-7). 18.95 (978-1-4197-1175-6(X), Abrams Bks. for Young Readers) Abrams, Inc.

Henty, George Alfred. Wulf the Saxon: A Story of the Norman Conquest. Peacock, Ralph, illus. 2010. (Dover Children's Classics Ser.). (ENG.). 352p. (YA). (gr. 3-8). pap. 8.95 (978-0-486-47595-0(6)) Dover Pubns., Inc.

Higgins, M. G. The Soldier. 2014. (Red Rhino Ser.). (J). lib. bdg. 18.40 (978-0-606-36204-7(5)) Turtleback Bks.

Hoffman, Mary. The Twelve Dancing Princesses. Clara, Miss, illus. 2013. (ENG.). 40p. (J). (gr. 1-5). 17.99 (978-1-84686-966-2(8)) Barefoot Bks., Inc.

Holmes, Sara. Operation Yes. 2009. 234p. (J). pap. (978-0-545-20418-7(6)) Scholastic, Inc.

Holsey, Chanda Nicole. Precious Pete, Will You Remember Me, When I Am Out to Sea? A Salute to All Navy Dads. 2011. 20p. 11.99 (978-1-4520-9651-3(1)) AuthorHouse.

Holsey, Dr Chanda Nicole & Holsey, Chanda Nicole. Savvie Sunshine, Will You Remember Daddy When I Am Out to Sea? A Salute to All Navy Dads. 2010. 24p. pap. 13.50 (978-1-4490-7729-7(3)) AuthorHouse.

Hopkinson, Deborah. Billy & the Rebel: Based on a True Civil War Story. Floca, Brian, illus. 2005. 44p. (J). lib. bdg. 15.00 (978-1-4242-1148-7(4)) Fitzgerald Bks.

—Billy & the Rebel: Based on a True Civil War Story. Floca, Brian, illus. 2006. (Ready-to-Read Ser.). 44p. (gr. 1-3). 14.00 (978-0-7569-6390-3(7)) Perfection Learning Corp.

—Billy & the Rebel: Based on a True Civil War Story. Floca, Brian, illus. 2006. (Ready-To-Reads Ser.). (ENG.). 48p. (J). (gr. 1-3). pap. 3.99 (978-0-689-83396-0(2), Simon Spotlight) Simon Spotlight.

—Billy & the Rebel: Based on a True Civil War Story. Anderson, Bethanne & Floca, Brian, illus. 2005. (Ready-to-Reads Ser.). (ENG.). 48p. (J). (gr. 1-3). 16.99 (978-0-689-83964-1(2), Simon Spotlight) Simon Spotlight.

—From Slave to Soldier: Based on a True Civil War Story. Floca, Brian, illus. (Ready-To-Reads Ser.). (ENG.). 48p. (J). (gr. 1-3). 2007. pap. 3.99 (978-0-689-83966-5(9)) 2005. 16.99 (978-0-689-83965-8(0)) Simon Spotlight. (Simon Spotlight).

Howe, Peter. Warriors of the Black Shroud. 2012. (ENG.). 272p. (J). (gr. 3-7). 16.99 (978-0-06-172987-4(6)) HarperCollins Pubs.

Huggins-Cooper, Lynn & Hayward, Ian Benfold. One Boy's War. 2014. (ENG., Illus.). 32p. (J). (gr. 2-6). pap. 8.99 (978-1-84780-126-5(9), Frances Lincoln) Quarto Publishing Group UK GBR. Dist: Hachette Bk. Group.

Hughes, Dean. The Dean Hughes Collection: Soldier Boys; Search & Destroy; Missing in Action. 2015. (ENG., Illus.). 752p. (YA). (gr. 7). pap. 29.99 (978-1-4814-3997-8(9), Atheneum Bks. for Young Readers) Simon & Schuster Children's Publishing.

—Four-Four-Two. 2016. (ENG., Illus.). 272p. (YA). (gr. 7). 17.99 (978-1-4814-6252-5(0), Atheneum Bks. for Young Readers) Simon & Schuster Children's Publishing.

—Soldier Boys. 2004. 230p. (gr. 7-12). 17.00 (978-0-7569-4566-4(6)) Perfection Learning Corp.

—Soldier Boys. 2015. (ENG., Illus.). 240p. (YA). (gr. 7). pap. 10.99 (978-1-4814-2704-3(0), Atheneum Bks. for Young Readers) Simon & Schuster Children's Publishing.

Hulme-Cross, Benjamin. The Spartan's March. 2016. (Warrior Heroes Ser.). (ENG., Illus.). 176p. (J). (gr. 6-9). (978-0-7787-2865-8(X)) Crabtree Publishing Co.

Hutton, Keely. Soldier Boy. 2017. (ENG.). 336p. (YA). 17.99 (978-0-374-30563-5(3), 9780374305635, Farrar, Straus & Giroux (BYR)) Farrar, Straus & Giroux.

Ibbott, Penny. Scarcode. 2013. 358p. pap. (978-1-78299-864-8(0)) FeedARead.com.

Jackson, Corrine. If I Lie. (ENG.). 288p. (YA). (gr. 9). 2013. pap. 12.99 (978-1-4424-4000-5(7)) 2012. 16.99 (978-1-4424-5413-2(X)) Simon Pulse. (Simon Pulse).

Johnson, Nancy. A Sweet-Sounding Place: A Civil War Story. 2008. (ENG.). 128p. (J). (gr. 3-7). pap. 10.95 (978-0-89272-770-4(5)) Down East Bks.

Johnston, K. E. M. The Witness Tree & the Shadow of the Noose: Mystery, Lies, & Spies in Manassas. 2009. 111p. (J). (gr. 5-7). pap. 8.95 (978-1-57249-397-1(6), White Mane Kids) White Mane Publishing Co., Inc.

Jones, Patrick. Combat Zone. 2015. (ENG.). 96p. (YA). (gr. 6-12). pap. 7.99 (978-1-4677-8094-0(4)) Lerner Publishing Group.

Jones Yang, Dori. Daughter of Xanadu. 2012. (ENG.). 352p. (YA). (gr. 7). pap. 9.99 (978-0-385-73924-5(9), Ember) Random Hse. Children's Bks.

Jorgensen, Norman. In Flanders Fields. Harrison-Lever, Brian, illus. 2003. (ENG.). 32p. (J). (gr. -1-3). 16.95 (978-1-894965-01-9(9)) Simply Read Bks. CAN. Dist: Ingram Publisher Services.

Jorgensen, Norman & Harrison-Lever, Brian. In Flanders Fields. 2004. (Illus.). 32p. pap. 13.50 (978-1-920731-03-8(2)) Fremantle Pr. AUS. Dist: Independent Pubs. Group.

Kantorek, Keith A. A Soldier's Choice. 2009. 108p. 24.50 (978-0-557-10928-9(0)); pap. 9.50 (978-0-557-10764-3(4)) Lulu Pr., Inc.

Karesh, Tracy Ann. Brave Little Soldier. 2005. (J). pap. 15.00 (978-0-8059-6742-5(7)) Dorrance Publishing Co., Inc.

Kidd, Virginia Bates. The Children's Escape. 2011. 90p. pap. 19.95 (978-1-4560-5406-9(6)) America Star Bks.

Krensky, Stephen. Davy Crockett A Life on the Frontier. Dacey, Bob & Bandelin, Debra, illus. 2005. (Ready-to-Read Ser.). 48p. (J). lib. bdg. 15.00 (978-1-59054-959-9(7)) Fitzgerald Bks.

Laureano, C. E. Beneath the Forsaken City. 2015. (Song of Seare Ser.: 2). (ENG., Illus.). 416p. (YA). pap. 14.99 (978-1-61291-631-6(7)) Tyndale Hse. Pubs.

Le Feuvre, Amy. Teddy's Button. 2007. 92p. per. (978-1-4065-2383-6(6)) Dodo Pr.

—Teddy's Button. 2004. reprint ed. pap. 1.99 (978-1-4192-5094-1(9)); pap. 15.95 (978-1-4191-5094-4(4)) Kessinger Publishing, LLC.

LeSourd, Nancy. Secrets of Civil War Spies, 1 vol. 2008. (Liberty Letters Ser.). (ENG.). 224p. (J). pap. 7.99 (978-0-310-71390-6(0)) Zonderkidz.

Lewis, Ellen Parry. An Unremarkable Girl. 2011. 434p. (YA). pap. 19.99 (978-0-9843437-8-2(4)) Metal Lunchbox Publishing.

Lewis, Floyd. The Foundered Mule. 2006. (YA). 9.95 (978-0-9788283-2-5(1)) Acacia Publishing, Inc.

Lieberman Hackelberg, Lori. Shep & the Wounded Soldier. 2012. pap. 11.95 (978-0-7414-7353-0(4)) Infinity Publishing.

London, C. Alexander. Prisoners of War. 2014. (Dog Tags Ser.: 3). (ENG.). 192p. (J). (gr. 5-9). pap. 5.99 (978-0-545-47706-2(9), Scholastic Paperbacks) Scholastic, Inc.

Lu, Marie. Legend. aut. ltd. collector's ed. 2013. (Legend Trilogy: Bk. 1). (Illus.). 306p. (YA). mass mkt. 100.00 net. (978-1-934267-38-7(4)) Gauntlet, Inc.

—Legend. 2011. (Legend Trilogy: Bk. 1). (ENG.). (YA). (gr. 8-12). 54.99 (978-1-61657-044-6(X), Penguin AudioBooks) Penguin Publishing Group.

—Legend. (Legend Ser.: 1). (ENG.). (YA). (gr. 7). 2013. 352p. pap. 9.99 (978-0-14-242207-6(X), Speak) 2011. 320p. 17.99 (978-0-399-25675-2(X), G.P. Putnam's Sons Books for Young Readers) Penguin Young Readers Group.

—Legend. l.t. ed. 2012. (Legend Trilogy: Bk. 1). (ENG.). 394p. (J). (gr. 7-12). 23.99 (978-1-4104-4606-0(9)) Thorndike Pr.

—Legend. (Legend Graphic Novels Ser.: 1). 2015. lib. bdg. 26.95 (978-0-606-38424-7(3)) 2013. lib. bdg. 20.85 (978-0-606-31701-6(5), Turtleback) Turtleback Bks.

—Prodigy. 2013. (Legend Trilogy: Bk. 2). (ENG.). 384p. (YA). (gr. 7). 18.99 (978-0-399-25676-9(8), G.P. Putnam's Sons Books for Young Readers) Penguin Publishing Group.

—Prodigy. 2014. (Legend Ser.: 2). (ENG., Illus.). 416p. (YA). (gr. 7). pap. 10.99 (978-0-14-242755-2(1), Speak) Penguin Young Readers Group.

—Prodigy. l.t. ed. 2013. (Legend Trilogy: Bk. 2). (ENG.). 486p. 23.99 (978-1-4104-5512-3(2)) Thorndike Pr.

—Prodigy. 2014. (Legend Ser.: 2). lib. bdg. 20.85 (978-0-606-35716-6(5)) Turtleback Bks.

—Prodigy: The Graphic Novel. 2016. (Legend Trilogy: Bk. 2). (ENG.). 160p. (YA). (gr. 7). pap. 14.99 (978-0-399-17190-1(8), G.P. Putnam's Sons Books for Young Readers) Penguin Young Readers Group.

Lynch, Chris. Casualties of War. 2013. (Vietnam Ser.: 4). (ENG.). 192p. (J). (gr. 5-9). pap. 7.99 (978-0-545-27024-3(3), Scholastic Pr.) Scholastic, Inc.

—Free-Fire Zone. 2012. (Vietnam Ser.). (J). (ENG.). 192p. (gr. 5-9). 16.99 (978-0-545-27025-0(1)); 183p. (978-0-545-49427-4(3)) Scholastic, Inc. (Scholastic Pr.).

—Free-Fire Zone. 2013. (Vietnam Ser.: 3). lib. bdg. 18.40 (978-0-606-31963-8(8), Turtleback) Turtleback Bks.

—I Pledge Allegiance. 2011. 183p. (YA). (978-0-545-38415-5(X)) Scholastic, Inc.

—I Pledge Allegiance. 2013. (Vietnam Ser.: 1). lib. bdg. 17.20 (978-0-606-31961-4(1), Turtleback) Turtleback Bks.

—The Right Fight. 2014. 189p. (YA). (978-0-545-63728-2(7), Scholastic Pr.) Scholastic, Inc.

—Sharpshooter. (J). 2013. (Vietnam Ser.: 2). (ENG.). 192p. (gr. 5-9). pap. 7.99 (978-0-545-27027-4(8)) 2012. (978-0-545-43650-2(8)) Scholastic, Inc. (Scholastic Pr.).

—Sharpshooter. 2013. (Vietnam Ser.: 2). lib. bdg. 18.40 (978-0-606-31962-1(X), Turtleback) Turtleback Bks.

—Vietnam #1: I Pledge Allegiance. 2013. (Vietnam Ser.: 1). (ENG.). 192p. (J). (gr. 5-9). pap. 7.99 (978-0-545-27030-4(8), Scholastic Paperbacks) Scholastic, Inc.

—Walking Wounded, Bk. 5. (Vietnam Ser.: 5). (ENG.). 208p. (J). (gr. 5-9). 2016. pap. 7.99 *(978-0-545-64016-9(4))* 2014. 17.99 *(978-0-545-64013-8(X))* Scholastic, Inc. (Scholastic Pr.).

—World War II Book 1: the Right Fight. 2014. (World War II Ser.). (ENG.). 192p. (J). (gr. 5-9). 18.99 *(978-0-545-52294-6(3)*, Scholastic Pr.) Scholastic, Inc.

Lynch, Keven R. What's a Buffalo Soldier? The Historical Adventures of Amber & Trevor. 2005. (J). pap. 12.00 *(978-0-8059-6750-0(8))* Dorrance Publishing Co., Inc.

Mac, Carrie. Storm. 2009. (ENG.). 304p. (J). (gr. k-12). 14.00 *(978-0-14-305115-2(6)*, Puffin Canada) Penguin Random House Canada Young Readers CAN. Dist: Penguin Random Hse. LLC.

MacKenzie, Ross. My Sailor Dad. 2008. (J). pap. 12.95 *(978-1-934666-34-0(3))* High-Pitched Hum Inc.

Maddox, Joseph & Maddox, Diana. See You in Hell. 2004. 215p. (YA). pap. 14.95 *(978-0-7414-1872-2(X))* Infinity Publishing.

Mafi, Tahereh. Ignite Me. 2014. (Shatter Me Ser.). (ENG.). 352p. (J). (gr. 9). 17.99 *(978-0-06-208557-3(3))* HarperCollins Pubs.

—Shatter Me. (Shatter Me Ser.: 1). (ENG.). (YA). (gr. 9). 2012. 464p. pap. 9.99 *(978-0-06-208550-4(6))* 2011. 352p. 17.99 *(978-0-06-208548-1(4))* HarperCollins Pubs.

—Shatter Me. 2012. (Shatter Me Ser.: 1). (YA). lib. bdg. 20.85 *(978-0-606-26868-4(5)*, Turtleback) Turtleback Bks.

—Unravel Me. 2013. (Shatter Me Ser.: 2). (ENG.). (YA). (gr. 9). 496p. pap. 9.99 *(978-0-06-208554-2(9))*; 480p. 17.99 *(978-0-06-208553-5(0))* HarperCollins Pubs.

—Unravel Me. 2013. (Shatter Me Ser.: 2). (YA). lib. bdg. 20.85 *(978-0-606-35049-5(7)*, Turtleback) Turtleback Bks.

Manning, Matthew K. EOD Soldiers, 4 vols. Lima, Rico & Lima, Dijo, illus. 2016. (EOD Soldiers Ser.). (ENG.). 40p. (gr. 4-8). lib. bdg. 106.60 *(978-1-4965-3415-6(8))* Stone Arch Bks.

—Go Slow. Lima, Dijjo & Furuzono, Carlos, illus. 2016. (EOD Soldiers Ser.). (ENG.). 40p. (gr. 4-8). lib. bdg. 26.65 *(978-1-4965-3109-4(4))* Stone Arch Bks.

—The List. Lima, Rico et al, illus. 2016. (EOD Soldiers Ser.). (ENG.). 40p. (gr. 4-8). lib. bdg. 26.65 *(978-1-4965-3110-0(8))* Stone Arch Bks.

Massey, David. Taken. 2014. 311p. (YA). *(978-0-545-66129-4(3))*; (ENG.). 320p. (J). (gr. 9). 18.99 *(978-0-545-66128-7(5)*, Chicken Hse., The) Scholastic, Inc.

—Torn. 2013. (ENG.). 288p. (J). (gr. 9). 17.99 *(978-0-545-49645-2(4))* Scholastic, Inc.

Mattick, Lindsay. Finding Winnie: The True Story of the World's Most Famous Bear. Blackall, Sophie, illus. 2015. (ENG.). 56p. (J). (gr. -1-1). 18.00 *(978-0-316-32490-8(6))* Little Brown & Co.

McCormick, Patricia. Never Fall Down. 224p. (YA). (gr. 9). 2013. (ENG.). pap. 9.99 *(978-0-06-173095-5(5))* 2012. (ENG.). 17.99 *(978-0-06-173093-1(9))* 2012. lib. bdg. 18.89 *(978-0-06-173094-8(7))* HarperCollins Pubs.

—Purple Heart. (ENG.). (YA). (gr. 8). 2011. 224p. pap. 9.99 *(978-0-06-173092-4(0))* 2009. 208p. 16.99 *(978-0-06-173090-0(4))* HarperCollins Pubs.

McElroy, Lisa Tucker. Love, Lizzie: Letters to a Military Mom. Paterson, Diane, illus. (ENG.). 32p. (J). (gr. 1-3). 2009. pap. 6.99 *(978-0-8075-4778-6(6))* 2005. lib. bdg. 16.99 *(978-0-8075-4777-9(8))* Whitman, Albert & Co.

McKay, Sharon E. & Lafrance, Daniel. War Brothers: The Graphic Novel. Lafrance, Daniel, illus. 2013. (ENG., Illus.). 176p. (YA). (gr. 9-12). 2nd ed. 27.95 *(978-1-55451-489-2(4)*, 9781554514892) 3rd ed. pap. 18.95 *(978-1-55451-488-5(6)*, 9781554514885) Annick Pr., Ltd. CAN. Dist: Publishers Group West (PGW).

McLeese, Don. Spartans. 2009. (ENG., Illus.). 32p. (gr. 4-8). pap. 9.95 *(978-1-60694-545-2(9))* Rourke Educational Media.

Meehan, William. Fife. 2006. (ENG.). 180p. (YA). (gr. 4-6). per. 12.95 *(978-0-595-39223-0(7))* iUniverse, Inc.

Metzenthen, David. Dreaming the Enemy. 2017. (ENG.). 304p. pap. 14.95 ***(978-1-76011-225-7(9))*** Allen & Unwin AUS. Dist: Independent Pubs. Group.

Millhouse, Jackie. The Tiger & the General. Girouard, Patrick, illus. 2007. (J). *(978-1-932911-32-9(4))* World Tribune Pr.

Monte, Diane E. Coming Home: Welcome Home at Last. 2012. 24p. pap. 17.99 *(978-1-4772-5713-5(6))* AuthorHouse.

Morpurgo, Michael. Private Peaceful. 2006. 18.00 *(978-0-7569-6630-0(2))* Perfection Learning Corp.

—Private Peaceful. 2006. (YA). 1.25 *(978-1-4193-2976-0(6))* Recorded Bks., Inc.

—Private Peaceful. 2006. (After Words Ser.). (ENG., Illus.). 224p. (J). (gr. 7-12). per. 7.99 *(978-0-439-63653-7(1)*, Scholastic Paperbacks) Scholastic, Inc.

Moverley, Richard. The Reluctant Rajput. Dean, David, illus. 2005. (Yellow Go Bananas Ser.). (ENG.). 48p. (J). (gr. 3-4). lib. bdg. *(978-0-7787-2723-1(8))* Crabtree Publishing Co.

Murdock, Catherine Gilbert. Wisdom's Kiss. 2013. (ENG.). 320p. (YA). (gr. 7). pap. 8.99 *(978-0-547-85540-0(0))* Houghton Mifflin Harcourt Publishing Co.

Myers, Walter Dean. Invasion. 2015. (ENG.). 224p. (J). (gr. 6). pap. 8.99 *(978-0-545-38429-2(X))* 2013. (YA). *(978-0-545-57659-8(8))* 2013. (ENG.). 224p. (J). (gr. 7). 17.99 *(978-0-545-38428-5(1))* Scholastic, Inc. (Scholastic Pr.).

—Patrol: An American Soldier in Vietnam. 2005. 17.00 *(978-0-7569-5428-4(2))* Perfection Learning Corp.

Nelson, Birgitta. The Sacking of Visby. 2011. 150p. 30.00 *(978-1-257-05686-6(7))*; pap. 14.99 *(978-1-257-05680-4(8))* Lulu Pr., Inc.

Nix, Garth. Sir Thursday. 2007. (Keys to the Kingdom Ser.: No. 4). 344p. (gr. 4-7). 18.00 *(978-0-7569-8121-1(2))* Perfection Learning Corp.

—Sir Thursday. 2007. (Keys to the Kingdom Ser.: 4). (ENG.). 352p. (J). (gr. 3-7). pap. 7.99 *(978-0-439-43657-1(5)*, Scholastic Paperbacks) Scholastic, Inc.

Oelschlager, Vanita. Postcards from a War. Blanc, Mike & Bauknight, Wilfred, illus. 2009. (ENG.). 40p. (J). (gr. 1-4). 15.95 *(978-0-9800162-9-1(0))*; pap. 8.95 *(978-0-9819714-0-7(7))* VanitaBooks.

Oh, Ellen. Prophecy. 2013. (Prophecy Ser.: 1). (ENG., Illus.). 320p. (YA). (gr. 8). 17.99 *(978-0-06-209109-3(3)*, HarperTeen) HarperCollins Pubs.

—Warrior. 2015. (Prophecy Ser.: 2). (ENG.). 352p. (YA). (gr. 8). pap. 9.99 *(978-0-06-209113-0(1)*, HarperTeen) HarperCollins Pubs.

Orzechowski, Shawneen. Sarah's Secret: Civil War Deserter at Fredericksburg. 2011. 104p. (J). pap. 8.95 *(978-1-57249-400-8(X)*, White Mane Kids) White Mane Publishing Co., Inc.

Parry, Rosanne. Second Fiddle. 2012. (ENG.). 240p. (J). (gr. 3-7). 6.99 *(978-0-375-86166-6(1)*, Yearling) Random Hse. Children's Bks.

Patterson, Valerie O. Operation Oleander. (ENG.). 192p. (J). (gr. 5-7). 2015. pap. 7.99 *(978-0-544-43935-1(X)*, HMH Books For Young Readers) 2013. 16.99 *(978-0-547-24437-2(1))* Houghton Mifflin Harcourt Publishing Co.

Paulsen, Gary. A Soldier's Heart. 2004. 128p. (J). (gr. 7-18). pap. 29.00 incl. audio *(978-0-8072-8301-1(0)*, Listening Library) Random Hse. Audio Publishing Group.

—Woods Runner. 2011. (ENG.). 176p. (YA). (gr. 7). pap. 7.99 *(978-0-375-85908-3(X)*, Lamb, Wendy Bks.) Random Hse. Children's Bks.

Phillips, Dee. Blast, 1 vol. unabr. ed. 2011. (Right Now! Ser.). (ENG.). 45p. (YA). (gr. 9-12). pap. 8.95 *(978-1-61651-245-3(8))* Saddleback Educational Publishing, Inc.

—Over the Top. 2014. (Yesterday's Voices Ser.). (YA). lib. bdg. 19.60 *(978-0-606-35582-7(0))* Turtleback Bks.

Polacco, Patricia. Tucky Jo & Little Heart. Polacco, Patricia, illus. 2015. (ENG., Illus.). 48p. (J). (gr. -1-3). 17.99 *(978-1-4814-1584-2(0)*, Simon & Schuster Bks. For Young Readers) Simon & Schuster Bks. For Young Readers.

Remarque, Erich-Maria. All Quiet on the Western Front: With Related Readings. Wheen, A. W., tr. from GER. 2003. (EMC Masterpiece Series Access Editions). (Illus.). xxv, 249p. (YA). 13.96 *(978-0-8219-2420-4(6))* EMC/Paradigm Publishing.

Robbins, Dennis L. A Soldier's Christmas. 2011. 44p. pap. 21.99 *(978-1-4653-4097-9(1))* Xlibris Corp.

Ruth, Greg. Coming Home. Ruth, Greg, illus. 2014. (ENG., Illus.). 32p. (J). (gr. -1-2). 16.99 *(978-1-250-05547-7(4)*, 9781250055477) Feiwel & Friends.

Sarah Taylor. The Teddy That Went to Iraq. Baker, David, illus. 2011. 28p. pap. 24.95 *(978-1-4560-8382-3(1))* America Star Bks.

Saxon, Lucy. The Almost King. 2016. (ENG., Illus.). 400p. (YA). (gr. 7-12). 17.99 *(978-1-61963-627-9(1)*, 9781619636279, Bloomsbury USA Childrens) Bloomsbury Publishing USA.

Schlitz, Laura Amy. The Bearskinner: A Tale of the Brothers Grimm. Grafe, Max, illus. 2007. (ENG.). 40p. (J). (gr. 4-7). 16.99 *(978-0-7636-2730-0(5))* Candlewick Pr.

Schmidt, Gary D. Anson's Way. 2009. (ENG.). 224p. (J). (gr. 2-5). pap. 15.95 *(978-0-547-23761-9(8))* Houghton Mifflin Harcourt Publishing Co.

Schwabach, Karen. The Storm Before Atlanta. 2011. (ENG.). 320p. (J). (gr. 3-7). pap. 6.99 *(978-0-375-85867-3(9)*, Yearling) Random Hse. Children's Bks.

Sherman, M. Zachary. Blood Brotherhood, 1 vol. Casas, Fritz, illus. 2011. (Bloodlines Ser.). (ENG.). 88p. (gr. 4-8). pap. 6.95 *(978-1-4342-3098-0(8))*; 26.65 *(978-1-4342-2559-7(3))* Stone Arch Bks.

—Control under Fire, 1 vol. Casas, Fritz, illus. 2011. (Bloodlines Ser.). (ENG.). 88p. (gr. 4-8). pap. 6.95 *(978-1-4342-3100-0(3))*; lib. bdg. 26.65 *(978-1-4342-2561-0(5))* Stone Arch Bks.

—Fighting Phantoms, 1 vol. Casas, Fritz, illus. 2011. (Bloodlines Ser.). (ENG.). 88p. (gr. 4-8). lib. bdg. 26.65 *(978-1-4342-2560-3(7))* Stone Arch Bks.

—The Heart of War. 2013. (Bloodlines Ser.). (ENG.). 240p. (gr. 4-8). pap. 7.95 *(978-1-62370-002-7(7))* Stone Arch Bks.

—A Time for War, 1 vol. Casas, Fritz, illus. 2011. (Bloodlines Ser.). (ENG.). 88p. (gr. 4-8). pap. 6.95 *(978-1-4342-3097-3(X))*; 26.65 *(978-1-4342-2558-0(5))* Stone Arch Bks.

Shinn, Sharon. General Winston's Daughter. 2009. (ENG.). 352p. (YA). (gr. 7-18). 7.99 *(978-0-14-241346-3(1)*, Speak) Penguin Young Readers Group.

Shoulders, Michael. Crossing the Dead Line: Stephen's Journey Through the Civil War. 2016. (ENG.). 384p. (YA). (gr. 4-7). 16.99 *(978-1-58536-951-5(9)*, 204098) Sleeping Bear Pr.

Simmons, Kristen. Article 5. 2012. (Article 5 Ser.: 1). (ENG.). 368p. (YA). (gr. 8-12). 17.99 *(978-0-7653-2958-5(1)*, 9780765329585, Tor Teen) Doherty, Tom Assocs., LLC.

Smith, Annie Laura. Saving da Vinci. 2005. (YA). mass mkt. 6.99 *(978-0-9753367-6-2(2))* Onstage Publishing, LLC.

Smith, W. J. Gorte 2: The Awakening. 2010. 174p. pap. *(978-1-84748-452-9(2))* Athena Pr.

Sorman, Joy. Waterloo & Trafalgar. Tallec, Olivier, illus. 2012. (ENG.). 64p. (J). (gr. k). 17.95 *(978-1-59270-127-8(2))* Enchanted Lion Bks., LLC.

Stewart-Goodair, Madonna. Key to the Golden Gates: The Mystic Soldier, Book 1, 1 vol. 2009. 48p. pap. 16.95 *(978-1-61582-625-4(4))* PublishAmerica, Inc.

—The Mystic Soldier: Warlock of Fire, 1 vol. 2009. 57p. pap. 16.95 *(978-1-61546-840-9(4))* PublishAmerica, Inc.

Stratemeyer, Edward. Marching on Niagara: The Soldier Boys of the Old Frontier. 2011. 191p. (YA). pap. *(978-0-9843717-2-3(9))* Gask Castle Pr.

—With Washington in the West: A Soldier Boy's Battles in the Wilderness. 2011. 198p. (J). pap. *(978-0-9843717-1-6(0))* Gask Castle Pr.

Stratford, Anne Margaret. My Daddy Is A Soldier. 2008. (Illus.). 40p. (J). 17.99 *(978-0-9817938-0-1(0))* Diamond Fly Publishing, Inc.

Styles, Showell. The Flying Ensign: Greencoats Against Napoleon. 2003. (Budget Bks.). Orig. Title: Greencoat Against Napoleon. 297p. (YA). pap. 14.95 *(978-1-883937-70-6(1))* Bethlehem Bks.

Sullivan, Jacqueline Levering. Annie's War. 2007. (Illus.). 183p. (J). (gr. 3-7). 15.00 *(978-0-8028-5325-7(0)*, Eerdmans Bks For Young Readers) Eerdmans, William B. Publishing Co.

Sutcliff, Rosemary. The Eagle. movie tie-in ed. 2011. (Roman Britain Trilogy Ser.: 1). (ENG.). 240p. (YA). (gr. 5). pap. 9.99 *(978-0-312-56434-6(1)*, 9780312564346) Square Fish.

—The Eagle of the Ninth. 2010. (Roman Britain Trilogy Ser.: 1). (ENG.). 240p. (YA). (gr. 7). pap. 9.99 *(978-0-312-64429-1(9)*, 9780312644291) Square Fish.

Sykes, Shelley & Szymanski, Lois. The Soldier in the Cellar. 2011. (Gettysburg Ghost Gang Ser.: Vol. 5). 96p. (J). pap. 7.95 *(978-1-57249-299-8(6)*, White Mane Kids) White Mane Publishing Co., Inc.

Tak, Bibi Dumon & Dumon Tak, Bibi. Soldier Bear. Hopman, Philip, illus. 2011. (ENG.). 158p. (J). 13.00 *(978-0-8028-5375-2(7)*, Eerdmans Bks For Young Readers) Eerdmans, William B. Publishing Co.

Teacher Created Resources Staff & Collins, Susan. A Guide for Using Time Soldiers in the Classroom. 2009. (ENG.). 48p. pap. 9.99 *(978-1-4206-2003-0(7))* Teacher Created Resources, Inc.

Tintera, Amy. Rebel. (Reboot Ser.: 2). 352p. (YA). (gr. 8). 2015. (ENG.). pap. 9.99 *(978-0-06-221711-0(9))* 2014. pap. 12.00 *(978-0-06-233790-0(4))* HarperCollins Pubs. (HarperTeen).

—Reboot. 2013. (Reboot Ser.: 1). (ENG.). 384p. (YA). (gr. 8). 17.99 *(978-0-06-221707-3(0)*, HarperTeen) HarperCollins Pubs.

Tischler, Tracey. Heroes in the Sandbox. 2009. 28p. pap. 13.95 *(978-1-4490-5502-8(0))* AuthorHouse.

To Keep Me SAFE! A Story for Children Affected by Military Deployments. 2003. (J). 12.00 *(978-0-9740289-0-3(8))* State of Growth Publishing Co.

Turner, Megan Whalen. The King of Attolia. (Queen's Thief Ser.: 3). (ENG.). (YA). (gr. 8). 2017. 432p. pap. 9.99 *(978-0-06-264298-1(7))* 2007. 432p. pap. 7.99 *(978-0-06-083579-8(6))* 2006. 400p. 17.99 *(978-0-06-083577-4(X))* HarperCollins Pubs. (Greenwillow Bks.).

—The King of Attolia. 2007. (Queen's Thief Ser.: BK.3). 387p. (YA). 18.00 *(978-0-7569-8106-8(9))* Perfection Learning Corp.

—The King of Attolia. (YA). 2008. (Queen's Thief Ser.: BK.3). (ENG.). 84.49 *(978-1-4281-8027-7(3))* 2007. (Attolia Ser.: 3). 119.75 *(978-1-4281-1722-8(9))* 2007. (Queen's Thief Ser.: BK.3). (ENG.). 92.75 *(978-1-4281-1716-7(4))* 2006. (Queen's Thief Ser.: BK.3). (ENG.). 90.75 *(978-1-4281-1718-1(0))* 2006. (Queen's Thief Ser.: BK.3). (ENG.). 122.75 *(978-1-4281-1720-4(2))* 2006. (Queen's Thief Ser.: BK.3). (ENG.). 251.75 *(978-1-4281-1717-4(2))* 2006. (Queen's Thief Ser.: BK.3). 281.75 *(978-1-4281-1721-1(0))* 2006. (Queen's Thief Ser.: BK.3). (ENG.). 1.25 *(978-1-4281-1713-6(X))* Recorded Bks., Inc.

Verne, Jules. The Secret of the Island. Kingston, W. H. G., tr. 2008. 160p. 24.95 *(978-1-60664-753-0(9))* Rodgers, Alan Bks.

Warner, Susan & Wetherell, Elizabeth. Daisy in the Field. 2011. 272p. 29.95 *(978-1-4638-9964-6(5))*; pap. 16.95 *(978-1-4638-0163-2(7))* Rodgers, Alan Bks.

Weston Woods Staff, creator. Stone Soup. 2011. 38.75 *(978-0-439-84572-4(6))*; 29.95 *(978-0-439-74595-6(0))* Weston Woods Studios, Inc.

Wiechman, Kathy Cannon. Like a River. 2015. (ENG.). 336p. (J). (gr. 3). 17.95 *(978-1-62979-209-5(8)*, Calkins Creek) Boyds Mills Pr.

William Murray Hogben. Johnny & Mr Reb: A Civil War Tale. 2009. 40p. pap. 18.99 *(978-1-4389-4326-8(1))* AuthorHouse.

Wills, Cheryl. The Emancipation of Grandpa Sandy Wills. Pearson, Randell, illus. 2016. (ENG.). 48p. (J). pap. 18.63 *(978-1-61717-886-3(1))* Sussman Sales Co.

Wilson, John. Flames of the Tiger. 2003. (ENG., Illus.). 176p. (J). (gr. 13-18). 6.95 *(978-1-55337-619-4(6))* Kids Can Pr., Ltd. CAN. Dist: Hachette Bk. Group.

Winders, Gertrude Hecker. Jeb Stuart: Boy in the Saddle. Doremus, Robert, illus. 2011. 202p. 44.95 *(978-1-258-08155-3(5))* Literary Licensing, LLC.

Wolfer, Dianne & Harrison-Lever, Brian. Photographs in the Mud. 2007. (Illus.). 32p. pap. 15.50 *(978-1-921361-04-3(2))* Fremantle Pr. AUS. Dist: Independent Pubs. Group.

Wooten, Laura. With My Little Box of Crayons. Pennington, Kelly, illus. 2008. 50p. pap. 18.95 *(978-1-4251-7103-2(6))* Trafford Publishing.

Wright, Caleb E. Marcus Blair A Story of Provincial Times. 2006. pap. 22.95 *(978-1-4286-6303-9(7))* Kessinger Publishing, LLC.

Wulffson, Don L. & Wulffson, Don. Soldier X. 2003. (ENG.). 240p. (YA). (gr. 7-18). 6.99 *(978-0-14-250073-6(9)*, Speak) Penguin Young Readers Group.

Wynne-Jones, Tim. The Emperor of Any Place. 2015. (ENG.). 336p. (YA). (gr. 9). 17.99 *(978-0-7636-6973-7(3))* Candlewick Pr.

Young, Miriam. Miss Suzy. Lobel, Arnold, illus. (J). 40th anniv. ed. 2004. 44p. 18.95 *(978-1-930900-28-8(7))* 50th ed. 2014. (ENG.). 40p. (gr. -1-3). 18.95 *(978-1-930900-75-2(9))* Purple Hse. Pr.

SOLDIERS—UNITED STATES

see also African American Soldiers

Ades, Audrey. Ethan Allen & the Green Mountain Boys. 2017. 25.70 *(978-1-61228-952-6(5))* Mitchell Lane Pubs., Inc.

Anderson, Dale. A Soldier's Life in the Civil War. 2004. (World Almanac Library of the Civil War). (Illus.). 48p. (gr. 5-12). pap. 14.05 *(978-0-8368-5595-1(7))*; lib. bdg. 31.00 *(978-0-8368-5586-9(8))* Stevens, Gareth Publishing LLLP. (Gareth Stevens Secondary Library).

Beller, Susan Provost. Billy Yank & Johnny Reb: Soldiering in the Civil War. rev. ed. 2007. (Soldiers on the Battlefront Ser.). (ENG., Illus.). 112p. (gr. 6-8). lib. bdg. 33.26 *(978-0-8225-6803-2(9))* Lerner Publishing Group.

—The Doughboys over There: Soldiering in World War I. 2007. (Soldiers on the Battlefront Ser.). (ENG., Illus.). 112p. (J). (gr. 6-8). lib. bdg. 33.26 *(978-0-8225-6295-5(2))* Lerner Publishing Group.

—Yankee Doodle & the Redcoats: Soldiering in the Revolutionary War. rev. ed. 2007. (Soldiers on the Battlefront Ser.). (ENG., Illus.). 112p. (gr. 6-8). lib. bdg. 33.26 *(978-0-8225-6655-7(9))* Lerner Publishing Group.

Bryfonski, Dedria. Veterans. 2015. (Opposing Viewpoints Ser.). (ENG., Illus.). 224p. (gr. 10-12). pap. 33.80 *(978-0-7377-7299-9(9)*, Greenhaven Pr., Inc.) Cengage Gale.

Burns, Heidi A., contrib. by. U. S. Army True Stories: Tales of Bravery. 2014. (Courage under Fire Ser.). (ENG.). 32p. (gr. 3-4). lib. bdg. 27.99 *(978-1-4765-9938-0(6))* Capstone Press of Coughlan Cos.

Castrovilla, Selene. By the Sword. Farnsworth, Bill, illus. 2007. (ENG.). 40p. (J). (gr. 5-7). 17.95 *(978-1-59078-427-3(8))* Boyds Mills Pr.

Cefrey, Holly. One Life to Lose for My Country: The Arrest & Execution of Nathan Hale. (Great Moments in American History Ser.). 32p. 2009. (gr. 3-3). 47.90 *(978-1-61513-135-8(3))* 2004. (Illus.). (gr. 4-8). lib. bdg. 22.50 *(978-0-8239-4371-5(2)*, Rosen Reference) Rosen Publishing Group, Inc., The.

Collier, Peter. Choosing Courage: Inspiring Stories of What It Means to Be a Hero. (ENG., Illus.). (J). 2016. 272p. (gr. 4-6). pap. 8.95 *(978-1-57965-705-5(2))* 2015. 240p. 18.95 *(978-1-57965-596-9(3))* Artisan.

Cooke, Tim. The U. S. Civil War on the Front Lines, 1 vol. 2014. (Life on the Front Lines Ser.). (ENG., Illus.). 32p. (gr. 3-4). 27.99 *(978-1-4914-0842-1(1)*, Edge Bks.) Capstone Press of Coughlan Cos.

—World War II on the Front Lines, 1 vol. 2014. (Life on the Front Lines Ser.). (ENG., Illus.). 32p. (gr. 3-4). lib. bdg. 27.99 *(978-1-4914-0844-5(8))* Capstone Press of Coughlan Cos.

Curtis, Suzanne. John Wesley Powell: American Hero. 2013. (ENG & SPA., Illus.). 78p. (J). pap. 8.95 *(978-0-86541-178-4(6))* Filter Pr., LLC.

Davis, Daniel K. Miles Standish. 2010. (Leaders of the Colonial Era Ser.). 120p. (gr. 5-8). 35.00 *(978-1-60413-739-2(8)*, Chelsea Hse.) Facts On File, Inc.

Dell, Pamela & Raatma, Lucia. The Science of Soldiers, 1 vol. 2012. (Science of War Ser.). (ENG.). 48p. (gr. 5-6). pap. 9.10 *(978-0-7565-4526-0(9))*; lib. bdg. 33.99 *(978-0-7565-4460-7(2))* Compass Point Bks. (CPB Grades 4-8).

DeVillier, Christy. Nathan Hale, 1 vol. 2004. (First Biographies Set Iv Ser.). (ENG., Illus.). 32p. (gr. k-4). 27.07 *(978-1-59197-513-7(1)*, Buddy Bks.) ABDO Publishing Co.

Dixon Jr., John T. Mommy, What Is a POW/MIA? 2008. 48p. pap. 24.95 *(978-1-60474-029-5(9))* PublishAmerica, Inc.

Doeden, Matt. Can You Survive in the Special Forces? An Interactive Survival Adventure. 2012. (You Choose: Survival Ser.). (ENG.). 112p. (gr. 3-4). pap. 41.70 *(978-1-4296-9481-0(5)*, You Choose Bks.) Capstone Press of Coughlan Cos.

Doyle, Bill H. Behind Enemy Lines: Under Fire in the Middle East. 2011. 136p. (J). pap. *(978-0-545-33463-1(2))* Scholastic, Inc.

Ellis, Edward S. The Life of Kit Carson: Hunter, Trapper, Guide, Indian Agent & Colonel U. S. A. 2007. 176p. per. *(978-1-4065-2477-2(8))* Dodo Pr.

The G. I. Series: The Illustrated History of the American Soldier, His Uniform, & His Equipment, 21. 2005. (G. I. Ser.). 84p. (gr. 6-12). 495.00 *(978-0-7910-8077-1(3)*, Chelsea Hse.) Facts On File, Inc.

Gauch, Patricia Lee. The Impossible Major Rogers. Parker, Robert Andrew, illus. 2008. (J). *(978-1-59078-334-4(4))* Boyds Mills Pr.

Goldish, Meish. Army: Civilian to Soldier. 2010. (Becoming a Soldier Ser.). 24p. (YA). (gr. 3-6). lib. bdg. 22.61 *(978-1-936088-11-9(8))* Bearport Publishing Co., Inc.

Gonzalez, Lissette. The U. S. Military: Defending the Nation. (Dangerous Jobs Ser.). 24p. 2009. (gr. 2-3). 42.50 *(978-1-61512-137-3(4)*, PowerKids Pr.) 2007. (Illus.). (J). (gr. 3-7). lib. bdg. 22.60 *(978-1-4042-3777-3(1))* Rosen Publishing Group, Inc., The.

Gourley, Catherine. The Horrors of Andersonville: Life & Death Inside a Civil War Prison. 2010. (ENG.). 192p. (gr. 9-12). lib. bdg. 38.60 *(978-0-7613-4212-0(5))* Lerner Publishing Group.

Grossi, Craig. Craig & Fred: the True Story of a Marine & His Dog. 2017. 256p. (J). (gr. 3). 16.99 ***(978-0-06-269335-8(2))*** HarperCollins Pubs.

Gunderson, Jessica. U. S. Navy True Stories: Tales of Bravery. 2014. (Courage under Fire Ser.). (ENG.). 32p. (gr. 3-4). lib. bdg. 27.99 *(978-1-4765-9937-3(8))* Capstone Press of Coughlan Cos.

Hart, Joyce. Frequently Asked Questions about Being Part of a Military Family. 2009. (FAQ: Teen Life Ser.). (Illus.). 64p. (J). (gr. 5-6). lib. bdg. 31.95 *(978-1-4358-5328-7(8))* Rosen Publishing Group, Inc., The.

Henrickson, Beth. The Marquis de Lafayette & Other International Champions of the American Revolution. 2015. (Spotlight on American History Ser.). (ENG., Illus.). 24p. (J). (gr. 4-6). pap. 10.00 *(978-1-4994-1745-6(4)*, PowerKids Pr.) Rosen Publishing Group, Inc., The.

Hollmann, Robert E. William Barret Travis. 2012. (ENG.). 130p. pap. 9.95 *(978-0-9779863-9-2(X))* Fireside Pr., Inc.

Kann, Bob. Cordelia Harvey: Civil War Angel. 2011. (Badger Biographies Ser.). (ENG., Illus.). 128p. (J). pap. 12.95 *(978-0-87020-458-6(0))* Wisconsin Historical Society.

Koestler-Grack, Rachel A. Nathan Hale: Courageous Spy. 2005. (Leaders of the American Revolution Ser.). (Illus.). 100p. (gr. 5-8). lib. bdg. 30.00 *(978-0-7910-8623-0(2))* Facts On File, Inc.

Levy, Janey. The Battle of the Alamo. 2009. (Real Life Readers Ser.). 32p. (gr. 4-5). pap. 10.00 *(978-1-4358-0167-7(9)*, Rosen Classroom); (gr. 4-4). 47.90 *(978-1-61511-369-9(X)*, PowerKids Pr.); (J). (gr. 3-4). lib. bdg. 25.25 *(978-1-4358-2991-6(3)*, PowerKids Pr.) Rosen Publishing Group, Inc., The.

Liberston, Jody. Nathan Hale: Heroe de la guerra de Independencia. 2004. (Grandes personajes en la historia de los Estados Unidos Ser.). (SPA.). 32p. (gr. 3-6). pap. 10.00 *(978-0-8239-4235-0(X)*, Rosen Classroom) Rosen Publishing Group, Inc., The.

Libertson, Jody. Nathan Hale: Hero of the American Revolution. 2009. (Primary Sources of Famous People in American History Ser.). 32p. (gr. 2-3). 47.90 *(978-1-60851-709-1(8))* Rosen Publishing Group, Inc., The.

—Nathan Hale: Héroe revolucionario / Hero of the American Revolution. 2009. (Famous People in American History/Grandes personajes en la historia de los Estados Unidos Ser.). (ENG & SPA.). 32p. (gr. 2-3). 47.90 *(978-1-61512-552-4(3)*, Editorial Buenas Letras) Rosen Publishing Group, Inc., The.

—Nathan Hale: Héroe revolucionario (Nathan Hale: Hero of the American Revolution) 2009. (Grandes personajes en la historia de los Estados Unidos (Famous People in American History) Ser.). (SPA.). 32p. (gr. 2-3). 47.90 *(978-1-61512-805-1(0)*, Editorial Buenas Letras) Rosen Publishing Group, Inc., The.

S

Markovics, Joyce L. & Pushies, Fred J. Today's Army Heroes. 2012. (Acts of Courage: Inside America's Military Ser.). 32p. (J). (gr. 2-7). lib. bdg. 25.27 (978-1-61772-445-9(9)) Bearport Publishing Co., Inc.

Marx, Mandy R. Amazing U. S. Marine Facts. 2016. (Amazing Military Facts Ser.). (ENG., Illus.). 24p. (gr. k-1). lib. bdg. 26.65 (978-1-5157-0954-1(X), Pebble Plus) Capstone Press of Coughlan Cos.

Maynard, Charles W. John Wesley Powell: Soldier, Scientist, & Explorer. 2009. (Famous Explorers of the American West Ser.). 24p. (gr. 3-4). 42.50 (978-1-61512-505-0(1), PowerKids Pr.) Rosen Publishing Group, Inc., The.

McNab, Chris. Learning Mental Endurance for Survival. Carney, John, ed. 2014. (Extreme Survival in the Military Ser.: 12). 64p. (J). (gr. 7-18). lib. bdg. 23.95 (978-1-4222-3082-4(1)) Mason Crest.

Micklos, John. Why We Won the American Revolution — Through Primary Sources. 2013. (American Revolution Through Primary Sources Ser.). 48p. (J). (gr. 4-18). 25.27 (978-0-7660-4134-9(4)) Enslow Pubs., Inc.

Miller, Adam, et al. Courage under Fire: True Stories of Bravery from the U. S. Army, Navy, Air Force, & Marines, 1 vol. 2014. (Courage under Fire Ser.). (ENG., Illus.). 112p. (gr. 3-4). pap. 9.95 (978-1-4914-1065-3(5)) Capstone Press of Coughlan Cos.

Miller, Reagan & Claus, J. Matteson. Life on a Civil War Battlefield. 2011. (ENG.). 48p. (J). pap. (978-0-7787-5357-5(3)); lib. bdg. (978-0-7787-5340-7(9)) Crabtree Publishing Co.

Moss, Marissa. Nurse, Soldier, Spy: The Story of Sarah Edmonds, a Civil War Hero. Hendrix, John, illus. 2011. (ENG.). 48p. (J). (gr. 3-7). 19.95 (978-0-8109-9735-6(5), Abrams Bks. for Young Readers) Abrams, Inc.

Norfolk, Sherry & Norfolk, Bobby. The Virginia Giant: The True Story of Peter Francisco. Brennan, Cait, illus. 2014. (ENG.). 160p. (J). (gr. 4-7). 16.99 (978-1-62619-117-4(4), History Pr., The) Arcadia Publishing.

Olson, Nathan. Nathan Hale: Revolutionary Spy. Martin, Cynthia & Schoonover, Brent, illus. 2005. (Graphic Biographies Ser.). (ENG.). 32p. (gr. 3-4). 30.65 (978-0-7368-4968-5(8), Graphic Library) Capstone Press of Coughlan Cos.

Olson, Nathan & Glaser, Jason. Nathan Hale: Revolutionary Spy, 1 vol. Martin, Cynthia & Schoonover, Brent, illus. 2006. (Graphic Biographies Ser.). (ENG.). 32p. (gr. 3-4). per. 8.10 (978-0-7368-6199-1(8), Graphic Library) Capstone Press of Coughlan Cos.

Peppas, Lynn. Why Sam Houston Matters to Texas. 2014. (Illus.). 32p. (J). lib. bdg. 26.25 (978-1-4777-0912-2(6)) Rosen Publishing Group, Inc., The.

Porterfield, Jason. The Third Amendment: The Right to Privacy in the Home. 2011. (Amendments to the United States Constitution: the Bill of Rights Ser.). (Illus.). 64p. (YA). (gr. 5-9). lib. bdg. 31.95 (978-1-4488-1256-1(9)) Rosen Publishing Group, Inc., The.

—Third Amendment: Upholding the Right to Privacy. 2011. (Amendments to the United States Constitution: the Bill of Rights Ser.). (ENG.). 64p. (YA). pap. 12.95 (978-1-4488-2304-8(8), Rosen Reference) Rosen Publishing Group, Inc., The.

Ratliff, Thomas. How to Be a Revolutionary War Soldier. 2008. (How to Be Ser.). (ENG., Illus.). 32p. (J). (gr. 4-7). pap. 5.95 (978-1-4263-0247-3(9), National Geographic Children's Bks.) National Geographic Society.

—You Wouldn't Want to Be a Civil War Soldier! A War You'd Rather Not Fight. Antram, David, illus. 2013. (You Wouldn't Want to... Ser.). (ENG.). 32p. (J). 29.00 (978-0-531-25947-4(1), Watts, Franklin) Scholastic Library Publishing.

—You Wouldn't Want to Be a Civil War Soldier! A War You'D Rather Not Fight. 2013. (You Wouldn't Want To... Ser.). lib. bdg. 20.80 (978-0-606-31627-9(2), Turtleback) Turtleback Bks.

—You Wouldn't Want to Be a Civil War Soldier! A War You'd Rather Not Fight. Antram, David, illus. rev. ed. 2013. (You Wouldn't Want to... Ser.). (ENG.). 40p. (J). pap. 9.95 (978-0-531-24503-3(9), Watts, Franklin) Scholastic Library Publishing.

Raum, Elizabeth. At Battle in the Revolutionary War: An Interactive Battlefield Adventure. 2015. (You Choose: Battlefields Ser.). (ENG., Illus.). 112p. (gr. 3-4). pap. 6.95 (978-1-4914-2392-9(7), You Choose Bks.) Capstone Press of Coughlan Cos.

Rice, Earle. The Life & Times of the Brothers Custer: Galloping to Glory. 2008. (Profiles in American History Ser.). (Illus.). 48p. (J). (gr. 4-8). lib. bdg. 29.95 (978-1-58415-665-9(1)) Mitchell Lane Pubs., Inc.

Sanford, William R. & Green, Carl R. Kit Carson: Courageous Mountain Man. 2012. (Courageous Heroes of the American West Ser.). 48p. (J). pap. 8.95 (978-1-4644-0094-0(6)) Enslow Pubs., Inc.

Shoup, Kate. Life As a Soldier in the Civil War. 2016. (Life As... Ser.). (ENG., Illus.). 32p. (J). (gr. 3-3). pap. 10.58 (978-1-5026-1083-6(3)) Cavendish Square Publishing.

Siddons, Brian. Crispus Attucks & African American Patriots of the American Revolution. 2015. (Spotlight on American History Ser.). (ENG., Illus.). 24p. (J). (gr. 4-6). pap. 10.00 (978-1-4994-1739-5(X), PowerKids Pr.) Rosen Publishing Group, Inc., The.

Silvey, Anita. I'll Pass for Your Comrade: Women Soldiers in the Civil War. 2008. (ENG., Illus.). 128p. (J). (gr. 5-7). 19.99 (978-0-618-57491-9(3)) Houghton Mifflin Harcourt Publishing Co.

Simons, Lisa M. Bolt. Soldados del Ejército de EE. UU. 2010. (Gente de Las Fuerzas Armadas de EE. UU. /People of the Armed Forces Ser.).Tr. of Soldiers of the U. S. Army. (MUL, SPA & ENG.). 24p. (gr. k-1). lib. bdg. 26.65 (978-1-4296-6118-8(6)) Capstone Press of Coughlan Cos.

Smithson, Ryan. *Ghosts of War: The True Story of a 19-Year-Old GI.* 2010. (ENG.). 352p. (YA). (gr. 9). pap. 9.99 (978-0-06-166471-7(5), Collins) HarperCollins Pubs.

Souza, Dorothy M. John Wesley Powell. 2004. (Watts Library). (ENG., Illus.). 64p. (J). (gr. 5-7). pap. 8.95 (978-0-531-16653-6(8), Watts, Franklin) Scholastic Library Publishing.

Stewart, Gail B. Life of a Soldier in Washington's Army. 2003. (American War Library). (ENG., Illus.). 112p. (J). 30.85 (978-1-59018-215-4(4), Lucent Bks.) Cengage Gale.

Stout, Glenn. Soldier Athletes. 2011. (Good Sports Ser.). (ENG.). 112p. (J). (gr. 5-7). pap. 6.99 (978-0-547-41729-5(2)) Houghton Mifflin Harcourt Publishing Co.

Thornton, Jeremy. Foreign-Born Champions of the American Revolution. (Building America's Democracy Ser.). 24p. 2009. (gr. 3-3). 42.50 (978-1-61511-764-2(4)) 2003. (Illus.). (J). lib. bdg. 22.60 (978-0-8239-6277-8(6)) Rosen Publishing Group, Inc., The. (PowerKids Pr.).

Vonne, Mira. Gross Facts about the American Civil War. 2017. (Gross History Ser.). (ENG., Illus.). 32p. (gr. 1-2). lib. bdg. 26.65 (978-1-5157-4155-8(9)) Capstone Press of Coughlan Cos.

Walsh, Steve. Zebulon Montgomery Pike: Explorer & Military Officer. 2011. (ENG & SPA., Illus.). 54p. (J). pap. 8.95 (978-0-86541-123-4(9)) Filter Pr., LLC.

Williams, Jack S. Soldiers & Their Families of the California Mission Frontier. 2009. (People of the California Missions Ser.). 64p. (gr. 4-4). 58.50 (978-1-60851-160-0(X), PowerKids Pr.) Rosen Publishing Group, Inc., The.

Yomtov, Nelson. Courage on the Battlefield: True Tales of Survival in the Military. 2015. (True Stories of Survival Ser.). (ENG., Illus.). 32p. (gr. 3-4). lib. bdg. 30.65 (978-1-4914-6571-4(9)) Capstone Press of Coughlan Cos.

Zullo, Allan. Battle Heroes. 2014. (10 True Tales Ser.). (ENG.). 160p. (J). (gr. 3-7). pap. 5.99 (978-0-545-81810-0(9), Scholastic Nonfiction) Scholastic, Inc.

—War Heroes: Voices from Iraq. 2009. 48p. (J). pap. (978-0-545-09026-1(1)) Scholastic, Inc.

SOLDIERS, AFRICAN AMERICAN

see African American Soldiers

SOLDIERS IN ART

Bergin, Mark. Soldiers. 2012. (How to Draw Ser.). (ENG.). 32p. (J). (gr. 4-6). pap. 11.75 (978-1-4488-6473-7(9)); lib. bdg. 26.50 (978-1-4488-6463-8(1)) Rosen Publishing Group, Inc., The. (PowerKids Pr.).

O'Connor, Jane. Hidden Army: Clay Soldiers of Ancient China. 2011. (All Aboard Reading Ser.). (ENG.). 48p. (J). (gr. 1-3). mass mkt. 3.99 (978-0-448-45580-8(3), Grosset & Dunlap) Penguin Young Readers Group.

SOLDIERS' LIFE

see Soldiers

SOLID GEOMETRY

see Geometry

SOLO, HAN (FICTITIOUS CHARACTER)—FICTION

ABDO Publishing Company Staff & Wood, Brian. Star Wars: In the Shadow of Yavin. D'Anda, Carlos, illus. 2014. (Star Wars: in the Shadow of Yavin Ser.: 6). (ENG.). 24p. (J). (gr. 9-14). lib. bdg. 145.26 (978-1-61479-285-7(2), Graphic Planet) Magic Wagon.

Angleberger, Tom. Star Wars - Return of the Jedi: Beware the Power of the Dark Side! McCaig, Iain, illus. 2015. (ENG.). 432p. (J). (gr. 3-7). 17.99 (978-1-4847-0913-9(6), Disney Lucasfilm Press) Disney Publishing Worldwide.

Barlow, Jeremy & Soriano, Carlo. Star Wars Adventures: Princess Leia & the Royal Ransom, 1 vol. 2012. (Star Wars Digests Ser.). (ENG., Illus.). 80p. (J). (gr. 4-7). 27.07 (978-1-59961-902-6(4)) Spotlight.

Bracken, Alexandra. Star Wars - A New Hope: The Princess, the Scoundrel, & the Farm Boy. McCaig, Iain, illus. 2015. (ENG.). 336p. (J). (gr. 3-7). 17.99 (978-1-4847-0912-2(8), 1384321, Disney Lucasfilm Press) Disney Publishing Worldwide.

Disney Book Group. Star Wars the Force Awakens. 2016. (Read-Along Storybook & CD Ser.). (ENG.). 32p. (J). (gr. 1-3). pap. 6.99 (978-1-4847-3149-9(2)) Disney Pr.

Disney Book Group. Trapped in the Death Star! 2016. (Star Wars: World of Reading Ser.). (J). lib. bdg. 14.75 **(978-0-606-39174-0(6))** Turtleback Bks.

Dorling Kindersley Publishing Staff & Kent, Lindsay. The Adventures of Han Solo, Level 2. 2011. (DK Readers Ser.). (ENG.). 32p. (J). (gr. -1-1). 3.99 (978-0-7566-8252-1(5), DK Children) Dorling Kindersley Publishing, Inc.

Fry, Jason. Star Wars the Force Awakens Chapter Book. 2016. (ENG.). 128p. (J). (gr. 1-3). pap. 5.99 (978-1-4847-7409-0(4), Disney Lucasfilm Press) Disney Publishing Worldwide.

LucasFilm Press. Star Wars Han & the Rebel Rescue. 2017. (ENG.). 24p. (J). (gr. 1-3). pap. 4.99 (978-1-368-00352-0(4), Disney Lucasfilm Press) Disney Publishing Worldwide.

LucasFilm Press Staff & Rucka, Greg. Smuggler's Run: A Han Solo Adventure. Noto, Phil, illus. 2015. (ENG.). 192p. (J). (gr. 5-9). 12.99 (978-1-4847-2495-8(X), Disney Lucasfilm Press) Disney Publishing Worldwide.

Wang, Holman & Wang, Jack. Star Wars Epic Yarns: A New Hope. 2015. (ENG., Illus.). 24p. (J). (gr. -1 — 1). 9.95 (978-1-4521-3393-5(X)) Chronicle Bks. LLC.

—Star Wars Epic Yarns: Return of the Jedi. 2015. (ENG., Illus.). 24p. (J). (gr. -1 — 1). 9.95 (978-1-4521-3500-7(2)) Chronicle Bks. LLC.

—Star Wars Epic Yarns: The Empire Strikes Back. 2015. (ENG., Illus.). 24p. (J). (gr. -1 — 1). 9.95 (978-1-4521-3499-4(5)) Chronicle Bks. LLC.

SOLOMON, KING OF ISRAEL

Myers, Glenn, illus. Solomon Builds the Temple: 1 Kings 5:1-8:66. 2005. (Little Learner Bible Story Books). 16p. (J). pap. 2.29 (978-0-7586-0944-1(2)) Concordia Publishing Hse.

Steinberg, Sari. King Solomon Figures It Out. Taulo, Tuija, illus. 2005. 32p. (J). (gr. k-3). 9.95 (978-965-465-004-5(5), Devora Publishing) Simcha Media Group.

Woodman, Ros. The Wise King: A Puzzle Book about Solomon. rev. ed. 2008. (Puzzle Ser.). (ENG.). 24p. (J). 4.99 (978-1-84550-404-5(6), bde9e1c9-e7ee-4d1c-98a1-0b3c87149528) Christian Focus *Pubns. GBR. Dist: Bookmasters Distribution.*

SOLOMON, KING OF ISRAEL—FICTION

Biers-Ariel, Matt. Solomon & the Trees. Silverberg-Kiss, Esti, illus. 2004. (J). (gr. k-3). 13.95 (978-0-8074-0749-3(6), 101055) URJ Pr.

Haggard, H. Rider. Las Minas del Rey Salomon.Tr. of King Solomon's Mines. (SPA., Illus.). 184p. (YA). 11.95 (978-84-7281-094-5(1), AF1094) Auriga, Ediciones S.A. ESP. Dist: Continental Bk. Co., Inc.

—Las Minas del Rey Salomon. Eric, F. Rowe, illus. 5th ed. (Coleccion Clasicos en Accion).Tr. of King Solomon's Mines. (SPA.). 80p. (YA). (gr. 5-8). 12.76 (978-84-241-5779-1(6)) Everest Editora ESP. Dist: Lectorum Pubns., Inc.

Jules, Jacqueline. The Princess & the Ziz. Kahn, Katherine Janus, illus. 2008. 32p. (J). (gr. -1-3). lib. bdg. 17.95 (978-0-8225-7377-7(6)); (ENG.). pap. 7.95 (978-0-8225-7382-1(2)) Lerner Publishing Group. (Kar-Ben Publishing).

SOMME, 1ST BATTLE OF THE, FRANCE, 1916

Ridley, Sarah. The Somme. 2016. (ENG., Illus.). 48p. (J). (gr. 7-11). 18.99 (978-1-4451-4690-4(8), Franklin Watts) Hachette Children's Group GBR. Dist: Hachette Bk. Group.

SONG BOOKS

see Songbooks

SONGBOOKS

see also School Songbooks

Barretta, Gene, illus. On Top of Spaghetti: A Silly Song Book. 2005. 12p. (J). 12.95 (978-1-58117-331-4(8), Intervisual/Piggy Toes) Bendon, Inc.

Big's Big Baby. (Looney Tunes Song & Sound Bks.). (Illus.). 16p. (J). (gr. -1-k). 7.98 (978-0-7853-1608-4(6), PI10) Publications International, Ltd.

Boytim, Joan Frey. Daffodils, Violets & Snowflakes: 24 Classical Songs for Young Women, Ages Ten to Mid-Teens. 2003. (ENG.). 88p. pap. 16.99 (978-0-634-06212-4(3), 0634062123) Leonard, Hal Corp.

Boytim, Joan Frey, ed. Daffodils, Violets & Snowflakes: 24 Classical Songs for Young Women, Ages 10 to Mid-Teens. 2003. (ENG.). 88p. (gr. 5-18). pap. 16.99 (978-0-634-06181-3(X), 063406181X) Leonard, Hal Corp.

Diaper Days Songs. (Baby Looney Tunes Song Bks.). (Illus.). 16p. (J). (gr. -1). 7.98 (978-0-7853-1612-1(4), PI112) Publications International, Ltd.

Dockery, L. D. The Multiplication Song Book. 2012. 24p. pap. 17.99 (978-1-4772-6900-8(2)) AuthorHouse.

Frosty the Snowman: Songs of the Season: 5-Button Song Book. (Illus.). 10p. (J). (gr. -1-2). 7.98 (978-0-7853-2067-8(9), PI27) Publications International, Ltd.

Glazer, Tom. Tom Glazer's Treasury of Songs for Children. Seiden, Art, illus. 2nd ed. 2003. 256p. (J). (gr. 3-6). pap. 20.00 (978-1-58690-003-8(X)) Empire Publishing Service.

Goldstein, Rose B. Songs to Share. Schloss, E., illus. (ENG & HEB.). 64p. (J). (gr. -1-5). 2.95 (978-0-8381-0720-1(6), 10-720) United Synagogue of America Bk. Service.

Grant, Carrie and David. Elephant's Birthday Bells: Jump up & Join In. Busby, Ailie, illus. 2013. 32p. (J). pap. 7.99 (978-1-61067-181-1(3)) Kane Miller.

—Lion's Speedy Sauce: Jump up & Join In. Busby, Ailie, illus. 2013. 32p. (J). pap. 7.99 (978-1-61067-180-4(5)) Kane Miller.

Hal Leonard Corp. Staff, creator. The Easy Disney Fake Book. 2012. (ENG.). 216p. pap. 19.99 (978-1-4584-4514-8(3), 1458445143) Leonard, Hal Corp.

Hal Leonard Music Books Staff. Still More Disney Solos for Kids: Voice & Piano with Online Recorded Performances & Accompaniments. 2010. (ENG.). 44p. pap. 19.99 (978-1-4234-8333-5(2), 1423483332) Leonard, Hal Corp.

Hop! Hop! Hop! (J). 15.95 (978-0-8126-0086-5(X)) Open Court Publishing Co.

Merrill, Bob & Trapani, Iza. How Much Is That Doggie in the Window? 2004. (ENG., Illus.). 32p. (J). (gr. k-k). pap. 7.95 (978-1-58089-030-4(X)) Charlesbridge Publishing, Inc.

Mickey's Favorites. (Sing-Along Ser.). (J). 11.99 incl. audio (978-1-55723-962-4(2)) Walt Disney Records.

Miller, Carolyn. Teaching Little Fingers to Play More Broadway Songs: 10 Mid to Later Elementary Show Tunes for Piano. 2012. (ENG.). 32p. pap. 6.99 (978-1-4584-1767-1(0), 1458417670) Willis Music Co.

Okun, Milton, ed. Cliff Eberhardt Songbook. Date not set. 56p. (YA). pap. 15.95 (978-0-89524-957-9(X)) Cherry Lane Music Co.

—Just for Kids. 32p. (YA). pap. 7.95 (978-0-89524-950-0(2), 02505506) Cherry Lane Music Co.

Pingry, Patricia A. O Little Town of Bethlehem. 2008. (ENG., Illus.). 16p. (J). bds. 12.99 (978-0-8249-6566-2(3), Ideal Pubns.) Worthy Publishing.

Publications International Ltd. Staff, ed. Disney Princess: Canciones the Princesas. 2011. 24p. (J). 17.98 (978-1-4508-1615-1(0)) Publications International, Ltd.

—Disney Princess: Magical Princess Songs. 2011. 14p. (J). bds. 17.98 (978-1-4508-1132-3(9)) Publications International, Ltd.

—Disney Princess: Royal Recital. 2011. 14p. (J). bds. 17.98 (978-1-4508-1006-7(3)) Phoenix International Publications, Inc.

—Disney Princess: Songs to Treasure: Little Pop-Up Song Book. 2013. 10p. (J). (gr. k-4). bds. 10.99 (978-1-4508-6225-7(X), d48145fd-2550-4549-b020-98778a694300) Phoenix International Publications, Inc.

—Hello Kitty: Hello Songs: Play-A-Sound Digital Music Player Book. 2013. 14p. (J). (gr. k-4). bds. 22.98 (978-1-4508-6605-7(0), 4d3710ac-97b9-4b41-a7cd-23b43c501ffa) Phoenix International Publications, Inc.

—Minnie Mouse: Pretty Piano Play-Along: Piano Book. 2013. (Illus.). 14p. (J). (gr. k-3). bds. 18.98 (978-1-4508-6770-2(7), a4f2852b-3a90-4b10-ac4c-e802ee4cfa50) Phoenix International Publications, Inc.

—Minnie Mouse: Surprise, Surprise! Play-A-Sound Book. 2012. 10p. (J). (gr. k-3). bds. 7.99 (978-1-4508-6848-8(7), 0897e306-d7d1-4df0-a08f-afd88e1cfa82) Phoenix International Publications, Inc.

—Nickelodeon Dora the Explorer: Follow the Music. 2011. 14p. (J). 18.98 (978-1-4508-0712-8(7)) Phoenix International Publications, Inc.

—Rudolph the Red-Nosed Reindeer: Little Pop-Up Song Book. 2013. 10p. (J). (gr. k-4). bds. 18.98 (978-1-4508-5363-7(3), e80b43a2-a0ce-4d2a-8c6e-90c92a828ab9) Phoenix International Publications, Inc.

—Sofia the First: Princess in Training: Play-A-Sound Book. 2013. 12p. (J). (gr. k-3). bds. 10.99 (978-1-4508-6278-3(0), 8d870699-8d28-476c-b7fd-49589bc268a4) Phoenix International Publications, Inc.

—Thomas & Friends: Play-a-Tune Puzzle Book. 2010. 10p. (J). bds. 13.98 (978-1-60553-756-6(X)) Publications International, Ltd.

Seuss, Dr. The Cat in the Hat Songbook. 2017. (Classic Seuss Ser.). (ENG., Illus.). 72p. (J). (gr. k-12). 16.99 (978-0-394-81695-1(1), Random Hse. Bks. for Young Readers) Random Hse. Children's Bks.

Shake It up! Songbook. 120p. (J). 16.99 (978-0-8307-2769-8(8), Gospel Light) Gospel Light Pubns.

Shrubshall & Free. Around the Pind in 80 Days: A Musical for Children. 2011. 47p. (978-0-573-08130-9(1)) French, Samuel Ltd.

Sweet Dreams Lullabies. (Baby Looney Tunes Song Bks.). (Illus.). 16p. (J). (gr. -1). 7.98 (978-0-7853-1613-8(2), PI13) Publications International, Ltd.

Taz TV. (Looney Tunes Song & Sound Bks.). (Illus.). 16p. (J). (gr. -1-k). 7.98 (978-0-7853-1609-1(4), PI9) Publications International, Ltd.

SONGS

see also Ballads; Carols; Folk Songs; Hymns; Lullabies; National Songs; Popular Music; School Songbooks; Songbooks

A&C Black, A&C. Apusskidu: Songs for Children. 2017. (ENG.). 98p. (J). pap. 29.95 **(978-1-4729-2991-4(8))** HarperCollins Pubs. Ltd. GBR. Dist: Independent Pubs. Group.

—Take One Song: Years 1-2. 2017. (ENG.). 64p. (J). pap. 29.95 **(978-1-4729-3460-4(1))** HarperCollins Pubs. Ltd. GBR. Dist: Independent Pubs. Group.

Ableman, Aaron & Room, Dave. Pacha's Pajamas: A Story Written by Nature. 2016. (ENG.). 200p. (J). pap. 12.95 (978-1-63047-704-2(4)) Morgan James Publishing.

Albee, Sarah. Elmo's 12 Days of Christmas. Swanson, Maggie, illus. 2003. (Big Bird's Favorites Board Bks.). (ENG.). 24p. (J). (gr. k — 1). bds. 4.99 (978-0-375-82506-4(1), Random Hse. Bks. for Young Readers) Random Hse. Children's Bks.

Albrecht, Sally K., et al. I SIng, You Sing, Too! 30 Echo Songs for Young Singers. 2008. (ENG.). 68p. pap. 44.95 (978-0-7390-5257-0(8)) Alfred Publishing Co., Inc.

Albrecht, Sally K. & Althouse, Jay. I SIng, You Sing, Too! 30 Echo Songs for Young Singers. 2008. (ENG.). 68p. pap. 19.95 (978-0-7390-5259-4(4)) Alfred Publishing Co., Inc.

—Rhythm All Around! 10 Songs That Explore Rhythm in Our World. 2007. (ENG.). 72p. pap. 29.95 (978-0-7390-4643-2(8)) Alfred Publishing Co., Inc.

Alderman, Daniel, et al. Rub a Dub Dub. 2013. (ENG., Illus.). 32p. (J). (gr. -1-3). pap. 8.95 (978-1-58089-575-0(1)) Charlesbridge Publishing, Inc.

Alexander, Martha. A You're Adorable. Alexander, Martha, illus. 2011. (ENG., Illus.). 20p. (J). (gr. -1 — 1). bds. 6.99 (978-0-7636-5332-3(2)) Candlewick Pr.

Allingham, William. Rhymes for the Young Folk. unabr. ed. 2012. (Illus.). 81p. 39.99 (978-1-4622-9303-2(4)) Repressed Publishing LLC.

Almeida, Artie. Recorder Express (Soprano Recorder Method for Classroom or Individual Use) Soprano Recorder Method for Classroom or Individual Use, Book & CD. 2007. (ENG.). 48p. pap. 14.95 (978-0-7390-4726-2(4)) Alfred Publishing Co., Inc.

Amador Family Staff & Barefoot Books Staff. The Wheels on the Bus. Williamson, Melanie, illus. 2014. 24p. (J). 16.99 (978-1-84686-787-3(8)) Barefoot Bks., Inc.

AMSCO Publications Staff & Hal Leonard Corp. Staff, creators. The Super Songbook for Kids. 2007. (ENG., Illus.). 80p. pap. 14.95 (978-0-8256-3464-2(4), 0825634644, Amsco Music) Music Sales Corp.

Antonini, Gabriele, illus. Wheels on the Bus. 2012. 22p. (J). (978-1-4508-3332-5(2)) Publications International, Ltd.

Apusskidu: Songs for Children (2016 Edition), 1 vol. 3rd ed. 2017. (ENG.). 96p. (J). pap. 39.95 **(978-1-4729-3269-3(2))** HarperCollins Pubs. Ltd. GBR. Dist: Independent Pubs. Group.

Archambault, John & Plummer, David. Two Birds SAT upon a Stone. Hollander, Sarah, illus. 2006. (J). pap. (978-1-58669-187-5(2)) Childcraft Education Corp.

Arrullos. (SPA & ENG.). (J). (gr. -1-3). 10.00 net. (978-1-57417-032-0(5), AC30087) Arcoiris Records, Inc.

Audio & Kidzup Productions Staff. Best Toddler Songbook. 2003. (Toddler Ser.). (J). pap. 12.99 incl. audio (978-1-894281-76-8(4)) Kidzup Productions.

Axford, Elizabeth C. & compiled by. Kidtunes Songbook & Activity Guide Axford, Elizabeth C., compiled by. 2003. (ENG., Illus.). 52p. (J). 14.95 (978-1-931844-01-7(1), PP1013) Piano Pr.

Ayotte-Irwin, Tracy & Jordan, Sara. Bilingual Songs - English-French, 2 vols., Vol. 2. 2003. (Bilingual Song English-French Ser.: 2). (FRE., Illus.). 48p. (J). 17.95 (978-1-894262-80-4(8), 1894262808) Jordan, Sara Publishing.

The B-I-B-L-E Online Children Song. 2.00 (978-0-687-07975-9(6)) Abingdon Pr.

Baby Signing Time. 2005. (J). Bk. 1. bds. (978-1-933543-06-2(X))Bk. 2. bds. (978-1-933543-07-9(8)) Two Little Hands Productions LLC.

Baker, Clara Belle & Kohlsaat, Caroline. Songs for the Little Child. 2005. reprint ed. pap. 19.95 (978-1-4179-3304-4(6)) Kessinger Publishing, LLC.

Bangs, Edward. Yankee Doodle. Squier, Robert, illus. 2010. (Favorite Children's Songs Ser.). (ENG.). 16p. (J). (gr. -1-2). 25.64 (978-1-60253-534-3(5), 200116) Child's World, Inc., The.

Barker, Dan. Mary Had a Little Lamb Songbook. 2003. 44p. (J). 5.00 (978-1-58302-239-9(2)) One Way St., Inc.

Baron, Andrew, illus. The Adventures of Octopus Rex. 2003. (J). per. 17.95 (978-0-9760348-0-3(8)) BaHart Pubns. / Eight Legs Publishing.

Bauer, Marion Dane. Love Song for a Baby. Andreasen, Dan, illus. 2011. (Classic Board Bks.). (ENG.). 40p. (J). (gr. -1 — 1). bds. 7.99 (978-1-4169-6395-0(2), Little Simon) Little Simon.

Baxter, Nicola. Sing-Along Songs for Children: Join in with Your Free CD. Finn, Rebecca, illus. 2014. (ENG.). 12p. (J). (gr. -1-k). bds. 14.99 (978-1-84322-892-9(0), Armadillo) Anness Publishing GBR. Dist: National Bk. Network.

Beall, Pamela Conn & Nipp, Susan Hagen. The Best of Wee Sing, 1 vol. 13th ed. 2007. (Wee Sing Ser.). (ENG., Illus.). 64p. (J). (gr. -1-2). 10.99 *(978-0-8431-2184-1(X)*, Price Stern Sloan) Penguin Young Readers Group.

—Wee Sing & Play, 1 vol. 2006. (Wee Sing Ser.). (ENG., Illus.). 64p. (J). (gr. -1-2). 10.99 *(978-0-8431-2003-5(7)*, Price Stern Sloan) Penguin Young Readers Group.

—Wee Sing Bible Songs, 1 vol. 2005. (Wee Sing Ser.). (ENG.). 64p. (J). (gr. -1-2). 10.99 *(978-0-8431-1300-6(6)*, Price Stern Sloan) Penguin Young Readers Group.

—Wee Sing Children's Songs & Fingerplays, 1 vol. 2005. (Wee Sing Ser.). (ENG.). 64p. (J). (gr. -1-2). 10.99 *(978-0-8431-1362-4(6)*, Price Stern Sloan) Penguin Young Readers Group.

—Wee Sing Dinosaurs, 1 vol. 2006. (Wee Sing Ser.). (ENG., Illus.). 64p. (J). (gr. -1-2). 10.99 *(978-0-8431-2097-4(5)*, Price Stern Sloan) Penguin Young Readers Group.

—Wee Sing in the Car, 1 vol. 2005. (Wee Sing Ser.). (ENG.). 64p. (J). (gr. -1-2). 10.99 *(978-0-8431-1339-6(1)*, Price Stern Sloan) Penguin Young Readers Group.

—Wee Sing Silly Songs, 1 vol. 2006. (Wee Sing Ser.). (ENG., Illus.). 64p. (J). (gr. -1-2). 10.99 *(978-0-8431-2004-2(5)*, Price Stern Sloan) Penguin Young Readers Group.

—Wee Sing Sing-Alongs, 1 vol. 2005. (Wee Sing Ser.). Orig. Title: Wee Sing Around the Campfire. (ENG.). 64p. (J). (gr. -1-2). 10.99 *(978-0-8431-1361-7(8)*, Price Stern Sloan) Penguin Young Readers Group.

Beall, Pamela Conn, et al. Wee Sing Around the World, 1 vol. Chauncey, G., illus. 2006. (Wee Sing Ser.). (ENG.). 64p. (J). (gr. -1-2). 10.99 *(978-0-8431-2005-9(3)*, Price Stern Sloan) Penguin Young Readers Group.

—Wee Sing for Baby, 1 vol. 2005. (Wee Sing Ser.). (ENG.). 64p. (J). (gr. -1-2). 10.99 *(978-0-8431-1338-9(3)*, Price Stern Sloan) Penguin Young Readers Group.

Beaton, Clare & Kietter, Dana. Mrs. Moon: Lullabies for Bedtime. 2007. (ENG., Illus.). 48p. (J). 19.99 *(978-1-84686-067-6(9))* Barefoot Bks., Inc.

Beaumont. Miss Polly Wolly Doodle from T. (J). 15.95 *(978-0-8118-4825-1(6))* Chronicle Bks. LLC.

Bee, Kati. Mrs. Flutterbee & the Funny Farm. 2007. (Illus.). 32p. (J). 15.99 *(978-0-9793760-0-9(9))* Kati Bee & Friends Publishing.

Berkner, Laurie. The Laurie Berkner Songbook. 2006. (ENG., Illus.). 56p. pap. 16.95 incl. audio compact disk *(978-0-8256-3544-1(6)*, 0825635446, Amsco Music) Music Sales Corp.

—We Are the Dinosaurs. Clanton, Ben, illus. 2017. (ENG.). 40p. (J). (gr. -1-3). 17.99 *(978-1-4814-6463-5(9)*, Simon & Schuster Bks. For Young Readers) Simon & Schuster Bks. For Young Readers.

Berlin, Irving. Easter Parade. McCue, Lisa, illus. 2003. 32p. (J). 16.89 *(978-0-06-029126-6(5))* HarperCollins Pubs.

—White Christmas. Hague, Michael, illus. 2010. (ENG.). 32p. (J). 16.99 *(978-0-06-029123-5(0))* HarperCollins Pubs.

Big Animal Songbook. 2009. pap. 12.95 *(978-1-84772-546-2(5)*, AM993553) Wise Pubns. GBR. Dist: Music Sales Corp.

Birchard, C. C. Boy Scout Song Book. 2004. reprint ed. pap. 20.95 *(978-1-4179-5741-5(7))* Kessinger Publishing, LLC.

Birt, Catherine & MacGregor, Helen. Singing Phonics, 1 vol. 2008. (Singing Phonics Ser.). (ENG., Illus.). 80p. (J). pap. 32.95 incl. audio compact disk ***(978-1-4081-0472-9(5))*** HarperCollins Pubs. Ltd. GBR. Dist: Independent Pubs. Group.

Black, Joe. Boker Tov! Good Morning! Brown, Rick, illus. 2009. (Kar-Ben Favorites Ser.). (ENG.). 24p. (J). (gr. -1 — 1). 16.95 *(978-0-7613-3950-2(7))*; pap. 8.95 *(978-0-7613-3951-9(5))* Lerner Publishing Group. (Kar-Ben Publishing).

Blomgren, Jennifer. Why Do I Sing? Animal Songs of the Pacific Northwest. Gabriel, Andrea, illus. 2015. (ENG.). 20p. (J). (— 1). bds. 9.99 *(978-1-63217-020-0(5)*, Little Bigfoot) Sasquatch Bks.

Bower, Gary. Jingle in My Pocket. Bower, Jan, illus. 2009. 32p. 11.99 *(978-0-9704621-9-0(0))* Storybook Meadow Publishing.

Boynton, Sandra. Blue Moo: 17 Jukebox Hits from Way Back Never. 2007. (ENG., Illus.). 64p. (J). (gr. k — 1). 16.95 *(978-0-7611-4775-6(6)*, 14775) Workman Publishing Co., Inc.

—Frog Trouble: And Eleven Other Pretty Serious Songs. 2013. (ENG., Illus.). 70p. (gr. k-4). 16.95 *(978-0-7611-7176-8(2)*, 17176) Workman Publishing Co., Inc.

—Rhinoceros Tap. Boynton, Sandra, illus. 2004. (ENG., Illus.). 64p. (J). 16.95 *(978-0-7611-3323-0(2)*, 13323) Workman Publishing Co., Inc.

Brady, Janeen. I Have a Song for You Vol. 1: About People & Nature. rev. ed. (Illus.). (J). (gr. -1-4). pap., stu. ed. 9.95 incl. audio *(978-0-944803-01-1(6))* Brite Music, Inc.

Brannon, Tom, illus. I Love You Valentine Songs. 2012. (J). *(978-1-4508-3303-5(9))* Phoenix International Publications, Inc.

Brighter Minds, creator. My Little Pony Sing & Play: Follow-Th-Lights Paino Songbook. gif. ed. 2005. (Illus.). 24p. (J). (gr. -1-4). bds. 13.99 *(978-1-57791-192-0(X))* Brighter Minds Children's Publishing.

Brimhall, John. My Favorite Classics: Level One. 120p. (J). (gr. 3-6). 13.95 *(978-0-8494-2180-8(2)*, 0114) Hansen, Charles Educational Music & Bks., Inc.

Brooks, Amy. Home Songs for Little Darlings: Children. 2005. pap. 24.95 *(978-1-4179-9169-3(0))* Kessinger Publishing, LLC.

Brown, Greg. Down at the Sea Hotel: A Greg Brown Song. LeVert, Mireille, illus. 2007. (ENG.). 36p. (J). (gr. -1-2). 16.95 *(978-2-923163-34-5(6))* La Montagne Secrete CAN. Dist: Independent Pubs. Group.

Brown, Linda Kayse. Jerboth Weaves a Song. Noble, Penny, illus. 2007. (ENG.). 20p. (J). pap. 9.95 *(978-0-9769742-0-8(7))* Bay Villager, The.

Brown, Margaret Wise. A Celebration of the Seasons. 2015. (ENG., Illus.). 36p. (J). (gr. -1-k). 17.95 *(978-1-4549-0447-2(X))* Sterling Publishing Co., Inc.

Brumfield, Susan. Over the Garden Wall: Children's Songs & Games from England. 2010. (ENG.). 160p. pap. 34.99 incl. audio compact disk *(978-1-4234-7337-4(X)*, 142347337X) Leonard, Hal Corp.

Bryan, Ashley, illus. & selected by. All Night, All Day: A Child's First Book of African-American Spirituals. Bryan, Ashley, selected by. 2004. (ENG.). 48p. (J). (gr. -1-3). 7.99 *(978-0-689-86786-6(7)*, Atheneum Bks. for Young Readers) Simon & Schuster Children's Publishing.

Bucchino, John. Grateful: A Song of Giving Thanks. Hakkarainen, Anna-Liisa, illus. (Julie Andrews Collection). 40p. (J). (gr. -1-3). 2006. pap. 6.99 *(978-0-06-051635-2(6)*, Julie Andrews Collection) 2003. (ENG.). 17.99 *(978-0-06-051633-8(X))* HarperCollins Pubs.

Buchanan, Colin. Remember the Lord. 2007. (ENG., Illus.). 32p. (J). 14.99 *(978-1-84550-293-5(0)*, 45e54d0c-5b2e-4255-b3d8-509d58f4a1d7) Christian Focus Pubns. GBR. Dist: Bookmasters Distribution.

Burrows, Mark. The Ultimate Gettin' down with Mama Goose: Your Favorite Rhymes in One Big Musical Collection! 2012. (ENG.). 88p. pap. 24.99 incl. audio compact disk *(978-1-4584-1090-0(0)*, 1458410900) Shawnee Pr., Inc.

Busy Bees: Cassette. (Song Box Ser.). (gr. 1-2). 8.50 incl. audio *(978-0-7802-2269-4(5))* Wright Group/McGraw-Hill.

Cabrera, Jane. Here We Go Round the Mulberry Bush. Cabrera, Jane, illus. 2010. (ENG., Illus.). 32p. (J). (gr. -1-k). 16.95 *(978-0-8234-2288-3(7))* Holiday Hse., Inc.

—If You're Happy & You Know It! Cabrera, Jane, illus. 2010. (Illus.). 24p. (J). (gr. -1). bds. 7.95 *(978-0-8234-2227-2(5))* Holiday Hse., Inc.

—Row, Row, Row Your Boat. (ENG., Illus.). 32p. (J). (gr. -1-k). 2015. 6.99 *(978-0-8234-3302-5(1))* 2014. 16.95 *(978-0-8234-3050-5(2))* Holiday Hse., Inc.

—Ten in the Bed. Cabrera, Jane, illus. (ENG., Illus.). (J). (gr. -1). 2010. 24p. bds. 7.95 *(978-0-8234-2258-6(5))* 2006. 32p. 16.95 *(978-0-8234-2027-8(2))* Holiday Hse., Inc.

Cabrera, Mirna Y., et al, eds. A La Rueda, Rueda: Traditional Latin American Folk Songs for Children. Jones, Juan Luis, illus. 2010. (LAT & ENG.). 64p. pap. 29.99 incl. audio compact disk *(978-1-4234-7797-6(9)*, 1423477979) Leonard, Hal Corp.

Cameron, Andrea. The 10 Most Revolutionary Songs. 2008. 14.99 *(978-1-55448-493-5(6))* Scholastic Library Publishing.

La Cancion del Rey. (SPA.). (J). 3.99 *(978-0-7899-0482-9(9)*, 495652) Editorial Unilit.

Canciones de Mi Tierra Española: Songs of My Spanish Land: Canary Islands. 2005. 32p. *(978-0-9766568-0-7(9))* ERPublishing, LLC.

Cantos al maiz: un poeta hopi habla del Maiz: 6 Softcover Books. (Saludos Ser.: Vol. 2). (SPA.). (gr. 3-5). 31.00 *(978-0-7635-1813-4(1))* Rigby Education.

Canyon, Christopher, illus. John Denver's Take Me Home, Country Roads, 1 vol. 2005. (John Denver & Kids! Ser.). (ENG.). 36p. (J). (gr. -1-3). 8.95 *(978-1-58469-073-3(9))* Dawn Pubns.

Canyon, Christopher, illus. & adapted by. John Denver's Take Me Home, Country Roads, 1 vol. Canyon, Christopher, adapted by. 2005. (John Denver & Kids! Ser.). (ENG.). 36p. (J). (gr. -1-3). 19.95 *(978-1-58469-072-6(0))* Dawn Pubns.

Carpenter-Pezoldt, Wendy. Grandma's Unique Birthday Songs. 2012. 40p. pap. 24.95 *(978-1-4626-8945-3(0))* America Star Bks.

Carpenter, Stephen, illus. I've Been Burping in the Classroom. 2007. (Giggle Poetry Ser.). (ENG.). 32p. (J). (gr. 1-6). 9.95 *(978-1-4169-2946-8(0))* Meadowbrook Pr.

Cartwright, Amy, illus. Dreidel, Dreidel, Dreidel. 2010. (ENG.). 10p. (J). (gr. -1-k). 7.99 *(978-0-8431-9899-7(0)*, Price Stern Sloan) Penguin Young Readers Group.

Cartwright, Stephen, illus. Children's Songbook - Internet Referenced. 2004. (Songbooks Ser.). 32p. (J). pap. 6.95 *(978-0-7945-0710-7(7)*, Usborne) EDC Publishing.

Carus, Marianne. Higglety Pigglety Pop! Or There Must Be More to Life. (J). 19.95 incl. audio *(978-0-8126-0057-5(6))* Open Court Publishing Co.

—Sing, Clap, & Dance with Ladybug. (J). 19.95 incl. audio *(978-0-8126-0053-7(3))* Open Court Publishing Co.

—Sing Together with Ladybug. (J). 19.95 incl. audio *(978-0-8126-0081-0(9))* Open Court Publishing Co.

Caswell, Kelly, illus. Hickory Dickory Dock. 2015. (Classic Books with Holes Ser.). (ENG.). 16p. (J). pap. incl. audio compact disk *(978-1-84643-677-2(X))* Child's Play International Ltd.

Catrow, David. Monster Mash. 2012. (ENG.). 40p. (J). (gr. -1-3). 16.99 *(978-0-545-21479-7(3)*, Orchard Bks.) Scholastic, Inc.

Champagne, Melanie, illus. My Aunt Came Back. 2008. (First Steps in Music Ser.). (ENG.). 32p. (J). (gr. -1-k). 16.95 *(978-1-57999-680-2(9))* G I A Pubns., Inc.

Chapin, Tom & Forster, John. The Backwards Birthday Party. Groenink, Chuck, illus. 2015. (ENG.). 40p. (J). (gr. -1-3). 17.99 *(978-1-4424-6798-9(3)*, Atheneum Bks. for Young Readers) Simon & Schuster Children's Publishing.

Children's Press, contrib. by. The Ants Go Marching. 2009. (Rookie Preschool-NEW Ser.). (ENG.). 24p. (J). pap. 6.95 *(978-0-531-24581-1(0)*, Children's Pr.) Scholastic Library Publishing.

—Sing a Song of Seasons. 2009. (Rookie Preschool Ser.). (ENG.). 24p. (J). (gr. -1). lib. bdg. 23.00 *(978-0-531-24409-8(1)*, Children's Pr.) Scholastic Library Publishing.

Childrens Press Staff. The Ants Go Marching. 2009. (Rookie Preschool Ser.). (ENG.). 24p. (J). (gr. -1). 23.00 *(978-0-531-24406-7(7)*, Children's Pr.) Scholastic Library Publishing.

Clement, Debbie, et al. You're Wonderful. 2004. (Illus.). (J). *(978-0-9705987-4-5(2))* Rainbows Within Reach.

Clement, Gary, illus. Swimming, Swimming, 1 vol. 2015. (ENG.). 48p. (J). (gr. -1-2). 18.95 *(978-1-55498-449-7(1))* Groundwood Bks. CAN. Dist: Publishers Group West (PGW).

Clydesdale, David T., contrib. by. King of the Jungle: The God of Creation Is Lord of My Heart. 2007. (Illus.). 116p. pap. 6.95 *(978-5-557-71505-8(3)*, Word Music) Word Entertainment.

Cohan, George M. & Schwaeber, Barbie. Give My Regards to Broadway. Newsom, Carol, illus. 2008. (American Favorites Ser.). (ENG.). 32p. (J). (gr. -1-3). 8.95 *(978-1-59249-727-0(6))*; 14.95 *(978-1-59249-726-3(8))* Soundprints.

Colandro, Lucille. There Was an Old Lady Who Swallowed a Shell! Lee, Jared, illus. 2008. (ENG.). 32p. (J). (gr. -1-3). pap. 6.99 *(978-0-439-87380-2(0)*, Cartwheel Bks.) Scholastic, Inc.

Coleccion A, Level A. (De Canciones A Cuentos Ser.). (SPA.). (gr. k-18). 444.07 *(978-1-56334-873-0(X))* CENGAGE Learning.

Coleccion B, Level B. (De Canciones A Cuentos Ser.). (SPA.). (gr. 1-18). 434.56 *(978-1-56334-991-1(4))* CENGAGE Learning.

Coleccion C, Level C. (De Canciones A Cuentos Ser.). (SPA.). (gr. 2-18). 406.81 *(978-0-7362-0440-8(7))* CENGAGE Learning.

Connors, Stompin' Tom. Hockey Night Tonight, 1 vol. Jones, Brenda, illus. 2010. (ENG.). 24p. (J). (gr. -1-k). bds. 12.95 *(978-1-55109-733-6(8))* Nimbus Publishing, Ltd. CAN. Dist: Orca Bk. Pubs. USA.

Coots, J. Fred. Santa Claus Is Comin' to Town. Kellogg, Steven, illus. 2004. 40p. (J). (gr. -1-3). 16.89 *(978-0-06-623849-4(8))* HarperCollins Pubs.

Court, Shirley, et al. Singing Sherlock Vol. 2: The Complete Singing Resorce for Primary Schools. 2004. (ENG.). 88p. pap. 79.00 incl. audio compact disk *(978-0-85162-353-5(0)*, 0851623530) Leonard, Hal Corp.

Crabtree, Sally. Magic Train Ride. Esplugas, Sonia, illus. 2012. (ENG.). 32p. (J). (gr. -1-2). 9.99 *(978-1-84686-657-9(X))* Barefoot Bks., Inc.

Crews, Nina. The Neighborhood Sing-Along. Crews, Nina, illus. 2011. (ENG., Illus.). 64p. (J). (gr. -1-3). 17.99 *(978-0-06-185063-9(2)*, Greenwillow Bks.) HarperCollins Pubs.

Crisp, Dan, illus. Five Little Men in a Flying Saucer. 2005. (Classic Books with Holes Soft Cover Ser.). (ENG.). 16p. (J). pap. *(978-1-904550-30-3(4))* Child's Play International Ltd.

Dalmatian Press Staff. On Top of Spaghetti. 2008. (ENG.). 6p. (J). bds. 4.95 *(978-1-58117-720-6(8)*, Intervisual/Piggy Toes) Bendon, Inc.

Dalton, Pamela, illus. Under the Silver Moon: Lullabies, Night Songs, & Poems. 2017. (ENG.). 48p. (J). 17.99 *(978-1-4521-1673-0(3))* Chronicle Bks. LLC.

Dann, Penny. Eensy Weensy Spider. 2003. (ENG., Illus.). 16p. (J). bds. 4.99 *(978-0-7641-5662-5(4))* Barron's Educational Series, Inc.

Dansicker, Michael, ed. Kids' Musical Theatre Audition. 2007. (ENG.). 40p. pap. 19.99 incl. audio compact disk *(978-1-4234-2877-0(3)*, 1423428773) Leonard, Hal Corp.

—Kid's Theatre Audition Songs - Boys Edition. 2007. (ENG.). 40p. pap. 19.95 incl. audio compact disk *(978-1-4234-2880-0(3)*, 1423428803) Leonard, Hal Corp.

Dathini, Desiré. Memez: Songs to Make You Shout & Dance. 2012. 24p. pap. 15.99 *(978-1-4691-8597-2(0))* Xlibris Corp.

Davis, Jimmie. The More We Get Together. Church, Caroline Jayne, illus. 2011. (ENG.). 12p. (J). (— 1). bds. 6.99 *(978-0-545-28146-1(6)*, Cartwheel Bks.) Scholastic, Inc.

de La Cour, Gary, et al, illus. Wheels on the Bus. rev. ed. 2007. (ENG.). 24p. (J). (gr. -1-3). 4.99 *(978-1-59069-562-3(3))* Studio Mouse LLC.

Dean, James. The Wheels on the Bus. Dean, James, illus. 2013. (Pete the Cat Ser.). (ENG., Illus.). 32p. (J). (gr. -1-3). 9.99 *(978-0-06-219871-6(8))* HarperCollins Pubs.

Decker, William. Songs That Honor America. 2012. (InfoMax Readers Ser.). (ENG., Illus.). 24p. (J). (gr. 1-2). pap. 8.25 *(978-1-4488-9037-8(3)*, Rosen Classroom) Rosen Publishing Group, Inc., The.

Denver, John. Ancient Rhymes, a Dolphin Lullaby, 1 vol. Canyon, Christopher, illus. 2004. (Sharing Nature with Children Book Ser.). (ENG.). 36p. (J). (gr. -1-6). pap. 8.95 *(978-1-58469-065-8(8))* Dawn Pubns.

—For Baby (For Bobbie) Mason, Janeen, illus. 2009. (ENG.). 32p. (J). (gr. -1-6). 19.95 *(978-1-58469-120-4(4))*; pap. 8.95 *(978-1-58469-121-1(2))* Dawn Pubns.

—Grandma's Feather Bed, 1 vol. Canyon, Christopher, illus. 2007. (Sharing Nature with Children Book Ser.). (ENG.). 36p. (J). (gr. -1-18). pap. 8.95 *(978-1-58469-096-2(8))* Dawn Pubns.

—John Denver's Grandma's Feather Bed. Canyon, Christopher, illus. 2007. (Sharing Nature with Children Book Ser.). 36p. (J). (gr. -1-3). 19.95 incl. audio compact disk *(978-1-58469-095-5(X))* Dawn Pubns.

—Sunshine on My Shoulders, 1 vol. Canyon, Christopher, illus. 2004. (ENG.). 32p. 19.95 *(978-1-58469-048-1(8))* Dawn Pubns.

Deters, Kevin, illus. Care Bears Sing & Play: Follow-the-Lights Piano Songbook. 2006. (Care Bears Ser.). 24p. (J). (gr. -1-3). bds. 13.99 *(978-1-57791-300-9(0))* Brighter Minds Children's Publishing.

Diamond, Eileen. Everyday Songbook: 29 Bright & Happy Songs & Activities for Children. 2008. (Faber Edition Ser.). (ENG., Illus.). 63p. pap. 30.25 *(978-0-571-52887-5(2))* Faber & Faber, Ltd. GBR. Dist: Alfred Publishing Co., Inc.

Dickens, Charles & Sims, Lesley. A Christmas Carol. gif. ed. 2004. 64p. (Orig.). (J). (gr. 2-18). 8.95 *(978-0-7945-0584-4(8)*, Usborne) EDC Publishing.

Disney Storybook Artists Staff, contrib. by. Princess Songs. 2011. (Illus.). 12p. (J). bds. *(978-1-4508-2074-5(3)*, 1450820743) Publications International, Ltd.

Dobbins, Jan. A Farmer's Life for Me. Huliska-Beith, Laura, illus. 2013. (ENG.). 24p. (J). (gr. -1-2). 9.99 *(978-1-84686-791-0(6))*; (gr. k-3). 16.99 *(978-1-84686-790-3(8))* Barefoot Bks., Inc.

Dobbins, Jan & Bernal, Natalia. Vivamos la Granja! Huliska-Beith, Laura, illus. 2013. (SPA.). 24p. (J). (gr. -1-1). 9.99 *(978-1-84686-860-3(2))* Barefoot Bks., Inc.

Dobbins, Jan & Songs, Steve. Driving My Tractor. Sim, David, illus. 2012. (ENG.). 32p. (J). (gr. -1-2). 9.99 *(978-1-84686-664-7(2))* Barefoot Bks., Inc.

Donaldson, Julia. Songbook Treasury. Scheffler, Axel, illus. 2016. (ENG.). 96p. (J). (gr. -1-k). 24.99 *(978-1-4472-8271-6(X))* Pan Macmillan GBR. Dist: Independent Pubs. Group.

Dorenkamp, Michelle. The Bear Went over the Mountain. Dorenkamp, Michelle, illus. 2011. (Favorite Children's Songs Ser.). (ENG., Illus.). 16p. (J). (gr. -1-2). lib. bdg. 25.64 *(978-1-60954-295-5(9)*, 200099) Child's World, Inc., The.

Dorn, Susy. Cantemos en Español Song-Book: Spanish Learning Song-Book for Children. Carbajal, Diego, illus. 2006. (SPA.). (J). *(978-0-9764010-6-3(1))* Susy Dorn Productions, LLC.

—Sal y Pimienta Song-Book: Spanish Learning Song-Book for Children. Carbajal, Diego, illus. 2006. (SPA.). (J). *(978-0-9764010-7-0(X))* Susy Dorn Productions, LLC.

Downes, Belinda. Baby Days: A Quilt of Rhymes & Pictures. Downes, Belinda, illus. 2006. (ENG., Illus.). 32p. (J). (— 1). 14.99 *(978-0-7636-2786-7(0))* Candlewick Pr.

Duder, Tessa, ed. A Book of Pacific Lullabies. Hagin, Sally, illus. 2003. 32p. (J). pap. *(978-1-86950-393-2(7))* HarperCollins Pubs. New Zealand.

Duebber, Carol. Praise Power for Kids. 2005. pap. 40.99 *(978-1-4208-7465-5(9))* AuthorHouse.

Dylan, Bob. Blowin' in the Wind. Muth, Jon J., illus. 2011. (ENG.). 28p. (J). (gr. k-3). 17.95 *(978-1-4027-8002-8(8))* Sterling Publishing Co., Inc.

—If Dogs Run Free. Campbell, Scott, illus. 2013. (ENG.). 40p. (J). (gr. -1-3). 17.99 *(978-1-4516-4879-9(0))* Simon & Schuster Children's Publishing.

—Man Gave Names to All the Animals. Arnosky, Jim, illus. 2015. (ENG.). 32p. (J). (gr. -1). pap. 6.95 *(978-1-4549-1576-8(5))* Sterling Publishing Co., Inc.

Egielski, Richard. Itsy Bitsy Spider. Egielski, Richard, illus. 2012. (ENG., Illus.). 12p. (J). (gr. -1-1). 19.99 *(978-1-4169-9895-2(0)*, Atheneum Bks. for Young Readers) Simon & Schuster Children's Publishing.

Elementary Piggyback Song Book. 2003. (J). *(978-0-9745630-4-6(8))* F & S Music KS Publishing Co.

Elkins, Stephen. Little Dongs for Little Souls: Sharing God's Love. Davis, Lynne, illus. 2005. 32p. (J). 9.99 incl. audio compact disk *(978-0-8054-2673-1(6))* B&H Publishing Group.

S

—Little Songs for Little Souls: God Cares for Me. Davis, Lynne, illus. 2005. 32p. (J). 9.99 incl. audio compact disk *(978-0-8054-2675-5(2))* B&H Publishing Group.

—Little Songs for Little Souls: I Can Be Happy in Jesus. Davis, Lynne, illus. 2005. 32p. (J). 9.99 incl. audio compact disk *(978-0-8054-2676-2(0))* B&H Publishing Group.

—Little Songs for Little Souls: I Can Praise the Lord. Davis, Lynne, illus. 2005. 32p. (J). 9.99 incl. audio compact disk *(978-0-8054-2677-9(9))* B&H Publishing Group.

—LullaBible: A Musical Treasury for Mother & Baby. 2004. (Illus.). 224p. (J). 21.99 incl. audio compact disk *(978-0-8054-2390-7(7))* B&H Publishing Group.

—The LullaBible: A Musical Treasury for Mother & Baby. 2004. (Illus.). (J). 9.99 *(978-0-8054-2391-4(5))* B&H Publishing Group.

—The LullaBible: A Musical Treasury for Mother & Baby. Colton, Ellie, illus. 2004. (J). (gr. -1). 223p. 14.99 *(978-0-8054-2388-4(5))*; 224p. 19.99 incl. audio *(978-0-8054-2389-1(3))* B&H Publishing Group.

—Lullabies for Babies. Colton, Ellie, illus. 2005. (Jesus Loves Me Ser.). (ENG.). 32p. (J). (gr. -1-2). 6.99 *(978-1-4169-0843-2(9)*, Little Simon) Little Simon.

—My Sing-Along Bible: 50 Easy-Read Stories + 50 Fun Bible Songs. Reagan, Susan, illus. 2015. (ENG.). 96p. (J). 12.99 *(978-1-4964-0543-2(9))* Tyndale Hse. Pubs.

—100 Ways to Know God Loves Me, 100 Songs to Love Him Back, 1 vol. 2008. (ENG., Illus.). 208p. 19.99 *(978-1-4003-1157-6(8))* Nelson, Thomas Inc.

Elliott, Rebecca, et al, illus. Five Little Monkeys: And Other Counting Rhymes. 2004. (Mother Goose Ser.). (ENG.). 36p. (J). 15.95 *(978-1-59249-523-8(0)*, 1D026) Soundprints.

Ellwand, David, photos by. The Wheels on the Bus. 2016. (ENG., Illus.). 14p. (J). bds. 14.99 *(978-1-62686-652-2(X)*, Silver Dolphin Bks.) Readerlink Distribution Services, LLC.

Elwell, Ellen Banks. The Toddler's Songbook. Elwell, Ellen Banks & Turk, Caron, illus. 2009. 48p. (J). 14.99 incl. audio compact disk *(978-1-4335-0595-9(9))* Crossway.

Elwell, Ellen Banks & Turk, Caron, illus. The Toddler's Songbook. 2009. (J). *(978-1-4335-0597-3(5))* Crossway.

Emberley, Rebecca & Emberley, Ed. If You're a Monster & You Know It... Emberley, Ed, illus. 2010. (ENG., Illus.). 32p. (J). (gr. -1-k). 17.99 *(978-0-545-21829-0(2)*, Orchard Bks.) Scholastic, Inc.

Emerson, Roger. Cover Your Sneeze, Please! A Short Musical Play about Kids' Healthy Habits. 2013. (ENG.). 32p. pap. 39.99 *(978-1-4803-3393-2(X)*, 148033393X) Leonard, Hal Corp.

Engvick, William. Lullabies & Night Songs. Sendak, Maurice, illus. 2004. (Sendak Reissues Ser.). 80p. (J). 40.00 *(978-0-06-029733-6(6))* HarperCollins Pubs.

Essential Audition Songs for Kids. (J). 21.95 incl. audio compact disk *(978-1-85909-867-7(3)*, Warner Bros. Pubns.) Alfred Publishing Co., Inc.

Faber, Nancy, et al. BigTime Kids' Songs: Level 4. 2012. (ENG.). 40p. pap. 7.99 *(978-1-61677-629-9(3)*, 1616776293) Faber Piano Adventures(r).

Fallon, Kathy Reilly & Pellegrino, Frank. Heavenly Skies & Lullabies: Illustrated Songbook & CD. Kelly, Becky, illus. 2006. (J). (gr. -1-3). 29.95 incl. audio compact disk *(978-1-933626-06-2(2)*, Llumina Pr.) Aeon Publishing Inc.

Fatus, Sophie. Here We Go Round the Mulberry Bush. 2007. (J). *(978-1-84686-036-2(9))* Barefoot Bks., Inc.

Fatus, Sophie & Penner, Fred. Here We Go Round the Mulberry Bush. 2011. (ENG., Illus.). 24p. (J). (gr. -1-2). 9.99 *(978-1-84686-656-2(1))* Barefoot Bks., Inc.

—Here We Go Round the Mulberry Bush. Fatus, Sophie, illus. 2007. (ENG., Illus.). 24p. (J). (gr. -1-2). 16.99 *(978-1-84686-035-5(0))* Barefoot Bks., Inc.

Feierabend, John M. The Book of Finger Plays & Action Songs. 2003. (First Steps in Music Ser.). (ENG., Illus.). 88p. (J). (gr. -1-2). pap. 14.95 *(978-1-57999-212-5(9))* G I A Pubns., Inc.

—The Book of Song Dances. 2015. (First Steps in Music Ser.). (ENG., Illus.). 122p. (J). (gr. 2-4). pap. 17.95 *(978-1-62277-086-1(2))* G I A Pubns., Inc.

—The Book of Song Tales for Upper Grades. 2015. (First Steps in Music Ser.). (ENG., Illus.). 144p. (J). (gr. 4-7). pap. 18.95 *(978-1-62277-087-8(0))* G I A Pubns., Inc.

—The Book of Songs & Rhymes with Beat Motions: Let's Clap Our Hands Together. 2004. (First Steps in Music Ser.). (ENG., Illus.). 142p. (J). (gr. -1-2). pap. 18.95 *(978-1-57999-267-5(6)*, G-5879) G I A Pubns., Inc.

—The Other Day I Met a Bear. Miller, Julia Love, illus. 2014. (First Steps in Music Ser.). (ENG.). 32p. (J). (gr. -1-k). 16.95 *(978-1-62277-076-2(5))* G I A Pubns., Inc.

—Over in the Meadow. Napoletano, Marissa, illus. 2016. (First Steps in Music Ser.). (ENG.). 32p. (J). (gr. k-2). 16.95 (978-1-62277-178-3(8)) G I A Pubns., Inc.

Feldman, Jean. Birdies Lap Book. 2009. pap. 8.99 (978-1-60689-099-8(9)) Creative Teaching Pr., Inc.

—Color Train Lap Book. 2009. pap. 8.99 (978-1-60689-094-3(8)) Creative Teaching Pr., Inc.

—Dinosaur Boogie Lap Book. 2009. (J). pap. 8.99 (978-1-60689-097-4(2)) Creative Teaching Pr., Inc.

—Five Little Monkeys Lap Book. 2009. pap. 8.99 (978-1-60689-095-0(6)) Creative Teaching Pr., Inc.

—I Know an Old Lady Who Swallowed A One Lap Book. 2009. pap. 8.99 (978-1-60689-102-5(2)) Creative Teaching Pr., Inc.

—May There Always Be Sunshine Lap Book. 2009. pap. 8.99 (978-1-60689-101-8(4)) Creative Teaching Pr., Inc.

—My Hands on My Head Lap Book. 2009. pap. 8.99 (978-1-60689-105-6(7)) Creative Teaching Pr., Inc.

—My Mother Is A Baker Lap Book. 2009. pap. 8.99 (978-1-60689-104-9(9)) Creative Teaching Pr., Inc.

—Nursey Rhyme Rally Lap Book. 2009. pap. 8.99 (978-1-60689-100-1(6)) Creative Teaching Pr., Inc.

—Rules Rap Lap Book. 2009. pap. 8.99 (978-1-60689-098-1(0)) Creative Teaching Pr., Inc.

—Twinkle Friends Lap Book. 2009. pap. 8.99 (978-1-60689-103-2(0)) Creative Teaching Pr., Inc.

Feldman, Jean & Karapetkova, Holly. Math Songs. unabr. ed. 2010. (ENG.). 16p. (gr. -1-k). 12.99 (978-1-61741-588-3(X)) Rourke Educational Media.

Feldman, Jean R. & Karapetkova, Holly. Addition Pokey (Tune, Hokey Pokey) Lap Book. 2010. (ENG., Illus.). 12p. (gr. -1-k). 9.95 (978-1-61590-198-2(1)) Rourke Educational Media.

Fletcher, Terri. Scrumpy's Educational Kid Songs. 2003. (Illus.). 16p. (J). (gr. -1-1). pap. 12.95 incl. audio compact disk (978-0-9672279-1-7(7)) Scrumps Entertainment, Inc.

Flor Ada, Alma & Zubizarreta, Rosalma, trs. Uncle Nacho's Hat Reisberg, Mira, illus. 2013.Tr. of El Sombrero Del Tío Nacho. (ENG & SPA.). 32p. (J). (gr. 1-18). pap. 8.95 (978-0-89239-043-4(3), CBP0433S) Lee & Low Bks., Inc.

Flores, Carolyn Dee. Canta, Rana, Canta. Rosales-Yeomans, Natalia, tr. from SPA. Flores, Carolyn Dee, illus. 2013.Tr. of Sing, Froggie, Sing. (ENG & SPA., Illus.). 32p. (J). 16.95 (978-1-55885-764-3(8), Piñata Books) Arte Publico Pr.

Freeman-Hines, Laura. If You're Happy & You Know It. 2010. (Favorite Children's Songs Ser.). (ENG., Illus.). 16p. (J). (gr. -1-2). 25.64 (978-1-60253-531-2(0), 200113) Child's World, Inc., The.

Freeman, Laura. Here We Go Looby Loo. Freeman, Laura, illus. 2011. (Favorite Children's Songs Ser.). (ENG., Illus.). 16p. (J). (gr. -1-2). lib. bdg. 25.64 (978-1-60954-291-7(6), 200095) Child's World, Inc., The.

Friedman, Debbie. Lullaby. Bubar, Lorraine, illus. 2014. (ENG.). 32p. (J). 18.99 (978-1-58023-807-6(6), 9781580238076, Jewish Lights Publishing) LongHill Partners, Inc.

Friedman, Randee & Lander, Donna, eds. The New Rabbi Joe Black Songbook: Selected Songs from Aleph Bet Boogie, Everybody's Got A Little Music, Leave A Little Bit Undone, Sabbatical. 2004. (ENG & HEB.). 111p. (YA). per. 25.95 (978-1-890161-52-1(7)) Sounds Write Productions, Inc.

Fyke, Laurie & Sinclair, Kerrie. Songs. Stephen, Lib, illus. 2005. (ENG.). (J). pap. 17.50 incl. audio compact disk (978-1-84414-079-4(2), Jolly Learning) Jolly Learning, Ltd. GBR. Dist: American International Distribution Corp.

G-Mo. Shmu Songs. 2008. 81p. pap. 19.95 (978-1-60672-098-1(8)) America Star Bks.

Gallina, Jill, et al. Dino Soaring! A Prehistoric Musical Adventure for Cross-Curricular Fun in the Classroom. 2012. (ENG.). 64p. pap. 24.99 incl. audio compact disk (978-1-4584-2532-4(0), 1458425320) Shawnee Pr., Inc.

—Happy, the High-Tech Snowman: A One-Act Musical. 2012. (ENG.). 48p. pap. 19.99 (978-1-4584-2076-3(0), 1458420760); 56p. pap. 19.99 (978-1-4584-2075-6(2), 1458420752) Shawnee Pr., Inc.

—Kitty Cat Capers. 2012. (ENG.). 52p. pap. 49.99 incl. audio compact disk (978-1-4584-1976-7(2), 1458419762) Shawnee Pr., Inc.

—The Rhythm Band Strikes AGAIN! 2012. (ENG.). 64p. pap. 49.99 incl. audio compact disk (978-1-4584-1088-7(9), 1458410889) Shawnee Pr., Inc.

—Snoozy Snowflake: Singin' & Swingin' at the K-2 Chorale Series. 2011. (ENG.). 48p. pap. 49.99 (978-1-4234-9891-9(7), 1423498917) Shawnee Pr., Inc.

Gallina, Michael, et al. Sing & Play about the USA! 2007. (ENG.). 48p. (gr. k-4). pap. 29.95 (978-1-59235-184-8(0), 1592351840) Shawnee Pr., Inc.

Galvin, Laura Gates. Oh Where, Oh Where Has My Little Dog Gone? Villnave, Erica Pelton, illus. 2008. (ENG.). 32p. (J). (gr. -1-2). 17.95 (978-1-59249-859-8(0)) Soundprints.

García Lorca, Federico. Canciones (1921-1924) (SPA.). 96p. (J). 13.25 (978-84-206-6106-3(6), AZ6106) Alianza Editorial, S. A. ESP. Dist: Continental Bk. Co., Inc.

—Canciones y Poemas para Ninos. (Coleccion Poemas Juvenil). (SPA., Illus.). 96p. (J). 9.50 (978-84-335-8401-4(4), DD4014) Labor, Editorial S. A. ESP. Dist: Continental Bk. Co., Inc.

—Canciones y Poemas para Ninos. (SPA., Illus.). 64p. (J). (gr. 4-6). pap. 6.95 net. (978-1-887578-59-2(5), SQ0128) SpanPress, Inc.

Gardner, Louise, et al, illus. Old MacDonald & Other Sing-along Rhymes. 2006. (Mother Goose Ser.). (ENG.). 36p. (J). 12.95 (978-1-59249-525-2(7), 1D028) Soundprints.

The Ghosts Go Haunting. 2014. (ENG., Illus.). 32p. (J). (gr. -1-3). 16.99 (978-0-8075-2852-5(8)) Whitman, Albert & Co.

Gillespie, Haven & Coots, J. Fred. Santa Claus Is Comin' to Town. Kellogg, Steven, tr. Kellogg, Steven, illus. 2004. (ENG.). 40p. (J). (gr. -1-3). 15.99 (978-0-688-14938-3(3)) HarperCollins Pubs.

Gitarren Songs. 2004. (YA). cd-rom (978-1-891155-20-8(2)) EMedia Corp.

Gobo Books Staff. Sleepytime Songs. 2007. (Baby Sing & Play Ser.). 8p. (J). (gr. -1). bds. 12.95 incl. audio compact disk (978-1-932915-42-6(7)) Sandvik Innovations, LLC.

God Is with You in Sleep. Date not set. 44p. (J). (gr. -1-5). 16.99 incl. audio compact disk (978-0-9702219-0-2(8)) Bowden Music Co.

Goebel, Jenny & dePaola, Tomie. Foreman Frankie Is Handy. Mack, Steve, illus. 2015. (ENG.). 32p. (J). (gr. -1-k). bds. 3.99 (978-0-448-48099-2(9), Grosset & Dunlap) Penguin Young Readers Group.

Golio, Gary. Strange Fruit: Billie Holiday & the Power of a Protest Song. Riley-Webb, Charlotte, illus. 2017. (ENG.). 40p. (J). (gr. 3-6). 19.99 (978-1-4677-5123-0(5), Millbrook Pr.) Lerner Publishing Group.

Goodman, Steve. The Train They Call the City of New Orleans. McCurdy, Michael, illus. pap. incl. audio compact disk (978-1-59112-905-9(2)); pap. 18.95 incl. audio compact disk (978-1-59112-903-5(6)); pap. 16.95 incl. audio (978-1-59112-899-1(4)); pap. incl. audio (978-1-59112-901-1(X)) Live Oak Media.

Gott, Barry, illus. Head, Shoulders, Knees, & Toes. 2006. (J). (978-1-58987-056-7(5)) Kindermusik International.

Graham, Pat, et al. A Children's Songbook Companion. Grover, Nina, illus. 2005. per. (978-0-88290-795-6(6), Horizon Pubs.) Cedar Fort, Inc./CFI Distribution.

Graves, Harmon. I'm Only Three, & Look at All the Things That I Can Do! Ritchie, Scot, illus. 2013. 30p. pap. 13.95 (978-1-4349-3729-2(1)) Dorrance Publishing Co., Inc.

Greene, Carol. The 13 Days of Halloween. Raglin, Tim, illus. 2009. (ENG.). 32p. (J). (gr. k-3). 14.99 (978-1-4022-3096-7(6), 9781402230967, Sourcebooks Jabberwocky) Sourcebooks, Inc.

Greenfield, Howard. Dinosaur Pet. Bowers, Tim, illus. 2012. (ENG.). 28p. (J). (gr. -1-3). 17.95 (978-1-936140-36-7(5)) Charlesbridge Publishing, Inc.

Group/McGraw-Hill, Wright. The Song Box Social Studies Songs: 1 Each of 4 Big Books. (Song Box Ser.). (gr. 1-2). 124.95 (978-0-322-03797-7(2)) Wright Group/McGraw-Hill.

—The Song Box Social Studies Songs: 1 Each of 4 Cassettes. (Song Box Ser.). (gr. 1-2). 33.95 (978-0-322-03795-3(6)) Wright Group/McGraw-Hill.

—The Song Box Social Studies Songs: 1 Each of 4 Student Books. (Song Box Ser.). (gr. 1-2). 18.95 (978-0-322-03961-2(4)) Wright Group/McGraw-Hill.

—The Song Box Social Studies Songs: 6 Each of 4 Student Books. (Song Box Ser.). (gr. 1-2). 116.50 (978-0-322-03796-0(4)) Wright Group/McGraw-Hill.

Gullible, Ru. The Phantom. 2008. 24p. pap. 14.50 (978-1-4389-0229-6(8)) AuthorHouse.

Guthrie, Arlo. Me & My Goose. Garren, Kathy, illus. 2014. (ENG.). (J). 15.00 (978-0-9915370-6-8(8)) Rising Son International, Ltd.

Guthrie, Woody. Enviarme a Ti, Level 2. Flor Ada, Alma, tr. Rosenberry, Vera, illus. 2003. (Dejame Leer Ser.). (SPA.). 8p. (J). (gr. -1-1). 6.50 (978-0-673-36301-5(5), Good Year Bks.) Celebration Pr.

—Riding in My Car. 2012. (ENG., Illus.). 16p. (J). (gr. k-17). 17.99 (978-0-316-05216-0(7)) Little, Brown Bks. for Young Readers.

Haas, Peter Michael. Geschichten Für Akkordeon - 25 Lustige und Wehmütige Kinderstücke. 2009.Tr. of Squeeze Box Fairy Tales - 25 Amusing & Wistful Children's Songs. (ENG.). 48p. 16.99 (978-3-89922-124-4(9)) AMA Verlag GmbH DEU. Dist: Mel Bay Pubns., Inc.

Hal Leonard Corp. Staff. Children's Songs: Budget Books, 1 vol. 2009. (ENG.). 304p. pap. 12.99 (978-1-4234-8033-4(3), 1423480333) Leonard, Hal Corp.

Hal Leonard Corp. Staff, creator. Disney's My First Songbook: A Treasury of Favorite Songs to Sing & Play. 2003. (Easy Piano Songbook Ser.). (ENG., Illus.). 88p. pap. 14.95 (978-0-634-04792-3(2), 0634047922) Leonard, Hal Corp.

—Disney's My First Songbook - Volume 4. 2011. (ENG.). 96p. pap. 14.99 (978-1-4584-0698-9(9), 1458406989) Leonard, Hal Corp.

—The Fantastic Big Book of Children's Songs. 2004. (ENG., Illus.). 240p. pap. 17.95 (978-0-634-06820-1(2), 0634068202) Leonard, Hal Corp.

—Great Songs for Children. 2009. (ENG.). 268p. pap. 19.99 (978-1-60378-129-9(3), 1603781293) Cherry Lane Music Co.

—The Kids' Collection: Recorder Fun! 3-Book Bonus Pack. 2006. (ENG., Illus.). 96p. (J). pap. 12.95 (978-1-4234-1843-6(3), 1423418433) Leonard, Hal Corp.

—Kids' Fun Songs: Learn & Play Recorder Pack. 2012. (ENG.). (J). pap. 19.99 (978-1-4768-1507-7(0), 1476815070) Leonard, Hal Corp.

—Songs Children Can Sing! Pro Vocal Boys' & Girls' Edition Volume 1. 2012. (ENG.). 40p. pap. 14.99 incl. audio compact disk (978-1-4584-2367-2(0), 1458423670) Leonard, Hal Corp.

—Songs for Kids - Audition Songs: Piano/Vocal/Guitar Arrangements with CD Backing Tracks. 2016. (ENG.). 48p. pap. 14.99 incl. audio compact disk (978-1-4234-8955-9(1), 1423489551) Music Sales Corp.

—Teaching Little Fingers to Play Broadway Songs. 2012. (ENG.). 32p. pap. 12.99 incl. audio compact disk (978-1-4584-1766-4(2), 1458417662); pap. 7.99 (978-1-4584-1765-7(4), 1458417654) Willis Music Co.

—Worship Together Favorites for Kids. 2007. (ENG.). 72p. pap. 12.95 (978-1-4234-2541-0(3), 1423425413) Leonard, Hal Corp.

—15 Recital Songs in English. 2008. (ENG.). 48p. pap. 18.99 (978-1-4234-4113-7(3), 1423441133) Boosey & Hawkes, Inc.

Hammerstein. In My Own Little Corner. 2007. (ENG., Illus.). 32p. (J). (gr. -1-3). 12.99 (978-1-4169-6140-6(2), Simon & Schuster/Paula Wiseman Bks.) Simon & Schuster/Paula Wiseman Bks.

Hanby, Benjamin Russell. Up on the Housetop. Snyder, Robert, illus. 2007. (ENG.). 26p. (J). (gr. -1-3). bds. 12.99 (978-0-8249-6714-7(3), Ideal Pubns.) Worthy Publishing.

Harburg, E. Y. Over the Rainbow. Noonan, Julia, illus. Date not set. 32p. (J). 5.99 (978-0-06-443677-9(2)) HarperCollins Pubs.

Harburg, E. Y. & Arlen, Harold. Over the Rainbow. Puybaret, Eric, illus. 2014. (ENG.). 22p. (J). (gr. k-4). bds. 7.95 (978-1-62354-044-9(5)) Charlesbridge Publishing, Inc.

—Over the Rainbow. Noonan, Julia, illus. 2004. 24p. (J). (gr. 4-8). reprint ed. 16.00 (978-0-7567-7340-3(7)) DIANE Publishing Co.

Harnick, Sheldon. Sunrise, Sunset. Schoenherr, Ian, illus. 2005. 32p. (J). (gr. -1-1). lib. bdg. 16.89 (978-0-06-051527-0(9)) HarperCollins Pubs.

Harris, Charisse N. Mama Please. 2009. (J). 6.95 (978-1-61584-843-0(6)) Independent Pub.

Harter, Debbie. The Animal Boogie. Harter, Debbie, illus. (Illus.). 32p. pap. 6.99 (978-1-84148-996-4(4)) Barefoot Bks., Inc.

—The Animal Boogie. 2005. (ENG., Illus.). 32p. (J). (gr. -1-2). 9.99 (978-1-905236-22-0(0)) Barefoot Bks., Inc.

—The Animal Boogie. Harter, Debbie, illus. 2005. (ENG., Illus.). 32p. (J). (gr. -1-2). 6.99 (978-1-905236-60-2(3)) Barefoot Bks., Inc.

Hayes, Larry E. My Name Starts with A (Library Version) 2004. (My Name Starts With Ser.). (Illus.). 32p. (J). lib. bdg. 12.95 (978-0-9725292-7-3(6)) Inspire Pubns.

Henneberg, Susan. What Is a Song?, 1 vol. 2015. (ENG., Illus.). 32p. (J). 23.45 (978-1-62275-664-3(9), Britannica Educational Publishing) Rosen Publishing Group, Inc., The.

Heras, Theo. What Will We Do with the Baby-O? Herbert, Jennifer, illus. 2004. (ENG.). 32p. (J). (gr. k-k). 12.95 (978-0-88776-689-3(7), Tundra Bks.) Tundra Bks. CAN. Dist: Penguin Random Hse. LLC.

Heyge, Lorna Lutz. Music Garden for Babies from Birth to 18 Months: Songbook 1. 2003. (ENG.). 40p. pap. 20.95 incl. audio compact disk (978-3-937315-00-3(4), 3937315004) Schott Music Corp.

Highlights, creator. Old MacDonald Had a Farm. 2016. (Highlights(tm) Song & Puzzle Bks.). (ENG.). 48p. (J). (gr. -1-k). pap. 4.99 (978-1-62979-609-3(3), Highlights) Boyds Mills Pr.

Hilderbrand, Karen Mitzo & Thompson, Kim Mitzo. Essential Preschool Skills. 2008. (J). 44.99 (978-1-59922-321-6(X)) Findaway World, LLC.

Hills, Tad & Savage, Lauren. Duck & Goose, Let's Dance! Hills, Tad, illus. 2016. (Duck & Goose Ser.). (ENG., Illus.). 26p. (J). (gr. -1-2). bds. 8.99 (978-0-385-37245-9(0), Schwartz & Wade Bks.) Random Hse. Children's Bks.

Hinkler Studios Staff., ed. Jack & the Beanstalk. 2011. (Fairytale Pop-Ups Ser.). 12p. (J). 12.99 (978-1-74185-087-1(8)) Hinkler Bks. Pty. Ltd. AUS. Dist: Ideals Pubns.

His Fleece Was White As Snow: Songbook. 2003. 66p. (YA). 5.00 (978-1-58302-243-6(0)) One Way St., Inc.

Hoberman, Mary Ann. The Eensy-Weensy Spider. Westcott, Nadine Bernard, illus. 2004. (ENG.). 32p. (J). (gr. -1-1). pap. 7.99 (978-0-316-73412-7(8)) Little, Brown Bks. for Young Readers.

Hodges, Lynn & Buchanan, Sue. I Love You This Much, 1 vol. Bendall-Brunello, John, illus. 2010. (ENG.). 36p. (J). pap. 6.99 (978-0-310-72265-6(9)) Zonderkidz.

Hodges, Lynn, et al. I Love You This Much, 1 vol. Bendall-Brunello, John, illus. 2005. (Songs of Gods Love Ser.). (ENG.). 16p. (J). (gr. -1). bds. 6.99 (978-0-310-70961-9(X)) Zonderkidz.

Holiday, Billie. God Bless the Child. Pinkney, Jerry, illus. 2004. 32p. (J). lib. bdg. 17.89 (978-0-06-029487-8(6), Amistad) HarperCollins Pubs.

Holiday, Billie & Herzog, Arthur, Jr. God Bless the Child. Pinkney, Jerry, illus. 2008. (ENG.). 40p. (J). (gr. -1-3). per. 7.99 (978-0-06-443646-5(2)) HarperCollins Pubs.

Hollingworth, Denise, et al. Jammin' in the Jungle! 2013. (ENG.). 64p. pap. 39.99 incl. audio compact disk (978-1-4584-1749-7(2), 1458417492) Shawnee Pr., Inc.

Hook, Dianne J., creator. All about Me: Creative Scrapbooking Templates & Clip Art for Classroom & Home. 2005. (Illus.). 64p. pap. 22.99 incl. cd-rom (978-1-59441-191-5(3), DJ-604010, DJ Inkers) Carson-Dellosa Publishing, LLC.

Hop! Hop! Hop! (J). 19.95 incl. audio (978-0-8126-0088-9(6)) Open Court Publishing Co.

Hort, Lenny. Seals on the Bus. Karas, G. Brian & Karas, G., illus. 2008. (ENG.). 32p. (J). (gr. -1-k). pap. 26.99 (978-0-8050-8678-2(1), 9780805086782, Holt, Henry & Co. Bks. For Young Readers) Holt, Henry & Co.

—The Seals on the Bus. Karas, G. Brian, illus. rev. ed. 2003. (ENG.). 32p. (J). (gr. -1-k). pap. 7.99 (978-0-8050-7263-1(2), 9780805072631) Square Fish.

Houston, Scott. Play Piano in a Flash Fake Book for Kids! A song book for kids in lead sheet Format. 1. l.t. ed. 2006. 88p. (J). spiral bd. 24.95 (978-0-9712861-2-2(4), 75) Houston Enterprises.

Houston, Scott & Sowash, Bradley. Play Piano in a Flash! the Next Step. l.t. ed. 2006. 100p. spiral bd. 24.95 (978-0-9712861-3-9(2)) Houston Enterprises.

How Much Wood Could a Woodchuck Chuck? unabr. ed. 2007. (J). (gr. -1-k). 17.00 incl. audio compact disk (978-0-9705773-4-4(6)) Kids At Our House, Inc., The.

Howe, Maggy G. & Bagby, Susan. Magical Future Song. 2012. 28p. pap. 19.99 (978-1-4772-6833-9(2)) AuthorHouse.

Hull, Bunny. Happy, Happy Kwanzaa: Kwanzaa for the World. Saint-James, Synthia, illus. 2003. 24p. (J). (gr. k-5). pap. 16.95 incl. audio compact disk (978-0-9721478-1-1(0), KCC/HHKCD810, Kid's Creative Classics) BrassHeart Music.

Hyams, Tor, et al. A World of Happiness: Book & CD. 2008. (ENG.). 116p. pap. 24.95 (978-0-7390-5446-8(5)) Alfred Publishing Co., Inc.

If You're Happy: Individual Title Six-Packs. (Literatura 2000 Ser.). (gr. 1-2). 28.00 (978-0-7635-0137-2(9)) Rigby Education.

In My Daughter's Eyes. 2006. (Illus.). 20p. (J). 9.99 incl. audio compact disk (978-1-57791-218-7(7)) Brighter Minds Children's Publishing.

Ingram, Scott. The Writing of The Star-Spangled Banner. 2004. (Landmark Events in American History Ser.). (Illus.). 48p. (gr. 5-12). pap. 14.05 (978-0-8368-5418-3(7), Gareth Stevens Secondary Library) Stevens, Gareth Publishing LLLP.

Itsy Bitsy Spider. 2004. (J). per. (978-1-57657-427-0(X)) Paradise Pr., Inc.

I've Been Working on the Railroad. (Song Box Ser.). (gr. 1-2). 31.50 (978-0-7802-0936-7(2)); 8.50 incl. audio (978-0-7802-0938-1(9)) Wright Group/McGraw-Hill.

I've Been Working on the Railroad: 1 Big Book, 6 Each of 1 Student Book, & 1 Cassette. (Song Box Ser.). (gr. 1-2). 68.95 (978-0-7802-0939-8(7)) Wright Group/McGraw-Hill.

I've Been Working on the Railroad: 6 Each of 1 Student Book, 6 vols. (Song Box Ser.). (gr. 1-2). 29.50 (978-0-7802-0937-4(0)) Wright Group/McGraw-Hill.

J, Harris. Salam Alaikum: A Message of Peace. Jenkins, Ward, illus. 2017. (ENG.). 40p. (J). (gr. -1-3). 17.99 (978-1-4814-8938-6(0), Salaam Reads) Simon & Schuster Bks. For Young Readers.

Jacobs, Paul DuBois & Swender, Jennifer. Children's Songbag. 2005. (ENG., Illus.). 112p. (gr. 3-4). spiral bd. 12.99 (978-1-58685-356-3(2)) Gibbs Smith, Publisher.

Jacobson, John. ImagiBOP: Creative Movement & Songs for Grades K-2. 2011. (ENG.). 48p. pap. 29.99 (978-1-61774-284-2(8), 1617742848) Leonard, Hal Corp.

Jacobson, John, et al. Say Hello Wherever You Go: Music Strategies, Songs & Activities for Grades K-2. 2010. (ENG.). 40p. pap. 19.99 incl. audio compact disk (978-1-4234-8824-8(5), 1423488245) Leonard, Hal Corp.

Jensema, Marissa, illus. ASL Songs for Kids - 1: With Songs in American Sign Language. 2003. (J). cd-rom 29.95 (978-0-9752933-1-7(1)) Institute for Disabilities Research & Training, Inc.

Jesus Loves Me. (Illus.). 16p. (J). pap. 1.50 (978-0-87162-970-8(4), E4983) Warner Pr., Inc.

Jewel. Sweet Dreams. Bates, Amy June, illus. 2013. (ENG.). 32p. (J). (gr. -1-k). 17.99 (978-1-4424-8931-8(6), Simon & Schuster/Paula Wiseman Bks.) Simon & Schuster/Paula Wiseman Bks.

Joachimowski, Paula L. Swamp Band Lullaby. McGrath, Ryan, illus. 2008. 32p. 17.99 (978-1-59879-433-5(7)) Lifevest Publishing, Inc.

Jordan, Sara. Fonetica Funky y Algo Mas, 2 vols., Kit. 2007. (SPA.). 48p. (J). (gr. k-4). 17.95 (978-1-55386-080-8(2), 1553860802) Jordan, Sara Publishing.

Joseph M. Martin. The Light Before Christmas. 2013. (ENG.). 72p. pap. 6.95 (978-1-4803-1494-8(3), 1480314943) Shawnee Pr., Inc.

Joshua, Aaron, illus. There Was a Man & He Was Mad. 2008. (First Steps in Music Ser.). (ENG.). 24p. (J). (gr. -1-k). 16.95 (978-1-57999-681-9(7)) G I A Pubns., Inc.

Kaiser, Cecily. On the First Night of Chanukah. Schatell, Brian, illus. 2007. (ENG.). 24p. (J). (gr. -1-3). pap. 3.99 (978-0-439-75802-4(5), Cartwheel Bks.) Scholastic, Inc.

Kanzler, John. Rock-a -Bye Baby. Tiger Tales Staff, ed. Kanzler, John, illus. 2011. (ENG., Illus.). 24p. (J). (gr. -1-k). bds. 8.95 (978-1-58925-853-2(3)) Tiger Tales.

Kanzler, John, tr. & illus. The Big Rock Candy Mountain. Kanzler, John, illus. 2004. 24p. (J). 15.95 (978-1-59336-062-7(2)); pap. (978-1-59336-063-4(0)) Mondo Publishing.

Katz, Alan. Are You Quite Polite? Silly Dilly Manners Songs. Catrow, David, illus. 2006. (ENG.). 32p. (J). (gr. -1-3). 17.99 (978-0-689-86970-9(3), McElderry, Margaret K. Bks.) McElderry, Margaret K. Bks.

—Going, Going, Gone! And Other Silly Dilly Sports Songs. Catrow, David, illus. 2009. (ENG.). 32p. (J). (gr. -1-3). 16.99 (978-1-4169-0696-4(7), McElderry, Margaret K. Bks.) McElderry, Margaret K. Bks.

—I'm Still Here in the Bathtub: Brand New Silly Dilly Songs. Catrow, David, illus. 2003. (ENG.). 32p. (J). (gr. -1-3). 17.99 (978-0-689-84551-2(0), McElderry, Margaret K. Bks.) McElderry, Margaret K. Bks.

—Mosquitoes Are Ruining My Summer! And Other Silly Dilly Camp Songs. Catrow, David, illus. 2011. (ENG.). 32p. (J). (gr. -1-3). 16.99 (978-1-4169-5568-9(2), McElderry, Margaret K. Bks.) McElderry, Margaret K. Bks.

—On Top of the Potty: And Other Get-up-and-Go Songs. Catrow, David, illus. 2008. (ENG.). 32p. (J). (gr. -1-3). 17.99 (978-0-689-86215-1(6), McElderry, Margaret K. Bks.) McElderry, Margaret K. Bks.

—Smelly Locker: Silly Dilly School Songs. Catrow, David, illus. (ENG.). 32p. (J). (gr. -1-3). 2010. 7.99 (978-1-4424-0251-5(2)) 2008. 16.99 (978-1-4169-0695-7(9)) McElderry, Margaret K. Bks. (McElderry, Margaret K. Bks.).

—Too Much Kissing! And Other Silly Dilly Songs about Parents. Catrow, David, illus. 2009. (ENG.). 32p. (J). (gr. -1-2). 16.99 (978-1-4169-4199-6(1), McElderry, Margaret K. Bks.) McElderry, Margaret K. Bks.

Katz, Karen. The Babies on the Bus. Katz, Karen, illus. 2013. (ENG., Illus.). 28p. (J). (gr. -1-k). bds. 7.99 (978-0-8050-9779-5(1), 9780805097795, Holt, Henry & Co. Bks. For Young Readers) Holt, Henry & Co.

Kemp, Moira. I'm a Little Teapot. Kemp, Moira, illus. 2009. (Favorite Children's Songs Ser.). (ENG., Illus.). 16p. (J). (gr. -1-2). 25.64 (978-1-60253-192-5(7), 200103) Child's World, Inc., The.

—Knock at the Door. Kemp, Moira, illus. 2009. (Favorite Children's Songs Ser.). (ENG., Illus.). 16p. (J). (gr. -1-2). 25.64 (978-1-60253-193-2(5), 200104) Child's World, Inc., The.

Kempf, Joe & Pescarino, Cathy. Faith-Filled Lullabies with Big Al & Annie. Sharp, Chris, illus. 2012. 32p. (J). (978-1-61278-689-6(8)) Our Sunday Visitor, Publishing Div.

Kim, Daeshin. A Horse with Wings: And Other Songs for Children Sung by Characters from Shakespeare with CD. 2012. 25.95 (978-0-7414-8050-7(6)) Infinity Publishing.

Kraft, Tamera & Colkmire, Lance. Kid Konnection: Kids Entering the Presence of God, Vol. 5. 2003. (Illus.). 112p. ring bd. 69.99 (978-0-87148-383-6(1)) Pathway Pr.

Krauss, Gene & adapted by. Awesome Performance Music & Tracks. Krauss, Gene, adapted by. 2nd ed. 2005. (YA). spiral bd. 20.00 (978-0-9785992-0-1(9)) GuitarVoyager Inc.

Kubler, Annie, illus. If You're Happy & You Know It... /Si Te Sientes Bien Contento... 2009. (Baby Board Bks.). (SPA & ENG.). 12p. (J). bds. (978-1-84643-310-8(X)) Child's Play International Ltd.

—Ten Little Fingers/Tengo Diez Deditos. 2009. (Baby Board Bks.). (SPA & ENG.). 12p. (J). bds. (978-1-84643-312-2(6)) Child's Play International Ltd.

Kurtz, John. What Belongs? Baby Looney Tunes. Shively, Julie, illus. 2004. 12p. bds. 6.95 (978-0-8249-6560-0(4), Ideal Pubns.) Worthy Publishing.

Kwasi: a Storysong: Six-Pack. (Greetings Ser.: Vol. 2). 24p. (gr. 2-3). 31.00 (978-0-7635-9415-2(6)) Rigby Education.

Laing, Robin. The Whisky Muse: Collected & Introduced by Robin Laing. Dewar, Bob, illus. 2nd ed. 2003. (ENG.). 224p. per. 19.95 (978-1-84282-041-4(9)) Luath Pr. Ltd. GBR. Dist: Midpoint Trade Bks., Inc.

Lait, Alain le. It's So Good, 1 bk & 1 CD. 2003. (Illus.). 28p. (J). audio compact disk 15.95 (978-0-9747122-0-8(5), ENG100) Yadeeda.com.

Lakeshore Learning Materials Staff, contrib. by. Big Book of Learning Songs. 2007. (J). 19.95 *(978-1-59746-016-3(8))* Lakeshore Learning Materials.

Lamb, Amy And Chris. The Our World Series: Friends around our Home. 2010. (Illus.). 32p. pap. 14.49 *(978-1-4490-8098-3(7))* AuthorHouse.

Langham, Tony. Creepy Crawly Calypso. Harter, Debbie, illus. 2007. (ENG.). 32p. (J). pap. 6.99 *(978-1-84686-133-8(0))* Barefoot Bks., Inc.

Langham, Tony & Harter, Debbie. Mira Quien Toca Calipso! Harter, Debbie, illus. 2009. (SPA., Illus.). 32p. (J). (gr. -1-2). pap. 7.99 *(978-1-84686-281-6(7))* Barefoot Bks., Inc.

Lansky, Bruce, ed. I've Been Burping in the Classroom: And Other Silly Sing-along Songs. Carpenter, Stephen, illus. 2007. 32p. (J). *(978-0-88166-521-5(5))* Meadowbrook Pr.

Larsen, Donna R. In My Own Backyard. Reilly, Michelle, illus. 2011. 30p. (J). *(978-0-615-52915-8(1))* DeuxRay Productions.

Law, Jessica. A Hole in the Bottom of the Sea. McDonald, Jill, illus. 2013. (ENG.). 24p. (J). (gr. -1-2). 9.99 *(978-1-84686-862-7(9))*; (gr. k-3). 16.99 *(978-1-84686-861-0(0))* Barefoot Bks., Inc.

Le Lait, Alain. Parapluie: Fabulous French Songs for Children. Le Lait, Alain, . 2006. (FRE.). (J). pap. 15.95 incl. audio compact disk *(978-0-9747122-5-3(6))* Yadeeda.com.

LeBuis, Peter. Character Building Songs, 2 vols., Kit. 2009. (ENG.). 48p. (J). 17.95 *(978-1-55386-104-1(3)*, 1553861043) Jordan, Sara Publishing.

Lennon, John. Imagine. Jullien, Jean, illus. 2017. (ENG.). 32p. (J). (gr. -1-3). 18.99 ***(978-1-328-80865-3(3)***, Clarion Bks.) Houghton Mifflin Harcourt Trade & Reference Pubs.

Lettice, Jenna. The 12 Days of Halloween. Madden, Colleen M., illus. 2017. (Pictureback(R) Ser.). (ENG.). 24p. (J). (gr. -1-2). pap. 4.99 *(978-0-399-55731-6(8)*, Random Hse. Bks. for Young Readers) Random Hse. Children's Bks.

—The 12 Days of Kindergarten. Madden, Colleen M., illus. 2017. (Pictureback(R) Ser.). (ENG.). 24p. (J). (gr. -1-2). pap. 4.99 *(978-0-399-55733-0(4)*, Random Hse. Bks. for Young Readers) Random Hse. Children's Bks.

Lichfield, Wilma B. Pocketful of Melodies. 2007. (J). per. 17.95 *(978-1-60002-236-4(7))* Mountain Valley Publishing, LLC.

Light, John. Are These Rhymes Nonsense? 2005. (Illus.). 60p. 12.00 *(978-0-907759-71-3(8))* KT Pubns. GBR. Dist: Photon Pr.

Linn, Jennifer. The Hungry Spider. 2003. 4p. pap. 2.50 *(978-0-634-05819-6(3))* Leonard, Hal Corp.

Lithgow, John. I Got Two Dogs. Neubecker, Robert, illus. 2008. (ENG.). 32p. (J). (gr. -1-1). 18.99 *(978-1-4169-5881-9(9)*, Simon & Schuster Bks. For Young Readers) Simon & Schuster Bks. For Young Readers.

—Never Play Music Right Next to the Zoo. Hernandez, Leeza, illus. 2013. (ENG.). 40p. (J). (gr. -1-1). 18.99 *(978-1-4424-6743-9(6)*, Simon & Schuster Bks. For Young Readers) Simon & Schuster Bks. For Young Readers.

Little Song Book. (De Canciones A Cuentos Ser.). (SPA.). (gr. 1-18). 8.91 *(978-1-56334-892-1(6))* CENGAGE Learning.

Litton, Jonathan. Big Fish Little Fish. Galloway, Fhiona, illus. 2016. (My Little World Ser.). (ENG.). 16p. (J). (gr. -1-k). bds. 7.99 *(978-1-58925-215-8(2))* Tiger Tales.

Loeb, Lisa. Lisa Loeb's Silly Sing-Along: The Disappointing Pancake & Other Zany Songs. O'Rourke, Ryan, illus. 2011. (ENG.). 24p. (J). (gr. -1-2). 14.95 *(978-1-4027-6915-3(6))* Sterling Publishing Co., Inc.

Loeb, Lisa & O'Rourke, Ryan. Lisa Loeb's Songs for Movin' & Shakin': the Air Band Song & Other Toe-Tapping Tunes. 2013. (ENG., Illus.). 24p. (J). (gr. -1-2). 14.95 *(978-1-4027-6916-0(4))* Sterling Publishing Co., Inc.

Logan, Laura, illus. Jesus Loves Me. 2009. 20p. (J). (gr. -1-k). 6.99 *(978-0-8249-1839-2(8)*, Ideal Pubns.) Worthy Publishing.

Loggins, Kenny. Footloose. Bowers, Tim, illus. 2016. (ENG.). 28p. (J). (gr. -1-1). 17.95 *(978-1-63322-118-5(0)*, Moondance) Quarto Publishing Group USA.

Long, Ethan. The Croaky Pokey! Long, Ethan, illus. 2011. (ENG., Illus.). 32p. (J). (gr. -1-1). 14.95 *(978-0-8234-2291-3(7))* Holiday Hse., Inc.

Lowitz, Sadyebeth & Lowitz, Anson. Mr Key's Song: The Star Spangled Banner. 2011. 58p. 36.95 *(978-1-258-10511-2(X))* Literary Licensing, LLC.

Lowry, Mark & Greene, Buddy. Mary, Did You Know? Bond, Denny, illus. 2005. 24p. (J). (gr. -1-k). bds. 9.99 incl. audio compact disk *(978-1-57791-176-0(8))* Brighter Minds Children's Publishing.

MacDonald, Margaret Read & Jaeger, Winifred. The Round Book: Rounds Kids Love to Sing. Davis, Yvonne LeBrun, illus. 2006. (ENG.). 136p. (J). (gr. -1-3). per. 18.95 *(978-0-87483-786-5(3))* August Hse. Pubs., Inc.

MacGregor, Helen & Chadwick, Stephen. Singing Spanish (Book + CD) 22 Photocopiable songs & chants for learning Spanish, 1 vol. Harding, Emma & Gosney, Joy, illus. 2008. (Singing Languages Ser.). (SPA & ENG.). 64p. (J). (gr. 2-6). pap. 32.95 incl. audio compact disk ***(978-0-7136-8880-1(7))*** HarperCollins Pubs. Ltd. GBR. Dist: Independent Pubs. Group.

Madonna, Marissa, illus. There's a Hole in the Bucket! 2013. (First Steps in Music Ser.). (ENG.). 32p. (J). (gr. k-2). 16.95 *(978-1-57999-970-4(0))* G I A Pubns., Inc.

Mahoney, Judy & Mahoney, Anne. Teach Me... French Spiritual Songs. 2005. (FRE., Illus.). 24p. (J). 15.95 *(978-0-934633-50-5(9))* Teach Me Tapes, Inc.

Marks, Anthony. The Usborne Farmyard Tales Songbook. Tyler, Jenny, ed. Cartwright, Stephen, illus. 2005. 31p. (J). (gr. -1-7). per. 6.95 *(978-0-7945-0918-7(5)*, Usborne) EDC Publishing.

Marley, Cedella. One Love. Brantley-Newton, Vanessa, illus. 2014. (ENG.). 24p. (J). (gr. -1-k). bds. 7.99 *(978-1-4521-3855-8(9))* Chronicle Bks. LLC.

Marley, Cedella & Marley, Bob. One Love: Based on the Song by Bob Marley. Newton, Vanessa, illus. 2011. (ENG.). 32p. (J). (gr. -1-1). 16.99 *(978-1-4521-0224-5(4))* Chronicle Bks. LLC.

Marsh, Kathryn. The Musical Playground: Global Tradition & Change in Children's Songs & Games. 2009. (ENG., Illus.). 464p. pap. 35.95 *(978-0-19-530898-3(0))* Oxford Univ. Pr., Inc.

Martin, Joseph M., et al. Sing & Celebrate! Sacred Songs for Young Voices. 2012. (ENG.). 56p. pap. 39.99 incl. audio compact disk *(978-1-4584-2103-6(1)*, 1458421031) Shawnee Pr., Inc.

Matz, Carol, contrib. by. The Best of Strawberry Shortcake: Early Elementary. 2007. (ENG.). 24p. (J). pap. 7.95 *(978-0-7390-4957-0(7))* Alfred Publishing Co., Inc.

—Strawberry Shortcake: Berry Merry Christmas: Early Elementary. 2007. (ENG.). 16p. (J). pap. 6.95 *(978-0-7390-4849-8(X))* Alfred Publishing Co., Inc.

McCabe, Larry. Easiest Mandolin Tunes for Children, 1 vol. 2007. (ENG.). 32p. 14.99 *(978-0-7866-7535-7(7))* Mel Bay Pubns., Inc.

McCarthy, John. Only Chord Book You Will Ever Need. 2007. (ENG.). 160p. pap. 19.99 *(978-0-9764347-8-8(4)*, 0976434784, Rock Hse. Method, The) Russell, Fred Publishing.

McDermott, Tom. The Ghouls Come Haunting One by One, 1 vol. McGrath, Liz, illus. 2010. (ENG.). 32p. (J). (gr. k-k). 16.99 *(978-1-58980-786-0(3))* Pelican Publishing Co., Inc.

McKay-Lawton, Toni. Family Favourites. Manning, Eddie, illus. 2007. (Just in Rhyme Ser.). (ENG.). 12p. (J). (gr. -1-3). pap. *(978-1-84167-028-7(6))* Ransom Publishing Ltd.

—Under the Sea. Manning, Eddie, illus. 2007. (Just in Rhyme Ser.). (ENG.). 12p. (J). (gr. -1-3). pap. *(978-1-84167-027-0(8))* Ransom Publishing Ltd.

McQuinn, Anna. If You're Happy & You Know It. Fatus, Sophie, illus. 2011. (ENG.). 80p. (J). pap. 6.99 *(978-1-84686-434-6(8))* Barefoot Bks., Inc.

McQuinn, Anna & Fatus, Sophie. If You're Happy & You Know It. 2009. (ENG., Illus.). (J). (gr. k-2). 16.99 *(978-1-84686-288-5(4))* Barefoot Bks., Inc.

—If You're Happy & You Know It! Fatus, Sophie, illus. 2011. (ENG., Illus.). 24p. (J). (gr. -1-2). 9.99 *(978-1-84686-619-7(7))* Barefoot Bks., Inc.

Mendoza, Javier, et al. El Mundo. 2008. (SPA., Illus.). 32p. (J). pap. 7.99 *(978-1-84686-209-0(4))* Barefoot Bks., Inc.

Metzger, Steve. The Leaves Are Falling One by One. Sagasti, Miriam, illus. 2007. (J). *(978-0-439-02444-0(7))* Scholastic, Inc.

Michels-Boyce, Steven, illus. When Jesus Was A Kid Like Me: A Counting Song about Jesus When He Was a Kid Like You & Me. 2005. (J). 15.95 *(978-0-9761477-0-1(X))* SoJam Pr.

Miles, Sandy. Birthday: Words by John Lennon & Paul Mccartney. 2009. 20p. pap. 11.25 *(978-1-4389-4951-2(0))* AuthorHouse.

Miller, J. Philip & Greene, Sheppard M. We All Sing with the Same Voice. Meisel, Paul, illus. 2005. (ENG.). 32p. (J). (gr. -1-2). reprint ed. pap. 6.99 *(978-0-06-073900-3(2))* HarperCollins Pubs.

Mills, J. Elizabeth. The Spooky Wheels on the Bus. Mantle, Ben, illus. 2010. (ENG.). 24p. (J). (gr. -1-k). pap. 3.99 *(978-0-545-17480-0(5)*, Cartwheel Bks.) Scholastic, Inc.

Mitchell, Loretta. One, Two, Three... Echo Me! Ready-to-Use Songs, Games & Activities to Help Children Sing in Tune. 2003. (Illus.). 203p. pap. 29.95 *(978-0-89328-157-1(3)*, 30/1800H) Heritage Music Pr.

Miyares, Daniel, illus. Waking up Is Hard to Do. 2010. (Book & CD Ser.). (ENG.). 26p. (J). (gr. k-4). 17.95 *(978-1-936140-13-8(6))* Charlesbridge Publishing, Inc.

Moore, Felicia. Children, Sing along & Learn with Me in Support of Antibullying Awareness! 2012. 16p. pap. 12.68 *(978-1-4669-4831-0(0))* Trafford Publishing.

Murphy, Claire Rudolf. My Country, 'Tis of Thee: How One Song Reveals the History of Civil Rights. Collier, Bryan, illus. 2014. (ENG.). 48p. (J). (gr. k-4). 17.99 *(978-0-8050-8226-5(3)*, 9780805082265, Holt, Henry & Co. Bks. For Young Readers) Holt, Henry & Co.

Naji, Jamilla. Musical Storyland: A Sing-A-Long Book with Musical Disc. l.t. ed. 2004. (Illus.). 32p. (J). per. 19.99 *(978-0-9745568-0-2(7))* Worlds In Ink Publishing, Inc.

Nelson, Kadir. He's Got the Whole World in His Hands. 2010. (ENG.). 32p. (J). pap. 6.99 *(978-0-14-241635-8(5)*, Puffin) Penguin Publishing Group.

Nelson, Steve & Rollins, Jack. Here Comes Peter Cottontail! Levy, Pamela R., illus. 2015. (J). *(978-0-8249-1948-1(3)*, Ideal Pubns.) Worthy Publishing.

—Here Comes Peter Cottontail! 2014. (Illus.). 16p. (J). bds. 12.99 *(978-0-8249-1927-6(0)*, Ideal Pubns.) Worthy Publishing.

—Here Comes Peter Cottontail! Levy, Pamela R., illus. (ENG.). 26p. (J). 2007. bds. 12.99 *(978-0-8249-6701-7(1))* 2003. (gr. -1-k). bds. 6.95 *(978-0-8249-4149-9(7))* Worthy Publishing. (Ideal Pubns.).

Norworth, Jack. Take Me Out to the Ball Game. Hirao, Amiko, illus. 2016. (ENG.). 24p. (J). (— 1). bds. 7.95 *(978-1-62354-071-5(2))* Charlesbridge Publishing, Inc.

—Take Me Out to the Ball Game. Huntington, Amy, illus. 2011. (Favorite Children's Songs Ser.). (ENG.). 16p. (J). (gr. -1-2). lib. bdg. 25.64 *(978-1-60954-294-8(0)*, 200098) Child's World, Inc., The.

—Take Me Out to the Ball Game. Meyers, Mark, illus. 2011. 16p. (J). (gr. -1-k). bds. 10.99 *(978-0-8249-1852-1(5)*, Ideal Pubns.) Worthy Publishing.

Numeroff, Laura Joffe. Mouse Stroller Songs. Date not set. (J). 9.99 *(978-0-694-01420-0(6))* HarperCollins Pubs.

Okun, Milton, ed. All My Life - Karla Bonoff (Piano - Vocal) (Illus.). 64p. (Orig.). (YA). pap. 14.95 *(978-0-89524-707-0(0))* Cherry Lane Music Co.

—From the Heart - 30 Love Songs. 117p. (Orig.). (YA). pap. 14.95 *(978-0-89524-864-0(6)*, 02502146) Cherry Lane Music Co.

Omoto, Garrett, illus. Na Waihooluu. 2006.Tr. of Colors. (HAW & ENG.). 16p. (J). 8.95 *(978-1-933835-00-6(1))* Partners in Development Foundation.

Orozco, Jose-Luis. Diez Deditos. 2014. 18.00 *(978-1-63419-695-6(3))* Perfection Learning Corp.

Pagnoni, Roberta & Rigo, Laura, illus. The Twelve Days of Christmas. 2013. (ENG.). 24p. (J). (gr. -1 — 1). bds. 10.99 *(978-0-7641-6622-8(0))* Barron's Educational Series, Inc.

Pair, Karma A. On My Way to the Market. Pressey, Deborah, illus. 2009. 24p. pap. 15.00 *(978-1-4389-6299-3(1))* AuthorHouse.

Pancho Claus con Jose-Luis Orozco - Christmas with Jose-Luis Orozco. (SPA & ENG.). (J). (gr. k-3). 10.00 *(978-1-57417-031-3(7))* Arcoiris Records, Inc.

Parisi, Bettie. Lullabies of Love. 2009. 28p. pap. 13.00 *(978-1-4269-1016-6(9))* Trafford Publishing.

Partin, Judith E. Songs in the Night: (A Collection of Hymns, Choruses, & Songs...) 2004. 211p. (YA). 25.00 *(978-0-9748494-1-6(3))* Omega Publishing.

Paul, Ellis. The Hero in You. Padrón, Angela, illus. 2014. (ENG.). 32p. (J). (gr. 2-5). 16.99 *(978-0-8075-3238-6(X))* Whitman, Albert & Co.

Pax Lodge Songbook. 2005. (J). *(978-0-88441-690-6(9))* Girl Scouts of the USA.

Paxton, Tom. The Jungle Baseball Game. Schmidt, Karenlee, illus. 2005. 30p. (J). (gr. -1-2). reprint ed. 16.00 *(978-0-7567-8932-9(X))* DIANE Publishing Co.

Penner, Fred. Here We Go Round the Mulberry Bush. Fatus, Sophie, illus. 2008. (ENG.). 24p. (J). 9.99 *(978-1-84686-079-9(2))* Barefoot Bks., Inc.

Perkins, Jill E. Cherubs Chatter: A Collection of Original Songs & Poems. 2004. (Illus.). 88p. (J). per. 7.95 *(978-0-9749862-2-7(4))* Theragogy.com.

Perry, Rex, illus. Over the River & Through the Woods. 2004. 24p. (J). lib. bdg. 8.00 *(978-1-4242-0640-7(5))* Fitzgerald Bks.

Person, Jill. Early Concepts Sing-Along Flip Chart: 25 Delightful Congs Set to Favorite Tunes That Help Children Learn Colors, Shapes & Sizes. 2006. (Sing-along Flip Chart & CD Ser.). (ENG., Illus.). 26p. (gr. -1-1). 24.99 *(978-0-439-72160-8(1)*, Teaching Resources) Scholastic, Inc.

Petersen, George & Jenkins, J. J. Crazy Campsongs. Davis, Jack, illus. 2003. 64p. (J). bds. 9.99 *(978-0-9726794-9-7(9))* Jenpet Publishing.

Pingry, Patricia A. Jesus Loves Me. 2010. 22p. bds. 6.99 *(978-0-8249-1893-4(2)*, Ideal Pubns.) Worthy Publishing.

Pingry, Patricia A. & Urbano, Aide. One Baby Jesus/Un Nino Dios. Edelson, Wendy, illus. 2003. (ENG & SPA.). 30p. (J). pap. 3.95 *(978-0-8249-5472-7(6)*, Ideal Pubns.) Worthy Publishing.

Playaway, creator. Praise Songs for Kids. 2008. (Playaway Children Ser.). (J). 59.99 *(978-1-59922-326-1(0))* Findaway World, LLC.

—Scripture Memory Songs. 2008. (Playaway Adult Nonfiction Ser.). (J). (gr. -1-3). 59.99 *(978-1-59922-325-4(2))* Findaway World, LLC.

Pooh Songs. (Play-A-Song Ser.). (Illus.). 20p. (J). pap. 15.98 *(978-0-7853-1326-7(5))* Publications International, Ltd.

The Predator. (Song Box Ser.). (gr. 1-2). 8.50 incl. audio *(978-0-7802-2261-8(X))* Wright Group/McGraw-Hill.

The Predator: 1 Big Book, 6 Each of 1 Student Book, & 1 Cassette. (Song Box Ser.). (gr. 1-2). 68.95 *(978-0-7802-3205-1(4))* Wright Group/McGraw-Hill.

The Predator: Big Book. (Song Box Ser.). (gr. 1-2). 31.50 *(978-0-7802-2260-1(1))* Wright Group/McGraw-Hill.

Prévert, Jacques. Chanson des Escargotsqui Vont l'Enterrement. 2004. (Illus.). (J). (gr. 1-6). spiral bd. *(978-0-616-07265-3(1))* Canadian National Institute for the Blind/Institut National Canadien pour les Aveugles.

Priddy, Roger. First Songs Library. 2010. (ENG.). 32p. (J). (gr. -1 — 1). 14.99 *(978-0-312-50873-9(5)*, Priddy Bks.) St. Martin's Pr.

—Songs. 2009. (Sing-Along Ser.). (ENG.). 30p. (J). (gr. -1 — 1). bds. 12.95 *(978-0-312-50648-3(1)*, 9780312506483, Priddy Bks.) St. Martin's Pr.

Print Music Staff. Party. 2006. (Wiggles Ser.). (ENG., Illus.). 40p. pap. 9.95 *(978-1-921029-01-1(3)*, 1921029013) Music Sales Corp.

Public Domain Staff. Away in a Manger. Kinkade, Thomas, illus. 2009. (ENG.). 32p. (J). (gr. -1-3). pap. 7.99 *(978-0-06-078734-9(1))* HarperCollins Pubs.

Publications International Ltd. Staff. Dora Ballerina Little Music Note Sound. 2010. 12p. bds. 9.98 *(978-1-4508-1018-0(7))* Phoenix International Publications, Inc.

—Enchanted Songs. (Disney Princess Ser.). (Illus.). 10p. (J). bds. 9.98 *(978-0-7853-8279-9(8)*, 7182300) Publications International, Ltd.

—Lenticular 1 Button Sesame Street. 2010. (SPA.). 12p. (J). bds. 10.98 *(978-1-4127-4468-3(7)*, PIL Kids) Publications International, Ltd.

—Lenticular 1 Button Thomas. 2010. 12p. (J). bds. 10.98 *(978-1-4127-4543-7(8)*, PIL Kids) Publications International, Ltd.

—My Little Pony Magic Friendship Songs. 2013. 10p. (J). (gr. k-4). bds. 10.99 *(978-1-4508-6352-0(3)*, e11c6844-0b70-40b4-a490-b56ef2e7ed9f) Phoenix International Publications, Inc.

Publications International Ltd. Staff, creator. Dora the Explorer Laugh-along Sing-along. 2007. (Play-A-Song Ser.). (Illus.). bds. 15.98 *(978-1-4127-7417-8(9))* Publications International, Ltd.

—Help along Sing a Song. 2007. (Play-A-Song Ser.). (Illus.). bds. 15.98 *(978-1-4127-7419-2(5))* Publications International, Ltd.

—Learning Songs. 2007. (Take-along Songs Ser.). (Illus.). 16p. (J). (gr. -1). bds. 9.98 incl. audio compact disk *(978-1-4127-7437-6(3))* Publications International, Ltd.

—Magic Songs. 2007. (Play-A-Song Ser.). (Illus.). (gr. -1-k). bds. 15.98 *(978-1-4127-8813-7(7))* Publications International, Ltd.

—Scooby Doo!: Spooky Scooby Songs. 2007. (Play-A-Song Ser.). (Illus.). (J). (gr. -1-3). 16.98 *(978-1-4127-7408-6(X))* Publications International, Ltd.

—Songs That Go. 2007. (Take-along Songs Ser.). (Illus.). 14p. (J). (gr. -1-3). bds. 9.98 incl. audio compact disk *(978-1-4127-7440-6(3))* Publications International, Ltd.

Publications International Ltd. Staff, ed. All the World's Asleep. 2010. 14p. (J). bds. 7.98 net. *(978-1-4127-4496-6(2)*, 1412744962, PIL Kids) Publications International, Ltd.

—Barney: I Love You Songs. 2011. 14p. (J). bds. 22.98 *(978-1-4508-1249-8(X))* Publications International, Ltd.

—Car Tunes. 2010. 12p. (J). bds. 14.98 *(978-1-60553-400-8(5)*, PIL Kids) Publications International, Ltd.

—Disney(r) Mickey Mouse Clubhouse I Can Play Christmas Songs! 2014. 12p. (J). bds. *(978-1-4508-8515-7(2)*, 1450885152) Publications International, Ltd.

—Disney Mickey Mouse Clubhouse Let's Sing! Play-A-Sound Book & Cuddly Mickey. 2014. 6p. (J). bds. 19.98 *(978-1-4508-7451-9(7)*, cbf92671-51dc-428b-801c-1493d85def5e) Publications International, Ltd.

—Disney Pixar Cars: Radiator Springs Sings. 2011. 14p. (J). bds. 17.98 *(978-1-60553-389-6(0))* Publications International, Ltd.

—Disney Princess. 2010. 14p. (J). bds. 19.98 *(978-1-60553-621-7(0))* Phoenix International Publications, Inc.

—Dora Digital Music Player. 2010. 14p. (J). bds. 9.39 net. *(978-1-4508-1437-9(9)*, 1450814379) Phoenix International Publications, Inc.

—Elmos Garden Little Sound Book. 2005. (Play-a-Sound Ser.). (Illus.). 10p. (J). bds. 10.50 *(978-1-4127-3291-8(3)*, 7244300) Publications International, Ltd.

—Friendship Songs. 2010. 24p. (J). 17.98 *(978-1-60553-399-5(8)*, PIL Kids) Publications International, Ltd.

—Hello Kitty Sweet Songs: Play-A-Sound. 2013. 12p. (J). bds. 9.98 *(978-1-4508-6167-0(9)*, 1450861679) Phoenix International Publications, Inc.

—Holiday Easter Play a Song Disney Bunnies. 2010. 10p. (J). bds. 12.98 *(978-1-4127-9887-7(6))* Phoenix International Publications, Inc.

—Mickey Mouse 10 Song Sound. 2011. 24p. (J). 17.98 *(978-1-4508-1472-0(7))* Publications International, Ltd.

—Mickey Mouse Clubhouse: Play Day Songs. 2011. (Illus.). 12p. (J). bds. 15.98 *(978-1-4508-0925-2(1))* Publications International, Ltd.

—Mickey's Clubhouse Drum Song Sound. 2011. 14p. (J). bds. 20.98 *(978-1-4508-1240-5(6))* Phoenix International Publications, Inc.

—Move to the Music. 2011. 14p. (J). bds. 20.98 *(978-1-4508-1242-9(2))* Phoenix International Publications, Inc.

—Play & Learn Piano Elmo. 2011. 24p. (J). 17.98 *(978-1-4508-0871-2(9))* Phoenix International Publications, Inc.

—Record a Song Old Mac Donald. 2011. 18p. 17.98 *(978-1-4508-2179-7(0))* Phoenix International Publications, Inc.

—Sesame Street: Potty Time Songs. 2011. 12p. (J). bds. *(978-1-4508-0401-1(2))* Phoenix International Publications, Inc.

—Sing-Along Songs. 2010. 14p. (J). bds. 17.98 *(978-1-4127-4553-6(5))* Phoenix International Publications, Inc.

—Starry Sky Songs. 2010. 14p. (J). bds. 17.98 *(978-1-4127-4497-3(0))* Phoenix International Publications, Inc.

—Sunny Sing-Along Songs. 2010. 10p. (J). bds. 12.98 *(978-1-4127-4493-5(8)*, PIL Kids) Publications International, Ltd.

—Thomas & Friends: Sing-Along Songs. 2011. 14p. (J). bds. 17.98 *(978-1-4508-1130-9(2))* Phoenix International Publications, Inc.

—Winnie the Pooh: Sing along with Pooh (Little Pop-up Songbook) 2011. 10p. (J). bds. *(978-1-60553-145-8(6))* Publications International, Ltd.

—The World of Eric Carle: Merry Christmas: Play-A-Sound Book. 2012. 14p. (J). (gr. k-3). bds. 16.99 *(978-1-4508-6623-1(9)*, df3db359-6e89-4107-9d94-fec814a161da) Phoenix International Publications, Inc.

—9 Button Record Song Mickey'S Christmas. 2011. 18p. 19.98 *(978-1-4508-1985-5(0))* Publications International, Ltd.

—9 Button Record Song Thomas Sing Along. 2011. 12p. (J). bds. 17.98 *(978-1-4508-1995-4(8)*, 1450819958) Phoenix International Publications, Inc.

—9 Button Record Story Elmo Silly Stories. 2011. 18p. 19.98 *(978-1-4508-1986-2(9))* Publications International, Ltd.

Puybaret, Eric, illus. Over the Rainbow. 2010. (Book & CD Ser.). (ENG.). 26p. (J). (gr. k-4). 17.95 *(978-1-936140-00-8(4))* Charlesbridge Publishing, Inc.

Racknor & Morrow. Wordszart. 2011. 92p. pap. 29.99 *(978-0-557-55589-5(2))* Lulu Pr., Inc.

Raposo, Joe. Sing. Lichtenheld, Tom, illus. 2013. (ENG.). 40p. (J). (gr. -1-3). 16.99 *(978-0-8050-9071-0(1)*, 9780805090710, Holt, Henry & Co. Bks. For Young Readers) Holt, Henry & Co.

Rappin' Heart Rhyme. (Song Box Ser.). (gr. 1-2). 8.50 incl. audio *(978-0-322-00248-7(6))* Wright Group/McGraw-Hill.

Rappin' Heart Rhyme: 1 Big Book, 6 Each of 1 Student Book, & 1 Cassette. (Song Box Ser.). (gr. 1-2). 68.95 *(978-0-322-00274-6(5))* Wright Group/McGraw-Hill.

Rappin' Heart Rhyme: 6 Each of 1 Student Book, 6 vols. (Song Box Ser.). (gr. 1-2). 29.50 *(978-0-322-00270-8(2))* Wright Group/McGraw-Hill.

Rappin' Heart Rhyme: Big Book. (Song Box Ser.). (gr. 1-2). 31.50 *(978-0-322-00265-4(6))* Wright Group/McGraw-Hill.

Rauenhorst, Linda. Frohliche Weihnachten: Learning Songs & Traditions in German. Collier, Roberta, illus. 2007. (Teach Me Ser.). (GER & ENG.). 32p. (J). (gr. -1-3). 19.95 *(978-1-59972-063-0(9))* Teach Me Tapes, Inc.

Reasoner, Charles. Inside Old MacDonald's Barn. 2014. (Illus.). (J). *(978-1-4351-5467-4(3))* Barnes & Noble, Inc.

Reeder Eubank, Patricia. The Gifts They Gave. 2013. (ENG., Illus.). 32p. (J). (gr. -1-k). 9.95 *(978-1-4549-0508-0(5)*, 1364142) Sterling Publishing Co., Inc.

Rescek, Sanja, et al, illus. Itsy Bitsy Spider & Other Clap-along Rhymes. 2004. (Clap-Alongs Ser.). (ENG.). 36p. (J). (gr. -1-k). 12.95 *(978-1-59249-522-1(2)*, 1D025) Soundprints.

Rey, H. A. My First Nursery Songs. 2010. (Curious Baby Curious George Ser.). (ENG., Illus.). 14p. (J). (gr. k — 1). bds. 8.99 *(978-0-547-27938-1(8))* Houghton Mifflin Harcourt Publishing Co.

Rice, Ruth Mason & Villar, Rose. Cycle, Children's Games & Other Songs. Browne, Anita, illus. 2012. 56p. 36.95 *(978-1-258-23019-7(4))*; pap. 21.95 *(978-1-258-24214-5(1))* Literary Licensing, LLC.

Riggs Vetter, Jennifer. Down by the Station. Remkiewicz, Frank, illus. 2009. (ENG.). 32p. (J). (gr. -1-2). 15.99 *(978-1-58246-243-1(7)*, Tricycle Pr.) Random Hse. Children's Bks.

Roberts, Sheena. Birds & Beasts: Animal songs, games & Activities. Price, David & Ursell, Martin, illus. 2006. (Classroom Music Ser.). (ENG.). 80p. (J). (gr. 1-6). *(978-0-7136-5653-4(0)*, A&C Black) Bloomsbury Publishing Plc.

S

—We All Go Traveling By. Bell, Siobhan, illus. 2011. (ENG.). 24p. (J). (gr. -1-2). 9.99 (978-1-84686-655-5(3)) Barefoot Bks., Inc.

Rojo, Andrea Szekasy & Bardsley, Maggie. I Love Spanish Songs: Songbook & CD. 2003. (SPA., Illus.). 30p. (J). (gr. -1-2). pap. 15.99 (978-0-9671053-7-6(4)) Language Adventure Pubns.

Rollins, Jack & Nelson, Steve. Frosty the Snowman. Reed, Lisa, illus. 2014. 22p. (J). bds. 6.99 (978-0-8249-1935-1(1), Ideal Pubns.) Worthy Publishing.

—Frosty the Snowman. Thornburgh, Rebecca McKillip, illus. 2003. (ENG.). 24p. (J). bds. 6.95 (978-0-8249-6500-6(0), Ideal Pubns.) Worthy Publishing.

Romendik, Irena, illus. The Musical Muffin Man. 2003. (Rub a Dub Books Ser.). 8p. (J). (gr. -1-k). vinyl bd. 7.00 (978-1-883043-45-2(X)) Straight Edge Pr., The.

Romendik, Irene, illus. I've Been Working on the Railroad: Musical Book. 2003. (J). 6.49 (978-1-883043-48-3(4)) Straight Edge Pr., The.

Rothero, Chris, illus. Strawberry Fair. 2004. 96p. (gr. 1-6). 14.95 (978-0-7136-2676-6(3), A&C Black) Bloomsbury Publishing Plc GBR. Dist: Consortium Bk. Sales & Distribution.

Ruesga, Rita Rosa & Scholastic, Inc. Staff. Cantaba la Rana. Sebastián, Soledad, illus. 2011. (SPA.). 32p. (J). (gr. -1-3). pap. 6.99 (978-0-545-27357-2(9), Scholastic en Espanol) Scholastic, Inc.

Rupprecht, Karen & Minor, Pamela. Months of Music & More. 2005. (Illus.). 28p. (J). per. 18.95 (978-0-9704184-3-2(4)) Pennypack Productions, Inc.

Sabol, Elizabeth, illus. Day Is Done: A Lullaby l.t. ed. 2004. 26p. (J). pap. incl. audio compact disk (978-0-9747382-0-8(4)) LeDor Publishing.

Sadlier We Believe Program Songbook. 2003. (J). per. (978-0-8215-5448-7(4), Sadlier) Sadlier, William H. Inc.

Salgado. Nuevas Canciones Infantiles.Tr. of New Children's Songs. (SPA.). (J). 7.98 (978-968-403-664-2(7)) Selector, S.A. de C.V. MEX. Dist: AIMS International Bks., Inc.

Salmon, Shirley. Hello Children: A Collection of Songs & Related Activities for Children Aged 4-9. 2007. (ENG.). 48p. pap. 21.95 (978-1-84761-052-2(8), 1847610528) Schott Music Corp.

Sangam Songbook (Revised) 2005. (J). (978-0-88441-689-0(5)) Girl Scouts of the USA.

Save a Tree for Me: 1 Big Book, 6 Each of 1 Student Book, & 1 Cassette. (Song Box Ser.). (gr. 1-2). 68.95 (978-0-7802-3206-8(2)) Wright Group/McGraw-Hill.

Sawyer, Louise. The Phantom. 2003. (YA). 12.95 (978-0-9719842-1-9(2)) Martin & Brothers.

Schiller, David. All American Car-I-Oke. 2003. (ENG., Illus.). 64p. (J). 14.95 (978-0-7611-3068-0(3), 13068) Workman Publishing Co., Inc.

Schmicker, Michael. Old Mcdonald-San's Farm. Kenyon, Tony, illus. 2004. 19p. (J). (gr. -1-5). pap. 13.95 incl. audio (978-0-9631154-4-7(8)) Watermark Publishing, LLC.

Schnetzler, Pattie. Earth Day Birthday. Wallace, Chad, illus. 2004. (Sharing Nature with Children Book Ser.). 32p. (J). 16.95 (978-1-58469-053-5(4)); 8.95 (978-1-58469-054-2(2)) Dawn Pubns.

Scholastic, Inc. Staff, contrib. by. The Wheels on the Truck Go 'Round & 'Round. 2012. (Rookie Toddler Ser.). (ENG.). 12p. (J). bds. 6.95 (978-0-531-20855-7(9), Children's Pr.) Scholastic Library Publishing.

Schumacher, Bev. Patterns (Chinese/English) 2012. 20p. (J). pap. 8.95 (978-1-935292-48-7(X)) Learning Props.

Schwaeber, Barbie. Make New Friends. Brooks, Nan, illus. (American Favorites Ser.). (ENG.). 32p. (J). (gr. -1-3). 2008. 14.95 (978-1-59249-728-7(4)) 2007. 8.95 (978-1-59249-729-4(2)) Soundprints.

Schwaeber, Barbie H. She'll Be Comin Round the Mountain. Beaky, Suzanne, illus. 2007. (American Favorites Ser.). (ENG.). 32p. (J). (gr. -1-3). 9.85 (978-1-59249-688-4(1)) Soundprints.

Schwaeber, Barbie H., ed. She'll Be Comin' Round the Mountain. Beaky, Suzanne, illus. 2007. (American Favorites Ser.). (ENG.). 32p. (J). (gr. -1-3). 14.95 (978-1-59249-687-7(3)) Soundprints.

Schwortz, Anna M. A B C Rhymetime. Schwortz, Anna M., ed. Schwortz, Anna M., illus. 2005. (Illus.). 48p. (J). (gr. k-3). pap. (978-0-9769719-0-0(9)) AnnArt Pr.

Scribens, Sunny & Barefoot Books Staff. Space Song Rocket Ride. 2014. (Illus.). 24p. (J). 16.99 (978-1-78285-097-7(X)) Barefoot Bks., Inc.

Scruggs, Kathy. Espanol Con Senora Scruggs! 2003. (Illus.). 46p. (J). spiral bd. (978-0-9747272-0-2(2)) Permiso Por Favor Publishing Co.

Seasons & Celebrations. 2003. (Toddler Ser.). (Illus.). 36p. (J). pap. 12.99 (978-1-894677-48-6(X)) Kidzup Productions.

Sehgal, Kabir & Sehgal, Surishtha. The Wheels on the Tuk Tuk. Golden, Jess, illus. 2016. (ENG.). 40p. (J). (gr. -1-k). 17.99 (978-1-4814-4831-4(5), Beach Lane Bks.) Beach Lane Bks.

Sharp, Cecil James. English Folk-Chanteys: With Pianoforte Accompaniment, Introduction & Notes. unabr. ed. 2012. (Illus.). 91p. 39.99 (978-1-4622-9398-8(0)) Repressed Publishing LLC.

Sherab, Chodzin & Langham, Tony. Creepy Crawly Calypso. 2012. (ENG., Illus.). 32p. (J). (gr. -1-2). 9.99 (978-1-84686-828-3(9)) Barefoot Bks., Inc.

Shyu, Theresa. Bilingual Songs - English-Mandarin-Chinese, 2 vols., Vol. 1. 2009. (Bilingual Songs English Mandarin Ser.: 1). (MAN, ENG & CHI.). 48p. (J). 17.95 (978-1-55386-107-2(8), 1553861078) Jordan, Sara Publishing.

Sickler, Jonas. Frere Jacques: Hey Baby! Look Where Jacques is Sleeping — and Dreaming — in Paris! Sickler, Jonas & Pixton, Kaaren, illus. 2011. (Indestructibles Ser.). (ENG.). 12p. (J). (gr. k — 1). pap. 5.95 (978-0-7611-5923-0(1), 15923) Workman Publishing Co., Inc.

Sign2Me, creator. Pick Me up! (Music & ASL) Fun Songs for Learning Signs. 2003. (ENG., Illus.). 64p. act. bk. ed. 36.95 incl. audio compact disk (978-0-9668367-8-3(2), Sign2Me) Sign2Me Early Learning / Northlight Communications, Inc.

Simon, Carly. Take Me Out to the Ball Game. Hirao, Amiko, illus. 2011. (ENG.). 26p. (J). (gr. k-12). 17.95 (978-1-936140-26-8(8)) Charlesbridge Publishing, Inc.

Smart Kidz, creator. Jesus Loves the Little Children. 2013. (Bible Sing along Bks.). (ENG., Illus.). 12p. (gr. -1). bds. 12.99 (978-1-891100-34-5(3), Smart Kids) Penton Overseas, Inc.

Smith, Janet Kay. Sing A Song of Science: Lyrics for Kids From 1-99. 2005. (Illus.). 27p. (J). spiral bd. (978-0-9768786-0-5(7)) Kay, Janet Consulting.

Smithsonian Institution Staff. Home on the Range. Schwaeber, Barbie H., ed. Magnuson, Diana, illus. 2007. (ENG.). 32p. (J). (gr. -1-3). 9.85 (978-1-59249-686-0(5)) Soundprints.

The Song Box Science Songs: 1 Each of 12 Big Books. (Song Box Ser.). (gr. 1-2). 375.50 (978-0-322-02962-0(7)) Wright Group/McGraw-Hill.

The Song Box Science Songs: 1 Each of 12 Cassettes. (Song Box Ser.). (gr. 1-2). 101.95 (978-0-322-02963-7(5)) Wright Group/McGraw-Hill.

The Song Box Science Songs: 1 Each of 12 Student Books. (Song Box Ser.). (gr. 1-2). 57.95 (978-0-322-02959-0(7)) Wright Group/McGraw-Hill.

The Song Box Science Songs: 6 Each of 12 Student Books. (Song Box Ser.). (gr. 1-2). 349.95 (978-0-322-02960-6(0)) Wright Group/McGraw-Hill.

Songs to the Corn: A Hopi Poet Writes about Corn, 6 packs. (Greetings Ser.: Vol. 2). (gr. 3-5). 31.00 (978-0-7635-1808-0(5)) Rigby Education.

Soundprints Staff. Make New Friends. Schwaeber, Barbie Heit & Williams, Tracee, eds. Brooks, Nan, illus. 2008. (ENG.). 24p. (J). (gr. -1). 4.99 (978-1-59069-651-4(4)) Studio Mouse LLC.

Soussana, Nathalie, et al. Songs from the Garden of Eden: Jewish Lullabies & Nursery Rhymes. Alemagna, Beatrice, illus. 2009. (ENG & MUL.). 52p. (J). (gr. -1-2). 16.95 (978-2-923163-46-8(X)) La Montagne Secrete CAN. Dist: Independent Pubs. Group.

Stein, Kristen. Oh Sweet Child of Mine. 2009. 32p. pap. 16.50 (978-0-557-09407-3(0)) Lulu Pr., Inc.

SteveSongs Staff. The Shape Song Singalong. Sim, David, illus. 2011. (ENG.). 36p. (J). 16.99 (978-1-84686-671-5(5)) Barefoot Bks., Inc.

—Shape Song Singalong. Sim, David, illus. 2011. (ENG.). 24p. (J). (gr. -1-2). 9.99 (978-1-84686-679-1(0)) Barefoot Bks., Inc.

Stotts, Stuart. We Shall Overcome: A Song That Changed the World. Cummings, Terrance, illus. 2010. (ENG.). 80p. (J). (gr. 5-7). 18.00 (978-0-547-18210-0(4)) Houghton Mifflin Harcourt Publishing Co.

Strauss, Kurt & Strauss, Kim. Little Boy's Lullaby: A Songbook. 2005. (J). 35.00 (978-0-9760929-0-2(5)); DVD, audio compact disk 35.00 (978-0-9760929-3-3(X)) Blanket Street Publishing.

Stroniarz, Christina V., illus. Let's Sing & Celebrate! 105 Original Songs for Seasons & Festivals. 2003. 224p. pap. 24.95 (978-0-9720913-9-8(4)) Songbird Pr.

Studio Mouse, creator. Let's Play: Nursery Rhymes for Playing & Learning. 2005. (Read-Aloud Book Ser.). (ENG., Illus.). 36p. (J). 7.95 (978-1-59249-535-1(4), 1D205) Soundprints.

Sullivan, Carolyn Rose, illus. The Music Box: Songs, Rhymes, & Games for Young Children, 1 box. 2006. 200p. (J). 49.95 (978-0-9772717-1-9(4)) ELZ Publishing.

Sullivan, James Kevin, illus. What Went RIght Today? Journal: WWRT Journal. 2007. 72p. (J). spiral bd. 12.95 (978-0-9766990-1-9(X)) Buz-Land Presentations, Inc.

Tagore, Rabindranath. Gitanjali - Song Offerings. 2007. 52p. per. 11.99 (978-1-59547-773-6(X)) NuVision Pubns., LLC.

Taylor, Michaelle. Singing Across the Old North State: Story-Songs of North Carolina. 2004. 44p. (J). pap. (978-1-880970-89-8(9)) Aerial Photography Services, Inc.

Temporin, Elena, illus. The Usborne Book of Christmas Lullabies. 2006. (Christmas Lullabies Ser.). 8p. (J). bds. 14.99 incl. audio compact disk (978-0-7945-1469-3(3), Usborne) EDC Publishing.

Thiele, Bob & Weiss, George David. What a Wonderful World. Hopgood, Tim, illus. 2014. (ENG.). 32p. (J). (gr. -1-k). 17.99 (978-1-62779-254-7(6), 9781627792547, Holt, Henry & Co. Bks. For Young Readers) Holt, Henry & Co.

Thomas: It's Great to Be an Engine. 2004. (Little Music Note Ser.). (Illus.). 10p. (J). bds. (978-0-7853-9950-6(X), 7209400) Phoenix International Publications, Inc.

Thomas, Doni Zasloff & Lindberg, Eric. Sing-Along Alef Bet. Gilboa, Rinat, illus. 2016. (J). (978-1-68115-509-8(5)) Behrman Hse., Inc.

Thomas, Joyce Carol. Singing Mama's Songs. Date not set. 32p. (J). 16.00 (978-0-06-025379-0(7)); lib. bdg. 15.89 (978-0-06-025382-0(7)) HarperCollins Pubs.

Thompson, Kim Mitzo. Bible Songs. 2011. (J). (gr. k-1). audio compact disk 4.99 (978-1-59922-874-7(2)) Twin Sisters IP, LLC.

—The Easter Story. 2010. (J). (gr. k-2). pap. 4.99 (978-1-59922-494-7(1)) Twin Sisters IP, LLC.

Thompson, Kim Mitzo & Hilderbrand, Karen Mitzo. Alphabet. 2010. 12p. (J). (gr. k-2). bds. 8.99 (978-1-59922-569-2(7)) Twin Sisters IP, LLC.

—Counting. 2010. 12p. (J). (gr. k-2). bds. 8.99 (978-1-59922-570-8(0)) Twin Sisters IP, LLC.

—Multiplication Rap. 2008. (Playaway Children Ser.). (J). 44.99 (978-1-59922-324-7(4)) Findaway World, LLC.

Ticktock Media, Ltd. Staff. Itsy Bitsy Spider. 2011. (Sing-Along Songs Ser.). (ENG.). 10p. (J). (gr. k — 1). bds. 6.95 (978-1-84898-170-6(8), TickTock Books) Octopus Publishing Group GBR. Dist: Independent Pubs. Group.

—Old McDonald Had a Farm. 2011. (Sing-Along Songs Ser.). (ENG.). 10p. (J). (gr. k — 1). bds. 6.95 (978-1-84898-169-0(4), TickTock Books) Octopus Publishing Group GBR. Dist: Independent Pubs. Group.

—The Wheels on the Bus. 2011. (Sing-Along Songs Ser.). (ENG.). 10p. (J). (gr. k — 1). bds. 6.95 (978-1-84898-172-0(4), TickTock Books) Octopus Publishing Group GBR. Dist: Independent Pubs. Group.

Tiger Tales, ed. Jingle Bells: A Collection of Songs & Carols. Kolvanovic, Dubravka, illus. 2014. (ENG.). 22p. (J). (gr. -1-k). bds. 8.99 (978-1-58925-568-5(2)) Tiger Tales.

Time to Sign. Time to Sign with Children Infant/Toddler: Time to Sign with Music Infant/Toddler. 2003. Orig. Title: Time to Sign with Music Infant/Toddler. (Illus.). 42p. per. 19.95 (978-0-9713666-0-2(8)) Time to Sign, Incorporated.

Todd, Traci N. Wiggle Waggle Bee. Barner, Bob, illus. 2013. (J). (978-1-58987-327-8(0)) Kindermusik International.

Traditional Staff. Dayenu! A Favorite Passover Song. Latimer, Miriam, illus. 2012. (ENG.). 12p. (J). (gr. -1-k). bds. 7.99 (978-0-545-31236-3(1), Cartwheel Bks.) Scholastic, Inc.

Trapani, Iza. The Bear Went over the Mountain. Trapani, Iza, illus. 2012. (ENG., Illus.). 32p. (J). (gr. k-3). 16.95 (978-1-61608-510-0(X), 608510, Sky Pony Pr.) Skyhorse Publishing Co., Inc.

—Mary Had a Little Lamb. Trapani, Iza, illus. 2003. (ENG., Illus.). 32p. (J). (gr. -1-k). 7.95 (978-1-58089-090-8(3)) Charlesbridge Publishing, Inc.

—Shoo Fly! Trapani, Iza, illus. 2007. (ENG., Illus.). 32p. (J). (gr. k-3). per. 7.95 (978-1-58089-076-2(8)) Charlesbridge Publishing, Inc.

—Sing along with Iza & Friends: Row Row Row Your Boat. Trapani, Iza, illus. 2004. (Illus.). 32p. (J). pap. 11.95 incl. audio compact disk (978-1-58089-102-8(0)) Charlesbridge Publishing, Inc.

—Sing along with Iza & Friends: The Itsy Bitsy Spider. Trapani, Iza, illus. 2004. (Illus.). 32p. (J). pap. 11.95 incl. audio compact disk (978-1-58089-100-4(4)) Charlesbridge Publishing, Inc.

Tricia Lowenfield design. S Is for Shepherd. 2004. (Illus.). 32p. (J). per. 19.99 incl. audio compact disk (978-0-9747367-0-9(8)) Pumpkins Pansies Bunnies & Bears.

Twin Sisters(r) Staff. B-I-N-G-O. 2009. 16p. 4.99 (978-1-59922-368-1(6)) Twin Sisters IP, LLC.

—Bible Songs Workbook/CD Set. 2008. 96p. 10.99 (978-1-57583-897-7(4)) Twin Sisters IP, LLC.

—Down Through the Chimney. 2009. 16p. 4.99 (978-1-59922-413-8(5)) Twin Sisters IP, LLC.

—The Farmer in the Dell. 2009. 16p. 4.99 (978-1-59922-370-4(8)) Twin Sisters IP, LLC.

—Five Little Monkeys Jumping on the Bed. 2009. 16p. 4.99 (978-1-59922-372-8(4)) Twin Sisters IP, LLC.

—Jesus Loves the Little Children. 2010. (J). (gr. k-2). pap. 4.99 (978-1-59922-495-4(X)) Twin Sisters IP, LLC.

—Jolly Old St.Nicholas. 2009. 16p. 4.99 (978-1-59922-412-1(7)) Twin Sisters IP, LLC.

—The Lord Is My Shepherd. 2010. (J). (gr. k-1). 14.99 (978-1-59922-632-3(4)) Twin Sisters IP, LLC.

—Multiplication Workbook & Music CD. 2009. pap. 12.99 incl. audio compact disk (978-1-57583-894-6(X)) Twin Sisters IP, LLC.

—Old MacDonald Had a Farm. 2009. 16p. 4.99 (978-1-59922-369-8(4)) Twin Sisters IP, LLC.

—Old Testament Handlebox-4 books. 2009. 12.99 (978-1-59922-112-0(8)) Twin Sisters IP, LLC.

—Rise & Shine. 2010. (J). (gr. k-2). pap. 4.99 (978-1-59922-496-1(8)) Twin Sisters IP, LLC.

—Six Little Ducks. 2010. (J). (gr. k-1). 14.99 (978-1-59922-631-6(6)); pap. 4.99 (978-1-59922-504-3(2)) Twin Sisters IP, LLC.

—The Story of Jesus Handlebox-4books. 2009. 12.99 (978-1-59922-111-3(X)) Twin Sisters IP, LLC.

—Ten in the Bed. 2010. (J). (gr. k-2). pap. 4.99 (978-1-59922-503-6(4)) Twin Sisters IP, LLC.

—The Wheels on the Bus. 2009. 16p. 4.99 (978-1-59922-371-1(6)) Twin Sisters IP, LLC.

—When I Go Trick or Treating. 2009. 16p. 4.99 (978-1-59922-416-9(X)) Twin Sisters IP, LLC.

—120 Kids' Songs 4CD Digipack. 2008. (Illus.). 14.99 (978-1-59922-106-9(3)) Twin Sisters IP, LLC.

Twin Sisters(r) Staff, et al, adapted by. Six Little Ducks. 2010. (J). (gr. k-1). 14.99 (978-1-59922-423-7(2)) Twin Sisters IP, LLC.

Twin Sisters(r) Staff & Hilderbrand, Karen Mitzo, adapted by. Ten in the Bed. 2010. (J). (gr. k-1). 14.99 (978-1-59922-420-6(8)) Twin Sisters IP, LLC.

Twin Sisters(r) Staff, et al. I Thank God for You. 2010. (J). (gr. k-2). pap. 4.99 (978-1-59922-497-8(6)) Twin Sisters IP, LLC.

—It's Silly Time. 2010. (J). (gr. k-2). pap. 4.99 (978-1-59922-508-1(5)) Twin Sisters IP, LLC.

Vasilovich, Guy. The 13 Nights of Halloween. Vasilovich, Guy, illus. 2011. (ENG., Illus.). 40p. (J). (gr. -1-3). 16.99 (978-0-06-180445-8(2)) HarperCollins Pubs.

Vasylenko, Veronica, illus. Jingle Bells. 2007. (Padded Board Bks.). 18p. (J). (gr. -1-k). bds. 7.95 (978-1-58925-821-1(5)) Tiger Tales.

VBS Ready, Set, Gold! Music Guide. 2003. (J). pap. (978-0-8100-1528-9(5)) Northwestern Publishing Hse.

Vilsaint, Fequiere. Children Songs from Haiti: Chante Timoun Ayiti. Date not set. 28p. (J). (gr. 1-5). wbk. ed. 25.00 (978-1-881839-55-2(9)) Educa Vision Inc.

Wade, Connie Morgan. Bible Songs & Action Rhymes, Ages 3-6. 2016. (ENG., Illus.). 224p. (J). (gr. -1-3). per. 16.99 (978-0-7847-1781-3(8), 24190) Standard Publishing.

Walty, Margaret T., illus. Rock-a-Bye Baby: Lullabies for Bedtime. 2005. 40p. (J). (gr. k-4). reprint ed. 15.00 (978-0-7567-8555-0(3)) DIANE Publishing Co.

Wang, Margaret. Eency Weency Spider. Rueda, Claudia, illus. 2006. (ENG.). 22p. (J). (gr. -1-3). bds. 10.95 (978-1-58117-418-2(7), Intervisual/Piggy Toes) Bendon, Inc.

Warhola, James. If You're Happy & You Know It. 2007. (Illus.). (J). pap. (978-0-545-01981-1(8)) Scholastic, Inc.

Warhola, James & Scholastic, Inc. Staff. If You're Happy & You Know It. Geist, Ken, ed. Warhola, James, illus. 2007. (ENG., Illus.). 32p. (J). (gr. -1-k). 16.99 (978-0-439-72766-2(9), Orchard Bks.) Scholastic, Inc.

Weeks, Sarah. Don't Discover Me. Date not set. (J). (gr. -1-3). 15.99 (978-0-06-028139-7(1)) HarperCollins Pubs.

Welfing, Melanie Rook. Sing for Joy. 2005. (J). pap. 1.69 (978-1-59317-119-3(6)) Warner Pr., Inc.

Westerman, Robert. Santa We've Been Good: Sheet Music & Lyrics. 2006. (Illus.). 10p. (J). 6.95 (978-0-9761992-2-9(X)) Gold Boy Music & Pubn.

Weston Woods Staff, creator. Over in the Meadow. 2004. 18.95 (978-1-55592-809-4(9)); 29.95 (978-1-55592-852-0(8)); 38.75 (978-1-55592-759-2(9)) Weston Woods Studios, Inc.

Wilcox, Ella Wheeler. Historical Mother Goose: A Jingle Book O. 2006. pap. 15.95 (978-1-4179-7078-0(2)) Kessinger Publishing, LLC.

Williams, Pharrell. Happy! (ENG., Illus.). (J). (gr. -1 — 1). 2016. 30p. bds. 6.99 (978-0-399-54812-3(2)) 2015. 32p. 19.99 (978-0-399-17643-2(8)) Penguin Young Readers Group. (G.P. Putnam's Sons Books for Young Readers).

Williamson, Melanie, illus. Las Ruedas Del Autobús. 2017. (SPA.). 24p. (J). (gr. -1-1). pap. 9.99 incl. audio compact disk (978-1-84686-789-7(4)) Barefoot Bks., Inc.

Winter's Gift. (Song Box Ser.). (gr. 1-2). 31.50 (978-0-322-00267-8(2)) Wright Group/McGraw-Hill.

Winter's Gift: 6 Each of 1 Student Book, 6 vols. (Song Box Ser.). (gr. 1-2). 29.50 (978-0-322-00272-2(9)); 68.95 (978-0-322-00277-7(X)) Wright Group/McGraw-Hill.

Winter's Gift: Cassette. (Song Box Ser.). (gr. 1-2). 8.50 incl. audio (978-0-322-00251-7(6)) Wright Group/McGraw-Hill.

Wood, Hannah, illus. Old MacDonald Had a Farm: And Other Favorite Songs. 2012. (ENG.). 22p. (J). bds. (978-1-58925-874-7(6)) Tiger Tales.

Yarrow, Peter & Lipton, Lenny. Puff, the Magic Dragon. Puybaret, Eric, illus. (ENG.). (J). 2012. 24p. (gr. k — 1). bds. 7.95 (978-1-4549-0114-3(4)) 2010. 32p. (gr. k-2). cd-rom 9.95 (978-1-4027-7216-0(5)) 2007. 24p. (gr. -1-2). 16.95 (978-1-4027-4782-3(9)) Sterling Publishing Co., Inc.

Zahares, Wade, illus. Frosty the Snowman. 2013. (ENG.). 28p. (J). (gr. -1-3). 17.95 (978-1-62354-012-8(7)) Charlesbridge Publishing, Inc.

Zondervan Staff. Jesus Loves Me, 1 vol. Borlasca, Hector, illus. 2008. (I Can Read! / Song Ser.). (ENG.). 32p. (J). (gr. -1-3). pap. 3.99 (978-0-310-71619-8(5)) Zonderkidz.

—Jesus Loves the Little Children, 1 vol. Trasler, Janee, illus. 2008. (I Can Read! / Song Ser.). (ENG.). 32p. (J). (gr. -1-3). pap. 3.99 (978-0-310-71620-4(9)) Zonderkidz.

2005 VBS SongBook. 2005. (J). (978-1-58942-262-9(7)) R.H. Boyd Publishing Corp.

SONGS, AFRICAN AMERICAN

see African Americans—Music

SONGS, NATIONAL

see National Songs

SONGS, POPULAR

see Popular Music

SOOTHSAYING

see Divination

SOPORIFICS

see Narcotics

SORCERY

see Occultism; Witchcraft

SOSA, SAMMY, 1968-

Castle, George. Sammy Sosa: Slammin' Sammy. Rains, Rob, ed. 2003. (Superstar Ser.). (Illus.). 96p. (J). (gr. 4-7). pap. 4.95 (978-1-58261-029-0(0)) Sports Publishing, LLC.

Kirkpatrick, Rob. Sammy Sosa: Bateador de Home Runs (Home-Run Hitter) 2009. (Deportistas de Poder (Power Players) Ser.). (SPA.). 24p. (gr. 1-1). 42.50 (978-1-61512-160-1(9), Editorial Buenas Letras) Rosen Publishing Group, Inc., The.

—Sammy Sosa: Home Run Hitter/Bateador de home Runs. 2009. (Power Players / Deportistas de Poder Ser.). (ENG & SPA.). 24p. (gr. 1-2). 42.50 (978-1-60851-333-8(5), Editorial Buenas Letras) Rosen Publishing Group, Inc., The.

—Sammy Sosa, Home Run Hitter/Bateador de Home Runs. De Leon, Mauricio Velzaquez, tr. 2008. (Reading Power Ser.). (ENG., Illus.). 24p. (gr. 1-6). pap. 8.85 (978-1-4042-7541-6(X)) Rosen Publishing Group, Inc., The.

Malone, Julio. Sammy Sosa en 9 Innings. 2nd exp. ed. 2004. (SPA.). (YA). pap. 12.95 net. (978-0-9671705-0-3(8)) Editorial Miglo Inc.

—Sammy Sosa in 9 Innings. 2004. (YA). pap. 12.95 (978-0-9671705-1-0(6)) Editorial Miglo Inc.

Morrison, John. Sammy Sosa. 2006. (Great Hispanic Heritage Ser.). (Illus.). 112p. (gr. 6-12). lib. bdg. 35.00 (978-0-7910-8845-6(6), Chelsea Hse.) Facts On File, Inc.

Sammy Sosa - Sports Action Flipp Book. 2003. (J). mass mkt. 4.99 (978-0-9744443-3-8(2)) Flipp Sports.

Savage, Jeff. Sammy Sosa. 2005. (Amazing Athletes Ser.). (Illus.). 32p. (gr. 2-5). (J). per. 5.95 (978-0-8225-2041-2(9)); (ENG., lib. bdg. 25.26 (978-0-8225-3672-7(2)) Lerner Publishing Group.

—Sammy Sosa: Home Run Hero. (Sports Achievers Biographies Ser.). (Illus.). 2005. (SPA.). 80p. (gr. 7-12). lib. bdg. 22.60 (978-0-8225-3681-9(1)) 2003. 64p. (J). (gr. 4-9). 5.95 (978-0-8225-9858-9(2), Carolrhoda Bks.) Lerner Publishing Group.

Stewart, Mark. Sammy Sosa: Touching All the Bases. 2004. (American Literary Greats Ser.). (Illus.). 64p. (J). (gr. 5-18). lib. bdg. 25.26 (978-0-7613-2778-3(9), Millbrook Pr.) Lerner Publishing Group.

Torres, John Albert. Sports Great Sammy Sosa. 2003. (Sports Great Bks.). (Illus.). 64p. (J). (gr. 4-10). lib. bdg. 23.94 (978-0-7660-2065-8(7)) Enslow Pubs., Inc.

SOTO, HERNANDO DE, APPROXIMATELY 1500-1542

Brown, Janet Hubbard. Hernando de Soto & His Expeditions Across the Americas. Goetzmann, William H., ed. 2005. (Explorers of New Lands Ser.). (Illus.). 100p. (gr. 5-8). lib. bdg. 30.00 (978-0-7910-8610-0(0)) Facts On File, Inc.

Donohue, Moira Rose. Hernando de Soto. 2015. (Illus.). 24p. (J). (978-1-938813-20-7(0)) State Standards Publishing, LLC.

Goldberg, Jan. Hernando de Soto: Trailblazer of the American Southeast. (Library of Explorers & Exploration Ser.). 112p. (gr. 5-8). 2009. 66.50 (978-1-60853-607-8(6)) 2003. (Illus.). lib. bdg. 34.60 (978-0-8239-3623-6(6)) Rosen Publishing Group, Inc., The. (Rosen Reference).

Marsh, Carole. Hernando de Soto: First Discovered the Mississippi River: First Discovered the Mississippi River. 2003. 12p. (gr. k-4). 2.95 (978-0-635-02134-2(X)) Gallopade International.

Petrie, Kristin. Hernando de Soto, 1 vol. 2004. (Explorers Set 1 Ser.). (ENG.). 32p. (gr. k-6). 27.07 (978-1-59197-600-4(6), Checkerboard Library) ABDO Publishing Co.

Stein, R. Conrad. Hernando de Soto: A Life of Adventure. 2005. (Proud Heritage: the Hispanic Library). (ENG., Illus.). 40p. (J). (gr. 3-6). 29.93 (978-1-59296-385-0(4), 200010) Child's World, Inc., The.

Stuckey, Rachel. Explore with Hernando de Soto. 2016. (Travel with the Great Explorers Ser.). (ENG., Illus.). 32p. (J). (gr. 3-6). (978-0-7787-2849-8(8)) Crabtree Publishing Co.

Young, Jeff C. Hernando de Soto: Spanish Conquistador in the Americas. 2009. (Great Explorers of the World Ser.). (Illus.). 112p. (J). (gr. 7-12). lib. bdg. 33.27 (978-1-59845-104-7(9)) Enslow Pubs., Inc.

SOUND

see also High-Fidelity Sound Systems

Alinas, Marv. Red Ribbons: The Sound of R. 2016. (Consonants Ser.). (ENG.). 24p. (J). (gr. -1-2). 25.64 *(978-1-5038-0923-9(4),* 210758) Child's World, Inc., The.

Allen, Joy. Baby Sounds. 2012. (ENG.). 16p. (J). (gr. -1 — 1). bds. 6.99 *(978-0-8037-3831-7(5),* Dial Bks) Penguin Young Readers Group.

Amoroso, Cynthia. A Day with George: The Sound of Soft G. 2016. (Consonants Ser.). (ENG.). 24p. (J). (gr. -1-2). 25.64 *(978-1-5038-0931-4(5),* 210766) Child's World, Inc., The.

—Fun in the City: The Sound of Soft C. 2016. (Consonants Ser.). (ENG.). 24p. (J). (gr. -1-2). 25.64 *(978-1-5038-0930-7(7),* 210767) Child's World, Inc., The.

Amoroso, Cynthia & Ballard, Peg. Malls: The Sound of M. 2016. (Consonants Ser.). (ENG.). 24p. (J). (gr. -1-2). 25.64 *(978-1-5038-0909-3(9),* 210755) Child's World, Inc., The.

—Task Time: The Sound of T. 2016. (Consonants Ser.). (ENG.). 24p. (J). (gr. -1-2). 25.64 *(978-1-5038-0913-0(7),* 210760) Child's World, Inc., The.

Amoroso, Cynthia & Noyed, Bob. The Cabin: The Sound of Hard C. 2016. (Consonants Ser.). (ENG.). 24p. (J). (gr. -1-2). 25.64 *(978-1-5038-0914-7(5),* 210761) Child's World, Inc., The.

—Jump! The Sound of J. 2016. (Consonants Ser.). (ENG.). 24p. (J). (gr. -1-2). 25.64 *(978-1-5038-0917-8(X),* 210752) Child's World, Inc., The.

—Naps: The Sound of N. 2016. (Consonants Ser.). (ENG.). 24p. (J). (gr. -1-2). 25.64 *(978-1-5038-0918-5(8),* 210756) Child's World, Inc., The.

—Quack! The Sound of Q. 2016. (Consonants Ser.). (ENG.). 24p. (J). (gr. -1-2). 25.64 *(978-1-5038-0929-1(3),* 210757) Child's World, Inc., The.

At My Grandfather's, 6 Pcks. (gr. -1-2). 27.00 *(978-0-7635-9435-0(0))* Rigby Education.

AZ Books Staff. Buzzing Meadow. Tulup, Natalia, ed. 2012. (How We Speak Ser.). (ENG.). 12p. (J). (gr. -1-k). bds. 10.95 *(978-1-61889-095-5(6))* AZ Bks. LLC.

—Feathered Singers. Tulup, Natalia, ed. 2012. (How We Speak Ser.). (ENG.). 12p. (J). (gr. -1-k). bds. 10.95 *(978-1-61889-096-2(4))* AZ Bks. LLC.

—Loud Farm. Tulup, Natalia, ed. 2012. (How We Speak Ser.). (ENG.). 12p. (J). (-k). bds. 10.95 *(978-1-61889-093-1(X))* AZ Bks. LLC.

Baker, Wendy, et al. Sound. (Make It Work! (Eureka!) Ser.). (FRE., Illus.). (J). pap. 9.99 *(978-0-590-24631-6(3))* Scholastic, Inc.

Ballard, Carol. Exploring Sound. 2008. (How Does Science Work? Ser.). (Illus.). 32p. (J). (gr. 3-7). lib. bdg. 26.50 *(978-1-4042-4279-1(1))* Rosen Publishing Group, Inc., The.

Ballard, Peg. Gifts for Gus: The Sound of Hard G. 2016. (Consonants Ser.). (ENG.). 24p. (J). (gr. -1-2). 25.64 *(978-1-5038-0921-5(8),* 210749) Child's World, Inc., The.

—Vets: The Sound of V. 2016. (Consonants Ser.). (ENG.). 24p. (J). (gr. -1-2). 25.64 *(978-1-5038-0920-8(X),* 210762) Child's World, Inc., The.

Barchers, Suzanne I. I've Discovered Sound. 2008. (Eureka! Ser.). 32p. (gr. 4-18). lib. bdg. 28.50 *(978-0-7614-3207-4(8),* Benchmark Bks.) Marshall Cavendish Corp.

Barlex, David & Wadsworth, Pamela. Rhagor Am Sain a Cherddoriaeth. 2005. (WEL., Illus.). 24p. pap. *(978-1-85596-240-8(3))* Dref Wen.

—Sain a Cherddoriaeth. 2005. (WEL., Illus.). 24p. pap. *(978-1-85596-239-2(X))* Dref Wen.

Bateman, Graham, ed. Light & Sound. 2011. (FAYFT: Introducing Physics Ser.). 64p. (gr. 4-10). lib. bdg. 39.95 *(978-1-936333-06-6(6))* Brown Bear Bks.

Beech, Linda Ward. The Magic School Bus in the Haunted Museum: A Book about Sound. Duchesne, Lucie, tr. Schick, Joel, illus. (Magic School Bus Ser.). (FRE.). 32p. (J). (gr. 1-4). pap. 5.99 *(978-0-590-24657-6(7))* Scholastic, Inc.

Benchmark Education Co., LLC. What Is That Sound? Big Book. 2014. (Shared Reading Foundations Ser.). (J). (gr. -1). *(978-1-4509-9437-8(7))* Benchmark Education Co.

Benchmark Education Company, LLC Staff, compiled by. Light & Sound: Theme Set. 2006. (J). 215.00 *(978-1-4108-7121-3(5))* Benchmark Education Co.

Boothroyd, Jennifer. Loud or Soft? High or Low? A Look at Sound. 2011. (Lightning Bolt Books Exploring Physical Science Ser.). 32p. pap. 45.32 *(978-0-7613-7650-7(X));* (ENG.). pap. 7.95 *(978-0-7613-7107-6(9));* (ENG.). lib. bdg. 26.60 *(978-0-7613-6091-9(3))* Lerner Publishing Group.

—Sending Messages with Light & Sound. 2014. (First Step Nonfiction - Light & Sound Ser.). (Illus.). 24p. (gr. k-2). pap. 6.95 *(978-1-4677-4504-8(9));* (ENG., Illus.). lib. bdg. 23.93 *(978-1-4677-3913-9(8),* Lerner Pubns.) Lerner Publishing Group.

—Sensing Light & Sound. 2014. (First Step Nonfiction - Light & Sound Ser.). (ENG., Illus.). 24p. (gr. k-2). lib. bdg. 23.93 *(978-1-4677-3915-3(4),* Lerner Pubns.) Lerner Publishing Group.

—Vibrations Make Sound. 2014. (First Step Nonfiction - Light & Sound Ser.). (ENG., Illus.). 24p. (gr. k-2). lib. bdg. 23.93 *(978-1-4677-3910-8(3),* Lerner Pubns.) Lerner Publishing Group.

Brasch, Nicolas. Tricks of Sound & Light. 2010. (Science Behind Ser.). 32p. lib. bdg. 28.50 *(978-1-59920-564-9(5))* Black Rabbit Bks.

—Why Does Sound Travel? All about Sound. 2010. (Illus.). 24p. (J). 49.50 *(978-1-61531-909-1(3),* 1307169, PowerKids Pr.) Rosen Publishing Group, Inc., The.

—Why Is It So Loud? 2010. (Solving Science Mysteries Ser.). (Illus.). (J). pap. 8.25 *(978-1-61531-908-4(5),* PowerKids Pr.); (YA). (gr. 3-6). lib. bdg. 22.60 *(978-1-61531-888-9(7))* Rosen Publishing Group, Inc., The.

Braun, Eric. Simply Sound: Science Adventures with Jasper the Origami Bat, 1 vol. Christoph, Jamey, illus. 2014. (Origami Science Adventures Ser.). (ENG.). 24p. (gr. 3-4). lib. bdg. 27.32 *(978-1-4795-2187-6(6))* Picture Window Bks.

Burton, Margie, et al. I Hear! 2011. (Early Connections Ser.). (J). *(978-1-61672-294-4(0))* Benchmark Education Co.

Carlson Berne, Emma. Loud! Sound Energy. 2013. (Energy Everywhere Ser.). (ENG., Illus.). 24p. (J). (gr. 3-6). 22.60 *(978-1-4488-9648-6(7));* pap. 8.25 *(978-1-4488-9754-4(8))* Rosen Publishing Group, Inc., The. (PowerKids Pr.).

Casado, Dami & Casado, Alicia. El Sueño. 2005. (Sentidos y Algo Más). (SPA & ESP.). 16p. 8.99 *(978-84-272-6417-5(8))* Molino, Editorial ESP. Dist: Santillana USA Publishing Co., Inc.

Challoner, Jack. Sound: An Investigation. 2008. (Science Investigations Ser.). (Illus.). 32p. (YA). (gr. 4-7). lib. bdg. 26.50 *(978-1-4042-4285-2(6))* Rosen Publishing Group, Inc., The.

Claybourne, Anna. Ear-Splitting Sounds & Other Vile Noises. 2013. (ENG., Illus.). 32p. (J). *(978-0-7787-0925-1(6));* pap. *(978-0-7787-0951-0(5))* Crabtree Publishing Co.

—Light & Sound. 2017. (Mind Webs Ser.). (ENG., Illus.). 32p. (J). (gr. 4-6). pap. 11.99 *(978-0-7502-8959-7(7),* Wayland) Hachette Children's Group GBR. Dist: Hachette Bk. Group.

—Sound. 2013. (Physical Science Ser.). 48p. (J). (gr. 4-6). pap. 84.30 *(978-1-4339-9522-4(0));* pap. 14.05 *(978-1-4339-9521-7(2));* (ENG., Illus.). lib. bdg. 31.95 *(978-1-4339-9520-0(4))* Stevens, Gareth Publishing LLLP.

Coan, Sharon. How Sound Moves, 1 vol. (Science Readers: Content & Literacy Ser.). (ENG., Illus.). 24p. (gr. 1-1). 2015. (J). 22.96 *(978-1-4938-1151-9(7))* 2014. pap. 8.99 *(978-1-4807-4564-3(2))* Teacher Created Materials, Inc.

Cooper, Christopher. The Basics of Sound. 2014. (Core Concepts Ser.). (Illus.). 96p. (YA). (gr. 7-12). 35.60 *(978-1-4777-7766-4(0))* Rosen Publishing Group, Inc., The.

Dorling Kindersley Publishing Staff. Baby Beep! Beep! 2010. (ENG.). 16p. (J). (gr. -1 — 1). bds. 6.99 *(978-0-7566-7133-4(7),* DK Children) Dorling Kindersley Publishing, Inc.

—Baby Faces Peekaboo! 2009. (ENG.). 12p. (J). (gr. -1 — 1). bds. 9.99 *(978-0-7566-5506-8(4),* DK Children) Dorling Kindersley Publishing, Inc.

—Noisy Toys Peekaboo! 2016. (ENG., Illus.). 12p. (J). (— 1). bds. 12.99 *(978-1-4654-5423-2(3),* DK Children) Dorling Kindersley Publishing, Inc.

Dunne, Abbie. Sound. 2016. (Physical Science Ser.). (ENG., Illus.). 24p. (gr. k-1). lib. bdg. 26.65 *(978-1-5157-0940-4(X),* Pebble Plus) Capstone Press of Coughlan Cos.

Flanagan, Alice K. Dogs: The Sound of D. 2016. (Consonants Ser.). (ENG.). 24p. (J). (gr. -1-2). 25.64 *(978-1-5038-0916-1(1),* 210747) Child's World, Inc., The.

—Four Fish: The Sound of F. 2016. (Consonants Ser.). (ENG.). 24p. (J). (gr. -1-2). 25.64 *(978-1-5038-0919-2(6),* 210748) Child's World, Inc., The.

—Hats Can Help: The Sound of H. 2016. (Consonants Ser.). (ENG.). 24p. (J). (gr. -1-2). 25.64 *(978-1-5038-0915-4(3),* 210750) Child's World, Inc., The.

—I Like Bugs: The Sound of B. 2016. (Consonants Ser.). (ENG.). 24p. (J). (gr. -1-2). 25.64 *(978-1-5038-0911-6(0),* 210751) Child's World, Inc., The.

—Kids: The Sound of K. 2016. (Consonants Ser.). (ENG.). 24p. (J). (gr. -1-2). 25.64 *(978-1-5038-0928-4(5),* 210753) Child's World, Inc., The.

—Left: The Sound of L. 2016. (Consonants Ser.). (ENG.). 24p. (J). (gr. -1-2). 25.64 *(978-1-5038-0922-2(6),* 210754) Child's World, Inc., The.

—A Pet: The Sound of P. 2016. (Consonants Ser.). (ENG.). 24p. (J). (gr. -1-2). 25.64 *(978-1-5038-0910-9(2),* 210746) Child's World, Inc., The.

—Sam: The Sound of S. 2016. (Consonants Ser.). (ENG.). 24p. (J). (gr. -1-2). 25.64 *(978-1-5038-0912-3(9),* 210759) Child's World, Inc., The.

—Wish & Win: The Sound of W. 2016. (Consonants Ser.). (ENG.). 24p. (J). (gr. -1-2). 25.64 *(978-1-5038-0924-6(2),* 210763) Child's World, Inc., The.

—Yum! The Sound of Y. 2016. (Consonants Ser.). (ENG.). 24p. (J). (gr. -1-2). 25.64 *(978-1-5038-0926-0(9),* 210764) Child's World, Inc., The.

—Zigzag: The Sound of Z. 2016. (Consonants Ser.). (ENG.). 24p. (J). (gr. -1-2). 25.64 *(978-1-5038-0927-7(7),* 210765) Child's World, Inc., The.

Flesch Connors, Abigail. Exploring the Science of Sounds: 100 Musical Activities for Young Children. 2017. (ENG.). (gr. 13). pap. 16.95 ***(978-0-87659-731-6(2)***, Gryphon House Inc) Gryphon Hse., Inc.

Fonder, Toni. The Science of Sound. 2009. (Real Life Readers Ser.). 16p. (gr. 2-3). pap. 7.05 *(978-1-4358-0093-9(1),* Rosen Classroom) Rosen Publishing Group, Inc., The.

Frenkel, Karen A. Light & Sound Technology: Text Pairs. 2008. (Bridges/Navigators Ser.). (J). (gr. 4). 94.00 *(978-1-4108-8386-5(8))* Benchmark Education Co.

—Listening to Sound: Set Of 6. 2011. (Navigators Ser.). (J). pap. 48.00 net. *(978-1-4108-6227-3(5))* Benchmark Education Co.

—Listening to Sound: Text Pairs. 2008. (Bridges/Navigators Ser.). (J). (gr. 4). 94.00 *(978-1-4108-8387-2(6))* Benchmark Education Co.

Gardner, Jane P. Music Science, Vol. 11. Lewin, Russ, ed. 2015. (Science 24/7 Ser.). (Illus.). 48p. (J). (gr. 5). 20.95 *(978-1-4222-3412-9(6))* Mason Crest.

Gardner, Robert & Conklin, Joshua. A Kid's Book of Experiments about Sound. 2016. (Surprising Science Experiments Ser.). (ENG., Illus.). 48p. (J). (gr. 4-4). 27.93 *(978-0-7660-7209-1(6))* Enslow Pubs., Inc.

Gish, Melissa. Sound. 2005. (My First Look at Science Ser.). (Illus.). 24p. (J). (gr. k-3). lib. bdg. 15.95 *(978-1-58341-374-6(X),* Creative Education) Creative Co., The.

Gregoire, Maryellen. All Kinds of Sounds. 2011. (Wonder Readers Emergent Level Ser.). (ENG.). (gr. -1-1). 8p. pap. 35.94 *(978-1-4296-8217-6(5));* 32p. pap. 5.99 *(978-1-4296-7838-4(0))* Capstone Press of Coughlan Cos. (Wonder Readers).

Greve, Meg. Speakers. 2014. (ENG., Illus.). 24p. (gr. k-3). 28.50 *(978-1-62717-644-6(6))* Rourke Educational Media.

Hall, Pamela. Discover Sound. Yamada, Jane, illus. 2014. (Science Around Us Ser.). (ENG.). 24p. (J). (gr. -1-2). 25.64 *(978-1-62687-306-3(2),* 207147) Child's World, Inc., The.

Harkrader, Lisa. The Science of Sound. 2016. (Spring Forward Ser.). (J). (gr. 1). *(978-1-4900-9401-4(6))* Benchmark Education Co.

Hartman, Eve & Meshbesher, Wendy. Light & Sound. 2016. (Sci-Hi: Physical Science Ser.). (ENG.). 48p. (gr. 4-4). pap. 8.99 *(978-1-4109-8536-1(9),* Sci-Hi) Heinemann-Raintree.

Haslam, Andrew, et al. Sound. (Make It Work! Ser.). (Illus.). 48p. (J). pap. 7.99 *(978-0-590-24615-6(1))* Scholastic, Inc.

Herold, Vickey. Breaking the Sound Barrier. 2006. (J). pap. *(978-1-4108-6487-1(1))* Benchmark Education Co.

—Discover Sound. 2006. (J). pap. *(978-1-4108-6489-5(8))* Benchmark Education Co.

—Sound Is Energy. 2006. (J). pap. *(978-1-4108-6486-4(3))* Benchmark Education Co.

Hewitt, Sally. Amazing Sound. 2007. (Amazing Science Ser.). (ENG., Illus.). 32p. (J). (gr. 3-7). pap. *(978-0-7787-3629-5(6))* Crabtree Publishing Co.

Higgins, Nadia. Stupendous Sound, 1 vol. Ricci, Andres Martinez, illus. 2008. (Science Rocks Ser.). (ENG.). 32p. (gr. -1-4). 28.50 *(978-1-60270-280-6(2),* 1287328, Looking Glass Library- Nonfiction) Magic Wagon.

—Stupendous Sound CD+Book. Martinez Ricci, Andres, illus. 2010. (Science Rocks! Set 2 CD+Book Ser.). 32p. lib. bdg. 54.14 incl. cd-rom *(978-1-60270-995-9(5))* ABDO Publishing Co.

—Stupendous Sound Site CD+Book. Martinez Ricci, Andres, illus. 2010. (Science Rocks! Set 2 Site CD+Book Ser.). 32p. lib. bdg. 84.14 incl. cd-rom *(978-1-61641-012-4(4))* ABDO Publishing Co.

Hollar, Sherman. Sound. 2012. (Introduction to Physics Ser.). (ENG., Illus.). 80p. (gr. 7-12). (J). 31.70 *(978-1-61530-841-5(5));* (YA). 63.40 *(978-1-61530-849-1(0))* Rosen Publishing Group, Inc., The.

Holt, Rinehart and Winston Staff. Holt Science & Technology Chapter 21: Physical Science: The Nature of Sound. 5th ed. 2004. (Illus.). pap. 12.86 *(978-0-03-030436-1(9))* Holt McDougal.

Horne, Jane. Busy Baby Noisy Book. 2007. (Busy Baby Ser.). (Illus.). 12p. (gr. -1). per., bds. *(978-1-84610-434-3(3))* Make Believe Ideas.

Issa, Joanna. What Can I Hear?, 1 vol. 2014. (These Are My Senses Ser.). (ENG., Illus.). 24p. (gr. -1-1). pap. 5.99 *(978-1-4846-0433-5(4),* Acorn) Heinemann-Raintree.

Jankowski, Connie. All about Light & Sound, 1 vol. 2007. (Science Readers Ser.). (SPA & ENG.). 32p. (J). (gr. 4-4). pap. 8.99 *(978-0-7439-0579-4(2))* Shell Educational Publishing.

—Pioneers of Light & Sound, 1 vol. 2007. (Science Readers Ser.). (ENG.). 32p. (J). (gr. 3-3). pap. 8.99 *(978-0-7439-0580-0(6))* Shell Educational Publishing.

Jennings, Terry Catasús. Sounds of the Savanna, 1 vol. Saroff, Phyllis, illus. 2015. 32p. (J). (gr. k-3). (ENG.). pap. 9.95 *(978-1-62855-637-7(4));* (SPA & ENG.). pap. 9.95 *(978-1-62855-642-1(0))* Arbordale Publishing.

Johnson, Rebecca L. & National Geographic Learning Staff. The Magic of Light & Sound. 2006. (Nonfiction Reading & Writing Workshops Ser.). (ENG., Illus.). 32p. (J). pap. 17.95 *(978-0-7922-8886-2(6))* CENGAGE Learning.

Johnson, Robin. How Does Sound Change? 2014. (ENG., Illus.). 24p. (J). *(978-0-7787-0520-8(X))* Crabtree Publishing Co.

Jordan, Apple. Noisy Quiet. 2nd rev. ed. 2011. (Bookworms 2nd Edition: Opposites Ser.). 16p. (gr. k-1). 21.36 *(978-1-60870-421-7(1))* Marshall Cavendish Corp.

Kelly, Lynne. Simple Concepts in Physics: Sound & Light. (Illus.). 88p. (J). (gr. 5-6). pap. *(978-1-875739-69-1(6))* Wizard Bks.

Kenney, Karen Latchana. The Science of Music: Discovering Sound, 1 vol. 2016. (Science in Action Ser.). (ENG., Illus.). 32p. (J). (gr. 3-6). 27.07 *(978-1-62403-962-1(6))* ABDO Publishing Co.

Lawrence, Ellen. Sound. 2014. (Science Slam: FUN-Damentals Ser.). 24p. (J). (gr. -1-3). lib. bdg. 23.93 *(978-1-62724-094-9(2))* Bearport Publishing Co., Inc.

Light & Sound. 2010. (Science Foundations Ser.). (Illus.). 128p. (gr. 6-12). 35.00 *(978-1-60413-344-8(9),* Chelsea Hse.) Facts On File, Inc.

Llewellyn, Claire. Sound. 2005. (I Know That! Ser.). (Illus.). 24p. (J). (gr. 1-3). lib. bdg. 22.80 *(978-1-932889-37-6(X))* Sea-To-Sea Pubns.

—Sound & Hearing. 2011. (Start-Up Connections Ser.). (ENG., Illus.). 32p. (J). pap. 12.99 *(978-0-237-54364-8(8))* Evans Brothers, Ltd. GBR. Dist: Independent Pubs. Group.

Loria, Laura. What Is Sound Energy? 2017. (Let's Find Out! Forms of Energy Ser.). 32p. (gr. 6-8). pap. 12.90 ***(978-1-68048-713-8(2)***, Britannica Educational Publishing) Rosen Publishing Group, Inc., The.

Lowery, Lawrence F. Quiet As a Butterfly. 2017. (I Wonder Why Ser.). (ENG., Illus.). 36p. (J). (gr. k-2). pap. 11.95 *(978-1-68140-354-0(4))* National Science Teachers Assn.

—Sounds Are High, Sounds Are Low: I Wonder Why. Fraser, Betty, illus. 2014. (I Wonder Why Ser.). (ENG.). 36p. (J). (gr. k-3). pap. 11.95 *(978-1-941316-04-7(2))* National Science Teachers Assn.

Manolis, Kay. Sound. 2007. (First Science Ser.). (ENG., Illus.). 24p. (J). (gr. 2-5). lib. bdg. 25.95 *(978-1-60014-099-0(8))* Bellwether Media.

—Sound. 2007. (Blastoff! Readers Ser.). (ENG.). 24p. (J). (gr. k-2). 20.00 *(978-0-531-14728-3(2),* Children's Pr.) Scholastic Library Publishing.

Mason, Adrienne. Lost & Found. Cupples, Pat, illus. 2008. (Kids Can Read Ser.). (ENG.). 32p. (J). (gr. 1-2). 14.95 *(978-1-55453-251-3(5));* pap. 3.95 *(978-1-55453-252-0(3))* Kids Can Pr., Ltd. CAN. Dist: Hachette Bk. Group.

Maurer, Daniel D. Do You Really Want to Yell in a Cave? A Book about Sound. Alberini, Teresa, illus. 2016. (Adventures in Science Ser.). (ENG.). 24p. (J). (gr. k-3). 20.95 *(978-1-60753-956-8(X))* Amicus Publishing.

Max and Sid Staff, illus. My First Sounds. 2016. (My First Ser.). (ENG.). 12p. (J). (gr. -1 — 1). bds. 5.99 *(978-1-4998-0187-3(4))* Little Bee Books Inc.

McGregor, Harriet. Sound. 2010. (Sherlock Bones Looks at Physical Science Ser.). (ENG.). 32p. (YA). (gr. 3-6). lib. bdg. 25.25 *(978-1-61533-215-1(4))* Windmill Bks.

Mendez, Horatio. Understanding Sound. 2013. (InfoMax Readers Ser.). (ENG.). 24p. (J). (gr. 2-3). pap. 49.50 *(978-1-4777-2394-4(3));* (Illus.). pap. 8.25 *(978-1-4777-2393-7(5))* Rosen Publishing Group, Inc., The. (Rosen Classroom).

Midthun, Joseph & Hiti, Samuel. Gravity. 2012. (Illus.). 32p. (J). *(978-0-7166-1420-3(0))* World Bk., Inc.

Milios, Rita. Sound in the Real World. 2013. (Science in the Real World EBook Ser.). (ENG.). 48p. (J). pap. 15.64 *(978-1-61783-794-4(6),* Core Library); (gr. 3-6). lib. bdg. 32.79 *(978-1-61783-744-9(X))* ABDO Publishing Co.

Mortensen, Lori. What's That Sound? 2016. (Spring Forward Ser.). (J). (gr. 1). *(978-1-4900-9387-1(7))* Benchmark Education Co.

Murray, Julie. Sound & Hearing, 1 vol. 2006. (First Science Ser.). (ENG., Illus.). 24p. (gr. k-4). 25.65 *(978-1-59679-831-1(9),* Buddy Bks.) ABDO Publishing Co.

Nsrc, prod. Science & Technology for Children BOOKS: Sound. 2008. 64p. (J). *(978-1-933008-42-4(3),* Science and Technology Concepts (STC)) Smithsonian Science Education Ctr. (SSEC).

O'Hara, Nicholas. Sonidos / Sort It by Sound. de la Vega, Eida, tr. 2015. (Vamos a Agrupar Por... / Sort It Out! Ser.). (ENG & SPA.). 24p. (J). (gr. k-1). lib. bdg. 22.60 *(978-1-4824-3221-3(8))* Stevens, Gareth Publishing LLLP.

—Sort It by Sound. 2015. (Sort It Out! Ser.). (ENG., Illus.). 24p. (J). (gr. k-1). 22.60 *(978-1-4824-2579-6(3))* Stevens, Gareth Publishing LLLP.

Orr, Tamra B. Understanding Sound. 2015. (Explorer Library: Science Explorer Ser.). (ENG., Illus.). 32p. (J). (gr. 4-8). pap. 14.21 *(978-1-63362-421-4(8),* 206993) Cherry Lake Publishing.

Peterson, Megan Cooley. Scooby-Doo! a Science of Sound Mystery: A Song for Zombies. 2016. (Scooby-Doo Solves It with S. T. E. M. Ser.). (ENG., Illus.). 32p. (gr. 3-4). 27.99 *(978-1-5157-2593-0(6))* Capstone Press of Coughlan Cos.

Prentice Hall Direct Education Staff. Science Explorer - Sound & Light. 2004. (ENG.). (gr. 6-8). stu. ed. 14.97 *(978-0-13-115101-7(0),* Prentice Hall) Pearson Schl.

Prentice-Hall Staff. Sound & Light. 2nd ed. (J). stu. ed. 7.97 *(978-0-13-400565-2(1));* pap., act. bk. ed. *(978-0-13-400581-2(3))* Prentice Hall (Schl. Div.).

Publications International Ltd. Staff, creator. Baby Einstein Animal Melodies. 2005. (Baby Einstein Ser.). (Illus.). 10p. (J). (gr. -1-k). 10.50 *(978-1-4127-3495-0(9),* 7262600) Publications International, Ltd.

Randolph, Joanne. Sounds in My World. (My World of Science Ser.). 24p. 2009. (gr. 2-2). 37.50 *(978-1-61514-729-8(2))* 2006. (Illus.). (J). (gr. 3-7). lib. bdg. 18.75 *(978-1-4042-3287-7(7))* Rosen Publishing Group, Inc., The. (PowerKids Pr.).

—Sounds in My World: Los Sonidos en Mi Mundo. 2006. (My World of Science/ Mi mundo y la Ciencia Ser.). (ENG & SPA.). (J). (gr. k-3). 16.00 *(978-1-4042-3318-8(0))* Rosen Publishing Group, Inc., The.

—Sounds in My World/Los sonidos en mi Mundo. 2009. (My World of Science/la ciencia en mi mundo Ser.). (ENG & SPA.). 48p. (gr. 2-2). 37.50 *(978-1-61514-741-0(1),* Editorial Buenas Letras) Rosen Publishing Group, Inc., The.

Riley, Peter. Changing Sounds. 2007. (Essential Science/Watts Ser.). (Illus.). 32p. (YA). (gr. 3-6). lib. bdg. 28.50 *(978-1-59920-023-1(6))* Black Rabbit Bks.

—Sound. 2016. (Moving up with Science Ser.). 00032p. (J). (gr. 3-4). pap. 10.00 *(978-1-4994-3157-5(0),* PowerKids Pr.) Rosen Publishing Group, Inc., The.

Riley, Peter D. Sound. 2011. (Real Scientist Investigates Ser.). (Illus.). 32p. (J). (gr. 3-5). lib. bdg. 28.50 *(978-1-59771-283-5(3))* Sea-To-Sea Pubns.

Ritchie, Scot. My House Is Alive! The Weird & Wonderful Sounds Your House Makes. 2016. (ENG., Illus.). 40p. (J). (gr. -1-3). 16.95 *(978-1-77147-136-7(0),* Owlkids) Owlkids Bks. Inc. CAN. Dist: Publishers Group West (PGW).

Rogers, K. Light, Sound & Electricity. 2004. (Library of Science Ser.). 64p. (J). lib. bdg. 17.95 *(978-1-58086-376-6(0))* EDC Publishing.

Rooney, Anne. Audio Engineering & the Science of Soundwaves. 2013. (ENG., Illus.). 32p. (J). *(978-0-7787-1196-4(X));* pap. *(978-0-7787-1229-9(X))* Crabtree Publishing Co.

Rosinsky, Natalie M. El Sonido: Fuerte, Suave, Alto y Bajo, 1 vol. Robledo, Sol, tr. from ENG. John, Matthew, illus. 2007. (Ciencia Asombrosa Ser.). (SPA.). 24p. (gr. k-4). per. 8.19 *(978-1-4048-2493-5(6))* Picture Window Bks.

Rosinsky, Natalie M. & Picture Window Books Staff. El Sonido: Fuerte, Suave, Alto y Bajo, 1 vol. Robledo, Sol, tr. from ENG. John, Matthew, illus. 2007. (Ciencia Asombrosa Ser.). (SPA.). 24p. (gr. k-4). 26.65 *(978-1-4048-3229-9(7))* Picture Window Bks.

Royston, Angela. All about Sound. 2016. (All about Science Ser.). (ENG., Illus.). 32p. (gr. 1-3). lib. bdg. 27.32 *(978-1-4846-2691-7(5),* Heinemann First Library) Heinemann-Raintree.

—Sound & Hearing. 2012. (Science Corner Ser.). (Illus.). 24p. (J). (gr. 1-3). lib. bdg. 22.60 *(978-1-4488-5259-8(5))* Rosen Publishing Group, Inc., The.

Science Stories Foss Spanish Physics of Sound EA CR05. 2005. (J). *(978-1-59242-587-7(9))* Delta Education, LLC.

Sian Revision Sound Vibrations. 2004. (J). *(978-1-59242-075-9(3))* Delta Education, LLC.

Silverman, Buffy. The Amazing Facts about Sound. 2012. (ENG.). 24p. (gr. 4-5). pap. 8.95 *(978-1-61810-242-3(7))* Rourke Educational Media.

Sohn, Emily & Timmons, Anne. Adventures in Sound with Max Axiom, Super Scientist, 1 vol. Martin, Cynthia, illus. 2007. (Graphic Science Ser.). (ENG.). 32p. (gr. 3-4). per. 8.10 *(978-0-7368-7889-0(0),* Graphic Library) Capstone Press of Coughlan Cos.

Sohn, Emily & Wright, Pam. Sound: Music to Your Ears. 2011. (iScience Readers Ser.). 32p. (J). (gr. 3-4). lib. bdg. 22.60 *(978-1-59953-419-0(3))* Norwood Hse. Pr.

Solway, Andrew. From Crashing Waves to Music Download: An Energy Journey Through the World of Sound. 2015. (Energy Journeys Ser.). (ENG.). 48p. (gr. 3-6). 33.32 *(978-1-4846-0883-8(6),* Heinemann InfoSearch) Heinemann-Raintree.

Somervill, Barbara A. Ticks: Digging for Blood. 2007. (Bloodsuckers Ser.). (Illus.). 24p. (gr. 2-5). lib. bdg. 22.60 *(978-1-4042-3800-8(X))* Rosen Publishing Group, Inc., The.

Sound. (Make It Work Ser.). 42p. (J). (gr. 4-8). pap. *(978-1-882210-46-6(8))* Action Publishing, Inc.

Spilsbury, Louise. The Science of Sound. 2016. (Flowchart Smart Ser.). (ENG.). 48p. (J). (gr. 4-5). pap. 14.05 *(978-1-4824-4150-5(0))* Stevens, Gareth Publishing LLLP.

Spilsbury, Louise & Spilsbury, Richard. Exploring Sound, 1 vol. 2014. (Exploring Sound Ser.). (ENG.). 32p. (gr. 2-4). lib. bdg. 122.60 *(978-1-4109-6003-0(X),* Raintree Perspectives) Heinemann-Raintree.

S

—Light & Sound, 1 vol. 2013. (Essential Physical Science Ser.). (ENG.). 48p. (gr. 4-6). 33.32 (978-1-4329-8146-4(3), Heinemann InfoSearch) Heinemann-Raintree.

—Turn It up!; Turn It down!: Volume, 1 vol. HL Studios Staff, illus. 2014. (Exploring Sound Ser.). (ENG.). 32p. (gr. 2-4). lib. bdg. 30.65 (978-1-4109-6001-6(3), Raintree Perspectives) Heinemann-Raintree.

—Why Can't I Hear That?: Pitch & Frequency, 1 vol. HL Studios Staff, illus. 2014. (Exploring Sound Ser.). (ENG.). 32p. (gr. 2-4). lib. bdg. 30.65 (978-1-4109-6000-9(5), Raintree Perspectives) Heinemann-Raintree.

Stiegemeyer, Julie. Things I Hear in Church. Mitter, Kathy, illus. 2003. 20p. (J). bds. 5.49 (978-0-7586-0125-4(5)) Concordia Publishing Hse.

Stradling, Jan. Sounds all Around: Level K, 6 vols.; Vol. 2. (First Explorers Ser.). 24p. (gr. 1-2). 34.95 (978-0-7699-1464-0(0)) Shortland Pubns. (U. S. A.) Inc.

Sundance/Newbridge LLC Staff. Sound. 2007. (Early Science Ser.). (gr. k-3). 18.95 (978-1-4007-6395-5(9)); pap. 6.10 (978-1-4007-6391-7(6)) Sundance/Newbridge Educational Publishing.

—What's That Sound? 2004. (Reading PowerWorks Ser.). (gr. 1-3). 37.50 (978-0-7608-9807-9(3)); pap. 6.10 (978-0-7608-9808-6(1)) Sundance/Newbridge Educational Publishing.

Trumbauer, Lisa. All about Sound. 2004. (Rookie Read-About Science Ser.). (ENG.). 32p. (J). (gr. 1-2). pap. 4.95 (978-0-516-25847-8(8), Children's Pr.) Scholastic Library Publishing.

Vogel, Julia. Your Sensational Sense of Hearing. Squier, Robert, illus. 2011. (Sensational Senses Ser.). (ENG.). 32p. (J). (gr. k-3). lib. bdg. 27.07 (978-1-60954-286-3(X), 200815) Child's World, Inc., The.

Wacholtz, Anthony. Mummies & Sound, 6 vols. Mallea, Cristian, illus. 2013. (Monster Science Ser.). (ENG.). 32p. (gr. 3-4). 47.70 (978-1-62065-819-2(4)); 30.65 (978-1-4296-9930-3(2)) Capstone Press of Coughlan Cos. (Graphic Library).

Wadsworth, Pamela. Golwg Gyntaf Ar Sain a Cherddoriaeth. 2005. (WEL., Illus.). 24p. pap. (978-1-85596-247-7(0)) Dref Wen.

Walker, Sally M. Investigating Sound. 2011. (Searchlight Books How Does Energy Work Ser.). (ENG., Illus.). (gr. 3-5). pap. 51.01 (978-0-7613-8410-6(3)); 40p. pap. 8.95 (978-0-7613-7876-1(6)); 40p. lib. bdg. 27.93 (978-0-7613-5777-3(7)) Lerner Publishing Group.

—El Sonido. Translations.com Staff, tr. from ENG. King, Andy, photos by. 2007. (Libros de Energía para madrugadores (Early Bird Energy) Ser.). (SPA., Illus.). 48p. (gr. 2-5). lib. bdg. 26.60 (978-0-8225-7722-5(4)) Lerner Publishing Group.

—El Sonido; Sound. 2008. pap. 52.95 (978-0-8225-9867-1(1)) Lerner Publishing Group.

What Is Noisy?, 6 Packs. (gr. 1-2). 22.00 (978-0-7635-9095-6(9)) Rigby Education.

Winnick, Neil. Hearing. 2009. (World of Wonder Ser.). (Illus.). 24p. (J). (gr. 2-4). pap. 8.95 (978-1-60596-055-5(1)) Weigl Pubs., Inc.

Winnick, Nick. Hearing. 2009. (World of Wonder Ser.). (Illus.). 24p. (J). (gr. 2-4). lib. bdg. 24.45 (978-1-60596-054-8(3)) Weigl Pubs., Inc.

Winterberg, Jenna. Sound Waves & Communication. 2015. (Science Readers: Content & Literacy Ser.). (ENG., Illus.). 32p. (gr. 4-4). pap. 8.99 (978-1-4807-4684-8(3)) Teacher Created Materials, Inc.

World Book, Inc Staff, contrib. by. Sound. 2011. (J). (978-0-7166-1430-2(8)) World Bk., Inc.

SOUND—EXPERIMENTS

Angliss, Sarah, et al. Hands-On Science: Sound & Light. 2013. (Hands-On Science Ser.). (ENG., Illus.). 32p. (J). (gr. 2-5). pap. 7.99 (978-0-7534-6974-3(X), 9780753469743, Kingfisher) Roaring Brook Pr.

Baker, Wendy, et al. Sound. (Make It Work! Ser.). (Illus.). 48p. (J). pap. 15.95 (978-0-590-74522-2(0)) Scholastic, Inc.

Canavan, Thomas. Super Experiments with Light & Sound. Linley, Adam, illus. 2017. (Mind-Blowing Science Experiments Ser.). 32p. (gr. 4-5). pap. 63.00 **(978-1-5382-0733-8(8))** Stevens, Gareth Publishing LLLP.

Clark, John & Walker, Richard. Light & Sound. 2006. (Real World Science Ser.). (Illus.). 32p. (gr. 2-6). lib. bdg. 26.00 (978-0-8368-6306-2(2), Gareth Stevens Learning Library) Stevens, Gareth Publishing LLLP.

Claybourne, Anna. Make It Boom!, 1 vol. Scott, Kimberly & Dean, Venetia, illus. 2014. (Whiz Kid Science Ser.). (ENG.). 32p. (gr. 2-4). 29.99 (978-1-4109-6745-9(X), Read Me!) Heinemann-Raintree.

—Make It Zoom!, 1 vol. Scott, Kimberly & Dean, Venetia, illus. 2014. (Whiz Kid Science Ser.). (ENG.). 32p. (gr. 2-4). 29.99 (978-1-4109-6750-3(6), Read Me!) Heinemann-Raintree.

Cobb, Allan B. Super Science Projects about Sound. 2005. (Psyched for Science Ser.). (Illus.). 48p. (YA). (gr. 5-8). lib. bdg. 29.25 (978-0-8239-3176-7(5), SCSOUN) Rosen Publishing Group, Inc., The.

Cobb, Vicki. Bangs & Twangs: Science Fun with Sound. Haefele, Steve, illus. 2007. (Science Fun with Vicki Cobb Ser.). 48p. (J). (gr. 4-7). per. 7.95 (978-0-8225-7022-6(X), First Avenue Editions) Lerner Publishing Group.

Cook, Trevor. Experiments with Light & Sound. 2009. (Science Lab Ser.). (J). (ENG., Illus.). 32p. (gr. 4-6). pap. 10.00 (978-1-4358-3221-3(3)); lib. bdg. 26.50 (978-1-4358-2808-7(9)) Rosen Publishing Group, Inc., The. (PowerKids Pr.).

Gardner, Robert. Experimenting with Sound Science Projects. 2013. (Exploring Hands-On Science Projects Ser.). 128p. (J). (gr. 5-18). lib. bdg. 27.94 (978-0-7660-4148-6(4)) Enslow Pubs., Inc.

—Jazzy Science Projects with Sound & Music. LaBaff, Tom, illus. 2006. (Fantastic Physical Science Experiments Ser.). 48p. (J). (gr. 4-7). lib. bdg. 25.27 (978-0-7660-2588-2(8), Enslow Elementary) Enslow Pubs., Inc.

—Light, Sound, & Waves Science Fair Projects: Using Sunglasses, Guitars, CDs, & Other Stuff. 2004. (Physics! Best Science Projects Ser.). (Illus.). 128p. (J). lib. bdg. 27.94 (978-0-7660-2126-6(2)) Enslow Pubs., Inc.

—Light, Sound, & Waves Science Fair Projects, Revised & Expanded Using the Scientific Method. 2010. (Physics Science Projects Using the Scientific Method Ser.). (Illus.). 160p. (J). (gr. 5-18). 35.94 (978-0-7660-3416-7(X)) Enslow Pubs., Inc.

—Sound Experiments in Your Own Music Lab. 2015. (Design, Build, Experiment Ser.). (ENG.). 128p. (J). (gr. 7-7). lib. bdg. 37.27 (978-0-7660-6960-2(5)) Enslow Pubs., Inc.

—Sound Projects with a Music Lab You Can Build. 2008. (Build-A-Lab! Science Experiments Ser.). (Illus.). 128p. (J). (gr. 3-7). lib. bdg. 33.27 (978-0-7660-2809-8(7)) Enslow Pubs., Inc.

Gardner, Robert & Conklin, Joshua. A Kid's Book of Experiments with Sound. 2016. (Surprising Science Experiments Ser.). (ENG.). 48p. (J). (gr. 4-4). pap. 11.70 (978-0-7660-7207-7(X)) Enslow Pubs., Inc.

Hagler, Gina. Sound. 2016. (J). (978-1-4896-5292-8(2)) Weigl Pubs., Inc.

—Step-by-Step Experiments with Sound. Ostrom, Bob, illus. 2012. (Step-By-Step Experiments Ser.). (ENG.). 32p. (J). (gr. 1-4). lib. bdg. 29.93 (978-1-60973-593-7(5), 201239) Child's World, Inc., The.

Hawkins, Jay. Super Sonic: The Science of Sound. 2013. (Big Bang Science Experiments Ser.). (ENG., Illus.). 32p. (gr. 3-6). 26.50 (978-1-4777-0325-0(X)); pap. 11.75 (978-1-4777-0370-0(5)) Windmill Bks.

Kuskowski, Alex. Science Experiments with Sight & Sound, 1 vol. 2013. (More Super Simple Science Ser.). (ENG.). 32p. (gr. k-4). lib. bdg. 27.07 (978-1-61783-854-5(3), Super SandCastle) ABDO Publishing Co.

—Super Simple Phonograph Projects: Inspiring & Educational Science Activities, 1 vol. 2016. (ENG., Illus.). 32p. (J). (978-1-62403-731-3(3)) ABDO Publishing Co.

Madgwick, Wendy. First Science Library: Sound Magic. 2014. (ENG., Illus.). 32p. (J). (gr. k-2). 8.99 (978-1-86147-353-0(2), Armadillo) Anness Publishing GBR. Dist: National Bk. Network.

Merrill, Amy French. Everyday Physical Science Experiments with Light. 2006. (Tony Stead Nonfiction Independent Reading Collection). (ENG.). 24p. (gr. 3-6). pap. 8.85 (978-1-4042-5679-8(2)) Rosen Publishing Group, Inc., The.

—Everyday Physical Science Experiments with Light & Sound. 2009. (Science Surprises Ser.). 24p. (gr. 3-3). 42.50 (978-1-60853-061-8(2), PowerKids Pr.) Rosen Publishing Group, Inc., The.

Navarro, Paula & Jimenez, Angels. Surprising Experiments with Sound. Cuxart, Bernadette, illus. 2014. (Magic Science Ser.). (ENG.). 36p. (J). (gr. 1-6). pap. 7.99 (978-1-4380-0425-9(7)) Barron's Educational Series, Inc.

Oxlade, Chris. Experiments with Sound & Light, 1 vol. 2015. (ENG., Illus.). 32p. (J). lib. bdg. 27.50 (978-1-4777-5965-3(4), PowerKids Pr.) Rosen Publishing Group, Inc., The.

Oxlade, Chris. Super Science Light & Sound Experiments: 10 Amazing Experiments with Step-By-Step Photographs. 2016. (ENG., Illus.). (J). pap. **(978-1-78209-421-0(0))** Miles Kelly Publishing, Ltd.

Rompella, Natalie. Experiments in Light & Sound with Toys & Everyday Stuff. 2015. (Fun Science Ser.). (ENG., Illus.). 24p. (gr. 1-2). lib. bdg. 25.32 (978-1-4914-5033-8(9)) Capstone Press of Coughlan Cos.

Rowe, Brooke. Making a Telephone. Bane, Jeff, illus. 2016. (My Early Library: My Science Fun Ser.). (ENG.). 24p. (J). (gr. k-1). 28.50 (978-1-63471-029-9(0), 208196) Cherry Lake Publishing.

—Playing Musical Bottles. Bane, Jeff, illus. 2016. (My Early Library: My Science Fun Ser.). (ENG.). 24p. (J). (gr. k-1). 28.50 (978-1-63471-028-2(2), 208192) Cherry Lake Publishing.

Spilsbury, Richard & Spilsbury, Louise. What Is Sound? Exploring Science with Hands-on Activities. 2008. (In Touch with Basic Science Ser.). (Illus.). 32p. (J). (gr. 3-4). lib. bdg. 23.94 (978-0-7660-3098-5(9), Enslow Elementary) Enslow Pubs., Inc.

Taylor-Butler, Christine. Super Cool Science Experiments: Sound. 2009. (Explorer Library: Science Explorer Ser.). (ENG., Illus.). 32p. (gr. 4-8). lib. bdg. 28.50 (978-1-60279-532-7(0), 200301) Cherry Lake Publishing.

Thomas, Isabel. Experiments with Sound. 2015. (Read & Experiment Ser.). (ENG., Illus.). 32p. (gr. 2-4). 30.65 (978-1-4109-6836-4(7), Raintree Perspectives) Heinemann-Raintree.

Woodford, Chris. Experiments with Sound & Hearing. 2010. (Cool Science Ser.). (Illus.). 32p. (J). (gr. 5-6). pap. 10.50 (978-1-4339-3457-5(4)); lib. bdg. 28.00 (978-1-4339-3456-8(6), 1309305) Stevens, Gareth Publishing LLLP. (Gareth Stevens Learning Library).

SOUND—FICTION

Ann, Sharrie. Granddaughter & King Green Warts. 2008. 24p. pap. 12.99 (978-1-4343-9470-5(0)) AuthorHouse.

Arthur, Clint. Bleep Blop Bloop, 1. Schedeen, Minnie, illus. 2006. 24p. (J). per. 8.99 net. (978-1-4276-0218-3(2)) Aardvark Global Publishing.

AZ Books Staff. Babbling Pond. Tulup, Natalia, ed. 2012. (How We Speak Ser.). (ENG.). 12p. (J). (gr. -1-k). bds. 10.95 (978-1-61889-097-9(2)) AZ Bks. LLC.

—My Farm. Yaroshevich, Angelica, ed. 2012. (Open the Book-I Am Alive Ser.). (ENG.). 8p. (J). (— 1). bds. 5.95 (978-1-61889-043-6(3)) AZ Bks. LLC.

—My Forest. Yaroshevich, Angelica, ed. 2012. (Open the Book-I Am Alive Ser.). (ENG.). 8p. (J). (— 1). bds. 5.95 (978-1-61889-042-9(5)) AZ Bks. LLC.

—My Pets. Yaroshevich, Angelica, ed. 2012. (Open the Book-I Am Alive Ser.). (ENG.). 8p. (J). (— 1). bds. 5.95 (978-1-61889-045-0(X)) AZ Bks. LLC.

—My Zoo. Yaroshevich, Angelica, ed. 2012. (Open the Book-I Am Alive Ser.). (ENG.). 8p. (J). (— 1). bds. 5.95 (978-1-61889-044-3(1)) AZ Bks. LLC.

Beauregard, Lynda. The Whispering Lake Ghosts: A Mystery about Sound. Torres, German, illus. 2013. (Summer Camp Science Mysteries Ser.: 6). (ENG.). 48p. (gr. 3-6). pap. 6.95 (978-1-4677-0734-3(1)); lib. bdg. 29.27 (978-1-4677-0168-6(8)) Lerner Publishing Group. (Graphic Universe™).

Beil, Karen Magnuson. Mooove Over! A Book about Counting by Twos. Meisel, Paul, tr. Meisel, Paul, illus. 2004. (ENG.). 32p. (J). (gr. k-3). tchr. ed. 16.95 (978-0-8234-1736-0(0)) Holiday Hse., Inc.

Bentley, Dawn. Disney Pixar Cars Rhymes on the Go. Schwaeber, Barbie Heit, ed. 2011. (Carry a Tune Ser.). (ENG., Illus.). 22p. (J). (gr. -1-1). pap. 4.99 incl. audio compact disk (978-1-60727-306-6(3)) Studio Mouse LLC.

Berg, Jean Horton & dePaola, Tomie. The Noisy Clock Shop. Seiden, Art, illus. 2015. (G&d Vintage Ser.). (ENG.). 32p. (J). (gr. -1-k). bds. 7.99 (978-0-448-48216-3(9), Grosset & Dunlap) Penguin Young Readers Group.

Berry, Ron. Can You Roar Like a Lion? Sharp, Chris, illus. 2009. (ENG.). 14p. bds. 10.99 (978-0-8249-1433-2(3), Ideal Pubns.) Worthy Publishing.

Berry, Ron & Mead, David. All Aboard! Charlie the Can-Do Choo Choo. Sharp, Chris, illus. 2009. (ENG.). 8p. 12.99 (978-0-8249-1420-2(1), Ideal Pubns.) Worthy Publishing.

Boynton, Sandra. Sandra Boynton's Moo, Baa, la la La! Boynton, Sandra, illus. 2009. (ENG., Illus.). 16p. (J). bds. 16.99 (978-1-4169-5035-6(4), Little Simon) Little Simon.

Brown, Margaret Wise. The Noisy Book Board Book. Weisgard, Leonard, illus. 2017. 36p. (J). (gr. -1 — 1). bds. 7.99 **(978-0-06-248465-9(6)**, HarperFestival) HarperCollins Pubs.

Burleigh, Robert. Clang! Clang! Beep! Beep! Listen to the City. Giacobbe, Beppe, illus. 2009. (ENG.). 32p. (J). (gr. -1-2). 17.99 (978-1-4169-4052-4(9), Simon & Schuster/Paula Wiseman Bks.) Simon & Schuster/Paula Wiseman Bks.

—Zoom! Zoom! Sounds of Things That Go in the City. Carpenter, Tad, illus. 2014. (ENG.). 32p. (J). (gr. -1-3). 17.99 (978-1-4424-8315-6(6), Simon & Schuster Bks. For Young Readers) Simon & Schuster Bks. For Young Readers.

Carle, Eric. My First Busy Book. Carle, Eric, illus. 2015. (World of Eric Carle Ser.). (ENG., Illus.). 12p. (J). bds. 14.99 (978-1-4814-5791-0(8), Little Simon) Little Simon.

Carlson, Lavelle. Eek! I Hear a Squeak & the Scurrying of Little Feet. Loehr, Jenny, illus. 2006. (ENG.). 28p. (J). (gr. -1-3). 19.95 incl. audio compact disk (978-0-9725803-8-0(7)) Children's Publishing.

Carluccio, Maria. The Sounds Around Town. Carluccio, Maria, illus. 2010. (ENG., Illus.). 13p. (J). 14.99 (978-1-84686-362-2(7)) Barefoot Bks., Inc.

—The Sounds Around Town. 2008. (ENG., Illus.). 24p. (J). (gr. -1-k). 16.99 (978-1-905236-28-2(X)) Barefoot Bks., Inc.

Carluccio, Maria, illus. The Sounds Around Town. 2011. (ENG.). 24p. (J). (gr. -1-3). pap. 7.99 (978-1-84686-430-8(5)) Barefoot Bks., Inc.

Choo Choo. 2011. (Dora the Explorer Ser.). (Illus.). 10p. (J). bds. 10.98 (978-0-7853-8278-2(X), 7182700) Publications International, Ltd.

Clayton, Darcy M. Making Mouth Sounds All Day Long. Freeswick, Jill, illus. 2013. 36p. pap. 9.95 (978-1-889131-90-0(3), Castlebridge Bks.) Big Tent Bks.

Colato Lainez, Rene. Vamonos! / Let's Go! 2016. (ENG & SPA.). lib. bdg. 17.20 (978-0-606-39166-5(5)) Turtleback Bks.

Cook, Sherry & Johnson, Terri. Susie Sound, 26. Kuhn, Jesse, illus. l.t. ed. 2006. 32p. (J). 7.99 (978-1-933815-18-3(3), Quirkles, The) Creative 3, LLC.

Cornwell, Charles Scott. The Bell. 2009. 24p. pap. 12.95 (978-1-60844-255-3(1)) Dog Ear Publishing, LLC.

Czekaj, Jef. Oink-a-Doodle-Moo. Czekaj, Jef, illus. 2012. (ENG., Illus.). 32p. (J). (gr. -1-1). 16.99 (978-0-06-206011-2(2)) HarperCollins Pubs.

Dipucchio, Kelly. Dinosnores. Goembel, Ponder, illus. 2005. 32p. (J). (gr. -1 — 1). 17.99 (978-0-06-051577-5(5)); lib. bdg. 16.89 (978-0-06-051578-2(3)) HarperCollins Pubs.

Disney Publishing Staff. What's That Sound?, 15 vols. 2003. (It's Fun to Learn Ser.). (Illus.). 32p. (J). (gr. -1-3). 3.99 (978-1-57973-132-8(5)) Advance Pubs. LLC.

Doyle, Malachy. Rory's Lost His Voice. Semple, David, illus. 2005. (ENG.). 24p. (J). lib. bdg. 23.65 (978-1-59646-714-9(2)) Dingles & Co.

Eggleton, Jill. Where Are You, Mouse? McGrath, Raymond, illus. 2003. (Rigby Sails Early Ser.). (ENG.). 16p. (gr. 1-2). pap. 6.95 (978-0-7578-8741-3(4)) Houghton Mifflin Harcourt Publishing Co.

Engineering is Elementary Team. Kwame's Sound: An Acoustical Engineering Story. 2005. (J). lib. bdg. 15.99 (978-0-9774084-2-9(6)) Engineering is Elementary.

Field, Elaine. Sounds (Cuddly Cuffs with Hang Tag) (Cuddly Cuffs Ser.). (Illus.). 12p. (J). tchr. ed. 5.95 (978-1-58925-708-5(1)) Tiger Tales.

Fleming, Denise. The Cow Who Clucked. 2007. (J). (gr. -1-1). 27.95 incl. audio (978-0-8045-6951-4(7)) Spoken Arts, Inc.

Forhan, Mary C. & Forhan, Mary C. Introduction to Letter Sounds: Fun, Active, Multisensory. 2003. (Illus.). 88p. spiral bd. 59.95 (978-0-9744575-0-5(7)) Butterfly Park Educational Materials, Inc.

Freedman, Claire. The Monster of the Woods!/By Claire Freedman & Russell Julian. Julian, Russell, illus. 2013. (J). (978-0-545-56837-1(4), Cartwheel Bks.) Scholastic, Inc.

Galloway, Fhiona, illus. Where's Frog? 2012. (Squeaky Bath Bks.). (ENG.). 8p. (J). (— 1). 9.99 (978-0-230-75868-1(1)) Pan Macmillan GBR. Dist: Independent Pubs. Group.

Galvin, Laura Gates. Quack's Masterpiece. 2006. (ENG., Illus.). 28p. (J). (gr. -1-3). pap. 2.99 (978-1-59249-550-4(8)) Soundprints.

—What's That Sound? 2006. (ENG., Illus.). 28p. (J). (gr. -1-3). pap. 2.99 (978-1-59249-553-5(2)) Soundprints.

Garcia, Emma. Tip Tip Dig Dig. 2013. (ENG., Illus.). 26p. (J). (— 1). bds. 6.95 (978-1-906250-82-9(0)) Boxer Bks., Ltd. GBR. Dist: Sterling Publishing Co., Inc.

—Toot Toot Beep Beep. 2013. (ENG., Illus.). 26p. (J). (— 1). bds. 6.95 (978-1-906250-84-3(7)) Boxer Bks., Ltd. GBR. Dist: Sterling Publishing Co., Inc.

Gershator, Phillis. Listen, Listen. Jay, Alison, illus. 2007. (ENG.). 32p. (J). (gr. -1-3). 16.99 (978-1-84686-084-3(9)) Barefoot Bks., Inc.

Goldsaito, Katrina. The Sound of Silence. Kuo, Julia, illus. 2016. (ENG.). 40p. (J). (gr. -1-3). 17.99 (978-0-316-20337-1(8)) Little Brown & Co.

Good Morning, Who's Snoring? Individual Title Six-Packs. (Story Steps Ser.). (gr. k-2). 32.00 (978-0-7635-9619-4(1)) Rigby Education.

Greenwell, Jessica. Noisy Body Book. 2012. (Noisy Bks). 10p. (J). ring bd. 18.99 (978-0-7945-3133-1(4), Usborne) EDC Publishing.

Harshman, Marc. All the Way to Morning. Dávalos, Felipe, illus. 2006. (J). per. 7.95 (978-1-891852-49-7(3)) Quarrier Pr.

Hays, Anna Jane. The Pup Speaks Up. Petrone, Valeria, illus. 2003. (Step into Reading Ser.). 32p. (gr. -1-1). 14.00 (978-0-7569-1696-1(8)) Perfection Learning Corp.

—The Pup Speaks Up. Petrone, Valeria, illus. 2003. (Step into Reading Ser.). (ENG.). 32p. (J). (gr. -1-1). pap. 3.99 (978-0-375-81232-3(6), Random Hse. Bks. for Young Readers) Random Hse. Children's Bks.

Hogan, Martina, illus. Roar! Shh! 2016. (Early Birds Ser.). (ENG.). 12p. (J). (gr. -1 — 1). bds. 6.99 (978-1-4998-0183-5(1)) Little Bee Books Inc.

Jay, Alison & Gershator, Phillis. Listen, Listen. 2008. (ENG., Illus.). 32p. (J). (gr. -1-k). 14.99 (978-1-84686-201-4(9)) Barefoot Bks., Inc.

Johnson, Errol. What's That Sound? 2006. (Neighborhood Readers Ser.). (Illus.). 12p. (gr. -1-3). pap. 5.90 (978-1-4042-6738-1(7), Rosen Classroom) Rosen Publishing Group, Inc., The.

Ka Hulu Kohukohu. 2003. (J). 11.95 (978-0-89610-463-1(X)) Island Heritage Publishing.

Kato, Yukiko. In the Meadow. Sakai, Komako, illus. 2011. (Being in the World Ser.). (ENG.). 32p. (J). (gr. k-k). 14.95 (978-1-59270-108-7(6)) Enchanted Lion Bks., LLC.

Kidd, Ron. Bookee Presents Colors, Shapes & Sounds. Nord, Mary, illus. (Talking Book Adventures Ser.). 12p. (J). (gr. -1-18). 16.95 (978-0-9627001-1-8(8)) Futech Educational Products, Inc.

Krensky, Stephen. Noah's Bark. Girard, Roger, illus. 2010. (ENG.). 32p. (J). (gr. -1-2). lib. bdg. 16.95 (978-0-8225-7645-7(7)) Lerner Publishing Group.

Laplante, Carole. Night Noises. Byrne-Walker, Mary Ann, illus. 2012. 40p. pap. 9.95 (978-1-62006-046-9(9)) Sunbury Press, Inc.

Lawrence, Mary. Que Es Ese Sonido? Adams, Lynn, illus. 2008. (Science Solves It! en Espanol Ser.). (SPA.). 32p. (J). (gr. -1-3). pap. 5.95 (978-1-57565-266-5(8)) Kane Press, Inc.

—¿Qué es Ese Sonido? (What's That Sound?) Adams, Lynn, illus. 2009. (Science Solves It! (r) en Espanol Ser.). (SPA.). (gr. k-2). pap. 33.92 (978-0-7613-4801-6(8)) Lerner Publishing Group.

Light, Steve. Boats Go. 2015. (ENG., Illus.). 16p. (J). (gr. -1 — 1). bds. 9.99 (978-1-4521-2900-6(2)) Chronicle Bks. LLC.

Long, Kathy. Christopher SAT Straight up in Bed. Cantor, Patricia, illus. 2013. (ENG.). 40p. (J). 16.00 (978-0-8028-5359-2(5), Eerdmans Bks For Young Readers) Eerdmans, William B. Publishing Co.

Lynn, Michelle. Fall Leaves. 2008. 17p. pap. 24.95 (978-1-60672-027-1(9)) America Star Bks.

Mack, Karen. Who Makes the Sound? 2008. 11p. pap. 24.95 (978-1-60610-852-9(2)) America Star Bks.

MacLeod, Elizabeth. I Heard a Little Baa. Phillips, Louise, illus. 2007. (ENG.). 30p. (J). (gr. -1 — 1). bds. 7.95 (978-1-55453-179-0(9)) Kids Can Pr., Ltd. CAN. Dist: Hachette Bk. Group.

Magsamen, Sandra. Baa, Moo, I Love You! A Book of Animal Sounds. 2014. (I Love Learning Ser.). (ENG., Illus.). 14p. (J). (gr. -1 — 1). bds. 7.99 (978-0-316-13358-6(2)) Little, Brown Bks. for Young Readers.

Mazza, Barbara. How the Short Vowels Got Their Sound. 2007. 28p. per. 17.32 (978-1-4257-2721-5(2)) Xlibris Corp.

McTaggart, Stephen & McTaggart, Debra. Bookee's Sounds Around. Nord, Mary, illus. (Talking Book Adventures Ser.). 12p. (J). (gr. -1-18). 16.95 (978-0-9627001-0-1(X)) Futech Educational Products, Inc.

Muller, Daniella L. Rumble, Rumble, Boom! 2009. 28p. pap. 12.99 (978-1-4389-7710-2(7)) AuthorHouse.

Mysak, Mary. Little Train! Stickley, Kelly, illus. 2004. 16p. (J). 7.50 (978-0-9762274-0-3(1)) Helping Hands Children's Bks.

O'Connell, Rebecca. The Baby Goes Beep. Wilson-Max, Ken, illus. 2010. (ENG.). 16p. (J). (gr. -1 — 1). bds. 7.99 (978-0-8075-0508-3(0)) Whitman, Albert & Co.

Ormerod, Jan, et al. Doing the Animal Bop. 2005. (Illus.). (J). (978-0-7641-8299-0(4)) Barron's Educational Series, Inc.

Palatini, Margie. Boo-Hoo Moo. Graves, Keith, illus. 2009. 32p. (J). (gr. -1-3). lib. bdg. 18.89 (978-0-06-114376-2(6)) HarperCollins Pubs.

—Moo Who? Graves, Keith, illus. (ENG.). 40p. (J). (gr. -1-2). 2007. pap. 6.99 (978-0-06-000107-0(0)) 2004. 16.99 (978-0-06-000105-6(4)) HarperCollins Pubs. (Tegen, Katherine Bks).

Pearson, Debora. Big City Song. Reed, Lynn Rowe, illus. 2006. (ENG.). 32p. (J). (gr. -1-3). 16.95 (978-0-8234-1988-3(6)) Holiday Hse., Inc.

Pearson, Tracey Campbell. Bob. Pearson, Tracey Campbell, illus. 2006. (ENG., Illus.). 32p. (J). (gr. -1-1). reprint ed. 8.99 (978-0-374-40871-8(8), 9780374408718) Square Fish.

Perkins, Al. The Ear Book. Payne, Henry, illus. 2007. (Bright & Early Books(R) Ser.). (ENG.). 36p. (J). (gr. k-k). 9.99 (978-0-375-84251-1(9), Random Hse. Bks. for Young Readers) Random Hse. Children's Bks.

Perkins, Lynne Rae. Snow Music. Perkins, Lynne Rae, illus. 2003. (Illus.). 40p. (J). lib. bdg. 16.89 (978-0-06-623958-3(3)) HarperCollins Pubs.

Perkins, Lynne Rae & Perkins, Lynne R. Snow Music. Perkins, Lynne Rae, illus. 2003. (ENG., Illus.). 40p. (J). (gr. -1-3). 16.99 (978-0-06-623956-9(7), Greenwillow Bks.) HarperCollins Pubs.

Peters, Polly. The Ding-Dong Bag. Stockham, Jess, illus. 2006. (Child's Play Library). (ENG.). 32p. (J). (gr. 2-2). (978-1-84643-015-2(1)) Child's Play International Ltd.

Pfeffer, Wendy. Sounds All Around. Chernyshova, Anna, illus. 2016. (Let's-Read-And-Find-Out Science 1 Ser.). 40p. (J). (gr. -1-3). pap. 6.99 (978-0-06-238669-4(7)) HarperCollins Pubs.

Pilney, Dovie. Charlie the Cocky Rooster: Another Adventure. 2008. 52p. pap. 20.95 (978-1-4389-3517-1(X)) AuthorHouse.

Play a Sound Sesame Street 3 Pack. 2010. (J). 12.98 (978-1-4127-8258-6(9)) Phoenix International Publications, Inc.

Pocahontas: Who's Making that Sound? (My First Read Along Ser.). (Illus.). (J). 7.99 incl. audio (978-1-55723-961-7(4)) Walt Disney Records.

Potter, Beatrix. The Tale of Peter Rabbit: A Sound Story Book. 2013. (Peter Rabbit Ser.). (ENG., Illus.). 10p. (J). (gr. -1-2). 12.99 (978-0-7232-6856-7(8), Warne) Penguin Young Readers Group.

Publications International Ltd. Staff, ed. Race Day. 2010. 10p. (J). bds. 11.98 *(978-1-4127-4931-2(X),* PIL Kids) Publications International, Ltd.

—Ring-a-Ling! A Friend Is Here. 2010. 12p. (J). 9.98 *(978-1-4127-7939-5(1))* Phoenix International Publications, Inc.

Rand, Paul & Rand, Ann. Listen! Listen! 2016. (ENG., Illus.). 32p. (J). (gr. -1-1). 17.95 *(978-1-61689-494-8(6))* Princeton Architectural Pr.

Rinker, Sherri Duskey. Steam Train, Dream Train Sound Book. Lichtenheld, Tom, illus. 2015. (ENG.). 12p. (J). (gr. -1-k). 12.99 *(978-1-4521-2825-2(1))* Chronicle Bks. LLC.

Rozen, Anna. The Merchant of Noises. Scarbrough, Carl W., tr. from FRE. Avril, Francois, illus. 2006. (ENG.). 28p. (J). (gr. 3-7). 18.95 *(978-1-56792-321-6(6))* Godine, David R. Pub.

Rubin, Susan Goldman. Jacob Lawrence in the City. 2009. (ENG., Illus.). 24p. (J). (gr. -1 — 1). bds. 7.99 *(978-0-8118-6582-1(7))* Chronicle Bks. LLC.

Scarry, Richard. Splish-Splash.Tr. of Splish-Splash. (SPA., Illus.). (J). pap. 6.95 *(978-950-04-0676-5(4))* Emecé Editores S.A. ARG. Dist: Planeta Publishing Corp.

Schoberle, Cecile. Morning Sounds, Evening Sounds. 2014. (ENG., Illus.). 24p. (J). (gr. -1-3). 13.99 *(978-1-4814-2538-4(2),* Simon & Schuster Bks. For Young Readers) Simon & Schuster Bks. For Young Readers.

Seuss. Gerald Mcboing Boing. Crawford, Mel, illus. 2017. (Classic Seuss Ser.). (ENG.). 40p. (J). (gr. k-4). 16.99 ***(978-1-5247-1635-6(9))***; lib. bdg. 19.99 ***(978-1-5247-1757-5(6))*** Random Hse. Children's Bks. (Random Hse. Bks. for Young Readers).

Seuss, Dr. Gerald McBoing Boing. Seuss, Dr., illus. 2004. (Little Golden Book Ser.). (ENG., Illus.). 24p. (J). (gr. -1-2). 4.99 *(978-0-375-82721-1(8),* Golden Bks.) Random Hse. Children's Bks.

—Mr. Brown Can Moo! Can You? 2014. (Big Bright & Early Board Book Ser.). (ENG., Illus.). 24p. (J). (-k). bds. 6.99 *(978-0-385-38712-5(1),* Random Hse. Bks. for Young Readers) Random Hse. Children's Bks.

Snow, Peggy. My Favorite Sounds from a to Z. 2007. (ENG.). 32p. (J). lib. bdg. 15.99 *(978-1-934277-02-7(9))* Mam Green Publishing, Inc.

Sohn, Emily & Timmons, Anne. Adventures in Sound with Max Axiom, Super Scientist. Martin, Cynthia & Timmons, Anne, illus. 2007. (Graphic Science Ser.). (ENG.). 32p. (gr. 3-4). 30.65 *(978-0-7368-6836-5(4),* Graphic Library) Capstone Press of Coughlan Cos.

Stute, Lela LaBree. The Big Bad Blonde, 1 vol. 2010. 18p. pap. 24.95 *(978-1-4489-9621-6(X))* PublishAmerica, Inc.

van Genechten, Guido. The Big Woods Orchestra. 2012. (ENG.). 24p. (J). (gr. -1-k). 17.95 *(978-1-60537-113-9(0))* Cobblestone Publishing Co.

Viau, Nancy. City Street Beat. 2015. (Illus.). 32p. (J). *(978-1-4896-3855-7(5))* Weigl Pubs., Inc.

—City Street Beat. Bakos, Barbara, illus. 2014. (ENG.). 32p. (J). (gr. -1-3). 16.99 *(978-0-8075-1164-0(1))* Whitman, Albert & Co.

Waring, Geoff. Oscar & the Bat: A Book about Sound. Waring, Geoff, illus. 2009. (Start with Science Ser.). (ENG., Illus.). 32p. (J). (gr. -1-3). pap. 6.99 *(978-0-7636-4513-7(3))* Candlewick Pr.

Watts, Kevin Bradley. Ben & the Mysterious Sound: Series: the Adventures of Tug Boat Ben. 2007. (Illus.). 32p. (J). *(978-0-9782625-2-5(2))*; pap. *(978-0-9782625-1-8(4))* Alderney Publishing, Inc.

Weiner, Marcella Bakur & Neimark, Jill. I Want Your Moo: A Story for Children about Self-Esteem. Adinolfi, JoAnn, illus. 2nd ed. 2009. 32p. (J). (gr. -1-3). 14.95 *(978-1-4338-0542-4(1))*; pap. 9.95 *(978-1-4338-0552-3(9))* American Psychological Assn. (Magination Pr.).

Whybrow, Ian & Warnes, Tim. Say Hello to the Animals, 2. 2008. (ENG., Illus.). 20p. (J). (gr. 1-5). bds. 14.95 *(978-0-230-52859-8(7),* Macmillan) Pan Macmillan GBR. Dist: Trans-Atlantic Pubns., Inc.

Willis Hudson, Cheryl. Sounds I Love to Hear. 2009. 24p. 3.99 *(978-1-60349-010-8(8),* Marimba Bks.) Hudson Publishing Group, The.

Wormell, Chris. Molly & the Night Monster. Wormell, Chris, illus. 2011. (ENG., Illus.). 32p. (J). (gr. -1-k). pap. 9.99 *(978-1-86230-185-6(9),* Red Fox) Random House Children's Books GBR. Dist: Independent Pubs. Group.

Ylvis & Løchstøer, Christian. What Does the Fox Say? Nyhus, Svein, illus. 2013. (ENG.). 32p. (J). (gr. -1-3). 17.99 *(978-1-4814-2223-9(5),* Simon & Schuster Bks. For Young Readers) Simon & Schuster Bks. For Young Readers.

Yuly, Toni. Night Owl. Yuly, Toni, illus. 2015. (ENG., Illus.). 40p. (J). (— 1). 15.99 *(978-1-250-05457-9(5),* 9781250054579) Feiwel & Friends.

SOUND—POETRY

Cleary, Brian P. Bow-Tie Pasta: Acrostic Poems. Rowland, Andy, illus. 2015. (ENG.). 32p. (J). (gr. 2-5). 26.65 *(978-1-4677-2046-5(1),* Millbrook Pr.) Lerner Publishing Group.

SOUND—RECORDING AND REPRODUCING

Ambrosek, Renee. Shawn Fanning: The Founder of Napster. (Internet Career Biographies Ser.). 112p. 2009. (gr. 8-8). 63.90 *(978-1-61513-600-1(2))* 2006. (Illus.). (YA). (gr. 7-12). lib. bdg. 34.60 *(978-1-4042-0720-2(1))* Rosen Publishing Group, Inc., The.

Anniss, Matt. The Music Industry. 2015. (Music Scene Ser.). (J). lib. bdg. 37.10 *(978-1-59920-911-1(X))* Black Rabbit Bks.

Anniss, Matthew. Recording & Promoting Your Music, 1 vol. 2014. (I'm in the Band Ser.). (ENG.). 48p. (gr. 6-6). 33.32 *(978-1-4109-6726-8(3))* Heinemann-Raintree.

Bailey, Diane. The Story of Interscope Records. 2012. (J). pap. *(978-1-4222-2128-0(8))*; 64p. (gr. 4). 22.95 *(978-1-4222-2115-0(6))* Mason Crest.

Baughan, Brian. The Story of Def Jam Records. 2012. (J). pap. *(978-1-4222-2127-3(X))*; 64p. (gr. 4). 22.95 *(978-1-4222-2114-3(8))* Mason Crest.

Bingham, Hettie. Will. I. Am. 2017. (Real-Life Stories Ser.). (ENG., Illus.). 32p. (J). (gr. 4-6). pap. 11.99 *(978-0-7502-8947-4(3),* Wayland) Hachette Children's Group GBR. Dist: Hachette Bk. Group.

Cole, Joanna. Inside the Human Body. Degen, Bruce, illus. 2011. (Magic School Bus Ser.). (ENG.). (J). (gr. 2-5). 9.99 *(978-0-545-24083-3(2))* Scholastic, Inc.

Colson, Mary & Throp, Claire. Digital Music: A Revolution in Music. 2010. (Culture in Action Ser.). (ENG.). 32p. (gr. 3-6). 30.65 *(978-1-4109-3915-9(4),* NA-r) Heinemann-Raintree.

Culp, Jennifer. Using Computer Science in Digital Music Careers. 2017. (Coding Your Passion Ser.). 80p. (gr. 12-12). 35.75 ***(978-1-5081-7517-9(9)***, Rosen Young Adult) Rosen Publishing Group, Inc., The.

Daniels, Leonard & Orr, Tamra. Web-Based Digital Presentations, 01 vols., 1. 2016. (Digital & Information Literacy Ser.). (ENG.). 48p. (J). pap. 11.75 *(978-1-4994-3773-7(0),* Rosen Central) Rosen Publishing Group, Inc., The.

Espejo, Roman. What Is the Future of the Music Industry? 2008. (At Issue Ser.). (ENG., Illus.). 80-128p. (gr. 10-12). 24.45 *(978-0-7377-4111-7(2))*; pap. 34.45 *(978-0-7377-4110-0(4))* Cengage Gale. (Greenhaven Pr., Inc.).

Finley, Toiya Kristen. Russell Simmons. 2009. (Sharing the American Dream Ser.). (Illus.). 64p. (YA). (gr. 7-12). 22.95 *(978-1-4222-0584-6(3))* Mason Crest.

Foy, Debbie. Simon Cowell: Global Music Mogul. 2011. (Famous Lives Ser.). (Illus.). 32p. (YA). (gr. 3-6). lib. bdg. 26.50 *(978-1-4488-3290-3(X))* Rosen Publishing Group, Inc., The.

Golus, Carrie. Biography Russell Simmons. 2007. (Biography Ser.). (Illus.). 112p. (J). (gr. -1). lib. bdg. *(978-0-8225-7158-2(7))* Twenty First Century Bks.

—Russell Simmons: From Def Jam to Super Rich. 2012. (USA TODAY Lifeline Biographies Ser.). (ENG., Illus.). 112p. (gr. 6-12). lib. bdg. 34.60 *(978-0-7613-8157-0(0))* Lerner Publishing Group.

Graham, Amy. Thomas Edison: Wizard of Light & Sound. 2007. (Inventors Who Changed the World Ser.). (Illus.). 128p. (J). (gr. 5-9). lib. bdg. 34.60 *(978-1-59845-052-1(2),* MyReportLinks.com Bks.) Enslow Pubs., Inc.

Hill, Z. B. Sean "Diddy" Combs. 2012. (J). pap. *(978-1-4222-2540-0(2))*; (Illus.). 48p. (gr. 3-4). 19.95 *(978-1-4222-2514-1(3))* Mason Crest.

Indovino, Shaina C. Russell Simmons: From Drug Dealer to Music Mogul. 2012. (Extraordinary Success with a High School Diploma or Less Ser.). 64p. (J). (gr. 7-8). 22.95 *(978-1-4222-2301-7(9))* Mason Crest.

—Simon Cowell: From the Mailroom to Idol Fame. 2012. (Extraordinary Success with a High School Diploma or Less Ser.). 64p. (J). (gr. 7-8). 22.95 *(978-1-4222-2296-6(9))* Mason Crest.

Indovino, Shaina Carmel. Russell Simmons: From Drug Dealer to Music Mogul. 2012. (J). pap. *(978-1-4222-2312-3(4))* Mason Crest.

—Simon Cowell: From the Mailroom to Idol Fame. 2012. pap. *(978-1-4222-2307-9(8))* Mason Crest.

Kallen, Stuart A. IPods & MP3 Players. 2009. (Technology 360 Ser.). (Illus.). 128p. (YA). (gr. 7-10). lib. bdg. 34.95 *(978-1-4205-0166-7(6),* LML02109-246078, Lucent Bks.) Cengage Gale.

Kowalski, Emma. The Story of Konvict Muzik. 2012. (J). pap. *(978-1-4222-2129-7(6))*; 64p. (gr. 4). 22.95 *(978-1-4222-2116-7(4))* Mason Crest.

—The Story of Mosley Music Group. 2012. (J). pap. *(978-1-4222-2130-3(X))*; 64p. (gr. 4). 22.95 *(978-1-4222-2117-4(2))* Mason Crest.

—The Story of Roc-A-Fella Records. 2012. (J). pap. *(978-1-4222-2132-7(6))*; 64p. (gr. 4). 22.95 *(978-1-4222-2119-8(9))* Mason Crest.

Lommel, Cookie. Russell Simmons. 2007. (Hip-Hop Stars Ser.). (Illus.). 104p. (YA). (gr. 7-12). lib. bdg. 30.00 *(978-0-7910-9467-9(7))* Facts On File, Inc.

Mara, Wil. Sound Engineer. 2015. (21st Century Skills Library: Cool STEAM Careers Ser.). (ENG., Illus.). 32p. (J). (gr. 4-7). 29.93 *(978-1-63362-563-1(X),* 206436) Cherry Lake Publishing.

Mintzer, Richard. The Story of So So Def Records. 2012. (J). pap. *(978-1-4222-2133-4(4))*; 64p. (gr. 4). 22.95 *(978-1-4222-2120-4(2))* Mason Crest.

Pickney, Andrea Davis. Rhythm Ride: A Road Trip Through the Motown Sound. 2015. (ENG., Illus.). 176p. (J). (gr. 5-9). 22.99 *(978-1-59643-973-3(4),* 9781596439733) Roaring Brook Pr.

Sturm, Jeanne. MP3 Players. 2008. (Let's Explore Science Ser.). (Illus.). 48p. (J). (gr. 4-8). lib. bdg. 31.36 *(978-1-60472-332-8(7))* Rourke Educational Media.

Traugh, Susan. Sean Combs. 2010. (People in the News Ser.). (ENG., Illus.). 104p. 33.95 *(978-1-4205-0237-4(9),* Lucent Bks.) Cengage Gale.

Whiting, Jim. The Story of No Limit Records. 2012. (J). pap. *(978-1-4222-2131-0(8))*; 64p. (gr. 4). 22.95 *(978-1-4222-2118-1(0))* Mason Crest.

Witmer, Scott. Recording, 1 vol. 2009. (Rock Band Ser.). (ENG., Illus.). 32p. (YA). (gr. 4-7). 27.07 *(978-1-60453-694-2(2))* ABDO Publishing Co.

Wooster, Patricia. Music Producer. 2011. (21st Century Skills Library: Cool Arts Careers Ser.). (ENG.). 32p. (gr. 4-8). lib. bdg. 28.50 *(978-1-61080-133-1(4),* 201144) Cherry Lake Publishing.

SOUND EFFECTS

see Sounds

SOUND WAVES

see also Ultrasonic Waves

Boothroyd, Jennifer. Loud or Soft? High or Low? A Look at Sound. 2011. (Lightning Bolt Books Exploring Physical Science Ser.). 32p. pap. 45.32 *(978-0-7613-7650-7(X))*; (ENG.). pap. 7.95 *(978-0-7613-7107-6(9))*; (ENG.). lib. bdg. 26.60 *(978-0-7613-6091-9(3))* Lerner Publishing Group.

Coan, Sharon. How Sound Moves, 1 vol. rev. ed. 2014. (Science Readers: Content & Literacy Ser.). (ENG., Illus.). 24p. (gr. 1-1). pap. 8.99 *(978-1-4807-4564-3(2))* Teacher Created Materials, Inc.

Corsaro, Nicola. What Are Sound Waves? 2013. (Rosen Readers Ser.). (ENG.). 24p. (J). (gr. 2-3). pap. 8.25 *(978-1-4777-2397-5(8))*; pap. 49.50 *(978-1-4777-2398-2(6))* Rosen Publishing Group, Inc., The. (Rosen Classroom).

Duke, Shirley. Waves of Light & Sound. 2014. (ENG.). 48p. (gr. 4-6). 35.64 *(978-1-62717-749-8(3))* Rourke Educational Media.

Gardner, Jane P. Music Science, Vol. 11. Lewin, Russ, ed. 2015. (Science 24/7 Ser.). (Illus.). 48p. (J). (gr. 5). 20.95 *(978-1-4222-3412-9(6))* Mason Crest.

Hagler, Gina. Step-by-Step Experiments with Sound. Ostrom, Bob, illus. 2012. (Step-By-Step Experiments Ser.). (ENG.). 32p. (J). (gr. 1-4). lib. bdg. 29.93 *(978-1-60973-593-7(5),* 201239) Child's World, Inc., The.

Hawkins, Jay. Super Sonic: The Science of Sound. 2013. (Big Bang Science Experiments Ser.). (ENG., Illus.). 32p. (gr. 3-6). 26.50 *(978-1-4777-0325-0(X))*; pap. 11.75 *(978-1-4777-0370-0(5))* Windmill Bks.

Jennings, Terry Catasús. Sounds of the Savanna, 1 vol. Saroff, Phyllis, illus. 2015. 32p. (J). (gr. k-3). (ENG.). pap. 9.95 *(978-1-62855-637-7(4))*; (SPA & ENG.). pap. 9.95 *(978-1-62855-642-1(0))* Arbordale Publishing.

Jennings, Terry J. Sound. 2009. (J). 28.50 *(978-1-59920-275-4(1))* Black Rabbit Bks.

Johnson, Robin. How Does Sound Change? 2014. (ENG., Illus.). 24p. (J). *(978-0-7787-0520-8(X))* Crabtree Publishing Co.

—The Science of Sound Waves. 2017. (Illus.). 32p. (J). ***(978-0-7787-2941-9(9))*** Crabtree Publishing Co.

Johnson, Robin. What Are Sound Waves? 2014. (ENG.). 24p. (J). *(978-0-7787-0522-2(6))* Crabtree Publishing Co.

Kenney, Karen Latchana. Sound & Light Waves Investigations. 2017. (Key Questions in Physical Science Ser.). (ENG.). 32p. (J). (gr. 3-6). 27.99 ***(978-1-5124-4004-1(3))*** Lerner Publishing Group.

Kuskowski, Alex. Super Simple Phonograph Projects: Inspiring & Educational Science Activities, 1 vol. 2016. (ENG., Illus.). 32p. (J). *(978-1-62403-731-3(3))* ABDO Publishing Co.

Lilly, Melinda. Sound up & Down. Thompson, Scott M., illus. 2003. 24p. (J). 20.64 *(978-1-58952-644-0(9))* Rourke Educational Media.

Mahaney, Ian F. Sound Waves. (Energy in Action Ser.). 24p. (gr. 3-3). 2009. 42.50 *(978-1-61512-263-9(X))* 2007. (ENG., Illus.). pap. 7.05 *(978-0-7787-4042-2189-5(1))* 2007. (Illus.). (J). lib. bdg. 21.25 *(978-1-4042-3480-2(2))* Rosen Publishing Group, Inc., The. (PowerKids Pr.).

Riley, Peter. Changing Sounds. 2007. (Essential Science/Watts Ser.). (Illus.). 32p. (YA). (gr. 3-6). lib. bdg. 28.50 *(978-1-59920-023-1(6))* Black Rabbit Bks.

Rooney, Anne. Audio Engineering & the Science of Soundwaves. 2013. (ENG., Illus.). 32p. (J). *(978-0-7787-1196-4(X))*; pap. *(978-0-7787-1229-9(X))* Crabtree Publishing Co.

Wacholtz, Anthony. Mummies & Sound, 1 vol. Mallea, Cristian, illus. 2013. (Monster Science Ser.). (ENG.). 32p. (gr. 3-4). pap. 8.10 *(978-1-62065-818-5(6),* Graphic Library) Capstone Press of Coughlan Cos.

Walker, Sally M. Investigating Sound. 2011. (Searchlight Books How Does Energy Work Ser.). (ENG., Illus.). 40p. (gr. 3-5). lib. bdg. 27.93 *(978-0-7613-5777-3(7))* Lerner Publishing Group.

Winterberg, Jenna. Sound Waves & Communication. 2015. (Science Readers: Content & Literacy Ser.). (ENG., Illus.). 32p. (gr. 4-4). pap. 8.99 *(978-1-4807-4684-8(3))* Teacher Created Materials, Inc.

SOUNDS

Adivina Lo Que Es: Individual 6-packs, Level 4. 2003. 23.95 *(978-0-673-57868-6(2))* Celebration Pr.

AZ Books. Our Planet. 2013. (Sounds Around Us Ser.). (ENG.). 16p. (J). (gr. 1-3). bds. 17.95 *(978-1-61889-282-9(7))* AZ Bks. LLC.

Baggott, Stella. Baby's Very First Noisy Book. Baggott, Stella, illus. 2010. (Illus.). 10p. (J). bds. 14.99 *(978-0-7945-2653-5(5),* Usborne) EDC Publishing.

Bullard, Lisa. Loud & Quiet [Scholastic]: An Animal Opposites Book. 2009. (Animal Opposites Ser.). 32p. (gr. 1-2). pap. 1.00 *(978-1-4296-4232-3(7),* Aplus Bks.) Capstone Press of Coughlan Cos.

Burton, Margie, et al. Sounds. 2011. (Early Connections Ser.). (J). *(978-1-61672-506-8(0))* Benchmark Education Co.

Cardenas, Ernesto A. Sounds. 2009. pap. 4.95 *(978-1-60698-090-3(4))* Milo Educational Bks. & Resources.

Chapman, Jared & Smeldt, H. W. Farts in the Wild: A Spotter's Guide. 2012. (ENG., Illus.). 24p. (J). (gr. -1-17). 15.99 *(978-1-4521-0631-1(2))* Chronicle Bks. LLC.

Claybourne, Anna. Make It Boom!, 1 vol. Scott, Kimberly & Dean, Venetia, illus. 2014. (Whiz Kid Science Ser.). (ENG.). 32p. (gr. 2-4). 29.99 *(978-1-4109-6745-9(X),* Read Me!) Heinemann-Raintree.

Crick, Sharon. Sounds. 2014. 20p. pap. 16.00 *(978-1-4828-9215-4(4))* Partridge Pub.

—Sounds. 2012. 20p. pap. 16.00 *(978-1-4669-2832-9(8))* Trafford Publishing.

Cricket Magazine Editors. Oink-Oink: And Other Animal Sounds. Conteh-Morgan, Jane, illus. 2007. (ENG.). 20p. (J). (gr. k-k). bds. 7.95 *(978-0-8126-7934-2(2))* Cricket Bks.

Dalmatian Press Staff. Say Moo! 2008. (ENG.). 5p. (J). bds. 4.95 *(978-1-58117-722-0(4),* Intervisual/Piggy Toes) Bendon, Inc.

Dobson, Jolie. Beep Beep Choo Choo. 2014. (Snappy Sounds Ser.). (ENG., Illus.). 22p. (J). (gr. -1 — 1). bds. 5.95 *(978-1-77085-436-9(3),* 9781770854369) Firefly Bks., Ltd.

—Ring Ring Pop Pop. 2014. (Snappy Sounds Ser.). (ENG., Illus.). 22p. (J). (gr. -1 — 1). bds. 5.95 *(978-1-77085-437-6(1),* 9781770854376) Firefly Bks., Ltd.

—Snap Snap Woof Woof. 2014. (Snappy Sounds Ser.). (ENG., Illus.). 22p. (J). (gr. -1 — 1). bds. 5.95 *(978-1-77085-435-2(5),* 9781770854352) Firefly Bks., Ltd.

Dorling Kindersley Publishing Staff. Noisy Playhouse Peekaboo! 2016. (ENG., Illus.). 12p. (J). (— 1). bds. 12.99 *(978-1-4654-4408-0(4),* DK Children) Dorling Kindersley Publishing, Inc.

Doudna, Kelly. Tick Tock, 1 vol. 2004. (Sound Words Ser.). (ENG., Illus.). 24p. (J). (gr. k-3). lib. bdg. 24.21 *(978-1-59197-455-0(0),* SandCastle) ABDO Publishing Co.

Gardner, Robert. Experimenting with Sound Science Projects. 2013. (Exploring Hands-On Science Projects Ser.). 128p. (J). (gr. 5-12). pap. 10.95 *(978-1-4644-0225-8(6))* Enslow Pubs., Inc.

Gold-Vukson, Marji. The Sounds of My Jewish Year. Urban, Suzanne, illus. 2003. (Very First Board Bks.). (ENG.). 12p. (J). (gr. -1 — 1). 5.95 *(978-1-58013-047-9(X),* Kar-Ben Publishing) Lerner Publishing Group.

Golden Books Staff. Animal Sounds. Battaglia, Aurelius, illus. 2005. (Golden Sturdy Book Ser.). (ENG.). 26p. (J). (gr. k — 1). bds. 7.99 *(978-0-375-83278-9(5),* Golden Bks.) Random Hse. Children's Bks.

Goodman, Andy. It Was So Quiet I Could Hear a Pin Drop. 2016. (ENG., Illus.). 34p. (J). (gr. -1-1). 15.95 *(978-1-61689-480-1(6))* Princeton Architectural Pr.

Greenwell, Jessica. Noisy Monsters. Wildish, Lee, illus. 2010. (Busy Sounds Board Bks). 10p. (J). bds. 18.99 *(978-0-7945-2769-3(8),* Usborne) EDC Publishing.

Hal Leonard Corp. Staff. Mickey's Found Sounds: A Musical Exploration Storybook. 2017. (ENG.). 32p. 14.99 *(978-1-4950-6478-4(6),* 1495064786) Leonard, Hal Corp.

Hewitt, Sally. Hear This! 2008. (Let's Start Science Ser.). (ENG., Illus.). 24p. (J). (gr. 3-7). pap. *(978-0-7787-4058-2(7))* Crabtree Publishing Co.

Himmelman, John. Noisy Bug Sing-Along, 1 vol. Himmelman, John, illus. 2013. (ENG., Illus.). 32p. (J). (gr. -1-4). 16.95 *(978-1-58469-191-4(3))*; pap. 8.95 *(978-1-58469-192-1(1))* Dawn Pubns.

Jennings, Terry J. Sound. 2009. (J). 28.50 *(978-1-59920-275-4(1))* Black Rabbit Bks.

Killen, Nicola. Animal Noises. 2014. (Nicola Killen Animals Ser.). (ENG., Illus.). 10p. (J). (— 1). bds. 8.99 *(978-1-4052-6287-3(7))* Egmont Bks., Ltd. GBR. Dist: Independent Pubs. Group.

Lowery, Lawrence F. What Makes Different Sounds? 2012. (I Wonder Why Ser.). (ENG., Illus.). 32p. (J). (gr. k-3). pap. 11.95 *(978-1-936959-44-0(5))* National Science Teachers Assn.

Marchesani, Laura & Grosset and Dunlap Staff. Who Says? Aikins, Dave, illus. 2013. (Sassy Ser.). (ENG.). 12p. (J). (gr. -1 — 1). bds. 6.99 *(978-0-448-47789-3(0),* Grosset & Dunlap) Penguin Young Readers Group.

Marsalis, Wynton. Squeak, Rumble, Whomp! Whomp! Whomp! Rogers, Paul, illus. 2012. (ENG.). 40p. (J). (gr. -1-3). 15.99 *(978-0-7636-3991-4(5))* Candlewick Pr.

Matthews, Derek. Animales de la Granja. 2005. (Escucha y Aprende Ser.). (SPA., Illus.). 10p. (J). (gr. -1-1). *(978-970-718-300-1(4),* Silver Dolphin en Español) Advanced Marketing, S. de R. L. de C. V.

—Animales de la Selva. 2005. (Escucha y Aprende Ser.). (SPA., Illus.). 10p. (J). (gr. -1-1). *(978-970-718-298-1(9),* Silver Dolphin en Español) Advanced Marketing, S. de R. L. de C. V.

—Escucha y Aprende - Mascotas. 2005. (Escucha y Aprende Ser.). (SPA., Illus.). 10p. (J). (gr. -1-k). *(978-970-718-299-8(7),* Silver Dolphin en Español) Advanced Marketing, S. de R. L. de C. V.

—Tráfico: Con Graciosos Sonidos de vehículos. 2005. (Escucha y Aprende Ser.). (SPA., Illus.). 10p. (J). (gr. -1-1). *(978-970-718-297-4(0),* Silver Dolphin en Español) Advanced Marketing, S. de R. L. de C. V.

Parker, Ant, illus. Amazing Machines First Concepts: Sounds. 2015. (ENG.). 12p. (J). (gr. -1-1). bds. 5.99 *(978-0-7534-7232-3(5),* 9780753472323, Kingfisher) Roaring Brook Pr.

Perkins, Al. The Ear Book. Payne, Henry, illus. 2008. (Bright & Early Board Books(TM) Ser.). (ENG.). 24p. (J). (— 1). bds. 4.99 *(978-0-375-84279-5(9),* Random Hse. Bks. for Young Readers) Random Hse. Children's Bks.

Sounds Great! Complete Set. (gr. k-2). incl. cd-rom *(978-0-7327-2785-7(5))* McGraw-Hill Australia.

Spilsbury, Louise & Spilsbury, Richard. Making Noise!: Making Sounds, 1 vol. 2014. (Exploring Sound Ser.). (ENG., Illus.). 32p. (gr. 2-4). lib. bdg. 30.65 *(978-1-4109-5999-7(6),* Raintree Perspectives) Heinemann-Raintree.

—Shhh! Listen!: Hearing Sounds, 1 vol. HL Studios, H. L., illus. 2014. (Exploring Sound Ser.). (ENG.). 32p. (gr. 2-4). lib. bdg. 30.65 *(978-1-4109-6002-3(1),* Raintree Perspectives) Heinemann-Raintree.

Taplin, Sam. Noisy Spooky Book. 2012. (Noisy Bks). 10p. (J). bds. 19.99 *(978-0-7945-2913-0(5),* Usborne) EDC Publishing.

Twist, Clint. Light & Sound. 2010. (Science Everywhere! Ser.). 24p. 24.25 *(978-1-84898-297-0(6))* Black Rabbit Bks.

What's That Sound? (Peek A Boo Pockets Ser.). (Illus.). 12p. (J). bds. *(978-2-89393-877-6(9))* Phidal Publishing, Inc./Editions Phidal, Inc.

SOUPS

Goss, Gary. Blue Moon Soup: A Family Cookbook. Dyer, Jane, illus. 2013. (ENG.). 72p. (J). (gr. 1-4). 16.95 *(978-1-62087-990-0(5),* 620990, Sky Pony Pr.) Skyhorse Publishing Co., Inc.

Kuskowski, Alex. Cool Soups & Stews, 1 vol. 2014. (Cool Home Cooking Ser.). (ENG.). 32p. (gr. 3-6). 28.50 *(978-1-62403-504-3(3))* ABDO Publishing Co.

SOUTH, THE

see Southern States

SOUTH AFRICA

Here are entered works on the Republic of South Africa. Works on the area south of the countries of Zaire and Tanzania are entered under Africa, Southern.

Aloian, Molly. Cultural Traditions in South Africa. 2014. (ENG., Illus.). 32p. (J). *(978-0-7787-0304-4(5))* Crabtree Publishing Co.

Angelou, Maya. My Painted House, My Friendly Chicken, & Me. Courtney-Clarke, Margaret, illus. 2003. (ENG.). 48p. (J). (gr. -1-2). pap. 7.99 *(978-0-375-82567-5(3),* Crown Books For Young Readers) Random Hse. Children's Bks.

—My Painted House, My Friendly Chicken, & Me. 2003. (gr. k-3). lib. bdg. 18.40 *(978-0-613-71911-7(5),* Turtleback) Turtleback Bks.

Barraclough, John. South Africa. (World Focus Ser.). (Illus.). 31p. (J). (gr. 3-7). pap. 3.99 *(978-0-431-07268-5(X))* Oxfam Publishing GBR. Dist: Stylus Publishing, LLC.

Blauer, Ettagale & Laure, Jason. South Africa. (Enchantment of the World™, Second Ser.). (ENG.). 144p. (J). 2013. 40.00 *(978-0-531-25603-9(0))* 2006. (Illus.). (gr. 5-9). 37.00 *(978-0-516-24853-0(7))* Scholastic Library Publishing. (Children's Pr.).

Bouma, Paddy, illus. Nelson Mandela: Long Walk to Freedom. 2009. (ENG.). 64p. (J). (gr. 2-6). 18.99 *(978-1-59643-566-7(6),* 9781596435667) Roaring Brook Pr.

Bowden, Rob. Cape Town. Maconachie, Roy, photos by. 2006. (Global Cities Ser.). (Illus.). 61p. (gr. 5-8). 30.00 *(978-0-7910-8856-2(1),* Chelsea Hse.) Facts On File, Inc.

Clark, Domini. South Africa: The Culture. 3rd rev. ed. 2008. (Lands, Peoples, & Cultures Ser.). (ENG., Illus.). 32p. (J). (gr.

S

3-9). lib. bdg. (978-0-7787-9292-5(7)) Crabtree Publishing Co.

—South Africa: The Land. 3rd rev. ed. 2008. (Lands, Peoples, & Cultures Ser.). (ENG., Illus.). 32p. (J). (gr. 3-9). lib. bdg. (978-0-7787-9290-1(0)) Crabtree Publishing Co.

—South Africa: The People. 3rd rev. ed. 2008. (Lands, Peoples, & Cultures Ser.). (ENG., Illus.). 32p. (J). (gr. 3-9). pap. (978-0-7787-9659-6(0)) Crabtree Publishing Co.

—South Africa - The Culture. 3rd rev. ed. 2008. (Lands, Peoples, & Cultures Ser.). (ENG., Illus.). 32p. (J). (gr. 3-9). pap. (978-0-7787-9660-2(4)) Crabtree Publishing Co.

—South Africa - The Land. 3rd rev. ed. 2008. (Lands, Peoples, & Cultures Ser.). (ENG., Illus.). 32p. (J). (gr. 3-9). pap. (978-0-7787-9658-9(2)) Crabtree Publishing Co.

—South Africa - The People. 3rd rev. ed. 2008. (Lands, Peoples, & Cultures Ser.). (ENG., Illus.). 32p. (J). (gr. 3-9). lib. bdg. (978-0-7787-9291-8(9)) Crabtree Publishing Co.

Clarke, Nadine. Get Bushwise: on Safari Desert, River, Bushveld: A Young Explorer's Guide. 2013. 192p. pap. 23.00 (978-1-4317-0206-0(4)) Penguin Random House Grupo Editorial ESP. Dist: Casemate Pubs. & Bk. Distributors, LLC.

Conley, Kate. South Africa. 2015. (One World, Many Countries Ser.). (ENG.). 32p. (J). (gr. 1-4). 28.50 (978-1-63407-056-0(9), 208887) Child's World, Inc., The.

Cottrell, Robert C. South Africa: A State of Apartheid. Matray, James I., ed. 2005. (Arbitrary Borders Ser.). (Illus.). 112p. (C). (gr. 9-13). 35.00 (978-0-7910-8257-7(1), Chelsea Hse.) Facts On File, Inc.

Gagne, Tammy. We Visit South Africa. 2012. (J). lib. bdg. 33.95 (978-1-61228-308-1(X)) Mitchell Lane Pubs., Inc.

Gallagher, Michael. South Africa. 2007. (Countries in the News/Watts Ser.). (Illus.). 32p. (YA). (gr. 4-7). lib. bdg. 27.10 (978-1-59920-020-0(1)) Black Rabbit Bks.

Ganeri, Anita. South Africa. 2016. (Journey Through Ser.). (ENG., Illus.). 32p. (J). (gr. 4-6). 16.99 (978-1-4451-3684-4(8), Franklin Watts) Hachette Children's Group GBR. Dist: Hachette Bk. Group.

—South Africa: A Benjamin Blog & His Inquisitive Dog Guide, 1 vol. Isik, Semur, illus. 2014. (Country Guides, with Benjamin Blog & His Inquisitive Dog Ser.). (ENG.). 32p. (gr. 1-3). 29.99 (978-1-4109-6668-1(2)); pap. 7.99 (978-1-4109-6677-3(1)) Heinemann-Raintree. (Read Me!).

Green, Jen. Focus on South Africa. 2007. (World in Focus Ser.). (Illus.). 64p. (gr. 5-12). lib. bdg. 34.00 (978-0-8368-6738-1(6), Gareth Stevens Secondary Library) Stevens, Gareth Publishing LLLP.

—South Africa. 2017. (Living In Ser.). (ENG., Illus.). 24p. (J). (gr. k-2). 16.99 (978-1-4451-4868-7(4), Franklin Watts) Hachette Children's Group GBR. Dist: Hachette Bk. Group.

Hanks, Karoline. Exploring Our Biomes (Boxed Set) South Africa, 5 vols. 2010. (ENG., Illus.). 370p. (J). (gr. 4-7). pap. 108.00 (978-1-77009-679-0(5)) Jacana Media ZAF. Dist: Independent Pubs. Group.

Haskins, Jim & Benson, Kathleen. Count Your Way Through South Africa. Neibert, Alissa, illus. 2006. (Count Your Way Ser.). (ENG.). 24p. (gr. 2-5). lib. bdg. 19.93 (978-1-57505-883-2(9), Millbrook Pr.) Lerner Publishing Group.

Hollingsworth, Tamara. Nelson Mandela: Leading the Way, 1 vol. 2nd rev. ed. 2013. (Nonfiction Readers Ser.). (ENG., Illus.). 48p. (J). (gr. 4-4). pap. 29.96 (978-1-4807-1116-7(0)) Shell Educational Publishing.

Jones, Moses. South Africa. 2016. (Real Ser.). (ENG., Illus.). 48p. (J). (gr. 4-6). pap. 12.99 (978-1-4451-4907-3(9), Franklin Watts) Hachette Children's Group GBR. Dist: Hachette Bk. Group.

Kalman, Bobbie. Spotlight on South Africa. 2011. (Spotlight on My Country Ser.: No. 19). (ENG.). 32p. (J). (gr. k-3). pap. (978-0-7787-3490-1(0)) Crabtree Publishing Co.

Koosman, Melissa. Meet Our New Student from South Africa. 2009. (Meet Our New Student Ser.). (Illus.). 47p. (J). (gr. 2-5). lib. bdg. 29.95 (978-1-58415-781-6(X)) Mitchell Lane Pubs., Inc.

Langley, Andrew. Cape Town. 2005. (Great Cities of the World Ser.). (Illus.). 48p. (gr. 5-12). lib. bdg. 31.00 (978-0-8368-5045-1(9), Gareth Stevens Secondary Library) Stevens, Gareth Publishing LLLP.

Mace, Virginia. National Geographic Countries of the World - South Africa. 2008. (National Geographic Countries of the World Ser.). (ENG., Illus.). 64p. (J). (gr. 5-9). lib. bdg. 27.90 (978-1-4263-0203-9(7), National Geographic Children's Bks.) National Geographic Society.

Matthews, Sheelagh. South Africa. 2016. (J). (978-1-5105-1907-7(6)) SmartBook Media, Inc.

—South Africa. 2014. (J). (978-1-4896-1030-0(8)) Weigl Pubs., Inc.

Mis, Melody S. How to Draw South Africa's Sights & Symbols. 2009. (Kid's Guide to Drawing the Countries of the World Ser.). 48p. (gr. 4-4). 53.00 (978-1-61511-125-1(5), PowerKids Pr.) Rosen Publishing Group, Inc., The.

Noonan, Sheila Smith. South Africa. Rotberg, Robert I., ed. 2012. (Evolution of Africa's Major Nations Ser.). (Illus.). 88p. (J). (gr. 7). 22.95 (978-1-4222-2184-6(9)) Mason Crest.

—South Africa. 2011. (J). pap. (978-1-4222-2212-6(8)) Mason Crest.

Oluonye, Mary. South Africa. 2009. pap. 52.95 (978-0-7613-4735-4(6)) Lerner Publishing Group.

Oluonye, Mary N. South Africa. 2008. (Country Explorers Ser.). (ENG.). 48p. (gr. 2-4). 29.27 (978-0-8225-9411-6(0)) Lerner Publishing Group.

Owings, Lisa. South Africa. 2011. (Exploring Countries Ser.). (ENG., Illus.). 32p. (YA). (gr. 3-7). lib. bdg. 26.95 (978-1-60014-623-7(6), Blastoff! Readers) Bellwether Media.

Perkins, Chloe. Living in ... South Africa. Woolley, Tom, illus. 2016. (Living In... Ser.). (ENG.). 32p. (J). (gr. k-2). pap. 3.99 (978-1-4814-7092-6(2), Simon Spotlight) Simon Spotlight.

Petersen, Christine. South Africa. 2009. (J). (978-1-58415-786-1(0)) Mitchell Lane Pubs., Inc.

Pugliano-Martin, Carol. Cape Town, South Africa. 2006. (J). pap. (978-1-4108-6422-2(7)) Benchmark Education Co.

—Discover Cape Town. 2006. (J). pap. (978-1-4108-6425-3(1)) Benchmark Education Co.

Ritter, Christie Rose. South Africa, 1 vol. 2011. (Countries of the World Set 1 Ser.). (ENG., Illus.). 144p. (J). (gr. 6-12). lib. bdg. 37.07 (978-1-61783-118-8(2)) ABDO Publishing Co.

Savery, Annabel. South Africa. 2011. (ENG., Illus.). 32p. (J). pap. 10.95 (978-1-77092-027-9(7)) Saunders Bk. Co. CAN. Dist: RiverStream Publishing.

Senker, Cath. South Africa. 2014. (My Country Ser.). 24p. (gr. k-3). lib. bdg. 28.50 (978-1-59920-907-4(1)) Black Rabbit Bks.

Sheen, Barbara, ed. Foods of South Africa. 2012. (Taste of Culture Ser.). (ENG., Illus.). 64p. (gr. 3-6). lib. bdg. 30.45 (978-0-7377-5952-5(6), Kidhaven) Cengage Gale.

Shoup, Kate. South Africa. 2017. (J). pap. 19.95 (978-1-5026-2507-6(5)) Cavendish Square Publishing.

South Africa. 2003. (Modern World Nations Ser.). (Illus.). 150p. (gr. 6-12). 35.00 (978-0-7910-7610-1(5), Chelsea Hse.) Facts On File, Inc.

Taylor, Trace. South Africa. 2010. pap. 39.62 (978-1-61541-131-3(3)) American Reading Co.

Taylor, Trace & SáNchez, LucíA M. South Africa. 2010. pap. 39.62 (978-1-61541-154-2(2)) American Reading Co.

Taylor, Trace & Sánchez, Lucía M. South Africa. 2010. (1Y Nuestro Mundo Ser.). (SPA.). 16p. (J). (gr. k-1). pap. 6.99 (978-1-61541-153-5(4)) American Reading Co.

Throp, Claire. South Africa, 1 vol. 2012. (Countries Around the World Ser.). (ENG.). 48p. (gr. 3-6). pap. 9.95 (978-1-4329-6138-1(1), NA-h) Heinemann-Raintree.

Venter, Sahm. Human Rights Day March 21. 2008. (Exploring Our National Days Ser.). (ENG.). 70p. 20.95 (978-1-77009-321-8(4)) Jacana Media ZAF. Dist: Independent Pubs. Group.

—Youth Day June 16. 2007. (Exploring Our National Days Ser.). (ENG., Illus.). 72p. (gr. 4-7). 20.95 (978-1-77009-235-8(8)) Jacana Media ZAF. Dist: Independent Pubs. Group.

Ward, Chris. Discover South Africa. 2010. (Illus.). 32p. (J). 63.60 (978-1-61532-300-5(7), 1307266); pap. 10.60 (978-1-61532-299-2(X)) Rosen Publishing Group, Inc., The. (PowerKids Pr.).

Wilson, Rosie & Ward, Chris. Discover South Africa. 2010. (Discover Countries Ser.). (Illus.). 32p. (J). (gr. 3-5). 26.50 (978-1-61532-289-3(2)) Rosen Publishing Group, Inc., The.

SOUTH AFRICA—BIOGRAPHY

Abrams, Dennis. Thabo Mbeki. 2007. (Modern World Leaders Ser.). (Illus.). 126p. (YA). (gr. 7-12). lib. bdg. 30.00 (978-0-7910-9443-3(X)) Facts On File, Inc.

Baptiste, Tracey. Nelson Mandela: Nobel Peace Prize-Winning Champion for Hope & Harmony. 2015. (Britannica Beginner Bios Ser.). (ENG.). 32p. (J). (gr. 2-3). 46.90 (978-1-62275-943-9(5), Britannica Educational Publishing) Rosen Publishing Group, Inc., The.

—Nelson Mandela: Nobel Peace Prize-Winning Warrior for Hope & Harmony. 2015. (Britannica Beginner Bios Ser.). (ENG., Illus.). 32p. (J). 23.45 (978-1-62275-941-5(9), Britannica Educational Publishing) Rosen Publishing Group, Inc., The.

Barnham, Kay. Nelson Mandela: Revolutionary President. 2017. (Inspirational Lives Ser.). (ENG., Illus.). 32p. (J). (gr. 4-6). pap. 12.99 (978-0-7502-9311-2(X), Wayland) Hachette Children's Group GBR. Dist: Hachette Bk. Group.

Belviso, Meg & Pollack, Pam. Who Is Nelson Mandela? 2014. (Who Was... ? Ser.). lib. bdg. 16.00 (978-0-606-34158-5(7), Turtleback) Turtleback Bks.

Boothroyd, Jennifer. Nelson Mandela: A Life of Persistence. (Pull Ahead Books-Biographies Ser.). (ENG., Illus.). 32p. (gr. k-3). 2007. pap. 7.95 (978-0-8225-6434-8(3)) 2006. lib. bdg. 22.60 (978-0-8225-6385-3(1)) Lerner Publishing Group. (Lerner Pubns.).

Capozzi, Suzy. Nelson Mandela: From Prisoner to President. Tadgell, Nicole, illus. 2016. (Step into Reading Ser.). (ENG.). 48p. (J). (gr. 2-4). 12.99 (978-0-375-97467-0(9), Random Hse. Bks. for Young Readers) Random Hse. Children's Bks.

Dakers, Diane. Nelson Mandela: South Africa's Anti-Apartheid Revolutionary. 2014. (ENG., Illus.). 112p. (J). (978-0-7787-1241-1(9)) Crabtree Publishing Co.

Denenberg, Barry. Nelson Mandela: No Easy Walk to Freedom. 2014. (ENG.). 240p. (J). (gr. 3-7). pap. 7.99 (978-0-545-66911-5(1)) Scholastic, Inc.

Gormley, Beatrice. Nelson Mandela: South African Revolutionary. 2015. (Real-Life Story Ser.). (ENG., Illus.). 256p. (J). (gr. 3-7). 17.99 (978-1-4814-2059-4(3), Aladdin) Simon & Schuster Children's Publishing.

Green, Sara. Elon Musk. 2014. (Tech Icons Ser.). (ENG., Illus.). 24p. (J). (gr. 3-8). lib. bdg. 25.95 (978-1-60014-988-7(X), Pilot Bks.) Bellwether Media.

Hollingsworth, Tamara. Nelson Mandela: Marcando el Camino. 2017. (TIME for Kids en Español - Level 4 Ser.). (SPA., Illus.). 48p. (gr. 4-4). lib. bdg. 31.99 (978-1-5157-5145-8(7)) Time for Kids Inc AUS. Dist: Capstone Pub.

Ingram, Doreen. My Sanctuary, a Place I Call Home. 2010. (Illus.). 54p. pap. 17.50 (978-1-60911-480-0(9), Eloquent Bks.) Strategic Book Publishing & Rights Agency (SBPRA).

Josephson, Judith Pinkerton. Nelson Mandela. 2009. (History Maker Biographies Ser.). (ENG.). 48p. (gr. 3-6). 27.93 (978-1-58013-703-4(2), Lerner Pubns.) Lerner Publishing Group.

Kallen, Stuart A. Elon Musk & Tesla. 2015. (ENG., Illus.). 80p. (J). lib. bdg. (978-1-60152-870-4(1)) ReferencePoint Pr., Inc.

Keller, Bill. Tree Shaker: The Life of Nelson Mandela. 2013. (New York Times Ser.). (ENG., Illus.). 128p. (J). (gr. 5-9). pap. 9.99 (978-1-59643-533-9(X), 9781596435339) Square Fish.

—Tree Shaker: The Story of Nelson Mandela. 2013. (ENG., Illus.). 128p. (J). (gr. 7-12). 17.99 (978-0-7534-7184-5(1), 9780753471845, Kingfisher) Roaring Brook Pr.

Kramer, Ann. Mandela: The Hero Who Led His Nation to Freedom. 2008. (National Geographic World History Biographies Ser.). (ENG., Illus.). 64p. (J). (gr. 3-7). pap. 7.99 (978-1-4263-0173-5(1), National Geographic Children's Bks.) National Geographic Society.

Magoon, Kekla. Nelson Mandela: A Leader for Freedom, 1 vol. 2008. (Essential Lives Set 2 Ser.). (ENG., Illus.). 112p. (J). (gr. 6-12). lib. bdg. 35.64 (978-1-60453-038-4(3)) ABDO Publishing Co.

Meyer, Susan. Nelson Mandela: South African President & Anti-Apartheid Activist. 2017. (J). (978-1-5383-8089-5(7), Rosen Young Adult) Rosen Publishing Group, Inc., The.

Nelson, Kadir. Nelson Mandela. Nelson, Kadir, illus. 2013. (Illus.). 40p. (J). (gr. -1-3). (ENG.). 17.99 (978-0-06-178374-6(9)); lib. bdg. 18.89 (978-0-06-178376-0(5)) HarperCollins Pubs. (Tegen, Katherine Bks).

—Nelson Mandela. 2014. (SPA.). (J). (gr. 2-4). 21.99 (978-84-261-4069-2(6)) Juventud, Editorial ESP. Dist: Lectorum Pubns., Inc.

Rajczak, Kristen. Nelson Mandela. 2015. (Heroes of Black History Ser.). (ENG., Illus.). 32p. (J). (gr. 3-4). pap. 10.50 (978-1-4824-2908-4(X)) Stevens, Gareth Publishing LLLP.

Riggs, Kate. The Release of Nelson Mandela. 2009. (Days of Change Ser.). (Illus.). 48p. (YA). (gr. 4-7). 22.95 (978-1-58341-736-2(2)) Creative Co., The.

Rodriguez, Ann Graham Gaines. Nelson Mandela & the End of Apartheid. 2016. (People & Events That Changed the World Ser.). (ENG., Illus.). 128p. (J). (gr. 7-8). 37.27 (978-0-7660-7300-5(9)) Enslow Pubs., Inc.

Rose, Simon. Nelson Mandela. 2010. (Remarkable People Ser.). (Illus.). 24p. (J). (gr. 3-5). lib. bdg. 25.70 (978-1-61690-172-1(1)); (gr. 4-6). pap. 11.95 (978-1-61690-173-8(X)) Weigl Pubs., Inc.

Senker, Cath. Nelson Mandela. 2015. (Against the Odds Biographies Ser.). (ENG., Illus.). 48p. (gr. 3-6). 33.32 (978-1-4846-2465-4(3)) Heinemann-Raintree.

Stamper, G. C. Nelson Mandela. 2005. (Illus.). 32p. (J). pap. (978-0-7367-2922-2(4)) Zaner-Bloser, Inc.

Trussell-Cullen, Alan. Nelson Mandela. 2009. pap. 13.25 (978-1-60559-067-7(3)) Hameray Publishing Group, Inc.

Vandegrift, Tom. 24 New Moons. 2003. 429p. (YA). pap. 20.95 (978-0-7414-1503-5(8)) Infinity Publishing.

Wilcox, Christine. Oscar Pistorius. 2014. (People in the News Ser.). (ENG., Illus.). 128p. (gr. 7-10). 39.40 (978-1-4205-1041-6(X), Lucent Bks.) Cengage Gale.

SOUTH AFRICA—FICTION

Benjamin, Ruth. Yesterday's Child. Cohen, Deene, illus. (YA). 16.95 (978-1-56062-176-8(1), CFR122H); pap. 13.95 (978-1-56062-177-5(X), CFR122S) C I S Communications, Inc.

Beverley, Naidoo. Journey to Jo'Burg: A South African Story. 97th rev. ed. 2014. (ENG.). 96p. (J). (gr. k-4). 10.24 (978-1-63245-264-1(2)) Lectorum Pubns., Inc.

Bildner, Phil. The Soccer Fence: A Story of Friendship, Hope, & Apartheid in South Africa. Watson, Jesse Joshua, illus. 2014. (ENG.). 40p. (J). (gr. 1-3). 16.99 (978-0-399-24790-3(4), G.P. Putnam's Sons Books for Young Readers) Penguin Young Readers Group.

Bulbring, Edyth. Cornelia Button & the Globe of Gamagion. 2009. (ENG.). 208p. (J). (gr. 4-7). pap. 18.00 (978-1-77009-501-4(2)) Jacana Media ZAF. Dist: Independent Pubs. Group.

Callen, Sharon. Anna Goes to Zambia, 1 vol. rev. ed. 2013. (Fiction Readers Ser.). (ENG., Illus.). 20p. (J). (gr. 1-1). pap. 15.96 (978-1-4807-1151-8(9)); pap. 4.99 (978-1-4333-5495-3(0)) Shell Educational Publishing.

Coman, Carolyn. Many Stones. 2009. (ENG.). 160p. (YA). pap. 12.95 (978-1-59078-782-3(X), Front Street) Boyds Mills Pr.

—Many Stones. 2011. 14.12 (978-0-7848-3598-2(5), Everbind) Marco Bk. Co.

Craig, Colleen. Afrika. 2008. (ENG.). 240p. (J). (gr. 7). pap. 9.95 (978-0-88776-807-1(5), Tundra Bks.) Tundra Bks. CAN. Dist: Penguin Random Hse. LLC.

Cumberland, Wendy. Inkwelo Mountain: A Child's Adventure in Kwa Zulu, South Africa. 2013. 46p. pap. 10.95 (978-1-62857-135-6(7), Strategic Bk. Publishing) Strategic Book Publishing & Rights Agency (SBPRA).

Daly, Niki. The Herd Boy. 2012. (ENG., Illus.). 32p. (J). 17.00 (978-0-8028-5417-9(6), Eerdmans Bks For Young Readers) Eerdmans, William B. Publishing Co.

—A Song for Jamela. Daly, Niki, illus. 2014. (ENG., Illus.). 36p. (J). (gr. -1-2). pap. 8.99 (978-1-84780-429-7(2), Frances Lincoln) Quarto Publishing Group UK GBR. Dist: Hachette Bk. Group.

Deeks, Graham. Ratrigues & the Invisible Intelligence. 2011. 264p. 27.08 (978-1-4269-7019-1(6)); pap. 17.08 (978-1-4269-7020-7(X)) Trafford Publishing.

Driftin' Aarong. Claude Henry, the Iditarod Mouse ~3: The Great Castaway Adventure. 2009. 92p. pap. 9.95 (978-1-4401-1949-1(X)) iUniverse, Inc.

Garisch, Dawn. Babyshoes. 2004. (ENG.). 288p. (J). pap. 9.99 (978-0-689-83778-4(X)) Simon & Schuster, Ltd. GBR. Dist: Simon & Schuster, Inc.

Hart, Sue. Tales of the Full Moon. Harvey, Chris, illus. 2006. (ENG.). 96p. (J). (gr. 2-4). pap. 16.95 (978-1-55591-582-7(5), 800.992.2908) Fulcrum Publishing.

Hartley, A. J. Steeplejack. 2016. (Steeplejack Ser.: 1). (ENG.). 336p. (YA). 17.99 (978-0-7653-8342-6(X), 9780765383426, Tor Teen) Doherty, Tom Assocs., LLC.

Heale, Jay. African Animal Tales. 2004. (Illus.). 96p. (978-1-86872-704-9(1)) Penguin Random House South Africa.

Henty, George Alfred. With Buller in Natal: Or a Born Leader. 2007. (ENG.). 290p. pap. 21.99 (978-1-4264-9358-4(4)); 324p. pap. 24.99 (978-1-4264-9739-1(3)) Creative Media Partners, LLC.

Hichens, Joanne. Stained. 2008. (Cutting Edge Ser.). (ENG.). 200p. pap. (978-1-84167-715-6(9)) Ransom Publishing Ltd.

Hildahl, Violetta R. Peacock of Taj Mahal. 2011. 28p. (gr. -1). pap. 13.59 (978-1-4520-0259-0(2)) AuthorHouse.

Irwin, Bindi & Black, Jess. Rescue! Bindi Wildlife Adventures. 2011. (Bindi's Wildlife Adventures Ser.: 2). (ENG.). 112p. (gr. 3-6). pap. 4.99 (978-1-4022-5517-5(9), Sourcebooks Jabberwocky) Sourcebooks, Inc.

Javaherbin, Mina. Goal! Ford, A. G., illus. 2012. (ENG.). 40p. (J). (gr. 1-4). pap. 6.99 (978-0-7636-5822-9(7)) Candlewick Pr.

Kent, Trilby. Stones for My Father. 2011. (ENG.). 176p. (YA). (gr. 5-18). 19.95 (978-1-77049-252-3(6), Tundra Bks.) Tundra Bks. CAN. Dist: Penguin Random Hse. LLC.

Khoury, Jessica. Kalahari. 2015. (ENG.). 368p. (YA). (gr. 7). 17.99 (978-1-59514-765-3(9), Razorbill) Penguin Young Readers Group.

Kowen, Dorothy. The Gift of Gold. Mathew, Gillian, illus. 2011. (ENG.). 24p. 13.95 (978-1-77009-796-4(1)) Jacana Media ZAF. Dist: Independent Pubs. Group.

—Thando Rocker. Sherrell, Craig, illus. 2012. (ENG.). 24p. (J). (gr. k-2). pap. 7.95 (978-1-4314-0087-4(4)) Jacana Media ZAF. Dist: Independent Pubs. Group.

Kramer, Berri, photos by & text. Mbali: A story from South Africa. Kramer, Berri, text. 2nd ed. 2006. (Illus.). (J). per. (978-0-9706901-1-1(8)) Rotaplast Pr.

Krueger, Anton. Sunnyside Sal. 2010. 120p. pap. (978-0-9584915-6-3(9)) Deep South Bks.

Marsh, Carole. The Rip-Roaring Mystery on the African Safari. 2009. (Around the World in 80 Mysteries Ser.). (J). (gr. 2-9). lib. bdg. 18.99 (978-0-635-06835-4(4)); (Illus.). 133p. (gr. 4-7). pap. 7.99 (978-0-635-06829-3(X), Marsh, Carole Bks.) Gallopade International.

Mbuyazi, Phiwayinkosi G. The Wiby Kids - How It All Began. 2011. 204p. pap. 12.99 (978-1-61667-337-6(0)) Raider Publishing International.

McMiller, Theresa R. Bessie Goes All over the World. 2012. 28p. pap. 24.95 (978-1-4626-9464-8(0)) America Star Bks.

Moodley, Ermila. Path to My African Eyes. 2007. 173p. (J). (gr. 6-13). per. 15.95 (978-1-933491-09-7(4)) Just Us Bks., Inc.

Naidoo, Beverley. No Turning Back. 2017. (ENG.). 208p. (YA). (gr. 9). pap. 12.99 (978-0-14-136890-0(X)) Penguin Bks., Ltd. GBR. Dist: Independent Pubs. Group.

—Out of Bounds: Seven Stories of Conflict & Hope. 2008. (ENG.). 208p. (J). (gr. 5). pap. 6.99 (978-0-06-050801-2(9)) HarperCollins Pubs.

Nelson, Marilyn. Ostrich & Lark. Artists of the Kuru Art Project in Botswana, San, illus. 2012. (ENG.). 32p. (J). (gr. k-4). 16.95 (978-1-59078-702-1(1)) Boyds Mills Pr.

The Other Side of the Invisible Fence. 2006. (YA). per. 9.95 (978-0-9787783-8-5(3)) Romain, Trevor Co., The.

Patel, T. M. The Immigrant: Stargazer. 2013. 290p. (J). pap. (978-1-78299-385-8(1)) FeedARead.com.

Pegler, Robin. Having Fun Together: A Collection of Children's Stories. 2010. 514p. pap. 23.95 (978-1-60693-817-1(7), Eloquent Bks.) Strategic Book Publishing & Rights Agency (SBPRA).

Pennels, Geraldine. The School Shenanigans of Amy & Nontand. 2009. 152p. pap. 33.50 (978-1-60860-496-8(9), Strategic Bk. Publishing) Strategic Book Publishing & Rights Agency (SBPRA).

Penning, L. & Nelson, Marietjie. The Hero of Spionkop. 2006. (Illus.). 166p. (YA). pap. (978-1-894666-92-3(5)) Inheritance Pubns.

—The Lion of Moddersspruit. 2004. (Illus.). 142p. (YA). pap. (978-1-894666-91-6(7)) Inheritance Pubns.

Powers, J. L. This Thing Called the Future. 2011. (FRS & ENG.). 208p. (J). (gr. 7-11). 16.95 (978-1-933693-95-8(9)) Cinco Puntos Pr.

Raina, Arushi. When Morning Comes, 1 vol. 2017. (ENG., Illus.). 232p. (J). (gr. 8-12). pap. 10.95 (978-1-926890-14-2(0)) Tradewind Bks. CAN. Dist: Orca Bk. Pubs. USA.

Reid, Mayne. Young Yagers or A Narrative of Hunting A. 2006. (Illus.). pap. 31.95 (978-1-4286-2205-0(5)) Kessinger Publishing, LLC.

Remza, Freddie. Ride the Wave. 2011. 272p. pap. 16.95 (978-1-4327-6642-9(2)) Outskirts Pr., Inc.

Rupert, Rona. Straw Sense. 2013. (ENG., Illus.). 36p. (J). (gr. k-3). 17.99 (978-1-4814-0151-7(3), Simon & Schuster Bks. For Young Readers) Simon & Schuster Bks. For Young Readers.

Schermbrucker, Reviva. An African Christmas Cloth. 2007. (ENG.). 36p. 27.95 (978-1-77009-081-1(9)) Jacana Media ZAF. Dist: Independent Pubs. Group.

Shepherd, J. A., illus. Old Hendrik's Tales - 13 South African Folk Tales. 2013. 198p. pap. (978-1-909302-15-0(5)) Abela Publishing.

Smith, E. The Adventures of Sir Ambrose Elephant: A Visit to the City. Apa, Ivy Marie, illus. 2012. 19p. pap. 9.95 (978-1-4691-8378-7(1)) Xlibris Corp.

Smith, Pieter Ernst. A Donkey Is Not Stupid, a Donkey Can Think. Shirley-Smith, Sanette, illus. 2011. 24p. pap. 11.50 (978-1-61204-039-4(X), Eloquent Bks.) Strategic Book Publishing & Rights Agency (SBPRA).

St. John, Lauren. The Elephant's Tale. 2011. (ENG.). 240p. (J). (gr. 3-7). 6.99 (978-0-14-241879-6(X), Puffin Books) Penguin Young Readers Group.

—The White Giraffe. 2008. (ENG., Illus.). 208p. (J). (gr. 2-5). 7.99 (978-0-14-241152-0(3), Puffin Books) Penguin Young Readers Group.

Swedeen, Staci. Tombi-Ende & the Frog: A Fairy Tale from Southern Africa. 2006. (J). pap. (978-1-4108-7151-0(7)) Benchmark Education Co.

Tlali, Miriam. Between Two Worlds. 2004. (ENG.). 222p. reprint ed. pap. (978-1-55111-605-1(7)) Broadview Pr.

True, J. J. Billy Brite: Africa & Beyond. 2011. (Illus.). 112p. pap. 14.03 (978-1-4567-7281-9(3)) AuthorHouse.

Tutu, Desmond. Desmond & the Very Mean Word. Ford, A. G., illus. 2012. (ENG.). 32p. (J). (gr. 1-4). 15.99 (978-0-7636-5229-6(6)) Candlewick Pr.

Uncle Markie. Piglettė & Bobo in Sud Africa. 2003. (YA). ring bd. 9.95 (978-1-933129-15-0(8)) Studio 403.

—Piglettė & Bobo on Safari. 2003. (YA). ring bd. 9.95 (978-1-933129-16-7(6)) Studio 403.

van de Ruit, John. Spud. 2005. 300p. pap. (978-0-14-302484-2(1)) Penguin Publishing Group.

—Spud. 2008. (ENG.). 336p. (YA). (gr. 7-18). 9.99 (978-1-59514-187-3(1), Razorbill) Penguin Young Readers Group.

Van De Ruit, John. Spud - The Madness Continues. 2009. (ENG.). 352p. (YA). (gr. 7-18). 9.99 (978-1-59514-245-0(2), Razorbill) Penguin Young Readers Group.

Waddilove, Guy. Dancing with the Dragleon. 2013. (Illus.). 222p. pap. (978-1-78036-196-3(3)) Peach Publishing.

Williams, Geoffrey T. The Great White Red Alert. Artful Doodlers, illus. Campbell, Tom, photos by. 2008. (Save Our Seas Adventure Bks.). (ENG.). 64p. (J). (gr. 4-7). 8.95 (978-0-9800444-0-9(5)) Save Our Seas, Ltd.

Wood, Amanda. Rainbow. 2009. 208p. pap. 13.50 (978-1-60860-343-5(1), Strategic Bk. Publishing) Strategic Book Publishing & Rights Agency (SBPRA).

Wulf, Linda Press. The Night of the Burning. 2007. (ENG.). 224p. pap. (978-0-7475-9051-4(6)) Bloomsbury Publishing Plc.

SOUTH AFRICA—RACE RELATIONS

Cruden, Alex & Bryfonski, Dedria. The End of Apartheid. 2009. (Perspectives on Modern World History Ser.). (Illus.). 224p. (YA). (gr. 10-12). 42.45 (978-0-7377-4557-3(6), Greenhaven Pr., Inc.) Cengage Gale.

The End of Apartheid in South Africa. 2010. (Milestones in World History Ser.). (Illus.). 120p. (C). (gr. 9-18). 35.00 *(978-1-60413-409-4(7)*, Chelsea Hse.) Facts On File, Inc.
Finlayson, Reggie. Nelson Mandela. 2005. (Just the Facts Biographies Ser.). (ENG., Illus.). 112p. (gr. 5-12). lib. bdg. 27.93 *(978-0-8225-2644-5(1)*, Lerner Pubns.) Lerner Publishing Group.
Koosman, Melissa. The Fall of Apartheid in South Africa. 2009. (Monumental Milestones Ser.). 48p. (YA). (gr. 4-7). lib. bdg. 29.95 *(978-1-58415-736-6(4))* Mitchell Lane Pubs., Inc.
Magoon, Kekla. Nelson Mandela: A Leader for Freedom, 1 vol. 2008. (Essential Lives Set 2 Ser.). (ENG., Illus.). 112p. (J). (gr. 6-12). lib. bdg. 35.64 *(978-1-60453-038-4(3))* ABDO Publishing Co.
Malaspina, Ann. Nelson Mandela: Fighting to Dismantle Apartheid. 2017. (Rebels with a Cause Ser.). 128p. (YA). (gr. 8-8). lib. bdg. 37.27 ***(978-0-7660-8517-6(1))*** Enslow Pubs., Inc.
Rodriguez, Ann Graham Gaines. Nelson Mandela & the End of Apartheid. 2016. (People & Events That Changed the World Ser.). (ENG., Illus.). 128p. (J). (gr. 7-8). 37.27 *(978-0-7660-7300-5(9))* Enslow Pubs., Inc.
World Book, Inc Staff, contrib. by. South Africa's Anti-Apartheid Movement. 2010. (Illus.). 62p. (J). *(978-0-7166-1507-1(X))* World Bk., Inc.

SOUTH AFRICAN WAR, 1899-1902

Slavicek, Louise Chipley. The Boer War. 2011. (Milestones in Modern World History Ser.). (Illus.). 128p. (C). (gr. 9). 35.00 *(978-1-60413-458-2(5)*, Chelsea Hse.) Facts On File, Inc.

SOUTH AMERICA

Aloian, Molly & Kalman, Bobbie. Explore South America. rev. ed. 2007. (Explore the Continents Ser.). (ENG., Illus.). 32p. (J). (gr. 1-5). pap. *(978-0-7787-3090-3(5))* Crabtree Publishing Co.
Banting, Erinn. South America. (J). 2016. ***(978-1-4896-5728-2(2))*** 2005. (Illus.). 32p. (gr. -1-7). pap. 9.95 *(978-1-59036-329-4(9))* 2005. (Illus.). 32p. (gr. 4-6). lib. bdg. 26.00 *(978-1-59036-322-5(1))* Weigl Pubs., Inc.
Benchmark Education Co., LLC. Ancient Cultures of South America. 2014. (PRIME Ser.). (J). (gr. 6-8). pap. *(978-1-4509-9485-9(7))* Benchmark Education Co.
—The Geography of North & South America. 2014. (PRIME Ser.). (J). (gr. 6-8). pap. *(978-1-4509-9505-4(5))* Benchmark Education Co.
Carr, Joaquin. Habitats of South America: Set Of 6. 2010. (Navigators Ser.). (J). pap. 44.00 net. *(978-1-4108-5073-7(0))* Benchmark Education Co.
Delacre, Lulu. ¡Olinguito, de la A a la Z!: Descubriendo el Bosque Nublado: Olinguito, from A to Z!: Unveiling the Cloud Forest. Delacre, Lulu, illus. 2016. (ENG & SPA., Illus.). 40p. (J). 18.95 *(978-0-89239-327-5(0))* Lee & Low Bks., Inc.
Donaldson, Madeline. South America. 2005. (Pull Ahead Bks.). (Illus.). 32p. (gr. k-3). (J). lib. bdg. 22.60 *(978-0-8225-4723-5(6))*; (ENG., pap. 7.95 *(978-0-8225-2495-3(3))* Lerner Publishing Group.
Encyclopaedia Britannica, Inc. Staff, compiled by. My First Britannica: The Americas. 2008. (gr. 7-12). *(978-1-59339-409-7(8))* Encyclopaedia Britannica, Inc.
Encyclopaedia Britannica Publishers, Inc. Staff. Views of the Americas. 2003. (Britannica Learning Library). (Illus.). 14.95 *(978-1-59339-012-9(2))* Encyclopaedia Britannica, Inc.
Gibson, Karen Bush. South America. 2016. (Seven Continents Ser.). (ENG.). 24p. (gr. 2-3). pap. 7.45 *(978-1-5157-4217-3(2)*, Bridgestone Bks.) Capstone Press of Coughlan Cos.
—Spotlight on South America. (Spotlight on the Continents Ser.). (ENG.). 24p. (gr. 1-2). 2016. pap. 7.99 *(978-1-5157-6148-8(7))* 2010. lib. bdg. 25.32 *(978-1-4296-6622-0(6))* Capstone Press of Coughlan Cos. (First Facts).
Gorrell, Gena K. In the Land of the Jaguar: South America & Its People. Krystoforski, Andrej, illus. 2007. (ENG.). 160p. (J). (gr. 4-7). 22.95 *(978-0-88776-756-2(7)*, Tundra Bks.) Tundra Bks. CAN. Dist: Penguin Random Hse. LLC.
Henderson, James D., ed. Discovering South America, 13 vols., Set. (Illus.). 64p. (YA). (gr. 5-18). lib. bdg. *(978-1-59084-284-3(7))* Mason Crest.
Hernández, Roger E. South America: Facts & Figures. (South America Today Ser.). 64p. (gr. 4-7). 2009. (Illus.). (J). 21.95 *(978-1-4222-0640-9(8))* 2007. (YA). pap. 9.95 *(978-1-4222-0707-9(2))* Mason Crest.
Hirschmann, Kristine. Geography of South America: Set Of 6. 2011. (Navigators Ser.). (J). pap. 50.00 net. *(978-1-4108-6264-8(X))* Benchmark Education Co.
Hovanec, Erin M. An Online Visit to South America. 2009. (Internet Field Trips Ser.). 24p. (gr. 3-3). 45.00 *(978-1-61513-607-0(X)*, PowerKids Pr.) Rosen Publishing Group, Inc., The.
Koponen, Libby. South America. (True Bks.). (ENG., Illus.). 48p. (J). 2009. pap. 6.95 *(978-0-531-21831-0(7)*, Children's Pr.) 2008. (gr. 2-5). 29.00 *(978-0-531-16869-1(7))* Scholastic Library Publishing.
Marsh, Carole. South America: A Continent of Countries of Amazing Proportions! 2009. (It's Your World Ser.). 48p. (J). (gr. 2-9). pap. 7.99 *(978-0-635-06822-4(2))* Gallopade International.
McIntosh, Kenneth & McIntosh, Marsha. The Flight from Turmoil. 2007. (Hispanic Heritage Ser.). (Illus.). 112p. (YA). lib. bdg. 22.95 *(978-1-59084-930-9(2))* Mason Crest.
Nelson, Maria. The Pan-American Highway. 2016. (Road Trip Ser.). (Illus.). 24p. (J). (gr. 3-2). 22.60 *(978-1-4824-4669-2(3))* Stevens, Gareth Publishing LLLP.
Proujan, Carl & National Geographic Learning Staff. South America - Geography & Environments. 2007. (Reading Expeditions Ser.). (ENG., Illus.). 64p. (J). pap. 25.95 *(978-0-7922-4382-3(X))* CENGAGE Learning.
Sayre, April Pulley. South America, Surprise! 2003. 32p. (J). (gr. 2-5). pap. 7.95 *(978-0-7613-1989-4(1))*; (Illus.). lib. bdg. 21.90 *(978-0-7613-2123-1(3))* Lerner Publishing Group. (Millbrook Pr.).
Scoones, Simon. South America. 2005. (Continents of the World Ser.). (Illus.). 64p. (gr. 5-12). pap. 14.05 *(978-0-8368-5922-5(7))*; lib. bdg. 34.00 *(978-0-8368-5915-7(4))* Stevens, Gareth Publishing LLLP. (Gareth Stevens Secondary Library).
Tarbox, A. D. A Rainforest Food Chain: Nature's Bounty. 2nd ed. 2015. (Illus.). 80p. (J). *(978-1-60818-543-6(5)*, Creative Education) Creative Co., The.
Vierow, Wendy. South America. 2004. (Atlas of the Seven Continents Ser.). (ENG.). 24p. (J). lib. bdg. 22.60 *(978-0-8239-6693-6(3)*, PowerKids Pr.) Rosen Publishing Group, Inc., The.
Wojahn, Rebecca Hogue & Wojahn, Donald. A Rain Forest Food Chain: A Who-Eats-What Adventure in South America. 2009. (Follow That Food Chain Ser.). (ENG.). 64p. (gr. 3-5). 30.60 *(978-0-8225-7497-2(7))* Lerner Publishing Group.
Woods, Michael & Woods, Mary B. Seven Natural Wonders of Central & South America. 2009. (Seven Wonders Ser.). (Illus.). 80p. (YA). (gr. 5-9). lib. bdg. 33.26 *(978-0-8225-9070-5(0))* Twenty First Century Bks.

SOUTH AMERICA—DESCRIPTION AND TRAVEL

Harasymiw, Mark. Mapping South America. 2013. (Mapping the World Ser.). 24p. (J). (gr. 2-5). pap. 48.90 *(978-1-4339-9121-9(7))*; (ENG., Illus.). pap. 8.15 *(978-1-4339-9120-2(9))* Stevens, Gareth Publishing LLLP.
Harasymiw, Mark & Harasymiw, Mark J. Mapping South America. 2013. 24p. (J). (gr. 2-5). 22.60 *(978-1-4339-9119-6(5))* Stevens, Gareth Publishing LLLP.
Lee, James, ed. South America in Charts & Graphs. 2004. (YA). cd-rom 25.00 *(978-0-9749905-0-7(7))* JLM CD-ROM Publishing Co.
Lonely Planet Publications Staff. South America: Everything You Ever Wanted to Know, 1 vol. 2013. (Lonely Planet Kids Ser.). (ENG., Illus.). 96p. (J). pap. 12.99 *(978-1-74321-916-4(4)*, 4634) Lonely Planet Pubns.
Rockett, Paul. Mapping South America. 2016. (Illus.). 32p. (J). *(978-0-7787-2617-3(7))* Crabtree Publishing Co.
Vierow, Wendy. South America. 2009. (Atlas of the Seven Continents Ser.). 24p. (J). (gr. 3-3). 42.50 *(978-1-61511-484-9(X)*, PowerKids Pr.) Rosen Publishing Group, Inc., The.
Zronik, John Paul & Zronik, John. Francisco Pizarro: Journeys Through Peru & South America. 2005. (In the Footsteps of Explorers Ser.). (ENG., Illus.). 32p. (J). (gr. -1-9). pap. *(978-0-7787-2447-6(6))* Crabtree Publishing Co.

SOUTH AMERICA—DISCOVERY AND EXPLORATION

see America—Discovery and Exploration

SOUTH AMERICA—FICTION

Appleton, Victor. Tom Swift in Captivity or A Daring Escap. 2006. pap. *(978-1-4065-0914-4(0))* Dodo Pr.
Baldini-Chavez, Cecilia. The Silver-Golden Feather Secreted at el Dorado, 1 vol. 2009. 92p. pap. 19.95 *(978-1-60813-664-3(7))* America Star Bks.
Ballantyne, R. M. The Lighthouse. 2006. pap. *(978-1-4065-0531-3(5))* Dodo Pr.
Breckenridge, Gerald. The Radio Boys Search for the Inca's Treasure. 2011. 282p. pap. *(978-1-907256-99-8(7))* Abela Publishing.
Brenchley, Chaz & Doyle, Arthur Conan. The Lost World. Bennett, Felix, illus. 2009. (Real Reads Ser.). 64p. (J). (gr. 4-8). pap. 13.55 *(978-1-60754-395-4(8))*; lib. bdg. 29.25 *(978-1-60754-394-7(X))* Windmill Bks.
C.M.M. A Life of Many Forms. 2012. 52p. pap. 16.95 *(978-1-62709-318-7(4))* America Star Bks.
Day, Williamson. The Pretorius Stories. 2011. 96p. pap. 9.99 *(978-1-4634-7430-0(X))* AuthorHouse.
De Matos, Isabel Freire. Una Carta de Monica. Saez, Sofia, illus. 2004. (SPA.). 32p. (gr. k-3). pap. 8.95 *(978-1-57581-574-9(5))* Santillana USA Publishing Co., Inc.
Fawcett, Jack & Rimes, Raleigh. Dinosaurology. 2013. (Ologies Ser.). (ENG.). 30p. (J). (gr. 3-7). 21.99 *(978-0-7636-6739-9(0))* Candlewick Pr.
Fraggalosch, Audrey. Land of the Wild Llama: A Story of the Patagonian Andes. Denman, Michael & Huiett, William J., illus. 2005. (Wild Habitats Ser.). (ENG.). (J). (gr. 1-4). 32p. 19.95 *(978-1-931465-83-0(5)*, BC7022); 36p. 15.95 *(978-1-931465-81-6(9)*, B7022) Soundprints.
—Land of the Wild Llama: A Story of the Patagonian Andes, Including 10" Toy. Denman, Michael & Huiett, William J., illus. 2005. (Wild Habitats Ser.). (ENG.). 36p. (J). (gr. 1-4). 17.95 *(978-1-931465-86-1(X)*, PS7022) Soundprints.
Garis, Howard R. The Curlytops & Their Pets. 2009. 120p. 22.95 *(978-1-60664-609-0(5))*; pap. 10.95 *(978-1-60664-341-9(X))* Rodgers, Alan Bks.
Graham-Morgan, Ivet. Peter the Parrot Misses Home: Misses Home. 2011. 16p. 9.98 *(978-1-4343-9791-1(2))* AuthorHouse.
Hayes, Celeste. Cacao & the Jaded Orb: A Sphinx & Trevi Adventure. 2011. (Illus.). 62p. (J). pap. 22.95 *(978-0-9785695-2-5(0))* Adam's Creations Publishing, LLC.
Hergé. The Broken Ear. (Illus.). 62p. (J). 24.95 *(978-0-8288-5086-5(0))* French & European Pubns., Inc.
—L' Oreille Cassee.Tr. of Broken Ear. (FRE., Illus.). 62p. (J). 19.95 *(978-0-8288-5054-4(2))* French & European Pubns., Inc.
Jones, Allan Frewin. Legend of the Anaconda King. 2006. 186p. (J). pap. *(978-0-439-85670-6(1))* Scholastic, Inc.
Kavanagh, Shannon & McKay, Jeffrey. Safari Jeff & Shannon Visit South America. 2005. (Great Green Adventure Ser.). (Illus.). 46p. 14.95 *(978-0-9734409-1-1(0))* Croctalk Publishing CAN. Dist: Hushion Hse. Publishing, Ltd.
King Sr., Billy. The Story. 2010. 73p. pap. 11.95 *(978-0-557-25606-8(2))* Lulu Pr., Inc.
Krebs, Laurie. We're Sailing to Galapagos: A Week in the Pacific. Restelli, Grazia, illus. 2007. (ENG.). 32p. (J). (gr. k-1). pap. 8.99 *(978-1-84686-102-4(0))* Barefoot Bks., Inc.
Marsh, Carole. The Mystery in the Amazon Rainforest: South America. 2009. (Around the World in 80 Mysteries Ser.). (Illus.). 131p. (J). lib. bdg. 18.99 *(978-0-635-07017-3(0)*, Marsh, Carole Mysteries) Gallopade International.
Mattassi, Ezio. Pepito the Penguin, 1 vol. Mattassi, Ezio, illus. 2009. (Illus.). 15p. pap. 24.95 *(978-1-61582-731-2(5))* PublishAmerica, Inc.
Mitton, Tony. Rainforest Adventure. 2015. (Amazing Animals Ser.). (ENG., Illus.). 24p. (J). (gr. -1-1). pap. 4.99 *(978-0-7534-7227-9(9)*, 9780753472279, Kingfisher) Roaring Brook Pr.
O'Neill, Katrina. Key of the Mayan Kingdom. 2007. (Illus.). 52p. (J). pap. *(978-1-4207-0717-5(5))* Sundance/Newbridge Educational Publishing.
Paterson, John B., Jr. & Paterson, John B., Sr. Roberto's Trip to the Top. Alarcao, Renato, illus. 2009. (ENG.). 40p. (J). (gr. -1-3). 16.99 *(978-0-7636-2708-9(9))* Candlewick Pr.
Paulding, Steve. The Wonderful Adventures of Bradley the Bat. Schmidt, Caleb & Schmidt, Carter, illus. 2013. 70p. pap. 18.95 *(978-0-615-74591-6(1))* Slow on the Draw Productions.
Peet, Mal. The Penalty. 2016. (ENG.). 272p. (J). (gr. 7). pap. 8.99 *(978-0-7636-8747-2(2))* Candlewick Pr.
Pierson, Rich. Adventures of Fred the Donkey. 2012. 48p. pap. 21.99 *(978-1-4691-7343-6(3))* Xlibris Corp.
Rockwood, Roy. Jack North's Treasure Hunt: Or, Daring Adventures in South America. 2007. (ENG.). 142p. pap. 18.99 *(978-1-4264-2654-4(2))*; 146p. pap. 19.99 *(978-1-4264-2711-4(5))* Creative Media Partners, LLC.
Rollins, Janice. Bunny's Dream. 2009. 56p. pap. 23.99 *(978-1-4389-9146-7(0))* AuthorHouse.
Sherrow, Victoria. Galapagos Fur Seal. 2012. (ENG.). 24p. (J). pap. 3.95 *(978-1-60727-725-5(5))* Soundprints.
Wagner, Lori. Gateway of the Sun. 2007. 120p. pap. 9.95 *(978-0-9798627-2-4(8))* Affirming Faith.
Watson, Myrtle. Kite Flying in the Village: A Guyanese Girl's Story. 2011. 20p. 10.03 *(978-1-4520-8632-3(X))* AuthorHouse.
Winter, Barbara. The Golden Scarab. 2007. (Illus.). 48p. (J). lib. bdg. 15.00 *(978-1-4242-1617-8(6))* Dingles & Co.

SOUTH AMERICA—HISTORY

ABDO Publishing Company Staff. South American Animals. 2014. (South American Animals Ser.: 6). (ENG.). 32p. (gr. 2-5). lib. bdg. 171.00 *(978-1-62403-188-5(9)*, Big Buddy Bks.) ABDO Publishing Co.
Adamson, Thomas K. Learning about South America. 2015. (ENG., Illus.). 40p. (J). (gr. 3-5). 29.32 *(978-1-4677-8021-6(9)*, Lerner Pubns.) Lerner Publishing Group.
Aloian, Molly & Kalman, Bobbie. Explora America del Sur. 2007. (Explora Los Continentes Ser.). (SPA & ENG., Illus.). 32p. (J). (gr. 3-7). pap. *(978-0-7787-8301-5(4))* Crabtree Publishing Co.
Banting, Erinn. South America. 2012. (J). *(978-1-61913-453-9(5))*; pap. *(978-1-61913-454-6(3))* Weigl Pubs., Inc.
Barnett, Tracy. Immigration from South America. 2005. (Changing Face of North America Ser.). (Illus.). 112p. (YA). lib. bdg. 24.95 *(978-1-59084-687-2(7))* Mason Crest.
Boyd, Judy. South America, Vol. 10. 2016. (Social Progress & Sustainability Ser.). (Illus.). 80p. (J). (gr. 7). 24.95 *(978-1-4222-3499-0(1))* Mason Crest.
Brown, Risa. South America, 1 vol. 2013. (Continents Ser.). (ENG.). 48p. (J). (gr. 3-6). lib. bdg. 32.79 *(978-1-61783-934-4(5))* ABDO Publishing Co.
Colleen Madonna Flood Williams. Suriname, Vol. 13. Henderson, James D., ed. 2015. (Discovering South America: History, Politics, & Culture Ser.). (Illus.). 64p. (J). (gr. 7). lib. bdg. 22.95 *(978-1-4222-3304-7(9))* Mason Crest.
Cooke, Tim. The Exploration of South America. 2013. (Explorers Discovering the World Ser.). (Illus.). 48p. (gr. 4-6). 31.95 *(978-1-4339-8627-7(2))*; pap. 14.05 *(978-1-4339-8628-4(0))* Stevens, Gareth Publishing LLLP. (Gareth Stevens Learning Library).
Cruz, Bárbara C. Simón Bolívar: Fighting for Latin American Liberation. 2017. (Rebels with a Cause Ser.). 128p. (J). (gr. 8-8). lib. bdg. 37.27 ***(978-0-7660-8952-5(5))*** Enslow Pubs., Inc.
DePietro, Frank. South American Immigrants. 2013. (Illus.). 64p. (J). pap. *(978-1-4222-2346-8(9))* Mason Crest.
—South American Immigrants. Limón, José E., ed. 2012. (Hispanic Americans: Major Minority Ser.). (Illus.). 64p. (J). (gr. 4). 22.95 *(978-1-4222-2329-1(9))* Mason Crest.
Doane, Beth. From the Jungle: Stories & Original Art from Children Living in Rainforests. 2012. 40p. pap. 15.95 *(978-1-4525-6090-8(0))* Balboa Pr.
Ganeri, Anita. Introducing South America, 1 vol. 2013. (Introducing Continents Ser.). (ENG.). 32p. (gr. 1-3). 27.32 *(978-1-4329-8044-3(0))*; pap. 8.95 *(978-1-4329-8052-8(1))* Heinemann-Raintree. (Heinemann First Library).
Gillenwater, Chadwick & Dunn, Mary R. South American Animals. 2012. (South American Animals Ser.). (ENG.). 24p. (gr. k-1). lib. bdg. 133.25 *(978-1-4296-8114-8(4)*, Pebble Plus) Capstone Press of Coughlan Cos.
Hernandez, Roger E. South America: Facts & Figures, Vol. 13. Henderson, James D., ed. 2015. (Discovering South America: History, Politics, & Culture Ser.). (Illus.). 64p. (J). (gr. 7). lib. bdg. 22.95 *(978-1-4222-3303-0(0))* Mason Crest.
Hirsch, Rebecca E. South America. 2012. (Rookie Read-About(tm) Geography — Continents Ser.). (ENG., Illus.). 32p. (J). lib. bdg. 25.00 *(978-0-531-28981-5(8))*; pap. 5.95 *(978-0-531-29281-5(9))* Scholastic Library Publishing.
Hirschmann, Kristine. Geography of South America: Text Pairs. 2008. (Bridges/Navigators Ser.). (J). (gr. 6). 81.00 *(978-1-4108-8440-4(6))* Benchmark Education Co.
In North & South America. (J). (gr. 5). 3.80 *(978-0-8374-1454-6(7)*, 405) Weekly Reader Corp.
Kalman, Bobbie. L'Amérique du Sud. 2012. (FRE.). 32p. (J). pap. 9.95 *(978-2-89579-461-5(8))* Bayard Canada CAN. Dist: Crabtree Publishing Co.
Kennedy, Mike & Stewart, Mark. Soccer in South America. 2011. (Smart about Soccer Ser.). 24p. (J). (gr. k-3). lib. bdg. 22.60 *(978-1-59953-446-6(0))* Norwood Hse. Pr.
Kuskowski, Alex. Super Simple South & Central American Art: Fun & Easy Art from Around the World, 1 vol. 2012. (ENG.). 32p. 27.07 *(978-1-61783-215-4(4)*, Super SandCastle) ABDO Publishing Co.
Lynette, Rachel. South American Tapirs. 2013. (Jungle Babies of the Amazon Rain Forest Ser.). 24p. (J). (gr. -1-3). lib. bdg. 21.32 *(978-1-61772-759-7(8))* Bearport Publishing Co., Inc.
McClish, Bruce. New World Continents & Land Bridges: North & South America. 2016. (Continents Ser.). (ENG.). 32p. (gr. 4-6). pap. 8.99 *(978-1-4846-3639-8(2)*, NA-h) Heinemann-Raintree.
National Geographic Learning. South America - People & Places. 2007. (Reading Expeditions Ser.). (ENG.). 64p. pap. 25.95 *(978-0-7922-4383-0(8))* National Geographic School Publishing, Inc.
Oachs, Emily Rose. South America. (South America Ser.). 24p. (J). (gr. k-3). 2017. pap. 6.99 ***(978-1-61891-260-2(7))*** 2016. (ENG., Illus.). lib. bdg. 25.95 *(978-1-62617-329-3(X))* Bellwether Media. (Blastoff! Readers).
Roumanis, Alexis. Exploring Continents: South America. 2015. 24p. pap. 12.95 *(978-1-4896-3049-0(X))* Weigl Pubs., Inc.
—South America. 2014. (Illus.). 24p. (J). *(978-1-4896-3046-9(5))* Weigl Pubs., Inc.
Schaffer, David. Discovering South America's Land, People, & Wildlife: A MyReportLinks. com Book. 2004. (Continents of the World Ser.). (Illus.). 48p. (J). lib. bdg. 26.60 *(978-0-7660-5208-6(7)*, MyReportLinks.com Bks.) Enslow Pubs., Inc.
Simon Bolivar. 2010. (Great Hispanic Heritage Ser.). (Illus.). 120p. (J). (gr. 6-12). 35.00 *(978-1-60413-731-6(2)*, Chelsea Hse.) Facts On File, Inc.
Sirota, Lyn A. South America. 2014. (J). *(978-1-4896-0958-8(X))* Weigl Pubs., Inc.
South America: Regions of the World. 2003. spiral bd. 16.95 *(978-1-56004-158-0(7))* Social Studies Schl. Service.
Tylers, Michael. Predators of South America & Antarctica. 2015. (J). lib. bdg. *(978-1-62713-550-4(2))* Cavendish Square Publishing.
Waxman, Malcolm & Porter, Malcolm. Atlas of South America & Antarctica. 2009. (Atlases of the World Ser.). (Illus.). 48p. (YA). (gr. 5-8). 29.25 *(978-1-4358-8459-5(0)*, Rosen Reference) Rosen Publishing Group, Inc., The.
World Book, Inc Staff, contrib. by. Endangered Animals of the World. 2014. (J). *(978-0-7166-5620-3(5))* World Bk., Inc.
Zocchi, Judith Mazzeo. In South Africa. Brodie, Neale, illus. 2008. (J). *(978-1-59646-642-5(1))*; pap. *(978-1-59646-643-2(X))* Dingles & Co.

SOUTH ATLANTIC STATES

see Atlantic States

SOUTH CAROLINA

Berri, Victoria L. South Carolina: A MyReportLinks. Com Book. 2003. (States Ser.). (Illus.). 48p. (J). lib. bdg. 25.26 *(978-0-7660-5139-3(0)*, MyReportLinks.com Bks.) Enslow Pubs., Inc.
Columbia in Pictures. 2004. (Illus.). lib. bdg. 27.93 *(978-0-8225-1996-6(8))* Lerner Publishing Group.
Crane, Carol. Net Numbers: A South Carolina Numbers Book. Palmer, Gary, illus. 2006. (Count Your Way Across the U. S. A. Ser.). (ENG.). 40p. (J). (gr. -1-3). 17.95 *(978-1-58536-202-8(6))* Sleeping Bear Pr.
Dykstra, Mary. South Carolina. 2006. (Portraits of the States Ser.). (Illus.). 32p. (gr. 2-6). pap. 10.50 *(978-0-8368-4694-2(X))*; lib. bdg. 26.00 *(978-0-8368-4675-1(3))* Stevens, Gareth Publishing LLLP. (Gareth Stevens Learning Library).
Fredeen, Charles. South Carolina. 2012. (J). lib. bdg. 25.26 *(978-0-7613-4556-5(6)*, Lerner Pubns.) Lerner Publishing Group.
Hoffman, Nancy & Hart, Joyce. South Carolina. 2nd rev. ed. 2009. (Celebrate the States 9 Ser.). 144p. (gr. 6). 42.79 *(978-0-7614-4034-5(8))* Marshall Cavendish Corp.
Kovacik, Charles F. & Steinke, Theodore R., eds. South Carolina: An Atlas. 2005. (Illus.). 40p. (YA). 9.95 *(978-0-9768247-0-1(1))* South Carolina Geographic Alliance.
Marsh, Carole. South Carolina Current Events Projects: 30 Cool, Activities, Crafts, Experiments & More for Kids to Do to Learn about Your State! 2003. (South Carolina Experience Ser.). 32p. (gr. k-8). pap. 5.95 *(978-0-635-02059-8(9)*, Marsh, Carole Bks.) Gallopade International.
—South Carolina Geography Projects: 30 Cool, Activities, Crafts, Experiments & More for Kids to Do to Learn about Your State! 2003. (South Carolina Experience Ser.). 32p. (gr. k-5). pap. 5.95 *(978-0-635-01859-5(4)*, Marsh, Carole Bks.) Gallopade International.
—South Carolina Government Projects: 30 Cool, Activities, Crafts, Experiments & More for Kids to Do to Learn about Your State! 2003. (South Carolina Experience Ser.). 32p. (gr. k-5). pap. 5.95 *(978-0-635-01959-2(0)*, Marsh, Carole Bks.) Gallopade International.
—South Carolina People Projects: 30 Cool, Activities, Crafts, Experiments & More for Kids to Do to Learn about Your State! 2003. (South Carolina Experience Ser.). 32p. (gr. k-5). pap. 5.95 *(978-0-635-02009-3(2)*, Marsh, Carole Bks.) Gallopade International.
—South Carolina Symbols & Facts Projects: 30 Cool, Activities, Crafts, Experiments & More for Kids to Do to Learn about Your State! 2003. (South Carolina Experience Ser.). 32p. (gr. k-5). pap. 5.95 *(978-0-635-01909-7(4)*, Marsh, Carole Bks.) Gallopade International.
Murray, Julie. South Carolina, 1 vol. 2006. (United States Ser.). (ENG., Illus.). 32p. (gr. 2-4). 27.07 *(978-1-59197-699-8(5)*, Buddy Bks.) ABDO Publishing Co.
O'Neill, Elizabeth. Alfred Visits South Carolina. 2007. (Illus.). 24p. (J). (gr. -1-3). pap. 12.00 *(978-0-9790240-5-4(6))* Global Business Information Strategies, Inc.
Parker, Bridget. South Carolina. 2016. (States Ser.). (ENG., Illus.). 32p. (gr. 3-4). lib. bdg. 27.32 *(978-1-5157-0428-7(9))* Next Page Pr., The.
Parker, Janice. South Carolina: The Palmetto State. 2016. (J). ***(978-1-5105-2093-6(7))*** SmartBook Media, Inc.
Schuetz, Kristin. South Carolina. 2013. (Exploring the States Ser.). (ENG., Illus.). 32p. (J). (gr. 3-7). lib. bdg. 26.95 *(978-1-62617-040-7(1)*, Blastoff! Readers) Bellwether Media.
South Carolina. 2003. (Switched on Schoolhouse Ser.). cd-rom 24.95 *(978-0-7403-0664-8(2))* Alpha Omega Pubns., Inc.
Stroud, Cynthia. Carolina Children: The Sandhills. 2007. (Illus.). 30p. pap. 17.99 *(978-0-9794580-0-2(5))* Carolina Children.
Sullivan, E. J. S Is for South Carolina. Eldredge, Ernie, illus. 2007. (State Alphabet Bks.). 20p. *(978-1-58173-626-7(6))* Sweetwater Pr.
Way, Jennifer. South Carolina. 2009. (Bilingual Library of the United States of America Ser.). (ENG & SPA.). 32p. (gr. 2-2). 47.90 *(978-1-60853-385-5(9)*, Editorial Buenas Letras) Rosen Publishing Group, Inc., The.
—South Carolina/Carolina del Sur. Brusca, Maria Cristina, tr. 2006. (Bilingual Library of the United States of America Ser.: Set 2). (ENG & SPA., Illus.). 32p. (J). (gr. 3-6). lib. bdg. 25.25 *(978-1-4042-3106-1(4))* Rosen Publishing Group, Inc., The.
Weatherly, Myra S. South Carolina. 2008. (ENG.). 80p. (J). pap. 7.95 *(978-0-531-20813-7(3)*, Children's Pr.) Scholastic Library Publishing.

S

Weintraub, A. How to Draw South Carolina's Sights & Symbols. 2009. (Kid's Guide to Drawing America Ser.). 32p. (gr. k-k). 50.50 (978-1-61511-094-0(1), PowerKids Pr.) Rosen Publishing Group, Inc., The.

SOUTH CAROLINA—FICTION

Adams, Michelle. Sarah Boone: A Lowcountry Girl, 1 vol. Brewster, Jane, illus. 2009. (ENG.). 152p. (J). (gr. 3-6). 15.95 (978-1-58980-657-3(3)) Pelican Publishing Co., Inc.

Alexander, Scott L. My Dog Named Whatever. 2007. 68p. per. 10.95 (978-1-4327-1572-4(0)) Outskirts Pr., Inc.

Alger, Horatio & Stratemeyer, Edward. Young Captain Jack: The Son of a Soldier. 2007. (ENG.). 180p. pap. 19.99 (978-1-4346-5115-0(0)); 192p. pap. 21.99 (978-1-4346-5116-7(9)) Creative Media Partners, LLC.

Alice Turner Curtis. A Yankee Girl at Fort Sumter. 2007. (ENG.). 128p. per. 18.99 (978-1-4346-3775-8(1)); 140p. per. 19.99 (978-1-4346-3887-8(1)) Creative Media Partners, LLC.

Anderson, T. Neill. Ocean of Fire: The Burning of Columbia 1865. 2014. (ENG., Illus.). 176p. (YA). (gr. 7). 16.95 (978-1-58089-516-3(6)) Charlesbridge Publishing, Inc.

Antle, Bhagavan. Suryia & Roscoe: The True Story of an Unlikely Friendship. Antle, Bhagavan & Bland, Barry, illus. 2011. (ENG.). 32p. (J). (gr. -1-3). 18.99 (978-0-8050-9316-2(8), 9780805093162, Holt, Henry & Co. Bks. For Young Readers) Holt, Henry & Co.

Arrington, Linda. Ugly Trees. Arrington, Linda, photos by. 2012. (Illus.). 24p. pap. 24.95 (978-1-4626-8925-5(6)) America Star Bks.

Asim, Jabari. The Road to Freedom: A Story of the Reconstruction. 2004. 131p. (J). lib. bdg. 16.92 (978-1-4242-0765-7(7)) Fitzgerald Bks.

Baisley, Tilda. Crabbing. Wyrick, Monica, illus. 2016. (Young Palmetto Bks.). (ENG.). 32p. (J). 18.99 (978-1-61117-640-7(9)) Univ. of South Carolina Pr.

Black, Chuck. Rise of the Fallen: Wars of the Realm, Book 2. 2015. (Wars of the Realm Ser.). (ENG.). 320p. (YA). (gr. 7). pap. 11.99 (978-1-60142-504-1(X), Multnomah Bks.) Crown Publishing Group.

Blue, Rose, et al. Ron's Big Mission. Tate, Don, illus. 2009. (ENG.). 32p. (J). (gr. 1-3). 16.99 (978-0-525-47849-2(3), Dutton Books for Young Readers) Penguin Young Readers Group.

Boone, Martina. Illusion. 2016. (Heirs of Watson Island Ser.). (ENG., Illus.). 480p. (YA). (gr. 9). 17.99 (978-1-4814-1128-8(4), Simon Pulse) Simon Pulse.

—Persuasion. 2015. (Heirs of Watson Island Ser.). (ENG., Illus.). 464p. (YA). (gr. 9). 17.99 (978-1-4814-1125-7(X), Simon Pulse) Simon Pulse.

Brian, Kate. Endless (a Shadowlands Novel) 2014. (Shadowlands Ser.). (ENG.). 336p. (YA). (gr. 7-12). 17.99 (978-1-4231-6485-2(7)) Hyperion Bks. for Children.

—Hereafter (a Shadowlands Novel) 2014. (Shadowlands Ser.). (ENG.). 336p. (YA). (gr. 9-17). pap. 9.99 (978-1-4231-6526-2(8)) Hyperion Bks. for Children.

—Shadowlands. 2013. (Shadowlands Ser.). (ENG.). 352p. (YA). (gr. 9-17). pap. 9.99 (978-1-4231-6525-5(X)) Hyperion Pr.

Brown, Monica. Waiting for the Biblioburro. Parra, John, illus. 2011. (ENG.). 32p. (J). (gr. k-3). 16.99 (978-1-58246-353-7(0), Tricycle Pr.) Random Hse. Children's Bks.

Carmen & Thane Johnson. Dogs Don't Wear Underwear. Bianca & Annie West, illus. 2009. 20p. pap. 12.99 (978-1-4389-4128-8(5)) AuthorHouse.

Charley's Columbia Backyard. 2006. (J). 14.95 (978-0-9793808-0-8(4)) Backyard Ambassador Reader Publishing Co.

Clamp, Janet. The Adventures of Lilly the Bloodhound & Her Friends: Lilly Gets a New Home & Family. 2013. 20p. pap. 17.99 (978-1-4817-0057-3(X)) AuthorHouse.

Crouse, Donna J. The Ruby Ring: The Whispering Cove Kids Club. 2005. 114p. pap. 12.99 (978-0-9765339-0-0(1)) Crouse, Donna J.

Davies, Anna. Wrecked. (ENG., Illus.). 336p. (YA). (gr. 9). 2013. pap. 9.99 (978-1-4424-3279-6(9)) 2012. 16.99 (978-1-4424-3278-9(0)) Simon & Schuster Bks. For Young Readers. (Simon & Schuster Bks. For Young Readers).

Deriso, Christine Hurley. Thirty Sunsets. 2014. (ENG.). 240p. (YA). pap. 9.99 (978-0-7387-3991-5(X), Flux) North Star Editions.

Draper, Sharon M. Copper Sun. 2014. (ENG.). 336p. (YA). 14.24 (978-1-63245-110-1(7)) Lectorum Pubns., Inc.

—Copper Sun. 2011. 11.04 (978-0-7848-3373-5(7), Everbind) Marco Bk. Co.

—Copper Sun. (ENG.). (YA). 2008. 336p. (gr. 9-12). pap. 10.99 (978-1-4169-5348-7(5)) 2006. 320p. (gr. 8-18). 19.99 (978-0-689-82181-3(6)) Simon & Schuster Children's Publishing. (Atheneum Bks. for Young Readers).

—Copper Sun. l.t. ed. 2006. 358p. (YA). (gr. 8-18). 22.95 (978-0-7862-8948-6(1)) Thorndike Pr.

—Copper Sun. 2008. lib. bdg. 22.10 (978-1-4177-9702-8(9), Turtleback) Turtleback Bks.

Echols, Jennifer. Such a Rush. 2012. (ENG.). 336p. pap. 20.99 (978-1-4516-5802-6(8), Gallery Bks.) Gallery Bks.

Ellison, Joy D. Carol & Connie. 2008. 28p. per. 24.95 (978-1-4241-9276-2(5)) America Star Bks.

Flood, Pansie Hart. Secret Holes. Marshall, Felicia, illus. 2004. 128p. (J). (gr. 3-6). 15.95 (978-0-87614-923-2(9), Carolrhoda Bks.) Lerner Publishing Group.

—Sometimey Friend. Marshall, Felicia, illus. 2005. 124p. (J). (gr. 3-7). 15.95 (978-1-57505-866-5(9)) Lerner Publishing Group.

—Sylvia & Miz Lula Maye. Marshall, Felicia, illus. 2003. (Middle Grade Fiction Ser.). 120p. (J). (gr. 3-6). 15.95 (978-0-87614-204-2(8), Carolrhoda Bks.) Lerner Publishing Group.

Fuqua, Jonathon Scott. Darby. 2006. (ENG.). 256p. (J). (gr. 5-7). per. 7.99 (978-0-7636-2290-9(7)) Candlewick Pr.

Garcia, Kami & Stohl, Margaret. Beautiful Chaos. (Beautiful Creatures Ser.: 3). (ENG.). 528p. (YA). (gr. 7-17). 2012. pap. 13.99 (978-0-316-12351-8(X)) 2011. 18.99 (978-0-316-12352-5(8)) Little, Brown Bks. for Young Readers.

—Beautiful Creatures. 2009. (Beautiful Creatures Ser.: 1). (ENG.). 576p. (YA). (gr. 7-17). 17.99 (978-0-316-04267-3(6)) Little Brown & Co.

—Beautiful Creatures. (Beautiful Creatures Ser.: 1). (ENG.). 592p. (YA). (gr. 7-17). 2010. pap. 12.99 (978-0-316-07703-3(8)) 2012. mass mkt. 7.99 (978-0-316-23165-7(7)) 2012. pap. 10.99 (978-0-316-23167-1(3)) Little, Brown Bks. for Young Readers.

—Beautiful Creatures. 2013. (ENG., Illus.). 240p. (gr. 8-17). 20.00 (978-0-316-18271-3(0), Yen Pr.) Orbit.

—Beautiful Creatures. 2010. (Beautiful Creatures Ser.: 1). (YA). lib. bdg. 23.30 (978-0-606-26699-4(2), Turtleback) Turtleback Bks.

—Beautiful Darkness. 2010. (Beautiful Creatures Ser.: Bk. 2). (YA). 59.99 (978-1-60941-036-0(X)) Findaway World, LLC.

—Beautiful Darkness. (Beautiful Creatures Ser.: 2). 2011. (ENG.). 528p. (YA). (gr. 7-17). pap. 12.99 (978-0-316-07704-0(6)) 2010. (ENG.). 512p. (YA). (gr. 7-17). 17.99 (978-0-316-07705-7(4)) 2010. 512p. pap. 17.99 (978-0-316-09861-8(2)) Little, Brown Bks. for Young Readers.

—Beautiful Darkness. 2011. (Beautiful Creatures Ser.: 2). (YA). lib. bdg. 24.50 (978-0-606-26700-7(X), Turtleback) Turtleback Bks.

—Beautiful Redemption. (Beautiful Creatures Ser.: 4). (ENG.). (YA). (gr. 7-17). 2013. 496p. pap. 13.99 (978-0-316-12356-3(0)) 2012. 464p. 18.99 (978-0-316-12353-2(6)) 2012. 576p. pap. 9.99 (978-0-316-22519-9(3)) Little, Brown Bks. for Young Readers.

—Beautiful Redemption. 2013. (Beautiful Creatures Ser.: 4). (YA). lib. bdg. 24.50 (978-0-606-32282-9(5), Turtleback) Turtleback Bks.

Hampton, Patrick. Down by the Mulberry Tree, 1 vol. 2009. 15p. pap. 24.95 (978-1-60703-672-2(X)) America Star Bks.

Haskins, James. The March on Washington. 2004. (Illus.). 192p. (J). (gr. 5-18). pap. 10.95 (978-0-940975-93-4(9), Sankofa Bks.) Just Us Bks., Inc.

Hay, Angela. Grace S Incredible! Unforgettable! Summer! 2012. 38p. pap. 19.99 (978-1-62419-562-4(8)) Salem Author Services.

Himes, Rachel. Princess & the Peas. Himes, Rachel, illus. 2017. (ENG., Illus.). 32p. (J). (gr. k-3). 16.99 (978-1-58089-718-1(5)) Charlesbridge Publishing, Inc.

Ingle, Sheila. Courageous Kate: A Daughter of the American Revolution. 2006. (ENG.). 130p. pap. 11.95 (978-1-891885-52-5(9)) Hub City Pr.

Jacobs, Lily. The Littlest Bunny in South Carolina: An Easter Adventure. Dunn, Robert, illus. 2015. (ENG.). 32p. (J). (-3). 9.99 (978-1-4926-1195-0(6), Sourcebooks Jabberwocky) Sourcebooks, Inc.

James, Eric. A Halloween Scare in South Carolina. Le Ray, Marina, illus. 2015. (ENG.). 32p. (J). (-5). 9.99 (978-1-4926-2860-6(3), 9781492628606, Sourcebooks Jabberwocky) Sourcebooks, Inc.

—A Halloween Scare in the Carolinas. Le Ray, Marina, illus. 2014. (ENG.). 32p. (J). (-5). 9.99 (978-1-4926-0576-8(X), 9781492605768, Sourcebooks Jabberwocky) Sourcebooks, Inc.

—Santa's Sleigh Is on Its Way to South Carolina. Dunn, Robert, illus. 2015. (ENG.). 32p. (J). (-2). 12.99 (978-1-4926-2757-9(7), Sourcebooks Jabberwocky) Sourcebooks, Inc.

Jones, Joyce Elaine. For Such a Journey. 2005. (J). 5.99 (978-0-9766559-0-9(X)) Treorca Pr.

Joyce, S. E. Silas Saves the Friendly Crab: A Low Country Tale. 2011. 28p. (gr. 1-2). pap. 14.99 (978-1-4634-0285-3(6)) AuthorHouse.

Karr, Kathleen. Worlds Apart, 0 vols. unabr. ed. 2013. (ENG.). 208p. (J). (gr. 5-7). pap. 9.99 (978-1-4778-1710-0(7), 9781477817100, Amazon Children's Publishing) Amazon Publishing.

Long, Melinda. The Twelve Days of Christmas in South Carolina. Mai-Wyss, Tatjana, illus. (Twelve Days of Christmas in America Ser.). (ENG.). (J). (— 1). 2016. 22p. bds. 7.95 (978-1-4549-2058-8(0)) 2010. 40p. 12.95 (978-1-4027-6672-5(6)) Sterling Publishing Co., Inc.

Luddy, Karon. Spelldown: The Big-Time Dreams of a Small-Town Word Whiz. 2008. (Mix Ser.). (ENG.). 224p. (J). (gr. 4-8). pap. 10.99 (978-1-4169-5452-1(X), Simon & Schuster/Paula Wiseman Bks.) Simon & Schuster/Paula Wiseman Bks.

Matthew-Barnes, David. Wonderland. 2013. (ENG.). 264p. (gr. 7). pap. 11.95 (978-1-60282-788-2(5)) Bold Strokes Bks.

McKinney-Whitaker, Courtney. The Last Sister: A Novel. 2014. (Young Palmetto Bks.). (ENG.). 232p. (YA). 39.95 (978-1-61117-429-8(5)) Univ. of South Carolina Pr.

Mosier, Pamela. Elizabeth, the Eastern Gray Squirrel. 2008. 44p. pap. 18.95 (978-1-4357-5407-2(7)) Lulu Pr., Inc.

Moulder, Holly. Eyes of the Calusa. 2007. 111p. (J). pap. 8.95 (978-0-9790405-0-4(7)) White Pelican Pr.

Mullinax, Jerry. Enoree. 2009. (YA). pap. (978-0-88092-646-1(5)) Royal Fireworks Publishing Co.

Muschla, Gary Robert. The Sword & the Cross. 2009. (YA). pap. (978-0-88092-472-6(1)) Royal Fireworks Publishing Co.

Myers, Walter Dean. The Glory Field. 2008. (ENG.). 400p. (J). (gr. 7). pap. 9.99 (978-0-545-05575-8(X), Scholastic Paperbacks) Scholastic, Inc.

Myracle, Lauren. Thirteen Plus One. 2011. (Winnie Years Ser.). (ENG.). 304p. (J). (gr. 5-18). 7.99 (978-0-14-241901-4(X), Puffin Books) Penguin Young Readers Group.

Nolan, Lea. Allure. 2013. (Hoodoo Apprentice Ser.: 2). (ENG.). 304p. (YA). (gr. 7-12). pap. 9.99 (978-1-62266-022-3(6), 9781622660223) Entangled Publishing, LLC.

O'Connor, Barbara. On the Road to Mr. Mineo's, 1 vol. 2012. (ENG.). 192p. (J). (gr. 3-7). 16.99 (978-0-374-38002-1(3), 9780374380021, Farrar, Straus & Giroux (BYR)) Farrar, Straus & Giroux.

—On the Road to Mr. Mineo's. 2014. (ENG., Illus.). 208p. (J). (gr. 3-7). pap. 7.99 (978-1-250-03993-4(2), 9781250039934) Square Fish.

—The Small Adventure of Popeye & Elvis. 2011. (ENG.). 176p. (J). (gr. 3-7). pap. 7.99 (978-0-312-65932-5(6), 9780312659325) Square Fish.

Reichs, Kathy. Code. 2013. (Virals Ser.: 3). (ENG.). 432p. (J). (gr. 5). pap. 8.99 (978-1-59514-572-7(9), Puffin Books) Penguin Young Readers Group.

—Virals. 2014. lthr. 79.00 (978-1-62715-582-3(1)) Leatherbound Bestsellers.

—Virals. (Virals Ser.: 1). (ENG.). (J). (gr. 5-18). 2011. 480p. 10.99 (978-1-59514-426-3(9), Puffin Books) 2010. 464p. 17.99 (978-1-59514-342-6(4), Razorbill) Penguin Young Readers Group.

—Virals. 2011. 20.00 (978-1-61383-226-4(5)) Perfection Learning Corp.

Reichs, Kathy & Reichs, Brendan. Code. 2013. (Virals Ser.: 3). lib. bdg. 19.65 (978-0-606-32140-2(3), Turtleback) Turtleback Bks.

—Terminal. 2015. (Virals Ser.: 5). (ENG.). 432p. (J). (gr. 5). 17.99 (978-1-59514-528-4(1), G.P. Putnam's Sons Books for Young Readers) Penguin Young Readers Group.

—Virals. 2011. (Virals Ser.: 1). lib. bdg. 20.85 (978-0-606-23069-8(6), Turtleback) Turtleback Bks.

Rinaldi, Ann. Cast Two Shadows: The American Revolution in the South. 2004. (Great Episodes Ser.). (ENG., Illus.). 304p. (YA). (gr. 7-8). pap. 7.99 (978-0-15-205077-1(9)) Houghton Mifflin Harcourt Publishing Co.

Rivers, Susan. The Second Mrs. Hockaday: A Novel. 2017. (ENG.). 272p. 25.95 (978-1-61620-581-2(4)) Algonquin Bks. of Chapel Hill.

Rubin, Sarah. Someday Dancer. 2012. (J). (978-0-545-39379-9(5)); (ENG.). 256p. (gr. 7-7). 16.99 (978-0-545-39378-2(7), Chicken Hse., The) Scholastic, Inc.

Silvano, Wendi. Love Is All Around South Carolina. Czernichowska, Joanna, illus. 2016. (ENG.). 32p. (J). (-6). 12.99 (978-1-4926-2960-3(X), Sourcebooks Jabberwocky) Sourcebooks, Inc.

Skelton, Vonda Skinner. Bitsy & the Mystery at Hilton Head Island. 2008. 192p. (J). (gr. 4-7). pap. 8.95 (978-1-57072-325-4(7)) Overmountain Pr.

Smallman, Steve. Santa Is Coming to South Carolina. Dunn, Robert, illus. 2014. (ENG.). 32p. (J). (-3). 9.99 (978-1-4926-0685-7(5), Sourcebooks Jabberwocky) Sourcebooks, Inc.

—Santa Is Coming to the Carolinas. Dunn, Robert, illus. 2012. (ENG.). 32p. (J). (-3). 9.99 (978-1-4022-7586-9(2), Sourcebooks Jabberwocky) Sourcebooks, Inc.

Teaster, Gerald Fred. Spirit up the People: Four Days to the Cowpens. 2006. (Illus.). 236p. per. 12.95 (978-0-9744556-2-4(8)) Junior History Pr.

Thompson, J. E. The Girl from Felony Bay. 2013. (Felony Bay Mysteries Ser.: 1). (ENG.). 384p. (J). (gr. 3-7). 16.99 (978-0-06-210446-5(2), Walden Pond Pr.) HarperCollins Pubs.

Todd, Anne. Teddy Powers: The Stone Keepers. 2012. 394p. pap. 13.99 (978-1-938993-00-8(4)) Keogh, Anne.

Victoria & the Baby Tree. 2005. pap. 14.95 (978-1-59526-525-8(2)) Aeon Publishing Inc.

Vrabel, Beth. A Blind Guide to Stinkville. (ENG.). (J). (gr. 2-7). 2016. 280p. pap. 7.99 (978-1-5107-0382-7(9)) 2015. 264p. 16.99 (978-1-63450-157-6(8)) Skyhorse Publishing Co., Inc. (Sky Pony Pr.).

Weston, Elise. The Coastwatcher, 1 vol. 2009. (ENG.). 160p. (J). (gr. 3-7). pap. 7.95 (978-1-56145-484-6(2)) Peachtree Pubs.

SOUTH CAROLINA—HISTORY

Aluri, Rao. Backcountry Fury: A Sixteen-Year-Old Patriot in the Revolutionary War. 2010. (J). pap. 19.95 (978-1-59712-409-6(5)) Catawba Publishing Co.

Bodie, Idella. The Wizard Owl. 2003. (Illus.). 86p. (J). pap. 6.95 (978-0-87844-167-9(0)) Sandlapper Publishing Co., Inc.

Boehm Jerome, Kate. Columbia & the State of South Carolina: Cool Stuff Every Kid Should Know. 2011. (Arcadia Kids Ser.). (ENG., Illus.). 48p. (J). (gr. 3-6). pap. 9.99 (978-1-4396-0090-0(2)) Arcadia Publishing.

Born, Mark Alan. TIDELOG 2003 Graphic Almanac for Southeastern States: Covering the Entire South Carolina Coast, North to Wilmington NC, & South to Brunswick, Ga. Escher, M. C., illus. 2004. 144p. spiral bd. 14.95 (978-1-933120-05-8(3)) Pacific Pubs.

Crane, Carol. Little South Carolina. Monroe, Michael Glenn & Tsairis, Jeannie Brett, illus. 2011. (My Little State Ser.). (ENG.). 22p. (J). 9.95 (978-1-58536-486-2(X)) Sleeping Bear Pr.

Cunningham, Kevin. The South Carolina Colony. 2011. (True Book-the Thirteen Colonies Ser.). (ENG., Illus.). 48p. (J). lib. bdg. 29.00 (978-0-531-25398-4(8)); (gr. 3-5). pap. 6.95 (978-0-531-26611-3(7)) Scholastic Library Publishing. (Children's Pr.).

Ditchfield, Christin. Exploring the South Carolina Colony. 2016. (Exploring the 13 Colonies Ser.). (ENG., Illus.). 48p. (gr. 3-4). lib. bdg. 31.99 (978-1-5157-2230-4(9)) Capstone Press of Coughlan Cos.

Doak, Robin. South Carolina, 1540-1776. 2007. (National Geographic Voices from ColonialAmerica Ser.). (ENG., Illus.). 112p. (J). (gr. 5-9). 21.95 (978-1-4263-0066-0(2)); lib. bdg. 32.90 (978-1-4263-0067-7(0)) National Geographic Society. (National Geographic Children's Bks.).

Doherty, Craig A. & Doherty, Katherine M. South Carolina. 2005. (Thirteen Colonies Ser.). (Illus.). 144p. (gr. 5-8). 35.00 (978-0-8160-5409-1(6)) Facts On File, Inc.

Felix, Rebecca. What's Great about South Carolina? 2015. (Our Great States Ser.). (ENG., Illus.). 32p. (gr. 2-5). pap. 7.95 (978-1-4677-6085-0(4)); lib. bdg. 26.60 (978-1-4677-3861-3(1), Lerner Pubns.) Lerner Publishing Group.

Gamble, Adam, et al. Good Night South Carolina. 2014. (Good Night Our World Ser.). (ENG.). 20p. (J). (— 1). bds. 9.95 (978-1-60219-190-7(5)) Good Night Bks.

Gilbert, Sara. South Carolina. 2009. (This Land Called America Ser.). 32p. (YA). (gr. 3-6). 19.95 (978-1-58341-793-5(1)) Creative Co., The.

Harmon, Daniel E. Lower Atlantic: Florida, Georgia, South Carolina, Vol. 19. 2015. (Let's Explore the States Ser.). (Illus.). 64p. (J). (gr. 5). 23.95 (978-1-4222-3325-2(1)) Mason Crest.

—South Carolina: Past & Present. 2010. (United States: Past & Present Ser.). (ENG.). 48p. (YA). pap. 11.75 (978-1-4358-9522-5(3)); lib. bdg. 29.25 (978-1-4358-9495-2(2)) Rosen Publishing Group, Inc., The. (Rosen Reference).

Hasan, Heather. A Primary Source History of the Colony of South Carolina. (Primary Sources of the Thirteen Colonies & the Lost Colony Ser.). 64p. 2009. (gr. 5-8). 58.50 (978-1-60851-889-0(2)) 2006. (Illus.). (YA). (gr. 4-7). lib. bdg. 31.95 (978-1-4042-0436-2(9)) 2006. (ENG., Illus.). (gr. 4-8). per. 12.95 (978-1-4042-0667-0(1)) Rosen Publishing Group, Inc., The.

Hawk, Frank. The Story of the H. L. Hunley & Queenie's Coin. Nance, Dan, illus. 2004. (ENG.). 40p. (J). (gr. k-6). 16.95 (978-1-58536-218-9(2)) Sleeping Bear Pr.

Hess, Debra & McGeveran, William. South Carolina. 2nd rev. ed. 2011. (It's My State! 2 Ser.). 80p. (gr. 3). 31.36 (978-1-60870-526-9(9)) Marshall Cavendish Corp.

Hess, Debra, et al. South Carolina. 2016. (ENG., Illus.). 80p. (J). 34.21 (978-1-62713-175-9(2)) Cavendish Square Publishing.

Jerome, Kate B. Lucky to Live in South Carolina. 2017. (Arcadia Kids Ser.). (ENG., Illus.). 32p. (J). 16.99 **(978-0-7385-2794-9(7))** Arcadia Publishing.

—The Wise Animal Handbook South Carolina. 2017. (Arcadia Kids Ser.). (ENG., Illus.). 32p. (J). 16.99 **(978-0-7385-2841-0(2))** Arcadia Publishing.

Kauffman, Scott. Francis Marion: Swamp Fox of South Carolina. 2006. (Forgotten Heroes of the American Revolution Ser.). (Illus.). 88p. (YA). (gr. 5-11). lib. bdg. 23.95 (978-1-59556-014-8(9)) OTTN Publishing.

Kelly Edwards Elementary School (Williston, S.C.) Staff, contrib. by. The ABCs of Williston History. 2007. (J). pap. (978-0-87844-185-3(9)) Sandlapper Publishing Co., Inc.

Krebs, Laurie. A Day in the Life of a Colonial Indigo Planter. (Library of Living & Working in Colonial Times Ser.). 24p. 2009. (gr. 3-3). 42.50 (978-1-60853-732-7(3), PowerKids Pr.) 2004. (Illus.). (J). lib. bdg. 19.95 (978-0-8239-6229-7(6)) Rosen Publishing Group, Inc., The.

Marsh, Carole. Exploring South Carolina Through Project-Based Learning: Geography, History, Government, Economics & More. 2016. (South Carolina Experience Ser.). (ENG.). (J). pap. 9.99 (978-0-635-12364-0(9)) Gallopade International.

—South Carolina History Projects: 30 Cool, Activities, Crafts, Experiments & More for Kids to Do to Learn about Your State! 2003. (South Carolina Experience Ser.). 32p. (gr. k-5). pap. 5.95 (978-0-635-01809-0(8), Marsh, Carole Bks.) Gallopade International.

Maynard, Charles W. Fort Sumter. 2009. (Famous Forts Throughout American History Ser.). 24p. (gr. 3-4). 42.50 (978-1-61512-520-3(5), PowerKids Pr.) Rosen Publishing Group, Inc., The.

Mis, Melody S. The Colony of South Carolina: A Primary Source History. 2007. (Primary Source Library of the Thirteen Colonies & the Lost Colony Ser.). (ENG., Illus.). 24p. (J). (gr. 3-7). lib. bdg. 22.60 (978-1-4042-3438-3(1), PowerKids Pr.) Rosen Publishing Group, Inc., The.

Olhoff, Jim. South Carolina, 1 vol. 2009. (United States Ser.). (ENG., Illus.). 48p. (YA). (gr. 2-5). 27.07 (978-1-60453-676-8(4)) ABDO Publishing Co.

Parker, Janice. South Carolina. 2011. (Guide to American States Ser.). (Illus.). 48p. (YA). (gr. 3-6). 29.99 (978-1-61690-813-3(0)); (J). (978-1-61690-489-0(5)) Weigl Pubs., Inc.

—South Carolina: The Palmetto State. 2016. (J). (978-1-4896-4938-6(7)) Weigl Pubs., Inc.

Pohl, Amelia J. Savannah River. 2009. (J). (978-1-935077-58-9(9)); pap. (978-1-935077-65-7(1)) State Standards Publishing, LLC.

Rockwell, Anne F. Hey, Charleston! The True Story of the Jenkins Orphanage Band. Bootman, Colin, illus. 2013. (ENG.). 32p. (J). (gr. 2-5). lib. bdg. 16.95 (978-0-7613-5565-6(0), Carolrhoda Bks.) Lerner Publishing Group.

Somervill, Barbara A. South Carolina (Revised Edition) 2014. (America the Beautiful, Third Ser. (Revised Edition) Ser.). (ENG.). 144p. (J). lib. bdg. 40.00 (978-0-531-28292-2(9)) Scholastic Library Publishing.

Tieck, Sarah. South Carolina, 1 vol. 2012. (Explore the United States Ser.). (ENG.). 32p. (J). (gr. 2-5). lib. bdg. 28.50 (978-1-61783-379-3(7), Big Buddy Bks.) ABDO Publishing Co.

Vierow, Wendy. The Assault on Fort Wagner: Black Union Soldiers Make a Stand in South Carolina Battle. 2009. (Headlines from History Ser.). 24p. (gr. 3-3). 42.50 (978-1-61513-240-9(6), PowerKids Pr.) Rosen Publishing Group, Inc., The.

Walker, Sally M. Shipwreck Search: Discovery of the H. L. Hunley. Verstraete, Elaine, illus. (On My Own Science Ser.). (ENG.). 48p. (gr. 2-4). 2007. per. 6.95 (978-0-8225-6449-2(1), First Avenue Editions) 2006. lib. bdg. 25.26 (978-1-57505-878-8(2), Millbrook Pr.) Lerner Publishing Group.

Winter, Jeanette. Biblioburro: A True Story from Colombia. Winter, Jeanette, illus. 2010. (ENG., Illus.). 32p. (J). (gr. 1-4). 17.99 (978-1-4169-9778-8(4), Beach Lane Bks.) Beach Lane Bks.

Yasuda, Anita. South Carolina: The Palmetto State. 2012. (J). (978-1-61913-401-0(2)); pap. (978-1-61913-402-7(0)) Weigl Pubs., Inc.

Zepke, Terrance. Pirates of the Carolinas for Kids. 2009. (Carolinas for Kids Ser.). (ENG.). 71p. (J). (gr. 4-18). pap. 9.95 (978-1-56164-459-9(5)) Pineapple Pr., Inc.

SOUTH DAKOTA

Bjorklund, Ruth. South Dakota. 2013. (It's My State 2nd Ed 4 Ser.). 80p. (J). (gr. 4-8). pap. 17.64 (978-1-62712-097-5(1)) Cavendish Square Publishing.

Brown, Jonatha A. South Dakota. 2006. (Portraits of the States Ser.). 32p. (gr. 2-6). pap. 10.50 (978-0-8368-4725-3(3)); (Illus.). lib. bdg. 26.00 (978-0-8368-4708-6(3)) Stevens, Gareth Publishing LLLP. (Gareth Stevens Learning Library).

Brown, Vanessa. South Dakota/Dakota del Sur. Brusca, Maria Cristina, tr. from ENG. 2006. (Bilingual Library of the United States of America Ser.: Set 2). (ENG & SPA., Illus.). 32p. (J). (gr. 3-6). lib. bdg. 25.25 (978-1-4042-3107-8(2)) Rosen Publishing Group, Inc., The.

Bryan, Dale-Marie. South Dakota. 2006. (Rookie Read-About Geography Ser.). (ENG., Illus.). 32p. (J). (gr. 1-2). lib. bdg. 20.50 (978-0-516-25444-9(8)) Scholastic Library Publishing.

Glaser, Jason. South Dakota: The Mount Rushmore State. 2010. (Our Amazing States Ser.). (ENG.). 24p. (J). pap. 8.25 (978-1-4358-9774-8(9)); lib. bdg. 22.60 (978-1-4358-9343-6(3)) Rosen Publishing Group, Inc., The. (PowerKids Pr.).

Hirschmann, Kris. South Dakota. 2003. (World Almanac Library of the States). (Illus.). 48p. (gr. 4-9). lib. bdg. 31.00

(978-0-8368-5160-1(9), Gareth Stevens Learning Library) Stevens, Gareth Publishing LLLP.

—South Dakota: The Mount Rushmore State. 2003. (World Almanac Library of the States). (Illus.). 48p. (gr. 4-9). pap. 14.05 *(978-0-8368-5331-5(8)*, Gareth Stevens Learning Library) Stevens, Gareth Publishing LLLP.

Marsh, Carole. South Dakota Current Events Projects: 30 Cool, Activities, Crafts, Experiments & More for Kids to Do to Learn about Your State! 2003. (South Dakota Experience Ser.). 32p. (gr. k-8). pap. 5.95 *(978-0-635-02060-4(2)*, Marsh, Carole Bks.) Gallopade International.

—South Dakota Geography Projects: 30 Cool, Activities, Crafts, Experiments & More for Kids to Do to Learn about Your State! 2003. (South Dakota Experience Ser.). 32p. (gr. k-5). pap. 5.95 *(978-0-635-01875-5(6)*, Marsh, Carole Bks.) Gallopade International.

—South Dakota Government Projects: 30 Cool, Activities, Crafts, Experiments & More for Kids to Do to Learn about Your State! 2003. (South Dakota Experience Ser.). 32p. (gr. k-5). pap. 5.95 *(978-0-635-01960-8(4)*, Marsh, Carole Bks.) Gallopade International.

—South Dakota People Projects: 30 Cool, Activities, Crafts, Experiments & More for Kids to Do to Learn about Your State! 2003. (South Dakota Experience Ser.). 32p. (gr. k-5). pap. 5.95 *(978-0-635-02010-9(6)*, Marsh, Carole Bks.) Gallopade International.

—South Dakota Symbols & Facts Projects: 30 Cool, Activities, Crafts, Experiments & More for Kids to Do to Learn about Your State! 2003. (South Dakota Experience Ser.). 32p. (gr. k-5). pap. 5.95 *(978-0-635-01910-3(8)*, Marsh, Carole Bks.) Gallopade International.

McDaniel, Melissa. South Dakota. 2nd rev. ed. 2006. (Celebrate the States Ser.). (Illus.). 144p. (gr. 6-7). lib. bdg. 42.79 *(978-0-7614-2156-6(4)*, Benchmark Bks.) Marshall Cavendish Corp.

Murray, Julie. South Dakota, 1 vol. 2006. (United States Ser.). (ENG., Illus.). 32p. (gr. 2-4). 27.07 *(978-1-59197-700-1(2)*, Buddy Bks.) ABDO Publishing Co.

Parker, Bridget. South Dakota. 2016. (States Ser.). (ENG., Illus.). 32p. (gr. 3-4). lib. bdg. 27.32 *(978-1-5157-0429-4(7))* Next Page Pr., The.

Peters, S. True. How to Draw South Dakota's Sights & Symbols. 2009. (Kid's Guide to Drawing America Ser.). 32p. (gr. k-k). 50.50 *(978-1-61511-095-7(X)*, PowerKids Pr.) Rosen Publishing Group, Inc., The.

Peterson, Sheryl. North Dakota. 2009. (This Land Called America Ser.). 32p. (YA). (gr. 3-6). 19.95 *(978-1-58341-794-2(X))* Creative Co., The.

Savage, Jeff. South Dakota: A MyReportLinks. Com Book. 2003. (States Ser.). (Illus.). 48p. (J). lib. bdg. 25.26 *(978-0-7660-5116-4(1)*, MyReportLinks.com Bks.) Enslow Pubs., Inc.

Schuler, Harold H. Fort Sisseton. 2012. (Prairie Plains Ser.: No. 5). (Illus.). 283p. (Orig.). reprint ed. pap. 22.95 *(978-0-931170-62-1(1))* Ctr. for Western Studies.

Sirvaitis, Karen. South Dakota. 2nd exp. rev. ed. 2003. (Hello U. S. A. Ser.). (Illus.). 84p. (J). (gr. 3-6). pap. 6.95 *(978-0-8225-4139-4(4))* Lerner Publishing Group.

Townsley, Janet Howe. Dakota Dreams: Fannie Sabra Howe's Own Story, 1881-1884. 2003. (Illus.). 77p. (J). 19.95 *(978-0-9715171-4-1(2))* South Dakota State Historical Society Pr.

Turnipseed, Susan. South Dakota: A Journey Through Time Student Workbook. Heers, Matt & Heers, Nate, illus. 2003. 28p. (J). pap. *(978-1-57579-268-2(0))* Pine Hill Pr.

—South Dakota: A Journey Through Time Student Workbook Answer Key. Heers, Matt & Heers, Nate, illus. 2003. 28p. (J). pap. *(978-1-57579-269-9(9))* Pine Hill Pr.

Waldman, Nomi J. Deadwood, South Dakota: A Frontier Community: Text Pairs. 2008. (Bridges/Navigators Ser.). (J). (gr. 3). 81.00 *(978-1-4108-8358-2(2))* Benchmark Education Co.

SOUTH DAKOTA—FICTION

Anderson, William. M Is for Mount Rushmore: A South Dakota Alphabet. Harness, Cheryl, illus. 2005. (Discover America State by State Ser.). (ENG.). 40p. (J). 17.95 *(978-1-58536-141-0(0))* Sleeping Bear Pr.

Baum, L. Frank. The Discontented Gopher: A Prairie Tale. Conahan, Carolyn Digby, illus. 2006. (Prairie Tales Ser.). 40p. (J). (gr. 3-7). 14.95 *(978-0-9749195-9-1(4)*, South Dakota State Historical Society Pr.) South Dakota State Historical Society Pr.

Black HIlls Summer. 2003. (YA). per. *(978-0-9740718-0-0(3))* Strathmoor Pr.

Brezenoff, Steve. The Mount Rushmore Face That Couldn't See, 1 vol. Calo, Marcos, illus. 2012. (Field Trip Mysteries Ser.). (ENG.). 88p. (gr. 2-3). pap. 6.10 *(978-1-4342-4199-3(8))* Stone Arch Bks.

Brown, Jeff. The Mount Rushmore Calamity. Pamintuan, Macky, illus. 2009. (Flat Stanley's Worldwide Adventures Ser.: 1). (ENG.). 96p. (J). (gr. 2-5). 15.99 *(978-0-06-142991-0(0))*; pap. 4.99 *(978-0-06-142990-3(2))* HarperCollins Pubs.

Cartwright, Nancy & Jones, Joanna. Henry's Adventure at the Franklin Hotel. Feterl, Bill, illus. 2011. (YA). lib. bdg. *(978-0-913062-44-9(8))* Fenwyn Pr.

Chace, Rebecca. June Sparrow & the Million-Dollar Penny. Schwartz, Kacey, illus. 2017. 352p. (J). (gr. 3-7). 16.99 *(978-0-06-246498-9(1))* HarperCollins Pubs.

Eastman, Charles A. & Eastman, Elaine Goodale. The Raccoon & the Bee Tree. Susan, Turnbull, illus. 2013. 32p. (J). *(978-0-9860355-4-8(8))* South Dakota State Historical Society Pr.

Erickson, Mary Ellen. What Happened to the Deer? Peanut Butter Club Mysteries. 2007. 182p. (J). 23.95 *(978-0-595-68396-3(7))*; per. 13.95 *(978-0-595-42799-4(5))* iUniverse, Inc.

Glaser, Linda. Hannah's Way. Gustavson, Adam, illus. 2012. (Shabbat Ser.). 32p. (J). (gr. k-3). lib. bdg. 17.95 *(978-0-7613-5137-5(X)*, Kar-Ben Publishing) Lerner Publishing Group.

Hardesty, Ann A. Lucy's Trials in the Black Hills. 2009. 104p. pap. 10.99 *(978-1-4490-5368-0(8))* AuthorHouse.

Hobbs, Will. Go Big or Go Home. 2009. (ENG.). 208p. (J). (gr. 5). pap. 6.99 *(978-0-06-074143-3(0))* HarperCollins Pubs.

House, Peggy. Prairie Anna. 2012. (J). *(978-1-60682-395-8(7))* BJU Pr.

Jacobs, Lily. The Littlest Bunny in South Dakota: An Easter Adventure. Dunn, Robert, illus. 2015. (ENG.). 32p. (J). (-3). 9.99 *(978-1-4926-1198-1(0)*, Sourcebooks Jabberwocky) Sourcebooks, Inc.

James, Eric. A Halloween Scare in South Dakota. Le Ray, Marina, illus. 2015. (ENG.). 32p. (J). (-5). 9.99 *(978-1-4926-2400-4(4)*, 9781492624004, Sourcebooks Jabberwocky) Sourcebooks, Inc.

—Santa's Sleigh Is on Its Way to South Dakota: A Christmas Adventure. Dunn, Robert, illus. 2016. (ENG.). 32p. (J). (-2). 12.99 *(978-1-4926-4355-5(6)*, 9781492643555, Sourcebooks Jabberwocky) Sourcebooks, Inc.

Kropp, Joseph P. Hickok's Gold. 2006. (J). 11.95 *(978-1-890905-25-5(9))* Day to Day Enterprises.

McNeely, Marian Hurd. The Jumping-Off Place. Siegel, William, illus. 2017. (ENG.). 320p. pap. 9.95 *(978-0-486-81568-8(4))* Dover Pubns., Inc.

—The Jumping-off Place. Siegel, William, illus. 2008. 321p. (J). 15.95 *(978-0-9798940-4-6(2)*, South Dakota State Historical Society Pr.) South Dakota State Historical Society Pr.

Mehnert, Robert. Spelunkers. 2012. 108p. pap. 19.95 *(978-1-62709-036-0(3))* America Star Bks.

Meierhenry, Mark & Volk, David. The Mystery of the Pheasants. Turnbull, Susan, illus. 2012. 44p. (J). 14.95 *(978-0-9845041-9-0(2))* South Dakota State Historical Society Pr.

Meierhenry, Mark V. & Volk, David. The Mystery of the Maize. Two Bulls, Marty Grant, illus. 2010. (J). *(978-0-9822749-1-0(2)*, South Dakota State Historical Society Pr.) South Dakota State Historical Society Pr.

Meyer, Deanna. Buffalo on the Ridge. 2010. pap. 12.95 *(978-0-7414-6103-2(X))* Infinity Publishing.

Moore, Ted. Eagle Eye & the Fall of Creek Canyon. 2007. 112p. per. 10.95 *(978-0-595-43133-5(X))* iUniverse, Inc.

Neal, Michael. Bonnie's Rescue: A Courageous Critters« Series Book. 2009. 56p. pap. 8.95 *(978-1-4401-1237-9(1))* iUniverse, Inc.

Peterson, Esther Allen. Will Spring Come? 2009. (Illus.). 157p. (J). *(978-0-88092-768-0(2))* Royal Fireworks Publishing Co.

Rey, H. A. Curious George & the Hot Air Balloon. 2011. (Curious George Ser.). (ENG., Illus.). 24p. (J). (gr. -1-3). pap. 4.99 *(978-0-547-54745-9(5))* Houghton Mifflin Harcourt Publishing Co.

Schurch, Maylan Henry. The Meatless Mayhem Mystery. 2003. (Justin Case Adventures Ser.: 5). 121p. (J). pap. 7.99 *(978-0-8280-1615-5(1)*, 133-650) Review & Herald Publishing Assn.

Silvano, Wendi. Love Is All Around South Dakota. Czernichowska, Joanna, illus. 2016. (ENG.). 32p. (J). (-6). 12.99 *(978-1-4926-2961-0(8)*, Sourcebooks Jabberwocky) Sourcebooks, Inc.

Smallman, Steve. Santa Is Coming to Rapid City. Dunn, Robert, illus. 2015. (ENG.). 32p. (J). (-3). 9.99 *(978-1-4926-2658-9(9)*, Sourcebooks Jabberwocky) Sourcebooks, Inc.

—Santa Is Coming to Sioux Falls. Dunn, Robert, illus. 2015. (ENG.). 32p. (J). (-3). 9.99 *(978-1-4926-2650-3(3)*, Sourcebooks Jabberwocky) Sourcebooks, Inc.

—Santa Is Coming to South Dakota. Dunn, Robert, illus. 2013. (ENG.). 32p. (J). (-3). 9.99 *(978-1-4022-9021-3(7)*, Sourcebooks Jabberwocky) Sourcebooks, Inc.

Stilton, Geronimo. Run for the Hills, Geronimo! 2011. (Geronimo Stilton Ser.: Bk. 47). (ENG.). 128p. (J). (gr. 2-5). pap. 7.99 *(978-0-545-33132-6(3)*, Scholastic Paperbacks) Scholastic, Inc.

Wilder, Laura Ingalls. The First Four Years. Williams, Garth, illus. (Little House Ser.: 9). (ENG.). 160p. (J). (gr. 3-7). 2008. pap. 7.99 *(978-0-06-440031-2(X))* 2004. pap. 8.99 *(978-0-06-058188-6(3))* HarperCollins Pubs.

—Little Town on the Prairie. Williams, Garth, illus. (Little House Ser.: 7). 320p. (J). 2008. (ENG.). (gr. 3-7). pap. 8.99 *(978-0-06-440007-7(7))* 2004. (ENG.). (gr. 3-7). pap. 8.99 *(978-0-06-058186-2(7))* 2003. pap. 5.99 *(978-0-06-052242-1(9))* HarperCollins Pubs.

—The Long Winter. Williams, Garth, illus. (Little House Ser.: 6). (ENG.). 352p. (J). (gr. 3-7). 2008. pap. 8.99 *(978-0-06-440006-0(9))* 2004. pap. 8.99 *(978-0-06-058185-5(9))* HarperCollins Pubs.

—These Happy Golden Years. 2007. (Little House Ser.). (ENG.). 304p. (J). (gr. 3-7). pap., pap. 6.99 *(978-0-06-088544-1(0)*, Harper Trophy) HarperCollins Pubs.

—These Happy Golden Years. Williams, Garth, illus. (Little House Ser.: 8). (ENG.). 304p. (J). (gr. 3-7). 2004. pap. 8.99 *(978-0-06-058187-9(5))* 2008. pap. 7.99 *(978-0-06-440008-4(5))* HarperCollins Pubs.

—These Happy Golden Years. l.t. ed. (J). (gr. 3-6). 35.95 *(978-1-58118-102-9(7))* LRS.

SOUTH DAKOTA—HISTORY

Bjorklund, Ruth, et al. South Dakota. 2016. (It's My State! (r) Ser.). (Illus.). 80p. (J). (gr. 4-4). 34.21 *(978-1-62713-222-0(8))* Cavendish Square Publishing.

Burgan, Michael. South Dakota (Revised Edition) 2014. (America the Beautiful, Third Ser. (Revised Edition) Ser.). (ENG., Illus.). 144p. (J). lib. bdg. 40.00 *(978-0-531-28293-9(7))* Scholastic Library Publishing.

Dell, Pamela. Last Battle: Causes & Effects of the Massacre at Wounded Knee. 2015. (Cause & Effect: American Indian History Ser.). (ENG., Illus.). 32p. (gr. 3-4). lib. bdg. 27.32 *(978-1-4914-4835-9(0))* Capstone Press of Coughlan Cos.

Gabriel, Luke. Mount Rushmore. 2014. (United States Landmarks Ser.). (ENG.). 24p. (J). (gr. 1-4). 27.07 *(978-1-62323-955-8(9)*, 206730) Child's World, Inc., The.

Gitlin, Martin. Wounded Knee Massacre, 1 vol. 2010. (Landmarks of the American Mosaic Ser.). 185p. (C). (gr. 7-18). 39.00 *(978-1-59884-409-2(1)*, A2840C, Greenwood) ABC-CLIO, LLC.

Goldsworthy, Kaite. El Monte Rushmore. 2013. (Iconos Americanos Ser.). (SPA., Illus.). 24p. (J). (gr. k-2). lib. bdg. 27.13 *(978-1-62127-621-0(X)*, AV2 by Weigl) Weigl Pubs., Inc.

—Mount Rushmore. 2014. (Illus.). 24p. (J). *(978-1-62127-465-0(9))* Weigl Pubs., Inc.

Horn, Geoffrey M. & Bjorklund, Ruth. South Dakota. 2nd ed. 2013. 80p. (J). (gr. 4-8). 31.36 *(978-1-60870-884-0(5))* Cavendish Square Publishing.

Jerome, Kate B. The Wise Animal Handbook South Dakota. 2017. (Arcadia Kids Ser.). (ENG., Illus.). 32p. (J). 16.99 ***(978-0-7385-2842-7(0))*** Arcadia Publishing.

Kopp, Megan. South Dakota: Mount Rushmore State. 2012. (J). *(978-1-61913-403-4(9))*; pap. *(978-1-61913-404-1(7))* Weigl Pubs., Inc.

Marsh, Carole. Exploring South Dakota Through Project-Based Learning: Geography, History, Government, Economics & More. 2016. (South Dakota Experience Ser.). (ENG.). (J). pap. 9.99 *(978-0-635-12365-7(7))* Gallopade International.

—I'm Reading about Mount Rushmore. 2016. (I'm Reading about Mount Rushmore Ser.). (ENG., Illus.). (J). lib. bdg. 24.99 *(978-0-635-12215-5(4))* Gallopade International.

—I'm Reading about South Dakota. 2014. (South Dakota Experience Ser.). (ENG., Illus.). (J). pap., pap. 8.99 *(978-0-635-11316-0(3))* Gallopade International.

—South Dakota History Projects: 30 Cool, Activities, Crafts, Experiments & More for Kids to Do to Learn about Your State! 2003. (South Dakota Experience Ser.). 32p. (gr. k-5). pap. 5.95 *(978-0-635-01810-6(1)*, Marsh, Carole Bks.) Gallopade International.

Mattern, Joanne. Mount Rushmore. 2014. (ENG.). 32p. (gr. 3-6). 32.79 *(978-1-62717-741-2(8))* Rourke Educational Media.

Meinking, Mary. What's Great about South Dakota? 2015. (Our Great States Ser.). (ENG., Illus.). 32p. (J). (gr. 2-5). lib. bdg. 26.60 *(978-1-4677-3869-9(7)*, Lerner Pubns.) Lerner Publishing Group.

Ollhoff, Jim. South Dakota, 1 vol. 2009. (United States Ser.). (ENG., Illus.). 48p. (YA). (gr. 2-4). 27.07 *(978-1-60453-677-5(2))* ABDO Publishing Co.

Pearson, Jaci Conrad. Adams A to Z. Nelson, Darrel, illus. 2011. 51p. (J). *(978-0-9793584-3-2(4))* TDG Communications, Inc.

Petersen, Christine. South Dakota: Past & Present. 2010. (United States: Past & Present Ser.). (ENG., Illus.). 48p. (J). pap. 11.75 *(978-1-4358-9523-2(1))*; lib. bdg. 29.25 *(978-1-4358-9496-9(0))* Rosen Publishing Group, Inc., The. (Rosen Reference).

Strudwick, Leslie. South Dakota. 2011. (Guide to American States Ser.). (Illus.). 48p. (YA). (gr. 3-6). 29.99 *(978-1-61690-814-0(9))*; (J). 29.99 *(978-1-61690-490-6(9))* Weigl Pubs., Inc.

—South Dakota: The Mount Rushmore State. 2016. (J). *(978-1-4896-4941-6(7))* Weigl Pubs., Inc.

Tieck, Sarah. South Dakota, 1 vol. 2012. (Explore the United States Ser.). (ENG.). 32p. (J). (gr. 2-5). lib. bdg. 28.50 *(978-1-61783-380-9(0)*, Big Buddy Bks.) ABDO Publishing Co.

Waldman, Nomi J. Deadwood, South Dakota A Frontier Community: Set Of 6. 2011. (Navigators Ser.). (J). pap. 44.00 net. *(978-1-4108-6247-1(X))* Benchmark Education Co.

Westcott, Jim. Upper Plains: Montana, North Dakota, South Dakota, Vol. 19. 2015. (Let's Explore the States Ser.). (Illus.). 64p. (J). (gr. 5). 23.95 *(978-1-4222-3336-8(7))* Mason Crest.

Yacowitz, Caryn. South Dakota. 2009. (From Sea to Shining Sea, Second Ser.). (ENG.). 80p. (J). pap. 7.95 *(978-0-531-21143-4(6)*, Children's Pr.) Scholastic Library Publishing.

SOUTH POLE

Bluthenthal, Todd. The South Pole. 2017. (Where on Earth? Mapping Parts of the World Ser.). 24p. (J). (gr. 1-2). pap. 8.15 ***(978-1-4824-6433-7(0))***; pap. 48.90 ***(978-1-4824-6434-4(9))*** Stevens, Gareth Publishing LLLP.

Bodden, Valerie. To the South Pole. (Great Expeditions Ser.). 48p. (J). 2012. (ENG.). (gr. 4-7). pap. 12.00 *(978-0-89812-667-9(3)*, Creative Paperbacks) 2011. (Illus.). 35.65 *(978-1-60818-069-1(7)*, Creative Education) Creative Co., The.

Cooke, Tim. The Exploration of the North & South Poles. 2013. (Explorers Discovering the World Ser.). (Illus.). 48p. (J). (gr. 4-6). 31.95 *(978-1-4339-8631-4(0))*; pap. 14.05 *(978-1-4339-8632-1(9))* Stevens, Gareth Publishing LLLP. (Gareth Stevens Learning Library).

Dickmann, Nancy. The South Pole, 1 vol. 2012. (Explorer Tales Ser.). (ENG.). 32p. (gr. 1-3). 29.99 *(978-1-4109-4785-7(8))*; pap. 8.29 *(978-1-4109-4792-5(0))* Heinemann-Raintree. (Read Me!).

Llanas, Sheila Griffin. Who Reached the South Pole First? (Race for History Ser.). (ENG.). 32p. (gr. 3-4). 2011. pap. 47.70 *(978-1-4296-6413-4(4))* 2010. lib. bdg. 27.32 *(978-1-4296-3344-4(1))* Capstone Press of Coughlan Cos. (Fact Finders).

Mason, Theodore. The South Pole Ponies. 2007. 232p. (gr. 7). per. 18.00 *(978-1-59048-251-3(4))* Long Riders' Guild Pr., The.

Worth, Bonnie. Ice Is Nice! All about the North & South Poles. Ruiz, Aristides & Mathieu, Joe, illus. 2010. (Cat in the Hat's Learning Library). (ENG.). 48p. (J). (gr. -1-3). 9.99 *(978-0-375-82885-0(0)*, Random Hse. Bks. for Young Readers) Random Hse. Children's Bks.

Yomtov, Nel. Roald Amundsen Explores the South Pole. 2015. (Extraordinary Explorers Ser.). (ENG., Illus.). 24p. (J). (gr. 3-7). lib. bdg. 29.95 *(978-1-62617-295-1(1)*, Black Sheep) Bellwether Media.

SOUTH POLE—FICTION

Berenstain, Stan, et al. Nothing Ever Happens at the South Pole. Berenstain, Jan & Berenstain, Mike, illus. 2012. (ENG.). 40p. (J). (gr. -1-3). 10.99 *(978-0-06-207532-1(2))* HarperCollins Pubs.

Burks, James. Bird & Squirrel on Ice. 2014. (Bird & Squirrel Ser.). (ENG.). 128p. (J). (gr. 2-5). pap. 8.99 *(978-0-545-56318-5(6)*, Graphix) Scholastic, Inc.

Coyle, Carmela Lavigna. Thank You, Aunt Tallulah! MacPherson, Bruce, illus. 2006. (ENG.). 32p. (J). (gr. -1-3). 15.95 *(978-0-87358-891-1(6))* Cooper Square Publishing Llc.

Hooper, Meredith & Quarto Generic Staff. Ponko & the South Pole. Ormerod, Jan, illus. 2012. (ENG.). 32p. (J). (gr. -1-1). pap. 8.99 *(978-1-84780-403-7(9)*, Frances Lincoln) Quarto Publishing Group UK GBR. Dist: Hachette Bk. Group.

Kimmel, Elizabeth Cody. My Penguin Osbert in Love. Lewis, H. B., illus. 2010. (ENG.). 48p. (J). (gr. -1-3). 7.99 *(978-0-7636-5001-8(3))* Candlewick Pr.

Kimmel, Elizabeth Cody & Buck, Lewis. My Penguin Osbert in Love, Set. Lewis, H. B., illus. 2008. (ENG.). 48p. (J). (gr. -1-3). 16.99 *(978-0-7636-3032-4(2))* Candlewick Pr.

Lawrence, Iain. The Winter Pony. 2012. (ENG., Illus.). 256p. (J). (gr. 4-7). 7.99 *(978-0-440-23972-7(9)*, Yearling) Random Hse. Children's Bks.

Rockwood, Roy. Under the Ocean to the South Pole. 2007. 120p. per. *(978-1-4068-3972-2(8))* Echo Library.

—Under the Ocean to the South Pole. 2009. 152p. 24.95 *(978-1-60664-626-7(5))*; pap. 12.95 *(978-1-60664-365-5(7))* Rodgers, Alan Bks.

—Under the Ocean to the South Pole or the Strange Cruise of the Submarine Wonder. 2007. 180p. 95.99 *(978-1-4280-7589-4(5))*; per. 89.99 *(978-1-4280-7588-7(7))* IndyPublish.com.

Spinelli, Eileen. Something to Tell the Grandcows. Slavin, Bill, illus. 2004. 32p. (J). 16.00 *(978-0-8028-5236-6(X))*; (gr. -1-3). 8.00 *(978-0-8028-5304-2(8)*, Eerdmans Bks For Young Readers) Eerdmans, William B. Publishing Co.

SOUTH SEA ISLANDS

see Islands of the Pacific

SOUTHEAST ASIA

Here are entered works dealing collectively with the mainland and insular regions of Asia lying south of China and east of India, including Burma, Thailand, Laos, Cambodia, Vietnam, Malaysia, Singapore, Brunei, Indonesia, East Timor, and the Philippines.

Boomgaard, Peter & Stoll, Mark. Southeast Asia: An Environmental History, 1 vol. 2006. (Nature & Human Societies Ser.). (Illus.). 377p. (C). 94.00 *(978-1-85109-419-6(9)*, SASIAC) ABC-CLIO, LLC.

Chandler, Julia. The Colonial & Postcolonial Experience in East & Southeast Asia. 2016. (Colonial & Postcolonial Experience Ser.). 00128p. (J). (gr. 10-10). 54.00 *(978-1-5081-0438-4(7))* Rosen Publishing Group, Inc., The.

Fry, Gerald W. The Association of Southeast Asian Nations. 2008. (Global Organizations Ser.). (Illus.). 144p. (YA). (gr. 7-12). 35.00 *(978-0-7910-9609-3(2))* Facts On File, Inc.

Orr, Tamra. Brunei. 2008. (Cultures of the World Ser.). 144p. (gr. 6-18). lib. bdg. 42.79 *(978-0-7614-3121-3(7)*, Benchmark Bks.) Marshall Cavendish Corp.

Phillips, Douglas A. Southeast Asia. 2005. (Modern World Cultures Ser.). (Illus.). 136p. (gr. 6-12). lib. bdg. 30.00 *(978-0-7910-8149-5(4)*, Chelsea Hse.) Facts On File, Inc.

Robbins, Gerald. Azerbaijan. 2006. (Growth & Influence of Islam in the Nations of Asia & Central Asia Ser.). (Illus.). 128p. (YA). lib. bdg. 25.95 *(978-1-59084-878-4(0))* Mason Crest.

Southeast Asia: Regions of the World. 2003. spiral bd. 16.95 *(978-1-56004-159-7(5))* Social Studies Schl. Service.

SOUTHEAST ASIA—FICTION

Coburn, Jewell Reinhart & Lee, Tzexa Cherta. Jouanah: A Hmong Cinderella. O'Brien, Anne Sibley, illus. 2014. (ENG.). 32p. (J). pap. 9.95 *(978-1-885008-41-1(4)*, Shen's Bks.) Lee & Low Bks., Inc.

Cornwell, Autumn. Carpe Diem. 2009. (ENG.). 368p. (YA). (gr. 7-12). pap. 12.99 *(978-0-312-56129-1(6)*, 9780312561291) Square Fish.

Kingston, William H. In the Eastern Seas. 2013. 396p. pap. *(978-3-943850-66-6(8))* weitsüchtig. in Europäischer Hochschulverlag GmbH & Co. KG.

Lewis, Gill. Moon Bear. Gottardo, Alessandro, illus. 2015. (ENG.). 384p. (J). (gr. 3-7). 16.99 *(978-1-4814-0094-7(0))* Simon & Schuster Children's Publishing.

Meloy, Maile. The Apprentices. Schoenherr, Ian, illus. 2013. (Apothecary Ser.: 2). (ENG.). 416p. (J). (gr. 5). 16.99 *(978-0-399-16245-9(3)*, G.P. Putnam's Sons Books for Young Readers) Penguin Young Readers Group.

SOUTHERN STATES

Andrews, Barbara. Discover the Southeast Region. 2006. (J). pap. *(978-1-4108-6435-2(9))* Benchmark Education Co.

Bethea, Nikole Brooks. G Is for Grits: A Southern Alphabet, 1 vol. Lyne, Alison Davis, illus. 2012. (ENG.). 32p. (J). (gr. k-3). 16.99 *(978-1-4556-1698-5(2))* Pelican Publishing Co., Inc.

Currie, Stephen. A Peculiar Institution: Slavery in the Plantation South. 2005. (Lucent Library of Black History). (ENG., Illus.). 112p. (YA). (gr. 7-10). lib. bdg. 33.45 *(978-1-59018-704-3(0)*, Lucent Bks.) Cengage Gale.

Davidson, Tish. East South-Central States: Kentucky & Tennessee, Vol. 19. 2015. (Let's Explore the States Ser.). (Illus.). 64p. (J). (gr. 5). 23.95 *(978-1-4222-3322-1(7))* Mason Crest.

Dunn, Mary. My Adventure in the Southeast: Advanced My Adventure. 2007. 44p. (J). pap. 8.99 *(978-1-59092-436-5(3))* Blue Forge Pr.

Erickson, Paul. Daily Life on a Southern Plantation. Gabbey, Terry, illus. Slingsby, Miki, photos by. 2006. 48p. (J). (gr. 2-5). reprint ed. pap. 8.00 *(978-1-4223-5727-9(9))* DIANE Publishing Co.

Goldberg, Jan. Hernando de Soto: Trailblazer of the American Southeast. 2003. (Library of Explorers & Exploration Ser.). (Illus.). 112p. (gr. 5-8). lib. bdg. 34.60 *(978-0-8239-3623-6(6)*, Rosen Reference) Rosen Publishing Group, Inc., The.

Gullo, Jim. A Travel Guide to the Plantation South. 2005. (Travel Guide To Ser.). (ENG., Illus.). 112p. (J). (gr. 5-8). lib. bdg. 30.85 *(978-1-59018-360-1(6)*, Lucent Bks.) Cengage Gale.

Johnson, Michael & Clarke, Duncan. Native Tribes of the Southeast. 2004. (Native Tribes of North America Ser.). (Illus.). 64p. (gr. 5-12). lib. bdg. 34.00 *(978-0-8368-5614-9(7)*, Gareth Stevens Secondary Library) Stevens, Gareth Publishing LLLP.

Micklos, John, Jr. People & Places of the Southeast. 2016. (United States by Region Ser.). (ENG., Illus.). 32p. (gr. 3-4). lib. bdg. 27.32 *(978-1-5157-2443-8(3)*, Fact Finders) Capstone Press of Coughlan Cos.

Rikson, Paule. Daily Life on a Southern Plantation 1853. 2004. (Illus.). 48p. (J). (gr. 4-8). reprint ed. 17.00 *(978-0-7567-7709-8(7))* DIANE Publishing Co.

The South. 2014. (Land That I Love: Regions of the United States Ser.). (Illus.). 32p. (J). (gr. 3-6). lib. bdg. 26.25 *(978-1-4777-6857-0(2)*, PowerKids Pr.) Rosen Publishing Group, Inc., The.

U. S. National Geographic Society Staff, contrib. by. The Southeast Today. 2007. (Reading Expeditions Ser.). (ENG.,

Illus.). 32p. (J). pap. 17.95 (978-0-7922-4533-9(4)) CENGAGE Learning.
Yannuzzi, Della A. The Life of Zora Neale Hurston: Author & Folklorist. 2015. (Legendary African Americans Ser.). 96p. (J). (gr. 6-12). 27.94 (978-0-7660-6275-7(9)) Enslow Pubs., Inc.

SOUTHERN STATES—FICTION

Battle-Lavert, Gwendolyn. Papa's Mark. Bootman, Colin, illus. 2003. (ENG.). 32p. (J). (gr. k-3). tchr. ed. 17.95 (978-0-8234-1650-9(X)) Holiday Hse., Inc.
Birtha, Becky. Grandmama's Pride. Bootman, Colin, illus. 2005. (ENG.). 32p. (J). (gr. 2-3). 16.99 (978-0-8075-3028-3(X)) Whitman, Albert & Co.
Burg, Ann E. Unbound. 2016. (ENG.). 352p. (J). (gr. 4-6). 16.99 (978-0-545-93427-5(3), Scholastic Pr.) Scholastic, Inc.
Carter, Noni. Good Fortune. (ENG.). 496p. (YA). (gr. 7). 2011. pap. 9.99 (978-1-4169-8481-8(X)) 2010. 16.99 (978-1-4169-8480-1(1)) Simon & Schuster Bks. For Young Readers. (Simon & Schuster Bks. For Young Readers).
Cline-Ransome, Lesa. Light in the Darkness: A Story about How Slaves Learned in Secret. Ransome, James E., illus. 2013. (ENG.). 40p. (J). (gr. k-3). 16.99 (978-1-4231-3495-4(8), Jump at the Sun) Hyperion Bks. for Children.
Davis, David. Ten Redneck Babies: A Southern Counting Book, 1 vol. Ward, Sue Marshall, illus. 2004. (ENG.). 32p. (J). (gr. k-k). 16.99 (978-1-58980-232-2(2)) Pelican Publishing Co., Inc.
DeLong, Lucianne. A Tall Southern Tale. Ungureanu, Dan Paul, illus. l.t. ed. 2013. (Possum Squat Ser.). (ENG.). 40p. (J). 15.95 (978-0-9833237-1-6(2)) Krullstone Publishing, LLC.
—Whiskers Takes a Walk: A Possum Squat Tale. Ungureanu, Dan Paul, illus. 2013. (Possum Squat Ser.). (ENG.). 40p. (J). 15.95 (978-0-9833237-3-0(9)) Krullstone Publishing, LLC.
DiCamillo, Kate. Gracias a Winn-Dixie. 2010.Tr. of Because of Winn-Dixie. (SPA.). 152p. (gr. 4-6). pap. 12.99 (978-84-279-3265-4(0)) Noguer y Caralt Editores, S. A. ESP. Dist: Lectorum Pubns., Inc.
Evans, Freddi Williams. Hush Harbor: Praying in Secret. Banks, Erin, illus. 2008. (ENG.). 32p. (J). (gr. k-3). 16.95 (978-0-8225-7965-6(0), Carolrhoda Bks.) Lerner Publishing Group.
Finley, Martha. Elsie's Kith & Kin. 2006. 28.95 (978-1-4218-2994-4(0)); pap. 13.95 (978-1-4218-3094-0(9)) 1st World Publishing, Inc.
—Elsie's Motherhood. 2006. 29.95 (978-1-4218-2995-1(9)); pap. 14.95 (978-1-4218-3095-7(7)) 1st World Publishing, Inc.
—Elsie's Motherhood. l.t. ed. 2007. 286p. pap. 23.99 (978-1-4264-8102-4(0)) Creative Media Partners, LLC.
Flake, Sharon. Unstoppable Octobia May. 2014. (ENG.). 288p. (J). (gr. 3-7). 16.99 (978-0-545-60960-9(7), Scholastic Pr.) Scholastic, Inc.
Friedman, Aimee. Sea Change. (ENG.). (J). (gr. 7). 2010. 320p. 8.99 (978-0-439-92230-2(5)) 2009. 304p. 16.99 (978-0-439-92228-9(3)) Scholastic, Inc.
Gutman, Dan. You Only Die Twice. 2013. (Genius Files Ser.: 3). (J). (gr. 3-7). (ENG.). 320p. pap. 6.99 (978-0-06-182772-3(X)); (ENG., Illus.). 304p. 16.99 (978-0-06-182770-9(3)); (Illus.). 304p. lib. bdg. 17.89 (978-0-06-182771-6(1)) HarperCollins Pubs.
—You Only Die Twice. 2013. (Genius Files Ser.: 3). (J). lib. bdg. 17.20 (978-0-606-35043-3(8), Turtleback) Turtleback Bks.
Hamilton, Martha & Weiss, Mitch. The Hidden Feast: A Folktale from the American South. Tate, Don, illus. 2006. (ENG.). 32p. (J). (gr. k-3). 16.95 (978-0-87483-758-2(8)) August Hse. Pubs., Inc.
Harrington, Janice N. Going North. Lagarrigue, Jerome, illus. 2004. (ENG.). 40p. (J). (gr. k-3). 18.99 (978-0-374-32681-4(9), 9780374326814, Farrar, Straus & Giroux (BYR)) Farrar, Straus & Giroux.
Johnson, Allen, Jr. My Brother's Story. McMorris, Kelley, illus. 2014. (Blackwater Novels Ser.: Vol. 1). (ENG.). 191p. (J). (gr. 4-7). 14.99 (978-1-933725-37-6(0)) Premium Pr. America.
Kendall, Jane F. Tennessee Rose. Sheckels, Astrid, illus. 2012. (Horse Diaries). (ENG.). 160p. (J). (gr. 3-7). pap. 7.99 (978-0-375-87006-4(7), Random Hse. Bks. for Young Readers) Random Hse. Children's Bks.
Kidd, Ronald. Night on Fire. 2015. (ENG.). 288p. (J). (gr. 3-7). 16.99 (978-0-8075-7024-1(9)) Whitman, Albert & Co.
LaFaye, A. Stella Stands Alone. 2010. (ENG.). 256p. (YA). (gr. 7). pap. 7.99 (978-1-4169-8647-8(2), Simon & Schuster Bks. For Young Readers) Simon & Schuster Bks. For Young Readers.
Lambe, Jennifer Holloway & National Geographic Learning Staff. Kudzu Chaos, 1 vol. Lyne, Alison Davis, illus. 2003. (ENG.). 32p. (J). (gr. k-3). 16.99 (978-1-58980-157-8(1)) Pelican Publishing Co., Inc.
Lawson, Jessica. Waiting for Augusta. 2016. (ENG., Illus.). 336p. (J). (gr. 3-7). 16.99 (978-1-4814-4839-0(0), Simon & Schuster Bks. For Young Readers) Simon & Schuster Bks. For Young Readers.
Mitchell, Margaree King. When Grandmama Sings. Ransome, James E., illus. 2012. (ENG.). 40p. (J). (gr. k-4). 16.99 (978-0-688-17563-4(5), Amistad) HarperCollins Pubs.
Optic, Oliver, pseud. Watch & Wait; or, the Young Fugitives a Story for Young People by Oliver Optic [Pseud]. 2006. 284p. per. 23.99 (978-1-4255-2683-2(7)) Michigan Publishing.
Patrick, Denise Lewis. A Matter of Souls. 2014. 192p. (YA). (gr. 6-12). 16.95 (978-0-7613-9280-4(7), Carolrhoda Lab™) Lerner Publishing Group.
Payne, C. C. The Thing about Leftovers. 2016. (ENG.). 288p. (J). (gr. 5). 16.99 (978-0-399-17204-5(1), Nancy Paulsen Books) Penguin Young Readers Group.
Phillips, Lyda. Mr Touchdown. 2008. 184p. 23.95 (978-1-4401-0976-8(1)); pap. 13.95 (978-1-60528-029-5(1)) iUniverse, Inc. (iUniverse Star).
Ramsnips, Tunder. The Hardly Boys. 2010. 196p. pap. 15.95 (978-0-557-38767-0(1)) Lulu Pr., Inc.
Sam's Last Summer. 2006. (J). per. 5.95 (978-0-9790796-3-4(2)) PJR Assocs., Ltd.
San Souci, Robert D. & San Souci, Daniel, illus. Sister Tricksters: Rollicking Tales of Clever Females. 2006. (ENG.). 70p. (J). (gr. 3-7). 19.95 (978-0-87483-791-9(X)) August Hse. Pubs., Inc.
Schronk, Julie. The Grass Grows Green. 2007. 208p. per. 24.95 (978-1-60441-057-0(4)) America Star Bks.
Sorensen. Curious Missie C. 2003. (J). (978-0-15-204717-7(4)) Harcourt Trade Pubs.
—Curious Missie P. 2003. (J). pap. (978-0-15-204716-0(6)) Harcourt Trade Pubs.
Standish, Burt L. Frank Merriwell down South. Rudman, Jack, ed. (Frank Merriwell Ser.). (YA). (gr. 9-18). 29.95 (978-0-8373-9305-6(1)); 2003. pap. 9.95 (978-0-8373-9005-5(2), FM-005) Merriwell, Frank Inc.
Taylor, Mildred D. The Friendship. 2014. (ENG.). 56p. (J). (gr. 3-7). 11.24 (978-1-63245-342-6(8)) Lectorum Pubns., Inc.
Twain, Mark, pseud. The Adventures of Tom Sawyer. Ingpen, Robert R., illus. 2010. (Sterling Illustrated Classics Ser.). (ENG.). 240p. (J). (gr. 5-18). 19.95 (978-1-4027-6762-3(5)) Sterling Publishing Co., Inc.
Whelan, Gloria. The Listeners. Benny, Mike, illus. 2009. (Tales of Young Americans Ser.). (ENG.). 32p. (J). (gr. k-6). 17.95 (978-1-58536-419-0(3)) Sleeping Bear Pr.
Wiles, Deborah. Each Little Bird That Sings. 2006. (ENG., Illus.). 288p. (J). (gr. 2-5). reprint ed. pap. 7.99 (978-0-15-205657-5(2)) Houghton Mifflin Harcourt Publishing Co.
—Freedom Summer. Lagarrigue, Jerome, illus. 2005. (ENG.). 32p. (J). (gr. -1-3). reprint ed. 7.99 (978-0-689-87829-9(X), Aladdin) Simon & Schuster Children's Publishing.

SOUTHERN STATES—HISTORY

Anderson, Dale. The Aftermath of the Civil War. 2004. (World Almanac Library of the Civil War). (Illus.). 48p. (gr. 5-12). pap. 14.05 (978-0-8368-5597-5(3)); lib. bdg. 31.00 (978-0-8368-5588-3(4)) Stevens, Gareth Publishing LLLP. (Gareth Stevens Secondary Library).
Aretha, David. Sit-Ins & Freedom Rides. 2009. (Civil Rights Movement Ser.). 128p. (J). (gr. 4-7). 28.95 (978-1-59935-098-1(X)) Reynolds, Morgan Inc.
—The Story of the Civil Rights Freedom Rides in Photographs. 2014. (Story of the Civil Rights Movement in Photographs Ser.). 48p. (J). lib. bdg. 25.27 (978-0-7660-4236-0(7)) Enslow Pubs., Inc.
Bartley, Niccole. The South. 2014. (Land That I Love: Regions of the United States Ser.). 32p. (J). (gr. 3-6). pap. 60.00 (978-1-4777-6636-1(7), PowerKids Pr.) Rosen Publishing Group, Inc., The.
Chandler, Matt. Ghosts of the Alamo & Other Hauntings of the South, 1 vol. 2014. (Haunted America Ser.). (ENG.). 32p. (gr. 3-4). lib. bdg. 27.99 (978-1-4765-3914-0(6), Edge Bks.) Capstone Press of Coughlan Cos.
Connors, Kathleen. Let's Explore the Southeast. 2013. (Road Trip: Exploring America's Regions Ser.). 24p. (J). (gr. 2-5). pap. 8.15 (978-1-4339-9145-5(4)); (ENG., Illus.). lib. bdg. 22.60 (978-1-4339-9144-8(6)) Stevens, Gareth Publishing LLLP.
Harkrader, Lisa. Reconstruction & Aftermath of the Civil War: A MyReportLinks. com Book. 2004. (American Civil War Ser.). (Illus.). 48p. (J). lib. bdg. 25.26 (978-0-7660-5265-9(6), MyReportLinks.com Bks.) Enslow Pubs., Inc.
Hazelton, Amie. Hernando de Soto: An Explorer of the Southeast. 2017. (World Explorers Ser.). (ENG., Illus.). 32p. (gr. 3-4). lib. bdg. 27.32 (978-1-5157-4204-3(0)) Capstone Press of Coughlan Cos.
Hernández, Roger E. Early Explorations: The 1500s. 2008. (Hispanic America Ser.). 80p. (gr. 5-18). lib. bdg. 34.21 (978-0-7614-2937-1(9), Benchmark Bks.) Marshall Cavendish Corp.
Hinton, Kerry. Sit-Ins & Nonviolent Protest. 2017. (J). pap. **(978-1-5383-8064-2(1)**, Rosen Young Adult) Rosen Publishing Group, Inc., The.
Jameson, W. C. Buried Treasures of the South: Legends of Lost, Buried, & Forgotten Treasures, from Tidewater Virginia to Coastal Carolina to Cajun Louisiana. 2006. (Buried Treasure Ser.). (ENG., Illus.). 192p. (J). (gr. 4-17). pap. 14.95 (978-0-87483-286-0(1)) August Hse. Pubs., Inc.
LaClair, Teresa. The Southern Colonies: The Search for Wealth (1600-1770) 2012. (J). pap. (978-1-4222-2412-0(0)) Mason Crest.
—The Southern Colonies: The Search for Wealth (1600-1770) Rakove, Jack N., ed. 2012. (How America Became America Ser.). 48p. (J). (gr. 3-4). 19.95 (978-1-4222-2398-7(1)) Mason Crest.
Lemay, Violet. Southern Baby. Lemay, Violet, illus. 2015. (ENG., Illus.). 22p. (gr. k — 1). bds. 8.95 (978-1-938093-45-6(3), Duo Pr. Llc (US)) Duo Pr. LLC.
Let's Explore the Southeast. 2013. (Road Trip: Exploring America's Regions Ser.). 24p. (J). (gr. 2-5). pap. 48.90 (978-1-4339-9146-2(2)) Stevens, Gareth Publishing LLLP.
Maloof, Torrey. Reconstruction: Freedom Delayed. 2017. (Primary Source Readers Ser.). (Illus.). 32p. (J). (gr. 4-5). pap. 8.99 (978-1-4938-3806-6(7)) Teacher Created Materials, Inc.
Marsico, Katie. It's Cool to Learn about the United States Southeast. 2011. (Explorer Library: Social Studies Explorer Ser.). (ENG.). 48p. (gr. 4-8). pap. 15.64 (978-1-61080-303-8(5), 201199) Cherry Lake Publishing.
—Southeast. 2011. (Explorer Library: Social Studies Explorer Ser.). (ENG.). 48p. (gr. 4-8). lib. bdg. 31.36 (978-1-61080-181-2(4), 201156) Cherry Lake Publishing.
Meachen-Rau, Dana. The Southeast. 2012. (True Book Ser.). (ENG., Illus.). 48p. (J). pap. 6.95 (978-0-531-28327-1(5), Children's Pr.) Scholastic Library Publishing.
Nelson, Sheila. The Southern Colonies: The Quest for Prosperity. 2006. (How America Became America Ser.). (Illus.). 96p. (YA). lib. bdg. 22.95 (978-1-59084-902-6(7)) Mason Crest.
Rau, Dana Meachen. The Southeast. 2012. (True Book Ser.). (ENG., Illus.). 48p. (J). 29.00 (978-0-531-24852-2(6), Children's Pr.) Scholastic Library Publishing.
Santella, Andrew. Mountain Men. 2003. (Cornerstones of Freedom Ser.). (ENG., Illus.). 48p. (YA). (gr. 4-7). 26.00 (978-0-516-24216-3(4)) Scholastic Library Publishing.
Streissguth, Thomas. Perspectives on Reconstruction. 2018. (ENG.). 32p. (gr. 3-6). **(978-1-63235-403-7(9)**, 12-Story Library) Pr. Room Editions LLC.
Thompson, Gare. The Southeast: Its History & People. 2007. (Reading Expeditions Ser.). (ENG., Illus.). 32p. (J). pap. 17.95 (978-0-7922-8613-4(8)) CENGAGE Learning.
Wiseman, Blaine. The Southeast. 2016. (Illus.). 48p. (J). (978-1-5105-1140-8(7)) SmartBook Media, Inc.

SOUTHERN STATES—RACE RELATIONS

Coles, Robert. The Story of Ruby Bridges. 2009. 8.44 (978-0-7848-3016-1(9), Everbind) Marco Bk. Co.
—The Story of Ruby Bridges. 2011. 17.00 (978-1-61383-173-1(0)) Perfection Learning Corp.
—The Story of Ruby Bridges. Ford, George, illus. 50th anniv. ed. 2010. (ENG.). 32p. (J). (gr. -1-3). pap. 6.99 (978-0-439-47226-5(1), Scholastic Paperbacks) Scholastic, Inc.
—The Story of Ruby Bridges. 2010. lib. bdg. 17.20 (978-0-606-23189-3(7), Turtleback) Turtleback Bks.
Crayton, Lisa A. Freedom Riders. 2017. (J). pap. **(978-1-5383-8026-0(9))** Rosen Publishing Group, Inc., The.
Fremon, David K. The Jim Crow Laws & Racism in United States History. 2014. (In United States History Ser.). (Illus.). 96p. (J). (gr. 5-12). pap. 10.95 (978-0-7660-6093-7(4)) Enslow Pubs., Inc.
Herr, Melody. Sitting for Equal Service: Lunch Counter Sit-Ins, United States, 1960s. 2010. (Civil Rights Struggles around the World Ser.). (ENG.). 160p. (gr. 9-12). lib. bdg. 38.60 (978-0-8225-8970-9(2)) Lerner Publishing Group.
Hinton, Kerry. Sit-Ins & Nonviolent Protest. 2017. (J). pap. **(978-1-5383-8064-2(1)**, Rosen Young Adult) Rosen Publishing Group, Inc., The.
Hunter-Gault, Charlayne. To the Mountaintop: My Journey Through the Civil Rights Movement. 2014. (New York Times Ser.). (ENG., Illus.). 224p. (YA). (gr. 7). pap. 12.99 (978-1-250-04062-6(0), 9781250040626) Square Fish.
Hussey, Maria. The Rise of the Jim Crow ERA. 2015. (African American Experience: from Slavery to the Presidency Ser.). (ENG., Illus.). 80p. (J). (gr. 7-8). 32.90 (978-1-68048-042-9(1), Britannica Educational Publishing) Rosen Publishing Group, Inc., The.
Hussey, Maria, ed. The Rise of the Jim Crow Era. 2015. (African American Experience: from Slavery to the Presidency Ser.). (ENG.). 80p. (YA). (gr. 7-8). 65.80 (978-1-68048-043-6(X), Britannica Educational Publishing) Rosen Publishing Group, Inc., The.
Latta, Susan M. Reconstruction Era, 1 vol. 2014. (African-American History Ser.). (ENG.). 48p. (gr. 8-12). lib. bdg. 32.79 (978-1-62403-147-2(1)) ABDO Publishing Co.
Levy, Debbie. Slaves on a Southern Plantation. 2004. (Daily Life Ser.). (ENG., Illus.). 48p. (J). 27.50 (978-0-7377-1827-0(7), Greenhaven Pr., Inc.) Cengage Gale.
Maloof, Torrey. Reconstruction: Freedom Delayed. 2017. (Primary Source Readers Ser.). (Illus.). 32p. (J). (gr. 4-5). pap. 8.99 (978-1-4938-3806-6(7)) Teacher Created Materials, Inc.
Miller, Jake. Sit-Ins & Freedom Rides: The Power of Nonviolent Resistance. (Library of the Civil Rights Movement Ser.). 24p. 2009. (gr. 3-3). 42.50 (978-1-60853-892-8(3)) 2004. (Illus.). (J). lib. bdg. 22.60 (978-0-8239-6253-2(9)) Rosen Publishing Group, Inc., The. (PowerKids Pr.).
Mortensen, Lori. Voices of the Civil Rights Movement. 2015. (We Shall Overcome Ser.). (ENG.). 32p. (gr. 3-4). lib. bdg. 27.32 (978-1-4914-2044-7(8)) Capstone Press of Coughlan Cos.
Muldoon, Kathleen M. Jim Crow Era, 1 vol. 2014. (African-American History Ser.). (ENG.). 48p. (gr. 8-12). lib. bdg. 32.79 (978-1-62403-146-5(3)) ABDO Publishing Co.
Pinkney, Andrea Davis. Sit-In: How Four Friends Stood up by Sitting Down. 2010. (ENG., Illus.). 40p. (J). (gr. 1-17). 18.99 (978-0-316-07016-4(5)) Little, Brown Bks. for Young Readers.
Rappaport, Doreen. Free at Last! Stories & Songs of Emancipation. Evans, Shane W., illus. 2006. (ENG.). 64p. (J). (gr. 4-7). pap. 9.99 (978-0-7636-3147-5(7)) Candlewick Pr.
Sapet, Kerrily. John Lewis. 2009. (Political Profiles Ser.). 100p. (YA). (gr. 5-9). 28.95 (978-1-59935-130-8(7)) Reynolds, Morgan Inc.
Tisdale, Rachel. The Freedom Riders, 1 vol., 1: 2014. (We Shall Overcome Ser.). (ENG.). 32p. (J). (gr. 3-6). 26.25 (978-1-4777-6061-1(X), PowerKids Pr.) Rosen Publishing Group, Inc., The.
Welch, Catherine A. Children of the Civil Rights Era. 2005. (Picture the American Past Ser.). (Illus.). 48p. (J). (gr. 2-5). lib. bdg. 22.60 (978-1-57505-481-0(7)) Lerner Publishing Group.
Worth, Richard. African Americans During Reconstruction. Schwarz, Philip, ed. 2006. (Slavery in the Americas Ser.). (Illus.). 112p. (gr. 5-8). 35.00 (978-0-8160-6139-6(4)) Facts On File, Inc.
—Slave Life on the Plantation: Prisons Beneath the Sun. 2004. (Slavery in American History Ser.). (Illus.). 128p. (J). lib. bdg. 27.94 (978-0-7660-2152-5(1)) Enslow Pubs., Inc.

SOUTHWEST, NEW

Here are entered works on that part of the United States which roughly corresponds to the old Spanish province of New Mexico, including the present Arizona, New Mexico, southern Colorado, Utah, Nevada and California.

Alagna, Magdalena. Wyatt Earp: Lawman of the American West. 2009. (Primary Sources of Famous People in American History Ser.). 32p. (gr. 2-3). 47.90 (978-1-60851-747-3(0)) Rosen Publishing Group, Inc., The.
—Wyatt Earp: Lawman of the American West / Sheriff del oeste Americano. 2009. (Famous People in American History/Grandes personajes en la historia de los Estados Unidos Ser.). (ENG & SPA.). 32p. (gr. 2-3). 47.90 (978-1-61512-558-6(2), Editorial Buenas Letras) Rosen Publishing Group, Inc., The.
—Wyatt Earp: Sheriff del oeste americano (Wyatt Earp: Lawman of the American West) 2009. (Grandes personajes en la historia de los Estados Unidos (Famous People in American History) Ser.). (SPA.). 32p. (gr. 2-3). 47.90 (978-1-61512-811-2(5), Editorial Buenas Letras) Rosen Publishing Group, Inc., The.
Aldridge, Rebecca. The Hoover Dam. 2009. (Building America Ser.). (Illus.). 120p. (gr. 5-8). 35.00 (978-1-60413-069-0(5), Chelsea Hse.) Facts On File, Inc.
Alpers, Jody. T Is for Tortilla: A Southwestern Alphabet Book. Johnson, Celeste, illus. 2006. (J). (gr. -1-3). (978-1-929115-14-3(8)) Azro Pr., Inc.
Anderson, Dale. The Anasazi Culture at Mesa Verde. 2003. (Landmark Events in American History Ser.). (Illus.). 48p. (gr. 5-12). lib. bdg. 31.00 (978-0-8368-5371-1(7), Gareth Stevens Secondary Library) Stevens, Gareth Publishing LLLP.
Andrews, Barbara. The Southwest Region. 2006. (J). pap. (978-1-4108-6433-8(2)) Benchmark Education Co.
Billy the Kid. 2010. (Legends of the Wild West Ser.). (Illus.). 104p. (gr. 6-12). 35.00 (978-1-60413-596-1(4), Chelsea Hse.) Facts On File, Inc.
Connors, Kathleen. Let's Explore the Great Basin. 2013. (Road Trip: Exploring America's Regions Ser.). 24p. (J). (gr. 2-5). pap. 8.15 (978-1-4339-9125-7(X)); pap. 48.90 (978-1-4339-9126-4(8)); (ENG., Illus.). lib. bdg. 22.60 (978-1-4339-9124-0(1)) Stevens, Gareth Publishing LLLP.
—Let's Explore the Southwest. 2013. (Road Trip: Exploring America's Regions Ser.). 24p. (J). (gr. 2-5). pap. 8.15 (978-1-4339-9150-9(0)); (ENG., Illus.). lib. bdg. 22.60 (978-1-4339-9149-3(7)) Stevens, Gareth Publishing LLLP.
Cooke, Tim. Billy the Kid: A Notorious Gunfighter of the Wild West. 2016. (Wanted! Famous Outlaws Ser.). (ENG., Illus.). 48p. (J). (gr. 6-8). pap. 14.05 (978-1-4824-4243-4(4)) Stevens, Gareth Publishing LLLP.
—Explore with Francisco Vazquez de Coronado. 2016. (Travel with the Great Explorers Ser.). (ENG., Illus.). 32p. (J). (gr. 3-6). (978-0-7787-2847-4(1)) Crabtree Publishing Co.
Cunningham, Kevin & Benoit, Peter. The Ute. 2011. (True Bk Ser.). 48p. (J). pap. 6.95 (978-0-531-29307-2(6)); (gr. 3-5). 29.00 (978-0-531-20765-9(X)) Scholastic Library Publishing. (Children's Pr.).
Dean, Arlan. The Old Spanish Trail: From Santa Fe, New Mexico to Los Angeles, California. (Famous American Trails Ser.). 24p. 2009. (gr. 3-3). 42.50 (978-1-61512-489-3(6), PowerKids Pr.) 2003. (Illus.). (J). lib. bdg. 22.60 (978-0-8239-6480-2(9)) Rosen Publishing Group, Inc., The.
—The Santa Fe Trail: From Independence, Missouri to Santa Fe, New Mexico. (Famous American Trails Ser.). 24p. 2009. (gr. 3-3). 42.50 (978-1-61512-492-3(6)) 2003. (Illus.). (J). lib. bdg. 22.60 (978-0-8239-6481-9(7)) Rosen Publishing Group, Inc., The. (PowerKids Pr.).
Dewey, Jennifer Owings. The Shaman & the Water Serpent. Yazzie, Benton, illus. 2007. (ENG.). 40p. (J). 19.95 (978-0-8263-4211-9(6)) Univ. of New Mexico Pr.
Glasscock, Sarah. The Southwest: Set Of 6. 2011. (Navigators Ser.). (J). pap. 48.00 net. (978-1-4108-5104-8(4)) Benchmark Education Co.
—The Southwest: Text Pairs. 2008. (Bridges/Navigators Ser.). (J). (gr. 4). 89.00 (978-1-4108-8397-1(3)) Benchmark Education Co.
Goodman, Michael E. Wyatt Earp. 2005. (Legends of the West Ser.). (Illus.). 48p. (J). (gr. 5-9). lib. bdg. 21.95 (978-1-58341-339-5(1), Creative Education) Creative Co., The.
Green, Carl R. & Sanford, William R. Billy the Kid. rev. ed. 2008. (Outlaws & Lawmen of the Wild West, Revised Edition Ser.). (Illus.). 48p. (J). (gr. 5-18). lib. bdg. 25.27 (978-0-7660-3173-9(X)) Enslow Pubs., Inc.
—Wyatt Earp. rev. ed. 2008. (Outlaws & Lawmen of the Wild West, Revised Edition Ser.). (Illus.). 48p. (J). (gr. 5-18). lib. bdg. 25.27 (978-0-7660-3174-6(8)) Enslow Pubs., Inc.
Hall, Margaret C. & Hall, Margaret. Venom & Visions: Art of the Southwest. 2007. (Shockwave: Arts & Culture Ser.). (ENG., Illus.). 36p. (J). (gr. 4-8). 25.00 (978-0-531-17788-4(2), Children's Pr.) Scholastic Library Publishing.
Hazleton, Amie. Francisco Vasquez de Coronado: An Explorer of the Southwest. 2017. (World Explorers Ser.). (ENG., Illus.). 32p. (gr. 3-4). lib. bdg. 27.32 (978-1-5157-4203-6(2)) Capstone Press of Coughlan Cos.
Healy, Nick. Billy the Kid. 2005. (Legends of the West (Creative Education) Ser.). (Illus.). 48p. (J). (gr. 5-9). lib. bdg. 21.95 (978-1-58341-335-7(9), Creative Education) Creative Co., The.
HELMAN, Wolfe Jecan. C Is for Coyote: A Southwest Alphabet Book, Vol. 2017. (ENG., Illus.). 32p. (J). (gr. k-3). 7.95 (978-1-63076-300-8(4)) Muddy Boots Pr.
Hernández, Roger E. Early Explorations: The 1500s. 2008. (Hispanic America Ser.). 80p. (gr. 5-18). lib. bdg. 34.21 (978-0-7614-2937-1(9), Benchmark Bks.) Marshall Cavendish Corp.
Katchur, Matthew & Sterngass, Jon. Spanish Settlement in North America: 1822-1898. Overmyer-Velazquez, Mark, ed. 2006. (Latino-American History Ser.). (Illus.). 106p. (YA). (gr. 5-9). lib. bdg. 35.00 (978-0-8160-6442-7(3)) Facts On File, Inc.
Kavanagh, James. Southwest Desert Wildlife Nature. Leung, Raymond, illus. 2nd ed. 2011. (Nature Activity Book Ser.). (ENG.). 32p. (J). (gr. 4-7). act. bk. ed. 6.95 (978-1-58355-585-9(4)) Western National Parks Assn.
Let's Explore the Southwest. 2013. (Road Trip: Exploring America's Regions Ser.). 24p. (J). (gr. 2-5). pap. 48.90 (978-1-4339-9151-6(9)) Stevens, Gareth Publishing LLLP.
Magoon, Kekla. The Zebulon Pike Expedition, 1 vol. 2009. (Essential Events Set 3 Ser.). (ENG., Illus.). 112p. (J). (gr. 6-12). lib. bdg. 35.64 (978-1-60453-518-1(0)) ABDO Publishing Co.
Maynard, Charles W. Zebulon Pike: Soldier-Explorer of the American Southwest. 2009. (Famous Explorers of the American West Ser.). 24p. (gr. 3-4). 42.50 (978-1-61512-506-7(X), PowerKids Pr.) Rosen Publishing Group, Inc., The.
McNeese, Tim. Santa Fe. 2007. (Colonial Settlements in America Ser.). (Illus.). 116p. (YA). (gr. 5-9). lib. bdg. 30.00 (978-0-7910-9332-0(8)) Facts On File, Inc.
Miller, Reagan & Peppas, Lynn. What's in the Southwest? Crabtree Publishing Staff, ed. 2011. (All Around the U.S. Ser.: No. 4). (ENG.). 32p. (J). (gr. 3-6). pap. (978-0-7787-1832-1(8)) Crabtree Publishing Co.
Mountjoy, Shane. Francisco Coronado & the Seven Cities of Gold. Goetzmann, William H., ed. 2005. (Explorers of New Lands Ser.). (Illus.). 160p. (gr. 5-8). lib. bdg. 30.00 (978-0-7910-8631-5(3)) Facts On File, Inc.
Peppas, Lynn. Why Francisco Coronado Matters to Texas. 2014. (Illus.). 32p. (J). lib. bdg. 26.25 (978-1-4777-0909-2(6)) Rosen Publishing Group, Inc., The.
Perritano, John. Spanish Missions. 2010. (True Book(tm), a — Spanish Missions Ser.). (Illus.). 48p. (J). (gr. 2-5). 31.00 (978-0-531-20575-4(4)); pap. 6.95 (978-0-531-21238-7(6)) Scholastic Library Publishing.

Smith-Llera, Danielle. People & Places of the Southwest. 2016. (United States by Region Ser.). (ENG., Illus.). 32p. (gr. 3-4). lib. bdg. 27.32 *(978-1-5157-2442-1(5)*, Fact Finders) Capstone Press of Coughlan Cos.

Steele, Christy. California & the Southwest Join the United States. 2005. (America's Westward Expansion Ser.). (Illus.). 48p. (gr. 5-12). lib. bdg. 31.00 *(978-0-8368-5786-3(0)*, Gareth Stevens Secondary Library) Stevens, Gareth Publishing LLLP.

Stein, R. Conrad. Spanish Missionaries: Bringing Spanish Culture to the Americas. 2005. (Proud Heritage: the Hispanic Library). (ENG., Illus.). 40p. (J). (gr. 3-6). 29.93 *(978-1-59296-387-4(0)*, 200014) Child's World, Inc., The.

Tarbox, A. D. A Desert Food Chain: Nature's Bounty. 2nd ed. 2015. (Illus.). 80p. *(978-1-60818-539-9(7)*, Creative Education) Creative Co., The.

Thompson, Paul B. Billy the Kid: It Was a Game of Two & I Got There First. 2010. (Americans—the Spirit of a Nation Ser.). (Illus.). 128p. (J). lib. bdg. 33.27 *(978-0-7660-3480-8(1))* Enslow Pubs., Inc.

U. S. National Geographic Society Staff, contrib. by. The Southwest Today. 2007. (Nonfiction Reading & Writing Workshops Ser.). (ENG., Illus.). 32p. (J). pap. 17.95 *(978-0-7922-4535-3(0))* CENGAGE Learning.

Urban, William. Wyatt Earp: The O. K. Corral & the Law of the American West. 2009. (Library of American Lives & Times Ser.). 112p. (gr. 5-5). 69.20 *(978-1-60853-512-5(6))* Rosen Publishing Group, Inc., The.

Walsh, Steve. Zebulon Montgomery Pike: Explorer & Military Officer. 2011. (ENG & SPA., Illus.). 54p. (J). pap. 8.95 *(978-0-86541-123-4(9))* Filter Pr., LLC.

Weisberg, Barbara & Haley, Alex. Coronado's Golden Quest. Eagle, Mike, illus. 2009. (Steck-Vaughn Stories of America Ser.). (ENG.). 88p. (gr. 3-8). pap. 14.20 *(978-0-8114-8072-7(0))* Houghton Mifflin Harcourt Publishing Co.

Wiewandt, Thomas A. Hidden Life of the Desert. 2nd ed. 2010. (J). *(978-0-87842-555-6(1))* Mountain Pr. Publishing Co., Inc.

Wiseman, Blaine. The Southwest. 2016. (Illus.). 48p. (J). *(978-1-5105-1142-2(3))* SmartBook Media, Inc.

World Book, Inc Staff, contrib. by. Indians of the Southwest. 2009. (J). *(978-0-7166-2142-3(8))* World Bk., Inc.

Worth, Richard. Independence for Latino America. 2006. (Latino-American History Ser.). 112p. (YA). (gr. 5-9). 35.00 *(978-0-8160-6441-0(5))* Facts On File, Inc.

—The Texas War of Independence. 2008. (Hispanic America Ser.). 80p. (gr. 5-18). lib. bdg. 34.21 *(978-0-7614-2934-0(4)*, Benchmark Bks.) Marshall Cavendish Corp.

Wyatt Earp. 2010. (Legends of the Wild West Ser.). (Illus.). 112p. (gr. 6-12). 35.00 *(978-1-60413-597-8(2)*, Chelsea Hse.) Facts On File, Inc.

SOUTHWEST, NEW—FICTION

Allred, Sylvester. Jabber the Steller's Jay. Iverson, Diane, illus. 2017. (ENG.). 32p. (J). (gr. k-3). 16.99 *(978-1-943328-89-5(7)*, West Winds Pr.) Graphic Arts Ctr. Publishing Co.

Brimner, Larry Dane. Trick or Treat, Old Armadillo. Catalano, Dominic, illus. 2010. (ENG.). 32p. (J). (gr. k-2). 16.95 *(978-1-59078-758-8(7))* Boyds Mills Pr.

Browne, Vee. The Stone Cutter & the Navajo Maiden. Manavi, Lorraine Begay, tr. from ENG. Brycelea, Clifford & Yazzie, Johnson, illus. 2008. (NAV & ENG.). 32p. (J). (gr. -1-3). 17.95 *(978-1-893354-92-0(X))* Salina Bookshelf Inc.

Bruchac, Joseph. Killer of Enemies, 1 vol. 2013. (Killer of Enemies Ser.). (ENG.). 400p. (YA). 19.95 *(978-1-62014-143-4(4)*, Tu Bks.) Lee & Low Bks., Inc.

—Trail of the Dead, 1 vol. 2015. (Killer of Enemies Ser.). (ENG.). 400p. (YA). 19.95 *(978-1-62014-261-5(9))* Lee & Low Bks., Inc.

Cantor, Jillian. The Life of Glass. 2010. (ENG.). 352p. (YA). (gr. 8-18). 16.99 *(978-0-06-168651-1(4)*, HarperTeen) HarperCollins Pubs.

Carrillo, P. S. Desert Passage. 2008. (ENG.). 192p. (YA). (gr. 6-18). pap. 10.95 *(978-1-55885-517-5(3)*, Piñata Books) Arte Publico Pr.

Córdova, Amy. Abuelita's Heart. Córdova, Amy, illus. 2008. (ENG., Illus.). 32p. (J). (gr. -1-3). 13.99 *(978-1-4169-7576-2(4)*, Simon & Schuster/Paula Wiseman Bks.) Simon & Schuster/Paula Wiseman Bks.

Crum, Sally. Race to the River: The Ancient Journey Continues. 2009. (YA). pap. 12.95 *(978-1-932738-72-8(X))* Western Reflections Publishing Co.

Fitzmaurice, Kathryn. A Diamond in the Desert. 2013. (ENG.). 272p. (J). (gr. 5). pap. 6.99 *(978-0-14-242437-7(4)*, Puffin Books) Penguin Young Readers Group.

Gutman, Dan. From Texas with Love. 2014. (ENG.). (J). (gr. 3-7). (Genius Files Ser.: 4). 304p. pap. 6.99 *(978-0-06-182775-4(4))*; (Genius Files Ser.: Bk. 4). (Illus.). 288p. 16.99 *(978-0-06-182773-0(8))* HarperCollins Pubs.

—From Texas with Love. 2014. (Genius Files Ser.: 4). (J). lib. bdg. 17.20 *(978-0-606-36462-1(5))* Turtleback Bks.

—The Genius Files #4: from Texas with Love. 2014. (Genius Files Ser.: 4). 288p. (J). (gr. 3-7). lib. bdg. 17.89 *(978-0-06-182774-7(6))* HarperCollins Pubs.

Hobbs, Will. The Big Wander. 2004. (Illus.). 181p. (J). (gr. 5-9). 13.65 *(978-0-7569-4970-9(X))* Perfection Learning Corp.

Jennings, Terry Catasús. Vivian & the Legend of the Hoodoos. Saroff, Phyllis, illus. 2017. (ENG & SPA.). 32p. (J). (gr. k-3). 17.95 *(978-1-62855-957-6(8))* Arbordale Publishing.

—Viviana y la Leyenda de Los Hoodoos. Saroff, Phyllis, illus. 2017. (SPA.). 32p. (J). (gr. k-3). pap. 9.95 *(978-1-62855-959-0(4))* Arbordale Publishing.

La Farge, Oliver. Cochise of Arizona. 2014. 222p. pap. 24.95 *(978-0-86534-675-8(5))* Sunstone Pr.

Lamadrid, Enrique R. Amadito & the Hero Children: Amadito y los Ninos Heroes. Cordova, Amy, illus. 2011. (SPA & ENG.). 60p. (J). 19.95 *(978-0-8263-4979-8(X))* Univ. of New Mexico Pr.

—Amadito & the Hero Children: Amadito y Los Niños Héroes. Córdova, Amy, illus. 2011. (SPA & ENG.). (J). *(978-0-8263-4980-4(3))*; *(978-0-8263-4978-1(1))* Univ. of New Mexico Pr.

Lowell, Susan. A Very Hairy Christmas. Harris, Jim, illus. 2012. (J). *(978-1-933855-80-6(0))* Rio Nuevo Pubs.

McCormack, Caren McNelly. The Fiesta Dress: A Quinceanera Tale, 0 vols. Aviles, Martha, illus. 2012. (ENG.). 42p. (J). (gr. k-4). pap. 7.99 *(978-0-7614-6236-1(8)*, 9780761462361, Amazon Children's Publishing) Amazon Publishing.

Muldoon, Kathleen M. The Runaway Skeleton. Hilliker, Phillip, illus. 2008. (Vortex Bks.). (ENG.). 112p. (gr. 2-3). 26.65 *(978-1-4342-0800-2(1)*, Vortex Bks.) Stone Arch Bks.

Muller, Seth. Keepers of the WindClaw Chronicles: The Day of Storms, 3 vols., Vol. 2. Dubay, Tayloe, ed. Whitethorne, Bahe, Jr., illus. 2nd ed. 2010. 224p. (J). pap. 12.95 *(978-1-893354-10-4(5))* Salina Bookshelf Inc.

—Keepers of the WindClaw Chronicles: The Mockingbird's Manual. Tayloe, McConnell Dubay, ed. Whitethorne, Bahe, Jr., illus. 2009. (ENG.). 128p. (J). (gr. 4-7). pap. 12.95 *(978-1-893354-04-3(0))* Salina Bookshelf Inc.

O'Dell, Scott. Sing down the Moon. 2010. (ENG.). 144p. (J). (gr. 2-5). pap. 7.99 *(978-0-547-40632-9(0))* Houghton Mifflin Harcourt Publishing Co.

—Sing down the Moon. 2011. 9.00 *(978-0-7848-3596-8(9)*, Everbind) Marco Bk. Co.

Parpan, Justin, illus. Gwango's Lonesome Trail. 2006. 32p. (J). (gr. -1-3). 15.95 *(978-1-60108-004-2(2))* Red Cygnet Pr.

Polette, Keith. Isabel & the Hungry Coyote/Isabel y el Coyote Hambriento. Raven Tree Press Staff, ed. Szegedy, Esther, illus. 2004.Tr. of Isabel y el coyote Hambriento. (SPA & ENG.). 32p. (J). (gr. -1-3). 16.95 *(978-0-9724973-0-5(7)*, 626999, Raven Tree Pr.) Continental Sales, Inc.

Randles, Slim & Montoya, Jerry, illus. Ol' Jimmy Dollar. 2015. 42p. (J). *(978-1-936744-40-4(6))* LPD Pr.

Rivera-Ashford, Roni Capin & Johnson, Richard. Hip Hip Hooray, It's Monsoon Day! 2007. (ENG & SPA.). (YA). pap. 15.95 *(978-1-886679-36-8(3))* Arizona Sonora Desert Museum Pr.

Roach, Joyce Gibson. Horned Toad Canyon. Shaw, Charles, illus. 2003. (ENG.). 48p. (J). (gr. 2-4). 17.95 *(978-1-931721-01-1(7)*, c2d211ff-dcbc-4d55-8600-9edaa91d316d) Bright Sky Pr.

Spady, Angela & Thomas Nelson Publishing Staff. Channing o'Banning & the Turquoise Trail, 1 vol. 2015. (ENG., Illus.). 128p. (J). pap. 6.99 *(978-0-7180-3236-4(5))* Nelson, Thomas Inc.

Wells, Rosemary. Ivy Takes Care. LaMarche, Jim, illus. 2015. (ENG.). 208p. (J). (gr. 3-7). pap. 6.99 *(978-0-7636-7660-5(8))* Candlewick Pr.

SOUTHWEST, OLD

Here are entered works on the section which comprised the southwestern part of the United States before the cessions of land from Mexico following the Mexican War. It includes Louisiana, Texas, Arkansas, Tennessee, Kentucky and Missouri.

Gallagher, Derek, text. Ancient Dwellings of the Southwest. 2004. (Illus.). 10p. (J). 16.95 *(978-1-58369-048-2(4))* Western National Parks Assn.

SOUTHWEST, OLD—FICTION

Ts'o, Pauline. Whispers of the Wolf. 2015. (ENG., Illus.). 40p. (J). (gr. k-3). 16.95 *(978-1-937786-45-8(5)*, Wisdom Tales) World Wisdom, Inc.

SOVEREIGNS

see Kings, Queens, Rulers, etc.

SOVIET UNION

Baker, Lawrence W. Cold War Reference Library Cumulative Index. 2003. (Cold War Reference Library). (ENG.). 85p. (J). 5.00 *(978-0-7876-7667-4(5)*, UXL) Cengage Gale.

—Immigration & Migration Reference. 2004. (US Immigration & Migration Reference Library). (ENG.). (J). 5.00 *(978-0-7876-7734-3(5)*, UXL) Cengage Gale.

Hanes, Sharon M., et al. Cold War: Almanac, 2 vols. 2003. (U-X-L Cold War Reference Library). (Illus.). (J). *(978-0-7876-9087-8(2))*; (ENG., 376p. lib. bdg. 191.00 *(978-0-7876-9089-2(9))* Cengage Gale. (UXL).

Kallen, Stuart A. Primary Sources. 2003. (American War Library). (ENG., Illus.). 112p. (J). 30.85 *(978-1-59018-243-7(X)*, Lucent Bks.) Cengage Gale.

Márquez, Herón. Russia in Pictures. 2nd ed. 2003. (Visual Geography Series, Second Ser.). (ENG., Illus.). 80p. (gr. 5-12). 31.93 *(978-0-8225-0937-0(7))* Lerner Publishing Group.

SOVIET UNION—BIOGRAPHY

The Collapse of the Soviet Union. 2010. (Milestones in World History Ser.). (Illus.). 128p. (C). (gr. 9-18). 35.00 *(978-1-60413-493-3(3)*, Chelsea Hse.) Facts On File, Inc.

Feldman, Heather. Valentina Tereshkova: The First Woman in Space. 2009. (Space Firsts Ser.). 24p. (gr. 3-4). 42.50 *(978-1-60853-114-1(7)*, PowerKids Pr.) Rosen Publishing Group, Inc., The.

Glaser, Jason. Maria Sharapova. 2008. (Sports Idols Ser.). (Illus.). 24p. (J). (gr. 2-5). lib. bdg. 22.60 *(978-1-4042-4181-7(7))* Rosen Publishing Group, Inc., The.

Goldstein, Margaret J. V. I. Lenin. 2007. (Biography Ser.). (Illus.). 112p. (J). (gr. 3-7). lib. bdg. 29.27 *(978-0-8225-5977-1(3)*, Twenty-First Century Bks.) Lerner Publishing Group.

Hubbard, Ben. Yuri Gagarin & the Race to Space. 2015. (Adventures in Space Ser.). (ENG., Illus.). 48p. (gr. 4-6). 33.32 *(978-1-4846-2514-9(5))* Heinemann-Raintree.

McCollum, Sean. Joseph Stalin. 2010. (Wicked History Ser.). (ENG.). 128p. (J). (gr. 6-12). pap. 5.95 *(978-0-531-22355-0(8))*; (Illus.). 31.00 *(978-0-531-20755-0(2))* Scholastic Library Publishing. (Watts, Franklin).

Resnick, Abraham. Lenin: Founder of the Soviet Union. 2004. 132p. (YA). pap. 13.95 *(978-0-595-30701-2(9)*, Authors Choice Pr.) iUniverse, Inc.

Stewart, Mark. Maria Sharapova. 2009. (Today's Superstars Ser.). 48p. (J). (gr. 5-8). pap. 14.05 *(978-1-4339-2160-5(X))*; lib. bdg. 31.95 *(978-1-4339-1967-1(2))* Stevens, Gareth Publishing LLLP.

SOVIET UNION—FICTION

Abadzis, Nick. Laika. 2014. (YA). lib. bdg. 22.10 *(978-0-606-36130-9(8))* Turtleback Bks.

Appleton, Victor. Tom Swift & his Air Glider. 2005. 26.95 *(978-1-4218-1500-8(1)*, 1st World Library - Literary Society) 1st World Publishing, Inc.

Blaine, John. Boy Scouts in Russia. 2006. 25.95 *(978-1-4218-2968-5(1))*; pap. 10.95 *(978-1-4218-3068-1(X))* 1st World Publishing, Inc.

Blue, Sebastien. Liquid Diamond. 2013. 176p. *(978-1-4602-3345-0(X))* FriesenPress.

Bridges, Robin. The Katerina Trilogy, Vol. I: the Gathering Storm. 2012. (ENG.). 400p. (YA). (gr. 7). pap. 9.99 *(978-0-385-74023-4(9)*, Ember) Random Hse. Children's Bks.

—The Katerina Trilogy, Vol. II: the Unfailing Light. 2013. (ENG.). 320p. (YA). (gr. 7). pap. 9.99 *(978-0-385-74025-8(5)*, Ember) Random Hse. Children's Bks.

Carson, John E. & Carson, Marlene R. Ramblin' Rose: The Porcelain Mines in Russia. 2007. (Ramblin' Rose Ser.). 191p. (J). (gr. 8-12). per. 8.99 *(978-0-9776043-7-1(3))* Beast Stew.

Celenza, Anna Harwell. Pictures at an Exhibition. Kitchel, JoAnn E., illus. 2016. (Once upon a Masterpiece Ser.). (ENG.). 32p. (J). (gr. 1-4). lib. bdg. 16.95 *(978-1-58089-528-6(X))* Charlesbridge Publishing, Inc.

Constable, Cathryn. The Wolf Princess. (ENG.). 320p. (J). (gr. 5-9). 2014. pap. 6.99 *(978-0-545-52841-2(0))* 2013. 16.99 *(978-0-545-52839-9(9))* Scholastic, Inc. (Chicken Hse., The).

Durbin, William. The Darkest Evening. 2011. (Fesler-Lampert Minnesota Heritage Ser.). (ENG.). 248p. pap. 11.95 *(978-0-8166-7568-5(6))* Univ. of Minnesota Pr.

Edmondson, Nathan. Black Widow - The Finely Woven Thread, Vol. 1. 2014. (ENG., Illus.). 144p. (YA). (gr. 8-17). pap. 17.99 *(978-0-7851-8819-3(3))* Marvel Worldwide, Inc.

Flannigan, Liz. Starlight Grey. Docampo, Valeria, illus. 2013. (Magic Stories Ser.). (ENG.). 48p. (J). (gr. 1-4). pap. 8.99 *(978-1-84686-778-1(9))* Barefoot Bks., Inc.

Grant, Myrna. Ivan & the American Journey. 2006. (Flamingo Fiction 9-13s Ser.). (ENG., Illus.). 144p. (J). (gr. 4-7). per. 6.99 *(978-1-84550-131-0(4)*, 219b73c2-7f68-49a8-b40f-d5dbfb745039) Christian Focus Pubns. GBR. Dist: Bookmasters Distribution.

—Ivan & the Hidden Bible. 2006. (Flamingo Fiction 9-13s Ser.). (ENG., Illus.). 144p. (J). (gr. 4-7). per. 6.99 *(978-1-84550-133-4(0)*, 9394aef3-942b-4824-b0b8-0ae3449d32e0) Christian Focus Pubns. GBR. Dist: Bookmasters Distribution.

—Ivan & the Informer. 2013. (Flamingo Fiction 9-13s Ser.). (ENG., Illus.). 128p. (J). (gr. 1-8). per. 6.99 *(978-1-84550-134-1(9)*, a4873bb8-0b7a-4393-a40a-6315d03042d2) Christian Focus Pubns. GBR. Dist: Bookmasters Distribution.

—Ivan & the Secret in the Suitcase. 2006. (Flamingo Fiction 9-13s Ser.). (ENG., Illus.). 144p. (J). (gr. 4-7). per. 6.99 *(978-1-84550-136-5(5)*, 90ba43f9-c4f3-4eac-aa9d-e552a2ffb74d) Christian Focus Pubns. GBR. Dist: Bookmasters Distribution.

Hergé. The Calculus Affair. (Illus.). 62p. (J). 19.95 *(978-0-8288-5014-8(3))* French & European Pubns., Inc.

—Tintin in the Land of the Soviets. 2007. (Adventures of Tintin: Original Classic Ser.). (ENG., Illus.). 144p. (gr. 3-17). pap. 13.99 *(978-0-316-00374-2(3))* Little, Brown Bks. for Young Readers.

Horowitz, Anthony. Russian Roulette. 2014. (Alex Rider Ser.: 10). lib. bdg. 19.65 *(978-0-606-36189-7(8))* Turtleback Bks.

—Russian Roulette: The Story of an Assassin. 2014. (Alex Rider Ser.). (ENG.). 432p. (J). (gr. 5). pap. 8.99 *(978-0-14-751231-4(X)*, Puffin Books) Penguin Young Readers Group.

Howell, Gill. Snow King. Cann, Helen, illus. 2005. (ENG.). 24p. (J). lib. bdg. 23.65 *(978-1-59646-742-2(8))* Dingles & Co.

Johnson, Vargie. Catherine the Great the Victorious: What Made Them Famous? 2006. 156p. (J). per. 15.00 *(978-1-931195-96-6(X))* KiwE Publishing, Ltd.

Katz, Gwen C. Among the Red Stars. 2017. 384p. (YA). (gr. 8). 17.99 ***(978-0-06-264274-5(X)***, HarperTeen) HarperCollins Pubs.

Kiem, Elizabeth. Dancer, Daughter, Traitor, Spy. 2014. (Bolshoi Saga Ser.: 1). (ENG., Illus.). 292p. (YA). (gr. 9). pap. 10.99 *(978-1-61695-422-2(1)*, Soho Teen) Soho Pr., Inc.

King, Dedie. I See the Sun in Russia. Ossipova, Irina, tr. Inglese, Judith, illus. 2012. (I See the Sun Ser.: 0). (RUS & ENG.). 40p. (J). (gr. 1-2). 12.95 *(978-1-935874-08-9(X))* Satya Hse. Pubns.

Ludmila's Way - Teaching Guide. 2003. (J). 17.95 *(978-1-55942-192-8(4))* Witcher Productions.

Maguire, Gregory. Egg & Spoon. (ENG.). 496p. (YA). (gr. 7). 2015. pap. 11.99 *(978-0-7636-8016-9(8))* 2014. (Illus.). 17.99 *(978-0-7636-7220-1(3))* Candlewick Pr.

Optic, Oliver, pseud. Northern Lands: Or, Young America in Russia & Prussia; A Story of Travel & Adventure / by William T. Adams (Oliver Optic). 2006. 384p. per. 26.99 *(978-1-4255-4074-6(0))* Michigan Publishing.

Pierce, Nicola. City of Fate. 2014. (ENG.). 272p. (J). pap. 11.00 ***(978-1-84717-337-9(3))*** O'Brien Pr., Ltd., The IRL. Dist: Dufour Editions, Inc.

Ransome, Arthur. Old Peter's Russian Tales. 2007. 180p. per. 12.95 *(978-1-60312-321-1(0))*; 24.95 *(978-1-60312-739-4(9))* Aegypan.

—Old Peter's Russian Tales. 2007. (ENG.). 200p. pap. 19.99 *(978-1-4346-0606-8(6))*; 222p. pap. 22.99 *(978-1-4346-0681-5(3))* Creative Media Partners, LLC.

—Old Peter's Russian Tales. 2005. 35.00 *(978-1-55742-465-5(9))*; pap. 15.95 *(978-1-55742-456-3(X))* Wildside Pr., LLC.

Stilton, Thea. Thea Stilton & the Lost Letters. 2015. (Thea Stilton Ser.: 21). (Illus.). 159p. (J). lib. bdg. 18.40 *(978-0-606-37061-5(7))* Turtleback Bks.

Vermeulen, Mariska. Anton & Boris Finger Puppet Book. van de Leijgraaf, Deborah, illus. 2016. (My Best Friend & Me Ser.). (ENG.). 10p. (J). (gr. -1-k). bds., bds. 6.99 *(978-0-7641-6831-4(2))* Barron's Educational Series, Inc.

Wang, Jack & Wang, Holman. Leo Tolstoy's War & Peace. 2016. (ENG., Illus.). 24p. (J). (gr. -1 — 1). bds. 9.95 *(978-1-4521-5245-5(4))* Chronicle Bks. LLC.

Wilke, Daria & Schwartz, Marian. Playing a Part. 2015. (ENG.). 176p. (J). (gr. 7). 18.99 *(978-0-545-72607-8(7))* Scholastic, Inc.

Yehoshua, A. B. & Dostoyevsky, Fyodor. The Story of Crime & Punishment. Schoffman, Stuart, tr. from HEB. Bougaeva, Sonja, illus. 2016. (Save the Story Ser.). (ENG.). 104p. (J). (gr. 3-7). 19.95 *(978-1-78269-014-6(X)*, Pushkin Press) Steerforth Pr.

Yelchin, Eugene. Breaking Stalin's Nose. 2013. (J). lib. bdg. 18.40 *(978-0-606-32308-6(2)*, Turtleback) Turtleback Bks.

SOVIET UNION—HISTORY

Anderson, M. T. Symphony for the City of the Dead: Dmitri Shostakovich & the Siege of Leningrad. 2017. (ENG.). 464p. (YA). (gr. 9). 26.95 *(978-0-606-39102-3(9))* Turtleback Bks.

Blomquist, Christopher. A Primary Source Guide to Russia. 2005. (Countries of the World). (Illus.). 24p. (J). (gr. k-5). lib. bdg. 22.60 *(978-1-4042-2756-9(3)*, PowerKids Pr.) Rosen Publishing Group, Inc., The.

Burgan, Michael. Miracle on Ice: How a Stunning Upset United a Country. 2016. (Captured History Sports Ser.). (ENG.). 64p. (gr. 5-7). pap. 8.95 *(978-0-7565-5294-7(X)*, CPB Grades 4-8) Compass Point Bks.

The Collapse of the Soviet Union. 2010. (Milestones in World History Ser.). (Illus.). 128p. (C). (gr. 9-18). 35.00 *(978-1-60413-493-3(3)*, Chelsea Hse.) Facts On File, Inc.

Dunn, Joeming & Dunn, Ben. Laika: The 1st Dog in Space, 1 vol. 2011. (Famous Firsts: Animals Making History Ser.). (ENG., Illus.). 32p. (YA). (gr. 3-6). 28.50 *(978-1-61641-641-6(6))* Magic Wagon.

Feldman, Heather. Valentina Tereshkova: The First Woman in Space. 2003. (Space Firsts Ser.). (Illus.). 24p. (J). lib. bdg. 22.60 *(978-0-8239-6246-4(6)*, PowerKids Pr.) Rosen Publishing Group, Inc., The.

Gay, Kathlyn. The Aftermath of the Russian Revolution. 2009. (Aftermath of History Ser.). (ENG.). 160p. (gr. 9-12). 38.60 *(978-0-8225-9092-7(1))* Lerner Publishing Group.

Goodman, Michael E. Spies Around the World: the KGB & Other Russian Spies. 2014. (Spies Around the World Ser.). (ENG., Illus.). 48p. (J). (gr. 4-7). pap. 12.00 *(978-0-89812-970-0(2)*, Creative Paperbacks) Creative Co., The.

Harkins, Susan Sales & Harkins, William H. The Fall of the Soviet Union 1991. 2007. (Monumental Milestones Ser.). (Illus.). 48p. (YA). (gr. 4-7). lib. bdg. 29.95 *(978-1-58415-539-3(6))* Mitchell Lane Pubs., Inc.

Hunt, Jilly. Russia, 1 vol. 2012. (Countries Around the World Ser.). (ENG.). 48p. (gr. 3-6). pap. 9.95 *(978-1-4329-6136-7(5))*; lib. bdg. 33.32 *(978-1-4329-6110-7(1))* Heinemann-Raintree. (NA-h).

Murray, Laura K. Spies in the KGB. 2016. (Illus.). 24p. (J). *(978-1-60818-617-4(2)*, Creative Education) Creative Co., The.

Price, Sean. Ivan the Terrible: Tsar of Death. 2008. (Wicked History Ser.). (ENG.). 128p. (J). (gr. 6-18). pap. 5.95 *(978-0-531-20500-6(2)*, Watts, Franklin) Scholastic Library Publishing.

Russell, Henry & National Geographic Kids Staff. Russia. 2008. (Countries of the World Ser.). (ENG., Illus.). 64p. (J). (gr. 5). lib. bdg. 27.90 *(978-1-4263-0259-6(2)*, National Geographic Children's Bks.) National Geographic Society.

The Russian Federation: Then & Now. 2014. (The Former Soviet Union: Then & Now). (ENG., Illus.). 80p. (J). lib. bdg. *(978-1-60152-692-2(X))* ReferencePoint Pr., Inc.

Suib, Stella. Inside Russia's SVR: The Foreign Intelligence Service. 2005. (Illus.). 63p. (YA). reprint ed. 26.00 *(978-0-7567-8668-7(1))* DIANE Publishing Co.

Todd, Allan. The Soviet Union & Post-Soviet Russia (1924-2000) 2nd rev. ed. 2016. (IB Diploma Ser.). (ENG., Illus.). 334p. pap. 35.63 *(978-1-316-50369-0(0))* Cambridge Univ. Pr.

Waller, Sally. Imperial Russia, Revolution & the Establishment of the Soviet Union (1855-1924) 2nd rev. ed. 2016. (IB Diploma Ser.). (ENG.). 294p. pap. 30.31 *(978-1-316-50366-9(6))* Cambridge Univ. Pr.

Wittrock, Jeni. Laika the Space Dog: First Hero in Outer Space, 1 vol. Toth, Shannon, illus. 2014. (Animal Heroes Ser.). (ENG.). 32p. (gr. k-2). 28.65 *(978-1-4795-5463-8(4))* Picture Window Bks.

Wittrock, Jeni, et al. Animal Heroes, 1 vol. 2014. (Animal Heroes Ser.). (ENG.). 32p. (gr. k-2). 114.60 *(978-1-4795-5555-0(X))* Picture Window Bks.

SOVIET UNION—HISTORY—FICTION

Barrow, Randi. Saving Zasha. 2013. (ENG.). 256p. (J). (gr. 3-7). pap. 6.99 *(978-0-545-20633-4(2)*, Scholastic Paperbacks) Scholastic, Inc.

Dueck, Adele. Nettie's Journey, 1 vol. 2005. (From Many Peoples Ser.). (ENG., Illus.). 216p. (J). (gr. 4-7). per. 7.95 *(978-1-55050-322-7(7))* Coteau Bks. CAN. Dist: Orca Bk. Pubs. USA.

Durbin, William. The Darkest Evening. 2011. (Fesler-Lampert Minnesota Heritage Ser.). (ENG.). 248p. pap. 11.95 *(978-0-8166-7568-5(6))* Univ. of Minnesota Pr.

Haar, Jaap Ter & Mearns, Martha. Boris. Poortvliet, Rien, illus. 2009. (J). pap. *(978-0-921100-72-0(8))* Inheritance Pubns.

Haddix, Margaret Peterson. Risked. 2013. (Missing Ser.: Bk. 6). (ENG., Illus.). 320p. (J). (gr. 3-7). 16.99 *(978-1-4169-8984-4(6)*, Simon & Schuster Bks. For Young Readers) Simon & Schuster Bks. For Young Readers.

—Risked. 2014. (Missing Ser.: 6). lib. bdg. 19.65 *(978-0-606-36096-8(4))* Turtleback Bks.

Hood, Ann. Anastasia Romanov: The Last Grand Duchess. Zilber, Denis, illus. 2014. (Treasure Chest Ser.: 10). (ENG.). 240p. (J). (gr. 3-7). 15.99 *(978-0-448-46770-2(4))*;No. 10. 6.99 *(978-0-448-46771-9(2))* Penguin Young Readers Group. (Grosset & Dunlap).

Kiem, Elizabeth. Orphan, Agent, Prima, Pawn. 2017. (Bolshoi Saga Ser.: 3). (ENG.). 320p. (YA). (gr. 9). 18.99 ***(978-1-61695-655-4(0)***, Soho Teen) Soho Pr., Inc.

Lasky, Kathryn. Broken Song. 2007. (ENG.). 160p. (J). (gr. 5-18). 6.99 *(978-0-14-240741-7(0)*, Puffin Books) Penguin Young Readers Group.

—The Night Journey. 2005. (ENG., Illus.). 160p. (J). (gr. 3-7). pap. 5.99 *(978-0-14-240322-8(9)*, Puffin Books) Penguin Young Readers Group.

—The Night Journey. 2005. 151p. (gr. 3-7). 16.00 *(978-0-7569-5062-0(7))* Perfection Learning Corp.

Meyer, Carolyn. Anastasia & Her Sisters. 2015. (ENG., Illus.). 320p. (YA). (gr. 7). 17.99 *(978-1-4814-0326-9(5)*, Simon & Schuster Bks. For Young Readers) Simon & Schuster Bks. For Young Readers.

Miller, Sarah. The Lost Crown. 2012. (ENG., Illus.). 448p. (YA). (gr. 7). pap. 9.99 *(978-1-4169-8341-5(4)*, Atheneum Bks. for Young Readers) Simon & Schuster Children's Publishing.

Patrick, J. Nelle. Tsarina. 2014. (ENG.). 336p. (YA). (gr. 7). 17.99 *(978-1-59514-693-9(8)*, Razorbill) Penguin Young Readers Group.

S

Sedgwick, Marcus. Blood Red, Snow White. 2016. (ENG.). 320p. (YA). 17.99 (978-1-62672-547-8(0), 9781626725478) Roaring Brook Pr.

Sepetys, Ruta. Between Shades of Gray. 2009. 10.36 (978-0-7848-3779-5(1), Everbind) Marco Bk. Co.

—Between Shades of Gray. (ENG., (YA). (gr. 7-18). 2012. Illus.). 384p. pap. 9.99 (978-0-14-242059-1(X), Speak) 2011. 352p. 17.99 (978-0-399-25412-3(9), Philomel Bks.) Penguin Young Readers Group.

—Between Shades of Gray. l.t. ed. 2011. (ENG.). 420p. (YA). 23.99 (978-1-4104-4083-9(4)) Thorndike Pr.

—Between Shades of Gray. 2012. lib. bdg. 20.85 (978-0-606-26089-3(7), Turtleback) Turtleback Bks.

Standiford, Natalie. The Boy on the Bridge. 2013. (ENG.). 256p. (J). (gr. 9). 17.99 (978-0-545-33481-5(0), Scholastic Pr.) Scholastic, Inc.

Tildes, Phyllis Limbacher. The Magic Babushka. Tildes, Phyllis Limbacher, illus. 2009. (ENG., Illus.). 32p. (J). (gr. k-3). pap. 7.95 (978-1-58089-225-4(6)) Charlesbridge Publishing, Inc.

Verne, Jules. Michael Strogoff. 2006. 408p. pap. 26.45 (978-1-59462-432-2(1), Book Jungle) Standard Pubns., Inc.

—Miguel Strogoff. (SPA., Illus.). 176p. (YA). 11.95 (978-84-7281-109-6(3), AF1109) Auriga, Ediciones S.A. ESP. Dist: Continental Bk. Co., Inc.

Verne, Jules & Verne, Julio. Miguel Strogoff. (Coleccion Clasicos de la Juventud). (SPA., Illus.). 236p. (J). 12.95 (978-84-7189-106-8(9), ORT305) Ortells, Alfredo Editorial S.L. ESP. Dist: Continental Bk. Co., Inc.

Whelan, Gloria. Angel on the Square. 2004. 288p. (gr. 5-9). 20.00 (978-0-7569-4062-1(1)) Perfection Learning Corp.

—Burying the Sun. 2004. 224p. (J). (gr. 5-18). (ENG.). 15.99 (978-0-06-054112-5(1)); lib. bdg. 16.89 (978-0-06-054113-2(X)) HarperCollins Pubs.

Wulffson, Don L. & Wulffson, Don. Soldier X. 2003. (ENG.). 240p. (YA). (gr. 7-18). 6.99 (978-0-14-250073-6(9), Speak) Penguin Young Readers Group.

Yelchin, Eugene. Arcady's Goal. Yelchin, Eugene, illus. 2014. (ENG., Illus.). 240p. (J). (gr. 4-7). 15.99 (978-0-8050-9844-0(5), 9780805098440, Holt, Henry & Co. Bks. For Young Readers) Holt, Henry & Co.

—Arcady's Goal. Yelchin, Eugene, illus. 2015. (ENG., Illus.). 256p. (J). (gr. 4-7). pap. 7.99 (978-1-250-06814-9(2), 9781250068149) Square Fish.

—Breaking Stalin's Nose. Yelchin, Eugene, illus. 2011. (ENG., Illus.). 160p. (J). (gr. 4-7). 15.99 (978-0-8050-9216-5(1), 9780805092165, Holt, Henry & Co. Bks. For Young Readers) Holt, Henry & Co.

—Breaking Stalin's Nose. Yelchin, Eugene, illus. 2013. (ENG., Illus.). 176p. (J). (gr. 4-7). pap. 7.99 (978-1-250-03410-6(8), 9781250034106) Square Fish.

SOVIET UNION—HISTORY—1689-1800

Catherine the Great & the Enlightenment in Russia. 2005. (World Leaders Ser.). (Illus.). 160p. (gr. 6-12). lib. bdg. 28.95 (978-1-931798-27-3(3)) Reynolds, Morgan Inc.

Gibson, Karen Bush. The Life & Times of Catherine the Great. 2005. (Biography from Ancient Civilizations Ser.). (Illus.). 48p. (J). (gr. 4-7). lib. bdg. 29.95 (978-1-58415-347-4(4)) Mitchell Lane Pubs., Inc.

Vincent, Zu. Catherine the Great: Empress of Russia. 2009. (Wicked History Ser.). (ENG., Illus.). 128p. (J). (gr. 6-12). 31.00 (978-0-531-21802-0(3), Watts, Franklin) Scholastic Library Publishing.

SOVIET UNION—HISTORY—REVOLUTION, 1905-1907

Engdahl, Sylvia. Bolshevik Revolution. Greenhaven Press Editors, ed. 2013. (Perspectives on Modern World History Ser.). (ENG., Illus.). 224p. (gr. 10-12). lib. bdg. 47.80 (978-0-7377-6363-8(9), Greenhaven Pr., Inc.) Cengage Gale.

SOVIET UNION—HISTORY—1917-1991

Choices Program - Brown University. The Russian Revolution, 2 vols. 2005. (ENG., Illus.). 124p. pap., lab manual ed. 34.00 (978-1-891306-79-2(0)) Choices Program, Watson Institute, Brown Univ.

Joihnson, Robert, compiled by. Lenin, Stalin & Communist Russia: The Myth & Reality of Communism. 2003. (Studymates Ser.). (Illus.). 132p. (C). pap. 27.50 (978-1-84285-039-8(3)) GLMP Ltd. GBR. Dist: Chicago Distribution Ctr.

Sherman, Josepha. The Cold War. 2004. (Chronicle of America's Wars Ser.). (Illus.). 96p. (J). (gr. 5-12). 27.93 (978-0-8225-0150-3(3)) Lerner Publishing Group.

SOVIET UNION—HISTORY—REVOLUTION, 1917-1921

Adcock, Michael. Cambridge Checkpoints VCE History - Russian Revolution 2014-16 & Quiz Me More. 2013. (Cambridge Checkpoints Ser.). (ENG.). pap., stu. ed. (978-1-107-66979-6(0)) Cambridge Univ. Pr.

The Bolshevik Revolution. 2010. (Milestones in World History Ser.). (Illus.). 120p. (J). (gr. 9-18). 35.00 (978-1-60413-279-3(5), Chelsea Hse.) Facts On File, Inc.

Edwards, Judith & Schmermund, Elizabeth. Vladamir Lenin & the Russian Revolution. 2016. (People & Events That Changed the World Ser.). (ENG., Illus.). 128p. (J). (gr. 7-8). 37.27 (978-0-7660-7414-9(5)) Enslow Pubs., Inc.

Fleming, Candace. The Family Romanov: Murder, Rebellion, & the Fall of Imperial Russia. 2014. (ENG., Illus.). 304p. (YA). (gr. 7). 19.99 (978-0-375-86782-8(1)); lib. bdg. 21.99 (978-0-375-96782-5(6)) Random Hse. Children's Bks. (Schwartz & Wade Bks.).

O'Neill, Joseph R. The Bolshevik Revolution, 1 vol. 2009. (Essential Events Set 3 Ser.). (ENG., Illus.). 112p. (J). (gr. 6-12). lib. bdg. 35.64 (978-1-60453-511-2(3)) ABDO Publishing Co.

Trenton, Russell. The Russian Revolution: The Fall of the Tsars & the Rise of Communism. 2015. (Age of Revolution Ser.). (ENG., Illus.). 128p. (J). (gr. 9-10). 35.25 (978-1-68048-032-0(4), Britannica Educational Publishing) Rosen Publishing Group, Inc., The.

Whiting, Jim. The Russian Revolution 1917. 2007. (Monumental Milestones Ser.). (Illus.). 48p. (YA). (gr. 4-7). lib. bdg. 29.95 (978-1-58415-537-9(X)) Mitchell Lane Pubs., Inc.

SOVIET UNION—HISTORY—1925-1953

Joihnson, Robert, compiled by. Lenin, Stalin & Communist Russia: The Myth & Reality of Communism. 2003. (Studymates Ser.). (Illus.). 132p. (C). pap. 27.50 (978-1-84285-039-8(3)) GLMP Ltd. GBR. Dist: Chicago Distribution Ctr.

Jukes, Geoffrey & O'Neill, Robert John. World War II: The Eastern Front 1941-1945. 2010. (World War II: Essential Histories Ser.). (Illus.). 96p. (YA). (gr. 9-12). lib. bdg. 33.25 (978-1-4358-9134-0(1)) Rosen Publishing Group, Inc., The.

McCollum, Sean. Joseph Stalin. 2010. (Wicked History Ser.). (ENG.). 128p. (J). (gr. 6-12). pap. 5.95 (978-0-531-22355-0(8)); (Illus.). 31.00 (978-0-531-20755-0(2)) Scholastic Library Publishing. (Watts, Franklin).

Zuehlke, Jeffrey. Joseph Stalin. 2006. (Biography Ser.). (Illus.). 112p. (J). (gr. 3-7). lib. bdg. 27.93 (978-0-8225-3421-1(5), Twenty-First Century Bks.) Lerner Publishing Group.

SOVIET UNION—KINGS AND RULERS

Price, Sean. Ivan the Terrible: Tsar of Death. 2008. (Wicked History Ser.). (ENG.). 128p. (J). (gr. 6-18). pap. 5.95 (978-0-531-20500-6(2), Watts, Franklin) Scholastic Library Publishing.

SOVIET UNION—POLITICS AND GOVERNMENT

The Collapse of the Soviet Union. 2010. (Milestones in World History Ser.). (Illus.). 128p. (C). (gr. 9-18). 35.00 (978-1-60413-493-3(3), Chelsea Hse.) Facts On File, Inc.

Immell, Myra. The Dissolution of the Soviet Union. 2010. (Perspectives on Modern World History Ser.). (Illus.). 224p. (YA). (gr. 10-12). 42.45 (978-0-7377-4794-2(3), Greenhaven Pr., Inc.) Cengage Gale.

Marcovitz, Hal. Cause & Effect the Fall of the Soviet Union: The Fall of the Soviet Union. 2015. (ENG., Illus.). 80p. (J). lib. bdg. (978-1-60152-792-9(6)) ReferencePoint Pr., Inc.

O'Neill, Joseph R. The Bolshevik Revolution, 1 vol. 2009. (Essential Events Set 3 Ser.). (ENG., Illus.). 112p. (J). (gr. 6-12). lib. bdg. 35.64 (978-1-60453-511-2(3)) ABDO Publishing Co.

Roxburgh, Ellis. John F. Kennedy vs. Nikita Khrushchev. 2015. (History's Greatest Rivals Ser.). (ENG., Illus.). 48p. (J). (gr. 6-8). lib. bdg. 31.95 (978-1-4824-2221-4(2)) Stevens, Gareth Publishing LLLP.

Sasley, Brent. The Cold War in the Middle East, 1950-1991. 2009. (Making of the Middle East Ser.). (Illus.). 80p. (YA). (gr. 7-18). lib. bdg. 22.95 (978-1-4222-0173-2(2)) Mason Crest.

Small, Cathleen. The Collapse of Communism & the Break up of the Soviet Union. 2017. (J). **(978-1-5026-2728-5(0))** Cavendish Square Publishing.

SPACE, OUTER

see Outer Space

SPACE AND TIME

see also Cyberspace; Relativity (Physics); Time Travel

Asimov, Isaac & Hantula, Richard. Space Junk. 2005. (Isaac Asimov's 21st Century Library of the Universe). (Illus.). 32p. (gr. 2-6). lib. bdg. 26.00 (978-0-8368-3983-8(8), Gareth Stevens Learning Library) Stevens, Gareth Publishing LLLP.

Butterfield, Moira. Space. Biggin, Gary & Lipscombe, Nick, illus. 32p. (J). mass mkt. 8.99 (978-0-590-24424-4(8)) Scholastic, Inc.

Hoban, Tana. Over, under & Through. Hoban, Tana, illus. 2008. (ENG., Illus.). 32p. (J). (gr. -1-2). 8.99 (978-1-4169-7541-0(1), Simon & Schuster/Paula Wiseman Bks.) Simon & Schuster/Paula Wiseman Bks.

Jacklin, Karl. A Space in Time. (Illus.). (J). (gr. 3-6). pap. (978-1-876367-04-6(0)) Wizard Bks.

Kagayame, Johnny & Sherman, Josepha. Discovering the Construct of Time. 2011. (Scientist's Guide to Physics Ser.). (YA). (gr. 7-12). lib. bdg. 34.60 (978-1-4488-4703-7(6)) Rosen Publishing Group, Inc., The.

O'Byrne, John, ed. Space. 2007. (Little Guides). (Illus.). 320p. pap. 7.98 (978-1-74089-348-0(4)) Fog City Pr.

Perrin, Clotilde. At the Same Moment, Around the World. 2014. (ENG., Illus.). 36p. (J). (gr. k-3). 17.99 (978-1-4521-2208-3(3)) Chronicle Bks. LLC.

Rand, Casey. Time, 1 vol. 2010. (Measure It! Ser.). (ENG., Illus.). 32p. (gr. 3-6). 33.32 (978-1-4329-3766-9(9)); pap. 8.29 (978-1-4329-3772-0(3)) Heinemann-Raintree. (Heinemann InfoSearch).

Rebman, Nick. What Is on Top? A Book about Positions. 2016. (Concept Fun Ser.). (ENG.). 16p. (J). (gr. -1-2). 25.64 (978-1-5038-0769-3(X), 210617) Child's World, Inc., The.

The Science of Space. 2016. (Illus.). 48p. (J). (978-1-4222-3515-7(7)) Mason Crest.

The Science of Time. 2016. (Illus.). 48p. (J). (978-1-4222-3516-4(5)) Mason Crest.

Wadsworth, Pamela. Amser a Gofod. 2005. (WEL., Illus.). 24p. pap. (978-1-85596-241-5(1)) Dref Wen.

—Golwg Gyntaf Ar Amser a Gofod. 2005. (WEL., Illus.). 24p. pap. (978-1-85596-248-4(9)) Dref Wen.

—Rhagor Am Amser a Gofod. 2005. (WEL., Illus.). 24p. pap. (978-1-85596-242-2(X)) Dref Wen.

Whiting, Jim. Mysteries of the Universe: Space & Time. 2013. (Mysteries of the Universe Ser.). (ENG., Illus.). 48p. (J). (gr. 4-7). pap. 12.00 (978-0-89812-917-5(6), Creative Paperbacks) Creative Co., The.

—Space & Time. 2012. (Mysteries of the Universe Ser.). (Illus.). 48p. (J). (gr. 5-12). 23.95 (978-1-60818-192-6(8), Creative Education) Creative Co., The.

SPACE AND TIME—FICTION

Abela, Deborah. Hollywood. O'Connor, George, illus. 2007. (Spy Force Ser.: 4). (ENG.). 240p. (J). (gr. 3-7). pap. 10.99 (978-1-4169-3969-6(5), Aladdin) Simon & Schuster Children's Publishing.

Adlington, L. J. Glittering Eye. 2009. (ENG.). 320p. (J). (gr. 4-6). pap. 8.99 (978-0-340-95681-6(X)) Hodder & Stoughton GBR. Dist: Hachette Bk. Group.

Ali, Khayyam Esab. The Wormhole Kids Visit President Kennedy. 2004. (ENG., Illus.). 56p. (J). per. 7.95 (978-1-59526-231-8(8)) Aeon Publishing Inc.

Alton, Steve. The Firehills. 2005. (ENG.). 192p. (YA). (gr. 5-12). 15.95 (978-1-57505-798-9(0), Carolrhoda Bks.) Lerner Publishing Group.

—The Malifex. 2003. (Middle Readers Ser.). (Illus.). 182p. (J). (gr. 3-7). 14.95 (978-0-8225-0959-2(8)) Lerner Publishing Group.

Angelini, Josephine. Trail of Tears. 2015. (Worldwalker Trilogy Ser.: 2). (SPA & ENG.). 352p. (YA). (gr. 7). 17.99 (978-1-250-05090-8(1), 9781250050908) Feiwel & Friends.

Baltazar, Art & Aureliani, Franco. Titans in Space, 1 vol. Baltazar, Art & Aureliani, Franco, illus. 2013. (Tiny Titans Ser.). (ENG., Illus.). 32p. (gr. 1-2). lib. bdg. 22.60 (978-1-4342-4698-1(1)) Stone Arch Bks.

Banks, Lynne Reid. The Indian in the Cupboard. 181p. (J). (Indian in the Cupboard Ser.: No. 1). (gr. 4-7). pap. 4.99 (978-0-8072-1433-6(7)); 2004. (Indian in the Cupboard Ser.). (gr. 3-7). pap. 36.00 incl. audio (978-0-8072-7308-1(2), YA809SP) Random Hse. Audio Publishing Group. (Listening Library).

—The Key to the Indian. 2004. (Indian in the Cupboard Ser.: 5). (J). (gr. 3-6). lib. bdg. 17.20 (978-0-613-23006-3(X), Turtleback) Turtleback Bks.

—The Secret of the Indian. 2010. (Indian in the Cupboard Ser.). (ENG.). 192p. (J). (gr. 3-7). 6.99 (978-0-375-85524-5(6), Yearling) Random Hse. Children's Bks.

—Secret of the Indian. 2003. (ENG., Illus.). 160p. pap. (978-0-00-714900-1(X), Collins) HarperCollins Pubs. Ltd.

Barker, Clive. Abarat. 119.90 (978-0-06-056894-8(1)) HarperCollins Pubs.

—Abarat. Barker, Clive, illus. (Abarat Ser.: 1). (ENG., Illus.). (YA). (gr. 8). 2011. 528p. pap. 9.99 (978-0-06-209410-0(6)) 2004. 496p. reprint ed. pap. 8.99 (978-0-06-059637-8(6)) HarperCollins Pubs.

—Abarat: Days of Magic, Nights of War, 4 vols., Vol. 2. Barker, Clive, illus. ltd. num. aut. ed. 2004. (Illus.). 493p. 175.00 (978-1-890885-17-5(7)) Trice, B.E. Publishing.

—Absolute Midnight. Barker, Clive, illus. 2013. (Abarat Ser.: 3). (ENG., Illus.). 640p. (YA). (gr. 8). pap. 9.99 (978-0-06-440933-9(3)) HarperCollins Pubs.

—Days of Magic, Nights of War. Barker, Clive, illus. (Abarat Ser.: 2). (ENG., Illus.). (YA). (gr. 8). 2011. 624p. pap. 9.99 (978-0-06-209411-7(4)) 2006. 576p. reprint ed. pap. 7.99 (978-0-06-059638-5(4)) HarperCollins Pubs.

Bernstein, Nina. Magic by the Book, 4 vols. unabr. ed. 2005. (J). 65.75 (978-1-4193-3607-2(X), 42048) Recorded Bks., Inc.

Birney, Betty G. The Princess & the Peabodys. 2007. (ENG.). 256p. (J). (gr. 5-9). 15.99 (978-0-06-084720-3(4)) HarperCollins Pubs.

Boné, Thomas H., illus. The Teacher Who Would Not Retire Discovers a New Planet. 2009. (J). 17.95 (978-0-9792918-3-8(6)) Blue Marlin Pubns.

Boston, Lucy M. The Children of Green Knowe Collection. 2013. (ENG., Illus.). 368p. (J). 12.95 (978-0-571-30347-2(1)) Faber & Faber, Inc.

British Broadcasting Corporation Children's Books Staff & Richards, Justin. The American Adventures. 2016. (ENG.). 192p. (J). 14.99 (978-1-4059-2872-4(7), 9781405928724) Penguin Bks., Ltd. GBR. Dist: Diamond Comic Distributors, Inc.

Brody, Jessica. Unchanged. 2015. (Unremembered Trilogy Ser.: 3). (ENG.). 432p. (YA). (gr. 7). 17.99 (978-0-374-37989-6(0), 9780374379896, Farrar, Straus & Giroux (BYR)) Farrar, Straus & Giroux.

—Unremembered. 2013. (Unremembered Trilogy Ser.: 1). (ENG.). 320p. (YA). (gr. 7). 17.99 (978-0-374-37991-9(2), 9780374379919, Farrar, Straus & Giroux (BYR)) Farrar, Straus & Giroux.

—Unremembered. 2014. (Unremembered Trilogy Ser.: 1). (ENG.). 352p. (YA). (gr. 7). pap. 9.99 (978-1-250-04002-2(7), 9781250040022) Square Fish.

Buckingham, Will. Lucy & the Rocket Dog. Arnaldo, Monica, illus. 2017. (ENG.). 160p. (J). (gr. 3-7). 16.99 **(978-0-399-55432-2(7))**; lib. bdg. 19.99 **(978-0-399-55433-9(5))** Random Hse. Children's Bks. (Knopf Bks. for Young Readers).

Bullen, Alexandra. Wishful Thinking. 2011. (ENG.). 256p. (J). (gr. 9-9). 17.99 (978-0-545-13907-6(4)) Scholastic, Inc.

Carter, Mike. Access to the Universe. 2005. (Illus.). 160p. (Orig.). pap. (978-0-7344-0696-5(7), Lothian Children's Bks.) Hachette Australia.

Caterer, Claire M. The Key & the Flame. (ENG.). (J). (gr. 3-7). 2015. 496p. pap. 7.99 (978-1-4424-5742-3(2)) 2013. 480p. 17.99 (978-1-4424-5741-6(4)) McElderry, Margaret K. Bks. (McElderry, Margaret K. Bks.).

Caveney, Philip. Space Blasters. 2013. (ENG.). 256p. (J). (gr. 4-6). pap. 10.99 (978-1-84939-572-4(1)) Andersen Pr. GBR. Dist: Independent Pubs. Group.

Christopher, John. Dragon Dance. 2015. (Fireball Trilogy Ser.: 3). (ENG., Illus.). 224p. (J). (gr. 4-8). pap. 7.99 (978-1-4814-2015-0(1), Aladdin) Simon & Schuster Children's Publishing.

Cockcroft, Jason. Counter Clockwise. 2009. 208p. (J). lib. bdg. 16.89 (978-0-06-125555-7(6)); (ENG., Illus.). (gr. 5-18). 15.99 (978-0-06-125554-0(8)) HarperCollins Pubs. (Tegen, Katherine Bks).

Cody, Matthew. The Dead Gentleman. 2012. (ENG.). 288p. (J). (gr. 5). 6.99 (978-0-375-84490-4(2), Yearling) Random Hse. Children's Bks.

Cole, Frank L. Hashbrown Winters & Whiz-Tastrophe. 2013. pap. 14.99 (978-1-4621-1056-8(8), Bonneville Bks.) Cedar Fort, Inc./CFI Distribution.

Colfer, Eoin. Artemis Fowl & the Atlantis Complex. 2012. (ENG.). 384p. (J). (gr. 5-9). pap. 8.99 (978-1-4231-2972-1(5)) Hyperion Pr.

—The Atlantis Complex. 2010. (Artemis Fowl Ser.: 7). (ENG.). 368p. (J). (gr. 5-9). 17.99 (978-1-4231-2819-9(2)) Hyperion Pr.

—The Atlantis Complex. 2012. (Artemis Fowl Ser.: 7). (J). lib. bdg. 19.65 (978-0-606-23614-0(7), Turtleback) Turtleback Bks.

—The Last Guardian. 2012. (Artemis Fowl Ser.). (ENG.). 336p. (J). (gr. 5-9). 18.99 (978-1-4231-6161-5(0)) Hyperion Pr.

—The Last Guardian. 2014. (Artemis Fowl Ser.: 8). (J). lib. bdg. 19.65 (978-0-606-32288-1(4), Turtleback) Turtleback Bks.

—The Lost Colony. rev. ed. 2009. (Artemis Fowl Ser.). (ENG.). 432p. (J). (gr. 5-9). pap. 8.99 (978-1-4231-2494-8(4)) Hyperion Pr.

—The Time Paradox. 2009. (Artemis Fowl Ser.). (ENG.). 448p. (J). (gr. 5-9). pap. 8.99 (978-1-4231-0837-5(X)) Hyperion Pr.

—The Time Paradox. 2009. (Artemis Fowl Ser.: 6). (J). lib. bdg. 19.65 (978-0-606-10579-8(4), Turtleback) Turtleback Bks.

Collins, Renee. Until We Meet Again. 2015. (ENG.). 336p. (YA). (gr. 8-12). 16.99 (978-1-4926-2116-4(1), 9781492621164) Sourcebooks, Inc.

Cooper, Susan. The Dark Is Rising. 2007. (YA). 1.25 (978-1-4193-7923-9(2)) Recorded Bks., Inc.

Corlett, William. The Door in the Tree. 2010. (Magician's House Quartet Ser.: 2). (ENG.). 304p. (YA). (gr. 5-8). pap. 13.99 (978-1-4424-1414-3(6), Simon Pulse) Simon Pulse.

—The Steps up the Chimney. 2011. (Magician's House Quartet Ser.: 1). (ENG.). 288p. (YA). (gr. 7). pap. 13.99 (978-1-4424-2935-2(6), Simon Pulse) Simon Pulse.

Corp, Carey & Langdon, Lorie. Doon, 1 vol. 2014. (Doon Novel Ser.). (ENG.). 416p. (YA). pap. 12.99 (978-0-310-74239-5(0)) Blink.

Cotterill, Colin. Average Alan. 2013. 150p. pap. (978-616-7503-18-9(4)) Asia Document Bureau, Ltd.

Crashland. 2014. (Twinmaker Ser.: 2). (ENG.). 480p. (YA). (gr. 8). 17.99 (978-0-06-220324-3(X)) HarperCollins Pubs.

Curley, Marianne. The Dark. 2010. (Guardians of Time Ser.). (ENG.). 352p. (YA). (gr. 7). pap. 8.99 (978-1-59990-544-0(2), 9781599905440, Bloomsbury USA Childrens) Bloomsbury Publishing USA.

Dalton, Annie. Feeling the Vibes: Babysit a Buddha! 2008. (Mel Beeby Agent Angel Ser.). (ENG.). 208p. (J). (gr. 4-7). pap. 6.95 (978-0-00-716140-9(9)) HarperCollins Pubs. Ltd. GBR. Dist: Independent Pubs. Group.

Dashner, James. The Blade of Shattered Hope. 2010. (13th Reality Ser.: Bk. 3). 432p. (J). 18.99 (978-1-60641-239-8(6), Shadow Mountain) Shadow Mountain Publishing.

—The Blade of Shattered Hope. Dorman, Brandon, illus. 2011. (13th Reality Ser.: 3). (ENG.). 528p. (J). (gr. 3-7). pap. 8.99 (978-1-4424-0871-5(5), Aladdin) Simon & Schuster Children's Publishing.

—The Hunt for Dark Infinity. Beus, Bryan, illus. 2009. (13th Reality Ser.: Bk. 2). 446p. (J). 18.95 (978-1-60641-034-9(2), Shadow Mountain) Shadow Mountain Publishing.

—The Hunt for Dark Infinity. Beus, Bryan, illus. 2010. (13th Reality Ser.: 2). (ENG.). 544p. (J). (gr. 3-7). pap. 8.99 (978-1-4169-9153-3(0), Aladdin) Simon & Schuster Children's Publishing.

—The Journal of Curious Letters. Beus, Bryan, illus. 2008. (13th Reality Ser.: Bk. 1). 434p. (J). (gr. 4-7). 17.95 (978-1-59038-831-0(3), Shadow Mountain) Shadow Mountain Publishing.

—The Journal of Curious Letters. Beus, Bryan, illus. 2009. (13th Reality Ser.: 1). (ENG.). 528p. (J). (gr. 3-7). pap. 8.99 (978-1-4169-9152-6(2), Aladdin) Simon & Schuster Children's Publishing.

—The Void of Mist & Thunder. Dorman, Brandon, illus. 2013. (13th Reality Ser.: 4). (ENG.). 496p. (J). (gr. 3-7). pap. 8.99 (978-1-4424-0873-9(1), Aladdin) Simon & Schuster Children's Publishing.

—The 13th Reality: The Blade of Shattered Hope; the Void of Mist & Thunder. Dorman, Brandon, illus. 2015. (13th Reality Ser.). (ENG.). 976p. (YA). (gr. 7-7). pap. 12.99 (978-1-4814-5702-6(0), Simon & Schuster/Paula Wiseman Bks.) Simon & Schuster/Paula Wiseman Bks.

—The 13th Reality: The Journal of Curious Letters; the Hunt for Dark Infinity. Beus, Bryan, illus. 2015. (13th Reality Ser.). (ENG.). 1024p. (YA). (gr. 7-7). pap. 12.99 (978-1-4814-5315-8(7), Simon & Schuster/Paula Wiseman Bks.) Simon & Schuster/Paula Wiseman Bks.

Dateno, Maria Grace. Braving the Storm, 6 vols., Vol. 2. Cunningham, Paul, illus. 2013. 70p. (J). pap. 5.95 (978-0-8198-1204-9(8)) Pauline Bks. & Media.

—Shepherds to the Rescue, 6 vols., Vol. 1. Cunningham, Paul, illus. 2013. 71p. (J). pap. 5.95 (978-0-8198-7251-7(2)) Pauline Bks. & Media.

Davis, Bryan. From the Mouth of Elijah. 2012. (Children of the Bard Ser.: 2). (ENG.). 512p. (YA). (gr. 7). pap. 14.99 (978-0-89957-881-1(0)) AMG Pubs.

Davis, Heather. The Clearing. 2010. (ENG., Illus.). 224p. (YA). (gr. 9). pap. 8.99 (978-0-547-26367-0(8)) Houghton Mifflin Harcourt Publishing Co.

De Laurentiis, Giada. Hong Kong! #3. Gambatesa, Francesca, illus. 2014. (Recipe for Adventure Ser.: 3). (ENG.). 144p. (J). (gr. 2-5). 6.99 (978-0-448-46258-5(3)); 16.99 (978-0-448-48040-4(9)) Penguin Young Readers Group. (Grosset & Dunlap).

De Laurentiis, Giada, et al. Hawaii! #6. Gambatesa, Francesca, illus. 2015. (Recipe for Adventure Ser.: 6). (ENG.). 160p. (J). (gr. 2-4). bds. 6.99 (978-0-448-48391-7(2), Grosset & Dunlap) Penguin Young Readers Group.

—Rio de Janeiro! #5. Gambatesa, Francesca, illus. 2015. (Recipe for Adventure Ser.: 5). (ENG.). 160p. (J). (gr. 2-4). bds. 6.99 (978-0-448-48204-0(5), Grosset & Dunlap) Penguin Young Readers Group.

Doty, Jean Slaughter. Can I Get There by Candlelight? 2012. (ENG.). 128p. (YA). (gr. 7). pap. 7.99 (978-1-4424-8608-9(2), Simon & Schuster Bks. For Young Readers) Simon & Schuster Bks. For Young Readers.

Downey, Jen Swann. The Ninja Librarians: The Accidental Keyhand. 2015. (Ninja Librarians Ser.: 1). (ENG.). 400p. (J). (gr. 4-7). pap. 8.99 (978-1-4926-0180-7(2), Sourcebooks Jabberwocky) Sourcebooks, Inc.

Duey, Kathleen. Arthur. Gould, Robert, photos by. 2006. (Time Soldiers Ser.). (ENG., Illus.). 96p. (gr. -1-4). 24.21 (978-1-59961-224-9(0)) Spotlight.

—Rex. Epstein, Eugene, illus. Gould, Robert, photos by. 2006. (Time Soldiers Ser.: Bk. 1). (ENG.). 96p. (gr. -1-7). 24.21 (978-1-59961-226-3(7)) Spotlight.

—Rex. Epstein, Eugene, illus. Epstein, Eugene, photos by. 2006. (Time Soldiers Ser.: Bk. 1). (ENG.). 96p. (gr. 4-7). 24.21 (978-1-59961-225-6(9)) Spotlight.

Edge, Christopher. The Many Worlds of Albie Bright. 2017. (ENG.). 176p. (J). (gr. 4-7). 16.99 **(978-1-5247-1357-7(0))**; lib. bdg. 19.99 **(978-1-5247-1359-1(7))** Random Hse. Children's Bks. (Delacorte Bks. for Young Readers).

Elaine Vanier. Crystal Lights: Awaken the Power. 2009. 116p. pap. 10.95 (978-1-4401-8357-7(0)) iUniverse, Inc.

Engdahl, Sylvia. Enchantress from the Stars. 2003. (ENG.). 304p. (YA). (gr. 7-18). pap. 8.99 (978-0-14-250037-8(2), Firebird) Penguin Young Readers Group.

Ephron, Delia. Frannie in Pieces. Beckerman, Chad, illus. 2007. 374p. (YA). (gr. 7-12). lib. bdg. 17.89 (978-0-06-074717-6(X), HarperTeen) HarperCollins Pubs.

Fisher, Catherine. Darkhenge. 2006. 340p. (YA). (gr. 7-12). 15.99 (978-0-06-078582-6(9)) HarperCollins Pubs.

Flavin, Teresa. The Blackhope Enigma. 2011. (ENG., Illus.). 304p. (J). (gr. 4-7). 15.99 (978-0-7636-5694-2(1), Templar) Candlewick Pr.

—The Crimson Shard. (ENG.). (J). (gr. 4-7). 2015. 288p. pap. 6.99 *(978-0-7636-7172-3(X))* 2012. (Illus.). 256p. 15.99 *(978-0-7636-6093-2(0))* Candlewick Pr. (Templar).
Fox Mazer, Norma. Saturday, the Twelfth of October. 2015. (ENG.). 274p. (J). (gr. 3). pap. 13.95 *(978-1-939601-31-5(2))* Ig Publishing, Inc.
Gaiman, NEil. Fortunately, the Milk. Young, Skottie, illus. (ENG.). 128p. (J). (gr. 3-7). 2014. pap. 5.99 *(978-0-06-222408-8(5))* 2013. 14.99 *(978-0-06-222407-1(7))* HarperCollins Pubs.
—Fortunately, the Milk. 2014. (J). lib. bdg. 16.00 *(978-0-606-35965-8(6))* Turtleback Bks.
Gaiman, NEil & Reaves, Michael. Interworld. (InterWorld Trilogy Ser.: 1). (ENG.). (YA). (gr. 8). 2013. 304p. pap. 9.99 *(978-0-06-212530-9(3),* HarperTeen) 2008. 256p. pap. 9.99 *(978-0-06-123898-7(8))* HarperCollins Pubs.
—Interworld. 2008. (Illus.). 181p. (J). (gr. 5-9). 60.00 *(978-1-59606-173-6(1))* Subterranean Pr.
Gaiman, NEil, et al. Eternity's Wheel. (InterWorld Trilogy Ser.: 3). 288p. (YA). (gr. 8). 2016. pap. 9.99 *(978-0-06-206800-2(8))* 2015. (ENG.). 17.99 *(978-0-06-206799-9(0))* HarperCollins Pubs. (HarperTeen).
—The Silver Dream. (InterWorld Trilogy Ser.: 2). (ENG.). (YA). (gr. 8). 2015. 272p. pap. 9.99 *(978-0-06-206797-5(4))* 2013. 256p. 18.99 *(978-0-06-206796-8(6))* HarperCollins Pubs. (HarperTeen).
Garner, Alan. The Owl Service. 2006. (Odyssey Classics Ser.). (ENG., Illus.). 240p. (J). (gr. 7-12). pap. 14.95 *(978-0-15-205618-6(1))* Houghton Mifflin Harcourt Publishing Co.
—Red Shift. 2011. (ENG.). 232p. pap. 14.00 *(978-1-59017-443-2(7),* NYRB Classics) New York Review of Bks., Inc., The.
Germano, Yveta. Bring Me Back. 2013. 298p. 27.99 *(978-1-938516-75-7(3));* 318p. pap. 13.99 *(978-1-938516-17-7(6))* Midnight Hologram, LLC.
Graham, Judith A. The Didley-Doo's Go on an Adventure, 1 vol. 2009. 33p. pap. 24.95 *(978-1-60749-897-1(9))* America Star Bks.
Gray, Claudia. Ten Thousand Skies above You. (Firebird Ser.: 2). (YA). (gr. 9). 2016. 448p. pap. 9.99 *(978-0-06-227900-2(9),* HarperTeen) 2015. (ENG.). 432p. 17.99 *(978-0-06-227899-9(1))* HarperCollins Pubs.
Haarsma, P. J. Awakening on Orbis 4. 2010. (Softwire Ser.: 4). (ENG., Illus.). 368p. (YA). (gr. 7-18). 16.99 *(978-0-7636-2712-6(7))* Candlewick Pr.
Haddix, Margaret Peterson. Caught. (Missing Ser.: 5). (ENG., (J). (gr. 3-7). 2013. Illus.). 368p. pap. 7.99 *(978-1-4169-8983-7(8))* 2012. 352p. 16.99 *(978-1-4169-8982-0(X))* Simon & Schuster Bks. For Young Readers. (Simon & Schuster Bks. For Young Readers).
—Redeemed. 2015. (Missing Ser.: 8). (ENG.). 416p. (J). (gr. 3-7). 17.99 *(978-1-4424-9756-6(4),* Simon & Schuster Bks. For Young Readers) Simon & Schuster Bks. For Young Readers.
—Redeemed. 2016. (Missing Ser.: 8). lib. bdg. 18.40 *(978-0-606-39234-1(3))* Turtleback Bks.
—Sabotaged. (Missing Ser.: 3). (ENG.). (J). (gr. 3-7). 2011. 400p. pap. 8.99 *(978-1-4169-5425-5(2))* 2010. 384p. 17.99 *(978-1-4169-5424-8(4))* Simon & Schuster Bks. For Young Readers. (Simon & Schuster Bks. For Young Readers).
—Sent. (Missing Ser.: 2). (YA). 2011. 82.75 *(978-1-4407-2678-1(7))* 2009. 98.75 *(978-1-4407-2675-0(2))* 2009. 1.25 *(978-1-4407-2679-8(5))* 2009. 218.75 *(978-1-4407-2670-5(1))* Recorded Bks., Inc.
—Sent. (Missing Ser.: 2). (ENG.). (J). (gr. 3-7). 2010. 336p. pap. 7.99 *(978-1-4169-5423-1(6))* 2009. 320p. 16.99 *(978-1-4169-5422-4(8))* Simon & Schuster Bks. For Young Readers. (Simon & Schuster Bks. For Young Readers).
—Sent. abr. ed. 2009. *(978-1-4424-0767-1(0))* Simon & Schuster Children's Publishing.
—Sent. l.t. ed. 2010. (Missing Ser.: Bk. 2). (ENG.). 346p. 23.99 *(978-1-4104-3245-2(9))* Thorndike Pr.
—Sent. 2010. (Missing Ser.: 2). lib. bdg. 18.40 *(978-0-606-14699-9(7),* Turtleback) Turtleback Bks.
Hamel, Mike. Dragon's Lair, 5. 2007. (Matterhorn the Brave Ser.: 5). (ENG.). 192p. (J). (gr. 5-11). per. 9.99 *(978-0-89957-837-8(3))* AMG Pubs.
—Jewel Heist, 4. 2007. (Matterhorn the Brave Ser.: 4). (ENG.). 192p. (gr. 8-7). per. 9.99 *(978-0-89957-836-1(5))* AMG Pubs.
—Pyramid Scheme. 2007. (Matterhorn the Brave Ser.: 3). (ENG.). 176p. (J). (gr. 5-7). per. 9.99 *(978-0-89957-835-4(7))* AMG Pubs.
—Rylan the Renegade, 6. 2007. (Matterhorn the Brave Ser.: 6). (ENG.). 192p. (J). (gr. 8-7). per. 9.99 *(978-0-89957-838-5(1))* AMG Pubs.
—The Sword & the Flute. 2007. (Matterhorn the Brave Ser.: 1). (ENG.). 176p. (J). (gr. 5-12). per. 9.99 *(978-0-89957-833-0(0))* AMG Pubs.
—Talis Hunters, Vol. 2. 2007. (Matterhorn the Brave Ser.: 2). (ENG.). 176p. (J). (gr. 5-12). per. 9.99 *(978-0-89957-834-7(9))* AMG Pubs.
Hapgood, Harriet Reuter & Peppermint Frog Limited. The Square Root of Summer. 2016. (ENG.). 304p. (YA). 17.99 *(978-1-62672-373-3(7),* 9781626723733) Roaring Brook Pr.
Hautman, Pete. The Cydonian Pyramid. (Klaatu Diskos Ser.). (ENG.). 368p. (YA). (gr. 7). 2014. pap. 8.99 *(978-0-7636-6933-1(4))* 2013. 16.99 *(978-0-7636-5404-7(3))* Candlewick Pr.
—The Klaatu Terminus. (Klaatu Diskos Ser.). (ENG.). 368p. (YA). (gr. 7). 2015. pap. 8.99 *(978-0-7636-7675-9(6))* 2014. 16.99 *(978-0-7636-5405-4(1))* Candlewick Pr.
—The Obsidian Blade. 2012. (Klaatu Diskos Ser.). (ENG., Illus.). 320p. (YA). (gr. 7). 16.99 *(978-0-7636-5403-0(5))* Candlewick Pr.
Hering, Marianne & Sanders, Nancy I. Captured on the High Seas. 2014. (AIO Imagination Station Bks.: 14). (ENG.). 144p. (J). pap. 4.99 *(978-1-58997-775-4(0))* Tyndale Hse. Pubs.
Hering, Marianne, et al. Doomsday in Pompeii. 2015. (AIO Imagination Station Bks.: 16). (ENG., Illus.). 144p. (J). pap. 4.99 *(978-1-58997-803-4(X))* Focus on the Family Publishing.
Herrick, Amy. The Time Fetch. 2013. (ENG.). 320p. (J). (gr. 4-7). 16.95 *(978-1-61620-220-0(3),* 73220) Algonquin Bks. of Chapel Hill.
Hoffman, Mary. City of Secrets. (Stravaganza Ser.). (ENG.). (YA). 2010. 416p. (gr. 7). pap. 8.99 *(978-1-59990-451-1(9),* 9781599904511) 2008. 400p. (gr. 5-18). 17.99 *(978-1-59990-202-9(8),* 9781599902029) Bloomsbury Publishing USA. (Bloomsbury USA Childrens).
—City of Ships. 2010. (Stravaganza Ser.). (ENG.). 368p. (YA). (gr. 7-18). 17.99 *(978-1-59990-491-7(8),* 9781599904917, Bloomsbury USA Childrens) Bloomsbury Publishing USA.
—Stravaganza: City of Ships. 2012. (Stravaganza Ser.). (ENG.). 384p. (YA). (gr. 7). pap. 9.99 *(978-1-59990-832-8(8),* 9781599908328, Bloomsbury USA Childrens) Bloomsbury Publishing USA.
—Stravaganza: City of Swords. 2012. (Stravaganza Ser.). (ENG.). 368p. (YA). (gr. 7-12). 18.99 *(978-1-59990-842-7(5),* 9781599908427, Bloomsbury USA Childrens) Bloomsbury Publishing USA.
Hood, Ann. Jewel of the East. Kwasny, Karl et al, illus. 2012. (Treasure Chest Ser.: 3). (ENG.). 208p. (J). (gr. 3-7). 15.99 *(978-0-448-45473-3(4));* pap. 6.99 *(978-0-448-45469-6(6))* Penguin Young Readers Group. (Grosset & Dunlap).
Hood, Ann & Altmann, Scott. Alexander Hamilton: Little Lion. Kwasney, Karl & Zilber, Denis, illus. 2012. (Treasure Chest Ser.: 2). (ENG.). 224p. (J). (gr. 3-7). pap. 6.99 *(978-0-448-45468-9(8),* Grosset & Dunlap) Penguin Young Readers Group.
House, David James. The Key to Space. 2006. (ENM.). 364p. (YA). 24.95 *(978-0-9777086-0-4(8))* House, David.
Howe, Katherine. The Appearance of Annie Van Sinderen. 2015. (ENG.). 400p. (YA). (gr. 7). 18.99 *(978-0-399-16778-2(1),* G.P. Putnam's Sons Books for Young Readers) Penguin Young Readers Group.
Hubbard, L. Ron, contrib. by. The Crossroads: Literature Guide for Teachers & Librarians, Based on Common Core ELA Standards for Classrooms 6-9. 2013. (Stories from the Golden Age Ser.). (ENG.). 35p. (gr. 6-9). pap., tchr. ed. 14.95 *(978-1-59212-810-5(6))* Galaxy Pr., LLC.
Hubert, Jerry. They Were Not Gods: A Space-Age Fairytale. 2003. 170p. (YA). 23.95 *(978-0-595-66091-9(6));* pap. 13.95 *(978-0-595-29970-6(9))* iUniverse, Inc.
Hulme, John & Wexler, Michael. The Glitch in Sleep. 2007. (Seems Ser.). (ENG., Illus.). 288p. (YA). (gr. 5-18). 16.95 *(978-1-59990-129-9(3),* 9781599901299, Bloomsbury USA Childrens) Bloomsbury Publishing USA.
—The Seems: The Lost Train of Thought. 2010. (Seems Ser.). (ENG., Illus.). 304p. (YA). (gr. 3-6). pap. 7.99 *(978-1-59990-300-2(8),* 9781599903002, Bloomsbury USA Childrens) Bloomsbury Publishing USA.
Jacques, Brian. The Angel's Command. Elliot, David & Schoenherr, Ian, illus. 2005. (ENG.). 384p. (J). (gr. 3-7). 7.99 *(978-0-14-240285-6(0),* Firebird) Penguin Young Readers Group.
—The Angel's Command. 2003. (Castaways of the Flying Dutchman Ser.: No. 2). 1.00 *(978-1-4175-5393-8(6))* Recorded Bks., Inc.
—Voyage of Slaves: A Tale from the Castaways of the Flying Dutchman. 2007. (ENG.). 320p. (gr. 12-18). 7.99 *(978-0-441-01526-3(X),* Ace Bks.) Penguin Publishing Group.
Jaffe, Charlotte & Doherty, Barbara. The Space Race. 2003. (Illus.). (J). (gr. 2-3). 60.00 *(978-1-57336-395-2(2),* I5077) Interaction Pubs., Inc.
James, J. Alison. Sing for a Gentle Rain. 2012. (ENG.). 224p. (J). (gr. 3-7). pap. 10.99 *(978-1-4424-7483-3(1),* Atheneum Bks. for Young Readers) Simon & Schuster Children's Publishing.
James, Nick. Skyship Academy: Strikeforce. 2013. (Skyship Academy Ser.: 3). (ENG.). 360p. (YA). pap. 9.99 *(978-0-7387-3637-2(6),* Flux) North Star Editions.
Jansen, Patty. The Far Horizon. 2012. 176p. pap. *(978-0-9872009-4-5(1))* Capricornica Pubns.
Johnson, Cara. Looking Forward Back: The Dream Travelers Book Three. 2008. 162p. (J). per. 9.99 *(978-0-9768870-3-4(7))* Whirling Dirvish Publishing.
Johnson, Jane. Legends of the Shadow World: The Secret Country; the Shadow World; Dragon's Fire. Stower, Adam, illus. 2010. (ENG.). 1120p. (J). (gr. 3-7). pap. 14.99 *(978-1-4169-9082-6(8),* Simon & Schuster Bks. For Young Readers) Simon & Schuster Bks. For Young Readers.
—The Secret Country. Stower, Adam, illus. 2007. (Eidolon Chronicles Ser.: 1). (ENG.). 336p. (J). (gr. 3-7). per. 15.99 *(978-1-4169-3815-6(X),* Simon & Schuster Bks. For Young Readers) Simon & Schuster Bks. For Young Readers.
Kenney, Cindy. Cool Hand Cuke Vol. 5: A Lesson in Giving, 1 vol. Moore, Michael, illus. 2006. (Big Idea Books / VeggieTown Values Ser.: Bk. 5). (ENG.). 32p. (J). (gr. -1-3). pap. 3.99 *(978-0-310-70738-7(2))* Zonderkidz.
Kenney, Cindy, et al. Veggietown Voyage, 1 vol. Moore, Michael, illus. 2013. (Big Idea Books / VeggieTales Ser.). (ENG.). 96p. (J). 7.99 *(978-0-310-72352-3(3))* Zonderkidz.
Kirsch, R. A. The Big One: (A Bicycle Tale), 1 vol. 2009. 191p. pap. 24.95 *(978-1-60703-341-7(0))* PublishAmerica, Inc.
Klass, David. Firestorm. 2008. (Caretaker Trilogy Ser.: 1). (ENG.). 320p. (YA). (gr. 9-13). pap. 11.99 *(978-0-312-38018-2(6),* 9780312380182) Square Fish.
—Firestorm. rev. l.t. ed. 2007. (Caretaker Trilogy: Bk. 1). 435p. (YA). (gr. 9). 23.95 *(978-0-7862-9364-3(0))* Thorndike Pr.
—Whirlwind. 2009. (Caretaker Trilogy Ser.: 2). (ENG.). 320p. (YA). (gr. 9-12). pap. 18.99 *(978-0-312-38429-6(7),* 9780312384296) Square Fish.
Klingele, Lindsey. The Broken World. 2017. 432p. (YA). (gr. 8). 17.99 ***(978-0-06-238036-4(2),*** HarperTeen) HarperCollins Pubs.
Kuykendall, Roger. All Day September. 2011. 28p. 12.95 *(978-1-4638-9782-6(0));* pap. 6.95 *(978-1-4638-0109-0(2))* Rodgers, Alan Bks.
Larbalestier, Justine. Magic's Child. 2007. (Magic or Madness Trilogy). 291p. (YA). *(978-1-4287-3603-0(4),* Razorbill) Penguin Publishing Group.
Laurie, Victoria. The Curse of Deadman's Forest. 2011. (ENG.). 432p. (J). (gr. 3-7). 8.99 *(978-0-440-42259-4(0),* Yearling) Random Hse. Children's Bks.
—Oracles of Delphi Keep. 2010. (Oracles of Delphi Keep Ser.). (ENG.). 576p. (J). (gr. 3-7). 7.99 *(978-0-440-42258-7(2),* Yearling) Random Hse. Children's Bks.
Lawrence, Michael. A Crack in the Line. 2004. (Withern Rise Ser.). (ENG.). 336p. (J). 15.99 *(978-0-06-072477-1(3))* HarperCollins Pubs.
—A Crack in the Line. 2005. (Withern Rise Trilogy). 323p. (YA). (gr. 9). 16.65 *(978-0-7569-5739-1(7))* Perfection Learning Corp.
—Small Eternities. (Withern Rise Ser.). 336p. 2006. (Illus.). (J). (gr. 7). pap. 7.99 *(978-0-06-072482-5(X),* HarperTeen) 2005. (YA). 16.89 *(978-0-06-072481-8(1))* 2005. (ENG.). (J). (gr. 8). 15.99 *(978-0-06-072480-1(3),* Greenwillow Bks.) HarperCollins Pubs.
—The Underwood See. 2007. (Withern Rise Ser.). (gr. 9). (ENG.). 384p. (J). pap. 7.99 *(978-0-06-072485-6(4),* Greenwillow Bks.); 372p. (YA). 16.99 *(978-0-06-072483-2(8))* HarperCollins Pubs.
L'Engle, Madeleine. An Acceptable Time. 2007. (Wrinkle in Time Quintet Ser.: 5). (ENG.). 384p. (J). (gr. 5-9). per. 6.99 *(978-0-312-36858-6(5),* 9780312368586) Square Fish.
Lindbergh, Anne M. The People in Pineapple Place. 2011. (ENG.). 176p. (J). pap. 12.95 *(978-1-56792-411-4(5))* Godine, David R. Pub.
Lipsyte, Robert. The Twin Powers. 2014. (ENG.). 256p. (J). (gr. 5-7). 16.99 *(978-0-547-97335-7(7))* Houghton Mifflin Harcourt Publishing Co.
—The Twinning Project. (ENG.). (J). (gr. 5-7). 2014. 288p. pap. 6.99 *(978-0-544-22522-0(8),* HMH Books For Young Readers) 2012. 272p. 16.99 *(978-0-547-64571-1(6))* Houghton Mifflin Harcourt Publishing Co.
MacHale, D. J. Pendragon: The Merchant of Death; The Lost City of Fear; The Never War; The Reality Bug; Black Water. 2013. (Pendragon Ser.). (ENG., Illus.). 1968p. (J). (gr. 5-9). pap. 49.99 *(978-1-4424-9926-3(5),* Simon & Schuster/Paula Wiseman Bks.) Simon & Schuster/Paula Wiseman Bks.
—The Pilgrims of Rayne. 2008. (Pendragon Ser.: 8). (ENG.). 576p. (J). (gr. 5-9). pap. 9.99 *(978-1-4169-1417-4(X),* Aladdin) Simon & Schuster Children's Publishing.
—The Soldiers of Halla. (Pendragon Ser.: 10). (ENG.). 608p. (J). (gr. 5-9). 2010. pap. 9.99 *(978-1-4169-1421-1(8))* 2009. 17.99 *(978-1-4169-1420-4(X))* Simon & Schuster Children's Publishing. (Aladdin).
McCool, Ben. Souljacker: #2. Rousseau, Craig, illus. 2012. (Captain America: the Korvac Saga Ser.). 24p. (J). (gr. 3-5). lib. bdg. 24.21 *(978-1-61479-020-4(5))* Spotlight.
—The Star Lord: #4. Rousseau, Craig, illus. 2012. (Captain America: the Korvac Saga Ser.). 24p. (J). (gr. 3-5). lib. bdg. 24.21 *(978-1-61479-022-8(1))* Spotlight.
—Strange Days: #1. Rousseau, Craig, illus. 2012. (Captain America: the Korvac Saga Ser.). 24p. (J). (gr. 3-5). lib. bdg. 24.21 *(978-1-61479-019-8(1))* Spotlight.
—The Traveler: #3. Rousseau, Craig, illus. 2012. (Captain America: the Korvac Saga Ser.). 24p. (J). (gr. 3-5). lib. bdg. 24.21 *(978-1-61479-021-1(3))* Spotlight.
McCusker, Paul. Out of Time, 1 vol. 2009. (Time Thriller Trilogy Ser.: Bk. 2). (ENG., Illus.). 240p. (YA). (gr. 8-11). pap. 9.99 *(978-0-310-71437-8(0))* Zondervan.
McDonald, Joyce. Shades of Simon Gray. 2003. (Readers Circle Ser.). 245p. (YA). 14.15 *(978-0-7569-1880-4(4))* Perfection Learning Corp.
McKinty, Adrian. The Lighthouse Keepers. 2008. (ENG.). 400p. (YA). (gr. 7-11). 17.95 *(978-0-8109-7070-0(8),* Amulet Bks.) Abrams, Inc.
—The Lighthouse War. 2007. (ENG.). 414p. (J). (gr. 7-17). 16.95 *(978-0-8109-9354-9(6))* Abrams, Inc.
McOmber, Rachel B., ed. McOmber Phonics Storybooks: The Time Box. rev. ed. (Illus.). (J). *(978-0-944991-52-7(1))* Swift Learning Resources.
McQuerry, Maureen Doyle. Time Out of Time. 2015. (Time Out of Time Ser.). (ENG., Illus.). 368p. (J). (gr. 5-9). 16.95 *(978-1-4197-1494-8(5),* Amulet Bks.) Abrams, Inc.
—Time Out of Time: Book One: Beyond the Door. 2015. (Time Out of Time Ser.). (ENG., Illus.). 400p. (J). (gr. 5-9). pap. 7.95 *(978-1-4197-1493-1(7),* Amulet Bks.) Abrams, Inc.
—Time Out of Time: Book Two: the Telling Stone. 2016. (ENG., Illus.). 376p. (J). (gr. 3-7). pap. 8.95 *(978-1-4197-1916-5(5),* Amulet Bks.) Abrams, Inc.
—Time Out of Time Bk. 1: Beyond the Door. 2014. (Time Out of Time Ser.). (ENG., Illus.). 384p. (J). (gr. 3-7). 16.95 *(978-1-4197-1016-2(8),* Amulet Bks.) Abrams, Inc.
Mebus, Scott. Gods of Manhattan, 1 vol. 2009. (ENG.). 368p. (J). (gr. 3-7). 8.99 *(978-0-14-241307-4(0),* Puffin Books) Penguin Young Readers Group.
—The Sorcerer's Secret, Bk. 3. 2011. (ENG.). 384p. (J). (gr. 5-18). 8.99 *(978-0-14-241878-9(1),* Puffin Books) Penguin Young Readers Group.
—Spirits in the Park. 2009. (Gods of Manhattan Ser.: No. 2). (J). *(978-0-525-47963-5(5),* Dutton Juvenile) Penguin Publishing Group.
—Spirits in the Park, Vol. 2. 2010. (ENG.). 400p. (J). (gr. 3-7). 8.99 *(978-0-14-241645-7(2),* Puffin Books) Penguin Young Readers Group.
Miller, Chris & Miller, Allan. Hunter Brown & the Consuming Fire, 3 bks., Bk.2. 2009. (ENG., Illus.). 352p. (J). pap. 13.99 *(978-1-59317-357-9(1))* Warner Pr., Inc.
Miller, Christopher & Miller, Allan. Hunter Brown & the Eye of Ends, 3 bks., Bk.3. 2011. (J). pap. 13.99 *(978-1-59317-400-2(4))* Warner Pr., Inc.
—Hunter Brown & the Secret of the Shadow, 3 bks., Bk.1. 2008. (ENG., Illus.). 384p. (J). (gr. 9-18). pap. 13.99 *(978-1-59317-328-9(8))* Warner Pr., Inc.
Monson, Marianne. The Enchanted Tunnel Vol. 3: Journey to Jerusalem. Burr, Dan, illus. 2011. (J). (gr. 3-6). pap. 7.99 *(978-1-60908-068-6(8))* Deseret Bk. Co.
—The Enchanted Tunnel Vol. 4: Wandering in the Wilderness. Burr, Dan, illus. 2011. 85p. (YA). (gr. 3-6). pap. 7.99 *(978-1-60908-069-3(6))* Deseret Bk. Co.
—Escape from Egypt. 2010. (J). *(978-1-60641-670-9(7))* Deseret Bk. Co.
Moreau, Chris. The Professor's Telescope. Marek, Jane, illus. 2006. (YA). 10.95 *(978-0-9785399-0-0(7));* cd-rom 7.95 *(978-0-9785399-2-4(3))* Windows of Discovery.
Morris, Chad. Cragbridge Hall, Book 2: The Avatar Battle. 2014. (Cragbridge Hall Ser.: 2). (ENG., Illus.). 360p. (J). (gr. 3-9). 17.99 *(978-1-60907-809-6(8),* Shadow Mountain) Shadow Mountain Publishing.
—Cragbridge Hall, Book 3: The Impossible Race. 2015. (Cragbridge Hall Ser.: 3). (ENG., Illus.). 432p. (J). (gr. 3-9). 18.99 *(978-1-60907-979-6(5),* Shadow Mountain) Shadow Mountain Publishing.
Mull, Brandon. Chasing the Prophecy. (Beyonders Ser.: 3). (ENG.). (J). (gr. 3-7). 2014. 528p. pap. 8.99 *(978-1-4169-9797-9(0))* 2013. 512p. 19.99 *(978-1-4169-9796-2(2))* Simon & Schuster Children's Publishing. (Aladdin).
—Seeds of Rebellion. (Beyonders Ser.: 2). (ENG., Illus.). (J). (gr. 3-7). 2013. 528p. pap. 8.99 *(978-1-4169-9795-5(4))* 2012. 512p. 19.99 *(978-1-4169-9794-8(6))* Simon & Schuster Children's Publishing. (Aladdin).
—Seeds of Rebellion. 2012. (Beyonders Ser.: Bk. 2). (ENG., Illus.). 512p. (J). pap. 10.99 *(978-1-4424-4965-7(9),* Simon & Schuster/Paula Wiseman Bks.) Simon & Schuster/Paula Wiseman Bks.
—Seeds of Rebellion. 2013. (Beyonders Ser.: 2). lib. bdg. 19.65 *(978-0-606-27030-4(2),* Turtleback) Turtleback Bks.
—A World Without Heroes. (J). 2011. (Beyonders Ser.: 1). 1.25 *(978-1-4640-0920-4(1))* (Beyonders Ser.: 1). 92.75 *(978-1-4618-0338-6(1))* 2011. (Beyonders Ser.: 1). 124.75 *(978-1-4618-0353-9(5))* 2011. 122.75 *(978-1-4618-0363-8(2))* Recorded Bks., Inc.
—A World Without Heroes. (Beyonders Ser.: 1). (ENG.). (J). (gr. 3-7). 2012. 496p. pap. 8.99 *(978-1-4169-9793-1(8))* 2011. 464p. 19.99 *(978-1-4169-9792-4(X))* Simon & Schuster Children's Publishing. (Aladdin).
—A World Without Heroes. 2011. (Beyonders Ser.: Bk. 1). (ENG.). 464p. (J). pap. 10.99 *(978-1-4424-3530-8(5),* Simon & Schuster/Paula Wiseman Bks.) Simon & Schuster/Paula Wiseman Bks.
—A World Without Heroes. 2012. (Beyonders Ser.: 1). lib. bdg. 19.65 *(978-0-606-23675-1(9),* Turtleback) Turtleback Bks.
—A World Without Heroes; Seeds of Rebellion; Chasing the Prophecy, Set. 2013. (Beyonders Ser.). (ENG., Illus.). 1456p. (J). (gr. 3-7). 59.99 *(978-1-4424-8593-8(0),* Aladdin) Simon & Schuster Children's Publishing.
Natl Children's Book & Literacy Alliance. The Exquisite Corpse Adventure. 2011. (ENG., Illus.). 288p. (J). (gr. 4-7). pap. 7.99 *(978-0-7636-5773-4(5))* Candlewick Pr.
Neimark, Gillian. The Golden Rectangle. (ENG., 160p. (J). (gr. 3-7). 2014. Illus.). pap. 6.99 *(978-1-4169-8043-8(1))* 2013. 15.99 *(978-1-4169-8042-1(3))* Simon & Schuster Children's Publishing. (Aladdin).
—The Secret Spiral. 2013. (ENG.). 224p. (J). (gr. 3-7). pap. 5.99 *(978-1-4169-8041-4(5),* Aladdin) Simon & Schuster Children's Publishing.
New York Hall of Science Staff. Charlie & Kiwi: An Evolutionary Adventure. Reynolds, Peter H. & Fable Vision Studios Staff, illus. 2011. (ENG.). 48p. (J). (gr. -1-3). 16.99 *(978-1-4424-2112-7(6),* Atheneum Bks. for Young Readers) Simon & Schuster Children's Publishing.
Nichols, Amy K. Now That You're Here. (Duplexity Ser.). (ENG.). (YA). (gr. 7). 2016. 608p. pap. 12.99 *(978-0-385-75396-8(9),* Ember) 2014. 304p. 16.99 *(978-0-385-75389-0(6),* Knopf Bks. for Young Readers) Random Hse. Children's Bks.
—While You Were Gone (Duplexity, Part II) 2015. (Duplexity Ser.). (ENG.). 304p. (YA). (gr. 7). 17.99 *(978-0-385-75392-0(6),* Knopf Bks. for Young Readers) Random Hse. Children's Bks.
Nix, Garth. Sir Thursday. 2007. (Keys to the Kingdom Ser.: No. 4). 344p. (gr. 4-7). 18.00 *(978-0-7569-8121-1(2))* Perfection Learning Corp.
—Sir Thursday. 2007. (Keys to the Kingdom Ser.: 4). (ENG.). 352p. (J). (gr. 3-7). pap. 7.99 *(978-0-439-43657-1(5),* Scholastic Paperbacks) Scholastic, Inc.
—Superior Saturday. 2010. (Keys to the Kingdom Ser.: 6). (ENG.). 288p. (J). (gr. 3-7). 7.99 *(978-0-439-43659-5(1),* Scholastic Paperbacks) Scholastic, Inc.
Norris, Christine. The Sword of Danu. 2012. (J). 268p. (gr. 3-7). pap. 14.99 *(978-1-61271-095-2(6));* *(978-1-61271-096-9(4));* *(978-1-61271-097-6(2))* Zumaya Pubns. LLC.
Osborne, Mary Pope. El Invierno Del Hechicero Del Hielo. 2015. (Casa De árbol Ser.: 32). (SPA., Illus.). 144p. (J). (gr. 2-4). pap. 5.99 *(978-1-63245-535-2(8))* Lectorum Pubns., Inc.
—A Perfect Time for Pandas. Murdocca, Sal, illus. 2014. (Magic Tree House Merlin Mission Ser.: No. 20). (ENG.). 144p. (J). (gr. 2-5). pap. 5.99 *(978-0-375-86798-9(8),* Random Hse. Bks. for Young Readers) Random Hse. Children's Bks.
—A Perfect Time for Pandas. 2014. (Magic Tree House Merlin Missions Ser.: 20). lib. bdg. 16.00 *(978-0-606-35564-3(2))* Turtleback Bks.
—Tigers at Twilight. unabr. ed. 2004. (Magic Tree House Ser.: No. 19). 72p. (J). (gr. k-3). pap. 17.00 incl. audio *(978-0-8072-0928-8(7),* S FTR 251 SP, Listening Library) Random Hse. Audio Publishing Group.
—Vacation under the Volcano. unabr. ed. 2004. (Magic Tree House Ser.: No. 13). 74p. (J). (gr. k-3). pap. 17.00 incl. audio *(978-0-8072-0782-6(9),* LFTR 241 SP, Listening Library) Random Hse. Audio Publishing Group.
Osborne, Mary Pope, et al. Perros Salvajes a la Hora de la Cena. Murdocca, Sal, illus. 2008. (Casa del Arbol Ser.: 20).Tr. of Dingoes at Dinnertime. (SPA.). (J). (gr. 2-4). pap. 5.99 *(978-1-933032-50-4(2))* Lectorum Pubns., Inc.
—Tigres Al Anochecer. Murdocca, Sal, illus. 2008. (Casa del Arbol Ser.: 19).Tr. of Tigers at Twilight. (SPA.). (J). (gr. 2-4). pap. 5.99 *(978-1-933032-49-8(9))* Lectorum Pubns., Inc.
Paul, Donita K. Two Renegade Realms, 1 vol. 2014. (Realm Walkers Ser.). (ENG.). 416p. (YA). pap. 13.99 *(978-0-310-73581-6(5))* Zondervan.
Paulsen, Gary. The Time Hackers. 2006. (ENG.). 96p. (J). (gr. 3-7). 5.99 *(978-0-553-48788-6(4),* Yearling) Random Hse. Children's Bks.
Peterson, Doug. Ben Hurry: A Lesson in Patience, 1 vol. Moore, Michael, illus. 2006. (Big Idea Books / VeggieTown Values Ser.: Bk. 8). (ENG.). 32p. (J). (gr. -1-3). pap. 3.99 *(978-0-310-70743-1(9))* Zonderkidz.
Pilkington, Linda Rash. Arthur Collins & the Three Wishes: Arthur the Brave! 322p. (YA). (gr. 4-18). 2009. pap. 13.95 *(978-0-615-26743-2(2))* 2008. 20.95 *(978-0-615-22213-4(7))* City Castles Publishing.
Pinkwater, Daniel M. The Yggyssey: How Iggy Wondered What Happened to All the Ghosts, Found Out Where They Went, & Went There. 2010. (ENG., Illus.). 256p. (J). (gr. 5-7).

S

pap. 6.99 (978-0-547-32865-2(6)) Houghton Mifflin Harcourt Publishing Co.

Prince, Maggie. The House on Hound Hill. 2003. (ENG.). 256p. (J). (gr. 5-7). pap. 15.95 (978-0-618-33124-6(7)) Houghton Mifflin Harcourt Publishing Co.

Rebecca, Stead. When You Reach Me. 2014. (ENG.). 208p. (J). (gr. 12-12). 11.24 (978-1-63245-235-1(9)) Lectorum Pubns., Inc.

Revealed. 2014. (Missing Ser.: 7). (ENG., Illus.). 448p. (J). (gr. 3-7). 18.99 (978-1-4169-8986-8(2), Simon & Schuster Bks. For Young Readers) Simon & Schuster Bks. For Young Readers.

Rockwell, Carey. Sabotage in Space. 2007. (ENG.). 162p. pap. 19.99 (978-1-4264-9345-4(2)); 184p. pap. 21.99 (978-1-4264-9726-1(1)) Creative Media Partners, LLC.

Rockwood, Roy. Through Space to Mars. 2008. 128p. (gr. 4-7). pap. 11.95 (978-1-60664-173-6(5)) Aegypan.

Rodda, Emily. The Wizard of Rondo. 2009. (ENG.). 400p. (J). (gr. 3-7). 16.99 (978-0-545-11516-2(7), Scholastic Pr.) Scholastic, Inc.

Rollins, James. Jake Ransom & the Howling Sphinx. 2012. (Jake Ransom Ser.: 2). (ENG.). 384p. (J). (gr. 5). pap. 7.99 (978-0-06-147384-5(7)) HarperCollins Pubs.

Rust, Ned. Patrick Griffin's First Birthday on Ith. 2017. (Patrick Griffin & the Three Worlds Ser.: 2). (ENG.). 304p. (J). 16.99 (978-1-62672-344-3(3), 9781626723443) Roaring Brook Pr.

—Patrick Griffin's Last Breakfast on Earth. 2016. (Patrick Griffin & the Three Worlds Ser.: 1). (ENG.). 416p. (J). 16.99 (978-1-62672-342-9(7), 9781626723429) Roaring Brook Pr.

Salerni, Dianne K. The Inquisitor's Mark. 2015. (Eighth Day Ser.: 2). (ENG.). 352p. (J). (gr. 3-7). 16.99 (978-0-06-227218-8(7)) HarperCollins Pubs.

Sanders, Ted. The Box & the Dragonfly. Bruno, Iacopo, illus. 2015. (Keepers Ser.: No. 1). 534p. (J). (978-0-06-239019-6(8)) Harper & Row Ltd.

—The Box & the Dragonfly. Bruno, Iacopo, illus. 2015. (Keepers Ser.: 1). (ENG.). 544p. (J). (gr. 3-7). 16.99 (978-0-06-227582-0(8)) HarperCollins Pubs.

Santat, Dan, illus. Are We There Yet? 2016. (ENG.). 40p. (J). (gr. -1-3). 17.99 (978-0-316-19999-5(0)) Little Brown & Co.

Sappenfield, Heather. Life at the Speed of Us. 2016. (ENG.). 384p. (YA). pap. 11.99 (978-0-7387-4730-9(0), Flux) North Star Editions.

Schmatz, Pat. Circle the Truth. 2007. (Exceptional Reading & Language Arts Titles for Intermediate Grades Ser.). (ENG.). 192p. (YA). (gr. 7-12). 16.95 (978-0-8225-7268-8(0)) Lerner Publishing Group.

Sedgwick, Marcus. The Ghosts of Heaven. 2015. (ENG.). 336p. (YA). (gr. 7-12). 17.99 (978-1-62672-125-8(4), 9781626721258) Roaring Brook Pr.

—The Ghosts of Heaven. 2016. (ENG.). 384p. (YA). pap. 9.99 (978-1-250-07367-9(7), 9781250073679) Square Fish.

Shinn, Sharon. Gateway. 2009. (ENG.). 288p. (YA). (gr. 7-18). 17.99 (978-0-670-01178-0(9), Viking Books for Young Readers) Penguin Young Readers Group.

Shire, Poppy. Jewel the Midnight Pony. Berg, Ron, illus. 2008. (Magic Pony Carousel Ser.: 4). (ENG.). 96p. (J). (gr. 2-5). pap. 3.99 (978-0-06-083788-4(8)) HarperCollins Pubs.

—Sparkle the Circus Pony. Berg, Ron, illus. 2007. (Magic Pony Carousel Ser.: 1). (ENG.). 96p. (J). (gr. 2-5). pap. 3.99 (978-0-06-083779-2(9)) HarperCollins Pubs.

—Star the Western Pony. Berg, Ron, illus. 2007. (Magic Pony Carousel Ser.: 3). (ENG.). 96p. (J). (gr. 2-5). pap. 3.99 (978-0-06-083785-3(3)) HarperCollins Pubs.

Signorino, John. Billy & the Aliens of Alpha-C, 1 vol. 2008. (ENG.). 36p. pap. 24.95 (978-1-60474-882-6(6)) America Star Bks.

Sividious Stark & the Stadium Between Worlds. 2013. (ENG.). 236p. (YA). pap. 12.99 (978-1-62108-273-6(3)) Covenant Communications, Inc.

Snyder, Laurel. Any Which Wall. Pham, LeUyen, illus. 2010. (ENG.). 256p. (J). (gr. 3-7). pap. 7.99 (978-0-375-85561-0(0), Yearling) Random Hse. Children's Bks.

—Seven Stories Up. 2015. (ENG.). 240p. (J). (gr. 3-7). 6.99 (978-0-375-87326-3(0), Yearling) Random Hse. Children's Bks.

Sorrells, Aaron. A Trip through the Solar System. 2010. 34p. pap. 16.00 (978-0-557-49151-3(7)) Lulu Pr., Inc.

Starmer, Aaron. The Riverman. 2015. (Riverman Trilogy Ser.: 1). (ENG.). 336p. (YA). (gr. 5-9). pap. 8.99 (978-1-250-05685-6(3), 9781250056856) Square Fish.

Stead, Rebecca. Cuando Me Alcances. 2011.Tr. of When You Reach Me. (SPA.). 294p. pap. (978-958-45-3215-2(4)) Norma S.A.

—When You Reach Me. (ENG.). (J). (gr. 3-7). 2010. 224p. 7.99 (978-0-375-85086-8(4), Yearling) 2009. 208p. 16.99 (978-0-385-73742-5(4), Lamb, Wendy Bks.) Random Hse. Children's Bks.

—When You Reach Me. 2010. lib. bdg. 18.40 (978-0-606-15179-5(6), Turtleback) Turtleback Bks.

Stephens, Berin L. Time Gangsters. 2012. pap. 14.99 (978-1-59955-966-7(8)) Cedar Fort, Inc./CFI Distribution.

Stephens, John. The Black Reckoning. 2015. (Books of Beginning Ser.). (ENG.). 432p. (J). (gr. 3-7). 17.99 (978-0-375-86872-6(0), Knopf Bks. for Young Readers) Random Hse. Children's Bks.

—The Emerald Atlas. (Books of Beginning Ser.). (ENG.). (J). (gr. 3-7). 2012. 448p. 7.99 (978-0-375-87271-6(X), Yearling) 2011. 432p. 17.99 (978-0-375-86870-2(4), Knopf Bks. for Young Readers) Random Hse. Children's Bks.

—The Emerald Atlas. l.t. ed. 2012. (Books of Beginning Ser.). (ENG.). 548p. (J). (gr. 4-7). 23.99 (978-1-4104-4234-5(9)) Thorndike Pr.

—The Fire Chronicle. 2012. (Illus.). 437p. (J). (978-0-449-81015-6(1)) Knopf, Alfred A. Inc.

—The Fire Chronicle. (Books of Beginning Ser.). (ENG.). 448p. (J). (gr. 3-7). 2013. 7.99 (978-0-375-87272-3(8), Yearling) 2012. (Illus.). 17.99 (978-0-375-86871-9(2), Knopf Bks. for Young Readers) Random Hse. Children's Bks.

Stevenson, Patricia. The Z Family Coloring Book. 2012. 60p. (gr. -1). pap. 8.99 (978-1-4582-0242-0(9), Abbott Pr.) Author Solutions, Inc.

Stone, Tamara Ireland. Time after Time. 2014. (ENG.). 368p. (YA). (gr. 7-12). pap. 9.99 (978-1-4231-5981-0(0)) Hyperion Bks. for Children.

Stories Beyond Time & Space. (J). pap. 15.50 (978-0-8359-0158-1(0)) Globe Fearon Educational Publishing.

Studio Mouse Staff. Space Adventure. rev. ed. 2008. (ENG., Illus.). (J). 12.99 (978-1-59069-609-5(3)) Studio Mouse LLC.

Tanigawa, Nagaru. The Disappearance of Haruhi Suzumiya. 2010. (Haruhi Suzumiya Ser.: 4). (ENG., Illus.). 192p. (YA). (gr. 10-17). pap. 18.00 (978-0-316-03889-8(X)) Little, Brown Bks. for Young Readers.

Teague, David. Henry Cicada's Extraordinary Elktonium Escapade. 2016. 320p. (J). (gr. 3-7). 16.99 (978-0-06-237745-6(0)) HarperCollins Pubs.

Teague, Mark & Scholastic, Inc. Staff. The Doom Machine. Teague, Mark, illus. 2009. (ENG., Illus.). 384p. (J). (gr. 3-7). 17.99 (978-0-545-15142-9(2), Blue Sky Pr., The) Scholastic, Inc.

Thompson, Kate. The New Policeman. 2008. (New Policeman Trilogy Ser.: 1). (ENG., Illus.). 464p. (YA). (gr. 8-12). pap. 9.99 (978-0-06-117429-2(7), Greenwillow Bks.) HarperCollins Pubs.

—The New Policeman. pap. 1.00 (978-1-4074-4550-2(2)) Recorded Bks., Inc.

A Thousand Pieces of You. 2014. (Firebird Ser.: 1). (ENG.). 368p. (YA). (gr. 9). 17.99 (978-0-06-227896-8(7)) HarperCollins Pubs.

Toft, Di. Wolven, Bk. 1. 2011. (Wolven Ser.: 1). (ENG.). 352p. (J). (gr. 3-7). pap. 7.99 (978-0-545-17110-6(5), Chicken Hse., The) Scholastic, Inc.

Turetsky, Bianca. The Time-Traveling Fashionista at the Palace of Marie Antoinette. 2013. (Time-Traveling Fashionista Ser.: 2). (ENG., Illus.). 272p. (J). (gr. 3-7). pap. 9.00 (978-0-316-10535-4(X), Poppy) Little, Brown Bks. for Young Readers.

Uttley, Alison & Singh, Mahendra. A Traveller in Time. Bray, Phyllis, illus. 2011. (ENG.). 336p. (J). (gr. 4-7). 17.95 (978-1-59017-388-6(0), NYR Children's Collection) New York Review of Bks., Inc., The.

Valentine, James. The Past Is Gone. 2007. (TimeJumpers Ser.: 1). (ENG.). 288p. (J). (gr. 3-7). pap. 13.99 (978-1-4169-3955-9(5), Simon & Schuster/Paula Wiseman Bks.) Simon & Schuster/Paula Wiseman Bks.

Warner, Michael N. The Titanic Game. Ordaz, Frank, illus. 2007. (ENG.). 208p. (J). pap. 11.95 (978-0-9744446-2-8(6)) All About Kids Publishing.

Webb, Philip. Six Days. 2011. (ENG.). 352p. (J). (gr. 5-9). 17.99 (978-0-545-31767-2(3), Chicken Hse., The) Scholastic, Inc.

Wells, H. G. The Time Machine, 1 vol. Dunn, Ben, illus. 2007. (Graphic Classics). (ENG.). 32p. (gr. 4-7). 28.50 (978-1-60270-054-3(0), Graphic Planet- Fiction) ABDO Publishing Co.

Wells, Rosemary. On the Blue Comet. Ibatoulline, Bagram, illus. (ENG.). 336p. (J). (gr. 5). 2012. pap. 8.99 (978-0-7636-5815-1(4)) 2010. 16.99 (978-0-7636-3722-4(X)) Candlewick Pr.

West, Jacqueline. The Second Spy. Bernatene, Poly, illus. 2013. (Books of Elsewhere Ser.: 3). (ENG.). 320p. (J). (gr. 5). pap. 7.99 (978-0-14-242608-1(3), Puffin Books) Penguin Young Readers Group.

—The Second Spy. 2013. (Books of Elsewhere Ser.: 3). lib. bdg. 18.40 (978-0-606-31698-9(1), Turtleback) Turtleback Bks.

—The Second Spy, Vol. 3. Bernatene, Poly, illus. 2012. (Books of Elsewhere Ser.: 3). (ENG.). 304p. (J). (gr. 5-18). 16.99 (978-0-8037-3689-4(4), Dial Bks) Penguin Young Readers Group.

—The Shadows. 2011. (Books of Elsewhere Ser.: 1). (ENG.). 272p. (J). (gr. 5-7). 7.99 (978-0-14-241872-7(2), Puffin Books) Penguin Young Readers Group.

—The Shadows. Bernatene, Poly, illus. 2010. (Books of Elsewhere Ser.: 1). (ENG.). 256p. (J). (gr. 5-18). 16.99 (978-0-8037-3440-1(9), Dial Bks) Penguin Young Readers Group.

—The Shadows. l.t. ed. 2010. (Books of Elsewhere Ser.: Vol. 1). (ENG.). 268p. 23.99 (978-1-4104-3139-4(8)) Thorndike Pr.

—The Shadows. 2011. (Books of Elsewhere Ser.: 1). lib. bdg. 17.20 (978-0-606-23070-4(X), Turtleback) Turtleback Bks.

—Spellbound, 2 vols. (Books of Elsewhere Ser.: 2). (ENG.). (J). (gr. 5-18). 2012. 320p. pap. 7.99 (978-0-14-242102-4(2), Puffin Books) Vol. 2. 2011. (Illus.). 304p. 16.99 (978-0-8037-3441-8(7), Dial Bks) Penguin Young Readers Group.

—Still Life: The Books of Elsewhere: Volume 5. Bernatene, Poly, illus. 2015. (Books of Elsewhere Ser.: 5). (ENG.). 352p. (J). (gr. 5). 7.99 (978-0-14-242297-7(5), Puffin Books) Penguin Young Readers Group.

—The Strangers. Bernatene, Poly, illus. (Books of Elsewhere Ser.: 4). (ENG.). (J). (gr. 5). 2014. 336p. pap. 7.99 (978-0-14-242575-6(3), Puffin Books) 2013. 320p. 16.99 (978-0-8037-3690-0(8), Dial Bks) Penguin Young Readers Group.

—The Strangers. 2014. (Books of Elsewhere Ser.: 4). lib. bdg. 18.40 (978-0-606-35680-0(0)) Turtleback Bks.

Weyn, Suzanne. The Renaissance Kids. Graves, Linda Dockey, illus. 2003. (ENG.). 56p. (J). (gr. 6-8). pap. 7.97 net. (978-0-7652-3277-9(4), Celebration Pr.) Pearson Schl.

White, Dorine. The Emerald Ring (Cleopatra's Legacy) 2013. 183p. (YA). pap. 13.99 (978-1-4621-1133-6(5), Horizon Pubs.) Cedar Fort, Inc./CFI Distribution.

Williams, Sean. Hollowgirl: A Twinmaker Novel. 2015. (Twinmaker Ser.: 3). (ENG.). 512p. (YA). (gr. 8). 17.99 (978-0-06-220327-4(4)) HarperCollins Pubs.

—Twinmaker. 2013. (Twinmaker Ser.: 1). (ENG.). 496p. (YA). (gr. 8). 17.99 (978-0-06-220321-2(5), HarperTeen) HarperCollins Pubs.

Willis, Jeanne. Shamanka. 2009. (J). pap. (978-0-7636-3767-5(X)) Candlewick Pr.

Wilson, N. D. The Chestnut King. 2011. (100 Cupboards Ser.: 3). (ENG., Illus.). 512p. (J). (gr. 3-7). 8.99 (978-0-375-83886-6(4), Yearling) Random Hse. Children's Bks.

—Dandelion Fire. 2009. (100 Cupboards Ser.: 2). (ENG.). 480p. (J). (gr. 3-7). 8.99 (978-0-375-83884-2(8), Yearling) Random Hse. Children's Bks.

—The Door Before (100 Cupboards Prequel) 2017. (ENG.). 240p. (J). (gr. 3-7). lib. bdg. 19.99 (978-0-449-81678-3(8), Random Hse. Bks. for Young Readers) Random Hse. Children's Bks.

—100 Cupboards. 2008. (100 Cupboards Ser.: 1). (ENG.). 320p. (J). (gr. 3-7). 7.99 (978-0-375-83882-8(1), Yearling) Random Hse. Children's Bks.

Winters, Jeffrey. Mystic Uncle & the Magical Bridge. 2005. 116p. (J). (gr. 3-7). pap. 10.95 (978-1-59526-167-0(2), Llumina Pr.) Aeon Publishing Inc.

Wood, Maryrose. How I Found the Perfect Dress. 2008. (ENG.). 240p. (YA). (gr. 9-18). 11.00 (978-0-425-21939-3(9), Berkley) Penguin Publishing Group.

Woodruff, Elvira. George Washington's Spy. (Time Travel Adventures Ser.). (ENG.). 240p. (J). (gr. 3-7). 2012. pap. 6.99 (978-0-545-10488-3(2), Scholastic Paperbacks) 2010. 16.99 (978-0-545-10487-6(4), Scholastic Pr.) Scholastic, Inc.

—George Washington's Spy. 2012. lib. bdg. 17.20 (978-0-606-26216-3(4), Turtleback) Turtleback Bks.

SPACE EXPLORATION (ASTRONAUTICS)

see Outer Space—Exploration

SPACE FLIGHT

see also Interplanetary Voyages; Outer Space—Exploration; Space Stations

Aldrin, Buzz. Look to the Stars. Minor, Wendell, illus. 2009. (ENG.). 40p. (J). (gr. 1-3). 17.99 (978-0-399-24721-7(1), G.P. Putnam's Sons Books for Young Readers) Penguin Young Readers Group.

Baker, David. Living in Space. 2008. (Exploring Space Ser.). (Illus.). 32p. (J). (gr. 4-6). lib. bdg. 26.00 (978-1-59036-769-8(3)) Weigl Pubs., Inc.

Baker, David & Kissock, Heather. Living in Space. 2008. (Exploring Space Ser.). (Illus.). 32p. (J). (gr. 4-6). pap. 9.95 (978-1-59036-770-4(7)) Weigl Pubs., Inc.

Benoit, Peter. The Space Race. 2012. (Cornerstones of Freedom, Third Ser.). (ENG.). 64p. (J). pap. 8.95 (978-0-531-28165-9(5)); (gr. 4-6). lib. bdg. 30.00 (978-0-531-23065-7(1)) Scholastic Library Publishing. (Children's Pr.).

Biskup, Agnieszka. Amazing Story of Space Travel. Pop Art Properties Staff, illus. 2013. (STEM Adventures Ser.). (ENG.). 32p. (gr. 3-4). 30.65 (978-1-4765-0124-6(6), Graphic Library) Capstone Press of Coughlan Cos.

Blast off with Ellen Ochoa! (Greetings Ser.: Vol. 3). 24p. (gr. 2-3). 31.00 (978-0-7635-5861-1(3)) Rigby Education.

Blast off with Ellen Ochoa! 6 Small Books. (Greetings Ser.: Vol. 3). 24p. (gr. 2-3). 31.00 (978-0-7635-9432-9(6)) Rigby Education.

Bortz, Fred. Envisioning Outer Space: Where Science & Fiction Meet. 2015. (J). (978-1-4677-6305-9(5)); lib. bdg. (978-1-4677-3740-1(2)) Twenty First Century Bks.

Carroll, Jillian. Where to Stay. 2003. (J). pap. (978-1-58417-233-8(9)) Lake Street Pubs.

Carson, Mary Kay. The Mission to Pluto: The First Visit to an Ice Dwarf & the Kuiper Belt. Uhlman, Tom, photos by. 2017. (Scientists in the Field Ser.). (ENG., Illus.). 80p. (J). (gr. 5-7). 18.99 (978-0-544-41671-0(6), HMH Books For Young Readers) Houghton Mifflin Harcourt Publishing Co.

Clark, Julie. The 10 Greatest Breakthroughs in Space Exploration. 2008. (J). 14.99 (978-1-55448-520-8(7)) Scholastic Library Publishing.

Dalmatian Press Staff. My Race into Space! 2008. (ENG.). 9p. bds. 4.95 (978-1-58117-717-6(8), Intervisual/Piggy Toes) Bendon, Inc.

DeYoe, Aaron. Space Travel, 1 vol. 2015. (ENG., Illus.). 24p. (J). (978-1-62403-745-0(3), 1391272) ABDO Publishing Co.

Dubbs, Chris. Space Dogs: Pioneers of Space Travel. 2003. 102p. (YA). pap. 11.95 (978-0-595-26735-4(1), Writer's Showcase Pr.) iUniverse, Inc.

Farnighetti, Robert, et al. How Does a Spacecraft Reach the Moon? 2009. (Science in the Real World Ser.). (Illus.). 32p. (gr. 4-6). 28.00 (978-1-60413-470-4(4), Chelsea Clubhouse) Facts On File, Inc.

Feldman, Heather. Dennis Tito: The First Space Tourist. 2009. (Space Firsts Ser.). 24p. (gr. 3-4). 42.50 (978-1-60853-112-7(0), PowerKids Pr.) Rosen Publishing Group, Inc., The.

—Dennis Tito, the First Space Tourist. 2003. (Space Firsts Ser.). (Illus.). 24p. (J). lib. bdg. 22.60 (978-0-8239-6249-5(0), PowerKids Pr.) Rosen Publishing Group, Inc., The.

From Earth to the Stars. 2017. (From Earth to the Stars Ser.). 48p. (gr. 10-12). 107.40 **(978-1-5081-0527-5(8))**; pap. 56.20 **(978-1-5081-0529-9(4))** Rosen Publishing Group, Inc., The. (Britannica Educational Publishing).

Gardner, Jane P. Travel Science, Vol. 11. Lewin, Russ, ed. 2015. (Science 24/7 Ser.). (Illus.). 48p. (J). (gr. 5). 20.95 (978-1-4222-3415-0(0)) Mason Crest.

Goldstein, Margaret J. Astronauts: A Space Discovery Guide. 2017. (Space Discovery Guides). (ENG.). 48p. (J). (gr. 4-6). 16.99 **(978-1-5124-3800-0(6)**, Lerner Pubns.); 47.99 **(978-1-5124-3801-7(4)**, Lerner Pubns.); 47.99 **(978-1-5124-2793-6(4)**, Lerner Pubns.); (Illus.). 31.99 (978-1-5124-2588-8(5)) Lerner Publishing Group.

The Great Space Race. (Color & Learn Ser.). 36p. (J). (gr. 1-5). pap. (978-1-882210-15-2(8)) Action Publishing, Inc.

Gross, Miriam J. All about Space Missions. 2009. (Blast Off! Ser.). 24p. (J). (gr. 2-5). (ENG.). pap. 8.25 (978-1-4358-3138-4(1)); lib. bdg. 22.60 (978-1-4358-2740-0(6)) Rosen Publishing Group, Inc., The. (PowerKids Pr.).

Hansen, Ole Steen. Space Flight. 2003. (Story of Flight Ser.). (ENG., Illus.). 32p. (J). (gr. 2-9). lib. bdg. (978-0-7787-1207-7(9)) Crabtree Publishing Co.

Holcroft, John & Candlewick Press Staff. Space Exploration: Panorama Pops. Holcroft, John, illus. 2015. (ENG., Illus.). 30p. (J). (gr. k-4). 8.99 (978-0-7636-7699-5(3)) Candlewick Pr.

Houran, Lori Haskins. A Trip into Space: An Adventure to the International Space Station. Marquez, Francisca, illus. 2014. (ENG.). 24p. (J). (gr. -1-3). 15.99 (978-0-8075-8091-2(0)) Whitman, Albert & Co.

Jones, Tom. Ask the Astronaut: A Galaxy of Astonishing Answers to Your Questions on Spaceflight. 2016. (ENG., Illus.). 224p. (YA). (gr. 5-12). pap. 12.95 (978-1-58834-537-0(8), Smithsonian Bks.) Smithsonian Institution Scholarly Pr.

Kemoun, Hubert Ben & Grenier, Christian. Half & Half-Voyage into Space. Moutarde & Blanchin, Matthieu, illus. 2008. 48p. (J). 9.95 (978-1-60115-209-1(4)); pap. 4.99 (978-1-60115-210-7(8)) Treasure Bay, Inc.

Ladybird. Space, Level 4. 2016. (Ladybird Readers Ser.). (ENG.). 16p. (J). (gr. 2-4). pap., act. bk. ed. 5.99 (978-0-241-25377-9(2)) Penguin Bks., Ltd. GBR. Dist: Independent Pubs. Group.

Lakin, Patricia. The Stellar Story of Space Travel. Burroughs, Scott, illus. 2016. (History of Fun Stuff Ser.). (ENG.). 48p. (J). (gr. 1-3). pap. 3.99 (978-1-4814-5623-4(7), Simon Spotlight) Simon Spotlight.

Lassieur, Allison. International Space Station: An Interactive Space Exploration Adventure. 2016. (You Choose: Space Ser.). (ENG., Illus.). 112p. (gr. 3-4). lib. bdg. 31.99 (978-1-4914-8104-2(8), You Choose Bks.) Capstone Press of Coughlan Cos.

Launch into Space! 2015. (Launch into Space! Ser.). (ENG.). 32p. (J). (gr. 3-4). pap., pap., pap. 63.12 (978-0-7660-7056-1(5)) Enslow Pubs., Inc.

Llimós, Anna. Space Adventure Crafts. 2010. (Fun Adventure Crafts Ser.). (Illus.). 32p. (J). pap. 7.95 (978-0-7660-3733-5(9), Enslow Elementary) Enslow Pubs., Inc.

Llimós, Anna & Library Association Staff. Space Adventure Crafts. 2010. (Fun Adventure Crafts Ser.). (Illus.). 32p. (J). 23.94 (978-0-7660-3732-8(0), Enslow Elementary) Enslow Pubs., Inc.

Lubka, S. Ruth. Pupniks: The Story of Two Space Dogs, 1 vol. 2003. (ENG., Illus.). 32p. (J). (gr. k-3). 16.95 (978-0-7614-5137-2(4)) Marshall Cavendish Corp.

Meet NASA Inventor Masahiro Ono & His Team's Asteroid-Harpooning Hitcher. 2017. (J). **(978-0-7166-6161-0(6))** World Bk., Inc.

Miles, Lisa & Smith, Alastair. Astronomy & Space. 2003. (Complete Bks.). (ENG., Illus.). 1p. (YA). (gr. 3-18). pap. 14.95 (978-0-7460-3104-9(1)) EDC Publishing.

Miller, Gary. The Outer Limits: The Future of Space Exploration. 2009. (Current Science Ser.). (ENG.). 48p. (gr. 4-7). (YA). lib. bdg. 31.00 (978-1-4339-2242-8(8)); (J). pap. 8.95 (978-1-4339-2246-6(0), Gareth Stevens Learning Library) Stevens, Gareth Publishing LLLP.

Newland, Sonya. Space Exploration: Triumphs & Tragedies. 2016. (ENG., Illus.). 48p. (J). pap. (978-0-7787-2231-1(7)) Crabtree Publishing Co.

Parker, Steve & Snedding, Robert. A Brief Illustrated History of Space Exploration. 2017. (Brief Illustrated History Ser.). (ENG.). 32p. (gr. 3-5). lib. bdg. 27.32 (978-1-5157-2519-0(7), Fact Finders) Capstone Press of Coughlan Cos.

Porterfield, Jason. The Benefits of Spaceflight & Space Exploration. 2017. (From Earth to the Stars Ser.). 48p. (gr. 10-12). pap. 14.05 **(978-1-68048-661-2(6)**, Britannica Educational Publishing) Rosen Publishing Group, Inc., The.

Randolph, Joanne. Dennis Tito: First Space Tourist. 2009. (Reading Room Collection 2 Ser.). 24p. (gr. 3-4). 42.50 (978-1-60851-962-0(7), PowerKids Pr.) Rosen Publishing Group, Inc., The.

—Dennis Tito, First Space Tourist. 2003. (Reading Room Collection 2 Ser.). (Illus.). 24p. (J). lib. bdg. 22.60 (978-0-8239-3699-1(6)) Rosen Publishing Group, Inc., The.

Rice, William. Despegar Hacia el Campamento Espacial. 2017. (TIME for Kids en Español - Level 3 Ser.). (SPA.). 32p. (gr. 3-3). lib. bdg. 31.99 **(978-1-5157-5180-9(5))** Time for Kids Inc AUS. Dist: Capstone Pub.

Rice, William B. & Wolfe, Hillary. Blast off to Space Camp, 1 vol. 2nd rev. ed. 2012. (Nonfiction Readers Ser.). (ENG.). 32p. (J). (gr. 3-3). pap. 8.99 (978-1-4333-3673-7(1)) Teacher Created Materials, Inc.

Roby, Cynthia A. Building Aircraft & Spacecraft: Aerospace Engineers, 01 vols., 1. 2016. (Engineers Rule Ser.). (ENG., Illus.). 32p. (J). pap. 11.75 (978-1-5081-4528-8(8), PowerKids Pr.) Rosen Publishing Group, Inc., The.

Rooney, Anne. A Math Journey Through Space. 2014. (ENG.). 32p. (J). (978-0-7787-0730-1(X)) Crabtree Publishing Co.

Royston, Angela. Space Blog. 2010. (ENG., Illus.). 32p. (J). (978-0-7787-9910-8(7)); pap. (978-0-7787-9931-3(X)) Crabtree Publishing Co.

Shaughnessy, Mara. LEGO Man in Space: A True Story. 2013. (ENG., Illus.). 32p. (J). (gr. -1-3). 14.95 (978-1-62087-544-5(6), 620544, Sky Pony Pr.) Skyhorse Publishing Co., Inc.

Sibila, Tom. SpaceShipOne: Making Dreams Come True. 2005. (High Five Reading - Blue Ser.). (ENG., Illus.). 48p. (gr. 3-4). per. 9.00 (978-0-7368-5744-4(3), High Five Reading (RBL)) Capstone Press of Coughlan Cos.

Snedden, Robert. Exploring Space. 2016. (Sci-Hi: Earth & Space Science Ser.). (ENG.). 48p. (gr. 4-4). pap. 8.99 (978-1-4109-8522-4(9), Sci-Hi) Heinemann-Raintree.

Space Exploration: Science Technology Engineering. 2014. (Calling All Innovators: a Career for You Ser.). (ENG.). 64p. (J). lib. bdg. 32.00 (978-0-531-20615-7(7)) Scholastic Library Publishing.

Space Missions. (Illus.). (J). (gr. k-5). 119.70 (978-0-8239-7142-8(2)) Rosen Publishing Group, Inc., The.

Spilsbury, Louise & Spilsbury, Richard. Fly to Mars! Forces in Space. 2015. (Feel the Force Ser.). (ENG., Illus.). 48p. (gr. 3-6). 33.32 (978-1-4846-2600-9(1)) Heinemann-Raintree.

Top That Publishing Staff, ed. Lets Explore Space. 2004. (Fun Kits Ser.). (Illus.). 48p. (J). (978-1-84510-244-9(4)) Top That! Publishing PLC.

A Trip into Space: Individual Title Six-Pack. (Story Steps Ser.). (gr. k-2). 23.00 (978-0-7635-9614-9(0)) Rigby Education.

West, David. Spacecraft. West, David, illus. 2017. (What's Inside? Ser.). (Illus.). 24p. (gr. k-3). 28.50 **(978-1-62588-404-6(4)**, Smart Apple Media) Black Rabbit Bks.

West, David. Ten of the Best Adventures in Space. 2015. (Ten of the Best: Stories of Exploration & Adventure Ser.). (ENG., Illus.). 24p. (J). (gr. 3-6). (978-0-7787-1836-9(0)) Crabtree Publishing Co.

Williams, Dave & Cunti, Loredana. To Burp or Not to Burp: A Guide to Your Body in Space. Key, Theodore, illus. 2016. (Dr. Dave — Astronaut Ser.). (ENG.). 56p. (J). (gr. 1-5). pap. 12.95 (978-1-55451-853-1(9)) Annick Pr., Ltd. CAN. Dist: Publishers Group West (PGW).

Woods, David & Harland, David M. Inside Gemini. 2017. (Geek's Guide to Space Ser.). 192p. (J). (gr. 12-14). 44.60 **(978-1-4994-6697-3(8)**, Rosen Young Adult) Rosen Publishing Group, Inc., The.

World Book, Inc Staff, contrib. by. Human Space Exploration. 2010. (J). *(978-0-7166-9543-1(X))* World Bk., Inc.

Zelon, Helen. The Endeavor Mission STS-61: Fixing the Hubble Space Telescope. 2009. (Space Missions Ser.). 24p. (gr. 3-4). 42.50 *(978-1-60853-117-2(1)*, PowerKids Pr.) Rosen Publishing Group, Inc., The.

SPACE FLIGHT—FICTION

Alafaci, Marie. Zelda's Big Adventure. McG, Shane, illus. 2017. (ENG.). 32p. (J). (gr. -1-3). 16.99 ***(978-1-328-66081-7(8)**, Clarion Bks.)* Houghton Mifflin Harcourt Trade & Reference Pubs.

Alley, R. W. Mitchell on the Moon. 2016. (ENG., Illus.). 32p. (J). (gr. -1-3). 14.99 *(978-0-547-90703-1(6))* Houghton Mifflin Harcourt Publishing Co.

Anderson, Jodi Lynn. Midnight at the Electric. 2017. 272p. (YA). (gr. 9). 17.99 *(978-0-06-239354-8(5)*, HarperTeen) HarperCollins Pubs.

Applegate, K. A., pseud. Survival. 2003. (Remnants Ser.: No. 13). 165p. (J). (gr. 4-8). 12.65 *(978-0-7569-5301-0(4))* Perfection Learning Corp.

Appleton, Victor. The Alien Probe. (Tom Swift Ser.). (J). (gr. 3-7). 20.95 *(978-0-88411-464-2(3))* Amereon Ltd.

—The Rescue Mission. (Tom Swift Ser.). (J). (gr. 3-7). 20.95 *(978-0-88411-458-1(9))* Amereon Ltd.

—Terror on the Moons of Jupiter. (Tom Swift Ser.). (J). (gr. 3-7). 20.95 *(978-0-88411-460-4(0))* Amereon Ltd.

Arnold, Tedd. Green Wilma, Frog in Space. Arnold, Tedd, illus. 2009. (ENG., Illus.). 32p. (J). (gr. -1-3). 16.99 *(978-0-8037-2698-7(8)*, Dial Bks) Penguin Young Readers Group.

Aston, Dianna Hutts. The Moon over Star. Pinkney, Jerry, illus. 2008. (ENG.). 32p. (J). (gr. 1-3). 17.99 *(978-0-8037-3107-3(8)*, Dial Bks) Penguin Young Readers Group.

Barbini, F. T. Tijaran Tales: White Child. 2011. 214p. pap. *(978-0-7552-1349-8(1))* Authors OnLine, Ltd.

Barnes, John. Losers in Space. 2012. (ENG.). 448p. (YA). (gr. 9-18). 18.99 *(978-0-670-06156-3(5)*, Viking Books for Young Readers) Penguin Young Readers Group.

Bell, David. Pyjamas in Space. 2007. (Dawn Gray Ser.). (ENG.). 260p. pap. *(978-1-84167-580-0(6))* Ransom Publishing Ltd.

Bennett, Jeffrey. Max Goes to the Moon: A Science Adventure with Max the Dog. Okamoto, Alan, illus. 2nd ed. 2012. (Science Adventures with Max the Dog Ser.). (ENG.). 32p. (J). (gr. 2-4). 15.00 *(978-1-937548-20-9(1))* Big Kid Science.

Bergman, Mara. Oliver Who Would Not Sleep! Maland, Nick, illus. 2007. (J). *(978-0-439-92827-4(3)*, Levine, Arthur A. Bks.) Scholastic, Inc.

Blake Savage. Rip Foster Rides the Gray Planet. 2007. (ENG.). 172p. per. 19.99 *(978-1-4346-3762-8(X))*; 188p. per. 21.99 *(978-1-4346-3776-5(X))* Creative Media Partners, LLC.

Brallier, Max. Galactic Hot Dogs 2: The Wiener Strikes Back. Maguire, Rachel & Kelley, Nichole, illus. 2016. (Galactic Hot Dogs Ser.: 2). (ENG.). 288p. (J). (gr. 3-7). 13.99 *(978-1-4814-2496-7(3)*, Aladdin) Simon & Schuster Children's Publishing.

Brockington, Drew. CatStronauts: Race to Mars. 2017. (CatStronauts Ser.: 2). (ENG.). 184p. (J). (gr. 1-5). 16.99 *(978-0-316-30748-2(3))* Little, Brown Bks. for Young Readers.

Brooks, Walter R. Freddy & the Space Ship. Wiese, Kurt, illus. 2011. (ENG.). 266p. (gr. 2-18). 10.99 *(978-1-59020-469-6(7))* Overlook Pr., The.

Brown, Jeff. Stanley in Space. Pamintuan, Macky, illus. 2009. (Flat Stanley Ser.). (ENG.). 128p. (J). (gr. 2-5). pap. 4.99 *(978-0-06-442174-4(0))* HarperCollins Pubs.

—Stanley in Space. Nash, Scott, illus. 2009. (Flat Stanley Ser.: 3). (J). (gr. k-3). lib. bdg. 14.75 *(978-0-613-66735-7(2)*, Turtleback) Turtleback Bks.

Buckeridge, Anthony. According to Jennings. 2008. (Jennings Ser.: 6). (ENG.). 190p. (J). (gr. 4-7). pap. 12.95 *(978-0-7551-0165-8(0))* House of Stratus, Inc. GBR. Dist: Gardners Bks. Ltd.

Burns, Dal. The Adventures of Phoo. 2006. 148p. pap. 24.95 *(978-1-4241-1773-4(9))* PublishAmerica, Inc.

Cameron, Eleanor. Stowaway to the Mushroom Planet. 2003. (J). (gr. 4-8). 21.50 *(978-0-8446-7237-3(8))* Smith, Peter Pub., Inc.

Card, Orson Scott. Pathfinder. (ENG.). 672p. (YA). (gr. 7). 2011. pap. 12.99 *(978-1-4169-9179-3(4))* 2010. 19.99 *(978-1-4169-9176-2(X))* Simon Pulse. (Simon Pulse).

—Pathfinder. l.t. ed. 2011. (Pathfinder Ser.). (ENG.). 802p. 23.99 *(978-1-4104-3681-8(0))* Thorndike Pr.

Chad, Jon. Leo Geo & the Cosmic Crisis. Chad, Jon, illus. 2013. (ENG., Illus.). 40p. (J). (gr. 2-6). 16.99 *(978-1-59643-822-4(3)*, 9781596438224) Roaring Brook Pr.

Courtenay, L. A. Space Penguins Galaxy Race! Davies, James, illus. 2015. (Space Penguins Ser.). (ENG.). 112p. (gr. 2-3). lib. bdg. 22.65 *(978-1-4342-9783-9(7))* Stone Arch Bks.

—Space Penguins Meteor Madness! Davies, James, illus. 2015. (Space Penguins Ser.). (ENG.). 112p. (gr. 2-3). lib. bdg. 22.65 *(978-1-4342-9782-2(9))* Stone Arch Bks.

Dare, Danni. Jake Jett: Adventures in Space. 2010. 32p. pap. 12.99 *(978-1-4520-4981-6(5))* AuthorHouse.

Deluca, Alison. Christmas O'Clock: A Collection. Daly, Lisa, illus. 2013. 198p. pap. 9.99 *(978-1-939296-98-6(6))* Myrddin Publishing Group.

Disney Book Group. Miles from Tomorrowland Spaceship Invader. Disney Storybook Art Team, illus. 2016. (ENG.). 24p. (J). (gr. -1-k). pap. 4.99 *(978-1-4847-1911-4(5))* Disney Pr.

Dixon, Andy. Star Quest. Brooks, Felicity, ed. Harris, Nick, illus. 2006. (Usborne Fantasy Puzzle Bks.). 32p. (YA). (gr. 7). lib. bdg. 15.99 *(978-1-58086-906-5(8)*, Usborne) EDC Publishing.

Draper, Sharon M. The Space Mission Adventure. Watson, Jesse Joshua, illus. 2012. (Clubhouse Mysteries Ser.: 4). (ENG.). 112p. (J). (gr. 3-7). 15.99 *(978-1-4424-4225-2(5))*; pap. 5.99 *(978-1-4424-4226-9(3))* Simon & Schuster Children's Publishing. (Aladdin).

DuPrau, Jeanne. Voyagers: Escape the Vortex (Book 5) 2016. (Voyager Ser.). (ENG.). 208p. (J). (gr. 3-7). 12.99 *(978-0-385-38670-8(2)*, Random Hse. Bks. for Young Readers) Random Hse. Children's Bks.

Epstein, Adam Jay & Jacobson, Andrew. Starbounders. McClellan, David, illus. 2013. (Starbounders Ser.: 1). (ENG.). 320p. (J). (gr. 3-7). 16.99 *(978-0-06-212022-9(0))* HarperCollins Pubs.

—Starbounders Vol. 2: Rebellion. 2014. (Starbounders Ser.: 2). (ENG.). 304p. (J). (gr. 3-7). 16.99 *(978-0-06-212027-4(1))* HarperCollins Pubs.

Espluga, Maria. I, Astronaut: Yo, Astronauta. 2009. (SPA & ENG.). 28p. (J). 13.95 *(978-1-931398-56-5(9))* Me+Mi Publishing.

Fyfe, H. b. & Fyfe, H. B. The Outbreak of Peace. 2011. 18p. 13.95 *(978-1-4638-9705-5(7))* Rodgers, Alan Bks.

Ganz-Schmitt, Sue. Planet Kindergarten. Prigmore, Shane, illus. 2016. (ENG.). 36p. (J). (gr. -1-k). 7.99 *(978-1-4521-5644-6(1))* Chronicle Bks. LLC.

—Planet Kindergarten: 100 Days in Orbit. Prigmore, Shane, illus. 2016. (ENG.). 36p. (J). (gr. -1-k). 16.99 *(978-1-4521-3776-6(5))* Chronicle Bks. LLC.

Gehrt, Linda. My Trip, My Spaceship. 2004. 26p. pap. 24.95 *(978-1-4137-3392-1(1))* PublishAmerica, Inc.

Gibbs, Stuart. Space Case. 2015. (Moon Base Alpha Ser.). (ENG., Illus.). 368p. (J). (gr. 3-7). pap. 7.99 *(978-1-4424-9487-9(5)*, Simon & Schuster Bks. For Young Readers) Simon & Schuster Bks. For Young Readers.

—Space Case. 2015. (Moon Base Alpha Ser.: 1). lib. bdg. 18.40 *(978-0-606-37883-3(9))* Turtleback Bks.

Goulbourne, Nathaniel. The Aliens Zoo. 2013. (Illus.). 28p. pap. 21.35 *(978-1-4817-8198-5(7))* AuthorHouse.

Handford, Martin. Where's Waldo? Spaer Adventure: The Great Space Adventure. (Illus.). 24p. (J). (gr. k-18). 19.95 *(978-0-9627001-4-9(2))* Futech Educational Products, Inc.

Harstad, Johan & Chace, Tara. 172 Hours on the Moon. 2012. (ENG.). 368p. (gr. 7-17). 17.99 *(978-0-316-18288-1(5))* Little Brown & Co.

Hawking, Lucy & Hawking, Stephen W. George's Cosmic Treasure Hunt. Parsons, Garry, illus. 2011. (George's Secret Key Ser.). (ENG.). 352p. (J). (gr. 3-7). pap. 11.99 *(978-1-4424-2175-2(4)*, Simon & Schuster Bks. For Young Readers) Simon & Schuster Bks. For Young Readers.

Hawking, Stephen & Hawking, Lucy. George & the Unbreakable Code. Parsons, Garry, illus. 2016. (George's Secret Key Ser.). (ENG.). 352p. (J). (gr. 3-7). 18.99 *(978-1-4814-6627-1(5)*, Simon & Schuster Bks. For Young Readers) Simon & Schuster Bks. For Young Readers.

Hawking, Stephen W. & Hawking, Lucy. George's Cosmic Treasure Hunt. Parsons, Garry, illus. 2009. (George's Secret Key Ser.). (ENG.). 320p. (J). (gr. 3-7). 19.99 *(978-1-4169-8671-3(5)*, Simon & Schuster Bks. For Young Readers) Simon & Schuster Bks. For Young Readers.

Hayes, Vicki C. Space Trip, 1 vol. 2015. (Red Rhino Ser.). (ENG.). 72p. (J). (gr. 3-6). mass mkt. 7.95 *(978-1-62250-965-2(X))* Saddleback Educational Publishing, Inc.

Hergé. Destination Moon.Tr. of Objectif Lune. (J). (gr. 3-8). ring bd. 19.95 *(978-0-8288-5026-1(7))*; (Illus.). 62p. 19.95 *(978-0-8288-5027-8(5))* French & European Pubns., Inc.

—Objectif Lune.Tr. of Destination Moon. (FRE., Illus.). (J). (gr. 7-9). ring bd. 19.95 *(978-0-8288-5051-3(8))* French & European Pubns., Inc.

—On a Marche sur la Lune. (Tintin Ser.).Tr. of Explorers on the Moon. (FRE.). (J). pap. 21.95 *(978-2-203-00116-9(X))* Casterman, Editions FRA. Dist: Distribooks, Inc.

—On a Marche sur la Lune.Tr. of Explorers on the Moon. (FRE., Illus.). (J). (gr. 7-9). ring bd. 19.95 *(978-0-8288-5053-7(4))* French & European Pubns., Inc.

Hillert, Margaret. Up, up, & Away. Spinks, Scott, illus. 2016. (BeginningtoRead Ser.). (ENG.). 32p. (J). (gr. 1-2). 22.60 *(978-1-59953-806-8(7))* Norwood Hse. Pr.

Jeapes, Ben. His Majesty's Starship. 2013. 348p. pap. *(978-1-909016-18-7(7))* Monico.

Jeffers, Oliver. The Way Back Home. Jeffers, Oliver, illus. 2008. (ENG., Illus.). 32p. (J). (gr. -1-3). 17.99 *(978-0-399-25074-3(3)*, Philomel Bks.) Penguin Young Readers Group.

Jones, Allan Frewin. Starship. (Hunter & Moon Mystery Ser.: Vol. 5). 169p. (J). pap. 8.99 *(978-0-340-70964-1(2))* Hodder & Stoughton GBR. Dist: Trafalgar Square Publishing.

Kaczynski, Heather. Dare Mighty Things. 2017. 384p. (YA). (gr. 8). 17.99 ***(978-0-06-247986-0(5)**, HarperTeen)* HarperCollins Pubs.

Kaufman, Amie. Illuminae. 2017. lib. bdg. 24.50 ***(978-0-606-39847-3(3))*** Turtleback Bks.

Kaufman, Amie & Kristoff, Jay. Illuminae. 2015. (Illuminae Files Ser.). (ENG., Illus.). 608p. (YA). (gr. 9). lib. bdg. 21.99 *(978-0-553-49912-4(2))*; 18.99 *(978-0-553-49911-7(4))* Random Hse. Children's Bks. (Knopf Bks. for Young Readers).

Kelly, Mark. Astrotwins — Project Rescue. 2016. (Astrotwins Ser.). (ENG., Illus.). 256p. (J). (gr. 3-7). 16.99 *(978-1-4814-2458-5(0)*, Simon & Schuster/Paula Wiseman Bks.) Simon & Schuster/Paula Wiseman Bks.

—Mousetronaut Goes to Mars. Payne, C. F., illus. 2013. (ENG.). 40p. (J). (gr. -1-3). 16.99 *(978-1-4424-8426-9(8)*, Simon & Schuster/Paula Wiseman Bks.) Simon & Schuster/Paula Wiseman Bks.

Kerr, P. B., pseud. One Small Step. 2009. (ENG.). 320p. (J). (gr. 3-9). pap. 8.99 *(978-1-4169-4214-6(9)*, McElderry, Margaret K. Bks.) McElderry, Margaret K. Bks.

King, Wesley. The Incredible Space Raiders from Space! 2015. (ENG., Illus.). 304p. (J). (gr. 3-7). 16.99 *(978-1-4814-2319-9(3)*, Simon & Schuster Bks. For Young Readers) Simon & Schuster Bks. For Young Readers.

Korda, Lerryn & Korda, Lerryn. Rocket to the Moon. Korda, Lerryn & Korda, Lerryn, illus. 2010. (Playtime with Little Nye Ser.). (ENG., Illus.). 32p. (J). (— 1). 8.99 *(978-0-7636-4652-3(0))* Candlewick Pr.

Kristoff, Amie Kaufman/Jay. ILLUMINAE. EXPEDIENTE_01 (ILLUMINAE 1) 2016. (SPA.). 592p. (J). (gr. 6). pap. 17.95 *(978-84-204-8355-9(9)*, Alfaguara Juvenil) Santillana USA Publishing Co., Inc.

Landers, Ace. Anakin: Space Pilot. White, David A., illus. 2011. (Lego Star Wars Ser.). (ENG.). 16p. (J). (gr. -1-3). 12.99 *(978-0-545-30440-5(7))* Scholastic, Inc.

Lavoie, Rejean. Des Legumes Pour Frank Einstein. Begin, Jean-Guy, illus. 2004. (Des 9 Ans. Ser.: Vol. 44). (FRE.). 120p. (J). 8.95 *(978-2-89599-006-2(9))* Editions de la Paix CAN. Dist: World of Reading, Ltd.

Layne, Steven L. Thomas's Sheep & the Spectacular Science Project, 1 vol. Board, Perry, illus. 2004. (ENG.). 32p. (J). (gr. k-3). 16.99 *(978-1-58980-210-0(1))* Pelican Publishing Co., Inc.

Litton, Jonathan. Planet Pop-Up: Monkey on the Moon. Anderson, Nicola, illus. 2015. (Planet Pop-Up Ser.). (ENG.). 12p. (J). (gr. -1). 12.95 *(978-1-62686-372-9(5)*, Silver Dolphin Bks.) Readerlink Distribution Services, LLC.

Mak, D P. Invisible Pill. 2005. 44p. pap. *(978-1-84401-210-7(7))* Athena Pr.

Mansfield, Andy. Journey to the Moon. 2015. (ENG., Illus.). 14p. (J). (gr. -1-2). 12.99 *(978-1-4998-0072-2(X))* Little Bee Books Inc.

Mansfield, Keith. Star Blaze. 2010. (Johnny Mackintosh,Johnny Mackintosh Trilogy Ser.: 2). (ENG.). 276p. (J). (gr. 4-6). pap. 8.99 *(978-1-84916-126-8(7))* Quercus GBR. Dist: Hachette Bk. Group.

Marazano, Richard. The Sons of Ares, 2 vols. Ponzio, Jean-Michel, illus. 2009. (Chimpanzee Complex Ser.: 1). (ENG.). 56p. pap. 13.95 *(978-1-84918-002-3(4))* CineBook GBR. Dist: National Bk. Network.

Marbury, Stephanie. Off to the Moon! Leigh, Tom, illus. 2006. 20p. (J). *(978-1-59939-100-7(7)*, Reader's Digest Young Families, Inc.) Studio Fun International.

Marshall, Sandra K. Tom's Space Adventure. 2007. 60p. per. 16.95 *(978-1-4241-7840-7(1))* America Star Bks.

Martin, Carrie Waddington. Ham the Astrochimp: Anything Is Possible. 2012. 52p. (-18). pap. 24.99 *(978-1-4797-1059-1(8))* Xlibris Corp.

Mass, Wendy. Voyagers: the Seventh Element (Book 6) 2016. (Voyager Ser.). (ENG.). 208p. (J). (gr. 3-7). 12.99 *(978-0-385-38673-9(7)*, Random Hse. Bks. for Young Readers) Random Hse. Children's Bks.

Moesta, Rebecca, et al. Star Challengers Trilogy. 2013. (J). pap. 18.99 *(978-1-61475-124-3(2)*, WordFire Pr.) WordFire Pr.

Moncure, Jane Belk. The Magic Moon Machine: A Counting Adventure. Rooney, Ronnie, illus. 2013. (Magic Castle Readers Ser.). (ENG.). 32p. (J). (gr. -1-2). 25.64 *(978-1-62323-580-2(4)*, 206316) Child's World, Inc., The.

Montgomery, R. A. War with the Evil Power Master. 2005. (Illus.). 123p. (J). pap. *(978-0-7608-9700-3(X))* Sundance/Newbridge Educational Publishing.

—War with the Evil Power Master. Millet, Jason, illus. 2006. (Choose Your Own Adventure Ser.: No. 12). 144p. (J). (gr. 4-8). per. 6.99 *(978-1-933390-12-3(3)*, CHCL12) Chooseco LLC.

Munzel, Alexander. Where the Holy Thistle Blooms. 2003. (Illus.). 98p. (J). per. *(978-0-9672566-1-0(5))* Technical Software, Inc.

North, Phoebe. Starglass. 2013. (Starglass Sequence Ser.). (ENG., Illus.). 448p. (YA). (gr. 7). 17.99 *(978-1-4424-5953-3(0)*, Simon & Schuster Bks. For Young Readers) Simon & Schuster Bks. For Young Readers.

Nosy Crow Staff. Bizzy Bear: Space Rocket. Davies, Benji, illus. 2015. (Bizzy Bear Ser.). (ENG.). 8p. (J). (— 1). bds. 6.99 *(978-0-7636-8003-9(6)*, Nosy Crow) Candlewick Pr.

Olivas, John D. Endeavour's Long Journey/la Larga Travesia de Endeavour. Roski, Gayle G., illus. 2016. (SPA.). 40p. (J). 19.95 ***(978-0-9973947-2-6(2))*** East West Discovery Pr.

Parker, Emma. The Space Rocket. 2010. (Illus.). pap. *(978-1-877547-87-4(5))* First Edition Ltd.

Patchett, Mary E. Flight to the Misty Planet. 2011. 236p. 46.95 *(978-1-258-07100-4(2))* Literary Licensing, LLC.

Pati, Geeta. Finny's Voyage Through the Universe: Nebula, Supernova, Open Star Cluster. 2007. 100p. per. 11.95 *(978-1-59526-422-0(1)*, Llumina Pr.) Aeon Publishing Inc.

Random House Staff. Outer-Space Chase (Team Umizoomi) Fruchter, Jason, illus. 2013. (Step into Reading Ser.). (ENG.). 32p. (J). (gr. -1-1). 3.99 *(978-0-449-81890-9(X)*, Random Hse. Bks. for Young Readers) Random Hse. Children's Bks.

Rau, Dana. Moon Walk. Buchs, Thomas, illus. 3rd ed. 2003. (Soundprints' Read-and-Discover Ser.). (ENG.). 48p. (J). (gr. -1-3). pap. 4.35 *(978-1-59249-015-8(8)*, S2006) Soundprints.

Rau, Dana Meachen. Moon Walk. Buchs, Thomas, illus. 2004. (Soundprints' Read-and-Discover Ser.). 48p. (gr. -1-3). 13.95 *(978-0-7569-3370-8(6))* Perfection Learning Corp.

Reed, Lynn Rowe. Oliver, the Spaceship, & Me. 2009. (ENG., Illus.). 32p. (J). (gr. -1-3). 16.95 *(978-0-8234-2193-0(7))* Holiday Hse., Inc.

Revis, Beth. Across the Universe. 2012. (Across the Universe Trilogy: Bk. 1). (ENG.). (YA). (gr. 7-12). 54.99 *(978-1-61587-857-4(2)*, Penguin AudioBooks) Penguin Publishing Group.

—Across the Universe. 2011. (Across the Universe Ser.: Bk. 1). (ENG.). (YA). (gr. 9-18). 448p. 9.99 *(978-1-59514-467-6(6))*; 416p. 17.99 *(978-1-59514-397-6(1))* Penguin Young Readers Group. (Razorbill).

—Across the Universe. 2011. (Across the Universe Trilogy: 1). lib. bdg. 20.85 *(978-0-606-23139-8(0)*, Turtleback) Turtleback Bks.

Robinson, Alise. Shining Stars: A Colors Book. Reich, Carin, illus. 2005. (Space Craze Ser.). 16p. (J). (gr. -1-k). per., bds. 6.95 *(978-1-58117-392-5(X)*, Intervisual/Piggy Toes) Bendon, Inc.

Rockwell, Carey. The Revolt on Venus. 2007. 120p. per. *(978-1-4068-3961-6(2))* Echo Library.

—Sabotage in Space. 2007. 108p. per. *(978-1-4068-3959-3(0))* Echo Library.

—The Space Pioneers. 2007. 120p. per. *(978-1-4068-3962-3(0))* Echo Library.

Rockwood, Roy. Lost on the Moon. 2008. 132p. pap. 10.95 *(978-1-60664-236-8(7))* Rodgers, Alan Bks.

—Through Space to Mars. 2008. 128p. (gr. 4-7). 23.95 *(978-1-60664-801-8(2))* Aegypan.

Ryan, Candace. Zoo Zoom! Pamintuan, Macky, illus. 2015. (ENG.). 32p. (J). (gr. -1-1). 16.99 *(978-1-61963-357-5(4)*, 9781619633575, Bloomsbury USA Childrens) Bloomsbury Publishing USA.

Sander, Sonia. 3, 2, 1, Liftoff! 2011. (Lego City Ser.). (ENG.). 32p. (J). (gr. -1-k). pap. 3.99 *(978-0-545-33167-8(6))* Scholastic, Inc.

Schindler, Roslyn. Zeon. Schindler, Roslyn, illus. 2013. (Illus.). 28p. pap. 13.95 *(978-1-61493-192-8(5))* Peppertree Pr., The.

The Secret Life of Jack O' Lanterns. 2004. 32p. 15.00 *(978-1-883211-35-6(2))* Laughing Elephant.

Shaw, Nancy E. Sheep Blast Off! Apple, Margot, illus. 2011. (ENG.). 32p. (J). (gr. -1-3). pap. 5.99 *(978-0-547-52025-4(5))* Houghton Mifflin Harcourt Publishing Co.

Sloane, William, ed. Space, Space, Space: Stories about the Time When Men Will Be Adventuring to the Stars. 2011. 288p. 48.95 *(978-1-258-10156-5(4))* Literary Licensing, LLC.

Snyder, Lavinia Branca. Mission in Space: Softi's Adventures. 2003. (Illus.). (J). mass mkt. *(978-1-932233-35-3(0))* Aurora Libris Corp.

Space Case. 2014. (Moon Base Alpha Ser.). (ENG., Illus.). 352p. (J). (gr. 3-7). 17.99 *(978-1-4424-9486-2(7)*, Simon & Schuster Bks. For Young Readers) Simon & Schuster Bks. For Young Readers.

Stanek, Robert, pseud. Bugville Critters Explore the Solar System. 2011. (Illus.). 42p. pap. 5.99 *(978-1-57545-262-3(6)*, Reagent Pr. Bks. for Young Readers) RP Media.

Stilton, Geronimo & Mckeon, Kathryn. Mouse in Space! 2013. (Geronimo Stilton Ser.: 52). lib. bdg. 18.40 *(978-0-606-31525-8(X)*, Turtleback) Turtleback Bks.

Terrell, Brandon. Mars for Humanity. Foti, Anthony J., illus. 2015. (Exploring Space & Beyond Ser.). (ENG.). 96p. (gr. 3-4). lib. bdg. 26.65 *(978-1-4965-0502-6(6))* Stone Arch Bks.

Tesler, Monica. Bounders. 2016. (Bounders Ser.: 1). (ENG., Illus.). 384p. (J). (gr. 5-9). 16.99 *(978-1-4814-4593-1(6)*, Aladdin) Simon & Schuster Children's Publishing.

Testa, Dom. The Web of Titan. 2010. (Galahad Ser.: 2). (ENG.). 272p. (YA). (gr. 8-12). pap. 8.99 *(978-0-7653-6078-6(0)*, 9780765360786, Tor Teen) Doherty, Tom Assocs., LLC.

Verba, Joan Marie. Action Alert. 2008. 176p. (YA). pap. 15.95 *(978-0-9653575-8-6(9))* FTL Pubns.

Walker, Peter Lancaster. Space Travelers Land at Buckingham Palace. Dixit, Rama, illus. 2007. 275p. (J). 19.95 *(978-1-934138-12-0(6))* Bouncing Ball Bks., Inc.

Welsh, C. E. L. Space Race. Jones, K. L., illus. 2011. (Campfire Graphic Novels Ser.). (ENG.). 68p. (YA). (gr. 5-12). pap. 9.99 *(978-93-80028-62-0(8)*, Campfire) Steerforth Pr.

Westerfeld, Scott. The Manual of Aeronautics: An Illustrated Guide to the Leviathan Series. Thompson, Keith, illus. 2012. (ENG.). 64p. (YA). (gr. 7). 19.99 *(978-1-4169-7179-5(3)*, Simon Pulse) Simon Pulse.

Wheeler, Kim. Jonny Plumb's New Adventures... 2013. 172p. pap. *(978-0-7552-1569-0(9)*, Bright Pen) Authors OnLine, Ltd.

Young, J. E. Horror in Space. Huddleston, Courtney, illus. 2011. (Twisted Journeys (r) Ser.: 18). (ENG.). 112p. (J). (gr. 4-7). lib. bdg. 27.93 *(978-0-8225-9265-5(7)*, Graphic Universe™) Lerner Publishing Group.

Zakour, John. Baxter Moon Galactic Scout. 2008. 198p. (J). (gr. 5-10). per. 8.95 *(978-0-9768126-9-2(X))* Brown Barn Bks.

SPACE FLIGHT, MANNED

see Manned Space Flight

SPACE FLIGHT—POETRY

Carthew, Mark. Footprints on the Moon: Poems about Space, 1 vol. 2013. (Fiction Readers Ser.). (ENG., Illus.). 28p. (J). (gr. 2-2). pap. 6.99 *(978-1-4333-5564-6(7))* Shell Educational Publishing.

SPACE FLIGHT TO MARS

Aldrin, Buzz & Dyson, Marianne J. Welcome to Mars: Making a Home on the Red Planet. 2015. (ENG., Illus.). 96p. (J). (gr. 3-7). lib. bdg. 28.90 *(978-1-4263-2207-5(0)*, National Geographic Children's Bks.) National Geographic Society.

Anderson, Rane. Stem: Mission to Mars: Problem Solving (Grade 3) 2017. (Mathematics Readers Ser.). (Illus.). 32p. (gr. 3-3). 8.99 ***(978-1-4807-5801-8(9))*** Teacher Created Materials, Inc.

Bellisario, Gina. To Mars! Moran, Mike, illus. 2017. (Cloverleaf Books (tm) — Space Adventures Ser.). (ENG.). 24p. (J). (gr. k-2). 25.32 *(978-1-5124-2539-0(7))*; 6.99 ***(978-1-5124-3888-8(X))***; 38.65 ***(978-1-5124-2832-2(9))***; 38.65 ***(978-1-5124-3887-1(1))*** Lerner Publishing Group. (Millbrook Pr.).

Hartman, Eve & Meshbesher, Wendy. Mission to Mars, 1 vol. 2011. (Science Missions Ser.). (ENG.). 56p. (gr. 3-3). 34.65 *(978-1-4109-3989-0(8)*, Raintree Freestyle Express) Heinemann-Raintree.

Leedy, Loreen & Schuerger, Andrew. Messages from Mars. Leedy, Loreen, illus. 2006. (ENG., Illus.). 40p. (J). (gr. 3-7). 16.95 *(978-0-8234-1954-8(1))* Holiday Hse., Inc.

Silverman, Buffy. Mars Missions: A Space Discovery Guide. 2017. (Space Discovery Guides). (ENG.). 48p. (J). (gr. 4-6). 16.99 ***(978-1-5124-3809-3(X)**, Lerner Pubns.)*; 47.99 ***(978-1-5124-3810-9(3)**, Lerner Pubns.)*; 47.99 ***(978-1-5124-2795-0(0)**, Lerner Pubns.)*; (Illus.). 31.99 *(978-1-5124-2585-7(0))* Lerner Publishing Group.

SPACE FLIGHT TO THE MOON

see also Moon—Exploration; Project Apollo (U.S.)

Adamson, Thomas K. Apollo 11 Moon Landing: An Interactive Space Exploration Adventure. 2016. (You Choose: Space Ser.). (ENG., Illus.). 112p. (gr. 3-4). lib. bdg. 31.99 *(978-1-4914-8103-5(X)*, You Choose Bks.) Capstone Press of Coughlan Cos.

—The First Moon Landing, 1 vol. Purcell, Gordon & Beatty, Terry, illus. 2006. (Graphic History Ser.). (ENG.). 32p. (gr. 3-4). per. 8.10 *(978-0-7368-9654-2(6)*, Graphic Library) Capstone Press of Coughlan Cos.

Aldrin, Buzz. Reaching for the Moon. Minor, Wendell, illus. (ENG.). 40p. (J). (gr. 1-4). 2008. 6.99 *(978-0-06-055447-7(9)*, Collins) 2005. 17.99 *(978-0-06-055445-3(2))* HarperCollins Pubs.

—Reaching for the Moon. Minor, Wendell, illus. unabr. ed. 2005. (Picture Book Readalong Ser.). (gr. k-4). 28.95 incl. audio compact disk *(978-1-59519-582-1(3))* Live Oak Media.

Anderson, Dale. The First Moon Landing. 2003. (Landmark Events in American History Ser.). (Illus.). 48p. (gr. 5-12). pap. 14.05 *(978-0-8368-5406-0(3)*, Gareth Stevens Secondary Library) Stevens, Gareth Publishing LLLP.

Anderson, Dale & Goff, Elizabeth Hudson. The First Moon Landing. Floor, Guus & Spay, Anthony, illus. 2006. (Graphic Histories Ser.). 32p. (gr. 5-8). lib. bdg. 27.00 *(978-0-8368-6203-4(1))* Stevens, Gareth Publishing LLLP.

Bailey, Gerry & Foster, Karen. Armstrong's Moon Rock. Radford, Karen & Noyes, Leighton, illus. 2008. (Stories of Great People Ser.). (ENG.). 40p. (J). (gr. 3-8). lib. bdg. (978-0-7787-3684-4(9)); (gr. 5-8). pap. (978-0-7787-3706-3(3)) Crabtree Publishing Co.

Bodden, Valerie. Man Walks on the Moon. 2009. (Days of Change Ser.). 48p. (YA). (gr. 4-7). 22.95 (978-1-58341-735-5(4)) Creative Co., The.

—Man Walks on the Moon: Days of Change. 2015. (Illus.). 80p. (J). (978-1-60818-528-3(1), Creative Education) Creative Co., The.

—Man Walks on the Moon: Odysseys in History. 2016. (Odysseys in History Ser.). (ENG.). 80p. (J). (gr. 7-10). pap. 14.99 (978-1-62832-129-6(6), Creative Paperbacks) Creative Co., The.

—To the Moon. (Great Expeditions Ser.). (Illus.). 48p. (J). 2012. (ENG.). (gr. 4-7). pap. 12.00 (978-0-89812-666-2(5)) 2011. 35.65 (978-1-60818-068-4(9)) Creative Co., The. (Creative Education).

Burleigh, Robert. One Giant Leap. Wimmer, Mike, illus. (ENG.). 40p. (J). (gr. 1-3). 2014. 8.99 (978-0-14-751165-2(8), Puffin Books) 2009. 16.99 (978-0-399-23883-3(2), Philomel Bks.) Penguin Young Readers Group.

Chambers, Catherine. Neil Armstrong, 1 vol. 2014. (Science Biographies Ser.). (ENG.). 32p. (gr. 2-4). lib. bdg. 30.65 (978-1-4109-6237-9(7), Raintree Perspectives) Heinemann-Raintree.

Close, Edward. Moon Missions, 1 vol., 1. 2014. (Discovery Education: Earth & Space Science Ser.). (ENG.). 32p. (gr. 3-6). 26.25 (978-1-4777-6178-6(0), PowerKids Pr.) Rosen Publishing Group, Inc., The.

Dell, Pamela. Man on the Moon: How a Photograph Made Anything Seem Possible, 1 vol. 2011. (Captured History Ser.). (ENG.). 64p. (gr. 5-7). pap. 9.10 (978-0-7565-4447-8(5), CPB Grades 4-8) Compass Point Bks.

Dunn, Joe. Moon Landing, 1 vol. Espinosa, Rod et al, illus. 2007. (Graphic History Ser.). (ENG.). 32p. (gr. 3-6). 28.50 (978-1-60270-078-9(8), Graphic Planet- Nonfiction) ABDO Publishing Co.

Dyer, Alan. Mission to the Moon. 2009. (ENG., Illus.). 80p. (J). (gr. 3-7). 19.99 (978-1-4169-7935-7(2), Simon & Schuster Bks. For Young Readers) Simon & Schuster Bks. For Young Readers.

Engdahl, Sylvia, ed. The Apollo 11 Moon Landing. 2011. (Perspectives on Modern World History Ser.). (Illus.). 224p. (J). (gr. 9-12). 42.45 (978-0-7377-5785-9(X), 1330286) Cengage Gale.

Feinstein, Stephen. Read about Neil Armstrong. 2005. (I Like Biographies! Ser.). (Illus.). 24p. (J). lib. bdg. 22.60 (978-0-7660-2593-6(4), Enslow Elementary) Enslow Pubs., Inc.

Floca, Brian. Moonshot: The Flight of Apollo 11. Floca, Brian, illus. 2009. (ENG., Illus.). 48p. (J). (gr. -1-5). 19.99 (978-1-4169-5046-2(X), Atheneum/Richard Jackson Bks.) Simon & Schuster Children's Publishing.

Goff, Elizabeth Hudson & Anderson, Dale. The First Moon Landing. 2006. (Graphic Histories Ser.). (Illus.). 32p. (gr. 5-8). pap. 10.50 (978-0-8368-6255-3(4)) Stevens, Gareth Publishing LLLP.

Goff, Elizabeth Hudson, et al. El Primer Alunizaje. 2007. (Historias Graficas (Graphic Histories) Ser.). (SPA., Illus.). 32p. (gr. 5-8). pap. 10.50 (978-0-8368-7904-9(X)); lib. bdg. 27.00 (978-0-8368-7897-4(3)) Stevens, Gareth Publishing LLLP.

Graham, Ian. You Wouldn't Want to Be on Apollo 13! A Mission You'd Rather Not Go On. Antram, David, illus. 2003. (You Wouldn't Want to Ser.). (ENG.). 32p. (J). (gr. 2-5). pap. 9.95 (978-0-531-16650-5(3), Watts, Franklin) Scholastic Library Publishing.

Green, Carl R. Apollo 11 Rockets to First Moon Landing: A MyReportLinks. com Book. 2004. (Space Flight Adventures & Disasters Ser.). (Illus.). 48p. (J). lib. bdg. 25.26 (978-0-7660-5164-5(1), MyReportLinks.com Bks.) Enslow Pubs., Inc.

—Walking on the Moon: The Amazing Apollo 11 Mission. 2012. (American Space Missions — Astronauts, Exploration, & Discovery Ser.). (Illus.). 48p. (J). (gr. 5-18). 25.27 (978-0-7660-4076-2(3)) Enslow Pubs., Inc.

Higgins, Nadia. Moon Landing, 1 vol. 2007. (Essential Events Set 1 Ser.). (ENG., Illus.). 112p. (J). (gr. 6-12). lib. bdg. 35.64 (978-1-59928-854-3(0)) ABDO Publishing Co.

Holden, Henry M. Triumph over Disaster Aboard Apollo 13: A MyReportLinks. com Book. 2004. (Space Flight Adventures & Disasters Ser.). (Illus.). 48p. (J). lib. bdg. 26.60 (978-0-7660-5167-6(6), MyReportLinks.com Bks.) Enslow Pubs., Inc.

Hubbard, Ben. Neil Armstrong & Getting to the Moon. 2015. (Adventures in Space Ser.). (ENG., Illus.). 48p. (gr. 4-6). 33.32 (978-1-4846-2515-6(3)) Heinemann-Raintree.

Hunter, Nick. Christopher Columbus & Neil Armstrong. 2015. (Comparing People from the Past Ser.). (ENG., Illus.). 32p. (gr. 3-3). pap. 6.49 (978-1-4846-0920-0(4), Heinemann First Library) Heinemann-Raintree.

Irwin, James. Destination Moon. 15th anniv. ed. 2004. 52p. 16.00 (978-1-929241-98-9(4)) Send The Light Distribution LLC.

Kelly, Nigel & Tames, Richard. Point of Impact Series, 7 bks., Set 1. (Illus.). (J). (gr. 5-7). lib. bdg. 169.54 (978-1-57572-419-5(7)) Heinemann-Raintree.

Koestler-Grack, Rachel A. Moon Landing, 1 vol. 2005. (American Moments Ser.). (ENG., Illus.). 48p. (gr. 4-8). 27.07 (978-1-59197-932-6(3), Abdo & Daughters) ABDO Publishing Co.

—Neil Armstrong. 2009. (People We Should Know Ser.). 48p. (J). (gr. 3-5). pap. 10.50 (978-1-4339-2147-6(2)); lib. bdg. 31.00 (978-1-4339-1948-0(6)) Stevens, Gareth Publishing LLLP. (Gareth Stevens Learning Library).

Malam, John. Man Walks on the Moon. 2003. (Dates with History Ser.). 45p. (J). lib. bdg. 28.50 (978-1-58340-407-2(4)) Black Rabbit Bks.

McNulty, Faith. If You Decide to Go to the Moon. Kellogg, Steven, illus. 2010. (Rise & Shine Ser.). (ENG.). 48p. (C). (gr. -1-3). 30.95 (978-0-590-48359-9(5)) National Geographic School Publishing, Inc.

McReynolds, Linda. Eight Days Gone. O'Rourke, Ryan, illus. 2012. (ENG.). 40p. (J). (gr. k-3). 16.95 (978-1-58089-364-0(3)) Charlesbridge Publishing, Inc.

Morris, Neil. Who Traveled to the Moon?, 1 vol. 2014. (Primary Source Detectives Ser.). (ENG.). 64p. (gr. 7-8). lib. bdg. 35.99 (978-1-4329-9605-5(3)) Heinemann-Raintree.

Nagelhout, Ryan. The First Moon Walk. 2015. (Incredible True Adventures Ser.). (ENG.). 32p. (J). (gr. 3-4). pap. 10.50 (978-1-4824-2038-8(4)) Stevens, Gareth Publishing LLLP.

—Neil Armstrong in His Own Words. 2016. (Eyewitness to History Ser.). (ENG., Illus.). 32p. (J). (gr. 4-5). pap. 10.50 (978-1-4824-4078-2(4)) Stevens, Gareth Publishing LLLP.

Ollhoff, Jim. Neil Armstrong. 2013. (Great Explorers Ser.). 32p. (J). (gr. 5-9). lib. bdg. 27.07 (978-1-61783-963-4(9), Abdo & Daughters) ABDO Publishing Co.

Oxlade, Chris. The Moon. 2010. (Eye on Space Ser.). 24p. (J). pap. 8.25 (978-1-61532-546-7(8), PowerKids Pr.); (ENG.). lib. bdg. 22.60 (978-1-61532-541-2(7)) Rosen Publishing Group, Inc., The.

Paris, Stephanie. Siglo Xx: Carrera Hacia la Luna. 2016. (TIME for Kids en Español - Level 5 Ser.). (SPA.). 64p. (gr. 5-5). lib. bdg. 31.99 (978-1-5157-2938-9(9)) Time for Kids Inc AUS. Dist: Capstone Pub.

Riley, Christopher & Dolling, Phil. Inside Apollo 11. 2017. (Geek's Guide to Space Ser.). 192p. (J). (gr. 12-14). 44.60 **(978-1-4994-6696-6(X)**, Rosen Young Adult) Rosen Publishing Group, Inc., The.

Scott, Elaine. Our Moon: New Discoveries about Earth's Closest Companion. 2016. (ENG., Illus.). 72p. (J). (gr. 5-7). 18.99 (978-0-547-48394-8(5), Clarion Bks.) Houghton Mifflin Harcourt Trade & Reference Pubs.

Stefoff, Rebecca. Space Race: An Interactive Space Exploration Adventure. 2016. (You Choose: Space Ser.). (ENG.). 112p. (gr. 3-4). lib. bdg. 31.99 (978-1-4914-8101-1(3), You Choose Bks.) Capstone Press of Coughlan Cos.

Tan, Sheri. Handshake in Space: The Apollo-Soyuz Test Project. Bond, Higgins, illus. 2009. 32p. (J). (gr. 1-5). pap. 9.95 incl. audio (978-1-60727-104-8(4)); (ENG.). 9.95 (978-1-60727-115-4(X)); (ENG.). 17.95 (978-1-60727-114-7(1)); pap. 9.95 incl. reel tape (978-1-59249-203-9(7)) Soundprints.

Thimmesh, Catherine. Team Moon: How 400,000 People Landed Apollo 11 on the Moon. 2006. (ENG., Illus.). 80p. (J). (gr. 5-7). 19.95 (978-0-618-50757-3(4)) Houghton Mifflin Harcourt Publishing Co.

Watts, Franklin & Howell, Izzi. Neil Armstrong & the Moon Landings. 2016. (ENG., Illus.). 32p. (J). (gr. 1-3). 17.99 (978-1-4451-4841-0(2), Franklin Watts) Hachette Children's Group GBR. Dist: Hachette Bk. Group.

Weakland, Mark. When Neil Armstrong Built a Wind Tunnel. Lozano, Luciano, illus. 2017. (Leaders Doing Headstands Ser.). (ENG.). 32p. (gr. 2-3). lib. bdg. 27.99 **(978-1-5158-1575-4(7))** Picture Window Bks.

Wilkinson, Philip. Spacebusters: Race to the Moon. 2012. (DK Readers Ser.). (ENG.). 48p. (J). (gr. 2-4). 3.99 (978-0-7566-9084-7(6), DK Children) Dorling Kindersley Publishing, Inc.

Wishinsky, Frieda. Could We Live on the Moon? 2004. (ENG., Illus.). 24p. (J). (gr. 2-2). pap. 10.92 (978-0-7652-5178-7(7), Celebration Pr.) Pearson Schl.

Yomtov, Nel. The Apollo 11 Moon Landing: July 20 1969, 1 vol. 2014. (24-Hour History Ser.). (ENG.). 48p. (gr. 3-5). pap. 8.95 (978-1-4329-9298-9(8)); (Illus.). lib. bdg. 33.32 (978-1-4329-9292-7(9)) Heinemann-Raintree. (NA-h).

Zemlicka, Shannon. Neil Armstrong. 2003. (History Maker Bios Ser.). (Illus.). 48p. (J). (gr. 2-4). 26.60 (978-0-8225-0395-8(6), Lerner Pubns.) Lerner Publishing Group.

SPACE MEDICINE

see also Life Support Systems (Space Environment); Manned Space Flight

Linde, Barbara M. Rocket Scientists, 01 vols., 1. 2016. (Out of the Lab: Extreme Jobs in Science Ser.). (ENG., Illus.). 32p. (J). pap. 10.00 (978-1-4994-1855-2(8), PowerKids Pr.) Rosen Publishing Group, Inc., The.

SPACE PROBES

see also Lunar Probes

also names of space vehicles and space projects, e.g. Mariner project; etc.

Angelo, Joseph A., Jr. Robot Spacecraft. 2006. (Frontiers in Space Ser.). (Illus.). 320p. (C). (gr. 9). 45.00 (978-0-8160-5773-3(7)) Facts On File, Inc.

—Spacecraft for Astronomy. 2006. (Frontiers in Space Ser.). (Illus.). 304p. (C). (gr. 9). 45.00 (978-0-8160-5774-0(5)) Facts On File, Inc.

Asimov, Isaac & Hantula, Richard. Exploring Outer Space. 2005. (Isaac Asimov's 21st Century Library of the Universe). (Illus.). 32p. (gr. 2-6). lib. bdg. 26.00 (978-0-8368-3981-4(1), Gareth Stevens Learning Library) Stevens, Gareth Publishing LLLP.

Baker, David & Kissock, Heather. Probing Space. 2009. (Exploring Space Ser.). (Illus.). 32p. (J). (gr. 2-4). pap. 9.95 (978-1-60596-026-5(8)); lib. bdg. 26.00 (978-1-60596-025-8(X)) Weigl Pubs., Inc.

Furstinger, Nancy. Robots in Space. 2014. (Lightning Bolt Books Robots Everywhere! Ser.). (Illus.). 32p. (gr. k-2). (J). lib. bdg. 26.60 (978-1-4677-4055-5(1), Lerner Pubns.); pap. 7.95 (978-1-4677-4510-9(3)) Lerner Publishing Group.

Gross, Miriam. All about Space Missions. 2009. (Blast Off! Ser.). 24p. (gr. 2-3). 42.50 (978-1-61511-623-2(0), PowerKids Pr.) Rosen Publishing Group, Inc., The.

Gross, Miriam J. All about Space Missions. 2009. (Blast Off! Ser.). 24p. (J). (gr. 2-5). (ENG.). pap. 8.25 (978-1-4358-3138-4(1)); lib. bdg. 22.60 (978-1-4358-2740-0(6)) Rosen Publishing Group, Inc., The. (PowerKids Pr.).

Hamilton, S. L. Exploration. 2011. (Xtreme Space Ser.). (Illus.). 32p. (gr. 3-9). 27.07 (978-1-61714-737-1(0), A&D Xtreme) ABDO Publishing Co.

Jefferis, David. Space Probes: Exploring Beyond Earth. 2008. (Exploring our Solar System Ser.). (ENG., Illus.). 32p. (J). (gr. 3-8). pap. (978-0-7787-3741-4(1)) Crabtree Publishing Co.

Jemison, Mae & Rau, Dana Meachen. Journey Through Our Solar System. 2013. (True Book™—Dr. Mae Jemison & 100 Year Starship™ Ser.). (ENG., Illus.). 48p. (J). pap. 6.95 (978-0-531-24061-8(4)); lib. bdg. 29.00 (978-0-531-25501-8(8)) Scholastic Library Publishing.

Meet NASA Inventor Kendra Short & Her Printable Probes & Cosmic Confetti. 2017. (J). **(978-0-7166-6158-0(6))** World Bk., Inc.

Miller, Ron. Robot Explorers. 2007. (Space Innovations Ser.). (ENG., Illus.). 112p. (gr. 6-8). lib. bdg. 31.93 (978-0-8225-7152-0(8)) Lerner Publishing Group.

Mills, Nathan & Stiegler, Lorraine. Space Probes. 2012. (Rosen Readers Ser.). (ENG., Illus.). 24p. (J). (gr. 1-2). pap. 8.25 (978-1-4488-8869-6(7), Rosen Classroom) Rosen Publishing Group, Inc., The.

O'Hearn, Michael. Awesome Space Robots. 2013. (Robots Ser.). (ENG.). 32p. (gr. 3-4). pap. 47.70 (978-1-62065-779-9(1), Edge Bks.); lib. bdg. 27.99 (978-1-4296-9918-1(3)); (Illus.). pap. 8.29 (978-1-62065-778-2(3)) Capstone Press of Coughlan Cos.

Saunders-Smith, Gail. Robots in Space, 1 vol. 2014. (Cool Robots Ser.). (ENG., Illus.). 24p. (gr. k-1). 26.65 (978-1-4914-0585-7(6), Pebble Plus) Capstone Press of Coughlan Cos.

Shea, Therese. Gareth's Guide to Building a Space Probe. 2017. (Gareth Guides to an Extraordinary Life Ser.). 32p. (gr. 4-5). pap. 63.00 **(978-1-5382-0337-8(5))** Stevens, Gareth Publishing LLLP.

Sparrow, Giles. Destination Mars. (Illus.). 32p. (J). 2010. pap. 10.00 (978-1-4358-3459-0(3)) 2009. (ENG., lib. bdg. 25.25 (978-1-4358-3443-9(7)) Rosen Publishing Group, Inc., The. (PowerKids Pr.).

—Destination Mercury. 32p. (J). 2010. (Illus.). pap. 10.00 (978-1-4358-3455-2(0)) 2009. (ENG.). lib. bdg. 25.25 (978-1-4358-3441-5(0)) Rosen Publishing Group, Inc., The. (PowerKids Pr.).

Stiegler, Lorraine. Space Probes. 2012. (Exploring Earth & Space Ser.). (ENG., Illus.). 24p. (J). (gr. 1-3). 22.60 (978-1-4488-8580-0(9), PowerKids Pr.) Rosen Publishing Group, Inc., The.

Telescopes & Space Probes. 2006. (World Book's Solar System & Space Exploration Library). (Illus.). 63p. (J). (978-0-7166-9510-3(3)) World Bk., Inc.

World Book, Inc Staff, contrib. by. Telescopes & Space Probes. (J). 2010. (978-0-7166-9541-7(3)) 2nd ed. 2006. (Illus.). 64p. (978-0-7166-9520-2(0)) World Bk., Inc.

SPACE RESEARCH

see Outer Space—Exploration; Space Sciences

SPACE SCIENCES

see also Astronautics; Astronomy; Geophysics; Outer Space; Space Medicine

Anderson, Amy & Anderson, Brian. Space Dictionary for Kids: The Everything Guide for Kids Who Love Space. 2016. (ENG., Illus.). 200p. (J). (gr. 4-7). 13.95 (978-1-61821-515-4(9), 9781618215154) Prufrock Pr.

Asimov, Isaac & Hantula, Richard. Global Space Programs: Past & Present. 2005. (Isaac Asimov's 21st Century Library of the Universe). (Illus.). 32p. (gr. 2-6). lib. bdg. 26.00 (978-0-8368-3982-1(X), Gareth Stevens Learning Library) Stevens, Gareth Publishing LLLP.

Becklake, Sue & Parker, Steve. Astronomy. 2013. (Illus.). 48p. (J). (978-1-4351-5086-7(4)) Barnes & Noble, Inc.

Benchmark Education Company, LLC Staff, compiled by. Earth & Space Science. 2006. spiral bd. 365.00 (978-1-4108-6946-3(6)) 2006. spiral bd. 695.00 (978-1-4108-6942-5(3)) 2006. spiral bd. 365.00 (978-1-4108-6939-5(3)) 2006. spiral bd. 235.00 (978-1-4108-6934-0(2)) 2006. spiral bd. 80.00 (978-1-4108-6927-2(X)) 2006. spiral bd. 365.00 (978-1-4108-6925-8(3)) 2005. spiral bd. 675.00 (978-1-4108-5851-1(0)) 2005. spiral bd. 950.00 (978-1-4108-5441-4(8)) 2005. spiral bd. 1025.00 (978-1-4108-5440-7(X)) 2005. spiral bd. 870.00 (978-1-4108-4518-4(4)) 2005. spiral bd. 55.00 (978-1-4108-3874-2(9)) 2005. spiral bd. 75.00 (978-1-4108-3870-4(6)) 2005. spiral bd. 220.00 (978-1-4108-3859-9(5)) 2005. spiral bd. 220.00 (978-1-4108-3851-3(X)) 2005. spiral bd. 305.00 (978-1-4108-3850-6(1)) 2005. spiral bd. 335.00 (978-1-4108-3829-2(3)) 2005. spiral bd. 580.00 (978-1-4108-3826-1(9)) 2005. spiral bd. 405.00 (978-1-4108-5852-8(9)) 2005. spiral bd. 370.00 (978-1-4108-3858-2(7)) Benchmark Education Co.

—Science Theme: Earth & Space Science. 2005. spiral bd. 340.00 (978-1-4108-5314-1(4)) Benchmark Education Co.

Bortz, Fred. Astrobiology. 2008. pap. 52.95 (978-0-8225-9326-3(2)) 2007. (ENG., Illus.). 48p. (gr. 4-8). lib. bdg. 27.93 (978-0-8225-6771-4(7), Lerner Pubns.) Lerner Publishing Group.

Carson, Mary Kay. The Universe: From the Big Bang to Deep Space. 2014. (ENG.). 24p. (gr. k-3). 28.50 (978-1-62717-731-3(0)) Rourke Educational Media.

Chapman, Cindy. What Is in the Sky?, 6 vols., Set. 2003. (Phonics Readers 1-36 Ser.). (ENG.). 8p. (gr. k-1). pap. 29.70 (978-0-7368-3202-1(5), Phonics Readers) Capstone Press of Coughlan Cos.

Cientificos! 9: Ciencias Terrestres y del Espacio. (SPA.). (J). 60.00 (978-958-04-6348-1(4)) Norma S.A. COL. Dist: Distribuidora Norma, Inc.

Daynes, Katie. Living in Space. Wray, Zoe & Fox, Christyan, illus. 2006. (Beginners Nature: Level 2 Ser.). 32p. (J). (gr. 1-3). 4.99 (978-0-7945-1339-9(5), Usborne) EDC Publishing.

Dickmann, Nancy. Exploring Comets, Asteroids, & Other Objects in Space. 2015. (Spectacular Space Science Ser.). (ENG., Illus.). 48p. (J). (gr. 5-6). 30.25 (978-1-4994-3637-2(8), Rosen Central) Rosen Publishing Group, Inc., The.

Dowswell, Paul. First Encyclopedia of Space. 2004. (First Encyclopedia Ser.). (SPA & ENG., Illus.). (J). (gr. 3-18). 1p. pap. 9.99 (978-0-7945-0035-1(8), Usborne); 64p. lib. bdg. 17.95 (978-1-58086-357-5(4)) EDC Publishing.

Earth & Space Science. 2011. (Earth & Space Science Ser.). (ENG.). 24p. (gr. k-1). pap. 166.80 (978-1-4296-7148-4(3)); pap. 27.80 (978-1-4296-7147-7(5)); lib. bdg. 53.30 (978-1-4296-6836-1(9)) Capstone Press of Coughlan Cos. (Pebble Plus).

Elish, Dan. Kaleidoscope Space Gorup 2, 4 bks., Set. Incl. Galaxies. 20.95 (978-0-7614-2047-7(9)); NASA. lib. bdg. 20.95 (978-0-7614-2046-0(0)); Satellites. lib. bdg. 20.95 (978-0-7614-2098-9(3)); Sun. lib. bdg. 20.95 (978-0-7614-2048-4(7)); (Illus.). 48p. (gr. 3-7). 2006. 2007. Set lib. bdg. 119.71 (978-0-7614-2045-3(2), Benchmark Bks.) Marshall Cavendish Corp.

Encyclopaedia Britannica, Inc. Staff, compiled by. Science & Nature. 2003. (Britannica Learning Library). (Illus.). (gr. 2-5). 14.95 (978-1-59339-002-0(5), 049903-EN-REF) Encyclopaedia Britannica, Inc.

—Technology & Inventions. 2003. (Britannica Learning Library). (Illus.). (gr. 2-5). 14.95 (978-1-59339-003-7(3), 049904-EN-REF) Encyclopaedia Britannica, Inc.

Erickson, John R., et al. AfterSchool KidzScience: Earth & Space Science: Sunlight Science Kit. 2013. (J). 225.00 (978-1-61003-142-4(3)) Center for the Collaborative Classroom.

Exploracion del Espacio, 6 vols., Vol. 3. (Explorers. Exploradores Nonfiction Sets Ser.). (SPA.). (gr. 3-6). (978-0-7699-0653-9(2)) Shortland Pubns. (U. S. A.) Inc.

Explore Space! Classroom Library. (gr. 2-5). lib. bdg. 22.95 (978-0-7368-9250-6(8)) Red Brick Learning.

Explore Space! II Classroom Library. (gr. 2-5). lib. bdg. 22.95 (978-0-7368-4536-6(4)) Red Brick Learning.

Exploring Space: Level Q, 6 vols., Vol. 3. (Explorers Ser.). 32p. (gr. 3-6). 44.95 (978-0-7699-0617-1(6)) Shortland Pubns. (U. S. A.) Inc.

Feldman, Heather. Skylab: The First American Space Station. 2003. (Space Firsts Ser.). (Illus.). 24p. (J). lib. bdg. 22.60 (978-0-8239-6248-8(2), PowerKids Pr.) Rosen Publishing Group, Inc., The.

Gardner, Robert & Goodstein, Madeline P. Ace Your Space Science Project: Great Science Fair Ideas. 2009. (Ace Your Science Project Ser.). (Illus.). 128p. (J). (gr. 5-9). lib. bdg. 33.27 (978-0-7660-3230-9(2)) Enslow Pubs., Inc.

Gibson, Brylee. The World Beyond Earth. 2007. (Connectors Ser.). (gr. 2-5). pap. (978-1-877453-11-3(0)) Global Education Systems Ltd.

Goldsmith, Mike. The Kingfisher Space Encyclopedia. 2017. (Kingfisher Encyclopedias Ser.). (ENG.). 160p. (J). pap. 13.99 (978-0-7534-7353-5(4), 9780753473535, Kingfisher) Roaring Brook Pr.

Goodman, Susan E. Ultimate Field Trip #5: Blasting off to Space Academy. Doolittle, Michael J., illus. 2011. (ENG.). 48p. (J). (gr. 3-7). pap. 19.99 (978-1-4424-4345-7(6), Atheneum Bks. for Young Readers) Simon & Schuster Children's Publishing.

Graham, Ian & Jones, Geriant. H. Exploring Science: Space an Amazing Fact File & Hands-On Project Book. 2015. (ENG., Illus.). 64p. (J). (gr. -1-6). 12.99 (978-1-86147-386-8(9), Armadillo) Anness Publishing GBR. Dist: National Bk. Network.

Grant, Donald. Atlas of Space. 2012. (ENG., Illus.). 36p. (J). (gr. -1-k). 14.99 (978-1-85103-407-9(2)) Moonlight Publishing, Ltd. GBR. Dist: Independent Pubs. Group.

Grolier Educational Staff, contrib. by. Space Science, 8 vols. 2004. (Illus.). (J). 309.00 (978-0-7172-5825-3(4), Grolier) Scholastic Library Publishing.

Hamilton, S. L. Xtreme Space, 6 vols., Set. Incl. Astronaut Firsts. 27.07 (978-1-61714-736-4(2)); Exploration. 27.07 (978-1-61714-737-1(0)); Robots & Rovers. 27.07 (978-1-61714-738-8(9)); Sky Watch. 27.07 (978-1-61714-739-5(7)); Solar System. 27.07 (978-1-61714-740-1(0)); Stars. 27.07 (978-1-61714-741-8(9)); (gr. 3-9). (Xtreme Space Ser.). (Illus.). 32p. 2011. 162.42 (978-1-61714-735-7(4), A&D Xtreme) ABDO Publishing Co.

Harris, Tim. Space Science. 2015. (Science Q & A Ser.). (ENG., Illus.). 32p. (J). (gr. 5-5). pap. 10.58 (978-1-5026-0612-9(7)) Cavendish Square Publishing.

Hewitt, Sally. Earth & Space. (Illus.). 32p. (YA). (gr. 2-18). lib. bdg. 27.10 (978-1-932333-31-2(2)) Chrysalis Education.

Higgins, Nadia. Dwarf Planets: Pluto & the Lesser Planets. 2014. (ENG.). 24p. (gr. k-3). 28.50 (978-1-62717-729-0(9)) Rourke Educational Media.

—Solar Systems: Planets, Stars, & Orbits. 2014. (ENG.). 24p. (gr. k-3). 28.50 (978-1-62717-730-6(2)) Rourke Educational Media.

Holden, Henry M. The Coolest Job in the Universe: Working Aboard the International Space Station. 2012. (American Space Missions — Astronauts, Exploration, & Discovery Ser.). (Illus.). 48p. (J). (gr. 5-18). lib. bdg. 25.27 (978-0-7660-4074-8(7)) Enslow Pubs., Inc.

Holt, Rinehart and Winston Staff. Holt Science & Technology Chapter 19: Earth Science: Stars, the Galaxy, & the Universe. 5th ed. 2004. (Illus.). pap. 12.86 (978-0-03-030336-4(2)) Holt McDougal.

—Holt Science & Technology Chapter 22: Earth Science: Exploring Space. 5th ed. 2004. (Illus.). pap. 12.86 (978-0-03-030351-7(6)) Holt McDougal.

Hunter, Dru. What Is Out There? Think Like a Scientist. 2016. (Think Like a Scientist Ser.). (ENG.). 48p. (J). (gr. 5-9). pap. 12.00 (978-1-62832-199-9(7), Creative Paperbacks) Creative Co., The.

Hutson, Matt. What Do You Want to Be? Explore Aerospace. 2005. (J). 6.00 (978-0-9753920-7-2(7)) Sally Ride Science.

Ivey, Catherine. Totally Amazing Careers in Space Sciences. 2006. (J). 7.80 (978-1-933798-00-4(9)) Sally Ride Science.

Johnson, Rose. Discoveries in Earth & Space Science That Changed the World, 1 vol. 2015. (ENG.). 48p. (YA). 30.25 (978-1-4777-8609-3(0), Rosen Reference) Rosen Publishing Group, Inc., The.

Kawa, Katie. Freaky Space Stories. 2015. (Freaky True Science Ser.). (ENG., Illus.). 32p. (J). (gr. 4-5). 26.60 (978-1-4824-2958-9(6)) Stevens, Gareth Publishing LLLP.

Khan, Hena & Dyson, Marianne J. The Space Explorer's Guide to Out-Of-This-World Science. 2004. (Space University Ser.). (Illus.). 48p. (J). (978-0-439-55747-4(X)) Scholastic, Inc.

Koellhoffer, Tara, ed. Space & Astronomy. 2006. (Science News for Kids Ser.). (Illus.). 136p. (gr. 4-6). lib. bdg. 30.00 (978-0-7910-9125-8(2), Chelsea Clubhouse) Facts On File, Inc.

Kruesi, Liz. Discover Space Exploration. 2016. (Searchlight Books (tm) — What's Cool about Science? Ser.). (ENG., Illus.). 40p. (J). (gr. 3-5). 30.65 (978-1-5124-0811-9(5)) Lerner Publishing Group.

Let's Find Out! Space. 2014. (Let's Find Out! Ser.). 32p. (J). (gr. 3-6). 140.70 (978-1-62275-486-1(7)) Rosen Publishing Group, Inc., The.

Macmillan Reference USA, ed. Space Sciences: 4 Volume Set, 4 vols. 2nd ed. 2012. (Macmillan Science Library). (ENG., Illus.). 761.00 *(978-0-02-866214-5(8)*, Macmillan Reference USA) Cengage Gale.
McDougal-Littell Publishing Staff. Modules: Physical Science - Space Science. 2004. (McDougal Littell Science Ser.). (ENG.). 64p. (gr. 6-8). pap., lab manual ed. 15.30 *(978-0-618-43734-4(7)*, 2-01227) Great Source Education Group, Inc.
Michael, Allaby. El Planeta Tierra.Tr. of Planet Earth. (SPA.). 96p. (YA). (gr. 5-8). 18.36 *(978-84-241-1994-2(0))* Everest Editora ESP. Dist: Lectorum Pubns., Inc.
Milbourne, Anna. On the Moon. 2004. (On the Moon Ser.). 24p. (J). 9.95 *(978-0-7945-0617-9(8)*, Usborne) EDC Publishing.
Modules: Earth Science; Space Science TE. 2005. (gr. 6-12). *(978-0-618-33422-3(X)*, 2-01012) Holt McDougal.
Newton, David E. Chemistry of Space. 2007. (New Chemistry Ser.). (Illus.). 256p. (gr. 6-12). 35.00 *(978-0-8160-5274-5(3))* Facts On File, Inc.
Out in Space. 2005. (Earth & Outer Space Ser.). (YA). (gr. k-3). 118.80 *(978-0-7368-4211-2(X)*, Pebble Bks.) Capstone Press of Coughlan Cos.
Owen, Ruth. Space Survival Guide. 2010. (ENG., Illus.). 32p. (J). pap. *(978-0-7787-7553-9(4))*; lib. bdg. *(978-0-7787-7531-7(3))* Crabtree Publishing Co.
Parker. Space Mysteries - Space Busters. 2004. (YA). pap. 48.30 *(978-1-4109-0293-1(5))* Harcourt Schl. Pubs.
Parker, Steve. Probes to the Planets. West, David, illus. 2015. (Story of Space Ser.). (ENG.). 32p. (J). (gr. 3-6). 31.35 *(978-1-62588-077-2(4))* Black Rabbit Bks.
Parks, Peggy J. Space Research. 2010. (Inside Science Ser.). (Illus.). 96p. (J). (gr. 7-12). 26.95 *(978-1-60152-111-8(1)*, 1316146) ReferencePoint Pr., Inc.
Pebble Books: Earth & Outer Space. 2005. (YA). (gr. k-3). 594.00 *(978-0-7368-4222-8(5)*, Pebble Bks.) Capstone Press of Coughlan Cos.
Perritano, John. Space Science, Vol. 10. 2016. (Stem in Current Events Ser.). (Illus.). 64p. (J). (gr. 7). 23.95 *(978-1-4222-3595-9(5))* Mason Crest.
Pinna, Lorenzo. La Conquista del Espacio. (SPA.). 88p. (YA). (gr. 5-8). *(978-84-7131-926-5(8))* Editex, Editorial S.A. ESP. Dist: Lectorum Pubns., Inc.
Rauf, Don & Vescia, Monique. Choose Your Own Career Adventure at NASA. 2016. (Bright Futures Press: Choose Your Own Career Adventure Ser.). (ENG., Illus.). 32p. (J). (gr. 4-6). 29.93 *(978-1-63471-913-1(1)*, 208973) Cherry Lake Publishing.
Rice, Dona Herweck, et al. Let's Explore Earth & Space Science, Grades 4-5. 2015. (Science Readers: Content & Literacy Ser.). (ENG., Illus.). 32p. (gr. 4-5). 89.90 *(978-1-4938-1423-7(0))* Shell Educational Publishing.
Rich, Mari. Space, Vol. 10. Gilmore, Malinda & Pouson, Mel, eds. 2016. (Black Achievement in Science Ser.). (Illus.). 64p. (J). (gr. 7). 23.95 *(978-1-4222-3563-8(7))* Mason Crest.
Rosen Publishing Staff. Spotlight on Space Science, 1 vol. 2014. (Spotlight on Space Science Ser.). (ENG.). 32p. (J). (gr. 5-5). lib. bdg. 367.50 *(978-1-4994-0438-8(7)*, PowerKids Pr.) Rosen Publishing Group, Inc., The.
Rudy, Lisa Jo. Eyes in the Sky: Satellite Spies Are Watching You! 2007. (24/7: Science Behind the Scenes Ser.). (ENG., Illus.). 64p. (J). (gr. 8-12). 29.00 *(978-0-531-12082-8(1)*, Watts, Franklin) Scholastic Library Publishing.
Scholastic News Nonficiton Readers - Space Science, 12 vols., Set. Incl. Jupiter. Taylor-Butler, Christine. 22.00 *(978-0-531-14696-5(0))*; Mars. Chrismer, Melanie. 22.00 *(978-0-531-14697-2(9))*; Mercury. Taylor-Butler, Christine. 22.00 *(978-0-531-14698-9(7))*; Neptune. Chrismer, Melanie. 22.00 *(978-0-531-14750-4(9))*; Pluto: Dwarf Planet. Taylor-Butler, Christine. 22.00 *(978-0-531-14751-1(7))*; Saturn. Taylor-Butler, Christine. 22.00 *(978-0-531-14752-8(5))*; Uranus. Taylor-Butler, Christine. 22.00 *(978-0-531-14754-2(1))*; Venus. Chrismer, Melanie. 22.00 *(978-0-531-14755-9(X))*; (Illus.). 24p. (J). (gr. 1-2). 2007. 2007. Set lib. bdg. 240.00 o.p. *(978-0-531-18674-9(1)*, Children's Pr.) Scholastic Library Publishing.
The Science of Space. 2016. (Illus.). 48p. (J). *(978-1-4222-3515-7(7))* Mason Crest.
Spectacular Space Science. 2015. (Spectacular Space Science Ser.). (ENG.). 48p. (J). (gr. 5-6). pap., pap., pap. 423.00 *(978-1-4777-8623-9(6)*, Rosen Central) Rosen Publishing Group, Inc., The.
Steinkraus, Kyla. Giant Gas Planets: Jupiter, Saturn, Uranus, & Neptune. 2014. (ENG.). 24p. (gr. k-3). 28.50 *(978-1-62717-728-3(0))* Rourke Educational Media.
—Rocky Planets: Mercury, Venus, Earth, & Mars. 2014. (ENG.). 24p. (gr. k-3). 28.50 *(978-1-62717-727-6(2))* Rourke Educational Media.
Steps To Literacy Staff, compiled by. Explore Space Collection: Capv220. 2005. (ENG., Illus.). (J). pap. *(978-1-60015-016-6(0))* Steps To Literacy, LLC.
Stiefel, Chana. Comets & Meteors: Shooting Through Space. 2014. (ENG.). 24p. (gr. k-3). 28.50 *(978-1-62717-732-0(9))* Rourke Educational Media.
Stott, Carole. I Wonder Why Stars Twinkle. 2011. (I Wonder Why Ser.). (ENG., Illus.). 32p. (J). (gr. k-3). pap. 6.99 *(978-0-7534-6520-2(5)*, 9780753465202, Kingfisher) Roaring Brook Pr.
Teacher Created Materials Staff, ed. Earth & Space Science: Add-on Pack. 2007. (Science Readers Ser.). 89.99 *(978-1-4333-0067-7(2))* Teacher Created Materials, Inc.
Top That Publishing Staff, ed. Space. 2004. (Stickertastic Ser.). (Illus.). (J). 24p. pap. *(978-1-84510-114-5(6))*; 48p. pap. *(978-1-84510-026-1(3))*; 48p. per. *(978-1-84510-012-4(3))* Top That! Publishing PLC.
Wadsworth, Pamela. Golwg Gyntaf Ar Amser a Gofod. 2005. (WEL., Illus.). 24p. pap. *(978-1-85596-248-4(9))* Dref Wen.
What Is in Space?, 6 vols. (Sunshinetm Science Ser.). 24p. (gr. 1-2). 31.50 *(978-0-7802-0292-4(9))* Wright Group/McGraw-Hill.
Willett, Edward. Space. 2009. (Science Q & A Ser.). (Illus.). 48p. (YA). (gr. 5-8). pap. 10.95 *(978-1-60596-073-9(X))*; lib. bdg. 29.05 *(978-1-60596-072-2(1))* Weigl Pubs., Inc.
World Book, Inc Staff, contrib. by. Encyclopedia of Space. 2013. (J). *(978-0-7166-7523-5(4))* World Bk., Inc.
Zuchora-Walske, Christine. Key Discoveries in Earth & Space Science. 2015. (Science Discovery Timelines Ser.). (ENG., Illus.). 48p. (J). (gr. 6-8). pap. 8.99 *(978-1-4677-6157-4(5))*; lib. bdg. 30.65 *(978-1-4677-5787-4(X))* Lerner Publishing Group. (Lerner Pubns.).

SPACE SCIENCES—HISTORY

Hall, Derek. Chemistry, Earth, & Space Sciences. 2010. (Facts at Your Fingertips Ser.). (YA). (gr. 7-12). 35.65 *(978-1-933834-47-4(1))* Brown Bear Books.
Space Firsts. (Illus.). (J). (gr. k-5). 119.70 *(978-0-8239-7268-5(2))* Rosen Publishing Group, Inc., The.
Space Missions. (Illus.). (J). (gr. k-5). 119.70 *(978-0-8239-7142-8(2))* Rosen Publishing Group, Inc., The.

SPACE SHIPS—PILOTS

see Astronauts

SPACE SHUTTLES

Amato, William. The Space Shuttle. 2009. (High-Tech Vehicles Ser.). 24p. (gr. 2-3). 42.50 *(978-1-61513-308-6(9)*, PowerKids Pr.) Rosen Publishing Group, Inc., The.
—Transbordadores Espaciales. 2004. (Vehículos de Alta Tecnología (High-Tech Vehicles) Ser.). (SPA & ENG., Illus.). 24p. (J). (gr. 3-6). lib. bdg. 22.60 *(978-0-8239-6885-5(5)*, Editorial Buenas Letras) Rosen Publishing Group, Inc., The.
—Transbordadores espaciales (the Space Shuttle) 2009. (Vehículos de alta tecnología (High-Tech Vehicles) Ser.). (SPA.). 24p. (gr. 2-3). 42.50 *(978-1-60854-721-0(3)*, Editorial Buenas Letras) Rosen Publishing Group, Inc., The.
Baker, David. Living in Space. 2008. (Exploring Space Ser.). (Illus.). 32p. (J). (gr. 4-6). lib. bdg. 26.00 *(978-1-59036-769-8(3))* Weigl Pubs., Inc.
—The Shuttle. 2008. (Exploring Space Ser.). (Illus.). 32p. (J). (gr. 4-6). lib. bdg. 26.00 *(978-1-59036-767-4(7))* Weigl Pubs., Inc.
Baker, David & Kissock, Heather. Living in Space. 2008. (Exploring Space Ser.). (Illus.). 32p. (J). (gr. 4-6). pap. 9.95 *(978-1-59036-770-4(7))* Weigl Pubs., Inc.
—The Shuttle. 2008. (Exploring Space Ser.). (Illus.). 32p. (J). (gr. 4-6). pap. 9.95 *(978-1-59036-768-1(5))* Weigl Pubs., Inc.
Braun, Eric. Fatal Faults: The Story of the Challenger Explosion. 2015. (Tangled History Ser.). (ENG., Illus.). 112p. (gr. 3-4). lib. bdg. 31.99 *(978-1-4914-7077-0(1))* Capstone Press of Coughlan Cos.
Channing, Margot. Space & Other Flying Machines. 2015. (Inside Eye Ser.). (Illus.). 32p. (gr. 3-6). 31.35 *(978-1-906370-79-4(6))* Book Hse. GBR. Dist: Black Rabbit Bks.
Cole, Michael D. The Columbia Space Shuttle Disaster: From First Liftoff to Tragic Final Flight. 2003. (Countdown to Space Ser.). (Illus.). 48p. (J). lib. bdg. 25.27 *(978-0-7660-2295-9(1))* Enslow Pubs., Inc.
Dahl, Michael. On the Launch Pad: A Counting Book about Rockets, 1 vol. Alderman, Derrick & Shea, Denise, illus. 2004. (Know Your Numbers Ser.). (ENG.). 24p. (gr. -1-2). per. 8.95 *(978-1-4048-1119-5(2))* Picture Window Bks.
Englert, Christoph. Destination: Space. Clohosy Cole, Tom, illus. 2016. (ENG.). 40p. (J). 19.99 *(978-1-84780-824-0(7)*, Wide Eyed Editions) Quarto Publishing Group UK GBR. Dist: Littlehampton Bk Services, Ltd.
Fahey, Kathleen. Challenger & Columbia. 2005. (Disasters Ser.). (Illus.). 32p. (gr. 2-6). lib. bdg. 26.00 *(978-0-8368-4496-2(3)*, Gareth Stevens Learning Library) Stevens, Gareth Publishing LLLP.
Feldman, Heather. Columbia: The First Space Shuttle. 2003. (Space Firsts Ser.). (Illus.). 24p. (J). lib. bdg. 22.60 *(978-0-8239-6247-1(4)*, PowerKids Pr.) Rosen Publishing Group, Inc., The.
Graham, Ian. Slide & Discover: Space. 2013. (Slide & Discover Ser.). (ENG., Illus.). 24p. (J). (gr. 1). 19.95 *(978-1-60710-585-5(3)*, Silver Dolphin Bks.) Readerlink Distribution Services, LLC.
Gross, Miriam. All about Space Shuttles. 2009. (Blast Off! Ser.). 24p. (gr. 2-5). (Illus.). (J). pap. 8.25 *(978-1-4358-3136-0(5))*; 42.50 *(978-1-61511-626-3(5))* Rosen Publishing Group, Inc., The. (PowerKids Pr.).
Gross, Miriam J. All about Space Shuttles. 2009. (Blast Off! Ser.). 24p. (J). (gr. 2-5). lib. bdg. 22.60 *(978-1-4358-2738-7(4)*, PowerKids Pr.) Rosen Publishing Group, Inc., The.
Herrod, Robin & Kerrod, Robin. Space Shuttles. 2004. (History of Space Exploration Ser.). (Illus.). 48p. (gr. 5-12). lib. bdg. 31.00 *(978-0-8368-5709-2(7)*, Gareth Stevens Secondary Library) Stevens, Gareth Publishing LLLP.
Holden, Henry M. Space Shuttle Disaster: The Tragic Mission of the Challenger. 2012. (American Space Missions — Astronauts, Exploration, & Discovery Ser.). (Illus.). 48p. (J). (gr. 5-18). 25.27 *(978-0-7660-4073-1(9))* Enslow Pubs., Inc.
—The Tragedy of the Space Shuttle Challenger: A MyReportLinks. com Book. 2004. (Space Flight Adventures & Disasters Ser.). (Illus.). 48p. (J). lib. bdg. 25.26 *(978-0-7660-5165-2(X)*, MyReportLinks.com Bks.) Enslow Pubs., Inc.
Koestler-Grack, Rachel A. Space Shuttle Columbia Disaster, 1 vol. 2004. (American Moments Ser.). (ENG.). 48p. (gr. 4-8). 27.07 *(978-1-59197-659-2(6)*, Abdo & Daughters) ABDO Publishing Co.
Krumm, Brian. Shuttle in the Sky: The Story of the Space Shuttle Columbia. 2015. (Exploring Space & Beyond Ser.). (ENG., Illus.). 48p. (gr. 3-4). lib. bdg. 29.32 *(978-1-4914-4161-9(5))* Capstone Press of Coughlan Cos.
Langley, Andrew. Sally Ride & the Shuttle Missions. 2015. (Adventures in Space Ser.). (ENG., Illus.). 48p. (gr. 4-6). 33.32 *(978-1-4846-2516-3(1))* Heinemann-Raintree.
Littlejohn, Randy. Life in Outer Space. (Life in Extreme Environments Ser.). 64p. (gr. 5-8). 2009. 53.00 *(978-1-61514-269-9(X))* 2004. (Illus.). lib. bdg. 31.95 *(978-0-8239-3989-3(8))* Rosen Publishing Group, Inc., The. (Rosen Reference).
Morey, Allan. Space Shuttles. 2017. (Space Tech Ser.). (ENG., Illus.). 24p. (J). (gr. 3-7). lib. bdg. 25.95 ***(978-1-62617-706-2(6)***, Epic Bks.) Bellwether Media.
Murray, Julie. Spaceships, 1 vol. 2014. (Transportation Ser.). (ENG.). 24p. (J). (gr. 4-8). lib. bdg. 28.50 *(978-1-62970-081-6(9))* ABDO Publishing Co.
Murray, Julie, et al. Naves Espaciales. 2015. (Medios de Transporte Ser.). (SPA., Illus.). 24p. (gr. k-1). pap. 7.95 *(978-1-4966-0493-4(8))* Capstone Classroom.
Rees, Peter. Secrets of the Space Shuttle. 2007. (Shockwave: Technology & Manufacturing Ser.). (ENG., Illus.). 36p. (J). (gr. 4-6). lib. bdg. 25.00 *(978-0-531-17590-3(1)*, Children's Pr.) Scholastic Library Publishing.
Roza, Greg. The Hubble Space Telescope: Understanding & Representing Numbers in the Billions. 2005. (PowerMath: Proficiency Plus Ser.). (Illus.). 32p. (J). (gr. 3-6). lib. bdg. 25.25 *(978-1-4042-2931-0(0)*, PowerKids Pr.) Rosen Publishing Group, Inc., The.
—The Hubble Space Telescope: Understanding & Representing Numbers up to 1 Billion. 2009. (Math for the REAL World Ser.). (ENG., Illus.). 32p. (gr. 5-6). pap. 10.00 *(978-1-4042-5129-8(4))* Rosen Publishing Group, Inc., The.
Sofer, Barbara. Ilan Ramon: Israel's Space Hero. 2003. (Illus.). 64p. (J). (gr. 3-6). 16.95 *(978-1-58013-115-5(8))*; pap. 6.95 *(978-1-58013-116-2(6))* Lerner Publishing Group. (Kar-Ben Publishing).
Space Firsts. (Illus.). (J). (gr. k-5). 119.70 *(978-0-8239-7268-5(2))* Rosen Publishing Group, Inc., The.
Stone, Adam. The Challenger Explosion. 2014. (Disaster Stories Ser.). (ENG., Illus.). 24p. (J). (gr. 3-8). 29.95 *(978-1-62617-151-0(3)*, Black Sheep) Bellwether Media.
A Trip into Space: Individual Title Six-Pack. (Story Steps Ser.). (gr. k-2). 23.00 *(978-0-7635-9614-9(0))* Rigby Education.
Waxman, Laura Hamilton. Terrific Transportation Inventions. 2013. (Awesome Inventions You Use Every Day Ser.). (ENG., Illus.). 32p. (gr. 3-6). lib. bdg. 26.60 *(978-1-4677-1096-1(2)*, Lerner Pubns.) Lerner Publishing Group.
Weil, Ann. Space Disasters, 1 vol. unabr. ed. 2012. (Disasters Ser.). (ENG.). 92p. (YA). (gr. 9-12). 8.95 *(978-1-61651-934-6(7))* Saddleback Educational Publishing, Inc.
Zelon, Helen. The Endeavor SRTM: Mapping the Earth. 2009. (Space Missions Ser.). 24p. (gr. 3-4). 42.50 *(978-1-60853-118-9(X)*, PowerKids Pr.) Rosen Publishing Group, Inc., The.
Zuehlke, Jeffrey. The Space Shuttle. (Pull Ahead Books-Mighty Movers Ser.). (Illus.). 32p. 2007. (ENG.). (gr. k-3). pap. 7.95 *(978-0-8225-6426-3(2)*, First Avenue Editions) 2006. (J). (gr. 3-7). lib. bdg. 22.60 *(978-0-8225-6420-1(3)*, Lerner Pubns.) Lerner Publishing Group.

SPACE SHUTTLES—FICTION

Arnett, Mindee. Avalon. 2014. (Avalon Ser.: 1). (ENG.). 432p. (YA). (gr. 8). 17.99 *(978-0-06-223559-6(1))* HarperCollins Pubs.
Bannister, Bram. Rupert, the Alien & the Bank Robbery. 2007. 56p. per. 8.95 *(978-0-595-44839-5(9))* iUniverse, Inc.
Barth, Kathleen E. The Amazing Adventures of Quigley D Pigley & His Friends. 2009. 16p. pap. 8.49 *(978-1-4389-8322-6(0))* AuthorHouse.
Bennett, Jeffrey, et al. Max Goes to Jupiter: A Science Adventure with Max the Dog. Carroll, Michael, illus. 2008. (Science Adventures with Max the Dog Ser.). (ENG.). 32p. (J). (gr. 2-4). 16.95 *(978-0-9721819-3-8(8))* Big Kid Science.
Colvin, Denise Marie. Suzy's Big Dream Comes True. 2007. 61p. pap. 19.95 *(978-1-4241-8157-5(7))* America Star Bks.
Douglas, Atom. Mathew's Space Ship. Douglas, Atom, . 2007. (Illus.). 32p. (J). 6.50 *(978-0-9798316-0-7(1))* JaxPublishing.net.
Edick, Grant. Space Station. 2004. (Two Boys Adventure Story Ser.). 98p. (J). (gr. 3-6). 15.95 *(978-0-9677839-9-4(2))* Wysteria Publishing.
Gentry, Stephen. Journey to the Stars & Back. 2005. 52p. (J). pap. 16.49 *(978-1-4116-5985-8(6))* Lulu Pr., Inc.
Greenburg, Dan. Dude, Where's My Spaceship? Parnintuan, Macky, illus. 2006. (Weird Planet Ser.: No. 1). (ENG.). 96p. (J). (gr. 1-4). 3.99 *(978-0-375-83344-1(7)*, Random Hse. Bks. for Young Readers) Random Hse. Children's Bks.
Kelly, Mark. Mousetronaut: Based on a (Partially) True Story. Payne, C. F., illus. 2012. (ENG.). 40p. (J). (gr. -1-3). 17.99 *(978-1-4424-5824-6(0)*, Simon & Schuster/Paula Wiseman Bks.) Simon & Schuster/Paula Wiseman Bks.
Martin, Justin McCory. The Planet Without Pronouns. Lee, Jared, illus. 2004. (Grammar Tales Ser.). (ENG.). 16p. (J). (gr. 3-7). pap. 3.25 *(978-0-439-45820-7(X))* Scholastic, Inc.
Olivas, John D. Endeavour's Long Journey: Celebrating 19 Years of Space Exploration. Roski, Gayle Garner, illus. 2013. (J). pap. *(978-0-9856237-3-9(X))* East West Discovery Pr.
Olivas, John D. Endeavour's Long Journey/la Larga Travesía de Endeavour. Roski, Gayle G., illus. 2016. (SPA.). 40p. (J). 19.95 ***(978-0-9973947-2-6(2))*** East West Discovery Pr.
Rigby Education Staff. The Space Cat. (Sails Literacy Ser.). (Illus.). 16p. (gr. 2-3). 27.00 *(978-0-7635-9949-2(2)*, 699492C99) Rigby Education.
Rockwell, Carey. On the Trail of Space Pirates. Ley, Willy, ed. 2007. 140p. per. 11.95 *(978-1-60312-283-2(4))* Aegypan.
Steele, Andrew. The Galaxy Boys & the Sphere. 2008. (ENG.). 285p. (J). (gr. 4-7). pap. *(978-1-85756-687-1(4))* Janus Publishing Co.
Turner, Paul. ULYSSES: the Pegasi Incident. 2007. 216p. pap. 15.95 *(978-1-84753-642-6(5))* Lulu Pr., Inc.
West, Robert. There's a Spaceship in My Tree!, 1 vol. 2008. (Star-Fighters of Murphy Street Ser.). (ENG., Illus.). 144p. (J). (gr. 4-7). pap. 6.99 *(978-0-310-71425-5(7))* Zonderkidz.
Woodsonrick. Poodles in Space. 2012. 24p. 24.95 *(978-1-4626-5333-1(2))* America Star Bks.
Wyre, Yvonne. The Further Adventures of Cuthbert the Coal Lorry & all His Friends. 2007. (Illus.). 204p. pap. *(978-1-84401-801-7(6))* Athena Pr.
Zakour, John. Baxter Moon Galactic Scout. 2008. 198p. (J). (gr. 5-10). per. 8.95 *(978-0-9768126-9-2(X))* Brown Barn Bks.

SPACE STATIONS

Here are entered works dealing with manned installations existing for specific functions, such as servicing space ships, etc., in orbit around the earth or other natural extraterrestrial bodies.

Baker, David. Inside the International Space Station. 2017. (Geek's Guide to Space Ser.). 192p. (J). (gr. 12-14). 44.60 ***(978-1-4994-6698-0(6)***, Rosen Young Adult) Rosen Publishing Group, Inc., The.
Baker, David. The International Space Station. 2009. 32p. 26.00 *(978-1-59036-775-9(8))* Weigl Pubs., Inc.
Baker, David & Kissock, Heather. The International Space Station. (J). 2016. ***(978-1-4896-5824-1(6)***, AV2 by Weigl) 2009. (Illus.). 32p. (gr. 2-4). pap. 9.95 *(978-1-60596-024-1(1))* 2009. (Illus.). 32p. (gr. 2-4). lib. bdg. 26.00 *(978-1-60596-023-4(3))* Weigl Pubs., Inc.
Brown, Carron. Space Station. Johnson, Bee, illus. 2016. (ENG.). 36p. (J). 12.99 *(978-1-61067-411-9(1))* Kane Miller.
Buckley, James & Bader, Bonnie. Home Address - ISS: The International Space Station. 2015. (Smithsonian Ser.). (ENG., Illus.). 48p. (J). (gr. 3-4). 3.99 *(978-0-448-48709-0(8)*, Penguin Young Readers) Penguin Young Readers Group.
Carroll, Jillian. Where to Stay. 2003. (J). lib. bdg. *(978-1-58417-232-1(0))* Lake Street Pubs.
Clay, Kathryn. Living in Space. 2017. (Little Astronauts Ser.). (ENG., Illus.). 32p. (gr. 1-2). lib. bdg. 27.99 *(978-1-5157-3657-8(1))* Capstone Press of Coughlan Cos.
Dyson, Marianne J. Space Station Science. Klug, Dave, illus. 2nd ed. 2004. 128p. (J). pap. 11.95 *(978-0-89317-059-2(3)*, WW-0593, Windward Publishing) Finney Co., Inc.
Einspruch, Andrew. Life on a Space Station. 2012. (Discovery Education: Technology Ser.). (ENG., Illus.). 32p. (J). (gr. 3-6). pap. 10.00 *(978-1-4488-7966-3(3))*; lib. bdg. 25.25 *(978-1-4488-7884-0(5))* Rosen Publishing Group, Inc., The. (PowerKids Pr.).
Faust, Daniel R. Más Allá de la Tierra: Vivir en Otro Planeta. 2009. (Historietas Juveniles: Peligros Del Medioambiente (Jr. Graphic Environmental Dangers) Ser.). (SPA., Illus.). 24p. (gr. 3-6). (YA). lib. bdg. 25.25 *(978-1-4358-8471-7(X))*; pap. 10.60 *(978-1-4358-8472-4(8))* Rosen Publishing Group, Inc., The.
Feldman, Heather. Skylab: The First American Space Station. (Space Firsts Ser.). 24p. 2009. (gr. 3-4). 42.50 *(978-1-60853-113-4(9))* 2003. (Illus.). (J). lib. bdg. 22.60 *(978-0-8239-6248-8(2))* Rosen Publishing Group, Inc., The. (PowerKids Pr.).
Gross, Miriam. All about Space Stations. 2009. (Blast Off! Ser.). 24p. (gr. 2-3). 42.50 *(978-1-61511-629-4(X))*; (J). lib. bdg. 22.60 *(978-1-4358-2737-0(6))* Rosen Publishing Group, Inc., The. (PowerKids Pr.).
Gross, Miriam J. All about Space Stations. 2009. (Blast Off! Ser.). (Illus.). 24p. (J). (gr. 2-5). pap. 8.25 *(978-1-4358-3135-3(7)*, PowerKids Pr.) Rosen Publishing Group, Inc., The.
Holden, Henry M. The Coolest Job in the Universe: Working Aboard the International Space Station. 2012. (American Space Missions — Astronauts, Exploration, & Discovery Ser.). (Illus.). 48p. (J). (gr. 5-18). lib. bdg. 25.27 *(978-0-7660-4074-8(7))* Enslow Pubs., Inc.
—Living & Working Aboard the International Space Station: A MyReportLinks. com Book. 2004. (Space Flight Adventures & Disasters Ser.). (Illus.). 48p. (J). lib. bdg. 25.26 *(978-0-7660-5168-3(4)*, MyReportLinks.com Bks.) Enslow Pubs., Inc.
Jenkins, Martin. Exploring Space: from Galileo to the Mars Rover & Beyond. Biesty, Stephen, illus. 2017. (ENG.). 64p. (J). (gr. 3-7). 17.99 *(978-0-7636-8931-5(9))* Candlewick Pr.
Kerrod, Robin. Space Stations. 2004. (History of Space Exploration Ser.). (Illus.). 48p. (gr. 5-12). lib. bdg. 31.00 *(978-0-8368-5710-8(0)*, Gareth Stevens Secondary Library) Stevens, Gareth Publishing LLLP.
Lassieur, Allison. International Space Station: An Interactive Space Exploration Adventure. 2016. (You Choose: Space Ser.). (ENG., Illus.). 112p. (gr. 3-4). lib. bdg. 31.99 *(978-1-4914-8104-2(8)*, You Choose Bks.) Capstone Press of Coughlan Cos.
Littlejohn, Randy. Life in Outer Space. (Life in Extreme Environments Ser.). 64p. (gr. 5-8). 2009. 53.00 *(978-1-61514-269-9(X))* 2004. (Illus.). lib. bdg. 31.95 *(978-0-8239-3989-3(8))* Rosen Publishing Group, Inc., The. (Rosen Reference).
Morey, Alla. The International Space Station. 2017. (Space Tech Ser.). (ENG., Illus.). 24p. (J). (gr. 3-7). lib. bdg. 25.95 ***(978-1-62617-701-7(5)***, Epic Bks.) Bellwether Media.
Owen, Ruth. Space Stations, 1 vol. 2015. (Objects in Space Ser.). (ENG.). 32p. (J). 26.25 *(978-1-4777-5869-4(0)*, PowerKids Pr.) Rosen Publishing Group, Inc., The.
Parker, Steve. Space Stations. West, David, illus. 2015. (Story of Space Ser.). (ENG.). 32p. (gr. 3-6). 31.35 *(978-1-62588-081-9(2))* Black Rabbit Bks.
Rustad, Martha E. H. Space Stations. 2012. (Exploring Space Ser.). (ENG.). 24p. (gr. k-1). pap. 41.70 *(978-1-4296-8330-2(9))*; lib. bdg. 26.65 *(978-1-4296-7579-6(9))* Capstone Press of Coughlan Cos. (Pebble Plus).
Sexton, Colleen. Space Stations. 2010. (Exploring Space Ser.). (ENG., Illus.). 24p. (J). (gr. k-3). lib. bdg. 25.95 *(978-1-60014-295-6(8)*, Blastoff! Readers) Bellwether Media.
Tagliaferro, Linda. Who Walks in Space? Working in Space. 2010. (Wild Work Ser.). (ENG.). 32p. (gr. 1-2). 29.99 *(978-1-4109-3849-7(2)*, Read Me!) Heinemann-Raintree.
Throp, Claire. Fantasy Science Field Trips, 1 vol. 2014. (Fantasy Science Field Trips Ser.). (ENG.). 32p. (gr. 1-3). lib. bdg. 119.96 *(978-1-4109-6201-0(6)*, Read Me!) Heinemann-Raintree.
—A Visit to a Space Station: Fantasy Science Field Trips, 1 vol. 2014. (Fantasy Science Field Trips Ser.). (ENG.). 32p. (gr. 1-3). pap. 8.95 *(978-1-4109-6202-7(4))*; lib. bdg. 29.99 *(978-1-4109-6197-6(4))* Heinemann-Raintree. (Read Me!).
Waxman, Laura Hamilton. Exploring the International Space Station. 2011. (Searchlight Books Whats Amazing about Space Ser.). (ENG., Illus.). (J). (gr. 3-5). pap. 51.01 *(978-0-7613-8416-8(2))*; 40p. pap. 8.95 *(978-0-7613-7879-2(0))*; 40p. lib. bdg. 27.93 *(978-0-7613-5443-7(3))* Lerner Publishing Group.
Yes Magazine Editors. The Amazing International Space Station. Cowles, Rose, illus. 2003. (ENG.). 48p. (J). (gr. 3-7). 9.95 *(978-1-55337-523-4(8))* Kids Can Pr., Ltd. CAN. Dist: Hachette Bk. Group.
Zappa, Marcia. Space Stations, 1 vol. 2011. (Universe Set 2 Ser.). (ENG., Illus.). 32p. (gr. 3-5). 27.07 *(978-1-61714-693-0(5)*, Buddy Bks.) ABDO Publishing Co.

SPACE STATIONS—FICTION

Appleton, Victor. The Space Hotel. 2007. (Tom Swift, Young Inventor Ser.). (ENG.). 160p. (gr. 4-7). 27.07 *(978-1-59961-353-6(0))* Spotlight.
Bean, Raymond. The Curse of Mars. 2016. (Out of This World Ser.). (ENG., Illus.). 112p. (gr. 2-5). lib. bdg. 32.65 *(978-1-4965-3615-0(0))* Out of this World GBR. Dist: Capstone Pub.
—First Family in Space. 2016. (Out of This World Ser.). (ENG., Illus.). 112p. (gr. 2-5). lib. bdg. 32.65 *(978-1-4965-3617-4(7))* Out of this World GBR. Dist: Capstone Pub.

S

—Journey to the Moon. 2016. (Out of This World Ser.). (ENG., Illus.). 112p. (gr. 2-5). lib. bdg. 32.65 *(978-1-4965-3616-7(9))* Out of this World GBR. Dist: Capstone Pub.

—Trouble on Venus. 2016. (Out of This World Ser.). (ENG., Illus.). 112p. (gr. 2-5). lib. bdg. 32.65 *(978-1-4965-3614-3(2))* Out of this World GBR. Dist: Capstone Pub.

Beecroft, Simon. DK Readers L3: Star Wars: Death Star Battles. 2016. (DK Readers Ser.). (ENG.). 48p. (J). (gr. 2-4). pap. 3.99 *(978-1-4654-6004-2(7)*, DK Children) Dorling Kindersley Publishing, Inc.

Brouwer, Sigmund. Death Trap. 2009. (Robot Wars Ser.: 1). (ENG.). 288p. (YA). pap. 7.99 *(978-1-4143-2309-1(3)*, Tyndale Kids) Tyndale Hse. Pubs.

Cahill, Byron. Space Pox. 2005. (J). pap. *(978-1-4108-4220-6(7))* Benchmark Education Co.

Castellucci, Cecil. Tin Star. 2014. (Tin Star Ser.: 1). (ENG.). 240p. (YA). (gr. 7). 16.99 *(978-1-59643-775-3(8)*, 9781596437753) Roaring Brook Pr.

Childress, Jamie. Lost Universe. Braun, Chris, illus. 2015. (ENG.). 100p. (J). (gr. 4-7). per. 4.99 *(978-1-931882-74-3(6))* Adventures Unlimited Pr.

Daley, Michael J. Rat Trap. 2008. (ENG.). 272p. (J). (gr. 3-7). 16.95 *(978-0-8234-2093-3(0))* Holiday Hse., Inc.

—Space Station Rat. 2008. (ENG., Illus.). 181p. (J). (gr. 4-7). 6.95 *(978-0-8234-2151-0(1))* Holiday Hse., Inc.

Dean, James. Out of This World. 2017. (Pete the Cat (HarperCollins) Ser.). lib. bdg. 14.75 ***(978-0-606-40077-0(X))*** Turtleback Bks.

Edick, Grant. Space Station. 2004. (Two Boys Adventure Story Ser.). 98p. (J). (gr. 3-6). 15.95 *(978-0-9677839-9-4(2))* Wysteria Publishing.

Geiger, Beth & Fuerst, Jeffrey B. Return to Earth. Wolk-Stanley, Jessica, illus. 2004. (Reader's Theater Ser.). (J). pap. *(978-1-4108-2306-9(7)*, A23067) Benchmark Education Co.

Hench, Larry. Boing-Boing the Bionic Cat & the Space Station. Morgan-Jones, Tom, illus. 2011. (Boing-Boing the Bionic Cat Ser.: 5). (ENG.). 96p. (J). (gr. 2-4). pap. 8.99 *(978-1-904872-07-8(7)*, Can of Worms Kids Pr.) Can of Worms Pr. GBR. Dist: Independent Pubs. Group.

Holt, K. A. Mike Stellar: Nerves of Steel. 2010. (ENG.). 272p. (J). (gr. 3-7). 7.99 *(978-0-375-84557-4(7)*, Yearling) Random Hse. Children's Bks.

Kaufman, Amie & Kristoff, Jay. Gemina. Lu, Marie, illus. 2016. (Illuminae Files Ser.). (ENG.). 672p. (YA). (gr. 9). 19.99 *(978-0-553-49915-5(7))*; lib. bdg. 22.99 *(978-0-553-49916-2(5))* Random Hse. Children's Bks. (Knopf Bks. for Young Readers).

Leo. The Group, 3 vols., Vol. 2. 2009. (Aldebaran Ser.: 2). (ENG., Illus.). 96p. pap. 19.95 *(978-1-905460-70-0(8))* CineBook GBR. Dist: National Bk. Network.

Levigne, Michelle. Commonwealth Universe: Modern Era. 2013. 110p. pap. *(978-1-922066-31-2(1))*; 134p. pap. *(978-1-922066-32-9(X))*; 146p. pap. *(978-1-922066-33-6(8))*; 110p. pap. *(978-1-922066-35-0(4))* Writers Exchange E-Publishing.

Marsh, Carole. The Mission Possible Mystery at Space Center Houston. 2009. 160p. (J). 18.99 *(978-0-635-06833-0(8)*, Marsh, Carole Bks.) Gallopade International.

Murray, Leinster. Space Tug. 2007. 152p. pap. 19.99 *(978-1-4264-9420-8(3))*; 172p. pap. 21.99 *(978-1-4264-9801-5(2))* Creative Media Partners, LLC.

Rey, H. A. Curious George Discovers Space (science Storybook) 2015. (Curious George Ser.). (ENG., Illus.). 32p. (J). (gr. -1-3). 6.99 *(978-0-544-50028-0(8)*, HMH Books For Young Readers) Houghton Mifflin Harcourt Publishing Co.

Rockwell, Carey. The Revolt on Venus: The TOM CORBETT Space Cadet Adventure. 2007. (ENG.). 180p. pap. 19.99 *(978-1-4264-9548-9(X))*; 202p. pap. 22.99 *(978-1-4264-9929-6(9))* Creative Media Partners, LLC.

Seegert, Scott & Martin, John. Sci-Fi Junior High. 2017. (Sci-Fi Junior High Ser.: 1). (ENG., Illus.). 320p. (J). (gr. 3-7). 13.99 *(978-0-316-31516-6(8)*, Jimmy Patterson) Little Brown & Co.

Seigel, Jonathan & Rother, Beverly S. Myrtle the Turtle & Popeye the Mouse: Learning about Our Solar System. 2012. 40p. pap. 24.95 *(978-1-4626-6587-7(X))* America Star Bks.

Williams, Allen. Claude the Backward-Jumping Bullfrog: Space Shuttle Commander. 2009. 32p. pap. 17.99 *(978-1-4490-0479-8(2))* AuthorHouse.

SPACE SUITS

see Astronauts—Clothing

SPACE TELECOMMUNICATION

see Interstellar Communication

SPACE TRAVEL

see Interplanetary Voyages; Manned Space Flight; Space Flight

SPACE VEHICLES

see also Artificial Satellites; Space Probes; Space Stations

Angelo, Joseph A. Frontiers in Space Set, 6-Volumes. 2007. (Frontiers in Space Ser.). 384p. (C). (gr. 9). 225.00 *(978-0-8160-7429-7(1))* Facts On File, Inc.

Avera, Randy. The Truth about Challenger. 2003. (Illus.). 344p. 34.00 *(978-1-932258-00-4(0)*, SAN # 254-9522) Randolph Publishing.

Baxter, Roberta. Challenger Explosion. 2013. (Illus.). 48p. (J). 15.64 *(978-1-62403-019-2(X)*, 1360919, Core Library); (ENG., (gr. 3-6). lib. bdg. 32.79 *(978-1-61783-954-2(X)*, 1360919) ABDO Publishing Co.

Bortz, Fred. Seven Wonders of Space Technology. 2011. (Seven Wonders Ser.). (ENG., Illus.). 80p. (gr. 5-8). 33.26 *(978-0-7613-5453-6(0))* Lerner Publishing Group.

Brasch, Nicolas. Machines of Speed & Flight. 2011. (Technology Behind Ser.). 32p. (YA). (gr. 3-6). 28.50 *(978-1-59920-568-7(8))* Black Rabbit Bks.

Bricker, Sandra D. Challenger. Miller, Zachary N., ed. Taylor, Marjorie, illus. rev. ed. 2003. (Take Ten Ser.). 47p. (J). (gr. 4-18). pap. 4.95 *(978-1-58659-021-5(9))* Artesian Pr.

Buller, Laura & Kosara, Tori. DK Readers L3: Star Wars: Star Pilot: Star Wars: Star Pilot. 2015. (DK Readers Ser.). (ENG., Illus.). 64p. (J). (gr. 2-4). 14.99 *(978-1-4654-3387-9(2)*, DK Children) Dorling Kindersley Publishing, Inc.

Caper, William. The Challenger Space Shuttle Explosion. 2007. (Code Red Ser.). (Illus.). 32p. (YA). (gr. 2-5). lib. bdg. 25.27 *(978-1-59716-367-5(8))* Bearport Publishing Co., Inc.

DeYoe, Aaron. Space Travel, 1 vol. 2015. (ENG., Illus.). 24p. (J). *(978-1-62403-745-0(3)*, 1391272) ABDO Publishing Co.

Fahey, Kathleen. Challenger & Columbia. 2005. (Disasters Ser.). (Illus.). 32p. (gr. 2-6). lib. bdg. 26.00 *(978-0-8368-4496-2(3)*, Gareth Stevens Learning Library) Stevens, Gareth Publishing LLLP.

Furniss. Spacecraft 6-Pack. 2004. (Illus.). (J). pap. 48.30 *(978-1-4109-1203-9(5))* Harcourt Schl. Pubs.

The Geek's Guide to Space. 2017. (Geek's Guide to Space Ser.). 192p. (gr. 12-14). 223.00 ***(978-1-4994-6664-5(1)***, Rosen Young Adult) Rosen Publishing Group, Inc., The.

Gilpin, Daniel & Pang, Alex. Spacecraft. 2010. (Machines Close-Up Ser.). 32p. (J). (gr. 4-7). 28.50 *(978-1-60870-112-4(3))* Marshall Cavendish Corp.

Goldberg, Jan. James Lovell: The Rescue of Apollo 13. (Library of Astronaut Biographies Ser.). 112p. (gr. 5-8). 2009. 63.90 *(978-1-60853-522-4(3))* 2004. (Illus.). lib. bdg. 34.60 *(978-0-8239-4459-0(X))* Rosen Publishing Group, Inc., The. (Rosen Reference).

Graham, Ian. In Space. 2008. (QEB Machines at Work Ser.). (Illus.). 36p. (YA). (gr. 4-7). 19.95 *(978-1-59566-318-4(5))* QEB Publishing Inc.

—You Wouldn't Want to Be on Apollo 13! (Revised Edition) 2017. (You Wouldn't Want to... American History Ser.). (ENG., Illus.). 32p. (J). lib. bdg. 29.00 *(978-0-531-23835-6(0)*, Watts, Franklin) Scholastic Library Publishing.

Hamilton, John. Spaceships, 1 vol. 2006. (World of Science Fiction Ser.). (ENG., Illus.). 32p. (gr. 4-7). 27.07 *(978-1-59679-995-0(1)*, Abdo & Daughters) ABDO Publishing Co.

Hamilton, Tracy Brown. All about Spacecraft. 2016. (Let's Find Out! Ser.). 32p. (J). (gr. 3-2). lib. bdg. 24.45 *(978-1-68048-445-8(1))* Rosen Publishing Group, Inc., The.

Harper, Benjamin. Ships of the Galaxy. 2015. (ENG.). 42p. (J). (gr. 1-2). 11.99 *(978-0-7944-3477-9(0))* Studio Fun International.

Hofer, Charles. Spacecraft. (World's Fastest Machines Ser.). 24p. 2009. (gr. 2-3). 42.50 *(978-1-60854-855-2(4))* 2008. (Illus.). lib. bdg. 22.60 *(978-1-4042-4178-7(7))* Rosen Publishing Group, Inc., The. (PowerKids Pr.).

Holden, Henry M. Triumph over Disaster Aboard Apollo 13: A MyReportLinks. com Book. 2004. (Space Flight Adventures & Disasters Ser.). (Illus.). 48p. (J). lib. bdg. 26.60 *(978-0-7660-5167-6(6)*, MyReportLinks.com Bks.) Enslow Pubs., Inc.

Jackson, Tom. Spacecraft. 2015. (Technology Timelines Ser.). (Illus.). 32p. (gr. 3-6). 31.35 *(978-1-78121-237-0(6))* Brown Bear Bks.

Kortenkamp, Steve. Mars Exploration Rovers: An Interactive Space Exploration Adventure. 2016. (You Choose: Space Ser.). (ENG., Illus.). 112p. (gr. 3-4). lib. bdg. 31.99 *(978-1-4914-8106-6(4)*, You Choose Bks.) Capstone Press of Coughlan Cos.

Krumm, Brian. Shuttle in the Sky: The Story of the Space Shuttle Columbia. 2015. (Exploring Space & Beyond Ser.). (ENG., Illus.). 48p. (gr. 3-4). lib. bdg. 29.32 *(978-1-4914-4161-9(5))* Capstone Press of Coughlan Cos.

Land-Sailing Venus Rover: Meet NASA Inventor Geoffrey Landis & His Team's. 2017. (J). ***(978-0-7166-6160-3(8))*** World Bk., Inc.

Laser-Sailing Starships: Meet NASA Inventor Philip Lubin & His Team's. 2017. (J). ***(978-0-7166-6159-7(4))*** World Bk., Inc.

Lemke, Donald & Lemke, Donald B. The Apollo 13 Mission, 1 vol. Tucker, Keith, illus. 2006. (Disasters in History Ser.). (ENG.). 32p. (gr. 3-4). 30.65 *(978-0-7368-5476-4(2)*, Graphic Library) Capstone Press of Coughlan Cos.

Maxwell, Scott & Chambers, Catherine. Mars Rover Driver. 2013. (Coolest Jobs on the Planet Ser.). (ENG., Illus.). 48p. (gr. 5-8). 32.65 *(978-1-4109-5483-1(8))*; pap. 8.99 *(978-1-4109-5488-6(9))* Heinemann-Raintree.

McMahon, Peter. Space Tourism. Mora, Andy, illus. 2011. (Machines of the Future Ser.). (ENG.). 40p. (J). (gr. 4-7). 16.95 *(978-1-55453-368-8(6))* Kids Can Pr., Ltd. CAN. Dist: Hachette Bk. Group.

McReynolds, Linda. Eight Days Gone. O'Rourke, Ryan, illus. 2012. (ENG.). 40p. (J). (gr. k-3). 16.95 *(978-1-58089-364-0(3))* Charlesbridge Publishing, Inc.

Meet NASA Inventor Robert Hoyt & His Team's Web-Spinning Space Spiders. 2017. (J). ***(978-0-7166-6157-3(8))*** World Bk., Inc.

Micklos, John, Jr. The Challenger Explosion: Core Events of a Space Tragedy. 2015. (What Went Wrong? Ser.). (ENG.). 32p. (gr. 3-4). lib. bdg. 27.32 *(978-1-4914-2046-1(4))* Capstone Press of Coughlan Cos.

Morey, Allan. The Hubble Space Telescope. 2017. (Space Tech Ser.). (ENG., Illus.). 24p. (J). (gr. 3-7). lib. bdg. 25.95 ***(978-1-62617-700-0(7)***, Epic Bks.) Bellwether Media.

Olson, Tod. Lost in Outer Space: The Incredible Journey of Apollo 13. 2017. (Lost Ser.: 2). (ENG.). 224p. (J). (gr. 3-7). 12.99 *(978-0-545-92815-1(X)*, Scholastic Nonfiction) Scholastic, Inc.

Omoth, Tyler. Building a Spacecraft, 1 vol. 2014. (See How It's Made Ser.). (ENG.). 32p. (gr. 1-2). lib. bdg. 26.65 *(978-1-4765-3979-9(0)*, Blazers) Capstone Press of Coughlan Cos.

Owen, Ruth. Saturn. 2013. (Explore Outer Space Ser.). 32p. (J). (gr. 3-6). 25.25 *(978-1-61533-727-9(X))*; pap. 60.00 *(978-1-61533-772-9(5))*; pap. 10.00 *(978-1-61533-771-2(7))* Windmill Bks.

—Spacecraft, 1 vol. 2015. (Objects in Space Ser.). (ENG., Illus.). 32p. (J). pap. 10.00 *(978-1-4777-5875-5(5)*, PowerKids Pr.) Rosen Publishing Group, Inc., The.

Oxlade, Chris & West, David. The Apollo Missions & Other Adventures in Space. 2011. (Incredible True Adventures Ser.). (ENG., Illus.). 48p. (YA). (gr. 5-8). pap. 11.75 *(978-1-4488-6664-9(2))*; lib. bdg. 29.25 *(978-1-4488-6660-1(X))* Rosen Publishing Group, Inc., The. (Rosen Reference).

Parker, Steve. Space Exploration. 2010. (How It Works Ser.). 40p. (J). (gr. 3-18). lib. bdg. 19.95 *(978-1-4222-1799-3(X))* Mason Crest.

Perritano, John. Space Machines. 2013. (Machines in Motion Ser.). 48p. (J). (gr. 3-5). pap. 84.30 *(978-1-4339-9614-6(6))*; pap. 14.05 *(978-1-4339-9613-9(8))*; (ENG., Illus.). lib. bdg. 31.95 *(978-1-4339-9612-2(X))* Stevens, Gareth Publishing LLLP.

Pierce, Alan. Apollo 13, 1 vol. 2005. (American Moments Set II Ser.). (ENG.). 48p. (gr. 4-8). 27.07 *(978-1-59197-726-1(6)*, Abdo & Daughters) ABDO Publishing Co.

Radomski, Kassandra. The Apollo 13 Mission: Core Events of a Crisis in Space, 1 vol. 2014. (What Went Wrong? Ser.). (ENG.). 32p. (gr. 3-4). pap. 7.95 *(978-1-4765-5130-2(8))*; lib. bdg. 27.32 *(978-1-4765-4181-5(7))* Capstone Press of Coughlan Cos.

Roza, Greg. The Hubble Space Telescope: Understanding & Representing Numbers in the Billions. 2009. (PowerMath: Proficiency Plus Ser.). 32p. (gr. 4-5). 47.90 *(978-1-60851-422-9(6)*, PowerKids Pr.) Rosen Publishing Group, Inc., The.

Rustad, Martha E. H. Space Vehicles. 2012. (Exploring Space Ser.). (ENG.). 24p. (gr. k-1). pap. 41.70 *(978-1-4296-8331-9(7))*; (Illus.). lib. bdg. 26.65 *(978-1-4296-7580-2(2))* Capstone Press of Coughlan Cos. (Pebble Plus).

Scott, Elaine. Space, Stars, & the Beginning of Time: What the Hubble Telescope Saw. 2011. (ENG., Illus.). 72p. (J). (gr. 5-7). 17.99 *(978-0-547-24189-0(5))* Houghton Mifflin Harcourt Publishing Co.

Silverman, Buffy. How Do Space Vehicles Work? 2013. (Lightning Bolt Books (tm) — How Flight Works). (ENG., Illus.). 32p. (gr. k-2). pap. 7.95 *(978-1-4677-0788-6(0))*; lib. bdg. 26.60 *(978-0-7613-8971-2(7)*, Lerner Pubns.) Lerner Publishing Group.

Simon, Seymour. Destination - Space. 2006. (ENG., Illus.). 32p. (J). (gr. k-4). pap. 6.99 *(978-0-06-087723-1(5)*, Collins) HarperCollins Pubs.

—Destination Space. 2006. (Illus.). 32p. (gr. k-4). 17.00 *(978-0-7569-6746-8(5))* Perfection Learning Corp.

Solar-Wind-Riding Electric Sail: Meet NASA Inventor Bruce Wiegmann & His Team's. 2017. (J). ***(978-0-7166-6162-7(4))*** World Bk., Inc.

Space Systems. 2016. (Space Systems Ser.). 112p. (YA). lib. bdg. 256.74 *(978-1-5026-2404-8(4))* Cavendish Square Publishing.

Sparrow, Giles. Exploring the Universe. 2006. (Secrets of the Universe Ser.). (Illus.). 48p. (gr. 6-12). lib. bdg. 31.00 *(978-0-8368-7276-7(2)*, Gareth Stevens Secondary Library) Stevens, Gareth Publishing LLLP.

Spizzirri, Linda, ed. Space Craft. Spizzirri, Peter M., illus. 32p. (J). (gr. 1-8). pap. 4.98 incl. audio *(978-0-86545-036-3(6))* Spizzirri Pr., Inc.

Thimmesh, Catherine. Team Moon: How 400,000 People Landed Apollo 11 on the Moon. 2006. (ENG., Illus.). 80p. (J). (gr. 5-7). 19.95 *(978-0-618-50757-3(4))* Houghton Mifflin Harcourt Publishing Co.

Vallejo, Harry. Dropping Clues from the Sky. 2011. 48p. (gr. 10-12). 19.89 *(978-1-4269-9297-1(1))*; pap. 9.89 *(978-1-4269-9296-4(3))* Trafford Publishing.

Visca, Curt. How to Draw Cartoon Spacecraft & Astronauts in Action. 2009. (Kid's Guide to Drawing Ser.). 24p. (gr. 3-3). 47.90 *(978-1-61511-019-3(4)*, PowerKids Pr.) Rosen Publishing Group, Inc., The.

Visca, Curt & Visca, Kelley. How to Draw Cartoon Spacecraft & Astronauts in Action. 2004. (Kid's Guide to Drawing Ser.). (Illus.). 24p. (J). lib. bdg. 25.25 *(978-0-8239-6729-2(8)*, PowerKids Pr.) Rosen Publishing Group, Inc., The.

Vogt, Gregory L. Disasters in Space Exploration. rev. ed. 2003. (Worlds Beyond Ser.). (Illus.). 80p. (gr. 5-8). lib. bdg. 25.90 *(978-0-7613-2895-7(5)*, Twenty-First Century Bks.) Lerner Publishing Group.

West, David. Spacecraft. West, David, illus. 2017. (What's Inside? Ser.). (Illus.). 24p. (gr. k-3). 28.50 ***(978-1-62588-404-6(4)***, Smart Apple Media) Black Rabbit Bks.

—Spacecraft. 2015. (Mechanic Mike's Machines (continuation) Ser.). (Illus.). 24p. (J). (gr. k-3). 27.10 *(978-1-62588-067-3(7))* Black Rabbit Bks.

Zelon, Helen. The Apollo 13 Mission: Surviving an Explosion in Space. 2009. (Space Missions Ser.). 24p. (gr. 3-4). 42.50 *(978-1-60853-116-5(3)*, PowerKids Pr.) Rosen Publishing Group, Inc., The.

Zobel, Derek. The Hubble Telescope. 2010. (Exploring Space Ser.). (ENG., Illus.). 24p. (J). (gr. k-3). lib. bdg. 25.95 *(978-1-60014-296-3(6)*, Blastoff! Readers) Bellwether Media.

Zoehfeld, Kathleen Weidner. Apollo 13. Lowe, Wesley, illus. 2015. (Totally True Adventures Ser.). (ENG.). 112p. (J). (gr. 2-5). pap. 4.99 *(978-0-385-39125-2(0)*, Random Hse. Bks. for Young Readers) Random Hse. Children's Bks.

SPACE VEHICLES—MODELS

Boekhoff, P. M. Nifty Thrifty Space Crafts. Ponte, June, illus. 2007. (Nifty Thrifty Crafts for Kids Ser.). 32p. (J). (gr. 3-4). lib. bdg. 23.94 *(978-0-7660-2783-1(X)*, Enslow Elementary) Enslow Pubs., Inc.

SPAIN

Bader, Bonnie. Who Was Christopher Columbus? Harrison, Nancy, illus. 2013. (Who Was? Ser.). (ENG.). 112p. (J). (gr. 3-7). pap. 5.99 *(978-0-448-46333-9(4)*, Grosset & Dunlap) Penguin Young Readers Group.

Blomquist, Christopher. A Primary Source Guide to Spain. (Countries of the World). 24p. 2009. (gr. 2-3). 42.50 *(978-1-61512-045-1(9))* 2005. (Illus.). (J). (gr. k-5). lib. bdg. 22.60 *(978-1-4042-2757-6(1))* Rosen Publishing Group, Inc., The. (PowerKids Pr.).

Brooks, Susie. Let's Visit Spain. 2009. (Around the World Ser.). (Illus.). 32p. (J). (ENG.). pap. 10.00 *(978-1-4358-8608-7(9))*; (gr. 2-5). lib. bdg. 25.25 *(978-1-4358-3027-1(X))* Rosen Publishing Group, Inc., The. (PowerKids Pr.).

Burlingame, Jeff. Soccer Star Andrés Iniesta. 2014. (Goal! Latin Stars of Soccer Ser.). 48p. (J). (gr. 4-9). pap. 8.95 *(978-1-62285-226-0(5))* Enslow Pubs., Inc.

Campbell, Polly, et al. Focus on Spain. 2006. (World in Focus Ser.). (Illus.). 64p. (gr. 5-12). pap. 14.05 *(978-0-8368-6730-5(0))*; lib. bdg. 34.00 *(978-0-8368-6723-7(8))* Stevens, Gareth Publishing LLLP. (Gareth Stevens Secondary Library).

Cefrey, Holly. The Pinckney Treaty: America Wins the Right to Travel the Mississippi River. 2009. (Life in the New American Nation Ser.). 32p. (gr. 4-4). 47.90 *(978-1-61514-286-6(X))* Rosen Publishing Group, Inc., The.

Donaldson, Madeline. Spain. 2011. (Country Explorers Ser.). (ENG., Illus.). 48p. (gr. 2-4). lib. bdg. 29.27 *(978-0-7613-6410-8(2))* Lerner Publishing Group.

Dyan, Penelope. The Rain in Spain — -A Kid's Guide to Barcelona, Spain. Weigand, John D., photos by. 2011. (Illus.). 38p. pap. 12.95 *(978-1-935630-56-2(3))* Bellissima Publishing, LLC.

Elgin, Kathy. Spain. 2008. (Costume Around the World Ser.). (Illus.). 32p. (gr. 4-6). 28.00 *(978-0-7910-9772-4(2)*, Chelsea Clubhouse) Facts On File, Inc.

Faiella, Graham. Spain: A Primary Source Cultural Guide. 2009. (Primary Sources of World Cultures Ser.). 128p. (gr. 4-5). 79.90 *(978-1-60851-930-9(9))* Rosen Publishing Group, Inc., The.

Feinstein, Stephen. Columbus: Opening up the New World. 2009. (Great Explorers of the World Ser.). (Illus.). 112p. (J). (gr. 7-12). lib. bdg. 33.27 *(978-1-59845-101-6(4))* Enslow Pubs., Inc.

Flynn, Claire E. Running with the Bulls. 2013. (Thrill Seekers Ser.). (Illus.). 32p. (J). (gr. 3-6). pap. 10.50 *(978-1-4824-3294-7(3))* Rosen Publishing Group, Inc., The.

Goldberg, Jan. Hernando de Soto: Trailblazer of the American Southeast. 2009. (Library of Explorers & Exploration Ser.). 112p. (gr. 5-8). 66.50 *(978-1-60853-607-8(6)*, Rosen Reference) Rosen Publishing Group, Inc., The.

Graham, Ian. Spain. 2003. (Country Files Ser.). 32p. (J). lib. bdg. 24.25 *(978-1-58340-240-5(3))* Black Rabbit Bks.

Hoogenboom, Lynn. Amerigo Vespucci. 2009. (Primary Source Library of Famous Explorers Ser.). 24p. (gr. 4-4). 42.50 *(978-1-60854-118-8(5)*, PowerKids Pr.) Rosen Publishing Group, Inc., The.

James, Yolanda. In Spain. Brodie, Neale, illus. 2008. (J). *(978-1-59646-772-9(X))* Dingles & Co.

Kent, Su. Living in Spain. Hampton, David, photos by. 2006. (Living In- Ser.). (Illus.). 32p. (J). (gr. 4-7). lib. bdg. 27.10 *(978-1-59771-048-0(2))* Sea-To-Sea Pubns.

Kenyon, John. Spain. 2004. (QEB Travel Through Ser.). (Illus.). 32p. (J). lib. bdg. 18.95 *(978-1-59566-061-9(5))* QEB Publishing Inc.

Kohen, Elizabeth. Spain. 2013. (Cultures of the World 4 Ser.). 144p. (J). (gr. 6-9). pap. 23.51 *(978-1-62712-162-0(5))* Cavendish Square Publishing.

Kohen, Elizabeth & Graff, Marie Louise. Spain. 2nd ed. 2003. (Illus.). 144p. (gr. 5-18). lib. bdg. 42.79 *(978-0-7614-1501-5(7)*, Marshall Cavendish Reference Bks.) Marshall Cavendish Corp.

Lusted, Marcia Amidon. Spain, 1 vol. 2013. (Countries of the World Set 2 Ser.). (ENG.). 144p. (J). (gr. 6-12). lib. bdg. 37.07 *(978-1-61783-637-4(0)*, Essential Library) ABDO Publishing Co.

Markovics, Joyce. Spain. 2017. (Countries We Come From Ser.). (ENG.). 32p. (J). (gr. k-3). 19.95 ***(978-1-68402-251-9(7))*** Bearport Publishing Co., Inc.

Mattern, Joanne. Spain. 2016. (Exploring World Cultures Ser.). 32p. (J). pap. 10.58 *(978-1-5026-2146-7(0))* Cavendish Square Publishing.

Peppas, Lynn. Why Francisco Coronado Matters to Texas. 2014. (Illus.). 32p. (J). lib. bdg. 26.25 *(978-1-4777-0909-2(6))* Rosen Publishing Group, Inc., The.

Powell, Jillian. Descubramos Espana. 2007. (Descubramos paises del mundo (Looking at Countries) Ser.). (SPA., Illus.). 32p. (gr. 1-5). lib. bdg. 26.00 *(978-0-8368-7952-0(X)*, Gareth Stevens Learning Library) Stevens, Gareth Publishing LLLP.

—Looking at Spain. 2007. (Looking at Countries Ser.). (Illus.). 32p. (gr. 1-5). pap. 10.50 *(978-0-8368-7679-6(2))*; lib. bdg. 26.00 *(978-0-8368-7672-7(5))* Stevens, Gareth Publishing LLLP. (Gareth Stevens Learning Library).

Reis, Ronald A. Christopher Columbus & the Age of Exploration for Kids: With 21 Activities. 2013. (For Kids Ser.). (ENG., Illus.). 160p. (J). (gr. 4). pap. 16.95 *(978-1-61374-674-5(1))* Chicago Review Pr., Inc.

Rice, Simon & Campbell, Polly. Discover Spain. 2010. (Discover Countries Ser.). (Illus.). 32p. (J). (gr. 3-5). lib. bdg. 26.50 *(978-1-61532-301-2(5))* Rosen Publishing Group, Inc., The.

Savery, Annabel. Spain. 2011. (ENG., Illus.). 32p. (J). pap. 10.95 *(978-1-77092-028-6(5))* Saunders Bk. Co. CAN. Dist: RiverStream Publishing.

Schon, Isabel. The Best of Latino Heritage, 1996-2002: A Guide to the Best Juvenile Books about Latino People, Vol. 2003. (ENG., Illus.). 272p. 70.00 *(978-0-8108-4669-2(1))* Scarecrow Pr., Inc.

Stewart, Mark. Rafael Nadal. 2009. (Today's Superstars Ser.). (ENG.). 48p. (J). (gr. 5-8). lib. bdg. 31.95 *(978-1-4339-1965-7(6))* Stevens, Gareth Publishing LLLP.

Taus-Bolstad, Stacy. Spain in Pictures. 2nd rev. expurg. ed. 2004. (Visual Geography Series, Second Ser.). (ENG., Illus.). 80p. (gr. 5-12). 31.93 *(978-0-8225-1993-5(3))* Lerner Publishing Group.

Teacher Created Resources Staff. Travel Through - Spain: Come on a Journey of Discovery. 2008. (Qeb Travel Through Ser.). (ENG., Illus.). 32p. (gr. 4-7). pap. 7.99 *(978-1-4206-8286-1(5))* Teacher Created Resources, Inc.

Thompson, Linda. The Spanish in America. 2005. (Expansion of America II Ser.). (Illus.). 48p. (J). (gr. 4-8). lib. bdg. 31.36 *(978-1-59515-514-6(7))* Rourke Educational Media.

SPAIN—FICTION

Albo, Pablo. The Glutton. 2007. (ENG., Illus.). 48p. (J). 18.95 *(978-84-96788-91-6(1))* OQO, Editora ESP. Dist: Baker & Taylor Bks.

Alonso, Manuel L. Tiempo de Nubes Negras. 4th ed. 2004. Tr. of Time for Black Clouds. (SPA., Illus.). 88p. (J). (gr. 6-8). pap. 12.99 *(978-84-207-7770-2(6))* Grupo Anaya, S.A. ESP. Dist: Lectorum Pubns., Inc.

Angel, Ido. Vipo in Madrid: Billy Must Win! 2015. (AV2 Animated Storytime Ser.). (ENG.). (J). lib. bdg. 29.99 *(978-1-4896-3893-9(8)*, AV2 by Weigl) Weigl Pubs., Inc.

Bentley, Sue. Sunshine Shimmers. 2014. (Magic Puppy Ser.: 12). lib. bdg. 14.75 *(978-0-606-34141-7(2)*, Turtleback) Turtleback Bks.

Bostick, B. k. Huber Hill & the Brotherhood of Coronado. 2012. 14.99 *(978-1-59955-981-0(1))* Cedar Fort, Inc./CFI Distribution.

Butcher, Nicholas. The Hand above the Gate. 2008. 204p. pap. *(978-1-84923-348-4(9))* YouWriteOn.

El Cid. (SPA., Illus.). 128p. (J). 11.95 *(978-84-7281-098-3(4),* AF1098) Auriga, Ediciones S.A. ESP. Dist: Continental Bk. Co., Inc.
de Trevino, Elizabeth Borton. I, Juan de Pareja. 3rd ed. pap. 3.95 *(978-0-13-800129-2(4))* Prentice Hall (Schl. Div.).
—I, Juan de Pareja. 2008. (ENG.). 192p. (YA). (gr. 7-12). pap. 7.99 *(978-0-312-38005-2(4),* 9780312380052) Square Fish.
—I, Juan de Pareja. l.t. ed. 2005. 244p. 20.95 *(978-0-7862-7666-0(5))* Thorndike Pr.
Elmokadem, Shirley. Serena & The Moor's Last Sigh. 2007. 80p. per. *(978-1-84549-229-8(3))* arima publishing.
Following Isabella - Evaluation Guide: Evaluation Guide. 2006. (J). *(978-1-55942-406-6(0))* Witcher Productions.
Galdós, Benito Pérez. Tristana. Jull Costa, Margaret, tr. from FRE. 2014. (NYRB Classics Ser.). (ENG.). 192p. pap. 14.95 *(978-1-59017-765-5(7),* NYRB Classics) New York Review of Bks., Inc., The.
Gerber, Linda. Lights, Camera, Cassidy - Celebrity. 2012. (Lights, Camera, Cassidy Ser.: 1). (ENG.). 240p. (J). (gr. 3-7). 6.99 *(978-0-14-241814-7(5),* Puffin Books) Penguin Young Readers Group.
Gray, Kes. Daisy & the Trouble with Kittens. Sharratt, Nick & Parsons, Garry, illus. 2010. (Daisy Ser.). (ENG.). 256p. (J). (gr. 2-4). pap. 11.99 *(978-0-86230-834-3(9),* Red Fox) Random House Children's Books GBR. Dist: Independent Pubs. Group.
Green, Elaine. The Adventures of Abigale Green in Spain. Alston, Brad, illus. 2012. 38p. (J). 14.95 *(978-1-937406-10-3(5))* Mascot Bks., Inc.
I, Juan de Pareja. 3rd ed. (J). pap., stu. ed. *(978-0-13-667452-8(6))* Prentice Hall (Schl. Div.).
Jellen, Michelle. Spain or Shine. 2005. (S. A. S. S. Ser.). (ENG., Illus.). 224p. (YA). (gr. 7-7). 7.99 *(978-0-14-240368-6(7),* Speak) Penguin Young Readers Group.
Jiménez, Juan Ramón. Platero y Yo. (SPA.). 192p. (J). 13.95 *(978-84-206-1851-7(9),* AZ1851); (Illus.). 159p. 15.95 *(978-84-206-3408-1(5))* Alianza Editorial, S. A. ESP. Dist: Continental Bk. Co., Inc., Distribooks, Inc.
—Platero y Yo. (SPA.). (J). pap. 9.95 *(978-968-432-357-5(3),* PM223) Editorial Porrua MEX. Dist: Continental Bk. Co., Inc.
—Platero y Yo. annot. ed. (SPA., Illus.). 232p. (J). 15.95 *(978-84-207-2636-6(2),* ANY010) Grupo Anaya, S.A. ESP. Dist: Continental Bk. Co., Inc.
—Platero y Yo (Platero & I) (SPA.). (J). pap. 9.95 *(978-968-416-022-4(4),* AOR01) Fernandez USA Publishing.
Johnson, Jane. La Princesa y el Pintor. Johnson, Jane, illus. 2003.Tr. of Princess & the Painter. (SPA., Illus.). 32p. (J). (gr. -1-3). pap. 14.95 *(978-1-56014-618-6(4),* SAN6184) Santillana USA Publishing Co., Inc.
Kephart, Beth. Small Damages. 2013. (ENG., Illus.). 304p. (YA). (gr. 9). pap. 8.99 *(978-0-14-242641-8(5),* Speak) Penguin Young Readers Group.
Krantz, Hazel. In the Garden of the Caliph. 2012. 132p. (gr. 4-6). 23.14 *(978-1-4669-2888-6(3))*; (J). pap. 13.14 *(978-1-4669-2886-2(7))* Trafford Publishing.
Kurlansky, Mark. The Girl Who Swam to Euskadi: Euskadiraino Igerian Joan Zen Neska. Kurlansky, Mark, illus. 2005. (ENG & BAQ., Illus.). 32p. (J). (gr. -1-3). 18.95 *(978-1-877802-54-6(9))* Ctr. for Basque Studies.
Lindo, Elvira. Manolito Four-Eyes, 0 vols. Emilio, Urberuaga & Urberuaga, Emilio, illus. 2010. (Manolito Four-Eyes Ser.: 1). (ENG.). 155p. (J). (gr. 3-7). pap. 9.99 *(978-0-7614-5729-9(1),* 9780761457299, Amazon Children's Publishing) Amazon Publishing.
—Manolito Four-Eyes: the 2nd Volume of the Great Encyclopedia of My Life: The 2nd Volume of the Great Encyclopedia of My Life, 0 vols. Urberuaga, Emilio, illus. unabr. ed. 2013. (Manolito Four-Eyes Ser.: 2). (ENG.). 162p. (J). (gr. 3-7). pap. 9.99 *(978-1-4778-1700-1(X),* 9781477817001, Amazon Children's Publishing) Amazon Publishing.
—Manolito Gafotas, 0 vols. Urberuaga, Emilio, illus. 2010. (SPA & ENG.). 192p. (J). (gr. 3-7). pap. 9.99 *(978-0-7614-5730-5(5),* 9780761457305, Amazon Children's Publishing) Amazon Publishing.
Maglia. EL LIBRO DE DON QUIJOTE PARA NIÑOS: NUEVA EDICIÓN) 2016. (SPA., Illus.). 114p. *(978-84-16075-98-0(0))* Ediciones B.
Martínez, Rueben. Once upon a Time: Traditional Latin American Tales. Unger, David, tr. from SPA. Colón, Raúl, illus. 2010. (ENG & SPA.). 96p. (J). (gr. k-5). 19.99 *(978-0-06-146895-7(9),* Rayo) HarperCollins Pubs.
McDougal-Littell Publishing Staff. Literature Connections Spanish: Yo, Juan de Pareja (I, Juan de Pareja) 2004. (McDougal Littell Literature Connections Ser.). (SPA.). 256p. (gr. 7-7). 16.90 *(978-0-395-84375-8(8),* 2-70788) Great Source Education Group, Inc.
Morningstar, Jeremy. Penalty Kick. 2005. 56p. pap. 9.00 *(978-1-4116-6572-9(4))* Lulu Pr., Inc.
Muñiz-Huberman, Angelina & Menton, Seymour. Dreaming of Safed. 2014. 126p. (YA). pap. *(978-1-935604-61-7(9))* Gaon Bks.
Narváez, Concha López. El Fuego de los Pastores.Tr. of Shepherds' Fire. (SPA.). (YA). (gr. 5). pap. *(978-84-395-0902-8(2))* Espasa Calpe, S.A. ESP. Dist: Lectorum Pubns., Inc.
Pearson, Harry. Alicia. 2008. (Clique Ser.). (ENG., Illus.). 144p. (YA). (gr. 7-17). pap. 6.99 *(978-0-316-02753-3(7),* Poppy) Little, Brown Bks. for Young Readers.
Pérez Galdós, Benito. Marianela. 2003. (SPA.). 159p. (YA). 12.95 *(978-968-6966-08-4(0))* EDITER'S Publishing Hse. MEX. Dist: EDITER'S Publishing Hse.
—Marianela. 9th ed. (SPA., Illus.). 240p. 18.50 *(978-84-376-0380-3(3),* CT1174) Ediciones Cátedra ESP. Dist: Continental Bk. Co., Inc.
—Marianela. 10th ed. 2003. (SPA., Illus.). 208p. *(978-84-207-3415-6(2),* GS1219) Grupo Anaya, S.A. ESP. Dist: Lectorum Pubns., Inc.
Pinter, Karin. Niki Owl: Leap of Faith. 2012. 172p. (gr. 4-6). 27.99 *(978-1-4772-8023-2(5))*; pap. 16.95 *(978-1-4772-8024-9(3))* AuthorHouse.
Sedgwick, Julian. The Palace of Memory. Moffett, Patricia, illus. 2017. (Mysterium Ser.: 2). (ENG.). 352p. (J). (gr. 4-8). 18.99 *(978-1-4677-7568-7(1),* Carolrhoda Bks.) Lerner Publishing Group.
Servi Machlin, Edda. My Puppy Marrano. 2007. (YA). 19.95 *(978-1-878857-13-2(4))* Giro Pr.
Sierra, Judy. The Beautiful Butterfly: A Folktale from Spain. Chess, Victoria, illus. 2005. 32p. (J). (gr. k-4). reprint ed. 19.00 *(978-0-7567-9593-1(1))* DIANE Publishing Co.
Song-i, Yoon. Saint Teresa of Avila, God's Troublemaker. 2014. (ENG., Illus.). 208p. (J). pap. 14.95 *(978-0-8198-9038-2(3))* Pauline Bks. & Media.
Staley, Samuel. The Pirate of Panther Bay Classroom Guide. 2007. 75p. spiral bd. 15.00 *(978-0-9764684-2-4(5))* IZS, Inc.
Stilton, Thea. The Spanish Dance Mission. 2013. (Thea Stilton Ser.: 16). (ENG., Illus.). 176p. (J). (gr. 2-5). pap. 8.99 *(978-0-545-55626-2(0),* Scholastic Paperbacks) Scholastic, Inc.
Strange, Derek & Pearson Longman Staff. Girl Meets Boy. 2nd ed. 2008. (ENG., Illus.). 32p. pap. 11.99 *(978-1-4058-6971-3(2))* Pearson Education.
Suguitan, Jazel A. We're Moving?! Shari Tucker's Wacky World #1. 2010. 124p. 20.95 *(978-1-4502-6874-5(9))*; pap. 10.95 *(978-1-4502-6871-4(4))* iUniverse, Inc.
Terrell, Brandon. Harmony & Hoops. Max, Iman & Garcia, Eduardo, illus. 2016. (Time Machine Magazine Ser.). (ENG.). 128p. (gr. 3-4). lib. bdg. 22.65 *(978-1-4965-2596-3(5))* Capstone Press of Coughlan Cos.
Terry, Alana. What Hurricane? My Solar-Powered History on a Supply Ship to the Jamestown Colony. Steffen, Jeremy, illus. 2013. 136p. pap. 12.99 *(978-1-937848-05-7(1))* Do Life Right, Inc.
Tulien, Sean & Poe, Edgar Allen. The Pit & the Pendulum, 1 vol. Fabul, J. C. & Calero, Dennis, illus. 2013. (Edgar Allan Poe Graphic Novels Ser.). (ENG.). 72p. (gr. 2-3). pap. 6.10 *(978-1-4342-4260-0(9))*; lib. bdg. 27.99 *(978-1-4342-4024-8(X))* Stone Arch Bks.
Waller, Stephen & Pearson Education Staff. Run for Your Life, Level 1. 2nd ed. 2009. (ENG., Illus.). 32p. pap. 11.99 *(978-1-4058-6970-6(4))* Pearson Education.
Wilson, John. Broken Arrow, 1 vol. 2014. (Seven Sequels Ser.). (ENG., Illus.). 240p. (J). (gr. 5-10). pap. 10.95 *(978-1-4598-0540-8(2))* Orca Bk. Pubs. USA.
—Lost Cause, 1 vol. 2012. (Seven (the Series) Ser.). (ENG., Illus.). 224p. (J). (gr. 5-10). pap. 9.95 *(978-1-55469-944-5(4))* Orca Bk. Pubs. USA.
Wojciechowska, Maia. Shadow of a Bull. 2011. 8.32 *(978-0-7848-3457-2(1),* Everbind) Marco Bk. Co.

SPAIN—HISTORY

Anderson, Wayne. The ETA: Spain's Basque Terrorists. (Inside the World's Most Infamous Terrorist Organizations Ser.). 64p. 2009. (gr. 5-5). 58.50 *(978-1-61513-578-3(2))* 2005. (Illus.). (YA). (gr. 7-12). lib. bdg. 31.95 *(978-0-8239-3818-6(2))* Rosen Publishing Group, Inc., The.
Bader, Bonnie. Who Was Christopher Columbus? 2013. (Who Was... ? Ser.). lib. bdg. 16.00 *(978-0-606-31684-2(1),* Turtleback) Turtleback Bks.
Baicker, Karen. Conquistador: Francisco Pizarro Ravages the Inca Empire. 2011. (J). pap. *(978-0-545-32940-8(X))* Scholastic, Inc.
Barker, Catherine. Spain. 2010. (Countries of the World Ser.). (ENG., Illus.). 64p. (J). (gr. 5-18). 27.90 *(978-1-4263-0633-4(4),* National Geographic Children's Bks.) National Geographic Society.
Behar, Yvonne. Out of Spain Vol. 3: Celebrating Sephardi Culture. Brooks, Andree Aelion, ed. (Illus.). 58p. (J). (gr. 5-7). pap. 4.95 *(978-0-9702700-3-0(8))* Brooks, Andree Aelion.
Berne, Emma Carlson. Did Christopher Columbus Really Discover America? And Other Questions about the New World. 2015. (Good Question! Ser.). (ENG., Illus.). 40p. (J). (gr. 2). 12.95 *(978-1-4549-1258-3(8))* Sterling Publishing Co., Inc.
Bodden, Valerie. Conquistadors. 2013. 24p. pap. *(978-1-60818-467-5(6))* Creative Co., The.
Bridges, Shirin Yim. Isabella of Castile. Nguyen, Albert, illus. 2010. (Thinking Girl's Treasury of Real Princesses Ser.). (ENG.). 24p. (J). (gr. 3-8). 18.95 *(978-0-9845098-4-3(4))* Goosebottom Bks. LLC.
Cohen, Robert Z. Hernando de Soto. 2016. (Spotlight on Explorers & Colonization Ser.). 00048p. (J). (gr. 6-6). pap. 11.75 *(978-1-5081-7210-9(2))* Rosen Publishing Group, Inc., The.
Cultures of the Past - Group 6, 4 bks. 119.71 *(978-0-7614-1491-9(6),* Benchmark Bks.) Marshall Cavendish Corp.
DiConsiglio, John. Francisco Pizarro: Destroyer of the Inca Empire. 2008. (Wicked History Ser.). (ENG., Illus.). 128p. (J). 31.00 *(978-0-531-18551-3(6),* Watts, Franklin) Scholastic Library Publishing.
Donohue, Moira Rose. Christopher Columbus. 2013. (Illus.). 24p. (J). *(978-1-938813-04-7(9))*; pap. *(978-1-938813-08-5(1))* State Standards Publishing, LLC.
—Hernando de Soto. 2015. (Illus.). 24p. (J). *(978-1-938813-20-7(0))* State Standards Publishing, LLC.
—Juan Ponce de León. 2013. (Illus.). 24p. (J). *(978-1-938813-06-1(5))* State Standards Publishing, LLC.
Dyan, Penelope. Around Corners — -A Kid's Guide to Malaga, Spain. Weigand, John D., photos by. 2012. (Illus.). 34p. pap. 11.95 *(978-1-61477-032-9(8))* Bellissima Publishing, LLC.
—¡Hola Córdoba! a Kid's Guide to Córdoba, Spain. Weigand, John D., photos by. 2012. (Illus.). 34p. pap. 11.95 *(978-1-61477-035-0(2))* Bellissima Publishing, LLC.
—¡Hola Madrid! a Kid's Guide to Madrid, Spain. Weigand, John D., photos by. 2012. (Illus.). 34p. pap. 11.95 *(978-1-61477-031-2(X))* Bellissima Publishing, LLC.
—I Remember Still, a Kid's Guide to Seville, Spain. Weigand, John D., photos by. 2012. (Illus.). 34p. pap. 11.95 *(978-1-61477-034-3(4))* Bellissima Publishing, LLC.
—A Lot o' Granada, a Kid's Guide to Granada, Spain. Weigand, John D., photos by. 2012. (Illus.). 34p. pap. 11.95 *(978-1-61477-033-6(6))* Bellissima Publishing, LLC.
Ganeri, Anita. Spain - Jouney Through. Isik, Semur, illus. 2015. (Country Guides, with Benjamin Blog & His Inquisitive Dog Ser.). (ENG.). 32p. (gr. 1-3). 29.99 *(978-1-4109-7996-4(2),* Read Me!) Heinemann-Raintree.
Greene, Meg. The Transcontinental Treaty 1819: A Primary Source Examination of the Treaty Between the United States & Spain over the American West. (Primary Sources of American Treaties Ser.). 64p. 2009. (gr. 5-8). 58.50 *(978-1-60851-514-1(1))* 2006. (Illus.). (J). (gr. k-3). lib. bdg. 31.95 *(978-1-4042-0439-3(3))* Rosen Publishing Group, Inc., The.
Guillain, Charlotte. Spain, 1 vol. 2012. (Countries Around the World Ser.). (ENG.). 48p. (gr. 3-6). pap. 9.95 *(978-1-4329-6137-4(3),* NA-h) Heinemann-Raintree.
Gunderson, Jessica. Christopher Columbus: New World Explorer or Fortune Hunter?, 1 vol. 2013. (Perspectives on History Ser.). (ENG.). 32p. (gr. 3-4). 27.32 *(978-1-4765-0242-7(0))*; pap. 7.95 *(978-1-4765-3406-0(3))* Capstone Press of Coughlan Cos. (Fact Finders).
Hernández, Roger E. Early Explorations: The 1500s. 2008. (Hispanic America Ser.). 80p. (gr. 5-18). lib. bdg. 34.21 *(978-0-7614-2937-1(9),* Benchmark Bks.) Marshall Cavendish Corp.
Hilliam, David. Philip II: King of Spain & Leader of the Counter-Reformation. 2009. (Rulers, Scholars, & Artists of the Renaissance Ser.). 112p. (gr. 5-8). 66.50 *(978-1-60852-944-5(4),* Rosen Reference) Rosen Publishing Group, Inc., The.
Kallen, Stuart A. A Journey with Christopher Columbus. 2017. (Primary Source Explorers Ser.). (ENG.). 40p. (J). (gr. 3-5). lib. bdg. 30.65 *(978-1-5124-0772-3(0))* Lerner Publishing Group.
Lee, Michelle. Guggenheim Museum. 2015. (How Did They Build That? Ser.). (ENG., Illus.). 32p. (gr. 3-8). 27.99 *(978-1-62920-563-2(X))* Scobre Pr. Corp.
Malam, John. You Wouldn't Want to Sail in the Spanish Armada! An Invasion You'd Rather Not Launch. Antram, David, illus. 2006. (You Wouldn't Want to Ser.). (ENG.). 32p. (J). (gr. 2-5). 29.00 *(978-0-531-14974-4(9))* Scholastic Library Publishing.
Martin, Carme & Herrero, Teresa. Gaudí. 2010. (Me Llamo... Ser.). (SPA., Illus.). 63p. (J). pap. *(978-84-342-3337-9(1))* Parramon Ediciones S.A.
Matthews, Rupert. Conquistadors. 2015. (History's Fearless Fighters Ser.). (ENG., Illus.). 48p. (J). (gr. 5-6). pap. 14.05 *(978-1-4824-3161-2(0))* Stevens, Gareth Publishing LLLP.
Nagelhout, Ryan. Vasco Núñez de Balboa. 2016. (Spotlight on Explorers & Colonization Ser.). 48p. (J). (gr. 6-6). pap. 11.75 *(978-1-4777-8828-8(X))* Rosen Publishing Group, Inc., The.
Nardo, Don. The Spanish Conquistadors. 2009. (World History Ser.). (ENG.). 128p. (J). (gr. 7-10). 34.95 *(978-1-4205-0133-9(X),* Lucent Bks.) Cengage Gale.
O'Brien, Cynthia. Explore with Francisco Pizarro. 2015. (Travel with the Great Explorers Ser.). (ENG., Illus.). 32p. (J). (gr. 3-6). *(978-0-7787-1700-3(3))* Crabtree Publishing Co.
—Explore with Ponce de León. 2014. (ENG., Illus.). 32p. (J). *(978-0-7787-1429-3(2))* Crabtree Publishing Co.
Ollhoff, Jim. Christopher Columbus. 2013. (Great Explorers Ser.). 32p. (J). (gr. 5-9). lib. bdg. 27.07 *(978-1-61783-964-1(7),* Abdo & Daughters) ABDO Publishing Co.
—The Conquistadors, 1 vol. 2011. (Hispanic American History Ser.). (ENG., Illus.). 32p. (YA). (gr. 5-9). 27.07 *(978-1-61783-055-6(0))* ABDO Publishing Co.
Owens, L. L. A Journey with Hernán Cortés. 2017. (Primary Source Explorers Ser.). (ENG.). 40p. (J). (gr. 3-5). 30.65 *(978-1-5124-0777-8(1))* Lerner Publishing Group.
Parker, Lewis K. Spanish Colonies in the Americas. (European Colonies in the Americas Ser.). 24p. 2009. (gr. 2-2). 42.50 *(978-1-61512-320-9(2))* 2003. (Illus.). (J). lib. bdg. 22.60 *(978-0-8239-6471-0(X))* Rosen Publishing Group, Inc., The. (PowerKids Pr.).
Pavlovic, Zoran, et al. Spain. 2nd rev. ed. 2011. (Modern World Nations Ser.). (gr. 6-12). 35.00 *(978-1-61753-047-0(6),* Chelsea Hse.) Facts On File, Inc.
Pelleschi, Andrea. Juan Ponce de Leon. 2013. (Jr. Graphic Famous Explorers Ser.). (ENG., Illus.). 24p. (J). (gr. 3-6). pap. 10.60 *(978-1-4777-0131-7(1))*; lib. bdg. 25.25 *(978-1-4777-0073-0(0))* Rosen Publishing Group, Inc., The. (PowerKids Pr.).
Peppas, Lynn. Why Cabeza de Vaca Matters to Texas. 2014. (Illus.). 32p. (J). lib. bdg. 26.25 *(978-1-4777-0913-9(4))* Rosen Publishing Group, Inc., The.
Ramen, Fred. Albucasis (Abu al-Qasim Al-Zahrawi) Renowned Muslim Surgeon of the Tenth Century. 2009. (Great Muslim Philosophers & Scientists of the Middle Ages Ser.). 112p. (gr. 6-6). 66.50 *(978-1-61513-178-5(7),* Rosen Reference) Rosen Publishing Group, Inc., The.
—Hernán Cortés: The Conquest of Mexico & the Aztec Empire. 2009. (Library of Explorers & Exploration Ser.). 112p. (gr. 5-8). 66.50 *(978-1-60853-606-1(8),* Rosen Reference) Rosen Publishing Group, Inc., The.
Ray, Michael, ed. Portugal & Spain. 2013. (Britannica Guide to Countries of the European Union Ser.). 344p. (YA). (gr. 9-12). 53.00 *(978-1-61530-967-2(5))* Rosen Publishing Group, Inc., The.
Rice, Simon. Discover Spain. 2010. (Illus.). 32p. (J). 63.60 *(978-1-61532-303-6(1))*; pap. 10.60 *(978-1-61532-302-9(3))* Rosen Publishing Group, Inc., The. (PowerKids Pr.).
Roberts, Steven. Francisco Vasquez de Coronado. 2013. (Jr. Graphic Famous Explorers Ser.). (ENG., Illus.). 24p. (J). (gr. 3-6). pap. 10.60 *(978-1-4777-0125-6(7))*; lib. bdg. 25.25 *(978-1-4777-0070-9(6))* Rosen Publishing Group, Inc., The. (PowerKids Pr.).
Ryan, Sean. Spain in Our World. 2010. (Countries in Our World Ser.). 32p. (gr. 4-7). lib. bdg. 31.35 *(978-1-59920-438-3(X))* Black Rabbit Bks.
Sammons, Sandra Wallus. Ponce de Leon & the Discovery of Florida. 2013. (ENG., Illus.). 72p. (J). (gr. 4-6). 12.95 *(978-1-56164-592-3(3))*; pap. 9.95 *(978-1-56164-593-0(1))* Pineapple Pr., Inc.
Sebastian, Emily. The Colonial & Postcolonial Experience in Latin America & the Caribbean. 2016. (Colonial & Postcolonial Experience Ser.). 00128p. (J). (gr. 10-10). 54.00 *(978-1-5081-0439-1(5))* Rosen Publishing Group, Inc., The.
Sexton, Colleen & Grack, Rachel. Spain. 2010. (Exploring Countries Ser.). (ENG., Illus.). 32p. (J). (gr. 3-7). lib. bdg. 26.95 *(978-1-60014-489-9(6),* Blastoff! Readers) Bellwether Media.
Sheen, Barbara. Foods of Spain. 2007. (Taste of Culture Ser.). (ENG., Illus.). 64p. (J). (gr. 3-5). lib. bdg. 30.45 *(978-0-7377-3539-0(2),* Kidhaven) Cengage Gale.
Simons, Rae & Indovino, Shaina C. Spain. Bruton, John, ed. 2012. (Major European Union Nations Ser.). 64p. (J). (gr. 7). 22.95 *(978-1-4222-2259-1(4))* Mason Crest.
Simons, Rae & Indovino, Shaina Carmel. Spain. 2012. (J). pap. *(978-1-4222-2290-4(X))* Mason Crest.
Somervill, Barbara A. Spain. 2012. (ENG., Illus.). 144p. (J). 40.00 *(978-0-531-27546-7(9),* Children's Pr.) Scholastic Library Publishing.
Sonneborn, Liz. The Acquisition of Florida: America's Twenty-Seventh State. 2009. (Milestones in American History Ser.). (Illus.). 120p. (gr. 6-12). 35.00 *(978-1-60413-054-6(7),* Chelsea Hse.) Facts On File, Inc.
Sutherland, Katrice. Spanish Explorers. 2016. (J). ***(978-1-5105-1872-8(X))*** SmartBook Media, Inc.
Thomson, Ruth. Spain. 2011. (Countries Ser.). (Illus.). 24p. (J). (gr. k-3). lib. bdg. 22.60 *(978-1-4488-3278-1(0))* Rosen Publishing Group, Inc., The.
Tieck, Sarah. Spain, 1 vol. 2013. (Explore the Countries Ser.). (ENG.). 40p. (J). (gr. 2-5). lib. bdg. 29.93 *(978-1-61783-818-7(7),* Big Buddy Bks.) ABDO Publishing Co.
Urrutia, Maria Christina & Libura, Krystyna. Ecos de la Conquista. 2005. (SPA.). (J). pap. 14.25 *(978-968-7381-21-3(3))* Tecolote, Ediciones, S.A. de C.V. MEX. Dist: Iaconi, Mariuccia Bk. Imports.
Usborne Books Staff & Doherty, Gillian. 1001 Cosas Que Buscar en el Pasado. 2004. (SPA., Illus.). 32p. (J). (gr. -1-18). lib. bdg. 14.95 *(978-1-58086-286-8(1),* EU1375) EDC Publishing.
Wade, Mary Dodson. Christopher Columbus. 2014. (Rookie Biographies(r) Ser.). (ENG., Illus.). 32p. (J). pap. 5.95 *(978-0-531-21202-8(5))* Scholastic Library Publishing.
Williams, Jack S. Soldiers & Their Families of the California Mission Frontier. 2009. (People of the California Missions Ser.). 64p. (gr. 4-4). 58.50 *(978-1-60851-160-0(X),* PowerKids Pr.) Rosen Publishing Group, Inc., The.
Woog, Adam. Life During the Spanish Inquisition. 2014. (Living History Ser.). (ENG., Illus.). 96p. (J). lib. bdg. *(978-1-60152-722-6(5))* ReferencePoint Pr., Inc.
Worth, Richard. Independence for Latino America. 2006. (Latino-American History Ser.). 112p. (YA). (gr. 5-9). 35.00 *(978-0-8160-6441-0(5))* Facts On File, Inc.

SPAIN—HISTORY—FICTION

Aiken, Joan. The Teeth of the Gale. 2007. (ENG., Illus.). 352p. (YA). (gr. 7). pap. 18.99 *(978-0-15-206070-1(7))* Houghton Mifflin Harcourt Publishing Co.
Collingwood, Harry. Across the Spanish Main. 2009. 204p. pap. 14.95 *(978-1-60664-390-7(8))* Rodgers, Alan Bks.
Eiseman, Joan. Ricardo & the Fisherman. Eiseman, Joan, illus. 2007. (Illus.). 32p. (J). per. 12.95 *(978-0-9786745-4-0(5))* Marble Hse. Editions.
Gibbs, Stuart. Traitor's Chase. 2012. (Last Musketeer Ser.: 2). (ENG.). 256p. (J). (gr. 3-7). 16.99 *(978-0-06-204841-7(4))* HarperCollins Pubs.
Gonzalez, Christina Diaz. A Thunderous Whisper. 2013. (ENG., Illus.). 320p. (J). (gr. 5). pap. 7.99 *(978-0-375-87371-3(6),* Yearling) Random Hse. Children's Bks.
Greene, Jacqueline Dembar. The Secret Shofar of Barcelona. Chayka, Doug, illus. 2009. (High Holidays Ser.). (ENG.). 32p. (J). (gr. k-3). 17.95 *(978-0-8225-9915-9(5),* Kar-Ben Publishing) Lerner Publishing Group.
—The Secret Shofar of Barcelona. Chayka, Douglas, illus. 2009. (High Holidays Ser.). (ENG.). 32p. (J). (gr. k-3). pap. 7.95 *(978-0-8225-9944-9(9),* Kar-Ben Publishing) Lerner Publishing Group.
Henty, George Alfred. With Moore at Corunna: A Tale of the Peninsular War. 2007. (ENG.). 334p. pap. 23.99 *(978-1-4264-3149-4(X))*; 372p. pap. 26.99 *(978-1-4264-3242-2(9))* Creative Media Partners, LLC.
—With Moore at Corunna: A Tale of the Peninsular War. 2004. reprint ed. pap. 30.95 *(978-1-4191-9445-0(3))*; pap. 1.99 *(978-1-4192-9445-7(8))* Kessinger Publishing, LLC.
Hoffman, Alice. Incantation. rev. ed. 2007. (ENG., Illus.). 192p. (YA). (gr. 7-17). per. 10.00 *(978-0-316-15428-4(8))* Little, Brown Bks. for Young Readers.
Holub, Joan. Isabel Saves the Prince: Based on a True Story of Isabel I of Spain. Aleshina, Nonna, illus. 2007. (Young Princesses Around the World Ser.). (ENG.). 48p. (J). (gr. 1-3). pap. 13.99 *(978-0-689-87197-9(X),* Simon Spotlight) Simon Spotlight.
Jules, Jacqueline. Never Say a Mean Word Again: A Tale from Medieval Spain. Bernhard, Durga Yael, illus. 2014. (ENG.). 32p. (J). (gr. -1-3). 16.95 *(978-1-937786-20-5(X),* Wisdom Tales) World Wisdom, Inc.
Miklowitz, Gloria D. Secrets in the House of Delgado. 2004. 192p. (J). (gr. 4-18). pap. 8.00 *(978-0-8028-5210-6(6))* Eerdmans, William B. Publishing Co.
Muschla, Gary Robert. The Sword & the Cross. 2009. (YA). lib. bdg. *(978-0-88092-471-9(3))* Royal Fireworks Publishing Co.
Narvaez, Concha Lopez. La Colina de Edeta. (SPA.). 124p. (YA). (gr. 5-8). *(978-84-239-9050-4(8),* EC3401) Espasa Calpe, S.A. ESP. Dist: Lectorum Pubns., Inc.
Narváez, Concha López. El Tiempo y la Promesa.Tr. of Time & the Promise. (SPA.). (YA). (gr. 5-8). 164p. *(978-84-216-2558-3(6),* BU7323); 9th ed. (Illus.). 208p. *(978-84-216-1538-6(6),* BU6188) Bruño, Editorial ESP. Dist: Lectorum Pubns., Inc.
Orgad, Dorit. The Boy from Seville. Silverston, Sondra, tr. from HEB. Katz, Avi, illus. 2007. (Kar-Ben for Older Readers Ser.). (ENG.). 200p. (J). (gr. 5-7). lib. bdg. 16.95 *(978-1-58013-253-4(7),* Kar-Ben Publishing) Lerner Publishing Group.
Ricci, Dorothy. Through Goya's Eyes: The World of the Spanish Painter & His Friend & Mentor, Gaspar Jovellanos. 2008. (YA). pap. *(978-0-88092-763-5(1))*; lib. bdg. *(978-0-88092-762-8(3))* Royal Fireworks Publishing Co.
Robinson, Whitney A. Horse Diaries #14: Calvino. Sanderson, Ruth, illus. 2017. (Horse Diaries: 12). (ENG.). 160p. (J). (gr. 3-7). pap. 7.99 *(978-1-101-93779-2(3),* Random Hse. Bks. for Young Readers) Random Hse. Children's Bks.
Rollason, Jane. Freddie's War Level 6 Advanced. 2010. (ENG.). 128p. pap. 14.50 *(978-84-8323-909-4(4))* Cambridge Univ. Pr.
—Freddie's War Level 6 Advanced Book with CD-ROM & Audio CDs (3), 1 vol. 2010. (ENG.). 128p. cd-rom, audio compact disk 18.25 *(978-84-8323-662-8(1))* Cambridge Univ. Pr.
Styles, Showell. The Flying Ensign: Greencoats Against Napoleon. 2003. (Budget Bks.). Orig. Title: Greencoat

S

Against Napoleon. 297p. (YA). pap. 14.95 (978-1-883937-70-6(1)) Bethlehem Bks.
Wilson, John. Lost in Spain. 2009. (ENG., Illus.). 216p. (YA). (gr. 7-18). pap. (978-1-55470-177-3(5)) Me to We.
Wiseman, Eva. The Last Song. 2012. (ENG., Illus.). 228p. (YA). (gr. 5). 17.95 (978-0-88776-979-5(9), Tundra Bks.) Tundra Bks. CAN. Dist: Penguin Random Hse. LLC.
Zafón, Carlos Ruiz. Marina. 2014. (ENG.). 336p. (YA). (gr. 7-17). 19.00 (978-0-316-04471-4(7)) Little, Brown Bks. for Young Readers.

SPAIN—HISTORY—CIVIL WAR, 1936-1939

Byers, Ann. Strategic Inventions of the Spanish Civil War. 2016. (Tech in the Trenches Ser.). 112p. (J). lib. bdg. 42.79 (978-1-5026-2355-3(2)) Cavendish Square Publishing.
Griffiths, Katie. The Spanish Civil War. 2017. (J). **(978-1-5026-2719-3(1))** Cavendish Square Publishing.
Katz, William Loren & Crawford, Marc. The Lincoln Brigade: A Picture History. 2013. 96p. pap. 12.00 (978-1-62032-901-6(8), Wipf and Stock) Wipf & Stock Pubs.

SPANISH AMERICA

see Latin America

SPANISH-AMERICAN WAR, 1898

Baker, Brynn. Roosevelt's Rough Riders: Fearless Cavalry of the Spanish-American War. 2015. (Military Heroes Ser.). (ENG., Illus.). 32p. (gr. 3-4). lib. bdg. 27.32 (978-1-4914-4840-3(7)) Capstone Press of Coughlan Cos.
Clinton, Greg. Puerto Rico & the Spanish-American War. 2016. (Expanding America Ser.). (ENG., Illus.). 96p. (J). (gr. 8-8). 42.79 (978-1-5026-0972-4(X)) Cavendish Square Publishing.
Golay, Michael. Spanish-American War. 3rd rev. ed. 2010. (America at War Ser.). (Illus.). 192p. (gr. 6-12). 45.00 (978-0-8160-8189-9(1), Chelsea Hse.) Facts On File, Inc.
Hendrickson, Kenneth E. & Hendrickson, Kenneth E., Jr. Primary Source Accounts of the Spanish-American War. 2006. (America's Wars Through Primary Sources Ser.). (Illus.). 128p. (J). (gr. 4-7). lib. bdg. 34.60 (978-1-59845-007-1(7), MyReportLinks.com Bks.) Enslow Pubs., Inc.
Hernández, Roger E. The Spanish-American War. 2009. (Hispanic America 2 Ser.). 80p. (gr. 5). 34.21 (978-0-7614-4174-8(3)) Marshall Cavendish Corp.
Johanson, Paula. The Spanish-American War. 2016. (United States at War Ser.). (ENG., Illus.). 128p. (J). (gr. 6-6). 37.27 (978-0-7660-7665-5(2)) Enslow Pubs., Inc.
McGowen, Tom. The Spanish-American War & Teddy Roosevelt in American History. 2003. (In American History Ser.). (Illus.). 128p. (J). lib. bdg. 26.60 (978-0-7660-1987-4(X)) Enslow Pubs., Inc.
McNeese, Tim. Remember the Maine! The Spanish-American War Begins. 2004. (First Battles Ser.). (Illus.). 112p. (YA). (gr. 6-12). 23.95 (978-1-883846-79-4(X), First Biographies) Reynolds, Morgan Inc.
Poulakidas, Georgene. The Spanish-American War. (Primary Sources of American Wars Ser.). 24p. 2009. (gr. 3-4). 42.50 (978-1-60851-528-8(1), PowerKids Pr.) 2006. (Illus.). (YA). (gr. 4-7). lib. bdg. 22.60 (978-1-4042-2685-2(0)) Rosen Publishing Group, Inc., The.
Rice, Katelyn. The Spanish-American War. 2016. (Primary Source Readers Ser.). 32p. (J). (gr. 4-4). pap. 8.99 (978-1-4938-3541-6(6)) Teacher Created Materials, Inc.
Spanish American War. 2003. (ENG., Illus.). 264p. (J). 106.00 (978-0-7876-6561-6(4), UXL) Cengage Gale.

SPANISH-AMERICAN WAR, 1898—FICTION

Finley, Martha. Elsie's Young Folks. 2008. 296p. 34.99 (978-1-58960-287-8(0)) Sovereign Grace Pubs., Inc.
Loughrey, Eithne. Annie Moore: New York City Girl. l.t. ed. 2006. (Dales Ser.). 208p. 23.99 (978-1-84262-448-7(2)) Dales Large Print Bks. GBR. Dist: Ulverscroft Large Print Bks., Ltd.
Morrison, Harry Steele. The Adventures of A Boy Reporter. 2004. reprint ed. pap. 1.99 (978-1-4192-5137-5(6)); pap. 20.95 (978-1-4191-5137-8(1)) Kessinger Publishing, LLC.
Munroe, Kirk. 'Forward, March' 2007. 148p. per. 11.95 (978-1-60312-029-6(7)) Aegypan.

SPANISH LANGUAGE

La Abeja Trabajadora. 2003. (J). 23.95 (978-0-673-77796-6(0)) Celebration Pr.
Ace Academics, ed. Spanish: A Whole Course in a Box! 2007. (Exambusters Ser.). 384p. (gr. 7-18). 12.95 (978-1-881374-97-8(1), Exambusters) Ace Academics, Inc.
Aigner-Clark, Julie. La Guarderia de Idiomas (The Guarderia Language) 2004. (Baby Einstein Ser.). (SPA., Illus.). 16p. (J). bds. (978-970-718-153-3(2), Silver Dolphin en Español) Advanced Marketing, S. de R. L. de C. V.
Amery, H. First Thousand Words. 2004. (SPA.). 70p. (J). pap. 9.99 (978-0-7945-0463-2(9)) EDC Publishing.
—First Thousand Words in Spanish IL. rev. ed. 2004. (First Thousand Words Ser.). (SPA & ENG.). 64p. (J). 12.99 (978-0-7945-0284-3(9)); lib. bdg. 20.99 (978-1-58086-564-7(X)) EDC Publishing.
Amery, H. & Cartwright, S. First Spanish Word Book. 2004. (Treasury of Farmyard Tales Ser.). (SPA & ENG.). 48p. (J). 10.95 (978-0-7945-0476-2(0)) EDC Publishing.
Anaya, Rudolfo A. How Chile Came to New Mexico. Nasario, Garcia, tr. from ENG. Nicolas, Otero, illus. 2014. (SPA & ENG.). 48p. (J). (gr. -1-3). 24.95 (978-1-936744-20-6(1), Rio Grande Bks.) LPD Pr.
Anderson, Jill, ed. Let's Go on Safari!/Vamos de Safari! Utton, Peter, illus. 2005. (Word Play/Juegos con Pala Ser.). (ENG & SPA.). 20p. (J). (gr. -1-17). bds. 6.95 (978-1-58728-522-6(3)) Cooper Square Publishing Llc.
Appleby, Alex. Lo Que Oigo / What I Hear. 2014. (Mis Cinco Sentidos / My Five Senses Ser.). (SPA.). 24p. (J). (gr. k-2). 22.60 (978-1-4824-0869-0(4)) Stevens, Gareth Publishing LLLP.
La Arana. 2003. 23.95 (978-0-673-77156-8(3)) Celebration Pr.
Baker, Mary. English - Spanish Counting Book. Mason, Alfonso & Mason, Ruth, illus. 2008. 24p. pap. 24.95 (978-1-60672-035-6(X)) America Star Bks.
Barfell, Judith A. Learn & Sign Funtime-Beginnings-Spanish. 2005. (Beginnings Ser.: Bk. 1). (SPA.). (J). per. 14.95 (978-0-9753717-2-5(X)) Learn & Sign Funtime Bks.
Bauman, Carey. God Controls the Storm. Bauman, Carey, tr. 2007. (Little Jewel Book Ser.). (Illus.). 24p. (J). (gr. 2). pap. 2.70 (978-0-7399-2396-2(X)) Rod & Staff Pubs., Inc.
Baylis, Aless. ABC Spanish: Take a Fun Journey Through the Alphabet & Learn Some Spanish! 2017. (Little Concepts Ser.). (ENG, EST & SPA., Illus.). 36p. (J). (gr. -1-1). 12.95 (978-1-63322-283-0(7), Walter Foster) Quarto Publishing Group USA.
Beaton, Clare, illus. English-Spanish Bilingual First Books, 6 bks. (J). lib. bdg. 86.70 (978-1-56674-944-2(1)) Forest Hse. Publishing Co., Inc.
Beck, Jeanine. Los Animales: An Introduction to Commonly Used Spanish Words & Phrases about Animal Friends, with More Than 425 Lively Photographs. 2016. (ENG & SPA., Illus.). 64p. 12.99 (978-1-86147-633-3(7), Armadillo) Anness Publishing GBR. Dist: National Bk. Network.
—Mi Casa: An Introduction to Commonly Used Spanish Words & Phrases Around the Home, with 500 Lively Photographs. (Illus.). 64p. 2016. (ENG & SPA.). (J). (gr. -1-12). 12.99 (978-1-86147-697-5(3), Armadillo) 2008. (SPA & ENG., pap. 7.99 (978-1-84476-525-6(3)) Anness Publishing GBR. Dist: National Bk. Network.
Berendes, Mary. Actions/Las Acciones. Petelinsek, Kathleen, illus. 2008. (WordBooks/Libros de Palabras Ser.). (SPA & ENG.). 24p. (J). (gr. k-3). 25.64 (978-1-59296-987-6(9), 201085) Child's World, Inc., The.
—Careers/Las Carreras. Petelinsek, Kathleen, illus. 2008. (WordBooks/Libros de Palabras Ser.). (SPA & ENG.). 24p. (J). (gr. k-3). 25.64 (978-1-59296-988-3(7), 201088) Child's World, Inc., The.
—Clothes/la Ropa. Petelinsek, Kathleen, illus. 2008. (WordBooks/Libros de Palabras Ser.). (SPA & ENG.). 24p. (J). (gr. k-3). 25.64 (978-1-59296-989-0(5), 201089) Child's World, Inc., The.
—Days & Times (Los Días y Las Horas) Petelinsek, Kathleen, illus. 2008. (WordBooks/Libros de Palabras Ser.). (ENG.). 24p. (J). (gr. k-3). 25.64 (978-1-59296-990-6(9), 201090) Child's World, Inc., The.
—Holidays & Celebrations (Los Días de Fiestas y Las Celebraciones) Petelinsek, Kathleen, illus. 2008. (WordBooks/Libros de Palabras Ser.). (SPA & ENG.). 24p. (J). (gr. k-3). 25.64 (978-1-59296-991-3(7), 201093) Child's World, Inc., The.
—House/la Casa. Petelinsek, Kathleen, illus. 2008. (WordBooks/Libros de Palabras Ser.). (SPA & ENG.). 24p. (J). (gr. k-3). 25.64 (978-1-59296-992-0(5), 201094) Child's World, Inc., The.
Berkes, Marianne. The Tortoise & Hare's Amazing Race, 1 vol. Morrison, Cathy, illus. 2015. (ENG & SPA.). 32p. (J). (gr. k-3). 17.95 (978-1-62855-635-3(8)) Arbordale Publishing.
Berlitz Publishing Staff, ed. 1000 Spanish Words. 2nd rev. ed. 2005. (1000 Words Ser.). (SPA & ENG., Illus.). 64p. (J). pap. 9.99 (978-981-246-528-3(6), 465286) APA Publications Services SGP. Dist: Ingram Publisher Services.
Berry, Shilo. E-Mails Home. 2008. (Illus.). 24p. (J). pap. 10.95 (978-1-59646-565-7(4)) Dingles & Co.
Beullens-Maoui, Nathalie, ed. Animals Habitats: Spanish, 01 vols., 1. 2016. (Our Wonderful World Ser.). (ENG & SPA.). 8p. (J). pap. 9.35 (978-1-5081-1251-8(7), Rosen Classroom) Rosen Publishing Group, Inc., The.
Brandenberg, Aliki & Aliki. La Fiesta Medieval. (SPA.). 32p. 15.95 (978-84-261-2696-2(0)) Juventud, Editorial ESP. Dist: Distribooks, Inc.
Brooks, Felicity. Easy Spanish Words Sticker Book. 2012. (First Sticker Language Bks). 24p. (J). pap. 6.99 (978-0-7945-3323-6(X), Usborne) EDC Publishing.
—Everyday Words in Spanish. Litchfield, Jo, illus. rev. ed. 2004. (Everyday Words Ser.). 48p. (J). pap. 9.95 (978-0-7945-0881-4(2), Usborne) EDC Publishing.
—My First Spanish Word Book. 2015. (My First Word Bks.). (ENG.). 20p. (J). 9.99 (978-0-7945-3493-6(7), Usborne) EDC Publishing.
Budds, Sam. 1000 First Words in Spanish. Lacome, Susie, illus. 2013. (ENG & SPA.). 96p. (J). (gr. k-4). 12.99 (978-1-84322-959-9(5)) Anness Publishing GBR. Dist: National Bk. Network.
Burke, David. GOLDILOCKS (Spanish to English - Level 2) Learn ENGLISH Through Fairy Tales. 2007. (SPA & ENG.). (J). per. 14.95 incl. audio compact disk (978-1-891888-96-0(X)) Slangman Publishing.
Camarena, Cathy & Ruff, Gloria B. Valeria y Víctor. 2006. (Primeros Sonidos Ser.). (J). pap. 48.42 (978-1-59679-908-0(0)) ABDO Publishing Co.
—Valeria y Víctor, 1 vol. 2006. (Primeros Sonidos Ser.). (ENG & SPA., Illus.). 24p. (J). (gr. k-3). lib. bdg. 24.21 (978-1-59679-907-3(2), SandCastle) ABDO Publishing Co.
Canetti, Yanitzia. Colores escolares/School Colors: A World of Color. 2010. (ENG & SPA.). 24p. (J). pap. 6.99 (978-1-59835-272-6(5), BrickHouse Education) Cambridge BrickHouse, Inc.
—Colorful Shapes/Figuras de Colores: A World of Color. 2010. (SPA & ENG.). 24p. (J). pap. 6.99 (978-1-59835-278-8(4), BrickHouse Education) Cambridge BrickHouse, Inc.
—Colorful Sights Paisajes de Colores: A World of Color. 2010. (SPA & ENG.). 24p. (J). pap. 6.99 (978-1-59835-280-1(6), BrickHouse Education) Cambridge BrickHouse, Inc.
—Colors on Colors/Colores Sobre Colores: A World of Color. 2010. (SPA & ENG.). 24p. (J). pap. 6.99 (978-1-59835-276-4(8), BrickHouse Education) Cambridge BrickHouse, Inc.
—Tasty Colors/Colores de Sabores: A World of Color. 2010. (SPA & ENG.). 24p. (J). pap. 6.99 (978-1-59835-270-2(9), BrickHouse Education) Cambridge BrickHouse, Inc.
Carole Marsh. Uh,Oh,Amigo! Spanish for Kids. 2004. (Little Linguist Ser.). 32p. (gr. 2-6). pap. 5.95 (978-0-635-02428-2(4)) Gallopade International.
Carson, Jana. We Both Read Bilingual Edition-About Space/Acerca Del Espacio. 2011. (SPA., Illus.). 44p. (J). pap. 4.99 (978-1-60115-052-3(0)) Treasure Bay, Inc.
Chagollan, Samantha. Lift-A-Flap Language Learners: the Enchanted Forest: An English/Spanish Lift-A-Flap Fairy Tale Adventure. Golubeva, Evgenia, illus. 2017. (Lift-A-Flap Language Learners Ser.). (ENG, EST & SPA.). 16p. (J). (gr. -1-1). 16.95 (978-1-63322-242-7(X), Walter Foster Jr) Quarto Publishing Group USA.
Chano: Individual Title Six-Packs. (Literatura 2000 Ser.). (gr. 2-3). 33.00 (978-0-7635-0194-5(8)) Rigby Education.
Chappell, Jackie. Our School Is Like A Family. 2007. (ENG., Illus.). 16p. (gr. k-2). 28.50 (978-1-60472-110-2(3)) Rourke Educational Media.
Charlie: Individual Title Six-Packs. (Literatura 2000 Ser.). (gr. 2-3). 33.00 (978-0-7635-0221-8(9)) Rigby Education.
La Charreada. 2003. 23.95 (978-0-673-77782-9(0)) Celebration Pr.
Chiquilibros: Activity Masters. (SPA.). (gr. -1-1). 26.00 (978-0-7635-2366-4(6)); 21.00 (978-0-7635-2557-6(X)) Rigby Education.
Chiquilibros: Add-to Packs. (SPA.). (gr. k-1). 30.00 (978-0-7635-8584-6(X)); 30.00 (978-0-7635-8585-3(8)); 30.00 (978-0-7635-8586-0(6)); 61.00 (978-0-7635-8587-7(4)) Rigby Education.
Chiquilibros: Chiquicuentos Complete Package. (SPA.). (gr. -1-1). 250.00 (978-0-7635-8571-6(8)) Rigby Education.
Chiquilibros: Chiquicuentos Grupo A Add-to Pack. (SPA.). (gr. -1-1). 125.00 (978-0-7635-8568-6(8)) Rigby Education.
Chiquilibros: Chiquicuentos Grupo B Add-to Pack. (SPA.). (gr. -1-1). 125.00 (978-0-7635-8569-3(6)) Rigby Education.
Chiquilibros: Cuentos listos Complete Packages. (SPA.). (gr. k-1). 114.00 (978-0-7635-8581-5(5)); 114.00 (978-0-7635-8580-8(7)); 114.00 (978-0-7635-8582-2(3)); 203.00 (978-0-7635-8583-9(1)) Rigby Education.
Chiquilibros: Grupo A Activity Guide. (SPA.). (gr. k-1). 18.00 (978-0-7635-2400-5(X)) Rigby Education.
Chiquilibros: Grupo B Activity Guide. (SPA.). (gr. k-1). 18.00 (978-0-7635-2401-2(8)) Rigby Education.
Chiquilibros: Grupo C Activity Guide. (SPA.). (gr. k-1). 18.00 (978-0-7635-2402-9(6)) Rigby Education.
Chiquilibros: Grupo D Activity Guide. (SPA.). (gr. k-1). 18.00 (978-0-7635-2403-6(4)) Rigby Education.
Chiquilibros: Grupos consonanticos Add-to Pack. (SPA.). (gr. -1-1). 38.00 (978-0-7635-8579-2(3)) Rigby Education.
Chiquilibros: Grupos consonanticos Complete Package. (SPA.). (gr. -1-1). 166.00 (978-0-7635-8578-5(5)) Rigby Education.
Chiquilibros: Silabas Add-to Pack. (SPA.). (gr. -1-1). 78.00 (978-0-7635-8576-1(9)) Rigby Education.
Chiquilibros: Silabas Complete Package. (SPA.). (gr. -1-1). 307.00 (978-0-7635-8577-8(7)) Rigby Education.
Ciencia Física (Physical Science) 2011. (Ciencia Física/Physical Science Ser.). (MUL.). 24p. (gr. k-1). lib. bdg. 106.60 (978-1-4296-6908-5(X)) Capstone Press of Coughlan Cos.
Clothes-Ropa Bilingual Board Book. 2008. (ENG & SPA.). (J). pap. 5.99 (978-0-9727886-9-4(7)) Osmosis, LLC.
El Coqui. 2003. 23.95 (978-0-673-77382-1(5)) Celebration Pr.
El Coqui: Poems, Rhymes, & Songs Listening Packs. 2003. 34.50 (978-0-673-58630-8(8)) Celebration Pr.
Coupe, Robert. Antiguo Egipto/Acient Egypt. 2011. 16p. pap. (978-607-404-320-4(5), Silver Dolphin en Español) Advanced Marketing, S. de R. L. de C. V.
Cuaderno Suenos y Palabras. (SPA.). (J). (gr. k-6). wbk. ed. 18.00 (978-958-04-7094-6(4)); Vol. 2. (gr. k-6). wbk. ed. 18.00 (978-958-04-7095-3(2)); Vol. 3. (gr. k-6). wbk. ed. 18.00 (978-958-04-7096-0(0)); Vol. 4. (gr. k-6). wbk. ed. 18.00 (978-958-04-7737-2(X)); Vol. 5. (gr. k-6). wbk. ed. 18.00 (978-958-04-7738-9(8)); Vol. 6. (gr. k-6). wbk. ed. 18.00 (978-958-04-7739-6(6)); Vol. 7. (gr. 7-12). wbk. ed. 18.00 (978-958-04-5653-7(4)); Vol. 8. (gr. 7-12). wbk. ed. 18.00 (978-958-04-5654-4(2)); Vol. 9. (gr. 7-12). wbk. ed. 18.00 (978-958-04-5655-1(0)); Vol. 10. (gr. 7-12). wbk. ed. 18.00 (978-958-04-5956-9(8)); Vol. 11. (gr. 7-12). wbk. ed. 18.00 (978-958-04-5958-3(4)); Vol. 12. (gr. 7-12). wbk. ed. 18.00 (978-958-04-5960-6(6)) Norma S.A. COL. Dist: Distribuidora Norma, Inc.
Cuando el senor Rey ronco: When Mr Quinn Snored. 2005. (Take-Home Bks.). (SPA.). (YA). (gr. -1-3). 15.75 (978-0-8215-1207-4(2)) Sadlier, William H. Inc.
Cuidando a los animales/Keeping Baby Animals Safe. 2005. (Libros en Espanol Para Ninos Ser.). (SPA.). (YA). (gr. -1-1). 11.97 (978-0-8215-0996-8(9)) Sadlier, William H. Inc.
Dayton, Connor. Tricks with Bikes/Trucos con la Moto. Alaman, Eduardo, tr. from ENG. 2007. (Motorcycles Made for Speed / Motocicletas a Toda Velocidad Ser.). (SPA., Illus.). 24p. (J). (gr. 2-5). lib. bdg. 22.60 (978-1-4042-7615-4(7)) Rosen Publishing Group, Inc., The.
Deacon, Carol. Manualidades Divertidas. 2003. (SPA.). 64p. 12.98 (978-1-4054-1483-8(9)) Parragon, Inc.
Dee, Nora. Spanish Words at the Zoo, Vol. 1. 2014. (Learn My Language! Spanish Ser.). 24p. (J). (gr. 1-2). (ENG.). pap. 8.15 (978-1-4824-0358-9(7)); 22.60 (978-1-4824-0355-8(2)) Stevens, Gareth Publishing LLLP.
Denmark-Allen, Eva. I Was, I Am, I Will Be! - Yo Fui! Yo soy! Yo Sere! 2007. (ENG & SPA., Illus.). 56p. (J). per. 12.00 (978-0-9792016-8-4(3)) Professional Publishing Hse. LLC.
Dingles, Molly. Blue as a Blueberry/Azul como un Arandano. Velez, Walter, illus. 2003. (SPA.). 32p. (J). lib. bdg. 21.65 (978-1-891997-28-0(9)) Dingles & Co.
—Brown as an Acorn. Velez, Walter, illus. 2004. (Community of Color Ser.). 32p. (J). pap. 10.95 (978-1-59646-346-2(5)) Dingles & Co.
—Brown as an Acorn/Marrón como una Bellota. Velez, Walter, illus. 2004. (Community of Color Ser.).Tr. of Marrón como una Bellota. (ENG & SPA.). 32p. (J). lib. bdg. 21.65 (978-1-891997-37-2(8)) Dingles & Co.
—Gray as a Dolphin. Velez, Walter, illus. 2004. (Community of Color Ser.). 32p. (J). pap. 10.95 (978-1-59646-342-4(2)) Dingles & Co.
—Gray as a Dolphin/Gris como un Delfín. Velez, Walter, illus. 2004. (Community of Color Ser.).Tr. of Gris como un Delfín. (ENG & SPA.). 32p. (J). pap. 10.95 (978-1-59646-092-8(X)); lib. bdg. 21.65 (978-1-891997-58-7(0)) Dingles & Co.
—Green as a Frog/Verde como una Rana. Velez, Walter, illus. 2003. (Community of Color Ser.). (SPA.). 32p. (J). lib. bdg. 21.65 (978-1-891997-29-7(7)) Dingles & Co.
—Green as a Frog/Vert comme une Grenouille. Velez, Walter, illus. 2004. (Community of Color Ser.).Tr. of Vert comme une Grenouille. (ENG & FRE.). 32p. (J). lib. bdg. 21.65 (978-1-891997-71-6(8)) Dingles & Co.
—Red as a Fire Truck/Rojo como un camion de Bomberos. Velez, Walter, illus. 2003. (Community of Color Ser.).Tr. of Rojo Como un Camion de Bomberos. (SPA.). 32p. (J). lib. bdg. 21.65 (978-1-891997-27-3(0)) Dingles & Co.
—Yellow as a Lemon/Amarillo como un Limon. Velez, Walter, illus. 2003. (Community of Color Ser.). (SPA.). 32p. (J). lib. bdg. 21.65 (978-1-891997-30-3(0)) Dingles & Co.
Dorling Kindersley Publishing Staff. 10 Minutes a Day: Spanish, Beginner. 2016. (ENG & SPA., Illus.). 80p. (J). (gr. 3-7). pap. 9.99 (978-1-4654-4410-3(6), 1403605, DK Children) Dorling Kindersley Publishing, Inc.
Dorling Kindersley Smart Steps: DK Smart Steps Complete Package. 2003. cd-rom 123.95 (978-0-673-61614-2(2)) Celebration Pr.
Dorn, Susy. Cantemos en Español Song-Book: Spanish Learning Song-Book for Children. Carbajal, Diego, illus. 2006. (SPA.). (J). (978-0-9764010-6-3(1)) Susy Dorn Productions, LLC.
—Sal y Pimienta Song-Book: Spanish Learning Song-Book for Children. Carbajal, Diego, illus. 2006. (SPA.). (J). (978-0-9764010-7-0(X)) Susy Dorn Productions, LLC.
Downing, Julie, illus. All the Ways I Love You (bilingual Edition) 2005. (SPA & ENG.). 10p. (J). 8.95 (978-1-58117-335-2(0), Intervisual/Piggy Toes) Bendon, Inc.
Drawing Conclusions & Inferences Spanish Version, Gr. 1-3. 2005. (J). per. (978-1-58232-148-6(5)) ECS Learning Systems, Inc.
Drawing Conclusions & Inferences Spanish Version, Gr. 4-5. 2005. (J). per. (978-1-58232-143-1(4)) ECS Learning Systems, Inc.
Egan, Tracie. Cynthia Ann Parker: Cautiva de los Comanches. Gonzalez, Tomas, tr. 2004. (Grandes Personajes en la Historia de Los Estados Unidos Ser.). (ENG & SPA.). 32p. (gr. 3-6). pap. 10.00 (978-0-8239-4225-1(2)) Rosen Publishing Group, Inc., The.
Ellis, Martyn & Martin, Rosa Maria. Aventura Nueva, Bk. 1. 2003. (SPA., Illus.). 224p. pap., stu. ed. 42.50 (978-0-340-86880-5(5)) Hodder Education Group GBR. Dist: Trans-Atlantic Pubns., Inc.
Elya, Susan Middleton. La Princesa & the Pea. Martinez-Neal, Juana, illus. 2017. (ENG.). 32p. (J). (gr. -1-3). 16.99 **(978-0-399-25156-6(1)**, G.P. Putnam's Sons Books for Young Readers) Penguin Young Readers Group.
—Say Hola to Spanish at the Circus. Lopez, Loretta, illus. 2013. (ENG.). 32p. (J). (gr. -1-5). pap. 8.95 (978-1-58430-042-7(6)) Lee & Low Bks., Inc.
—Say Hola to Spanish, Otra Vez (Again!) Lopez, Loretta, illus. 2013. (SPA & ENG.). 32p. (J). (gr. -1-5). pap. 9.95 (978-1-880000-64-9(4)); pap. 9.95 (978-1-880000-83-0(0)) Lee & Low Bks., Inc.
Emberley, Rebecca. My Big Book of Spanish Words. 2008. (SPA & ENG., Illus.). 14p. (J). (gr. -1-1). bds. 9.99 (978-0-316-11803-3(6)) Little, Brown Bks. for Young Readers.
En el Bosque. 2003. 23.95 (978-0-673-77175-9(X)) Celebration Pr.
En el Mercado. 2003. 23.95 (978-0-673-77790-4(1)) Celebration Pr.
En Mi Jardin. 2003. 23.95 (978-0-673-77131-5(8)) Celebration Pr.
El Enanito Malolgoloso. 2003. (J). (gr. -1-2). 28.95 (978-0-673-77377-7(9)) Celebration Pr.
Entin, Cindy. Los Marines. Boldman, Craig, illus. 2014. (ENG & SPA.). 10p. (J). bds. 5.99 (978-1-60433-458-6(4), Applesauce Pr.) Cider Mill Pr. Bk. Pubs., LLC.
Estoy Enojado. 2003. (J). (gr. -1-2). 23.95 (978-0-673-77391-3(4)) Celebration Pr.
Estrada, Altamira Perea. Un Abecedario Muy Sabroso. (SPA.). (J). pap. 4.76 net. (978-0-590-93319-3(1)) Scholastic, Inc.
Fact & Opinion Spanish Version, Gr. 1-3. 2005. (J). per. (978-1-58232-149-3(3)) ECS Learning Systems, Inc.
Fact & Opinion Spanish Version, Gr. 4-5. 2005. (Spanish Version Ser.). (J). per. (978-1-58232-144-8(2)) ECS Learning Systems, Inc.
Fatus, Sophie & Paris, Mertxe. My Big Barefoot Book of Spanish & English Words. 2016. (SPA & ENG.). (J). pap. (978-1-78285-275-9(1)) Barefoot Bks., Inc.
Fedoruk, Dennis, prod. Bilingual Baby - Flashcard Set - Spanish. 2013. (SPA.). (J). 7.99 (978-1-892703-75-0(0)) Small Fry Beginnings.
First Explorers Primeros Exploradores Set 1: Spanish - 1 Each of 12 Student Books. (First Explorers. Primeros Exploradores Nonfiction Sets Ser.). (gr. 1-2). 59.95 (978-0-7699-1370-4(9)) Shortland Pubns. (U. S. A.) Inc.
First Explorers Primeros Exploradores Set 1: Spanish - 1 Each of 12 Student Books, 1 Each of 12 Lesson Plans. (First Explorers. Primeros Exploradores Nonfiction Sets Ser.). (gr. 1-2). 107.95 (978-0-7699-1368-1(7)) Shortland Pubns. (U. S. A.) Inc.
First Explorers Primeros Exploradores Set 1: Spanish - 6 Each of 12 Student Books, 1 Each of 12 Lesson Plans. (First Explorers. Primeros Exploradores Nonfiction Sets Ser.). (SPA.). (gr. 1-2). 407.50 (978-0-7699-1372-8(5)) Shortland Pubns. (U. S. A.) Inc.
First Explorers Primeros Exploradores Set 2: Spanish - 1 Each of 12 Student Books. (First Explorers. Primeros Exploradores Nonfiction Sets Ser.). (gr. 1-2). 67.50 (978-0-7699-1371-1(7)) Shortland Pubns. (U. S. A.) Inc.
First Explorers Primeros Exploradores Set 2: Spanish - 1 Each of 12 Student Books, 1 Each of 12 Lesson Plans. (First Explorers. Primeros Exploradores Nonfiction Sets Ser.). (gr. 1-2). 115.50 (978-0-7699-1369-8(5)) Shortland Pubns. (U. S. A.) Inc.
First Explorers Primeros Exploradores Set 2: Spanish - 6 Each of 12 Student Books, 1 Each of 12 Lesson Plans. (First Explorers. Primeros Exploradores Nonfiction Sets Ser.). (SPA.). (gr. 1-2). 452.50 (978-0-7699-1373-5(3)) Shortland Pubns. (U. S. A.) Inc.
First Explorers Primeros Exploradores Sets 1-2: Spanish - 1 Each of 24 Student Books, 1 Each of 24 Lesson Plans. (First Explorers. Primeros Exploradores Nonfiction Sets Ser.). (gr. 1-2). 223.50 (978-0-7699-1358-2(X)) Shortland Pubns. (U. S. A.) Inc.
First Explorers Primeros Exploradores Sets 1-2: Spanish - 6 Each of 24 Student Books, 1 Each of 24 Lesson Plans. (First Explorers. Primeros Exploradores Nonfiction Sets Ser.). (SPA.). (gr. 1-2). 816.95 (978-0-7699-1367-4(9)) Shortland Pubns. (U. S. A.) Inc.
Flor Ada, Alma & Campoy, F. Isabel, contrib. by. Steps. (Literature Collection of Gateways to the Sun Ser.). 32p. (J). (gr. k-6). pap. 13.95 (978-1-59437-716-7(2)) Santillana USA Publishing Co., Inc.
Friends Are Forever: Individual Title Six-Packs. (Literatura 2000 Ser.). (gr. 2-3). 33.00 (978-0-7635-0169-3(7)) Rigby Education.

Fui Al Mar. 2003. 23.95 (978-0-673-77162-9(8)) Celebration Pr.

Fulcher, Roz. Color & Learn Easy Spanish Phrases for Kids. 2015. (Dover Little Activity Bks.). (ENG.). 64p. (J). (gr. k-3). pap. 1.99 (978-0-486-79759-5(7)) Dover Pubns., Inc.

Ganeri, Anita. Volcanes y terremotos/Earthquakes & Volcanoes. 2011. 16p. pap. (978-607-404-319-8(1), Silver Dolphin en Español) Advanced Marketing, S. de R. L. de C. V.

George, Patrick & PatrickGeorge. Contrarios. 2012. (SPA.). 26p. (J). (gr. -1-1). pap. 19.99 (978-84-261-3885-9(3)) Juventud, Editorial ESP. Dist: Lectorum Pubns., Inc.

Getting the Sequence Spanish Version, Gr. 1-3. 2005. (J). per. (978-1-58232-146-2(9)) ECS Learning Systems, Inc.

Getting the Sequence Spanish Version, Gr. 4-5. 2005. (J). per. (978-1-58232-141-7(8)) ECS Learning Systems, Inc.

Gibbons, Gail. De Sol a Sol.Tr. of Sun Up, Sun Down. (SPA., Illus.). (J). (gr. 1-3). pap. 3.96 net. (978-0-590-46903-6(7), SO30343, Scholastic en Espanol) Scholastic, Inc.

Glencoe McGraw-Hill Staff. Glencoe Middle School Spanish: ¿Cómo Te Va? B Nivel Azul. 2005. (Glencoe Spanish Ser.). (ENG.). (gr. 6-8). stu. ed. 120.96 incl. cd-rom (978-0-07-874279-8(X), 007874279X) McGraw-Hill Higher Education.

Glencoe McGraw-Hill Staff, creator. Repaso: A Review Workbook for Grammar, Communication, & Culture. 2nd ed. 2004. (SPA., Illus.). 719p. (gr. 6-12). per., wbk. ed. 26.64 (978-0-07-846050-0(6), 9780078460500) Glencoe/McGraw-Hill.

Gómez, Carlos Humberto. Workbook 1. (Coleccion Nos Comunicamos). (SPA & ENG.). (J). (gr. 1). pap., wbk. ed. 11.50 (978-958-04-2074-3(2), 01021255) Norma S.A. COL. Dist: Continental Bk. Co., Inc.

—Workbook 2. (Coleccion Nos Comunicamos). (SPA & ENG.). (J). (gr. 2). pap., wbk. ed. 11.50 (978-958-04-2075-0(0), 01021256) Norma S.A. COL. Dist: Continental Bk. Co., Inc.

—Workbook 3. (Coleccion Nos Comunicamos). (SPA & ENG.). (J). (gr. 3). pap., wbk. ed. 11.50 (978-958-04-2076-7(9), 01021257) Norma S.A. COL. Dist: Continental Bk. Co., Inc.

—Workbook 4. (Coleccion Nos Comunicamos). (SPA & ENG.). (J). (gr. 4). pap., wbk. ed. 11.50 (978-958-04-1784-2(9), 01021258) Norma S.A. COL. Dist: Continental Bk. Co., Inc.

—Workbook 6. (Coleccion Nos Comunicamos). (SPA & ENG.). (J). (gr. 6). pap., wbk. ed. 11.50 (978-958-04-1791-0(1), 01021260) Norma S.A. COL. Dist: Continental Bk. Co., Inc.

—Workbook Kindergarten. (Coleccion Nos Comunicamos). (SPA & ENG.). (J). pap., wbk. ed. 11.50 (978-958-04-2035-4(1), 01021254) Norma S.A. COL. Dist: Continental Bk. Co., Inc.

Gose, Senora. Flip Flop Spanish: Ages 3-5: Level 2. 2008. (Illus.). 108p. (J). spiral bd. 29.95 (978-0-9801772-0-6(0)) Flip n Flop Learning, LLC.

Grades 1-2 Complete Pinata/Mas Pinata Package. 2003. 1943.95 (978-0-673-58717-6(7)) Celebration Pr.

Guy, Ginger Foglesong & Guy, Ginger F. ¡Perros! ¡Perros! Glick, Sharon, illus. 2006. (ENG & SPA.). 32p. (J). (gr. -1-3). 16.99 (978-0-06-083574-3(5), Greenwillow Bks.) HarperCollins Pubs.

Harte, May. Halloween. Gonzalez, Tomas, tr. from ENG. 2004. (My Library of Holidays). (SPA & ENG., Illus.). 24p. (J). (gr. 1-2). lib. bdg. 16.00 (978-1-4042-7529-4(0), 1219514, PowerKids Pr.) Rosen Publishing Group, Inc., The.

Harvey, William C. Spanish Every Day: A Learning Adventure for Young Readers. 2nd rev. ed. 2011. (ENG & SPA.). 216p. 21.99 (978-1-4380-7050-6(0)); pap. 14.99 (978-0-7641-4596-4(7)) Barron's Educational Series, Inc.

Hayhurst, Chris. Toro Sentado: Jefe Sioux. 2004. (Grandes personajes en la historia de los Estados Unidos Ser.). (ENG & SPA.). 32p. (gr. 3-6). pap. 10.00 (978-0-8239-4238-1(4)) Rosen Publishing Group, Inc., The.

Hazan, Maurice, creator. El Camino: Practicing Everyday Vocabulary. (SPA.). (J). 124.95 (978-1-932770-44-5(5), SG5) Symtalk, Inc.

—The Conversation Game for Spanish. (SPA.). (YA). 124.95 (978-1-932770-47-6(X), SG8) Symtalk, Inc.

—Dime quien Es: Spanish Dialogues Level 1. (SPA.). (J). 134.95 (978-1-932770-43-8(7), SG4) Symtalk, Inc.

—Dime quien Es: Spanish Dialogues Level 2. (SPA.). (J). 134.95 (978-1-932770-45-2(3), SG6) Symtalk, Inc.

—Dime quien Es: Spanish Dialogues Level 3. (SPA.). (YA). 199.95 (978-1-932770-55-1(0), SG16) Symtalk, Inc.

—Frases y Fotos: Long Sentence Bingo. (SPA.). (YA). 124.95 (978-1-932770-46-9(1), SG7) Symtalk, Inc.

—Object, Color & Number Bingo. (SPA.). (J). 124.95 (978-1-932770-41-4(0), SG2) Symtalk, Inc.

—Los Perdidos: Directions in the City. (SPA.). (YA). 199.95 (978-1-932770-54-4(2), SG15) Symtalk, Inc.

—The Prom Game for Spanish. (YA). 44.95 (978-1-932770-51-3(8), SG12) Symtalk, Inc.

—Resto Presto. (SPA.). (J). 169.95 (978-1-932770-42-1(9), SG3) Symtalk, Inc.

Heller, Daryl. Hanukkah/Januca. 2004. (My Library of Holidays). (SPA & ENG., Illus.). 24p. (J). (gr. k-1). lib. bdg. 16.00 (978-1-4042-7525-6(8), PowerKids Pr.) Rosen Publishing Group, Inc., The.

Holland, Gini. Alive & Not Alive (Vivo y no Vivo) 2007. (I Know Opposites/Conceptos Contrarios Ser.). (SPA & ENG., Illus.). 16p. (gr. -1-3). lib. bdg. 19.00 (978-0-8368-8303-9(9), Weekly Reader Leveled Readers) Stevens, Gareth Publishing LLLP.

—Alive & Not Alive/Vivo y No Vivo. 2007. (I Know Opposites/Conceptos Contrarios Ser.). (SPA & ENG., Illus.). 16p. (gr. -1-3). pap. 5.30 (978-0-8368-8308-4(X), Weekly Reader Leveled Readers) Stevens, Gareth Publishing LLLP.

—Hot & Cold/Caliente y Frio. 2007. (I Know Opposites/Conceptos Contrarios Ser.). (SPA & ENG.). 16p. (gr. -1-3). lib. bdg. 19.00 (978-0-8368-8304-6(7), Weekly Reader Leveled Readers) Stevens, Gareth Publishing LLLP.

Holt, Rinehart and Winston Staff. Expresate: Premier Online Edition. 6th ed. Date not set. (SPA.). 76.80 (978-0-03-074564-5(0));Level 1. 75.13 (978-0-03-074563-8(2)) Holt McDougal.

HOP, LLC. Hooked on Spanish. 2006. 64.99 (978-1-931020-92-3(2)); 99.99 (978-1-931020-75-6(2)) HOP, LLC.

—Hooked on Spanish Beginning Spanish. 2006. 24.99 (978-1-933863-14-6(5)) HOP, LLC.

Howard, Linda & Dockray, Tracy Arah, illus. Mi Gran Libro de Palabras Play-Doh. 2006. (SPA.). 10p. (J). (gr. -1-4). reprint ed. 10.00 (978-1-4223-5586-2(1)) DIANE Publishing Co.

Hudson, Amanda & Nations, Susan. This Is My Ball/Ésta Es Mi Pelota. 2008. (Our Toys/Nuestros Juguetes Ser.). (SPA & ENG., Illus.). 16p. (J). (gr. -1-2). lib. bdg. 19.00 (978-0-8368-9256-7(9), Weekly Reader Leveled Readers) Stevens, Gareth Publishing LLLP.

—This Is My Bear: Éste Es Mi Oso. 2008. (Our Toys/Nuestros Juguetes Ser.). (SPA.). 16p. (gr. -1-2). pap. 5.30 (978-0-8368-9356-4(5), Weekly Reader Leveled Readers) Stevens, Gareth Publishing LLLP.

—This Is My Bear/Éste Es Mi Oso. 2008. (Our Toys/Nuestros Juguetes Ser.). (SPA & ENG., Illus.). 16p. (J). (gr. -1-2). lib. bdg. 19.00 (978-0-8368-9257-4(7), Weekly Reader Leveled Readers) Stevens, Gareth Publishing LLLP.

Humbach. Expresate: Premier Online Edition. 6th ed. Date not set. (SPA.). Level 1. stu. ed. 19.93 (978-0-03-040457-3(6))Level 1a. stu. ed. 14.60 (978-0-03-040449-8(5))Level 1b. 14.60 (978-0-03-040453-5(3))Level 2. stu. ed. 19.93 (978-0-03-040459-7(2))Level 3. stu. ed. 19.93 (978-0-03-040463-4(0)) Holt McDougal.

—Ven Conmigo: Online Edition, Level 3. 3rd ed. 2003. (SPA.). 71.40 (978-0-03-036149-4(4)) Holt McDougal.

Hutchins, J. Spanish First Words - Primeras Palabras en Español. 2013. (SPA & ENG., Illus.). 32p. (J). (gr. -1-3). pap. 4.99 (978-0-545-56328-4(3), Scholastic en Espanol) Scholastic, Inc.

—Spanish First Words (Primeras Palabras en Espanol) 2013. (SPA & ENG.). lib. bdg. 14.75 (978-0-606-32400-7(3), Turtleback) Turtleback Bks.

I'm Learning Spanish, Vol. 3. 2005. (J). 12.99 (978-1-894677-77-6(3)) Kidzup Productions.

Johnson, J. Bradley. Surround Yourself with Essential Vacation Spanish. 2005. per. 49.99 (978-0-9765236-2-8(0)) Innovative Language, LLC.

—Surround Yourself with Spanish: Beginner Level. 2005. (ENG & SPA.). 156p. (C). per. 99.99 (978-0-9765236-0-4(4)) Innovative Language, LLC.

—Surround Yourself with Spanish Conversations, Vol. 1. 2005. (ENG & SPA.). 92p. (C). per. 39.99 (978-0-9765236-1-1(2)) Innovative Language, LLC.

Jordan, Sara. Fonetica Funky y Algo Mas, 2 vols., Kit. 2007. (SPA.). 48p. (J). (gr. k-4). 17.95 (978-1-55386-080-8(2), 1553860802) Jordan, Sara Publishing.

Jordan, Sara & Gomez, Patricia. Bilingual Beginners: English-Spanish, 2 vols. abr. ed. 2010. (ENG & SPA.). 48p. (J). 17.95 (978-1-55386-114-0(0), 1553861140) Jordan, Sara Publishing.

Kelley, Michelle. Rules, Rules, Rules. 2007. (ENG., Illus.). 16p. (gr. k-2). 28.50 (978-1-60472-111-9(1)) Rourke Educational Media.

Kennedy, Robert. Spanish Words in the House, Vol. 1. 2014. (Learn My Language! Spanish Ser.). 24p. (J). (gr. 1-2). (ENG.). 22.60 (978-1-4824-0360-2(9)); pap. 8.15 (978-1-4824-0363-3(3)) Stevens, Gareth Publishing LLLP.

Kidzup Productions Staff. I'm Learning Spanish. 2005. (J). Vol. 1. 12.99 (978-1-894677-75-2(7)) Vol. 2. 12.99 (978-1-894677-76-9(5)) Kidzup Productions.

Kim, illus. Colors All Around. 2008. (SPA & ENG.). 28p. (J). pap. 8.95 (978-1-60448-009-2(2)) Lectura Bks.

Kratky, Lada Josefa. Alfarrimas: Guia Del Maestro. 2005. (Alfarrimas Ser.). (SPA & ENG., Illus.). 8p. (C). pap. 36.95 (978-0-7362-2659-2(1)) CENGAGE Learning.

Leigh, Johanna. Spanish Words at the Park, Vol. 1. 2014. (Learn My Language! Spanish Ser.). 24p. (J). (gr. 1-2). (ENG.). pap. 8.15 (978-1-4824-0345-9(5)); 22.60 (978-1-4824-0346-6(3)) Stevens, Gareth Publishing LLLP.

Leonard, Marcia. Mi Dia de Campamento; My Camp Out. 2008. pap. 34.95 (978-0-8225-9496-3(X)) Lerner Publishing Group.

Levine, Julia Pimsleur. Little Pim: Numbers. 2012. (ENG.). 10p. (J). (gr. -1-k). bds. 8.95 (978-1-4197-0175-7(4)) Abrams, Inc.

Listen & Learn First Spanish Words. 2017. (Listen & Learn First Words Ser.). (ENG.). (J). bds. 19.99 **(978-0-7945-3886-6(X)**, Usborne) EDC Publishing.

Litchfield, Jo, illus. Very First Words in Spanish. 2009. (Very First Words in Spanish Ser.). (SPA & ENG.). 18p. (J). (gr. -1). bds. 7.99 (978-0-7945-2446-3(X), Usborne) EDC Publishing.

LiveABC (Firm) Staff & McGraw-Hill Companies Staff, contrib. by. McGraw-Hill's Spanish Illustrated Dictionary. 2011. (ENG & SPA., Illus.). iv, 140p. (J). cd-rom (978-0-07-174916-9(0)) McGraw-Hill Cos., The.

Lome, Emilio Angel. Lottery of Riddles. Martinez, Enrique, illus. 2011. 46p. (gr. 2-5). pap. 6.95 (978-968-19-0663-4(2)) Aguilar, Altea, Taurus, Alfaguara, S.A. de C.V MEX. Dist: Santillana USA Publishing Co., Inc.

Lonely Planet Publications Staff. Lonely Planet First Words - Spanish, 1 vol. 2017. (Lonely Planet Kids Ser.). (ENG., Illus.). 208p. (J). pap. 12.99 **(978-1-78657-317-9(2)**, 5403) Lonely Planet Pubns.

Long, Sara. nexos Multimedia: Used with ... Long-Nexos: Introductory Spanish. 2004. cd-rom 2.76 (978-0-618-06865-4(1), 334239) CENGAGE Learning.

The Lost Feet. 2003. 28.95 (978-0-673-78113-0(5)) Celebration Pr.

Macken, JoAnn Early. Penguins/Los Pingüinos. 2003. (Weekly Reader Early Learning Library). (ENG & SPA., Illus.). 24p. (J). (gr. k-3). pap. 8.15 (978-0-8368-4006-3(2), Weekly Reader Leveled Readers) Stevens, Gareth Publishing LLLP.

Main Idea & Details Spanish Version, Gr. 4-5. 2005. (J). per. (978-1-58232-142-4(6)) ECS Learning Systems, Inc.

El Maiz De Quetzalcoatl. 2003. 28.95 (978-0-673-78095-9(3)) Celebration Pr.

Maldonado, Premier. Animales. 2006. (SPA.). 14.99 (978-0-9727886-5-6(4)) Osmosis, LLC.

—Cuerpo. 2006. (SPA., Illus.). 14.99 (978-0-9727886-4-9(6)) Osmosis, LLC.

El Mariachi. 2003. 23.95 (978-0-673-77788-1(X)) Celebration Pr.

Mariachi Tradition Videotape: Videotape Packages. 2003. (Share the Music Ser.). (gr. 1-8). (978-0-02-295488-8(0)) Macmillan/McGraw-Hill Schl. Div.

Marsh, Carole. Uh, Oh, Amigo! Spanish for Kids. Beard, Chad, ed. 2004. (Little Linguist Ser.). (Illus.). 32p. 29.95 (978-0-635-02436-7(5)) Gallopade International.

Martin, Dayna. The Toddler's Handbook: Bilingual (English / Spanish) (Ingles / Espanol) Numbers, Colors, Shapes, Sizes, ABC Animals, Opposites, & Sounds, with over 100 Words That Every Kid Should Know (Engage Early Readers: Children's Learning Books) Roumanis, A. r., ed. l.t. ed. 2015. (SPA & ENG., Illus.). 48p. (J). pap. (978-1-77226-225-4(0)) AD Classic.

Martin, Jane. Spanish. Trotter, Stuart, illus. 3rd rev. unabr. ed. 2006. (ENG & SPA.). 32p. (J). pap. 6.99 (978-0-330-32871-5(9), Pan) Pan Macmillan GBR. Dist: Trafalgar Square Publishing.

Martín, Rosa Maria & Ellis, Martyn. Nueva. 2004. (SPA & ENG., Illus.). 208p. pap. 42.50 (978-0-340-86887-4(2)) Hodder Education Group GBR. Dist: Trans-Atlantic Pubns., Inc.

Maurice, creator. The Spanish Question Game. (SPA.). (YA). 134.95 (978-1-932770-48-3(8), SG9) Symtalk, Inc.

Maze, Stephanie, ed. Healthy Foods from A to Z: Comida Sana de la a a la Z. Comet, Renee, photos by. 2012. (SPA & ENG., Illus.). 32p. (J). (gr. -1-k). 15.95 (978-0-9834983-1-5(8)) Moonstone Pr., LLC.

Mazxzeo, J. L. Xavia's X Book (BL) el libro X de Xavia (PB), 24 vols. 2007. (My Letter Library Ser.: 24). (SPA., Illus.). (J). pap. 10.95 (978-1-59646-558-9(1)) Dingles & Co.

Mazzeo, J. L. Bebe's B Book/ el libro B de Bebé, 2 vols. 2007. (My Letter Library Ser.: 2). (SPA & ENG., Illus.). (J). pap. 10.95 (978-1-59646-426-1(7)); lib. bdg. 23.60 (978-1-59646-425-4(9)) Dingles & Co.

—Delia's D Book /el libro D de Delia, 4 vols. 2007. (My Letter Library Ser.: 4). (SPA., Illus.). (J). pap. 10.95 (978-1-59646-438-4(0)); lib. bdg. 23.60 (978-1-59646-437-7(2)) Dingles & Co.

—Emma's E-Book / El Libro E de Emma, 5 vols. 2007. (My Letter Library Ser.: 5). (SPA & ENG.). (J). pap. 10.95 (978-1-59646-444-5(5)); lib. bdg. 23.60 (978-1-59646-443-8(7)) Dingles & Co.

—Faye's F Book (BL) el libro F de Faye (PB), 6 vols. 2007. (My Letter Library Ser.: 6). (SPA.). (J). pap. 10.95 (978-1-59646-450-6(X)) Dingles & Co.

—George's G Book (BL) el libro G de George, 7 vols. 2007. (My Letter Library Ser.: 7). (J). lib. bdg. 23.60 (978-1-59646-455-1(0)) Dingles & Co.

—George's G Book (BL) el libro G de George (PB), 7 vols. 2007. (My Letter Library Ser.: 7). (SPA.). (J). pap. 10.95 (978-1-59646-456-8(9)) Dingles & Co.

—Henry's H Book (BL) el libro H de Henry, 8 vols. 2007. (My Letter Library Ser.: 8). (J). lib. bdg. 23.60 (978-1-59646-461-2(5)) Dingles & Co.

—Henry's H Book (BL) el libro H de Henry (PB), 8 vols. 2007. (My Letter Library Ser.: 8). (SPA.). (J). pap. 10.95 (978-1-59646-462-9(3)) Dingles & Co.

—Izzy's I Book (BL) el libro I de Izzy, 9 vols. 2007. (My Letter Library Ser.: 9). (SPA.). (J). lib. bdg. 23.60 (978-1-59646-467-4(4)) Dingles & Co.

—Izzy's I Book (BL) el libro I de Izzy (PB), 9 vols. 2007. (My Letter Library Ser.: 9). (SPA.). (J). pap. 10.95 (978-1-59646-468-1(2)) Dingles & Co.

—Jade's J Book (BL) el libro J de Jade, 10 vols. 2007. (My Letter Library Ser.: 10). (SPA.). (J). lib. bdg. 23.60 (978-1-59646-473-5(9)) Dingles & Co.

—Jade's J Book (BL) el libro J de Jade (PB), 10 vols. 2007. (My Letter Library Ser.: 10). (SPA.). (J). pap. 10.95 (978-1-59646-474-2(7)) Dingles & Co.

—Jade's J Book (PB), 10 vols. 2007. (My Letter Library Ser.: 10). (J). pap. 10.95 (978-1-59646-471-1(2)) Dingles & Co.

—Kelsey's K Book (BL) el libro K de Kelsey, 11 vols. 2007. (My Letter Library Ser.: 11). (SPA.). (J). lib. bdg. 23.60 (978-1-59646-479-7(8)) Dingles & Co.

—Kelsey's K Book (BL) el libro K de Kelsey (PB), 11 vols. 2007. (My Letter Library Ser.: 11). (SPA.). (J). pap. 10.95 (978-1-59646-480-3(1)) Dingles & Co.

—El Libro F de Faye, 5 vols. 2007. (My Letter Library Ser.: 6).Tr. of Faye's F Book. (SPA.). (J). lib. bdg. 23.60 (978-1-59646-449-0(6)) Dingles & Co.

—Logan's L Book (BL) el libro L de Logan, 12 vols. 2007. (My Letter Library Ser.: 12). (SPA.). (J). lib. bdg. 23.60 (978-1-59646-485-8(2)) Dingles & Co.

—Logan's L Book (BL) el libro L de Logan (PB), 12 vols. 2007. (My Letter Library Ser.: 12). (SPA.). (J). pap. 10.95 (978-1-59646-486-5(0)) Dingles & Co.

—Mia's M Book (BL) el libro M de Mia, 13 vols. 2007. (My Letter Library Ser.: 13). (SPA.). (J). lib. bdg. 23.60 (978-1-59646-491-9(7)) Dingles & Co.

—Mia's M Book (BL) el libro M de Mia (PB), 13 vols. 2007. (My Letter Library Ser.: 13). (SPA.). (J). pap. 10.95 (978-1-59646-492-6(5)) Dingles & Co.

—Nate's N Book (BL) el libro N de Nate, 14 vols. 2007. (My Letter Library Ser.: 14). (SPA.). (J). lib. bdg. 23.60 (978-1-59646-497-1(6)) Dingles & Co.

—Nate's N Book (BL) el libro N de Nate (PB), 14 vols. 2007. (My Letter Library Ser.: 14). (SPA.). (J). pap. 10.95 (978-1-59646-498-8(4)) Dingles & Co.

—Owen's O Book (BL) el libro O de Owen, 15 vols. 2007. (My Letter Library Ser.: 15). (SPA.). (J). lib. bdg. 23.60 (978-1-59646-503-9(4)) Dingles & Co.

—Owen's O Book (BL) el libro O de Owen (PB), 15 vols. 2007. (My Letter Library Ser.: 15). (SPA.). (J). pap. 10.95 (978-1-59646-504-6(2)) Dingles & Co.

—Owen's O Book (PB), 15 vols. 2007. (My Letter Library Ser.: 15). (J). pap. 10.95 (978-1-59646-501-5(8)) Dingles & Co.

—Peter's P Book (BL) el libro P de Peter, 16 vols. 2007. (My Letter Library Ser.: 16). (SPA.). (J). lib. bdg. 23.60 (978-1-59646-509-1(3)) Dingles & Co.

—Peter's P Book (BL) el libro P de Peter (PB), 16 vols. 2007. (My Letter Library Ser.: 16). (SPA.). (J). pap. 10.95 (978-1-59646-510-7(7)) Dingles & Co.

—Quinn's Q Book (BL) el libro Q de Quinn, 17 vols. 2007. (My Letter Library Ser.: 17). (SPA.). (J). lib. bdg. 23.60 (978-1-59646-515-2(8)) Dingles & Co.

—Quinn's Q Book (BL) el libro Q de Quinn (PB), 17 vols. 2007. (My Letter Library Ser.: 17). (SPA.). (J). pap. 10.95 (978-1-59646-516-9(6)) Dingles & Co.

—Rosie's R Book (BL) el libro R de Rosie, 18 vols. 2007. (My Letter Library Ser.: 18). (SPA.). (J). lib. bdg. 23.60 (978-1-59646-521-3(2)) Dingles & Co.

—Rosie's R Book (BL) el libro R de Rosie (PB), 18 vols. 2007. (My Letter Library Ser.: 18). (SPA.). (J). pap. 10.95 (978-1-59646-522-0(0)) Dingles & Co.

—Sofie's S Book (BL) el libro S de Sofie, 19 vols. 2007. (My Letter Library Ser.: 19). (SPA.). (J). lib. bdg. 23.60 (978-1-59646-527-5(1)) Dingles & Co.

—Sofie's S Book (BL) el libro S de Sofie (PB), 19 vols. 2007. (My Letter Library Ser.: 19). (SPA.). (J). pap. 10.95 (978-1-59646-528-2(X)) Dingles & Co.

—Tad's T Book (BL) el libro T de Tad, 20 vols. 2007. (My Letter Library Ser.: 20). (SPA.). (J). lib. bdg. 23.60 (978-1-59646-533-6(6)) Dingles & Co.

—Tad's T Book (BL) el libro T de Tad (PB), 20 vols. 2007. (My Letter Library Ser.: 20). (SPA.). (J). pap. 10.95 (978-1-59646-534-3(4)) Dingles & Co.

—Uri's U Book (BL) el libro U de Uri, 21 vols. 2007. (My Letter Library Ser.: 21). (SPA.). (J). lib. bdg. 23.60 (978-1-59646-539-8(5)) Dingles & Co.

—Uri's U Book (BL) el libro U de Uri (PB), 21 vols. 2007. (My Letter Library Ser.: 21). (SPA.). (J). pap. 10.95 (978-1-59646-540-4(9)) Dingles & Co.

—Vera's V Book (BL) el libro V de Vera, 22 vols. 2007. (My Letter Library Ser.: 22). (SPA & ENG., Illus.). (J). lib. bdg. 23.60 (978-1-59646-545-9(X)) Dingles & Co.

—Vera's V Book (BL) el libro V de Vera (PB), 22 vols. 2007. (My Letter Library Ser.: 22). (SPA & ENG., Illus.). (J). pap. 10.95 (978-1-59646-546-6(8)) Dingles & Co.

—Will's W Book (BL) el libro W de Will, 23 vols. 2007. (My Letter Library Ser.: 23). (SPA.). (J). lib. bdg. 23.60 (978-1-59646-551-0(4)) Dingles & Co.

—Will's W Book (BL) el libro W de Will (PB), 23 vols. 2007. (My Letter Library Ser.: 23). (SPA.). (J). pap. 10.95 (978-1-59646-552-7(2)) Dingles & Co.

—Xavia's X Book (BL) el libro X de Xavia, 24 vols. 2007. (My Letter Library Ser.: 24). (SPA., Illus.). (J). lib. bdg. 23.60 (978-1-59646-557-2(3)) Dingles & Co.

—Yola's Y Book (BL) el libro Y de Yola, 25 vols. 2007. (My Letter Library Ser.: 25). (SPA.). (J). lib. bdg. 23.60 (978-1-59646-563-3(8)) Dingles & Co.

—Yola's Y Book (BL) el libro Y de Yola (PB), 25 vols. 2007. (My Letter Library Ser.: 25). (SPA.). (J). pap. 10.95 (978-1-59646-564-0(6)) Dingles & Co.

McKay, Sindy. We Both Read Bilingual Edition-About Dinosaurs/Acerca de Los Dinosaurios. Walters, Robert, illus. 2011. (SPA.). 44p. (J). pap. 4.99 (978-1-60115-050-9(4)) Treasure Bay, Inc.

Mi Amigo. 2003. stu. ed. 35.50 (978-0-8136-8135-1(9)) Modern Curriculum Pr.

Milet Publishing Staff. Animals - My First Bilingual Book. 2011. (My First Bilingual Book Ser.). (SPA & ENG., Illus.). 24p. (J). (gr. k — 1). bds. 8.99 (978-1-84059-620-5(1)) Milet Publishing.

—Bilingual Visual Dictionary. 2011. (Milet Multimedia Ser.). (SPA & ENG., Illus.). 1p. (J). (gr. k-2). cd-rom 19.95 (978-1-84059-592-5(2)) Milet Publishing.

—Home - My First Bilingual Book. 2011. (My First Bilingual Book Ser.). (SPA & ENG., Illus.). 24p. (J). (gr. k — 1). bds. 8.99 (978-1-84059-652-6(X)) Milet Publishing.

—Jobs Profesiones. 2012. (My First Bilingual Book Ser.). (SPA & ENG., Illus.). 24p. (J). (gr. k — 1). bds. 7.99 (978-1-84059-712-7(7)) Milet Publishing.

—Milet Interactive for Kids - Spanish for English Speakers. 2012. (Milet Interactive for Kids Ser.). (SPA & ENG., Illus.). 1p. (J). (gr. k-2). cd-rom 24.95 (978-1-84059-678-6(3)) Milet Publishing.

—My Bilingual Book-Sight (English-Spanish) 2014. (My Bilingual Book Ser.). (ENG & SPA., Illus.). 28p. (J). (gr. -1-k). 9.95 (978-1-84059-800-1(X)) Milet Publishing.

—My Bilingual Book-Smell. 2014. (My Bilingual Book Ser.). (ENG & SPA., Illus.). 28p. (J). (gr. -1-k). 9.95 (978-1-84059-816-2(6)) Milet Publishing.

—My Bilingual Book-Touch. 2014. (My Bilingual Book Ser.). (ENG & SPA., Illus.). 28p. (J). (gr. -1-k). 9.95 (978-1-84059-848-3(4)) Milet Publishing.

—My First Bilingual Book-Fruit (English-Spanish) 2011. (My First Bilingual Book Ser.). (SPA & ENG., Illus.). 24p. (J). (gr. k — 1). bds. 7.99 (978-1-84059-636-6(8)) Milet Publishing.

—My First Bilingual Book-Vegetables (English-Spanish) 2011. (My First Bilingual Book Ser.). (SPA & ENG., Illus.). 24p. (J). (gr. k — 1). bds. 8.99 (978-1-84059-668-7(6)) Milet Publishing.

Mis Primeras Palabras (My First Words) (SPA.). (J). 6.95 (978-970-05-0284-7(8)) Grijalbo, Editorial MEX. Dist: AIMS International Bks., Inc.

Mlawer, Teresa, tr. What Do I Feel? / ¿Qué Siento? Kubler, Annie, illus. 2015. (Small Senses Bilingual Ser.: 5). (ENG & SPA.). 12p. (J). bds. (978-1-84643-721-2(0)) Child's Play International Ltd.

Monckeberg, Paulina. Artilugia Spanish 2008. 2007. (Pascualina Family of Products Ser.). 114p. (J). spiral bd. 14.95 (978-956-8222-58-1(8)) Pascualina Producciones S.A.

Mora, Pat, et al. Water Rolls, Water Rises, 1 vol. So, Meilo, illus. 2014. (SPA & ENG.). 32p. (J). 18.95 (978-1-60060-899-5(X)) Lee & Low Bks., Inc.

My Español Book Level I. 2005. pap. (978-0-9767837-0-1(3)) Linguatechnics Publishing.

My Español Book, Level II. 2005. pap. (978-0-9767837-1-8(1)); pap., tchr. ed. (978-0-9767837-3-2(8)) Linguatechnics Publishing.

My First Coloring Book of Spansih Words. 1000th ed. 2003. (ENG & SPA., Illus.). 34p. (J). 5.95 (978-0-9722999-0-9(4)) Three Sisters Pr.

Nance, Kimberly A. & Rivera, Isidro J. Aprendizaje: Tecnicas de Composicion. 2nd ed. 2003. (SPA., Illus.). 196p. tchr. ed. (978-0-618-23127-0(7)) CENGAGE Learning.

Nelson, Robin. Empujar Y Jalar; Push & Pull. 2008. pap. 34.95 (978-0-8225-9895-4(7)) Lerner Publishing Group.

Nextext, creator. Ana Maria Matute. 2006. (Spanish Readers Ser.). (SPA., Illus.). 223p. (YA). (gr. 8-12). (978-0-618-04826-7(X)) Holt McDougal.

Nickelodeon Staff, ed. Words - Dora the Explorer. 2010. (Write, Slide & Learn Ser.). 14p. (J). (gr. -1-1). 9.99 (978-1-74184-519-8(X), Ideal Pubns.) Worthy Publishing.

Ninos Aprenden Ingles Corp. Children Learning Spanish. 2005. (Illus.). 119p. (J). pap. 19.95 (978-1-934665-04-6(5)) Ninos Aprenden Ingles Corp.

No Diga Si Cuando Quiera Decir No (Don't Say Yes When You Mean No) (SPA.). pap. (978-968-419-347-5(5)) Grijalbo, Editorial.

Nunn, Daniel. Colors in Spanish: Los Colores, 1 vol. 2012. (World Languages - Colors Ser.). (ENG, SPA & MUL.). 24p. (gr. 1-3). pap. 6.29 (978-1-4329-6659-1(6), Acorn) Heinemann-Raintree.

—Families in Spanish: Las Familias, 1 vol. 2013. (World Languages - Families Ser.). (ENG, MUL & SPA., Illus.). 24p. (gr. 1-3). pap. 6.29 (978-1-4329-7180-9(8)); lib. bdg. 22.65 (978-1-4329-7173-1(5)) Heinemann-Raintree. (Acorn).

—Numbers in Spanish: Los Números, 1 vol. 2012. (World Languages - Numbers Ser.). (ENG, SPA & MUL.). 24p. (gr. 1-3). pap. 6.29 (978-1-4329-6680-5(4)); lib. bdg. 22.65 (978-1-4329-6673-7(1)) Heinemann-Raintree. (Acorn).

Oliver, Stephen, photos by. Tamanos. 2005. (Coleccion Primeras Imagenes).Tr. of My First Look at Sizes. (SPA., Illus.). (J). (gr. -1-18). pap. 7.95 (978-950-11-0907-8(0), SGM9070) Sigmar ARG. Dist: Continental Bk. Co., Inc.

Oquendo, Lisa, illus. Abecedario. 2006. (SPA.). bds. 5.99 (978-1-934113-04-2(2)) Little Cubans, LLC.

Orero, Maria Jesus. Nico y Sus Trajes. 2006. (Nico Collection). (SPA & ESP., Illus.). 12p. (gr. -1-2). per., bds. 6.99 (978-84-272-6152-5(7)) Molino, Editorial ESP. Dist: Santillana USA Publishing Co., Inc.

Ortells, Estela. En el Bosque. (Coleccion Pequeno Simon). (SPA., Illus.). 32p. (J). 7.95 (978-84-7189-166-2(2), ORT347) Ortells, Alfredo Editorial S.L. ESP. Dist: Continental Bk. Co., Inc.

Un Pajarito. 2003. 23.95 (978-0-673-77778-2(2)) Celebration Pr.

Paradis, Anne. Caillou, My First Spanish Word Book. Brignaud, Pierre & Sévigny, Éric, illus. 2016. (My First Dictionary Ser.). (ENG & SPA.). 24p. (J). (gr. -1-k). bds. 9.99 (978-2-89718-306-6(3)) Caillouet, Gerry.

Parish, Ellen. Spanish: Level 2. 2003. (Skill Builders Ser.). 80p. 2.95 (978-1-932210-15-6(6)) Rainbow Bridge Publishing.

Parker, Helen. Trace, Stick Learn Borrar Primeras Palabras/Wipe Clean First Words. 2007. (Trace, Stick & Learn Ser.). (Illus.). 12p. (gr. -1-k). pap. (978-1-84610-645-3(1)) Make Believe Ideas.

Parnell, Declan. Luis Speaks Spanish, 01 vols., 1. 2016. (Rosen REAL Readers: Social Studies Nonfiction / Fiction: Family, Community, & the World Ser.). (ENG.). 12p. (J). pap. 6.33 (978-1-5081-1776-6(4), Rosen Classroom) Rosen Publishing Group, Inc., The.

El parque de Juegos, 2 Packs. (Chiquilibros Ser.). (SPA.). (gr. -1-1). 12.00 (978-0-7635-8548-8(3)) Rigby Education.

El paseo en Trineo: Individual Title Two-Packs. (Chiquilibros Ser.). (SPA.). (gr. -1-1). 12.00 (978-0-7635-8546-4(7)) Rigby Education.

Patrick, Roman. Spanish Words at the Post Office, Vol. 1. 2014. (Learn My Language! Spanish Ser.). (ENG & SPA., Illus.). 24p. (J). (gr. 1-2). 22.60 (978-1-4824-0350-3(1)) Stevens, Gareth Publishing LLLP.

Patterson, Irania & McElvane, Catherine. Wings & Dreams (Alas y Suenos) The Legend of Angel Falls (La Leyenda del Salto Angel) 2010. (ENG & SPA.). 40p. (J). (gr. 1-3). 19.95 (978-0-9815192-4-1(5)) Novello Festival Pr.

El Payaso, 6 Packs. (Chiquilibros Ser.). (SPA.). (gr. k-1). 23.00 (978-0-7635-8785-7(0)) Rigby Education.

Pebble Soup Exploraciones: Pebble Soup Exploraciones Extra Ingredients. 239.00 (978-0-7578-3342-7(X)) Rigby Education.

El Pequenito Tonito. 2003. 23.95 (978-0-673-77368-5(X)) Celebration Pr.

Phillips, Larissa. Cochise: Jefe Apache. de la Vega, Eida, tr. from ENG. 2004. (Grandes Personajes en la Historia de Los Estados Unidos Ser.). (ENG & SPA., Illus.). 32p. (gr. 3-6). pap. 10.00 (978-0-8239-4223-7(6)) Rosen Publishing Group, Inc., The.

Pisonero, Isidoro, et al. Pasacalle 2: Curso de Espanol para Ninos. (SPA & ENG.). (J). (gr. 3-7). 96p. tchr. ed. (978-84-7143-715-0(5)); 96p. stu. ed. (978-84-7143-708-2(2)); 64p. wbk. ed. (978-84-7143-709-9(0)) Sociedad General Espanola de Libreria.

Portavoz. Libro Abc-dario. 2004. (Sabio Y Prudente Ser.).Tr. of ABC Book. (SPA.). 32p. (J). pap. 2.50 (978-0-8254-0925-7(X)) Kregel Pubns.

Potey Mollina, José Luis. El pergamino de Zenit y el descubrimiento de los sellos Divinos. 2010. (SPA.). 224p. (YA). pap. 18.99 (978-1-59835-099-9(4), CBH Bks.) Cambridge BrickHouse, Inc.

Publications International Ltd. Staff. Little English Spanish Sound Diego. 2007. 12p. (J). 10.98 (978-1-4127-6738-5(5)) Publications International, Ltd.

Publications International Ltd. Staff, ed. Baby Einstein. 2007. (J). 10.98 (978-1-4127-7467-3(5)) Publications International, Ltd.

Que Sigue? 2003. 23.95 (978-0-673-77129-2(6)) Celebration Pr.

Que Soy? 2003.Tr. of What Am I? (J). (gr. -1-2). 23.95 (978-0-673-77408-8(2)) Celebration Pr.

Que Soy? Big Book Packages. 2003. 64.95 (978-0-673-58600-1(6)) Celebration Pr.

Que Susto Me Dio! 2003. (J). (gr. -1-2). 23.95 (978-0-673-77397-5(3)) Celebration Pr.

Quetzalcoalt's Corn. 2003. 28.95 (978-0-673-78116-1(X)) Celebration Pr.

Quien Vive Aqui? 2003. (J). (gr. -1-2). 23.95 (978-0-673-77396-8(5)) Celebration Pr.

Quien Vive Aqui? Big Book Packages. 2003. 64.95 (978-0-673-58601-8(4)) Celebration Pr.

Randolph, Joanne. All about A Months/Los Meses. Brusca, Maria Cristina, tr. 2007. (It's about Time / Los Libros Del Tiempo Ser.). (SPA., Illus.). 24p. (J). (gr. k-2). lib. bdg. 22.60 (978-1-4042-7628-4(9)) Rosen Publishing Group, Inc., The.

Random House Staff. 500 Palabras Nuevas Para Ti. Kest, Kristin, illus. 2005. (Pictureback(R) Ser.). (ENG & SPA.). 32p. (J). (gr. -1-2). pap. 3.99 (978-0-375-83308-3(0), Random House Para Ninos) Random Hse. Children's Bks.

—500 Words to Grow On. Kest, Kristin, illus. 2005. (Pictureback(R) Ser.). (ENG.). 32p. (J). (gr. -1-k). pap. 3.99 (978-0-375-83307-6(2), Random Hse. Bks. for Young Readers) Random Hse. Children's Bks.

El Rebozo: Big Book Packages. 2003. 64.95 (978-0-673-58595-0(6)) Celebration Pr.

El Recreo. 2003. 23.95 (978-0-673-77180-3(6)) Celebration Pr.

El Renacuajo. 2003. 23.95 (978-0-673-77169-8(5)) Celebration Pr.

Robleda, Margarita. Jugando con Las Vocales. Suarez, Maribel, illus. 2006. (Rana, Rema, Rimas Ser.).Tr. of Playing with Vowels. (SPA.). 12p. (J). (gr. -1-k). 7.95 (978-1-59820-210-6(3), Alfaguara) Santillana USA Publishing Co., Inc.

Rojo, Andrea Szekasy. Arcoiris, Level 1 Activity Book: Spanish for Children. 2003. (SPA., Illus.). 48p. (Orig.). (J). (gr. 1-6). pap., act. bk. ed. 10.99 (978-0-9671053-5-2(8), 0510) Language Adventure Pubns.

Rosa-Mendoza, Gladys. English-Spanish Foundations Series: The Alphabet; Numbers; Colors & Shapes. Cifuentes, Carolina, ed. Noiset, Michele, illus. 2004. (Spanish Foundations Ser.). (ENG & SPA.). (J). bds. 19.95 (978-0-9679748-1-1(X)) Me+Mi Publishing.

—Let's Go to the Zoo!/Vamos Al Zoolgico! Elkerton, Andy, illus. 2007. (English Spanish Foundations Ser.). (ENG & SPA.). 20p. (J). (gr. -1-k). bds. 6.95 (978-1-931398-20-6(8)) Me+Mi Publishing.

—Lupe Lupita, Where Are You?/Lupe Lupita Donde Estas? Ochoa, Ana, illus. 2007. (English Spanish Foundations Ser.). 20p. (gr. -1-k). pap. 19.95 (978-1-931398-82-4(8)) Me+Mi Publishing.

—My House/Mi Casa. Borlasca, Hector, illus. (English Spanish Foundations Ser.). (gr. -1-1). 2007. per. 19.95 (978-1-931398-84-8(4)) 2006. (ENG & SPA.). 20p. (J). bds. 6.95 (978-1-931398-18-3(6)) Me+Mi Publishing.

—My School/Mi Escuela. Murphy, Terri, illus. 2007. (English Spanish Foundations Ser.). (ENG & SPA.). (J). (gr. -1-k). bds. 6.95 (978-1-931398-23-7(2)) Me+Mi Publishing.

—My Senses/Mis Sentidos. Merer, Laura, illus. 2007. (English Spanish Foundations Ser.). (ENG & SPA.). 20p. (J). (gr. -1-k). bds. 6.95 (978-1-931398-21-3(6)) Me+Mi Publishing.

—My Week/Mi Semana. Wesley, Milliana, ed. Grosshauser, Peter, illus. 2007. (English Spanish Foundations Ser.). (gr. -1-k). bds. 6.95 (978-1-931398-25-1(9)) Me+Mi Publishing.

—Opposites/Opuestos. Cifuentes, Carolina, ed. McGeehan, Dan, illus. 2008. (English-Spanish Foundations Ser.). (gr. -1-k). bds. 6.95 (978-1-931398-04-6(6)) Me+Mi Publishing.

—When I Am/Cuando Estoy. Regan, Dana, illus. 2007. (English Spanish Foundations Ser.). 20p. (gr. -1-k). pap. 19.95 (978-1-931398-83-1(6)) Me+Mi Publishing.

—Who Lives in the Sea?/Qui'n Vive en el Mar? O'Neil, Sharron, illus. 2007. (English Spanish Foundations Ser.). (ENG & SPA.). 20p. (J). (gr. -1-k). bds. 6.95 (978-1-931398-24-4(0)) Me+Mi Publishing.

Rosa y Sus Amigos. 2003. 23.95 (978-0-673-77793-5(6)) Celebration Pr.

Rosier, Michelle. Elementary Spanish - Worktext Step 1. 2006. 72p. per. 15.00 (978-1-59166-276-1(1)) BJU Pr.

—Elementary Spanish — Worktext Step 2. 2006. 72p. per. 15.00 (978-1-59166-277-8(X)) BJU Pr.

—Elementary Spanish — Worktext Step 3. 2006. 72p. per. 15.00 (978-1-59166-278-5(8)) BJU Pr.

Ryan, Pam Muñoz. Nuestra California. López, Rafael, illus. 2008.Tr. of Our California. (SPA & ENG.). 48p. (J). (gr. 1-4). 17.95 (978-1-58089-226-1(4)) Charlesbridge Publishing, Inc.

Salazar, Julia. Spanish Words on the Road, Vol. 1. 2014. (Learn My Language! Spanish Ser.). (ENG & SPA., Illus.). 24p. (J). (gr. 1-2). 22.60 (978-1-4824-0365-7(X)) Stevens, Gareth Publishing LLLP.

Saludos! Complete Blue Level Packages. 697.00 (978-0-7635-9510-4(1)) Rigby Education.

Santiago, Carmen. Fun & Easy Spanish for You, Vol. 2. 2003. 48p. (J). per. 29.95 (978-1-56167-794-8(9)) American Literary Pr.

Santiago, Carmen Angelica. Fun & Easy Spanish for You. 2003. (SPA.). 50p. (J). Vol. 1. per. 29.95 (978-1-56167-793-1(0)) Vol. 3. (Illus.). per. 29.95 (978-1-56167-795-5(7)) American Literary Pr.

Sara, Sarita. 2003. (SPA.). 23.95 (978-0-673-77366-1(3)) Celebration Pr.

Scarry, Richard. Richard Scarry's Best Word Book Ever. 2004. (SPA, ENG & MUL., Illus.). 64p. (J). (gr. -1-2). 16.95 (978-0-87358-873-7(8)) Cooper Square Publishing Llc.

—Richard Scarry's Best Word Book Ever. Scarry, Richard, illus. 2004. (SPA, ENG & MUL., Illus.). 64p. (J). (gr. -1-2). pap. 10.95 (978-0-87358-874-4(6)) Cooper Square Publishing Llc.

Schmitt, et al. Glencoe Middle School Spanish: Cómo te va? Intro Nivel Rojo. 2003. (Middle School Spanish Intro Ser.). (SPA.). (gr. 6-8). stu. ed. 61.96 (978-0-07-861026-4(5), 0078610265) Glencoe/McGraw-Hill.

Schmitt, Conrad J. ¿Cómo Te Va? 2003. (Middle School Spanish Intro Ser.). (SPA., Illus.). 72p. (gr. 6-8). spiral bd., wbk. ed. 10.44 (978-0-07-860542-0(3), 0078605423) McGraw-Hill Higher Education.

—Como Te Va?, B: Glencoe Middle School Spanish. 2003. (Glencoe Spanish Ser.). (SPA., Illus.). 128p. (gr. 6-8). pap., wbk. ed. 17.04 (978-0-07-860556-7(3), 0078605563) McGraw-Hill Education.

Schmitt, Conrad J. & McGraw-Hill Education Editors. Glencoe Middle School Spanish - ¿Cómo Te Va? 2003. (Middle School Spanish Intro Ser.). (SPA., Illus.). 144p. (gr. 6-8). stu. ed. 61.96 (978-0-07-860350-1(1), 0078603501) McGraw-Hill Higher Education.

Schmitt, Conrad J. & Woodford. Cómo te va? B Nivel Azul. 2003. (Glencoe Spanish Ser.). (SPA & ENG.). (gr. 6-8). stu. ed. 91.08 (978-0-07-861025-7(7), 0078610257) Glencoe/McGraw-Hill.

Schmitt, Conrad J., et al. Glencoe Middle School Spanish: ¿Cómo Te Va? A Nivel Verde. 2003. (Glencoe Spanish Ser.). (SPA & ENG.). (gr. 6-8). stu. ed. 88.36 (978-0-07-861024-0(9), 0078610249) Glencoe/McGraw-Hill.

School Zone Publishing Company Staff. Bilingual Preschool Big Get Ready! 2005. (ENG.). 320p. (J). (gr. k). pap. 9.99 (978-1-58947-493-2(7)) School Zone Publishing Co.

Schumacher, Bev. Where Will You Find Me? / Donde Me Encontraras. 2008. (SPA.). 20p. (J). lib. bdg. 9.95 (978-1-935292-07-4(2)) Learning Props.

Segal, Robin. ABC in Albuquerque. 2009. (All 'Bout Cities Ser.). (ENG.). 32p. (J). (gr. -1-k). (978-1-935139-01-0(0)) Murray Hill Bks., LLC.

—ABC in San Antonio. 2009. (All 'Bout Cities Ser.). (ENG.). 32p. (J). (gr. -1-k). (978-1-935139-04-1(5)) Murray Hill Bks., LLC.

Segal, Robin & Adler, Tasha. ABC in Los Angeles: And la County. 2009. (All 'Bout Cities Ser.). (ENG.). 32p. (J). (gr. -1-k). (978-1-935139-02-7(9)) Murray Hill Bks., LLC.

Senor Cascaron. 2003. (SPA.). 23.95 (978-0-673-77170-4(9)) Celebration Pr.

Senor Cascaron: Poems, Rhymes, & Songs Listening Packs. 2003. (SPA.). 34.50 (978-0-673-58623-0(5)) Celebration Pr.

Seuss, Dr. The Cat in the Hat/el Gato Ensombrerado: Bilingual Edition. 2015. (Classic Seuss Ser.). (ENG & SPA.). 72p. (J). (gr. -1-2). 15.00 (978-0-553-52443-7(7), Random Hse. Bks. for Young Readers) Random Hse. Children's Bks.

Sierra i Fabra, Jordi. Aydin. 97th ed. 2003. (SPA., Illus.). 144p. pap. 23.40 (978-84-236-3708-9(5), ED6264) Harcourt Schl. Pubs.

Sombreros. 2003. (SPA.). 23.95 (978-0-673-77798-0(7)) Celebration Pr.

Sosa, Carlos. Celebrations. 2007. (Familia Banderas Ser.). (Illus.). 48p. (J). (gr. 3-7). per. 9.95 (978-1-933669-11-3(X)) Literary Architects, LLC.

—Cultures. 2007. (Familia Banderas Ser.). (Illus.). 48p. (J). (gr. 3-7). per. 9.95 (978-1-933669-12-0(8)) Literary Architects, LLC.

Soy la Cafetera. 2003. 23.95 (978-0-673-77386-9(8)) Celebration Pr.

Soy La Cafetera: Poems, Rhymes, & Songs Listening Packs. 2003. 34.50 (978-0-673-58634-6(0)) Celebration Pr.

Spanish II, Set. 2004. (YA). (gr. 9-12). 99.95 (978-0-7403-0241-1(8), ES9915, Lifepac) Alpha Omega Pubns., Inc.

Spanish Intro Kit. 2004. (ENG & SPA.). (J). 44.99 (978-0-943343-76-1(3)) Learning Wrap-Ups, Inc.

Spanish School Thesaurus: Sinonimos, Antonimos, Paronimos. 2004th ed. 2004. 380p. pap. 9.95 (978-950-11-1158-3(X)) Los Andes Publishing Co.

Spanish/English Desk Cards. 2004. (J). 8.95 (978-1-56911-177-2(4)) Learning Resources, Inc.

Sterling Publishing Co., Inc. First Words/Primeras Palabras. 2013. (Say & Play Ser.). (ENG & SPA., Illus.). 28p. (J). (— 1). bds. 4.95 (978-1-4549-1039-8(9)) Sterling Publishing Co., Inc.

Stillman, David. Repaso: Answer Key. 2004. (SPA & ENG.). 416p. (gr. 6-12). pap. 8.95 (978-0-8442-7422-5(4), NTC4224) Glencoe/McGraw-Hill.

Stokes, Jeffery D. !Qué Bien Suena! Text. 2004. 224p. (YA). pap. 104.76 incl. cd-rom (978-0-618-23502-5(7), 354274) CENGAGE Learning.

Suenos y Palabras. (SPA.). (J). (gr. k-6). 30.00 (978-958-04-7091-5(X)); 30.00 (978-958-04-7090-8(1)); Vol. 2. 30.00 (978-958-04-7092-2(8)); Vol. 3. 30.00 (978-958-04-7093-9(6)); Vol. 4. (978-958-04-7734-1(5)); Vol. 5. (978-958-04-7735-8(3)); Vol. 6. (978-958-04-7736-5(1)) Norma S.A. COL. Dist: Distribuidora Norma, Inc.

Suenos y Palabras 1. (J). 26.50 (978-958-04-4036-9(0)) Norma S.A. COL. Dist: Distribuidora Norma, Inc.

Suenos y Palabras 10. (SPA.). (J). (gr. 7-12). 40.00 (978-958-04-5955-2(X)) Norma S.A. COL. Dist: Distribuidora Norma, Inc.

Suenos y Palabras 11. (SPA.). (J). (gr. 7-12). 45.00 (978-958-04-5957-6(6)) Norma S.A. COL. Dist: Distribuidora Norma, Inc.

Suenos y Palabras 12. (SPA.). (J). (gr. 7-12). 50.00 (978-958-04-5959-0(2)) Norma S.A. COL. Dist: Distribuidora Norma, Inc.

Suenos y Palabras 2. (SPA.). (J). 26.50 (978-958-04-4037-6(9)) Norma S.A. COL. Dist: Distribuidora Norma, Inc.

Suenos y Palabras 3. (SPA.). (J). 26.50 (978-958-04-4038-3(7)) Norma S.A. COL. Dist: Distribuidora Norma, Inc.

Suenos y Palabras 4. (SPA.). (J). 26.50 (978-958-04-4039-0(5)) Norma S.A. COL. Dist: Distribuidora Norma, Inc.

Suenos y Palabras 5. (SPA.). (J). 26.50 (978-958-04-4040-6(9)) Norma S.A. COL. Dist: Distribuidora Norma, Inc.

Suenos y Palabras 6. (SPA.). (J). 26.50 (978-958-04-4041-3(7)) Norma S.A. COL. Dist: Distribuidora Norma, Inc.

Suenos y Palabras 7, Vol. 7. (SPA.). (J). (gr. 7-12). 35.00 (978-958-04-5650-6(X)) Norma S.A. COL. Dist: Distribuidora Norma, Inc.

Suenos y Palabras 8. (SPA.). (J). (gr. 7-12). 35.00 (978-958-04-5651-3(8)) Norma S.A. COL. Dist: Distribuidora Norma, Inc.

Suenos y Palabras 9. (SPA.). (J). (gr. 7-12). 40.00 (978-958-04-5652-0(6)) Norma S.A. COL. Dist: Distribuidora Norma, Inc.

Suenos y Palabras K. (SPA.). (J). 26.50 (978-958-04-4355-1(6)) Norma S.A. COL. Dist: Distribuidora Norma, Inc.

Taylor, Trace & Sánchez, Lucía M. Delfines: Dolphins. 2010. (2G Animales Marinos Ser.). (SPA.). 12p. (J). (gr. k-2). pap. 6.99 (978-1-61541-282-2(4)) American Reading Co.

Teckentrup, Britta, illus. Fast & Slow Spanish. 2013. (ENG & SPA.). 14p. (J). (gr. -1-k). bds. 6.99 (978-1-78285-035-9(X)) Barefoot Bks., Inc.

TestWorks. 2004. (Scott Foresman Reading Ser.). (gr. k-18). cd-rom 99.00 (978-0-328-02541-1(0)); (gr. 1-18). tchr. ed. 99.00 incl. cd-rom (978-0-673-62281-5(9)); (gr. 2-18). cd-rom 99.00 (978-0-673-62282-2(7)); (gr. 3-18). cd-rom 99.00 (978-0-673-62283-9(5)); (gr. 4-18). tchr. ed. 99.00 incl. cd-rom (978-0-673-62284-6(3)); (gr. 5-18). tchr. ed. 99.00 incl. cd-rom (978-0-673-62285-3(1)); (gr. 6-18). tchr. ed. 99.00 incl. cd-rom (978-0-673-62286-0(X)) Addison-Wesley Educational Pubs., Inc.

Tipton, Stacey. The Complete Musical Spanish: With New Bonus Verbs Learning CD, 1. 2nd ed. 2005. (SPA., Illus.). 112p. 49.99 (978-0-9706829-7-0(2)) Musical Linguist, The.

Todos Somos Amigos. 2003. 23.50 (978-0-673-77190-2(3)) Celebration Pr.

Travis, Joelle & Figueras, Ligaya, eds. Los Animales y los Verbos. Hazan, Maurice, illus. 2003. (SPA.). 89p. (J). per. 20.00 (978-1-932770-16-2(X), SWLB1) Symtalk, Inc.

Traynor, Tracy & Pérez, María. Spanish with Abby & Zak. Hambleton, Laura, illus. 2008. (Abby & Zak Ser.). (SPA & ENG.). 48p. (J). (gr. k-2). pap. 16.95 (978-1-84059-515-4(9)) Milet Publishing.

Tremaine, Jon. Tangrams: Magnéticos. 2011. (SPA.). 48p. (J). (gr. -1-k). 17.95 (978-84-9825-434-1(5)) Combel Editorial, S.A. ESP. Dist: Independent Pubs. Group.

Tu Amigo, Jorge. 2003. 28.95 (978-0-673-78106-2(2)) Celebration Pr.

Uriz, Francisco J. & Harling, Birgit. En el Mundo Hispanico. stu. ed. 19.95 (978-0-8219-2324-5(2), 70376); pap., tchr.'s training gde. ed. 15.95 (978-0-8219-2325-2(0), 70865) EMC/Paradigm Publishing.

Vargo, Sharon Hawkins. Senor Felipes Alphabet Adventure: El Alfabeto Espanol. 2003. (Single Titles Ser.: Vol. 3). 32p. (J). (gr. -1). 7.95 (978-0-7613-1897-2(6)) Lerner Publishing Group.

El Viaje de Carlos y Ceci. 2003. (Illus.). (J). 28.95 (978-0-673-78103-1(8)) Celebration Pr.

Villafane-Leon, Ines. A Story for All Seasons: Un Cuento Para Cada Estacion: Immigration of One. 2004. (ENG & SPA.). xiii, 367p. (YA). pap. 22.95 (978-1-882897-78-0(1)) Lost Coast Pr.

Way, Jennifer. The Running Book: Correr. 2004. (Let's Get Moving / Diviértete en Movimiento Ser.). (ENG & SPA., Illus.). 24p. (J). (gr. -1-1). lib. bdg. 22.60 (978-1-4042-7512-6(6), Editorial Buenas Letras) Rosen Publishing Group, Inc., The.

Who Is Michael Ramirez? 2003. (J). 28.95 (978-0-673-78107-9(0)) Celebration Pr.

Williams-Ashe, Marcella Norton. Granny Says. Williams Jr., Anthony, illus. 2012. 46p. pap. 12.00 (978-0-9764198-4-6(X)) Allecram Publishing.

Wilson, Natashya. Bears: Osos. Beullens, Nathalie, tr. 2004. (My World of Animals Ser.). (ENG & SPA., Illus.). 24p. (J). (gr. k-1). lib. bdg. 16.00 (978-1-4042-7518-8(5), PowerKids Pr.) Rosen Publishing Group, Inc., The.

Ya Llego el Mariachi! 2003. (J). 28.95 (978-0-673-78104-8(6)) Celebration Pr.

Ya Mero Llegamos, Mami? 2003. 23.95 (978-0-673-78081-2(3)) Celebration Pr.

Yellow Umbrella Spanish Big Books [Kaplan]. 2011. (Big Book - Spanish Edition Ser.). (SPA.). 16p. 149.70 (978-1-4296-6642-8(0), Yellow Umbrella en espanol) Capstone Press of Coughlan Cos.

Yo Bailo! 2003. (J). 23.95 (978-0-673-77781-2(2)) Celebration Pr.

Yo Tengo una Tia. 2003. (J). 23.95 (978-0-673-78059-1(7)) Celebration Pr.

Yo Vivo Aqui. 2003. (J). 23.95 (978-0-673-77792-8(8)) Celebration Pr.

Zaz! 2003. 23.95 (978-0-673-77367-8(1)) Celebration Pr.

Zoo-Zológico Bilingual Board Book. 2008. (ENG & SPA., Illus.). (J). pap. 5.99 (978-0-9727886-8-7(9)) Osmosis, LLC.

Zorzi, Gina & Sánchez, Lucía M. Bosques: This Is a Forest. 2011. (2G Ecosistemas Ser.). (SPA.). 28p. (J). (gr. k-2). pap. 6.99 (978-1-61541-426-0(6)) American Reading Co.

The 5 W's & H Spanish Version, Gr. 4-5. 2005. (Spanish Version Ser.). (J). per. (978-1-58232-140-0(X)) ECS Learning Systems, Inc.

The 5 W's Spanish Version, Gr. 1-3. 2005. (J). per. (978-1-58232-145-5(0)) ECS Learning Systems, Inc.

SPANISH LANGUAGE—CONVERSATION AND PHRASE BOOKS

Brooks, Felicity & Mackinnon, Mairi. Spanish Words & Phrases - Internet Referenced. 2008. (First Picture Spanish Ser.). (Illus.). 50p. (J). 9.99 (978-0-7945-2229-2(7), Usborne) EDC Publishing.

Bruzzone, Catherine & Martineau, Susan. Hide & Speak Spanish. Comfort, Louise, illus. 2003. (Hide & Speak Ser.). (SPA & ENG.). 32p. (J). pap. 9.99 (978-0-7641-2589-8(3)) Barron's Educational Series, Inc.

Dorling Kindersley Publishing Staff. Spanish Language Learner. 2011. (ENG.). 160p. (J). (gr. 5-12). 19.99 (978-0-7566-8256-9(8), DK Children) Dorling Kindersley Publishing, Inc.

Gose, Senora. Flip Flop Spanish: Ages 3-5: Level 1. 2008. (Illus.). 84p. (J). spiral bd. 29.95 (978-0-9801772-1-3(9)) Flip n Flop Learning, LLC.

Kalz, Jill. My First Spanish Phrases, 1 vol. Translations.com Staff, tr. Fabbri, Daniele, illus. 2012. (Speak Another Language! Ser.). (SPA, ENG & MUL.). 32p. (gr. 1-3). pap. 8.95 (978-1-4048-7247-9(7)) Picture Window Bks.

—My First Spanish Phrases, 1 vol. Advocate-Art Staff & Translations.com Staff, trs. Fabbri, Daniele, illus. 2012. (Speak Another Language! Ser.). (SPA, ENG & MUL.). 32p. (gr. 1-3). lib. bdg. 26.65 (978-1-4048-7152-6(7)) Picture Window Bks.

Mahoney, Judy. Teach Me Everyday Spanish: Celebrating the Seasons, 22 vols., Vol. 2. Girouard, Patrick, illus. adapted ed. 2009. (SPA & ENG.). 32p. (J). (gr. -1-2). lib. bdg. 19.95 incl. audio compact disk (978-1-59972-202-3(X)) Teach Me Tapes, Inc.

—Teach Me Everyday Spanish Vol 1, Volume 1. Girouard, Patrick, illus. 2008. (SPA & ENG.). 32p. (J). (gr. -1). 19.95 (978-1-59972-102-6(3)) Teach Me Tapes, Inc.

Pirz, Therese Slevin. Language Helper Spanish: Helping You Speak More Spanish. 2006. (Language Helper Ser.). (Illus.). 218p. (J). pap. 20.00 (978-0-9716605-8-8(1)) Chou Chou Pr.

Reyes, Raquel, et al. I May Bien! Level E. 2005. (I May Bien! Ser.).Tr. of Very Good. (SPA.). 130p. (J). 22.95 (978-0-9718696-9-1(3)) Double R Publishing, LLC.

Schmitt, Conrad J. Glencoe Middle School Spanish Level a Como Te Va? 2003. (Glencoe Spanish Ser.). (SPA & ENG., Illus.). 48p. (gr. 6-8). spiral bd. 9.04 (978-0-07-860550-5(4), 0078605504) Glencoe/McGraw-Hill.

Schmitt, Conrad J. & McGraw-Hill Education Editors. ¿Cómo Te Va? 2003. (Glencoe Spanish Ser.). (SPA., Illus.). 40p. (gr. 6-8). pap. 8.96 (978-0-07-860557-4(1), 0078605571) McGraw-Hill Higher Education.

Spanish for Business: Beginning Level. (J). (gr. k-6). suppl. ed. 59.00 (978-0-8219-0144-1(3), 70036) EMC/Paradigm Publishing.

Spanish for Business Interm: Intermediate Level. (J). (gr. k-6). suppl. ed. 59.00 (978-0-8219-0145-8(1), 70037) EMC/Paradigm Publishing.

Tulip, Jenny. My First Spanish Word Book. 2004. (ENG & SPA., Illus.). 48p. (J). 5.99 *(978-1-85854-394-9(0))* Brimax Books Ltd. GBR. Dist: Byeway Bks.

Vaamonde, Conchita, tr. My First Spanish Words. Tulip, Jenny, illus. 2004. (SPA.). 12p. (J). bds. 7.99 *(978-1-85854-512-7(9))* Brimax Books Ltd. GBR. Dist: Byeway Bks.

Watson, Carol, et al. Let's Learn Spanish. 2003. (Let's Learn Ser.). (ENG., Illus.). 32p. pap. 9.95 *(978-0-7818-1013-5(2))* Hippocrene Bks., Inc.

SPANISH LANGUAGE—DICTIONARIES

Brooks, Felicity & MacKinnon, Mairi. The Usborne Picture Dictionary in Spanish. rev. ed. 2007. (Picture Dictionaries Ser.). (Illus.). 111p. (J). 16.99 *(978-0-7945-1608-6(4),* Usborne) EDC Publishing.

Bruzzone, Catherine. Spanish-English Picture Dictionary. 2011. (First Bilingual Picture Dictionaries Ser.). (SPA & ENG., Illus.). 48p. (J). (gr. -1-3). pap. 7.99 *(978-0-7641-4661-9(0))* Barron's Educational Series, Inc.

Davies, H. Spanish Dictionary for Beginners. 2004. (Beginner's Dictionaries Ser.). (SPA & ENG.). 128p. (J). pap. 12.99 *(978-0-7945-0288-1(1))* EDC Publishing.

Davies, Helen. Spanish Dictionary for Beginners. Irving, Nicole, ed. Shackell, John, illus. 2003. (Beginner's Dictionaries Ser.). (SPA.). 128p. lib. bdg. 20.99 *(978-1-58086-488-6(0))* EDC Publishing.

Diaz-Cubero, Jose H. Practicas de Ortografia: 3 Grado. (SPA & ENG.). (J). (gr. 3). 9.95 *(978-84-357-0127-3(1),* CPR88) Ediciones y Distribuciones Codice, S.A. ESP. Dist: Continental Bk. Co., Inc.

Diccionario de la Lengua Espanola Basico. (SPA., Illus.). (J). 5.95 *(978-958-04-4116-8(2))* Norma S.A. COL. Dist: Distribuidora Norma, Inc.

Diccionario de la Lengua Espanola Mini. (SPA.). (J). 2.50 *(978-958-04-4584-5(2))* Norma S.A. COL. Dist: Distribuidora Norma, Inc.

Diccionario de Primaria de la Lengua Española. 2nd ed. 2003. (SPA., Illus.). 1006p. (J). (gr. 3-7). *(978-84-8332-061-7(4))* Bibliograf, S.A.

Diccionario Didactico de Espanol Elemental (Didactic Dictionary of Elementary Spanish) Edicion Mexicana (Mexican Edition) (SPA., Illus.). 880p. *(978-84-348-4715-6(9),* SM1932) SM Ediciones.

Diccionario Esencial. (SPA.). 1376p. 19.95 *(978-84-294-3415-6(1))* Santillana USA Publishing Co., Inc.

Diccionario Inicial de la Lengua Espanola. (SPA., Illus.). 336p. (J). 8.95 *(978-84-7153-199-5(2),* VX992) Bibliograf, S.A. ESP. Dist: Continental Bk. Co., Inc.

Diccionario Usual Larousse.Tr. of Handy Larousse Spanish Dictionary. (SPA.). 782p. pap. *(978-970-22-0126-7(8))* Larousse, Ediciones, S. A. de C. V.

Dorling Kindersley Publishing Staff. Spanish Picture Dictionary. Wilson, Hannah & Ferris, Julie, eds. 2005. (SPA & ENG., Illus.). 128p. (J). (gr. 5-12). 16.99 *(978-0-7566-1370-9(1),* DK Children) Dorling Kindersley Publishing, Inc.

Enciclopedia Juvenil, 4 vols., Set. (J). 59.00 *(978-84-272-5995-9(6),* MO501) Molino, Editorial ESP. Dist: Continental Bk. Co., Inc.

Equipo Staff. Dicionario Inicial Everest. Jorge, Gutiérrez Sahagún, illus. (SPA.). 336p. *(978-84-241-1013-0(7))* Everest Editora ESP. Dist: Lectorum Pubns., Inc.

—Everest Diccionario Cima de la Lengua Espanola.Tr. of Everest Cima Dictionary of the Spanish Language. (SPA.). 566p. 19.95 *(978-84-241-1027-7(7),* EV6705); 868p. 22.95 *(978-84-241-1036-9(6),* EV7041) Everest Editora ESP. Dist: Lectorum Pubns., Inc.

Equipo Staff & Equipo Lexicográfico Everest. Everest Diccionario Practico de Sinonimos y Antonimos.Tr. of Everest Practical Thesaurus. (SPA.). 576p. 12.99 *(978-84-241-1508-1(2),* EV7151) Everest Editora ESP. Dist: Lectorum Pubns., Inc.

Goodman, Marlene. Let's Learn Spanish Picture Dictionary. 2004. 80p. 9.95 *(978-0-07-140828-8(2))* McGraw-Hill/Contemporary.

Harpercollins Staff & Collins Dictionaries Staff. Collins Very First Spanish Dictionary. 2nd ed. 2014. (Collins Primary Dictionaries Ser.). (SPA & ENG., Illus.). 80p. (J). (gr. 1-4). pap. 9.95 *(978-0-00-758355-3(9))* HarperCollins Pubs. Ltd. GBR. Dist: Independent Pubs. Group.

Liccioni, Tina. The Clownfish/el Pez Payaso: An English/Spanish Bilingual Book. Vesazquez, Gloria, tr. 2013. (ENG.). 36p. (J). pap. 21.95 *(978-1-4327-9060-8(9))* Outskirts Pr., Inc.

Magic Spanish Picture Dictionary. 2009. (ENG.). 144p. pap. 9.99 *(978-1-4231-2265-4(8))* Disney Pr.

McGraw-Hill Education Staff. McGraw-Hill's Spanish Picture Dictionary. 2004. (SPA & ENG., Illus.). 96p. (J). 15.00 *(978-0-07-142812-5(7),* 0071428127) McGraw-Hill Cos., The.

Merriam-Webster. Merriam-Webster's Illustrated Spanish-English Student Dictionary. 2012. (ENG., Illus.). 495p. (gr. 4-8). 21.95 *(978-0-87779-177-5(5))* Merriam-Webster, Inc.

Norma Staff. Mi Primer Vocabulario (My First Vocabulary Dict.), 2 vols., Set. (SPA.). (J). 50.00 *(978-958-04-3093-3(4))* Norma S.A. COL. Dist: AIMS International Bks., Inc.

Rey, Alain. Robert junior Poche. pap. 29.95 *(978-2-85036-687-1(0))* Le Robert FRA. Dist: Distribooks, Inc.

Richmond Concise Dictionary. (SPA.). 716p. (J). (gr. 3-8). pap. 30.95 *(978-970-29-0661-2(X))* Santillana USA Publishing Co., Inc.

Santillana. Pictodiccionario: Diccionario en Im Genes. Sangregorio, Fernando et al, illus. 2003.Tr. of Child's First Spanish Dictionary. (SPA.). 144p. (gr. k-3). 29.95 *(978-1-58105-973-1(6),* Santillana) Santillana USA Publishing Co., Inc.

Schmitt, Conrad J., et al. El Español para Nosotros, Level 2: Curso para Hispanohablantes. 2005. (Spanish Heritage Speaker Ser.). (SPA.). (gr. 9-12). stu. ed., per., wbk. ed. 26.16 *(978-0-07-867656-7(8),* 0078676568) McGraw-Hill Education.

SPANISH LANGUAGE—DICTIONARIES—ENGLISH

Amery, Heather. First Hundred Words in Spanish II. 2015. (First Hundred Words Ser.). (ENG.). 32p. (J). pap. 6.99 *(978-0-7945-3513-1(5),* Usborne) EDC Publishing.

Brooks, Felicity. Very First Dictionary in Spanish - Internet Referenced. 2008. (Very First Dictionaries Ser.). 80p. (J). 11.99 *(978-0-7945-2104-2(5),* Usborne) EDC Publishing.

Collins Dictionaries. Collins Spanish School Dictionary. 3rd rev. ed. 2015. (SPA & ENG.). 640p. (J). (gr. 2). pap. 10.99 *(978-0-00-756933-5(5))* HarperCollins Pubs. Ltd. GBR. Dist: Independent Pubs. Group.

—Spanish School Dictionary. 3rd rev. ed. 2015. (SPA & ENG.). 640p. (YA). (gr. 6-11). pap. 7.99 *(978-0-00-756930-4(0))* HarperCollins Pubs. Ltd. GBR. Dist: Independent Pubs. Group.

Collins Dictionaries Staff. Collins Primary Illustrated Spanish Dictionary. 2015. (SPA & ENG., Illus.). 640p. (J). (gr. 3-6). 14.95 *(978-0-00-811196-0(0))* HarperCollins Pubs. Ltd. GBR. Dist: Independent Pubs. Group.

Collins Dictionary Staff. Collins Spanish School Dictionary. 2nd ed. 2011. (SPA & ENG.). 640p. (J). pap. 9.95 *(978-0-00-736784-9(8))* HarperCollins Pubs. Ltd. GBR. Dist: Independent Pubs. Group.

Diccionario Basico Ingles/Espanol (1540) 2003. (SPA & ENG.). 528p. pap. 5.98 *(978-970-22-0480-0(1))* Larousse, Ediciones, S. A. de C. V. MEX. Dist: Giron Bks.

Diccionario Bilingue Basico. (SPA & ENG.). (J). 5.95 *(978-958-04-4118-2(9))* Norma S.A. COL. Dist: Distribuidora Norma, Inc.

Dorling Kindersley Publishing Staff. Spanish Language Learner. 2011. (ENG.). 160p. (J). (gr. 5-12). 19.99 *(978-0-7566-8256-9(8),* DK Children) Dorling Kindersley Publishing, Inc.

Hanson, Tracie, des. New World Baby - Spanish. 2007. (ENG, SPA, FRE, GER & ITA., Illus.). 28p. (J). 14.00 *(978-0-9799185-0-6(2))* Hanson, Tracie.

Hippocrene Books Staff, creator. Children's Picture Dictionary. 2006. (Hippocrene Children's Illustrated Dictionaries Ser.). (ENG & SPA., Illus.). 108p. (J). (gr. 3-7). pap. 14.95 *(978-0-7818-1130-9(9))* Hippocrene Bks., Inc.

Hochstatter, Daniel J. Just Look 'n Learn Spanish Picture Dictionary. 2004. 96p. 11.95 *(978-0-07-140829-5(0))* McGraw-Hill/Contemporary.

Kudela, Katy R. My First Book of Spanish Words, 1 vol. 2009. (Bilingual Picture Dictionaries Ser.). (SPA, ENG & MUL.). 32p. (gr. 1-2). lib. bdg. 27.32 *(978-1-4296-3298-0(4),* Aplus Bks.) Capstone Press of Coughlan Cos.

Laud, Valerie. The Picture Book Dictionary: The Essential Source for Bilingual Families, English-Spanish Edition. Latushkin, Valentin, illus. I.t. ed. 2005. (ENG & SPA.). 96p. (J). *(978-0-9747387-0-3(0))* EKADOO Publishing Group.

Lipton, Gladys C. Spanish Beginner's Bilingual Dictionary. 4th rev. ed. 2009. (Barron's Beginner's Bilingual Dictionaries Ser.). (ENG & SPA., Illus.). 456p. pap. 8.99 *(978-0-7641-3968-0(1))* Barron's Educational Series, Inc.

Merriam-Webster Editors. Merriam-Webster's Spanish-English Dictionary. 2014. (SPA.). (gr. 7-12). lib. bdg. 17.20 *(978-0-613-09430-6(1),* Turtleback) Turtleback Bks.

Merriam-Webster, Inc. Staff, ed. Merriam-Webster's Notebook Spanish-English Dictionary. 2004. (SPA & ENG.). 112p. (gr. 5). pap. 4.95 *(978-0-87779-672-5(6),* MER-672) Merriam-Webster, Inc.

O'Sullivan, Jill Korey. Picture Dictionary for Children. 2007. (ENG.). 176p. (C). pap. 32.95 *(978-1-4240-0876-6(X))* Cengage Heinle.

Pearson Longman Staff & Pearson Education Staff. Longman Diccionario Pocket, Ingles-Espanol, Espanol-Ingles: Para Estudiantes Mexicanos. 2004. (ENG & SPA., Illus.). 832p. (C). pap. 27.27 *(978-0-582-51157-6(7))* Pearson Education.

Richmond Advanced Dictionary: Spanish/English, English/Spanish. (ENG & SPA.). 720p. (J). (gr. 9-12). 30.95 *(978-84-294-9861-5(3),* Richmond) Santillana USA Publishing Co., Inc.

Richmond Pocket Dictionary: Spanish-English, English-Spanish. (SPA & ENG.). 806p. (J). (gr. 6-12). pap. 10.95 *(978-84-294-9860-8(5))* Santillana USA Publishing Co., Inc.

Sauri, Trudy. Gift of Yucatan Nouns A-Z. 2008. (ENG & SPA., Illus.). 64p. (J). per. 18.00 *(978-0-9797637-3-1(8))* Your Culture Gifts.

Spanish-English Picture Dictionary. 2003. (SPA & ENG.). (J). per. *(978-1-884907-30-2(X))* Paradise Pr., Inc.

Thomas, Mar Andres. Mi Primer Libro Bilingue: la Comida/My First Bilingual Book: Food. 2013. (ENG & SPA., Illus.). 69p. (J). (gr. -1-3). pap. 14.95 *(978-1-938690-43-3(5))* Salem Author Services.

York, M. J. Learn Spanish Words. Petelinsek, Kathleen, illus. 2014. (Foreign Language Basics Ser.). (ENG.). 24p. (J). (gr. 2-5). 27.07 *(978-1-62687-379-7(8),* 207126) Child's World, Inc., The.

SPANISH LANGUAGE—GRAMMAR

ABC. 2003. (J). per. *(978-1-884907-44-9(X));* per. *(978-1-884907-40-1(7))* Paradise Pr., Inc.

ABC. 2003. (First Concepts Book Ser.). 32p. (J). 3.98 *(978-0-7525-8892-6(3))* Parragon, Inc.

ABC. (Coleccion Picaros Peluchines). (SPA.). (J). 5.50 *(978-950-11-0398-4(6),* SGM398) Sigmar ARG. Dist: Continental Bk. Co., Inc.

La Abeja Trabajadora. 2003. (J). 23.95 *(978-0-673-77796-6(0))* Celebration Pr.

Acento 8: Cuaderno de Ortografia. (SPA.). (J). (gr. 1-9). 16.00 *(978-958-04-3831-1(5))* Norma S.A. COL. Dist: Distribuidora Norma, Inc.

Acento 9: Cuaderno de Ortografia. (SPA., Illus.). (J). (gr. 1-9). 16.00 *(978-958-04-3832-8(3))* Norma S.A. COL. Dist: Distribuidora Norma, Inc.

Advina Quien Soy? 2003. 23.95 *(978-0-673-77182-7(2))* Celebration Pr.

Al Juego! 2003. 23.95 *(978-0-673-77777-5(4))* Celebration Pr.

Ana Y Tito. 2003. 23.95 *(978-0-673-77783-6(9))* Celebration Pr.

Los Animales Nos Ayudan. 2003. 23.95 *(978-0-673-77393-7(0))* Celebration Pr.

Antonio Y Su Poncho. 2003. 28.95 *(978-0-673-78086-7(4))* Celebration Pr.

El Apartamento. 2003. 23.95 *(978-0-673-77183-4(0))* Celebration Pr.

La Arana. 2003. 23.95 *(978-0-673-77156-8(3))* Celebration Pr.

El Arco Iris. 2003. 23.95 *(978-0-673-77128-5(8))* Celebration Pr.

Ashley, Moana. Wonders of the Worlds. 2008. (Illus.). 24p. (J). pap. 10.95 *(978-1-59646-541-1(7))* Dingles & Co.

Ay, Caramba! 2003. 28.95 *(978-0-673-78097-3(X))* Celebration Pr.

Los Ayudantes. 2003. 23.95 *(978-0-673-77164-3(4))* Celebration Pr.

Borreguita Negra: Poems, Rhymes, & Songs Listening Packs. 2003. 34.50 *(978-0-673-58629-2(4))* Celebration Pr.

Brilla, Brilla, Estrellita. 2003. 23.95 *(978-0-673-77365-4(5))* Celebration Pr.

Brinca La Tablita: Big Book Packages. 2003. 64.95 *(978-0-673-58603-2(0))* Celebration Pr.

Las Buenas Noches. 2003. 23.95 *(978-0-673-77392-0(2))* Celebration Pr.

El Caldo. 2003. 23.95 *(978-0-673-77773-7(1))* Celebration Pr.

Camarena, Cathy & Ruff, Gloria B. Carmen y Carlos, 1 vol. 2006. (Primeros Sonidos Ser.). (Illus.). (J). (gr. k-3). (ENG & SPA.). 24p. lib. bdg. 24.21 *(978-1-59679-847-2(5),* SandCastle); (SPA., 23p. pap. 48.42 *(978-1-59679-848-9(3))* ABDO Publishing Co.

—Cindi y Cesar, 1 vol. 2006. (Primeros Sonidos Ser.). (ENG & SPA., Illus.). 24p. (J). (gr. k-3). lib. bdg. 24.21 *(978-1-59679-851-9(3),* SandCastle) ABDO Publishing Co.

—Cindi y César. 2006. (Primeros Sonidos Ser.). (SPA., Illus.). 23p. (J). pap. 48.42 *(978-1-59679-852-6(1))* ABDO Publishing Co.

—Crisma y Cristián. 2006. (Primeros Sonidos Ser.). (SPA., Illus.). 23p. (J). pap. 48.42 *(978-1-59679-850-2(5))* ABDO Publishing Co.

—Ema y Eduardo, 1 vol. 2006. (Primeros Sonidos Ser.). (J). (gr. k-3). (ENG & SPA., Illus.). 24p. lib. bdg. 24.21 *(978-1-59679-857-1(2),* SandCastle); pap. 48.42 *(978-1-59679-858-8(0))* ABDO Publishing Co.

—Fey y Felix, 1 vol. 2006. (Primeros Sonidos Ser.). (ENG & SPA., Illus.). 24p. (J). (gr. k-3). lib. bdg. 24.21 *(978-1-59679-859-5(9),* SandCastle) ABDO Publishing Co.

—Fey y Félix. 2006. (Primeros Sonidos Ser.). (SPA., Illus.). 23p. (J). pap. 48.42 *(978-1-59679-860-1(2))* ABDO Publishing Co.

—Florinda y Flavio, 1 vol. 2006. (Primeros Sonidos Ser.). (Illus.). (J). (gr. k-3). (ENG & SPA.). 24p. lib. bdg. 24.21 *(978-1-59679-861-8(0),* SandCastle); (SPA., 23p. pap. 48.42 *(978-1-59679-862-5(9))* ABDO Publishing Co.

—Gilda y Gilberto, 1 vol. 2006. (Primeros Sonidos Ser.). (Illus.). (J). (gr. k-3). (ENG & SPA.). 24p. lib. bdg. 24.21 *(978-1-59679-869-4(6),* SandCastle); (SPA., 23p. pap. 48.42 *(978-1-59679-870-0(X))* ABDO Publishing Co.

—Isabel E Ivan, 1 vol. 2006. (Primeros Sonidos Ser.). (ENG & SPA., Illus.). 24p. (J). (gr. k-3). lib. bdg. 24.21 *(978-1-59679-875-5(0),* SandCastle) ABDO Publishing Co.

—Isabel e Iván. 2006. (Primeros Sonidos Ser.). (SPA., Illus.). 23p. (J). pap. 48.42 *(978-1-59679-876-2(9))* ABDO Publishing Co.

—Kelli y Avellino, 1 vol. 2006. (Primeros Sonidos Ser.). (Illus.). (J). (gr. k-3). (ENG & SPA.). 24p. lib. bdg. 24.21 *(978-1-59679-881-6(5),* SandCastle); (SPA., 23p. pap. 48.42 *(978-1-59679-882-3(3))* ABDO Publishing Co.

—Oliva y Oscar, 1 vol. Flores-Hanson, Lourdes & Rosso-White, Gloria, eds. 2006. (Primeros Sonidos Ser.). (ENG & SPA., Illus.). 24p. (J). (gr. k-3). lib. bdg. 24.21 *(978-1-59679-889-2(0),* SandCastle) ABDO Publishing Co.

—Olivia y Oscar. 2006. (Primeros Sonidos Ser.). (J). pap. 48.42 *(978-1-59679-890-8(4))* ABDO Publishing Co.

—Tonis y Tono, 1 vol. 2006. (Primeros Sonidos Ser.). (ENG & SPA., Illus.). 24p. (J). (gr. k-3). lib. bdg. 24.21 *(978-1-59679-887-8(4),* SandCastle) ABDO Publishing Co.

—Toñis y Toño. 2006. (Primeros Sonidos Ser.). (SPA., Illus.). 23p. (J). pap. 48.42 *(978-1-59679-888-5(2))* ABDO Publishing Co.

Celebramos las Fiestas. 2003. 23.95 *(978-0-673-77389-0(2))* Celebration Pr.

La Charreada. 2003. 23.95 *(978-0-673-77782-9(0))* Celebration Pr.

Los Cinco Hermanos. 2003. 23.95 *(978-0-673-77192-6(X))* Celebration Pr.

Los Cinco Sentidos. 2003. 23.95 *(978-0-673-77126-1(1))* Celebration Pr.

El Conejo Magico. 2003. 23.95 *(978-0-673-77191-9(1))* Celebration Pr.

Conozco una Viejita. 2003. 23.95 *(978-0-673-77364-7(7))* Celebration Pr.

Los Contrarios (Opposites) (SPA.). (J). 6.95 *(978-968-419-087-0(5))* Grijalbo, Editorial MEX. Dist: AIMS International Bks., Inc.

El Coqui: Big Book Packages. 2003. 64.95 *(978-0-673-58596-7(4))* Celebration Pr.

El Correo: Individual Title Two-Packs. (Chiquilibros Ser.). (SPA.). (gr. -1-1). 12.00 *(978-0-7635-8561-7(0))* Rigby Education.

Cual Contiene Mas? 2003. 23.95 *(978-0-673-77400-2(7))* Celebration Pr.

Cuando Me Bano. 2003. 23.95 *(978-0-673-77160-5(1))* Celebration Pr.

Cuando Sea Grande. 2003. 23.95 *(978-0-673-77388-3(4))* Celebration Pr.

Cuantos Hay? 2003. 23.95 *(978-0-673-77159-9(8))* Celebration Pr.

La Cucaracha: Big Book Packages. 2003. 64.95 *(978-0-673-58594-3(8))* Celebration Pr.

De Colores: Big Book Packages. 2003. 64.95 *(978-0-673-58602-5(2))* Celebration Pr.

Denne, B. & Irving, N. Easy Spanish. 2004. (Easy Languages Ser.). (SPA., Illus.). 128p. (J). (gr. 6-18). lib. bdg. 20.95 *(978-1-58086-431-2(7))* EDC Publishing.

Diaz-Cubero, Jose H. Practicas de Ortografia: 2 Grado. (SPA & ENG.). (J). (gr. 2). 9.95 *(978-84-357-0128-0(X),* CPR86) Ediciones y Distribuciones Codice, S.A. ESP. Dist: Continental Bk. Co., Inc.

Diez Ositos. 2003. 23.95 *(978-0-673-77362-3(0))* Celebration Pr.

Los Dinosaurios. 2003.Tr. of Great Dinosaur Search. 28.95 *(978-0-673-77403-3(1))* Celebration Pr.

Donde Aprendo Yo. 2003. (J). (gr. -1-2). 23.95 *(978-0-673-77390-6(6))* Celebration Pr.

Donde Juego Yo. 2003. 23.95 *(978-0-673-77185-8(7))* Celebration Pr.

Emberley, Rebecca. My Room/Mi Cuarto. 2005. (SPA & ENG., Illus.). 10p. (J). (gr. -1 — 1). bds. 6.99 *(978-0-316-00052-9(3))* Little, Brown Bks. for Young Readers.

En el Mercado. 2003. 23.95 *(978-0-673-77790-4(1))* Celebration Pr.

En Mi Jardin. 2003. 23.95 *(978-0-673-77131-5(8))* Celebration Pr.

Las Estaciones. 2003. 23.95 *(978-0-673-77127-8(X))* Celebration Pr.

Estoy Enojado. 2003. (J). (gr. -1-2). 23.95 *(978-0-673-77391-3(4))* Celebration Pr.

Fabulas Fabulosas. 2006. (SPA.). (J). *(978-1-933485-24-9(8))* Publicaciones Puertorriquenas, Inc.

Figueras, Ligaya, ed. En Plena Vista Level 1. Hazan, Maurice, illus. 5th ed. 2003. (SPA.). 140p. per. 22.00 *(978-1-932770-98-8(4),* SHB-SM) Symtalk, Inc.

Las Figuras Geometricas. 2003. 23.95 *(978-0-673-77123-0(7))* Celebration Pr.

Fui Al Mar. 2003. 23.95 *(978-0-673-77162-9(8))* Celebration Pr.

Gordon, Ronni L. & Stillman, David M. Cuaderno 2: An Intermediate Workbook for Grammar & Communication: Answer Key & Progress Checks, Vol. 2. 2004. (ENG & SPA.). (J). (gr. 6-12). pap., suppl. ed. *(978-0-8442-7927-5(7),* EC79277) Glencoe/McGraw-Hill.

Grades 1-2 Complete Pinata/Mas Pinata Package. 2003. 1943.95 *(978-0-673-58717-6(7))* Celebration Pr.

Hazan, Maurice. Saber, Deber, Querer, Poder: Symtalk Verb + Verb Infinitive Game for Spanish. (SPA.). (YA). 134.95 *(978-1-932770-49-0(6),* SG10) Symtalk, Inc.

Hazan, Maurice, creator. Spanish Conjugating Cards. (SPA.). 149.95 *(978-1-932770-86-5(0),* SCC) Symtalk, Inc.

—Los Verbos: Symtalk Verb Bingo. (SPA.). (J). 124.95 *(978-1-932770-40-7(2),* SG1) Symtalk, Inc.

Holt, Rinehart and Winston Staff. Ven Conmigo! Level 1: Cuaderno de Grammar. 3rd ed. 2003. (Â¡Ven Conmigo! Ser.). (SPA & ENG.). 112p. (gr. 6-6). pap. 16.10 *(978-0-03-064982-0(X))* Houghton Mifflin Harcourt Publishing Co.

—Ven Conmigo! Level 1: Cuaderno/Act. 3rd ed. 2003. (SPA.). pap., tchr. ed. 22.93 *(978-0-03-064981-3(1))* Holt McDougal.

—Ven Conmigo! Level 1: Cuadero/Hispanic. 3rd ed. 2003. (Holt ?Ven Conmigo! Ser.). (SPA & ENG.). 64p. (gr. 6-6). pap. 16.20 *(978-0-03-065538-8(2))* Houghton Mifflin Harcourt Publishing Co.

—Ven Conmigo! Level 2: Cuaderno de Act. 3rd ed. 2003. (Â¡Ven Conmigo! Ser.). (SPA & ENG.). 160p. (gr. 8-8). pap. 20.15 *(978-0-03-064986-8(2))* Houghton Mifflin Harcourt Publishing Co.

—Ven Conmigo! Level 2: Cuaderno de Grammar. 3rd ed. 2003. (Â¡Ven Conmigo! Ser.). (SPA & ENG.). 112p. (gr. 8-8). pap. 16.55 *(978-0-03-064983-7(8))* Houghton Mifflin Harcourt Publishing Co.

—Ven Conmigo! Level 2: Cuadero/Hispanic. 3rd ed. 2003. (SPA.). pap. 14.60 *(978-0-03-065546-3(3))* Holt McDougal.

A La Cama! 2003. 23.95 *(978-0-673-77399-9(X))* Celebration Pr.

Lakeshore Learning Materials Staff, contrib. by. Spanish Alphabet Big Book. 2006. (SPA.). (J). pap. 19.95 *(978-1-59746-000-2(1))* Lakeshore Learning Materials.

Lasetras. 2003. 23.95 *(978-0-673-77167-4(9))* Celebration Pr.

Leeme un Cuento. 2003. 23.95 *(978-0-673-77189-6(X))* Celebration Pr.

Lengua Espanola: Cuarto Grado. (SPA & ENG.). (J). (gr. 4). 21.95 *(978-84-357-0027-6(5),* CPR76) Ediciones y Distribuciones Codice, S.A. ESP. Dist: Continental Bk. Co., Inc.

Lengua Espanola: Quinto Grado. (SPA & ENG.). (J). (gr. 5). 22.00 *(978-84-357-0171-6(9),* CPR78) Ediciones y Distribuciones Codice, S.A. ESP. Dist: Continental Bk. Co., Inc.

Lengua Espanola: Segundo Grado. (SPA & ENG.). (J). (gr. 2). 17.95 *(978-84-357-0137-2(9),* CPR72) Ediciones y Distribuciones Codice, S.A. ESP. Dist: Continental Bk. Co., Inc.

Lengua Espanola: Sexto Grado. (SPA & ENG.). (J). (gr. 6). 22.00 *(978-84-357-0170-9(0),* CPR80) Ediciones y Distribuciones Codice, S.A. ESP. Dist: Continental Bk. Co., Inc.

Lengua Espanola: Tercer Grado. (SPA & ENG.). (J). (gr. 3). 17.95 *(978-84-357-0028-3(3),* CPR74) Ediciones y Distribuciones Codice, S.A. ESP. Dist: Continental Bk. Co., Inc.

Lo Que Sale De un Huevo. 2003. 23.95 *(978-0-673-77161-2(X))* Celebration Pr.

Looking for Insects. 2003. (J). 28.95 *(978-0-673-78112-3(7))* Celebration Pr.

Los Tres Deseos. 2003. 23.95 *(978-0-673-77193-3(8))* Celebration Pr.

Lupita Y David. 2003. (J). (gr. -1-2). 28.95 *(978-0-673-77380-7(9))* Celebration Pr.

Las Maquinas. 2003. (J). (gr. -1-2). 28.95 *(978-0-673-77401-9(5))* Celebration Pr.

La Mariposa. 2003.Tr. of Butterfly. 23.95 *(978-0-673-77125-4(3))* Celebration Pr.

Las Mariposas de Alicia. 2003. 28.95 *(978-0-673-78105-5(4))* Celebration Pr.

La Mariquita Triste. 2003. 23.95 *(978-0-673-77795-9(2))* Celebration Pr.

Mazzeo, J. L. Aimee's A Book (BL) el libro A de Aimée, 1. 2007. (My Letter Library Ser.: 1). (SPA., Illus.). (J). pap. 10.95 *(978-1-59646-420-9(8));* lib. bdg. 23.60 *(978-1-59646-419-3(4))* Dingles & Co.

—Cassie's C Book (BL) el libro C de Cassie: S, 3 vols. 2007. (My Letter Library Ser.: 3). (SPA & ENG., Illus.). (J). lib. bdg. 23.60 *(978-1-59646-431-5(3))* Dingles & Co.

—Cassie's C Book (BL) el libro C de Cassie (PB), 3 vols. 2007. (My Letter Library Ser.: 3). (SPA & ENG., Illus.). (J). pap. 10.95 *(978-1-59646-432-2(1))* Dingles & Co.

—Zach's Z Book (BL) el libro Z de Zach, 26 vols. 2007. (My Letter Library Ser.: 26). (SPA & ENG., Illus.). (J). lib. bdg. 23.60 *(978-1-59646-569-5(7))* Dingles & Co.

—Zach's Z Book (BL) el libro Z de Zach (PB), 26 vols. 2007. (My Letter Library Ser.: 26). (SPA & ENG., Illus.). (J). pap. 10.95 *(978-1-59646-570-1(0))* Dingles & Co.

S

Me Encontre una Piedra. 2003. 23.95 *(978-0-673-77158-2(X))* Celebration Pr.
Me Siento Feliz. 2003. (J). (gr. -1-2). 23.95 *(978-0-673-77394-4(9))* Celebration Pr.
Mi Bicicleta. 2003. 23.95 *(978-0-673-77775-1(6))* Celebration Pr.
Mi Camion. 2003. 23.95 *(978-0-673-77780-5(4))* Celebration Pr.
Mi Casa Nueva. 2003. 23.95 *(978-0-673-77172-8(5))* Celebration Pr.
Mi Cuerpo. 2003. 23.95 *(978-0-673-77124-7(5))* Celebration Pr.
Mi Dia. 2003. 23.95 *(978-0-673-77165-0(2))* Celebration Pr.
Mi Gatito Fachoso. 2003. 23.95 *(978-0-673-77176-6(8))* Celebration Pr.
Mi Libro de Cocina. 2003. (Illus.). 28.95 *(978-0-673-78085-0(6))* Celebration Pr.
Mi Mama Trabaja. 2003. 23.95 *(978-0-673-77184-1(9))* Celebration Pr.
A Mi Me Gusta. 2003. 23.95 *(978-0-673-77387-6(6))* Celebration Pr.
Mi Mejor Amigo. 2003. 23.95 *(978-0-673-77181-0(4))* Celebration Pr.
Mi Mundo. 2003. (J). (gr. -1-2). 23.95 *(978-0-673-77406-4(6))* Celebration Pr.
Mi Muneco De Nieve. 2003. 23.95 *(978-0-673-77779-9(0))* Celebration Pr.
Mi Nana Chalita. 2003. 23.95 *(978-0-673-77171-1(7))* Celebration Pr.
Milet Publishing Staff. Music - English-Spanish. 2012. (My First Bilingual Book Ser.). (SPA & ENG., Illus.). 24p. (J). (gr. k — 1). bds. 7.99 *(978-1-84059-728-8(3))* Milet Publishing.
—My First Bilingual Book-Sports (English-Spanish) 2012. (My First Bilingual Book Ser.). (SPA & ENG., Illus.). 24p. (J). (gr. k — 1). bds. 7.99 *(978-1-84059-760-8(7))* Milet Publishing.
Mis Cinco Perritos. 2003. 23.95 *(978-0-673-77363-0(9))* Celebration Pr.
Mis Comidas Favoritas. 2003. (SPA.). 23.95 *(978-0-673-77799-7(5))* Celebration Pr.
Mis Mascotas. 2003. 23.95 *(978-0-673-77177-3(6))* Celebration Pr.
Mis Zapatos Ruevos. 2003. 23.95 *(978-0-673-77188-9(1))* Celebration Pr.
More Pizza. 2003. 28.95 *(978-0-673-78111-6(9))* Celebration Pr.
Muchos Frijoles. 2003. 23.95 *(978-0-673-77774-4(X))* Celebration Pr.
La Muneca Azul. 2003. (J). (gr. -1-2). 23.95 *(978-0-673-77383-8(3))* Celebration Pr.
La Muneca Azul: Poems, Rhymes, & Songs Listening Packs. 2003. 34.50 *(978-0-673-58631-5(6))* Celebration Pr.
My Grandma's Memory Trunk. 2003. 28.95 *(978-0-673-78110-9(0))* Celebration Pr.
Necesito Mi Desayuno. 2003. 23.95 *(978-0-673-77178-0(4))* Celebration Pr.
No Les Tengo Miedo. 2003. 23.95 *(978-0-673-77130-8(X))* Celebration Pr.
No Me Quiero Banar. 2003. (J). (gr. -1-2). 23.95 *(978-0-673-77395-1(7))* Celebration Pr.
No Quiero Ir Al Dentista. 2003. 23.95 *(978-0-673-77174-2(1))* Celebration Pr.
Oscar. 2003. 23.95 *(978-0-673-77369-2(8))* Celebration Pr.
A Paco. 2003. 23.95 *(978-0-673-77797-3(9))* Celebration Pr.
Palencia, Ramon. Uso de la Gramatica Junior Avanzado. (SPA.). 128p. 24.95 *(978-84-7711-555-7(9))* Edelsa Grupo Didascalia, S.A. ESP. Dist: Distribooks, Inc.
Las Partes De una Planta. 2003. (J). (gr. -1-2). 23.95 *(978-0-673-77402-6(3))* Celebration Pr.
Pattis, Anne-Francoise. Let's Learn Spanish Coloring Book. 2003. (SPA & ENG., Illus.). 64p. pap. 9.00 *(978-0-07-142142-3(4),* 0071421424) McGraw-Hill Education.
Pedro, Pedrito. 2003. (J). (gr. -1-2). 23.95 *(978-0-673-77384-5(1))* Celebration Pr.
Pedro, Pedrito: Big Book Packages. 2003. 64.95 *(978-0-673-58598-1(0))* Celebration Pr.
Pedro, Pedrito: Poems, Rhymes, & Songs Listening Packs. 2003. 34.50 *(978-0-673-58632-2(4))* Celebration Pr.
La Primavera. 2003. (J). (gr. -1-2). 23.95 *(978-0-673-77385-2(X))* Celebration Pr.
La Primavera: Poems, Rhymes, & Songs Listening Packs. 2003. 34.50 *(978-0-673-58633-9(2))* Celebration Pr.
Primer Dia de Clases. 2003. 23.95 *(978-0-673-77187-2(3))* Celebration Pr.
Que Alegria! 2003. 23.95 *(978-0-673-77173-5(3))* Celebration Pr.
Que Comes Tu? 2003. 23.95 *(978-0-673-77186-5(5))* Celebration Pr.
Que Dia Es Hoy? 2003. 23.95 *(978-0-673-77157-5(1))* Celebration Pr.
Que Mala Suerte! 2003. (J). (gr. -1-2). 23.95 *(978-0-673-77398-2(1))* Celebration Pr.
Que Me Pongo? 2003. (J). (gr. -1-2). 23.95 *(978-0-673-77407-1(4))* Celebration Pr.
Que Me Pongo? Big Book Packages. 2003. 64.95 *(978-0-673-58599-8(9))* Celebration Pr.
Que Miedo! 2003. 23.95 *(978-0-673-77794-2(4))* Celebration Pr.
Ranchetti, Sebastiano. Animal Opposites/Opuestos Animales. 2008. (Learn with Animals/Aprende con los Animales Ser.). (SPA & ENG., Illus.). 24p. (gr. -1-2). lib. bdg. 22.00 *(978-0-8368-9038-9(8),* Weekly Reader Leveled Readers) Stevens, Gareth Publishing LLLP.
—Opuestos Animales. 2008. (Learn with Animals;Aprende con los animales Ser.). (SPA & ENG., Illus.). 24p. (gr. -1-2). pap. 8.15 *(978-0-8368-9043-3(4),* Weekly Reader Leveled Readers) Stevens, Gareth Publishing LLLP.
Saber Es Poder: A Basic Grammar Book, Easy, Fun & Practical. (ENG & SPA.). 45.00 *(978-0-944356-08-1(7))* Alegria Hispana Pubns.
Sigmar Staff. Sinonimos - Ant - Paraonimos (Synonyms - Ant - Homonyms) (SPA.). (J). 9.95 *(978-950-11-0639-8(X))* Sigmar ARG. Dist: AIMS International Bks., Inc.
La Sirenita. 2003. (SPA.). 28.95 *(978-0-673-77379-1(5))* Celebration Pr.
Thayer, Tanya. La Primavera. Translations.com Staff, tr. 2005. (Mi Primer Paso Al Mundo Real Las Estaciones Del Ano (First Step Nonfiction - Seasons) Ser.).Tr. of Spring. (SPA., Illus.). 24p. (gr. k-2). lib. bdg. 23.93 *(978-0-8225-3165-4(8));* per. 6.95 *(978-0-8225-3158-6(5))* Lerner Publishing Group.
Thomas, Keith A. The Idioms. Thomas, Keith A., illus. (ENG & SPA., Illus.). 44p. (J). (gr. 3-18). pap. *(978-0-9617451-4-1(2))* KALEXT Productions, LLC.
La Tostada. 2003. 23.95 *(978-0-673-77800-0(2))* Celebration Pr.
Travis, Joelle & Figueras, Ligaya, eds. Numeros, Colores, Verbos y Frases. Hazan, Maurice, illus. 2003. (SPA.). 112p. (J). per. 20.00 *(978-1-932770-17-9(8),* SWLB2) Symtalk, Inc.
Tulip, Jenny. My First Spanish Word Book. 2004. (ENG & SPA., Illus.). 48p. (J). 5.99 *(978-1-85854-394-9(0))* Brimax Books Ltd. GBR. Dist: Byeway Bks.
Vaamonde, Conchita, tr. My First Spanish Words. Tulip, Jenny, illus. 2004. (SPA.). 12p. (J). bds. 7.99 *(978-1-85854-512-7(9))* Brimax Books Ltd. GBR. Dist: Byeway Bks.
Wise, Sue. Cómo se Dice... ? Coirault, Christine, illus. 2006. (How I Say That? Ser.). (ENG & SPA.). 32p. (gr. k-4). lib. bdg. 26.00 *(978-0-8368-6259-1(7),* Gareth Stevens Learning Library) Stevens, Gareth Publishing LLLP.
—How Do I Say That? (¿Cómo se Dice?) Coirault, Christine, illus. 2006. (How Do I Say That?/ Como se dice? Ser.). (ENG & SPA.). 32p. (gr. k-4). pap. 10.50 *(978-0-8368-6583-7(9),* Gareth Stevens Learning Library) Stevens, Gareth Publishing LLLP.
With addition of Elefonetica Phonics Storybooks Green & Orange Collections. (De Canciones A Cuentos Ser.). (SPA.). (gr. 1-18). 987.10 *(978-0-7362-0703-4(1))* CENGAGE Learning.
Zocchi, Judith Mazzeo. Will's W Book: El Libro "W" de Will. 2005. (ENG & SPA., Illus.). *(978-1-59646-553-4(0))* Dingles & Co.
Zocchi, Judith Mazzeo, et al. Aimee's a Book: El Libro a de Aimee. Revutsky, Helen Ross, illus. 2005. (J). *(978-1-59646-421-6(6))* Dingles & Co.
—Bebe's "B" Book: El Libro "B" de Bibi. Revutsky, Helen Ross, illus. 2005. (SPA & ENG.). (J). *(978-1-59646-427-8(5))* Dingles & Co.
—Delia's D Book: El Libro D de Delia. Revutsky, Helen Ross, illus. 2005. (SPA.). (J). *(978-1-59646-439-1(9))* Dingles & Co.
—Tad's "T" Book: El Libro "T" de Tad. 2005. (ENG & SPA., Illus.). (J). *(978-1-59646-535-0(2))* Dingles & Co.
—Vera's "V" Book: El Libro "V" de Vera. 2005. (ENG & SPA., Illus.). (J). *(978-1-59646-547-3(6))* Dingles & Co.
—Xavia's "X" Book: El Libro "X" de Xavia. Revutsky, Helen Ross, illus. 2005. (SPA.). *(978-1-59646-559-6(X))* Dingles & Co.
Zocchi, Judy. Cassie's "C" Book: El Libro "C" de Cassie. 2005. (SPA & ENG., Illus.). (J). *(978-1-59646-433-9(X))* Dingles & Co.

SPANISH LANGUAGE—READERS

Abrapalabra! (SPA.). (gr. -1-1). 161.67 *(978-0-7362-2592-2(7))* CENGAGE Learning.
Abuelita y Yo. (Spanish Early Intervention Levels Ser.). (SPA.). 23.10 *(978-1-56334-777-1(6))* CENGAGE Learning.
Acento 1: Cuaderno de Ortografia. (SPA.). (J). (gr. 1-9). 16.00 *(978-958-04-3823-6(4))* Norma S.A. COL. Dist: Distribuidora Norma, Inc.
Acento 2: Cuaderno de Ortografia. (SPA.). (J). 16.00 *(978-958-04-3822-9(6))* Norma S.A. COL. Dist: Distribuidora Norma, Inc.
Acento 3: Cuaderno de Ortografia. (SPA.). (J). (gr. 1-9). 16.00 *(978-958-04-3821-2(8))* Norma S.A. COL. Dist: Distribuidora Norma, Inc.
Acento 4: Cuaderno de Ortografia. (SPA.). (J). (gr. 1-9). 16.00 *(978-958-04-3820-5(X))* Norma S.A. COL. Dist: Distribuidora Norma, Inc.
Acento 5: Cuaderno de Ortografia. (SPA.). (J). (gr. 1-9). 16.00 *(978-958-04-3819-9(6))* Norma S.A. COL. Dist: Distribuidora Norma, Inc.
Acento 6: Cuaderno de Ortografia. (SPA.). (J). (gr. 1-9). 16.00 *(978-958-04-3829-8(3))* Norma S.A. COL. Dist: Distribuidora Norma, Inc.
Acento 7: Cuaderno de Ortografia. (SPA.). (J). (gr. 1-9). 16.00 *(978-958-04-3830-4(7))* Norma S.A. COL. Dist: Distribuidora Norma, Inc.
Adivinalo!, 6, Pack. (Literatura 2000 Ser.). (SPA.). (gr. k-1). 28.00 *(978-0-7635-1009-1(2))* Rigby Education.
El Aeropuerto, 2, Pack. (Chiquilibros Ser.). (SPA.). (gr. -1-1). 12.00 *(978-0-7635-8557-0(2))* Rigby Education.
Aguilar, Jose. Jovenes piratas/Youngs Pirates. 2008. 36p. *(978-84-934160-7-2(X))* Atalante.
Ahumada. Juguemos a Leer-Texto.Tr. of Lets Play to Read. (SPA.). (J). 7.98 *(978-968-24-5631-2(2))* Trillas Editorial, S. A. MEX. Dist: Continental Bk. Co., Inc.
Al Circo, Al Circo! 2003. 63.50 *(978-0-8136-8085-9(9));* suppl. ed. 8.95 *(978-0-8136-8082-8(4))* Modern Curriculum Pr.
Alagna, Magdalena. Wyatt Earp: Lawman of the American West / Sheriff del oeste Americano. 2009. (Famous People in American History/Grandes personajes en la historia de los Estados Unidos Ser.). (ENG & SPA.). 32p. (gr. 2-3). 47.90 *(978-1-61512-558-6(2),* Editorial Buenas Letras) Rosen Publishing Group, Inc., The.
—Wyatt Earp: Sheriff del oeste americano (Wyatt Earp: Lawman of the American West) 2009. (Grandes personajes en la historia de los Estados Unidos (Famous People in American History) Ser.). (SPA.). 32p. (gr. 2-3). 47.90 *(978-1-61512-811-2(5),* Editorial Buenas Letras) Rosen Publishing Group, Inc., The.
Alcántara, Ricardo. Cuenta Estrellas.Tr. of Counting Stars. (SPA.). 64p. (J). (gr. 3-5). 6.36 *(978-84-261-2146-2(2))* Juventud, Editorial ESP. Dist: Lectorum Pubns., Inc.
Alfaro Sifontes, Manuel Guillermo. Alboroto en un Lugar Remoto. 2005. (Illus.). 32p. (J). *(978-1-58018-052-8(3))* Cambridge BrickHouse, Inc.
Allsop, Marcus. Nos gustan nuestros dientes / we like our Teeth. 2011th alt. ed. 2012. (We Like Toi Ser.). (ENG.). 32p. pap. 10.95 *(978-1-935826-09-5(3))* Kalindi Pr.
Aloian, Molly. Columbus Day. 2010. (ENG., Illus.). 32p. (J). *(978-0-7787-4760-4(3));* pap. *(978-0-7787-4778-9(6))* Crabtree Publishing Co.
Alphabet Sorting Box. (gr. -1-12). 22.40 *(978-0-7362-1095-9(4))* CENGAGE Learning.
Alvarez, Julia. Devolver Al Remitente. 2010.Tr. of Return to Sender. (SPA & ENG.). 368p. (J). (gr. 3-7). 7.99 *(978-0-375-85124-7(0),* Yearling) Random Hse. Children's Bks.
Alvarez, Mrinali, illus. Pon, Pon: ¡A Jugar con el Bebé! 2005. (SPA.). 28p. (J). 8.95 *(978-0-8477-1550-3(7))* Univ. of Puerto Rico Pr.
Amanecer Grade K: Student Anthology. (Nuevos Horizontes Ser.). (SPA.). (J). 9.95 *(978-1-56014-499-1(8))* Santillana USA Publishing Co., Inc.
Ambrus, Victor G. Busca a Dracula (Search for Dracula) (J). 5.95 *(978-950-08-1288-7(6))* Atlantida ARG. Dist: AIMS International Bks., Inc.
—Cuenta con Dracula (Count with Dracula) (J). 5.95 *(978-950-08-1286-3(X))* Atlantida ARG. Dist: AIMS International Bks., Inc.
—Lee Con Dracula (Read with Dracula) (J). 5.95 *(978-950-08-1287-0(8))* Atlantida ARG. Dist: AIMS International Bks., Inc.
—Que Hora Es, Dracula? (What Time Is It, Dracula?) (J). 5.95 *(978-950-08-1285-6(1))* Atlantida ARG. Dist: AIMS International Bks., Inc.
Amigos, 6 vols., Pack. (Literatura 2000 Ser.). (SPA.). (gr. k-1). 28.00 *(978-0-7635-1010-7(6))* Rigby Education.
Los amigos del Mono, 6 Pack. (Literatura 2000 Ser.). (SPA.). (gr. 1-2). 28.00 *(978-0-7635-1033-6(5))* Rigby Education.
Amigos para Siempre: Individual Title Six-Packs. (Literatura 2000 Ser.). (SPA.). (gr. 2-3). 33.00 *(978-0-7635-1081-7(5))* Rigby Education.
El Amor de Beatriz. (SPA.). pap. 5.95 *(978-88-8148-806-3(X))* EMC/Paradigm Publishing.
Anastasio, Dina. How Raven Became Black & Owl Got Its Spots & Por qué el cuervo es negro y el búho tiene Manchitas: 6 English, 6 Spanish Adaptations. 2011. (ENG & SPA.). (J). 75.00 net. *(978-1-4108-5626-5(7))* Benchmark Education Co.
Anaya Publishers Staff. Aprender a Vivir 1. (SPA.). 56p. (J). *(978-84-207-7136-6(8))* Grupo Anaya, S.A.
—Aprender a Vivir 2. (SPA.). (J). *(978-84-207-7190-8(2))* Grupo Anaya, S.A.
—Aprender a Vivir 3. (SPA.). 88p. (J). *(978-84-207-6555-6(4))* Grupo Anaya, S.A.
—Aprender a Vivir 3: Propuesta Didactica. (SPA.). 128p. (J). *(978-84-207-6556-3(2))* Grupo Anaya, S.A.
—Aprender a Vivir 4. (SPA.). 88p. (J). *(978-84-207-6557-0(0))* Grupo Anaya, S.A.
—Aprender a Vivir 4: Propuesta Didactica. (SPA.). 128p. (J). *(978-84-207-6558-7(9))* Grupo Anaya, S.A.
—Aprender a Vivir 5. (SPA.). 88p. (J). *(978-84-207-6559-4(7))* Grupo Anaya, S.A.
—Aprender a Vivir 5: Propuesta Didactica. (SPA.). 128p. (J). *(978-84-207-6560-0(0))* Grupo Anaya, S.A.
—Aprender a Vivir 6. (SPA.). 88p. (J). *(978-84-207-6561-7(9))* Grupo Anaya, S.A.
—Aprender a Vivir 6: Propuesta Didactica. (SPA.). 128p. (J). *(978-84-207-6562-4(7))* Grupo Anaya, S.A.
Anaya, Rudolfo. The First Tortilla: A Bilingual Story. Lamadrid, Enrique R., tr. Córdova, Amy, illus. 2012. (ENG & SPA.). 32p. (J). pap. 16.95 *(978-0-8263-4215-7(9))* Univ. of New Mexico Pr.
Anaya, Rudolfo A. La Llorona: The Crying Woman. Lamadrid, Enrique R., tr. Córdova, Amy, illus. 2011. (SPA & ENG.). 40p. (J). 19.95 *(978-0-8263-4460-1(7))* Univ. of New Mexico Pr.
Andersen, Hans Christian. Princess & the Pea (La Princesa y el Guisante) Estrada, Pau, illus. 2013. (Bilingual Fairy Tales Ser.). (SPA & ENG.). 32p. (J). (gr. 1-4). lib. bdg. 28.50 *(978-1-60753-357-3(X))* Amicus Publishing.
El Apicultor, 6 vols., Pack. (Literatura 2000 Ser.). (SPA.). (gr. 2-3). 33.00 *(978-0-7635-1083-1(1))* Rigby Education.
Appleby, Alex. It's Sunny! / Est Soleado! 2013. (What's the Weather? / Qu Tiempo Hace? Ser.). (SPA & ENG., Illus.). 24p. (J). (gr. k-2). 22.60 *(978-1-4339-9454-8(2))* Stevens, Gareth Publishing LLLP.
—It's Windy! / Est Ventoso! 2013. (What's the Weather? / Qu Tiempo Hace? Ser.). (SPA & ENG., Illus.). 24p. (J). (gr. k-2). 22.60 *(978-1-4339-9452-4(6))* Stevens, Gareth Publishing LLLP.
—Lo Que Toco / What I Touch. 2014. (Mis Cinco Sentidos / My Five Senses Ser.). (SPA.). 24p. (J). (gr. k-2). 22.60 *(978-1-4824-0877-5(5))* Stevens, Gareth Publishing LLLP.
April, Elyse. We Like to Move - Spanish / English Edition: Exercise Is Fun. 2012. (We Like To Ser.). (SPA & ENG., Illus.). 32p. pap. 10.95 *(978-1-935826-08-8(5))* Kalindi Pr.
Aquel que Escucha: Individual Title Six-Packs. (Literatura 2000 Ser.). (SPA.). (gr. 2-3). 33.00 *(978-0-7635-1084-8(X))* Rigby Education.
Aquellos Dias de Dinosaurios: Little Book, Level 14, Vol. 14. 2003. (Fonolibros Ser.). 35.50 *(978-0-7652-0124-9(0))* Modern Curriculum Pr.
El arbol de Diego: Individual Title Six-Packs. (Literatura 2000 Ser.). (SPA.). (gr. 1-2). 28.00 *(978-0-7635-1034-3(3))* Rigby Education.
El arbol de la Miel: Individual Title Six-Packs. (Literatura 2000 Ser.). (SPA.). (gr. 2-3). 33.00 *(978-0-7635-1254-5(0))* Rigby Education.
Are We There Yet, Mama? 2003. 23.95 *(978-0-673-78136-9(4))* Celebration Pr.
Arnold, George. Los Gatos of the CIA. 2005. (SPA & ENG., Illus.). 225p. pap. 22.95 *(978-1-57168-861-3(7),* Nortex Pr.) Eakin Pr.
Arrugas: Individual Title Six-Packs. (Literatura 2000 Ser.). (SPA.). (gr. 1-2). 28.00 *(978-0-7635-1035-0(1))* Rigby Education.
Aventuras Infantiles/Adventures for Kids. (ENG & SPA.). 80p. (J). 17.00 *(978-0-944356-04-3(4))* Alegria Hispana Pubns.
Avignon, Marie-Claude. Mi Primer Larousse de las Ciencias: De la Vida y de la Tierra. Larousse Staff, ed. 2006. (Mi Primer Larousse Ser.). (SPA., Illus.). 160p. (gr. -1-3). 19.95 *(978-970-22-1231-7(6))* Larousse, Ediciones, S. A. de C. V. MEX. Dist: Houghton Mifflin Harcourt Publishing Co.
Ayer Vino Santa Clos: Individual, 6-packs. 2003. 23.95 *(978-0-673-77137-7(7))* Celebration Pr.
AZ Books Staff. Animales - Farm Animals: Farm Animals. Gorbachenok, Ekaterina, ed. 2012. (Spanish for Kids Ser.). (ENG & SPA.). 10p. (J). (gr. -1-k). 11.95 *(978-1-61889-135-8(9))* AZ Bks. LLC.
—Colores - Colorful Animals: Colorful Animals. Gorbachenok, Ekaterina, ed. 2012. (Spanish for Kids Ser.). (ENG & SPA.). 10p. (J). (gr. -1-k). bds. 11.95 *(978-1-61889-136-5(7))* AZ Bks. LLC.
—Numeros - Count the Toys: Count the Toys. Gorbachenok, Ekaterina, ed. 2012. (Spanish for Kids Ser.). (ENG & SPA.). 10p. (J). (-k). bds. 11.95 *(978-1-61889-137-2(5))* AZ Bks. LLC.
Baca, Ana. Tia's Tamales. Chilton, Noel, illus. (ENG & SPA.). 32p. 2012. (J). pap. 16.95 *(978-0-8263-5027-5(5))* 2011. (YA). (gr. 4-18). 16.95 *(978-0-8263-5026-8(7))* Univ. of New Mexico Pr.
Bain, Michelle. The Adventures of Thumbs up Johnnie Rules of Thumb for Going Green: Rules of Thumb for Going Green. Lizana, Lorenzo, illus. 2008. 18p. (J). pap. 5.95 *(978-0-9795832-4-7(1))* Pixie Stuff LLC.
—Las aventuras de Juanito el Pulgarcito Zipp, Pequeño Dígito, las señales y las Señas: Zipp, Pequeño Digito, las señales y las Señas. Lizana, Lorenzo, illus. 2007.Tr. of Zipp, Digit & the Happy Signs! (SPA.). 28p. (J). *(978-0-9795832-3-0(3))* Pixie Stuff LLC.
El bano de Benito. (Spanish Early Intervention Levels Ser.). (SPA.). 21.30 *(978-0-7362-0824-6(0))* CENGAGE Learning.
El Bano de Papa, 6, Pack. (Literatura 2000 Ser.). (SPA.). (gr. 1-2). 28.00 *(978-0-7635-1058-9(0))* Rigby Education.
Bansch, Helga. Petra. 2010. (SPA., Illus.). 48p. (J). 15.95 *(978-84-9871-003-8(0))* OQO, Editora ESP. Dist: Baker & Taylor Bks.
Barker, Henry. Vino Del Espacio (It Came from Outer Space) Gott, Barry, illus. 2009. (Science Solves It! (r) en Espanol Ser.). (SPA.). (gr. 1-3). pap. 33.92 *(978-1-58013-771-3(7))* Lerner Publishing Group.
Barner, Bob. The Day of the Dead (El Día de los Muerto) Mlawer, Teresa, tr. Barner, Bob, illus. 2011. (ENG., Illus.). 32p. (J). pap. 7.99 *(978-0-8234-2381-1(6))* Holiday Hse., Inc.
Barredo, Jose Eduardo. Mundo Azul. (Torre de Papel Ser.). (SPA.). 284p. (YA). (gr. 7-18). 7.95 *(978-958-04-4522-7(2))* Norma S.A. COL. Dist: Distribuidora Norma, Inc.
Un Barrio Muy Especial. (Coleccion Leo Con Figuras). (SPA., Illus.). 14p. (J). pap. 4.50 *(978-950-11-0928-3(3),* SGM293) Sigmar ARG. Dist: Continental Bk. Co., Inc.
Barry, Frances. Salvemos a Los Animales. 2012. (SPA.). 26p. (J). (gr. k-1). pap. 23.99 *(978-84-261-3856-9(X))* Juventud, Editorial ESP. Dist: Lectorum Pubns., Inc.
Beaton, Clare & Blackstone, Stella. Un Alce, Veinte Ratones. Beaton, Clare, illus. 2006.Tr. of One Moose, Twenty Mice. (ENG., Illus.). 32p. (J). (gr. -1-k). bds. 6.99 *(978-1-84686-019-5(9))* Barefoot Bks., Inc.
Beaude, Pierre Marie. Flora, la Desconocida del Espacio. (Torre de Papel Ser.). (SPA.). (YA). (gr. 6-18). 7.95 *(978-958-04-1033-1(X))* Norma S.A. COL. Dist: Distribuidora Norma, Inc.
Beck, Paul. El Cuerpo Humano. Fairman, Jennifer, illus. 2007. (SPA.). 48p. (J). (gr. k-5). *(978-970-718-436-7(1),* Silver Dolphin en Español) Advanced Marketing, S. de R. L. de C. V.
Beckstrand, Karl. Crumbs on the Stairs - Migas en Las Escaleras: A Mystery. Beckstrand, Karl, illus. 2011. (Mini-Mysteries for Minors Ser.: 2).Tr. of Migas en Las Escaleras. (ENG & SPA., Illus.). 24p. (J). pap. 14.95 *(978-0-9776065-9-7(7),* Gozo Bks.) Premio Publishing & Gozo Bks., LLC.
Beltran, Andrea. Juliet's Day. 2009. 34p. pap. 24.20 *(978-0-557-18983-0(7))* Lulu Pr., Inc.
Benchmark Education Company, LLC Staff. Spanish Emergent Supplement. 2005. (BookRoom Collection Ser.). (J). spiral bd. 880.00 *(978-1-4108-5613-5(5))* Benchmark Education Co.
Benchmark Education Company, LLC Staff, compiled by. Spanish Early/Fluent Supplement. 2005. spiral bd. 1350.00 *(978-1-4108-5661-6(5))* Benchmark Education Co.
—Spanish Grade 3 Small Group Set. 2005. spiral bd. 4000.00 *(978-1-4108-5667-8(4));* spiral bd. 1000.00 *(978-1-4108-5668-5(2))* Benchmark Education Co.
—Spanish Grade 4 Small Group Set. 2005. spiral bd. 1000.00 *(978-1-4108-5670-8(4));* spiral bd. 4000.00 *(978-1-4108-5669-2(0))* Benchmark Education Co.
—Spanish Grade 5 Small Group Set. 2005. spiral bd. 1000.00 *(978-1-4108-4960-1(0))* Benchmark Education Co.
Benegas, Candela. Una Rayuela: Level 1. (SPA & ENG.). 128p. (J). (gr. 3-7). stu. ed. 21.95 *(978-84-7143-804-1(6),* SGS8046) Sociedad General Espanola de Libreria ESP. Dist: Continental Bk. Co., Inc.
Benoist, Cathy & Gilmore, Cathy. El Conejito de Pascua: El Cuento de un Dia Extraordinario. Sundy, Jonathan, illus. 2014. (SPA.). 40p. (J). (gr. 4-7). 16.99 *(978-0-7648-2456-2(2),* Libros Liguori) Liguori Pubns.
Berkes, Marianne. El árbol Que Trepó el Oso, 1 vol. Rietz, Kathleen, illus. 2012. (SPA.). 32p. (J). (gr. -1-3). 17.95 *(978-1-60718-679-3(9))* Arbordale Publishing.
Bernier-Grand, Carmen T. Shake It, Morena! And Other Folklore from Puerto Rico. Delacre, Lulu, illus. 2007. 48p. (J). (gr. -1-3). per. 6.95 *(978-0-8225-7026-4(2),* First Avenue Editions) Lerner Publishing Group.
Bertrand, Diane Gonzales. El Momento de Trino. Sanmiguel, Rosario, tr. from ENG. 2006. (SPA.). 181p. (J). (gr. 3-7). per. 9.95 *(978-1-55885-473-4(8),* Piñata Books) Arte Publico Pr.
Bertrand, Diane Gonzales & Ventura, Gabriela Baeza. The Party for Papá Luis/La Fiesta para Papá Luis. Galindo, Alejandro, illus. 2010. (ENG.). 32p. (J). (gr. -1-3). 16.95 *(978-1-55885-532-8(7))* Arte Publico Pr.
Biblioteca Saltamontes Spanish Chapter Books Coleccion Viva Chivito! Classroom Set & Manipulatives. (SPA.). (gr. 1-2). 521.25 incl. reel tape *(978-0-7362-1589-3(1));* 517.82 incl. audio compact disk *(978-0-7362-1591-6(3))* CENGAGE Learning.
La Bicicross de Alex: Individual Title Six-Packs. (Literatura 2000 Ser.). (SPA.). (gr. 1-2). 28.00 *(978-0-7635-1036-7(X))* Rigby Education.
Biello, David. Portaaviones: Por dentro y por fuera (Aircraft Carriers: Inside & Out) 2009. (Tecnología: Mapas para el Futuro Ser.). (SPA.). 48p. (gr. 4-4). 53.00 *(978-1-60853-287-2(9),* Editorial Buenas Letras) Rosen Publishing Group, Inc., The.
Bienvenidos! (Illus.). 96p. (J). (gr. k-5). Level 1. (ENG & SPA.). pap., wbk. ed. 18.95 *(978-88-8148-038-8(7))*Level 2. (SPA & ENG., pap., wbk. ed. 18.95 *(978-88-8148-045-6(X))*Level 3. (SPA & ENG., pap., wbk. ed. 18.95 *(978-88-8148-046-3(8))* European Language Institute ITA. Dist: Distribooks, Inc.

Blackaby, Susan. El Lugar de Luis, 1 vol. Ruiz, Carlos, tr. from ENG. Gallagher-Cole, Mernie, illus. 2006. (Read-It! Readers en Español: Story Collection).Tr. of Place for Mike. (SPA.). 24p. (gr. -1-3). 21.32 *(978-1-4048-1688-6(7)*, Easy Readers) Picture Window Bks.

—El Patito Feo. Ruiz, Carlos, tr. from ENG. Delage, Charlene, illus. 2006. (Read-It! Readers en Español: Cuentos de Hadas Ser.). (SPA.). 32p. (gr. k-3). 21.32 *(978-1-4048-1644-2(5)*, Easy Readers) Picture Window Bks.

—La Princesa Del Guisante: Versión Del Cuento de Hans Christian Anderson. Abello, Patricia, tr. from ENG. Delage, Charlene, illus. 2006. (Read-It! Readers en Español: Cuentos de Hadas Ser.).Tr. of Princess & the Pea - A Retelling of the Grimm's Fairy Tale. (SPA.). 32p. (gr. k-3). 21.32 *(978-1-4048-1634-3(8)*, Easy Readers) Picture Window Bks.

—El Traje Nuevo Del Emperador. Abello, Patricia, tr. from ENG. Delage, Charlene, illus. 2006. (Read-It! Readers en Español: Cuentos de Hadas Ser.). (SPA.). 32p. (gr. k-3). 21.32 *(978-1-4048-1629-9(1)*, Easy Readers) Picture Window Bks.

Blackaby, Susan & Jones, Christianne C. El Cuadro de Mary, 1 vol. Ruiz, Carlos, tr. Haugen, Ryan, illus. 2006. (Read-It! Readers en Español: Story Collection).Tr. of Mary's Art. (SPA.). 32p. (gr. -1-3). 21.32 *(978-1-4048-1649-7(6)*, Easy Readers) Picture Window Bks.

Blackstone, Stella. Bear at Work. Harter, Debbie, illus. 2011. (ENG & SPA.). 24p. (J). (gr. -1-k). pap. 6.99 *(978-1-84686-554-1(9))* Barefoot Bks., Inc.

—Bear at Work (Oso en el Trabajo) 2012. (ENG & SPA., Illus.). (J). 6.99 *(978-1-84686-769-9(X))* Barefoot Bks., Inc.

—La Familia Ocupada de Oso. 2012. (ENG & SPA.). (J). 6.99 *(978-1-84686-771-2(1))* Barefoot Bks., Inc.

Blackstone, Stella & Barefoot Books. Bear on a Bike (Oso en Bicicleta) Harter, Debbie, illus. 2014. (ENG & SPA.). 32p. (J). (gr. -1-1). pap. 6.99 *(978-1-78285-079-3(1))* Barefoot Bks., Inc.

Blackstone, Stella & Scribens, Sunny. Mis Primeras Palabras. 2017. (SPA.). 30p. (J). (gr. -1-k). bds. 14.99 ***(978-1-78285-325-1(1))*** Barefoot Bks., Inc.

Blair, Eric. El Cuervo y la Jarra: Versión de la Fábula de Esopo. Abello, Patricia, tr. Silverman, Dianne, illus. 2006. (Read-It! Readers en Español: Fábulas Ser.).Tr. of Crow & the Pitcher - A Retelling of Aesop's Fable. (SPA.). 24p. (gr. k-3). 21.32 *(978-1-4048-1618-3(6)*, Easy Readers) Picture Window Bks.

—El Lobo y los Siete Cabritos. Abello, Patricia, tr. from ENG. Petrusek, Brett, illus. 2006. (Read-It! Readers en Español: Cuentos de Hadas Ser.). (SPA.). 32p. (gr. k-3). 21.32 *(978-1-4048-1645-9(3)*, Easy Readers) Picture Window Bks.

—El Ninito de Jengibre, 1 vol. Abello, Patricia, tr. from ENG. Peterson, Ben, illus. 2006. (Read-It! Readers en Español: Cuentos Folclóricos Ser.).Tr. of Gingerbread Man. (SPA.). 32p. (gr. k-3). 21.32 *(978-1-4048-1647-3(X)*, Easy Readers) Picture Window Bks.

—El Pastorcito Mentiroso: Versión de la Fábula de Esopo. Abello, Patricia, tr. from ENG. Silverman, Dianne, illus. 2006. (Read-It! Readers en Español: Fábulas Ser.).Tr. of Boy Who Cried Wolf - A Retelling of Aesop's Fable. (SPA.). 24p. (gr. k-3). 21.32 *(978-1-4048-1616-9(X)*, Easy Readers) Picture Window Bks.

—El Pescador y Su Mujer: Versión del Cuento de los Hermanos Grimm. Abello, Patricia, tr. Ouren, Todd, illus. 2006. (Read-It! Readers en Español: Cuentos de Hadas Ser.). (SPA.). 32p. (gr. k-3). 21.32 *(978-1-4048-1630-5(5)*, Easy Readers) Picture Window Bks.

—El Principe Encantado. Abello, Patricia, tr. from ENG. Ouren, Todd, illus. 2006. (Read-It! Readers en Español: Cuentos de Hadas Ser.).Tr. of Frog Prince. (SPA.). 32p. (gr. k-3). 21.32 *(978-1-4048-1631-2(3)*, Easy Readers) Picture Window Bks.

—El Raton de Campo y el Raton de Ciudad: Versión de la Fábula de Esopo. Abello, Patricia, tr. from ENG. Silverman, Dianne, illus. 2006. (Read-It! Readers en Español: Fábulas Ser.).Tr. of Country Mouse & the City Mouse - A Retelling of Aesop's Fable. (SPA.). 24p. (gr. k-3). 21.32 *(978-1-4048-1617-6(8)*, Easy Readers) Picture Window Bks.

Blake, Stephanie. No Quiero Ir a la Escuela. 2007. (SPA., Illus.). 40p. (gr. k-2). 17.99 *(978-84-8470-268-9(5))* Corimbo, Editorial S.L. ESP. Dist: Lectorum Pubns., Inc.

Blue Collection. (Elefonetica Ser.). (SPA.). (gr. 1-2). 373.22 *(978-0-7362-0795-9(3))* CENGAGE Learning.

La Boda, 6, Pack. 2003. 23.95 *(978-0-673-77138-4(5))* Celebration Pr.

La Boda, 6 pack. (Literatura 2000 Ser.). (SPA.). (gr. k-1). 28.00 *(978-0-7635-1011-4(4))* Rigby Education.

La Boda de Trazo y Rayita. (SPA.). (J). 12.00 *(978-958-02-1364-2(X))* Editorial Voluntad S.A. COL. Dist: Distribuidora Norma, Inc.

Boie, Kirsten. King-Kong, el Conejillo de Indias Viajeros. (Torre de Papel Ser.). (SPA.). (J). (gr. 2). 7.95 *(978-958-04-1311-0(8))* Norma S.A. COL. Dist: Distribuidora Norma, Inc.

Bojunga, Lygia. La Casa de la Madrina. (Torre de Papel Ser.). (SPA.). (J). (gr. 4-18). 8.95 *(978-958-04-3396-5(8)*, NR30562) Norma S.A. COL. Dist: Distribuidora Norma, Inc., Lectorum Pubns., Inc.

—La Cuerda Floja. (Torre de Papel Ser.).Tr. of Tightrope. (SPA.). (J). (gr. 4-18). 8.95 *(978-958-04-4527-2(3))* Norma S.A. COL. Dist: Distribuidora Norma, Inc.

Boo! Matching English, 6 Pack. 2003. 23.95 *(978-0-673-76188-0(6))* Celebration Pr.

Bornemann, Elsa. El Libro de los Chicos Enamorados. (SPA.). (J). (gr. 5-8). 8.95 *(978-958-04-3454-2(9)*, NR7681) Norma S.A. COL. Dist: Distribuidora Norma, Inc., Lectorum Pubns., Inc.

—El Ultimo Mago de Bilembambudin. (Torre de Papel Ser.). (SPA.). (J). (gr. 4-18). 8.95 *(978-958-04-3455-9(7))* Norma S.A. COL. Dist: Distribuidora Norma, Inc.

Borreguita Negra. 2003. 23.95 *(978-0-673-77381-4(7))* Celebration Pr.

El bosque de Miel. (Saludos Ser.: Vol. 1). (SPA.). (gr. 2-3). 31.00 *(978-0-7635-5731-7(5))* Rigby Education.

El bosque de Miel: 6 Small Books. (Saludos Ser.: Vol. 1). (SPA.). (gr. 2-3). 31.00 *(978-0-7635-9538-8(1))* Rigby Education.

Bowen, Anne. Que Hacen los Maestros? (Despues de Que Te Vas de la Escuela) Gott, Barry, illus. 2007. (Ediciones Lerner Single Titles Ser.). (SPA.). 32p. (J). (gr. k-3). 16.95 *(978-0-8225-6264-1(2)*, Ediciones Lerner) Lerner Publishing Group.

Bowman, Crystal. Mommy, May I Hug the Fish?, 1 vol. Christensen, Donna, illus. 2009. (I Can Read! / ¡Yo Sé Leer! Ser.).Tr. of Mamá, Puedo Abrazar Al Pez? (ENG & SPA.). 32p. (J). pap. 3.99 *(978-0-310-71868-0(6))* Vida Pubs.

Bravo, Queta!, 6 pack. 2003. 23.95 *(978-0-673-78072-0(4))* Celebration Pr.

Brinca la Tablita. 2003. 28.95 *(978-0-673-78091-1(0))* Celebration Pr.

Brooks, Felicity & MacKinnon, Mairi. First Picture Spanish. Litchfield, Jo, illus. 2006. (First Picture Flap Bks.). 18p. (J). (gr. 1-4). bds. 14.99 *(978-0-7945-1384-9(0)*, Usborne) EDC Publishing.

Brown, Jonatha A. La Piel y el Pelo de los Animales. 2006. (En que se diferencian los animales (Why Animals Look Different) Ser.). (SPA., Illus.). 24p. (J). (gr. 1-4). lib. bdg. 22.00 *(978-0-8368-7415-0(3)*, Weekly Reader Leveled Readers) Stevens, Gareth Publishing LLLP.

Brown, Monica. Marisol Mcdonald & the Monster: Marisol Mcdonald y el Monstruo. Palacios, Sara, illus. 2016. (Marisol Mcdonald Ser.). (ENG & SPA.). 32p. (J). (gr. k-3). 18.95 *(978-0-89239-326-8(2))* Lee & Low Bks., Inc.

—Marisol Mcdonald Doesn't Match / Marisol Mcdonald no Combina. Palacios, Sara, illus. 2013. (Marisol Mcdonald Ser.). (SPA & ENG.). 32p. (J). (gr. -1-3). 17.95 *(978-0-89239-235-3(5))* Lee & Low Bks., Inc.

Brown, Monica & Dominguez, Adriana. Maya's Blanket, 1 vol. Diaz, David, illus. 2015. (SPA & ENG.). 32p. (J). 17.95 *(978-0-89239-292-6(4))* Lee & Low Bks., Inc.

Brown, Monica & Ventura, Gabriela Baeza. Clara & the Curandera / Clara y la Curandera. Muraida, Thelma, illus. 2011. (J). 16.95 *(978-1-55885-700-1(1)*, Piñata Books) Arte Publico Pr.

Brunell, Heather. Bedtime Monster/A Dormir, Monstruito! Del Risco, Eida & de la Vega, Eida, trs. 2010. (ENG & SPA., Illus.). 32p. (J). (gr. -1-3). pap. 7.95 *(978-1-932748-81-9(4)*, Raven Tree Pr.,Csi) Continental Sales, Inc.

—Bedtime Monster/A Dormir, Monstruito! de la Vega, Eida, tr. Adamson, Bonnie, illus. 2010. (ENG & SPA.). 32p. (J). (gr. -1-3). lib. bdg. 16.95 *(978-1-932748-80-2(6)*, Raven Tree Pr.,Csi) Continental Sales, Inc.

Bruzzone, Catherine. First Spanish with Supergato: Learn Spanish the Super-Fun Way Through Games, Activities & Songs. Beaton, Clare, illus. 2007. (ENG.). 32p. (gr. -1-3). 13.95 *(978-0-07-147931-8(7)*, 0071479317) McGraw-Hill Cos., The.

—Spanish on the Move for Kids: Lively Songs & Games for Busy Kids. 2nd rev. ed. 2005. (SPA & ENG., Illus.). 24p. audio compact disk 14.00 *(978-0-07-145689-0(9)*, 0071456899) McGraw-Hill Cos., The.

Buceando en el Misterio. (SPA., Illus.). 70p. (YA). (gr. 8-10). pap. *(978-88-8148-333-4(5))* EMC/Paradigm Publishing.

Un buen Lugar. (Spanish Early Intervention Levels Ser.). (SPA.). 31.14 *(978-0-7362-0326-5(5))* CENGAGE Learning.

Buen Viaje Pinguinos! (Coleccion Leo Con Figuras). (SPA., Illus.). 14p. (J). pap. 4.50 *(978-950-11-0929-0(1)*, SGM291) Sigmar ARG. Dist: Continental Bk. Co., Inc.

Buenas noches, Hermanito: Individual Title Six-Packs. (Literatura 2000 Ser.). (SPA.). (gr. 1-2). 28.00 *(978-0-7635-1037-4(8))* Rigby Education.

A Bully Named Laura Sue: Social/Emotional Lap Book. (Pebble Soup Explorations Ser.). (SPA.). (gr. -1-18). 16.00 *(978-0-7635-7568-7(2))* Rigby Education.

Burke, David. Beauty & the Beast: Level 3: Learn Spanish Through Fairy Tales. Sandoval, Migs, illus. 2006. (Learn Spanish Through Fairy Tales Ser.). (ENG & SPA.). 29p. (J). (gr. -1-3). pap. 14.95 incl. audio compact disk *(978-1-891888-86-1(2))* Slangman Publishing.

—Cinderella: Level 1: Learn Spanish Through Fairy Tales. Bobrick, Julie, ed. Redoles, Marcela, tr. Sandoval, Migs, illus. 2006. (Learn Spanish Through Fairy Tales Ser.). (ENG & SPA.). 29p. pap. 14.95 incl. audio compact disk *(978-1-891888-74-8(9))* Slangman Publishing.

—Goldilocks & the 3 Bears: Level 2: Learn Spanish Through Fairy Tales. Sandoval, Migs, illus. 2006. (Learn Spanish Through Fairy Tales Ser.). (ENG & SPA.). 29p. (J). (gr. -1-3). pap. 14.95 incl. audio compact disk *(978-1-891888-80-9(3))* Slangman Publishing.

Burton, Margie, et al. Clean Beaches & Playas Limpias: 6 English, 6 Spanish Adaptations. 2011. (J). spiral bd. 75.00 net. *(978-1-4108-5625-8(9))* Benchmark Education Co.

Cabal, Graciela Beatriz. Toby. (Torre de Papel Ser.). (SPA., Illus.). (J). (gr. 4-18). 8.95 *(978-958-04-4222-6(3))* Norma S.A. COL. Dist: Distribuidora Norma, Inc.

Caballero, D., tr. Que? Como? Por Que?: Autos y Camiones. Weller, Ursula, illus. 2007. (Junior (Silver Dolphin) Ser.). 16p. (J). (gr. -1). *(978-970-718-490-9(6)*, Silver Dolphin en Español) Advanced Marketing, S. de R. L. de C. V.

El Caballo Blanco, 6 Pack. (Literatura 2000 Ser.). (SPA.). (gr. 2-3). 33.00 *(978-0-7635-1255-2(9))* Rigby Education.

El Caballo Comilon, 6 Pack. (Literatura 2000 Ser.). (SPA.). (gr. 1-2). 28.00 *(978-0-7635-1038-1(6))* Rigby Education.

El caballo Mecanico, 6 Pack. (Chiquilibros Ser.). (SPA.). (gr. k-1). 23.00 *(978-0-7635-8613-3(7))* Rigby Education.

Cae una Nuez. (Spanish Early Intervention Levels Ser.). 28.38 *(978-0-7362-0838-3(0))* CENGAGE Learning.

Caicedo, Maria Victoria. En la Casa con la Abuelita. (SPA.). (J). 8.95 *(978-958-04-7445-6(1))* Norma S.A. COL. Dist: Distribuidora Norma, Inc.

Cajas: Individual Title Six-Packs. (Literatura 2000 Ser.). (SPA.). (gr. 1-2). 28.00 *(978-0-7635-1059-6(9))* Rigby Education.

El Calcetin. (Spanish Early Intervention Levels Ser.). (SPA.). 23.10 *(978-0-7362-0324-1(9))* CENGAGE Learning.

Camila y la Anciana-del-Barro: 6 Softcover Books. (Saludos Ser.: Vol. 1). (SPA.). (gr. 3-5). 31.00 *(978-0-7635-1752-6(6))* Rigby Education.

Caminando: Individual Title Six-Packs. (Literatura 2000 Ser.). (SPA.). (gr. 2-3). 33.00 *(978-0-7635-1085-5(8))* Rigby Education.

Caminata en la Ciudad, 6 Packs. (Chiquilibros Ser.). (SPA.). (gr. -1-1). 12.00 *(978-0-7635-8553-2(X))* Rigby Education.

Una Caminata Por el Bosque, 2 pack. (Chiquilibros Ser.). (SPA.). (gr. -1-1). 12.00 *(978-0-7635-8547-1(5))* Rigby Education.

La Camisa de Guerrero, 6 Pack. (Saludos Ser.: Vol. 2). (SPA.). (gr. 2-3). 31.00 *(978-0-7635-9523-4(3))* Rigby Education.

Campbell, Eric. El Lugar de los Leones. (Torre de Papel Ser.).Tr. of Where Lions Live Wild. (SPA.). (YA). (gr. 6-18). 8.95 *(978-958-04-3150-3(7))* Norma S.A. COL. Dist: Distribuidora Norma, Inc.

Campbell, Kathy. Let's Draw a Bear with Squares / Vamos a dibujar un oso usando Cuadrados. 2009. (Let's Draw with Shapes / Vamos a dibujar con figuras Ser.). (ENG & SPA.). 24p. (gr. k-1). 42.50 *(978-1-61514-220-0(7)*, Editorial Buenas Letras) Rosen Publishing Group, Inc., The.

—Let's Draw a Fish with Triangles / Vamos a dibujar un pez usando Triángulos. 2009. (Let's Draw with Shapes / Vamos a dibujar con figuras Ser.). (ENG & SPA.). 24p. (gr. k-1). 42.50 *(978-1-61514-222-4(3)*, Editorial Buenas Letras) Rosen Publishing Group, Inc., The.

—Let's Draw a Frog with Ovals / Vamos a dibujar una rana Usando óvalos. 2009. (Let's Draw with Shapes / Vamos a dibujar con figuras Ser.). (ENG & SPA.). 24p. (gr. k-1). 42.50 *(978-1-61514-223-1(1)*, Editorial Buenas Letras) Rosen Publishing Group, Inc., The.

Candela, Pilar. Una Rayuela Bk. A: Level 1. (SPA & ENG.). 96p. (J). (gr. 3-7). wbk. ed. 12.95 *(978-84-7143-810-2(0)*, SGS8100) Sociedad General Espanola de Libreria ESP. Dist: Continental Bk. Co., Inc.

—Una Rayuela Bk. B: Level 1. (SPA & ENG.). 98p. (J). (gr. 3-7). wbk. ed. 12.95 *(978-84-7143-811-9(9)*, SGS8119) Sociedad General Espanola de Libreria ESP. Dist: Continental Bk. Co., Inc.

Canetti, Yanitzia. Abecedario Nutritivo. 2009. (SPA.). 40p. (J). pap. 8.99 *(978-1-59835-115-6(X)*, BrickHouse Education) Cambridge BrickHouse, Inc.

El cangrejo al fondo del Mar: Individual Title Six-Packs. (Literatura 2000 Ser.). (SPA.). (gr. 1-2). 28.00 *(978-0-7635-1060-2(2))* Rigby Education.

Canizares, Susan & Chessen, Betsey. Storms: Tormentas. 2004. (Science Emergent Readers Ser.). (ENG & SPA., Illus.). (J). *(978-0-439-66392-2(X))* Scholastic, Inc.

Cann, Kate. Viviendo Juntos. (SPA.). (YA). 9.95 *(978-958-04-6873-8(7))* Norma S.A. COL. Dist: Distribuidora Norma, Inc.

Cano, Carles & Cano Peiró, Carles. El Arbol de las Hojas Din A-4. (SPA., Illus.). 28p. (J). (gr. k-2). *(978-84-8464-027-1(2)*, KA30310) Kalandraka Editora, S.L. ESP. Dist: Lectorum Pubns., Inc.

Caraballo, Samuel. My Big Sister / Mi Hermana Mayor. Muraida, Thelma, illus. 2012. (ENG & SPA.). (J). (gr. 3-8). 16.95 *(978-1-55885-750-6(8)*, Piñata Books) Arte Publico Pr.

Caritas. (Spanish Early Intervention Levels Ser.). 23.10 *(978-1-56334-785-6(7))* CENGAGE Learning.

Carle, Eric. Amigos. Carle, Eric, illus. 2016. (SPA., Illus.). 22p. (J). (— 1). bds. 7.99 *(978-0-399-54506-1(9)*, Philomel Bks.) Penguin Young Readers Group.

—My Very First Book of Numbers (Mi Primer Libro de Numeros) Carle, Eric, illus. 2013. (SPA & ENG., Illus.). 20p. (J). (gr. -1 — 1). bds. 5.99 *(978-0-399-16141-4(4)*, Philomel Bks.) Penguin Young Readers Group.

—My Very First Book of Shapes / Mi Primer Libro de Figuras: Bilingual Edition. Carle, Eric, illus. 2013. (SPA & ENG., Illus.). 20p. (J). (gr. -1 — 1). bds. 5.99 *(978-0-399-16142-1(2)*, Philomel Bks.) Penguin Young Readers Group.

Carlitos: Individual Title Six-Packs. (Literatura 2000 Ser.). (SPA.). (gr. 2-3). 33.00 *(978-0-7635-1256-9(7))* Rigby Education.

Carr, Elias. Jo y la Sopa Lenta. Garton, Michael, illus. 2016. (SPA.). (J). ***(978-1-5064-2097-4(4)***, Sparkhouse Pr.) Spark Hse.

Carson-Dellosa Publishing Staff. Everyday Words in Spanish: Photographic. 2004. (ENG.). 104p. (gr. -1-8). 7.49 *(978-1-936022-83-0(4))* Carson-Dellosa Publishing, LLC.

La casa de Calabaza: Individual Title Six-Packs. (Literatura 2000 Ser.). (SPA.). (gr. 2-3). 33.00 *(978-0-7635-1086-2(6))* Rigby Education.

La casa de Tita: Individual Title Six-Packs. (Literatura 2000 Ser.). (SPA.). (gr. 2-3). 33.00 *(978-0-7635-1257-6(5))* Rigby Education.

La casa nueva de los Ortega: Individual Title Six-Packs. (Literatura 2000 Ser.). (SPA.). (gr. 1-2). 28.00 *(978-0-7635-1061-9(0))* Rigby Education.

Una casa para Sergin: Six-Pack. (Saludos Ser.: Vol. 2). (SPA.). (gr. 2-3). 31.00 *(978-0-7635-9542-5(X))* Rigby Education.

Casado, Dami & Casado, Alicia. La Nieve. 2005. (Yo Te Hablare De... Ser.). (SPA., Illus.). 14p. (J). per., bds. 8.99 *(978-84-272-7297-2(9))* Molino, Editorial ESP. Dist: Santillana USA Publishing Co., Inc.

Casanueva, Idilian. I Like to Flap My Hands. 2009. 32p. pap. 12.95 *(978-1-60844-001-6(X))* Dog Ear Publishing, LLC.

Casas. (Spanish Early Intervention Levels Ser.). (SPA.). 23.10 *(978-1-56334-774-0(1))* CENGAGE Learning.

Chamberlain, Mary, et al. Las Crepes de Mama Panya: Un Relato de Kenia. Cairns, Julia, illus. 2016. (SPA.). 40p. (J). (gr. k-5). pap. 8.99 *(978-1-78285-072-4(4))* Barefoot Bks., Inc.

Chano: Individual Title Six-Packs. (Literatura 2000 Ser.). (SPA.). (gr. 2-3). 33.00 *(978-0-7635-1087-9(4))* Rigby Education.

Chiles. (Spanish Early Intervention Levels Ser.). 23.10 *(978-1-56334-778-8(4))* CENGAGE Learning.

Chiquilibros: Letras Add-to Pack. (SPA.). (gr. -1-1). 103.00 *(978-0-7635-8575-4(0))* Rigby Education.

Chiquilibros: Letras Complete Package. (SPA.). (gr. -1-1). 374.00 *(978-0-7635-8574-7(2))* Rigby Education.

Chirridos!, 6, Pack. (Literatura 2000 Ser.). (SPA.). (gr. 1-2). 28.00 *(978-0-7635-1039-8(4))* Rigby Education.

El chivo Comilon. (Spanish Early Intervention Levels Ser.). (SPA.). 23.10 *(978-1-56334-767-2(9))* CENGAGE Learning.

Christelow, Eileen. Cinco Monitos Hacen un Pastel de Cumpleanos. 2014. (Five Little Monkeys Story Ser.).Tr. of Five Little Monkeys Bake a Birthday Cake. (ENG & SPA., Illus.). 30p. (J). (— 1). bds. 7.99 *(978-0-544-08899-3(9)*, HMH Books For Young Readers) Houghton Mifflin Harcourt Publishing Co.

—Cinco Monitos Sin Nada Que Hacer. 2014. (Five Little Monkeys Story Ser.).Tr. of Five Little Monkeys with Nothing to Do. (ENG & SPA., Illus.). 32p. (J). (— 1). bds. 7.99 *(978-0-544-08889-4(1)*, HMH Books For Young Readers) Houghton Mifflin Harcourt Publishing Co.

—Five Little Monkeys Jumping on the Bed. Ortiz, Victoria, tr. 2014. (Five Little Monkeys Story Ser.). (ENG & SPA., Illus.). 30p. (J). (— 1). bds. 7.99 *(978-0-544-08900-6(6)*, HMH Books For Young Readers) Houghton Mifflin Harcourt Publishing Co.

El Circo: Individual Title Six-Packs. (Literatura 2000 Ser.). (SPA.). (gr. -1-1). 28.00 *(978-0-7635-1188-3(9))* Rigby Education.

Cirilo, el gallo Desafinado. (Spanish Early Intervention Levels Ser.). (SPA.). 28.38 *(978-0-7362-0840-6(2))* CENGAGE Learning.

The City Walk: Individual Title Two-Packs. (Chiquilibros Ser.). (gr. -1-1). 12.00 *(978-0-7635-8533-4(5))* Rigby Education.

Una ciudad, una escuela, muchas Comidas: 6 Small Books. (Saludos Ser.: Vol. 1). (SPA.). (gr. 3-5). 31.00 *(978-0-7635-1805-9(0))* Rigby Education.

Clark, Sarah Kartchner. ¡En Equipo Con el Sr. Supercoyote!, 1 vol. rev. ed. 2007. (Building Fluency Through Reader's Theater Ser.).Tr. of Teaming with Mr. Cool! (SPA., Illus.). 24p. (J). (gr. 3-4). pap. 6.99 *(978-1-4333-0025-7(7))* Teacher Created Materials, Inc.

Claro que Sí! (Spanish Early Intervention Levels Ser.). 28.38 *(978-0-7362-0844-4(5))* CENGAGE Learning.

Clavel, Bernard. Leyendas de Montanas. (Torre de Papel Ser.). (SPA.). (YA). (gr. 6-18). 7.95 *(978-958-04-1529-9(3))* Norma S.A. COL. Dist: Distribuidora Norma, Inc.

—Leyendas del Mar. (Torre de Papel Ser.). (SPA.). (YA). (gr. 6-18). 8.95 *(978-958-04-1387-5(8))* Norma S.A. COL. Dist: Distribuidora Norma, Inc.

Cochinita bien Vestida. (Spanish Early Intervention Levels Ser.). 21.30 *(978-0-7362-0830-7(5))* CENGAGE Learning.

La Cocina: Individual Title Two-Packs. (Chiquilibros Ser.). (SPA.). (gr. -1-1). 12.00 *(978-0-7635-8560-0(2))* Rigby Education.

El cocinero Feroz: Individual Title Six-Packs. (Literatura 2000 Ser.). (SPA.). (gr. 2-3). 33.00 *(978-0-7635-1258-3(3))* Rigby Education.

Cofer, Judith Ortiz. Animal Jamboree / La Fiesta de los Animales: Latino Folktales / Leyendas Latinas. Rosales-Yeomans, Natalia, tr. 2012. (SPA & ENG.). (J). pap. 9.95 *(978-1-55885-743-8(5)*, Piñata Books) Arte Publico Pr.

Colasanti, Marina. Lejos Como Mi Querer y Otros Cuentos. (SPA.). (YA). 8.95 *(978-958-04-3651-5(7))* Norma S.A. COL. Dist: Distribuidora Norma, Inc.

Cole, Babette. El Principe Ceniciento.Tr. of Prince Cinders. (SPA.). 32p. (J). 12.95 *(978-84-233-1687-8(4))* Ediciones Destino ESP. Dist: Planeta Publishing Corp.

Cole, Carol A. La Dama de Los Pingüinos, 1 vol. Rogers, Sherry, illus. 2012. (SPA & ENG.). 32p. (J). (gr. -1-3). 17.95 *(978-1-60718-697-7(7))* Arbordale Publishing.

Los Collaros. 2003. 23.95 *(978-0-673-77776-8(6))* Celebration Pr.

Collins, Kathleen. Sojourner Truth: Defensora de los derechos civiles (Sojourner Truth: Equal Rights Advocate) 2009. (Grandes personajes en la historia de los Estados Unidos (Famous People in American History) Ser.). (SPA.). 32p. (gr. 2-3). 47.90 *(978-1-61512-808-2(5)*, Editorial Buenas Letras) Rosen Publishing Group, Inc., The.

—Sojourner Truth: Equal Rights Advocate. 2009. (Primary Sources of Famous People in American History Ser.). 32p. (gr. 2-3). 47.90 *(978-1-60851-727-5(6))* Rosen Publishing Group, Inc., The.

—Sojourner Truth: Equal Rights Advocate / Defensora de los derechos Civiles. 2009. (Famous People in American History/Grandes personajes en la historia de los Estados Unidos Ser.). (ENG & SPA.). 32p. (gr. 2-3). 47.90 *(978-1-61512-556-2(6)*, Editorial Buenas Letras) Rosen Publishing Group, Inc., The.

Come See My Farm. 2003. 23.95 *(978-0-673-78129-1(1))* Celebration Pr.

Comida Magica: Individual Title-Six Packs. (Chiquilibros Ser.). (SPA.). (gr. k-1). 23.00 *(978-0-7635-8615-7(3))* Rigby Education.

Una Comida Tradicional. 2003. 28.95 *(978-0-673-78092-8(9))* Celebration Pr.

Como funciona? Interactive Packages: A rodar, a Rodar. (Pebble Soup Exploraciones Ser.). (SPA.). (gr. -1-18). 52.00 *(978-0-7578-5268-8(8))* Rigby Education.

Como funciona? Interactive Packages: Mirandolo Bien. (Pebble Soup Exploraciones Ser.). (SPA.). (gr. -1-18). 52.00 *(978-0-7578-5270-1(X))* Rigby Education.

Compartiendo: Individual Title Six-Packs. (Literatura 2000 Ser.). (SPA.). (gr. k-1). 28.00 *(978-0-7635-1013-8(0))* Rigby Education.

Complete Spanish, Set. 2004. 13.99 incl. audio compact disk *(978-1-57583-299-9(2))* Twin Sisters IP, LLC.

Complete Spanish DRA Pack, 96 vols. (Spanish Dra Levels Ser.). (SPA.). 353.75 *(978-0-7362-0993-9(X))* CENGAGE Learning.

Complete Spanish Guided Reading Pack, 96 vols. (Spanish Guided Reading Levels Ser.). (SPA.). 353.75 *(978-0-7362-0991-5(3))* CENGAGE Learning.

Complete Spanish Lexile Pack, 92 vols. (Spanish Lexile Levels Ser.). (SPA.). 339.89 *(978-0-7362-1512-1(3))* CENGAGE Learning.

Conklin, Wendy. Dos Amigos Planos Viajan por el Mundo, 1 vol. rev. ed. 2007. (Building Fluency Through Reader's Theater Ser.).Tr. of Two Flat Friends Travel the World. (SPA.). 24p. (J). (gr. 3-4). pap. 6.99 *(978-1-4333-0022-6(2))* Teacher Created Materials, Inc.

Conoce las Nubes. 2006. (Real Readers en español Ser.). (J). pap. 24.95 *(978-1-4042-2486-5(6)*, Rosen Classroom) Rosen Publishing Group, Inc., The.

Contro, Arturo. Rafael Marquez. 2009. (World Soccer Stars / Estrellas del fútbol mundial Ser.). (ENG & SPA.). 24p. (gr. 2-2). 42.50 *(978-1-60854-849-1(X)*, Editorial Buenas Letras) Rosen Publishing Group, Inc., The.

Cooper, Lynne. Alien Invaders. Leick, Bonnie, illus. 2010. (ENG.). 32p. (J). (gr. 4-7). *(978-1-934960-83-7(7))* Continental Sales.

El corderito mas Chiquito: Lap Book. (Pebble Soup Exploraciones Ser.). (SPA.). 16p. (gr. -1-18). 21.00 *(978-0-7578-1678-9(9))* Rigby Education.

El corderito mas Chiquito: Small Book. (Pebble Soup Exploraciones Ser.). (SPA.). 16p. (gr. -1-18). 5.00 *(978-0-7578-1718-2(1))* Rigby Education.

El coro de Gatos: Individual Title Six-Packs. (Literatura 2000 Ser.). (SPA.). (gr. 2-3). 33.00 *(978-0-7635-1088-6(2))* Rigby Education.

S

El Correo: Individual Title Two-Packs. (Chiquilibros Ser.). (SPA.). (gr. -1-1). 12.00 *(978-0-7635-8561-7(0))* Rigby Education.

Costales, Amy. Abuelo Vivia Solo/Grandpa Used to Live Alone. Gama, Esperanza, illus. 2010. (ENG.). 32p. (J). (gr. -1-3). 16.95 *(978-1-55885-531-1(9))* Arte Publico Pr.

—Lupe Vargas & Her Super Best Friend/Lupe Vargas y Su Super Mejor Amiga. 2006. (ENG, SPA & MUL., Illus.). 32p. (J). (gr. -1-3). 15.95 *(978-0-87358-888-1(6))* Cooper Square Publishing Llc.

Cowan, Catherine & Buehner, Mark. Mi Vida con la Ola. Rubio, Esther, tr. Buehner, Mark, illus. 2004. (SPA., Ilus.). 29p. (J). 19.99 *(978-84-88342-45-4(4))* S.A. Kokinos ESP. Dist: Lectorum Pubns., Inc.

Cowen-Fletcher, Jane. Se Necesita Todo un Pueblo. 2003. (SPA., Illus.). (J). pap. 4.76 net. *(978-0-590-29394-5(X),* SO30915) Scholastic, Inc.

Creo que Si! (Spanish Early Intervention Levels Ser.). (SPA.). 31.14 *(978-0-7362-0332-6(X))* CENGAGE Learning.

Crisp, Dan. Trabajo/ Work. 2007. 14p. 10.95 *(978-84-263-6452-4(7))* Vives, Luis Editorial (Edelvives) ESP. Dist: Baker & Taylor Bks.

Cronin, Doreen. Dubi Dubi Muu. Jimenez Rioja, Alberto, tr. from ENG. 2007.Tr. of Dooby Dooby Moo. (SPA., Illus.). 35p. (J). (gr. -1-1). 15.95 *(978-1-933032-33-7(2))* Lectorum Pubns., Inc.

Crow, Melinda Melton. Camiones Amigos/Truck Buddies, 1 vol. Heck, Claudia M., tr. from ENG. Rooney, Ronnie, illus. 2012. (Camiones Amigos/Truck Buddies Ser.). (ENG, SPA & MUL.). 32p. (gr. -1-1). pap. 5.05 *(978-1-4342-3913-6(6))*; lib. bdg. 22.65 *(978-1-4342-3774-3(5))* Stone Arch Bks. (Bilingual Stone Arch Readers).

—Carrera en la Carretera. Heck, Claudia M., tr. Rooney, Ronnie, illus. 2012. (Camiones Amigos/Truck Buddies Ser.).Tr. of Road Race. (ENG, SPA & MUL.). 32p. (gr. -1-1). pap. 5.05 *(978-1-4342-3915-0(2),* Bilingual Stone Arch Readers) Stone Arch Bks.

Cual es el Mio? (Spanish Early Intervention Levels Ser.). (SPA.). 23.10 *(978-1-56334-791-7(1))* CENGAGE Learning.

Cuando estaba Enferma: Individual Title Six-Packs. (Literatura 2000 Ser.). (SPA.). (gr. 1-2). 28.00 *(978-0-7635-1040-4(8))* Rigby Education.

Cuando sea mas Grande: Individual Title Six-Packs. (Literatura 2000 Ser.). (SPA.). (gr. 1-2). 28.00 *(978-0-7635-1063-3(7))* Rigby Education.

Cuando tienes Susto: Social/Emotional Lap Book. (Pebble Soup Exploraciones Ser.). (SPA.). (gr. -1-18). 16.00 *(978-0-7578-1792-2(0))* Rigby Education.

Cuatro Ardillitas. (Spanish Early Intervention Levels Ser.). (SPA.). 31.14 *(978-0-7362-0336-4(2))* CENGAGE Learning.

La Cucaracha: Individual 6-packs. 2003. 23.95 *(978-0-673-78071-3(6))* Celebration Pr.

Cuenta con la Familia. (Spanish Early Intervention Levels Ser.). (SPA.). 23.10 *(978-1-56334-758-0(X))* CENGAGE Learning.

Cuentitos mios Classroom Set: Green Series. (Rimas Y Risas Ser.). (SPA.). (gr. -1-2). 352.70 *(978-0-7362-0057-8(6))* CENGAGE Learning.

Cuentitos Mios Classroom Set: Green Series with addition of Manipulatives. (Rimas Y Risas Ser.). (SPA.). (gr. -1-2). 477.31 *(978-0-917837-96-8(7))* CENGAGE Learning.

El cuento de Dona Chila: 6 Softcover Books. (Saludos Ser.: Vol. 3). (SPA.). (gr. 3-5). 31.00 *(978-0-7635-1780-9(1))* Rigby Education.

Cuentos de Muchos Mundos/Stories of Many Worlds. (ENG & SPA.). 160p. 20.00 *(978-0-944356-19-7(2))* Alegria Hispana Pubns.

Cuentos Favoritos/Favorite Tales. (ENG & SPA.). 80p. 15.00 *(978-0-944356-01-2(X))* Alegria Hispana Pubns.

Cuentos Matematicos/Math Tales. (ENG & SPA.). 80p. 17.00 *(978-0-944356-05-0(2))* Alegria Hispana Pubns.

Cuidado! Individual Title Six-Packs. (Literatura 2000 Ser.). (SPA.). (gr. -1-1). 28.00 *(978-0-7635-1189-0(7))* Rigby Education.

El cumpleanos de Alisa: Individual Title Six-Packs. (Literatura 2000 Ser.). (SPA.). (gr. k-1). 28.00 *(978-0-7635-1014-5(9))* Rigby Education.

El cumpleanos de Bruno: Individual Title Six-Packs. (Literatura 2000 Ser.). (SPA.). (gr. 1-2). 28.00 *(978-0-7635-1041-1(6))* Rigby Education.

El cumpleanos de mi Abuelito: Individual Title Six-Packs. (Literatura 2000 Ser.). (SPA.). (gr. 2-3). 33.00 *(978-0-7635-1089-3(0))* Rigby Education.

Cuno, Sabine. Abre, Cierra y Aprende! Caballero, D., tr. Senner, Katja, illus. 2007. 14p. (J). (gr. -1). *(978-970-718-489-3(2),* Silver Dolphin en Español) Advanced Marketing, S. de R. L. de C. V.

Curry, Don L. En Mi Patio. Brown, Erin O'Leary, illus. 2011. (Rookie Ready to Learn Español Ser.). (SPA.). 32p. (J). pap. 5.95 *(978-0-531-26784-4(9),* Children's Pr.) Scholastic Library Publishing.

Curry, Don L. & O'Leary Brown, Erin. En Mi Patio. O'Leary Brown, Erin, illus. 2011. (Rookie Ready to Learn Español Ser.). (SPA., Illus.). 32p. (J). lib. bdg. 23.00 *(978-0-531-26116-3(6),* Children's Pr.) Scholastic Library Publishing.

Curtis, Christopher Paul & Jiménez Rioja, Alberto. Me Llamo Bud, No Buddy. 2016. (SPA.). 240p. (J). (gr. 5-12). pap. 12.99 ***(978-1-63245-639-7(7))*** Lectorum Pubns., Inc.

Cusimano Love, Maryann & Ichikawa, Satomi. You Are My Miracle (Tú Eres Mi Milagro) 2016. (SPA & ENG., Illus.). 28p. (J). (— 1). bds. 7.99 *(978-0-399-54734-8(7),* Philomel Bks.) Penguin Young Readers Group.

Da Vacaciones. (Mi Primer Diccionario Illustrado Espanol Ser.). (SPA.). pap. 4.95 *(978-88-8148-844-5(2))* EMC/Paradigm Publishing.

Daniel: Individual Title Six-Packs. (Literatura 2000 Ser.). (SPA.). (gr. 1-2). 28.00 *(978-0-7635-1064-0(5))* Rigby Education.

Danziger, Paula. Es Dia de Feria, Ambar Dorado. Ross, Tony, illus. 2007. (de Ámbar / a Is for Amber Easy-To-Read Ser.).Tr. of It's a Fair Day, Amber Brown. (SPA.). 48p. (gr. k-3). pap. 8.95 *(978-1-59820-596-1(X))* Santillana USA Publishing Co., Inc.

—Segundo Grado Es Increible, Ambar Dorado. Ross, Tony, illus. 2007. (de Ámbar / a Is for Amber Easy-To-Read Ser.).Tr. of Second Grade Rules, Amber Brown. (SPA.). 48p. (gr. k-3). pap. 8.95 *(978-1-59820-594-7(3))* Santillana USA Publishing Co., Inc.

de Alba, Laura, tr. Caritas Felices. 2007. (Disney Winnie the Pooh (SilverDolphin) Ser.). (Illus.). 8p. (J). (gr. -1). bds. *(978-970-718-391-9(8),* Silver Dolphin en Español) Advanced Marketing, S. de R. L. de C. V.

De Anda, Diane. The Patchwork Garden. Ventura, Gabriela Baeza, tr. Kemarskaya, Oksana, illus. 2013.Tr. of Pedacitos de Huerto. (ENG & SPA.). 32p. (J). 16.95 *(978-1-55885-763-6(X),* Piñata Books) Arte Publico Pr.

De Compras. (Spanish Early Intervention Levels Ser.). 23.10 *(978-1-56334-784-9(9))* CENGAGE Learning.

de Lambana, Martha Lucia Martinez. Grafias 4 4: Escritura Asociativa Script: Ejercitacion. (SPA.). (J). (gr. k-6). 12.00 *(978-958-04-5329-1(2))* Norma S.A. COL. Dist: Distribuidora Norma, Inc.

—Grafias 5 5: Escritura Asociativa Script: Intermedio. (SPA.). (J). (gr. k-6). 12.00 *(978-958-04-5330-7(6))* Norma S.A. COL. Dist: Distribuidora Norma, Inc.

—Grafias 6 6: Escritura Asociativa Script: Avanzada. (SPA.). (J). (gr. k-6). 12.00 *(978-958-04-5331-4(4))* Norma S.A. COL. Dist: Distribuidora Norma, Inc.

—Grafias K: Escritura Asociativa Script: Aprestamiento. (SPA.). (J). (gr. k-6). 12.00 *(978-958-04-5316-1(0))* Norma S.A. COL. Dist: Distribuidora Norma, Inc.

De lo Que Contaron - Fraile (What They Told the Friar (XVI)) 2005. (SPA.). (J). pap. *(978-968-7381-04-6(3))* Tecolote, Ediciones, S.A. de C.V.

De padre a Hijo: 6 Small Books. (Saludos Ser.: Vol. 1). (SPA.). (gr. 3-5). 31.00 *(978-0-7635-1755-7(0))* Rigby Education.

De Safari: Individual Title-Six Packs. (Chiquilibros Ser.). (SPA.). (gr. k-1). 23.00 *(978-0-7635-8605-8(6))* Rigby Education.

De Valdenebro, Eladio. Tono y el Bosque. (Torre de Papel Ser.). (SPA.). (J). (gr. 4-18). 8.95 *(978-958-04-3397-2(6))* Norma S.A. COL. Dist: Distribuidora Norma, Inc.

Debajo de la Cama, 6 Packs. (Chiquilibros Ser.). (SPA.). (gr. k-1). 23.00 *(978-0-7635-8619-5(6))* Rigby Education.

Del Moral, S., tr. Animales. 2006. (Disney Learning (Silver Dolphin en Espanol) Ser.). (Illus.). 22p. (J). (gr. -1). *(978-970-718-431-2(0),* Silver Dolphin en Español) Advanced Marketing, S. de R. L. de C. V.

—Colores. 2006. (Disney Learning (Silver Dolphin en Espanol) Ser.). (Illus.). 22p. (J). (gr. -1). *(978-970-718-430-5(2),* Silver Dolphin en Español) Advanced Marketing, S. de R. L. de C. V.

—Contrarios. 2006. (Disney Learning (Silver Dolphin en Espanol) Ser.). (Illus.). 22p. (J). (gr. -1). *(978-970-718-428-2(0),* Silver Dolphin en Español) Advanced Marketing, S. de R. L. de C. V.

—Formas. 2006. (Disney Learning (Silver Dolphin en Espanol) Ser.). (Illus.). 22p. (J). (gr. -1). *(978-970-718-429-9(9),* Silver Dolphin en Español) Advanced Marketing, S. de R. L. de C. V.

Del Moral, Susana. Baby Da Vinci, Mi Cuerpo. Zaidi, Nadeem, illus. 2006. (Baby Einstein Ser.). (SPA.). 6p. (J). (gr. -1-k). bds. *(978-970-718-455-8(8),* Silver Dolphin en Español) Advanced Marketing, S. de R. L. de C. V.

del Moral Zavariz, Susana & Zaidi, Nadeem. El Concurso: Un Libro con Espejos. 2006. (SPA., Illus.). 5p. (J). (gr. -1-k). bds. *(978-970-718-458-9(2),* Silver Dolphin en Español) Advanced Marketing, S. de R. L. de C. V.

Delacre, Lulu. Rafi y Rosi. Delacre, Lulu, illus. 2016. (Rafi & Rosi Ser.).Tr. of Rafi & Rosi. (SPA., Illus.). (J). pap. 8.95 *(978-0-89239-378-7(5))* Lee & Low Bks., Inc.

—Rafi y Rosi ¡Carnaval!, 1 vol. 2016. (Rafi & Rosi Ser.).Tr. of Rafi & Rosi Carnival. (SPA & ENG., Illus.). 64p. (J). pap. 8.95 *(978-0-89239-380-0(7))* Lee & Low Bks., Inc.

Demado. En Avant: Enhanced Online Edition. 4th ed. 2003. (SPA.). cd-rom 54.80 *(978-0-03-031974-7(9))* Holt McDougal.

Demasiada Ropa, 6 Pack. (Literatura 2000 Ser.). (SPA.). (gr. k-1). 28.00 *(978-0-7635-1015-2(7))* Rigby Education.

DeMolay, Jack. El Triángulo de las Bermudas: La desaparición del vuelo 19 (the Bermuda Triangle:the Disappearance of Flight 19) 2009. (Historietas Juveniles: Misterios (Jr. Graphic Mysteries) Ser.). (SPA.). 24p. (gr. 2-3). 47.90 *(978-1-61513-348-2(8),* Editorial Buenas Letras) Rosen Publishing Group, Inc., The.

Den Vueltas, 6 Packs. (Literatura 2000 Ser.). (SPA.). (gr. 1-2). 28.00 *(978-0-7635-1065-7(3))* Rigby Education.

El Dentista, 2 Packs. (Chiquilibros Ser.). (SPA.). (gr. -1-1). 12.00 *(978-0-7635-8565-5(3))* Rigby Education.

DeRubertis, Barbara. Cuenta con Pablo: Math Matters en Espanol. Thornburgh, Rebecca, illus. 2005. 32p. pap. 5.95 *(978-1-57565-151-4(3))* Kane Press, Inc.

Desmazieres, Sandra. Emma y Sus Amigos: Un Libro Sobre los Colores. 2006. (Picture Bks.). (SPA., Illus.). 28p. (gr. k-3). lib. bdg. 24.00 *(978-0-8368-6998-9(2),* Gareth Stevens Learning Library) Stevens, Gareth Publishing LLLP.

Despegue con Ellen Ochoa! 6 Small Books. (Saludos Ser.: Vol. 3). (SPA.). (gr. 2-3). 31.00 *(978-0-7635-9548-7(9))* Rigby Education.

Despegue con Ellen Ochoa! Big Book. (Saludos Ser.: Vol. 3). (SPA.). (gr. 2-3). 31.00 *(978-0-7635-5863-5(X))* Rigby Education.

El dia de Escuela, 2 packs. (Chiquilibros Ser.). (SPA.). (gr. -1-1). 12.00 *(978-0-7635-8562-4(9))* Rigby Education.

El Dia de los Muertos: 6 Small Books. (Saludos Ser.: Vol. 1). (SPA.). 24p. (gr. 2-3). 31.00 *(978-0-7635-9520-3(9))* Rigby Education.

El Dia lluvioso, 2 packs. (Chiquilibros Ser.). (SPA.). (gr. -1-1). 12.00 *(978-0-7635-8552-5(1))* Rigby Education.

Diario de una Marquesa (Diary of a Marchioness) 2005. (SPA.). (J). pap. *(978-968-7381-05-3(1))* Tecolote, Ediciones, S.A. de C.V.

El Diario de Val. (SPA., Illus.). 70p. (YA). (gr. 7-9). pap. *(978-88-8148-328-0(9))* EMC/Paradigm Publishing.

Dias de Alegria. (Spanish Early Intervention Levels Ser.). (SPA.). 23.10 *(978-1-56334-781-8(4))* CENGAGE Learning.

Diaz, Nelbaliz. Laura y Su Caja de Sorpresas. 2007. (SPA.). 48p. 14.95 *(978-0-8477-0452-1(1))* Univ. of Puerto Rico Pr.

Dickens, Charles. Las Campanas.Tr. of Chimes. (SPA.). 7.75 *(978-958-04-2124-5(2))* Norma S.A. COL. Dist: Distribuidora Norma, Inc.

Diez Ositos: Big Book Packages. 2003. 64.95 *(978-0-673-58578-3(6))* Celebration Pr.

Dime como te Sientes: Big Book. (Pebble Soup Exploraciones Ser.). (SPA.). 16p. (gr. -1-18). 31.00 *(978-0-7578-1685-7(1))* Rigby Education.

Dime como te Sientes: Small Book. (Pebble Soup Exploraciones Ser.). (SPA.). 16p. (gr. -1-18). 5.00 *(978-0-7578-1725-0(4))* Rigby Education.

Los Dinosaurios: Big Book Packages. 2003. 64.95 *(978-0-673-58597-4(2))* Celebration Pr.

La diosa del Volcan: 6 Small Books. (Saludos Ser.: Vol. 1). (SPA.). (gr. 3-5). 31.00 *(978-0-7635-2055-7(1))* Rigby Education.

Disfraces, 6 Pack. (Chiquilibros Ser.). (SPA.). (gr. k-1). 23.00 *(978-0-7635-8601-0(3))* Rigby Education.

Disher, Garry. Flaminio, el Piano. (Torre de Papel Ser.). (SPA.). (J). (gr. 4-18). 8.95 *(978-958-04-4139-7(1))* Norma S.A. COL. Dist: Distribuidora Norma, Inc.

Disney Enterprises Inc. Staff, creator. Caritas Felices. 2007. (Disney Princesa (Silver Dolphin) Ser.). (Illus.). 8p. (J). (gr. -1). bds. *(978-970-718-389-6(6),* Silver Dolphin en Español) Advanced Marketing, S. de R. L. de C. V.

—Disney Caritas Felices: Simba. 2007. (Illus.). 8p. (J). (gr. -1). *(978-970-718-392-6(6),* Silver Dolphin en Español) Advanced Marketing, S. de R. L. de C. V.

El doctor Buscapistas: Social/Emotional Lap Book. (Pebble Soup Exploraciones Ser.). (SPA.). (gr. -1-18). 16.00 *(978-0-7578-1790-8(4))* Rigby Education.

Dominguez, Angela. María Tenía una Llamita. Dominguez, Angela, illus. 2013.Tr. of Maria Had a Little Llama. (SPA & ENG., Illus.). 32p. (J). (gr. -1-2). 17.99 *(978-0-8050-9333-9(8),* 9780805093339, Holt, Henry & Co. Bks. For Young Readers) Holt, Henry & Co.

Dominguez, Ramon Garcia. El Grillo del Tercer Milenium. (SPA.). (J). 8.95 *(978-958-04-6266-8(6))* Norma S.A. COL. Dist: Distribuidora Norma, Inc.

Dona Coneja. (Spanish Early Intervention Levels Ser.). (SPA.). 21.30 *(978-0-7362-0826-0(7))* CENGAGE Learning.

Dona Flora's Flowers. 2003. 23.95 *(978-0-673-78133-8(X))* Celebration Pr.

Donde esta Claudia? Individual Title Six-Packs. (Literatura 2000 Ser.). (SPA.). (gr. k-1). 28.00 *(978-0-7635-1017-6(3))* Rigby Education.

Donde esta mi Mascota? Individual Title-Six Packs. (Chiquilibros Ser.). (SPA.). (gr. k-1). 23.00 *(978-0-7635-8624-9(2))* Rigby Education.

Donde vivimos Interactive Packages: En mi Vecindario. (Pebble Soup Exploraciones Ser.). (SPA.). (gr. -1-18). 52.00 *(978-0-7578-5258-9(0))* Rigby Education.

Donde vivimos Interactive Packages: Los Trabajos. (Pebble Soup Exploraciones Ser.). (SPA.). (gr. -1-18). 52.00 *(978-0-7578-5256-5(4))* Rigby Education.

Donde Vivo Yo: Individual 6-packs. 2003. 23.95 *(978-0-673-77136-0(9))* Celebration Pr.

Doro, el Potrillo. (Coleccion Leo Con Figuras). (SPA., Illus.). 14p. (J). pap. 5.50 *(978-950-11-0841-5(4),* SGM414) Sigmar ARG. Dist: Continental Bk. Co., Inc.

Dos gatos Tontos, 6 Packs. (Literatura 2000 Ser.). (SPA.). (gr. 2-3). 33.00 *(978-0-7635-1090-9(4))* Rigby Education.

Los Dos Volcanes. 2003. 28.95 *(978-0-673-78100-0(3))* Celebration Pr.

Doudna, Kelly. La Lana de la Oveja, 1 vol. Chawla, Neena, illus. 2007. (Cuentos de Animales Ser.).Tr. of Lamb Chops. (SPA & ENG.). 24p. (J). (gr. k-3). lib. bdg. 24.21 *(978-1-59928-661-7(0),* SandCastle) ABDO Publishing Co.

—Las Orejas del Conejo, 1 vol. Nobens, C. A., illus. 2007. (Cuentos de Animales Ser.).Tr. of Rabbit Ears. (SPA & ENG.). 24p. (J). (gr. k-3). lib. bdg. 24.21 *(978-1-59928-669-3(6),* SandCastle) ABDO Publishing Co.

—El Peinado Del Gallo, 1 vol. Haberstroh, Anne, illus. 2007. (Cuentos de Animales Ser.).Tr. of Rooster Combs. (SPA & ENG.). 24p. (J). (gr. k-3). lib. bdg. 24.21 *(978-1-59928-663-1(7),* SandCastle) ABDO Publishing Co.

—La Rata Coleccionista, 1 vol. Chawla, Neena, illus. 2007. (Cuentos de Animales Ser.).Tr. of Pack Rat. (SPA & ENG.). 24p. (J). (gr. k-3). lib. bdg. 24.21 *(978-1-59928-671-6(8),* SandCastle) ABDO Publishing Co.

El dragon Grunon. (Spanish Early Intervention Levels Ser.). (SPA.). 31.14 *(978-0-7362-0338-8(9))* CENGAGE Learning.

Droop, Constanza. Que? Como? Por Que?: Las Estaciones del Ano. Caballero, D., tr. Droop, Constanza, illus. 2007. (Junior (Silver Dolphin) Ser.). (Illus.). 16p. (J). (gr. -1). *(978-970-718-492-3(2),* Silver Dolphin en Español) Advanced Marketing, S. de R. L. de C. V.

Dugan, Christine. Marcha Hacia Delante, 1 vol. rev. ed. 2007. (Building Fluency Through Reader's Theater Ser.). (SPA., Illus.). 20p. (J). (gr. 1-2). pap. 6.99 *(978-1-4333-0019-6(2))* Teacher Created Materials, Inc.

—Muchas Manos Ayudan, 1 vol. rev. ed. 2007. (Building Fluency Through Reader's Theater Ser.). (SPA.). 20p. (J). (gr. 1-2). pap. 6.99 *(978-1-4333-0017-2(6))* Teacher Created Materials, Inc.

Los Dulces. 2003. 23.95 *(978-0-673-77163-6(6))* Celebration Pr.

Dulces Recuerdos. 2003. 28.95 *(978-0-673-78102-4(X))* Celebration Pr.

Duncan, E. E. Ralph Carr: Defender of Japanese Americans. 2011. (ENG & SPA., Illus.). 66p. (J). pap. 8.95 *(978-0-86541-116-6(6))* Filter Pr., LLC.

Durmiendo: Individual Title Six-Packs. (Literatura 2000 Ser.). (SPA.). (gr. 1-2). 28.00 *(978-0-7635-1043-5(2))* Rigby Education.

Dussling, Jennifer. El problema de 100 Libras: Math Matters en Espanol. Thornburgh, Rebecca, illus. 2005. 32p. (J). pap. 5.95 *(978-1-57565-154-5(8))* Kane Press, Inc.

Each Big Book Set: Green Series. (Rimas Y Risas Ser.). (SPA.). (gr. -1-2). 212.23 *(978-1-56334-004-8(6))* CENGAGE Learning.

Each Big Book Set: Green Series with addition of Manipulatives. (Rimas Y Risas Ser.). (SPA.). (gr. -1-2). 344.62 *(978-0-7362-0054-7(1))* CENGAGE Learning.

East, Jacqueline. No Quiero comer Eso! (SPA.). (J). 8.95 *(978-958-04-7345-9(5))* Norma S.A. COL. Dist: Distribuidora Norma, Inc.

Eastman, P. D. El Mejor Nido. Mlawer, Teresa, tr. from ENG. 2005.Tr. of Best Nest. (SPA., Illus.). 64p. (J). (gr. k-2). 9.99 *(978-1-930332-84-3(X),* LC33270) Lectorum Pubns., Inc.

El/Dibujo de Maria: Individual Title, 6 packs. (Literatura 2000 Ser.). (SPA.). (gr. 1-2). 28.00 *(978-0-7635-1042-8(4))* Rigby Education.

Elena y el Monito. (Spanish Early Intervention Levels Ser.). (SPA.). 21.30 *(978-0-7362-0807-9(0))* CENGAGE Learning.

Ellis, Catherine. Cars & Trucks/Autos y Camiones. 2009. (Mega Military Machines/Megamaquinas militares Ser.). (ENG & SPA.). 24p. (gr. 1-1). 42.50 *(978-1-61514-639-0(3),* Editorial Buenas Letras) Rosen Publishing Group, Inc., The.

—Helicopters/Helicópteros. 2009. (Mega Military Machines/Megamaquinas militares Ser.). (ENG & SPA.). 24p. (gr. 1-1). 42.50 *(978-1-61514-640-6(7),* Editorial Buenas Letras) Rosen Publishing Group, Inc., The.

Elsa's Shawl. 2003. 23.95 *(978-0-673-78130-7(5))* Celebration Pr.

En Busca De Insectos. 2003. 28.95 *(978-0-673-78096-6(1))* Celebration Pr.

En Busca del Amigo Desaparecido. (SPA., Illus.). 70p. (YA). (gr. 6-8). *(978-88-8148-323-5(8))* EMC/Paradigm Publishing.

En casa de mis Padrinos. (Spanish Early Intervention Levels Ser.). (SPA.). 28.38 *(978-0-7362-0847-5(X))* CENGAGE Learning.

En Donde Marchan los Elefantes? (Pebble Soup Exploraciones Ser.). (SPA.). 16p. (gr. -1-18). 31.00 *(978-0-7578-1679-6(7))* Rigby Education.

En donde marchan los Elefantes? Small Book. (Pebble Soup Exploraciones Ser.). (SPA.). 16p. (gr. -1-18). 5.00 *(978-0-7578-1719-9(X))* Rigby Education.

En el cielo de Medianoche: Big Book. (Pebble Soup Exploraciones Ser.). (SPA.). 16p. (gr. -1-18). 31.00 *(978-0-7578-1693-2(2))* Rigby Education.

En el cielo de Medianoche: Small Book. (Pebble Soup Exploraciones Ser.). (SPA.). 16p. (gr. -1-18). 5.00 *(978-0-7578-1733-5(5))* Rigby Education.

En el Jardin: Individual Title Six-Packs. (Literatura 2000 Ser.). (SPA.). (gr. 1-2). 28.00 *(978-0-7635-1067-1(X))* Rigby Education.

En el Mundo. (Spanish Early Intervention Levels Ser.). (SPA.). 23.10 *(978-1-56334-794-8(6))* CENGAGE Learning.

En el Rancho, 6, Pack. (Literatura 2000 Ser.). (SPA.). (gr. k-1). 28.00 *(978-0-7635-1018-3(1))* Rigby Education.

En el restaurante de mis Tios. (Spanish Early Intervention Levels Ser.). (SPA.). 23.10 *(978-1-56334-780-1(6))* CENGAGE Learning.

En el Supermercado, 6, Pack. (Chiquilibros Ser.). (SPA.). (gr. k-1). 23.00 *(978-0-7635-8617-1(X))* Rigby Education.

En el Zoologico, 6, Pack. 2003. 23.95 *(978-0-673-77146-9(6))* Celebration Pr.

En la Ciudad. (Spanish Early Intervention Levels Ser.). (SPA.). 23.10 *(978-1-56334-776-4(8))* CENGAGE Learning.

En la ciudad de Roma: Individual Title Six-Packs. (Literatura 2000 Ser.). (SPA.). (gr. 2-3). 33.00 *(978-0-7635-1091-6(2))* Rigby Education.

En la ciudad de San Antonio: Lap Book. (Pebble Soup Exploraciones Ser.). (SPA.). 16p. (gr. -1-18). 21.00 *(978-0-7578-1680-2(0))* Rigby Education.

En la ciudad de San Antonio: Small Book. (Pebble Soup Exploraciones Ser.). (SPA.). 16p. (gr. -1-18). 5.00 *(978-0-7578-1720-5(3))* Rigby Education.

En la Mananita. (Spanish Early Intervention Levels Ser.). (SPA.). 23.10 *(978-1-56334-796-2(2))* CENGAGE Learning.

En la oscuridad Interactive Packages: Duermete, mi Amor. (Pebble Soup Exploraciones Ser.). (SPA.). (gr. -1-18). 52.00 *(978-0-7578-5271-8(8))* Rigby Education.

En La Playa, 6 Pks. 2003. 23.95 *(978-0-673-77135-3(0))* Celebration Pr.

En la Playa, 6, Pack. (Chiquilibros Ser.). (SPA.). (gr. k-1). 23.00 *(978-0-7635-8618-8(8))* Rigby Education.

En mi Cama, 6 Pks. (Literatura 2000 Ser.). (SPA.). (gr. k-1). 28.00 *(978-0-7635-1019-0(X))* Rigby Education.

En mi Cuarto: Individual Title Six-Packs. (Literatura 2000 Ser.). (SPA.). (gr. k-1). 28.00 *(978-0-7635-1020-6(3))* Rigby Education.

En mi Escuela. (Spanish Early Intervention Levels Ser.). (SPA.). 23.10 *(978-1-56334-757-3(1))* CENGAGE Learning.

En Mi Jardin: Big Book Packages. 2003. 64.95 *(978-0-673-58579-0(4))* Celebration Pr.

Encuentros. (Nuevos Horizontes Ser.). (SPA.). (J). (gr. 5). wbk. ed. 9.95 *(978-1-56014-523-3(4))* Santillana USA Publishing Co., Inc.

Encuentros: Evaluations, Grade 5. (Nuevos Horizontes Ser.). (SPA.). (J). 22.50 *(978-1-56014-524-0(2))* Santillana USA Publishing Co., Inc.

Encuentros: Student Anthology. (Nuevos Horizontes Ser.). (SPA.). (J). (gr. 5). 19.95 *(978-1-56014-522-6(6))* Santillana USA Publishing Co., Inc.

English-Spanish Book Set 800937, 4 vols. 2005. (J). bds. *(978-1-59794-096-2(8))* Environments, Inc.

La Ensalada, 6 Packs. 2003. 23.95 *(978-0-673-77147-6(4))* Celebration Pr.

Es Mejor Dar Que Recibir. 2003. 28.95 *(978-0-673-78099-7(6))* Celebration Pr.

Es Mia! Social/Emotional Lap Book. (Pebble Soup Exploraciones Ser.). (SPA.). (gr. -1-18). 16.00 *(978-0-7578-1786-1(6))* Rigby Education.

Es un Elefante? (Spanish Early Intervention Levels Ser.). (SPA.). 21.30 *(978-0-7362-0800-0(3))* CENGAGE Learning.

Escalando: Individual Title Six-Packs. (Literatura 2000 Ser.). (SPA.). (gr. k-1). 28.00 *(978-0-7635-1021-3(1))* Rigby Education.

El Escondite: Individual Title, 6 pack. (Chiquilibros Ser.). (SPA.). (gr. k-1). 23.00 *(978-0-7635-8625-6(0))* Rigby Education.

Escudos Rotos (Broken Shields (XVI Century)) 2005. (SPA.). (J). pap. *(978-968-7381-00-8(0))* Tecolote, Ediciones, S.A. de C.V.

Espanol Correcto. (SPA.). (J). 29.00 *(978-958-04-5925-5(8))* Norma S.A. COL. Dist: Distribuidora Norma, Inc.

Espluga, Maria. I, Astronaut: Yo, Astronauta. 2009. (SPA & ENG.). 28p. (J). 13.95 *(978-1-931398-56-5(9))* Me+Mi Publishing.

—I, Ballerina: Yo, Bailarina. 2009. (ENG & SPA.). 28p. (J). 13.95 *(978-1-931398-55-8(0))* Me+Mi Publishing.

—I, Sailor: Yo, Marinero. 2009. (SPA & ENG.). 28p. (J). 13.95 *(978-1-931398-53-4(4))* Me+Mi Publishing.

Estados Unidos: Formacion, Desarrollo y Transformacion. (SPA.). (J). *(978-958-04-7743-3(4))* Norma S.A. COL. Dist: Distribuidora Norma, Inc.

Estice, Rose Mary & Fried, Mary. Big Keep Books- Spanish Emergent Reader 1: Mira como Juego; ¡Curitas!; Los Animales del Zoológico; Construyendo una Casa; la Alberca; ¡Agua y Jabón!; Me Visto; Mi Gato, 8 bks., Set. Elías, Annette, tr. Simon, Sue A. et al, illus. 2005.Tr. of Emergent Reader 1. (SPA.). 8p. (J). 20.00 *(978-1-893986-42-8(X))* Keep Bks.

Evan-Moor. Spanish / English Read & nderstand Science Grades 4-6. 2007. (Spanish/English Read & Understand Ser.). (ENG., Illus.). 304p. (J). (gr. 4-6). pap. 29.99 *(978-1-59673-077-9(3)*, EMC 5312) Evan-Moor Educational Pubs.

—Spanish/English Read & Understand Nonfiction: Grades 4-6. 2007. (Spanish/English Read & Understand Ser.). (ENG.). 304p. (J). (gr. 4-6). pap. 29.99 *(978-1-59673-076-2(5)*, EMC 5311) Evan-Moor Educational Pubs.

Expertas en Terremotos. (Saludos Ser.: Vol. 2). (SPA.). (gr. 3-5). 31.00 *(978-0-7635-3235-2(5))* Rigby Education.

Expertas en Terremotos: 6 Small Books. (Saludos Ser.: Vol. 2). (SPA.). (gr. 3-5). 31.00 *(978-0-7635-2066-3(7))* Rigby Education.

Falconer, Ian. Olivia y Las Princesas. 2012. (SPA., Illus.). 32p. (J). (gr. -1-1). 17.99 *(978-1-933032-82-5(0))* Lectorum Pubns., Inc.

La Familia Ruidosa: Lap Book. (Pebble Soup Exploraciones Ser.). 16p. (gr. -1-18). 21.00 *(978-0-7578-1671-0(1))* Rigby Education.

La Familia Ruidosa: Small Book. (Pebble Soup Exploraciones Ser.). 16p. (gr. -1-18). 5.00 *(978-0-7578-1711-3(4))* Rigby Education.

Fantasia Bilingüe/Bilingual Fantasy. (ENG & SPA.). 80p. 15.00 *(978-0-944356-02-9(8))* Alegria Hispana Pubns.

Feeling Scared: Social/Emotional Lap Book. (Pebble Soup Explorations Ser.). (SPA.). (gr. -1-18). 16.00 *(978-0-7635-7573-1(9))* Rigby Education.

Felipa y el Dragon: Individual Title Six-Packs. (Literatura 2000 Ser.). (SPA.). (gr. 1-2). 28.00 *(978-0-7635-1069-5(6))* Rigby Education.

Feliz Ano Nuevo. 2003. 23.95 *(978-0-673-78079-9(1))* Celebration Pr.

Fente, et al. Curso Intensivo de Espanol: Ejercicios Practicos: Nivel de Iniciacion y Elemental. (SPA.). 288p. stu. ed. 26.95 *(978-84-85786-43-5(2)*, SGS694) Edelsa Grupo Didascalia, S.A. ESP. Dist: Continental Bk. Co., Inc.

La Feria. (Spanish Early Intervention Levels Ser.). (SPA.). 23.10 *(978-1-56334-770-2(9))* CENGAGE Learning.

Fernández de Lizardi, José Joaquín. El Periquillo Sarniento. 2003. (SPA.). 351p. (YA). 12.95 *(978-968-6966-10-7(2))* EDITER'S Publishing Hse. MEX. Dist: EDITER'S Publishing Hse.

Fernández, Jesús, et al. Curso Intensivo de Espanol: Niveles Elemental e Intermedio: Clave. (SPA.). 32p. *(978-84-7143-416-6(4))* Sociedad General Espanola de Libreria.

—Curso Intensivo de Espanol: Niveles Intermedio y Superior: Clave. (SPA.). 64p. *(978-84-7143-418-0(0))* Sociedad General Espanola de Libreria.

Fernandez, Joyce. Little Bird - Pajarito. 2010. 31p. 15.95 *(978-0-615-23709-1(6))* My Second Language Publishing, USA.

Fernández, Mayra. Los Colores de Mi Mundo (Rainbow Kids) (SPA & ENG., Illus.). 20p. (J). pap. 6.95 *(978-1-887578-01-1(3)*, STK1SP) SpanPress, Inc.

Fiction & Nonfiction Packs: Combo Packs. (SPA.). (gr. k-2). 85.92 *(978-1-56334-403-9(3))* CENGAGE Learning.

Fiction & Nonfiction Packs: Jumbo Packs. (SPA.). (gr. k-2). 438.19 *(978-1-56334-400-8(9))* CENGAGE Learning.

La fiesta de Cumpleanos. (Spanish Early Intervention Levels Ser.). (SPA.). 23.10 *(978-1-56334-759-7(8))* CENGAGE Learning.

Fiesta de Dinosaurios, 6 Pks. (Chiquilibros Ser.). (SPA.). (gr. k-1). 23.00 *(978-0-7635-8786-4(9))* Rigby Education.

La Fiesta Monstruosa, 6 Pks. (Chiquilibros Ser.). (SPA.). (gr. k-1). 23.00 *(978-0-7635-8600-3(5))* Rigby Education.

Fiol, Maria A., tr. Eating the Rainbow (Spanish/English), 1 vol. 2010. (Libro de Comidas de Colores/Colorful Food Bks.). (ENG., Illus.). 16p. (J). bds. 6.95 *(978-1-59572-203-4(3))* Star Bright Bks., Inc.

—Que Sabroso Arco Iris!, 1 vol. 2010. (Libro de Comidas de Colores Ser.).Tr. of Eating the Rainbow. (SPA., Illus.). 32p. (J). bds. 6.95 *(978-1-59572-225-6(4))* Star Bright Bks., Inc.

Fisher, Doris & Sneed, Dani. Un dia Non, 1 vol. Lee, Karen, illus. 2006. (SPA.). 32p. (J). (gr. -1-3). 17.95 *(978-1-60718-694-6(2))* Arbordale Publishing.

—Mi dia Par, 1 vol. Lee, Karen, illus. 2007. (SPA & ENG.). 32p. (J). (gr. -1-3). 17.95 *(978-1-60718-692-2(6))* Arbordale Publishing.

"Fisher" Suedmeyer, Paul A. The 12 Eternals on the Great Voyage. 2013. 40p. pap. *(978-1-4602-1731-3(4))* FriesenPress.

Fito, el Perro. (Coleccion Leo Con Figuras). (SPA., Illus.). 14p. (J). pap. 5.50 *(978-950-11-0840-8(6)*, SGM410) Sigmar ARG. Dist: Continental Bk. Co., Inc.

Fleming, Candace. Nam! Nam! Nam! Schmidt, Alejandra, tr. from ENG. Karas, G. Brian, illus. 2007. (SPA.). 32p. (J). (gr. -1-2). 15.95 *(978-1-933032-35-1(9))* Lectorum Pubns., Inc.

Flip Chart. 2003. (Scott Foresman Science Ser.). (gr. k-18). suppl. ed. 294.00 *(978-0-673-59350-4(9))*; (gr. 1-18). suppl. ed. 435.75 *(978-0-673-59351-1(7))*; (gr. 2-18). suppl. ed. 435.75 *(978-0-673-59352-8(5))* Addison-Wesley Educational Pubs., Inc.

Flor Ada, Alma. Celebra el Ano Nuevo Chino con la Familia Fong. 2006. (Cuentos para Celebrar / Stories to Celebrate Ser.). (Illus.). 30p. (gr. k-6). per. 11.95 *(978-1-59820-114-7(X)*, Alfaguara) Santillana USA Publishing Co., Inc.

—Celebra el Cinco de Mayo con un Jarabe Tapatio. Gomez, Marcela & Silva, David, illus. 2006. (Cuentos para Celebrar / Stories to Celebrate Ser.). 30p. (gr. k-6). per. 11.95 *(978-1-59820-118-5(2))* Ediciones Alfaguara ESP. Dist: Santillana USA Publishing Co., Inc.

Flor Ada, Alma & Campoy, F. Isabel. ¡Muu, Moo! Rimas de Animales. Escrivá, Viví, illus. 2010. (SPA & ENG.). 48p. (J). (gr. -1-2). 16.99 *(978-0-06-134613-2(6)*, Rayo) HarperCollins Pubs.

—Muu, Moo! Rimas de Animales - Animal Nursery Rhymes. Escrivá, Viví, illus. 2010. (SPA & ENG.). 48p. (J). (gr. -1-2). lib. bdg. 17.89 *(978-0-06-134614-9(4)*, Rayo) HarperCollins Pubs.

—Ten Little Puppies/Diez Perritos. Wensell, Ulises, illus. 2011. (SPA & ENG.). 32p. (J). (gr. -1-3). 16.99 *(978-0-06-147043-1(0)*, Rayo) HarperCollins Pubs.

Flor Ada, Alma & Zubizarreta, Gabriel M. Con Cariño, Amalia. (SPA., Illus.). (J). (gr. 3-7). 2013. 160p. pap. 6.99 *(978-1-4424-2406-7(0))* 2012. 144p. 15.99 *(978-1-4424-2405-0(2)*, Atheneum Bks. for Young Readers) Simon & Schuster Children's Publishing.

Las Flores De Dona Flora: Individual 6-packs. 2003. 23.95 *(978-0-673-78073-7(2))* Celebration Pr.

Focas. (Spanish Early Intervention Levels Ser.). (SPA.). 21.30 *(978-0-7362-0827-7(5))* CENGAGE Learning.

Fonolibros Series: Complete Stage One. 2003. (SPA.). 1230.95 *(978-0-7652-1052-4(5))* Modern Curriculum Pr.

Fonolibros Series: Complete Stage Two. 2003. (SPA.). 895.50 *(978-0-7652-1053-1(3))* Modern Curriculum Pr.

Fontes, Justine. Daniel el Descortes: Rude Ralph. Jordan, Charles, illus. 2005. (Rookie Reader Español Ser.). 32p. (gr. k-2). 19.50 *(978-0-516-24444-0(2)*, Children's Pr.) Scholastic Library Publishing.

Fontes, Justine & Jordan, Charles. Daniel el Descortés. Jordan, Charles, illus. 2011. (Rookie Ready to Learn Español Ser.). (SPA., Illus.). 40p. (J). pap. 5.95 *(978-0-531-26790-5(3))*; lib. bdg. 23.00 *(978-0-531-26122-4(0))* Scholastic Library Publishing. (Children's Pr.).

Franks, Katie. Dirt Bikes. 2009. (Motorcycles Made for Speed/Motocicletas a toda velocidad Ser.). (ENG & SPA.). 24p. (gr. 1-1). 42.50 *(978-1-61514-672-7(5)*, Editorial Buenas Letras) Rosen Publishing Group, Inc., The.

Fraser, Janine M. La Mariposa de Abdullah. (Torre de Papel Ser.). (SPA., Illus.). (J). (gr. 2). 7.95 *(978-958-04-4917-1(1))* Norma S.A. COL. Dist: Distribuidora Norma, Inc.

Freddy the Fish. 2003. 23.95 *(978-0-673-78128-4(3))* Celebration Pr.

Freed, Herb. Sing & Learn Spanish. 2004. 271p. (J). pap. 14.95 *(978-0-9760472-0-9(9))* Global Village Kids, LLC.

French, Cathy. Make an Animal Mobile & Haz un móvil de Animales: 6 English, 6 Spanish Adaptations. 2011. (SPA & ENG.). (J). 75.00 net. *(978-1-4108-5619-7(4))* Benchmark Education Co.

—Make an Island & Haz una Isla: 6 English, 6 Spanish Adaptations. 2011. (ENG & SPA.). (J). 75.00 net. *(978-1-4108-5632-6(1))* Benchmark Education Co.

Friedman, Laurie. A Clases Otra Vez, Mallory. Anaya, Josefina, tr. from ENG. Schmitz, Tamara, illus. 2008. (Mallory en español (Mallory in Spanish) Ser.).Tr. of Back to School, Mallory. (SPA & ENG.). 176p. (J). (gr. 2-5). pap. 5.95 *(978-0-7613-3904-5(3))* Lerner Publishing Group.

Fruits & Vegetables I Like to Eat - Spanish Take Home Book. 2007. (Journeys Ser.). (J). pap. 49.95 *(978-1-4042-5513-5(3)*, Rosen Classroom) Rosen Publishing Group, Inc., The.

La Fruta. (Spanish Early Intervention Levels Ser.). (SPA.). 23.10 *(978-1-56334-762-7(8))* CENGAGE Learning.

Galindo-Leal, Carlos. De dos mundos = of Two Worlds: Las ranas, sapos y salamandras de la Península de Yucatán, México = the Frogs, Toads & Salamanders of the Yucatan Peninsula, Mexico. Arreola Alemón, Roberto, illus. 2003. (SPA & ENG.). 152p. pap. 19.95 *(978-1-929165-52-0(8))* PANGAEA.

La Gallinita Roja: Lap Book. (Pebble Soup Exploraciones Ser.). (SPA.). 16p. (gr. -1-18). 21.00 *(978-0-7578-1684-0(3))* Rigby Education.

La Gallinita Roja: Small Book. (Pebble Soup Exploraciones Ser.). (SPA.). 16p. (gr. -1-18). 5.00 *(978-0-7578-1724-3(6))* Rigby Education.

La Gallinita Roja: Video Tape. (ENG & SPA.). (gr. k-1). 26.00 *(978-0-7635-6276-2(9))* Rigby Education.

Gamblin, Rose Tooley & Hernández, Oscar. Bill's Lunch: El Almuerzo de Bill. 2010. (ENG & SPA., Illus.). 32p. (J). *(978-0-8127-0472-3(X))* Review & Herald Publishing Assn.

Game Time: Matching English 6-packs. 2003. 23.95 *(978-0-673-57558-6(6))* Celebration Pr.

García Márquez, Gabriel. La Siesta del Martes.Tr. of Tuesday's Siesta. (SPA.). 28p. 10.50 *(978-958-04-5574-5(0))* Norma S.A. COL. Dist: Distribuidora Norma, Inc.

Garcia, Nasario. Grandpa Lolo & Trampa: A Story of Surprise & Mystery = Abuelito Lolo y Trampa: Un Cuento de Sorpresa y Misterio. Montoya, Jeremy, illus. 2014. (SPA & ENG.). (J). 9.99 *(978-1-936744-30-5(9))* LPD Pr.

—Grandpa Lolo's Navajo Saddle Blanket: La Tilma de Abuelito Lolo. Moeller, Richard, illus. Moeller, Richard, photos by. 2012. (J). *(978-0-8263-5078-7(X))*; 61p. pap. *(978-0-8263-5080-0(1))* Univ. of New Mexico Pr.

Gartando, Luigi. Un Gran Equipo: Gol 1. 2012. (Vintage Espanol Ser.). (SPA.). 160p. (J). (gr. 2-5). pap. 8.95 *(978-0-345-80422-8(8)*, Vintage Espanol) Knopf Doubleday Publishing Group.

—¡Nos Vamos a Brasil! ¡Gol! 2013. (Vintage Espanol Ser.). (SPA.). 144p. (J). (gr. 2-5). pap. 9.95 *(978-0-345-80423-5(6)*, Vintage Espanol) Knopf Doubleday Publishing Group.

La gatita Presumida. (Spanish Early Intervention Levels Ser.). (SPA.). 28.38 *(978-0-7362-0846-8(1))* CENGAGE Learning.

Gatitos: Individual Title Six-Packs. (Literatura 2000 Ser.). (SPA.). (gr. -1-1). 28.00 *(978-0-7635-1195-1(1))* Rigby Education.

Gedovius, Juan. Purple Cubed. Gedovius, Juan, illus. (Illus.). 32p. (J). (gr. k-6). 13.95 *(978-968-19-0751-8(5))* Santillana USA Publishing Co., Inc.

Ghigna, Charles. Veo el Invierno. Jatkowska, Ag, illus. 2012. (Bilingual I See Ser.).Tr. of I See Winter. (ENG, SPA & MUL.). 24p. (gr. -1 — 1). lib. bdg. 22.65 *(978-1-4048-7310-0(4)*, I See) Picture Window Bks.

El gigante Solitario: Individual Title Six-Packs. (Literatura 2000 Ser.). (SPA.). (gr. 2-3). 33.00 *(978-0-7635-1092-3(0))* Rigby Education.

Glencoe McGraw-Hill Staff. !Buen Viaje! 2005. (Glencoe Spanish Ser.). (ENG & SPA.). (gr. 8-12). cd-rom 152.28 *(978-0-07-868623-8(7)*, 0078686237) McGraw-Hill Higher Education.

—¡Buen Viaje!, Level 3. 2004. (Glencoe Spanish Ser.). (ENG & SPA.). (gr. 9-12). stu. ed. 152.28 incl. cd-rom *(978-0-07-868624-5(5)*, 0078686245) McGraw-Hill Education.

—¡Buen Viaje!, Level 1. 2005. (Glencoe Spanish Ser.). (ENG & SPA.). (gr. 7-12). stu. ed. 150.52 incl. cd-rom *(978-0-07-868622-1(9)*, 0078686229) McGraw-Hill Education.

Gol! (Spanish Early Intervention Levels Ser.). (SPA.). 23.10 *(978-0-7362-0323-4(0))* CENGAGE Learning.

Gol!, 6, Pack. 2003. 23.95 *(978-0-673-78064-5(3))* Celebration Pr.

Gómez, Carlos Humberto. Nos Comunicamos 1. (Coleccion Nos Comunicamos). (SPA & ENG.). (J). (gr. 1). pap. 23.50 *(978-958-04-1580-0(3)*, 15017309) Norma S.A. COL. Dist: Continental Bk. Co., Inc.

—Nos Comunicamos 2. (Coleccion Nos Comunicamos). (SPA & ENG.). (J). (gr. 2). pap. 23.50 *(978-958-04-1581-7(1)*, 15017310) Norma S.A. COL. Dist: Continental Bk. Co., Inc.

—Nos Comunicamos 4. (Coleccion Nos Comunicamos). (SPA & ENG.). (J). (gr. 4). pap. 23.50 *(978-958-04-1583-1(8)*, 1021251) Norma S.A. COL. Dist: Continental Bk. Co., Inc.

—Nos Comunicamos 6. (Coleccion Nos Comunicamos). (SPA & ENG.). (J). (gr. 6). pap. 23.50 *(978-958-04-1585-5(4)*, 1021253) Norma S.A. COL. Dist: Continental Bk. Co., Inc.

—Nos Comunicamos Kindergarten. (Coleccion Nos Comunicamos). (SPA & ENG.). (J). 23.50 *(978-958-04-1579-4(X)*, NOR5794) Norma S.A. COL. Dist: Continental Bk. Co., Inc.

Gonzalez, Maya Christina. My Colors, My World. Gonzalez, Maya Christina, illus. 2013.Tr. of Mis Colores, Mi Mundo. (ENG & SPA., Illus.). 32p. (J). pap. 9.95 *(978-0-89239-278-0(9)*, Children's Book Press) Lee & Low Bks., Inc.

Gonzalez, Maya Christina & Goldberg, Dana. Llámame Árbol. 2014.Tr. of Call Me Tree. (SPA & ENG.). 24p. (J). 19.95 *(978-0-89239-294-0(0))* Lee & Low Bks., Inc.

La Granja De Don Manuel: Individual 6-packs. 2003. 23.95 *(978-0-673-77151-3(2))* Celebration Pr.

Granny Says. 2005. (Illus.). (J). pap. 11.00 *(978-0-9764198-0-8(7))* Allecram Publishing.

Green Collection. (Elefonetica Ser.). (SPA.). (gr. 1-2). 324.85 *(978-0-7362-0784-3(8))* CENGAGE Learning.

Greene, Inez. Adonde Esta Me Topito?, Level 1. Flor Ada, Alma, tr. 2003. (Dejame Leer Ser.). (SPA., Illus.). (J). (gr. -1-3). 6.50 *(978-0-673-36328-2(7)*, Good Year Bks.) Celebration Pr.

Gregorio El Gallo, 6 Pack. 2003. 23.95 *(978-0-673-78078-2(3))* Celebration Pr.

The Grocery Store: Individual Title Two-Packs. (Chiquilibros Ser.). (gr. -1-1). 12.00 *(978-0-7635-8539-6(4))* Rigby Education.

El grupo musical Lac Hong: 6 Small Books. (Saludos Ser.: Vol. 1). (SPA.). (gr. 3-5). 31.00 *(978-0-7635-1757-1(7))* Rigby Education.

El Guerito Travieso, 6 Packs. 2003. 23.95 *(978-0-673-77154-4(7))* Celebration Pr.

Guy, Ginger Foglesong. Fiesta! Moreno, Rene King, illus. 2007. (SPA.). 32p. (J). (gr. -1-3). 6.99 *(978-0-06-088226-6(3)*, Greenwillow Bks.) HarperCollins Pubs.

Hanson, Anders. Los Pantaloncillos del Canguro, 1 vol. Nobens, C. A., illus. 2007. (Cuentos de Animales Ser.). (SPA & ENG.). 24p. (J). (gr. k-3). lib. bdg. 24.21 *(978-1-59928-655-6(6)*, SandCastle) ABDO Publishing Co.

—La Tuba del Rinoceronte, 1 vol. Nobens, C. A., illus. 2007. (Cuentos de Animales Ser.). (SPA & ENG.). 24p. (J). (gr. k-3). lib. bdg. 24.21 *(978-1-59928-665-5(3)*, SandCastle) ABDO Publishing Co.

Harris, Dorothy Joan. Un Perro Muy Diferente. Rioja, Alberto Jimenez, tr. from ENG. LaFave, Kim, illus. 2006. (SPA.). 28p. (J). (gr. 5-6). pap. 7.99 *(978-1-933032-04-7(9))* Lectorum Pubns., Inc.

Harvey, Sarah N. El Blanco, 1 vol. 2010. (Spanish Soundings Ser.). (SPA.). 128p. (YA). (gr. 8-12). pap. 9.95 *(978-1-55469-317-7(9))* Orca Bk. Pubs. USA.

Has visto al jabali que anda por Aqui? Individual Title Six-Packs. (Literatura 2000 Ser.). (SPA.). (gr. 2-3). 33.00 *(978-0-7635-1093-0(9))* Rigby Education.

Hay un esqueleto en el Autobus: Individual Title Six-Packs. (Literatura 2000 Ser.). (SPA.). (gr. 2-3). 33.00 *(978-0-7635-1094-7(7))* Rigby Education.

Hayes, Joe. The Coyote under the Table (El Coyote Debajo de la Mesa) Castro L., Antonio, illus. 2011. (ENG & SPA.). 144p. (J). (gr. 1-7). pap. 12.95 *(978-1-935955-06-1(3))* Cinco Puntos Pr.

—Dance, Nana, Dance (Baila, Nana, Baila) Trenard Sayago, Mauricio, illus. 2010. (ENG & SPA.). 128p. (J). (gr. 3-6). pap. 12.95 *(978-1-933693-61-3(4))* Cinco Puntos Pr.

—El Día que Nevaron Tortillas. Hayes, Joe, tr. Lopez, Antonio Castro & Castro L., Antonio, illus. 2003.Tr. of Day It Snowed Tortillas. (SPA & ENG.). 160p. (J). (gr. 4-6). pap. 12.95 *(978-0-938317-76-0(8))* Cinco Puntos Pr.

—Don't Say a Word, Mama / No Digas Nada, Mama. 2013. (Illus.). 32p. (gr. -1-3). (ENG & SPA.). 17.95 *(978-1-935955-29-0(2))*; (SPA & ENG., (J). pap. 8.95 *(978-1-935955-45-0(4))* Cinco Puntos Pr.

Hayhurst, Chris. John Sutter: California Pioneer / Pionero de California. 2009. (Famous People in American History/Grandes personajes en la historia de los Estados Unidos Ser.). (ENG & SPA.). 32p. (gr. 2-3). 47.90 *(978-1-61512-549-4(3)*, Editorial Buenas Letras) Rosen Publishing Group, Inc., The.

—John Sutter: Pionero de California (John Sutter: California Pioneer) 2009. (Grandes personajes en la historia de los Estados Unidos (Famous People in American History) Ser.). (SPA.). 32p. (gr. 2-3). 47.90 *(978-1-61512-803-7(4)*, Editorial Buenas Letras) Rosen Publishing Group, Inc., The.

—Sitting Bull / Toro Sentado: Sioux War Chief / Jefe Sioux. 2009. (Famous People in American History/Grandes personajes en la historia de los Estados Unidos Ser.). (SPA.). 32p. (gr. 2-3). 47.90 *(978-1-61512-555-5(8)*, Editorial Buenas Letras) Rosen Publishing Group, Inc., The.

Hecho en Corea: 6 Small Books. (Saludos Ser.: Vol. 3). (SPA.). (gr. 3-5). 31.00 *(978-0-7635-1830-1(1))* Rigby Education.

Hector tiene Hipo. (Spanish Early Intervention Levels Ser.). 21.30 *(978-0-7362-0833-8(X))* CENGAGE Learning.

Henderson, Sara & Zenz, Aaron. Howie Wants to Play, 1 vol. Henderson, Sara & Zenz, Aaron, illus. 2009. (I Can Read! / Howie Series / ¡Yo Sé Leer! / Serie: Fido Ser.). (ENG., Illus.). 32p. (J). pap. 3.99 *(978-0-310-71875-8(9))* Zonderkidz.

Hermoso, A. S., et al. Curso Practico de la Gramatica de Espanol Lengua Extranjera: Curso Practico I. 2nd ed. (SPA.). 116p. wbk. ed. 18.95 *(978-84-7711-073-6(5)*, EDI0735) Edelsa Grupo Didascalia, S.A. ESP. Dist: Continental Bk. Co., Inc.

—Curso Practico de la Gramatica de Espanol Lengua Extranjera: Curso Practico II. (SPA.). 116p. wbk. ed. 18.95 *(978-84-7711-074-3(3)*, EDI0743) Edelsa Grupo Didascalia, S.A. ESP. Dist: Continental Bk. Co., Inc.

—Curso Practico de la Gramatica de Espanol Lengua Extranjera: Curso Practico III. (SPA., Illus.). 128p. wbk. ed. 24.95 *(978-84-7711-075-0(1)*, EDI0751) Edelsa Grupo Didascalia, S.A. ESP. Dist: Continental Bk. Co., Inc.

Herrera, Juan Felipe. The Upside down Boy. Gómez, Elizabeth, illus. 2011. (Rise & Shine Ser.).Tr. of Nino de Cabeza. (SPA & ENG.). 32p. (C). (gr. k-3). per. 14.95 *(978-0-89239-217-9(7))* National Geographic School Publishing, Inc.

Hill, Eric. Donde Esta Spot? (SPA.). pap. 10.95 *(978-950-07-1960-5(6))* Editorial Sudamericana S.A. ARG. Dist: Distribooks, Inc.

Hillert, Margaret. Dear Dragon Goes to the Library (Querido Dragon Va a la Biblioteca) Del Risco, Eida, tr. from ENG. Schimmel, David, illus. 2010. (BeginningtoRead Ser.). (SPA & ENG.). 32p. (J). (gr. k-2). lib. bdg. 22.60 *(978-1-59953-361-2(8))* Norwood Hse. Pr.

—Dear Dragon's Day with Father (Querido Dragon Pasa el Dia con Papa) Del Risco, Eida, tr. from ENG. Schimmel, David, illus. 2010. (BeginningtoRead Ser.). (SPA & ENG.). 32p. (J). (gr. k-2). lib. bdg. 22.60 *(978-1-59953-360-5(X))* Norwood Hse. Pr.

—Es Primavera, Querido Dragón/It's Spring, Dear Dragon. Schimmell, David, illus. 2011. (BeginningtoRead Ser.). 32p. (J). (-2). pap. 11.94 *(978-1-60357-555-3(3))* Norwood Hse. Pr.

—Es Primavera, Querido Dragón/It's Spring, Dear Dragon. del Risco, Eida, tr. from ENG. Schimmell, David, illus. 2011. (BeginningtoRead Ser.). 32p. (J). (gr. k-2). lib. bdg. 22.60 *(978-1-59953-471-8(1))* Norwood Hse. Pr.

—Es un Buen Juego, Querido Dragón/It's a Good Game, Dear Dragon. Schimmell, David, illus. 2010. (BeginningtoRead Ser.). 32p. (J). (-2). pap. 11.94 *(978-1-60357-550-8(2))* Norwood Hse. Pr.

—It's a Good Game, Dear Dragon (Es un Buen Juego, Querido Dragon) Del Risco, Eida, tr. from ENG. Schimmell, David, illus. 2010. (BeginningtoRead Ser.). (SPA & ENG.). 32p. (J). (gr. k-2). lib. bdg. 22.60 *(978-1-59953-362-9(6))* Norwood Hse. Pr.

—Juega, Juega, Juega, Querido Dragón/Play, Play, Play, Dear Dragon. del Risco, Eida, tr. Schimmell, David, illus. 2010. (BeginningtoRead Ser.). 32p. (J). (-2). pap. 11.94 *(978-1-60357-551-5(0))* Norwood Hse. Pr.

—Play, Play, Play, Dear Dragon (Juega, Juega, Juega, Querido Dragon) Del Risco, Eida, tr. Schimmell, David, illus. 2010. (BeginningtoRead Ser.). (SPA & ENG.). 32p. (J). (gr. k-2). lib. bdg. 22.60 *(978-1-59953-363-6(4))* Norwood Hse. Pr.

Hipp, Andrew. El Girasol: Por dentro y por fuera (Sunflower:Inside & Out) 2009. (Explora la Naturaleza (Getting into Nature) Ser.). (SPA.). 32p. (gr. 3-4). 47.90 *(978-1-61512-336-0(9)*, Editorial Buenas Letras) Rosen Publishing Group, Inc., The.

—El Maiz: Por dentro y por fuera (Corn: Inside & Out) 2009. (Explora la Naturaleza (Getting into Nature) Ser.). (SPA.). 32p. (gr. 3-4). 47.90 *(978-1-61512-337-7(7)*, Editorial Buenas Letras) Rosen Publishing Group, Inc., The.

—El Roble: Por dentro y por fuera (Oak Tree: Inside & Out) 2009. (Explora la Naturaleza (Getting into Nature) Ser.). (SPA.). 32p. (gr. 3-4). 47.90 *(978-1-61512-338-4(5)*, Editorial Buenas Letras) Rosen Publishing Group, Inc., The.

Hoffman, Mary Ann. LeBron James: Basketball Star. 2009. (Sports Superstars Ser.). 24p. (gr. 1-1). 42.50 *(978-1-60853-178-3(3)*, PowerKids Pr.) Rosen Publishing Group, Inc., The.

Hola! (Spanish Early Intervention Levels Ser.). (SPA.). 23.10 *(978-1-56334-761-0(X))* CENGAGE Learning.

Hola y Adios, 6 Packs. (Literatura 2000 Ser.). (SPA.). (gr. k-1). 28.00 *(978-0-7635-1023-7(8))* Rigby Education.

Holt, Rinehart and Winston Staff. En Avant: Online Edition. 4th ed. 2003. 43.86 *(978-0-03-031718-7(5))* Holt McDougal.

—Ven Conmigo! Level 1: Storytelling Book. 3rd ed. 2003. (Holt Spanish Ser.). (SPA.). pap. 14.60 *(978-0-03-065474-9(2))* Holt McDougal.

El Hombrecito de pan de Jengibre. (ENG & SPA.). (gr. k-1). 26.00 incl. VHS *(978-0-7635-6277-9(7))* Rigby Education.

Las Horas. (Coleccion Libritos Acordeon). (SPA., Illus.). 10p. (J). pap. 5.50 *(978-950-11-0827-9(9)*, SGM279) Sigmar ARG. Dist: Continental Bk. Co., Inc.

La Hormiga y el Saltamontes: Lap Book. (Pebble Soup Exploraciones Ser.). (SPA.). 16p. (gr. -1-18). 21.00 *(978-0-7578-1682-6(7))* Rigby Education.

La hormiga y el Saltamontes: Small Book. (Pebble Soup Exploraciones Ser.). (SPA.). 16p. (gr. -1-18). 5.00 *(978-0-7578-1722-9(X))* Rigby Education.

Houghton, Gillian. Abejas: Por dentro y por fuera (Bees: Inside & Out) 2009. (Explora la Naturaleza (Getting into Nature) Ser.). (SPA.). 32p. (gr. 3-4). 47.90 *(978-1-61512-333-9(4)*, Editorial Buenas Letras) Rosen Publishing Group, Inc., The.

Hudson, Amanda & Nations, Susan. This Is My Ball/Ésta es mi Pelota. 2008. (Our Toys/Nuestros Juguetes Ser.). (SPA.). 16p. (gr. -1-2). pap. 5.30 *(978-0-8368-9355-7(7)*, Weekly Reader Leveled Readers) Stevens, Gareth Publishing LLLP.

Huevo rojo y Jengibre: Six-Pack. (Saludos Ser.: Vol. 1). (SPA.). (gr. 2-3). 31.00 *(978-0-7635-9518-0(7))* Rigby Education.

Hunt, Angela Elwell. Los Tres Árboles: Cento Tradicional. Jonke, Tim, illus. 2010. Orig. Title: The Tale of Three Trees - A Traditional Folktale. (SPA & ENG.). 32p. (J). 5.99 *(978-1-4143-3737-1(X))* Tyndale Hse. Pubs.

Huracan a la Vista! 6 Small Books. (Saludos Ser.: Vol. 2). (SPA.). (gr. 3-5). 31.00 *(978-0-7635-2069-4(1))* Rigby Education.

S

Hurt-Newton, Tania. Vamos de Paseo. (SPA.). pap. 7.95 (978-950-07-2027-4(2)) Editorial Sudamericana S.A. ARG. Dist: Distribooks, Inc.

I Dance 6 Packs: Matching English. 2003. 23.95 (978-0-673-57559-3(4)) Celebration Pr.

I Live Here: Matching English, 6 Packs. 2003. 23.95 (978-0-673-57560-9(8)) Celebration Pr.

The Ice Cream Shop: Individual Title, 2 Packs. (Chiquilibros Ser.). (gr. -1-1). 12.00 (978-0-7635-8534-1(3)) Rigby Education.

Igual a mi Abuelo: Individual Title, 6 Packs. (Literatura 2000 Ser.). (SPA.). (gr. 1-2). 28.00 (978-0-7635-1045-9(9)) Rigby Education.

In the Dark Interactive Packages: Bedtime. (Pebble Soup Explorations Ser.). (SPA.). (gr. -1-18). 52.00 (978-0-7578-5247-3(5)) Rigby Education.

In the Dark Interactive Packages: Nighttime Jobs. (Pebble Soup Explorations Ser.). (SPA.). (gr. -1-18). 52.00 (978-0-7578-5250-3(5)) Rigby Education.

In the Midnight Sky. (Pebble Soup Explorations Ser.). (SPA.). 16p. (gr. -1-18). 31.00 (978-0-7578-1669-7(X)) Rigby Education.

In the Midnight Sky: Small Book. (Pebble Soup Explorations Ser.). (SPA.). 16p. (gr. -1-18). 5.00 (978-0-7578-1709-0(2)) Rigby Education.

Infante, Begona. Fatima Yo Soy de El Salvador.Tr. of I'm from El Salvador. (SPA.). 48p. (J). 12.95 (978-84-246-9403-6(1)) La Galera, S.A. Editorial ESP. Dist: AIMS International Bks., Inc.

El Ingles Animado por Walt Disney.Tr. of Animated English by Walt Disney. (SPA.). (978-970-22-0098-7(9)) Larousse, Ediciones, S. A. de C. V.

Inkiow, Dimiter. Yo, Clara y el Papagayo Pipo. (Torre de Papel Ser.). (SPA.). (J). (gr. 2). 7.95 (978-958-04-2072-9(6)) Norma S.A. COL. Dist: Distribuidora Norma, Inc.

—Yo, Clara y el Poni Miguelin. (SPA., Illus.). 7.95 (978-958-04-2389-8(X)) Norma S.A. COL. Dist: Distribuidora Norma, Inc.

Insectos, Insectos, 6 Packs. 2003. 23.95 (978-0-673-78070-6(8)) Celebration Pr.

Insects, Insects. 2003. 23.95 (978-0-673-78132-1(1)) Celebration Pr.

The Iron Horse, 6 Packs. (Chiquilibros Ser.). (gr. k-1). 23.00 (978-0-7635-0443-4(2)) Rigby Education.

Iturralde, Edna. Conoce a Miguel de Cervantes: Get to Know Miguel de Cervantes. 2014. (Personajes Del Mundo Hispnico Ser.). (ENG & SPA., Illus.). 32p. (J). (gr. -1-3). 15.95 (978-1-61435-352-2(2), Alfaguara) Santillana USA Publishing Co., Inc.

Izquierdo, Ana, tr. Caritas Felices: Winnie-the-Pooh. 2007. (Disney Winnie the Pooh (SilverDolphin) Ser.). (SPA., Illus.). 10p. (J). (gr. -1). bds. (978-970-718-393-3(4), Silver Dolphin en Español) Advanced Marketing, S. de R. L. de C. V.

Jackson, Nikki. Georgia & Reed's: My Potty & Me. 2012. 16p. pap. 15.99 (978-1-4772-4516-3(2)) AuthorHouse.

—Georgia & Reeds: The AL-PHA-BET Book. 2012. 20p. pap. 17.99 (978-1-4772-2939-2(6)) AuthorHouse.

Jarkins, Sheila. The Adventures of Marco Flamingo in the Jungle. Jarkins, Sheila, illus. 2012. (Illus.). 32p. (J). 1.99 (978-1-936299-31-7(3), Raven Tree Pr.) Delta Systems Company, Inc.

Jeffries, Joyce. Meet the Mayor / Conoce a Los Alcaldes. 2013. (People Around Town / Gente de Mi Ciudad Ser.). (SPA & ENG., Illus.). 24p. (J). (gr. k-2). 22.60 (978-1-4339-9470-8(4)) Stevens, Gareth Publishing LLLP.

—Meet the Pilot / Conoce a Los Pilotos. 2013. (People Around Town / Gente de Mi Ciudad Ser.). (SPA.). 24p. (J). (gr. k-2). 22.60 (978-1-4339-9472-2(0)) Stevens, Gareth Publishing LLLP.

Jenkins, Jerry B. & Fabry, Chris. El Libro del Rey. 2008. (Lombricero Ser.: 1).Tr. of Book of the King. (SPA.). 304p. (J). pap. 7.99 (978-1-4143-2216-2(X), Tyndale Espanol) Tyndale Hse. Pubs.

Johansen, Heidi. What I Look Like When I am Angry / Cómo me veo cuando estoy Enojado. 2009. (Let's Look at Feelings / un vistazo a los sentimientos Ser.). (ENG & SPA.). 24p. (gr. k-1). 42.50 (978-1-61514-245-3(2), Editorial Buenas Letras) Rosen Publishing Group, Inc., The.

—What I Look Like When I am Happy / Cómo me veo cuando estoy Contento. 2009. (Let's Look at Feelings / un vistazo a los sentimientos Ser.). (ENG & SPA.). 24p. (gr. k-1). 42.50 (978-1-61514-244-6(4), Editorial Buenas Letras) Rosen Publishing Group, Inc., The.

Johnson, Bruce & McKay, Sindy. We Both Read Bilingual Edition-About Dogs/Acerca de Los Perros. 2011. (ENG & SPA., Illus.). 44p. (J). pap. 4.99 (978-1-60115-048-6(2)) Treasure Bay, Inc.

Johnson, Gee & Sánchez, Lucía M. El Pulpo. 2011. (2G Vida Marina Ser.). (SPA., Illus.). 20p. (J). (gr. k-2). pap. 6.99 (978-1-61541-452-9(5)) American Reading Co.

Jones, Christianne C. Un Cuarto para Dos, 1 vol. Ruíz, Carlos, tr. Trover, Zachary, illus. 2006. (Read-It! Readers en Español: Story Collection).Tr. of Room to Share. (SPA.). 24p. (gr. -1-3). 21.32 (978-1-4048-1694-7(1), Easy Readers) Picture Window Bks.

—Dani el Dinosaurio, 1 vol. Lozano, Clara, tr. from ENG. Epstein, Len, illus. 2006. (Read-It! Readers en Español: Story Collection). (SPA.). 24p. (gr. -1-3). lib. bdg. 21.32 (978-1-4048-2706-6(4), Easy Readers) Picture Window Bks.

—Eric No Juega, 1 vol. Ruíz, Carlos, tr. Demski, James, Jr., illus. 2006. (Read-It! Readers en Español: Story Collection).Tr. of Eric Won't Do It. (SPA.). 24p. (gr. -1-3). 21.32 (978-1-4048-1683-1(6), Easy Readers) Picture Window Bks.

—Pollita Pequenita, 1 vol. Abello, Patricia, tr. from ENG. Hermanson, Kyle, illus. 2006. (Read-It! Readers en Español: Cuentos Folclóricos Ser.).Tr. of Chicken Little. (SPA.). 32p. (gr. k-3). 21.32 (978-1-4048-1646-6(1), Easy Readers) Picture Window Bks.

—Pruebalo, 1 vol. Ruíz, Carlos, tr. Yi, Hye Won, illus. 2006. (Read-It! Readers en Español: Story Collection).Tr. of Just Try it. (SPA.). 24p. (gr. -1-3). 21.32 (978-1-4048-1692-3(5), Easy Readers) Picture Window Bks.

Juan y Paula en la Granja. (Coleccion Leo Con Figuras). (SPA.). 14p. (J). pap. 4.50 (978-950-11-0837-8(6), SGM376) Sigmar ARG. Dist: Continental Bk. Co., Inc.

Juego de Dedos. (Spanish Early Intervention Levels Ser.). (SPA.). 21.30 (978-0-7362-0805-5(4)) CENGAGE Learning.

Juez por un Dia: 6 Small Books. (Saludos Ser.: Vol. 1). (SPA.). (gr. 3-5). 31.00 (978-0-7635-1802-8(6)) Rigby Education.

Juez por un Dia: Big Book. (Saludos Ser.: Vol. 1). (SPA.). (gr. 3-5). 31.00 (978-0-7635-3172-0(3)) Rigby Education.

Juguemos con la Musica.Tr. of Let's Play with Music. (SPA.). (J). (gr. k-2). pap., stu. ed. 11.16 (978-968-24-3081-7(X)) Trillas Editorial, S. A. MEX. Dist: Lectorum Pubns., Inc.

Jung, Scott. Verdades bíblicas eternas (Timeless Bible Truths) 2011. 32p. pap. 6.99 (978-0-7586-2680-6(0)) Concordia Publishing Hse.

—Verdades bíblicas eternas (Timeless Bible Truths) - Bilingual. 2011. 64p. pap. 7.99 (978-0-7586-2681-3(9)) Concordia Publishing Hse.

Just Bunny & Me: Big Book. (Pebble Soup Explorations Ser.). (SPA.). 16p. (gr. -1-18). 31.00 (978-0-7578-1666-6(5)) Rigby Education.

Just Bunny & Me: Small Book. (Pebble Soup Explorations Ser.). (SPA.). 16p. (gr. -1-18). 5.00 (978-0-7578-1706-9(8)) Rigby Education.

Kalman, Bobbie & Johnson, Robin. El Ciclo de Vida Del Pinguino Emperador. 2007. (Libro de Bobbie Kalman Ser.). (SPA., Illus.). 32p. (J). (978-1-4287-3238-4(1)) Crabtree Publishing Co.

Kanellos, Nicolás. El Torneo de Trabalenguas / the Tongue Twister Tournament. Vega, Anne, illus. 2016. (SPA & ENG.). 32p. (J). (gr. k-4). 17.95 (978-1-55885-832-9(6), Piñata Books) Arte Publico Pr.

Kassirer, Sue. La feria musical de Matematicas: Math Matters en Espanol. Smath, Jerry, illus. 2005. 32p. (J). pap. 5.95 (978-1-57565-153-8(X)) Kane Press, Inc.

—Que Sigue, Nina? Math Matters en Espanol. O'Rourke, Page Eastburn, illus. 2005. 32p. (J). pap. 5.95 (978-1-57565-152-1(1)) Kane Press, Inc.

Kasza, Keiko. El Mas Poderoso. (SPA.). (J). 8.95 (978-958-04-6490-7(1)) Norma S.A. COL. Dist: Distribuidora Norma, Inc.

Katz, Karen. ¡Cu-Cú, Bebé! Katz, Karen, illus. 2009. (SPA., Illus.). 14p. (J). (gr. -1 — 1). bds. 7.99 (978-1-4169-7938-8(7), Libros Para Ninos) Libros Para Ninos.

Kaut, Ellis. El Duende del Carpintero. (Torre de Papel Ser.). (SPA.). (J). (gr. 4-18). 7.95 (978-958-04-2889-3(1)) Norma S.A. COL. Dist: Distribuidora Norma, Inc.

Kelly, Harold G. El Sol por dentro (Inside the Sun) 2009. (Reading Room Collection: Spanish Ser.). (SPA.). 24p. (gr. 3-4). 42.50 (978-1-60854-177-5(0), Editorial Buenas Letras) Rosen Publishing Group, Inc., The.

Khu, Jannel. Let's Draw a School Bus with Shapes/Vamos a dibujar un autobus escolar usando Figuras. 2009. (Let's Draw with Shapes / Vamos a dibujar con figuras Ser.). (ENG & SPA.). 24p. (gr. k-1). 42.50 (978-1-61514-218-7(5), Editorial Buenas Letras) Rosen Publishing Group, Inc., The.

Kique el Taxista. (Spanish Early Intervention Levels Ser.). (SPA.). 21.30 (978-0-7362-0835-2(6)) CENGAGE Learning.

The Kitchen: Individual Title Two-Packs. (Chiquilibros Ser.). (gr. -1-1). 12.00 (978-0-7635-8540-2(8)) Rigby Education.

Kittinger, Jo S. Cuando sea Grande: When I Grow Up. Lucas, Margeaux, illus. 2005. (Rookie Reader Español Ser.). 24p. (gr. k-2). 19.50 (978-0-516-24443-3(4), Children's Pr.) Scholastic Library Publishing.

Klein, Adria F. Max Celebra el Ano Nuevo Chino, 1 vol. Robledo, Sol, tr. from ENG. Gallagher-Cole, Mernie, illus. 2007. (Read-It! Readers en Español: la Vida de Max Ser.). (SPA.). 24p. (gr. -1-3). lib. bdg. 21.32 (978-1-4048-3794-2(9), Easy Readers) Picture Window Bks.

—Max Come Al Aire Libre, 1 vol. Robledo, Sol, tr. from ENG. Gallagher-Cole, Mernie, illus. 2007. (Read-It! Readers en Español: la Vida de Max Ser.). (SPA.). 24p. (gr. -1-3). lib. bdg. 21.32 (978-1-4048-3795-9(7), Easy Readers) Picture Window Bks.

—Max Se Queda a Dormir, 1 vol. Robledo, Sol, tr. from ENG. Gallagher-Cole, Mernie, illus. 2007. (Read-It! Readers en Español: la Vida de Max Ser.). (SPA.). 24p. (gr. -1-3). lib. bdg. 21.32 (978-1-4048-3797-3(3), Easy Readers) Picture Window Bks.

—Max y la Fiesta de Adopcion, 1 vol. Robledo, Sol, tr. from ENG. Gallagher-Cole, Mernie, illus. 2007. (Read-It! Readers en Español: la Vida de Max Ser.). (SPA.). 24p. (gr. -1-3). lib. bdg. 21.32 (978-1-4048-3793-5(0), Easy Readers) Picture Window Bks.

Kline, Trish & Donev, Mary. Celebration of Letters A & B: Busy Preschoolers. 2007. (Illus.). 16p. (J). per. 20.00 (978-1-934307-04-5(1)) Ghost Hunter Productions.

—Celebration of Letters C & D: Busy Preschoolers. 2007. (Illus.). 16p. (J). per. 20.00 (978-1-934307-05-2(X)) Ghost Hunter Productions.

—Celebration of Letters E & F: Busy Preschoolers. 2007. (Illus.). 16p. (J). per. 20.00 (978-1-934307-06-9(8)) Ghost Hunter Productions.

—Celebration of Letters G & H: Busy Preschoolers. 2007. (Illus.). 16p. (J). per. 20.00 (978-1-934307-07-6(6)) Ghost Hunter Productions.

—Celebration of Letters I & J: Busy Preschoolers. 2007. (Illus.). 16p. (J). per. 20.00 (978-1-934307-08-3(4)) Ghost Hunter Productions.

—Celebration of Letters K & L: Busy Preschoolers. 2007. (Illus.). 16p. (J). per. 20.00 (978-1-934307-09-0(2)) Ghost Hunter Productions.

—Celebration of Letters M & N: Busy Preschoolers. 2007. (Illus.). 16p. (J). per. 20.00 (978-1-934307-10-6(6)) Ghost Hunter Productions.

—Celebration of Letters O & Q: Busy Preschoolers. 2007. (Illus.). 16p. (J). per. 20.00 (978-1-934307-11-3(4)) Ghost Hunter Productions.

—Celebration of Letters P & R: Busy Preschoolers. 2007. (Illus.). 16p. (J). per. 20.00 (978-1-934307-12-0(2)) Ghost Hunter Productions.

—Celebration of Letters S & T: Busy Preschoolers. 2007. (Illus.). 16p. (J). per. 20.00 (978-1-934307-13-7(0)) Ghost Hunter Productions.

—Celebration of Letters U & V: Busy Preschoolers. 2007. (Illus.). 16p. (J). per. 20.00 (978-1-934307-14-4(9)) Ghost Hunter Productions.

—Celebration of Letters W & X: Busy Preschoolers. 2007. (Illus.). 16p. (J). per. 20.00 (978-1-934307-15-1(7)) Ghost Hunter Productions.

—Celebration of Letters Y & Z: Busy Preschoolers. 2007. (Illus.). 16p. (J). per. 20.00 (978-1-934307-16-8(5)) Ghost Hunter Productions.

Klingel, Cynthia & Noyed, Robert B. Hair. 2010. (Let's Read about Our Bodies Ser.). (Illus.). 24p. (gr. k-3). pap. 8.15 (978-1-4339-3363-9(2)) Stevens, Gareth Publishing LLLP.

—Hair / el Cabello. 2010. (Let's Read about Our Bodies / Hablemos del cuerpo humano Ser.). (SPA., Illus.). 24p. (gr. k-3). pap. 8.15 (978-1-4339-3739-2(5)) Stevens, Gareth Publishing LLLP.

—Hair/el Cabello. 2010. (Let's Read about Our Bodies / Hablemos del cuerpo humano Ser.). (SPA., Illus.). 24p. (J). (gr. k-3). lib. bdg. 22.00 (978-1-4339-3738-5(7)) Stevens, Gareth Publishing LLLP.

—Hands. 2010. (Let's Read about Our Bodies Ser.). (Illus.). 24p. (gr. k-3). pap. 8.15 (978-1-4339-3366-0(7)); (J). lib. bdg. 22.00 (978-1-4339-3365-3(9)) Stevens, Gareth Publishing LLLP.

—Hands / Las Manos. 2010. (Let's Read about Our Bodies / Hablemos del cuerpo humano Ser.). (SPA., Illus.). 24p. (gr. k-3). pap. 8.15 (978-1-4339-3742-2(5)) Stevens, Gareth Publishing LLLP.

—Hands/Las Manos. 2010. (Let's Read about Our Bodies / Hablemos del cuerpo humano Ser.). (SPA., Illus.). 24p. (J). (gr. k-3). lib. bdg. 22.00 (978-1-4339-3741-5(7)) Stevens, Gareth Publishing LLLP.

—Nose. 2010. (Let's Read about Our Bodies Ser.). (Illus.). 24p. (gr. k-3). pap. 8.15 (978-1-4339-3372-1(1)); (J). lib. bdg. 22.00 (978-1-4339-3371-4(3)) Stevens, Gareth Publishing LLLP.

—Nose / la Nariz. 2010. (Let's Read about Our Bodies / Hablemos del cuerpo humano Ser.). (SPA., Illus.). 24p. (gr. k-3). pap. 8.15 (978-1-4339-3748-4(4)) Stevens, Gareth Publishing LLLP.

—Nose/la Nariz. 2010. (Let's Read about Our Bodies / Hablemos del cuerpo humano Ser.). (SPA., Illus.). 24p. (J). (gr. k-3). lib. bdg. 22.00 (978-1-4339-3747-7(6)) Stevens, Gareth Publishing LLLP.

—Skin. 2010. (Let's Read about Our Bodies Ser.). (Illus.). 24p. (gr. k-3). pap. 8.15 (978-1-4339-3375-2(6)); (J). lib. bdg. 22.00 (978-1-4339-3374-5(8)) Stevens, Gareth Publishing LLLP.

—Skin / la Piel. 2010. (Let's Read about Our Bodies / Hablemos del cuerpo humano Ser.). (SPA., Illus.). 24p. (gr. k-3). pap. 8.15 (978-1-4339-3751-4(4)) Stevens, Gareth Publishing LLLP.

—Skin/la Piel. 2010. (Let's Read about Our Bodies / Hablemos del cuerpo humano Ser.). (SPA., Illus.). 24p. (J). (gr. k-3). lib. bdg. 22.00 (978-1-4339-3750-7(6)) Stevens, Gareth Publishing LLLP.

Kondrchek, Jamie. A Day in the Life (Un Dia en la Vida), 4 vols., Set. Vega, Eida de la, tr. Rasemas, Joe, illus. Incl. My Favorite Time of Day (Mi Hora Preferida del Dia) lib. bdg. 25.70 (978-1-58415-837-0(9)); On My Way to School (De Camino a la Escuela) Rasemas, Joe. 25.70 (978-1-58415-840-0(9)); What Day Is It? (Que Dia Es Hoy?) Rasemas, Joe. 25.70 (978-1-58415-838-7(7)); What Should I Wear Today? (Que Ropa Me Pondre Hoy?) Rasemas, Joe. 25.70 (978-1-58415-839-4(5)); (Illus.). 32p. (J). (gr. -1-1). 2009. (ENG & SPA.). 2009. Set lib. bdg. 102.80 (978-1-58415-844-8(1)) Mitchell Lane Pubs., Inc.

Koontz, Robin. Zelda la Cenicienta. 2012. (SPA & ENG.). 24p. (gr. 2-3). pap. 8.95 (978-1-61810-544-8(2)) Rourke Educational Media.

Kranz, Linda. Only One You. Mlawer, Teresa, tr. from ENG. 2014. (ENG & SPA., Illus.). 32p. (J). (gr. -1-1). 12.95 (978-1-63076-023-6(4)) Taylor Trade Publishing.

—You Be You. Mlawer, Teresa, tr. from ENG. 2014. (ENG & SPA., Illus.). 32p. (J). (gr. -1-1). 12.95 (978-1-63076-021-2(8)) Taylor Trade Publishing.

Kwasi: un cuento Cancion: 6 Small Books. (Saludos Ser.: Vol. 2). (SPA.). 24p. (gr. 2-3). 31.00 (978-0-7635-9525-8(X)) Rigby Education.

Lab Manual. 2003. (Scott Foresman Science Ser.). (gr. 1-18). tchr. ed., lab manual ed. 13.25 (978-0-673-59344-3(4)); (gr. 2-18). tchr. ed., lab manual ed. 13.25 (978-0-673-59345-0(2)); (gr. 3-18). tchr. ed., lab manual ed. 13.25 (978-0-673-59346-7(0)); (gr. 4-18). tchr. ed., lab manual ed. 13.25 (978-0-673-59347-4(9)); (gr. 5-18). tchr. ed., lab manual ed. 13.25 (978-0-673-59348-1(7)) Addison-Wesley Educational Pubs., Inc.

Lachtman, Ofelia Dumas. Pepita Packs Up: Pepita Empaca. Ventura, Gabriela Baeza, tr. from ENG. Delange, Alex Pardo, illus. 2005. 48p. (J). (gr. -1-k). lib. bdg. 16.95 (978-1-55885-431-4(2), Piñata Books) Arte Publico Pr.

El Ladron: Individual Title-Six Packs. (Chiquilibros Ser.). (SPA.). (gr. k-1). 23.00 (978-0-7635-8606-5(4)) Rigby Education.

Laínez, René Colato. Mamá the Alien: Mamá la Extraterrestre. Lacámara, Laura, illus. 2016. (ENG & SPA.). 32p. (J). (gr. 1-4). 17.95 (978-0-89239-298-8(3)) Lee & Low Bks., Inc.

Lakeshore Learning Materials Staff, contrib. by. Spanish Emergent Readers: Set of 8 Books. 2007. (SPA.). (J). 44.95 (978-1-59746-020-0(6)) Lakeshore Learning Materials.

Lamadrid, Enrique R. Amadito & the Hero Children: Amadito y los Ninos Heroes. Cordova, Amy, illus. 2011. (SPA & ENG.). 60p. (J). 19.95 (978-0-8263-4979-8(X)) Univ. of New Mexico Pr.

—Amadito & the Hero Children: Amadito y Los Niños Héroes. Córdova, Amy, illus. 2011. (SPA & ENG.). (J). (978-0-8263-4980-4(3)); (978-0-8263-4978-1(1)) Univ. of New Mexico Pr.

Landrón, Rafael & Landrón, José Rafael. Beba y la Isla Nena: Beba & the Little Island. Ordóñez, María Antonia, illus. 2010. (SPA & ENG.). 32p. (J). (978-1-934370-05-6(3), Campanita Bks.) Editorial Campana.

Larousse Mexico Staff, ed. Buenas Noche. Desplanche, Vincent, illus. 2006. (SPA & ENG.). 33p. (gr. -1-3). pap. 3.95 (978-970-22-1190-7(5)) Larousse, Ediciones, S. A. de C. V. MEX. Dist: Houghton Mifflin Harcourt Publishing Co.

—Mi Pequena Encicopedia Larousse el Zoologico. 2006. (SPA., Illus.). 38p. (gr. -1 — 1). pap. 3.95 (978-970-22-1193-8(X)) Larousse, Ediciones, S. A. de C. V. MEX. Dist: Houghton Mifflin Harcourt Publishing Co.

Las dos Hermanas: Lap Book. (Pebble Soup Exploraciones Ser.). (SPA.). 16p. (gr. -1-18). 21.00 (978-0-7578-1692-5(4)) Rigby Education.

Las dos Hermanas: Small Book. (Pebble Soup Exploraciones Ser.). (SPA.). 16p. (gr. -1-18). 5.00 (978-0-7578-1732-8(7)) Rigby Education.

Las Escondidas. (Spanish Early Intervention Levels Ser.). (SPA.). 31.14 (978-0-7362-0337-1(0)) CENGAGE Learning.

Las huellas Verdes: Individual Title Six-Packs. (Literatura 2000 Ser.). (SPA.). (gr. 1-2). 28.00 (978-0-7635-1044-2(0)) Rigby Education.

Las Ovejitas. (Spanish Early Intervention Levels Ser.). (SPA.). 21.30 (978-0-7362-0825-3(9)) CENGAGE Learning.

Las Pinatas. (Spanish Early Intervention Levels Ser.). (SPA.). 21.30 (978-0-7362-0808-6(9)) CENGAGE Learning.

Las Visitas: Individual Title Six-Packs. (Literatura 2000 Ser.). (SPA.). (gr. k-1). 28.00 (978-0-7635-1032-9(7)) Rigby Education.

Lavaca BLANCA de botas NEGRAS. (SPA.). (J). 12.00 (978-958-02-1235-5(X)) Editorial Voluntad S.A. COL. Dist: Distribuidora Norma, Inc.

Lawton, Wendy. A La Sombra de Su Mano, 1 vol. 2009. Orig. Title: Shadow of His Hand. (SPA.). 160p. pap. 4.99 (978-0-8254-1379-7(6), Editorial Portavoz) Kregel Pubns.

Le Guillou, Philippe. Jesús. Pérez, Berta Herreros, tr. Pommier, Maurice, illus. 2008. (Tras Los Pasos de ... Ser.). (SPA.). 128p. (J). (gr. 4-7). pap. 14.95 (978-84-9801-197-5(3)) Blume ESP. Dist: Independent Pubs. Group.

Lebscky, Ibi. Albert. Cardoni, Paolo, illus. (Coleccion Seran Famosos).Tr. of Little Albert Einstein. (SPA.). 28p. (J). (gr. 2-4). 10.36 (978-84-233-1400-3(6)) Ediciones Destino ESP. Dist: Lectorum Pubns., Inc.

Lechermeier, Philippe & Dautremer, Rebecca. Princesas/ Princesses: Mini Album. 2008. (SPA.). 108p. 15.95 (978-84-263-6701-3(1)) Vives, Luis Editorial (Edelvives) ESP. Dist: Lectorum Pubns., Inc.

Lectura en Familia: Spanish Easy Reading Combo. (SPA.). (gr. -1-2). 122.04 (978-1-56334-402-2(5)) CENGAGE Learning.

Lectura en Familia: Spanish Phonics Grade 1 Combo. (SPA.). (gr. 1-18). 200.04 (978-0-7362-1490-2(9)) CENGAGE Learning.

Lectura en Familia: Spanish Phonics Grade 2 Combo. (SPA.). (gr. 2-18). 114.18 (978-0-7362-1491-9(7)) CENGAGE Learning.

Leo 1. (SPA.). (J). 16.00 (978-958-04-5657-5(7)) Norma S.A. COL. Dist: Distribuidora Norma, Inc.

Leo 2. (SPA.). (J). 16.00 (978-958-04-5658-2(5)) Norma S.A. COL. Dist: Distribuidora Norma, Inc.

Leo 3. (SPA.). (J). 16.00 (978-958-04-5659-9(3)) Norma S.A. COL. Dist: Distribuidora Norma, Inc.

Leo 4. (SPA.). (J). 16.00 (978-958-04-5660-5(7)) Norma S.A. COL. Dist: Distribuidora Norma, Inc.

Leo 5. (SPA.). (J). 16.00 (978-958-04-5661-2(5)) Norma S.A. COL. Dist: Distribuidora Norma, Inc.

Leo 6. (SPA.). (J). 16.00 (978-958-04-5662-9(3)) Norma S.A. COL. Dist: Distribuidora Norma, Inc.

Leonard, Marcia. El Hombre de Hojalata. Handelman, Dorothy, photos by. 2005. (ENG & SPA., Illus.). 32p. (J). (gr. -1-1). pap. 4.99 (978-0-8225-3310-8(3)) Lerner Publishing Group.

Leonard, Marcia & Handelman, Dorothy. The Pet Vet. Handelman, Dorothy, illus. Leonard, Marcia, photos by. 2005. (ENG & SPA., Illus.). 32p. (J). (gr. -1-1). pap. 4.99 (978-0-8225-3299-6(9)) Lerner Publishing Group.

Levine, Julia Pimsleur. Little Pim - Feelings. 2011. (ENG, FRE & SPA., Illus.). 10p. (J). (gr. -1 — 1). bds. 8.95 (978-1-4197-0018-7(9), Abrams Bks. for Young Readers) Abrams, Inc.

Levy, Janice & Arisa, Miguel. I Remember Abuelito: A Day of the Dead Story. Lopez, Loretta, illus. 2012.Tr. of Yo Recuerdo a Abuelito - Un Cuento del Dia de los Muertos. (SPA & ENG.). (J). (978-1-61913-114-9(5)) Weigl Pubs., Inc.

Levy, Robert. Not Just Mustard & Ketchup/ No Solo Mostaza y Salsa de Tomate. 2007. 58p. pap. 9.95 (978-0-7414-4304-5(X)) Infinity Publishing.

La Leyenda del Dorado. (SPA.). (J). 12.00 (978-958-02-1355-0(0)) Editorial Voluntad S.A. COL. Dist: Distribuidora Norma, Inc.

Libertson, Jody. Nathan Hale: Hero of the American Revolution. 2009. (Primary Sources of Famous People in American History Ser.). 32p. (gr. 2-3). 47.90 (978-1-60851-709-1(8)) Rosen Publishing Group, Inc., The.

—Nathan Hale: Héroe revolucionario / Hero of the American Revolution. 2009. (Famous People in American History/Grandes personajes en la historia de los Estados Unidos Ser.). (ENG & SPA.). 32p. (gr. 2-3). 47.90 (978-1-61512-552-4(3), Editorial Buenas Letras) Rosen Publishing Group, Inc., The.

—Nathan Hale: Héroe revolucionario (Nathan Hale: Hero of the American Revolution) 2009. (Grandes personajes en la historia de los Estados Unidos (Famous People in American History) Ser.). (SPA.). 32p. (gr. 2-3). 47.90 (978-1-61512-805-1(0), Editorial Buenas Letras) Rosen Publishing Group, Inc., The.

Libritos Mios staff, et al. Spanish Emergent Reader 1: Mira como Juego; ¡Curitas!; Los Animales del Zoológico; Construyendo una Casa; la Alberca; ¡Agua y Jabón!; Me Visto; Mi Gato, 8 bks. Elías, Annette, tr. Clayman, Fillys et al, illus. 2003.Tr. of Emergent Reader 1. (SPA.). 8p. (J). 120.00 (978-1-893986-24-4(1)) Keep Bks.

Libritos para Mi: Blue Set. (SPA.). (gr. k-2). 129.00 (978-0-7362-0711-9(2)) CENGAGE Learning.

Libritos para Mi: Green Set. (SPA.). (gr. k-2). 129.00 (978-0-7362-0709-6(0)) CENGAGE Learning.

Libritos para Mi: Orange Set. (SPA.). (gr. k-2). 129.00 (978-0-7362-0710-2(4)) CENGAGE Learning.

Libritos para Mi: Purple Set. (SPA.). (gr. k-2). 129.00 (978-0-7362-0708-9(2)) CENGAGE Learning.

Libritos para Mi: Red Set. (SPA.). (gr. k-2). 129.00 (978-0-7362-0707-2(4)) CENGAGE Learning.

Lillegard, Dee. Papas el Martes, Level 1. 2003. (Dejame Leer Ser.). (SPA., Illus.). (J). (gr. -1-3). 6.50 (978-0-673-36327-5(9), Good Year Bks.) Celebration Pr.

Linari, Adrian. Los Cuentos de Aguara. (SPA.). (J). 8.95 (978-958-04-5031-3(5)) Norma S.A. COL. Dist: Distribuidora Norma, Inc.

Lionni, Leo. A Color of His Own: (Spanish-English Bilingual Edition) Lionni, Leo, illus. 2016. (ENG & SPA., Illus.). 32p.

(J). (gr. -1-k). bds. 7.99 *(978-0-553-53873-1(X)*, Knopf Bks. for Young Readers) Random Hse. Children's Bks.
Lisansky, Sue, illus. Cinderella. 2011. (First Fairy Tales Ser.). (ENG.). 20p. (J). (gr. -1-3). pap. 4.99 *(978-1-934004-19-7(7))* Byeway Bks.
El Liston. (Spanish Early Intervention Levels Ser.). (SPA.). 23.10 *(978-1-56334-773-3(3))* CENGAGE Learning.
Little Books Collection: Includes 18 Little Books. 2003. 83.50 *(978-0-7652-0130-0(5))* Modern Curriculum Pr.
Llega la Abuelita: 6 Small Books. (Saludos Ser.: Vol. 2). (SPA.). (gr. 2-3). 31.00 *(978-0-7635-9544-9(6))* Rigby Education.
La Llegada del Virrey (Arrival of the Viceroy) 2005. (SPA.). (J). pap. *(978-968-7381-01-5(9))* Tecolote, Ediciones, S.A. de C.V.
Llego la Banda (E) (Spanish Early Intervention Levels Ser.). (SPA.). 21.30 *(978-0-7362-0831-4(3))* CENGAGE Learning.
Llorente, Maria Isabel Molina. El Misterio del Hombre Que Desaparecio. (Torre de Papel Ser.). (SPA.). (J). (gr. 4-18). 7.95 *(978-958-04-0729-4(0))* Norma S.A. COL. Dist: Distribuidora Norma, Inc.
Lo mas Importante. (Spanish Early Intervention Levels Ser.). (SPA.). 31.14 *(978-0-7362-0340-1(0))* CENGAGE Learning.
Lo mas quieto que Puedo: 6 Small Books. (Saludos Ser.: Vol. 3). (SPA.). (gr. 2-3). 31.00 *(978-0-7635-9549-4(7))* Rigby Education.
Lo Que Sale De Un Huevo: Big Book Packages. 2003. 64.95 *(978-0-673-58590-5(5))* Celebration Pr.
Lodge, Jo. La Casa del Senor Coc/ The House of Mr Coc. 2007. 8p. bds. 36.95 *(978-84-263-6454-8(3))* Vives, Luis Editorial (Edelvives) ESP. Dist: Baker & Taylor Bks.
—Imita Al Senor Coc/ Imitate Mr Coc. 2007. 22p. bds. 18.95 *(978-84-263-6221-6(4))* Vives, Luis Editorial (Edelvives) ESP. Dist: Baker & Taylor Bks.
Lolita Y Su Familia: Individual 6-packs. 2003. 23.95 *(978-0-673-78062-1(7))* Celebration Pr.
Lolita's Family, 6 Packs. 2003. 23.95 *(978-0-673-78126-0(7))* Celebration Pr.
Los animales Astutos: Individual Title Six-Packs. (Literatura 2000 Ser.). (SPA.). (gr. 2-3). 33.00 *(978-0-7635-1082-4(3))* Rigby Education.
Los animalitos de Oaxaca: Lap Book. (Pebble Soup Exploraciones Ser.). (SPA.). 16p. (gr. -1-18). 21.00 *(978-0-7578-1688-8(6))* Rigby Education.
Los animalitos de Oaxaca: Small Book. (Pebble Soup Exploraciones Ser.). (SPA.). 16p. (gr. -1-18). 5.00 *(978-0-7578-1728-1(9))* Rigby Education.
Los cinco Pollitos: Individual Title Six-Packs. (Literatura 2000 Ser.). (SPA.). (gr. 1-2). 28.00 *(978-0-7635-1062-6(9))* Rigby Education.
Los Comilones: Individual Title Six-Packs. (Literatura 2000 Ser.). (SPA.). (gr. k-1). 28.00 *(978-0-7635-1012-1(2))* Rigby Education.
A los dos Anos: 6 Small Books. (SPA.). (gr. k-1). 20.00 *(978-0-7635-6254-0(8))* Rigby Education.
Los fideos de Papa: Individual Title Six-Packs. (Literatura 2000 Ser.). (SPA.). (gr. 1-2). 28.00 *(978-0-7635-1070-1(X))* Rigby Education.
Los recuerdos de mi Abuelita: Individual Title Six-Packs. (Literatura 2000 Ser.). (SPA.). (gr. 1-2). 28.00 *(978-0-7635-1077-0(7))* Rigby Education.
Los regalos de mi Abuelito. (Spanish Early Intervention Levels Ser.). (SPA.). 23.10 *(978-1-56334-790-0(3))* CENGAGE Learning.
Los Sentidos. (Spanish Early Intervention Levels Ser.). (SPA.). 23.10 *(978-1-56334-787-0(3))* CENGAGE Learning.
Los tres chivos Vivos: Video Tape. (ENG & SPA.). (gr. k-1). 26.00 *(978-0-7635-6280-9(7))* Rigby Education.
Los tres Cochinitos: Video Tape. (ENG & SPA.). (gr. k-1). 26.00 *(978-0-7635-6228-1(9))* Rigby Education.
Los trucos de Paco: Individual Title Six-Packs. (Literatura 2000 Ser.). (SPA.). (gr. 1-2). 28.00 *(978-0-7635-1056-5(4))* Rigby Education.
Losantos, Cristina, illus. Beauty & the Beast: La Bella y la Bestia. 2007. (Bilingual Fairy Tales Ser.: BILI). (ENG & SPA.). 32p. (J). (gr. -1-3). pap. 6.95 *(978-0-8118-5970-7(3))* Chronicle Bks. LLC.
—Beauty & the Beast (La Bella y la Bestia) 2013. (Bilingual Fairy Tales Ser.). (SPA & ENG.). 32p. (J). (gr. 1-4). lib. bdg. 28.50 *(978-1-60753-355-9(3))* Amicus Publishing.
—Bella y la Bestia. 2007. (Bilingual Fairy Tales Ser.: BILI).Tr. of Beauty & the Beast. (ENG & SPA.). 32p. (J). (gr. -1-3). 14.95 *(978-0-8118-5969-1(X))* Chronicle Bks. LLC.
Louise, Cristina & McIlroy, Michelle. Where Is Paco Now? Louise, Cristina & McIlroy, Michelle, illus. 2012. (SPA & ENG., Illus.). (J). *(978-1-934370-26-1(6)*, Campanita Bks.) Editorial Campana.
Love, Maryann Cusimano. You Are My I Love You / Tú Eres Mi Te Quiero. Ichikawa, Satomi, illus. 2012. (SPA & ENG.). 28p. (J). (gr. -1 — 1). bds. 6.99 *(978-0-399-24396-7(8)*, Philomel Bks.) Penguin Young Readers Group.
Lozano, José. Little Chanclas. 2015. (ENG & SPA., Illus.). 32p. (J). (gr. k-3). 16.95 *(978-1-935955-85-6(3))* Cinco Puntos Pr.
—Once Around the Block (Una Vuelta a la Manzana) Crosthwaite, Luis Humberto, tr. 2009. (SPA & ENG., Illus.). 32p. (J). (gr. -1-4). 16.95 *(978-1-933693-57-6(6))* Cinco Puntos Pr.
Lucia encuentra un Dragon: Individual Title, 6 packs. (Literatura 2000 Ser.). (SPA.). (gr. 2-3). 33.00 *(978-0-7635-1095-4(5))* Rigby Education.
Luis y la Mariposa: Individual Title Six-Packs. (Literatura 2000 Ser.). (SPA.). (gr. 2-3). 33.00 *(978-0-7635-1263-7(X))* Rigby Education.
MacHado, Ana Maria. Eso No Me lo Quita Nadie.Tr. of No One Can Take That Away from Me. (SPA.). (YA). (gr. 7-8). 8.95 *(978-958-04-4530-2(3)*, NR4358) Norma S.A. COL. Dist: Distribuidora Norma, Inc., Lectorum Pubns., Inc.
Maddox, Jake. Definición por Penales. Heck, Claudia M., tr. from ENG. Tiffany, Sean, illus. 2012. (Jake Maddox en Español Ser.). (SPA.). 72p. (gr. 2-3). 25.32 *(978-1-4342-3814-6(8))* Stone Arch Bks.
—El Lanzador Bajo Presión. Heck, Claudia M., tr. from ENG. Tiffany, Sean, illus. 2012. (Jake Maddox en Español Ser.). (SPA.). 72p. (gr. 2-3). 25.32 *(978-1-4342-3815-3(6))* Stone Arch Bks.
—El Rebelde de la Patineta, 1 vol. Heck, Claudia, tr. from ENG. Tiffany, Sean, illus. 2012. (Jake Maddox en Español Ser.). (SPA.). 72p. (gr. 2-3). 25.32 *(978-1-4342-3816-0(4))* Stone Arch Bks.
—El Tramposo de BMX, 1 vol. Heck, Claudia M., tr. from ENG. Tiffany, Sean, illus. 2012. (Jake Maddox en Español Ser.). (SPA.). 72p. (gr. 2-3). 25.32 *(978-1-4342-3817-7(2))* Stone Arch Bks.
Mahoney, Judy. Teach Me Even More Spanish Book Box: Twenty-One Songs to Sing & a Story about Pen Pals. (Foreign Language Ser.). (SPA.). (J). incl. audio NewSound, LLC.
Mami, Mami! (Spanish Early Intervention Levels Ser.). (SPA.). 21.30 *(978-0-7362-0801-7(1))* CENGAGE Learning.
La Manana: Individual Title Two-Packs. (Chiquilibros Ser.). (SPA.). (gr. -1-1). 12.00 *(978-0-7635-8551-8(3))* Rigby Education.
Manushkin, Fran & Lyon, Tammie. Adiós a Goldie. Lyon, Tammie, illus. 2012. (Katie Woo en Español Ser.). (SPA., Illus.). 32p. (gr. k-2). pap. 6.95 *(978-1-4048-7676-7(6))*; lib. bdg. 21.32 *(978-1-4048-7524-1(7))* Picture Window Bks.
—Basta de Burlas, 1 vol. Lyon, Tammie, illus. 2012. (Katie Woo en Español Ser.). (SPA., Illus.). 32p. (gr. k-2). pap. 6.95 *(978-1-4048-7677-4(4))*; lib. bdg. 21.32 *(978-1-4048-7525-8(5))* Picture Window Bks.
—La Gran Mentira, 1 vol. Lyon, Tammie, illus. 2012. (Katie Woo en Español Ser.). (SPA., Illus.). 32p. (gr. k-2). pap. 6.95 *(978-1-4048-7678-1(2))*; lib. bdg. 21.32 *(978-1-4048-7522-7(0))* Picture Window Bks.
—La Jefa Del Mundo, 1 vol. Lyon, Tammie, illus. 2012. (Katie Woo en Español Ser.). (SPA., Illus.). 32p. (gr. k-2). pap. 6.95 *(978-1-4048-7679-8(0))*; lib. bdg. 21.32 *(978-1-4048-7523-4(9))* Picture Window Bks.
Many Hats: Matching English, 6-packs. 2003. 23.95 *(978-0-673-57561-6(6))* Celebration Pr.
La maquina de Imprimir: Individual Title Six-Packs. (Literatura 2000 Ser.). (SPA.). (gr. 1-2). 28.00 *(978-0-7635-1046-6(7))* Rigby Education.
La Marca en la Roca. (SPA., Illus.). 70p. (YA). (gr. 8-10). pap. *(978-88-8148-466-9(8))* EMC/Paradigm Publishing.
El Mariachi: Big Book Packages. 2003. 64.95 *(978-0-673-58585-1(9))* Celebration Pr.
Mariachi 6 Packs: Matching English. 2003. 23.95 *(978-0-673-57562-3(4))* Celebration Pr.
Marianela. (Coleccion Centro Literario). (SPA.). (J). pap., stu. ed. 7.95 *(978-958-02-0483-1(7)*, CAR017) Editorial Voluntad S.A. COL. Dist: Continental Bk. Co., Inc.
Mariconda, Barbara. ¡Clasificalo! Rogers, Sherry, illus. 2008.Tr. of Sort it Out! (SPA.). 32p. (J). (gr. k-4). 17.95 *(978-1-60718-695-3(0))* Arbordale Publishing.
Marina la Ballena. 2003. 28.95 *(978-0-673-78090-4(2))* Celebration Pr.
Mariño, Ricardo. Lo Unico del Mundo. (Torre de Papel Ser.). (SPA.). (YA). (gr. 6-18). 8.95 *(978-958-04-3812-0(9))* Norma S.A. COL. Dist: Distribuidora Norma, Inc.
Marshall, Linda Elovitz. Rainbow Weaver/Tejedora del Arcoíris. Chavarri, Elisa, illus. 2016. (ENG & SPA.). 40p. (J). (gr. 1-4). 18.95 *(978-0-89239-374-9(2))* Lee & Low Bks., Inc.
Martin, Ann M. Claudia y la Nueva Alumna. Peraire del Molino, C., tr. (Club de Las Canguro Ser.: Vol. 12).Tr. of Claudia & the New Girl. (SPA.). 156p. (J). 11.95 *(978-84-272-3662-2(X))* Molino, Editorial ESP. Dist: AIMS International Bks., Inc.
—Claudia y la Triste Despedida. Peraire del Molino, Conchita, tr. (El Club de las Canguro Ser.: Vol. 26).Tr. of Claudia & the Sad Good-Bye. (SPA.). 150p. (J). 11.95 *(978-84-272-3676-9(X))* Molino, Editorial ESP. Dist: AIMS International Bks., Inc.
—Kristy y el Secreto de Susan. (El Club de las Canguro Ser.: Vol. 32).Tr. of Kristy & the Susan's Secret. (SPA.). 150p. (J). 11.95 *(978-84-272-3682-0(4))* Molino, Editorial ESP. Dist: AIMS International Bks., Inc.
—Kristy y los Esnobs. (Club de Las Canguro Ser.: Vol. 11).Tr. of Kristy & the Snobs. (SPA.). 158p. (J). 11.95 *(978-84-272-3661-5(1))* Molino, Editorial ESP. Dist: AIMS International Bks., Inc.
—Mala Suerte de Mary Anne. Peraire del Molino, Conchita, tr. (Club de Las Canguro Ser.: Vol. 17).Tr. of Mary Anne's Bad-Luck Mystery. (SPA.). 142p. (J). 11.95 *(978-84-272-3667-7(0))* Molino, Editorial ESP. Dist: AIMS International Bks., Inc.
Martin, Bill, Jr. Oso Panda, Oso Panda, ¿Qué Ves Ahí? Mlawer, Teresa, tr. Carle, Eric, illus. 2009. (Brown Bear & Friends Ser.).Tr. of Brown Bear, Brown Bear, What Do You See? (SPA & ENG.). 26p. (J). (gr. -1-k). 9.99 *(978-0-8050-8756-7(7)*, 9780805087567, Holt, Henry & Co. Bks. For Young Readers) Holt, Henry & Co.
Mas Pizza! 2003. 28.95 *(978-0-673-78089-8(9))* Celebration Pr.
Masters, Susan Rowan. La Vida Secreta de Hubie Hatzel. (Torre de Papel Ser.). (SPA.). (J). (gr. 4-18). 7.95 *(978-958-04-1900-6(0))* Norma S.A. COL. Dist: Distribuidora Norma, Inc.
Mattern, Joanne. Sojourner Truth: Early Abolitionist. 2009. (Women Who Shaped History Ser.). 24p. (gr. 2-3). 42.50 *(978-1-60854-821-7(X)*, PowerKids Pr.) Rosen Publishing Group, Inc., The.
Matthias, Catherine & Sharp, Gene. Demasiados Globos. Sharp, Gene, illus. 2011. (Rookie Ready to Learn Español Ser.). (SPA., Illus.). 40p. (J). pap. 5.95 *(978-0-531-26792-9(X))*; lib. bdg. 23.00 *(978-0-531-26124-8(7))* Scholastic Library Publishing. (Children's Pr.).
Mayra y el baile de Disfraces: Individual Title Six-Packs. (Literatura 2000 Ser.). (SPA.). (gr. 2-3). 33.00 *(978-0-7635-1096-1(3))* Rigby Education.
McDonald, Megan. Judy Moody & Stink: La Loca, Loca Busqueda del Tesoro. Reynolds, Peter, illus. 2011. (SPA.). 256p. (J). (gr. 2-5). pap. 14.95 *(978-1-61605-137-2(X))* Ediciones Alfaguara ESP. Dist: Two Rivers Distribution.
—Stink y los Tenis Más Apestosos del Mundo. 2008. (SPA.). 208p. (J). (gr. 3-5). pap. 7.95 *(978-1-60396-195-0(X)*, Alfaguara) Santillana USA Publishing Co., Inc.
McQuinn, Anna & Calvo, Carlos E. Lola Planta un Jardin. Beardshaw, Rosalind, illus. 2017. (SPA.). 28p. (J). (-k). pap. 7.99 *(978-1-58089-786-0(X))* Charlesbridge Publishing, Inc.
Me Encontre Una Piedra: Big Book Packages. 2003. 64.95 *(978-0-673-58591-2(3))* Celebration Pr.
Me gusta Leer. (Spanish Early Intervention Levels Ser.). (SPA.). 21.30 *(978-0-7362-0806-2(2))* CENGAGE Learning.
Meachen Rau, Dana. Cansada de Esperar, 1 vol. Ruiz, Carlos, tr. Fitzpatrick, Brad, illus. 2006. (Read-It! Readers en Español: Story Collection).Tr. of Tired of Waiting. (SPA.). 32p. (gr. -1-3). 21.32 *(978-1-4048-1695-4(X)*, Easy Readers) Picture Window Bks.
—En el Parque. 2007. (¡A Divertimos! Ser.). (SPA., Illus.). 24p. (gr. k-1). lib. bdg. 15.95 *(978-0-7614-2775-9(9)*, Benchmark Bks.) Marshall Cavendish Corp.
—En el Parque de Atracciones. 2007. (¡A Divertimos! Ser.). (SPA., Illus.). 24p. (gr. k-1). lib. bdg. 15.95 *(978-0-7614-2749-0(X)*, Benchmark Bks.) Marshall Cavendish Corp.
—En el Zoologico. 2007. (¡A Divertimos! Ser.). (SPA., Illus.). 24p. (gr. k-1). lib. bdg. 15.95 *(978-0-7614-2777-3(5)*, Benchmark Bks.) Marshall Cavendish Corp.
—En la Granja. 2007. (¡A Divertimos! Ser.). (SPA., Illus.). 24p. (gr. k-1). lib. bdg. 15.95 *(978-0-7614-2778-0(3)*, Benchmark Bks.) Marshall Cavendish Corp.
—A Rodar! 2006. (En Movimiento Ser.). (SPA., Illus.). 24p. (gr. k-1). lib. bdg. 15.95 *(978-0-7614-2419-2(9)*, Benchmark Bks.) Marshall Cavendish Corp.
Mead, Richelle. Vampire Academy. 2010. (SPA.). 256p. (gr. 8-12). pap. 16.99 *(978-607-11-0456-4(4)*, Alfaguara) Santillana USA Publishing Co., Inc.
Meddaugh, Susan. Fireworks for All. 2011. (Martha Speaks Ser.). (SPA & ENG., Illus.). 24p. (J). (gr. -1-3). pap. 3.99 *(978-0-547-55620-8(9))* Houghton Mifflin Harcourt Publishing Co.
—Martha Habla: Conoce a Martha/Martha Speaks: Meet Martha Bilingual Reader. 2015. (Martha Speaks Ser.). (SPA & ENG., Illus.). 24p. (J). (gr. -1-3). 12.99 *(978-0-544-43508-7(7)*, HMH Books For Young Readers) Houghton Mifflin Harcourt Publishing Co.
Medina, Conni. Haz Papel Picado, 1 vol. 2nd rev. ed. 2012. (Nonfiction Readers Ser.).Tr. of Make Papel Picado. (SPA.). 20p. (J). (gr. 1-1). pap. 4.99 *(978-1-4333-4425-1(4))* Teacher Created Materials, Inc.
—Haz un Dragón del Año Nuevo Chino, 1 vol. 2nd rev. ed. 2012. (Nonfiction Readers Ser.). (SPA.). 20p. (J). (gr. 1-1). pap. 4.99 *(978-1-4333-4426-8(2))* Teacher Created Materials, Inc.
—Haz un Muñequito de Jengibre, 1 vol. 2nd rev. ed. 2012. (Nonfiction Readers Ser.). (SPA.). 20p. (J). (gr. 1-1). pap. 4.99 *(978-1-4333-4427-5(0))* Teacher Created Materials, Inc.
Medina, Meg. Tia Isa Quiere un Carro. Munoz, Claudio, illus. 2012.Tr. of Tia Isa Wants a Car. (SPA.). 32p. (J). (gr. -1-2). pap. 6.99 *(978-0-7636-5751-2(4))* Candlewick Pr.
—Tía Isa Quiere un Carro. 2012.Tr. of Tia Isa Wants a Car. (SPA.). lib. bdg. 17.20 *(978-0-606-23801-4(8)*, Turtleback) Turtleback Bks.
Meister, Cari. Moopy el Monstruo Subterráneo/Moopy the Underground Monster. Heck, Claudia M., tr. from ENG. Messner, Dennis, illus. 2012. (Los Amigos Monstruos/Monster Friends Ser.). (SPA & MUL.). 32p. (gr. 2-3). lib. bdg. 22.65 *(978-1-4342-3785-9(0)*, Bilingual Stone Arch Readers) Stone Arch Bks.
—Ora - El Monstruo Marino. Heck, Claudia M., tr. from ENG. Messner, Dennis, illus. 2012. (Los Amigos Monstruos/Monster Friends Ser.).Tr. of Ora - The Sea Monster. (MUL & SPA.). 32p. (gr. 2-3). lib. bdg. 22.65 *(978-1-4342-3784-2(2)*, Bilingual Stone Arch Readers) Stone Arch Bks.
—Snorp el Monstruo de la Ciudad/Snorp the City Monster, 1 vol. Heck, Claudia M., tr. from ENG. Messner, Dennis, illus. 2012. (Los Amigos Monstruos/Monster Friends Ser.). (MUL & SPA.). 32p. (gr. 2-3). lib. bdg. 22.65 *(978-1-4342-3783-5(4)*, Bilingual Stone Arch Readers) Stone Arch Bks.
Mejías, Mónica. Aprendiendo a Leer con Mili y Molo: Learn How to Read in Spanish. Mejías, Mónica, illus. 2004.Tr. of Lernen Sie Spanish Lesen, Impara a leggere in Spagnolo, Aprenda a ler Espanhol, Apprenez à lire L'espagnol. (Illus.). 40p. (J). audio compact disk 12.00 *(978-0-9753799-0-5(9))* Ediciones Alas, Inc.
El mejor regalo de Cumpleanos: Individual Title Six-Packs. (Literatura 2000 Ser.). (SPA.). (gr. 2-3). 33.00 *(978-0-7635-1264-4(8))* Rigby Education.
El mensaje de las Estrellas: Lap Book. (Pebble Soup Exploraciones Ser.). (SPA.). 16p. (gr. -1-18). 21.00 *(978-0-7578-1677-2(0))* Rigby Education.
Los Meses Del Ano. 2003. 23.95 *(978-0-673-77168-1(7))* Celebration Pr.
Mi amiga Laura. (Spanish Early Intervention Levels Ser.). (SPA.). 31.14 *(978-0-7362-0329-6(X))* CENGAGE Learning.
Mi Amigo. 2003. 35.50 *(978-0-8136-8137-5(5))*; 63.50 *(978-0-8136-8139-9(1))* Modern Curriculum Pr.
Mi Caballito. (Spanish Early Intervention Levels Ser.). (SPA.). 23.10 *(978-1-56334-775-7(X))* CENGAGE Learning.
Mi Caja: Individual Title-Six Packs. (Chiquilibros Ser.). (SPA.). (gr. k-1). 23.00 *(978-0-7635-8604-1(8))* Rigby Education.
Mi conejito y Yo: Big Book. (Pebble Soup Exploraciones Ser.). (SPA.). 16p. (gr. -1-18). 31.00 *(978-0-7578-1690-1(8))* Rigby Education.
Mi Dia. (Spanish Early Intervention Levels Ser.). (SPA.). 23.10 *(978-1-56334-771-9(7))* CENGAGE Learning.
Mi Escuelita: Individual 6-packs. 2003. 23.95 *(978-0-673-77142-1(3))* Celebration Pr.
Mi Familia. (Spanish Early Intervention Levels Ser.). (SPA.). 31.14 *(978-0-7362-0327-2(3))* CENGAGE Learning.
Mi Familia: Individual 6-packs. 2003. 23.95 *(978-0-673-77133-9(4))* Celebration Pr.
Mi Hermanita: Individual Title Six-Packs. (Literatura 2000 Ser.). (SPA.). (gr. -1-1). 28.00 *(978-0-7635-1196-8(X))* Rigby Education.
Mi Hermanito. (Spanish Early Intervention Levels Ser.). (SPA.). 23.10 *(978-1-56334-772-6(5))* CENGAGE Learning.
Mi Hogar: Individual Title-Six Packs. (Chiquilibros Ser.). (SPA.). (gr. k-1). 23.00 *(978-0-7635-8621-8(8))* Rigby Education.
Mi Maestra, 6 Packs. 2003. 23.95 *(978-0-673-77148-3(2))* Celebration Pr.
Mi Mami: Individual 6-packs. 2003. 23.95 *(978-0-673-77143-8(1))* Celebration Pr.
Mi Perrita Chata, 6 Packs. 2003. 23.95 *(978-0-673-77149-0(0))* Celebration Pr.
Mi Tata Chuy, 6 Packs. 2003. 23.95 *(978-0-673-77139-1(3))* Celebration Pr.
Milet Publishing Staff. Colors. 2010. (My First Bilingual Book Ser.). (SPA & ENG., Illus.). 24p. (J). (gr. k — 1). bds. 7.99 *(978-1-84059-539-0(6))* Milet Publishing.
—My First Bilingual Book - Numbers. 2010. (My First Bilingual Book Ser.). (SPA & ENG., Illus.). 24p. (J). (gr. k — 1). bds. 8.99 *(978-1-84059-545-1(0))* Milet Publishing.
Mira el Dinosaurio! (Spanish Early Intervention Levels Ser.). (SPA.). 31.14 *(978-0-7362-0334-0(6))* CENGAGE Learning.
Mira lo que hizo Tomas, 6 vols., Pack. (Literatura 2000 Ser.). (SPA.). (gr. 1-2). 28.00 *(978-0-7635-1072-5(6))* Rigby Education.
Mis Animalitos: Individual Title Six-Packs. (Literatura 2000 Ser.). (SPA.). (gr. k-1). 28.00 *(978-0-7635-1024-4(6))* Rigby Education.
Mis Cinco Perritos: Big Book Packages. 2003. 64.95 *(978-0-673-58580-6(8))* Celebration Pr.
Mis Cumpleanos: Individual 6-packs. 2003. 23.95 *(978-0-673-77150-6(4))* Celebration Pr.
Mis Juguetes, 6 Packs. 2003. 23.95 *(978-0-673-77141-4(5))* Celebration Pr.
Mis Quehaceres, 6 Packs. 2003. 23.95 *(978-0-673-77145-2(8))* Celebration Pr.
Mlawer, Teresa, tr. What Do I Hear? / ¿Qué Oigo? Kubler, Annie, illus. 2015. (Small Senses Bilingual Ser.: 5). (ENG & SPA.). 12p. (J). bds. *(978-1-84643-724-3(5))* Child's Play International Ltd.
—What Do I See? / ¿Qué Veo? Kubler, Annie, illus. 2015. (Small Senses Bilingual Ser.: 5). (ENG & SPA.). 12p. (J). bds. *(978-1-84643-725-0(3))* Child's Play International Ltd.
—What Do I Smell? / ¿Qué Huelo? Kubler, Annie, illus. 2015. (Small Senses Bilingual Ser.: 5). (ENG & SPA.). 12p. (J). bds. *(978-1-84643-723-6(7))* Child's Play International Ltd.
—What Do I Taste? / ¿Qué Saboreo? Kubler, Annie, illus. 2015. (Small Senses Bilingual Ser.: 5). (ENG & SPA.). 12p. (J). bds. *(978-1-84643-722-9(9))* Child's Play International Ltd.
El Modelo: Individual Title Six-Packs. (Chiquilibros Ser.). (SPA.). (gr. k-1). 23.00 *(978-0-7635-8596-9(3))* Rigby Education.
Molina, Angeles. El Principe Que No Queria Ser Principe. 2007. (SPA.). 64p. 14.95 *(978-0-8477-0455-2(6))* Univ. of Puerto Rico Pr.
Los Monstruos, 6 packs. 2003. 23.95 *(978-0-673-77144-5(X))* Celebration Pr.
La Montana que Llora. (Saludos Ser.: Vol. 1). (SPA.). (gr. 3-5). 31.00 *(978-0-7635-3221-5(5))* Rigby Education.
La Montana que Llora: 6 Small Books. (Saludos Ser.: Vol. 1). (SPA.). (gr. 3-5). 31.00 *(978-0-7635-1848-6(4))* Rigby Education.
Montes, Marisa. A Crazy Mixed-Up Spanglish Day. Cepeda, Joe, illus. 2004. (Get Ready for Gabi Ser.: 1). 120p. (gr. 2-5). 14.00 *(978-0-7569-3403-3(6))* Perfection Learning Corp.
Montoya, Martha, creator. Cenando con el Monstruo: Take-Home. 2005. (Los Kitos Ser.). (SPA.). (YA). (gr. 1-3). 15.00 *(978-0-8215-8813-0(3))* Sadlier, William H. Inc.
—Mi heroe Favorito: Take-Home. 2005. (Los Kitos Ser.). (SPA.). (YA). (gr. 1-3). 15.00 *(978-0-8215-8811-6(7))* Sadlier, William H. Inc.
—No, no a la Biblioteca! Take-Home. 2005. (Los Kitos Ser.). (SPA.). (YA). (gr. 1-3). 15.00 *(978-0-8215-8812-3(5))* Sadlier, William H. Inc.
Mora, Pat, et al. La Hermosa Señora: Nuestra Señora de Guadalupe. Johnson, Steve & Fancher, Lou, illus. 2012. (SPA & ENG.). 40p. (J). (gr. k-3). pap. 8.99 *(978-0-375-86840-5(2)*, Dragonfly Bks.) Random Hse. Children's Bks.
La Mosquita Lista. 2003. 23.95 *(978-0-673-77122-3(9))* Celebration Pr.
Multicultural Activities Blackline Masters: Fuerzas de la Naturaleza. (Saludos Ser.). (SPA.). (gr. 3-5). 21.00 *(978-0-7635-2228-5(7))* Rigby Education.
Multicultural Activities Blackline Masters: Regalos de la Tierra. (Saludos Ser.). (SPA.). (gr. 3-5). 21.00 *(978-0-7635-2227-8(9))* Rigby Education.
Multicultural Activities Blackline Masters: Vivan las Tradiciones. (Saludos Ser.). (SPA.). (gr. 3-5). 21.00 *(978-0-7635-2226-1(0))* Rigby Education.
El mundo de los Pajaros. (Spanish Early Intervention Levels Ser.). (SPA.). 23.10 *(978-0-7362-0325-8(7))* CENGAGE Learning.
La Muneca De Galleta: Individual 6-packs. 2003. 23.95 *(978-0-673-77152-0(0))* Celebration Pr.
El muneco de Nieve, 6 vols., Pack. (Chiquilibros Ser.).Tr. of Little Snowman. (SPA.). (gr. k-1). 23.00 *(978-0-7635-8592-1(0))* Rigby Education.
Murphy, Stuart J. ¡Bien Hecho, Ajay! 2011. (I See I Learn Ser.).Tr. of Good Job, Ajay! (SPA., Illus.). 32p. (J). (-k). 14.95 *(978-1-58089-486-9(0))*; pap. 6.95 *(978-1-58089-487-6(9))* Charlesbridge Publishing, Inc.
—Camille y Su Equipo. 2012. (I See I Learn Ser.). (SPA & ENG., Illus.). 32p. (J). (-k). 14.95 *(978-1-58089-490-6(9))*; pap. 6.95 *(978-1-58089-491-3(7))* Charlesbridge Publishing, Inc.
—Emma Hace Amigos. 2011. (I See I Learn Ser.). (SPA & ENG., Illus.). 32p. (J). (-k). 14.95 *(978-1-58089-482-1(8))*; pap. 6.95 *(978-1-58089-483-8(6))* Charlesbridge Publishing, Inc.
—En Busca de Freda. Mlawer, Teresa, tr. from ENG. Jones, Tim, illus. 2012. (I See I Learn Ser.). (SPA & ENG.). 32p. (J). (-k). 14.95 *(978-1-58089-494-4(1))*; pap. 6.95 *(978-1-58089-495-1(X))* Charlesbridge Publishing, Inc.
—Freda Organiza una Merienda. 2011. (I See I Learn Ser.). (SPA & ENG., Illus.). 32p. (J). (-k). 14.95 *(978-1-58089-488-3(7))*; pap. 6.95 *(978-1-58089-489-0(5))* Charlesbridge Publishing, Inc.
—Percy Juega con Cuidado. 2011. (I See I Learn Ser.). (SPA & ENG., Illus.). 32p. (J). (-k). 14.95 *(978-1-58089-484-5(4))*; pap. 6.95 *(978-1-58089-485-2(2))* Charlesbridge Publishing, Inc.
—Percy Se Enoja. 2012. (I See I Learn Ser.). (SPA & ENG., Illus.). 32p. (J). (-k). 14.95 *(978-1-58089-492-0(5))*; pap. 6.95 *(978-1-58089-493-7(3))* Charlesbridge Publishing, Inc.
Murphy, Stuart J. & Mlawer, Teresa. Carlos Escribe Su Nombre! Jones, Tim, illus. 2014. (I See I Learn Ser.). (SPA.).

S

32p. (J). (-k). 14.95 *(978-1-58089-496-8(8))*; pap. 6.95 *(978-1-58089-497-5(6))* Charlesbridge Publishing, Inc.

Muy bien, Mayra! (Spanish Early Intervention Levels Ser.). (SPA.). 28.38 *(978-0-7362-0836-9(4))* CENGAGE Learning.

My Cook Book. 2003. 28.95 *(978-0-673-78108-6(9))* Celebration Pr.

My Family Set - Spanish 800799, 6. 2005. (J). bds. *(978-1-59794-043-6(7))* Environments, Inc.

My Snowman: Matching English 6-packs. 2003. 23.95 *(978-0-673-57563-0(2))* Celebration Pr.

Nada Extra: Individual Title Six-Packs. (Literatura 2000 Ser.). (SPA.). (gr. 1-2). 28.00 *(978-0-7635-1048-0(3))* Rigby Education.

Nelson, Mary Beth & Linn, Laurent, illus. Elmo's Big Word Book/el Libro Grande de Palabras de Elmo. Barrett, John E., photos by. 2006. (Elmo's Big Word Book/el Libro Grande de Palabras de Elmo Ser.). (SPA, ENG, MUL & ANG.). 12p. (J). (gr. -1 — 1). bds. 8.95 *(978-0-87358-906-2(8))* Cooper Square Publishing Llc.

Nelson, Robin. El Ciclo Del Agua. 2003. (SPA.). 23p. (J). pap. 5.95 *(978-0-8225-4824-9(0)*, Lerner Pubns.) Lerner Publishing Group.

—Usamos el Agua. 2003. (Primeros Pasos Ser.). (SPA., Illus.). 23p. (J). pap. 6.95 *(978-0-8225-4825-6(9)*, Lerner Pubns.) Lerner Publishing Group.

Niebisch, Jackie. La Escuela de los Vampiritos. (SPA.). (J). (gr. 4-18). 8.95 *(978-958-04-5042-9(0))* Norma S.A. COL. Dist: Distribuidora Norma, Inc.

—La Escuela de los Vampiritos - Examen. (SPA.). (J). 8.95 *(978-958-04-5641-4(0))* Norma S.A. COL. Dist: Distribuidora Norma, Inc.

La Nina Del Poncho. 2003. (J). (gr. -1-2). 28.95 *(978-0-673-77378-4(7))* Celebration Pr.

El Nino que fue al Viento Norte: Individual Title, 6 packs. (Literatura 2000 Ser.). (SPA.). (gr. 2-3). 33.00 *(978-0-7635-1266-8(4))* Rigby Education.

Niven, David. Los 100 Secretos de la Gente Feliz: Lo que los Cientificos han Descubierto y como Puede Aplicarlo a su Vida. (SPA.). (J). 12.00 *(978-958-04-7180-6(0))* Norma S.A. COL. Dist: Distribuidora Norma, Inc.

No, Chayito, No: Individual 6-packs. 2003. 23.95 *(978-0-673-78074-4(0))* Celebration Pr.

No Les Tengo Miedo: Big Book Packages. 2003. 64.95 *(978-0-673-58581-3(6))* Celebration Pr.

No te dejes de Laura Sue: Social/Emotional Lap Book. (Pebble Soup Exploraciones Ser.). (SPA.). (gr. -1-18). 16.00 *(978-0-7578-1793-9(9))* Rigby Education.

No te Preocupes: Individual Title, 6 packs. (Literatura 2000 Ser.). (SPA.). (gr. 2-3). 33.00 *(978-0-7635-1098-5(X))* Rigby Education.

Noël, Alyson. Desafío: Quinto Libro de la Serie de Los Inmortales. 2012. (Vintage Espanol Ser.). (SPA.). 336p. (YA). (gr. 7). pap. 10.95 *(978-0-307-95147-2(2)*, Vintage Espanol) Knopf Doubleday Publishing Group.

Nonfiction Packs. (SPA.). 288.75 *(978-0-7362-2578-6(1))* CENGAGE Learning.

Nonfiction Packs: Spanish Nonfiction Pack, 33 vols. 117.53 *(978-0-7362-1511-4(5))* CENGAGE Learning.

North, Sherry. Champ's Story: Dogs Get Cancer Too!, 1 vol. Rietz, Kathleen, illus. 2010. (ENG.). 32p. (J). (gr. -1-4). 16.95 *(978-1-60718-077-7(4))*; pap. 8.95 *(978-1-60718-088-3(X))* Arbordale Publishing.

—La Historia de Campeona: ¡a Los Perros También les Da Cáncer!, 1 vol. Rietz, Kathleen, illus. 2010. (SPA & ENG.). 32p. (J). (gr. -1-4). 17.95 *(978-1-60718-681-6(0))* Arbordale Publishing.

Nos traen Agua. (Saludos Ser.: Vol. 3). (SPA.). (gr. 3-5). 31.00 *(978-0-7635-3268-0(1))* Rigby Education.

Nos traen Agua: 6 Small Books. (Saludos Ser.: Vol. 3). (SPA.). (gr. 3-5). 31.00 *(978-0-7635-1827-1(1))* Rigby Education.

Nosotros Interactive Packages: Aqui me Tienen. (Pebble Soup Exploraciones Ser.). (gr. -1-18). 52.00 *(978-0-7578-5251-0(3))* Rigby Education.

Nöstlinger, Christine. Las Enfermedades de Franz. (Torre de Papel Ser.). (SPA.). (J). 7.95 *(978-958-04-1930-3(2))* Norma S.A. COL. Dist: Distribuidora Norma, Inc.

—Franz Se Mete en Problemas de Amor. (Torre de Papel Ser.). (SPA.). (J). 7.95 *(978-958-04-2697-4(X))* Norma S.A. COL. Dist: Distribuidora Norma, Inc.

—El Lobo y los Siete Cabritos. (Torre de Papel Ser.). (SPA., Illus.). (J). (gr. 2). 7.95 *(978-958-04-4532-6(X))* Norma S.A. COL. Dist: Distribuidora Norma, Inc.

—Un Marido para Mamá. 2011. (Torre de Papel Ser.). (SPA.). 184p. (gr. 6-8). pap. 12.99 *(978-958-04-2382-9(2))* Norma S.A. COL. Dist: Lectorum Pubns., Inc.

—Las Vacaciones de Franz. (Torre de Papel Ser.). (SPA.). (J). (gr. 2). 7.95 *(978-958-04-1931-0(0))* Norma S.A. COL. Dist: Distribuidora Norma, Inc.

Nuestra casa de Adobe: 6 Small Books. (Saludos Ser.: Vol. 2). (SPA.). (gr. 2-3). 31.00 *(978-0-7635-9543-2(8))* Rigby Education.

Nuestras geniales Orejas. (Spanish Early Intervention Levels Ser.). (SPA.). 28.38 *(978-0-7362-0841-3(0))* CENGAGE Learning.

Nuestro Mundo. (Nuevos Horizontes Ser.). (SPA.). (J). (gr. 1). No. 1. wbk. ed. 7.95 *(978-1-56014-504-2(8))*No. 2. wbk. ed. 7.95 *(978-1-56014-505-9(6))* Santillana USA Publishing Co., Inc.

Nuestro Mundo: Evaluations, Grade 1. (Nuevos Horizontes Ser.). (SPA.). (J). 22.50 *(978-1-56014-506-6(4))* Santillana USA Publishing Co., Inc.

Nuestro Mundo No. 1: Student Anthology. (Nuevos Horizontes Ser.). (SPA.). (J). (gr. 1). 14.95 *(978-1-56014-502-8(1))* Santillana USA Publishing Co., Inc.

Nuestro Mundo No. 2: Student Anthology. (Nuevos Horizontes Ser.). (SPA.). (J). (gr. 1). 14.95 *(978-1-56014-503-5(X))* Santillana USA Publishing Co., Inc.

Nuestro perro Sam 6 Packs. Individual Title. (Literatura 2000 Ser.). (SPA.). (gr. k-1). 28.00 *(978-0-7635-1025-1(4))* Rigby Education.

Nuestro viaje hacia la Libertad: 6 Small Books. (Saludos Ser.: Vol. 3). (SPA.). (gr. 3-5). 31.00 *(978-0-7635-1782-3(8))* Rigby Education.

Nuevas Aventuras. (Nuevos Horizontes Ser.). (SPA.). (J). (gr. 3). wbk. ed. 8.95 *(978-1-56014-515-8(3))* Santillana USA Publishing Co., Inc.

Nuevas Aventuras: Evaluations, Grade 3. (Nuevos Horizontes Ser.). (SPA.). (J). 22.50 *(978-1-56014-516-5(1))* Santillana USA Publishing Co., Inc.

Nuevas Aventuras: Student Anthology. (Nuevos Horizontes Ser.). (SPA.). (J). (gr. 3). 18.95 *(978-1-56014-514-1(5))* Santillana USA Publishing Co., Inc.

Nuevas Fronteras. (Nuevos Horizontes Ser.). (SPA.). (J). (gr. 4). wbk. ed. 8.95 *(978-1-56014-519-6(6))* Santillana USA Publishing Co., Inc.

Nuevas Fronteras: Evaluations, Grade 4. (Nuevos Horizontes Ser.). (SPA.). (J). 22.50 *(978-1-56014-520-2(X))* Santillana USA Publishing Co., Inc.

Nuevas Fronteras: Student Anthology. (Nuevos Horizontes Ser.). (SPA.). (J). (gr. 4). 18.95 *(978-1-56014-518-9(8))* Santillana USA Publishing Co., Inc.

Obregón, José María. Nevada. 2009. (Bilingual Library of the United States of America Ser.). (ENG & SPA.). 32p. (gr. 2-2). 47.90 *(978-1-60853-372-5(7)*, Editorial Buenas Letras) Rosen Publishing Group, Inc., The.

—New York / Nueva York. 2009. (Bilingual Library of the United States of America Ser.). (ENG & SPA.). 32p. (gr. 2-2). 47.90 *(978-1-60853-376-3(X)*, Editorial Buenas Letras) Rosen Publishing Group, Inc., The.

Ohara, Maricarmen. Amiguitos. (SPA., Illus.). 144p. (J). (gr. k-3). 23.00 *(978-0-944356-22-7(2))* Alegria Hispana Pubns.

—Capullitos. (SPA., Illus.). 70p. (J). (gr. k-3). 15.00 *(978-0-944356-03-6(6))* Alegria Hispana Pubns.

—Tesoro de Poesia Juvenil. (SPA.). 144p. 20.00 *(978-0-944356-09-8(5))* Alegria Hispana Pubns.

Ojos, Orejas y Pecas. (SPA.). (J). 12.00 *(978-958-02-1236-2(8))* Editorial Voluntad S.A. COL. Dist: Distribuidora Norma, Inc.

Olivas, Daniel. Benjamin & the Word: Benjamín y la Palabra. Baeza Ventura, Gabriela, tr. Dyen, Don, illus. 2011. 32p. (J). pap. 7.95 *(978-1-55885-687-5(0)*, Piñata Books) Arte Publico Pr.

On Safari: Individual Title-Six Packs. (Chiquilibros Ser.). (gr. k-1). 23.00 *(978-0-7635-0434-2(3))* Rigby Education.

Once upon a Time Spanish Version-Little Red Riding Hood. 2005. (J). *(978-1-57022-562-8(1))* ECS Learning Systems, Inc.

Once upon a Time Spanish Version-the Boy Who Cried Wolf. 2005. (J). *(978-1-57022-557-4(5))* ECS Learning Systems, Inc.

Once upon a Time Spanish Version-the Elves & the Shoemaker. 2005. (J). *(978-1-57022-559-8(1))* ECS Learning Systems, Inc.

Once upon a Time Spanish Version-the Gingerbread Man. 2005. (J). *(978-1-57022-556-7(7))* ECS Learning Systems, Inc.

Once upon a Time Spanish Version-the Little Red Hen. 2005. (J). *(978-1-57022-561-1(3))* ECS Learning Systems, Inc.

Once upon a Time Spanish Version-the Three Bears. 2005. (J). *(978-1-57022-563-5(X))* ECS Learning Systems, Inc.

Once upon a Time Spanish Version-the Three Billy Goats Gruff. 2005. (J). *(978-1-57022-564-2(8))* ECS Learning Systems, Inc.

Once upon a Time Spanish Version-the Three Little Pigs. 2005. (J). *(978-1-57022-565-9(6))* ECS Learning Systems, Inc.

Onetti, Juan Carlos. Los Adioses. (SPA.). (J). 9.00 *(978-958-04-7258-2(0))* Norma S.A. COL. Dist: Distribuidora Norma, Inc.

Onieva Morales, Juan Luis. Como Dominar la Ortografia: Ortografia Moderna. (SPA.). 176p. 18.95 *(978-84-359-0467-4(9)*, ARG502) Playor, Editorial, S.A. ESP. Dist: Continental Bk. Co., Inc.

Oppenheim, Joanne F. & Barefoot Books Staff. El Principe No Duerme. Latimer, Miriam, illus. 2014. (SPA.). 32p. (J). (gr. -1-1). pap. 7.99 *(978-1-78285-077-9(5))* Barefoot Bks., Inc.

Orange Collection. (Elefonetica Ser.). (SPA.). (gr. 1-2). 296.76 *(978-0-7362-0790-4(2))* CENGAGE Learning.

Orejas. (Spanish Early Intervention Levels Ser.). (SPA.). 23.10 *(978-1-56334-783-2(0))* CENGAGE Learning.

Orlev, Uri. La Pequena Nina Grande. Gleich, Jacky, illus. (Buenas Noches Ser.). (SPA.). (J). 8.95 *(978-958-04-4902-7(3))* Norma S.A. COL. Dist: Distribuidora Norma, Inc.

Osborne, Mary Pope, et al. Carnaval a Media Luz. Murdocca, Sal, illus. 2016. (SPA.). (J). (gr. 2-4). pap. 5.99 ***(978-1-63245-643-4(5))*** Lectorum Pubns., Inc.

—La Estación de Las Tormentas de Arena. Murdocca, Sal, illus. 2016. (SPA.). (J). (gr. 2-4). pap. 5.99 ***(978-1-63245-644-1(3))*** Lectorum Pubns., Inc.

—La Noche de los Nuevos Magos. Murdocca, Sal, illus. 2016. (SPA.). (J). (gr. 2-4). pap. 5.99 ***(978-1-63245-645-8(1))*** Lectorum Pubns., Inc.

—Tormenta de Nieve en Luna Azul. Murdocca, Sal, illus. 2016. (SPA.). (J). (gr. 2-4). pap. 5.99 ***(978-1-63245-646-5(X))*** Lectorum Pubns., Inc.

El Oso Meno, 6 Packs. 2003. 23.95 *(978-0-673-78067-6(8))* Celebration Pr.

Los Osos. 2003. (J). (gr. -1-2). 28.95 *(978-0-673-77404-0(X))* Celebration Pr.

Palabras. (Coleccion Libritos Acordeon). (SPA., Illus.). 10p. (J). pap. 5.50 *(978-950-11-0824-8(4)*, SGM244) Sigmar ARG. Dist: Continental Bk. Co., Inc.

Palermo, Miguel Angel. Lo Que Cuentan los Tehuelches. (Cuentamerica Ser.). (SPA.). (YA). (gr. 4-18). pap. *(978-950-07-1405-1(1)*, SA30067) Editorial Sudamericana S.A. ARG. Dist: Lectorum Pubns., Inc.

—Lo Que Cuentan los Wichis. (Cuentamerica Ser.). (SPA.). (YA). (gr. 4-18). *(978-950-07-1616-1(X)*, SA30068) Editorial Sudamericana S.A. ARG. Dist: Lectorum Pubns., Inc.

Pan y Canela. (SPA.). (gr. k-2). 519.49 *(978-1-56334-643-9(5)*, SE8103); (gr. k-2). 500.86 *(978-1-56334-642-2(7)*, SE8102); (gr. k-2). 1533.42 *(978-0-7362-0446-0(6)*, PA8220); (gr. k-2). 426.37 *(978-1-56334-543-2(9)*, CO8206); (gr. k-2). 426.37 *(978-1-56334-542-5(0)*, CO8205);Level C. (gr. 2-18). 738.56 *(978-0-7362-0705-8(8)*, SU8100) CENGAGE Learning.

Pan y Canela: Collection C. (SPA.). (gr. k-2). 522.85 *(978-0-7362-0342-5(7))*; 615.30 *(978-0-7362-0343-2(5))* CENGAGE Learning.

A Papa no le Molesto: Individual Title Six-Packs. (Literatura 2000 Ser.). (SPA.). (gr. 1-2). 28.00 *(978-0-7635-1057-2(2))* Rigby Education.

Papa salvo la Fiesta: Six-Pack. (Saludos Ser.: Vol. 3). (SPA.). (gr. 2-3). 31.00 *(978-0-7635-9528-9(4))* Rigby Education.

Papas. (Spanish Early Intervention Levels Ser.). (SPA.). 21.30 *(978-0-7362-0802-4(X))* CENGAGE Learning.

Papi y Yo. (Spanish Early Intervention Levels Ser.). (SPA.). 23.10 *(978-1-56334-786-3(5))* CENGAGE Learning.

Paquito y los frijoles Magicos: Video Tape. (ENG & SPA.). (gr. k-1). 26.00 *(978-0-7635-6278-6(5))* Rigby Education.

Parker, David & Lyon, Tammie. ¡Soy Optimista! Lyon, Tammie, illus. 2011. (SPA., Illus.). (J). *(978-0-545-27356-5(0))* Scholastic, Inc.

Parramón, José María. Mi Calle. Borday, Irene, illus. (Coleccion Estoy En...).Tr. of My Street. (SPA.). 32p. (J). (gr. k-3). 6.36 *(978-84-342-1003-5(7))* Parramon Ediciones S.A. ESP. Dist: Lectorum Pubns., Inc.

—Mi Casa. Borday, Irene, illus. (Coleccion Estoy En...).Tr. of My House. (SPA.). 32p. (J). (gr. k-3). 6.36 *(978-84-342-1002-8(9))* Parramon Ediciones S.A. ESP. Dist: Lectorum Pubns., Inc.

—Mi Jardin. Borday, Irene, illus. (Coleccion Estoy En...).Tr. of My Garden. (SPA.). 32p. (J). (gr. k-3). 6.36 *(978-84-342-1005-9(3))* Parramon Ediciones S.A. ESP. Dist: Lectorum Pubns., Inc.

Parramón, José María & Bordoy, Irene. Mi Calle.Tr. of My Street. (SPA., Illus.). (J). (gr. -1-1). 6.95 *(978-958-04-1277-9(4))* Norma S.A. COL. Dist: Distribuidora Norma, Inc.

Pastel de Lodo: Individual Title Six-Packs. (Literatura 2000 Ser.). (SPA.). (gr. -1-1). 28.00 *(978-0-7635-1000-8(9))* Rigby Education.

Patas, 6 Packs. (Literatura 2000 Ser.). (SPA.). (gr. 1-2). 28.00 *(978-0-7635-1049-7(1))* Rigby Education.

El patito y los Gusanos. (Spanish Early Intervention Levels Ser.). (SPA.). 21.30 *(978-0-7362-0811-6(9))* CENGAGE Learning.

Patricelli, Leslie. Faster! Faster!/Mas Rapido! Mas Rapido! Patricelli, Leslie, illus. 2013. (Leslie Patricelli Board Bks.). (ENG., Illus.). 30p. (J). (-k). bds. 6.99 *(978-0-7636-6611-8(4))* Candlewick Pr.

Paty la Pequenita, 6 Packs. (Literatura 2000 Ser.). (SPA.). (gr. 1-2). 28.00 *(978-0-7635-1050-3(5))* Rigby Education.

Pebble Soup Exploraciones: Complete Pebble Soup Exploraciones Package. 1650.00 *(978-0-7578-3315-1(2))* Rigby Education.

El Pececito Andres: Individual 6-packs. 2003. 23.95 *(978-0-673-78065-2(1))* Celebration Pr.

Penn, Sarah. Nat Love: African American Cowboy / Vaquero Afroamericano. 2009. (Famous People in American History/Grandes personajes en la historia de los Estados Unidos Ser.). (ENG & SPA.). 32p. (gr. 2-3). 47.90 *(978-1-61512-551-7(5)*, Editorial Buenas Letras) Rosen Publishing Group, Inc., The.

Pennac, Daniel. La Mirada del Lobo. (Torre de Papel Ser.). (SPA.). (J). (gr. 4-18). 8.95 *(978-958-04-4145-8(6))* Norma S.A. COL. Dist: Distribuidora Norma, Inc.

Penner, Lucille Recht. Donde esta ese Hueso? Math Matters en Espanol. Adams, Lynne, illus. 2005. 32p. (J). pap. 5.95 *(978-1-57565-156-9(4))* Kane Press, Inc.

Penovi, Celina. Alboroto a la Hora Del Desayuno / Scrambled Breakfast. 2009. 20p. pap. 14.99 *(978-1-4490-2743-8(1))* AuthorHouse.

Pensando. (Coleccion Mil Preguntas). (SPA., Illus.). 24p. (J). pap. 5.50 *(978-950-11-0661-9(6)*, SGM629) Sigmar ARG. Dist: Continental Bk. Co., Inc.

Pepe El Panadero, 6 Packs. 2003. 23.95 *(978-0-673-78061-4(9))* Celebration Pr.

Pérez-Mercado, Mary Margaret. ¡Zas! Torrey, Richard L., illus. 2011. (Rookie Ready to Learn Español Ser.). (SPA.). 40p. (J). pap. 5.95 *(978-0-531-26788-2(1)*, Children's Pr.) Scholastic Library Publishing.

Pérez-Mercado, Mary Margaret & Torrey, Rich. ¡Zas! Torrey, Rich, illus. 2011. (Rookie Ready to Learn Español Ser.). (SPA., Illus.). 40p. (J). lib. bdg. 23.00 *(978-0-531-26120-0(4)*, Children's Pr.) Scholastic Library Publishing.

Perrault, Charles. Cinderella (Cenicienta) Fransoy, Monse, illus. 2013. (Bilingual Fairy Tales Ser.). (ENG & SPA.). 32p. (gr. 1-4). lib. bdg. 28.50 *(978-1-60753-356-6(1))* Amicus Publishing.

Perrin. (Spanish Early Intervention Levels Ser.). (SPA.). 21.30 *(978-0-7362-0834-5(8))* CENGAGE Learning.

Perritos, 6 Packs. 2003. 23.95 *(978-0-673-78063-8(5))* Celebration Pr.

Pesce, Elena. La Cola de los Ingleses. (SPA.). (J). (gr. 4-18). 7.95 *(978-958-04-5033-7(1))* Norma S.A. COL. Dist: Distribuidora Norma, Inc.

Peters, Elisa. It's a Bird! / ¡Es un Ave! 2009. (Everyday Wonders / Maravillas de todos los días Ser.). (ENG & SPA.). 24p. (gr. 1-1). 42.50 *(978-1-61512-327-8(X)*, Editorial Buenas Letras) Rosen Publishing Group, Inc., The.

—It's a Caterpillar! / ¡Es una Oruga! 2009. (Everyday Wonders / Maravillas de todos los días Ser.). (ENG & SPA.). 24p. (gr. 1-1). 42.50 *(978-1-61512-328-5(8)*, Editorial Buenas Letras) Rosen Publishing Group, Inc., The.

—It's a Dragonfly! / ¡Es una Libélula! 2009. (Everyday Wonders / Maravillas de todos los días Ser.). (ENG & SPA.). 24p. (gr. 1-1). 42.50 *(978-1-61512-329-2(6)*, Editorial Buenas Letras) Rosen Publishing Group, Inc., The.

—It's a Sunflower! / ¡Es un Girasol! 2009. (Everyday Wonders / Maravillas de todos los días Ser.). (ENG & SPA.). 24p. (gr. 1-1). 42.50 *(978-1-61512-330-8(X)*, Editorial Buenas Letras) Rosen Publishing Group, Inc., The.

—It's an Apple Tree! / ¡Es un Manzano! 2009. (Everyday Wonders / Maravillas de todos los días Ser.). (ENG & SPA.). 24p. (gr. 1-1). 42.50 *(978-1-61512-331-5(8)*, Editorial Buenas Letras) Rosen Publishing Group, Inc., The.

—It's Snow! / ¡la Nieve! 2009. (Everyday Wonders / Maravillas de todos los días Ser.). (ENG & SPA.). 24p. (gr. 1-1). 42.50 *(978-1-61512-332-2(6)*, Editorial Buenas Letras) Rosen Publishing Group, Inc., The.

Petersen, Kathleen C. Null. ¿Poesía? ¡Qué Horror!, 1 vol. rev. ed. 2007. (Building Fluency Through Reader's Theater Ser.). (SPA.). 20p. (J). (gr. 1-2). pap. 6.99 *(978-1-4333-0020-2(6))* Teacher Created Materials, Inc.

Phillips, Larissa. Cochise: Apache Chief. 2009. (Primary Sources of Famous People in American History Ser.). 32p. (gr. 2-3). 47.90 *(978-1-60851-660-5(1))* Rosen Publishing Group, Inc., The.

—Cochise: Apache Chief / Cochise: Jefe Apache. 2009. (Famous People in American History/Grandes personajes en la historia de los Estados Unidos Ser.). (ENG & SPA.). 32p. (gr. 2-3). 47.90 *(978-1-61512-540-1(X)*, Editorial Buenas Letras) Rosen Publishing Group, Inc., The.

—Cochise: Jefe apache (Cochise: Apache Chief) 2009. (Grandes personajes en la historia de los Estados Unidos (Famous People in American History) Ser.). (SPA.). 32p. (gr. 2-3). 47.90 *(978-1-61512-792-4(5)*, Editorial Buenas Letras) Rosen Publishing Group, Inc., The.

Phonics Songs & Rhymes Flip Chart. 2004. (gr. k-18). suppl. ed. 109.15 *(978-0-328-02213-7(6))*; (gr. 3-18). suppl. ed. 109.50 *(978-0-673-59718-2(0))* Addison-Wesley Educational Pubs., Inc.

Pin uno, pin dos, pin Tres: Individual Title Six-Packs. (Literatura 2000 Ser.). (SPA.). (gr. 2-3). 33.00 *(978-0-7635-1269-9(9))* Rigby Education.

La Pinata, 6 Packs. 2003. 23.95 *(978-0-673-77134-6(2))* Celebration Pr.

Pinata: Mas Pinata Package. 2003. 1744.95 *(978-0-673-58718-3(5))* Celebration Pr.

Pinguete y Miguela. (Spanish Early Intervention Levels Ser.). (SPA.). 28.38 *(978-0-7362-0842-0(9))* CENGAGE Learning.

Pinto, Pinto. (Spanish Early Intervention Levels Ser.). (SPA.). 23.10 *(978-1-56334-769-6(5))* CENGAGE Learning.

Pisa Y Ve! Little Books, Level 6, Vol. 10. 2003. (Fonolibros Ser.). 25.50 *(978-0-7652-0087-7(2))* Modern Curriculum Pr.

Pitt, Marilyn, et al. Perro en Apuros: Let Me In. Bianchi, John & Taylor, Trace, illus. 2010. (1G Our World Ser.). (ENG.). 24p. (J). pap. 5.99 *(978-1-61541-170-2(4))* American Reading Co.

La Playa: Individual Title Six-Packs. (Literatura 2000 Ser.). (SPA.). (gr. -1-1). 28.00 *(978-0-7635-1001-5(7))* Rigby Education.

Polacco, Patricia. Gracias, Senor Falker. 2006. (SPA., Illus.). 34p. (J). (gr. 2-3). per. 7.99 *(978-1-933032-02-3(2)*, LC34004) Lectorum Pubns., Inc.

Polette, Keith. Moon over the Mountain. 2009. (ENG.). 32p. (J). (gr. -1-3). 16.95 *(978-1-934960-07-3(1)*, Raven Tree Pr.,Csi) Continental Sales, Inc.

—Moon over the Mountain/Luna Sobre la Montana. 2009. (ENG & SPA.). 32p. (J). (gr. -1-3). 16.95 *(978-1-932748-85-7(7))*; pap. 7.95 *(978-1-932748-84-0(9))* Continental Sales, Inc. (Raven Tree Pr.,Csi).

Pollack, Pam & Belviso, Meg. I Can't Sit Still! Living with ADHD. Fabrega, Marta, illus. 2009. (Live & Learn Ser.). (ENG.). 36p. (J). (gr. -1-2). pap. 6.99 *(978-0-7641-4419-6(7))* Barron's Educational Series, Inc.

—¡No Puedo Estar Quieto! Mi Vida con ADHD. Fabrega, Marta, illus. 2009. (Viva y Aprende Ser.). (SPA.). 36p. (J). (gr. -1-2). pap. 6.99 *(978-0-7641-4420-2(0))* Barron's Educational Series, Inc.

La pollita Vivita: Video Tape. (ENG & SPA.). (gr. k-1). 26.00 *(978-0-7635-6279-3(3))* Rigby Education.

El Pollito Huerfanito: Individual 6-packs. 2003. 23.95 *(978-0-673-77153-7(9))* Celebration Pr.

Los Pollitos. 2003. (J). (gr. -1-2). 28.95 *(978-0-673-77405-7(8))* Celebration Pr.

Por amor a las Tortugas: Six-Pack. (Saludos Ser.: Vol. 1). (SPA.). (gr. 2-3). 31.00 *(978-0-7635-9537-1(3))* Rigby Education.

Por Que? (Coleccion Mil Preguntas). (SPA., Illus.). 24p. (J). pap. 5.50 *(978-950-11-0611-4(X)*, SGM11X) Sigmar ARG. Dist: Continental Bk. Co., Inc.

Por que el conejo tiene las orejas tan Largas? Lap Book. (Pebble Soup Exploraciones Ser.). (SPA.). 16p. (gr. -1-18). 21.00 *(978-0-7578-1691-8(6))* Rigby Education.

Por que el conejo tiene las orejas tan Largas? Small Book. (Pebble Soup Exploraciones Ser.). (SPA.). 16p. (gr. -1-18). 5.00 *(978-0-7578-1731-1(9))* Rigby Education.

Por que el mar es Salado: Individual Title Six-Packs. (Literatura 2000 Ser.). (SPA.). (gr. 2-3). 33.00 *(978-0-7635-1270-5(2))* Rigby Education.

Por que los conejos tienen las orejas Largas: Individual Title Six-Packs. (Literatura 2000 Ser.). (SPA.). (gr. 2-3). 33.00 *(978-0-7635-1271-2(0))* Rigby Education.

Por que soplan los vientos Salvajes: 6 Softcover Books. (Saludos Ser.: Vol. 1). (SPA.). (gr. 3-5). 31.00 *(978-0-7635-1845-5(X))* Rigby Education.

Porque los elefantes tienen narices Largas: Individual Title Six-Packs. (Literatura 2000 Ser.). (SPA.). (gr. 1-2). 28.00 *(978-0-7635-1073-2(4))* Rigby Education.

Preparandose para la Fiesta, 6 Packs. (Literatura 2000 Ser.). (SPA.). (gr. -1-1). 28.00 *(978-0-7635-1002-2(5))* Rigby Education.

Price, Mara & Ventura, Gabriela Baeza. Grandma's Chocolate/El Chocolate de Abuelita. Fields, Lisa, illus. 2010. (SPA.). 32p. (J). (gr. -1-3). 16.95 *(978-1-55885-587-8(4)*, Piñata Books) Arte Publico Pr.

Price, Mathew. Vueltas y Vueltas en Patin. (SPA.). pap. 3.95 *(978-950-07-2062-5(0))* Editorial Sudamericana S.A. ARG. Dist: Distribooks, Inc.

Prieto, Iliana. La Princesa del Retrato y el Dragon Rey. (Torre de Papel Ser.). (SPA.). (J). (gr. 4-18). 8.95 *(978-958-04-4219-6(3))* Norma S.A. COL. Dist: Distribuidora Norma, Inc.

La Princesa De Verdad. 2003. 28.95 *(978-0-673-78087-4(2))* Celebration Pr.

El problema de Ema, 6 Packs. (Literatura 2000 Ser.). (SPA.). (gr. 1-2). 28.00 *(978-0-7635-1074-9(2))* Rigby Education.

Publications International Ltd. Staff, ed. PNO BK Spa Disney Princess. 2009. 12p. 15.98 *(978-1-4127-9243-1(6))* Phoenix International Publications, Inc.

Puedo Salir? 2003. (Coleccion Parvulitos). 63.50 *(978-0-8136-8103-0(0))* Modern Curriculum Pr.

Puedo Salir? Big Book. 2003. 35.50 *(978-0-8136-8101-6(4))* Modern Curriculum Pr.

Puertas al sol / Gold Set. (SPA.). (J). (gr. 3-5). 65.00 *(978-1-59437-849-2(5))* Santillana USA Publishing Co., Inc.

Puertas al sol / Silver Set. (SPA.). (J). (gr. k-2). 65.00 *(978-1-59437-848-5(7))* Santillana USA Publishing Co., Inc.

Pullman, Philip. Luces del Norte. (SPA.). (YA). 2007. 672p. pap. 8.95 *(978-84-666-1635-5(7))* 8th ed. 2005. (Illus.). 379p. (gr. 7-11). 13.95 *(978-84-406-3296-8(7))* Ediciones B ESP. Dist: Spanish Pubs., LLC, Independent Pubs. Group.

—Luces del Norte. (SPA.). 672p. 18.95 *(978-84-663-0673-7(0))* Suma de Letras, S.L. ESP. Dist: Distribooks, Inc.

Puppies. 2003. 23.95 *(978-0-673-78127-7(5))* Celebration Pr.

Puppies. 10.95 *(978-3-8238-4703-8(1))* teNeues Publishing Co.

Puzo, Mario. Las Extranas Vacaciones de Davie Shaw. (SPA.). 124p. (YA). (gr. 5-18). *(978-84-279-3318-7(5)*, NG2827) Noguer y Caralt Editores, S. A. ESP. Dist: Lectorum Pubns., Inc.

Que agarro Rigo? Individual Title Six-Packs. (Literatura 2000 Ser.). (SPA.). (gr. k-1). 28.00 *(978-0-7635-1027-5(0))* Rigby Education.

Que debes decir? Que debes Hacer? Social/Emotional Lap Book. (Pebble Soup Exploraciones Ser.). (SPA.). (gr. -1-18). 16.00 *(978-0-7578-1791-5(2))* Rigby Education.

Que es Chiquito? (Spanish Early Intervention Levels Ser.). (SPA.). 23.10 *(978-1-56334-760-3(1))* CENGAGE Learning.

Que es Rojo? (Spanish Early Intervention Levels Ser.). (SPA.). 31.14 *(978-0-7362-0339-5(7))* CENGAGE Learning.

Que Es un Murcielago? Individual Title Six-Packs. (Literatura 2000 Ser.). (SPA.). (gr. 1-2). 28.00 *(978-0-7635-1051-0(3))* Rigby Education.

Que hay a la vuelta de la Esquina? Individual Title Six-Packs. (Literatura 2000 Ser.). (SPA.). (gr. 1-2). 28.00 *(978-0-7635-1075-6(0))* Rigby Education.

Que hizo Zoe Zapata? (Spanish Early Intervention Levels Ser.). (SPA.). 21.30 *(978-0-7362-0828-4(3))* CENGAGE Learning.

Que puede Volar? Individual Title Six-Packs. (Literatura 2000 Ser.). (SPA.). (gr. k-1). 28.00 *(978-0-7635-1028-2(9))* Rigby Education.

Que puedo yo Hacer? 6 Small Books. (Saludos Ser.: Vol. 1). (SPA.). (gr. 2-3). 31.00 *(978-0-7635-9539-5(X))* Rigby Education.

Que quiere Beto? Individual Title-Six Packs. (Chiquilibros Ser.). (SPA.). (gr. k-1). 23.00 *(978-0-7635-8610-2(2))* Rigby Education.

Que quieren Ellos? Individual Title-Six Packs. (Chiquilibros Ser.). (SPA.). (gr. k-1). 23.00 *(978-0-7635-8611-9(0))* Rigby Education.

Que Revoltijo! Individual Title Six-Packs. (Chiquilibros Ser.). (SPA.). (gr. k-1). 23.00 *(978-0-7635-8593-8(9))* Rigby Education.

Que sale de las Semillas? (Spanish Early Intervention Levels Ser.). (SPA.). 23.10 *(978-1-56334-768-9(7))* CENGAGE Learning.

Que Sera? 2003. 28.95 *(978-0-673-78093-5(7))* Celebration Pr.

Que Sera? Big Book. (Pebble Soup Exploraciones Ser.). (SPA.). 16p. (gr. -1-18). 31.00 *(978-0-7578-1689-5(4))* Rigby Education.

Que Sera? Small Book. (Pebble Soup Exploraciones Ser.). (SPA.). 16p. (gr. -1-18). 5.00 *(978-0-7578-1729-8(7))* Rigby Education.

Que Sigue? Big Book Packages. 2003. 64.95 *(978-0-673-58584-4(0))* Celebration Pr.

Que suerte Tengo! Individual Title Six-Packs. (Literatura 2000 Ser.). (SPA.). (gr. 1-2). 28.00 *(978-0-7635-1076-3(9))* Rigby Education.

Que va en la Tina? Individual Title Six-Packs. (Literatura 2000 Ser.). (SPA.). (gr. k-1). 28.00 *(978-0-7635-1029-9(7))* Rigby Education.

Querida Abuelita: 6 Small Books. (Saludos Ser.: Vol. 2). (SPA.). (gr. 3-5). 31.00 *(978-0-7635-1770-0(4))* Rigby Education.

Querida Gilda. (Spanish Early Intervention Levels Ser.). (SPA.). 23.10 *(978-0-7362-0322-7(2))* CENGAGE Learning.

Querido Santa, 6 Packs. (Literatura 2000 Ser.). (SPA.). (gr. k-1). 28.00 *(978-0-7635-1030-5(0))* Rigby Education.

Quien? (Coleccion Mil Preguntas). (SPA., Illus.). 24p. (J). pap. 5.50 *(978-950-11-0607-7(1)*, SGM110) Sigmar ARG. Dist: Continental Bk. Co., Inc.

Quien es Michael Ramirez? 2003. 28.95 *(978-0-673-78084-3(8))* Celebration Pr.

A quien le gusta la Noche? (Spanish Early Intervention Levels Ser.). (SPA.). 31.14 *(978-0-7362-0330-2(3))* CENGAGE Learning.

Quien paso por Aqui? (Spanish Early Intervention Levels Ser.). (SPA.). 23.10 *(978-1-56334-788-7(1))* CENGAGE Learning.

Quien soy Yo? (Spanish Early Intervention Levels Ser.). (SPA.). 23.10 *(978-1-56334-793-1(8))* CENGAGE Learning.

Quienes Son Tus Amigos? 2003. 35.50 *(978-0-8136-8047-7(6))* Modern Curriculum Pr.

Quieres Jugar? Big Book. (Pebble Soup Exploraciones Ser.). 16p. (gr. -1-18). 31.00 *(978-0-7578-1672-7(X))* Rigby Education.

Quieres Jugar? Small Book. (Pebble Soup Exploraciones Ser.). 16p. (gr. -1-18). 5.00 *(978-0-7578-1712-0(2))* Rigby Education.

Rabbits: Individual Title Six-Packs. (Literatura 2000 Ser.). (gr. 2-3). 33.00 *(978-0-7635-0235-5(9))* Rigby Education.

Rabe, Tish. ¡Te Amo, Te Abrazo, Leo Contigo!/Love You, Hug You, Read to You! Endersby, Frank, illus. 2015. (SPA & ENG.). 32p. (J). (gr. -1 — 1). bds. 7.99 *(978-1-101-93657-3(6)*, Random Hse. Bks. for Young Readers) Random Hse. Children's Bks.

Ramos, et al. La Nueva Casa. (SPA.). 32p. (J). 10.00 *(978-84-342-2517-6(4))* Parramon Ediciones S.A. ESP. Dist: Distribuidora Norma, Inc.

Ramos, Maria Cristina. De Barrio Somos. (Torre de Papel Ser.). (SPA.). (J). (gr. 4). 7.95 *(978-958-04-4221-9(5))* Norma S.A. COL. Dist: Distribuidora Norma, Inc.

La rana que se creia Caballo: Individual Title Six-Packs. (Literatura 2000 Ser.). (SPA.). (gr. 2-3). 33.00 *(978-0-7635-1272-9(9))* Rigby Education.

El Ranchito. (Spanish Early Intervention Levels Ser.). (SPA.). 23.10 *(978-1-56334-764-1(4))* CENGAGE Learning.

El Rancho: Individual Title Six-Packs. (Literatura 2000 Ser.). (SPA.). (gr. -1-1). 28.00 *(978-0-7635-1006-0(8))* Rigby Education.

Randolph, Joanne. Fire Trucks. 2009. (To the Rescue! Ser.). 24p. (gr. 1-1). 42.50 *(978-1-60854-397-7(8)*, PowerKids Pr.) Rosen Publishing Group, Inc., The.

—Fire Trucks/Camiones de Bomberos. 2009. (To the Rescue! / ¡Al rescate! Ser.). (ENG & SPA.). 24p. (gr. 1-1). 42.50 *(978-1-60854-403-5(6)*, Editorial Buenas Letras) Rosen Publishing Group, Inc., The.

—Gases in My World. 2007. (Journeys Ser.). (ENG.). 24p. (gr. k-8). pap. 7.05 *(978-1-4042-8419-7(2)*, Rosen Classroom) Rosen Publishing Group, Inc., The.

—Gears in My World. 2007. (Journeys Ser.). (ENG.). 24p. (gr. k-8). pap. 7.05 *(978-1-4042-8423-4(0)*, Rosen Classroom) Rosen Publishing Group, Inc., The.

—Let's Draw a Butterfly with Circles / Vamos a dibujar una mariposa usando Círculos. 2009. (Let's Draw with Shapes / Vamos a dibujar con figuras Ser.). (ENG & SPA.). 24p. (gr. k-1). 42.50 *(978-1-61514-221-7(5)*, Editorial Buenas Letras) Rosen Publishing Group, Inc., The.

—Let's Draw a Horse with Rectangles / Vamos a dibujar un caballo usando Rectángulos. 2009. (Let's Draw with Shapes / Vamos a dibujar con figuras Ser.). (ENG & SPA.). 24p. (gr. k-1). 42.50 *(978-1-61514-224-8(X)*, Editorial Buenas Letras) Rosen Publishing Group, Inc., The.

—Police Cars. 2009. (To the Rescue! Ser.). 24p. (gr. 1-1). 42.50 *(978-1-60854-398-4(6)*, PowerKids Pr.) Rosen Publishing Group, Inc., The.

—Police Cars/Patruallas. 2009. (To the Rescue! / ¡Al rescate! Ser.). (ENG & SPA.). 24p. (gr. 1-1). 42.50 *(978-1-60854-404-2(4)*, Editorial Buenas Letras) Rosen Publishing Group, Inc., The.

—Wedges in My World. 2007. (Journeys Ser.). (ENG.). 24p. (gr. k-8). pap. 7.05 *(978-1-4042-8426-5(5)*, Rosen Classroom) Rosen Publishing Group, Inc., The.

—What I Look Like When I am Confused / Cómo me veo cuando estoy Confundido. 2009. (Let's Look at Feelings / un vistazo a los sentimientos Ser.). (ENG & SPA.). 24p. (gr. k-1). 42.50 *(978-1-61514-246-0(0)*, Editorial Buenas Letras) Rosen Publishing Group, Inc., The.

—Wheels & Axels in My World/Ejes y ruedas en mi Mundo. 2009. (My World of Science/la ciencia en mi mundo Ser.). (ENG & SPA.). 48p. (gr. 2-2). 37.50 *(978-1-61514-743-4(8)*, Editorial Buenas Letras) Rosen Publishing Group, Inc., The.

—Whose Back Is This? / ¿de quién es esta Espalda? 2009. (Animal Clues / ¿Adivina de Quién Es? Ser.). (ENG & SPA.). 24p. (gr. 1-1). 42.50 *(978-1-61511-437-5(8)*, Editorial Buenas Letras) Rosen Publishing Group, Inc., The.

—Whose Eyes Are These? / ¿de quién son estos Ojos? 2009. (Animal Clues / ¿Adivina de Quién Es? Ser.). (ENG & SPA.). 24p. (gr. 1-1). 42.50 *(978-1-61511-438-2(6)*, Editorial Buenas Letras) Rosen Publishing Group, Inc., The.

—Whose Nose Is This? / ¿de quién es esta Nariz? 2009. (Animal Clues / ¿Adivina de Quién Es? Ser.). (ENG & SPA.). 24p. (gr. 1-1). 42.50 *(978-1-61511-439-9(4)*, Editorial Buenas Letras) Rosen Publishing Group, Inc., The.

—Whose Teeth Are These? / ¿de quién son estos Dientes? 2009. (Animal Clues / ¿Adivina de Quién Es? Ser.). (ENG & SPA.). 24p. (gr. 1-1). 42.50 *(978-1-61511-440-5(8)*, Editorial Buenas Letras) Rosen Publishing Group, Inc., The.

—Whose Toes Are Those? / ¿de quién son estas Patas? 2009. (Animal Clues / ¿Adivina de Quién Es? Ser.). (ENG & SPA.). 24p. (gr. 1-1). 42.50 *(978-1-61511-441-2(6)*, Editorial Buenas Letras) Rosen Publishing Group, Inc., The.

—Whose Tongue Is This? / ¿de quién es esta Lengua? 2009. (Animal Clues / ¿Adivina de Quién Es? Ser.). (ENG & SPA.). 24p. (gr. 1-1). 42.50 *(978-1-61511-442-9(4)*, Editorial Buenas Letras) Rosen Publishing Group, Inc., The.

Los Raspados. 2003. 23.95 *(978-0-673-77786-7(3))* Celebration Pr.

Ratita y Raton. (Spanish Early Intervention Levels Ser.). (SPA.). 21.30 *(978-0-7362-0810-9(0))* CENGAGE Learning.

El raton Audaz. (Spanish Early Intervention Levels Ser.). (SPA.). 28.38 *(978-0-7362-0839-0(9))* CENGAGE Learning.

Reach for Reading: Reaching up en espanol Self-Training Package. (SPA.). (gr. 1-3). 675.00 *(978-0-7578-5933-5(X))* Rigby Education.

Reaching up en espanol Additional Resources: Additional Tutor's Manual. (Reach for Reading Ser.). (SPA.). (gr. 1-3). 31.00 *(978-0-7635-7622-6(0))* Rigby Education.

Reaching up en espanol Additional Resources: Spanish Books (75 Titles) (Reach for Reading Ser.). (SPA.). (gr. 1-3). 205.00 *(978-0-7578-4878-0(8))* Rigby Education.

Reaching up en espanol Additional Workstations: With Books. (Reach for Reading Ser.). (SPA.). (gr. 1-3). 390.00 *(978-0-7635-3711-1(X))* Rigby Education.

Reaching up en espanol Additional Workstations: Without Books. (Reach for Reading Ser.). (SPA.). (gr. 1-3). 285.00 *(978-0-7578-3544-5(9))* Rigby Education.

Read & Understand Spanish / English, Fiction. 2005. (J). 29.99 *(978-1-59673-075-5(7)*, EMC 5310) Evan-Moor Educational Pubs.

Reading 2000 Phonics Songs & Rhymes Flip Chart. 2004. (gr. 2-18). suppl. ed. 109.15 *(978-0-673-59717-5(2))* Addison-Wesley Educational Pubs., Inc.

El Rebozo De Elsa, 6 packs. 2003. 23.95 *(978-0-673-78068-3(6))* Celebration Pr.

Recortes. (Spanish Early Intervention Levels Ser.). (SPA.). 23.10 *(978-1-56334-779-5(2))* CENGAGE Learning.

Recuerdos: Individual Title Six-Packs. (Literatura 2000 Ser.). (SPA.). (gr. 2-3). 33.00 *(978-0-7635-1099-2(8))* Rigby Education.

Un Regalo del Mar, 6 Packs. (Literatura 2000 Ser.). (SPA.). (gr. 2-3). 33.00 *(978-0-7635-1273-6(7))* Rigby Education.

Regalos de Navidad, 6 Packs. (Literatura 2000 Ser.). (SPA.). (gr. 1-2). 28.00 *(978-0-7635-1052-7(1))* Rigby Education.

Reiser, Lynn. My Way(A Mi Manera) A Margaret & Margarita Story(Un Cuento de Margarita y Margaret) Reiser, Lynn, illus. 2007. (ENG & SPA., Illus.). 32p. (J). (gr. -1-k). 16.99 *(978-0-06-084101-0(X)*, Greenwillow Bks.) HarperCollins Pubs.

El Renacuajo: Big Book Packages. 2003. 64.95 *(978-0-673-58587-5(5))* Celebration Pr.

Reno ensucia: Messy Moose. 2005. (Take-Home Bks.). (SPA.). (YA). (gr. -1-3). 15.75 *(978-0-8215-1201-2(3))* Sadlier, William H. Inc.

Reno ensucia/Messy Moose. 2005. (Libros en Espanol Para Ninos Ser.). (SPA.). (YA). (gr. -1-1). 11.97 *(978-0-8215-0991-3(8))* Sadlier, William H. Inc.

El rey de la Laguna. (Spanish Early Intervention Levels Ser.). (SPA.). 31.14 *(978-0-7362-0328-9(1))* CENGAGE Learning.

Rey, H. A. ¡Eres Curioso Todo el Tiempo! 2012. (Curious George Ser.).Tr. of Curious You on Your Way! (ENG & SPA.). 32p. (J). (gr. -1-3). 9.99 *(978-0-547-79368-9(5))* Houghton Mifflin Harcourt Publishing Co.

—Jorge el Curioso el Baile. 2013. (Curious George Ser.). (SPA & ENG., Illus.). 24p. (J). (gr. -1-3). pap. 3.99 *(978-0-547-96822-3(1))* Houghton Mifflin Harcourt Publishing Co.

Rice, Dona Herweck. Agua, 1 vol. 2nd rev. ed. 2011. (Nonfiction Readers Ser.). (SPA.). 12p. (J). (gr. 1-1). pap. 4.99 *(978-1-4333-4415-2(7))* Teacher Created Materials, Inc.

—Casas Alrededor Del Mundo, 1 vol. 2nd rev. ed. 2012. (Nonfiction Readers Ser.).Tr. of Homes Around the World. (SPA., Illus.). 20p. (J). (gr. 1-1). pap. 4.99 *(978-1-4333-4431-2(9))* Teacher Created Materials, Inc.

—Colores, 1 vol. 2nd rev. ed. 2011. (Nonfiction Readers Ser.). (SPA.). 12p. (J). (gr. 1-1). pap. 4.99 *(978-1-4333-4405-3(X))* Teacher Created Materials, Inc.

—Comer Bien, 1 vol. 2nd rev. ed. 2012. (Nonfiction Readers Ser.). (SPA.). 20p. (J). (gr. 1-1). pap. 4.99 *(978-1-4333-4430-5(0))* Teacher Created Materials, Inc.

—Cómo Crecen las Plantas, 1 vol. 2nd rev. ed. 2011. (Nonfiction Readers Ser.). (SPA.). 12p. (J). (gr. 1-1). pap. 4.99 *(978-1-4333-4416-9(5))* Teacher Created Materials, Inc.

—Cosas con Alas, 1 vol. 2nd rev. ed. 2012. (Nonfiction Readers Ser.). (SPA.). 20p. (J). (gr. 1-1). pap. 4.99 *(978-1-4333-4422-0(X))* Teacher Created Materials, Inc.

—A Dónde Ir, 1 vol. 2nd rev. ed. 2011. (Nonfiction Readers Ser.). (SPA.). 12p. (J). (gr. 1-1). pap. 4.99 *(978-1-4333-4412-1(2))* Teacher Created Materials, Inc.

—Esta Soy Yo, 1 vol. 2nd rev. ed. 2011. (Nonfiction Readers Ser.). (SPA.). 12p. (J). (gr. 1-1). pap. 4.99 *(978-1-4333-4407-7(6))* Teacher Created Materials, Inc.

—Figuras, 1 vol. 2nd rev. ed. 2011. (Nonfiction Readers Ser.). (SPA.). 12p. (J). (gr. 1-1). pap. 4.99 *(978-1-4333-4406-0(8))* Teacher Created Materials, Inc.

—Grande y Pequeño, 1 vol. 2nd rev. ed. 2011. (Nonfiction Readers Ser.). (SPA.). 12p. (J). (gr. 1-1). pap. 4.99 *(978-1-4333-4404-6(1))* Teacher Created Materials, Inc.

—Lugares del Mundo, 1 vol. 2nd rev. ed. 2012. (Nonfiction Readers Ser.).Tr. of Places Around the World. (SPA.). 20p. (J). (gr. 1-1). pap. 4.99 *(978-1-4333-4433-6(5))* Teacher Created Materials, Inc.

—Madres Animales y Sus Crías, 1 vol. 2nd rev. ed. 2011. (Nonfiction Readers Ser.). (SPA., Illus.). 12p. (J). (gr. 1-1). pap. 4.99 *(978-1-4333-4418-3(1))* Teacher Created Materials, Inc.

—Mantenerse en Forma con Deportes, 1 vol. 2nd rev. ed. 2012. (Nonfiction Readers Ser.). (SPA.). 20p. (J). (gr. 1-1). pap. 4.99 *(978-1-4333-4429-9(7))* Teacher Created Materials, Inc.

—Mantenerse Sano, 1 vol. 2nd rev. ed. 2012. (Nonfiction Readers Ser.).Tr. of Staying Healthy. (SPA., Illus.). 20p. (J). (gr. 1-1). pap. 4.99 *(978-1-4333-4428-2(9))* Teacher Created Materials, Inc.

—Mi Gran Familia, 1 vol. 2nd rev. ed. 2011. (Nonfiction Readers Ser.). (SPA.). 12p. (J). (gr. 1-1). pap. 4.99 *(978-1-4333-4409-1(2))* Teacher Created Materials, Inc.

—En Movimiento, 1 vol. 2nd rev. ed. 2011. (Nonfiction Readers Ser.). (SPA.). 12p. (J). (gr. 1-1). pap. 4.99 *(978-1-4333-4410-7(6))* Teacher Created Materials, Inc.

—Niños Alrededor del Mundo, 1 vol. 2nd rev. ed. 2012. (Nonfiction Readers Ser.). (SPA.). 20p. (J). (gr. 1-1). pap. 4.99 *(978-1-4333-4432-9(7))* Teacher Created Materials, Inc.

—Ojos de Animales, 1 vol. 2nd rev. ed. 2011. (Nonfiction Readers Ser.). (SPA.). 12p. (J). (gr. 1-1). pap. 4.99 *(978-1-4333-4417-6(3))* Teacher Created Materials, Inc.

—Terreno, 1 vol. 2nd rev. ed. 2011. (Nonfiction Readers Ser.). (SPA.). 12p. (J). (gr. 1-1). pap. 4.99 *(978-1-4333-4413-8(0))* Teacher Created Materials, Inc.

—El Tiempo, 1 vol. 2nd rev. ed. 2011. (Nonfiction Readers Ser.). (SPA.). 12p. (J). (gr. 1-1). pap. 4.99 *(978-1-4333-4414-5(9))* Teacher Created Materials, Inc.

—Trabajadores, 1 vol. 2nd rev. ed. 2011. (Nonfiction Readers Ser.). (SPA.). 12p. (J). (gr. 1-1). pap. 4.99 *(978-1-4333-4411-4(4))* Teacher Created Materials, Inc.

—La Vida de una Abeja, 1 vol. 2nd rev. ed. 2012. (Nonfiction Readers Ser.). (SPA.). 20p. (J). (gr. 1-1). pap. 4.99 *(978-1-4333-4421-3(1))* Teacher Created Materials, Inc.

—La Vida de una Mariposa, 1 vol. 2nd rev. ed. 2012. (Nonfiction Readers Ser.). (SPA.). 20p. (J). (gr. 1-1). pap. 4.99 *(978-1-4333-4420-6(3))* Teacher Created Materials, Inc.

—La Vida de Una Rana, 1 vol. 2nd rev. ed. 2012. (Nonfiction Readers Ser.).Tr. of Frog's Life. (SPA.). 20p. (J). (gr. 1-1). pap. 4.99 *(978-1-4333-4419-0(X))* Teacher Created Materials, Inc.

—La Vida Marina, 1 vol. 2nd rev. ed. 2012. (Nonfiction Readers Ser.). (SPA.). 20p. (J). (gr. 1-1). pap. 4.99 *(978-1-4333-4423-7(8))* Teacher Created Materials, Inc.

—Yo Sé, 1 vol. 2nd rev. ed. 2011. (Nonfiction Readers Ser.). (SPA.). 12p. (J). (gr. 1-1). pap. 4.99 *(978-1-4333-4408-4(4))* Teacher Created Materials, Inc.

Rice, Dona Herweck & Rice, Dona. ¡Locos por Insectos y Arañas!, 1 vol. 2nd rev. ed. 2012. (Nonfiction Readers Ser.).Tr. of Going Buggy. (SPA.). 20p. (J). (gr. 1-1). pap. 4.99 *(978-1-4333-4424-4(6))* Teacher Created Materials, Inc.

Ridell, Chris. Ottoline va al colegio/ Ottolina Goes To School. 2008. (SPA.). 172p. (J). 13.95 *(978-84-263-6833-1(6))* Vives, Luis Editorial (Edelvives) ESP. Dist: Baker & Taylor Bks.

—Ottoline y la gata amarilla/ Ottolina & the Yellow Cat. 2008. (SPA.). 172p. (J). 13.95 *(978-84-263-6832-4(8))* Vives, Luis Editorial (Edelvives) ESP. Dist: Baker & Taylor Bks.

El Rio: Big Book. (Pebble Soup Exploraciones Ser.). (SPA.). 16p. (gr. -1-18). 31.00 *(978-0-7578-1683-3(5))* Rigby Education.

El Rio: Small Book. (Pebble Soup Exploraciones Ser.). (SPA.). 16p. (gr. -1-18). 5.00 *(978-0-7578-1723-6(8))* Rigby Education.

El rio es mi Vida: 6 Small Books. (Saludos Ser.: Vol. 3). (SPA.). (gr. 3-5). 31.00 *(978-0-7635-1829-5(8))* Rigby Education.

Riqui y el Carnaval. (Spanish Early Intervention Levels Ser.). (SPA.). 21.30 *(978-0-7362-0832-1(1))* CENGAGE Learning.

Risley, Jacqueline & Tim. Alpha's ABC's Games: Spanish & English Ages 2-6. Risley, Jacqueline & Tim, illus. 2007.Tr. of Alfa y sus Juegos de la A a la Z. (SPA & ENG., Illus.). 32p. (J). 6.99 *(978-0-9791680-0-0(7))* Alpha Learning World, Inc.

Rivas, Spelile. The Cucuy Stole My Cascarones / el Coco Me Robó Los Cascarones. Baeza Ventura, Gabriela, tr. Cervantes, Valeria, illus. 2013. (SPA & ENG.). 32p. (J). 17.95 *(978-1-55885-771-1(0)*, Piñata Books) Arte Publico Pr.

Rivas, Spelile & Plascencia, Amira. No Time for Monsters/No Hay Tiempo para Monstruos. Cervantes, Valeria, illus. 2010. (SPA & ENG.). 32p. (J). (gr. -1-3). 16.95 *(978-1-55885-445-1(2))* Arte Publico Pr.

Rivera-Ashford, Roni Capin. My Tata's Remedies - Los Remedios de Mi Tata. Castro L., Antonio, illus. 2015. (ENG & SPA.). 40p. (J). (gr. 1-6). pap. 8.95 *(978-1-935955-89-4(6))* Cinco Puntos Pr.

Rivera, Jose E. La Voragine (The Vortex) (Coleccion Centro Literario). (SPA.). (J). pap., stu. ed. 7.95 *(978-958-02-0502-9(7)*, CAR027) Editorial Voluntad S.A. COL. Dist: Continental Bk. Co., Inc.

Rivera, Lassen. Mi Silla de Ruedas. Alvarez, Mrinali, illus. 2006. (SPA.). 28p. 8.95 *(978-0-8477-1568-8(X))* Univ. of Puerto Rico Pr.

—Soy Gordito. Alvarez, Mrinali, illus. 2006. (SPA.). 28p. 8.95 *(978-0-8477-1565-7(5))* Univ. of Puerto Rico Pr.

El Robot, 6, Pack. (Chiquilibros Ser.). (SPA.). (gr. k-1). 23.00 *(978-0-7635-8612-6(9))* Rigby Education.

Rockhill, Dennis. Sueno Polar. 2008. (ENG.). 32p. (J). (gr. -1-3). 16.95 *(978-1-932748-76-5(8)*, Raven Tree Pr.,Csi) Continental Sales, Inc.

Rodriguez, Angelica. Mia y Primos/Mia & Cousins: Yo grito,corro y grito / I scream, run & Scream. 2009. 24p. pap. 12.49 *(978-1-4389-7095-0(1))* AuthorHouse.

Rodríguez, Ed. Kiki Kokí: La Leyenda Encantada del Coquí. 2015.Tr. of Kiki Kokí - The Enchanted Legend of the Coquí Frog. (SPA & ENG., Illus.). 40p. (J). (gr. -1-3). 17.99 *(978-1-62672-104-3(1)*, 9781626721043) Roaring Brook Pr.

Rodríguez, Orlando A. Valores Morales y Buenos Hábitos — Rangel, Mario Hugo, illus. (SPA.). 32p. (J). 2004. *(978-0-311-38596-6(6))* 2004. *(978-0-311-38597-3(4))* 2003. *(978-0-311-38595-9(8))* Baptist Spanish Publishing Hse./Casa Bavtista de Publicaciones: Mundo Hispano.

Rojas, Emilio. Ortografía Real de la Lengua Española: Libro con Ejercicios. 2003. 328p. (YA). (gr. 5-18). 17.95 *(978-968-6966-15-2(3))* EDITER'S Publishing Hse. MEX. Dist: EDITER'S Publishing Hse.

El Rompecabezas: Individual Title-Six Packs. (Chiquilibros Ser.). (SPA.). (gr. k-1). 23.00 *(978-0-7635-8614-0(5))* Rigby Education.

Rosa-Mendoza, Gladys. Animals at the Farm/Animales de la Granja Big Book. 2009. (ENG & SPA.). 20p. (J). pap. 19.95 *(978-1-931398-89-3(5))* Me+Mi Publishing.

—Jobs Around My Neighborhood/Oficios en Mi Vecindario. Iosa, Ann, illus. 2007. (English Spanish Foundations Ser.). 20p. (gr. -1-k). pap. 19.95 *(978-1-931398-81-7(X))* Me+Mi Publishing.

Rosa-Mendoza, Gladys, creator. I Can! 2004. (English-Spanish Foundations Ser.: Vol. 11).Tr. of Yo Puedo! (SPA & ENG., Illus.). 20p. (J). bds. 6.95 *(978-1-931398-11-4(9))* Me+Mi Publishing.

Rossetti-Shustak, Bernadette. I Love You Through & Through (Te Quiero, Yo Te Quiero) Church, Caroline Jayne, illus. 2013. (Caroline Jayne Church Ser.). (ENG & SPA.). 24p. (J). (— 1). bds. 8.95 *(978-0-545-58416-6(7))* Scholastic, Inc.

Ruedas. (Spanish Early Intervention Levels Ser.). (SPA.). 23.10 *(978-1-56334-789-4(X))* CENGAGE Learning.

Ruedas, 6 Packs. (Literatura 2000 Ser.). (SPA.). (gr. k-1). 28.00 *(978-0-7635-1031-2(9))* Rigby Education.

Ruffin, Fran. Whales / Ballenas. 2009. (My World of Animals / Yo y los animales Ser.). (ENG & SPA.). 24p. (gr. 1-1). 37.50 *(978-1-61514-719-9(5)*, Editorial Buenas Letras) Rosen Publishing Group, Inc., The.

Ruiz-Flores, Lupe. Lupita's First Dance / el Primer Baile de Lupita. Baeza Ventura, Gabriela, tr. Utomo, Gabhor, illus. 2013. (SPA.). 32p. (J). 17.95 *(978-1-55885-772-8(9)*, Piñata Books) Arte Publico Pr.

Ruiz-Flores, Lupe & Rosales-Yeomans, Natalia. Let's Salsa. Rosales-Yeomans, Natalia, tr. Casilla, Robert, illus. 2013.Tr. of Bailemos Salsa. (SPA & ENG.). 32p. (J). 17.95 *(978-1-55885-762-9(1)*, Piñata Books) Arte Publico Pr.

Ruiz, Olivia, et al. La Amiga Nueva De Roberto: Guias De Observacion, Level 12. 2003. 3.95 *(978-0-673-61538-1(3))* Celebration Pr.

—Las Cajas De Zapatos: Guias De Observacion, Level 10. 2003. 3.95 *(978-0-673-61537-4(5))* Celebration Pr.

—Debes Ser Atento Con Jesefina: Resumen Del Cuento, Level 34. 2003. 3.95 *(978-0-673-61562-6(6))* Celebration Pr.

—Debes Ser Atento Con Josefina: Guias De Observacion, Level 34. 2003. (SPA.). 3.95 *(978-0-673-61546-6(4))* Celebration Pr.

—El Dia Mas Maravilloso: Guias De Observacion, Level 24. 2003. 3.95 *(978-0-673-61543-5(X))* Celebration Pr.

—Donde Esta Mi Gorra? Guias De Observacion, Level 4. 2003. 3.95 *(978-0-673-61534-3(0))* Celebration Pr.

—Duque: Guias De Observacion, Level 8. 2003. 3.95 *(978-0-673-61536-7(7))* Celebration Pr.

—Evaluacion Del Desarrollo De la Lectura Package. 2003. 123.50 *(978-0-673-61724-8(6))* Celebration Pr.

—Un Gigante En El Bosque: Guias De Observacion, Level 18. 2003. 3.95 *(978-0-673-61541-1(3))* Celebration Pr.

—Mas Astuto Que El Viejo Camilo Canoso: Guias De Observacion, Level 40. 2003. 3.95 *(978-0-673-61548-0(0))* Celebration Pr.

—La Olla De Oro: Guias De Observacion, Level 16. 2003. 3.95 *(978-0-673-61540-4(5))* Celebration Pr.

—Peligro En las Profundidades: Guias De Observacion, Level 44. 2003. 3.95 *(978-0-673-61549-7(9))* Celebration Pr.

—Por Que Paramos? Guias De Observacion, Level 6. 2003. 3.95 *(978-0-673-61535-0(9))* Celebration Pr.

—Que Te Gusta? Guias De Observacion, Level 3. 2003. 3.95 *(978-0-673-61533-6(2))* Celebration Pr.

—Reni la Rana: Guias De Observacion, Level 20. 2003. 3.95 *(978-0-673-61542-8(1))* Celebration Pr.

—Sabes Cantar? Mira Lo Que Se Va: Registro De la Lectura Oral. 2003. (SPA.). 3.95 *(978-0-673-61566-4(9))* Celebration Pr.

—Sabes Cantar? Mira Lo Que Se Va Yo Veo: Guias De Observacion, Level 2. 2003. (SPA.). 3.95 *(978-0-673-61532-9(4))* Celebration Pr.

—El Vagon: Guias De Observacion, Level 14. 2003. (SPA.). 3.95 *(978-0-673-61539-8(1))* Celebration Pr.

—Yo No Te Veo Hermosa: Guias De Observacion, Level 28. 2003. (SPA.). 3.95 *(978-0-673-61544-2(8))* Celebration Pr.

—Yo Veo Que Te Gusta? Registro De la Lectura Oral, Level 3. 2003. (SPA.). 3.95 (978-0-673-61567-1(7)) Celebration Pr.

Rusty the Rooster. 2003. 23.95 (978-0-673-78134-5(8)) Celebration Pr.

Rylant, Cynthia. El Caso de la Perezosa Dormilona. (SPA.). (J). 7.95 (978-958-04-7539-2(3)) Norma S.A. COL. Dist: Distribuidora Norma, Inc.

El sacudon de San Francisco: 6 Small Books. (Saludos Ser.: Vol. 3). (SPA.). (gr. 3-5). 31.00 (978-0-7635-2081-6(0)) Rigby Education.

Sad Ladybug: Matching English 6-packs. 2003. 23.95 (978-0-673-57564-7(0)) Celebration Pr.

Sáenz, Benjamin Alire. La Perrita Que le Encantaban las Tortillas. Garcia, Geronimo, illus. 2009. (Little Diego Book Ser.).Tr. of Dog Who Loved Tortillas. (SPA & ENG.). 40p. (J). (gr. 1-4). 17.95 (978-1-933693-54-5(1)) Cinco Puntos Pr.

Sal, Solecito. (Spanish Early Intervention Levels Ser.). (SPA.). 23.10 (978-0-7362-0321-0(4)) CENGAGE Learning.

Saldaña, René. Dancing with the Devil & Other Tales from Beyond / Bailando con el Diablo y Otros Cuentos del Más Allá. Baeza Ventura, Gabriela, tr. from ENG. 2012. (SPA & ENG.). (YA). pap. 9.95 (978-1-55885-744-5(3), Piñata Books) Arte Publico Pr.

Sale un Patito. (Spanish Early Intervention Levels Ser.). (SPA.). 21.30 (978-0-7362-0804-8(6)) CENGAGE Learning.

Saludos! Add-to Pack. (SPA.). 47.00 (978-0-7635-9515-9(2)) Rigby Education.

Saludos! Complete Blue Level Packages. (ENG & SPA.). 1279.00 (978-0-7635-9511-1(X)); (SPA.). 697.00 (978-0-7635-9509-8(8)) Rigby Education.

Saludos! Complete Pasado valioso, futuro Brillante. (SPA.). 385.00 (978-0-7635-9512-8(8)) Rigby Education.

Saludos! Complete Pasado valioso, futuro brillante Rich Past, Bright Future Theme Packages. (ENG & SPA.). 693.00 (978-0-7635-9514-2(4)) Rigby Education.

Saludos! Rich Past, Bright Future Theme Packages. 385.00 (978-0-7635-9513-5(6)) Rigby Education.

Salzmann, Mary Elizabeth. El Caracol de la Tortuga, 1 vol. Nobens, C. A., illus. 2007. (Cuentos de Animales Ser.). (SPA & ENG.). 24p. (J). (gr. k-3). lib. bdg. 24.21 (978-1-59928-657-0(2), SandCastle) ABDO Publishing Co.

Sánchez, Isidro. Mi Gato. Ruis, Maria, illus. (Coleccion Mis Animales Preferidos).Tr. of My Cat. (SPA.). 32p. (J). (gr. k-3). 6.36 (978-84-342-1127-8(0), PR0482) Parramon Ediciones S.A. ESP. Dist: Lectorum Pubns., Inc.

—Mi Hamster. Ruis, Maria, illus. (Coleccion Mis Animales Preferidos).Tr. of My Hamster. (SPA.). 32p. (J). (gr. k-3). 6.36 (978-84-342-1129-2(7), PR0485) Parramon Ediciones S.A. ESP. Dist: Lectorum Pubns., Inc.

—Mi Pajaro. Ruis, Maria, illus. (Coleccion Mis Animales Preferidos).Tr. of My Bird. (SPA.). 32p. (J). (gr. k-3). 6.36 (978-84-342-1128-5(9), PR0483) Parramon Ediciones S.A. ESP. Dist: Lectorum Pubns., Inc.

—Mi Perro. Ruis, Maria, illus. (Coleccion Mis Animales Preferidos).Tr. of My Dog. (SPA.). 32p. (J). (gr. k-3). (978-84-342-1126-1(2), PR0481) Parramon Ediciones S.A. ESP. Dist: Lectorum Pubns., Inc.

Sánchez, Lucía M. & Taylor, Trace. Chocolate (Spanish) Taylor, Trace, illus. 2012. (2G Necesidades Ser.). (SPA., Illus.). 24p. (J). pap. 6.99 (978-1-61406-170-0(X)) American Reading Co.

La Sandia. (Spanish Early Intervention Levels Ser.). (SPA.). 23.10 (978-1-56334-795-5(4)) CENGAGE Learning.

Sandviks HOP, Inc. Staff. Learn to Read: Localized Spanish for U. S. 2007. (J). (gr. k). 64.99 (978-1-60143-890-4(7)); (gr. k-1). 139.99 (978-1-60143-889-8(3)); (gr. 1). 64.99 (978-1-60143-891-1(5)) HOP, LLC.

Sastrias, Martha. Como Motivar a los Ninos a Leer: Lecto-Juegos y Algo Mas. 2005. (SPA & ENG., Illus.). 180p. (gr. 2-4). per. 11.95 (978-968-860-449-6(6)) Editorial Pax MEX. Dist: Independent Pubs. Group.

Scheunemann, Pam. El Boligrafo del Cerdo, 1 vol. Nobens, C. A., illus. 2007. (Cuentos de Animales Ser.). (SPA & ENG.). 24p. (J). (gr. k-3). lib. bdg. 24.21 (978-1-59928-659-4(9), SandCastle) ABDO Publishing Co.

Schreiber-Wicke, Edith. Cuando Decir No. (SPA.). (J). 8.95 (978-958-04-6534-8(7)) Norma S.A. COL. Dist: Distribuidora Norma, Inc.

Schuette, Sarah L. Rectángulos: Rectángulos a Nuestro Alrededor. 2012. (Figuras Geométricas/Shapes Ser.).Tr. of Rectangles - Seeing Rectangles All Around Us. (MUL & SPA.). 32p. (gr. 1-2). pap. 8.10 (978-1-4296-8531-3(X)); pap. 47.70 (978-1-4296-8532-0(8)) Capstone Press of Coughlan Cos. (A+ Bilingue/Bilingual).

Schwartz, David M. Cuanto Es un Millon? Kellogg, Steven, illus. 2003. (SPA.). (J). (gr. k-3). pap. 3.96 net. (978-0-590-47393-4(X), SO30942) Scholastic, Inc.

Scott, Ann Herbert. En Las Piernas de Mamá. Coalson, Glo, illus. 2007.Tr. of On Mother's Lap. (SPA & ENG.). 14p. (J). (gr. k — 1). bds. 5.95 (978-0-618-75247-8(1)) Houghton Mifflin Harcourt Publishing Co.

Scott Foresman Family Reading Guide. 2004. (gr. k-18). 13.25 (978-0-673-63394-1(2)); (gr. 1-18). 13.25 (978-0-673-63395-8(0)); (gr. 2-18). 13.25 (978-0-673-63396-5(9)); (gr. 3-18). 13.50 (978-0-673-63397-2(7)); (gr. 4-18). 13.50 (978-0-673-63398-9(5)); (gr. 5-18). 13.50 (978-0-673-63399-6(3)) Addison-Wesley Educational Pubs., Inc.

Scotti, Alberto Douglas. Cocina y Ciencia. 2012. 44p. (J). (gr. 3-5). pap. 23.99 (978-958-30-3715-3(X)) Juventud, Editorial ESP. Dist: Lectorum Pubns., Inc.

Se venden Pasteles. (Spanish Early Intervention Levels Ser.). (SPA.). 31.14 (978-0-7362-0333-3(8)) CENGAGE Learning.

Segal, John. Sopa de Zanahoria. Mlawer, Teresa, tr. from ENG. 2006. (Illus.). (gr. -1-k). 12.99 (978-1-933032-13-9(8)) Lectorum Pubns., Inc.

Un Segundo Cumpleanos: 6 Small Books. (Saludos Ser.: Vol. 2). (SPA.). 24p. (gr. 2-3). 31.00 (978-0-7635-9524-1(1)) Rigby Education.

Seki, Sunny. The Tale of the Lucky Cat. Seki, Sunny, illus. 2008. (ENG & SPA., Illus.). 32p. (J). 18.95 (978-0-9669437-9-5(1)) East West Discovery Pr.

Senor Cascaron: Big Book Packages. 2003. (SPA.). 64.95 (978-0-673-58592-9(1)) Celebration Pr.

La Senora Audaz, 6 Pack. (Literatura 2000 Ser.). (SPA.). (gr. 1-2). 28.00 (978-0-7635-1053-4(X)) Rigby Education.

Set of 10 Titles, Vol. 4. (Spanish Early Intervention Levels Ser.). (SPA.). 37.00 (978-0-7362-1180-2(2)) CENGAGE Learning.

Set of 10 Titles: Levels 14-18. (Spanish Early Intervention Levels Ser.). (SPA.). 51.44 (978-0-7362-1184-0(5)) CENGAGE Learning.

Set of 11 Titles, Vol. 3. (Spanish Early Intervention Levels Ser.). (SPA.). 41.15 (978-0-7362-1179-6(9)) CENGAGE Learning.

Set of 11 Titles: Levels 19-20. (Spanish Early Intervention Levels Ser.). (SPA.). 52.03 (978-0-7362-1185-7(3)) CENGAGE Learning.

Set of 14 Titles: Levels 5-7. (Spanish Early Intervention Levels Ser.). (SPA.). 52.10 (978-0-7362-1181-9(0)) CENGAGE Learning.

Set of 20 Titles: Level B. (Spanish Guided Reading Levels Ser.). (SPA.). 75.80 (978-0-7362-1195-6(0)) CENGAGE Learning.

Set of 8 Titles. (Spanish Early Intervention Levels Ser.). (SPA.). 30.80 (978-0-7362-1010-2(5)) CENGAGE Learning.

Set of 9 Titles: Levels 10-13. (Spanish Early Intervention Levels Ser.). (SPA.). 42.09 (978-0-7362-1183-3(7)) CENGAGE Learning.

Set of 9 Titles: Levels 8-9. (Spanish Early Intervention Levels Ser.). (SPA.). 33.75 (978-0-7362-1182-6(9)) CENGAGE Learning.

Seuss, Dr. Un Pez, Dos Peces, Pez Rojo. Canetti, Yanitzia, tr. from ENG. 2005. 64p. (J). 8.99 (978-1-930332-83-6(1)) Lectorum Pubns., Inc.

Sh! Sh! 2003. 23.95 (978-0-673-78060-7(0)) Celebration Pr.

Shaw, Diana. Dias de Terror. (Torre de Papel Ser.). (SPA.). (YA). (gr. 6-18). 8.95 (978-958-04-1504-6(8)) Norma S.A. COL. Dist: Distribuidora Norma, Inc.

Shepherd, Joanne. What I Look Like When I am Scared / Cómo me veo cuando estoy Asustado. 2009. (Let's Look at Feelings / un vistazo a los sentimientos Ser.). (ENG & SPA.). 24p. (gr. k-1). 42.50 (978-1-61514-248-4(7), Editorial Buenas Letras) Rosen Publishing Group, Inc., The.

—What I Look Like When I am Surprised / Cómo me veo cuando estoy Sorprendido. 2009. (Let's Look at Feelings / un vistazo a los sentimientos Ser.). (ENG & SPA.). 24p. (gr. k-1). 42.50 (978-1-61514-249-1(5), Editorial Buenas Letras) Rosen Publishing Group, Inc., The.

Si Camino Por Laz Ciudad... 2003. (SPA.). 35.50 (978-0-8136-8089-7(1)) Modern Curriculum Pr.

Sierra i Fabra, Jordi. El Disco Magico. (SPA.). (YA). 8.95 (978-958-04-6264-4(X)) Norma S.A. COL. Dist: Distribuidora Norma, Inc.

—Martes XXIII. (SPA.). (YA). 9.95 (978-958-04-6025-1(6)) Norma S.A. COL. Dist: Distribuidora Norma, Inc.

Silate, Jennifer. Betsy Ross: Creator of the American Flag. 2009. (Primary Sources of Famous People in American History Ser.). 32p. (gr. 2-3). 47.90 (978-1-60851-657-5(1)) Rosen Publishing Group, Inc., The.

Silver Dolphin en Español Editors. Disney Tesoro de libros de Calcomanias: Disney Sticker Book Treasury, Spanish-Language Edition. 2007. (Illus.). 48p. (J). (978-970-718-447-3(7), Silver Dolphin en Español) Advanced Marketing, S. de R. L. de C. V.

Silver Dolphin en Español Staff, creator. El Gusto. 2007. (Baby Senses (Silver Dolphin en Espanol) Ser.). (Illus.). 10p. (J). (gr. -1). bds. (978-970-718-473-2(6), Silver Dolphin en Español) Advanced Marketing, S. de R. L. de C. V.

—El Olfato. 2007. (Baby Senses (Silver Dolphin en Espanol) Ser.). (Illus.). 10p. (J). (gr. 5). bds. (978-970-718-471-8(X), Silver Dolphin en Español) Advanced Marketing, S. de R. L. de C. V.

—La Vista. 2007. (Baby Senses (Silver Dolphin en Espanol) Ser.). (Illus.). 8p. (J). (gr. -1). bds. (978-970-718-472-5(8), Silver Dolphin en Español) Advanced Marketing, S. de R. L. de C. V.

Silver Dolphin Staff, creator. Disney Caritas Felices: Dumbo. 2007. (Illus.). 8p. (J). (gr. -1). bds. (978-970-718-394-0(2), Silver Dolphin en Español) Advanced Marketing, S. de R. L. de C. V.

Sinon Sinonimo y Horacio Contrario. (SPA.). (J). 12.00 (978-958-02-1238-6(4)) Editorial Voluntad S.A. COL. Dist: Distribuidora Norma, Inc.

La Sirenita. (SPA & ENG., Illus.). (J). (gr. -1-5). pap. 5.95 incl. audio compact disk (978-88-8148-363-1(7)) EMC/Paradigm Publishing.

Skinner, Daphne. Tod el Apretado: Math Matters en Espanol. Nez, John, illus. 2005. (SPA.). 32p. (J). pap. 5.95 (978-1-57565-155-2(6)) Kane Press, Inc.

Small Book Classroom Set: Green Series. (Rimas Y Risas Ser.). (SPA.). (gr. -1-2). 337.22 (978-1-56334-129-8(8)) CENGAGE Learning.

Small Book Classroom Set: Green Series with addition of Manipulatives. (Rimas Y Risas Ser.). (SPA.). (gr. -1-2). 461.82 (978-0-7362-0882-6(8)) CENGAGE Learning.

Smith, Michael. Thomas the T. Rex: The Journey of a Young Dinosaur to Los Angeles. Roski, Gayle Garner, illus. 2011. (J). (978-0-9832278-4-7(5)) East West Discovery Pr.

Smith, Michael & Roski, Gayle Garner. Thomas the T. Rex: The Journey of a Young Dinosaur to Los Angeles. Roski, Gayle Garner, illus. 2011. (SPA & ENG., Illus.). (J). (978-0-9832278-2-3(9)) East West Discovery Pr.

El Soldadito de Plomo.Tr. of Staunch Tin Soldier. (SPA & ENG., Illus.). (J). (gr. -1-5). pap. 5.95 incl. audio compact disk (978-88-8148-293-1(2)) EMC/Paradigm Publishing.

Solomon, Sharon. A Walk With Grandpa/Un Paseo con el Abuelo. Del Risco, Eida, tr. Barcita, Pamela, illus. 2009. (ENG & SPA.). 32p. (J). (gr. -1-3). 16.95 (978-1-932748-91-8(1), Raven Tree Pr.,Csi) Continental Sales, Inc.

El Sombrero de Juan: Harry's Hat. 2005. (Take-Home Bks.). (SPA.). (YA). (gr. -1-3). 15.75 (978-0-8215-1203-6(X)) Sadlier, William H. Inc.

El Sombrero de Juan/Harry's Hat. 2005. (Libros en Espanol Para Ninos Ser.). (SPA.). (YA). (gr. -1-1). 11.97 (978-0-8215-0993-7(4)) Sadlier, William H. Inc.

Sommer, Carl. Can You Help Me Find My Smile? Me Puedes Ayudar a Encontrar Mi Sonrisa? Budwine, Greg, illus. 2009. (Another Sommer-Time Story Bilingual Ser.). (SPA & ENG.). 48p. (J). lib. bdg. 16.95 (978-1-57537-150-4(2)) Advance Publishing, Inc.

—Dare to Dream! ¡Atrévete a Soñar! Martínez, Jorge et al, illus. 2009. 48p. (J). 26.95 incl. audio compact disk (978-1-57537-176-4(6)) Advance Publishing, Inc.

—Dream (Sueña) Martínez, Jorge et al, illus. 2009. (Quest for Success Bilingual Ser.). (SPA & ENG.). 104p. (YA). (gr. 6-18). lib. bdg. 14.95 (978-1-57537-226-6(6)) Advance Publishing, Inc.

—Fast Forward(Avance Acelarado) Budwine, Greg, illus. 2009. (Quest for Success Bilingual Ser.). (SPA & ENG.). 104p. (YA). lib. bdg. 14.95 (978-1-57537-227-3(4)) Advance Publishing, Inc.

—The Great Deception(El Gran Engaño) Noé, illus. 2009. (Quest for Success Bilingual Ser.). (ENG & SPA.). 72p. (YA). lib. bdg. 14.95 (978-1-57537-228-0(2)) Advance Publishing, Inc.

—The Great Royal Race(La Gran Carrera Real) Westbrook, Dick, illus. 2009. (Another Sommer-Time Story Bilingual Ser.). (SPA & ENG.). 48p. (J). lib. bdg. 16.95 (978-1-57537-152-8(9)) Advance Publishing, Inc.

—I Am a Lion!(Yo Soy un León!) Budwine, Greg, illus. 2009. (Another Sommer-Time Story Bilingual Ser.). (SPA & ENG.). 48p. (J). lib. bdg. 16.95 (978-1-57537-153-5(7)) Advance Publishing, Inc.

—If Only I Were...(Si Yo Fuese...) James, Kennon, illus. 2009. (Another Sommer-Time Story Bilingual Ser.). (SPA & ENG.). 48p. (J). lib. bdg. 16.95 (978-1-57537-154-2(5)) Advance Publishing, Inc.

—It's Not Fair!(No Es Justo) ! Budwine, Greg, illus. 2009. (Another Sommer-Time Story Bilingual Ser.). (SPA & ENG.). 48p. (J). lib. bdg. 16.95 (978-1-57537-155-9(3)) Advance Publishing, Inc.

—King of the Pond(El Rey Del Estanque) Budwine, Greg, illus. 2009. (Another Sommer-Time Story Bilingual Ser.). (SPA & ENG.). 48p. (J). lib. bdg. 16.95 (978-1-57537-156-6(1)) Advance Publishing, Inc.

—Light Your Candle(Enciende Tu Vela) James, Kennon, illus. 2009. (Another Sommer-Time Story Bilingual Ser.). (SPA & ENG.). 48p. (J). lib. bdg. 16.95 (978-1-57537-157-3(X)) Advance Publishing, Inc.

—The Little Red Train(El Trenecito Rojo) James, Kennon, illus. 2009. (Another Sommer-Time Story Bilingual Ser.). (SPA & ENG.). 48p. (J). lib. bdg. 16.95 (978-1-57537-158-0(8)) Advance Publishing, Inc.

—Lost & Found(Perdida y Encontrada) Budwine, Greg, illus. 2009. (Quest for Success Bilingual Ser.). (ENG & SPA.). 96p. (YA). lib. bdg. 14.95 (978-1-57537-229-7(0)) Advance Publishing, Inc.

—Mayor for a Day: Alcalde Por un Dia. Westbrook, Dick, illus. 2009. (Another Sommer-Time Story Bilingual Ser.). (SPA & ENG.). 48p. (J). lib. bdg. 16.95 (978-1-57537-159-7(6)) Advance Publishing, Inc.

—Miserable Millie(La Pobrecita Mili) Vignolo, Enrique, illus. 2009. (Another Sommer-Time Story Bilingual Ser.). (SPA & ENG.). 48p. (J). lib. bdg. 16.95 (978-1-57537-160-3(X)) Advance Publishing, Inc.

—No Longer a Dilly Dally(¡Nunca Mas a Troche y Moche) James, Kennon, illus. 2009. (Another Sommer-Time Story Bilingual Ser.). (SPA & ENG.). 48p. (J). lib. bdg. 16.95 (978-1-57537-162-7(6)) Advance Publishing, Inc.

—No One Will Ever Know(Nadie Se Va a Enterar) Westbrook, Dick, illus. 2009. (Another Sommer-Time Story Bilingual Ser.). (SPA & ENG.). 48p. (J). lib. bdg. 16.95 (978-1-57537-163-4(4)) Advance Publishing, Inc.

—Noise! Noise! Noise!(Ruido! Ruido! Ruido!) James, Kennon, illus. 2009. (Another Sommer-Time Story Bilingual Ser.). (SPA & ENG.). 48p. (J). lib. bdg. 16.95 (978-1-57537-161-0(8)) Advance Publishing, Inc.

—Proud Rooster & Little Hen(Gallito Orgulloso y Gallinita) Budwine, Greg, illus. 2009. (Another Sommer-Time Story Bilingual Ser.). (SPA & ENG.). 48p. (J). 16.95 (978-1-57537-164-1(2)) Advance Publishing, Inc.

—The Race(La Carrera) Budwine, Greg, illus. 2009. (Quest for Success Bilingual Ser.). (SPA & ENG.). 104p. (YA). lib. bdg. 14.95 (978-1-57537-230-3(4)) Advance Publishing, Inc.

—The Rebel(El Rebelde) Vignolo, Enrique, illus. 2009. (Quest for Success Bilingual Ser.). (ENG & SPA.). 104p. (YA). lib. bdg. 14.95 (978-1-57537-231-0(2)) Advance Publishing, Inc.

—The Revolt(La Revuelta) Budwine, Greg, illus. 2009. (Quest for Success Bilingual Ser.). (SPA & ENG.). 104p. (YA). lib. bdg. 14.95 (978-1-57537-232-7(0)) Advance Publishing, Inc.

—The Roar(El Rugido) Budwine, Greg, illus. 2009. (Quest for Success Bilingual Ser.). (SPA & ENG.). 96p. (YA). lib. bdg. 14.95 (978-1-57537-233-4(9)) Advance Publishing, Inc.

—The Runaway(La Escapada) Vignolo, Enrique, illus. 2009. (Quest for Success Bilingual Ser.). (SPA & ENG.). 104p. (YA). lib. bdg. 14.95 (978-1-57537-234-1(7)) Advance Publishing, Inc.

—The Sly Fox & the Chicks(El Zorro Astuto y los Pollitos) James, Kennon, illus. 2009. (Another Sommer-Time Story Bilingual Ser.). (SPA & ENG.). 48p. (J). lib. bdg. 16.95 (978-1-57537-166-5(9)) Advance Publishing, Inc.

—Spike the Rebel!(pua, el Rebelde!) Vignolo, Enrique, illus. 2009. (Another Sommer-Time Story Bilingual Ser.). (SPA & ENG.). 48p. (J). lib. bdg. 16.95 (978-1-57537-167-2(7)) Advance Publishing, Inc.

—Three Little Pigs(Los Tres Cerditos) Budwine, Greg & Vignolo, Enrique, illus. 2009. (Another Sommer-Time Story Bilingual Ser.). (SPA & ENG.). 48p. (J). lib. bdg. 16.95 (978-1-57537-168-9(5)) Advance Publishing, Inc.

—Tied up in Knots(Enredados) Budwine, Greg, illus. 2009. (Another Sommer-Time Story Bilingual Ser.). (SPA & ENG.). 48p. (J). lib. bdg. 16.95 (978-1-57537-169-6(3)) Advance Publishing, Inc.

—Time Remote!(El Control Del Tiempo!) Budwine, Greg, illus. 2009. (Another Sommer-Time Story Bilingual Ser.). (SPA & ENG.). 48p. (J). lib. bdg. 16.95 (978-1-57537-170-2(7)) Advance Publishing, Inc.

—The Ugly Caterpillar(La Oruga Fea) Budwine, Greg, illus. 2009. (Another Sommer-Time Story Bilingual Ser.). (SPA & ENG.). 48p. (J). (gr. k-3). lib. bdg. 16.95 (978-1-57537-171-9(5)) Advance Publishing, Inc.

—You Move You Lose(El Que Se Mueva, Pierde) James, Kennon, illus. 2009. (Another Sommer-Time Story Bilingual Ser.). (SPA & ENG.). 48p. (J). lib. bdg. 16.95 (978-1-57537-172-6(3)) Advance Publishing, Inc.

—Your Job Is Easy(Tu Trabajo Es Facil) James, Kennon, illus. 2009. (Another Sommer-Time Story Bilingual Ser.). (SPA & ENG.). 48p. (J). lib. bdg. 16.95 (978-1-57537-173-3(1)) Advance Publishing, Inc.

Sommer, Carl & Aesop. Divide to Conquer(Divide y Venceras) Mercado, Jorge, illus. 2009. (Quest for Success Bilingual Ser.). (ENG & SPA.). 72p. (YA). lib. bdg. 14.95 (978-1-57537-225-9(8)) Advance Publishing, Inc.

—The Silent Scream(El Grito Silencioso) Bogdan, Enache, illus. 2009. (Quest for Success Bilingual Ser.). (SPA & ENG.). 72p. (YA). lib. bdg. 14.95 (978-1-57537-235-8(5)) Advance Publishing, Inc.

—Tiny Giant(La Gigante Pequeña) Mercado, Jorge, illus. 2009. (Quest for Success Bilingual Ser.). (ENG & SPA.). 72p. (YA). lib. bdg. 14.95 (978-1-57537-236-5(3)) Advance Publishing, Inc.

Somos Amigos. (Spanish Early Intervention Levels Ser.). (SPA.). 23.10 (978-1-56334-763-4(6)) CENGAGE Learning.

La sopa Especial: Individual Title, 6 packs. (Literatura 2000 Ser.). (SPA.). (gr. 1-2). 28.00 (978-0-7635-1054-1(8)) Rigby Education.

Una sorpresa para Monica: 6 Small Books. (Saludos Ser.: Vol. 2). (SPA.). (gr. 3-5). 31.00 (978-0-7635-1816-5(6)) Rigby Education.

Spanish Board Book Set 800782, 7. 2005. (J). bds. (978-1-59794-017-7(8)) Environments, Inc.

Spanish Book Set #2 800875, 8 vols. 2005. (J). pap. (978-1-59794-053-5(4)) Environments, Inc.

Spanish DRA Levels, 7 bks., Set. (Spanish Dra Levels Ser.). (SPA.). Level 1. 26.65 (978-0-7362-1213-7(2))Level 10-14. 49.19 (978-0-7362-1219-9(1))Level 16-18. 35.41 (978-0-7362-1220-5(5))Level 20-28. 68.06 (978-0-7362-1221-2(3))Level A. 18.65 (978-0-7362-1212-0(4)) Vol. 2. 61.00 (978-0-7362-1214-4(0)) Vol. 3. 49.15 (978-0-7362-1215-1(9)) Vol. 4. 33.15 (978-0-7362-1216-8(7)) Vol. 6. 22.20 (978-0-7362-1217-5(5)) Vol. 8. 29.60 (978-0-7362-1218-2(3)) CENGAGE Learning.

Spanish-English Books 800878, 4 vols. 2005. (J). bds. (978-1-59794-056-6(9)) Environments, Inc.

Spanish Guided Reading Levels, 28 bks., Set. (Spanish Guided Reading Levels Ser.). (SPA.). Level C. 105.10 (978-0-7362-1196-3(9))Level D. 14.80 (978-0-7362-1197-0(7))Level A. 15.40 (978-0-7362-1194-9(2))Levels E-F. 46.78 (978-0-7362-1198-7(5))Levels G-J. 77.96 (978-0-7362-1199-4(3))Levels K-M. 57.22 (978-0-7362-1200-7(0)) Vol. 2. 52.70 (978-0-7362-1178-9(0)) CENGAGE Learning.

Spanish Guided Reading Levels Series, 96 vols. (Spanish Early Intervention Levels Ser.). (SPA.). 393.06 (978-0-7362-1177-2(2)) CENGAGE Learning.

Spanish Paperbacks 800718, 10. 2005. (J). (978-1-59794-016-0(X)) Environments, Inc.

Spanish TAKS MASTER Reading Grade 3. 2004. (978-1-57022-464-5(1)) ECS Learning Systems, Inc.

Spanish TAKS MASTER Reading Grade 4. 2004. (978-1-57022-465-2(X)) ECS Learning Systems, Inc.

Spencer, Mignon. I'm Living My Dream: An inspirationsl Rhyme for all Ages in English & Spanish. Mack, Travis, illus. 2008.Tr. of Hago mi sueno Realidad. (ENG & SPA.). 32p. (J). 12.99 (978-0-9763871-2-1(3)) Solomon's Bks.

Stalcup. La Loncheria. Arroyo, illus. 2008. (SPA & ENG.). 28p. (J). pap. 8.95 (978-1-60448-006-1(8)) Lectura Bks.

—La Loncheria. Arroyo, illus. 2008. (SPA & ENG.). 28p. (J). 15.95 (978-1-60448-005-4(X)) Lectura Bks.

Stanley, Diane. El Caballero y la Doncella.Tr. of Gentleman & the Kitchen Maid. (SPA.). 30p. (J). (gr. 3-5). 11.96 (978-84-261-2876-8(9)) Juventud, Editorial ESP. Dist: Lectorum Pubns., Inc.

Steinsiek, Sabra Brown. The Tale of the Pronghorned Cantaloupe. Chilton, Noel Dora, illus. 2013. 48p. 24.95 (978-1-936744-11-4(2), Rio Grande Bks.) LPD Pr.

Sterling Publishing Co., Inc. Things That Go/Cosas Que Se Mueven. 2013. (Say & Play Ser.). (ENG & SPA., Illus.). 28p. (J). (— 1). bds. 4.95 (978-1-4549-1042-8(9)) Sterling Publishing Co., Inc.

Street, Sesame. Elmo's Guessing Game about Colors/Elmo y Su Juego de Adivinar Los Colores. 2006. (Elmo's Guessing Game about Colors / Elmo y Su Juego de Adivinar Los Colores Ser.). (SPA, ENG & MUL., Illus.). 10p. (J). (gr. -1 — 1). bds. 5.95 (978-0-87358-905-5(X)) Cooper Square Publishing Llc.

Student Pack. (Cuentacuentos Ser.). (SPA.). (gr. k-18). 83.31 (978-1-56334-798-6(9)) CENGAGE Learning.

Suen, Anastasia. Hábitat para la Humanidad (Habitat for Humanity) 2009. (Organizaciones de ayuda (Helping Organizations) Ser.). (SPA.). 24p. (gr. 2-2). 42.50 (978-1-60851-145-7(6), Editorial Buenas Letras) Rosen Publishing Group, Inc., The.

Suenos y Fantasias. (Nuevos Horizontes Ser.). (SPA.). (J). (gr. 2). No. 1. wbk. ed. 8.95 (978-1-56014-510-3(2))No. 2. wbk. ed. 8.95 (978-1-56014-511-0(0)) Santillana USA Publishing Co., Inc.

Suenos y Fantasias: Evaluations, Grade 2. (Nuevos Horizontes Ser.). (SPA.). (J). 22.50 (978-1-56014-512-7(9)) Santillana USA Publishing Co., Inc.

Suenos y Fantasias No. 1: Student Anthology. (Nuevos Horizontes Ser.). (SPA.). (J). (gr. 2). 14.95 (978-1-56014-508-0(0)) Santillana USA Publishing Co., Inc.

Suenos y Fantasias No. 2: Student Anthology. (Nuevos Horizontes Ser.). (SPA.). (J). (gr. 2). 16.95 (978-1-56014-509-7(9)) Santillana USA Publishing Co., Inc.

Super Classroom Set. (Elefonetica Ser.). (SPA.). (gr. 1-2). 939.56 (978-0-7362-0782-9(1)) CENGAGE Learning.

Superflaco! (Spanish Early Intervention Levels Ser.). (SPA.). 28.38 (978-0-7362-0843-7(7)) CENGAGE Learning.

Susaeta, Equipo. La Bella Durmiente -Sleeping Beauty. Susaeta Publishing, Inc., Staff, ed. 2011. (Cuentos Bilingües Ser.). (SPA & ENG.). 34p. (J). (gr. k-2). 6.95 (978-84-305-2453-2(3)) Susaeta Ediciones, S.A. ESP. Dist: Independent Pubs. Group.

—LAS BRUJAS. (SPA.). (J). 3.48 (978-84-305-9406-1(X)) Susaeta Ediciones, S.A. ESP. Dist: AIMS International Bks., Inc.

—Leo y Veo, las Hadas.Tr. of I Read & See, the Fairies. (SPA.). 24p. (J). 3.48 (978-84-305-9408-5(6)) Susaeta Ediciones, S.A. ESP. Dist: AIMS International Bks., Inc.

—Leo y Veo, los Gnomos.Tr. of I Read & See, the Elves. (SPA.). 24p. (J). 3.48 *(978-84-305-9407-8(8))* Susaeta Ediciones, S.A. ESP. Dist: AIMS International Bks., Inc.
—LOS GIGANTES. (SPA.). 24p. (J). 3.48 *(978-84-305-9409-2(4))* Susaeta Ediciones, S.A. ESP. Dist: AIMS International Bks., Inc.
Susaeta Publishing, Inc., Staff, ed. BLANCANIEVES/SNOW WHITE. 2011. (Cuentos Bilingües Ser.). (SPA & ENG.). 34p. (J). (gr. k-2). 6.95 *(978-84-305-2454-9(1))* Susaeta Ediciones, S.A. ESP. Dist: Independent Pubs. Group.
TAKS Reading Preparation Grade 3 - Spanish. 2004. (SPA.). per., wbk. ed. *(978-1-932524-91-8(6))* Region IV Education Service Ctr.
TAKS Reading Preparation Grade 4 - Spanish. 2004. (SPA.). stu. ed., per., wbk. ed. *(978-1-932524-92-5(4))* Region IV Education Service Ctr.
TAKS Reading Preparation Grade 5 - Spanish. 2004. (SPA.). stu. ed., per., wbk. ed. *(978-1-932524-93-2(2))* Region IV Education Service Ctr.
El Taller de Piñatas. 2003. (SPA.). 23.95 *(978-0-673-78082-9(1))* Celebration Pr.
Los Tamales. 2003. 23.95 *(978-0-673-77132-2(6))* Celebration Pr.
Tan Set. (Dias y Dias de Poesia Ser.). (SPA.). (gr. -1-6). 207.23 *(978-1-56334-271-4(5)*, DI8631); 293.52 *(978-1-56334-272-1(3)*, DI8632) CENGAGE Learning.
Taylor, Mildred D. Lloro por la Tierra. (SPA.). (YA). 10.95 *(978-958-04-1838-2(1))* Norma S.A. COL. Dist: AIMS International Bks., Inc.
Taylor, Trace. Afghanistan. 2010. pap. 39.62 *(978-1-61541-135-1(6))* American Reading Co.
Taylor, Trace & SáNchez, LucíA M. Afghanistan. 2010. pap. 39.62 *(978-1-61541-158-0(5))* American Reading Co.
Taylor, Trace & Sánchez, Lucía M. Ballenas: Whales. 2010. (2G Animales Marinos Ser.). (SPA.). 12p. (J). (gr. k-2). pap. 6.99 *(978-1-61541-280-8(8))* American Reading Co.
—Pingüinos de la AntáRtida: Antarctic Penguins. 2010. (2G Animales Marinos Ser.). (ENG & SPA.). 12p. (J). (gr. k-2). pap. 6.99 *(978-1-61541-274-7(3))* American Reading Co.
Taylor, Trace & Sanchez, Lucia M. Vamos de acampada (Let's Go Camping) 2011. (Lugares adonde voy Ser.). (SPA.). 16p. pap. 39.62 *(978-1-61541-418-5(5))* American Reading Co.
Taylor, Trace, et al. Vamos de Acampada: Let's Go Camping. 2011. (2Y Lugares Adonde Voy Ser.). (SPA.). 16p. (J). (gr. k-2). pap. 6.99 *(978-1-61541-417-8(7))* American Reading Co.
El tesoro de Tono: Individual Title Six-Packs. (Literatura 2000 Ser.). (SPA.). (gr. 2-3). 33.00 *(978-0-7635-1252-1(4))* Rigby Education.
Tesoro Escondido, 6, Pack. (Chiquilibros Ser.). (SPA.). (gr. k-1). 23.00 *(978-0-7635-8589-1(0))* Rigby Education.
Theme Library, 10 vols. (High Point Ser.). (gr. 6-12). Level C. 74.53 *(978-0-7362-0983-0(2))*Level B. (Illus.). 91.19 *(978-0-7362-0951-9(4))* CENGAGE Learning.
Thompson, Lauren. Cuaquito (Little Quack) Anderson, Derek, illus. 2010. (SPA.). 34p. (J). (gr. -1-1). bds. 7.99 *(978-1-4169-9894-5(2)*, Libros Para Ninos) Libros Para Ninos.
Thompson, Michael. Los Otros Osos / the Other Bears. Thompson, Michael, illus. 2013. (ENG & SPA., Illus.). (J). 16.99 *(978-1-59572-644-5(6))* Star Bright Bks., Inc.
La tia Rosalia: Individual Title Six-Packs. (Literatura 2000 Ser.). (SPA.). (gr. 1-2). 28.00 *(978-0-7635-1079-4(3))* Rigby Education.
Tibo, Gilles. Corre, Nicolas, Corre! Rioja, Alberto Jimenez, tr. from FRE. St. Aubin, Bruno, illus. 2009. (SPA & ENG.). 32p. (J). (gr. 2-4). pap. 6.99 *(978-1-933032-57-3(X))* Lectorum Pubns., Inc.
Tiburones. 2003.Tr. of Sharks. (SPA.). 23.95 *(978-0-673-78080-5(5))* Celebration Pr.
El Tiempo: Individual Title Six-Packs. (Chiquilibros Ser.). (SPA.). (gr. k-1). 23.00 *(978-0-7635-8588-4(2))* Rigby Education.
El tigre Comilon, 6, Pack. (Literatura 2000 Ser.). (SPA.). (gr. -1-1). 28.00 *(978-0-7635-1007-7(6))* Rigby Education.
Time for Bed: Individual Title Six-Packs. (Chiquilibros Ser.). (gr. k-1). 23.00 *(978-0-7635-0425-0(4))* Rigby Education.
A Tina le gustan las Herramientas: Lap Book. (Pebble Soup Exploraciones Ser.). (SPA.). 16p. (gr. -1-18). 21.00 *(978-0-7578-1686-4(X))* Rigby Education.
A Tina le gustan las Herramientas: Small Book. (Pebble Soup Exploraciones Ser.). (SPA.). 16p. (gr. -1-18). 5.00 *(978-0-7578-1726-7(2))* Rigby Education.
Titanes de la Literatura Infantil.Tr. of Infant Literature. (SPA.). (J). *(978-968-15-0412-0(7))* Editores Mexicanos Unidos.
A Tocar! Individual 6-packs. 2003. 23.95 *(978-0-673-78075-1(9))* Celebration Pr.
Toconayo. 2003. 28.95 *(978-0-673-78101-7(1))* Celebration Pr.
Todas las Mananas: Lap Book. (Pebble Soup Exploraciones Ser.). 16p. (gr. -1-18). 21.00 *(978-0-7578-1673-4(8))* Rigby Education.
Todas las Mananas: Small Book. (Pebble Soup Exploraciones Ser.). 16p. (gr. -1-18). 5.00 *(978-0-7578-1713-7(0))* Rigby Education.
Todo cambia Interactive Packages: El agua Cambia. (Pebble Soup Exploraciones Ser.). (SPA.). (gr. -1-18). 52.00 *(978-0-7578-5263-3(7))* Rigby Education.
Todo cambia Interactive Packages: Los Sentimientos. (Pebble Soup Exploraciones Ser.). (SPA.). (gr. -1-18). 52.00 *(978-0-7578-5266-4(1))* Rigby Education.
Todo Rojo. (Spanish Early Intervention Levels Ser.). (SPA.). 21.30 *(978-0-7362-0803-1(8))* CENGAGE Learning.
Todos Enojados: Social/Emotional Lap Book. (Pebble Soup Exploraciones Ser.). (SPA.). (gr. -1-18). 16.00 *(978-0-7578-1788-5(2))* Rigby Education.
Todos Somos Amigos: Big Book Packages. 2003. 64.95 *(978-0-673-58593-6(X))* Celebration Pr.
Tolstoi, Leo. La Muerte de Ivan Ilich. (SPA.). 6.25 *(978-958-04-2126-9(9))* Norma S.A. COL. Dist: Distribuidora Norma, Inc.
Tomas: Individual Title Six-Packs. (Literatura 2000 Ser.). (SPA.). (gr. 1-2). 28.00 *(978-0-7635-1055-8(6))* Rigby Education.
Tomas's Tops. 2003. 23.95 *(978-0-673-78131-4(3))* Celebration Pr.
Torres, Jennifer. Finding the Music, 1 vol. Alarcão, Renato, illus. 2015.Tr. of En Pos de la Música. (ENG & SPA.). 40p. (J). 18.95 *(978-0-89239-291-9(6))* Lee & Low Bks., Inc.
Tostada: Matching English 6-packs. 2003. 23.95 *(978-0-673-57565-4(9))* Celebration Pr.
El Traje Perdido. (Spanish Early Intervention Levels Ser.). (SPA.). 31.14 *(978-0-7362-0335-7(4))* CENGAGE Learning.
Trapp, Kyrima. Que? Como? Por Que?: Los Colores. 2007. (Illus.). 16p. (J). (gr. -1). *(978-970-718-491-6(4)*, Silver Dolphin en Español) Advanced Marketing, S. de R. L. de C. V.
Los tres Bobos: Individual Title, 6 Packs. (Literatura 2000 Ser.). (SPA.). (gr. 2-3). 33.00 *(978-0-7635-1274-3(5))* Rigby Education.
Los tres Cerditos: Lap Book. (Pebble Soup Exploraciones Ser.). (SPA.). 16p. (gr. -1-18). 21.00 *(978-0-7578-1674-1(6))* Rigby Education.
Los Tres Cerditos Desobedientes: Individual 6-packs. 2003. 23.95 *(978-0-673-77155-1(5))* Celebration Pr.
Los tres Magos: Individual Title, 6 Packs. (Literatura 2000 Ser.). (SPA.). (gr. 2-3). 33.00 *(978-0-7635-1275-0(3))* Rigby Education.
Los Trillizos: Individual Title, 6 Packs. (Literatura 2000 Ser.). (SPA.). (gr. 2-3). 33.00 *(978-0-7635-1253-8(2))* Rigby Education.
Los Trompos De Tomas, 6 packs. 2003. 23.95 *(978-0-673-78069-0(4))* Celebration Pr.
Tu, Alice. A Fair Is Fun, 6 vols., Set. 2003. (Phonics Readers 1-36 Ser.). (ENG.). 8p. (gr. k-1). pap. 29.70 *(978-0-7368-3203-8(3)*, Phonics Readers) Capstone Press of Coughlan Cos.
Tullet, Hervé & Perez, Peter L. Presiona Aqui. Perez, Peter L., illus. 2012. (SPA & ENG., Illus.). 56p. (J). (gr. -1-3). 15.99 *(978-1-4521-1287-9(8))* Chronicle Bks. LLC.
Tuminelly, Nancy. Los Zapatos de la Potranca, 1 vol. Nobens, C. A., illus. 2007. (Cuentos de Animales Ser.). (SPA & ENG.). 24p. (J). (gr. k-3). lib. bdg. 24.21 *(978-1-59928-677-8(7)*, SandCastle) ABDO Publishing Co.
Twin Sisters(r) Staff. Kids Learn Spanish Handlebox- 4 books. 2009. 12.99 *(978-1-59922-110-6(1))* Twin Sisters IP, LLC.
Twine, Alice. Puppies/Cachorros. 2009. (Baby Animals/Animales bebé Ser.). (ENG & SPA.). 24p. (gr. 1-1). 42.50 *(978-1-61511-507-5(2)*, Editorial Buenas Letras) Rosen Publishing Group, Inc., The.
Two Volcanoes. 2003. 28.95 *(978-0-673-78117-8(8))* Celebration Pr.
Los uniformes Amarillos: Individual Title, 6 Packs. (Literatura 2000 Ser.). (SPA.). (gr. 2-3). 33.00 *(978-0-7635-1276-7(1))* Rigby Education.
Uno, dos, tres y Cuatro. (Spanish Early Intervention Levels Ser.). (SPA.). 23.10 *(978-1-56334-792-4(X))* CENGAGE Learning.
Urraca, Maraca, Urraca: Little Books, Level 1, Vol. 13. 2003. (Fonolibros Ser.). 25.50 *(978-0-7652-0090-7(2))* Modern Curriculum Pr.
Usen la Cabeza: Social/Emotional Lap Book. (Pebble Soup Exploraciones Ser.). (SPA.). (gr. -1-18). 16.00 *(978-0-7578-1784-7(X))* Rigby Education.
Valentin, Karen. Allie's World: Abuela & Abuelo Move: Abuela & Abuelo Move. 2009. 32p. 6.95 *(978-1-60349-021-4(3)*, Marimba Bks.) Hudson Publishing Group, The.
Vamos! (Spanish Early Intervention Levels Ser.). (SPA.). 21.30 *(978-0-7362-0809-3(7))* CENGAGE Learning.
Vamos De Viaje. 2003. (SPA.). 23.95 *(978-0-673-77179-7(2))* Celebration Pr.
Vamos, Samantha R. The Cazuela That the Farm Maiden Stirred. López, Rafael, illus. 2013. (ENG & SPA.). 32p. (J). (gr. k-3). pap. 8.95 *(978-1-58089-243-8(4))* Charlesbridge Publishing, Inc.
Vaughan, Richard. Levantemos el Cielo, Level 3. 2003. (Dejame Leer Ser.). (SPA., Illus.). (J). (gr. -1-3). 4.50 *(978-0-673-36332-9(5)*, Good Year Bks.) Celebration Pr.
—El Universo, Level 2. 2003. (Dejame Leer Ser.). (SPA., Illus.). (J). (gr. -1-3). 6.50 *(978-0-673-36329-9(5)*, Good Year Bks.) Celebration Pr.
Vaughn, Inés. Potatoes/Papas. 2009. (Native Foods of Latin America / Alimentos indígenas de Latino América Ser.). (ENG & SPA.). 24p. (gr. 2-3). 42.50 *(978-1-61514-798-4(5)*, Editorial Buenas Letras) Rosen Publishing Group, Inc., The.
Vázquez-Figueroa, Alberto. Anaconda. (SPA.). 400p. 12.95 *(978-84-01-46951-0(1))* Plaza & Janes Editories, S.A. ESP. Dist: Distribooks, Inc.
El Veliz De los Recuerdos. 2003. 28.95 *(978-0-673-78088-1(0))* Celebration Pr.
El venado de Mario. (Spanish Early Intervention Levels Ser.). (SPA.). 28.38 *(978-0-7362-0837-6(2))* CENGAGE Learning.
El venado y el Cocodrilo: Individual Title Six-Packs. (Literatura 2000 Ser.). (SPA.). (gr. 1-2). 28.00 *(978-0-7635-1080-0(7))* Rigby Education.
Veo, veo Colas. (Spanish Early Intervention Levels Ser.). (SPA.). 23.10 *(978-1-56334-766-5(0))* CENGAGE Learning.
Vestimos con Orgullo: 6 Small Books. (Saludos Ser.: Vol. 2). (SPA.). (gr. 3-5). 31.00 *(978-0-7635-1769-4(0))* Rigby Education.
El viaje de la abuelita Jenny: 6 Small Books. (Saludos Ser.: Vol. 3). (SPA.). (gr. 3-5). 31.00 *(978-0-7635-1783-0(6))* Rigby Education.
El viento Bravo. (Spanish Early Intervention Levels Ser.). (SPA.). 28.38 *(978-0-7362-0845-1(3))* CENGAGE Learning.
Villasenor, Victor. The Stranger & the Red Rooster: El Forastero y el Gallo Rojo. Ventura, Gabriela Baeza, tr. Jara, Jose, illus. 2005. (ENG & SPA.). 26p. (J). (gr. -1-2). 16.95 *(978-1-55885-420-8(7)*, Piñata Books) Arte Publico Pr.
Vingan A Ver Mi Rancho! Individual 6-packs. 2003. 23.95 *(978-0-673-78066-9(X))* Celebration Pr.
Viva la Musica! (Spanish Early Intervention Levels Ser.). (SPA.). 31.14 *(978-0-7362-0331-9(1))* CENGAGE Learning.
Viva el Midsommar! (Saludos Ser.: Vol. 1). (SPA.). 24p. (gr. 2-3). 31.00 *(978-0-7635-5719-5(6))* Rigby Education.
Viva el Midsommar! 6 Small Books. (Saludos Ser.: Vol. 1). (SPA.). 24p. (gr. 2-3). 31.00 *(978-0-7635-9519-7(5))* Rigby Education.
Las Vocales: Big Book Packages. 2003. 64.95 *(978-0-673-58588-2(3))* Celebration Pr.
Vogel, Elizabeth. ¡A hacer ejercicio! (Let's Exercise) 2009. (Limpieza y salud todo el día (Clean & Healthy All Day Long) Ser.). (SPA.). 24p. (gr. 1-1). 37.50 *(978-1-61514-291-0(6)*, Editorial Buenas Letras) Rosen Publishing Group, Inc., The.
—¡A lavarse las manos! (Washing My Hands) 2009. (Limpieza y salud todo el día (Clean & Healthy All Day Long) Ser.). (SPA.). 24p. (gr. 1-1). 37.50 *(978-1-61514-292-7(4)*, Editorial Buenas Letras) Rosen Publishing Group, Inc., The.
—¡Al agua patos! (Taking My Bath) 2009. (Limpieza y salud todo el día (Clean & Healthy All Day Long) Ser.). (SPA.). 24p. (gr. 1-1). 37.50 *(978-1-61514-294-1(0)*, Editorial Buenas Letras) Rosen Publishing Group, Inc., The.
—¡el cuidado de tu cabello! (Taking Care of My Hair) 2009. (Limpieza y salud todo el día (Clean & Healthy All Day Long) Ser.). (SPA.). 24p. (gr. 1-1). 37.50 *(978-1-61514-295-8(9)*, Editorial Buenas Letras) Rosen Publishing Group, Inc., The.
Volver a Empezar: 6 Softcover Books. (Saludos Ser.: Vol. 3). (SPA.). (gr. 3-5). 31.00 *(978-0-7635-2079-3(9))* Rigby Education.
Wall Chart. 2003. (gr. k-18). suppl. ed. 81.90 *(978-0-673-59354-2(1))*; (gr. 1-18). suppl. ed. 81.90 *(978-0-673-59355-9(X))* Addison-Wesley Educational Pubs., Inc.
Washington, Joi. Wasps. 2011. (Predator Bugs Ser.). 16p. pap. 39.62 *(978-1-61541-352-2(9))* American Reading Co.
Watson, Jude. The 39 Clues # 6: En Las Profundidades. 2012. (SPA.). 208p. (J). (gr. 5-8). pap. 14.99 *(978-84-08-10768-2(2))* Noguer y Caralt Editores, S. A. ESP. Dist: Lectorum Pubns., Inc.
Wax, Wendy A. Musica en Casa: Libro de Cuentos. de Alba, Arlette, tr. 2005. (Disney Princess Ser.). (SPA., Illus.). 38p. (J). (gr. -1-7). incl. audio compact disk *(978-970-718-289-9(X)*, Silver Dolphin en Español) Advanced Marketing, S. de R. L. de C. V.
The Wedding: Individual Title Six-Packs. (Literatura 2000 Ser.). (gr. k-1). 28.00 *(978-0-7635-0071-9(2))* Rigby Education.
Weinhold, Angela. El Bosque. 2007. (Junior (Silver Dolphin) Ser.). (Illus.). 16p. (J). (gr. -1). *(978-970-718-493-0(0)*, Silver Dolphin en Español) Advanced Marketing, S. de R. L. de C. V.
Werther, Scott P. Powerboats / Lanchas Motorizadas. 2009. (Extreme Machines / Máquinas extremas Ser.). (ENG & SPA.). 24p. (gr. 1-2). 42.50 *(978-1-61512-448-0(9)*, Editorial Buenas Letras) Rosen Publishing Group, Inc., The.
What's in the Box? 2003. 28.95 *(978-0-673-78114-7(3))* Celebration Pr.
The White Horse: Individual Title Six-Packs. (Literatura 2000 Ser.). (gr. 2-3). 33.00 *(978-0-7635-0244-7(8))* Rigby Education.
White, Mark. El Leon y el Raton: Versión de la Fábula de Esopo. Abello, Patricia, tr. from ENG. Pérez, Sara Rojo, illus. 2006. (Read-It! Readers en Español: Fábulas Ser.).Tr. of Lion & the Mouse - A Retelling of Aesop's Fable. (SPA.). 24p. (gr. k-3). 21.32 *(978-1-4048-1623-7(2)*, Easy Readers) Picture Window Bks.
Wilde, Oscar. El Fantasma de Canterville: Y otros Cuentos. (SPA.). (YA). 8.75 *(978-958-04-6746-5(3))* Norma S.A. COL. Dist: Distribuidora Norma, Inc.
Willems, Mo. El Conejito Knuffle: Un Cuento Aleccionador. Willems, Mo, illus. rev. ed. 2007. (Knuffle Bunny Ser.). (ENG & SPA., Illus.). 40p. (J). (gr. -1-k). pap. 7.99 *(978-1-4231-0567-1(2))* Hyperion Pr.
Williamson, Melanie. El magnífico plan de Lobo/ Wolf's Magnificent Plan. Williamson, Melanie, illus. 2008. (SPA., Illus.). 29p. 20.95 *(978-84-263-6837-9(9))* Vives, Luis Editorial (Edelvives) ESP. Dist: Baker & Taylor Bks.
With addition of Elefonetica & Pan y Canela. (De Canciones A Cuentos Ser.). (SPA.). (gr. 1-18). 1413.46 *(978-0-7362-0704-1(X))*; (gr. 2-18). 1261.41 *(978-0-7362-0706-5(6))* CENGAGE Learning.
A With Addition of Pan y Canela Collection. (Cuentacuentos Ser.). (SPA.). (gr. k-18). 1238.34 *(978-1-56334-801-3(2))* CENGAGE Learning.
A With Addition of Pan y Canela Little Reader Collection. (De Canciones A Cuentos Ser.). (SPA.). (gr. k-18). 870.44 *(978-1-56334-571-5(4))* CENGAGE Learning.
With Addition of Pan y Canela Little Reader Collection B. (De Canciones A Cuentos Ser.). (SPA.). (gr. 1-18). 860.93 *(978-1-56334-993-5(0))* CENGAGE Learning.
With addition of Pan y Canela Little Reader Collection C. (De Canciones A Cuentos Ser.). (SPA.). (gr. 2-18). 929.66 *(978-0-7362-0442-2(3))* CENGAGE Learning.
Witte, Anna. El Fandango de Lola. Archer, Micha, illus. 2011. (SPA.). 32p. (J). (gr. k-5). 9.99 *(978-1-84686-359-2(7))* Barefoot Bks., Inc.
Wolff, Ashley. The Baby Chicks Are Singing: Sing along in English & Spanish! Wolff, Ashley, illus. 2005. (ENG., Illus.). 22p. (J). (gr. -1 — 1). bds. 7.99 *(978-0-316-06732-4(6))* Little, Brown Bks. for Young Readers.
Word Pocket with Letras Moviles. (SPA.). (gr. 2-18). 7.40 *(978-0-7362-0853-6(4))* CENGAGE Learning.
Y Ahora, Que Leo? 2003. (J). 28.95 *(978-0-673-78098-0(8))* Celebration Pr.
Yo Me Visto Solo, 6-packs. 2003. (J). 23.95 *(978-0-673-77140-7(7))* Celebration Pr.
Yo quiero Ser. (Spanish Early Intervention Levels Ser.). (SPA.). 23.10 *(978-1-56334-782-5(2))* CENGAGE Learning.
Yo Vivo Aqui: Big Book Packages. 2003. (J). 64.95 *(978-0-673-58586-8(7))* Celebration Pr.
Your Friend, Jorge. 2003. 28.95 *(978-0-673-78118-5(6))* Celebration Pr.
El yoyo de Mayito. (Spanish Early Intervention Levels Ser.). (SPA.). 21.30 *(978-0-7362-0829-1(1))* CENGAGE Learning.
Zepeda, Gwendolyn. Level up / Paso de Nivel. Baeza Ventura, Gabriela, tr. from ENG. Torrecilla, Pablo, illus. 2012. (SPA & ENG.). (J). (gr. 5-9). 16.95 *(978-1-55885-747-6(8)*, Piñata Books) Arte Publico Pr.
Zepeda, Gwendolyn & Ventura, Gabriela Baeza. Growing up with Tamales: Los Tamales de Ana. Ward, April, illus. 2008. (SPA & ENG.). 32p. (J). (gr. -1-2). 16.95 *(978-1-55885-493-2(2)*, Piñata Books) Arte Publico Pr.
Ziegler, Argentina Palacios, tr. Dora y la Princesa de la Nieve (Dora Saves the Snow Princess) Aikins, Dave, illus. 2008. (Dora la Exploradora Ser.). (SPA.). 24p. (J). (gr. -1-2). pap. 3.99 *(978-1-4169-5870-3(3)*, Libros Para Ninos) Libros Para Ninos.
Zimmermann, Natalie. Un Principe para Lila. (Torre de Papel Ser.). (SPA., Illus.). (J). 7.95 *(978-958-04-5051-1(X))* Norma S.A. COL. Dist: Distribuidora Norma, Inc.
Un Zoologico, 6 Packs. (Literatura 2000 Ser.). (SPA.). (gr. -1-1). 28.00 *(978-0-7635-1008-4(4))* Rigby Education.
Zusak, Markus. Cartas Cruzadas. 2012. (Vintage Espanol Ser.). (SPA.). 384p. (YA). (gr. 7). pap. 14.95 *(978-0-307-95145-8(6)*, Vintage Espanol) Knopf Doubleday Publishing Group.
6-Pack Collection: Includes 180 books (30 6-Packs) 2003. (J). 769.95 *(978-0-7652-0558-2(0))* Modern Curriculum Pr.

SPANISH LITERATURE

Pascal, Francine. Rebelde con Causa. Orig. Title: Taking Charge. (SPA.). 136p. (J). 6.95 *(978-84-272-3796-4(0))* Molino, Editorial ESP. Dist: AIMS International Bks., Inc.

SPANISH MAIN

Malam, John. Do You Want to Be a Pirate? 2015. (Do You Want to Be... Ser.). (Illus.). 32p. (gr. 3-6). 28.50 *(978-1-909645-36-3(2))* Book Hse. GBR. Dist: Black Rabbit Bks.
—You Wouldn't Want to... Be a Pirate's Prisoner! Antram, David, illus. rev. ed. 2012. (ENG.). 32p. (J). lib. bdg. 29.00 *(978-0-531-27502-3(7))* Scholastic Library Publishing.
—You Wouldn't Want to Be a Pirate's Prisoner! Horrible Things You'd Rather Not Know. Antram, David, illus. rev. ed. 2012. (You Wouldn't Want to...: History of the World Ser.). (ENG.). 40p. (J). pap. 9.95 *(978-0-531-28027-0(6))* Scholastic Library Publishing.

SPANISH MAIN—FICTION

Batson, Wayne Thomas. Isle of Fire, 1 vol. 2009. (ENG.). 352p. pap. 9.99 *(978-1-4003-1512-3(3))* Nelson, Thomas Inc.
—Isle of Swords, 1 vol. 2008. (ENG.). 352p. pap. 9.99 *(978-1-4003-1363-1(5))* Nelson, Thomas Inc.
Henty, George Alfred. Under Drake's Flag: A Tale of the Spanish Main. 2007. (ENG.). 290p. pap. 21.99 *(978-1-4346-3056-8(0))*; 322p. pap. 24.99 *(978-1-4346-3070-4(6))* Creative Media Partners, LLC.
—Under Drake's Flag: A Tale of the Spanish Main. 2011. 316p. pap. 19.95 *(978-1-61179-182-2(0))* Fireship Pr.

SPANISH POETRY—COLLECTIONS

Medina, Jane & Median, Jane. The Dream on Blanca's Wall: Poems in English & Spanish. Casilla, Robert, illus. 2004. (SPA & ENG.). 32p. (J). (gr. 2-4). pap. 9.95 *(978-1-59078-264-4(X))* Boyds Mills Pr.
Polo, Eduardo. Chamario. Ballester, Arnal, illus. 2005. (SPA.). 48p. (J). 8.99 *(978-980-257-278-6(0))* Ekare, Ediciones VEN. Dist: Iaconi, Mariuccia Bk. Imports.

SPARRING

see Boxing

SPARROWS

Amstutz, Lisa J. House Sparrows. 2015. (Backyard Birds Ser.). (ENG., Illus.). 24p. (gr. k-1). lib. bdg. 26.65 *(978-1-4914-6109-9(8))* Capstone Press of Coughlan Cos.
Post, Hans & Heij, Kees. Sparrows. Goede, Irene, illus. 2008. (ENG.). 32p. (J). (gr. -1-3). 16.95 *(978-1-59078-570-6(3))* Lemniscaat USA.
Vail, Grace. A Bird Watcher's Guide to Sparrows. 2016. (Backyard Bird Watchers Ser.). (ENG., Illus.). 32p. (J). (gr. 2-3). pap. 10.50 *(978-1-4824-3911-3(5))* Stevens, Gareth Publishing LLLP.
Webster, Christine. Sparrows. 2007. (Backyard Animals Ser.). (Illus.). 24p. (J). (gr. -1-3). lib. bdg. 24.45 *(978-1-59036-681-3(6))* Weigl Pubs., Inc.
—Sparrows. Hudak, Heather C., ed. 2007. (Backyard Animals Ser.). (Illus.). 24p. (J). (gr. -1-3). pap. 8.95 *(978-1-59036-682-0(4))* Weigl Pubs., Inc.

SPARROWS—FICTION

Adams, Michelle Medlock. The Sparrow's Easter Song. Eldridge, Marion, illus. 2003. (ENG.). 32p. (J). 14.95 *(978-0-8249-5470-3(X)*, Ideal Pubns.) Worthy Publishing.
Albright, Ann. Samuel Sparrow & the Tree of Light. Albright, Ann, illus. 2nd ed. 2003. (ENG., Illus.). 28p. (J). pap. *(978-0-9715472-5-4(4))* Ascension Lutheran Church.
Barnes, Kenneth Edward. In Search of A Golden Sparrow. 2011. 124p. (gr. 2-4). 21.23 *(978-1-4634-0878-7(1))*; pap. 12.01 *(978-1-4634-0879-4(X))* AuthorHouse.
Bischoff, Marlene A. Charming Chirp. 2013. 26p. pap. 13.95 *(978-1-4796-0132-5(2))* TEACH Services, Inc.
Dalton, Sherry A. Do Indians Eat Soup? 2011. 32p. pap. 24.95 *(978-1-4560-7463-0(6))* America Star Bks.
Doney, Meryl. The Very Worried Sparrow. Hansen, Gaby, illus. 2008. (J). (gr. -1-3). 12.95 *(978-0-8198-8038-3(8))* Pauline Bks. & Media.
DuFalla, Anita, illus. Sumac & the Magic Lake. 2004. (Reader's Theater Ser.). (J). pap. *(978-1-4108-2291-8(5)*, A22915) Benchmark Education Co.
Ebers, Georg. A Question. 2005. 96p. pap. 10.95 *(978-1-4218-0443-9(3)*, 1st World Library - Literary Society) 1st World Publishing, Inc.
Glass, Stephen. Sara Sparrow. 2006. (J). per. 14.95 *(978-1-59858-065-5(5))* Dog Ear Publishing, LLC.
Graham, Bob. Vanilla Ice Cream. Graham, Bob, illus. 2014. (ENG., Illus.). 40p. (J). (gr. -1-1). 16.99 *(978-0-7636-7377-2(3))* Candlewick Pr.
Grandmother Sparrow: Copyright TXu1-280-697. 2007. (J). *(978-0-9792641-0-8(3))* Shelle, Carole Creative Arts.
Griffin, Molly Beth. Silhouette of a Sparrow. 2013. (Milkweed Prize for Children's Literature Ser.). (ENG., Illus.). 208p. pap. 8.00 *(978-1-57131-704-9(X))* Milkweed Editions.
Hicks, Constance. Florabelle Bunny & the Sparrow. 2011. 24p. pap. 12.99 *(978-1-4490-9969-5(6))* AuthorHouse.
Himes, John. Beauty. 2012. 24p. pap. 17.99 *(978-1-4772-9440-6(6))* AuthorHouse.
Howell, Julie Ann. The Tooth Be Told. Cotton, Sue Lynn, illus. 2011. 24p. 18.95 *(978-1-61493-061-7(9))* Peppertree Pr., The.
Kasbarian, Lucine. The Greedy Sparrow: An Armenian Tale, 0 vols. Zaikina, Maria, illus. 2011. (ENG.). 32p. (J). (gr. -1-3). 17.99 *(978-0-7614-5821-0(2)*, 9780761458210, Amazon Children's Publishing) Amazon Publishing.
Kassel, Roger de. Mr P & the Bully Birds. 2013. (Illus.). 12p. pap. 8.75 *(978-1-78035-677-8(3)*, Fastprint Publishing) Upfront Publishing Ltd. GBR. Dist: Printondemand-worldwide.com.
—Mr P & the Red Poppy. 2013. (Illus.). 22p. pap. 8.75 *(978-1-78035-707-2(9)*, Fastprint Publishing) Upfront Publishing Ltd. GBR. Dist: Printondemand-worldwide.com.

S

Kerven, Rosalind. Sparrow, the Crow & the Pearl. Williamson, Melanie, illus. 2005. (ENG.). 24p. (J). lib. bdg. 23.65 *(978-1-59646-754-5(1))* Dingles & Co.

Kidd, Rob. The Age of Bronze, 1 vol. Orpinas, Jean-Paul, illus. 2009. (Pirates of the Caribbean, Jack Sparrow Ser.: Bk. 5). (ENG.). 144p. (gr. 3-6). 24.21 *(978-1-59961-527-1(4))* Spotlight.

—The Coming Storm, 1 vol. Orpinas, Jean-Paul, illus. 2009. (Pirates of the Caribbean, Jack Sparrow Ser.: Bk. 1). (ENG.). 144p. (gr. 3-6). 24.21 *(978-1-59961-523-3(1))* Spotlight.

—The Pirate Chase, 1 vol. Orpinas, Jean-Paul, illus. 2009. (Pirates of the Caribbean, Jack Sparrow Ser.: Bk. 3). (ENG.). 128p. (gr. 3-6). 24.21 *(978-1-59961-525-7(8))* Spotlight.

—The Siren Song, 1 vol. Orpinas, Jean-Paul, illus. 2009. (Pirates of the Caribbean, Jack Sparrow Ser.: Bk. 2). (ENG.). 128p. (gr. 3-6). 24.21 *(978-1-59961-524-0(X))* Spotlight.

—The Sword of Cortes, 1 vol. Orpinas, Jean-Paul, illus. 2009. (Pirates of the Caribbean, Jack Sparrow Ser.: Bk. 4). (ENG.). 128p. (gr. 3-6). 24.21 *(978-1-59961-526-4(6))* Spotlight.

Kircher, Jean. Bertie Can't Fly. 2007. 24p. pap. 24.95 *(978-1-4241-8477-4(0))* America Star Bks.

Lampley, David Gerald. Shorty's Dilemm. 2011. 74p. pap. 19.95 *(978-1-4560-4189-2(4))* America Star Bks.

Lee, Y. J. The Little Moon Princess. Lee, Y. J., illus. 2010. (ENG., Illus.). 32p. (J). (gr. -1-3). 16.99 *(978-0-06-154736-2(0))* HarperCollins Pubs.

Lewis, C. A. Harold the Sparrow & His Bellybutton. 2013. 48p. pap. *(978-1-4602-1117-5(0))* FriesenPress.

Maguire, Thomas Aquinas. A Growling Place. 2007. (ENG., Illus.). 32p. (J). (gr. -1-3). 16.95 *(978-1-894965-74-3(4))* Simply Read Bks. CAN. Dist: Ingram Publisher Services.

Michael J. Larson, J. Larson & Michael J. Larson. The Easter Sparrows. 2010. 28p. pap. 10.95 *(978-1-4497-0012-6(8),* WestBow Pr.) Author Solutions, Inc.

Mitchell, Ronnie & May, Leslie. Catching the Wind: Beanie's First Flight. 2011. 24p. pap. 12.79 *(978-1-4567-5613-0(3))* AuthorHouse.

Moore, Sherry. The Crab Is Back in Town. 2007. (ENG.). 100p. (J). per. *(978-1-894936-78-1(7))* Saga Bks.

Narváez, Concha López & Concha, López Narváez. El Cernicalo Porque. Salmeron, Rafael, illus. (Pajaros de Cuento Coleccion). (SPA.). 84p. (YA). (gr. 5-8). *(978-84-241-7927-4(7))* Everest Editora ESP. Dist: Lectorum Pubns., Inc.

Otenbaker, Audrey Lee. God's Jewel. 2009. 48p. (J). pap. 17.95 *(978-1-4327-3340-7(0))* Outskirts Pr., Inc.

Paiva, Teresa & Pinto, Helena Rebelo. My Friend, Sleep. 2011. (Illus.). 68p. pap. 35.25 *(978-1-4567-8990-9(2));* 60p. (gr. 1-2). pap. 14.95 *(978-1-4567-8952-7(X))* AuthorHouse.

Parker, Jake. Little Bot & Sparrow. Parker, Jake, illus. 2016. (ENG., Illus.). 40p. (J). 17.99 *(978-1-62672-367-2(2),* 9781626723672) Roaring Brook Pr.

Pennypacker, Sara. Sparrow Girl. Tanaka, Yoko, illus. 2009. (ENG.). 40p. (J). (gr. k-4). 16.99 *(978-1-4231-1187-0(7))* Hyperion Pr.

Pugliano-Martin, Carol. The Very Mean King & el rey Malo: 6 English, 6 Spanish Adaptations. 2011. (ENG & SPA.). (J). 75.00 net. *(978-1-4108-5648-7(8))* Benchmark Education Co.

Santilli, Shirley. Trouble in Treeville. Santilli Wolfinger, Lorrie, illus. 2013. 42p. 19.99 *(978-0-9910962-0-6(7))* Aperture Pr., LLC.

Sargent, Dave & Sargent, David M. Cindy Sparrow: Respect the Property of Others, 19 vols., Vol. 6. Lenoir, Jane, illus. 2003. (Feather Tales Ser.: 6). 42p. (J). pap. 10.95 *(978-1-56763-730-4(2));* 2nd ed. lib. bdg. 20.95 *(978-1-56763-729-8(9))* Ozark Publishing.

Sharp, Euan. Diggedy Dozer in Treetop Troubles. 2008. 34p. 15.95 *(978-1-4357-0982-9(9))* Lulu Pr., Inc.

Thompson, Anne. Arrow Sparrow. 2009. (Illus.). 32p. pap. *(978-1-84549-369-1(9),* Swirl) arima publishing.

Urbain, Christophe, photos by. Emma in Paris. 2013. (ENG., Illus.). 56p. (J). (gr. k). 17.95 *(978-1-59270-139-1(6))* Enchanted Lion Bks., LLC.

Von Michaelis, Carol. Magpie Grows Up. 2012. 16p. pap. 15.99 *(978-1-4772-6115-6(X))* AuthorHouse.

Wittenbach, Jennie. Little Stories for Little Folks. 2011. 36p. pap. 21.99 *(978-1-4628-8818-4(6))* Xlibris Corp.

SPARTA (EXTINCT CITY)—HISTORY—FICTION

McLeese, Don. Spartans. 2009. (ENG., Illus.). 32p. (gr. 4-8). pap. 9.95 *(978-1-60694-545-2(9))* Rourke Educational Media.

SPASTIC PARALYSIS

see Cerebral Palsy

SPEAKING

see Debates and Debating; Public Speaking; Rhetoric; Voice

SPECIAL EFFECTS (CINEMATOGRAPHY)

see Cinematography—Special Effects

SPECIE

see Money

SPECIMENS, PRESERVATION OF

see Taxidermy; Zoological Specimens—Collection and Preservation

SPECTACLES

see Eyeglasses

SPECTERS

see Apparitions; Ghosts

SPEECH

see also Language and Languages; Phonetics; Voice

Apel, Melanie Ann. Coping with Stuttering. 2005. (Coping Ser.). (Illus.). 192p. (YA). (gr. 7-12). lib. bdg. 34.60 *(978-0-8239-2970-2(1),* COSTUT) Rosen Publishing Group, Inc., The.

Beaumont, Susanna. Baby Senses Speech: Look! I'm Talking! 2005. (Baby Senses Ser.). (Illus.). 16p. (gr. -1-k). bds. *(978-1-905051-52-6(2))* Make Believe Ideas.

Carillo, Christina Martin. Come Smile with Me. 2011. 40p. pap. 24.95 *(978-1-4560-8297-0(3))* America Star Bks.

Dow, Kathy & Dow, Danica, illus. Low-Down Dirty Words. 2004. 28p. (J). *(978-0-9749886-0-3(X))* KayStar Publishing.

First Experiences - Going to the Doctor. 2005. (J). per. 8.95 *(978-1-59566-130-2(1))* QEB Publishing Inc.

Galvin, Kathleen M., et al. The Basics of Speech: Learning to Be a Competent Communicator. 4th ed. 2004. (Ntc: Basics of Speech Ser.). (ENG., Illus.). 606p. (gr. 6-12). stu. ed. 99.00 *(978-0-07-861620-4(4),* 0078616204) McGraw-Hill Higher Education.

Hodson, Sarah E. Wh- Questions. 2012. (Illus.). (J). *(978-0-7606-1382-5(6))* LinguiSystems, Inc.

Holzer, Angela. Fat Freddy. Tucker, Barclay, illus. 2009. 36p. (J). lib. bdg. 8.99 *(978-0-9821563-4-6(0))* Good Sound Publishing.

—Gooey Gummy Geese. Smith, Ashley, illus. 2008. (ENG.). (J). lib. bdg. 8.99 *(978-0-9821563-1-5(6))* Good Sound Publishing.

—My Dog, Eddie. Funk, Debbie, illus. 2009. 36p. (J). lib. bdg. 8.99 *(978-0-9821563-5-3(9))* Good Sound Publishing.

Lenny's Lost Spots. 2005. (J). per. 8.95 *(978-1-59566-131-9(X))* QEB Publishing Inc.

Libal, Joyce. Finding My Voice: Youth with Speech Impairment. 2003. (Youth with Special Needs Ser.). (Illus.). 127p. (YA). pap. 14.95 *(978-1-4222-0422-1(7))* Mason Crest.

—Speech Impairment. Albers, Lisa et al, eds. 2014. (Living with a Special Need Ser.: 16). 128p. (J). (gr. 7-18). 25.95 *(978-1-4222-3043-5(0))* Mason Crest.

Life Cycles - from Seed to Sunflower. 2005. (J). per. 8.95 *(978-1-59566-145-6(X))* QEB Publishing Inc.

Life Cycles: From Caterpillar to Butterfly. 2005. (J). per. 8.95 *(978-1-59566-129-6(8))* QEB Publishing Inc.

LoGiudice, Carolyn & McConnell, Nancy. Room 28 a Social Language Program. 2004. (YA). per. 25.95 *(978-0-7606-0530-1(0))* LinguiSystems, Inc.

MagneTalk Match-Up Adventure Kit (with Barrier) Gb181. 2006. (J). 59.99 *(978-1-58650-616-2(1))* Super Duper Pubns.

MagneTalk Match-Up Adventure Kit (without Barrier) Gb182. 2006. (J). 59.99 *(978-1-58650-653-7(6))* Super Duper Pubns.

Matheson, Hughena. The 10 Most Historic Speeches. 2007. 14.99 *(978-1-55448-478-2(2))* Scholastic Library Publishing.

McCutcheon, Randall, et al. Glencoe Speech. 3rd ed. 2004. (Ntc: Speech Comm Matters Ser.). (ENG., Illus.). 605p. (gr. 9-12). stu. ed. 104.56 *(978-0-07-861618-1(2),* 0078616182) McGraw-Hill Higher Education.

O'Connor, Frances. Frequently Asked Questions about Stuttering. 2007. (FAQ: Teen Life Ser.). (Illus.). 64p. (YA). (gr. 7-12). lib. bdg. 31.95 *(978-1-4042-1931-1(5))* Rosen Publishing Group, Inc., The.

Rembisz, Linda. Count with Balloons. Liebeck, Lisa, illus. 2009. 28p. pap. 12.49 *(978-1-4490-1989-1(7))* AuthorHouse.

Sleeper, Amanda A. Speech & Language. 2007. (Gray Matter Ser.). (Illus.). 123p. (YA). (gr. 9-12). lib. bdg. 35.00 *(978-0-7910-8952-1(5))* Facts On File, Inc.

Sparks, Sarah Constance. Omfg: Owning My Future Greatness. 2010. 56p. pap. 21.99 *(978-1-4520-2684-8(X))* AuthorHouse.

SPEECH, LIBERTY OF

see Freedom of Speech

SPEECH THERAPY

Buesser, Jeanne. He Talks Funny: A Heartwarming Story of Everyday Life. 2010. 28p. 12.49 *(978-1-4520-2595-7(9))* AuthorHouse.

Cottrell, Sue. Can I Tell You about Stammering? A Guide for Friends, Family & Professionals. Khan, Sophie, illus. 2013. (Can I Tell You About...? Ser.). (ENG.). 48p. (C). pap. 13.95 *(978-1-84905-415-7(0),* 2484) Kingsley, Jessica Pubs. GBR. Dist: Macmillan Distribution Ltd.

—Can I Tell You about Stuttering? A Guide for Friends, Family, & Professionals. Khan, Sophie, illus. 2013. (Can I Tell You About...? Ser.). (ENG.). 48p. pap. 13.95 *(978-1-84905-435-5(5),* 2486) Kingsley, Jessica Pubs. GBR. Dist: Macmillan Distribution Ltd.

Flath, Camden. Therapy Jobs in Educational Settings: Speech, Physical, Occupational & Audiology. 2010. (New Careers for the 21st Century Ser.). (Illus.). 64p. (YA). (gr. 7-18). pap. 9.95 *(978-1-4222-2047-4(8));* lib. bdg. 22.95 *(978-1-4222-1826-6(0))* Mason Crest.

Gustafson, Monica. Quick Make Artic Activities. 2006. (J). per. 27.95 *(978-0-7606-0656-8(0))* LinguiSystems, Inc.

Kaufman, Nancy R. Kaufman Speech Praxis Workout Book. 2005. (Illus.). 127p. (J). pap. *(978-0-9765497-1-0(9))* Northern Speech Services.

Libal, Joyce. Finding My Voice: Youth with Speech Impairment. 2004. (Youth with Special Needs Ser.). (Illus.). 128p. (YA). 24.95 *(978-1-59084-738-1(5))* Mason Crest.

—Finding My Voice: Youth with Speech Impairment. 2003. (Youth with Special Needs Ser.). (Illus.). 127p. (YA). pap. 14.95 *(978-1-4222-0422-1(7))* Mason Crest.

Reinert, Linda M. Talking Is Hard for Me! Encouraging Communication in Children with Speech-Language Difficulties. Lynch, Emily S., illus. 2013. (ENG.). 54p. pap. 18.95 *(978-1-60613-192-3(3))* Woodbine Hse.

Sargisson, Lisa. Quick Connect Articulation 1. 2006. (J). 15.95 *(978-0-7606-0661-2(7))* LinguiSystems, Inc.

Sarrgisson, Lisa. Quick Connect Articulaton 2. 2006. (J). 15.95 *(978-0-7606-0662-9(5))* LinguiSystems, Inc.

Simon, Samantha. Speech Pathologists & Audiologists. 2017. (Careers in Healthcare Ser.: Vol. 13). (ENG.). (YA). (gr. 7-12). 23.95 ***(978-1-4222-3806-6(7))*** Mason Crest.

Wojcicki, Ronda M. Speech Class Rules: An Introduction to Speech Therapy for Children. 2007. (Illus.). 32p. (J). 19.95 *(978-0-9794102-0-8(7))* Speech Place Publishing, The.

SPEECH THERAPY—FICTION

Carillo, Christina. Life Can Be A Smile. 2010. 30p. pap. 21.99 *(978-1-4500-2848-6(9))* Xlibris Corp.

Feiffer, Jules. Bark, George. 2004. 29.95 *(978-1-55592-700-4(9))* Weston Woods Studios, Inc.

Gutman, Dan. Miss Laney Is Zany! Paillot, Jim, illus. 2010. (My Weird School Daze Ser.: 8). 112p. (J). (gr. 1-5). (ENG.). pap. 4.99 *(978-0-06-155415-5(4));* lib. bdg. 15.89 *(978-0-06-155417-9(0))* HarperCollins Pubs.

—Miss Laney Is Zany! 2010. (My Weird School Daze Ser.: 8). (J). lib. bdg. 14.75 *(978-0-606-10112-7(8),* Turtleback) Turtleback Bks.

Patterson, Nancy Ruth. The Shiniest Rock of All. 2009. 84p. pap. 8.95 *(978-1-4401-1620-9(2))* iUniverse, Inc.

SPEED

Adamson, Heather. Animals with Speed. 2010. (Our Animal World Ser.). 24p. (J). 25.65 *(978-1-60753-007-7(4))* Amicus Publishing.

Armentrout, David & Armentrout, Patricia. Speed Demons. 2008. (Illus.). 32p. (J). 28.50 *(978-1-60472-305-2(X))* Rourke Educational Media.

Baer, T. H. Measuring Speed. 2016. (Measure It! Ser.). (ENG.). 24p. (J). (gr. 1-2). pap. 8.15 *(978-1-4824-3864-2(X))* Stevens, Gareth Publishing LLLP.

Barkan, Joanne. What Is Velocity? 2005. (Rookie Read-About Science Ser.). (ENG., Illus.). 32p. (J). (gr. 1-2). pap. 4.95 *(978-0-516-24664-2(X),* Children's Pr.) Scholastic Library Publishing.

Butterfield, Moira, et al. Record Breakers & Other Speed Machines. (ENG., Illus.). 32p. (J). mass mkt. 8.99 *(978-0-590-24653-8(4))* Scholastic, Inc.

Caes, Charles J. Discovering the Speed of Light. 2011. (Scientist's Guide to Physics Ser.). (Illus.). 112p. (YA). (gr. 7-12). lib. bdg. 34.60 *(978-1-4488-4699-3(4))* Rosen Publishing Group, Inc., The.

—How Do We Know the Speed of Light? 2009. (Great Scientific Questions & the Scientists Who Answered Them Ser.). 112p. (gr. 7-12). 63.90 *(978-1-61513-207-2(4))* Rosen Publishing Group, Inc., The.

Cruschiform. Full Speed Ahead! 2014. (ENG., Illus.). 64p. (J). (gr. k-2). 18.95 *(978-1-4197-1338-5(8),* Abrams Bks. for Young Readers) Abrams, Inc.

Dintiman, George Blough. Speed Improvement for Young Athletes: How to Sprint Faster in Your Sport in 30 Workouts. rev. ed. 2006. (Illus.). 153p. pap. 17.95 *(978-0-938074-26-7(1))* National Assn. of Speed & Explosion.

Enz, Tammy. Outrunning Bullets: Superman & the Science of Speed. 2016. (Superman Science Ser.). (ENG., Illus.). 32p. (gr. 3-4). lib. bdg. 27.32 *(978-1-5157-0915-2(9),* DC Super Heroes) Stone Arch Bks.

—The Science Behind Superman's Speed. 2017. (Science Behind Superman Ser.). (ENG.). 24p. (gr. 1-2). lib. bdg. 25.32 *(978-1-5157-5096-3(5),* DC Super Heroes) Stone Arch Bks.

Frederick, Shane. Speed Training for Teen Athletes: Exercises to Take Your Game to the Next Level. 2012. (Sports Training Zone Ser.). (ENG.). 48p. (gr. 4-5). pap. 47.70 *(978-1-4296-8487-3(9));* lib. bdg. 31.99 *(978-1-4296-7678-6(7))* Capstone Press of Coughlan Cos.

Gardner, Robert. Bicycle Science Fair Projects. 2015. (Prize-Winning Science Fair Projects Ser.). (ENG.). 128p. (J). (gr. 7-7). lib. bdg. 37.27 *(978-0-7660-7016-5(6))* Enslow Pubs., Inc.

—Bicycle Science Projects: Physics on Wheels. 2004. (Science Fair Success Ser.). (Illus.). 112p. (J). lib. bdg. 27.94 *(978-0-7660-1630-9(7))* Enslow Pubs., Inc.

—How Fast Is Fast? Science Projects with Speed. 2015. (Hot Science Experiments Ser.). 48p. (J). (gr. 3-4). 25.27 *(978-0-7660-6615-1(0));* pap. 8.95 *(978-0-7660-6616-8(9),* Enslow Elementary) Enslow Pubs., Inc.

—Split-Second Science Projects with Speed: How Fast Does It Go? 2003. (Sensational Science Experiments Ser.). (Illus.). 48p. (J). (gr. 1-4). lib. bdg. 25.27 *(978-0-7660-2017-7(7))* Enslow Pubs., Inc.

Gordon, Sharon. Fast/Slow. 2007. (J). pap. 6.99 *(978-0-7614-3281-4(7))* Marshall Cavendish Corp.

—Fast/Slow/Rapido/Lento. 2006. (Bookworms Ser.). (ENG & SPA., Illus.). 24p. (gr. k-1). lib. bdg. 15.95 *(978-0-7614-2447-5(4))* Marshall Cavendish Corp.

—Rapido Lento. 2006. (Bookworms Ser.). (SPA & ENG., Illus.). 24p. (gr. k-1). lib. bdg. 15.95 *(978-0-7614-2367-6(2))* Marshall Cavendish Corp.

Greathouse, Lisa. Farm Animals: Classifying & Sorting. rev. ed. 2011. (Mathematics Readers Ser.). (ENG.). 32p. (J). (gr. k-k). pap. 8.99 *(978-1-4333-3442-9(9))* Teacher Created Materials, Inc.

—Wild Animals, Level K. rev. ed. 2011. (Mathematics Readers Ser.). (ENG.). 32p. (J). (gr. k-k). pap. 8.99 *(978-1-4333-3443-6(7))* Teacher Created Materials, Inc.

Gregoire, Maryellen. Moving Fast. 2011. (Wonder Readers Emergent Level Ser.). (ENG.). (gr. -1-1). 16p. pap. 35.94 *(978-1-4296-8130-8(6));* 32p. pap. 5.99 *(978-1-4296-8060-8(1))* Capstone Press of Coughlan Cos. (Wonder Readers).

Group/McGraw-Hill, Wright. Speed: Magazine Anthology: Level 6, 6 vols. (Comprehension Strand Ser.). (gr. 4-8). 54.00 *(978-0-322-06040-1(0))* Wright Group/McGraw-Hill.

Harrison, Paul. Speed Machines. (Up Close Ser.). 24p. 2009. (gr. 3-3). 47.90 *(978-1-60854-705-0(1))* 2008. (Illus.). (J). (gr. 4-7). lib. bdg. 25.25 *(978-1-4042-4222-7(8))* Rosen Publishing Group, Inc., The. (PowerKids Pr.).

Hile, Lori, et al. The Science of Speed, 1 vol. 2014. (Science of Speed Ser.). (ENG.). 48p. (gr. 3-4). lib. bdg. 127.96 *(978-1-4765-6207-0(5))* Capstone Press of Coughlan Cos.

Holden, Pam. So Fast, 6 pack. Webb, Philip, illus. 2009. (Red Rocket Readers Ser.). (ENG.). 16p. (gr. -1-1). pap. *(978-1-877363-20-7(0),* Red Rocket Readers) Flying Start Bks.

Hyde, Natalie. Speeding up, Slowing Down. 2014. (ENG., Illus.). 24p. (J). *(978-0-7787-0530-7(7))* Crabtree Publishing Co.

Ipcizade, Catherine. The Fastest Animals, 1 vol. (Extreme Animals Ser.). (ENG., 24p. (gr. k-1). 2011. Illus.). pap. 7.29 *(978-1-4296-6208-6(5))* 2011. pap. 41.70 *(978-1-4296-6377-9(4))* 2010. lib. bdg. 26.65 *(978-1-4296-5311-4(6))* Capstone Press of Coughlan Cos. (Pebble Plus).

—The Slowest Animals, 1 vol. (Extreme Animals Ser.). (ENG., 24p. (gr. k-1). 2011. Illus.). pap. 7.29 *(978-1-4296-6209-3(3))* 2011. pap. 41.70 *(978-1-4296-6379-3(0))* 2010. lib. bdg. 26.65 *(978-1-4296-5310-7(8))* Capstone Press of Coughlan Cos. (Pebble Plus).

KociendaGenevieve. FAST: THE NEED FOR SPEED HIGH BEGINNING BOOK WITH ONLINE ACCESS. 2014. (ENG., Illus.). 24p. pap. 9.50 *(978-1-107-68068-5(9))* Cambridge Univ. Pr.

Kramer, Nash. What Goes Fastest? 2014. (Little Books of Answers: Level B Ser.). (Illus.). 16p. (gr. k-2). pap. 7.95 *(978-1-927136-19-5(9))* Three Crows Media NZL. Dist: RiverStream Publishing.

Labrecque, Ellen. Speed: Get Quick!, 1 vol. 2012. (Exercise! Ser.). (ENG.). 32p. (J). (gr. 1-3). 27.32 *(978-1-4329-6732-1(0));* pap. 8.29 *(978-1-4329-6739-0(8))* Heinemann-Raintree. (Heinemann First Library).

Lindeen, Mary. Speed. 2017. (BeginningtoRead Ser.). (ENG.). 32p. (J). (-2). 22.60 ***(978-1-59953-880-8(6));*** pap. 11.94 ***(978-1-68404-099-5(X))*** Norwood Hse. Pr.

Loughran, Donna & Brunner-Jass, Renata. Field of Play: Measuring Distance, Rate, & Time. 2013. (iMath Ser.). (Illus.). 48p. (J). (gr. 5-6). pap. 11.94 *(978-1-60357-510-2(3));* lib. bdg. 23.94 *(978-1-59953-571-5(8))* Norwood Hse. Pr.

Mapua, Jeff. Extreme Motorsports. 2015. (Sports to the Extreme Ser.). (ENG., Illus.). 48p. (J). (gr. 5-6). 30.25 *(978-1-4994-3549-8(5),* Rosen Central) Rosen Publishing Group, Inc., The.

Mason, Paul. Improving Speed. 2011. (Training for Sports Ser.). (Illus.). 32p. (YA). (gr. 5-9). 26.50 *(978-1-4488-3302-3(7))* Rosen Publishing Group, Inc., The.

Meyer, Eileen R. Who's Faster? Animals on the Move. Bergum, Constance Rummel, illus. 2012. (J). *(978-0-87842-592-1(6))* Mountain Pr. Publishing Co., Inc.

Minden, Cecilia. Fast & Slow. 2016. (21st Century Basic Skills Library: Animal Opposites Ser.). (ENG., Illus.). 24p. (J). (gr. k-3). 24.21 *(978-1-63470-472-4(X),* 207619) Cherry Lake Publishing.

Murray, Julie. Fastest Animals, 1 vol. 2010. (That's Wild!: A Look at Animals Ser.). (ENG.). 32p. (J). (gr. 2-5). 28.50 *(978-1-60453-978-3(X))* ABDO Publishing Co.

—Slowest Animals, 1 vol. 2010. (That's Wild!: A Look at Animals Ser.). (ENG.). 32p. (J). (gr. 2-5). 28.50 *(978-1-60453-979-0(8))* ABDO Publishing Co.

Orme, David. Speed. 2008. (Trailblazers Ser.). (ENG., Illus.). 36p. pap. *(978-1-84167-647-0(0))* Ransom Publishing Ltd.

—Speed. 2009. (Fact to Fiction Ser.). (Illus.). 36p. (J). 16.95 *(978-0-7569-9283-5(4));* pap. 6.95 *(978-0-7891-7906-7(7))* Perfection Learning Corp.

Owen, Ruth. Speed Machines, 1 vol., 1. 2014. (DIY for Boys Ser.). (ENG.). 32p. (J). (gr. 3-6). 27.50 *(978-1-4777-6274-5(4),* PowerKids Pr.) Rosen Publishing Group, Inc., The.

—Top 10 Fastest. 2010. (Crabtree Contact Ser.). (ENG., Illus.). 32p. (J). (gr. 3-6). pap. *(978-0-7787-7509-6(7),* 1308102); lib. bdg. *(978-0-7787-7488-4(0),* 1308102) Crabtree Publishing Co.

—Top 10 Slowest. 2010. (ENG., Illus.). 32p. (J). pap. *(978-0-7787-7511-9(9));* lib. bdg. *(978-0-7787-7490-7(2))* Crabtree Publishing Co.

Parham, Jerrill. Thrills & Spills: Fast Sports. 2007. (Shockwave: the Human Experience Ser.). (ENG., Illus.). 36p. (J). (gr. 3-5). 25.00 *(978-0-531-17762-4(9),* Children's Pr.) Scholastic Library Publishing.

Paris, Stephanie. ¡Brumm! Velocidad y Aceleración. 2016. (TIME for Kids en Español - Level 5 Ser.). (SPA.). 64p. (gr. 5-5). lib. bdg. 31.99 *(978-1-5157-2932-7(X))* Time for Kids Inc AUS. Dist: Capstone Pub.

—Vroom! Speed & Acceleration, 1 vol. 2nd rev. ed. 2013. (Nonfiction Readers Ser.). (ENG.). 64p. (J). (gr. 5-5). pap. 10.99 *(978-1-4333-4938-6(8));* (Illus.). pap. 31.96 *(978-1-4333-7437-1(4))* Teacher Created Materials, Inc.

Roza, Greg. Severe Storms: Measuring Velocity. (Math for the Real World Ser.). 32p. 2009. (ENG., Illus.). (gr. 6-7). pap. 10.00 *(978-1-4042-6085-6(4))* 2009. (gr. 5-5). 47.90 *(978-1-60851-365-9(3),* PowerKids Pr.) 2006. (Illus.). (YA). (gr. 5-9). lib. bdg. 25.25 *(978-1-4042-3366-9(0))* Rosen Publishing Group, Inc., The.

Schaefer, Lola M. Run for Your Life! Predators & Prey on the African Savanna. Meisel, Paul, illus. 2016. (ENG.). 32p. (J). 16.95 *(978-0-8234-3555-5(5))* Holiday Hse., Inc.

Schuh, Mari C. Full Speed Ahead: The Science of Going Fast. 2007. (Shockwave: Earth & Physical Science Ser.). (ENG., Illus.). 36p. (J). (gr. 4-8). 25.00 *(978-0-531-17792-1(0),* Children's Pr.) Scholastic Library Publishing.

Schwartz, Heather E. The Science of a Race Car: Reactions in Action. 2010. (Action Science Ser.). (ENG.). 32p. (gr. 3-4). pap. 47.70 *(978-1-4296-5074-8(5),* Fact Finders) Capstone Press of Coughlan Cos.

Slade, Suzanne, et al. The Science of Speed, 1 vol. 2014. (Science of Speed Ser.). (ENG.). 48p. (gr. 3-4). pap. 39.80 *(978-1-4765-6208-7(3))* Capstone Press of Coughlan Cos.

Somervill, Barbara A. Speed & Acceleration, 1 vol. 2010. (Measure It! Ser.). (ENG., Illus.). 32p. (gr. 3-6). 33.32 *(978-1-4329-3764-5(2));* pap. 8.29 *(978-1-4329-3770-6(7))* Heinemann-Raintree. (Heinemann InfoSearch).

Starke, John. Speed Machines: Mission Xtreme 3D. 2004. (Mission Xtreme 3D Ser.). (Illus.). 18p. (J). pap. 5.95 *(978-1-902626-50-5(8))* Red Bird Publishing GBR. Dist: Weatherhill, Inc.

Sullivan, Navin. Speed. 2006. (Measure Up! Ser.). (Illus.). 48p. (gr. 4-7). lib. bdg. 31.36 *(978-0-7614-2325-6(7),* Benchmark Bks.) Marshall Cavendish Corp.

Tan, Richard. Fast & Slow. 2015. (Rosen REAL Readers: STEM & STEAM Collection). (ENG.). 8p. pap. 5.46 *(978-1-4994-9652-9(4),* Rosen Classroom) Rosen Publishing Group, Inc., The.

Weakland, Mark. Zoom! Wile E. Coyote Experiments with Speed & Velocity. Sordo, Paco, illus. 2017. (Wile E. Coyote, Physical Science Genius Ser.). (ENG.). 32p. (gr. 3-5). lib. bdg. 30.65 *(978-1-5157-3734-6(9))* Capstone Press of Coughlan Cos.

Wells, Robert E. What's Faster Than a Speeding Cheetah? 2012. (J). *(978-1-61913-153-8(6))* Weigl Pubs., Inc.

What Is Fast?, 6 Packs. (gr. 1-2). 22.00 *(978-0-7635-9104-5(1))* Rigby Education.

Woodford, Chris. Speed. 2012. (Measure up Math Ser.). (Illus.). 32p. (J). (gr. 4-6). 26.60 *(978-1-4339-7445-8(2));* pap. 10.50 *(978-1-4339-7446-5(0))* Stevens, Gareth Publishing LLLP. (Gareth Stevens Learning Library).

Woods, Bob. Wild Racers. 2009. (Racing Mania Ser.). 48p. (gr. 4-18). lib. bdg. 31.36 *(978-0-7614-4389-6(4))* Marshall Cavendish Corp.

SPEED, SUPERSONIC

see Aerodynamics, Supersonic

SPELEOLOGY

see Caves

SPELLERS

Cundy, David. Animals Spell Love. 2016. (Illus.). 40p. (J). *(978-1-56792-586-9(3))* Godine, David R. Pub.

Grambs, David L. & Levine, Ellen S. So You Think You Can Spell? Killer Quizzes for the Incurably Competitive & Overly Confident. 2009. (ENG.). 288p. (gr. 12-18). 13.95 *(978-0-399-53528-4(4)*, TarcherPerigee) Penguin Publishing Group.

Siede Preis Photography (Firm) Staff & Brian Warling Photography (Firm) Staff, contrib. by. First Words. 2003. (Lift-A-Flap Ser.). (Illus.). 12p. (J). bds. 12.98 *(978-0-7853-8624-7(6)*, 7188400) Publications International, Ltd.

SPELLING

see names of languages with the subdivision Spelling, e.g. English Language—Spelling

The Battle of Bowling Street: Level 4, 6 vols. (Fluency Strand Ser.). (gr. 4-8). 45.00 *(978-1-4045-1224-5(1))* Wright Group/McGraw-Hill.

Bohrer, Erica. 20 Super Spelling Centers: Fun, Ready-to-Go Activities That Help Kids Master the Words on Their Spelling Lists. 2012. (ENG.). 80p. (gr. k-2). pap. 12.99 *(978-0-545-37489-7(8)*, Teaching Resources) Scholastic, Inc.

Carson-Dellosa Publishing Staff. Spelling & Writing for Beginners, Grade 1. 2010. (Home Workbooks Ser.). (ENG.). 64p. (gr. 1-1). pap. 4.49 *(978-1-60418-788-5(3))* Carson-Dellosa Publishing, LLC.

Diaz-Cubero, Jose H. Practicas de Ortografia: 6 Grado. (SPA & ENG.). (J). (gr. 6). 9.95 *(978-84-357-0124-2(7)*, CPR94) Ediciones y Distribuciones Codice, S.A. ESP. Dist: Continental Bk. Co., Inc.

Disney Staff, contrib. by. Write, Slide & Learn Disney Princess: Spelling. 2011. (Disney Write, Slide & Learn Ser.). 12p. (J). 9.99 *(978-1-74183-852-7(5))* Hinkler Bks. Pty. Ltd. AUS. Dist: Ideals Pubns.

Dr Awkward: Level 6, 6 vols. (Fluency Strand Ser.). (gr. 4-8). 45.00 *(978-1-4045-1239-9(X))* Wright Group/McGraw-Hill.

Herbold, Marvin. Marvin Teaches Fingerspelling. 2003. (YA). cd-rom 19.95 *(978-0-9752933-3-1(8))* Institute for Disabilities Research & Training, Inc.

Hinkler Studios Staff., ed. Disney Princess: Counting & Spelling. 2011. 12p. 9.99 *(978-1-74183-871-8(1))* Hinkler Bks. Pty. Ltd. AUS. Dist: Ideals Pubns.

Holt, Rinehart and Winston Staff. Elements of Language: Spelling - Grade 6. 2003. (Elements of Language Ser.). 13.86 *(978-0-03-056326-3(7))* Holt McDougal.

HOP, LLC. Hooked on Spelling. 2006. 64.99 *(978-1-60143-000-7(0))*; 99.99 *(978-1-933863-98-6(6))*; 24.99 *(978-1-60143-001-4(9))* HOP, LLC.

Howard, Cheryl Lee. Daisy Dustbunny Seven Days a Week: Learning to spell the days of the week Is fun with Daisy Dustbunny. 2011. 24p. pap. 24.95 *(978-1-4560-6777-9(X))* America Star Bks.

Just Around the Block. (J). (gr. k-2). 75.00 *(978-0-669-13448-3(1))*; pap. 9.90 *(978-0-669-15288-3(9))* Houghton Mifflin Harcourt School Pubs.

Learning Company Books Staff, ed. Reader Rabbit Spelling Challenge. 2004. (Illus.). 64p. (J). (gr. 1-18). pap. *(978-0-7630-7740-2(2))*; (gr. 2-18). pap. *(978-0-7630-7741-9(0))* Magma.

Marcel Meringue: Level 2, 6 vols. (Fluency Strand Ser.). (gr. 4-8). 45.00 *(978-1-4045-1212-2(8))* Wright Group/McGraw-Hill.

More Spelling. 2004. (Help with Homework Ser.). 32p. (J). (gr. 1-4). wbk. ed. 3.99 *(978-1-904586-27-2(9))* Byeway Bks.

Night Mare Trip: Level 5, 6 vols. (Fluency Strand Ser.). (gr. 4-8). 45.00 *(978-1-4045-1230-6(6))* Wright Group/McGraw-Hill.

Olo: Level 6, 6 vols. (Fluency Strand Ser.). (gr. 4-8). 45.00 *(978-1-4045-1237-5(3))* Wright Group/McGraw-Hill.

Once, Twice, Boom: Level 7, 6 vols. (Fluency Strand Ser.). (gr. 4-8). 45.00 *(978-1-4045-1240-5(3))* Wright Group/McGraw-Hill.

Pulse- Fun with Vocabulary & Spelling. 2006. cd-rom 4.99 *(978-1-60245-041-7(2))* GDL Multimedia, LLC.

Rechtschreibung und Wortkunde. (Duden-Schuelerduden Ser.). (GER.). 384p. (YA). (gr. 4-18). pap. *(978-3-411-05175-5(2))* Bibliographisches Institut & F. A. Brockhaus AG DEU. Dist: International Bk. Import Service, Inc.

Rieder, E. & Toth, M. Das ABC-Haus: Arbeitsheft 1. (Illus.). 64p. pap. *(978-3-12-675645-7(X))* Klett, Ernst, Verlag GmbH DEU. Dist: International Bk. Import Service, Inc.

—Das ABC-Haus: Schuelerbuch. (Illus.). 96p. (J). pap. *(978-3-12-675644-0(1))* Klett, Ernst, Verlag GmbH DEU. Dist: International Bk. Import Service, Inc.

—Das ABC-Haus. Arbeitsheft 2: Deutsch als Fremd- oder Zweitsprache mit wenigen oder keinen Vorkenntnissen. (Illus.). 64p. pap. *(978-3-12-675648-8(4))* Klett, Ernst, Verlag GmbH DEU. Dist: International Bk. Import Service, Inc.

School Zone Publishing. Spelling Puzzles. 2003. (Language Arts Ser.). (ENG.). cd-rom 19.99 *(978-1-58947-914-2(9))* School Zone Publishing Co.

Schwartz, Linda. Conquer Spelling: Word Lists, Roles, & Activities to Help Kids Become Spelling Heros. Scott, Kelly, ed. Armstrong, Beverly & Grayson, Rick, illus. 2003. 112p. (J). pap. 13.99 *(978-0-88160-362-0(7)*, LW-420, Learning Works, The) Creative Teaching Pr., Inc.

Spelling & Vocabulary, Set. 2004. (gr. 2). 38.95 *(978-0-7403-0219-0(1)*, Horizons) Alpha Omega Pubns., Inc.

Spelling Words & Sentences. 2011. (Spelling by Sound & Structure Ser.). 87p. (J). (gr. 2-8). pap. 4.35 *(978-0-7399-0708-5(5))* Rod & Staff Pubs., Inc.

Spelling Workout. (J). Bk. A. 3rd ed. (gr. 1). 11.95 net. *(978-0-8136-2815-8(6))*Bk. F. 3rd ed. (gr. 6). 11.95 net. *(978-0-8136-2820-2(2))*Bk. G. 3rd ed. (gr. 7). 11.95 net. *(978-0-8136-2821-9(0))*Bk. H. 3rd ed. (gr. 8). 11.95 net. *(978-0-8136-2822-6(9))*Bk. H. 3rd ed. (gr. 8). 12.50 net. *(978-0-8136-2847-9(4))*Rev. B. (gr. 2). *(978-0-8136-2808-0(3))* Modern Curriculum Pr.

Stella, Heather & Lima, Athena Anna. Get Ready for First Grade: Spelling, Writing & Reading. 2012. (Get Ready for School Ser.). (ENG., Illus.). 320p. (J). (gr. -1-17). 17.95 *(978-1-57912-896-8(3)*, 81896, Black Dog & Leventhal Pubs. Inc.) Hachette Bks.

Studio Mouse Staff. Spelling Fun. 2011. (Cars Ser.). (Illus.). 28p. (J). 15.99 *(978-1-59069-938-6(6))* Studio Mouse LLC.

Terror Bear Canyon: Level 5, 6 vols. (Fluency Strand Ser.). (gr. 4-8). 45.00 *(978-1-4045-1225-2(X))* Wright Group/McGraw-Hill.

To Catch a Thief: Level 3, 6 vols. (Fluency Strand Ser.). (gr. 4-8). 45.00 *(978-1-4045-1219-1(5))* Wright Group/McGraw-Hill.

Trocki, Phillip. Spelling Workout. rev. ed. 2003. (Illus.). (J). Level C. (gr. 3). tchr. ed. 10.50 *(978-0-7652-2490-3(9))*Level A. (gr. 1). tchr. ed. 10.50 *(978-0-7652-2488-0(7))*Level B. (gr. 2). tchr. ed. 10.50 *(978-0-7652-2489-7(5))* Modern Curriculum Pr.

Unccor: Level 5, 6 vols. (Fluency Strand Ser.). (gr. 4-8). 45.00 *(978-1-4045-1231-3(4))* Wright Group/McGraw-Hill.

Vinopol, Corinne. Spell Well: CD-ROM American Sign Language Spelling Game. 2003. (YA). cd-rom 19.95 *(978-0-9752933-0-0(3))* Institute for Disabilities Research & Training, Inc.

Zone Zoomers: Level 2, 6 vols. (Fluency Strand Ser.). (gr. 4-8). 45.00 *(978-1-4045-1213-9(6))* Wright Group/McGraw-Hill.

SPELLS

see Charms

SPHERICAL TRIGONOMETRY

see Trigonometry

SPICES

Rodger, Ellen. The Biography of Spices. 2005. (How did That Get There? Ser.). (ENG., Illus.). 32p. (J). (gr. 4-5). pap. *(978-0-7787-2520-6(0))*; lib. bdg. *(978-0-7787-2484-1(0))* Crabtree Publishing Co.

Wells, Donald. The Spice Trade. 2005. (Great Journeys Ser.). (Illus.). 32p. (J). (gr. 6-7). lib. bdg. 26.00 *(978-1-59036-208-2(X))* Weigl Pubs., Inc.

SPIDER-MAN (FICTITIOUS CHARACTER)—FICTION

Andrews, Kaare. Spider-Man Legend of the Spider-Clan, 3 vols. Young, Skott, illus. 2003. (Mangaverse Ser.: Vol. 3). 128p. (YA). pap. 11.99 *(978-0-7851-1114-6(X))* Marvel Worldwide, Inc.

Bagley, Mark, illus. Irresponsible, 8 vols., Vol. 7. 2006. (ENG.). 144p. (J). (gr. -1-17). pap. 12.99 *(978-0-7851-1092-7(5))* Marvel Worldwide, Inc.

—Public Scrutiny, 5, Vol. 5. 2007. (ENG.). 120p. (J). (gr. 4-17). pap. 11.99 *(978-0-7851-1087-3(9))* Marvel Worldwide, Inc.

—Ultimate Spider-Man Vol. 11: Carnage. 2007. (ENG.). 144p. (J). (gr. -1-17). pap. 12.99 *(978-0-7851-1403-1(3))* Marvel Worldwide, Inc.

Behling, Steve. Spider-Man Retro. Panosian, Dan, illus. 2017. (ENG.). 48p. (J). (gr. 1-3). 10.99 *(978-1-4847-4928-9(6)*, Marvel Pr.) Disney Publishing Worldwide.

Bendis, Brian Michael. Ultimate Spider-Man Ultimate Collection, Bk. 3. 2010. (ENG., Illus.). 296p. (J). (gr. 4-17). pap. 29.99 *(978-0-7851-4919-4(8))* Marvel Worldwide, Inc.

Berrios, Frank. The Amazing Spider-Man (Marvel: Spider-Man) Gurihiru Staff et al, illus. 2012. (Little Golden Book Ser.). (ENG.). 24p. (J). (gr. k-k). 4.99 *(978-0-307-93107-8(2)*, Golden Bks.) Random Hse. Children's Bks.

—High Voltage! (Marvel: Spider-Man) Golden Books Staff et al, illus. 2016. (Little Golden Book Ser.). (ENG.). 24p. (J). (-k). 4.99 *(978-0-385-37427-9(5)*, Golden Bks.) Random Hse. Children's Bks.

—Night of the Vulture! (Marvel: Spider-Man) Legramandi, Francesco & Scolari, Silvano, illus. 2017. (Little Golden Book Ser.). (ENG.). 24p. (J). (-k). 4.99 ***(978-1-5247-1728-5(2)***, Golden Bks.) Random Hse. Children's Bks.

Berrios, Frank. Trapped by the Green Goblin! (Marvel: Spider-Man) Cagol, Andrea & Legramandi, Francesco, illus. 2016. (Little Golden Book Ser.). (ENG.). 24p. (J). (-k). 4.99 *(978-0-307-97655-0(6)*, Golden Bks.) Random Hse. Children's Bks.

Berrios, Frank & Wrecks, Billy. Marvel Spider-Man, Vol. 2. 2016. (Little Golden Book Favorites Ser.). (ENG., Illus.). 80p. (J). (-k). 7.99 *(978-0-307-97659-8(9)*, Golden Bks.) Random Hse. Children's Bks.

Bright, J. E. Super Hero Adventures: the Amazing Chase: A Move-Along Adventure. Laufman, Derek, illus. 2017. (ENG.). 12p. (J). (gr. -1-k). bds. 8.99 ***(978-1-4847-8886-8(9)***, Marvel Pr.) Disney Publishing Worldwide.

Bright, J. E. & West, Alexandra. Super Hero Adventures: Save the Day! Laufman, Derek, illus. 2017. (ENG.). 14p. (J). (gr. -1-k). bds. 10.99 ***(978-1-4847-8859-2(1)***, Marvel Pr.) Disney Publishing Worldwide.

Caramagna, Joe, text. Amazing Spider-Man, Vol. 4. 2012. (ENG., Illus.). 96p. (J). (gr. -1-17). pap. 6.99 *(978-0-7851-6613-9(0))* Marvel Worldwide, Inc.

Casey, Joe & Reed, Brian. The Amazing Spider-Man: The One & Only. Weeks, Lee et al, illus. 2014. (ENG.). 168p. (J). (gr. 4-17). pap. 16.99 *(978-0-7851-9010-3(4))* Marvel Worldwide, Inc.

Cruz, Roger, illus. Spider-Man: Friendly Neighborhood Spider-Man by Peter David - the Complete Collection. 2017. (ENG.). 480p. (J). (gr. 4-17). pap. 39.99 ***(978-1-302-90436-4(1))*** Marvel Worldwide, Inc.

David, Peter, text. Spider-Man 2099 Vol. 6. 2017. (ENG., Illus.). 112p. (J). (gr. 4-17). pap. 15.99 ***(978-1-302-90282-7(2))*** Marvel Worldwide, Inc.

David, Peter, et al. Amazing Spider-Man Epic Collection: Ghosts of the Past. Buscema, Sal & Frenz, Ron, illus. 2014. (ENG.). 472p. (J). (gr. 4-17). pap. 34.99 *(978-0-7851-8916-9(5))* Marvel Worldwide, Inc.

—Wizard Spiderman, Vol. 11. 2006. (Illus.). 272p. (YA). 50.00 *(978-0-9743253-6-1(8))* Diamond Comic Distributors, Inc.

Davis, Alan. Killraven. Davis, Alan, illus. 2003. (Spider-Man Ser.). (Illus.). 144p. (YA). pap. 16.99 *(978-0-7851-1083-5(6))* Marvel Worldwide, Inc.

Defalco, Tom. Spider-Man Bk. 1: The Complete Alien Costume Saga. Leonardi, Rick et al, illus. 2014. (ENG.). 488p. (J). (gr. 4-17). pap. 44.99 *(978-0-7851-8867-4(3))* Marvel Worldwide, Inc.

Defalco, Tom, et al. Thor Epic Collection: War of the Pantheons. Frenz, Ron et al, illus. 2013. (ENG.). 472p. (J). (gr. 4-17). pap. 34.99 *(978-0-7851-8788-2(X))* Marvel Worldwide, Inc.

DeMatteis, J. M. & Kleid, Neil, texts. Spider-Man: Kraven's Last Hunt. 2014. (ENG., Illus.). 288p. (YA). (gr. 8-17). 24.99 *(978-0-7851-8970-1(X))* Marvel Worldwide, Inc.

DeMatteis, J. M., et al. Son of the Goblin. 2004. (Spider-Man Ser.). (Illus.). 144p. (YA). pap. 15.99 *(978-0-7851-1563-2(3))* Marvel Worldwide, Inc.

Disney Book Group. 5-Minute Spider-Man Stories. Disney Book Group, illus. 2013. (5-Minute Stories Ser.). (ENG., Illus.). 192p. (J). (gr. 1-3). 12.99 *(978-1-4231-7786-9(X))* Marvel Worldwide, Inc.

Disney Book Group & Marvel Book Group. Spider-Man: Love Bug. 2015. (Marvel 8x8s Ser.). (J). lib. bdg. 16.00 *(978-0-606-37542-9(2))* Turtleback Bks.

Disney Book Group Staff. The Story of Spider-Man (Level 2) 2012. (World of Reading Ser.). (ENG.). 32p. (J). (gr. 1-3). pap. 3.99 *(978-1-4231-5409-9(6))* Marvel Worldwide, Inc.

—This Is Spider-Man, Level 1. 2012. (World of Reading Ser.). (ENG.). 32p. (J). (gr. -1-k). pap. 3.99 *(978-1-4231-5408-2(8)*, Marvel Pr.) Disney Publishing Worldwide.

Dorling Kindersley Publishing Staff. Spider-Man: Inside the World of Your Friendly Neighborhood Hero. 2012. (ENG.). 200p. (J). (gr. 3-7). 24.99 *(978-0-7566-9089-2(7)*, DK Children) Dorling Kindersley Publishing, Inc.

Dougall, Alastair & Dorling Kindersley Publishing Staff. Spider-Man - Glow in the Dark. 2006. (Ultimate Sticker Bks.). (ENG., Illus.). 16p. (J). (gr. k-3). pap. 6.99 *(978-0-7566-1999-2(8)*, DK Children) Dorling Kindersley Publishing, Inc.

Duggan, Gerry. Spider-Man/Deadpool Vol. 2. Brown, Reilly et al, illus. 2017. (ENG.). 120p. (YA). (gr. 8-17). pap. 16.99 ***(978-0-7851-9992-2(6))*** Marvel Worldwide, Inc.

Egan, Kate. Evil Comes in Pairs. Merkel, Joe F., illus. 2009. (Spider-Man Ser.). 64p. (J). (gr. 2-5). pap. 4.99 *(978-0-06-162625-8(2)*, HarperFestival) HarperCollins Pubs.

Figueroa, Acton. Spider-Man 2: Everyday Hero. Vasquez, Ivan & Redondo, Jesus, illus. movie tie-in ed. 2004. (Festival Reader Ser.). 32p. (J). (gr. -1-2). pap. 3.99 *(978-0-06-057363-8(5)*, HarperFestival) HarperCollins Pubs.

Gunter, Jacob Ben, et al. The Daily Bugle Stories. 2004. (Spider-Man 2 Ser.). (Illus.). 144p. pap. *(978-0-00-717815-5(8)*, HarperCollins Entertainment) HarperCollins Pubs. Ltd.

Jenkins, Paul. Here There Be the Monsters, Vol. 3. Scott, Damion, illus. 2004. (Spider-Man Ser.). 144p. (YA). 9.99 *(978-0-7851-1333-1(9))* Marvel Worldwide, Inc.

Lime, Harry. Spider-Man 3: Meet the Heroes & Villains. Gordon, Steven E., illus. 2007. (I Can Read Bks.). 32p. (J). pap. 3.99 *(978-0-06-083721-1(7)*, Harper Trophy) HarperCollins Pubs.

Loeb, Jeph. Blue. Sale, Tim, illus. 2003. (Spider-Man Ser.). 160p. (YA). 21.99 *(978-0-7851-1062-0(3))* Marvel Worldwide, Inc.

Marvel. Meet Spidey. 2017. (ENG., Illus.). 32p. (J). (gr. -1-3). pap. 4.99 ***(978-0-316-43834-6(0))*** Little, Brown Bks. for Young Readers.

Marvel & Busse, R. R. The Tangled Web of Super Tech. 2017. (ENG., Illus.). 32p. (J). (gr. -1-3). pap. 5.99 ***(978-0-316-43822-3(7))*** Little, Brown Bks. for Young Readers.

Marvel & May, Tallulah. Mayhem at the Monument. 2017. (ENG., Illus.). 32p. (J). (gr. -1-3). pap. 4.99 ***(978-0-316-43831-5(6))*** Little, Brown Bks. for Young Readers.

Marvel & McCann, Jim. The Stick-Like-Spidey. 2017. (ENG.). 160p. (J). (gr. 3-7). 9.99 ***(978-0-316-43818-6(9))***; pap. 6.99 ***(978-0-316-43817-9(0))*** Little, Brown Bks. for Young Readers.

Marvel Book Group. Ultimate Spider-Man - Spider-Man vs Dracula. 2014. (ENG.). 24p. (J). (gr. 3-7). pap. 5.99 *(978-1-4847-1110-1(6)*, Marvel Pr.) Disney Publishing Worldwide.

Marvel Book Group & Macri, Thomas. This Is Spider-Man. 2012. (Marvel World of Reading Level 1 Ser.). (J). lib. bdg. 13.55 *(978-0-606-23787-1(9)*, Turtleback) Turtleback Bks.

Marvel Book Group Staff. Ultimate Spider-Man Halloween. 2014. (Marvel 8x8s Ser.). (J). lib. bdg. 16.00 *(978-0-606-35286-4(4))* Turtleback Bks.

Marvel Comics. Spider-Man: Homecoming - the Art of the Movie. 2017. (ENG., Illus.). 240p. (J). (gr. -1-17). 50.00 ***(978-1-302-90275-9(X))*** Marvel Worldwide, Inc.

Marvel Press Book Group. Spider-Man: an Amazing Book & Magnetic Play Set: Book & Magnetic Play Set. Marvel Press Book Group, illus. 2016. (Magnetic Dress-Up Book Ser.). (ENG., Illus.). 32p. (J). (gr. -1-k). 15.99 *(978-1-4847-6168-7(5)*, Marvel Pr.) Disney Publishing Worldwide.

—Spider-Man Storybook Collection. 2016. (Storybook Collection). (ENG.). 304p. (J). (gr. 1-3). 16.99 *(978-1-4847-3215-1(4)*, Marvel Pr.) Disney Publishing Worldwide.

Marvel Press Book Group Staff. 5-Minute Spider-Man Stories. 2017. (5-Minute Stories Ser.). (ENG.). 192p. (J). (gr. 1-3). 12.99 ***(978-1-4847-8142-5(2)***, Marvel Pr.) Disney Publishing Worldwide.

McDonnell, David, ed. Spiderman & Other Amazing Heroes. 2004. (Starlog Movie Magic Ser.). (YA). pap. *(978-0-88013-065-3(2))* Profile Entertainment, Inc.

McVeigh, Mark W. The Lizard's Legacy. Sazaklis, John, illus. 2009. (Spider-Man Ser.). 64p. (J). (gr. 2-5). pap. 4.99 *(978-0-06-162627-2(9)*, HarperFestival) HarperCollins Pubs.

Mosier, Scott & Son, Eugene, illus. Marvel Universe Ultimate Spider-Man Volume 6. 2014. (ENG.). 88p. (J). (gr. -1-17). pap. 9.99 *(978-0-7851-8815-5(0))* Marvel Worldwide, Inc.

Palacios, Tomas. Ultimate Spider-Man: the Really Big Sticker Book! Disney Book Group Staff, illus. 2014. (Really Big Sticker Book Ser.). (ENG.). 88p. (J). (gr. -1-k). pap. 12.99 *(978-1-4231-9850-5(6)*, Marvel Pr.) Disney Publishing Worldwide.

Publications International Ltd. Staff, ed. Spider Sense Spider-Man: Super Villain Showdown. 2010. 12p. (J). bds. 12.98 *(978-1-4127-9911-9(2))* Phoenix International Publications, Inc.

Ramos, Humberto, et al, illus. Spider-Man - Trouble on the Horizon. 2013. (ENG.). 112p. (J). (gr. 4-17). pap. 16.99 *(978-0-7851-6004-5(3))* Marvel Worldwide, Inc.

Reynolds, Jason. Miles Morales. Nelson, Kadir, illus. 2017. (Marvel YA Novel Ser.). (ENG.). 272p. (YA). (gr. 7-12). 17.99 ***(978-1-4847-8748-9(X)***, Marvel Pr.) Disney Publishing Worldwide.

Sazaklis, John, retold by. Marvel Ultimate Spider-Man: Spider-Man & His Amazing Friends. 2016. (ENG.). 80p. (J). (gr. 1-4). pap. 6.99 *(978-0-7944-3391-8(X))* Studio Fun International.

Slott, Dan & Busiek, Kurt. Spider-Man - Lizard: No Turning Back. Frenz, Ron, illus. 2013. (ENG.). 112p. (J). (gr. 4-17). pap. 16.99 *(978-0-7851-6008-3(6)*, Marvel Pr.) Disney Publishing Worldwide.

Slott, Dan & Caselli, Stefano. Ends of the Earth. Silas, Thony et al, illus. 2013. (ENG.). 192p. (J). (gr. 4-17). pap. 24.99 *(978-0-7851-6006-9(X))* Marvel Worldwide, Inc.

Slott, Dan & Waid, Mark. The Amazing Spider-Man - Flying Blind. Camuncoli, Giuseppe et al, illus. 2012. (ENG.). 120p. (J). (gr. 4-17). pap. 16.99 *(978-0-7851-6002-1(7))* Marvel Worldwide, Inc.

Spider-Man & Friends. 2003. (J). per. *(978-1-57657-858-2(5))* Paradise Pr., Inc.

Stern, Roger, et al. Spider-Man by Roger Stern Omnibus. Zeck, Mike et al, illus. 2014. (ENG.). 1296p. (J). (gr. 4-17). 125.00 *(978-0-7851-8827-8(4))* Marvel Worldwide, Inc.

Straczynski, J. Michael. Best of Spider-Man, Vol. 3. Youngquist, Jeff, ed. 2004. (Spider-Man Ser.). (Illus.). 368p. (YA). 29.99 *(978-0-7851-1339-3(8))* Marvel Worldwide, Inc.

—The Book of Ezekiel, Vol. 7. Romita, John, Jr., illus. 2004. (Spider-Man Ser.). 144p. (YA). pap. 12.99 *(978-0-7851-1525-0(0))* Marvel Worldwide, Inc.

Teitelbaum, Michael. The Secret Life of Black Cat. Sazaklis, John, illus. 2009. (Spider-Man Ser.). 64p. (J). (gr. 2-5). pap. 4.99 *(978-0-06-162626-5(0)*, HarperFestival) HarperCollins Pubs.

Thomas, Rich. The Amazing Spider-Man: An Origin Story, 1 vol. Clark, Jeff, illus. 2012. (Marvel Origins Ser.). (ENG.). 48p. (J). (gr. -1-4). lib. bdg. 24.21 *(978-1-61479-007-5(8))* Spotlight.

Thomas, Rich, Jr. Spider-Man: An Origin Story. Olliffe, Pat et al, illus. 2nd ed. 2013. (ENG.). 48p. (J). (gr. 1-3). 8.99 *(978-1-4231-8306-8(1))* Marvel Worldwide, Inc.

Thomas, Rich. Spider-Man: Attack of the Heroes. 2014. (Mighty Marvel Chapter Bks.). (J). lib. bdg. 16.00 *(978-0-606-35271-0(6))* Turtleback Bks.

—Spider-Man: Attack of the Heroes: A Marvel Chapter Book. Disney Book Group, illus. 2014. (Mighty Marvel Chapter Book Ser.: 1). (ENG.). 128p. (J). (gr. 1-3). pap. 5.99 *(978-1-4231-4301-7(9)*, Marvel Pr.) Disney Publishing Worldwide.

Tobin, Paul. Spider-Man & the Secret Wars GN. Scherberger, Patrick, illus. 2010. (ENG.). 128p. pap. 14.99 *(978-0-7851-4443-4(9))* Marvel Worldwide, Inc.

Weisman, Greg. Vulture & Morbius. Quinones, Joe et al, illus. 2010. (ENG.). 136p. (J). (gr. 4-17). pap. 14.99 *(978-0-7851-4612-4(1))* Marvel Worldwide, Inc.

SPIDERS

Allen, Judy. Are You a Spider? Humphries, Tudor, illus. 2003. (Backyard Bks.). (ENG.). 31p. (J). (gr. k-3). pap. 6.99 *(978-0-7534-5609-5(5)*, 9780753456095, Kingfisher) Roaring Brook Pr.

—Are You a Spider? 2003. (Backyard Bks.). (J). (gr. -1-2). lib. bdg. 17.20 *(978-0-613-90776-7(0)*, Turtleback) Turtleback Bks.

Allman, Toney. From Spider Webs to Man-Made Silk. 2005. (Imitating Nature Ser.). (ENG., Illus.). 32p. (J). (gr. 4-8). lib. bdg. 26.20 *(978-0-7377-3124-8(9)*, Greenhaven Pr., Inc.) Cengage Gale.

Amstutz, Lisa J. Creepy Crawlers. 2013. (Creepy Crawlers Ser.). (ENG.). 24p. (gr. k-1). lib. bdg. 159.90 *(978-1-4765-3694-1(5)*, Pebble Plus) Capstone Press of Coughlan Cos.

Amstutz, Lisa J. Spiders. 2017. (Little Critters Ser.). (ENG.). 24p. (gr. k-1). lib. bdg. 21.99 ***(978-1-5157-7826-4(6))*** Capstone Press of Coughlan Cos.

Anderson, Catherine. Daddy Longlegs. 2003. (Bug Bks.). (Illus.). (J). 32p. lib. bdg. 22.79 *(978-1-4034-0763-4(0))*; (ENG., 24p. pap. 6.50 *(978-1-4034-0994-2(3))* Heinemann-Raintree.

Archer, Claire. Araña Lobo, 1 vol. 2014. (Arañas Ser.). (SPA.). 24p. (J). (gr. 4-8). lib. bdg. 28.50 *(978-1-62970-370-1(2))* ABDO Publishing Co.

—Bird-Eating Spiders, 1 vol. 2014. (Spiders Ser.). (ENG.). 24p. (J). (gr. 4-8). lib. bdg. 28.50 *(978-1-62970-071-7(1))* ABDO Publishing Co.

—Black Widow Spiders, 1 vol. 2014. (Spiders Ser.). (ENG.). 24p. (J). (gr. 4-8). lib. bdg. 28.50 *(978-1-62970-072-4(X))* ABDO Publishing Co.

—Jumping Spiders, 1 vol. 2014. (Spiders Ser.). (ENG.). 24p. (J). (gr. 4-8). lib. bdg. 28.50 *(978-1-62970-073-1(8))* ABDO Publishing Co.

—Tarantula Spiders, 1 vol. 2014. (Spiders Ser.). (ENG.). 24p. (J). (gr. 4-8). lib. bdg. 28.50 *(978-1-62970-074-8(6))* ABDO Publishing Co.

—Trapdoor Spiders, 1 vol. 2014. (Spiders Ser.). (ENG.). 24p. (J). (gr. 4-8). lib. bdg. 28.50 *(978-1-62970-075-5(4))* ABDO Publishing Co.

—Wolf Spiders, 1 vol. 2014. (Spiders Ser.). (ENG.). 24p. (J). (gr. 4-8). lib. bdg. 28.50 *(978-1-62970-076-2(2))* ABDO Publishing Co.

Archer, Claire, et al. Arañas Lobo. 2015. (Arañas Ser.). (SPA., Illus.). 24p. (gr. k-1). pap. 7.95 *(978-1-4966-0387-6(7))* Capstone Classroom.

—Arañas Saltarinas. 2015. (Arañas Ser.). (SPA.). 24p. (gr. k-1). pap. 7.95 *(978-1-4966-0389-0(3))* Capstone Classroom.

—Arañas Tramperas. 2015. (Arañas Ser.). (SPA., Illus.). 24p. (gr. k-1). pap. 7.95 *(978-1-4966-0391-3(5))* Capstone Classroom.

—Arañas Viuda Negra. 2015. (Arañas Ser.). (SPA., Illus.). 24p. (gr. k-1). pap. 7.95 *(978-1-4966-0393-7(1))* Capstone Classroom.

—Tarántulas. 2015. (Arañas Ser.). (SPA., Illus.). 24p. (gr. k-1). pap. 7.95 *(978-1-4966-0395-1(8))* Capstone Classroom.

—Tarántulas Goliat. 2015. (Arañas Ser.). (SPA., Illus.). 24p. (gr. k-1). pap. 7.95 *(978-1-4966-0397-5(4))* Capstone Classroom.

Arnosky, Jim. Creep & Flutter: The Secret World of Insects & Spiders. (ENG., Illus.). (J). (gr. 1-5). 2016. 32p. pap. 6.95 *(978-1-4549-1910-0(8))* 2012. 40p. 14.95 *(978-1-4027-7766-0(3))* Sterling Publishing Co., Inc.

Barton, Bethany. I'm Trying to Love Spiders. Barton, Bethany, illus. 2015. (ENG., Illus.). 40p. (J). (gr. -1-3). 16.99 *(978-0-670-01693-8(4)*, Viking Books for Young Readers) Penguin Young Readers Group.

Berger, Melvin. Spinning Spiders. Schindler, S. D., illus. 2015. 40p. pap. 6.00 *(978-1-61003-617-7(4))* Center for the Collaborative Classroom.

—Spinning Spiders. Schindler, S. D., illus. 2003. (Let's-Read-and-Find-Out-Science Ser.: Vol. 2). 40p. (J). (gr. k-4). lib. bdg. 16.89 *(978-0-06-028697-2(0))* HarperCollins Pubs.

—Spinning Spiders. Schindler, S. D., illus. 2003. (Let's-Read-and-Find-Out Science Ser.). 33p. (gr. k-4). 16.00 *(978-0-7569-1449-3(3))* Perfection Learning Corp.

Biel, Timothy Levi. Aranas. Rountree, Monica, tr. 2003. (Zoobooks Ser.). Orig. Title: Spiders. (SPA., Illus.). 24p. (J). (gr. 1-7). lib. bdg. 15.95 *(978-1-888153-82-8(2))* Wildlife Education, Ltd.

Bishop, Celeste. Scrambling Spiders. 2015. (Icky Animals! Small & Gross Ser.). (ENG.). 24p. (J). (gr. 1-1). pap. 8.25 *(978-1-4994-0717-4(3)*, PowerKids Pr.) Rosen Publishing Group, Inc., The.

Bishop, Nic. NIC Bishop - Spiders. Bishop, Nic, photos by. 2012. (Scholastic Reader Level 2 Ser.). (ENG., Illus.). 32p. (J). (gr. k-2). pap. 3.99 *(978-0-545-23757-4(2)*, Scholastic Paperbacks) Scholastic, Inc.

—Spiders. Bishop, Nic, photos by. 2007. (Nic Bishop Ser.). (ENG., Illus.). 48p. (J). (gr. -1-3). 17.99 *(978-0-439-87756-5(3)*, Scholastic Nonfiction) Scholastic, Inc.

—Spiders. 2012. (Scholastic Reader Level 2 Ser.). lib. bdg. 13.55 *(978-0-606-26742-7(5)*, Turtleback) Turtleback Bks.

Black, Nessa. Spiders. 2017. (Spot Creepy Crawlies Ser.). (ENG.). 16p. (gr. k-3). 17.95 ***(978-1-68151-110-8(X))*** Amicus Publishing.

Bodden, Valerie. Grow with Me: Spider. 2015. (Grow with Me Ser.). (ENG.). 32p. (J). (gr. 3-5). pap. 9.99 *(978-0-89812-993-9(1)*, Creative Paperbacks) Creative Co., The.

—Spider. 2014. (Illus.). 32p. (J). *(978-1-60818-407-1(2)*, Creative Education) Creative Co., The.

—Spiders. 2011. (Creepy Creatures Ser.). 24p. (J). (gr. 1-3). (ENG.). pap. 7.99 *(978-0-89812-569-6(3)*, Creative Paperbacks); 24.25 *(978-1-58341-996-0(9)*, Creative Education) Creative Co., The.

—Spiders. 2010. (ENG., Illus.). 24p. (J). 8.95 *(978-1-926853-76-5(8))* Saunders Bk. Co. CAN. Dist: Creative Co., The.

Books Are Fun 8 Title Animal Lives Set: Spiders. 2006. (J). *(978-1-59566-313-9(4))* QEB Publishing Inc.

Borgert-Spaniol, Megan. Black Widow Spiders. 2016. (Creepy Crawlies Ser.). (ENG., Illus.). 24p. (J). (gr. k-3). lib. bdg. 25.95 *(978-1-62617-299-9(4)*, Blastoff! Readers) Bellwether Media.

—Spiders. 2013. (Backyard Wildlife Ser.). (ENG., Illus.). 24p. (J). (gr. k-3). lib. bdg. 25.95 *(978-1-60014-921-4(9)*, Blastoff! Readers) Bellwether Media.

Bredeson, Carmen. Hair-Shooting Tarantulas & Other Weird Spiders. 2009. (I Like Weird Animals! Ser.). (Illus.). 24p. (J). (gr. 1-3). lib. bdg. 22.60 *(978-0-7660-3127-2(6)*, Enslow Elementary) Enslow Pubs., Inc.

—Tarantulas up Close. (Zoom in on Animals! Ser.). (Illus.). 24p. (J). 2012. (gr. k-18). pap. 7.95 *(978-1-59845-421-5(8))* 2008. (gr. 3-7). lib. bdg. 22.60 *(978-0-7660-3076-3(8))* Enslow Pubs., Inc. (Enslow Elementary).

Breene, Robert G., III. A Widow Spider in Its Web. 2003. (Where Do Animals Live? Ser.). (J). *(978-1-58417-186-7(3))*; pap. *(978-1-58417-187-4(1))* Lake Street Pubs.

Britton, Tamara L. Bird-Eating Spiders, 1 vol. 2011. (Spiders Set 1 *2011 Ser.). (ENG.). 24p. 25.65 *(978-1-61613-439-6(9)*, Checkerboard Library) ABDO Publishing Co.

—Black Widow Spiders, 1 vol. 2011. (Spiders Set 1 *2011 Ser.). (ENG.). 24p. 25.65 *(978-1-61613-440-2(2)*, Checkerboard Library) ABDO Publishing Co.

—Jumping Spiders, 1 vol. 2011. (Spiders Set 1 *2011 Ser.). (ENG.). 24p. 25.65 *(978-1-61613-441-9(0)*, Checkerboard Library) ABDO Publishing Co.

—Tarantula Spiders, 1 vol. 2011. (Spiders Set 1 *2011 Ser.). (ENG.). 24p. 25.65 *(978-1-61613-442-6(9)*, Checkerboard Library) ABDO Publishing Co.

—Wolf Spiders, 1 vol. 2011. (Spiders Set 1 *2011 Ser.). (ENG.). 24p. 25.65 *(978-1-61613-444-0(5)*, Checkerboard Library) ABDO Publishing Co.

Buckley, James, et al. Discovery Bugopedia. 2015. (J). lib. bdg. 33.00 *(978-0-606-36892-6(2))* Turtleback Bks.

Camisa, Kathryn. Hairy Tarantulas. 2008. (No Backbone! Ser.). (Illus.). 24p. (J). (gr. k-3). lib. bdg. 21.28 *(978-1-59716-704-8(5)*, 1284308) Bearport Publishing Co., Inc.

Canetti, Yanitzia. Canta y Cuenta Las Arañas. 2010. (J). *(978-1-59835-226-9(1))* Cambridge BrickHouse, Inc.

—1-2-3 Do, Re, Mi Spiders. 2010. (J). *(978-1-59835-225-2(3))* Cambridge BrickHouse, Inc.

Caputo, Christine A. Insects & Spiders. 2012. (Illus.). 32p. (J). *(978-0-545-46703-2(9))* Scholastic, Inc.

Carle, Eric. My Own Very Busy Spider Coloring Book. Carle, Eric, illus. 2004. (ENG., Illus.). 32p. (J). (gr. -1-k). 5.99 *(978-0-399-24309-7(7)*, Philomel Bks.) Penguin Young Readers Group.

Charner, Kathy, ed. Learn Every Day about Bugs & Spiders: 100 Best Ideas from Teachers. 2010. (Learn Every Day Ser.). (ENG.). 128p. pap. 12.95 *(978-0-87659-128-4(4)*, Gryphon House Inc) Gryphon Hse., Inc.

Christiansen, Per. Poisonous Spiders. 2008. (Nature's Monsters Ser.). (Illus.). 32p. (J). (gr. 3-6). lib. bdg. 26.00 *(978-0-8368-9219-2(4))* Stevens, Gareth Publishing LLLP.

Clapper, Nikki Bruno. Camel Spiders. 2015. (Creepy Crawlers Ser.). (ENG., Illus.). 24p. (gr. k-1). lib. bdg. 26.65 *(978-1-4914-6216-4(7))* Capstone Press of Coughlan Cos.

Clark, Willow. Black Widow Spider! 2010. (Animal Danger Zone Ser.). (ENG.). 24p. (J). (gr. k-3). lib. bdg. 22.60 *(978-1-60754-959-8(X))*; (Illus.). pap. 8.15 *(978-1-60754-968-0(9))* Windmill Bks.

Colson, Rob. Spider. 2017. (Pet to Get Ser.). (ENG., Illus.). 32p. (J). (gr. 4-6). pap. 12.99 *(978-0-7502-8941-2(4)*, Wayland) Hachette Children's Group GBR. Dist: Hachette Bk. Group.

Cooper, Jason. Black Widow Spiders. 2005. (Rourke Discovery Library). (Illus.). 24p. (J). (gr. 2-5). lib. bdg. 22.79 *(978-1-59515-445-3(0))* Rourke Educational Media.

—Black Widows. Rourke Publishing Staff, ed. 2009. 24p. (J). pap. 3.99 *(978-0-8249-5141-2(7)*, Ideal Pubns.) Worthy Publishing.

—Fishing Spiders. 2005. (Rourke Discovery Library). (Illus.). 24p. (J). (gr. 2-5). lib. bdg. 22.79 *(978-1-59515-446-0(9))* Rourke Educational Media.

—Garden Spiders. 2005. (Rourke Discovery Library). (Illus.). 24p. (J). (gr. 2-5). lib. bdg. 14.95 *(978-1-59515-447-7(7))* Rourke Educational Media.

—Jumping Spiders. 2005. (Rourke Discovery Library). (Illus.). 24p. (J). (gr. 2-5). lib. bdg. 22.79 *(978-1-59515-448-4(5))* Rourke Educational Media.

—Jumping Spiders. Rourke Publishing Staff, ed. 2009. 24p. (J). pap. 3.99 *(978-0-8249-5142-9(5)*, Ideal Pubns.) Worthy Publishing.

—Tarantulas. 2005. (Spiders Discovery Ser.). (Illus.). 24p. (J). (gr. 2-5). lib. bdg. 14.95 *(978-1-59515-449-1(3))* Rourke Educational Media.

—Tarantulas. Rourke Publishing Staff, ed. 2009. 24p. (J). pap. 3.99 *(978-0-8249-5143-6(3)*, Ideal Pubns.) Worthy Publishing.

Creepy Crawly Creatures. 2007. (ENG., Illus.). 14p. (J). (gr. -1-3). 16.95 *(978-1-58117-623-0(6)*, Intervisual/Piggy Toes) Bendon, Inc.

De Nijs, Erika. A Spider's Web. 2016. (Animal Builders Ser.). 24p. (J). pap. 8.22 *(978-1-5026-2071-2(5))* Cavendish Square Publishing.

Dell, Pamela. Arachnids. 2017. (My First Animal Kingdom Encyclopedias Ser.). (ENG., Illus.). 32p. (gr. 1-2). lib. bdg. 27.32 *(978-1-5157-3924-1(4)*, Aplus Bks.) Capstone Press of Coughlan Cos.

Dellaccio, Tanya. Spiders Lived with the Dinosaurs! 2016. (Living with the Dinosaurs Ser.). 00024p. (J). pap. 8.15 ***(978-1-4824-5681-3(8))*** Stevens, Gareth Publishing LLLP.

Dinaberg, Leslie. Spider Life. 2006. (Reading Rocks! Ser.). (ENG., Illus.). 32p. (J). (gr. 2-5). 28.50 *(978-1-59296-737-7(X)*, 200723) Child's World, Inc., The.

Dorling Kindersley Publishing Staff & Buckley, Jim. Spiders & Other Deadly Animals. 2016. (DK Readers Ser.). (ENG., Illus.). 96p. (J). (gr. 3-7). lib. bdg. 14.99 *(978-1-4654-5211-5(7)*, DK Children) Dorling Kindersley Publishing, Inc.

Editors of Kingfisher. Scary Spiders. 2016. (It's All About... Ser.). (ENG., Illus.). 32p. (J). pap. 5.99 *(978-0-7534-7265-1(1)*, 9780753472651, Kingfisher) Roaring Brook Pr.

Ethan, Eric. Black Widow Spiders. 2003. (Dangerous Spiders Ser.). (Illus.). 24p. (gr. 1-4). lib. bdg. 23.00 *(978-0-8368-3765-0(7)*, Gareth Stevens Learning Library) Stevens, Gareth Publishing LLLP.

—Brown Recluse Spiders. 2003. (Dangerous Spiders Ser.). (Illus.). 24p. (gr. 1-4). lib. bdg. 23.00 *(978-0-8368-3766-7(5)*, Gareth Stevens Learning Library) Stevens, Gareth Publishing LLLP.

—Funnel Web Spiders. 2003. (Dangerous Spiders Ser.). (Illus.). 24p. (gr. 1-4). lib. bdg. 23.00 *(978-0-8368-3767-4(3)*, Gareth Stevens Learning Library) Stevens, Gareth Publishing LLLP.

—Hobo Spiders. 2003. (Dangerous Spiders Ser.). (Illus.). 24p. (gr. 1-4). lib. bdg. 23.00 *(978-0-8368-3768-1(1)*, Gareth Stevens Learning Library) Stevens, Gareth Publishing LLLP.

—Tarantulas. 2003. (Dangerous Spiders Ser.). (Illus.). 24p. (gr. 1-4). lib. bdg. 23.00 *(978-0-8368-3769-8(X)*, Gareth Stevens Learning Library) Stevens, Gareth Publishing LLLP.

—Yellow Sac Spiders. 2003. (Dangerous Spiders Ser.). (Illus.). 24p. (gr. 1-4). lib. bdg. 23.00 *(978-0-8368-3770-4(3)*, Gareth Stevens Learning Library) Stevens, Gareth Publishing LLLP.

Evans, Arthur V., et al. Grzimek's Student Animal Life Resource, 2 vols. 2005. (Illus.). l, 442p. (J). *(978-0-7876-9245-2(X))*; *(978-0-7876-9244-5(1))* Cengage Gale. (UXL).

Evans, Barbara Greene. Oscar, the Inquisitive Spider. Greene, Kelly Evelyn, illus. 2013. (ENG.). 45p. (J). pap. 24.95 *(978-1-4787-1779-9(3))* Outskirts Pr., Inc.

Farndon, John. Incredible Bugs. Portolano, Cristina, illus. 2016. (Animal Bests Ser.). (ENG.). 32p. (J). (gr. 3-6). lib. bdg. 26.65 *(978-1-5124-0640-5(6))* Lerner Publishing Group.

Franchino, Vicky. Tarantulas. 2012. (Nature's Children Ser.). (ENG., Illus.). 48p. (J). pap. 6.95 *(978-0-531-21083-3(9))*; (gr. 3-5). lib. bdg. 28.00 *(978-0-531-20908-0(3))* Scholastic Library Publishing. (Children's Pr.).

Franks, Katie. Spiders up Close. (Nature up Close Ser.). 24p. 2009. (gr. k-1). 42.50 *(978-1-61514-828-8(0))* 2008. (Illus.). (J). (gr. -1-3). lib. bdg. 22.60 *(978-1-4042-4138-1(8))* Rosen Publishing Group, Inc., The. (PowerKids Pr.).

—Spiders up Close / Las Aranas. 2009. (Nature up Close / la naturaleza de cerca Ser.). (ENG & SPA.). 24p. (gr. k-1). 42.50 *(978-1-61514-834-9(5)*, Editorial Buenas Letras) Rosen Publishing Group, Inc., The.

—Spiders up Close/Las Aranas. Sanz, Pilar, tr. from ENG. 2008. (Nature up Close / la Naturaleza de Cerca Ser.). (Illus.). 24p. (J). (gr. -1-3). lib. bdg. 22.60 *(978-1-4042-7679-6(3)*, Editorial Buenas Letras) Rosen Publishing Group, Inc., The.

Fridell, Ron & Walsh, Patricia. La Araña, 1 vol. 2010. (Ciclo de Vida Ser.).Tr. of Spider. (SPA & ENG.). 32p. (gr. 1-3). 27.32 *(978-1-4329-4372-1(3))*; pap. 8.29 *(978-1-4329-4389-9(8))* Heinemann-Raintree.

Furstinger, Nancy. Spiders Are Awesome. 2018. (ENG.). 32p. (gr. 3-6). 31.35 ***(978-1-63235-441-9(1)***, 12-Story Library) Pr. Room Editions LLC.

Gallagher, Debbie. Spiders. 2011. (Mighty Minibeasts Ser.). 32p. (J). (gr. 2). 28.50 *(978-1-60870-547-4(1))* Marshall Cavendish Corp.

Ganeri, Anita. Tarantula, 1 vol. 2010. (Day in the Life: Rain Forest Animals Ser.). (ENG.). 24p. (gr. k-2). 23.32 *(978-1-4329-4109-3(7)*, Heinemann Read & Learn) Heinemann-Raintree.

Gareth Stevens Publishing Staff, contrib. by. Spiders. 2004. (All about Wild Animals Ser.). (Illus.). 32p. (gr. k-4). lib. bdg. 26.00 *(978-0-8368-4172-5(7)*, Gareth Stevens Learning Library) Stevens, Gareth Publishing LLLP.

Gilpin, Rebecca. Spiders. Kushii, Tetsuo & Wright, David, illus. 2006. (Usborne Beginners Ser.). 32p. (J). (gr. 1). lib. bdg. 12.99 *(978-1-58086-946-1(7)*, Usborne) EDC Publishing.

—Spiders. Kushii, Tetsuo et al, illus. 2006. (Beginners Nature: Level 1 Ser.). 32p. (J). (gr. k-2). 4.99 *(978-0-7945-1398-6(0)*, Usborne) EDC Publishing.

Giulieri, Anne. The Banana Spider, 1 vol. 2012. (Engage Literacy Blue Ser.). (ENG.). 32p. (gr. k-2). pap. 5.99 *(978-1-4296-8982-3(X)*, Engage Literacy) Capstone Press of Coughlan Cos.

Goldish, Meish. Jumping Spiders. 2008. (No Backbone! Ser.). (Illus.). 24p. (J). (gr. k-3). lib. bdg. 21.28 *(978-1-59716-705-5(3)*, 1284307) Bearport Publishing Co., Inc.

—Spider-Tizers & Other Creepy Treats. 2009. (Extreme Cuisine Ser.). (Illus.). 24p. (J). (gr. 1-4). lib. bdg. 22.61 *(978-1-59716-759-8(2))* Bearport Publishing Co., Inc.

—Spooky Wolf Spiders. 2008. (No Backbone! Ser.). (Illus.). 24p. (J). (gr. k-3). lib. bdg. 21.28 *(978-1-59716-706-2(1)*, 1284306) Bearport Publishing Co., Inc.

—Tricky Trapdoor Spiders. 2008. (No Backbone! Ser.). (Illus.). 24p. (J). (gr. k-3). lib. bdg. 21.28 *(978-1-59716-707-9(X)*, 1284305) Bearport Publishing Co., Inc.

Gordon, Sharon. Guess Who Spins. 2004. (Bookworms: Guess Who Ser.). (SPA & ENG., Illus.). 31p. (J). (gr. 3-7). lib. bdg. 21.36 *(978-0-7614-1768-2(0)*, Benchmark Bks.) Marshall Cavendish Corp.

—Guess Who Spins: Adivina Quién Teje. 2007. (Bookworms Ser.). (SPA & ENG.). 32p. (gr. k-2). 15.95 *(978-0-7614-2871-8(2))*; 15.95 *(978-0-7614-2887-9(9))* Marshall Cavendish Corp.

Graham, Chris. Spiders! 2008. (Real Readers - Upper Emergent Ser.). (ENG., Illus.). 12p. (gr. 1-2). pap. 5.90 *(978-0-8239-8198-4(3))* Rosen Publishing Group, Inc., The.

Gravel, Élise. The Spider. (Disgusting Critters Ser.). (ENG., Illus.). 32p. (J). (gr. 1-4). 2016. pap. 5.99 *(978-1-101-91854-8(3))* 2015. 10.99 *(978-1-77049-664-4(5))* Tundra Bks. CAN. (Tundra Bks.). Dist: Penguin Random Hse. LLC.

Gregory, Josh. Wolf Spiders. 2013. (ENG.). 48p. (J). 28.00 *(978-0-531-23363-4(4))*; pap. 6.95 *(978-0-531-25161-4(6))* Scholastic Library Publishing.

Group/McGraw-Hill, Wright. Spider & Buffalo: Level N, 6 vols. (Summer Skies Ser.). 128p. (gr. 3-6). 36.95 *(978-0-322-05887-3(2))* Wright Group/McGraw-Hill.

Guillain, Charlotte. Super Spiders, 1 vol. 2013. (Walk on the Wild Side Ser.). (ENG.). 32p. (gr. 1-3). 29.99 *(978-1-4109-5219-6(3))*; pap. 8.95 *(978-1-4109-5226-4(6))* Heinemann-Raintree. (Read Me!).

Hamilton, Robert M. Ticks. 2015. (Freaky Freeloaders: Bugs That Feed on People Ser.). (ENG., Illus.). 24p. (J). (gr. 2-3). 23.60 *(978-1-4994-0770-9(X)*, PowerKids Pr.) Rosen Publishing Group, Inc., The.

Hamilton, S. L. Spiders. 2013. (Xtreme Pets Ser.). (Illus.). 32p. (J). (gr. 3-9). lib. bdg. 27.07 *(978-1-61783-975-7(2)*, Abdo & Daughters) ABDO Publishing Co.

Harris, Monica. Black Widow Spider. 2003. (Bug Bks.). (Illus.). 32p. (J). lib. bdg. 22.79 *(978-1-4034-0762-7(2))* Heinemann-Raintree.

—Tarantula. 2003. (Bug Bks.). (Illus.). 32p. (J). lib. bdg. 22.79 *(978-1-4034-0764-1(9))* Heinemann-Raintree.

Hayes, Amy. Funnel-Web Spiders. 2017. (Spiders: Eight-Legged Terrors Ser.). 24p. (J). (gr. 2-3). pap. 8.15 ***(978-1-5382-0205-0(0))*** Stevens, Gareth Publishing LLLP.

Heos, Bridget. Stronger Than Steel: Spider Silk DNA & the Quest for Better Bulletproof Vests, Sutures, & Parachute Rope. Comins, Andy, illus. 2013. (Scientists in the Field Ser.). (ENG.). 80p. (J). (gr. 5-7). 18.99 *(978-0-547-68126-9(7))* Houghton Mifflin Harcourt Publishing Co.

Herrington, Lisa M. It's a Good Thing There Are Spiders. 2014. (Rookie Read-About(r) Science — It's a Good Thing... Ser.). (ENG.). 32p. (J). pap. 5.95 *(978-0-531-22832-6(0))*; lib. bdg. 25.00 *(978-0-531-22360-4(4))* Scholastic Library Publishing.

Hesper, Sam. Black Widow Spiders, 1 vol. 2015. (ENG., Illus.). 24p. (J). lib. bdg. 23.60 *(978-1-4777-5745-1(7)*, PowerKids Pr.) Rosen Publishing Group, Inc., The.

Hileman, Jane. Spiders Are Hunters. 2015. (2B Wild Animals Ser.). (ENG., Illus.). 32p. (J). pap. 5.99 *(978-1-63437-124-7(0))* American Reading Co.

Hirschmann, Kris. Deadliest Spiders. 2016. (ENG.). 80p. (J). (gr. 5-12). lib. bdg. *(978-1-68282-058-2(0))* ReferencePoint Pr., Inc.

Houghton, Gillian. Abejas: Por Dentro y Por Fuera. Velazquez De Leon, Mauricio, tr. Studio Stalio, illus. 2004. (Explora la Naturaleza (Getting into Nature) Ser.). (SPA.). 32p. (YA). (gr. 3-6). lib. bdg. 25.25 *(978-1-4042-2862-7(4))* Rosen Publishing Group, Inc., The.

—Aranas: Por Dentro y Por Fuera. Gonzalez, Tomas, tr. Studio Stalio, illus. 2004. (Explora la Naturaleza (Getting into Nature) Ser.). (SPA.). 27p. (YA). (gr. 3-6). lib. bdg. 25.25 *(978-1-4042-2867-2(5))* Rosen Publishing Group, Inc., The.

—Aranas: Por dentro y por fuera (Spiders: Inside & Out) 2009. (Explora la Naturaleza (Getting into Nature) Ser.). 32p. (gr. 3-4). 47.90 *(978-1-61512-334-6(2)*, Editorial Buenas Letras) Rosen Publishing Group, Inc., The.

—Spider. 2004. (Getting into Nature Ser.). (Illus.). 32p. (J). lib. bdg. 25.25 *(978-0-8239-4209-1(0))* Rosen Publishing Group, Inc., The.

—Spiders: Inside & Out. 2009. (Getting into Nature Ser.). 32p. (gr. 3-4). 47.90 *(978-1-61512-725-2(9)*, PowerKids Pr.) Rosen Publishing Group, Inc., The.

How Spiders Live, 6 vols. (Sunshinetm Science Ser.). 24p. (gr. 1-2). 36.95 *(978-0-7802-0534-5(0))*; 31.50 *(978-0-7802-0283-2(X))* Wright Group/McGraw-Hill.

Huggins-Cooper, Lynn. Minibeasts. 2003. (Starters Ser.). 24p. (J). lib. bdg. 21.35 *(978-1-58340-263-4(2))* Black Rabbit Bks.

—Scary Spiders. 2006. (Killer Nature! Ser.). (Illus.). 32p. (J). (gr. 3-5). lib. bdg. 28.50 *(978-1-58340-935-0(1))* Black Rabbit Bks.

Impey, Rose. Spiders. 2009. (Wild Reads Ser.). (ENG., Illus.). 32p. (YA). (gr. k). pap. 4.95 *(978-0-19-911933-2(3))* Oxford Univ. Pr., Inc.

Ingram, Kevin. Spider. 2017. (Up Close & Scary Ser.). (Illus.). 32p. (gr. 2-5). 31.35 ***(978-1-911242-06-2(7))*** Book Hse. GBR. Dist: Black Rabbit Bks.

Insects & Spiders. (Action Bks.). 64p. (J). (gr. 3-7). pap. *(978-1-882210-67-1(0))* Action Publishing, Inc.

Iorio, Nicole & Time for Kids Editors. Spiders! 2005. (Time for Kids Science Scoops Ser.). (ENG., Illus.). 48p. (J). 14.99 *(978-0-06-057635-6(9))*; (gr. 1-3). pap. 3.99 *(978-0-06-057634-9(0))* HarperCollins Pubs.

Ives, Penny & Hilb, Nora, illus. Itsy Bitsy Spider. 2017. (Classic Books with Holes 8x8 Ser.). (ENG.). 16p. (J). pap. ***(978-1-84643-974-2(4))*** Child's Play International Ltd.

Jackson, Tom. Spiders. 2008. (Nature's Children. Set 3 Ser.). (Illus.). 52p. (J). *(978-0-7172-6287-8(1))* Grolier, Ltd.

—Spooky Spiders. 2010. (Dangerous Animals Ser.). (ENG.). 32p. (J). (gr. 2-6). pap. 10.50 *(978-1-4339-4050-7(7)*, Gareth Stevens Learning Library); (YA). (gr. 3-6). lib. bdg. 26.60 *(978-1-4339-4049-1(3))* Stevens, Gareth Publishing LLLP.

Kalman, Bobbie & Smithyman, Kathryn. El Ciclo de Vida de la Araña. 2006. (Ciclos de Vida Ser.). (SPA., Illus.). 32p. (J). (gr. 3-7). pap. *(978-0-7787-8714-3(1))* Crabtree Publishing Co.

—El Ciclo de Vida de la Arana. 2006. (Ciclos de Vida Ser.). (SPA., Illus.). 32p. (J). (gr. 3-7). lib. bdg. *(978-0-7787-8668-9(4))* Crabtree Publishing Co.

Kenney, Karen Latchana. Spin with the Spiders, 1 vol. Hedicker, Lisa, illus. 2010. (Bug's World Ser.). (ENG.). 32p. 28.50 *(978-1-60270-789-4(8)*, Looking Glass Library-Nonfiction) Magic Wagon.

Keppeler, Jill. Black Widows. 2017. (Spiders: Eight-Legged Terrors Ser.). 24p. (J). (gr. 2-3). pap. 8.15 ***(978-1-4824-6495-5(0))*** Stevens, Gareth Publishing LLLP.

Khu, Jannell. Spiders. 2009. (My World of Animals Ser.). 24p. (gr. 1-1). 37.50 *(978-1-61514-713-7(6)*, PowerKids Pr.) Rosen Publishing Group, Inc., The.

—Spiders / Arañas. 2009. (My World of Animals / Yo y los animales Ser.). (ENG & SPA.). 24p. (gr. 1-1). 37.50 *(978-1-61514-718-2(7)*, Editorial Buenas Letras) Rosen Publishing Group, Inc., The.

—Spiders/Aranas. Beullens, Nathalie, tr. 2004. (My World of Animals Ser.). (ENG & SPA., Illus.). 24p. (J). (gr. k-1). lib. bdg. 16.00 *(978-1-4042-7523-2(1)*, PowerKids Pr.) Rosen Publishing Group, Inc., The.

Klepeis, Alicia Z. Assassin Bug vs. Ogre-Faced Spider: When Cunning Hunters Collide. 2016. (Bug Wars Ser.). (ENG., Illus.). 32p. (gr. 3-4). lib. bdg. 27.99 *(978-1-4914-8065-6(3)*, Edge Bks.) Capstone Press of Coughlan Cos.

Kolpin, Molly. Black Widow Spiders, 1 vol. 2010. (Spiders Ser.). (ENG.). 24p. (gr. 1-2). lib. bdg. 25.32 *(978-1-4296-4519-5(9)*, First Facts) Capstone Press of Coughlan Cos.

—Daddy Long-Leg Spiders, 1 vol. 2010. (Spiders Ser.). (ENG.). 24p. (gr. 1-2). lib. bdg. 25.32 *(978-1-4296-5390-9(6)*, First Facts) Capstone Press of Coughlan Cos.

—Tarantulas, 1 vol. 2010. (Spiders Ser.). (ENG.). 24p. (gr. 1-2). lib. bdg. 25.32 *(978-1-4296-4520-1(2)*, First Facts) Capstone Press of Coughlan Cos.

—Trapdoor Spiders, 1 vol. 2010. (Spiders Ser.). (ENG.). 24p. (gr. 1-2). lib. bdg. 25.32 *(978-1-4296-4521-8(0)*, First Facts) Capstone Press of Coughlan Cos.

Kopp, Megan. Black Widow Spiders. 2011. (gr. 2-4). (J). pap. 12.95 *(978-1-61690-628-3(6)*, AV2 by Weigl); (Illus.). 24p. (YA). 27.13 *(978-1-61690-622-1(7))* Weigl Pubs., Inc.

Kubler, Annie, illus. Incey Wincey Spider. 2005. (ENG.). 12p. (J). bds. *(978-1-904550-03-7(7))* Child's Play International Ltd.

Kuskowski, Alex. Tricky Tarantulas, 1 vol. Nobens, C. A., illus. 2013. (Unusual Pets Ser.). (ENG.). 24p. (J). (gr. -1-3). 24.21 *(978-1-61783-402-8(5))* ABDO Publishing Co.

Ladybird. Minibeasts. 2016. (Read It Yourself with Ladybird Ser.). (ENG., Illus.). 48p. (J). 5.99 *(978-0-241-23737-3(8))* Penguin Bks., Ltd. GBR. Dist: Independent Pubs. Group.

Landau, Elaine. Creepy Spiders. 2003. (Fearsome, Scary, & Creepy Animals Ser.). (Illus.). 48p. (J). (gr. 1-4). lib. bdg. 23.93 *(978-0-7660-2059-7(2))* Enslow Pubs., Inc.

Lawrence, Ellen. A Spider's Life. 2012. (Animal Diaries: Life Cycles Ser.). 24p. (J). (gr. -1-3). lib. bdg. 23.93 *(978-1-61772-414-5(9))* Bearport Publishing Co., Inc.

Leavitt, Amie Jane. Care for a Pet Tarantula. 2007. (How to Convince Your Parents You Can ... Ser.). (Illus.). 32p. (J). (gr. 1-4). lib. bdg. 25.70 *(978-1-58415-603-1(1))* Mitchell Lane Pubs., Inc.

Levy, Janey. Bird-Eating Spiders. 2017. (Spiders: Eight-Legged Terrors Ser.). 24p. (gr. 2-3). pap. 48.90 ***(978-1-4824-6485-6(3))*** Stevens, Gareth Publishing LLLP.

Lewis, Clare. Bug Body Parts. 2015. (J). *(978-1-4846-2555-2(2))* Heinemann-Raintree.

Llewellyn, Claire, et al. Spiders: Deadly Predators. 7th ed. 2014. (Kingfisher Readers Ser.). (ENG., Illus.). 32p. (J). (gr. k-3). 12.99 *(978-0-7534-7150-0(7)*, 9780753471500, Kingfisher) Roaring Brook Pr.

—Spiders - Kingfisher Readers: Deadly Predators. 2014. (Kingfisher Readers Ser.). (ENG., Illus.). 32p. (J). (gr. k-3). pap. 3.99 *(978-0-7534-7151-7(5)*, 9780753471517, Kingfisher) Roaring Brook Pr.

Lomberg, Michelle. Caring for Your Spider. 2004. (Caring for Your Pet Ser.). (Illus.). 32p. (J). (gr. 4-7). per. 9.95 *(978-1-59036-155-9(5))*; lib. bdg. 26.00 *(978-1-59036-120-7(2))* Weigl Pubs., Inc.

—Spider. 2009. (My Pet Ser.). (Illus.). 32p. (J). (gr. 3-5). pap. 9.95 *(978-1-60596-095-1(0))*; lib. bdg. 26.00 *(978-1-60596-094-4(2))* Weigl Pubs., Inc.

Lomberg, Michelle & Gillespie, Katie. Spider. 2015. (J). *(978-1-4896-2970-8(X))* Weigl Pubs., Inc.

Lunis, Natalie. Deadly Black Widows. (No Backbone! Spiders Ser.). 24p. (J). (gr. k-3). 2016. (ENG.). pap. 7.95 ***(978-1-944998-44-8(6))*** 2008. (Illus.). lib. bdg. 21.28 *(978-1-59716-667-6(7)*, 1284310) Bearport Publishing Co., Inc.

—Inside the Spider's Web. 2013. (Science Slam: Snug As a Bug-Where Bugs Live Ser.). 24p. (J). (gr. -1-3). lib. bdg. 23.93 *(978-1-61772-903-4(5))* Bearport Publishing Co., Inc.

—Inside the Tarantula's Burrow. 2013. (Science Slam: Snug As a Bug-Where Bugs Live Ser.). 24p. (J). (gr. -1-3). lib. bdg. 23.93 *(978-1-61772-907-2(8))* Bearport Publishing Co., Inc.

Lynette, Rachel. Tarantulas. 2013. (Monsters of the Animal Kingdom Ser.). (ENG., Illus.). 24p. (J). (gr. k-5). pap. 8.25 *(978-1-4488-9720-9(3))*; lib. bdg. 22.60 *(978-1-4488-9632-5(0))* Rosen Publishing Group, Inc., The. (PowerKids Pr.).

Machajewski, Sarah. Brown Recluse Spiders. 2017. (Spiders: Eight-Legged Terrors Ser.). 24p. (J). (gr. 2-3). pap. 8.15 ***(978-1-5382-0202-9(6))*** Stevens, Gareth Publishing LLLP.

Macheske, Felicia. Hairy Hunter. 2016. (Guess What Ser.). (ENG.). 24p. (J). (gr. k-2). 28.50 *(978-1-63470-722-0(2),* 207599) Cherry Lake Publishing.

Markle, Sandra. Black Widows: Deadly Biters. 2011. (Arachnid World Ser.). (ENG., Illus.). 48p. (J). (gr. 4-8). lib. bdg. 29.27 *(978-0-7613-5038-5(1))* Lerner Publishing Group.

—Crab Spiders: Phantom Hunters. 2012. (Arachnid World Ser.). (ENG.). 48p. (gr. 4-8). lib. bdg. 29.27 *(978-0-7613-5045-3(4))* Lerner Publishing Group.

—Fishing Spiders: Water Ninjas. 2012. (Arachnid World Ser.). (ENG., Illus.). 48p. (gr. 4-8). lib. bdg. 29.27 *(978-0-7613-5044-6(6))* Lerner Publishing Group.

—Jumping Spiders: Gold-Medal Stalkers. 2012. (Arachnid World Ser.). (ENG.). 48p. (gr. 4-8). lib. bdg. 29.27 *(978-0-7613-5047-7(0))* Lerner Publishing Group.

—Orb Weavers: Hungry Spinners. 2011. (Arachnid World Ser.). (ENG.). 48p. (gr. 4-8). 29.27 *(978-0-7613-5039-2(X))* Lerner Publishing Group.

—Spiders: Biggest! Littlest! Pollard, Simon, photos by. 2011. (Biggest! Littlest! Ser.). (ENG., Illus.). 32p. (J). pap. 10.95 *(978-1-59078-875-2(3))* Boyds Mills Pr.

—Wolf Spiders: Mothers on Guard. 2011. (Arachnid World Ser.). (ENG.). 48p. (gr. 4-8). lib. bdg. 29.27 *(978-0-7613-5040-8(3))* Lerner Publishing Group.

Marsh, Laura. National Geographic Readers: Spiders. 2011. (Readers Ser.). (ENG., Illus.). 32p. (J). (gr. k-3). lib. bdg. 13.90 *(978-1-4263-0852-9(3),* National Geographic Children's Bks.) National Geographic Society.

—Spiders. 2011. (Readers Ser.). (ENG., Illus.). 32p. (J). (gr. k-3). pap. 3.99 *(978-1-4263-0851-2(5),* National Geographic Children's Bks.) National Geographic Society.

Marshall Cavendish Corporation Staff, contrib. by. Insects & Spiders of the World, 11 vols., Set. 2003. (Illus.). 704p. lib. bdg. 471.36 *(978-0-7614-7334-3(3),* Marshall Cavendish Reference Bks.) Marshall Cavendish Corp.

Marsico, Katie. Black Widow Spiders. 2014. (Nature's Children Ser.). (ENG.). (J). lib. bdg. 28.00 *(978-0-531-21225-7(4))* Scholastic Library Publishing.

—Spiders Weave Webs. 2015. (Tell Me Why Library). (ENG., Illus.). 24p. (J). (gr. 2-5). 27.07 *(978-1-63362-617-1(2),* 206652) Cherry Lake Publishing.

Mattern, Joanne. Water Spiders, 1 vol. 2010. (Spiders Ser.). (ENG.). 24p. (gr. 1-2). lib. bdg. 25.32 *(978-1-4296-4522-5(9),* First Facts) Capstone Press of Coughlan Cos.

McAneney, Caitie. Scorpion vs. Black Widow. 2015. (Bizarre Beast Battles Ser.). (ENG., Illus.). 24p. (J). (gr. 2-3). pap. 8.15 *(978-1-4824-2792-9(3))* Stevens, Gareth Publishing LLLP.

McEvey, Shane F. & Australian Museum Archives Staff. Insects & Spiders Series, 6 bks. Incl. Moths & Butterflies. (Illus.). (J). (gr. 4-18). 2001. 16.95 *(978-0-7910-6598-3(7),* 010555, Chelsea Hse.); (Illus.). 101.70 *(978-0-7910-6594-5(4),* 010550S, Chelsea Hse.) Facts On File, Inc.

McFee, Shane. Deadly Spiders. 2009. (Poison! Ser.). 24p. (gr. 2-3). 42.50 *(978-1-60851-323-9(8),* PowerKids Pr.) Rosen Publishing Group, Inc., The.

McGavin, George C. Amazing Insects & Spiders. 2008. (Amazing Life Cycles Ser.). (Illus.). 32p. (gr. 2-6). lib. bdg. 26.00 *(978-0-8368-8899-7(5),* Gareth Stevens Learning Library) Stevens, Gareth Publishing LLLP.

McGinty, Alice B. The Jumping Spider. 2009. (Library of Spiders Ser.). 24p. (gr. 3-3). 42.50 *(978-1-60853-872-0(9),* PowerKids Pr.) Rosen Publishing Group, Inc., The.

—The Tarantula. 2009. (Library of Spiders Ser.). 24p. (gr. 3-3). 42.50 *(978-1-60853-873-7(7),* PowerKids Pr.) Rosen Publishing Group, Inc., The.

—The Wolf Spider. 2009. (Library of Spiders Ser.). 24p. (gr. 3-3). 42.50 *(978-1-60853-874-4(5),* PowerKids Pr.) Rosen Publishing Group, Inc., The.

McNab, Chris & Sutherland, Jonathan. Dangerous Insects & Spiders. 2006. (Nature's Monsters Ser.). (Illus.). 32p. (gr. 2-6). lib. bdg. 26.00 *(978-0-8368-6848-7(X),* Gareth Stevens Learning Library) Stevens, Gareth Publishing LLLP.

—Giant Spiders & Insects. 2006. (Nature's Monsters Ser.). (Illus.). 32p. (gr. 2-6). lib. bdg. 26.00 *(978-0-8368-6850-0(1),* Gareth Stevens Learning Library) Stevens, Gareth Publishing LLLP.

Meachen Rau, Dana. Spin, Spider, Spin! 2007. (Go, Critter, Go! Ser.). (Illus.). 24p. (gr. k-1). lib. bdg. 15.95 *(978-0-7614-2653-0(1),* Benchmark Bks.) Marshall Cavendish Corp.

—Spin, Spider, Spin!/Teje Arana, Teje! 2007. (Go, Critter, Go!/¡Vamos Criaturita, Vamos! Ser.). (SPA & ENG., Illus.). 24p. (gr. k-1). lib. bdg. 15.95 *(978-0-7614-2818-3(6),* Benchmark Bks.) Marshall Cavendish Corp.

—Teje Arana, Teje! 2007. (¡Vamos Criaturita, Vamos! Ser.). (SPA & ENG., Illus.). 24p. (gr. k-1). lib. bdg. 15.95 *(978-0-7614-2794-0(5),* Benchmark Bks.) Marshall Cavendish Corp.

Mehta, Baldev. I Like Spiders. 2009. (Illus.). 24p. pap. 11.49 *(978-1-4490-2879-4(9))* AuthorHouse.

Meinking, Mary. Tarantula vs. Bird, 1 vol. 2011. (Predator vs. Prey Ser.). (ENG., Illus.). 32p. (gr. 1-2). pap. 8.29 *(978-1-4109-3947-0(2),* Read Me!) Heinemann-Raintree.

Merlino, Kim. Insects & Spiders: Grades 2 & 3. (Illus.). (J). pap., wbk. ed. 4.99 *(978-0-88743-960-5(8))* School Zone Publishing Co.

Miller, Jake. Cobweb Weavers. (Library of Spiders Ser.). 24p. 2009. (gr. 3-3). 42.50 *(978-1-60853-866-9(4),* PowerKids Pr.) 2004. (Illus.). (YA). (gr. 2-5). lib. bdg. 22.60 *(978-0-8239-6708-7(5))* Rosen Publishing Group, Inc., The.

—Fishing Spiders. (Library of Spiders Ser.). 24p. 2009. (gr. 3-3). 42.50 *(978-1-60853-868-3(0))* 2004. (Illus.). (J). lib. bdg. 22.60 *(978-0-8239-6711-7(5))* Rosen Publishing Group, Inc., The. (PowerKids Pr.).

—Funnel Weavers. (Library of Spiders Ser.). 24p. 2009. (gr. 3-3). 42.50 *(978-1-60853-869-0(9))* 2004. (Illus.). (J). lib. bdg. 22.60 *(978-0-8239-6709-4(3))* Rosen Publishing Group, Inc., The. (PowerKids Pr.).

—Trap-Door Spiders. 2009. (Library of Spiders Ser.). 24p. (gr. 3-3). 42.50 *(978-1-60853-875-1(3),* PowerKids Pr.) Rosen Publishing Group, Inc., The.

—Trap Door Spiders. 2004. (Library of Spiders Ser.). (Illus.). 24p. (J). lib. bdg. 22.60 *(978-0-8239-6710-0(7),* PowerKids Pr.) Rosen Publishing Group, Inc., The.

Mitchell, Susan K. Biggest vs. Smallest Creepy, Crawly Creatures. 2010. (Biggest vs. Smallest Animals Ser.). (Illus.). 24p. (J). 22.60 *(978-0-7660-3581-2(6),* Enslow Elementary) Enslow Pubs., Inc.

Montgomery, Sy. The Tarantula Scientist. Bishop, Nic, photos by. 2007. (Scientists in the Field Ser.). (ENG., Illus.). 80p. (J). (gr. 5-7). pap. 9.99 *(978-0-618-91577-4(X))* Houghton Mifflin Harcourt Publishing Co.

Morgan, Emily. Next Time You See a Spiderweb. 2016. (Next Time You See Ser.). (ENG., Illus.). 32p. (J). (gr. k-2). pap. 12.95 *(978-1-938946-34-9(0))* National Science Teachers Assn.

Morgan, Sally. Spiders. 2010. (Amazing Animal Hunters Ser.). 32p. (J). 28.50 *(978-1-60753-048-0(1))* Amicus Publishing.

—Spiders. 2004. (QEB Animal Lives Ser.). (Illus.). 32p. (J). lib. bdg. 18.95 *(978-1-59566-036-7(4))* QEB Publishing Inc.

—Spiders. 2012. (Illus.). 32p. (gr. 3-5). pap. 8.95 *(978-1-926722-52-8(3))* Saunders Bk. Co. CAN. Dist: RiverStream Publishing.

Morley, Christine. Freaky Facts about Spiders. 2007. (Freaky Facts Ser.). (ENG., Illus.). 32p. (J). (gr. 2-5). 13.95 *(978-1-58728-596-7(7));* pap. 8.95 *(978-1-58728-597-4(5))* Cooper Square Publishing Llc.

Murawski, Darlyne A. Spiders & Their Webs. Murawski, Darlyne A., photos by. 2007. (Illus.). 31p. (J). reprint ed. 17.00 *(978-1-4223-6813-8(0))* DIANE Publishing Co.

—Spiders & Their Webs. 2004. (ENG., Illus.). 32p. (J). (gr. 1-4). 25.90 *(978-0-7922-6994-6(2));* 16.95 *(978-0-7922-6979-3(9))* National Geographic Society. (National Geographic Children's Bks.).

Murray, Julie. Black Widow Spiders, 1 vol. 2003. (Buddy Book Ser.). (ENG.). 24p. (J). (gr. 1-4). 25.65 *(978-1-57765-728-6(4))* ABDO Publishing Co.

—Jumping Spiders, 1 vol. 2005. (Animal Kingdom Set Ii Ser.). (ENG., Illus.). 24p. (J). (gr. k-4). 25.65 *(978-1-59197-323-2(6),* Buddy Bks.) ABDO Publishing Co.

—Tarantula Spiders, 1 vol. 2003. (Buddy Book Ser.). (ENG.). 24p. (gr. k-4). 25.65 *(978-1-57765-729-3(2),* Buddy Bks.) ABDO Publishing Co.

—Wolf Spiders, 1 vol. 2005. (Animal Kingdom Set Ii Ser.). (ENG., Illus.). 24p. (gr. k-4). 25.65 *(978-1-59197-339-3(2),* Buddy Bks.) ABDO Publishing Co.

Murray, Laura K. Spiders. 2015. (Illus.). 24p. (J). *(978-1-60818-584-9(2),* Creative Education) Creative Co., The.

—Spiders: Seedlings. 2016. (Seedlings Ser.). (ENG.). 24p. (J). (gr. k-2). pap. 7.99 *(978-1-62832-189-0(X),* Creative Paperbacks) Creative Co., The.

O'Brien, Lindsy. Tarantula vs. Tarantula Hawk: Clash of the Giants. 2016. (Bug Wars Ser.). (ENG., Illus.). 32p. (gr. 3-4). lib. bdg. 27.99 *(978-1-4914-8064-9(5),* Edge Bks.) Capstone Press of Coughlan Cos.

Orme, David. Bugs & Spiders. 2010. (Fact to Fiction Grafx Ser.). (Illus.). 36p. (J). lib. bdg. 16.95 *(978-1-60686-465-4(3))* Perfection Learning Corp.

Owen, Ruth. Science & Craft Projects with Insects, Spiders, & Other Minibeasts. 2013. (Get Crafty Outdoors Ser.). (ENG., Illus.). 32p. (J). (gr. k-3). 26.50 *(978-1-4777-0245-1(8));* pap. 11.75 *(978-1-4777-0253-6(9))* Rosen Publishing Group, Inc., The. (PowerKids Pr.).

Pallotta, Jerry. Tarantula vs. Scorpion. Bolster, Robert, illus. 2016. (Who Would Win? Ser.). (ENG.). 32p. (J). (gr. 1-3). pap. 3.99 *(978-0-545-30172-5(6))* Scholastic, Inc.

Parker, Steve. Insects & Spiders. 2015. (100 Facts You Should Know Ser.). (ENG., Illus.). 48p. (J). (gr. 4-5). pap. 14.05 *(978-1-4824-3203-9(X))* Stevens, Gareth Publishing LLLP.

—Spiders. Draper, Richard, illus. 2010. (I Love Animals Ser.). (ENG.). 24p. (J). (gr. 1-5). pap. 8.15 *(978-1-61533-256-4(1));* lib. bdg. 22.60 *(978-1-61533-250-2(2))* Windmill Bks.

—10 Things You Should Know about Spiders. Gallagher, Belinda & Borton, Paula, eds. Draper, Richard, illus. 2004. (10 Things You Should Know Ser.). 24p. (J). 6.99 *(978-1-84236-122-1(8))* Miles Kelly Publishing, Ltd. GBR. Dist: Independent Pubs. Group.

Petrie, Kristin. Tarantulas, 1 vol. 2012. (Unique Pets Ser.). (ENG.). 24p. (J). (gr. 3-6). lib. bdg. 25.65 *(978-1-61783-444-8(0),* Checkerboard Library) ABDO Publishing Co.

Pixton, Kaaren. Creep! Crawl! Hey Baby! Look at These Animals on the Ground! 2009. (Indestructibles Ser.). (ENG., Illus.). 12p. (J). (gr. k — 1). pap. 5.95 *(978-0-7611-5696-3(8),* 15696) Workman Publishing Co., Inc.

Platt, Richard. Spiders' Secrets. 2010. (DK Readers Ser.). (ENG., Illus.). 48p. (J). (gr. 2-4). 3.99 *(978-0-7566-6283-7(4),* DK Children) Dorling Kindersley Publishing, Inc.

Powell, Patricia Hruby. Zinnia: How the Corn Was Saved. Ruffenach, Jessie, ed. Thomas, Peter, tr. from NAV. Benally, Kendrick, illus. 2004. (ENG & NAV.). 32p. (J). (gr. -1-3). 17.95 *(978-1-893354-38-8(5))* Salina Bookshelf Inc.

Randolph, Joanne. Black Widow Spiders, 1 vol., 1. 2014. (Nightmare Creatures: Spiders! Ser.). (ENG.). 24p. (J). (gr. k-5). 23.60 *(978-1-4777-2888-8(0),* PowerKids Pr.) Rosen Publishing Group, Inc., The.

—Crab Spiders, 1 vol., 1. 2014. (Nightmare Creatures: Spiders! Ser.). (ENG.). 24p. (J). (gr. k-5). 23.60 *(978-1-4777-2892-5(9),* PowerKids Pr.) Rosen Publishing Group, Inc., The.

—Jumping Spiders, 1 vol., 1. 2014. (Nightmare Creatures: Spiders! Ser.). (ENG.). 24p. (J). (gr. k-5). 23.60 *(978-1-4777-2889-5(9),* PowerKids Pr.) Rosen Publishing Group, Inc., The.

—Orb-Weaver Spiders, 1 vol., 1. 2014. (Nightmare Creatures: Spiders! Ser.). (ENG., Illus.). 24p. (J). (gr. k-5). 23.60 *(978-1-4777-2893-2(7),* PowerKids Pr.) Rosen Publishing Group, Inc., The.

—Tarantulas. (Classroom Pets Ser.). 2009. 24p. (gr. 2-3). 42.50 *(978-1-61511-860-1(8))* 2007. 28p. (gr. 3-7). pap. 21.25 *(978-1-4358-3835-2(1))* 2007. (Illus.). 24p. (J). (gr. 3-7). lib. bdg. 22.60 *(978-1-4042-3678-3(3))*1. 2014. (ENG.). 24p. (J). (gr. k-5). 23.60 *(978-1-4777-2891-8(0))* Rosen Publishing Group, Inc., The. (PowerKids Pr.).

—Wolf Spiders, 1 vol., 1. 2014. (Nightmare Creatures: Spiders! Ser.). (ENG.). 24p. (J). (gr. k-5). 23.60 *(978-1-4777-2890-1(2),* PowerKids Pr.) Rosen Publishing Group, Inc., The.

Raum, Elizabeth. Black Widow Spiders. 2015. (Poisonous Animals Ser.). (ENG., Illus.). 32p. (J). (gr. 2-4). 19.95 *(978-1-60753-784-7(2))* Amicus Publishing.

Reher, Matt. All about Spiders. 2015. (2G Bugs Ser.). (ENG., Illus.). 24p. (J). pap. 5.99 *(978-1-63437-096-7(1))* American Reading Co.

René, Ellen. Investigating Spiders & Their Webs. 2009. (Science Detectives Ser.). 24p. (gr. 2-3). 42.50 *(978-1-60853-013-7(2),* PowerKids Pr.); (Illus.). (J). lib. bdg. 22.60 *(978-1-4042-4482-5(4))* Rosen Publishing Group, Inc., The.

Reynolds, Toby & Calver, Paul. Insects & Spiders. 2016. (Visual Explorers Ser.). (ENG., Illus.). 32p. (J). (gr. 3-7). pap. 6.99 *(978-1-4380-0827-1(9))* Barron's Educational Series, Inc.

Rice, Dona Herweck. Going Buggy!, 1 vol. 2nd rev. ed. 2013. (Nonfiction Readers Ser.). (ENG., Illus.). 20p. (J). (gr. 1-1). pap. 19.96 *(978-1-4807-1024-5(5))* Shell Educational Publishing.

Riley, Joelle. Hairy Tarantulas. 2009. pap. 40.95 *(978-0-8225-9318-8(1))* 2007. (ENG., Illus.). 32p. (J). (gr. -1-3). per. 6.95 *(978-0-8225-6705-9(9),* First Avenue Editions) 2007. (ENG., Illus.). 32p. (J). (gr. k-3). lib. bdg. 22.60 *(978-0-8225-6702-8(4),* Lerner Pubns.) Lerner Publishing Group.

Rin, Bo. Insects & Spiders. Cowley, Joy, ed. Garrido & Do, Gam, illus. 2015. (Science Storybooks Ser.). (ENG.). 32p. (J). (gr. k-3). 26.65 *(978-1-925233-61-2(8))* Lerner Publishing Group.

Ripley's Believe It Or Not! Staff & Ripley's Believe It Or Not! Editors. Ripley Twists: Spiders & Scary Creepy Crawlies. 2014. (Twist Ser.: 12). (ENG.). 48p. (J). 12.95 *(978-1-60991-115-7(6))* Ripley Entertainment, Inc.

Robb, Jackie & Stringle, Berny. The Story of Spider. Duncan, Karen & Stringle, Sam, illus. 2004. (Bang on the Door Ser.). 32p. (YA). pap. *(978-1-85602-318-4(4),* Pavilion Children's Books) Pavilion Bks.

Robbins, Lynette. Jumping Spiders. 2012. (J). 49.50 *(978-1-4488-5166-9(1),* PowerKids Pr.); pap. 8.25 *(978-1-4488-5165-2(3),* PowerKids Pr.); lib. bdg. 22.60 *(978-1-4488-5016-7(9))* Rosen Publishing Group, Inc., The.

Rodriguez, Ana Maria. The Secret of the Scuba Diving Spider... & More! 2017. (Animal Secrets Revealed! Ser.). 48p. (J). (gr. 4-4). lib. bdg. 27.93 ***(978-0-7660-8629-6(1))*** Enslow Pubs., Inc.

Ross, Michael Elsohn. Spiderology. Erickson, Darren, illus. Grogan, Brian, photos by. (Backyard Buddies Ser.). 48p. (gr. 3-6). 2005. lib. bdg. 19.93 *(978-1-57505-387-5(X))* 2003. (YA). 6.95 *(978-1-57505-438-4(8),* Carolrhoda Bks.) Lerner Publishing Group.

Roza, Greg. Deadly Black Widows. 2011. (Small but Deadly Ser.). 24p. (J). (gr. 2-5). pap. 8.15 *(978-1-4339-5732-1(9));* lib. bdg. 22.60 *(978-1-4339-5730-7(2))* Stevens, Gareth Publishing LLLP. (Gareth Stevens Learning Library).

—Strange Spiders. 2011. (World of Bugs Ser.). (Illus.). 24p. (gr. k-2). 69.20 *(978-1-4339-6145-8(8));* (J). (gr. -1-2). lib. bdg. 22.60 *(978-1-4339-4611-0(4));* (J). (gr. k-2). pap. 8.15 *(978-1-4339-4612-7(2))* Stevens, Gareth Publishing LLLP.

Rupert, Matthews. Visual Factfinder Bugs. 2008. 512p. pap. *(978-1-84810-079-4(5))* Miles Kelly Publishing, Ltd.

Rustad, Martha E. H. Stunning Spiders. 2017. (Bugs Are Beautiful! Ser.). (ENG., Illus.). 32p. (gr. 1-2). lib. bdg. 27.32 *(978-1-5157-4500-6(7),* Aplus Bks.) Capstone Press of Coughlan Cos.

School Zone Publishing Company Staff. Insects & Spiders. (Illus.). (J). 19.99 incl. audio compact disk *(978-0-88743-977-3(2));* 19.99 incl. audio compact disk *(978-0-88743-944-5(6))* School Zone Publishing Co.

Schuetz, Kari. Tarantulas. 2015. (Creepy Crawlies Ser.). (ENG., Illus.). 24p. (J). (gr. k-3). lib. bdg. 25.95 *(978-1-62617-227-2(7),* Blastoff! Readers) Bellwether Media.

Seeley, M. H. Trap-Door Spiders. 2017. (Spiders: Eight-Legged Terrors Ser.). 24p. (J). (gr. 2-3). pap. 8.15 ***(978-1-5382-0213-5(1))*** Stevens, Gareth Publishing LLLP.

Shea, Therese. Spider Biters. (Big Bad Biters Ser.). 24p. 2009. (gr. 2-3). 42.50 *(978-1-61511-565-5(X))* 2006. (Illus.). (J). (gr. 3-7). lib. bdg. 22.60 *(978-1-4042-3521-2(3))* Rosen Publishing Group, Inc., The. (PowerKids Pr.).

—We Need Spiders. 2015. (Creatures We Can't Live Without Ser.). (ENG.). 24p. (J). (gr. 3-4). 23.60 *(978-1-4994-1044-0(1),* PowerKids Pr.) Rosen Publishing Group, Inc., The.

—20 Fun Facts about Spiders. 2013. (Fun Fact File: Bugs! Ser.). (Illus.). 32p. (gr. 2-5). 25.25 *(978-1-4339-8245-3(5));* pap. 10.50 *(978-1-4339-8246-0(3))* Stevens, Gareth Publishing LLLP. (Gareth Stevens Learning Library).

Shofner, Melissa Raé. Giant Huntsman Spiders. 2017. (Spiders: Eight-Legged Terrors Ser.). 24p. (J). (gr. 2-3). pap. 8.15 ***(978-1-5382-0209-8(3))*** Stevens, Gareth Publishing LLLP.

Sill, Cathryn P., et al. About Arachnids: A Guide for Children, 1 vol. Sill, Cathryn P. & Sill, John, illus. 2003. (About...Ser.). (ENG.). 40p. (J). (gr. k-3). 16.95 *(978-1-56145-038-1(3))* Peachtree Pubs.

Silverstein, Alvin, et al. Tarantulas: Cool Pets! Kelley, Gerald, illus. 2012. (Far-Out & Unusual Pets Ser.). 48p. (J). (gr. 3-4). pap. 8.95 *(978-1-4644-0128-2(4),* Enslow Elementary) Enslow Pubs., Inc.

Simon, Seymour. Spiders. (Illus.). 32p. (J). (gr. k-4). 2007. (ENG.). pap. 6.99 *(978-0-06-089103-9(3),* Collins) 2003. lib. bdg. 17.89 *(978-0-06-028392-6(0))* HarperCollins Pubs.

Simons, Lisa M. B. From Egg to Spider. 2003. (Grow up! Ser.). (J). pap. *(978-1-58417-178-2(2));* lib. bdg. *(978-1-58417-172-0(3))* Lake Street Pubs.

Siy, Alexandra. Spidermania: Friends on the Web. Kunkel, Dennis, photos by. 2015. (ENG., Illus.). 48p. (J). (gr. 1-5). 17.95 *(978-0-8234-2871-7(0))* Holiday Hse., Inc.

Slade, Suzanne. Do All Bugs Have Wings? And Other Questions Kids Have about Bugs, 1 vol. Pillo, Cary, illus. 2010. (Kids' Questions Ser.). (ENG.). 24p. (gr. 1-2). lib. bdg. 26.65 *(978-1-4048-5761-2(3))* Picture Window Bks.

Smith, Sian. Spiders, 1 vol. 2012. (Creepy Critters Ser.). (ENG.). 24p. (gr. -1-k). pap. 9.95 *(978-1-4109-4823-6(4));* lib. bdg. 25.32 *(978-1-4109-4810-6(2))* Heinemann-Raintree.

The Spider Bank: Individual Title Six-Packs. (Story Steps Ser.). (gr. k-2). 32.00 *(978-0-7635-9845-7(3))* Rigby Education.

Spiders. (Eyes on Nature Ser.). 32p. (J). (gr. 1). pap. *(978-1-882210-59-6(X))* Action Publishing, Inc.

Spiders. (Eyes on Nature Ser.). (Illus.). 32p. (J). (gr. 1-18). 7.95 *(978-1-56156-462-0(1))* Kidsbooks, LLC.

Spiders: Eight-Legged Terrors. 2017. (Spiders: Eight-Legged Terrors Ser.). 24p. (gr. 2-3). pap. 48.90 ***(978-1-5382-0489-4(4));*** lib. bdg. 135.60 ***(978-1-5382-0475-7(4))*** Stevens, Gareth Publishing LLLP.

Spiders: Level I, 6 vols. (Wonder Worldtm Ser.). 16p. 29.95 *(978-0-7802-1237-4(1))* Wright Group/McGraw-Hill.

Spiders & their Webs, 6 vols. (Sunshinetm Science Ser.). 24p. (gr. 1-2). 36.95 *(978-0-7802-0535-2(9));* 31.50 *(978-0-7802-0284-9(8))* Wright Group/McGraw-Hill.

Spiders are Special Animals, 6 vols. (Sunshinetm Science Ser.). 24p. (gr. 1-2). 31.50 *(978-0-7802-0285-6(6));* 36.95 *(978-0-7802-0536-9(7))* Wright Group/McGraw-Hill.

Stewart, Melissa. How Do Spiders Make Webs? 2008. (Tell Me Why, Tell Me How Ser.). (Illus.). 32p. (gr. 3-18). lib. bdg. 29.93 *(978-0-7614-2920-3(4),* Benchmark Bks.) Marshall Cavendish Corp.

—Insect or Spider? How Do You Know? 2011. (Which Animal Is Which? Ser.). (Illus.). 24p. (J). (gr. k-18). pap. 7.95 *(978-1-59845-237-2(1),* Enslow Elementary); lib. bdg. 22.60 *(978-0-7660-3681-9(2))* Enslow Pubs., Inc.

Stradling, Jan. Spy on Spiders: Level K, 6 vols., Vol. 2. (First Explorers Ser.). 24p. (gr. 1-2). 34.95 *(978-0-7699-1465-7(9))* Shortland Pubns. (U. S. A.) Inc.

Strother, Ruth. Tarantula, 1 vol. 2013. (Great Predators Ser.). (ENG., Illus.). 48p. (J). (gr. 3-6). lib. bdg. 32.79 *(978-1-61783-952-8(3))* ABDO Publishing Co.

—Tarantula Paperback. 2013. (Illus.). 48p. (J). pap. 15.64 *(978-1-62403-017-8(3),* Core Library) ABDO Publishing Co.

Sullivan, Laura. Insects & Arachnids Explained. 2016. (Distinctions in Nature Ser.). 32p. (J). pap. 10.58 *(978-1-5026-2189-4(4))* Cavendish Square Publishing.

Sundance/Newbridge LLC Staff. Spinning a Web. 2007. (Early Science Ser.). (gr. k-3). 18.95 *(978-1-4007-6233-0(2));* pap. 6.10 *(978-1-4007-6229-3(4))* Sundance/Newbridge Educational Publishing.

Tait, Noel. Insects & Spiders. 2008. (Insiders Ser.). (ENG.). 64p. (J). (gr. 3-7). 17.99 *(978-1-4169-3868-2(0),* Simon & Schuster Bks. For Young Readers) Simon & Schuster Bks. For Young Readers.

Taylor, Barbara. Exploring Nature - Sensational Spiders: A Comprehensive Guide to Some of the Most Intriguing Creatures in the Animal Kingdom, with over 220 Pictures. 2013. (ENG., Illus.). 64p. (J). (gr. k-8). 12.99 *(978-1-84322-854-7(8),* Armadillo) Anness Publishing GBR. Dist: National Bk. Network.

Taylor-Butler, Christine. Insects & Spiders. 2013. (ENG.). 48p. (J). 29.00 *(978-0-531-21753-5(1));* pap. 6.95 *(978-0-531-22338-3(8))* Scholastic Library Publishing.

Taylor, Trace. Jumping Spiders. Taylor, Trace, illus. 2014. (1-3Y Bugs Ser.). (ENG., Illus.). 20p. (J). pap. 5.99 *(978-1-61406-687-3(6))* American Reading Co.

Taylor, Trace & Rupp, Kristina. Tarantulas (English) 2015. (2G Bugs Ser.). (ENG., Illus.). 20p. (J). pap. 5.99 *(978-1-61406-692-7(2))* American Reading Co.

Taylor, Trace & Sanchez, Lucia M. Tarántulas (Tarantulas) 2011. (poder de 100 - Bichos Ser.). (SPA.). 12p. pap. 33.92 *(978-1-61541-291-4(3))* American Reading Co.

Truett, Trudi Strain. Spiders. (Backyard Safari Ser.). 2011. 32p. (gr. 3). 28.50 *(978-1-60870-249-7(9))* 2009. 24p. (gr. k-1). 15.95 *(978-0-7614-3965-3(X))* Marshall Cavendish Corp.

Turner, Matt. Deadly Spiders. Calle, Santiago, illus. 2017. (Crazy Creepy Crawlers Ser.). (ENG.). 32p. (J). (gr. 3-6). 26.65 *(978-1-5124-1553-7(7));* 7.99 ***(978-1-5124-3597-9(X));*** 39.99 ***(978-1-5124-2713-4(6));*** 39.99 ***(978-1-5124-3596-2(1))*** Lerner Publishing Group.

Underwater Spiders: Early Level Satellite Individual Title Six-Packs. (Sails Literacy Ser.). 16p. (gr. 1-2). 27.00 *(978-0-7578-3162-1(1))* Rigby Education.

Uttridge, Sarah. Spiders & Bugs Around the World. 2014. (Animals Around the World Ser.). (Illus.). 32p. (gr. 2-5). 31.35 *(978-1-62588-198-4(3))* Black Rabbit Bks.

Washington, Joi. Jumping Spiders. 2011. (Predator Bugs Ser.). 16p. pap. 39.62 *(978-1-61541-356-0(1))* American Reading Co.

—The Wolf Spider. 2011. (Power 50 - Predator Bugs Ser.). 32p. (J). (gr. k-2). pap. 7.95 *(978-1-61541-379-9(0))* American Reading Co.

Washington, Joi & Sanchez, Lucia M. ArañAs Saltadoras: Jumping Spiders. 2011. (Bichos depredadores (Predator Bugs) Ser.). 16p. (J). pap. 6.95 *(978-1-61541-357-7(X))* American Reading Co.

Waxman, Laura Hamilton. Web-Spinning Spiders. 2016. (First Step Nonfiction — Backyard Critters Ser.). (ENG., Illus.). 24p. (J). (gr. k-2). 23.99 *(978-1-5124-0884-3(0))* Lerner Publishing Group.

Weber, Valerie J. Por Qué Algunos Animales Tejen Telarañas. 2008. (Donde viven los animales (Where Animals Live) Ser.). (SPA.). 24p. (gr. 1-4). pap. 8.15 *(978-0-8368-8819-5(7),* Weekly Reader Leveled Readers) Stevens, Gareth Publishing LLLP.

—Por Qué Algunos Animales Tejen Telarañas. 2008. (Donde viven los animales (Where Animals Live) Ser.). (SPA., Illus.). 24p. (gr. 1-4). lib. bdg. 22.00 *(978-0-8368-8812-6(X),* Weekly Reader Leveled Readers) Stevens, Gareth Publishing LLLP.

—Why Animals Live in Webs. 2008. (Where Animals Live Ser.). 24p. (gr. 1-4). pap. 8.15 *(978-0-8368-8805-8(7),* Weekly Reader Leveled Readers) Stevens, Gareth Publishing LLLP.

—Why Animals Live in Webs. 2008. (Where Animals Live Ser.). (Illus.). 24p. (gr. 1-4). lib. bdg. 22.00 *(978-0-8368-8798-3(0),* Weekly Reader Leveled Readers) Stevens, Gareth Publishing LLLP.

What's This Spider Doing? Individual Title Six-Packs. (Story Steps Ser.). (gr. k-2). 32.00 *(978-0-7635-9617-0(5))* Rigby Education.

Wheeler, Jill C. Crab Spiders, 1 vol. 2006. (Spiders Set 2 Ser.). (ENG., Illus.). 24p. (gr. k-6). 25.65 *(978-1-59679-292-0(2),* Checkerboard Library) ABDO Publishing Co.

—Daddy Longlegs Spiders, 1 vol. 2006. (Spiders Set 2 Ser.). (ENG., Illus.). 24p. (gr. k-6). 25.65 *(978-1-59679-293-7(0),* Checkerboard Library) ABDO Publishing Co.

S

—Funnel-Web Spiders, 1 vol. 2006. (Spiders Set 2 Ser.). (ENG., Illus.). 24p. (gr. k-6). 25.65 *(978-1-59679-294-4(9)*, Checkerboard Library) ABDO Publishing Co.
—Hobo Spiders, 1 vol. 2006. (Spiders Set 2 Ser.). (ENG.). 24p. (gr. k-6). 25.65 *(978-1-59679-295-1(7)*, Checkerboard Library) ABDO Publishing Co.
—Recluse Spiders, 1 vol. 2006. (Spiders Set 2 Ser.). (ENG., Illus.). 24p. (gr. k-6). 25.65 *(978-1-59679-296-8(5)*, Checkerboard Library) ABDO Publishing Co.
—White-Tailed Spiders, 1 vol. 2006. (Spiders Set 2 Ser.). (ENG., Illus.). 24p. (gr. k-6). 25.65 *(978-1-59679-297-5(3)*, Checkerboard Library) ABDO Publishing Co.
White, Nancy. Crafty Garden Spiders. 2008. (No Backbone! Ser.). (Illus.). 24p. (YA). (gr. k-3). lib. bdg. 21.28 *(978-1-59716-703-1(7))* Bearport Publishing Co., Inc.
Wilson, Emily. Trap-Door Spiders. 2016. (Dig Deep! Bugs That Live Underground Ser.). (Illus.). 24p. (J). (gr. 3-3). pap. 8.25 *(978-1-4994-2066-1(8)*, PowerKids Pr.) Rosen Publishing Group, Inc., The.
Wimmer, Teresa. Spiders. 2006. (My First Look at Insects Ser.). (Illus.). 24p. (J). (gr. k-2). 15.95 *(978-1-58341-456-9(8)*, Creative Education) Creative Co., The.
Wittrock, Jeni. Tarantulas, 1 vol. 2013. (Creepy Crawlers Ser.). (ENG., Illus.). 24p. (gr. k-1). lib. bdg. 26.65 *(978-1-4765-2458-0(0)*, Pebble Plus) Capstone Press of Coughlan Cos.
Wood, Selina. Spiders. 2009. (Extreme Pets Ser.). (YA). (gr. 4-7). 28.50 *(978-1-59920-234-1(4))* Black Rabbit Bks.
Woodward, John. Spider. 2010. (Garden Minibeasts up Close Ser.). 32p. (gr. 2-4). 30.00 *(978-1-60413-895-5(5)*, Chelsea Clubhouse) Facts On File, Inc.
World Book, Inc Staff, contrib. by. Animal Lives, 7 vols. 2009. (Illus.). 336p. (J). (gr. 3-5). 139.00 *(978-0-7166-0401-3(9))* World Bk., Inc.
—Insects & Spiders. (J). 2011. *(978-0-7166-1789-1(7))* 2009. *(978-0-7166-0405-1(1))* World Bk., Inc.
—Insects, Spiders, & Creepy Crawlers: A Supplement to Childcraft, the How & Why Library. 2007. (J). *(978-0-7166-0618-5(6))* World Bk., Inc.
—Pinktoes & Other Tarantulas. 2007. (World Book's Animals of the World Ser.). (Illus.). 64p. (J). *(978-0-7166-1332-9(8))* World Bk., Inc.
Zabludoff, Marc. Spiders. 2005. (Animalways Ser.). (Illus.). 112p. (J). (gr. 3-7). lib. bdg. *(978-0-7614-1747-7(8)*, Benchmark Bks.) Marshall Cavendish Corp.
Zondervan Staff. Spiders, Snakes, Bees, & Bats, 1 vol. 2010. (I Can Read! / Made by God Ser.). (ENG., Illus.). 32p. (J). (gr. -1-2). pap. 3.99 *(978-0-310-72007-2(9))* Zonderkidz.

SPIDERS—FICTION

Abbott Orloff, Chrissy. Lady Humming Fly's Lesson on Staying Safe. 2009. 80p. pap. 28.99 *(978-1-4389-9938-8(0))* AuthorHouse.
Alexander, R. W. Spider Fight. 2010. (J). pap. 9.95 *(978-0-7414-5924-4(8))* Infinity Publishing.
Allen, Jean M. A Tangled Web. 2012. 26p. 24.95 *(978-1-4512-9475-0(1))* America Star Bks.
Anderson, Jane. Anansi the Spider & the Sky King: A Tale from Africa. 2006. (J). pap. *(978-1-4108-6175-7(9))* Benchmark Education Co.
Anderson, Michael. Woolly Bargains: A Scary Story for Young People. 2013. (ENG.). 27p. (J). pap. 22.95 *(978-1-4787-0654-0(6))* Outskirts Pr., Inc.
Archer, Dosh. Itsy Bitsy Spider. Archer, Dosh, illus. (Urgency Emergency! Ser.). (ENG., Illus.). 48p. (J). (gr. -1-3). 2015. pap. 9.99 *(978-0-8075-8360-9(X))* 2013. 12.99 *(978-0-8075-8358-6(8))* Whitman, Albert & Co.
Arkhurst, Joyce Cooper. The Further Adventures of Spider: West African Folktales. Pinkney, Jerry, illus. 2012. (Passport to Reading Level 4 Ser.). (ENG.). 32p. (J). (gr. -1-3). pap. 4.99 *(978-0-316-20345-6(9))* Little, Brown Bks. for Young Readers.
Arrington, H. Anansi's Narrow Waist: A Tale from Ghana, 1 vol. Allin, Nicole, illus. 2017. (ENG.). 32p. (J). (gr. k-3). 16.99 *(978-1-4556-2216-0(8))* Pelican Publishing Co., Inc.
Austrian, J. J. Worm Loves Worm. Curato, Mike, illus. 2016. 32p. (J). (gr. -1-3). 17.99 *(978-0-06-238633-5(6))* HarperCollins Pubs.
Baldwin., C. R. Henry the Spider. 2011. (Illus.). 44p. pap. 16.76 *(978-1-4567-8649-6(0))* AuthorHouse.
Baldwin, Kevin. Beetle Dan & the Big Purple Slide: A Beetle Dan Story. 2006. (Beetle Dan Story Ser.). (ENG., Illus.). 32p. (J). (gr. -1-2). 14.99 *(978-1-59185-921-5(2)*, Creation Hse.) Charisma Media.
Bass, Guy. The Spider's Lair. Williamson, Pete, illus. 2015. (Stitch Head Ser.). (ENG.). 208p. (gr. 3-4). 10.95 *(978-1-62370-192-5(9))* Capstone Young Readers of Coughlan Cos.
Beeson, Jan. Mysterious World of the Puffins the Treasure Hunt Book 1. 2013. 74p. pap. 19.99 *(978-0-9890482-0-0(9))* Beeson, Jan.
Bentley, Dawn. Three Hungry Spiders & One Fat Fly! Twinem, Neecy, illus. 2010. (Stretchies Book Ser.). 16p. (J). (gr. -1-k). 8.99 *(978-0-8249-1460-8(0)*, Ideal Pubns.) Worthy Publishing.
Berger, Melvin. Spinning Spiders. Schindler, S. D., illus. 2003. (Let's-Read-and-Find-Out Science Ser.). (ENG.). 40p. (J). (gr. k-4). 15.99 *(978-0-06-028696-5(2))*; pap. 5.99 *(978-0-06-445207-6(7))* HarperCollins Pubs.
Beus, Bryan. Westly: A Spider's Tale. Beus, Bryan, illus. 2015. (Illus.). 171p. (J). 15.99 *(978-1-62972-068-5(2)*, Shadow Mountain) Deseret Bk. Co.
Blocker, Adam P. Joshua & the Spider. Taylor, Josh, illus. 2013. (ENG.). 72p. 17.99 *(978-1-939418-08-1(9))* Writer of the Round Table Pr.
Bolander, Sharon Miller. At the Stroke of Midnight. 2012. 40p. pap. 24.95 *(978-1-4626-8905-7(1))* America Star Bks.
Boniface, William. Lights Out, Night's Out. Kirkova, Milena, illus. 2011. (ENG.). 24p. (J). pap. 6.99 *(978-1-4494-0236-5(4))* Andrews McMeel Publishing.
Bonnell, Kris. Spiders. 2009. (J). pap. 7.95 *(978-1-60892-000-6(3))* Reading Reading Bks., LLC.
Bowman, Chaliece. Sarah's Camping Trip. 2012. 20p. pap. 17.99 *(978-1-4772-5531-5(1))* AuthorHouse.
Brewis, Alan. Boris Returns A Hero! 2008. 72p. pap. 12.50 *(978-1-4357-4377-9(6))* Lulu Pr., Inc.
Brightwood, Laura, illus. Anansi & the Turtle. Brightwood, Laura, . 2006. (J). *(978-0-9779290-0-9(0))* 3-C Institute for Social Development.
Brooks, Donna. The Golden Spindle. 2010. 112p. pap. 30.00 *(978-1-60860-852-2(2)*, Eloquent Bks.) Strategic Book Publishing & Rights Agency (SBPRA).
Cairo, Anna. The Spider in My Shower. 2012. 28p. pap. 16.99 *(978-1-4634-8768-3(1))* AuthorHouse.
Callen, Sharon. Happy Faces Leave Home, 1 vol. 2013. (Fiction Readers Ser.). (ENG., Illus.). 28p. (J). (gr. 2-2). pap. 6.99 *(978-1-4333-5560-8(4))* Shell Educational Publishing.
Carle, Eric. La Arana Muy Ocupada. Carle, Eric, illus. 2004.Tr. of Very Busy Spider. (SPA & ENG., Illus.). 32p. (J). (gr. -1-k). 21.99 *(978-0-399-24241-0(4)*, Philomel Bks.) Penguin Young Readers Group.
—The Very Busy Spider. Carle, Eric, illus. (Penguin Young Readers, Level 2 Ser.). (ENG., Illus.). (J). 2014. 32p. (gr. 1-2). pap. 3.99 *(978-0-448-48052-7(2)*, Penguin Young Readers) 2011. 24p. (gr. -1 — 1). bds. 15.99 *(978-0-399-25601-1(6)*, Philomel Bks.) Penguin Young Readers Group.
—The Very Busy Spider. 2006. (World of Eric Carle Ser.). (ENG., Illus.). 24p. (J). (gr. -1-k). 6.99 *(978-0-448-44421-5(6)*, Grosset & Dunlap) Penguin Young Readers Group.
Carlson, Melody. Bitsy's Harvest Party. Reagan, Susan Joy, illus. 2005. 32p. (J). (gr. -1-4). 12.99 *(978-0-8054-2684-7(1))* B&H Publishing Group.
Chapman, Keith. Itsy Bitsy Spider. Tickle, Jack, illus. (Tiger Tales Ser.). (J). 2008. 24p. (gr. -1-2). pap. 6.95 *(978-1-58925-407-7(4))* 2006. 32p. 15.95 *(978-1-58925-055-0(9))* Tiger Tales.
Charlesworth, Liza & Scholastic Canada Ltd. Staff. Eight Legs Are Great! Snider, Jackie, illus. 2005. (Number Tales Ser.). (ENG.). 16p. (J). (gr. -1-1). pap. 2.99 *(978-0-439-69019-5(6))* Scholastic, Inc.
Child's Play Staff. Itsy Bitsy Spider. Hilb, Nora, illus. 2017. (Classic Books with Holes 8x8 with CD Ser.). (ENG.). 16p. (J). pap. incl. audio compact disk ***(978-1-78628-079-4(5))*** Child's Play International Ltd.
Coffman, Dan. Titu Miata's Spider. 2012. (ENG.). pap. *(978-1-4675-2424-7(7))* Independent Pub.
Cook, Beatrice. A Journey with the Spider & Snake to Arizona. Campis, Adrian, Jr., illus. 2007. (J). 14.95 *(978-0-9795867-0-5(4))* Travel America Bks.
Cook, Sherry & Johnson, Terri. Susie Sound. 26. Kuhn, Jesse, illus. l.t. ed. 2006. 32p. (J). 7.99 *(978-1-933815-18-3(3)*, Quirkles, The) Creative 3, LLC.
Cox, Tracey M. Arachnabet- an Alphabet of Spiders. 2013. 20p. pap. 9.95 *(978-1-61633-362-1(6))* Guardian Angel Publishing, Inc.
Cronin, Doreen. Diary of a Spider. Bliss, Harry, illus. (ENG.). 40p. (J). (gr. -1-3). 2013. 9.99 *(978-0-06-223300-4(9))* 2005. 16.99 *(978-0-06-000153-7(4))* HarperCollins Pubs.
—Diary of a Spider. Bliss, Harry, illus. unabr. ed. 2006. (Picture Book Readalong Ser.). (J). (gr. -1-2). 28.95 incl. audio compact disk *(978-1-59519-486-2(X))* Live Oak Media.
—Diary of a Spider. Bliss, Harry, illus. unabr. ed. 2006. (J). (gr. -1-3). 29.95 *(978-0-439-90579-4(6))* Weston Woods Studios, Inc.
Czajak, Paul & Brothers Hilts Staff. Seaver the Weaver. Hilts, Ben, illus. 2015. (ENG.). 32p. (J). (-k). 15.95 *(978-1-938063-57-2(0)*, Mighty Media Kids) Mighty Media Pr.
Danley, Jerry J. Billy Black Ant's Exciting Adventures. Hilley, Thomas, illus. 2012. 56p. pap. 12.99 *(978-0-9885180-5-6(8))* Mindstir Media.
Delessert, Etienne. Spartacus the Spider. 2010. (ENG., Illus.). 32p. (J). (gr. 1-3). 17.95 *(978-1-56846-213-4(1)*, Creative Editions) Creative Co., The.
Diaz, S. Jemmy & the Little Spider of Hope. 2012. 40p. pap. 20.99 *(978-1-4772-7032-5(9))* AuthorHouse.
Dj Caz. Spiders & Cupcakes. 2009. 28p. pap. 12.49 *(978-1-4389-7243-5(1))* AuthorHouse.
Dodd, Emma. I Love Bugs. Dodd, Emma, illus. 2011. (ENG., Illus.). 32p. (J). pap. 6.95 *(978-0-8234-2345-3(X))* Holiday Hse., Inc.
Dodson, Emma. Speckle the Spider. Dodson, Emma, illus. 2010. (ENG., Illus.). 32p. (J). (gr. -1-2). 14.99 *(978-0-7636-4778-0(0))* Candlewick Pr.
Donaldson, Julia. Spinderella. Pichon, Liz, illus. 2005. (Blue Go Bananas Ser.). (ENG.). 48p. (J). (gr. 1-2). lib. bdg. *(978-0-7787-2628-9(2))* Crabtree Publishing Co.
Donbavand, Tommy. Heart of the Mummy. Bk. 3. Cartoon Saloon Staff, illus. 2010. (Scream Street Ser.: 3). (ENG.). 128p. (J). (gr. 3-7). pap. 5.99 *(978-0-7636-4636-3(9))* Candlewick Pr.
—Heart of the Mummy: Book 3, 1 vol. Cartoon Saloon, illus. 2012. (ENG.). 120p. (J). 24.21 *(978-1-59961-994-1(6)*, Chapter Bks.) Spotlight.
Dyan, Penelope. Mikey & Me & the Spider — -the Continuing Story of a Girl & Her Dog. Dyan, Penelope, illus. 2010. (Illus.). 50p. pap. 14.95 *(978-1-935118-95-4(1))* Bellissima Publishing, LLC.
Eddy, Olivia. The Hatchling. 2008. 112p. pap. 9.99 *(978-1-60693-546-0(1)*, Strategic Bk. Publishing) Strategic Book Publishing & Rights Agency (SBPRA).
El-Magazy, Rowaa & Stratford, Stevan. Ali & the Spider. 2016. (ENG., Illus.). 18p. (J). (gr. -1-2). 8.95 *(978-0-86037-325-4(8))* Kube Publishing Ltd. GBR. Dist: Consortium Bk. Sales & Distribution.
Ewers, Hans Heinz. The Spider. 2004. reprint ed. pap. 1.99 *(978-1-4192-8326-0(X))* Kessinger Publishing, LLC.
Farahay, Michael L. The Butterfly, The Bee & The Spider. Farahay, Naomi E., ed. 2007. 80p. pap. 36.95 *(978-1-4303-2623-6(9))* Lulu Pr., Inc.
Finn, Isobel. La Mariquita Perezosa. 2003. (SPA., Illus.). 26p. (J). *(978-84-8418-029-6(8)*, ZZ4475) Zendrera Zariquiey, Editorial ESP. Dist: Lectorum Pubns., Inc.
Fletcher, Ralph. Spider Boy. 2009. (ENG.). 192p. (J). (gr. 5-7). pap. 6.99 *(978-0-547-24820-2(2))* Houghton Mifflin Harcourt Publishing Co.
Flores, Vanessa. Tasha Tries to Fly: If... Then. 2017. (Computer Science for the Real World Ser.). 12p. (gr. 6-7). pap. 7.05 ***(978-1-5383-5178-9(1)***, Rosen Classroom) Rosen Publishing Group, Inc., The.
Fogelin, Adrian. Sister Spider Knows All, 1 vol. 2003. (ENG.). 224p. (J). (gr. 3-7). 14.95 *(978-1-56145-290-3(4)*, Q35925) Peachtree Pubs.
Fogwill, Joyce Graham. Bubs the Bumblebee & the Spider's Web. 2012. (ENG.). 24p. (J). pap. 12.95 *(978-1-4327-9586-3(4))* Outskirts Pr., Inc.
Freeman, Don. Manuelo the Playing Mantis. 2006. (ENG., Illus.). 32p. (J). (gr. -1-2). reprint ed. pap. 6.99 *(978-0-14-240560-4(4)*, Puffin Books) Penguin Young Readers Group.
Friar, Christine. Anansi & the Scarecrow. 2011. 32p. pap. 15.99 *(978-1-4568-7143-7(9))* Xlibris Corp.
Fuerst, Jeffrey B. The Itsy Bity Spider. Collins, Daryll, illus. 2010. (Rising Readers Ser.). (J). 3.49 *(978-1-60719-689-1(1))* Newmark Learning LLC.
Georgiana, Vanessa. Lulu: And the Garden of Life. 2013. 104p. (gr. 4-6). pap. 8.99 *(978-1-4582-0936-8(9)*, Abbott Pr.) Author Solutions, Inc.
Greens, Olivia. My Dream. 2012. 28p. pap. 21.99 *(978-1-4797-1305-9(8))* Xlibris Corp.
Guillain, Charlotte. Why the Spider Has Long Legs: An African Folk Tale, 1 vol. Dorado, Steve, illus. 2014. (Folk Tales from Around the World Ser.). (ENG.). 24p. (gr. 1-3). pap. 6.95 *(978-1-4109-6701-5(8)*, NA-r) Heinemann-Raintree.
Harney Jr., Robert. The Clumsiest Spider. Scott, Jennifer, illus. 2011. 44p. pap. 24.95 *(978-1-4626-2166-8(X))* America Star Bks.
Hart, Teresa. The Ant & the Lost Spider, 1 vol. 2009. 76p. pap. 19.95 *(978-1-60749-296-2(2))* America Star Bks.
Harwell, Andrew. The Spider Ring. 2015. (ENG.). 224p. (J). (gr. 3-7). 16.99 *(978-0-545-68290-9(8)*, Scholastic Pr.) Scholastic, Inc.
Hilb, Nora, illus. Itsy Bitsy Spider. (Classic Books with Holes Ser.). (ENG.). (J). 2015. 16p. pap. incl. audio compact disk *(978-1-84643-676-5(1))* 2012. 14p. bds. *(978-1-84643-509-6(9))* 2012. 16p. pap. *(978-1-84643-498-3(X))* Child's Play International Ltd.
Hilton, Marcel. The Magical Web. 2007. 38p. 19.50 *(978-1-4303-2678-6(6))* Lulu Pr., Inc.
Holden, Pam. Sneaky Spider, 6 pack. Storey, Jim, illus. 2009. (Red Rocket Readers Ser.). (ENG.). 16p. (gr. 2-2). pap. *(978-1-877363-83-2(9))* Flying Start Bks.
Holub, Joan. More Snacks! A Thanksgiving Play. Terry, Will, illus. 2006. (Ant Hill Ser.: 1). (ENG.). 24p. (J). (gr. -1-k). pap. 3.99 *(978-1-4169-0954-5(0))*; lib. bdg. 11.89 *(978-1-4169-2559-0(7))* Simon Spotlight. (Simon Spotlight).
—Picnic! A Day in the Park. Terry, Will, illus. 2008. (Ant Hill Ser.). (ENG.). 24p. (J). (gr. -1-k). pap. 3.99 *(978-1-4169-5133-9(4)*, Simon Spotlight) Simon Spotlight.
Hopgood, Tim. Walter's Wonderful Web. 2016. (ENG., Illus.). 32p. (J). 16.99 *(978-0-374-30352-5(5)*, 9780374303525, Farrar, Straus & Giroux (BYR)) Farrar, Straus & Giroux.
Hord, Colleen. Itsy Bitsy Spider. Poole, Helen, illus. 2012. (ENG.). 24p. (gr. 1-2). pap. 8.95 *(978-1-61810-310-9(5))* Rourke Educational Media.
Housel, Debra. Charlotte's Web: An Instructional Guide for Literature. rev. ed. 2015. (Great Works). (ENG., Illus.). 72p. (gr. 3-5). pap. 9.99 *(978-1-4807-6995-3(9))* Shell Educational Publishing.
Hulme-Cross, Benjamin. The House of Memories. Evergreen, Nelson, illus. 2015. (Dark Hunter Ser.). (ENG.). 64p. (J). (gr. 4-8). pap. 4.99 *(978-1-4677-8085-8(5))* Lerner Publishing Group.
ImageBooks Staff & Chronicle Books Staff. Little Spider Finger Puppet Book. van der Put, Klaartje, illus. 2007. (Little Finger Puppet Board Bks.: FING). (ENG.). 12p. (J). (gr. -1 — 1). bds. 6.99 *(978-0-8118-6104-5(X))* Chronicle Bks. LLC.
Jarman, Julia. Harry the Clever Spider at School. Fowkes, Charlie, illus. 2007. (Collins Big Cat Ser.). (ENG.). 128p. (J). (gr. 1-2). pap. 6.99 *(978-0-00-718670-9(3))* HarperCollins Pubs. Ltd. GBR. Dist: Independent Pubs. Group.
Jenkins, Steven. The Spider House: Battle for the Wall. 2007. 264p. 26.95 *(978-0-595-69910-0(3))*; per. 16.95 *(978-0-595-44488-5(1))* iUniverse, Inc.
Johnson, Gerald J. Miss Spinny, the Spider. Miltenberger, Jeri & Miltenberger, Dave, illus. 2012. 24p. 24.95 *(978-1-4626-6488-7(1))* America Star Bks.
Johnson, Myrna. Let's Take a Hike. 2013. (ENG., Illus.). 32p. (gr. -1-1). pap. 13.95 *(978-1-936205-79-0(3))* Austin, Stephen F. State Univ. Pr.
Kear, Nicole C. The Fix-It Friends: Have No Fear! Dockray, Tracy, illus. 2017. (Fix-It Friends Ser.). (ENG.). 144p. (J). 16.99 *(978-1-250-11577-5(9)*, 9781250115775) Imprint IND. Dist: Macmillan.
Kelly, Martin & Legris, Phil. Itsy Bitsy Spider. (Illus.). 6p. (J). 4.95 *(978-1-929766-25-3(4))* Handprint Bks.
Kemp, Dane. Imaginary Tales. 2011. 186p. pap. 24.95 *(978-1-4560-4686-6(1))* America Star Bks.
Khan, Aliyah. The Adventures of Solomon Spider: Solomon Sees the City. 2011. 28p. (gr. -1 — 1). pap. 14.09 *(978-1-4490-1546-6(8))* AuthorHouse.
Kimmel, Eric A. Anansi Series. Stevens, Janet, illus. 2003. pap. 68.95 incl. audio compact disk *(978-1-59112-840-3(4))*;Set. (J). pap. 61.95 incl. audio *(978-0-87499-469-8(1))* Live Oak Media.
Kirk, Bill. There's a Spider in My Sink! Brown, Suzy, illus. 2008. 16p. pap. 9.95 *(978-1-935137-25-2(5))* Guardian Angel Publishing, Inc.
Kirk, David. Bedtime Story. 2006. (Illus.). 32p. (J). *(978-0-448-44514-4(X))* Penguin Publishing Group.
—Captain Sunny Patch. 2006. (Illus.). 32p. (J). *(978-0-448-44515-1(8))* Callaway Editions, Inc.
—Miss Spider's Sunny Patch Surprise. 2005. (Play-a-Sound Ser.). (Illus.). 24p. (J). 16.98 *(978-1-4127-3558-2(0)*, 7262900) Publications International, Ltd.
Kompelien, Tracy. Spider Web, 1 vol. Haberstroh, Anne, illus. 2007. (Critter Chronicles Ser.). (ENG.). 24p. (J). (gr. k-3). lib. bdg. 24.21 *(978-1-59928-474-3(X)*, SandCastle) ABDO Publishing Co.
Krenina, Katya, illus. The Spider's Gift: A Ukrainian Christmas Story. 2005. (ENG.). 32p. (J). (gr. -1-3). 16.95 *(978-0-8234-1743-8(3))* Holiday Hse., Inc.
Kroupa, Robert J. Just Like You. 2011. (J). *(978-0-9825503-4-2(0))* IGI Pr.
Krumwiede, Lana. Just Itzy. Pizzoli, Greg, illus. 2015. (ENG.). 40p. (J). (-k). 15.99 *(978-0-7636-5811-3(1))* Candlewick Pr.
Lancaster, Melinda. Tyler & the Spider. Gillen, Rosemarie, illus. 2010. 32p. (J). pap. 9.95 *(978-1-935706-08-3(X))* Wiggles Pr.
Lane, Jeanette, et al. The Magic School Bus Gets Caught in a Web. Enik, Ted, illus. 2007. (Scholastic Reader Ser.). (J). *(978-0-545-03587-3(2))* Scholastic, Inc.
Lasky, Kathryn. Felix Takes the Stage. Gilpin, Stephen, illus. (Deadlies Ser.). (ENG.). 144p. (J). (gr. 2-5). 2011. pap. 5.99 *(978-0-545-11730-2(5)*, Scholastic Paperbacks) 2010. 15.99 *(978-0-545-11681-7(3)*, Scholastic Pr.) Scholastic, Inc.
—Spiders on the Case. Gilpin, Stephen, illus. (Deadlies Ser.). (ENG.). 176p. (J). (gr. 2-5). 2012. pap. 5.99 *(978-0-545-11731-9(3))*Bk. 2. 2011. 15.99 *(978-0-545-11682-4(1))* Scholastic, Inc. (Scholastic Pr.).
Lindsay, Sierra. Spindly the Spider. Lindsay, Sierra, illus. 2012. (Illus.). 20p. pap. 10.99 *(978-0-9836641-9-2(6))* Kids At Heart Publishing, LLC.
Lobo, Julia. Eek! That's Creepy! Look & Find. Cavallini, Linda, illus. 2010. 24p. (J). 7.98 *(978-1-60553-898-3(1))* Publications International, Ltd.
London, Jonathan. Dream Weaver. Baviera, Rocco, illus. 2010. (Rise & Shine Ser.). (ENG.). 32p. (C). (gr. -1-3). 29.95 *(978-0-15-200944-1(2))* National Geographic School Publishing, Inc.
Lucado, Max & Schmidt, Troy. Webster, the Scaredy Spider. 2005. 32p. (J). pap. 3.99 *(978-1-4003-0665-7(5))* Nelson, Thomas Inc.
Lyssenko, Taras. Wendy's Fear of Heights. 2003. 14p. (J). *(978-0-9740542-0-9(8))* Prairie Shore Creative, Inc.
Magsamen, Sandra. Itsy-Bitsy I Love You! Magsamen, Sandra, illus. 2016. (Heart-Felt Bks.). (ENG., Illus.). 10p. (J). (— 1). 7.99 *(978-0-545-46841-1(8)*, Cartwheel Bks.) Scholastic, Inc.
Make Believe Ideas. Incy Wincy Spider. 2015. (ENG.). 12p. (J). bds. 8.99 *(978-1-78393-533-8(2))* Make Believe Ideas GBR. Dist: Nelson, Thomas Inc.
Marchi, Mary V. The Web in the Halo: A Tale of a Spider Who Learns about Christmas. 2012. 32p. pap. 19.99 *(978-1-4685-6624-6(5))* AuthorHouse.
Marshall, Geraldine Ann. Spider's Gift: A Christmas Story. Sorge, Rebecca, illus. 2016. 40p. (J). pap. 14.95 *(978-0-8198-9058-0(8))* Pauline Bks. & Media.
Matt & Dave. Yuck's Amazing Underpants. Baines, Nigel, illus. 2012. (Yuck Ser.). (ENG.). 112p. (J). (gr. 2-5). 14.99 *(978-1-4424-5121-6(1))*; pap. 4.99 *(978-1-4424-5122-3(X))* Simon & Schuster/Paula Wiseman Bks. (Simon & Schuster/Paula Wiseman Bks.).
—Yuck's Slime Monster. Baines, Nigel, illus. 2012. (Yuck Ser.). (ENG.). 112p. (J). (gr. 2-5). 14.99 *(978-1-4424-5124-7(6))*; pap. 4.99 *(978-1-4424-5126-1(2))* Simon & Schuster/Paula Wiseman Bks. (Simon & Schuster/Paula Wiseman Bks.).
Max, Jill, compiled by. Spider Spins a Story: Fourteen Legends from Native America. 2007. (ENG.). 72p. (J). (gr. 3-7). pap. 8.95 *(978-0-87358-936-9(X))* Cooper Square Publishing Llc.
Miceli, Mary Anne. Boston North Shore's. 2011. 44p. pap. 21.99 *(978-1-4568-1135-8(5))* Xlibris Corp.
Miller, John. Red Spider Hero. Cucco, Giuliano, illus. 2015. (ENG.). 40p. (J). (gr. -1-3). 16.95 *(978-1-59270-176-6(0))* Enchanted Lion Bks., LLC.
Miss Spider Activity Kit. 2005. (Illus.). (J). *(978-0-448-44063-7(6)*, Grosset & Dunlap) Penguin Publishing Group.
Monks, Lydia. Aaaarrgghh! Spider! 2004. (Illus.). 32p. (J). *(978-1-4052-0688-4(8))* Egmont Bks., Ltd.
—Aaaarrgghh! Spider! 2007. (ENG., Illus.). 32p. (J). (gr. -1-3). 9.99 *(978-0-618-73751-2(0))* Houghton Mifflin Harcourt Publishing Co.
Monks, Lydia, illus. Aaaarrgghh, Spider! 2004. (ENG.). 32p. (J). pap. 10.99 *(978-1-4052-1044-7(3))* Egmont Bks., Ltd.
Moore, James W. & Moore, Eileen. Dark at the Foot of the Stairs. (Illus.). 92p. (J). pap. *(978-0-340-64873-5(2))* Hodder & Stoughton.
Morgan, C. M. Silver Doorway #2: Dwarves in the Dark. 2003. 104p. (J). pap. *(978-0-9702189-3-3(1))* Sabledrake Enterprises.
Morley, Farah, illus. The Spider & the Doves: The Story of the Hijra. 2012. (ENG.). 30p. (J). (gr. -1-2). 8.95 *(978-0-86037-449-7(1))* Kube Publishing Ltd. GBR. Dist: Consortium Bk. Sales & Distribution.
Moulton, Mark K. A Royal Wedding. Good, Karen H., illus. 2007. (ENG.). 32p. (J). (gr. k-3). 14.99 *(978-0-8249-8677-3(6)*, Ideal Pubns.) Worthy Publishing.
Moulton, Mark Kimball. One Enchanted Evening. Crouch, Karen Hillard, illus. 2003. 32p. (J). 14.95 *(978-0-8249-5480-2(7)*, Ideal Pubns.) Worthy Publishing.
Nagda, Ann Whitehead. Tarantula Power! 2007. (ENG., Illus.). 96p. (J). (gr. 2-5). 15.95 *(978-0-8234-1991-3(6))* Holiday Hse., Inc.
Nanny, B. The Spider who Lived in our Grandads Car. 2011. (Illus.). 12p. 10.17 *(978-1-4567-7645-9(2))* AuthorHouse.
Niddrie, June. Sweetpea & His Friends. 2010. 36p. pap. 17.30 *(978-0-557-31853-7(X))* Lulu Pr., Inc.
Norfolk, Bobby & Norfolk, Sherry. Anansi & the Pot of Beans. Hoffmire, Baird, illus. 2006. (Story Cove Ser.). (ENG.). 32p. (J). (gr. -1-3). 4.95 *(978-0-87483-811-4(8))* August Hse. Pubs., Inc.
Oaklee, Mammy. My Keyboard Was Hi~Jacked! 2013. 40p. pap. *(978-1-4602-2616-2(X))* FriesenPress.
Oguneye, Kunle. Sikulu & Harambe by the Zambezi River: An African Vversion of the Good Samaritan Story. McCorkindale, Bruce & Youtsey, Scott, illus. 2008. 32p. (J). (gr. -1-5). 14.99 *(978-0-9777382-4-3(8))* Blue Brush Media.
Olson, Kevin Noel. Eerey Tocsin in the Cryptoid Zoo. Hammack, Debi, illus. 2006. (ENG.). 176p. (YA). per. 15.95 *(978-1-887560-17-7(3)*, Cornerstone Bk. Publishers) Poll, Michael Publishing.
Orme, David. Bugs & Spiders. Mongiovi, Jorge, illus. 2010. (Fact to Fiction Ser.). 36p. pap. 7.45 *(978-0-7891-7990-6(3))* Perfection Learning Corp.
Osborne, Mary Pope. The Mysteries of Spider Kane. 2006. (ENG.). 240p. (J). (gr. 3-7). 6.99 *(978-0-440-42097-2(0)*, Yearling) Random Hse. Children's Bks.
Osei, Leah. Why Anansi Has Eight Thin Legs: A Tale from West Africa, 1 vol. 2013. (Fiction Readers Ser.). (ENG., Illus.). 24p. (J). (gr. 2-2). pap. 6.99 *(978-1-4333-5524-0(8))* Shell Educational Publishing.
Pandya, Ashish. Ping the Spider: The journey Begins... 2008. 16p. pap. 12.99 *(978-1-4343-9261-9(9))* AuthorHouse.

The check digit for ISBN-10 appears in parentheses after the full ISBN-13

Pantelides, Sherry. Make A Choice to Rejoice! A Story about Being Cheerful. Perez, Debi, illus. 2007. 32p. (J). 12.99 *(978-0-9771076-2-9(0))* Lacey Productions.

Perry, Tally. Saving Sunny Stream, a Wormie Wormald Adventure. 2009. 60p. pap. 22.00 *(978-1-60860-296-4(6),* Eloquent Bks.) Strategic Book Publishing & Rights Agency (SBPRA).

Phillips, Gina & Martin, Stuart. Ants & Caterpillars. 2003. (Busy Bugs Ser.). 12p. (J). bds. 14.95 *(978-1-74047-240-1(3))* Book Co. Publishing Pty, Ltd., The AUS. Dist: Penton Overseas, Inc.

Pollock, Terry. A Spider Like Me. 2011. 28p. pap. 21.99 *(978-1-4628-6791-2(X))* Xlibris Corp.

Pryce, Trevor. An Army of Frogs. Greene, Sanford, illus. 2013. (Kulipari Ser.). (ENG.). 288p. (J). (gr. 3-7). 15.95 *(978-1-4197-0172-6(X),* Amulet Bks.) Abrams, Inc.

Pryce, Trevor & Naftali, Joel. An Army of Frogs. Greene, Sanford, illus. 2014. (Kulipari Ser.). (ENG.). 304p. (J). (gr. 3-7). pap. 8.95 *(978-1-4197-1381-1(7),* Amulet Bks.) Abrams, Inc.

Publications International Ltd. Staff, ed. Sesame Street: The Itsy Bitsy Spider. 2011. 10p. (J). bds. 7.98 *(978-1-4508-0858-3(1),* 6461bf3e-ab03-4ebc-81c6-091daf4fbc8e) Phoenix International Publications, Inc.

Ray, Michelle. A Huntsman Spider in My House... Ashford, Sylvie, illus. 2014. (ENG.). 34p. pap. 8.95 *(978-1-61448-842-2(8),* 9781614488422) Morgan James Publishing.

Raye, Donna. Edison the Firefly & Sierra the Special Spider. 2013. 28p. pap. 9.99 *(978-0-9910324-9-5(7))* Mindstir Media.

Razi, Michaele. Frank the Seven-Legged Spider. 2017. (ENG.). 32p. (J). (gr. -1-3). 16.99 ***(978-1-63217-128-3(7),*** Little Bigfoot) Sasquatch Bks.

Read, Laurie. Blacky Longlegs Meets Freddy the Fly. 2008. 20p. pap. 14.00 *(978-1-4389-1231-8(5))* AuthorHouse.

Redepenning, George. The Adventures of Webster. 2008. pap. 9.00 *(978-0-8059-8629-7(4))* Dorrance Publishing Co., Inc.

Reed, Len. Monsters at My Bed. 2011. 16p. (gr. 1-2). pap. 8.49 *(978-1-4567-6786-0(0))* AuthorHouse.

ReWalt, Nancy E. Aerial: A Spider's Tale. Cranford, Darren, illus. 2009. 32p. (J). 16.95 *(978-0-9821110-0-0(2))* Ronan Enterprises, Inc.

—Aerial: A Trip to Remember. Cranford, Darren, illus. 2010. 32p. (J). 16.95 *(978-0-9821110-1-7(0))* Ronan Enterprises, Inc.

Rewalt, Nancy E. Aerial Meets Farmer Fedamore. Cranford, Darren, illus. 2012. 64p. (J). 17.95 *(978-0-9821110-3-1(7))* Ronan Enterprises, Inc.

Rhatigan, Joe. The Itsy Bitsy Spider. Farias, Carolina, illus. 2017. (Classic Nursery Rhymes Retold Ser.). (ENG.). 32p. (J). (gr. -1-k). 12.95 *(978-1-63322-160-4(1),* Moondance) Quarto Publishing Group USA.

Rivera, Monica O. Lola the Spider & the Purple Crayon. 2009. 20p. pap. 15.00 *(978-1-4389-7487-3(6))* AuthorHouse.

Roark, Algernon Michael. Graylinger Grotto. Triplett, Ginger, illus. 2011. (ENG.). 94p. (J). pap. 22.95 *(978-1-59299-631-5(0))* Inkwater Pr.

Roberts, Pauline. Miss Spider Misses Supper. 2012. 28p. pap. 16.09 *(978-1-4669-5264-5(4))* Trafford Publishing.

Rogers, Buddy & Avery, Ben. Power Play, 1 vol. Wong, Scott, illus. 2008. (Z Graphic Novels / TimeFlyz Ser.). (ENG.). 160p. (J). pap. 6.99 *(978-0-310-71365-4(X))* Zondervan.

Rouss, Sylvia. Sammy Spider's First Haggadah. Kahn, Katherine, illus. 2007. (Passover Ser.). (ENG.). 32p. (J). (gr. -1-3). per. 6.95 *(978-1-58013-230-5(8),* Kar-Ben Publishing) Lerner Publishing Group.

—Sammy Spider's First Mitzvah. Janus Kahn, Katherine, illus. 2014. (ENG.). 24p. (J). (gr. -1-3). 17.95 *(978-1-4677-1947-6(1),* Kar-Ben Publishing) Lerner Publishing Group.

Rouss, Sylvia A. A Sammy Spider Hanukkah Colors. Kahn, Katherine, illus. 2017. (ENG.). 12p. (gr. -1 — 1). bds. 5.99 *(978-1-4677-5238-1(X),* Kar-Ben Publishing) Lerner Publishing Group.

—A Sammy Spider Passover. Kahn, Katherine & Kahn, Katherine Janus, illus. 2017. (ENG.). 12p. (gr. -1 — 1). 5.99 *(978-1-4677-7970-8(9),* Kar-Ben Publishing) Lerner Publishing Group.

—Sammy Spider Series, 11 vols., Set. Kahn, Katherine Janus, illus. 2003. (J). (gr. -1-3). 70.61 *(978-1-58013-046-2(1),* Kar-Ben Publishing) Lerner Publishing Group.

—Sammy Spider's First Bar Mitzvah. Kahn, Katherine Janus, illus. 2016. (ENG.). 32p. (J). (gr. -1-3). 17.99 *(978-1-4677-8931-8(3),* Kar-Ben Publishing) Lerner Publishing Group.

—Sammy Spider's First Day of School. Kahn, Katherine, illus. 2009. (Kar-Ben Favorites Ser.). (ENG.). 32p. (J). (gr. -1-2). 16.95 *(978-0-8225-8583-1(9),* Kar-Ben Publishing) Lerner Publishing Group.

—Sammy Spider's First Day of School. Kahn, Katherine Janus, illus. 2009. (Kar-Ben Favorites Ser.). (ENG.). 32p. (J). (gr. -1-2). pap. 7.95 *(978-0-8225-8584-8(7),* Kar-Ben Publishing) Lerner Publishing Group.

—Sammy Spider's First Shavuot. Kahn, Katherine Janus, illus. 2008. (Sammy Spider's First Bks.). (ENG.). 32p. (J). (gr. -1-3). lib. bdg. 15.95 *(978-0-8225-7224-4(9));* per. 7.95 *(978-0-8225-7225-1(7))* Lerner Publishing Group. (Kar-Ben Publishing).

—Sammy Spider's First Simchat Torah. Kahn, Katherine Janus, illus. 2010. (Sukkot & Simchat Torah Ser.). (ENG.). 32p. (J). (gr. -1-2). pap. 7.95 *(978-0-7613-3966-3(3),* Kar-Ben Publishing) Lerner Publishing Group.

—Sammy Spider's First Simchat Torah. Kahn, Katherine, illus. 2010. (Sukkot & Simchat Torah Ser.). (ENG.). 32p. (J). (gr. -1-2). lib. bdg. 15.95 *(978-0-7613-3965-6(5),* Kar-Ben Publishing) Lerner Publishing Group.

—Sammy Spider's First Sukkot. Kahn, Katherine Janus, illus. 2004. (ENG.). 32p. (J). (gr. -1-3). 17.95 *(978-1-58013-142-1(5));* pap. 7.95 *(978-1-58013-083-7(6))* Lerner Publishing Group. (Kar-Ben Publishing).

—Sammy Spider's First Yom Kippur. 2013. (Illus.). 32p. (J). pap. 16.95 *(978-1-4677-1639-0(1))* Lerner Publishing Group.

—Sammy Spider's First Yom Kippur. Kahn, Katherine Janus, illus. 2013. (High Holidays Ser.). (ENG.). 32p. (J). (gr. -1-3). 7.95 *(978-0-7613-9196-8(7),* Kar-Ben Publishing) Lerner Publishing Group.

—Sammy Spider's First Yom Kippur. Kahn, Katherine, illus. 2013. (High Holidays Ser.). (ENG.). 32p. (J). (gr. -1-3). lib. bdg. 16.95 *(978-0-7613-9195-1(9),* Kar-Ben Publishing) Lerner Publishing Group.

—Sammy Spider's New Friend. Kahn, Katherine, illus. 2012. (Kar-Ben Favorites Ser.). (ENG.). 32p. (J). (gr. -1-2). lib. bdg. 17.95 *(978-0-7613-6663-8(6),* Kar-Ben Publishing) Lerner Publishing Group.

Rouss, Sylvia A. Sammy Spider's Passover Shapes. Kahn, Katherine Janus, illus. 2017. (Passover Ser.). (ENG.). 12p. (gr. -1 — 1). 23.99 ***(978-1-5124-2727-1(6),*** Kar-Ben Publishing) Lerner Publishing Group.

Rouss, Sylvia A. & Janus Kahn, Katherine. Sammy Spider's New Friend. 2012. (Kar-Ben Favorites Ser.). (ENG., Illus.). 32p. (J). (gr. -1-3). 7.95 *(978-0-7613-6664-5(4),* Kar-Ben Publishing) Lerner Publishing Group.

Rouss, Sylvia A. & Kahn, Katherine Janus. Sammy Spider's Israel Fun Book. 2004. (ENG., Illus.). 24p. (J). (gr. -1-2). pap. 4.95 *(978-1-58013-119-3(0),* Kar-Ben Publishing) Lerner Publishing Group.

Rouss, Sylvia A. & Lanton, Sandy. Lots of Latkes: A Hanukkah Story. Kahn, Katherine Janus & Redenbaugh, Vicki Jo, illus. 2003. (ENG.). 32p. (J). (gr. -1-3). pap. 6.95 *(978-1-58013-061-5(5),* Kar-Ben Publishing) Lerner Publishing Group.

Sanders, Terri L. Rainbow Spider. 2003. E-Book 4.95 incl. cd-rom *(978-1-59201-011-0(3))* Bks. Unbound E-Publishing Co.

Satterfield, April. Leah Bug & Her Flying Friends. Guthrie, Lewis, illus. 2011. 20p. pap. 24.95 *(978-1-4560-8422-6(4))* America Star Bks.

Schandle, Julie. Little Wishes Big Dreams: Around the World. 2005. (Illus.). 22p. (J). 11.95 *(978-0-9771868-0-8(6),* 303-503-3289) Big Dreams Publishing.

Schmickl, Angela. The Matador Who Ran Away from the Spider. 2013. 24p. pap. 10.96 *(978-1-4251-9190-0(8))* Trafford Publishing.

Schweizer, Chris. Tricky Spider Tales. Huddleston, Courtney, illus. 2011. (Tricky Journeys Ser.: 5). (ENG.). (J). (gr. 2-4). pap. 39.62 *(978-0-7613-8629-2(7));* 64p. pap. 6.95 *(978-0-7613-7864-8(2));*No. 5. 64p. lib. bdg. 27.93 *(978-0-7613-6609-6(1))* Lerner Publishing Group.

Scorpions. 2003. 50p. (YA). tchr. ed., ring bd. *(978-1-58049-470-0(6),* TU226) Prestwick Hse., Inc.

Seuling, Barbara. Robert & the Attack of the Giant Tarantula. Brewer, Paul, illus. 2003. (Oh No, It's Robert Ser.). (ENG.). 64p. (J). pap. 3.99 *(978-0-439-23545-7(6),* Scholastic Paperbacks) Scholastic, Inc.

Shan, Darren, pseud. Trials of Death. 2004. (Cirque du Freak Ser.: 5). (ENG., Illus.). 224p. (J). (gr. 7-17). pap. 10.99 *(978-0-316-60395-9(3))* Little, Brown Bks. for Young Readers.

Sherlock, Philip. Anansi & the Alligator Eggs y Los Huevos Del Caimán. Rickham, Elethia, tr. Judah, Susan, illus. 2nd ed. 2013. 42p. pap. 15.00 *(978-976-95510-6-0(6))* Minna Pr.

Simpon, Tj. Tiny Paul the Tarantula Takes a Walk, 1 vol. Register, J. R., illus. 2010. 70p. pap. 19.95 *(978-1-60703-117-8(5))* America Star Bks.

Smart Kidz, creator. The Itsy Bitsy Spider. 2013. (Sing N Play Songs Ser.). (ENG., Illus.). 12p. (J). (gr. -1). bds. 12.99 *(978-1-891100-56-7(4),* Smart Kidz) Penton Overseas, Inc.

Smith, Kim. Leroy's Long Journey: Leroy Baxter, the near-Sighted Spider Volume I, 4 vols., Vol. 1. 2009. (Leroy Baxter, the Near-Sighted Spider Ser.: Vol. 1). (Illus.). 28p. (J). (gr. k-3). pap. 8.99 *(978-0-9818190-0-6(1),* Candy Cane Bks.) Sunlight Publishing.

Smith, Pamela Colman. Annancy Stories. 2006. (YA). reprint ed. pap. 19.99 *(978-0-9769612-2-2(9))* Darker Intentions Pr.

Snyder, Robert. Itsy Bitsy Spider. Snyder, Robert, illus. 2009. (ENG., Illus.). 20p. (J). 12.99 *(978-0-8249-1821-7(5),* Ideal Pubns.) Worthy Publishing.

Soileau, Hodges, illus. The Black Widow Spider Mystery. 2004. (Boxcar Children Special Ser.). 130p. (gr. 2-7). 15.50 *(978-0-7569-3266-4(1))* Perfection Learning Corp.

Sorenson, Jack R. Eibhlin & Her Dragon, 1 vol. 2009. 131p. pap. 24.95 *(978-1-60749-634-2(8))* America Star Bks.

Soundprints Staff. Itsy Bitsy Spider: And Other Favorites. 2005. (Meet Mother Goose Ser.). (ENG., Illus.). 36p. (J). 10.95 *(978-1-931465-31-1(2),* MD1100); 14.95 *(978-1-931465-51-9(7),* MPD1100) Soundprints.

Sparkes, Ali. Spider Stampede. Collins, Ross, illus. 2013. (S. W. I. T. C. H. Ser.: 1). (ENG.). 104p. (J). (gr. 2-5). lib. bdg. 27.93 *(978-0-7613-9199-9(1))* Lerner Publishing Group.

Spider Night! (Early Intervention Levels Ser.). 28.38 *(978-0-7362-0411-8(3))* CENGAGE Learning.

The Spider Who Never Gave Up. 2004. (J). *(978-0-9759077-0-2(0))* Flores, Travis.

Spinelli, Eileen. Sophie's Masterpiece: A Spider's Tale. Dyer, Jane, illus. 2004. (ENG.). 32p. (J). (gr. -1-2). reprint ed. 7.99 *(978-0-689-86680-7(1),* Simon & Schuster Bks. For Young Readers) Simon & Schuster Bks. For Young Readers.

St. Romain, Rose Anne. Monsieur Durand's Grosse Affaire, 1 vol. Waites, Joan, illus. 2011. (ENG.). 32p. (J). (gr. k-3). 16.99 *(978-1-58980-808-9(8))* Pelican Publishing Co., Inc.

Stadelmann, Amy Marie. The Not-So Itty-Bitty Spiders. 2015. (Olive & Beatrix Ser.: 1). (ENG., Illus.). 80p. (J). (gr. k-2). pap. 4.99 *(978-0-545-81480-5(4))* Scholastic, Inc.

Stoh, Emily. Roger Meets Sam. Stoh, Judy, illus. 2009. 24p. pap. 9.95 *(978-1-935105-41-1(8))* Avid Readers Publishing Group.

Stoner, Eileen M. Inky & Dinky: Mindy .... A Tale of Change. 2009. 48p. pap. 17.49 *(978-1-4490-0488-0(1))* AuthorHouse.

Sydor, Colleen. Raising a Little Stink. Constantin, Pascale, illus. 2006. (ENG.). 32p. (J). (gr. -1-2). 16.95 *(978-1-55337-896-9(2))* Kids Can Pr., Ltd. CAN. Dist: Hachette Bk. Group.

.T. Ozzie the Spider. 2013. 24p. pap. 11.95 *(978-1-4575-2025-9(7))* Dog Ear Publishing, LLC.

Tandy, Clive. Quarry Grove. 2008. 60p. per. 11.59 *(978-1-4251-4974-1(X))* Trafford Publishing.

Thomas, Susan. Beyond the Mist: Sequel to Mist on the Window. 2012. 352p. pap. 24.34 *(978-1-4772-4627-6(4))* AuthorHouse.

Thompson, Chad. The Itsy Bitsy Spider, 1 vol. 2009. (Early Childhood Themes Ser.). (ENG., Illus.). 16p. (J). (gr. -1-2). pap. 19.99 *(978-1-4333-1455-1(X))* Shell Educational Publishing.

—The Itsy Bitsy Spider, 1 vol. 2009. (Early Childhood Themes Ser.). (ENG., Illus.). 16p. (J). (gr. -1-2). pap. 6.99 *(978-1-4333-1454-4(1))* Teacher Created Materials, Inc.

Toms, Kate & Make Believe Ideas Staff. Itsy Bitsy Spider. 2009. (Kate Toms Ser.). (Illus.). 26p. (gr. -1-k). bds. 7.99 *(978-1-84610-974-4(4))* Make Believe Ideas GBR. Dist: Nelson, Thomas Inc.

Trapani, Iza. Sing along with Iza & Friends: The Itsy Bitsy Spider. Trapani, Iza, illus. 2004. (Illus.). 32p. (J). pap. 11.95 incl. audio compact disk *(978-1-58089-100-4(4))* Charlesbridge Publishing, Inc.

Treviño, Hilda L. Ladybugs on a Mission. 2013. 70p. (gr. 4-6). pap. 8.95 *(978-1-4759-7762-2(X))* iUniverse, Inc.

Troupe, Thomas Kingsley. The Big Hairy Secret, 1 vol. Gilpin, Stephen, illus. 2013. (Furry & Flo Ser.). (ENG.). 128p. (gr. 2-3). 8.95 *(978-1-62370-033-1(7));* lib. bdg. 25.32 *(978-1-4342-3858-0(X))* Stone Arch Bks.

Vermeulen, Thomas. Gabangani Guinea Fowl & Huzu the Bird Eating Spider. 2009. 50p. pap. 19.50 *(978-1-60693-741-9(3),* Eloquent Bks.) Strategic Book Publishing & Rights Agency (SBPRA).

Wakefield, Beth. The Cleaner. 2010. 151p. pap. 14.50 *(978-1-4457-6809-0(7))* Lulu Pr., Inc.

Wang, Margaret. Eency Weency Spider. Rueda, Claudia, illus. 2006. (ENG.). (J). 12p. bds. 5.95 *(978-1-58117-505-9(1));* 22p. (gr. -1-3). bds. 10.95 *(978-1-58117-418-2(7))* Bendon, Inc. (Intervisual/Piggy Toes).

West, Robert. Escape from the Drooling Octopod!, 1 vol. 2008. (Star-Fighters of Murphy Street Ser.). (ENG., Illus.). 144p. (J). (gr. 4-7). pap. 6.99 *(978-0-310-71427-9(3))* Zonderkidz.

Weston Woods Staff, creator. Anansi the Spider. 2011. 18.95 *(978-0-439-88174-6(9));* 38.75 *(978-0-439-84573-1(4))* Weston Woods Studios, Inc.

Whincup, Sara. The St John's Cross Spider. Yapsangco, Kenn, illus. 2015. (ENG.). 28p. (J). pap. 28.22 *(978-1-5035-0985-6(0))* Xlibris Corp.

White. Tela di Carlotta. pap. 13.95 *(978-88-04-46241-5(8))* Mondadori ITA. Dist: Distribooks, Inc.

White, E. B. Charlotte's Web. Williams, Garth, illus. 2005. (Charming Classics). 192p. (J). pap. 7.99 *(978-0-06-084594-0(5),* HarperFestival) HarperCollins Pubs.

—Charlotte's Web. movie tie-in ed. 2006. (Charlotte's Web Ser.). (ENG., Illus.). 192p. (J). (gr. 4-7). per. 7.99 *(978-0-06-112026-8(X))* HarperCollins Pubs.

—Charlotte's Web. Williams, Garth, illus. movie tie-in ed. 2006. (Charlotte's Web Ser.). (J). 192p. mass mkt. 7.99 *(978-0-06-122874-2(5),* Harper Trophy);Set. pap. 19.99 *(978-0-06-121502-5(3))* HarperCollins Pubs.

—Charlotte's Web. Williams, Garth, illus. 2004. (CHI.). 158p. (YA). pap. *(978-957-08-2568-8(5))* Linking Publishing Co., Ltd.

—Charlotte's Web. Williams, Garth, illus. 184p. (J). pap. 5.95 *(978-0-8072-8305-9(3),* Listening Library) Random Hse. Audio Publishing Group.

—Charlotte's Web. unabr. ed. 2004. 184p. (J). (gr. 3-7). pap. 36.00 incl. audio *(978-0-8072-8304-2(5),* YYA156SP, Listening Library) Random Hse. Audio Publishing Group.

—Charlotte's Web. 2012. (J). (gr. 3-6). 18.40 *(978-0-8085-3772-4(5),* Turtleback) Turtleback Bks.

—Wilbur's Adventure: A Charlotte's Web Picture Book. Kneen, Maggie, illus. 2008. (Charlotte's Web Ser.). 32p. (J). (gr. k-2). lib. bdg. 17.89 *(978-0-06-078165-1(3))* HarperCollins Pubs.

White, E. B. & DiCamillo, Kate. Charlotte's Web. Williams, Garth, illus. (ENG.). 192p. (J). (gr. 3-7). 2012. 16.99 *(978-0-06-026385-0(7))* 2012. 8.99 *(978-0-06-112495-2(8))* 2012. pap. 8.99 *(978-0-06-440055-8(7))* 2006. 16.99 *(978-0-06-088261-7(1))* HarperCollins Pubs.

Wilson, George H. The Message of the Writing Spider. 2010. (Illus.). 50p. (J). 15.00 *(978-0-9778477-1-6(3))* A Story Plus Children Bks.

Winter, Barbara. Spider Saga. 2004. (Amazing Dictionary Ser.). (Illus.). 64p. pap. *(978-0-921156-96-3(0))* Rubicon Publishing, Inc.

Zimmerman, Carol. Charlie the Spider. 2011. 32p. pap. 13.95 *(978-1-4567-9523-8(6))* AuthorHouse.

SPIES

see also Secret Service; World War, 1939-1945—Underground Movements

see also subdivisions Secret Service and Underground Movements under individual wars, e.g. World War, 1939-1945—Secret Service; World War, 1939-1945—Underground Movements.

Allen, Thomas B. George Washington, Spymaster: How the Americans Outspied the British & Won the Revolutionary War. Harness, Cheryl, illus. 2007. (ENG.). 192p. (J). (gr. 5-7). per. 7.95 *(978-1-4263-0041-7(7),* National Geographic Children's Bks.) National Geographic Society.

Anniss, Matt. Espionage. 2013. (Crime Science Ser.). 48p. (J). (gr. 4-8). pap. 84.30 *(978-1-4339-9490-6(9));* pap. 14.05 *(978-1-4339-9489-0(5));* (ENG., Illus.). lib. bdg. 31.95 *(978-1-4339-9488-3(7))* Stevens, Gareth Publishing LLLP.

Baden-Powell, Robert. My Adventures as a Spy. 2014. (ENG., Illus.). 128p. pap. 13.95 *(978-1-4456-3610-8(7))* Amberley Publishing GBR. Dist: Independent Pubs. Group.

Bearce, Stephanie. The American Revolution: Spies, Secret Missions, & Hidden Facts from the American Revolution. 2014. (Top Secret Files of History Ser.: 0). (ENG.). 125p. (J). (gr. 4-7). pap. 8.95 *(978-1-61821-247-4(8))* Prufrock Pr.

—Top Secret Files - The Cold War Spies: Secrets, Special Missions, & Hidden Facts about the CIA, KGB, & MI6. rev. ed. 2015. (Top Secret Files of History Ser.: 0). (ENG., Illus.). 125p. (J). (gr. 4-7). pap. 8.95 *(978-1-61821-419-5(5))* Prufrock Pr.

—World War I: Spies, Secret Missions, & Hidden Facts from World War I. 2014. (Top Secret Files of History Ser.: 0). (ENG.). 125p. (J). (gr. 4-7). pap. 8.95 *(978-1-61821-241-2(9))* Prufrock Pr.

—World War II: Spies, Secret Missions, & Hidden Facts from World War II. 2014. (Top Secret Files of History Ser.: 0). (ENG.). 125p. (J). (gr. 4-7). pap. 8.95 *(978-1-61821-244-3(3))* Prufrock Pr.

Beck, Esther. Cool Spy Supplies: Fun Top Secret Science Projects, 1 vol. 2008. (Cool Science Ser.). (ENG.). 32p. (YA). (gr. 2-5). 28.50 *(978-1-59928-911-3(3))* ABDO Publishing Co.

Blake, Spencer. Spyology. Steer, Dugald A., ed. Blake, Spencer et al, illus. 2008. (Ologies Ser.: 7). (ENG.). 32p. (J). (gr. 3-7). 25.99 *(978-0-7636-4048-4(4))* Candlewick Pr.

Botones para el General Washington (Buttons for General Washington) 2006. (J). pap. 6.95 *(978-0-8225-6617-5(6),* Ediciones Lerner) Lerner Publishing Group.

Brian, Sarah Jane. Brainiac's Secret Agent: Fun Activities for Spies of All Ages. 2005. (Activity Journal Ser.). 128p. act. bk. ed. 12.99 *(978-0-88088-446-4(0))* Peter Pauper Pr. Inc.

Brook, Henry. Spying. Frith, Alex, ed. Johnson, Staz & Roots, Adrian, illus. 2014. (ENG.). 80p. (J). (gr. 4-7). pap. 8.99 *(978-0-7945-2809-6(0),* Usborne) EDC Publishing.

Brown, Alex. Secret Missions. 2009. (Difficult & Dangerous Ser.). (Illus.). 32p. (J). pap. *(978-1-897563-26-7(4))* Saunders Bk. Co.

Buranelli, Vincent. American Spies & Traitors. 2004. (Collective Biographies Ser.). (Illus.). 112p. (J). lib. bdg. 26.60 *(978-0-7660-2006-1(1))* Enslow Pubs., Inc.

Burgan, Michael. Spies of the Civil War: An Interactive History Adventure. 2015. (You Choose: Spies Ser.). (ENG., Illus.). 112p. (gr. 3-4). pap. 6.95 *(978-1-4914-5932-4(8),* You Choose Bks.) Capstone Press of Coughlan Cos.

—Spies of World War I: An Interactive History Adventure. 2015. (You Choose: Spies Ser.). (ENG., Illus.). 112p. (gr. 3-4). pap. 6.95 *(978-1-4914-5933-1(6),* You Choose Bks.) Capstone Press of Coughlan Cos.

—World War II Spies, 1 vol. 2013. (You Choose: World War II Ser.). (ENG., Illus.). 112p. (gr. 3-4). pap. 6.95 *(978-1-62065-722-5(8),* You Choose Bks.) Capstone Press of Coughlan Cos.

—World War II Spies: An Interactive History Adventure. 2013. (You Choose: World War II Ser.). (ENG.). 112p. (gr. 3-4). pap. 41.70 *(978-1-62065-723-2(6),* You Choose Bks.) Capstone Press of Coughlan Cos.

—World War II Spies: An Interactive History Adventure, 1 vol. 2013. (You Choose: World War II Ser.). (ENG.). 112p. (gr. 3-4). lib. bdg. 31.99 *(978-1-4296-9898-6(5),* You Choose Bks.) Capstone Press of Coughlan Cos.

Burgan, Michael & Raum, Elizabeth. You Choose: Spies. 2015. (You Choose: Spies Ser.). (ENG.). 112p. (gr. 3-4). 127.96 *(978-1-4914-6970-5(6),* You Choose Bks.) Capstone Press of Coughlan Cos.

Caravantes, Peggy. The Many Faces of Josephine Baker: Dancer, Singer, Activist, Spy. 2015. (Women of Action Ser.). (ENG., Illus.). 208p. (YA). (gr. 7). 19.95 *(978-1-61373-034-8(9))* Chicago Review Pr., Inc.

—Petticoat Spies: Six Women Spies of the US Civil War. 2004. (Notable Americans Ser.). (Illus.). 112p. (YA). (gr. 6-12). 23.95 *(978-1-883846-88-6(9),* First Biographies) Reynolds, Morgan Inc.

Cefrey, Holly. One Life to Lose for My Country: The Arrest & Execution of Nathan Hale. (Great Moments in American History Ser.). 32p. 2009. (gr. 3-3). 47.90 *(978-1-61513-135-8(3))* 2004. (Illus.). (gr. 4-8). lib. bdg. 22.50 *(978-0-8239-4371-5(2),* Rosen Reference) Rosen Publishing Group, Inc., The.

Cerasini, Marc, et al. Keep It Hidden! The Best Places to Stash Your Stuff. 2007. (Illus.). 32p. (J). pap. *(978-0-439-90850-4(7))* Scholastic, Inc.

—Spy to Spy: Sharing Your Secrets Safely. 2007. (Illus.). 32p. (J). *(978-0-545-01560-8(X))* Scholastic, Inc.

Chaline, Eric. Secret Heroes of World War II: Tales of Courage from the Worlds of Espionage & Resistance. 2016. (Illus.). 224p. (YA). ***(978-1-4351-6251-8(X))*** Metro Bks.

Cordello, Red, et al. The Stakeout: Spying & Secret Surveillance. 2007. 32p. (J). *(978-0-439-90851-1(5))* Scholastic, Inc.

Cornioley, Pearl Witherington & Atwood, Kathryn J. Code Name Pauline: Memoirs of a World War II Special Agent. 2013. (Women of Action Ser.). (ENG., Illus.). 208p. (YA). (gr. 6). 19.95 *(978-1-61374-487-1(0))* Chicago Review Pr., Inc.

Costain, Meredith. Spies Revealed. 2013. (Discovery Education: Sensational True Stories Ser.). (ENG., Illus.). 32p. (J). (gr. 3-6). pap. 10.00 *(978-1-4777-0103-4(6));* lib. bdg. 25.25 *(978-1-4777-0059-4(5))* Rosen Publishing Group, Inc., The. (PowerKids Pr.).

Curley, Robert. Spy Agencies, Intelligence Operations, & the People Behind Them. Curley, Robert, ed. 2013. 120p. (YA). (gr. 9-12). 32.90 *(978-1-62275-035-1(7))* Rosen Publishing Group, Inc., The.

De Winter, James. Amazing Tricks of Real Spies. 2010. (Extreme! Ser.). (ENG.). 32p. (gr. 3-4). pap. 47.70 *(978-1-4296-5118-9(0),* Fact Finders) Capstone Press of Coughlan Cos.

Denton, Gill. A Mysterious Case of Spying & Espionage: Techniques & Tales of Master Spies. 2013. (ENG.). 48p. (J). (gr. 3-7). 16.99 *(978-1-4380-7367-5(4))* Barron's Educational Series, Inc.

DeVillier, Christy. Nathan Hale, 1 vol. 2004. (First Biographies Set Iv Ser.). (ENG., Illus.). 32p. (gr. k-4). 27.07 *(978-1-59197-513-7(1),* Buddy Bks.) ABDO Publishing Co.

Doak, Robin S. National Intelligence. 2012. (Cornerstones of Freedom, Third Ser.). (ENG., Illus.). 64p. (J). pap. 8.95 *(978-0-531-28161-1(2));* lib. bdg. 30.00 *(978-0-531-23061-9(9))* Scholastic Library Publishing.

Dowswell, P. Secret Agent Spy. 2009. (Kid Kits Ser.). 144p. (J). 16.99 *(978-1-60130-153-6(7));* 16.99 *(978-1-60130-152-9(9))* EDC Publishing. (Usborne).

Dowswell, Paul & Fleming, Fergus. Spies. 2008. (Usborne True Stories Ser.). (Illus.). 139p. (J). pap. 4.99 *(978-0-7945-1842-4(7),* Usborne) EDC Publishing.

—True Spy Stories. 2004. (True Adventure Stories Ser.). (J). 144p. pap. 4.95 *(978-0-7945-0088-7(9));* (Illus.). 139p. (gr. 5). lib. bdg. 12.95 *(978-1-58086-682-8(4))* EDC Publishing. (Usborne).

Doyle, Bill H. Behind Enemy Lines. 2009. 135p. (J). pap. *(978-0-545-14705-7(0))* Scholastic, Inc.

Earnest, Peter. The Real Spy's Guide to Becoming a Spy. Harper, Suzanne, illus. 2009. (ENG.). 144p. (J). (gr. 3-7). 19.95 *(978-0-8109-8329-8(X),* Abrams Bks. for Young Readers) Abrams, Inc.

Francis, Suzanne, et al. Spy by Night: Stealth & Secrets after Dark. 2007. (Illus.). 32p. (J). pap. *(978-0-545-01557-8(X))* Scholastic, Inc.

S

Friddell, Claudia. George Washington's Spies. Lowe, Wesley, illus. 2016. (Totally True Adventures Ser.). (ENG.). 112p. (J). (gr. 2-5). pap. 4.99 (978-0-399-55077-5(1), Random Hse. Bks. for Young Readers) Random Hse. Children's Bks.
Fridell, Ron. Spy Technology. 2006. (Cool Science Ser.). (ENG., Illus.). 48p. (gr. 4-8). lib. bdg. 27.93 (978-0-8225-5934-4(X), Lerner Pubns.) Lerner Publishing Group.
Gifford, Clive. Spies & Spying. 2013. (Illus.). 128p. (J). (978-1-4351-5016-4(3)) Barnes & Noble, Inc.
Gilbert, Adrian. Spy Files: Secret Agents. 2009. (Spy Files Ser.). (ENG., Illus.). 32p. (J). (gr. 3-12). pap. 6.95 (978-1-55407-574-4(2), 9781554075744) Firefly Bks., Ltd.
—Spy School. 2009. (Spy Files Ser.). (ENG., Illus.). 32p. (J). (gr. 3-12). pap. 6.95 (978-1-55407-575-1(0), 9781554075751) Firefly Bks., Ltd.
—Top Technology. 2009. (Spy Files Ser.). (ENG., Illus.). 32p. (J). (gr. 3-12). pap. 6.95 (978-1-55407-576-8(9), 9781554075768) Firefly Bks., Ltd.
Goodman, Michael. World War I Spies. 2015. (Illus.). 48p. (J). (978-1-60818-602-0(4), Creative Education) Creative Co., The.
Goodman, Michael E. The CIA & Other American Spies. 2012. (Spies Around the World Ser.). (Illus.). 48p. (J). (gr. 5-12). 23.95 (978-1-60818-226-8(6)) Creative Co., The.
—Civil War Spies. 2015. (Illus.). 48p. (J). (978-1-60818-598-6(2), Creative Education) Creative Co., The.
—Civil War Spies: Wartime Spies. 2016. (Wartime Spies Ser.). (ENG.). 48p. (J). (gr. 5-9). pap. 12.00 (978-1-62832-203-3(9), Creative Paperbacks) Creative Co., The.
—Cold War Spies. 2015. (Illus.). 48p. (J). (978-1-60818-599-3(0), Creative Education) Creative Co., The.
—Cold War Spies: Wartime Spies. 2016. (Wartime Spies Ser.). (ENG.). 48p. (J). (gr. 5-9). pap. 12.00 (978-1-62832-204-0(7), Creative Paperbacks) Creative Co., The.
—The KGB & Other Russian Spies. 2012. (Spies Around the World Ser.). (Illus.). 48p. (J). (gr. 5-12). 23.95 (978-1-60818-227-5(4), Creative Education) Creative Co., The.
—Modern Spies. 2015. (Illus.). 48p. (J). (978-1-60818-600-6(8), Creative Education) Creative Co., The.
—Modern Spies: Wartime Spies. 2016. (Wartime Spies Ser.). (ENG., Illus.). 48p. (J). (gr. 5-9). pap. 12.00 (978-1-62832-205-7(5), Creative Paperbacks) Creative Co., The.
—Revolutionary War Spies. 2015. (Illus.). 48p. (J). (978-1-60818-601-3(6), Creative Education) Creative Co., The.
—Revolutionary War Spies: Wartime Spies. 2016. (Wartime Spies Ser.). (ENG.). 48p. (J). (gr. 5-9). pap. 12.00 (978-1-62832-206-4(3), Creative Paperbacks) Creative Co., The.
—The SIS & Other British Spies. 2012. (Spies Around the World Ser.). (Illus.). 48p. (J). (gr. 5-12). 23.95 (978-1-60818-229-9(0), Creative Education) Creative Co., The.
—Spies Around the World: the CIA & Other American Spies. 2014. (Spies Around the World Ser.). (ENG., Illus.). 48p. (J). (gr. 4-7). pap. 12.00 (978-0-89812-969-4(9), Creative Paperbacks) Creative Co., The.
—Spies Around the World: the KGB & Other Russian Spies. 2014. (Spies Around the World Ser.). (ENG., Illus.). 48p. (J). (gr. 4-7). pap. 12.00 (978-0-89812-970-0(2), Creative Paperbacks) Creative Co., The.
—Spies Around the World: the Mossad & Other Israeli Spies. 2014. (Spies Around the World Ser.). (ENG., Illus.). 48p. (J). (gr. 4-7). pap. 12.00 (978-0-89812-971-7(0), Creative Paperbacks) Creative Co., The.
—Spies Around the World: the SIS & Other British Spies. 2014. (Spies Around the World Ser.). (ENG., Illus.). 48p. (J). (gr. 4-7). pap. 12.00 (978-0-89812-972-4(9), Creative Paperbacks) Creative Co., The.
—World War I Spies: Wartime Spies. 2016. (Wartime Spies Ser.). (ENG., Illus.). 48p. (J). (gr. 5-9). pap. 12.00 (978-1-62832-207-1(1), Creative Paperbacks) Creative Co., The.
—World War II Spies. 2015. (Illus.). 48p. (J). (978-1-60818-603-7(2), Creative Education) Creative Co., The.
—World War II Spies: Wartime Spies. 2016. (Wartime Spies Ser.). (ENG.). 48p. (J). (gr. 5-9). pap. 12.00 (978-1-62832-208-8(X), Creative Paperbacks) Creative Co., The.
Guillain, Charlotte. Sneaky Spies, 1 vol. 2011. (War Stories Ser.). (ENG.). 32p. (gr. 3-6). 30.65 (978-1-4329-4833-7(4), NA-h) Heinemann-Raintree.
Hale, Nathan. One Dead Spy. 2012. (Nathan Hale's Hazardous Tales Ser.). (ENG., Illus.). 128p. (J). (gr. 3-7). 12.95 (978-1-4197-0396-6(X), Amulet Bks.) Abrams, Inc.
Harmon, Daniel E. Special Ops: Military Intelligence, 1 vol. 2015. (ENG.). 64p. (J). 32.95 (978-1-4777-7587-5(0), Rosen Reference) Rosen Publishing Group, Inc., The.
Harvey, Gill. True Stories of Crime & Detection. 2004. (True Adventure Stories Ser.). 144p. (J). lib. bdg. 12.95 (978-1-58086-644-6(1), Usborne) EDC Publishing.
—True Stories of Crime & Detection. Chisholm, Jane, ed. 2004. (True Adventure Stories Ser.). 144p. (J). pap. 4.95 (978-0-7945-0613-1(5), Usborne) EDC Publishing.
Hastedt, Glenn. Espionage: A Reference Handbook, 1 vol. Vasan, Mildred, ed. 2003. (Contemporary World Issues Ser.). (Illus.). 225p. (C). 50.00 (978-1-57607-950-8(3), ESPIONC) ABC-CLIO, LLC.
Head, Honor. Famous Spies. 2010. (Spies & Spying Ser.). (J). (gr. 4-7). 28.50 (978-1-59920-358-4(8)) Black Rabbit Bks.
Hunt, Elizabeth Singer. The Secret Agent Training Manual: How to Make & Break Top Secret Messages: a Companion to the Jack & Max Stalwart Adventure Series. Williamson, Brian, illus. 2017. (Secret Agents Jack & Max Stalwart Nonfiction Ser.: 1). (ENG.). 112p. (J). (gr. 2-7). pap. 6.99 **(978-1-60286-339-2(3)**, Weinstein Bks.) Perseus Bks. Group.
Hunter, Ryan Ann. In Disguise! Stories of Real Women Spies. 2004. (Illus.). 133p. (J). (gr. 4-7). per. 9.95 (978-1-58270-095-3(8)) Beyond Words Publishing, Inc.
—In Disguise! Undercover with Real Women Spies. Little, Jeanette, illus. 2013. (ENG.). 176p. (J). (gr. 3-7). 17.99 (978-1-58270-383-1(3)); pap. 9.99 (978-1-58270-382-4(5)) Aladdin/Beyond Words.
Hyde, Natalie. Classified: Spies at Work. 2014. (ENG., Illus.). 48p. (J). (978-0-7787-1335-7(0)) Crabtree Publishing Co.
Janeczko, Paul B. The Dark Game: True Spy Stories from Invisible Ink to CIA Moles. 2012. (ENG.). 256p. (YA). (gr. 5-9). pap. 9.99 (978-0-7636-6066-6(3)) Candlewick Pr.
Jeffrey, Gary. Secret Agents. 2009. (Graphic Careers Ser.). (ENG.). 48p. (YA). (gr. 5-5). 58.50 (978-1-61512-891-4(3), Rosen Reference) Rosen Publishing Group, Inc., The.
—Secret Agents. Riley, Terry, illus. 2008. (Graphic Careers Ser.). (ENG.). 48p. (gr. 5-8). per. 14.05 (978-1-4042-1465-1(8)); (YA). lib. bdg. 31.95 (978-1-4042-1464-4(X)) Rosen Publishing Group, Inc., The.
Jones, Carrie. Sarah Emma Edmonds Was a Great Pretender: The True Story of a Civil War Spy. Oldroyd, Mark, illus. 2011. (Carolrhoda Picture Bks.). (ENG.). 32p. (J). (gr. 2-5). 17.95 (978-0-7613-5399-7(2)) Lerner Publishing Group.
Kallen, Stuart A. Primary Sources. 2003. (American War Library). (ENG., Illus.). 112p. (J). 30.85 (978-1-59018-243-7(X), Lucent Bks.) Cengage Gale.
Kelley, K. C. How Spies Work. 2010. (Spies & Spying Ser.). (J). (gr. 4-7). 28.50 (978-1-59920-359-1(6)) Black Rabbit Bks.
Kim, F. S. Undercover Women: History's Greatest Spies. 2015. (Illus.). 32p. (J). pap. (978-0-545-59146-1(5)) Scholastic, Inc.
Koestler-Grack, Rachel A. Nathan Hale: Courageous Spy. 2005. (Leaders of the American Revolution Ser.). (Illus.). 100p. (gr. 5-8). lib. bdg. 30.00 (978-0-7910-8623-0(2)) Facts On File, Inc.
Kudlinski, Kathleen V. Rebel with a Cause: The Daring Adventure of Dicey Langston, Girl Spy of the American Revolution. Faber, Rudy, illus. 2015. (Encounter: Narrative Nonfiction Picture Bks.). (ENG.). 40p. (gr. 3-4). lib. bdg. 28.65 (978-1-4914-6073-3(3)) Encounter Bks.
Landau, Elaine. Assassins, Traitors, & Spies. 2013. (ShockZone (tm) — Villains Ser.). (ENG., Illus.). 32p. (gr. 5-8). pap. 8.95 (978-1-4677-0894-4(1)) Lerner Publishing Group.
—Assassins/Traitors/Spies. 2013. (ShockZone (tm) — Villains Ser.). (ENG., Illus.). 32p. (gr. 5-8). lib. bdg. 26.60 (978-1-4677-0608-7(6), Lerner Pubns.) Lerner Publishing Group.
Langley, Andrew. Wartime Spies. 2010. (Spies & Spying Ser.). (J). (gr. 4-7). 28.50 (978-1-59920-362-1(6)) Black Rabbit Bks.
Langston-George, Rebecca. Deep-Cover Spies & Double-Crossers of the Cold War. 2017. (Spies! Ser.). (ENG., Illus.). 64p. (gr. 5-6). lib. bdg. 33.99 (978-0-7565-5497-2(7), CPB Grades 4-8) Compass Point Bks.
—Fearless Spies & Daring Deeds of World War II. 2017. (Spies! Ser.). (ENG., Illus.). 64p. (gr. 5-6). lib. bdg. 33.99 (978-0-7565-5500-9(0), CPB Grades 4-8) Compass Point Bks.
Lassieur, Allison. Courageous Spies & International Intrigue of World War I. 2017. (Spies! Ser.). (ENG., Illus.). 64p. (gr. 5-6). lib. bdg. 33.99 (978-0-7565-5499-6(3), CPB Grades 4-8) Compass Point Bks.
—Cyber Spies & Secret Agents of Modern Times. 2017. (Spies! Ser.). (ENG., Illus.). 64p. (gr. 5-6). lib. bdg. 33.99 (978-0-7565-5498-9(5), CPB Grades 4-8) Compass Point Bks.
Lassieur, Allison & Langston-George, Rebecca. Spies! 2017. (Spies! Ser.). (ENG.). 64p. (gr. 5-6). 135.96 (978-0-7565-5518-4(3), CPB Grades 4-8) Compass Point Bks.
LeBoutillier, Linda. Secrets of the U. S. Civil War. 2017. (Top Secret Files Ser.). (ENG., Illus.). 32p. (gr. 3-4). lib. bdg. 27.99 (978-1-5157-4138-1(9), Edge Bks.) Capstone Press of Coughlan Cos.
Liberston, Jody. Nathan Hale: Heroe de la guerra de Independencia. 2004. (Grandes personajes en la historia de los Estados Unidos Ser.). (SPA.). 32p. (gr. 3-6). pap. 10.00 (978-0-8239-4235-0(X), Rosen Classroom) Rosen Publishing Group, Inc., The.
Libertson, Jody. Nathan Hale: Hero of the American Revolution. (Primary Sources of Famous People in American History Ser.). 32p. 2009. (gr. 2-3). 47.90 (978-1-60851-709-1(8)) 2004. (ENG., Illus.). (gr. 4-8). pap. 10.00 (978-0-8239-4189-6(2)) Rosen Publishing Group, Inc., The.
—Nathan Hale: Héroe revolucionario / Hero of the American Revolution. 2009. (Famous People in American History/Grandes personajes en la historia de los Estados Unidos Ser.). (ENG & SPA.). 32p. (gr. 2-3). 47.90 (978-1-61512-552-4(3), Editorial Buenas Letras) Rosen Publishing Group, Inc., The.
—Nathan Hale: Héroe revolucionario (Nathan Hale: Hero of the American Revolution) 2009. (Grandes personajes en la historia de los Estados Unidos (Famous People in American History) Ser.). (SPA.). 32p. (gr. 2-3). 47.90 (978-1-61512-805-1(0), Editorial Buenas Letras) Rosen Publishing Group, Inc., The.
Lockwood, Brad. Domestic Spying & Wiretapping. 2009. (In the News Ser.). 64p. (gr. 6-6). 58.50 (978-1-61513-465-6(4)) Rosen Publishing Group, Inc., The.
Lonely Planet Publications Staff. How to Be an International Spy: Your Training Manual, Should You Choose to Accept It, 1 vol. 2015. (Lonely Planet Kids Ser.). (ENG., Illus.). 160p. (J). 17.99 (978-1-74360-773-2(3), 4979) Lonely Planet Pubns.
McCollum, Sean. Secrets of World War I. 2017. (Top Secret Files Ser.). (ENG., Illus.). 32p. (gr. 3-4). lib. bdg. 27.99 (978-1-5157-4139-8(7), Edge Bks.) Capstone Press of Coughlan Cos.
—Secrets of World War II. 2017. (Top Secret Files Ser.). (ENG., Illus.). 32p. (gr. 3-4). lib. bdg. 27.99 (978-1-5157-4140-4(0), Edge Bks.) Capstone Press of Coughlan Cos.
McCormick, Patricia. The Plot to Kill Hitler: Dietrich Bonhoeffer: Pastor, Spy, Unlikely Hero. 2016. (Illus.). 192p. (J). (gr. 3). 18.99 (978-0-06-241108-2(X)) HarperCollins Pubs.
Mendez, Antonio J. & Mendez, Jonna. Gathering Info: Getting the Scoop by Using Your Wits. 2007. (Illus.). 32p. (J). (978-0-439-90849-8(3)) Scholastic, Inc.
Micklos, John. The Brave Women & Children of the American Revolution. 2008. (Revolutionary War Library). (Illus.). 48p. (J). (gr. 3-4). lib. bdg. 25.27 (978-0-7660-3019-0(9), Enslow Elementary) Enslow Pubs., Inc.
—Courageous Children & Women of the American Revolution: Through Primary Sources. 2013. (American Revolution Through Primary Sources Ser.). 48p. (J). (gr. 4-18). 25.27 (978-0-7660-4131-8(X)) Enslow Pubs., Inc.
—How the Revolutionary War Was Won. 2008. (Revolutionary War Library). (Illus.). 48p. (J). (gr. 3-4). lib. bdg. 25.27 (978-0-7660-3016-9(4), Enslow Elementary) Enslow Pubs., Inc.
—Why We Won the American Revolution — Through Primary Sources. 2013. (American Revolution Through Primary Sources Ser.). 48p. (J). (gr. 4-18). 25.27 (978-0-7660-4134-9(4)) Enslow Pubs., Inc.
—Why We Won the American Revolution—Through Primary Sources. 2013. (American Revolution Through Primary Sources Ser.). 48p. (J). (gr. 4-10). pap. 8.95 (978-1-4644-0192-3(6)) Enslow Pubs., Inc.
Mitchell, Susan K. The Secret World of Spy Agencies. 2011. (Secret World of Spies Ser.). (Illus.). 48p. (J). (gr. 2-5). lib. bdg. 25.27 (978-0-7660-3714-4(2)); (gr. 4-18). pap. 8.95 (978-1-59845-352-2(1)) Enslow Pubs., Inc.
—Spies & Lies-Famous & Infamous Spies. 2011. (Secret World of Spies Ser.). (Illus.). 48p. (J). (gr. 4-18). pap. 8.95 (978-1-59845-349-2(1)) Enslow Pubs., Inc.
—Spies, Double Agents, & Traitors. 2011. (Secret World of Spies Ser.). (Illus.). 48p. (J). (gr. 2-5). lib. bdg. 25.27 (978-0-7660-3711-3(8)); (gr. 4-18). pap. 8.95 (978-1-59845-351-5(3)) Enslow Pubs., Inc.
—Spy Codes & Ciphers. 2011. (Secret World of Spies Ser.). (Illus.). 48p. (J). (gr. 2-5). lib. bdg. 25.27 (978-0-7660-3709-0(6)); (gr. 4-18). pap. 8.95 (978-1-59845-353-9(X)) Enslow Pubs., Inc.
—Spy Gizmos & Gadgets. 2011. (Secret World of Spies Ser.). (Illus.). 48p. (J). (gr. 2-5). lib. bdg. 25.27 (978-0-7660-3710-6(X)); (gr. 4-18). pap. 8.95 (978-1-59845-354-6(8)) Enslow Pubs., Inc.
—Spy Tech — Digital Dangers. 2011. (Secret World of Spies Ser.). (Illus.). 48p. (J). (gr. 2-5). lib. bdg. 25.27 (978-0-7660-3712-0(6)) Enslow Pubs., Inc.
—Spy Tech-Digital Dangers. 2011. (Secret World of Spies Ser.). (Illus.). 48p. (J). (gr. 4-18). pap. 8.95 (978-1-59845-350-8(5)) Enslow Pubs., Inc.
Moss, Marissa. Nurse, Soldier, Spy: The Story of Sarah Edmonds, a Civil War Hero. Hendrix, John, illus. 2011. (ENG.). 48p. (J). (gr. 3-7). 19.95 (978-0-8109-9735-6(5), Abrams Bks. for Young Readers) Abrams, Inc.
Murray, Laura K. Spies in the CIA. 2016. 24p. (J). (978-1-60818-616-7(4), Creative Education) Creative Co., The.
—Spies in the KGB. 2016. (Illus.). 24p. (J). (978-1-60818-617-4(2), Creative Education) Creative Co., The.
—Spies in the Mossad. 2016. (Illus.). 24p. (J). (978-1-60818-618-1(0), Creative Education) Creative Co., The.
—Spies in the SIS. 2016. (Illus.). 24p. (J). (978-1-60818-619-8(9), Creative Education) Creative Co., The.
Narayan, Natasha. Spies, Secret Agents & Spooks of London. 2004. (Of London Ser.). (ENG., Illus.). 96p. (J). pap. 8.99 (978-1-904153-14-6(3)) Tempus ESP. Dist: Independent Pubs. Group.
Olson, Nathan. Nathan Hale: Revolutionary Spy. Martin, Cynthia & Schoonover, Brent, illus. 2005. (Graphic Biographies Ser.). (ENG.). 32p. (gr. 3-4). 30.65 (978-0-7368-4968-5(8), Graphic Library) Capstone Press of Coughlan Cos.
Olson, Nathan & Glaser, Jason. Nathan Hale: Revolutionary Spy, 1 vol. Martin, Cynthia & Schoonover, Brent, illus. 2006. (Graphic Biographies Ser.). (ENG.). 32p. (gr. 3-4). per. 8.10 (978-0-7368-6199-1(8), Graphic Library) Capstone Press of Coughlan Cos.
Omoth, Tyler. Secrets of the American Revolution. 2017. (Top Secret Files Ser.). (ENG., Illus.). 32p. (gr. 3-4). lib. bdg. 27.99 (978-1-5157-4137-4(0), Edge Bks.) Capstone Press of Coughlan Cos.
Orme, David. Spies. 2008. (Trailblazers Ser.). (ENG., Illus.). 36p. pap. (978-1-84167-695-1(0)) Ransom Publishing Ltd.
—Spies. 2010. (Fact to Fiction Grafx Ser.). (Illus.). 36p. (J). lib. bdg. 16.95 (978-1-60686-473-9(4)) Perfection Learning Corp.
Owen, David. Spies: The Undercover World of Secrets, Gadgets & Lies. 2004. (ENG., Illus.). 128p. (J). (gr. 5-9). pap. 9.95 (978-1-55297-794-1(3), 9781552977941) Firefly Bks., Ltd.
Owen, Ruth. The Superspy Handbook, 1 vol., 1. 2014. (DIY for Boys Ser.). (ENG.). 32p. (J). (gr. 3-6). 27.50 (978-1-4777-6282-0(5), PowerKids Pr.) Rosen Publishing Group, Inc., The.
Payne, Matt. Secret Agent Gear: Spy Tools & Tech: Past, Present, & Future. 2013. (Illus.). 32p. (J). pap. (978-0-545-59143-0(0)) Scholastic, Inc.
Pender, Lionel. Spy vs. Spy: Intelligence Organizations. 2016. (Law Enforcement & Intelligence Gathering Ser.). 00104p. (YA). (gr. 8-8). lib. bdg. 36.25 (978-1-5081-0370-7(4), Britannica Educational Publishing) Rosen Publishing Group, Inc., The.
Perrin, Pat & Coleman, Wim. The Mystery of the Murdered Playwright. 2004. (Cover-To-Cover Books). (Illus.). 56p. pap. 9.00 (978-0-7891-6001-0(3)); (gr. 4-7). lib. bdg. 17.95 (978-0-7569-1353-3(5)) Perfection Learning Corp.
Phillips, Larissa. Women Civil War Spies of the Confederacy. (American Women at War Ser.). 112p. 2009. (gr. 8-8). 63.90 (978-1-61511-402-3(5)) 2004. (Illus.). (gr. 7-12). lib. bdg. 34.60 (978-0-8239-4451-4(4)) Rosen Publishing Group, Inc., The.
Pipe, Jim. Spies: Behind Enemy Lines. 2012. (Mission Impossible Ser.). 32p. (gr. 4-8). lib. bdg. 31.35 (978-1-936333-29-5(5)) Brown Bear Bks.
Platt, Richard. Spy. 2009. (DK Eyewitness Bks.). (ENG.). 72p. (J). (gr. 3-7). 19.99 (978-0-7566-5035-3(6), DK Children) Dorling Kindersley Publishing, Inc.
Polette, Nancy. The Spy with the Wooden Leg: The Story of Virginia Hall. 2012. (ENG.). 160p. (J). pap. 12.95 (978-1-934617-16-8(4)); 16.95 (978-1-934617-15-1(6)) Elva Resa Publishing, LLC. (Alma Little).
Poole, Hazel. Spies & Detectives. 2008. (Factastic Journey Ser.). (Illus.). 32p. (J). (gr. k-7). pap. 8.95 (978-1-59905-243-4(1)) Saddleback Educational Publishing, Inc.
Portalupi, Laura. Spies! Real People, Real Stories. 2003. (High Five Reading - Green Ser.). (ENG., Illus.). 48p. (gr. 3-4). per. 9.00 (978-0-7368-2830-7(3), High Five Reading (RBL)) Capstone Press of Coughlan Cos.
Price, Sean. Modern Spies. 2014. pap. (978-1-4765-3593-7(0)) Capstone Press of Coughlan Cos.
Price, Sean Stewart. Modern Spies, 1 vol. 2013. (Classified Ser.). (ENG.). 48p. (gr. 3-4). 31.99 (978-1-4765-0123-9(8)) Capstone Press of Coughlan Cos.
—World War II Spies, 1 vol. 2013. (Classified Ser.). (ENG.). 48p. (gr. 3-4). 31.99 (978-1-4765-0122-2(X)) Capstone Press of Coughlan Cos.
Purcell, Martha Sias. Spies of the American Revolution. 2003. (Reading Essentials in Social Studies). (Illus.). 48p. pap. 9.00 (978-0-7891-5854-3(X)) Perfection Learning Corp.
Rauf, Don. Killer Lipstick: And Other Spy Gadgets. 2007. (24/7: Science Behind the Scenes Ser.). (ENG., Illus.). 64p. (J). (gr. 8-12). 29.00 (978-0-531-12084-2(8)); pap. 7.95 (978-0-531-17536-1(7)) Scholastic Library Publishing. (Watts, Franklin).
Raum, Elizabeth. Spies of the American Revolution: An Interactive Espionage Adventure. 2015. (You Choose: Spies Ser.). (ENG., Illus.). 112p. (gr. 3-4). lib. bdg. 31.99 (978-1-4914-5858-7(5), You Choose Bks.) Capstone Press of Coughlan Cos.
—Stealing Nazi Secrets in World War II: An Interactive Espionage Adventure. 2015. (You Choose: Spies Ser.). (ENG., Illus.). 112p. (gr. 3-4). pap. 6.95 (978-1-4914-5934-8(4), You Choose Bks.) Capstone Press of Coughlan Cos.
Rigby Education Staff. Spy Manual. (Sails Literacy Ser.). (Illus.). 16p. (gr. 2-3). 27.00 (978-0-7635-9938-6(7), 699387C99) Rigby Education.
Riordan, Rick & Scholastic, Inc. Staff. The Black Book of Buried Secrets. 2010. (39 Clues Ser.). (ENG.). 192p. (J). (gr. 3-7). 12.99 (978-0-545-28504-9(6)) Scholastic, Inc.
Rockwell, Anne. A Spy Called James: The True Story of James Lafayette, Revolutionary War Double Agent. Cooper, Floyd, illus. 2016. (ENG.). 32p. (gr. 2-5). lib. bdg. 17.99 (978-1-4677-4933-6(8)); 35.99 (978-1-4677-6178-9(8)) Lerner Publishing Group. (Carolrhoda Bks.).
Rooney, Anne. Spies. 2003. (Wicked Wallets Ser.). (Illus.). 24p. (YA). (978-1-84347-036-6(5), Pavilion Children's Books) Pavilion Bks.
Roop, Peter & Roop, Connie. Botones Para el General Washington. Hanson, Peter E., illus. 2006. (Yo Solo - Historia (on My Own - History) Ser.).Tr. of Buttons for General Washington. (SPA.). 48p. (gr. 2-4). lib. bdg. 25.26 (978-0-8225-6261-0(8)) Lerner Publishing Group.
Rose, Alexa. Spy Games. 2014. (PACKtivities Ser.: 3). (ENG.). 48p. (J). 11.99 (978-1-935703-38-9(2)) Downtown Bookworks.
Sakany, Lois. Women Civil War Spies of the Union. (American Women at War Ser.). 112p. 2009. (gr. 8-8). 63.90 (978-1-61511-403-0(3)) 2004. (Illus.). (gr. 7-12). lib. bdg. 34.60 (978-0-8239-4450-7(6)) Rosen Publishing Group, Inc., The.
Samuels, Charlie. Spying & Security. 2012. (World War II Sourcebook Ser.). 48p. (gr. 5-12). lib. bdg. 37.10 (978-1-936333-25-7(2)) Brown Bear Bks.
Sodaro, Craig. Civil War Spies. 2013. 48p. pap. 9.95 (978-1-4765-3590-6(6)) Capstone Press of Coughlan Cos.
The Spy, 6 vols., Pack. (Sails Literacy Ser.). 16p. (gr. k-18). 27.00 (978-0-7635-4437-9(X)) Rigby Education.
Spy Files Set, 6 vols., Set. Incl. Bioterror: Deadly Invisible Weapons. Rudy, Lisa Jo. (gr. 9-12). 29.00 (978-0-531-12080-4(5)); Eyes in the Sky: Satellite Spies Are Watching You! Rudy, Lisa Jo. (gr. 8-12). 29.00 (978-0-531-12082-8(1)); Killer Lipstick: And Other Spy Gadgets. Rauf, Don. (gr. 8-12). 29.00 (978-0-531-12084-2(8)); Micro Spies: Spy Planes the Size of Birds! Rudy, Lisa Jo. (gr. 8-12). 29.00 (978-0-531-12083-5(X)); 64p. (J)., Watts, Franklin (24/7: Science Behind the Scenes Ser.). (Illus.). 2007. 174.00 (978-0-531-12477-2(0)) Scholastic Library Publishing.
Stemple, Heidi E. Y. Ready for Anything! Training Your Brain for Expert Espionage. 2006. (Illus.). 32p. (J). (978-0-439-90504-6(4)) Scholastic, Inc.
Stewart, James. Spies & Traitors. 2008. (Amazing History Ser.). (Illus.). 32p. (J). (gr. 2-6). pap. 28.50 (978-1-59920-109-2(7)) Black Rabbit Bks.
—Spies & Traitors. 2009. (Amazing History Ser.). (Illus.). 32p. (J). pap. 7.95 (978-1-59920-210-5(7)) Black Rabbit Bks.
Sullivan, Laura L. Life As a Spy in the American Revolution. 2016. (Life As... Ser.). (ENG., Illus.). 32p. (J). (gr. 3-3). 28.50 (978-1-5026-1081-2(7)) Cavendish Square Publishing.
Swanson, Jennifer. Top Secret Science: Projects You Aren't Supposed to Know About, 1 vol. 2014. (Scary Science Ser.). (ENG.). 32p. (gr. 3-4). lib. bdg. 27.32 (978-1-4765-3926-3(X), Fact Finders) Capstone Press of Coughlan Cos.
Throp, Claire. Spies & Codebreakers. 2015. (Heroes of World War II Ser.). (ENG., Illus.). 48p. (gr. 4-6). 32.65 (978-1-4109-8047-2(2)) Heinemann-Raintree.
Tracy, Kathleen. Nathan Hale. 2006. (Profiles in American History Ser.). (Illus.). 48p. (J). (gr. 3-7). lib. bdg. 29.95 (978-1-58415-447-1(0)) Mitchell Lane Pubs., Inc.
Wiese, Jim & Melton, H. Keith. The Spy's Guide to Counterintelligence. 2003. (Illus.). 48p. (J). (978-0-439-33646-8(5)) Scholastic, Inc.
Wilson, Camilla. Civil War Spies: Behind Enemy Lines. 2010. vii, 104p. (J). pap. (978-0-545-13002-8(6)) Scholastic, Inc.
Yomtov, Nel. Revolutionary War Spies, 1 vol. 2013. (Classified Ser.). (ENG.). 48p. (gr. 3-4). 31.99 (978-1-4296-9977-8(9)) Capstone Press of Coughlan Cos.

Yomtov, Nel, et al. Classified. 2013. (Classified Ser.). (ENG.). 48p. (gr. 3-4). lib. bdg. 127.96 *(978-1-4296-9978-5(7))* Capstone Press of Coughlan Cos.

Zullo, Allan. The Secret Agent & Other Spy Kids. 2006. 147p. (J). pap. *(978-0-439-84835-0(0))* Scholastic, Inc.

SPIES—FICTION

Aaron, Chester. Alex, Who Won His War. 2014. 225p. (YA). *(978-1-936144-26-6(3))* Zumaya Pubns. LLC.

Abela, Deborah. Hollywood. O'Connor, George, illus. 2007. (Spy Force Ser.: 4). (ENG.). 240p. (J). (gr. 3-7). pap. 10.99 *(978-1-4169-3969-6(5),* Aladdin) Simon & Schuster Children's Publishing.

—In Search of the Time & Space Machine. Murphy, Jobi, illus. 2005. (Spy Force Ser.). 256p. (Orig.). (J). 14.95 *(978-1-74051-765-2(2),* Simon & Schuster Bks. For Young Readers) Simon & Schuster Bks. For Young Readers.

Allen, Elise & Daryle Connors. Gabby Duran & the Unsittables. 2016. (Gabby Duran Ser.: 1). (J). lib. bdg. 18.40 *(978-0-606-39443-7(5))* Turtleback Bks.

Allison, Jennifer. The Dead Drop. (Gilda Joyce Ser.). (ENG.). 320p. (J). (gr. 5-18). 2010. 9.99 *(978-0-14-241638-9(X),* Puffin Books) 2009. 16.99 *(978-0-525-47980-2(5),* Dutton Books for Young Readers) Penguin Young Readers Group.

Anderson, Danny. Santa's Spy. 2012. 28p. pap. 15.99 *(978-1-4771-1007-2(0))* Xlibris Corp.

Anderson, Laurie Halse. Chains. l.t. ed. 2017. (Seeds of America Ser.). (ENG.). 442p. 22.99 ***(978-1-4104-9917-2(0))*** Cengage Gale.

—Chains. 2014. (Seeds of America Trilogy). (ENG.). 336p. (J). 12.24 *(978-1-63245-094-4(1))* Lectorum Pubns., Inc.

—Chains. 2009. 9.00 *(978-0-7848-3678-1(7),* Everbind) Marco Bk. Co.

—Chains. (Seeds of America Trilogy Ser.). (ENG., Illus.). (J). (gr. 5-9). 2010. 336p. pap. 8.99 *(978-1-4169-0586-8(3))* 2008. 320p. 18.99 *(978-1-4169-0585-1(5))* Simon & Schuster Children's Publishing. (Atheneum Bks. for Young Readers).

—Chains. l.t. ed. 2009. (ENG.). 390p. (YA). 23.95 *(978-1-4104-1425-0(6))* Thorndike Pr.

—Chains. 2010. (Seeds of America Trilogy Ser.: 1). lib. bdg. 19.65 *(978-0-606-14520-6(6),* Turtleback) Turtleback Bks.

Anderson, M. T. Agent Q, or the Smell of Danger! Cyrus, Kurt, illus. (Pals in Peril Tale Ser.). (ENG.). (J). (gr. 5-9). 2011. 320p. pap. 6.99 *(978-1-4424-2640-5(3))* 2010. 304p. 16.99 *(978-1-4169-8640-9(5))* Beach Lane Bks. (Beach Lane Bks.).

Anstey, Cindy & Anstey, Cynthia. Love, Lies & Spies. 2016. (ENG.). 368p. (YA). pap. 10.99 *(978-1-250-08403-3(2),* 9781250084033) Feiwel & Friends.

Arena, Felice & Kettle, Phil. Secret Agent Heroes. Vane, Mitch, illus. 2004. (J). pap. *(978-1-59336-355-0(9))* Mondo Publishing.

Avi. Sophia's War: A Tale of the Revolution. 2012. (ENG., Illus.). 320p. (J). (gr. 3-7). 17.99 *(978-1-4424-1441-9(3),* Beach Lane Bks.) Beach Lane Bks.

—Sophia's War: A Tale of the Revolution. 2013. (ENG., Illus.). 336p. (J). (gr. 3-7). pap. 7.99 *(978-1-4424-1442-6(1))* Simon & Schuster Children's Publishing.

—The Traitors' Gate. Raude, Karina, illus. 2007. (ENG.). 368p. (J). (gr. 5-8). 17.99 *(978-0-689-85335-7(1),* Atheneum/Richard Jackson Bks.) Simon & Schuster Children's Publishing.

Backues, E. Sharol. Stories of a Dragonfly Spy, a Dog Named Droop & a Little Calf That Wondered Why? 2011. 28p. pap. 21.99 *(978-1-4653-6343-5(2))* Xlibris Corp.

Baldwin, Kathleen. A School for Unusual Girls. 2015. (Stranje House Ser.: 1). (ENG.). 352p. (YA). (gr. 8-12). 17.99 *(978-0-7653-7600-8(8),* 9780765376008, Tor Teen) Doherty, Tom Assocs., LLC.

The Balloon Ride, 6, Pack. (Sails Literacy Ser.). 16p. (gr. k-18). 27.00 *(978-0-7635-4427-0(2))* Rigby Education.

The Balloon Ride: KinderConcepts Individual Title Six-Packs. (Kinderstarters Ser.). 8p. (gr. -1-1). 21.00 *(978-0-7635-8736-9(2))* Rigby Education.

Barba, Rick. The Secret of Stoneship Woods. Steccati, Eve, illus. 2006. (Spy Gear Adventures Ser.: 1). (ENG.). 160p. (J). (gr. 3-7). pap. 8.99 *(978-1-4169-0887-6(0),* Simon & Schuster/Paula Wiseman Bks.) Simon & Schuster/Paula Wiseman Bks.

Barchers, Suzanne I. Spy It!, 1 vol. 2011. (Targeted Phonics Ser.). (ENG., Illus.). 16p. (J). (gr. k-2). pap. 5.99 *(978-1-4333-2910-4(7))* Teacher Created Materials, Inc.

Barnes, Jennifer Lynn. Perfect Cover. 2008. (The Squad). (ENG.). 288p. (YA). (gr. 7). mass mkt. 7.99 *(978-0-385-73454-7(9),* Laurel Leaf) Random Hse. Children's Bks.

Becker, Helaine. Dirk Daring, Secret Agent, 1 vol. 2014. (Dirk Daring, Secret Agent Ser.: 1). (ENG., Illus.). 208p. (J). (gr. 3-6). pap. 9.95 *(978-1-4598-0683-2(2))* Orca Bk. Pubs. USA.

Beil, Michael D. Agents of the Glass: a New Recruit. 2016. (ENG.). 400p. (J). (gr. 4-7). 16.99 *(978-0-385-75321-0(7),* Knopf Bks. for Young Readers) Random Hse. Children's Bks.

Bell, Michele Ashman. Dragon's Jaw: A Heart-Pounding Adventure. 2005. 241p. (J). *(978-1-59156-880-3(3))* Covenant Communications.

—Spyhunt: A Heart-Pounding Adventure: A Novel. 2004. 187p. (J). *(978-1-59156-457-7(3))* Covenant Communications.

Benway, Robin. Going Rogue. 2015. (Also Known As Ser.). (ENG.). 320p. (YA). (gr. 7). pap. 9.99 *(978-0-8027-3786-1(2),* 9780802737861, Bloomsbury USA Childrens) Bloomsbury Publishing USA.

Bernstein, Jonathan. Bridget Wilder: Spy-In-Training. 2016. (Bridget Wilder Ser.: 1). (J). lib. bdg. 17.20 *(978-0-606-38746-0(3))* Turtleback Bks.

—Bridget Wilder: Spy-In-Training. (Bridget Wilder Ser.: 1). 320p. (J). (gr. 3-7). 2016. pap. 6.99 *(978-0-06-238267-2(5))* 2015. (ENG.). 16.99 *(978-0-06-238266-5(7))* HarperCollins Pubs. (Tegen, Katherine Bks).

Berry, Nina. City of Spies. 2016. (Pagan Jones Ser.: 2). (ENG.). 448p. 18.99 *(978-0-373-21189-0(9),* Harlequin Teen) Harlequin Enterprises, Ltd. CAN. Dist: HarperCollins Pubs.

Black Friday. 2014. (ENG.). 400p. (gr. 7). 10.99 *(978-0-340-99924-0(1))* Hodder & Stoughton GBR. Dist: Hachette Bk. Group.

Blakemore, Megan Frazer. The Spy Catchers of Maple Hill. 2014. (ENG.). 320p. (YA). (gr. 3-6). 16.99 *(978-1-61963-348-3(5),* 9781619633483, Bloomsbury USA Childrens) Bloomsbury Publishing USA.

Boyd, David. Hidden Message. Alward, Jeff, illus. 2007. 48p. (J). lib. bdg. 23.08 *(978-1-4242-1637-6(0))* Fitzgerald Bks.

Bradbury, Jennifer. Wrapped. 2011. (ENG., Illus.). 320p. (YA). (gr. 7-18). 16.99 *(978-1-4169-9007-9(0),* Atheneum Bks. for Young Readers) Simon & Schuster Children's Publishing.

Bradley, F. T. The Alias Men. 2015. (Double Vision Ser.: 3). (ENG.). 256p. (J). (gr. 3-7). pap. 6.99 *(978-0-06-210444-1(6))* HarperCollins Pubs.

—Double Vision. (Double Vision Ser.: 1). (ENG.). (J). (gr. 3-7). 2013. 272p. pap. 6.99 *(978-0-06-210438-0(1))* 2012. (Illus.). 256p. 16.99 *(978-0-06-210437-3(3))* HarperCollins Pubs.

—Double Vision: The Alias Men. 2014. (Double Vision Ser.: 3). (ENG.). 256p. (J). (gr. 3-7). 16.99 *(978-0-06-210443-4(8))* HarperCollins Pubs.

—Double Vision - Code Name 711. 2013. (Double Vision Ser.: 2). (ENG.). 256p. (J). (gr. 3-7). 16.99 *(978-0-06-210440-3(3))* HarperCollins Pubs.

Bradley, Kimberly Brubaker. For Freedom: The Story of a French Spy. 2005. 181p. 16.00 *(978-0-7569-5091-0(0))* Perfection Learning Corp.

—For Freedom: The Story of a French Spy. 2005. (ENG.). 192p. (YA). (gr. 7-9). mass mkt. 5.99 *(978-0-440-41831-3(3),* Laurel Leaf) Random Hse. Children's Bks.

Brennan, Herbie. The Doomsday Box: A Shadow Project Adventure. 2011. (Shadow Project Ser.: 2). (ENG.). 352p. (J). (gr. 5). pap. 6.99 *(978-0-06-175650-4(4))* HarperCollins Pubs.

Broad, Michael. Ghost Diamond!, No. 1. Broad, Michael, illus. 2011. (Agent Amelia Ser.: 1). (ENG., Illus.). 144p. (J). (gr. 2-5). pap. 5.95 *(978-0-7613-8060-3(4),* Darby Creek); lib. bdg. 22.60 *(978-0-7613-8056-6(6))* Lerner Publishing Group.

—Hypno Hounds!, No. 3. Broad, Michael, illus. 2011. (Agent Amelia Ser.: 3). (ENG., Illus.). 144p. (J). (gr. 2-5). pap. 5.95 *(978-0-7613-8062-7(0),* Darby Creek); lib. bdg. 22.60 *(978-0-7613-8058-0(2))* Lerner Publishing Group.

—Spooky Ballet!, No. 4. Broad, Michael, illus. 2011. (Agent Amelia Ser.: 4). (ENG., Illus.). 144p. (J). (gr. 2-5). pap. 5.95 *(978-0-7613-8064-1(7),* Darby Creek); lib. bdg. 22.60 *(978-0-7613-8059-7(0))* Lerner Publishing Group.

—Zombie Cows! Broad, Michael, illus. 2011. (Agent Amelia Ser.: 2). (ENG., Illus.). 144p. (J). (gr. 2-5). pap. 5.95 *(978-0-7613-8066-5(3),* Darby Creek);No. 2. lib. bdg. 22.60 *(978-0-7613-8057-3(4))* Lerner Publishing Group.

—#1 Ghost Diamond! 2011. (Agent Amelia Ser.). pap. 33.92 *(978-0-7613-8341-3(7),* Darby Creek) Lerner Publishing Group.

—#2 Zombie Cows! 2011. (Agent Amelia Ser.). pap. 33.92 *(978-0-7613-8342-0(5),* Darby Creek) Lerner Publishing Group.

—#3 Hypno Hounds! 2011. (Agent Amelia Ser.). pap. 33.92 *(978-0-7613-8343-7(3),* Darby Creek) Lerner Publishing Group.

—#4 Spooky Ballet! 2011. (Agent Amelia Ser.). pap. 33.92 *(978-0-7613-8344-4(1),* Darby Creek) Lerner Publishing Group.

Brooks, Walter R. Freddy & the Flying Saucer Plans. Wiese, Kurt, illus. 2013. (ENG.). 256p. (gr. 4-13). pap. 10.99 *(978-1-4683-0319-3(8),* 460319) Overlook Pr., The.

Brown, Teri. Velvet Undercover. 2015. (ENG.). 336p. (YA). (gr. 8). 17.99 *(978-0-06-232127-5(7))* HarperCollins Pubs.

Bruchac, Joseph. Code Talker: A Novel about the Navajo Marines of World War Two. 2005. (ENG.). 240p. (YA). (gr. 7-18). 17.99 *(978-0-8037-2921-6(9),* Dial Bks) Penguin Young Readers Group.

—Wolf Mark, 1 vol. 2013. (ENG.). 392p. (J). 17.95 *(978-1-60060-661-8(X),* Tu Bks.) Lee & Low Bks., Inc.

Buckeridge, Anthony. Just Like Jennings. 2008. (Jennings Ser.: 12). (ENG.). 184p. (J). (gr. -1-12). pap. 12.95 *(978-0-7551-0170-2(7))* House of Stratus, Inc. GBR. Dist: Gardners Bks. Ltd.

Buckingham, Royce Scott. The Terminals. 2014. (ENG.). 288p. (YA). (gr. 9). 18.99 *(978-1-250-01155-8(8),* 9781250011558, Dunne, Thomas Bks.) St. Martin's Pr.

Buckley, Michael. Attack of the Bullies. (Nerds Ser.). (ENG.). (gr. 3-7). 2013. 336p. (YA). 16.95 *(978-1-4197-0857-2(0))*Bk. 5. 2014. (Illus.). 352p. (J). pap. 7.95 *(978-1-4197-1222-7(5))* Abrams, Inc. (Amulet Bks.).

—The Cheerleaders of Doom, Bk. 3. 2012. (Nerds Ser.). (ENG.). 304p. (YA). (gr. 3-7). pap. 7.95 *(978-1-4197-0414-7(1),* Amulet Bks.) Abrams, Inc.

—The Cheerleaders of Doom. 2012. (Nerds Ser.: 3). (YA). lib. bdg. 18.40 *(978-0-606-26927-8(4),* Turtleback) Turtleback Bks.

—M Is for Mama's Boy. Beavers, Ethen, illus. 2010. (Nerds Ser.). (ENG.). 288p. (J). (gr. 3-7). 16.95 *(978-0-8109-8986-3(7),* Amulet Bks.) Abrams, Inc.

—M Is for Mama's Boy, Bk. 2. 2011. (Nerds Ser.). (ENG., Illus.). 304p. (J). (gr. 3-7). pap. 7.95 *(978-1-4197-0023-1(5),* Amulet Bks.) Abrams, Inc.

—NERDS: National Espionage, Rescue, & Defense Society, 5 vols. 2009. (N. E. R. D. S. Ser.: 1). (J). 71.75 *(978-1-4407-4235-4(9));* 190.75 *(978-1-4407-4234-7(0));* 1.25 *(978-1-4407-4243-9(X));* 88.75 *(978-1-4407-4237-8(5));* 86.75 *(978-1-4407-4239-2(1));* 73.75 *(978-1-4407-4233-0(2))* Recorded Bks., Inc.

—NERDS Bk. 1: National Espionage, Rescue, & Defense Society. 2010. (Nerds Ser.). (ENG., Illus.). 352p. (J). (gr. 3-7). pap. 7.95 *(978-0-8109-8985-6(9),* Amulet Bks.) Abrams, Inc.

—Nerds Bk. 1: National Espionage, Rescue, & Defense Society. Beavers, Ethen, illus. 2009. (Nerds Ser.). (ENG.). 336p. (J). (gr. 3-7). 16.95 *(978-0-8109-4324-7(7),* Amulet Bks.) Abrams, Inc.

—NERDS - National Espionage, Rescue, & Defense Society. 2010. (Nerds Ser.: 1). (J). lib. bdg. 18.40 *(978-0-606-15084-2(6),* Turtleback) Turtleback Bks.

—NERDS 2: M für Muttersöhnchen. 2011. (SPA.). 260p. (J). (gr. 6-8). pap. 10.99 *(978-987-612-335-8(1))* V&R Editoras.

—The Villain Virus. 2013. (Nerds Ser.). (ENG.). 304p. (YA). (gr. 3-7). pap. 7.95 *(978-1-4197-0975-3(5),* Amulet Bks.) Abrams, Inc.

Burchett, Jan & Vogler, Sara. Deadly Storm & Fatal Voyage. 2017. (Spy Master Ser.). (ENG.). 400p. (J). (gr. 4-6). 7.99 ***(978-1-4440-1074-9(3),*** Orion Children's Bks.) Hachette Children's Group GBR. Dist: Hachette Bk. Group.

Butcher, A. J. Chaos Rising. 2004. (ENG., Illus.). 240p. (J). (gr. 5-8). pap. 18.99 *(978-0-316-73765-4(8))* Little, Brown Bks. for Young Readers.

—The Serpent Scenario. 2004. (ENG.). 224p. (J). (gr. 5-8). pap. 18.99 *(978-0-316-73766-1(6))* Little, Brown Bks. for Young Readers.

—Spy High Mission One. 2004. (ENG.). 224p. (J). (gr. 5-8). pap. 17.99 *(978-0-316-73760-9(7))* Little, Brown Bks. for Young Readers.

Cage, Elizabeth. Covert Affairs: License to Thrill; Live & Let Spy; Nobody Does It Better. 2014. (ENG., Illus.). 704p. (YA). (gr. 7). pap. 12.99 *(978-1-4424-8227-2(3),* Simon Pulse) Simon Pulse.

—Covert Affairs 2: Spy Girls Are Forever; Dial V for Vengeance; If Looks Could Kill. 2014. (ENG., Illus.). 640p. (YA). (gr. 7). pap. 12.99 *(978-1-4424-8229-6(X),* Simon Pulse) Simon Pulse.

—Dial V for Vengeance. 2013. (Spy Girls Ser.: 5). (ENG., Illus.). 192p. (YA). (gr. 7). pap. 13.99 *(978-1-4814-2084-6(4),* Simon Pulse) Simon Pulse.

—If Looks Could Kill. 2013. (Spy Girls Ser.: 6). (ENG., Illus.). 192p. (YA). (gr. 7). pap. 13.99 *(978-1-4814-2085-3(2),* Simon Pulse) Simon Pulse.

—License to Thrill. 2013. (Spy Girls Ser.: 1). (ENG., Illus.). 192p. (YA). (gr. 7). pap. 13.99 *(978-1-4814-2078-5(X),* Simon Pulse) Simon Pulse.

—Live & Let Spy. 2013. (Spy Girls Ser.: 2). (ENG., Illus.). 192p. (YA). (gr. 7). pap. 13.99 *(978-1-4814-2079-2(8),* Simon Pulse) Simon Pulse.

—Nobody Does It Better. 2013. (Spy Girls Ser.: 3). (ENG., Illus.). 192p. (YA). (gr. 7). pap. 13.99 *(978-1-4814-2080-8(1),* Simon Pulse) Simon Pulse.

—Spy Girls Are Forever. 2013. (Spy Girls Ser.: 4). (ENG., Illus.). 192p. (YA). (gr. 7). pap. 13.99 *(978-1-4814-2082-2(8),* Simon Pulse) Simon Pulse.

Calkhoven, Laurie. Daniel at the Siege of Boston 1776. 2011. (Boys of Wartime Ser.: 1). (ENG.). 224p. (J). (gr. 4-7). 6.99 *(978-0-14-241750-8(5),* Puffin Books) Penguin Young Readers Group.

Carey, John. Cook Spies. 2005. 34p. (J). per. *(978-0-9773723-2-4(4))* Trent's Prints.

Carriger, Gail. Curtsies & Conspiracies. (Finishing School Ser.: 2). (ENG.). (YA). (gr. 7-17). 2014. 336p. pap. 10.00 *(978-0-316-19020-6(9))* 2013. 320p. 18.00 *(978-0-316-19011-4(X))* Little, Brown Bks. for Young Readers.

—Etiquette & Espionage. 2013. (Finishing School Ser.: 1). (ENG.). 320p. (YA). (gr. 7-17). 18.99 *(978-0-316-19008-4(X))* Little Brown & Co.

—Etiquette & Espionage. 2013. (Finishing School Ser.: 1). (ENG.). 336p. (YA). (gr. 7-17). pap. 10.99 *(978-0-316-19010-7(1))* Little, Brown Bks. for Young Readers.

—Waistcoats & Weaponry. 2014. (Finishing School Ser.: 3). (ENG.). 304p. (YA). (gr. 7-17). 18.00 *(978-0-316-19027-5(6))* Little Brown & Co.

—Waistcoats & Weaponry. 2015. (Finishing School Ser.: 3). (ENG.). 320p. (YA). (gr. 7-17). pap. 10.00 *(978-0-316-19025-1(X))* Little, Brown Bks. for Young Readers.

Carter, Ally. Cross My Heart & Hope to Spy. 2016. (Gallagher Girls Ser.: 2). (J). lib. bdg. 20.85 *(978-0-606-38296-0(8))* Turtleback Bks.

—Cross My Heart & Hope to Spy (10th Anniversary Edition) 2016. (Gallagher Girls Ser.). (ENG.). 256p. (J). (gr. 5-9). pap. 9.99 *(978-1-4847-8503-4(7))* Hyperion Bks. for Children.

—I'd Tell You I Love You, but Then I'd Have to Kill You (10th Anniversary Edition) 2016. (Gallagher Girls Ser.). (ENG.). 304p. (J). (gr. 5-9). pap. 9.99 *(978-1-4847-8505-8(3))* Hyperion Bks. for Children.

—Only the Good Spy Young (10th Anniversary Edition) 2016. (Gallagher Girls Ser.). (ENG.). 288p. (J). (gr. 5-9). pap. 9.99 *(978-1-4847-8506-5(1))* Hyperion Bks. for Children.

—Out of Sight, Out of Time. 2016. (Gallagher Girls Ser.: 5). (YA). lib. bdg. 20.85 *(978-0-606-38299-1(2))* Turtleback Bks.

—Out of Sight, Out of Time (10th Anniversary Edition) 2016. (Gallagher Girls Ser.). (ENG.). 320p. (YA). (gr. 5-9). pap. 9.99 *(978-1-4847-8507-2(X))* Hyperion Bks. for Children.

—United We Spy. 2013. (Gallagher Girls Ser.: Bk. 6). (ENG.). 296p. (YA). (gr. 7-17). 17.99 *(978-1-4231-6599-6(3))* Hyperion Pr.

—United We Spy. 2016. (Gallagher Girls Ser.: 6). (YA). lib. bdg. 20.85 *(978-0-606-38300-4(X))* Turtleback Bks.

—United We Spy (10th Anniversary Edition) 2016. (Gallagher Girls Ser.). (ENG.). 320p. (YA). (gr. 5-9). pap. 9.99 *(978-1-4847-8508-9(8))* Hyperion Bks. for Children.

Catlow, Nikalas. Spies vs. Giant Slugs in the Jungle. Wesson, Tim, illus. 2012. (Mega Mash-Up Ser.). (ENG.). 96p. (J). (gr. 2-5). pap. 6.99 *(978-0-7636-5902-8(9),* Nosy Crow) Candlewick Pr.

Cherub: The Recruit; the Dealer; Maximum Security. 2013. (Cherub Ser.). (ENG.). 1008p. (YA). (gr. 7). pap. 29.99 *(978-1-4424-8376-7(8),* Simon Pulse) Simon Pulse.

Child, Lauren. Ruby Redfort Feel the Fear. Child, Lauren, illus. 2016. (Ruby Redfort Ser.). (ENG., Illus.). 528p. (J). (gr. 5-9). 16.99 *(978-0-7636-5470-2(1))* Candlewick Pr.

Clements, Andrew. The Whites of Their Eyes. Stower, Adam, illus. (Benjamin Pratt & the Keepers of the School Ser.: 3). (ENG.). (J). (gr. 2-5). 2013. 240p. pap. 6.99 *(978-1-4169-3909-2(1))* 2012. 224p. 14.99 *(978-1-4169-3888-0(5))* Simon & Schuster Children's Publishing. (Atheneum Bks. for Young Readers).

Cope, Andrew. Captured! 2nd ed. 2006. (Spy Dog Ser.: 2). (ENG., Illus.). 176p. (J). (gr. 2-7). pap. 7.99 *(978-0-14-131885-1(6))* Penguin Bks., Ltd. GBR. Dist: Independent Pubs. Group.

—The Gunpowder Plot. 2017. (Spy Dog Ser.: 12). (ENG., Illus.). 176p. (J). (gr. 2-7). pap. 7.99 ***(978-0-14-136999-0(X))*** Penguin Bks., Ltd. GBR. Dist: Independent Pubs. Group.

—Rollercoaster! 7th ed. 2015. (Spy Dog Ser.). (ENG., Illus.). 160p. (J). (gr. 2-7). pap. 7.99 *(978-0-14-133882-8(2))* Penguin Bks., Ltd. GBR. Dist: Independent Pubs. Group.

—Safari. 3rd ed. 2016. (ENG., Illus.). 160p. (J). (gr. 2-7). pap. 7.99 *(978-0-14-135718-8(5))* Penguin Bks., Ltd. GBR. Dist: Independent Pubs. Group.

—Spy Dog. Wallace, Tig, ed. 2005. (Spy Dog Ser.: 1). (ENG., Illus.). 176p. (J). (gr. 2-7). pap. 7.99 *(978-0-14-131884-4(8))* Penguin Bks., Ltd. GBR. Dist: Independent Pubs. Group.

—Spy Dog & Captured!, 2 bks. in 1. 2014. (Spy Dog Ser.). (ENG., Illus.). 352p. (J). (gr. 2-7). 14.99 *(978-0-14-135097-4(0))* Penguin Bks., Ltd. GBR. Dist: Independent Pubs. Group.

—Spy Dog Unleashed. 3rd ed. 2007. (Spy Dog Ser.: 3). (ENG., Illus.). 160p. (J). (gr. 2-7). pap. 7.99 *(978-0-14-132123-3(7))* Penguin Bks., Ltd. GBR. Dist: Independent Pubs. Group.

—Storm Chaser. 10th ed. 2015. (Spy Dog Ser.: 11). (ENG., Illus.). 160p. (J). (gr. 2-7). pap. 7.99 *(978-0-14-135715-7(0))* Penguin Bks., Ltd. GBR. Dist: Independent Pubs. Group.

—Superbrain. 4th ed. 2008. (Spy Dog Ser.: 4). (ENG., Illus.). 160p. (J). (gr. 2-7). pap. 7.99 *(978-0-14-132244-5(6))* Penguin Bks., Ltd. GBR. Dist: Independent Pubs. Group.

—Survival Camp. 5th ed. 2015. (Spy Pups Ser.: 5). (ENG., Illus.). 160p. (J). (gr. 2-7). pap. 7.99 *(978-0-14-133880-4(6))* Penguin Bks., Ltd. GBR. Dist: Independent Pubs. Group.

—Teacher's Pet. 7th ed. 2011. (Spy Dog Ser.: 6). (ENG., Illus.). 160p. (J). (gr. 2-7). pap. 7.99 *(978-0-14-133620-6(X))* Penguin Bks., Ltd. GBR. Dist: Independent Pubs. Group.

—Training School. 6th ed. 2015. (Spy Pups Ser.: 6). (ENG., Illus.). 144p. (J). (gr. 2-7). pap. 7.99 *(978-0-14-133881-1(4))* Penguin Bks., Ltd. GBR. Dist: Independent Pubs. Group.

Crane, Laura Dent. The Automobile Girls at Washington. rev. ed. 2006. (ENG.). 196p. 26.95 *(978-1-4218-2096-5(X),* 1st World Library - Literary Society) 1st World Publishing, Inc.

Croall, Marie P. & Jolley, Dan. Agent Mongoose & the Attack of the Giant Insects. Wendt, Matt, illus. 2010. (Twisted Journeys (r) Ser.: 15). (ENG.). 112p. (J). (gr. 4-7). lib. bdg. 27.93 *(978-0-8225-9251-8(7))* Lerner Publishing Group.

Cross, Julie. Tempest. 2012. (Tempest Trilogy Ser.: 1). (ENG.). (YA). (gr. 9-12). 368p. pap. 9.99 *(978-1-250-01120-6(5),* 9781250011206); 352p. 17.99 *(978-0-312-56889-4(4),* 9780312568894) St. Martin's Pr. (St. Martin's Griffin).

—Timestorm: A Tempest Novel. 2014. (Tempest Trilogy Ser.: 3). (ENG.). 368p. (YA). (gr. 9-12). 18.99 *(978-0-312-56891-7(6),* 9780312568917, St. Martin's Griffin) St. Martin's Pr.

—Vortex. 2013. (Tempest Trilogy Ser.: 2). (ENG.). 368p. (YA). (gr. 9-12). 18.99 *(978-0-312-56890-0(8),* 9780312568900, St. Martin's Griffin) St. Martin's Pr.

—Vortex: A Tempest Novel. 2013. (Tempest Trilogy Ser.: 2). (ENG.). 384p. (YA). (gr. 9-12). pap. 9.99 *(978-1-250-04478-5(2),* 9781250044785, St. Martin's Griffin) St. Martin's Pr.

Cuffaro, Anna. Gatwick Bear & the Secret Plans. Anguissola, Anna, illus. 2009. (ENG.). 189p. (J). 18.00 *(978-1-907230-02-8(5))* Sparkling Bks. GBR. Dist: Silvermine International Bks., LLC.

Daneshvari, Gitty. The League of Unexceptional Children. 2015. (League of Unexceptional Children Ser.: 1). (ENG., Illus.). 240p. (J). (gr. 3-7). 17.00 *(978-0-316-40570-6(1))* Little Brown & Co.

—The League of Unexceptional Children. 2016. (League of Unexceptional Children Ser.: 1). (ENG., Illus.). 256p. (J). (gr. 3-7). pap. 6.99 *(978-0-316-40568-3(X))* Little, Brown Bks. for Young Readers.

Daneshvari, Gitty, ed. Get Smart-Ish. 2016. (League of Unexceptional Children Ser.: 2). (ENG., Illus.). 240p. (J). (gr. 3-7). 16.99 *(978-0-316-40574-4(4))* Little, Brown Bks. for Young Readers.

Davis, Tim, illus. The Case of the Purple Diamonds. 2011. 88p. pap. 9.95 *(978-1-934606-07-0(3))* TAG Publishing, LLC.

Del Toro, Gladys. The Mutation of Black Cat, 1 vol. 2009. 76p. pap. 16.95 *(978-1-61546-487-6(5))* PublishAmerica, Inc.

Dietrich, Cale. The Love Interest. 2017. (ENG.). 384p. (YA). 17.99 *(978-1-250-10713-8(X),* 9781250107138) Feiwel & Friends.

Disney Press Staff & Disney Book Group Staff. The Best School Day Ever. 2011. (ENG.). 24p. (J). (gr. 1-2). pap. 5.99 *(978-1-4231-3731-3(0))* Disney Pr.

—Cars 2. 2011. (Read-Along Storybook & CD Ser.). (ENG.). 32p. (J). (gr. -1-2). pap. 6.99 *(978-1-4231-4179-2(2))* Disney Pr.

Divine Madness. (Cherub Ser.: 5). (ENG.). (YA). (gr. 7). 2013. 400p. pap. 11.99 *(978-1-4424-1364-1(6))* 2012. 384p. 16.99 *(978-1-4169-9944-7(2))* Simon Pulse. (Simon Pulse).

Domanska, Mary Ann. Emic Rizzle, Tinkerer. 2016. (J). pap. ***(978-1-59021-777-1(2))*** Lethe Pr.

Duble, Kathleen Benner. Quest. 2008. (ENG.). 256p. (J). (gr. 5-9). 17.99 *(978-1-4169-3386-1(7),* McElderry, Margaret K. Bks.) McElderry, Margaret K. Bks.

Duggan, Olive. Spy Kitties Create a Better World. 2013. 158p. pap. 7.95 *(978-1-62137-257-8(X))* Virtualbookworm.com Publishing, Inc.

Durham, Victor G. Submarine Boys & the Spies. 2006. 27.95 *(978-1-4218-3008-7(6));* pap. 12.95 *(978-1-4218-3108-4(2))* 1st World Publishing, Inc.

Edmondson, Nathan. Where Is Jake Ellis? 2016. (ENG., Illus.). 124p. (YA). pap. 14.99 *(978-1-60706-744-3(7),* 9781607067443) Image Comics.

—Who Is Jake Ellis?, Vol. 1. 2011. (ENG., Illus.). 136p. (YA). pap. 16.99 *(978-1-60706-459-6(6),* 9781607064596) Image Comics.

Eisenstein, Ann. Fallen Prey, a Sean Gray Junior Special Agent Mystery. Waugh, Leslie, ed. 2013. 190p. pap. 9.99 *(978-1-935711-31-5(8))* Peak City Publishing, LLC.

Enna, Bruno. Double Duck. Soffritti, Donald, illus. 2010. (ENG.). 112p. (J). pap. 9.99 *(978-1-60886-545-1(2))* Boom! Studios.

Ericson, Helen. Harriet Spies Again. 2004. 240p. (J). (gr. 3-7). pap. 36.00 incl. audio *(978-0-8072-2091-7(4),* Listening Library) Random Hse. Audio Publishing Group.

Ericson, Helen & Fitzhugh, Louise. Harriet Spies Again. 2003. (ENG.). 256p. (J). (gr. 3-7). mass mkt. 7.99 *(978-0-440-41688-3(4),* Yearling) Random Hse. Children's Bks.

The Fall. 2014. (Cherub Ser.: 7). (ENG., Illus.). 368p. (YA). (gr. 7). pap. 11.99 *(978-1-4424-9947-8(8),* Simon Pulse) Simon Pulse.

Farrant, Natasha. What We Did for Love: Resistance, Heartbreak, Betrayal. 2014. 208p. 18.95 *(978-1-62324-028-8(X))* Enslow Pubs., Inc.

S

Fisher, Linda C. A Will of Her Own. 2006. (YA). pap. *(978-0-88092-641-6(4))*; lib. bdg. *(978-0-88092-640-9(6))* Royal Fireworks Publishing Co.

Fitzhugh, Louise. Harriet l Espionne. (FRE.). pap. 19.95 *(978-2-07-058141-2(1))* Gallimard, Editions FRA. Dist: Distribooks, Inc.

—Harriet the Spy. 298p. (J). (gr. 3-5). pap. 5.95 *(978-0-8072-1535-7(X)*, Listening Library) Random Hse. Audio Publishing Group.

—Harriet the Spy. 50th anniv. ed. 2014. (ENG.). 336p. (J). (gr. 3-7). 17.99 *(978-0-385-37610-5(3)*, Delacorte Bks. for Young Readers) Random Hse. Children's Bks.

Fortune, Emil. Root. 2014. (ENG.). 288p. (J). (gr. 6). pap. 10.99 *(978-0-552-56635-3(7))* Transworld Publishers Ltd. GBR. Dist: Independent Pubs. Group.

Francia, Giada, ed. Ballooning over Italy: An Extraordinary Voyage Packed with Games & Fantastic Adventures; Special Agents. Ezrin, Amy, tr. Colombo, Angelo, illus. 2007. (Alex & Penny Ser.). (ENG.). 80p. (J). (gr. 2-5). 14.95 *(978-88-544-0160-0(9)*, White Star) Rizzoli International Pubns., Inc.

Frederick, Heather Vogel. The Black Paw. 2013. (Spy Mice Ser.: 1). (ENG., Illus.). 224p. (J). (gr. 3-6). pap. 7.99 *(978-1-4424-6701-9(0)*, Simon & Schuster Bks. For Young Readers) Simon & Schuster Bks. For Young Readers.

—For Your Paws Only. 2013. (Spy Mice Ser.: 2). (ENG., Illus.). 240p. (J). (gr. 3-6). pap. 6.99 *(978-1-4424-6703-3(7)*, Simon & Schuster Bks. For Young Readers) Simon & Schuster Bks. For Young Readers.

—For Your Paws Only. Comport, Sally Wern, illus. 2006. (Spy Mice Ser.: 2). (ENG.). 272p. (J). (gr. 3-6). pap. 5.99 *(978-1-4169-4025-8(1)*, Simon & Schuster Bks. For Young Readers) Simon & Schuster Bks. For Young Readers.

—Goldwhiskers. 2013. (Spy Mice Ser.: 3). (ENG., Illus.). 272p. (J). (gr. -1-6). pap. 6.99 *(978-1-4424-6705-7(3)*, Simon & Schuster Bks. For Young Readers) Simon & Schuster Bks. For Young Readers.

Freeman, Martha. The Case of the Bug on the Run. 2014. (First Kids Mystery Ser.: 6). (ENG.). 144p. (J). (gr. 2-7). pap. 6.99 *(978-0-8234-3188-5(6))* Holiday Hse., Inc.

—The Case of the Bug on the Run: First Kids Mystery #6. 2013. (First Kids Mystery Ser.: 6). (ENG.). 144p. (J). (gr. 2-7). 16.95 *(978-0-8234-2872-4(9))* Holiday Hse., Inc.

Gagnon, Michelle & Gangsei, Jan. Zero Day. 2016. (ENG., Illus.). 364p. (YA). (gr. 7-12). 17.99 *(978-1-4847-2226-8(4))* Hyperion Bks. for Children.

Gale, Emily. My Explosive Diary. Dreidemy, Joëlle, illus. 2014. (Eliza Boom Ser.: 1). (ENG.). 128p. (J). (gr. 1-4). 15.99 *(978-1-4814-0650-5(7)*, Simon & Schuster/Paula Wiseman Bks.) Simon & Schuster/Paula Wiseman Bks.

Gamble, Paul. The Ministry of S. U. I. T. S. 2016. (Ministry of SUITs Ser.: 1). (ENG.). 384p. (J). 16.99 *(978-1-250-07682-3(X)*, 9781250076823) Feiwel & Friends.

Gibbs, Stuart. Evil Spy School. 2015. (Spy School Ser.). (ENG., Illus.). 336p. (J). (gr. 3-7). 17.99 *(978-1-4424-9489-3(1)*, Simon & Schuster Bks. For Young Readers) Simon & Schuster Bks. For Young Readers.

—Spy Camp. (Spy School Ser.). (ENG., Illus.). (J). (gr. 3-7). 2014. 352p. pap. 7.99 *(978-1-4424-5754-6(6))* 2013. 336p. 17.99 *(978-1-4424-5753-9(8))* Simon & Schuster Bks. For Young Readers. (Simon & Schuster Bks. For Young Readers).

—Spy School. (Spy School Ser.). (ENG., (J). (gr. 3-7). 2013. Illus.). 320p. pap. 7.99 *(978-1-4424-2183-7(5))* 2012. 304p. 17.99 *(978-1-4424-2182-0(7))* Simon & Schuster Bks. For Young Readers. (Simon & Schuster Bks. For Young Readers).

—Spy School Secret Service. 2017. (J). pap. ***(978-1-4814-7783-3(8)***, Simon & Schuster Bks. For Young Readers) Simon & Schuster Bks. For Young Readers.

Gibbs, Stuart. Spy Ski School. 2016. (Spy School Ser.). (ENG., Illus.). 368p. (J). (gr. 3-7). 16.99 *(978-1-4814-4562-7(6)*, Simon & Schuster Bks. For Young Readers) Simon & Schuster Bks. For Young Readers.

Glass, George. Black-Tie Spy. 2013. 94p. (J). pap. *(978-0-545-47271-5(7))* Scholastic, Inc.

Gold, Maya & Fitzhugh, Louise. Harriet the Spy, Double Agent. 2007. (Harriet the Spy Adventures Ser.). (ENG.). 160p. (J). (gr. 3-7). 6.99 *(978-0-440-41691-3(4)*, Yearling) Random Hse. Children's Bks.

Golden Books Staff & Tillworth, Mary. Barbie Spy Squad. 2016. (Big Golden Book Ser.). (ENG., Illus.). 48p. (J). (gr. -1-2). 9.99 *(978-0-553-53917-2(5)*, Golden Bks.) Random Hse. Children's Bks.

Gonzalez, Christina Diaz. A Thunderous Whisper. 2013. (ENG., Illus.). 320p. (J). (gr. 5). pap. 7.99 *(978-0-375-87371-3(6)*, Yearling) Random Hse. Children's Bks.

Goodwin, Archie. Secret Agent Corrigan, 1977-1980, 5 vols., Vol. 5. Williamson, Al, illus. 2013. (X-9 Ser.). (ENG.). 288p. 49.99 *(978-1-61377-542-4(3)*, 9781613775424) Idea & Design Works, LLC.

Gratz, Alan. Projekt 1065: A Novel of World War II. 2016. (ENG.). 320p. (J). (gr. 4-7). 16.99 *(978-0-545-88016-9(5)*, Scholastic Pr.) Scholastic, Inc.

Greene, Stephanie. Owen Foote, Super Spy. Weston, Martha, illus. 2005. (ENG.). 96p. (J). (gr. 1-4). pap. 8.95 *(978-0-618-55159-0(X))* Houghton Mifflin Harcourt Publishing Co.

Greenland, Shannon. Down to the Wire. 2007. (Specialists Ser.: Vol. 2). (ENG.). 224p. (YA). (gr. 7-18). pap. 7.99 *(978-0-14-240917-6(0)*, Speak) Penguin Young Readers Group.

—The Winning Element, Vol. 3. 2008. (Specialists Ser.). (ENG.). 224p. (YA). (gr. 7-18). 6.99 *(978-0-14-241052-3(7)*, Speak) Penguin Young Readers Group.

Griffis, Molly Levite. The Rachel Resistance. 224p. 8.95 *(978-1-57168-553-7(7))* Eakin Pr.

Griffith, A. J. America's Child. 2008. (J). pap. 9.99 *(978-0-88092-493-1(4))* Royal Fireworks Publishing Co.

Gutman, Dan. Mrs. Cooney Is Loony! Paillot, Jim, illus. 2005. (My Weird School Ser.: 7). (ENG.). 112p. (J). (gr. 1-5). pap. 4.99 *(978-0-06-074522-6(3))* HarperCollins Pubs.

Guzman, Lila & Guzman, Rick. Lorenzo's Revolutionary Quest. 2003. 176p. (J). pap. 9.95 *(978-1-55885-392-8(8)*, Piñata Books) Arte Publico Pr.

Hale, Bruce. Ends of the Earth. Dorman, Brandon, illus. 2015. (School for Spies Novel Ser.). (ENG.). 304p. (J). (gr. 3-7). 16.99 *(978-1-4231-6852-2(6))* Disney Pr.

—School for SPIES Book 2 Thicker Than Water. Dorman, Brandon, illus. 2014. (School for Spies Novel Ser.). (ENG.). 352p. (J). (gr. 3-7). 16.99 *(978-1-4231-6851-5(8))* Hyperion Bks. for Children.

—School for SPIES Book One Playing with Fire. Dorman, Brandon, illus. 2014. (School for Spies Novel Ser.). (ENG.). 336p. (J). (gr. 3-7). pap. 6.99 *(978-1-4231-7105-8(5))* Hyperion Bks. for Children.

—School for SPIES Thicker Than Water. Dorman, Brandon, illus. 2015. (ENG.). 368p. (J). (gr. 3-7). pap. 6.99 *(978-1-4231-7106-5(3))* Hyperion Bks. for Children.

Hale, Shannon. River Secrets. (Books of Bayern Ser.). (ENG., Illus.). (YA). (gr. 7). 2008. 320p. 9.99 *(978-1-59990-293-7(1)*, 9781599902937) 2006. 304p. 18.99 *(978-1-58234-901-5(0)*, 9781582349015) Bloomsbury Publishing USA. (Bloomsbury USA Childrens).

Harlow, Joan Hiatt. Midnight Rider. 2006. (ENG.). 384p. (J). (gr. 4-9). pap. 8.99 *(978-0-689-87010-1(8)*, McElderry, Margaret K. Bks.) McElderry, Margaret K. Bks.

Hayner, Linda K. Ellanor's Exchange. 2005. 195p. (YA). 8.99 *(978-1-59166-462-8(4))* BJU Pr.

Higgins, Jack & Richards, Justin. Death Run. 2009. (Rich & Jade Ser.: Bk. 2). (ENG.). 288p. (YA). (gr. 7-18). 8.99 *(978-0-14-241475-0(1)*, Speak) Penguin Young Readers Group.

—First Strike. 2011. (Rich & Jade Ser.: Bk. 4). (ENG.). 240p. (YA). (gr. 7-18). 8.99 *(978-0-14-241909-0(5)*, Speak) Penguin Young Readers Group.

—Sharp Shot. 2010. (Rich & Jade Ser.: Bk. 3). (ENG.). 240p. (YA). (gr. 7-18). 8.99 *(978-0-14-241730-0(0)*, Speak) Penguin Young Readers Group.

—Sure Fire. 2008. (Rich & Jade Ser.: Bk. 1). (ENG.). 272p. (YA). (gr. 7-18). 8.99 *(978-0-14-241213-8(9)*, Speak) Penguin Young Readers Group.

Higgins, Simon. Moonshadow: Rise of the Ninja. 2011. (Moonshadow Ser.: 1). (ENG.). 352p. (J). (gr. 3-7). pap. 6.99 *(978-0-316-05532-1(8))* Little, Brown Bks. for Young Readers.

Hildebrand, Jens. Team 002: The Abduction of the Queen. Garcia, Juan F., illus. 2013. 224p. pap. *(978-3-929892-46-8(4))* Hildebrand, Jutta Warped Tomato Publishing.

—Team 002 und das Utopia-Element. Garcia, Juan F., illus. 2013. 270p. pap. *(978-3-929892-39-0(1))* Hildebrand, Jutta Warped Tomato Publishing.

—Team 002 und Die Entführung der Queen. Garcia, Juan F., illus. 2013. 240p. pap. *(978-3-929892-37-6(5))* Hildebrand, Jutta Warped Tomato Publishing.

Holm, Jennifer L. & Hamel, Jonathan. The Postman Always Brings Mice. Weinman, Brad, illus. 2005. (Stink Files Ser.: No. 1). 129p. (J). 12.65 *(978-0-7569-6529-7(2))* Perfection Learning Corp.

—To Scratch a Thief. Weinman, Brad, illus. (Stink Files Ser.: No. 2). 144p. 2005. pap. 4.99 *(978-0-06-052984-0(9)*, Harper Trophy) 2004. (J). 14.99 *(978-0-06-052982-6(2))* 2004. (J). lib. bdg. 15.89 *(978-0-06-052983-3(0))* HarperCollins Pubs.

Horowitz, Anthony. Ark Angel. (Alex Rider Ser.: Bk. 6). (ENG.). (J). (gr. 5-18). 2007. 352p. 8.99 *(978-0-14-240738-7(0)*, Puffin Books) 2006. 336p. 17.99 *(978-0-399-24152-9(3)*, Philomel Bks.) Penguin Young Readers Group.

—Ark Angel. 2007. (Alex Rider Ser.: Bk. 6). 326p. (gr. 5-9). 19.00 *(978-0-7569-8134-1(4))* Perfection Learning Corp.

—Ark Angel. 2007. (Alex Rider Ser.: 6). 326p. lib. bdg. 19.65 *(978-1-4177-7664-1(1)*, Turtleback) Turtleback Bks.

—Crocodile Tears. (Alex Rider Ser.: Bk. 8). (ENG.). (J). (gr. 5-18). 2010. 416p. 8.99 *(978-0-14-241719-5(X)*, Puffin Books) 2009. 400p. 18.99 *(978-0-399-25056-9(5)*, Philomel Bks.) Penguin Young Readers Group.

—Crocodile Tears, 9 vols. 2010. (Alex Rider Adventure Ser.: 8). (J). 81.75 *(978-1-4407-5451-7(9))*; 79.75 *(978-1-4407-5453-1(5))*; 102.75 *(978-1-4407-5456-2(X))*; 1.25 *(978-1-4407-5459-3(4))*; 100.75 *(978-1-4407-5458-6(6))* Recorded Bks., Inc.

—Crocodile Tears. 2010. (Alex Rider Ser.: 8). lib. bdg. 19.65 *(978-0-606-23639-3(2)*, Turtleback) Turtleback Bks.

—Eagle Strike. (Alex Rider Ser.). (ENG.). (J). (gr. 5-18). 2006. 368p. 8.99 *(978-0-14-240613-7(9)*, Puffin Books) 2004. (Illus.). 272p. 17.99 *(978-0-399-23979-3(0)*, Philomel Bks.) Penguin Young Readers Group.

—The Falcon's Malteser. 2004. (Diamond Brothers Ser.: No. 1). (ENG.). 208p. (J). (gr. 3-7). 6.99 *(978-0-14-240219-1(2)*, Puffin Books) Penguin Young Readers Group.

—Point Blanc. 2004. (Alex Rider Ser.: Bk. 2). (SPA.). 264p. pap. 7.95 *(978-84-414-1410-5(6))* Editorial Edaf, S.L. ESP. Dist: Spanish Pubs., LLC.

—Point Blank. 2006. (Alex Rider Ser.). (ENG.). 320p. (J). (gr. 5-18). 8.99 *(978-0-14-240612-0(0)*, Puffin Books) Penguin Young Readers Group.

—Russian Roulette: The Story of an Assassin. 2013. (Alex Rider Ser.). (ENG.). 384p. (J). (gr. 6-9). 17.99 *(978-0-399-25441-3(2)*, Philomel Bks.) Penguin Publishing Group.

—Scorpia. (Alex Rider Ser.). (ENG.). (J). (gr. 5-18). 2006. 416p. pap. 8.99 *(978-0-14-240578-9(7)*, Puffin Books) 2005. 336p. 17.99 *(978-0-399-24151-2(5)*, Philomel Bks.) Penguin Young Readers Group.

—Scorpia Rising. (Alex Rider Ser.). (ENG.). (J). (gr. 5-18). 2012. 432p. 8.99 *(978-0-14-241985-4(0)*, Puffin Books) 2011. 416p. 17.99 *(978-0-399-25057-6(3)*, Philomel Bks.) Penguin Young Readers Group.

—Scorpia Rising, 9 vols. (J). 2012. 90.75 *(978-1-4561-3363-4(2))* 2012. 256.75 *(978-1-4561-3362-7(4))* 2012. 1.25 *(978-1-4640-0577-0(X))* 2011. 122.75 *(978-1-4561-3365-8(9))* 2011. 120.75 *(978-1-4561-3367-2(5))* Recorded Bks., Inc.

—Scorpia Rising. 2012. (Alex Rider Ser.: 9). lib. bdg. 19.65 *(978-0-606-23638-6(4)*, Turtleback) Turtleback Bks.

—Skeleton Key. Kanako & Yuzuru, illus. 2009. (Alex Rider Ser.: Bk. 3). (ENG.). 176p. (J). (gr. 5-18). pap. 14.99 *(978-0-399-25418-5(8)*, Philomel Bks.) Penguin Young Readers Group.

—Skeleton Key. (Alex Rider Ser.: Bk. 3). (ENG.). (J). (gr. 5-18). 2006. 368p. 8.99 *(978-0-14-240614-4(7)*, Puffin Books) 2003. 240p. 17.99 *(978-0-399-23777-5(1)*, Philomel Bks.) Penguin Young Readers Group.

—Snakehead. (Alex Rider Ser.: Bk. 7). (ENG.). (J). (gr. 5-18). 2008. 432p. (J). pap. 8.99 *(978-0-14-241212-1(0)*, Puffin Books) 2007. 400p. (YA). 17.99 *(978-0-399-24161-1(2)*, Philomel Bks.) Penguin Young Readers Group.

—Stormbreaker. Damerum, Kanako et al, illus. 2006. (Alex Rider Ser.). (ENG.). 144p. (J). (gr. 5-18). pap. 14.99 *(978-0-399-24633-3(9)*, Philomel Bks.) Penguin Young Readers Group.

—Stormbreaker. 2006. (Alex Rider Ser.: Bk. 1). (ENG.). 304p. (J). (gr. 5-18). 8.99 *(978-0-14-240611-3(2)*, Puffin Books) Penguin Young Readers Group.

—Stormbreaker. 2004. (Alex Rider Ser.: Bk. 1). 208p. (J). (gr. 4-7). pap. 38.00 incl. audio *(978-0-8072-2277-5(1)*, Listening Library) Random Hse. Audio Publishing Group.

Howard, Kate, adapted by. Spy vs. Spy. 2015. (Illus.). 32p. (J). *(978-1-4806-9048-6(1))* Scholastic, Inc.

Hunsaker, Joan. A Dagger in Time - the Web of Spies. 2010. 200p. 25.99 *(978-1-58930-247-1(8))*; pap. 15.99 *(978-1-58930-248-8(6))* Selah Publishing Group, LLC.

Hunt, Elizabeth Singer. The Search for the Sunken Treasure Bk. 2: Australia. 2007. (Illus.). 110p. (J). *(978-1-4242-4190-3(1)*, Weinstein Bks.) Perseus Bks. Group.

Hunter, John P. Red Thunder: Secrets, Spies, & Scoundrels at Yorktown. 2006. 234p. (YA). (gr. 6-8). 7.95 *(978-0-87935-231-8(0))* Colonial Williamsburg Foundation.

I Spy: Individual Title Six-Packs. (Story Steps Ser.). (gr. k-2). 29.00 *(978-0-7635-9571-5(3))* Rigby Education.

Jacobs, Edgar P. The Mystery of the Great Pyramid. (Blake & Mortimer Ser.: 2). (ENG., Illus.). Pt. 1. 2007. 72p. pap. 15.95 *(978-1-905460-37-3(6))*Pt. 2. 2008. 56p. pap. 15.95 *(978-1-905460-38-0(4))* CineBook GBR. Dist: National Bk. Network.

—S. O. S. Meteors. 2009. (Blake & Mortimer Ser.: 6). (ENG., Illus.). 64p. pap. 15.95 *(978-1-905460-97-7(X))* CineBook GBR. Dist: National Bk. Network.

—The Yellow "M" 2007. (Blake & Mortimer Ser.: 1). (ENG., Illus.). 72p. per. 15.95 *(978-1-905460-21-2(X))* CineBook GBR. Dist: National Bk. Network.

Jacobson, Ryan. The Case of the Florida Freeze, 1 vol. Belkholm, Erica, illus. l.t. ed. 2005. (Santa Claus: Super Spy Ser.). (ENG.). 80p. (J). per. 4.99 *(978-0-9774122-0-4(2)*, Getchu Bks.) Lake 7 Creative, LLC.

James, Brian. Port of Spies. Zivoin, Jennifer, illus. 2007. (Pirate School Ser.: 4). (ENG.). 64p. (J). (gr. 1-3). pap. 3.99 *(978-0-448-44646-2(4)*, Grosset & Dunlap) Penguin Young Readers Group.

Johnston, K. E. M. The Witness Tree & the Shadow of the Noose: Mystery, Lies, & Spies in Manassas. 2009. 111p. (J). (gr. 5-7). pap. 8.95 *(978-1-57249-397-1(6)*, White Mane Kids) White Mane Publishing Co., Inc.

Jolley, Dan. Agent Mongoose & the Hypno-Beam Scheme. Wendt, Matt, illus. 2009. (Twisted Journeys (r) Ser.: 9). (ENG.). 112p. (J). (gr. 4-7). 27.93 *(978-0-8225-6203-0(0))*; pap. 7.95 *(978-0-8225-6204-7(9))* Lerner Publishing Group.

Jolley, Dan & Croall, Marie P. Agent Mongoose & the Attack of the Giant Insects. Wendt, Matt, illus. 2010. (Twisted Journeys (r) Ser.: 15). (ENG.). 112p. (J). (gr. 4-7). pap. 7.95 *(978-0-8225-9257-0(6)*, Graphic Universe™) Lerner Publishing Group.

—Agent Mongoose & the Attack of the Giant Insects. 15th rev. ed. 2010. (Twisted Journeys (r) Ser.: 15). (ENG.). (J). (gr. 4-7). pap. 45.32 *(978-0-7613-6998-1(8))* Lerner Publishing Group.

Jones, Allan & Frewin, Jones. In the Zone. 2012. (ENG.). 128p. (J). (gr. 4-6). pap. 6.99 *(978-1-4440-0545-5(6)*, Orion Children's Bks.) Hachette Children's Group GBR. Dist: Hachette Bk. Group.

Jones, Allan Frewin. Burning Sky. 2012. (ENG.). 208p. (J). (gr. 4-6). pap. 6.99 *(978-1-4440-0547-9(2)*, Orion Children's Bks.) Hachette Children's Group GBR. Dist: Hachette Bk. Group.

Jones, Ena. Clayton Stone, at Your Service. 2015. (ENG.). 224p. (J). (gr. 2-6). 16.95 *(978-0-8234-3389-6(7))* Holiday Hse., Inc.

—Clayton Stone, Facing Off. 2016. (ENG.). 224p. (J). 16.95 *(978-0-8234-3648-4(9))* Holiday Hse., Inc.

Kehoe, Tim. Furious Jones & the Assassin's Secret. 2014. (ENG., Illus.). 336p. (J). (gr. 3-7). 16.99 *(978-1-4424-7337-9(1)*, Simon & Schuster Bks. For Young Readers) Simon & Schuster Bks. For Young Readers.

Kelly, Katy. Melonhead & the Undercover Operation. Johnson, Gillian, illus. 2012. (Melonhead Ser.). (ENG.). 256p. (J). (gr. 3-7). 7.99 *(978-0-375-84528-4(3)*, Yearling) Random Hse. Children's Bks.

Kidd, Ronald. Undercover Kid: The Comic Book King. Sklar, Andy, illus. 2007. (All Aboard Mystery Reader Ser.). (ENG.). 48p. (J). pap. 3.99 *(978-0-448-44438-3(0)*, Grosset & Dunlap) Penguin Publishing Group.

Kiem, Elizabeth. Dancer, Daughter, Traitor, Spy. 2014. (Bolshoi Saga Ser.: 1). (ENG., Illus.). 292p. (YA). (gr. 9). pap. 10.99 *(978-1-61695-422-2(1)*, Soho Teen) Soho Pr., Inc.

Kindt, Matt. Super Spy. 2007. (Super Spy Ser.). (ENG., Illus.). 304p. pap. 19.95 *(978-1-891830-96-9(1)*, 9781891830969) Top Shelf Productions.

Korman, Gordon. Showoff. 2012. (Swindle Ser.: 4). (ENG.). 256p. (J). (gr. 3-7). 16.99 *(978-0-545-32059-7(3)*, Scholastic Pr.) Scholastic, Inc.

Lagonegro, Melissa. Super Agents. 2016. (Step into Reading Ser.). (ENG., Illus.). 24p. (J). (gr. -1-1). pap. 4.99 *(978-1-101-93140-0(X)*, Random Hse. Bks. for Young Readers) Random Hse. Children's Bks.

Lantigua, Lizette M. Mission Libertad. 2012. (ENG.). 192p. (YA). pap. 9.95 *(978-0-8198-4900-7(6))* Pauline Bks. & Media.

Larry, H. I. Deep Waters. Oswald, Ash, illus. 2008. (Zac Power Ser.: 2). (ENG.). 96p. (J). (gr. 3-6). pap. 5.99 *(978-0-312-34655-3(7)*, 9780312346553) Square Fish.

—Frozen Fear. Oswald, Ash, illus. 2008. (Zac Power Ser.: 4). (ENG.). 96p. (J). (gr. 3-6). pap. 4.99 *(978-0-312-34656-0(5)*, 9780312346560) Square Fish.

—Mind Games. Oswald, Ash, illus. 2008. (Zac Power Ser.: 3). (ENG.). 96p. (J). (gr. 3-6). pap. 4.99 *(978-0-312-34657-7(3)*, 9780312346577) Square Fish.

—Poison Island. Oswald, Ash, illus. 2008. (Zac Power Ser.: 1). (ENG.). 96p. (J). (gr. 3-6). pap. 5.99 *(978-0-312-34659-1(X)*, 9780312346591) Square Fish.

Lasky, Kathryn. The Shattering. 2004. (Guardians of Ga'hoole Ser.: 5). (ENG., Illus.). 192p. (J). (gr. 3-7). 6.99 *(978-0-439-40561-4(0)*, Scholastic Paperbacks) Scholastic, Inc.

Lee, M. C. Like I Know Jack. 2016. (ENG., Illus.). (YA). 27.99 ***(978-1-63533-042-7(4))***; 260p. (J). pap. *(978-1-63476-807-8(8))* Dreamspinner Pr. (Harmony Ink Pr.).

Leonard, Julia Platt. Cold Case. 2012. (ENG.). 288p. (J). (gr. 3-7). pap. 5.99 *(978-1-4424-2010-6(3)*, Simon & Schuster/Paula Wiseman Bks.) Simon & Schuster/Paula Wiseman Bks.

—Cold Case. Mauro, Tony, illus. 2011. (ENG.). 288p. (J). (gr. 3-7). 15.99 *(978-1-4424-2009-0(X)*, Simon & Schuster/Paula Wiseman Bks.) Simon & Schuster/Paula Wiseman Bks.

LeSourd, Nancy. Secrets of Civil War Spies, 1 vol. 2008. (Liberty Letters Ser.). (ENG.). 224p. (J). pap. 7.99 *(978-0-310-71390-6(0))* Zonderkidz.

Logsted, Greg. Alibi Junior High. (ENG.). 256p. (J). (gr. 5-9). 2011. pap. 6.99 *(978-1-4169-4814-8(7))* 2009. (Illus.). 16.99 *(978-1-4169-7959-3(X))* Simon & Schuster/Paula Wiseman Bks. (Simon & Schuster/Paula Wiseman Bks.).

Long, Angela Pullam. Salvador the Spy in the Case of the Missing Cats. 2008. 32p. pap. 24.95 *(978-1-60672-724-9(9))* America Star Bks.

Long, Loren & Bildner, Phil. Blastin' the Blues. Long, Loren, illus. 2011. (Sluggers Ser.: 5). (ENG., Illus.). 448p. (J). (gr. 3-7). pap. 8.99 *(978-1-4169-1891-2(4)*, Simon & Schuster Bks. For Young Readers) Simon & Schuster Bks. For Young Readers.

Lord, Gabrielle. Black Ops Hunted: Conspiracy 365. 2014. 192p. (J). 10.99 *(978-1-61067-171-2(6))* Kane Miller.

—Black Ops Missing: Conspiracy 365. 2014. 192p. (J). 10.99 *(978-1-61067-168-2(6))* Kane Miller.

Lorentz, Dayna. No Easy Way Out, Bk. 2. 2nd ed. 2014. (No Safety in Numbers Ser.: 2). (ENG.). 480p. (YA). (gr. 7). pap. 9.99 *(978-0-14-242524-4(9)*, Speak) Penguin Young Readers Group.

Lorimer, Janet. A Deadly Game (Spy), 1 vol. 2017. (Pagetumers Ser.). (ENG.). 80p. (YA). (gr. 9-12). 8.95 ***(978-1-68021-398-0(9))*** Saddleback Educational Publishing, Inc.

—An Eye for an Eye (Spy), 1 vol. 2017. (Pagetumers Ser.). (ENG.). 76p. (YA). (gr. 9-12). 8.95 ***(978-1-68021-399-7(7))*** Saddleback Educational Publishing, Inc.

—Scavenger Hunt (Spy), 1 vol. 2017. (Pagetumers Ser.). (ENG.). 80p. (YA). (gr. 9-12). 8.95 ***(978-1-68021-401-7(2))*** Saddleback Educational Publishing, Inc.

—Tuesday Raven (Spy), 1 vol. 2017. (Pagetumers Ser.). (ENG.). 80p. (YA). (gr. 9-12). 8.95 ***(978-1-68021-402-4(0))*** Saddleback Educational Publishing, Inc.

Lu, Marie. Warcross, 9 vols. 2017. (ENG.). (YA). 170.91 ***(978-0-525-48674-9(7))***; 368p. (gr. 7). 18.99 ***(978-0-399-54796-6(7))*** Penguin Young Readers Group. (G.P. Putnam's Sons Books for Young Readers).

Lubar, David. Dead Guy Spy. 2010. (Nathan Abercrombie, Accidental Zombie Ser.: 2). (ENG.). 176p. (J). (gr. 3-7). pap. 8.99 *(978-0-7653-2507-5(1)*, 9780765325075, Starscape) Doherty, Tom Assocs., LLC.

Luper, Eric. The Spy's Secret. 2016. (Key Hunters Ser.: 2). (ENG.). 128p. (J). (gr. 2-5). pap. 4.99 *(978-0-545-82206-0(8))* Scholastic, Inc.

Macauley, Jo. Inferno, 1 vol. 2014. (Secrets & Spies Ser.). (ENG.). 224p. (gr. 4-7). 26.65 *(978-1-4342-9595-8(8))* Stone Arch Bks.

—New World, 1 vol. 2014. (Secrets & Spies Ser.). (ENG.). 224p. (gr. 4-7). 26.65 *(978-1-4342-9596-5(6))* Stone Arch Bks.

—Plague, 1 vol. 2014. (Secrets & Spies Ser.). (ENG.). 224p. (gr. 4-7). pap. 8.95 *(978-1-62370-053-9(1))* Capstone Young Readers of Coughlan Cos.

—Plague, 1 vol. 2014. (Secrets & Spies Ser.). (ENG.). 224p. (gr. 4-7). 26.65 *(978-1-4342-7947-7(2))* Stone Arch Bks.

—Secrets & Spies, 1 vol. 2014. (Secrets & Spies Ser.). (ENG.). 224p. (gr. 4-7). 53.30 *(978-1-4342-8770-0(X))* Stone Arch Bks.

—Treason, 1 vol. 2014. (Secrets & Spies Ser.). (ENG., Illus.). 224p. (gr. 4-7). pap. 8.95 *(978-1-62370-052-2(3))* Capstone Young Readers of Coughlan Cos.

—Treason. 2014. (J). pap. *(978-1-4342-7944-6(8))*; (ENG.). 224p. (gr. 4-7). 26.65 *(978-1-4342-7946-0(4))* Stone Arch Bks.

MacLean, Alistair. Circus. (J). 24.95 *(978-0-89190-672-8(X))* Amereon Ltd.

—Circus. 2009. (ENG., Illus.). 288p. mass mkt. 9.99 *(978-0-00-616735-8(7))* HarperCollins Pubs.

Mad Dogs. 2014. (Cherub Ser.: 8). (ENG., Illus.). 416p. (YA). (gr. 7). pap. 11.99 *(978-1-4424-9954-6(0))*; 17.99 *(978-1-4424-9953-9(2))* Simon Pulse. (Simon Pulse).

Mah, Adeline Yen. Chinese Cinderella & the Secret Dragon Society. 2006. (ENG., Illus.). 256p. (J). (gr. 5-9). pap. 7.99 *(978-0-06-056736-1(8))* HarperCollins Pubs.

Mahle, Melissa & Dennis, Kathryn. Camp Secret. Wong, Liz, illus. 2013. (Junior Spies Ser.: 1). (ENG.). 268p. (J). pap. 10.99 *(978-0-9852273-4-0(6))* SpyGirls Pr.

Maid of Deception. 2014. (Maids of Honor Ser.). (ENG., Illus.). 416p. (YA). (gr. 7). 17.99 *(978-1-4424-4141-5(0))*, Simon & Schuster Bks. For Young Readers) Simon & Schuster Bks. For Young Readers.

Man vs. Beast. 2013. (Cherub Ser.: 6). (ENG., (YA). (gr. 7). Illus.). 352p. pap. 11.99 *(978-1-4424-1365-8(4))*; 336p. 16.99 *(978-1-4169-9945-4(0))* Simon Pulse. (Simon Pulse).

Marathon. When You're Having Fun, Vol. 4. 2005. (Totally Spies! Ser.). (Illus.). pap. 14.99 *(978-1-59532-818-2(1)*, Tokyopop Kids) TOKYOPOP, Inc.

Marsh, Carole. The Counterfeit Constitution Mystery. 2008. (Real Kids, Real Places Ser.). (Illus.). 144p. (J). (gr. 3-5). 14.95 *(978-0-635-06517-9(7))*; per. 5.95 *(978-0-635-06512-4(6))* Gallopade International.

Martinek, Frank V. Don Winslow Breaks the Spy Net. Warren, F., illus. 2011. 226p. 44.95 *(978-1-258-07858-4(9))* Literary Licensing, LLC.

—Don Winslow Saves the Secret Formul. Warren, F., illus. 2011. 226p. 44.95 *(978-1-258-07446-3(X))* Literary Licensing, LLC.

Martinek, Frank Victor. Don Winslow: Face to Face with the Scorpion. Warren, F., illus. 2011. 224p. 44.95 *(978-1-258-07493-7(1))* Literary Licensing, LLC.

Marzollo, Jean. I Spy Lightning in the Sky. Wick, Walter, illus. 2005. (Scholastic Reader Level 1 Ser.). (ENG.). 32p. (J). (gr. -1-3). pap. 3.99 *(978-0-439-68052-3(2),* Cartwheel Bks.) Scholastic, Inc.

Marzollo, Jean & Scholastic / LeapFrog. I Spy Imagine That! Wick, Walter, illus. 2008. (J). 13.99 *(978-1-59319-933-3(3))* LeapFrog Enterprises, Inc.

Mason, Adrienne. Secret Spies. Cupples, Patricia & Cupples, Pat, illus. 2008. (Kids Can Read Ser.). (ENG.). 32p. (J). (gr. 1-2). 14.95 *(978-1-55453-276-6(0));* pap. 3.95 *(978-1-55453-277-3(9))* Kids Can Pr., Ltd. CAN. Dist: Hachette Bk. Group.

Mason, Jane B. & Hines-Stephens, Sarah. Disguised & Dangerous. Phillips, Craig, illus. 2011. 92p. (J). *(978-0-545-37469-9(3))* Scholastic, Inc.

Mason, Jane B. & Stephens, Sarah Hines. A Dog & His Girl Mysteries #3: Cry Woof. 2013. (ENG.). 208p. (J). (gr. 3-7). pap. 5.99 *(978-0-545-43626-7(5),* Scholastic Paperbacks) Scholastic, Inc.

Mass, Wendy & Brawer, Michael. The Galactic B. U. R. P. 2016. (Space Taxi Ser.: 4). (ENG., Illus.). 128p. (J). (gr. 1-5). 14.99 *(978-0-316-24331-5(0));* pap. 5.99 *(978-0-316-24330-8(2))* Little, Brown Bks. for Young Readers.

Mayer, Kirsten. Despicable Me 2 - Undercover Super Spies. 2013. (ENG.). 24p. (J). (gr. -1-3). 4.99 *(978-0-316-23446-7(X))* Little, Brown Bks. for Young Readers.

McCaffrey, Laura Williams. Marked. 2017. (ENG.). 368p. (YA). (gr. 7). pap. 9.99 *(978-0-544-93884-7(4),* HMH Books For Young Readers) Houghton Mifflin Harcourt Publishing Co.

McDavid-Jones, Elizabeth. The Night Flyers. 2009. (Mysteries Through Time Ser.). 144 - 176p. (YA). (gr. 4-8). 31.95 *(978-1-60754-197-4(1));* pap. 15.25 *(978-1-60754-198-1(X))* Windmill Bks.

McDivitt, Barry. The Youngest Spy. 2007. (ENG.). 176p. (YA). (gr. 3-9). per. 12.95 *(978-1-897235-17-1(8))* Thistledown Pr., Ltd. CAN. Dist: Univ. of Toronto Pr.

McGee, Ron. Ryan Quinn & the Rebel's Escape. Samnee, Chris, illus. 2016. (Ryan Quinn Ser.: 1). 368p. (J). (gr. 3-7). 16.99 *(978-0-06-242164-7(6))* HarperCollins Pubs.

McGowan, Jennifer. Maid of Secrets. (Maids of Honor Ser.). (ENG.). (YA). (gr. 7). 2014. 432p. pap. 9.99 *(978-1-4424-4139-2(9))* 2013. 416p. 17.99 *(978-1-4424-4138-5(0))* Simon & Schuster Bks. For Young Readers. (Simon & Schuster Bks. For Young Readers).

—Maid of Wonder. 2015. (Maids of Honor Ser.). (ENG., Illus.). 336p. (YA). (gr. 7). 17.99 *(978-1-4814-1826-3(2))* Simon & Schuster Children's Publishing.

McMullen, Beth. Mrs. Smith's Spy School for Girls. 2017. (Mrs. Smith's Spy School for Girls Ser.: 1). (ENG., Illus.). 304p. (J). (gr. 4-8). 16.99 ***(978-1-4814-9020-7(6),*** Aladdin) Simon & Schuster Children's Publishing.

—Mrs. Smith's Spy School for Girls. 2017. (J). pap. ***(978-1-4814-9021-4(4),*** Simon & Schuster/Paula Wiseman Bks.) Simon & Schuster/Paula Wiseman Bks.

Menotti, Andrea. Operation Fowl Play. Kennedy, Kelly, illus. 2004. (Spy Five Ser.). 92p. (J). *(978-0-439-70349-9(2))* Scholastic, Inc.

—Operation Master Mole. Kennedy, Kelly, illus. 2004. (Spy Five Ser.). 93p. (J). *(978-0-439-70351-2(4))* Scholastic, Inc.

Meyer, L. A. My Bonny Light Horseman: Being an Account of the Further Adventures of Jacky Faber, in Love & War. (Bloody Jack Adventures Ser.: 6). (ENG., Illus.). 448p. (YA). (gr. 7). 2010. pap. 9.99 *(978-0-547-32794-5(3))* 2008. 17.00 *(978-0-15-206187-6(8))* Houghton Mifflin Harcourt Publishing Co.

—Rapture of the Deep: Being an Account of the Further Adventures of Jacky Faber, Soldier, Sailor, Mermaid, Spy. 2011. (Bloody Jack Adventures Ser.: 7). (ENG.). 464p. (YA). (gr. 9). pap. 9.99 *(978-0-547-55120-3(7))* Houghton Mifflin Harcourt Publishing Co.

—Viva Jacquelina! Being an Account of the Further Adventures of Jacky Faber, over the Hills & Far Away. (Bloody Jack Adventures Ser.: 10). (ENG.). (YA). (gr. 9). 2014. 384p. pap. 9.99 *(978-0-544-23439-0(1),* HMH Books For Young Readers) 2012. 368p. 16.99 *(978-0-547-76350-7(6))* Houghton Mifflin Harcourt Publishing Co.

Monroe, Ella. Secrets & Lies: A Capital Girls Novel. 2012. (Capital Girls Ser.: 2). (ENG.). 320p. (YA). (gr. 8). pap. 21.99 *(978-0-312-62305-0(4),* St. Martin's Griffin) St. Martin's Pr.

Monsell, Mary Elise. The Spy Who Came North from the Pole: Vol. III. 2016. (ENG.). 66p. (J). pap. 8.99 *(978-1-5040-2966-7(6))* Open Road Integrated Media, Inc.

Morley, Elizabeth. Let Sleeping Hedgehogs Spy. 2013. (Illus.). 154p. pap. *(978-1-78299-107-6(7))* FeedARead.com.

Moss, Marissa. Emma's Journal. 2004. (Young American Voice Bks.). (Illus.). (gr. 3-7). 17.00 *(978-0-7569-4110-9(5))* Perfection Learning Corp.

Moss, Marissa, illus. Mira's Diary: Bombs over London. 2014. (ENG.). 190p. (J). (gr. 2-8). 12.99 *(978-1-939547-12-5(1))* Creston Bks.

Muchamore, Robert. Brigands M. C. 2010. (ENG.). 416p. (YA). (gr. 7-17). pap. 10.99 *(978-0-340-95646-5(1))* Hodder & Stoughton GBR. Dist: Hachette Bk. Group.

—Brigands M. C. 2016. (Cherub Ser.: 11). (ENG., Illus.). 416p. (YA). (gr. 9). 17.99 *(978-1-4814-5671-5(7),* Simon Pulse) Simon Pulse.

—The Dealer. (Cherub Ser.: 2). (ENG.). (YA). (gr. 7). 2011. 336p. pap. 11.99 *(978-1-4424-1361-0(1))* 2010. 320p. 18.99 *(978-1-4169-9941-6(8))* Simon Pulse. (Simon Pulse).

—Eagle Day. 2nd ed. 2009. (ENG., Illus.). 432p. (J). (gr. 7-17). 10.99 *(978-0-340-95649-6(6))* Hodder & Stoughton GBR. Dist: Hachette Bk. Group.

—The General. 2013. (ENG.). 352p. (J). (gr. 7-17). pap. 10.99 *(978-0-340-93184-4(1))* Hodder & Stoughton GBR. Dist: Hachette Bk. Group.

—The Killing. 2012. (Cherub Ser.: 4). (ENG.). 336p. (YA). (gr. 7). pap. 10.99 *(978-1-4424-1363-4(8));* 16.99 *(978-1-4169-9943-0(4))* Simon Pulse. (Simon Pulse).

—Mad Dogs. 2007. (ENG.). 400p. (J). (gr. 7-17). pap. 10.99 *(978-0-340-91171-6(9))* Hodder & Stoughton GBR. Dist: Hachette Bk. Group.

—Maximum Security. (Cherub Ser.: 3). (ENG.). 320p. (YA). (gr. 7). 2012. pap. 9.99 *(978-1-4424-1362-7(X))* 2011. lib. bdg. 17.99 *(978-1-4169-9942-3(6))* Simon Pulse. (Simon Pulse).

—New Guard, Bk. 17. 2017. (Cherub 2. 0 Ser.). (ENG.). 320p. (J). (gr. 7-17). 10.99 ***(978-1-4449-1414-6(6))*** Hachette Children's Group GBR. Dist: Hachette Bk. Group.

—The Recruit. Aggs, John, illus. 2012. (ENG.). 176p. (YA). (gr. 7-17). pap. 12.99 *(978-1-4449-0318-8(7))* Hodder & Stoughton GBR. Dist: Hachette Bk. Group.

—The Recruit. 2010. (Cherub Ser.: 1). (ENG.). 352p. (YA). (gr. 7). pap. 11.99 *(978-1-4424-1360-3(3));* 17.99 *(978-1-4169-9940-9(X))* Simon Pulse. (Simon Pulse).

—Secret Army. 2010. (ENG., Illus.). 384p. (YA). (gr. 7-17). pap. 10.99 *(978-0-340-95650-2(X),* Hodder Children's Books) Hachette Children's Group GBR. Dist: Hachette Bk. Group.

—Shadow Wave. 2011. (ENG.). 352p. (J). (gr. k-17). 10.99 *(978-0-340-99974-5(8))* Hodder & Stoughton GBR. Dist: Hachette Bk. Group.

—The Sleepwalker. 2008. (ENG.). 336p. (J). (gr. 7-17). pap. 10.99 *(978-0-340-93183-7(3))* Hodder & Stoughton GBR. Dist: Hachette Bk. Group.

—The Sleepwalker. 2015. (Cherub Ser.: 9). (ENG., Illus.). 336p. (YA). (gr. 7). 17.99 *(978-1-4814-5663-0(6),* Simon Pulse) Simon Pulse.

My Super-Spy Diary. 2014. (Eliza Boom Ser.: 2). (ENG., Illus.). 128p. (J). (gr. 1-4). pap. 5.99 *(978-1-4814-0652-9(3),* Aladdin) Simon & Schuster Children's Publishing.

Myklusch, Matt. The Lost Prince. 2015. (Seaborne Ser.: No. 1). (ENG.). 400p. (J). (gr. 3-7). 16.99 *(978-1-60684-525-7(X),* Carolrhoda Bks.) Lerner Publishing Group.

—Strangers in Atlantis. 2017. (Seaborne Ser.: 2). (ENG.). 280p. (gr. 3-6). (J). 18.99 *(978-1-5124-1375-5(5));* 38.65 ***(978-1-5124-2691-5(1))*** Lerner Publishing Group. (Carolrhoda Bks.).

Nayeri, Daniel and Dina. Another Faust. 2010. (ENG., Illus.). 400p. (YA). (gr. 9). pap. 8.99 *(978-0-7636-4834-3(5))* Candlewick Pr.

Nick Barry. Revenge of Poseidon's Trident: An Ethan Sparks Adventure. 2010. 176p. 23.95 *(978-1-4502-1090-4(2));* pap. 13.95 *(978-1-4502-1088-1(0))* iUniverse, Inc.

Nielsen, Jennifer A. Behind Enemy Lines. 2016. (Infinity Ring Ser.: 6). (ENG.). 192p. (J). (gr. 3-7). pap. 6.99 *(978-0-545-90121-5(9),* Scholastic Pr.) Scholastic, Inc.

—Behind Enemy Lines. 2016. (Infinity Ring Ser.: 6). lib. bdg. 17.20 *(978-0-606-38623-4(8))* Turtleback Bks.

Noble, Trinka Hakes. The Scarlet Stockings Spy. Papp, Robert, illus. 2004. (Tales of Young Americans Ser.). (ENG.). 48p. (J). (gr. 1-7). 16.95 *(978-1-58536-230-1(1))* Sleeping Bear Pr.

O'Brien, Jack. Silver Chief's Revenge. Wiese, Kurt, illus. 2011. 222p. 44.95 *(978-1-258-09709-7(5))* Literary Licensing, LLC.

Oelschlager, Vanita & Durrant, Lynda. Ariel Bradley, Spy for General Washington. Rossi, Joe, illus. 2013. (ENG.). 56p. (J). (gr. 1-5). 9.99 *(978-0-9832904-9-0(0))* VanitaBooks.

O'Hely, Eileen. P. E. P. Squad. 2014. (ENG.). 320p. (J). 16.00 *(978-1-78117-195-0(5))* Mercier Pr., Ltd., The IRL. Dist: Dufour Editions, Inc.

O'Malley, Kevin. Herbert Fieldmouse, Secret Agent. 2003. (Illus.). 32p. (J). pap. *(978-1-59336-043-6(6));* (gr. 1-6). 15.95 *(978-1-59336-042-9(8))* Mondo Publishing.

Orme, David. Spies. Martin, Jan, illus. 2010. (Fact to Fiction Grafx Ser.). 36p. pap. 7.45 *(978-0-7891-7998-2(9))* Perfection Learning Corp.

Osborne, Erin. Spy Recruit, 1 vol. Simmons, Bethany, illus. 2010. (ENG.). 216p. (J). (gr. 3-6). pap. 8.95 *(978-1-58980-782-2(0))* Pelican Publishing Co., Inc.

Parker, Jake. Rescue on Tankium, No. 3. 2011. (Missile Mouse Ser.: 2). (ENG.). 160p. (J). (gr. 3-7). pap. 10.99 *(978-0-545-11717-3(8),* Graphix) Scholastic, Inc.

—Rescue on Tankium3. 2011. (Missile Mouse Ser.: 2). (ENG.). 160p. (J). (gr. 3-7). 21.99 *(978-0-545-11716-6(X),* Graphix) Scholastic, Inc.

Parkinson, Curtis. Man Overboard! 2012. (ENG., Illus.). 152p. (J). (gr. 4-7). pap. 9.95 *(978-1-77049-298-1(4),* Tundra Bks.) Tundra Bks. CAN. Dist: Penguin Random Hse. LLC.

Paulsen, Gary. Woods Runner. 2011. (ENG.). 176p. (YA). (gr. 7). pap. 7.99 *(978-0-375-85908-3(X),* Lamb, Wendy Bks.) Random Hse. Children's Bks.

Pearce, Jackson. The Doublecross: (And Other Skills I Learned As a Superspy) (ENG.). 304p. 2016. (J). pap. 7.99 *(978-1-61963-939-3(4),* 9781619639393) 2015. (YA). (gr. 3-6). 16.99 *(978-1-61963-414-5(7),* 9781619634145) Bloomsbury Publishing USA. (Bloomsbury USA Childrens).

—The Doublecross: (And Other Skills I Learned As a Superspy) 2016. (J). lib. bdg. 18.40 *(978-0-606-38555-8(X))* Turtleback Bks.

—The Inside Job: (and Other Skills I Learned As a Superspy) 2016. (ENG.). 272p. (J). 16.99 *(978-1-61963-420-6(1),* 9781619634206, Bloomsbury USA Childrens) Bloomsbury Publishing USA.

Perlman, Rhea. Canyon Catastrophe. Santat, Dan, illus. 2006. (Otto Undercover Ser.). 128p. (J). (gr. 4-7). 14.99 *(978-0-06-075498-3(2))* HarperCollins Pubs.

Peterfreund, Diana. Across a Star-Swept Sea. (Stars Ser.: 2). (ENG.). 464p. (YA). (gr. 8). 2014. pap. 9.99 *(978-0-06-200617-2(7))* 2013. 17.99 *(978-0-06-200616-5(9))* HarperCollins Pubs.

Pierpoint, Eric. The Secret Mission of William Tuck. 2015. (ENG.). 320p. (J). (gr. 4-7). pap. 7.99 *(978-1-4022-8174-7(9),* 9781402281747, Sourcebooks Jabberwocky) Sourcebooks, Inc.

Platt, Richard & Gifford, Clive. Spies Revealed. 2008. (ENG., Illus.). 32p. (J). (gr. 1-7). 21.99 *(978-1-4169-7113-9(0),* Atheneum Bks. for Young Readers) Simon & Schuster Children's Publishing.

Plum-Ucci, Carol. Fire Will Fall. 2011. (ENG.). 492p. (YA). (gr. 9). pap. 25.99 *(978-0-547-55007-7(3))* Houghton Mifflin Harcourt Publishing Co.

Ponnay, Brenda. Secret Agent Josephine in Paris. Ponnay, Brenda, illus. 2013. (Illus.). 32p. 19.99 *(978-1-62395-524-3(6))* Xist Publishing.

Ponnay, Brenda & Ponnay, Brenda. Secret Agent Josephine in Paris. 2013. 32p. pap. 9.99 *(978-1-62395-552-6(1))* Xist Publishing.

Preus, Margi. Shadow on the Mountain. 2014. (ENG., Illus.). 320p. (YA). (gr. 3-7). pap. 8.95 *(978-1-4197-1159-6(8),* Amulet Bks.) Abrams, Inc.

Prins, Piet. The Grim Reaper. 2006. (Illus.). 130p. (J). pap. *(978-1-894666-74-9(7))* Inheritance Pubns.

Publications International Ltd. Staff, ed. Mater Saves the Day. 2011. 12p. (J). bds. 10.98 *(978-1-4508-0695-4(3))* Phoenix International Publications, Inc.

Rash, Andy. Agent A to Agent Z. 2004. (Illus.). (J). *(978-0-439-36883-4(9),* Levine, Arthur A. Bks.) Scholastic, Inc.

Readler, Blaine C. Under the Radar: The Spy Drone Adventure. 2006. (ENG.). 248p. (J). (gr. 7-12). per. *(978-1-933255-18-7(8))* DNA Pr.

Reeve, Philip. Starcross: A Stirring Adventure of Spies, Time Travel & Curious Hats. Wyatt, David, illus. 2007. (ENG.). 384p. (YA). (gr. 5-18). 16.95 *(978-1-59990-121-3(8),* 9781599901213, Bloomsbury USA Childrens) Bloomsbury Publishing USA.

Regan, Peter. Riverside: The Spy. 2007. (ENG.). 112p. (J). pap. 10.95 *(978-1-901737-53-0(5))* Anvil Bks., Ltd. IRL. Dist: Dufour Editions, Inc.

Reid, Roger. Space. 2008. (ENG.). 160p. (J). 19.95 *(978-1-58838-230-6(3),* NewSouth Bks.) NewSouth, Inc.

Richards, Justin. Licence to Fish, Vol. 3. 2011. (Agent Alfie Ser.). (ENG., Illus.). 176p. (J). (gr. 2-4). 6.99 *(978-0-00-727359-1(2))* HarperCollins Pubs. Ltd. GBR. Dist: Independent Pubs. Group.

—Thunder Raker, 1. 2008. (Agent Alfie Ser.: 1). (ENG., Illus.). 144p. (J). (gr. 2-4). pap. 6.99 *(978-0-00-727357-7(6),* HarperCollins Children's Bks.) HarperCollins Pubs. Ltd. GBR. Dist: HarperCollins Pubs.

Richler, Mordecai. First Spy Case. Eyolfson, Norman, illus. 2003. (Jacob Two-Two Ser.). (ENG.). 144p. (J). (gr. 3-7). pap. 6.95 *(978-0-88776-694-7(3))* Tundra Bks. CAN. Dist: Random Hse., Inc.

—Jacob Two-Two's First Spy Case. Petricic, Dusan, illus. 2009. (Jacob Two-Two Ser.). (ENG.). 168p. (J). (gr. 4-7). 10.95 *(978-0-88776-927-6(6))* Tundra Bks. CAN. Dist: Random Hse., Inc.

Richmond, Caroline Tung. Darkest Hour. 2016. (ENG.). 320p. (J). (gr. 7). 17.99 *(978-0-545-80127-0(3),* Scholastic Pr.) Scholastic, Inc.

Rinaldi, Ann. Finishing Becca: A Story about Peggy Shippen & Benedict Arnold. 2004. (Great Episodes Ser.). (ENG.). 384p. (YA). (gr. 7-8). pap. 17.95 *(978-0-15-205079-5(5))* Houghton Mifflin Harcourt Publishing Co.

—The Secret of Sarah Revere. 2003. (Great Episodes Ser.). (ENG.). 336p. (J). (gr. 5-7). pap. 8.99 *(978-0-15-204684-2(4))* Houghton Mifflin Harcourt Publishing Co.

Roberts, Daniel. Douglas Diggly Super Spy. 2012. 180p. pap. 12.50 *(978-1-105-49212-9(5))* Lulu Pr., Inc.

Rogers, Meghan. Crossing the Line. 2016. (Raven Files Ser.). (ENG.). 368p. (YA). (gr. 7). 17.99 *(978-0-399-17617-3(9),* Philomel Bks.) Penguin Young Readers Group.

—Enemy Exposure. 2017. (Raven Files Ser.: 2). (ENG.). 320p. (YA). (gr. 7). 17.99 *(978-0-399-17618-0(7),* Philomel Bks.) Penguin Young Readers Group.

Roop, Peter & Roop, Connie. The Top-Secret Adventure of John Darragh, Revolutionary War Spy. 2010. pap. 51.02 *(978-0-7613-6923-3(6))* Lerner Publishing Group.

—The Top-Secret Adventure of John Darragh, Revolutionary War Spy. Trover, Zachary, illus. 2010. (History's Kid Heroes Ser.). (ENG.). 32p. (gr. 3-5). pap. 8.95 *(978-0-7613-6193-0(6),* Graphic Universe™); lib. bdg. 26.60 *(978-0-7613-6174-9(X))* Lerner Publishing Group.

Rosenberg, Madelyn. Nanny X. 2015. (ENG., Illus.). 128p. (J). (gr. 2-5). 16.95 *(978-0-8234-3533-3(4))* Holiday Hse., Inc.

Roy, Ron. A Spy in the White House. Bush, Timothy, tr. Bush, Timothy, illus. 2004. (Capital Mysteries Ser.: No. 4). (ENG.). 96p. (J). (gr. 1-4). 4.99 *(978-0-375-82557-6(6),* Random Hse. Bks. for Young Readers) Random Hse. Children's Bks.

Rylander, Chris. Codename Zero. 2014. (Codename Conspiracy Ser.: 1). (ENG.). 368p. (J). (gr. 3-7). 16.99 *(978-0-06-212008-3(5),* Waldon Pond Pr.) HarperCollins Pubs.

—Countdown Zero. 2015. (Codename Conspiracy Ser.: 2). (ENG.). 368p. (J). (gr. 3-7). 16.99 *(978-0-06-212011-3(5),* Waldon Pond Pr.) HarperCollins Pubs.

Sabel, Lauren. Lies I Live By. 2016. 432p. (YA). (gr. 8). 17.99 *(978-0-06-223198-7(7),* Tegen, Katherine Bks) HarperCollins Pubs.

Sala, George Augustus. Captain Dangerous. 2011. 130p. 24.95 *(978-1-4638-9899-1(1));* 130p. pap. 10.95 *(978-1-4638-0140-3(8));* 126p. pap. 10.95 *(978-1-4638-0141-0(6));* 124p. pap. 10.95 *(978-1-4638-0142-7(4))* Rodgers, Alan Bks.

Salisbury, Graham. Hunt for the Bamboo Rat. 2014. (ENG., Illus.). 336p. (YA). (gr. 7). 16.99 *(978-0-375-84266-5(7),* Lamb, Wendy Bks.) Random Hse. Children's Bks.

Scholastic, Inc. Staff & Howard, Kate. Spy vs. Spy. 2015. (Lego Ninjago Ser.: 13). (ENG., Illus.). 32p. (J). (gr. 1-3). pap. 3.99 *(978-0-545-82553-5(9))* Scholastic, Inc.

Schreiber, Joe. Game over, Pete Watson. Rash, Andy, illus. 2014. (ENG.). 224p. (J). (gr. 5-7). 16.99 *(978-0-544-15756-9(7),* HMH Books For Young Readers) Houghton Mifflin Harcourt Publishing Co.

Scieszka, Jon. Spaceheadz. Prigmore, Shane, illus. (Spaceheadz Ser.: 3). (ENG.). (J). (gr. 2-5). 2012. 224p. pap. 7.99 *(978-1-4169-7956-2(5))* 2011. 224p. 15.99 *(978-1-4169-7955-5(7))* 2010. 176p. 14.99 *(978-1-4169-7951-7(4))*Set. 2013. 864p. pap. 23.99 *(978-1-4424-9858-7(7))* Simon & Schuster Bks. For Young Readers. (Simon & Schuster Bks. For Young Readers).

—SPHDZ 4 Life! Prigmore, Shane, illus. 2013. (Spaceheadz Ser.: 4). (ENG.). 192p. (J). (gr. 2-5). pap. 5.99 *(978-1-4169-7958-6(1));*Bk. 4. 16.99 *(978-1-4169-7957-9(3))* Simon & Schuster Bks. For Young Readers. (Simon & Schuster Bks. For Young Readers).

—SPHDZ Book #2! Prigmore, Shane, illus. (Spaceheadz Ser.: 2). (ENG.). (J). (gr. 2-5). 2011. 256p. pap. 7.99 *(978-1-4169-7954-8(9))* 2010. 240p. 14.99 *(978-1-4169-7953-1(0))* Simon & Schuster Bks. For Young Readers. (Simon & Schuster Bks. For Young Readers).

Scorched Earth. 2013. (ENG., Illus.). 336p. (YA). (gr. 7-17). pap. 10.99 *(978-1-4449-0233-4(4))* Hodder & Stoughton GBR. Dist: Hachette Bk. Group.

Scott, Kate. Spies in Disguise: Boy in Tights. 2016. (ENG., Illus.). 192p. (J). (gr. 1-5). pap. 7.99 *(978-1-63450-689-2(8),* Sky Pony Pr.) Skyhorse Publishing Co., Inc.

Sealed with a Lie. 2014. (ENG., Illus.). 256p. (YA). (gr. 9). 17.99 *(978-1-4814-0052-7(5),* Simon & Schuster Bks. For Young Readers) Simon & Schuster Bks. For Young Readers.

Sharmat, Marjorie Weinman & Sharmat, Mitchell. The Sly Spy. Brunkus, Denise, illus. 2005. (Olivia Sharp: Agent for Secrets Ser.). (ENG.). 80p. (J). (gr. 3-7). per. 5.99 *(978-0-440-42062-0(8),* Yearling) Random Hse. Children's Bks.

Sherman, M. Zachary & Lee, Raymund. Depth Charge, 1 vol. Bermudez, Raymund, illus. 2012. (Bloodlines Ser.). (ENG.). 88p. (gr. 4-8). pap. 6.95 *(978-1-4342-3876-4(8));* lib. bdg. 26.65 *(978-1-4342-3764-4(8))* Stone Arch Bks.

Shugaar, Antony & International Spy Museum Staff. I Lie for a Living: Greatest Spies of All Time. Guarnaccia, Steven, illus. 2006. (ENG.). 192p. (J). per. 14.95 *(978-0-7922-5316-7(7))* National Geographic Society.

Singleton, Linda Joy. Kelsey the Spy. 2016. (Curious Cat Spy Club Ser.: 3). (ENG.). (J). (gr. 3-7). 304p. pap. 9.99 *(978-0-8075-1384-2(9));* 288p. 14.99 *(978-0-8075-1380-4(6))* Whitman, Albert & Co.

Skead, Robert A. & Skead, Robert J. Patriots, Redcoats & Spies, 1 vol. 2015. (American Revolutionary War Adventures Ser.). (ENG.). 192p. (J). 14.99 *(978-0-310-74841-0(0))* Zonderkidz.

Skillchecks for Spy. 2005. (Double Fastback Ser.). (J). (gr. 6-12). 64p. pap. 5.95 *(978-0-13-024475-8(9));* 32p. pap. 5.95 *(978-0-13-024458-1(9))* Globe Fearon Educational Publishing.

Slade, Arthur. Island of Doom: Hunchback Assignments 4. 2013. (Hunchback Assignments Ser.). (ENG.). 320p. (YA). (gr. 7). pap. 9.99 *(978-0-375-85406-4(1),* Ember) Random Hse. Children's Bks.

Slade, Arthur G. The Dark Deeps. 2011. (Hunchback Assignments Ser.: Vol. 2). (ENG.). 320p. (YA). (gr. 7). pap. 9.99 *(978-0-375-85404-0(5),* Ember) Random Hse. Children's Bks.

—Empire of Ruins. 2012. (Hunchback Assignments Ser.). (ENG.). 300p. (YA). (gr. 7). pap. 8.99 *(978-0-375-85405-7(3),* Ember) Random Hse. Children's Bks.

Smith, Annie Laura. The Legacy of Bletchley Park. 2004. (YA). mass mkt. 6.99 *(978-0-9753367-1-7(1))* Onstage Publishing, LLC.

Smith, Icy. Three Years & Eight Months. Kindert, Jennifer C., illus. 2013. (J). *(978-0-9856237-8-4(0))* East West Discovery Pr.

Smith, Lindsay. Skandal. 2015. (Sekret Ser.: Vol. 2). (ENG.). 336p. (YA). (gr. 7-12). 17.99 *(978-1-62672-005-3(3),* 9781626720053) Roaring Brook Pr.

—Skandal. 2016. (Sekret Ser.: 2). (ENG.). 352p. (YA). pap. 9.99 *(978-1-250-07369-3(3),* 9781250073693) Square Fish.

Smith, Roland. Independence Hall. (I, Q Ser.: Bk. 1). (ENG., 312p. (gr. 5-9). 2009. Illus.). (J). 15.95 *(978-1-58536-468-8(1))* 2008. (YA). pap. 8.95 *(978-1-58536-325-4(1))* Sleeping Bear Pr.

—The White House. 2010. (I, Q Ser.: Bk. 2). (ENG.). 256p. (YA). (gr. 6-8). 15.95 *(978-1-58536-478-7(9),* 202191); pap. 8.95 *(978-1-58536-456-5(8),* 202378) Sleeping Bear Pr.

Smith, Roland & Spradlin, Michael P. The Windy City, Bk.5. 2014. (I, Q Ser.). (ENG.). 240p. (YA). (gr. 5-7). 9.99 *(978-1-58536-823-5(7),* 202902) Sleeping Bear Pr.

Sobol, Donald J. Secret Agents Four. Shortall, Leonard W., illus. 2003. (Adventure Library). 133p. (J). pap. 10.95 *(978-1-883937-65-2(5))* Bethlehem Bks.

Soup, Cuthbert. A Whole Nother Story. Timmins, Jeffrey Stewart, illus. 2010. (Whole Nother Story Ser.). (ENG.). 288p. (YA). (gr. 3-6). pap. 7.99 *(978-1-59990-518-1(3),* 9781599905181, Bloomsbury USA Childrens) Bloomsbury Publishing USA.

Speer, Cindy Lynn. Unbalanced. 2010. pap. *(978-1-934841-90-7(0))* Zumaya Pubns. LLC.

Spradlin, Michael P. Live & Let Shop. 2005. (Spy Goddess Ser.: Bk. 1). (ENG., Illus.). 224p. (gr. 7-18). 15.99 *(978-0-06-059407-7(1))* HarperCollins Pubs.

Spradlin, Michael P. & Smith, Roland. Alcatraz. 2014. (I, Q Ser.). (ENG.). 272p. (J). (gr. 5-7). 16.99 *(978-1-58536-826-6(1),* 203667); pap. 9.99 *(978-1-58536-825-9(3),* 203727) Sleeping Bear Pr.

Spy, 10 vols. 2005. (Double Fastback Ser.). (J). (gr. 6-12). 64p. pap. 54.95 *(978-0-13-024468-0(6));* 32p. pap. 44.95 *(978-0-13-024440-6(6))* Globe Fearon Educational Publishing.

The Spy down the Street, 6 vols., Vol. 2. (Woodland Mysteriestm Ser.). 133p. (gr. 3-7). 42.50 *(978-0-7802-7938-4(7))* Wright Group/McGraw-Hill.

Stead, Rebecca. Liar & Spy. (ENG.). (J). (gr. 3-7). 2013. 208p. 7.99 *(978-0-375-85087-5(2),* Yearling) 2012. 192p. 15.99 *(978-0-385-73743-2(2),* Lamb, Wendy Bks.) Random Hse. Children's Bks.

Stone, Sonja. Desert Dark. (ENG.). (YA). (gr. 7). 2017. 344p. pap. 7.99 *(978-0-8234-3766-5(3))* 2016. 336p. 17.95 *(978-0-8234-3562-3(8))* Holiday Hse., Inc.

Strange, Spencer. Operation Billion Gazillion. 2005. (Spy Five Ser.). 93p. *(978-0-439-70352-9(2))* Scholastic, Inc.

Sutherland, Jon, et al. The Spy Master. 2005. (F. E. A. R. Adventures S. Ser.). (ENG., Illus.). 128p. (J). 8.00 *(978-1-84046-692-8(8),* Wizard Books) Icon Bks., Ltd. GBR. Dist: Publishers Group Canada.

Swendson, Shanna. Rebel Mechanics. 2015. (ENG.). 320p. (YA). (gr. 7). 18.99 *(978-0-374-30009-8(7),* 9780374300098, Farrar, Straus & Giroux (BYR)) Farrar, Straus & Giroux.

Taylor, Mary Ann. Spies: A Gander's Cove Mystery. Casteel, Kay, illus. 2006. (J). mass mkt. 5.99 *(978-0-9753367-7-9(0))* Onstage Publishing, LLC.

—Traitors: A Gander's Cove Mystery. Casteel, Kay, illus. 2006. (J). mass mkt. 5.99 *(978-0-9753367-9-3(7))* Onstage Publishing, LLC.

Thomas, Jane Resh. The Counterfeit Princess. 2005. 197p. (J). *(978-0-618-93780-6(3),* Clarion Bks.) Houghton Mifflin Harcourt Trade & Reference Pubs.

Thompson, Paul B. Liberty's Son: A Spy Story of the American Revolution. (Historical Fiction Adventures (HFA) Ser.). 160p. (J). 2012. pap. 10.95 *(978-0-7660-3654-3(5))* 2009. (Illus.).

S

(gr. 3-6). lib. bdg. 29.27 (978-0-7660-3309-2(0)) Enslow Pubs., Inc.

Tra, Frank. Spy School. O'Reilly, Sean Patrick, ed. 2011. (Illus.). 76p. (YA). pap. 14.95 (978-1-926914-27-5(9)) Arcana Studio, Inc.

Two Lies & a Spy. 2014. (ENG., Illus.). 272p. (YA). (gr. 9). pap. 11.99 (978-1-4424-8173-2(0), Simon & Schuster Bks. For Young Readers) Simon & Schuster Bks. For Young Readers.

Universal. Gru's Gadget Guide. 2017. (ENG., Illus.). 24p. (J). (gr. -1-3). pap. 5.99 **(978-0-316-50773-8(3))** Little, Brown Bks. for Young Readers.

Van Draanen, Wendelin. Enemy Spy. Biggs, Brian, illus. 2006. (Shredderman Ser.: Bk. 4). (ENG.). 192p. (J). (gr. 1-4). 6.99 (978-0-440-41915-0(8), Yearling) Random Hse. Children's Bks.

Van Hamme, Jean. The Strange Encounter, Vol. 5. 2009. (Blake & Mortimer Ser.: 5). (ENG., Illus.). 66p. pap. 15.95 (978-1-905460-75-5(9)) CineBook GBR. Dist: National Bk. Network.

Van King, L. The Dwarf in the Drawer: A Mischievous Parody. Gonzales, Chuck, illus. 2013. (ENG.). 32p. (J). 19.99 (978-1-250-04143-2(0), 9781250041432) Square Fish.

Vaughan, M. M. Mindscape. Bruno, Iacopo, illus. 2015. (Ability Ser.). (ENG.). 336p. (YA). (gr. 3-7). pap. 7.99 (978-1-4424-5205-3(6), McElderry, Margaret K. Bks.) McElderry, Margaret K. Bks.

Vaughan, M. M. & Caletti, Deb. The Last Forever. Bruno, Iacapo, illus. 2016. (ENG.). 352p. (YA). (gr. 7-7). pap. 10.99 (978-1-4424-5002-8(9), Simon & Schuster Bks. For Young Readers) Simon & Schuster Bks. For Young Readers.

Vigenère, Sator & Alberti, Enigma. Mary Bowser & the Civil War Spy Ring. Cliff, Tony, illus. 2016. (Spy on History Ser.). (ENG.). 96p. (J). (gr. 4). 12.95 (978-0-7611-8739-4(1)) Workman Publishing Co., Inc.

Viorst, Judith. Lulu's Mysterious Mission. Smith, Lane, illus. 2015. (ENG.). 192p. (J). (gr. 1-5). pap. 7.99 (978-1-4424-9747-4(5)) Simon & Schuster Children's Publishing.

Walden, Mark. Rogue. (H. I. V. E. Ser.: 5). (ENG.). (J). (gr. 3-7). 2012. 320p. pap. 8.99 (978-1-4424-1369-6(7)) 2011. 304p. 16.99 (978-1-4424-2187-5(8)) Simon & Schuster Bks. For Young Readers. (Simon & Schuster Bks. For Young Readers).

Walters, Eric. Sleeper, 1 vol. 2014. (Seven Sequels Ser.). (ENG., Illus.). 240p. (J). (gr. 5-10). pap. 10.95 (978-1-4598-0543-9(7)) Orca Bk. Pubs. USA.

Warner, Penny. The Hunt for the Missing Spy. 2016. (Code Busters Club Ser.: 5). (ENG.). 168p. (gr. 3-6). (J). 16.99 (978-1-5124-0304-6(0)); 33.32 (978-1-5124-0305-3(9)) Lerner Publishing Group.

Webb, Robert N. We Were There at the Boston Tea Party. Ward, E. F., illus. 2013. (ENG.). 192p. (J). (gr. 3-8). pap. 6.99 (978-0-486-49260-5(5)) Dover Pubns., Inc.

Wein, Elizabeth. Code Name Verity. (ENG.). (YA). (gr. 9-17). 2013. 368p. pap. 9.99 (978-1-4231-5288-0(3)) 2012. 352p. 16.99 (978-1-4231-5219-4(0)) Hyperion Pr.

—Code Name Verity. 2013. (YA). lib. bdg. 20.85 (978-0-606-31760-3(0), Turtleback) Turtleback Bks.

Whelan, Gloria. Parade of Shadows. 2007. 304p. (J). (gr. 5-18). lib. bdg. 16.89 (978-0-06-089029-2(0)) HarperCollins Pubs.

Wickstrom, Lois June & Darling, Lucrecia. The Orange Forest Rabbit Mysteries: Book One. 2003. (J). per. 13.95 (978-0-916176-23-5(1)) Gripper Products.

Wild, Kate. Firefight. 2009. (ENG.). 352p. (J). (gr. 3-7). 16.99 (978-0-439-87176-1(X), Chicken Hse., The) Scholastic, Inc.

Wolfe, Jack & Wolfe, Jennifer. The Tales of Spy Dogs Archie & Hazel. 2011. 44p. pap. 16.59 (978-1-4567-6244-5(3)) AuthorHouse.

Woodruff, Elvira. George Washington's Spy. (Time Travel Adventures Ser.). (ENG.). 240p. (J). (gr. 3-7). 2012. pap. 6.99 (978-0-545-10488-3(2), Scholastic Paperbacks) 2010. 16.99 (978-0-545-10487-6(4), Scholastic Pr.) Scholastic, Inc.

—George Washington's Spy. 2012. lib. bdg. 17.20 (978-0-606-26216-3(4), Turtleback) Turtleback Bks.

Young, Jessica. Spy Guy: The Not-So-Secret Agent. Santoso, Charles, illus. 2015. (ENG.). 40p. (J). (gr. -1-3). 16.99 (978-0-544-20859-9(5), HMH Books For Young Readers) Houghton Mifflin Harcourt Publishing Co.

Zettel, Sarah. Assassin's Masque. 2017. (Palace of Spies Ser.: 3). (ENG.). 432p. (YA). (gr. 7). pap. 8.99 (978-0-544-81317-5(0), HMH Books For Young Readers) Houghton Mifflin Harcourt Publishing Co.

—Palace of Spies. (Palace of Spies Ser.: 1). (ENG.). (YA). (gr. 7). 2014. 384p. pap. 8.99 (978-0-544-33617-9(8), HMH Books For Young Readers) 2013. 368p. 16.99 (978-0-544-07411-8(4)) Houghton Mifflin Harcourt Publishing Co.

Zindel, Paul & Zindel, Paul. The Gadget. 2003. (ENG., Illus.). 192p. (YA). (gr. 7). mass mkt. 6.99 (978-0-440-22951-3(0), Laurel Leaf) Random Hse. Children's Bks.

SPINAL PARALYSIS, ANTERIOR

see Poliomyelitis

SPIRIT OF ST. LOUIS (AIRPLANE)

Koestler-Grack, Rachel A. Spirit of St. Louis, 1 vol. 2005. (American Moments Ser.). (ENG., Illus.). 48p. (gr. 4-8). 27.07 (978-1-59197-940-1(4), Abdo & Daughters) ABDO Publishing Co.

SPIRITS

see also Angels; Apparitions; Ghosts; Witchcraft

Cox, Barbara & Forbes, Scott. Spooky Spirits & Creepy Creatures, Vol. 1. 2014. (Creepy Chronicles Ser.). (ENG., Illus.). 32p. (J). (gr. 5-6). 26.60 (978-1-4824-0243-8(2)) Stevens, Gareth Publishing LLLP.

Felix, Rebecca. Ghosts: The Truth Behind History's Spookiest Spirits. 2015. (Monster Handbooks Ser.). (ENG., Illus.). 32p. (gr. 3-4). lib. bdg. 27.99 (978-1-4914-4249-4(2)) Capstone Press of Coughlan Cos.

Howard, Ian T. One Love, Two Worlds. Bishop, Tracey, illus. 2010. 36p. pap. 14.75 (978-1-60911-771-9(9), Eloquent Bks.) Strategic Book Publishing & Rights Agency (SBPRA).

Juettner, Bonnie. Genies. 2010. (Monsters Ser.). (ENG., Illus.). 48p. (gr. 4-8). 35.20 (978-0-7377-5051-5(0), Kidhaven) Cengage Gale.

Krensky, Stephen. Zombies. 2007. (Monster Chronicles Ser.). (ENG., Illus.). 48p. (gr. 4-7). lib. bdg. 26.60 (978-0-8225-6759-2(8), Lerner Pubns.) Lerner Publishing Group.

netzley, patricia. Paranormal Activity. 2011. (Mysterious & Unknown Ser.). 96p. (YA). (gr. 7-12). lib. bdg. 37.27 (978-1-60152-240-5(1)) ReferencePoint Pr., Inc.

SPIRITUAL HEALING

Ferguson, Isabel, et al. A World More Bright: The Life of Mary Baker Eddy. 2013. (Illus.). vi, 279p. (J). (978-0-87510-494-2(0)) Christian Science Publishing Society.

Galloway, Tammy. I Am Healed: Praying God's Word for Children. 2010. 28p. 13.95 (978-1-4497-0428-5(X), WestBow Pr.) Author Solutions, Inc.

Ives, Pastor Carla. Healed from the Inside Out! 2010. 32p. pap. 12.99 (978-1-4490-3000-1(9)) AuthorHouse.

Taylor, Mary J. God's Miracle Process: Trauma Transformed into Treasures 2005. (Illus.). 144p. per. 12.95 (978-0-9768530-0-8(0)) Choices International.

Walker, Kathryn. Mysterious Healing. 2009. (Unsolved! Ser.). (ENG., Illus.). 32p. (J). (gr. 3-5). pap. (978-0-7787-4163-3(X)); (gr. 4-6). lib. bdg. (978-0-7787-4150-3(8)) Crabtree Publishing Co.

SPIRITUAL HEALING—FICTION

Bruce, Ann Elizabeth. Inspire Your Spirit. 2007. 48p. per. (978-1-897312-54-4(7)) Adlibbed Ltd.

Conley, Autumn. Colby's Peace. 2005. 197p. pap. 24.95 (978-1-4137-8937-9(4)) America Star Bks.

Corley, Theresa. The Journey Home: The Story of Michael Thomas & the Seven Angels. 2003. (ENG.). 240p. pap. 16.95 (978-1-56170-987-8(5)) Hay Hse., Inc.

Harris, Janice. The Journey: Subtle Lessons in Spiritual Awakening. 2007. 180p. per. 19.95 (978-1-4327-0795-8(7)) Outskirts Pr., Inc.

Harwell, Wiley D. Knowing Truth by Name: The Stories of White Bear. 2006. 144p. per. (978-1-59298-130-4(5)) Beaver's Pond Pr., Inc.

An Inner Child Speaks. 2006. (J). 17.99 (978-0-9779130-0-8(7)) Zy Iman Pubng.

Kolb, Joseph J. Reservation Dreams. 2004. 185p. pap. 24.95 (978-1-4137-3054-8(X)) America Star Bks.

Lansdowne, Marcella. The Adventures of Patty & Annabel: The Monsoon & the Auric Field. 2009. 28p. pap. 15.95 (978-1-4389-4786-0(0)) AuthorHouse.

Richardson, Faith. Tree Root & River Rat. 2003. (Illus.). 248p. (J). pap. 12.95 (978-0-9744989-5-9(5)) Fox Song Bks.

Sanderson, Whitney. Golden Sun. Sanderson, Ruth, illus. 2010. (Horse Diaries). (ENG.). 160p. (J). (gr. 3-7). pap. 7.99 (978-0-375-86194-9(7), Random Hse. Bks. for Young Readers) Random Hse. Children's Bks.

Thompson, John & Thompson, Susan. The Lilychild. 2011. 256p. 35.95 (978-1-4497-1331-7(9)); pap. 19.95 (978-1-4497-1330-0(0)) Author Solutions, Inc. (WestBow Pr.).

SPIRITUAL LIFE

see also Christian Life; Faith

Allah in Person, Royall. The Center Page, Volume 1. 2003. (Illus.). 241p. 51.00 (978-0-9768502-0-5(6)) United Nation of Islam, The.

Anderson, Carolyn B. Exchanging God's Glory for the Pleasures of the Flesh. 2004. 120p. (YA). per. 8.95 (978-0-9718249-8-0(3)) Anderson Publishing.

Armbrecht, Doug, compiled by. Quiet Time Prepack for Families (Quiet Time Devotionals), 21. 2006. (Illus.). (YA). per. 347.79 (978-1-931235-53-2(8), gbookpack) Word of Life Fellowship, Inc.

Arons, Marsha. Teen Miracles: Extraordinary Life-Changing Stories by America's Teenagers. 2004. (Illus.). 256p. pap. 9.95 (978-1-58062-758-0(7)) Adams Media Corp.

Artworks. Faith, Hope & Love. 2004. (YA). 16.95 (978-1-57938-856-0(6)) Artworks International.

Bewes, Richard & Thompson, Ian. Top 100 Questions Remix: Spiritual Answers to Real Questions. 2010. (ENG.). 224p. (gr. 7-12). pap. 14.99 (978-1-84550-191-4(8), 422120b2-6629-493b-8158-752e891c001a) Christian Focus Pubns. GBR. Dist: Bookmasters Distribution.

Blosser, Connie S. Destiny's Trouble: A True Story. 2013. 20p. pap. 24.95 (978-1-4626-9341-2(5)) America Star Bks.

Bowman, Crystal. Is God Always with Me? Kucharik, Elena, illus. 2006. (Little Blessings Ser.). (ENG.). 64p. (J). 9.99 (978-1-4143-0287-4(8)) Tyndale Hse. Pubs.

Box, Su. You Are Very Special. Poole, Susie, illus. 2003. 32p. (J). pap. 6.95 (978-0-8198-8807-5(9), 332-417) Pauline Bks. & Media.

Cardero, Patrick & JFA Productions Staff. Hello It's Me: An Ineterview with God. 2003. 225p. pap. 19.95 (978-0-9723024-0-1(9)) JFA Productions.

Carr, Dan. God, I Need to Talk to You about Lying. Clark, Bartholomew & Clark, Bill, illus. 16p. (J). 1.19 (978-0-7586-0512-2(9)) Concordia Publishing Hse.

—God, I Need to Talk to You about Sharing. Clark, Bartholomew & Clark, Bill, illus. 16p. (J). 1.19 (978-0-7586-0511-5(0)) Concordia Publishing Hse.

—God, I Need to Talk to You about Stealing. Clark, Bartholomew & Clark, Bill, illus. 16p. (J). 1.19 (978-0-7586-0509-2(9)) Concordia Publishing Hse.

—God, I Need to Talk to You about Vandalism. Clark, Bartholomew & Clark, Bill, illus. 16p. (J). 1.19 (978-0-7586-0510-8(2)) Concordia Publishing Hse.

Chopra, Deepak. Fire in the Heart: A Spiritual Guide for Teens. 2006. (ENG., Illus.). 208p. (YA). (gr. 7-12). pap. 14.99 (978-0-689-86217-5(2), Simon & Schuster Bks. For Young Readers) Simon & Schuster Bks. For Young Readers.

—Teens Ask Deepak: All the Right Questions. Barchowsky, Damien, illus. 2006. (ENG.). 208p. (YA). (gr. 7). pap. 15.99 (978-0-689-86218-2(0), Simon Pulse) Simon Pulse.

Christensen, Catherine. The Holy Ghost Is My Friend. 2017. (ENG.). (J). (gr. -1-2). 14.99 **(978-1-4621-2083-3(0))** Cedar Fort, Inc./CFI Distribution.

Cummings Moore, Thelma Wyatt. Living with a Passion. 2003. 103p. (YA). (gr. 8-18). pap. 5.95 (978-0-942683-40-0(4)) Publishing Assocs., Inc.

Dent, Jenny. The Giant Jigsaw Puzzle: Democratic Committee Assignments in the Modern House. (Spiritual Teachings for Children Ser.). (Illus.). 32p. (J). (gr. k-9). 17.95 (978-0-85487-053-0(9)) White Eagle Publishing Trust GBR. Dist: DeVorss & Co.

Dobson, Shirley. God Helps Me Share: Coloring Book about Abigail & David. 2004. (Illus.). 12p. pap. 1.49 (978-0-8307-2894-7(5), Gospel Light) Gospel Light Pubns.

—God Made the World Coloring Book. 2004. (Illus.). 16p. 1.49 (978-0-8307-2487-1(7), Gospel Light) Gospel Light Pubns.

—God Made the World Coloring Book: 100-Unit Counter Merchandiser. 2004. 16p. 99.00 (978-0-8307-2488-8(5), Gospel Light) Gospel Light Pubns.

—God's Little Helper Coloring Book. 2004. (Illus.). 16p. pap. 1.49 (978-0-8307-2188-7(6), Gospel Light) Gospel Light Pubns.

Dobson, Shirley, contrib. by. God Gives Me Joy Coloring Book. 2004. 16p. 1.49 (978-0-8307-3054-4(0), Gospel Light) Gospel Light Pubns.

Dunagan, Cindy. Journaling Toward Moral Excellence Volume Four for Young Adults: A Character Building Workbook of 100 Thought-Provoking Questions to Help the Young Discover the Value of Moral Strength. 2004. (Journaling Toward Moral Excellence Ser.: Vol. 4). 107p. (YA). (gr. 11-18). 11.95 (978-0-9759871-3-1(5)) Straight Paths Pr.

—Journaling Toward Moral Excellence Volume Three for Teenagers: A Character Building Workbook of 100 Thought-Provoking Questions to Help the Young Discover the Value of Moral Strength. 2004. (Journaling Toward Moral Excellence Ser.: Vol. 3). 107p. (YA). (gr. 8-10). 11.95 (978-0-9759871-2-4(7)) Straight Paths Pr.

—Journaling Toward Moral Excellence Volume Two for Pre-Teens Vol. 2: A Character Building Workbook of 100 Thought-Provoking Questions to Help the Young Discover the Value of Moral Strength. 2004. (Journaling Toward Moral Excellence Ser.: Vol. 2). 107p. (J). (gr. 5-7). 11.95 (978-0-9759871-1-7(9)) Straight Paths Pr.

Eagle, Golden. It's Good to Laugh at Yourself (Coyote Medicine. l.t. ed. 2004. (Illus.). 22p. (J). per. 12.99 (978-1-932338-36-2(5)) Lifevest Publishing, Inc.

Enloe, Rochelle & Enloe, Tim. Kid-Power! How Kids Can Get the Holy Spirit's Power! 2007. (Illus.). (J). per. 5.99 (978-0-9794331-0-8(X)) E M Pubns.

Fear Not My Child, I Am Here: Emerging from the Spiral of Fear the Practical Mystic's Guide for Embracing Your Heart's Desire. 2003rd ed. 2003. 240p. per. 15.95 (978-0-9742213-0-4(9)) Community Works!

Feinberg, Margaret & Gillespie, Natalie. Text Messages from God for Kids. 2005. (Instant Messages Ser.). 160p. mass mkt. 9.99 (978-1-59379-040-0(6)) White Stone Bks.

Fernandez, Mayte. Secrets of Your Guardian Angels. 2013. 68p. pap. 24.45 (978-1-4525-6765-5(4)) Balboa Pr.

Fischer, Jean. 3-Minute Devotions for Little Hearts. 2017. (3-Minute Devotions Ser.). (ENG.). 192p. (J). pap. 7.99 **(978-1-68322-221-7(0)**, Barbour Bks.) Barbour Publishing, Inc.

Fitzhugh, Steve. Who Will Survive: The Teenager's Ultimate Struggle for Survival. 2003. (YA). per. 10.00 (978-0-9748298-0-7(3)) PowerMoves.

Foster, Kathryn Joy. Always Room for One More. l.t. ed. 2004. (Illus.). 12p. (J). spiral bd. 13.00 (978-0-9728779-6-1(7), TBK-21007) Read All Over Publishing.

Gilven, Edwin. Blubaugh, Spiritually Speaking. 2005. 27p. spiral bd. 13.58 (978-1-4116-4623-0(1)) Lulu Pr., Inc.

Hallinan, P. K. A Love Letter from God. Watson, Laura, illus. 2014. 24p. (J). 12.99 (978-0-8249-5662-2(1), Ideal Pubns.) Worthy Publishing.

Haskins, Jim & Benson, Kathleen. African American Religious Leaders. 2008. (Black Stars Ser.: 7). (ENG., Illus.). 168p. (J). (gr. 4-8). 24.95 (978-0-471-73632-5(5), Wiley) Wiley, John & Sons, Inc.

Havergal, Frances Ridley. Little Pillows & Morning Bells: Good-Night Thoughts & Waking Thoughts for the Little Ones. 2004. 200p. (J). per. 14.95 (978-1-932474-25-1(0)) Solid Ground Christian Bks.

Hemry, Melanie & Lynnes, Gina. Anointing for Children w/ anointing oil Vial. 2007. (Illus.). 192p. 14.99 (978-0-88368-686-7(4), 776867) Whitaker Hse.

Hodgson, Joan. Hullo Sun. Ripper, Peter, illus. 2003. 32p. (gr. -1-3). 8.95 (978-0-85487-072-1(5)) White Eagle Publishing Trust GBR. Dist: DeVorss & Co.

How to Hear the Voice of God Today! 2003. 52p. per. (978-1-932833-09-6(9)) Dickow, Gregory Ministries.

Jackson, Vanessa Wyse. Recipes for Life: Fifty Ready-To-Use Spiritual Talks for Children. 2012. (ENG., Illus.). 134p. pap. 15.95 (978-1-84730-360-8(9)) Veritas Pubns. IRL. Dist: Dufour Editions, Inc.

Jones, Nona C. When the Soul Won't Let Go: No-Nonsense Answers to a Broken Woman's Questions. 2004. 90p. (YA). pap. 10.00 (978-0-9762770-0-2(X)) TNJ Ministries.

Liebenow, Todd & VonSeggen, Liz. Join the Hall of Faith. 2004. 20p. (J). 18.00 (978-1-58302-256-6(2)) One Way St., Inc.

Lucado, Max & Lucado, Jenna. Redefining Beautiful: What God Sees When God Sees You, 1 vol. 2009. (ENG.). 240p. (gr. 7-12). pap. 14.99 (978-1-4003-1428-7(3)) Nelson, Thomas Inc.

The Man of Destiny. 2005. (YA). per. 8.95 (978-1-59872-161-4(5)) Instant Pub.

Mattern, Joanne. Mystics & Psychics. 2011. (World Religions & Beliefs Ser.). 128p. (gr. 7-12). 28.95 (978-1-59935-148-3(X)) Reynolds, Morgan Inc.

McCarroll, Tolbert. A Winter Walk. Beebee, Dorothy, illus. 2006. (ENG.). 160p. 14.95 (978-0-8245-2416-6(0)) Crossroad Publishing Co., The.

Meyer, Richard. This Faith Is Mine. 2005. 176p. 10.49 (978-0-7586-0727-0(X)) Concordia Publishing Hse.

Monge, Marlyn. Mary & the Little Shepherds of Fatima. Lopez, Maria Joao, illus. 2017. (ENG.). (J). 14.95 **(978-0-8198-4959-5(6))** Pauline Bks. & Media.

Montgomery, Sharon, text. Your Invisible Bodies: A Reference Book for Children & Adults about Human Energy Fields. 2011. (Illus.). (978-0-9811089-2-6(X)) Words By Montgomery.

Nagaraja, Dharmachari. The Buddha's Apprentice at Bedtime: Tales of Compassion & Kindness for You to Read with Your Child - To Delight & Inspire. 2013. (ENG., Illus.). 128p. (J). (gr. -1-3). pap. 16.95 (978-1-78028-514-6(0), Watkins Publishing) Watkins Media Limited GBR. Dist: Penguin Random Hse. LLC.

Oaks, Kristen M. & Phillips, JoAnn. The Testimony Glove. Burr, Dan, illus. 2010. (J). (gr. -1-4). 17.99 (978-1-60641-151-3(9)) Deseret Bk. Co.

Overstreet, Betty. The Lord Still Speaks - Are You Listening?, 1 book. 2004. 113p. (YA). per. 14.95 (978-0-9746253-0-0(2)) Overstreet Pub. & Mktg.

Parr, Susan Sherwood. 30 Days Out of Depression. 2004. (ENG., Illus.). 58p. 3.95 (978-0-9728590-5-9(5)) Word Prodns.

Pope Francis. Anointed: Gifts of the Holy Spirit. 2017. (ENG.). (J). 18.95 **(978-0-8198-0653-6(6))** Pauline Bks. & Media.

Power Twins Handbook Volume One. 2006. (J). spiral bd. (978-0-9742355-1-6(2)) Brda, Tracy.

Promiseland. 2008. (J). per. 8.00 (978-0-9664736-0-5(4)) Grace Walk Resources, LLC.

Rees, Rebecca. It Is Good to Be a Part of All This: Stories of a Small Part in the Great Work. 2011. 122p. pap. 19.99 (978-1-4568-8875-6(7)) Xlibris Corp.

Selby, John. Meditation the Cool Way to Calm: Solve Your Problems, Find Peace of Mind, & Discover the Real You. 2004. (ENG.). 1p. pap. 10.95 (978-0-8048-3486-5(5)) Tuttle Publishing.

Simmons, Judy. Where Is Heaven? 2009. 32p. pap. 12.99 (978-1-4389-5900-9(1)) AuthorHouse.

Sisters of Notre Dame, Chardon, Ohio. God Cares for Us: Grade 2. 2008. (Christ Our Life 2009 Ser.). (ENG.). 222p. (gr. 1-8). pap., stu. ed. 15.20 (978-0-8294-2407-2(5)) Loyola Pr.

—We Believe: Grade 3. 2008. (Christ Our Life 2009 Ser.). (ENG.). 252p. (gr. 1-8). pap., stu. ed. 15.20 (978-0-8294-2410-2(5)) Loyola Pr.

SL Resources Staff, prod. Inhabit Student Book. 2010. 47p. (YA). 3.99 (978-1-935040-77-4(4)) SL Resources.

—SEQUENCE Student Work Book. 2009. 47p. (YA). 3.99 (978-1-935040-74-3(X)) SL Resources.

Spiritual Leaders & Thinkers. 2005. (Spiritual Leaders & Thinkers Ser.). 120p. (C). (gr. 9). 270.00 (978-0-7910-8734-3(4), Chelsea Hse.) Facts On File, Inc.

Stillman, Sarah. Soul Searching: A Girl's Guide to Finding Herself. Gross, Susan, illus. 2012. (ENG.). 176p. (YA). (gr. 7). pap. 9.99 (978-1-58270-303-9(5)) Simon Pulse/Beyond Words.

Terpstra, Marcia J. Splinters from My Rocking Chair: A Journey Through Incest Survival. 2011. 128p. pap. 14.99 (978-1-4634-3928-6(8)) AuthorHouse.

Urne, Anne. A Spiritual Trilogy. Hudson, David W., photos by. 2003. (ENG., Illus.). 352p. (YA). pap. 21.00 (978-0-9727967-0-5(3), 77707) Bois Pubns.

Valeri, Jennifer. God from A-Z: A Child's Guide to Learning about God. 2009. 32p. pap. 15.00 (978-1-60860-761-7(5), Eloquent Bks.) Strategic Book Publishing & Rights Agency (SBPRA).

Vukelic, Deneen. Soaring - a Teen's Guide to Spirit & Spirituality. 2015. (ENG., Illus.). 209p. pap. 19.95 (978-1-78279-874-3(9), Soul Rocks Bks.) Hunt, John Publishing Ltd. GBR. Dist: National Bk. Network.

Walker, Peggy, illus. My First Book of Buddhist Treasures. 2003. 38p. (J). 8.95 (978-0-915678-81-5(0)) World Tribune Pr.

Walsch, Neale Donald. The Little Soul & the Earth: A Children's Parable Adapted from Conversations with God. Riccio, Frank, illus. 2005. (ENG.). 32p. (J). 20.00 (978-1-57174-451-7(7)) Hampton Roads Publishing Co., Inc.

Walsh, Sheila. Where Do I Find Jesus? Horne, Sarah, illus. 2017. (ENG.). 32p. (J). (gr. -1-3). 14.99 (978-1-4336-8806-5(9), B&H Kids) B&H Publishing Group.

Watson, W. Hamp, Jr. Frederick Wilson Still Speaks - Big Words for Our Time. Watson, W. Hamp, Jr., ed. l.t. ed. 2004. (J). per. 12.95 (978-0-9746976-0-4(5)) Cambridge Way Publishing.

SPIRITUALS (SONGS)

Bryan, Ashley. Let It Shine: Three Favorite Spirituals. Bryan, Ashley, illus. 2007. (ENG., Illus.). 40p. (J). (gr. -1-3). 18.99 (978-0-689-84732-5(7), Atheneum Bks. for Young Readers) Simon & Schuster Children's Publishing.

Corr, Christopher, illus. Whole World: PB with CD. 2010. (ENG.). 32p. (J). (gr. -1-2). 9.99 (978-1-84686-085-0(7)) Barefoot Bks., Inc.

Corr, Christopher & Penner, Fred. Whole World. Corr, Christopher, illus. 2007. (ENG., Illus.). 32p. (J). (gr. -1-4). 16.99 (978-1-84686-043-0(1)) Barefoot Bks., Inc.

—Whole World. 2007. (ENG., Illus.). 32p. (J). (gr. -1-3). 9.99 (978-1-84686-092-8(X)) Barefoot Bks., Inc.

Edmunds, Kate, illus. Dry Bones. 2007. (Classic Books with Holes Board Book Ser.). (ENG.). (J). 14p. (gr. -1-1). bds. (978-1-84643-112-8(3)); 16p. (gr. 1-1). pap. (978-1-84643-108-1(5)) Child's Play International Ltd.

Giovanni, Nikki. On My Journey Now: Looking at African-American History Through the Spirituals. (ENG., Illus.). 128p. (J). (gr. 7-9). 2009. pap. 9.99 (978-0-7636-4380-5(7)) 2007. 18.99 (978-0-7636-2885-7(9)) Candlewick Pr.

Holiday, Billie. God Bless the Child. Pinkney, Jerry, illus. 2004. 32p. (J). lib. bdg. 17.89 (978-0-06-029487-8(6), Amistad) HarperCollins Pubs.

Holiday, Billie & Herzog, Arthur, Jr. God Bless the Child. Pinkney, Jerry, illus. 2008. (ENG.). 40p. (J). (gr. -1-3). per. 7.99 (978-0-06-443646-5(2)) HarperCollins Pubs.

Penner, Fred & Corr, Christopher. Whole World. 2012. (ENG., Illus.). 32p. (J). (gr. -1-2). 9.99 (978-1-84686-832-0(7)) Barefoot Bks., Inc.

Pinkney, Gloria Jean. Music from Our Lord's Holy Heaven. Pinkney, Jerry et al, illus. 2005. 48p. (J). (gr. -1-18). lib. bdg. 18.89 incl. audio compact disk (978-0-06-000769-0(9)) HarperCollins Pubs.

Twin Sisters(r), et al. Bible Songs for Little Hearts. 2017. (Let's Share a Story Ser.). (ENG.). 14p. (J). (-5). bds. 9.99 (978-1-68322-072-5(2)) Barbour Publishing, Inc.

SPLICING

see Knots and Splices

SPONGEBOB SQUAREPANTS (FICTITIOUS CHARACTER)—FICTION

Aikins, Dave. Haunted Houseboat. 2013. (SpongeBob Squarepants 8X8 Ser.). lib. bdg. 13.55 (978-0-606-32220-1(5), Turtleback) Turtleback Bks.

Artifact Group Staff & Artifact Group, The. Atlantis SquarePants. 2007. (SpongeBob SquarePants Ser.). (ENG., Illus.). 24p. (J). (gr. k-3). pap. 3.99 *(978-1-4169-3799-9(4)*, Simon Spotlight/Nickelodeon) Simon Spotlight/Nickelodeon.

Banks, Steven. The Art Contest: No Cheating Allowed! Dress, Robert, illus. 2006. (SpongeBob SquarePants Ser.: 12). (ENG.). 24p. (J). (gr. -1-3). pap. 3.99 *(978-1-4169-0667-4(3)*, Simon Spotlight/Nickelodeon) Simon Spotlight/Nickelodeon.

—Lost in Time. The Artifact Group, illus. 2006. 22p. (J). lib. bdg. 15.00 *(978-1-4242-0977-4(3))* Fitzgerald Bks.

—The Song That Never Ends. DePorter, Vince, illus. 2005. 32p. (J). lib. bdg. 15.00 *(978-1-59054-984-1(8))* Fitzgerald Bks.

—SpongeBob Goes to the Doctor. Saunders, Zina, illus. 2005. (SpongeBob SquarePants Ser.: 9). (ENG.). 24p. (J). pap. 3.99 *(978-1-4169-0359-8(3)*, Simon Spotlight/Nickelodeon) Simon Spotlight/Nickelodeon.

—Spongebob Goes to the Doctor. Saunders, Zina, illus. 2005. 22p. (J). lib. bdg. 15.00 *(978-1-4242-0976-7(5))* Fitzgerald Bks.

—Stop the Presses! DePorter, Vince, illus. 2005. 22p. (J). lib. bdg. 15.00 *(978-1-4242-0973-6(0))* Fitzgerald Bks.

Bond, Clint & Clark, Andy, illus. The Great Snail Race. 2005. (SpongeBob SquarePants Ser.). (ENG.). 24p. (J). pap. 3.99 *(978-0-689-87313-3(1)*, Simon Spotlight/Nickelodeon) Simon Spotlight/Nickelodeon.

Carbone, Courtney. Food Fight! Random House Editors & Aikins, Dave, illus. 2015. (Step into Reading Ser.). (ENG.). 24p. (J). (gr. -1-1). pap. 4.99 *(978-0-385-38773-6(3)*, Random Hse. Bks. for Young Readers) Random Hse. Children's Bks.

—Food Fight! 2015. (Spongebob Squarepants Step into Reading Ser.). lib. bdg. 14.75 *(978-0-606-36398-3(X))* Turtleback Bks.

—Somebunny Special (SpongeBob SquarePants) Golden Books Staff, illus. 2013. (Holographic Sticker Book Ser.). (ENG.). 48p. (J). (gr. -1-2). pap. 3.99 *(978-0-307-98104-2(5)*, Golden Bks.) Random Hse. Children's Bks.

Chipponeri, Kelli. The Big Win. Aikins, Dave, illus. 2008. (SpongeBob SquarePants Ser.: 13). (ENG.). 32p. (J). (gr. k-2). pap. 3.99 *(978-1-4169-4938-1(0)*, Simon Spotlight/Nickelodeon) Simon Spotlight/Nickelodeon.

Dart, Allan, ed. SpongeBob SquarePants & Other TV Tunes, No. 2. 2003. (Illus.). 16p. (J). pap. 3.99 *(978-0-88013-060-8(1))* Profile Entertainment, Inc.

David, Erica. Christmas with Krabby Klaws. Martinez, Heather, illus. 2010. (SpongeBob SquarePants Ser.). (ENG.). 16p. (J). pap. 5.99 *(978-1-4424-0805-0(7)*, Simon Spotlight/Nickelodeon) Simon Spotlight/Nickelodeon.

David, Erica & Artifact Group Staff. Good Times! 10th anniv. ed. 2009. (SpongeBob SquarePants Ser.). (ENG.). 32p. (J). (gr. k-2). pap. 3.99 *(978-1-4169-8500-6(X)*, Simon Spotlight/Nickelodeon) Simon Spotlight/Nickelodeon.

Eliot, Chip & Lewman, David. Funny-Side Up! A SpongeBob Joke Book. 2014. lib. bdg. 16.00 *(978-0-606-36279-5(7))* Turtleback Bks.

Giddy Up Staff. SpongeBob Abraca Dazzle. 2006. 24p. 4.99 *(978-1-59524-079-8(9))* Giddy Up, LLC.

Goldberg, Barry, illus. Bubble Blowers, Beware! 2004. (SpongeBob SquarePants Ser.). (ENG.). 24p. (J). pap. 3.99 *(978-0-689-86862-7(6)*, Simon Spotlight/Nickelodeon) Simon Spotlight/Nickelodeon.

Golden Books. Extreme Team! (SpongeBob SquarePants) Golden Books, illus. 2013. (Deluxe Coloring Book Ser.). (ENG., Illus.). 96p. (J). (gr. k-3). pap. 3.99 *(978-0-307-98227-8(0)*, Golden Bks.) Random Hse. Children's Bks.

—Plank-Ton's Big Plan! Golden Books, illus. movie tie-in ed. 2015. (Big Coloring Book Ser.). (ENG., Illus.). 48p. (J). (gr. -1-2). pap. 6.99 *(978-0-553-50827-7(X)*, Golden Bks.) Random Hse. Children's Bks.

—SpongeBob SquarePants 400th Episode Big Golden Book (SpongeBob SquarePants) Golden Books, illus. 2017. (Big Golden Book Ser.). (ENG., Illus.). 32p. (J). (gr. -1-2). 9.99 *(978-1-5247-1430-7(5)*, Golden Bks.) Random Hse. Children's Bks.

—SpongeBob Squarepants Movie Tie-In. Golden Books & Meurer, Caleb, illus. 2015. (Little Golden Book Ser.). (ENG.). 24p. (J). (-k). 4.99 *(978-0-553-49775-5(8)*, Golden Bks.) Random Hse. Children's Bks.

Golden Books, illus. Nickelodeon Little Golden Book Library (Nickelodeon), 5 vols. 2015. (ENG.). 120p. (J). (-k). 24.95 *(978-0-553-50797-3(4)*, Golden Bks.) Random Hse. Children's Bks.

Golden Books Staff. Let's Get Happy! Golden Books Staff, illus. 2016. (Color Plus 1,000 Stickers Ser.). (ENG., Illus.). 64p. (J). (gr. -1-2). pap. 9.99 *(978-1-101-93848-5(X)*, Golden Bks.) Random Hse. Children's Bks.

—Private Eyes (SpongeBob SquarePants) 2012. (3-D Coloring Book Ser.). (ENG.). 32p. (J). (gr. -1-2). pap. 4.99 *(978-0-307-92994-5(9)*, Golden Bks.) Random Hse. Children's Bks.

—SpongeBob for President! (SpongeBob SquarePants) Golden Books Staff & Aikins, Dave, illus. 2012. (Color Plus Chunky Crayons Ser.). (ENG.). 48p. (J). (gr. -1-2). pap. 3.99 *(978-0-307-97634-5(3)*, Golden Bks.) Random Hse. Children's Bks.

—SpongeBob's Best Days! Golden Books Staff, illus. 2010. (Jumbo Coloring Book Ser.). (ENG., Illus.). 224p. (J). (gr. -1-2). pap. 5.99 *(978-0-375-86351-6(6)*, Golden Bks.) Random Hse. Children's Bks.

Harvey, Alex. Dancing with the Star. 2013. (Spongebob Squarepants Step into Reading Ser.). lib. bdg. 13.55 *(978-0-606-23687-4(2)*, Turtleback) Turtleback Bks.

Hillenburg, Stephen. SpongeBob Comics: Book 1: Silly Sea Stories. 2017. (SpongeBob Comics Ser.). (ENG., Illus.). 112p. (J). (gr. 3-7). pap. 10.95 ***(978-1-4197-2319-3(7)***, Amulet Bks.) Abrams, Inc.

—SpongeBob Comics: Book 2: Aquatic Adventurers, Unite! 2017. (SpongeBob Comics Ser.). (ENG., Illus.). 112p. (J). (gr. 3-7). pap. 10.95 ***(978-1-4197-2320-9(0)***, Amulet Bks.) Abrams, Inc.

Hillenburg, Steven. SpongeBob SquarePants, Vol. 7. 2005. (SpongeBob SquarePants Ser.). (Illus.). 89p. pap. 14.99 *(978-1-59532-678-2(2)*, Tokyopop Kids) TOKYOPOP, Inc.

—SpongeBob SquarePants: Another Day Another Dollar, Vol. 5. 2004. (Nickelodeon Ser.). (Illus.). 96p. pap. 14.99 *(978-1-59532-209-8(4)*, Tokyopop Kids) TOKYOPOP, Inc.

Hillenburg, Steven, creator. Crime & Funishment Vol. 4, 7 vols. 2004. (Illus.). 96p. (gr. 2-5). pap. 14.99 *(978-1-59182-576-0(8)*, Tokyopop Kids) TOKYOPOP, Inc.

—SpongeBob SquarePants Vol. 1: Krusty Krab Adventures, 2 vols. 2003. (Illus.). 96p. (J). pap. 14.99 *(978-1-59182-398-8(6)*, Tokyopop Kids) TOKYOPOP, Inc.

—SpongeBob SquarePantsTM: Friends Forever. 2003. (Illus.). 96p. pap. 14.99 *(978-1-59182-399-5(4)*, Tokyopop Kids) TOKYOPOP, Inc.

Killeen, James. Top of the Class! Martinez, Heather, illus. 2011. (Little Golden Book Ser.). (ENG.). 24p. (J). (gr. -1-2). 3.99 *(978-0-375-86568-8(3)*, Golden Bks.) Random Hse. Children's Bks.

Krulik, Nancy. Ice-Cream Dreams. Martinez, Heather, illus. 2004. 22p. (J). lib. bdg. 15.00 *(978-1-4242-0975-0(7))* Fitzgerald Bks.

Lewman, David. The Case of the Vanished Squirrel. Moore, Harry, illus. 2008. (SpongeBob SquarePants Ser.). (ENG.). 16p. (J). (gr. -1-3). pap. 5.99 *(978-1-4169-4939-8(9)*, Simon Spotlight/Nickelodeon) Simon Spotlight/Nickelodeon.

—Double Trouble: The Case of the Missing Spatula - The Case of the Vanished Squirrel. Moore, Harry, Jr., illus. 2010. (SpongeBob SquarePants Ser.). (ENG.). 36p. (J). bds. 10.99 *(978-1-4424-1337-5(9)*, Simon Spotlight/Nickelodeon) Simon Spotlight/Nickelodeon.

—Oh, Barnacles! SpongeBob's Handbook for Bad Days. Style Guide Staff, illus. 2005. (SpongeBob SquarePants Ser.). (ENG.). 48p. (J). pap. 3.99 *(978-1-4169-0641-4(X)*, Simon Spotlight/Nickelodeon) Simon Spotlight/Nickelodeon.

—SpongeBob, Soccer Star! Reed, Stephen, illus. 2010. (SpongeBob SquarePants Ser.). (ENG.). 24p. (J). (gr. -1-3). pap. 3.99 *(978-1-4169-9445-9(9)*, Simon Spotlight/Nickelodeon) Simon Spotlight/Nickelodeon.

—SpongeBob's Slap Shot. Moore, Harry, illus. 2008. (SpongeBob SquarePants Ser.). (ENG.). 24p. (J). (gr. -1-3). pap. 3.99 *(978-1-4169-6153-6(4)*, Simon Spotlight/Nickelodeon) Simon Spotlight/Nickelodeon.

—Spongebob's Slap Shot. 2014. (SpongeBob Squarepants 8X8 Ser.). lib. bdg. 13.55 *(978-0-606-36280-1(0))* Turtleback Bks.

Lewman, David & Gomez, Yuliana. Batter up!/¡a Batear!(SpongeBob SquarePants) Random House, illus. 2014. (Pictureback Ser.). (ENG.). 24p. (J). (gr. -1-2). 3.99 *(978-0-385-38436-0(X)*, Random Hse. Bks. for Young Readers) Random Hse. Children's Bks.

Miglis, Jenny. And the Winner Is... Meurer, Caleb, illus. 2005. (SpongeBob SquarePants Ser.: 4). 22p. (J). lib. bdg. 15.00 *(978-1-59054-824-0(8))* Fitzgerald Bks.

—New Student Starfish. Martinez, Heather, illus. 2003. (SpongeBob SquarePants Ser.). (ENG.). 64p. (J). pap. 3.99 *(978-0-689-86164-2(8)*, Simon Spotlight/Nickelodeon) Simon Spotlight/Nickelodeon.

Nickelodeon. SpongeBob SquarePants: Goodnight Lagoon. 2014. (ENG.). 32p. (J). (-3). 15.99 *(978-1-4926-1669-6(9)*, Sourcebooks Jabberwocky) Sourcebooks, Inc.

—Surf's Up, SpongeBob! 2013. (SpongeBob Squarepants 8X8 Ser.). lib. bdg. 14.75 *(978-0-606-31934-8(4)*, Turtleback) Turtleback Bks.

Nickelodeon Staff. Party Time! 2013. (Spongebob Squarepants Step into Reading Ser.). lib. bdg. 13.55 *(978-0-606-32221-8(3)*, Turtleback) Turtleback Bks.

Nickelodeon Staff & Nickelodeon / LeapFrog. SpongeBob SquarePants: The Tour de Bikini Bottom. 2008. (J). 13.99 *(978-1-59319-926-5(0))* LeapFrog Enterprises, Inc.

Ostrow, Kim. The Great Snail Race. Bond, Clint & Clark, Andy, illus. 2005. (SpongeBob SquarePants Ser.: No. 6). 22p. (J). lib. bdg. 15.00 *(978-1-59054-830-1(2))* Fitzgerald Bks.

Pass, Erica. Hooray for Dads! 2014. (SpongeBob Squarepants 8X8 Ser.). lib. bdg. 14.75 *(978-0-606-35560-5(X))* Turtleback Bks.

—SpongeBob LovePants. Schigiel, Gregg, illus. 2006. (Ready-to-Read Ser.). (ENG.). 32p. (J). (gr. k-2). pap. 3.99 *(978-1-4169-1758-8(6)*, Simon Spotlight/Nickelodeon) Simon Spotlight/Nickelodeon.

Publications International Ltd. Staff, ed. Nickelodeon(tm) Spongebob Squarepants: Look & Find(r). 2014. 24p. (J). *(978-1-4508-9354-1(6)*, 1450893546) Publications International, Ltd.

—Spongebob Clock It's Time Sound Book. 2004. 10p. (J). bds. 16.98 *(978-1-4127-3030-3(9)*, 7226500) Publications International, Ltd.

—SpongeBob Squarepants (Little Look & Find) 2010. 24p. (J). 2.98 *(978-1-4508-0205-5(2))* Phoenix International Publications, Inc.

Random House. Five Playtime Tales (Nick, Jr.) Random House, illus. 2015. (Step into Reading Ser.). (ENG., Illus.). 160p. (J). (gr. -1-1). 7.99 *(978-0-553-50859-8(8)*, Random Hse. Bks. for Young Readers) Random Hse. Children's Bks.

—Five Undersea Stories (SpongeBob SquarePants) Random House, illus. 2015. (Step into Reading Ser.). (ENG., Illus.). 160p. (J). (gr. -1-1). 7.99 *(978-0-553-50860-4(1)*, Random Hse. Bks. for Young Readers) Random Hse. Children's Bks.

—The Great Train Mystery. 2013. (Spongebob Squarepants Step into Reading Ser.). lib. bdg. 13.55 *(978-0-606-35116-4(7))* Turtleback Bks.

—Hooray for Dads! (SpongeBob SquarePants) Random House, illus. 2014. (Pictureback(R) Ser.). (ENG., Illus.). 24p. (J). (gr. -1-2). 4.99 *(978-0-385-37607-5(3)*, Random Hse. Bks. for Young Readers) Random Hse. Children's Bks.

—Plankton's Christmas Surprise! (SpongeBob SquarePants) Martinez, Heather, illus. 2013. (Pictureback(R) Ser.). (ENG.). 16p. (J). (gr. -1-2). 4.99 *(978-0-449-81851-0(9)*, Random Hse. Bks. for Young Readers) Random Hse. Children's Bks.

—SpongeBob's Slap Shot (SpongeBob SquarePants) Random House, illus. 2014. (Pictureback(R) Ser.). (ENG., Illus.). 24p. (J). (gr. -1-2). 3.99 *(978-0-385-37852-9(1)*, Random Hse. Bks. for Young Readers) Random Hse. Children's Bks.

Random House & Wilson, Sarah. Moms Are the Best! (SpongeBob SquarePants) Random House, illus. 2014. (Step into Reading Ser.). (ENG., Illus.). 32p. (J). (gr. -1-1). 3.99 *(978-0-385-37499-6(2)*, Random Hse. Bks. for Young Readers) Random Hse. Children's Bks.

Random House Dictionary Staff. You're Fired! (SpongeBob SquarePants) Random House Dictionary Staff & Aikins, Dave, illus. 2014. (Pictureback(R) Ser.). (ENG.). 24p. (J). (gr. -1-2). 3.99 *(978-0-385-37431-6(3)*, Random Hse. Bks. for Young Readers) Random Hse. Children's Bks.

Random House Editors. Don't Be a Jerk, It's Christmas! Random House Editors, illus. 2013. (Big Golden Book Ser.). (ENG., Illus.). 40p. (J). (gr. -1-2). 12.99 *(978-0-449-81766-7(0)*, Random Hse. Bks. for Young Readers) Random Hse. Children's Bks.

Random House Staff. Dancing with the Star (SpongeBob SquarePants) Random House Staff, illus. 2013. (Step into Reading Ser.). (ENG., Illus.). 32p. (J). (gr. -1-1). pap. 3.99 *(978-0-449-81438-3(6)*, Random Hse. Bks. for Young Readers) Random Hse. Children's Bks.

—Demolition Derby/Class Confusion (SpongeBob SquarePants) Aikins, Dave, illus. 2013. (Pictureback(R) Ser.). (ENG.). 32p. (J). (gr. -1-2). 4.99 *(978-0-449-81756-8(3)*, Random Hse. Bks. for Young Readers) Random Hse. Children's Bks.

—The Great Train Mystery (SpongeBob SquarePants) Random House Staff, illus. 2013. (Step into Reading Ser.). (ENG., Illus.). 32p. (J). (gr. -1-1). pap. 3.99 *(978-0-449-81441-3(6)*, Random Hse. Bks. for Young Readers) Random Hse. Children's Bks.

—Happiness to Go! (SpongeBob SquarePants) Random House Staff, illus. 2013. (Pictureback(R) Ser.). (ENG., Illus.). 144p. (J). (gr. -1-2). 11.99 *(978-0-449-81479-6(3)*, Random Hse. Bks. for Young Readers) Random Hse. Children's Bks.

—Haunted Houseboat (SpongeBob SquarePants) Random House Staff & Aikins, Dave, illus. 2013. (Pictureback(R) Ser.). (ENG.). 24p. (J). (gr. -1-2). 3.99 *(978-0-449-81759-9(8)*, Random Hse. Bks. for Young Readers) Random Hse. Children's Bks.

—Party Time! (SpongeBob SquarePants) Random House Staff & Moore, Harry, illus. 2013. (Step into Reading Ser.). (ENG.). 32p. (J). (gr. -1-1). 3.99 *(978-0-449-81875-6(6)*, Random Hse. Bks. for Young Readers) Random Hse. Children's Bks.

—SpongeBob's Easter Parade (SpongeBob SquarePants) Random House Staff, illus. 2013. (Pictureback(R) Ser.). (ENG., Illus.). 24p. (J). (gr. -1-2). pap. 3.99 *(978-0-449-81444-4(0)*, Random Hse. Bks. for Young Readers) Random Hse. Children's Bks.

—You're Fired! 2014. (SpongeBob Squarepants 8X8 Ser.). lib. bdg. 13.55 *(978-0-606-35204-8(X))* Turtleback Bks.

Random House Staff & Wilson, Sarah. Moms Are the Best! (SpongeBob SquarePants) Random House Staff, illus. 2014. (Step into Reading Ser.). (ENG., Illus.). 32p. (J). (gr. -1-1). lib. bdg. 12.99 *(978-0-385-37500-9(X)*, Random Hse. Bks. for Young Readers) Random Hse. Children's Bks.

Reader's Digest Editors. Nickelodeon My Pal SpongeBob: Pose-a-Book. 2012. (Nickelodeon Spongebob Ser.). (ENG., Illus.). 10p. (J). (gr. -1-k). bds. 12.99 *(978-0-7944-2289-9(6))* Reader's Digest Assn., Inc., The.

Reisner, Molly, et al. Nickelodeon Little Golden Book Collection (Nickelodeon) Golden Books, illus. 2012. (Little Golden Book Treasury Ser.). (ENG.). 224p. (J). (gr. -1-2). 10.99 *(978-0-375-85120-9(8)*, Golden Bks.) Random Hse. Children's Bks.

Richards, Kitty. SpongeBob Airpants: The Lost Episode. Martinez, Heather, illus. 2003. (SpongeBob SquarePants Ser.). (ENG.). 64p. (J). pap. 3.99 *(978-0-689-86163-5(X)*, Simon Spotlight/Nickelodeon) Simon Spotlight/Nickelodeon.

Schigiel, Gregg. Feel the Love. 2013. (SpongeBob Squarepants 8X8 Ser.). lib. bdg. 14.75 *(978-0-606-35559-9(6))* Turtleback Bks.

Silverhardt, Lauryn. SpongeBob SpookyPants. Style Guide Staff, illus. 2004. (SpongeBob SquarePants Ser.). (ENG.). 16p. (J). bds. 5.99 *(978-0-689-87320-1(4)*, Simon Spotlight/Nickelodeon) Simon Spotlight/Nickelodeon.

SpongeBob Squarepants WOW! Scratchers. 2005. 4p. (J). 6.99 *(978-1-59524-031-6(4))* Giddy Up, LLC.

SpongeBob WOW Paper Scribble & Giggle Pad. 2004. 36p. (J). 7.99 *(978-1-59524-006-4(3))* Giddy Up, LLC.

SpongeBob WOW! Surprise & Shine. 2005. 4p. (J). 6.99 *(978-1-59524-049-1(7))* Giddy Up, LLC.

SpongeBob's Box of Books. 2005. (SpongeBob SquarePants Ser.). (ENG.). 144p. (J). pap. 10.99 *(978-1-4169-1186-9(3)*, Simon Spotlight/Nickelodeon) Simon Spotlight/Nickelodeon.

Taylor, Nicole & Watts, Michael. SpongeBob Squarepants: Wormy. 2014. 32p. (J). pap. incl. audio compact disk *(978-1-909221-71-0(6))* Glasgow, Mary Pubns.

Willson, Sarah. Behold, No Cavities! A Visit to the Dentist. Moore, Harry, illus. 2007. (SpongeBob SquarePants Ser.: 15). (ENG.). 24p. (J). (gr. -1-3). pap. 3.99 *(978-1-4169-3566-7(5)*, Simon Spotlight/Nickelodeon) Simon Spotlight/Nickelodeon.

—Just Say Please! Moore, Harry, illus. 2007. (SpongeBob SquarePants Ser.). (ENG.). 32p. (J). (gr. k-2). pap. 3.99 *(978-1-4169-4129-3(0)*, Simon Spotlight/Nickelodeon) Simon Spotlight/Nickelodeon.

—Mother Knows Best. Dress, Robert, illus. 2006. (SpongeBob SquarePants Chapter Bks.: Vol. 11). (ENG.). 64p. (J). (gr. 3-7). pap. 4.99 *(978-1-4169-0793-0(9)*, Simon Spotlight/Nickelodeon) Simon Spotlight/Nickelodeon.

Wygand, Melissa. Where the Pirates Arrgh! (SpongeBob SquarePants) Martinez, Heather, illus. 2013. (Little Golden Book Ser.). (ENG.). 24p. (J). (-k). 3.99 *(978-0-307-98174-5(6)*, Golden Bks.) Random Hse. Children's Bks.

SPORTS

see also Aeronautical Sports; Amusements; Aquatic Sports; Athletics; Coaching (Athletics); Games; Gymnastics; Olympics; Outdoor Life; Physical Education and Training; Rodeos; School Sports; Winter Sports

also names of sports, e.g. baseball; etc.

ABDO. Sports' Best Ever, 1 vol. 2014. (Sports' Best Ever Ser.: 6). (ENG.). 64p. (gr. 3-6). lib. bdg. 196.74 *(978-1-62403-616-3(3)*, SportsZone) ABDO Publishing Co.

ABDO Publishing. Legendary World of Sports. 2016. (Legendary World of Sports Ser.: 6). (ENG.). 48p. (J). (gr. 3-6). lib. bdg. 196.74 *(978-1-62403-987-4(1)*, SportsZone) ABDO Publishing Co.

Abdo Publishing. Sports' Great Championships, 1 vol. 2013. (Sports' Great Championships Ser.: 8). (ENG.). 64p. (J). (gr. 4-6). lib. bdg. 262.32 *(978-1-61783-668-8(0)*, SportsZone) ABDO Publishing Co.

ABDO Publishing. Sports Trivia. 2016. (Sports Trivia Ser.: 6). (ENG.). 48p. (J). (gr. 3-9). lib. bdg. 196.74 *(978-1-68078-000-0(X)*, SportsZone) ABDO Publishing Co.

ABDO Publishing Company. Girls' SportsZone: Set Of 8. 2013. (Girls' SportsZone Ser.: 8). (ENG.). 48p. (J). (gr. 3-6). lib. bdg. 262.32 *(978-1-61783-983-2(3)*, SportsZone) ABDO Publishing Co.

ABDO Publishing Company Staff. Issues in Sports. 2014. (Issues in Sports Ser.: 6). (ENG.). 64p. (gr. 5-8). lib. bdg. 196.74 *(978-1-62403-119-9(6)*, SportsZone) ABDO Publishing Co.

ABDO Publishing Company Staff & Salzmann, Mary Elizabeth. Sports Gear. 2012. (Sports Gear Ser.: 6). (ENG., Illus.). 24p. (J). (gr. k-3). lib. bdg. 145.26 *(978-1-61714-821-7(0)*, SandCastle) ABDO Publishing Co.

Adamson, Thomas K. The Kids' Guide to Sports Design & Engineering, 1 vol. 2014. (SI Kids Guide Bks.). (ENG.). 48p. (gr. 4-9). lib. bdg. 31.99 *(978-1-4765-4155-6(8))* Capstone Press of Coughlan Cos.

Adamson, Thomas K. & Frederick, Shane. Sports Math. 2011. (Sports Math Ser.). (ENG.). 48p. (gr. 5-6). pap. 190.80 *(978-1-4296-7324-2(9))*; pap. 31.80 *(978-1-4296-7323-5(0))*; lib. bdg. 127.96 *(978-1-4296-6571-1(8))* Capstone Press of Coughlan Cos.

Adamson, Thomas K., et al. High-Tech Sports. 2013. (High-Tech Sports Ser.). (ENG.). 48p. (gr. 3-9). pap. 214.80 *(978-1-62065-915-1(8))* Capstone Press of Coughlan Cos.

Aksomitis, Linda. Sports Champions. 2008. (Science Solves It Ser.). (ENG., Illus.). 32p. (J). (gr. 3-7). pap. *(978-0-7787-4179-4(6))*; lib. bdg. *(978-0-7787-4172-5(9))* Crabtree Publishing Co.

Alcraft, Rob. Four Desert Challenge. 2015. (Collins Big Cat Ser.). (ENG., Illus.). 48p. (J). (gr. 3-4). pap. 9.95 *(978-0-00-812781-7(6))* HarperCollins Pubs. Ltd. GBR. Dist: Independent Pubs. Group.

Alexander, Kwame. The Playbook: 52 Rules to Aim, Shoot, & Score in This Game Called Life. Neave, Thai, photos by. 2017. (ENG., Illus.). 176p. (J). (gr. 5-7). 14.99 *(978-0-544-57097-9(9)*, HMH Books For Young Readers) Houghton Mifflin Harcourt Publishing Co.

—The Playbook: 52 Rules to Aim, Shoot, & Score in This Game Called Life. Neave, Thai, photos by. 2017. (ENG., Illus.). (J). (gr. 5-7). lib. bdg. 26.95 ***(978-0-606-39814-5(7))*** Turtleback Bks.

All-Star Sports Stars, 6 bks. Incl. Gridiron Greats: 8 of Today's Hottest NFL Stars. Collie, Ashley Jude. lib. bdg. 33.25 *(978-0-8239-3691-5(0))*; Ken Griffey, Jr. Superstar Centerfielder. Rolfe, John. lib. bdg. 33.25 *(978-0-8239-3687-8(2))*; Sports Superstars: 8 of Today's Hottest Athletes. Knotts, Bob. lib. bdg. 33.25 *(978-0-8239-3692-2(9))*; (YA). (gr. 7-12). (Illus.). 176p. 2005. Set lib. bdg. 164.85 *(978-0-8239-9732-9(4))* Rosen Publishing Group, Inc., The.

The All-Time Best of Sports. (All-Time Best of Sports Ser.). (ENG.). 64p. (gr. 3-4). 2011. pap. 214.80 *(978-1-4296-6456-1(8))* 2010. pap. 35.80 *(978-1-4296-6329-8(4))* Capstone Press of Coughlan Cos.

The All-Time Best of Sports, 4 vols., Set. Incl. Best of Everything Basketball Book. LeBoutillier, Nate. lib. bdg. 34.65 *(978-1-4296-5468-5(6))*; Best of Everything Football Book. Frederick, Shane. lib. bdg. 34.65 *(978-1-4296-5466-1(X))*; Best of Everything Hockey Book. Frederick, Shane. lib. bdg. 34.65 *(978-1-4296-5469-2(4))*; (gr. 3-4). (All-Time Best of Sports Ser.). (ENG.). 64p. 2010. Set lib. bdg. 103.95 *(978-1-4296-5470-8(8))* Capstone Press of Coughlan Cos.

Anniss, Matt. The Impact of Technology in Sports. 2015. (Impact of Technology Ser.). (ENG., Illus.). 56p. (gr. 6-9). pap. 9.49 *(978-1-4846-2641-2(9))* Heinemann-Raintree.

Aretha, David. Top 10 Worst Injuries in Football. 2016. (Sports Greats Ser.). 48p. (J). pap. 11.70 *(978-0-7660-8300-4(4))* Enslow Pubs., Inc.

Atlantic, Leonard. We Play Sports! 2017. (Ways to Play Ser.). 24p. (gr. k-k). pap. 8.15 ***(978-1-4824-6353-8(9))*** Stevens, Gareth Publishing LLLP.

Barber, Nicola. Ancient Roman Sports & Pastimes. 2010. (Ancient Communities: Roman Life Ser.). 32p. (J). (ENG.). pap. 10.60 *(978-1-61532-315-9(5))*; (Illus.). (gr. 3-6). lib. bdg. 26.50 *(978-1-61532-306-7(6))* Rosen Publishing Group, Inc., The. (PowerKids Pr.).

Barceló, Josefina. Vamos a Jugar. Álvarez, Mrinali, illus. 2006. (SPA.). (J). 8.95 *(978-0-8477-1560-2(4))* Univ. of Puerto Rico Pr.

Barker, Geoff. Sports & Leisure Careers. 2010. (In the Workplace Ser.). 48p. (J). 35.65 *(978-1-60753-094-7(5))* Amicus Publishing.

Barker, Geoff & Savery, Annabel. Sports & Leisure Careers. 2011. (Been There! Ser.). 32p. (gr. 3-6). lib. bdg. 31.35 *(978-1-59920-474-1(6))* Black Rabbit Bks.

Be a Plant Scientist: Level L, 6 vols. (Take-Twostm Ser.). 16p. 36.95 *(978-0-322-03403-7(5))* Wright Group/McGraw-Hill.

BeaverSimon. SPORT, GAME OR HOBBY? LOW INTERMEDIATE BOOK WITH ONLINE ACCESS. 2014. (ENG., Illus.). 48p. (J). pap. 9.50 *(978-1-107-68658-8(X))* Cambridge Univ. Pr.

Benched: Dealing with Sports Injuries. 2016. (Benched: Dealing with Sports Injuries Ser.). 24p. (gr. 3-2). pap. 48.90 *(978-1-4824-5311-9(8))*; lib. bdg. 135.60 *(978-1-4824-4593-0(X))* Stevens, Gareth Publishing LLLP.

Berendes, Mary. Sports & Games/Los Deportes y Los Juegos. Petelinsek, Kathleen, illus. 2007. (WordBooks/Libros de Palabras Ser.). (SPA & ENG.). 24p. (J). (gr. k-3). 25.64 *(978-1-59296-802-2(3)*, 201099) Child's World, Inc., The.

Berman, Len. And Nobody Got Hurt! The World's Weirdest, Wackiest True Sports Stories. Gamble, Kent, illus. 2005. (ENG.). 128p. (J). (gr. 3-7). per. 7.99 *(978-0-316-01029-0(4))* Little, Brown Bks. for Young Readers.

—And Nobody Got Hurt 2! The World's Weirdest, Wackiest Most Amazing True Sports Stories. Gamble, Kent, illus. rev. ed. 2007. (ENG.). 144p. (J). (gr. 3-7). per. 16.99 *(978-0-316-06705-8(9))* Little, Brown Bks. for Young Readers.

Berman, Ron. Sports. 2012. (Urban Entrepreneurs Ser.). (ENG., Illus.). 40p. (gr. 3-8). pap. 9.95 *(978-1-61570-519-1(8))* Scobre Pr. Corp.

S

Berry, Joy. Help Me Be Good about Being a Bad Sport. 2009. (Help Me Be Good Ser.). 40p. pap. 7.95 *(978-1-60577-108-3(2))* Berry, Joy Enterprises.

—Help Me Be Good Being a Bad Sport. Bartholomew, illus. 2010. (Help Me Be Good Ser.). (ENG.). 32p. (J). (gr. -1-2). pap. 4.99 *(978-1-60577-139-7(2))* Berry, Joy Enterprises.

The Best of the Best. 2011. (Best of the Best Ser.). (ENG.). 32p. (gr. 1-2). pap. 32.40 *(978-1-4296-7255-9(2))*; pap. 286.20 *(978-1-4296-7256-6(0))*; lib. bdg. 133.25 *(978-1-4296-6503-2(3))* Capstone Press of Coughlan Cos. (Blazers).

Best Young Players in Sports, 6 bks. Incl. Rising Stars: The 10 Best Young Players in Baseball. Schwarz, Alan. lib. bdg. 33.25 *(978-0-8239-3576-5(0))*; Rising Stars: The 10 Best Young Players in the NHL. Brehm, Mike & Russo, Michael. lib. bdg. 33.25 *(978-0-8239-3575-8(2))*; Shaquille O'Neal: Superhero at Center. Smith, Pohla & Wilson, Steve. lib. bdg. 33.25 *(978-0-8239-3577-2(9))*; (YA). (gr. 7-12). (Illus.). 176p. 2005. Set lib. bdg. 183.75 *(978-0-8239-9731-2(6))* Rosen Publishing Group, Inc., The.

Bethea, Nikole Brooks. The Science of Basketball with Max Axiom, Super Scientist. 2015. (Science of Sports with Max Axiom Ser.). (ENG., Illus.). 32p. (gr. 3-4). lib. bdg. 30.65 *(978-1-4914-6084-9(9))* Capstone Press of Coughlan Cos.

—The Science of Football with Max Axiom, Super Scientist. 2015. (Science of Sports with Max Axiom Ser.). (ENG., Illus.). 32p. (gr. 3-4). lib. bdg. 30.65 *(978-1-4914-6085-6(7))* Capstone Press of Coughlan Cos.

Bethea, Nikole Brooks, et al. The Science of Sports with Max Axiom. Cacau, Caio, illus. 2015. (Science of Sports with Max Axiom Ser.). (ENG.). 32p. (gr. 3-4). pap. 31.80 *(978-1-4914-7342-9(8)*, Graphic Library) Capstone Press of Coughlan Cos.

Big Time. 64p. (YA). (gr. 6-12). pap. *(978-0-8224-2390-4(1))* Globe Fearon Educational Publishing.

Bildner, Phil. Martina & Chrissie: The Greatest Rivalry in the History of Sports. Helquist, Brett, illus. 2017. (ENG.). 40p. (J). (gr. 2-5). 16.99 *(978-0-7636-7308-6(0))* Candlewick Pr.

Binkow, Howard. Howard B. Wigglebottom Learns about Sportsmanship: Winning Isn't Everything. Cornelison, Susan F., illus. 2012. (Howard B. Wigglebottom Ser.). 32p. (J). (gr. -1-2). 15.00 *(978-0-9826165-6-7(2)*, We Do Listen) We Do Listen Foundation.

Birmingham, Maria. Weird Zone: Sports. Bennett, Jamie & Owlkids Books Inc. Staff, illus. 2013. (Weird Zone Ser.). (ENG.). 128p. (J). (gr. 3-6). pap. 12.95 *(978-1-926973-61-6(5))* Owlkids Bks. Inc. CAN. Dist: Publishers Group West (PGW).

Blomquist, Christopher. Motocross in the X Games. 2003. (Kid's Guide to the X Games Ser.). (Illus.). 24p. (J). lib. bdg. 22.60 *(978-0-8239-6303-4(9)*, PowerKids Pr.) Rosen Publishing Group, Inc., The.

—Wakeboarding in the X Games. 2003. (Kid's Guide to the X Games Ser.). (Illus.). 24p. (J). lib. bdg. 22.60 *(978-0-8239-6301-0(2)*, PowerKids Pr.) Rosen Publishing Group, Inc., The.

Bloomquist, Christopher. Skateboarding in the X Games. 2003. (Kid's Guide to the X Games Ser.). (Illus.). 24p. (J). lib. bdg. 22.60 *(978-0-8239-6300-3(4)*, PowerKids Pr.) Rosen Publishing Group, Inc., The.

—Street Luge in the X Games. 2003. (Kid's Guide to the X Games Ser.). (Illus.). 24p. (J). lib. bdg. 22.60 *(978-0-8239-6299-0(7)*, PowerKids Pr.) Rosen Publishing Group, Inc., The.

Borth, Teddy. Great Sports, 1 vol. 2014. (Great Sports Ser.: 6). (ENG.). 24p. (J). (gr. 2-4). lib. bdg. 171.00 *(978-1-62970-686-3(8))* ABDO Publishing Co.

Bourassa, Barbara. Sports Club. 2012. (Illus.). 120p. (J). *(978-1-4351-4414-9(7))* Barnes & Noble, Inc.

Bowker, Paul. Playing Pro Football. 2014. (Playing Pro Sports Ser.). (ENG.). 64p. (gr. 4-8). lib. bdg. 26.60 *(978-1-4677-3844-6(1)*, Lerner Pubns.) Lerner Publishing Group.

Branon, Dave. Heads Up! Sports Devotions for All-Star Kids, 1 vol. rev. ed. 2012. (ENG.). 346p. (J). pap. 9.99 *(978-0-310-72544-2(5))* Zondervan.

Braun, Eric. The Guys' Guide to Making Sports More Awesome, 1 vol. 2014. (Guys' Guides). (ENG.). 32p. (gr. 3-4). lib. bdg. 27.99 *(978-1-4765-3921-8(9)*, Edge Bks.) Capstone Press of Coughlan Cos.

Brocker, Susan. Sports Legends: Set Of 6. 2011. (Navigators Ser.). (J). pap. 44.00 net. *(978-1-4108-0406-8(2))* Benchmark Education Co.

Brush, Jim. Extreme Summer Sports. 2013. (Illus.). 46p. (J). 35.65 *(978-1-59771-407-5(0))* Sea-To-Sea Pubns.

Bryan, Gayle. Virtual Apprentice: Professional Athlete. 2009. (Virtual Apprentice Ser.). 64p. (gr. 4-9). pap. 9.95 *(978-0-8160-7896-7(3)*, Checkmark Bks.) Facts On File, Inc.

Buckley, James, Jr. Scholastic Year in Sports 2016. 2015. lib. bdg. 20.85 *(978-0-606-37763-8(8))* Turtleback Bks.

—Scholastic Year in Sports 2017. 2016. (ENG.). 192p. (J). (gr. 3-7). 20.85 *(978-0-606-39153-5(3))* Turtleback Bks.

Buckley, James. Sports Media Relations, Vol. 10. Ferrer, Al, ed. 2015. (Careers off the Field Ser.). (Illus.). 64p. (J). (gr. 7). lib. bdg. 23.95 *(978-1-4222-3269-9(7))* Mason Crest.

—STEM in Sports. 2015. (STEM in Sports Ser.). (Illus.). 64p. (J). (gr. 7). 23.95 *(978-1-4222-3232-3(8))* Mason Crest.

Burdick, Jeff. Super Sports Trivia. 2013. (Ultimate Trivia Challenge Ser.). 32p. (J). (gr. 2-5). pap. 10.50 *(978-1-4339-8301-6(X))*; pap. 63.00 *(978-1-4339-8302-3(8))*; (ENG., Illus.). lib. bdg. 25.25 *(978-1-4339-8300-9(1))* Stevens, Gareth Publishing LLLP.

Burgan, Michael. Working in College Sports, Vol. 10. Ferrer, Al, ed. 2015. (Careers off the Field Ser.). (Illus.). 64p. (J). (gr. 7). lib. bdg. 23.95 *(978-1-4222-3274-3(3))* Mason Crest.

Burgan, Michael & Nardo, Don. Captured History Sports. 2016. (Captured History Sports Ser.). (ENG.). 64p. (gr. 5-7). 138.60 *(978-0-7565-5309-8(1)*, CPB Grades 4-8) Compass Point Bks.

Bussell, Linda. Vamos a Usar la División en el Campamento de Deportes. 2008. (Matemáticas en Nuestro Mundo - Nivel 3 (Math in Our World - Level 3) Ser.). (SPA.). 24p. (gr. 2-5). (J). lib. bdg. 22.00 *(978-0-8368-9296-3(8))*; pap. 8.15 *(978-0-8368-9395-3(6))* Stevens, Gareth Publishing LLLP. (Weekly Reader Leveled Readers).

Butterfield, Moira & Hachette Children's Group. The Olympics Scandals. 2011. (Olympics Ser.). 32p. (YA). (gr. 4-7). 28.50 *(978-1-59771-320-7(1))* Sea-To-Sea Pubns.

Canetti, Yanitzia. Sporty Colors/Colores Deportivos: A World of Color. 2010. (ENG & SPA.). 24p. (J). pap. 6.99 *(978-1-59835-268-9(7)*, BrickHouse Education) Cambridge BrickHouse, Inc.

Capstone Press. Passport to World Sports. 2010. (Passport to World Sports Ser.). (ENG.). 32p. lib. bdg. 159.90 *(978-1-4296-5917-8(3)*, Edge Bks.) Capstone Press of Coughlan Cos.

—Play Like the Pros, 1 vol. 2010. (Play Like the Pros (Sports Illustrated for Kids) Ser.). (ENG.). 32p. lib. bdg. 101.28 *(978-1-4296-5916-1(5))* Capstone Press of Coughlan Cos.

—Ultimate Pro Team Guides, 1 vol. 2010. (Ultimate Pro Team Guides (Sports Illustrated for Kids) Ser.). (ENG.). 32p. lib. bdg. 133.28 *(978-1-4296-5900-0(9))* Capstone Press of Coughlan Cos.

—Wild Outdoors. 2010. (Wild Outdoors Ser.). (ENG.). 32p. lib. bdg. 101.28 *(978-1-4296-5904-8(1)*, Blazers) Capstone Press of Coughlan Cos.

Carr, Aaron. BMX. 2013. *(978-1-62127-627-2(9))* Weigl Pubs., Inc.

—Esqui. 2013. (Deportes de Moda Ser.). (SPA., Illus.). 24p. (J). (gr. k-2). lib. bdg. 27.13 *(978-1-62127-633-3(3)*, AV2 by Weigl) Weigl Pubs., Inc.

—Moto X. 2012. (Cool Sports (Av2) Ser.). (ENG., Illus.). 24p. (J). lib. bdg. 27.13 *(978-1-61913-511-6(6)*, AV2 by Weigl) Weigl Pubs., Inc.

—Moto X with Code. 2012. (Cool Sports (Av2) Ser.). (ENG., Illus.). 24p. (J). (gr. k-2). pap. 12.95 *(978-1-61913-517-8(5)*, AV2 by Weigl) Weigl Pubs., Inc.

Carter, André & Nicholls, Shawn. You Call That a Sport? Strange Sports from Around the Globe. 2003. (J). 3.99 *(978-1-930623-32-3(1))* Sports Illustrated For Kids.

Champion, Neil. Orienteering. 2009. (Get Outdoors Ser.). (Illus.). 32p. (ENG.). (J). pap. 10.00 *(978-1-4358-3052-3(0)*, PowerKids Pr.); (YA). (gr. 4-7). lib. bdg. 25.25 *(978-1-4358-3044-8(X))* Rosen Publishing Group, Inc., The.

Chandler, Matt & Nicolai, Gregory. Top 10 Science. 2016. (Top 10 Science Ser.). (ENG.). 32p. (gr. 3-4). 111.96 *(978-1-4914-8731-0(3))* Capstone Press of Coughlan Cos.

Chandler, Matt, et al. All-Star Goofball Trivia: Weird & Wild Sports Trivia. 2017. (Sports Illustrated Kids Ser.). (ENG., Illus.). 144p. (gr. 3-4). pap. 9.95 *(978-1-62370-778-1(1))* Capstone Press of Coughlan Cos.

—Wacky Sports Trivia. 2016. (Wacky Sports Trivia Ser.). (ENG.). 32p. (gr. 3-4). 139.95 *(978-1-5157-2013-3(6))* Capstone Press of Coughlan Cos.

Chastain, Zachary. Rooting for the Home Team: Sports in The 1800s. 2009. (Daily Life in America in the 1800s Ser.). 64p. (YA). (gr. 7-18). pap. 9.95 *(978-1-4222-1859-4(7))*; lib. bdg. 22.95 *(978-1-4222-1786-3(8))* Mason Crest.

Cherry Lake Publishing Staff, compiled by. Heathly for Life. 2007. 32p. lib. bdg. 159.60 *(978-1-60279-105-3(8)*, 200028) Cherry Lake Publishing.

Child's World Staff & Watson, S. B. Weird Sports of the World. 2011. (Weird Sports Ser.). (ENG., Illus.). 24p. (J). (gr. 2-5). lib. bdg. 28.50 *(978-1-60954-378-5(5)*, 201056) Child's World, Inc., The.

Child's World Staff, The & Kelley, K. C. Weird Races. 2011. (Weird Sports Ser.). (ENG., Illus.). 24p. (J). (gr. 2-5). lib. bdg. 28.50 *(978-1-60954-376-1(9)*, 201054) Child's World, Inc., The.

—Weird Sports Moments. 2011. (Weird Sports Ser.). (ENG., Illus.). 24p. (J). (gr. 2-5). lib. bdg. 28.50 *(978-1-60954-377-8(7)*, 201055) Child's World, Inc., The.

Child's World Staff, The & Watson, S. B. Weird Animal Sports. 2011. (Weird Sports Ser.). (ENG., Illus.). 24p. (J). (gr. 2-5). lib. bdg. 28.50 *(978-1-60954-375-4(0)*, 201053) Child's World, Inc., The.

—Weird Throwing & Kicking Sports. 2011. (Weird Sports Ser.). (ENG., Illus.). 24p. (J). (gr. 2-5). lib. bdg. 28.50 *(978-1-60954-379-2(3)*, 201057) Child's World, Inc., The.

Ching, Jacqueline. Adventure Racing. 2009. (Ultra Sports Ser.). 64p. (gr. 5-8). 58.50 *(978-1-60854-606-0(3)*, Rosen Reference) Rosen Publishing Group, Inc., The.

Clark, Jeff. Dad's Masterpiece: The Patricia Masotto Story. 2009. 112p. 22.50 *(978-1-60693-873-7(8)*, Strategic Bk. Publishing) Strategic Book Publishing & Rights Agency (SBPRA).

Clay, Kathryn & Czeskleba, Abby. Datos Geniales Sobre Deportes/Cool Sports Facts. Strictly Spanish LLC. Staff, tr. 2012. (Datos Geniales Sobre Deportes/Cool Sports Facts Ser.). (MUL.). 24p. (gr. k-1). lib. bdg. 79.95 *(978-1-4296-9218-2(9))* Capstone Press of Coughlan Cos.

Clay, Kathryn, et al. Cool Sports Facts. (Cool Sports Facts Ser.). (ENG.). 24p. (gr. k-1). 2011. pap. 21.87 *(978-1-4296-7398-3(2))* 2011. pap. 166.80 *(978-1-4296-6375-5(8))* 2010. pap. 21.87 *(978-1-4296-6206-2(9))* 2010. lib. bdg. 106.60 *(978-1-4296-5306-0(X))* Capstone Press of Coughlan Cos. (Pebble Plus).

Cohn, Jessica. On the Job in the Game. Scheuer, Lauren, illus. 2016. (Core Content Social Studies — on the Job Ser.). (ENG.). 32p. (J). (gr. 2-5). lib. bdg. 26.65 *(978-1-63440-111-1(5))* Red Chair Pr.

Colich, Abby. Women in Sports. 2016. (Women in Sports Ser.). (ENG.). 24p. (gr. k-1). 159.90 *(978-1-4914-8716-7(X)*, Pebble Plus) Capstone Press of Coughlan Cos.

Cool Sports Facts. 2011. (Cool Sports Facts Ser.). (ENG.). 24p. (gr. k-1). pap. 375.30 *(978-1-4296-7401-0(6)*, Pebble Plus) Capstone Press of Coughlan Cos.

Corrigan, Delia Stubbs & Tighe, Elizabeth. Go Team! Mascots of the SEC. 2008. (Illus.). 64p. (J). pap. 10.99 *(978-0-9797040-0-0(6))* Go Team, LLC.

Crabtree Publishing, creator. Sports Starters. 2008. pap. *(978-0-7787-3166-5(9))* Crabtree Publishing Co.

Creighton, Jayne. Sports. 2009. (Science Q & A Ser.). (Illus.). 48p. (YA). (gr. 5-8). pap. 10.95 *(978-1-60596-071-5(3))*; lib. bdg. 29.05 *(978-1-60596-070-8(5))* Weigl Pubs., Inc.

Crossingham, John. Lacrosse in Action. 2003. (Sports in Action Ser.). (ENG., Illus.). 32p. (J). (gr. 4). pap. *(978-0-7787-0349-5(5))* Crabtree Publishing Co.

Currie, Stephen. Cheating. 2007. (Ripped from the Headlines Ser.). (YA). (gr. 7-12). 23.95 *(978-1-60217-011-7(8))* Erickson Pr.

Dahl, Michael. Sports Illustrated Kids Bedtime Books. Forshay, Christina E., illus. 2015. (Sports Illustrated Kids Bedtime Bks.). (ENG.). 32p. (gr. -1-2). 67.80 *(978-1-4795-8261-7(1))* Capstone Press of Coughlan Cos.

Daredevil Sports. 2015. (Daredevil Sports Ser.). (ENG.). 32p. (J). (gr. 1-1). pap., pap., pap. 63.00 *(978-1-4824-3451-4(2))* Stevens, Gareth Publishing LLLP.

Davies, Monika. No Way! Spectacular Sports Stories (Grade 7) 2017. (TIME for KIDS(r) Nonfiction Readers Ser.). (Illus.). 48p. (J). (gr. 7-7). pap. 9.99 ***(978-1-4938-3609-3(9))*** Teacher Created Materials, Inc.

DeGezelle, Terri, et al. Deportes y Actividades. 2012. (Deportes y Actividades/Sports & Activities Ser.).Tr. of Sports & Activities. (MUL.). 24p. (gr. k-1). 79.95 *(978-1-4296-8248-0(5))* Capstone Press of Coughlan Cos.

Deportes Atleticos, 6 vols., Vol. 2. (Explorers. Exploradores Nonfiction Sets Ser.). (SPA.). 32p. (gr. 3-6). 44.95 *(978-0-7699-0648-5(6))* Shortland Pubns. (U. S. A.) Inc.

Deportes Con Pelota, 6 vols., Vol. 3. (Explorers. Exploradores Nonfiction Sets Ser.). (SPA.). (gr. 3-6). *(978-0-7699-0660-7(5))* Shortland Pubns. (U. S. A.) Inc.

Doeden, Matt, et al. Sports Rivalries. 2015. (Sports Rivalries Ser.). (ENG.). 32p. (gr. 3-4). lib. bdg. 111.96 *(978-1-4914-2545-9(8)*, Edge Bks.) Capstone Press of Coughlan Cos.

Donovan, Sandy. Keep Your Eye on the Ball: And Other Expressions about Sports. 2012. (It's Just an Expression Ser.). (ENG., Illus.). 32p. (J). (gr. 4-6). lib. bdg. 26.60 *(978-0-7613-7889-1(8)*, Lerner Pubns.) Lerner Publishing Group.

—Sports Top Tens. 2014. (Entertainment's Top 10 Ser.). (ENG., Illus.). 32p. (gr. 5-8). lib. bdg. 26.60 *(978-1-4677-3842-2(5)*, Lerner Pubns.) Lerner Publishing Group.

Doudna, Kelly. Play Fair!, 1 vol. 2007. (Character Concepts Ser.). (ENG., Illus.). 24p. (J). (gr. k-3). lib. bdg. 24.21 *(978-1-59928-739-3(0)*, SandCastle) ABDO Publishing Co.

Downey, Glen R. The 10 Greatest Sports Showdowns. 2008. 14.99 *(978-1-55448-535-2(5))* Scholastic Library Publishing.

—The 10 Most Shocking Sports Scandals. 2007. 14.99 *(978-1-55448-505-5(3))* Scholastic Library Publishing.

Dreier, David L. & Hoena, Blake. The Science of Sports with Max Axiom. Cacau, Caio, illus. 2015. (Science of Sports with Max Axiom Ser.). (ENG.). 32p. (gr. 3-4). 122.60 *(978-1-4914-6914-9(5)*, Graphic Library) Capstone Press of Coughlan Cos.

Duncan, David A. Dude, Where's Your Helmet?, 1 vol. 2009. (ENG., Illus.). 48p. (J). pap. *(978-1-897522-59-2(2))* RMB Rocky Mountain Bks.

Dyan, Penelope. The Rain in Spain — -A Kid's Guide to Barcelona, Spain. Weigand, John D., photos by. 2011. (Illus.). 38p. pap. 12.95 *(978-1-935630-56-2(3))* Bellissima Publishing, LLC.

Editors of TIME For Kids Magazine. Amazing Sports & Science. 2014. (TIME for Kids Big Books of WHY Ser.). (ENG., Illus.). 48p. (J). (gr. 3-17). mass mkt. 4.99 *(978-1-60320-986-1(7))* Time Inc. Bks.

Egendorf, Laura K. Girls & Sports. 2012. (Issues That Concern You Ser.). (ENG., Illus.). 144p. (gr. 7-10). lib. bdg. 42.00 *(978-0-7377-5693-7(4))* Cengage Gale.

—Performance Enhancing Drugs. 2007. (Compact Research Ser.). (Illus.). 96p. (YA). (gr. 7-12). lib. bdg. 25.95 *(978-1-60152-003-6(4))* ReferencePoint Pr., Inc.

El-Hewie, Mohamed F. Essentials of Weightlifting & Strength Training. 2nd rev. exp. ed. 2005. (Illus.). 700p. lib. bdg. 85.00 *(978-0-9719581-9-7(X))* Shaymaa Publishing Corp.

Eliot, Hannah. Turkeys Strike Out. Spurgeon, Aaron, illus. 2016. (Did You Know? Ser.). (ENG.). 32p. (J). (gr. -1-3). 17.99 *(978-1-4814-5169-7(3))*; pap. 6.99 *(978-1-4814-5168-0(5))* Little Simon. (Little Simon).

Encarnacion, Elizabeth. Sports Stadiums. 2007. (Qeb Buildings at Work Ser.). (Illus.). 36p. (J). (gr. 4-7). lib. bdg. 19.95 *(978-1-59566-372-6(X))* QEB Publishing Inc.

Entrenamiento Deportivo Series, 6 bks., Set. 2003. (Entrenamiento Deportivo Ser.). (SPA & ENG., Illus.). (J). 103.50 *(978-0-8239-6913-5(4)*, Editorial Buenas Letras) Rosen Publishing Group, Inc., The.

ESPN Staff. The ESPN Book, No. 9. 2005. (ENG.). 96p. (J). pap. 3.99 *(978-0-7868-1261-5(3))* Hyperion Pr.

Evans, Gwydion, et al. Ar Dîm Duw: Cyfres o Sesiynau Sydd Yn Defnyddio Byd Chwaraeon I Son Am y Ffydd Gristnogol. 2005. (WEL., Illus.). 24p. pap. *(978-1-85994-036-5(6))* Cyhoeddiadau'r Gair.

Extreme! 2010. (Extreme! Ser.). (ENG.). 32p. (gr. 3-4). pap. 1526.40 *(978-1-4296-5204-9(7)*, Fact Finders) Capstone Press of Coughlan Cos.

Extreme Sports, 6 bks. Incl. In-Line Skating. Woods, Bob. lib. bdg. 23.00 *(978-0-8368-3722-3(3))*; Mountain Biking. Kelley, K. C. lib. bdg. 23.00 *(978-0-8368-3723-0(1))*; Skateboarding. Kelley, K. C. lib. bdg. 23.00 *(978-0-8368-3724-7(X))*; Snowboarding. Woods, Bob. lib. bdg. 23.00 *(978-0-8368-3725-4(8))*; Stunt Bicycle Riding. Kelley, K. C. (J). lib. bdg. 23.00 *(978-0-8368-3726-1(6))*; Water Sports. Woods, Bob. lib. bdg. 23.00 *(978-0-8368-3727-8(4))*; 24p. (gr. 2-5). 2003., Gareth Stevens Learning Library (Illus.). 2003. Set lib. bdg. 127.60 o.p. *(978-0-8368-3721-6(5))* Stevens, Gareth Publishing LLLP.

The Extreme Sports Collection, 8 bks. Incl. Bicycle Stunt Riding! Catch Air. Hayhurst, Chris. (YA). 2000. lib. bdg. 31.95 *(978-0-8239-3011-1(4)*, EXBIST); In-Line Skating! Get Aggressive. Kaminker, Laura. (YA). 1999. lib. bdg. 31.95 *(978-0-8239-3012-8(2)*, EXSKAT, Rosen Reference); Mountain Biking! Get on the Trail. Hayhurst, Chris. (YA). 2000. lib. bdg. 31.95 *(978-0-8239-3013-5(0)*, EXMOBI, Rosen Reference); Rock & Ice Climbing! Top the Tower. Roberts, Jeremy. (YA). 2000. lib. bdg. 31.95 *(978-0-8239-3009-8(2)*, EXROIC, Rosen Reference); Skateboarding! Surf the Pavement. Burke, L. M. (J). 2000. lib. bdg. 31.95 *(978-0-8239-3014-2(9)*, EXSKBO, Rosen Reference); Skydiving! Take the Leap. Roberts, Jeremy. (YA). 1999. lib. bdg. 31.95 *(978-0-8239-3015-9(7)*, EXSKDI, Rosen Reference); Snowboarding! Shred the Powder. Hayhurst, Chris. (YA). 1999. lib. bdg. 31.95 *(978-0-8239-3010-4(6)*, EXSNBO, Rosen Reference); Wakeboarding! Throw a Tantrum. Hayhurst, Chris. (YA). 2000. lib. bdg. 31.95 *(978-0-8239-3008-1(4)*, EXWABO, Rosen Reference); 64p. (gr. 5-8). (Illus.). Set lib. bdg. 212.00 o.p. *(978-0-8239-9038-2(9)*, EXSPCO, Rosen Reference) Rosen Publishing Group, Inc., The.

Felix, Rebecca. Patterns in Sports. 2015. (21st Century Basic Skills Library: Patterns All Around Ser.). (ENG., Illus.). 24p. (J). (gr. k-3). 24.21 *(978-1-63188-921-9(4)*, 206008) Cherry Lake Publishing.

—They Won One! 2015. (Hear Homophones Here Ser.). 16p. (J). 25.65 *(978-1-60753-573-7(4))* Amicus Publishing.

Ferguson. Coaches & Fitness Professionals. 2nd rev. ed. 2008. (Careers in Focus Ser.). 188p. (gr. 6-12). 32.95 *(978-0-8160-7284-2(1)*, Ferguson Publishing Co.) Facts On File, Inc.

—Sports. 4th rev. ed. 2008. (Careers in Focus Ser.). 204p. (gr. 6-12). 32.95 *(978-0-8160-7287-3(6)*, Ferguson Publishing Co.) Facts On File, Inc.

Fisher, Doris & Gibbs, D. L. Bowling Alley Adjectives. Angle, Scott & Chandler, Jeff, illus. 2008. (Grammar All-Stars Ser.). 32p. (J). (gr. 2-5). lib. bdg. 26.00 *(978-0-8368-8901-7(0)*, Gareth Stevens Learning Library) Stevens, Gareth Publishing LLLP.

—Bowling Alley Adjectives, 6 vols. Chandler, Jeff, illus. 2008. (Grammar All-Stars: the Parts of Speech Ser.). 32p. (gr. 2-5). pap. 10.50 *(978-0-8368-8908-6(8)*, Gareth Stevens Learning Library) Stevens, Gareth Publishing LLLP.

—Grammar All-Stars: Parts of Speech, 6 vols. Angle, Scott, illus. 2008. (Grammar All-Stars Ser.). 32p. (gr. 2-5). pap. 10.50 *(978-0-8368-8913-0(4))*; pap. 10.50 *(978-0-8368-8910-9(X))*; pap. 10.50 *(978-0-8368-8912-3(6))* Stevens, Gareth Publishing LLLP. (Gareth Stevens Learning Library).

—Hole-in-One Adverbs. Chandler, Jeff, illus. 2008. (Grammar All-Stars Ser.). 32p. (J). (gr. 2-5). lib. bdg. 26.00 *(978-0-8368-8902-4(9)*, Gareth Stevens Learning Library) Stevens, Gareth Publishing LLLP.

—Hole-in-One Adverbs. Angle, Scott, illus. 2008. (Grammar All-Stars Ser.). 32p. (gr. 2-5). pap. 10.50 *(978-0-8368-8909-3(6)*, Gareth Stevens Learning Library) Stevens, Gareth Publishing LLLP.

—Home Run Verbs. Angle, Scott & Roper, Robert, illus. 2008. (Grammar All-Stars Ser.). 32p. (J). (gr. 2-5). lib. bdg. 26.00 *(978-0-8368-8903-1(7)*, Gareth Stevens Learning Library) Stevens, Gareth Publishing LLLP.

—Slam Dunk Pronouns. Chandler, Jeff, photos by. 2008. (Grammar All-Stars Ser.). (Illus.). 32p. (J). (gr. 2-5). lib. bdg. 26.00 *(978-0-8368-8904-8(5)*, Gareth Stevens Learning Library) Stevens, Gareth Publishing LLLP.

—Slam dunk Pronouns, 6 vols. Angle, Scott, illus. 2008. (Grammar All-Stars Ser.). 32p. (gr. 2-5). pap. 10.50 *(978-0-8368-8911-6(8)*, Gareth Stevens Learning Library) Stevens, Gareth Publishing LLLP.

—Tennis Court Conjunctions. Rose, Drew, illus. 2008. (Grammar All-Stars Ser.). 32p. (J). (gr. 2-5). lib. bdg. 26.00 *(978-0-8368-8905-5(3)*, Gareth Stevens Learning Library) Stevens, Gareth Publishing LLLP.

—Touchdown Nouns. Angle, Scott, illus. 2008. (Grammar All-Stars Ser.). 32p. (J). (gr. 2-5). lib. bdg. 26.00 *(978-0-8368-8906-2(1)*, Gareth Stevens Learning Library) Stevens, Gareth Publishing LLLP.

Fitzpatrick, Tom & Grogan, Jerry. All about Gaelic Football. 2004. (ENG., Illus.). 32p. pap. 15.95 *(978-0-86278-892-6(7))* O'Brien Pr., Ltd., The IRL. Dist: Dufour Editions, Inc.

Forest, Christopher. The Kids' Guide to Sports Ethics, 1 vol. 2014. (SI Kids Guide Bks.). (ENG.). 48p. (gr. 4-9). lib. bdg. 31.99 *(978-1-4765-4153-2(1))* Capstone Press of Coughlan Cos.

Frederick, Shane. The Kids' Guide to Sports Media, 1 vol. 2014. (SI Kids Guide Bks.). (ENG.). 48p. (gr. 4-9). lib. bdg. 31.99 *(978-1-4765-4152-5(3))* Capstone Press of Coughlan Cos.

—Stamina Training for Teen Athletes: Exercises to Take Your Game to the Next Level, 1 vol. 2012. (Sports Training Zone Ser.). (ENG.). 48p. (gr. 4-5). pap. 8.19 *(978-1-4296-8001-1(6))*; lib. bdg. 31.99 *(978-1-4296-7679-3(5))* Capstone Press of Coughlan Cos.

Frederick, Shane & Braun, Eric. Sports Stats & Stories. 2016. (Sports Stats & Stories Ser.). (ENG.). 48p. (gr. 4-6). 127.96 *(978-1-4914-8724-2(0))* Capstone Press of Coughlan Cos.

Frederick, Shane & Hetrick, Hans. Record Breakers. 2017. (Record Breakers Ser.). (ENG.). 32p. (gr. 3-4). 109.28 *(978-1-5157-3801-5(9))* Capstone Press of Coughlan Cos.

Frederick, Shane, et al. For the Record. 2012. (For the Record Ser.). (ENG.). 64p. (gr. 4-6). pap. 17.90 *(978-1-4296-9436-0(X))*; pap. 214.80 *(978-1-4296-9437-7(8))*; lib. bdg. 138.60 *(978-1-4296-9181-9(6))* Capstone Press of Coughlan Cos.

—High-Tech Sports. 2013. (High-Tech Sports Ser.). (ENG.). 48p. (gr. 3-9). pap. 35.80 *(978-1-62065-914-4(X))* Capstone Press of Coughlan Cos.

Free Spirit Publishing. Character in Sports: Quotes, Prompts, & Stories about Being Your Best — On & off the Field. 2015. (In a Jar(r) Ser.). (ENG.). (J). (gr. 3-7). 9.99 *(978-1-57542-489-7(4))* Free Spirit Publishing, Inc.

Freedman, Jeri. Dream Jobs in Sports Management & Administration. 2012. (Great Careers in the Sports Industry Ser.). (ENG., Illus.). 136p. (J). (gr. 7-12). lib. bdg. 39.95 *(978-1-4488-6901-5(3))* Rosen Publishing Group, Inc., The.

Fridell, Ron. Sports Technology. 2009. pap. 52.95 *(978-0-7613-4785-9(2))* 2008. (ENG.). 48p. (gr. 4-8). 27.93 *(978-0-8225-7587-0(6))* Lerner Publishing Group.

Furgang, Kathy. Dream Jobs in Sports Law. 2014. (Great Careers in the Sports Industry Ser.). (Illus.). 160p. (J). (gr. 7-12). 40.95 *(978-1-4777-7527-1(7))* Rosen Publishing Group, Inc., The.

Furgang, Kathy & Furgang, Adam. Dream Jobs in Stadium & Sports Facility Operations. 2014. (Great Careers in the Sports Industry Ser.). (Illus.). 160p. (J). (gr. 7-12). 40.95 *(978-1-4777-7529-5(3))* Rosen Publishing Group, Inc., The.

Gaarder-Juntti, Oona. Shapes in Sports, 1 vol. 2013. (Shapes Everywhere Ser.). (ENG.). 24p. (gr. k-4). lib. bdg. 25.65 *(978-1-61783-415-8(7)*, Super SandCastle) ABDO Publishing Co.

Galvin, Laura. Oh Where, Oh Where Has My Little Dog Gone? Villnave, Erica Pelton, illus. 2008. (ENG.). 32p. (J). (gr. -1-2). 9.95 *(978-1-59249-860-4(4))* Soundprints.

Game Day: From the Locker Room to the Press Box (and Everything in Between) (Game Day (Sports Illustrated for Kids) Ser.). (ENG.). 32p. (gr. 3-4). 2011. pap. 190.80

(978-1-4296-6451-6(7)) 2010. pap. 31.80
(978-1-4296-6287-1(5)) Capstone Press of Coughlan Cos.

Gane, Declan. So You Want to Be Captain? Top Tips from Sporting Heroes. 2012. (ENG., Illus.). 96p. (J). 14.95 (978-1-4081-3183-1(8), 9781408131831, Bloomsbury Sport) Bloomsbury Publishing USA.

Gardner, Jane P. Sports Science, Vol. 11. Lewin, Russ, ed. 2015. (Science 24/7 Ser.). (Illus.). 48p. (J). (gr. 5). lib. bdg. 20.95 (978-1-4222-3414-3(2)) Mason Crest.

Gardner, Robert. The Physics of Sports Science Projects. 2013. (Exploring Hands-On Science Projects Ser.). 128p. (J). (gr. 5-12). pap. 10.95 (978-1-4644-0222-7(1)); lib. bdg. 27.94 (978-0-7660-4146-2(8)) Enslow Pubs., Inc.

Gardner, Robert, et al. Ace Your Sports Science Project: Great Science Fair Ideas. 2009. (Ace Your Physics Science Project Ser.). (Illus.). 128p. (J). (gr. 5-18). lib. bdg 33.27 (978-0-7660-3229-3(9)) Enslow Pubs., Inc.

Gerber, Larry. Dream Jobs in Sports Refereeing. 2014. (Great Careers in the Sports Industry Ser.). (Illus.). 160p. (J). (gr. 7-12). 40.95 (978-1-4777-7525-7(0)) Rosen Publishing Group, Inc., The.

Gifford, Clive. Sports. 2010. (Healthy Lifestyles Ser.). 48p. (J). 35.65 (978-1-60753-088-6(0)) Amicus Publishing.

—Teamwork in Soccer. 2010. (Spotlight on Soccer Ser.). (Illus.). 32p. (J). (gr. 3-6). lib. bdg. 25.25 (978-1-61532-609-9(X), PowerKids Pr.) Rosen Publishing Group, Inc., The.

—Tell Me about Sports, 8 vols., Set. Incl. Baseball. 28.50 (978-0-7614-4453-4(X)); Basketball. 28.50 (978-0-7614-4455-8(6)); Football. 28.50 (978-0-7614-4456-5(4)); Martial Arts. 28.50 (978-0-7614-4457-2(2)); Running. 28.50 (978-0-7614-4459-6(9)); Soccer. 28.50 (978-0-7614-4460-2(2)); Swimming. (Illus.). (J). 28.50 (978-0-7614-4462-6(9)); Tennis. 28.50 (978-0-7614-4463-3(7)); 32p. (gr. 3-5). (Tell Me about Sports Ser.). 2009. Set lib. bdg. 228.00 o.p. (978-0-7614-4452-7(1)) Marshall Cavendish Corp.

Gigliotti, Jim. Animal Sports, 1 vol. 2011. (Extreme Sports Ser.). (ENG., Illus.). 32p. (gr. 1-2). pap. 8.29 (978-1-4109-4223-4(6)); 29.99 (978-1-4109-4216-6(3)) Heinemann-Raintree. (Read Me!).

—Sports Arena & Event Management, Vol. 10. Ferrer, Al, ed. 2015. (Careers off the Field Ser.). (Illus.). 64p. (J). (gr. 7). lib. bdg. 23.95 (978-1-4222-3266-8(2)) Mason Crest.

—STEM in Sports. 2015. (STEM in Sports Ser.). (Illus.). 64p. (J). (gr. 7). 23.95 (978-1-4222-3233-0(6)) Mason Crest.

Ginsburg, Richard D., et al. Whose Game Is It, Anyway? A Guide to Helping Your Child Get the Most from Sports, Organized by Age & Stage. 2006. (ENG.). 336p. pap. 18.95 (978-0-618-47460-8(9)) Houghton Mifflin Harcourt Publishing Co.

Girls Join the Team. 2016. (Girls Join the Team Ser.). 24p. (gr. 3-3). 141.60 (978-1-5081-4900-2(3)); pap. 49.50 (978-1-4994-2472-0(8)) Rosen Publishing Group, Inc., The. (PowerKids Pr.).

Gitlin, Martin. Dream Jobs in Sports Finance & Administration. 2014. (Great Careers in the Sports Industry Ser.). (Illus.). 160p. (YA). (gr. 7-12). 40.95 (978-1-4777-7520-2(X)) Rosen Publishing Group, Inc., The.

—Dream Jobs in Sports Scouting. 2014. (Great Careers in the Sports Industry Ser.). (Illus.). 160p. (YA). (gr. 7-12). 40.95 (978-1-4777-7518-9(8)) Rosen Publishing Group, Inc., The.

—Playing Pro Basketball. 2014. (Playing Pro Sports Ser.). (ENG., Illus.). 64p. (gr. 4-8). lib. bdg. 26.60 (978-1-4677-3845-3(X), Lerner Pubns.) Lerner Publishing Group.

—Referee. 2013. (Earning $50,000 - $100,000 with a High School Diploma or Less Ser.: 14). 64p. (J). (gr. 7-18). 22.95 (978-1-4222-2899-9(1)) Mason Crest.

Gitlin, Martin, et al. Winner Takes All. 2012. (Winner Takes All Ser.). (ENG.). 32p. (gr. 3-4). pap. 14.38 (978-1-4296-9446-9(7)) Capstone Press of Coughlan Cos.

Gitlin, Marty. A Dream Job As a Sports Statistician. 2017. (J). **(978-1-5383-8138-0(9))** Rosen Publishing Group, Inc., The.

Goh, Michelle. The 10 Best Cinderella Stories in Sports. 2008. 14.99 (978-1-55448-495-9(2)) Scholastic Library Publishing.

Going Pro. 2015. (Going Pro Ser.). (ENG.). 32p. (J). (gr. 3-4). 159.60 (978-1-4824-1647-3(6)) Stevens, Gareth Publishing LLLP.

Gonzalez, Tony & Brown, Greg. Tony Gonzalez: Catch & Connect. 2004. (Football Ser.). (Illus.). 48p. (J). 15.95 (978-0-9634650-8-5(2)) Positively for Kids, Inc.

Goodstein, Madeline. Sports Science Fair Projects. 2015. (Prize-Winning Science Fair Projects Ser.). (ENG.). 128p. (J). (gr. 7-7). lib. bdg. 37.27 (978-0-7660-7026-4(3)) Enslow Pubs., Inc.

Goossens, Jesse. Right to Play. 2011. (ENG., Illus.). 144p. (J). (gr. 5). pap. 20.95 (978-1-935954-10-1(5), 9781935954101) Lemniscaat USA.

Goranson, Christopher D. Danny Harf: Wakeboarding Superstar. 2005. (Extreme Sports Biographies Ser.). (Illus.). 64p. (YA). (gr. 5-9). lib. bdg. 31.95 (978-1-4042-0066-1(5)) Rosen Publishing Group, Inc., The.

Gordon, Sharon. Somos un Equipo. 2006. (Bookworms Ser.). (SPA & ENG., Illus.). 24p. (gr. k-1). lib. bdg. 15.95 (978-0-7614-2357-7(5), Benchmark Bks.) Marshall Cavendish Corp.

—We Are a Team. 2005. (Bookworms Ser.). (ENG & SPA., Illus.). 24p. (J). (gr. 3-7). lib. bdg. 22.79 (978-0-7614-1994-5(2), Benchmark Bks.) Marshall Cavendish Corp.

—We Are a Team/Somos un Equipo. 2006. (Bookworms Ser.). (ENG & SPA., Illus.). 24p. (gr. k-1). lib. bdg. 15.95 (978-0-7614-2436-9(9)) Marshall Cavendish Corp.

Gordon, Sharon & National Geographic Learning Staff. We Are a Team. 2010. (Rise & Shine Ser.). (ENG.). (C). pap. 15.95 (978-0-7614-3271-5(X)) National Geographic School Publishing, Inc.

Gorman, Jacqueline Laks. The Playground: El Parque. 2005. (I Like to Visit/ Me gusta visitar Ser.). (ENG & SPA., Illus.). 24p. (gr. k-3). pap. 8.15 (978-0-8368-4605-8(2), Weekly Reader Leveled Readers) Stevens, Gareth Publishing LLLP.

Gorman, Jacqueline Laks & Laks Gorman, Jacqueline. The Playground/El Parque. 2005. (I Like to Visit/Me Gusta Visitar Ser.). (SPA & ENG., Illus.). 24p. (gr. k-3). lib. bdg. 22.00 (978-0-8368-4598-3(6), Weekly Reader Leveled Readers) Stevens, Gareth Publishing LLLP.

Gosman, Gillian. Simple Machines in Sports. 2014. (Simple Machines Everywhere Ser.). (Illus.). 24p. (J). (gr. k-3). 23.60 (978-1-4777-6829-7(7), PowerKids Pr.) Rosen Publishing Group, Inc., The.

Graubart, Norman D. The Science of Basketball. 2015. (Sports Science Ser.). (ENG., Illus.). 32p. (J). (gr. 4-5). pap. 10.00 (978-1-4994-1064-8(6), PowerKids Pr.) Rosen Publishing Group, Inc., The.

Great Careers in the Sports Industry: Set 2. 2014. (Great Careers in the Sports Industry Ser.). 160p. (YA). (gr. 7-12). 245.70 (978-1-4777-7522-6(6)) Rosen Publishing Group, Inc., The.

Great Careers in the Sports Industry: Sets 1-2. 2014. (Great Careers in the Sports Industry Ser.). 160p. (YA). (gr. 7-12). 409.50 (978-1-4777-8098-5(X)) Rosen Publishing Group, Inc., The.

Great Record-Breakers in Sports. (Illus.). (J). (gr. k-5). (978-0-8239-7066-7(3)) Rosen Publishing Group, Inc., The.

Greathead, Helen. Supersports. 2016. (What Would You Choose? Ser.). 00032p. (J). pap. 10.50 **(978-1-4824-6118-3(8))** Stevens, Gareth Publishing LLLP.

Green, Sara. Nike. (Nike Ser.). 24p. (J). (gr. 3-8). 2017. pap. 7.99 **(978-1-61891-250-3(X))** 2015. (ENG., Illus.). 25.95 (978-1-62617-210-4(2)) Bellwether Media. (Pilot Bks.).

Greenhaven Press Editors & Schwartz, Heather E. Cheerleading. 2012. (Science Behind Sports Ser.). (ENG., Illus.). 128p. (gr. 7-10). lib. bdg. 39.40 (978-1-4205-0818-5(0), Lucent Bks.) Cengage Gale.

Group/McGraw-Hill, Wright. Take-Twos Sports Vol. 2: Early Fluency - Complete Kit. (gr. 2-18). 420.50 (978-0-322-09173-3(X)) Wright Group/McGraw-Hill.

—Take-Twos Sports Vol. 2: Early Fluency - Student Book Set - 1 Each of 12 Titles. (gr. 2-18). 69.95 (978-0-322-09301-0(5)) Wright Group/McGraw-Hill.

Guillain, Charlotte. Extreme Athletes: True Stories of Amazing Sporting Adventurers, 1 vol. 2014. (Ultimate Adventurers Ser.). (ENG., Illus.). 48p. (gr. 6-6). lib. bdg. 29.99 (978-1-4109-5418-3(8)) Heinemann-Raintree.

—Sports, 1 vol. 2012. (Jobs If You Like... Ser.). (ENG.). 32p. (gr. 1-3). pap. 8.29 (978-1-4329-6823-6(8), Heinemann First Library) Heinemann-Raintree.

Gutman, Dan. My Weird School Fast Facts: Sports. Paillot, Jim, illus. 2016. (My Weird School Fast Facts Ser.). 176p. (J). (gr. 1-5). pap. 5.99 (978-0-06-230617-3(0)) HarperCollins Pubs.

Haldy, Emma E. Florence Griffith Joyner. Bane, Jeff, illus. 2016. (My Early Library: My Itty-Bitty Bio Ser.). (ENG.). 24p. (J). (gr. k-1). 28.50 (978-1-63471-019-0(3), 208156) Cherry Lake Publishing.

Hamilton, S. L. Base Jumping. 2010. (Xtreme Sports Ser.). 32p. (gr. 3-9). 27.07 (978-1-61613-001-5(6), A&D Xtreme) ABDO Publishing Co.

Hamilton, Tracy Brown. Dream Jobs in Sports Equipment Design. 2017. (J). **(978-1-5383-8140-3(0))** Rosen Publishing Group, Inc., The.

Hammelef, Danielle S. Behind-The-Scenes Pro Sports Careers. 2017. (Behind the Glamour Ser.). (ENG.). 64p. (gr. 4-5). lib. bdg. 31.32 (978-1-5157-4896-0(0)) Capstone Press of Coughlan Cos.

Hammond, Tim & Dorling Kindersley Publishing Staff. Sports. 2005. (DK Eyewitness Bks.). (ENG., Illus.). 72p. (J). (gr. 3-7). 16.99 (978-0-7566-1390-7(6), DK Children) Dorling Kindersley Publishing, Inc.

Harris, Tim. Sport: Almost Everything You Ever Wanted to Know. 2009. (ENG., Illus.). 960p. pap. 24.95 (978-0-224-08021-7(0)) Random Hse. GBR. Dist: Independent Pubs. Group.

Hay DeSimone, Corkey. Future Sports Legend Board Book: An Early Introduction to Sports in Maryland. Hay DeSimone, Corkey, illus. 2006. (Illus.). (J). bds. 4.99 (978-0-9747921-5-6(2)) Gentle Giraffe Pr.

Heling, Kathryn & Hembrook, Deborah. Clothesline Clues to Sports People Play. Davies, Andy Robert, illus. 2015. (ENG.). 40p. (J). (gr. -1-2). lib. bdg. 14.95 (978-1-58089-602-3(2)) Charlesbridge Publishing, Inc.

Herweck, Diana. En el Juego: La Vida de un Atleta. 2017. (TIME for Kids en Español - Level 4 Ser.). (SPA., Illus.). 48p. (gr. 4-4). lib. bdg. 31.99 (978-1-5157-5129-8(5)) Time for Kids Inc AUS. Dist: Capstone Pub.

—In the Game: An Athlete's Life, 1 vol. 2nd rev. ed. 2013. (Nonfiction Readers Ser.). (ENG., Illus.). 48p. (J). (gr. 4-4). pap. 29.96 (978-1-4807-1100-6(4)) Shell Educational Publishing.

Herzog, Brad. Inspiring Stories of Sportsmanship. 2014. (Count on Me: Sports Ser.). (ENG., Illus.). 96p. (J). (gr. 4-7). pap. 9.99 (978-1-57542-455-2(X)) Free Spirit Publishing, Inc.

—A Is for Amazing Moments: A Sports Alphabet. Rose, Melanie, illus. 2008. (Sports Ser.). (ENG.). 40p. (J). (gr. -1-5). 17.95 (978-1-58536-360-5(X)) Sleeping Bear Pr.

—A Is for Amazing Moments: A Sports Alphabet. Rose, Melanie, illus. 2015. (Av2 Fiction Readalong 2016 Ser.). (ENG.). (J). (gr. 1-4). lib. bdg. 34.28 (978-1-4896-3729-1(X), AV2 by Weigl) Weigl Pubs., Inc.

—Remarkable Stories of Teamwork in Sports. 2014. (Count on Me: Sports Ser.). (ENG., Illus.). 96p. (J). (gr. 4-7). pap. 9.99 (978-1-57542-479-8(7)) Free Spirit Publishing, Inc.

Hetrick, Hans. Breaking Barriers. 2017. (Real Heroes of Sports Ser.). (ENG., Illus.). 32p. (gr. 3-4). lib. bdg. 25.99 (978-1-5157-4434-4(5)) Capstone Press of Coughlan Cos.

—This Book's Got Game: A Collection of Awesome Sports Trivia, 1 vol. 2012. (Super Trivia Collection). (ENG.). 32p. (gr. 3-4). 27.99 (978-1-4296-7656-4(6), Edge Bks.) Capstone Press of Coughlan Cos.

Hetrick, Hans, et al. Winner Takes All. 2012. (Winner Takes All Ser.). (ENG.). 32p. (gr. 3-4). lib. bdg. 111.96 (978-1-4296-6576-6(9)) Capstone Press of Coughlan Cos.

High Five Reading: Sports / Adventure [Really Good Stuff]. 2010. (High Five Reading Ser.). pap. 90.00 (978-1-4296-5360-2(4)) Red Brick Learning.

Highlights for Children, compiled by. Good Sports. 2009. (Hidden Pictures Playground Ser.). (ENG., Illus.). 32p. (J). (gr. -1-1). pap. 5.49 (978-0-87534-320-4(1)) Highlights for Children.

Hoena, B. A. The Science of Hockey with Max Axiom, Super Scientist. 2015. (Science of Sports with Max Axiom Ser.). (ENG., Illus.). 32p. (gr. 3-4). lib. bdg. 30.65 (978-1-4914-6086-3(5)) Capstone Press of Coughlan Cos.

Hofer, Charles. Motorcycles. 2008. (World's Fastest Machines Ser.). (Illus.). 24p. (J). (gr. 3-7). lib. bdg. 22.60 (978-1-4042-4177-0(9), PowerKids Pr.) Rosen Publishing Group, Inc., The.

Hogenkamp, S. All Sorts of Sports: Learning the or Sound. 2009. (PowerPhonics Ser.). 24p. (gr. 1-1). 39.90 (978-1-60851-431-1(5), PowerKids Pr.) Rosen Publishing Group, Inc., The.

Holden, Pam. We Like Sports. 2015. (ENG., Illus.). 16p. (-1). pap. (978-1-77654-120-1(0), Red Rocket Readers) Flying Start Bks.

Holder, Sherie. More Amazing Sports Photos: More Funny, Famous, & Fantastic Photographs from the World of Sports. rev. ed. Date not set. 32p. (J). pap. 3.95 (978-1-886749-13-9(2)) Sports Illustrated For Kids.

Hollow, Michele C. Nifty Thrifty Sports Crafts. Ponte, June, illus. 2007. (Nifty Thrifty Crafts for Kids Ser.). 32p. (J). (gr. 3-4). lib. bdg. 23.94 (978-0-7660-2782-4(1), Enslow Elementary) Enslow Pubs., Inc.

Horn, Geoffrey M. Sports Therapist. 2008. (Cool Careers Ser.). 32p. (gr. 5-8). pap. 10.50 (978-0-8368-9329-8(8)); lib. bdg. 26.00 (978-0-8368-9196-6(1)) Stevens, Gareth Publishing LLLP.

Hot Shots: Grandes Idolos Set 3.Tr. of Grandes idolos. (ENG & SPA., Illus.). (J). (gr. 3-6). 103.50 (978-0-8239-7199-2(6), Editorial Buenas Letras) Rosen Publishing Group, Inc., The.

Howell, Brian. Playing Pro Baseball. 2014. (Playing Pro Sports Ser.). (ENG., Illus.). 64p. (gr. 4-8). lib. bdg. 26.60 (978-1-4677-3846-0(8), Lerner Pubns.) Lerner Publishing Group.

—Sports, 1 vol. 2011. (Inside the Industry Ser.). (ENG., Illus.). 112p. (J). (gr. 6-12). lib. bdg. 35.64 (978-1-61714-804-0(0), Essential Library) ABDO Publishing Co.

Howse, Jennifer. Sports: African American History. 2011. (J). (gr. 5-8). pap. 14.95 (978-1-61690-664-1(2), AV2 by Weigl); (Illus.). 48p. (YA). (gr. 1-4). 29.99 (978-1-61690-660-3(X)) Weigl Pubs., Inc.

Hudson, Amanda & Nations, Susan. This Is My Ball/Ésta Es Mi Pelota. 2008. (Our Toys/Nuestros Juguetes Ser.). (SPA & ENG., Illus.). 16p. (J). (gr. -1-2). lib. bdg. 19.00 (978-0-8368-9256-7(9), Weekly Reader Leveled Readers) Stevens, Gareth Publishing LLLP.

Hughes, Morgan. Cheerleading. 2005. (Junior Sports Ser.). (Illus.). 32p. (gr. 2-4). 19.95 (978-1-59515-194-0(X)) Rourke Educational Media.

Hurley, Michael. Fantastic Sports Facts. 2013. (Fantastic Sports Facts Ser.). (ENG.). 32p. (gr. 1-3). pap. 47.94 (978-1-4109-5116-8(2)); lib. bdg. 149.95 (978-1-4109-5109-0(X)) Heinemann-Raintree. (Read Me!).

Ingham, Anne. The Ball Book. 2012. 28p. pap. 21.99 (978-1-4691-8747-1(7)) Xlibris Corp.

Ivy, Darlene Sigda. Working in Sports. 2018. (ENG.). 32p. (gr. 3-6). **(978-1-63235-449-5(7)**, 12-Story Library) Pr. Room Editions LLC.

Jacobson, Ryan. Exciting Entertainment Inventions. 2013. (Awesome Inventions You Use Every Day Ser.). (ENG., Illus.). 32p. (gr. 3-6). lib. bdg. 26.60 (978-1-4677-1094-7(6), Lerner Pubns.) Lerner Publishing Group.

Johanson, Paula. Supercharged Sports. 2017. 32p. (J). **(978-0-7787-3603-5(2))** Crabtree Publishing Co.

Johnson, Jeremy. Unusual & Awesome Jobs in Sports: Pro Team Mascot, Pit Crew Member, & More. 2015. (You Get Paid for THAT? Ser.). (ENG.). 32p. (gr. 3-4). lib. bdg. 27.99 (978-1-4914-2032-4(4), Edge Bks.) Capstone Press of Coughlan Cos.

Jones, Rob Lloyd. Look Inside Sports. 2012. (Look Inside Board Bks). 16p. (J). bds. 15.99 (978-0-7945-3250-5(0), Usborne) EDC Publishing.

Jones, Tammy. I Like to Play Sports. 2009. (Sight Word Readers Set A Ser.). (J). 3.49 net. (978-1-60719-135-3(0)) Newmark Learning LLC.

Kallen, Stuart A. Careers If You Like Sports. 2017. (Career Discovery Ser.). (ENG.). 80p. (YA). (gr. 5-12). **(978-1-68282-142-8(0))** ReferencePoint Pr., Inc.

Kamberg, Mary-Lane. A Dream Job As a Sports Agent. 2017. (J). **(978-1-5383-8136-6(2))** Rosen Publishing Group, Inc., The.

Katz, Ben & Nyman, Debbie. The 10 Greatest Sports Dynasties. 2008. 14.99 (978-1-55448-525-3(8)) Scholastic Library Publishing.

Kaufman, Gabriel. Sporting Events: From Baseball to Skateboarding. 2006. (Which Came First? Ser.). (Illus.). 32p. (YA). (gr. 3-6). lib. bdg. 25.27 (978-1-59716-132-9(2)) Bearport Publishing Co., Inc.

Kawa, Katie. Mujeres en Los Deportes (Women in Sports) 2015. (Ellas Abrieron Camino (Women Groundbreakers) Ser.). (ENG & SPA.). 32p. (J). (gr. 4-5). 26.25 (978-1-4994-0518-7(9), PowerKids Pr.) Rosen Publishing Group, Inc., The.

—Staying Fit with Sports! 2013. (Rosen Readers Ser.). (ENG.). 24p. (J). (gr. 3-4). pap. 8.25 (978-1-4777-2590-0(3)); pap. 49.50 (978-1-4777-2592-4(X)) Rosen Publishing Group, Inc., The. (Rosen Classroom).

—Women in Sports. 2015. (Women Groundbreakers Ser.). (ENG., Illus.). 32p. (J). (gr. 4-5). 26.25 (978-1-4994-1095-2(6), PowerKids Pr.) Rosen Publishing Group, Inc., The.

Kelly, David A. Miracle Mud: Lena Blackburne & the Secret Mud That Changed Baseball. Dominguez, Oliver, illus. 2013. (ENG.). 32p. (J). (gr. 2-5). lib. bdg. 16.95 (978-0-7613-8092-4(2), Millbrook Pr.) Lerner Publishing Group.

Kenney, Karen Latchana. Cool Sports Parties: Perfect Party Planning for Kids, 1 vol. 2012. (Cool Parties Ser.). (ENG., Illus.). 32p. (J). (gr. 3-6). 28.50 (978-1-61714-977-1(2)) ABDO Publishing Co.

Kerr, Jim. Sports. 2010. (Media Power Ser.). 48p. (YA). (gr. 5-9). 35.65 (978-1-60753-115-9(1)) Amicus Publishing.

Kleist, Nick. Super Sports Numbers: Understand Place Value. 2014. (Math Masters: Number & Operations in Base Ten Ser.). 24p. (J). (gr. 2-3). 23.60 (978-1-4777-6401-5(1)); (ENG.). pap. 8.25 (978-1-4777-4666-0(8)) Rosen Publishing Group, Inc., The. (Rosen Classroom).

Kortemeier, Tom. Pro Sports by the Numbers. 2016. (Pro Sports by the Numbers Ser.). (ENG.). 32p. (gr. 3-4). 111.96 (978-1-4914-9073-0(X), Edge Bks.) Capstone Press of Coughlan Cos.

Koya, Lena & La Bella, Laura. Women Athletes. 2017. (J). **(978-1-5081-7718-0(X))** Rosen Publishing Group, Inc., The.

Kreisman, Rachelle. Things We Do: A Kids' Guide to Community Activity. Haggerty, Tim, illus. 2015. (Start Smart: Community Ser.). (ENG.). 32p. (gr. 1-3). 26.65 (978-1-937529-51-2(7)) Red Chair Pr.

Kurtz, Kevin. What Makes Sports Gear Safer? 2015. (ENG., Illus.). 32p. (gr. 4-6). (J). 26.65 (978-1-4677-7915-9(6)); 26.65 (978-1-4677-8650-8(0), Lerner Pubns.) Lerner Publishing Group.

Kuskowski, Alex. Know Your Numbers: Sports, 1 vol. 2014. (Numbers 1-20 Ser.). (ENG.). 24p. (J). (gr. k-3). lib. bdg. 24.21 (978-1-62403-268-4(0), SandCastle) ABDO Publishing Co.

La Bella, Laura. Women & Sports. 2012. (Young Woman's Guide to Contemporary Issues Ser.). (ENG., Illus.). 112p. (YA). (gr. 9-12). lib. bdg. 34.60 (978-1-4488-8398-1(9)) Rosen Publishing Group, Inc., The.

Lancaster, Scott B. Fair Play: Making Organized Sports a Great Experience for Your Kids. 2004. 194p. reprint ed. pap. 15.00 (978-0-7567-8419-5(0)) DIANE Publishing Co.

Lang, Elizabeth. Sports Safety. 2013. (Healthy Kids Ser.). (ENG.). 24p. (J). (gr. 1-4). 28.50 (978-1-62323-541-3(3), 206274) Child's World, Inc., The.

Latimer, Clay. Game Day: From the Locker Room to the Press Box (and Everything in Between), 4 vols., Set. Incl. VIP Pass to a Pro Baseball Game Day: From the Locker Room to the Press Box (and Everything in Between) lib. bdg. 27.99 (978-1-4296-5462-3(7)); VIP Pass to a Pro Basketball Game Day: From the Locker Room to the Press Box (and Everything in Between) lib. bdg. 27.99 (978-1-4296-5463-0(5)); VIP Pass to a Pro Hockey Game Day: From the Locker Room to the Press Box (and Everything in Between) lib. bdg. 27.99 (978-1-4296-5464-7(3)); (gr. 3-4). (Game Day (Sports Illustrated for Kids) Ser.). (ENG.). 32p. 2010. Set lib. bdg. 83.97 (978-1-4296-5465-4(1)) Capstone Press of Coughlan Cos.

LeBoutillier, Nate. Ultimate Pro Team Guides, 1 vol., Set. Incl. Ultimate Guide to Pro Basketball Teams. (ENG.). 72p. (gr. 3-4). 2010. lib. bdg. 34.65 (978-1-4296-4821-9(X)); (Ultimate Pro Team Guides (Sports Illustrated for Kids) Ser.). (ENG.). 72p. 2010. Set lib. bdg. 138.60 o.p. (978-1-4296-4823-3(6)) Capstone Press of Coughlan Cos.

Lee, Tony. Greatest Rivalries in Sports, 1 vol. 2013. (Sports' Biggest Moments Ser.). (ENG., Illus.). 64p. (J). (gr. 3-6). lib. bdg. 32.79 (978-1-61783-925-2(6), SportsZone) ABDO Publishing Co.

Let's Talk Sports! 2016. (Let's Talk Sports! Ser.). 00032p. (J). pap. 63.00 **(978-1-4824-5836-7(5))** Stevens, Gareth Publishing LLLP.

Levete, Sarah. Maker Projects for Kids Who Love Sports. 2017. (Be a Maker! Ser.). (ENG.). 32p. (J). (gr. 4-7). **(978-0-7787-2877-1(3))**; (Illus.). pap. **(978-0-7787-2891-7(9))** Crabtree Publishing Co.

Libal, Joyce & Simons, Rae. Professional Athlete & Sports Official. Riggs, Ernestine G. & Gholar, Cheryl, eds. 2013. (Careers with Character Ser.: 18). 96p. (J). (gr. 7-18). 22.95 (978-1-4222-2763-3(4)) Mason Crest.

Lindeen, Mary & Kesselring, Susan. Being Safe on Wheels. McGeehan, Dan & Moore, David, illus. 2011. (Be Safe Ser.). (ENG.). 24p. (J). (gr. k-3). lib. bdg. 27.07 (978-1-60954-371-6(8), 200082) Child's World, Inc., The.

Living Legends of Sports. 2015. (Living Legends of Sports Ser.). (ENG.). 48p. (J). (gr. 5-6). 413.60 (978-1-68048-196-9(7), Britannica Educational Publishing) Rosen Publishing Group, Inc., The.

Living with Sports Injuries. 2010. (Teen's Guides). 208p. (gr. 6-12). 34.95 (978-0-8160-7848-6(3)) Facts On File, Inc.

Loader, Mandy. Amazing Young Sports People, Level 1, 1 vol., Pack. 2009. (ENG.). 48p. pap. 13.25 (978-84-8323-568-3(4)) Cambridge Univ. Pr.

—Amazing Young Sports People Level 1 Beginner/Elementary. 2010. (ENG.). 48p. pap. 11.00 (978-84-8323-572-0(2)) Cambridge Univ. Pr.

Loh-Hagan, Virginia. Extreme Cliff Diving. 2016. (Nailed It! Ser.). (ENG., Illus.). 32p. (J). (gr. 4-8). 29.93 (978-1-63471-089-3(4), 208467, 45th Parallel Press) Cherry Lake Publishing.

—Extreme Downhill Ski Racing. 2016. (Nailed It! Ser.). (ENG., Illus.). 32p. (J). (gr. 4-8). 29.93 (978-1-63471-092-3(4), 208479, 45th Parallel Press) Cherry Lake Publishing.

—Extreme MotoGP. 2016. (Nailed It! Ser.). (ENG., Illus.). 32p. (J). (gr. 4-8). 29.93 (978-1-63471-091-6(6), 208475, 45th Parallel Press) Cherry Lake Publishing.

—Stadiums. 2017. (21st Century Junior Library: Extraordinary Engineering Ser.). (ENG., Illus.). 24p. (J). (gr. 2-5). lib. bdg. 27.07 (978-1-63472-166-0(7), 209236) Cherry Lake Publishing.

Long, Dustin. Greatest Comebacks in Sports, 1 vol. 2013. (Sports' Biggest Moments Ser.). (ENG.). 64p. (gr. 3-6). lib. bdg. 32.79 (978-1-61783-924-5(8), SportsZone) ABDO Publishing Co.

Louck, Cheryl. The ABC's of Motocross. Zielinski, Dave, photos by. 2003. (Illus.). 24p. (J). per. 14.95 (978-0-9744230-0-5(9)) Louck, Cheryl.

Luke, Andrew. Lacrosse, Vol. 13. 2016. (Inside the World of Sports Ser.: Vol. 13). (ENG., Illus.). 80p. (J). (gr. 7-12). 24.95 (978-1-4222-3464-8(9)) Mason Crest.

MacDonald, Margaret. What Does the Referee Do? 2011. (Learn-Abouts Ser.). (Illus.). 16p. (J). pap. 7.95 (978-1-59920-632-5(3)) Black Rabbit Bks.

Mack, Gail. Kickboxing. 2011. (Martial Arts in Action 2 Ser.). 48p. (gr. 6). lib. bdg. 29.93 (978-0-7614-4936-2(1)) Marshall Cavendish Corp.

MacKinnon, Christopher. Canadian Sports Sites for Kids: Places Named for Speedsters, Scorers, & Other Sportsworld Citizens. 2012. (ENG., Illus.). 144p. (J). pap. 14.99 (978-1-4597-0705-4(2)) Dundurn CAN. Dist: Ingram Publisher Services.

—Canadian Sports Sites for Kids: Places Named for Speedsters, Scorers, & Other Sportsworld Citizens (Large Print 16pt) 2013. 208p. pap. (978-1-4596-6305-3(5)) ReadHowYouWant.com, Ltd.

S

MacNab, Chris. Weight Training. 2005. (Sports Injuries Ser.). (Illus.). 64p. (YA). lib. bdg. 19.95 *(978-1-59084-641-4(9))* Mason Crest.

marcovitz, hal. How Serious a Problem Is Drug Use in Sports? 2012. (Illus.). 80p. (J). lib. bdg. *(978-1-60152-448-5(X))* ReferencePoint Pr., Inc.

Marini, Matt. Analytics: Sports Stats & More, Vol. 10. Ferrer, Al, ed. 2015. (Careers off the Field Ser.). (Illus.). 64p. (J). (gr. 7). lib. bdg. 23.95 *(978-1-4222-3265-1(4))* Mason Crest.

Markegard, Blake. Rey Mysterio. 2017. (Rey Mysterio Ser.). 24p. (J). (gr. 3-7). pap. 7.99 ***(978-1-61891-239-8(9)***, Epic Bks.) Bellwether Media.

Marsico, Katie. Ball Game Math. 2014. (Math Everywhere! Ser.). (Illus.). 32p. (gr. 3-4). (J). lib. bdg. 26.60 *(978-1-4677-1885-1(8)*, Lerner Pubns.); pap. 7.95 *(978-1-4677-4512-3(X))* Lerner Publishing Group.

Martin, Oscar, Jr., creator. Sports Legends l.t. ed. 2003. (Illus.). 25p. (J). E-Book 19.95 incl. cd-rom *(978-0-9748416-6-3(8))* Build Your Story.

Marzilli, Alan. Drugs & Sports. 2008. (Point/Counterpoint Ser.). (Illus.). 144p. (C). (gr. 9). 35.00 *(978-0-7910-9553-9(3)*, Chelsea Hse.) Facts On File, Inc.

Mason, Paul. Passport to World Sports. 2011. (Passport to World Sports Ser.). (ENG.). 32p. (gr. 3-4). lib. bdg. 111.96 *(978-1-4296-6881-1(4))*; lib. bdg. 111.96 *(978-1-4296-6880-4(6))* Capstone Press of Coughlan Cos. (Edge Bks.).

—Sports Heroes of Ancient Greece. 2010. (ENG.). 32p. (J). (gr. 3-5). *(978-0-7787-9911-5(5))*; pap. *(978-0-7787-9932-0(8))* Crabtree Publishing Co.

—Training for Sports, 4 vols., Set. Incl. Improving Endurance. 26.50 *(978-1-4488-3300-9(0))*; Improving Flexibility. lib. bdg. 26.50 *(978-1-4488-3299-6(3))*; Improving Speed. 26.50 *(978-1-4488-3302-3(7))*; Improving Strength & Power. 26.50 *(978-1-4488-3301-6(9))*; (YA). (gr. 5-9). (Training for Sports Ser.). (Illus.). 32p. 2011. Set lib. bdg. 101.00 *(978-1-4488-3310-8(8)*, PowerKids Pr.) Rosen Publishing Group, Inc., The.

Mattern, Joanne. Famous Mystics & Psychics. 2004. (gr. 7-10). 27.45 *(978-1-59018-558-2(7))* Cengage Gale.

—So, You Want to Work in Sports? The Ultimate Guide to Exploring the Sports Industry. 2014. (Be What You Want Ser.). (ENG., Illus.). 224p. (J). (gr. 3-7). pap. 9.99 *(978-1-58270-448-7(1))* Aladdin/Beyond Words.

McDaniel, Melissa. Pushing the Limits: A Chapter Book. 2004. (True Tales Ser.). (ENG., Illus.). 48p. (J). 22.50 *(978-0-516-23734-3(9)*, Children's Pr.) Scholastic Library Publishing.

McDonnell, Vincent. The Story of the GAA. 2009. (ENG.). 146p. (J). pap. 13.95 *(978-1-905172-96-2(6))* Collins Pr., The IRL. Dist: Dufour Editions, Inc.

McFee, Shane. Whitewater Rafting. 2008. (Living on the Edge Ser.). (Illus.). 24p. (J). (gr. 2-5). lib. bdg. 22.60 *(978-1-4042-4218-0(X))* Rosen Publishing Group, Inc., The.

McKay, Lucia & Guscott, Maggie. Sports & Hobbies Math. 2005. (Practical Math in Context Ser.). (Illus.). 104p. per. 9.95 *(978-1-56254-766-0(6)*, SP7666) Saddleback Educational Publishing, Inc.

McLeish, Ewan. Sports Industry. 2010. (Closer Look: Global Industries Ser.). (ENG., Illus.). 48p. (J). lib. bdg. 29.25 *(978-1-4358-9634-5(3)*, Rosen Reference) Rosen Publishing Group, Inc., The.

McNeil, Niki, et al. HOCPP 1128 the History of Sports. 2006. spiral bd. 12.50 *(978-1-60308-128-3(3))* In the Hands of a Child.

McPherson, Stephanie Sammartino. Doping in Sports: Winning at Any Cost? 2016. (ENG., Illus.). 104p. (YA). (gr. 7-12). 51.99 *(978-1-4677-9576-0(3)*, Twenty-First Century Bks.) Lerner Publishing Group.

Meeks, Connor. Sports! Have Fun & Stay Healthy. 2013. (InfoMax Readers Ser.). (ENG.). 24p. (J). (gr. 3-4). pap. 49.50 *(978-1-4777-2647-1(0))*; pap. 8.25 *(978-1-4777-2646-4(2))* Rosen Publishing Group, Inc., The. (Rosen Classroom).

Mental X 2003. (Illus.). 32p. (YA). pap. 5.50 *(978-0-9745066-8-5(0))* Sports In Mind.

Milet Publishing Staff. My First Bilingual Book-Sports. 2012. (My First Bilingual Book Ser.). (ENG & TUR., Illus.). 24p. (J). (gr. k — 1). bds. 7.99 *(978-1-84059-761-5(5))* Milet Publishing.

—My First Bilingual Book-Sports (English-Bengali) 2012. (My First Bilingual Book Ser.). (ENG & BEN., Illus.). 24p. (J). (gr. k — 1). bds. 7.99 *(978-1-84059-749-3(6))* Milet Publishing.

—My First Bilingual Book-Sports (English-Farsi) 2012. (My First Bilingual Book Ser.). (ENG & PER., Illus.). 24p. (J). (gr. k — 1). bds. 7.99 *(978-1-84059-751-6(8))* Milet Publishing.

—My First Bilingual Book-Sports (English-German) 2012. (My First Bilingual Book Ser.). (ENG & GER., Illus.). 24p. (J). (gr. k — 1). bds. 7.99 *(978-1-84059-753-0(4))* Milet Publishing.

—My First Bilingual Book-Sports (English-Korean) 2012. (My First Bilingual Book Ser.). (ENG & KOR., Illus.). 24p. (J). (gr. k — 1). bds. 7.99 *(978-1-84059-755-4(0))* Milet Publishing.

—My First Bilingual Book-Sports (English-Polish) 2012. (My First Bilingual Book Ser.). (ENG, POL & POR., Illus.). 24p. (J). (gr. k — 1). bds. 7.99 *(978-1-84059-756-1(9))* Milet Publishing.

—My First Bilingual Book-Sports (English-Russian) 2012. (My First Bilingual Book Ser.). (ENG & RUS., Illus.). 24p. (J). (gr. k — 1). bds. 7.99 *(978-1-84059-758-5(5))* Milet Publishing.

—My First Bilingual Book-Sports (English-Spanish) 2012. (My First Bilingual Book Ser.). (SPA & ENG., Illus.). 24p. (J). (gr. k — 1). bds. 7.99 *(978-1-84059-760-8(7))* Milet Publishing.

—My First Bilingual Book-Sports (English-Urdu) 2012. (My First Bilingual Book Ser.). (ENG & URD., Illus.). 24p. (J). (gr. k — 1). bds. 7.99 *(978-1-84059-762-2(3))* Milet Publishing.

—My First Bilingual Book-Sports (English-Vietnamese) 2012. (My First Bilingual Book Ser.). (ENG & VIE., Illus.). 24p. (J). (gr. k — 1). bds. 7.99 *(978-1-84059-763-9(1))* Milet Publishing.

—Sports. 2012. (My First Bilingual Book Ser.). (ENG & ARA., Illus.). 24p. (J). (gr. k — 1). bds. 7.99 *(978-1-84059-748-6(8))*; bds. 7.99 *(978-1-84059-750-9(X))*; bds. 7.99 *(978-1-84059-757-8(7))* Milet Publishing.

—Sports - My First Bilingual Book. 2012. (My First Bilingual Book Ser.). (Illus.). 24p. (J). (gr. k — 1). (ENG & SOM.). bds. 7.99 *(978-1-84059-759-2(3))*; (FRE & ENG., bds. 7.99 *(978-1-84059-752-3(6))* Milet Publishing.

—Sports (English-Italian) 2012. (My First Bilingual Book Ser.). (ENG & ITA., Illus.). 24p. (J). (gr. k — 1). bds. 7.99 *(978-1-84059-754-7(2))* Milet Publishing.

Miller, Karen. Girls & Sports. 2009. (J). 29.45 *(978-0-7377-4811-6(7)*, Greenhaven Pr., Inc.); (Illus.). 240p. 29.45 *(978-0-7377-4517-7(7))* Cengage Gale.

—Girls & Sports. 2009. (Opposing Viewpoints Ser.). (ENG., Illus.). 224p. (gr. 10-12). 48.80 *(978-0-7377-4516-0(9))* Cengage Gale.

Miller, Ray, et al. Beat the Clock Sports. Thorp, Cameron, illus. 2007. 48p. (J). *(978-0-439-02189-0(8))* Scholastic, Inc.

Mis Deportes Favoritos / My Favorite Sports. 2014. (Mis Deportes Favoritos / My Favorite Sports Ser.). (SPA.). 24p. (J). (gr. k-2). 135.60 *(978-1-4824-1186-7(5))* Stevens, Gareth Publishing LLLP.

Mitchell-Hughes, Kimberley. The 10 Most Extreme Sports. 2008. 14.99 *(978-1-55448-555-0(X))* Scholastic Library Publishing.

Mooney, Carla. Dream Jobs in Sports Personnel. 2017. (J). ***(978-1-5383-8142-7(7))*** Rosen Publishing Group, Inc., The.

—For People Who Love Sports. 2016. (Cool Careers Without College Ser.). 00104p. (J). (gr. 7-7). 38.45 *(978-1-5081-7286-4(2))* Rosen Publishing Group, Inc., The.

Mooney, Carla. Using Math in Sports. 2017. (Math You Will Actually Use Ser.). 48p. (J). (gr. 10-10). pap. 11.75 ***(978-1-4994-3872-7(9)***, Rosen Central) Rosen Publishing Group, Inc., The.

Mooney, Carla, ed. African Americans in Sports. 2012. (Lucent Library of Black History Ser.). (ENG., Illus.). 128p. (gr. 7-10). lib. bdg. 34.80 *(978-1-4205-0675-4(7)*, Lucent Bks.) Cengage Gale.

Moore, Elizabeth. Sports Rules, 1 vol. (Wonder Readers Next Steps: Social Studies). (ENG.). (gr. -1-1). 2013. 20p. 22.65 *(978-1-4765-2364-4(9))* 2011. 16p. pap. 35.94 *(978-1-4296-8158-2(6))* 2011. 32p. pap. 5.99 *(978-1-4296-7871-1(2))* Capstone Press of Coughlan Cos. (Wonder Readers).

Moore, Tijon Adamson. Pigeon Toed. Baker, David, illus. 2011. 28p. pap. 24.95 *(978-1-4560-0607-5(X))* America Star Bks.

Morey, Allan, et al. Fantasy Sports Math. 2016. (Fantasy Sports Math Ser.). (ENG.). 32p. (gr. 3-4). 111.96 *(978-1-5157-2189-5(2))* Capstone Press of Coughlan Cos.

Mullins, Patty Rutland. All about Sports with Inspector McQ. Ebert, Len, illus. 2004. (Treasure Tree Ser.). 32p. (J). *(978-0-7166-1645-0(9))* World Bk., Inc.

Murphy, Bernadette & Surridge, Gerry. Sport Readiness. 2004. (Illus.). 160p. pap. 14.95 *(978-0-673-58914-9(5))* Good Year Bks.

Murphy, Glenn. Olympic Sport: The Whole Muscle-Flexing Story. unabr. ed. 2016. (ENG., Illus.). 176p. (J). (gr. k-2). pap. 9.99 *(978-1-4472-5468-3(6))* Pan Macmillan GBR. Dist: Independent Pubs. Group.

Murray, Stuart A. P. Score with Track & Field Math. 2013. (Score with Sports Math Ser.). 48p. (J). lib. bdg. 25.27 *(978-0-7660-4176-9(X))*; (gr. 3-4). pap. 8.95 *(978-1-4644-0291-3(4))* Enslow Pubs., Inc. (Enslow Elementary).

My Favorite Sports. 2014. (My Favorite Sports Ser.). 24p. (J). (gr. k-2). 135.60 *(978-1-4824-0773-0(6))*; pap. 48.90 *(978-1-4824-1575-9(5))* Stevens, Gareth Publishing LLLP.

Nagelhout, Ryan. Lacrosse: Who Does What? 2017. (Sports: What's Your Position? Ser.). 32p. (J). (gr. 3-4). lib. bdg. 26.60 ***(978-1-5382-0411-5(8))*** Stevens, Gareth Publishing LLLP.

Nagelhout, Ryan. The Science of Hockey. 2015. (Sports Science Ser.). (ENG., Illus.). 32p. (J). (gr. 4-5). pap. 10.00 *(978-1-4994-1070-9(0)*, PowerKids Pr.) Rosen Publishing Group, Inc., The.

Nardo, Don. Arts, Leisure, & Sport in Ancient Egypt. 2005. (Lucent Library of Historical Eras Ser.). (ENG., Illus.). 112p. (YA). (gr. 7-12). lib. bdg. 33.45 *(978-1-59018-706-7(7))* Cengage Gale.

—A Roman Gladiator. 2004. (Working Life Ser.). (ENG., Illus.). 112p. (J). 30.85 *(978-1-59018-480-6(7)*, Lucent Bks.) Cengage Gale.

Nasium, James. African Americans in Sports. 2012. (J). pap. *(978-1-4222-2394-9(9))* Mason Crest.

National Geographic Kids Staff. My Gold Medal Adventure. 2016. (NG Kids Funny Fill In Ser.). (ENG.). 48p. (J). (gr. 3-7). pap. 4.99 *(978-1-4263-2404-8(9)*, National Geographic Children's Bks.) National Geographic Society.

—Sports: 300 Wacky Facts about Awesome Athletics. 2016. (Weird but True Ser.). (ENG., Illus.). 208p. (J). (gr. 3-7). pap. 7.99 *(978-1-4263-2467-3(7)*, National Geographic Children's Bks.) National Geographic Society.

Newcomb, Tim. STEM in Sports: Engineering. 2015. (STEM in Sports Ser.). 64p. (J). (gr. 7). lib. bdg. 23.95 *(978-1-4222-3231-6(X))* Mason Crest.

Nitz, Kristin Wolden. Track. 2003. (Play-by-Play Ser.). (Illus.). 80p. (J). (gr. 5-18). pap. 7.95 *(978-0-8225-9873-2(6))* Lerner Publishing Group.

Nixon, James. Freerunning Champion. 2016. (ENG., Illus.). 32p. (J). (gr. 4-6). 17.99 *(978-1-4451-3626-4(0)*, Franklin Watts) Hachette Children's Group GBR. Dist: Hachette Bk. Group.

—Mountain Biking Champion. 2017. (How to Be a Champion Ser.). (ENG., Illus.). 32p. (J). (gr. 4-6). 17.99 *(978-1-4451-3605-9(8)*, Franklin Watts) Hachette Children's Group GBR. Dist: Hachette Bk. Group.

Omoth, Tyler. Bizarre Things We've Done for Sport. 2015. (History of the Bizarre Ser.). (ENG., Illus.). 32p. (gr. 3-4). lib. bdg. 27.99 *(978-1-4914-4267-8(0))* Capstone Press of Coughlan Cos.

—First Sports Source. 2016. (First Sports Source Ser.). (ENG.). 24p. (gr. 1-2). 101.28 *(978-1-4914-8677-1(5)*, First Facts) Capstone Press of Coughlan Cos.

Omoth, Tyler, et al. Six Degrees of Sports. 2015. (Six Degrees of Sports Ser.). (ENG.). 48p. (gr. 3-4). lib. bdg. 127.96 *(978-1-4914-2624-1(1))* Capstone Press of Coughlan Cos.

O'Neill, Dan. The Stubborn Gal: The True Story of an Undefeated Sled Dog Racer. Maisch, Klara, illus. 2015. 48p. 15.95 *(978-1-60223-272-3(5))* Univ. of Alaska Pr.

O'Shei, Tim. The World's Zaniest Sports. 2015. (Library of Weird Ser.). (ENG.). 32p. (gr. 3-4). lib. bdg. 27.99 *(978-1-4914-2020-1(0))* Capstone Press of Coughlan Cos.

Owens, L. L. Join a Team, 1 vol. Davidson, Chris, illus. 2010. (Let's Be Social Ser.). (ENG.). 32p. 28.50 *(978-1-60270-801-3(0)*, Looking Glass Library- Nonfiction) Magic Wagon.

Oxlade, Chris. Sports, 1 vol. 2012. (Science Behind Ser.). (ENG., Illus.). 32p. (gr. 3-3). pap. 8.29 *(978-1-4109-4500-6(6))*; lib. bdg. 30.65 *(978-1-4109-4489-4(1))* Heinemann-Raintree. (Raintree Perspectives).

Page, Jason. Cycling, Shooting, & Show Jumping: Archery, Weightlifting, & a Whole Lot More. 2008. (Olympic Sports Ser.). (ENG., Illus.). 32p. (J). (gr. 3-7). pap. *(978-0-7787-4030-8(7))*; (gr. 4-7). lib. bdg. *(978-0-7787-4013-1(7))* Crabtree Publishing Co.

Pawlett, Mark. The Tae Kwon Do Handbook. 2009. (Martial Arts Ser.). 256p. (gr. 8-8). 79.90 *(978-1-61514-370-2(X))* Rosen Publishing Group, Inc., The.

Pernu, Dennis. The Complete Guide to Sports. 2015. (Illus.). 144p. (J). *(978-1-4351-6166-5(1))* Barnes & Noble, Inc.

Perritano, John. Gnarly Sports Injuries, 1 vol. 2017. (Red Rhino Nonfiction Ser.). (ENG.). 60p. (J). (gr. 3-8). pap. 8.95 ***(978-1-68021-071-2(8))*** Saddleback Educational Publishing, Inc.

—Gnarly Sports Injuries. 2017. (Red Rhino Nonfiction Ser.). (J). lib. bdg. 19.60 ***(978-0-606-39893-0(7))*** Turtleback Bks.

Perritano, John. Sports Science. 2010. (Cool Science Ser.). 48p. (J). (gr. 3-6). 28.50 *(978-1-60870-081-3(X))* Marshall Cavendish Corp.

Peterson, Brian C. Sports Marketing: Careers off the Field, Vol. 10. Ferrer, Al, ed. 2015. (Careers off the Field Ser.). (Illus.). 64p. (J). (gr. 7). 23.95 *(978-1-4222-3272-9(7))* Mason Crest.

Petrie, Kristin. Food as Fuel: Nutrition for Athletes, 1 vol. 2012. (Mission: Nutrition Ser.). (ENG., Illus.). 32p. (YA). (gr. 3-6). 27.07 *(978-1-61783-081-5(X))* ABDO Publishing Co.

Pezzi, Bryan. Terry Fox. 2010. (Illus.). 24p. *(978-1-77071-598-1(3))*; pap. *(978-1-77071-604-9(1))* Weigl Educational Pubs. Ltd.

Phelan, Glen. Forces & Motion in Sports: Set Of 6. 2011. (Navigators Ser.). (J). pap. 50.00 net. *(978-1-4108-5088-1(9))* Benchmark Education Co.

—Forces & Motion in Sports: Text Pairs. 2008. (Bridges/Navigators Ser.). (J). (gr. 6). 81.00 *(978-1-4108-8435-0(X))* Benchmark Education Co.

Play Like the Pros. 2010. (Play Like the Pros (Sports Illustrated for Kids) Ser.). (ENG.). 32p. (gr. 3-4). pap. 27.80 *(978-1-4296-5740-2(5))* Capstone Press of Coughlan Cos.

Play Like the Pros, 1 vol., Set. Incl. Play Baseball Like a Pro: Key Skills & Tips. Hetrick, Hans. lib. bdg. 26.65 *(978-1-4296-4824-0(4))*; Play Basketball Like a Pro: Key Skills & Tips. LeBoutillier, Nate. lib. bdg. 26.65 *(978-1-4296-4826-4(0))*; Play Football Like a Pro: Key Skills & Tips. Doeden, Matt. lib. bdg. 26.65 *(978-1-4296-4825-7(2))*; Play Soccer Like a Pro: Key Skills & Tips. Forest, Christopher. lib. bdg. 26.65 *(978-1-4296-4827-1(9))*; (gr. 3-4). (Play Like the Pros (Sports Illustrated for Kids) Ser.). (ENG.). 32p. 2010. Set lib. bdg. 106.60 *(978-1-4296-4828-8(7))* Capstone Press of Coughlan Cos.

Play Like the Pros Classroom Collection. 2010. (Play Like the Pros (Sports Illustrated for Kids) Ser.). (ENG.). 32p. (gr. 3-4). pap. 166.80 *(978-1-4296-5743-3(X))* Capstone Press of Coughlan Cos.

Play Like the Pros Collection. 2010. (Play Like the Pros (Sports Illustrated for Kids) Ser.). (ENG.). 32p. (gr. 3-4). pap. 27.80 *(978-1-4296-5742-6(1))* Capstone Press of Coughlan Cos.

Pollard, Josephine. Winter Sports. 2012. (American Antiquarian Society Ser.). (ENG., Illus.). 28p. (gr. 1-5). 24.95 *(978-1-4290-9734-5(5))* Applewood Bks.

Polydoros, Lori. Motorcycle Racing, 1 vol. 2013. (Super Speed Ser.). (ENG.). 32p. (gr. 1-2). 26.65 *(978-1-4765-0121-5(1)*, Blazers) Capstone Press of Coughlan Cos.

—Strange but True Sports, 1 vol. 2010. (Strange but True Ser.). (ENG.). 32p. (gr. 1-2). lib. bdg. 26.65 *(978-1-4296-4550-8(4)*, Blazers) Capstone Press of Coughlan Cos.

Powerkids Press, creator. Personal Best Set. 2008. (J). 101.00 *(978-1-4358-2566-6(7)*, PowerKids Pr.) Rosen Publishing Group, Inc., The.

Powless, Justin, Neal and Giles & Benchmark Education Co. Staff. Lasting Legacies - America's First Game. 2014. (Text Connections Ser.). (J). (gr. 5). *(978-1-4900-1374-9(1))* Benchmark Education Co.

Price, Sean Stewart. Sports. Doty, Eldon, illus. 2010. (Truth & Rumors Ser.). (ENG.). 32p. (gr. 3-4). lib. bdg. 27.99 *(978-1-4296-4747-2(7)*, Edge Bks.) Capstone Press of Coughlan Cos.

Professional Athlete. 2009. (Virtual Apprentice Ser.). 64p. (gr. 4-9). 29.95 *(978-0-8160-6759-6(7)*, Ferguson Publishing Co.) Facts On File, Inc.

Publ, Griffin. Easy Olympic Sports Reader, 6 Bks, Set. 2004. (U. S. Olympic Committee Easy Olympic Sports Readers Ser.). (Illus.). 16p. (J). pap. 17.95 *(978-1-58000-116-8(5))* Griffin Publishing Group.

Publications International Ltd. Staff, ed. Pub Time Sports Trivia. 2013. 192p. *(978-1-4508-7827-2(X)*, 145087827X) Publications International, Ltd.

Raatma, Lucia. Sportsmanship. 2013. (21st Century Junior Library: Character Education Ser.). (ENG., Illus.). 24p. (J). (gr. 1-4). 25.64 *(978-1-62431-158-1(X)*, 202952); pap. 12.79 *(978-1-62431-290-8(X)*, 202954) Cherry Lake Publishing.

Raatma, Lucia & Sodaro, Craig. Unusual Histories. 2012. (Unusual Histories Ser.). (ENG.). 48p. (gr. 3-4). lib. bdg. 63.98 *(978-1-4296-8226-8(4))*; lib. bdg. 159.95 *(978-1-4296-8227-5(2))* Capstone Press of Coughlan Cos.

Rad Sports. 2005. (Illus.). 48p. (gr. 5-8). lib. bdg. 212.00 *(978-0-8239-4056-1(X))* Rosen Publishing Group, Inc., The.

Rappoport, Ken. Ladies First: Women Athletes Who Made a Difference, 1 vol. 2010. (ENG., Illus.). 192p. (J). pap. 8.95 *(978-1-56145-534-8(2))* Peachtree Pubs.

Raymos, Rick. STEM Jobs in Sports. 2014. (ENG.). 48p. (gr. 4-8). 35.64 *(978-1-62717-696-5(9))* Rourke Educational Media.

Real World Math: Sports, 8 vols. Incl. Baseball. Minden, Cecilia. (Illus.). lib. bdg. 28.50 *(978-1-60279-243-2(7)*, 200194); Basketball. Minden, Cecilia. (Illus.). lib. bdg. 28.50 *(978-1-60279-245-6(3)*, 200196); Football. Marsico, Katie. (Illus.). lib. bdg. 28.50 *(978-1-60279-247-0(X)*, 200198); Running. Marsico, Katie. (Illus.). lib. bdg. 28.50 *(978-1-60279-249-4(6)*, 200032); Soccer. Minden, Cecilia. (Illus.). lib. bdg. 28.50 *(978-1-60279-244-9(5)*, 200195); Speed Skating. Marsico, Katie. lib. bdg. 28.50 *(978-1-60279-250-0(X)*, 200128); Swimming. Minden, Cecilia. (Illus.). lib. bdg. 28.50 *(978-1-60279-246-3(1)*, 200197); Tennis. Marsico, Katie. (Illus.). lib. bdg. 28.50 *(978-1-60279-248-7(8)*, 200127); (gr. 4-8). 32p. 2008. Set lib. bdg. 159.60 *(978-1-60279-289-0(5)*, 200185) Cherry Lake Publishing.

Reeves, Diane Lindsey. Career Ideas for Kids Who Like Sports. Bond, Nancy, illus. 2nd rev. ed. 2007. (Career Ideas for Kids Ser.). 208p. (gr. 4-9). lib. bdg. 32.95 *(978-0-8160-6551-6(9)*, Checkmark Bks.) Facts On File, Inc.

Reeves, Diane Lindsey & Kelley, K. C. Choose Your Own Career Adventure at the Olympics. 2016. (Bright Futures Press: Choose Your Own Career Adventure Ser.). (ENG., Illus.). 32p. (J). (gr. 4-6). 29.93 *(978-1-63471-914-8(X)*, 208977) Cherry Lake Publishing.

—Choose Your Own Career Adventure at the Super Bowl. 2016. (Bright Futures Press: Choose Your Own Career Adventure Ser.). (ENG., Illus.). 32p. (J). (gr. 4-6). 29.93 *(978-1-63471-915-5(8)*, 208981) Cherry Lake Publishing.

Rice, Dona Herweck. Keeping Fit with Sports, 1 vol. 2nd rev. ed. 2014. (TIME for KIDS(r) Nonfiction Readers Ser.). (ENG., Illus.). 20p. (J). (gr. 1-1). pap. 19.96 *(978-1-4807-1029-0(6))* Shell Educational Publishing.

—Keeping Fit with Sports, 1 vol. 2nd rev. ed. 2011. (TIME for KIDS(r) Nonfiction Readers Ser.). (ENG.). 20p. (J). (gr. 1-1). 4.99 *(978-1-4333-3596-9(4))* Teacher Created Materials, Inc.

—Mantenerse en Forma con Deportes, 1 vol. 2nd rev. ed. 2012. (Nonfiction Readers Ser.). (SPA.). 20p. (J). (gr. 1-1). pap. 4.99 *(978-1-4333-4429-9(7))* Teacher Created Materials, Inc.

Richards, Jon. Art, Culture, & Sports. 2016. (Mapographica Ser.). (ENG., Illus.). 32p. (J). (gr. 3-6). *(978-0-7787-2655-5(X))* Crabtree Publishing Co.

Ridley, Sarah. Sport. 2016. (ENG., Illus.). 24p. (J). (gr. k-2). 17.99 *(978-1-4451-4007-0(1)*, Franklin Watts) Hachette Children's Group GBR. Dist: Hachette Bk. Group.

Riggs, Kate. The Great Recession. 2017. (Turning Points Ser.). (ENG.). 48p. (J). (gr. 7-12). pap. 12.00 *(978-1-62832-345-0(0)*, Creative Paperbacks) Creative Co., The.

Riggs, Thomas. Are Players' Unions Good for Professional Sports Leagues? 2012. (At Issue Ser.). (ENG.). 128p. (gr. 10-12). pap. 27.80 *(978-0-7377-6417-8(1))*; lib. bdg. 39.40 *(978-0-7377-6416-1(3))* Cengage Gale. (Greenhaven Pr., Inc.).

Ripley Publishing Staff & Mason Crest Publishers Staff, contrib. by. Extreme Endeavors. 2013. (Ripley's Believe It or Not! Enter If You Dare Ser.). (Illus.). 36p. (J). (gr. 4-18). pap. 9.95 *(978-1-4222-2797-8(9))* Mason Crest.

Ripley's Believe It Or Not! Staff. Extreme Endeavors. 2013. (Ripley's Believe It or Not! Enter If You Dare Ser.: 8). 36p. (J). (gr. 4-18). 19.95 *(978-1-4222-2780-0(4))* Mason Crest.

Rissman, Rebecca. Playing with Friends: Comparing Past & Present, 1 vol. 2014. (Comparing Past & Present Ser.). (ENG., Illus.). 24p. (gr. -1-1). lib. bdg. 22.65 *(978-1-4329-8993-4(6)*, Acorn) Heinemann-Raintree.

Rissman, Rebecca & Schwartz, Heather E. Top Sports Tips. 2017. (Top Sports Tips Ser.). (ENG.). 32p. (gr. 3-4). 167.94 *(978-1-5157-4749-9(2)*, Snap Bks.) Capstone Press of Coughlan Cos.

Rober, Harold. Starting a Sport. 2017. (Bumba Books (tm) — Fun Firsts Ser.). (ENG.). 24p. (J). (gr. -1-1). 12.99 ***(978-1-5124-3690-7(9))***; 38.65 ***(978-1-5124-2748-6(9))***; 38.65 ***(978-1-5124-3689-1(5))*** Lerner Publishing Group. (Lerner Pubns.).

Rober, Harold T. Starting a Sport. 2017. (Bumba Books (tm) — Fun Firsts Ser.). (ENG., Illus.). 24p. (J). (gr. -1-1). 25.32 *(978-1-5124-2552-9(4))* Lerner Publishing Group.

Robinson, Garrick & Kjeldsen, Neil. Having A Ball: Youth Sports Done Right, 1 book. 2006. (ENG & SPA., Illus.). 44p. (J). per. 14.95 *(978-0-9777437-0-4(5))* Zeus Sports Florida LLC.

Rosen, Michael J. Balls! Margeson, John, illus. 2006. 72p. (J). (gr. 4-8). 18.95 *(978-1-58196-030-3(1)*, Darby Creek) Lerner Publishing Group.

Rosen, Michael J. & Kassoy, Ben. Wacky Sports. Jones, Doug, illus. 2013. (No Way! Ser.). (ENG.). 32p. (gr. 3-5). lib. bdg. 26.60 *(978-0-7613-8982-8(2)*, Millbrook Pr.) Lerner Publishing Group.

Rosen Publishing Staff. Inside Sports: Set 2, 1 vol. 2015. (Inside Sports Ser.). (ENG.). 96p. (YA). 190.20 *(978-1-62275-598-1(7)*, Britannica Educational Publishing) Rosen Publishing Group, Inc., The.

—Sports Tips, Techniques, & Strategies: Set 2, 1 vol. 2015. (Sports Tips, Techniques, & Strategies Ser.). (ENG.). 48p. (YA). 181.50 *(978-1-4777-8097-8(1)*, Rosen Central) Rosen Publishing Group, Inc., The.

Ross, Stewart. Sport Technology. 2010. (New Technology Ser.). (ENG., Illus.). 48p. (J). 26.99 *(978-0-237-54077-7(0))* Evans Brothers, Ltd. GBR. Dist: Independent Pubs. Group.

Rowe, Brooke. What Kind of Sports Pro Are You? 2015. (Illus.). 32p. (J). *(978-1-63470-036-8(8))* Cherry Lake Publishing.

Royston, Angela. Win That Sprint! Forces in Sport. 2015. (Feel the Force Ser.). (ENG., Illus.). 48p. (gr. 3-6). 33.32 *(978-1-4846-2597-2(8))* Heinemann-Raintree.

Ruscoe, Michael. Kick Ball Capitalization. 2009. (Grammar All-Stars Ser.). 32p. (J). (gr. 2-5). lib. bdg. 26.00 *(978-1-4339-1942-8(7)*, Gareth Stevens Learning Library) Stevens, Gareth Publishing LLLP.

Rutherford, Kristina. Level the Playing Field: The Past, Present, & Future of Women's Pro Sports. 2016. (ENG., Illus.). 56p. (J). (gr. 3-7). 16.95 *(978-1-77147-160-2(3)*, Owlkids) Owlkids Bks. Inc. CAN. Dist: Publishers Group West (PGW).

Salas, Laura Purdie. Colors of Sports, 1 vol. (Colors All Around Ser.). (ENG.). 32p. (gr. 1-2). 2011. pap. 8.10 *(978-1-4296-6149-2(6))* 2011. pap. 47.70 *(978-1-4296-6150-8(X))* 2010. lib. bdg. 27.32 *(978-1-4296-5259-9(4))* Capstone Press of Coughlan Cos. (Aplus Bks.).

—S Is for Score! A Sports Alphabet. 2010. (Alphabet Fun Ser.). (ENG.). 32p. (gr. 1-2). pap. 47.70 *(978-1-4296-5087-8(7))*; lib. bdg. 27.32

(978-1-4296-3915-6(6)) Capstone Press of Coughlan Cos. (Aplus Bks.).
Salzmann, Mary Elizabeth. Angling to Zorbing: Sports from A to Z, 1 vol. 2007. (Let's See A to Z Ser.). (ENG., Illus.). 32p. (gr. 3-7). 27.07 *(978-1-59928-881-9(8),* Super SandCastle) ABDO Publishing Co.
Samuel, Adele. Wild World of Sports. 2007. (Steck-Vaughn BOLDPRINT Anthologies Ser.). (ENG., Illus.). 48p. (gr. 4-7). pap. 16.90 *(978-1-4190-4020-7(0))* Houghton Mifflin Harcourt Publishing Co.
Santillan, Jorge H., illus. Sports Illustrated Kids Victory School Superstars, 6 vols., Set. Incl. Five Fouls & You're Out! Priebe, Val. lib. bdg. 26.65 *(978-1-4342-2228-2(4));* It's a Wrestling Mat, Not a Dance Floor. Nickel, Scott. lib. bdg. 26.65 *(978-1-4342-2227-5(6));* There's a Hurricane in the Pool! Gunderson, Jessica. 26.65 *(978-1-4342-2230-5(6));* There's No Crying in Baseball. Yasuda, Anita. lib. bdg. 26.65 *(978-1-4342-2226-8(8));* Who Wants to Play Just for Kicks? Kreie, Chris. lib. bdg. 26.65 *(978-1-4342-2229-9(2));* You Can't Spike Your Serves. Gassman, Julie A. lib. bdg. 26.65 *(978-1-4342-2231-2(4));* (Illus.). (gr. 1-3). (Sports Illustrated Kids Victory School Superstars Ser.). (ENG.). 56p. 2011. Set lib. bdg. 159.90 *(978-1-4342-3126-0(7))* Stone Arch Bks.
Schaefer, Adam. Steroids. 2008. (21st Century Skills Library: Health at Risk Ser.). (ENG., Illus.). 32p. (gr. 4-8). lib. bdg. 28.50 *(978-1-60279-287-6(9),* 200136) Cherry Lake Publishing.
Schaub, Michelle. This or That Sports Debate: A Rip-Roaring Game of Either/or Questions. 2012. (This or That? Ser.). (ENG.). 32p. (gr. 3-4). pap. 47.70 *(978-1-4296-9277-9(4),* Edge Bks.); (Illus.). lib. bdg. 27.99 *(978-1-4296-8592-4(1))* Capstone Press of Coughlan Cos.
Schmidt, Debra. Careers in Sports & Fitness. 2016. (Exploring Careers Ser.). (ENG., Illus.). 80p. (J). (gr. 5-12). 38.60 *(978-1-60152-814-8(0))* ReferencePoint Pr., Inc.
Scholastic Library Publishing. Rookie Read-about(r) Sports. 2012. (Rookie Read-about Ser.). (J). (gr. -1-1). 92.00 *(978-0-531-26524-6(2),* Children's Pr.) Scholastic Library Publishing.
Schuette, Sarah L. Sports Zone: A Spot-It Challenge, 1 vol. 2012. (Spot It Ser.). (ENG.). 32p. (gr. 1-2). lib. bdg. 27.32 *(978-1-4296-8712-6(6))* Capstone Press of Coughlan Cos.
Schulz, Christian Dahl. Professional Sports Organizations. 2012. (Career Launcher Ser.). 130p. (C). (gr. 9). 34.95 *(978-0-8160-7964-3(1),* Ferguson Publishing Co.) Facts On File, Inc.
Schwaeber, Barbie Heit. Alphabet of Sports. Lowe, David, illus. (Alphabet Bks.). (ENG.). 40p. 2011. (J). (gr. -1-3). 9.95 *(978-1-60727-446-9(9))* 2009. 9.95 *(978-1-59249-994-6(5))* 2008. (J). (gr. k-2). 15.95 *(978-1-59249-769-0(1))* Soundprints.
The Science of Sports [Capstone Sole Source]. 2010. (Science of Sports (Sports Illustrated for Kids) Ser.). 48p. lib. bdg. 179.94 *(978-1-4296-5880-5(0))* Capstone Press of Coughlan Cos.
The Science of Sports [Kurtz]. 2010. (Science of Sports (Sports Illustrated for Kids) Ser.). 32p. pap. 59.70 *(978-1-4296-5961-1(0))* Capstone Press of Coughlan Cos.
Scott, Celicia. Sports & Fitness. Hart, Diane H., ed. 2014. (Integrated Life of Fitness Ser.). 64p. (J). (gr. 7-18). pap. 11.95 *(978-1-4222-3201-9(8));* 23.95 *(978-1-4222-3163-0(1))* Mason Crest.
Scott, John, text. Athletic Quest Total Sports System. 2004. (YA). 30.00 *(978-1-879498-82-2(0))* SportAmerica.
—Seniors: How to Get Recruited. 2004. (YA). 30.00 *(978-1-879498-77-8(4))* SportAmerica.
—Sophomore: How to Make the Team. 2004. (YA). 30.00 *(978-1-879498-79-2(0))* SportAmerica.
Seder, Rufus Butler. Swing! 2008. (Scanimation Ser.). (ENG., Illus.). 12p. (J). (gr. -1-3). 12.95 *(978-0-7611-5127-2(3),* 15127) Workman Publishing Co., Inc.
Shannon, Terry Miller. Good Sports. 2016. (Spring Forward Ser.). (J). (gr. 1). *(978-1-4900-2236-9(8))* Benchmark Education Co.
Shapiro, Simon. Faster, Higher, Smarter: Bright Ideas That Transformed Sports. 2016. (ENG., Illus.). 120p. (J). (gr. 5). pap. 12.95 *(978-1-55451-813-5(X))* Annick Pr., Ltd. CAN. Dist: Publishers Group West (PGW).
Shaw, Jessica. Dream Jobs in Sports Psychology. 2017. (J). ***(978-1-5383-8144-1(3))*** Rosen Publishing Group, Inc., The.
Side-By-Side Sports, 1 vol. 2014. (Side-By-Side Sports Ser.). (ENG.). 48p. (gr. 4-6). pap. 31.80 *(978-1-4765-6173-8(7))* Capstone Press of Coughlan Cos.
Simonds, Lucy. Indoor Sports. 2007. (Trackers-Math Ser.). (gr. 2-5). pap. 5.00 *(978-1-59055-921-5(5))* Pacific Learning, Inc.
Simons, Rae. Sports Math. 2013. (Math 24/7 Ser.: 10). 48p. (J). (gr. 5-18). 19.95 *(978-1-4222-2909-5(2))* Mason Crest.
Slade, Suzanne. The Kids' Guide to Money in Sports, 1 vol. 2014. (SI Kids Guide Bks.). (ENG.). 48p. (gr. 4-9). lib. bdg. 31.99 *(978-1-4765-4154-9(X))* Capstone Press of Coughlan Cos.
—Who Invented Basketball? And Other Questions Kids Have about Sports, 1 vol. Pillo, Cary, illus. 2011. (Kids' Questions Ser.). (ENG.). 24p. (gr. 1-2). pap. 7.49 *(978-1-4048-6730-7(9))* Picture Window Bks.
Slade, Suzanne, et al. High-Tech Sports. 2013. (High-Tech Sports Ser.). (ENG.). 48p. (gr. 3-9). lib. bdg. 127.96 *(978-1-4296-9957-0(4))* Capstone Press of Coughlan Cos.
—SI Kids Guide Books, 1 vol. 2014. (SI Kids Guide Bks.). (ENG.). 48p. (gr. 4-9). lib. bdg. 127.96 *(978-1-4765-6214-8(8))* Capstone Press of Coughlan Cos.
So Many Sports! (Girls' World Ser.). 16p. (J). *(978-2-7643-0143-2(X))* Phidal Publishing, Inc./Editions Phidal, Inc.
Sosieski, Shanti. Who's Next: The Hottest Young Stars in Action Sports. 2004. (J). 3.99 *(978-1-930623-34-7(8))* Sports Illustrated For Kids.
Sports. 2nd rev. ed. 2007. (What Can I Do Now? Ser.). 184p. (YA). (gr. 7-12). 32.95 *(978-0-8160-6034-4(7))* Facts On File, Inc.
Sports, 10 vols. 2005. (Double Fastback Ser.). (J). (gr. 6-12). 64p. pap. 54.95 *(978-0-13-024465-9(1));* 32p. pap. 44.95 *(978-0-13-024446-8(5))* Globe Fearon Educational Publishing.
Sports: What's Your Position? 2017. (Sports: What's Your Position? Ser.). 32p. (gr. 3-4). pap. 63.00 ***(978-1-5382-0490-0(8));*** lib. bdg. 159.60 ***(978-1-5382-0476-4(2))*** Stevens, Gareth Publishing LLLP.
Sports & Fitness (Gr. PreK-5) 2003. (J). *(978-1-58232-026-7(8))* ECS Learning Systems, Inc.
Sports Around the World, 6 vols. (Book2WebTM Ser.). (gr. 4-8). 36.50 *(978-0-322-02989-7(9))* Wright Group/McGraw-Hill.
Sports Families, 6 vols., Set. Incl. Archie, Peyton, & Eli Manning: Football's Royal Family. Nagle, Jeanne. lib. bdg. 29.25 *(978-1-4358-3550-4(6));* Calvin Hill & Grant Hill: One Family's Legacy in Football & Basketball. Porterfield, Jason. lib. bdg. 29.25 *(978-1-4358-3549-8(2));* Earnhardt NASCAR Dynasty: The Legacy of Dale Sr. & Dale Jr. Watson, Stephanie. lib. bdg. 29.25 *(978-1-4358-3551-1(4));* Ken Griffey Sr. & Ken Griffey Jr. Baseball Heroes. Mills, J. Elizabeth. lib. bdg. 29.25 *(978-1-4358-3554-2(9));* Ronde & Tiki Barber: Football Stars. Heos, Bridget. lib. bdg. 29.25 *(978-1-4358-3553-5(0));* Venus & Serena Williams: Tennis Champions. Bailey, Diane. lib. bdg. 29.25 *(978-1-4358-3552-8(2));* (YA). (gr. 4-7). 2010. (Illus.). 48p. 2010. Set lib. bdg. 159.00 *(978-1-4358-3601-3(4),* Rosen Reference) Rosen Publishing Group, Inc., The.
Sports for All: Level P, 6 vols., Vol. 2. (Explorers Ser.). 32p. (gr. 3-6). 44.95 *(978-0-7699-0612-6(5))* Shortland Pubns. (U. S. A.) Inc.
Sports from Coast to Coast. 2005. (Illus.). 48p. (gr. 5-8). lib. bdg. 159.00 *(978-1-4042-0347-1(8))* Rosen Publishing Group, Inc., The.
Sports from Coast to Coast, 6 bks., Set 2. Incl. Baseball: Rules, Tips, Strategy, & Safety. Porterfield, Jason. (J). (gr. 5-8). 2006. lib. bdg. 29.25 *(978-1-4042-0991-6(3));* Basketball: Rules, Tips, Strategy, & Safety. Ramen, Fred. (J). (gr. 3-7). 2007. lib. bdg. 29.25 *(978-1-4042-0992-3(1));* Football: Rules, Tips, Strategy, & Safety. Wingate, Brian. (J). (gr. 3-7). 2007. lib. bdg. 29.25 *(978-1-4042-0993-0(X));* Paintball: Rules, Tips, Strategy, & Safety. Roza, Greg. (YA). (gr. 5-8). 2006. lib. bdg. 29.25 *(978-1-4042-0994-7(8));* Soccer: Rules, Tips, Strategy, & Safety. Wingate, Brian. (J). (gr. 5-8). 2006. lib. bdg. 29.25 *(978-1-4042-0995-4(6));* Softball: Rules, Tips, Strategy, & Safety. Hofstetter, Adam B. (J). (gr. 5-8). 2006. lib. bdg. 29.25 *(978-1-4042-0996-1(4));* (Illus.). 48p. 2007. Set lib. bdg. 159.00 *(978-1-4042-1044-8(X))* Rosen Publishing Group, Inc., The.
Sports Illustrated for Kids: Year in Sports 2006. 2005. (J). 99.90 *(978-0-439-82763-8(9))* Scholastic, Inc.
Sports Illustrated for Kids Books. 2005. (Illus.). 176p. (gr. 7-12). lib. bdg. 388.65 *(978-0-8239-3925-1(1))* Rosen Publishing Group, Inc., The.
Sports Illustrated for Kids Editors. Sports Illustrated Kids Stats! The Greatest Numbers in Sports. 2013. (ENG.). 128p. (J). (gr. k-17). pap. 14.95 *(978-1-61893-039-2(7))* Time Inc. Bks.
Sports Illustrated Kids Magazine Staff. The Top 10 of Everything in Sports. 2013. (Sports Illustrated Kids Top 10 Lists Ser.). (ENG.). 96p. (J). (gr. 3-17). 19.95 *(978-1-61893-079-8(6))* Sports Illustrated For Kids.
Sports Reports, 50 bks., Set. (Illus.). (YA). (gr. 4-10). lib. bdg. 1047.50 *(978-0-89490-568-1(6))* Enslow Pubs., Inc.
Sports Science. 2015. (Sports Science Ser.). (ENG.). 32p. (J). (gr. 4-5). pap., pap., pap. 360.00 *(978-1-4994-1311-3(4),* PowerKids Pr.) Rosen Publishing Group, Inc., The.
Sports Tips, Techniques, & Strategies: Set 1. 2014. (Sports Tips, Techniques, & Strategies Ser.). 48p. (YA). (gr. 5-8). pap. 423.00 *(978-1-4777-8125-8(0));* pap. 70.50 *(978-1-4777-8124-1(2))* Rosen Publishing Group, Inc., The. (Rosen Reference).
SportsGirl, 8 bks. Incl. Competitive Basketball for Girls. Gettelman, Elizabeth. lib. bdg. 31.95 *(978-0-8239-3402-7(0));* Competitive Tennis for Girls. Guillermo-Newton, Judith. lib. bdg. 31.95 *(978-0-8239-3407-2(1));* Competitive Track & Field for Girls. Manley, Claudia B. lib. bdg. 31.95 *(978-0-8239-3408-9(X));* (YA). (gr. 5-9). (Illus.). 64p. 2005. Set lib. bdg. 212.00 *(978-0-8239-9426-7(0))* Rosen Publishing Group, Inc., The.
Staeger, Rob. Native American Sports & Games. Johnson, Troy, ed. 2013. (Native American Life Ser.: 15). 64p. (J). (gr. 5-18). 19.95 *(978-1-4222-2976-7(9))* Mason Crest.
Stephens, Ronald, ed. Sports. 2014. (Safety First Ser.: 11). 48p. (J). (gr. 5-18). 20.95 *(978-1-4222-3053-4(8))* Mason Crest.
Stewart, Mark. Classic Rivalries. 2009. (Ultimate 10: Sports Ser.). 48p. (ENG.). (J). (gr. 4-8). pap. 10.50 *(978-1-4339-2205-3(3));* (YA). (gr. 5-9). lib. bdg. 31.00 *(978-0-8368-9161-4(9))* Stevens, Gareth Publishing LLLP.
—The Ultimate 10: Sports - Fall 2009 Release Set, 6 vols. 2009. (Ultimate 10: Sports Ser.). (ENG.). 48p. (J). (gr. 3-8). pap. 53.70 *(978-1-4339-2209-1(6),* Gareth Stevens Hi-Lo Must Reads) Stevens, Gareth Publishing LLLP.
Stock Car Racers. (Cool Cars Ser.). 16p. (J). *(978-2-7643-0131-9(6))* Phidal Publishing, Inc./Editions Phidal, Inc.
Storden, Thom. Epic Sports Records, 1 vol. 2014. (Epic Sports Records Ser.). (ENG.). 32p. (gr. 1-2). 106.60 *(978-1-4914-0744-8(1),* Blazers) Capstone Press of Coughlan Cos.
Sullivan, Erin. Sports Math & Matemáticas en los Deportes: 6 English, 6 Spanish Adaptations, 122 vols., Vol. 2. 2011. (Navigators Ser.). (J). instr.'s gde. ed. 97.00 net. *(978-1-4108-1774-7(1),* 17741) Benchmark Education Co.
Super Racing. (Cool Cars Ser.). 16p. (J). *(978-2-7643-0002-2(6))* Phidal Publishing, Inc./Editions Phidal, Inc.
Super Speeders. (Cool Cars Ser.). 16p. (J). *(978-2-7643-0004-6(2))* Phidal Publishing, Inc./Editions Phidal, Inc.
Super Sports Star, 17 bks., Set. Incl. Super Sports Star Gary Payton. Mandell, Judith J. lib. bdg. 25.27 *(978-0-7660-1519-7(X));* Super Sports Star Grant Hill. Lowenstein, Felicia. lib. bdg. 23.93 *(978-0-7660-1517-3(3));* Super Sports Star Kevin Garnett. Thornley, Stew. lib. bdg. 23.93 *(978-0-7660-1515-9(7));* Super Sports Star Kobe Bryant. Thornley, Stew. lib. bdg. 23.93 *(978-0-7660-1514-2(9));* Super Sports Star Penny Hardaway. Rappoport, Ken. lib. bdg. 23.93 *(978-0-7660-1516-6(5));* Super Sports Star Tim Duncan. Thornley, Stew. lib. bdg. 23.93 *(978-0-7660-1513-5(0));* 48p. (J). (gr. 1-4). 2001. (Illus.). Set lib. bdg. 322.15 *(978-0-7660-1802-0(4))* Enslow Pubs., Inc.
Sutherland, Steve. Courage to Win. 2010. 94p. pap. 9.99 *(978-1-60860-804-1(2),* Eloquent Bks.) Strategic Book Publishing & Rights Agency (SBPRA).
Sylvester, Kevin. Sports Hall of Weird. Sylvester, Kevin, illus. 2005. (ENG., Illus.). 96p. (J). (gr. 2-6). 8.95 *(978-1-55337-635-4(8))* Kids Can Pr., Ltd. CAN. Dist: Hachette Bk. Group.
Tammen, Christina. C h u m P. 2010. 42p. pap. 13.95 *(978-1-935268-21-5(X))* Halo Publishing International.
Tardif, Benoît, illus. Sport-O-Rama. 2015. (ENG.). 56p. (J). (gr. -1-2). 17.95 *(978-1-77138-327-1(5))* Kids Can Pr., Ltd. CAN. Dist: Hachette Bk. Group.
Technosports: Individual Title, 6 packs. (Bookweb Ser.). 32p. (gr. 4-18). 34.00 *(978-0-7635-3746-3(2))* Rigby Education.
Teitelbaum, Michael. Sports Broadcasting. 2008. (21st Century Skills Innovation Library: Innovation in Entertainment Ser.). (ENG., Illus.). 32p. (gr. 4-8). lib. bdg. 28.50 *(978-1-60279-216-6(X),* 200147) Cherry Lake Publishing.
Tellier, Derek, et al. What's Your Dream? 2016. (What's Your Dream? Ser.). (ENG.). 96p. (gr. 3-4). 101.28 *(978-1-4965-3469-9(7))* Capstone Press of Coughlan Cos.
Thomas, Ron & Herran, Joe. Getting into Sports. 2005. (Getting into Sports Ser.). (Illus.). 32p. (gr. 4-6). 140.00 *(978-0-7910-9067-1(1),* Chelsea Clubhouse) Facts On File, Inc.
Tibballs, Geoff. Sports. 2010. (Ripley Twists Ser.). 48p. (J). (gr. 3-18). lib. bdg. 19.95 *(978-1-4222-1834-1(1))* Mason Crest.
Time Out: Star Athletes Who Shine off the Field. (Illus.). 32p. (J). (gr. 3-9). pap. 3.99 *(978-1-930623-19-4(4))* Sports Illustrated For Kids.
To the Extreme [Really Good Stuff]. 2010. (To the Extreme Ser.). 32p. pap. 79.50 *(978-1-4296-5362-6(0),* Blazers) Capstone Press of Coughlan Cos.
Torres, John. Critical Perspectives on Minors Playing High-Contact Sports. 2016. (Analyzing the Issues Ser.). 208p. (YA). lib. bdg. 47.93 *(978-0-7660-8137-6(0))* Enslow Pubs., Inc.
Torrisi, Cathy. Take a Stand. 2011. pap. 39.95 *(978-0-7664-3753-1(1))* Abrams & Co. Pubs., Inc.
Turnbull, Stephanie. Sports Horses. 2015. (ENG., Illus.). 24p. (J). pap. 8.95 *(978-1-77092-230-3(X))* RiverStream Publishing.
Ultimate Pro Team Guides Classroom Collection. 2010. (Ultimate Pro Team Guides (Sports Illustrated for Kids) Ser.). (ENG.). 72p. (gr. 3-4). pap. 214.80 *(978-1-4296-5739-6(1))* Capstone Press of Coughlan Cos.
Ultimate Sports Force Staff. Super Squad: Basketball's Superstars. 2003. (Illus.). 56p. (J). pap. 7.95 *(978-1-57243-601-5(8))* Triumph Bks.
Ultimate Trivia Challenge. 2013. (Ultimate Trivia Challenge Ser.). 32p. (J). (gr. 2-5). 126.25 *(978-1-4339-8308-5(7));* pap. 315.00 *(978-1-4339-9740-2(1));* pap. 52.50 *(978-1-4339-9739-6(8))* Stevens, Gareth Publishing LLLP.
Valat, Pierre-Marie. El Deporte. (Coleccion Mundo Maravilloso). (SPA., Illus.). 168p. (J). (gr. 2-4). 13.56 *(978-84-348-4486-5(9),* SM1438) SM Ediciones ESP. Dist: Lectorum Pubns., Inc.
Wacky World of Sports. 2014. (Wacky World of Sports Ser.). 32p. (J). (gr. 3-6). 159.60 *(978-1-4824-1176-8(8))* Stevens, Gareth Publishing LLLP.
Walsh, Kieran. Sports Math. 2005. (Math & My World Ser.). (Illus.). 48p. (J). (gr. 4-6). lib. bdg. 20.95 *(978-1-59515-495-8(7))* Rourke Educational Media.
Watkins, Christine. Sports & Athletes, No. 9. 2009. (Opposing Viewpoints Ser.). (ENG., Illus.). (gr. 10-12). 224p. 48.80 *(978-0-7377-4542-9(8),* LML01709-245987); 240p. (YA). 29.45 *(978-0-7377-4543-6(6),* LML01709-246015) Cengage Gale. (Greenhaven Pr., Inc.).
Watson, Stephanie. The Science Behind Soccer, Volleyball, Cycling, & Other Popular Sports. 2016. (Science of the Summer Olympics Ser.). (ENG., Illus.). 32p. (gr. 3-4). lib. bdg. 27.99 *(978-1-4914-8160-8(9),* Edge Bks.) Capstone Press of Coughlan Cos.
Watt, Fiona. Sports Sticker Book. 2011. (Sticker Activity Bks). 24p. (J). pap. 8.99 *(978-0-7945-3121-8(0),* Usborne) EDC Publishing.
Wells, Don. Lacrosse. 2005. (For the Love of Sports Ser.). (Illus.). 24p. (J). (gr. 4-6). lib. bdg. 24.45 *(978-1-59036-297-6(7))* Weigl Pubs., Inc.
What's Your Dream? 2016. (What's Your Dream? Ser.). (ENG.). 96p. (gr. 3-4). pap. 23.80 *(978-1-4965-3470-5(0))* Capstone Press of Coughlan Cos.
Whelon, Chuck. What to Doodle? All Sorts of Sports! 2009. (Dover Doodle Bks.). (ENG., Illus.). 64p. (J). (gr. 2-5). pap. 5.99 *(978-0-486-47267-6(1))* Dover Pubns., Inc.
Wild Outdoors, 1 vol. 2010. (Wild Outdoors Ser.). (ENG.). 32p. (gr. 1-2). lib. bdg. 53.30 *(978-1-4296-4813-4(9),* Blazers) Capstone Press of Coughlan Cos.
Wilder, K. C. Tour de You: Swirling Circles of Freedom. 2010. 24p. 11.49 *(978-1-4520-1099-1(4))* AuthorHouse.
Williams, Brian. Sport & Entertainment: Biggest & Best. 2003. (Biggest & Best Ser.). (Illus.). 40p. (J). pap. 7.95 *(978-1-84236-063-7(9))* Miles Kelly Publishing, Ltd. GBR. Dist: Independent Pubs. Group.
Wingate, Brian. Violence at Sports Events. (Violence & Society Ser.). 64p. 2009. (gr. 6-6). 58.50 *(978-1-60854-727-2(2))* 2008. (Illus.). (YA). (gr. 9-12). lib. bdg. 31.95 *(978-1-4042-1796-6(7))* Rosen Publishing Group, Inc., The.
Winning Sports for Girls Set, 6-Volumes. 2009. (Winning Sports for Girls Ser.). (gr. 6-12). 237.00 *(978-0-8160-8197-4(2),* Chelsea Hse.) Facts On File, Inc.
Witmer, Scott. Sports & Society, 1 vol. 2012. (Ethics of Sports Ser.). (ENG.). 64p. (gr. 6-10). pap. 9.00 *(978-1-4329-5984-5(0))* Heinemann-Raintree.
Wood, Alix. Sports on the Map. 2014. (Fun with Map Skills Ser.). (Illus.). 32p. (J). (gr. 3-6). lib. bdg. 26.25 *(978-1-4777-6972-0(2),* PowerKids Pr.) Rosen Publishing Group, Inc., The.
—Wacky Moments in Sports. 2014. (Wacky World of Sports Ser.). (Illus.). 32p. (J). (gr. 3-6). pap. 10.50 *(978-1-4824-1221-5(7))* Stevens, Gareth Publishing LLLP.
—Wacky Races. 2014. (Wacky World of Sports Ser.). 32p. (J). (gr. 3-6). pap. 10.50 *(978-1-4824-1222-2(5))* Stevens, Gareth Publishing LLLP.
—Wacky Team Sports. 2014. (Wacky World of Sports Ser.). (Illus.). 32p. (J). (gr. 3-6). pap. 10.50 *(978-1-4824-1224-6(1))* Stevens, Gareth Publishing LLLP.
—Wacky Throwing Sports. 2014. (Wacky World of Sports Ser.). 32p. (J). (gr. 3-6). pap. 63.00 *(978-1-4824-0876-8(7))* Stevens, Gareth Publishing LLLP.
Wunderlich, Rick. Math on the Job: Working in Sports. 2016. (ENG., Illus.). 32p. (J). *(978-0-7787-2362-2(3))* Crabtree Publishing Co.
Yomtov, Nel. The Science of a Carve Turn. 2015. (21st Century Skills Library: Full-Speed Sports Ser.). (ENG., Illus.). 32p. (J). (gr. 4-7). 29.93 *(978-1-63362-580-8(X),* 206504) Cherry Lake Publishing.
—The Science of a Cutback. 2015. (21st Century Skills Library: Full-Speed Sports Ser.). (ENG., Illus.). 32p. (J). (gr. 4-7). 29.93 *(978-1-63362-581-5(8),* 206508) Cherry Lake Publishing.
You Can Canoe! Individual Title Six-Packs. (Action Packs Ser.). 120p. (gr. 3-5). 44.00 *(978-0-7635-8393-4(6))* Rigby Education.
Young, Jeff C. Adrenaline Adventure, 1 vol., Set. Incl. Belaying the Line: Mountain, Rock, & Ice Climbing. (YA). 27.07 *(978-1-61613-547-8(6));* Dropping the Flag: Auto Racing. (YA). 27.07 *(978-1-61613-548-5(4));* Leading the Pack: Dogsled Racing. (YA). 27.07 *(978-1-61613-549-2(2));* Pulling the Rip Cord: Skydiving. (YA). 27.07 *(978-1-61613-550-8(6));* Running the Rapids: White-Water Rafting, Canoeing, & Kayaking. (J). 27.07 *(978-1-61613-551-5(4));* Shooting the Curl: Surfing. (YA). 27.07 *(978-1-61613-552-2(2));* (gr. 3-6). (Adrenaline Adventure Ser.: 6). (ENG., Illus.). 32p. 2011. 162.42 *(978-1-61613-546-1(8),* Checkerboard Library) ABDO Publishing Co.
Zuckerman, Gregory, et al. Rising Above: How 10 Athletes Overcame Challenges in Their Youth to Become Stars. 2016. (ENG.). 256p. (J). (gr. 3-7). 17.99 *(978-0-399-17382-0(X));* lib. bdg. 20.99 *(978-0-399-54570-2(0))* Penguin Young Readers Group. (Philomel Bks.).

SPORTS—BIOGRAPHY

Adams, Sean. Tim Duncan. 2004. (Sports Heroes & Legends Ser.). (ENG., Illus.). 112p. (gr. 5-12). lib. bdg. 30.60 *(978-0-8225-1793-1(0))* Lerner Publishing Group.
All-Star Players, 12 vols., Sets 1-2. Incl. Set. Rosen Publishing Group. 2007. lib. bdg. 143.70 *(978-1-4042-3601-1(5));* Set 2. Edwards, Ethan. 2008. lib. bdg. 143.70 *(978-1-4358-2564-2(0),* PowerKids Pr.); (J). (gr. 4-6). 2008. Set lib. bdg. 287.40 *(978-1-4358-2669-4(8))* Rosen Publishing Group, Inc., The.
Allyson, Jackie. Chris Jesus Ferguson. 2009. (Superstars of Poker Ser.). (Illus.). 64p. (YA). (gr. 4-7). lib. bdg. 22.95 *(978-1-4222-0218-0(6))* Mason Crest.
—Doyle Texas Dolly Brunson. 2009. (Superstars of Poker Ser.). (Illus.). 64p. (YA). (gr. 4-7). lib. bdg. 22.95 *(978-1-4222-0216-6(X))* Mason Crest.
—Gus the Great Dane Hansen. 2009. (Superstars of Poker Ser.). (Illus.). 64p. (YA). (gr. 4-7). lib. bdg. 22.95 *(978-1-4222-0219-7(4))* Mason Crest.
Anderson, Jennifer Joline. Wilma Rudolph: Track & Field Inspiration, 1 vol. 2011. (Legendary Athletes Ser.). (ENG., Illus.). 112p. (YA). (gr. 7-12). 34.22 *(978-1-61714-759-3(1))* ABDO Publishing Co.
Anthony, Carmelo & Brown, Greg. Carmelo Anthony: It's Just the Beginning. 2004. (Basketball Ser.). (Illus.). 48p. (J). 15.95 *(978-0-9634650-7-8(4))* Positively for Kids, Inc.
Armentrout, David & Armentrout, Patricia. Tony Hawk. 2005. (Discover the Life of a Sports Star Ser.). (Illus.). 24p. (gr. 1-4). 14.95 *(978-1-59515-129-2(X))* Rourke Educational Media.
Armstrong, Jesse. Big Show. 2017. (Big Show Ser.). 24p. (J). (gr. 3-7). pap. 7.99 ***(978-1-61891-246-6(1),*** Epic Bks.) Bellwether Media.
Benchmark All-Stars: Group 2, 6 Bks, Set. 2004. (J). 162.43 *(978-0-7614-1755-2(9))* Marshall Cavendish Corp.
Carter, Vince & Brown, Greg. Vince Carter: Choose Your Course. 2004. (Basketball Ser.). (Illus.). 48p. (J). 15.95 *(978-0-9634650-2-3(3))* Positively for Kids, Inc.
Christopher, Matt. Babe Ruth. 2015. (Great Americans in Sports Ser.). (J). lib. bdg. 16.00 *(978-0-606-37519-1(8))* Turtleback Bks.
—Mia Hamm. 2015. (Great Americans in Sports Ser.). (J). lib. bdg. 16.00 *(978-0-606-37520-7(1))* Turtleback Bks.
—On the Court with... Yao Ming. 2004. (ENG., Illus.). 112p. (J). (gr. 5-8). pap. 15.99 *(978-0-316-73574-2(4),* Tingley, Megan Bks.) Little, Brown Bks. for Young Readers.
Contro, Arturo. Gianluigi Buffon. Benson, Megan, tr. from SPA. 2008. (World Soccer Stars / Estrellas Del Fútbol Mundial Ser.). (SPA., Illus.). 24p. (J). (gr. 2-5). lib. bdg. 22.60 *(978-1-4042-7668-0(8))* Rosen Publishing Group, Inc., The.
—Landon Donovan. Benson, Megan, tr. 2008. (World Soccer Stars / Estrellas Del Fútbol Mundial Ser.). (SPA., Illus.). 24p. (J). (gr. 2-5). lib. bdg. 22.60 *(978-1-4042-7666-6(1))* Rosen Publishing Group, Inc., The.
Doeden, Matt. Shaun White. rev. ed. 2012. (Amazing Athletes Ser.). (ENG.). 32p. (gr. 2-5). pap. 7.95 *(978-0-7613-9067-1(7))* Lerner Publishing Group.
—Shaun White (Revised Edition) 2012. (Amazing Athletes Ser.). 32p. (J). (gr. 2-5). pap. 45.32 *(978-0-7613-9139-5(8))* Lerner Publishing Group.
Edwards, Ethan. All-Star Players, 6 bks., Set 2. Incl. Meet Albert Pujols: Baseball's Power Hitter. (YA). lib. bdg. 25.25 *(978-1-4042-4487-0(5));* Meet Derek Jeter: Captain of the New York Yankees. (YA). lib. bdg. 25.25 *(978-1-4042-4488-7(3));* Meet Kevin Garnett: Basketball's Big Ticket. (YA). lib. bdg. 25.25 *(978-1-4042-4490-0(5));* Meet LaDainian Tomlinson: Football's Fastest Running Back. (YA). lib. bdg. 25.25 *(978-1-4042-4491-7(3));* Meet Steve Nash: Basketball's Ultimate Team Player. (J). lib. bdg. 23.95 *(978-1-4042-4489-4(1),* PowerKids Pr.); Meet Tom Brady: Football's Famous Quarterback. (YA). lib. bdg. 25.25 *(978-1-4042-4492-4(1));* (Illus.). 32p. (gr. 4-7). 2009. 2008. Set lib. bdg. 143.70 *(978-1-4358-2564-2(0),* PowerKids Pr.) Rosen Publishing Group, Inc., The.
Extreme Sports Biographies. (Illus.). (J). (gr. k-5). 119.70 *(978-1-4042-2954-9(X));* 2005. 64p. (gr. 5-8). lib. bdg. 159.00 *(978-1-4042-0344-0(3))* Rosen Publishing Group, Inc., The.
Galán, Johnn. Luis Tejada -Vida Breve, Crítica Crónica. 2006. (SPA.). 192p. (YA). *(978-958-30-1692-9(6))* Panamericana Editorial.

S

Glaser, Jason. Sports Idols, 6 vols., Set. 2008. (J). (gr. 2-5). lib. bdg. 127.50 (978-1-4042-4239-5(2)) Rosen Publishing Group, Inc., The.

Golus, Carrie. Muhammad Ali. 2006. (Sports Heroes & Legends Ser.). (ENG., Illus.). 120p. (J). (gr. 5-12). lib. bdg. 30.60 (978-0-8225-5960-3(9)) Lerner Publishing Group.

Goranson, Christopher D. Danny Harf: Wakeboarding Superstar. 2005. (Extreme Sports Biographies Ser.). (Illus.). 64p. (YA). (gr. 5-9). lib. bdg. 31.95 (978-1-4042-0066-1(5)) Rosen Publishing Group, Inc., The.

Greenberg, Michael. Sword of a Champion: The Sharon Monplaisir Story. 2003. (Anything You Can Do. . .Ser.: Vol. 2). (Illus.). 96p. (J). (gr. 2-5). pap. 9.95 (978-1-930546-39-4(4)) Wish Publishing.

Greenhaven Press Editors. Lindsey Vonn. 2012. (People in the News Ser.). (ENG., Illus.). 128p. (YA). (gr. 7-12). lib. bdg. 33.95 (978-1-4205-0614-3(5)) Cengage Gale.

Hall, Kirsten. Kids in Sports. 2005. (True Tales Ser.). (ENG., Illus.). 48p. (J). (gr. 2-4). pap. 4.95 (978-0-516-24685-7(2), Children's Pr.) Scholastic Library Publishing.

Johnson, Brad & Brown, Greg. Brad Johnson: Play with Passion. 2004. (Football Ser.). (Illus.). 48p. (J). 15.95 (978-0-9634650-4-7(X)) Positively for Kids, Inc.

Jones, Jeremy V. Toward the Goal: The Kaka Story, 1 vol. rev. ed. 2014. (ZonderKidz Biography Ser.). (ENG.). 160p. (J). pap. 7.99 (978-0-310-73840-4(7)) Zonderkidz.

Kennedy, Mike. Tony Hawk. 2009. (People We Should Know Ser.). 48p. (J). (gr. 3-5). pap. 10.50 (978-1-4339-2191-9(X)); lib. bdg. 31.00 (978-1-4339-1952-7(4)) Stevens, Gareth Publishing LLLP. (Gareth Stevens Learning Library).

Kirkpatrick, Rob. Hot Shots, 6 bks. Incl. Dale Earnhardt, Jr. NASCAR Road Racer. lib. bdg. 17.25 (978-0-8239-5545-9(1), PKDAEA); Oscar de la Hoya: Gold-Medal Boxer. lib. bdg. 19.95 (978-0-8239-5543-5(5)); 24p. (J). (gr. 1). 2000. (Illus.). Set lib. bdg. 96.00 (978-0-8239-7001-8(9), PKPOHS, PowerKids Pr.) Rosen Publishing Group, Inc., The.

—Power Players, 6 bks. Incl. Doug Flutie: International Football Star. 2003. lib. bdg. 17.25 (978-0-8239-5537-4(0)); Grant Hill: Basketball All-Star. 2003. lib. bdg. 17.25 (978-0-8239-5538-1(9)); Kobe Bryant: "Slam Dunk" Champion. 2000. lib. bdg. 22.60 (978-0-8239-5539-8(7)); Sammy Sosa: Home Run Hitter. 2002. lib. bdg. 22.60 (978-0-8239-5534-3(6)); 24p. (J). (gr. 1). (Illus.). Set lib. bdg. 96.00 (978-0-8239-7000-1(0), PowerKids Pr.) Rosen Publishing Group, Inc., The.

Kjelle, Marylou Morano. Dwayne the Rock Johnson. 2008. (Robbie Reader Ser.). (Illus.). 32p. (YA). (gr. 2-5). lib. bdg. 25.70 (978-1-58415-722-9(4)) Mitchell Lane Pubs., Inc.

Lewis, Wendy A. Fire on the Water: The Red-Hot Career of Superstar Rower Ned Hanlan, 1 vol. 2007. (Lorimer Recordbooks Ser.). (ENG & GER., Illus.). 112p. (J). (gr. 4-6). 9.95 (978-1-55028-972-5(1), 9781550289725) Lorimer, James & Co., Ltd., Pubs. CAN. Dist: Casemate Pubs. & Bk. Distributors, LLC.

Lewis, Wendy A. & Lewis, Wendy. Fire on the Water: The Red-Hot Career of Superstar Rower Ned Hanlan. 2007. (Lorimer Recordbooks Ser.). (ENG., Illus.). 112p. (J). (gr. 4-6). 16.95 (978-1-55028-973-2(X), 9781550289732) Lorimer, James & Co., Ltd., Pubs. CAN. Dist: Casemate Pubs. & Bk. Distributors, LLC.

—Lacrosse Warrior: The Life of Mohawk Lacrosse Champion Gaylord Powless, 1 vol. 3rd ed. 2008. (Lorimer Recordbooks Ser.). (ENG., Illus.). 120p. (J). (gr. 7-12). 8.95 (978-1-55277-001-6(X), 9781552770016) Lorimer, James & Co., Ltd., Pubs. CAN. Dist: Casemate Pubs. & Bk. Distributors, LLC.

Lyon, Drew, et al. Real Heroes of Sports. 2017. (Real Heroes of Sports Ser.). (ENG.). 32p. (gr. 3-4). pap. 28.76 (978-1-5157-4464-1(7)) Capstone Press of Coughlan Cos.

Macrae, Sloan. The Greatest Records in Sports, 1 vol. 2015. (Greatest Records in Sports Ser.). (ENG.). 32p. (J). 60.00 (978-1-4994-0310-7(0), PowerKids Pr.) Rosen Publishing Group, Inc., The.

Mahaney, Ian. Tony Hawk: Skateboarding Champ. 2005. (Extreme Sports Biographies Ser.). (Illus.). 24p. (J). 22.60 (978-1-4042-2747-7(4), PowerKids Pr.) Rosen Publishing Group, Inc., The.

Mahaney, Ian F. Taig Khris: In-Line Skate Champion. 2005. (Extreme Sports Biographies Ser.). (Illus.). 24p. (J). 22.60 (978-1-4042-2746-0(6), PowerKids Pr.) Rosen Publishing Group, Inc., The.

Marx, Mandy R. & Schuh, Mari. Sports Stars, 1 vol. 2014. (Sports Stars Ser.). (ENG.). 24p. (gr. k-1). 53.30 (978-1-4914-0666-3(6), Pebble Plus) Capstone Press of Coughlan Cos.

McClellan, Ray. Undertaker. 2017. (Undertaker Ser.). 24p. (J). (gr. 3-7). pap. 7.99 **(978-1-61891-245-9(3)**, Epic Bks.) Bellwether Media.

Micklos, John. Muhammad Ali: "I Am the Greatest" 2010. (American Rebels Ser.). 160p. (J). (gr. 7-12). 35.94 (978-0-7660-3381-8(3)) Enslow Pubs., Inc.

Miller, Raymond H. Tony Hawk. 2004. (Stars of Sport Ser.). (ENG., Illus.). 48p. (J). 27.50 (978-0-7377-1568-2(5), Greenhaven Pr., Inc.) Cengage Gale.

Nagle, Jeanne. Top 101 Athletes, 1 vol., 1. 2014. (People You Should Know Ser.). (ENG.). 168p. (YA). (gr. 7-12). 35.25 (978-1-62275-136-5(1)) Rosen Publishing Group, Inc., The.

Obregon, Jose M. David Beckham. Benson, Megan, tr. 2008. (World Soccer Stars / Estrellas Del Fútbol Mundial Ser.). (SPA., Illus.). 24p. (J). (gr. 2-5). lib. bdg. 22.60 (978-1-4042-7665-9(3)) Rosen Publishing Group, Inc., The.

Obregón, José María. Freddy Adu. 2009. (World Soccer Stars / Estrellas Del Fútbol Mundial Ser.). (SPA, ENG & MUL., Illus.). 24p. (J). lib. bdg. 22.60 (978-1-4358-2730-1(9), Editorial Buenas Letras) Rosen Publishing Group, Inc., The.

Owens, Thomas. Muhammad Ali: Boxing Champ & Role Model, 1 vol. 2011. (Legendary Athletes Ser.). (ENG., Illus.). 112p. (YA). (gr. 7-12). 34.22 (978-1-61714-752-4(4), 1324107) ABDO Publishing Co.

Parham, Jerrill. Thrills & Spills: Fast Sports. 2007. (Shockwave: the Human Experience Ser.). (ENG., Illus.). 36p. (J). (gr. 3-5). 25.00 (978-0-531-17762-4(9), Children's Pr.) Scholastic Library Publishing.

Polydoros, Lori, et al. The Best of the Best. 2012. (Best of the Best Ser.). (ENG.). 32p. (gr. 1-2). lib. bdg. 53.30 (978-1-4296-9135-2(2), Blazers) Capstone Press of Coughlan Cos.

Rappoport, Ken. Profiles in Sports Courage, 1 vol. 2006. (ENG., Illus.). 160p. (J). (gr. 3-7). 15.95 (978-1-56145-368-9(4)) Peachtree Pubs.

Real Heroes of Sports. 2017. (Real Heroes of Sports Ser.). (ENG.). 32p. (gr. 3-4). 103.96 (978-1-5157-4463-4(9)) Capstone Press of Coughlan Cos.

Roberts, Jeremy. Tiger Woods. 2007. (Biography Ser.). (Illus.). 112p. (J). (gr. 4-7). per. 7.95 (978-0-8225-8563-3(4), First Avenue Editions) Lerner Publishing Group.

Rogers, Andy, et al. Who's Who of Pro Sports. 2015. (Who's Who of Pro Sports Ser.). (ENG.). 32p. (gr. 3-4). 111.96 (978-1-4914-6965-1(X)) Capstone Press of Coughlan Cos.

Rosen Publishing Staff. The Greatest Records in Sports, 1 vol. 2015. (Greatest Records in Sports Ser.). (ENG.). 32p. (J). 157.50 (978-1-4777-5743-7(0), PowerKids Pr.) Rosen Publishing Group, Inc., The.

Savage, Jeff. James Stewart. 2007. (Amazing Athletes Ser.). (ENG., Illus.). 32p. (gr. 2-5). lib. bdg. 25.26 (978-0-8225-7663-1(5)) Lerner Publishing Group.

—Marion Jones. 2005. (J). pap. 5.95 (978-0-8225-2040-5(0), First Avenue Editions); (Illus.). (gr. 3-4). lib. bdg. 22.60 (978-0-8225-3657-4(9)) Lerner Publishing Group.

—Usain Bolt. 2012. (Amazing Athletes Ser.). (ENG., Illus.). 32p. (gr. 2-5). pap. 7.95 (978-1-4677-1097-8(0)) Lerner Publishing Group.

Schraff, Anne. Wilma Rudolpn: The Greatest Woman Sprinter in History. 2004. (African-American Biographies Ser.). (Illus.). 112p. (J). lib. bdg. 26.60 (978-0-7660-2291-1(9)) Enslow Pubs., Inc.

Sherrow, Victoria. Wilma Rudolph. Johnson, Larry, illus. 2006. (Yo Solo Biografías Ser.). (ENG & SPA.). 48p. (J). (gr. 2-3). lib. bdg. 23.93 (978-0-8225-6260-3(X), Ediciones Lerner) Lerner Publishing Group.

Smithwick, John. All-Star Players, 6 bks., Set. Incl. Meet Alex Rodriguez: Baseball's Lightning Rod. lib. bdg. 25.25 (978-1-4042-3636-3(8)); Meet David Ortiz: Baseball's Top Slugger. lib. bdg. 25.25 (978-1-4042-3637-0(6)); Meet Dwyane Wade: Basketball's Rising Star. lib. bdg. 25.25 (978-1-4042-3639-4(2)); Meet Lebron James: Basketball's King James. lib. bdg. 25.25 (978-1-4042-3638-7(4)); Meet Shaun Alexander: Football's Top Running Back. lib. bdg. 25.25 (978-1-4042-3635-6(X)); (Illus.). 32p. (YA). (gr. 4-7). 2007. 2007. Set lib. bdg. 143.70 (978-1-4042-3601-1(5)) Rosen Publishing Group, Inc., The.

Snow, D. C. Champ Bailey. 2009. (Superstars of Pro Football Ser.). (Illus.). 64p. (YA). (gr. 7-12). lib. bdg. 22.95 (978-1-4222-0544-0(4)) Mason Crest.

Sporting Heroes. Date not set. 32p. (J). 3.98 (978-0-7525-9875-8(9)) Parragon, Inc.

Sports Star Champions: Set 2. 2017. (Sports Star Champions Ser.). 48p. (gr. 5-6). pap. 70.20 **(978-0-7660-8805-4(7))**; lib. bdg. 167.58 **(978-0-7660-8598-5(8))** Enslow Pubs., Inc.

Stewart, Mark. New Wave, 27 vols. Incl. Allen Iverson: Motion & Emotion. 2001. lib. bdg. 22.90 (978-0-7613-1958-0(1)); Andruw Jones: Love That Glove. 2001. lib. bdg. 22.90 (978-0-7613-1967-2(0)); Daunte Culpepper: Command & Control. 2002. lib. bdg. 22.90 (978-0-7613-2613-7(8)); Ichiro Suzuki: The Best in the West. 2002. lib. bdg. 22.90 (978-0-7613-2616-8(2)); Jackie Stiles: Gym Dandy. 2002. lib. bdg. 22.90 (978-0-7613-2614-4(6)); Jevon Kearse: Force of One. 2001. lib. bdg. 22.90 (978-0-7613-2269-6(8)); Kevin Garnett/Shake up the Game. 2002. lib. bdg. 22.90 (978-0-7613-2615-1(4)); Kurt Warner: Can't Keep Him Down. 2001. lib. bdg. 22.90 (978-0-7613-1953-5(0)); Scott Gomez: Open up the Ice. 2001. lib. bdg. 22.90 (978-0-7613-2268-9(X)); Todd Helton: The Hits Keep Coming. 2001. lib. bdg. 22.90 (978-0-7613-2271-9(X)); Vince Carter: The Fire Burns Bright. 2001. lib. bdg. 22.90 (978-0-7613-2270-2(1)); 48p. (gr. 4-18)., Millbrook Pr. (Illus.). 2004. 595.40 o.p. (978-0-7613-3080-6(1), Twenty-First Century Bks.) Lerner Publishing Group.

Streissguth, Tom. Wilma Rudolph. 2007. (Illus.). 110p. (YA). pap. 9.95 (978-0-8225-6693-9(1)) Lerner Publishing Group.

Tieck, Sarah. Eli Manning CD & Book. 2010. (Big Buddy Biographies CD+Book Ser.). 32p. (gr. 2-5). audio compact disk 57.00 (978-1-61613-309-2(0), Big Buddy Bks.) ABDO Publishing Co.

—Michael Phelps: The Greatest Olympian, 1 vol. 2013. (Big Buddy Biographies Set 9 Ser.). (ENG.). 32p. (J). (gr. 2-5). lib. bdg. 28.50 (978-1-61783-753-1(9), Big Buddy Bks.) ABDO Publishing Co.

Timblin, Stephen. MX Champions: The Stars of the Show - Past & Present. 2008. (MXplosion! Ser.). (ENG., Illus.). 32p. (J). (gr. 3-7). pap. (978-0-7787-4002-5(1)); lib. bdg. (978-0-7787-3989-0(9)) Crabtree Publishing Co.

Valay, Ana Patricia. Giovani Dos Santos. 2012. (Superstars of Soccer ENGLISH Ser.). (ENG., Illus.). 32p. (J). (gr. 4-7). lib. bdg. 19.95 (978-1-4222-2650-6(6)) Mason Crest.

Velázquez de León, Mauricio. 20 Soccer Legends. 2010. (World Soccer Books Ser.). (Illus.). 64p. (YA). (gr. 5-8). lib. bdg. 31.95 (978-1-4358-9136-4(8), Rosen Reference) Rosen Publishing Group, Inc., The.

Wade, Mary Dodson. Amazing Olympic Athlete Wilma Rudolph. 2009. (Amazing Americans Ser.). (Illus.). 24p. (J). (gr. 1-3). lib. bdg. 22.60 (978-0-7660-3282-8(5)) Enslow Pubs., Inc.

Who's Who in Sports 2003-2004: High School Edition. 26th ed. 2004. (YA). 39.95 (978-0-9724667-2-1(X), Who's Who In Sports) Guidry Assocs., Inc.

The World's Greatest Sports Stars [Kurtz]. 2010. (World's Greatest Sports Stars (Sports Illustrated for Kids) Ser.). 32p. pap. 35.80 (978-1-4296-5960-4(2)) Capstone Press of Coughlan Cos.

Wrestling Greats. 2005. (Illus.). 112p. (gr. 7-12). lib. bdg. 265.30 (978-0-8239-3911-4(1)) Rosen Publishing Group, Inc., The.

Zuehlke, Jeffrey. Ben Roethlisberger. 2007. (Amazing Athletes Ser.). (ENG., Illus.). 32p. (gr. 2-5). lib. bdg. 25.26 (978-0-8225-7660-0(0)) Lerner Publishing Group.

—Dirk Nowitzki. 2007. (Amazing Athletes Ser.). (ENG., Illus.). 32p. (gr. 2-5). lib. bdg. 25.26 (978-0-8225-7661-7(9)) Lerner Publishing Group.

SPORTS—FICTION

ABDO Publishing Company Staff. Comeback Kids. 2012. (Comeback Kids Ser.: 5). 176-192p. (J). (gr. 4-8). lib. bdg. 135.35 (978-1-59961-174-7(0)) Spotlight.

Adler, David A. Cam Jansen & the Sports Day Mysteries. Allen, Joy, illus. 2009. (Cam Jansen: A Super Special Ser.). 118p. 16.00 (978-1-60686-431-9(9)) Perfection Learning Corp.

—Cam Jansen & the Sports Day Mysteries: A Super Special. 2009. (Cam Jansen Ser.). lib. bdg. 16.00 (978-0-606-00110-6(7), Turtleback) Turtleback Bks.

—Cam Jansen the Sports Day Mysteries: A Super Special. Allen, Joy, illus. 2009. (Cam Jansen Ser.). (ENG.). 128p. (J). (gr. 2-5). 5.99 (978-0-14-241225-1(2), Puffin Books) Penguin Young Readers Group.

Adler, David A. Get a Hit, Mo! 2017. (Penguin Young Readers Level 2 Ser.). lib. bdg. 13.55 **(978-0-606-39770-4(1))** Turtleback Bks.

Alexander, Samantha. Team Spirit, Bk. 2. 2nd ed. (ENG.). 128p. (J). mass mkt. 6.99 (978-0-330-34534-7(6), Pan) Pan Macmillan GBR. Dist: Trafalgar Square Publishing.

Alonge, L. J. Janae. Allen, Raul, illus. 2016. (Blacktop Ser.: 2). (ENG.). 144p. (YA). (gr. 7). mass mkt. 6.99 (978-1-101-99564-8(5), Grosset & Dunlap) Penguin Young Readers Group.

Alonge, L. J. & dePaola, Tomie. Janae #2. Allen, Raul, illus. 2016. (Blacktop Ser.: 2). (ENG.). 144p. (YA). (gr. 7). bds. 15.99 (978-0-399-54276-3(0), Grosset & Dunlap) Penguin Young Readers Group.

Arena, Felice. Sporty Kids: Handball! Jarrett, Tom, illus. 6th ed. 2017. (Sporty Kids Ser.). (ENG.). 80p. (J). (gr. 1-3). 7.99 **(978-0-14-330890-4(4))** Random Hse. Australia AUS. Dist: Independent Pubs. Group.

Aretha, David. Rounding Third, Heading Home! 2012. (Champion Sports Story Ser.). 112p. (J). (gr. 3-18). 27.94 (978-0-7660-3876-9(9)) Enslow Pubs., Inc.

Aronson, Jeff & Aronson, Miriam. Little Mike & Maddie's First Motorcycle Ride. Aronson, Jeff & Zephyr, Jay, illus. 2007. 32p. (J). 16.00 (978-0-9795302-0-3(2), CrumbGobbler Pr.) Downtown Wetmore Pr.

Aronson, Sarah. Beyond Lucky. 2011. (ENG.). 256p. (J). (gr. 3-7). 16.99 (978-0-8037-3520-0(0), Dial Bks) Penguin Young Readers Group.

Aryal, Aimee. Hello, Brutus! De Angel, Miguel & Moore, D., illus. 2006. 24p. (J). lib. bdg. 14.95 (978-1-932888-51-5(9)) Mascot Bks., Inc.

—Hello, Paws! 2007. (YA). 14.95 (978-1-932888-74-4(8)) Mascot Bks., Inc.

—Let's Go, Giants! De Angel, Miguel, illus. 2007. 24p. (J). lib. bdg. 14.95 (978-1-932888-92-8(6)) Mascot Bks., Inc.

Aryal, Aimee & Halligan, Chris. Meet Cort the Sport. 2006. (Cort the Sport Adventures Ser.). (Illus.). 24p. (J). (gr. -1-3). per. 5.95 (978-1-932888-61-4(6), 91-100-01) Mascot Bks., Inc.

The Autumn Marathon. 2005. (J). 16.95 (978-0-9771495-0-6(1)) Artistic Ventures LLC.

Avivi, Karen. Shredded. 2013. 316p. pap. (978-0-9918079-3-2(6)) Avivi, Karen.

Axworthy, Anni. The Dragon Who Couldn't Do Sporty Things. Axworthy, Anni, illus. 2008. (Little Dragon Ser.). (ENG., Illus.). 32p. (J). (gr. -1-k). (978-1-84089-533-9(0)) Zero to Ten, Ltd.

Barber, Tiki & Barber, Ronde. Jump Shot. 2013. (Barber Game Time Bks.). (ENG., Illus.). 160p. (J). (gr. 3-7). 16.99 (978-1-4424-5729-4(5), Simon & Schuster/Paula Wiseman Bks.) Simon & Schuster/Paula Wiseman Bks.

Barbo, Maria S. & Preller, James. The Case of the Four-Leaf Clover. Smith, Jamie, illus. 2008. 104p. (J). pap. (978-0-545-03837-9(5)) Scholastic, Inc.

Barshaw, Ruth McNally. The Ellie McDoodle Diaries: Most Valuable Player. Barshaw, Ruth McNally, illus. 2013. (Ellie Mcdoodle Diaries). (ENG., Illus.). 192p. (YA). (gr. 3-6). 12.99 (978-1-61963-176-2(8), 9781619631762, Bloomsbury USA Childrens) Bloomsbury Publishing USA.

Barwin, Steven. Making Select, 1 vol. 2011. (Lorimer Sports Stories Ser.). (ENG.). 104p. (J). (gr. 4-8). 16.95 (978-1-55277-875-3(4), 9781552778753); pap. 9.95 (978-1-55277-874-6(6), 9781552778746) Lorimer, James & Co., Ltd., Pubs. CAN. Dist: Casemate Pubs. & Bk. Distributors, LLC.

—Sk8er, 1 vol. 2007. (Lorimer Sports Stories Ser.). (ENG., 128p. (J). (gr. 4-8). Illus.). 16.95 (978-1-55028-985-5(3), 9781550289855); 8.95 (978-1-55028-983-1(7), 9781550289831) Lorimer, James & Co., Ltd., Pubs. CAN. Dist: Casemate Pubs. & Bk. Distributors, LLC.

—Spiked, 1 vol. 2013. (Lorimer Sports Stories Ser.). (ENG.). 120p. (J). (gr. 4-8). pap. 9.95 (978-1-4594-0528-8(5), 9781459405288) Lorimer, James & Co., Ltd., Pubs. CAN. Dist: Casemate Pubs. & Bk. Distributors, LLC.

Beka. Why Are We Here Again? Poupard et al, illus. 2007. (Rugger Boys Ser.: 1). (ENG.). 48p. (J). (gr. 4-7). per. 9.99 (978-1-905460-33-5(3)) CineBook GBR. Dist: National Bk. Network.

Bently, Peter. The Yoga Ogre. Rickerty, Simon, illus. 2012. (ENG.). 32p. (J). 15.99 (978-1-84738-902-2(3)) Simon & Schuster, Ltd. GBR. Dist: Simon & Schuster, Inc.

Berenstain, Jan, et al. The Berenstain Bears Play a Good Game, 1 vol. 2009. (Berenstain Bears/Living Lights Ser.). (ENG., Illus.). 32p. (J). (gr. -1-2). pap. 3.99 (978-0-310-71252-7(1)) Zonderkidz.

Berenstain, Stan & Berenstain, Jan. The Berenstain Bears' Report Card Trouble. 2004. (Berenstain Bears First Time Bks.). (J). (gr. k-3). spiral bd. (978-0-616-11095-9(2)); spiral bd. (978-0-616-11096-6(0)) Canadian National Institute for the Blind/Institut National Canadien pour les Aveugles.

Berk, Josh. Say It Ain't So. (Lenny & the Mikes Ser.). (ENG.). 288p. (J). (gr. 3-7). 2015. pap. 7.99 (978-0-307-93007-1(6), Yearling) 2014. 16.99 (978-0-375-87009-5(1), Knopf Bks. for Young Readers) Random Hse. Children's Bks.

Bietz, Kara. Until I Break. 2016. (ENG.). 256p. (YA). (gr. 8-12). 16.99 (978-0-8075-7438-6(4)) Whitman, Albert & Co.

The Big Race, Level 2. 2016. (Ladybird Readers Ser.). (ENG.). 48p. (J). (gr. 2-4). pap. 9.99 (978-0-241-25448-6(5)) Penguin Bks., Ltd. GBR. Dist: Independent Pubs. Group.

Bildner, Phil. The Greatest Game Ever Played. Pullen, Zachary, illus. 2006. (ENG.). 40p. (J). (gr. k-3). 17.99 (978-0-399-24171-0(X), G.P. Putnam's Sons Books for Young Readers) Penguin Young Readers Group.

Bittmann, Suzy. Life with Molly Mcgee - Sports Chick: Caught in a Pickle. 2010. 211p. pap. 15.99 (978-0-557-46339-8(4)) Lulu Pr., Inc.

Bonehill, Ralph. Guns & Snowshoes or the Winter Outing of the Young Hunters. 2004. reprint ed. pap. 19.95 (978-1-4191-2252-1(5)); pap. 1.99 (978-1-4192-2252-8(X)) Kessinger Publishing, LLC.

BookSource Staff, compiled by. Sports Sabotage. 2012. (Hardy Boys: Secret Files Ser.: 8). lib. bdg. 16.00 (978-0-606-23673-7(2), Turtleback) Turtleback Bks.

Bossley, Michele Martin. Goon Squad, 1 vol. 2003. (Lorimer Sports Stories Ser.). (ENG.). 104p. (J). (gr. 4-8). 8.95 (978-1-55028-808-7(3), 9781550288087); 16.95 (978-1-55028-809-4(1), 9781550288094) Lorimer, James & Co., Ltd., Pubs. CAN. Dist: Casemate Pubs. & Bk. Distributors, LLC.

Bowe, Julie. Curve Ball. 2017. (Victoria Torres, Unfortunately Average Ser.). (ENG.). 160p. (gr. 4-4). lib. bdg. 26.65 (978-1-4965-3818-5(8)) Stone Arch Bks.

Bowen, Fred. Go for the Goal!, 1 vol. 2012. (Fred Bowen Sports Stories Ser.). (ENG.). 128p. (J). pap. 5.95 (978-1-56145-632-1(2)) Peachtree Pubs.

—Real Hoops, 1 vol. 2011. (Fred Bowen Sports Stories Ser.). (ENG.). 128p. (J). (gr. 2-7). pap. 5.95 (978-1-56145-566-9(0)) Peachtree Pubs.

Bridwell, Norman. Clifford's Sports Day. (Clifford, the Big Red Dog Ser.). (Illus.). 32p. (J). (gr. k-2). pap. 5.99 (978-0-590-16002-5(8)) Scholastic, Inc.

Brouwer, Sigmund & Gingras, Gaston. La Course-Poursuite des Loups Gris, 1 vol. Griffiths, Dean, illus. 2011. (Loups Gris Ser.). (FRE.). 72p. (J). (gr. 2-3). pap. 6.95 (978-1-4598-0009-0(5)) Orca Bk. Pubs. USA.

Brown, Dustin. The Sports Pages. Scieszka, Jon, ed. 2012. (Guys Read Ser.). (J). lib. bdg. 17.20 (978-0-606-26877-6(4), Turtleback) Turtleback Bks.

Bruchac, Joseph, et al. Sports Shorts. 2007. (Illus.). 127p. (J). per. 4.99 (978-1-58196-058-7(1), Darby Creek) Lerner Publishing Group.

—Sports Shorts: An Anthology of Short Stories. 2005. (Illus.). 127p. (J). (gr. 4-7). 15.95 (978-1-58196-040-2(9), Darby Creek) Lerner Publishing Group.

Buffington, Cecil. High School Super-Star: The Junior Year. 2008. 244p. pap. 16.95 (978-0-595-51914-9(8)) iUniverse, Inc.

Burroughs, Scott, illus. Sports Sabotage. 2012. (Hardy Boys: the Secret Files Ser.: 8). (ENG.). 112p. (J). (gr. 1-4). pap. 5.99 (978-1-4424-2316-9(1), Aladdin) Simon & Schuster Children's Publishing.

Burton, Jennifer. Christopher's Dilemma. 2003. (Topeka Heights Ser.). (YA). (gr. 9-12). pap. 10.99 (978-0-9724733-1-6(9)) ALEXZUS Bks.

Campbell, Tonie. The Highest Stand. 2005. (Dream Ser.). 150p. (gr. 3-8). pap. 9.95 (978-0-9708992-5-5(4)) Scobre Pr. Corp.

Casciano, Christie & Moziak, Rose Mary Casciano, illus. Haunted Hockey in Lake Placid. 2012. 72p. (J). pap. (978-1-59531-040-8(1)) North Country Bks., Inc.

—The Puck Hog. 2011. 44p. (J). pap. 9.95 (978-1-59531-037-8(1)) North Country Bks., Inc.

Cayen, Alise. Patty Pom-Poms. 2009. 36p. pap. 16.50 (978-1-60693-685-6(9), Strategic Bk. Publishing) Strategic Book Publishing & Rights Agency (SBPRA).

Chambers, Sam T., et al. Head Case Lacrosse Goalie: Sports Fiction with a Winning Edge. Collins, Don, illus. 2009. (ENG.). 95p. (gr. 4-7). pap. 9.95 (978-1-933979-40-3(2), b514b6ed-9361-4f2c-97bd-9aefd77b5e96) Bright Sky Pr.

Chapman, Megan Joy. Lion Heart & Alessio Book 2: Mission, Peace, Patience, Kindness. 2014. (ENG.). 192p. (J). (gr. 3-7). pap. 11.99 (978-1-62136-755-0(X), Creation Hse.) Charisma Media.

Christopher, Matt. Comeback of the Home Run Kid. 2006. (ENG.). 128p. (J). (gr. 2-5). per. 15.99 (978-0-316-05987-9(0)) Little, Brown Bks. for Young Readers.

—Lacrosse Face-Off. 2010. (Matt Christopher Sports Library). 128p. (J). (gr. 4-6). lib. bdg. 26.60 (978-1-59953-355-1(3)) Norwood Hse. Pr.

—Lacrosse Face-Off. 2006. (ENG.). 128p. (J). (gr. 3-7). per. 15.99 (978-0-316-79641-5(7)) Little, Brown Bks. for Young Readers.

—Making the Save. Vasconcellos, Daniel, illus. 11th ed. 2004. (ENG.). 64p. (J). (gr. 1-4). pap. 13.99 (978-0-316-73745-6(3)) Little, Brown Bks. for Young Readers.

Ciencin, Scott & Fuentes, Benny. End Zone Thunder, 1 vol. Sandoval, Gerardo, illus. 2010. (Sports Illustrated Kids Graphic Novels Ser.). (ENG.). 56p. (gr. 2-3). 26.65 (978-1-4342-2010-3(9)); pap. 7.19 (978-1-4342-2784-3(7)) Stone Arch Bks.

—Full Court Flash, 1 vol. Sandoval, Gerardo, illus. 2011. (Sports Illustrated Kids Graphic Novels Ser.). (ENG.). 56p. (gr. 2-3). pap. 7.19 (978-1-4342-3074-4(0)); lib. bdg. 26.65 (978-1-4342-2225-1(X)) Stone Arch Bks.

Collins, Terry. High-Flying Sam. Date not set. (Rocket Power Ready-to-Read Ser.: Vol. 5). (J). pap. 3.50 (978-0-689-86582-4(1), Simon Spotlight/Nickelodeon) Simon Spotlight/Nickelodeon.

Colman, Michelle Sinclair. Sporty Babies Wear Sweats. Dion, Nathalie, illus. 2010. (Urban Babies Wear Black Book Ser.). (ENG.). 20p. (J). (gr. -1 — 1). bds. 6.99 (978-1-58246-313-1(1), Tricycle Pr.) Random Hse. Children's Bks.

Connor, Lexi. The Runaway Spell. 2011. (B Magical Ser.: 3). (ENG.). 144p. (J). (gr. 3-7). pap. 5.99 (978-0-545-26552-2(5), Scholastic Paperbacks) Scholastic, Inc.

Cook, Julia. My Mom Thinks She's My Volleyball Coach... but She's Not! 2007. (J). pap. 9.95 (978-1-934073-09-4(1)); (YA). 15.95 (978-1-934073-10-0(5)) National Ctr. For Youth Issues.

—Teamwork Isn't My Thing, & I Don't Like to Share! De Weerd, Kelsey, illus. 2012. (ENG.). 32p. (J). pap. 10.95 (978-1-934490-35-8(0)) Boys Town Pr.

Coombs, Charles Ira. Indoor Sports Stories. Geer, Charles H., illus. 2011. 190p. 42.95 (978-1-258-09130-9(5)) Literary Licensing, LLC.

Coven, Wanda. Heidi Heckelbeck Tries Out for the Team. Burris, Priscilla, illus. 2017. (Heidi Heckelbeck Ser.: 19). (ENG.). 128p. (J). (gr. k-4). pap. 5.99 *(978-1-4814-7172-5(4),* Little Simon) Little Simon.

—Heidi Heckelbeck Tries Out for the Team. 2017. (Heidi Heckelbeck Ser.: 19). lib. bdg. 16.00 ***(978-0-606-39741-4(8))*** Turtleback Bks.

Cross, Julie. Off the Ice. 2017. (Juniper Falls Ser.). (ENG.). 370p. (YA). pap. 9.99 *(978-1-63375-655-7(6),* 9781633756557) Entangled Publishing, LLC.

Crutcher, Chris. Whale Talk. 2009. (ENG.). 304p. (YA). (gr. 8). pap. 9.99 *(978-0-06-177131-6(7),* Greenwillow Bks.) HarperCollins Pubs.

—Whale Talk. 2004. 224p. (J). (gr. 7-18). pap. 38.00 incl. audio *(978-0-8072-2289-8(5),* Listening Library) Random Hse. Audio Publishing Group.

Damman, Matthew. The Small Sports Take the Field! Eisenbraun, Patty, illus. 2nd ed. 2013. (ENG.). 32p. (J). 15.99 *(978-0-9856967-0-2(2))* MAP Creative LLC.

Darlison, A. Aim for the Top. 2016. (Netball Gems Ser.: 5). (ENG., Illus.). 160p. (J). (gr. 3-6). pap. 8.99 *(978-0-14-378114-1(6))* Random Hse. Australia AUS. Dist: Independent Pubs. Group.

Darlison, Aleesah. Willow's Victory Cancelled. Brailsford, Jill, illus. 2017. (Unicorn Riders Ser.). (ENG.). 112p. (gr. 3-5). pap. 5.95 *(978-1-4795-6557-3(1))* Picture Window Bks.

Deans, Sis Boulos. Racing the Past. 2005. (ENG.). 160p. (J). (gr. 3-7). reprint ed. 5.99 *(978-0-14-240308-2(3),* Puffin Books) Penguin Young Readers Group.

Delashmutt, Amy. Hello, Cy! Torgeson, Sarah, illus. 2007. 24p. (J). lib. bdg. 14.95 *(978-1-932888-53-9(5))* Mascot Bks., Inc.

deRubertis, Barbara. Rosie Raccoon's Rock & Roll Raft. Alley, R. W., illus. 2011. (Animal Antics A to Z Ser.). 32p. (J). pap. 45.32 *(978-0-7613-7664-4(X))* Kane Press, Inc.

Derubertis, Barbara. Tessa Tiger's Temper Tantrums. Alley, R. W., illus. 2011. (Animal Antics A to Z Set III Ser.). pap. 45.32 *(978-0-7613-8429-8(4))* Kane Press, Inc.

deRubertis, Barbara & DeRubertis, Barbara. Rosie Raccoon's Rock & Roll Raft. Alley, R. W., illus. 2012. (Animal Antics A to Z Ser.). 32p. (J). (gr. 2 — 1). cd-rom 7.95 *(978-1-57565-411-9(3))* Kane Press, Inc.

Devine, Eric. Press Play. 2014. (ENG.). 368p. (YA). (gr. 3-17). pap. 9.95 *(978-0-7624-5512-6(8),* Running Pr. Kids) Running Pr. Bk. Pubs.

Diersch, Sandra. Ceiling Stars, 1 vol. 2004. (Lorimer SideStreets Ser.). (ENG.). 144p. (YA). (gr. 9-12). 9.95 *(978-1-55028-834-6(2),* 9781550288346) Lorimer, James & Co., Ltd., Pubs. CAN. Dist: Casemate Pubs. & Bk. Distributors, LLC.

Diersch, Sandra & Moreira, Carol. Ceiling Stars, 1 vol. 2004. (Lorimer SideStreets Ser.). (ENG.). 144p. (YA). (gr. 9-12). 16.95 *(978-1-55028-835-3(0),* 9781550288353) Lorimer, James & Co., Ltd., Pubs. CAN. Dist: Casemate Pubs. & Bk. Distributors, LLC.

Dillard, Mary Gregory. The Days of My Youth. 2011. 184p. pap. 24.95 *(978-1-4560-7513-2(6))* America Star Bks.

Dixon, Amy. Marathon Mouse. Denlinger, Sam, illus. 2012. (ENG.). 32p. (J). (gr. -1-k). 16.95 *(978-1-61608-966-5(0),* 608966, Sky Pony Pr.) Skyhorse Publishing Co., Inc.

Drummond, Ree. Charlie Plays Ball. deGroat, Diane, illus. 2015. (Charlie the Ranch Dog Ser.). (ENG.). 40p. (J). (gr. -1-3). 17.99 *(978-0-06-229752-5(X))* HarperCollins Pubs.

Duane, Diane, et al. Death Match. 2003. (Net Force YA Ser.: 18). (ENG.). 192p. (Orig.). (YA). (gr. 7-18). 5.99 *(978-0-425-18448-6(X),* Berkley) Penguin Publishing Group.

Earhart, Kristin. Arctic Freeze. 2015. (Race the Wild Ser.: 3). lib. bdg. 14.75 *(978-0-606-37773-7(5))* Turtleback Bks.

Evans, Zoe. Bevan vs. Evan: And Other School Rivalries. Barrager, Brigette, illus. 2012. (Cheer! Ser.: 4). (ENG.). 224p. (J). (gr. 3-7). pap. 6.99 *(978-1-4424-3364-9(7),* Simon Spotlight) Simon Spotlight.

—Confessions of a Wannabe Cheerleader. Barrager, Brigette, illus. 2011. (Cheer! Ser.: 1). (ENG.). 240p. (J). (gr. 3-7). pap. 6.99 *(978-1-4424-2241-4(6),* Simon Spotlight) Simon Spotlight.

Farshtey, Greg & Scholastic, Inc. Staff. Zane - Ninja of Ice. 2011. (Lego Ninjago Ser.). (ENG.). 80p. (J). (gr. 2-5). pap. 4.99 *(978-0-545-34828-7(5))* Scholastic, Inc.

Ferguson, Donald. Chums of Scranton High on the Cinder Pat. 2006. 25.95 *(978-1-4218-2937-1(1));* pap. 10.95 *(978-1-4218-3037-7(X))* 1st World Publishing, Inc.

—The Chums of Scranton High on the Cinder Path. 2007. 124p. per. *(978-1-4065-2363-8(1))* Dodo Pr.

—Chums of Scranton High Out for the Penna. 2006. 25.95 *(978-1-4218-2938-8(X));* pap. 10.95 *(978-1-4218-3038-4(8))* 1st World Publishing, Inc.

—The Chums of Scranton High Out for the Pennant, or, in the Three Town League. 2007. 124p. per. *(978-1-4065-2364-5(X))* Dodo Pr.

Ferreira, Ninha. The Breakthrough: All Star Cheer Articles - Book 1. 2008. (ENG.). 194p. (YA). per. 13.95 *(978-0-9815202-0-9(0))* Higgins Publishing.

Flower, Graham Jessie. Grace Harlowe's Sophomore Year at High School: The Record of the Girl Chums in Work & Athletics. 2007. 154p. pap. 19.99 *(978-1-4264-8570-1(0));* (ENG.). 174p. pap. 21.99 *(978-1-4264-8627-2(8))* Creative Media Partners, LLC.

Freeman, Tor. Ambrose Goes for Gold. 2008. (ENG., Illus.). 32p. (J). (gr. 3-6). 24.50 *(978-0-230-53146-8(6),* Macmillan) Pan Macmillan GBR. Dist: Trans-Atlantic Pubns., Inc.

Froggatt, Sarah H. E. Leopard Spots: How the Clouded Leopard Got Her Spots. 2012. 32p. pap. 32.70 *(978-1-4771-3891-5(9))* Xlibris Corp.

Gallo, Lisa. A Picnic Adventure. Thomas, Laura, illus. 2010. (Strawberry Shortcake Ser.). (ENG.). 32p. (J). (gr. 1-3). mass mkt. 3.99 *(978-0-448-45345-3(2),* Penguin Young Readers) Penguin Young Readers Group.

Galloway, Priscilla. Atalante: La Coureuse la Plus Rapide au Monde. Cousineau, Normand, illus. 2006. (FRE.). 75p. (J). (gr. k-4). reprint ed. pap. 15.00 *(978-1-4223-5394-3(X))* DIANE Publishing Co.

Gassman, Julie A. Cheerleading Really Is a Sport, 1 vol. Santillan, Jorge H., illus. 2010. (Sports Illustrated Kids Victory School Superstars Ser.). (ENG.). 56p. (gr. 1-3). 26.65 *(978-1-4342-2130-8(X));* pap. 5.95 *(978-1-4342-2809-3(6))* Stone Arch Bks.

—I Am on Strike Against Softball, 1 vol. Santillan, Jorge H., illus. 2012. (Sports Illustrated Kids Victory School Superstars Ser.). (ENG.). 56p. (gr. 1-3). pap. 5.95 *(978-1-4342-3870-2(9));* lib. bdg. 26.65 *(978-1-4342-2247-3(0))* Stone Arch Bks.

—Nobody Wants to Play with a Ball Hog, 1 vol. Santillan, Jorge H., illus. 2010. (Sports Illustrated Kids Victory School Superstars Ser.). (ENG.). 56p. (gr. 1-3). 26.65 *(978-1-4342-2056-1(7));* pap. 5.95 *(978-1-4342-2806-2(1))* Stone Arch Bks.

—You Can't Spike Your Serves, 1 vol. Santillan, Jorge H., illus. 2011. (Sports Illustrated Kids Victory School Superstars Ser.). (ENG.). 56p. (gr. 1-3). pap. 5.95 *(978-1-4342-3080-5(5));* lib. bdg. 26.65 *(978-1-4342-2231-2(4))* Stone Arch Bks.

Gibbs, L. Netball Gems 2: Chase Your Goal. 2016. (Netball Gems Ser.: 2). (ENG.). 144p. (J). (gr. 4-7). pap. 8.99 *(978-0-85798-766-2(6))* Random Hse. Australia AUS. Dist: Independent Pubs. Group.

Gibbs, L. & Hellard, B. Defend to the End. 2016. (Netball Gems Ser.: 4). (ENG., Illus.). 144p. (J). (gr. 4-7). pap. 8.99 *(978-0-85798-770-9(4))* Random Hse. Australia AUS. Dist: Independent Pubs. Group.

—Hooked on Netball. Macinnes, Cat, illus. 2016. (Netball Gems Ser.: 1). (ENG.). 144p. (J). (gr. 4-7). 8.99 *(978-0-85798-763-1(1))* Random Hse. Australia AUS. Dist: Independent Pubs. Group.

Goodhart, Pippa. Fun Race. Mason, Sue, illus. 2013. (Start Reading Ser.). (ENG.). 24p. (gr. k-1). pap. 7.95 *(978-1-4765-4101-3(9))* Capstone Press of Coughlan Cos.

Gottesfeld, Jeff. Starstruck, 1 vol. 2015. (Red Rhino Ser.). (ENG.). 68p. (J). (gr. 4-6). pap. 7.95 *(978-1-62250-947-8(1))* Saddleback Educational Publishing, Inc.

Gray, Kes. Daisy & the Trouble with Sports Day. Sharratt, Nick, illus. 2014. (Daisy Ser.). (ENG.). 320p. (J). (gr. 2-4). pap. 11.99 *(978-1-78295-285-5(3),* Red Fox) Random House Children's Books GBR. Dist: Independent Pubs. Group.

Green, Tim. Kid Owner. 2016. (ENG.). 352p. (J). (gr. 3-7). 17.20 *(978-0-606-39256-3(4))* Turtleback Bks.

Hallinan, P. K. Let's Play As a Team. 2003. (ENG., Illus.). 28p. (J). 8.75 *(978-0-8249-5452-9(1),* Ideal Pubns.) Worthy Publishing.

Hancock, H. Irving. The High School Captain of the Team. 2006. (ENG.). 156p. pap. 19.99 *(978-1-4264-6386-0(3));* 172p. pap. 21.99 *(978-1-4264-6460-7(6))* Creative Media Partners, LLC.

—The High School Freshmen. rev. ed. 2006. 212p. 27.95 *(978-1-4218-1741-5(1));* pap. 12.95 *(978-1-4218-1841-2(8))* 1st World Publishing, Inc. (1st World Library - Literary Society).

—The High School Freshmen. 2007. 180p. per. *(978-1-4065-1988-4(X))* Dodo Pr.

—The High School Pitcher. rev. ed. 2006. 212p. 27.95 *(978-1-4218-1743-9(8));* pap. 12.95 *(978-1-4218-1843-6(4))* 1st World Publishing, Inc. (1st World Library - Literary Society).

Harding, David. Chance of a Lifetime. Fosdike, James, illus. 2015. (Israel Folau Ser.: 1). (ENG.). 192p. (J). (gr. 4-7). pap. 9.99 *(978-0-85798-661-0(9))* Random Hse. Australia AUS. Dist: Independent Pubs. Group.

—Reality Check. Fosdike, James, illus. 2015. (Israel Folau Ser.: 2). (ENG.). 192p. (J). (gr. 4-7). pap. 9.99 *(978-0-85798-663-4(5))* Random Hse. Australia AUS. Dist: Independent Pubs. Group.

Harris, Devon D. Yes I Can. 2006. (Illus.). 48p. (J). *(978-0-9764082-4-6(4))* Waterhouse Publishing.

Hartman, Mike. Take Your Dreams to the ICE. 2003. (Illus.). 60p. (YA). per. 9.99 *(978-0-9760419-1-7(X))* ThatsMyLife Co.

He, Xu. Happy Taichichuan. 2007. 60p. pap. 9.50 *(978-1-4303-2610-6(7))* Lulu Pr., Inc.

Health New England, creator. Sammie Sportz My Summer of Sports Safety. 2007. (Illus.). 16p. (J). 9.95 *(978-0-9777159-3-0(0))* Health New England.

Hegerhorst, Bethany. The Soccer Princess: Josephina & the Gown Fashion Runway Show, 13 bks., bk. 1. Abbott, Kristin, illus. 2011. 32p. (J). 17.99 *(978-0-615-35488-0(2))* Leo Publishing Works, Inc.

—The Soccer Princess: Josephina & the Gown Fashion Runway Show, 12. Abbott, Kristin, illus. 2011. 32p. (J). *(978-0-9803829-6-9(3))* Murray Bks.

Heidbreder, Robert. Crocodiles Play! Mate, Rae, illus. 2009. (ENG.). 32p. (J). (gr. -1-3). 16.95 *(978-1-894965-86-6(8))* Simply Read Bks. CAN. Dist: Ingram Publisher Services.

Hellard, B. Netball Gems Bindup 1. 2017. (Netball Gems Ser.). (ENG.). 304p. (J). (gr. 2-4). 17.99 ***(978-0-14-378088-5(3))*** Random Hse. Australia AUS. Dist: Independent Pubs. Group.

—Netball Gems Bindup 2. 2017. (Netball Gems Ser.). (ENG.). 304p. (J). (gr. 2-4). 17.99 ***(978-0-14-378090-8(5))*** Random Hse. Australia AUS. Dist: Independent Pubs. Group.

Hellard, B. Pivot & Win. 2016. (Netball Gems Ser.: 3). (ENG., Illus.). 144p. (J). (gr. 4-7). pap. 8.99 *(978-0-85798-768-6(2))* Random Hse. Australia AUS. Dist: Independent Pubs. Group.

Hellman, Charles. Fun Is... 2005. 124p. (gr. 4-7). per. 9.95 *(978-0-935938-16-6(8))* LuckySports.

Hellman, Charles S. Discovering Sportsland. Tiritilli, Robert A., illus. 2013. 44p. pap. 9.49 *(978-0-935938-51-7(6))* LuckySports.

—The Volleyball Bully. Tiritilli, Robert A., illus. 2013. 34p. pap. 9.25 *(978-0-935938-53-1(2))* LuckySports.

Hicks, Betty. Basketball Bats / Goof-Off Goalie. McCauley, Adam, illus. 2009. (Gym Shorts Ser.). (ENG.). 128p. (J). (gr. 2-5). pap. 10.99 *(978-0-312-58247-0(1),* 9780312582470) Square Fish.

Higgins, Kitty. Mushing in Alaska. 2005. (J). pap. *(978-1-4108-4228-2(2))* Benchmark Education Co.

Hitchhiking Flat Kid. 2004. (J). ring bd. 4.50 *(978-0-9763328-0-0(9),* Flat Kids) Smart Smiles Co., The.

Hoban, Russell. How Tom Beat Captain Najork & His Hired Sportsmen. Blake, Quentin, illus. 2006. (ENG.). 32p. (J). (gr. k-4). pap. 7.95 *(978-1-56792-322-3(4))* Godine, David R. Pub.

Hoese, Ray. My Dad Is an Ironman. Steinbach, Coreen, illus. 2004. (ENG.). 32p. (J). 15.00 *(978-1-891369-51-3(2))* Breakaway Bks.

Holm, Jennifer L. & Holm, Matthew. Captain Disaster. Holm, Jennifer L. & Holm, Matthew, illus. 2012. (Squish Ser.: No. 4). (ENG., Illus.). 96p. (J). (gr. 2-5). pap. 6.99 *(978-0-375-84392-1(2));* lib. bdg. 12.99 *(978-0-375-93786-6(2))* Random Hse. Children's Bks. (Random Hse. Bks. for Young Readers).

—Captain Disaster. 2012. (Squish Ser.: 4). lib. bdg. 17.20 *(978-0-606-26812-7(X),* Turtleback) Turtleback Bks.

Houran, Lori Haskins. Alien in the Outfield: Perseverance. Warrick, Jessica, illus. 2017. (How to Be an Earthling (r) Ser.: 6). (ENG.). 64p. (J). (gr. 1-3). lib. bdg. 22.65 *(978-1-57565-844-5(5))* Kane Press, Inc.

—Alien in the Outfield: Perseverance. Warrick, Jessica, illus. 2017. (How to Be an Earthling (r) Ser.: 6). (ENG.). 64p. (J). (gr. 1-3). 6.99 *(978-1-57565-848-3(8))* Kane Press, Inc.

Howling, Eric. Hoop Magic, 1 vol. 2013. (Lorimer Sports Stories Ser.). (ENG.). 136p. (J). (gr. 4-8). pap. 9.95 *(978-1-4594-0525-7(0),* 9781459405257) Lorimer, James & Co., Ltd., Pubs. CAN. Dist: Casemate Pubs. & Bk. Distributors, LLC.

Hutchins, Hazel. TJ & the Sports Fanatic, 1 vol. 2006. (Orca Young Readers Ser.). (ENG., Illus.). 144p. (J). (gr. 3-6). per. 5.95 *(978-1-55143-461-2(X))* Orca Bk. Pubs. USA.

I Play for Notre Dame. 2004. (J). bds. *(978-0-9749156-0-9(2))* Mandell, Ted.

Jeter, Derek. Change Up. 2016. (Jeter Publishing Ser.). (ENG., Illus.). 176p. (J). (gr. 3-7). 16.99 *(978-1-4814-6445-1(0),* Simon & Schuster/Paula Wiseman Bks.) Simon & Schuster/Paula Wiseman Bks.

Jones Beehler, Jayne J. Drop the Puck, It's Hockey Season. Dohm, Katrina G., illus. 2015. (Official Adventures Ser.). (ENG.). (J). (gr. 2-5). 17.95 *(978-1-59298-881-5(4))* Beaver's Pond Pr., Inc.

Jones, Christianne C. Rah-Rah Ruby!, 1 vol. Doerrfeld, Cori, illus. 2009. (My First Graphic Novel Ser.). (ENG.). 32p. (gr. k-2). pap. 6.25 *(978-1-4342-1412-6(5),* My First Graphic Novel) Stone Arch Bks.

Jones, Jasmine. Coach Carter. 2004. (Amistad Ser.). (ENG., Illus.). 144p. (J). (gr. 8-18). pap. 6.99 *(978-0-06-077252-9(2),* Amistad) HarperCollins Pubs.

Jones, Melanie Davis. Balls. Bronson, Linda, illus. 2011. (Rookie Ready to Learn - Numbers & Shapes Ser.). 32p. (J). (gr. -1-k). lib. bdg. 23.00 *(978-0-531-26445-4(9),* Children's Pr.) Scholastic Library Publishing.

Kaye, Marilyn. Teammates. 2014. (ENG., Illus.). 80p. (J). (gr. 3-7). pap. 13.99 *(978-1-4814-2887-3(X),* Simon & Schuster/Paula Wiseman Bks.) Simon & Schuster/Paula Wiseman Bks.

Kellerhals-Stewart, Heather. SAR: Powderhounds, 1 vol. 2013. (ENG.). 176p. (YA). (gr. 8-12). 19.95 *(978-1-4594-0518-9(8),* 9781459405189); pap. 12.95 *(978-1-4594-0519-6(6),* 9781459405196) Lorimer, James & Co., Ltd., Pubs. CAN. Dist: Casemate Pubs. & Bk. Distributors, LLC.

Kelli Hunter Beamon. Mommy, I Want to Be a Cheerleader! 2009. 16p. pap. 8.49 *(978-1-4389-7037-0(4))* AuthorHouse.

Kelly, David A. The Gold Medal Mess. Brundage, Scott, illus. 2016. (Most Valuable Players Ser.: 1). (ENG.). 128p. (J). (gr. 1-4). 4.99 *(978-0-553-51319-6(2),* Random Hse. Bks. for Young Readers) Random Hse. Children's Bks.

Kelsey, Stacy. Sprocket the Moto Dog, 1 vol. 2009. 40p. pap. 24.95 *(978-1-60749-899-5(5))* America Star Bks.

Kew, Trevor. Breakaway, 1 vol. 2011. (Lorimer Sports Stories Ser.). (ENG.). 144p. (J). (gr. 4-8). 16.95 *(978-1-55277-863-0(0),* 9781552778630); pap. 9.95 *(978-1-55277-862-3(2),* 9781552778623) Lorimer, James & Co., Ltd., Pubs. CAN. Dist: Casemate Pubs. & Bk. Distributors, LLC.

Kilby, Tracie. Gymnastics Gina. 2010. 32p. pap. 16.00 *(978-1-4520-6277-8(3))* AuthorHouse.

Kishimoto, Masashi. Naruto: Chapter Book, Vol. 2. Kishimoto, Masashi, illus. 2008. (ENG., Illus.). 80p. (J). (gr. 1-5). pap. 4.99 *(978-1-4215-2213-5(6))* Viz Media.

Klass, David. Losers Take All. 2015. (ENG.). 320p. (YA). (gr. 7). 17.99 *(978-0-374-30136-1(0),* 9780374301361, Farrar, Straus & Giroux (BYR)) Farrar, Straus & Giroux.

—Losers Take All. 2016. (YA). lib. bdg. 20.85 *(978-0-606-39480-2(X))* Turtleback Bks.

Koertge, Ron. Shakespeare Makes the Playoffs. 2012. (ENG., Illus.). 176p. (YA). (gr. 7). pap. 6.99 *(978-0-7636-5852-6(9))* Candlewick Pr.

Kosgei, William. The Talented & Gifted: African Writers Series. 2013. 106p. pap. 10.95 *(978-1-62516-165-9(4),* Strategic Bk. Publishing) Strategic Book Publishing & Rights Agency (SBPRA).

Krakow, Amy. The Matt & the Monster 60 Sking & Snowboarding. Williams, Steve, illus. 2005. 32p. (J). (gr. k-6). 15.00 *(978-0-9715224-2-8(1))* Wagging Tales Publishing.

Kreie, Chris. I Couldn't Land a Bunny Hop, 1 vol. Santillan, Jorge H., illus. 2012. (Sports Illustrated Kids Victory School Superstars Ser.). (ENG.). 56p. (gr. 1-3). pap. 5.95 *(978-1-4342-3865-8(2));* lib. bdg. 26.65 *(978-1-4342-3762-0(1))* Stone Arch Bks.

Kreie, Chris & Maese, Fares. Shot Clock Slam. Aburto, Jesus & Esparza, Andres, illus. 2010. (Sports Illustrated Kids Graphic Novels Ser.). (ENG.). 56p. (gr. 2-3). pap. 7.19 *(978-1-4342-2786-7(3))* Stone Arch Bks.

Krinsky, Lee. The Longest Fall. 2009. 228p. 25.95 *(978-0-595-71908-2(2));* pap. 15.95 *(978-0-595-42719-2(7))* iUniverse, Inc.

Krulik, Nancy & dePaola, Tomie. 'Snot Funny! Blecha, Aaron, illus. 2015. (George Brown, Class Clown Ser.: 14). (ENG.). 128p. (J). (gr. 2-4). bds. 4.99 *(978-0-448-48282-8(7),* Grosset & Dunlap) Penguin Young Readers Group.

Laks, Shan. The Tale of Brave Ritchie: Be Aware of Strangers; Beat the Bullies & Exercise Changes Health. 2012. 76p. pap. 42.05 *(978-1-4797-2882-4(9))* Xlibris Corp.

Landers, Ace. Race for Treasure. White, Dave, illus. 2011. 32p. (J). pap. *(978-0-545-33454-9(3))* Scholastic, Inc.

Lewis, Axel. Canyon Chaos, 1 vol. 2014. (Robot Racers Ser.). (ENG., Illus.). 160p. (gr. 2-4). pap. 6.95 *(978-1-4342-7936-1(7))* Stone Arch Bks.

—Rain Forest Rampage. 2014. (Robot Racers Ser.). (ENG., 160p. (gr. 2-4). Illus.). pap. 6.95 *(978-1-4342-7937-8(5));* 26.65 *(978-1-4342-6571-5(4))* Stone Arch Bks.

Ley, Mary. Tri-Son: The Little Triathlete. Ley, Mary, illus. 2003. (Illus.). per. *(978-0-9707547-1-4(X))* Woodburn Graphics, Inc.

Lin, Chris. Mandy & Pandy Play Sports. Villalta, Ingrid, illus. 2008. 20p. (J). (gr. -1-3). bds. 9.99 *(978-0-9800156-7-6(7))* Mandy & Pandy Bks., LLC.

London, Jonathan. Desolation Canyon. London, Sean, illus. 2015. (Aaron's Wilderness Ser.: 1). (ENG.). 168p. (YA). pap. 12.99 *(978-1-941821-29-9(4),* West Winds Pr.) Graphic Arts Ctr. Publishing Co.

London, Jonathan & Remkiewicz, Frank. Froggy Plays T-Ball. Remkiewicz, Frank, illus. 2009. (Froggy Ser.). (ENG., Illus.). 32p. (J). (gr. -1-k). pap. 6.99 *(978-0-14-241304-3(6),* Puffin Books) Penguin Young Readers Group.

Long, Loren & Bildner, Phil. Blastin' the Blues. Long, Loren, illus. 2011. (Sluggers Ser.: 5). (ENG., Illus.). 448p. (J). (gr. 3-7). pap. 8.99 *(978-1-4169-1891-2(4),* Simon & Schuster Bks. For Young Readers) Simon & Schuster Bks. For Young Readers.

Loughlin, Patrick. Super Sports Stories for Kids. Hart, James, illus. 2016. (ENG.). 208p. (J). (gr. 1-3). pap. 11.99 *(978-0-85798-966-6(9))* Random Hse. Australia AUS. Dist: Independent Pubs. Group.

Lubar, David. Lay Ups & Long Shots: Eight Short Stories. 2008. 128p. (YA). (gr. 5-8). 14.95 *(978-1-58196-078-5(6),* Darby Creek) Lerner Publishing Group.

Luciani, Brigitte. What a Team! Gauvin, Edward, tr. from FRE. Tharlet, Eve, illus. 2011. (Mr. Badger & Mrs. Fox Ser.: 3). (ENG.). 32p. (J). (gr. k-3). 25.26 *(978-0-7613-5627-1(4))* Lerner Publishing Group.

Lupica, Mike. Game Changers. 2013. (Game Changers Ser.: 1). (ENG.). 224p. (J). (gr. 3-7). pap. 6.99 *(978-0-545-38179-6(7),* Scholastic Pr.) Scholastic, Inc.

—Safe at Home, 1 vol. 2012. (Comeback Kids Ser.). (ENG.). 192p. (J). (gr. 4-8). lib. bdg. 27.07 *(978-1-59961-177-8(5))* Spotlight.

—True Legend. 2012. (ENG.). 304p. (J). (gr. 5). 17.99 *(978-0-399-25227-3(4),* Philomel Bks.) Penguin Young Readers Group.

Lynch, Chris. Slot Machine. 2003. 23.00 *(978-0-8446-7249-6(1))* Smith, Peter Pub., Inc.

Maccarone, Grace. Bunny Race! Long, Ethan, illus. 2009. (J). *(978-0-545-11290-1(7))* Scholastic, Inc.

Macdonald, Kelly. They Shoot! They Score! Life's Lessons on Ice. Luca, Bogdan, illus. 2005. 32p. 9.99 *(978-0-9736893-0-3(7))* MacDonald, Kelly CAN. Dist: Hushion Hse. Publishing, Ltd.

MacGregor, Roy. The Highest Number in the World. Despres, Genevieve, illus. 2014. (ENG.). 32p. (J). (gr. 1-4). 17.99 *(978-1-77049-575-3(4),* Tundra Bks.) Tundra Bks. CAN. Dist: Penguin Random Hse. LLC.

—The Night They Stole the Stanley Cup. 2013. (Screech Owls Ser.). (ENG.). 176p. (J). (gr. 4-7). pap. 8.99 *(978-1-77049-414-5(6),* Tundra Bks.) Tundra Bks. CAN. Dist: Penguin Random Hse. LLC.

Mack, W. C. Time-Out. 2014. (Athlete vs. Mathlete Ser.). (ENG.). 208p. (YA). (gr. 3-6). 16.99 *(978-1-61963-301-8(9),* 9781619633018, Bloomsbury USA Childrens) Bloomsbury Publishing USA.

Maddox, Jake. Caught Stealing. Aburtov, Jesus Aburto, illus. 2015. (Jake Maddox Sports Stories Ser.). (ENG.). 72p. (gr. 2-3). lib. bdg. 25.32 *(978-1-4965-0493-7(3))* Stone Arch Bks.

—Definición por Penales. Heck, Claudia M., tr. from ENG. Tiffany, Sean, illus. 2012. (Jake Maddox en Español Ser.). (SPA.). 72p. (gr. 2-3). 25.32 *(978-1-4342-3814-6(8))* Stone Arch Bks.

—En la línea de Ataque. Heck, Claudia M., tr. from ENG. Tiffany, Sean, illus. 2012. (Jake Maddox en Español Ser.). (SPA.). 72p. (gr. 2-3). 25.32 *(978-1-4342-3813-9(X))* Stone Arch Bks.

—Face-Off, 1 vol. Tiffany, Sean, illus. 2006. (Jake Maddox Sports Stories Ser.). (ENG.). 72p. (gr. 2-3). lib. bdg. 25.32 *(978-1-59889-063-1(8))* Stone Arch Bks.

—Free Climb. Tiffany, Sean, illus. 2008. (Jake Maddox Sports Stories Ser.). (ENG.). 72p. (gr. 2-3). 25.32 *(978-1-4342-0784-5(6));* pap. 5.95 *(978-1-4342-0880-4(X))* Stone Arch Bks.

—Gold Medal Swim, 1 vol. Garcia, Eduardo, illus. 2012. (Jake Maddox Sports Stories Ser.). (ENG.). 72p. (gr. 2-3). lib. bdg. 25.32 *(978-1-4342-3288-5(3))* Stone Arch Bks.

—Gridiron Showdown, 1 vol. Ray, Mike, illus. 2014. (Jake Maddox JV Ser.). (ENG.). 96p. (gr. 3-4). 25.99 *(978-1-4342-9155-4(3))* Stone Arch Bks.

—Impact Books, 10 bks., Set. Tiffany, Sean, illus. 2007. (Jake Maddox Sports Stories Ser.). (ENG.). 72p. (gr. 2-3). 253.20 *(978-1-59889-462-2(5))* Stone Arch Bks.

—Jake Maddox. 2013. (Jake Maddox Sports Stories Ser.). (ENG.). 72p. (gr. 2-3). lib. bdg. 1544.52 *(978-1-4342-6052-9(6))* Stone Arch Bks.

—Jake Maddox. Tiffany, Sean, illus. 2013. (Jake Maddox Sports Stories Ser.). (ENG.). 72p. (gr. 2-3). lib. bdg. 101.28 *(978-1-4342-6051-2(8))* Stone Arch Bks.

—Jake Maddox Girl Sport Stories. Wood, Katie, illus. (Jake Maddox Girl Sports Stories Ser.). (ENG.). 72p. (gr. 2-3). 2014. pap. 24.80 *(978-1-4342-8947-6(8))* 2013. 101.28 *(978-1-4342-4134-4(3))* Stone Arch Bks.

—Jake Maddox Girl Sports Stories, 1 vol. Wood, Katie, illus. (Jake Maddox Girl Sports Stories Ser.). (ENG.). 72p. (gr. 2-3). 2014. 101.28 *(978-1-4342-6402-2(5))* 2013. 708.96 *(978-1-4342-4847-3(X))* 2013. pap. 71.40 *(978-1-4342-4359-1(1))* 2013. pap. 23.80 *(978-1-4342-4358-4(3))* Stone Arch Bks.

—Jake Maddox Girls Sport Stories. Wood, Katie, illus. 2014. (Jake Maddox Girl Sports Stories Ser.). (ENG.). 72p. (gr. 2-3). pap. 96.20 *(978-1-4342-8948-3(6))* Stone Arch Bks.

—Jake Maddox Graphic Novels. 2017. (Jake Maddox Graphic Novels Ser.). (ENG.). 72p. (gr. 2-5). 106.60 *(978-1-4965-3747-8(5))* Stone Arch Bks.

—Jake Maddox JV. Ray, Mike, illus. 2015. (Jake Maddox JV Ser.). (ENG.). 96p. (gr. 3-4). 103.96 *(978-1-4965-0045-8(8))* Stone Arch Bks.

—Jake Maddox JV Girls. 2016. (Jake Maddox JV Girls Ser.). (ENG.). 96p. (gr. 3-4). 103.96 *(978-1-4965-3692-1(4))* Stone Arch Bks.

—Jake Maddox Sports Stories, 4 vols. (Jake Maddox Sports Stories Ser.). (ENG.). 72p. (gr. 2-3). 2015. 101.28 *(978-1-4965-2006-7(8))* 2013. pap. 255.85 *(978-1-4342-6316-2(9))* 2013. pap. 1499.40 *(978-1-4342-6315-5(0))* 2013. pap. 23.80 *(978-1-4342-6317-9(7))* Stone Arch Bks.

S

—Jump Serve. Mourning, Tuesday, illus. 2008. (Jake Maddox Girl Sports Stories Ser.). (ENG.). 72p. (gr. 2-3). lib. bdg. 25.32 (978-1-4342-0470-7(7)); per. 5.95 (978-1-4342-0520-9(7)) Stone Arch Bks.

—Lacrosse Attack. Tiffany, Sean, illus. 2008. (Jake Maddox Sports Stories Ser.). (ENG.). 72p. (gr. 2-3). 25.32 (978-1-4342-0776-0(5)); pap. 5.95 (978-1-4342-0872-9(9)) Stone Arch Bks.

—Lacrosse Laser. Aburtov, Jesus Aburto, illus. 2016. (Jake Maddox Sports Stories Ser.). (ENG.). 72p. (gr. 2-3). lib. bdg. 25.32 (978-1-4965-3051-6(9)) Stone Arch Bks.

—On the Line, 1 vol. Tiffany, Sean, illus. 2006. (Jake Maddox Sports Stories Ser.). (ENG.). 72p. (gr. 2-3). 25.32 (978-1-59889-062-4(X)) Stone Arch Bks.

—Over the Net, 1 vol. Mourning, Tuesday, illus. 2009. (Jake Maddox Girl Sports Stories Ser.). (ENG.). 72p. (gr. 2-3). 25.32 (978-1-4342-1213-9(0)) Stone Arch Bks.

—Paintball Boss. 2016. (Jake Maddox JV Ser.). (ENG.). 96p. (gr. 3-4). lib. bdg. 25.99 (978-1-4965-3982-3(6)) Stone Arch Bks.

—Pool Panic. Wood, Katie, illus. 2016. (Jake Maddox Girl Sports Stories Ser.). (ENG.). 72p. (gr. 2-3). lib. bdg. 25.32 (978-1-4965-2618-2(X)) Stone Arch Bks.

—Relay Race Breakdown, 1 vol. Garcia, Eduardo, illus. 2012. (Jake Maddox Sports Stories Ser.). (ENG.). 72p. (gr. 2-3). pap. 5.95 (978-1-4342-3903-7(9)); lib. bdg. 25.32 (978-1-4342-3289-2(1)) Stone Arch Bks.

—Soccer Shootout, 1 vol. Tiffany, Sean, illus. 2007. (Jake Maddox Sports Stories Ser.). (ENG.). 72p. (gr. 2-3). 25.32 (978-1-59889-844-6(2)) Stone Arch Bks.

—Tiro Libre, 1 vol. Heck, Claudia M., tr. from ENG. Tiffany, Sean, illus. 2012. (Jake Maddox en Español Ser.). (SPA.). 72p. (gr. 2-3). 25.32 (978-1-4342-3812-2(1)) Stone Arch Bks.

—El Tramposo de BMX, 1 vol. Heck, Claudia M., tr. from ENG. Tiffany, Sean, illus. 2012. (Jake Maddox en Español Ser.). (SPA.). 72p. (gr. 2-3). 25.32 (978-1-4342-3817-7(2)) Stone Arch Bks.

—Volleyball Dreams, 1 vol. Wood, Katie, illus. 2012. (Jake Maddox Girl Sports Stories Ser.). (ENG.). 72p. (gr. 2-3). pap. 5.95 (978-1-4342-3907-5(1)); lib. bdg. 25.32 (978-1-4342-3292-2(1)) Stone Arch Bks.

—Volleyball Victory. Wood, Katie, illus. 2016. (Jake Maddox Girl Sports Stories Ser.). (ENG.). 72p. (gr. 2-3). lib. bdg. 25.32 (978-1-4965-2619-9(8)) Stone Arch Bks.

—Whitewater Courage, 1 vol. Tiffany, Sean, illus. 2011. (Jake Maddox Sports Stories Ser.). (ENG.). 72p. (gr. 2-3). lib. bdg. 25.32 (978-1-4342-2530-6(5)) Stone Arch Bks.

Maddox, Jake & Berne, Emma Carlson. Soccer Surprise, 1 vol. Wood, Katie, illus. 2012. (Jake Maddox Girl Sports Stories Ser.). (ENG.). 72p. (gr. 2-3). pap. 5.95 (978-1-4342-3906-8(3)); lib. bdg. 25.32 (978-1-4342-3291-5(3)) Stone Arch Bks.

Magness, Vicki. Stephen: A Strong Man to Run a Race. 2012. 40p. pap. 21.99 (978-1-4771-2562-5(0)) Xlibris Corp.

Maiocco, Chris & Maiocco, Kimberly. Things My Father Taught Me Through Sports... Playing the Game of Baseball: Playing the Game of Baseball. Cox, Tom, illus. 2003. 20p. (J). 12.99 (978-0-9720417-0-6(2), 0-9720417-0-2) His Kids Publishing, Inc.

Manceau, Édouard. The Race, 0 vols. Owlkids Books Inc. Staff & Quinn, Sarah, trs. from FRE. 2014. (ENG & FRE., Illus.). 64p. (J). (gr. -1-4). 17.95 (978-1-77147-055-1(0), Owlkids) Owlkids Bks. Inc. CAN. Dist: Publishers Group West (PGW).

Mantell, Paul & Christopher, Matt. Snowboard Champ. 2005. (Matt Christopher Sports Ser.). 146p. (gr. 3-7). 16.00 (978-0-7569-5198-6(4)) Perfection Learning Corp.

Mantlo, Mickey A. & Cook, Darren A. Tennis Shoes & Toe Clips, 1 vol. 2010. 204p. pap. 24.95 (978-1-4512-9683-9(5)) America Star Bks.

Marsh, Carole. The Castaway Cheerleaders. 2006. 64p. (gr. 2-4). 14.95 (978-0-635-06224-6(0)); pap. 3.99 (978-0-635-06218-5(6)) Gallopade International.

—The Mystery on Alaska's Iditarod Trail. 2009. (Real Kids, Real Places Ser.). 145p. (J). 18.99 (978-0-635-06997-9(0), Marsh, Carole Mysteries) Gallopade International.

Martin, R. Pod Racer. 2017. (Level Up Ser.). (ENG.). (YA). (gr. 6-12). 120p. pap. 7.99 (**978-1-5124-5358-4(7)**); lib. bdg. 26.65 (**978-1-5124-3988-5(6)**) Lerner Publishing Group. (Darby Creek).

Mayer, Mercer. Fair Play. 2012. (Big Little Critter Ser.: 1). (ENG., Illus.). 98p. (J). 12.95 (978-1-60746-763-2(1), Premiere) FastPrncil, Inc.

McCann, James. Flying Feet, 1 vol. 2010. (Orca Sports Ser.). (ENG., Illus.). 152p. (YA). (gr. 6-10). pap. 9.95 (978-1-55469-290-3(3)) Orca Bk. Pubs. USA.

McCoy, Mary. Camp So-And-So. 2017. (ENG.). 424p. (YA). (gr. 8-12). 18.99 (978-1-5124-1597-1(9)); 9.99 (**978-1-5124-3428-6(0)**, Carolrhoda Lab™); 38.65 (**978-1-5124-3429-3(9)**, Carolrhoda Lab™); 38.65 (**978-1-5124-2693-9(8)**, Carolrhoda Lab™) Lerner Publishing Group.

McCully, Emily Arnold. Late Nate in a Race. McCully, Emily Arnold, illus. 2013. (I Like to Read(r) Ser.). (ENG., Illus.). 24p. (J). (gr. -1-3). pap. 6.99 (978-0-8234-2755-0(2)) Holiday Hse., Inc.

McDonald, Megan. Stink & the Ultimate Thumb-Wrestling Smackdown. Reynolds, Peter H., illus. 2013. (Stink Ser.: 6). (ENG.). 144p. (J). (gr. 1-4). pap. 4.99 (978-0-7636-6423-7(5));Bk. 6. 12.99 (978-0-7636-6393-3(X)) Candlewick Pr.

—Stink & the Ultimate Thumb-Wrestling Smackdown, 1 vol. Reynolds, Peter H., illus. 2012. (Stink Ser.: No. 2). (ENG.). 144p. (J). (gr. 2-5). 24.21 (978-1-59961-194-5(5)) Spotlight.

McDonnell, Vincent. Race Against Time. 2005. (SPA & ENG.). 96p. (J). pap. 11.95 (978-1-903464-62-5(5)) Collins Pr., The IRL. Dist: Dufour Editions, Inc.

McEwan, Jamie. Willy the Scrub. Kennedy, Victor, illus. 2004. (Junior Library Guild Selection Ser.). (ENG.). 64p. (J). (gr. 2-5). 11.95 (978-1-58196-010-5(7), Darby Creek) Lerner Publishing Group.

McKee, David. Elmer & the Whales. McKee, David, illus. 2014. (ENG., Illus.). 32p. (J). (gr. -1-3). 16.95 (978-1-4677-3453-0(5)) Lerner Publishing Group.

McKissack, Robert L. Try Your Best. Cepeda, Joe, illus. 2004. (Green Light Readers Level 2 Ser.). (ENG.). 24p. (J). (gr. -1-3). pap. 3.95 (978-0-15-205090-0(6)) Houghton Mifflin Harcourt Publishing Co.

—Try Your Best. Cepeda, Joe, illus. 2005. (Green Light Readers Level 2 Ser.). (gr. k-2). 13.95 (978-0-7569-5630-1(7)) Perfection Learning Corp.

McMahon, Kate. That Touch of Magic. 2009. (ENG.). 112p. (J). pap. 12.95 (978-1-901737-60-8(8)) Anvil Bks., Ltd. IRL. Dist: Dufour Editions, Inc.

McMullan, Kate. Go for the Gold, Atalanta! 2003. (Myth-o-Mania Ser.: No. 8). (Illus.). 160p. (J). 9.99 (978-0-7868-0864-9(0)) Hyperion Bks. for Children.

—Go for the Gold, Atalanta!, 1 vol. Zilber, Denis, illus. (Myth-O-Mania Ser.: Bk. 8). (ENG.). 192p. (gr. 4-8). 2011. pap. 5.95 (978-1-4342-3441-4(X)) 2010. lib. bdg. 25.32 (978-1-4342-3197-0(6)) Stone Arch Bks. (Myth-O-Mania).

McOmber, Rachel B., ed. McOmber Phonics Storybooks: A Game for Champions. rev. ed. (Illus.). (J). (978-0-944991-68-8(8)) Swift Learning Resources.

Meister, Cari. The Kickball Kids, 1 vol. Olson, Julie, illus. 2009. (My First Graphic Novel Ser.). (ENG.). 32p. (gr. k-2). pap. 6.25 (978-1-4342-1410-2(9)); lib. bdg. 24.65 (978-1-4342-1294-8(7)) Stone Arch Bks. (My First Graphic Novel).

Mills, Tricia. Heartbreak River. 2009. (YA). (978-1-59514-220-7(7), Razorbill) Penguin Publishing Group.

Moceanu, Dominique & Thompson, Alicia. Reaching High. 2012. (Go-For-Gold Gymnasts Ser.). (ENG.). 224p. (J). (gr. 5-9). pap. 5.99 (978-1-4231-3657-6(8)) Hyperion Pr.

Montalbano, Andrea. Lily Out of Bounds. 2012. (ENG.). 132p. (J). pap. 8.99 (978-0-9858956-1-7(6)) In This Together Media.

Montgomery, R. A. Always Picked Last. 2009. 64p. (J). pap. 7.99 (978-1-933390-38-3(7)) Chooseco LLC.

Moore, Stephanie Perry. Keep Jumping/No Hating. 2012. (Lockwood Lions Ser.). (YA). lib. bdg. 26.90 (978-0-606-26494-5(9), Turtleback) Turtleback Bks.

—Prayed Up, 4 vols. 2008. (ENG., Illus.). 208p. (YA). (gr. 8-12). 15.00 (978-0-7582-2538-2(5), K-Teen/Dafina) Kensington Publishing Corp.

—Settle down/Be Real. 2012. (Lockwood Lions Ser.). (YA). lib. bdg. 26.90 (978-0-606-26495-2(7), Turtleback) Turtleback Bks.

Moore, Stephanie Perry & Moore, Derrick. Real Diva/Man Up. 2014. (Grovehill Giants Ser.). (YA). lib. bdg. 26.90 (978-0-606-31879-2(8), Turtleback) Turtleback Bks.

—Scream Loud/Quiet Strength. 2014. (Grovehill Giants Ser.). (YA). lib. bdg. 26.90 (978-0-606-31880-8(1), Turtleback) Turtleback Bks.

Moore, Steve. King of the Bench: No Fear! Moore, Steve, illus. 2017. (King of the Bench Ser.: 1). (Illus.). 224p. (J). (gr. 3-7). 13.99 (978-0-06-220330-4(4)) HarperCollins Pubs.

Morgan, Alex. Under Pressure. 2017. (Kicks Ser.). (ENG., Illus.). 128p. (J). (gr. 3-7). 16.99 (**978-1-4814-8150-2(9)**, Simon & Schuster Bks. For Young Readers) Simon & Schuster Bks. For Young Readers.

Morgan, Alex. Win or Lose. 2014. (Kicks Ser.). (ENG., Illus.). 160p. (J). (gr. 3-7). 15.99 (978-1-4424-8580-8(9), Simon & Schuster Bks. For Young Readers) Simon & Schuster Bks. For Young Readers.

Morningstar, Jeremy. My Own Special Angel. 2005. 24p. 7.00 (978-1-4116-6574-3(0)) Lulu Pr., Inc.

Murphy, Harriet. Diego in Action! Follow the Reader Level 2. 2007. (Go, Diego, Go! Ser.). (ENG., Illus.). 24p. (J). (gr. -1-2). 24.99 (978-1-4169-4993-0(3), Simon Scribbles) Simon Scribbles.

Murray, Stuart A. P. Matty in the Goal. 2012. (Champion Sports Story Ser.). 104p. (J). (gr. 3-18). pap. 10.95 (978-1-4644-0003-2(2)); 27.94 (978-0-7660-3877-6(7)) Enslow Pubs., Inc.

Myers, Walter Dean. Game. (ENG.). (YA). (gr. 8). 2009. 240p. pap. 9.99 (978-0-06-058296-3(0)) 2008. 224p. 17.99 (978-0-06-058294-4(4)) HarperCollins Pubs. (HarperTeen).

Neighbors, Jared. Rivals, 1 vol. 2009. 73p. pap. 19.95 (978-1-61582-021-4(3)) America Star Bks.

New Coach Blues. 2003. (Illus.). pap. 5.60 (978-0-7398-7509-4(4)) Steck-Vaughn.

Nickel, Scott. I Could Be a One-Man Relay, 1 vol. Santillan, Jorge H., illus. 2012. (Sports Illustrated Kids Victory School Superstars Ser.). (ENG.). 56p. (gr. 1-3). pap. 5.95 (978-1-4342-3867-2(9)); lib. bdg. 26.65 (978-1-4342-2246-6(2)) Stone Arch Bks.

Norman, Kimberly. Ten on the Sled. Woodruff, Liza, illus. 2010. (ENG.). 26p. (J). (gr. -1). 14.95 (978-1-4027-7076-0(6)) Sterling Publishing Co., Inc.

Olivas, Daniel. Benjamin & Word Benjamin Y la Palabra. (SPA & ENG., Illus.). 32p. 15.95 (978-1-55885-413-0(4), Piñata Books) Arte Publico Pr.

O'Neal, Shaquille. Little Shaq. Taylor, Theodore, III, illus. 2015. (ENG.). 80p. (J). (gr. k-2). 9.99 (978-1-61963-721-4(9), 9781619637214, Bloomsbury USA Childrens) Bloomsbury Publishing USA.

Owen, Frank, ed. Teenage Winter Sports Stories. Ricketts, William, illus. 2011. 254p. 46.95 (978-1-258-10167-1(X)) Literary Licensing, LLC.

Parish, Herman. Amelia Bedelia Chapter Book #5. Avril, Lynne, illus. 2014. (Amelia Bedelia Ser.). (ENG.). 160p. (J). (gr. 1-5). 9.99 (978-0-06-233399-5(2), Greenwillow Bks.) HarperCollins Pubs.

—Amelia Bedelia Shapes Up! Avril, Lynne, illus. 2014. (Amelia Bedelia Ser.). (ENG.). 160p. (J). (gr. 1-5). pap. 4.99 (978-0-06-233396-4(8), Greenwillow Bks.) HarperCollins Pubs.

Pattison, Darcy. The Scary Slopes, 1 vol. Harpster, Steve, illus. 2011. (My First Graphic Novel Ser.). (ENG.). 32p. (gr. k-2). lib. bdg. 24.65 (978-1-4342-2534-4(8), My First Graphic Novel) Stone Arch Bks.

Pee-Wee T-Ball. 2003. (J). per. (978-1-57657-942-8(5)) Paradise Pr., Inc.

Peirce, Lincoln. Big Nate: Thunka, Thunka, Thunka. 2016. (Big Nate Ser.: Vol. 14). (ENG., Illus.). (J). (gr. 3-6). 29.99 (**978-1-4494-7581-9(7)**) Andrews McMeel Publishing.

Peirce, Lincoln. Big Nate: Thunka, Thunka, Thunka. 2016. (ENG., Illus.). 176p. (J). (gr. 3-6). pap. 9.99 (978-1-4494-6227-7(8)) Andrews McMeel Publishing.

Peltola, Anne. Boing Boing. 2009. (ENG., Illus.). 32p. (J). (gr. -1-1). 12.95 (978-1-59270-085-1(3)) Enchanted Lion Bks., LLC.

Peschke, Marci. Football Queen, 1 vol. Mourning, Tuesday, illus. 2012. (Kylie Jean Ser.). (ENG.). 112p. (gr. 2-3). pap. 5.95 (978-1-4048-7210-3(8)); lib. bdg. 22.65 (978-1-4048-6799-4(6)) Picture Window Bks. (Kylie Jean).

Petrillo, Genevieve & Lyon, Lea. Keep Your Ear on the Ball, 1 vol. Lyon, Lea07/, illus. 2009. (ENG.). 32p. (gr. 2-6). pap. 7.95 (978-0-88448-324-3(X), 884324) Tilbury Hse. Pubs.

Phillips, Lyda. Mr Touchdown. 2008. 184p. 23.95 (978-1-4401-0976-8(1)); pap. 13.95 (978-1-60528-029-5(1)) iUniverse, Inc. (iUniverse Star).

Popalis, Amy. Everyone Plays Sports. 2015. (ENG.). 24p. (gr. k-3). 28.50 (978-1-63430-362-0(8)) Rourke Educational Media.

Posada, Jorge. Sí, Puedes. Colón, Raúl, illus. 2010.Tr. of Play Ball! (SPA.). 32p. (J). (gr. 1-5). 6.99 (978-1-4169-9826-6(8), Simon & Schuster/Paula Wiseman Bks.) Simon & Schuster/Paula Wiseman Bks.

Poulsen, David A. Blind Date. 2nd rev. ed. 2008. (Lawrence High Yearbook Ser.). (ENG.). 96p. (J). (gr. 2-7). pap. (978-1-55263-933-7(9)) Me to We.

—Wild Thing. 2008. (Lawrence High Yearbook Ser.). (ENG.). 96p. (gr. 2-7). pap. (978-1-55263-931-3(2)) Me to We.

Raczka, Bob. Joy in Mudville. Dibley, Glin, illus. 2014. (ENG.). 32p. (J). (gr. -1-3). 17.95 (978-0-7613-6015-5(8), Carolrhoda Bks.) Lerner Publishing Group.

Random House Staff. Blaze of Glory (Blaze & the Monster Machines) Foley, Niki, illus. 2015. (Pictureback(R) Ser.). (ENG.). 16p. (J). (gr. -1-2). 4.99 (978-0-553-52457-4(7), Random Hse. Bks. for Young Readers) Random Hse. Children's Bks.

Rayburn, Tricia. Maggie Bean Stays Afloat. 2008. (ENG.). 320p. (J). (gr. 4-8). pap. 6.99 (978-1-4169-3347-2(6), Aladdin) Simon & Schuster Children's Publishing.

Rayner, Robert. Just for Kicks, 1 vol. 2004. (Lorimer Sports Stories Ser.). (ENG.). 152p. (J). (gr. 4-8). 16.95 (978-1-55028-825-4(3), 9781550288254) Lorimer, James & Co., Ltd., Pubs. CAN. Dist: Casemate Pubs. & Bk. Distributors, LLC.

Ricci, Christine. The Super Soccer Game. Hall, Susan & Roper, Robert, illus. 2007. (J). pap. (978-1-4127-8926-4(5)) Publications International, Ltd.

Richardson, Charisse K. The Real Slam Dunk. Nelson, Kadir, illus. 2005. (ENG.). 96p. (J). (gr. k-3). 5.99 (978-0-14-240212-2(5), Puffin Books) Penguin Young Readers Group.

Riley, Zach. Down for the Count. Ricci, Andrés, illus. 2012. (Zach Riley Ser.). 80p. (J). (gr. 3-6). lib. bdg. 27.07 (978-1-61783-533-9(1)) Magic Wagon.

—Quarterback Crisis. Ricci, Andrés, illus. 2012. (Zach Riley Ser.). 80p. (J). (gr. 3-6). lib. bdg. 27.07 (978-1-61783-534-6(X)) Magic Wagon.

Rippin, Sally. The Soccer Star. Fukuoka, Aki, illus. 2012. 44p. (J). (978-1-61067-133-0(3)) Kane Miller.

Robins, Eleanor. Back-Up Quarterback, 1 vol. unabr. ed. 2011. (Carter High Chronicles Ser.). (ENG.). 52p. (YA). (gr. 9-12). pap. 7.95 (978-1-61651-303-0(9)) Saddleback Educational Publishing, Inc.

—Don't Blame Me 2011, 1 vol. unabr. ed. 2011. (Carter High Chronicles Ser.). (ENG.). 51p. (YA). (gr. 9-12). pap. 7.95 (978-1-61651-306-1(3)) Saddleback Educational Publishing, Inc.

—One More Chance, 1 vol. unabr. ed. 2011. (Carter High Senior Year Ser.). (ENG.). 51p. (YA). (gr. 9-12). pap. 7.95 (978-1-61651-327-6(6)) Saddleback Educational Publishing, Inc.

Rocking & Rolling Along, 6 vols., Set B. 32p. (gr. 1-3). 26.50 (978-0-7802-8053-3(9)) Wright Group/McGraw-Hill.

Roddy, Lee. Escape down the Raging Rapids. 2008. (D. J. Dillon Adventure Ser.: No. 10). (J). 7.99 (978-0-88062-274-5(1)) Mott Media.

Ross, Jeff. The Drop, 1 vol. 2011. (Orca Sports Ser.). (ENG.). 168p. (YA). (gr. 6-10). pap. 9.95 (978-1-55469-392-4(6)) Orca Bk. Pubs. USA.

Rosselson, Leon. Gordon & the Giantkillers. (Illus.). 127p. (J). pap. 7.99 (978-0-340-64072-2(3)) Hodder & Stoughton GBR. Dist: Trafalgar Square Publishing.

Roza, Greg. Goal! 2006. (Neighborhood Readers Ser.). (ENG.). 16p. (gr. 1-3). pap. 6.50 (978-1-4042-7046-6(9), Rosen Classroom) Rosen Publishing Group, Inc., The.

Rud, Jeff. High & Inside, 1 vol. 2006. (ENG.). 180p. (J). (gr. 3-7). per. 7.95 (978-1-55143-532-9(2)) Orca Bk. Pubs. USA.

Saddleback Educational Publishing Staff, ed. Back-Up Quarterback. 2011. (Carter High Chronicles Ser.). (ENG.). 16p. (YA). (gr. 9-12). tchr. ed. 7.95 incl. cd-rom (978-1-61651-313-9(6)) Saddleback Educational Publishing, Inc.

—Don't Blame Me. 2011. (Carter High Chronicles Ser.). (ENG.). 16p. (YA). (gr. 9-12). tchr. ed. 7.95 incl. cd-rom (978-1-61651-317-7(9)) Saddleback Educational Publishing, Inc.

—The Easy Way. 2011. (Carter High Chronicles Ser.). (ENG.). 16p. (YA). (gr. 9-12). tchr. ed. 7.95 incl. cd-rom (978-1-61651-316-0(0)) Saddleback Educational Publishing, Inc.

—The Fastest Runner. 2011. (Carter High Chronicles Ser.). (ENG.). 16p. (YA). (gr. 9-12). cd-rom 7.95 (978-1-61651-318-4(7)) Saddleback Educational Publishing, Inc.

—It Does Matter. 2011. (Carter High Senior Year Ser.). (ENG.). 16p. (YA). (gr. 9-12). tchr. ed. 7.95 incl. cd-rom (978-1-61651-334-4(9)) Saddleback Educational Publishing, Inc.

—It Is Not a Date. 2011. (Carter High Chronicles Ser.). (ENG.). 16p. (YA). (gr. 9-12). cd-rom 7.95 (978-1-61651-319-1(5)) Saddleback Educational Publishing, Inc.

—Just Be Yourself. 2011. (Carter High Senior Year Ser.). (ENG.). 16p. (YA). (gr. 9-12). cd-rom 7.95 (978-1-61651-335-1(7)) Saddleback Educational Publishing, Inc.

—One Date Too Many. 2011. (Carter High Chronicles Ser.). (ENG.). 16p. (YA). (gr. 9-12). tchr. ed. 7.95 incl. cd-rom (978-1-61651-320-7(9)) Saddleback Educational Publishing, Inc.

—One More Chance. 2011. (Carter High Senior Year Ser.). (ENG.). 16p. (YA). (gr. 9-12). cd-rom 7.95 (978-1-61651-337-5(3)) Saddleback Educational Publishing, Inc.

—Right Kind of Win. 2011. (Carter High Chronicles Ser.). (ENG.). 16p. (YA). (gr. 9-12). cd-rom 7.95 (978-1-61651-321-4(7)) Saddleback Educational Publishing, Inc.

—Someone to Count On. 2011. (Carter High Senior Year Ser.). (ENG.). 16p. (YA). (gr. 9-12). cd-rom 7.95 (978-1-61651-338-2(1)) Saddleback Educational Publishing, Inc.

—Time to Move. 2011. (Carter High Senior Year Ser.). (ENG.). 16p. (YA). (gr. 9-12). tchr. ed. 7.95 incl. cd-rom (978-1-61651-339-9(X)) Saddleback Educational Publishing, Inc.

—Too Late. 2011. (Carter High Chronicles Ser.). (ENG.). 16p. (YA). (gr. 9-12). cd-rom 7.95 (978-1-61651-322-1(5)) Saddleback Educational Publishing, Inc.

Schultz Nicholson, Lorna. Big Air, 1 vol. 2013. (Lorimer Podium Sports Academy Ser.). (ENG.). 144p. (YA). (gr. 8-12). pap. 9.95 (978-1-4594-0531-8(5), 9781459405318) Lorimer, James & Co., Ltd., Pubs. CAN. Dist: Casemate Pubs. & Bk. Distributors, LLC.

Scieszka, Jon, et al. The Sports Pages. Santat, Dan, illus. 2012. (Guys Read Ser.: 3). (ENG.). 272p. (J). (gr. 3-7). pap. 6.99 (978-0-06-196377-3(1), Walden Pond Pr.) HarperCollins Pubs.

Sharifi, David & Sharifi, Jason. Moonlight Valley: The Great Race. 2008. 28p. pap. 13.99 (978-1-4389-1865-5(8)) AuthorHouse.

Shaw, Mary. Brady Brady & the Big Mistake, 11vols. Temple, Chuck, illus. l.t. ed. 2004. 32p. (J). per. (978-0-9735557-4-5(2)) Brady Brady, Inc.

—Brady Brady & the Great Exchange, 11 vols. Temple, Chuck, illus. l.t. ed. 2003. 32p. (J). per. (978-0-9735557-5-2(0)) Brady Brady, Inc.

Shaw, Michael. Slider: The Leo Butterburger Story. 2004. per. 14.95 (978-0-9747666-4-5(X)) American Retrospects, LLC.

Siggins, Gerard. Rugby Runner: Ancient Roots, Modern Boots. 2017. (ENG.). 208p. (J). 13.00 (**978-1-84717-913-5(4)**) O'Brien Pr., Ltd., The IRL. Dist: Dufour Editions, Inc.

Sikes, Richard. Laughing with Uncle Adolph. 2008. pap. 14.95 (978-0-9745854-2-0(4)) Old Bay Publishing.

Skillchecks for Sports. 2005. (Double Fastback Ser.). (J). (gr. 6-12). 64p. pap. 5.95 (978-0-13-024471-0(6)); 32p. pap. 5.95 (978-0-13-024454-3(6)) Globe Fearon Educational Publishing.

Skuy, David. Striker, 1 vol. 2013. (ENG.). 216p. (J). (gr. 4-7). 19.95 (978-1-4594-0512-7(9), 9781459405127); pap. 12.95 (978-1-4594-0513-4(7), 9781459405134) Lorimer, James & Co., Ltd., Pubs. CAN. Dist: Casemate Pubs. & Bk. Distributors, LLC.

Slam Dunk. Date not set. 9.95 (978-0-89868-289-2(4)); pap. 3.95 (978-0-89868-288-5(6)) ARO Publishing Co.

Smith, Bryan. If Winning Isn't Everything, Why Do I Hate to Lose? Martin, Brian, illus. 2015. (ENG.). 32p. (J). pap. 10.95 (978-1-934490-85-3(7)) Boys Town Pr.

Snyder, Betsy E., illus. I Can Play. 2015. (ENG.). 14p. (J). (gr. -1 — 1). bds. 8.99 (978-1-4521-2905-1(3)) Chronicle Bks. LLC.

Sporteller Staff. Race to Win (Auto Racing) 64p. (YA). (gr. 6-12). pap. 10.95 (978-0-8224-6479-2(9)) Globe Fearon Educational Publishing.

Sports Day: Individual Title Six-Packs. (gr. -1-2). 23.00 (978-0-7635-8804-5(0)) Rigby Education.

Sports Double Fastbacks, 10 bks. (YA). (gr. 6-12). pap. 59.95 (978-0-8224-2389-8(8)) Globe Fearon Educational Publishing.

Sports Illustrated Kids Graphic Novels, 6 vols., Set. 2010. (Sports Illustrated Kids Graphic Novels Ser.). (ENG.). (gr. 3-8). pap. 41.70 (978-1-4342-2483-5(X)) Stone Arch Bks.

Sports Illustrated Kids Graphic Novels Fall 2010 Set, 1 vol., Set. 2010. (Sports Illustrated Kids Graphic Novels Ser.). (ENG.). 56p. (gr. 2-3). 133.25 (978-1-4342-2692-1(1)) Stone Arch Bks.

Standish, Burt L. Dick Merriwell at Fardale. Rudman, Jack, ed. 2003. (Frank Merriwell Ser.). 29.95 (978-0-8373-9376-6(0)) Merriwell, Frank Inc.

—Dick Merriwell, Freshman. Rudman, Jack, ed. 2003. (Frank Merriwell Ser.). pap. 9.95 (978-0-8373-9142-7(3)) Merriwell, Frank Inc.

—Dick Merriwell in the Wilds. Rudman, Jack, ed. 2003. (Frank Merriwell Ser.). pap. 9.95 (978-0-8373-9167-0(9)) Merriwell, Frank Inc.

—Dick Merriwell on the Gridiron. Rudman, Jack, ed. 2003. (Frank Merriwell Ser.). pap. 9.95 (978-0-8373-9102-1(4)) Merriwell, Frank Inc.

—Dick Merriwell, the Wizard. Rudman, Jack, ed. 2003. (Frank Merriwell Ser.). pap. 9.95 (978-0-8373-9126-7(1)) Merriwell, Frank Inc.

—Dick Merriwell's Ability. Rudman, Jack, ed. 2003. (Frank Merriwell Ser.). 29.95 (978-0-8373-9390-2(6)); pap. 9.95 (978-0-8373-9090-1(7)) Merriwell, Frank Inc.

—Dick Merriwell's Assurance. Rudman, Jack, ed. 2003. (Frank Merriwell Ser.). pap. 9.95 (978-0-8373-9109-0(1)) Merriwell, Frank Inc.

—Dick Merriwell's Backers. Rudman, Jack, ed. 2003. (Frank Merriwell Ser.). pap. 9.95 (978-0-8373-9149-6(0)) Merriwell, Frank Inc.

—Dick Merriwell's Backstop. Rudman, Jack, ed. 2003. (Frank Merriwell Ser.). 29.95 (978-0-8373-9396-4(5)); pap. 9.95 (978-0-8373-9096-3(6)) Merriwell, Frank Inc.

—Dick Merriwell's Best Work. Rudman, Jack, ed. 2003. (Frank Merriwell Ser.). pap. 9.95 (978-0-8373-9150-2(4)) Merriwell, Frank Inc.

—Dick Merriwell's Black Star. Rudman, Jack, ed. 2003. (Frank Merriwell Ser.). pap. 9.95 (978-0-8373-9158-8(X)) Merriwell, Frank Inc.

—Dick Merriwell's Cleverness. Rudman, Jack, ed. 2003. (Frank Merriwell Ser.). pap. 9.95 (978-0-8373-9124-3(5)) Merriwell, Frank Inc.

—Dick Merriwell's Close Call. Rudman, Jack, ed. 2003. (Frank Merriwell Ser.). pap. 9.95 (978-0-8373-9156-4(3)) Merriwell, Frank Inc.

—Dick Merriwell's Dare. Rudman, Jack, ed. 2003. (Frank Merriwell Ser.). pap. 9.95 (978-0-8373-9136-6(9)) Merriwell, Frank Inc.

—Dick Merriwell's Dash. Rudman, Jack, ed. 2003. (Frank Merriwell Ser.). 29.95 (978-0-8373-9389-6(2)); pap. 9.95 (978-0-8373-9089-5(3)) Merriwell, Frank Inc.

—Dick Merriwell's Day. Rudman, Jack, ed. 2003. (Frank Merriwell Ser.). pap. 9.95 (978-0-8373-9114-4(8)) Merriwell, Frank Inc.
—Dick Merriwell's Debt. Rudman, Jack, ed. 2003. (Frank Merriwell Ser.). pap. 9.95 (978-0-8373-9152-6(0)) Merriwell, Frank Inc.
—Dick Merriwell's Defense. Rudman, Jack, ed. 2003. (Frank Merriwell Ser.). 29.95 (978-0-8373-9392-6(2)); pap. 9.95 (978-0-8373-9092-5(3)) Merriwell, Frank Inc.
—Dick Merriwell's Delivery. Rudman, Jack, ed. 2003. (Frank Merriwell Ser.). 29.95 (978-0-8373-9384-1(1)); pap. 9.95 (978-0-8373-9084-0(2)) Merriwell, Frank Inc.
—Dick Merriwell's Diamond. Rudman, Jack, ed. 2003. (Frank Merriwell Ser.). 29.95 (978-0-8373-9387-2(6)); pap. 9.95 (978-0-8373-9087-1(7)) Merriwell, Frank Inc.
—Dick Merriwell's Disguise. Rudman, Jack, ed. 2003. (Frank Merriwell Ser.). pap. 9.95 (978-0-8373-9103-8(2)) Merriwell, Frank Inc.
—Dick Merriwell's Distrust. Rudman, Jack, ed. 2003. (Frank Merriwell Ser.). pap. 9.95 (978-0-8373-9151-9(2)) Merriwell, Frank Inc.
—Dick Merriwell's Downfall. Rudman, Jack, ed. 2003. (Frank Merriwell Ser.). pap. 9.95 (978-0-8373-9116-8(4)) Merriwell, Frank Inc.
—Dick Merriwell's Example. Rudman, Jack, ed. 2003. (Frank Merriwell Ser.). pap. 9.95 (978-0-8373-9166-3(0)) Merriwell, Frank Inc.
—Dick Merriwell's Five. Rudman, Jack, ed. 2003. (Frank Merriwell Ser.). pap. 9.95 (978-0-8373-9130-4(X)) Merriwell, Frank Inc.
—Dick Merriwell's Glory. Rudman, Jack, ed. 2003. (Frank Merriwell Ser.). 29.95 (978-0-8373-9377-3(9)); pap. 9.95 (978-0-8373-9077-2(X)) Merriwell, Frank Inc.
—Dick Merriwell's Grit. Rudman, Jack, ed. 2003. (Frank Merriwell Ser.). pap. 9.95 (978-0-8373-9108-3(3)) Merriwell, Frank Inc.
—Dick Merriwell's Home Run. Rudman, Jack, ed. 2003. (Frank Merriwell Ser.). pap. 9.95 (978-0-8373-9135-9(0)) Merriwell, Frank Inc.
—Dick Merriwell's Honors. Rudman, Jack, ed. 2003. (Frank Merriwell Ser.). pap. 9.95 (978-0-8373-9173-1(3)) Merriwell, Frank Inc.
—Dick Merriwell's Influence. Rudman, Jack, ed. 2003. (Frank Merriwell Ser.). pap. 9.95 (978-0-8373-9141-0(5)) Merriwell, Frank Inc.
—Dick Merriwell's Joke. Rudman, Jack, ed. 2003. (Frank Merriwell Ser.). pap. 9.95 (978-0-8373-9144-1(X)) Merriwell, Frank Inc.
—Dick Merriwell's Long Slide. Rudman, Jack, ed. 2003. (Frank Merriwell Ser.). pap. 9.95 (978-0-8373-9110-6(5)) Merriwell, Frank Inc.
—Dick Merriwell's Magnetism. Rudman, Jack, ed. 2003. (Frank Merriwell Ser.). pap. 9.95 (978-0-8373-9148-9(2)) Merriwell, Frank Inc.
—Dick Merriwell's Marked Money. Rudman, Jack, ed. 2003. (Frank Merriwell Ser.). pap. 9.95 (978-0-8373-9100-7(8)) Merriwell, Frank Inc.
—Dick Merriwell's Mastery. Rudman, Jack, ed. 2003. (Frank Merriwell Ser.). pap. 9.95 (978-0-8373-9153-3(9)) Merriwell, Frank Inc.
—Dick Merriwell's Model. Rudman, Jack, ed. 2003. (Frank Merriwell Ser.). 29.95 (978-0-8373-9393-3(0)); pap. 9.95 (978-0-8373-9093-2(1)) Merriwell, Frank Inc.
—Dick Merriwell's Mystery. Rudman, Jack, ed. 2003. (Frank Merriwell Ser.). 29.95 (978-0-8373-9394-0(9)); pap. 9.95 (978-0-8373-9094-9(X)) Merriwell, Frank Inc.
—Dick Merriwell's Narrow Escape. Rudman, Jack, ed. 2003. (Frank Merriwell Ser.). 29.95 (978-0-8373-9380-3(9)); pap. 9.95 (978-0-8373-9080-2(X)) Merriwell, Frank Inc.
—Dick Merriwell's Persistence. Rudman, Jack, ed. 2003. (Frank Merriwell Ser.). pap. 9.95 (978-0-8373-9113-7(X)) Merriwell, Frank Inc.
—Dick Merriwell's Polo Team. Rudman, Jack, ed. 2003. (Frank Merriwell Ser.). pap. 9.95 (978-0-8373-9132-8(6)) Merriwell, Frank Inc.
—Dick Merriwell's Pranks. Rudman, Jack, ed. 2003. (Frank Merriwell Ser.). pap. 9.95 (978-0-8373-9120-5(2)) Merriwell, Frank Inc.
—Dick Merriwell's Promise. Rudman, Jack, ed. 2003. (Frank Merriwell Ser.). 29.95 (978-0-8373-9378-0(7)); pap. 9.95 (978-0-8373-9078-9(8)) Merriwell, Frank Inc.
—Dick Merriwell's Racket. Rudman, Jack, ed. 2003. (Frank Merriwell Ser.). 29.95 (978-0-8373-9381-0(7)); pap. 9.95 (978-0-8373-9081-9(8)) Merriwell, Frank Inc.
—Dick Merriwell's Regret. Rudman, Jack, ed. 2003. (Frank Merriwell Ser.). pap. 9.95 (978-0-8373-9147-2(4)) Merriwell, Frank Inc.
—Dick Merriwell's Reputation. Rudman, Jack, ed. 2003. (Frank Merriwell Ser.). pap. 9.95 (978-0-8373-9171-7(7)) Merriwell, Frank Inc.
—Dick Merriwell's Rescue. Rudman, Jack, ed. 2003. (Frank Merriwell Ser.). 29.95 (978-0-8373-9379-7(5)); pap. 9.95 (978-0-8373-9079-6(6)) Merriwell, Frank Inc.
—Dick Merriwell's Resource. Rudman, Jack, ed. 2003. (Frank Merriwell Ser.). pap. 9.95 (978-0-8373-9129-8(6)) Merriwell, Frank Inc.
—Dick Merriwell's Return. Rudman, Jack, ed. 2003. (Frank Merriwell Ser.). pap. 9.95 (978-0-8373-9128-1(8)) Merriwell, Frank Inc.
—Dick Merriwell's Revenge. Rudman, Jack, ed. 2003. (Frank Merriwell Ser.). 29.95 (978-0-8373-9382-7(5)); pap. 9.95 (978-0-8373-9082-6(6)) Merriwell, Frank Inc.
—Dick Merriwell's Ruse. Rudman, Jack, ed. 2003. (Frank Merriwell Ser.). 29.95 (978-0-8373-9383-4(3)); pap. 9.95 (978-0-8373-9083-3(4)) Merriwell, Frank Inc.
—Dick Merriwell's Stanchness. Rudman, Jack, ed. 2003. (Frank Merriwell Ser.). pap. 9.95 (978-0-8373-9161-8(X)) Merriwell, Frank Inc.
—Dick Merriwell's Stand. Rudman, Jack, ed. 2003. (Frank Merriwell Ser.). pap. 9.95 (978-0-8373-9163-2(6)) Merriwell, Frank Inc.
—Dick Merriwell's Staying Power. Rudman, Jack, ed. 2003. (Frank Merriwell Ser.). pap. 9.95 (978-0-8373-9143-4(1)) Merriwell, Frank Inc.
—Dick Merriwell's Stroke. Rudman, Jack, ed. 2003. (Frank Merriwell Ser.). pap. 9.95 (978-0-8373-9127-4(X)) Merriwell, Frank Inc.
—Dick Merriwell's Team Mate. Rudman, Jack, ed. 2003. (Frank Merriwell Ser.). pap. 9.95 (978-0-8373-9138-0(5)) Merriwell, Frank Inc.
—Dick Merriwell's Test. Rudman, Jack, ed. 2003. (Frank Merriwell Ser.). pap. 9.95 (978-0-8373-9104-5(0)) Merriwell, Frank Inc.
—Frank Merriwell as Coach. Rudman, Jack, ed. 2003. (Frank Merriwell Ser.). 29.95 (978-0-8373-9372-8(8)); pap. 9.95 (978-0-8373-9072-7(9)) Merriwell, Frank Inc.
—Frank Merriwell Facing His Foes. Rudman, Jack, ed. 2003. (Frank Merriwell Ser.). pap. 9.95 (978-0-8373-9160-1(1)) Merriwell, Frank Inc.
—Frank Merriwell in Camp. Rudman, Jack, ed. 2003. (Frank Merriwell Ser.). (YA). (gr. 9-18). 29.95 (978-0-8373-9324-7(8)); pap. 9.95 (978-0-8373-9024-6(9), FM-024) Merriwell, Frank Inc.
—Frank Merriwell in Maine. Rudman, Jack, ed. 2003. (Frank Merriwell Ser.). (YA). (gr. 9-18). 29.95 (978-0-8373-9328-5(0)); pap. 9.95 (978-0-8373-9028-4(1), FM-028) Merriwell, Frank Inc.
—Frank Merriwell's Alarm. Rudman, Jack, ed. 2003. (Frank Merriwell Ser.). (YA). (gr. 9-18). 29.95 (978-0-8373-9316-2(7)); pap. 9.95 (978-0-8373-9016-1(8), FM-016) Merriwell, Frank Inc.
—Frank Merriwell's Athletes. Rudman, Jack, ed. 2003. (Frank Merriwell Ser.). (YA). (gr. 9-18). 29.95 (978-0-8373-9317-9(5)); pap. 9.95 (978-0-8373-9017-8(6), FM-017) Merriwell, Frank Inc.
—Frank Merriwell's Champions. Rudman, Jack, ed. 2003. (Frank Merriwell Ser.). (YA). (gr. 9-18). 29.95 (978-0-8373-9319-3(1)); pap. 9.95 (978-0-8373-9019-2(2), FM-019) Merriwell, Frank Inc.
—Frank Merriwell's Chase. Rudman, Jack, ed. 2003. (Frank Merriwell Ser.). (YA). (gr. 9-18). 29.95 (978-0-8373-9327-8(2)); pap. 9.95 (978-0-8373-9027-7(3), FM-027) Merriwell, Frank Inc.
—Frank Merriwell's Courage. Rudman, Jack, ed. 2003. (Frank Merriwell Ser.). (YA). (gr. 9-18). 29.95 (978-0-8373-9314-8(0)); pap. 9.95 (978-0-8373-9014-7(1), FM-014) Merriwell, Frank Inc.
—Frank Merriwell's Double Shot. Rudman, Jack, ed. 2003. (Frank Merriwell Ser.). 29.95 (978-0-8373-9347-6(7)); pap. 9.95 (978-0-8373-9047-5(8)) Merriwell, Frank Inc.
—Frank Merriwell's Hard Luck. Rudman, Jack, ed. 2003. (Frank Merriwell Ser.). 29.95 (978-0-8373-9332-2(9)); pap. 9.95 (978-0-8373-9032-1(X)) Merriwell, Frank Inc.
—Frank Merriwell's Honor. Rudman, Jack, ed. 2003. (Frank Merriwell Ser.). 29.95 (978-0-8373-9386-5(8)); pap. 9.95 (978-0-8373-9086-4(9)) Merriwell, Frank Inc.
—Frank Merriwell's Leaguers. Rudman, Jack, ed. 2003. (Frank Merriwell Ser.). pap. 9.95 (978-0-8373-9139-7(3)) Merriwell, Frank Inc.
—Frank Merriwell's Lesson. Rudman, Jack, ed. 2003. (Frank Merriwell Ser.). pap. 9.95 (978-0-8373-9170-0(9)) Merriwell, Frank Inc.
—Frank Merriwell's Luck. Rudman, Jack, ed. 2003. (Frank Merriwell Ser.). 29.95 (978-0-8373-9356-8(6)); pap. 9.95 (978-0-8373-9056-7(7)) Merriwell, Frank Inc.
—Frank Merriwell's Marvel. Rudman, Jack, ed. 2003. (Frank Merriwell Ser.). 29.95 (978-0-8373-9374-2(4)); pap. 9.95 (978-0-8373-9074-1(5)) Merriwell, Frank Inc.
—Frank Merriwell's Mascot. Rudman, Jack, ed. 2003. (Frank Merriwell Ser.). 29.95 (978-0-8373-9357-5(4)); pap. 9.95 (978-0-8373-9057-4(5)) Merriwell, Frank Inc.
—Frank Merriwell's New Comedian. Rudman, Jack, ed. 2003. (Frank Merriwell Ser.). 29.95 (978-0-8373-9340-7(X)); pap. 29.95 (978-0-8373-9040-6(0)) Merriwell, Frank Inc.
—Frank Merriwell's Nomads. Rudman, Jack, ed. 2003. (Frank Merriwell Ser.). pap. 9.95 (978-0-8373-9101-4(6)) Merriwell, Frank Inc.
—Frank Merriwell's Opportunity. Rudman, Jack, ed. 2003. (Frank Merriwell Ser.). 29.95 (978-0-8373-9331-5(0)); pap. 9.95 (978-0-8373-9031-4(1)) Merriwell, Frank Inc.
—Frank Merriwell's Own Company. Rudman, Jack, ed. 2003. (Frank Merriwell Ser.). 29.95 (978-0-8373-9335-3(3)); pap. 9.95 (978-0-8373-9035-2(4)) Merriwell, Frank Inc.
—Frank Merriwell's Peril. Rudman, Jack, ed. 2003. (Frank Merriwell Ser.). pap. 9.95 (978-0-8373-9115-1(6)) Merriwell, Frank Inc.
—Frank Merriwell's Phantom. Rudman, Jack, ed. 2003. (Frank Merriwell Ser.). 29.95 (978-0-8373-9359-9(0)); pap. 9.95 (978-0-8373-9059-8(1)) Merriwell, Frank Inc.
—Frank Merriwell's Power. Rudman, Jack, ed. 2003. (Frank Merriwell Ser.). 29.95 (978-0-8373-9364-3(7)); pap. 9.95 (978-0-8373-9064-2(8)) Merriwell, Frank Inc.
—Frank Merriwell's Pride. Rudman, Jack, ed. 2003. (Frank Merriwell Ser.). pap. 9.95 (978-0-8373-9121-2(0)) Merriwell, Frank Inc.
—Frank Merriwell's Problem. Rudman, Jack, ed. 2003. (Frank Merriwell Ser.). 29.95 (978-0-8373-9338-4(8)); pap. 9.95 (978-0-8373-9038-3(9)) Merriwell, Frank Inc.
—Frank Merriwell's Prosperity. Rudman, Jack, ed. 2003. (Frank Merriwell Ser.). 29.95 (978-0-8373-9341-4(8)); pap. 9.95 (978-0-8373-9041-3(9)) Merriwell, Frank Inc.
—Frank Merriwell's Protege. Rudman, Jack, ed. 2003. (Frank Merriwell Ser.). 29.95 (978-0-8373-9333-9(7)); pap. 9.95 (978-0-8373-9033-8(8)) Merriwell, Frank Inc.
—Frank Merriwell's Pursuit. Rudman, Jack, ed. 2003. (Frank Merriwell Ser.). pap. 9.95 (978-0-8373-9117-5(2)) Merriwell, Frank Inc.
—Frank Merriwell's Races. 2007. (ENG.). 232p. per. 20.99 (978-1-4346-4433-6(2)); 256p. per. 23.99 (978-1-4346-4434-3(0)) Creative Media Partners, LLC.
—Frank Merriwell's Rescue. Rudman, Jack, ed. 2003. (Frank Merriwell Ser.). 29.95 (978-0-8373-9398-8(1)); pap. 9.95 (978-0-8373-9098-7(2)) Merriwell, Frank Inc.
—Frank Merriwell's Reward. Rudman, Jack, ed. 2003. (Frank Merriwell Ser.). 29.95 (978-0-8373-9358-2(2)); pap. 9.95 (978-0-8373-9058-1(3)) Merriwell, Frank Inc.
—Frank Merriwell's Rough Deal. Rudman, Jack, ed. 2003. (Frank Merriwell Ser.). pap. 9.95 (978-0-8373-9111-3(3)) Merriwell, Frank Inc.
—Frank Merriwell's Search. Rudman, Jack, ed. 2003. (Frank Merriwell Ser.). 29.95 (978-0-8373-9367-4(1)); pap. 9.95 (978-0-8373-9067-3(2)) Merriwell, Frank Inc.
—Frank Merriwell's Setback. Rudman, Jack, ed. 2003. (Frank Merriwell Ser.). 29.95 (978-0-8373-9366-7(3)); pap. 9.95 (978-0-8373-9066-6(4)) Merriwell, Frank Inc.
—Frank Merriwell's Shrewdness. Rudman, Jack, ed. 2003. (Frank Merriwell Ser.). 29.95 (978-0-8373-9365-0(5)); pap. 9.95 (978-0-8373-9065-9(6)) Merriwell, Frank Inc.
—Frank Merriwell's Sports Afield. Rudman, Jack, ed. (Frank Merriwell Ser.). (YA). (gr. 9-18). 29.95 (978-0-8373-9310-0(8)); pap. 9.95 (978-0-8373-9010-9(9), FM-010) Merriwell, Frank Inc.
—Frank Merriwell's Stage Hit. Rudman, Jack, ed. 2003. (Frank Merriwell Ser.). 29.95 (978-0-8373-9342-1(6)); pap. 9.95 (978-0-8373-9042-0(7)) Merriwell, Frank Inc.
—Frank Merriwell's Steadying Hand. Rudman, Jack, ed. 2003. (Frank Merriwell Ser.). pap. 9.95 (978-0-8373-9165-6(2)) Merriwell, Frank Inc.
—Frank Merriwell's Strategy. Rudman, Jack, ed. 2003. (Frank Merriwell Ser.). pap. 9.95 (978-0-8373-9106-9(7)) Merriwell, Frank Inc.
—Frank Merriwell's Strong Arm. Rudman, Jack, ed. 2003. (Frank Merriwell Ser.). 29.95 (978-0-8373-9371-1(X)); pap. 9.95 (978-0-8373-9071-0(0)) Merriwell, Frank Inc.
—Frank Merriwell's Support. Rudman, Jack, ed. 2003. (Frank Merriwell Ser.). 29.95 (978-0-8373-9375-9(2)); pap. 9.95 (978-0-8373-9075-8(3)) Merriwell, Frank Inc.
—Frank Merriwell's Talisman. Rudman, Jack, ed. 2003. (Frank Merriwell Ser.). pap. 9.95 (978-0-8373-9145-8(8)) Merriwell, Frank Inc.
—Frank Merriwell's Temptation. Rudman, Jack, ed. 2003. (Frank Merriwell Ser.). 29.95 (978-0-8373-9354-4(X)); pap. 9.95 (978-0-8373-9054-3(0)) Merriwell, Frank Inc.
—Frank Merriwell's Tigers. Rudman, Jack, ed. 2003. (Frank Merriwell Ser.). pap. 9.95 (978-0-8373-9131-1(8)) Merriwell, Frank Inc.
—Frank Merriwell's Tricks. Rudman, Jack, ed. 2003. (Frank Merriwell Ser.). 29.95 (978-0-8373-9353-7(1)); pap. 9.95 (978-0-8373-9053-6(2)) Merriwell, Frank Inc.
—Frank Merriwell's Triumph. Rudman, Jack, ed. 2003. (Frank Merriwell Ser.). pap. 9.95 (978-0-8373-9107-6(5)) Merriwell, Frank Inc.
—Frank Merriwell's Trump Card. Rudman, Jack, ed. 2003. (Frank Merriwell Ser.). pap. 9.95 (978-0-8373-9105-2(9)) Merriwell, Frank Inc.
—Frank Merriwell's Trust. Rudman, Jack, ed. 2003. (Frank Merriwell Ser.). 29.95 (978-0-8373-9369-8(8)); pap. 9.95 (978-0-8373-9069-7(9)) Merriwell, Frank Inc.
—Frank Merriwell's Victories. Rudman, Jack, ed. 2003. (Frank Merriwell Ser.). 29.95 (978-0-8373-9361-2(2)); pap. 9.95 (978-0-8373-9061-1(3)) Merriwell, Frank Inc.
—Frank Merriwell's Winners. Rudman, Jack, ed. 2003. (Frank Merriwell Ser.). 29.95 (978-0-8373-9388-9(4)); pap. 9.95 (978-0-8373-9088-8(5)) Merriwell, Frank Inc.
—Frank Merriwell's Wizard. Rudman, Jack, ed. 2003. (Frank Merriwell Ser.). pap. 9.95 (978-0-8373-9174-8(1)) Merriwell, Frank Inc.
—Frank Merriwell's Worst Boy. Rudman, Jack, ed. 2003. (Frank Merriwell Ser.). pap. 9.95 (978-0-8373-9155-7(5)) Merriwell, Frank Inc.
Stanwood Pier, Arthu. The Jester of St. Timothy's. 2006. pap. 14.95 (978-1-55742-546-1(9)) Wildside Pr., LLC.
Starin, Liz. Splashdance. Starin, Liz, illus. 2016. (ENG., Illus.). 32p. (J). 16.99 (978-0-374-30098-2(4), 9780374300982, Farrar, Straus & Giroux (BYR)) Farrar, Straus & Giroux.
Stevens, Eric & Maddox, Jake. Playing Forward. Tiffany, Sean, illus. 2010. (Jake Maddox Sports Story Ser.). 72p. pap. 0.60 (978-1-4342-3206-9(9), Impact Bks.) Stone Arch Bks.
Sticker Dolly Dressing Sports (Revised) 2017. (Sticker Dolly Dressing Ser.). (ENG.). (J). pap. 9.99 **(978-0-7945-3782-1(0)**, Usborne) EDC Publishing.
Stilton, Geronimo. The Great Mouse Race. 2014. (Geronimo Stilton Cavemice Ser.: 5). (ENG., Illus.). 128p. (J). (gr. 2-5). pap. 7.99 (978-0-545-64654-3(5), Scholastic Paperbacks) Scholastic, Inc.
Stine, R. L. Monster Blood for Breakfast! 2008. (Goosebumps Horrorland Ser.: 3). (ENG.). 144p. (J). (gr. 3-7). pap. 6.99 (978-0-439-91871-8(5), Scholastic Paperbacks) Scholastic, Inc.
Strasser, Todd. Close Out. 2004. (ENG.). 304p. (YA). (gr. 9). mass mkt. 5.99 (978-0-689-87031-6(0), Simon Pulse) Simon Pulse.
—Sidewayz Glory. Phillips, Craig, illus. 2006. (DriftX Ser.: 3). (ENG.). 208p. (YA). (gr. 9-12). pap. 10.99 (978-1-4169-0583-7(9), Simon Pulse) Simon Pulse.
Stroke of Luck (Swimming) 64p. (YA). (gr. 6-12). pap. 10.95 (978-0-8224-6482-2(9)) Globe Fearon Educational Publishing.
Swan, Bill. Corner Kick, 1 vol. 2004. (Lorimer Sports Stories Ser.: 66). (ENG.). 144p. (J). (gr. 4-6). 16.95 (978-1-55028-817-9(2), 9781550288179) Lorimer, James & Co., Ltd., Pubs. CAN. Dist: Casemate Pubs. & Bk. Distributors, LLC.
—Mud Happens, 1 vol. 2005. (Lorimer Sports Stories Ser.: 82). (ENG.). 112p. (J). (gr. 4-8). 16.95 (978-1-55028-899-5(7), 9781550288995); 8.95 (978-1-55028-898-8(9), 9781550288988) Lorimer, James & Co., Ltd., Pubs. CAN. Dist: Casemate Pubs. & Bk. Distributors, LLC.
—Road Rage, 1 vol. 2006. (Lorimer Sports Stories Ser.). (ENG.). 120p. (J). (gr. 4-8). 8.95 (978-1-55028-916-9(0), 9781550289169) Lorimer, James & Co., Ltd., Pubs. CAN. Dist: Casemate Pubs. & Bk. Distributors, LLC.
Swann, Stephen. The Blooter Boys. 2009. 42p. pap. 21.50 (978-1-4452-2665-1(0)) Lulu Pr., Inc.
Tammen, Christina. Chump li Every Team Has an Undiscovered Secret Weapon! 2013. 30p. pap. 14.95 (978-1-61244-081-1(9)) Halo Publishing International.
Tate, Nikki. Deadpoint. 2017. (Orca Sports Ser.). lib. bdg. 20.80 **(978-0-606-40454-9(6))** Turtleback Bks.
Terrell, Brandon. Grit & Gold. Max, Iman & Garcia, Eduardo, illus. 2016. (Time Machine Magazine Ser.). (ENG.). 128p. (gr. 3-4). lib. bdg. 22.65 (978-1-4965-2597-0(3)) Capstone Press of Coughlan Cos.
Thaler, Mike. The Field Day from the Black Lagoon. Lee, Jared, illus. 2008. (From the Black Lagoon Ser.). 64p. (gr. 2-5). 14.00 (978-0-7569-8801-2(2)) Perfection Learning Corp.
—The Field Day from the Black Lagoon. Lee, Jared, illus. 2008. (Black Lagoon Adventures Ser.: 6). (ENG.). 64p. (J). (gr. 2-5). pap. 4.99 (978-0-439-68076-9(X)) Scholastic, Inc.
—The Field Day from the Black Lagoon, 1 vol. Lee, Jared, illus. 2011. (Black Lagoon Adventures Ser.: No. 1). (ENG.). 64p. (gr. 3-6). 24.21 (978-1-59961-812-8(5)) Spotlight.
Thomas, Michelle. Bubble World & the Olympics. 2010. 28p. 12.49 (978-1-4520-1682-5(8)) AuthorHouse.
Tomlinson, Everett T. Winning His W. 2006. pap. (978-1-4068-1194-0(7)) Echo Library.
Truckey, Don. The Adventures of Caraway Kim... Southpaw. Macintyre, R P, ed. 2006. (ENG.). 192p. pap. 10.95 (978-1-894345-90-3(8)) Thistledown Pr., Ltd. CAN. Dist: Univ. of Toronto Pr.
Tulien, Sean & Maese, Fares. Paintball Punk, 1 vol. Aburto, Jesus & Esparza, Andres, illus. 2010. (Sports Illustrated Kids Graphic Novels Ser.). (ENG.). 56p. (gr. 2-3). 26.65 (978-1-4342-2219-0(5)); pap. 7.19 (978-1-4342-2788-1(X)) Stone Arch Bks.
Twigg, Aeres. The Green Hawk. 2003. (ENG., Illus.). 88p. (J). pap. 12.95 (978-1-85902-787-5(3)) Beekman Bks., Inc.
Wallace, Rich. The Ball Hogs, No. 1. Holder, Jimmy, illus. 2011. (Kickers Ser.: Bk. 1). (ENG.). 128p. (J). (gr. 1-4). 5.99 (978-0-375-85092-9(9), Yearling) Random Hse. Children's Bks.
—Fast Company. 3rd ed. 2005. (Winning Season Ser.: Bk. 3). (ENG.). 128p. (J). (gr. 3-7). 5.99 (978-0-14-240468-3(3), Puffin Books) Penguin Young Readers Group.
—Game Face. 2016. (Game Face Ser.: 4). (ENG.). 112p. (J). (gr. 3-7). lib. bdg. 108.28 (978-1-62402-131-2(X), Calico Chapter Bks.) ABDO Publishing Co.
—Sports Camp. 2012. (ENG.). 160p. (J). (gr. 4-7). 6.99 (978-0-440-23993-2(1), Yearling) Random Hse. Children's Bks.
Walters, Eric. Grind, 1 vol. 2004. (Orca Soundings Ser.). (ENG.). 128p. (YA). (gr. 8-12). pap. 9.95 (978-1-55143-317-2(6)) Orca Bk. Pubs. USA.
—Underdog, 1 vol. 2004. (Orca Young Readers Ser.). (ENG., Illus.). 176p. (J). (gr. 3-6). pap., tchr. ed. 6.95 (978-1-55143-302-8(8), 1234544) Orca Bk. Pubs. USA.
Ward, Stephen J. The GREATEST Togger Story Ever Told - Part 1: Thrifty's Stand. 2010. 66p. pap. 14.95 (978-1-4461-3060-5(6)) Lulu Pr., Inc.
—The GREATEST Togger Story Ever Told - Part 2: the Boot of All Evil. 2010. 84p. pap. 16.95 (978-1-4461-3069-8(X)) Lulu Pr., Inc.
—The GREATEST Togger Story Ever Told - Part 3: Far from the Screaming Crowd. 2010. 86p. pap. 16.95 (978-1-4461-3075-9(4)) Lulu Pr., Inc.
—The GREATEST Togger Story Ever Told - Part 4: the Raiders of Leaf. 2010. 170p. pap. 21.50 (978-1-4461-3076-6(2)) Lulu Pr., Inc.
West, Tracey. Enemy Rising. Phillips, Craig, illus. 2010. (Hiro's Quest Ser.: 1). (ENG.). 96p. (J). (gr. 2-5). 4.99 (978-0-545-16288-3(2), Scholastic Paperbacks) Scholastic, Inc.
Weston Woods Staff, creator. Clown of God. 2011. 38.75 (978-0-545-14915-0(0)) Weston Woods Studios, Inc.
Wheeler, Lee Alden. Bucking the Odds 2004. (YA). pap. 13.00 (978-0-9760824-0-8(3)) United Writers Pr.
Whyte, Janet M. Rescue Rider, 1 vol. 2011. (Lorimer Sports Stories Ser.). (ENG.). 136p. (J). (gr. 4-8). pap. 9.95 (978-1-55277-868-5(1), 9781552778685) Lorimer, James & Co., Ltd., Pubs. CAN. Dist: Casemate Pubs. & Bk. Distributors, LLC.
Wight, Eric. Frankie Pickle & the Pine Run 3000. Wight, Eric, illus. 2010. (Frankie Pickle Ser.). (ENG., Illus.). 96p. (J). (gr. 2-5). 9.99 (978-1-4169-6485-8(1), Simon & Schuster Bks. For Young Readers) Simon & Schuster Bks. For Young Readers.
Wilson, George. Arron the Royal Archer. 2010. (Illus.). 50p. (J). 15.00 (978-0-9778477-3-0(X)) A Story Plus Children Bks.
Winfield, Arthur M. Putnam Hall Champions or Bound to Win Ou. 2006. pap. 28.95 (978-1-4286-2346-0(9)) Kessinger Publishing, LLC.
Wisler, Joelle. Ariana Gold. 2016. (What's Your Dream? Ser.). (ENG., Illus.). 96p. (gr. 3-4). lib. bdg. 25.32 (978-1-4965-3442-2(5)) Capstone Press of Coughlan Cos.
Wyler, Melissa. The Adventures of Henry the Sports Bug: Book 1. 2012. 36p. pap. 19.99 (978-1-105-64532-7(0)) Lulu Pr., Inc.
Yasuda, Anita. Beach Volleyball Is No Joke, 1 vol. Santillan, Jorge H., illus. 2011. (Sports Illustrated Kids Victory School Superstars Ser.). (ENG.). 56p. (gr. 1-3). pap. 5.95 (978-1-4342-3393-6(6)) Stone Arch Bks.
Zullo, Allan. The Haunted Shortstop: True Ghostly Sports Stories. 2007. 128p. (J). pap. (978-0-439-88618-5(X)) Scholastic, Inc.

SPORTS—HISTORY

ABDO. Greatest Events in Sports History, 1 vol. 2014. (Greatest Events in Sports History Ser.: 6). (ENG.). 48p. (gr. 3-6). lib. bdg. 196.74 (978-1-62403-593-7(0), SportsZone) ABDO Publishing Co.
ABDO Publishing Company Staff. Sports' Biggest Moments. 2013. (Sports' Biggest Moments Ser.: 6). 64p. (gr. 3-6). lib. bdg. 196.74 (978-1-61783-920-7(5), SportsZone) ABDO Publishing Co.
Berman, Len. The Greatest Moments in Sports: Upsets & Underdogs. 2012. (ENG.). 128p. (J). (gr. 2-6). 19.99 (978-1-4022-7226-4(X), Sourcebooks Jabberwocky) Sourcebooks, Inc.
Brignall, Richard. Forever Champions: The Enduring Legacy of the Edmonton Grads, 1 vol. 2007. (Lorimer Recordbooks Ser.). (ENG., Illus.). 112p. (J). (gr. 4-8). 9.95 (978-1-55028-976-3(4), 9781550289763) Lorimer, James & Co., Ltd., Pubs. CAN. Dist: Casemate Pubs. & Bk. Distributors, LLC.
—Forever Champions: The Enduring Legacy of the Edmonton Grads Women's Basketball Team. 2007. (Recordbooks Ser.). (ENG., Illus.). 112p. (gr. 4-8). (978-1-55028-977-0(2)) Lorimer, James & Co., Ltd., Pubs. CAN. Dist: Casemate Pubs. & Bk. Distributors, LLC.
Christopher, Matt. The Greatest Sports Team Rivalries. 2012. (ENG., Illus.). 144p. (J). (gr. 3-7). pap. 5.99 (978-0-316-17687-3(7)) Little, Brown Bks. for Young Readers.

S

Craats, Rennay. Sports. 2008. (USA Past Present Future Ser.). (Illus.). 48p. (J). (gr. 4-6). pap. 10.95 *(978-1-59036-975-3(0))*; lib. bdg. 29.05 *(978-1-59036-974-6(2))* Weigl Pubs., Inc.

Davies, Monika. No Way! Spectacular Sports Stories. 2017. (Time for Kids Nonfiction Readers Ser.). lib. bdg. 20.85 ***(978-0-606-40272-9(1))*** Turtleback Bks.

Doeden, Matt. All about Sports. 2015. (All about Sports Ser.). (ENG.). 32p. (gr. 1-2). lib. bdg. 109.28 *(978-1-4914-2433-9(8)*, Aplus Bks.) Capstone Press of Coughlan Cos.

Ford, Jeanne Marie. The 12 Most Influential Athletes of All Time. 2018. (ENG.). 32p. (gr. 3-6). 31.35 ***(978-1-63235-407-5(1)***, 12-Story Library) Pr. Room Editions LLC.

Ford, Michael. You Wouldn't Want to Be a Greek Athlete! (Revised Edition) 2014. (You Wouldn't Want to... Ser.). (ENG.). 32p. (J). lib. bdg. 29.00 *(978-0-531-21175-5(4)*, Watts, Franklin) Scholastic Library Publishing.

Gatto, Steve. Da Curse of the Billy Goat: The Chicago Cubs, Pennant Races, & Curses. 2004. 144p. per. 19.95 *(978-0-9720910-4-6(1))* Protar Hse., LLC.

Gilpin, Daniel. Record-Breaking People. 2012. (Record Breakers Ser.). (Illus.). 32p. (J). lib. bdg. 26.50 *(978-1-4488-5293-2(5)*, PowerKids Pr.) Rosen Publishing Group, Inc., The.

Gitlin, Martin. Weirdest Moments in Sports, 1 vol. 2013. (Sports' Biggest Moments Ser.). (ENG.). 64p. (gr. 3-6). lib. bdg. 32.79 *(978-1-61783-926-9(4)*, SportsZone) ABDO Publishing Co.

Hawkins, Jeff. Biggest Chokes in Sports, 1 vol. 2013. (Sports' Biggest Moments Ser.). (ENG.). 64p. (gr. 3-6). lib. bdg. 32.79 *(978-1-61783-922-1(1)*, SportsZone) ABDO Publishing Co.

Historia de los Deportes Series, 6 bks., Set. 2003. (Historia de los Deportes Ser.). (SPA & ENG., Illus.). (J). 103.50 *(978-0-8239-6917-3(7)*, Editorial Buenas Letras) Rosen Publishing Group, Inc., The.

Hoblin, Paul. Biggest Blunders in Sports, 1 vol. 2013. (Sports' Biggest Moments Ser.). (ENG.). 64p. (gr. 3-6). lib. bdg. 32.79 *(978-1-61783-921-4(3)*, SportsZone) ABDO Publishing Co.

Howell, Brian. Masters, 1 vol. 2013. (Sports' Great Championships Ser.). (ENG.). 64p. (J). (gr. 4-6). lib. bdg. 32.79 *(978-1-61783-670-1(2)*, SportsZone) ABDO Publishing Co.

Krull, Kathleen. Lives of the Athletes: Thrills, Spills (and What the Neighbors Thought) Hewitt, Kathryn, illus. 2013. (Lives Of ... Ser.). (ENG.). 96p. (J). (gr. 5-7). pap. 8.99 *(978-0-544-24760-4(4))* Houghton Mifflin Harcourt Publishing Co.

Mathaler, Jon. Bad Days in Sports. 2017. (Whoops! a History of Bad Days Ser.). (ENG., Illus.). 48p. (gr. 5-8). lib. bdg. 33.32 *(978-1-4109-8564-4(4))* Capstone Press of Coughlan Cos.

Mattern, Joanne. Legendary Athletic Achievements. 2018. (ENG.). 32p. (gr. 3-6). 31.35 ***(978-1-63235-423-5(3)***, 12-Story Library) Pr. Room Editions LLC.

Miles, Liz. Sports: From Ancient Olympics to the Super Bowl. 2010. (Timeline History Ser.). (ENG.). 32p. (gr. 3-5). 29.99 *(978-1-4329-3805-5(3))*; pap. 8.95 *(978-1-4329-3813-0(4))* Heinemann-Raintree. (NA-h).

Monteverde, Matthew. Giants vs. Cowboys. 2014. (J). 49.50 *(978-1-4777-2783-6(3))*; pap. 8.25 *(978-1-4777-2782-9(5))*; 24p. (gr. 2-5). lib. bdg. 22.60 *(978-1-4777-2781-2(7))* Rosen Publishing Group, Inc., The. (PowerKids Pr.).

Morley, Jacqueline. How to Be an Ancient Greek Athlete. Antram, David, illus. 2008. (How to Be Ser.). (ENG.). 32p. (J). (gr. 3-7). pap. 5.95 *(978-1-4263-0278-7(9)*, National Geographic Children's Bks.) National Geographic Society.

Murray, Laura K. Lululemon: Built for Success. 2016. (Built for Success Ser.). (ENG., Illus.). 48p. (J). (gr. 5-9). pap. 12.00 *(978-1-62832-159-3(8)*, Creative Paperbacks) Creative Co., The.

Nasium, James. African Americans in Sports. Hill, Marc Lamont, ed. 2012. (Major Black Contributions from Emancipation to Civil Rights Ser.). 64p. (J). (gr. 5). 22.95 *(978-1-4222-2381-9(7))* Mason Crest.

Platt, Richard. They Played What?! The Weird History of Sports & Recreation. 2007. (Weird History Ser.). (ENG.). 48p. (J). (gr. 3-6). 16.95 *(978-1-58728-585-1(1))*; (Illus.). pap. 9.95 *(978-1-58728-586-8(X))* Cooper Square Publishing Llc.

Raatma, Lucia. The Curious, Captivating, Unusual History of Sports, 1 vol. 2012. (Unusual Histories Ser.). (ENG.). 48p. (gr. 3-4). lib. bdg. 31.99 *(978-1-4296-7537-6(3))* Capstone Press of Coughlan Cos.

Rappoport, Ken. Biggest Upsets in Sports, 1 vol. 2013. (Sports' Biggest Moments Ser.). (ENG.). 64p. (gr. 3-6). lib. bdg. 32.79 *(978-1-61783-923-8(X)*, SportsZone) ABDO Publishing Co.

Rice, Dona Herweck. Physical Feats & Failures, 1 vol. 2nd rev. ed. 2013. (Nonfiction Readers Ser.). (ENG., Illus.). 48p. (J). (gr. 4-4). pap. 29.96 *(978-1-4807-1122-8(5))* Shell Educational Publishing.

Samuel, Charlie. Entertainment in Colonial America. 2003. (Primary Sources of Everyday Life in Colonial America Ser.). (Illus.). 24p. (J). lib. bdg. 22.60 *(978-0-8239-6600-4(3)*, PowerKids Pr.) Rosen Publishing Group, Inc., The.

Scheppler, Bill. The Iron Man Triathlon. 2009. (Ultra Sports Ser.). 64p. (gr. 5-8). 58.50 *(978-1-60854-608-4(X)*, Rosen Reference) Rosen Publishing Group, Inc., The.

Smith-Llera, Danielle & Burgan, Michael. Captured History Sports. 2017. (Captured History Sports Ser.). (ENG.). 64p. (gr. 5-7). 277.20 *(978-0-7565-5550-4(7)*, CPB Grades 4-8) Compass Point Bks.

Sports Greats: Set 2. 2016. (Sports Greats Ser.). 48p. (gr. 6-5). pap. 70.20 *(978-0-7660-7972-4(4))*; lib. bdg. 167.58 *(978-0-7660-7500-9(1))* Enslow Pubs., Inc.

Sports in America, 1990-1999. 2nd rev. ed. 2010. (Sports in America Ser.). (Illus.). 96p. (YA). (gr. 7-12). 39.95 *(978-1-60413-456-8(9))* Facts On File, Inc.

Sports in America, 2000-2009. 2010. (Sports in America Ser.). (Illus.). 96p. (YA). (gr. 7-12). 39.95 *(978-1-60413-457-5(7))* Facts On File, Inc.

Stokes, Erica M. Sports of Mexico. (Mexico: Beautiful Land, Diverse People Ser.). 64p. (YA). (gr. 7-12). 2009. (Illus.). 21.95 *(978-1-4222-0654-6(8))* 2007. pap. 9.95 *(978-1-4222-0721-5(8))* Mason Crest.

Zweig, Eric. Everything Sports: All the Photos, Facts, & Fun to Make You Jump! 2016. (National Geographic Kids Everything Ser.). (ENG., Illus.). 64p. (J). (gr. 3-7). pap. 12.99 *(978-1-4263-2333-1(6)*, National Geographic Children's Bks.) National Geographic Society.

SPORTS—POETRY

Akister, Finola, et al, selected by. Sports Poems & Mouse Poems. 2008. (Illus.). 32p. (J). pap. 10.95 *(978-1-59646-619-7(7))* Dingles & Co.

Akister, Finola, et al. Sports Poems & Mouse Poems. 2008. (Illus.). 32p. (J). lib. bdg. 23.65 *(978-1-59646-618-0(9))* Dingles & Co.

Alvarez, Mrinali, illus. Pon, Pon: ¡A Jugar con el Bebé! 2005. (SPA.). 28p. (J). 8.95 *(978-0-8477-1550-3(7))* Univ. of Puerto Rico Pr.

Chatterjee, Debjani & Quarto Generic Staff. Let's Play! Poems about Sports & Games from Around the World. D'Arcy, Brian, ed. Adl, Shirin, illus. 2014. (ENG.). 56p. (J). (gr. 1-5). 19.99 *(978-1-84780-370-2(9)*, Frances Lincoln) Quarto Publishing Group UK GBR. Dist: Hachette Bk. Group.

Colson, Mary. Sports Poems, 1 vol. 2014. (Experiencing Poetry Ser.). (ENG.). 64p. (gr. 7-8). lib. bdg. 35.99 *(978-1-4329-9561-4(8))* Heinemann-Raintree.

Foster, John. Football Fever. 2010. (ENG., Illus.). 128p. (YA). pap. 10.95 *(978-0-19-276355-6(5))* Oxford Univ. Pr., Inc.

Gutman, Dan. Casey Back at Bat. Johnson, Steve & Fancher, Lou, illus. 2009. (ENG.). 32p. (J). (gr. -1-3). pap. 6.99 *(978-0-06-056027-0(4))* HarperCollins Pubs.

Hoyte, Carol-Ann. And the Crowd Goes Wild! A Global Gathering of Sports Poems. Roemer, Heidi Bee, ed. Sylvester, Kevin, illus. 2012. 80p. pap. *(978-1-77097-953-6(0))* FriesenPress.

Ipcizade, Catherine, et al. Pucks, Clubs, & Baseball Gloves: Reading & Writing Sports Poems, 1 vol. Loveridge, Matt et al, illus. 2014. (Poet in You Ser.). (ENG.). 32p. (gr. 2-4). pap. 9.95 *(978-1-4795-2947-6(8))*; lib. bdg. 27.32 *(978-1-4795-2196-8(5))* Picture Window Bks.

Lansky, Bruce. I Hope I Don't Strike Out! & Other Funny Sports Poems. Carpenter, Stephen, illus. 2008. 30p. *(978-0-88166-535-2(5))* Meadowbrook Pr.

Moses, Brian & Stevens, Roger. Olympic Poems - 100% Unofficial! 2016. (ENG., Illus.). 96p. (J). (gr. 4-7). pap. 8.99 *(978-1-5098-1224-0(5))* Pan Macmillan GBR. Dist: Independent Pubs. Group.

Smith, Charles R., Jr. Hoop Kings. 2007. (ENG., Illus.). 40p. (J). (gr. 3-7). pap. 6.99 *(978-0-7636-3560-2(X))* Candlewick Pr.

—Hoop Queens. 2007. (ENG., Illus.). 40p. (J). (gr. 3-7). pap. 6.99 *(978-0-7636-3561-9(8))* Candlewick Pr.

SPORTS—YEARBOOKS

Buckley, James, Jr. Scholastic Year in Sports 2017. 2016. (ENG., Illus.). 192p. (J). (gr. 3-7). pap. 9.99 *(978-1-338-03277-2(1))* Scholastic, Inc.

SPORTS IN ART

Antram, David. Extreme Sports. 2012. (How to Draw Ser.). (ENG.). 32p. (J). (gr. 4-6). pap. 11.75 *(978-1-4488-6465-2(8))*; lib. bdg. 26.50 *(978-1-4488-6459-1(3))* Rosen Publishing Group, Inc., The. (PowerKids Pr.).

Cook, Trevor & Miles, Lisa. Drawing Sports Figures. 2011. (Drawing Is Fun Ser.). (Illus.). 32p. (J). (gr. 1-3). pap. 10.50 *(978-1-4339-5074-2(X)*, Gareth Stevens Learning Library); lib. bdg. 26.60 *(978-1-4339-5028-5(6))* Stevens, Gareth Publishing LLLP.

Garbot, Dave. Silly Sports: Learn to Draw More Than 20 Amazingly Awesome Athletes. Garbot, Dave, illus. 2016. (Cartooning for Kids Ser.). (ENG., Illus.). 64p. (J). (gr. k-5). 33.32 *(978-1-939581-93-8(1)*, Walter Foster Jr) Quarto Publishing Group USA.

Kissock, Heather. Extreme Sports. 2012. (J). *(978-1-61913-239-9(7))*; pap. *(978-1-61913-244-3(3))* Weigl Pubs., Inc.

Reid, Emily. Sports Claymation. 2016. (Claymation Sensation Ser.). 32p. (gr. 3-3). pap. 11.75 *(978-1-4994-8104-4(7)*, Windmill Bks.) Rosen Publishing Group, Inc., The.

Wacholtz, Anthony. Drawing with Sports Illustrated Kids, 1 vol. Haya, Erwin & Ray, Mike, illus. 2013. (Drawing with Sports Illustrated Kids Ser.). (ENG.). 144p. (gr. 5-7). pap. 14.95 *(978-1-4765-3581-4(7))* Capstone Press of Coughlan Cos.

—Drawing with Sports Illustrated Kids. Ray, Mike & Haya, Erwin, illus. 2013. (Drawing with Sports Illustrated Kids Ser.). (ENG.). 64p. (gr. 5-7). 135.96 *(978-1-4765-3741-2(0))* Capstone Press of Coughlan Cos.

—Picture a Home Run: A Baseball Drawing Book, 1 vol. Haya, Erwin, illus. 2013. (Drawing with Sports Illustrated Kids Ser.). (ENG.). 64p. (gr. 5-7). 33.99 *(978-1-4765-3106-9(4))* Capstone Press of Coughlan Cos.

—Picture a Slam Dunk: A Basketball Drawing Book, 1 vol. Haya, Erwin, illus. 2013. (Drawing with Sports Illustrated Kids Ser.). (ENG.). 64p. (gr. 5-7). 33.99 *(978-1-4765-3107-6(2))* Capstone Press of Coughlan Cos.

—Picture a Slap Shot: A Hockey Drawing Book, 1 vol. Ray, Mike, illus. 2013. (Drawing with Sports Illustrated Kids Ser.). (ENG.). 64p. (gr. 5-7). 33.99 *(978-1-4765-3105-2(6))* Capstone Press of Coughlan Cos.

—Picture a Touchdown: A Football Drawing Book, 1 vol. Ray, Mike, illus. 2013. (Drawing with Sports Illustrated Kids Ser.). (ENG.). 64p. (gr. 5-7). 33.99 *(978-1-4765-3104-5(8))* Capstone Press of Coughlan Cos.

SPORTS JOURNALISM

Christopher, Dale. Behind the Desk with... Matt Christopher: The #1 Sportswriter for Kids. 2004. (ENG., Illus.). 128p. (J). (gr. 2-5). pap. 15.99 *(978-0-316-10952-9(5)*, Tingley, Megan Bks.) Little, Brown Bks. for Young Readers.

Marlowe, Christie. Announcer. 2013. (Earning $50,000 - $100,000 with a High School Diploma or Less Ser.: 14). 64p. (J). (gr. 7-18). 22.95 *(978-1-4222-2887-6(8))* Mason Crest.

Peterson, Brian C. Sports Marketing: Careers off the Field, Vol. 10. Ferrer, Al, ed. 2015. (Careers off the Field Ser.). (Illus.). 64p. (J). (gr. 7). 23.95 *(978-1-4222-3272-9(7))* Mason Crest.

Schwartzenberger, Tina. Don Cherry. 2010. (Illus.). 24p. *(978-1-77071-625-4(4))*; pap. *(978-1-77071-626-1(2))* Weigl Educational Pubs. Ltd.

Suen, Anastasia. Read & Write Sports: Readers Theatre & Writing Activities for Grades 3-8, 1 vol. 2011. 189p. (C). pap. 40.00 *(978-1-59884-631-7(0)*, A3166P) Pearson Education GBR. Dist: ABC-CLIO, LLC.

Thomas, Stephen, ed. Hot Summer Fun, Cool Summer Stars. Staake, Bob et al, illus. Date not set. 28p. (Orig.). (J). (gr. 3-7). pap. *(978-1-886749-26-9(4))* Sports Illustrated For Kids.

Tracy, Kathleen. Matt Christopher. 2008. (Classic Storytellers Ser.). (Illus.). 48p. (J). (gr. 4-7). lib. bdg. 29.95 *(978-1-58415-535-5(3))* Mitchell Lane Pubs., Inc.

Walters, John. Sports Broadcasting, Vol. 10. Ferrer, Al, ed. 2015. (Careers off the Field Ser.). (Illus.). 64p. (J). (gr. 7). 23.95 *(978-1-4222-3271-2(9))* Mason Crest.

—Sportswriting & Sports Photography, Vol. 10. Ferrer, Al, ed. 2015. (Careers off the Field Ser.). (Illus.). 64p. (J). (gr. 7). lib. bdg. 23.95 *(978-1-4222-3273-6(5))* Mason Crest.

SPRING

Aloian, Molly. How Do We Know It Is Spring? 2013. (ENG., Illus.). 24p. (J). *(978-0-7787-0959-6(0))*; pap. *(978-0-7787-0963-3(9))* Crabtree Publishing Co.

Amoroso, Cynthia & Noyed, Robert B. Spring. 2014. (Seasons of the Year Ser.). (ENG.). 24p. (J). (gr. -1-2). 25.64 *(978-1-62687-025-3(X)*, 206824) Child's World, Inc., The.

Anderson, Maxine & Berkenkamp, Lauri. Explore Spring! 25 Great Ways to Learn about Spring. Frederick-Frost, Alexis, illus. 2007. (Explore Your World Ser.). (ENG.). 96p. (J). (gr. k-4). per. 12.95 *(978-0-9785037-4-1(0))* Octavio Publishing.

Anderson, Sheila. Are You Ready for Spring? 2010. (Lightning Bolt Books (tm) — Our Four Seasons Ser.). (ENG.). 32p. (gr. k-2). pap. 7.95 *(978-0-7613-5670-7(3))*; lib. bdg. 26.60 *(978-0-7613-4584-8(1))* Lerner Publishing Group.

Appleby, Alex. Qu Sucede en Primavera? / What Happens in Spring?, Vol. 1. 2014. (Cuatro Estaciones Estupendas / Four Super Seasons Ser.). (SPA & BYN.). 24p. (J). (gr. k-k). 22.60 *(978-1-4824-0119-6(3))* Stevens, Gareth Publishing LLLP.

—What Happens in Spring?, Vol. 1. 2014. (Four Super Seasons Ser.). (ENG.). 24p. (J). (gr. k-k). 22.60 *(978-1-4824-0105-9(3))* Stevens, Gareth Publishing LLLP.

Barnham, Kay. Spring. 2010. (Seasons Ser.). (ENG.). 24p. (J). lib. bdg. 22.60 *(978-1-61532-569-6(7)*, PowerKids Pr.) Rosen Publishing Group, Inc., The.

Bekkering, Annalise. Spring. 2010. (J). pap. 9.95 *(978-1-61690-050-2(4))*; 24p. (gr. 2-4). lib. bdg. 25.70 *(978-1-61690-046-5(6))* Weigl Pubs., Inc.

—Spring: World of Wonder Seasons. 2010. (J). *(978-1-60596-766-0(1))* Weigl Pubs., Inc.

Brode, Robyn. April;abril. 2009. (Months of the Year/Meses del año Ser.). (ENG & SPA.). 24p. (J). (gr. -1-3). pap. 8.15 *(978-1-4339-2109-4(X)*, Weekly Reader Leveled Readers) Stevens, Gareth Publishing LLLP.

—April/Abril. 2009. (Months of the Year/Meses del año Ser.). (ENG & SPA.). 24p. (J). (gr. -1-3). lib. bdg. 22.00 *(978-1-4339-1932-9(X)*, Weekly Reader Leveled Readers) Stevens, Gareth Publishing LLLP.

—March;marzo. 2009. (Months of the Year/Meses del año Ser.). (ENG & SPA.). 24p. (J). (gr. -1-3). pap. 8.15 *(978-1-4339-2108-7(1)*, Weekly Reader Leveled Readers) Stevens, Gareth Publishing LLLP.

—March/Marzo. 2009. (Months of the Year/Meses del año Ser.). (ENG & SPA.). 24p. (J). (gr. -1-3). lib. bdg. 22.00 *(978-1-4339-1931-2(1)*, Weekly Reader Leveled Readers) Stevens, Gareth Publishing LLLP.

—May;mayo. 2009. (Months of the Year/Meses del año Ser.). (ENG & SPA.). 24p. (J). (gr. -1-3). pap. 8.15 *(978-1-4339-2110-0(3)*, Weekly Reader Leveled Readers) Stevens, Gareth Publishing LLLP.

—May/Mayo. 2009. (Months of the Year/Meses del año Ser.). (ENG & SPA.). 24p. (J). (gr. -1-3). lib. bdg. 22.00 *(978-1-4339-1933-6(8)*, Weekly Reader Leveled Readers) Stevens, Gareth Publishing LLLP.

Brode, Robyn & Nations, Susan. April. 2nd rev. ed. 2009. (Months of the Year Ser.). (ENG.). 24p. (J). (gr. -1-3). pap. 8.15 *(978-1-4339-2097-4(2))*; lib. bdg. 22.00 *(978-1-4339-1920-6(6))* Stevens, Gareth Publishing LLLP. (Weekly Reader Leveled Readers).

—March. 2nd rev. ed. 2009. (Months of the Year Ser.). (ENG.). 24p. (J). (gr. -1-3). pap. 8.15 *(978-1-4339-2096-7(4))*; lib. bdg. 22.00 *(978-1-4339-1919-0(2))* Stevens, Gareth Publishing LLLP. (Weekly Reader Leveled Readers).

—May. 2nd rev. ed. 2009. (Months of the Year Ser.). (ENG.). 24p. (J). (gr. -1-3). pap. 8.15 *(978-1-4339-2098-1(0))*; lib. bdg. 22.00 *(978-1-4339-1921-3(4))* Stevens, Gareth Publishing LLLP. (Weekly Reader Leveled Readers).

Bryant, Margaret A., et al. Learning about Spring with Children's Literature. 2006. (ENG., Illus.). 160p. (J). (gr. k-3). pap. 14.95 *(978-1-56976-206-6(6)*, Zephyr Pr.) Chicago Review Pr., Inc.

Burke, Betty & Finer, Susie. Activités de Printemps. (FRE.). 32p. pap. *(978-0-439-98520-8(X))* Scholastic Canada, Ltd.

Butterfield, Moira. Spring. James, Helen, illus. 2005. (Seasons (Smart Apple Media) Ser.). 32p. (YA). (gr. 2-4). lib. bdg. 27.10 *(978-1-58340-614-4(X))* Black Rabbit Bks.

Carr, Aaron. Spring. 2013. 25.00 *(978-1-62127-493-3(4))* Weigl Pubs., Inc.

Carter, David A. Spring: A Pop-up Book. 2016. (Seasons Pop-Up Ser.). (ENG., Illus.). 12p. (J). (gr. -1-k). 14.95 *(978-1-4197-1912-7(2)*, Abrams Appleseed) Abrams, Inc.

Casado, Dami & Casado, Alicia. La Primavera. 2005. (Brujita Mo y las Cuatro Estaciones Ser.). (SPA & ESP., Illus.). 14p. (J). (gr. k-4). per., bds. 7.99 *(978-84-272-6238-6(8))* Molino, Editorial ESP. Dist: Santillana USA Publishing Co., Inc.

Clay, Kathryn. Animals in Spring. 2016. (Celebrate Spring Ser.). (ENG., Illus.). 24p. (gr. k-1). lib. bdg. 21.99 *(978-1-4914-8302-2(4)*, Pebble Bks.) Capstone Press of Coughlan Cos.

—Celebrate Spring. 2016. (Celebrate Spring Ser.). (ENG.). 24p. (gr. k-1). 87.96 *(978-1-4914-8318-3(0)*, Pebble Bks.) Capstone Press of Coughlan Cos.

—Flowers. 2016. (Celebrate Spring Ser.). (ENG., Illus.). 24p. (gr. k-1). lib. bdg. 21.99 *(978-1-4914-8304-6(0)*, Pebble Bks.) Capstone Press of Coughlan Cos.

—Planting Seeds. 2016. (Celebrate Spring Ser.). (ENG., Illus.). 24p. (gr. k-1). lib. bdg. 21.99 *(978-1-4914-8305-3(9)*, Pebble Bks.) Capstone Press of Coughlan Cos.

Collinson, Clare. Spring. 2010. (Thinking about the Seasons Ser.). 32p. 28.50 *(978-1-59771-260-6(4))* Sea-To-Sea Pubns.

Declus, Jennifer. What Might I Find in a Geyser. Kalasea, illus. 2004. (J). *(978-0-9743690-0-6(4))* Britt Allcroft Productions.

DeGezelle, Terri. Exploring Spring, 1 vol. 2012. (Exploring the Seasons Ser.). (ENG.). 24p. (gr. k-1). pap. 7.29 *(978-1-4296-7910-7(7))*; pap. 41.70 *(978-1-4296-8351-7(1))* Capstone Press of Coughlan Cos. (Pebble Plus).

Dolphin, Colleen. Signs of Spring, 1 vol. 2012. (Signs of the Seasons Ser.). (ENG.). 24p. (J). (gr. k-3). lib. bdg. 24.21 *(978-1-61783-393-9(2)*, SandCastle) ABDO Publishing Co.

Endres, Hollie J. The Letter Ss Set: Spring & Summer, 6 vols. 2004. (Letter Bks.). (ENG.). 8p. (gr. k-1). pap. 29.70 *(978-0-7368-4118-4(0)*, Letter Bks.) Capstone Press of Coughlan Cos.

Enslow, Brian. Spring Colors. 2011. (All about Colors of the Seasons Ser.). (Illus.). 24p. (J). (gr. -1-18). pap. 7.95 *(978-1-59845-265-5(7)*, Enslow Elementary) Enslow Pubs., Inc.

Esbaum, Jill & National Geographic Kids Staff. Everything Spring. 2010. (ENG., Illus.). 16p. (J). (gr. -1-3). pap. 5.95 *(978-1-4263-0607-5(5)*, National Geographic Children's Bks.) National Geographic Society.

Fewer, Michael. Naturama. Doran, Melissa, illus. 2017. (ENG.). 96p. (J). 38.00 *(978-0-7171-6980-1(4))* M.H. Gill & Co. U. C. IRL. Dist: Dufour Editions, Inc.

Flatt, Lizann. Sorting Through Spring. Barron, Ashley, illus. 2013. (Math in Nature Ser.: 2). (ENG.). 32p. (J). (gr. 1-4). 15.95 *(978-1-926973-59-3(3)*, Owlkids) Owlkids Bks. Inc. CAN. Dist: Publishers Group West (PGW).

Fretland VanVoorst, Jenny. Animals in Spring. 2015. (Illus.). 24p. (J). lib. bdg. *(978-1-62031-234-6(4)*, Bullfrog Bks.) Jump! Inc.

—Birds in Spring. 2015. (Illus.). 24p. (J). lib. bdg. *(978-1-62031-235-3(2))* Jump! Inc.

—El Clima en la Primavera. 2015.Tr. of Weather in Spring. (SPA., Illus.). 24p. (J). lib. bdg. *(978-1-62031-252-0(2)*, Bullfrog Bks.) Jump! Inc.

—Gardens in Spring. 2015. (Illus.). 24p. (J). lib. bdg. *(978-1-62031-236-0(0))* Jump! Inc.

—Las Aves en la Primavera. 2015.Tr. of Birds in Spring. (SPA., Illus.). 24p. (J). lib. bdg. *(978-1-62031-250-6(6)*, Bullfrog Bks.) Jump! Inc.

—Los Animales en la Primavera. 2015.Tr. of Animals in Spring. (SPA., Illus.). 24p. (J). lib. bdg. *(978-1-62031-241-4(7)*, Bullfrog Bks.) Jump! Inc.

—Los árboles en la Primavera. 2015.Tr. of Trees in Spring. (SPA., Illus.). 24p. (J). lib. bdg. *(978-1-62031-251-3(4)*, Bullfrog Bks.) Jump! Inc.

—Los Jardines en la Primavera. 2015.Tr. of Gardens in Spring. (SPA., Illus.). 24p. (J). lib. bdg. *(978-1-62031-242-1(5)*, Bullfrog Bks.) Jump! Inc.

—Trees in Spring. 2015. (Illus.). 24p. (J). lib. bdg. *(978-1-62031-237-7(9)*, Bullfrog Bks.) Jump! Inc.

—Weather in Spring. 2015. (Illus.). 24p. (J). lib. bdg. *(978-1-62031-238-4(7)*, Bullfrog Bks.) Jump! Inc.

Ghigna, Charles. Hail to Spring! Watson, Laura, illus. 2015. (Springtime Weather Wonders Ser.). (ENG.). (gr. -1-2). 20p. bds. 7.99 *(978-1-4795-6041-7(3))*; 24p. lib. bdg. 21.99 *(978-1-4795-6029-5(4))* Picture Window Bks.

—Raindrops Fall All Around. Watson, Laura, illus. 2015. (Springtime Weather Wonders Ser.). (ENG.). 24p. (gr. -1-2). lib. bdg. 21.99 *(978-1-4795-6030-1(8))* Picture Window Bks.

—Springtime Weather Wonders. Watson, Laura, illus. 2015. (Springtime Weather Wonders Ser.). (ENG.). 24p. (gr. -1-2). lib. bdg. 87.96 *(978-1-4795-6045-5(6))* Picture Window Bks.

—Sunshine Brightens Springtime. Watson, Laura, illus. 2015. (Springtime Weather Wonders Ser.). (ENG.). (gr. -1-2). 20p. bds. 7.99 *(978-1-4795-6043-1(X))*; 24p. lib. bdg. 21.99 *(978-1-4795-6031-8(6))* Picture Window Bks.

—A Windy Day in Spring. Watson, Laura, illus. 2015. (Springtime Weather Wonders Ser.). (ENG.). 24p. (gr. -1-2). lib. bdg. 21.99 *(978-1-4795-6032-5(4))* Picture Window Bks.

Glaser, Rebecca. Spring. 2012. (ENG., Illus.). 24p. (J). lib. bdg. 25.65 *(978-1-62031-014-4(7))* Jump! Inc.

Gleisner, Jenna Lee. How's the Weather in Spring? 2014. (21st Century Basic Skills Library: Let's Look at Spring Ser.). (ENG., Illus.). 24p. (J). (gr. k-3). pap. 12.79 *(978-1-62431-681-4(6)*, 203129) Cherry Lake Publishing.

—What Blossoms in Spring? 2014. (21st Century Basic Skills Library: Let's Look at Spring Ser.). (ENG.). 24p. (J). (gr. k-3). 22.79 *(978-1-62431-659-3(X)*, 203148); pap. 12.79 *(978-1-62431-686-9(7)*, 203149) Cherry Lake Publishing.

—What Do Animals Do in Spring? 2014. (21st Century Basic Skills Library: Let's Look at Spring Ser.). (ENG., Illus.). 24p. (J). (gr. k-3). 22.79 *(978-1-62431-660-9(3)*, 203152) Cherry Lake Publishing.

—What Do People Do in Spring? 2014. (21st Century Basic Skills Library: Let's Look at Spring Ser.). (ENG., Illus.). 24p. (J). (gr. k-3). 22.79 *(978-1-62431-661-6(1)*, 203156) Cherry Lake Publishing.

Hedlund, Stephanie. Spring. Bauer, Stephanie, illus. 2013. (Seasons Ser.). 24p. (J). (gr. k-4). lib. bdg. 27.07 *(978-1-61641-993-6(8)*, Looking Glass Library- Nonfiction) Magic Wagon.

Henshaw, Lorne. Birds in Spring. 2016. (We Love Spring! Ser.). 00024p. (J). pap. 8.15 ***(978-1-4824-5477-2(7))*** Stevens, Gareth Publishing LLLP.

Here Comes Spring! 2003. (J). per. *(978-1-57657-968-8(9))* Paradise Pr., Inc.

Herriges, Ann. Spring. 2006. (Seasons Ser.). (ENG., Illus.). 24p. (J). (gr. k-3). lib. bdg. 25.95 *(978-1-60014-031-0(9))* Bellwether Media.

—Spring. 2011. (Blastoff! Readers Ser.). (ENG.). 24p. (J). pap. 5.95 *(978-0-531-26247-4(2)*, Children's Pr.) Scholastic Library Publishing.

Herrington, Lisa M. How Do You Know It's Spring? 2013. (ENG.). 32p. (J). 23.00 *(978-0-531-29947-0(3))*; pap. 5.95 *(978-0-531-22576-9(3))* Scholastic Library Publishing.

Hollow, Stanley. First Spring Flowers. 2016. (We Love Spring! Ser.). 00024p. (J). pap. 8.15 ***(978-1-4824-5489-5(0))*** Stevens, Gareth Publishing LLLP.

Jeffries, Joyce. Dinosaurs in the Spring. 2014. (Dinosaur School Ser.). 24p. (J). (gr. -1-1). pap. 8.15 *(978-1-4824-0622-1(5))* Stevens, Gareth Publishing LLLP.

Jones, Tammy. I Like the Spring! 2009. (Sight Word Readers Set A Ser.). (J). 3.49 net. *(978-1-60719-138-4(5))* Newmark Learning LLC.

Kalz, Jill. Spring. 2005. (My First Look at Seasons Ser.). (Illus.). 24p. (J). (gr. k-3). lib. bdg. 15.95 *(978-1-58341-363-0(4)*, Creative Education) Creative Co., The.

Latta, Sara L. ¿Qué Sucede en la Primavera? What Happens in Spring? 2010. (SPA.). (J). 23.94 *(978-0-7660-3242-2(6),* Enslow Elementary) Enslow Pubs., Inc.

—What Happens in Spring? 2006. (I Like the Seasons! Ser.). (Illus.). 24p. (J). (gr. 1-3). lib. bdg. 22.60 *(978-0-7660-2419-9(9),* Enslow Elementary) Enslow Pubs., Inc.

—Why Is It Spring? 2012. (Why Do We Have Seasons? Ser.). (Illus.). 24p. (J). (gr. k-18). pap. 7.95 *(978-1-59845-389-8(0),* Enslow Elementary); 22.60 *(978-0-7660-3986-5(2))* Enslow Pubs., Inc.

Lim, Annalees. 10-Minute Seasonal Crafts for Spring. 2014. (10-Minute Seasonal Crafts Ser.). 24p. (J). (gr. k-3). lib. bdg. 26.25 *(978-1-4777-9206-3(6))* Windmill Bks.

Lindeen, Mary. Spring! 2015. (BeginningtoRead Ser.). (ENG., Illus.). 32p. (J). (gr. k-2). lib. bdg. 22.60 *(978-1-59953-679-8(X))* Norwood Hse. Pr.

—Spring. 2015. (BeginningtoRead Ser.). (ENG., Illus.). 32p. (J). (gr. k-2). pap. 11.94 *(978-1-60357-739-7(4))* Norwood Hse. Pr.

Macken, JoAnn Early. Spring. 2006. (Seasons of the Year Ser.). (Illus.). 16p. (gr. -1-2). pap. 5.30 *(978-0-8368-6359-8(3));* lib. bdg. 19.00 *(978-0-8368-6354-3(2))* Stevens, Gareth Publishing LLLP. (Weekly Reader Leveled Readers).

—Spring (Primavera) 2006. (Seasons of the Year/ Las estaciones del ano Ser.). (SPA., Illus.). 16p. (gr. -1-2). pap. 5.30 *(978-0-8368-6538-7(3),* Weekly Reader Leveled Readers) Stevens, Gareth Publishing LLLP.

—Spring/Primavera. 2006. (Seasons of the Year/Las Estaciones del Ano Ser.). (ENG & SPA., Illus.). 16p. (gr. -1-2). lib. bdg. 19.00 *(978-0-8368-6533-2(2),* Weekly Reader Leveled Readers) Stevens, Gareth Publishing LLLP.

McGee, Randel. Fun & Festive Spring Crafts: Flower Puppets, Bunny Masks, & Mother's Day Pop-Up Cards. 2014. (Fun & Festive Crafts for the Seasons Ser.). (Illus.). 48p. (J). (gr. 3-4). lib. bdg. 25.27 *(978-0-7660-4318-3(5),* Enslow Elementary) Enslow Pubs., Inc.

Meister, Cari. Spring Is Special, 1 vol. Lingenfelter, Jim, illus. 2010. (First Graphics: Seasons Ser.). (ENG.). 24p. (gr. 1-2). pap. 6.29 *(978-1-4296-5621-4(2));* pap. 35.70 *(978-1-4296-5693-1(X));* lib. bdg. 23.99 *(978-1-4296-4729-8(9))* Capstone Press of Coughlan Cos.

Moon, Walt K. ¡La Primavera Es Divertida! 2017. (Bumba Books (tm) en Español — Diviértete con Las Estaciones (Season Fun) Ser.). (SPA., Illus.). 24p. (J). (gr. -1-1). 25.32 *(978-1-5124-2861-2(2))* Lerner Publishing Group.

—Spring Is Fun! 2016. (Bumba Books (tm) — Season Fun Ser.). (ENG., Illus.). 24p. (J). (gr. -1-1). 25.32 *(978-1-5124-1411-0(5))* Lerner Publishing Group.

Murray, Julie. La Primavera. 2016. (Las Estaciones Ser.). (SPA.). 24p. (J). (gr. k-5). pap. 7.95 *(978-1-4966-0709-6(0))* Capstone Classroom.

—Spring, 1 vol. 2016. (ENG., Illus.). 24p. *(978-1-62970-920-8(4),* 1391200) ABDO Publishing Co.

Owen, Ruth. How Do You Know It's Spring? (Signs of the Seasons Ser.). 24p. (J). 2016. (ENG.). (gr. k-3). pap. 7.95 *(978-1-944998-49-3(7))* 2012. (gr. -1-3). lib. bdg. 23.93 *(978-1-61772-398-8(3))* Bearport Publishing Co., Inc.

Priddy, Roger. Spring: Bright Baby Touch & Feel. 2011. (Bright Baby Touch & Feel Ser.). (ENG., Illus.). 12p. (J). (gr. -1 — 1). bds. 4.95 *(978-0-312-51006-0(3),* 9780312510060, Priddy Bks.) St. Martin's Pr.

Rose, Deborah Lee. The Twelve Days of Springtime: A School Counting Book. Armstrong-Ellis, Carey, illus. 2009. (ENG.). 32p. (J). (gr. -1-3). 15.95 *(978-0-8109-8330-4(3),* Abrams Bks. for Young Readers) Abrams, Inc.

Rotner, Shelley. Hello Spring! 2017. (ENG., Illus.). 32p. (J). (gr. -1-1). 16.95 *(978-0-8234-3752-8(3))* Holiday Hse., Inc.

Rustad, Martha E. H. All about Spring. 2012. (All about Spring Ser.). (ENG.). 24p. (gr. k-1). pap. 166.80 *(978-1-4296-9367-7(3));* pap. 27.80 *(978-1-4296-9366-0(5));* lib. bdg. 106.60 *(978-1-4296-9166-6(2))* Capstone Press of Coughlan Cos. (Pebble Plus).

—Animals in Spring. 2012. (All about Spring Ser.). (ENG.). 24p. (gr. k-1). pap. 41.70 *(978-1-4296-9360-8(6));* (Illus.). 26.65 *(978-1-4296-8655-6(3));* (Illus.). pap. 7.29 *(978-1-4296-9358-5(4))* Capstone Press of Coughlan Cos. (Pebble Plus).

—People in Spring. 2012. (All about Spring Ser.). (ENG.). 24p. (gr. k-1). pap. 41.70 *(978-1-4296-9359-2(2));* pap. 7.29 *(978-1-4296-9361-5(4));* (Illus.). lib. bdg. 26.65 *(978-1-4296-8657-0(X))* Capstone Press of Coughlan Cos. (Pebble Plus).

—Plants in Spring. 2012. (All about Spring Ser.). (ENG.). 24p. (gr. k-1). pap. 41.70 *(978-1-4296-9363-9(0));* pap. 7.29 *(978-1-4296-9362-2(2));* lib. bdg. 26.65 *(978-1-4296-8656-3(1))* Capstone Press of Coughlan Cos. (Pebble Plus).

—Weather in Spring. 2012. (All about Spring Ser.). (ENG.). 24p. (gr. k-1). pap. 41.70 *(978-1-4296-9365-3(7));* pap. 7.29 *(978-1-4296-9364-6(9));* (Illus.). lib. bdg. 26.65 *(978-1-4296-8654-9(5))* Capstone Press of Coughlan Cos. (Pebble Plus).

Shepherd, Jodie. Crayola Spring Colors. 2017. (Crayola (r) Seasons Ser.). (ENG.). 24p. (J). (gr. -1-3). 26.65 ***(978-1-5124-3292-3(X))*** Lerner Publishing Group.

Smith, Sian. What Can You See in Spring?, 1 vol. 2014. (Seasons Ser.). (ENG.). 24p. (gr. -1-1). pap. 5.99 *(978-1-4846-0354-3(0),* Acorn) Heinemann-Raintree.

Thayer, Tanya. Spring. 2005. (First Step Nonfiction Ser.). (Illus.). 24p. (gr. k-2). lib. bdg. 17.27 *(978-0-8225-1986-7(0))* Lerner Publishing Group.

Thayer, Tanya & National Geographic Learning Staff. Spring. 2010. (ENG., Illus.). 24p. (C). (gr. k-2). pap. 9.95 *(978-0-8225-1990-4(9))* National Geographic School Publishing, Inc.

Turnbull, Stephanie. Spring. 2013. (Seasons Ser.). (Illus.). 24p. (J). (gr. 1-4). 25.65 *(978-1-59920-847-3(4))* Black Rabbit Bks.

Urban, Chieu Anh. Hooray for Spring! Urban, Chieu Anh, illus. 2016. (Color Wonder Ser.). (ENG., Illus.). 14p. (J). (gr. -1 — 1). bds. 7.99 *(978-1-4814-8720-7(5),* Little Simon) Little Simon.

Wargin, Kathy-jo. K Is for Kite: God's Springtime Alphabet, 1 vol. Gatto, Kim, illus. 2010. (ENG.). 40p. (J). (gr. -1-2). 15.99 *(978-0-310-71662-4(4))* Zonderkidz.

We Love Spring! 2016. (We Love Spring! Ser.). 00024p. (J). pap. 48.90 ***(978-1-4824-5536-6(6))*** Stevens, Gareth Publishing LLLP.

Welch, Martha Mckeen. Close Looks in a Spring Woods. 2011. (J). *(978-0-396-07998-9(9))* Dodd, Mead & Co., U. S.

World Book, Inc Staff, contrib. by. Spring Celebrations. 2009. (Illus.). 46p. (J). *(978-0-7166-5042-3(8))* World Bk., Inc.

York, M. J. Plants in Spring. 2017. (Welcome, Spring! Ser.). (ENG.). 24p. (J). (gr. -1-2). lib. bdg. 27.07 *(978-1-5038-1654-1(0),* 211507) Child's World, Inc., The.

—Spring on the Farm. 2017. (Welcome, Spring! Ser.). (ENG.). 24p. (J). (gr. -1-2). lib. bdg. 27.07 *(978-1-5038-1657-2(5),* 211508) Child's World, Inc., The.

—Weather in Spring. 2017. (Welcome, Spring! Ser.). (ENG.). 24p. (J). (gr. -1-2). lib. bdg. 27.07 *(978-1-5038-1658-9(3),* 211509) Child's World, Inc., The.

SPRING—FICTION

Alexander, Liza. Splish-Splash Spring! 2016. lib. bdg. 14.75 *(978-0-606-38486-5(3))* Turtleback Bks.

—Splish-Splash Spring! (Sesame Street) Ewers, Joe, illus. 2016. (Pictureback Ser.). (ENG.). 24p. (J). (gr. -1-3). 4.99 *(978-1-101-93429-6(8),* Random Hse. Bks. for Young Readers) Random Hse. Children's Bks.

Allen, Elise & Stanford, Halle. Spring's Sparkle Sleepover. Pooler, Paige, illus. 2015. (Enchanted Sisters Ser.: 3). (J). lib. bdg. 16.00 *(978-0-606-36218-4(5))* Turtleback Bks.

Alley, R. W. Clark in the Deep Sea. 2016. (ENG., Illus.). 32p. (J). (gr. -1-3). 14.99 *(978-0-547-90692-8(7))* Houghton Mifflin Harcourt Publishing Co.

Armstrong, Jeannette C. Dancing with the Cranes. Hall, Ron, illus. 2nd rev. ed. 2009. (ENG.). 24p. pap. 10.95 *(978-1-894778-70-1(7))* Theytus Bks., Ltd. CAN. Dist: Univ. of Toronto Pr.

Barklem, Jill. Cuento de Primavera.Tr. of Spring Story. (SPA.). (J). pap. 8.95 *(978-84-233-2618-1(7))* Ediciones Destino ESP. Dist: Planeta Publishing Corp.

Bauer, Marion Dane. Crinkle, Crackle, Crack: It's Spring! Shelley, John, illus. 2015. (ENG.). 32p. (J). (gr. -1-3). 16.95 *(978-0-8234-2952-3(0))* Holiday Hse., Inc.

—In Like a Lion, Out Like a Lamb. McCully, Emily Arnold, illus. (ENG.). 32p. (J). 2012. pap. 6.95 *(978-0-8234-2432-0(4))* 2011. (gr. -1-3). 16.95 *(978-0-8234-2238-8(0))* Holiday Hse., Inc.

Berger, Carin. Finding Spring. Berger, Carin, illus. 2015. (ENG., Illus.). 40p. (J). (gr. -1-3). 17.99 *(978-0-06-225019-3(1),* Collins Design) HarperCollins Pubs.

Bond, Rebecca. Pig & Goose & the First Day of Spring. Bond, Rebecca, illus. 2017. (ENG., Illus.). 48p. (J). (gr. k-3). lib. bdg. 12.99 *(978-1-58089-594-1(8))* Charlesbridge Publishing, Inc.

Bonnell, Kris. Spring Is Coming! 2007. (J). pap. 6.95 *(978-1-933727-64-6(0))* Reading Reading Bks., LLC.

Brooks, Donna. The Amazing Apple Tree. 2011. 40p. pap. 16.95 *(978-1-61204-563-4(4),* Strategic Bk. Publishing) Strategic Book Publishing & Rights Agency (SBPRA).

Carlstrom, Nancy White. Raven & River. Van Zyle, Jon, illus. 2011. (ENG.). 32p. pap. 11.95 *(978-1-60223-150-4(8))* Univ. of Alaska Pr.

Carter, David A. Springtime in Bugland! Carter, David A., illus. 2012. (David Carter's Bugs Ser.). (ENG., Illus.). 24p. (J). (gr. -1-1). 15.99 *(978-1-4424-3892-7(4));* pap. 3.99 *(978-1-4424-3890-3(8))* Simon Spotlight. (Simon Spotlight).

Chaconas, Dori. Looking for Easter. Moore, Margie, illus. 2012. (J). 34.28 *(978-1-61913-120-0(X))* Weigl Pubs., Inc.

Chernesky, Felicia Sanzari. Sun above & Blooms Below: A Springtime of Opposites. Swan, Susan, illus. 2015. (ENG.). 32p. (J). (gr. -1-3). 16.99 *(978-0-8075-3632-2(6))* Whitman, Albert & Co.

Coe, Victoria J. Fenway & Hattie. 2016. (Fenway & Hattie Ser.). (ENG.). 176p. (J). (gr. 3-7). 15.99 *(978-0-399-17274-8(2),* G.P. Putnam's Sons Books for Young Readers) Penguin Young Readers Group.

Colandro, Lucille. There Was an Old Lady Who Swallowed a Frog! Lee, Jared D., illus. (J). 2015. *(978-0-545-83213-7(6))* 2014. (ENG.). 32p. pap. 6.99 *(978-0-545-69138-3(9),* Cartwheel Bks.) Scholastic, Inc.

Curry, Don L. En Mi Patio. Brown, Erin O'Leary, illus. 2011. (Rookie Ready to Learn Español Ser.). (SPA.). 32p. (J). pap. 5.95 *(978-0-531-26784-4(9),* Children's Pr.) Scholastic Library Publishing.

—In My Backyard. O'Leary Brown, Erin, illus. 2011. (Rookie Ready to Learn — Animals Ser.). 32p. (J). (gr. -1-k). lib. bdg. 25.00 *(978-0-531-26416-4(5));* pap. 5.95 *(978-0-531-26697-7(4))* Scholastic Library Publishing. (Children's Pr.).

Curry, Don L. & O'Leary Brown, Erin. En Mi Patio. O'Leary Brown, Erin, illus. 2011. (Rookie Ready to Learn Español Ser.). (SPA., Illus.). 32p. (J). lib. bdg. 23.00 *(978-0-531-26116-3(6),* Children's Pr.) Scholastic Library Publishing.

Cyrus, Kurt. Shake a Leg, Egg! Cyrus, Kurt, illus. 2017. (ENG., Illus.). 32p. (J). (gr. -1-3). 17.99 *(978-1-4814-5848-1(5),* Beach Lane Bks.) Beach Lane Bks.

Davis, Nancy & Davis, Kathryn Lynn. Wake Up! Wake Up! Davis, Nancy & Davis, Kathryn Lynn, illus. 2011. (ENG., Illus.). 14p. (J). (gr. -1 — 1). bds. 5.99 *(978-1-4424-1217-0(8),* Little Simon) Little Simon.

dePaola, Tomie. Four Friends in Summer. dePaola, Tomie, illus. 2003. (ENG., Illus.). 32p. (J). (gr. -1-3). reprint ed. 17.99 *(978-0-689-85693-8(8),* Simon & Schuster Bks. For Young Readers) Simon & Schuster Bks. For Young Readers.

Depken, Kristen. A Royal Spring. 2016. (Disney Princess Step into Reading Ser.). lib. bdg. 14.75 *(978-0-606-38466-7(9))* Turtleback Bks.

Depken, Kristen L. A Royal Spring (Disney Princess) Laguna, Fabio & Colletti, Marco, illus. 2016. (Step into Reading Ser.). (ENG.). 24p. (J). (gr. -1-1). 4.99 *(978-0-7364-3452-2(6),* RH/Disney) Random Hse. Children's Bks.

Disney Book Group Staff. The Easter Egg Hunt. 2010. (Read-Along Storybook & CD Ser.). (ENG.). 32p. (J). (gr. -1-2). pap. 6.99 *(978-1-4231-2087-2(6))* Disney Pr.

Disney Princess, Disney & Froeb, Lori C. Ice Is Nice. 2016. (ENG.). 20p. (J). (gr. -1-1). 10.99 *(978-0-7944-3573-8(4))* Studio Fun International.

Earhart, Kristin. Roscoe & the Pony Parade. Gurney, John Steven, illus. 2008. (Little Apple Ser.). 88p. (J). *(978-0-545-08094-1(0))* Scholastic, Inc.

Ergun, Erol. The Hearer & the Seer of All. 2011. (ENG., Illus.). 160p. pap. 9.95 *(978-1-59784-257-0(5))* Tughra Bks.

Ernst, Lisa Campbell. Wake up, It's Spring! Ernst, Lisa Campbell, illus. 2004. (ENG., Illus.). 40p. (J). (gr. -1-3). 16.99 *(978-0-06-008985-6(7))* HarperCollins Pubs.

Floyd, Jamie. The Spring Flower. 2008. 17p. pap. 24.95 *(978-1-60610-810-9(7))* America Star Bks.

Fogliano, Julie. And Then It's Spring. Stead, Erin E., illus. 2012. (ENG.). 32p. (J). (gr. -1-2). 17.99 *(978-1-59643-624-4(7),* 9781596436244) Roaring Brook Pr.

—And Then It's Spring. 2013. (J). (gr. k-3). *(978-0-545-57133-3(2))* Weston Woods Studios, Inc.

Francis-Harris, Annabel. The Other Side of the Forest. 2006. pap. 19.95 *(978-1-59526-458-9(2))* Aeon Publishing Inc.

Ghigna, Charles. I See Spring, 1 vol. Jatkowska, Ag, illus. 2011. (I See Ser.). (ENG.). 24p. (gr. -1 — 1). pap. 6.10 *(978-1-4048-6849-6(6));* lib. bdg. 22.65 *(978-1-4048-6587-7(X))* Picture Window Bks. (I See).

Giles, Mike, illus. Spring Showers Bring Flowers. 2014. (Yo Gabba Gabba! Ser.). (ENG.). 12p. (J). (gr. -1-k). bds. 5.99 *(978-1-4424-9572-2(3),* Simon Spotlight) Simon Spotlight.

Grandfather Pine & His Special Place: Book One - Spring. 2013. 48p. *(978-1-4602-2520-2(1))* FriesenPress.

Hale, Rachael. Somebunny Loves You. 2009. (Paw Pals Ser.). (ENG., Illus.). 20p. (J). (gr. -1 — 1). bds. 6.99 *(978-0-316-11370-0(0))* Little, Brown Bks. for Young Readers.

Hanson, Bonnie Compton. A Stormy Spring. 2004. (Ponytail Girls Ser.). (Illus.). 192p. (J). pap. 7.99 *(978-1-58411-032-3(5),* Legacy Pr.) Rainbow Pubs. & Legacy Pr.

Hapka, Catherine, pseud & Disney Book Group Staff. Pooh's Secret Garden. Disney Storybook Art Team, illus. 2012. (ENG.). 24p. (J). (gr. -1-k). pap. 4.99 *(978-1-4231-4845-6(2))* Disney Pr.

Harrod-Eagles, Cynthia. Hello Kitty: Garden Party. Hino, Sachiho, illus. 2015. 22p. (J). ***(978-0-545-73447-9(9))*** Scholastic, Inc.

Harrod-Eagles, Cynthia. It's Spring Time! Baccala, Gladys, illus. 2013. (ENG.). 16p. (gr. -1). bds. 8.95 *(978-1-58925-639-2(5))* Tiger Tales.

Hays, Anna Jane. Spring Surprises. Wittwer, Hala Swearingen, illus. 2010. (Step into Reading Ser.). (ENG.). 24p. (J). (gr. -1-1). pap. 3.99 *(978-0-375-85840-6(7),* Random Hse. Bks. for Young Readers) Random Hse. Children's Bks.

Heckt, Jackie. It's Spring. 2016. (Four Seasons Ser.). (ENG., Illus.). 24p. (gr. 1-1). pap. 8.25 *(978-1-5081-5183-8(0),* PowerKids Pr.) Rosen Publishing Group, Inc., The.

Henkes, Kevin. When Spring Comes. Dronzek, Laura, illus. 2016. 40p. (J). (gr. -1-3). 18.89 *(978-0-06-233140-3(X),* Collins Design) HarperCollins Pubs.

Hennessy, Mary L. Spring Breezes & Sneezes. 2012. 20p. pap. 17.99 *(978-1-4772-6042-5(0))* AuthorHouse.

Hillenbrand, Will. Spring Is Here. Hillenbrand, Will, illus. 2012. (ENG., Illus.). 32p. (J). pap. 7.99 *(978-0-8234-2431-3(6))* Holiday Hse., Inc.

Hillert, Margaret. Es Primavera, Querido Dragón/It's Spring, Dear Dragon. Schimmell, David, illus. 2011. (BeginningtoRead Ser.). 32p. (J). (-2). pap. 11.94 *(978-1-60357-555-3(3))* Norwood Hse. Pr.

—Es Primavera, Querido Dragón/It's Spring, Dear Dragon. del Risco, Eida, tr. from ENG. Schimmell, David, illus. 2011. (BeginningtoRead Ser.). 32p. (J). (gr. k-2). lib. bdg. 22.60 *(978-1-59953-471-8(1))* Norwood Hse. Pr.

—It's Spring, Dear Dragon. Schimmell, David, illus. 2009. (BeginningtoRead Ser.). 32p. (J). (gr. k-2). lib. bdg. 22.60 *(978-1-59953-312-4(X))* Norwood Hse. Pr.

Hive Enterprise Staff, contrib. by. Spring Bee. 2016. (Illus.). (J). ***(978-1-4844-7010-7(9),*** Grosset & Dunlap) Penguin Publishing Group.

Holub, Joan. Groundhog Weather School. Sorra, Kristin, illus. 2009. (ENG.). 32p. (J). (gr. k-3). 16.99 *(978-0-399-24659-3(2),* G.P. Putnam's Sons Books for Young Readers) Penguin Young Readers Group.

—Groundhog Weather School: Fun Facts about Weather & Groundhogs. Sorra, Kristin, illus. 2013. (ENG.). 32p. (J). (gr. k-3). 6.99 *(978-0-14-750945-1(9),* Puffin Books) Penguin Young Readers Group.

Hopgood, Tim. Hooray for Hoppy! 2015. (ENG., Illus.). 32p. (J). (gr. -1-k). 16.99 *(978-0-374-30129-3(8),* 9780374301293, Farrar, Straus & Giroux (BYR)) Farrar, Straus & Giroux.

Hubbell, Patricia. Hurray for Spring. Morley, Taia, illus. 2005. (Picture Book Ser.). (ENG.). 32p. (J). (gr. -1-k). 15.95 *(978-1-55971-913-1(3))* Cooper Square Publishing Llc.

Iriyama, Satoshi. Happy Spring, Chirp! 2015. (Chirp the Chick Ser.). (ENG., Illus.). 32p. (J). (— 1). 8.99 *(978-0-544-36150-8(4),* HMH Books For Young Readers) Houghton Mifflin Harcourt Publishing Co.

Iwamura, Kazuo. Hooray for Spring! Iwamura, Kazuo, illus. 2009. (ENG., Illus.). 32p. (J). (gr. -1-3). 16.95 *(978-0-7358-2228-3(X))* North-South Bks., Inc.

Johnson, Amy Crane. Cinnamon & the April Shower. Mommaerts, Robb, illus. 2009. (ENG.). 32p. (J). (gr. -1-3). 16.95 *(978-1-934960-54-7(3),* Raven Tree Pr.,Csi) Continental Sales, Inc.

Johnson, Crockett. Time for Spring. Johnson, Crockett, illus. 2016. (Illus.). 40p. (J). (gr. -1-3). 14.99 *(978-0-06-243033-5(5))* HarperCollins Pubs.

—Will Spring Be Early? or Will Spring Be Late? Johnson, Crockett, illus. 2016. (Illus.). 48p. (J). (gr. -1-3). 14.99 *(978-0-06-243037-3(8))* HarperCollins Pubs.

Jordan, Apple. The Sweetest Spring. Matta, Gabriella & Legramandi, Francesco, illus. 2008. (Step into Reading Ser.). (ENG.). 32p. (J). (gr. k-3). pap. 3.99 *(978-0-375-84810-0(X),* RH/Disney) Random Hse. Children's Bks.

Kann, Victoria. Fairy House. Kann, Victoria, illus. 2013. (I Can Read Level 1 Ser.). (ENG., Illus.). 32p. (J). (gr. -1-3). 16.99 *(978-0-06-218783-3(X))* HarperCollins Pubs.

—Fairy House. 2013. (Pinkalicious I Can Read Ser.). (J). lib. bdg. 13.55 *(978-0-606-27134-9(1),* Turtleback) Turtleback Bks.

Katschke, Judy. Bring on Spring! Elsom, Clare, illus. 2015. 32p. (J). pap. *(978-0-545-82337-1(4))* Scholastic, Inc.

Katz, Karen. Baby Loves Spring! Katz, Karen, illus. 2012. (ENG., Illus.). 14p. (J). (gr. -1 — 1). bds. 6.99 *(978-1-4424-2745-7(0),* Little Simon) Little Simon.

Kelley, Marty, illus. Spring Goes Squish: A Vibrant Volume of Vociferous Vernal Verse. 2008. (J). (gr. k-2). 14.95 *(978-1-55933-315-3(4))* Zino Pr. Children's Bks.

Kimura, ken. 999 Frogs Wake Up. 2013. (ENG., Illus.). 48p. (J). (gr. -1-3). 17.95 *(978-0-7358-4108-6(X))* North-South Bks., Inc.

Kirk, Daniel. The Thing about Spring. 2015. (ENG., Illus.). 32p. (J). (gr. -1-3). 16.95 *(978-1-4197-1492-4(9),* Abrams Bks. for Young Readers) Abrams, Inc.

Koontz, Robin Michal & Elliott, Rebecca. Butterfly Spring. 2009. (Rhyme Time Readers Ser.). (Illus.). (J). *(978-0-545-08359-1(1))* Scholastic, Inc.

Lagerlöf, Selma. The Further Adventures of Nils. Howard, Velma Swanston, tr. 2003. 284p. pap. 14.95 *(978-1-59224-320-4(7));* 32.95 *(978-1-59224-541-3(2))* Wildside Pr., LLC.

Lloyd, Jennifer. Taffy Time. Lee, Jacqui, illus. 2015. (ENG.). 40p. (J). (gr. -1-3). 16.95 *(978-1-927018-62-0(5))* Simply Read Bks. CAN. Dist: Ingram Publisher Services.

Luker, Lynne M. Mr Mushroom's Busy Day: Little Forest People. 2009. 32p. pap. 21.95 *(978-1-4389-8971-6(7))* AuthorHouse.

Mackall, Dandi. The Super Gifts of Spring: Easter. 2015. (Seasons Ser.). (ENG., Illus.). 32p. (J). (gr. -1-3). 9.99 *(978-1-4336-8233-9(8),* B&H Kids) B&H Publishing Group.

Marino Walters, Jennifer. Surprising Spring. Nez, John, illus. 2016. (Seasons Ser.). (ENG.). 24p. (J). (gr. -1-1). lib. bdg. 25.32 *(978-1-63440-047-3(X))* Red Chair Pr.

Marmon, Carol. When Mommy Bird Comes to Visit. 2007. 32p. (J). pap. 8.00 *(978-0-8059-7079-1(7))* Dorrance Publishing Co., Inc.

Mazur, Kathy. It's Springtime in My Backyard. 2005. (J). bds. 16.95 *(978-0-9761076-0-6(0))* Spring Ducks Bks., LLC.

McCue, Lisa. Quiet Bunny's Many Colors. 2011. (ENG., Illus.). 32p. (J). (gr. -1-1). 14.95 *(978-1-4027-7209-2(2))* Sterling Publishing Co., Inc.

Mcintyre, Gary P. Jake Fall & Winter. 2011. 198p. pap. 24.95 *(978-1-4560-4085-7(5))* America Star Bks.

Menconi, James Pasqual. Queen Mariella & the Fable of the Peony. 2011. 24p. (gr. -1). pap. 13.50 *(978-1-4567-3934-8(4))* AuthorHouse.

Nakagawa, Masafumi. Dr. Mouse's Mission. Perry, Mia Lynn, tr. Yamawaki, Yuriko, illus. 2007. (R. I. C. Story Chest Ser.). 27p. (J). (gr. -1-1). 14.95 incl. audio compact disk *(978-1-74126-051-9(5))* R.I.C. Pubns. AUS. Dist: SCB Distributors.

Neusner, Dena Wallenstein. Colors of Spring. McKee, Darren, illus. 2003. (Barney Ser.). (ENG.). 32p. (J). pap., act. bk. ed. 3.99 *(978-1-58668-305-4(5))* Scholastic, Inc.

Nicholas, Nicki. Spring Has Sprung for Peter & Lil. 2012. 24p. pap. 15.50 *(978-1-4669-2211-2(7))* Trafford Publishing.

Nolen, Jerdine. Bradford Street Buddies: Springtime Blossoms. Henninger, Michelle, illus. 2017. (Green Light Readers Level 3 Ser.). (ENG.). 48p. (J). (gr. 1-4). pap. 3.99 *(978-0-544-87390-2(4),* HMH Books For Young Readers) Houghton Mifflin Harcourt Publishing Co.

O'Brien, Anne Sibley. Abracadabra, It's Spring! Gal, Susan, illus. 2016. (Seasonal Magic Ser.). (ENG.). 24p. (J). (gr. -1-k). 14.95 *(978-1-4197-1891-5(6),* Abrams Appleseed) Abrams, Inc.

O'Connor, Jane. Spring Fashion Fling. Glasser, Robin Preiss, illus. 2015. (Fancy Nancy Ser.). (ENG.). 24p. (J). (gr. -1-3). pap. 4.99 *(978-0-06-226956-0(9),* HarperFestival) HarperCollins Pubs.

—Spring Fashion Fling. 2015. (Fancy Nancy Picture Bks.). (J). lib. bdg. 14.75 *(978-0-606-36476-8(5))* Turtleback Bks.

Page, Nick & Page, Claire. The King of Spring. Robert, Yannick, illus. 2006. (Read with Me (Make Believe Ideas) Ser.). 31p. (J). (gr. k-2). *(978-1-84610-169-4(7))* Make Believe Ideas.

Passchier, Anne, illus. Springtime Splash! 2017. (See-Through Stories Ser.). (ENG.). 10p. (J). (gr. -1-2). bds. 8.95 ***(978-1-4549-2500-2(0))*** Sterling Publishing Co., Inc.

Pickering, Jimmy. It's Spring. 2003. (Illus.). 32p. (J). 16.95 *(978-1-931290-22-7(9))* Tallfellow Pr.

Pugliano-Martin, Carol. See You in Spring! 2006. (Early Explorers Ser.). (J). pap. *(978-1-4108-6105-4(8))* Benchmark Education Co.

Rabbit's Spring Adventure. 2012. (Illus.). (J). *(978-1-4351-4584-9(4))* Barnes & Noble, Inc.

Random House Disney Staff. Welcome, Spring! (Disney Frozen) Random House Disney Staff, illus. 2016. (Pictureback(R) Ser.). (ENG., Illus.). 16p. (J). (gr. -1-2). 4.99 *(978-0-7364-3385-3(6),* RH/Disney) Random Hse. Children's Bks.

Random House Staff. The Spring Chicken! (Bubble Guppies) Random House Staff & Trover, Zachary, illus. 2013. (Step into Reading Ser.). (ENG.). 24p. (J). (gr. -1-1). pap. 3.99 *(978-0-449-81440-6(8),* Random Hse. Bks. for Young Readers) Random Hse. Children's Bks.

Rawlinson, Julia. Fletcher & the Springtime Blossoms. Beeke, Tiphanie, illus. 2009. (ENG.). 32p. (J). (gr. -1-2). 17.99 *(978-0-06-168855-3(X),* Greenwillow Bks.) HarperCollins Pubs.

—Fletcher & the Springtime Blossoms. 2011. (J). (gr. -1-2). 29.95 *(978-0-545-32738-1(5))* Weston Woods Studios, Inc.

Reinlein, Ann. The Adventures of Mister Squirrel Acorn. 2008. 32p. pap. 15.00 *(978-1-4389-1879-2(8))* AuthorHouse.

Remenar, Kristen. Groundhog's Dilemma. Faulkner, Matt, illus. 2015. (ENG.). 32p. (J). (gr. -1-2). lib. bdg. 16.95 *(978-1-58089-600-9(6))* Charlesbridge Publishing, Inc.

Rockwell, Anne. My Spring Robin. Rockwell, Harlow, illus. 2015. (ENG.). 24p. (J). (gr. -1-3). 16.99 *(978-1-4814-1137-0(3),* Aladdin) Simon & Schuster Children's Publishing.

Russell, Rachel Renée. Tales from a Not-So-Dorky Drama Queen, 3 vols. unabr. ed. 2015. (Dork Diaries: 8). (ENG.). 320p. (gr. 4-8). audio compact disk 14.99 *(978-1-4423-7023-4(8))* Simon & Schuster Audio.

—Tales from a Not-So-Dorky Drama Queen. Russell, Rachel Renée, illus. 2015. (Dork Diaries: Bk. 9). (ENG., Illus.). 352p. (J). (gr. 4-8). 13.99 *(978-1-4424-8769-7(0),* Aladdin Paperbacks) Simon & Schuster Children's Publishing.

Sanrio Company, Ltd. Staff. Hello Kitty, Hello Spring! Hirashima, Jean, illus. 2013. (ENG.). 14p. (J). (gr. -1 — 1). bds. 7.95 *(978-1-4197-0688-2(8),* Abrams Appleseed) Abrams, Inc.

Senior, Patricia. Pip & the Magic Flute. 2008. (Illus.). 40p. pap. 18.49 (978-1-4389-0023-0(6)) AuthorHouse.

Smith, Rosemary. Lizard Tales: Lizzie Walks on the Wild Side. 2010. 28p. pap. 12.50 (978-1-60911-082-6(X), Strategic Bk. Publishing) Strategic Book Publishing & Rights Agency (SBPRA).

Thompson, Lauren. Mouse's First Spring. Erdogan, Buket, illus. 2012. (Classic Board Bks.). (ENG.). 34p. (J). (gr. -1-3). bds. 7.99 (978-1-4424-3431-8(7), Little Simon) Little Simon.

—Mouse's First Spring. Erdogan, Buket, illus. 2005. (ENG.). 32p. (J). (gr. -1-3). 17.99 (978-0-689-85838-3(8), Simon & Schuster Bks. For Young Readers) Simon & Schuster Bks. For Young Readers.

Trover, Zachary. The Spring Chicken! 2013. (Step into Reading Level 2 Ser.). lib. bdg. 13.55 (978-0-606-26979-7(7), Turtleback) Turtleback Bks.

Urbanovic, Jackie. Happy Go Ducky. Urbanovic, Jackie & Mathieu, Joe, illus. 2012. (I Can Read Level 1 Ser.). (ENG.). 32p. (J). (gr. k-3). 16.99 (978-0-06-186440-7(4)); pap. 3.99 (978-0-06-186439-1(0)) HarperCollins Pubs.

von Olfers, Sibylle. Mother Earth & Her Children: A Quilted Fairy Tale. Zipes, Jack, tr. from GER. Schoen-Smith, Sieglinde, illus. 2015. (ENG.). 32p. (J). (— 1). 12.95 (978-1-933308-50-0(8)) Breckling Pr.

—Mother Earth & Her Children Coloring Book: Color the Wonderful World of Nature As You See It! 24 Magical, Mythical Coloring Scenes. Zipes, Jack, tr. Schoen-Smith, Sieglinde, illus. 2015. (ENG.). 24p. (J). (gr. 2-4). pap. 6.95 (978-1-933308-54-8(0)) Breckling Pr.

Voorheis, Tracy. Nibbles... a strawberry Tale. Voorheis, Tracy, illus. 2007. (Illus.). 60p. (J). per. 19.00 (978-0-9787113-0-6(0), Ithaca Pr.) Authors & Artists Publishers of New York, Inc.

Walton, Mildred D. Spring Reborn. 2012. 28p. pap. 21.99 (978-1-4691-2556-5(0)) Xlibris Corp.

Warfield, Laura Castillo. Daisy's Faith. 2011. 24p. pap. 15.99 (978-1-4568-8348-5(8)) Xlibris Corp.

Werber, Yael. Spring for Sophie. Hill, Jen, illus. 2017. (ENG.). 32p. (J). (gr. -1-3). 17.99 (978-1-4814-5134-5(0), Simon & Schuster Bks. For Young Readers) Simon & Schuster Bks. For Young Readers.

Williams, Nate & Snow, Virginia Brimhall. Spring Walk, 1 vol. 2015. (ENG., Illus.). 32p. (J). (gr. 2-3). 16.99 (978-1-4236-3879-7(4)) Gibbs Smith, Publisher.

Wilson, Karma. Dormouse Dreams. Liwska, Renata, illus. 2017. (ENG.). 40p. (J). (gr. -1-k). 16.99 (978-1-4231-7874-3(2)) Disney Pr.

Winnie the Pooh. Spring Cleaning. 2010. 32p. pap. 4.99 (978-1-4231-3072-7(3)) Disney Pr.

Yang, Belle. A Nest in Springtime: A Bilingual Book of Numbers. Yang, Belle, illus. 2012. (CHI & ENG., Illus.). 24p. (J). (gr. k — 1). bds. 6.99 (978-0-7636-5279-1(2)) Candlewick Pr.

Yee, Wong Herbert. Fine Feathered Friends. Yee, Wong Herbert, illus. 2011. (Mouse & Mole Story Ser.). (ENG., Illus.). 48p. (J). (gr. 1-4). pap. 3.99 (978-0-547-51977-7(X)) Houghton Mifflin Harcourt Publishing Co.

—Mouse & Mole, Fine Feathered Friends. Yee, Wong Herbert, illus. 2009. (Mouse & Mole Story Ser.). (ENG., Illus.). 48p. (J). (gr. 1-4). 15.00 (978-0-547-15222-6(1)) Houghton Mifflin Harcourt Publishing Co.

Young, Rebecca & Accord Publishing Staff. Hop, Pop, & Play: A Mini Animotion Book. 2011. (ENG.). 12p. (J). 9.99 (978-1-4494-0177-1(5)) Andrews McMeel Publishing.

Zimmerman, Amanda. The Spring Snowman. 2011. 48p. pap. 9.95 (978-1-4502-9816-2(8)) iUniverse, Inc.

Zipf, Sean. What Color Is Spring? Antkowski, Marygrace, illus. 2008. 36p. pap. 24.95 (978-1-60703-005-8(5)) America Star Bks.

SPRING—POETRY

Carr, Jan. Splish, Splash, Spring. Donohue, Dorothy, illus. 2005. (ENG.). 32p. (J). (gr. k-3). 6.95 (978-0-8234-1754-4(9)) Holiday Hse., Inc.

SPY FOX (FICTITIOUS CHARACTER)—FICTION

Kull, Cyndi. I Spy. 2011. 16p. pap. 8.50 (978-1-4634-2279-0(2)) AuthorHouse.

SQUANTO

Ghiglieri, Carol. Easy Reader Biographies: Squanto: A Friend to the Pilgrims. 2007. (ENG.). 16p. pap. 2.99 (978-0-439-77422-2(5), Teaching Resources) Scholastic, Inc.

Isbell, Hannah. Squanto. 2017. (J). pap. (978-0-7660-9065-1(5)) Enslow Pubs., Inc.

Kessel, Joyce K. Squanto & the First Thanksgiving. Donze, Lisa, illus. rev. ed. 2003. (On My Own Holidays Ser.). (ENG.). 48p. (gr. 2-4). pap. 6.95 (978-1-57505-585-5(6)); lib. bdg. 25.26 (978-0-87614-941-6(7)) Lerner Publishing Group.

—Squanto y el Primer Dia de Accion de Gracias. Donze, Lisa, illus. 2007. (Yo Solo - Festividades (on My Own - Holidays) Ser.). 48p. (J). (gr. 4-7). per. 6.95 (978-0-8225-7795-9(X)) Lerner Publishing Group.

—Squanto y el Primer Día de Acción de Gracias. Translations.com Staff, tr. from ENG. Donze, Lisa, illus. 2007. (Yo Solo - Festividades (on My Own - Holidays) Ser.). (SPA.). 48p. (gr. 2-4). lib. bdg. 25.26 (978-0-8225-7792-8(5)) Lerner Publishing Group.

—Squanto Y el Primer Dia de Accion de Gracias; Squanto & the First Thanksgiving. 2008. pap. 40.95 (978-0-8225-9678-3(4)) Lerner Publishing Group.

Metaxas, Eric. Squanto & the First Thanksgiving: The Legendary American Tale. Donato, Michael A., illus. 2004. 36p. (J). (gr. 3-8). reprint ed. 19.00 (978-0-7567-7123-2(4)) DIANE Publishing Co.

SQUANTO—FICTION

Bruchac, Joseph. Squanto's Journey: The Story of the First Thanksgiving. 2014. 17.00 (978-1-63419-743-4(7)) Perfection Learning Corp.

SQUIDS

Andover, Max. Octopuses & Squid. 2011. (Illus.). 16p. (J). pap. (978-0-545-24792-4(6)) Scholastic, Inc.

Coldiron, Deborah. Squid, 1 vol. 2007. (Underwater World Ser.). (ENG., Illus.). 32p. (J). (gr. 3-7). 27.07 (978-1-59928-816-1(8), Buddy Bks.) ABDO Publishing Co.

Dussling, Jennifer. Giant Squid: Mystery of the Deep. Johnson, Pamela, illus. 2004. (American Museum of Natural History Ser.). 48p. (gr. 1-3). 14.00 (978-0-7569-1981-8(9)) Perfection Learning Corp.

Fleming, Candace. Giant Squid. Rohmann, Eric, illus. 2016. (ENG.). 40p. (J). (gr. 1-5). 18.99 (978-1-59643-599-5(2), 9781596435995) Roaring Brook Pr.

Lunis, Natalie. Squirting Squids. 2007. (No Backbone! Ser.). (Illus.). 24p. (J). (gr. k-3). lib. bdg. 21.28 (978-1-59716-513-6(1)) Bearport Publishing Co., Inc.

Lunis, Natalie & Murphy, Bill. Squirting Squids. 2016. (No Backbone! Marine Invertebrates Ser.). (ENG.). 24p. (J). (gr. k-3). pap. 7.95 (978-1-944998-79-0(9)) Bearport Publishing Co., Inc.

Matsen, Bradford. The Incredible Hunt for the Giant Squid. 2003. (Incredible Deep-Sea Adventures Ser.). (Illus.). 48p. (J). lib. bdg. 25.27 (978-0-7660-2192-1(0)) Enslow Pubs., Inc.

Miller, Tori. Octopuses & Squid. 2009. (Freaky Fish Ser.). 24p. (ENG., Illus.). (J). (gr. 2-5). pap. 8.25 (978-1-4358-3174-2(8), PowerKids Pr.); (gr. 2-3). 42.50 (978-1-61512-640-8(6), PowerKids Pr.); (J). (gr. 1-4). lib. bdg. 22.60 (978-1-4358-2757-8(0)) Rosen Publishing Group, Inc., The.

Nyikos, Stacy Ann. Squirt. Sisneros, Shawn, illus. l.t. ed. 2005. 32p. (J). lib. bdg. 15.95 (978-0-9764199-0-7(4)) Stonehorse Publishing, LLC.

Owen, Ruth. Giant Squid & Octopuses, 1 vol., 1. 2014. (Real Life Sea Monsters Ser.). (ENG.). 32p. (J). (gr. k-5). 26.25 (978-1-4777-6261-5(2), PowerKids Pr.) Rosen Publishing Group, Inc., The.

Redmond, Shirley Raye. Tentacles! Tales of the Giant Squid. Barnard, Bryn, illus. 2005. (Step into Reading Ser.). (gr. k-2). 14.00 (978-0-7569-5576-2(9)) Perfection Learning Corp.

Schuh, Mari. Squids. 2015. (Illus.). 24p. (J). lib. bdg. (978-1-62031-193-6(3), Bullfrog Bks.) Jump! Inc.

Sexton, Colleen. Squids. 2008. (Oceans Alive Ser.). (ENG., Illus.). 24p. (J). (gr. k-3). lib. bdg. 25.95 (978-1-60014-175-1(7)) Bellwether Media.

Weber, Valerie J. Octopuses & Squids. 2008. (Animals That Live in the Ocean Ser.). (Illus.). 24p. (J). (gr. -1-3). lib. bdg. 22.60 (978-0-8368-9242-0(9), Weekly Reader Leveled Readers) Stevens, Gareth Publishing LLLP.

—Octopuses & Squids/Pulpos y Calamares. 2008. (Animals That Live in the Ocean/Animales Que Viven en el Oceano Ser.). (SPA & ENG.). 24p. (gr. -1-3). (J). lib. bdg. 22.60 (978-0-8368-9248-2(8)); pap. 8.15 (978-0-8368-9347-2(6)) Stevens, Gareth Publishing LLLP. (Weekly Reader Leveled Readers).

—Squids. 2005. (Weird Wonders of the Deep Ser.). (Illus.). 24p. (gr. 1-4). lib. bdg. 23.00 (978-0-8368-4564-8(1), Gareth Stevens Learning Library) Stevens, Gareth Publishing LLLP.

SQUIRRELS

Booth, Anita K. Squirrels!!! An Informative & Entertaining Book about Our Favorite Mountain Mammal. Booth, Anita K., illus. 2nd ed. 2004. (Illus.). 76p. 12.95 (978-0-9748702-1-2(8)) AKB Design.

Borgert-Spaniol, Megan. Baby Squirrels. 2015. (Super Cute! Ser.). (ENG., Illus.). 24p. (J). (gr. k-3). lib. bdg. 25.95 (978-1-62617-220-3(X), Blastoff! Readers) Bellwether Media.

Bowman, Chris. Red Squirrels. 2016. (North American Animals Ser.). (ENG., Illus.). 24p. (J). (gr. k-3). lib. bdg. 25.95 (978-1-62617-336-1(2), Blastoff! Readers) Bellwether Media.

Bradley, James V. The Squirrel. 2006. (Nature Walk Ser.). (Illus.). 64p. (gr. 4-6). lib. bdg. 28.00 (978-0-7910-9116-6(3), Chelsea Hse.) Facts On File, Inc.

Ciovacco, Justine. Squirrels. 2009. (Amazing Animals Ser.). 48p. (gr. 2-6). pap. 10.50 (978-1-4339-2029-5(8), Gareth Stevens Learning Library); (YA). (gr. 3-6). lib. bdg. 28.00 (978-0-8368-9112-6(0)) Stevens, Gareth Publishing LLLP.

—Squirrels. 2007. (J). (978-1-59939-133-5(3), Reader's Digest Young Families, Inc.) Studio Fun International.

Clark Sawyer, J. Las Ardillas de Tierra de Trece Franjas. 2014. (¿a dónde Van en Invierno? Ser.). (SPA.). 24p. (J). (gr. -1-3). lib. bdg. 23.93 (978-1-62724-459-6(X)) Bearport Publishing Co., Inc.

—Thirteen-Lined Ground Squirrels. 2015. (Illus.). 24p. (J). lib. bdg. (978-1-62724-317-9(8)) Bearport Publishing Co., Inc.

Dettman, Eileen. Determo: The true story of a very clever North Carolina red Squirrel. 2010. (J). 9.95 (978-0-615-38527-3(3)) Dettman Design Services.

Dieker, Wendy Strobel. La Ardilla. 2017. (Spot Backyard Animals Ser.). (SPA & ENG.). 16p. (gr. k-3). 17.95 (978-1-68151-277-8(7)) Amicus Publishing.

—Squirrels. 2017. (Spot Backyard Animals Ser.). (ENG.). 16p. (J). (gr. k-3). 17.95 (978-1-68151-097-2(9)) Amicus Publishing.

Diemer, Lauren. Squirrels. 2007. (Backyard Animals Ser.). (Illus.). 24p. (J). (gr. 2-4). lib. bdg. 24.45 (978-1-59036-671-4(9)) Weigl Pubs., Inc.

—Squirrels. Hudak, Heather C., ed. 2007. (Backyard Animals Ser.). (Illus.). 24p. (J). (gr. -1-3). pap. 8.95 (978-1-59036-672-1(7)) Weigl Pubs., Inc.

Gagne, Tammy. Backyard Jungle Safari Gray Squirrels: Grey Squirrels. 2015. (ENG., Illus.). 32p. (J). 26.50 (978-1-62469-104-1(8)) Purple Toad Publishing, Inc.

Gilkerson, Patricia. My Adventure with Squirrels. 2009. (ENG.). 44p. (J). 8.99 (978-1-59092-470-9(3)) Blue Forge Pr.

Glaser, Linda. Hello, Squirrels! Scampering Through the Seasons. Holland, Gay W., illus. 2006. (Linda Glaser's Classic Creatures Ser.). (ENG.). 32p. (gr. k-3). 22.60 (978-0-7613-2887-2(4), Millbrook Pr.) Lerner Publishing Group.

Hawksworth, Lorraine & Guzy, Adam. Fables from the Largetooth Animal Refuge. 2009. 52p. pap. 20.49 (978-1-4389-6508-6(7)) AuthorHouse.

Jackson, Tom. Squirrels. 2008. (Nature's Children Ser.). (Illus.). 52p. (J). (978-0-7172-6245-8(6)) Grolier, Ltd.

Jango-Cohen, Judith. Flying Squirrels. 2004. (Pull Ahead Books-Animals Ser.). (ENG., Illus.). 32p. (J). (gr. k-3). pap. 7.95 (978-0-8225-9886-2(8)) Lerner Publishing Group.

Lake, G. G. Gray Squirrels. 2016. (Woodland Wildlife Ser.). (ENG., Illus.). 24p. (gr. k-1). lib. bdg. 26.65 (978-1-5157-0818-6(7), Pebble Plus) Capstone Press of Coughlan Cos.

Leaf, Christina. Gray Squirrels. 2015. (North American Animals Ser.). (ENG., Illus.). 24p. (J). (gr. k-3). lib. bdg. 25.95 (978-1-62617-187-9(4), Blastoff! Readers) Bellwether Media.

Lundgren, Julie K. Squirrels. 2010. (ENG., Illus.). 24p. (gr. 1-4). pap. 8.95 (978-1-61590-549-2(9)) Rourke Educational Media.

McGill, Jordan. Ardillas. 2012. (SPA.). (J). (978-1-61913-197-2(8)) Weigl Pubs., Inc.

—Squirrels. 2011. (J). (978-1-61690-577-4(8)); (978-1-61690-931-4(5)) Weigl Pubs., Inc.

Nagelhout, Ryan. I See a Squirrel. 2013. (In My Backyard Ser.). (Illus.). 24p. (J). (gr. k-2). lib. bdg. 22.60 (978-1-4339-8559-1(4)) Stevens, Gareth Publishing LLLP.

Nagelhout, Ryan & Appleby, Alex. I See a Squirrel. 2013. (In My Backyard Ser.). (Illus.). 24p. (J). (gr. k-2). pap. 8.15 (978-1-4339-8560-7(8)) Stevens, Gareth Publishing LLLP.

—I See a Squirrel: Puedo Ver una Ardilla. 2013. (In My Backyard / en Mi Jardín Ser.). (SPA & ENG., Illus.). 24p. (J). (gr. k-2). lib. bdg. 22.60 (978-1-4339-8800-4(3)) Stevens, Gareth Publishing LLLP.

O'Brien, Lindsy. Squirrels. 2016. (Illus.). 24p. (J). (978-1-60818-702-7(0), Creative Education) Creative Co., The.

O'Brien, Lindsy J. Squirrels. 2017. (In My Backyard Ser.). (ENG., Illus.). 24p. (J). (gr. 1-3). pap. 8.99 (978-1-62832-298-9(5), Creative Paperbacks) Creative Co., The.

Otfinoski, Steven. Squirrels. 2010. (Animals Animals 11 Ser.). 48p. (gr. 3). 23.95 (978-0-7614-4843-3(8)) Marshall Cavendish Corp.

Owen, Ruth. Squirrel Kits. 2011. (Wild Baby Animals Ser.). 24p. (J). (gr. k-3). lib. bdg. 19.96 (978-1-61772-160-1(3)); lib. bdg., E-Book 39.93 (978-1-61772-244-8(8)) Bearport Publishing Co., Inc.

Petrie, Kristin. Squirrels, 1 vol. 2014. (Backyard Animals Ser.). (ENG.). 32p. (gr. 3-6). 27.07 (978-1-62403-663-7(5)) ABDO Publishing Co.

Roza, Greg. Your Neighbor the Squirrel. 2011. (City Critters Ser.). (ENG., Illus.). 24p. (J). (gr. k-5). pap. 8.25 (978-1-4488-5123-2(8)); lib. bdg. 22.60 (978-1-61533-383-7(5)) Windmill Bks.

Sayre, April Pulley. Squirrels Leap, Squirrels Sleep. Jenkins, Steve, illus. 2016. (ENG.). 40p. (J). 17.99 (978-0-8050-9251-6(X), 9780805092516, Holt, Henry & Co. Bks. For Young Readers) Holt, Henry & Co.

Schuh, Mari C. Squirrels. 2015. (Backyard Animals Ser.). (ENG.). 24p. (gr. k-1). lib. bdg. 26.65 (978-1-4914-2088-1(X), Pebble Plus) Capstone Press of Coughlan Cos.

Somervill, Barbara. Gray Squirrel. 2008. (21st Century Skills Library: Animal Invaders Ser.). (ENG.). 32p. (gr. 4-8). lib. bdg. 28.50 (978-1-60279-116-9(3), 200100) Cherry Lake Publishing.

Sundance/Newbridge LLC Staff. Squirrels All Year Long. 2007. (Early Science Ser.). (gr. k-3). 18.95 (978-1-4007-6404-4(1)); pap. 6.10 (978-1-4007-6400-6(9)) Sundance/Newbridge Educational Publishing.

Thomas, Isabel. Squirrel: City Safari, 1 vol. 2014. (City Safari Ser.). (ENG., Illus.). 24p. (gr. 1-1). lib. bdg. 23.32 (978-1-4329-8809-8(3), Heinemann Read & Learn) Heinemann-Raintree.

Trueit, Trudi Strain. Squirrels. 2011. (Backyard Safari Ser.). 32p. (gr. 3). 28.50 (978-1-60870-248-0(0)) Marshall Cavendish Corp.

Watanabe, Lynne M. Squirrels. 2016. (Illus.). 32p. (J). (978-0-87659-709-5(6)) Gryphon Hse., Inc.

Zappa, Marcia. Flying Squirrels, 1 vol. 2016. (ENG., Illus.). 32p. (J). (978-1-62403-775-7(5)) ABDO Publishing Co.

Zobel, Derek. Squirrels. 2010. (Backyard Wildlife Ser.). (ENG., Illus.). 24p. (J). (gr. k-3). lib. bdg. 25.95 (978-1-60014-447-9(0), Blastoff! Readers) Bellwether Media.

SQUIRRELS—FICTION

Abbott, Jacob. Rollo at Play. 2008. 124p. (gr. 3-7). 23.95 (978-1-60664-760-8(1)); pap. 10.95 (978-1-60664-132-3(8)) Aegypan.

—Rollo at Play. 2009. 148p. pap. 8.95 (978-1-59915-343-8(2)) Yesterday's Classics.

Alaniz, Joshua. The Unfortunate yet Fortunate Squirrel. 2013. 20p. pap. 24.95 (978-1-63004-271-4(4)) America Star Bks.

Alexander, Ron. And God Created Squirrels. 2007. 28p. per. 19.95 (978-1-4327-1512-0(7)) Outskirts Pr., Inc.

Allard, Toni. Anything but Nuts. 2007. 20p. per. 24.95 (978-1-4241-8796-6(6)) America Star Bks.

Allred, Sylvester. Rascal, the Tassel-Eared Squirrel. Iverson, Diane, illus. 2007. (ENG.). 64p. 16.95 (978-0-938216-88-9(0)) Grand Canyon Assn.

Allred, Sylvester & Iverson, Diane. Rascal, the Tassel-Eared Squirrel. 2007. (ENG., Illus.). 64p. pap. 9.95 (978-0-938216-44-5(9)) Grand Canyon Assn.

Anderson, Steven. Leap & Twirl. DeAnguelo Hout, Sarah, illus. 2012. 34p. (J). pap. 10.99 (978-0-692-01667-1(8)) BalletMet Dance Centre.

Ardagh, Philip. High in the Clouds. Dunbar, Geoff, illus. 2007. 93p. (J). 20.00 (978-1-4223-6720-9(7)) DIANE Publishing Co.

Aryal, Aimee. Hello Buzz! Moore, Danny, illus. 2004. 24p. (J). 19.95 (978-1-932888-27-0(6)) Mascot Bks., Inc.

Aschermann, Kurt. Bj & the Amazing Doctor Directions. 2008. 172p. pap. 11.99 (978-1-4343-7708-1(3)) AuthorHouse.

Atchison, David C. The Adventures of Black Bart: Dry Bones. 2008. 84p. pap. 7.94 (978-0-615-20238-9(1)) Black Bart Bks.

Avi. The Mayor of Central Park. Floca, Brian, illus. (ENG.). 208p. (J). (gr. 3-6). 2003. 15.99 (978-0-06-000682-2(X)) 2005. reprint ed. pap. 6.99 (978-0-06-051557-7(0)) HarperCollins Pubs.

—The Mayor of Central Park. Floca, Brian, illus. 2005. 193p. (J). (gr. 3-7). 13.65 (978-0-7569-5125-2(9)) Perfection Learning Corp.

Axe-Bronk, Susan. The Vanishing Gourds: A Sukkot Mystery. Monelli, Marta, illus. 2012. (Sukkot & Simchat Torah Ser.). (ENG.). 24p. (J). (gr. -1-3). 7.95 (978-0-7613-7504-3(X)); lib. bdg. 17.95 (978-0-7613-7503-6(1)) Lerner Publishing Group. (Kar-Ben Publishing).

AZ Books Staff. Squirrel Searches for a Home. 2012. (Plush Baby Ser.). (ENG., Illus.). 10p. (J). (gr. -1 — 1). bds. 11.95 (978-1-61889-220-1(7)) AZ Bks. LLC.

Bailey, Dawn Wentz. Joey & the Mighty Oak. 2008. 20p. pap. 24.95 (978-1-60813-377-2(X)) PublishAmerica, Inc.

Barba, Theresa. How Talia Met Tanner. 2012. 40p. pap. 20.99 (978-1-4772-1617-0(0)) AuthorHouse.

Barnard, Bobbie. The Fairies of the Big Forest. 2013. 16p. pap. 24.95 (978-1-63004-359-9(1)) America Star Bks.

Barnard, Lucy, illus. Squirrel's Busy Day. 2014. 24p. (J). (978-1-4351-5602-9(1)) Barnes & Noble, Inc.

Barone, Barbara. Leafy Trees & Bumbly Bees. 2012. 28p. pap. 16.09 (978-1-4669-6267-5(4)) Trafford Publishing.

Bauman, Jill, illus. The Tale of Squirrel Nutkin. 2006. (J). 6.99 (978-1-59939-017-8(5)) Cornerstone Pr.

Bellew, Steve C. The Great Walnut War. 2012. 24p. pap. 24.95 (978-1-4626-7623-1(5)) America Star Bks.

Beranek, Malinda. Rocky, the Country Squirrel. 2008. 12p. pap. 24.95 (978-1-60563-018-2(7)) America Star Bks.

Berglund, Andrea Lloyd. A Good Little Horse: Thunder's Morning Stroll. 2009. 36p. (J). pap. 19.95 (978-1-4327-3822-8(4)) Outskirts Pr., Inc.

Biederman, Judy. Bushy Tail Squirrel's First Day Out. 2004. (J). lib. bdg. (978-0-9725485-2-6(1)) Waterfall Ridge.

Billows, Denis. Down in Bluebell Wood. 2010. 164p. pap. 11.99 (978-1-4490-8822-4(8)) AuthorHouse.

Blevins-Counts, Charlotte. Squirrel, Where Are You? 2009. 24p. pap. 12.95 (978-1-59858-963-4(6)) Dog Ear Publishing, LLC.

Bonnell, Kris. A House for Squirrel. 2007. (J). pap. 5.95 (978-1-933727-46-2(2)) Reading Reading Bks., LLC.

Bowers, Tim. A New Home. 2003. (Green Light Readers Level 1 Ser.). (ENG., Illus.). 24p. (J). (gr. -1-3). pap. 3.95 (978-0-15-204848-8(0)) Houghton Mifflin Harcourt Publishing Co.

Bowlin, Serina. Wandering Sam. Thrasher, Brian, illus. 2011. 20p. pap. 9.97 (978-1-61204-280-0(5), Eloquent Bks.) Strategic Book Publishing & Rights Agency (SBPRA).

Bowman, Rachael Ann. Sammy the Karate Squirrel. 2013. 28p. pap. 13.95 (978-1-4624-0800-9(1), Inspiring Voices) Author Solutions, Inc.

Brown, Daniel. Chipper Learns a Lesson. 2013. 28p. pap. 5.99 (978-0-9897549-4-1(4)) Story and Logic Media Group.

Bruchac, Joseph. How Chipmunk Got His Stripes. 2003. (gr. k-3). lib. bdg. 17.20 (978-0-613-61631-7(6), Turtleback) Turtleback Bks.

Bryant, Phoebe. What Is That in the Air? A play date with Sayde. 2009. (Illus.). 28p. pap. 12.99 (978-1-4490-2209-9(X)) AuthorHouse.

Buckley, Michael. M Is for Mama's Boy, Bk. 2. 2011. (Nerds Ser.). (ENG., Illus.). 304p. (J). (gr. 3-7). pap. 7.95 (978-1-4197-0023-1(5), Amulet Bks.) Abrams, Inc.

—NERDS 2: M für Muttersöhnchen. 2011. (SPA.). 260p. (J). (gr. 6-8). pap. 10.99 (978-987-612-335-8(1)) V&R Editoras.

Buice, J. W. Silly Squirrel. 2011. 28p. pap. 15.99 (978-1-4568-3384-8(7)) Xlibris Corp.

Bunting, Sarah Clare. Why Are You So Lazy Owl? 2012. 16p. pap. 12.50 (978-1-4709-4837-5(0)) Lulu Pr., Inc.

Burch, Minnie Kirby. The Adventures of Squir Squirrel: A Story of Love & Trust. 2012. 64p. pap. 31.99 (978-1-4771-2043-9(2)) Xlibris Corp.

Burgess, Thornton W. The Adventures of Chatterer the Red Squirrel. (J). 18.95 (978-0-8488-0376-6(0)) Amereon Ltd.

—The Adventures of Chatterer the Red Squirrel. 2006. pap. 10.95 (978-1-59605-783-8(1), Cosimo Classics) Cosimo, Inc.

—The Adventures of Happy Jack. 2004. (Dover Children's Thrift Classics Ser.). (ENG., Illus.). 128p. (J). (gr. 3-8). pap. 4.00 (978-0-486-43321-9(8)) Dover Pubns., Inc.

—Happy Jack. 2011. 140p. 25.95 (978-1-4638-9558-7(5)) Rodgers, Alan Bks.

Burks, James. Bird & Squirrel on Fire. 2017. (Bird & Squirrel Ser.). (ENG.). 192p. (J). (gr. 2-5). 18.99 (978-0-545-80429-5(9), Graphix) Scholastic, Inc.

—Bird & Squirrel on Ice. 2014. (Bird & Squirrel Ser.). (ENG.). 128p. (J). (gr. 2-5). pap. 8.99 (978-0-545-56318-5(6), Graphix) Scholastic, Inc.

—Bird & Squirrel on the Edge! 2015. (Bird & Squirrel Ser.). (ENG., Illus.). 144p. (J). (gr. 2-5). 18.99 (978-0-545-80425-7(6), Graphix) Scholastic, Inc.

—Bird & Squirrel on the Run! 2012. (Bird & Squirrel Ser.). (ENG., Illus.). 128p. (J). (gr. 2-5). pap. 8.99 (978-0-545-31283-7(3), Graphix) Scholastic, Inc.

—Bird & Squirrel on the Run! 2012. (Bird Squirrel Ser.). (Illus.). 125p. (J). lib. bdg. 19.65 (978-0-606-26211-8(3), Turtleback) Turtleback Bks.

Byers, James. One Nutty Family. Collier, Kevin, illus. 2012. 16p. pap. 9.95 (978-1-61633-200-6(X)) Guardian Angel Publishing, Inc.

Cain, Karen L. Squirrel's Curl. 2011. 24p. 13.00 (978-1-4567-1466-6(X)) AuthorHouse.

Calvani, Mayra. Humberto, the Bookworm Hamster. Grady, Kit, illus. 2009. 20p. pap. 10.95 (978-1-935137-92-4(1)) Guardian Angel Publishing, Inc.

Carman, Patrick. The Walnut Cup. James, Steve, illus. 2009. (Elliot's Park Ser.: Bk. 3). 80p. (J). (gr. 1-5). 8.99 (978-0-545-01932-3(X), Orchard Bks.) Scholastic, Inc.

Case, Maggie. A Squirrel's Tale. 2011. 24p. (gr. -1). pap. 11.32 (978-1-4567-5118-0(2)) AuthorHouse.

Cavagnaro, Teresa Dunham. Sweet Sallie's Squirrel Scarf Factory. Cavagnaro, Larry, illus. 2012. 36p. 24.95 (978-1-4626-6126-8(2)) America Star Bks.

Chamberlain, Lyn. Quonby & the Tree Den. Weltner, Dave, illus. l.t. ed. 2004. 12p. (J). 7.95 (978-0-9706654-8-5(2)) Sprite Pr.

Chichester Clark, Emma, tr. & illus. Will & Squill. Chichester Clark, Emma, illus. 2006. 32p. (J). (gr. -1-k). 15.95 (978-1-57505-936-5(3), Carolrhoda Bks.) Lerner Publishing Group.

Chinnery, Karen. Secret Agent Squirrel. 2006. (ENG.). 48p. per. 16.95 (978-1-4241-5459-3(6)) America Star Bks.

Chuang, Emily. Francis' Tail. 2010. 32p. pap. 23.95 (978-0-557-73632-4(3)) Lulu Pr., Inc.

Clayton, Emily. If my Parents Only Knew... 2011. (Illus.). 28p. (gr. -1). pap. 14.09 (978-1-4567-7405-9(0)) AuthorHouse.

Collins, Paul. A Tale of Two Squirrels. 2008. 104p. pap. 9.95 (978-1-60693-204-9(7), Eloquent Bks.) Strategic Book Publishing & Rights Agency (SBPRA).

Conroe, Lindy. Rockafella Jones & the Hidden Treasure. Riette, Susanne, illus. 2011. 108p. (J). pap. 10.95 (978-1-935199-00-7(5)) Blue Mustang Pr.

Cook, Kacy. Nuts, 0 vols. 2012. (ENG.). 160p. (J). (gr. 3-7). pap. 7.99 (978-0-7614-6311-5(9), 9780761463115, Amazon Children's Publishing) Amazon Publishing.

Cook, Sherry & Johnson, Terri. Vinnie Volcano, 26. Kuhn, Jesse, illus. l.t. ed. 2006. (Quirkles — Exploring Phonics through Science Ser.: 22). 32p. (J). 7.99 (978-1-933815-21-3(3), Quirkles, The) Creative 3, LLC.

Cooper, D. C. Rascal the Baby Squirrel. 2013. 32p. (978-1-4602-2658-2(5)) FriesenPress.

Cooper, Helen S. Delicious! Cooper, Helen S., illus. 2007. (ENG., Illus.). 32p. (J). (gr. -1-3). 16.99 (978-0-374-31756-0(9), 9780374317560, Farrar, Straus & Giroux (BYR)) Farrar, Straus & Giroux.

—Pumpkin Soup, Set. unabr. ed. 2009. (ENG., Illus.). 32p. (J). (gr. -1-3). 9.99 (978-1-4272-0740-1(2), 9781427207401) Macmillan Audio.

Cortina, Janice. Grandpa Kolbe & the Squirrels. 2009. 32p. pap. 12.99 (978-1-4389-6762-2(4)) AuthorHouse.

Costa, Maria S. How to Find a Friend. 2017. (ENG., Illus.). 32p. (J). (gr. -1-3). 16.99 (978-0-544-92678-3(1)) Houghton Mifflin Harcourt Publishing Co.

Councilman, Janet H. Rocky & His Responsible Band of Cowboys, 1 vol. 2009. pap. 24.95 (978-1-60749-384-6(5)) America Star Bks.

Covey, Sean. Sammy & the Pecan Pie. Curtis, Stacy, illus. 2013. (7 Habits of Happy Kids Ser.: 4). (ENG.). 32p. (J). (gr. -1-1). 7.99 (978-1-4424-7647-9(8), Simon & Schuster Bks. For Young Readers) Simon & Schuster Bks. For Young Readers.

—Sophie & the Perfect Poem. Curtis, Stacy, illus. 2013. (7 Habits of Happy Kids Ser.: 6). (ENG.). 32p. (J). (gr. -1-1). 7.99 (978-1-4424-7651-6(6), Simon & Schuster Bks. For Young Readers) Simon & Schuster Bks. For Young Readers.

Craig, Joni. A Shoulder for Oscar. Haddad-Hamwi, Louise, illus. 2013. 40p. pap. 11.95 (978-0-9887836-6-9(5)) Taylor and Seale Publishing, LLC.

Crane Johnson, Amy. A Home for Pearl Squirrel: Una casa para la ardilla Perla, 4 vols. de la Vega, Eida, tr. Mommaerts, Robb, illus. rev. ed. 2004. (Solomon Raven Ser.: 1).Tr. of casa para la ardilla Perla. (SPA & ENG.). 32p. (J). (gr. 4-7). 16.95 (978-0-9724973-4-3(X), 626999, Raven Tree Pr.,Csi) Continental Sales, Inc.

Cronin, Doreen. The Chicken Squad. Cornell, Kevin, illus. 2014. 92p. (J). (978-0-605-90609-9(2)) Simon & Schuster Children's Publishing.

Cronin, Doreen. The Chicken Squad: The First Misadventure. Cornell, Kevin, illus. 2015. (Chicken Squad Ser.: 1). (ENG.). 112p. (J). (gr. 2-5). pap. 6.99 (978-1-4424-9677-4(0), Atheneum Bks. for Young Readers) Simon & Schuster Children's Publishing.

Crow, Marilee. A Short Tale about a Long Tail. Snider, K. C., illus. 2010. 16p. pap. 10.95 (978-1-61633-067-5(8)) Guardian Angel Publishing, Inc.

Cruea, Kim. Summer Falls Junior Rangers: The First Adventures. 2008. 73p. pap. 19.95 (978-1-60474-552-8(5)) America Star Bks.

Cummins, Judi, creator. It's Raining Acorns & Ladybugs. 2005. (Illus.). 28p. (J). per. (978-0-9760377-4-3(2)) Cummins, Judi.

Curtis, Jennifer Keats. Squirrel Rescue, 1 vol. Jacques, Laura, illus. 2012. (ENG.). 32p. (J). 16.99 (978-0-7643-4246-2(0), 9780764342462) Schiffer Publishing, Ltd.

Cusack, Bob. The Squirming Squirrel. 2009. 16p. pap. 12.99 (978-1-4389-5551-3(0)) AuthorHouse.

Cusick, N. L. Tales from Grey Squirrel Manor #1 - a Tale of Two Squirrels. 2013. 24p. pap. (978-1-4602-0814-4(5)) FriesenPress.

Dalton, Kippy. Cat & Squirrel. 2016. (Spring Forward Ser.). (J). (gr. 1). (978-1-4900-3714-1(4)) Benchmark Education Co.

Damjan, Mischa. Big Red Squirrel & the Little Rhinoceros. Steadman, Ralph, illus. 2010. (ENG.). 32p. (J). (gr. -1-k). 15.99 (978-1-84365-130-7(0), Pavilion) Pavilion Bks. GBR. Dist: Independent Pubs. Group.

Daniels, Cheri & Nicewander, Carol. Shadow Tail Meets the Gang. 2008. 24p. pap. 11.49 (978-1-4389-3259-0(6)) AuthorHouse.

Davenport, Eddie. Bunnyburg: The Newcomers. 2013. (ENG.). 30p. (J). pap. 14.95 (978-1-4787-2062-1(X)) Outskirts Pr., Inc.

Davies, Caroline & Martin, Sharon. Chwarae Cuddio. 2005. (WEL., Illus.). 12p. pap. (978-1-86101-080-3(X)) Acen Limited.

—Cotiau Newydd. 2005. (WEL., Illus.). 12p. pap. (978-1-86101-081-0(8)) Acen Limited.

—Y Frech Goch. 2005. (WEL., Illus.). 12p. pap. (978-1-86101-079-7(6)) Acen Limited.

Davis, Holly. Thankful Together. Sokolova, Valerie, illus. 2006. 36p. (J). 5.99 (978-0-7847-1436-2(3), 04077) Standard Publishing.

Degen, Bruce. Snow Joke. Degen, Bruce, illus. 2014. (I Like to Read(r) Ser.). (ENG., Illus.). 24p. (J). (gr. -1-3). 14.95 (978-0-8234-3065-9(0)) Holiday Hse., Inc.

—Snow Joke. 2014. 24p. pap. (978-0-8234-3223-3(8)) Holiday Hse., Inc.

Dhariwal, Radhika R. The Tale of a No-Name Squirrel. Benjaminsen, Audrey, illus. 2016. (ENG.). 384p. (J). (gr. 3-7). 16.99 (978-1-4814-4475-0(1), Simon & Schuster Bks. For Young Readers) Simon & Schuster Bks. For Young Readers.

DiCamillo, Kate. Flora & Ulysses: The Illuminated Adventures. Campbell, K. G., illus. (ENG.). (J). (gr. 3-7). 2016. pap. 6.99 (978-0-7636-8764-9(2)) 2013. 240p. 17.99 (978-0-7636-6040-6(X)) Candlewick Pr.

—Flora & Ulysses: The Illuminated Adventures. Campbell, K. G., illus. 2016. (ENG.). 256p. (J). (gr. 3-7). 17.20 (978-0-606-39100-9(2)) Turtleback Bks.

—Flora & Ulysses: The Illuminated Adventures. 2015. lib. bdg. 19.65 (978-0-606-36861-2(2)) Turtleback Bks.

Dillard, Mary Gregory. Jeepers Creepers! The Squirrels Are Coming. 2007. 85p. pap. 19.95 (978-1-4241-9951-8(4)) America Star Bks.

Dilley, Kristi. Squiggy the Squirrel Meets Wallis the Woodpecker. Dilley, Kristi, illus. 2013. (Illus.). 28p. pap. 9.99 (978-1-937165-47-5(7)) Orange Hat Publishing.

d'Lacey, Chris. The Fire Within. 2007. (Last Dragon Chronicles Ser.: 1). (ENG.). 352p. (J). (gr. 3-7). pap. 8.99 (978-0-439-67244-3(9), Orchard Bks.) Scholastic, Inc.

—Icefire. d'Lacey, Chris, illus. 2007. (Last Dragon Chronicles Ser.: 2). (Illus.). lib. bdg. 19.65 (978-1-4177-9138-5(1), Turtleback) Turtleback Bks.

Dobson, Donna. Timmy's First Adventure. 2012. 28p. pap. 24.95 (978-1-4626-7945-4(5)) America Star Bks.

Dodd, Melissa. Santa Sheds, 1 vol. 2009. 17p. pap. 24.95 (978-1-60749-208-5(3)) America Star Bks.

Doodle, Nanny. Divorced at Six. 2006. 158p. pap. 24.95 (978-1-4241-3963-7(5)) PublishAmerica, Inc.

Doudna, Kelly. Squirrel Hollow, 1 vol. Chawla, Neena, illus. 2006. (Animal Tales Ser.). 24p. (J). (gr. k-3). (ENG.). lib. bdg. 24.21 (978-1-59679-967-7(6), SandCastle); pap. 48.42 (978-1-59679-968-4(4)) ABDO Publishing Co.

Douglass, E. The Squirrel Friends Adventures: The Monster & the Great Storm. 2013. 100p. 19.95 (978-1-4759-6640-4(7)); pap. 9.95 (978-1-4759-6638-1(5)) iUniverse, Inc.

Dowler, Pattie. Suzie Squirrel & the Disappearing Pies. 2012. 24p. pap. 24.95 (978-1-4626-7636-1(7)) America Star Bks.

Duling, Astrid. The Guinea Pigs Twiggy & Molly. 2012. 134p. pap. (978-3-8423-1287-6(3)) Books on Demand GmbH.

Dunbar, Geoff & Ardagh, Philip. High in the Clouds. 2005. (Illus.). 91p. (J). (978-1-4156-2820-1(3), Dutton Juvenile) Penguin Publishing Group.

Duracell and the National Center for Missing & Exploited Children (NCMEC), creator. The Great Tomato Adventure: A Story about Smart Safety Choices. 2007. 0.00 (978-0-9795307-0-8(9)) Duracell & the National Ctr. for Missing & Exploited Children (NCMEC).

Earl the Squirrel & the Great Acorn Caper: None. 2003. (J). pap. 24.95 incl. cd-rom (978-0-9749041-0-8(4)) Big Lil' Bks.

Edwards, Jamee-Marie. But I Am a Cat! 2013. 44p. pap. 20.00 (978-1-4772-8231-1(9)) AuthorHouse.

Eller, Sylvia Klope. The Squirrel Who Hitchhiked to Atlanta. 2007. (Illus.). 32p. (J). pap. 8.00 (978-0-8059-7596-3(9)) Dorrance Publishing Co., Inc.

Elliott, Rebecca. Baxter Is Missing - A Branches Book. Elliott, Rebecca, illus. 2017. (Owl Diaries: 6). (ENG., Illus.). 80p. (J). (gr. k-2). pap. 4.99 (978-1-338-04284-9(X)) Scholastic, Inc.

Fisher, Stacey & Paner, Amy, Illustrator. No Nuts for Nutty. 2008. 26p. 14.95 (978-0-615-19778-4(7)) Fisher-Paner Publishing.

Fitzgerald, J. Rupert, the Sturdy Oak Tree: Who thought he was a little better than the other Trees. 2010. 16p. (J). pap. 14.95 (978-1-4327-5734-2(2)) Outskirts Pr., Inc.

Flaxenwick, Dim. Dobbin, Our Favourite Pony: Dobbin & the Little Red Squirrel. 2012. 44p. pap. 20.72 (978-1-4669-2179-5(X)) Trafford Publishing.

Flynn, Caren. Exceptional Elvis. 2010. (Illus.). 24p. pap. 12.00 (978-1-60844-481-6(3)) Dog Ear Publishing, LLC.

Freeman, Don. Earl the Squirrel. Freeman, Don, illus. 2008. (Illus.). (J). (gr. -1-2). pap. 16.95 incl. audio (978-1-4301-0411-7(2)) Live Oak Media.

—Earl the Squirrel. Freeman, Don, illus. 2007. (ENG., Illus.). 48p. (J). (gr. -1-2). pap. 6.99 (978-0-14-240893-3(X), Puffin Books) Penguin Young Readers Group.

Freeman, Don & Freeman, Roy. One More Acorn. 2010. (ENG., Illus.). 32p. (J). (gr. -1-k). 16.99 (978-0-670-01083-7(9), Viking Books for Young Readers) Penguin Young Readers Group.

Friend, Larry. Squirrelly the Squirrel & Starlett. 2012. (ENG.). 64p. pap. 10.95 (978-1-4327-8658-8(X)) Outskirts Pr., Inc.

Fyne, Olga. Squirrel Race. 2009. 28p. pap. 13.99 (978-1-4389-3676-5(1)) AuthorHouse.

Galjanic, Lisa. When Series 6 Volume Set, 6, 6. 2007. (Illus.). 100p. (J). 34.95 (978-1-933532-06-6(8)) LSG Pubns.

—When Squirrels Try. Hope, Michelle, illus. 2007. (J). 9.95 (978-1-933532-02-8(5)) LSG Pubns.

Gammage, Karen S. Nutty & Buddy. 2010. 32p. pap. 21.99 (978-1-4535-1182-4(2)) Xlibris Corp.

Gard, Don. The Adventures of Beezer. Giancanelli, Candace, illus. 2006. 100p. per. 12.95 (978-1-59858-157-7(0)) Dog Ear Publishing, LLC.

George, Lindsay Barrett. That Pup! George, Lindsay Barrett, illus. 2011. (ENG., Illus.). 32p. (J). (gr. -1-k). 16.99 (978-0-06-200413-0(1), Greenwillow Bks.) HarperCollins Pubs.

Giddens, Martha Anne. The Unluckiest Kid in the Universe. 2006. 56p. pap. 9.95 (978-1-4120-7935-8(7)) Trafford Publishing.

Gifford, Jerry. The Squirrel Highway. 2011. 32p. pap. 24.95 (978-1-4560-9397-6(5)) America Star Bks.

Godby, Michele. Mommy... Would You Still Love Me If I Was a Squirrel. 2012. 32p. pap. 21.99 (978-1-4797-6199-9(0)) Xlibris Corp.

Gordon, Pauline C. Animals in My Backyard! Joey, the Flying Squirrel. 2012. 28p. pap. 15.99 (978-1-4771-1961-7(2)) Xlibris Corp.

Graham, Janice C. The Little Country Girl & Frisky the Squirrel. Allen, S. Joan & Graham, Jerry L., illus. 2008. 32p. pap. 24.95 (978-1-60610-312-8(1)) America Star Bks.

Grambling, Lois G. & Grambling. Shoo! Scat!, 1 vol. Newman, Barbara Johansen, illus. 2004. (ENG.). 32p. (J). 16.95 (978-0-7614-5167-9(6)) Marshall Cavendish Corp.

Grandma. Harry's Adventure, 1 vol. 2009. 17p. pap. 24.95 (978-1-60836-943-0(9)) America Star Bks.

Green, Poppy. The Clover Curse. Bell, Jennifer A., illus. 2016. (Adventures of Sophie Mouse Ser.: 7). (ENG.). 128p. (J). (gr. k-4). 16.99 (978-1-4814-5184-0(7), Little Simon) Little Simon.

—The Emerald Berries. Bell, Jennifer A., illus. 2015. (Adventures of Sophie Mouse Ser.: 2). (ENG.). 128p. (J). (gr. k-4). pap. 5.99 (978-1-4814-2835-4(7), Little Simon) Little Simon.

Grossnickle, Mary. A Place in My Heart. Relyea, Alison, illus. 2014. (ENG.). 36p. 15.95 (978-1-84905-771-4(0), 3958) Kingsley, Jessica Pubs. GBR. Dist: Macmillan Distribution Ltd.

Grove, Malachai. The Return of Malachai. 2011. 24p. pap. 14.99 (978-1-4567-6257-5(5)) AuthorHouse.

Guillain, Charlotte. Rumplesnakeskin, 1 vol. Beacon, Dawn, illus. 2014. (Animal Fairy Tales Ser.). (ENG.). 24p. (gr. 1-2). lib. bdg. 23.99 (978-1-4109-6111-2(7), NA-r) Heinemann-Raintree.

Hagler, Chris E. Big Jim & the Squirrel. 2012. 28p. 24.95 (978-1-4626-6085-8(1)) America Star Bks.

Hall, Pamela. Miss You Like Crazy. Bell, Jennifer A., illus. 2014. (ENG.). 32p. (J). (gr. -1-3). 15.99 (978-1-933718-91-0(9)) Tanglewood Pr.

Harrington, Geri. Gray Squirrel at Pacific Avenue. Roosevelt, Michele Chopin, illus. 2011. (Smithsonian's Backyard Ser.). (ENG.). 32p. (J). (gr. -1-3). 19.95 (978-1-60727-638-8(0)) Soundprints.

Harvey, Gwendolyn Fowlkes. The Backyard Plum Tree. 2009. (J). pap. (978-1-61623-481-2(4)) Independent Pub.

Hasan, Jamal I. A Journey to Remember. 2007. 64p. per. 8.95 (978-0-595-43375-9(8)) iUniverse, Inc.

Head, Murray. I Can Run. 2017. (I Like to Read(r) Ser.). (ENG.). 32p. (J). (gr. -1-3). 6.99 (978-0-8234-3846-4(5)); 14.95 (978-0-8234-3831-0(7)) Holiday Hse., Inc.

Heigh, Stephen. Mr. George & the Red Hat. Burton, Kevin, ed. Heigh, Stephen, illus. 2004. (Illus.). 32p. (J). 18.95 (978-0-9745715-2-2(0)) KRBY Creations, LLC.

Hein, Connie L. Toliver in Time; for a Journey West: History in a Nutshell. Theobald, Denise, illus. l.t. ed. 2005. 28p. (J). lib. bdg. 17.95 (978-0-9740855-6-2(1)); per. 9.95 (978-0-9740855-7-9(X)) Still Water Publishing.

Hill, Chris. Lucky. 2016. (ENG.). 208p. (J). (gr. 2-5). 16.99 (978-0-545-83977-8(7), Chicken Hse., The) Scholastic, Inc.

Hoffer, Rod. The Strange Christmas Dream. 2012. 64p. pap. 24.99 (978-1-4772-5949-8(X)) AuthorHouse.

Holland, Francis. KoKo's New Home. 2008. 32p. pap. 24.95 (978-1-60474-706-5(4)) America Star Bks.

Holliday, Andrea. Squissy, the Little Grey Squirrel That Got a Second Chance. 2013. 28p. pap. 24.95 (978-1-4626-9788-5(7)) America Star Bks.

Holmes, Andy. Building God's Kingdom - Diggit Saves the Day, 1 vol. de Giorgi, Sergio, illus. 2014. (ENG.). 22p. (J). bds. 9.99 (978-0-529-11100-5(4)) Nelson, Thomas Inc.

Horn, Mildred D. Teeny the Squirrel Meets the Outside World. 2009. 15.95 (978-1-61623-107-1(6)) Independent Pub.

Houser, Marlin. The Secret of Squirrel Meadow. 2006. (Adventures of Little Fox Ser.). (Illus.). 171p. (J). 16.95 (978-0-9752703-4-9(6)); per. 7.95 (978-0-9752703-5-6(4)) Marhouse, Inc.

Howells, Angela. The Tails of Victoria Way. 2009. (Illus.). 32p. pap. 12.99 (978-1-4490-4432-9(8)) AuthorHouse.

Hughes, Diane Marie. Meet Wilbur the Squirrel. 2004. 21p. pap. 24.95 (978-1-4137-2758-6(1)) PublishAmerica, Inc.

Humphreys, Dolores, illus. The Adventures of J. G. & Echo: The Land of All Creatures & the Swamp Creature, 1. 2003. 81p. (J). per. 16.00 (978-0-9727415-2-1(6)) Cuccia, Louis.

Iverson, Diane. Rascal, the Tassel Eared Squirrel. 2007. 64p. pap. 9.95 (978-0-932821-64-5(2)) Grand Canyon Assn.

Iwamura, Kazuo. Bedtime in the Forest. 2010. (ENG., Illus.). 32p. (J). (gr. -1-3). 16.95 (978-0-7358-2310-5(3)) North-South Bks., Inc.

Jackson, Glenda K. Friends of the Hills. 2012. 20p. pap. 17.99 (978-1-4685-4082-6(3)) AuthorHouse.

Jacques, Brian. Rakkety Tam, 17 vols. 2005. (Redwall Ser.: 17). (ENG.). 384p. (J). (gr. 5-18). mass mkt. 8.99 (978-0-441-01318-0(X), Ace Bks.) Penguin Publishing Group.

—Rakkety Tam. Elliot, David, illus. 2006. (Redwall Ser.). (ENG.). 384p. (J). (gr. 5-18). 8.99 (978-0-14-240683-0(X), Firebird) Penguin Young Readers Group.

—Rakkety Tam. 2004. (Redwall Ser.). 1.00 (978-1-4175-5517-8(3)) Recorded Bks., Inc.

Jasnoch, Dorothy. The Adventures of Oskar: Oskar's New School. Korzeniowski, Samson O., ed. Jasnoch, Dorothy, illus. 2013. (Illus.). 32p. 18.99 (978-1-937752-27-9(5)) Owl About Bks. Pub., Inc.

Jeanfield. Twinkle, a Christmas Story. 2009. 36p. pap. 13.95 (978-1-60693-745-7(6), Eloquent Bks.) Strategic Book Publishing & Rights Agency (SBPRA).

Jenkins, Henry A. The Adventures of Monkey Squirrel & Frogman: Sand Trap. 2009. 16p. pap. 8.49 (978-1-4343-7827-9(6)) AuthorHouse.

John, Clement. Best Friends: A Bedtime Story. 2011. (Illus.). 40p. pap. 21.93 (978-1-4520-7922-6(6)) AuthorHouse.

Johnson, Amy Crane. A Home for Pearl Squirrel. Mommaerts, Robb, illus. 2009. (ENG.). 32p. (J). (gr. -1-3). 16.95 (978-1-934960-58-5(6), Raven Tree Pr.,Csi) Continental Sales, Inc.

Johnson, Donna. The Story of the Little Red Leaf. Johnson, Emily, illus. l.t. ed. 2006. (ENG.). 22p. (J). 25.00 (978-0-9778774-0-9(X)) Choice Point Editions.

Jones, Janey Louise. Sonny the Daring Squirrel. Poh, Jennie, illus. 2016. (Superfairies Ser.). (ENG.). 56p. (gr. k-3). lib. bdg. 23.99 (978-1-5158-0433-8(X)) Picture Window Bks.

Jules, Jacqueline. Freddie Ramos Zooms to the Rescue, Bk. 3. Benitez, Miguel, illus. 2011. (Zapato Power Ser.: Book 3). (ENG.). 96p. (J). (gr. 1-5). 14.99 (978-0-8075-9482-7(2)) Whitman, Albert & Co.

Kabir, Shohag. Mice & Squirrel. 2009. 24p. pap. 13.99 (978-1-4389-9164-1(9)) AuthorHouse.

Keller, George. Squirrelly Whirly & the Haunted House. 2005. 21p. 7.45 (978-1-4116-4425-0(5)) Lulu Pr., Inc.

Kiick, Lisa. Bailey & Friends. Stouch, Ryan, illus. 2008. 40p. pap. 14.95 (978-1-59858-743-2(9)) Dog Ear Publishing, LLC.

Kinger, Rachit. Zapp: The Squirrel Who Wanted to Fly. 2015. (ENG.). 100p. pap. 7.95 (978-81-8328-137-9(0)) Wisdom Tree IND. Dist: SCB Distributors.

Kirkpatrick, Teresa. Roscoe's Forest Adventures. 2008. 177p. pap. 24.95 (978-1-60672-328-9(6)) America Star Bks.

Kreidler, Shannon. The Adventures of Sally the Squirrel: Interactive... Educational & Earn Gold Stars. 2013. 28p. pap. 15.99 (978-1-4797-7674-0(2)) Xlibris Corp.

Lang, Valerie E. Jet's Day: A Whisker Team Story. 2011. 32p. pap. 13.00 (978-1-61204-178-0(7), Strategic Bk. Publishing) Strategic Book Publishing & Rights Agency (SBPRA).

Lawson, Tanya. Pawpaw Harry & the Baby Squirrel. 2011. 24p. pap. 12.00 (978-1-4567-4616-2(2)) AuthorHouse.

Lease, Janice. Marigold Little Squirrel in a Cactus Patch. 2008. 48p. pap. 19.95 (978-0-9800762-0-2(X)) Cinnamon Ridge Publishing.

Leatham, Marc Vincent. The Race. 2007. (Illus.). (J). (gr. -1-3). per. 15.99 (978-1-59879-274-4(1)) Lifevest Publishing, Inc.

—The Story of the Five Squirrels. Leatham, Marc Vincent, illus. 2007. (Illus.). (J). (gr. -1-3). per. 15.99 (978-1-59879-275-1(X)) Lifevest Publishing, Inc.

Lechner, John. Sticky Burr: Adventures in Burrwood Forest. Lechner, John, illus. 2008. (ENG., Illus.). 56p. (J). (gr. 1-4). pap. 7.99 (978-0-7636-3567-1(7)) Candlewick Pr.

Leist, Christina, illus. Jack the Bear. 2009. (ENG.). 40p. (J). (gr. -1-3). 16.95 (978-1-894965-97-2(3)) Simply Read Bks. CAN. Dist: Ingram Publisher Services.

Levy, Elizabeth. The Mixed-Up Mask Mystery: A Fletcher Mystery. Gorstein, Mordicai, illus. unabr. ed. 2006. (First Chapter Bks.). (J). (gr. 2-4). pap. 20.95 incl. audio compact disk (978-1-59519-711-5(7)); pap. 17.95 incl. audio (978-1-59519-710-8(9)) Live Oak Media.

Lewellyn, Natalie. Nutty to Meet You! Dr. Peanut Book #1. 2008. (Illus.). 32p. (J). 11.95 (978-0-9777082-0-8(9)) One Monkey Bks.

Lipe, Riki. Hanging with Yum-Yum & Yuck. 2007. (Illus.). (J). 10.00 (978-0-9659381-6-7(6)) Hoot N' Cackle Pr.

Lithgow, John. Micawber. Payne, C. F., illus. 2005. (ENG.). 40p. (J). (gr. -1-3). reprint ed. 8.99 (978-0-689-83542-1(6), Simon & Schuster Bks. For Young Readers) Simon & Schuster Bks. For Young Readers.

Lloyd-Jones, Sally. Just Because You're Mine. Endersby, Frank, illus. 2011. (ENG.). 32p. (J). (gr. -1-2). 16.99 (978-0-06-201476-4(5)) HarperCollins Pubs.

Loughead, Deb. A Pocketful of Fur. Birke, Lisa, tr. 2005. (Illus.). 60p. (J). (gr. 2-4). 6.95 (978-0-9730831-6-3(6)) Hodgepog Bks. CAN. Dist: Fitzhenry & Whiteside, Ltd.

Lowery, Marie Hayes. Beau & Friends. 2012. 20p. pap. 17.99 (978-1-4817-0106-8(1)) AuthorHouse.

Luberto, Bradley. Clide & Druce: A Repulsive Tale of Trolls & Tax Money. 2006. (ENG.). 48p. per. 16.95 (978-1-4241-5012-0(4)) PublishAmerica, Inc.

Lush, Nella. Gracie & Belle Never Again! 2007. 20p. per. 24.95 (978-1-4241-8373-9(1)) America Star Bks.

Mabry, Virginia. Jolly Ollie from Olney. 2012. 16p. pap. 10.00 (978-1-937260-25-5(9)) Sleepytown Pr.

MacVicar, Andrea. Tales of Zoftic. Morse, Patti, illus. 2007. 58p. (J). per. 16.95 (978-0-9798395-0-4(5)) Inspiration Pr. Inc.

Mae, Darcie. Sammy & Robert. 2008. 24p. pap. 24.95 (978-1-60474-811-6(7)) America Star Bks.

The Magical Adventures of Samuel the Squirrel & Oscar the Owl Journey to Mars. 2005. (J). per. 12.95 (978-0-9762929-0-6(4)) Morning Glory Pubns.

Marinaro, Stacy. Carter the Acorn Collecting Cutie. 2008. 20p. pap. 10.50 (978-0-615-20807-7(X)) Marinaro, Stacy.

Matthews, Ian. Albert the Big Eyed Squirrel. 2011. 25p. (J). pap. 15.95 (978-1-4327-5904-9(3)) Outskirts Pr., Inc.

Mayer, Marvin S. Sammy Squirrel & the Sunflower Seeds. Johns, Dick, illus. 2008. 73p. pap. 19.95 (978-1-60672-193-3(3)) America Star Bks.

McAdams, Susan. Shubert. McAdams, Caleb, illus. 2008. 16p. per. 24.95 (978-1-4241-9756-9(2)) America Star Bks.

McClurkan, Rob. Aw, Nuts! McClurkan, Rob, illus. 2014. (ENG., Illus.). 32p. (J). (gr. -1-3). 17.99 (978-0-06-231729-2(6)) HarperCollins Pubs.

McCorkle, Barbara. Bandit Raccoon. Taylor, David A., illus. l.t. ed. 2006. 39p. (J). 19.95 (978-1-59879-170-9(2)); per. 13.99 (978-1-59879-123-5(0)) Lifevest Publishing, Inc.

—Brutis' New Friend. Taylor, David A., illus. 2007. 30p. (J). 13.99 (978-1-59879-439-7(6)) Lifevest Publishing, Inc.

—Brutis' New Friend. 2005. (Illus.). 23p. (J). (gr. -1-3). per. 8.99 (978-1-932338-60-7(8)) Lifevest Publishing, Inc.

McFarland, Myndie. Squigley the Squirrel. 2012. 46p. pap. 12.95 (978-1-886057-11-1(7)) Warren Publishing, Inc.

McKelvey, Lonnie. Ralph & His New Friends. 2007. (J). (978-0-9796519-1-5(3)) Mirror Publishing.

McLeod, Laura. George the Squirrel. 2015. (ENG., Illus.). (J). 15.99 (978-1-58169-548-9(9), Evergreen Pr.) Genesis Communications, Inc.

McNease, Mitzy. Chester's Presents. Cox, Kim, illus. 2006. 28p. (J). 10.95 (978-0-9779488-0-2(3)) Blancmange Publishing LLC.

McQueen, Todd. Bob & Rob & Corn on the Cob. McQueen, Todd, illus. 2014. (ENG., Illus.). 32p. (J). (gr. -1-k). 16.95 (978-1-62873-591-8(0), Sky Pony Pr.) Skyhorse Publishing Co., Inc.

Meadows, Daisy. Sophie Flufftail's Brave Plan. 2016. (Magic Animal Friends Ser.: 5). (ENG., Illus.). 112p. (J). (gr. 2-5). pap. 4.99 (978-0-545-90741-5(1), Scholastic Paperbacks) Scholastic, Inc.

Meaker, Mary. Quinton, Brewster & Chaley. 2011. 64p. (gr. -1). pap. 9.99 (978-1-4634-3023-8(X)) AuthorHouse.

Meisel, Paul, illus. Good Night, Bat! Good Morning, Squirrel! 2016. (ENG.). 40p. (J). (gr. -1-3). 16.95 (978-1-62979-495-2(3)) Boyds Mills Pr.

Meschenmoser, Sebastian. Mr. Squirrel & the Moon. 2015. (ENG., Illus.). 48p. (J). 18.95 (978-0-7358-4156-7(X)) North-South Bks., Inc.

—Waiting for Winter. Meschenmoser, Sebastian, illus. 2015. (ENG., Illus.). 58p. (J). (gr. k-3). 10.99 (978-1-61067-435-5(9)) Kane Miller.

Meyer, Linda. Jones & the Great Act. 2009. 118p. pap. 9.99 (978-0-557-17339-6(6)) Lulu Pr., Inc.

Miller, Donna C. Me & Mister Squirrel. 2005. (J). pap. 8.00 (978-0-8059-6523-0(8)) Dorrance Publishing Co., Inc.

Miller, Jennifer. Christmas Tails. Knight, Vanessa, illus. 2009. 56p. pap. 17.26 (978-1-4251-8987-7(3)) Trafford Publishing.

Miller, Pat. Squirrel's New Year's Resolution. Ember, Kathi, illus. 2012. (J). 34.28 (978-1-61913-135-4(8)) Weigl Pubs., Inc.

—Squirrel's New Year's Resolution. Ember, Kathi, illus. (ENG.). 32p. (J). (gr. k-2). 2017. pap. 7.99 (978-0-8075-7592-5(5)) 2010. 16.99 (978-0-8075-7591-8(7)) Whitman, Albert & Co.

Mjolhus, Joy. Squirrel Babies & Friends. 2008. 16p. pap. 24.95 (978-1-4241-8562-7(9)) America Star Bks.

Morgan, Allen. Matthew & the Midnight Hospital. 2004. (Illus.). (J). (gr. k-3). spiral bd. (978-0-616-01529-2(1)) Canadian National Institute for the Blind/Institut National Canadien pour les Aveugles.

Moser, Lisa. Squirrel's Fun Day. Gorbachev, Valeri, illus. 2015. (Candlewick Sparks Ser.). (ENG.). 48p. (J). (gr. k-4). pap. 3.99 (978-0-7636-7789-3(2)) Candlewick Pr.

—Squirrel's World. Gorbachev, Valeri, illus. 2013. (Candlewick Sparks Ser.). (ENG.). 48p. (J). (gr. k-4). pap. 3.99 (978-0-7636-6644-6(0)) Candlewick Pr.

Mosier, Pamela. Elizabeth, the Eastern Gray Squirrel. 2008. 44p. pap. 18.95 (978-1-4357-5407-2(7)) Lulu Pr., Inc.

Muir, Leslie. C. R. Mudgeon. Hector, Julian, illus. 2012. (ENG.). 32p. (J). (gr. -1-3). 15.99 (978-1-4169-7906-7(9), Atheneum Bks. for Young Readers) Simon & Schuster Children's Publishing.

Mullican, Norma Waldon & Zivney, Missy Mullican. A Collection of Squirrel Tales: Something to Crow About. 2009. 84p. pap. 10.99 (978-1-60791-702-1(5)) Salem Author Services.

Munroe, C. K. Attack of the Mutant Squirrels. 2011. (Illus.). 118p. pap. *(978-1-908147-55-4(5))* YouWriteOn.

Music for Little People, contrib. by. Let's Go Chipper! into the Great Outdoors. 2011. (ENG.). audio compact disk 9.98 *(978-1-56628-474-5(0))* Music for Little People, Inc.

Nair, Anita. Adventures of Nonu, the Skating Squirrel. 2006. (Illus.). 44p. (J). *(978-81-291-0892-0(5))* Rupa & Co.

Nicholas, Nicki. Peter & Lil on a Winter's Day. 2011. 24p. pap. *(978-1-4269-7316-1(0))* Trafford Publishing (UK) Ltd.

—Peter & Lil's Amazing Autumn Day. 2011. 24p. (gr. 1-2). pap. 15.50 *(978-1-4269-6047-5(6))* Trafford Publishing.

—Peter & Lil's Summer Day Adventure. 2011. 24p. pap. 15.50 *(978-1-4269-5358-3(5))* Trafford Publishing.

Nick, Papa. Never Ending Stories. 2011. 44p. pap. 24.95 *(978-1-4626-3792-8(2))* America Star Bks.

Nolan, Lucy. Smarter Than Squirrels, 0 vols. Reed, Mike, illus. unabr. ed. 2009. (Down Girl & Sit Ser.: 1). (ENG.). 68p. (J). (gr. 1-4). pap. 9.99 *(978-0-7614-5571-4(X)*, 9780761455714, Amazon Children's Publishing) Amazon Publishing.

Nona Theresa Perez - Bayanin. Nadia Mei's First Spring: A Season of Growth. 2012. 32p. pap. 21.99 *(978-1-4771-1006-5(2))* Xlibris Corp.

O'Brien, Richard. Christopher & Joshua Go Fishing. 2012. (Illus.). 38p. pap. 11.00 *(978-1-78035-257-2(3)*, Fastprint Publishing) Upfront Publishing Ltd. GBR. Dist: Printondemand-worldwide.com.

Ohi, Debbie Ridpath. Where Are My Books? Ohi, Debbie Ridpath, illus. 2015. (ENG., Illus.). 40p. (J). (gr. -1-3). 17.99 *(978-1-4424-6741-5(X)*, Simon & Schuster Bks. For Young Readers) Simon & Schuster Bks. For Young Readers.

Ohi, Ruth. Fox & Squirrel. Ohi, Ruth, illus. 2013. (ENG., Illus.). 32p. (gr. -1-2). *(978-1-4431-1914-6(8))* Scholastic Canada, Ltd.

OHora, Zachariah. My Cousin Momo. 2015. (ENG., Illus.). 32p. (J). (gr. -1-k). 17.99 *(978-0-8037-4011-2(5)*, Dial Bks) Penguin Young Readers Group.

Osuna, Rosa, illus. No es Facil, Pequena Ardilla. 2004.Tr. of It's Not Easy, Little Squirrel. (SPA.). (J). 15.99 *(978-84-8464-202-2(X))* Kalandraka Editora, S.L. ESP. Dist: Lectorum Pubns., Inc.

Ottitoloju/Blazing Ideas ltd, Ololade/Adewunmi, retold by. Kunkuru, Jaba Da Kurege: The Tortoise, the Rat & the Squirrel. 2008. (YOR & ENG., Illus.). 36p. 16.00 *(978-0-9801243-7-8(9))* Blazing Ideas Ltd.

—Mbe, Nkapi na Osa. 2008. (YOR & ENG., Illus.). 36p. 16.00 *(978-0-9801243-3-0(6))* Blazing Ideas Ltd.

Page, Frank. Sometimes a Squirrel Is Just a Squirrel. 2005. 106p. pap. 9.99 *(978-1-4116-6062-5(5))* Lulu Pr., Inc.

Paner, Amy & Fisher, Stacey. Nutty Scurries to School. 2008. 25p. 14.95 *(978-0-615-23931-6(5))* Fisher-Paner Publishing.

Parker, Emma. Bill Hides Acorns. 2010. (Illus.). 24p. pap. *(978-1-877561-33-7(9))* First Edition Ltd.

Parker-Quayle, Eric. Eric Quayle's Tiny Tales. 2015. (ENG., Illus.). 60p. (J). (gr. 2-3). pap. 13.95 *(978-1-78455-867-3(2)*, f25c391c-ecc9-472d-a9fd-362a8bf7e971) Austin, Stan AUS. Dist: Bookmasters Distribution.

Pearson, Iris & Merrill, Mike. The Adventures of Lady: The Big Storm. Pearson, Iris, ed. Project Firefly Animation Studios, illus. rev. ed. 2007. 34p. (J). 11.99 *(978-0-9789984-2-4(1))* Adventures of Lady LLC, The.

—The Adventures of Lady: The Big Storm Coloring Book. Pearson, Iris, ed. Project Firefly Animation Studios, illus. 2007. 34p. (J). pap. 5.49 *(978-0-9789984-3-1(X))* Adventures of Lady LLC, The.

Peck, Steven L. The Rifts of Rime (Quickened Chronicles) 2012. pap. 14.99 *(978-1-59955-967-4(6))* Cedar Fort, Inc./CFI Distribution.

Pedersen, Peggy A. Jasmine & the Magic Squirrel. 2008. 12p. pap. 24.95 *(978-1-60474-052-3(3))* America Star Bks.

Pellant, Terry. The Real Valentine's Story. 2004. 27p. (J). pap. 24.95 *(978-1-4137-2146-1(X))* PublishAmerica, Inc.

Perkins, Lynne Rae. Nuts to You. Perkins, Lynne Rae, illus. 2014. (ENG., Illus.). 272p. (J). (gr. 3-7). 16.99 *(978-0-06-009275-7(0)*, Greenwillow Bks.) HarperCollins Pubs.

Pernikoff, Doug. So What If Im a Bully. 2009. 40p. 11.99 *(978-0-9816923-3-3(8))* Cochran, Russ Co., The.

Pigott, Louise. Squirrel Me Timbers. 2016. (Fiction Picture Bks.). (ENG., Illus.). 24p. (gr. k-1). lib. bdg. 24.65 *(978-1-4795-9177-0(7)*, Fiction Picture Bks.) Picture Window Bks.

Pilutti, Deb. Bear & Squirrel Are Friends ... Yes, Really! Pilutti, Deb, illus. 2015. (ENG., Illus.). 40p. (J). (gr. -1-3). 17.99 *(978-1-4814-2913-9(2)*, Simon & Schuster Bks. For Young Readers) Simon & Schuster Bks. For Young Readers.

Pittman, Michael. Mackey's first Adventure. 2011. 24p. pap. 14.93 *(978-1-4269-5175-6(2))* Trafford Publishing.

Potter, Beatrix. The Tale of Squirrel Nutkin. Rasmussen, Wendy, illus. 2009. (Classic Tales by Beatrix Potter Ser.). (ENG.). 24p. (J). (gr. k-3). 28.50 *(978-1-60253-296-0(6)*, 200122) Child's World, Inc., The.

—The Tale of Squirrel Nutkin. (Beatrix Potter Bookmark Board Book Ser.). (Illus.). 6p. (J). bds. 3.95 *(978-1-58989-203-3(8))* Thurman Hse., LLC.

Powell, Jimmie. The Squirrel the Worm & the Nut Trees. 2007. 48p. per. 15.95 *(978-1-4327-1326-3(4))* Outskirts Pr., Inc.

Ramoutar, Christine L. Tales from the Pine Forest. 2012. 108p. pap. 10.95 *(978-1-4620-7030-5(2))* iUniverse, Inc.

Randy. The Adventures of Rico. 2010. 28p. pap. 13.79 *(978-1-4490-8353-3(6))* AuthorHouse.

Ray, J. Hamilton. Squirrels on Skis. Lemaitre, Pascal, illus. 2013. (Beginner Books Ser.). (ENG.). 64p. (J). (gr. k-3). 9.99 *(978-0-449-81081-1(X)*, Random Hse. Bks. for Young Readers) Random Hse. Children's Bks.

Reimiller, Diane L. Ike & Jamie. Jastrzebski, Brandy, illus. 2008. 32p. pap. 24.95 *(978-1-60610-227-5(3))* America Star Bks.

Reinlein, Ann. The Adventures of Mister Squirrel Acorn. 2008. 32p. pap. 15.00 *(978-1-4389-1879-2(8))* AuthorHouse.

Rey, H. A. *Jorge el Curioso Siembra Una Semilla. Zappy*, Erica, ed. Canetti, Yanitzia, tr. 2007. (Curious George Ser.). (ENG & SPA., Illus.). 24p. (J). (gr. -1-3). mass mkt. 3.99 *(978-0-618-89688-2(0))* Houghton Mifflin Harcourt Publishing Co.

Rey, H. A. & Rey, Margret. Lost & Found. 2008. (Curious George Ser.). (ENG., Illus.). 24p. (J). (gr. -1-3). pap. 3.99 *(978-0-618-89197-9(8))* Houghton Mifflin Harcourt Publishing Co.

Richardson, Lin Douglas. The Meaning of Me. 2011. 28p. pap. 24.95 *(978-1-4626-2891-9(5))* America Star Bks.

Ringler, Matt. It's Fall! Shearing, Leonie, illus. 2006. 28p. (J). pap. *(978-0-439-87146-4(8))* Scholastic, Inc.

Ringley, Patrick & Brown, Anne Corbett. The Adventures of the Nutters, the Tree Highway. Cotton, Sue Lynn, illus. 2013. 48p. pap. 19.95 *(978-1-61493-207-9(7))* Peppertree Pr., The.

Ritch, Catherine. Zipper Finds a Job. Trexler, Jennifer Suther, illus. 2014. (White Squirrel Parables Ser.: Vol. 2). (ENG.). 32p. (J). (gr. -1-3). 13.95 *(978-1-933341-40-8(8))* CRM.

Roberton, Fiona. A Tale of Two Beasts. Roberton, Fiona, illus. 2015. (ENG., Illus.). 32p. (J). pap. 12.99 *(978-1-61067-361-7(1))* Kane Miller.

Rockas, Leo. Mice Make War. 2007. 53p. 16.95 *(978-1-4241-5708-2(0))* America Star Bks.

Rogers, Diana. Critters of Grassy Green Plains: Got to Get the Critters Counted. 2012. 20p. pap. 24.95 *(978-1-4626-7562-3(X))* America Star Bks.

Rose, Chloe Gayle & Rose, Tammy Marie. The Snake That Eats Cake. 2012. 28p. pap. 24.95 *(978-1-4626-9882-0(4))* America Star Bks.

Rose, Nancy. Merry Christmas, Squirrels! 2015. (ENG., Illus.). 32p. (J). (gr. -1-3). 17.00 *(978-0-316-30257-9(0))* Little, Brown Bks. for Young Readers.

—The Secret Life of Squirrels: A Love Story. (ENG., Illus.). 32p. (J). (gr. -1-3). 2016. 16.99 *(978-0-316-27263-6(9))* 2014. 17.00 *(978-0-316-37027-1(4))* Little, Brown Bks. for Young Readers.

Rottgen, Barbara. A Friend Like You. Julian, Sean, illus. 2016. (ENG.). 32p. (J). (gr. -1-2). 16.99 *(978-1-68010-031-0(9))* Tiger Tales.

Rubin, Adam. Those Darn Squirrels! Salmieri, Daniel, illus. (ENG.). 32p. (J). (gr. -1-3). 2011. pap. 7.99 *(978-0-547-57681-7(1))* 2008. 17.99 *(978-0-547-00703-8(5))* Houghton Mifflin Harcourt Publishing Co.

—Those Darn Squirrels & the Cat Next Door. Salmieri, Daniel, illus. 2011. (ENG.). 32p. (J). (gr. -1-3). 17.99 *(978-0-547-42922-9(3))* Houghton Mifflin Harcourt Publishing Co.

—Those Darn Squirrels Fly South. Salmieri, Daniel, illus. 2012. (ENG.). 32p. (J). (gr. -1-3). 17.99 *(978-0-547-67823-8(1))* Houghton Mifflin Harcourt Publishing Co.

Ruiz, John. The Squirrel, the Eagle & the Red Hawk. 2012. 32p. pap. 21.99 *(978-1-4691-7970-4(9))* Xlibris Corp.

Rylant, Cynthia. Gooseberry Park. Howard, Arthur, illus. 2007. (ENG.). 144p. (J). (gr. 2-5). pap. 6.99 *(978-0-15-206159-3(2))* Houghton Mifflin Harcourt Publishing Co.

Sackanay, Kathleen. Adventures in the Forest. Wood, Morgan, illus. 2007. 24p. (J). pap. 8.45 *(978-0-9791276-2-5(9))* Athanatos Publishing Group.

Saldivar, Jose A. The Adventures of Oskar: Oskar's New School. Nilsson, Janet Busbey, ed. Jasnoch, Dorothy, illus. 2013. 32p. pap. 13.99 *(978-1-937752-14-9(3))*; (ENG.). pap. 13.99 *(978-1-937752-07-1(0))* Owl About Bks. Pub., Inc.

Salmon, Peg. Percy & His Family. 2007. 44p. per. 15.95 *(978-1-4327-0841-2(4))* Outskirts Pr., Inc.

Salten, Felix. Perri. Mussey, Barrows, tr. from GER. 2015. (Bambi's Classic Animal Tales Ser.). (ENG., Illus.). 256p. (J). (gr. 3-7). pap. 8.99 *(978-1-4424-8760-4(7)*, Aladdin) Simon & Schuster Children's Publishing.

Sargent, Dave & Sargent, David M. Cindy Sparrow: Respect the Property of Others, 19 vols., Vol. 6. Lenoir, Jane, illus. 2003. (Feather Tales Ser.: 6). 42p. (J). pap. 10.95 *(978-1-56763-730-4(2))*; 2nd ed. lib. bdg. 20.95 *(978-1-56763-729-8(9))* Ozark Publishing.

Satterly, Denise B. The Adventures of Icky & Weezy: Fall Has Arrived. 2011. 20p. (gr. -1 — 1). pap. 10.03 *(978-1-4520-2046-4(9))* AuthorHouse.

Scheber, George. Earl Joins the Circus. Spicer, Bridgett, illus. l.t. ed. 2005. (Adventures of Earl the Squirrel Ser.). 32p. (J). (gr. -1-3). 12.95 *(978-1-878847-01-0(5))* Make Me A Story Pr.

—Earl the Squirrel. Spicer, Bridgett, illus. l.t. ed. 2005. (Adventures of Earl the Squirrel Ser.). 32p. (J). (gr. -1-2). 12.95 *(978-1-878847-00-3(7))* Make Me A Story Pr.

Schwartz, Virginia Frances. Nutz!, 1 vol. Leist, Christina, illus. 2012. (ENG.). 152p. (J). (gr. 3-6). pap. 12.95 *(978-1-896580-87-6(4))* Tradewind Bks. CAN. Dist: Orca Bk. Pubs. USA.

Scott, Dee Mary. The Adventures of Charles & Camilla Chinchilla. 2012. (Illus.). 46p. pap. 6.99 *(978-1-78035-389-0(8)*, Fastprint Publishing) Upfront Publishing Ltd. GBR. Dist: Printondemand-worldwide.com.

Seymour, Mary Sue. Friends in a Storm. Flynn, Samantha, illus. 2013. 20p. pap. 9.95 *(978-1-61633-376-8(6))* Guardian Angel Publishing, Inc.

Shelton, Ricky V. Quacker Meets His Dad the Squirrel: Tales from a Duck Named Quacker. Williams, Shan, illus. Date not set. (J). (gr. -1-1). pap. 7.00 *(978-0-9634257-3-7(0))* RVS Bks., Inc.

Shepherd, Melissa L. On Mother's Day. 2012. 24p. pap. 14.93 *(978-1-4669-1165-9(4))* Trafford Publishing.

Shields, Kathleen J. Hamilton Troll Meets Chatterton Squirrel. Klug, Leigh A. & Bryant, Carol W., illus. 4th ed. 2013. 42p. 14.00 *(978-0-9882745-3-2(1))* Erin Go Bragh Publishing.

Shongo Jr., Earl. Chippie the Squirrel. 2012. 20p. pap. 14.99 *(978-1-4772-8252-6(1))* AuthorHouse.

Sica, Diane. The Adventures of Sammy & Vinney. 2012. 48p. pap. 11.95 *(978-1-4685-6883-7(3))* AuthorHouse.

Simon, Mary Manz. Squirrel Says Thank You. Couri, Kathy & Clearwater, Linda, illus. 2006. (First Virtues for Toddlers Ser.). 20p. (J). 5.99 *(978-0-7847-1415-7(0)*, 04067) Standard Publishing.

Simpson, Richard. The Squirrel Who Was Afraid to Climb Trees. Hoch, Kevin, illus. 2003. 55p. (J). pap. 9.95 *(978-0-7414-1825-8(8))* Infinity Publishing.

Singhose, Rose. Granny's giggles book Four. 2010. 38p. pap. 16.95 *(978-0-557-59965-3(2))* Lulu Pr., Inc.

—Granny's GIGGLES BOOK SIX. 2010. 34p. pap. 16.95 *(978-0-557-61003-7(6))* Lulu Pr., Inc.

—Granny's giggles book Three. 2010. 33p. pap. 16.95 *(978-0-557-59768-0(4))* Lulu Pr., Inc.

Singhose, Rose & StGermain, Annetta. Gramma's Sure Fire Cure for Insomnia in the Very Young. 2010. 67p. pap. 27.50 *(978-0-557-08697-9(3))* Lulu Pr., Inc.

Skidmore, Marlene. In Trouble Again! 2010. 24p. pap. 9.99 *(978-0-9845208-9-3(9))* Faithful Life Pubs.

—Wesley's Swoo-Foo. 2008. 28p. pap. 9.99 *(978-0-9821408-5-7(1))* Faithful Life Pubs.

Slegers, Liesbet. Fall Leaves. 2012. (Clavis Toddler: Daily Life Ser.). (ENG.). 12p. (J). (gr. k — 1). bds. 5.95 *(978-1-60537-122-1(X))* Cobblestone Publishing Co.

Smith, Sharon. Speedy the Squirrel. 2012. 32p. pap. 17.25 *(978-1-4669-6438-9(3))* Trafford Publishing.

Smythe, Katie. Squirrel Gets Ready. 2015. (Rosen REAL Readers: STEM & STEAM Collection). (ENG.). 8p. pap. 5.46 *(978-1-4994-9611-6(7)*, Rosen Classroom) Rosen Publishing Group, Inc., The.

Snider, Kc. Silence. Snider, Kc, illus. 2013. (Illus.). 28p. 19.95 *(978-1-61633-437-6(1))* Guardian Angel Publishing, Inc.

The Snowman, 6 vols., Pack. (Chiquilibros Ser.). (gr. k-1). 23.00 *(978-0-7635-0417-5(3))* Rigby Education.

The Snowman: Individual Title Six-Pack. (Story Steps Ser.). (gr. k-2). 20.00 *(978-0-7635-9578-4(0))* Rigby Education.

Sommer, Carl. No One Will Ever Know. Budwine, Greg, illus. 2014. (J). pap. *(978-1-57537-962-3(7))* Advance Publishing, Inc.

—No One Will Ever Know. 2003. (Another Sommer-Time Story Ser.). (Illus.). 48p. (J). (gr. 1-4). 16.95 incl. audio *(978-1-57537-555-7(9))* Advance Publishing, Inc.

—No One Will Ever Know. Westbrook, Dick, illus. 2003. (Another Sommer-Time Story Ser.). (ENG.). 48p. (J). (gr. 1-4). 16.95 incl. audio compact disk *(978-1-57537-506-9(0))* Advance Publishing, Inc.

—No One Will Ever Know(Nadie Se Va a Enterar) Westbrook, Dick, illus. 2009. (Another Sommer-Time Story Bilingual Ser.). (SPA & ENG.). 48p. (J). lib. bdg. 16.95 *(978-1-57537-163-4(4))* Advance Publishing, Inc.

Sparks, Joanne. Mr. Squirrel. Sparks, Jolene, illus. 2009. 29p. pap. 24.95 *(978-1-61546-375-6(5))* America Star Bks.

Spellman, Frankie. Pinky & Bubs' Stinky Night Out. Spellman, Susan, illus. 2005. (ENG.). 32p. (J). (gr. -1-3). per. 12.95 *(978-1-933002-16-3(6))* PublishingWorks.

Stauffacher, Sue. Show Time. Lamont, Priscilla, illus. 2011. (Animal Rescue Team Ser.). (ENG.). 160p. (J). (gr. 3-7). 5.99 *(978-0-375-85134-6(8)*, Yearling) Random Hse. Children's Bks.

Stein, David Ezra. Ol' Mama Squirrel. Stein, David Ezra, illus. 2013. (ENG., Illus.). 32p. (J). (gr. -1-k). 16.99 *(978-0-399-25672-1(5)*, Nancy Paulsen Books) Penguin Young Readers Group.

Steiner, Dawn. The Silver Squirrel & Friends: The Original Book. 2009. 16p. pap. 8.99 *(978-1-4389-2944-6(7))* AuthorHouse.

—Silver Squirrel & Friends I Can Read Edition: For Beginner Readers. 2009. 16p. pap. 8.99 *(978-1-4389-2916-3(1))* AuthorHouse.

Stone, Chuck. Squizzy the Black Squirrel: A Fabulous Fable of Friendship. Jackson, Jeannie, tr. Jackson, Jeannie, illus. 2003. 30p. (J). 16.95 *(978-0-940880-71-9(7))* Open Hand Publishing, LLC.

Summerville, Justin. Forgetful Freddie. 2013. 44p. 17.99 *(978-0-9890288-1-3(X))* Mindstir Media.

Swallow, Pamela Curtis & Swallow, Pamela C. Groundhog Gets a Say. Bunkus, Denise, illus. 2007. (ENG.). 40p. (J). (gr. k-3). pap. 6.99 *(978-0-14-240896-4(4)*, Puffin Books) Penguin Young Readers Group.

Tafuri, Nancy. The Busy Little Squirrel. Tafuri, Nancy, illus. 2010. (Classic Board Bks.). (ENG., Illus.). 34p. (J). (gr. -1 — 1). bds. 7.99 *(978-1-4424-0721-3(2)*, Little Simon) Little Simon.

—The Busy Little Squirrel. Tafuri, Nancy, illus. 2007. (ENG., Illus.). 32p. (J). (gr. -1-3). 17.99 *(978-0-689-87341-6(7)*, Simon & Schuster Bks. For Young Readers) Simon & Schuster Bks. For Young Readers.

Taher, Amr. Jimmy the Squirrel. Taher, Layal, ed. Graphics, Nataly, illus. 2011. 36p. (J). 14.99 *(978-1-4567-3526-5(8))* AuthorHouse.

Tatsuyama, Sayuri. Happy Happy Clover, Vol. 4. Tatsuyama, Sayuri, illus. 2010. (ENG., Illus.). 192p. (J). pap. 7.99 *(978-1-4215-2735-2(9))* Viz Media.

Taylor, Anna. Sophia's Favorite Squirrel Browny. 2013. 24p. pap. 9.95 *(978-0-9891694-7-9(2))* Barringer Publishing.

Taylor, Pat Eytcheson. Scamper Tangles with Christmas. 2012. 56p. pap. 15.00 *(978-0-9845630-4-3(0))* Catch-A-Winner Publishing.

Tela, Carl M. Squnky's Big Awakening. Tela, Donna L., illus. 2009. 140p. pap. 14.99 *(978-1-4251-8145-1(7))* Trafford Publishing.

Terrell, Andrea M. The Adventures of Sammy the Squirrel: Buying Shoes. Mitchell, Anthony W., illus. 2008. (ENG.). 28p. pap. 13.99 *(978-1-4343-5608-6(6))* AuthorHouse.

Theodoridou, Despoina. Lola, the Lonely Doctor. 2012. (Illus.). 24p. pap. 15.99 *(978-1-4691-6637-7(2))* Xlibris Corp.

Thomson, Malcolm. Let's Go Nuts. 2012. (Illus.). 48p. pap. 24.40 *(978-1-4772-3913-1(8))* AuthorHouse.

Thorpe, Linda W. Teeny-Weeny's Two Front Teeth. 2007. (Illus.). 16p. (J). 6.95 *(978-0-9799671-0-8(4))* ThunderBolt Publishing.

Tollefson, Carol. McTavich That Rascal Squirrel. 2015. (ENG., Illus.). 20p. pap. 12.00 *(978-1-62288-101-7(X))* Austin, Stephen F. State Univ. Pr.

Tossell, David H. Charlie & Chippo Meet a Ghost. Pritchard, Louise, illus. 2012. 24p. pap. *(978-1-908773-25-8(1))* Iponymous Publishing, Ltd.

Utsler, Elaine. The Black Cherry Forest: Storybook 1. Wendle, Stan, ed. Jeannotte, Lawrence, illus. 2nd ed. 2003. 48p. (J). per. 6.95 *(978-0-9727787-1-8(3)*, BCF1B) EV Publishing Corp.

van Genechten, Guido. Ricky & the Squirrel. van Genechten, Guido, illus. 2010. (Ricky Ser.). (ENG., Illus.). 30p. (J). (gr. -1-k). 16.95 *(978-1-60537-078-1(9))* Cobblestone Publishing Co.

Vande Velde, Vivian. Squirrel in the House. Björkman, Steve, illus. (ENG.). 80p. (J). 2017. pap. 6.99 ***(978-0-8234-3877-8(5))*** 2016. 15.95 *(978-0-8234-3633-0(0))* Holiday Hse., Inc.

Vil, Steve. Arvid & Hornschwatz Go Skunk Scoffing. Witt, Eddie, illus. 2011. 32p. pap. 24.95 *(978-1-4560-6043-5(0))* America Star Bks.

Voake, Steve. Daisy Dawson & the Secret Pond. Meserve, Jessica, illus. 2010. (Daisy Dawson Ser.: 2). (ENG.). 96p. (J). (gr. 1-4). pap. 5.99 *(978-0-7636-4730-8(6))* Candlewick Pr.

Wall, Billy James. The Mystery of Marcy & the Stony Squirrel. 2009. 40.00 *(978-1-61584-580-4(1))* Independent Pub.

Wallace, Nancy K. The Haunted Sleepover, 1 vol. Chronister, Amanda, illus. 2013. (Abby & the Book Bunch Ser.). (ENG.). 80p. (J). (gr. 2-5). 27.07 *(978-1-61641-913-4(X))* Magic Wagon.

Walter-Goodspeed, Dee Dee. Friends Will Be There Forever. Jones, Ayanna, illus. 2012. 26p. (J). (-18). pap. 15.99 *(978-1-933846-36-1(4))* Fairwood Pr.

Watt, Mélanie. Scaredy Squirrel. Watt, Mélanie, illus. (ENG., Illus.). 40p. (J). (gr. -1-3). 2008. pap. 7.95 *(978-1-55453-023-6(7))* 2006. 16.95 *(978-1-55337-959-1(4))* Kids Can Pr., Ltd. CAN. Dist: Hachette Bk. Group.

—Scaredy Squirrel. 2011. (J). (gr. -1-3). 18.95 *(978-0-545-32752-7(0))*; 29.95 *(978-0-545-32740-4(7))*;Set. 38.75 *(978-0-545-32759-6(8))* Weston Woods Studios, Inc.

—Scaredy Squirrel at Night. Watt, Mélanie, illus. 2009. (ENG., Illus.). 32p. (J). (gr. -1-3). 16.95 *(978-1-55453-288-9(4))* Kids Can Pr., Ltd. CAN. Dist: Hachette Bk. Group.

—Scaredy Squirrel at the Beach. Watt, Mélanie, illus. 2012. (ENG., Illus.). 32p. (J). (gr. -1-3). pap. 7.95 *(978-1-55453-462-3(3))* Kids Can Pr., Ltd. CAN. Dist: Hachette Bk. Group.

—Scaredy Squirrel at the Beach. Watt, Mélanie, illus. 2008. (ENG., Illus.). 32p. (J). (gr. -1-3). 15.95 *(978-1-55453-225-4(6))* Kids Can Pr., Ltd. CAN. Dist: Hachette Bk. Group.

—Scaredy Squirrel Goes Camping. Watt, Mélanie, illus. 2013. (ENG., Illus.). 32p. (J). (gr. -1-3). pap. 16.95 *(978-1-894786-86-7(6))* Kids Can Pr., Ltd. CAN. Dist: Hachette Bk. Group.

—Scaredy Squirrel Has a Birthday Party, 0 vols. Watt, Mélanie, illus. (ENG., Illus.). 32p. (J). (gr. -1-3). 2014. pap. 7.95 *(978-1-55453-716-7(9))* 2011. 16.95 *(978-1-55453-468-5(2))* Kids Can Pr., Ltd. CAN. Dist: Hachette Bk. Group.

—Scaredy Squirrel Makes a Friend. Watt, Mélanie, illus. 2007. (ENG., Illus.). 32p. (J). (gr. -1-3). 16.95 *(978-1-55453-181-3(0))* Kids Can Pr., Ltd. CAN. Dist: Hachette Bk. Group.

—Scaredy Squirrel Prepares for Christmas. Watt, Mélanie, illus. 2012. (ENG., Illus.). 80p. (J). (gr. -1-3). 17.95 *(978-1-55453-469-2(0))* Kids Can Pr., Ltd. CAN. Dist: Hachette Bk. Group.

—Scaredy Squirrel Prepares for Halloween. Watt, Mélanie, illus. 2013. (ENG., Illus.). 64p. (J). (gr. -1-3). 17.95 *(978-1-894786-87-4(4))* Kids Can Pr., Ltd. CAN. Dist: Hachette Bk. Group.

West, Karen L. Tommy the Squirrel Wants to Be Human. 2009. 24p. pap. 12.99 *(978-1-4389-8096-6(5))* AuthorHouse.

Wheat, Tiffany. There's a Gopher in My Garden! 2013. (ENG., Illus.). (J). (gr. -1-3). pap. 9.95 *(978-1-62086-463-0(0))* Mascot Bks., Inc.

Willett, Christie. Isabella. 2011. 52p. (gr. -1). pap. 19.39 *(978-1-4269-6387-2(4))* Trafford Publishing.

Williamgoldenpen. Quacker's Bedtime Stories. 2006. 49p. pap. 16.95 *(978-1-4241-2236-3(8))* PublishAmerica, Inc.

Williams, Antonio. A Day in the World of Todd the Squirrel. 2011. 28p. pap. 12.82 *(978-1-4634-4408-2(7))* AuthorHouse.

Williams, Greg. Airmont the Flying Squirrel. 2011. 30p. pap. 19.00 *(978-1-60746-219-4(2))* FastPrncil, Inc.

Williams, Levester. The Adventures od Crunchy & Munchy Squirrel: Field Nuts. 2005. pap. *(978-0-9774418-0-8(6))* L.Patrick Publishing.

Williams, M. Ed. Friends in the Meadow - Squirrels the Frolics of Scamp & Scooter. 2013. 72p. pap. *(978-1-77067-429-5(2))* FriesenPress.

Windhorst, Brenda. Do You Want a Henry Story? 2011. 24p. pap. 15.99 *(978-1-4628-8796-5(1))* Xlibris Corp.

Wright, Craig. Silly Squirrel. 2010. (ENG., Illus.). 20p. 4.81 *(978-0-19-440076-3(X))* Oxford Univ. Pr., Inc.

Yalmeh, Jacklin. Scruffy & the Blue Hazelnut Tree. 2013. 38p. pap. 10.95 *(978-0-9885898-1-0(8))* i ZGOOL Media.

—Scruffy & the Walnuts. 2013. 38p. pap. 10.95 *(978-0-9885898-2-7(6))* i ZGOOL Media.

Yang, Stella, illus. The Snowman, 6 vols., Pack. (Sails Literacy Ser.). 16p. (gr. k-18). 27.00 *(978-0-7635-4439-3(6))* Rigby Education.

Yolen, Jane. Trash Mountain. Monroe, Chris, illus. 2015. (J). 17.32 *(978-1-4677-7170-2(8))*; (ENG.). 184p. (gr. 3-6). 16.99 *(978-1-4677-1234-7(5))* Lerner Publishing Group. (Carolrhoda Bks.).

Young, Miriam. Miss Suzy. Lobel, Arnold, illus. (J). 40th anniv. ed. 2004. 44p. 18.95 *(978-1-930900-28-8(7))* 50th ed. 2014. (ENG.). 40p. (gr. -1-3). 18.95 *(978-1-930900-75-2(9))* Purple Hse. Pr.

Young, Sandra M. Daniel, the Little Red Squirrel: Learns His Lessons. 2008. 40p. pap. 18.49 *(978-1-4389-1844-0(5))* AuthorHouse.

Youngberg, Yvette M. The Tooting Squirrel. 2009. (Illus.). 20p. pap. 10.95 *(978-1-4389-1967-6(0))* AuthorHouse.

SRI LANKA

Berlatsky, Noah. Sri Lanka. Greenhaven Press Editors & Gale Editors, eds. 2014. (Genocide & Persecution Ser.). (ENG., Illus.). 240p. (gr. 10-12). lib. bdg. 42.00 *(978-0-7377-6900-5(9)*, Greenhaven Pr., Inc.) Cengage Gale.

Hoffmann, Sara. Sri Lanka in Pictures. 2006. (Visual Geography Series, Second Ser.). (ENG., Illus.). 80p. (gr. 5-12). lib. bdg. 31.93 *(978-0-8225-3481-5(9))* Lerner Publishing Group.

O'Brien, Cynthia. Cultural Traditions in Sri Lanka. 2017. 32p. (J). ***(978-0-7787-8099-1(6))*** Crabtree Publishing Co.

SRI LANKA—FICTION

Isbell, Tessa J. Animal Adventures: Goosey & Beauty Take a Mystery Magic Carpet Ride to Jamaica. 2013. 48p. pap. 21.99 *(978-1-4669-7217-9(3))* Trafford Publishing.

Lipp, Frederick J. Tea Leaves. Coloma, Lester, tr. Coloma, Lester, illus. 2003. (J). 32p. (gr. 1-6). 15.95 *(978-1-59034-998-4(9))*; 33p. pap. *(978-1-59034-999-1(7))* Mondo Publishing.

Selvadurai, Shyam. Swimming in the Monsoon Sea. 2007. (ENG.). 280p. (YA). (gr. 9-12). per. 12.95 (978-0-88776-834-7(2), Tundra Bks.) Tundra Bks. CAN. Dist: Penguin Random Hse. LLC.

Wamasuriya, Chandrani. Favorite Folktales of Sri Lank. 2007. 108p. per. 19.95 (978-1-4241-9965-5(4)) America Star Bks.

STABILIZATION IN INDUSTRY

see Economic History

STAGE

see Acting; Actors and Actresses; Theater

STAGE SCENERY

see Theaters—Stage Setting and Scenery

STAGE SETTING

see Theaters—Stage Setting and Scenery

STAINED GLASS

see Glass Painting and Staining

STAIRCASES

Hicks, Kelli. Escalators. 2014. (ENG., Illus.). 24p. (J). (gr. k-3). 28.50 (978-1-62717-647-7(0)) Rourke Educational Media.

STALIN, JOSEPH, 1879-1953

Benchmark Education Company. Three Twentieth Century Dictators (Teacher Guide) 2004. (978-1-4108-2593-3(0)) Benchmark Education Co.

Joihnson, Robert, compiled by. Lenin, Stalin & Communist Russia: The Myth & Reality of Communism. 2003. (Studymates Ser.). (Illus.). 132p. (C). pap. 27.50 (978-1-84285-039-8(3)) GLMP Ltd. GBR. Dist: Chicago Distribution Ctr.

Jukes, Geoffrey & O'Neill, Robert John. World War II: The Eastern Front 1941-1945. 2010. (World War II: Essential Histories Ser.). (Illus.). 96p. (YA). (gr. 9-12). lib. bdg. 33.25 (978-1-4358-9134-0(1)) Rosen Publishing Group, Inc., The.

McCollum, Sean. Joseph Stalin. 2010. (Wicked History Ser.). (ENG.). 128p. (J). (gr. 6-12). pap. 5.95 (978-0-531-22355-0(8)); (Illus.). 31.00 (978-0-531-20755-0(2)) Scholastic Library Publishing. (Watts, Franklin).

Ruby, India. Three Twentieth Century Dictators: Set Of 6. 2011. (Navigators Ser.). (J). pap. 50.00 net. (978-1-4108-2578-0(7)) Benchmark Education Co.

Zuehlke, Jeffrey. Joseph Stalin. 2006. (Biography Ser.). (Illus.). 112p. (J). (gr. 3-7). lib. bdg. 27.93 (978-0-8225-3421-1(5), Twenty-First Century Bks.) Lerner Publishing Group.

STALINGRAD, BATTLE OF, VOLGOGRAD, RUSSIA, 1942-1943

Wilson, John. Four Steps to Death. 2005. (ENG.). 208p. (YA). (gr. 7-9). 7.95 (978-1-55337-705-4(2)) Kids Can Pr., Ltd. CAN. Dist: Hachette Bk. Group.

STAMINA, PHYSICAL

see Physical Fitness

STAMPS, POSTAGE

see Postage Stamps

STANDARD OF VALUE

see Money

STANDARD TIME

see Time

STANDISH, MYLES, 1584?-1656

Davis, Daniel K. Miles Standish. 2010. (Leaders of the Colonial Era Ser.). 120p. (gr. 5-8). 35.00 (978-1-60413-739-2(8), Chelsea Hse.) Facts On File, Inc.

Harness, Cheryl. The Adventurous Life of Myles Standish & the Amazing-but-True Survival Story of Plymouth Colony. Harness, Cheryl, illus. 2006. (Cheryl Harness Histories Ser.). (ENG., Illus.). 144p. (J). (gr. 5-9). 16.95 (978-0-7922-5918-3(1)); lib. bdg. 25.90 (978-0-7922-5919-0(X)) National Geographic Society. (National Geographic Children's Bks.).

STANLEY, HENRY M. (HENRY MORTON), 1841-1904

Henry Stanley & the Quest for the Source of the Nile. 2014. (ENG.). 176p. (J). (gr. 3-7). pap. 13.95 (978-1-59077-348-2(9)) Evans, M. & Co., Inc.

O'Brien, Cynthia. Explore with Stanley & Livingstone. 2016. (Travel with the Great Explorers Ser.). (ENG., Illus.). 32p. (J). (gr. 3-6). (978-0-7787-2848-1(X)) Crabtree Publishing Co.

STANTON, ELIZABETH CADY, 1815-1902

Adiletta, Dawn. Elizabeth Cady Stanton: Women's Suffrage & the First Vote. (Library of American Lives & Times Ser.). 112p. 2009. (gr. 5-5). 69.20 (978-1-60853-479-1(0)) 2005. (Illus.). (J). (gr. -1-3). lib. bdg. 34.60 (978-1-4042-2647-0(8)) Rosen Publishing Group, Inc., The.

Bohannon, Lisa Frederiksen. Women's Rights & Nothing Less: The Story of Elizabeth Cady Stanton. 2004. (Feminist Voices Ser.). (Illus.). 112p. (YA). (gr. 6-12). 23.95 (978-1-883846-66-4(8), First Biographies) Reynolds, Morgan Inc.

Frey, Wendy. Citizen Heroes. 2007. (Illus.). 68p. (J). (978-1-4105-0888-1(9)); (978-1-4105-0887-4(0)) Johnston, Don Inc.

Fry, Erin. The Power of Friendship. 2005. (Illus.). 16p. (J). pap. (978-0-7367-2920-8(8)) Zaner-Bloser, Inc.

Isecke, Harriet. Susan B. Anthony & Elizabeth Cady Stanton: Early Suffragists, 1 vol. 2011. (Primary Source Readers Ser.). (ENG., Illus.). 32p. (J). (gr. 4-4). pap. 8.99 (978-1-4333-1506-0(8)) Teacher Created Materials, Inc.

Kent, Deborah. Elizabeth Cady Stanton: Founder of the Women's Suffrage Movement. 2016. (Heroes of the Women's Suffrage Movement Ser.). 128p. (J). (gr. 6-6). 37.27 (978-0-7660-7889-5(2)) Enslow Pubs., Inc.

—Elizabeth Cady Stanton: Woman Knows the Cost of Life. 2010. (Americans—the Spirit of a Nation Ser.). (Illus.). 128p. (J). lib. bdg. 33.27 (978-0-7660-3357-3(0)) Enslow Pubs., Inc.

Marigorz, Juliet. Elizabeth Cady Stanton & the Fight for Equal Rights. 2009. (Real Life Readers Ser.). 32p. (gr. 4-6). pap. 10.00 (978-1-4358-0233-9(0), Rosen Classroom) Rosen Publishing Group, Inc., The.

Mattern, Joanne. Elizabeth Cady Stanton & Susan B. Anthony: Fighting Together for Women's Rights. (Women Who Shaped History Ser.). 24p. 2009. (gr. 2-3). 42.50 (978-1-60854-818-7(X)) 2003. (Illus.). (J). lib. bdg. 22.60 (978-0-8239-6503-8(1)) Rosen Publishing Group, Inc., The. (PowerKids Pr.).

Rappaport, Doreen. Elizabeth Started All the Trouble. Faulkner, Matt, illus. 2016. (ENG.). 40p. (J). (gr. 1-3). 17.99 (978-0-7868-5142-3(2)) Disney Pr.

Shea, Nicole. Elizabeth Cady Stanton in Her Own Words. 2014. (Eyewitness to History Ser.). 32p. (J). (gr. 4-6). pap. 63.00 (978-1-4824-1201-7(2)) Stevens, Gareth Publishing LLLP.

Stone, Tanya Lee. Elizabeth Leads the Way: Elizabeth Cady Stanton & the Right to Vote. Gibbon, Rebecca, illus. 2008. (ENG.). 32p. (J). (gr. 1-5). 18.99 (978-0-8050-7903-6(3), 9780805079036, Holt, Henry & Co. Bks. For Young Readers) Holt, Henry & Co.

—Elizabeth Leads the Way: Elizabeth Cady Stanton & the Right to Vote. Gibbon, Rebecca, illus. 2010. (ENG.). 32p. (J). (gr. 1-5). pap. 8.99 (978-0-312-60236-9(7), 9780312602369) Square Fish.

STANTON, WILL (FICTITIOUS CHARACTER)—FICTION

Cooper, Susan. The Dark Is Rising. 2009. 7.64 (978-0-7848-2212-8(3), Everbind) Marco Bk. Co.

—The Dark Is Rising. 15.85 (978-0-7569-8464-9(5)) Perfection Learning Corp.

—The Dark Is Rising. (Dark Is Rising Sequence Ser.). 244p. (YA). (gr. 5-18). pap. 4.99 (978-0-8072-1533-3(3), Listening Library) Random Hse. Audio Publishing Group.

STARFISHES

Coldiron, Deborah. Starfish, 1 vol. 2007. (Underwater World Ser.). (ENG., Illus.). 32p. (J). (gr. 3-7). 27.07 (978-1-59928-813-0(3), Buddy Bks.) ABDO Publishing Co.

Fish, Lori Flying. One Shining Starfish. Fish, Lori Flying, illus. 2010. (Illus.). 16p. pap. 9.95 (978-1-936343-12-6(6)) Peppertree Pr., The.

Gay, Marie-Louise. Stella, l'Etoile de Mer. braille ed. 2004. (FRE.). (J). (gr. -1-3). spiral bd. (978-0-616-03072-1(X)) Canadian National Institute for the Blind/Institut National Canadien pour les Aveugles.

Gibbs, Maddie. Sea Stars. 2013. (PowerKids Readers: Fun Fish Ser.). 24p. (J). (gr. k-2). 22.60 (978-1-4777-0760-9(3)); pap. 49.50 (978-1-4777-0854-5(5)); pap. 8.25 (978-1-4777-0853-8(7)) Rosen Publishing Group, Inc., The. (PowerKids Pr.).

—Sea Stars / Las Estrellas de Mar. De La Vega, Eida, ed. 2013. (PowerKids Readers: Fun Fish / Peces Divertidos Ser.). (ENG & SPA.). 24p. (J). (gr. k-2). 22.60 (978-1-4777-1218-4(6), PowerKids Pr.) Rosen Publishing Group, Inc., The.

Gray, Susan H. Sea Star. 2014. (21st Century Skills Library: Exploring Our Oceans Ser.). (ENG., Illus.). 32p. (J). (gr. 3-6). 28.50 (978-1-63188-023-0(3), 205499) Cherry Lake Publishing.

Halfmann, Janet. Star of the Sea: A Day in the Life of a Starfish. Paley, Joan, illus. 2011. (ENG.). 32p. (J). (gr. k-2). 17.99 (978-0-8050-9073-4(8), 9780805090734, Holt, Henry & Co. Bks. For Young Readers) Holt, Henry & Co.

Herriges, Ann. Sea Stars. 2006. (Oceans Alive Ser.). (ENG., Illus.). 24p. (J). (gr. k-3). lib. bdg. 25.95 (978-1-60014-021-1(1)) Bellwether Media.

James, Helen Foster. Discover Sea Stars. 2015. (21st Century Basic Skills Library: Splash! Ser.). (ENG., Illus.). 24p. (J). (gr. 2-4). pap. 12.79 (978-1-63362-696-6(2), 206609) Cherry Lake Publishing.

Jones, Tammy. At the Shore. 2009. (Sight Word Readers Set A Ser.). (J). 3.49 net. (978-1-60719-137-7(7)) Newmark Learning LLC.

Kenan, Tessa. Look, a Starfish! 2016. (Bumba Books (tm) — I See Ocean Animals Ser.). (ENG., Illus.). 24p. (J). (gr. -1-1). 25.32 (978-1-5124-1423-3(9)) Lerner Publishing Group.

—¡Mira, una Estrella de Mar! (Look, a Starfish!) 2017. (Bumba Books (tm) en Español — Veo Animales Marinos (I See Ocean Animals) Ser.). (SPA., Illus.). 24p. (J). (gr. -1-1). 25.32 (978-1-5124-2869-8(8)) Lerner Publishing Group.

Laughlin, Kara L. Sea Stars. 2017. (In the Deep Blue Sea Ser.). (ENG.). 24p. (J). (gr. k-3). lib. bdg. 27.07 (978-1-5038-1693-0(1), 211527) Child's World, Inc., The.

Lunis, Natalie. Prickly Sea Stars. (No Backbone! Marine Invertebrates Ser.). 24p. (J). (gr. k-3). 2016. (ENG.). pap. 7.95 (**978-1-944998-77-6(2)**) 2007. (Illus.). lib. bdg. 21.28 (978-1-59716-508-2(5)) Bearport Publishing Co., Inc.

Meister, Cari. Sea Stars. 2012. (ENG., Illus.). 24p. (J). lib. bdg. 25.65 (978-1-62031-012-0(0)) Jump! Inc.

Metz, Lorijo. Discovering Starfish. 2012. (Along the Shore Ser.). (Illus.). 24p. (J). (gr. k-3). lib. bdg. 22.60 (978-1-4488-4996-3(9)) Rosen Publishing Group, Inc., The.

Mitchell, Susan K. Biggest vs. Smallest Sea Creatures. 2010. (Biggest vs. Smallest Animals Ser.). (Illus.). 24p. (J). 22.60 (978-0-7660-3580-5(8), Enslow Elementary) Enslow Pubs., Inc.

Nagelhout, Ryan. Sea Stars. 2013. (Underwater World Ser.). (Illus.). 24p. (J). (gr. k-2). pap. 8.15 (978-1-4339-8572-0(1)); lib. bdg. 22.60 (978-1-4339-8571-3(3)) Stevens, Gareth Publishing LLLP.

—Sea Stars: Estrellas de Mar. 2013. (Underwater World / el Mundo Submarino Ser.). (SPA & ENG., Illus.). 24p. (J). (gr. k-2). lib. bdg. 22.60 (978-1-4339-8782-3(1)) Stevens, Gareth Publishing LLLP.

Pettiford, Rebecca. Sea Stars. (Sea Stars Ser.). 24p. (J). (gr. k-3). 2017. pap. 6.99 (**978-1-61891-268-8(2)**) 2016. (ENG., Illus.). 25.95 (978-1-62617-421-4(0)) Bellwether Media. (Blastoff! Readers).

Schaefer, Lola M. Sea Stars [Scholastic]. 2009. (Ocean Life Ser.). 24p. (gr. k-1). pap. 2.99 (978-1-4296-3678-0(5), Pebble Bks.) Capstone Press of Coughlan Cos.

Schuh, Mari C. Sea Stars. 2015. (Sea Life Ser.). (ENG., Illus.). 24p. (gr. k-1). lib. bdg. 26.65 (978-1-4914-6044-3(X)) Capstone Press of Coughlan Cos.

Stone, Lynn M. Sea Stars. 2005. (Rourke Discovery Library). (Illus.). 24p. (J). (gr. -1-3). lib. bdg. 21.36 (978-1-59515-442-2(6)) Rourke Educational Media.

Sullivan, Jody. Sea Stars [Scholastic]. 2010. (Under the Sea Ser.). 24p. pap. 0.50 (978-1-4296-5066-3(4), Pebble Plus) Capstone Press of Coughlan Cos.

Trueit, Trudi Strain. Starfish. 2010. (Benchmark Rebus: Ocean Life Ser.). 24p. (gr. k-1). 15.95 (978-0-7614-4894-5(2)) Marshall Cavendish Corp.

Zuchora-Walske, Christine. Spiny Sea Stars. 2003. (Pull Ahead Bks.). (Illus.). 32p. (J). (gr. k-2). pap. 6.95 (978-0-8225-3770-0(2)) Lerner Publishing Group.

STARLINGS

Bronson, Wilfrid S., illus. Starlings. 2008. 84p. (J). pap. 18.95 (978-0-86534-649-9(5)) Sunstone Pr.

Gray, Susan H. Starling. 2008. (21st Century Skills Library: Animal Invaders Ser.). (ENG.). 32p. (gr. 4-8). lib. bdg. 28.50 (978-1-60279-113-8(9), 200109) Cherry Lake Publishing.

STARR, BELLE, 1848-1899

Green, Carl R. & Sanford, William R. Belle Starr. rev. ed. 2008. (Outlaws & Lawmen of the Wild West, Revised Edition Ser.). (Illus.). 48p. (J). (gr. 5-18). lib. bdg. 25.27 (978-0-7660-3176-0(4)) Enslow Pubs., Inc.

Rau, Margaret. Belle of the West: The True Story of Belle Starr. 2004. (Women of the Frontier Ser.). (Illus.). 160p. (YA). (gr. 6-12). 23.95 (978-1-883846-68-8(4), First Biographies) Reynolds, Morgan Inc.

Sargent, Dave & Sargent, Pat. Lily: (Lilac Dun) A Second Chance, 30 vols., Vol. 38. Lenoir, Jane, illus. 2003. (Saddle up Ser.: Vol. 38). 42p. (J). pap. 10.95 (978-1-56763-698-7(5)); lib. bdg. 23.60 (978-1-56763-697-0(7)) Ozark Publishing.

STARR, EMILY (FICTITIOUS CHARACTER)—FICTION

see Starr, Emily Byrd (Fictitious Character)—Fiction

STARR, EMILY BYRD (FICTITIOUS CHARACTER)—FICTION

Montgomery, L. M. Emily Climbs. 2014. (ENG.). 384p. (J). (gr. 4-9). pap. 10.99 (978-1-84408-989-5(4), Virago Press) Little, Brown Book Group Ltd. GBR. Dist: Hachette Bk. Group.

—Emily of New Moon. 2014. (ENG.). 416p. (J). (gr. 4-9). pap. 10.99 (978-1-84408-988-8(6), Virago Press) Little, Brown Book Group Ltd. GBR. Dist: Hachette Bk. Group.

—Emily's Quest. 2014. (ENG.). 272p. (J). (gr. 4-9). pap. 10.99 (978-1-84408-987-1(8), Virago Press) Little, Brown Book Group Ltd. GBR. Dist: Hachette Bk. Group.

STARS

see also Astrology; Astronomy; Astrophysics; Meteors; Planets; Solar System

Adamson, Thomas K. Stars [Scholastic]. 2011. (Exploring the Galaxy Ser.). 24p. pap. 0.50 (978-1-4296-6291-8(3), Pebble Plus) Capstone Press of Coughlan Cos.

Anderson, Michael. The Sun, Stars, & Galaxies. 2011. (Illus.). 96p. (J). lib. bdg. 31.70 (978-1-61530-519-3(X)) Rosen Publishing Group, Inc., The.

Asimov, Isaac & Hantula, Richard. The Life & Death of Stars. 2005. (Isaac Asimov's 21st Century Library of the Universe). (Illus.). 32p. (gr. 2-6). lib. bdg. 26.00 (978-0-8368-3967-8(6), Gareth Stevens Learning Library) Stevens, Gareth Publishing LLLP.

—A Stargazer's Guide. 2005. (Isaac Asimov's 21st Century Library of the Universe). (Illus.). 32p. (gr. 2-6). lib. bdg. 26.00 (978-0-8368-3953-1(6), Gareth Stevens Learning Library) Stevens, Gareth Publishing LLLP.

Aspen-Baxter, Linda & Kissock, Heather. Las Estrellas. 2012. (Mirando Al Cielo Ser.). (SPA., Illus.). 24p. (J). (gr. k-2). lib. bdg. 27.13 (978-1-61913-218-4(4), AV2 by Weigl) Weigl Pubs., Inc.

Asselin, Kristine Carlson. Stars, 1 vol. 2011. (Solar System & Beyond Ser.). (ENG., 32p. (gr. 3-4). Illus.). pap. 8.10 (978-1-4296-6243-7(3)); pap. 47.70 (978-1-4296-6411-0(8)) Capstone Press of Coughlan Cos. (Fact Finders).

Austen, Mary. Andromeda. 2015. (Constellation Collection). (ENG., Illus.). 24p. (J). (gr. 3-3). pap. 8.25 (978-1-4994-0931-4(1), PowerKids Pr.) Rosen Publishing Group, Inc., The.

Bellisario, Gina. To the Stars! Moran, Mike, illus. 2017. (Cloverleaf Books (tm) — Space Adventures Ser.). (ENG.). 24p. (J). (gr. k-2). 25.32 (978-1-5124-2537-6(0)); 6.99 (**978-1-5124-3897-0(9)**); 38.65 (**978-1-5124-3896-3(0)**); 38.65 (**978-1-5124-2834-6(5)**) Lerner Publishing Group. (Millbrook Pr.).

Berger, Melvin & Berger, Gilda. Planets. 2010. (Scholastic True or False Ser.: 9). (ENG.). 48p. (J). (gr. 2-5). pap. 4.99 (978-0-545-20204-6(3), Scholastic Paperbacks) Scholastic, Inc.

Berne, Emma Carlson. Totally Wacky Facts about Planets & Stars. 2015. (Mind Benders Ser.). (ENG., Illus.). 112p. (gr. 1-3). lib. bdg. 23.32 (978-1-4914-6523-3(9)) Capstone Press of Coughlan Cos.

Bredeson, Carmen. What Are Stars? 2008. (I Like Space! Ser.). (Illus.). 32p. (J). (gr. 3-7). lib. bdg. 23.94 (978-0-7660-2943-9(3), Enslow Elementary) Enslow Pubs., Inc.

Bredeson, Carmen & Dyson, Marianne. Exploring the Stars. 2015. (Launch into Space! Ser.). (ENG.). 32p. (J). (gr. 3-4). pap. 10.52 (978-0-7660-6829-2(3)) Enslow Pubs., Inc.

Bredeson, Carmen, et al. Exploring the Stars. 2015. (Launch into Space! Ser.). (ENG., Illus.). 32p. (J). (gr. 3-4). 25.27 (978-0-7660-6831-5(5)) Enslow Pubs., Inc.

Buchanan, Shelly. Stars. 2015. (Science Readers: Content & Literacy Ser.). (Illus.). 32p. (gr. 5-5). pap. 8.99 (978-1-4807-4728-9(9)) Teacher Created Materials, Inc.

Burton, Margie, et al. Counting Stars. 2011. (Early Connections Ser.). (J). (978-1-61672-519-8(2)) Benchmark Education Co.

Capstone Press Staff. The Story of Cassiopeia: A Roman Constellation Myth, 1 vol. Squier, Robert, illus. 2012. (Night Sky Stories Ser.). (ENG.). 24p. (gr. 2-3). lib. bdg. 26.65 (978-1-4048-7376-6(7)) Picture Window Bks.

Channing, Margot. Stars & Planets. 2014. (Closer Look At... Ser.). (Illus.). 32p. (gr. 3-6). 31.35 (978-1-905087-08-2(X), 1374553) Book Hse. GBR. Dist: Black Rabbit Bks.

Crabtree Editors & Wimbush, Jeff. The Stars. 2012. (Journey Through Space Ser.). (ENG.). 24p. (J). (gr. 3-6). lib. bdg. (978-0-7787-5308-7(5)) Crabtree Publishing Co.

Cram101 Textbook Reviews Staff. Outlines & Highlights for in Quest of the Stars & Galaxies by Theo Koupelis, Isbn: 9780763766306. 2014. (ENG.). 214p. (C). pap. 30.95 (978-1-61812-145-5(6)) Cram101 Inc.

Demuth, Patricia Brennan. The Sun: Our Amazing Star. 2016. (Penguin Core Concepts Ser.). (ENG., Illus.). 32p. (J). (gr. -1-1). pap. 3.99 (978-0-448-48828-8(0), Grosset & Dunlap) Penguin Young Readers Group.

Deutsch, Stacia & Cohon, Rhody. Life of a Star: Set Of 6. 2010. (Navigators Ser.). (J). pap. 50.00 net. (978-1-4108-6241-9(0)) Benchmark Education Co.

—Life of a Star: Text Pairs. 2008. (Bridges/Navigators Ser.). (J). (gr. 6). 89.00 (978-1-4108-8444-2(9)) Benchmark Education Co.

Dickmann, Nancy. Exploring Beyond the Solar System. 2015. (Spectacular Space Science Ser.). (ENG., Illus.). 48p. (J). (gr. 5-6). 30.25 (978-1-4994-3641-9(6), Rosen Central) Rosen Publishing Group, Inc., The.

Dilkes, D. H. I See Stars. 2010. (All about Shapes Ser.). (Illus.). 24p. (J). lib. bdg. 22.60 (978-0-7660-3803-5(3), Enslow Elementary) Enslow Pubs., Inc.

Dorling Kindersley Publishing Staff. DK Readers L2: Stars & Galaxies. 2017. (DK Readers Ser.). (ENG., Illus.). 48p. (J). (gr. k-2). pap. 3.99 (978-1-4654-5863-6(8), DK Children) Dorling Kindersley Publishing, Inc.

—Space! 2015. (ENG., Illus.). 208p. (J). (gr. 5-12). 24.99 (978-1-4654-3806-5(8), DK Children) Dorling Kindersley Publishing, Inc.

—Stars & Planets: Glow in the Dark. 2014. (ENG.). 24p. (J). (gr. k-4). 19.99 (978-1-4654-1420-5(7), DK Children) Dorling Kindersley Publishing, Inc.

—Universo. 2016. (SPA., Illus.). 208p. (J). (gr. 5-12). 24.99 (978-1-4654-6088-2(8), DK Children) Dorling Kindersley Publishing, Inc.

Driscoll, Michael. A Child's Introduction to the Night Sky: The Story of the Stars, Planets & Constellations - And How You Can Find Them in the Sky. Hamilton, Meredith, illus. 2004. (ENG.). 96p. (J). (gr. 3-7). tchr. ed. 19.99 (978-1-57912-366-6(X), 81366, Black Dog & Leventhal Pubs. Inc.) Hachette Bks.

Duffey, Gary. Windows. 2012. 16p. pap. 7.95 (978-1-4582-0512-4(6), Abbott Pr.) Author Solutions, Inc.

Dusek, Jiri & Pisala, Jan. Space Atlas. Tuma, Tomas, illus. 2014. (ENG.). 34p. (J). (gr. 1-3). 16.95 (978-1-4549-1237-8(5)) Sterling Publishing Co., Inc.

Las Estrellas. (SPA.). (J). 10.00 (978-84-342-1469-9(5)) Parramon Ediciones S.A. ESP. Dist: Distribuidora Norma, Inc.

Evert, Laura. Planets, Moons, & Stars. Garrow, Linda, illus. 2003. (Take along Guides). (ENG.). 48p. (J). (gr. 2-5). pap. 7.95 (978-1-55971-842-4(0)) Cooper Square Publishing Llc.

Farndon, John. What Do We Know about Stars & Galaxies?, 1 vol. 2011. (Earth, Space, & Beyond Ser.). (ENG.). 48p. (gr. 3-3). pap. 9.49 (978-1-4109-4186-2(8), Raintree Freestyle Express); (gr. 6-6). pap. 9.49 (978-1-4109-4168-8(X), Raintree Freestyle); (gr. 3-3). 34.65 (978-1-4109-4180-0(9), Raintree Freestyle Express); (gr. 6-6). 34.65 (978-1-4109-4162-6(0), Raintree Freestyle) Heinemann-Raintree.

Finton, Nancy. Explore the Solar System! 2010. (Illus.). 29p. (J). (978-0-545-28884-2(3)) Scholastic, Inc.

Fried, Ellen. Stars & Galaxies. 2007. (Reading Expeditions Ser.). (ENG., Illus.). 32p. (J). pap. 17.95 (978-0-7922-4574-2(1)) CENGAGE Learning.

Galat, Joan Marie. Black Holes & Supernovas, 1 vol. 2011. (Solar System & Beyond Ser.). (ENG.). 32p. (gr. 3-4). pap. 8.10 (978-1-4296-7225-2(0)); pap. 47.70 (978-1-4296-7226-9(9)) Capstone Press of Coughlan Cos. (Fact Finders).

Gardner, Robert & Conklin, Joshua. A Kid's Book of Experiments with Stars. 2016. (Surprising Science Experiments Ser.). (ENG.). 48p. (J). (gr. 4-4). pap. 11.70 (978-0-7660-7268-8(1)) Enslow Pubs., Inc.

Gendell, Megan & O'Dea, Tierney. Shoot for the Stars: Everything You Wanted to Know about Astronomy, Stars, & Constellations. 2008. (Illus.). 32p. (J). (978-0-545-04458-5(8)) Scholastic, Inc.

George, Michael. Stars: Beacons in the Sky. 2003. (LifeViews Ser.). (Illus.). 32p. (J). lib. bdg. (978-1-58341-250-3(6), Creative Education) Creative Co., The.

Gifford, Clive. Stars, Galaxies, & the Milky Way. 2015. (Watch This Space! Ser.). (ENG., Illus.). 32p. (J). (gr. 3-7). lib. bdg. (978-0-7787-2022-5(5)) Crabtree Publishing Co.

Goldsmith, Mike. Stars & Planets. 2011. (Navigators Ser.). (ENG., Illus.). 48p. (J). (gr. 4-7). pap. 8.99 (978-0-7534-6682-7(1), 9780753466827, Kingfisher) Roaring Brook Pr.

Goldstein, Margaret. Stars. 2009. pap. 6.95 (978-0-8225-4759-4(7)) Lerner Publishing Group.

Goldstein, Margaret J. Stars. 2003. (Our Universe Ser.). (ENG., Illus.). 32p. (gr. 2-4). lib. bdg. 22.60 (978-0-8225-4646-7(9)) Lerner Publishing Group.

Goldsworthy, Steve. Constellations. 2016. (J). (**978-1-4896-5809-8(2)**, AV2 by Weigl) Weigl Pubs., Inc.

Graham, Ian. Galaxies & Stars. 2015. (Space Ser.). (Illus.). 24p. (gr. 3-6). lib. bdg. 28.50 (978-1-62588-208-0(4)) Black Rabbit Bks.

Graun, Ken. Our Constellations & Their Stars. 2004. (Twenty-First Century Astronomy Ser.: 3). (Illus.). 36p. (J). 15.95 (978-1-928771-09-8(2)) Ken Pr.

Griffin, Ingrid. The Story of the Great Bear. 2015. (Stories in the Stars Ser.). (ENG., Illus.). 24p. (J). (gr. 1-2). pap. 8.15 (978-1-4824-2665-6(X)) Stevens, Gareth Publishing LLLP.

Guillain, Charlotte. Stars, 1 vol. 2009. (Space Ser.). (ENG.). 24p. (gr. -1-1). 21.99 (978-1-4329-2748-6(5), Acorn) Heinemann-Raintree.

Hamilton, S. L. Stars. 2011. (Xtreme Space Ser.). (Illus.). 32p. (gr. 3-9). 27.07 (978-1-61714-741-8(9), A&D Xtreme) ABDO Publishing Co.

Hansen, Rosanna. Seven Wonders of the Sun & Other Stars. 2011. (Seven Wonders Ser.). (ENG.). 80p. (gr. 5-8). 33.26 (978-0-7613-5450-5(6)) Lerner Publishing Group.

Harcourt School Publishers Staff. How the Sky Got Its Starr. 3rd ed. 2004. (Trophies Reading Program Ser.). (Illus.). (gr. k). pap. 11.50 (978-0-15-340895-3(2)) Harcourt Schl. Pubs.

Harrod-Eagles, Cynthia. Stars & Constellations. 2007. (Illus.). 16p. (J). (978-0-545-00734-4(8)) Scholastic, Inc.

How Are Stars Born? 2013. (Space Mysteries Ser.). 32p. (J). (gr. 2-5). pap. 63.00 (978-1-4339-9220-9(5)) Stevens, Gareth Publishing LLLP.

Howard, Fran. Stars, 1 vol. 2008. (Universe Ser.). (ENG.). 32p. (gr. k-4). 27.07 (978-1-59928-931-1(8), Buddy Bks.) ABDO Publishing Co.

Hunter, Nick. Stars & Constellations, 1 vol. 2013. (Night Sky: & Other Amazing Sights in Space Ser.). (ENG.). 32p. (gr. 1-3). 27.32 (978-1-4329-7517-3(X)); pap. 8.95 (978-1-4329-7522-7(6)) Heinemann-Raintree. (Heinemann First Library).

Hutmacher, Kimberly. The Night Sky. 2012. (ENG.). 24p. (gr. 3-4). pap. 8.95 (978-1-61810-225-6(7)) Rourke Educational Media.

S

Jacobson, Ryan. Constellations Activity Book, 1 vol. Nitzsche, Shane, illus. 2012. (Color & Learn Ser.). (ENG.). 64p. (J). (gr. k-5). pap. 6.95 (978-1-59193-325-0(0)) Adventure Pubns.

Jefferis, David. Black Holes: And Other Bizarre Space Objects. 2006. (Science Frontiers Ser.). (ENG., Illus.). 32p. (J). (gr. 4-7). pap. (978-0-7787-2870-2(6), 1253434) Crabtree Publishing Co.

—The Stars: Glowing Spheres in the Sky. 2008. (Exploring our Solar System Ser.). (ENG., Illus.). 32p. (J). (gr. 3-8). pap. (978-0-7787-3743-8(8)) Crabtree Publishing Co.

Kenney, Karen Latchana. The Science of Stars: Exploring Matter, 1 vol. 2016. (Science in Action Ser.). (ENG., Illus.). 32p. (J). (gr. 3-6). 27.07 (978-1-62403-965-2(0)) ABDO Publishing Co.

Keranen, Rachel. The Composition of the Universe: The Evolution of Stars & Galaxies. 2016. (Space Systems Ser.). 112p. (J). 42.79 (978-1-5026-2285-3(8)) Cavendish Square Publishing.

Kim, Flora. Constellations. 2009. (True Book(tm), A — Space Ser.). (ENG.). 48p. (J). (gr. 2-5). 31.00 (978-0-531-16895-0(6)) Scholastic Library Publishing.

Kimmelman, Leslie. Star Pictures. 2005. (IOpeners Ser.). (Illus.). 8p. (J). pap. 7.56 (978-0-7652-5134-3(5)) Celebration Pr.

Kissock, Heather. Stars. 2011. (J). (978-1-61690-601-6(4)); (ENG.). lib. bdg. 27.13 (978-1-61690-955-0(2)) Weigl Pubs., Inc.

Koupelis, Theo. In Quest of the Stars & Galaxies. rev. ed. 2010. (ENG.). 457p. (J). pap. 149.95 (978-0-7637-6630-6(5)) Jones & Bartlett Learning, LLC.

Kubuitsile, Lauri. Stars Yellow Band. 2016. (Cambridge Reading Adventures Ser.). (ENG.). 16p. pap. 6.56 (978-1-316-50315-7(1)) Cambridge Univ. Pr.

Kuskowski, Alex. Stargazing, 1 vol. 2015. (ENG., Illus.). 24p. (J). (978-1-62403-746-7(1)) ABDO Publishing Co.

Lacey, Saskia. Art & Culture: The Stories of Constellations: Shapes (Grade 3) 2017. (Mathematics Readers Ser.). (Illus.). 32p. (gr. 3-3). 8.99 **(978-1-4807-5812-4(4))** Teacher Created Materials, Inc.

Lawrence, Ellen. The Sun: The Star of Our Solar System. 2013. (Zoom into Space Ser.). (Illus.). 24p. (J). (gr. -1-3). lib. bdg. 23.93 (978-1-909673-00-7(5)) Ruby Tuesday Books Limited GBR. Dist: Bearport Publishing Co., Inc.

little bee books, little bee. Listopia: Space. 2016. (ENG., Illus.). 208p. (J). (gr. 2-4). pap. 9.99 (978-1-4998-0280-1(3)) Little Bee Books Inc.

Lois, Lowry. Number the Stars. 2004. 144p. (J). (gr. 5-9). pap. 29.00 incl. audio (978-1-4000-8637-5(X), Listening Library) Random Hse. Audio Publishing Group.

Low, Chen-Chen-Chen. Lizzie May the Immortal. 2008. 70p. pap. 29.99 (978-1-4092-4579-7(9)) Lulu Pr., Inc.

Mack, Gail. The Stars. 2009. (Space!). 64p. (gr. 5-18). lib. bdg. 32.79 (978-0-7614-4250-9(2)) Marshall Cavendish Corp.

Marsh, Laura. National Geographic Readers: Night Sky. 2017. (Readers Ser.). (ENG.). 32p. (J). (gr. k-3). pap. 3.99 **(978-1-4263-2815-2(X)**, National Geographic Children's Bks.) National Geographic Society.

Martin, Justin McCory. Stars. 2010. (Illus.). 16p. (J). (978-0-545-13736-2(5)) Scholastic, Inc.

Massey, Steve. Space, Stars & Planets. 2009. (Young Reed Ser.). (ENG.). 1p. (J). 14.95 (978-1-921073-06-9(3)) New Holland Pubs. Pty, Ltd. AUS. Dist: Tuttle Publishing.

Meachen Rau, Dana. Spots of Light: A Book about Stars, 1 vol. Shea, Denise, illus. 2005. (Amazing Science: Exploring the Sky Ser.). (ENG.). 24p. (J). (gr. k-4). lib. bdg. 25.99 (978-1-4048-1139-3(7), Nonfiction Picture Bks.) Picture Window Bks.

Miller, Ron. Stars & Galaxies. 2006. (Worlds Beyond Ser.). (Illus.). 96p. (J). (gr. 5-9). 27.93 (978-0-7613-3466-8(1), Twenty-First Century Bks.) Lerner Publishing Group.

Mistral, Gabriela. Ronda de Astros. 3rd ed. (SPA., Illus.). 128p. (YA). (gr. 5). 9.95 (978-84-239-9019-1(2), EC5264) Espasa Calpe, S.A. ESP. Dist: Libros Sin Fronteras, Lectorum Pubns., Inc.

Mitchell, Melanie S. Stars. 2004. (First Step Nonfiction). (ENG., Illus.). 24p. (gr. k-2). lib. bdg. 23.93 (978-0-8225-5138-6(1)) Lerner Publishing Group.

—The Stars. 2003. (First Step Nonfiction Ser.). (Illus.). 22p. (J). pap. 5.95 (978-0-8225-3592-8(0), Lerner Pubns.) Lerner Publishing Group.

Mitton, Jacqueline. Once upon a Starry Night: A Book of Constellations. Balit, Christina, illus. 2009. (ENG.). 32p. (J). (gr. 1-4). pap. 8.95 (978-1-4263-0391-3(2), National Geographic Children's Bks.) National Geographic Society.

—Zoo in the Sky: A Book of Animal Constellations. Balit, Christina, illus. 2006. (ENG.). 32p. (J). (gr. 1-4). pap. 7.95 (978-0-7922-5935-0(1), National Geographic Children's Bks.) National Geographic Society.

Mitton, Jacqueline & Balit, Christina. Once upon a Starry Night: A Book of Constellations. 2004. (ENG., Illus.). 32p. (J). (gr. 1-4). 16.95 (978-0-7922-6332-6(4), National Geographic Children's Bks.) National Geographic Society.

Moon, Walt K. Let's Explore the Stars. 2017. (Bumba Books (tm) — a First Look at Space Ser.). (ENG.). 24p. (J). (gr. -1-1). 25.32 **(978-1-5124-3347-0(0))** Lerner Publishing Group.

Moore, David. Expl on Your Own Stories in the Stars. 2009. (Explore on Your Own Ser.). (ENG.). 12p. (C). pap. 7.95 (978-0-7362-5593-6(1)) National Geographic School Publishing, Inc.

Moore, Patrick. First Book of Stars. 2010. (ENG., Illus.). 96p. pap. 22.95 (978-1-84868-291-7(3)) Amberley Publishing GBR. Dist: Independent Pubs. Group.

Nadeau, Isaac. Learning about the Movement of the Sun & Other Stars with Graphic Organizers. 2006. (Graphic Organizers in Science Ser.). (ENG., Illus.). 24p. (gr. 4-6). pap. 8.25 (978-1-4042-5040-6(9), PowerKids Pr.) Rosen Publishing Group, Inc., The.

Nicolson, Cynthia. Discover the Stars. Slavin, Bill, illus. 2006. 32p. (J). lib. bdg. 15.38 (978-1-4242-1196-8(4)) Fitzgerald Bks.

Orr, Tamra. I Spy in the Sky the Stars. 2011. (Randy's Corner Ser.). (Illus.). 32p. (J). (gr. k-3). lib. bdg. 25.70 (978-1-58415-975-9(8)) Mitchell Lane Pubs., Inc.

Owen, Ruth. Supernovas. 2012. (Explore Outer Space Ser.). (ENG., Illus.). 32p. (J). (gr. 3-6). pap. 10.00 (978-1-4488-8119-2(6)); lib. bdg. 25.25 (978-1-4488-8078-2(5)) Windmill Bks.

Parker, Steve. Beyond the Solar System: From Red Giants to Black Holes. 2007. (Earth & Space Ser.). (Illus.). 48p. (YA). (gr. 5-9). lib. bdg. 29.25 (978-1-4042-3739-1(9)) Rosen Publishing Group, Inc., The.

Pasachoff, Jay M. Peterson First Guide to Astronomy. 2nd ed. 2014. (Peterson First Guide Ser.). (ENG., Illus.). 128p. pap. 7.95 (978-0-544-16562-5(4)) Houghton Mifflin Harcourt Publishing Co.

Peddicord, Jane Ann. Night Wonders. 2005. (ENG., Illus.). 32p. (J). (gr. 1-4). pap. 7.95 (978-1-57091-878-0(3)) Charlesbridge Publishing, Inc.

Peters, Elisa. Stars. 2012. (PowerKids Readers: the Universe Ser.). (ENG., Illus.). 24p. (J). (gr. k-2). pap. 8.25 (978-1-4488-7534-4(X)); lib. bdg. 22.60 (978-1-4488-7388-3(6)) Rosen Publishing Group, Inc., The. (PowerKids Pr.).

—Stars: Las Estrellas. 2012. (PowerKids Readers: the Universe / el universo Ser.). (SPA & ENG., Illus.). 24p. (J). (gr. k-2). lib. bdg. 22.60 (978-1-4488-7824-6(1), PowerKids Pr.) Rosen Publishing Group, Inc., The.

Peters, Stephanie. Andromeda. 2003. (Library of Constellations Ser.). (Illus.). 24p. (YA). (gr. 2-5). lib. bdg. 21.25 (978-0-8239-6165-8(6)) Rosen Publishing Group, Inc., The.

—Gemini. 2003. (Library of Constellations Ser.). (Illus.). 24p. (J). lib. bdg. 21.25 (978-0-8239-6167-2(2), PowerKids Pr.) Rosen Publishing Group, Inc., The.

—The Little Dipper. 2003. (Library of Constellations Ser.). (Illus.). 24p. (J). lib. bdg. 21.25 (978-0-8239-6163-4(X), PowerKids Pr.) Rosen Publishing Group, Inc., The.

—Orion. 2003. (Library of Constellations Ser.). (Illus.). 24p. (J). lib. bdg. 21.25 (978-0-8239-6164-1(8), PowerKids Pr.) Rosen Publishing Group, Inc., The.

—Pisces. 2003. (Library of Constellations Ser.). (Illus.). 24p. (J). lib. bdg. 21.25 (978-0-8239-6166-5(4), PowerKids Pr.) Rosen Publishing Group, Inc., The.

Peters, Stephanie True. Andromeda. 2009. (Library of Constellations Ser.). 24p. (gr. 3-4). 45.00 (978-1-60853-573-6(8), PowerKids Pr.) Rosen Publishing Group, Inc., The.

—Gemini. 2009. (Library of Constellations Ser.). 24p. (gr. 3-4). 45.00 (978-1-60853-574-3(6), PowerKids Pr.) Rosen Publishing Group, Inc., The.

—The Little Dipper. 2009. (Library of Constellations Ser.). 24p. (gr. 3-4). 45.00 (978-1-60853-577-4(0), PowerKids Pr.) Rosen Publishing Group, Inc., The.

Phelan, Glen & National Geographic Learning Staff. Stars. 2007. (Language, Literacy, & Vocabulary - Reading Expeditions Ser.). (ENG., Illus.). 36p. (J). pap. 18.95 (978-0-7922-5433-1(3)) CENGAGE Learning.

Prokos, Anna. Star Light, Star Bright: Exploring Our Solar System. Clegg, Dave, illus. 2017. (Imagine That! Ser.). (ENG.). 32p. (J). (gr. 2-4). lib. bdg. 26.65 (978-1-63440-152-4(2)); 39.99 **(978-1-63440-164-7(6))** Red Chair Pr.

Rajczak, Kristen. 20 Fun Facts about Stars. 2014. (Fun Fact File: Space! Ser.). (Illus.). 32p. (J). (gr. 2-5). 25.25 (978-1-4824-1013-6(3)); pap. 10.50 (978-1-4824-1014-3(1)) Stevens, Gareth Publishing LLLP.

Rao, Joe. Looking Up! The Science of Stargazing. Borgions, Mark, illus. 2017. (Science of Fun Stuff Ser.). (ENG.). 48p. (J). (gr. 1-3). pap. 3.99 (978-1-4814-7917-2(2), Simon Spotlight) Simon Spotlight.

Reilly, Carmel. The Stars. 2011. (Sky Watching Ser.). 32p. (gr. 2-4). 28.50 (978-1-60870-583-2(8)) Marshall Cavendish GBR. Dist: Marshall Cavendish Corp.

Ridpath, Ian. Facts on File Stars & Planets Atlas: New Edition. 3rd rev. ed. 2005. (Facts on File Atlas Ser.). 96p. (gr. 4-6). 18.95 (978-0-8160-6294-2(3), Checkmark Bks.) Facts On File, Inc.

Roesser, Blanche. The Story of Pegasus. 2015. (Stories in the Stars Ser.). (ENG., Illus.). 24p. (J). (gr. 1-2). pap. 8.15 (978-1-4824-2677-9(3)) Stevens, Gareth Publishing LLLP.

—The Story of Perseus. 2015. (Stories in the Stars Ser.). (ENG., Illus.). 24p. (J). (gr. 1-2). 22.60 (978-1-4824-2683-0(8)) Stevens, Gareth Publishing LLLP.

Rogers, Amy B. Orion. 2015. (Constellation Collection). (ENG., Illus.). 24p. (J). (gr. 3-3). 23.60 (978-1-4994-0990-1(7), PowerKids Pr.) Rosen Publishing Group, Inc., The.

Romero, Libby. Discover Stars. 2006. (J). pap. (978-1-4108-6509-0(6)) Benchmark Education Co.

—Stars. 2006. (J). pap. (978-1-4108-6506-9(1)) Benchmark Education Co.

Rose, Simon. Andromeda: The Myth & Science. 2015. (Illus.). 24p. (J). (978-1-5105-0265-9(3)) SmartBook Media, Inc.

—Andromeda: The Myth & Science. 2015. (J). (978-1-4896-3316-3(2)) Weigl Pubs., Inc.

—Cygnus the Swan: The Myth & Science. 2015. (Illus.). 24p. (J). pap. (978-1-5105-0266-6(1)) SmartBook Media, Inc.

—Cygnus the Swan: The Myth & Science. 2015. (J). (978-1-4896-3320-0(0)) Weigl Pubs., Inc.

—Hercules: The Myth & Science. 2015. (Illus.). 24p. (J). pap. (978-1-5105-0267-3(X)) SmartBook Media, Inc.

—Hercules: The Myth & Science. 2015. (J). (978-1-4896-3324-8(3)) Weigl Pubs., Inc.

—Orion: The Myth & Science. 2015. (Illus.). 24p. (J). pap. (978-1-5105-0268-0(8)) SmartBook Media, Inc.

—Orion: The Myth & Science. 2015. (J). (978-1-4896-3328-6(6)) Weigl Pubs., Inc.

—Pegasus: The Myth & Science. 2015. (J). (978-1-4896-3332-3(4)) Weigl Pubs., Inc.

Royal Observatory Greenwich Staff & Collins Maps Staff. Stars & Planets. 2013. (ENG., Illus.). 32p. (YA). (gr. 4-10). 31.99 (978-0-00-753226-1(1)) HarperCollins Pubs. Ltd. GBR. Dist: Independent Pubs. Group.

Roza, Greg. How Are Stars Born? 2013. 32p. (J). (gr. 2-5). 25.25 (978-1-4339-9218-6(3)); pap. 10.50 (978-1-4339-9219-3(1)) Stevens, Gareth Publishing LLLP.

Rustad, Martha E. H. Constellations, 1 vol. 2012. (Exploring Space Ser.). (ENG.). 24p. (gr. k-1). pap. 7.29 (978-1-4296-7892-6(5)); pap. 41.70 (978-1-4296-8327-2(9)) Capstone Press of Coughlan Cos. (Pebble Plus).

—Does the Sun Sleep? Noticing Sun, Moon, & Star Patterns. Conger, Holli, illus. 2015. (ENG.). 24p. (J). (gr. k-2). 25.32 (978-1-4677-8560-0(1), Millbrook Pr.) Lerner Publishing Group.

—Las Estrellas. (En el Espacio/Out in Space Ser.).Tr. of The Stars. 24p. (gr. k-1). 2012. (MUL.). pap. 35.70 (978-1-4296-8551-1(4)) 2010. (SPA, ENG & MUL.). lib. bdg. 21.99 (978-1-4296-5342-8(6)) Capstone Press of Coughlan Cos.

—Las Estrellas. 2012. (En el Espacio/Out in Space Ser.). Orig. Title: The Stars. (MUL & SPA.). 24p. (gr. k-1). pap. 5.95 (978-1-4296-8550-4(6)) Capstone Press of Coughlan Cos.

—The Milky Way. 2012. (Exploring Space Ser.). (ENG.). 24p. (gr. k-1). pap. 41.70 (978-1-4296-8328-9(7), Pebble Plus) Capstone Press of Coughlan Cos.

—The Stars. rev. ed. 2008. (Out in Space Ser.). (ENG., Illus.). 24p. (gr. k-1). pap. 6.29 (978-1-4296-2816-7(2), 1284183, Pebble Bks.) Capstone Press of Coughlan Cos.

—The Stars [Scholastic]. 2009. (Out in Space Ser.). 24p. (gr. k-1). pap. 2.50 (978-1-4296-4051-0(0), Pebble Bks.) Capstone Press of Coughlan Cos.

Ryback, Carol. The Stars. 2006. (In the Sky Ser.). (Illus.). 24p. (gr. 1-4). pap. 8.15 (978-0-8368-6350-5(X)); lib. bdg. 22.00 (978-0-8368-6345-1(3)) Stevens, Gareth Publishing LLLP. (Weekly Reader Leveled Readers).

—The Sun. 2006. (In the Sky Ser.). (Illus.). 24p. (gr. 1-4). pap. 8.15 (978-0-8368-6351-2(8)); lib. bdg. 22.00 (978-0-8368-6346-8(1)) Stevens, Gareth Publishing LLLP. (Weekly Reader Leveled Readers).

Shadick, Stan. Skywatcher's Companion: Constellations & Their Mythology, 1 vol. 2007. (Starry Starry Night Discovery Book Ser.). (ENG., Illus.). 48p. (J). (gr. 4-7). pap. 9.95 (978-1-894974-36-3(0)) Heritage Hse. CAN. Dist: Orca Bk. Pubs. USA.

Sian revision Planets&stars. 2004. (J). (978-1-59242-057-5(5)) Delta Education, LLC.

Simon, Seymour. Stars. 2006. (ENG., Illus.). 32p. (J). (gr. k-4). pap. 6.99 (978-0-06-089001-8(0), Collins) HarperCollins Pubs.

—Stars. 2006. (Illus.). 31p. (gr. k-4). 17.00 (978-0-7569-6747-5(3)) Perfection Learning Corp.

—Stars & Constellations. 2007. (Illus.). 24p. (J). (978-0-545-00403-9(9)) Scholastic, Inc.

Sohn, Emily & Harter, Adam. Sun, Moon, & Stars: A Cosmic Case. 2011. (IScience Readers Ser.). 32p. (J). (gr. 3-4). lib. bdg. 22.60 (978-1-59953-421-3(5)) Norwood Hse. Pr.

Sparrow, Giles. Stars & Galaxies. 2006. (Secrets of the Universe Ser.). (Illus.). 48p. (gr. 6-12). lib. bdg. 31.00 (978-0-8368-7280-4(0), Gareth Stevens Secondary Library) Stevens, Gareth Publishing LLLP.

—The Sun & Stars. 2011. (Exploring Space: Space Travel Guides). 32p. (gr. 3-6). lib. bdg. 31.35 (978-1-59920-666-0(8)) Black Rabbit Bks.

Sparrow, Giles & John, Judith. Stars & Galaxies. 2016. (Discoveries in Space Science Ser.). (ENG., Illus.). 80p. (YA). (gr. 9-9). lib. bdg. 35.64 (978-1-5026-1020-1(5), 1398741) Cavendish Square Publishing.

Squier, Robert, illus. The Story of Cassiopeia: A Roman Constellation Myth, 1 vol. 2012. (Night Sky Stories Ser.). (ENG.). 24p. (gr. 2-3). pap. 8.95 (978-1-4048-7716-0(9)) Picture Window Bks.

Stars. 2nd rev. ed. 2008. (New Solar System Ser.). 32p. (YA). (gr. 3-6). 23.00 (978-1-60413-206-9(X)) Facts On File, Inc.

Stegenga, Wil. Spectacular Star Designs. 2009. (Dover Design Coloring Bks.). (ENG., Illus.). 32p. (gr. 3-5). pap. 3.99 (978-0-486-46993-5(X)) Dover Pubns., Inc.

Stiefel, Chana. Lives of Stars: From Supernovas to Black Holes. 2014. (ENG.). 24p. (gr. k-3). 28.50 (978-1-62717-733-7(7)) Rourke Educational Media.

Stories in the Stars. 2015. (Stories in the Stars Ser.). (ENG.). 24p. (J). (gr. 1-2). 135.60 (978-1-4824-2542-0(4)); pap., pap., pap. 293.40 (978-1-4824-3495-8(4)); pap., pap., pap. 48.90 (978-1-4824-3504-7(7)) Stevens, Gareth Publishing LLLP.

The Sun & Other Stars Instructional Guide. 2009. (Grade 8: Science Exit Project Kits Ser.). spiral bd. (978-1-4042-4026-1(8), Rosen Classroom) Rosen Publishing Group, Inc., The.

Than, Ker. Stars. (True Book(tm), A — Space Ser.). (ENG.). 48p. (J). 2009. (gr. 2-5). 31.00 (978-0-531-16899-8(9)) 2010. (Illus.). pap. 6.95 (978-0-531-22806-7(1), Children's Pr.) Scholastic Library Publishing.

Thomas, Isabel. Stars & Galaxies, 1 vol. 2012. (Astronaut Travel Guides). (ENG.). 48p. (gr. 3-6). lib. bdg. 32.65 (978-1-4109-4573-0(1), NA-r) Heinemann-Raintree.

Thomson, Sarah L. Extreme Stars! Q&A. 2006. (ENG., Illus.). 48p. (J). (gr. k-4). pap. 6.99 (978-0-06-089933-2(6), Collins) HarperCollins Pubs.

Tomecek, Steve. Stars. Guida, Liisa C., illus. 2003. (Jump into Science Ser.). (J). 16.95 (978-0-7922-8203-7(5)) CENGAGE Learning.

—Stars. 2006. (Jump into Science Ser.). (ENG., Illus.). 32p. (J). (gr. -1-3). per. 6.95 (978-0-7922-5581-9(X), National Geographic Children's Bks.) National Geographic Society.

—Stars. Yoshikawa, Sachiko, illus. 2003. (Jump into Science Ser.). (ENG.). 32p. (J). (gr. -1-3). 16.95 (978-0-7922-6955-7(1), National Geographic Children's Bks.) National Geographic Society.

Turnbull, Stephanie. Sun, Moon & Stars. Chen, Kuo Kang & Mayer, Uwe, illus. 2006. (Beginners Nature: Level 2 Ser.). 32p. (J). (gr. 1-3). 4.99 (978-0-7945-1399-3(9), Usborne) EDC Publishing.

Vaughan, Jenny & Collins UK Staff. Super Stars. 2016. (ENG.). 48p. (J). (gr. 3-4). pap. 9.95 (978-0-00-816393-8(6)) HarperCollins Pubs. Ltd. GBR. Dist: Independent Pubs. Group.

Vigil, Angel. Papi, How Many Stars Are in the Sky? Ahmad, Aadil & James, Martin, illus. 2010. (J). (978-1-60617-151-6(8)) Teaching Strategies, LLC.

Vogt, Gregory. Stars. 2010. (Early Bird Astronomy Ser.). (ENG.). 48p. (gr. 2-5). lib. bdg. 26.60 (978-0-7613-3873-4(X)) Lerner Publishing Group.

What Is a Sun? 2014. (Let's Find Out! Ser.). 32p. (J). (gr. 3-6). 23.45 (978-1-62275-461-8(1)) Rosen Publishing Group, Inc., The.

Whiting, Jim. Mysteries of the Universe: Stars. 2013. (Mysteries of the Universe Ser.). (ENG.). 48p. (J). (gr. 4-7). pap. 12.00 (978-0-89812-918-2(4), Creative Paperbacks) Creative Co., The.

—Stars. 2012. (Mysteries of the Universe Ser.). (Illus.). 48p. (J). (gr. 5-12). 23.95 (978-1-60818-193-3(6), Creative Education) Creative Co., The.

Wimbush, Jeff. The Stars. 2012. (ENG.). 24p. (J). pap. (978-0-7787-5313-1(1)) Crabtree Publishing Co.

World Book, contrib. by. The Sun & Other Stars. 2nd ed. 2006. (Illus.). 64p. (J). (978-0-7166-9521-9(9)) World Bk., Inc.

World Book, Inc Staff, contrib. by. Stars — Birth & Death. 2010. (J). (978-0-7166-9548-6(0)) World Bk., Inc.

—Stars — the Inside Story. 2010. (J). (978-0-7166-9547-9(2)) World Bk., Inc.

—The Sun & Other Stars. (J). 2010. (978-0-7166-9539-4(1)) 2006. 63p. (978-0-7166-9501-1(4)) World Bk., Inc.

Wright, Holly. Star. 2004. (J). pap. 3.75 (978-0-9743690-6-8(3)) Britt Allcroft Productions.

STARS, FALLING

see Meteors

STARS—FICTION

All the Stars. 2008. (Looney Tunes Giant Floor Pad Ser.). 80p. pap. (978-1-4075-2897-7(1)) Parragon, Inc.

Ayasta, Ayasta. Star. 2007. 117p. 34.95 (978-1-4303-1520-9(2)) Lulu Pr., Inc.

Barichella, Thomas. The Star Snatcher's Planet. 2013. (Little Prince Ser.: 5). (ENG., Illus.). 56p. (J). (gr. 4-8). pap. 7.95 (978-1-4677-0737-4(6), Graphic Universe™) Lerner Publishing Group.

Batson, Susann. Sparkie: A Star Afraid of the Dark. Batson, Susann, illus. 2008. (Illus.). 16p. pap. 7.95 (978-1-935137-01-6(8)) Guardian Angel Publishing, Inc.

Bauman, Boomer. One Star at a Time. 2009. 68p. pap. 20.50 (978-1-60860-571-2(X), Eloquent Bks.) Strategic Book Publishing & Rights Agency (SBPRA).

Baumgart, Klaus. Laura's Secret. Waite, Judy, tr. from GER. 2003. (Illus.). 32p. (J). (gr. -1-2). tchr. ed. 16.95 (978-1-58925-031-4(1)) Tiger Tales.

Baxter, Nicola. Josie the Giraffe & the Starry Night. Fox, Lisa, illus. 2016. (ENG.). 16p. (J). (gr. -1-12). 7.99 (978-0-85723-526-8(5), Armadillo) Anness Publishing GBR. Dist: National Bk. Network.

—The Mermaid & the Star. Rigby, Deborah, illus. 2025. 14p. (J). bds. (978-1-84322-907-0(2), Armadillo) Anness Publishing.

Beavin, John. The Parable of the Stars. 2009. 24p. pap. 11.50 (978-1-60693-368-8(X), Strategic Bk. Publishing) Strategic Book Publishing & Rights Agency (SBPRA).

Benjamin, Sigalit. Garland of Stars. 2009. 26p. pap. 14.50 (978-1-60860-345-9(8), Eloquent Bks.) Strategic Book Publishing & Rights Agency (SBPRA).

Bennett, Deborah. The Christmas Star. 2013. 24p. pap. 24.95 (978-1-63000-934-2(2)) America Star Bks.

Bickford-Smith, Coralie. The Fox & the Star. 2015. (ENG., Illus.). 64p. (J). 20.00 (978-0-14-310867-2(0), Penguin Books) Penguin Publishing Group.

Bobbie, Gramma. The Bright Stars. 2009. 20p. pap. 11.49 (978-1-4490-3474-0(8)) AuthorHouse.

Bowman, Crystal. A Star for Jesus, 1 vol. 2014. (ENG.). 14p. (J). bds. 6.99 (978-0-310-73826-8(1)) Zonderkidz.

Brooke, Samantha. Lalaloopsy: Star of the Show. 2014. (Lalaloopsy Ser.). (ENG., Illus.). 24p. (J). (gr. -1-3). pap. 3.99 (978-0-545-62985-0(3)) Scholastic, Inc.

Brown, Carl & Brown, Kay. The Little Star. 2006. 123p. (J). pap. 15.99 (978-1-4120-9079-7(2)) Trafford Publishing.

Brownlie, Marion. Star Is Happy. 2013. 36p. pap. (978-0-9875551-4-4(6)) Aurora House.

Burris, Shana Renee. Bailey the Bear: Sees Stars Everywhere! 2012. (ENG.). 31p. (J). pap. 12.95 (978-1-4327-9011-0(0)) Outskirts Pr., Inc.

Cara al Cielo Vol.3: Six-Pack. (Saludos Ser.: Vol. 3). (SPA.). (gr. 2-3). 31.00 (978-0-7635-9547-0(0)) Rigby Education.

Carrie C Yakola. Lucy's Shooting Star. 2009. 32p. pap. 15.99 (978-1-4343-5276-7(5)) AuthorHouse.

Caviezel, Giovanni. The Christmas Star. Pagnoni, Roberta, illus. 2013. (ENG.). 10p. (J). (gr. -1 — 1). bds. 6.99 (978-0-7641-6624-2(7)) Barron's Educational Series, Inc.

Cherobin. Zoomy Boomy & the Moon: Zoomy & the Moon Learn the Strength of Love. 2009. 24p. pap. 14.99 (978-1-4490-2069-9(0)) AuthorHouse.

Cherobin & Cherobin. Zoomy Boomy Lights the Night: Zoomy Conquers Shyness. 2009. 24p. pap. 14.49 (978-1-4490-2068-2(2)) AuthorHouse.

Clark, Brenda. Spiro Goes West: More Adventures of Spiro the Shooting Star. 2008. 57p. pap. 16.95 (978-1-60474-770-6(6)) America Star Bks.

Clontz, Jay F. The Tiny Star. 2004. 39p. pap. 16.95 (978-1-4137-2339-7(X)) America Star Bks.

Coats, Vivian. His Star. 2009. 24p. pap. 11.49 (978-1-4490-3885-4(9)) AuthorHouse.

cordone-warner, debra. Starzzee & A Day of Play. 2010. 40p. pap. 18.99 (978-0-557-54780-7(6)) Lulu Pr., Inc.

Côté, Yvonne. Bago the Adventurer: A Star's Help Book 2. 2012. 28p. (-18). pap. 19.99 (978-1-4772-8822-1(8)) AuthorHouse.

Cumming, Hannah. The Lost Stars. Cumming, Hannah, illus. 2011. (Child's Play Library). (ENG., Illus.). 32p. (J). (978-1-84643-416-7(5)) Child's Play International Ltd.

Dale, Jenny. Little Star. Reid, Mick, illus. 2003. 109p. (J). (978-0-439-54363-7(0)) Scholastic, Inc.

Dalmatian Press Staff. Star Light, Star Bright. 2008. (ENG.). 6p. bds. 4.95 (978-1-58117-723-7(2), Intervisual/Piggy Toes) Bendon, Inc.

Das, Christina. Swinging under the Stars. l.t. ed. 2005. (Illus.). 32p. (J). 15.95 (978-0-9763082-1-8(5), A JuneOne Production) JuneOne Publishing Hub.

Davis, Darren. Atlas Gt Planets. 2006. (ENG.). 16p. (J). (gr. -1-12). bds. 5.99 (978-1-59559-103-6(6)) Left Field,Angel Gate.

Dean, James. Twinkle, Twinkle, Little Star. Dean, James, illus. 2014. (Pete the Cat Ser.). (ENG., Illus.). 32p. (J). (gr. -1-3). 9.99 (978-0-06-230416-2(X)) HarperCollins Pubs.

DeStefano, Anthony. Little Star. Elliott, Mark, illus. 2013. (ENG.). 36p. (J). 14.99 (978-0-7369-5859-2(2)) Harvest Hse. Pubs.

Disney Book Group. Star Darlings a Wisher's Guide to Starland. Disney Storybook Art Team, illus. 2016. (Star Darlings Ser.). (ENG.). 176p. (J). (gr. 3-7). 14.99 (978-1-4847-1799-8(6)) Disney Pr.

—Star Darlings Good Wish Gone Bad. Disney Storybook Art Team, illus. 2016. (Star Darlings Ser.). (ENG.). 320p. (J). (gr. 3-7). 13.99 (978-1-4847-5351-4(8)) Disney Pr.

Dukovich, Amanda J. A Star Named Little One (Boy) Pride, Matthew, illus. l.t. ed. 2006. 32p. (J). (gr. -1). 15.99 (978-1-59879-189-1(3)) Lifevest Publishing, Inc.

—A Star Named Little One (Girl) Pride, Matthew, illus. l.t. ed. 2006. 32p. (J). (gr. -1-k). 15.99 (978-1-59879-090-0(0)) Lifevest Publishing, Inc.

Dyan, Penelope. A Thousand Stars. Dyan, Penelope, illus. 2012. (Illus.). 34p. pap. 11.95 (978-1-61477-049-7(2)) Bellissima Publishing, LLC.

Edmonds, Lin. Patric the Pony & the Shining Star. 2010. 36p. pap. 17.49 (978-1-4520-7389-7(9)) AuthorHouse.

Ehrmantraut, Brenda. Night Catch. Wehrman, Vicki, illus. 2014. (J). pap. (978-1-934617-28-1(8)) Elva Resa Publishing, LLC.

Elisabeth, Megan. A Star's Journey from Twinkle to Shine. 2012. 28p. pap. 24.95 (978-1-62709-789-5(9)) America Star Bks.

Elliot, David. Henry's Stars. Elliot, David, illus. 2015. (ENG., Illus.). 40p. (J). (gr. k-3). 16.99 (978-0-399-17116-1(9), Philomel Bks.) Penguin Young Readers Group.

Face to the Sky, 6 pack. (Greetings Ser.: Vol. 3). 24p. (gr. 2-3). 31.00 (978-0-7635-9431-2(8)) Rigby Education.

Facklam, Margery. Only a Star. Carpenter, Nancy, illus. 2004. 32p. (J). (gr. -1-3). pap. 8.00 (978-0-8028-5174-1(6)) Eerdmans, William B. Publishing Co.

Faghih, Parisa. The Sign of Green Stars. 2008. 45p. pap. 24.95 (978-1-4241-8967-0(5)) America Star Bks.

Fanny, Nanny. Touch the Stars: A Children's Book. Nanny Fanny, illus. 2013. 32p. pap. 12.99 (978-1-61204-275-6(9), Strategic Bk. Publishing) Strategic Book Publishing & Rights Agency (SBPRA).

Ferraro, Lynn. Joey Discovers Astronomy. Leslie, Melissa, illus. 2005. (ENG.). 23p. per. 12.99 (978-1-4134-9624-6(5)) Xlibris Corp.

Fischer, Jean & Thomas Nelson Publishing Staff. A Star for Me, 1 vol. Steele-Morgan, Alexandra, illus. 2014. (ENG.). 20p. (J). bds. 14.99 (978-0-529-11212-5(4)) Nelson, Thomas Inc.

Fischer, Kelly. The Moon Throws a Birthday Party. Duckworth, Michelle, illus. 2011. (ENG.). 32p. (J). 19.50 (978-1-58385-237-8(9)) ktf-writers-studio.

Foster, Patricia. Where Did You Come from, Tiny Drop? 2008. 24p. pap. 24.95 (978-1-60610-224-4(9)) America Star Bks.

Fox, Adrienne. Starstruck. 2012. 126p. 27.45 (978-1-4772-3558-4(2)); pap. 15.18 (978-1-4772-3556-0(6)) AuthorHouse.

Frank, Connie. Sadie & the Night Sky, 1 vol. 2009. 24p. pap. 24.95 (978-1-60703-911-2(7)) America Star Bks.

Galaxy X: Book One in the Galaxy X Trilogy, Bk. 1. 2009. (Hardy Boys (All New) Undercover Brothers Ser.: 28). (ENG.). 160p. (J). (gr. 3-7). pap. 5.99 (978-1-4169-7801-5(1), Aladdin) Simon & Schuster Children's Publishing.

Galloway, Teresa A. The Tiny Star Birth of a Soul. 2009. 36p. pap. 15.95 (978-1-4389-3857-8(8)) AuthorHouse.

Garrett, Christine. Dream Bunny's Tales - Saving the Land of Dreams. 2009. (Illus.). 48p. pap. 13.95 (978-1-60860-451-7(9), Eloquent Bks.) Strategic Book Publishing & Rights Agency (SBPRA).

Gasior, Julie. Samy the Star. 2008. 46p. 27.95 (978-0-615-18884-3(2)) Gasior, Julie.

Geffert, Karen L. A Falling Star Is the Beginning of a Wish. 2012. 32p. pap. 19.99 (978-1-4772-5649-7(0)) AuthorHouse.

Ginolfi, Art. The Tiny Star. 2005. 32p. (J). pap. 3.99 (978-1-4003-0683-1(3)) Nelson, Thomas Inc.

Gooch, T. It Was My Star. 2003. (Illus.). 32p. 19.97 (978-0-9726119-0-9(8)) Dancing Force, The.

Grizzell, Larry. The Star: A Christmas Song. 2006. (Illus.). 25p. (J). 19.95 (978-0-9759542-2-5(9)) Adventures Galore.

Guillet, Jean-Pierre. La Puce Cosmique et le Rayon Bleuge. Guillet, Francois, illus. 2004. (Des 9 Ans. Ser.). (FRE.). 120p. (J). (978-2-922565-98-0(X)) Editions de la Paix CAN. Dist: World of Reading, Ltd.

Harmening, Gail. How Did Clancey Get His Color?, 1 vol. 2009. 45p. pap. 24.95 (978-1-60836-440-4(2)) America Star Bks.

Hayes, Vicki C. Zuze & the Star, 1 vol. 2014. (Red Rhino Ser.). (ENG.). 68p. (J). (gr. 4-6). pap. 7.95 (978-1-62250-915-7(3)) Saddleback Educational Publishing, Inc.

He Who Listens: Individual Title Six-Packs. (Literatura 2000 Ser.). (gr. 2-3). 33.00 (978-0-7635-0171-6(9)) Rigby Education.

Heine, Theresa & Tavares, Victor. Star Seeker: A Journey to Outer Space. Tavares, Victor, illus. 2006. (ENG., Illus.). 32p. (J). (gr. -1-3). 16.99 (978-1-905236-36-7(0)) Barefoot Bks., Inc.

Henkes, Kevin. Wemberly's Ice-Cream Star. Henkes, Kevin, illus. 2003. (ENG., Illus.). 24p. (J). (gr. -1-k). bds. 6.99 (978-0-06-050405-2(6), Greenwillow Bks.) HarperCollins Pubs.

Hill, Harriet. The Star That Could Not Twinkle. 2010. 30p. 18.95 (978-1-4452-2689-7(8)) Lulu Pr., Inc.

Hoehn, Ron. The Windy Night: It happened one Night. 2011. 23p. (J). pap. 16.95 (978-1-4327-6408-1(X)) Outskirts Pr., Inc.

Holston-Holloway, Angela M. The Apple Pie Kids. 2006. (J). pap. 8.00 (978-0-8059-6899-6(7)) Dorrance Publishing Co., Inc.

Holub, Joan. Twinkle, Star of the Week. Nicholls, Paul, illus. 2012. (J). (978-1-61913-137-8(4)) Weigl Pubs., Inc.

Hopkins, Lee Bennett. Full Moon & Star. Hall, Marcellus, illus. 2011. (ENG.). 32p. (J). (gr. -1-k). 16.95 (978-1-4197-0013-2(8), Abrams Bks. for Young Readers) Abrams, Inc.

Horácek, Petr. Suzy Goose & the Christmas Star. Horácek, Petr, illus. 2009. (ENG., Illus.). 32p. (J). (gr. -1-2). 15.99 (978-0-7636-4487-1(0)) Candlewick Pr.

—Suzy Goose & the Christmas Star: Midi Edition. Horácek, Petr, illus. 2010. (ENG., Illus.). 32p. (J). (gr. -1-2). 7.99 (978-0-7636-5000-1(5)) Candlewick Pr.

Hotz, Donna. The Christmas Star. 2009. 24p. pap. 12.99 (978-1-4490-2387-4(8)) AuthorHouse.

Hughes, Suz. The Night the Stars Went Out. 2016. (Fiction Picture Bks.). (ENG.). 32p. (gr. 1-2). lib. bdg. 23.32 (978-1-5158-0214-3(0), Fiction Picture Bks.) Picture Window Bks.

Hyde, Catherine. The Star Tree. 2016. (ENG., Illus.). 32p. (J). (gr. -1-3). 19.99 (978-1-84780-672-7(4), Frances Lincoln Children's Bks.) Quarto Publishing Group UK GBR. Dist: Hachette Bk. Group.

Ibarrola, Begonia. Crisol & His Star. Herranz, Yésica, ed. Pita, Lorena, illus. 2013. (ENG.). 40p. (J). (gr. k-2). 13.95 (978-84-95923-50-9(5)) Primera Persona ESP. Dist: Independent Pubs. Group.

Ives, Suzanne Lintz. Bob, the Tree who Became a Star. 2010. 16p. (J). pap. 14.95 (978-1-4327-2748-2(6)) Outskirts Pr., Inc.

Jeffers, Oliver. How to Catch a Star. Jeffers, Oliver, illus. 2004. (ENG., Illus.). 32p. (J). (gr. -1-2). 17.99 (978-0-399-24286-1(4), Philomel Bks.) Penguin Young Readers Group.

Johnson-Carrigan, Ettarose. Old Rugged: How the Tree Became the Cross. 2008. 24p. pap. 11.99 (978-1-4389-2781-7(9)) AuthorHouse.

Jordan, Apple. Star Song. 2016. (Step into Reading Ser.). (ENG., Illus.). 24p. (J). (gr. -1-1). 4.99 (978-1-101-93986-4(9), Random Hse. Bks. for Young Readers) Random Hse. Children's Bks.

Kaye, Shannie. O, Little Star. 2012. 24p. 24.95 (978-1-62709-965-3(4)); pap. 24.95 (978-1-4626-9157-9(9)) America Star Bks.

Kazimierski, Diana. The Star. 2009. 24p. pap. 11.99 (978-1-4389-3799-1(7)) AuthorHouse.

Kiker, Jean. The Story of Misty: The star who became the most famous star of All. 2011. 20p. 11.59 (978-1-4269-5627-0(4)) Trafford Publishing.

Kowalik, Susie. Lumen: The Star That Shone for the Visit of the Composer-Conductor. 2013. 24p. pap. 10.99 (978-1-4624-0539-8(8), Inspiring Voices) Author Solutions, Inc.

Krishnaswami, Uma. Bright Sky, Starry City, 1 vol. Sicuro, Aimée, illus. 2015. (ENG.). 32p. (J). (gr. k-4). 17.95 (978-1-55498-405-3(X)) Groundwood Bks. CAN. Dist: Publishers Group West (PGW).

The Land Beyond Forever. 2006. 25.00 (978-0-9785570-0-3(X)) Three Sisters Publishing Hse., Ltd.

Lasky, Kathryn. Star Rise. 2015. (Horses of the Dawn Ser.: 2). (ENG.). 208p. (J). (gr. 3-7). pap. 6.99 (978-0-545-39731-5(6), Scholastic Pr.) Scholastic, Inc.

Lee, Y. J. The Little Moon Princess. Lee, Y. J., illus. 2010. (ENG., Illus.). 32p. (J). (gr. -1-3). 16.99 (978-0-06-154736-2(0)) HarperCollins Pubs.

Lemieux, Jean. Toby Shoots for Infinity. Cummins, Sarah, tr. from FRE. Casson, Sophie, illus. 2005. (Formac First Novels Ser.: 55). (ENG.). 64p. (J). (gr. 2-5). 14.95 (978-0-88780-685-8(6), 9780887806858) Formac Publishing Co., Ltd. CAN. Dist: Casemate Pubs. & Bk. Distributors, LLC.

—Toby Shoots for Infinity, 1 vol. Cummins, Sarah, tr. from FRE. Casson, Sophie, illus. 2005. (Formac First Novels Ser.: 55). (ENG.). 64p. (J). (gr. 2-5). 4.95 (978-0-88780-684-1(8), 9780887806841) Formac Publishing Co., Ltd. CAN. Dist: Casemate Pubs. & Bk. Distributors, LLC.

Leonard, Krystian. Shining Scars. Kelly, Lucas, illus. 2013. (ENG.). 31p. (J). 16.95 (978-0-938467-72-4(7)) Headline Bks., Inc.

Levasseur, Jody Rogers. The Forever Star. 2011. 28p. pap. 24.95 (978-1-4626-2729-5(3)) America Star Bks.

Lin, Grace, illus. Star Baby. 2017. (J). **(978-0-316-40448-8(9))** Little Brown & Co.

Lobel, Gill. Little Bear's Special Wish. Hansen, Gaby, illus. 2004. 32p. (J). tchr. ed. 16.95 (978-1-58925-034-5(6)) Tiger Tales.

Lois, Lowry. Number the Stars. 2004. 144p. (J). (gr. 5-9). pap. 29.00 incl. audio (978-1-4000-8637-5(X), Listening Library) Random Hse. Audio Publishing Group.

Lyon, George Ella. My Friend, the Starfinder. Gammell, Stephen, illus. 2008. (ENG.). 40p. (J). (gr. -1-2). 17.99 (978-1-4169-2738-9(7), Atheneum/Richard Jackson Bks.) Simon & Schuster Children's Publishing.

MacDonald, George. The Princess & the Goblin. 2010. 222p. pap. 13.95 (978-0-557-47296-3(2)) Lulu Pr., Inc.

Maguire, Thomas Aquinas. Three Little Dreams, 3 vols. 2010. (ENG., Illus.). 36p. (J). (gr. -1). 16.95 (978-1-894965-79-8(5)) Simply Read Bks. CAN. Dist: Ingram Publisher Services.

Mansfield, Keith. Star Blaze. 2010. (Johnny Mackintosh,Johnny Mackintosh Trilogy Ser.: 2). (ENG.). 276p. (J). (gr. 4-6). pap. 8.99 (978-1-84916-126-8(7)) Quercus GBR. Dist: Hachette Bk. Group.

March-Settle, Michelle. A Shining Star: A Journey for All Ages. 2004. (J). pap. 8.00 (978-0-8059-6368-7(5)) Dorrance Publishing Co., Inc.

McLellan, Dora. Stevie Star... the Star That Was Afraid to Shine. 2010. 21p. 14.99 (978-0-557-30108-9(4)) Lulu Pr., Inc.

Meadows, Daisy. Stella the Star Fairy. Ripper, Georgie, illus. 2008. (Rainbow Magic Ser.). (ENG.). 192p. (J). (gr. -1-3). pap. 6.99 (978-0-545-06776-8(6), Scholastic Paperbacks) Scholastic, Inc.

Meehan, Kelly. A Star Named Symphony. 2009. 24p. pap. 12.99 (978-1-4389-6652-6(0)) AuthorHouse.

The Message in the Stars: Lap Book. (Pebble Soup Explorations Ser.). 16p. (gr. -1-18). 21.00 (978-0-7578-2113-4(8)) Rigby Education.

The Message in the Stars: Small Book. (Pebble Soup Explorations Ser.). 16p. (gr. -1-18). 5.00 (978-0-7578-2114-1(6)) Rigby Education.

Mincin, Sabrina. Catching a Shooting Star. 2012. 28p. pap. 12.95 (978-1-4575-0862-2(1)) Dog Ear Publishing, LLC.

Morgan, Beverly. Gregory & the Stars: A Little Story about Independence. Joyful Noise, ed. 2005. (Illus.). 26p. (J). 4.95 (978-0-9772109-0-9(1)) Joyful Noise.

Muldoon Zappa, Shana & Zappa, Ahmet. Leona's Unlucky Mission. Disney Storybook Art Team, illus. 2016. (Star Darlings Ser.: 3). (ENG.). 176p. (J). (gr. 3-7). pap. 6.99 (978-1-4231-7768-5(1)) Disney Pr.

Nelson, S. D. The Star People: A Lakota Story. 2003. (ENG., Illus.). 36p. (J). (gr. -1-3). 18.95 (978-0-8109-4584-5(3)) Abrams, Inc.

O'Connor, Jane. Fancy Nancy Sees Stars. Glasser, Robin Preiss, illus. 2017. (I Can Read Level 1 Ser.). 40p. (J). (gr. -1-3). 9.99 (978-0-06-257275-2(X)) HarperCollins Pubs.

—Stellar Stargazer! Glasser, Robin Preiss, illus. 2011. (Fancy Nancy Ser.). (ENG.). 32p. (J). (gr. -1-2). 12.99 (978-0-06-191523-9(8)) HarperCollins Pubs.

Olsen, Bevan. Bethlehem's Star. 2008. 16p. pap. 2.99 (978-1-59955-181-4(0)) Cedar Fort, Inc./CFI Distribution.

Owings, Lisa. The Constellation Cassiopeia: The Story of the Queen. Morrow, J. T., illus. 2013. (Constellations Ser.). (ENG.). 32p. (J). (gr. 2-5). 29.93 (978-1-62323-484-3(0), 206252) Child's World, Inc., The.

—The Constellation Ursa Major: The Story of the Big Bear. Morrow, J. T., illus. 2013. (Constellations Ser.). (ENG.). 32p. (J). (gr. 2-5). 29.93 (978-1-62323-489-8(1), 206257) Child's World, Inc., The.

—The Constellation Ursa Minor: The Story of the Little Bear. Morrow, J. T., illus. 2013. (Constellations Ser.). (ENG.). 32p. (J). (gr. 2-5). 29.93 (978-1-62323-490-4(5), 206258) Child's World, Inc., The.

Pangalos, Carol B. Gabriella & the Magic Stars. 2011. 36p. (gr. -1). pap. 15.14 (978-1-4634-1108-4(1)) AuthorHouse.

Penado, Martha. Star Stuff. 2009. 47p. pap. 24.95 (978-1-60813-991-0(3)) America Star Bks.

Penelope Panda's Shooting Star. 2008. (Illus.). 32p. (J). (gr. k-3). pap. 14.99 (978-0-9717290-3-2(4)) Adrema Pr.

Peredo, Roberto. Acoyani: El Nino y el Poeta. Sanchez, Andres & Arte Y Diseno, Tane, illus. 2nd rev. ed. 2006. (Castillo de la Lectura Naranja Ser.). (SPA & ENG.). 166p. (J). (gr. 4-7). pap. 7.95 (978-970-20-0146-1(3)) Castillo, Ediciones, S. A. de C. V. MEX. Dist: Macmillan.

Phifer, Larry & Phifer. World on a String. 2013. (ENG.). 17.95 (978-0-9886984-0-6(4)) Storytime Works.

Phyllis Stella Jadosh. Well Then, You Must Be Lucky. 2011. 24p. pap. 11.95 (978-1-935268-70-3(8)) Halo Publishing International.

Pilon, Cindy Jett. Joni & the Fallen Star: Helping Children Learn Teamwork. Hazard, John, illus. 2011. (Let's Talk Ser.). (ENG.). 48p. (J). (gr. -1-2). pap. 9.95 (978-0-88282-353-9(1)) New Horizon Pr. Pubs., Inc.

Pinkney, Jerry. Twinkle, Twinkle, Little Star. 2016. (ENG., Illus.). 30p. (gr. -1 — 1). bds. 7.99 (978-0-316-40693-2(7)) Little, Brown Bks. for Young Readers.

Pitman, Sandra. 10 Busy Bumble Bees, 1 vol. Sizemore, Carmen, illus. 2009. 20p. pap. 24.95 (978-1-60749-683-0(6)) America Star Bks.

Pohlemann, Terri. She Lives in the Stars. 2012. 24p. pap. 24.95 (978-1-4626-6190-9(4)) America Star Bks.

Priddy, Roger. Shiny Stars: My Christmas Star. 2016. (Shiny Shapes Ser.). (ENG.). 10p. (J). bds. 7.99 (978-0-312-52052-6(2), 9780312520526, Priddy Bks.) St. Martin's Pr.

Randolph, Tammy. Cricket's Starry Night. 2011. 28p. pap. 15.99 (978-1-4568-4506-3(3)) Xlibris Corp.

Ranson, Erin. A Bright New Star: With Color-Changing Star Light. Crisp, Dan, illus. 2007. (Story Book Ser.). 16p. (J). (gr. -1-3). bds. (978-1-84666-161-7(7), Tide Mill Pr.) Top That! Publishing PLC.

Ray, Mary Lyn & Frazee, Marla. Stars. 2011. (ENG., Illus.). 40p. (J). (gr. -1-3). 17.99 (978-1-4424-2249-0(1), Beach Lane Bks.) Beach Lane Bks.

Rey, H. A. Curious George Discovers the Stars (science Storybook) 2016. (Curious George Ser.). (ENG., Illus.). 32p. (J). (gr. -1-3). 14.99 (978-0-544-65162-3(6), HMH Books For Young Readers) Houghton Mifflin Harcourt Publishing Co.

Reynolds, Peter H., illus. Star Bright: A Christmas Story. 2014. (ENG.). 40p. (J). (gr. -1-3). 17.99 (978-1-4169-5858-1(4), Atheneum Bks. for Young Readers) Simon & Schuster Children's Publishing.

Ringstad, Arnold. The Constellation Scorpius: The Story of the Scorpion. Morrow, J. T., illus. 2013. (Constellations Ser.). (ENG.). 32p. (J). (gr. 2-5). 29.93 (978-1-62323-488-1(3), 206251) Child's World, Inc., The.

—The Constellation Taurus: The Story of the Bull. Morrow, J. T., illus. 2013. (Constellations Ser.). (ENG.). 32p. (J). (gr. 2-5). 29.93 (978-1-62323-483-6(2), 206256) Child's World, Inc., The.

Roberg, Robert & Whiting, Chuck. The Littlest Star: A Musical Story. 2003rd gif. l.t. ed. 2003. (Illus.). 40p. 10.95 incl. audio compact disk (978-0-9712398-0-7(0)) Shine Time Records & Bks.

Roberts, Phyllis. Teeny Tiny Star. 2007. (Illus.). 30p. (J). lib. bdg. 19.95 (978-1-933732-40-4(7)) Big Ransom Studio.

Rose, Robin. Reaching for the Stars. 2008. 24p. pap. 11.95 (978-1-4389-2299-7(X)) AuthorHouse.

Runnells, Treesha. Five Wishing Stars: Disappearing Die Cut. Dillard, Sarah, illus. 2005. (ENG.). 12p. (J). 14.95 (978-1-58117-265-2(6), Intervisual/Piggy Toes) Bendon, Inc.

Runton, Andy. Owly & Wormy, Bright Lights & Starry Nights. Runton, Andy, illus. 2012. (ENG., Illus.). 40p. (J). (gr. -1-3). 17.99 (978-1-4169-5775-1(8), Atheneum Bks. for Young Readers) Simon & Schuster Children's Publishing.

San Giacomo, Renee. Herbie's Star. 2012. 24p. pap. 24.95 (978-1-4626-7596-8(4)) America Star Bks.

Santillo, LuAnn. The Wish. Santillo, LuAnn, ed. 2003. (Half-Pint Kids Readers Ser.). (Illus.). 7p. (J). (gr. -1-1). pap. 1.00 (978-1-59256-048-6(2)) Half-Pint Kids, Inc.

Scholastic, Inc. Staff & Boyd, Dee. Only the Stars. Rich, Anna, illus. 2004. (Just for You Ser.). (ENG.). 32p. pap. 3.99 (978-0-439-56862-3(5), Teaching Resources) Scholastic, Inc.

Schram, Peninnah & Davis, Rachayl Eckstein. The Apple Tree's Discovery. Lee, Wendy W., illus. 2012. (Kar-Ben Favorites Ser.). (ENG.). 24p. (J). (gr. -1-2). pap. 7.95 (978-0-7613-5132-0(9)); lib. bdg. 16.95 (978-0-7613-5130-6(2)) Lerner Publishing Group. (Kar-Ben Publishing).

Sierra i Fabra, Jordi. El Nino Que Vivia en las Estrellas. (SPA.). 120p. (YA). (gr. 5-8). 8.95 (978-84-204-4429-1(4)) Ediciones Alfaguara ESP. Dist: Santillana USA Publishing Co., Inc.

Sills, Elizabeth & Patrice, Elena. Nana Star. Saker, Linda, illus. 2004. 32p. (J). (gr. -1-3). (978-0-9753843-0-5(9)) Elfstone Press.

—Nana Star. Saker, Linda, illus. 2007. 32p. (J). (gr. -1-3). 15.95 (978-0-9753843-5-0(X)) ee publishing & productions, inc.

—Nana Star & the Moonman. Saker, Linda, illus. 2008. 32p. (J). (gr. -1-3). 15.95 (978-0-9753843-6-7(8)) ee publishing & productions, inc.

Silver Dolphin en Español Staff, creator. Mis Figuras Geometricas, Srita Estrella. 2005. (Mis figuras Geometricas Ser.). (SPA., Illus.). 6p. (J). (gr. -1-k). (978-970-718-295-0(4), Silver Dolphin en Español) Advanced Marketing, S. de R. L. de C. V.

Sklyar, Igor. King & the Star. 2005. (Illus.). 50p. pap. (978-1-84401-048-6(1)) Athena Pr.

Slate, Joseph & Slate. The Secret Stars, 1 vol. Dávalos, Felipe, illus. 2005. (ENG.). 32p. (J). pap. 5.95 (978-0-7614-5152-5(8)) Marshall Cavendish Corp.

Solomon, Philippa. Settle down for Storytime. 2009. (Illus.). 64p. pap. 23.49 (978-1-4389-6032-6(8)) AuthorHouse.

Spires, Sharlene. The Grandsisters. 2010. 56p. pap. 15.99 (978-1-4535-3004-7(5)) Xlibris Corp.

Sprenkle, Connie L. My Shining Star. 2011. 24p. pap. 15.99 (978-1-4568-2168-5(7)) Xlibris Corp.

Stark, Ulf. When Dad Showed Me the Universe. Eriksson, Eva, illus. 2015.Tr. of Nar Pappa Visade Mej Varldsalltet. (ENG.). 32p. (J). (gr. 2-4). 16.99 (978-1-927271-81-0(9)) Gecko Pr. NZL. Dist: Lerner Publishing Group.

Stars of the Sky. 2004. (Illus.). 32p. (J). 12.95 (978-0-9759468-0-0(3)) Balanced Families.

Symington, Martha M. Global Heart Warming: Dream Believe Achieve Series. Sanderson, Jessica B., illus. 2009. 36p. pap. (978-1-897435-34-2(7)) Agio Publishing Hse.

Tiger Tales, ed. The Gingerbread Man. Latimer, Miriam, illus. 2016. (My First Fairy Tales Ser.). (ENG.). 32p. (J). (gr. -1-2). pap. 7.99 (978-1-58925-477-0(5)) Tiger Tales.

—Ten Twinkly Stars. Julian, Russell, illus. 2016. (ENG.). 28p. (J). (gr. -1-k). mass mkt. 3.99 (978-1-58925-475-6(9)) Tiger Tales.

Titchenell, Elsa-Brita. Once Round the Sun. Gruelle, Justin C., illus. 2011. 62p. 36.95 (978-1-258-03323-1(2)) Literary Licensing, LLC.

Toms, Kate. Twinkle Twinkle Box Set. 2007. (Illus.). 26p. (gr. -1). per. (978-1-84610-672-9(9)) Make Believe Ideas.

—Twinkle, Twinkle, Little Star. 2007. (Kate Toms Ser.). (Illus.). 26p. (gr. -1). bds. 7.99 (978-1-84610-485-5(8)) Make Believe Ideas GBR. Dist: Nelson, Thomas Inc.

Torres, Christopher S. Salma & the Christmas Star. Hildebrandt, Lowell, illus. 2010. 24p. 12.99 (978-1-4490-8981-8(X)) AuthorHouse.

Trapani, Iza. Sing along with Iza & Friends: Twinkle, Twinkle Little Star. Trapani, Iza, illus. 2004. (Illus.). 32p. (J). pap. 11.95 incl. audio compact disk (978-1-58089-101-1(2)) Charlesbridge Publishing, Inc.

—Twinkle, Twinkle, Little Star. Trapani, Iza, illus. 2008. (ENG., Illus.). 26p. (J). (gr. -1 — 1). bds. 7.95 (978-1-58089-015-1(6)) Charlesbridge Publishing, Inc.

Twinkle Twinkle Little Star. 2005. (J). bds. 6.99 (978-0-9753127-3-5(1)) Family Bks. at Home.

Valdez-Moore, Pura J. Tippy the Special Star. 2008. 24p. pap. 24.95 (978-1-4241-9943-3(3)) America Star Bks.

Vela, Eugenio H. Twinkle, Twinkle Little Harold. 2012. 28p. pap. 24.95 (978-1-4560-0901-4(X)) America Star Bks.

Venditti, Stacey Marie. Stashi the Rainbow Star: Her Journey Home. Provenzano, Jeannine, illus. 2008. 52p. pap. 24.95 (978-1-60474-786-7(2)) America Star Bks.

Wallace, Nancy Elizabeth. Stars! Stars! Stars!, 0 vols. Wallace, Nancy Elizabeth, illus. 2009. (ENG., Illus.). 40p. (J). (gr. -1-3). 17.99 (978-0-7614-5612-4(0), 9780761456124, Amazon Children's Publishing) Amazon Publishing.

Warden, Kristina. Sparkle: A Star's Story. 2009. (Nature Stories Ser.). (Illus.). 24p. (J). (gr. -1-2). pap. 8.15 (978-1-60754-087-8(8)); lib. bdg. 22.60 (978-1-60754-086-1(X)) Windmill Bks.

Where Do the Stars Go? 2007. (J). 19.95 (978-0-9795877-1-9(9)) Pitcher, Jan.

Williamson, Ray A. & Monroe, Jean Guard. They Dance in the Sky: Native American Star Myths. Stewart, Edgar, illus. 2007. (ENG.). 144p. (J). (gr. 5-7). pap. 8.95 (978-0-618-80912-7(0)) Houghton Mifflin Harcourt Publishing Co.

Willson, Sarah & Thompson Bros. Estrellita. Thompson Brothers Studio Staff, illus. 2003. (Dora la Exploradora Ser.).Tr. of Little Star. (SPA.). 24p. (J). pap. 3.99 (978-0-689-86307-3(1), Libros Para Ninos) Libros Para Ninos.

Wilson, Jessica. Stary's Secret. Tintjer, Birgit, illus. 2007. 28p. pap. 24.95 (978-1-4241-9089-8(4)) America Star Bks.

Wisenrich, Athena. Sitar: Legend of the Morning Star. 2012. 32p. pap. 18.95 (978-1-4525-5351-1(3)) Balboa Pr.

Witschen, Kay. Clinker's Christmas Star. Witschen, Kay, illus. 2004. (Illus.). 24p. (J). 6.95 (978-0-9741352-1-2(6)) Dwitt Publishing.

Wolf, Mari. An Empty Bottle. 2011. 30p. 13.95 (978-1-4638-9995-0(5)) Rodgers, Alan Bks.

Wolfel, Ursula. Fliegender Stern. pap. 14.95 (978-3-570-26064-7(X)) Bertelsman, Verlagsgruppe C. GmbH DEU. Dist: Distribooks, Inc.

Woodall, Karen. Listen to the Stars. 2013. (ENG.). 34p. (J). 18.95 (978-1-4787-1446-0(8)) Outskirts Pr., Inc.

Woolf, Julia, illus. Special Star. 2008. (ENG.). 10p. (J). bds. 4.95 (978-1-58117-815-9(8), Intervisual/Piggy Toes) Bendon, Inc.

York, M. J. The Constellation Hercules: The Story of the Hero. Morrow, J. T., illus. 2013. (Constellations Ser.). (ENG.). 32p. (J). (gr. 2-5). 29.93 (978-1-62323-486-7(7), 206254) Child's World, Inc., The.

Zappa, Ahmet & Zappa, Shane Muldoon. Sage & the Journey to the Wish World. Bonatakis, Shannon & Disney Storybook Art Team, illus. 2015. (Star Darlings Ser.: 1). (ENG.). 176p. (J). (gr. 3-7). pap. 6.99 (978-1-4231-6643-6(4)) Disney Pr.

Zappa, Shana Muldoon. Star Darlings Bind up #1: Sage/Libby/Leona. Disney Storybook Art Team, illus. 2016. (Star Darlings Ser.). (ENG.). 480p. (J). (gr. 3-7). pap. 12.99 (978-1-4847-8295-8(X)) Disney Pr.

—Star Darlings Bind up #2: Vega/Scarlet/Cassie. Disney Storybook Art Team, illus. 2016. (Star Darlings Ser.). (ENG.). 464p. (J). (gr. 3-7). pap. 12.99 (978-1-4847-8296-5(8)) Disney Pr.

—Star Darlings Bind up #3: Piper/Astra/Tessa. Disney Storybook Art Team, illus. 2016. (Star Darlings Ser.). (ENG.).

464p. (J). (gr. 3-7). pap. 12.99 *(978-1-4847-8297-2(6))* Disney Pr.

—Star Darlings Collection Vol. 4: Adora Finds a Friend; Clover's Parent Fix-Up; Gemma & the Worst Wish Ever. Disney Storybook Art Team, illus. 2016. (Star Darlings Ser.). (ENG.). 464p. (J). (gr. 3-7). pap. 12.99 *(978-1-4847-8293-4(3))* Disney Pr.

Zappa, Shana Muldoon & Zappa, Ahmet. Cassie Comes Through. Disney Storybook Art Team, illus. 2016. (Star Darlings Ser.: 6). (ENG.). 176p. (J). (gr. 3-7). pap. 6.99 *(978-1-4847-1425-6(3))* Disney Pr.

—Piper's Perfect Dream. Disney Storybook Art Team, illus. 2016. (Star Darlings Ser.: 7). (ENG.). 176p. (J). (gr. 3-7). pap. 6.99 *(978-1-4847-1426-3(1))* Disney Pr.

—Star Darlings Astra's Mixed-Up Mission. Disney Storybook Art Team, illus. 2016. (Star Darlings Ser.: 8). (ENG.). 176p. (J). (gr. 3-7). pap. 6.99 *(978-1-4847-1427-0(X))* Disney Pr.

—Star Darlings Gemma & the Worst Wish Ever. Disney Storybook Art Team, illus. 2016. (Star Darlings Ser.: 12). (ENG.). 176p. (J). (gr. 3-7). pap. 6.99 *(978-1-4847-1431-7(8))* Disney Pr.

—Star Darlings Tessa's Lost & Found. Disney Storybook Art Team, illus. 2016. (Star Darlings Ser.: 9). (ENG.). 176p. (J). (gr. 3-7). pap. 6.99 *(978-1-4847-1428-7(8))* Disney Pr.

Zee, Amy Van. The Constellation Draco: The Story of the Dragon. Morrow, J. T., illus. 2013. (Constellations Ser.). (ENG.). 32p. (J). (gr. 2-5). 29.93 *(978-1-62323-485-0(9),* 206253) Child's World, Inc., The.

STARS—POETRY

Pinkney, Jerry. Twinkle, Twinkle, Little Star. 2011. (ENG., Illus.). 40p. (gr. -1 — 1). 16.99 *(978-0-316-05696-0(0))* Little, Brown Bks. for Young Readers.

Taylor, Jane. Twinkle, Twinkle, Little Star. Holm, Sharon Lane, illus. 2010. (Favorite Children's Songs Ser.). (ENG.). 16p. (J). (gr. -1-2). 25.64 *(978-1-60253-533-6(7),* 200115) Child's World, Inc., The.

Trapani, Iza. Twinkle, Twinkle, Little Star. Trapani, Iza, illus. 2008. (ENG., Illus.). 26p. (J). (gr. -1 — 1). bds. 7.95 *(978-1-58089-015-1(6))* Charlesbridge Publishing, Inc.

STATE AND CHURCH

see Church and State

STATE AND EDUCATION

see Education and State

STATE BIRDS

Tait, Leia. Birds. 2008. (U. S. Sites & Symbols Ser.). (Illus.). 48p. (J). (gr. 3-5). pap. 10.95 *(978-1-59036-891-6(6));* lib. bdg. 29.05 *(978-1-59036-890-9(8))* Weigl Pubs., Inc.

Talbott, Hudson. United Tweets of America: 50 State Birds Their Stories, Their Glories. Talbott, Hudson, illus. (ENG., Illus.). 64p. (J). (gr. 1-3). 2015. 8.99 *(978-0-14-751557-5(2),* Puffin Books) 2008. 17.99 *(978-0-399-24520-6(0),* G.P. Putnam's Sons Books for Young Readers) Penguin Young Readers Group.

STATE CHURCH

see Church and State

STATE FLOWERS

Tait, Leia. Flowers. 2008. (U. S. Sites & Symbols Ser.). (Illus.). 48p. (J). (gr. 3-5). pap. 10.95 *(978-1-59036-895-4(9));* lib. bdg. 29.05 *(978-1-59036-894-7(0))* Weigl Pubs., Inc.

STATE GOVERNMENTS

see also Governors

also names of states with the subdivision Politics and Government, e.g. New York (State)—Politics and government; etc.

Benchmark Education Company. Local & State Government (Teacher Guide) 2005. *(978-1-4108-4639-6(3))* Benchmark Education Co.

Benchmark Education Company, LLC Staff, compiled by. Social Studies Theme: GOVT & Citizenship. 2005. spiral bd. 115.00 *(978-1-4108-5331-8(4))* Benchmark Education Co.

Brannon, Barbara. Discover Local & State Government. 2005. (J). pap. *(978-1-4108-5145-1(1))* Benchmark Education Co.

Hurtig, Jennifer. Capitals. 2008. (U. S. Sites & Symbols Ser.). (Illus.). 48p. (J). (gr. 3-5). lib. bdg. 29.05 *(978-1-59036-896-1(7));* (gr. 4-6). pap. 10.95 *(978-1-59036-897-8(5))* Weigl Pubs., Inc.

Johnson, Etta. Local & State Government. 2005. (J). pap. *(978-1-4108-4591-7(5))* Benchmark Education Co.

Kenney, Karen. State Government. 2014. (ENG.). 24p. (gr. 3-5). 28.50 *(978-1-62717-683-5(7))* Rourke Educational Media.

LeVert, Suzanne. How States Make Laws. 2003. (Kaleidoscope Ser.). (Illus.). 48p. (gr. 3-18). lib. bdg. 20.95 *(978-0-7614-1595-4(5),* Benchmark Bks.) Marshall Cavendish Corp.

—State Government. 2003. (Kaleidoscope Ser.). (Illus.). 48p. (gr. 3-18). lib. bdg. 20.95 *(978-0-7614-1596-1(3),* Benchmark Bks.) Marshall Cavendish Corp.

Machajewski, Sarah. What Are State & Local Government? 2015. (Let's Find Out! Government Ser.). (ENG., Illus.). 32p. (J). (gr. 2-3). 23.45 *(978-1-62275-986-6(9),* Britannica Educational Publishing) Rosen Publishing Group, Inc., The.

Mahoney, Emily Jankowski. Becoming a State Governor. 2016. (Who's Your Candidate? Choosing Government Leaders Ser.). (ENG., Illus.). 32p. (J). (gr. 3-4). pap. 10.50 *(978-1-4824-4047-8(4))* Stevens, Gareth Publishing LLLP.

Manning, Jack. The State Governor, 1 vol. 2014. (Our Government Ser.). (ENG.). 24p. (gr. 1-2). lib. bdg. 25.32 *(978-1-4914-0335-8(7))* Capstone Press of Coughlan Cos.

Marsh, Carole. Alabama Government Projects: 30 Cool, Activities, Crafts, Experiments & More for Kids to Do to Learn about Your State! 2003. (Alabama Experience Ser.). 32p. (gr. k-5). pap. 5.95 *(978-0-635-01920-2(5),* Marsh, Carole Bks.) Gallopade International.

—Alaska Government Projects: 30 Cool, Activities, Crafts, Experiments & More for Kids to Do to Learn about Your State! 2003. (Alaska Experience Ser.). 32p. (gr. k-5). pap. 5.95 *(978-0-635-01921-9(3),* Marsh, Carole Bks.) Gallopade International.

—Arizona Government Projects: 30 Cool, Activities, Crafts, Experiments & More for Kids to Do to Learn about Your State! 2003. (Arizona Experience Ser.). 32p. (gr. k-5). pap. 5.95 *(978-0-635-01922-6(1),* Marsh, Carole Bks.) Gallopade International.

—Arkansas Government Projects: 30 Cool, Activities, Crafts, Experiments & More for Kids to Do to Learn about Your State! 2003. (Arkansas Experience Ser.). 32p. (gr. k-5). pap. 5.95 *(978-0-635-01923-3(X),* Marsh, Carole Bks.) Gallopade International.

—California Government Projects: 30 Cool, Activities, Crafts, Experiments & More for Kids to Do to Learn about Your State! 2003. (California Experience Ser.). 32p. (gr. k-5). pap. 5.95 *(978-0-635-01924-0(8),* Marsh, Carole Bks.) Gallopade International.

—Colorado Government Projects: 30 Cool, Activities, Crafts, Experiments & More for Kids to Do to Learn about Your State! 2003. (Colorado Experience Ser.). 32p. (gr. k-5). pap. 5.95 *(978-0-635-01925-7(6),* Marsh, Carole Bks.) Gallopade International.

—Connecticut Government Projects: 30 Cool, Activities, Crafts, Experiments & More for Kids to Do to Learn about Your State! 2003. (Connecticut Experience Ser.). 32p. (gr. k-5). pap. 5.95 *(978-0-635-01926-4(4),* Marsh, Carole Bks.) Gallopade International.

—Delaware Government Projects: 30 Cool, Activities, Crafts, Experiments & More for Kids to Do to Learn about Your State! 2003. (Delaware Experience Ser.). 32p. (gr. k-5). pap. 5.95 *(978-0-635-01927-1(2),* Marsh, Carole Bks.) Gallopade International.

—Florida Government Projects: 30 Cool, Activities, Crafts, Experiments & More for Kids to Do to Learn about Your State! 2003. (Florida Experience Ser.). 32p. (gr. k-5). pap. 5.95 *(978-0-635-01928-8(0),* Marsh, Carole Bks.) Gallopade International.

—Georgia Government Projects: 30 Cool, Activities, Crafts, Experiments & More for Kids to Do to Learn about Your State! 2003. (Georgia Experience Ser.). 32p. (gr. k-5). pap. 5.95 *(978-0-635-01929-5(9),* Marsh, Carole Bks.) Gallopade International.

—Hawaii Government Projects: 30 Cool, Activities, Crafts, Experiments & More for Kids to Do to Learn about Your State! 2003. (Hawaii Experience Ser.). 32p. (gr. k-5). pap. 5.95 *(978-0-635-01930-1(2),* Marsh, Carole Bks.) Gallopade International.

—Idaho Government Projects: 30 Cool, Activities, Crafts, Experiments & More for Kids to Do to Learn about Your State! 2003. (Idaho Experience Ser.). 32p. (gr. k-5). pap. 5.95 *(978-0-635-01931-8(0),* Marsh, Carole Bks.) Gallopade International.

—Illinois Government Projects: 30 Cool, Activities, Crafts, Experiments & More for Kids to Do to Learn about Your State! 2003. (Illinois Experience Ser.). 32p. (gr. k-5). pap. 5.95 *(978-0-635-01932-5(9),* Marsh, Carole Bks.) Gallopade International.

—Indiana Government Projects: 30 Cool, Activities, Crafts, Experiments & More for Kids to Do to Learn about Your State! 2003. (Indiana Experience Ser.). 32p. (gr. k-5). pap. 5.95 *(978-0-635-01933-2(7),* Marsh, Carole Bks.) Gallopade International.

—Iowa Government Projects: 30 Cool, Activities, Crafts, Experiments & More for Kids to Do to Learn about Your State! 2003. (Iowa Experience Ser.). 32p. (gr. k-5). pap. 5.95 *(978-0-635-01934-9(5),* Marsh, Carole Bks.) Gallopade International.

—Kansas Government Projects: 30 Cool, Activities, Crafts, Experiments & More for Kids to Do to Learn about Your State! 2003. (Kansas Experience Ser.). 32p. (gr. k-5). pap. 5.95 *(978-0-635-01935-6(3),* Marsh, Carole Bks.) Gallopade International.

—Kentucky Government Projects #4: 30 Cool Activities, Crafts, Experiments & More for Kids to Do! 2003. (Kentucky Experience Ser.). (Illus.). 32p. (J). (gr. k-5). pap. 5.95 *(978-0-635-01936-3(1),* Marsh, Carole Bks.) Gallopade International.

—Louisiana Government Projects: 30 Cool, Activities, Crafts, Experiments & More for Kids to Do to Learn about Your State! 2003. (Louisiana Experience Ser.). 32p. (gr. k-5). pap. 5.95 *(978-0-635-01937-0(X),* Marsh, Carole Bks.) Gallopade International.

—Maine Government Projects: 30 Cool, Activities, Crafts, Experiments & More for Kids to Do to Learn about Your State! 2003. (Maine Experience Ser.). 32p. (gr. k-5). pap. 5.95 *(978-0-635-01938-7(8),* Marsh, Carole Bks.) Gallopade International.

—Maryland Government Projects: 30 Cool, Activities, Crafts, Experiments & More for Kids to Do to Learn about Your State! 2003. (Maryland Experience Ser.). 32p. (gr. k-5). pap. 5.95 *(978-0-635-01939-4(6),* Marsh, Carole Bks.) Gallopade International.

—Massachusetts Government Projects: 30 Cool, Activities, Crafts, Experiments & More for Kids to Do to Learn about Your State! 2003. (Massachusetts Experience Ser.). 32p. (gr. k-5). pap. 5.95 *(978-0-635-01940-0(X),* Marsh, Carole Bks.) Gallopade International.

—Michigan Government Projects: 30 Cool, Activities, Crafts, Experiments & More for Kids to Do to Learn about Your State! 2003. (Michigan Experience Ser.). 32p. (gr. k-5). pap. 5.95 *(978-0-635-01941-7(8),* Marsh, Carole Bks.) Gallopade International.

—Minnesota Government Projects: 30 Cool, Activities, Crafts, Experiments & More for Kids to Do to Learn about Your State! 2003. (Minnesota Experience Ser.). 32p. (gr. k-5). pap. 5.95 *(978-0-635-01942-4(6),* Marsh, Carole Bks.) Gallopade International.

—Mississippi Government Projects: 30 Cool, Activities, Crafts, Experiments & More for Kids to Do to Learn about Your State! 2003. (Mississippi Experience Ser.). 32p. (gr. k-5). pap. 5.95 *(978-0-635-01943-1(4),* Marsh, Carole Bks.) Gallopade International.

—Missouri Government Projects: 30 Cool, Activities, Crafts, Experiments & More for Kids to Do to Learn about Your State! 2003. (Missouri Experience Ser.). 32p. (gr. k-5). pap. 5.95 *(978-0-635-01944-8(2),* Marsh, Carole Bks.) Gallopade International.

—Montana Government Projects: 30 Cool, Activities, Crafts, Experiments & More for Kids to Do to Learn about Your State! 2003. (Montana Experience Ser.). 32p. (gr. k-5). pap. 5.95 *(978-0-635-01945-5(0),* Marsh, Carole Bks.) Gallopade International.

—Nebraska Government Projects: 30 Cool, Activities, Crafts, Experiments & More for Kids to Do to Learn about Your State! 2003. (Nebraska Experience Ser.). 32p. (gr. k-5). pap. 5.95 *(978-0-635-01946-2(9),* Marsh, Carole Bks.) Gallopade International.

—Nevada Government Projects: 30 Cool, Activities, Crafts, Experiments & More for Kids to Do to Learn about Your State! 2003. (Nevada Experience Ser.). 32p. (gr. k-5). pap. 5.95 *(978-0-635-01947-9(7),* Marsh, Carole Bks.) Gallopade International.

—New Hampshire Government Projects: 30 Cool, Activities, Crafts, Experiments & More for Kids to Do to Learn about Your State! 2003. (New Hampshire Experience Ser.). 32p. (gr. k-5). pap. 5.95 *(978-0-635-01948-6(5),* Marsh, Carole Bks.) Gallopade International.

—New Jersey Government Projects: 30 Cool, Activities, Crafts, Experiments & More for Kids to Do to Learn about Your State! 2003. (New Jersey Experience Ser.). 32p. (gr. k-5). pap. 5.95 *(978-0-635-01949-3(3),* Marsh, Carole Bks.) Gallopade International.

—New Mexico Government Projects: 30 Cool, Activities, Crafts, Experiments & More for Kids to Do to Learn about Your State! 2003. (New Mexico Experience Ser.). 32p. (gr. k-5). pap. 5.95 *(978-0-635-01950-9(7),* Marsh, Carole Bks.) Gallopade International.

—North Carolina Government Projects: 30 Cool, Activities, Crafts, Experiments & More for Kids to Do to Learn about Your State! 2003. (North Carolina Experience Ser.). 32p. (gr. k-5). pap. 5.95 *(978-0-635-01952-3(3),* Marsh, Carole Bks.) Gallopade International.

—North Dakota Government Projects: 30 Cool, Activities, Crafts, Experiments & More for Kids to Do to Learn about Your State! 2003. (North Dakota Experience Ser.). 32p. (gr. k-5). pap. 5.95 *(978-0-635-01953-0(1),* Marsh, Carole Bks.) Gallopade International.

—Ohio Government Projects: 30 Cool, Activities, Crafts, Experiments & More for Kids to Do to Learn about Your State! 2003. (Ohio Experience Ser.). 32p. (gr. k-5). pap. 5.95 *(978-0-635-01954-7(X),* Marsh, Carole Bks.) Gallopade International.

—Oklahoma Government Projects: 30 Cool, Activities, Crafts, Experiments & More for Kids to Do to Learn about Your State! 2003. (Oklahoma Experience Ser.). 32p. (gr. k-5). pap. 5.95 *(978-0-635-01955-4(8),* Marsh, Carole Bks.) Gallopade International.

—Oregon Government Projects: 30 Cool, Activities, Crafts, Experiments & More for Kids to Do to Learn about Your State! 2003. (Oregon Experience Ser.). 32p. (gr. k-5). pap. 5.95 *(978-0-635-01956-1(6),* Marsh, Carole Bks.) Gallopade International.

—Pennsylvania Government Projects: 30 Cool, Activities, Crafts, Experiments & More for Kids to Do to Learn about Your State! 2003. (Pennsylvania Experience Ser.). 32p. (gr. k-5). pap. 5.95 *(978-0-635-01957-8(4),* Marsh, Carole Bks.) Gallopade International.

—Rhode Island Government Projects: 30 Cool, Activities, Crafts, Experiments & More for Kids to Do to Learn about Your State! 2003. (Rhode Island Experience Ser.). 32p. (gr. k-5). pap. 5.95 *(978-0-635-01958-5(2),* Marsh, Carole Bks.) Gallopade International.

—South Carolina Government Projects: 30 Cool, Activities, Crafts, Experiments & More for Kids to Do to Learn about Your State! 2003. (South Carolina Experience Ser.). 32p. (gr. k-5). pap. 5.95 *(978-0-635-01959-2(0),* Marsh, Carole Bks.) Gallopade International.

—South Dakota Government Projects: 30 Cool, Activities, Crafts, Experiments & More for Kids to Do to Learn about Your State! 2003. (South Dakota Experience Ser.). 32p. (gr. k-5). pap. 5.95 *(978-0-635-01960-8(4),* Marsh, Carole Bks.) Gallopade International.

—Tennessee Government Projects: 30 Cool, Activities, Crafts, Experiments & More for Kids to Do to Learn about Your State! 2003. (Tennessee Experience Ser.). 32p. (gr. k-5). pap. 5.95 *(978-0-635-01961-5(2),* Marsh, Carole Bks.) Gallopade International.

—Texas Government Projects: 30 Cool, Activities, Crafts, Experiments & More for Kids to Do to Learn about Your State! 2003. (Texas Experience Ser.). 32p. (gr. k-5). pap. 5.95 *(978-0-635-01962-2(0),* Marsh, Carole Bks.) Gallopade International.

—Utah Government Projects: 30 Cool, Activities, Crafts, Experiments & More for Kids to Do to Learn about Your State! 2003. (Utah Experience Ser.). 32p. (gr. k-5). pap. 5.95 *(978-0-635-01963-9(9),* Marsh, Carole Bks.) Gallopade International.

—Vermont Government Projects: 30 Cool, Activities, Crafts, Experiments & More for Kids to Do to Learn about Your State! 2003. (Vermont Experience Ser.). 32p. (gr. k-5). pap. 5.95 *(978-0-635-01964-6(7),* Marsh, Carole Bks.) Gallopade International.

—Virginia Government Projects: 30 Cool, Activities, Crafts, Experiments & More for Kids to Do to Learn about Your State! 2003. (Virginia Experience Ser.). 32p. (gr. k-5). pap. 5.95 *(978-0-635-01965-3(5),* Marsh, Carole Bks.) Gallopade International.

McAuliffe, Bill. State & Local Government. (By the People Ser.). (Illus.). 48p. (J). 2017. (ENG.). (gr. 7-11). pap. 12.00 *(978-1-62832-270-5(5),* Creative Paperbacks) 2016. 39.95 *(978-1-60818-674-7(1),* Creative Education) Creative Co., The.

Nagelhout, Ryan. Standing in a Governor's Shoes. 2015. (My Government Ser.). (ENG., Illus.). 32p. (J). (gr. 4-4). pap. 10.58 *(978-1-5026-0475-0(2))* Cavendish Square Publishing.

Othello: Activity Pack. 2003. 156p. (YA). pap. *(978-1-58049-631-5(8),* PA6318) Prestwick Hse., Inc.

STATE PLANNING

see Social Policy

STATE TREES

Watson, Galadriel Findlay. Trees. 2008. (U. S. Sites & Symbols Ser.). (Illus.). 48p. (J). (gr. 3-5). pap. 10.95 *(978-1-59036-889-3(4));* lib. bdg. 29.05 *(978-1-59036-888-6(6))* Weigl Pubs., Inc.

STATEN ISLAND (NEW YORK, N.Y.)—FICTION

Mercaldo, David. Little Boy Boo: The Adventures of A Yorkshire Terrier Who Thought He Was a Boy. 2009. 112p. pap. 11.99 *(978-1-61579-099-9(3))* Salem Author Services.

STATESMEN

see also Diplomats

Adams, Colleen. Benjamin Franklin: American Inventor. 2009. (Reading Room Collection 2 Ser.). 24p. (gr. 3-4). 42.50 *(978-1-60851-959-0(7),* PowerKids Pr.) Rosen Publishing Group, Inc., The.

Adler, David A. A Picture Book of Benjamin Franklin. Wallner, John & Wallner, Alexandra, illus. 2008. (Picture Book Biography Ser.). (J). (gr. k-3). 28.95 incl. audio compact disk *(978-1-4301-0340-0(X))* Live Oak Media.

—A Picture Book of Benjamin Franklin. 2008. (J). (gr. k-3). pap. 39.95 incl. audio compact disk *(978-1-4301-0341-7(8))* Live Oak Media.

—A Picture Book of Benjamin Franklin, 4 bks., Set. Wallner, John & Wallner, Alexandra, illus. 2008. (Picture Book Biography Ser.). (J). (gr. k-3). pap. 37.95 incl. audio *(978-1-4301-0338-7(8))* Live Oak Media.

Adler, David A. & Adler, Peter S. Heroes of the Revolution. 2003. (ENG., Illus.). 32p. (J). (gr. 1-5). tchr. ed. 17.95 *(978-0-8234-1471-0(X))* Holiday Hse., Inc.

Aldridge, Rebecca. Ban Ki-Moon: United Nations Secretary-General. 2009. (Modern World Leaders Ser.). 128p. (YA). (gr. 7-12). 30.00 *(978-1-60413-070-6(9))* Facts On File, Inc.

American Political Biographies, 3 vols., Set. 2010. (Political Biographies Ser.). (C). (gr. 9). 255.00 *(978-0-8160-8310-7(X))* Facts On File, Inc.

Anderson, Dale. Leaders of the American Revolution. 2005. (World Almanac Library of the American Revolution Ser.). 48p. (gr. 5-12). pap. 14.05 *(978-0-8368-5940-9(5));* lib. bdg. 31.00 *(978-0-8368-5931-7(6))* Stevens, Gareth Publishing LLLP. (Gareth Stevens Secondary Library).

Aretha, David A. Jefferson Davis. 2009. (Leaders of the Civil War Era Ser.). (Illus.). 144p. (gr. 6-12). 35.00 *(978-1-60413-297-7(3),* Chelsea Hse.) Facts On File, Inc.

Baldwin, James. Four Great Americans. 2006. pap. *(978-1-4065-0509-2(9))* Dodo Pr.

Benge, Janet & Benge, Geoff. Heroes of History - Benjamin Franklin: Live Wire. 2005. (Heroes of History Ser.). (ENG., Illus.). 208p. (YA). (gr. 5). pap. 9.99 *(978-1-932096-14-9(0))* Emerald Bks.

Bennett, Doraine & Scott, Clark C. Benjamin Franklin. 2012. (Illus.). 24p. (J). *(978-1-935884-38-5(7));* pap. *(978-1-935884-47-7(6))* State Standards Publishing, LLC.

Boekhoff, P. M. & Kallen, Stuart A. Benjamin Franklin. 2006. (Illus.). 48p. (J). (gr. 4-8). 17.00 *(978-1-4223-5322-6(2))* DIANE Publishing Co.

Boyer, Marilyn. For you they Signed. 2010. (YA). lib. bdg. 34.99 *(978-0-89051-598-3(0))* Master Bks.

Brandt, Keith & Macken, JoAnn Early. Paul Revere, Son of Liberty. Livingston, Francis, illus. 2007. 50p. (J). *(978-0-439-02017-6(4))* Scholastic, Inc.

Brockenbrough, Martha. Alexander Hamilton, Revolutionary. 2017. (ENG.). 384p. (YA). 19.99 ***(978-1-250-12319-0(4),*** 9781250123190) Feiwel & Friends.

Burch, Joann J. Jefferson Davis: Soldier & President of the Confederacy. 2015. (Legendary American Biographies Ser.). 96p. (J). (gr. 6-12). 27.94 *(978-0-7660-6465-2(4));* pap. 10.95 *(978-0-7660-6466-9(2))* Enslow Pubs., Inc.

Byrd, Robert. Electric Ben: The Amazing Life & Times of Benjamin Franklin. 2012. (ENG.). 40p. (J). (gr. k-3). 17.99 *(978-0-8037-3749-5(1),* Dial Bks) Penguin Young Readers Group.

Chemerka, William R. Juan Seguin. Collins, Don, illus. 2012. (ENG.). 64p. (J). 16.95 *(978-1-933979-79-3(8),* 9781933979793) Bright Sky Pr.

Colbert, David. Benjamin Franklin. 2008. (10 Days Ser.). (ENG.). 160p. (J). (gr. 3-8). pap. 8.99 *(978-1-4169-6446-9(0),* Simon & Schuster/Paula Wiseman Bks.) Simon & Schuster/Paula Wiseman Bks.

Collard, Sneed B., III. Benjamin Franklin: The Man Who Could Do Just about Anything. 2006. (American Heroes Ser.). (Illus.). 48p. (gr. 3-7). lib. bdg. 29.93 *(978-0-7614-2161-0(0),* Benchmark Bks.) Marshall Cavendish Corp.

Collins, Kathleen. El Marques de Lafayette: Heroe Frances de la Guerra de Independencia. 2004. (Grandes personajes en la historia de los Estados Unidos Ser.). (SPA.). 32p. (gr. 3-6). pap. 10.00 *(978-0-8239-4233-6(3),* Rosen Classroom) Rosen Publishing Group, Inc., The.

Conklin, Wendy. Benjamin Franklin, 1 vol. 2004. (Primary Source Readers Ser.). (ENG.). 24p. (J). (gr. 4-4). pap. 8.99 *(978-0-7439-8755-4(1))* Shell Educational Publishing.

Cook, Diane. Mohandas Gandhi: Spiritual Leader. 2013. (People of Importance Ser.: 21). (Illus.). 32p. (J). (gr. 4-18). 19.95 *(978-1-4222-2852-4(5))* Mason Crest.

Cooper, Meghan. Sun Tzu. 2017. (J). ***(978-1-5026-2867-1(8))*** Cavendish Square Publishing.

Crawford, Laura. Benjamin Franklin from A to Z, 1 vol. Hierstein, Judith, illus. 2013. (ENG.). 32p. (J). (gr. k-3). 16.99 *(978-1-4556-1713-5(X))* Pelican Publishing Co., Inc.

Crompton, Samuel Willard. Thomas More: And His Struggles of Conscience. 2005. (Makers of the Middle Ages & Renaissance Ser.). (Illus.). 152p. (J). (gr. 5-8). lib. bdg. 32.95 *(978-0-7910-8636-0(4),* Chelsea Hse.) Facts On File, Inc.

Davies, Monika. True Life: Alexander Hamilton. 2016. (TIME for KIDS(r) Nonfiction Readers Ser.). (Illus.). 48p. (J). (gr. 8-8). pap. 9.99 ***(978-1-4938-3633-8(1))*** Teacher Created Materials, Inc.

DeCarolis, Lisa. Alexander Hamilton: Federalist & Founding Father. (Library of American Lives & Times Ser.). 112p. 2009. (gr. 5-5). 69.20 *(978-1-60853-470-8(7))* 2005. (Illus.). (J). (gr. 4-8). lib. bdg. 34.60 *(978-0-8239-5735-4(7))* Rosen Publishing Group, Inc., The.

DeGraw, Aleine. Alexander Hamilton: American Statesman. 2009. (Primary Sources of Famous People in American History Ser.). 32p. (gr. 2-3). 47.90 *(978-1-60851-646-9(6))* Rosen Publishing Group, Inc., The.

—Alexander Hamilton: American Statesman / Estadista Estadounidense. 2009. (Famous People in American History/Grandes personajes en la historia de los Estados Unidos Ser.). (SPA.). 32p. (gr. 2-3). 47.90 *(978-1-61512-536-4(1),* Editorial Buenas Letras) Rosen Publishing Group, Inc., The.

—Alexander Hamilton: Estadista Estadounidense. 2004. (Grandes Personajes en la Historia de Los Estados Unidos Ser.). (SPA., Illus.). 32p. (gr. 5-8). pap. 10.00 *(978-0-8239-4219-0(8))* Rosen Publishing Group, Inc., The.

—Alexander Hamilton: Estadista estadounidense (Alexander Hamilton: American Statesman) 2009. (Grandes personajes en la historia de los Estados Unidos (Famous People in American History) Ser.). 32p. (gr. 2-3). 47.90 *(978-1-61512-788-7(7),* Editorial Buenas Letras) Rosen Publishing Group, Inc., The.

Doeden, Matt. Darkness Everywhere: The Assassination of Mohandas Gandhi. 2013. 80p. pap. 31.93 *(978-1-4677-1659-8(6))* Lerner Publishing Group.

—Mohandas Gandhi. 2011. (J). lib. bdg. *(978-0-7613-5483-3(2))* Twenty First Century Bks.

Edwards, Roberta. Who Was Paul Revere? Harrison, Nancy & O'brien, John, illus. 2011. (Who Was? Ser.). (ENG.). 112p. (J). (gr. 3-7). pap. 5.99 *(978-0-448-45715-4(6),* Grosset & Dunlap) Penguin Young Readers Group.

Espinosa, Rod. Benjamin Franklin, 1 vol. Espinosa, Rod, illus. 2007. (Bio-Graphics Ser.). (ENG., Illus.). 32p. (gr. 3-6). 28.50 *(978-1-60270-066-6(4),* Graphic Planet- Nonfiction) ABDO Publishing Co.

EZ Comics, ed. James A. Baker, III: The Authorised Comic Book Biography. 2009. (ENG., Illus.). 44p. (YA). *(978-0-9795887-3-0(1))* EZ Comics.

Feinstein, Stephen. Colin Powell. 2007. (African-American Heroes Ser.). (Illus.). 24p. (J). (gr. 1-3). lib. bdg. 22.60 *(978-0-7660-2761-9(9),* Enslow Elementary) Enslow Pubs., Inc.

—Read about Benjamin Franklin. 2006. (I Like Biographies! Ser.). (Illus.). 24p. (J). (gr. 1-3). lib. bdg. 22.60 *(978-0-7660-2596-7(9),* Enslow Elementary) Enslow Pubs., Inc.

Fingeroth, Danny. Democracy's Signature: Benjamin Franklin & the Declaration of Independence. 2009. (Great Moments in American History Ser.). 32p. (gr. 3-3). 47.90 *(978-1-61513-141-9(8))* Rosen Publishing Group, Inc., The.

Finlayson, Reggie. Colin Powell. 2005. (Biography Ser.). (Illus.). 112p. (gr. 6-12). lib. bdg. 27.93 *(978-0-8225-4966-6(2))* Lerner Publishing Group.

Fleming, Candace. Ben Franklin's Almanac: Being a True Account of the Good Gentleman's Life. 2003. (ENG., Illus.). 128p. (J). (gr. 5-9). 21.99 *(978-0-689-83549-0(3),* Atheneum Bks. for Young Readers) Simon & Schuster Children's Publishing.

Fleming, Thomas. Ben Franklin: Inventing America. (Great Leaders & Events Ser.). (ENG.). 208p. (J). (gr. 4-8). 2017. lib. bdg. 35.99 ***(978-1-942875-23-9(1))*** 2016. (Illus.). pap. 12.99 *(978-0-7603-5228-1(3))* Quarto Publishing Group USA. (Voyageur Pr.).

Ford, Barbara. Paul Revere: American Patriot. 2015. (Legendary American Biographies Ser.). 96p. (J). (gr. 6-12). 27.94 *(978-0-7660-6485-0(9));* pap. 10.95 *(978-0-7660-6486-7(7))* Enslow Pubs., Inc.

Ford, Nick. Niccolo Machiavelli: Florentine Statesman, Playwright, & Poet. 2004. (Rulers, Scholars, & Artists of the Renaissance Ser.). (J). lib. bdg. 34.60 *(978-1-4042-0316-7(8))* Rosen Publishing Group, Inc., The.

—Niccolò Machiavelli: Florentine Statesman, Playwright, & Poet. 2009. (Rulers, Scholars, & Artists of the Renaissance Ser.). 112p. (gr. 5-8). 66.50 *(978-1-60852-943-8(6),* Rosen Reference) Rosen Publishing Group, Inc., The.

Forsyth, Fiona. Cicero: Defender of the Republic. 2009. (Ancient Leaders Ser.). 112p. (gr. 5-8). 66.50 *(978-1-61511-420-7(3),* Rosen Reference) Rosen Publishing Group, Inc., The.

Foster, Leila Merrell. Benjamin Franklin: Statesman & Inventor. 2015. (Legendary American Biographies Ser.). 96p. (J). (gr. 6-12). 27.94 *(978-0-7660-6445-4(X));* pap. 10.95 *(978-0-7660-6446-1(8))* Enslow Pubs., Inc.

Fradin, Dennis Brindell. The Signers: The 56 Stories Behind the Declaration of Independence. McCurdy, Michael, illus. 2003. (ENG.). 176p. (J). (gr. 5-18). 24.95 *(978-0-8027-8849-8(1),* 9780802788498, Bloomsbury USA Childrens) Bloomsbury Publishing USA.

—Who Was Ben Franklin? O'brien, John, illus. 2003. (Who Was... ? Ser.). 105p. (gr. 4-7). 15.00 *(978-0-7569-1589-6(9))* Perfection Learning Corp.

Franklin, Benjamin. Benjamin Franklin's Wise Words. Harper, Fred, illus. 2017. (ENG.). 128p. (J). (gr. 3-7). 16.99 *(978-1-4263-2699-8(8));* lib. bdg. 26.90 *(978-1-4263-2700-1(5))* National Geographic Society. (National Geographic Children's Bks.).

Freedman, Russell. Becoming Ben Franklin: How a Candle-Maker's Son Helped Light the Flame of Liberty. 2013. (ENG.). 96p. (J). (gr. 5). 24.95 *(978-0-8234-2374-3(3))* Holiday Hse., Inc.

Fritz, Jean. Alexander Hamilton: The Outsider. 2012. (ENG.). 144p. (J). (gr. 3-7). 8.99 *(978-0-14-241986-1(9),* Puffin Books) Penguin Young Readers Group.

Furgang, Kathy. The Declaration of Independence & Benjamin Franklin of Pennsylvania. 2009. (Framers of the Declaration of Independence Ser.). 24p. (gr. 3-3). 42.50 *(978-1-61512-629-3(5),* PowerKids Pr.) Rosen Publishing Group, Inc., The.

—The Declaration of Independence & Robert Livingston of New York. 2009. (Framers of the Declaration of Independence Ser.). 24p. (gr. 3-3). 42.50 *(978-1-61512-631-6(7),* PowerKids Pr.) Rosen Publishing Group, Inc., The.

Gagne, Tammy. Who Were the Signers of the Declaration of Independence? 2017. (Young America Ser.). (gr. 3-6). 29.95 *(978-1-61228-983-0(5))* Mitchell Lane Pubs., Inc.

Gandhi, Arun & Hegedus, Bethany. Be the Change: A Grandfather Gandhi Story. Turk, Evan, illus. 2016. (ENG.). 48p. (J). (gr. -1-3). 18.99 *(978-1-4814-4265-7(1))* Simon & Schuster Children's Publishing.

—Grandfather Gandhi. Turk, Evan, illus. 2014. (ENG.). 48p. (J). (gr. -1-3). 17.99 *(978-1-4424-2365-7(X))* Simon & Schuster Children's Publishing.

Gaustad, Edwin S. Benjamin Franklin: Inventing America. 2006. 143p. (J). (gr. 4-8). reprint ed. 22.00 *(978-1-4223-5227-4(7))* DIANE Publishing Co.

Giblin, James Cross. The Amazing Life of Benjamin Franklin. Dooling, Michael, illus. 2006. 48p. (gr. -1-3). 18.00 *(978-0-7569-6551-8(9))* Perfection Learning Corp.

Gilman, Sarah. Ben Franklin. 2016. (Explore Colonial America Ser.). (Illus.). 48p. (J). (gr. 5-4). 27.93 *(978-0-7660-7873-4(6))* Enslow Pubs., Inc.

Gimpel, Lee. Fighting Wars, Planning for Peace: The Story of George C. Marshall. 2005. (World Leaders Ser.). (Illus.). 176p. (J). (gr. 6-12). lib. bdg. 26.95 *(978-1-931798-66-2(4))* Reynolds, Morgan Inc.

Glass, Maya. Benjamin Franklin: Early American Genius. (Primary Sources of Famous People in American History Ser.). 32p. 2009. (gr. 2-3). 47.90 *(978-1-60851-654-4(7))* 2004. (ENG., Illus.). (gr. 4-8). pap. 10.00 *(978-0-8239-4175-9(2))* Rosen Publishing Group, Inc., The.

—Benjamin Franklin: Early American Genius / Político e inventor Estadounidense. 2009. (Famous People in American History/Grandes personajes en la historia de los Estados Unidos Ser.). (ENG & SPA.). 32p. (gr. 2-3). 47.90 *(978-1-61512-538-8(8),* Editorial Buenas Letras) Rosen Publishing Group, Inc., The.

—Benjamin Franklin: Político e inventor Estadounidense. 2004. (Grandes personajes en la historia de los Estados Unidos Ser.). (SPA.). 32p. (gr. 5-8). pap. 10.00 *(978-0-8239-4221-3(X),* Rosen Classroom) Rosen Publishing Group, Inc., The.

—Benjamin Franklin: Político e inventor estadounidense (Benjamin Franklin: Early American Genius) 2009. (Grandes personajes en la historia de los Estados Unidos (Famous People in American History) Ser.). (SPA.). 32p. (gr. 2-3). 47.90 *(978-1-61512-790-0(9),* Editorial Buenas Letras) Rosen Publishing Group, Inc., The.

Goddu, Krystyna Poray. What's Your Story, Paul Revere? 2016. (Cub Reporter Meets Famous Americans Ser.). (ENG., Illus.). 32p. (J). (gr. k-3). pap. 8.99 *(978-1-4677-9641-5(7),* Lerner Pubns.) Lerner Publishing Group.

Golden, Nancy. The British Are Coming! The Midnight Ride of Paul Revere. 2009. (Great Moments in American History Ser.). 32p. (gr. 3-3). 47.90 *(978-1-61513-136-5(1))* Rosen Publishing Group, Inc., The.

Gosman, Gillian. Benjamin Franklin. 2011. (Life Stories Ser.). (Illus.). 24p. (J). pap. 8.25 *(978-1-4488-2759-6(0));* (gr. 1-4). lib. bdg. 22.60 *(978-1-4488-2585-1(7))* Rosen Publishing Group, Inc., The. (PowerKids Pr.).

Gould, Jane H. Alexander Hamilton. 2012. (Jr. Graphic Founding Fathers Ser.). (ENG., Illus.). 24p. (J). (gr. 3-6). pap. 10.60 *(978-1-4488-7989-2(2));* lib. bdg. 25.25 *(978-1-4488-7895-6(0))* Rosen Publishing Group, Inc., The. (PowerKids Pr.).

—Benjamin Franklin. 2012. (Jr. Graphic Founding Fathers Ser.). (ENG., Illus.). 24p. (J). (gr. 3-6). pap. 10.60 *(978-1-4488-7990-8(6));* lib. bdg. 25.25 *(978-1-4488-7896-3(9))* Rosen Publishing Group, Inc., The. (PowerKids Pr.).

Greene, Victor. The Life of Benjamin Franklin. 2012. (InfoMax Readers Ser.). (ENG., Illus.). 24p. (J). (gr. 1-2). pap. 8.25 *(978-1-4488-8992-1(8),* Rosen Classroom) Rosen Publishing Group, Inc., The.

Haldy, Emma E. Benjamin Franklin. Bane, Jeff, illus. 2016. (My Early Library: My Itty-Bitty Bio Ser.). (ENG.). 24p. (J). (gr. k-1). 28.50 *(978-1-63470-478-6(9),* 207643) Cherry Lake Publishing.

Hale, Sarah Elder, ed. Jefferson Davis & the Confederacy. 2005. (ENG., Illus.). 48p. (J). (gr. 3-9). 17.95 *(978-0-8126-7908-3(3))* Cobblestone Publishing Co.

Hancock, Lee. Lorenzo de' Medici: Florence's Great Leader & Patron of the Arts. (Rulers, Scholars, & Artists of the Renaissance Ser.). 112p. 2009. (gr. 5-8). 66.50 *(978-1-60852-942-1(8),* Rosen Reference) 2004. (Illus.). (J). lib. bdg. 34.60 *(978-1-4042-0315-0(X))* Rosen Publishing Group, Inc., The.

Harmon, Daniel E. Ayatollah Ruhollah Khomeini. 2004. (Spiritual Leaders & Thinkers Ser.). (Illus.). 120p. (J). (gr. 9-13). 30.00 *(978-0-7910-7865-5(5),* Chelsea Hse.) Facts On File, Inc.

Harness, Cheryl. The Remarkable Benjamin Franklin. 2008. (ENG., Illus.). 48p. (J). (gr. 2-5). 7.95 *(978-1-4263-0297-8(5),* National Geographic Children's Bks.) National Geographic Society.

—The Remarkable Benjamin Franklin. Harness, Cheryl, illus. 2005. (National Geographic Ser.). (ENG., Illus.). 48p. (J). (gr. 2-5). 17.95 *(978-0-7922-7882-5(8),* National Geographic Children's Bks.) National Geographic Society.

—The Remarkable Benjamin Franklin. 2005. (ENG., Illus.). 48p. (J). (gr. 2-5). 27.90 *(978-0-7922-7884-9(4),* National Geographic Children's Bks.) National Geographic Society.

Hesleden, Michael. Benjamin Franklin: American Diplomat. 2015. (Spotlight on American History Ser.). (ENG., Illus.). 24p. (J). (gr. 4-6). pap. 10.00 *(978-1-4994-1782-1(9),* PowerKids Pr.) Rosen Publishing Group, Inc., The.

Heuston, Kimberley. Mao Zedong. 2010. (Wicked History Ser.). (ENG.). 128p. (J). (gr. 6-12). pap. 5.95 *(978-0-531-22356-7(6),* Watts, Franklin) Scholastic Library Publishing.

—Otto von Bismarck: Iron Chancellor of Germany. (Wicked History Ser.). (ENG., Illus.). 128p. (YA). 2010. (gr. 6-12). pap. 5.95 *(978-0-531-22824-1(X),* Watts, Franklin) 2009. (gr. 5-9). 31.00 *(978-0-531-21278-3(5))* Scholastic Library Publishing.

Heuston, Kimberley Burton. Mao Zedong. 2010. (Wicked History Ser.). (ENG., Illus.). 128p. (J). (gr. 5-8). 31.00 *(978-0-531-20756-7(0))* Scholastic Library Publishing.

Hicks, Dwayne. Paul Revere: American Patriot. 2012. (Beginning Biographies Ser.). (ENG., Illus.). 24p. (J). (gr. 1-3). 22.60 *(978-1-4488-8599-2(X),* PowerKids Pr.) Rosen Publishing Group, Inc., The.

Hilliam, David. Thomas Becket: English Saint & Martyr. 2009. (Leaders of the Middle Ages Ser.). 112p. (gr. 5-8). 66.50 *(978-1-61513-902-6(8),* Rosen Reference) Rosen Publishing Group, Inc., The.

Hirschfeld, Leila & Hirschfeld, Tom. You Decide, Ben Franklin! Weber, Lisa K., illus. 2016. (J). pap. *(978-0-553-50952-6(7),* Salamander Bks.) Pavilion Bks.

Hollander, Barbara Gottfried. Harvey Milk: The First Openly Gay Elected Official in the United States. 2017. (J). ***(978-1-5383-8093-2(5),*** Rosen Young Adult) Rosen Publishing Group, Inc., The.

Howell, Izzi. Samuel Pepys. 2016. (Fact Cat: History Ser.). (ENG., Illus.). 24p. (J). (gr. k-2). 14.99 *(978-1-5263-0097-3(4),* Wayland) Hachette Children's Group GBR. Dist: Hachette Bk. Group.

Hughes, Chris. The Constitutional Convention. 2005. (People at the Center of Ser.). (Illus.). 48p. (J). (gr. -1-7). lib. bdg. 24.95 *(978-1-56711-918-3(2),* Blackbirch Pr., Inc.) Cengage Gale.

Jeffrey, Gary. Paul Revere & His Midnight Ride. 2011. (Graphic Heroes of the American Revolution Ser.). 24p. (J). (gr. 3-6). lib. bdg. 23.95 *(978-1-4339-6019-2(2));* pap. 8.15 *(978-1-4339-6020-8(6),* Gareth Stevens Learning Library) Stevens, Gareth Publishing LLLP.

—Thomas Jefferson & the Declaration of Independence. 2011. (Graphic Heroes of the American Revolution Ser.). (Illus.). 24p. (J). (gr. 3-6). 23.95 *(978-1-4339-6025-3(7));* pap. 8.15 *(978-1-4339-6026-0(5),* Gareth Stevens Learning Library) Stevens, Gareth Publishing LLLP.

Juarez, Christine. José Antonio Navarro. 2016. (Great Hispanic & Latino Americans Ser.). (ENG.). 24p. (gr. k-1). lib. bdg. 21.99 *(978-1-5157-1889-5(1),* Pebble Bks.) Capstone Press of Coughlan Cos.

Keller, Susanna. Alexander Hamilton: America's First Treasury Secretary. 2017. (J). pap. ***(978-1-68048-808-1(2));*** lib. bdg. ***(978-1-68048-809-8(0))*** Rosen Publishing Group, Inc., The. (Britannica Educational Publishing).

Keller, Susanna. The True Story of Paul Revere's Ride. 2013. (What Really Happened? Ser.). (ENG., Illus.). 24p. (J). (gr. 3-6). pap. 8.25 *(978-1-4488-9838-1(2));* lib. bdg. 22.60 *(978-1-4488-9690-5(8))* Rosen Publishing Group, Inc., The. (PowerKids Pr.).

Kelley, K. C. Alexander Hamilton: American Hero. 2017. (Rookie Biographies(tm) Ser.). (ENG., Illus.). 32p. (J). lib. bdg. 25.00 *(978-0-531-22290-4(X))* Scholastic Library Publishing.

Kelly, Jack. Benjamin Franklin. Tafalla, Ortiz, illus. 2005. (Heroes of America Ser.). 239p. (gr. 3-8). 27.07 *(978-1-59679-257-9(4),* Abdo & Daughters) ABDO Publishing Co.

Kenison, Misti. Cheer up, Ben Franklin! 2017. (ENG.). 28p. (J). bds. 9.99 ***(978-1-4926-5247-2(4),*** Sourcebooks Jabberwocky) Sourcebooks, Inc.

Kent, Zachary. Alexander Hamilton: Creating a Nation. 2004. (America's Founding Fathers Ser.). (Illus.). 128p. (J). lib. bdg. 26.60 *(978-0-7660-2181-5(5))* Enslow Pubs., Inc.

Koestler-Grack, Rachel A. Kofi Annan: Guiding the United Nations. 2007. (Modern Peacemakers Ser.). (Illus.). 119p. (YA). (gr. 9-12). lib. bdg. 30.00 *(978-0-7910-8996-5(7))* Facts On File, Inc.

Kuhn, Betsy. The Force Born of Truth: Mohandas Gandhi & the Salt March, India, 1930. 2010. (Civil Rights Struggles around the World Ser.). (ENG., Illus.). 160p. (gr. 9-12). lib. bdg. 38.60 *(978-0-8225-8968-6(0))* Lerner Publishing Group.

Kulling, Monica. Alexander Hamilton: From Orphan to Founding Father. 2017. (Step into Reading Ser.). (ENG., Illus.). 48p. (J). (gr. k-3). pap. 3.99 *(978-1-5247-1698-1(7),* Random Hse. Bks. for Young Readers) Random Hse. Children's Bks.

Lace, William W. Benjamin Franklin. 2010. (Leaders of the Colonial Era Ser.). (Illus.). 120p. (gr. 5-8). 35.00 *(978-1-60413-737-8(1),* Chelsea Hse.) Facts On File, Inc.

Landau, Elaine. Meet Ben Franklin with Elaine Landau. 2006. (Explore Colonial America with Elaine Landau Ser.). (Illus.). 48p. (J). (gr. 3-4). lib. bdg. 25.27 *(978-0-7660-2555-4(1),* Enslow Elementary) Enslow Pubs., Inc.

Let's Call It America! Meet Our Founding Fathers. 2013. (Illus.). 32p. (J). *(978-0-545-53539-7(5))* Scholastic, Inc.

Lowery, Zoe & Forsyth, Fiona. Cicero. 2016. (Leaders of the Ancient World Ser.). 00112p. (J). (gr. 6-6). 37.10 *(978-1-5081-7258-1(7))* Rosen Publishing Group, Inc., The.

Lucas, Eileen. Mahatma Gandhi: Fighting for Indian Independence. 2017. (Rebels with a Cause Ser.). 128p. (J). (gr. 8-8). lib. bdg. 37.27 ***(978-0-7660-8513-8(9))*** Enslow Pubs., Inc.

Mack, Molly. The Life of Paul Revere. 2012. (InfoMax Readers Ser.). (ENG., Illus.). 24p. (J). (gr. 1-2). pap. 8.25 *(978-1-4488-9049-1(7),* Rosen Classroom) Rosen Publishing Group, Inc., The.

Major World Leaders. 2005. (Major World Leaders Ser.). 144p. (gr. 6-12). 270.00 *(978-0-7910-8410-6(8),* Chelsea Hse.) Facts On File, Inc.

Makers of the Middle Ages & Renaissance. 2005. (Makers of the Middle Ages & Renaissance Ser.). (Illus.). 100p. (gr. 5-8). 329.50 *(978-0-7910-9064-0(7),* Chelsea Hse.) Facts On File, Inc.

Malaspina, Ann. Mahatma Gandhi & India's Independence. 2016. (People & Events That Changed the World Ser.). (ENG., Illus.). 128p. (J). (gr. 7-8). lib. bdg. 37.27 *(978-0-7660-7262-6(2))* Enslow Pubs., Inc.

Mara, Wil. Benjamin Franklin. (Rookie Biographies(r) Ser.). (Illus.). (J). 2014. (ENG.). 32p. pap. 5.95 *(978-0-531-21201-1(7))* 2014. (ENG., 32p. lib. bdg. 25.00 *(978-0-531-20558-7(4))* 2007. 31p. (gr. 1-2). pap. 4.95 *(978-0-531-12591-5(2),* Children's Pr.) Scholastic Library Publishing.

—Paul Revere. (Rookie Biographies(r) Ser.). (ENG., Illus.). 32p. (J). 2015. pap. 5.95 *(978-0-531-20597-6(5))* 2005. (gr. 1-2). pap. 4.95 *(978-0-516-25820-1(6))* Scholastic Library Publishing. (Children's Pr.).

Marcovitz, Hal. Benjamin Franklin: Scientist, Inventor, Printer, & Statesman. 2006. (Leaders of the American Revolution Ser.). (Illus.). 100p. (gr. 5-8). lib. bdg. 30.00 *(978-0-7910-9219-4(4),* Chelsea Hse.) Facts On File, Inc.

Marsh, Carole. Jefferson Davis, Civil War Hero. 2004. 12p. (gr. k-4). 2.95 *(978-0-635-02366-7(0))* Gallopade International.

Marston, Elsa. The Compassionate Warrior: Abd el-Kader of Algeria. 2013. (ENG., Illus.). 184p. (J). (gr. 8-12). pap. 16.95 *(978-1-937786-10-6(2),* Wisdom Tales) World Wisdom, Inc.

Marti, Jose. Jose Marti: Cuatro cuentos Infantiles. Martinez, Enrique & Graullera, Fabiola, illus. (SPA.). 28p. (J). (gr. 3-5). 9.95 *(978-970-29-0522-6(2))* Santillana, Editorial, S.A. de C.V. MEX. Dist: Santillana USA Publishing Co., Inc.

Mattern, Joanne. Sam Houston: Un Estadista Audaz. 2013. (Primary Source Readers Ser.). (SPA.). lib. bdg. 19.65 *(978-0-606-31869-3(0),* Turtleback) Turtleback Bks.

McCarthy, Rose. Dictatorship: A Primary Source Analysis. 2009. (Primary Sources of Political Systems Ser.). 64p. (gr. 5-8). 58.50 *(978-1-60851-837-1(X))* Rosen Publishing Group, Inc., The.

—Paul Revere: Freedom Rider. 2009. (Primary Sources of Famous People in American History Ser.). 32p. (gr. 2-3). 47.90 *(978-1-60851-714-5(4))* Rosen Publishing Group, Inc., The.

—Paul Revere: Freedom Rider / Jinete de la causa Revolucionaria. 2009. (Famous People in American History/Grandes personajes en la historia de los Estados Unidos Ser.). (ENG & SPA.). 32p. (gr. 2-3). 47.90 *(978-1-61512-553-1(1),* Editorial Buenas Letras) Rosen Publishing Group, Inc., The.

—Paul Revere: Jinete de la causa revolucionaria (Paul Revere: Freedom Rider) 2009. (Grandes personajes en la historia de los Estados Unidos (Famous People in American History) Ser.). (SPA.). 32p. (gr. 2-3). 47.90 *(978-1-61512-806-8(9),* Editorial Buenas Letras) Rosen Publishing Group, Inc., The.

—Paul Revere: Jinete de la guerra de Independencia. 2004. (Grandes personajes en la historia de los Estados Unidos Ser.). (SPA.). 32p. (gr. 3-6). pap. 10.00 *(978-0-8239-4236-7(8),* Rosen Classroom) Rosen Publishing Group, Inc., The.

McCollum, Sean. The Chairman: Mao Unleashes Chaos in China. 2011. (J). pap. *(978-0-545-32935-4(3))* Scholastic, Inc.

—Joseph Stalin. 2010. (Wicked History Ser.). (ENG.). 128p. (J). (gr. 6-12). pap. 5.95 *(978-0-531-22355-0(8));* (Illus.). 31.00 *(978-0-531-20755-0(2))* Scholastic Library Publishing. (Watts, Franklin).

McCurdy, Michael. So Said Ben. 2007. (ENG., Illus.). 32p. (J). (gr. 1-3). 17.95 *(978-1-56846-147-2(X),* Creative Editions) Creative Co., The.

McDonnell, Vincent. Michael Collins: Most Wanted Man. 2009. (ENG.). 136p. (J). pap. 15.95 *(978-1-905172-62-7(1))* Collins Pr., The IRL. Dist: Dufour Editions, Inc.

McDowell, Pamela. Benjamin Franklin. 2013. *(978-1-62127-307-3(5));* pap. *(978-1-62127-313-4(X))* Weigl Pubs., Inc.

McGrath, Brian. Aaron Burr: More Than a Villain (Alexander Hamilton) 2017. (Primary Source Readers Focus On Ser.). (Illus.). 32p. (J). (gr. 4-8). pap. 8.99 ***(978-1-4258-6355-5(8))*** Teacher Created Materials, Inc.

McLeese, Don. Alexander Hamilton. 2004. (Heroes of the American Revolution Ser.). (Illus.). 32p. (gr. 2-5). lib. bdg. *(978-1-59515-219-0(9))* Rourke Educational Media.

—Benjamin Franklin. 2005. (Heroes of the American Revolution Ser.). (Illus.). 32p. (gr. 2-5). 19.95 *(978-1-59515-216-9(4))* Rourke Educational Media.

McNeese, Tim. Alexander Hamilton: Framer of the Constitution. 2005. (Leaders of the American Revolution Ser.). (Illus.). 100p. (gr. 5-8). lib. bdg. 30.00 *(978-0-7910-8616-2(X))* Facts On File, Inc.

Melton, Buckner F. Aaron Burr: The Rise & Fall of an American Politician. 2009. (Library of American Lives & Times Ser.). 112p. (gr. 5-5). 69.20 *(978-1-60853-468-5(5))* Rosen Publishing Group, Inc., The.

Miller, Brandon Marie. Benjamin Franklin, American Genius: His Life & Ideas with 21 Activities. 2009. (For Kids Ser.). (ENG., Illus.). 144p. (J). (gr. 4-7). pap. 16.95 *(978-1-55652-757-9(8))* Chicago Review Pr., Inc.

Mills, Clifford W. Angela Merkel. 2007. (Modern World Leaders Ser.). (Illus.). 120p. (YA). (gr. 7-12). lib. bdg. 30.00 *(978-0-7910-9496-9(0))* Facts On File, Inc.

Mills, Nathan & Coleridge, Margaret. Who Was Benjamin Franklin? 2012. (Rosen Readers Ser.). (ENG., Illus.). 24p. (J). (gr. 1-2). pap. 8.25 *(978-1-4488-8773-6(9),* Rosen Classroom) Rosen Publishing Group, Inc., The.

Mills, Nathan & Hicks, Dwayne. Paul Revere: American Patriot. 2012. (Rosen Readers Ser.). (ENG., Illus.). 24p. (J). (gr. 1-2). pap. 8.25 *(978-1-4488-8836-8(0),* Rosen Classroom) Rosen Publishing Group, Inc., The.

Min, Ellen. The Midnight Ride of Paul Revere: One If by Land, Two If by Sea. 2015. (Spotlight on American History Ser.). (ENG., Illus.). 24p. (J). (gr. 4-6). pap. 10.00 *(978-1-4994-1734-0(9),* PowerKids Pr.) Rosen Publishing Group, Inc., The.

Mooney, Brian. Great Leaders. 2012. (Great People in History Ser.). (ENG., Illus.). 128p. (YA). (gr. 8-12). lib. bdg. 34.60 *(978-1-4777-0403-5(5))* Rosen Publishing Group, Inc., The.

Morlock, Theresa. 20 Fun Facts about Benjamin Franklin. 2017. (Fun Fact File: Founding Fathers Ser.). 32p. (gr. 2-3). pap. 63.00 ***(978-1-5382-0271-5(9))*** Stevens, Gareth Publishing LLLP.

Murphy, John A. Ali Khamenei. 2007. (Modern World Leaders Ser.). (Illus.). 143p. (YA). (gr. 7-12). lib. bdg. 30.00 *(978-0-7910-9517-1(7))* Facts On File, Inc.

Nagle, Jeanne, ed. Top 101 World Leaders, 1 vol., 1. 2014. (People You Should Know Ser.). (ENG.). 184p. (YA). (gr. 7-12). 35.25 *(978-1-62275-124-2(8))* Rosen Publishing Group, Inc., The.

Nardo, Don. Pericles: Great Leader of Ancient Athens. 2006. (Rulers of the Ancient World Ser.). (Illus.). 160p. (YA). (gr. 6-12). lib. bdg. 29.27 *(978-0-7660-2561-5(6))* Enslow Pubs., Inc.

Nelson, Maria. The Life of Ben Franklin. 2012. (Famous Lives Ser.). (ENG.). 24p. (J). (gr. k-3). lib. bdg. 22.60 *(978-1-4339-6345-2(0));* (gr. 1-4). pap. 8.15 *(978-1-4339-6347-6(7))* Stevens, Gareth Publishing LLLP.

—The Life of Ben Franklin / la Vida de BenjamíN Franklin. 2012. (Famous Lives / Vidas extraordinarias Ser.). (ENG & SPA., Illus.). 24p. (J). (gr. k-3). 22.60 *(978-1-4339-6653-8(0))* Stevens, Gareth Publishing LLLP.

—The Life of Paul Revere. 2012. (Famous Lives Ser.). (ENG.). 24p. (J). (gr. k-3). lib. bdg. 22.60 *(978-1-4339-6353-7(1));* (gr. 1-4). pap. 8.15 *(978-1-4339-6355-1(8))* Stevens, Gareth Publishing LLLP.

Newton, Michael E. Alexander Hamilton: The Formative Years. 2015. (ENG., Illus.). 774p. 40.00 *(978-0-9826040-3-8(3))* Eleftheria Publishing.

Niz, Xavier & Niz, Xavier W. Paul Revere's Ride. Bascle, Brian, illus. 2005. (Graphic History Ser.). (ENG.). 32p. (gr. 3-4). 30.65 *(978-0-7368-4965-4(3),* Graphic Library) Capstone Press of Coughlan Cos.

Otfinoski, Steven. Patriots & Redcoats: Stories of American Revolutionary War Leaders. 2015. (Revolutionary War Ser.). (ENG.). 48p. (gr. 3-4). pap. 8.95 *(978-1-4914-2158-1(4))* Capstone Press of Coughlan Cos.

Owens, L. L. Benjamin Franklin, 1 vol. 2007. (Essential Lives Set 1 Ser.). (ENG., Illus.). 112p. (J). (gr. 6-12). lib. bdg. 35.64 *(978-1-59928-840-6(0))* ABDO Publishing Co.

S

Peppas, Lynn. Why José Antonio Navarro Matters to Texas. 2014. (Illus.). 32p. (J). lib. bdg. 26.25 *(978-1-4777-0936-8(3))* Rosen Publishing Group, Inc., The.

Phan, Sandy. Cecil Rhodes: The Man Who Expanded an Empire, 1 vol. 2012. (Primary Source Readers Ser.). (ENG.). 32p. (J). (gr. 4-4). pap. 8.99 *(978-1-4333-5016-0(5))* Teacher Created Materials, Inc.

Pollack, Pam & Belviso, Meg. Who Was Alexander Hamilton? Putra, Dede, illus. 2017. (Who Was? Ser.). (ENG.). 112p. (J). (gr. 3-7). 5.99 ***(978-0-399-54427-9(5))***; lib. bdg. 15.99 ***(978-0-399-54429-3(1))*** Penguin Young Readers Group. (Penguin Workshop).

Price, Sean Stewart. Adolf Hitler. 2010. (Wicked History Ser.). (ENG., Illus.). 128p. (J). 31.00 *(978-0-531-20757-4(9))*, Watts, Franklin) Scholastic Library Publishing.

Proudfit, Benjamin. Benjamin Franklin. 2015. (What You Didn't Know about History Ser.). (ENG., Illus.). 24p. (J). (gr. 2-3). pap. 8.15 *(978-1-4824-1926-9(2))* Stevens, Gareth Publishing LLLP.

Publishers, Chelsea House, creator. Leaders of the American Revolution Set, 11-Volumes. 2006. (Leaders of the American Revolution Ser.). 100p. (gr. 5-8). 270.00 *(978-0-7910-9320-7(4)*, Chelsea Hse.) Facts On File, Inc.

Randolph, Joanne. The Call of Liberty: Marquis de Lafayette & the American Revolution. 2009. (Great Moments in American History Ser.). 32p. (gr. 3-3). 47.90 *(978-1-61513-152-5(3))* Rosen Publishing Group, Inc., The.

Randolph, Ryan P. Benjamin Franklin: Inventor, Writer & Patriot. 2005. (Library of American Lives & Times). (Illus.). 112p. (YA). (gr. 4-8). lib. bdg. 34.60 *(978-0-8239-5751-4(9))* Rosen Publishing Group, Inc., The.

—Benjamin Franklin: Inventor, Writer, & Patriot. 2009. (Library of American Lives & Times Ser.). 112p. (gr. 5-5). 69.20 *(978-1-60853-472-2(3))* Rosen Publishing Group, Inc., The.

Ransom, Candice. John Hancock. 2005. (History Maker Bios Ser.). (Illus.). 48p. (J). (gr. 3-4). 26.60 *(978-0-8225-1547-0(4)*, Lerner Pubns.) Lerner Publishing Group.

Rau, Dana Meachen. Who Was Gandhi? Hoare, Jerry & Harrison, Nancy, illus. 2014. (Who Was? Ser.). (ENG.). 112p. (J). (gr. 3-7). pap. 5.99 *(978-0-448-48235-4(5)*, Grosset & Dunlap) Penguin Young Readers Group.

Rausch, Monica. Benjamin Franklin. 2007. (Grandes personajes (Spanish- Great Americans) Ser.). 24p. (gr. 1-4). (ENG & SPA.). pap. 8.15 *(978-0-8368-7988-9(0))*; (Illus.). pap. 8.15 *(978-0-8368-7689-5(X))*; (Illus.). lib. bdg. 22.00 *(978-0-8368-7682-6(2))* Stevens, Gareth Publishing LLLP. (Weekly Reader Leveled Readers).

Rausch, Monica L. Benjamin Franklin. 2007. (Grandes personajes (Great Americans) Ser.). (ENG & SPA., Illus.). 24p. (gr. 1-4). lib. bdg. 22.00 *(978-0-8368-7981-0(3)*, Weekly Reader Leveled Readers) Stevens, Gareth Publishing LLLP.

Rice, Dona. Mohandas Gandhi, 1 vol. 2nd rev. ed. 2014. (TIME for KIDS(r) Nonfiction Readers Ser.). (ENG., Illus.). 32p. (J). (gr. 3-3). pap. 25.96 *(978-1-4807-1091-7(1))* Shell Educational Publishing.

Rice, William & Rice, Dona. Mohandas Gandhi. 2017. (TIME for Kids en Español - Level 3 Ser.). (SPA.). 32p. (gr. 3-3). lib. bdg. 31.99 ***(978-1-5157-5189-2(9))*** Time for Kids Inc AUS. Dist: Capstone Pub.

Riley, Gail Blasser. Benjamin Franklin & Electricity. 2004. (Cornerstones of Freedom Ser.). (ENG., Illus.). 48p. (YA). (gr. 4-7). 26.00 *(978-0-516-24240-8(7))* Scholastic Library Publishing.

Riley, John B. Benjamin Franklin: A Photo Biography. l.t. ed. 2004. (First Biographies Ser.). (Illus.). 24p. (YA). (gr. 5-18). 16.95 *(978-1-883846-64-0(1)*, First Biographies) Reynolds, Morgan Inc.

Rinaldo, Denise. Julius Caesar: Dictator for Life. 2010. (Wicked History Ser.). (ENG.). 128p. (J). (gr. 6-12). pap. 5.95 *(978-0-531-22822-7(3)*, Watts, Franklin) Scholastic Library Publishing.

Rivera, Sheila. Mohandas Gandhi: A Life of Integrity. 2006. (Pull Ahead Bks.). (Illus.). 32p. (J). (gr. 3-7). lib. bdg. 22.60 *(978-0-8225-6383-9(5)*, Lerner Pubns.) Lerner Publishing Group.

—Mohandas Ghandi: A Life of Integrity. 2007. (Pull Ahead Books-Biographies Ser.). (ENG., Illus.). 32p. (gr. k-3). pap. 7.95 *(978-0-8225-6432-4(7))* Lerner Publishing Group.

Ryckman, Tatiana. Alexander Hamilton: The First Secretary of Treasury & an Author of the Federalist Papers. 2016. (Great American Thinkers Ser.). (Illus.). 128p. (J). (gr. 9-9). 45.64 *(978-1-5026-1934-1(2))* Cavendish Square Publishing.

Salzmann, Mary Elizabeth. Benjamin Franklin, 1 vol. 2016. (ENG., Illus.). 24p. (J). *(978-1-68078-157-1(X))* ABDO Publishing Co.

Santillan, Beatriz & Aird, Hamish. Pericles: Athenian Statesman & Patron of the Arts. 2017. (Leaders of the Ancient World Ser.). 112p. (J). (gr. 12-11). 37.10 ***(978-1-5081-7487-5(3)***, Rosen Young Adult) Rosen Publishing Group, Inc., The.

Santillian, Beatriz & Randall, Bernard. Solon: Athenian Statesman & Poet. 2017. (Leaders of the Ancient World Ser.). 112p. (J). (gr. 12-11). 37.10 ***(978-1-5081-7493-6(8)***, Rosen Young Adult) Rosen Publishing Group, Inc., The.

Satterfield, Kathryn Hoffman. Benjamin Franklin A Man of Many Talents. 2005. 44p. (J). lib. bdg. 15.00 *(978-1-4242-0846-3(7))* Fitzgerald Bks.

Sawyer, Kem Knapp. Mohandas Gandhi. 2011. (Champion of Freedom Ser.). 144p. (gr. 7-12). 28.95 *(978-1-59935-166-7(8))* Reynolds, Morgan Inc.

Schroeder, Alan. Ben Franklin: His Wit & Wisdom from A to Z. O'brien, John, illus. 2011. (ENG.). 32p. (J). (gr. 1-5). 16.95 *(978-0-8234-1950-0(9))* Holiday Hse., Inc.

—Ben Franklin: His Wit & Wisdom from A-Z. O'brien, John, illus. 2012. (ENG.). 32p. (J). pap. 7.95 *(978-0-8234-2435-1(9))* Holiday Hse., Inc.

Seeley, M. H. 20 Fun Facts about Aaron Burr. 2017. (Fun Fact File: Founding Fathers Ser.). 32p. (gr. 2-3). 25.25 ***(978-1-5382-0281-4(6))*** Stevens, Gareth Publishing LLLP.

—20 Fun Facts about Alexander Hamilton. 2017. (Fun Fact File: Founding Fathers Ser.). 32p. (gr. 2-3). pap. 10.50 ***(978-1-5382-0288-3(3))*** Stevens, Gareth Publishing LLLP.

Shaw, Maura D. Gandhi: India's Great Soul. Marchesi, Stephen, illus. 2003. (ENG.). 32p. (J). (gr. 1-3). 12.95 *(978-1-893361-91-1(8)*, 9781893361911, Skylight Paths Publishing) LongHill Partners, Inc.

Shea, Therese M. Alexander Hamilton: Founding Father & Treasury Secretary. 2017. (J). pap. ***(978-0-7660-9045-3(0))*** Enslow Pubs., Inc.

Smith, Andrea P. A Day in the Life of Colonial Silversmith Paul Revere. 2012. (Illus.). 24p. (J). 63.60 *(978-1-4488-5217-8(X))*; pap. 10.60 *(978-1-4488-5216-1(1))*; lib. bdg. 25.25 *(978-1-4488-5189-8(0))* Rosen Publishing Group, Inc., The. (PowerKids Pr.).

Streissguth, Tom. Benjamin Franklin. 2005. (Bios for Challenged Readers Ser.). (Illus.). 112p. (J). (gr. 6-12). lib. bdg. 27.93 *(978-0-8225-2210-2(1))* Lerner Publishing Group.

Tarman, Mel. Judah: The Story of Judah P. Benjamin, Confederate Statesman. 2013. 46p. pap. 6.95 *(978-1-929919-50-5(6))* Camp Pope Publishing.

Thayer, William Makepeace. The Bobbin Boy: Or, How Nat Got His Learning. 2007. (ENG.). 210p. pap. 20.99 *(978-1-4346-3420-7(5))*; 228p. pap. 22.99 *(978-1-4346-3421-4(3))* Creative Media Partners, LLC.

—From Boyhood to Manhood: Life of Benjamin Franklin. 2006. pap. *(978-1-4068-0906-0(3))* Echo Library.

Tieck, Sarah. Paul Revere, 1 vol. 2006. (First Biographies Ser.). (ENG., Illus.). 32p. (gr. -1-3). 27.07 *(978-1-59679-787-1(8)*, Buddy Bks.) ABDO Publishing Co.

Time for Kids Editors. Benjamin Franklin - A Man of Many Talents. 2005. (Time for Kids Ser.). (ENG., Illus.). 48p. (J). (gr. 2-4). pap. 3.99 *(978-0-06-057609-7(X))* HarperCollins Pubs.

Todd, Anne M. Mohandas Gandhi. 2004. (Spiritual Leaders & Thinkers Ser.). (Illus.). 120p. (C). (gr. 9-13). 30.00 *(978-0-7910-7864-8(7)*, Chelsea Hse.) Facts On File, Inc.

Tracy, Kathleen. The Life & Times of Cicero. 2006. (Biography from Ancient Civilizations Ser.). (Illus.). 48p. (J). (gr. 4-8). lib. bdg. 29.95 *(978-1-58415-510-2(8))* Mitchell Lane Pubs., Inc.

Troupe, Thomas Kingsley. Paul Revere's Ride: a Fly on the Wall History. Tejido, Jomike, illus. 2017. (Fly on the Wall History Ser.). (ENG.). 32p. (gr. 1-3). lib. bdg. 27.32 *(978-1-4795-9785-7(6))* Picture Window Bks.

A True Book & Trade - Biographies. 2013. (True Book™—Biographies Ser.). (J). 116.00 *(978-0-531-28024-9(1)*, Children's Pr.) Scholastic Library Publishing.

Trussell-Cullen, Alan. Mahatma Gandhi. 2009. pap. 13.25 *(978-1-60559-064-6(9))* Hameray Publishing Group, Inc.

Uschan, Michael V. Fidel Castro. 2008. (Twentieth Century's Most Influencial Hispanics Ser.). (ENG., Illus.). 104p. (J). (gr. 7-10). lib. bdg. 33.45 *(978-1-4205-0059-2(7)*, LML02109-240047, Lucent Bks.) Cengage Gale.

Vander Hook, Sue. Colin Powell: General & Statesman, 1 vol. 2010. (Military Heroes Ser.). (ENG.). 112p. (J). (gr. 6-12). lib. bdg. 35.64 *(978-1-60453-965-3(8))* ABDO Publishing Co.

—Mahatma Gandhi: Proponent of Peace, 1 vol. 2010. (Essential Lives Set 5 Ser.). (ENG.). 112p. (J). (gr. 6-12). lib. bdg. 35.64 *(978-1-61613-515-7(8))* ABDO Publishing Co.

Venezia, Mike. Benjamin Franklin: Electrified the World with New Ideas. Venezia, Mike, illus. 2009. (Getting to Know the World's Greatest Inventors & Scientists Ser.). (ENG., Illus.). 32p. (J). (gr. 2-5). 28.00 *(978-0-531-23701-4(X))* Scholastic Library Publishing.

Vescia, Monique & Nicholson, Michael. Mahatma Gandhi: Champion of the Indian Independence Movement. 2017. (J). ***(978-1-5383-8084-0(6))***; pap. ***(978-1-5383-8083-3(8))*** Rosen Publishing Group, Inc., The. (Rosen Young Adult).

Wagner, Heather Lehr. Machiavelli: Renaissance Political Analyst & Author. 2005. (Makers of the Middle Ages & Renaissance Ser.). (Illus.). 136p. (gr. 5-8). lib. bdg. 32.95 *(978-0-7910-8629-2(1)*, Chelsea Hse.) Facts On File, Inc.

—Paul Revere: Messenger for Freedom. 2005. (Leaders of the American Revolution Ser.). (Illus.). 128p. (gr. 5-8). lib. bdg. 30.00 *(978-0-7910-8624-7(0))* Facts On File, Inc.

Wallace, Susan Helen & Jablonski, Patricia E. Saint Thomas More: Courage, Conscience, & the King. Lachuk, Dani, illus. 2014. (ENG.). 144p. (J). pap. 8.95 *(978-0-8198-9021-4(9))* Pauline Bks. & Media.

Waxman, Laura Hamilton. Colin Powell. 2005. (History Maker Bios Ser.). 48p. (J). pap. 8.95 *(978-0-8225-5463-9(1))*; (ENG., Illus.). (gr. 3-6). lib. bdg. 27.93 *(978-0-8225-2433-5(3)*, Lerner Pubns.) Lerner Publishing Group.

Weston Woods Staff, creator. Where Was Patrick Henry on the 29th of May? 2011. 38.75 *(978-1-55592-485-0(9))* 2004. 29.95 *(978-1-55592-484-3(0))* 2004. 18.95 *(978-1-55592-483-6(2))* Weston Woods Studios, Inc.

White, Casey. John Jay: Diplomat of the American Experiment. 2005. (Library of American Thinkers Ser.). (Illus.). 112p. (YA). (gr. 5-9). lib. bdg. 34.60 *(978-1-4042-0507-9(1))* Rosen Publishing Group, Inc., The.

Whiting, Jim. Benjamin Franklin. 2006. (Profiles in American History Ser.). (Illus.). 48p. (J). (gr. 3-7). lib. bdg. 29.95 *(978-1-58415-435-8(7))* Mitchell Lane Pubs., Inc.

—The Life & Times of Pericles. 2005. (Biography from Ancient Civilizations Ser.). (Illus.). 48p. (J). (gr. -1-7). lib. bdg. 29.95 *(978-1-58415-339-9(3))* Mitchell Lane Pubs., Inc.

Willett, Edward. Ayatollah Khomeini. 2009. (Middle East Leaders Ser.). 112p. (gr. 5-8). 66.50 *(978-1-61514-645-1(8)*, Rosen Reference) Rosen Publishing Group, Inc., The.

Winter, Jonah. Paul Revere & the Bell Ringers. Dodson, Bert, illus. 2003. (Ready-To-read COFA Ser.). (ENG.). 32p. (J). (gr. k-2). pap. 3.99 *(978-0-689-85535-8(0)*, Simon Spotlight) Simon Spotlight.

World Leaders Set, vols. 8, vol. 8. Incl. Adolf Hitler & Nazi Germany. (Illus.). 176p. (gr. 3-7). 2006. lib. bdg. 28.95 *(978-1-931798-78-5(8))*; Alexander the Great: Conqueror of the Known World. Nardo, Don. (Illus.). 100p. (J). 2009. 28.95 *(978-1-59935-126-1(9))*; Che Guevara: In Search of Revolution. Miller, Calvin Craig. (Illus.). 192p. (J). (gr. 6-12). 2006. lib. bdg. 26.95 *(978-1-931798-93-8(1))*; Cleopatra: Ruler of Egypt. (Illus.). 176p. (gr. 6-12). 2007. lib. bdg. 27.95 *(978-1-59935-035-6(1))*; Empire in the East: The Story of Genghis Khan. Rice, Earle, Jr. (Illus.). 160p. (gr. 3-7). 2005. 28.95 *(978-1-931798-62-4(1))*; Fidel Castro & the Cuban Revolution. Naden, Corinne J. & Blue, Rose. (Illus.). 144p. (J). (gr. 3-7). 2006. lib. bdg. 27.95 *(978-1-59935-029-5(7))*; Fighting Wars, Planning for Peace: The Story of George C. Marshall. Gimpel, Lee. (Illus.). 176p. (J). (gr. 6-12). 2005. lib. bdg. 26.95 *(978-1-931798-66-2(4))*; Hugo Chavez: Leader of Venezuela. (Illus.). 128p. 2007. lib. bdg. 27.95 *(978-1-59935-068-4(8))*; Joseph Stalin & the Soviet Union. (Illus.). 208p. (J). (gr. 6-12). 2006. lib. bdg. 26.95 *(978-1-931798-94-5(X))*; Mao Zedong & the Chinese Revolution. Naden, Corinne J. 144p. (YA). (gr. 6-9). 2008. lib. bdg. 28.95 *(978-1-59935-100-1(5))*; Velvet Revolution: Vaclav Havel & the Fall of Communism. Duberstein, John. (Illus.). 160p. (gr. 6-12). 2006. lib. bdg. 28.95 *(978-1-931798-85-3(0))*; Woodrow Wilson & the Progressive Era. Lukes, Bonnie L. (Illus.). 192p. (J). (gr. 6-10). 2006. lib. bdg. 26.95 *(978-1-931798-79-2(6))*; 2009. Set lib. bdg. 247.60 *(978-1-59935-013-4(0))* Reynolds, Morgan Inc.

Wyborny, Sheila. Kim Jong Il. 2009. (People in the News Ser.). (ENG., Illus.). 128p. (gr. 7-10). lib. bdg. 39.40 *(978-1-4205-0091-2(0)*, LML02109-242095, Lucent Bks.) Cengage Gale.

Yero, Judith Lloyd. The Declaration of Independence. 2007. (Reading Expeditions Ser.). (ENG., Illus.). 32p. (J). pap. 17.95 *(978-0-7922-4554-4(7))* CENGAGE Learning.

Zamosky, Lisa. Government Leaders Then & Now, 1 vol. 2006. (Primary Source Readers Ser.). (ENG.). 32p. (J). (gr. 2-2). pap. 8.99 *(978-0-7439-9386-9(1))* Shell Educational Publishing.

STATISTICS

see also Probabilities

also general subjects and names of countries, cities, etc. with the subdivision Statistics, e.g. U. S.—Statistics; etc.

Aboff, Marcie. Analyzing Doggie Data. 2011. (Data Mania Ser.). (ENG.). 24p. (gr. 1-2). pap. 41.70 *(978-1-4296-6465-3(7)*, First Facts) Capstone Press of Coughlan Cos.

Adams, Colleen. The Everglades: Analyzing Graphs, Tables, & Charts. (PowerMath Ser.). 32p. 2009. (ENG.). (gr. 5-6). pap. 10.00 *(978-1-4042-5127-4(8))* 2009. (gr. 4-5). 47.90 *(978-1-60851-420-5(X))* 2005. (Illus.). (J). (gr. 3-6). lib. bdg. 25.25 *(978-1-4042-2933-4(7))* Rosen Publishing Group, Inc., The. (PowerKids Pr.).

Alaina, Maria. Estimating, 1 vol. 2013. (Wonder Readers Next Steps: Math Ser.). (ENG.). 20p. (gr. -1-1). 22.65 *(978-1-4765-2367-5(3)*, Wonder Readers) Capstone Press of Coughlan Cos.

Arvoy, Marsha & Nardi, Dorianne. Percentage. 2010. (ENG., Illus.). 24p. (J). *(978-0-7787-5246-2(1))*; pap. *(978-0-7787-5293-6(3))* Crabtree Publishing Co.

Bodach, Vijaya Khisty. Pictografías. 2010. (Hacer Gráficas/Making Graphs Ser.). (MUL, SPA & ENG.). 32p. (gr. 1-2). lib. bdg. 27.32 *(978-1-4296-6101-0(1)*, A+ Bilingue/Bilingual) Capstone Press of Coughlan Cos.

Boswell, Kelly. Graphs, Graphs, Graphs!, 1 vol. 2013. (Displaying Information Ser.). (ENG.). 32p. (gr. 1-2). 27.32 *(978-1-4765-0259-5(5))*; pap. 8.95 *(978-1-4765-3336-0(9))* Capstone Press of Coughlan Cos. (Aplus Bks.).

Brookie, Anna, et al. Mathematics & Statistics for the New Zealand Curriculum Year 9. 2nd ed. 2013. (ENG.). pap., stu. ed. *(978-1-107-62840-3(7))* Cambridge Univ. Pr.

Burrill, Gail F., et al. Exploring Regression. (Data-Driven Mathematics Ser.). 96p. (YA). (gr. 7-12). pap., stu. ed. 18.95 *(978-1-57232-245-5(4))* Seymour, Dale Pubns.

Burton, Margie, et al. We All Scream for Ice Cream. 2011. (Early Connections Ser.). (J). *(978-1-61672-544-0(3))* Benchmark Education Co.

Bussell, Linda. Trabajemos con Números en Las Noticias. 2008. (Las matemáticas en nuestro mundo - Nivel 3 (Math in Our World - Level 3) Ser.). (SPA.). 24p. (gr. 2-5). pap. 8.15 *(978-0-8368-9391-5(3)*, Weekly Reader Leveled Readers) Stevens, Gareth Publishing LLLP.

—Trabajemos con Números en las Noticias. 2008. (Matemáticas en Nuestro Mundo - Nivel 3 (Math in Our World - Level 3) Ser.). (SPA.). 24p. (J). (gr. 2-5). lib. bdg. 22.00 *(978-0-8368-9292-5(5)*, Weekly Reader Leveled Readers) Stevens, Gareth Publishing LLLP.

—Working with Numbers in the News. 2008. (Math in Our World - Level 3 Ser.). (Illus.). 24p. (J). (gr. 2-5). pap. 8.15 *(978-0-8368-9383-0(2))*; lib. bdg. 22.00 *(978-0-8368-9284-0(4))* Stevens, Gareth Publishing LLLP. (Weekly Reader Leveled Readers).

Colson, Rob. What Are the Chances? Probability, Statistics, Ratios, & Proportions. 2017. (Math Everywhere Ser.). (ENG.). 32p. (J). pap. 8.95 ***(978-0-531-23321-4(9))***; lib. bdg. 27.00 ***(978-0-531-22885-2(1))*** Scholastic Library Publishing. (Children's Pr.).

D'Anna, Cindy. Field Day! 2013. (Core Math Skills: Measurement & Geometry Ser.). 24p. (J). (gr. 1-2). 22.60 *(978-1-4777-2229-9(7))*; (ENG.). pap. 8.25 *(978-1-4777-2046-2(4))* Rosen Publishing Group, Inc., The. (Rosen Classroom).

—Field Day! Represent & Interpret Data. 2013. (Rosen Math Readers Ser.). (ENG.). 24p. (J). (gr. 1-2). pap. 49.50 *(978-1-4777-2047-9(2)*, Rosen Classroom) Rosen Publishing Group, Inc., The.

Dase, Pam. Tonight's Concert. rev. ed. 2012. (Mathematics Readers Ser.). (ENG.). 32p. (J). (gr. 6-6). pap. 8.99 *(978-1-4333-3464-1(X))* Teacher Created Materials, Inc.

Dowdy, Penny. Estimation. 2008. (My Path to Math Ser.). (ENG., Illus.). 24p. (J). (gr. k-3). lib. bdg. *(978-0-7787-4337-8(3))* Crabtree Publishing Co.

Drawing Conclusions & Inferences (Gr. 4-5) 2004. (J). *(978-1-58232-134-9(5))* ECS Learning Systems, Inc.

Edgar, Sherra G. Tally Charts. 2013. (21st Century Basic Skills Library: Let's Make Graphs Ser.). (ENG., Illus.). 24p. (J). (gr. k-3). 22.79 *(978-1-62431-395-0(7)*, 202700); pap. 12.79 *(978-1-62431-471-1(6)*, 202702) Cherry Lake Publishing.

Exploring Statistics. (J). (gr. k-2). 9.90 *(978-0-669-15890-8(9))* Houghton Mifflin Harcourt School Pubs.

Faulkner, Nicholas & Gregersen, Erik. Statistics & Probability. 2017. (J). lib. bdg. ***(978-1-68048-779-4(5)***, Britannica Educational Publishing) Rosen Publishing Group, Inc., The.

Flatt, Lizann. Collecting Data. 2016. (Get Graphing! Building Data Literacy Skills Ser.). (ENG., Illus.). 24p. (J). (gr. k-3). *(978-0-7787-2633-3(9))* Crabtree Publishing Co.

Freudenthal. Insights into Data. 3rd ed. 2003. (Math in Context Ser.). (Illus.). 7.86 *(978-0-03-071699-7(3))* Holt McDougal.

Gitlin, Marty. A Dream Job As a Sports Statistician. 2017. (J). ***(978-1-5383-8138-0(9))*** Rosen Publishing Group, Inc., The.

Gnanadesikan, Mrudulla. Art & Technique of Simulation. (YA). (gr. 7-12). pap., stu. ed. 12.95 *(978-0-86651-336-4(1)*, DSO1704) Globe Fearon Educational Publishing.

Heinrich, Erik. This or That Survival Debate: A Rip-Roaring Game of Either/or Questions. 2012. (This or That? Ser.). (ENG.). 32p. (gr. 3-4). pap. 47.70 *(978-1-4296-9279-3(0)*, Edge Bks.) Capstone Press of Coughlan Cos.

Kompelien, Tracy. You Can Estimate, Thats Really Great!, 1 vol. 2007. (Math Made Fun Ser.). (ENG., Illus.). 24p. (J). (gr. k-3). lib. bdg. 24.21 *(978-1-59928-551-1(7)*, SandCastle) ABDO Publishing Co.

MacGillivray, Helen & Petocz, Peter. Statistics & Probability in the Australian Curriculum Years 9 And 10. 2013. (ENG.). pap. *(978-1-107-65599-7(4))* Cambridge Univ. Pr.

Marsico, Katie. Mountains. 2009. (21st Century Skills Library: Real World Math Ser.). (ENG.). 32p. (gr. 4-8). lib. bdg. 28.50 *(978-1-60279-492-4(8)*, 200316) Cherry Lake Publishing.

Martin, Steve, et al. The Wacky & Wonderful World Through Numbers: Over 2,000 Figures & Facts. 2015. (ENG., Illus.). 128p. (J). (gr. 3-7). pap. 11.99 *(978-1-4380-0590-4(3))* Barron's Educational Series, Inc.

Mineo, Kate. Compare with Bears. 2011. (Animal Math Ser.). (Illus.). 24p. (J). (gr. 1-3). pap. 8.15 *(978-1-4339-5660-7(8))*; lib. bdg. 22.60 *(978-1-4339-5658-4(6))* Stevens, Gareth Publishing LLLP.

Peters, Elisa. Statistics & Probability, 1 vol. 2015. (ENG.). 64p. (YA). 31.70 *(978-1-62275-533-2(2)*, Britannica Educational Publishing) Rosen Publishing Group, Inc., The.

Puritz, Christian. Venture Mathematics Worksheets - Statistics & Extra Investigations: Helping to Stretch the More Able 11 to 16 Year Olds. 2007. (ENG.). 40p. (J). pap. 21.00 *(978-1-899618-72-9(4))* Parkwest Pubns., Inc.

Robinson, C. L. MATH1on1 Statistics Foundation. 2006. (YA). per. 9.99 *(978-0-9786767-9-7(3))* Robinson, Consuelo.

Steffora, Tracey. Animal Math: Comparing & Measuring, 1 vol. 2014. (Animal Math Ser.). (ENG.). 32p. (gr. -1-1). 29.99 *(978-1-4846-0062-7(2)*, NA-h) Heinemann-Raintree.

Tallman, Teresa. Fun with Statistics. 2016. (ENG., Illus.). (J). pap. 9.95 ***(978-1-55571-832-9(9)***, Grid Pr.) L & R Publishing, LLC.

Understandable Statistics, Concepts & Methods. 7th ed. 2003. (gr. 11-12). instr.'s gde. ed. *(978-0-618-20560-8(8)*, 3-07006); cd-rom *(978-0-618-20563-9(2)*, 3-07010) CENGAGE Learning.

Visto, Joy. What Are the Chances? Making Math Work. 2016. (Making Math Work Ser.). (ENG.). 48p. (J). (gr. 5-9). pap. 12.00 *(978-1-62832-174-6(1)*, Creative Paperbacks) Creative Co., The.

Wingard-Nelson, Rebecca. Data, Graphing, & Statistics. 2004. (Math Success Ser.). (Illus.). 64p. (J). lib. bdg. 23.94 *(978-0-7660-2567-7(5))* Enslow Pubs., Inc.

STATISTICS—GRAPHIC METHODS

Arias, Lisa. Scrumptious Statistics: Show & Recognizie Statistics. 2014. (ENG.). 32p. (gr. 3-6). 32.79 *(978-1-62717-722-1(1))* Rourke Educational Media.

Burstein, John. Collecting Data: Pick a Pancake. Destiny Images Staff, illus. 2003. (Math Monsters Ser.). 24p. (J). (gr. k-4). lib. bdg. 21.00 *(978-0-8368-3805-3(X)*, Weekly Reader Leveled Readers) Stevens, Gareth Publishing LLLP.

Cocca, Lisa Colozza. Bar Graphs. 2013. (Explorer Junior Library: Math Explorer Junior Ser.). (ENG.). 24p. (gr. 1-4). 28.50 *(978-1-61080-911-5(4)*, 202623); pap. 12.79 *(978-1-61080-936-8(X)*, 202625) Cherry Lake Publishing.

—Pictographs. 2013. (Explorer Junior Library: Math Explorer Junior Ser.). (ENG.). 24p. (gr. 1-4). 28.50 *(978-1-61080-913-9(0)*, 202631); pap. 12.79 *(978-1-61080-938-2(6)*, 202633) Cherry Lake Publishing.

—Tally Charts. 2013. (Explorer Junior Library: Math Explorer Junior Ser.). (ENG.). 24p. (gr. 1-4). 28.50 *(978-1-61080-916-0(5)*, 202643); pap. 12.79 *(978-1-61080-941-2(6)*, 202645) Cherry Lake Publishing.

Edgar, Sherra G. Pictographs. 2013. (21st Century Basic Skills Library: Let's Make Graphs Ser.). (ENG., Illus.). 24p. (J). (gr. k-3). 22.79 *(978-1-62431-393-6(0)*, 202692); pap. 12.79 *(978-1-62431-469-8(4)*, 202694) Cherry Lake Publishing.

Harris, Nancy. Mashed Potatoes: Collecting & Reporting Data. 2007. (Math Focal Points (Discovery Library) Ser.). (Illus.). 24p. (J). (gr. -1-3). lib. bdg. 22.79 *(978-1-60044-640-5(X))* Rourke Educational Media.

Rupert, Matthews. Visual Factfinder Bugs. 2008. 512p. pap. *(978-1-84810-079-4(5))* Miles Kelly Publishing, Ltd.

Wilson, Natashya. The Census & America's People: Analyzing Data Using Line Graphs & Tables. (PowerMath Ser.). (ENG., 32p. (gr. 4-5). 2009. Illus.). pap. 10.00 *(978-0-8239-8903-4(8)*, PowerKids Pr.) 2004. 47.50 *(978-0-8239-7647-8(5))* Rosen Publishing Group, Inc., The.

STATUE OF LIBERTY (NEW YORK, N.Y.)

Bauer, Marion Dane. The Statue of Liberty. Wallace, John, illus. 2007. (Wonders of America Ser.). (ENG.). 32p. (J). (gr. -1-1). pap. 3.99 *(978-1-4169-3479-0(0)*, Simon Spotlight) Simon Spotlight.

Behrens, Janice. What Is the Statue of Liberty? 2009. (Scholastic News Nonfiction Readers Ser.). (Illus.). 24p. (J). (gr. 1-2). 22.00 *(978-0-531-21091-8(X))* Scholastic Library Publishing.

Blake, Kevin. Statue of Liberty. 2016. (American Places: from Vision to Reality Ser.). (ENG.). 32p. (J). (gr. 2-7). lib. bdg. 19.95 *(978-1-944102-41-8(8))* Bearport Publishing Co., Inc.

Braithwaite, Jill. La Estatua de la Libertad. 2005. (Libros para Avanzar (Pull Ahead Bks.)). (SPA., Illus.). 32p. (J). (gr. k-3). per. 6.95 *(978-0-8225-3137-1(2)*, Ediciones Lerner) Lerner Publishing Group.

—The Statue of Liberty. 2010. pap. 45.32 *(978-0-7613-6993-6(7))* 2010. (ENG.). 32p. pap. 7.95 *(978-0-7613-6052-0(2))* 2010. (ENG., Illus.). 32p. lib. bdg. 26.60 *(978-0-7613-6020-9(4)*, Lerner Pubns.) 2004. (Illus.). 32p. (J). lib. bdg. 22.60 *(978-0-8225-3802-8(4))* 2003. (ENG.). 32p. pap. 7.95 *(978-0-8225-3756-4(7))* Lerner Publishing Group.

Brannon, Cecelia H. Zoom in on the Statue of Liberty. 2016. (Zoom in on American Symbols Ser.). (Illus.). 24p. (J). pap. 9.35 *(978-0-7660-8450-6(7))* Enslow Pubs., Inc.

Burke, Michelle Prater. The Story of the Statue of Liberty. Mitchell, Kathy, illus. 2016. (J). *(978-0-8249-1985-6(8)*, Ideal Pubns.) Worthy Publishing.

Curlee, Lynn. Liberty. Curlee, Lynn, illus. 2003. (ENG., Illus.). 48p. (J). (gr. 2-7). 9.99 *(978-0-689-85683-9(0)*, Atheneum Bks. for Young Readers) Simon & Schuster Children's Publishing.

Douglas, Lloyd G. The Statue of Liberty. 2003. (Welcome Bks.). (ENG., Illus.). 24p. (J). (gr. -1-2). pap. 4.95 *(978-0-516-27877-3(0)*, Children's Pr.) Scholastic Library Publishing.

Eldridge, Alison & Eldridge, Stephen. The Statue of Liberty: An American Symbol. 2012. (All about American Symbols Ser.). (Illus.). 24p. (J). (gr. -1-1). pap. 7.95 *(978-1-4644-0051-3(2)*, Enslow Elementary) Enslow Pubs., Inc.

Fandel, Jennifer. The Statue of Liberty. 2005. (What in the World? Ser.). (Illus.). 48p. (J). (gr. 5-9). lib. bdg. 21.95 *(978-1-58341-377-7(4)*, Creative Education) Creative Co., The.

Faria, Joseph D. The Statue of Liberty & Ellis Island: A MyReportLinks.com Book. 2005. (Virtual Field Trips Ser.). (Illus.). 48p. (J). (gr. 4-10). lib. bdg. 26.60 *(978-0-7660-5226-0(5)*, MyReportLinks.com Bks.) Enslow Pubs., Inc.

Firestone, Mary. The Statue of Liberty, 1 vol. Skeens, Matthew, illus. 2006. (American Symbols Ser.). (ENG.). 24p. (gr. 1-2). 9.95 *(978-1-4048-2222-1(4))* Picture Window Bks.

Gamble, Adam & Jasper, Mark. Good Night Statue of Liberty. Kelly, Cooper, illus. 2017. (Good Night Our World Ser.). (ENG.). 20p. (J). (gr. -1 — 1). bds. 9.95 ***(978-1-60219-429-8(7))*** Good Night Bks.

Gaspar, Joe. The Statue of Liberty. 2013. (PowerKids Readers: American Symbols Ser.). (Illus.). 24p. (J). (gr. k-2). pap. 49.50 *(978-1-4777-0812-5(X))*; pap. 8.25 *(978-1-4777-0811-8(1))*; lib. bdg. 22.60 *(978-1-4777-0735-7(2))* Rosen Publishing Group, Inc., The. (PowerKids Pr.).

—The Statue of Liberty / la Estatua de la Libertad. Alamn, Eduardo, ed. 2013. (PowerKids Readers: American Symbols / Smbolos de Amrica Ser.). (ENG & SPA.). 24p. (J). (gr. k-2). 22.60 *(978-1-4777-1203-0(8)*, PowerKids Pr.) Rosen Publishing Group, Inc., The.

Glaser, Linda. Emma's Poem: The Voice of the Statue of Liberty. Nivola, Claire A., illus. (ENG.). 32p. (J). (gr. -1-3). 2013. pap. 7.99 *(978-0-544-10508-9(7))* 2010. 17.99 *(978-0-547-17184-5(6))* Houghton Mifflin Harcourt Publishing Co.

Goldsworthy, Steve. Estatua de la Libertad. 2013. (SPA.). (J). *(978-1-62127-623-4(6))* Weigl Pubs., Inc.

—Statue of Liberty with Code. 2012. (AV2 American Icons Ser.). (ENG., Illus.). 24p. (J). (gr. -1-3). pap. 12.95 *(978-1-61913-303-7(2)*, AV2 by Weigl) Weigl Pubs., Inc.

Healy, Nick. The Statue of Liberty. 2003. (J). pap. *(978-1-58417-117-1(0))*; lib. bdg. *(978-1-58417-054-9(9))* Lake Street Pubs.

Herrington, Lisa M. The Statue of Liberty. 2014. (Rookie Read-About(r) American Symbols Ser.). (ENG., Illus.). 32p. (J). pap. 5.95 *(978-0-531-21838-9(4))*; lib. bdg. 25.00 *(978-0-531-21565-4(2))* Scholastic Library Publishing.

Hicks, Terry Allan. Symbols of America Group 2, 6 bks., Set. Incl. Bald Eagle. (J). lib. bdg. 28.50 *(978-0-7614-2133-7(5))*; Capitol. lib. bdg. 20.95 *(978-0-7614-2132-0(7))*; Declaration of Independence. lib. bdg. 20.95 *(978-0-7614-2135-1(1))*; Ellis Island. lib. bdg. 20.95 *(978-0-7614-2134-4(3))*; Pledge of Allegiance. lib. bdg. 20.95 *(978-0-7614-2136-8(X))*; Uncle Sam. lib. bdg. 20.95 *(978-0-7614-2137-5(8))*; (Illus.). 40p. (gr. 3-7). 2006. 2007. Set lib. bdg. 171.00 *(978-0-7614-2130-6(0)*, Benchmark Bks.) Marshall Cavendish Corp.

Hochain, Serge. Building Liberty: A Statue Is Born. Hochain, Serge, illus. 2006. (Illus.). 46p. (J). (gr. 4-8). reprint ed. 25.00 *(978-1-4223-5181-9(5))* DIANE Publishing Co.

—Building Liberty: A Statue Is Born. 2004. (ENG., Illus.). 48p. (J). (gr. 3-7). 16.95 *(978-0-7922-6765-2(6))*; 25.90 *(978-0-7922-6969-4(1))* National Geographic Society. (National Geographic Children's Bks.).

Holub, Joan. What Is the Statue of Liberty? Mantha, John et al, illus. 2014. (What Was? Ser.). (ENG.). 112p. (J). (gr. 3-7). 5.99 *(978-0-448-47917-0(6)*, Grosset & Dunlap) Penguin Young Readers Group.

—What Is the Statue of Liberty? 2014. (What Is... ? Ser.). lib. bdg. 16.00 *(978-0-606-35687-9(8))* Turtleback Bks.

Hurtig, Jennifer. The Statue of Liberty. 2008. (Structural Wonders Ser.). (Illus.). 32p. (J). (gr. 4-6). pap. 9.95 *(978-1-59036-941-8(6))*; lib. bdg. 26.00 *(978-1-59036-940-1(8))* Weigl Pubs., Inc.

Hurtig, Jennifer & Kissock, Heather. The Statue of Liberty. 2014. (J). *(978-1-4896-1966-2(6))* Weigl Pubs., Inc.

Kent, Deborah. The Statue of Liberty. 2012. (Cornerstones of Freedom, Third Ser.). (ENG.). 64p. (J). pap. 8.95 *(978-0-531-28166-6(3))*; (gr. 4-6). lib. bdg. 30.00 *(978-0-531-23066-4(X))* Scholastic Library Publishing. (Children's Pr.).

Landau, Elaine. The Statue of Liberty. 2008. (True Bks.). (ENG., Illus.). 48p. (J). (gr. 4-6). pap. 6.95 *(978-0-531-14785-6(1)*, Children's Pr.) Scholastic Library Publishing.

Lewison, Wendy Cheyette. L Is for Liberty. Hines, Laura Freeman, illus. 2003. (Reading Railroad Ser.). (ENG.). 24p. (J). (gr. -1-3). mass mkt. 3.99 *(978-0-448-43228-1(5)*, Grosset & Dunlap) Penguin Young Readers Group.

Malam, John. Be a Worker on the Statue of Liberty! A Monument You'd Rather Not Build. Antram, David, illus. 2008. (You Wouldn't Want to...: American History Ser.). (ENG.). 32p. (J). 29.00 *(978-0-531-20700-0(5)*, Watts, Franklin) Scholastic Library Publishing.

—You Wouldn't Want to Be a Worker on the Statue of Liberty! A Monument You'd Rather Not Build. Antram, David, illus. 2008. (You Wouldn't Want to...: American History Ser.). (ENG.). 32p. (J). (gr. 3-18). pap. 9.95 *(978-0-531-21910-2(0)*, Watts, Franklin) Scholastic Library Publishing.

—You Wouldn't Want to Be a Worker on the Statue of Liberty! (Revised Edition) 2017. (You Wouldn't Want to... American History Ser.). (ENG., Illus.). 32p. (J). lib. bdg. 29.00 *(978-0-531-23833-2(4)*, Watts, Franklin) Scholastic Library Publishing.

Malaspina, Ann. Nathan & Nicole Learn about Nouns. Hamblin, George, illus. 2014. (Language Builders Ser.). (ENG.). 32p. (J). (gr. 2-4). lib. bdg. 25.27 *(978-1-59953-666-8(8))* Norwood Hse. Pr.

Mann, Elizabeth. Statue of Liberty: A Tale of Two Countries. Witschonke, Alan, illus. 2011. (Wonders of the World Ser.). (ENG.). 48p. (J). (gr. 3-18). 22.95 *(978-1-931414-43-2(2)*, 9781931414432) Mikaya Pr.

Marcovitz, Hal. Statue of Liberty: A Beacon of Welcome & Hope. Moreno, Barry, ed. 2014. (Patriotic Symbols of America Ser.: 20). 48p. (J). (gr. 4-18). 20.95 *(978-1-4222-3130-2(5))* Mason Crest.

Marsh, Carole. I'm Reading About the Statue of Liberty. 2016. (I'm Reading About Ser.). (ENG., Illus.). (J). lib. bdg. 24.99 ***(978-0-635-12207-0(3))***; pap. 7.99 ***(978-0-635-12208-7(1))*** Gallopade International.

Monroe, Tyler. Statue of Liberty. 2013. (U. S. Symbols Ser.). (ENG.). 24p. (gr. k-1). 26.65 *(978-1-4765-3088-8(2))*; pap. 7.95 *(978-1-4765-3537-1(X))* Capstone Press of Coughlan Cos. (Pebble Plus).

Moriarty, Siobhan. Visit the Statue of Liberty. 2012. (Landmarks of Liberty Ser.). (ENG., Illus.). 24p. (J). (gr. 2-5). pap. 8.15 *(978-1-4339-6402-2(3)*, Gareth Stevens Learning Library); lib. bdg. 22.60 *(978-1-4339-6400-8(7))* Stevens, Gareth Publishing LLLP.

Orr, Tamra B. The Statue of Liberty: Introducing Primary Sources. 2016. (Introducing Primary Sources Ser.). (ENG., Illus.). 32p. (gr. 1-2). lib. bdg. 27.99 *(978-1-4914-8223-0(0))* Capstone Press of Coughlan Cos.

Qaiser, Annie. The Story of the Statue of Liberty: A History Perspectives Book. 2013. (Perspectives Library). (ENG., Illus.). 32p. (J). (gr. 4-8). 28.50 *(978-1-62431-422-3(8)*, 202808); pap. 14.21 *(978-1-62431-498-8(8)*, 202810) Cherry Lake Publishing.

Rappaport, Doreen. Lady Liberty: A Biography. Tavares, Matt, illus. (Candlewick Biographies Ser.). (ENG.). (J). 2014. 48p. (gr. 3-7). 14.99 *(978-0-7636-7114-3(2))* 2011. 40p. (gr. 3-7). pap. 8.99 *(978-0-7636-5301-9(2))* 2008. 40p. (gr. 2-5). 19.99 *(978-0-7636-2530-6(2))* Candlewick Pr.

RJF Publishing Staff & Staton, Hilarie. The Statue of Liberty. 2009. (Symbols of American Freedom Ser.). 48p. (gr. 4-6). 30.00 *(978-1-60413-516-9(6)*, Chelsea Clubhouse) Facts On File, Inc.

Rustad, Martha. Why Is the Statue of Liberty Green? Conger, Holli, illus. 2014. (Cloverleaf Books — Our American Symbols Ser.). 24p. (gr. k-2). pap. 6.95 *(978-1-4677-4470-6(0)*, Millbrook Pr.) Lerner Publishing Group.

Rustad, Martha E. H. Why Is the Statue of Liberty Green? Conger, Holli, illus. 2014. (Cloverleaf Books — Our American Symbols Ser.). (ENG.). 24p. (J). (gr. k-2). lib. bdg. 23.93 *(978-1-4677-2139-4(5)*, Millbrook Pr.) Lerner Publishing Group.

Shea, Pegi Deitz. Liberty Rising: The Story of the Statue of Liberty. Zahares, Wade, illus. 2013. (ENG.). 44p. (J). (gr. k-4). 8.99 *(978-1-250-02720-7(9)*, 9781250027207) Square Fish.

Silate, Jennifer. The Statue of Liberty. (Primary Sources of American Symbols Ser.). 24p. 2009. (gr. 3-3). 42.50 *(978-1-60851-510-3(9)*, PowerKids Pr.) 2006. (Illus.). (J). (gr. -1-3). lib. bdg. 22.60 *(978-1-4042-2696-8(6))* Rosen Publishing Group, Inc., The.

Sipperley, Keli. Statue of Liberty. 2014. (ENG.). 32p. (gr. 3-6). 32.79 *(978-1-62717-743-6(4))* Rourke Educational Media.

Statue of Liberty. 2008. (Build it now Ser.). 16p. pap. *(978-1-4075-2249-4(3))* Parragon, Inc.

Stevenson, Harvey. Looking at Liberty. Stevenson, Harvey, illus. 2003. (Illus.). 40p. (J). (gr. -1-2). 17.89 *(978-0-06-000101-8(1))* HarperCollins Pubs.

Stille, Darlene R. The Statue of Liberty, 1 vol. Ouren, Todd, illus. 2008. (Our Nation's Pride Ser.). (ENG.). 32p. (gr. -1-3). 28.50 *(978-1-60270-115-1(6)*, Looking Glass Library-Nonfiction) Magic Wagon.

Wilson, Jon. The Statue of Liberty. 2014. (United States Landmarks Ser.). (ENG.). 24p. (J). (gr. 1-4). 27.07 *(978-1-62323-958-9(3)*, 206733) Child's World, Inc., The.

STEALING

see Theft

STEAM-ENGINES

Collier, James Lincoln. The Steam Engine. 2005. (Great Inventions Ser.). (Illus.). 112p. (YA). (gr. 8-12). lib. bdg. *(978-0-7614-1880-1(6)*, Benchmark Bks.) Marshall Cavendish Corp.

Kras, Sara Louise. Steam Engine. 2003. (Transforming Power of Technology Ser.). (Illus.). 112p. (C). (gr. 9-13). 30.00 *(978-0-7910-7453-4(6)*, Chelsea Hse.) Facts On File, Inc.

Lock, Deborah & Dorling Kindersley Publishing Staff. Train Travel, Level 1. 2013. (DK Readers Ser.). (ENG.). 32p. (J). (gr. k-4). pap. 3.99 *(978-1-4654-0892-1(4)*, DK Children) Dorling Kindersley Publishing, Inc.

Mattern, Joanne. The Steam Engine: Fueling the Industrial Revolution. 2003. (Technology That Changed the World Ser.). (Illus.). 24p. (J). lib. bdg. 22.60 *(978-0-8239-6490-1(6)*, PowerKids Pr.) Rosen Publishing Group, Inc., The.

Orr, Tamra B. The Steam Engine. 2006. (Inventions That Shaped the World Ser.). (Illus.). 80p. (J). (gr. 5-8). 17.60 *(978-0-7569-6862-5(3))* Perfection Learning Corp.

—The Steam Engine. 2005. (Inventions That Shaped the World Ser.). (ENG., Illus.). 80p. (J). (gr. 5-8). lib. bdg. 30.50 *(978-0-531-12400-0(2)*, Watts, Franklin) Scholastic Library Publishing.

STEAM SHOVELS—FICTION

Burton, Virginia Lee. Mike Mulligan & His Steam Shovel. 2007. (ENG., Illus.). 40p. (J). (gr. -1 — 1). bds. 7.99 *(978-0-618-84019-9(2))* Houghton Mifflin Harcourt Publishing Co.

—Mike Mulligan & His Steam Shovel, 1 vol. Burton, Virginia Lee, illus. 2006. (Read along Book & CD Ser.). (ENG., Illus.). 48p. (J). (gr. -1-3). audio compact disk 10.99 *(978-0-618-73756-7(1))* Houghton Mifflin Harcourt Publishing Co.

—Mike Mulligan & His Steam Shovel. 75th anniv. ed. 2014. (ENG., Illus.). 56p. (J). (gr. -1-3). 17.99 *(978-0-544-27992-6(1)*, HMH Books For Young Readers) Houghton Mifflin Harcourt Publishing Co.

—Mike Mulligan & His Steam Shovel. 2006. (Illus.). 48p. pap. *(978-1-84507-501-9(3)*, Frances Lincoln) Quarto Publishing Group UK.

Weston Woods Staff, creator. Mike Mulligan & His Steam Shovel. 2011. 18.95 *(978-0-439-72838-6(X))*; 38.75 *(978-0-439-72839-3(8))* Weston Woods Studios, Inc.

Zimmerman, Andrea & Clemesha, David. Digger Man. Zimmerman, Andrea & Clemesha, David, illus. 2007. (ENG., Illus.). 32p. (J). (gr. -1-k). pap. 7.99 *(978-0-8050-8203-6(4)*, 9780805082036) Square Fish.

STEAMBOATS

Boothroyd, Jennifer. Robert Fulton: A Life of Innovation. 2007. (Pull Ahead Bks.). (Illus.). 32p. (J). (gr. 3-7). lib. bdg. 22.60 *(978-0-8225-6458-4(0)*, Lerner Pubns.) Lerner Publishing Group.

Doeden, Matt. The Queen Mary: A Chilling Interactive Adventure. 2016. (You Choose: Haunted Places Ser.). (ENG., Illus.). 112p. (gr. 3-4). lib. bdg. 31.99 *(978-1-5157-2578-7(2)*, You Choose Bks.) Capstone Press of Coughlan Cos.

Ferut, Michael. RMS Queen Mary. 2014. (Scariest Places on Earth Ser.). (ENG., Illus.). 24p. (J). (gr. 3-7). lib. bdg. 25.95 *(978-1-60014-996-2(0)*, Torque Bks.) Bellwether Media.

Ford, Carin T. Robert Fulton: The Steamboat Man. 2004. (Famous Inventors Ser.). (Illus.). 32p. (J). lib. bdg. 23.94 *(978-0-7660-2248-5(X))* Enslow Pubs., Inc.

Gregory, Josh. If You Were a Kid Aboard the Titanic. 2017. (If You Were a Kid Ser.). (ENG., Illus.). 32p. (J). lib. bdg. 26.00 *(978-0-531-22382-6(5)*, Children's Pr.) Scholastic Library Publishing.

Haunted! the Queen Mary. 2013. (History's Most Haunted Ser.). 32p. (J). (gr. 3-6). pap. 63.00 *(978-1-4339-9260-5(4))* Stevens, Gareth Publishing LLLP.

Jordan, Shirley. Benjamin Brown & the Great Steamboat Race. Kemly, Kathleen, illus. 2011. (History Speaks: Picture Books Plus Reader's Theater Ser.). 48p. pap. 56.72 *(978-0-7613-7630-9(5))*; (ENG.). (gr. 2-4). pap. 9.95 *(978-0-7613-6133-6(2))* Lerner Publishing Group.

McLeese, Don. Robert Fulton. 2005. (Rourke Discovery Library). (Illus.). 24p. (J). (gr. 2-5). lib. bdg. *(978-1-59515-434-7(5)*, 1244323) Rourke Educational Media.

McVicker, Maryellen. Joseph Kinney: Steamboat Captain. Hare, John, illus. 2014. (ENG.). 48p. (J). lib. bdg. 24.00 *(978-1-61248-116-6(7))* Truman State Univ. Pr.

Murdico, Suzanne J. Railroads & Steamships: Important Developments in American Transportation. (America's Industrial Society in the 19th Century Ser.). 32p. 2009. (gr. 4-4). 47.90 *(978-1-61511-340-8(1))* 2004. (ENG., Illus.). (J). (gr. 5-8). pap. 10.00 *(978-0-8239-4278-7(3))* Rosen Publishing Group, Inc., The.

Parks, Peggy J. Robert Fulton: Innovator with Steam Power. 2003. (Giants of Science Ser.). (ENG., Illus.). (J). 28.35 *(978-1-56711-492-8(X)*, Blackbirch Pr., Inc.) Cengage Gale.

Pierce, Morris A. Robert Fulton & the Development of the Steamboat. (Library of American Lives & Times Ser.). 112p. 2009. (gr. 5-5). 69.20 *(978-1-60853-502-6(9))* 2005. (Illus.). (YA). (gr. 4-8). lib. bdg. 34.60 *(978-0-8239-5737-8(3))* Rosen Publishing Group, Inc., The.

Radford, James & Wooders, Dave. Adventures on the Queen Mary: ... tales of a Teenage Crew Member! 2015. (ENG., Illus.). 274p. pap. 25.00 *(978-0-692-54554-6(9))* Perfect Page, The.

Roberts, Steven. Robert Fulton. 2013. (Jr. Graphic American Inventors Ser.). (ENG., Illus.). 24p. (J). (gr. 3-6). pap. 10.60 *(978-1-4777-0139-3(7))*; lib. bdg. 25.25 *(978-1-4777-0077-8(3))* Rosen Publishing Group, Inc., The. (PowerKids Pr.).

Rogers, Kate. Robert Fulton Invents the Steamboat. 2013. (Rosen Readers Ser.). (ENG.). 24p. (J). (gr. 3-4). pap. 8.25 *(978-1-4777-2603-7(9))*; pap. 49.50 *(978-1-4777-2604-4(7))* Rosen Publishing Group, Inc., The. (Rosen Classroom).

Rosenberg, Pam. Robert Fulton: Engineer & Inventor. 2003. (Our People Ser.). (ENG., Illus.). 32p. (J). (gr. 3-6). 29.93 *(978-1-56766-448-5(2)*, 200651) Child's World, Inc., The.

Shea, Therese. Haunted! the Queen Mary. 2013. (History's Most Haunted Ser.). 32p. (J). (gr. 3-6). 26.60 *(978-1-4339-9258-2(2))*; pap. 10.50 *(978-1-4339-9259-9(0))* Stevens, Gareth Publishing LLLP.

Stone, Adam. The Titanic Disaster. 2014. (Disaster Stories Ser.). (ENG.). 24p. (J). (gr. 3-8). 29.95 *(978-1-62617-154-1(8)*, Black Sheep) Bellwether Media.

Youngblood, Wayne. Mark Twain along the Mississippi. 2006. (In the Footsteps of American Heroes Ser.). (Illus.). 64p. (gr. 5-12). pap. 14.05 *(978-0-8368-6435-9(2))*; lib. bdg. 34.00 *(978-0-8368-6430-4(1))* Stevens, Gareth Publishing LLLP. (Gareth Stevens Secondary Library).

STEAMSHIPS

see Steamboats

STEEL

see also Iron

also headings beginning with the word Steel

Kassinger, Ruth. Iron & Steel: From Thor's Hammer to the Space Shuttle. 2003. (Material World Ser.). (ENG., Illus.). 80p. (gr. 5-9). lib. bdg. 26.60 *(978-0-7613-2111-8(X)*, Twenty-First Century Bks.) Lerner Publishing Group.

STEEL-ENGRAVING

see Engraving

STEEL INDUSTRY AND TRADE

see also Iron Industry and Trade

Jarnow, Jesse. Oil, Steel, & Railroads: America's Big Businesses in the Late 1800s. (America's Industrial Society in the 19th Century Ser.). 32p. 2009. (gr. 4-4). 47.90 *(978-1-61511-337-8(1))* 2004. (ENG., Illus.). (J). (gr. 5-8). pap. 10.00 *(978-0-8239-4276-3(7))* Rosen Publishing Group, Inc., The.

Kent, Zachary. Andrew Carnegie: Industrialist & Philanthropist. 2015. (Legendary American Biographies Ser.). 96p. (J). (gr. 6-12). 27.94 *(978-0-7660-6435-5(2))*; pap. 10.95 *(978-0-7660-6436-2(0))* Enslow Pubs., Inc.

Parker, Lewis K. Andrew Carnegie & the Steel Industry. (American Tycoons Ser.). 24p. 2009. (gr. 3-3). 42.50 *(978-1-61511-338-0(6))* 2003. (Illus.). (J). lib. bdg. 22.60 *(978-0-8239-6448-2(5))* Rosen Publishing Group, Inc., The. (PowerKids Pr.).

Rajczak Nelson, Kristen. Andrew Carnegie & the Steel Industry. 2016. (Great Entrepreneurs in U. S. History Ser.). (Illus.). 32p. (J). (gr. 5-5). pap. 11.75 *(978-1-4994-2115-6(X)*, PowerKids Pr.) Rosen Publishing Group, Inc., The.

STEFANSSON, VILHJALMUR, 1879-1962

Montgomery, Richard. Pechuck. 2005. reprint ed. pap. 31.95 *(978-1-4179-9755-8(9))* Kessinger Publishing, LLC.

STEIN, GERTRUDE, 1874-1946

Shaughnessy, Nicola. Gertrude Stein. 2007. (ENG.). 148p. (C). pap. 19.95 *(978-0-7463-0906-3(6))* Northcote Hse. Publishers, Ltd. GBR. Dist: Casemate Academic.

Winter, Jonah. Gertrude Is Gertrude Is Gertrude Is Gertrude. Brown, Calef, illus. 2009. (ENG.). 40p. (J). (gr. -1-3). 16.99 *(978-1-4169-4088-3(X)*, Atheneum Bks. for Young Readers) Simon & Schuster Children's Publishing.

STEINBECK, JOHN, 1902-1968

Bloom, Harold, ed. John Steinbeck's of Mice & Men. 2006. (Bloom's Guides). 80p. (YA). (gr. 9-12). lib. bdg. 30.00 *(978-0-7910-8581-3(3))* Facts On File, Inc.

John Steinbeck: The Voice of the Land. 2014. (ENG.). 192p. (J). (gr. 3-7). pap. 13.95 *(978-1-59077-358-1(6))* Evans, M. & Co., Inc.

McArthur, Debra. John Steinbeck: The Grapes of Wrath & of Mice & Men. 2008. (Writers & Their Work Ser.). (Illus.). 144p. (J). (gr. 7-18). lib. bdg. 42.79 *(978-0-7614-2964-7(6)*, Benchmark Bks.) Marshall Cavendish Corp.

Newman, Gerald & Layfield, Eleanor Newman. A Student's Guide to John Steinbeck. 2004. (Understanding Literature Ser.). (Illus.). 176p. (YA). lib. bdg. 29.27 *(978-0-7660-2259-1(5))* Enslow Pubs., Inc.

Tracy, Kathleen. John Steinbeck. 2004. (Classic Storytellers Ser.). (Illus.). 48p. (J). (gr. 4-8). lib. bdg. 29.95 *(978-1-58415-271-2(0))* Mitchell Lane Pubs., Inc.

STENCIL WORK

see also Screen Process Printing

Cartwright, Stephen, illus. Christmas Stencil Book. 2005. (Usborne Farmyard Tales Ser.). 10p. (J). (gr. -1-3). bds. 9.95 *(978-0-7945-1142-5(2)*, Usborne) EDC Publishing.

Cleyet-Merle, Laurence, illus. Animal Stencil Book. 2006. (Stencil Bks.). 14p. (J). (gr. -1-3). bds. 12.99 *(978-0-7945-1140-1(6)*, Usborne) EDC Publishing.

Doherty, Gillian. Stencil Book. 2005. (Stencil Book Ser.). 14p. (J). 9.95 *(978-0-7945-0866-1(9)*, Usborne) EDC Publishing.

Gottesman, Eric. Fun with Wizards Stencils. 2003. (Dover Stencils Ser.). (ENG., Illus.). 6p. (J). (gr. -1-5). pap. 1.50 *(978-0-486-42633-4(5))* Dover Pubns., Inc.

Green, John. Fun with Horseback Riding Stencils. 2004. (Dover Stencils Ser.). (ENG., Illus.). 6p. (J). (gr. 1-4). pap. 1.99 *(978-0-486-43419-3(2))* Dover Pubns., Inc.

Hannigan, Paula. Stencil Art. Klutz Editors, ed. 2013. (ENG.). 48p. (J). (gr. 3). 19.99 *(978-0-545-56166-2(3))* Klutz.

Harper, Ellen. Fun with Egyptian Symbols Stencils. 2003. (Dover Stencils Ser.). (ENG., Illus.). 6p. (J). (gr. 1-4). pap. 1.99 *(978-0-486-43109-3(6))* Dover Pubns., Inc.

Kennedy, Paul E. Fun with Whales Stencils. 2008. (Dover Stencils Ser.). (ENG., Illus.). (J). (gr. -1-5). pap. 1.50 *(978-0-486-46687-3(6))* Dover Pubns., Inc.

Leonard, Barry, ed. Drawing Trucks & Diggers: A Book of 10 Stencils. 2004. (Illus.). 34p. (J). (gr. k-4). reprint ed. ring bd. 10.00 *(978-0-7567-8505-5(7))* DIANE Publishing Co.

Lovell, Katie, illus. Christmas Stencil Cards. 2007. (Christmas Stencil Cards Ser.). 16p. (J). 9.99 *(978-0-7945-1896-7(6)*, Usborne) EDC Publishing.

Noble, Marty. Fun with Christmas Ornaments Stencils. 2006. (Dover Stencils Ser.). (ENG., Illus.). 6p. (J). (gr. -1-5). pap. 1.50 *(978-0-486-44893-0(2))* Dover Pubns., Inc.

—Fun with Emergency Vehicles Stencils. 2003. (Dover Stencils Ser.). (ENG., Illus.). 6p. (J). (gr. -1-5). pap. 1.50 *(978-0-486-42634-1(3))* Dover Pubns., Inc.

—Fun with Fire Trucks Stencils. 2008. (Dover Stencils Ser.). (ENG., Illus.). 6p. (J). (gr. -1-5). pap. 1.50 *(978-0-486-46686-6(8))* Dover Pubns., Inc.

—Fun with Good Luck Symbols Stencils. 2004. (Dover Stencils Ser.). (ENG.). 6p. (J). (gr. -1-5). pap. 1.50 *(978-0-486-43692-0(6))* Dover Pubns., Inc.

—Fun with Mother Goose Stencils. 2003. (Dover Stencils Ser.). (ENG.). 6p. (J). (gr. -1-5). pap. 1.50 *(978-0-486-42351-7(4))* Dover Pubns., Inc.

—Fun with Noah's Ark Stencils. 2006. (Dover Stencils Ser.). (ENG., Illus.). 6p. (J). (gr. -1-5). pap. 1.50 *(978-0-486-44881-7(9))* Dover Pubns., Inc.

—Fun with Wedding Stencils. 2004. (Dover Stencils Ser.). (ENG.). 6p. (gr. -1-5). pap. 1.50 *(978-0-486-43683-8(7))* Dover Pubns., Inc.

Pearson, Maria, illus. Spooky Stencil Cards. 2008. (Stencil Cards Ser.). 16p. (J). 9.99 *(978-0-7945-2415-9(X)*, Usborne) EDC Publishing.

QEB Learn Art National Book Stores Edition: Stencils & Prints. 2006. (J). per. *(978-1-59566-283-5(9))* QEB Publishing Inc.

Robins, Deri. Stencils & Prints. 2006. (Art Smart Ser.). (ENG., Illus.). 32p. (J). (gr. 2-5). pap. 9.95 *(978-1-58728-544-8(4))* Cooper Square Publishing Llc.

Running Press Staff, ed. Wintery White: Draw Beautiful Sparkly Pictures. 2013. (ENG., Illus.). 24p. (J). (gr. -1-17). pap. 12.95 *(978-0-7624-5282-8(X)*, Running Pr. Kids) Running Pr. Bk. Pubs.

School Zone Staff. Fun & Festive. 2004. (ENG.). 32p. (J). 12.99 *(978-1-58947-471-0(6)*, 03602) School Zone Publishing Co.

—On the Farm. 2004. (ENG.). 32p. (J). 12.99 *(978-1-58947-470-3(8)*, 03601) School Zone Publishing Co.

—Things That Go. 2004. (ENG.). 32p. (J). 12.99 *(978-1-58947-472-7(4)*, 03603) School Zone Publishing Co.

Silver Dolphin en Español Editors. Libro de actividades con plantillas: Disney Animales: Animals Stencil. 2007. (Illus.). 10p. (J). bds. *(978-970-718-435-0(3)*, Silver Dolphin en Español) Advanced Marketing, S. de R. L. de C. V.

Silver Dolphin en Español Staff, creator. Disney Favoritos 2: Libro de Actividades con Plantillas. 2007. (Illus.). 20p. (J). (gr. -1). bds. *(978-970-718-433-6(7)*, Silver Dolphin en Español) Advanced Marketing, S. de R. L. de C. V.

—Disney Princesa Libro de Actividades con Plantillas. 2007. (Disney Princesa (Silver Dolphin) Ser.). (Illus.). 20p. (J). (gr. -1). bds. *(978-970-718-434-3(5)*, Silver Dolphin en Español) Advanced Marketing, S. de R. L. de C. V.

Stanley, Mandy. Stencils. 2016. (Arty Mouse Creativity Kits Ser.). (ENG., Illus.). 12p. (J). (gr. -1-2). pap. 16.99 *(978-1-78445-433-3(8))* Top That! Publishing PLC GBR. Dist: Independent Pubs. Group.

Stencils & Prints, 6 bks. 2005. (QEB Learn Art Ser.). (Illus.). 32p. (J). per. 8.95 *(978-1-59566-127-2(1))* QEB Publishing Inc.

Stowell, Louie & Pearcey, Alice. Diggers Stencil Book. Doherty, Gillian, ed. Tudor, Andy, illus. 2007. (Stencil Bks.). 14p. (J).

S

bds. 12.99 (978-0-7945-1576-8(2), Usborne) EDC Publishing.

Top That. Let's Stencil Things That Go. 2008. (978-1-84666-584-4(1)) Top That! Publishing PLC.

Tullet, Hervé. My Stencil Kit. 2016. (ENG., Illus.). 64p. (J). (gr. k-3). pap. 24.95 (978-0-500-65075-2(6), 565075) Thames & Hudson.

STENGEL, CASEY, 1891-1975

Winter, Jonah. You Never Heard of Casey Stengel?! Blitt, Barry, illus. 2016. (ENG.). 40p. (J). (gr. -1-3). 20.99 (978-0-375-97013-9(4)); 17.99 (978-0-375-87013-2(X)) Random Hse. Children's Bks. (Schwartz & Wade Bks.).

STEPFAMILIES

Beyl, Charles, illus. My Parents Are Divorced Too: A Book for Kids by Kids. 2nd ed. 2006. 71p. (J). (gr. 3-7). 14.95 (978-1-59147-241-4(5)); per. 9.95 (978-1-59147-242-1(3)) American Psychological Assn. (Magination Pr.).

Delessert, Etienne. A Glass. Delessert, Etienne, illus. 2013. (ENG., Illus.). 32p. (J). (gr. 4-7). 18.99 (978-1-56846-257-8(3), Creative Editions) Creative Co., The.

Gay, Kathlyn. Divorce: The Ultimate Teen Guide. 2014. (It Happened to Me Ser.: 41). (ENG., Illus.). 220p. 45.00 (978-0-8108-9238-5(3)) Rowman & Littlefield Publishers, Inc.

Hancock Ms Lsc, Dionna. Where Did My Half-Brother Come From: Book 1 of the Half-Brother/Step-Brother Children's Series. 2012. 28p. pap. 19.99 (978-1-4634-1244-9(4)) AuthorHouse.

Hewitt, Sally. My Stepfamily. 2009. (J). 28.50 (978-1-59920-229-7(8)) Black Rabbit Bks.

Leibowitz, Julie. Finding Your Place: A Teen Guide to Life in a Blended Family. 2005. (Divorce Resource Library). (Illus.). 64p. (YA). (gr. 7-12). lib. bdg. 31.95 (978-0-8239-3114-9(5), DIFIPL) Rosen Publishing Group, Inc., The.

MacGregor, Cynthia. Jigsaw Puzzle Family: The Stepkids' Guide to Fitting It Together. 2005. (Rebuilding Bks.). (ENG.). 120p. (J). (gr. 4-8). per. 12.95 (978-1-886230-63-7(3), Impact Pubs.) New Harbinger Pubns.

Myers, Nancy & Charles, Rodney. Where's My Brother Joshua? 2013. 20p. pap. 15.95 (978-1-935323-14-3(8)) Westry Wingate Group, Inc.

Peterman, Rosie L., et al. Divorce & Stepfamilies. 2012. (Teen Mental Health Ser.). (ENG., Illus.). 48p. (J). (gr. 7-12). lib. bdg. 27.95 (978-1-4488-6893-3(9)) Rosen Publishing Group, Inc., The.

Price, Elizabeth. Divorce & Teens: When a Family Splits Apart. 2004. (Teen Issues Ser.). (Illus.). 64p. (J). lib. bdg. 22.60 (978-0-7660-1670-5(6)) Enslow Pubs., Inc.

Schuette, Sarah L. Blended Families, 1 vol. 2010. (My Family Ser.). (ENG.). 24p. (gr. k-1). pap. 6.29 (978-1-4296-4835-6(X)); pap. 35.70 (978-1-4296-5158-5(X)) Capstone Press of Coughlan Cos. (Pebble Bks.).

Simons, Rae. Blended Families. 2010. (Changing Face of Modern Families Ser.). (Illus.). 64p. (YA). (gr. 6-18). 22.95 (978-1-4222-1492-3(3)) Mason Crest.

Stern, Zoe & Stern, Evan. Divorce Is Not the End of the World: Zoe's & Evan's Coping Guide for Kids. 2nd rev. ed. 2008. (ENG., Illus.). 112p. (J). (gr. 3-7). pap. 9.99 (978-1-58246-241-7(0), Tricycle Pr.) Random Hse. Children's Bks.

Weitzman, Elizabeth. Let's Talk about Living in a Blended Family. 2009. (Let's Talk Library). 24p. (gr. 2-3). 42.50 (978-1-60853-451-7(0), PowerKids Pr.) Rosen Publishing Group, Inc., The.

STEPFAMILIES—FICTION

Alender, Katie. Famous Last Words. 2014. (ENG.). 320p. (J). (gr. 7). 18.99 (978-0-545-63997-2(2)) Scholastic, Inc.

Arnold, David. Mosquitoland. 2015. (ENG.). 352p. (YA). (gr. 7). 17.99 (978-0-451-47077-5(X), Viking Books for Young Readers) Penguin Young Readers Group.

Baker, E. D. The Wish Fish. Manuzak, Lisa, illus. 2017. (ENG.). 128p. (J). pap. 5.99 (978-1-68119-143-0(1), 9781681191430, Bloomsbury USA Childrens) Bloomsbury Publishing USA.

Banks, Piper. Geek Abroad, 2 vols. 2008. (Geek High Ser.: 2). (ENG.). 256p. (YA). (gr. 9-18). 9.99 (978-0-451-22393-7(4), Berkley) Penguin Publishing Group.

—Revenge of the Geek. 2010. (Geek High Ser.: 4). (ENG.). 256p. (gr. 12-18). 9.99 (978-0-451-23134-5(1), Berkley) Penguin Publishing Group.

—Summer of the Geek. 2010. (Geek High Ser.: 3). (ENG.). 256p. (YA). (gr. 5-18). 9.99 (978-0-451-22984-7(3), Berkley) Penguin Publishing Group.

Barwin, Steven. Icebreaker, 1 vol. 2006. (Lorimer Sports Stories Ser.). (ENG.). 128p. (J). (gr. 4-8). 16.95 (978-1-55028-951-0(9), 9781550289510) Lorimer, James & Co., Ltd., Pubs. CAN. Dist: Casemate Pubs. & Bk. Distributors, LLC.

Bentley, Sue. Classroom Princess. 2013. (Magic Puppy Ser.: 9). lib. bdg. 16.00 (978-0-606-32122-8(5), Turtleback) Turtleback Bks.

—Classroom Princess #9. Swan, Angela, illus. 2013. (Magic Puppy Ser.: 9). (ENG.). 128p. (J). (gr. 1-3). 5.99 (978-0-448-46732-0(1), Grosset & Dunlap) Penguin Young Readers Group.

—Party Dreams, 5 vols. Farley, Andrew & Swan, Angela, illus. 2010. (Magic Puppy Ser.: 5). (ENG.). 128p. (J). (gr. 1-3). pap. 5.99 (978-0-448-45064-3(X), Grosset & Dunlap) Penguin Young Readers Group.

Bobrick, Julie, ed. Cinderella: Level 1: Learn Mandarin Chinese Through Fairy Tales. Peters, Li Li & Tao, Ming, trs. Sandoval, Migs, illus. 2006. (Learn Chinese Through Fairy Tales Ser.). (ENG & CHI.). 29p. pap. 14.95 incl. audio compact disk (978-1-891888-79-3(X)) Slangman Publishing.

Bodeen, S. A. Found. 2017. (Shipwreck Island Ser.: 4). (ENG.). 160p. (J). 16.99 (978-1-250-02783-2(7), 9781250027832) Feiwel & Friends.

—Lost. 2015. (Shipwreck Island Ser.: 2). (ENG.). 144p. (J). (gr. 5-8). 16.99 (978-1-250-02779-5(9), 9781250027795) Feiwel & Friends.

—Trapped. 2016. (Shipwreck Island Ser.: 3). (ENG.). 160p. (J). 16.99 (978-1-250-02781-8(0), 9781250027818) Feiwel & Friends.

Bowdish, Lynea. How to Be Nice — & Other Lessons I Didn't Learn. Gray, Leslie, illus. 2006. 47p. (J). pap. (978-1-59336-726-8(0)) Mondo Publishing.

Bowvayne. A Spell Behind Bars. Snow, Alan, illus. 2006. (Misadventures of Danny Cloke Ser.). 207p. (J). per. 4.99 (978-0-7945-1293-4(3), Usborne) EDC Publishing.

—A Turn in the Grave. Snow, Alan, illus. 2006. (Misadventures of Danny Cloke Ser.). 143p. (J). per. 4.99 (978-0-7945-1292-7(5), Usborne) EDC Publishing.

Bryant, Ann. Billie & the Parent Plan. 2007. (Billie & the Parent Plan Ser.). 191p. (J). (gr. 2-5). per. 4.99 (978-0-7945-1721-2(8), Usborne) EDC Publishing.

Bullard, Lisa. Trick-or-Treat on Milton Street. Oeltjenbruns, Joni, illus. 2003. (Picture Bks.). 32p. (J). (gr. -1-3). 15.95 (978-1-57505-158-1(3), Carolrhoda Bks.) Lerner Publishing Group.

Burke, David. Cinderella: Level 1: Learn German Through Fairy Tales. Bobrick, Julie, ed. Deese, Teut & Wirth, Petra, trs. Sandoval, Migs, illus. 2006. (Learn German Through Fairy Tales Ser.). (ENG & GER.). 29p. pap. 14.95 incl. audio compact disk (978-1-891888-76-2(5)) Slangman Publishing.

Buxbaum, Julie. Tell Me Three Things. (ENG.). (YA). (gr. 7). 2017. 352p. pap. 9.99 **(978-0-553-53567-9(6)**, Ember) 2016. 336p. 17.99 (978-0-553-53564-8(1), Delacorte Pr.) 2016. 336p. lib. bdg. 20.99 (978-0-553-53565-5(X), Delacorte Pr.) Random Hse. Children's Bks.

Cabot, Meg. Shadowland & Ninth Key. 2010. (Mediator Ser.). (ENG.). 544p. (YA). (gr. 8). pap. 9.99 (978-0-06-204020-6(0), HarperTeen) HarperCollins Pubs.

Caletti, Deb. Love Is All You Need: Wild Roses - The Nature of Jade. 2013. (ENG.). 608p. (YA). (gr. 7-7). pap. 11.99 (978-1-4424-6636-4(7), Simon Pulse) Simon Pulse.

Candau, Brittany. Cinderella. Godbey, Cory, illus. 2015. (ENG.). 40p. (J). (gr. -1-k). 16.99 (978-1-4847-2360-9(0)) Disney Pr.

Cartwright, Stephen, illus. Cinderella. 2006. (First Stories Sticker Bks.). 16p. (J). (gr. -1-3). pap. 6.99 (978-0-7945-1311-5(5), Usborne) EDC Publishing.

Chambers, Pamela G. My Mommy's Getting Married. Stewart, Muriel, illus. 2009. 32p. (gr. -1-3). 17.95 (978-0-9799487-0-1(3)) Infinity Publishing Co.

Chatterton, Martin. The Brain Full of Holes, 1 vol. 2010. (ENG.). 256p. (J). (gr. 5-9). 16.95 (978-1-56145-527-0(X)) Peachtree Pubs.

Childs, Tera Lynn & Childs, Tera. Oh. My. Gods. 2009. (ENG.). 288p. (YA). (gr. 7-18). 7.99 (978-0-14-241420-0(4), Speak) Penguin Young Readers Group.

Cinderella. unabr. ed. (Read-Along Ser.). (J). 7.99 incl. audio (978-1-55723-007-2(2)) Walt Disney Records.

Clifton, Lutricia. Freaky Fast Frankie Joe. (ENG.). 272p. (J). 2013. pap. 7.99 (978-0-8234-2867-0(2)) 2012. 16.95 (978-0-8234-2367-5(0)) Holiday Hse., Inc.

Cohen, Tish. Inside Out Girl. 2008. (P. S. Ser.). (ENG.). 352p. pap. 14.99 (978-0-06-145295-6(5), Harper Perennial) HarperCollins Pubs.

Cohn, Rachel. Shrimp, 7 vols. 2005. (YA). 171.75 (978-1-4193-5253-9(9)) Recorded Bks., Inc.

—Shrimp. 2006. (ENG.). 352p. (YA). (gr. 7-12). reprint ed. pap. 6.99 (978-0-689-86613-5(5), Simon & Schuster Bks. For Young Readers) Simon & Schuster Bks. For Young Readers.

—The Steps. 2004. (ENG.). 144p. (J). (gr. 3-7). reprint ed. pap. 6.99 (978-0-689-87414-7(6), Simon & Schuster Bks. For Young Readers) Simon & Schuster Bks. For Young Readers.

—Two Steps Forward. (ENG., Illus.). 240p. (YA). 2013. (gr. 7). pap. 11.99 (978-1-4424-9615-6(0)) 2006. 15.95 (978-0-689-86614-2(3)) Simon & Schuster Bks. For Young Readers. (Simon & Schuster Bks. For Young Readers).

Cohn, Rachel & Wattenberg, Jane. Gingerbread. 2003. (ENG., Illus.). 224p. (YA). (gr. 9). pap. 8.99 (978-0-689-86020-1(X), Simon & Schuster Bks. For Young Readers) Simon & Schuster Bks. For Young Readers.

Cook, Eileen. Unraveling Isobel. 2012. (ENG.). (YA). (gr. 9). 320p. pap. 9.99 (978-1-4424-1328-3(X)); 304p. 16.99 (978-1-4424-1327-6(1)) Simon Pulse. (Simon Pulse).

Cooper, Floyd. The Ring Bearer. Cooper, Floyd, illus. 2017. (ENG., Illus.). 32p. (J). (gr. -1-2). 16.99 (978-0-399-16740-9(4), Philomel Bks.) Penguin Young Readers Group.

Cooper, Ilene. The Worst Noel: A Novel. 2006. 143p. (J). (gr. 4-8). reprint ed. pap. 4.00 (978-1-4223-5411-7(3)) DIANE Publishing Co.

Cray, Jordan. Dead Man's Hand. 2009. (Danger. com Ser.: 8). (ENG.). 224p. (YA). (gr. 7). pap. 10.99 (978-1-4169-9852-5(7), Simon Pulse) Simon Pulse.

Cross, Frances. Marty's Diary. 2008. (Cutting Edge Ser.). (ENG.). 160p. pap. (978-1-84167-697-5(7)) Ransom Publishing Ltd.

Cumbie, Patricia. Where People Like Us Live. 2008. 224p. (YA). (gr. 7-18). lib. bdg. 17.89 (978-0-06-137598-9(5), Geringer, Laura Book) HarperCollins Pubs.

Daniels, Sara. Pieces of the Sky. 2005. 135p. pap. 15.99 (978-1-4116-4291-1(0)) Lulu Pr., Inc.

de Gramont, Nina. Meet Me at the River. 2014. (ENG., Illus.). 384p. (YA). (gr. 9). pap. 11.99 (978-1-4169-8016-2(4), Atheneum Bks. for Young Readers) Simon & Schuster Children's Publishing.

Deem, James M. 3 NBs of Julian Drew. 2004. (ENG.). 208p. (YA). (gr. 7-18). pap. 13.95 (978-0-618-43907-2(2)) Houghton Mifflin Harcourt Publishing Co.

Deriso, Christine Hurley. The Right-Under Club: Second Stage. 2010. (J). (978-0-385-73621-3(5)); lib. bdg. (978-0-385-90593-0(9)) Random House Publishing Group. (Delacorte Pr).

Dessen, Sarah. Along for the Ride. (ENG.). (YA). (gr. 7-18). 2011. 432p. pap. 10.99 (978-0-14-241556-6(1), Speak) 2009. 416p. 19.99 (978-0-670-01194-0(0), Viking Books for Young Readers) Penguin Young Readers Group.

—Along for the Ride. 2011. lib. bdg. 20.85 (978-0-606-15360-7(8), Turtleback) Turtleback Bks.

—This Lullaby. 2004. (ENG.). 368p. (YA). (gr. 7-18). reprint ed. pap. 10.99 (978-0-14-250155-9(7), Speak) Penguin Young Readers Group.

Disney Book Group Staff. Cinderella. Disney Storybook Artists Staff, illus. 2nd ed. 2012. (Read-Along Storybook & CD Ser.). (ENG.). 32p. (J). (gr. -1 — 1). pap. 6.99 (978-1-4231-6321-3(4)) Disney Pr.

Disney Book Group Staff & Green, Rico. Cinderella: A Night at the Ball. Disney Storybook Art Team & Disney Book Group Staff, illus. 2015. (ENG.). 24p. (J). (gr. -1-k). pap. 3.99 (978-1-4847-1111-8(4)) Disney Pr.

Disney Book Group Staff & Hapka, Catherine. Sofia the First. Lee, Grace, illus. 2012. (ENG.). 40p. (J). (gr. -1-k). 15.99 (978-1-4231-6986-4(7)) Disney Pr.

Dokey, Cameron. Before Midnight: A Retelling of Cinderella. 2007. (Once upon a Time Ser.). (ENG.). 208p. (YA). (gr. 7-12). mass mkt. 7.99 (978-1-4169-3471-4(5), Simon Pulse) Simon Pulse.

Draper, Sharon M. Forged by Fire. 2013. (Hazelwood High Trilogy Ser.: 2). (ENG., Illus.). 176p. (YA). (gr. 7). pap. 9.99 (978-1-4424-8914-1(6), Atheneum Bks. for Young Readers) Simon & Schuster Children's Publishing.

—Forged by Fire. 2013. (Hazelwood High Trilogy Ser.: 2). lib. bdg. 20.85 (978-0-606-32333-8(3), Turtleback) Turtleback Bks.

Dwyer, Mindy. The Salmon Princess: An Alaska Cinderella Story. 2004. (Paws IV Ser.). (ENG., Illus.). 32p. (J). (gr. -1-2). pap. 10.99 (978-1-57061-355-5(9), Little Bigfoot) Sasquatch Bks.

Ehrenhaft, Daniel. The After Life. 2006. (ENG.). 272p. (YA). (gr. 7-12). 8.99 (978-1-59514-080-7(8), Razorbill) Penguin Young Readers Group.

Evans, Clay Bonnyman. The Winter Witch. Bender, Robert, illus. 2005. (ENG.). 32p. (J). (gr. -1-3). 16.95 (978-0-8234-1615-8(1)) Holiday Hse., Inc.

Fowles, Shelley. Climbing Rosa. 2009. (ENG., Illus.). 32p. (J). (gr. -1-2). pap. 7.95 (978-1-84507-595-8(1), Frances Lincoln) Quarto Publishing Group UK GBR. Dist: Hachette Bk. Group.

Francis, Melissa. Bite Me! 2009. (ENG.). 304p. (YA). (gr. 9-18). pap. 8.99 (978-0-06-143098-5(6), HarperTeen) HarperCollins Pubs.

Francis, Melissa Mckenzie. Love Sucks! 2010. (ENG.). 288p. (YA). (gr. 9-18). pap. 8.99 (978-0-06-143099-2(4), HarperTeen) HarperCollins Pubs.

Frederick, Heather Vogel. Once upon a Toad. (ENG., Illus.). (J). (gr. 5-9). 2013. 288p. pap. 6.99 (978-1-4169-8479-5(8)) 2012. 272p. 16.99 (978-1-4169-8478-8(X)) Simon & Schuster Bks. For Young Readers. (Simon & Schuster Bks. For Young Readers).

Freymann-Weyr, Garret. After the Moment. 2010. (ENG.). 336p. (YA). (gr. 9). pap. 7.99 (978-0-547-33168-3(1)) Houghton Mifflin Harcourt Publishing Co.

Friend, Natasha. Where You'll Find Me. 2016. (ENG.). 272p. (YA). 16.99 (978-0-374-30230-6(8), 9780374302306, Farrar, Straus & Giroux (BYR)) Farrar, Straus & Giroux.

Friesen, Gayle. For Now. 2007. (ENG.). 248p. (J). (gr. 5-9). 7.95 (978-1-55453-133-2(0)) Kids Can Pr., Ltd. CAN. Dist: Hachette Bk. Group.

Gaetz, Dayle Campbell. Spoiled Rotten. 2006. (Orca Currents Ser.). 103p. (gr. 5-9). 19.95 (978-0-7569-6875-5(5)) Perfection Learning Corp.

Gervay, Susanne. Always Jack. Wilcox, Cathy, illus. 2013. 148p. (J). (978-1-61067-226-9(7)) Kane Miller.

—Super Jack. Wilcox, Cathy, illus. 2003. 192p. (978-0-207-19918-9(3)) HarperCollins Pubs. Australia.

—SuperJack. Wilcox, Cathy, illus. 2013. (ENG.). 192p. (J). pap. 5.99 (978-1-61067-129-3(5)) Kane Miller.

Greene, Stephanie. Falling into Place. 2006. (ENG.). 128p. (J). (gr. 5-7). pap. 8.95 (978-0-618-68928-6(1)) Houghton Mifflin Harcourt Publishing Co.

Guillain, Charlotte & Guillain, Adam. Cinderella & the Amazing Techno-Slippers. Moor, Becka, illus. 2016. (Fairy Tales Today Ser.). (ENG.). 24p. (gr. 1-2). 9.95 (978-1-4795-8750-6(8)) Picture Window Bks.

Hahn, Mary Downing. Look for Me by Moonlight. 2008. (ENG.). 208p. (YA). (gr. 7). pap. 7.99 (978-0-547-07616-4(9)) Houghton Mifflin Harcourt Publishing Co.

—Wait till Helen Comes: A Ghost Story. 2008. (ENG., Illus.). 192p. (J). (gr. 5-7). pap. 7.99 (978-0-547-02864-4(4)) Houghton Mifflin Harcourt Publishing Co.

Hapka, Catherine, pseud & Disney Book Group Staff. The Amulet & the Anthem. Disney Storybook Art Team, illus. 2013. (ENG.). 24p. (J). (gr. -1-k). pap. 4.99 (978-1-4231-8023-4(2)) Disney Pr.

Hapka, Cathy, pseud & Disney Book Group Staff. Sofia Makes a Friend. Disney Storybook Artists Staff, illus. 2013. (World of Reading Ser.). (ENG.). 32p. (J). (gr. -1-k). pap. 3.99 (978-1-4231-6408-1(3)) Disney Pr.

Hapka, Cathy, pseud, et al. The Royal Slumber Party. Disney Storybook Art Team, illus. 2013. (ENG.). 24p. (J). (gr. -1-k). pap. 3.99 (978-1-4231-6410-4(5)) Disney Pr.

Hicks, Betty. Out of Order. 2007. (ENG.). 176p. (J). (gr. 3-7). pap. 14.99 (978-0-312-37355-9(4), 9780312373559) Square Fish.

Hinton, S. E. Esto Ya Es Otra Historia. (SPA.). (J). 6.95 (978-84-204-4121-4(X)) Santillana USA Publishing Co., Inc.

Hodder, Bridget. The Rat Prince. 2016. (ENG.). 272p. (J). 16.99 (978-0-374-30213-9(8), 9780374302139, Farrar, Straus & Giroux (BYR)) Farrar, Straus & Giroux.

Hubbard, Kirsten. Watch the Sky. 2015. (ENG.). 272p. (J). (gr. 3-7). 16.99 (978-1-4847-0833-0(4)) Hyperion Bks. for Children.

Jeffers, Susan & Ehrlich, Amy. Cinderella. Battcock, Gregory, ed. Jeffers, Susan, illus. 2004. (ENG., Illus.). 32p. (J). (gr. -1-3). 18.99 (978-0-525-47345-9(9), Dutton Books for Young Readers) Penguin Young Readers Group.

Johnson, Lois Walfrid. The Creeping Shadows. 2009. (Orig.). (J). 8.99 (978-0-88062-277-6(6)) Mott Media.

—The Disappearing Stranger. 2009. (Orig.). (J). 8.99 (978-0-88062-275-2(X)) Mott Media.

Jones, Jen. Maren's New Family. Franco, Paula, illus. 2015. (Sleepover Girls Ser.). (ENG.). 128p. (gr. 3-5). lib. bdg. 22.65 (978-1-4965-0540-8(9)) Stone Arch Bks.

Kantor, Melissa. If I Have a Wicked Stepmother, Where's My Prince? 2005. 283p. (YA). (978-1-4156-2763-1(0)) Hyperion Pr.

Kats, Jewel. Cinderella's Magical Wheelchair: An Empowering Fairy Tale. Kinra, Richa, illus. 2012. (J). 24p. 29.95 (978-1-61599-113-6(1)); 20p. pap. 16.95 (978-1-61599-112-9(3)) Loving Healing Pr., Inc.

Kehoe, Tim. Vincent Shadow: Toy Inventor. Francis, Guy & Wohnoutka, Mike, illus. 2011. (Vincent Shadow Ser.: 1). (ENG.). 224p. (J). (gr. 3-7). pap. 6.99 (978-0-316-05666-3(9)) Little, Brown Bks. for Young Readers.

Lane, Bryan. Stepbrothers the New Arrival. 2012. 16p. pap. 15.00 (978-1-4685-7410-4(8)) AuthorHouse.

Langan, John. Search for Safety. 2006. (Bluford Ser.). 128p. (YA). (gr. 7-18). pap. 4.95 (978-1-59194-070-8(2)) Townsend Pr.

Lee, Kathy. Space Invaders. 2011. 144p. pap. (978-1-84427-507-6(8)) Scripture Union.

Les Becquets, Diane. Season of Ice. 2008. (ENG.). 288p. (YA). (gr. 9-13). 16.95 (978-1-59990-063-6(7), 9781599900636, Bloomsbury USA Childrens) Bloomsbury Publishing USA.

Levins, Sandra. Do You Sing Twinkle? A Story about Remarriage & New Family. Langdo, Bryan, illus. 2009. 32p. (J). (gr. -1-3). 14.95 (978-1-4338-0539-4(1)); pap. 9.95 (978-1-4338-0551-6(0)) American Psychological Assn. (Magination Pr.).

Lockwood, Cara. Wuthering High: At Boarding School, No One Can Hear Your Scream. 2006. (Bard Academy Ser.: 1). (ENG.). 272p. (gr. 8-12). pap. 17.99 (978-1-4165-2475-5(4), MTV Bks.) MTV Books.

Luciani, Brigitte. The Carnival. Tharlet, Eve, illus. 2014. (ENG.). 32p. (J). pap. 6.95 (978-1-4677-4204-7(X)); lib. bdg. 25.26 (978-1-4677-4203-0(1), Graphic Universe™) Lerner Publishing Group.

—A Hubbub. Gauvin, Edward, tr. from FRE. Tharlet, Eve, illus. 2010. (Mr. Badger & Mrs. Fox Ser.: 2). (ENG.). 32p. (J). (gr. k-3). pap. 6.95 (978-0-7613-5632-5(0), Graphic Universe™);Bk. 2. 25.26 (978-0-7613-5626-4(6)) Lerner Publishing Group.

—Peace & Quiet. Burrell, Carol, tr. Tharlet, Eve, illus. 2012. (Mr. Badger & Mrs. Fox Ser.: 4). (ENG.). 32p. (J). (gr. k-3). pap. 6.95 (978-0-8225-9163-4(4)); lib. bdg. 25.26 (978-0-7613-8520-2(7)) Lerner Publishing Group. (Graphic Universe™).

—What a Team! Gauvin, Edward, tr. from FRE. Tharlet, Eve, illus. 2011. (Mr. Badger & Mrs. Fox Ser.: 3). (ENG.). 32p. (J). (gr. k-3). 25.26 (978-0-7613-5627-1(4)); pap. 6.95 (978-0-7613-5633-2(9), Graphic Universe™) Lerner Publishing Group.

Lynn, Tracy. Snow: A Retelling of Snow White & the Seven Dwarfs. 2006. (Once upon a Time Ser.). (ENG.). 272p. (YA). (gr. 9-12). mass mkt. 7.99 (978-1-4169-4015-9(4), Simon Pulse) Simon Pulse.

Mancusi, Mari. Princesses, Inc. 2017. (Mix Ser.). (ENG., Illus.). 320p. (J). (gr. 4-8). pap. 7.99 **(978-1-4814-7900-4(8)**, Aladdin) Simon & Schuster Children's Publishing.

Mangum, Kay Lynn. When the Bough Breaks. 2007. 352p. (YA). pap. 15.95 (978-1-59038-748-1(1)) Deseret Bk. Co.

Manley, Candace. Skeeter's Dream. 2010. (ENG.). 192p. (J). (gr. 7-18). pap. 14.95 (978-0-9785634-8-6(4)) La Frontera Publishing.

Mansbach, Adam & Zweibel, Alan. Benjamin Franklin: Huge Pain in My... 2015. (Benjamin Franklin Ser.). (ENG., Illus.). 208p. (J). (gr. 5-9). 12.99 (978-1-4847-1304-4(4)) Hyperion Bks. for Children.

—Benjamin Franklin: Huge Pain in My... 2017. (Benjamin Franklin Ser.). (ENG.). 224p. (J). (gr. 5-9). pap. 7.99 (978-1-4847-2537-5(9)) Hyperion Bks. for Children.

Marciniak, Christine. Lights, Camera, Ali! 2013. 232p. pap. 13.99 (978-1-61271-214-7(2)) Zumaya Pubns. LLC.

—Reality Ali. 2012. (J). (978-1-61271-075-4(1)); (978-1-61271-076-1(X)); pap. 13.99 (978-1-61271-074-7(3)) Zumaya Pubns. LLC.

Maskame, Estelle. Did I Mention I Need You? 2016. (Did I Mention I Love You (DIMILY) Ser.: 2). (ENG.). 384p. (YA). (gr. 8-12). pap. 10.99 (978-1-4926-3218-4(X), 9781492632184) Sourcebooks, Inc.

McCahan, Erin. I Now Pronounce You Someone Else. 2010. (ENG.). 272p. (J). (gr. 7-18). 16.99 (978-0-545-08818-3(6), Levine, Arthur A. Bks.) Scholastic, Inc.

McCombie, Karen. My Big (Strange) Happy Family. Monks, Lydia, illus. 2009. (J). pap. (978-0-385-73597-1(9), Yearling) Random Hse. Children's Bks.

Meade, L. T. The Children's Pilgrimage. 2007. (ENG.). 254p. pap. 21.99 (978-1-4346-4863-1(X)); 280p. pap. 23.99 (978-1-4346-4864-8(8)) Creative Media Partners, LLC.

Meyer, Marissa. Cinder. 2012. (Lunar Chronicles Ser.: 1). (ENG.). 400p. (YA). (gr. 7-12). 19.99 (978-0-312-64189-4(3), 9780312641894) Feiwel & Friends.

—Cinder. 2013. (Lunar Chronicles Ser.: 1). (ENG.). 448p. (YA). (gr. 7-12). pap. 9.99 (978-1-250-00720-9(8), 9781250007209) Square Fish.

—Cinder. l.t. ed. 2012. (Lunar Chronicles: Bk. 1). (ENG.). 496p. (J). (gr. 7-12). 23.99 (978-1-4104-4607-7(7)) Thorndike Pr.

—Cinder. 2013. (Lunar Chronicles Ser.: 1). (YA). lib. bdg. 20.85 (978-0-606-28633-6(0), Turtleback) Turtleback Bks.

—Cinder. 2015. (Cinder Ser.: 1). (SPA.). 416p. (YA). (gr. 9-12). pap. 20.99 (978-987-612-927-5(9)) V&R Editoras.

Miles, Brenda & Sweet, Susan D. Cinderstella: A Tale of Planets Not Princes. Docampo, Valeria, illus. 2016. (J). (978-1-4338-2270-4(9), Magination Pr.) American Psychological Assn.

Miles, Cindy. Forevermore. 2013. (ENG.). 288p. (J). (gr. 7). pap. 9.99 (978-0-545-42622-0(7)) Scholastic, Inc.

Minh Quoc. Tam & Cam/Tam Cam: The Ancient Vietnamese Cinderella Story. Smith, William, tr. from VIE. Mai Long, illus. 2006. (ENG & VIE.). 32p. (J). (gr. 1-4). 16.95 (978-0-9701654-4-2(7)) East West Discovery Pr.

Minke, Shari. The Airplane Story: A Blended Family's Journey. 2010. pap. 12.99 (978-1-61579-944-2(3)) Salem Author Services.

Morgan, Melissa J. Extra Credit. 2009. (Camp Confidential Ser.: 22). (ENG.). 160p. (J). (gr. 4-7). pap. 4.99 (978-0-448-45216-6(2), Grosset & Dunlap) Penguin Young Readers Group.

Musilli Whitesell, Marjorie. I Have Four Parents. 2009. (Illus.). 20p. pap. 10.95 (978-1-60860-448-7(9), Eloquent Bks.) Strategic Book Publishing & Rights Agency (SBPRA).

Olsen, Sylvia. White Girl, 1 vol. 2004. (ENG., Illus.). 200p. (YA). (gr. 7-12). pap. 9.95 (978-1-55039-147-3(X)) Sono Nis Pr. CAN. Dist: Orca Bk. Pubs. USA.

Palmer, Robin. Girl vs. Superstar, Bk. 1. 2010. (Yours Truly, Lucy B. Parker Ser.: 1). (ENG.). 224p. (J). (gr. 5-18). 6.99 (978-0-14-241500-9(6), Puffin Books) Penguin Young Readers Group.

Palmer, Robin. Love You Like a Sister. 2017. (Mix Ser.). (ENG., Illus.). 256p. (J). (gr. 4-8). pap. 7.99 ***(978-1-4814-6642-4(9)***, Aladdin) Simon & Schuster Children's Publishing.

Payne, C. C. The Thing about Leftovers. 2016. (ENG.). 288p. (J). (gr. 5). 16.99 *(978-0-399-17204-5(1)*, Nancy Paulsen Books) Penguin Young Readers Group.

Peck, Dale. Drift House: The First Voyage. 2006. (ENG.). 464p. (YA). (gr. 5). per. 7.95 *(978-1-59990-005-6(X)*, 9781599900056, Bloomsbury USA Childrens) Bloomsbury Publishing USA.

Peloquin, Lili. The Innocents. 2013. (Innocents Ser.: 1). (ENG.). 288p. (YA). (gr. 7). pap. 9.99 *(978-1-59514-502-4(8)*, Razorbill) Penguin Young Readers Group.

Peters, Julie Anne. Keeping You a Secret. 2005. (ENG., Illus.). 272p. (YA). (gr. 10-17). pap. 10.00 *(978-0-316-00985-0(7)*, Tingley, Megan Bks.) Little, Brown Bks. for Young Readers.

Peterson, Esther Allen. The House That Cared. 2010. (J). pap. *(978-0-88092-505-1(1))* Royal Fireworks Publishing Co.

Probst, Jeff & Tebbetts, Chris. Stranded. 2013. (Stranded Ser.: 1). (ENG.). 208p. (J). (gr. 3-7). pap. 6.99 *(978-0-14-242424-7(2)*, Puffin Books) Penguin Young Readers Group.

—Stranded. 2013. (Stranded Ser.: 1). lib. bdg. 17.20 *(978-0-606-36788-2(8))* Turtleback Bks.

—Trial by Fire. 2013. (Stranded Ser.: 2). (ENG.). 192p. (J). (gr. 3). pap. 6.99 *(978-0-14-242425-4(0)*, Puffin Books) Penguin Publishing Group.

Probst, Jeff & Tebbetts, Christopher. Desperate Measures. 2016. (Stranded, Shadow Island Ser.: 3). lib. bdg. 17.20 *(978-0-606-37562-7(7))* Turtleback Bks.

—The Sabotage. 2015. (Stranded Ser.: 5). (ENG.). 224p. (J). (gr. 3-7). 6.99 *(978-0-14-751389-2(8)*, Puffin Books) Penguin Young Readers Group.

—Trial by Fire. 2013. 174p. (J). *(978-0-14-751195-9(X))* Penguin Publishing Group.

Rasheed, Leila. Diamonds & Deceit. 2014. (At Somerton Ser.). (ENG.). 432p. (YA). (gr. 7-12). 17.99 *(978-1-4231-7118-8(7))* Hyperion Bks. for Children.

Readler, Blaine C. Under the Radar: The Spy Drone Adventure. 2006. (ENG.). 248p. (J). (gr. 7-12). per. *(978-1-933255-18-7(8))* DNA Pr.

Reinhardt, Dana. How to Build a House. 2009. (ENG.). 240p. (YA). (gr. 9-11). pap. 8.99 *(978-0-375-84454-6(6)*, Ember) Random Hse. Children's Bks.

Reinhart, Matthew. Cinderella: A Pop-Up Fairy Tale. Reinhart, Matthew, illus. 2005. (ENG., Illus.). 12p. (J). (gr. -1-3). 34.99 *(978-1-4169-0501-1(4)*, Little Simon) Little Simon.

Reiss, Kathryn. Sweet Miss Honeywell's Revenge: A Ghost Story. 2005. (ENG.). 444p. (YA). (gr. 7-12). pap. 22.95 *(978-0-15-205471-7(5))* Houghton Mifflin Harcourt Publishing Co.

Ruby, Laura. Play Me. 2009. (ENG.). 336p. (YA). (gr. 9). pap. 9.99 *(978-0-06-124329-5(9)*, HarperTeen) HarperCollins Pubs.

Rudnick, Elizabeth. Cinderella. 2015. (ENG.). 176p. (J). (gr. 3-7). pap. 5.99 *(978-1-4847-1113-2(0))* Disney Pr.

Salenas, Bobbi. Cinderella Latina - Cinicienta Latina. La Madrid, Enriquee, tr. Salenas, Bobbi, illus. 2003. (SPA., Illus.). (YA). (gr. 3-12). 19.95 *(978-0-934925-06-8(2))* Pinata Pubns.

Salisbury, Graham. Lord of the Deep. braille ed. 2003. (J). (gr. 2). spiral bd. *(978-0-616-15872-2(6))* Canadian National Institute for the Blind/Institut National Canadien pour les Aveugles.

—Lord of the Deep. 2003. (ENG.). 192p. (YA). (gr. 7). mass mkt. 6.99 *(978-0-440-22911-7(1)*, Laurel Leaf) Random Hse. Children's Bks.

—Lord of the Deep: A Novel. 2006. 182p. (J). (gr. 6-10). reprint ed. 16.00 *(978-1-4223-5841-2(0))* DIANE Publishing Co.

Sandoval, Migs, illus. Cinderella: Level 1: Learn French Through Fairy Tales. 2006. (Learn French Through Fairy Tales Ser.). (ENG & FRE.). 29p. (J). (gr. -1-3). pap. 14.95 incl. audio compact disk *(978-1-891888-75-5(7))* Slangman Publishing.

Schroeder, Lisa. Far from You. (ENG.). (YA). 2010. 384p. (gr. 9). pap. 10.99 *(978-1-4169-7507-6(1))* 2008. 368p. (gr. 8-18). 15.99 *(978-1-4169-7506-9(3))* Simon Pulse. (Simon Pulse).

Scott, Mindi. Live Through This. 2012. (ENG.). 304p. (YA). (gr. 9). 17.99 *(978-1-4424-4059-3(7))*; pap. 9.99 *(978-1-4424-4060-9(0))* Simon Pulse. (Simon Pulse).

Sheinmel, Courtney. All the Things You Are. (ENG.). 256p. (J). (gr. 4-8). 2012. pap. 6.99 *(978-1-4169-9718-4(0))* 2011. 15.99 *(978-1-4169-9717-7(2))* Simon & Schuster Bks. For Young Readers. (Simon & Schuster Bks. For Young Readers).

—My So-Called Family. 2008. (ENG.). 208p. (J). (gr. 4-7). 15.99 *(978-1-4169-5785-0(5)*, Simon & Schuster Bks. For Young Readers) Simon & Schuster Bks. For Young Readers.

—Positively. 2010. (ENG.). 240p. (J). (gr. 4-9). pap. 6.99 *(978-1-4424-0622-3(4)*, Simon & Schuster Bks. For Young Readers) Simon & Schuster Bks. For Young Readers.

Shultz, Carrie. V. I. P. Stepkid. 2013. 24p. pap. 10.95 *(978-1-4908-0831-4(0)*, WestBow Pr.) Author Solutions, Inc.

Simon, Coco. Mia's Baker's Dozen. 2013. (Cupcake Diaries: 6). (ENG., Illus.). 160p. (J). (gr. 3-7). 17.99 *(978-1-4424-8566-2(3)*, Simon Spotlight) Simon Spotlight.

Smith, Roland & Spradlin, Michael P. The Windy City. Bk.5. 2014. (I, Q Ser.). (ENG.). 240p. (YA). (gr. 5-7). 9.99 *(978-1-58536-823-5(7)*, 202902) Sleeping Bear Pr.

Snowe, Olivia. The Glass Voice, 1 vol. Lamoreaux, Michelle, illus. 2014. (Twicetold Tales Ser.). (ENG.). 128p. (gr. 3-4). 25.32 *(978-1-4342-9148-6(0))* Stone Arch Bks.

Snyder, Zilpha Keatley. The Headless Cupid. Raible, Alton, illus. 2009. (Stanley Family Ser.). (ENG.). 224p. (J). (gr. 3-7). 16.99 *(978-1-4169-9532-6(3)*, Atheneum Bks. for Young Readers) Simon & Schuster Children's Publishing.

Spradlin, Michael P. & Smith, Roland. Alcatraz. 2014. (I, Q Ser.). (ENG.). 272p. (J). (gr. 5-7). 16.99 *(978-1-58536-826-6(1)*, 203667); pap. 9.99 *(978-1-58536-825-9(3)*, 203727) Sleeping Bear Pr.

Spykman, E. C. Terrible, Horrible Edie. 2010. (ENG.). 232p. (J). (gr. 4-7). 16.95 *(978-1-59017-353-4(8)*, NYR Children's Collection) New York Review of Bks., Inc., The.

St. Crow, Lili. Wayfarer. 2014. (Tales of Beauty & Madness Ser.). (ENG.). 352p. (YA). (gr. 7). pap. 9.99 *(978-1-59514-620-5(2)*, Razorbill) Penguin Young Readers Group.

Stockham, Jess, illus. Cinderella. 2007. (Flip-Up Fairy Tales Ser.). (ENG.). 24p. (J). (gr. -1-2). audio compact disk *(978-1-84643-091-6(7))* Child's Play International Ltd.

Tharp, Tim. The Spectacular Now. (ENG.). 304p. (YA). (gr. 9). 2010. pap. 8.99 *(978-0-375-86502-2(0)*, Knopf Bks. for Young Readers) 2013. pap. 9.99 *(978-0-385-75430-9(2)*, Ember) Random Hse. Children's Bks.

Thomas, Isabel. Cindy-Ella & the Incredible Techno-Slippers. Moor, Becka, illus. 2015. (Fairy Tales Today Ser.). (ENG.). 24p. (gr. 1-2). 23.99 *(978-1-4795-8616-5(1))* Picture Window Bks.

Tooke, Wes. Lucky: Maris, Mantle, & My Best Summer Ever. (ENG.). 192p. (J). (gr. 3-7). 2011. pap. 6.99 *(978-1-4169-8664-5(2))* 2010. 15.99 *(978-1-4169-8663-8(4))* Simon & Schuster Bks. For Young Readers. (Simon & Schuster Bks. For Young Readers).

Tucker, Charlotte Maria. Driven into Exile: A Story of the Huguenots. 2003. (Huguenot Inheritance Ser.: Vol. 5). (Illus.). 141p. (J). *(978-0-921100-66-9(3))* Inheritance Pubns.

Vail, Rachel. Kiss Me Again. 2012. (If We Kiss Ser.: 2). (ENG.). 256p. (YA). (gr. 8). 17.99 *(978-0-06-194717-9(2)*, HarperTeen) HarperCollins Pubs.

Ventresca, Yvonne. Black Flowers, White Lies. 2016. (ENG.). 272p. (YA). (gr. 6). 16.99 *(978-1-5107-0988-1(6)*, Sky Pony Pr.) Skyhorse Publishing Co., Inc.

West, Carly Anne. The Bargaining. 2015. (ENG., Illus.). 416p. (YA). (gr. 9). 17.99 *(978-1-4424-4182-8(8)*, Simon Pulse) Simon Pulse.

Wilhite, Becca. Bright Blue Miracle. 2009. 176p. (J). pap. 8.99 *(978-1-60641-031-8(8)*, Shadow Mountain) Shadow Mountain Publishing.

STEPPARENTS

Hancock, Rusty. Dedicated Dads: Stepfathers of Famous People. Van Kampen, Megan, illus. 2004. 138p. *(978-0-934981-12-5(4))* Lawells Publishing.

MacGregor, Cynthia. Jigsaw Puzzle Family: The Stepkids' Guide to Fitting It Together. 2005. (Rebuilding Bks.). (ENG.). 120p. (J). (gr. 4-8). per. 12.95 *(978-1-886230-63-7(3)*, Impact Pubs.) New Harbinger Pubns.

Riggs, Kate. Wicked Stepmothers. 2013. (Happily Ever After Ser.). (ENG., Illus.). 24p. (J). (gr. k-3). 25.65 *(978-1-60818-245-9(2)*, Creative Education) Creative Co., The.

Wells, Sherry A. Warm & Wonderful Stepmothers of Famous People. Van Kampen, Megan, illus. 2004. 131p. 20.00 *(978-0-934981-10-1(8))* Lawells Publishing.

STEPPARENTS—FICTION

Alger, Horatio. Frank & Fearless or the Fortunes of Jasper Kent. 2007. 228p. 20.99 *(978-1-4280-7465-1(1))*; per. 14.99 *(978-1-4280-7470-5(8))* IndyPublish.com.

Appelt, Kathi. When Otis Courted Mama. Szekeres, Cyndy & McElmurry, Jill, illus. 2015. (ENG.). 40p. (J). (gr. -1-3). 16.99 *(978-0-15-216688-5(2)*, HMH Books For Young Readers) Houghton Mifflin Harcourt Publishing Co.

Ashworth, Sherry. Close-Up. 2006. (ENG.). 256p. (J). (gr. 7). pap. 11.95 *(978-1-4169-0474-8(3)*, Simon & Schuster Children's) Simon & Schuster, Ltd. GBR. Dist: Simon & Schuster, Inc.

Banting, Celia. I Only Said I Had No Choice. 2006. (I Only Said Ser.). (Illus.). 202p. (YA). pap. 14.99 *(978-0-9786648-0-0(9))* Wighita Pr.

Beitia, Sara. The Last Good Place of Lily Odilon. 2010. (ENG.). 312p. (YA). (gr. 8-18). pap. 9.95 *(978-0-7387-2068-5(2)*, Flux) North Star Editions.

Billingsley, Franny. Chime. 2012. (ENG.). 384p. (YA). (gr. 7-18). 8.99 *(978-0-14-242092-8(1)*, Speak) Penguin Young Readers Group.

Bodeen, S. A. Shipwreck Island. 2014. (Shipwreck Island Ser.: 1). (ENG.). 192p. (J). (gr. 5-8). 16.99 *(978-1-250-02777-1(2)*, 9781250027771) Feiwel & Friends.

Bowvayne. A Spell Behind Bars. Snow, Alan, illus. 2006. (Misadventures of Danny Cloke Ser.). 208p. (J). (gr. 6). lib. bdg. 12.99 *(978-1-58086-926-3(2)*, Usborne) EDC Publishing.

Bradman, Tony. The Wicked Stepmother Helps Out, 1 vol. Warburton, Sarah, illus. 2014. (After Happily Ever After Ser.). (ENG.). 56p. (gr. 2-3). lib. bdg. 25.32 *(978-1-4342-7951-4(0)*, After Happily Ever After) Stone Arch Bks.

Brooks, Martha. Being with Henry, 1 vol. (ENG.). 174p. pap. 8.95 *(978-0-88899-502-5(4))* Groundwood Bks. CAN. Dist: Publishers Group West (PGW).

Caletti, Deb. Wild Roses. (ENG.). (YA). (gr. 7-12). 2008. 320p. pap. 8.99 *(978-1-4169-5782-9(0))* 2005. (Illus.). 304p. 15.95 *(978-0-689-86766-8(2))* Simon Pulse. (Simon Pulse).

Connor, Leslie. Waiting for Normal. 2008. (ENG.). 304p. (J). (gr. 5-18). 16.99 *(978-0-06-089088-9(6)*, Tegen, Katherine Bks) HarperCollins Pubs.

Couloumbis, Audrey. Not Exactly a Love Story. 2014. (ENG.). 288p. (YA). (gr. 7). pap. 9.99 *(978-0-375-86606-7(X)*, Ember) Random Hse. Children's Bks.

—Say Yes. 2003. (ENG.). 208p. (J). (gr. 3-7). pap. 7.99 *(978-0-14-250186-3(7)*, Speak) Penguin Young Readers Group.

Crystian, Carol Payne. Ebony Black & The 7. 2012. 28p. pap. 24.95 *(978-1-4626-9728-1(3))* America Star Bks.

Cullen, Lynn. Diary of Nelly Vandom. Date not set. 128p. (gr. 3-18). mass mkt. 4.99 *(978-0-06-440926-1(0))* HarperCollins Pubs.

Cullen-Skowronski, Fiona. The Smugglers' Caves. 2009. 284p. pap. 19.99 *(978-1-84923-435-1(3))* YouWriteOn.

Dickens, Charles. David Copperfield. 2006. (ENG.). 130p. per. 18.95 *(978-1-84002-570-5(0))* Consortium Bk. Sales & Distribution.

—David Copperfield. 2008. (Bring the Classics to Life Ser.). (Illus.). 72p. (gr. 4-12). pap., act. bk. ed. 10.95 *(978-1-55576-322-0(7)*, EDCTR-408B) EDCON Publishing Group.

—David Copperfield. 2009. 186p. pap. 19.99 *(978-1-4590-4328-2(6))* General Bks. LLC.

—David Copperfield. 2009. (Foundation Classics Ser.). 56p. (J). (gr. 5-9). lib. bdg. 27.95 *(978-1-60754-852-2(6))* Windmill Bks.

—David Copperfield. 2006. (Oxford Progressive English Readers Ser.). (ENG., Illus.). 103p. (J). (gr. 4-7). per. *(978-0-19-597140-8(X))* Oxford Univ. Pr.

Dickerson, Melanie. The Fairest Beauty, 1 vol. 2013. (Fairy Tale Romance Ser.). (ENG.). 336p. (YA). pap. 12.99 *(978-0-310-72439-1(2))* Zondervan.

Dolenz, Ami. Harold & Agatha: The Mysterious Jewel. 2013. 176p. *(978-1-4602-0520-4(0))*; pap. *(978-1-4602-0420-7(4))* FriesenPress.

Elkeles, Simone. Better Than Perfect. 2014. (Wild Cards Ser.). (ENG.). 352p. (YA). (gr. 9). pap. 9.99 *(978-0-8027-3725-0(0)*, 9780802737250, Bloomsbury USA Childrens) Bloomsbury Publishing USA.

Ferguson, Tina. The Day i Disappeared. 2005. 83p. pap. 16.95 *(978-1-4137-9243-0(X))* PublishAmerica, Inc.

French, Simon. Where in the World. 2003. 208p. (J). (gr. 3-7). 14.95 *(978-1-56145-292-7(0)*, Q34443) Peachtree Pubs.

Frost, Helen. When My Sister Started Kissing. 2017. (ENG.). 208p. (J). 16.99 *(978-0-374-30303-7(7)*, 9780374303037, Farrar, Straus & Giroux (BYR)) Farrar, Straus & Giroux.

Furniss, Clare. The Year of the Rat. 2015. (ENG.). 304p. (YA). (gr. 7). pap. 10.99 *(978-1-4814-2100-3(X)*, McElderry, Margaret K. Bks.) McElderry, Margaret K. Bks.

Galvin, Laura Gates & Studio Mouse Editorial. Cinderella: Dreams Do Come True. 2008. (Illus.). 36p. (J). (gr. -1). 7.99 *(978-1-59069-436-7(8))* Studio Mouse LLC.

Geras, Adèle. Pictures of the Night. 2005. (ENG.). 192p. (YA). (gr. 7-12). pap. 11.95 *(978-0-15-205543-1(6))* Houghton Mifflin Harcourt Publishing Co.

Gilani, Fawzia. Cinderella: An Islamic Tale. 2011. (ENG., Illus.). 44p. (J). (gr. k-5). 14.00 *(978-0-86037-473-2(4))* Kube Publishing Ltd. GBR. Dist: Consortium Bk. Sales & Distribution.

Grabenstein, Chris. The Crossroads. 2009. (Haunted Mystery Ser.: 1). (ENG.). 352p. (J). (gr. 3-7). 7.99 *(978-0-375-84698-4(0)*, Yearling) Random Hse. Children's Bks.

Grimm, Jacob & Grimm, Wilhelm. Hansel & Gretel, 1 vol. Archipova, Anastasiya, illus. 2008. (ENG.). 32p. (J). (gr. -1-3). *(978-0-86315-623-6(1))* Floris Bks.

Hanson-Roberts, Mary, illus. Cinderella: A Tale of Kindness. 2006. (J). 6.99 *(978-1-59939-001-7(9))* Cornerstone Pr.

Hayes, Vicki C. The Garden Troll, 1 vol. 2015. (Red Rhino Ser.). (ENG.). 68p. (J). (gr. 4-6). pap. 7.95 *(978-1-62250-916-4(1))* Saddleback Educational Publishing, Inc.

Heathfield, Lisa. Paper Butterflies. 2017. (ENG.). 272p. (YA). (gr. 7-12). 18.99 ***(978-1-5124-8241-6(2)***, Carolrhoda Bks.) Lerner Publishing Group.

Helget, Nicole. The End of the Wild. 2017. (ENG., Illus.). 272p. (J). (gr. 3-7). 16.99 *(978-0-316-24511-1(9))* Little, Brown Bks. for Young Readers.

Hendry, Frances. Quest for a Queen: The Falcon. 2006. pap. *(978-1-905665-06-8(7))* Pollinger In Print.

Hunt, Lynda Mullaly. One for the Murphys. (ENG.). (J). (gr. 5). 2013. 256p. pap. 7.99 *(978-0-14-242652-4(0)*, Puffin Books) 2012. 288p. 16.99 *(978-0-399-25615-8(6)*, Nancy Paulsen Books) Penguin Young Readers Group.

Jackson, Ellen B. Cinnamon Brown & the Seven Dwarfs. Brown, Elbrite, illus. 2006. (J). *(978-0-670-06106-8(9)*, Viking Adult) Penguin Publishing Group.

Johnson, Angela. Bird. 2006. 133p. (gr. 3-7). 16.00 *(978-0-7569-6660-7(4))* Perfection Learning Corp.

Jukes, Mavis. Like Jake & Me. 2005. (ENG., Illus.). 64p. (J). (gr. 1-4). 6.99 *(978-0-440-42122-1(5)*, Yearling) Random Hse. Children's Bks.

Kelly, Erin Entrada. The Land of Forgotten Girls. 2016. 304p. (J). (gr. 3-7). 16.99 *(978-0-06-223864-1(7)*, Greenwillow Bks.) HarperCollins Pubs.

Konigsburg, E. L. Journey to an 800 Number. 2008. (ENG.). 160p. (J). (gr. 4-8). pap. 6.99 *(978-1-4169-5875-8(4)*, Atheneum Bks. for Young Readers) Simon & Schuster Children's Publishing.

LaFaye, A. Nissa's Place. 2010. (ENG.). 256p. (J). (gr. 2-8). pap. 8.00 *(978-1-57131-697-4(3))* Milkweed Editions.

Lake, Susan. Ebony & the Five Dwarfs. 2007. 56p. per. 10.00 *(978-1-4257-7841-5(0))* Xlibris Corp.

Little Reader Digital Storybook: Cinderella. 2005. (J). cd-rom 8.99 *(978-0-9767657-7-6(2))* Mullings Media.

MacLachlan, Patricia. Sarah, Plain & Tall. 30th anniv. ed. 2015. (Sarah, Plain & Tall Ser.: 1). (ENG.). 112p. (J). (gr. 1-5). pap. 6.99 *(978-0-06-239952-6(7)*, Tegen, Katherine Bks) HarperCollins Pubs.

Matheson, Shirlee Smith. Gambler's Daughter. 2009. (ENG.). 144p. (YA). pap. 11.99 *(978-1-55002-718-1(2)*, Sandcastle Bks.) Dundurn CAN. Dist: Ingram Publisher Services.

McClintock, Norah. Tell, 1 vol. 2006. (Orca Soundings Ser.). (ENG.). 128p. (YA). (gr. 8-12). per. 9.95 *(978-1-55143-511-4(X))* Orca Bk. Pubs. USA.

—Tell. 2007. (Orca Soundings Ser.). 100p. (gr. 4-7). 19.95 *(978-0-7569-8069-6(0))* Perfection Learning Corp.

McGowan, Maureen. Cinderella: Ninja Warrior. 2010. 320p. pap. 8.95 *(978-1-60747-778-5(5)*, Pickwick Pr.) Phoenix Bks., Inc.

McKinty, Adrian. Deviant. 2011. (ENG.). 368p. (YA). (gr. 9-17). 16.95 *(978-0-8109-8420-2(2)*, Amulet Bks.) Abrams, Inc.

Meade, L. T. The Children's Pilgrimage. 2004. reprint ed. pap. 1.99 *(978-1-4192-5659-2(9))*; pap. 24.95 *(978-1-4191-5659-5(4))* Kessinger Publishing, LLC.

Messner, Kate. Spitfire. 2007. (J). *(978-1-59531-018-7(5))* North Country Bks., Inc.

Meyer, Marissa. Winter. 2015. (Lunar Chronicles Ser.: 4). (ENG.). 832p. (YA). (gr. 7-12). 22.99 *(978-0-312-64298-3(9)*, 9780312642983) Feiwel & Friends.

Meyers, Susan A. Callie & the Stepmother. Gauss, Rose, illus. l.t. ed. 2005. (ENG.). 64p. (J). (gr. -1-3). pap. 6.95 *(978-0-9718348-0-4(6))* Blooming Tree Pr.

Monstrata, Nessi. Monster High Diaries: Draculaura & the New Stepmomster. 2015. (Monster High Diaries: 1). (ENG.). 160p. (J). (gr. 3-7). 9.99 *(978-0-316-30084-1(5))* Little, Brown Bks. for Young Readers.

Nadin, Joanna. The Stepmonster: Blue Banana. Ceulemans, Eglantine, illus. 2015. (Blue Banana Ser.). (ENG.). 48p. (J). (gr. k-2). pap. 8.99 *(978-1-4052-7541-5(3))* Egmont Bks., Ltd. GBR. Dist: Independent Pubs. Group.

Narsimhan, Mahtab. The Third Eye. 2007. (Tara Trilogy Ser.: 1). (ENG.). 240p. (YA). (gr. 5-7). pap. 12.99 *(978-1-55002-750-1(6)*, Boardwalk Bks.) Dundurn CAN. Dist: Ingram Publisher Services.

Naylor, Phyllis Reynolds. Alice on Her Way. 2006. (Alice McKinley Ser.: No. 17). 322p. (gr. 9-12). 17.00 *(978-0-7569-6909-7(3))* Perfection Learning Corp.

—Alice on Her Way. 2006. (Alice Ser.: No. 17). (ENG.). 352p. (YA). (gr. 9-12). mass mkt. 6.99 *(978-0-689-87091-0(4)*, Simon Pulse) Simon Pulse.

Nixon, Joan Lowery. Nancy's Story, 1765. 2004. (J). *(978-0-87935-225-7(6))* Colonial Williamsburg Foundation.

Nussbaum, Ben & Studio Mouse Editorial. Snow White: A New Beginning. 2008. (ENG., Illus.). 36p. (J). (gr. -1). 7.99 *(978-1-59069-437-4(6))* Studio Mouse LLC.

Patricia, MacLachlan. Sarah, Plain & Tall. 2014. (Sarah, Plain & Tall Ser.). (ENG.). 96p. (J). 10.24 *(978-1-63245-125-5(5))* Lectorum Pubns., Inc.

Paulin, Chrita. Let's Bake a Family. Burns, Rosalyn, ed. Richards, Tanya, illus. 2009. (ENG.). 32p. (J). pap. 12.95 *(978-0-9763400-1-0(1))* Coal Under Pressure Pubns.

Peralta, Joaquin. Emma Snow: At the Edge of the World. 2009. 206p. (J). pap. 17.00 *(978-1-934376-19-5(1))* Balona Bks.

Polak, Monique. Home Invasion, 1 vol. 2005. (Orca Soundings Ser.). (ENG.). 128p. (YA). (gr. 8-12). per. 9.95 *(978-1-55143-482-7(2))* Orca Bk. Pubs. USA.

—Home Invasion. 2006. (Orca Soundings Ser.). 105p. (gr. 7-11). 19.95 *(978-0-7569-6871-7(2))* Perfection Learning Corp.

Rinaldi, Ann. Keep Smiling Through. 2005. (ENG.). 208p. (J). (gr. 2-5). pap. 13.95 *(978-0-15-205399-4(9))* Houghton Mifflin Harcourt Publishing Co.

Rollins, Ellie. Zip. 2013. (ENG.). 336p. (J). (gr. 3-7). pap. 7.99 *(978-1-59514-571-0(0)*, Razorbill) Penguin Young Readers Group.

Rorby, Ginny. How to Speak Dolphin. 2015. (ENG.). 272p. (J). (gr. 3-7). 16.99 *(978-0-545-67605-2(3)*, Scholastic Pr.) Scholastic, Inc.

Salisbury, Graham. Lord of the Deep. 2003. 182p. (J). (gr. 5-9). 13.65 *(978-0-7569-1455-4(8))* Perfection Learning Corp.

Sanchez, Alex. Bait. 2010. (ENG.). 256p. (YA). (gr. 7). pap. 12.99 *(978-1-4169-3774-6(9)*, Simon & Schuster Bks. For Young Readers) Simon & Schuster Bks. For Young Readers.

Schroeder, Lisa. Falling for You. 2013. (ENG.). 368p. (YA). (gr. 9). 16.99 *(978-1-4424-4399-0(5)*, Simon Pulse) Simon Pulse.

Sherrard, Valerie. Three Million Acres of Flame. 2007. (ENG.). 200p. (YA). pap. 10.99 *(978-1-55002-727-3(1)*, Boardwalk Bks.) Dundurn CAN. Dist: Ingram Publisher Services.

Stone Arch Books Staff. Cinderella: The Graphic Novel, 1 vol. Timmins, Jeffrey Stewart, illus. 2008. (Graphic Spin Ser.). (ENG.). 40p. (gr. 1-3). pap. 5.95 *(978-1-4342-0860-6(5)*, Graphic Revolve) Stone Arch Bks.

Sullivan, Derek E. Biggie. 2015. (ENG.). 272p. (YA). (gr. 8-12). 16.99 *(978-0-8075-0727-8(X))* Whitman, Albert & Co.

Tavner, Gill & Dickens, Charles. David Copperfield. Donnelly, Karen, illus. 2009. (Real Reads Ser.). 64p. (J). (gr. 4-8). pap. 13.55 *(978-1-60754-383-1(4))* Windmill Bks.

Timmins, Jeffrey Stewart, illus. Cinderella: The Graphic Novel, 1 vol. 2008. (Graphic Spin Ser.). (ENG.). 40p. (gr. 1-3). 25.32 *(978-1-4342-0764-7(1)*, Graphic Revolve) Stone Arch Bks.

Tullson, Diane. Red Sea, 1 vol. 2005. (ENG.). 176p. (YA). (gr. 8-12). per. 13.00 *(978-1-55143-331-8(1))* Orca Bk. Pubs. USA.

Urbain, Catherine. Manuel & the Lobsterman. 2008. (ENG.). 214p. (J). (gr. 4-7). 16.95 *(978-1-59078-516-4(9)*, Front Street) Boyds Mills Pr.

Weston Woods Staff, creator. James Marshall's Cinderella. 2011. 38.75 *(978-0-439-84886-2(5))* Weston Woods Studios, Inc.

Whitten, A. J. The Well. 2009. (ENG., Illus.). 336p. (YA). (gr. 7-18). pap. 18.95 *(978-0-547-23229-4(2))* Houghton Mifflin Harcourt Publishing Co.

STEROIDS

Aretha, David. Steroids & Other Performance-Enhancing Drugs: A MyReportLinks. com Book. 2005. (Drugs Ser.). (Illus.). 48p. (J). lib. bdg. 26.60 *(978-0-7660-5277-2(X)*, MyReportLinks.com Bks.) Enslow Pubs., Inc.

Benjamin, Daniel. Steroids. 2013. 64p. (J). (gr. 6-9). 34.21 *(978-1-60870-826-0(8))*; pap. 15.28 *(978-1-62712-062-3(9))* Cavendish Square Publishing.

Fretland VanVoorst, Jennifer. Performance-Enhancing Risks: The Science of Steroids, 1 vol. 2010. (Headline Science Ser.). (ENG.). 48p. (gr. 7-8). lib. bdg. 29.32 *(978-0-7565-4373-0(8)*, Headline Science) Compass Point Bks.

Friedman, Lauri S. Steroids. 2008. (Writing the Critical Essay Ser.). (ENG., Illus.). 128p. (gr. 10-12). lib. bdg. 38.30 *(978-0-7377-4267-1(4)*, LML02109-243179) Cengage Gale.

Gerber, Larry. The Truth about Steroids. 2013. (Drugs & Consequences Ser.). (Illus.). 64p. (J). (gr. 7-12). 31.95 *(978-1-4777-1895-7(8))* Rosen Publishing Group, Inc., The.

Honders, Christine & Roleff, Tamara L. Steroids & Other Performance-Enhancing Drugs. 2017. (Drug Education Library). 112p. (YA). (gr. 7-7). lib. bdg. 37.45 ***(978-1-5345-6003-1(3)***, Lucent Pr.) Greenhaven Publishing LLC.

Latta, Sara L. Investigate Steroids & Performance Drugs. 2014. (Investigate Drugs Ser.). (Illus.). 112p. (J). (gr. 5-12). lib. bdg. 33.27 *(978-0-7660-4240-7(5))* Enslow Pubs., Inc.

LeVert, Suzanne & Whiting, Jim. The Facts about Steroids. 2009. (Benchmark Rockets: Drug Facts Ser.). 32p. (YA). (gr. 5-9). 28.50 *(978-0-7614-4352-0(5))* Marshall Cavendish Corp.

May, Suellen & Triggle, David J. Steroids & Other Performance-Enhancing Drugs. 2011. (Understanding Drugs Ser.). (Illus.). 112p. (C). (gr. 9-12). 34.95 *(978-1-60413-552-7(2))* Facts On File, Inc.

Mintzer, Rich. Steroids = Busted! 2006. (Busted! Ser.). (Illus.). 112p. (J). (gr. 6). lib. bdg. 33.27 *(978-0-7660-2471-7(7))* Enslow Pubs., Inc.

Monroe, Judy. Steroids, Sports, & Body Image: The Risks of Performance-Enhancing Drugs. 2004. (Issues in Focus Ser.). (Illus.). 128p. (J). lib. bdg. 26.60 *(978-0-7660-2160-0(2))* Enslow Pubs., Inc.

Schaefer, Adam. Steroids. 2008. (21st Century Skills Library: Health at Risk Ser.). (ENG., Illus.). 32p. (gr. 4-8). lib. bdg. 28.50 *(978-1-60279-287-6(9)*, 200136) Cherry Lake Publishing.

S

Silverman, Steve. Performance-Enhancing Drugs, 1 vol. 2008. (Essential Viewpoints Set 3 Ser.). (ENG.). 112p. (J). (gr. 6-12). lib. bdg. 35.64 *(978-1-60453-111-4(8))* ABDO Publishing Co.

Sterngass, Jon. Steroids. 2010. (Controversy! 2 Ser.). 112p. (gr. 7). 37.07 *(978-0-7614-4903-4(5))* Marshall Cavendish Corp.

West, Krista, et al. Steroids & Other Performance-Enhancing Drugs. 2nd rev. ed. 2008. (Junior Drug Awareness Ser.). (Illus.). 120p. (gr. 5-8). 30.00 *(978-0-7910-9748-9(X)*, Chelsea Hse.) Facts On File, Inc.

STEVENSON, ROBERT LOUIS, 1850-1894

Hamilton, John. Man-Made Horrors, 1 vol. 2007. (World of Horror Ser.). (ENG.). 32p. (gr. 4-8). 27.07 *(978-1-59928-769-0(2)*, Abdo & Daughters) ABDO Publishing Co.

Murphy, Jim. Across America on an Emigrant Train. 2003. (ENG., Illus.). 168p. (J). (gr. 5-7). pap. 10.95 *(978-0-395-76483-1(1))* Houghton Mifflin Harcourt Publishing Co.

Saddleback Educational Publishing Staff, ed. Dr. Jekyll & Mr. Hyde. 2011. (Timeless Classics Ser.). (ENG.). 48p. (YA). (gr. 9-12). pupil's gde. ed. 19.95 incl. cd-rom *(978-1-61651-133-3(8))* Saddleback Educational Publishing, Inc.

—Kidnapped. 2011. (Timeless Classics Ser.). (ENG.). 48p. (YA). (gr. 9-12). pupil's gde. ed. 19.95 incl. cd-rom *(978-1-61651-141-8(9))* Saddleback Educational Publishing, Inc.

—Treasure Island. 2011. (Timeless Classics Ser.). (ENG.). 48p. (YA). (gr. 9-12). pupil's gde. ed. 19.95 incl. cd-rom *(978-1-61651-155-5(9))* Saddleback Educational Publishing, Inc.

STILTON, GERONIMO (FICTITIOUS CHARACTER)—FICTION

Geronimo Stilton 12: 12-Copy Solid Prepack. 2004. (J). *(978-0-439-64102-9(0)*, Scholastic Paperbacks) Scholastic, Inc.

Geronimo Stilton Staff. The Cheese Experiment. 2016. (Geronimo Stilton Ser.: 63). (ENG.). 128p. (J). (gr. 2-5). pap. 7.99 *(978-0-545-87252-2(9)*, Scholastic Paperbacks) Scholastic, Inc.

—Sea Monster Surprise. 2016. (Geronimo Stilton Cavemice Ser.: 11). (ENG.). 128p. (J). (gr. 2-5). pap. 6.99 *(978-0-545-87248-5(0)*, Scholastic Paperbacks) Scholastic, Inc.

Heim, Julia & Dami, Elisabetta. The Little Book of Happiness. Bluecheese, Wally, illus. 2013. 42p. (J). pap. *(978-0-545-48255-4(0))* Scholastic, Inc.

Scholastic, Inc. Staff, contrib. by. Geronimo Stilton 12: 12-copy Solid Self Shipper. 2004. (ENG.). (J). pap. *(978-0-439-64101-2(2)*, Scholastic Paperbacks) Scholastic, Inc.

Stilton, Geronimo. All Because of a Cup of Coffee. Wolf, Matt, illus. 2004. (Geronimo Stilton Ser.: 10). (ENG.). 128p. (J). (gr. 2-5). pap. 7.99 *(978-0-439-55972-0(3)*, Scholastic Paperbacks) Scholastic, Inc.

—Attack of the Bandit Cats. Wolf, Matt, illus. 2004. (Geronimo Stilton Ser.: 8). (ENG.). 128p. (J). (gr. 2-5). pap. 7.99 *(978-0-439-55970-6(7)*, Scholastic Paperbacks) Scholastic, Inc.

—Back in Time. 2015. (Geronimo Stilton Special Edition: the Journey Through Time Ser.: 2). (ENG.). 320p. (J). (gr. 2-5). 14.99 *(978-0-545-74618-2(3)*, Scholastic Paperbacks) Scholastic, Inc.

—Cat & Mouse in a Haunted House. Wolf, Matt & Keys, Larry, illus. 2004. (Geronimo Stilton Ser.: 3). (ENG.). 128p. (J). (gr. -1-3). pap. 7.99 *(978-0-439-55965-2(0)*, Scholastic Paperbacks) Scholastic, Inc.

—Cat & Mouse in a Haunted House. 2004. (Geronimo Stilton Ser.: 3). (gr. 3-6). lib. bdg. 18.40 *(978-0-613-72224-7(8)*, Turtleback) Turtleback Bks.

—Cavemice: Surfing for Secrets. 2015. (Geronimo Stilton Cavemice Ser.: 8). (ENG., Illus.). 128p. (J). (gr. 2-5). pap. 7.99 *(978-0-545-74617-5(5)*, Scholastic Paperbacks) Scholastic, Inc.

—Christmas Catastrophe. 2007. (Geronimo Stilton Ser.). (Illus.). 93p. (J). (gr. 2-5). 14.65 *(978-0-7569-8804-3(7))* Perfection Learning Corp.

—A Christmas Tale. 2005. (Geronimo Stilton Special Edition Ser.). (ENG., Illus.). 64p. (J). (gr. 2-5). 7.99 *(978-0-439-79131-1(6)*, Scholastic Paperbacks) Scholastic, Inc.

—The Curse of the Cheese Pyramid. Wolf, Matt & Keys, Larry, illus. 2004. (Geronimo Stilton Ser.: 2). (ENG.). 128p. (J). (gr. 2-5). pap. 7.99 *(978-0-439-55964-5(2))* Scholastic, Inc.

—The Curse of the Cheese Pyramid. 2004. (Geronimo Stilton Ser.: 2). (gr. 3-6). lib. bdg. 18.40 *(978-0-613-72223-0(X)*, Turtleback) Turtleback Bks.

—Dinosaurs in Action. Cooper-McGuinness, Nanette, tr. from ITA. 2011. (Geronimo Stilton Graphic Novels Ser.). (ENG., Illus.). 56p. (J). (gr. 2-6). 9.99 *(978-1-59707-239-7(7)*, 9781597072397) Papercutz.

—Down & Out down Under. 2007. (Geronimo Stilton Ser.: 29). lib. bdg. 18.40 *(978-1-4177-7837-9(7)*, Turtleback) Turtleback Bks.

—The Dragon Prophecy. 2012. (Geronimo Stilton & the Kingdom of Fantasy Ser.: Bk. 4). (ENG.). 320p. (J). (gr. 2-5). 14.99 *(978-0-545-39351-5(5)*, Scholastic Paperbacks) Scholastic, Inc.

—The Enormouse Pearl Heist. 2012. (ENG.). 128p. (J). (gr. 2-5). pap. 7.99 *(978-0-545-34103-5(5)*, Scholastic Paperbacks) Scholastic, Inc.

—The Enormouse Pearl Heist. 2012. (Geronimo Stilton Ser.: 51). lib. bdg. 18.40 *(978-0-606-26756-4(5)*, Turtleback) Turtleback Bks.

—A Fabumouse School Adventure. 2009. (Geronimo Stilton Ser.: 38). (ENG.). 128p. (J). (gr. 2-5). pap. 7.99 *(978-0-545-02138-8(3)*, Scholastic Paperbacks) Scholastic, Inc.

—A Fabumouse Vacation for Geronimo. Keys, Larry, illus. 2004. (Geronimo Stilton Ser.: 9). (ENG.). 128p. (J). (gr. 2-5). pap. 7.99 *(978-0-439-55971-3(5)*, Scholastic Paperbacks) Scholastic, Inc.

—Field Trip to Niagara Falls. Keys, Larry et al, illus. 2005. (Geronimo Stilton Ser.: No. 24). 121p. (J). lib. bdg. 18.46 *(978-1-4242-0293-5(0))* Fitzgerald Bks.

—Field Trip to Niagara Falls. 2006. (Geronimo Stilton Ser.: 24). (ENG., Illus.). 128p. (J). (gr. 2-5). pap. 7.99 *(978-0-439-69146-8(X)*, Scholastic Paperbacks) Scholastic, Inc.

—The First Samurai. Cooper-McGuinness, Nanette, tr. from ITA. 2013. (Geronimo Stilton Graphic Novels Ser.). (ENG., Illus.). 56p. (J). (gr. 2-6). 9.99 *(978-1-59707-385-1(7)*, 9781597073851) Papercutz.

—Flight of the Red Bandit. 2014. (ENG., Illus.). 128p. (J). (gr. 2-5). pap. 7.99 *(978-0-545-55630-9(9)*, Scholastic Paperbacks) Scholastic, Inc.

—Flight of the Red Bandit. 2014. (Geronimo Stilton Ser.: 56). lib. bdg. 18.40 *(978-0-606-35195-9(7))* Turtleback Bks.

—Following the Trail of Marco Polo, No. 4. Cooper-McGuinness, Nanette, tr. 2010. (Geronimo Stilton Graphic Novels Ser.). (ENG., Illus.). 56p. (J). (gr. 2-6). 9.99 *(978-1-59707-188-8(9)*, 9781597071888) Papercutz.

—Four Mice Deep in the Jungle. Wolf, Matt & Keys, Larry, illus. 2004. (Geronimo Stilton Ser.: 5). (ENG.). 128p. (J). (gr. 2-5). pap. 7.99 *(978-0-439-55967-6(7)*, Scholastic Paperbacks) Scholastic, Inc.

—Geronimo Stilton 12-Copy Prepack. 2004. (J). 71.88 *(978-0-439-70121-1(X)*, Scholastic Paperbacks) Scholastic, Inc.

—Geronimo Stilton Boxed Set: Vol. #4 - 6. 2011. (Geronimo Stilton Graphic Novels Ser.). (ENG., Illus.). 168p. (J). (gr. 2-6). 29.99 *(978-1-59707-271-7(0)*, 9781597072717) Papercutz.

—Geronimo Stilton Cavemice Bk. 7: I¿m a Scaredy-Mouse! 2015. (Geronimo Stilton Cavemice Ser.: 7). (ENG., Illus.). 128p. (J). (gr. 2-5). pap. 6.99 *(978-0-545-74616-8(7)*, Scholastic Paperbacks) Scholastic, Inc.

—Geronimo Stilton Saves the Olympics. Cooper-McGuinness, Nanette, tr. from ITA. 10th ed. 2012. (Geronimo Stilton Graphic Novels Ser.). (ENG., Illus.). 56p. (J). (gr. 2-6). 9.99 *(978-1-59707-319-6(9)*, 9781597073196) Papercutz.

—Geronimo's Valentine. 2009. (Geronimo Stilton Ser.: 36). (Illus.). 103p. (J). 18.40 *(978-1-4364-5051-5(9)*, Turtleback) Turtleback Bks.

—Ghost Pirate Treasure. 2012. (Creepella Von Cacklefur Ser.: 3). (ENG.). 128p. (J). (gr. 2-5). pap. 7.99 *(978-0-545-30744-4(9)*, Scholastic Paperbacks) Scholastic, Inc.

—Ghost Pirate Treasure. 2012. (Geronimo Stilton — Creepella Von Cacklefur Ser.: 3). lib. bdg. 18.40 *(978-0-606-23931-8(6)*, Turtleback) Turtleback Bks.

—The Golden Statue Plot. 2013. (Geronimo Stilton Ser.: 55). lib. bdg. 18.40 *(978-0-606-32380-2(5)*, Turtleback) Turtleback Bks.

—The Great Ice Age. Cooper-McGuinness, Nanette, tr. 2010. (Geronimo Stilton Graphic Novels Ser.). (ENG., Illus.). 56p. (J). (gr. 2-6). 9.99 *(978-1-59707-202-1(8)*, 9781597072021) Papercutz.

—The Haunted Castle. 2011. (ENG.). 128p. (J). (gr. 2-5). pap. 7.99 *(978-0-545-10374-9(6)*, Scholastic Paperbacks) Scholastic, Inc.

—The Hunt for the Secret Papyrus. 2016. (Geronimo Stilton Special Edition Ser.). (ENG.). 224p. (J). (gr. 2-5). 14.99 *(978-0-545-87250-8(2)*, Scholastic Paperbacks) Scholastic, Inc.

—I'm Too Fond of My Fur! Wolf, Matt & Keys, Larry, illus. 2004. (Geronimo Stilton Ser.: 4). (ENG.). 128p. (J). (gr. 2-5). pap. 7.99 *(978-0-439-55966-9(9)*, Scholastic Paperbacks) Scholastic, Inc.

—I'm Too Fond of My Fur! 2004. (Geronimo Stilton Ser.: 4). (gr. 3-6). lib. bdg. 18.40 *(978-0-613-72225-4(6)*, Turtleback) Turtleback Bks.

—It's Halloween, You 'Fraidy Mouse! Wolf, Matt, illus. 2004. (Geronimo Stilton Ser.: 11). (ENG.). 128p. (J). (gr. 2-5). pap. 7.99 *(978-0-439-55973-7(1)*, Scholastic Paperbacks) Scholastic, Inc.

—Journey Through Time. 2014. (Geronimo Stilton Special Edition Ser.). (ENG.). 320p. (J). (gr. 2-5). 14.99 *(978-0-545-55623-1(6)*, Scholastic Paperbacks) Scholastic, Inc.

—The Karate Mouse. 2010. (Geronimo Stilton Ser.: 40). lib. bdg. 18.40 *(978-0-606-06847-5(3)*, Turtleback) Turtleback Bks.

—Kingdom of Fantasy. 2009. (Kingdom of Fantasy Ser.: No. 1). 320p. 14.99 *(978-0-439-69148-2(6)*, Scholastic Paperbacks) Scholastic, Inc.

—The Kingdom of Fantasy. 2009. (Geronimo Stilton & the Kingdom of Fantasy Ser.: 1). (ENG., Illus.). 288p. (J). (gr. 2-5). 14.99 *(978-0-545-98025-8(9))* Scholastic, Inc.

—Lost Treasure of the Emerald Eye. Wolf, Matt & Keys, Larry, illus. 2004. (Geronimo Stilton Ser.: 1). (ENG.). 128p. (J). (gr. 2-5). pap. 7.99 *(978-0-439-55963-8(4)*, Scholastic Paperbacks) Scholastic, Inc.

—Meet Me in Horrorwood. 2011. (Creepella Von Cacklefur Ser.: 2). (ENG., Illus.). 128p. (J). (gr. 2-5). pap. 7.99 *(978-0-545-30743-7(0)*, Scholastic Paperbacks) Scholastic, Inc.

—Merry Christmas, Geronimo! Wolf, Matt, illus. 2004. (Geronimo Stilton Ser.: 12). (ENG.). 128p. (J). (gr. 2-5). pap. 7.99 *(978-0-439-55974-4(X)*, Scholastic Paperbacks) Scholastic, Inc.

—The Mona Mousa Code. Wolf, Matt, illus. 2005. (Geronimo Stilton Ser.: No. 15). 113p. (J). lib. bdg. 10.00 *(978-1-4242-0284-3(1))* Fitzgerald Bks.

—The Mouse Island Marathon. 2007. (Geronimo Stilton Ser.: 30). lib. bdg. 18.40 *(978-1-4177-7839-3(3)*, Turtleback) Turtleback Bks.

—The Mummy with No Name. 2006. (Geronimo Stilton Ser.: 26). (ENG., Illus.). 128p. (J). (gr. 2-5). pap. 7.99 *(978-0-439-84117-7(8)*, Scholastic Paperbacks) Scholastic, Inc.

—My Name Is Stilton, Geronimo Stilton. 2005. (Geronimo Stilton Ser.: 19). (ENG., Illus.). 128p. (J). (gr. 2-5). pap. 7.99 *(978-0-439-69142-0(7)*, Scholastic Paperbacks) Scholastic, Inc.

—The Mysterious Cheese Thief. 2007. (Geronimo Stilton Ser.). (Illus.). 111p. (J). (gr. 2-5). 14.65 *(978-0-7569-8303-1(7))* Perfection Learning Corp.

—The Mysterious Cheese Thief. 2007. (Geronimo Stilton Ser.: 31). (Illus.). 111p. (J). (gr. 4-7). 18.40 *(978-1-4177-9646-5(4)*, Turtleback) Turtleback Bks.

—The Mystery in Venice. 2012. (Geronimo Stilton Ser.: Bk. 48). (ENG.). 128p. (J). (gr. 2-5). pap. 7.99 *(978-0-545-34097-7(7)*, Scholastic Paperbacks) Scholastic, Inc.

—The Mystery in Venice. 2012. (Geronimo Stilton Ser.: 48). lib. bdg. 18.40 *(978-0-606-23729-1(1)*, Turtleback) Turtleback Bks.

—Paws Off, Cheddarface! Wolf, Matt & Keys, Larry, illus. 2004. (Geronimo Stilton Ser.: 6). (ENG.). 128p. (J). (gr. 2-5). pap. 7.99 *(978-0-439-55968-3(5))* Scholastic, Inc.

—The Phantom of the Subway. 2004. (Geronimo Stilton Ser.: No. 13). (ENG., Illus.). 128p. (J). (gr. 2-5). pap. 7.99 *(978-0-439-66162-1(5)*, Scholastic Paperbacks) Scholastic, Inc.

—Play It Again, Mozart! Cooper-McGuinness, Nanette, tr. 2011. (Geronimo Stilton Graphic Novels Ser.). (ENG., Illus.). 56p. (J). (gr. 2-6). 9.99 *(978-1-59707-276-2(1)*, 9781597072762) Papercutz.

—The Race Across America. 2009. (Geronimo Stilton Ser.: 37). lib. bdg. 18.40 *(978-0-606-00228-8(6)*, Turtleback) Turtleback Bks.

—Red Pizzas for a Blue Count. Wolf, Matt & Keys, Larry, illus. 2004. (Geronimo Stilton Ser.: 7). (ENG.). 128p. (J). (gr. 2-5). pap. 7.99 *(978-0-439-55969-0(3))* Scholastic, Inc.

—Ride for Your Life! 2014. (Creepella Von Cacklefur Ser.: 6). (ENG., Illus.). 128p. (J). (gr. 2-5). pap. 7.99 *(978-0-545-64659-8(6)*, Scholastic Paperbacks) Scholastic, Inc.

—Ride for Your Life! 2014. (Geronimo Stilton — Creepella Von Cacklefur Ser.: 6). lib. bdg. 18.40 *(978-0-606-35847-7(1))* Turtleback Bks.

—Rumble in the Jungle. 2013. (Geronimo Stilton Ser.: 53). lib. bdg. 18.40 *(978-0-606-31527-2(6)*, Turtleback) Turtleback Bks.

—Run for the Hills, Geronimo! 2011. (Geronimo Stilton Ser.: Bk. 47). (ENG.). 128p. (J). (gr. 2-5). pap. 7.99 *(978-0-545-33132-6(3)*, Scholastic Paperbacks) Scholastic, Inc.

—Save the White Whale! 2011. (ENG.). 128p. (J). (gr. 2-5). pap. 7.99 *(978-0-545-10377-0(0)*, Scholastic Paperbacks) Scholastic, Inc.

—The Search for Sunken Treasure. Wolf, Matt, illus. 2006. (Geronimo Stilton Ser.: No. 25). 111p. (J). lib. bdg. 10.00 *(978-1-4242-1519-5(6))* Fitzgerald Bks.

—The Search for Treasure. 2014. (ENG.). 320p. (J). (gr. 2-5). 14.99 *(978-0-545-65604-7(4)*, Scholastic Paperbacks) Scholastic, Inc.

—Secret Agent. 2008. (Geronimo Stilton Ser.: 34). (ENG., Illus.). 128p. (J). (gr. 2-5). pap. 7.99 *(978-0-545-02134-0(0)*, Scholastic Paperbacks) Scholastic, Inc.

—Singing Sensation. 2009. (Geronimo Stilton Ser.: 39). lib. bdg. 18.40 *(978-0-606-00230-1(8)*, Turtleback) Turtleback Bks.

—The Stinky Cheese Vacation. 2014. (Geronimo Stilton Ser.: 57). lib. bdg. 18.40 *(978-0-606-35843-9(9))* Turtleback Bks.

—A Suitcase Full of Ghosts. 2015. (Creepella Von Cacklefur Ser.: 7). (ENG.). 128p. (J). (gr. 2-5). pap. 7.99 *(978-0-545-74611-3(6)*, Scholastic Paperbacks) Scholastic, Inc.

—The Super Chef Contest. 2014. (Geronimo Stilton Ser.: 58). lib. bdg. 18.40 *(978-0-606-36056-2(5))* Turtleback Bks.

—The Temple of the Ruby of Fire. 2004. (Geronimo Stilton Ser.: 14). (ENG., Illus.). 128p. (J). (gr. 2-5). pap. 7.99 *(978-0-439-66163-8(3)*, Scholastic Paperbacks) Scholastic, Inc.

—The Thirteen Ghosts. 2011. (Creepella Von Cacklefur Ser.: 1). (ENG., Illus.). 128p. (J). (gr. 2-5). pap. 7.99 *(978-0-545-30742-0(2)*, Scholastic Paperbacks) Scholastic, Inc.

—This Hotel Is Haunted! 2012. (Geronimo Stilton Ser.: Bk. 50). (ENG., Illus.). 128p. (J). (gr. 2-5). pap. 7.99 *(978-0-545-34102-8(7)*, Scholastic Paperbacks) Scholastic, Inc.

—This Hotel Is Haunted! 2012. (Geronimo Stilton Ser.: 50). lib. bdg. 18.40 *(978-0-606-26182-1(6)*, Turtleback) Turtleback Bks.

—The Treasure of Easter Island. 2015. (Geronimo Stilton Ser.: 6). (ENG., Illus.). 128p. (J). (gr. 2-5). pap. 7.99 *(978-0-545-74614-4(0)*, Scholastic Paperbacks) Scholastic, Inc.

—Valley of the Giant Skeletons. 2008. (Illus.). 111p. (J). lib. bdg. 15.38 *(978-1-4242-4303-7(3))* Fitzgerald Bks.

—Valley of the Giant Skeletons. 2008. (Geronimo Stilton Ser.). (Illus.). 110p. (gr. 2-5). 17.00 *(978-0-7569-8805-0(5))* Perfection Learning Corp.

—Valley of the Giant Skeletons. 2008. (Geronimo Stilton Ser.: 32). (ENG., Illus.). 128p. (J). (gr. 2-5). pap. 7.99 *(978-0-545-02132-6(4)*, Scholastic Paperbacks) Scholastic, Inc.

—Valley of the Giant Skeletons. 2008. (Geronimo Stilton Ser.: 32). lib. bdg. 18.40 *(978-1-4364-2713-5(4))* Turtleback Bks.

—The Volcano of Fire. 2013. (Geronimo Stilton & the Kingdom of Fantasy Ser.: Bk. 5). (ENG., Illus.). 320p. (J). (gr. 2-5). 14.99 *(978-0-545-55625-5(2)*, Scholastic Paperbacks) Scholastic, Inc.

—Watch Your Tail! 2013. (Geronimo Stilton Cavemice Ser.: 2). lib. bdg. 18.40 *(978-0-606-31998-0(0)*, Turtleback) Turtleback Bks.

—The Way of the Samurai. 2012. (Geronimo Stilton Ser.: No. 49). (ENG.). 128p. (J). (gr. 2-5). pap. 7.99 *(978-0-545-34101-1(9)*, Scholastic Paperbacks) Scholastic, Inc.

—The Way of the Samurai. 2012. (Geronimo Stilton Ser.: 49). lib. bdg. 18.40 *(978-0-606-26094-7(3)*, Turtleback) Turtleback Bks.

—The Weird Book Machine. Cooper-McGuinness, Nanette, tr. from ITA. 2012. (Geronimo Stilton Graphic Novels Ser.). (ENG., Illus.). 56p. (J). (gr. 2-6). 9.99 *(978-1-59707-295-3(8)*, 9781597072953) Papercutz.

—Who Stole the Mona Lisa? Cooper-McGuinness, Nanette, tr. 2010. (Geronimo Stilton Graphic Novels Ser.). (ENG., Illus.). 56p. (J). (gr. 2-6). 9.99 *(978-1-59707-221-2(4)*, 9781597072212) Papercutz.

—You're Mine, Captain! 2014. (Geronimo Stilton Spacemice Ser.: 2). (ENG., Illus.). 128p. (J). (gr. 2-5). pap. 7.99 *(978-0-545-64652-9(9)*, Scholastic Paperbacks) Scholastic, Inc.

Stilton, Geronimo & Dami, Elisabetta. The Enchanted Charms: The Seventh Adventure in the Kingdom of Fantasy. Barozzi, Danilo, illus. 2015. (ENG.). 320p. (J). (gr. 2-5). 14.99 *(978-0-545-74615-1(9))* Scholastic, Inc.

Stilton, Geronimo & Mckeon, Kathryn. Mouse in Space! 2013. (Geronimo Stilton Ser.: 52). lib. bdg. 18.40 *(978-0-606-31525-8(X)*, Turtleback) Turtleback Bks.

Stilton, Geronimo & Stilton, Thea. Thea Stilton & the Ghost of the Shipwreck. 2010. (Thea Stilton Ser.: 3). lib. bdg. 19.65 *(978-0-606-06843-7(0)*, Turtleback) Turtleback Bks.

—Thea Stilton & the Ice Treasure. 2011. (Thea Stilton Ser.: 9). (ENG., Illus.). 176p. (J). (gr. 2-5). pap. 8.99 *(978-0-545-33134-0(X)*, Scholastic Paperbacks) Scholastic, Inc.

Stilton, Geronimo, et al. The Journey Through Time. 2014. (Illus.). 94p. (J). *(978-0-545-61129-9(6))* Scholastic, Inc.

Stilton, Thea. Thea Stilton & the Missing Myth. 2014. (Thea Stilton Ser.: 20). lib. bdg. 19.65 *(978-0-606-36058-6(1))* Turtleback Bks.

Stilton, Thea & Stilton, Geronimo. Secret of the Snow: A Geronimo Stilton Adventure. 2014. (Thea Stilton Special Edition Ser.). (ENG.). 320p. (J). (gr. 2-5). 14.99 *(978-0-545-65605-4(2)*, Scholastic Paperbacks) Scholastic, Inc.

STOCK EXCHANGES

see also Bonds; Investments; Stocks

Connolly, Sean. The Stock Market. 2010. (World Economy Explained Ser.). 48p. (YA). (gr. 7-12). 35.65 *(978-1-60753-082-4(1))* Amicus Publishing.

—The Stock Market. 2012. (Illus.). 48p. (gr. 6-10). pap. 9.95 *(978-1-926722-80-1(9))* Saunders Bk. Co. CAN. Dist: RiverStream Publishing.

Connolly, Sean & Pipe, Jim. The Stock Market. 2011. (On the Edge Ser.). 32p. (YA). (gr. 3-6). 28.50 *(978-1-59920-518-2(1))* Black Rabbit Bks.

Crayton, Lisa A. & Furang, Kathy. The Stock Market: What It Is & How It Works. 2016. (Economics in the 21st Century Ser.). (ENG.). 96p. (J). (gr. 8-8). 34.60 *(978-0-7660-7384-5(X))* Enslow Pubs., Inc.

Crewe, Sabrina & Ingram, Scott. The Stock Market Crash of 1929. 2005. (Events That Shaped America Ser.). (Illus.). 32p. (gr. 3-6). lib. bdg. 26.00 *(978-0-8368-3416-1(X)*, Gareth Stevens Learning Library) Stevens, Gareth Publishing LLLP.

Fuller, Donna Jo. The Stock Market. 2005. (How Economics Works). (ENG., Illus.). 48p. (gr. 3-5). lib. bdg. 25.26 *(978-0-8225-2635-3(2)*, Lerner Pubns.) Lerner Publishing Group.

Furgang, Kathy. How the Stock Market Works. 2010. (Real World Economics Ser.). (Illus.). 80p. (YA). (gr. 7-18). lib. bdg. 33.25 *(978-1-4358-9466-2(9))* Rosen Publishing Group, Inc., The.

Grant, R. G. Why Did the Great Depression Happen? 2010. (Moments in History Ser.). (Illus.). 48p. (YA). (gr. 5-9). lib. bdg. 31.95 *(978-1-4339-4169-6(4))*; (gr. 6-8). pap. 14.05 *(978-1-4339-4170-2(8)*, Gareth Stevens Secondary Library) Stevens, Gareth Publishing LLLP.

North, Charles & Caes, Charles J. The Stock Market. 2011. (J). 77.70 *(978-1-4488-4755-6(9))*; (J). pap. 12.95 *(978-1-4488-4723-5(0))*; (YA). (gr. 5-9). lib. bdg. 31.95 *(978-1-4488-4717-4(6))* Rosen Publishing Group, Inc., The.

Sepahban, Lois. 12 Things to Know about the Stock Market. 2015. (ENG., Illus.). 32p. (J). *(978-1-63235-034-3(3))* Pr. Room Editions LLC.

Thompson, Helen. Understanding the Stock Market. 2010. (Junior Library of Money). 64p. (YA). (gr. 7-18). lib. bdg. 22.95 *(978-1-4222-1773-3(6))* Mason Crest.

Zuravicky, Orli. The Stock Market: Understanding & Applying Ratios, Decimals, Fractions, & Percentages. (PowerMath Ser.). 32p. 2009. (ENG., Illus.). (gr. 5-6). pap. 10.00 *(978-1-4042-5121-2(9))* 2009. (gr. 4-5). 47.90 *(978-1-60851-426-7(9)*, PowerKids Pr.) 2005. (Illus.). (J). (gr. 3-6). lib. bdg. 25.25 *(978-1-4042-2929-7(9)*, PowerKids Pr.) Rosen Publishing Group, Inc., The.

STOCK MARKET

see Stock Exchanges

STOCK RAISING

see Livestock

STOCKS

see also Bonds; Investments; Stock Exchanges

Bateman, Katherine R. The Young Investor: Projects & Activities for Making Your Money Grow. 2nd ed. 2010. (ENG., Illus.). 144p. (J). (gr. 4). pap. 14.95 *(978-1-56976-546-3(4))* Chicago Review Pr., Inc.

Beach, Byron & Keck, Gayle. Stock Matters: An Introduction to Stock & Ownership for Kids. 2006. (Illus.). 72p. (J). pap. 6.99 *(978-0-9788438-0-9(0))* OneShare Educational Pr.

Connolly, Sean. The Stock Market. 2010. (World Economy Explained Ser.). 48p. (YA). (gr. 7-12). 35.65 *(978-1-60753-082-4(1))* Amicus Publishing.

—The Stock Market. 2012. (Illus.). 48p. (gr. 6-10). pap. 9.95 *(978-1-926722-80-1(9))* Saunders Bk. Co. CAN. Dist: RiverStream Publishing.

Connolly, Sean & Pipe, Jim. The Stock Market. 2011. (On the Edge Ser.). 32p. (YA). (gr. 3-6). 28.50 *(978-1-59920-518-2(1))* Black Rabbit Bks.

Fuller, Donna Jo. The Stock Market. 2005. (How Economics Works). (ENG., Illus.). 48p. (gr. 3-5). lib. bdg. 25.26 *(978-0-8225-2635-3(2)*, Lerner Pubns.) Lerner Publishing Group.

Furgang, Kathy. How the Stock Market Works. 2010. (Real World Economics Ser.). (Illus.). 80p. (YA). (gr. 7-18). lib. bdg. 33.25 *(978-1-4358-9466-2(9))* Rosen Publishing Group, Inc., The.

Gagne, Tammy. A Dividend Stock Strategy for Teens. 2013. (Illus.). 48p. (gr. 4-8). lib. bdg. 29.95 *(978-1-61228-426-2(4))* Mitchell Lane Pubs., Inc.

Healy, Aaron. Making the Trade: Stocks, Bonds, & Other Investments. 2011. (Global Marketplace Ser.). (ENG.). 56p. (gr. 6-9). pap. 9.95 *(978-1-4329-5478-9(4)*, NA-h) Heinemann-Raintree.

Minden, Cecilia. Investing: Making Your Money Work for You. 2007. (21st Century Skills Library: Real World Math Ser.). (ENG., Illus.). 32p. (gr. 4-8). lib. bdg. 28.50 *(978-1-60279-003-2(5)*, 200069) Cherry Lake Publishing.

Orr, Tamra. A Kid's Guide to Stock Market Investing. 2008. (Money Matters Ser.). (Illus.). 48p. (YA). (gr. 3-6). lib. bdg. 29.95 *(978-1-58415-642-0(2))* Mitchell Lane Pubs., Inc.

Pellittiere II, Michael. GROW MONEY - A Kid's Guide to Saving & Investing. 2007. 60p. (YA). pap. 10.40 *(978-0-615-14589-1(2))* Dakota Assocs., Inc.

—GROW MONEY II - A Teenager's Guide to Saving & Investing. 2008. 118p. (YA). pap. 11.42 *(978-0-615-18343-5(3))* Dakota Assocs., Inc.

Thompson, Helen. Understanding the Stock Market. 2010. (Junior Library of Money). 64p. (YA). (gr. 7-18). lib. bdg. 22.95 *(978-1-4222-1773-3(6))* Mason Crest.

STOCKYARDS

see Meat Industry and Trade

STONE

see also Masonry; Rocks

Auster, Michael A. Stone Is Strong! 2005. (Yellow Umbrella Fluent Level Ser.). (ENG., Illus.). 16p. (gr. k-1). pap. 35.70 *(978-0-7368-5300-2(6),* Yellow Umbrella Bks.) Capstone Press of Coughlan Cos.

deMarin, Layne. Built from Stone, 1 vol. (Wonder Readers: Science Ser.). (ENG.). (gr. -1-2). 2012. 20p. lib. bdg. 22.65 *(978-1-4296-9610-4(9))* 2011. 16p. pap. 35.94 *(978-1-4296-8074-5(1))* 2011. 32p. pap. 5.99 *(978-1-4296-7911-4(5))* Capstone Press of Coughlan Cos. (Wonder Readers).

Royston, Angela. Rock: Let's Look at a Pebble. 2005. (J). *(978-1-4109-1826-0(2));* (ENG.). 24p. pap. *(978-1-4109-1833-8(5))* Steck-Vaughn.

Storey, Rita. Rocks & Stones. 2007. (How We Use Materials/Watts Ser.). (Illus.). 30p. (J). (gr. 4-7). lib. bdg. 28.50 *(978-1-59920-006-4(6))* Black Rabbit Bks.

STONE AGE

see also Prehistoric Peoples

Bonner, Hannah. When Fish Got Feet, Sharks Got Teeth, & Bugs Began to Swarm: A Cartoon Prehistory of Life Long Before Dinosaurs. 2009. (ENG., Illus.). 48p. (J). (gr. 5). pap. 7.95 *(978-1-4263-0546-7(X),* National Geographic Children's Bks.) National Geographic Society.

Bruce, Julia. Hunt! Can You Survive the Stone Age? Dennis, Peter, illus. 2009. (Step into History Ser.). 32p. (J). (gr. 2-5). lib. bdg. 23.94 *(978-0-7660-3476-1(3))* Enslow Pubs., Inc.

Butterfield, Moira. Stone Age. 2017. (Britain in the Past Ser.). (ENG., Illus.). 32p. (J). (gr. 4-6). pap. 12.99 ***(978-1-4451-4052-0(7),*** Franklin Watts) Hachette Children's Group GBR. Dist: Hachette Bk. Group.

Dorling Kindersley Publishing Staff. DK Findout! Stone Age. 2017. (DK Find Out! Ser.). (ENG., Illus.). 64p. (J). (gr. 1-4). pap. 10.99 *(978-1-4654-5750-9(X),* DK Children) Dorling Kindersley Publishing, Inc.

Dyan, Penelope. High on a Hill! a Kid's Guide to Innsbruck, Austri. Weigand, John D., photos by. 2011. (Illus.). 40p. pap. 12.95 *(978-1-935630-76-0(8))* Bellissima Publishing, LLC.

Ganeri, Anita. How to Live Like a Stone-Age Hunter. Epelbaum, Mariano, illus. 2015. (How to Live Like... Ser.). (ENG.). 32p. (J). (gr. 3-6). pap. 7.99 *(978-1-4677-7207-5(0));* lib. bdg. 26.65 *(978-1-4677-6352-3(7))* Lerner Publishing Group.

Green, Jen. The Stone Age & Bronze Age. 2016. (Discover Through Craft Ser.). (ENG., Illus.). 32p. (J). (gr. 1-3). pap. 12.99 *(978-1-4451-3746-9(1),* Franklin Watts) Hachette Children's Group GBR. Dist: Hachette Bk. Group.

Hibbert, Clare. Stone Age to Iron Age. 2017. (History Detective Investigates Ser.). (ENG., Illus.). 32p. (J). (gr. 4-6). pap. 12.99 ***(978-0-7502-8197-3(9),*** Wayland) Hachette Children's Group GBR. Dist: Hachette Bk. Group.

Howell, Izzi. Stone Age to Iron Age. 2017. (Fact Cat: History: Early Britons Ser.). (ENG., Illus.). 24p. (J). (gr. k-2). pap. 9.99 *(978-0-7502-9938-1(X),* Wayland) Hachette Children's Group GBR. Dist: Hachette Bk. Group.

Hurdman, Charlotte. Hands-on History! Stone Age. 2013. (ENG., Illus.). 64p. (J). (gr. k-3). 12.99 *(978-1-84322-974-2(9),* Armadillo) Anness Publishing GBR. Dist: National Bk. Network.

Janulis, Klint. Stone Age. 2017. (Illus.). 64p. (J). ***(978-1-5364-0132-5(3))*** Dorling Kindersley Publishing, Inc.

Johanson, Paula. The Paleolithic Revolution. 2016. (First Humans & Early Civilizations Ser.). (ENG.). 64p. (J). (gr. 6-6). pap. 12.95 *(978-1-4994-6314-9(6))* Rosen Publishing Group, Inc., The.

Kerrigan, Juliet. The Stone Age. 2016. (ENG., Illus.). 32p. (J). (gr. 2-3). pap. 8.95 *(978-0-00-816380-8(4))* HarperCollins Pubs. Ltd. GBR. Dist: Independent Pubs. Group.

Meyer, Susan. The Neolithic Revolution. 2016. (First Humans & Early Civilizations Ser.). 64p. (J). (gr. 6-6). pap. 12.95 *(978-1-4994-6322-4(7))* Rosen Publishing Group, Inc., The.

Newland, Sonya. Stone, Bronze & Iron Ages. 2017. (Explore! Ser.). (ENG., Illus.). 32p. (J). (gr. 4-6). pap. 12.99 ***(978-0-7502-9736-3(0),*** Wayland) Hachette Children's Group GBR. Dist: Hachette Bk. Group.

Spizzirri, Linda, ed. Prehistoric Birds. Spizzirri, Peter M., illus. 32p. (J). (gr. 1-8). pap. 4.98 incl. audio *(978-0-86545-023-3(4))* Spizzirri Pr., Inc.

—Prehistoric Sea Life. Kohn, Arnie, illus. 32p. (J). (gr. 1-8). pap. 4.98 incl. audio *(978-0-86545-020-2(X))* Spizzirri Pr., Inc.

Stevens, Noel. In the Never-Never-Converse with an Archangel. 2008. 132p. pap. 13.95 *(978-0-595-52727-4(2))* iUniverse, Inc.

STONE AGE—FICTION

Beckhorn, Susan Williams. The Wolf's Boy. 2017. (ENG.). 240p. (J). (gr. 3-7). pap. 7.99 ***(978-1-4847-2555-9(7))*** Hyperion Bks. for Children.

Fidler, Kathleen. The Boy with the Bronze Axe. 3rd rev. ed. (ENG., Illus.). 176p. 11.95 *(978-0-86315-488-1(3))* Floris Bks. GBR. Dist: SteinerBooks, Inc.

Hart, John. Mammoth Boy: A Lad's Epic Journey to Find Mammoths in the Ice Age. 2012. (ENG.). 240p. pap. *(978-1-78088-174-4(6))* Troubador Publishing Ltd.

McDonnell, Vincent. Children of Stone. 2006. (ENG.). 206p. (J). pap. 11.95 *(978-1-903464-88-5(9))* Collins Pr., The IRL. Dist: Dufour Editions, Inc.

Randerath, Jeanette & Winterhager, Randerath -. ¡vuela, Yoa, Vuela! 2012. (SPA.). 32p. (J). (gr. 2-3). pap. 19.99 *(978-84-261-3918-4(3))* Juventud, Editorial ESP. Dist: Lectorum Pubns., Inc.

Scieszka, Jon. Your Mother Was a Neanderthal. Smith, Lane, illus. 2004. (Time Warp Trio Ser.: 4). (ENG.). 80p. (J). (gr. 2-4). pap. 5.99 *(978-0-14-240048-7(3),* Puffin Books) Penguin Young Readers Group.

Wood, Jacqui. Cliff Dreamers. 2017. (ENG.). 302p. (J). pap. 17.99 ***(978-1-78693-909-8(6),*** c6a96e5f-51f5-4a30-9049-4d533f30c109) Austin, Stan AUS. Dist: Bookmasters Distribution.

STONEHENGE (ENGLAND)

Coddington, Andrew. The Bermuda Triangle, Stonehenge, & Unexplained Places. 2017. (J). ***(978-1-5026-2843-5(0))*** Cavendish Square Publishing.

Dalgleish, Sharon. It's a Mystery. 2003. (Real Deal Ser.). (Illus.). 32p. (J). pap. *(978-0-7608-6692-4(9))* Sundance/Newbridge Educational Publishing.

Dunn, Mary. My Adventure at Stonehenge. 2006. 44p. (J). 8.99 *(978-1-59092-412-9(6))* Blue Forge Pr.

Henzel, Cynthia Kennedy. Stonehenge, 1 vol. 2011. (Troubled Treasures: World Heritage Sites Ser.). (ENG., Illus.). 32p. (YA). (gr. 3-6). 27.07 *(978-1-61613-567-6(0))* ABDO Publishing Co.

Kelley, True. Where Is Stonehenge? Hinderliter, John & Groff, David, illus. 2016. (Where Is? Ser.). (ENG.). 112p. (J). (gr. 3-7). pap. 5.99 *(978-0-448-48693-2(8));* lib. bdg. 15.99 *(978-0-399-54240-4(X))* Penguin Young Readers Group. (Grosset & Dunlap).

McDaniel, Sean. Stonehenge. 2011. (Unexplained Ser.). (ENG., Illus.). 24p. (J). (gr. 3-7). lib. bdg. 25.95 *(978-1-60014-645-9(7),* Torque Bks.) Bellwether Media.

Medina, Nico. Where Is the Great Barrier Reef? Hinderliter, John, illus. 2016. (Where Is? Ser.). (ENG.). 112p. (J). (gr. 3-7). lib. bdg. 15.99 *(978-0-399-54239-8(6),* Grosset & Dunlap) Penguin Young Readers Group.

Owings, Lisa. Stonehenge. 2015. (Unexplained Mysteries Ser.). (ENG., Illus.). 24p. (J). (gr. 3-7). lib. bdg. 25.95 *(978-1-62617-204-3(8),* Epic Bks.) Bellwether Media.

Parker-Pearson, Mike & Aronson, Marc. If Stones Could Speak: Unlocking the Secrets of Stonehenge. 2010. (ENG., Illus.). 64p. (J). (gr. 5-8). 26.90 *(978-1-4263-0600-6(8));* 17.95 *(978-1-4263-0599-3(0))* National Geographic Society. (National Geographic Children's Bks.).

Raum, Elizabeth. Stonehenge. 2015. (Ancient Wonders Ser.). (Illus.). 32p. (J). 28.50 *(978-1-60753-469-3(X))* Amicus Publishing.

Riggs, Kate. Stonehenge. 2009. (Places of Old Ser.). 24p. (J). (gr. 1-5). lib. bdg. 24.25 *(978-1-58341-711-9(7),* Creative Education) Creative Co., The.

Sabatino, Michael. ' 20 Fun Facts about Stonehenge, Vol. 1. 2014. (Fun Fact File: World Wonders! Ser.). (ENG.). 32p. (J). (gr. 2-3). 25.25 *(978-1-4824-0457-9(5))* Stevens, Gareth Publishing LLLP.

Shofner, Shawndra. Stonehenge. 2005. (Ancient Wonders of the World Ser.). (Illus.). 32p. (J). (gr. 4-7). lib. bdg. 18.95 *(978-1-58341-360-9(X),* Creative Education) Creative Co., The.

World Book, Inc Staff, contrib. by. The Mysteries of Stonehenge. 2014. (J). *(978-0-7166-2667-1(5))* World Bk., Inc.

STONES, PRECIOUS

see Precious Stones

STONEWARE

see Pottery

STORIES

see also Animals—Fiction; Ballet—Fiction; Bible Stories; Birds—Fiction; Christmas—Fiction; Fairy Tales; Horror Stories; Legends; Mystery and Detective Stories; Operas—Stories, Plots, Etc.; Sea Stories; Short Stories; Storytelling; Trees—Fiction

Alexander, Ian. Do You See a Dozen?, Vol. 2. Lt. ed. 2005. (Sadlier Phonics Reading Program). (Illus.). 8p. (gr. -1-1). 23.00 net. *(978-0-8215-7347-1(0))* Sadlier, William H. Inc.

Angela's Bookshelf Publishing Staff. Choice Stories for Children. Date not set. (Illus.). 144p. (J). pap. 6.95 *(978-1-878726-08-7(0))* A B Publishing.

Baldner, Jean V. Pebbles in the Wind. Webster, Carroll, illus. 52p. (Orig.). (YA). (gr. 7-18). pap. 5.95 *(978-0-9615317-0-6(3))* Baldner, Jean V.

Barber, Antonia & Quarto Generic Staff. Hidden Tales from Eastern Europe. Guild, Shena, ed. Hess, Paul, illus. 2004. (ENG.). 48p. (J). (gr. 2-17). 9.99 *(978-1-84507-147-9(6),* Frances Lincoln) Quarto Publishing Group UK GBR. Dist: Hachette Bk. Group.

Baum, L. Frank. Adventures of the Magical Monarch of Mo & His People. Date not set. (J). (gr. 5-6). lib. bdg. 20.95 *(978-0-88411-771-1(5))* Amereon Ltd.

Benchabbat, Edie C., et al. My Little Guardian Storybook. Date not set. (Illus.). 28p. (J). (gr. -1-5). pap. 5.99 *(978-0-9660879-0-1(9))* Little Guardians, Inc.

Berger, Melvin & Peck, Marshall H., III. A Whale Is Not a Fish & Other Animal Mix-Ups. (FRE., Illus.). 64p. (J). pap. 6.99 *(978-0-590-16026-1(5))* Scholastic, Inc.

Bertrand, Diane Gonzales. Upside down & Backwards. Hernandez, Karina, tr. 2004. (ENG & SPA., Illus.). 64p. (J). (gr. 2-5). pap. 9.95 *(978-1-55885-408-6(8),* Piñata Books) Arte Publico Pr.

Blyton, Enid. Mr Twiddle Stories. (Illus.). 224p. (J). pap. 5.95 *(978-0-09-965560-2(8))* Random Hse. GBR. Dist: Trafalgar Square Publishing.

—Well, Really, Mr Twiddle! 2nd ed. (ENG., Illus.). 111p. (J). pap. 6.95 *(978-0-7475-3852-3(2))* Bloomsbury Publishing Plc GBR. Dist: Trafalgar Square Publishing.

Brooks, Martha. Traveling on into the Light: And Other Stories. (J). 16.95 *(978-0-88899-220-8(3))* Groundwood Bks. CAN. Dist: Publishers Group West (PGW).

Capucilli, Alyssa Satin. Biscuit Storybook Collection. Schories, Pat, illus. 2004. (Biscuit Ser.). (ENG.). 192p. (J). (gr. -1-3). 11.99 *(978-0-06-075904-9(6),* HarperFestival) HarperCollins Pubs.

Castroviejo, Concha & Fedorchek, Robert M., trs. from SPA. The Garden with Seven Gates. 2003. (Illus.). 112p. (J). 32.50 *(978-0-8387-5559-4(3))* Bucknell Univ. Pr.

Cleary, Beverly. Jean & Johnny. 2007. (ENG.). 224p. (J). (gr. 5-18). pap. 10.99 *(978-0-380-72805-3(2))* HarperCollins Pubs.

Cooling, Wendy. The Puffin Book of Stories for Eight- Year-Olds. Cooling, Wendy, ed. Cox, Steve, illus. (ENG.). 160p. (J). (gr. 3). pap. 8.95 *(978-0-14-038052-1(3))* Penguin Bks., Ltd. GBR. Dist: Trafalgar Square Publishing.

Cuentos para Soñar. 2010. (SPA.). (J). *(978-970-718-864-8(2),* Silver Dolphin en Español) Advanced Marketing, S. de R. L. de C. V.

Dale, Jenny. Boomerang Bob. Reid, Mick, illus. 2003. 105p. (J). *(978-0-439-45348-6(8))* Scholastic, Inc.

—Homeward Bound. Reid, Mick, illus. 2003. 110p. (J). *(978-0-439-45354-7(2))* Scholastic, Inc.

Daley, Patrick Allen, et al. The Scholastic Read-Aloud Anthology: 35 Short, Riveting Read-Alouds That Build Comprehension, Listening, & Higher-Level Thinking Skills-And Keep Kids on the Edge of Their Seats. 2004. (ENG.). 128p. (gr. 5). pap. 18.99 *(978-0-439-04759-3(5),* Teaching Resources) Scholastic, Inc.

Disney Staff. La Belle et la Bete.Tr. of Beauty & the Beast. (FRE., Illus.). 96p. (J). (gr. -1-4). 11.95 *(978-2-89393-145-6(6))* Phidal Publishing, Inc./Editions Phidal, Inc. CAN. Dist: AIMS International Bks., Inc.

Elkins, Stephen. Special Times Bible Rhymes for Toddlers. 2005. (Special Times Ser.). (Illus.). 32p. (J). (gr. -1-18). 9.97 *(978-0-8054-2659-5(0))* B&H Publishing Group.

—Special Times Bible Stories for Toddlers. 2005. (Special Times Ser.). (Illus.). 32p. (J). (gr. -1-18). 9.97 *(978-0-8054-2681-6(7))* B&H Publishing Group.

—Stories That End with a Prayer. Menck, Kevin, illus. 32p. (J). (gr. k-8). 12.98 *(978-1-56919-003-6(8))* Wonder Workshop.

Encyclopaedia Britannica, Inc. Staff, compiled by. Legends, Myths, & Folktales. 2003. (Britannica Learning Library). (Illus.). (J). (gr. 2-5). 14.95 *(978-1-59339-006-8(8),* 049907-EN-REF) Encyclopaedia Britannica, Inc.

Fitzgerald, F. Scott. Bernice Bobs Her Hair & Other Stories. Date not set. (Nelson Readers Ser.). (Illus.). 86p. (J). pap. *(978-0-17-557051-5(5))* Addison-Wesley Longman, Inc.

Foster, Elizabeth Vincent. Lyrico: The Only Horse of His Kind. Buba, Joy, illus. 2nd ed. 2004. 230p. (gr. 6-8). reprint ed. 8.95 *(978-0-930407-21-6(0))* Parabola Bks.

Franco, Eloise. Little Stories. Bredius, Rein, illus. 2003. 66p. (gr. k-5). 5.95 *(978-0-87516-384-0(X),* Devorss Pubns.) DeVorss & Co.

Gavin, Fred. Bedtime Stories. Klemek, Ryan, illus. Date not set. 64p. (J). (gr. k-3). pap. *(978-0-935668-00-1(4))* Gavin, Fred Enterprises.

Glyman, Caroline A. Forest House Firsts: Supplemental Selected Early Childhood Stories, 2 bks. Biser, Dee, illus. (J). (gr. k-3). lib. bdg. 29.90 *(978-1-56674-910-7(7))* Forest Hse. Publishing Co., Inc.

Grandma's Magical Storybook. 2003. (Illus.). 256p. (J). 12.98 *(978-1-4054-0968-1(1))* Parragon, Inc.

Hamilton, Martha & Weiss, Mitch. How & Why Stories: World Tales Kids Can Read & Tell. Lyon, Carol, illus. 2005. (World Storytelling from August House Ser.). (ENG.). 96p. (J). (gr. 1-7). pap. 15.95 *(978-0-87483-561-8(5))* August Hse. Pubs., Inc.

HarperCollins Publishers Ltd. Staff. Charming Classics Box Set No. 3: Charming Horse Library. 2003. (Charming Classics). (J). (gr. 3-7). pap. 19.99 *(978-0-06-056141-3(6))* HarperCollins Pubs.

Hetzer, Michael. Footprints on the Ceiling: Your Child's Footprint Completes the Story. Clayton, Kim, illus. 2nd ed. 2005. 32p. (J). 18.95 *(978-0-9728222-2-0(4))* Webster Henrietta Publishing.

—Footprints on the Ceiling (Collector's Edition) Your Child's Footprint Completes the Story. Clayton, Kim, illus. 2004. 32p. (J). 18.95 *(978-0-9728222-1-3(6))* Webster Henrietta Publishing.

Homer, Larona. The Shore Ghosts & Other Stories of New Jersey. Bock, William Sauts, illus. 2005. 154p. (J). (gr. 4-8). pap. *(978-0-912608-82-2(X))* Middle Atlantic Pr.

Hughes, Shirley. The Big Alfie Out of Doors Storybook. Hughes, Shirley, illus. 2007. (Alfie Ser.). (ENG., Illus.). 64p. (J). (gr. -1-k). 15.95 *(978-0-925891-9(9),* Red Fox) Random House Children's Books GBR. Dist: Independent Pubs. Group.

Idaho Writers League Coeur d'Alene Chapter. Kaleidoscope: A Collection of Tantalizing Tales. 2003. (Illus.). (YA). (gr. 6-18). pap. 15.00 *(978-0-9740481-0-9(0))* Children's Village Foundation, Inc.

Iparraguirre, Sylvia, et al. Terminemos el Cuento. 2003. (SPA., Illus.). 128p. (YA). (gr. 9-12). 9.95 *(978-84-204-4965-4(2))* Ediciones Alfaguara ESP. Dist: Santillana USA Publishing Co., Inc.

Kelemen, Violet. Misty Finds a Family. 2008. 92p. pap. 11.95 *(978-0-615-19128-7(2))* Violet Bks.

Lansky, Bruce & Johnson, Martha. Girls to the Rescue, Bk. 5. 108p. (J). pap. *(978-0-88166-315-0(8))* Meadowbrook Pr.

LeapFrog Schoolhouse Staff. Read-It-All Books: 2nd Grade & Up. 2003. tchr. ed. 19.95 *(978-1-59319-016-3(6),* LeapFrog Schl. Hse.) LeapFrog Enterprises, Inc.

Leeson, Robert. All the Gold in the World. Leplar, Anna, illus. 2004. (ENG.). 96p. 8.95 *(978-0-7136-4059-5(6),* A&C Black) Bloomsbury Publishing Plc GBR. Dist: Consortium Bk. Sales & Distribution.

MacIntyre, R. P. The Blue Camaro. 2006. (ENG.). 160p. pap. 13.95 *(978-1-895449-23-5(5))* Thistledown Pr., Ltd. CAN. Dist: Univ. of Toronto Pr.

Marcovitz, Hal. Will Hobbs. 2005. (Who Wrote That? Ser.). (Illus.). 128p. (gr. 6-12). lib. bdg. 35.00 *(978-0-7910-8657-5(7),* Chelsea Hse.) Facts On File, Inc.

Marshall, Hallie. Winnie the Pooh's Many Adventures, Set. Kurtz, John, illus. 2003. 176p. (J). 15.99 *(978-0-7868-3440-2(4))* Disney Pr.

McOmber, Rachel B., ed. McOmber Phonics Storybooks: A Trip to China. rev. ed. (Illus.). (J). *(978-0-944991-70-1(X))* Swift Learning Resources.

—McOmber Phonics Storybooks: Choose Which One - 1. rev. ed. (Illus.). (J). *(978-0-944991-67-1(X))* Swift Learning Resources.

—McOmber Phonics Storybooks: Humps & Lumps. rev. ed. (Illus.). (J). *(978-0-944991-62-6(9))* Swift Learning Resources.

—McOmber Phonics Storybooks: Kim. rev. ed. (Illus.). (J). *(978-0-944991-07-7(6))* Swift Learning Resources.

—McOmber Phonics Storybooks: Razz. rev. ed. (Illus.). (J). *(978-0-944991-06-0(8))* Swift Learning Resources.

—McOmber Phonics Storybooks: Ten in the Hut. rev. ed. (Illus.). (J). *(978-0-944991-27-5(0))* Swift Learning Resources.

—McOmber Phonics Storybooks: The Bag. rev. ed. (Illus.). (J). *(978-0-944991-03-9(3))* Swift Learning Resources.

—McOmber Phonics Storybooks: The Big Deal. rev. ed. (Illus.). (J). *(978-0-944991-47-3(5))* Swift Learning Resources.

—McOmber Phonics Storybooks: The Big Hole. rev. ed. (Illus.). (J). *(978-0-944991-38-1(6))* Swift Learning Resources.

—McOmber Phonics Storybooks: The Bon-Bon Box. rev. ed. (Illus.). (J). *(978-0-944991-14-5(9))* Swift Learning Resources.

—McOmber Phonics Storybooks: The Box Mix. rev. ed. (Illus.). (J). *(978-0-944991-15-2(7))* Swift Learning Resources.

—McOmber Phonics Storybooks: The Fumes. rev. ed. (Illus.). (J). *(978-0-944991-39-8(4))* Swift Learning Resources.

—McOmber Phonics Storybooks: The Kit. rev. ed. (Illus.). (J). *(978-0-944991-08-4(4))* Swift Learning Resources.

—McOmber Phonics Storybooks: The Land of Morning. rev. ed. (Illus.). (J). *(978-0-944991-82-4(3))* Swift Learning Resources.

—McOmber Phonics Storybooks: The Map. rev. ed. (Illus.). (J). *(978-0-944991-05-3(X))* Swift Learning Resources.

—McOmber Phonics Storybooks: The Pit Kit. rev. ed. (Illus.). (J). *(978-0-944991-09-1(2))* Swift Learning Resources.

—McOmber Phonics Storybooks: The Prize. rev. ed. (Illus.). (J). *(978-0-944991-49-7(1))* Swift Learning Resources.

—McOmber Phonics Storybooks: The Quiz Is (1) rev. ed. (Illus.). (J). *(978-0-944991-34-3(3))* Swift Learning Resources.

—McOmber Phonics Storybooks: The Quiz Is (2) rev. ed. (Illus.). (J). *(978-0-944991-35-0(1))* Swift Learning Resources.

—McOmber Phonics Storybooks: The Rope. rev. ed. (Illus.). (J). *(978-0-944991-45-9(9))* Swift Learning Resources.

—McOmber Phonics Storybooks: The Tin Lid. rev. ed. (Illus.). (J). *(978-0-944991-10-7(6))* Swift Learning Resources.

—McOmber Phonics Storybooks: Tid Bits. rev. ed. (Illus.). (J). *(978-0-944991-36-7(X))* Swift Learning Resources.

Modern Staff. Kites in Flight & Mosquito Bites. (J). 7.95 *(978-0-8136-4839-2(4))* Modern Curriculum Pr.

Monster Stories. 2003. 256p. (J). 5.98 *(978-1-4054-1008-3(6))* Parragon, Inc.

No te dejes de Laura Sue: Social/Emotional Lap Book. (Pebble Soup Exploraciones Ser.). (SPA.). (gr. -1-18). 16.00 *(978-0-7578-1793-9(9))* Rigby Education.

Otfinoski, Steven. Our Freedom to Read Set, 4-Volumes. 2009. (Our Freedom to Read Ser.). (gr. 5-8). 160.00 *(978-1-60413-647-0(2),* Chelsea Hse.) Facts On File, Inc.

Reading Friends Staff. Benjamin. (J). pap. *(978-0-8136-3840-9(2))* Modern Curriculum Pr.

Rothman, Cynthia Anne. A Party for Nine. Lt. ed. 2005. (Sadlier Phonics Reading Program). (Illus.). 8p. (gr. -1-1). 23.00 net. *(978-0-8215-7349-5(7))* Sadlier, William H. Inc.

Selected Children's Stories Published in Other Lands, 7 bks. (Illus.). (J). (gr. k-3). lib. bdg. 101.65 *(978-1-56674-905-3(0))* Forest Hse. Publishing Co., Inc.

Stalcup, Ann & Politi, Leo. Leo Politi: Artist of the Angels. 2004. (gr. 4). 24.95 *(978-1-893110-38-0(9))* Silver Moon Pr.

Story Rhyme Staff. Self-Esteem: Stories, Poetry & Activity Pages. Story Rhyme Staff, illus. Date not set. (Illus.). 28p. (YA). (gr. 4-9). ring bd. 19.95 *(978-1-56820-107-8(9))* Story Time Stories That Rhyme.

Taylor, Roger. Seven Silly Stories. Date not set. (Illus.). pap. 129.15 *(978-0-582-18518-0(1))* Addison-Wesley Longman, Ltd. GBR. Dist: Trans-Atlantic Pubns., Inc.

We Read More Stories. (J). tchr. ed. 4.72 *(978-0-917186-12-7(5));* Set. pap. 10.62 *(978-0-917186-11-0(7))* McQueen Publishing Co.

Weinbach, Shaindel. Cartons in the Air & Other Stories. Dershowitz, Yosef, illus. (J). 14.99 *(978-0-89906-992-0(4),* CARH) Mesorah Pubns., Ltd.

—The Friendly Persuader & Other Stories. Dershowitz, Yosef, illus. (J). 14.99 *(978-0-89906-970-8(3),* FRIH) Mesorah Pubns., Ltd.

White, E. B. E. B. White: Charlotte's Web, Stuart Little, & the Trumpet of the Swan, 3 bks., Set. 2003. (Illus.). (J). pap. 14.99 *(978-0-06-055416-3(9))* HarperCollins Pubs.

Wilder, Laura Ingalls. Little House, Set. Williams, Garth, illus. Incl. By the Shores of Silver Lake. 304p. pap. 7.99 *(978-0-06-440005-3(0));* Farmer Boy. 384p. pap. 7.99 *(978-0-06-440003-9(4));* First Four Years. MacBride, Roger Lea, intro. 160p. pap. 7.99 *(978-0-06-440031-2(X));* Little House in the Big Woods. 256p. pap. 7.99 *(978-0-06-440001-5(8));* Little House on the Prairie. 352p. pap. 7.99 *(978-0-06-440002-2(6));* Little Town on the Prairie. 320p. pap. 8.99 *(978-0-06-440007-7(7));* (J). (gr. 3-7). 2008. (Little House Ser.). (ENG., Illus.). 2008. reprint ed. Set pap. 62.99 *(978-0-06-440040-4(9))* HarperCollins Pubs.

Young, Richard & Dockrey Young, Judy. Favorite Scary Stories of American Children. Bell, Don, illus. rev. ed. 2005. (ENG.). 128p. (J). (gr. 3-6). pap. 8.95 *(978-0-87483-563-2(1))* August Hse. Pubs., Inc.

STORIES IN RHYME

Abolade, Caroline, told to. I'm Going to Be a Big Brother. 2003. 14p. 9.44 *(978-1-4116-0123-9(8))* Lulu Pr., Inc.

Accord Publishing Staff. What Do You See? A Lift-The-Flap Book. 2014. (ENG.). 12p. (J). (-k). bds. 6.99 *(978-1-4494-4385-6(0))* Andrews McMeel Publishing.

Ackerman, Jill. Hey, Diddle Diddle! Berg, Michelle, illus. 2011. (Little Scholastic Ser.). (ENG.). 6p. (J). (gr. k — 1). 12.99 *(978-0-545-35113-3(8),* Cartwheel Bks.) Scholastic, Inc.

Adam, Guillain & Guillain, Charlotte. School for Dads. Grey, Ada, illus. 2016. (ENG.). 32p. (J). (gr. -1-k). pap. 9.99 ***(978-1-4052-7749-5(1))*** Egmont Bks., Ltd. GBR. Dist: Independent Pubs. Group.

Adam, Guillain & Guillain, Charlotte. Treats for a T. Rex. Wildish, Lee, illus. 2nd ed. 2016. (George's Amazing Adventures Ser.). (ENG.). 32p. (J). (gr. -1-k). pap. 10.99 *(978-1-4052-7362-6(3))* Egmont Bks., Ltd. GBR. Dist: Independent Pubs. Group.

Adams, Diane. I Can Do It Myself!, 1 vol. Hayashi, Nancy, illus. (ENG.). 32p. (J). (gr. -1-1). 2013. 7.95 *(978-1-56145-725-0(6))* 2009. 15.95 *(978-1-56145-471-6(0))* Peachtree Pubs.

S

—Love Is. Keane, Claire, illus. 2017. (ENG.). 32p. (J). 15.99 *(978-1-4521-3997-5(0))* Chronicle Bks. LLC.

—Teacher's Little Helper, 1 vol. Hayashi, Nancy, illus. 2012. (ENG.). 32p. (J). 15.95 *(978-1-56145-630-7(6))* Peachtree Pubs.

—Two Hands to Love You. Davis, Jon & Keiser, Paige, illus. 2014. (ENG.). 40p. (J). (gr. -1 — 1). 15.99 *(978-0-8118-7797-8(3))* Chronicle Bks. LLC.

—Zoom!, 1 vol. Luthardt, Kevin, illus. (ENG.). 32p. (J). 2013. (gr. -1-1). pap. 7.95 *(978-1-56145-683-3(7))* 2005. (gr. k-1). 15.95 *(978-1-56145-332-0(3))* Peachtree Pubs.

Adams, Michelle Medlock. How Much Does God Love You? Keiser, Paige, illus. 2010. 22p. (J). (gr. -1-k). 6.99 *(978-0-8249-1848-4(7),* Ideal Pubns.) Worthy Publishing.

—Little Colt's Palm Sunday. Parmenter, Wayne, illus. 2005. (ENG.). 28p. (J). 14.95 *(978-0-8249-5503-8(X),* Ideal Pubns.) Worthy Publishing.

—The Sparrow's Easter Song. Eldridge, Marion, illus. 2003. (ENG.). 32p. (J). 14.95 *(978-0-8249-5470-3(X),* Ideal Pubns.) Worthy Publishing.

—What Is Halloween? Wummer, Amy, illus. 2007. (ENG.). 26p. (J). (gr. -1-3). bds. 6.99 *(978-0-8249-6712-3(7),* Ideal Pubns.) Worthy Publishing.

Adams, Pam, illus. There Was an Old Lady Who Swallowed the Sea. 2007. (Classic Books with Holes Board Book Ser.). (ENG.). 14p. (J). (gr. -1-k). bds. *(978-1-84643-073-2(9))* Child's Play International Ltd.

Adams, Richard. The Tyger Voyage. Bayley, Nicola, illus. 2013. 32p. (J). 15.95 net. *(978-1-56792-491-6(3))* Godine, David R. Pub.

Adeney, Anne. Five Teddy Bears. Shimmen, Cathy, illus. 2008. (Tadpoles Ser.). (ENG.). 24p. (J). (gr. -1-k). pap. *(978-0-7787-3884-8(1));* lib. bdg. *(978-0-7787-3853-4(1))* Crabtree Publishing Co.

Adler, Victoria. All of Baby Nose to Toes. Nakata, Hiroe, illus. 2011. (ENG.). 30p. (J). (gr. k — 1). bds. 6.99 *(978-0-8037-3531-6(6),* Dial Bks) Penguin Young Readers Group.

Adlerman, Daniel. Rock-a-Bye Baby. Adlerman, Kimberly M., illus. 2004. 32p. (J). 15.95 *(978-1-58089-082-3(2))* Charlesbridge Publishing, Inc.

Adoff, Arnold. Black Is Brown Is Tan. McCully, Emily Arnold, illus. 2004. (ENG.). 40p. (J). (gr. -1-3). reprint ed. pap. 6.99 *(978-0-06-443644-1(6),* Amistad) HarperCollins Pubs.

Agee, Jon. It's Only Stanley. 2015. (J). 49.99 *(978-1-63379-786-4(4));* 14.99 *(978-1-63379-787-1(2))* Dreamscape Media, LLC.

—It's Only Stanley. 2015. (ENG., Illus.). 32p. (J). (gr. k-3). 17.99 *(978-0-8037-3907-9(9),* Dial Bks) Penguin Young Readers Group.

Ahlberg, Janet & Ahlberg, Allan. Each Peach Pear Plum. 2009. 7.64 *(978-0-7848-2266-1(2),* Everbind) Marco Bk. Co.

Aigner-Clark, Julie. Baby Einstein: on the Farm. Zaidi, Nadeem, illus. 2007. (Baby Einstein Ser.). (ENG.). *(978-0-7634-2150-2(2))* Walt Disney Records.

Aiken, Zora & Aiken, David. A to Z: Pick What You'll Be. Aiken, David, illus. 2011. (ENG., Illus.). 32p. (J). 14.99 *(978-0-7643-3701-7(7),* 9780764337017, Schiffer Publishing Ltd) Schiffer Publishing, Ltd.

Ain, Beth. Izzy Kline Has Butterflies. 2017. (ENG.). 176p. (J). (gr. 3-7). 16.99 *(978-0-399-55080-5(1),* Random Hse. Bks. for Young Readers) Random Hse. Children's Bks.

Aizen, Marina, illus. Mary Had a Little Lamb. 2012. (Classic Books with Holes Board Book Ser.). (ENG.). 14p. bds. *(978-1-84643-512-6(9));* 16p. pap. *(978-1-84643-501-0(3))* Child's Play International Ltd.

Akley, Jason. Sweet Pea & the Bumblebee. 2007. (ENG.). 36p. (J). per. 16.95 *(978-1-4327-0341-7(2))* Outskirts Pr., Inc.

Albee, Sarah. Hello, Cat, Hello, Dog. Leigh, Tom, illus. 2006. (Step-By-Step Readers Ser.). (J). pap. *(978-1-59939-054-3(X),* Reader's Digest Young Families, Inc.) Studio Fun International.

—Hic! Brannon, Tom, illus. 2006. (Step-By-Step Readers Ser.). (J). pap. *(978-1-59939-061-1(2),* Reader's Digest Young Families, Inc.) Studio Fun International.

Alborough, Jez. Billy the Goat's Big Breakfast. Alborough, Jez, illus. 2014. (ENG., Illus.). 32p. (J). 12.99 *(978-1-61067-190-3(2))* Kane Miller.

Alda, Arlene. Here a Face, There a Face. 2008. (ENG., Illus.). 32p. (J). (gr. k-k). 14.95 *(978-0-88776-845-3(8),* Tundra Bks.) Tundra Bks. CAN. Dist: Penguin Random Hse. LLC.

Aldis, Dorothy & Collins, Heather. Hiding. (FRE.). (J). pap. 7.99 *(978-0-590-24195-3(8))* Scholastic, Inc.

Alexander, Kayla M. H. He Was No Magician. 2017. (ENG., Illus.). 29p. (J). pap. 13.95 ***(978-1-78612-128-8(X),*** 551d1209-7b83-41e9-932f-fff4571bc3e3) Austin, Stan AUS. Dist: Bookmasters Distribution.

Alexander, Kwame. Acoustic Rooster & His Barnyard Band. Bowers, Tim, illus. 2011. (ENG.). 32p. (gr. k-5). lib. bdg. 15.95 *(978-1-58536-688-0(9))* Sleeping Bear Pr.

—Booked. 2016. (ENG.). 320p. (J). (gr. 5-7). 16.99 *(978-0-544-57098-6(7),* HMH Books For Young Readers) Houghton Mifflin Harcourt Publishing Co.

—Booked. 2016. lib. bdg. 29.40 *(978-0-606-37992-2(4))* Turtleback Bks.

—The Crossover. 2014. (ENG.). (J). (gr. 4-7). E-Book 16.99 *(978-1-306-46985-2(6))* Harcourt Trade Pubs.

—The Crossover. 2014. (ENG.). 240p. (J). (gr. 4-7). 16.99 *(978-0-544-10771-7(3),* HMH Books For Young Readers) Houghton Mifflin Harcourt Publishing Co.

—The Crossover. 2014. lib. bdg. 29.40 *(978-0-606-37975-5(4))* Turtleback Bks.

Alexander, Liza. Splish-Splash Spring! 2016. lib. bdg. 14.75 *(978-0-606-38486-5(3))* Turtleback Bks.

Allen, Constance. Elmo's Mother Goose Rhymes (Sesame Street) Swanson, Maggie, illus. 2017. (Little Golden Book Ser.). (ENG.). 24p. (J). (-k). 4.99 *(978-1-101-93994-9(X),* Golden Bks.) Random Hse. Children's Bks.

Allen, Joy. Princess Party. Allen, Joy, illus. 2009. (ENG., Illus.). 32p. (J). (gr. -1-k). 16.99 *(978-0-399-25259-4(2),* G.P. Putnam's Sons Books for Young Readers) Penguin Young Readers Group.

Allen, Kathryn Madeline. A Kiss Means I Love You. Futran, Eric, photos by. 2016. (ENG., Illus.). 16p. (J). (gr. -1 — 1). bds. 7.99 *(978-0-8075-4189-0(3))* Whitman, Albert & Co.

—A Kiss Means I Love You. Futran, Eric, illus. Futran, Eric, photos by. 2012. (ENG.). 24p. (J). (gr. -1-3). 15.99 *(978-0-8075-4186-9(9))* Whitman, Albert & Co.

—Show Me Happy. Futran, Eric, photos by. 2015. (ENG., Illus.). 24p. (J). (gr. -1-3). 15.99 *(978-0-8075-7349-5(3))* Whitman, Albert & Co.

Allen, Lisa & Sharp, Julia. Time for Bed - The Secret of Shadows: Shadow Theater Inside. Johnson, Vickie, illus. 26p. (J). (gr. -1-2). pap. *(978-1-56021-355-0(8),* 206) W.J. Fantasy, Inc.

Almy, Judy. My Name Is Ick: A Rhyming Story of an Alaska Caribou. 2003. 9.95 *(978-1-59433-009-4(3))* Publication Consultants.

Amato, Gaetano. Upside Right: A Children's Guide to Movement. 2010. (J). 19.95 *(978-0-615-38545-7(1))* Amato, G. J.

Amerikaner, Susan. Goofy at Bat. 2013. (Mickey & Friends World of Reading Ser.). (J). lib. bdg. 13.55 *(978-0-606-27117-2(1),* Turtleback) Turtleback Bks.

Amundson, Susan D. Three Little Lambs — Somewhere. Geiken, Brenda Joy, illus. 2006. 40p. (J). *(978-1-59984-002-4(2))* Bluedoor, llc.

Anastas, Margaret. A Hug for You. Winter, Susan, photos by. 2005. (ENG., Illus.). 32p. (J). (gr. -1-1). 15.99 *(978-0-06-623613-1(4))* HarperCollins Pubs.

—Mommy's Best Kisses. Winter, Susan, illus. 2003. (ENG.). 32p. (J). (gr. -1-1). 17.99 *(978-0-06-623601-8(0))* HarperCollins Pubs.

Anderson, Airlie, illus. Cows in the Kitchen. 2009. (Classic Books with Holes Big Book Ser.). (ENG.). 16p. (J). (gr. -1-1). *(978-1-84643-208-8(1))* Child's Play International Ltd.

—Cows in the Kitchen W/ 2009. (Classic Books with Holes US Soft Cover with CD Ser.). (ENG.). 16p. (J). pap. incl. audio compact disk *(978-1-84643-257-6(X))* Child's Play International Ltd.

Anderson, Derek. Ten Hungry Pigs: An Epic Lunch Adventure. Anderson, Derek, illus. 2016. (ENG., Illus.). 40p. (J). (gr. -1-k). 16.99 *(978-0-545-16848-9(1))* Scholastic, Inc.

—Ten Pigs: An Epic Bath Adventure. Anderson, Derek, illus. 2015. (ENG., Illus.). 40p. (J). (gr. -1-k). 16.99 *(978-0-545-16846-5(5))* Scholastic, Inc.

Anderson, Derek, et al. Over the River: A Turkey's Tale. 2005. (ENG., Illus.). 40p. (J). (gr. -1-3). 15.99 *(978-0-689-87635-6(1),* Simon & Schuster Bks. For Young Readers) Simon & Schuster Bks. For Young Readers.

Anderson, Georgia Lee. Bullying Is Wrong. Fox, Tom Paul, illus. 2012. (ENG.). 26p. pap. 14.95 *(978-1-57258-882-0(9),* Aspect Bk.) TEACH Services, Inc.

Anderson, Lena & Sandin, Joan. Hedgehog, Pig, & the Sweet Little Friend. Sandin, Joan, tr. from SWE. 2007. (Illus.). 32p. (J). (gr. -1-1). 16.00 *(978-91-29-66742-4(9))* R & S Bks. SWE. Dist: Macmillan.

Anderson, Peggy Perry. Chuck's Band. 2017. (Green Light Readers Level 1 Ser.). (ENG., Illus.). 32p. (J). (gr. -1-3). 12.99 *(978-0-544-92620-2(X),* HMH Books For Young Readers) Houghton Mifflin Harcourt Publishing Co.

—Chuck's Truck. 2017. (Green Light Readers Level 1 Ser.). (ENG., Illus.). 32p. (J). (gr. -1-3). 12.99 *(978-0-544-92618-9(8),* HMH Books For Young Readers) Houghton Mifflin Harcourt Publishing Co.

—I Can Help! 2015. (Green Light Readers Level 1 Ser.). (ENG., Illus.). 32p. (J). (gr. 1-4). pap. 3.99 *(978-0-544-52801-7(8),* HMH Books For Young Readers) Houghton Mifflin Harcourt Publishing Co.

—Joe on the Go. 2012. (Green Light Readers Level 1 Ser.). (ENG., Illus.). 32p. (J). (gr. -1-3). pap. 3.99 *(978-0-547-74563-3(X))* Houghton Mifflin Harcourt Publishing Co.

—Joe on the Go. 2012. (Green Light Readers — Level 1 Ser.: 1). lib. bdg. 13.55 *(978-0-606-24018-5(7),* Turtleback) Turtleback Bks.

—Let's Clean Up! 2012. (Green Light Readers Level 1 Ser.). (ENG., Illus.). 32p. (J). (gr. -1-3). pap. 3.99 *(978-0-547-74562-6(1))* Houghton Mifflin Harcourt Publishing Co.

—Let's Clean Up! 2012. (Green Light Readers — Level 1 Ser.). lib. bdg. 13.55 *(978-0-606-24024-6(1),* Turtleback) Turtleback Bks.

—Out to Lunch. 2015. (Green Light Readers Level 1 Ser.). (ENG., Illus.). 32p. (J). (gr. 1-4). pap. 3.99 *(978-0-544-52858-1(1),* HMH Books For Young Readers) Houghton Mifflin Harcourt Publishing Co.

—Time for Bed, the Babysitter Said. 2012. (Green Light Readers Level 1 Ser.). (ENG., Illus.). 32p. (J). (gr. -1-3). pap. 3.99 *(978-0-547-85061-0(1))* Houghton Mifflin Harcourt Publishing Co.

—To the Tub. 2012. (Green Light Readers Level 1 Ser.). (ENG., Illus.). 32p. (J). (gr. -1-3). pap. 3.99 *(978-0-547-85053-5(0))* Houghton Mifflin Harcourt Publishing Co.

Anderson, Sara. Noisy City Day (2015 Board Book) Anderson, Sara, illus. 2015. (ENG., Illus.). 12p. (J). (gr. -1-1). bds. 10.95 *(978-1-943459-00-1(2))* Sara Anderson Children's Bks.

—Noisy City Night (2015 Board Book) Anderson, Sara, illus. 2015. (ENG., Illus.). 12p. (J). (gr. -1-1). bds. 10.95 *(978-1-943459-01-8(0))* Sara Anderson Children's Bks.

Anderson, Shannon. Coasting Casey: A Tale of Busting Boredom in School. Madden, Colleen, illus. 2016. (ENG.). 48p. (J). (gr. k-4). 15.99 *(978-1-63198-088-6(2))* Free Spirit Publishing, Inc.

Andreae, Giles. Giraffes Can't Dance. Parker-Rees, Guy, illus. (J). (gr. -1-k). 2008. (ENG.). 9.99 *(978-0-545-09738-3(X))* 2007. 24.95 incl. audio *(978-0-439-02733-5(0))* Scholastic, Inc.

—Giraffes Can't Dance. Parker-Rees, Guy, illus. unabr. ed. 2011. (J). (gr. -1-1). 29.95 *(978-0-439-02734-2(9))* Weston Woods Studios, Inc.

—Giraffes Can't Dance: Number Rumba. Parker-Rees, Guy, illus. 2014. (ENG.). 12p. (J). (gr. -1 — 1). bds. 7.99 *(978-0-545-63996-5(4),* Cartwheel Bks.) Scholastic, Inc.

—Heaven Is Having You. Cabban, Vanessa, illus. 2007. (Padded Board Bks.). 18p. (J). (gr. -1-1). bds. 7.95 *(978-1-58925-820-4(7))* Tiger Tales.

—I Love My Grandma. Dodd, Emma, illus. 2016. (ENG.). 32p. (J). (gr. -1-k). 16.99 *(978-1-4847-3407-0(6))* Disney Pr.

—I Love My Mommy. Dodd, Emma, illus. 2013. (ENG.). 26p. (J). (gr. -1-k). bds. 6.99 *(978-1-4231-6825-6(9))* Hyperion Pr.

—I Love You, Baby. Dodd, Emma, illus. 2015. (ENG.). 32p. (J). (gr. -1-k). 15.99 *(978-1-4847-2230-5(2))* Disney Publishing Worldwide.

—I Love You Father Christmas. Dodd, Emma, illus. 2016. (ENG.). 24p. (J). (gr. -1 — 1). bds. 8.99 *(978-1-4083-3808-7(4),* Orchard Bks.) Hachette Children's Group GBR. Dist: Hachette Bk. Group.

—Keep Love in Your Heart, Little One. Vulliamy, Clara, illus. 2007. 32p. (J). (gr. -1-3). 15.95 *(978-1-58925-066-6(4))* Tiger Tales.

—Love Is a Handful of Honey. Cabban, Vanessa, illus. 2004. 32p. (J). (gr. -1-k). 5.95 *(978-1-58925-353-7(1));* tchr. ed. 15.95 *(978-1-58925-003-1(6))* Tiger Tales.

—Rumble in Jungle. 2011. (ENG.). 24p. (J). bds. 9.95 *(978-1-58925-864-8(9))* Tiger Tales.

Andrews, Andy. Henry Hodges Needs a Friend, 1 vol. 2015. (ENG., Illus.). 32p. (J). 14.99 *(978-0-529-11576-8(X))* Nelson, Thomas Inc.

Angel, Ido. Vipo in London: The Ravens of the London Tower. 2015. (AV2 Animated Storytime Ser.). (ENG.). (J). lib. bdg. 29.99 *(978-1-4896-3911-0(X),* AV2 by Weigl) Weigl Pubs., Inc.

Anglemyer, Jordan, illus. Grandpa's Favorites: A collection of quotes, things to ponder, stories, bits of verse, & Humor. 2007. 77p. (YA). per. 10.95 *(978-0-9796251-2-1(2))* Robertson Publishing.

Anholt, Laurence. The Big Book of Love. Anholt, Catherine, illus. 2017. (ENG.). 32p. (J). (gr. -1-k). pap. 9.99 *(978-1-4083-3598-7(0),* Orchard Bks.) Hachette Children's Group GBR. Dist: Hachette Bk. Group.

—The Big Book of Love. Anholt, Catherine, illus. 2015. (ENG.). 32p. (J). (gr. -1-k). 13.99 *(978-1-4083-3597-0(2))* Hodder & Stoughton GBR. Dist: Hachette Bk. Group.

—Two Nests. Coplestone, Jim, illus. 2013. (ENG.). 32p. (J). (gr. -1-1). 17.99 *(978-1-84780-323-8(7),* Frances Lincoln) Quarto Publishing Group UK GBR. Dist: Hachette Bk. Group.

—We Love Bears. Anholt, Catherine, illus. 2012. (ENG.). 32p. (J). (gr. -1-k). pap. 10.99 *(978-1-4083-1169-1(0))* Hodder & Stoughton GBR. Dist: Hachette Bk. Group.

Ansell, Liz. The Unforgettable Snow Lady: And Other Memorable Short Stories, Songs & Rhymes. 2012. (Illus.). 40p. (-18). pap. 22.88 *(978-1-4772-3533-1(7))* AuthorHouse.

Appelt, Kathi. Bat Jamboree. Sweet, Melissa, illus. 2004. 17.00 *(978-0-7569-4074-4(5))* Perfection Learning Corp.

—Brand-New Baby Blues. Murphy, Kelly, illus. 2009. (ENG.). 32p. (J). (gr. -1-1). 16.99 *(978-0-06-053233-8(5))* HarperCollins Pubs.

—Counting Crows. Dunlavey, Rob, illus. 2015. (ENG.). 40p. (J). (gr. -1-3). 17.99 *(978-1-4424-2327-5(7))* Simon & Schuster Children's Publishing.

—Incredible Me! Karas, G. Brian, illus. 2003. (ENG.). 32p. (J). (gr. -1-3). 16.99 *(978-0-06-028622-4(9))* HarperCollins Pubs.

—Oh My Baby, Little One. Dyer, Jane, illus. 2006. (ENG.). 32p. (J). (gr. -1 — 1). pap. 3.99 *(978-0-15-206031-2(6))* Houghton Mifflin Harcourt Publishing Co.

Appleby, Danny. Ella & the Balloons in the Sky. Pirie, Lauren & Laurence, Laurence, illus. 2013. (ENG.). 32p. (J). (gr. k-4). 15.95 *(978-1-77049-528-9(2),* Tundra Bks.) Tundra Bks. CAN. Dist: Penguin Random Hse. LLC.

Archambault, John. Boom Chicka Rock. Chitwood, Suzanne Tanner & Chitwood, Suzanne, illus. 2004. (ENG.). 32p. (J). (gr. -1-k). 16.99 *(978-0-399-23587-0(6),* Philomel Bks.) Penguin Young Readers Group.

—By the Baobab Tree. Bender, Robert, illus. 2005. (J). *(978-1-58669-164-6(3))* Childcraft Education Corp.

—Cat in the Tree. Cooper, Stephanie, illus. 2007. (J). *(978-1-58669-230-8(5))* Childcraft Education Corp.

Archambault, John & Martin, Bill, Jr. Here Are My Hands. Rand, Ted, illus. 2007. (ENG.). 32p. (J). (gr. -1-k). pap. 26.99 *(978-0-8050-8119-0(4),* 9780805081190, Holt, Henry & Co. Bks. For Young Readers) Holt, Henry & Co.

Argueta, Jorge & Perez, Lucia Angela. Hablando Con Madre Tierra, 1 vol. 2006.Tr. of Talking with Mother Earth. (ENG & SPA., Illus.). 36p. (J). (gr. k-3). 17.95 *(978-0-88899-626-8(8))* Groundwood Bks. CAN. Dist: Publishers Group West (PGW).

Arias De Cordoba, Heather & Arias de Cordoba, Kaiya. A Year Full of Fairies. 2011. (Illus.). 28p. pap. 19.99 *(978-1-257-74775-7(4))* Lulu Pr., Inc.

Armstrong, Aldona. Every Family Is Special. 2013. (Illus.). 20p. pap. 11.59 *(978-1-4669-8913-9(0))* Trafford Publishing.

Armstrong-Ellis, Carey F. I Love You More Than Moldy Ham. 2015. (ENG., Illus.). 32p. (J). (gr. -1-3). 14.95 *(978-1-4197-1646-1(8),* Abrams Bks. for Young Readers) Abrams, Inc.

Armstrong-Ellis, Carey F. Ten Creepy Monsters. (ENG., Illus.). 32p. (J). (gr. k-2). 2017. pap. 4.95 ***(978-1-4197-2741-2(9))*** 2012. 15.95 *(978-1-4197-0433-8(8))* Abrams, Inc. (Abrams Bks. for Young Readers).

Armstrong, Robert W. The Big Blue Lake. Broxon, Janet, illus. 2015. (ENG.). 32p. (J). (gr. -1). 13.95 *(978-0-9801468-3-7(6))* All About Kids Publishing.

Arnold, Tedd. Dirty Gert. Arnold, Tedd, illus. (ENG., Illus.). (J). (gr. 2-5). 2014. 32p. 6.99 *(978-0-8234-3054-3(5))* 2013. 40p. 16.95 *(978-0-8234-2404-7(9))* Holiday Hse., Inc.

—Even More Parts. Arnold, Tedd, illus. 2007. (ENG., Illus.). 40p. (J). (gr. -1-3). pap. 7.99 *(978-0-14-240714-1(3),* Puffin Books) Penguin Young Readers Group.

—Green Wilma, Frog in Space. Arnold, Tedd, illus. 2009. (ENG., Illus.). 32p. (J). (gr. -1-3). 16.99 *(978-0-8037-2698-7(8),* Dial Bks) Penguin Young Readers Group.

—More Parts. 2003. (ENG., Illus.). 32p. (J). (gr. -1-3). pap. 7.99 *(978-0-14-250149-8(2),* Puffin Books) Penguin Young Readers Group.

Arnosky, Jim. I'm a Turkey! 2009. (Illus.). (J). *(978-0-545-22631-8(7),* Scholastic Pr.) Scholastic, Inc.

Aronson, Deborah. Dragons from Mars. Jack, Colin, illus. 2016. 32p. (J). (gr. -1-3). 17.99 *(978-0-06-236850-8(8))* HarperCollins Pubs.

—Where's My Tushy? Stevanovic, Ivica, illus. 2014. (ENG.). 24p. (J). (gr. -1-3). 17.95 *(978-1-4677-1197-5(7),* Carolrhoda Bks.) Lerner Publishing Group.

Artell, Mike. Jacques & de Beanstalk. Harris, Jim, illus. 2010. (ENG.). 32p. (J). (gr. k-3). 18.99 *(978-0-8037-2816-5(6),* Dial Bks) Penguin Young Readers Group.

—Petite Rouge. Harris, Jim, illus. 2003. (ENG.). 32p. (J). (gr. k-3). 6.99 *(978-0-14-250070-5(4),* Puffin Books) Penguin Young Readers Group.

—Petite Rouge. 2004. (J). 27.75 *(978-1-4193-1631-9(1))* Recorded Bks., Inc.

Ashburn, Boni. The Class. Gee, Kimberly, illus. 2016. (ENG.). 40p. (J). (gr. -1-3). 17.99 *(978-1-4424-2248-3(3),* Beach Lane Bks.) Beach Lane Bks.

—The Fort That Jack Built. Helquist, Brett, illus. 2013. (ENG.). 32p. (J). (gr. k-2). 18.95 *(978-1-4197-0795-7(7),* Abrams Bks. for Young Readers) Abrams, Inc.

Ashman, Linda. Henry Wants More! Hughes, Brooke Boynton, illus. 2016. (ENG.). 32p. (J). (gr. -1-2). 20.99 *(978-0-375-97348-2(6),* Random Hse. Bks. for Young Readers) Random Hse. Children's Bks.

—How to Make a Night. Tusa, Tricia, illus. Date not set. 32p. (J). (gr. -1-3). pap. 5.99 *(978-0-06-443699-1(3))* HarperCollins Pubs.

—Just Another Morning. Muñoz, Claudio, illus. 2004. (ENG.). 32p. (J). (gr. -1-3). 15.99 *(978-0-06-029053-5(6))* HarperCollins Pubs.

—Mama's Day. Ormerod, Jan, illus. 2011. (ENG.). 32p. (J). (gr. -1-1). pap. 16.99 *(978-1-4424-5233-6(1),* Simon & Schuster Bks. For Young Readers) Simon & Schuster Bks. For Young Readers.

—Peace, Baby! Lew-Vriethoff, Joanne, illus. 2013. (ENG.). 32p. (J). (gr. -1-k). 15.99 *(978-1-4521-0613-7(4))* Chronicle Bks. LLC.

—Rock-a-Bye Romp. Mulazzani, Simona, illus. 2016. (ENG.). 36p. (J). (— 1). 16.99 *(978-0-399-17150-5(9),* Nancy Paulsen Books) Penguin Young Readers Group.

—Sailing off to Sleep. Winter, Susan, illus. 2010. (ENG.). 32p. (J). (gr. -1-1). pap. 9.99 *(978-1-4424-1435-8(9),* Simon & Schuster Bks. For Young Readers) Simon & Schuster Bks. For Young Readers.

—Samantha on a Roll. Davenier, Christine, illus. 2011. (ENG.). 40p. (J). (gr. -1-4). 17.99 *(978-0-374-36399-4(4),* 9780374363994, Farrar, Straus & Giroux (BYR)) Farrar, Straus & Giroux.

—When I Was King. McPhail, David, illus. 2008. 32p. (J). (gr. -1-3). 17.89 *(978-0-06-029052-8(8))* HarperCollins Pubs.

Ashman, Linda & Airgood, Ellen. Little Baby Buttercup. Byun, You, illus. 2015. (ENG.). 32p. (J). (— 1). 16.99 *(978-0-399-16763-8(3),* Nancy Paulsen Books) Penguin Young Readers Group.

Ashton, Anna. Molly & Ben. 2007. (Illus.). 76p. per. *(978-1-84401-178-0(X))* Athena Pr.

Asim, Jabari. Whose Knees Are These? Pham, LeUyen, illus. 2006. (ENG.). 24p. (J). (gr. -1 — 1). bds. 6.99 *(978-0-316-73576-6(0))* Little, Brown Bks. for Young Readers.

—Whose Toes Are Those? Pham, LeUyen, illus. 2006. (ENG.). 11p. (J). (gr. -1 — 1). bds. 6.99 *(978-0-316-73609-1(0))* Little, Brown Bks. for Young Readers.

Asquith, Ros & Quarto Generic Staff. It's Not Fairy. 2013. (ENG., Illus.). 32p. (J). (gr. -1-3). 17.99 *(978-1-84780-236-1(2),* Frances Lincoln) Quarto Publishing Group UK GBR. Dist: Hachette Bk. Group.

Atkins, Jeannine. Stone Mirrors: The Sculpture & Silence of Edmonia Lewis. 2017. (ENG., Illus.). 176p. (J). (gr. 7). 17.99 *(978-1-4814-5905-1(8),* Atheneum Bks. for Young Readers) Simon & Schuster Children's Publishing.

Atlas, Ron. Ten Pigs Fiddling. Flint, Stacie, illus. 2nd rev. ed. 2006. (ENG.). 32p. (J). (gr. -1-k). 17.95 *(978-0-9630243-3-6(7))* Amberwood Pr.

Atwood, Margaret. Up in the Tree, 1 vol. 2010. (ENG., Illus.). 32p. (J). (gr. k-k). 19.95 *(978-1-55498-080-2(1))* Groundwood Bks. CAN. Dist: Publishers Group West (PGW).

Aucoin, Lee. Todo Sobre Mí, 1 vol. rev. ed. 2010. (Early Childhood Themes Ser.). (SPA., Illus.). 16p. (J). (gr. -1-2). pap. 19.99 *(978-1-4333-1943-3(8))* Shell Educational Publishing.

—Todo Sobre Mi, 1 vol. rev. ed. 2010. (Early Childhood Themes Ser.). (SPA., Illus.). 16p. (J). (gr. -1-2). pap. 6.99 *(978-1-4333-1942-6(X))* Shell Educational Publishing.

Augustine, Kristen. Can I Tell You? 2005. 9.00 *(978-0-8059-8071-4(7))* Dorrance Publishing Co., Inc.

Aulbach, Kathy. Flower Sprouts: Let's have a Fest! 2009. 29p. 15.95 *(978-0-615-21683-6(8))* Flower Sprouts.

Awdry, W. Go, Go, Thomas! 2013. (Thomas & Friends 8X8 Ser.). lib. bdg. 14.75 *(978-0-606-26992-6(4),* Turtleback) Turtleback Bks.

—Thomas & Friends - Go, Thomas Go! 2007. (Bright & Early Playtime Bks.). (ENG., Illus.). 14p. (J). (gr. k-k). 10.99 *(978-0-375-83983-2(6),* Random Hse. Bks. for Young Readers) Random Hse. Children's Bks.

Awdry, Wilbert V. Blue Train, Green Train. Stubbs, Tommy, illus. 2006. (Bright & Early Books(R) Ser.). (ENG.). 36p. (J). (gr. k-k). 8.99 *(978-0-375-83463-9(X),* Random Hse. Bks. for Young Readers) Random Hse. Children's Bks.

—Fast Train, Slow Train. Stubbs, Tommy, illus. 2009. (Bright & Early Books(R) Ser.). (ENG.). 36p. (J). (gr. -1-2). 8.99 *(978-0-375-85689-1(7),* Golden Bks.) Random Hse. Children's Bks.

—Fast Train, Slow Train (Thomas & Friends) 2014. (Big Bright & Early Board Book Ser.). (ENG., Illus.). 24p. (J). (— 1). bds. 6.99 *(978-0-385-37408-8(9),* Random Hse. Bks. for Young Readers) Random Hse. Children's Bks.

—Trains, Cranes & Troublesome Trucks. Stubbs, Tommy, illus. 2008. (Beginner Books Ser.). (ENG.). 36p. (J). (gr. -1-1). 8.99 *(978-0-375-84977-0(7),* Random Hse. Bks. for Young Readers) Random Hse. Children's Bks.

Awdry, Wilbert V. & Awdry, W. Blue Train, Green Train. Stubbs, Tommy, illus. 2007. (Bright & Early Board Books(TM) Ser.). (ENG.). 24p. (J). (— 1). bds. 4.99 *(978-0-375-83984-9(4),* Random Hse. Bks. for Young Readers) Random Hse. Children's Bks.

Awdry, Wilbert V. & Hooke, R. Schuyler. Railway Rhymes. Courtney, Richard, illus. 2005. (Lap Library). (ENG.). 36p. (J). (gr. k — 1). bds. 11.99 *(978-0-375-83175-1(4),* Random Hse. Bks. for Young Readers) Random Hse. Children's Bks.

Aylesworth, Jim. Cock-a-Doodle-Doo, Creak, Pop-Pop, Moo. Sneed, Brad, illus. 2012. (ENG.). 32p. (J). 16.95 *(978-0-8234-2356-9(5))* Holiday Hse., Inc.

—Cock-a-Doodle-Doo, Creak, Pop-Pop, Moo. Sneed, Brad, illus. 2013. (ENG.). 32p. (J). pap. 7.99 *(978-0-8234-2754-3(4))* Holiday Hse., Inc.
—Naughty Little Monkeys. Cole, Henry, illus. 2006. (ENG.). 32p. (J). (gr. -1-2). reprint ed. 6.99 *(978-0-14-240562-8(0),* Puffin Books) Penguin Young Readers Group.
Ayres, Katherine. Up, down, & Around. Westcott, Nadine Bernard, illus. 2008. (Big Bks.). (ENG.). 32p. (J). (-k). pap. 24.99 *(978-0-7636-4018-7(2));* 6.99 *(978-0-7636-4017-0(4))* Candlewick Pr.
Baa, Baa Black Sheep. 2003. (J). per. *(978-1-57657-799-8(6))* Paradise Pr., Inc.
Bach, Annie. Monster Party! 2014. (ENG., Illus.). 32p. (J). (gr. -1-k). 9.95 *(978-1-4549-1051-0(8))* Sterling Publishing Co., Inc.
—Night-Night, Forest Friends. Bach, Annie, illus. 2013. (ENG., Illus.). 24p. (J). (gr. -1-k). bds. 8.99 *(978-0-8431-7278-2(9),* Grosset & Dunlap) Penguin Young Readers Group.
Baer, Edith. Words are like Faces, 1 vol. Teis, Kyra, illus. 2007. (ENG.). 32p. (J). 15.95 *(978-1-59572-108-2(8))* Star Bright Bks., Inc.
Baghcheban, Samineh. Zendigiye Koodakan. 2012. 44p. pap. 12.00 *(978-0-9790573-7-3(X))* Urtext.
Baines, Andy. I Know a Goldfish That Can't Swim. 2012. 72p. (-18). pap. *(978-1-909395-50-3(1))* Legend Pr.
Bair, Sheila. Rock, Brock, & the Savings Shock. Gott, Barry, illus. (ENG.). 32p. (J). 2017. (gr. -1-3). pap. 7.99 ***(978-0-8075-7095-1(8))*** 2006. (gr. 1-3). 16.99 *(978-0-8075-7094-4(X))* Whitman, Albert & Co.
Baker, Amanda, illus. The Cheesehead Night Before Christmas. 2007. 40p. (J). per. 19.95 *(978-0-9797781-0-0(7))* Dreams 2 Wings LLC.
Baker, Keith. Big Fat Hen Big Book. Baker, Keith, illus. 2010. (ENG., Illus.). 32p. (J). (gr. -1-3). 26.99 *(978-0-547-32859-1(1))* Houghton Mifflin Harcourt Publishing Co.
—Hap-Pea All Year! Baker, Keith, illus. 2016. (Peas Ser.). (ENG., Illus.). 40p. (J). (gr. -1-3). 17.99 *(978-1-4814-5854-2(X),* Beach Lane Bks.) Beach Lane Bks.
—Little Green Peas: A Big Book of Colors. Baker, Keith, illus. 2014. (Peas Ser.). (ENG., Illus.). 40p. (J). (gr. -1-3). 17.99 *(978-1-4424-7660-8(5),* Beach Lane Bks.) Beach Lane Bks.
—LMNO Pea-Quel. Baker, Keith, illus. 2017. (Peas Ser.). (ENG., Illus.). 40p. (J). (gr. -1-3). 17.99 ***(978-1-4814-5856-6(6),*** Beach Lane Bks.) Beach Lane Bks.
—LMNO Peas. Baker, Keith, illus. 2010. (Peas Ser.). (ENG., Illus.). 40p. (J). (gr. -1-3). 17.99 *(978-1-4169-9141-0(7),* Beach Lane Bks.) Beach Lane Bks.
—LMNO Peas. Baker, Keith, illus. 2014. (Peas Ser.). (ENG., Illus.). 36p. (J). (gr. -1-k). bds. 7.99 *(978-1-4424-8978-3(2),* Little Simon) Little Simon.
—My Octopus Arms. Baker, Keith, illus. 2013. (ENG., Illus.). 40p. (J). (gr. -1-3). 16.99 *(978-1-4424-5843-7(7),* Beach Lane Bks.) Beach Lane Bks.
—No Two Alike. Baker, Keith, illus. 2011. (ENG., Illus.). 40p. (J). (gr. -1-2). 16.99 *(978-1-4424-1742-7(0),* Beach Lane Bks.) Beach Lane Bks.
—Peas in a Pod! Baker, Keith, illus. 2013. (ENG., Illus.). 80p. (J). (gr. -1-3). 33.99 *(978-1-4424-9991-1(5),* Beach Lane Bks.) Beach Lane Bks.
—1-2-3 Peas. Baker, Keith, illus. 2012. (Peas Ser.). (ENG., Illus.). 40p. (J). (gr. -1-3). 17.99 *(978-1-4424-4551-2(3),* Beach Lane Bks.) Beach Lane Bks.
Baker, Liza. I Love You Because You're You. McPhail, David, illus. 2008. (ENG.). 24p. (J). (gr. -1-k). bds. 8.99 *(978-0-545-02931-5(7),* Cartwheel Bks.) Scholastic, Inc.
Baker, Ryan. How I Would Paint the World? 2006. (ENG.). 48p. per. 15.95 *(978-1-59800-969-9(9))* Outskirts Pr., Inc.
Bakos, Lisa M. Too Many Moose! Chambers, Mark, illus. 2016. (ENG.). 40p. (J). (-4). 16.99 *(978-1-4926-0935-3(8),* 9781492609353, Sourcebooks Jabberwocky) Sourcebooks, Inc.
Balaam, Lisa & Balaam, Steven. Abbey the Cavi in Miami Beach. 2006. 52p. (J). 19.95 *(978-1-4196-1004-2(X))* CreateSpace Independent Publishing Platform.
Ballard, George Anne. Flowers along the Way. Ballard, George Anne & Bolton, Georgia Helen, illus. 2012. 26p. pap. 12.00 *(978-0-9855312-2-5(3))* Bolton Publishing LLC.
Ballard, Peg & Amoroso, Cynthia. Fun! The Sound of Short U. 2015. (Long & Short Vowels Ser.). (ENG.). 24p. (J). (gr. -1-2). 25.64 *(978-1-63407-022-5(4),* 208857) Child's World, Inc., The.
Ballentine, Joyce. Nana's Nursery Rhymes 2. 2003. (J). pap. 12.00 *(978-0-8059-9211-3(1),* RoseDog Bks.) Dorrance Publishing Co., Inc.
Ballinger, Bryan. Animal Gas. 2015. (ENG., Illus.). 32p. (J). (gr. -1-2). 12.95 *(978-1-4549-1616-1(8))* Sterling Publishing Co., Inc.
Balsley, Tilda. ABC Hanukkah Hunt. Poole, Helen, illus. 2013. 32p. 17.95 *(978-1-4677-1637-6(5));* (ENG.). (J). (gr. -1-2). 7.95 *(978-1-4677-0421-2(0),* Kar-Ben Publishing); (ENG.). (J). (gr. -1-2). lib. bdg. 17.95 *(978-1-4677-0420-5(2),* Kar-Ben Publishing) Lerner Publishing Group.
—Soo's Boo-Boos: She's Got 10! McNicholas, Shelagh, illus. 2013. (ENG.). 32p. (J). (gr. -1-2). 12.95 *(978-1-58925-118-2(0))* Tiger Tales.
Banana-Tail. 2003. lib. bdg. 13.95 *(978-0-9727681-0-8(6))* Active Media Publishing, LLC.
Bandsuh, Jim. Helmet Hank. 2007. (Illus.). (J). per. 15.99 *(978-1-933156-19-4(8),* Visikid Bks.) GSVQ Publishing.
Bannister, Emily, illus. Itsy Bitsy Spider. 2016. (ENG.). 10p. (J). bds. 7.99 *(978-1-62686-764-2(X),* Silver Dolphin Bks.) Readerlink Distribution Services, LLC.
Barad, Alexis. Puppy Love. East, Jacqueline, illus. 2013. (J). *(978-0-545-47733-8(6))* Scholastic, Inc.
Barash, Chris. Is It Hanukkah Yet? Psacharopulo, Alessandra, illus. 2015. (ENG.). 32p. (J). (gr. -1-3). 16.99 *(978-0-8075-3384-0(X))* Whitman, Albert & Co.
—Is It Passover Yet? Psacharopulo, Alessandra, illus. 2015. (ENG.). 32p. (J). (gr. -1-3). 16.99 *(978-0-8075-6330-4(7))* Whitman, Albert & Co.
—Is It Sukkot Yet? Psacharopulo, Alessandra, illus. 2016. (ENG.). 32p. (J). (gr. -1-3). 16.99 *(978-0-8075-3388-8(2))* Whitman, Albert & Co.
—One Fine Shabbat. Mai-Wyss, Tatjana, illus. 2016. (ENG.). 12p. (gr. -1 — 1). 23.99 *(978-1-4677-9614-9(X),* Kar-Ben Publishing) Lerner Publishing Group.
Bardaus, Anna W. Bounce, Bounce, Baby! Grove, Christine, illus. 2013. (J). *(978-0-545-61897-7(5))* Scholastic, Inc.
—Dance, Dance, Baby! Grove, Christine, illus. 2013. (J). *(978-0-545-61899-1(1))* Scholastic, Inc.
—Reach, Reach, Baby! Grove, Christine, illus. 2013. (J). *(978-0-545-61900-4(9))* Scholastic, Inc.
—Read, Read, Baby! Grove, Christine, illus. 2013. (J). *(978-0-545-61898-4(3))* Scholastic, Inc.
Bardhan-Quallen, Sudipta. Chicks Run Wild. Jenkins, Ward, illus. 2011. (ENG.). 32p. (J). (gr. -1-1). 15.99 *(978-1-4424-0673-5(9),* Simon & Schuster Bks. For Young Readers) Simon & Schuster Bks. For Young Readers.
—Hampire! Fine, Howard, illus. 2011. (ENG.). 32p. (J). (gr. -1-3). 16.99 *(978-0-06-114239-0(5))* HarperCollins Pubs.
—The Pirate Princess. McElmurry, Jill, illus. 2012. (ENG.). 40p. (J). (gr. -1-3). 17.99 *(978-0-06-114242-0(5))* HarperCollins Pubs.
—Quackenstein Hatches a Family. Jones, Brian T., illus. 2010. (ENG.). 32p. (J). (gr. k-2). 15.95 *(978-0-8109-8973-3(5),* Abrams Bks. for Young Readers) Abrams, Inc.
—Snoring Beauty. Manning, Jane, illus. 2014. (J). *(978-0-06-087405-6(8))* Harper & Row Ltd.
—Snoring Beauty. Manning, Jane, illus. 2014. (ENG.). 32p. (J). (gr. -1-3). 17.99 *(978-0-06-087403-2(1))* HarperCollins Pubs.
—Tyrannosaurus Wrecks! OHora, Zachariah, illus. 2014. (ENG.). 32p. (J). (gr. k-2). 14.95 *(978-1-4197-1035-3(4),* Abrams Bks. for Young Readers) Abrams, Inc.
—The Worst Twelve Days of Christmas. Wood, Ryan, illus. 2011. (ENG.). 32p. (J). (gr. k-2). 15.95 *(978-1-4197-0033-0(2),* Abrams Bks. for Young Readers) Abrams, Inc.
Barker, Stephen. I Want to Be a Farmer. 2015. (ENG., Illus.). 10p. (J). (gr. -1-k). bds. 10.99 *(978-1-4052-7565-1(0))* Egmont Bks., Ltd. GBR. Dist: Independent Pubs. Group.
Barner, Bob. Parade Day: Marching Through the Calendar Year. 2003. (ENG., Illus.). 32p. (J). (gr. k-3). tchr. ed. 16.95 *(978-0-8234-1690-5(9))* Holiday Hse., Inc.
Barnes, Cheryl Shaw & Barnes, Peter W., illus. Liberty Lee's Tail of Independence. 2012. (ENG.). 36p. (J). (gr. k-3). 16.95 *(978-1-59698-792-0(8),* Little Patriot Pr.) Regnery Publishing, Inc., An Eagle Publishing Co.
Barnes, Peter W. Marshall, the Courthouse Mouse: A Tail of the U. S. Supreme Court. Barnes, Cheryl S., illus. 2012. (ENG.). 40p. (J). (gr. k). 16.95 *(978-1-59698-789-0(8),* Little Patriot Pr.) Regnery Publishing, Inc., An Eagle Publishing Co.
—Woodrow, the White House Mouse. Barnes, Cheryl Shaw, illus. 2012. (ENG.). 40p. (J). (gr. k-3). 16.95 *(978-1-59698-788-3(X),* Little Patriot Pr.) Regnery Publishing, Inc., An Eagle Publishing Co.
Barnes, Peter W. & Barnes, Cheryl. Woodrow for President: A Tail of Voting, Campaigns, & Elections. 2012. (ENG.). 32p. (J). (gr. k-3). 16.95 *(978-1-59698-786-9(3))* Regnery Publishing, Inc., An Eagle Publishing Co.
Baron Cohen, H. V. The Story of Joe & His Magic Snout: An Operetta of Nursery Fairytales for 2 to 10 years Olds. 2009. 106p. pap. 19.27 *(978-1-4251-3582-9(X))* Trafford Publishing.
Barrow, Shelley. My Life: The Story of a NFL Child. 2007. (J). 16.99 *(978-0-9792647-0-2(7))* Mikenzi's Kardz & Bks. Llc.
Barry, Cotter. The Adventures of Morgan Morgan the Rhymester. 2010. 16p. 12.99 *(978-1-4520-0116-6(2))* AuthorHouse.
—By the Numbers. 2010. 16p. 12.99 *(978-1-4520-1476-0(0))* AuthorHouse.
—The Morgan's Family Circle. 2010. 16p. 12.99 *(978-1-4520-0114-2(6))* AuthorHouse.
—The Rhymester Morgan Morgan In: Elephants Don't Fly. 2010. 16p. 12.99 *(978-1-4520-0115-9(4))* AuthorHouse.
Barry, Debra R. Let's Go to the Market. 2012. 26p. 24.95 *(978-1-62709-916-5(6));* 28p. pap. 24.95 *(978-1-4626-8533-2(1))* America Star Bks.
Barry, Robert. Mr. Willowby's Christmas Tree. Date not set. 32p. (J). 16.95 *(978-0-8488-2206-4(4))* Amereon Ltd.
Bartalos, Michael. Shadowville. 2013. (ENG., Illus.). 32p. (J). (gr. -1-2). 16.95 *(978-1-57687-645-9(4),* powerHouse Bks.) powerHouse Cultural Entertainment, Inc.
Bartoletti, Susan Campbell. Naamah & the Ark at Night. Meade, Holly, illus. 2011. (ENG.). 32p. (J). (gr. -1-3). 16.99 *(978-0-7636-4242-6(8))* Candlewick Pr.
Barton, Jen. If Chocolate Were Purple. Matsuoka, Yoko, illus. gif. ed. 2013. (ENG.). 28p. (J). pap., instr.'s hndbk. ed. 10.89 *(978-0-615-78343-7(0),* Flickerfawn) Barton Bks.
Base, Graeme, et al. Dinosaurs in Your Backyard: The Coolest, Scariest Creatures Ever Found in the USA! 2009. (ENG., Illus.). 32p. (J). (gr. 1-4). 16.95 *(978-0-8109-7099-1(6),* Abrams Bks. for Young Readers) Abrams, Inc.
Baskwill, Jane. If Peace Is... Carter, Stephanie, illus. 2003. (J). 23p. pap. 7.95 *(978-1-59034-449-1(9));* 24p. (gr. 11-18). 15.95 *(978-1-59034-448-4(0))* Mondo Publishing.
Bass, L. G. & Geringer, Laura. Boom Boom Go Away! Ibatoulline, Bagram, illus. 2010. (ENG.). 40p. (J). (gr. -1-1). 15.99 *(978-0-689-85093-6(X),* Atheneum Bks. for Young Readers) Simon & Schuster Children's Publishing.
Bateman, Teresa. April Foolishness. Westcott, Nadine Bernard, illus. 2004. (ENG.). 32p. (J). (gr. k-3). 6.99 *(978-0-8075-0405-5(X))* Whitman, Albert & Co.
—Fluffy: Scourge of the Sea. Chesworth, Michael, illus. 2006. (ENG.). 32p. (J). (gr. -1-2). pap. 7.95 *(978-1-58089-152-3(7))* Charlesbridge Publishing, Inc.
—Hunting the Daddyosaurus. Huang, Benrei, illus. 2004. 29p. (J). (gr. k-4). reprint ed. 16.00 *(978-0-7567-7796-8(8))* DIANE Publishing Co.
—A Plump & Perky Turkey, 0 vols. Shelly, Jeff, illus. 2013. (ENG.). 32p. (J). (gr. k-4). pap. 9.99 *(978-0-7614-5188-4(9),* 9780761451884, Amazon Children's Publishing) Amazon Publishing.
Bauer, Marion Dane. How Do I Love You? / ¿Cómo Te Quiero? Church, Caroline Jayne, illus. 2014. (SPA & ENG.). 24p. (J). (gr. -1-k). bds. 8.99 *(978-0-545-66525-4(6),* Scholastic en Espanol) Scholastic, Inc.
—In Like a Lion, Out Like a Lamb. McCully, Emily Arnold, illus. (ENG.). 32p. (J). 2012. pap. 6.95 *(978-0-8234-2432-0(4))* 2011. (gr. -1-3). 16.95 *(978-0-8234-2238-8(0))* Holiday Hse., Inc.
—Little Cat's Luck. Bell, Jennifer A., illus. 2016. (ENG.). 224p. (J). (gr. 3-7). 17.99 *(978-1-4814-2488-2(2),* Simon & Schuster Bks. For Young Readers) Simon & Schuster Bks. For Young Readers.
—Little Dog, Lost. Bell, Jennifer A., illus. 2012. (ENG.). 208p. (J). (gr. 3-7). 16.99 *(978-1-4424-3423-3(6),* Atheneum Bks. for Young Readers) Simon & Schuster Children's Publishing.
—My Mother Is Mine. Elwell, Peter, illus. 2009. (Classic Board Bks.). (ENG.). 36p. (J). (gr. -1-k). bds. 7.99 *(978-1-4169-6090-4(2),* Little Simon) Little Simon.
—My Mother Is Mine. Elwell, Peter, illus. 2004. (ENG.). 40p. (J). (gr. -1-k). reprint ed. 7.99 *(978-0-689-86695-1(X),* Simon & Schuster Bks. For Young Readers) Simon & Schuster Bks. For Young Readers.
—The Very Best Daddy of All. Wu, Leslie, illus. 2011. (Classic Board Bks.). (ENG.). 34p. (J). (gr. -1 — 1). bds. 7.99 *(978-1-4169-8517-4(4),* Little Simon) Little Simon.
—The Very Best Daddy of All. Wu, Leslie, illus. 2007. (ENG.). 40p. (J). (gr. -1-3). 6.99 *(978-1-4169-2736-5(0),* Simon & Schuster Bks. For Young Readers) Simon & Schuster Bks. For Young Readers.
—Why Do Kittens Purr? Cole, Henry, illus. 2007. (ENG.). 32p. (J). (gr. -1-2). 9.99 *(978-1-4169-6850-4(4),* Aladdin) Simon & Schuster Children's Publishing.
Baum, L. Frank. Mother Goose in Prose. l.t. ed. 2005. 268p. pap. *(978-1-84637-097-7(3))* Echo Library.
Bea, Holly. Lucy Goose Goes to Texas. Boddy, Joe, illus. 2005. (ENG.). 32p. (J). (gr. -1-5). 15.95 *(978-1-932073-15-7(9))* New World Library.
Beardsley, Martyn. Five Naughty Kittens. East, Jacqueline, illus. 2005. (Reading Corner Ser.). 24p. (J). (gr. k-3). lib. bdg. 22.80 *(978-1-59771-006-0(7))* Sea-To-Sea Pubns.
Beaton, Clare, illus. Daisy Gets Dressed. 2005. 24p. (J). 15.99 *(978-1-84148-794-6(5))* Barefoot Bks., Inc.
Beaton, Clare & Blackstone, Stella. Cerdota Grandota. Beaton, Clare, illus. 2006.Tr. of How Big Is a Pig. (ENG., Illus.). 24p. (J). (gr. -1-k). bds. 6.99 *(978-1-84686-018-8(0))* Barefoot Bks., Inc.
Beaty, Andrea. Ada Twist, Scientist. Roberts, David, illus. 2016. (ENG.). 32p. (J). (gr. k-2). 17.95 *(978-1-4197-2137-3(2),* Abrams Bks. for Young Readers) Abrams, Inc.
—Hide & Sheep. Mayer, Bill, illus. 2011. (ENG.). 32p. (J). (gr. -1-3). 15.99 *(978-1-4169-2544-6(9),* McElderry, Margaret K. Bks.) McElderry, Margaret K. Bks.
—Iggy Peck, Architect. Roberts, David, illus. 2007. (ENG.). 32p. (J). (gr. k-17). 17.95 *(978-0-8109-1106-2(X),* Abrams Bks. for Young Readers) Abrams, Inc.
—Iggy Peck, Architect. Roberts, David, illus. 2010. (ENG.). 32p. (J). (gr. k-17). pap. 7.95 *(978-0-8109-8928-3(X))* UK Abrams Bks. for Young Readers.
—Rosie Revere, Engineer. Roberts, David, illus. 2013. (ENG.). 32p. (J). (gr. k-17). 17.95 *(978-1-4197-0845-9(7),* Abrams Bks. for Young Readers) Abrams, Inc.
Beaumont, Karen. Dini Dinosaur. Roode, Daniel, illus. 2012. (ENG.). 32p. (J). (gr. -1-k). 14.99 *(978-0-06-207299-3(4),* Greenwillow Bks.) HarperCollins Pubs.
—Doggone Dogs! Catrow, David, illus. 2008. (ENG.). 40p. (J). (gr. -1-k). 16.99 *(978-0-8037-3157-8(4),* Dial Bks) Penguin Young Readers Group.
—Duck, Duck, Goose! (A Coyote's on the Loose!) Aruego, Jose & Dewey, Ariane, illus. 2004. 32p. (J). (gr. -1-2). lib. bdg. 18.89 *(978-0-06-050804-3(3))* HarperCollins Pubs.
—Duck, Duck, Goose! A Coyote's on the Loose! Aruego, Jose & Dewey, Ariane, illus. 2004. (ENG.). 32p. (J). (gr. -1-2). 17.99 *(978-0-06-050802-9(7))* HarperCollins Pubs.
—Hats off to You! Pham, LeUyen, illus. 2017. (ENG.). 40p. (J). (gr. -1-3). 16.99 *(978-0-545-47423-8(X),* Scholastic Pr.) Scholastic, Inc.
—I Ain't Gonna Paint No More! Catrow, David, illus. (ENG.). (J). (gr. -1 — 1). 2012. 30p. bds. 11.99 *(978-0-547-87035-9(3))* 2005. 32p. 17.99 *(978-0-15-202488-8(3))* Houghton Mifflin Harcourt Publishing Co.
—I Like Myself! Catrow, David, illus. (ENG.). 32p. (J). (gr. -1 — 1). 2010. bds. 11.99 *(978-0-547-40163-8(9))* 2004. 17.99 *(978-0-15-202013-2(6))* Houghton Mifflin Harcourt Publishing Co.
—Move over, Rover! Dyer, Jane, illus. 2016. (ENG.). 40p. (J). (gr. -1-3). 7.99 *(978-0-544-80900-0(9),* HMH Books For Young Readers) Houghton Mifflin Harcourt Publishing Co.
—No Sleep for the Sheep! Urbanovic, Jackie, illus. 2011. (ENG.). 32p. (J). (gr. -1-3). 17.99 *(978-0-15-204969-0(X))* Houghton Mifflin Harcourt Publishing Co.
—Shoe-la-La! Pham, LeUyen, illus. 2011. (ENG.). 40p. (J). (gr. -1-3). 16.99 *(978-0-545-06705-8(7),* Scholastic Pr.) Scholastic, Inc.
—Shoe-la-La! A Storyplay Book. Leuyen, Pham, illus. 2016. (ENG.). 40p. (J). (gr. -1-k). 5.99 *(978-1-338-11555-0(3),* Cartwheel Bks.) Scholastic, Inc.
—Who Ate All the Cookie Dough? Yelchin, Eugene, illus. 2008. (ENG.). 32p. (J). (gr. -1-k). 18.99 *(978-0-8050-8267-8(0),* 9780805082678, Holt, Henry & Co. Bks. For Young Readers) Holt, Henry & Co.
—Wild about Us! Stevens, Janet, illus. 2015. (ENG.). 40p. (J). (gr. -1-3). 17.99 *(978-0-15-206294-1(7),* HMH Books For Young Readers) Houghton Mifflin Harcourt Publishing Co.
Beck, Carolyn. Richard Was a Picker, 1 vol. Hodson, Ben, illus. 2010. (ENG.). 32p. (J). (gr. -1-3). 19.95 *(978-1-55469-088-6(9))* Orca Bk. Pubs. USA.
Becker, Laura. The Wonder of a Summer Day. Steffen, Jennifer, illus. 2008. (ENG.). 40p. (J). (gr. -1-3). lib. bdg. *(978-1-934363-25-6(1))* Zoe Life Publishing.
Becker, Shelly. Even Superheroes Have Bad Days. Kaban, Eda, illus. 2016. (ENG.). 40p. (J). (gr. -1-4). 14.95 *(978-1-4549-1394-8(0))* Sterling Publishing Co., Inc.
Beckerman, Menucha. The Candy Kids. 2004. (My Smiling World Ser.: No. 3). (Illus.). 32p. (J). 11.95 *(978-1-931681-54-4(6))* Israel Bookshop Pubns.
Beckman, Chris & Beckman, Kelly. It's Not Scary You See... 2012. (ENG.). (J). pap. *(978-1-4675-3871-8(X))* Independent Pub.
Beilenson, Evelyn. The Zoo Is Closed Today! Kennedy, Anne, illus. 2014. (ENG.). 32p. (J). 16.99 *(978-1-4413-1526-7(8),* 9781441315267) Peter Pauper Pr. Inc.
Beiser, Tim. Little Chicken Duck. Slavin, Bill, illus. 2013. (ENG.). 24p. (J). (gr. -1-2). 17.95 *(978-1-77049-392-6(1),* Tundra Bks.) Tundra Bks. CAN. Dist: Penguin Random Hse. LLC.
Bell, Hilary & Pesenti, Antonia. Numerical Street. 2016. (ENG., Illus.). 32p. (J). (gr. -1-3). 24.99 *(978-1-74223-228-7(0),* UNSW Press) NewSouth Publishing AUS. Dist: Independent Pubs. Group.
Bell-Jackson, Sylvia. Bree's Bubble Gum Adventures: The Pajamas from the Bahamas. 2012. 36p. pap. 13.97 *(978-1-61204-299-2(6),* Strategic Bk. Publishing) Strategic Book Publishing & Rights Agency (SBPRA).
Bell, Juliet Clare. The Kite Princess. Chapman, Laura-Kate, illus. 2012. (ENG.). 32p. (J). pap. 9.99 *(978-1-84686-830-6(0))* Barefoot Bks., Inc.
Bell, Juliet Clare & Chapman, Laura Kate. The Kite Princess. 2012. (ENG., Illus.). (J). 16.99 *(978-1-84686-803-0(3))* Barefoot Bks., Inc.
Bell, Liz. Amarie & Her Family. 2011. 24p. pap. 24.95 *(978-1-4560-5430-4(9))* America Star Bks.
—Chickee Chickee Chew & Whoo Whoo Whoo. 2011. 16p. pap. 24.95 *(978-1-4626-3588-7(1))* America Star Bks.
Bell, Lucy & Everett, Melissa. Do Your Ears Hang Low? Doss, Andrea, illus. 2014. (ENG.). 20p. (J). (gr. -1-2). bds. 8.99 *(978-1-4867-0358-6(5))* Flowerpot Children's Pr. Inc. CAN. Dist: Cardinal Pubs. Group.
Bell, Lucy J. God Made Feelings. Rimmington, Natasha, illus. 2017. 10p. (J). 6.99 ***(978-1-5064-1782-0(5),*** Sparkhouse Family) Augsburg Fortress, Pubs.
Bell-Martin, Janelle. Head & Shoulders, 1 vol. 2011. (Early Childhood Themes Ser.). (ENG.). 16p. (J). (gr. -1-2). pap. 19.99 *(978-1-4333-2372-0(9));* pap. 6.99 *(978-1-4333-2371-3(0))* Teacher Created Materials, Inc.
—Mary Had a Little Lamb, 1 vol. 2011. (Early Childhood Themes Ser.). (ENG.). 16p. (J). (gr. -1-2). pap. 6.99 *(978-1-4333-2357-7(5));* pap. 19.99 *(978-1-4333-2358-4(3))* Teacher Created Materials, Inc.
—Oh, Mr. Sun, 1 vol. 2012. (Early Childhood Themes Ser.). (ENG.). 16p. (J). (gr. -1-2). pap. 6.99 *(978-1-4333-3471-9(2))* Teacher Created Materials, Inc.
Bell, Philip. Jack & Boo's Dinosaur Island. Bell, Eleanor, illus. 2013. 32p. pap. *(978-0-9562980-3-4(6))* Beachy Bks.
Bell, Samantha. The Perfect Pet, 1 vol. 2013. (SPA.). 32p. (J). (gr. -1-3). pap. 9.95 *(978-1-60718-701-1(9))* Arbordale Publishing.
Belloc, Hilaire. Cautionary Tales for Children. 2009. 48p. (gr. 4-7). pap. 7.75 *(978-1-60459-576-5(0))* Wilder Pubns., Corp.
Bemelmans, Ludwig. Madeline: Edicion en Espanol. Anasal, Arshes, ed. 2005. (SPA., Illus.). 44p. (J). (gr. k-4). reprint ed. 16.00 *(978-0-7567-8842-1(0))* DIANE Publishing Co.
—Madeline 75th Anniversary Edition. 2014. (Madeline Ser.). (ENG.). 56p. (J). (gr. -1-2). 25.00 *(978-0-670-78540-7(7),* Viking Books for Young Readers) Penguin Young Readers Group.
—Madeline Christmas Activity Book. 2013. (Madeline Ser.). (ENG.). 16p. (J). (gr. -1-2). pap. 7.99 *(978-0-670-01568-9(7),* Viking Books for Young Readers) Penguin Young Readers Group.
—Madeline's Christmas, 1 vol. Bemelmans, Ludwig, illus. 2007. (Madeline Ser.). (ENG., Illus.). 15p. (J). (gr. -1-2). 9.99 *(978-0-14-240897-1(2),* Puffin Books) Penguin Young Readers Group.
—Madeline's Rescue. 2004. (J). (gr. -1-2). spiral bd. *(978-0-616-11864-1(3))* Canadian National Institute for the Blind/Institut National Canadien pour les Aveugles.
—Madeline's Rescue, 1 vol. 2009. (Madeline Ser.). (ENG.). 15p. (J). (gr. -1-2). 9.99 *(978-0-14-241444-6(1),* Puffin Books) Penguin Young Readers Group.
Ben-Gur, Naomi. The Cricket & the Ant: A Shabbat Story. Kober, Shahar, illus. 2016. (ENG.). 32p. (gr. -1-3). lib. bdg. 17.99 *(978-1-4677-8935-6(6),* Kar-Ben Publishing) Lerner Publishing Group.
Benaglia, Fred, illus. Hug This Book! 2016. (ENG.). 32p. (gr. -1-k). 16.95 *(978-0-7148-7284-1(9))* Phaidon Pr., Inc.
Benenfeld, Rikki. I Go Visiting. 2007. (Toddler Experience Ser.). (Illus.). 32p. (J). (gr. -1-k). 10.95 *(978-1-929628-33-9(1))* Hachai Publishing.
—Let's Go to the Park. 2015. (ENG., Illus.). 36p. (J). 10.95 *(978-1-929628-82-7(X))* Hachai Publishing.
—Let's Meet Community Helpers. Benenfeld, Rikki, illus. 2013. (Illus.). 32p. (J). 10.95 *(978-1-929628-75-9(7))* Hachai Publishing.
Bennett, Artie. The Butt Book. Lester, Mike, illus. 2010. (ENG.). 32p. (J). (gr. k-2). 17.99 *(978-1-59990-311-8(3),* 9781599903118, Bloomsbury USA Childrens) Bloomsbury Publishing USA.
Bennett, Kelly. Dance Y'all, Dance. Murphy, Terri, illus. 2010. (ENG.). 32p. (J). (gr. k-2). 16.95 *(978-1-933979-65-6(8))* Bright Sky Pr.
—One Day I Went Rambling. Murphy, Terri, illus. 2012. (ENG.). 24p. (J). (gr. k-3). 17.95 *(978-1-936474-06-6(9))* Bright Sky Pr.
Benson, Nicky. I Love You More & More. Lambert, Jonny, illus. 2016. (ENG.). 24p. (J). (gr. -1-k). bds. 9.99 *(978-1-58925-227-1(6))* Tiger Tales.
Bentley, Dawn. Three Hungry Spiders & One Fat Fly! Twinem, Neecy, illus. 2010. (Stretchies Book Ser.). 16p. (J). (gr. -1-k). 8.99 *(978-0-8249-1460-8(0),* Ideal Pubns.) Worthy Publishing.
—Three Stretchy Frogs. Wallis, Becky, illus. 2010. (Stretchies Book Ser.). 16p. (J). 8.99 *(978-0-8249-1459-2(7))* Hinkler Bks. Pty, Ltd. AUS. Dist: Ideals Pubns.
Bentley, Peter. Push-Pull-Turn! Construction Site. Bucco, Joe, illus. 2017. (ENG.). 20p. (J). (gr. -1). 15.99 *(978-1-62686-837-3(9),* Silver Dolphin Bks.) Readerlink Distribution Services, LLC.
Bently, Peter. Captain Jack & the Pirates. Oxenbury, Helen, illus. 2016. (ENG.). 32p. (J). (-k). 17.99 *(978-0-525-42950-0(6),* Dial Bks) Penguin Young Readers Group.
—The Cat, the Mouse, & the Runaway Train. Cox, Steve, illus. 2013. (J). *(978-1-4351-4968-7(8))* Barnes & Noble, Inc.
—Dustbin Dad. Ayto, Russell, illus. 2014. (ENG.). 32p. (J). 15.99 *(978-1-84738-873-5(6))* Simon & Schuster, Ltd. GBR. Dist: Simon & Schuster, Inc.
—The Great Balloon Hullaballoo. Matsuoka, Mei, illus. 2014. (ENG.). 32p. (J). (gr. -1-3). 16.95 *(978-1-4677-3449-3(7))* Lerner Publishing Group.

S

—The Great Dog Bottom Swap. Matsuoka, Mei, illus. 2011. (ENG.). 32p. (J). (gr. -1-k). pap. 12.99 *(978-1-84270-988-7(7))* Andersen Pr. GBR. Dist: Independent Pubs. Group.

—The Great Sheep Shenanigans. Matsuoka, Mei, illus. 2012. (Andersen Press Picture Bks). (ENG.). 32p. (J). (gr. -1-3). 16.95 *(978-0-7613-8990-3(3))* Lerner Publishing Group.

—King Jack & the Dragon. Oxenbury, Helen, illus. 2011. (ENG.). 32p. (J). (gr. -1-k). 17.99 *(978-0-8037-3698-6(3),* Dial Bks) Penguin Young Readers Group.

—King Jack & the Dragon Board Book. Oxenbury, Helen, illus. 2013. (ENG.). 14p. (J). (gr. -1 — 1). bds. 7.99 *(978-0-8037-3987-1(7),* Dial Bks) Penguin Young Readers Group.

—Meet the Parents. Ogilvie, Sara, illus. 2014. (ENG.). 32p. (J). (gr. -1-3). 17.99 *(978-1-4814-1483-8(6),* Simon & Schuster/Paula Wiseman Bks.) Simon & Schuster/Paula Wiseman Bks.

—The Prince & the Porker. Roberts, David, illus. 2017. (ENG.). 32p. (J). (gr. k-2). 16.95 *(978-1-4197-2312-4(X),* Abrams Bks. for Young Readers) Abrams, Inc.

—A Recipe for Bedtime. Massini, Sarah, illus. 2016. (ENG.). 32p. (J). (— 1). 16.99 *(978-0-399-17625-8(X),* G.P. Putnam's Sons Books for Young Readers) Penguin Young Readers Group.

—Rich Witch, Poor Witch. Field, Jim, illus. 2014. (ENG.). 32p. (J). (gr. -1-k). pap. 8.99 *(978-1-4472-2018-3(8))* Pan Macmillan GBR. Dist: Independent Pubs. Group.

—Royal Visit. 2017. (Tooth Fairy Ser.). (ENG., Illus.). 32p. (J). (gr. -1-k). 17.99 *(978-1-4449-2853-2(8))* Hachette Children's Group GBR. Dist: Hachette Bk. Group.

—Those Magnificent Sheep in Their Flying Machine. Bently, Peter, illus. 2014. (ENG., Illus.). 32p. (J). (gr. -1-3). 16.95 *(978-1-4677-4935-0(4))* Lerner Publishing Group.

—The Tooth Fairy's Christmas. Parsons, Garry, illus. 2014. (J). *(978-1-4351-5739-2(7))* Barnes & Noble, Inc.

—The Yoga Ogre. Rickerty, Simon, illus. 2012. (ENG.). 32p. (J). 15.99 *(978-1-84738-902-2(3))* Simon & Schuster, Ltd. GBR. Dist: Simon & Schuster, Inc.

Benton, Jim. Five Stinky Socks: A Counting Book. 2015. (ENG.). 16p. (J). (— 1). bds. 5.99 *(978-0-545-64784-7(3),* Cartwheel Bks.) Scholastic, Inc.

—Piggy Paints. 2015. (ENG.). 16p. (J). (— 1). bds. 5.99 *(978-0-545-64785-4(1),* Cartwheel Bks.) Scholastic, Inc.

—Robot Kitties: An up & down Book. 2015. (ENG.). 16p. (J). (— 1). bds. 5.99 *(978-0-545-64786-1(X),* Cartwheel Bks.) Scholastic, Inc.

—Where Did All the Dinos Go? Benton, Jim, illus. 2016. (ENG., Illus.). 18p. (J). (— 1). bds. 7.99 *(978-0-545-64789-2(4),* Cartwheel Bks.) Scholastic, Inc.

Berenstain, Jan & Berenstain, Mike. God Made the Colors, 1 vol. 2013. (I Can Read! / Berenstain Bears / Living Lights Ser.). (ENG.). 32p. (J). pap. 3.99 *(978-0-310-72507-7(0))* Zonderkidz.

—Let the Bible Be Your Guide. 2011. (Berenstain Bears/Living Lights Ser.). (ENG., Illus.). 40p. (J). 6.99 *(978-0-310-72714-9(6))* Zonderkidz.

Berenstain, Jan & Berenstain, Stan. The Big Book of Berenstain Bears Beginner Books. 2011. (Beginner Books(R) Ser.). (ENG., Illus.). 320p. (J). (gr. -1-2). 16.99 *(978-0-375-87366-9(X),* Random Hse. Bks. for Young Readers) Random Hse. Children's Bks.

Berenstain, Jan, et al. The Berenstain Bears Save Christmas. Berenstain, Mike, illus. 2003. (Berenstain Bears Ser.). (ENG.). 48p. (J). (gr. -1-3). 14.99 *(978-0-06-052670-2(X),* HarperFestival) HarperCollins Pubs.

Berenstain, Stan & Berenstain, Jan. The Berenstain Bears(r) & the Talent Show. 2014. (ENG.). 32p. (J). (-3). 9.99 *(978-1-4022-9095-4(0),* Sourcebooks Jabberwocky) Sourcebooks, Inc.

—The Berenstain Bears down on the Farm. Berenstain, Stan & Berenstain, Jan, illus. 2006. (I Can Read Level 1 Ser.). (ENG., Illus.). 32p. (J). (gr. k-3). pap. 3.99 *(978-0-06-058351-4(7))* HarperCollins Pubs.

—The Berenstain Bears' Family Reunion. 2009. (Berenstain Bears — I Can Read Ser.). (J). lib. bdg. 13.55 *(978-0-606-04776-0(X),* Turtleback) Turtleback Bks.

—Berenstain Bears' Home Sweet Tree. 2013. (ENG.). 32p. (J). (-3). 9.99 *(978-1-4022-9085-5(3),* Sourcebooks Jabberwocky) Sourcebooks, Inc.

—The Berenstain Bears Out West. Berenstain, Stan & Berenstain, Jan, illus. 2006. (I Can Read Level 1 Ser.). (ENG., Illus.). 32p. (J). (gr. k-3). pap. 3.99 *(978-0-06-058354-5(1))* HarperCollins Pubs.

—The Berenstain Bears' Pet Show. 2014. (ENG.). 32p. (J). (-3). 9.99 *(978-1-4022-9090-9(X),* Sourcebooks Jabberwocky) Sourcebooks, Inc.

—We Like Kites. 2004. (Step into Reading Level 1 Ser.). (gr. -1-2). lib. bdg. 13.55 *(978-0-613-87779-4(9),* Turtleback) Turtleback Bks.

Berenstain, Stan, et al. The Berenstain Bears' Christmas Tree, 1 vol. 2009. (Berenstain Bears/Living Lights Ser.). (ENG., Illus.). 72p. (J). (gr. -1-2). 9.99 *(978-0-310-71940-3(2))* Zonderkidz.

—The Berenstain Bears Discover God's Creation, 1 vol. 2010. (Berenstain Bears/Living Lights Ser.). (ENG.). 40p. (J). (gr. -1-2). 6.99 *(978-0-310-71936-6(4))* Zonderkidz.

—The Berenstain Bears Do Their Best, 1 vol. 2010. (Berenstain Bears/Living Lights Ser.). (ENG.). 40p. (J). (gr. -1-2). 6.99 *(978-0-310-71937-3(2))* Zonderkidz.

—The Berenstain Bears Learn to Share, 1 vol. 2010. (Berenstain Bears/Living Lights Ser.). (ENG.). 40p. (J). (gr. -1-2). 6.99 *(978-0-310-71939-7(9))* Zonderkidz.

Berger, Samantha. Boo-La-La Witch Spa. Roxas, Isabel, illus. 2015. (ENG.). 32p. (J). (gr. -1-k). 16.99 *(978-0-8037-3886-7(2),* Dial Bks) Penguin Young Readers Group.

—Snoozefest. Litten, Kristyna, illus. 2015. (ENG.). 34p. (J). (gr. -1-k). 16.99 *(978-0-8037-4046-4(8),* Dial Bks) Penguin Young Readers Group.

Berger, Samantha & Chanko, Pamela. It's Spring! Sweet, Melissa, illus. 2003. (ENG.). 30p. (J). (gr. -1-3). bds. 6.99 *(978-0-439-44238-1(9),* Cartwheel Bks.) Scholastic, Inc.

Berggren, Joyce D. The Hustle & Bustle of Poor Mrs. Tustle. Muellner, Nancy, illus. 2010. 32p. pap. 12.95 *(978-0-9819860-5-0(6))* Amber Skye Publishing LLC.

Bergman, Mara. Best Friends. Slater, Nicola, illus. 2015. (ENG.). 32p. (J). (gr. -1-k). pap. 10.99 *(978-1-4449-1420-7(0))* Hodder & Stoughton GBR. Dist: Hachette Bk. Group.

—Oliver Who Would Not Sleep! Maland, Nick, illus. 2007. (J). *(978-0-439-92827-4(3),* Levine, Arthur A. Bks.) Scholastic, Inc.

Berkes, Marianne. El árbol Que Trepó el Oso, 1 vol. Rietz, Kathleen, illus. 2012. (SPA.). 32p. (J). (gr. -1-3). 17.95 *(978-1-60718-679-3(9))* Arbordale Publishing.

—Marsh Morning. Noreika, Robert, illus. 2011. (ENG.). 32p. (J). (gr. k-3). pap. 6.95 *(978-0-7613-7462-6(0),* Millbrook Pr.) Lerner Publishing Group.

—Marsh Music. Noreika, Robert, illus. 2011. (ENG.). 32p. (J). (gr. k-3). pap. 6.95 *(978-0-7613-7461-9(2),* Millbrook Pr.) Lerner Publishing Group.

—Over in Australia: Amazing Animals down Under, 1 vol. Dubin, Jill, illus. 2011. (ENG.). 32p. (J). (gr. -1-3). 16.95 *(978-1-58469-135-8(2));* pap. 8.95 *(978-1-58469-136-5(0))* Dawn Pubns.

—Over in the Arctic: Where the Cold Winds Blow, 1 vol. Dubin, Jill, illus. 2008. (ENG.). 32p. (J). (gr. -1-2). 16.95 *(978-1-58469-109-9(3));* pap. 8.95 *(978-1-58469-110-5(7))* Dawn Pubns.

—Over in the Forest: Come & Take a Peek, 1 vol. Dubin, Jill, illus. 2012. (ENG.). 32p. (J). 16.95 *(978-1-58469-162-4(X));* pap. 8.95 *(978-1-58469-163-1(8))* Dawn Pubns.

—Over in the Grasslands: On an African Savanna, 1 vol. Dubin, Jill, illus. 2016. (ENG.). 32p. (J). (gr. -1-2). 16.95 *(978-1-58469-567-7(6))* Dawn Pubns.

—Over on a Mountain: Somewhere in the World, 1 vol. Dubin, Jill, illus. 2015. (ENG.). 32p. (J). (gr. -1-3). 16.95 *(978-1-58469-518-9(8))* Dawn Pubns.

—The Swamp Where Gator Hides, 1 vol. Baird, Roberta, illus. 2014. (ENG.). 32p. (J). (gr. k-4). 16.95 *(978-1-58469-470-0(X));* pap. 8.95 *(978-1-58469-471-7(8))* Dawn Pubns.

—The Tree That Bear Climbed, 1 vol. Rietz, Kathleen, illus. 2012. 32p. (J). (gr. -1-3). (ENG & SPA.). 17.95 *(978-1-60718-528-4(8));* (SPA.). pap. 9.95 *(978-1-62855-426-7(6));* (ENG & SPA.). pap. 9.95 *(978-1-60718-537-6(7))* Arbordale Publishing.

Berkes, Marianne Collins. Over on the Farm. Morrison, Cathy, illus. 2016. (ENG.). 32p. (J). (gr. -1-2). 16.95 *(978-1-58469-548-6(X))* Dawn Pubns.

Berlin, Bill & Berlin, Susan Isakoff. The Kvetch Who Stole Hanukkah, 1 vol. Welling, Peter J., illus. 2010. (ENG.). 32p. (J). (gr. k-3). 16.99 *(978-1-58980-798-3(7))* Pelican Publishing Co., Inc.

Bernal, Mitchell. Skelanimals: Dead Animals Need Love Too Bernal, Mitchell, illus. l.t. ed. 2005. (Illus.). 22p. (J). per. 12.95 *(978-0-9766621-0-5(8),* 818 554-8965) Kreations.

Berne, Jennifer. Nighty-Night, Sleep Tight. Walker, David, illus. 2015. (Snuggle Time Stories Ser.). (ENG.). 24p. (J). (gr. -1-k). bds. 6.95 *(978-1-4549-1390-0(8))* Sterling Publishing Co., Inc.

Bernstrom, Daniel. One Day in the Eucalyptus, Eucalyptus Tree. Wenzel, Brendan, illus. 2016. 32p. (J). (gr. -1-3). 17.99 *(978-0-06-235485-3(X),* Tegen, Katherine Bks) HarperCollins Pubs.

Berry, Lynne. What Floats in a Moat? Cordell, Matthew, illus. 2013. (ENG.). 48p. (J). (gr. k-4). 17.99 *(978-1-4169-7653-4(6),* Simon & Schuster Bks. For Young Readers) Simon & Schuster Bks. For Young Readers.

Berry, Ron. Can You Make Peter Rabbit Giggle? Sharp, Chris, illus. 2012. 10p. (J). bds. 10.99 *(978-0-8249-1418-9(X),* Ideal Pubns.) Worthy Publishing.

Berry, Ron & Mead, David. All Aboard! Charlie the Can-Do Choo Choo. Sharp, Chris, illus. 2009. (ENG.). 8p. 12.99 *(978-0-8249-1420-2(1),* Ideal Pubns.) Worthy Publishing.

Berthiaume, Donna M. Our Cool School Zoo Revue. Jirak, Tracey, illus. 2008. 36p. pap. 24.95 *(978-1-60672-672-3(2))* America Star Bks.

Bertram, Debbie & Bloom, Susan. The Best Book to Read. Garland, Michael, illus. 2011. (ENG.). 32p. (J). (gr. -1-2). pap. 7.99 *(978-0-375-87300-3(7),* Dragonfly Bks.) Random Hse. Children's Bks.

—The Best Place to Read. 2007. lib. bdg. 18.40 *(978-1-4177-9097-5(0),* Turtleback) Turtleback Bks.

Bessesen, Brooke. Zachary Z. Packrat & His Amazing Collections. Campbell, Jenney, illus. 2008. 40p. pap. 19.95 *(978-1-932082-83-8(2))* Arizona Highways.

Bianchini, Bob. Charlie Rides: Planes, Trains, Bikes, & More! 2017. (ENG., Illus.). 20p. (J). (gr. -1-k). bds. 8.95 *(978-1-4197-2292-9(1),* Abrams Appleseed) Abrams, Inc.

Bicknell, Joanna & Page, Nick. Finger Friends Tickle Monsters. Saunders, Katie, illus. 2007. (Finger Puppet Books Ser.). 12p. (gr. -1). bds. *(978-1-84610-427-5(0))* Make Believe Ideas.

Big Davie. The Lady & Her Cat As Told by Bigdavie: A simple easy reading bedtime story that will leave children with delightful images while drifting off to S. 2009. (Illus.). 28p. pap. 12.49 *(978-1-4389-3124-1(7))* AuthorHouse.

The Biggest Kiss. 2014. (ENG., Illus.). 28p. (J). (gr. -1 — 1). bds. 7.99 *(978-1-4814-1751-8(7),* Little Simon) Little Simon.

Billet, Marion, illus. Scooter Bug. 2014. (Whizzy Wheels Ser.). (ENG.). 10p. (J). (gr. -1-k). bds. 9.99 *(978-1-4472-5763-9(4))* Pan Macmillan GBR. Dist: Independent Pubs. Group.

Bingham, Kelly. Formerly Shark Girl. 2015. (ENG.). 352p. (YA). (gr. 7). pap. 8.99 *(978-0-7636-7673-5(X))* Candlewick Pr.

—Shark Girl. 2010. (ENG., Illus.). 288p. (YA). (gr. 7). pap. 8.99 *(978-0-7636-4627-1(X))* Candlewick Pr.

Binkley, Carolyn. The Errand: And Stinkbugs & Grasshoppers Green. 2012. 24p. pap. 15.99 *(978-1-4691-6096-2(X))* Xlibris Corp.

Bird, Roy & Harp, Kim. Hark! I Hear a Meadowlark! Battis, Gwen, illus. 2013. 34p. 16.99 *(978-1-939054-08-1(7));* 36p. pap. 10.99 *(978-1-939054-07-4(9))* Rowe Publishing and Design.

Bird, Shelia May. My Auntie Susan. Postgate, Daniel, illus. 2008. (Tadpoles Ser.). (ENG.). 24p. (J). (gr. -1-3). pap. *(978-0-7787-3889-3(2));* lib. bdg. *(978-0-7787-3858-9(2))* Crabtree Publishing Co.

Blabey, Aaron. Pig the Pug. 2016. (ENG., Illus.). 32p. (J). (gr. -1-k). 14.99 *(978-1-338-11245-0(7),* Scholastic Pr.) Scholastic, Inc.

—Pig the Winner. 2017. (Pig the Pug Ser.). (ENG.). 32p. (J). (gr. -1-k). 14.99 *(978-1-338-13638-8(0),* Scholastic Pr.) Scholastic, Inc.

Black, Joe. Afikomen Mambo. Prater, Linda, illus. 2011. (ENG.). 24p. (J). (gr. -1 — 1). pap. 8.95 *(978-0-7613-5639-4(8),* Kar-Ben Publishing) Lerner Publishing Group.

—Afikomen Mambo. Brown, Richard E. & Prater, Linda, illus. 2011. (Passover Ser.). (ENG.). 24p. (J). (gr. -1 — 1). lib. bdg. 17.95 *(978-0-7613-5638-7(X),* Kar-Ben Publishing) Lerner Publishing Group.

Black, Michael Ian. Chicken Cheeks. Hawkes, Kevin, illus. 2009. (ENG.). 40p. (J). (gr. -1-3). 17.99 *(978-1-4169-4864-3(3),* Simon & Schuster Bks. For Young Readers) Simon & Schuster Bks. For Young Readers.

Black, Robyn Hood. Sir Mike. Murphy, David, illus. 2006. (Rookie Reader Skill Set Ser.). (ENG.). 32p. (J). (gr. k-2). per. 4.95 *(978-0-516-25020-5(5),* Children's Pr.) Scholastic Library Publishing.

Blackmore, Jeanne C. How Does Sleep Come? Sayles, Elizabeth, illus. 2012. (ENG.). 32p. (J). (-3). 16.99 *(978-1-4022-7105-2(0),* Sourcebooks Jabberwocky) Sourcebooks, Inc.

Blackstone, Stella. Alligator Alphabet. Bauer, Stephanie, illus. (ENG.). (J). (gr. -1-k). 2007. 32p. 8.99 *(978-1-84686-073-7(3))* 2005. 48p. 16.99 *(978-1-84148-494-5(6))* Barefoot Bks., Inc.

—Bear about Town (Oso en las Ciudad) Harter, Debbie, illus. 2010. (ENG, SPA & FRE.). 24p. (J). (gr. -1-1). pap. 6.99 *(978-1-84686-377-6(5))* Barefoot Bks., Inc.

—Bear at Home (Oso en Casa) Harter, Debbie, illus. 2010. (ENG & SPA.). 24p. (J). (gr. -1-1). pap. 6.99 *(978-1-84686-422-3(4))* Barefoot Bks., Inc.

—Bear at Work. Harter, Debbie, illus. 2011. (ENG & SPA.). 24p. (J). (gr. -1-k). pap. 6.99 *(978-1-84686-554-1(9))* Barefoot Bks., Inc.

—Bear at Work (Oso en el Trabajo) 2012. (ENG & SPA., Illus.). (J). 6.99 *(978-1-84686-769-9(X))* Barefoot Bks., Inc.

—Bear's Birthday. Harter, Debbie, illus. 2011.Tr. of El Cumpleanos de Oso. (ENG.). 24p. (J). (gr. -1-1). pap. 6.99 *(978-1-84686-515-2(8))* Barefoot Bks., Inc.

—Cleo in the Snow. Mockford, Caroline, illus. 2013. (ENG.). 24p. (J). 6.99 *(978-1-78285-055-7(4));* 6.99 *(978-1-78285-054-0(6))* Barefoot Bks., Inc.

—Cleo on the Move. Mockford, Caroline, illus. 2013. (ENG.). 24p. (J). 6.99 *(978-1-78285-056-4(2))* Barefoot Bks., Inc.

—Cleo's Color Book. Mockford, Caroline, illus. 2006. 0032p. (J). 15.99 *(978-1-905236-30-5(1))* Barefoot Bks., Inc.

—A Dragon on the Doorstep. Harter, Debbie, illus. (ENG.). 32p. (J). 2012. (gr. -1-2). 9.99 *(978-1-84686-826-9(2))* 2006. pap. 9.99 *(978-1-905236-66-4(2))* 2006. (gr. -1-k). pap. 6.99 *(978-1-84686-032-4(6))* 2005. (gr. -1-1). 15.99 *(978-1-84148-227-9(7))* Barefoot Bks., Inc.

—La Familia Activa de Oso. Sarfatti, Esther, tr. Harter, Debbie, illus. 2003. (Bear Ser.). (SPA.). 24p. (J). pap. 6.99 *(978-1-84148-777-9(5))* Barefoot Bks., Inc.

—La Familia Ocupada de Oso. 2012. (ENG & SPA.). (J). 6.99 *(978-1-84686-771-2(1))* Barefoot Bks., Inc.

—La Famille Active de l'Ours. 2012.Tr. of Bear's Busy Family. (FRE & ENG.). (J). pap. 6.99 *(978-1-84686-772-9(X))* Barefoot Bks., Inc.

—I Dreamt I Was a Dinosaur. Beaton, Clare, illus. 2005. (ENG.). 32p. (J). (gr. -1-3). 15.99 *(978-1-84148-238-5(2))* Barefoot Bks., Inc.

—I Spy the Sun in the Sky. 2009. (ENG., Illus.). (J). 14.99 *(978-1-84686-276-2(0))* Barefoot Bks., Inc.

—An Island in the Sun. 2016. (ENG.). 32p. (J). (gr. -1-k). bds. 14.99 *(978-1-78285-285-8(9))* Barefoot Bks., Inc.

—Jump into January. Carluccio, Maria, illus. 2004. 32p. (J). 15.99 *(978-1-84148-629-1(9))* Barefoot Bks., Inc.

—L'Ours au Travail. 2012.Tr. of Bear at Work. (FRE & ENG.). (J). 6.99 *(978-1-84686-770-5(3))* Barefoot Bks., Inc.

—My Granny Went to Market: A Round-the-World Counting Rhyme. Corr, Christopher, illus. 2005. (ENG.). 24p. (J). 16.99 *(978-1-84148-792-2(9))* Barefoot Bks., Inc.

—On y Danse les Saisons. Carluccio, Maria, illus. 2016. (FRE.). (J). pap. *(978-1-78285-298-8(0))* Barefoot Bks., Inc.

—Oso Bajo el Sol. Sarfatti, Esther, tr. Harter, Debbie, illus. 2003. (Bear Ser.). (SPA.). 24p. (J). pap. 6.99 *(978-1-84148-778-6(3))* Barefoot Bks., Inc.

—Oso en Bicicleta. Sarfatti, Esther, tr. Harter, Debbie, illus. 2003. (Bear Ser.). (SPA.). 32p. (J). pap. 6.99 *(978-1-84148-775-5(9))* Barefoot Bks., Inc.

—Oso en Casa. Sarfatti, Esther, tr. Harter, Debbie, illus. 2003. (Bear Ser.). (SPA.). 24p. (J). pap. 6.99 *(978-1-84148-779-3(1))* Barefoot Bks., Inc.

—Oso en la Ciudad. Sarfatti, Esther, tr. Harter, Debbie, illus. 2003. (Bear Ser.). (SPA.). 24p. (J). pap. 6.99 *(978-1-84148-776-2(7))* Barefoot Bks., Inc.

—Oso en un Cuadrado. Sarfatti, Esther, tr. Harter, Debbie, illus. 2003. (Bear Ser.). (SPA.). 24p. (J). pap. 6.99 *(978-1-84148-774-8(0))* Barefoot Bks., Inc.

—Secret Seahorse. Beaton, Clare, illus. 2005. (J). (gr. -1-2). 24p. bds. 7.99 *(978-1-905236-15-2(8));* 24p. 15.99 *(978-1-84148-704-5(X));* 32p. pap. 7.99 *(978-1-84148-937-7(9))* Barefoot Bks., Inc.

—Ship Shapes. Bell, Siobhan, illus. 2006. (J). 0024p. 15.99 *(978-1-905236-34-3(4)); (978-1-4156-6474-2(9))* Barefoot Bks., Inc.

—Ship Shapes. 2012. lib. bdg. 17.20 *(978-0-606-23826-7(3),* Turtleback) Turtleback Bks.

—Talk with Me! Mockford, Caroline, illus. 2009. (ENG.). 14p. (J). (gr. -1). 7.99 *(978-1-84686-180-2(2))* Barefoot Bks., Inc.

—Walk with Me! Mockford, Caroline, illus. 2009. (ENG.). 14p. (J). (gr. -1). bds. 7.99 *(978-1-84686-179-6(9))* Barefoot Bks., Inc.

—Walking Through the Jungle. Harter, Debbie, illus. 2004. (ENG.). 32p. (J). (gr. -1-k). pap. 6.99 *(978-1-84148-548-5(9))* Barefoot Bks., Inc.

—Walking Through the Jungle. Harter, Debbie, illus. 2004. 32p. (J). 9.99 *(978-1-84148-182-1(3))* Barefoot Bks., Inc.

—Who Are You, Baby Kangaroo? Beaton, Clare, illus. 2004. 32p. (J). 14.99 *(978-1-84148-217-0(X))* Barefoot Bks., Inc.

—Who Are You Baby Kangaroo? Beaton, Clare, illus. 2011. (ENG.). 32p. (J). (gr. -1-2). pap. 6.99 *(978-1-84686-190-1(X))* Barefoot Bks., Inc.

Blackstone, Stella & Barefoot Books. Bear on a Bike (Oso en Bicicleta) Harter, Debbie, illus. 2014. (ENG & SPA.). 32p. (J). (gr. -1-1). pap. 6.99 *(978-1-78285-079-3(1))* Barefoot Bks., Inc.

Blackstone, Stella & Barefoot Books Staff. An Island in the Sun. Ceccoli, Nicoletta, illus. 2005. (ENG.). 24p. (J). pap. 6.99 *(978-1-84148-079-4(7))* Barefoot Bks., Inc.

Blackstone, Stella & Bass, Jules. Hay una Vaca Entre las Coles. Beaton, Clare, illus. 2003.Tr. of There's a Cow in the Cabbage Patch. (SPA.). 32p. (J). (gr. k-2). pap. 6.99 *(978-1-84148-965-0(4))* Barefoot Bks., Inc.

Blackstone, Stella & Bauer, Stephanie. Octopus Opposites. Bauer, Stephanie, illus. 2010. (ENG., Illus.). 32p. (J). (gr. -1). 16.99 *(978-1-84686-328-8(7))* Barefoot Bks., Inc.

Blackstone, Stella & Carluccio, Maria. Un Recorrido Por Las Estaciones. Carluccio, Maria, illus. 2009. (SPA., Illus.). 32p. (J). (gr. -1-2). pap. 7.99 *(978-1-84686-291-5(4))* Barefoot Bks., Inc.

—Skip Through the Seasons. Carluccio, Maria, illus. 2006. (Seek-and-Find Bks.). (ENG., Illus.). 32p. (J). (gr. -1-k). 7.99 *(978-1-905236-71-8(9))* Barefoot Bks., Inc.

Blackstone, Stella & Corr, Christopher. My Granny Went to Market: A Round-the-World Counting Rhyme. 2006. (ENG., Illus.). 24p. (J). (gr. -1-2). 6.99 *(978-1-905236-62-6(X))* Barefoot Bks., Inc.

Blackstone, Stella & Harter, Debbie. Bear at Work. Harter, Debbie, illus. 2008. (Bear Ser.). (ENG., Illus.). 24p. (J). (gr. -1-1). pap. 6.99 *(978-1-84686-110-9(1))* Barefoot Bks., Inc.

—Bear Takes a Trip. 2012. (ENG., Illus.). 24p. (J). (gr. -1-1). pap. 6.99 *(978-1-84686-756-9(8))* Barefoot Bks., Inc.

—Who Are You? Harter, Debbie, illus. 2003. (ENG., Illus.). 24p. (J). (gr. k-2). bds. 6.99 *(978-1-84148-609-3(4))* Barefoot Bks., Inc.

Blackstone, Stella & Meza-Riedewald, Leticia. Oso Bajo el Sol. Harter, Debbie, illus. 2009. (SPA & ENG.). 24p. (J). (gr. -1-1). pap. 6.99 *(978-1-84686-389-9(9))* Barefoot Bks., Inc.

—Oso en un Cuadrado. Harter, Debbie, illus. 2009. (SPA & ENG.). 24p. (J). (gr. -1-k). pap. 6.99 *(978-1-84686-387-5(2))* Barefoot Bks., Inc.

Blackstone, Stella & Parker, Elizabeth. L'Ours Fait un Voyage. Harter, Debbie, illus. 2013.Tr. of Bear Takes a Trip. (FRE & ENG.). 24p. (J). (gr. k-1). pap. 6.99 *(978-1-84686-946-4(3))* Barefoot Bks., Inc.

Blahitka, Vira. Joad the Toad. 2013. 32p. pap. *(978-1-4602-1881-5(7))* FriesenPress.

Blake, Quentin. Quentin Blake's ABC. 2014. lib. bdg. 24.50 *(978-0-606-31770-2(8),* Turtleback) Turtleback Bks.

Blake, Stephanie J. My Rotten Friend. Epelbaum, Mariano, illus. 2015. (ENG.). 32p. (J). (gr. -1-3). 16.99 *(978-0-8075-5327-5(1))* Whitman, Albert & Co.

Bland, Nick. Some Dads. 2017. (ENG., Illus.). 24p. (J). (gr. -1-1). 9.95 *(978-0-7624-6199-8(3),* Running Pr.) Running Pr. Bk. Pubs.

—The Very Cranky Bear. Bland, Nick, illus. 2014. (ENG., Illus.). 32p. (J). (gr. -1-k). 16.99 *(978-0-545-61269-2(1),* Orchard Bks.) Scholastic, Inc.

Blatt, Jane. Books Always Everywhere. 2014. (ENG., Illus.). 32p. (J). (gr. -1-2). 16.99 *(978-0-385-37506-1(9),* Random Hse. Bks. for Young Readers) Random Hse. Children's Bks.

—Books Always Everywhere. Massini, Sarah, illus. 2013. (J). *(978-0-385-37535-1(2))* Random Hse., Inc.

Blechman, Nicholas. Night Light. 2013. (ENG.). 48p. (J). (gr. -1-k). 16.99 *(978-0-545-46263-1(0))* Scholastic, Inc.

Blevins, James. The Crones. Whittaker, Stephen, illus. 2008. 36p. pap. 24.95 *(978-1-60610-259-6(1))* America Star Bks.

Bliss, Ryan T. Mooseclumps. Bliss, Ryan T., illus. 2013. (Illus.). 58p. 15.99 *(978-0-615-75521-2(6))* Artsy Bee, LLC.

Blomgren, Jennifer. Where Do I Sleep? A Pacific Northwest Lullaby. Gabriel, Andrea, illus. 2008. (ENG.). 20p. (J). (gr. k-k). pap. 10.99 *(978-1-57061-593-1(4),* Little Bigfoot) Sasquatch Bks.

Bloom, Susan & Bertram, Debbie. The Best Place to Read. Garland, Michael, illus. 2007. (ENG.). 32p. (J). (gr. -1-2). pap. 7.99 *(978-0-375-83757-9(4),* Dragonfly Bks.) Random Hse. Children's Bks.

Bloom, Suzanne. We Keep a Pig in the Parlor. 2004. (ENG., Illus.). 24p. (J). (gr. k-2). reprint ed. pap. 9.95 *(978-1-59078-084-8(1))* Boyds Mills Pr.

Bloom, Suzanne, illus. Number Slumber. 2016. (ENG.). 40p. (J). (gr. -1-k). 16.95 *(978-1-62979-557-7(7))* Boyds Mills Pr.

Blowers, Norman. Christmas with Carly. 2008. 16p. pap. 11.50 *(978-1-60693-337-4(X),* Strategic Bk. Publishing) Strategic Book Publishing & Rights Agency (SBPRA).

Bloxam, Frances. Beau Beaver Goes to Town. Sollers, Jim, illus. 2009. (ENG.). 32p. (J). (gr. -1-3). 16.95 *(978-0-89272-792-6(6))* Down East Bks.

Bluemle, Elizabeth. Dogs on the Bed. Wilsdorf, Anne, illus. 2013. (ENG.). 32p. (J). (gr. -1-2). pap. 6.99 *(978-0-7636-6736-8(6))* Candlewick Pr.

—How Do You Wokka-Wokka? Cecil, Randy, illus. 2012. (ENG.). 32p. (J). (gr. -1-2). pap. 6.99 *(978-0-7636-6085-7(X))* Candlewick Pr.

—Tap Tap Boom Boom. Karas, G. Brian, illus. 2014. (ENG.). 32p. (J). (gr. -1-2). 16.99 *(978-0-7636-5696-6(8))* Candlewick Pr.

Blum, Denise. Anything Is Possible: The Ben Carson Story. Rea, Nathan, illus. 2015. (ENG.). 28p. (J). pap. 10.00 *(978-0-9899479-1-6(2))* Mainstay Publishing.

Bock, Suzanne, illus. Meet the Angels l.t. ed. 2004. 10p. (J). bds. 12.99 *(978-0-9758709-4-5(7),* 13401) Journey Stone Creations, LLC.

Bodoh, Tony. Hannah's Animal Farm. 2008. 28p. pap. 14.95 *(978-1-4327-2046-9(5))* Outskirts Pr., Inc.

Boedoe, Geefwee. Arrowville. Boedoe, Geefwee, illus. 2004. (Illus.). 40p. (J). (gr. -1-2). 16.89 *(978-0-06-055599-3(8),* Geringer, Laura Book) HarperCollins Pubs.

Bogart, Jo Ellen. Count Your Chickens. Smith, Lori Joy, illus. 2017. (ENG.). 32p. (J). (-k). 16.99 *(978-1-77049-792-4(7),* Tundra Bks.) Tundra Bks. CAN. Dist: Penguin Random Hse. LLC.

Bolam, Emily, illus. Under the Sea. 2013. (Peekabooks Ser.). (ENG.). 8p. (J). (gr. -1 — 1). bds. 5.99 *(978-0-7641-6630-3(1))* Barron's Educational Series, Inc.

Bompart, Juanita A. Anna Pinnelope Poolah. 2011. 32p. pap. 16.95 *(978-1-4497-2335-4(7),* WestBow Pr.) Author Solutions, Inc.

Bond, Juliana. Pixie Tales the Wobbly Tooth. 2005. 30p. spiral bd. 12.08 *(978-1-4116-6046-5(3))* Lulu Pr., Inc.
—Salad Cream. 2005. 31p. spiral bd. 12.28 *(978-1-4116-6047-2(1))* Lulu Pr., Inc.
Bond, Michael. Paddington Bear Goes to Market. Alley, R. W., illus. 2014. (Paddington Ser.). (ENG.). 14p. (J). (gr. -1-3). bds. 6.99 *(978-0-06-231722-3(9)*, HarperFestival) HarperCollins Pubs.
Boniface, William. The Adventures of Max the Minnow. Sullivan, Don, illus. 2015. (ENG.). 26p. (J). bds. 9.99 *(978-1-4494-6490-5(4))* Andrews McMeel Publishing.
Bonnett-Rampersaud, Louise. Never Ask a Bear. Barrette, Doris, illus. 2009. (ENG.). 32p. (J). (gr. -1-1). 16.99 *(978-0-06-112876-9(7))* HarperCollins Pubs.
Bookins, Daddy. Outside with Lil Boo. Piotti, Dania, illus. 2012. 38p. pap. 13.50 *(978-0-9848019-3-0(6))* Inkwell Books LLC.
Boom Boom. 2014. (ENG., Illus.). 40p. (J). (gr. -1-3). 17.99 *(978-1-4424-3412-7(0)*, Beach Lane Bks.) Beach Lane Bks.
Bostrom, Kathleen Long. The View at the Zoo. Francis, Guy, illus. 2011. 32p. (J). (gr. -1-3). 14.99 *(978-0-8249-5629-5(X)*, Ideal Pubns.) Worthy Publishing.
—A View at the Zoo. Francis, Guy, illus. 2015. (J). pap. *(978-0-8249-5669-1(9)*, Ideal Pubns.) Worthy Publishing.
Bousquet, Anthea. Counting St. Lucian Style: A delightfully illustrated counting rhyme set in the Caribbean island of St. Lucia. Sandiford, Ted, illus. 2011. 16p. (J). pap. *(978-976-8238-01-6(1))* Maryli Pubs.
Bove, Candace Scobie. Calypso: A Day in the Life of a Puppy. 2012. 24p. 24.95 *(978-1-4626-4122-2(9))* America Star Bks.
Bowen, Anne. I Know an Old Teacher. Gammell, Stephen, illus. 2008. (ENG.). 32p. (J). (gr. k-3). 16.95 *(978-0-8225-7984-7(7)*, Carolrhoda Bks.) Lerner Publishing Group.
—Que Hacen los Maestros? (Despues de Que Te Vas de la Escuela) Gott, Barry, illus. 2007. (Ediciones Lerner Single Titles Ser.). (SPA.). 32p. (J). (gr. k-3). 16.95 *(978-0-8225-6264-1(2)*, Ediciones Lerner) Lerner Publishing Group.
—What Do Teachers Do (After You Leave School)? Gott, Barry, illus. 2006. (ENG.). 32p. (J). (gr. k-3). 16.95 *(978-1-57505-922-8(3)*, Carolrhoda Bks.) Lerner Publishing Group.
Bower, Kevin. Gilbert Grumble. 2009. (Illus.). 28p. pap. 13.99 *(978-1-4490-3841-0(7))* AuthorHouse.
Bowes, Lisa. Lucy Tries Short Track, 1 vol. Hearne, James, illus. 2016. (Lucy Tries Sports Ser.). (ENG.). 32p. (J). (gr. -1-3). pap. 12.95 *(978-1-4598-1025-9(2))* Orca Bk. Pubs. USA.
Bowie, C. W. Busy Fingers. Willingham, Fred, illus. 2004. (ENG.). 28p. (J). (gr. -1 — 1). bds. 7.95 *(978-1-58089-048-9(2))* Charlesbridge Publishing, Inc.
Bowles, Coy. When You're Feeling Sick. Elkerton, Andy, illus. 2017. (ENG.). 32p. (J). (gr. -1-2). 12.99 *(978-0-399-55286-1(3)*, Doubleday Bks. for Young Readers) Random Hse. Children's Bks.
Bowman, Crystal. The Best Thing about My Birthday. 2014. (Happy Day Ser.). (ENG.). 16p. (J). pap. 2.49 *(978-1-4143-9485-5(3))* Tyndale Hse. Pubs.
—My Christmas Stocking: Filled with God's Love, 1 vol. Gevry, Claudine, illus. 2015. (ENG.). 14p. (J). bds. 6.99 *(978-0-310-73823-7(7))* Zonderkidz.
—My Happy Pumpkin: God's Love Shining Through Me, 1 vol. 2014. (ENG.). 14p. (J). bds. 6.99 *(978-0-310-73828-2(8))* Zonderkidz.
—Thank You, God, for This Day. Fletcher, Rusty, illus. 2014. (Happy Day Ser.). (ENG.). 16p. (J). pap. 2.49 *(978-1-4143-9486-2(1))* Tyndale Hse. Pubs.
Bowman, Crystal, et al. My Read & Rhyme Bible Storybook. Engel, Christiane, illus. 2009. (ENG.). 368p. (J). (gr. -1-2). 17.99 *(978-1-4143-2016-8(7)*, Tyndale Kids) Tyndale Hse. Pubs.
Boynton, Colin. Tommy & the Dust Devils. 2010. 19p. 16.50 *(978-0-9559931-2-1(1))* Boynton, Colin GBR. Dist: Lulu Pr., Inc.
Boynton, Sandra. Are You a Cow? Boynton, Sandra, illus. 2012. (ENG., Illus.). 16p. (J). (gr. -1-k). bds. 5.99 *(978-1-4424-1733-5(1)*, Little Simon) Little Simon.
—Barnyard Dance! (Lap Edition) 2011. (ENG., Illus.). 22p. (J). (gr. k — 1). bds. 11.95 *(978-0-7611-6616-0(5)*, 16616) Workman Publishing Co., Inc.
—Belly Button Book! (Lap Edition) 2011. (ENG., Illus.). 24p. (J). (gr. k — 1). bds. 11.95 *(978-0-7611-6618-4(1)*, 16618) Workman Publishing Co., Inc.
—The Bunny Rabbit Show! Boynton, Sandra, illus. 2014. (ENG., Illus.). 24p. (J). (gr. -1). bds. 6.95 *(978-0-7611-8060-9(5)*, 18060) Workman Publishing Co., Inc.
—Eek! Halloween! 2016. (ENG., Illus.). 24p. (J). bds. 6.95 *(978-0-7611-9300-5(6))* Workman Publishing Co., Inc.
—The Going to Bed Book. Boynton, Sandra, illus. (ENG., Illus.). (J). 2006. 14p. bds. 12.95 *(978-1-4169-2794-5(8))* 30th anniv. ed. 2012. 18p. (gr. -1-3). bds. 7.99 *(978-1-4424-5409-5(1))* Little Simon. (Little Simon).
—Hey! Wake Up! 2004. (Illus.). (J). (gr. -1-18). spiral bd., bds. *(978-0-616-14611-8(6))* Canadian National Institute for the Blind/Institut National Canadien pour les Aveugles.
—Hippos Go Berserk! Boynton, Sandra, illus. 2009. (ENG., Illus.). 32p. (J). 9.99 *(978-1-4169-9619-4(2)*, Little Simon) Little Simon.
—Moo, Baa, la la La! Boynton, Sandra, illus. 2012. (ENG., Illus.). 18p. (J). (gr. -1 — 1). bds. 7.99 *(978-1-4424-5410-1(5)*, Little Simon) Little Simon.
—Moo, Baa, La La La! braille ed. 2004. (J). (gr. 1). spiral bd., bds. *(978-0-616-03082-0(7))* Canadian National Institute for the Blind/Institut National Canadien pour les Aveugles.
—Muu - Beee - iAsi Fue! Boynton, Sandra, illus. 2003. (SPA., Illus.). 14p. (J). (gr. -1 — 1). bds. 5.99 *(978-0-689-86302-8(0)*, Libros Para Ninos) Libros Para Ninos.
—Pajama Time! (Lap Edition) 2011. (ENG., Illus.). 20p. (J). (gr. k — 1). bds. 11.95 *(978-0-7611-6617-7(3)*, 16617) Workman Publishing Co., Inc.
—Sandra Boynton's Moo, Baa, la la La! Boynton, Sandra, illus. 2009. (ENG., Illus.). 16p. (J). bds. 16.99 *(978-1-4169-5035-6(4)*, Little Simon) Little Simon.
—Snuggle Puppy! 2003. (ENG., Illus.). 24p. (J). (gr. k — 1). bds. 6.95 *(978-0-7611-3067-3(5)*, 13067) Workman Publishing Co., Inc.
—Tickle Time! 2012. (ENG., Illus.). 24p. (J). (gr. k-1). bds. 6.95 *(978-0-7611-6883-6(4)*, 16883) Workman Publishing Co., Inc.
Bradford, William. Jeremy Mcbright Was Afraid of the Night. 2006. (Illus.). 36p. (J). lib. bdg. 13.95 *(978-0-9672585-2-2(9))* CyPress Pubns.
Bradley, Timothy. Teddy Bear, Teddy Bear, Say Good Night, 1 vol. Medina, Conni & Stark, Kristy, eds. 2009. (Early Childhood Themes Ser.). (ENG., Illus.). 16p. (J). (gr. -1-2). pap. 19.99 *(978-1-4333-1472-8(X))* Shell Educational Publishing.
Bradley, Timothy J. Teddy Bear, Teddy Bear, Say Good Night, 1 vol. 2009. (Early Childhood Themes Ser.). (ENG., Illus.). 16p. (J). (gr. -1-2). pap. 6.99 *(978-1-4333-1471-1(1))* Teacher Created Materials, Inc.
Brady, Karen. God Is Great: A Collection of 13 Story Book Poems, 1. l.t. ed. 2004. (Illus.). 20p. (J). 12.50 *(978-0-9754169-0-7(1))* Bradybooks.biz.
Braeuner, Shellie. The Great Dog Wash. Neubecker, Robert, illus. 2009. (ENG.). 32p. (J). (gr. -1-1). 15.99 *(978-1-4169-7116-0(5)*, Simon & Schuster Bks. For Young Readers) Simon & Schuster Bks. For Young Readers.
Bramsen, Carin. Hey, Duck! 2013. (ENG., Illus.). 40p. (J). (gr. -1-2). 17.99 *(978-0-375-86990-7(5)*, Random Hse. Bks. for Young Readers) Random Hse. Children's Bks.
Bramwell, Wendie, et al. The Friendship Alphabet. Ziegler, Michael, illus. Ziegler, Michael, photos by. 2003. 32p. (J). pap. *(978-0-9741388-3-1(5))* Committee for Children.
Brannon, Pat. Has a Donkey Ever Brought You Breakfast in Bed? Demming, Karen, illus. 2012. 38p. pap. 10.00 *(978-1-938634-90-1(X))* Freedom of Speech Publishing, Inc.
Brantz, Loryn. Feminist Baby. Brantz, Loryn, illus. 2017. (ENG., Illus.). 22p. (J). (gr. -1 — 1). 12.99 *(978-1-4847-7858-6(8))* Disney Pr.
Braud, Alexis. Parade, 1 vol. 2016. (ENG., Illus.). 32p. (J). (gr. -1-3). 16.99 *(978-1-4556-2148-4(X))* Pelican Publishing Co., Inc.
Braun, Sebastien. I Love You More. Braun, Sebastien, illus. 2013. (ENG., Illus.). 20p. (J). (gr. -1). bds. 8.95 *(978-1-58925-620-0(4))* Tiger Tales.
—One Sleepy Night. 2013. (Padded Board Books Ser.). (ENG.). 20p. (J). bds. 8.95 *(978-1-58925-619-4(0))* Tiger Tales Pubns.
Breathed, Berkeley. Edwurd Fudwupper Fibbed Big. Breathed, Berkeley, illus. 2003. (ENG., Illus.). 40p. (J). (gr. 1-4). pap. 8.00 *(978-0-316-14425-4(8))* Little, Brown Bks. for Young Readers.
Bremmer, Patricia A. The Christmas Westie. 2007. 48p. (J). kivar 17.99 *(978-0-9745884-5-2(8))* Windcall Publishing.
Bremner-Lewis, P. L. My Friend, the Unicorn. 2009. 28p. pap. 12.95 *(978-1-4389-8966-2(0))* AuthorHouse.
Brennan, Eileen. Bad Astrid. Dunnick, Regan, illus. 2013. (ENG.). 40p. (J). (gr. -1-2). 15.99 *(978-0-375-85580-1(7)*, Random Hse. Bks. for Young Readers) Random Hse. Children's Bks.
—Bad Astrid. Dunnick, Regan, illus. 2013. (J). *(978-0-449-81427-7(0))* Random Hse., Inc.
Brennan, Martin. I Saw It in the Garden. Monroe, Michael Glenn, illus. 2006. 32p. (J). (gr. -1-3). 17.95 *(978-1-58726-296-8(7)*, Mitten Pr.) Ann Arbor Editions LLC.
Brennan-Nelson, Denise. Buzzy the Bumblebee. Monroe, Michael Glenn, illus. 2003. (ENG.). 32p. (J). (gr. k-6). pap. 6.95 *(978-1-58536-166-3(6))* Sleeping Bear Pr.
—He's Been a Monster All Day. Moore, Cyd, illus. 2013. (ENG.). 32p. (J). (gr. -1-1). 14.99 *(978-1-58536-827-3(X)*, 202363) Sleeping Bear Pr.
Brennan, Sarah. A Dirty Story. Harrison, Harry, illus. 2012. (ENG.). 24p. (J). 21.95 *(978-1-937160-26-5(2))* Eliassen Creative.
—An Even Dirtier Story. Harrison, Harry, illus. 2012. (ENG.). 24p. (J). 21.95 *(978-1-937160-27-2(0))* Eliassen Creative.
—The Tale of a Dark Horse. 2013. (ENG., Illus.). 32p. (J). 24.95 *(978-1-937160-57-9(2))* Eliassen Creative.
—The Tale of Chester Choi. Harrison, Harry, illus. 2013. (ENG.). 32p. (J). 24.95 *(978-1-937160-16-6(5))* Eliassen Creative.
—The Tale of Oswald Ox. Harrison, Harry, illus. 2012. (ENG.). 32p. (J). *(978-1-937160-24-1(6))* Auspicious Times.
—The Tale of Pin Yin Panda. Harrison, Harry, illus. 2012. (ENG.). 32p. (J). 24.95 *(978-1-937160-15-9(7))* Eliassen Creative.
—The Tale of Rhonda Rabbit. Harrison, Harry, illus. 2012. (ENG.). 32p. (J). 24.95 *(978-1-937160-22-7(X))* Eliassen Creative.
—The Tale of Rodney Ram. Harrison, Harry, illus. 2014. (J). ***(978-1-937160-60-9(2))*** Eliassen Creative.
—The Tale of Run Run Rat. Harrison, Harry, illus. 2012. (ENG.). 32p. (J). 24.95 *(978-1-937160-25-8(4))* Eliassen Creative.
—The Tale of Temujin. Harrison, Harry, illus. 2012. (ENG.). 32p. (J). *(978-1-937160-23-4(8))* Auspicious Times.
Brenner, Barbara. Good Morning, Garden. Ortakales, Denise, illus. 2004. (ENG.). 32p. (J). (gr. -1-k). 15.95 *(978-1-55971-888-2(9))* Cooper Square Publishing Llc.
Brenner, Barbara & Sweet, Melissa. The Plant That Kept on Growing. 2015. (ENG., Illus.). 34p. (J). pap. 11.95 *(978-1-899694-59-4(5)*, ipicturebooks) ibooks, Inc.
Brenner, Emily. On the First Day of Grade School. Whatley, Bruce, illus. 2004. 32p. (J). (gr. -1-1). lib. bdg. 16.89 *(978-0-06-051041-1(2))* HarperCollins Pubs.
Brett, Jan. The Twelve Days of Christmas. Brett, Jan, illus. 2004. (ENG., Illus.). 32p. (J). (gr. -1 — 1). bds. 7.99 *(978-0-399-24329-5(1)*, G.P. Putnam's Sons Books for Young Readers) Penguin Young Readers Group.
BrickHouse Education. Guess Who: Whose Silhouette Is This? 2010. (J). pap. 8.99 *(978-1-59835-139-2(7))* Cambridge BrickHouse, Inc.
BrickHouse Education & Colón, Priscilla. Wild ABC's. 2009. 40p. (J). 8.99 *(978-1-59835-116-3(8))* Cambridge BrickHouse, Inc.
Briggs-Greenberg, Ruthie. Felicity the Dragon. 2015. (ENG., Illus.). 32p. (J). (gr. -1-2). 15.95 *(978-1-63076-062-5(5))* Taylor Trade Publishing.
Briggs, Kelly Paul. Lighthouse Lullaby. 2008. (ENG., Illus.). 32p. (J). (gr. -1-17). pap. 9.95 *(978-0-89272-549-6(4))* Down East Bks.
Bright, Rachel. The Lion Inside. Field, Jim, illus. 2016. (ENG.). 32p. (J). (gr. -1-k). 16.99 *(978-0-545-87350-5(9)*, Scholastic Pr.) Scholastic, Inc.
—Side by Side. Gliori, Debi, illus. 2015. (ENG.). 32p. (J). (gr. -1-k). 17.99 *(978-0-545-81326-6(3)*, Scholastic Pr.) Scholastic, Inc.
Briley, Randy W. Big Pigs & Sock Dances. 2013. 36p. pap. 10.99 *(978-0-9896269-2-7(X))* Raven Mad Studios.
Brimhall Snow, Virginia. Summer Walk, 1 vol. 2016. (ENG., Illus.). 32p. (J). 16.99 *(978-1-4236-4215-2(5))* Gibbs Smith, Publisher.
Brimner, Larry Dane. Monkey Math. Kulka, Joe, illus. 2007. (Rookie Reader Skill Set Ser.). (ENG.). 32p. (J). (gr. k-2). pap. 4.95 *(978-0-531-13850-2(X))* Scholastic Library Publishing.
Brisson, Pat. Before We Eat: From Farm to Table, 1 vol. Azarian, Mary, illus. 2014. (ENG.). 32p. (gr. k-3). 16.95 *(978-0-88448-352-6(5)*, 884352) Tilbury Hse. Pubs.
Britland, Jan. The Adventures of Rodger Dodger Dog. Swaim, Michael, illus. 2009. 40p. pap. 15.95 *(978-1-936051-23-6(0))* Peppertree Pr., The.
Broach, Elise. Barnyard Baby. Doerrfeld, Cori, illus. 2013. (Baby Seasons Ser.). (ENG.). 14p. (J). (gr. -1 — 1). bds. 7.99 *(978-0-316-21203-8(2))* Little, Brown Bks. for Young Readers.
—Seashore Baby. 2010. (Baby Seasons Ser.). (ENG., Illus.). 14p. (J). (gr. -1 — 1). bds. 7.99 *(978-0-316-04303-8(6))* Little, Brown Bks. for Young Readers.
Broadbent, Tom & Kosmo, Lisa. Henrietta. 2009. pap. *(978-1-61623-033-3(9))* Independent Pub.
Brochmann, Holly & Bowen, Leah. A Feel Better Book for Little Worriers. Ng-Benitez, Shirley, illus. 2017. 32p. (J). 15.95 ***(978-1-4338-2718-1(2)***, Magination Pr.) American Psychological Assn.
Brodsky, Kathy. A CatFish Tale. Bennett, Cameron, illus. 2012. (ENG.). (J). 19.99 *(978-0-9828529-3-4(2))* Helpingwords.
—Just Sniffing Around. Bennett, Cameron, illus. 2009. (ENG.). 40p. 19.99 *(978-0-578-03620-5(7))* Helpingwords.
—My Bent Tree. Bennett, Cameron, illus. 2008. (ENG.). 44p. (J). 19.95 *(978-0-615-16066-5(2))* Helpingwords.
Brody, Lazer. The Worry Worm. Shapiro, Rebecca, illus. 2007. 26p. (J). 26.95 *(978-0-9797530-1-5(5))* Kalcom Publishing.
Brooks, David. You Can Count at the Ocean. 2005. (You Can Count Ser.). (ENG., Illus.). 24p. (J). (gr. -1 — 1). bds. 7.95 *(978-1-55971-930-8(3))* Cooper Square Publishing Llc.
—You Can Count in the Jungle. 2005. (You Can Count Ser.). (ENG., Illus.). 24p. (J). (gr. -1 — 1). bds. 6.95 *(978-1-55971-931-5(1))* Cooper Square Publishing Llc.
Brosnan, Paris. Billy Bee - Sugarplums & Honey. 2017. (ENG., Illus.). 27p. (J). pap. 13.95 ***(978-1-78710-075-6(8)***, 4d1efa56-0d47-487a-bc8e-b11fdf88ec5d) Austin, Stan AUS. Dist: Bookmasters Distribution.
Brouillard, Anne. The Bathtub Prima Donna. Brouillard, Anne, illus. 2004. (Illus.). 24p. (J). (gr. k-4). reprint ed. 13.00 *(978-0-7567-7755-5(0))* DIANE Publishing Co.
Brown, Calef. Boy Wonders. Brown, Calef, illus. 2011. (ENG., Illus.). 40p. (J). (gr. -1-3). 16.99 *(978-1-4169-7877-0(1)*, Atheneum Bks. for Young Readers) Simon & Schuster Children's Publishing.
—Pirateria: The Wonderful Plunderful Pirate Emporium. Brown, Calef, illus. 2012. (ENG., Illus.). 40p. (J). (gr. -1-3). 16.99 *(978-1-4169-7878-7(X)*, Atheneum Bks. for Young Readers) Simon & Schuster Children's Publishing.
Brown, Gina Bates. Zen & Bodhi's Snowy Day. Hinder, Sarah Jane, illus. 2014. (ENG.). 24p. (J). 15.95 *(978-1-61429-165-7(9))* Wisdom Pubns.
Brown, Jahla. Nathan Is Nathan. 2009. (ENG., Illus.). 20p. (J). pap. 19.95 *(978-0-9778083-8-0(6))* Everlasting Publishing.
Brown, Jason Robert. Tickety Tock. GrandPré, Mary, illus. 2008. 32p. (J). (gr. -1-3). lib. bdg. 18.89 *(978-0-06-078753-0(8)*, Geringer, Laura Book) HarperCollins Pubs.
Brown, Margaret Wise. Christmas in the Barn. Dewdney, Anna, illus. 2016. 40p. (J). (gr. -1-3). 17.99 *(978-0-06-237986-3(0))* HarperCollins Pubs.
—Christmas in the Barn. Goode, Diane, illus. 2007. (ENG.). 32p. (J). (gr. -1-3). per. 7.99 *(978-0-06-052636-8(X))* HarperCollins Pubs.
—The Golden Bunny. Weisgard, Leonard, illus. 2015. (ENG.). 32p. (J). (-k). 16.99 *(978-0-385-39274-7(5)*, Golden Bks.) Random Hse. Children's Bks.
—Goodnight Moon. Hurd, Clement, illus. (J). (gr. -1 — 1). 2012. (ENG.). 8p. pap. 14.99 *(978-0-06-076224-7(1)*, HarperFestival) 2007. (ENG.). 32p. pap. 24.99 *(978-0-06-111977-4(6)*, HarperFestival) 2005. 32p. lib. bdg. 18.89 *(978-0-06-077586-5(6))* 60th anniv. ed. 2007. (ENG.). 32p. 18.99 *(978-0-06-077585-8(8))* HarperCollins Pubs.
—Goodnight Moon. 2007. (J). (gr. -1-2). lib. bdg. 18.40 *(978-0-8085-9386-7(2)*, Turtleback) Turtleback Bks.
—Goodnight Moon 123: A Counting Book. Hurd, Clement, illus. 2007. (J). (ENG.). 32p. (gr. -1-k). 16.99 *(978-0-06-112593-5(8))*; 32p. (gr. -1-k). lib. bdg. 17.89 *(978-0-06-112594-2(6))*; *(978-1-4287-4853-8(9))* HarperCollins Pubs.
—Goodnight Moon 123/Buenas Noches, Luna 123: A Counting Book/un Libro para Contar. Hurd, Clement, illus. 2007. (ENG & SPA.). 32p. (J). (gr. -1-k). 16.99 *(978-0-06-117325-7(8)*, Rayo) HarperCollins Pubs.
—Margaret Wise Brown's the Golden Bunny. Weisgard, Leonard, illus. 2015. (ENG.). 32p. (J). (-k). lib. bdg. 19.99 *(978-0-375-97372-7(9)*, Golden Bks.) Random Hse. Children's Bks.
—Sleepy ABC. Katz, Karen, illus. 2009. (ENG.). 40p. (J). (gr. -1-3). 16.99 *(978-0-06-128863-0(2))* HarperCollins Pubs.
—Sleepy ABC Board Book. Katz, Karen, illus. 2016. 32p. (J). (gr. -1 — 1). bds. 7.99 *(978-0-06-233793-1(9)*, HarperFestival) HarperCollins Pubs.
—Two Little Trains. Dillon, Leo & Dillon, Diane, illus. 2003. (ENG.). 32p. (J). (gr. -1-k). pap. 7.99 *(978-0-06-443568-0(7))* HarperCollins Pubs.
—Where Have You Been? Dillon, Leo & Dillon, Diane, illus. 2004. (ENG.). 32p. (J). (gr. -1-1). 16.99 *(978-0-06-028378-0(5))* HarperCollins Pubs.
—Wish upon a Dream. Cooke, Charlotte, illus. 2014. (ENG.). 24p. (J). (gr. -1-3). 7.99 *(978-1-4723-4531-8(2))* Parragon, Inc.
Brown, Skila. To Stay Alive: Mary Ann Graves & the Tragic Journey of the Donner Party. 2016. (ENG., Illus.). 304p. (J). (gr. 5-9). 17.99 *(978-0-7636-7811-1(2))* Candlewick Pr.
Brown, Tameka Fryer. Around Our Way on Neighbors' Day. Riley-Webb, Charlotte, illus. 2010. (ENG.). 32p. (J). (gr. k-2). 16.95 *(978-0-8109-8971-9(9)*, Abrams Bks. for Young Readers) Abrams, Inc.
—My Cold Plum Lemon Pie Bluesy Mood. Evans, Shane, illus. 2013. (ENG.). 40p. (J). (gr. -1-2). 16.99 *(978-0-670-01285-5(8)*, Viking Books for Young Readers) Penguin Young Readers Group.
Brown, Tricia. Musher's Night Before Christmas, 1 vol. Dubac, Debra, illus. 2011. (Night Before Christmas Ser.). (ENG.). 32p. (J). (gr. k-3). 16.99 *(978-1-58980-843-0(6))* Pelican Publishing Co., Inc.
Brown-Wood, Janay & Burris, Priscilla. Grandma's Tiny House. 2017. (ENG., Illus.). 32p. (J). (-k). lib. bdg. 16.99 *(978-1-58089-712-9(6))* Charlesbridge Publishing, Inc.
Brownlow, Michael. Ten Little Princesses. Rickerty, Simon, illus. 2014. (J). *(978-1-4351-5735-4(4))* Barnes & Noble, Inc.
Brownlow, Mike. Ten Little Dinosaurs. Rickerty, Simon, illus. 2016. (Ten Little Ser.). (ENG.). 32p. (J). (gr. -1-k). pap. ***(978-1-4083-3401-0(1)***, Orchard Bks.) Hachette Children's Group GBR. Dist: Hachette Bk. Group.
Broyles, Beverly Ashley, illus. Grandmother's Alligator/Burukenge Wa Nyanya Activity Guide. 2005. (ENG & SWA.). (J). 12.95 *(978-0-9703632-7-5(3))* Wakefield Connection, The.
Bruel, Nick. A Bad Kitty Christmas. Bruel, Nick, illus. 2011. (Bad Kitty Ser.). (ENG., Illus.). 40p. (J). (gr. -1-3). 16.99 *(978-1-59643-668-8(9)*, 9781596436688) Roaring Brook Pr.
—Bad Kitty Christmas Storytime Set. unabr. ed. 2014. (ENG.). (J). 12.99 *(978-1-4272-5230-2(0)*, 9781427252302) Macmillan Audio.
—Little Red Bird. Bruel, Nick, illus. 2008. (ENG., Illus.). 32p. (J). (gr. -1-1). 17.99 *(978-1-59643-339-7(6)*, 9781596433397) Roaring Brook Pr.
Brug, Sandra Gilbert. Soccer Beat. Moseng, Elisabeth, illus. 2012. (ENG.). 32p. (J). (gr. -1-1). 16.99 *(978-1-4424-8610-2(4)*, McElderry, Margaret K. Bks.) McElderry, Margaret K. Bks.
Brunette, Steffan. Cough, Achoo, & Roar! 2013. 16p. pap. 7.99 *(978-1-4624-0632-6(7)*, Inspiring Voices) Author Solutions, Inc.
Bruton, W., illus. The Dogs' Grand Dinner Party. 2011. (American Antiquarian Society Ser.). (ENG.). 16p. (gr. 1). 24.95 *(978-1-4290-9738-3(8))* Applewood Bks.
Bryan, Ashley. Can't Scare Me! Bryan, Ashley, illus. 2013. (ENG., Illus.). 40p. (J). (gr. -1-3). 16.99 *(978-1-4424-7657-8(5)*, Atheneum Bks. for Young Readers) Simon & Schuster Children's Publishing.
—Who Built the Stable? A Nativity Poem. Bryan, Ashley, illus. 2012. (ENG., Illus.). 40p. (J). (gr. -1-3). 16.99 *(978-1-4424-0934-7(7)*, Atheneum Bks. for Young Readers) Simon & Schuster Children's Publishing.
Bryan, Sean. A Boy & His Bunny. Murphy, Tom, illus. 2011. (ENG.). 32p. (J). (gr. -1-k). 14.95 *(978-1-61145-023-1(3)*, 611023, Arcade Publishing) Skyhorse Publishing Co., Inc.
—A Girl & Her Gator. Murphy, Tom, illus. 2011. (ENG.). 32p. (J). (gr. -1-k). 14.95 *(978-1-61145-032-3(2)*, 611032, Arcade Publishing) Skyhorse Publishing Co., Inc.
—The Juggling Pug. Murphy, Tom, illus. (ENG.). 32p. (J). 2014. (-k). 12.95 *(978-1-62873-596-3(1))* 2011. (gr. -1-k). 12.95 *(978-1-61608-329-8(8)*, 608329) Skyhorse Publishing Co., Inc. (Sky Pony Pr.).
Bryan, Sean & Thomas, Evan. A Bear & His Boy. Murphy, Tom, illus. 2011. (ENG.). 32p. (J). (gr. -1-k). 14.95 *(978-1-61145-027-9(6)*, 611027, Arcade Publishing) Skyhorse Publishing Co., Inc.
Bryant, Janine. Yucky Green Beans. l.t. ed. 2005. 12p. (J). per. 5.00 *(978-0-9703474-8-0(0))* Pinnini Pubs.
Bryant, Jen. Kaleidoscope Eyes. 2010. (ENG.). 272p. (J). (gr. 3-7). 7.99 *(978-0-440-42190-0(X)*, Yearling) Random Hse. Children's Bks.
Bryant, Phoebe. What Is That in the Air? A play date with Sayde. 2009. (Illus.). 28p. pap. 12.99 *(978-1-4490-2209-9(X))* AuthorHouse.
Buble, Brandee. O'Shae the Octopus. Liska, Eliska, illus. 2014. (ENG.). 32p. (J). (gr. -1-3). 15.95 *(978-1-927018-56-9(0))* Simply Read Bks. CAN. Dist: Ingram Publisher Services.
Buchanan, Pendella. Layers. 2011. (Illus.). 16p. pap. 12.52 *(978-1-4567-8749-3(7))* AuthorHouse.
Buchanan, Sue, et al. Mud Pie Annie, 1 vol. Allen, Joy, illus. 2008. (I Can Read! Ser.). (ENG.). 32p. (J). (gr. -1-1). pap. 3.99 *(978-0-310-71572-6(5))* Zonderkidz.
Buckley, Richard. The Foolish Tortoise. Carle, Eric, illus. (World of Eric Carle Ser.). (ENG.). 24p. (J). (gr. -1-3). 2013. pap. 9.99 *(978-1-4424-6638-8(3))* 2009. bds. 7.99 *(978-1-4169-7916-6(6))* Little Simon. (Little Simon).
—The Foolish Tortoise. Carle, Eric, illus. 2015. (World of Eric Carle Ser.). (ENG.). 24p. (J). (gr. k-2). pap. 3.99 *(978-1-4814-3577-2(9)*, Simon Spotlight) Simon Spotlight.
—The Foolish Tortoise: Lap Edition. Carle, Eric, illus. 2013. (World of Eric Carle Ser.). (ENG.). 24p. (J). (gr. -1-k). bds. 12.99 *(978-1-4424-8990-5(1)*, Little Simon) Little Simon.
—The Greedy Python. Carle, Eric, illus. 2012. (World of Eric Carle Ser.). (ENG.). 24p. (J). (gr. -1-1). 16.99 *(978-1-4424-4577-2(7))*; pap. 3.99 *(978-1-4424-4576-5(9))* Simon Spotlight. (Simon Spotlight).
—The Greedy Python. 2012. (Eric Carle Ready-To-Read Ser.). lib. bdg. 13.55 *(978-0-606-26357-3(8)*, Turtleback) Turtleback Bks.
—The Greedy Python: Lap Edition. Carle, Eric, illus. 2013. (World of Eric Carle Ser.). (ENG.). 24p. (J). (gr. -1-k). bds. 12.99 *(978-1-4424-8991-2(X)*, Little Simon) Little Simon.
Buckner, Andrew. Grand Poppa's Favorite Chair: No One Is As Special As You. Welker, Matthew S., illus. 2011. 48p. pap. 24.95 *(978-1-4560-8294-9(9))* America Star Bks.
Budde, Nadia. Bristly Hair & I Don't Care! 2015. (ENG., Illus.). 40p. (J). 15.95 *(978-0-7358-4205-2(1))* North-South Bks., Inc.
Budds, Laura. Have You Ever Seen a Bear with a Purple Smile? Zimmerman, Kadie, illus. 2013. 16p. (J). 16.95 *(978-1-59152-114-3(9))* Farcountry Pr.

S

Budge, Robyn E. Whoda Thunkit: Rhyming Tales for the Young & Not So. 2013. 180p. pap. 15.95 *(978-1-4787-2097-3(2))* Outskirts Pr., Inc.

Buehner, Caralyn. Merry Christmas, Mr. Mouse. Buehner, Mark, illus. 2015. (ENG.). 40p. (J). (gr. -1-k). 17.99 *(978-0-8037-4010-5(7),* Dial Bks) Penguin Young Readers Group.

—Snowmen All Year. Buehner, Mark, illus. 2010. (ENG.). 32p. (J). (gr. -1-2). 16.99 *(978-0-8037-3383-1(6),* Dial Bks) Penguin Young Readers Group.

—Snowmen All Year Board Book. Buehner, Mark, illus. 2012. (ENG.). 28p. (J). (gr. -1-k). bds. 6.99 *(978-0-8037-3905-5(2),* Dial Bks) Penguin Young Readers Group.

—Snowmen at Christmas. Buehner, Mark, illus. (ENG.). (J). (gr. -1-k). 2010. 28p. bds. 6.99 *(978-0-8037-3551-4(0))* 2005. 32p. 16.99 *(978-0-8037-2995-7(2))* Penguin Young Readers Group. (Dial Bks).

—Snowmen at Night. Buehner, Mark, illus. 2004. (ENG.). 26p. (J). (gr. -1-k). bds. 6.99 *(978-0-8037-3041-0(1),* Dial Bks) Penguin Young Readers Group.

—Snowmen at Play. Buehner, Mark, illus. 2013. (ENG.). 16p. (J). (gr. -1-k). 6.99 *(978-0-448-47782-4(3),* Grosset & Dunlap) Penguin Young Readers Group.

—Snowmen at Work. Buehner, Mark, illus. 2012. (ENG.). 32p. (J). (gr. -1-2). 16.99 *(978-0-8037-3579-8(0),* Dial Bks) Penguin Young Readers Group.

Buell, Janet. Sail Away, Little Boat. Ishida, Jui, illus. 2006. 32p. (J). 15.95 *(978-1-57505-821-4(9),* Carolrhoda Bks.) Lerner Publishing Group.

Bugbird, Tim. Molly the Muffin Fairy. 2015. (ENG.). 32p. (J). 15.99 *(978-1-78393-466-9(2))* Make Believe Ideas GBR. Dist: Nelson, Thomas Inc.

Buhlig Meister, Victoria. Tell Me a Story, Please, Mi-Mi! 2009. 36p. pap. 16.99 *(978-1-4389-2430-4(5))* AuthorHouse.

Bullard, Lisa. Not Enough Beds! A Christmas Alphabet Book. Oeltjenbruns, Joni, illus. 2004. (Picture Bks.). 32p. (J). (gr. -1-3). 15.95 *(978-1-57505-356-1(X),* Carolrhoda Bks.) Lerner Publishing Group.

Buller, Jon & Schade, Susan. I Love You, Good Night: Lap Edition. Pons, Bernadette, illus. 2013. (ENG.). 28p. (J). (gr. -1 — 1). bds. 12.99 *(978-1-4424-8539-6(6),* Little Simon) Little Simon.

Bunting, Eve. The Baby Shower. Love, Judy, illus. 2007. (ENG.). 28p. (J). (gr. -1-2). 15.95 *(978-1-58089-139-4(X))* Charlesbridge Publishing, Inc.

—The Bones of Fred McFee. Cyrus, Kurt, illus. 2005. (ENG.). 32p. (J). (gr. -1-3). pap. 7.99 *(978-0-15-205423-6(5))* Houghton Mifflin Harcourt Publishing Co.

—Flower Garden. Hewitt, Kathryn, illus. 2004. 28p. (gr. -1-2). 17.00 *(978-0-7569-4113-0(X))* Perfection Learning Corp.

—Girls A to Z. Bloom, Suzanne, illus. 2013. (ENG.). 32p. (J). (gr. k-2). pap. 6.95 *(978-1-62091-028-3(4))* Boyds Mills Pr.

—Have You Seen My New Blue Socks? Ruzzier, Sergio, illus. 2013. (ENG.). 32p. (J). (gr. -1-3). 16.99 *(978-0-547-75267-9(9))* Houghton Mifflin Harcourt Publishing Co.

—Hey Diddle Diddle. Fraser, Mary Ann, illus. 2011. (ENG.). 32p. (J). (gr. -1-k). 16.95 *(978-1-59078-768-7(4))* Boyds Mills Pr.

—Scary, Scary Halloween, 1 vol. Brett, Jan, illus. 2013. (ENG.). 40p. (J). (gr. -1-3). audio compact disk 10.99 *(978-0-544-11114-1(1))* Houghton Mifflin Harcourt Publishing Co.

—Scary, Scary Halloween Gift Edition. Brett, Jan, illus. 2017. (ENG.). 40p. (J). (gr. -1-3). 8.99 *(978-0-544-88034-4(X),* HMH Books For Young Readers) Houghton Mifflin Harcourt Publishing Co.

—Whose Shoe? Ruzzier, Sergio, illus. 2015. (ENG.). 32p. (J). (gr. -1-3). 16.99 *(978-0-544-30210-5(9))* Houghton Mifflin Harcourt Publishing Co.

Burchfield, Cindy. Gimme, Gimme Moocher Marmots. Burchfield, Cindy, illus. 2007. (Illus.). 48p. per. 18.95 *(978-1-59858-457-8(X))* Dog Ear Publishing, LLC.

Burfoot, Ella. Betty & the Yeti. 2nd ed. 2013. (ENG., Illus.). 32p. (J). (gr. -1-k). pap. 11.99 *(978-0-330-51117-9(3))* Pan Macmillan GBR. Dist: Independent Pubs. Group.

—How to Bake a Book. 2014. (ENG., Illus.). 32p. (J). (-2). 16.99 *(978-1-4926-0651-2(0),* 9781492606512, Sourcebooks Jabberwocky) Sourcebooks, Inc.

Burg, Ann E. All the Broken Pieces. 2009. (ENG.). 240p. (J). (gr. 5-9). 16.99 *(978-0-545-08092-7(4),* Scholastic Pr.) Scholastic, Inc.

Burgess, Karin Whiting. It's Always a Good Day for Crabbing. 2005. (J). 16.95 *(978-0-9718303-4-9(7))* Flat Hammock Pr.

Burgess, Thornton W. The Adventures of Paddy the Beaver. 2008. 108p. per. 9.95 *(978-1-60312-502-4(7))* Aegypan.

Burkart, Jeff. Once Upon a Clear Dark Night. 2011. 16p. pap. 2.49 *(978-0-7586-2579-3(0))* Concordia Publishing Hse.

Burke, Arlene Avery & Hamilton, Phyllis McAllister. Grandma's Fairy Tale Museum. 2009. 40p. pap. 21.99 *(978-1-4415-0607-8(1))* Xlibris Corp.

Burke, Zoe. Charley Harper's What's in the Coral Reef? A Nature Discovery Book. 2014. 3. (ENG., Illus.). 34p. (J). 14.95 *(978-0-7649-6846-4(7))* Pomegranate Communications, Inc.

—Charley Harper's What's in the Rain Forest? A Nature Discovery Book. Harper, Charley, illus. 2013. 34p. (J). 14.95 *(978-0-7649-6584-5(0))* Pomegranate Communications, Inc.

—Charley Harper's What's in the Woods? A Nature Discovery Book. Harper, Charley, illus. 2013. (ENG.). 32p. (J). 14.95 *(978-0-7649-6453-4(4))* Pomegranate Communications, Inc.

Burleigh, Robert. Clang! Clang! Beep! Beep! Listen to the City. Giacobbe, Beppe, illus. 2009. (ENG.). 32p. (J). (gr. -1-2). 17.99 *(978-1-4169-4052-4(9),* Simon & Schuster/Paula Wiseman Bks.) Simon & Schuster/Paula Wiseman Bks.

—I Love Going Through This Book. Yaccarino, Dan, illus. Date not set. 40p. (J). (gr. -1-3). pap. 5.99 *(978-0-06-443647-2(0))* HarperCollins Pubs.

—Messenger, Messenger. Root, Barry, illus. 2011. (ENG.). 32p. (J). (gr. -1-3). pap. 16.99 *(978-1-4424-5335-7(4), Atheneum Bks. for Young Readers) Simon & Schuster Children's Publishing.*

—Night Train, Night Train. Minor, Wendell, illus. 2017. (J). lib. bdg. ***(978-1-58089-717-4(7))*** Charlesbridge Publishing, Inc.

Burleigh, Robert. Zoom! Zoom! Sounds of Things That Go in the City. Carpenter, Tad, illus. 2014. (ENG.). 32p. (J). (gr. -1-3). 17.99 *(978-1-4424-8315-6(6),* Simon & Schuster Bks. For Young Readers) Simon & Schuster Bks. For Young Readers.

Burnham, Janet Hayward. The Dragoness Mess. 2003. (Illus.). 32p. (J). (gr. k-1). pap. 12.95 *(978-0-9740743-1-3(4))* My Little Jessie Pr.

Burns, Joanne. Abigail Is a Big Girl Now. 2005. 20p. (J). 8.99 *(978-1-4116-2042-1(9))* Lulu Pr., Inc.

—Annibelle Is a Big Girl Now Weaning Two Year-Olds. 2005. 20p. 8.99 *(978-1-4116-2044-5(5))* Lulu Pr., Inc.

—No Says the Baby When You Say Yes, a book about the terrible Twos. 2005. 1p. 5.68 *(978-1-4116-3386-5(5))* Lulu Pr., Inc.

—What Is Heaven Like? 2005. 35p. (J). 10.99 *(978-1-4116-3360-5(1))* Lulu Pr., Inc.

Burow, Ginger. The Night That Was Christmas, 1 vol. 2009. 21p. pap. 24.95 *(978-1-4489-9842-5(5))* America Star Bks.

Burris, Priscilla. The Ants Go Marching: Count-and-Sing. Burris, Priscilla, illus. 2016. (ENG., Illus.). 16p. (J). (— 1). bds. 6.99 *(978-0-545-82504-7(0),* Cartwheel Bks.) Scholastic, Inc.

Burroway, Janet & Lord, John Vernon. The Giant Jam Sandwich. Lord, John Vernon, illus. 2009. (ENG., Illus.). 28p. (J). (gr. -1-3). bds. 7.99 *(978-0-547-15077-2(6))* Houghton Mifflin Harcourt Publishing Co.

—The Giant Jam Sandwich, 1 vol. 2007. (Read along Book & CD Ser.). (ENG., Illus.). 32p. (J). (gr. -1-3). audio compact disk 10.99 *(978-0-618-83952-0(6))* Houghton Mifflin Harcourt Publishing Co.

Burrows, Mark. I'll Take My Chances, 1 vol. Springer, Sally, illus. 2015. (ENG.). 32p. (J). (gr. -1-3). 16.99 *(978-1-4556-2106-4(4))* Pelican Publishing Co., Inc.

Burton, Jeffrey. The Itsy Bitsy Pilgrim. Rescek, Sanja, illus. 2016. (Itsy Bitsy Ser.). (ENG.). 16p. (J). (gr. -1 — 1). bds. 5.99 *(978-1-4814-6852-7(9),* Little Simon) Little Simon.

Burton, Katherine. One Gray Mouse. Fernandes, Kim, illus. 2006. (ENG.). 24p. (J). (gr. -1 — 1). bds. 7.95 *(978-1-55453-026-7(1))* Kids Can Pr., Ltd. CAN. Dist: Hachette Bk. Group.

Burton, Linda & Burton, Carl. Pay Attention, Emily Brown! Burton, Linda & Burton, Carl, illus. 2011. (Illus.). 32p. (J). *(978-1-60613-027-8(7))* Woodbine Hse.

Burton M.Sc., Kathryn Mac. Diarmid. Haley Honeybee: Finds the Magic Rose. Cox, Glendyne Dewhurst, illus. 2013. 50p. pap. *(978-0-9917941-0-2(9))* Burton, K. Publishing.

Burwitz, Patrick. Mia's Dogcow. 2009. 28p. pap. 13.00 *(978-1-4343-8580-2(9))* AuthorHouse.

Bush, Randall. The Caterbury Tails. Watson, Ben, illus. 2013. 60p. pap. 13.99 *(978-1-936670-75-8(5))* BorderStone Pr., LLC.

Bushar, Carol. Robby the Lion Doesn't Eat Meat. 2006. 30p. 12.96 *(978-1-4116-9113-1(0))* Lulu Pr., Inc.

Butchart, Pamela. Yikes, Ticklysaurus! Lloyd, Sam, illus. 2015. (ENG.). 32p. (J). (gr. -1-1). 18.99 *(978-1-4088-3969-0(5),* 9781408839690, Bloomsbury USA Childrens) Bloomsbury Publishing USA.

Butler, John. Bedtime in the Jungle. Butler, John, illus. 2009. (Illus.). 32p. (J). (gr. -1-1). 16.95 *(978-1-56145-486-0(9))* Peachtree Pubs.

—Can You Cuddle Like a Koala? Butler, John, illus. (Illus.). (J). (gr. k-1). 2005. (ENG.). 20p. bds. 6.95 *(978-1-56145-347-4(1))* 2003. 32p. 15.95 *(978-1-56145-298-9(X))* Peachtree Pubs.

—Can You Growl Like a Bear? Butler, John, illus. (Illus.). (J). 2012. 20p. bds. 6.95 *(978-1-56145-667-3(5))* 2007. (ENG., 32p. 15.95 *(978-1-56145-396-2(X),* Peachtree Junior) Peachtree Pubs.

—Hush, Little Ones. Butler, John, illus. 2003. (Illus.). 24p. (J). (gr. k-k). bds. 6.95 *(978-1-56145-297-2(1))* Peachtree Pubs.

Butler, John, illus. If Your Dreams Take off & Fly. 2013. (J). *(978-1-4351-4769-0(3))* Barnes & Noble, Inc.

Butler, Kristi T. A Big Surprise. Paparone, Pamela, illus. 2005. (Green Light Readers Level 1 Ser.). (ENG.). 24p. (J). (gr. -1-3). pap. 3.95 *(978-0-15-205141-9(4))* Houghton Mifflin Harcourt Publishing Co.

Butlin, Ron. Here Come the Trolls! Hutcheson, Jim, illus. 2016. (ENG.). 32p. (J). (gr. -1-2). pap. *(978-1-78027-295-5(2))* Birlinn, Ltd.

Byous, Shawn. Because I Stubbed My Toe, 1 vol. 2014. (ENG.). 32p. (gr. -1-3). pap. 6.95 *(978-1-4795-3808-9(6),* Fiction Picture Bks.) Picture Window Bks.

Cabral, Noel. Rachel's Four-Legged Friend. 2012. 24p. 24.95 *(978-1-4626-6089-6(4))* America Star Bks.

Cabrera, Jane. Baa, Baa, Black Sheep. Cabrera, Jane, illus. 2016. (ENG., Illus.). 24p. (J). (gr. -1-k). bds. 7.99 *(978-0-8234-3631-6(4))* Holiday Hse., Inc.

—Baa, Baa, Black Sheep. 2015. (ENG., Illus.). 32p. (J). (gr. -1-k). 16.95 *(978-0-8234-3388-9(9))* Holiday Hse., Inc.

—One, Two, Buckle My Shoe. 2009. (ENG., Illus.). 32p. (J). (gr. -1-k). 16.95 *(978-0-8234-2230-2(5))* Holiday Hse., Inc.

—There Was an Old Woman Who Lived in a Shoe. (ENG.). 32p. (J). (gr. -1-k). 2017. 6.99 *(978-0-8234-3771-9(X))* 2016. (Illus.). 16.95 *(978-0-8234-3554-8(7))* Holiday Hse., Inc.

Cail, Carol. It's a Zoo Around Here. 2012. (Illus.). 36p. pap. 8.99 *(978-1-60820-567-7(3))* MLR Pr., LLC.

Caldecott, Randolph. A Frog He Would A-Wooing Go. 2006. pap. *(978-1-4065-1224-3(9))* Dodo Pr.

Calmenson, Stephanie. Birthday at the Panda Palace. Cushman, Doug, illus. 2007. 32p. (J). (gr. -1-3). 15.99 *(978-0-06-052663-4(7))* HarperCollins Pubs.

—Jazzmatazz! Degen, Bruce, illus. 2008. 32p. (J). (gr. -1). lib. bdg. 17.89 *(978-0-06-077290-1(5))* HarperCollins Pubs.

—Late for School! Yoshikawa, Sachiko, illus. 2008. (ENG.). 32p. (J). (gr. -1-2). lib. bdg. 16.95 *(978-1-57505-935-8(5))* Lerner Publishing Group.

—Look! Fish! Pinillos, Puy, illus. 2016. (Look! Ser.). (ENG.). 24p. (J). (gr. -1-1). 7.99 *(978-1-4998-0166-8(1))* Little Bee Books Inc.

—No Honking Allowed. Ferrari, Antongionata, illus. 2017. (ENG.). 40p. (J). 16.95 ***(978-0-8234-3672-9(1))*** Holiday Hse., Inc.

Calmenson, Stephanie. Oopsy, Teacher! Yoshikawa, Sachiko, illus. 2012. (Carolrhoda Picture Bks.). (ENG.). 32p. (J). (gr. -1-2). lib. bdg. 16.95 *(978-0-7613-5894-7(3))* Lerner Publishing Group.

Calvert, Deanna. Las Sombras. Lester, Mike, illus. 2005. (Rookie Reader Español Ser.). (SPA & ESP.). 23p. (J). (gr. k-2). per. 4.95 *(978-0-516-24697-0(6),* Children's Pr.) Scholastic Library Publishing.

—Shadows. Lester, Mike, illus. 2004. (Rookie Readers Ser.). 23p. (J). 12.60 *(978-0-7569-4333-2(7))* Perfection Learning Corp.

Camacho, Hector, Jr. & Warburton, Dustin. Macho Dad. Monroe, Daniel, illus. 2014. (ENG.). (J). 19.99 *(978-0-9960374-3-3(8))* Dragonbrush Arts.

Cameron, Kristy. Behind the Door of Timothy Moore. Schickle, Ian, illus. 2013. 28p. pap. *(978-0-9859790-1-0(1))* LP Publishing.

Camille, Diana, illus. A Treasury of Goops: Timeless Manners for Every Generation. 2005. Orig. Title: Goops & How to Be Them. (ENG.). 45p. (J). 19.95 *(978-0-9712368-5-1(2),* 8006811891) Goops Unlimited.

Canetti, Yanitzia. ABC's of Plants. 2010. (ENG.). 40p. (J). pap. 8.99 *(978-1-59835-118-7(4),* BrickHouse Education) Cambridge BrickHouse, Inc.

—Abecedario de Plantas. 2010. (SPA.). 40p. (J). pap. 8.99 *(978-1-59835-119-4(2),* BrickHouse Education) Cambridge BrickHouse, Inc.

—Abecedario de Profesiones y Oficios. 2009. (SPA.). 40p. (J). pap. 8.99 *(978-1-59835-122-4(2),* BrickHouse Education) Cambridge BrickHouse, Inc.

—Abecedario Nutritivo. 2009. (SPA.). 40p. (J). pap. 8.99 *(978-1-59835-115-6(X),* BrickHouse Education) Cambridge BrickHouse, Inc.

—ABeCedario Salvaje. 2009. (SPA.). 40p. (J). (gr. -1-3). pap. 7.99 *(978-1-59835-117-0(6))* Cambridge BrickHouse, Inc.

—Yummy ABC's. 2010. (ENG.). 40p. (J). pap. 8.99 *(978-1-59835-114-9(1),* BrickHouse Education) Cambridge BrickHouse, Inc.

Cannella, Nicole DeRosa. The Ribbit Exhibit: One frog's tale of a leap of Faith. 2011. 28p. pap. 13.59 *(978-1-4634-2435-0(3))* AuthorHouse.

Cannon, Sherrill S. Manner-Man. 2013. 28p. pap. 12.50 *(978-1-62212-478-7(2),* Strategic Bk. Publishing) Strategic Book Publishing & Rights Agency (SBPRA).

—Santa's Birthday Gift. 2009. 24p. pap. 11.50 *(978-1-60860-824-9(7),* Eloquent Bks.) Strategic Book Publishing & Rights Agency (SBPRA).

Cantrell, Caley. You're Bringing Me a Baby?! 2013. (Illus.). 40p. (J). 15.95 *(978-0-9859358-7-0(1),* Belle Isle Bks.) Brandylane Pubs., Inc.

Capucilli, Alyssa Satin. Biscuit's 123. Schories, Pat & Berlin, Rose Mary, illus. 2012. (Biscuit Ser.). (ENG.). 16p. (J). (gr. -1-1). pap. 6.99 *(978-0-06-162523-7(X),* HarperFestival) HarperCollins Pubs.

—Hannah Is a Big Sister. Stott, Dorothy, illus. 2014. (Hannah & Henry Ser.). (ENG.). 32p. (J). (gr. -1-k). 5.99 *(978-0-7641-6750-8(2))* Barron's Educational Series, Inc.

—Henry Is a Big Brother. Stott, Dorothy, illus. 2014. (Hannah & Henry Ser.). (ENG.). 32p. (J). (gr. -1-k). 5.99 *(978-0-7641-6749-2(9))* Barron's Educational Series, Inc.

—Monkey Play. 2012. (Step into Reading Ser.). (ENG., Illus.). 32p. (J). (gr. -1-1). pap. 3.99 *(978-0-375-86993-8(X),* Random Hse. Bks. for Young Readers) Random Hse. Children's Bks.

—My Dad & Me. Mitchell, Susan, illus. 2009. (ENG.). 16p. (J). (gr. -1-1). 7.99 *(978-1-4169-5828-4(2),* Little Simon) Little Simon.

—My Mom & Me. Mitchell, Susan, illus. 2009. (ENG.). 16p. (J). (gr. -1-1). 7.99 *(978-1-4169-5829-1(0),* Little Simon) Little Simon.

—Panda Kisses. Widdowson, Kay, illus. 2008. (Step into Reading Ser.). (ENG.). 32p. (J). (gr. -1-1). pap. 3.99 *(978-0-375-84562-8(3),* Random Hse. Bks. for Young Readers) Random Hse. Children's Bks.

Carey, Mariah. All I Want for Christmas Is You. Madden, Colleen, illus. 2015. (ENG.). 32p. (J). (gr. -1-2). 17.99 *(978-0-399-55139-0(5),* Doubleday Bks. for Young Readers) Random Hse. Children's Bks.

Carigiet, Alois, illus. A Bell for Ursli: A Story from the Engadine in Switzerland. 2007. 44p. (J). *(978-0-86315-614-4(2))* Floris Bks.

Carle, Eric & Mack, Jeff. The Nonsense Show. Carle, Eric, illus. 2015. (ENG., Illus.). 40p. (J). (gr. -1-2). bds. 18.99 *(978-0-399-17687-6(X),* Philomel Bks.) Penguin Young Readers Group.

Carlson, Melody. Farmer Brown's Field Trip. Björkman, Steve, illus. 2004. 40p. (gr. -1-3). 9.99 *(978-1-58134-142-3(3))* Crossway.

—Forgive Others. Reagan, Susan Joy, illus. 2004. (Just Like Jesus Said Ser.). 32p. (J). (gr. -1-5). 12.99 *(978-0-8054-2365-3(0))* B&H Publishing Group.

—Goodnight, Angels, 1 vol. Allsopp, Sophie, illus. 2011. (ENG.). 32p. (J). 15.99 *(978-0-310-71687-7(X))* Zonderkidz.

Carlstrom, Nancy White. It's Your First Day of School, Annie Claire. Moore, Margie, illus. 2009. (ENG.). 32p. (J). (gr. k-2). 16.95 *(978-0-8109-4057-4(4),* Abrams Bks. for Young Readers) Abrams, Inc.

—Where Is Christmas, Jesse Bear? Degen, Bruce, illus. 2003. (ENG.). 32p. (J). (gr. -1-1). 13.99 *(978-0-689-86233-5(4),* Aladdin) Simon & Schuster Children's Publishing.

Carluccio, Maria. The Sounds Around Town. Carluccio, Maria, illus. 2010. (ENG., Illus.). 13p. (J). 14.99 *(978-1-84686-362-2(7))* Barefoot Bks., Inc.

—The Sounds Around Town. 2008. (ENG., Illus.). 24p. (J). (gr. -1-k). 16.99 *(978-1-905236-28-2(X))* Barefoot Bks., Inc.

Carluccio, Maria, illus. The Sounds Around Town. 2011. (ENG.). 24p. (J). (gr. -1-3). pap. 7.99 *(978-1-84686-430-8(5))* Barefoot Bks., Inc.

Carney, Karin. Prince Braden's Animal Kingdom. 2011. 40p. pap. 18.95 *(978-1-4357-9406-1(0))* Lulu Pr., Inc.

—Princess Bailey & Her Animal Friends. 2011. (Illus.). 46p. pap. 18.95 *(978-0-557-95745-3(1))* Lulu Pr., Inc.

Carney, Larry, adapted by. The Three Bears Christmas. 2009. (ENG., Illus.). 24p. (J). 6.95 *(978-1-60072-112-0(5))* PC Treasures, Inc.

Carolan, Dr. Where Are My Slippers? A Book of Colors. Carolan, Joanna F., illus. 2007. 32p. 17.95 *(978-0-9715333-7-0(7))* Banana Patch Pr.

Carr, Crystal. Ram, Ham, Strawberry Jam: Identifying Nouns. 2007. 24p. per. 13.95 *(978-1-4327-0512-1(1))* Outskirts Pr., Inc.

Carson, Penny & Hess, Amy. Simon Goes Camping. 2008. 19p. 10.95 *(978-1-4357-1560-8(8))* Lulu Pr., Inc.

—Simon's Day of Rain. 2008. 17p. 10.94 *(978-1-4357-2168-5(3))* Lulu Pr., Inc.

Carta, Karla K. Chocolate in My Pocket. 2006. 21p. (J). 10.68 *(978-1-4116-9312-8(4))* Lulu Pr., Inc.

Carter, Anne Laurel. Night Boy, 1 vol. Pelletier, Ninon, illus. 2012. (ENG.). 32p. (J). (gr. -1-3). 19.95 *(978-1-55469-402-0(7))* Orca Bk. Pubs. USA.

Carter, David A. Bedtime Bugs. Carter, David A., illus. 2010. (David Carter's Bugs Ser.). (ENG., Illus.). 18p. (J). (gr. -1-2). 12.99 *(978-1-4169-9960-7(4),* Little Simon) Little Simon.

—Bugs at the Beach. Carter, David A., illus. 2016. (David Carter's Bugs Ser.). (ENG., Illus.). 24p. (J). (gr. -1-1). pap. 3.99 *(978-1-4814-4050-9(0),* Simon Spotlight) Simon Spotlight.

—Busy Bug Builds a Fort. Carter, David A., illus. 2016. (David Carter's Bugs Ser.). (ENG., Illus.). 24p. (J). (gr. -1-1). pap. 3.99 *(978-1-4814-4047-9(0),* Simon Spotlight) Simon Spotlight.

—Colors: A Bugs Pop-Up Concept Book. Carter, David A., illus. 2010. (David Carter's Bugs Ser.). (ENG., Illus.). 16p. (J). (gr. -1-1). 8.99 *(978-1-4424-0830-2(8),* Little Simon) Little Simon.

—Feely Bugs. Carter, David A., illus. 2005. (David Carter's Bugs Ser.). (ENG., Illus.). 14p. (J). (gr. -1-2). 12.99 *(978-1-4169-0326-0(7),* Little Simon) Little Simon.

—A Snowy Day in Bugland! Carter, David A., illus. 2012. (David Carter's Bugs Ser.). (ENG., Illus.). 24p. (J). (gr. -1-1). 15.99 *(978-1-4424-3895-8(9));* pap. 3.99 *(978-1-4424-3894-1(0))* Simon Spotlight. (Simon Spotlight).

—Springtime in Bugland! Carter, David A., illus. 2012. (David Carter's Bugs Ser.). (ENG., Illus.). 24p. (J). (gr. -1-1). 15.99 *(978-1-4424-3892-7(4));* pap. 3.99 *(978-1-4424-3890-3(8))* Simon Spotlight. (Simon Spotlight).

Carter, Grant Matthew. The Disaster Caster. Morling, Donovan, illus. 2012. 38p. pap. 16.00 *(978-1-4349-8432-6(X),* RoseDog Bks.) Dorrance Publishing Co., Inc.

Casale, Roberto, illus. Little Binky Bear. 2009. (ENM & ENG.). 18p. (J). 7.99 *(978-0-9825700-0-5(7))* Siebler Corp.

Casale, Roberto, illus. El Osito Binky. 2017.Tr. of Little Binky Bear. (J). 7.99 ***(978-0-9986498-0-1(5))*** Show n' Tell Publishing.

Casanova, Mary. One-Dog Canoe. Hoyt, Ard, illus. 2003. (ENG.). 32p. (J). (gr. -1-1). 18.99 *(978-0-374-35638-5(6),* 9780374356385, Farrar, Straus & Giroux (BYR)) Farrar, Straus & Giroux.

—One-Dog Canoe. Hoyt, Ard, illus. 2009. (ENG.). 32p. (J). (gr. -1-1). pap. 7.99 *(978-0-312-56118-5(0),* 9780312561185) Square Fish.

—One-Dog Sleigh. Hoyt, Ard, illus. 2013. (ENG.). 32p. (J). (gr. k-3). 16.99 *(978-0-374-35639-2(4),* 9780374356392, Farrar, Straus & Giroux (BYR)) Farrar, Straus & Giroux.

Cash, John Carter. The Cat in the Rhinestone Suit. Nash, Scott, illus. 2012. (ENG.). 32p. (J). (gr. -1-3). 17.99 *(978-1-4169-7483-3(0),* Little Simon Inspirations) Little Simon Inspirations.

—Daddy Loves His Little Girl. Burckhardt, Marc, illus. 2010. (ENG.). 32p. (J). (gr. -1-3). 16.99 *(978-1-4169-7482-6(2),* Little Simon Inspirations) Little Simon Inspirations.

Cash, M. A. Edward of Canterbury & the King of Red. Adams, Craig, illus. 2003. (J). *(978-0-9772711-0-8(2))* Jama Kids.

Casteel, Seth. Puppy Pool Party! An Underwater Dogs Adventure. 2016. (ENG., Illus.). 40p. (J). (gr. -1-3). 16.99 *(978-0-316-37633-4(7))* Little Brown & Co.

Caswell, Deanna. Beach House. Bates, Amy June, illus. 2015. (ENG.). 32p. (J). (gr. -1-k). 16.99 *(978-1-4521-2408-7(6))* Chronicle Bks. LLC.

Caudle, P. L. The Tale of Strawberry Snow, 1 vol. Simmonds, Frank H., illus. 2012. (ENG.). 48p. (J). 16.99 *(978-0-7643-4076-5(X),* 9780764340765) Schiffer Publishing, Ltd.

Cavanaugh, Wendy. Pumpkin in the Sky: Let's bake a pie together, you & I, with Auntie Wendy. Cavanaugh, Wendy & LeVesque, Sherry, photos by. 2011. (Illus.). 32p. (J). spiral bd. 20.00 *(978-0-9743121-1-8(8))* Eastlight Pr.

Celia, Shannon Casey. Nature's Music: Musical Colors Series 2003. (ENG., Illus.). 12p. (J). spiral bd. 10.95 *(978-1-931844-07-9(0),* PP1019) Piano Pr.

Centeio, Tara Jaye. Mommy Loves Her Baby. Date not set. 32p. (J). (gr. -1-1). pap. 5.99 *(978-0-06-443715-8(9))* HarperCollins Pubs.

Cerf, Christopher & Peterson, Paige. Blackie: the Horse Who Stood Still: The Horse Who Stood Still. 2014. (ENG., Illus.). 64p. (J). (gr. 1-4). 16.95 *(978-1-59962-130-2(4),* Welcome Bks) Rizzoli International Pubns., Inc.

Cervi, Isaac. Pockets. 2008. 20p. pap. 12.50 *(978-1-4389-0368-2(5))* AuthorHouse.

Cesak, Jerry. My Personal Panther. Naughton, Terry, illus. 2012. (J). *(978-0-578-10507-9(1))* U. S. ISBN Agency.

Cesler, Margaret E. The Bread Book. 2013. 12p. pap. 10.97 *(978-1-62212-527-2(4),* Strategic Bk. Publishing) Strategic Book Publishing & Rights Agency (SBPRA).

Cesmat, Brandon. When Pigs Fall in Love & Other Stories. 2010. 150p. pap. 15.00 *(978-0-9716383-8-9(1))* Lamp Post Inc.

Chaconas, Dori. Hurry down to Derry Fair. Tyler, Gillian, illus. 2011. (ENG.). 36p. (J). (gr. -1-2). 16.99 *(978-0-7636-3208-3(2))* Candlewick Pr.

Chall, Marsha Wilson. One Pup's Up. Cole, Henry, illus. 2010. (ENG.). 32p. (J). (gr. -1 — 1). 16.99 *(978-1-4169-7960-9(3),* McElderry, Margaret K. Bks.) McElderry, Margaret K. Bks.

—Pick a Pup. Henry, Jed, illus. 2011. (ENG.). 32p. (J). (gr. -1-k). 16.99 *(978-1-4169-7961-6(1),* McElderry, Margaret K. Bks.) McElderry, Margaret K. Bks.

—A Secret Keeps. 2012. (Carolrhoda Picture Bks.). (ENG., Illus.). 32p. (J). (gr. k-3). lib. bdg. 16.95 *(978-0-7613-5593-9(6))* Lerner Publishing Group.

Chaltas, Thalia. Because I Am Furniture. 2010. (ENG.). 368p. (YA). (gr. 7-18). 8.99 *(978-0-14-241510-8(3),* Speak) Penguin Young Readers Group.

Chambers, Veronica & Clampet, Jason. Papi's Bodega. Miyares, Daniel, illus. 2013. (J). *(978-1-4231-0125-3(1))* Disney Pr.

Chandler, Jeffery. The Christmas Santa Overslept. 2008. 13p. pap. 24.95 *(978-1-60703-421-6(2))* America Star Bks.

Chandler, Susan. What I Do with Vegetable Glue. Odriozola, Elena, illus. 2012. (ENG.). 24p. (J). (gr. k-3). 16.95

(978-1-61608-661-9(0), 608661, Sky Pony Pr.) Skyhorse Publishing Co., Inc.
Chapman, Cheryl. Pass the Fritters, Critters. Roth, Susan L., illus. 2007. (ENG.). 40p. (J). (gr. -1-2). 11.99 *(978-1-4169-6160-4(7)*, Simon & Schuster/Paula Wiseman Bks.) Simon & Schuster/Paula Wiseman Bks.
Chapman, Keith. Itsy Bitsy Spider. Tickle, Jack, illus. (Tiger Tales Ser.). (J). 2008. 24p. (gr. -1-2). pap. 6.95 *(978-1-58925-407-7(4))* 2006. 32p. 15.95 *(978-1-58925-055-0(9))* Tiger Tales.
Chapman, Mary Beth & Chapman, Steven Curtis. Shaoey & Dot: A Trip to Dr. Betterbee. 2005. 20p. (J). 6.99 *(978-1-4003-0568-1(3))* Nelson, Thomas Inc.
—Shaoey & Dot: Back in a Bug's Blink. 2005. 20p. (J). 6.99 *(978-1-4003-0569-8(1))* Nelson, Thomas Inc.
—Shaoey & Dot: Thunder & Lightning Bugs. 2005. 20p. (J). 6.99 *(978-1-4003-0570-4(5))* Nelson, Thomas Inc.
Charles, Faustin & Terry, Michael. The Selfish Crocodile Book of Nursery Rhymes. Terry, Michael, illus. 2008. (ENG., Illus.). 1p. (J). (gr. -1-k). 25.95 *(978-0-7475-9523-6(2))* Bloomsbury Publishing Plc GBR. Dist: Independent Pubs. Group.
Charles, Kaye Ellen. Macarthur & Martha. 2013. 56p. pap. 20.95 *(978-1-4525-8512-3(1)*, Balboa Pr.) Author Solutions, Inc.
Charlesworth, Liza. Six Silly Chicks: An Animal Friends Reader. Smith, Ian, illus. 2015. 16p. (J). pap. ***(978-0-545-85966-0(2))*** Scholastic, Inc.
Charley's Columbia Backyard. 2006. (J). 14.95 *(978-0-9793808-0-8(4))* Backyard Ambassador Reader Publishing Co.
Charlip, Remy. A Perfect Day. 2007. (Illus.). 40p. (J). (gr. -1). lib. bdg. 17.89 *(978-0-06-051973-5(8))* HarperCollins Pubs.
Chast, Roz. Around the Clock. Chast, Roz, illus. 2015. (ENG., Illus.). 32p. (J). (gr. -1-3). 18.99 *(978-1-4169-8476-4(3)*, Atheneum Bks. for Young Readers) Simon & Schuster Children's Publishing.
Cheetham, Stephen, illus. Off to the Park! 2014. (Tactile Bks.). (ENG.). 12p. (J). *(978-1-84643-502-7(1))* Child's Play International Ltd.
Chen, Sam. A Real Meal Table Fable. Peschel, Georgia, illus. 2007. 60p. (J). *(978-0-9800764-0-0(4))* Uncle Jim's Publishing.
Chernesky, Felicia Sanzari. Cheers for a Dozen Ears: A Summer Crop of Counting. Swan, Susan, illus. 2014. (ENG.). 32p. (J). (gr. -1-3). 16.99 *(978-0-8075-1130-5(7))* Whitman, Albert & Co.
—Pick a Circle, Gather Squares: A Fall Harvest of Shapes. Swan, Susan, illus. 2013. (ENG.). 32p. (J). (gr. -1-3). 16.99 *(978-0-8075-6538-4(5))* Whitman, Albert & Co.
—Sugar White Snow & Evergreens: A Winter Wonderland of Color. Swan, Susan, illus. 2014. (ENG.). 32p. (J). (gr. -1-3). 16.99 *(978-0-8075-7234-4(9))* Whitman, Albert & Co.
—Sun above & Blooms Below: A Springtime of Opposites. Swan, Susan, illus. 2015. (ENG.). 32p. (J). (gr. -1-3). 16.99 *(978-0-8075-3632-2(6))* Whitman, Albert & Co.
Cherobin. Zoomy Boomy & the Moon: Zoomy & the Moon Learn the Strength of Love. 2009. 24p. pap. 14.99 *(978-1-4490-2069-9(0))* AuthorHouse.
—Zoomy Boomy, the Moon, & the Earth: All in its Season, & Seasons Change. 2010. 24p. pap. 14.99 *(978-1-4490-2658-5(3))* AuthorHouse.
Cherobin & Cherobin. Zoomy Boomy Lights the Night: Zoomy Conquers Shyness. 2009. 24p. pap. 14.49 *(978-1-4490-2068-2(2))* AuthorHouse.
Chichester Clark, Emma. Mimi's Book of Opposites. Chichester Clark, Emma, illus. 2004. (Illus.). 24p. (J). 9.95 *(978-1-57091-574-1(1))* Charlesbridge Publishing, Inc.
—We Are Not Fond of Rat! Chichester Clark, Emma, illus. 2006. (Collins Big Cat Phonics Ser.). (ENG., Illus.). 16p. (J). (gr. -1-1). pap. 5.99 *(978-0-00-723590-2(9))* HarperCollins Pubs. Ltd. GBR. Dist: Independent Pubs. Group.
Chichester Clark, Emma, tr. & illus. Will & Squill. Chichester Clark, Emma, illus. 2006. 32p. (J). (gr. -1-k). 15.95 *(978-1-57505-936-5(3)*, Carolrhoda Bks.) Lerner Publishing Group.
Chiew, Suzanne. What a Wonderful World! McNaughton, Tina, illus. 2013. (ENG.). 32p. (J). (gr. -1-1). 16.95 *(978-1-58925-129-8(6))* Tiger Tales.
Children's Press, contrib. by. The Three Little Kittens Get Dressed. 2009. (Rookie Preschool-NEW Ser.). (ENG.). 24p. (J). pap. 6.95 *(978-0-531-24579-8(9)*, Children's Pr.) Scholastic Library Publishing.
Childrens Press Staff & Scholastic, Inc. Staff, contrib. by. Hide-and-Peek. 2010. (Rookie Toddler: First Concepts Ser.). (ENG.). 12p. (J). bds. 6.95 *(978-0-531-25235-2(3)*, Children's Pr.) Scholastic Library Publishing.
Childs, Mark. Jaloopa: Home of the Poobah Baloo. 2009. (Illus.). (J). 25.99 *(978-1-4415-0481-4(8))* Xlibris Corp.
Chin, Oliver Clyde. Harriet's Hairballs. Crawford, Gregory, tr. Crawford, Gregory, illus. 2003. 32p. (J). 15.95 *(978-1-58394-078-5(2)*, Frog Ltd.) North Atlantic Bks.
Christelow, Eileen. Five Little Monkeys Jumping on the Bed Big Book. 2006. (Five Little Monkeys Story Ser.). (ENG., Illus.). 32p. (J). (gr. -1-3). 26.99 *(978-0-618-83682-6(9))* Houghton Mifflin Harcourt Publishing Co.
—Five Little Monkeys Jumping on the Bed (board Book) 2017. (Five Little Monkeys Story Ser.). (ENG., Illus.). 30p. (J). (— 1). bds. 7.99 ***(978-1-328-88456-5(2)***, HMH Books For Young Readers) Houghton Mifflin Harcourt Publishing Co.
—Five Little Monkeys Play Hide & Seek. 2010. (Five Little Monkeys Story Ser.). (ENG., Illus.). 40p. (J). (gr. -1-3). pap. 6.99 *(978-0-547-33787-6(6))* Houghton Mifflin Harcourt Publishing Co.
—Five Little Monkeys Reading in Bed. (Five Little Monkeys Story Ser.). (ENG., Illus.). (J). 2014. 34p. (— 1). bds. 7.99 *(978-0-544-17330-9(9)*, HMH Books For Young Readers) 2011. 40p. (gr. -1-3). 16.99 *(978-0-547-38610-2(9))* Houghton Mifflin Harcourt Publishing Co.
—Five Little Monkeys Sitting in a Tree. 2014. (Five Little Monkeys Story Ser.). (ENG & SPA., Illus.). 28p. (J). (— 1). bds. 7.99 *(978-0-544-30218-1(4)*, HMH Books For Young Readers) Houghton Mifflin Harcourt Publishing Co.
—Five Little Monkeys Sitting in a Tree Book & CD, 1 vol. 2007. (Five Little Monkeys Story Ser.). (ENG., Illus.). 32p. (J). (gr. -1-3). 10.99 *(978-0-618-85284-0(0))* Houghton Mifflin Harcourt Publishing Co.
—Five Little Monkeys Trick-Or-Treat. 2015. (Five Little Monkeys Story Ser.). (ENG., Illus.). 36p. (J). (— 1). bds. 7.99 *(978-0-544-43062-4(X)*, HMH Books For Young Readers) Houghton Mifflin Harcourt Publishing Co.
—Five Little Monkeys Wash the Car. 2004. (Five Little Monkeys Story Ser.). (ENG., Illus.). 40p. (J). (gr. -1-3). 6.99 *(978-0-618-48602-1(X))* Houghton Mifflin Harcourt Publishing Co.
—Jumping on the Bed. 2017. (Five Little Monkeys Story Ser.). (ENG., Illus.). 30p. (J). (gr. -1 — 1). bds. 8.99 *(978-0-547-51075-0(6)*, HMH Books For Young Readers) Houghton Mifflin Harcourt Publishing Co.
Christensen, Catherine. Emily's Perfect Christmas Tree. 2015. (J). 14.99 *(978-1-4621-1750-5(3))* Cedar Fort, Inc./CFI Distribution.
Christie, Jacqueline. Alphabet Animals. 2012. 60p. pap. 37.37 *(978-1-4797-1567-1(0))* Xlibris Corp.
Chronicle Books Staff. New York, Baby! Jenkins, Ward, illus. 2012. (ENG.). 24p. (J). (gr. -1 — 1). 12.99 *(978-1-4521-0619-9(3))* Chronicle Bks. LLC.
—San Francisco, Baby! Jenkins, Ward, illus. 2012. (ENG.). 24p. (J). (gr. -1 — 1). 12.99 *(978-1-4521-0620-5(7))* Chronicle Bks. LLC.
Chronicle Books Staff & Image Books Staff. Little Cat: Finger Puppet Book. Put, Klaartje van der, illus. 2014. (Little Finger Puppet Board Bks.). (ENG.). 12p. (J). (gr. -1 — 1). bds. 6.99 *(978-1-4521-2916-7(9))* Chronicle Bks. LLC.
Chronicle Books Staff & ImageBooks Staff. Little Moose: Finger Puppet Book. Put, Klaartje van der, illus. 2015. (ENG.). 12p. (J). (gr. -1 — 1). bds. 6.99 *(978-1-4521-4231-9(9))* Chronicle Bks. LLC.
Chronicle Books Staff & Leuck, Laura. For Just One Day. Boutavant, Marc, illus. 2009. (ENG.). 32p. (J). (gr. -1 — 1). 16.99 *(978-0-8118-5610-2(0))* Chronicle Bks. LLC.
Chrustowski, Rick. My Little Fox. Chrustowski, Rick, illus. 2017. (ENG., Illus.). 40p. (J). (gr. -1-k). 17.99 ***(978-1-4814-6961-6(4)***, Beach Lane Bks.) Beach Lane Bks.
Chukovsky, Kornei. Doctor Ouch. Seabaugh, Jan, tr. from RUS. Seabaugh, Jan, illus. 2004. (Children's International Ser.: 1). Orig. Title: Aibolit. 43p. (J). pap. 6.99 *(978-0-9740551-0-7(7))* Smith, Viveca Publishing.
Church, Caroline Jayne. Goodnight, I Love You. Church, Caroline Jayne, illus. 2012. (ENG., Illus.). 20p. (J). (gr. -1-k). bds. 8.99 *(978-0-545-39215-0(2)*, Cartwheel Bks.) Scholastic, Inc.
—I Am a Big Brother! 2015. (SPA & ENG.). 24p. (J). (gr. -1 — 1). 6.99 *(978-0-545-84717-9(6)*, Scholastic en Espanol) Scholastic, Inc.
—I Am a Big Brother! Church, Caroline Jayne, illus. 2015. (ENG., Illus.). 24p. (J). (gr. -1 — 1). 6.99 *(978-0-545-68886-4(8)*, Cartwheel Bks.) Scholastic, Inc.
—I Am a Big Sister! 2015. (SPA & ENG.). 24p. (J). (gr. -1 — 1). 6.99 *(978-0-545-84718-6(4)*, Scholastic en Espanol) Scholastic, Inc.
—I Am a Big Sister! Church, Caroline Jayne, illus. 2015. (ENG., Illus.). 24p. (J). (gr. -1 — 1). 6.99 *(978-0-545-68898-7(1)*, Cartwheel Bks.) Scholastic, Inc.
—Sweet Child of Mine: A Caroline Jayne Church Treasury. Church, Caroline Jayne, illus. 2014. (ENG., Illus.). 26p. (J). (— 1). bds. 8.99 *(978-0-545-64771-7(1)*, Cartwheel Bks.) Scholastic, Inc.
Churchill, Vicki & Fuge, Charles. Sometimes I Like to Curl up in a Ball. 2003. (ENG., Illus.). 22p. (J). (gr. -1-k). bds. 5.95 *(978-1-4027-0870-1(X))* Sterling Publishing Co., Inc.
Ciundziewicki, Lech. Glupcio Zeglarz: Zbior Bajek I Wierszy. 2004. 114p. (J). per. *(978-1-59196-597-8(7))* Instant Pub.
Clark, Sally. Where's My Hug? Corke, Estelle, illus. 2015. (J). *(978-0-8249-1952-8(1)*, Ideal Pubns.) Worthy Publishing.
Clark, Seneca & Giardi, Sandy. The Yellowest Yellow Lab. Decedue, Julie, illus. 2005. 30p. (J). 11.95 *(978-0-9767276-2-0(5))* Three Bean Pr.
Clarke, Jane. Chewy Hughie. McConnell, Sarah, illus. 2006. (Collins Big Cat Ser.). (ENG.). 136p. (J). (gr. 2-2). pap. 6.99 *(978-0-00-718692-1(4))* HarperCollins Pubs. Ltd. GBR. Dist: Independent Pubs. Group.
—Dancing with the Dinosaurs. Wildish, Lee, illus. 2012. (ENG.). 32p. (J). (gr. -1-2). 12.95 *(978-1-936140-67-1(5))* Charlesbridge Publishing, Inc.
—Runny Honey. Zlatic, Tomislav, illus. 2008. (Tadpoles Ser.). (ENG.). 24p. (J). (gr. -1-3). pap. *(978-0-7787-3893-0(0))*; lib. bdg. *(978-0-7787-3862-6(0))* Crabtree Publishing Co.
Clarkson, Stephanie. Sleeping Cinderella & Other Princess Mix-Ups. Barrager, Brigette, illus. 2015. (ENG.). 40p. (J). (gr. -1-3). 17.99 *(978-0-545-56564-6(2)*, Orchard Bks.) Scholastic, Inc.
Clawson, Kimberly. Fun O' Licious. Bellomy, Gail, illus. 2007. (ENG.). 56p. per. 16.95 *(978-1-4241-5556-9(6))* America Star Bks.
Clayton, Dallas. An Awesome Book! Clayton, Dallas, illus. 2012. (Awesome Book Ser.). (ENG., Illus.). 64p. (J). (gr. k-3). 16.99 *(978-0-06-211468-6(9))* HarperCollins Pubs.
—An Awesome Book of Thanks!, 0 vols. unabr. ed. 2010. (ENG.). 86p. (gr. 4-6). 17.95 *(978-1-935597-37-7(X)*, 9781935597377, Two Lions) Amazon Publishing.
Cleary, Brian. The Sun Played Hide-And-Seek: A Personification Story. Crimmins, Carol, illus. 2017. (ENG.). (J). (gr. 2-5). lib. bdg. 26.65 ***(978-1-4677-2648-1(6)***, Millbrook Pr.) Lerner Publishing Group.
Cleary, Brian P. Eight Wild Nights: A Family Hanukkah. Udovic, David, illus. 2006. 24p. (J). (gr. -1-3). lib. bdg. 16.95 *(978-1-58013-152-0(2)*, Kar-Ben Publishing) Lerner Publishing Group.
—Eight Wild Nights: A Family Hanukkah Tale. Udovic, David, illus. 2006. (ENG.). 24p. (J). (gr. k-3). 8.95 *(978-1-58013-229-9(4)*, Kar-Ben Publishing) Lerner Publishing Group.
—Windows, Rings, & Grapes - A Look at Different Shapes. Gable, Brian, illus. 2011. (Math Is CATegorical Ser.). pap. 39.62 *(978-0-7613-8360-4(3)*, Millbrook Pr.) Lerner Publishing Group.
Clements, Andrew. The Handiest Things in the World. Jaramillo, Raquel, illus. 2010. (ENG.). 48p. (J). (gr. -1-3). 16.99 *(978-1-4169-6166-6(6)*, Atheneum Bks. for Young Readers) Simon & Schuster Children's Publishing.
Clennell, Bobby. Watch Me Do Yoga. 2010. (ENG., Illus.). 32p. (gr. -1-3). 15.95 *(978-1-930485-26-6(3))* Shambhala Pubns., Inc.
Cleofas-Moore, Ramona. Tiffany. 2008. 60p. pap. 16.95 *(978-1-60474-238-1(0))* America Star Bks.
Cleveland, Nicole K. Ode to a Fly. 2007. 56p. per. 16.95 *(978-1-4241-7977-0(7))* America Star Bks.
Clickard, Carrie. Magic for Sale. Shelley, John, illus. 2017. (ENG.). 32p. (J). 16.95 *(978-0-8234-3559-3(8))* Holiday Hse., Inc.
—Victricia Malicia: Book-Loving Buccaneer. Meyers, Mark, illus. 2012. (ENG.). 32p. (J). (gr. 2-4). 16.95 *(978-1-936261-12-3(X))* Flashlight Pr.
Clough, Paige. The Jumping Orie Story. Yates, Bridget & Ward, Karen, illus. 2015. (J). *(978-1-942945-24-6(8))* Bright Sky Pr.
—The Jumping Orie Story. Yates, Bridget & Ward, Karen, illus. 2015. (J). ***(978-0-9915511-2-5(5))*** Rule 2 Bks.
Cochran, Jean M. Off I Go! Gullens, Lee M., illus. 2008. (ENG.). 32p. (J). (gr. -1-k). 16.95 *(978-0-9792035-1-0(1))* Pleasant St. Pr.
Coffin, Douglas. One Maine Christmas Eve, 1 vol. Coffin, Douglas, illus. 2015. (ENG., Illus.). 32p. (gr. -1-12). 16.95 *(978-0-88448-469-1(6)*, 884469) Tilbury Hse. Pubs.
Cohen, Warren Lee. Dragon Baked Bread. Ssebulime, John, illus. 2005. 32p. (J). *(978-1-902636-70-2(8))* Clairview Bks.
Cohn, Arlen. Firsts. Vasconcellos, Daniel, illus. gif. ed. 2004. (ENG.). 28p. (J). bds. 9.99 *(978-1-57939-168-3(0))* Andrews McMeel Publishing.
Cohn, Scott M. Daddy Said a Word I Never Heard. 2015. (Daddy Ser.: 2). (ENG., Illus.). 32p. (J). (gr. -1-3). 15.00 *(978-0-316-40751-9(8))* Little Brown & Co.
—Daddy Sat on a Duck. 2015. (Daddy Ser.: 1). (ENG., Illus.). 32p. (J). (gr. -1-3). 15.00 *(978-0-316-40749-6(6))* Little Brown & Co.
Colandro, Lucille. There Was a Cold Lady Who Swallowed Some Snow! Lee, Jared, illus. 2006. (ENG.). (J). (gr. -1-3). 18.95 *(978-0-439-89841-6(2))*; 9.95 *(978-0-439-89556-9(1))* Scholastic, Inc.
—There Was a Cold Lady Who Swallowed Some Snow! 2003. (There Was an Old Lady Ser.). (gr. k-3). lib. bdg. 17.20 *(978-0-613-72229-2(9)*, Turtleback) Turtleback Bks.
—There Was an Old Lady Who Swallowed a Chick! Lee, Jared, illus. (ENG.). (J). (gr. -1-k). 2011. 9.99 *(978-0-545-27367-1(6))* 2010. 32p. pap. 6.99 *(978-0-545-16181-7(9)*, Cartwheel Bks.) Scholastic, Inc.
—There Was an Old Lady Who Swallowed a Chick! 2009. (Illus.). (J). *(978-0-545-06059-2(1))* Scholastic, Inc.
—There Was an Old Lady Who Swallowed a Chick! Lee, Jared, illus. 2010. (There Was an Old Lady... Ser.). lib. bdg. 17.20 *(978-0-606-06821-5(X)*, Turtleback) Turtleback Bks.
—There Was an Old Lady Who Swallowed a Frog! Lee, Jared D., illus. 2015. (J). *(978-0-545-83213-7(6))* Scholastic, Inc.
—There Was an Old Lady Who Swallowed Some Books! Lee, Jared, illus. 2012. (There Was an Old Lady Ser.). lib. bdg. 17.20 *(978-0-606-26208-8(3)*, Turtleback) Turtleback Bks.
—There Was an Old Lady Who Swallowed Some Leaves! Lee, Jared, illus. 2010. (ENG.). 32p. (J). (gr. -1-k). pap. 6.99 *(978-0-545-24198-4(7)*, Cartwheel Bks.) Scholastic, Inc.
Colby, Rebecca. Motor Goose. Kaminsky, Jef, illus. 2017. (ENG.). 32p. (J). 16.99 *(978-1-250-10193-8(X)*, 9781250101938) Feiwel & Friends.
Cole, Gina, illus. Adapt. 2005. 40p. (J). 17.00 *(978-0-9659538-3-2(1))* Soul Vision Works Publishing.
Coll, Ivar Da. Cinco Amigos. (SPA.). (J). bds. *(978-958-04-4909-6(0))* Norma S.A. COL. Dist: Lectorum Pubns., Inc.
Collins, Rachel. Fiddle Faddle Frog & Piddle Paddle Polliwog. 2010. 32p. pap. 16.95 *(978-0-557-53411-1(9))* Lulu Pr., Inc.
Collins, Suzanne. When Charlie McButton Lost Power. Lester, Mike, illus. 2007. (ENG.). 32p. (J). (gr. -1-3). pap. 6.99 *(978-0-14-240857-5(3)*, Puffin Books) Penguin Young Readers Group.
—When Charlie McButton Lost Power. Lester, Mike, illus. 2009. 32p. 16.00 *(978-1-60686-529-3(3))* Perfection Learning Corp.
Colman, Michelle Sinclair. Not That Tutu! Nakata, Hiroe, illus. 2013. (ENG.). 20p. (J). (— 1). bds. 7.99 *(978-0-307-97698-7(X)*, Robin Corey Bks.) Random Hse. Children's Bks.
Colors All Day. (J). 26.20 *(978-0-8136-8399-7(8))*; (gr. -1-3). 59.50 *(978-0-8136-7918-1(4))* Modern Curriculum Pr.
Comer, Brigitte Renee. The Little Hopping Frog. 2012. 24p. pap. 24.95 *(978-1-4626-8243-0(X))* America Star Bks.
Conan, Sally Anne. Sleepy Time Blessings. Rutten, Nicole, illus. 2009. (ENG.). 12p. (J). (gr. -1). 8.00 *(978-0-8028-5350-9(1))* Eerdmans, William B. Publishing Co.
Coniglio, John. The Cat Who Slept All Day: What Happens While the Cat Sleeps. Key, Pamela, illus. 2006. 24p. (J). per. 2.99 *(978-1-59958-004-3(7))* Journey Stone Creations, LLC.
Connelly, Wendy. Fiona the Firefly! 2003. (Illus.). (J). 12.95 *(978-1-929039-16-6(6))* Ambassador Bks., Inc.
Connolly, C J. The Boomerang. 2010. (Illus.). 32p. (J). 16.95 *(978-0-9825559-1-0(1))* Crosswinds Pr., Inc.
—Wil, Fitz, & a Flea Named T. 2009. (Illus.). 32p. (J). 16.95 *(978-0-9825559-0-3(3))* Crosswinds Pr., Inc.
conrad, catherine. The Lemonade Stand. 2008. (Illus.). 32p. (J). lib. bdg. 16.99 *(978-0-9799065-0-3(4))* Banana Pr.
Cook, Gary. The Best Saturday Ever! Sward, Adam, illus. 2013. (Robbie's Big Adventures Ser.). (ENG.). 40p. (J). (gr. k-3). 15.95 *(978-1-938063-25-1(2)*, Mighty Media Kids) Mighty Media Pr.
Cook, Julie Kidd. One Is Enough. Iwai, Melissa, illus. 2005. (Rookie Reader Skill Set Ser.). (ENG.). 24p. (J). (gr. 1-2). per. 4.95 *(978-0-516-25283-4(6)*, Children's Pr.) Scholastic Library Publishing.
Cook, Marisa. The Adventures of Ollie & Ronnie: Litter. 2012. 16p. (-18). pap. 12.68 *(978-1-4669-6630-7(0))* Trafford Publishing.
Coombs, Kate & Austen, Jane. Goodnight Mr. Darcy: A Babylit Parody, 1 vol. 2014. (ENG., Illus.). 32p. (J). 16.99 *(978-1-4236-3670-0(8))* Gibbs Smith, Publisher.
Copeland, Cynthia L. & Lewis, Alexandra P. Splashy Fins, Flashy Skins: Deep-Sea Rhymes to Make You Grin. 2003. (Silly Millies Ser.: 4). (Illus.). 32p. lib. bdg. 17.90 *(978-0-7613-2906-0(4)*, Millbrook Pr.) Lerner Publishing Group.
Corderoy, Tracey. Hubble Bubble, Granny Trouble. Berger, Joe, illus. 2012. (ENG.). 32p. (J). (gr. -1-2). 14.99 *(978-0-7636-5904-2(5)*, Nosy Crow) Candlewick Pr.
—Whizz! Pop! Granny, Stop! Berger, Joe, illus. 2013. (ENG.). 32p. (J). (gr. -1-2). 14.99 *(978-0-7636-6551-7(7)*, Nosy Crow) Candlewick Pr.
Cordsen, Carol Foskett. The Milkman. Jones, Douglas B., illus. 2007. (gr. -1-3). 17.00 *(978-0-7569-8148-8(4))* Perfection Learning Corp.
Corey, Shana. Monster Parade. Terry, Will, illus. 2009. (Step into Reading Ser.). (ENG.). 24p. (J). (gr. -1-1). 3.99 *(978-0-375-85638-9(2)*, Random Hse. Bks. for Young Readers) Random Hse. Children's Bks.
Corlyn, Ron. The House That Grew. 2013. 24p. pap. 24.95 *(978-1-63000-118-6(X))* America Star Bks.
Corso, Suzanne. Sammy & Sue Go Green Too! 2009. (Sammy & Sue Ser.: 0). (ENG.). 32p. 16.95 *(978-0-8253-0517-7(9))* Beaufort Bks., Inc.
Cortes, Mary. Where on Earth Did My Sock Go? 2006. (J). per. 15.95 *(978-0-9787788-3-5(9))* LUMEN-US Pubns.
Costain, Meredith. Daddies Are Awesome. Lovsin, Polona, illus. 2016. (ENG.). 32p. (J). 16.99 *(978-1-62779-452-7(2)*, 9781627794527, Holt, Henry & Co. Bks. For Young Readers) Holt, Henry & Co.
Costales, Amy. Hello Night/Hola Noche. McDonald, Mercedes, illus. 2007. (ENG, SPA & MUL.). 24p. (J). (gr. -1 — 1). 14.95 *(978-0-87358-927-7(0))* Cooper Square Publishing Llc.
Coster, Simon. My Dinosaur Is More Awesome! 2015. (ENG., Illus.). 48p. (J). (gr. -1-k). 16.99 *(978-1-63220-416-5(9)*, Sky Pony Pr.) Skyhorse Publishing Co., Inc.
Cote, Genevieve & Côté, Geneviève. Starring Me & You, 0 vols. Cote, Genevieve & Côté, Geneviève, illus. 2014. (Piggy & Bunny Ser.). (ENG., Illus.). 32p. (J). (gr. -1-k). 16.95 *(978-1-894786-39-3(4))* Kids Can Pr., Ltd. CAN. Dist: Hachette Bk. Group.
Cotter, Bill. Happy Face / Sad Face: All Kinds of Child Faces. 2017. (ENG., Illus.). 22p. (J). bds. 7.99 ***(978-1-4926-4981-6(3)***, Sourcebooks Jabberwocky) Sourcebooks, Inc.
Cotton, Katie. And the Cow Said. Gausden, Vicki, illus. 2015. (ENG.). 24p. (J). (gr. -1-1). 12.99 *(978-1-4998-0101-9(7))* Little Bee Books Inc.
—The Road Home. Jacoby, Sarah, illus. 2016. (ENG.). 32p. (J). 17.99 *(978-1-84780-803-5(4)*, Frances Lincoln Children's Bks.) Quarto Publishing Group UK GBR. Dist: Littlehampton Bk Services, Ltd.
—The Road Home. Jacoby, Sarah, illus. 2017. (ENG.). 32p. (J). (gr. k-2). 15.95 *(978-1-4197-2374-2(X)*, Abrams Bks. for Young Readers) Abrams, Inc.
—Ten Monsters in the Bed. Blecha, Aaron, illus. 2015. (ENG.). 24p. (J). (gr. -1-k). 12.99 *(978-1-4998-0067-8(3))* Little Bee Books Inc.
Cottswold, Wooley. Rose & the Bald-Headed Elephant. 2009. (Illus.). 28p. (J). 16.95 *(978-0-9779064-0-6(X))* Archie Publishing.
Cousins, Lucy. Hooray for Birds! 2017. (ENG.). 40p. (J). (-k). 15.99 *(978-0-7636-9265-0(4))* Candlewick Pr.
—Hooray for Fish! Cousins, Lucy, illus. (ENG., Illus.). (J). (— 1). 2017. 34p. bds. 8.99 *(978-0-7636-9352-7(9))* 2008. 34p. bds. 8.99 *(978-0-7636-3918-1(4))* 2005. 40p. 16.99 *(978-0-7636-2741-6(0))* Candlewick Pr.
—Maisy's First Colors: A Maisy Concept Book. Cousins, Lucy, illus. 2013. (Maisy Ser.). (ENG., Illus.). 14p. (J). (-k). bds. 6.99 *(978-0-7636-6804-4(4))* Candlewick Pr.
—Maisy's First Numbers: A Maisy Concept Book. Lucy Cousins, illus. 2013. (Maisy Ser.). (ENG.). 14p. (J). (-k). bds. 6.99 *(978-0-7636-6805-1(2))* Candlewick Pr.
Cowen-Fletcher, Jane. Baby Be Kind. Cowen-Fletcher, Jane, illus. 2012. (ENG., Illus.). 18p. (J). (gr. k — 1). bds. 5.99 *(978-0-7636-5647-8(X))* Candlewick Pr.
Cowley, Joy. The Bedtime Train. Odone, Jamison, illus. 2008. (ENG.). 32p. (J). (gr. k-2). 16.95 *(978-1-59078-493-8(6)*, Front Street) Boyds Mills Pr.
—Freddy Bear & the Beach. Webb, Philip, illus. 2016. (Freddy Bear Ser.). (ENG.). 20p. (J). (gr. -1-k). bds. 12.99 *(978-1-927262-56-6(9))* Upstart Pr. NZL. Dist: Independent Pubs. Group.
—Freddy Bear & the Green Peas. Webb, Philip, illus. 2016. (Freddy Bear Ser.). (ENG.). 20p. (J). (gr. -1-k). bds. 12.99 *(978-1-927262-57-3(7))* Upstart Pr. NZL. Dist: Independent Pubs. Group.
—Mrs. Wishy-Washy's Farm. Fuller, Elizabeth, illus. (ENG.). 32p. (J). (gr. -1-k). 2006. 5.99 *(978-0-14-240299-3(0)*, Puffin Books) 2003. 16.99 *(978-0-399-23872-7(7)*, Philomel Bks.) Penguin Young Readers Group.
Cox, Christine. Why the Zero Was Sad? 2008. 32p. pap. 14.49 *(978-1-4389-1056-7(8))* AuthorHouse.
Cox, Miss Karin & Cox, Karin. Pancakes on Sunday. Acar, Sinan, illus. 2012. 26p. pap. *(978-0-9873602-2-9(1))* Indelible Ink Pr.
Cox, Phil Roxbee. Fat Cat on a Mat. Tyler, Jenny, ed. Cartwright, Stephen, illus. rev. ed. 2006. (Phonics Readers Ser.). 16p. (J). (gr. -1-3). pap. 6.99 *(978-0-7945-1502-7(9)*, Usborne) EDC Publishing.
—Ted's Shed. Tyler, Jenny, ed. Cartwright, Stephen, illus. rev. ed. 2006. (Phonics Readers Ser.). 16p. (J). (gr. -1-3). pap. 6.99 *(978-0-7945-1511-9(8)*, Usborne) EDC Publishing.
Cox, Phil Roxbee & Cartwright, S. Goose on the Loose. 2004. (Easy Words to Read Ser.). 16p. (J). (gr. 1-18). pap. 6.95 *(978-0-7945-0036-8(6)*, Usborne) EDC Publishing.
Cox, Phil Roxbee & Cartwright, Stephen. Goose on the Loose. 2004. (Phonics Board Bks.). (Illus.). 10p. (J). 4.99 *(978-0-7945-0305-5(5)*, Usborne) EDC Publishing.
Coxall, Darcy. Where Is My Bear? Wittebrood, Menno, illus. 2015. (ENG.). 32p. (J). (gr. -1-1). pap. 8.99 *(978-1-907432-09-5(4))* Hogs Back Bks. GBR. Dist: Independent Pubs. Group.
Coyle, Carmela Lavigna. Do Princesses Have Best Friends Forever? Gordon, Mike & Gordon, Carl, illus. 2010. (J). *(978-1-58979-543-3(1))* Taylor Trade Publishing.
—Do Princesses Have Best Friends Forever? Gordon, Carl & Gordon, Mike, illus. 2010. (ENG.). 32p. (J). (gr. -1-3). 15.95 *(978-1-58979-542-6(3))* Taylor Trade Publishing.
—Do Princesses Make Happy Campers? Gordon, Mike, illus. 2015. (ENG.). 32p. (J). (gr. -1-2). 15.95 *(978-1-63076-054-0(4))* Taylor Trade Publishing.

S

—Do Princesses Really Kiss Frogs? Gordon, Mike & Gordon, Carl, illus. 2005. (ENG.). 32p. (J). (gr. -1-2). 15.95 *(978-0-87358-880-5(0))* Cooper Square Publishing Llc.

—Do Princesses Scrape Their Knees? 2006. (ENG., Illus.). 32p. (J). (gr. -1-2). 15.95 *(978-0-87358-909-3(2))* Cooper Square Publishing Llc.

—Do Princesses Scrape Their Knees? Keepsake Sticker Doodle Book. Gordon, Mike & Gordon, Carl, illus. 2014. (ENG.). 96p. (J). (gr. -1-2). 15.95 *(978-1-58979-948-6(8))* Taylor Trade Publishing.

—Do Princesses Wear Hiking Boots? Gordon, Mike & Gordon, Carl, illus. 2003. (ENG.). 32p. (J). (gr. -1-2). 15.95 *(978-0-87358-828-7(2))* Cooper Square Publishing Llc.

—Do Superheroes Have Teddy Bears? Gordon, Mike, illus. 2012. (ENG.). 32p. (J). (gr. -1-2). 15.95 *(978-1-58979-693-5(4))* Taylor Trade Publishing.

—The Tumbleweed Came Back. Rechin, Kevin, illus. 2013. 32p. (J). 15.95 *(978-1-933855-83-7(5),* Rio Nuevo Pubs.) Rio Nuevo Pubs.

Crabtree, Sally. Magic Train Ride. Esplugas, Sonia & Espulgas, Sonia, illus. 2007. (ENG.). 32p. (J). (gr. -1-k). 6.99 *(978-1-84686-132-1(2))* Barefoot Bks., Inc.

—Magic Train Ride. Esplugas, Sonia, illus. (Barefoot Singalongs Ser.). (J). 2007. (ENG.). 32p. (gr. -1-k). pap. 9.99 *(978-1-905236-91-6(3))* 2006. 0032p. 16.99 *(978-1-905236-52-7(2))* Barefoot Bks., Inc.

Craig, Lindsey. Dancing Feet! Brown, Marc, illus. 2010. (ENG.). 40p. (J). (gr. -1-2). 16.99 *(978-0-375-86181-9(5),* Knopf Bks. for Young Readers) Random Hse. Children's Bks.

—Dancing Feet! Brown, Marc, illus. 2012. (ENG.). 32p. (J). (gr. k-k). bds. 6.99 *(978-0-307-93081-1(5),* Knopf Bks. for Young Readers) Random Hse. Children's Bks.

—Farmyard Beat. Brown, Marc, illus. 2012. (ENG.). 32p. (J). (gr. k-k). bds. 6.99 *(978-0-307-93082-8(3),* Knopf Bks. for Young Readers) Random Hse. Children's Bks.

Craig, Sherryn. Locura de Medianoche en el Zoológico, 1 vol. Jones, Karen, illus. 2016. (SPA.). 32p. (J). (gr. k-3). pap. 9.95 *(978-1-62855-744-2(3))* Arbordale Publishing.

—Midnight Madness at the Zoo, 1 vol. Jones, Karen, illus. 2016. (ENG & SPA.). 32p. (J). (gr. k-3). 17.95 *(978-1-62855-730-5(3))* Arbordale Publishing.

Crawford, Georgina. Archie-Parchie-Piddley-Poo. 2009. (Illus.). 24p. pap. 12.99 *(978-1-4389-7307-4(1))* AuthorHouse.

Cree, Tahara, text. Bonnie the Bee. 2012. (ENG., Illus.). 13p. pap. 5.00 *(978-0-9824964-3-5(5))* Creative Education & Publishing.

Crimi, Carolyn. Pugs in a Bug. Buscema, Stephanie, illus. 2012. (ENG.). 32p. (J). (gr. -1-k). 16.99 *(978-0-8037-3320-6(8),* Dial Bks) Penguin Young Readers Group.

Crisp, Dan. Santa's Missing Reindeer. Crisp, Dan, illus. 2011. (ENG., Illus.). 12p. (J). (gr. -1-k). 12.99 *(978-0-230-71291-1(6))* Macmillan Pubs., Ltd. GBR. Dist: Independent Pubs. Group.

Crisp, Dan, illus. The Ants Go Marching! 2009. (Classic Books with Holes Big Book Ser.). (ENG.). 16p. (J). (gr. -1-1). *(978-1-84643-207-1(3));* pap. incl. audio compact disk *(978-1-84643-256-9(1))* Child's Play International Ltd.

Cronin, Doreen. Bounce. Menchin, Scott, illus. 2007. (ENG.). 40p. (J). (gr. -1-3). 17.99 *(978-1-4169-1627-7(X),* Atheneum Bks. for Young Readers) Simon & Schuster Children's Publishing.

—Clic, Clac, Plif, Plaf: Una Aventura de Contar. Lewin, Betsy, illus. 2006. (J). (gr. -1-k). per. 6.99 *(978-1-933032-03-0(0))* Lectorum Pubns., Inc.

—Clic, Clac, Plif, Plaf: Una Aventura de Contar. Rioja, Alberto Jimenez, tr. from ENG. Lewin, Betsy, illus. 2006. (J). (gr. 5-6). 12.99 *(978-1-933032-11-5(1))* Lectorum Pubns., Inc.

—Click, Clack, Splish, Splash: A Counting Adventure. Lewin, Betsy, illus. 2006. (Click, Clack Book Ser.). (ENG.). 24p. (J). (gr. -1-3). 17.99 *(978-0-689-87716-2(1),* Atheneum Bks. for Young Readers) Simon & Schuster Children's Publishing.

—Smick! Medina, Juana, illus. 2015. (ENG.). 34p. (J). (gr. -1-k). 16.99 *(978-0-670-78578-0(4),* Viking Books for Young Readers) Penguin Young Readers Group.

—Stretch. Menchin, Scott, illus. 2009. (ENG.). 40p. (J). (gr. -1-3). 17.99 *(978-1-4169-5341-8(8),* Atheneum Bks. for Young Readers) Simon & Schuster Children's Publishing.

—Wiggle. Menchin, Scott, illus. 2005. (ENG.). 40p. (J). (gr. -1-3). 16.99 *(978-0-689-86375-2(6),* Atheneum Bks. for Young Readers) Simon & Schuster Children's Publishing.

Cronin, Doreen & Lewin, Betsy. Click, Clack, Splish, Splash: A Counting Adventure, 1 vol. 2006. (Doreen Cronin: Click-Clack & More Ser.). (ENG.). 24p. (gr. -1-3). lib. bdg. 24.21 *(978-1-59961-090-0(6))* Spotlight.

Crossan, Sarah. One. 2015. (ENG.). 400p. (YA). (gr. 8). 17.99 *(978-0-06-211875-2(7),* Greenwillow Bks.) HarperCollins Pubs.

Crouse, Livingstone. Kisses for Kindergarten. Pamintuan, Macky, illus. 2017. (ENG.). 40p. (J). (gr. -1). 17.99 *(978-1-62686-703-1(8),* Silver Dolphin Bks.) Readerlink Distribution Services, LLC.

Crow, Kristyn. Bedtime at the Swamp. Pamintuan, Macky, illus. 2008. (ENG.). 32p. (J). (gr. -1-1). 16.99 *(978-0-06-083951-2(1))* HarperCollins Pubs.

—Skeleton Cat. Krall, Dan, illus. 2012. (ENG.). 32p. (J). (gr. -1-3). pap. 6.99 *(978-0-545-15385-0(9),* Scholastic Pr.) Scholastic, Inc.

—Skeleton Cat. 2012. lib. bdg. 17.20 *(978-0-606-26209-5(1),* Turtleback) Turtleback Bks.

—Zombelina: School Days. Idle, Molly, illus. (ENG.). (J). 2017. 40p. 16.99 *(978-1-61963-641-5(7),* 9781619636415) 2013. 32p. (gr. -1-3). 16.99 *(978-0-8027-2803-6(0),* 9780802728036) Bloomsbury Publishing USA. (Bloomsbury USA Childrens).

—Zombelina Dances the Nutcracker. Idle, Molly, illus. 2015. (ENG.). 40p. (J). (gr. -1-3). 16.99 *(978-1-61963-640-8(9),* 9781619636408, Bloomsbury USA Childrens) Bloomsbury Publishing USA.

Crow, Kristyn & Aesop. The Really Groovy Story of the Tortoise & the Hare. Forshay, Christina, illus. 2012. (J). *(978-1-61913-128-6(5))* Weigl Pubs., Inc.

Crow, Marilee & Foster, Jack. Once There Was a Monster. 2012. 20p. pap. 9.95 *(978-1-61633-331-7(6))* Guardian Angel Publishing, Inc.

Crow, Sara. Even Superheroes Have to Sleep. Record, Adam, illus. 2017. (ENG.). 32p. (J). (-k). 16.99 *(978-0-399-55806-1(3),* Doubleday Bks. for Young Readers) Random Hse. Children's Bks.

Crowder, Melanie. Audacity. 2016. (ENG.). 400p. (YA). (gr. 7). pap. 10.99 *(978-0-14-751249-9(2),* Speak) Penguin Young Readers Group.

Crowe, Caroline. Pirates in Pajamas. Knight, Tim, illus. 2015. (ENG.). 32p. (J). (gr. -1-3). 16.99 *(978-1-58925-190-8(3))* Tiger Tales.

Crowley, Peter. J T Seavey. 2012. (ENG.). 35p. (J). pap. 18.95 *(978-1-4327-8712-7(8))* Outskirts Pr., Inc.

Crown Peak Publishing. Just Be You. Crown Peak Publishing, illus. 2008. (ENG., Illus.). 40p. (J). 19.95 *(978-0-9645663-5-4(4))* Crown Peak Publishing.

Crownberry, Ethan. A Fish with a Wish. 2012. 84p. pap. 8.95 *(978-1-105-84560-4(5))* Lulu Pr., Inc.

Cruise, Robin. Only You. Chodos-Irvine, Margaret, illus. 2016. (ENG.). 40p. (J). (— 1). 7.99 *(978-0-544-66832-4(4),* HMH Books For Young Readers) Houghton Mifflin Harcourt Publishing Co.

Crummel, Susan Stevens. All in One Hour, 0 vols. Donohue, Dorothy, illus. 2009. (ENG.). 40p. (J). (gr. k-3). pap. 9.99 *(978-0-7614-5537-0(X),* 9780761455370, Amazon Children's Publishing) Amazon Publishing.

—Sherlock Bones & the Missing Cheese, 0 vols. Donohue, Dorothy, illus. 2012. (ENG.). 40p. (J). (gr. k-3). 17.99 *(978-0-7614-6186-9(8),* 9780761461869, Amazon Children's Publishing) Amazon Publishing.

Crystal, Billy. Grandpa's Little One. Porfirio, Guy, illus. 2006. 40p. (J). (gr. -1-k). lib. bdg. 17.89 *(978-0-06-078174-3(2))* HarperCollins Pubs.

—I Already Know I Love You. Sayles, Elizabeth, illus. (ENG.). 40p. (J). 2007. (gr. -1-3). pap. 6.99 *(978-0-06-059393-3(8))* 2004. 16.99 *(978-0-06-059391-9(1))* HarperCollins Pubs.

Cuartas, Jennifer M. So Many Things. 2012. 28p. 24.95 *(978-1-4626-6328-6(1))* America Star Bks.

Cummings, Pat. Harvey Moon, Museum Boy. Cummings, Pat, illus. 2008. (Illus.). 32p. (J). (gr. -1-3). lib. bdg. 18.89 *(978-0-06-057861-9(0))* HarperCollins Pubs.

Cummings, Priscilla. Beetle Boddiker, 1 vol. Ramsey, Marcy Dunn, illus. 2009. (ENG.). 30p. (J). (gr. k-7). 13.95 *(978-0-87033-602-7(9),* 9780870336027, Cornell Maritime Pr./Tidewater Pubs.) Schiffer Publishing, Ltd.

Cunningham, Sheila S. Willow's Walkabout: A Children's Guide to Boston. Kelleher, Kathie, illus. 2012. (ENG.). 32p. (J). (gr. 1-3). 17.95 *(978-1-59373-096-3(9))* Bunker Hill Publishing, Inc.

Curtis, Carolyn. I Took the Moon for a Walk. Jay, Alison, illus. (ENG.). 32p. (J). 2012. (gr. -1-2). 8.99 *(978-1-84148-803-5(8))* 2004. 16.99 *(978-1-84148-611-6(6))* Barefoot Bks., Inc.

Curtis, Carolyn, et al. Lleve a la Luna a Pasear. Jay, Alison, illus. 2014. (SPA.). 32p. (J). (gr. -1-2). pap. 8.99 *(978-1-78285-084-7(8))* Barefoot Bks., Inc.

Curtis, Jamie Lee. Big Words for Little People. Cornell, Laura, illus. 2008. (ENG.). 40p. (J). (gr. -1-3). 16.99 *(978-0-06-112759-5(0))* HarperCollins Pubs.

—I'm Gonna Like Me: Letting off a Little Self-Esteem. Cornell, Laura, illus. 2007. (ENG.). 32p. (J). (gr. -1-3). 16.99 *(978-0-06-028761-0(6))* HarperCollins Pubs.

—Is There Really a Human Race? Cornell, Laura, illus. 2006. (ENG.). 40p. (J). (gr. -1-3). 16.99 *(978-0-06-075346-7(3))* HarperCollins Pubs.

—It's Hard to Be Five: Learning How to Work My Control Panel. Cornell, Laura, illus. 40p. (J). (gr. -1-3). 2007. (ENG.). 16.99 *(978-0-06-008095-2(7))* 2004. lib. bdg. 17.89 *(978-0-06-008096-9(5),* Cotler, Joanna Books) HarperCollins Pubs.

—My Mommy Hung the Moon: A Love Story. Date not set. 32p. (J). (gr. -1-3). pap. 6.99 *(978-0-06-443696-0(9))* HarperCollins Pubs.

—My Mommy Hung the Moon: A Love Story. Cornell, Laura, illus. 2010. 40p. (J). (gr. -1-3). (ENG.). 16.99 *(978-0-06-029016-0(1));* lib. bdg. 17.89 *(978-0-06-029017-7(X))* HarperCollins Pubs.

—This Is Me: A Story of Who We Are & Where We Came From. Cornell, Laura, illus. 2016. (ENG.). 32p. (J). (gr. -1-3). 17.89 *(978-1-5235-0005-5(0));* 16.95 *(978-0-7611-8011-1(7))* Workman Publishing Co., Inc.

—Today I Feel Silly & Other Moods That Make My Day. Cornell, Laura, illus. 2007. (ENG.). 40p. (J). (gr. -1-3). 17.99 *(978-0-06-024560-3(3))* HarperCollins Pubs.

Cusimano Love, Maryann & Ichikawa, Satomi. You Are My Miracle (Tú Eres Mi Milagro) 2016. (SPA & ENG., Illus.). 28p. (J). (— 1). bds. 7.99 *(978-0-399-54734-8(7),* Philomel Bks.) Penguin Young Readers Group.

Cuyler, Margery. Best Friends. Walker, David L., illus. 2017. (Step into Reading Ser.). (ENG.). 32p. (J). (gr. -1-1). pap. 4.99 *(978-0-399-55369-1(X),* Random Hse. Bks. for Young Readers) Random Hse. Children's Bks.

—The Little Dump Truck. Kolar, Bob, illus. 2014. (Little Vehicles Ser.). (ENG.). 24p. (J). (gr. -1-1). bds. 7.99 *(978-0-8050-9990-4(5),* 9780805099904, Holt, Henry & Co. Bks. For Young Readers) Holt, Henry & Co.

—The Little School Bus. Kolar, Bob, illus. 2014. (Little Vehicles Ser.). (ENG.). 32p. (J). (gr. -1-1). 12.99 *(978-0-8050-9435-0(0),* 9780805094350, Holt, Henry & Co. Bks. For Young Readers) Holt, Henry & Co.

—Monster Mess! Schindler, S. D., illus. 2008. (ENG.). 32p. (J). (gr. -1-1). 14.99 *(978-0-689-86405-6(1),* McElderry, Margaret K. Bks.) McElderry, Margaret K. Bks.

—Princess Bess Gets Dressed. Malone, Heather Harms & Malone, Heather, illus. 2009. (ENG.). 32p. (J). (gr. -1-3). 15.99 *(978-1-4169-3833-0(8),* Simon & Schuster Bks. For Young Readers) Simon & Schuster Bks. For Young Readers.

—Tick Tock Clock. Neubecker, Robert, illus. 2012. (My First I Can Read Ser.). (ENG.). 32p. (J). (gr. -1 — 1). 16.99 *(978-0-06-136309-2(X));* pap. 3.99 *(978-0-06-136311-5(1))* HarperCollins Pubs.

Cyrus, Kurt. Billions of Bricks. Cyrus, Kurt, illus. 2016. (ENG., Illus.). 32p. (J). 17.99 *(978-1-62779-273-8(2),* 9781627792738, Holt, Henry & Co. Bks. For Young Readers) Holt, Henry & Co.

—Shake a Leg, Egg! Cyrus, Kurt, illus. 2017. (ENG., Illus.). 32p. (J). (gr. -1-3). 17.99 *(978-1-4814-5848-1(5),* Beach Lane Bks.) Beach Lane Bks.

—The Voyage of Turtle Rex. 2011. (ENG., Illus.). 40p. (J). (gr. -1-3). 16.99 *(978-0-547-42924-3(X))* Houghton Mifflin Harcourt Publishing Co.

Czajak, Paul. Monster Needs a Christmas Tree. Grieb, Wendy, illus. 2014. (Monster & Me Ser.). (ENG.). 32p. (J). (-k). 16.95 *(978-1-938063-46-6(5),* Mighty Media Kids) Mighty Media Pr.

—Monster Needs a Costume. Grieb, Wendy, illus. (Monster & Me Ser.). (ENG.). 32p. (J). (-k). 2014. 6.99 *(978-1-938063-38-1(4))* 2013. 16.95 *(978-1-938063-09-1(0))* Mighty Media Pr. (Mighty Media Kids).

—Monster Needs a Party. Grieb, Wendy, illus. 2015. (Monster & Me Ser.). (ENG.). 32p. (J). (-k). 16.95 *(978-1-938063-55-8(4),* Mighty Media Kids) Mighty Media Pr.

—Monster Needs His Sleep. Grieb, Wendy, illus. 2014. (Monster & Me Ser.). (ENG.). 32p. (J). (-k). 16.95 *(978-1-938063-26-8(0),* Mighty Media Kids) Mighty Media Pr.

—Monster Needs Your Vote. Grieb, Wendy, illus. 2015. (Monster & Me Ser.). (ENG.). 32p. (J). (gr. -1-3). 16.95 *(978-1-938063-63-3(5),* Mighty Media Kids) Mighty Media Pr.

Dacey, Richard. Spinner McClock & the Christmas Visit. Gillett, Hallie, illus. 2004. 32p. (J). 13.95 *(978-1-929039-24-1(7))* Ambassador Bks., Inc.

Dahl, Michael. Christmas. Ho, Jannie, illus. 2015. (Baby Face Ser.). (ENG.). 10p. (gr. -1 — 1). bds. 7.99 *(978-1-62370-292-2(5))* Capstone Young Readers of Coughlan Cos.

—Goodnight Baseball, 1 vol. Forshay, Christina, illus. 2013. (Sports Illustrated Kids Bedtime Bks.). (ENG.). 32p. (gr. -1-2). lib. bdg. 22.60 *(978-1-4048-7979-9(X))* Capstone Press of Coughlan Cos.

—Goodnight Hockey. Forshay, Christina, illus. 2015. (Sports Illustrated Kids Bedtime Bks.). (ENG.). 32p. (gr. -1-2). lib. bdg. 22.60 *(978-1-4795-6526-9(1))* Capstone Press of Coughlan Cos.

—Halloween. Ho, Jannie, illus. 2015. (Baby Face Ser.). (ENG.). 10p. (gr. -1 — 1). bds. 7.99 *(978-1-62370-293-9(3))* Capstone Young Readers of Coughlan Cos.

—Pirate. Ho, Jannie, illus. 2015. (Baby Face Ser.). (ENG.). 10p. (gr. -1 — 1). bds. 9.99 *(978-1-62370-294-6(1))* Capstone Young Readers of Coughlan Cos.

—Playdate for Panda. Vidal, Oriol, illus. 2016. (Hello Genius Ser.). (ENG.). 20p. (gr. 1-2). bds. 7.99 *(978-1-4795-8741-4(9))* Picture Window Bks.

—Princess. Ho, Jannie, illus. 2015. (Baby Face Ser.). (ENG.). 10p. (gr. -1 — 1). bds. 7.99 *(978-1-62370-295-3(X))* Capstone Young Readers of Coughlan Cos.

Dale, Elizabeth. Off to Market. Pal, Erika, illus. 2013. (ENG.). 32p. (J). (gr. -1-3). 17.99 *(978-1-84780-338-2(5),* Frances Lincoln) Quarto Publishing Group UK GBR. Dist: Hachette Bk. Group.

Dalmatian Press Staff. The Alphabet Song Book. 2008. (ENG.). 5p. (J). bds. 4.95 *(978-1-58117-726-8(7),* Intervisual/Piggy Toes) Bendon, Inc.

—Mommy, Is That You? 2008. (ENG.). 5p. bds. 4.95 *(978-1-58117-714-5(3),* Intervisual/Piggy Toes) Bendon, Inc.

Damon, Matt. The Fall of General Custard, or the Overthrow of a Leftover. Kendall, Gideon, illus. 2016. (HumanKIND Project Ser.). (ENG.). 32p. (J). (gr. k-6). 17.95 *(978-1-940468-33-4(7))* White Cloud Pr.

Damrell, John. The Flooring Family. 2008. 40p. pap. 24.95 *(978-1-60563-007-6(1))* America Star Bks.

Dane, Dichira A. Pathway of Pebbles. 2008. 20p. pap. 24.95 *(978-1-60703-801-6(3))* America Star Bks.

Danielson, Diane K. There Is a Mouse That Is Haunting Our House. 2012. (ENG.). 28p. (J). pap. 14.99 *(978-0-9885157-0-3(9))* SDP Publishing.

Danis, Naomi. Splish-Splash, into the Bath! Kreloff, Elliot, illus. 2007. 16p. (J). *(978-1-59354-609-0(2))* Handprint Bks.

Dannenbring, Cheryl. My Puppy Gave to Me, 1 vol. Kremsner, Cynthia, illus. 2014. (ENG.). 32p. (J). (gr. k-3). 16.99 *(978-1-4556-1943-6(4))* Pelican Publishing Co., Inc.

Danyi, Barb. The Maker of Heaven & Earth. 2011. 28p. (gr. -1). pap. 11.99 *(978-1-4634-1300-2(9))* AuthorHouse.

Danylyshyn, Greg. A Crash of Rhinos. Lomp, Stephan, illus. 2016. (ENG.). 40p. (J). (gr. -1-3). 16.99 *(978-1-4814-3150-7(1),* Little Simon) Little Simon.

Darby, Ada. Skip-Come-A-Lou. 2008. (ENG.). 252p. (J). pap. 17.95 *(978-1-55709-996-9(0))* Applewood Bks.

Darling, Helen. Hide-n-seek Monday. Glickstein, Jennifer, ed. Sona and Jacob, illus. 2007. (J). 10.00 *(978-0-9797674-0-1(7))* My Darling-Tots Pubns.

Darrow, Sharon. Trash. 2006. (ENG.). 160p. (YA). (gr. 7-12). 16.99 *(978-0-7636-2624-2(4))* Candlewick Pr.

Davick, Linda. I Love You, Nose! I Love You, Toes! Davick, Linda, illus. 2013. (ENG., Illus.). 32p. (J). (gr. -1-1). 17.99 *(978-1-4424-6037-8(7),* Beach Lane Bks.) Beach Lane Bks.

—Say Hello! Davick, Linda, illus. 2015. (ENG., Illus.). 40p. (J). (gr. -1-3). 17.99 *(978-1-4814-2867-5(5),* Beach Lane Bks.) Beach Lane Bks.

Davidge, Bud. The Mummer's Song, 1 vol. Wallace, Ian, illus. 2009. (ENG.). 32p. (J). (gr. k). 14.95 *(978-0-88899-960-3(7))* Groundwood Bks. CAN. Dist: Publishers Group West (PGW).

Davidson, Alice Joyce. St. Francis & the Animals. Swanson, Maggie, illus. 2006. 24p. (J). 7.95 *(978-0-88271-003-7(6))* Regina Pr., Malhame & Co.

Davies, Kate, illus. Little Squeak School. 2014. (J). *(978-1-4351-5582-4(3))* Barnes & Noble, Inc.

—Welcome to the Mouse House. 2014. (J). *(978-1-4351-5583-1(1))* Barnes & Noble, Inc.

Davies, Kathern. Bugs, Bugs, Bugs! Sorensen, Heather, illus. 2010. 24p. pap. 12.99 *(978-1-4520-1624-5(0))* AuthorHouse.

Davies, Timothy, Sr. The Polka-Dotted Elephant. 2007. (J). per. 12.00 *(978-0-9793207-0-5(4))* Wildlife Tales Publishing.

Davis, Darlene. God Made Everything. 2008. 28p. pap. 24.95 *(978-1-60672-183-4(6))* PublishAmerica, Inc.

Davis, David. Ten Texas Babies, 1 vol. Jackson, Shelley & Crosby, Jeff, illus. 2014. (ENG.). 32p. (J). (gr. k-3). 16.99 *(978-1-4556-1874-3(8))* Pelican Publishing Co., Inc.

Davis, Terrance. Mom & Me. 2012. 24p. (-18). pap. 24.95 *(978-1-4626-9502-7(7))* America Star Bks.

Davison, Gail. Prince Alexander. PellerinUndo, Joel Ray, illus. 2016. (ENG.). 28p. (J). pap. 28.22 ***(978-1-5245-1787-8(9))*** Xlibris Corp.

Dawnay, Gabby. London Calls. Barrow, Alex, illus. 2015. (ENG.). 32p. (gr. k-3). 13.95 *(978-1-84976-230-4(9))* Tate Publishing, Ltd. GBR. Dist: Abrams, Inc.

Day, Nancy Raines. On a Windy Night. Bates, George, illus. 2010. (ENG.). 40p. (J). (gr. k-2). 16.95 *(978-0-8109-3900-4(2),* Abrams Bks. for Young Readers) Abrams, Inc.

de Alba, Arlette, tr. Musica en Casa: Libro de Cuentos. 2005. (Disney Winnie the Pooh (SilverDolphin) Ser.). (SPA., Illus.). 38p. (J). (gr. -1-7). incl. audio compact disk *(978-970-718-290-5(3),* Silver Dolphin en Español) Advanced Marketing, S. de R. L. de C. V.

de Las Casas, Dianne. Dinosaur Mardi Gras, 1 vol. Gentry, Marita, illus. 2011. (ENG.). 32p. (J). (gr. k-3). 16.99 *(978-1-58980-966-6(1))* Pelican Publishing Co., Inc.

—Mama's Bayou, 1 vol. Stone-Barker, Holly, illus. 2010. (ENG.). 32p. (J). (gr. k-k). 16.99 *(978-1-58980-787-7(1))* Pelican Publishing Co., Inc.

Dealey, Erin. Goldie Locks Has Chicken Pox. 2004. (Illus.). (J). (gr. k-3). spiral bd. *(978-0-616-14572-2(1));* spiral bd. *(978-0-616-14573-9(X))* Canadian National Institute for the Blind/Institut National Canadien pour les Aveugles.

—Goldie Locks Has Chicken Pox. Wakiyama, Hanako, illus. 2005. (ENG.). 40p. (J). (gr. -1-2). reprint ed. 8.99 *(978-0-689-87610-3(6),* Aladdin) Simon & Schuster Children's Publishing.

Dean, James & Dean, Kimberly. Pete the Cat & the Bedtime Blues. Dean, James, illus. 2015. (Pete the Cat Ser.). (Illus.). 40p. (J). (gr. -1-3). (ENG.). 17.99 *(978-0-06-230430-8(5));* lib. bdg. 18.89 *(978-0-06-230431-5(3))* HarperCollins Pubs.

—Pete the Cat & the New Guy. Dean, James, illus. 2014. (Pete the Cat Ser.). (ENG., Illus.). 40p. (J). (gr. -1-3). 17.99 *(978-0-06-227560-8(7));* lib. bdg. 18.89 *(978-0-06-227561-5(5))* HarperCollins Pubs.

Debowski, Sharon. The Snowman, the Owl, & the Groundhog. 2007. (J). lib. bdg. 15.95 *(978-1-60227-468-6(1));* (Illus.). 32p. (gr. -1-4). 14.95 *(978-1-60227-470-9(3))* Above the Clouds Publishing.

Decola, Diane. Butterfly. 2008. 180p. pap. 15.99 *(978-1-4389-0715-4(X))* AuthorHouse.

Degen, Bruce. Jamberry. Degen, Bruce, illus. 25th enl. anniv. ed. 2008. (I Can Read Bks.). (ENG., Illus.). 32p. (J). (gr. -1-3). pap. 7.99 *(978-0-06-443068-5(5))* HarperCollins Pubs.

—Jamberry. 2006. (Illus.). (J). (gr. -1-3). 28.95 incl. audio compact disk *(978-1-59519-362-9(6));* pap. 39.95 incl. audio compact disk *(978-1-59519-323-0(5))* Live Oak Media.

—Nate Likes to Skate. Degen, Bruce, illus. 2016. (I Like to Read(r) Ser.). (ENG., Illus.). 24p. (J). (gr. -1-3). 6.99 *(978-0-8234-3543-2(1));* 14.95 *(978-0-8234-3456-5(7))* Holiday Hse., Inc.

Degman, Lori. Cock-A-Doodle-Oops! Zemke, Deborah, illus. 2014. (ENG.). 36p. (J). (gr. -1-4). 16.95 *(978-1-939547-07-1(5))* Creston Bks.

—1 Zany Zoo. Jack, Colin, illus. 2010. (ENG.). 32p. (J). (gr. -1-2). 17.99 *(978-1-4169-8990-5(0),* Simon & Schuster Bks. For Young Readers) Simon & Schuster Bks. For Young Readers.

Deich, Cheri Bivin. The Messy Monkey Tea Party. Genth, Christina, illus. 2007. 32p. (J). (gr. -1-3). 15.95 *(978-1-60108-006-6(9))* Red Cygnet Pr.

Del Moral, Susana. Las Rimas de Bard: Un Libro con Ventanas. Zaidi, Nadeem, illus. 2005. (Baby Einstein: Libros de Carton Ser.). (SPA.). 16p. (J). (gr. -1). bds. *(978-970-718-304-9(7),* Silver Dolphin en Español) Advanced Marketing, S. de R. L. de C. V.

DeLong, Lucianne. Mrs. Mumford's Missing. Richoll, Stephanie, illus. 2013. (Saloman Sawdust's Snappy Stories Ser.). (ENG.). 24p. (J). 4.99 *(978-0-9833237-5-4(5))* Krullstone Publishing, LLC.

Demarest, Chris L. Bus. 2017. (ENG., Illus.). 16p. (J). (— 1). bds. 6.99 *(978-0-544-87087-1(5),* HMH Books For Young Readers) Houghton Mifflin Harcourt Publishing Co.

Demas, Corinne & Roehrig, Artemis. Are Pirates Polite? Catrow, David, illus. 2016. (ENG.). 40p. (J). (gr. -1-k). 16.99 *(978-0-545-62874-7(1))* Scholastic, Inc.

Dempsey, Kristy. A Hop Is Up. Richmond, Lori, illus. 2016. (ENG.). 40p. (J). 16.99 *(978-1-61963-390-2(6),* 9781619633902, Bloomsbury USA Childrens) Bloomsbury Publishing USA.

—Me with You. Denise, Christopher, illus. 2013. (ENG.). 28p. (J). (gr. -1-k). bds. 7.99 *(978-0-399-16262-6(3),* Philomel Bks.) Penguin Young Readers Group.

—Mini Racer. Strevens-Marzo, Bridget, illus. 2011. (ENG.). 32p. (J). (gr. -1-k). 17.89 *(978-1-59990-591-4(4),* 9781599905914); 16.99 *(978-1-59990-170-1(6),* 9781599901701) Bloomsbury Publishing USA. (Bloomsbury USA Childrens).

—Surfer Chick. Cole, Henry, illus. 2012. (ENG.). 32p. (J). (gr. -1-k). 16.95 *(978-1-4197-0188-7(6),* Abrams Bks. for Young Readers) Abrams, Inc.

—Ten Little Fingers, Two Small Hands. Massey, Jane, illus. 2016. (ENG.). 32p. (J). (gr. -1-2). 16.99 *(978-1-4998-0229-0(3))* Little Bee Books Inc.

—Ten Little Toes, Two Small Feet. Massey, Jane, illus. 2016. (ENG.). 32p. (J). (gr. -1-2). 16.99 *(978-1-4998-0236-8(6))* Little Bee Books Inc.

Dena. Happi Baby, Happi Mommy. 2011. (Happi Baby Ser.). (ENG., Illus.). 12p. (J). (— 1). bds. 6.99 *(978-0-375-87399-7(6),* Random Hse. Bks. for Young Readers) Random Hse. Children's Bks.

Denise, Anika. Baking Day at Grandma's. Denise, Christopher, illus. 2014. (ENG.). 32p. (J). (gr. -1-k). 16.99 *(978-0-399-24244-1(9),* Philomel Bks.) Penguin Young Readers Group.

DePalma, Johnny. The Raindrop Keeper: (Limited Edition Hardcover) Crabapple, Molly, illus. 2006. 50p. (J). 16.50 *(978-0-9791127-8-2(8))* Umbrelly Bks.

DePalma, Mary Newell, illus. Bow-Wow Wiggle Waggle. 2012. (ENG.). 32p. (J). 14.00 *(978-0-8028-5408-7(7),* Eerdmans Bks For Young Readers) Eerdmans, William B. Publishing Co.

DePrisco, Dorothea. Lullaby & Good Night: Music & Lights. 2006. (ENG., Illus.). 12p. (gr. -1-k). 12.95 *(978-1-58117-450-2(0),* Intervisual/Piggy Toes) Bendon, Inc.

DeRosa Bodie, Leona. One Is Fun. Davis, Catherine Baptista, illus. 2007. 30p. (J). (gr. -1). bds. 12.95 *(978-1-4243-2961-8(2))* Independent Publisher Services.

Desai, Naina. Fun Jungle. 2009. 28p. pap. 13.99 *(978-1-4490-2058-3(5))* AuthorHouse.

Dewane, Patrick Ryan. What If the Rain Were Bugs? Konecny, John, illus. 2013. 24p. 14.99 *(978-1-937165-39-0(6))* Orange Hat Publishing.

Dewdney, Anna. Grumpy Gloria. Dewdney, Anna, illus. 2006. (ENG., Illus.). 28p. (J). (gr. -1-k). 16.99 *(978-0-670-06123-5(9),* Viking Books for Young Readers) Penguin Young Readers Group.

—Little Excavator. 2017. (ENG., Illus.). 44p. (J). (-k). 17.99 *(978-1-101-99920-2(9),* Viking Books for Young Readers) Penguin Young Readers Group.

—Llama Llama & the Bully Goat. 2013. (Llama Llama Ser.). (ENG., Illus.). 40p. (J). (gr. -1-k). 17.99 *(978-0-670-01395-1(1),* Viking Books for Young Readers) Penguin Young Readers Group.

—Llama Llama Easter Egg. Dewdney, Anna, illus. 2015. (Llama Llama Ser.). (ENG., Illus.). 14p. (J). (— 1). bds. 5.99 *(978-0-451-46982-3(8),* Viking Books for Young Readers) Penguin Publishing Group.

—Llama Llama Holiday Drama. 2010. (Llama Llama Ser.). (ENG.). 40p. (J). (gr. -1-k). 17.99 *(978-0-670-01161-2(4),* Viking Books for Young Readers) Penguin Young Readers Group.

—Llama Llama Home with Mama. 2011. (Llama Llama Ser.). (ENG.). 32p. (J). (gr. -1-k). 17.99 *(978-0-670-01232-9(7),* Viking Books for Young Readers) Penguin Young Readers Group.

—Llama Llama Hoppity-Hop! 2012. (Llama Llama Ser.). (ENG.). 14p. (J). (gr. -1 — 1). bds. 5.99 *(978-0-670-01329-6(3),* Viking Books for Young Readers) Penguin Young Readers Group.

—Llama Llama I Love You. 2014. (Llama Llama Ser.). (ENG., Illus.). 14p. (J). (gr. -1 — 1). bds. 5.99 *(978-0-451-46981-6(X),* Viking Books for Young Readers) Penguin Young Readers Group.

—Llama Llama Jingle Bells. Dewdney, Anna, illus. 2014. (Llama Llama Ser.). (ENG., Illus.). 14p. (J). (— 1). bds. 5.99 *(978-0-451-46980-9(1),* Viking Books for Young Readers) Penguin Young Readers Group.

—Llama Llama Mad at Mama. Dewdney, Anna, illus. 2007. (Llama Llama Ser.). (ENG., Illus.). 40p. (J). (gr. -1-k). 17.99 *(978-0-670-06240-9(5),* Viking Books for Young Readers) Penguin Young Readers Group.

—Llama Llama Misses Mama. 2009. (Llama Llama Ser.). (ENG., Illus.). 40p. (J). (gr. -1-k). 17.99 *(978-0-670-06198-3(0),* Viking Books for Young Readers) Penguin Young Readers Group.

—Llama Llama Nighty-Night. 2012. (Llama Llama Ser.). (ENG., Illus.). 14p. (J). bds. 5.99 *(978-0-670-01327-2(7),* Viking Books for Young Readers) Penguin Young Readers Group.

—Llama Llama Red Pajama. Dewdney, Anna, illus. (Llama Llama Ser.). (ENG., Illus.). 40p. (J). (gr. -1-k). 2014. 25.00 *(978-0-451-46990-8(9))* 2005. 17.99 *(978-0-670-05983-6(8))* Penguin Young Readers Group. (Viking Books for Young Readers).

—Llama Llama Red Pajama, 6 vols., Pack. gif. ed. 2014. (ENG.). (J). 107.94 *(978-0-451-47544-2(5),* Viking Books for Young Readers) Penguin Young Readers Group.

—Llama Llama Red Pajama. *(978-0-439-90665-4(2));* 2006. lp *(978-0-439-90679-1(2))* Scholastic, Inc.

—Llama Llama Time to Share. 2012. (Llama Llama Ser.). (ENG.). 40p. (J). (gr. -1-k). 17.99 *(978-0-670-01233-6(5),* Viking Books for Young Readers) Penguin Young Readers Group.

—Llama Llama Wakey-Wake. 2012. (Llama Llama Ser.). (ENG.). 14p. (J). (— 1). bds. 5.99 *(978-0-670-01326-5(9),* Viking Books for Young Readers) Penguin Young Readers Group.

—Llama Llama's Little Library. 2013. (Llama Llama Ser.). (ENG., Illus.). 56p. (J). (— 1). bds. 23.96 *(978-0-670-01648-8(9),* Viking Books for Young Readers) Penguin Young Readers Group.

—Nelly Gnu & Daddy Too. (ENG., Illus.). (J). 2017. 36p. (-k). bds. 9.99 *(978-0-425-28977-8(X))* 2014. 40p. (gr. -1-k). 17.99 *(978-0-670-01227-5(0))* Penguin Young Readers Group. (Viking Books for Young Readers).

—Nobunny's Perfect. (ENG.). 32p. (J). (gr. -1-k). 2012. bds. 6.99 *(978-0-670-01408-8(7),* Viking Books for Young Readers) 2010. pap. 6.99 *(978-0-14-241533-7(2),* Puffin Books) Penguin Young Readers Group.

Un Día de Escuela de Oso. 2014. (SPA., Illus.). (J). *(978-1-78285-087-8(2))* Barefoot Bks., Inc.

Diamond, Charlotte. Slippery Fish in Hawaii. Aardema, John, illus. 2013. (ENG.). 16p. (J). (gr. -1-1). bds. 7.95 *(978-1-933067-57-5(8))* Beachhouse Publishing, LLC.

Diaz-Pimienta, Alexis. Cuentos Clasicos en Verso.Tr. of Classic Stories in Verse. (SPA.). (J). (gr. 2-4). pap. 7.98 *(978-970-643-142-4(X))* Selector, S.A. de C.V. MEX. Dist: Lectorum Pubns., Inc.

DiCicco, Sue. Funny Bunnies: Morning, Noon, & Night. 2015. (Illus.). 32p. (J). *(978-1-4844-4595-2(3))* Scholastic, Inc.

Dickinson, Tom. Bob's Secret Hideaway. 2014. (Collins Big Cat Ser.). (ENG., Illus.). 32p. (J). (gr. k-1). pap. 6.99 *(978-0-00-753850-8(2))* HarperCollins Pubs. Ltd. GBR. Dist: Independent Pubs. Group.

Diesen, Deborah. The Not Very Merry Pout-Pout Fish. Hanna, Dan, illus. (Pout-Pout Fish Adventure Ser.). (ENG.). (J). 2017. 34p. bds. 7.99 *(978-0-374-30459-1(9),* 9780374304591) 2015. 32p. (gr. -1-1). 16.99 *(978-0-374-35549-4(5),* 9780374355494) Farrar, Straus & Giroux. (Farrar, Straus & Giroux (BYR)).

—The Pout-Pout Fish. Hanna, Dan, illus. (Pout-Pout Fish Adventure Ser.: 1). (ENG.). (J). (gr. -1 — 1). 2013. 36p. bds. 7.99 *(978-0-374-36097-9(9),* 9780374360979) 2008. 32p. 16.99 *(978-0-374-36096-2(0),* 9780374360962) Farrar, Straus & Giroux. (Farrar, Straus & Giroux (BYR)).

—The Pout-Pout Fish & the Bully-Bully Shark. Hanna, Dan, illus. 2017. (Pout-Pout Fish Adventure Ser.). (ENG.). 32p. (J). 16.99 ***(978-0-374-30402-7(5),*** 9780374304027, Farrar, Straus & Giroux (BYR)) Farrar, Straus & Giroux.

—The Pout-Pout Fish Book & CD Storytime Set. unabr. ed. 2013. (ENG.). (J). (gr. -1-1). 12.99 *(978-1-4272-3176-5(1),* 9781427231765) Macmillan Audio.

—The Pout-Pout Fish, Far, Far from Home. Hanna, Dan, illus. 2017. (Pout-Pout Fish Adventure Ser.). (ENG.). 32p. (J). 16.99 *(978-0-374-30194-1(8),* 9780374301941, Farrar, Straus & Giroux (BYR)) Farrar, Straus & Giroux.

—The Pout-Pout Fish Goes to School. Hanna, Dan, illus. 2014. (Pout-Pout Fish Adventure Ser.). (ENG.). 32p. (J). (gr. -1-k). 16.99 *(978-0-374-36095-5(2),* 9780374360955, Farrar, Straus & Giroux (BYR)) Farrar, Straus & Giroux.

—The Pout-Pout Fish in the Big-Big Dark. Hanna, Dan, illus. (Pout-Pout Fish Adventure Ser.: 2). (ENG.). (J). (gr. -1-1). 2015. 34p. bds. 7.99 *(978-0-374-30189-7(1),* 9780374301897) 2010. 32p. 16.99 *(978-0-374-30798-1(9),* 9780374307981) Farrar, Straus & Giroux. (Farrar, Straus & Giroux (BYR)).

—Smile, Pout-Pout Fish. Hanna, Dan, illus. 2014. (Pout-Pout Fish Mini Adventure Ser.). (ENG.). 12p. (J). (gr. -1 — 1). bds. 5.99 *(978-0-374-37084-8(2),* 9780374370848, Farrar, Straus & Giroux (BYR)) Farrar, Straus & Giroux.

Diggs, Taye. Mixed Me! Evans, Shane W., illus. 2015. (ENG.). 40p. (J). (gr. -1-3). 17.99 *(978-1-250-04719-9(6),* 9781250047199) Feiwel & Friends.

Dill, Mark. Maddie & Me: Go to the Zoo. 2012. 40p. pap. 20.99 *(978-1-4685-7481-4(7))* AuthorHouse.

Dillon-Butler, Marybeth. Myrtle the Hurdler: And Her Pink & Purple Polka-Dotted Girdle. Messing, David, illus. 2005. (ENG.). 32p. (J). (gr. -1-2). pap. 11.95 *(978-0-9785075-9-6(2),* Ferne Pr.) Nelson Publishing & Marketing.

Dillon, Leo & Dillon, Diane. Rap a Tap Tap: Here's Bojangles - Think of That! 2005. (J). 28.95 incl. audio compact disk *(978-1-59519-369-8(3))* Live Oak Media.

Dimplechin, Lord Reginald. Does a Wuzz. 2012. 38p. 24.95 *(978-1-4626-6151-0(3))* America Star Bks.

Dipucchio, Kelly. Dinosnores. Goembel, Ponder, illus. 2005. 32p. (J). (gr. -1 — 1). 17.99 *(978-0-06-051577-5(5));* lib. bdg. 16.89 *(978-0-06-051578-2(3))* HarperCollins Pubs.

—Littles: And How They Grow. Ford, A. G., illus. 2017. (ENG.). 32p. (J). (gr. -1 — 1). 17.99 ***(978-0-399-55526-8(9));*** lib. bdg. 20.99 ***(978-0-399-55527-5(7))*** Random Hse. Children's Bks. (Doubleday Bks. for Young Readers).

—Monster Makeovers. Pham, LeUyen, illus. 2006. (J). *(978-0-7868-5181-2(3))* Hyperion Bks. for Children.

—One Little, Two Little, Three Little Children. Lundquist, Mary, illus. 2016. 32p. (J). (gr. -1-3). 17.99 *(978-0-06-234866-1(3))* HarperCollins Pubs.

Disney & Studiomouse Staff. Give a Dog a Bone: Mother Goose. 2011. (ENG.). 20p. (J). *(978-1-59069-945-4(9))* Studio Mouse LLC.

Disney Book Group. Disney Princess Read-Along Storybook & CD Boxed Set. Disney Storybook Art Team, illus. 2017. (Read-Along Storybook & CD Ser.). (ENG.). 128p. (J). (gr. 1-3). pap. 12.99 *(978-1-368-00262-2(5))* Disney Pr.

—The Lion Guard Read-Along Storybook & CD the Power of the Roar. Disney Storybook Art Team, illus. 2017. (Read-Along Storybook & CD Ser.). (ENG.). 32p. (J). (gr. -1-k). pap. 6.99 *(978-1-4847-2950-2(1))* Disney Pr.

Disney Book Group Staff & Hapka, Catherine. Me & Our Mom. Disney Storybook Art Team, illus. 2015. (ENG.). 24p. (J). (gr. -1-k). pap. 4.99 *(978-1-4847-0688-6(9))* Disney Pr.

Disney, Pixar Cars, ed. Rhymes on the Go. 2009. (ENG.). 24p. 4.99 *(978-1-59069-776-4(6))* Studio Mouse LLC.

Disney, Sofia the First. Disney Guess Who, Sofia! 2014. (Guess Who Ser.: 1). (ENG.). 10p. (J). (gr. -1-k). 10.99 *(978-0-7944-3074-0(0),* Reader's Digest Children's Bks.) Studio Fun International.

Disney Storybook Art Team, illus. Frozen Fever Read-Along Storybook & CD. 2015. (Read-Along Storybook & CD Ser.). (ENG.). 32p. (J). (gr. 1-3). pap. 6.99 *(978-1-4847-4197-9(8))* Disney Pr.

DiTerlizzi, Angela. Baby Love. Hughes, Brooke Boynton, illus. 2015. (ENG.). 32p. (J). (gr. -1-3). 17.99 *(978-1-4424-3392-2(2),* Beach Lane Bks.) Beach Lane Bks.

—Say What? Chou, Joey, illus. 2011. (ENG.). 32p. (J). (gr. -1-k). 15.99 *(978-1-4169-8694-2(4),* Beach Lane Bks.) Beach Lane Bks.

—Some Bugs. Wenzel, Brendan, illus. 2014. (ENG.). 32p. (J). (gr. -1-3). 17.99 *(978-1-4424-5880-2(1),* Beach Lane Bks.) Beach Lane Bks.

—Some Pets. Wenzel, Brendan, illus. 2016. (ENG.). 32p. (J). (gr. -1-3). 17.99 *(978-1-4814-4402-6(6),* Beach Lane Bks.) Beach Lane Bks.

Dixon, Dallas L. Shelby's Shoes. Williams, Nancy E., ed. Cappoen, Jennifer Tipton, illus. 2013. 24p. (J). pap. 12.98 *(978-1-938526-33-6(3))* Laurus Bks.

Dixon, Pamela. A Windy Day Walk. Homer, Maree, illus. 2016. (ENG.). 32p. (J). (gr. 1-4). *(978-0-473-34486-3(6))* Lizzy Web Bks.

Dixon, Virginia. What Happened to Willie? Thomas, Tim, illus. 2007. 32p. (J). 16.00 *(978-0-9795386-0-5(2))* Grand Productions.

Dobbins, Jan. Driving My Tractor. Sim, David, illus. 2009. (ENG.). 32p. (J). (gr. -1-3). 16.99 incl. audio compact disk *(978-1-84686-358-5(9))* Barefoot Bks., Inc.

Dobkin, Bonnie. Crazy Pizza Day. Dey, Romi, illus. 2010. (J). *(978-1-60617-150-9(X))* Teaching Strategies, LLC.

Docherty, Helen. The Snatchabook. Docherty, Helen, illus. 2013. (ENG., Illus.). 32p. (J). (-2). 16.99 *(978-1-4022-9082-4(9),* 9781402290824, Sourcebooks Jabberwocky) Sourcebooks, Inc.

—The Storybook Knight. Docherty, Thomas, illus. 2016. (ENG.). 32p. (J). (-4). 16.99 *(978-1-4926-3814-8(5),* 9781492638148, Sourcebooks Jabberwocky) Sourcebooks, Inc.

Docherty, Thomas. Wash-A-Bye Bear. Docherty, Thomas, illus. 2013. (ENG., Illus.). 32p. (J). (gr. -1-2). 14.99 *(978-0-7636-6486-2(3),* Templar) Candlewick Pr.

Dodd, Emma. Happy. Dodd, Emma, illus. 2015. (Emma Dodd's Love You Bks.). (ENG., Illus.). 24p. (J). (-k). 12.99 *(978-0-7636-8008-4(7),* Nosy Crow) Candlewick Pr.

—When You Were Born. Dodd, Emma, illus. 2015. (Emma Dodd's Love You Bks.). (ENG., Illus.). 24p. (J). (-k). 12.99 *(978-0-7636-7405-2(2),* Templar) Candlewick Pr.

—Wish. Dodd, Emma, illus. 2015. (Emma Dodd's Love You Bks.). (ENG., Illus.). 24p. (J). (-k). 12.99 *(978-0-7636-8009-1(5),* Nosy Crow) Candlewick Pr.

Dodd, Lynley. Hairy Maclary's Caterwaul Caper. Dodd, Lynley, illus. 2009. (Hairy Maclary & Friends Ser.). (ENG., Illus.). 32p. (J). (gr. -1-2). pap. 6.99 *(978-0-58246-307-0(7),* Tricycle Pr.) Random Hse. Children's Bks.

—Schnitzel Von Krumm, Dogs Never Climb Trees. 2004. (Gold Star First Readers Ser.). (Illus.). 32p. (gr. -1-3). lib. bdg. 23.00 *(978-0-8368-4092-6(5),* Gareth Stevens Learning Library) Stevens, Gareth Publishing LLLP.

—Zachary Quack Minimonster. Dodd, Lynley, illus. 2006. (Gold Star First Readers Ser.). (Illus.). 32p. (gr. -1-3). lib. bdg. 23.00 *(978-0-8368-6187-7(6),* Gareth Stevens Learning Library) Stevens, Gareth Publishing LLLP.

Dodds, Dayle Ann. Full House: An Invitation to Fractions. Carter, Abby, illus. 2009. (ENG.). 32p. (J). (gr. 1-4). pap. 6.99 *(978-0-7636-4130-6(8))* Candlewick Pr.

—Minnie's Diner: A Multiplying Menu. Manders, John, illus. 2007. (ENG.). 40p. (J). (gr. k-3). pap. 6.99 *(978-0-7636-3313-4(5))* Candlewick Pr.

Doerrfeld, Cori. Little Bunny Foo Foo: The Real Story. 2016. (ENG., Illus.). 32p. (J). (-k). pap. 8.99 *(978-1-101-99774-1(5),* Puffin Books) Penguin Young Readers Group.

Doherty, Dave, illus. There Once Was a Place Called P.O.P. 2008. 93p. (J). 61.99 *(978-1-4363-6190-3(7))* Xlibris Corp.

Dominguez, Angela. Maria Tenía una Llamita. Dominguez, Angela, illus. 2013.Tr. of Maria Had a Little Llama. (SPA & ENG., Illus.). 32p. (J). (gr. -1-2). 17.99 *(978-0-8050-9333-9(8),* 9780805093339, Holt, Henry & Co. Bks. For Young Readers) Holt, Henry & Co.

Domney, Alexis. Splish, Splat!, 1 vol. Crawford, Alice, illus. 2011. (ENG.). 24p. (J). (gr. 1-3). 15.95 *(978-1-897187-88-3(2))* Second Story Pr. CAN. Dist: Orca Bk. Pubs. USA.

Donahue, Laurie. Mr. Blue a Job for You. Bryan, Hintz, illus. 2010. 32p. (J). 15.95 *(978-0-9799116-2-0(1))* LifeSong Pubs.

Donaldson, Julia. Animal Music. Sharratt, Nick, illus. (ENG.). (J). (-k). 2015. 20p. bds. 10.99 *(978-1-4472-7679-1(5))* 2014. 24p. pap. 9.99 *(978-1-4472-1095-5(6))* Pan Macmillan GBR. Dist: Independent Pubs. Group.

—The Fish Who Cried Wolf. Scheffler, Axel, illus. (J). 2017. (ENG.). 40p. (gr. -1-k). 17.99 *(978-0-439-92825-0(7))* 2008. pap. *(978-0-545-03454-8(X))* Scholastic, Inc. (Levine, Arthur A. Bks.).

—The Flying Bath. Roberts, David, illus. 2016. (ENG.). 32p. (J). (gr. -1-k). pap. 9.99 *(978-1-4472-7711-8(2))* Pan Macmillan GBR. Dist: Independent Pubs. Group.

—Freddie & the Fairy, 7. George, Karen, illus. 4th ed. 2012. (ENG.). 32p. (J). (gr. -1-k). 9.99 *(978-0-330-51118-6(1))* Pan Macmillan GBR. Dist: Independent Pubs. Group.

—Goat Goes to Playgroup. Sharratt, Nick, illus. (ENG.). (J). 2015. 24p. (-k). bds. 9.99 *(978-1-4472-8791-9(6))* 2014. 26p. bds. 9.99 *(978-1-4472-5484-3(8))*8. 2013. 32p. (gr. -1-k). pap. 9.99 *(978-1-4472-1094-8(8))* Pan Macmillan GBR. Dist: Independent Pubs. Group.

—A Gold Star for Zog. Scheffler, Axel, illus. 2012. (ENG.). 32p. (J). (gr. -1-3). 17.99 *(978-0-545-41724-2(4),* Levine, Arthur A. Bks.) Scholastic, Inc.

—The Gruffalo. Harris, Ben, tr. from ENG. Scheffler, Axel, illus. 2012. (LAT, SPA & ENG.). 32p. (J). (gr. -1-2). 19.99 *(978-0-230-75932-9(7))* Pan Macmillan GBR. Dist: Independent Pubs. Group.

—The Gruffalo. Scheffler, Axel, illus. (ENG.). (J). (gr. -1-2). 2006. 32p. pap. 7.99 *(978-0-14-240387-2(3),* Puffin Books) 2005. 26p. bds. 8.99 *(978-0-8037-3047-2(0),* Dial Bks) Penguin Young Readers Group.

—The Gruffalo. Scheffler, Axel, illus. 2005. (ENG.). 32p. (J). (gr. -1-2). 17.99 *(978-0-8037-3109-7(4),* Dial Bks) Penguin Young Readers Group.

—The Gruffalo. 2006. lib. bdg. 18.40 *(978-0-606-23141-1(2),* Turtleback) Turtleback Bks.

—The Gruffalo in Scots. Robertson, James, tr. from ENG. Scheffler, Axel, illus. 2012. (ENG.). 32p. (J). (-k). pap. 10.99 *(978-1-84502-503-8(2))* Black and White Publishing Ltd. GBR. Dist: Independent Pubs. Group.

—The Gruffalo's Child. Scheffler, Axel, illus. 2007. (ENG.). 32p. (J). (gr. -1-2). pap. 7.99 *(978-0-14-240754-7(2),* Puffin Books) Penguin Young Readers Group.

—The Highway Rat. Scheffler, Axel, illus. 2013. (ENG.). 32p. (J). (gr. -1-3). 16.99 *(978-0-545-47758-1(1),* Levine, Arthur A. Bks.) Scholastic, Inc.

—Jack & the Flumflum Tree. Roberts, David, illus. 2016. (ENG.). 30p. (J). (gr. -1-k). bds. 9.99 *(978-1-4472-8549-6(2))* Pan Macmillan GBR. Dist: Independent Pubs. Group.

—One Mole Digging A Hole. Sharratt, Nick, illus. 2015. (ENG.). 22p. (J). (-k). bds. 9.99 *(978-1-4472-8790-2(8))* Pan Macmillan GBR. Dist: Independent Pubs. Group.

—One Mole Digging a Hole, 2. Sharratt, Nick, illus. 2010. (ENG.). 32p. (J). (gr. k-k). pap. 8.99 *(978-0-230-70647-7(9))* Macmillan Pubs., Ltd. GBR. Dist: Independent Pubs. Group.

—One Ted Falls Out of Bed. Currey, Anna, illus. 2015. (ENG.). 32p. (J). (— 1). pap. 7.99 *(978-1-4472-6614-3(5))* Pan Macmillan GBR. Dist: Independent Pubs. Group.

—The Reiver Rat: The Highway Rat in Scots. Robertson, James, tr. from ENG. Scheffler, Axel, illus. 2015. (ENG.). 32p. (J). (-k). pap. 10.99 *(978-1-84502-996-8(8))* Black and White Publishing Ltd. GBR. Dist: Independent Pubs. Group.

—Room on the Broom. Scheffler, Axel, illus. 2003. (ENG.). 32p. (J). (gr. -1-2). pap. 6.99 *(978-0-14-250112-3(2),* Puffin Books) Penguin Young Readers Group.

—The Scarecrows' Wedding. Scheffler, Axel, illus. 2014. (ENG.). 32p. (J). (gr. -1-3). 17.99 *(978-0-545-72606-1(9),* Levine, Arthur A. Bks.) Scholastic, Inc.

—The Snail & the Whale. Scheffler, Axel, illus. (ENG.). 32p. (J). (gr. -1-2). 2004. 18.99 *(978-0-8037-2922-3(7),* Dial Bks) 2006. reprint ed. pap. 6.99 *(978-0-14-240580-2(9),* Puffin Books) Penguin Young Readers Group.

—A Squash & a Squeeze. Scheffler, Axel, illus. 2016. (ENG.). 32p. (J). (gr. -1-k). 16.99 *(978-1-338-05220-6(9))* Scholastic, Inc.

—Stick Man. Scheffler, Axel, illus. 2009. (ENG.). 32p. (J). (gr. -1-3). 16.99 *(978-0-545-15761-2(7),* Levine, Arthur A. Bks.) Scholastic, Inc.

—Superworm. Scheffler, Axel, illus. 2014. (ENG.). 32p. (J). (gr. -1-3). 16.99 *(978-0-545-59176-8(7),* Levine, Arthur A. Bks.) Scholastic, Inc.

—Tabby McTat: The Musical Cat. Scheffler, Axel, illus. 2012. (ENG.). 32p. (J). (gr. -1-3). 17.99 *(978-0-545-45168-0(X),* Levine, Arthur A. Bks.) Scholastic, Inc.

—What the Ladybug Heard. Monks, Lydia, illus. 2010. (ENG.). 32p. (J). (gr. -1-1). 18.99 *(978-0-8050-9028-4(2),* 9780805090284, Holt, Henry & Co. Bks. For Young Readers) Holt, Henry & Co.

—Where's My Mom? Scheffler, Axel, illus. 2008. (ENG.). 32p. (J). (gr. -1-2). 18.99 *(978-0-8037-3228-5(7),* Dial Bks) Penguin Young Readers Group.

—Whit the Clockleddy Heard. Robertson, James, tr. from ENG. Monks, Lydia, illus. 2015. (ENG.). 32p. (J). (-k). pap. 10.99 *(978-1-84502-957-9(7))* Black and White Publishing Ltd. GBR. Dist: Independent Pubs. Group.

Doodlemum & Smith, Justine. My Mummy Says. Stevens, Angie, illus. 2014. (Families & Friends Ser.). (ENG.). 16p. (J). (-k). bds. 9.99 *(978-1-4472-6097-4(X))* Pan Macmillan GBR. Dist: Independent Pubs. Group.

Doodler, Todd H. The Zoo I Drew. 2009. (ENG., Illus.). 56p. (J). (gr. -1-k). 14.99 *(978-0-375-85201-5(8),* Random Hse. Bks. for Young Readers) Random Hse. Children's Bks.

Dopirak, Kate. You're My Boo. Withrow, Lesley Breen, illus. 2016. (ENG.). 40p. (J). (gr. -1-3). 17.99 *(978-1-4424-4160-6(7),* Beach Lane Bks.) Beach Lane Bks.

Dorfman, Craig. I Knew You Could! A Book for All the Stops in Your Life. Ong, Cristina, illus. 2003. (Little Engine That Could Ser.). (ENG.). 32p. (J). (gr. -1-2). 11.99 *(978-0-448-43148-2(3),* Grosset & Dunlap) Penguin Young Readers Group.

Dorling Kindersley Publishing Staff. Baby Cheep! Cheep! 2015. (ENG.). 14p. (J). (gr. -1 — 1). bds. 5.99 *(978-1-4654-3184-4(5),* DK Children) Dorling Kindersley Publishing, Inc.

—Baby What's That? 2015. (ENG.). 14p. (J). (gr. -1 — 1). bds. 5.99 *(978-1-4654-3181-3(0),* DK Children) Dorling Kindersley Publishing, Inc.

—Farm. 2011. (ENG., Illus.). 12p. (J). (gr. -1 — 1). bds. 9.99 *(978-0-7566-7172-3(8),* DK Children) Dorling Kindersley Publishing, Inc.

—Pop-Up Peekaboo! - Playtime. 2011. (ENG.). 12p. (J). (gr. -1 — 1). bds. 9.99 *(978-0-7566-7171-6(X),* DK Children) Dorling Kindersley Publishing, Inc.

—Sophie Pop-Up Peekaboo! 2014. (ENG., Illus.). 12p. (J). (gr. -1 — 1). bds. 9.99 *(978-1-4654-2041-1(X),* DK Children) Dorling Kindersley Publishing, Inc.

Dorman, Brandon. Pirates of the Sea! Dorman, Brandon, illus. 2011. (ENG., Illus.). 32p. (J). (gr. -1-3). 16.99 *(978-0-06-204068-8(5),* Greenwillow Bks.) HarperCollins Pubs.

Las Dos Iguanas.Tr. of Two Iguanas. (SPA.). (J). 9.95 *(978-968-6044-78-2(7))* Corunda, Ediciones, S.A. de C.V. MEX. Dist: AIMS International Bks., Inc.

Dotlich, Rebecca Kai. Race Car Count. Slack, Michael, illus. (ENG.). 32p. (J). 2017. bds. 7.99 *(978-1-62779-934-8(6),* 9781627799348) 2015. (gr. -1-k). 14.99 *(978-1-62779-009-3(8),* 9781627790093) Holt, Henry & Co. (Holt, Henry & Co. Bks. For Young Readers).

Doughty, Rebecca. Before You. 2016. (ENG., Illus.). 32p. (J). (gr. -1-3). 14.99 *(978-0-544-46317-2(X),* HMH Books For Young Readers) Houghton Mifflin Harcourt Publishing Co.

Douglas, Atom. Mathew's Space Ship. Douglas, Atom, . 2007. (Illus.). 32p. (J). 6.50 *(978-0-9798316-0-7(1))* JaxPublishing.net.

Douglas, Babette. Curly Hare Gets It Straight. Williams, Ted, illus. 2006. (Kiss a Me Teacher Creature Stories Ser.). (J). (gr. -1-3). *(978-1-890343-35-4(8))* Kiss A Me Productions, Inc.

—Noreen: The Real King of the Jungle. Johnson, John, illus. 2006. (Kiss a Me Teacher Creature Stories Ser.). 20p. (J). (gr. -1-3). 9.99 *(978-1-890343-25-5(0))* Kiss A Me Productions, Inc.

Downing, Johnette. Down in Mississippi, 1 vol. Zecca, Katherine, illus. 2016. (ENG.). 32p. (J). 16.99 *(978-1-4556-2098-2(X))* Pelican Publishing Co., Inc.

—The Fifolet, 1 vol. Lindsley, Jennifer, illus. 2015. (ENG.). 32p. (J). (gr. k-3). 16.99 *(978-1-4556-2036-4(X))* Pelican Publishing Co., Inc.

—Macarooned on a Dessert Island, 1 vol. Wald, Christina, illus. 2014. (ENG.). 32p. (J). (gr. k-3). 16.99 *(978-1-4556-1936-8(1))* Pelican Publishing Co., Inc.

Downing, Sue. Cheep, Cheep! Baby Animal Sounds. 2016. (ENG., Illus.). 10p. (J). bds. 7.99 *(978-1-61963-833-4(9),* 9781619638334, Bloomsbury USA Childrens) Bloomsbury Publishing USA.

—Look, Look! Baby Animal Friends. 2016. (ENG., Illus.). 10p. (J). bds. 7.99 *(978-1-61963-832-7(0),* 9781619638327, Bloomsbury USA Childrens) Bloomsbury Publishing USA.

Downs, Jay & Downs, Jeanie. The Flutterfly. 2010. 68p. pap. 25.49 *(978-1-4520-1860-7(X))* AuthorHouse.

Downs, Mike. You See a Circus, I See... McGrory, Anik, illus. 2006. (ENG.). 32p. (J). (gr. -1-3). pap. 7.95 *(978-1-58089-155-4(1))* Charlesbridge Publishing, Inc.

Downs Webb, Michelle. What Color Is Love? 2005. 24p. 10.95 *(978-1-4116-2783-3(0))* Lulu Pr., Inc.

Doyen, Denise. Once upon a Twice. Moser, Barry, illus. 2013. (Picture Book Ser.). (ENG.). 32p. (J). (gr. -1-2). pap. 7.99 *(978-0-449-81794-0(6),* Dragonfly Bks.) Random Hse. Children's Bks.

Doyen, Denise. The Pomegranate Witch. Wheeler, Eliza, illus. 2017. (ENG.). 40p. (J). (gr. k-3). 16.99 ***(978-1-4521-4589-1(X))*** Chronicle Bks. LLC.

—The Pomegranate Witch. Moser, Barry, illus. 2013. (J). *(978-0-375-87057-6(1));* lib. bdg. *(978-0-375-97057-3(6))* Random Hse., Inc.

Dr. Seuss Enterprises Staff. Hop on Pop. 2004. (Bright & Early Board Books Ser.). (ENG., Illus.). 24p. (J). (gr. k-1). bds. 4.99 *(978-0-375-82837-9(0),* Random Hse. Bks. for Young Readers) Random Hse. Children's Bks.

Dragonwagon, Crescent. All the Awake Animals Are Almost Asleep. McPhail, David, illus. 2012. (ENG.). 40p. (J). (gr. -1-3). 16.99 *(978-0-316-07045-4(9))* Little Brown & Co.

—All the Awake Animals Are Almost Asleep. McPhail, David, illus. 2016. (ENG.). 30p. (J). (gr. -1 — 1). bds. 7.99

S

(978-0-316-33627-7(0)) Little, Brown Bks. for Young Readers.

Dreyer, Nicole E. The Parable of the Talents. Morris, Susan, illus. 2007. 16p. (J). (gr. k-4). 1.99 *(978-0-7586-1282-3(6))* Concordia Publishing Hse.

Drez, Jennifer & Burnstead, Robin. Goodnight Cowtown. Voight, Lisa, illus. 2012. 40p. (J). 17.95 *(978-0-615-54492-2(4))* Petit Chou Chou, LLC.

Driscoll, Laura. Thumper Goes A-Thumpin' Tyminski, Lori, illus. 2015. (ENG.). 12p. (J). (gr. -1 — 1). bds. 6.99 *(978-1-4847-0960-3(8))* Disney Pr.

—We Are Twins. Campion, Pascal, illus. 2012. (Penguin Young Readers, Level 1 Ser.). (ENG.). 32p. (J). (gr. k-1). mass mkt. 3.99 *(978-0-448-46157-1(9),* Penguin Young Readers) Penguin Young Readers Group.

—We Are Twins. 2012. (Penguin Young Readers Level 1 Ser.). lib. bdg. 13.55 *(978-0-606-26641-3(0),* Turtleback) Turtleback Bks.

Dromgoole, Glenn. Good Night Little Texan. Clack, Barbra, illus. 2012. (ENG.). 24p. (J). (gr. k-2). 15.95 *(978-1-936474-10-3(7),* 9781936474103) Bright Sky Pr.

Druvert, Hélène. Mary Poppins: Up, up & Away. 2017. (ENG., Illus.). 36p. (gr. k-4). 24.95 *(978-0-500-65104-9(3),* 565104) Thames & Hudson.

Dubosarsky, Ursula. The Terrible Plop. Joyner, Andrew, illus. 2009. (ENG.). 40p. (J). (gr. -1-1). 17.99 *(978-0-374-37428-0(7),* 9780374374280, Farrar, Straus & Giroux (BYR)) Farrar, Straus & Giroux.

Duddle, Jonny. The Pirate Cruncher. Duddle, Jonny, illus. 2010. (ENG., Illus.). 38p. (J). (gr. -1-2). 15.99 *(978-0-7636-4876-3(0),* Templar) Candlewick Pr.

—The Pirates Next Door. 2012. (ENG., Illus.). 44p. (J). (gr. -1-2). 15.99 *(978-0-7636-5842-7(1),* Templar) Candlewick Pr.

Dudley, Linda. Aunt Linda's Mommy & Me Book. 2003. (J). pap. 15.99 *(978-1-4134-3830-7(X))* Borders Personal Publishing.

Duffy, Carol Ann. The Skipping-Rope Snake. Monks, Lydia, illus. 2016. (ENG.). 32p. (J). (gr. -1-1). pap. 9.99 ***(978-1-5098-3245-3(9))*** Pan Macmillan GBR. Dist: Independent Pubs. Group.

Duffy, Jacqueline Ann. Dillon the Dog Finds His Family. 2008. 24p. pap. 24.95 *(978-1-60563-331-2(3))* America Star Bks.

Duksta, Laura. I Love You More. Keesler, Karen, illus. 2007. (ENG.). 34p. (J). (gr. k-2). 16.99 *(978-1-4022-1126-3(0),* Sourcebooks Jabberwocky) Sourcebooks, Inc.

—I'll Hug You More. Iwai, Melissa, illus. 2017. (ENG.). (J). 22p. bds. 8.99 *(978-1-4926-4187-2(1),* 9781492641872); 32p. 16.99 *(978-1-4926-2618-3(X),* 9781492626183) Sourcebooks, Inc. (Sourcebooks Jabberwocky).

Dunbar, Joyce. Pat-A-Cake Baby. Dunbar, Polly, illus. 2015. (ENG.). 40p. (J). (-k). 15.99 *(978-0-7636-7577-6(6))* Candlewick Pr.

Dunn, Jill. Littering Is for Losers. Hill, Bodhi, illus. 2012. 64p. (J). 21.99 *(978-0-9852146-2-3(7))* AM Ink Publishing.

Dunn, Opal. Number Rhymes to Say & Play! Gon, Adriano, illus. 2005. (ENG.). 32p. (J). (gr. -1 — 1). per. 7.95 *(978-1-84507-441-8(6),* Frances Lincoln) Quarto Publishing Group UK GBR. Dist: Hachette Bk. Group.

Dunphy, Madeleine. Here Is the Arctic Winter. Robinson, Alan James, illus. 2007. (Web of Life Ser.). (ENG.). 32p. (J). (gr. -1-3). 16.95 *(978-0-9777539-1-8(3));* pap. 9.95 *(978-0-9777539-0-1(5))* Web of Life Children's Bks.

Dunrea, Olivier. Me & Annie McPhee. Hillenbrand, Will, illus. 2016. (ENG.). 32p. (J). (gr. -1-2). 16.99 *(978-0-399-16808-6(7),* Philomel Bks.) Penguin Young Readers Group.

—Ollie's Halloween (reader) 2016. (Gossie & Friends Ser.). (ENG., Illus.). 32p. (J). (gr. -1-3). 12.99 *(978-0-544-64052-8(7),* HMH Books For Young Readers) Houghton Mifflin Harcourt Publishing Co.

Durango, Julia. Cha-Cha Chimps. Taylor, Eleanor, illus. 2010. (ENG.). 32p. (J). (gr. -1-3). 7.99 *(978-1-4169-9574-6(9),* Simon & Schuster Bks. For Young Readers) Simon & Schuster Bks. For Young Readers.

—Go-Go Gorillas. Taylor, Eleanor, illus. 2010. (ENG.). 32p. (J). (gr. -1-1). 15.99 *(978-1-4169-3779-1(X),* Simon & Schuster Bks. For Young Readers) Simon & Schuster Bks. For Young Readers.

—Pest Fest. Cyrus, Kurt, illus. 2012. (ENG.). 40p. (J). (gr. -1-2). 19.99 *(978-1-4424-3095-2(8),* Simon & Schuster Bks. For Young Readers) Simon & Schuster Bks. For Young Readers.

Durango, Julia & Trupiano, Katie Belle. Dream Away. Goldstrom, Robert, illus. 2011. (ENG.). 32p. (J). (gr. -1-3). 16.99 *(978-1-4169-8702-4(9),* Simon & Schuster Bks. For Young Readers) Simon & Schuster Bks. For Young Readers.

Durso, Diana T. Did You Know That's Not My Name? 2009. 52p. pap. 19.95 *(978-1-4389-3182-1(4))* AuthorHouse.

DuTemple, Leslie A. One Little Balsam Fir: A Northwoods Counting Book. Robinson, Susan, illus. 2006. 32p. (J). per. *(978-1-892384-37-9(X))* Avery Color Studios, Inc.

Dutson, Shelly. Jingle Jangle Jungle Jeepers. Christenson, Maren, illus. 2009. 24p. pap. 12.50 *(978-1-4490-1061-4(X))* AuthorHouse.

Duval, Kathy. A Bear's Year. Turley, Gerry, illus. 2015. (ENG.). 40p. (J). (gr. -1-2). 17.99 *(978-0-385-37011-0(3),* Schwartz & Wade Bks.) Random Hse. Children's Bks.

Dyer, Alyssa. When Whizzly Wanders. 2005. 15p. 6.78 *(978-1-4116-4667-4(3))* Lulu Pr., Inc.

Dwyer, Mindy. Sweet Dreams, Polar Bear. 2004. (ENG., Illus.). 32p. (J). 15.95 *(978-0-88240-554-4(3));* pap. 8.99 *(978-0-88240-555-1(1))* Graphic Arts Ctr. Publishing Co.

Dyan, Penelope. Animal Rescue, Book 2, Hanauma Bay, Hawaii. Weigand, John D., photos by. 2008. (Illus.). 56p. pap. 15.95 *(978-1-935118-43-5(9))* Bellissima Publishing, LLC.

—Arianna's Shoes. Dyan, Penelope, illus. 2008. (Illus.). 44p. pap. 11.95 *(978-1-935118-33-6(1))* Bellissima Publishing, LLC.

—Ba-Ba-Ba-Bad — -The Story of One Mean Moose. Dyan, Penelope, illus. 2012. (Illus.). 34p. pap. 11.95 *(978-1-61477-053-4(0))* Bellissima Publishing, LLC.

—Baylee's Giraffes! Sometimes Only a Giraffe Will Do. Dyan, Penelope, illus. 2013. (Illus.). 34p. pap. 11.95 *(978-1-61477-085-5(9))* Bellissima Publishing, LLC.

—Ben's Adventures — -Proof Positive That Boys Will Be Boys. Dyan, Penelope, illus. 2008. (Illus.). 44p. pap. 11.95 *(978-1-935118-40-4(4))* Bellissima Publishing, LLC.

—Bunny Love! a Book about Home & Bunnies. Dyan, Penelope, illus. 2013. (Illus.). 34p. pap. 11.95 *(978-1-61477-084-8(0))* Bellissima Publishing, LLC.

—Classy Nancy — A One of a Kind Girl. Dyan, Penelope, illus. 2009. (Illus.). 48p. pap. 11.95 *(978-1-935118-45-9(5))* Bellissima Publishing, LLC.

—Courtney's Beach. Dyan, Penelope, illus. 2008. (Illus.). 44p. pap. 11.95 *(978-1-935118-35-0(8))* Bellissima Publishing, LLC.

—Eileen Green the Recycling Queen. Dyan, Penelope, illus. 2009. 44p. pap. 11.95 *(978-1-935118-51-0(X))* Bellissima Publishing, LLC.

—The Fish That Got Away — -for Boys Only(r). Dyan, Penelope, illus. 2010. (Illus.). 34p. pap. 11.95 *(978-1-935630-29-6(6))* Bellissima Publishing, LLC.

—Frugal Frannie — and the Big Room Cleaning Day. Dyan, Penelope, illus. 2009. (Illus.). 44p. pap. 11.95 *(978-1-935118-47-3(1))* Bellissima Publishing, LLC.

—Gabriela's Dogs — -Because Happiness Really Is a Warm Puppy! Dyan, Penelope, illus. 2008. (Illus.). 44p. pap. 11.95 *(978-1-935118-37-4(4))* Bellissima Publishing, LLC.

—Grandma's Suitcase — -Where a Kid Can Always Find a Surprise! Dyan, Penelope, illus. 2008. (Illus.). 44p. pap. 11.95 *(978-1-935118-36-7(6))* Bellissima Publishing, LLC.

—I Like Football — for Boys Only(r). Dyan, Penelope, illus. 2010. (Illus.). 34p. pap. 11.95 *(978-1-935630-27-2(X))* Bellissima Publishing, LLC.

—I Love You! Dyan, Penelope, illus. 2012. (Illus.). 34p. pap. 11.95 *(978-1-61477-050-3(5))* Bellissima Publishing, LLC.

—Jordan's Hair — -the Big Dilemm. Dyan, Penelope, illus. 2008. (Illus.). 44p. pap. 11.95 *(978-1-935118-34-3(X))* Bellissima Publishing, LLC.

—Little Miss Chris & the Incredible Red Shoes. Dyan, Penelope, illus. 2009. (Illus.). 44p. pap. 11.95 *(978-1-935118-49-7(8))* Bellissima Publishing, LLC.

—Lovely Libby. Dyan, Penelope, illus. 2010. (Illus.). 34p. pap. 11.95 *(978-1-935630-28-9(8))* Bellissima Publishing, LLC.

—Mermaids & Wishes for Tails Like Fishes. Dyan, Penelope, illus. 2009. (Illus.). 44p. pap. 11.95 *(978-1-935118-50-3(1))* Bellissima Publishing, LLC.

—Mikey & Me & the Bees, the Continuing Story of a Girl & Her Dog. Dyan, Penelope, illus. 2010. (Illus.). 48p. pap. 14.95 *(978-1-935118-90-9(0))* Bellissima Publishing, LLC.

—Mikey & Me & the Fly — -the Continuing Story of a Girl & Her Dog. Dyan, Penelope, illus. 2010. (Illus.). 50p. pap. 14.95 *(978-1-935118-94-7(3))* Bellissima Publishing, LLC.

—Mikey & Me & the Spider — -the Continuing Story of a Girl & Her Dog. Dyan, Penelope, illus. 2010. (Illus.). 50p. pap. 14.95 *(978-1-935118-95-4(1))* Bellissima Publishing, LLC.

—Mikey & Me & the Valentines — -the Continuing Story of a Girl & Her Dog. Dyan, Penelope, illus. 2010. (Illus.). 50p. pap. 14.95 *(978-1-935118-96-1(X))* Bellissima Publishing, LLC.

—Molly Moose Is on the Loose. Dyan, Penelope, illus. 2012. (Illus.). 34p. pap. 11.95 *(978-1-61477-025-1(5))* Bellissima Publishing, LLC.

—My Mother Always Says. Dyan, Penelope, illus. 2010. (Illus.). 42p. pap. 11.95 *(978-1-935118-98-5(6))* Bellissima Publishing, LLC.

—Off to School. Dyan, Penelope, illus. 2010. (Illus.). 34p. pap. 11.95 *(978-1-935630-21-0(0))* Bellissima Publishing, LLC.

—Out of Deepest Africa — -Another of Ben's Big Adventures — -for Boys Only (r). Dyan, Penelope, illus. 2010. (Illus.). 34p. pap. 11.95 *(978-1-935630-13-5(X))* Bellissima Publishing, LLC.

—Tammy's Left Shoe — -As Opposed to Her Right. Dyan, Penelope, illus. 2008. (Illus.). 44p. pap. 11.95 *(978-1-935118-41-1(2))* Bellissima Publishing, LLC.

—There's a Flea in My Te. Dyan, Penelope, illus. 2012. (Illus.). 34p. pap. 11.95 *(978-1-61477-047-3(6))* Bellissima Publishing, LLC.

—There's a Skunk in My Trunk. Dyan, Penelope, illus. 2012. (Illus.). 34p. pap. 11.95 *(978-1-61477-045-9(X))* Bellissima Publishing, LLC.

—There's a Teddy Bear in My Heart! Dyan, Penelope, illus. 2012. (Illus.). 34p. pap. 11.95 *(978-1-61477-048-0(4))* Bellissima Publishing, LLC.

—Three Strikes — -Doesn't Really Mean You Are Out. Dyan, Penelope, illus. 2008. (Illus.). 44p. pap. 11.95 *(978-1-935118-39-8(0))* Bellissima Publishing, LLC.

—To See or Not to See — -the Story of Kourtney's Glasses. Dyan, Penelope, illus. 2008. (Illus.). 44p. pap. 11.95 *(978-1-935118-38-1(2))* Bellissima Publishing, LLC.

—Today I Am Two! I Am Two Years Old Today! Dyan, Penelope, illus. 2010. (Illus.). 34p. pap. 11.95 *(978-1-935630-14-2(8))* Bellissima Publishing, LLC.

—Who Deserves a Giant Chocolate Chip Cookie? Dyan, Penelope, illus. 2009. (Illus.). 44p. pap. 11.95 *(978-1-935118-56-5(0))* Bellissima Publishing, LLC.

—Why Angels Sing! Dyan, Penelope, illus. 2012. (Illus.). 34p. pap. 11.95 *(978-1-61477-065-7(4))* Bellissima Publishing, LLC.

—Work It Out! Dyan, Penelope, illus. 2012. (Illus.). 34p. pap. 11.95 *(978-1-61477-056-5(5))* Bellissima Publishing, LLC.

Eagle, Kim. It's Raining, It's Pouring. Davenier, Christine & Gilbert, Rob, illus. 2012. (ENG.). 32p. (J). (-k). 17.95 *(978-1-936140-77-0(2))* Charlesbridge Publishing, Inc.

Earhardt, Ainsley & Cristaldi, Kathryn. Take Heart, My Child: A Mother's Dream. Kim, Jaime, illus. 2016. (ENG.). 32p. (J). (gr. -1-3). 18.99 *(978-1-4814-6622-6(4),* Aladdin) Simon & Schuster Children's Publishing.

Eastman, P. D. Big Blue Book of Beginner Books. 2008. (Beginner Books(R) Ser.). (ENG., Illus.). 368p. (J). (gr. -1-2). 16.99 *(978-0-375-85552-8(1),* Random Hse. Bks. for Young Readers) Random Hse. Children's Bks.

Eastman, P. D., et al. The Big Red Book of Beginner Books. 2010. (Beginner Books(R) Ser.). (ENG., Illus.). 344p. (J). (gr. -1-2). 16.99 *(978-0-375-86531-2(4),* Random Hse. Bks. for Young Readers) Random Hse. Children's Bks.

Eaton, Seymour. The Roosevelt Bears Travels Adventures. 2013. (ENG.). 186p. pap. 17.95 *(978-1-4290-9805-2(8))* New-York Historical Society.

Ebbeler, Jeffrey, illus. Jingle Bells. 2009. (ENG.). 20p. (J). (gr. -1-k). bds. 6.99 *(978-0-8249-1827-9(4),* Ideal Pubns.) Worthy Publishing.

Eberhard, Phyllis Lunde Brees. Little Miss Neat-As-A-Pin. Jacoby, Nickolina Dye, illus. 2007. (J). *(978-0-9722741-7-3(0))* Publishing Factory, The.

Ecker, Rebecca. Miss Emmalou Strain & the Hunt for Hermie. 2008. 32p. pap. 12.95 *(978-1-4327-0182-6(7))* Outskirts Pr., Inc.

Edwards, Asasimone. What's a Mimi-Saurus? 2009. (Illus.). 36p. pap. 16.99 *(978-1-4389-7919-9(3))* AuthorHouse.

Edwards, Caroline. Who Took Poppy's Skates? 2010. (ENG., Illus.). 24p. pap. *(978-1-84876-392-0(1))* Troubador Publishing Ltd.

Edwards, Gareth. Never Ask a Dinosaur to Dinner. Parker-Rees, Guy, illus. 2015. (ENG.). 32p. (J). (gr. -1-k). 17.99 *(978-0-545-81296-2(8),* Scholastic Pr.) Scholastic, Inc.

Edwards, Pamela Duncan. Roar! A Noisy Counting Book. Cole, Henry, illus. Date not set. 32p. (J). (gr. -1-2). pap. 5.99 *(978-0-06-443572-7(5))* HarperCollins Pubs.

—Teddy Bear Hide-and-Seek. Birkett, Georgie, illus. 2008. (ENG.). 20p. (J). (gr. 2-5). 14.95 *(978-0-230-01442-8(9),* Macmillan) Pan Macmillan GBR. Dist: Trans-Atlantic Pubns., Inc.

Ehlert, Lois. Boo to You! Ehlert, Lois, illus. 2009. (ENG., Illus.). 42p. (J). (gr. -1-2). 17.99 *(978-1-4169-8625-6(1),* Beach Lane Bks.) Beach Lane Bks.

—Lots of Spots. Ehlert, Lois, illus. 2014. (Classic Board Bks.). (ENG., Illus.). 40p. (J). (gr. -1 — 1). bds. 7.99 *(978-1-4424-8927-1(8),* Little Simon) Little Simon.

—Oodles of Animals. 2008. (ENG., Illus.). 56p. (J). (gr. -1-2). 18.99 *(978-0-15-206274-3(2))* Houghton Mifflin Harcourt Publishing Co.

—Rain Fish. Ehlert, Lois, illus. 2016. (ENG., Illus.). 40p. (J). (gr. -1-3). 17.99 *(978-1-4814-6152-8(4),* Beach Lane Bks.) Beach Lane Bks.

—The Scraps Book: Notes from a Colorful Life. Ehlert, Lois, illus. 2014. (ENG., Illus.). 72p. (J). (gr. k-5). 17.99 *(978-1-4424-3571-1(2))* Simon & Schuster Children's Publishing.

Ehrhardt, Karen. This Jazz Man. Roth, R G, illus. 2006. (ENG.). 32p. (J). (gr. -1-3). 17.99 *(978-0-15-205307-9(7))* Houghton Mifflin Harcourt Publishing Co.

—This Jazz Man. Roth, R. G., illus. 2010. (J). (gr. 1-5). 28.95 incl. audio compact disk *(978-1-4301-0740-8(5))* Live Oak Media.

Ehrmantraut, Brenda. Night Catch. Wehrman, Vicki, illus. 2014. (J). pap. *(978-1-934617-28-1(8))* Elva Resa Publishing, LLC.

Eisen, Laura. Clouds for Breakfast. Cissna, Kent, illus. 2013. 60p. pap. 14.95 *(978-0-9882113-7-7(8))* StarryBks.

Elin Hirschman, Jessica & Bright, Bonnie. The Tangle Tower. Bright, Bonnie, illus. 2006. (Illus.). 32p. (J). (gr. k-2). 14.95 *(978-0-9701155-6-0(3))* Cookie Bear Pr., Inc.

Eliot, T. S. Macavity: The Mystery Cat. Robins, Arthur, illus. 75th ed. 2016. (Old Possum Picture Bks.). (ENG.). 32p. (J). (-k). pap. 9.95 *(978-0-571-30813-2(9))* Faber & Faber, Inc.

Eliot, T. S., et al. Macavity's Not There! A Lift-the-Flap Book. Robins, Arthur, illus. 2017. (Old Possum Picture Bks.). (ENG.). 16p. (-k). 14.95 *(978-0-571-32863-5(6))* Faber & Faber, Inc.

Elliott, David. And Here's to You! Cecil, Randy, illus. (ENG.). 32p. (J). (gr. -1-2). 2009. pap. 6.99 *(978-0-7636-4126-9(X))* 2004. 15.99 *(978-0-7636-1427-0(0))* Candlewick Pr.

—Bull. 2017. (ENG.). 200p. (YA). (gr. 9). 17.99 *(978-0-544-61060-6(1),* HMH Books For Young Readers) Houghton Mifflin Harcourt Publishing Co.

—One Little Chicken: A Counting Book. Long, Ethan, illus. 2007. (ENG.). 24p. (J). (gr. -1-3). 16.95 *(978-0-8234-1983-8(5))* Holiday Hse., Inc.

—What the Grizzly Knows. Grafe, Max, illus. 2008. (ENG.). 32p. (J). (gr. -1-2). 16.99 *(978-0-7636-2778-2(X))* Candlewick Pr.

Elliott, Zetta & Strickland, Shadra. Bird, 1 vol. 2008. (ENG., Illus.). 48p. (J). (gr. 3-7). 19.95 *(978-1-60060-241-2(X))* Lee & Low Bks., Inc.

Elliott, Zetta & Terasaki, Stanley Todd. Bird. Shinjo, Shelly, illus. 2016. (ENG.). 32p. (J). (gr. 2-5). pap. 9.95 ***(978-1-62014-350-6(X))*** Lee & Low Bks., Inc.

Ellis, Andy. When Lulu Went to the Zoo. Ellis, Andy, illus. 2010. (ENG., Illus.). 32p. (J). (gr. -1-3). 16.95 *(978-0-7613-5499-4(9))* Lerner Publishing Group.

Ellis, Dianne. Rusty Rumble & His Smelly Socks. 2012. 36p. pap. 32.70 *(978-1-4691-9914-6(9))* Xlibris Corp.

—Rusty Rumble's Day at the Beach. 2012. 40p. pap. 32.70 *(978-1-4797-0360-9(5))* Xlibris Corp.

Ellis, Libby. Midge & Max's Scavenger Hunt. Jonason, Dave, illus. 2005. 12p. (J). (gr. -1-3). act. bk. ed. 14.95 *(978-1-58117-109-9(9),* Intervisual/Piggy Toes) Bendon, Inc.

Elsohn Ross, Michael. Mama's Milk. Wolff, Ashley, illus. 2007. (ENG.). 32p. (J). (gr. -1-2). 12.95 *(978-1-58246-181-6(3),* Tricycle Pr.) Random Hse. Children's Bks.

—Mama's Milk / Mamá Me Alimenta. Wolff, Ashley, illus. 2016. (ENG & SPA.). 24p. (J). (-k). bds. 7.99 *(978-0-553-53874-8(8),* Tricycle Pr.) Random Hse. Children's Bks.

Elya, Susan Middleton. Bebé Goes Shopping. Salerno, Steven, illus. 2008. (ENG.). 36p. (J). (gr. -1-3). pap. 7.99 *(978-0-15-206142-5(8))* Houghton Mifflin Harcourt Publishing Co.

—Fire! Fuego! Brave Bomberos. Santat, Dan, illus. 2012. (ENG & SPA.). 40p. (J). (gr. -1-1). lib. bdg. 17.89 *(978-1-59990-759-8(3),* 9781599907598, Bloomsbury USA Childrens) Bloomsbury Publishing USA.

—Fire! ¡Fuego! Brave Bomberos. Dantat, Dan & Santat, Dan, illus. 2012. (ENG & SPA.). 40p. (J). (gr. -1-1). 16.99 *(978-1-59990-461-0(6),* 9781599904610, Bloomsbury USA Childrens) Bloomsbury Publishing USA.

—Little Roja Riding Hood. Guevara, Susan, illus. 2014. (ENG.). 32p. (J). (gr. k-3). 16.99 *(978-0-399-24767-5(X),* G.P. Putnam's Sons Books for Young Readers) Penguin Young Readers Group.

—Oh No, Gotta Go! Karas, G. Brian, illus. 2005. 29p. (J). (gr. k-4). reprint ed. 15.00 *(978-0-7567-8946-6(X))* DIANE Publishing Co.

—Oh No, Gotta Go! Karas, G. Brian, illus. 2003. (SPA & ENG.). 32p. (J). (gr. -1-2). 15.99 *(978-0-399-23493-4(4),* G.P. Putnam's Sons Books for Young Readers) Penguin Young Readers Group.

Elya, Susan Middleton. La Princesa & the Pea. Martinez-Neal, Juana, illus. 2017. (ENG.). 32p. (J). (gr. -1-3). 16.99 ***(978-0-399-25156-6(1),*** G.P. Putnam's Sons Books for Young Readers) Penguin Young Readers Group.

Emberley, Rebecca. Spare Parts. Emberley, Ed, illus. 2015. (ENG.). 32p. (J). (gr. -1-2). 17.99 *(978-1-59643-723-4(5),* 9781596437234) Roaring Brook Pr.

Emberley, Rebecca & Emberley, Edward R. Mice on Ice. Emberley, Rebecca & Emberley, Edward R., illus. 2012. (I Like to Read(r) Ser.). (ENG., Illus.). 24p. (J). (gr. -1-3). 14.95 *(978-0-8234-2576-1(2))* Holiday Hse., Inc.

Emmett, Jonathan. Through the Heart of the Jungle. Gomez, Elena, illus. 2003. 32p. (J). tchr. ed. 15.95 *(978-1-58925-029-1(X));* pap. 5.95 *(978-1-58925-380-3(9))* Tiger Tales.

Emzer, Counselor. Duane, You Must be Insane. 2005. 20p. 7.97 *(978-1-4116-3091-8(2))* Lulu Pr., Inc.

Engelbreit, Mary. Mary Engelbreit's A Merry Little Christmas: Celebrate from A to Z. Engelbreit, Mary, illus. 2006. (Illus.). 40p. (J). (gr. -1-3). lib. bdg. 17.89 *(978-0-06-074159-4(7))* HarperCollins Pubs.

—Mary Engelbreit's a Merry Little Christmas: Celebrate from A to Z. Engelbreit, Mary, illus. 2010. (ENG., Illus.). 40p. (J). (gr. -1-3). pap. 6.99 *(978-0-06-074160-0(0))* HarperCollins Pubs.

—Nursery Tales: A Treasury of Children's Classics. Engelbreit, Mary, illus. 2008. (ENG., Illus.). 136p. (J). (gr. 4-7). 19.99 *(978-0-06-073168-7(0))* HarperCollins Pubs.

England, Brooke. Guardian Fairies. 2006. 17p. 12.00 *(978-1-4116-7923-8(7))* Lulu Pr., Inc.

Engle, Margarita. Drum Dream Girl: How One Girl's Courage Changed Music. López, Rafael, illus. 2015. (ENG.). 48p. (J). (gr. -1-3). 16.99 *(978-0-544-10229-3(0),* HMH Books For Young Readers) Houghton Mifflin Harcourt Publishing Co.

—Forest World. 2017. (ENG., Illus.). 208p. (J). (gr. 5). 16.99 ***(978-1-4814-9057-3(5),*** Atheneum Bks. for Young Readers) Simon & Schuster Children's Publishing.

—Hurricane Dancers: The First Caribbean Pirate Shipwreck. 2014. (ENG.). 176p. (YA). (gr. 7-12). pap. 11.99 *(978-1-250-04010-7(8),* 9781250040107) Square Fish.

—The Lightning Dreamer: Cuba's Greatest Abolitionist. 2013. (ENG.). 192p. (YA). (gr. 7). 16.99 *(978-0-547-80743-0(0))* Houghton Mifflin Harcourt Publishing Co.

—Mountain Dog. Ivanov, Aleksey & Ivanov, Olga, illus. 2014. (ENG.). 240p. (J). (gr. 3-7). pap. 7.99 *(978-1-250-04424-2(3),* 9781250044242) Square Fish.

—Silver People: Voices from the Panama Canal. 2014. (ENG.). 272p. (J). (gr. 7-12). 17.99 *(978-0-544-10941-4(4),* HMH Books For Young Readers) Houghton Mifflin Harcourt Publishing Co.

Enik, Ted. Sticks 'N Stones 'N Dinosaur Bones. Newland, g. f., illus. 2013. 42p. pap. 12.99 *(978-1-939322-10-4(3))* Pixel Mouse Hse.

Epner, Paul. Herbert Hilligan & His Magical Adventure. Kuon, Vuthy & Nguyen, Duke, illus. 2003. 32p. (J). 15.95 *(978-0-9743335-0-2(6))* Imaginative Publishing, Ltd.

—Herbert Hilligan & His Magical Lunchbox. Kuon, Vuthy & Nguyen, Duke, illus. rev. ed. (Herbert Hilligan Ser.). 15.95 *(978-1-57168-549-0(9))* Eakin Pr.

—Herbert Hilligan's Lone Star Adventure. Kuon, Vuthy & Nguyen, Duke, illus. 2003. 32p. (J). 15.95 *(978-0-9743335-3-3(0))* Imaginative Publishing, Ltd.

—Herbert Hilligan's Tropical Adventure. Kuon, Vuthy & Nguyen, Duke, illus. 2003. 32p. (J). 15.95 *(978-0-9743335-2-6(2))* Imaginative Publishing, Ltd.

Erlich, Bev. Pink Roses Everywhere. gif. ed. 2004. (Illus.). 64p. (J). 14.95 *(978-0-9743913-0-4(1))* Snojoy Publishing.

Ernst, Lisa Campbell. This Is the Van That Dad Cleaned. Ernst, Lisa Campbell, illus. 2005. (ENG., Illus.). 40p. (J). (gr. -1-3). 18.99 *(978-0-689-86190-1(7),* Simon & Schuster Bks. For Young Readers) Simon & Schuster Bks. For Young Readers.

Errico, Daniel. The Journey of the Marmabill. Turrill, Tiffany, illus. 2013. (ENG.). 32p. (J). (gr. -1-k). 16.95 *(978-1-62087-736-4(8),* 620736, Sky Pony Pr.) Skyhorse Publishing Co., Inc.

—The Journey of the Noble Gnarble. Turrill, Tiffany, illus. 2013. (ENG.). 32p. (J). (gr. -1-k). 16.95 *(978-1-62087-732-6(5),* 620732, Sky Pony Pr.) Skyhorse Publishing Co., Inc.

Esbaum, Jill. I Am Cow, Hear Me Moo! Gordon, Gus, illus. 2014. (ENG.). 32p. (J). (gr. -1-k). 16.99 *(978-0-8037-3524-8(3),* Dial Bks) Penguin Young Readers Group.

Eubank, Patricia Reeder. ABCs of Halloween. Eubank, Patricia Reeder, illus. 2013. (Illus.). 32p. (J). pap. 4.99 *(978-0-8249-5658-5(3),* Ideal Pubns.) Worthy Publishing.

—Halloween 123s. Eubank, Patricia Reeder, illus. 2011. (Illus.). 22p. (J). bds. 6.99 *(978-0-8249-1868-2(1),* Ideal Pubns.) Worthy Publishing.

—Valentine ABCs. Eubank, Patricia Reeder, illus. 2009. (Illus.). 32p. (J). (gr. -1-3). 9.99 *(978-0-8249-5597-7(8),* Ideal Pubns.) Worthy Publishing.

Eubank, Patti Reeder, tr. ABCs of Halloween. 2003. (ENG., Illus.). 30p. (J). (gr. -1-k). 8.95 *(978-0-8249-5467-3(X),* Ideal Pubns.) Worthy Publishing.

Evans, Nate & Brown, Stephanie Gwyn. Bang! Boom! Roar! A Busy Crew of Dinosaurs. Santoro, Christopher, illus. 2012. (ENG.). 40p. (J). (gr. -1-2). 15.99 *(978-0-06-087960-0(2))* HarperCollins Pubs.

—Dinosaur ABC. Santoro, Christopher, illus. 2011. (J). lib. bdg. 16.89 *(978-0-06-087962-4(9))* HarperCollins Pubs.

Evans, Ruth Todd. The Panda Who Would Not Eat. Evans, Ruth Todd, illus. 2007. (Illus.). 32p. (J). (gr. -1-3). per. 9.95 *(978-0-932653-84-0(7))* Sunbelt Pubns., Inc.

Everson, Chance. Beginnings Vol. 2: Tales of the Mandrasaurs, Volume the Second. Geary, Steve, illus. 2004. cd-rom 9.95 *(978-0-9760303-1-7(4))* R.A.R.E. TALES.

—Discoveries: Tales of the Mandrasaurs, Volume the Third. Geary, Steve, illus. 2004. cd-rom 9.95 *(978-0-9760303-2-4(2))* R.A.R.E. TALES.

—Forever & a Day Vol. 1: Tales of the Mandrasaurs, Volume the First. Geary, Steve, illus. 2004. cd-rom 9.95 *(978-0-9760303-0-0(6))* R.A.R.E. TALES.

—Verlin's Magical Blunder: Tales of the Mandrasaurs, Volume the Seventh. Geary, Steve, illus. 2004. cd-rom 9.95 *(978-0-9760303-6-2(5))* R.A.R.E. TALES.

Ewert, Marcus. Mummy Cat. Brown, Lisa, illus. 2015. (ENG.). 48p. (J). (gr. 1-4). 16.99 *(978-0-544-34082-4(5),* Clarion Bks.) Houghton Mifflin Harcourt Trade & Reference Pubs.
Faber, Toni Tuso. The Poodle Tales: Book One. Rudd, Benton, illus. 2012. 26p. (-18). 16.99 *(978-0-9883162-9-4(3))* Mindstir Media.
—The Poodle Tales: Book Three. Rudd, Benton, illus. 2012. 24p. 16.99 *(978-0-9886409-9-3(6))*; pap. 10.99 *(978-0-9886409-8-6(8))* Mindstir Media.
—The Poodle Tales: Book Two. Rudd, Benton, illus. 2012. 24p. 16.99 *(978-0-9885180-9-4(0))*; pap. 10.99 *(978-0-9885180-8-7(2))* Mindstir Media.
Fagan, Cary. Directed by Kaspar Snit. 2007. (ENG.). 160p. (J). (gr. 3-7). per. 9.95 *(978-0-88776-753-1(2),* Tundra Bks.) Tundra Bks. CAN. Dist: Penguin Random Hse. LLC.
Fallon, Joe & Scarborough, Ken. Halfway Hank. Davis, Jack E., illus. 2005. 40p. (J). 15.99 *(978-0-06-623636-0(3))* HarperCollins Pubs.
Falwell, Cathryn. Gobble, Gobble, 1 vol. Falwell, Cathryn, illus. 2011. (ENG., Illus.). 32p. (J). 16.95 *(978-1-58469-148-8(4))*; pap. 8.95 *(978-1-58469-149-5(2))* Dawn Pubns.
—Mystery Vine. Falwell, Cathryn, illus. 2009. (Illus.). 32p. (J). lib. bdg. 17.89 *(978-0-06-177197-2(X),* Greenwillow Bks.) HarperCollins Pubs.
—Turtle Splash! Countdown at the Pond. Falwell, Cathryn, illus. 2008. (ENG., Illus.). 32p. (J). (gr. -1-3). pap. 6.99 *(978-0-06-142927-9(9),* Greenwillow Bks.) HarperCollins Pubs.
Farah, Mo, et al. Ready Steady Mo! 2017. (ENG., Illus.). 32p. (J). (gr. -1-k). pap. 8.99 ***(978-1-4449-3407-6(4))*** Hachette Children's Group GBR. Dist: Hachette Bk. Group.
Farnsworth-Simpson, Patricia Ann. Stories to Thrill & Delight. 2008. 142p. pap. 12.95 *(978-1-4357-3275-9(8))* Lulu Pr., Inc.
Farrell, Bill. Walter's Pond: The True Story of Three Brothers Who Went Fishing for Trouble. Julich, Jenniffer, illus. 2008. 16p. 8.95 *(978-0-9797790-0-8(6))* Lower Lane Publishing LLC.
Farrell, John. Dear Child. Manning, Maurie J., illus. 2008. (ENG.). 32p. (J). (gr. -1-k). 16.95 *(978-1-59078-495-2(2))* Boyds Mills Pr.
Fatus, Sophie, illus. A Hen, a Chick & a String Guitar. 2005. 32p. (J). 17.99 incl. audio compact disk *(978-1-84148-796-0(1))* Barefoot Bks., Inc.
Fehr, Signe. Mama Always Comes Back. 2008. 32p. pap. 14.99 *(978-1-4389-0036-0(8))* AuthorHouse.
Feierabend, John M. Momma, Buy Me a China Doll. Norton, Allyssa, illus. 2017. (First Steps in Music Ser.). (ENG.). 32p. (J). (— 1). 16.95 ***(978-1-62277-226-1(1))*** G I A Pubns., Inc.
Feierabend, John M. The Tailor & the Mouse. McGann, James, illus. 2012. (First Steps in Music Ser.). (ENG.). 32p. (J). (gr. -1-k). 16.95 *(978-1-57999-903-2(4))* G I A Pubns., Inc.
Feierabend, John M. & Poulin, Ashley. Risseldy, Rosseldy. 2012. (First Steps in Music Ser.). (ENG., Illus.). 32p. (J). (gr. k-2). 16.95 *(978-1-57999-902-5(6))* G I A Pubns., Inc.
Feit, Maureen. Letters & Laughs from a to Z. 2009. (Illus.). 52p. pap. 22.50 *(978-1-4490-2527-4(7))* AuthorHouse.
Feldman, Eve B. Billy & Milly, Short & Silly. Mourning, Tuesday, illus. 2009. (ENG.). 32p. (J). (gr. -1-k). 16.99 *(978-0-399-24651-7(7),* G.P. Putnam's Sons Books for Young Readers) Penguin Young Readers Group.
Fennell, Kristen & Petrucccelli, Jessica, illus. A World of Hope: Written by Hope's Parents Laurie & Mike. I.t. ed. 2005. 18p. (J). per. 9.99 *(978-1-59879-069-6(2))* Lifevest Publishing, Inc.
Fenske, Jonathan. Guppy Up! Fenske, Jonathan, illus. 2013. (Penguin Young Readers, Level 1 Ser.). (ENG., Illus.). 32p. (J). (gr. k-1). mass mkt. 3.99 *(978-0-448-49646-7(1),* Penguin Young Readers) Penguin Young Readers Group.
—Guppy Up! 2013. (Penguin Young Readers Level 1 Ser.). lib. bdg. 13.55 *(978-0-606-28736-4(1),* Turtleback) Turtleback Bks.
Fenton, Joe. What's under the Bed? Fenton, Joe, illus. 2008. (ENG., Illus.). 32p. (J). (gr. -1-2). 15.99 *(978-1-4169-4943-5(7),* Simon & Schuster Bks. For Young Readers) Simon & Schuster Bks. For Young Readers.
Fernandes, Eugenie. Kitten's Summer. Fernandes, Eugenie, illus. 2013. (ENG., Illus.). 24p. (J). (gr. -1 — 1). bds. 7.95 *(978-1-55453-721-1(5))* Kids Can Pr., Ltd. CAN. Dist: Hachette Bk. Group.
Ferrari, G. m. Lake, Sky, Dragonfly. 2009. 44p. pap. 16.99 *(978-1-4490-2895-4(0))* AuthorHouse.
Ferry, Beth. Stick & Stone. Lichtenheld, Tom, illus. 2015. (ENG.). 48p. (J). (gr. -1-3). 16.99 *(978-0-544-03256-9(X),* HMH Books For Young Readers) Houghton Mifflin Harcourt Publishing Co.
Ficocelli, Elizabeth. Kid Tea, 0 vols. Dibley, Glin, illus. 2013. (ENG.). 36p. (J). (gr. -1-k). pap. 9.99 *(978-1-4778-4738-1(3),* 9781477847381, Amazon Children's Publishing) Amazon Publishing.
—Kid Tea. Dibley, Glin, illus. 2009. 32p. (J). (gr. -1). bds. 7.99 *(978-0-7614-5533-2(7))* Marshall Cavendish Corp.
Fineman, Kelly Ramsdell. At the Boardwalk. Armino, Monica, illus. 2012. (ENG.). 32p. (J). *(978-1-58925-104-5(0))*; pap. *(978-1-58925-431-2(7))* Tiger Tales.
Finke, Margot. Kangaroo Clues. Delioglu, Mustafa, illus. 2013. 16p. pap. 9.95 *(978-1-61633-368-3(5))* Guardian Angel Publishing, Inc.
—Mama Grizzly Bear. Swan, Gloria, illus. 2012. 16p. (-18). pap. 9.95 *(978-1-61633-304-1(9))* Guardian Angel Publishing, Inc.
Finley, Ucal P. A Proper Place for Boogers. Stroud, Brenda D., illus. 2011. 54p. pap. 12.95 *(978-0-9834307-0-4(5))* G Publishing LLC.
Finn, Rebecca. Sammy the Snowman! 2013. (Sparkly Christmas Ser.). (ENG., Illus.). 12p. (J). (gr. -1-k). bds. 5.99 *(978-0-230-76062-2(7))* Pan Macmillan GBR. Dist: Independent Pubs. Group.
Finn, Rebecca, illus. Busy Beach. 2016. (Busy Bks.). (ENG.). 10p. (J). (gr. -1). bds. 8.95 *(978-1-4549-1941-4(8))* Sterling Publishing Co., Inc.
—Busy Fire Station. 2016. (Busy Bks.). (ENG.). 10p. (J). (gr. -1). bds. 8.95 *(978-1-4549-1942-1(6))* Sterling Publishing Co., Inc.
—Busy Park. 2016. (Busy Bks.). (ENG.). 10p. (J). (gr. -1). bds. 8.95 *(978-1-4549-1943-8(4))* Sterling Publishing Co., Inc.
Fischer, Kristen. Zoo Zen: A Yoga Story for Kids. Schaefer, Susi, illus. 2017. (ENG.). 32p. (J). (gr. -1-2). 17.95 *(978-1-62203-891-6(6))* Sounds True, Inc.
Fischer, Scott M. Jump! Fischer, Scott M., illus. 2010. (ENG., Illus.). 32p. (J). (gr. -1-3). 15.99 *(978-1-4169-7884-8(4),* Simon & Schuster Bks. For Young Readers) Simon & Schuster Bks. For Young Readers.
Fisher, Doris & Sneed, Dani. Un dia Non, 1 vol. Lee, Karen, illus. 2006. (SPA.). 32p. (J). (gr. -1-3). 17.95 *(978-1-60718-694-6(2))* Arbordale Publishing.
—Mi dia Par, 1 vol. Lee, Karen, illus. 2007. (SPA & ENG.). 32p. (J). (gr. -1-3). 17.95 *(978-1-60718-692-2(6))* Arbordale Publishing.
—My Even Day, 1 vol. Lee, Karen, illus. 2007. (Basic Math Numbers Ser.). (ENG.). 32p. (J). (gr. -1-3). pap. 8.95 *(978-1-934359-22-8(X))* Arbordale Publishing.
—One Odd Day, 1 vol., Vol. 1. Lee, Karen, illus. 2006. (Basic Math Numbers Ser.). (ENG.). 32p. (J). (gr. -1-3). pap. 8.95 *(978-1-934359-33-4(5))* Arbordale Publishing.
Fisher-Price Little People, Fisher-Price Little. Fisher-Price Little People Planes, Cars, Trucks & Trains! 2015. (Lift-The-Flap Ser.: 24). (ENG.). 10p. (J). (gr. -1-k). bds. 9.99 *(978-0-7944-3468-7(1))* Reader's Digest Assn., Inc., The.
Fisher, Rusty. Littlest Vampire's Story, 1 vol. 2014. (Story Time for Little Monsters Ser.). (ENG., Illus.). 24p. (J). (gr. -1-4). lib. bdg. 27.07 *(978-1-62402-020-9(8),* Looking Glass Library) Magic Wagon.
—Littlest Werewolf's Story, 1 vol. 2014. (Story Time for Little Monsters Ser.). (ENG.). 24p. (J). (gr. -1-4). lib. bdg. 27.07 *(978-1-62402-021-6(6),* Looking Glass Library) Magic Wagon.
—Littlest Witch's Story, 1 vol. 2014. (Story Time for Little Monsters Ser.). (ENG., Illus.). 24p. (J). (gr. -1-4). lib. bdg. 27.07 *(978-1-62402-022-3(4),* Looking Glass Library) Magic Wagon.
—Littlest Zombie's Story, 1 vol. 2014. (Story Time for Little Monsters Ser.). (ENG.). 24p. (J). (gr. -1-4). lib. bdg. 27.07 *(978-1-62402-023-0(2),* Looking Glass Library) Magic Wagon.
Fitzgerald, Paula. The ABCs of How I Love You! 2011. 16p. (J). (gr. -1-1). bds. 12.99 *(978-0-8249-1495-0(3),* Ideal Pubns.) Worthy Publishing.
Flaxman, Jessica & Hall, Kirsten. Who Says? Becker, Wayne, illus. 2003. (My First Reader Ser.). (ENG.). 32p. (J). 18.50 *(978-0-516-22958-4(3),* Children's Pr.) Scholastic Library Publishing.
Fleming, Candace. Oh, No! Rohmann, Eric, illus. 2012. (ENG.). 40p. (J). (gr. -1-2). 17.99 *(978-0-375-84271-9(3),* Schwartz & Wade Bks.) Random Hse. Children's Bks.
—Seven Hungry Babies. Yelchin, Eugene, illus. 2010. (ENG.). 40p. (J). (gr. -1-2). 16.99 *(978-1-4169-5402-6(3),* Atheneum Bks. for Young Readers) Simon & Schuster Children's Publishing.
—Who Invited You? Booth, George, illus. 2009. (ENG.). 36p. (J). (gr. -1-3). 10.99 *(978-1-4424-0219-5(9),* Atheneum Bks. for Young Readers) Simon & Schuster Children's Publishing.
Fleming, Denise. The First Day of Winter. Fleming, Denise, illus. 2012. (ENG., Illus.). 32p. (J). (gr. -1-1). 7.99 *(978-0-312-37138-8(1),* 9780312371388) Square Fish.
—In the Small, Small Pond. Fleming, Denise, illus. 2007. (ENG., Illus.). 32p. (J). (gr. -1-k). pap. 27.99 *(978-0-8050-8117-6(8),* 9780805081176, Holt, Henry & Co. Bks. For Young Readers) Holt, Henry & Co.
—In the Tall, Tall, Grass. 2015. 32p. pap. 8.00 *(978-1-61003-609-2(3))* Center for the Collaborative Classroom.
—Pumpkin Eye. 2009. (J). (gr. k-2). 27.95 incl. audio *(978-0-8045-6979-8(7))* Spoken Arts, Inc.
—Pumpkin Eye. Fleming, Denise, illus. rev. ed. 2005. (ENG., Illus.). 32p. (J). (gr. -1-k). reprint ed. pap. 7.99 *(978-0-8050-7635-6(2),* 9780805076356) Square Fish.
—UnderGROUND. Fleming, Denise, illus. 2012. (ENG., Illus.). 40p. (J). (gr. -1-3). 17.99 *(978-1-4424-5882-6(8),* Beach Lane Bks.) Beach Lane Bks.
Fleming, Denise, illus. 5 Little Ducks. 2016. (ENG.). 40p. (J). (gr. -1-3). 17.99 *(978-1-4814-2422-6(X),* Beach Lane Bks.) Beach Lane Bks.
Fleming, Meg. I Heart You. Wright, Sarah Jane, illus. 2016. (ENG.). 40p. (J). (gr. -1-3). 17.99 *(978-1-4424-8895-3(6),* Beach Lane Bks.) Beach Lane Bks.
—Ready, Set, Build! Jarvis, illus. 2017. (ENG.). 32p. (J). (gr. -1-3). 16.99 *(978-1-4998-0175-0(0))* Little Bee Books Inc.
Fliess, Sue. Calling All Cars. Beise, Sarah, illus. 2016. (ENG.). 32p. (J). (gr. -1-3). 14.99 *(978-1-4926-1881-2(0),* 9781492618812, Sourcebooks Jabberwocky) Sourcebooks, Inc.
—A Dress for Me!, 0 vols. Laughead, Mike, illus. 2012. (ENG.). 24p. (J). (gr. k-3). 12.99 *(978-0-7614-6148-7(5),* 9780761461487, Amazon Children's Publishing) Amazon Publishing.
—A Fairy Friend. Keane, Claire, illus. 2016. (ENG.). 32p. (J). 16.99 *(978-1-62779-081-9(0),* 9781627790819, Holt, Henry & Co. Bks. For Young Readers) Holt, Henry & Co.
—Goblin Hood. Thibodeau, Piper, illus. 2016. (ENG.). 32p. (J). (gr. -1-k). pap. 3.99 *(978-0-448-48933-9(3),* Grosset & Dunlap) Penguin Young Readers Group.
—Let's Build!, 0 vols. 2014. (ENG.). 24p. (J). (gr. -1-3). 14.99 *(978-1-4778-4724-4(3),* 9781477847244, Amazon Children's Publishing) Amazon Publishing.
—Race! Taylor, Edwardian, illus. 2017. (ENG.). 32p. (J). (gr. -1-3). 16.99 *(978-1-4998-0237-5(4))* Little Bee Books Inc.
—Robots, Robots Everywhere. Staake, Bob, illus. 2014. (Little Golden Board Book Ser.). (ENG.). 26p. (J). (-k). bds. 7.99 *(978-0-385-38924-2(8),* Random Hse. Bks. for Young Readers) Random Hse. Children's Bks.
—Shoes for Me!, 0 vols. Laughead, Mike, illus. 2011. (ENG.). 24p. (J). (gr. -1-3). 12.99 *(978-0-7614-5825-8(5),* 9780761458258, Amazon Children's Publishing) Amazon Publishing.
Flintham, Thomas. Animal Numbers. Flintham, Thomas, illus. 2016. (ENG., Illus.). 24p. (J). (gr. -1 — 1). bds. 7.99 *(978-1-4814-6937-1(1),* Little Simon) Little Simon.
Flor Ada, Alma. Celebra el Dia De3 San Patricio con Samantha y Lola. Lavandeira, Sandra, illus. 2006. (Cuentos para Celebrar / Stories to Celebrate Ser.). (SPA.). 30p. (gr. k-6). per. 11.95 *(978-1-59820-117-8(4),* Alfaguara) Santillana USA Publishing Co., Inc.
Flor Ada, Alma & Campoy, F. Isabel. Celebrate St. Patrick's Day with Samantha & Lola. Hayes, Joe & Franco, Sharon, trs. 2006. (Stories to Celebrate Ser.). (Illus.). 30p. (gr. k-6). per. 11.95 *(978-1-59820-129-1(8),* Alfaguara) Santillana USA Publishing Co., Inc.
Florian, Douglas. The Curious Cares of Bears. Sánchez, Sonia, illus. 2017. (ENG.). 32p. (J). (gr. -1-3). 16.99 ***(978-1-4998-0462-1(8))*** Little Bee Books Inc.
—How to Draw a Dragon. Florian, Douglas, illus. 2015. (ENG., Illus.). 42p. (J). (gr. -1-3). 17.99 *(978-1-4424-7399-7(1),* Beach Lane Bks.) Beach Lane Bks.
—I Love My Hat, 0 vols. Keiser, Paige, illus. 2014. (ENG.). 24p. (J). (gr. -1-2). 16.99 *(978-1-4778-4780-0(4),* 9781477847800, Amazon Children's Publishing) Amazon Publishing.
Flowers, Luke. Ninja on the Farm (Scholastic Reader, Level 1: Moby Shinobi) 2016. (Scholastic Reader, Level 1 Ser.). (ENG.). 32p. (J). (gr. -1-1). pap. 3.99 *(978-0-545-93537-1(7))* Scholastic, Inc.
Fluharty, Kristi & Fluharty, T. Lively. Fool Moon Rising. Fluharty, Kristi & Fluharty, T. Lively, illus. 2009. (Illus.). 40p. (J). 16.99 *(978-1-4335-0682-6(3))* Crossway.
Fogliano, Julie. Old Dog Baby Baby. Raschka, Chris, illus. 2016. (ENG.). 32p. (J). 17.99 *(978-1-59643-853-8(3),* 9781596438538) Roaring Brook Pr.
Follett, Ross C. Beebear 2. Sievers, Lee, illus. 2013. (ENG.). 52p. (J). (gr. -1-3). 15.95 *(978-0-9881748-0-1(4),* OddInt Media) Greenwood Hill Pr.
Fontanez, Edwin. En esta hermosa Isla. Fontanez, Edwin, illus. 2nd rev. ed. 2005. (SPA., Illus.). 32p. (J). 16.95 *(978-0-9640868-7-6(5))* Exit Studio.
Foreman, Jack. Say Hello. Foreman, Michael, illus. 2012. (ENG.). 40p. (J). (gr. -1-2). pap. 6.99 *(978-0-7636-6087-1(6))* Candlewick Pr.
Foreman, Jack & Foreman, Michael. Say Hello. 2015. 40p. pap. 7.00 *(978-1-61003-409-8(0))* Center for the Collaborative Classroom.
Foster, Chad. Dear God: Thank-You Notes to God from Baby Boys & Girls. 2004. (J). bds. 8.99 *(978-0-9644456-1-1(1))* Rising Bks.
Foster, Evelyn. Alan & the Animals. 2011. (Tadpoles Ser.). (ENG., Illus.). 24p. (J). (gr. k-2). *(978-0-7787-0573-4(0))*; pap. *(978-0-7787-0584-0(6))* Crabtree Publishing Co.
Foster, John. Dinosaur Rap. Harter, Debbie, illus. 2016. (ENG.). 32p. (J). (gr. -1-1). 16.99 *(978-1-78285-301-5(4))* Barefoot Bks., Inc.
Fox, Diane. Rain or Shine. Fox, Christyan, illus. 2013. (ENG.). 20p. (J). (gr. -1-k). pap. 9.99 *(978-1-4083-1613-9(7))* Hodder & Stoughton GBR. Dist: Hachette Bk. Group.
Fox, Mem. Baby Bedtime. 2014. (ENG., Illus.). 32p. (J). (gr. -1-3). 17.99 *(978-1-4814-2097-6(6),* Beach Lane Bks.) Beach Lane Bks.
—Diez Deditos de Las Manos y Diez Deditos de Los Pies / Ten Little Fingers & Ten Little Toes Bilingual Board Book. Oxenbury, Helen, illus. 2012. (ENG & SPA.). 38p. (J). (gr. k — 1). bds. 6.99 *(978-0-547-87006-9(X))* Houghton Mifflin Harcourt Publishing Co.
—Good Night, Sleep Tight. Horacek, Judy, illus. 2013. (ENG.). 32p. (J). (gr. -1-k). 16.99 *(978-0-545-53370-6(8),* Orchard Bks.) Scholastic, Inc.
—Hello Baby! Jenkins, Steve, illus. 2009. (ENG.). 32p. (J). (gr. -1-k). 17.99 *(978-1-4169-8513-6(1),* Beach Lane Bks.) Beach Lane Bks.
—Let's Count Goats! Thomas, Jan, illus. 2010. (ENG.). 40p. (J). (gr. -1-1). 16.99 *(978-1-4424-0598-1(8),* Beach Lane Bks.) Beach Lane Bks.
—Nellie Belle. Austin, Mike, illus. 2015. (ENG.). 32p. (J). (gr. -1-3). 17.99 *(978-1-4169-9005-5(4),* Beach Lane Bks.) Beach Lane Bks.
—Ten Little Fingers & Ten Little Toes. Oxenbury, Helen, illus. (ENG.). (J). 2010. 38p. (gr. k — 1). bds. 8.99 *(978-0-547-36620-3(5))* 2008. 40p. (gr. -1 — 1). 17.99 *(978-0-15-206057-2(X))* Houghton Mifflin Harcourt Publishing Co.
—Ten Little Fingers & Ten Little Toes Lap Board Book. Oxenbury, Helen, illus. 2011. (ENG.). 38p. (J). (gr. k — 1). bds. 11.99 *(978-0-547-58103-3(3))* Houghton Mifflin Harcourt Publishing Co.
—This & That. Horacek, Judy, illus. 2017. (ENG.). 32p. (J). (gr. -1-k). 17.99 *(978-1-338-03780-7(3),* Scholastic Pr.) Scholastic, Inc.
—Time for Bed: Lap-Sized Board Book. Dyer, Jane, illus. 2005. (ENG.). 28p. (J). (gr. k — 1). bds. 12.99 *(978-0-15-205349-9(2))* Houghton Mifflin Harcourt Publishing Co.
—Two Little Monkeys. Barton, Jill, illus. 2012. (ENG.). 32p. (J). (gr. -1-3). 16.99 *(978-1-4169-8687-4(1),* Beach Lane Bks.) Beach Lane Bks.
—Yoo-Hoo, Ladybug! Ljungkvist, Laura, illus. 2013. (ENG.). 32p. (J). (gr. -1-k). 16.99 *(978-1-4424-3400-4(7))* Simon & Schuster Children's Publishing.
Fox, Mem & Horacek, Judy. Where Is the Green Sheep? 2004. (ENG., Illus.). 32p. (J). (gr. -1-3). 16.99 *(978-0-15-204907-2(X))* Houghton Mifflin Harcourt Publishing Co.
—Where Is the Green Sheep? (¿Dónde Está la Oveja Verde?) Horacek, Judy, illus. 2010. (SPA & ENG., Illus.). 32p. (J). (gr. k — 1). bds. 4.99 *(978-0-547-39694-1(5))* Houghton Mifflin Harcourt Publishing Co.
Foxworthy, Jeff. Hide!!! Björkman, Steve, illus. 2010. (ENG.). 32p. (J). (gr. -1-2). 17.99 *(978-0-8253-0554-2(3))* Beaufort Bks., Inc.
Frampton, David. The Whole Night Through. Frampton, David, illus. Date not set. (Illus.). 32p. (J). (gr. -1-1). pap. 5.99 *(978-0-06-443652-6(7))* HarperCollins Pubs.
—The Whole Night Through: A Lullaby. Frampton, David, illus. 2004. (Illus.). 30p. (J). (gr. k-4). reprint ed. *(978-0-7567-7723-4(2))* DIANE Publishing Co.
Francis, JennaKay. The Ferry Boat. Woodward II, Ed, illus. 2013. 12p. pap. 8.95 *(978-1-61633-426-0(6))* Guardian Angel Publishing, Inc.
Franco, Betsy. Summer Beat. Middleton, Charlotte, illus. 2011. (ENG.). 36p. (J). (gr. -1-1). 14.99 *(978-1-4424-4339-6(1),* McElderry, Margaret K. Bks.) McElderry, Margaret K. Bks.
Frank, Connie. Sadie & the Night Sky, 1 vol. 2009. 24p. pap. 24.95 *(978-1-60703-911-2(7))* America Star Bks.
Frank, Janet & Golden Books Staff. Daddies. Gergely, Tibor, illus. 2011. (Little Golden Book Ser.). (ENG.). 24p. (J). (gr. -1-2). 4.99 *(978-0-375-86130-7(0),* Golden Bks.) Random Hse. Children's Bks.
Frankau, Gilbert. One of Us: A Novel in Verse. 2005. pap. 22.95 *(978-1-4179-6045-3(0))* Kessinger Publishing, LLC.
Frasconi, Antonio. The House That Jack Built: A Picture Book in Two Languages. 2017. (ENG & FRE., Illus.). 32p. 14.95 ***(978-0-486-81646-3(X))*** Dover Pubns., Inc.
Frazier, Kelly. The Red Sock Christmas. Matthes, Justice, illus. 2008. 25p. pap. 24.95 *(978-1-60610-704-1(6))* America Star Bks.
Frederick, Heather Vogel. Hide-and-Squeak. Payne, C. F., illus. 2011. (ENG.). 32p. (J). (gr. -1-1). 16.99 *(978-0-689-85570-2(2),* Simon & Schuster Bks. For Young Readers) Simon & Schuster Bks. For Young Readers.
Fredrickson, Lane. Monster Trouble. Robertson, Michael, illus. 2015. (ENG.). 32p. (J). (gr. -1-2). 14.95 *(978-1-4549-1345-0(2))* Sterling Publishing Co., Inc.
Freedman, Claire. Aliens in Underpants Save the World. Cort, Ben, illus. 2012. (Underpants Bks.). (ENG.). 32p. (J). (gr. -1-2). 17.99 *(978-1-4424-2768-6(X),* Simon & Schuster/Paula Wiseman Bks.) Simon & Schuster/Paula Wiseman Bks.
—Aliens Love Panta Claus. Cort, Ben, illus. 2011. (Underpants Bks.). (ENG.). 32p. (J). (gr. -1-2). 16.99 *(978-1-4424-2830-0(9),* Simon & Schuster/Paula Wiseman Bks.) Simon & Schuster/Paula Wiseman Bks.
—A Cuddle for Little Duck. Pedler, Caroline, illus. 2009. (ENG.). 20p. (J). (gr. -1-k). bds. 8.99 *(978-0-545-07797-2(4),* Cartwheel Bks.) Scholastic, Inc.
—Dragon Jelly. Hendra, Sue, illus. 2015. (ENG.). 32p. (J). (gr. k-3). 14.99 *(978-1-61963-682-8(4),* 9781619636828, Bloomsbury USA Childrens) Bloomsbury Publishing USA.
—I Love You, Baby! Abbot, Judi, illus. 2017. (ENG.). 32p. (J). (gr. -1-3). 17.99 ***(978-1-4814-9904-0(1),*** Simon & Schuster/Paula Wiseman Bks.) Simon & Schuster/Paula Wiseman Bks.
—Monstersaurus! Cort, Ben, illus. 2011. (ENG.). 32p. *(978-1-84738-904-6(X))* Simon & Schuster, Ltd.
—My Precious Little Bear. Scott, Gavin, illus. 2011. (ENG.). 20p. (J). (gr. k — 1). bds. 8.99 *(978-0-545-27432-6(X),* Cartwheel Bks.) Scholastic, Inc.
—Spider Sandwiches. Hendra, Sue, illus. 2014. (ENG.). 32p. (J). (gr. k-3). 14.99 *(978-1-61963-364-3(7),* 9781619633643, Bloomsbury USA Childrens) Bloomsbury Publishing USA.
Freeman, Anna Harber. Love You More Than Anything. Henry, Jed, illus. 2016. (Snuggle Time Stories Ser.). (ENG.). 24p. (J). (— 1). bds. 6.95 *(978-1-4549-1490-7(4))* Sterling Publishing Co., Inc.
Freeman, Chip. Why, Daddy, Why Are There Stars in the Sky? Perry, Lee Ann, illus. 2012. 20p. (-18). pap. 11.95 *(978-1-937770-23-5(0),* SPC Bks.) RPJ & Co., Inc.
French, Lisa S. Eco-Pig, 4 vols., Set. Gott, Barry, illus. Incl. Planet Called Home: Eco-Pig's Animal Protection. 28.50 *(978-1-60270-662-0(X))*; Terrible Trash Trail: Eco-Pig Stops Pollution. 28.50 *(978-1-60270-663-7(8))*; What Does It Mean to Be Green? Eco-Pig Explains Living Green. 28.50 *(978-1-60270-665-1(4))*; Who Turned up the Heat? Eco-Pig Explains Global Warming. 28.50 *(978-1-60270-664-4(6))*; (J). (gr. -1-2). (Eco-Pig Ser.). (Illus.). 32p. 2009. 114.00 *(978-1-60270-661-3(1),* Looking Glass Library) ABDO Publishing Co.
—A Planet Called Home: Eco-Pig's Animal Protection, 1 vol. Gott, Barry, illus. 2009. (Eco-Pig Ser.). (ENG.). 32p. (J). (gr. -1-2). 28.50 *(978-1-60270-662-0(X))* ABDO Publishing Co.
—The Terrible Trash Trail: Eco-Pig Stops Pollution, 1 vol. Gott, Barry, illus. 2009. (Eco-Pig Ser.). (ENG.). 32p. (J). (gr. -1-2). 28.50 *(978-1-60270-663-7(8))* ABDO Publishing Co.
—What Does It Mean to Be Green? Eco-Pig Explains Living Green, 1 vol. Gott, Barry, illus. 2009. (Eco-Pig Ser.). (ENG.). 32p. (J). (gr. -1-2). 28.50 *(978-1-60270-665-1(4))* ABDO Publishing Co.
—Who Turned up the Heat? Eco-Pig Explains Global Warming, 1 vol. Gott, Barry, illus. 2009. (Eco-Pig Ser.). (ENG.). 32p. (J). (gr. -1-2). 28.50 *(978-1-60270-664-4(6))* ABDO Publishing Co.
French, Vivian. If I Were an Alien. Williams, Lisa, illus. 2009. (Get Set Readers Ser.). 32p. (J). (gr. -1-2). lib. bdg. 22.60 *(978-1-60754-267-4(6))* Windmill Bks.
—Pig in Love. Archbold, Tim, illus. 2005. 32p. (J). lib. bdg. 9.00 *(978-1-4242-0889-0(0))* Fitzgerald Bks.
Freysinger, Karen. Adventures of Countess Pigula Her Royal Imagination. Freysinger, Karen, illus. 2006. (Illus.). (J). 15.95 *(978-0-9786729-0-4(9))* Aha! Elora Danan Productions.
Friedlander, Tim. The I Like Me Dance! Edwards, W M, illus. 2007. (Playdate Kids Musical Ser.). 27p. (J). (gr. -1-3). 14.95 incl. audio compact disk *(978-1-933721-07-1(3))* Playdate Kids Publishing.
Friedman, Laurie. Back-to-School Rules. Murfin, Teresa, illus. 2011. (Carolrhoda Picture Books Ser.). (ENG.). 32p. (J). (gr. k-3). lib. bdg. 16.95 *(978-0-7613-6070-4(0))* Lerner Publishing Group.
—I'm Not Afraid of This Haunted House. Murfin, Teresa, illus. 2005. (ENG.). 32p. (J). (gr. k-3). 16.95 *(978-1-57505-751-4(4),* Carolrhoda Bks.) Lerner Publishing Group.
—Love, Ruby Valentine. Cravath, Lynne Avril, illus. 2006. (ENG.). 32p. (J). (gr. k-3). lib. bdg. 16.95 *(978-1-57505-899-3(5),* Carolrhoda Bks.) Lerner Publishing Group.
—Merry Christmas, Mary Christmas! Durst, Kathryn, illus. 2017. (ENG.). 32p. (J). (gr. -1-3). lib. bdg. 17.99 ***(978-1-4677-9261-5(6),*** Carolrhoda Bks.) Lerner Publishing Group.
—Ruby Valentine & the Sweet Surprise. Avril, Lynne, illus. 2014. (ENG.). 32p. (J). (gr. k-3). 16.95 *(978-0-7613-8873-9(7),* Carolrhoda Bks.) Lerner Publishing Group.
—Ruby Valentine Saves the Day. Avril, Lynne, illus. 2010. (Carolrhoda Picture Bks.). (ENG.). 32p. (J). (gr. k-3). lib. bdg. 16.95 *(978-0-7613-4213-7(3))* Lerner Publishing Group.
—Thanksgiving Rules. Murfin, Teresa, illus. 2009. (Carolrhoda Picture Bks.). (ENG.). 32p. (J). (gr. k-3). 16.95 *(978-0-8225-7983-0(9))* Lerner Publishing Group.
Friedman, Laurie B. Birthday Rules. Murfin, Teresa, illus. 2015. (J). (gr. k-3). (ENG.). 32p. lib. bdg. 16.99

S

(978-0-7613-6071-1(9)); 17.32 *(978-1-4677-6177-2(X))* Lerner Publishing Group. (Carolrhoda Bks.).

Friend, David. With Any Luck, I'll Drive a Truck. Rex, Michael, illus. 2016. (ENG.). 32p. (J). (-k). 16.99 *(978-0-399-16956-4(3)*, Nancy Paulsen Books) Penguin Young Readers Group.

Fromental, Jean-Luc. Rapido's Next Stop. Jolivet, Joëlle, illus. 2012. (ENG.). 20p. (J). (gr. k-2). 17.95 *(978-1-4197-0195-5(9)*, Abrams Bks. for Young Readers) Abrams, Inc.

Frost, Helen. Applesauce Weather. Bates, Amy June, illus. 2016. (ENG.). 112p. (J). (gr. 3-7). 14.99 *(978-0-7636-7576-9(8))* Candlewick Pr.

—Crossing Stones. 2009. (ENG., Illus.). 192p. (YA). (gr. 7-18). 18.99 *(978-0-374-31653-2(8)*, 9780374316532, Farrar, Straus & Giroux (BYR)) Farrar, Straus & Giroux.

—When My Sister Started Kissing. 2017. (ENG.). 208p. (J). 16.99 *(978-0-374-30303-7(7)*, 9780374303037, Farrar, Straus & Giroux (BYR)) Farrar, Straus & Giroux.

Fry, Sonali. Where Are You, Blue? Clifton-Brown, Holly, illus. 2015. (Dot Town Ser.). (ENG.). 32p. (J). (gr. -1 — 1). bds. 8.99 *(978-1-4814-3589-5(2)*, Little Simon) Little Simon.

Fuller, Sandy Ferguson. My Cat, Coon Cat, 1 vol. Brett, Jeannie, illus. 2011. (ENG.). 36p. (J). 17.95 *(978-1-934031-32-2(1)*, 4251474a-88ba-4ed7-90df-8651e2bedb12) Islandport Pr., Inc.

Fulmer, Jeffrey. My Imagination Kit. Pickering, Jimmy, tr. Pickering, Jimmy, illus. 2003. (J). 24p. 15.95 *(978-1-59336-008-5(8))*; 23p. pap. *(978-1-59336-009-2(6))* Mondo Publishing.

Funk, Josh. Dear Dragon: A Pen Pal Tale. Montalvo, Rodolfo, illus. 2016. (ENG.). 40p. (J). (gr. -1-3). 16.99 *(978-0-451-47230-4(6)*, Viking Books for Young Readers) Penguin Young Readers Group.

—Lady Pancake & Sir French Toast. Kearney, Brendan, illus. 2015. (Lady Pancake & Sir French Toast Ser.). (ENG.). 40p. (J). (gr. k). 14.95 *(978-1-4549-1404-4(1)*, 1394148) Sterling Publishing Co., Inc.

—Pirasaurs! Slack, Michael H., illus. 2016. (ENG.). 40p. (J). (gr. -1-k). 14.99 *(978-0-545-75049-3(0)*, Orchard Bks.) Scholastic, Inc.

Fyleman, Rose. Mice. Ehlert, Lois, illus. 2012. (ENG.). 40p. (J). (gr. -1-k). 16.99 *(978-1-4424-5684-6(1)*, Beach Lane Bks.) Beach Lane Bks.

Gabriel, Andrea. My Favorite Bear. 2014. 32p. pap. 8.00 *(978-1-61003-310-7(8))* Center for the Collaborative Classroom.

—My Favorite Bear. Gabriel, Andrea, illus. 2004. (ENG., Illus.). 32p. (J). (-k). pap. 7.95 *(978-1-58089-039-7(3))* Charlesbridge Publishing, Inc.

Gaiman, NEil. Blueberry Girl. Vess, Charles, illus. (ENG.). 32p. (J). (gr. -1-3). 2011. pap. 7.99 *(978-0-06-083810-2(8))* 2009. 17.99 *(978-0-06-083808-9(6))* HarperCollins Pubs.

—Blueberry Girl. 2011. (J). lib. bdg. 17.20 *(978-0-606-15398-0(5)*, Turtleback) Turtleback Bks.

—Crazy Hair. McKean, Dave, illus. (ENG.). 40p. (J). (gr. -1-3). 2015. pap. 6.99 *(978-0-06-057910-4(2))* 2009. 18.99 *(978-0-06-057908-1(0))* HarperCollins Pubs.

—Crazy Hair. 2015. (J). lib. bdg. 17.20 *(978-0-606-36478-2(1))* Turtleback Bks.

—The Dangerous Alphabet. Grimly, Gris, illus. (ENG.). 32p. (J). (gr. k). 2010. pap. 6.99 *(978-0-06-078335-8(4))* 2008. 17.99 *(978-0-06-078333-4(8))* HarperCollins Pubs.

Gaither, Doug. The Lonely Mare, 1 vol. 2010. 22p. pap. 24.95 *(978-1-4489-5871-9(7))* PublishAmerica, Inc.

Galan, Alvaro. Billy Bully. Simpson, Steve, illus. 2009. (ENG.). 32p. (J). (gr. -1-3). pap. 3.99 *(978-0-545-11012-9(2))* Scholastic, Inc.

Galbraith, Kathryn O. Boo, Bunny! Mack, Jeff, illus. 2008. (ENG.). 40p. (J). (gr. -1-2). 16.00 *(978-0-15-216246-7(1))* Houghton Mifflin Harcourt Publishing Co.

—Boo, Bunny! Board Book. Mack, Jeff, illus. 2012. (ENG.). 32p. (J). (gr. -1 — 1). bds. 5.99 *(978-0-547-81850-4(5))* Houghton Mifflin Harcourt Publishing Co.

Galdone, Paul. Jack & the Beanstalk. 2013. (Folk Tale Classics Ser.). (ENG., Illus.). 40p. (J). (gr. -1-3). 8.99 *(978-0-544-06665-6(0))* Houghton Mifflin Harcourt Publishing Co.

Gall, Chris. Substitute Creacher. 2011. (ENG., Illus.). 40p. (J). (gr. -1-3). 16.99 *(978-0-316-08915-9(X))* Little, Brown Bks. for Young Readers.

Galliez, Roxane Marie. Give Me Moon. Delanssay, Cathy, illus. 2009. 44p. (J). (gr. -1-3). 14.99 *(978-0-8416-7138-6(9))* Hammond World Atlas Corp.

Galvin, Laura. I Love My Mommy. 2009. (I Love My... Ser.). (ENG., Illus.). 16p. (J). 12.95 *(978-1-59249-801-7(9))* Soundprints.

—I Love My Sister. 2008. (ENG., Illus.). 16p. (J). (gr. -1-k). bds. 6.95 *(978-1-59249-867-3(1))* Soundprints.

Galvin, Laura, told to. I Love My Mommy. 2007. (ENG., Illus.). 16p. (J). (gr. -1-k). bds. 6.95 *(978-1-59249-730-0(6))* Soundprints.

Galvin, Laura G. & Galvin, Laura. I Love My Mommy (with Download) 2011. (ENG.). 16p. (J). *(978-1-60727-345-5(4))* Soundprints.

Galvin, Laura Gates. I Love My Brother. Oughton, Taylor, illus. 2008. (ENG.). 16p. (J). (gr. -1-k). bds. 6.95 *(978-1-59249-866-6(3))* Soundprints.

—I Love My Daddy. 2011. (I Love My... Ser.). (ENG., Illus.). 16p. (J). (gr. -1-k). 6.95 *(978-1-60727-346-2(2))* Soundprints.

—I Love My Family. 2011. (ENG.). 16p. (J). *(978-1-60727-621-0(6))* Soundprints.

—I Love My Sister. Oughton, Taylor et al, illus. 2011. (I Love My... Ser.). (ENG.). 16p. (gr. -1-k). 6.95 *(978-1-60727-311-0(X))* Soundprints.

—Mickey Mouse Clubhouse Fun with Numbers & Shapes. 2008. (ENG.). 20p. (J). (gr. -1-3). 9.99 *(978-1-59069-655-2(7))* Studio Mouse LLC.

Gamble, Adam. Good Night Arizona. Veno, Joe & Hansen, Red, illus. 2008. (Good Night Our World Ser.). (ENG.). 20p. (J). (gr. k — 1). bds. 9.95 *(978-1-60219-000-9(3))* Good Night Bks.

—Good Night California. Kelly, Cooper, illus. 2008. (Good Night Our World Ser.). (ENG.). 26p. (J). (gr. k — 1). bds. 9.95 *(978-1-60219-021-4(6))* Good Night Bks.

—Good Night Tennessee. Veno, Joe, illus. 2007. (Good Night Our World Ser.). (ENG.). 20p. (J). (gr. k — 1). bds. 9.95 *(978-1-60219-019-1(4))* Good Night Bks.

—Good Night World. Kelly, Cooper, illus. 2009. (Good Night Our World Ser.). (ENG.). 28p. (J). (gr. k — 1). bds. 9.95 *(978-1-60219-030-6(5))* Good Night Bks.

Gandolfi, Claudine. The Night Before Dog-Mas. Anagost, Karen, illus. 2007. (Petite Plush Kit Ser.). 64p. (J). (gr. -1-3). 9.95 *(978-1-59359-883-9(1))* Peter Pauper Pr. Inc.

Garcia, Joan. Footsteps of Angels. 2003. 52p. (J). pap. 11.95 *(978-0-7414-1602-5(6))* Infinity Publishing.

A Garden Circus. 2003. (J). 9.99 *(978-0-9740847-5-6(1))* GiGi Bks.

Garden, Randa Sue. Penny the Penguin. 2003. 48p. per. 7.95 *(978-0-615-12322-6(8))* Garden, Randa.

Gardner, Louise, illus. Five Little Easter Eggs. (ENG.). 10p. (J). 2009. (gr. -1). 5.95 *(978-1-58117-849-4(2))* 2008. 9.95 *(978-1-58117-682-7(1))* Bendon, Inc. (Intervisual/Piggy Toes).

Garland, Michael. Big & Little: A Story of Two Friends. 2017. (ENG., Illus.). 32p. (J). (gr. -1-k). 14.99 *(978-0-545-87097-9(6))* Scholastic, Inc.

—Hooray José!, 1 vol. Garland, Michael, illus. 2007. (ENG., Illus.). 32p. (J). (gr. -1-3). 16.99 *(978-0-7614-5345-1(8))* Marshall Cavendish Corp.

Garriel, Barbara. I Know a Shy Fellow Who Swallowed a Cello. O'brien, John, illus. 2012. (ENG.). 32p. (J). (gr. k-2). pap. 6.95 *(978-1-59078-946-9(6))* Boyds Mills Pr.

Garriel, Barbara S. I Know a Shy Fellow Who Swallowed a Cello. O'brien, John, illus. 2004. (ENG.). 32p. (J). (gr. k-3). 17.95 *(978-1-59078-043-5(4))* Boyds Mills Pr.

Garza, Shelly S. Dancing Danica. Weinstein, Holly, illus. 2013. 24p. (J). 12.99 net. *(978-1-61254-138-9(0))* Brown Books Publishing Group.

Gassman, Julie. Do Not Bring Your Dragon to the Library. Elkerton, Andy, illus. 2016. (Fiction Picture Bks.). (ENG.). 32p. (gr. -1-2). lib. bdg. 21.32 *(978-1-4795-9175-6(0)*, Fiction Picture Bks.) Picture Window Bks.

—Do Not Bring Your Dragon to the Library. Elkerton, Andy, illus. 2016. (ENG.). 32p. (gr. -1-2). 14.95 *(978-1-62370-651-7(3))* Capstone Young Readers of Coughlan Cos.

Gassman, Julie. Do Not Take Your Dragon to Dinner. Elkerton, Andy, illus. 2017. (Fiction Picture Bks.). (ENG.). 32p. (gr. -1-2). lib. bdg. 21.32 ***(978-1-4795-9888-5(7))*** Picture Window Bks.

Gauthier, Lance C., text. The One-Eared Mouse of Pasture Hill. 2003. 55p. (J). per. 6.95 *(978-1-884540-70-7(8))* Haley's.

Gayzagian, Doris K. One White Wishing Stone: A Beach Day Counting Book. Swarner, Kristina, illus. 2006. (ENG.). 32p. (J). (gr. -1-2). 16.95 *(978-0-7922-5110-1(5))*; 25.90 *(978-0-7922-5573-4(9))* National Geographic Society. (National Geographic Children's Bks.).

Geddes, Anne. This Little Baby. 2014. (ENG., Illus.). 24p. (J). bds. 8.99 *(978-1-4022-9828-8(5))* Sourcebooks, Inc.

Gee, Lulu. Dolly's Wonderful New Life. 2009. (Illus.). 96p. pap. 31.99 *(978-1-4389-4433-3(0))* AuthorHouse.

Gehl, Laura. And Then Another Sheep Turned Up. Adele, Amy, illus. 2015. (J). 6.99 *(978-1-4677-1190-6(X))*; (ENG.). 32p. (gr. -1-3). lib. bdg. 17.95 *(978-1-4677-1188-3(8))* Lerner Publishing Group. (Kar-Ben Publishing).

Geiger, Lorraine Lynch. A Wild & Woolly Night. Vargo, Sharon, illus. 2007. (J). (gr. -1-3). 15.95 *(978-1-891795-25-1(2))* RGU Group, The.

Geist, Ken. Who's Who? Cole, Henry, illus. 2012. (ENG.). 28p. (J). (gr. -1 — 1). 16.99 *(978-0-312-64437-6(X)*, 9780312644376) Feiwel & Friends.

Gemmen, Heather. But It's True. Lagares, Luciano, illus. 2004. (Tough Stuff for Kids Ser.). 36p. (J). (gr. 4-7). pap., pap. 5.99 *(978-0-7814-4033-2(5)*, 0781440335) Cook, David C.

Genhart, Michael. So Many Smarts! Clifton-Brown, Holly, illus. 2017. (J). ***(978-1-4338-2722-8(0)***, Magination Pr.) American Psychological Assn.

George, Audra. Vagabonding. George, Audra, illus. 2006. (Illus.). 32p. (J). (gr. -1-3). 17.95 *(978-1-60108-010-3(7))* Red Cygnet Pr.

George, Olivia. Copy Cat. Hudson, Brett, illus. 2004. (My First Reader Ser.). (J). 18.50 *(978-0-516-24679-6(8)*, Children's Pr.) Scholastic Library Publishing.

Gerber, Carole. 10 Busy Brooms. Fleming, Michael, illus. 2016. (ENG.). 32p. (J). (gr. -1-2). 12.99 *(978-0-553-53341-5(X)*, Doubleday Bks. for Young Readers) Random Hse. Children's Bks.

Gerrard, K. A. My Family Is a Zoo. Dodd, Emma, illus. 2016. (ENG.). 32p. (J). 16.99 *(978-1-61963-851-8(7)*, 9781619638518, Bloomsbury USA Childrens) Bloomsbury Publishing USA.

Gershator, David. Where Did the Baby Go? Gershator, Phillis, illus. 2016. (J). pap. *(978-1-934370-57-5(6))* Editorial Campana.

Gershator, Phillis. Listen, Listen. Jay, Alison, illus. 2007. (ENG.). 32p. (J). (gr. -1-3). 16.99 *(978-1-84686-084-3(9))* Barefoot Bks., Inc.

—Time for a Nap. Walker, David, illus. 2017. (Snuggle Time Stories Ser.). (ENG.). 32p. (J). (gr. -1-k). 9.95 *(978-1-4549-1981-0(7))* Sterling Publishing Co., Inc.

Gershator, Phillis, illus. Little Lenty. 2014. (J). pap. *(978-1-934370-48-3(7))* Editorial Campana.

Gershator, Phillis & Green, Mim. Time for a Hug. Walker, David, illus. 2013. (Snuggle Time Stories Ser.). (ENG.). 22p. (J). (gr. -1-k). bds. 6.95 *(978-1-4549-0856-2(4))* Sterling Publishing Co., Inc.

Gershator, Phillis & Walker, David. Time for a Bath. 2014. (Snuggle Time Stories Ser.). (ENG., Illus.). 24p. (J). (gr. -1-k). 9.95 *(978-1-4549-1032-9(1))* Sterling Publishing Co., Inc.

Gershator, Phyllis. Who's in the Forest? McDonald, Jill, illus. 2010. (ENG.). 24p. (J). (gr. -1-k). bds. 14.99 *(978-1-84686-476-6(3))* Barefoot Bks., Inc.

Gershenson, Harold P. Freddy Flamingo & the Kindertown Five. Mills, Christopher, illus. 2005. 27p. (J). *(978-1-58987-070-3(0))* Kindermusik International.

—The Kindertown Fire Brigade. Mills, Christopher, illus. 2006. (J). *(978-1-58987-019-2(0))* Kindermusik International.

—Noodles from Scratch. Mills, Christopher, illus. 2006. (J). *(978-1-58987-007-9(7))* Kindermusik International.

Gerth, Melanie. Ten Little Ladybugs. Huliska-Beith, Laura, illus. 2007. (ENG.). 22p. (J). (gr. -1-3). bds. 15.95 *(978-1-58117-578-3(7)*, Intervisual/Piggy Toes) Bendon, Inc.

Gerver, Jane E. Bath Time. Ovresat, Laura, illus. 2004. (My First Reader Ser.). 31p. (J). 18.50 *(978-0-516-24677-2(1)*, Children's Pr.) Scholastic Library Publishing.

—Good Night. Flint, Gillian, illus. 2015. (ENG.). 14p. (J). (— 1). bds. 4.99 *(978-1-62979-415-0(5)*, Highlights) Boyds Mills Pr.

—I Love You. Brown, Jo, illus. 2015. (ENG.). 14p. (J). (— 1). bds. 4.99 *(978-1-62979-416-7(3)*, Highlights) Boyds Mills Pr.

—Wait for Me! Reid, Mick, illus. (My First Reader Ser.). (J). (gr. k-1). 2005. (ENG.). 32p. pap. 3.95 *(978-0-516-25116-5(3))* 2004. 31p. 18.50 *(978-0-516-24676-5(3))* Scholastic Library Publishing. (Children's Pr.).

Ghigna, Charles. I See Fall, 1 vol. Jatkowska, Ag, illus. 2011. (I See Ser.). (ENG.). 24p. (gr. -1 — 1). pap. 6.10 *(978-1-4048-6851-9(8))*; lib. bdg. 22.65 *(978-1-4048-6589-1(6))* Picture Window Bks. (I See).

—I See Spring, 1 vol. Jatkowska, Ag, illus. 2011. (I See Ser.). (ENG.). 24p. (gr. -1 — 1). pap. 6.10 *(978-1-4048-6849-6(6))*; lib. bdg. 22.65 *(978-1-4048-6587-7(X))* Picture Window Bks. (I See).

—I See Winter, 1 vol. Jatkowska, Ag, illus. 2011. (I See Ser.). (ENG.). 24p. (gr. -1 — 1). pap. 6.10 *(978-1-4048-6850-2(X))*; lib. bdg. 22.65 *(978-1-4048-6588-4(8))* Picture Window Bks. (I See).

—Little Seeds, 1 vol. Jatkowska, Ag, illus. 2012. (My Little Planet Ser.). (ENG.). 24p. (gr. -1 — 1). 6.95 *(978-1-4048-7226-4(4))*; lib. bdg. 22.65 *(978-1-4048-6790-1(2))* Picture Window Bks. (My Little Planet).

—Oh My, Pumpkin Pie! Spengler, Kenneth, illus. 2005. (Step into Reading Ser.). (ENG.). 32p. (J). (gr. -1-1). pap. 3.99 *(978-0-375-82945-1(8)*, Random Hse. Bks. for Young Readers) Random Hse. Children's Bks.

—Pick up the Park, 1 vol. Jatkowska, Ag, illus. 2012. (My Little Planet Ser.). (ENG.). 24p. (gr. -1 — 1). 6.95 *(978-1-4048-7228-8(0))*; lib. bdg. 22.65 *(978-1-4048-6793-2(7))* Picture Window Bks. (My Little Planet).

—Recycling Is Fun, 1 vol. Jatkowska, Ag, illus. 2012. (My Little Planet Ser.). (ENG.). 24p. (gr. -1 — 1). 6.95 *(978-1-4048-7229-5(9))*; lib. bdg. 22.65 *(978-1-4048-6791-8(0))* Picture Window Bks. (My Little Planet).

—Snow Wonder. Woolf, Julia, illus. 2008. (Step into Reading Ser.: Vol. 2). (ENG.). 24p. (J). (gr. -1-1). 3.99 *(978-0-375-85586-3(6)*, Random Hse. Bks. for Young Readers) Random Hse. Children's Bks.

—Veo el Invierno. Jatkowska, Ag, illus. 2012. (Bilingual I See Ser.).Tr. of I See Winter. (ENG, SPA & MUL.). 24p. (gr. -1 — 1). lib. bdg. 22.65 *(978-1-4048-7310-0(4)*, I See) Picture Window Bks.

—We Need Water, 1 vol. Jatkowska, Ag, illus. 2012. (My Little Planet Ser.). (ENG.). 24p. (gr. -1 — 1). 6.95 *(978-1-4048-7227-1(2))*; lib. bdg. 22.65 *(978-1-4048-6792-5(9))* Picture Window Bks. (My Little Planet).

Ghigna, Charles & Ghigna, Debra. Barn Storm. Greenseid, Diane, illus. 2010. (Step into Reading Ser.). (ENG.). 32p. (J). (gr. -1-1). pap. 3.99 *(978-0-375-86114-7(9)*, Random Hse. Bks. for Young Readers) Random Hse. Children's Bks.

Gibbs, Edward. Little Bee. 2012. (ENG.). 24p. (J). (gr. -1-17). bds. 8.99 *(978-0-316-12707-3(8))* Little, Brown Bks. for Young Readers.

Gibby, Bayne. You Mean the World to Me. Walker, David, illus. 2013. (ENG.). 16p. (J). (gr. -1-k). bds. 8.99 *(978-0-545-40570-6(X)*, Cartwheel Bks.) Scholastic, Inc.

Gibson, Ginger Foglesong. Tiptoe Joe. Rankin, Laura, illus. 2013. (ENG.). 32p. (J). (gr. -1-k). 17.99 *(978-0-06-177203-0(8)*, Greenwillow Bks.) HarperCollins Pubs.

Gibson, Mary, illus. Buried Treasure. 2007. 12p. (J). 5.95 *(978-0-9801269-0-7(8))* Scribe's Closet Pubns., The.

Gibson, Sherri L. In the Mind of a Child: Children's Stories. 2013. 36p. pap. 24.95 *(978-1-62709-750-5(3))* America Star Bks.

Gikow, Louise. I Can Read. Patience, John, illus. 2004. (My First Reader Ser.). 31p. (J). 18.50 *(978-0-516-24678-9(X)*, Children's Pr.) Scholastic Library Publishing.

Gile, John. El Primer Bosque. Kohen-Klieman, Clarita, tr. 2006.Tr. of First Forest. (SPA., Illus.). 40p. per. 9.95 *(978-0-910941-15-0(7))* JGC/United Publishing Corps.

Gill, Shelley. Kiana's Iditarod. Cartwright, Shannon, illus. 2008. (Paws IV Ser.). (ENG.). 32p. (J). (gr. -1-3). pap. 10.99 *(978-1-57061-589-4(6)*, Little Bigfoot) Sasquatch Bks.

—Prickly Rose. Cartwright, Shannon & Love, Judy, illus. 2014. (ENG.). 32p. (J). (gr. -1-3). pap. 7.95 *(978-1-57091-357-0(9))*; lib. bdg. 17.95 *(978-1-57091-356-3(0))* Charlesbridge Publishing, Inc.

—Sitka Rose. Cartwright, Shannon, illus. 2005. (ENG.). 32p. (J). (gr. -1-3). per. 7.95 *(978-1-57091-364-8(1))* Charlesbridge Publishing, Inc.

Gilland, Gary P. The Turtle Train Troop. 2011. 24p. pap. 24.95 *(978-1-4626-3210-7(6))* America Star Bks.

Gillingham, Sara. My Little Stocking. 2011. (ENG.). 12p. (J). (gr. -1 — 1). 9.99 *(978-1-4521-0225-2(2))* Chronicle Bks. LLC.

—My Little Sweetheart. 2011. (ENG.). 12p. (J). (gr. -1 — 1). 9.99 *(978-1-4521-0226-9(0))* Chronicle Bks. LLC.

Ginkel, Anne. I've Got an Elephant, 1 vol. Bynum, Janie, illus. (ENG.). 32p. (J). 2013. (gr. -1-3). 7.95 *(978-1-56145-685-7(3))* 2006. (gr. k-3). 16.95 *(978-1-56145-373-3(0))* Peachtree Pubs.

Giogas, Valarie. In My Backyard, 1 vol. Zecca, Katherine, illus. 2007. (ENG.). 32p. (J). (gr. -1-3). 15.95 *(978-0-9777423-1-8(8))* Arbordale Publishing.

Glass, Eleri. The Red Shoes. Spires, Ashley, illus. 2017. (ENG.). 40p. (J). (gr. -1-3). 8.99 *(978-1-927018-85-9(4))* Simply Read Bks. CAN. Dist: Ingram Publisher Services.

Glassman, Bruce. Zoolidays. Kiaulevicius, Rolandas, illus. 2006. 32p. (J). (gr. -1-3). 15.95 *(978-1-60108-011-0(5))* Red Cygnet Pr.

Gliori, Debi. Goodnight World. Gliori, Debi, illus. 2017. (ENG., Illus.). 32p. (J). 16.99 *(978-1-68119-363-2(9)*, 9781681193632, Bloomsbury USA Childrens) Bloomsbury Publishing USA.

—No Matter What. (ENG., Illus.). 24p. (J). (gr. -1 — 1). 2012. bds. 12.99 *(978-0-547-71905-4(1))* 2008. bds. 6.99 *(978-0-15-206343-6(9))* Houghton Mifflin Harcourt Publishing Co.

Gloria, Truitt. Baby Jesus Is Born. 2004. (Illus.). 16p. (J). 1.99 *(978-0-7586-0635-8(4))* Concordia Publishing Hse.

Glover, Clair. Fairy Penguin - the Penguin Who Loves to Play. 2013. 26p. pap. *(978-1-78222-119-7(0))* Paragon Publishing, Rothersthorpe.

Gmeyner, Elizabeth. The Key of the Kingdom: A Book of Stories & Poems for Children. Russell, Joyce, illus. 2004. 100p. (J). pap. 15.00 *(978-0-88010-549-1(6)*, Bell Pond Bks.) SteinerBooks, Inc.

Gobo, creator. Santa Baby. 2006. (Illus.). 10p. (gr. -1-k). 9.95 *(978-1-932915-30-3(3))* Sandvik Innovations, LLC.

Goddard, Mary Beth. How Would It Feel? Mycek-Wodecki, Anna, illus. 2005. (ENG.). 32p. (J). (gr. -1-6). 15.95 *(978-1-59143-050-6(X)*, Bear Cub Bks.) Bear & Co.

Godwin, Laura. The Flower Girl. Wallace, John, illus. 2017. (ENG.). 32p. (J). (gr. -1-k). 12.99 *(978-1-368-00828-0(3))* Hyperion Bks. for Children.

—One Moon, Two Cats. Tanaka, Yoko, illus. 2011. (ENG.). 32p. (J). (gr. -1-1). 16.99 *(978-1-4424-1202-6(X)*, Atheneum Bks. for Young Readers) Simon & Schuster Children's Publishing.

—This Is the Firefighter [Board Book]. Hector, Julian, illus. 2015. (ENG.). 24p. (J). (gr. -1 — 1). bds. 6.99 *(978-1-4847-0733-3(8))* Hyperion Bks. for Children.

Godwin, Laura & Buck, Nola. A Christmas Goodnight. Wright, Sarah Jane, illus. 2011. (ENG.). 24p. (J). (gr. -1-k). 12.99 *(978-0-06-166491-5(X)*, Tegen, Katherine Bks) HarperCollins Pubs.

Goebel, Jenny & dePaola, Tomie. The Firefighter. Psacharopulo, Alessandra, illus. 2015. (ENG.). 32p. (J). (gr. -1-k). bds. 3.99 *(978-0-448-48101-2(4)*, Grosset & Dunlap) Penguin Young Readers Group.

Goepel, Meg. Farting Is Fun. 2010. 16p. pap. 9.99 *(978-1-4490-2346-1(0))* AuthorHouse.

Gold, Gina. Disney Palace Pets Guess Who Castle Cuties. 2014. (Guess Who Ser.). (ENG.). 10p. (J). (gr. -1-k). 10.99 *(978-0-7944-3192-1(5)*, Reader's Digest Children's Bks.) Studio Fun International.

Gold-Vukson, Marji. Grandpa & Me on Tu B'Shevat. Evans, Leslie, illus. 2004. (ENG.). 32p. (J). (gr. -1-3). pap. 6.95 *(978-1-58013-122-3(0)*, Kar-Ben Publishing) Lerner Publishing Group.

Golda, Kata. Stories for Bedtime: A Keepsake Pocket & Tales to Cherish. 2011. (ENG.). 7p. (J). (gr. -1 — 1). 14.99 *(978-0-8118-7498-4(2))* Chronicle Bks. LLC.

Goldberg, Malky. What Else Do I Say? A Lift the Flap Book. Argoff, Patti, illus. 2007. (J). (gr. -1-k). bds. 9.95 *(978-1-929628-34-6(X))* Hachai Publishing.

Golden Books. Trains, Cranes & Troublesome Trucks (Thomas & Friends) 2015. (Big Bright & Early Board Book Ser.). (ENG., Illus.). 24p. (J). (— 1). bds. 6.99 *(978-0-385-37393-7(7)*, Random Hse. Bks. for Young Readers) Random Hse. Children's Bks.

Goldhawk, Emma. Snuggle Bunny. Lambert, Jonathan, illus. 2015. (Snuggle Puppet Ser.). (ENG.). 10p. (J). bds. 14.95 *(978-1-62686-327-9(X)*, Silver Dolphin Bks.) Readerlink Distribution Services, LLC.

Goldstein, Sam & Desisto, Allie. Some Kids Just Can't Sit Still! Desisto, Allie, illus. 2009. (ENG., Illus.). 32p. (J). (gr. 2-4). pap. 15.95 *(978-1-886941-73-1(4))* Specialty Pr., Inc.

Gollub, Matthew. Jazz Fly 2: The Jungle Pachanga. Hanke, Karen, illus. 2010. (J). 32p. (gr. -1-3). 17.95 incl. audio compact disk *(978-1-889910-44-4(9))*; *(978-1-889910-45-1(7))* Tortuga Pr.

—Ten Oni Drummers. Stone, Kazuko G., illus. 2013. (JPN & ENG.). 32p. (J). (gr. -1-3). 16.95 *(978-1-58430-011-3(6))* Lee & Low Bks., Inc.

—Ten Oni Drummers. Stone, Kazuko G., illus. 2017. (J). *(978-1-889910-51-2(1))* Tortuga Pr.

Gonzalez, Maya Christina & Goldberg, Dana. Llámame Árbol. 2014.Tr. of Call Me Tree. (SPA & ENG.). 24p. (J). 19.95 *(978-0-89239-294-0(0))* Lee & Low Bks., Inc.

Goode, Molly. Mama Loves. McCue, Lisa, illus. 2015. (Step into Reading Ser.). (ENG.). 32p. (J). (gr. -1-1). 4.99 *(978-0-553-53896-0(9)*, Random Hse. Bks. for Young Readers) Random Hse. Children's Bks.

Gooderham, Chris. Even More Wicked Rhymes. 2008. 68p. pap. 13.95 *(978-1-4092-1753-4(1))* Lulu Pr., Inc.

—More Wicked Rhymes. 2008. 68p. pap. 13.95 *(978-1-4092-1663-6(2))* Lulu Pr., Inc.

—Wicked Rhymes. 2008. 68p. pap. 13.95 *(978-1-4092-1662-9(4))* Lulu Pr., Inc.

Goodman, Larry. Clean up the Glup! 2007. 24p. per. 24.95 *(978-1-4241-9141-3(6))* America Star Bks.

—The Cowboy & Other Stories. 2008. 36p. pap. 24.95 *(978-1-60813-546-2(2))* America Star Bks.

Goodnight Football, 1 vol. 2014. (Sports Illustrated Kids Bedtime Bks.). (ENG., Illus.). 32p. (gr. -1-2). lib. bdg. 22.60 *(978-1-4795-5177-4(5))* Capstone Press of Coughlan Cos.

Goodrich, Carter & Moore, Clement C. A Creature Was Stirring: One Boy's Night Before Christmas. Goodrich, Carter, illus. 2006. (ENG., Illus.). 40p. (J). (gr. -1-3). 17.99 *(978-0-689-86399-8(3)*, Simon & Schuster Bks. For Young Readers) Simon & Schuster Bks. For Young Readers.

Gorey, Edward. The Wuggly Ump. Gorey, Edward, illus. 2007. (Illus.). 32p. 12.95 *(978-0-7649-4192-4(5)*, A142) Pomegranate Communications, Inc.

Gosline, Andrea Alban. The Happiness Tree: Celebrating the Gifts of Trees We Treasure. Bossi, Lisa Burnett, illus. 2008. (ENG.). 40p. (J). (gr. k-3). 17.99 *(978-0-312-37017-6(2)*, 9780312370176) Feiwel & Friends.

—Ten Little Wishes: A Baby Animal Counting Book. Bossi, Lisa Burnett, illus. 2007. 40p. (J). (gr. -1-k). 16.89 *(978-0-06-053411-0(7))* HarperCollins Pubs.

Goss, Leon. By the Light of the Moon. Luo, Shiyin Sean, illus. 2005. (J). pap. *(978-1-933156-12-5(0))*; per. 16.99 *(978-1-933156-05-7(8))* GSVQ Publishing. (VisionQuest Kids).

—I'm Good, I'm Beautiful, I'm Smart. Mailey, Maria C. & Neuburger, Jenny, illus. 2005. (J). per. *(978-1-933156-02-6(3)*, VisionQuest Kids) GSVQ Publishing.

—King for a Day. Nichols, Chris, illus. 2005. (J). pap. *(978-1-933156-09-5(0))*; per. 16.99 *(978-1-933156-01-9(5))* GSVQ Publishing. (VisionQuest Kids).
—Selfus Esteemus Personalitus Low. Tunell, Ken, illus. 2005. (J). pap. *(978-1-933156-08-8(2)*, VisionQuest Kids) GSVQ Publishing.
Goss, Leon, 3rd. Selfus Esteemus Personalitus Low. Tunell, Ken, illus. 2005. 32p. (J). per. 16.99 *(978-1-933156-00-2(7)*, VisionQuest Kids) GSVQ Publishing.
Gould, Terry. The Adventures of Sir Sniffsalot & His Friends. Proulx, Denis, illus. 2007. 48p. (gr. -1-3). pap. 15.99 *(978-0-9789057-3-6(3))* Huntington Ludlow Media Group.
—The Adventures of Sir Sniffsalot & His Friends. 2009. (Illus.). 48p. pap. 15.99 *(978-0-615-26181-2(7))* Write Away.
Grabill, Rebecca. Halloween Good Night. Okstad, Ella, illus. 2017. (ENG.). 32p. (J). (gr. -1-3). 17.99 *(978-1-4814-5061-4(1))* Simon & Schuster Children's Publishing.
Grady, Karen. It's Not My Fault, She Started It. 2005. (Illus.). (J). *(978-1-59975-127-6(5))* Independent Pub.
Graegin, Stephanie. Little Fox in the Forest. 2017. (ENG., Illus.). 40p. (J). (gr. -1-3). 17.99 *(978-0-553-53789-5(X)*, Schwartz & Wade Bks.) Random Hse. Children's Bks.
Graham, Bobby G. Jake the Snake. 2010. 24p. pap. 16.95 *(978-1-4497-0568-8(5)*, WestBow Pr.) Author Solutions, Inc.
Grandfeather Press. Roly Poly Napoleon Discovers Colors. 2011. (ENG., Illus.). 36p. (J). pap. 6.99 *(978-0-9832355-0-7(3))* Grandfeather Pr.
Granny J. Pinky Makes a New Friend: Pinky Frink's Adventures. 2012. 36p. pap. 17.99 *(978-1-105-82663-4(5))* Lulu Pr., Inc.
—Pinky Visits Outer Space: Pinky Frink's Adventures. 2012. 38p. pap. 17.99 *(978-1-300-06064-2(6))* Lulu Pr., Inc.
Grant, Callie. Mud Puddle Hunting Day. Magee, Melanie, illus. 2013. (ENG.). 20p. (J). bds. 8.99 *(978-0-9854090-0-5(2))* Blanchard, Graham.
Grant, Holly & Campbell, K. G. Wee Sister Strange. 2017. (ENG.). 40p. (J). (gr. -1-3). 17.99 ***(978-0-553-50879-6(2)***, Schwartz & Wade Bks.) Random Hse. Children's Bks.
Graves, Keith. The Monsterator. 2014. (ENG., Illus.). 40p. (J). (gr. 2-5). 17.99 *(978-1-59643-855-2(X)*, 9781596438552) Roaring Brook Pr.
Gravet & Donaldson, Julia. Cave Baby, 3. Gravett, Emily, illus. 2nd ed. 2011. (ENG.). 32p. (J). (gr. -1-k). 11.99 *(978-0-330-52276-2(0))* Pan Macmillan GBR. Dist: Independent Pubs. Group.
Gravett, Emily. Share! Gravett, Emily, illus. 2016. (Bear & Hare Ser.). (ENG., Illus.). 32p. (J). (gr. -1-3). 16.99 *(978-1-4814-6217-4(2)*, Simon & Schuster Bks. For Young Readers) Simon & Schuster Bks. For Young Readers.
—Tidy. Gravett, Emily, illus. 2017. (ENG., Illus.). 40p. (J). (gr. -1-3). 17.99 *(978-1-4814-8019-2(7)*, Simon & Schuster Bks. For Young Readers) Simon & Schuster Bks. For Young Readers.
Graw, Christine Werts. The Day I Gave My Stuff Away: The Story of Ashley Mae. 2011. 28p. pap. 13.95 *(978-1-4497-0981-5(8)*, WestBow Pr.) Author Solutions, Inc.
Gray, Jennifer & Copus, Julia. Hog in the Fog. Seo, Eunyoung, illus. 2016. (ENG.). 32p. (-k). 9.95 *(978-0-571-30721-0(3))* Faber & Faber, Inc.
Gray, Kes. Cluck O'Clock. McQuillan, Mary, tr. McQuillan, Mary, illus. 2004. (ENG.). 32p. (J). (gr. k-3). tchr. ed. 17.95 *(978-0-8234-1809-1(X))* Holiday Hse., Inc.
—Frog on a Log? Field, Jim, illus. 2015. (ENG.). 32p. (J). (gr. -1-k). 16.99 *(978-0-545-68791-1(8)*, Scholastic Pr.) Scholastic, Inc.
—Nuddy Ned. Parsons, Garry, illus. 2014. (ENG.). 32p. (J). (gr. -1-k). 13.99 *(978-1-4088-3659-0(9)*, 9781408836590, Bloomsbury USA Childrens) Bloomsbury Publishing USA.
—Nuddy Ned's Christmas. Parsons, Garry, illus. 2016. (ENG.). 32p. (J). 20.99 *(978-1-4088-6598-9(X)*, 9781408865989, Bloomsbury USA Childrens) Bloomsbury Publishing USA.
Gray, Kes & Gray, Claire. Dog on a Frog? Field, Jim, illus. 2017. (ENG.). 32p. (J). (gr. -1-k). 16.99 ***(978-1-338-11695-3(9)***, Scholastic Pr.) Scholastic, Inc.
Gray, Rita. When the World Is Dreaming. Pak, Kenard, illus. 2016. (ENG.). 32p. (J). (gr. -1-3). 17.99 *(978-0-544-58262-0(4)*, HMH Books For Young Readers) Houghton Mifflin Harcourt Publishing Co.
Green, Andi. The Monster Who Couldn't Decide. 2010. (WorryWoo Monsters Ser.). 98p. (J). 14.99 *(978-0-9792860-3-2(4))* Monsters in My Head, LLC, The.
Green, Babs Brumer, illus. Take Her Back: An Andy-Bear Tale. 2003. 19p. (J). pap. *(978-0-9753119-0-5(5))* ATU Golden Pubns.
Green, George & Brooke, Amy/ J. George Green's, the Lion Who Couldn't Roar. 2008. (Illus.). (J). per. 16.99 *(978-1-933156-14-9(7)*, Visikid Bks.) GSVQ Publishing.
Green, Lucyna A. M., illus. Love You Little Brother. 2006. (J). *(978-1-58669-185-1(6))*; *(978-1-58669-186-8(4))* Childcraft Education Corp.
Green, M. L. Underneath My Favorite Tree. 2008. 20p. pap. 24.95 *(978-1-60474-858-1(3))* America Star Bks.
Greenawalt, Kelly. I Am Truly. Rauscher, Amariah, illus. 2017. (ENG.). 40p. (J). (gr. -1-k). 16.99 *(978-1-338-16720-7(0)*, Orchard Bks.) Scholastic, Inc.
Greene, Rhonda Gowler. Firebears, the Rescue Team. Andreasen, Dan, illus. 2015. (ENG.). 30p. (J). (gr. -1 — 1). bds. 7.99 *(978-1-62779-240-0(6)*, 9781627792400, Holt, Henry & Co. Bks. For Young Readers) Holt, Henry & Co.
—Mail Monkeys. Bender, Robert, illus. 2006. (J). pap. *(978-1-58669-217-9(8))* Childcraft Education Corp.
—No Pirates Allowed! Said Library Lou. Ajhar, Brian, illus. 2013. (ENG.). 40p. (J). (gr. 1-3). 15.95 *(978-1-58536-796-2(6)*, 202364) Sleeping Bear Pr.
—Only God Can Make a Kitten, 1 vol. Bryant, Laura J., illus. 2016. (ENG.). 28p. (J). bds. 9.99 *(978-0-310-75008-6(3))* Zonderkidz.
—Only God Can Make a Kitten, 1 vol. 2015. (ENG.). 32p. (J). 14.99 *(978-0-310-73170-2(4))* Zonderkidz.
—Push! Dig! Scoop! A Construction Counting Rhyme. Kirk, Daniel, illus. 2016. (ENG.). 32p. (J). 16.99 *(978-0-8027-3506-5(1)*, 9780802735065, Bloomsbury USA Childrens) Bloomsbury Publishing USA.
—Santa's Stuck. Cole, Henry, illus. 2006. (ENG.). 32p. (J). (gr. -1-3). pap. 5.99 *(978-0-14-240686-1(4)*, Puffin Books) Penguin Young Readers Group.
—The Very First Thanksgiving Day. Gaber, Susan, illus. 2006. (ENG.). 32p. (J). (gr. -1-1). 6.99 *(978-1-4169-1916-2(3)*, Atheneum Bks. for Young Readers) Simon & Schuster Children's Publishing.
Gregory, Manju. Jill & the Beanstalk. Anstey, David, illus. 2004. (ENG & TUR.). (J). *(978-1-84444-495-3(3))* Mantra Lingua.
Griffis, Molly. The Buffalo in the Mall. Doner, Kim, illus. 32p. 8.95 *(978-1-57168-635-0(5))* Eakin Pr.
Griffiths, Andy. The Cat on the Mat Is Flat. Denton, Terry, illus. 2009. (ENG.). 192p. (J). (gr. -1-3). pap. 7.99 *(978-0-312-53584-1(8)*, 9780312535841) Square Fish.
—The Cat, the Rat, & the Baseball Bat. Denton, Terry, illus. 2013. (My Readers Ser.). (ENG.). 32p. (J). (gr. -1-1). pap. 3.99 *(978-1-250-02774-0(8)*, 9781250027740) Square Fish.
—Ed & Ted & Ted's Dog Fred. Denton, Terry, illus. 2014. (My Readers Ser.). (ENG.). 32p. (J). (gr. -1-1). 15.99 *(978-1-250-00447-1(2)*, 9781250044471) Square Fish.
—Ed & Ted & Ted's Dog Fred. 2014. (My Readers: Level 2 Ser.). (J). lib. bdg. 13.55 *(978-0-606-35525-4(1))* Turtleback Bks.
Grimes, Nikki. Danitra Brown, Class Clown. Lewis, E. B., illus. 2005. 32p. (J). lib. bdg. 17.89 *(978-0-688-17291-6(1))*; (ENG.). (gr. 3). 16.99 *(978-0-688-17290-9(3)*, Amistad) HarperCollins Pubs.
—Garvey's Choice. 2016. (ENG.). 120p. (J). (gr. 2-7). 16.95 *(978-1-62979-740-3(5)*, Wordsong) Boyds Mills Pr.
—Planet Middle School. 2011. (ENG.). 160p. (YA). 15.99 *(978-1-59990-284-5(2)*, 9781599902845, Bloomsbury USA Childrens) Bloomsbury Publishing USA.
Gross, S. D. Mugallumps. 2007. (Illus.). 32p. (J). per. 13.99 *(978-1-59879-303-1(9))* Lifevest Publishing, Inc.
Grossman, Bill. My Little Sister Ate One Hare. Hawkes, Kevin, illus. 2014. 32p. pap. 7.00 *(978-1-61003-374-9(4))* Center for the Collaborative Classroom.
—My Little Sister Hugged an Ape. Hawkes, Kevin, illus. 2008. (ENG.). 40p. (J). (gr. -1-2). pap. 6.99 *(978-0-385-73660-2(6)*, Dragonfly Bks.) Random Hse. Children's Bks.
Grove, Ella. A Surprise for Tommy. 2005. (Illus.). 24p. (gr. -1-5). 2.70 *(978-0-7399-2341-2(2)*, 2780) Rod & Staff Pubs., Inc.
Grover, Lorie Ann. On Pointe. 2008. (ENG.). 320p. (J). (gr. 3-7). pap. 14.99 *(978-1-4169-7826-8(7)*, McElderry, Margaret K. Bks.) McElderry, Margaret K. Bks.
Gruber, Daveda. Castle of Ice. 2008. 51p. pap. 10.94 *(978-1-4357-3251-3(0))* Lulu Pr., Inc.
Grubman, Bonnie. How Do You Get a Mouse to Smile?, 1 vol. Van Wright, Cornelius, illus. 2009. (ENG.). 32p. (J). (gr. -1-3). pap. 6.50 *(978-1-59572-167-9(3))* Star Bright Bks., Inc.
—Oy Vey! Life in a Shoe. Mottram, Dave, illus. 2016. (J). *(978-1-68115-515-9(X))* Behrman Hse., Inc.
Guarino, Deborah. Is Your Mama a Llama? Kellogg, Steven, illus. 2010. (Rise & Shine Ser.). (ENG.). 32p. (C). (gr. -1-3). pap. 11.95 *(978-0-439-59842-2(7))* National Geographic School Publishing, Inc.
—Is Your Mama a Llama? Kellogg, Steven, illus. 2006. (ENG.). (J). (gr. -1-3). 18.95 incl. audio compact disk *(978-0-439-87594-3(3))*; 9.99 *(978-0-439-87588-2(9))* Scholastic, Inc.
Guffrey, Lindsey. A Psalm for the Solar System. 2013. 24p. pap. 9.00 *(978-0-9896518-0-6(0))* Yorkshire Publishing Group.
Guidone, Thea. Drum City. Newton, Vanessa, illus. 2015. (ENG.). 32p. (J). (gr. -1-2). 7.99 *(978-0-553-52350-8(3)*, Dragonfly Bks.) Random Hse. Children's Bks.
Guiffre, William. Gramma's Glasses. Pippin, Barbara, illus. 2008. 32p. (J). (gr. -1-3). pap. 9.95 *(978-1-931650-35-9(7))* Bks. for Children Publishing.
Guiffre, William A. Gramma's Glasses. Pippin, Barbara, illus. 2008. 32p. (J). (gr. -1-7). lib. bdg. 17.95 *(978-1-931650-19-9(5))* Bks. for Children Publishing.
Guile, Gill, illus. Twinkle Twinkle Little Star. 2016. (ENG.). (J). 8.95 ***(978-1-58925-504-3(6))*** Tiger Tales.
Guillain, Adam. Marshmallows for Martians. Guillain, Charlotte & Wildish, Lee, illus. 2nd ed. 2014. (George's Amazing Adventures Ser.). (ENG.). 32p. (J). (-k). pap. 11.99 *(978-1-4052-6681-9(3))* Egmont Bks., Ltd. GBR. Dist: Independent Pubs. Group.
Guillain, Adam & Guillain, Charlotte. Doughnuts for a Dragon. Wildish, Lee, illus. 2nd ed. 2015. (George's Amazing Adventures Ser.). (ENG.). 32p. (J). (gr. -1-k). pap. 10.99 *(978-1-4052-7054-0(3))* Egmont Bks., Ltd. GBR. Dist: Independent Pubs. Group.
—Pizza for Pirates. Wildish, Lee, illus. 2nd ed. 2016. (George's Amazing Adventures Ser.). (ENG.). 32p. (J). (gr. -1-k). pap. 10.99 *(978-1-4052-7361-9(5))* Egmont Bks., Ltd. GBR. Dist: Independent Pubs. Group.
—Socks for Santa. Wildish, Lee, illus. 2nd ed. 2016. (George's Amazing Adventures Ser.). (ENG.). 32p. (J). (gr. -1-k). pap. 10.99 *(978-1-4052-7055-7(1))* Egmont Bks., Ltd. GBR. Dist: Independent Pubs. Group.
—Supermarket Gremlins. Chatterton, Chris, illus. 2016. (ENG.). 18p. (J). (gr. -1-k). pap. 11.99 *(978-1-4052-7713-6(0))* Egmont Bks., Ltd. GBR. Dist: Independent Pubs. Group.
Guillain, Charlotte & Guillain, Adam. Muffins for Mummies. Wildish, Lee, illus. 2017. (George's Amazing Adventures Ser.). (ENG.). 32p. (J). (gr. -1-k). pap. 10.99 ***(978-1-4052-7363-3(1))*** Egmont Bks., Ltd. GBR. Dist: Independent Pubs. Group.
Guillain, Charlotte & Guillain, Adam. Spaghetti with the Yeti. Wildish, Lee, illus. 2nd ed. 2014. (George's Amazing Adventures Ser.). (ENG.). 32p. (J). (gr. -1-k). pap. 10.99 *(978-1-4052-6351-1(2))* Egmont Bks., Ltd. GBR. Dist: Independent Pubs. Group.
Gulbis, Stephen, illus. Old MacDonald Had a Barn. 2003. 22p. (YA). *(978-1-85602-453-2(9)*, Pavilion Children's Books) Pavilion Bks.
—The Wheels on the Bus. 2003. 22p. (YA). *(978-1-85602-454-9(7)*, Pavilion Children's Books) Pavilion Bks.
Gurewitz, Samantha & Polay, Ellyn. Marvin Mcgunk & All of His Junk. 2012. (ENG.). 27p. (J). pap. 12.95 *(978-1-4327-9705-8(0))* Outskirts Pr., Inc.
Gutierrez, Lorna. Hello, Mr. Moon. Watkins, Laura, illus. 2016. (J). ***(978-1-4351-6412-3(1))*** Barnes & Noble, Inc.
Gutman, Dan. Rappy Goes to School. Bowers, Tim, illus. 2016. 40p. (J). (gr. -1-3). 17.99 *(978-0-06-229181-3(5))* HarperCollins Pubs.
—Rappy the Raptor. Bowers, Tim, illus. 2015. (ENG.). 40p. (J). (gr. -1-3). 17.99 *(978-0-06-229180-6(7))* HarperCollins Pubs.
Guy, Ginger Foglesong. Go Back to Bed! Bernardin, James, illus. 2006. (ENG.). 32p. (J). (gr. k-3). 16.95 *(978-1-57505-750-7(6)*, Carolrhoda Bks.) Lerner Publishing Group.
Haber, Tiffany Strelitz. The Monster Who Lost His Mean. Edmunds, Kirstie, illus. 2012. (ENG.). 40p. (J). (gr. -1-3). 17.99 *(978-0-8050-9375-9(3)*, 9780805093759, Holt, Henry & Co. Bks. For Young Readers) Holt, Henry & Co.
Haft, Sheryl. Baby Boo, I Love You. Massey, Jane, illus. 2017. (ENG.). 32p. (J). (-k). 16.99 *(978-0-399-54782-9(7)*, Nancy Paulsen Books) Penguin Young Readers Group.
Hahn, Daniel. Happiness Is a Watermelon on Your Head. Dreis, Stella, illus. 2013. (ENG.). 40p. (J). (gr. k-2). pap. 9.99 *(978-1-907912-05-4(3))* Phoenix Yard Bks. GBR. Dist: Independent Pubs. Group.
Haines, Genny, illus. Five Cute Kittens. 2016. (ENG.). 10p. (J). (gr. -1 — 1). bds. 8.99 *(978-1-4998-0218-4(8))* Little Bee Books Inc.
Hale, Aaron. Addy Gets Made. 2008. 27p. pap. 24.95 *(978-1-60610-339-5(3))* America Star Bks.
Hale, Rachael. Hugs & Kisses. 2012. (ENG., Illus.). 20p. (J). (gr. -1 — 1). bds. 6.99 *(978-0-316-13063-9(X))* Little, Brown Bks. for Young Readers.
—Somebunny Loves You. 2009. (Paw Pals Ser.). (ENG., Illus.). 20p. (J). (gr. -1 — 1). bds. 6.99 *(978-0-316-11370-0(0))* Little, Brown Bks. for Young Readers.
Hall, Hannah C. God Bless Our Fall, 1 vol. Whitlow, Steve, illus. 2015. (God Bless Book Ser.). (ENG.). 20p. (J). bds. 9.99 *(978-0-529-12333-6(9))* Nelson, Thomas Inc.
Hall, Kate W. Richmond Rocks! 2009. (Illus.). (J). 14.95 *(978-1-61623-975-6(1)*, Richmondmom.com Publishing) Palari Publishing LLP.
Hall, Kirsten. Birthday Beastie: All about Counting. Luedecke, Bev, illus. 2003. (Beastieville Ser.). 32p. (J). 19.50 *(978-0-516-22891-4(9)*, Children's Pr.) Scholastic Library Publishing.
—Buried Treasure: All about Using a Map. Luedecke, Bev, illus. 2003. (Beastieville Ser.). 32p. (J). 19.50 *(978-0-516-22894-5(3)*, Children's Pr.) Scholastic Library Publishing.
—Good Times: All about the Seasons. Luedecke, Bev, illus. 2004. (Beastieville Ser.). (J). 19.50 *(978-0-516-23648-3(2)*, Children's Pr.) Scholastic Library Publishing.
—Grandma's House. Calderas, Gloria, illus. 2004. (My First Reader Ser.). (ENG.). 32p. (J). (gr. k-1). pap. 3.95 *(978-0-516-25502-6(9)*, Children's Pr.) Scholastic Library Publishing.
—Help! All about Telling Time. Luedecke, Bev, illus. 2003. (Concept Bks.). 32p. (J). 19.50 *(978-0-516-22890-7(0)*, Children's Pr.) Scholastic Library Publishing.
—Hide-And-Seek: All about Location. Luedecke, Bev, illus. 2004. (Beastieville Ser.). (J). 19.50 *(978-0-516-23649-0(0)*, Children's Pr.) Scholastic Library Publishing.
—I'm a Princess. DeRosa, Dee, illus. 2004. (My First Reader Ser.). (ENG.). 32p. (J). (gr. k-1). pap. 3.95 *(978-0-516-24630-7(5)*, Children's Pr.) Scholastic Library Publishing.
—I'm Not Scared. Holub, Joan, illus. 2003. (My First Reader Ser.). (ENG.). 32p. (J). 18.50 *(978-0-516-22929-4(X)*, Children's Pr.) Scholastic Library Publishing.
—Let's Trade: All about Trading. Luedecke, Bev, illus. (Beastieville Ser.). (J). (gr. k-1). 2005. (ENG.). 32p. pap. 3.95 *(978-0-516-25520-0(7))* 2004. 19.50 *(978-0-516-22999-7(0))* Scholastic Library Publishing. (Children's Pr.).
—Little Lies: All about Math. Luedecke, Bev, illus. 2003. (Beastieville Ser.). 32p. (J). 19.50 *(978-0-516-22896-9(X)*, Children's Pr.) Scholastic Library Publishing.
—My New School. Gott, Barry, illus. 2004. (My First Reader Ser.). (ENG.). 32p. (J). (gr. k-1). pap. 3.95 *(978-0-516-25505-7(3)*, Children's Pr.) Scholastic Library Publishing.
—A Perfect Day: All about the Five Senses. Luedecke, Bev, illus. (Beastieville Ser.). (J). (gr. k-1). 2005. (ENG.). 32p. pap. 3.95 *(978-0-516-25521-7(5))* 2004. 19.50 *(978-0-516-24437-2(X))* Scholastic Library Publishing. (Children's Pr.).
—Slider's Pet: All about Nature. Luedecke, Bev, illus. 2004. (Beastieville Ser.). (J). 19.50 *(978-0-516-22898-3(6)*, Children's Pr.) Scholastic Library Publishing.
—Tug-of-War: All about Balance. Luedecke, Bev, illus. 2004. (Beastieville Ser.). 31p. (J). 19.50 *(978-0-516-22899-0(4)*, Children's Pr.) Scholastic Library Publishing.
—What a Mess! All about Numbers. Luedecke, Bev, illus. 2004. (Beastieville Ser.). (J). 19.50 *(978-0-516-23670-4(9)*, Children's Pr.) Scholastic Library Publishing.
Hall, Michael. Cat Tale. Hall, Michael, illus. 2012. (ENG., Illus.). 40p. (J). (gr. -1-k). 16.99 *(978-0-06-191516-1(5)*, Greenwillow Bks.) HarperCollins Pubs.
—My Heart Is Like a Zoo. Hall, Michael, illus. (Illus.). (J). (gr. -1-k). 2013. (ENG.). 34p. bds. 7.99 *(978-0-06-191512-3(2))* 2009. (ENG., 32p. 16.99 *(978-0-06-191510-9(6))* 2009. 32p. lib. bdg. 17.89 *(978-0-06-191511-6(4))* HarperCollins Pubs. (Greenwillow Bks.).
Hall, Shirley. Buggy Buggy. Ledger, Faye, illus. 2010. 20p. 12.00 *(978-1-4520-6787-2(2))* AuthorHouse.
Hallinan, P. K. ABC I Love You. 2003. (ENG., Illus.). 24p. (J). bds. 7.95 *(978-0-8249-5458-1(0)*, Ideal Pubns.) Worthy Publishing.
—Brothers Forever. Hallinan, P. K., illus. 2010. (Illus.). 20p. (J). (gr. -1-k). 7.99 *(978-0-8249-1847-7(9)*, Ideal Pubns.) Worthy Publishing.
—Forever Friends! 2003. (ENG., Illus.). 28p. (J). (gr. -1-k). bds. 7.95 *(978-0-8249-5454-3(8)*, Ideal Pubns.) Worthy Publishing.
—Grandma Loves You. 2008. (ENG., Illus.). 26p. (J). (gr. -1-k). bds. 7.99 *(978-0-8249-6728-4(3)*, Ideal Pubns.) Worthy Publishing.
—Grandma Loves You! Kirkland, Katherine, illus. 2014. 22p. (J). bds. 8.99 *(978-0-8249-1931-3(9)*, Ideal Pubns.) Worthy Publishing.
—Grandpa Loves You! Kirkland, Katherine, illus. 2014. 22p. (J). bds. 8.99 *(978-0-8249-1932-0(7)*, Ideal Pubns.) Worthy Publishing.
—Happy Birthday! 2003. (J). (ENG., Illus.). 26p. bds. 7.95 *(978-0-8249-5453-6(X))*; *(978-0-8249-6507-5(8))* Worthy Publishing. (Ideal Pubns.).
—Heartprints. 2004. (ENG., Illus.). 26p. (J). bds. 6.95 *(978-0-8249-6564-8(7)*, Ideal Pubns.) Worthy Publishing.
—How Do I Love You? Hallinan, P. K., illus. 2014. (Illus.). 24p. (J). bds. 8.99 *(978-0-8249-1944-3(0)*, Ideal Pubns.) Worthy Publishing.
—How Do I Love You? 2005. (ENG., Illus.). 32p. (J). (gr. -1-k). pap. 4.35 *(978-0-8249-5518-2(8)*, Ideal Pubns.) Worthy Publishing.
—How Do I Love You/Como Te Amo. 2008. (SPA & ENG., Illus.). 30p. (J). pap. 4.35 *(978-0-8249-5471-0(8)*, Ideal Pubns.) Worthy Publishing.
—I Know Jesus Loves Me. Hallinan, P. K., illus. 2014. (Illus.). 18p. (J). pap. 6.99 *(978-0-8249-5663-9(X)*, Ideal Pubns.) Worthy Publishing.
—I Know Jesus Loves Me. 2007. (ENG., Illus.). 28p. (J). (gr. -1-3). 8.99 *(978-0-8249-5553-3(6)*, Ideal Pubns.) Worthy Publishing.
—I'm Thankful Each Day!/Doy Gracias Cada Dia! 2008. (ENG., Illus.). 32p. (J). (gr. -1-3). per. 4.99 *(978-0-8249-5583-0(8)*, Ideal Pubns.) Worthy Publishing.
—Just Open a Book. (J). 24p. 7.95 *(978-0-8249-5353-9(3))*; (ENG.). 22p. pap. 6.55 *(978-0-8249-5354-6(1))*; 24p. lib. bdg. 11.00 *(978-0-8249-5355-3(X))*; 2004. (ENG., Illus.). 48p. pap. 9.95 *(978-0-8249-5490-1(4))* Worthy Publishing. (Ideal Pubns.).
—Let's Be Fit. 2012. (Illus.). 24p. (J). bds. 7.99 *(978-0-8249-1887-3(8)*, Ideal Pubns.) Worthy Publishing.
—Let's Be Friends. 2008. (ENG., Illus.). 26p. (J). (gr. -1-k). bds. 7.95 *(978-0-8249-6587-7(6)*, Ideal Pubns.) Worthy Publishing.
—Let's Be Happy. Hallinan, P. K., illus. 2005. (ENG., Illus.). 26p. (J). (gr. -1-1). bds. 7.95 *(978-0-8249-6588-4(4)*, Ideal Pubns.) Worthy Publishing.
—Let's Be Helpful. 2008. (ENG., Illus.). 26p. (J). bds. 7.95 *(978-0-8249-6563-1(9)*, Ideal Pubns.) Worthy Publishing.
—Let's Be Honest. (ENG., Illus.). 24p. (J). 2008. (gr. -1-3). lib. bdg. 8.99 *(978-0-8249-5580-9(3))* 2003. bds. 8.75 *(978-0-8249-5478-9(5))* Worthy Publishing. (Ideal Pubns.).
—Let's Be Kind. Hallinan, P. K., illus. 2008. (ENG., Illus.). 24p. (J). (gr. -1-2). 8.99 *(978-0-8249-5605-9(2)*, Ideal Pubns.) Worthy Publishing.
—Let's Be Kind. 2003. (ENG., Illus.). 24p. (J). bds. 7.95 *(978-0-8249-5477-2(7)*, Ideal Pubns.) Worthy Publishing.
—Let's Be Polite. (ENG., Illus.). (J). 2008. 24p. (gr. -1-3). lib. bdg. 8.99 *(978-0-8249-5579-3(X))* 2004. 26p. bds. 8.75 *(978-0-8249-6562-4(0))* Worthy Publishing. (Ideal Pubns.).
—Let's Be Safe. (Illus.). (J). 2012. 24p. bds. 7.99 *(978-0-8249-1888-0(6))* 2007. (ENG., 32p. (gr. -1-3). 8.99 *(978-0-8249-5529-8(3))* Worthy Publishing. (Ideal Pubns.).
—Let's Learn All We Can! (ENG., Illus.). (J). 24p. pap. 6.55 *(978-0-8249-5449-9(1))*; 2004. 48p. pap. 9.95 *(978-0-8249-5491-8(2))* Worthy Publishing. (Ideal Pubns.).
—Let's Play As a Team. 2003. (ENG., Illus.). 28p. (J). 8.75 *(978-0-8249-5452-9(1)*, Ideal Pubns.) Worthy Publishing.
—Let's Share. 2003. (ENG., Illus.). 24p. (J). bds. 8.75 *(978-0-8249-5451-2(3)*, Ideal Pubns.) Worthy Publishing.
—The Looking Book. Barton, Patrice, illus. (J). 2015. pap. *(978-0-8249-5670-7(2))* 2009. (ENG.). 32p. (gr. -1-2). 16.99 *(978-0-8249-5607-3(9))* Worthy Publishing. (Ideal Pubns.).
—My Brother & I. 2008. (ENG., Illus.). 24p. (J). (gr. -1-k). bds. 7.95 *(978-0-8249-5455-0(6)*, Ideal Pubns.) Worthy Publishing.
—My Daddy & I. 2005. (ENG., Illus.). 32p. (J). (gr. -1-k). pap. 3.95 *(978-0-8249-5521-2(8)*, Ideal Pubns.) Worthy Publishing.
—My Mommy & I. 2005. (ENG., Illus.). 32p. (J). (gr. k-3). pap. 3.95 *(978-0-8249-5520-5(X)*, Ideal Pubns.) Worthy Publishing.
—My Sister & I. 2008. (ENG., Illus.). 24p. (J). (gr. -1-k). bds. 7.95 *(978-0-8249-5456-7(4)*, Ideal Pubns.) Worthy Publishing.
—Sisters Forever. Hallinan, P. K., illus. 2014. (Illus.). 22p. (J). bds. 7.99 *(978-0-8249-1921-4(1)*, Ideal Pubns.) Worthy Publishing.
—Thank You, God. 2008. (ENG., Illus.). 28p. (J). (gr. -1-k). bds. 7.95 *(978-0-8249-5457-4(2)*, Ideal Pubns.) Worthy Publishing.
—Today Is Christmas! Hallinan, P. K., illus. 2008. (ENG., Illus.). 26p. (J). (gr. -1-k). bds. 6.99 *(978-0-8249-1804-0(5)*, Ideal Pubns.) Worthy Publishing.
—Today Is Thanksgiving! Hallinan, P. K., illus. 2008. (ENG., Illus.). 26p. (J). (gr. -1-k). bds. 6.99 *(978-0-8249-6727-7(5)*, Ideal Pubns.) Worthy Publishing.
Hallstrand, John & Sarah & Hawley, Karen. Zoey Helps the Mystery Dog Find a Home. 2011. 24p. pap. 11.99 *(978-1-4634-1094-0(8))* AuthorHouse.
Hallwood, Cheri L. Winter's First Snowflake. Rose, Patricia M., illus. l.t. ed. 2006. (ENG.). 32p. (J). 15.99 *(978-0-9774422-0-1(9))* Forever Young Pubs.
Halpern, Shari. Dinosaur Parade. Halpern, Shari, illus. 2014. (ENG., Illus.). 32p. (J). (gr. -1-k). 16.99 *(978-0-8050-9242-4(0)*, 9780805092424, Holt, Henry & Co. Bks. For Young Readers) Holt, Henry & Co.
Halsted, John David, ed. East of the Sun & West of the Moon & Other Moon Stories. 2012. (Illus.). 54p. pap. *(978-1-909302-02-0(3))* Abela Publishing.
Hamanaka, Sheila. Grandparents Song. Hamanaka, Sheila, illus. 2003. (Illus.). 32p. (J). 15.99 *(978-0-688-17852-9(9))* HarperCollins Pubs.
Hamburg, Jennifer. Monkey & Duck Quack Up! Fotheringham, Edwin, illus. 2015. (ENG.). 32p. (J). (gr. -1-3). 17.99 *(978-0-545-64514-0(X)*, Scholastic Pr.) Scholastic, Inc.
—A Moose That Says Moo. Truesdell, Sue, illus. 2013. (ENG.). 32p. (J). (gr. -1 — 1). 16.99 *(978-0-374-35058-1(2)*, 9780374350581, Farrar, Straus & Giroux (BYR)) Farrar, Straus & Giroux.
Hamburger, Carole. The Zippity-Do-Dot: The Dot Who Dared to Pick Her Knows. Hamburger, Carole, illus. 2008. (Illus.). 40p. (J). 16.95 *(978-0-9764921-1-5(3))* Cherry Street Pr.
Hamilton, Kersten. Blue Boat. Petrone, Valeria, illus. 2016. (ENG.). 32p. (J). (-k). 16.99 *(978-0-451-47141-3(5)*, Viking Books for Young Readers) Penguin Young Readers Group.

S

—Police Officers on Patrol. Alley, R. W., illus. 2009. (ENG.). 32p. (J). (gr. -1-k). 15.99 *(978-0-670-06315-4(0),* Viking Books for Young Readers) Penguin Young Readers Group.

—Red Truck. Petrone, Valeria, illus. 2012. (ENG.). 24p. (J). (gr. -1-k). bds. 6.99 *(978-0-670-01467-5(2),* Viking Books for Young Readers) Penguin Young Readers Group.

Hamilton, Kersten & Wells, Rosemary. Yellow Copter. Petrone, Valeria, illus. 2015. (ENG.). 32p. (J). (-k). bds. 16.99 *(978-0-451-46991-5(7),* Viking Books for Young Readers) Penguin Young Readers Group.

Hamilton, Libby & Haworth, Katie. Around the World. Shuttlewood, Craig, illus. 2015. (ENG.). 10p. (J). (gr. -1 — 1). bds. 6.99 *(978-1-4998-0075-3(4))* Little Bee Books Inc.

Hamlett, Martha. Bats in the Air, Bats in My Hair. 2008. 32p. pap. 13.99 *(978-1-4389-2358-1(9))* AuthorHouse.

Hamsa, Bobbie. Dirty Larry. Catanese, Donna, illus. rev. ed. 2003. (Rookie Reader Español Ser.). (ENG.). 24p. (J). (gr. k-2). pap. 4.95 *(978-0-516-27493-5(7),* Children's Pr.) Scholastic Library Publishing.

Hankey, Sandy. Sweet Little Girl. Gay, Maria T., illus. 2004. 20p. pap. 24.95 *(978-1-4137-3329-7(8))* PublishAmerica, Inc.

Hannigan, Paula. Hugs for You. Brown, Heather, illus. 2012. (ENG.). 10p. (J). (-k). bds. 7.99 *(978-1-4494-2192-2(X))* Andrews McMeel Publishing.

Hanson, Thor. Bartholomew Quill: A Crow Learns to Tell Who's Who in the Animal World. Amim, Dana, illus. 2016. (ENG.). 32p. (J). (gr. -1-3). 17.99 *(978-1-63217-046-0(9),* Little Bigfoot) Sasquatch Bks.

Hanson, Warren. Bugtown Boogie. Johnson, Steve & Fancher, Lou, illus. 2008. 32p. (J). (gr. -1-3). 17.89 *(978-0-06-059938-6(3),* Geringer, Laura Book) HarperCollins Pubs.

—It's Monday, Mrs. Jolly Bones! Tusa, Tricia, illus. 2013. (ENG.). 32p. (J). (gr. -1-1). 16.99 *(978-1-4424-1229-3(1),* Beach Lane Bks.) Beach Lane Bks.

—Kiki's Hats: Our Gifts Live on & On. Hanson, Warren, illus. 2007. (ENG., Illus.). 36p. (J). (gr. -1-3). 16.95 *(978-0-931674-94-5(8),* Waldman House Pr.) TRISTAN Publishing, Inc.

Hanton, Sophie, illus. Hugs: Tuck Each Baby into a Loving Hug. 2010. (ENG.). 12p. (J). (gr. -1 — 1). 9.99 *(978-1-60169-020-3(7))* Innovative Kids.

Hapka, Cathy, pseud. Pretend & Play Kitty: With Real Crown You Can Wear! Borlasca, Hector, illus. 2004. (Role Play Ser.). 10p. (J). (gr. -1-18). bds. 6.99 *(978-0-57151-742-5(1))* Playhouse Publishing.

Happpy Books. A Day at the Farm. 2012. (Day at ... Bks.). (ENG., Illus.). 8p. (J). bds. 6.99 *(978-0-7641-6532-0(1))* Barron's Educational Series, Inc.

Happy Books. A Day at the Circus. 2012. (Day at ... Bks.). (ENG., Illus.). 8p. (J). bds. 7.99 *(978-0-7641-6531-3(3))* Barron's Educational Series, Inc.

Harber Freeman, Anna. Love You More Than Anything. Henry, Jed, illus. 2014. (Snuggle Time Stories Ser.). (ENG.). 24p. (J). (gr. -1-k). 9.95 *(978-1-4549-0021-4(0))* Sterling Publishing Co., Inc.

Harby, Melanie. All Aboard for Dreamland! Valério, Geraldo, illus. 2012. (ENG.). 32p. (J). (gr. -1-k). 16.99 *(978-1-4424-3091-4(5),* Simon & Schuster Bks. For Young Readers) Simon & Schuster Bks. For Young Readers.

Harley, Bill. Dirty Joe the Pirate: A True Story. Davis, Jack E., illus. 2008. (ENG.). 32p. (J). (gr. k-3). 17.99 *(978-0-06-623780-0(7))* HarperCollins Pubs.

Harper, Jo. I Could Eat You Up! Chorao, Kay, illus. 2007. (ENG.). 32p. (J). (gr. -1-3). 16.95 *(978-0-8234-1733-9(6))* Holiday Hse., Inc.

Harrah, Judith. Come Inside the Ark. Foster, Jack, illus. 2012. (J). pap. 17.99 *(978-1-937331-12-2(1))* ShadeTree Publishing, LLC.

Harrington, Tim. Nose to Toes, You Are Yummy! Harrington, Tim, illus. 2015. (ENG., Illus.). 32p. (J). (gr. -1-3). 17.99 *(978-0-06-232816-8(6))* HarperCollins Pubs.

Harris, Christine. Four Tails: An Anthology of Four Tales for Children. 2011. (Illus.). 92p. (gr. -1). pap. 12.10 *(978-1-4520-7643-0(X))* AuthorHouse.

Harris, Jim. Dinosaur's Night Before Christmas, 1 vol. Harris, Jim, illus. 2010. (Night Before Christmas Ser.). (ENG., Illus.). 40p. (J). (gr. k-3). 16.99 *(978-1-58980-850-8(9))* Pelican Publishing Co., Inc.

Harris, Marian. Ten Little Kittens. Harris, Jim, illus. 2010. (ENG.). 28p. (J). (gr. k). 15.99 *(978-0-7407-9197-0(4))* Andrews McMeel Publishing.

Harris, Marian & Harris, Jim. Ten Little Kittens. 2011. (ENG., Illus.). 26p. (J). (gr. -1-k). bds. 9.99 *(978-1-4494-0175-7(9))* Andrews McMeel Publishing.

Harris, Robie H. Maybe a Bear Ate It (a StoryPlay Book) Emberley, Michael, illus. 2017. (StoryPlay Ser.). (ENG.). 40p. (J). (gr. -1-k). 5.99 ***(978-1-338-16110-6(5),*** Cartwheel Bks.) Scholastic, Inc.

Harris, Sally M. Color Me Happy. Paplinksie, Cecilia, illus. 2009. 24p. pap. 10.95 *(978-1-935137-75-7(1))* Guardian Angel Publishing, Inc.

Harris, Stephanie C. The Wonders of Monkey Mac! 2009. 302p. pap. 15.95 *(978-1-60693-257-5(8),* Eloquent Bks.) Strategic Book Publishing & Rights Agency (SBPRA).

Harris, Stephen. Ballroom Bonanza: A Hidden Pictures ABC Book. Rycroft, Nina, illus. 2010. (ENG.). 40p. (J). (gr. k-2). 16.95 *(978-0-8109-8842-2(9),* Abrams Bks. for Young Readers) Abrams, Inc.

Harris, Trudy. The Clock Struck One: A Time-Telling Tale. Hartman, Carrie, illus. 2009. (Math Is Fun! Ser.). (ENG.). 32p. (gr. k-2). 19.99 *(978-0-8225-9067-5(0),* Millbrook Pr.) Lerner Publishing Group.

—Jenny Found a Penny. Hovell, John, illus. 2007. (Math Is Fun! Ser.). (ENG.). 32p. (gr. k-3). lib. bdg. 23.93 *(978-0-8225-6725-7(3),* Millbrook Pr.) Lerner Publishing Group.

—Over, under, in, & Ouch! Haskamp, Steve, illus. 2003. (Silly Millies Level 2 Ser.). (ENG.). 32p. (gr. 1-3). lib. bdg. 21.27 *(978-0-7613-2912-1(9),* Millbrook Pr.) Lerner Publishing Group.

—Tally Cat Keeps Track. Harris, Andrew, illus. 2010. (Math Is Fun! Ser.). (ENG.). 32p. (gr. k-2). lib. bdg. 22.60 *(978-0-7613-4451-3(9),* Millbrook Pr.) Lerner Publishing Group.

Harrison, Kenny. Hide & Seek Harry at the Playground. Harrison, Kenny, illus. 2015. (ENG., Illus.). 20p. (J). (-k). bds. 6.99 *(978-0-7636-7347-5(1))* Candlewick Pr.

—Hide & Seek Harry on the Farm. Harrison, Kenny, illus. 2015. (ENG., Illus.). 20p. (J). (-k). bds. 6.99 *(978-0-7636-7370-3(6))* Candlewick Pr.

Harrison, Michael. Cop's Night Before Christmas, 1 vol. Miles, David, illus. 2010. (Night Before Christmas Ser.). (ENG.). 32p. (J). (gr. k-3). 16.99 *(978-1-58980-800-3(2))* Pelican Publishing Co., Inc.

Harrod-Eagles, Cynthia. The Biggest Pumpkin Ever! Woodruff, Liza, illus. 2007. (J). pap. *(978-0-545-00232-5(X))* Scholastic, Inc.

—It's Holiday Time! Baccala, Gladys, illus. 2012. (ENG.). 18p. (J). bds. *(978-1-58925-640-8(9))* Tiger Tales.

Harshman, Marc & Ryan, Cheryl. Red Are the Apples. Zahares, Wade, illus. 2007. (ENG.). 32p. (J). (gr. -1-3). pap. 6.99 *(978-0-15-206065-7(0))* Houghton Mifflin Harcourt Publishing Co.

Hart, Caryl. Catch That Rat. McLaughlin, Tom, illus. 2013. (ENG.). 32p. (J). pap. 8.99 *(978-1-84738-931-2(7),* Simon & Schuster Children's) Simon & Schuster, Ltd. GBR. Dist: Simon & Schuster, Inc.

—Don't Put Your Pants on Your Head, Fred! Hodgkinson, Leigh, illus. 2012. (ENG.). 32p. (J). (gr. -1-k). pap. 9.99 *(978-1-4083-0917-9(3))* Hodder & Stoughton GBR. Dist: Hachette Bk. Group.

—The Princess & the Peas. Warburton, Sarah, illus. 2013. (ENG.). 32p. (J). (gr. -1-2). 16.99 *(978-0-7636-6532-6(0),* Nosy Crow) Candlewick Pr.

Harter, Debbie. Animal Boogie. 2008. (ENG., Illus.). 32p. (J). 16.99 *(978-1-84686-231-1(0))* Barefoot Bks., Inc.

—Walking Through the Jungle. Harter, Debbie, illus. 2004. (ENG & PAN., Illus.). 32p. (J). pap. *(978-1-85269-851-5(9))* Mantra Lingua.

Harter, Debbie, illus. Walking Through the Jungle. 2004. 30p. (J). *(978-1-85269-886-7(1)); (978-1-85269-881-2(0)); (978-1-85269-876-8(4));* (ENG & SPA.). *(978-1-85269-871-3(3)); (978-1-85269-866-9(7)); (978-1-85269-861-4(6)); (978-1-85269-856-0(X)); (978-1-85269-846-1(2)); (978-1-85269-841-6(1)); (978-1-85269-831-7(4)); (978-1-85269-826-3(8)); (978-1-85269-811-9(X)); (978-1-85269-807-2(1))* Mantra Lingua.

Hartman, Sara. When Jesus Was Born. Mitter, Kathy, illus. 2007. 16p. (J). (gr. k-4). 1.99 *(978-0-7586-1281-6(8))* Concordia Publishing Hse.

Hartshorne, Holly L. School Time for the Three Little Fish, 1 vol. 2009. 12p. pap. 24.95 *(978-1-60749-404-1(3))* America Star Bks.

Harvey, Jeanne Walker. My Hands Sing the Blues: Romare Bearden's Childhood Journey, 0 vols. Zunon, Elizabeth, illus. 2011. (ENG.). 40p. (J). (gr. k-3). 17.99 *(978-0-7614-5810-4(7),* 9780761458104, Amazon Children's Publishing) Amazon Publishing.

Harvey, Matt. Shopping with Dad. Latimer, Miriam, illus. 2008. (ENG.). 32p. (J). (gr. -1-3). 16.99 *(978-1-84686-172-7(1))* Barefoot Bks., Inc.

Haskamp, Steven, illus. Eight Silly Monkeys. 2007. (ENG.). 18p. (J). (gr. -1-3). bds. 15.95 *(978-1-58117-577-6(9),* Intervisual/Piggy Toes) Bendon, Inc.

Hasling, Jack. Salamander the Great! 2006. (Illus.). (J). per. 10.00 *(978-0-9786988-1-2(9))* Hazel Street Productions.

Hasselbring, Janet. What Do You See, Mrs Night Heron? De Vries, Bruce, illus. 2010. 32p. pap. 12.95 *(978-1-936343-03-4(7))* Peppertree Pr., The.

Hatch, Morgan John. Where Dreams Are Made. 2011. 28p. pap. 24.95 *(978-1-4626-2896-4(6))* America Star Bks.

Hatton, Jenny. Swimming in the Sun. Rankin, Joan, illus. 2012. (Lucy Bks.). (ENG.). 32p. (J). (gr. -1-k). pap. 6.95 *(978-1-4314-0218-2(4))* Jacana Media ZAF. Dist: Independent Pubs. Group.

Havill, Juanita. Grow, 1 vol. Kodman, Stansislawa, illus. 2011. (ENG.). 160p. (J). (gr. 3-7). pap. 7.95 *(978-1-56145-575-1(X))* Peachtree Pubs.

—Grow, 1 vol. Kodman, Stanislawa, illus. 2008. (ENG.). 144p. (J). (gr. 3-7). 14.95 *(978-1-56145-441-9(9))* Peachtree Pubs.

—Jamaica's Find. O'Brien, Anne Sibley, illus. 2009. (ENG.). 32p. (J). (gr. -1-3). audio compact disk 10.99 *(978-0-547-11961-8(5))* Houghton Mifflin Harcourt Publishing Co.

Haws, Ileen. Feet are Neat. 2008. 40p. pap. 18.50 *(978-1-4357-4437-0(3))* Lulu Pr., Inc.

Hay DeSimone, Corkey. Dinosaur Explore Activity & Coloring Book: Dinosaurs designed for their littlest Fans. Hay DeSimone, Corkey, illus. 2006. (Illus.). (J). 4.95 *(978-0-9777394-0-0(6))* Gentle Giraffe Pr.

—Panda Promise Activity & Coloring Book. Hay DeSimone, Corkey, illus. 2006. (Illus.). (J). 4.95 *(978-0-9747921-9-4(5))* Gentle Giraffe Pr.

Hayes, Kate. All about Poop. Garnsworthy, Mario, ed. Vaughan, Brenna, illus. 2012. (ENG.). 38p. (J). pap. 14.95 *(978-0-9854248-0-0(X))* Pinwheel Bks.

Hayles, Marsha. Bunion Burt. Davis, Jack E., illus. 2009. (ENG.). 32p. (J). (gr. -1-3). 16.99 *(978-1-4169-4132-3(0),* McElderry, Margaret K. Bks.) McElderry, Margaret K. Bks.

Hays, Anna Jane. Here Comes Silent E! Adinolfi, JoAnn, illus. 2004. (Step into Reading Ser.). (ENG.). 32p. (J). (gr. -1-1). pap. 3.99 *(978-0-375-81233-0(4),* Random Hse. Bks. for Young Readers) Random Hse. Children's Bks.

—Kindergarten Countdown. Davick, Linda, illus. 2013. (ENG.). 24p. (J). (gr. -1-2). 6.99 *(978-0-385-75371-5(3),* Dragonfly Bks.) Random Hse. Children's Bks.

—Spring Surprises. Wittwer, Hala Swearingen, illus. 2010. (Step into Reading Ser.). (ENG.). 24p. (J). (gr. -1-1). pap. 3.99 *(978-0-375-85840-6(7),* Random Hse. Bks. for Young Readers) Random Hse. Children's Bks.

Hayward, Linda. It Takes Three. Koontz, Robin Michal, illus. 2003. (Silly Millies Ser.: 3). 32p. (J). (gr. 1-3). pap. 5.95 *(978-0-7613-1798-2(8));* lib. bdg. 17.90 *(978-0-7613-2902-2(1),* Millbrook Pr.) Lerner Publishing Group.

Hearn, Sam. Busy Builders. Hearn, Sam, illus. 2016. (ENG., Illus.). 16p. (J). (— 1). bds. 10.99 *(978-0-545-79957-7(0),* Cartwheel Bks.) Scholastic, Inc.

Hegarty, Patricia. Five Black Cats. Woolf, Julia, illus. 2013. (ENG.). 22p. (J). (gr. -1). bds. 8.95 *(978-1-58925-611-8(5))* Tiger Tales.

—Five Busy Elves. Woolf, Julia, illus. 2014. (ENG.). 22p. (J). (gr. -1-k). bds. 8.99 *(978-1-58925-561-6(5))* Tiger Tales.

Hegg, Tom & Hanson, Warren. Peef & the Baby Sister. Hegg, Tom & Hanson, Warren, illus. 2006. (ENG., Illus.). 36p. (J). (gr. -1-3). 16.95 *(978-0-931674-67-9(0),* Waldman House Pr.) TRISTAN Publishing, Inc.

Heiligman, Deborah. Cool Dog, School Dog, 0 vols. 2013. (ENG.). 32p. (J). (gr. -1-3). pap. 9.99 *(978-1-4778-1670-7(4),* 9781477816707, Amazon Children's Publishing) Amazon Publishing.

—Fun Dog, Sun Dog, 0 vols. Bowers, Tim, illus. 2011. (ENG.). 34p. (J). (gr. -1-2). pap. 7.99 *(978-0-7614-5836-4(0),* 9780761458364, Amazon Children's Publishing) Amazon Publishing.

Heine, Theresa & Tavares, Victor. Star Seeker: A Journey to Outer Space. Tavares, Victor, illus. 2006. (ENG., Illus.). 32p. (J). (gr. -1-3). 16.99 *(978-1-905236-36-7(0))* Barefoot Bks., Inc.

Heinz, Brian. The Great North Woods. Rothman, Michael, illus. 2016. (ENG.). 32p. (J). (gr. 1-3). 18.99 *(978-1-56846-275-2(1),* Creative Editions) Creative Co., The.

Heinz, Brian J. The Barnyard Cat. Lt. ed. 2003. (Illus.). 32p. (J). pap. 6.96 *(978-0-936335-07-0(6))* Ballyhoo BookWorks, Inc.

—Red Fox at McCloskey's Farm. Sheban, Chris, illus. 2006. 32p. (J). (gr. -1-3). 17.95 *(978-1-56846-195-3(X),* Creative Editions) Creative Co., The.

Helakoski, Leslie. Doggone Feet! Helakoski, Leslie, illus. 2013. (ENG., Illus.). 40p. (J). (gr. -1-2). 16.95 *(978-1-59078-933-9(4))* Boyds Mills Pr.

—Hoot & Honk Can't Sleep. 2017. (ENG., Illus.). 40p. (J). (gr. -1-k). 14.95 *(978-1-4549-2125-7(0))* Sterling Publishing Co., Inc.

Heling, Kathryn & Hembrook, Deborah. Ten Lucky Leprechauns. Johnson, Jay, illus. 2013. (ENG.). 24p. (J). (gr. -1-k). pap. 3.99 *(978-0-545-43648-9(6),* Cartwheel Bks.) Scholastic, Inc.

Helmore, Jim. Letterbox Lil: A Cautionary Tale. 2006. (Illus.). (J). *(978-1-4156-4110-1(2))* Book Wholesalers, Inc.

Helmore, Jim & Wall, Karen. Stripy Horse - Off We Go! 2014. (Stripy Horse Ser.). (ENG., Illus.). 12p. (J). (gr. -1-k). bds. 7.99 *(978-1-4052-5746-6(6))* Egmont Bks., Ltd. GBR. Dist: Independent Pubs. Group.

Henkel, Donald G. Painted Treasures or the Original 288 Tree Gnomes. Henkel, D. B., VIII, illus. 2006. (J). mass mkt. 20.50 *(978-0-9673504-1-7(7))* Quillpen.

Henning, Heather. Christmas. Bull, Nicola, ed. Chapman, Gillian, illus. 2007. (Touch & Feel Ser.). 14p. (J). (gr. -1-3). bds. 10.49 *(978-0-7586-1383-7(0))* Concordia Publishing Hse.

—Creation. Bull, Nicola, ed. Chapman, Gillian, illus. 2007. (Touch & Feel Ser.). 14p. (J). (gr. -1-3). bds. 10.49 *(978-0-7586-1384-4(9))* Concordia Publishing Hse.

Henry, Kristina. The Rat Tank, 1 vol. Ambler, Laura & Brown, Amanda, illus. 2011. (ENG.). 40p. (J). 16.99 *(978-0-7643-3842-7(0),* 9780764338427, Schiffer Publishing Ltd) Schiffer Publishing, Ltd.

—The Turtle Tank, 1 vol. Ambler, Laura & Brown, Amanda, illus. 2011. (ENG.). 32p. (J). 16.99 *(978-0-7643-3843-4(9),* 9780764338434, Schiffer Publishing Ltd) Schiffer Publishing, Ltd.

Henry, Nancy. Where's Papa? 2008. 24p. per. 24.95 *(978-1-60474-000-4(0))* America Star Bks.

Henry, Sandy. A Child's Bedtime Companion. Pavlova, Vera, illus. 2005. 26p. (J). (gr. -1-2). per. 12.95 *(978-1-929039-31-9(X))* Ambassador Bks., Inc.

Henson, Laura J. & Grooms, Duffy. Ten Little Elvi. Gorissen, Dean, illus. 2004. (ENG.). 30p. (J). (gr. -1-2). 12.99 *(978-1-58246-124-3(4),* Tricycle Pr.) Random Hse. Children's Bks.

Herman Horatio Hornblower III. 2005. (YA). per. 5.00 *(978-1-59872-239-0(5))* Instant Pub.

Hernandez, Peter. A New Day with Rhyming Robin. 2011. 32p. pap. *(978-1-4269-5817-5(X))* Trafford Publishing (UK) Ltd.

Herrera, Juan Felipe. SkateFate. 2015. 128p. (YA). (gr. 8). pap. 9.99 *(978-0-06-143289-7(X),* HarperTeen) HarperCollins Pubs.

Herrick, Steven. Cold Skin. 2009. (ENG.). 279p. (YA). (gr. 9-18). 18.95 *(978-1-59078-572-0(X),* Front Street) Boyds Mills Pr.

—The Simple Gift. 2004. (ENG.). 192p. (YA). (gr. 9). pap. 9.99 *(978-0-689-86867-2(7),* Simon Pulse) Simon Pulse.

Herzog, Pearl. The Pink Dollhouse. 2008. 112p. 29.99 *(978-1-58330-797-7(4))* Feldheim Pubs.

Hesse, Karen. My Thumb. Deas, Rich, illus. 2016. (ENG.). 32p. (J). 16.99 *(978-0-312-67120-4(2),* 9780312671204) Feiwel & Friends.

Hewitt, Hazel & Gillett, Chrissy. A Locust Ate My Daddy's Underwears. 2008. 24p. pap. 13.95 *(978-1-84799-261-1(7))* Lulu Pr., Inc.

Hicks, Barbara Jean. I Like Black & White. Prap, Lila, illus. 2006. 24p. (J). (gr. -1-3). 9.95 *(978-1-58925-056-7(7))* Tiger Tales.

—Monsters Don't Eat Broccoli. Hendra, Sue, illus. (ENG.). 40p. (J). (gr. -1-2). 2014. 7.99 *(978-0-385-75521-4(X),* Dragonfly Bks.) 2009. 16.99 *(978-0-375-85686-0(2),* Knopf Bks. for Young Readers) Random Hse. Children's Bks.

Hicks, Robert Z. Tommie Turtle's Secret. Rolseth, Ruthie, illus. 2007. (ENG.). 40p. (J). 16.95 *(978-0-9792031-0-7(4))* R.Z. Enterprises of Florida.

High, Linda Oatman. A Heart Like Ringo Starr, 1 vol. 2015. (Gravel Road Verse Ser.). (ENG.). (YA). (gr. 9-12). pap. 10.95 *(978-1-62250-968-3(4))* Saddleback Educational Publishing, Inc.

Highley, Rainey Marie. The Long Lost Tale of the Dragon & the Whale. 2013. 28p. pap. 16.95 *(978-1-4808-0151-6(8))* Archway Publishing.

Hilb, Nora, illus. Itsy Bitsy Spider. 2012. (Classic Books with Holes Board Book Ser.). (ENG.). (J). 14p. bds. *(978-1-84643-509-6(9));* 16p. pap. *(978-1-84643-498-3(X))* Child's Play International Ltd.

Hill, Annemarie. Meaty Treats. 2012. 16p. pap. 15.41 *(978-1-4669-3118-3(3))* Trafford Publishing.

Hill, Isabel. Building Stories, 1 vol. 2011. (ENG., Illus.). 32p. (J). 17.95 *(978-1-59572-279-9(3));* pap. 7.95 *(978-1-59572-280-5(7))* Star Bright Bks., Inc.

Hillert, Margaret. The Cow That Got Her Wish. (J). 4.95 *(978-0-87895-694-4(8))* Modern Curriculum Pr.

—The Cow That Got Her Wish. Prater, Linda, illus. 2016. (BeginningtoRead Ser.). (ENG.). 32p. (J). (gr. -1-2). pap. 11.94 *(978-1-60357-938-4(9));* (gr. 1-2). 22.60 *(978-1-59953-797-9(4))* Norwood Hse. Pr.

—Fun Days. (J). 4.95 *(978-0-87895-678-4(6))* Modern Curriculum Pr.

—Fun Days. Roraback, Robin, illus. 2016. (BeginningtoRead Ser.). (ENG.). 32p. (J). (gr. -1-2). 22.60 *(978-1-59953-815-0(6));* pap. 11.94 *(978-1-60357-977-3(X))* Norwood Hse. Pr.

—What Is It? Stalio, Ivan & Fabbrucci, Fabiano, illus. 2016. (BeginningtoRead Ser.). (ENG.). 32p. (J). (gr. k-2). 22.60 *(978-1-59953-807-5(5))* Norwood Hse. Pr.

Hilliard, Michael. Butter Bee Grows up Too Fast! 2010. 20p. pap. 12.49 *(978-1-4490-7300-8(X))* AuthorHouse.

Hills, Jodi. Hope-So. Bjornson, Barbara, illus. 2004. (ENG.). 36p. (J). 16.95 *(978-0-9726504-2-7(3))* TRISTAN Publishing, Inc.

Hindley, Judy. Do Like a Duck Does! Bates, Ivan, illus. 2007. (ENG.). 40p. (J). (gr. -1-2). 4.99 *(978-0-7636-3284-7(8))* Candlewick Pr.

—Do Like a Duck Does! Bates, Ivan, illus. 2007. (gr. -1-k). 15.00 *(978-0-7569-8127-3(1))* Perfection Learning Corp.

—Do Like A Duck Does! 2007. 14.75 *(978-1-4177-8331-1(1),* Turtleback) Turtleback Bks.

Hinkler Books Staff. CD Storybook: Beauty & the Beast; The Little Mermaid; Cinderella; Snow White. rev. ed. 2004. (Illus.). 128p. (J). (gr. 4-12). 14.95 incl. cd-rom *(978-1-86515-754-2(6))* Hinkler Bks. Pty, Ltd. AUS. Dist: Penton Overseas, Inc.

Hinman, Bobbie. The Fart Fairy. Adams, Mark Wayne, illus. 2010. (ENG.). 32p. (J). (gr. -1-1). 16.95 *(978-0-9786791-4-9(8))* Best Fairy Bks.

—The Knot Fairy. Bridgeman, Kristi, illus. 2010. (ENG.). 32p. (J). (gr. -1-1). 16.95 *(978-0-9786791-0-1(5))* Best Fairy Bks.

—The Sock Fairy. Bridgeman, Kristi, illus. 2008. (ENG.). 32p. (J). (gr. -1-1). 16.95 *(978-0-9786791-1-8(3))* Best Fairy Bks.

Hit Entertainment. Lost at Sea! Stubbs, Tommy, illus. 2010. (Pictureback(R) Ser.). (ENG.). 24p. (J). (gr. -1-2). pap. 3.99 *(978-0-375-84754-7(5),* Random Hse. Bks. for Young Readers) Random Hse. Children's Bks.

Hobbie, Nathaniel. Priscilla & the Pixie Princess. Hobbie, Jocelyn, illus. 2011. (ENG.). 32p. (J). (gr. -1-3). pap. 6.99 *(978-0-316-08349-2(6))* Little, Brown Bks. for Young Readers.

Hoberman, Mary Ann. A House Is a House for Me. Fraser, Betty, illus. 2007. (ENG.). 48p. (J). (gr. -1-1). pap. 7.99 *(978-0-14-240773-8(9),* Puffin Books) Penguin Young Readers Group.

—The Seven Silly Eaters. Frazee, Marla, illus. 2004. (J). (gr. k-3). spiral bd. *(978-0-616-14576-0(4))* Canadian National Institute for the Blind/Institut National Canadien pour les Aveugles.

Hochman, Marisa. A Walk in Pirate's Cove. Woodland, Bette, illus. 2012. (ENG.). 32p. (J). *(978-0-9865679-0-2(6))* Fitzhenry & Whiteside, Ltd.

Hodgkinson, Jo. The Talent Show. Hodgkinson, Jo, illus. 2011. (ENG., Illus.). 32p. (J). (gr. -1-3). 16.95 *(978-0-7613-7487-9(6))* Lerner Publishing Group.

Hodgkinson, Leigh. A Place to Read. 2017. (ENG., Illus.). 32p. (J). 16.99 *(978-1-68119-323-6(X),* 9781681193236, Bloomsbury USA Childrens) Bloomsbury Publishing USA.

Hodgman, Ann. Monsters Dance. Wood, Hannah, illus. 2013. (ENG.). 16p. (J). (gr. -1). bds. 8.95 *(978-1-58925-627-9(1))* Tiger Tales.

Hodgson, Karen J. Hugh's Blue Day. Collins, Ross, illus. 2010. (ENG.). 32p. (J). (gr. -1-k). pap. 9.99 *(978-1-907432-00-2(0))* Hogs Back Bks. GBR. Dist: Independent Pubs. Group.

Hodgson, Mona Gansberg. Bedtime in the Southwest. Graef, Renee, illus. 2004. (ENG.). 32p. (J). (gr. -1-k). 14.95 *(978-0-87358-871-3(1))* Cooper Square Publishing Llc.

Hoffman, Don. Abigail Is a Big Girl. Dakins, Todd, illus. 2nd ed. 2016. (Billy & Abby Ser.). (ENG.). 28p. (J). (gr. -1-k). pap. 3.99 *(978-1-943154-03-6(1))* Peek-A-Boo Publishing.

—Billy Is a Big Boy. Dakins, Todd, illus. 2nd ed. 2016. (Billy & Abby Ser.). (ENG.). 28p. (J). (gr. -1-k). pap. 3.99 *(978-1-943154-02-9(3))* Peek-A-Boo Publishing.

—Good Morning, Good Night Billy & Abigail. Dakins, Todd, illus. 2nd ed. 2016. (Billy & Abby Ser.). (ENG.). 24p. (J). (gr. -1-k). pap. 3.99 *(978-1-943154-09-8(0))* Peek-A-Boo Publishing.

Hoffman, Eric. A Dark, Dark Cave. Tabor, Corey R., illus. 2016. (ENG.). 40p. (J). (gr. -1-1). 17.99 *(978-0-670-01636-5(5),* Viking Books for Young Readers) Penguin Young Readers Group.

Hoffman, Peter. A ferret in a Garret. Olson, Cindy, illus. 2008. 36p. (J). 24.99 *(978-0-9790247-6-4(5))* Artpacks.

Hoffmann, Heinrich. Slovenly Betsy: the American Struwwelpeter: From the Struwwelpeter Library. Hayn, Walter, illus. 2013. (Dover Children's Classics Ser.). (ENG.). 96p. (J). (gr. 3-8). pap. 12.99 *(978-0-486-49828-7(X))* Dover Pubns., Inc.

Hogan, Robb Dragon Taz. Moonlight's Spell: Rhymes for Younger Readers by TAZ. 2003. (Illus.). 61p. (J). spiral bd. 9.95 *(978-0-9742178-1-9(6))* TazTales.

Holladay, Shirley. Gail the Snail. 2009. 28p. pap. 14.99 *(978-1-4389-8744-6(7))* AuthorHouse.

Hollon, Frank Turner, et al. Glitter Girl & the Crazy Cheese. Dulemba, Elizabeth O., illus. 2006. (ENG.). 32p. (J). (gr. -1-3). *(978-1-59692-137-5(4))* MacAdam/Cage Publishing, Inc.

Holmes, Kimberly. Digibots Classroom Adventures. Lawson, Devin, illus. 2004. (J). *(978-0-9755725-0-4(4),* 1238415) Digibots Corp.

Holt, Gretta Scott. The Reindeer Who Was Afraid to Fly. 2008. 24p. pap. 11.49 *(978-1-4389-1709-2(0))* AuthorHouse.

Holt, K. A. House Arrest. (ENG.). (J). (gr. 5-9). 2016. 312p. pap. 7.99 *(978-1-4521-5648-4(4))* 2015. 304p. 16.99 *(978-1-4521-3477-2(4))* Chronicle Bks. LLC.

Holub, Joan. Apple Countdown. Smith, Jan, illus. 2012. (J). *(978-1-61913-117-0(X))* Weigl Pubs., Inc.

—Apple Countdown. Smith, Jan, illus. 2009. (ENG.). 32p. (J). (gr. -1-3). 16.99 *(978-0-8075-0398-0(3))* Whitman, Albert & Co.
—Ballet Stars. McNicholas, Shelagh, illus. 2012. (Step into Reading Ser.). (ENG.). 24p. (J). (gr. -1-1). pap. 3.99 *(978-0-375-86909-9(3),* Random Hse. Bks. for Young Readers) Random Hse. Children's Bks.
—Ballet Stars. 2012. (Step into Reading Level 1 Ser.). lib. bdg. 13.55 *(978-0-606-26398-6(5),* Turtleback) Turtleback Bks.
—Big Heart! A Valentine's Day Tale. Terry, Will, illus. 2007. (Ant Hill Ser.). (ENG.). 24p. (J). (gr. -1-k). lib. bdg. 13.89 *(978-1-4169-2562-0(7),* Simon & Schuster/Paula Wiseman Bks.) Simon & Schuster/Paula Wiseman Bks.
—Big Heart! A Valentine's Day Tale. Terry, Will, illus. 2007. (Ant Hill Ser.). (ENG.). 24p. (J). (gr. -1-k). pap. 3.99 *(978-1-4169-0957-6(5),* Simon Spotlight) Simon Spotlight.
—Dig, Scoop, Ka-Boom! Gordon, David, illus. 2013. (Step into Reading Ser.). (ENG.). 24p. (J). (gr. -1-1). pap. 3.99 *(978-0-375-86910-5(7),* Random Hse. Bks. for Young Readers) Random Hse. Children's Bks.
—Good Luck! A St. Patrick's Day Story. Terry, Will, illus. 2007. (Ant Hill Ser.). (ENG.). 24p. (J). (gr. -1-k). lib. bdg. 11.89 *(978-1-4169-2560-6(0),* Aladdin Library) Simon & Schuster Children's Publishing.
—Good Luck! A St. Patrick's Day Story. Terry, Will, illus. 2007. (Ant Hill Ser.). (ENG.). 24p. (J). (gr. -1-k). pap. 3.99 *(978-1-4169-0955-2(9),* Simon Spotlight) Simon Spotlight.
—The Knights Before Christmas. Magoon, Scott, illus. 2015. (ENG.). 32p. (J). (gr. k-3). 16.99 *(978-0-8050-9932-4(8),* 9780805099324, Holt, Henry & Co. Bks. For Young Readers) Holt, Henry & Co.
—Mighty Dads. Dean, James, illus. 2014. (ENG.). 40p. (J). (gr. -1-k). 16.99 *(978-0-545-60968-5(2),* Scholastic Pr.) Scholastic, Inc.
—Scaredy-Pants! A Halloween Story. Terry, Will, illus. 2007. (Ant Hill Ser.). (ENG.). 24p. (J). (gr. -1-k). pap. 3.99 *(978-1-4169-0956-9(7),* Simon Spotlight/Nickelodeon) Simon Spotlight/Nickelodeon.
—Shampoodle. Bowers, Tim, illus. 2009. (Step into Reading Ser.). (ENG.). 32p. (J). (gr. -1-1). pap. 3.99 *(978-0-375-85576-4(9),* Random Hse. Bks. for Young Readers) Random Hse. Children's Bks.
—Snow Day! A Winter Tale. Terry, Will, illus. 2008. (Ant Hill Ser.). (ENG.). 24p. (J). (gr. -1-k). pap. 3.99 *(978-1-4169-5135-3(0),* Simon Spotlight) Simon Spotlight.
—Spring Is Here! A Story about Seeds. Terry, Will, illus. 2008. (Ant Hill Ser.). (ENG.). 24p. (J). (gr. -1-k). lib. bdg. 13.89 *(978-1-4169-5132-2(6),* Simon & Schuster/Paula Wiseman Bks.) Simon & Schuster/Paula Wiseman Bks.
—Spring Is Here! A Story about Seeds. Terry, Will, illus. 2008. (Ant Hill Ser.). (ENG.). 24p. (J). (gr. -1-k). pap. 3.99 *(978-1-4169-5131-5(8),* Simon Spotlight) Simon Spotlight.
—Vampoodle. Bowers, Tim, illus. 2017. (Step into Reading Ser.). (ENG.). 32p. (J). (gr. -1-1). pap. 3.99 *(978-1-101-93666-5(5),* Random Hse. Bks. for Young Readers) Random Hse. Children's Bks.
Holzer, Angela. Lovely Lily. Hansen, Angela, illus. 2009. (ENG.). 36p. (J). lib. bdg. 8.99 *(978-0-9821563-2-2(4))* Good Sound Publishing.
Hood, Susan. Leaps & Bounce. Cordell, Matthew, illus. 2016. (ENG.). 32p. (J). (gr. -1-k). 16.99 *(978-1-4231-5234-7(4))* Disney Pr.
—Tickly Toes. Barroux, Stéphane, illus. 2014. (ENG.). 24p. (J). (gr. -1 — 1). bds. 9.95 *(978-1-894786-52-2(1))* Kids Can Pr., Ltd. CAN. Dist: Hachette Bk. Group.
Hooke, R. Schuyler. Thomas' Night Before Christmas. Courtney, Richard, illus. 2013. (Little Golden Book Ser.). (ENG.). 24p. (J). (gr. -1-k). 4.99 *(978-0-449-81663-9(X),* Golden Bks.) Random Hse. Children's Bks.
Hope, Kathleen. Isiah Thomas & the Mysterious Castle Mcscary. 2012. (Illus.). 44p. pap. 24.40 *(978-1-4685-0496-5(7))* AuthorHouse.
Hopgood, Sally. See You Later, Alligator. Levey, Emma, illus. 2016. (ENG.). 32p. (J). (gr. -1-k). 16.99 *(978-1-5107-0484-8(1),* Sky Pony Pr.) Skyhorse Publishing Co., Inc.
—A Trip to Busy Town: A Pull-The-Tab Book. Hinton, Stephanie, illus. 2014. (J). *(978-1-4351-5690-6(0))* Barnes & Noble, Inc.
Hopkins, Ellen. Fallout. 2010. (ENG.). 672p. (YA). (gr. 9-18). 18.99 *(978-1-4169-5009-7(5),* McElderry, Margaret K. Bks.) McElderry, Margaret K. Bks.
—Impulse. 2008. (ENG.). 688p. (YA). (gr. 9-12). pap. 12.99 *(978-1-4169-0357-4(7),* McElderry, Margaret K. Bks.) McElderry, Margaret K. Bks.
—Tilt. (ENG., (YA). (gr. 9). 2014. Illus.). 624p. pap. 12.99 *(978-1-4169-8331-6(7))* 2012. 608p. 18.99 *(978-1-4169-8330-9(9))* McElderry, Margaret K. Bks. (McElderry, Margaret K. Bks.).
Hopkins, Jeanette. The Juggler. 2011. (Illus.). 32p. (J). 16.95 *(978-1-888160-58-1(6))* Ice Cube Pr., LLC.
Hopkinson, Deborah. Maria's Comet. Lanino, Deborah, illus. 2003. (ENG.). 32p. (J). (gr. -1-3). 8.99 *(978-0-689-85678-5(4),* Simon & Schuster/Paula Wiseman Bks.) Simon & Schuster/Paula Wiseman Bks.
Hopper, Karyn. There's a Monster in My Opu. 2006. (Illus.). 24p. (J). 11.95 *(978-1-57306-244-2(8))* Bess Pr., Inc.
Hopwood, Lolly & Kusters, YoYo. Move! Shea, Bob & Flowers, Luke, illus. 2016. (ENG.). 32p. (J). (gr. -1-1). bds. 12.95 *(978-0-7611-8733-2(2))* Workman Publishing Co., Inc.
Horacek, Judy. Yellow Is My Color Star. Horacek, Judy, illus. 2014. (ENG., Illus.). 32p. (J). (gr. -1-3). 16.99 *(978-1-4424-9299-8(6),* Beach Lane Bks.) Beach Lane Bks.
Horacek, Judy & Fox, Mem. Where Is the Green Sheep? alt. ed. 2009. (ENG., Illus.). 32p. (J). (gr. -1 — 1). bds. 6.99 *(978-0-15-206704-5(3))* Houghton Mifflin Harcourt Publishing Co.
Horácek, Petr. Jonathan & Martha. 2012. (ENG., Illus.). 40p. (gr. -1-1). 14.95 *(978-0-7148-6351-1(3))* Phaidon Pr., Inc.
Hord, Colleen. Itsy Bitsy Spider. Poole, Helen, illus. 2012. (ENG.). 24p. (gr. 1-2). pap. 8.95 *(978-1-61810-310-9(5))* Rourke Educational Media.
Horowitz, Dave. Five Little Gefiltes. Horowitz, Dave, illus. 2007. (ENG., Illus.). 32p. (J). (gr. -1-3). 15.99 *(978-0-399-24608-1(8),* G.P. Putnam's Sons Books for Young Readers) Penguin Young Readers Group.
—Humpty Dumpty Climbs Again. Horowitz, Dave, illus. 2011. (ENG., Illus.). 32p. (J). (gr. -1-k). pap. 6.99 *(978-0-14-241932-8(X),* Puffin Books) Penguin Young Readers Group.
—Twenty-Six Pirates: An Alphabet Book. Horowitz, Dave, illus. 2013. (ENG., Illus.). 32p. (J). (gr. -1-k). 16.99 *(978-0-399-25777-3(2),* Nancy Paulsen Books) Penguin Young Readers Group.
—Twenty-Six Princesses. Horowitz, Dave, illus. 2008. (ENG., Illus.). 32p. (J). (gr. -1-k). 15.99 *(978-0-399-24607-4(X),* G.P. Putnam's Sons Books for Young Readers) Penguin Young Readers Group.
—Twenty-Six Princesses: An Alphabet Story. Horowitz, Dave, illus. 2011. (ENG., Illus.). 32p. (J). (gr. -1-k). pap. 6.99 *(978-0-14-241536-8(7),* Puffin Books) Penguin Young Readers Group.
—The Ugly Pumpkin. Horowitz, Dave, illus. 2008. (ENG., Illus.). 40p. (J). (gr. -1-k). pap. 6.99 *(978-0-14-241145-2(0),* Puffin Books) Penguin Young Readers Group.
Horvath, James. Build, Dogs, Build: A Tall Tail. Horvath, James, illus. 2013. (ENG., Illus.). 40p. (J). (gr. -1-3). 15.99 *(978-0-06-218967-7(0))* HarperCollins Pubs.
—Work, Dogs, Work: A Highway Tail. Horvath, James, illus. 2014. (ENG., Illus.). 40p. (J). (gr. -1-3). 15.99 *(978-0-06-218970-7(0))* HarperCollins Pubs.
Hosford, Kate. Big Birthday. Clifton-Brown, Holly, illus. 2012. (Carolrhoda Picture Bks.). (ENG.). 32p. (J). (gr. k-2). lib. bdg. 16.95 *(978-0-7613-5410-9(7))* Lerner Publishing Group.
—Big Bouffant. Clifton-Brown, Holly, illus. 2011. (ENG.). 32p. (J). (gr. k-2). 16.95 *(978-0-7613-5409-3(3),* Carolrhoda Bks.) Lerner Publishing Group.
Hougue, Heather, ed. The Snowman Band. 2006. (Illus.). 22p. (J). spiral bd. 15.95 *(978-0-9764779-3-8(9))* Perennial Dreams Pubns.
Houran, Lori Haskins. I Will Keep You Safe & Sound. Brown, Petra, illus. 2013. (J). *(978-0-545-19752-6(X),* Scholastic Pr.) Scholastic, Inc.
Howard, Juliana. Catie the Copycat. 2010. 32p. (J). 17.00 *(978-1-59298-368-1(5))* Beaver's Pond Pr., Inc.
Howard, Mike. The Chronicles of Mike Bike Hall. Syder, Andrew, illus. 2016. (ENG.). (J). (gr. 1-5). pap. ***(978-1-78222-488-4(2))*** Paragon Publishing, Rothersthorpe.
Howard, Reginald. The Big, Big Wall. Dewey, Ariane & Aruego, Jose, illus. 2003. (Green Light Readers — Level 1 Ser.). (J). (gr. -1-3). 13.50 *(978-0-613-66350-2(0),* Turtleback) Turtleback Bks.
—The Big, Big Wall/No Puedo Bajar. Flor Ada, Alma & Campoy, F. Isabel, trs. Dewey, Ariane & Aruego, Jose, illus. 2009. (Green Light Readers Level 1 Ser.). (SPA & ENG.). 28p. (J). (gr. -1-3). pap. 3.99 *(978-0-547-25548-4(9))* Houghton Mifflin Harcourt Publishing Co.
Howatt, Sandra J. Sleepyheads. Wan, Joyce, illus. 2014. (ENG.). 32p. (J). (gr. -1-3). 17.99 *(978-1-4424-2266-7(1),* Beach Lane Bks.) Beach Lane Bks.
Howell, Julie Ann. Mrs Owl's Nest of Rhymes. LaGrange, Tiffany, illus. 2008. 24p. pap. 12.95 *(978-0-9818683-8-7(X))* Peppertree Pr., The.
Howland, Naomi. The Princess Says Goodnight. Small, David, illus. 2010. 32p. (J). (gr. -1-2). (ENG.). 16.99 *(978-0-06-145525-4(3));* lib. bdg. 17.89 *(978-0-06-145526-1(1))* HarperCollins Pubs.
Hsu, Stacey W. Old Mo. Ritter, Adam, illus. 2011. (Rookie Ready to Learn — Animals Ser.). 40p. (J). (gr. -1-k). lib. bdg. 25.00 *(978-0-531-26418-8(1));* pap. 5.95 *(978-0-531-26699-1(0))* Scholastic Library Publishing. (Children's Pr.).
Huang, Yu-Hsuan. Let's Play... Ice Skating. 2014. (Let's Play Ser.). (ENG.). 10p. (J). (gr. -1 — 1). 15.99 *(978-1-4472-7644-9(2))* Pan Macmillan GBR. Dist: Independent Pubs. Group.
Huang, Yu-Hsuan, illus. Let's Play Aliens in Space. 2016. (Let's Play Ser.). (ENG.). 10p. (J). (gr. -1-k). bds. 16.99 *(978-1-4472-8653-0(7))* Pan Macmillan GBR. Dist: Independent Pubs. Group.
Hubbard, Ben. My Very Own Kitten. Guile, Gill, illus. 2014. (ENG.). 12p. (J). (gr. -1). *(978-1-78244-602-6(8))* Top That! Publishing PLC.
—My Very Own Puppy. Guile, Gill, illus. 2014. (ENG.). 12p. (gr. -1). *(978-1-78244-603-3(6))* Top That! Publishing PLC.
Hubbell, Patricia. Black All Around! Tate, Don, illus. 2003. (ENG.). 32p. (J). 16.95 *(978-1-58430-048-9(5))* Lee & Low Bks., Inc.
—Boats: Speeding! Sailing! Cruising!, 0 vols. Halsey, Megan & Addy, Sean, illus. 2009. (ENG.). 32p. (J). (gr. -1-1). 17.99 *(978-0-7614-5524-0(8),* 9780761455240, Amazon Children's Publishing) Amazon Publishing.
—Cars: Rushing! Honking! Zooming!, 0 vols. Halsey, Megan & Addy, Sean, illus. 2010. (ENG.). 32p. (J). (gr. -1-1). pap. 6.99 *(978-0-7614-5616-2(3),* 9780761456162, Amazon Children's Publishing) Amazon Publishing.
—Check It Out! Reading, Finding, Helping, 0 vols. Speir, Nancy, illus. 2011. (ENG.). 32p. (J). (gr. -1-3). 16.99 *(978-0-7614-5803-6(4),* 9780761458036, Amazon Children's Publishing) Amazon Publishing.
—Firefighters! Speeding! Spraying! Saving!, 0 vols. Garofoli, Viviana, illus. 2012. (ENG.). 32p. (J). (gr. -1-2). pap. 7.99 *(978-0-7614-6245-3(7),* 9780761462453, Amazon Children's Publishing) Amazon Publishing.
—Firefighters! Speeing! Spraying! Saving!, 0 vols. Garofoli, Viviana, illus. 2009. (ENG.). 32p. (J). (gr. -1-2). bds. 7.99 *(978-0-7614-5615-5(5),* 9780761456155, Amazon Children's Publishing) Amazon Publishing.
—Hurray for Spring. Morley, Taia, illus. 2005. (Picture Book Ser.). (ENG.). 32p. (J). (gr. -1-k). 15.95 *(978-1-55971-913-1(3))* Cooper Square Publishing Llc.
—My First Airplane Ride, 0 vols. Speir, Nancy, illus. 2013. (ENG.). 42p. (J). (gr. -1-2). pap. 9.99 *(978-1-4778-1675-2(5),* 9781477816752, Amazon Children's Publishing) Amazon Publishing.
—Shaggy Dogs, Waggy Dogs, 0 vols. Wu, Donald, illus. 2011. (ENG.). 32p. (J). (gr. -1-3). 17.99 *(978-0-7614-5957-6(X),* 9780761459576, Amazon Children's Publishing) Amazon Publishing.
—Snow Happy! Nakata, Hiroe, illus. 2010. (ENG.). 32p. (J). (gr. -1-2). 15.99 *(978-1-58246-329-2(8),* Tricycle Pr.) Random Hse. Children's Bks.
—Teacher! Sharing, Helping, Caring, 0 vols. Speir, Nancy, illus. 2009. (ENG.). 32p. (J). (gr. -1-3). 16.99 *(978-0-7614-5574-5(4),* 9780761455745, Amazon Children's Publishing) Amazon Publishing.
—Trains: Steaming! Pulling! Huffing!, 0 vols. Addy, Sean & Halsey, Megan, illus. 2009. (ENG.). 34p. (J). (gr. -1-1). pap. 9.99 *(978-0-7614-5593-6(0),* 9780761455936, Amazon Children's Publishing) Amazon Publishing.
—Trucks: Whizz! Zoom! Rumble!, 0 vols. Halsey, Megan, illus. 2006. (ENG.). 32p. (J). (gr. -1-1). per. 9.99 *(978-0-7614-5328-4(8),* 9780761453284, Amazon Children's Publishing) Amazon Publishing.
Hubery, Julia. My Daddy. Elliot, Rebecca, illus. 2014. (J). *(978-1-4351-5507-7(6))* Barnes & Noble, Inc.
Hudgens, Melica, illus. Flim Flam & Other Such Gobbledygook. 2015. (J). 14.99 *(978-1-4621-1684-3(1))* Cedar Fort, Inc./CFI Distribution.
Hudson, Cheryl Willis. Clothes I Love to Wear. 2008. (Illus.). 24p. (J). (gr. -1-3). 3.99 *(978-1-60349-004-7(3),* Marimba Bks.) Hudson Publishing Group, The.
—Hands Can. Bourke, John-Francis, photos by. (ENG., Illus.). (J). (gr. k-k). 2012. 32p. pap. 24.99 *(978-0-7636-5819-9(7))* 2007. 24p. bds. 7.99 *(978-0-7636-3292-2(9))* Candlewick Pr.
—Hands Can. Bourke, John-Francis, illus. Bourke, John-Francis, photos by. 2003. (ENG.). 32p. (J). (gr. k-k). 16.99 *(978-0-7636-1667-0(2))* Candlewick Pr.
—Hands Can. 2013. lib. bdg. 14.75 *(978-0-606-31602-6(7),* Turtleback) Turtleback Bks.
—Las Manos. Bourke, John-Francis, illus. 2014. (ENG & SPA.). 32p. (J). (-k). pap. 4.99 *(978-0-7636-7392-5(7))* Candlewick Pr.
Hughes, Shirley. Alfie Weather. Hughes, Shirley, illus. 2007. (Alfie Ser.). (ENG., Illus.). 48p. (J). (gr. -1-k). pap. 9.99 *(978-0-09-940425-5(7),* Red Fox) Random House Children's Books GBR. Dist: Independent Pubs. Group.
Hull, Rod. Dr. Potts, My Pets Have Spots! PB. 2017. (Illus.). 32p. (J). (gr. -1-2). 8.99 ***(978-1-78285-324-4(3))*** Barefoot Bks., Inc.
Hulme, Joy N. Eerie Feary Feeling: A Hairy Scary Pop-up Book. Ely, Paul & Dudley, Dick, illus. 2006. 12p. (J). (gr. k-4). reprint ed. 14.00 *(978-1-4223-5171-0(8))* DIANE Publishing Co.
Hunt, Connie. Planting Love: A Tale of Love & Growing. 2012. 48p. 18.10 *(978-1-4669-0965-6(X));* pap. 8.10 *(978-1-4669-0967-0(6))* Trafford Publishing.
Hunt, Meg, illus. Interstellar Cinderella. 2015. (ENG.). 40p. (J). (gr. -1-k). 16.99 *(978-1-4521-2532-9(5))* Chronicle Bks. LLC.
Hurd, Thacher. Cat's Pajamas. 2015. (ENG., Illus.). 16p. (J). (gr. -1-k). 9.95 *(978-1-63076-030-4(7))* Taylor Trade Publishing.
Hutchins, Hazel J. I'd Know You Anywhere. 2004. (Illus.). (J). (gr. -1-18). spiral bd. *(978-0-616-14577-7(2));* spiral bd. *(978-0-616-14578-4(0))* Canadian National Institute for the Blind/Institut National Canadien pour les Aveugles.
Hutchins, Pat. Barn Dance! Hutchins, Pat, illus. 2007. (Illus.). 32p. (J). (gr. -1-k). lib. bdg. 17.89 *(978-0-06-089122-0(X),* Greenwillow Bks.) HarperCollins Pubs.
Hutton, John. Blanket: Baby Unplugged. Kang, Andrea, illus. 2011. (Baby Unplugged Ser.). (ENG.). 14p. (J). (— 1). bds. 7.99 *(978-1-936669-00-4(5))* Blue Manatee Press.
—Book: Baby Unplugged. Hutton, John, ed. Kang, Andrea, illus. 2012. (Baby Unplugged Ser.). (ENG.). 14p. (J). (— 1). bds. 7.99 *(978-1-936669-06-6(4))* Blue Manatee Press.
—Box: Baby Unplugged. Kang, Andrea, illus. 2012. (Baby Unplugged Ser.). (ENG.). 14p. (J). (— 1). bds. 7.99 *(978-1-936669-08-0(0))* Blue Manatee Press.
—Pets: Baby Unplugged. Kang, Andrea, illus. 2011. (Baby Unplugged Ser.). (ENG.). 14p. (J). (— 1). bds. 7.99 *(978-1-936669-02-8(1))* Blue Manatee Press.
—Yard: Baby Unplugged. Kang, Andrea, illus. 2011. (Baby Unplugged Ser.). (ENG.). 14p. (J). (— 1). bds. 7.99 *(978-1-936669-01-1(3))* Blue Manatee Press.
Iadonisi, Carmin & Word, Amanda. Whiny Whiny Rhino. Iadonisi, Carmin & Word, Amanda, illus. 2014. (ENG., Illus.). 32p. (J). 16.99 *(978-0-9903623-0-2(2))* Blue Blanket Publishing.
Ide, Laurie Shimizu. Okazu at the Zoo. Kanekuni, Daniel, illus. 2006. (J). *(978-1-56647-776-5(X))* Mutual Publishing LLC.
Igl, Janeane. Winter, Spring, Summer, Fall: (A Sing-Song Book) 2008. 20p. pap. 24.95 *(978-1-60563-279-7(1))* America Star Bks.
Image Books Staff. Little Chick: Finger Puppet Book. Put, Klaartje van der, illus. 2015. (ENG.). 12p. (J). (gr. -1 — 1). bds. 6.99 *(978-1-4521-2917-4(7))* Chronicle Bks. LLC.
—Little Chicken. Put, Klaartje van der, illus. 2012. (Little Finger Puppet Board Bks.: FING). (ENG.). 12p. (J). (gr. -1 — 1). bds. 6.99 *(978-1-4521-0811-7(0))* Chronicle Bks. LLC.
—Little Dolphin. Put, Klaartje van der, illus. 2012. (Little Finger Puppet Board Bks.: FING). (ENG.). 12p. (J). (gr. -1 — 1). bds. 6.99 *(978-1-4521-0816-2(1))* Chronicle Bks. LLC.
—Little Seal: Finger Puppet Book. Put, Klaartje van der, illus. 2012. (Little Finger Puppet Board Bks.: FING). (ENG.). 12p. (J). (gr. -1 — 1). bds. 6.99 *(978-1-4521-0812-4(9))* Chronicle Bks. LLC.
Image Books Staff & Chronicle Books Staff. Little Pig. Put, Klaartje van der, illus. 2012. (Little Finger Puppet Board Bks.). (ENG.). 12p. (J). (gr. -1 — 1). bds. 6.99 *(978-1-4521-0817-9(X))* Chronicle Bks. LLC.
ImageBooks Staff. Little Dog: Finger Puppet Book. 2014. (Little Finger Puppet Board Bks.). (ENG.). 12p. (J). (gr. -1 — 1). bds. 6.99 *(978-1-4521-2915-0(0))* Chronicle Bks. LLC.
—Little Horse: Finger Puppet Book. Put, Klaartje van der, illus. 2013. (Little Finger Puppet Board Bks.). (ENG.). 12p. (J). (gr. -1 — 1). bds. 6.99 *(978-1-4521-1249-7(5))* Chronicle Bks. LLC.
—Little Monkey. Put, Klaartje van der, illus. 2013. (Little Finger Puppet Board Bks.). (ENG.). 12p. (J). (gr. -1 — 1). bds. 6.99 *(978-1-4521-1250-3(9))* Chronicle Bks. LLC.
—Little Owl Finger Puppet Book. 2011. (Little Finger Puppet Board Bks.). (ENG.). 12p. (J). (gr. -1 — 1). bds. 6.99 *(978-1-4521-0221-4(X))* Chronicle Bks. LLC.
—Little Sea Turtle: Finger Puppet Book. 2014. (Little Finger Puppet Board Bks.). (ENG.). 12p. (J). (gr. -1 — 1). bds. 6.99 *(978-1-4521-2913-6(4))* Chronicle Bks. LLC.
—Little Shark: Finger Puppet Book. Put, Klaartje van der, illus. 2013. (Little Finger Puppet Board Bks.). (ENG.). 12p. (J). (gr. -1 — 1). bds. 6.99 *(978-1-4521-1251-0(7))* Chronicle Bks. LLC.
—Little Zebra. Put, Klaartje van der, illus. 2013. (Little Finger Puppet Board Bks.). (ENG.). 12p. (J). (gr. -1 — 1). bds. 6.99 *(978-1-4521-1252-7(5))* Chronicle Bks. LLC.
ImageBooks Staff & Chronicle Books Staff. Little Fox: Finger Puppet Book. Put, Klaartje van der, illus. 2015. (ENG.). 12p. (J). (gr. -1 — 1). bds. 6.99 *(978-1-4521-4230-2(0))* Chronicle Bks. LLC.
The Imaginary Zoo. 2007. (J). 16.95 *(978-0-9789880-0-5(0))* Wild About Learning, Inc.
Imbody, Amy E. & Imbody, Amy. Snug as a Bug, 1 vol. Gordon, Mike, illus. 2008. (I Can Read! Ser.). (ENG.). 32p. (J). (gr. -1-1). pap. 3.99 *(978-0-310-71575-7(X))* Zonderkidz.
Ingalls, Ann. Scholastic Reader Level 1: Biggety Bat: Hot Diggety, It's Biggety! Zenz, Aaron, illus. 2014. (Scholastic Reader Level 1 Ser.). (ENG.). 32p. (J). (gr. -1-2). pap. 3.99 *(978-0-545-66263-5(X))* Scholastic, Inc.
Ingle, L. G. Little Willy Wiggle & Johnny Amigo. 2012. 40p. pap. *(978-1-77097-479-1(2))* FriesenPress.
Inkpen, Mick. A Royal Lullabyhullaballoo! 2017. (ENG., Illus.). 40p. (J). (gr. -1-k). pap. 10.99 ***(978-1-4449-3051-1(6))*** Hachette Children's Group GBR. Dist: Hachette Bk. Group.
Inkpen, Mick. Wibbly Pig Has 10 Balloons. 2012. (ENG., Illus.). 32p. (J). (gr. -1-k). pap. 9.99 *(978-1-4449-0267-9(9))* Hodder & Stoughton GBR. Dist: Hachette Bk. Group.
Innovative Kids Staff, creator. Playful Penguins. 2012. (ENG.). 6p. (J). (gr. -1 — 1). 14.99 *(978-1-60169-266-5(8))* Innovative Kids.
Intrater, Roberta Grobel. Peek-a-Boo, You! Intrater, Roberta Grobel, photos by. 2nd rev. l.t. ed. 2005. (Illus.). 14p. (J). 14.99 *(978-0-9764985-0-6(2))* 1212 Pr.
Intriago, Patricia. Dot. Intriago, Patricia, illus. 2011. (ENG., Illus.). 36p. (J). (gr. -1-1). 14.99 *(978-0-374-31835-2(2),* 9780374318352, Farrar, Straus & Giroux (BYR)) Farrar, Straus & Giroux.
Ipcar, Dahlov, illus. Black & White. 2015. (Dahlov Ipcar Collection). (ENG.). 40p. (J). (gr. -1-2). 17.95 *(978-1-909263-44-4(3))* Flying Eye Bks. GBR. Dist: Consortium Bk. Sales & Distribution.
Ipcizade, Catherine. 'Twas the Day Before Zoo Day, 1 vol. Hodson, Ben, illus. 2008. (Basic Math Operations Ser.). (ENG.). 32p. (J). (gr. -1-2). 17.95 *(978-1-60718-585-7(7))* Arbordale Publishing.
Irly, I. R. Why Crocodile Does Not Smile. 2004. (Illus.). (J). bds. *(978-0-9753075-4-0(1))* M-Graphics Publishing.
Ismail, Yasmeen. Imagine That! 2017. (ENG., Illus.). 32p. (J). 16.99 *(978-1-68119-362-5(0),* 9781681193625, Bloomsbury USA Childrens) Bloomsbury Publishing USA.
Isom, Lori Boyd. Swoosh! Wise, Noreen, ed. 2004. (Illus.). 64p. (J). per. 6.95 *(978-1-58584-560-6(4))* Huckleberry Pr.
Isop, Laurie. How Do You Hug a Porcupine? Millward, Gwen, illus. 2011. (ENG.). 32p. (J). (gr. -1-1). 16.99 *(978-1-4424-1291-0(7),* Simon & Schuster Bks. For Young Readers) Simon & Schuster Bks. For Young Readers.
Ivy, Cheryl. Little Miss D: What did you SEE? 2011. 20p. pap. 11.49 *(978-1-4567-5739-7(3))* AuthorHouse.
J, Granny. Pinky Gets a New Puppy: Pinky Frink's Adventures. 2012. 38p. pap. 17.99 *(978-1-105-86479-7(0))* Lulu Pr., Inc.
Jackson, Alison. When the Wind Blew. Barrette, Doris, illus. 2014. (ENG.). 32p. (J). (gr. -1-2). 16.99 *(978-0-8050-8688-1(9),* 9780805086881, Holt, Henry & Co. Bks. For Young Readers) Holt, Henry & Co.
Jackson, Ann. Rags the Recycled Doll. O'Connor, Shannon, illus. 2004. 49p. 12.95 *(978-1-57197-405-1(9))* Pentland Pr., Inc.
Jackson, Byron & Jackson, Kathryn. A Day at the Seashore. 2010. (Little Golden Book Ser.). (ENG., Illus.). 24p. (J). (gr. -1-2). 4.99 *(978-0-375-85425-5(8),* Golden Bks.) Random Hse. Children's Bks.
Jackson, Ellen. Beastly Babies. Wenzel, Brendan, illus. 2015. (ENG.). 32p. (J). (gr. -1-3). 17.99 *(978-1-4424-0834-0(0),* Beach Lane Bks.) Beach Lane Bks.
Jackson, Ellen & Barden, Amy-Clare. Picky Eaters. 2017. (ENG., Illus.). 16p. (J). (gr. -1-2). bds. 7.95 *(978-1-4549-1901-8(9))* Sterling Publishing Co., Inc.
Jackson, Ellen B. The Ballad of Booster Bogg. Carolan, Christine, illus. 2011. (J). *(978-1-934860-07-6(7))* Shenanigan Bks.
Jackson, Richard. All Ears, All Eyes. Tillotson, Katherine, illus. 2017. (ENG.). 40p. (J). (gr. -1-3). 17.99 *(978-1-4814-1571-2(9))* Simon & Schuster Children's Publishing.
—Have a Look, Says Book. Hawkes, Kevin, illus. 2016. (ENG.). 48p. (J). (gr. -1-2). 17.99 *(978-1-4814-2105-8(0))* Simon & Schuster Children's Publishing.
Jackson, Richard. This Beautiful Day. Lee, Suzy, illus. 2017. (ENG.). 40p. (J). (gr. -1-3). 15.99 ***(978-1-4814-4139-1(6),*** Atheneum/Caitlyn Dlouhy Books) Simon & Schuster Children's Publishing.
Jacobs, Paul DuBois & Swender, Jennifer. Count on the Subway. Yaccarino, Dan, illus. 2014. (ENG.). 32p. (J). (-k). 14.99 *(978-0-307-97923-0(7));* lib. bdg. 17.99 *(978-0-307-97924-7(5))* Random Hse. Children's Bks. (Knopf Bks. for Young Readers).
—Fire Drill. Lee, Huy Voun, illus. 2010. (ENG.). 32p. (J). (gr. -1-2). 17.99 *(978-0-8050-8953-0(5),* 9780805089530, Holt, Henry & Co. Bks. For Young Readers) Holt, Henry & Co.
Jacobsen, Annie. The Terrible Troll Cat. Hanson, Susan Jo, illus. 2012. 32p. (J). 9.98 *(978-0-9778276-4-0(X))* Pickled Herring Pr.
Jacobson, Leonard. In Search of the Light. 2011. 32p. 16.99 *(978-1-890580-05-6(8))* Conscious Living Pubns.
Jacques, Florence Page. There Once Was a Puffin. Halpern, Shari, illus. 2016. (ENG.). 32p. (J). 15.95 *(978-0-7358-4245-8(0))* North-South Bks., Inc.
Jaeger, Elizabeth. It's Easter, Little Bunny! Boyer, Robin, illus. 2015. (ENG.). 16p. (J). bds. 12.99 *(978-0-8249-1949-8(1),* Ideal Pubns.) Worthy Publishing.
Jag, Shaani S. The Little Small Book of Pictures & Poems. 2011. 28p. pap. 32.70 *(978-1-4628-5109-6(6))* Xlibris Corp.
Jahn, Benny. Ah-Choo - God Bless You. Scott, Chelsey, illus. 2009. 24p. pap. 11.95 *(978-1-60844-178-5(4))* Dog Ear Publishing, LLC.
Jakary, Lin. I Lost My Sock. Olson, Ryan, illus. 2008. 40p. (J). (gr. -1-3). 16.99 *(978-1-934867-01-3(2))* Wocto Publishing.

S

Jakubowski, Kristan E. Paint the Town. 2008. 24p. pap. 11.85 (978-1-4343-6912-3(9)) AuthorHouse.

Jam, Teddy. Night Cars, 1 vol. Beddows, Eric, illus. 2006. (ENG.). 32p. (J). (gr. k — 1). bds. 11.95 (978-0-88899-748-7(5)) Groundwood Bks. CAN. Dist: Publishers Group West (PGW).

James, Dalton. The Sneakiest Pirates. 2008. 20p. pap. 10.95 (978-1-4327-2477-1(0)) Outskirts Pr., Inc.

James, Helen Foster. Grandma Loves You! Brown, Petra, illus. 2013. (ENG.). 32p. (J). (gr. -1 — 1). 14.99 (978-1-58536-836-5(9), 202884) Sleeping Bear Pr.

—Grandpa Loves You! Brown, Petra, illus. 2016. (ENG.). 32p. (J). (gr. -1-1). 15.99 (978-1-58536-940-9(3), 204032) Sleeping Bear Pr.

James, Karim. The Kids Time to Rhyme: Read & Rhyme at the same Time. 2009. 16p. pap. 14.99 (978-1-4490-0424-8(5)) AuthorHouse.

Jamesson, Christine. The Adventures of Samantha the Black Racer Snake. 2005. (ENG.). 28p. per. 18.00 (978-1-4208-1873-4(2)) AuthorHouse.

Jane, Pamela. Little Elfie One. Manning, Jane, illus. 2015. (ENG.). 32p. (J). (gr. -1-3). 17.99 (978-0-06-220673-2(7)) HarperCollins Pubs.

—Little Goblins Ten. Jane, Pamela & Manning, Jane, illus. 2011. (ENG.). 32p. (J). (gr. -1-3). 16.99 (978-0-06-176798-2(0)) HarperCollins Pubs.

—Monster Mischief. Rosenberry, Vera, illus. 2014. (ENG.). 32p. (J). (gr. -1-2). 16.99 (978-1-4814-2535-3(8), Atheneum Bks. for Young Readers) Simon & Schuster Children's Publishing.

Janni, Rebecca. Jammy Dance, 1 vol. Dockray, Tracy, illus. 2012. (ENG.). 40p. (J). (gr. -1-1). 16.99 (978-0-374-33680-6(6), 9780374336806, Farrar, Straus & Giroux (BYR)) Farrar, Straus & Giroux.

Jansson, Tove. The Book about Moomin, Mymble & Little My. Hannah, Sophie, tr. from SWE. 2009. (Moomin Ser.). Orig. Title: Boken om Mymlan, Mumintrollet och Lilla My. (ENG., Illus.). 20p. (J). (gr. k-5). 16.95 (978-1-897299-95-1(8), 9781897299951) Drawn & Quarterly Pubns. CAN. Dist: Macmillan.

Jantzen, Doug. Henry Hyena, Why Won't You Laugh? Claude, Jean, illus. 2015. (ENG.). 32p. (J). (gr. -1-2). 17.99 (978-1-4814-2822-4(5), Aladdin) Simon & Schuster Children's Publishing.

Janvier Gibeau, Claire. Here Comes Grandpa Now. 2009. 16p. pap. 8.49 (978-1-4490-3829-8(8)) AuthorHouse.

Jarman, Julia. Ants in Your Pants! Parker-Rees, Guy, illus. 2011. (ENG.). 32p. (J). (gr. -1-k). pap. 10.99 (978-1-4083-0525-6(9)) Hodder & Stoughton GBR. Dist: Hachette Bk. Group.

—The Best Kiss. Waters, Erica-Jane, illus. 2014. (ENG.). 32p. (J). (gr. -1-k). pap. 8.99 (978-1-4449-2091-8(X)) Hodder & Stoughton GBR. Dist: Hachette Bk. Group.

—Class Three at Sea. Chapman, Lynne, illus. 2008. (ENG.). 32p. (J). (gr. k-3). 16.95 (978-0-8225-7617-4(1), Carolrhoda Bks.) Lerner Publishing Group.

—Class Two at the Zoo. Chapman, Lynne, illus. 2007. (Carolrhoda Picture Bks.). (ENG.). 32p. (J). (gr. k-2). 16.95 (978-0-8225-7132-2(3), Carolrhoda Bks.) Lerner Publishing Group.

—Two Shy Pandas. Varley, Susan, illus. 2013. (ENG.). 32p. (J). (gr. -1-3). 16.95 (978-1-4677-1141-8(1)) Andersen Pr. GBR. Dist: Lerner Publishing Group.

Jarman, Julia & Sutcliffe, Mandy. Big Bouncy Bed. Reynolds, Adrian, illus. 2015. (ENG.). 32p. (J). (gr. -1-k). pap. 10.99 (978-1-4083-0544-7(5)) Hodder & Stoughton GBR. Dist: Hachette Bk. Group.

Jasper, Mark. Good Night Charleston. Kelly, Cooper, illus. 2007. (Good Night Our World Ser.). (ENG.). 20p. (J). (gr. k — 1). bds. 9.95 (978-1-60219-022-1(4)) Good Night Bks.

—Good Night Florida Keys. Rosen, Anne, illus. 2008. (Good Night Our World Ser.). (ENG.). 20p. (J). (gr. k — 1). bds. 9.95 (978-1-60219-020-7(8)) Good Night Bks.

Javernick, Ellen. The Birthday Pet, 0 vols. O'Malley, Kevin, illus. 2012. (ENG.). 34p. (J). (gr. k-3). pap. 7.99 (978-0-7614-6238-5(4), 9780761462385, Amazon Children's Publishing) Amazon Publishing.

Jay, Alison & Curtis, Carolyn. I Took the Moon for a Walk. 2008. (ENG., Illus.). 32p. (J). (gr. -1-2). 14.99 (978-1-84686-200-7(0)) Barefoot Bks., Inc.

Jay, Alison & Gershator, Phillis. Listen, Listen. 2008. (ENG., Illus.). 32p. (J). (gr. -1-k). 14.99 (978-1-84686-201-4(9)) Barefoot Bks., Inc.

Jenkins, Barbie. The Legend of the Christmas Kiss. 2010. (ENG.). 32p. pap. 11.99 (978-1-4391-9623-6(0), Howard Bks.) Howard Books.

Jenkins, Celeste. The Lost (and Found) Balloon. Bogade, Maria, illus. 2013. (ENG.). 32p. (J). (gr. -1-3). 16.99 (978-1-4424-6697-5(9), Aladdin) Simon & Schuster Children's Publishing.

Jenkins, Emily. A Greyhound, a Groundhog. Appelhans, Chris, illus. 2017. (ENG.). 32p. (J). (gr. -1-2). 17.99 (978-0-553-49805-9(3)); lib. bdg. 20.99 (978-0-553-49806-6(1)) Random Hse. Children's Bks. (Schwartz & Wade Bks.).

Jenkins-Greaves, Shenita. Raptown U. S. A. Rappers. 2013. 24p. pap. 14.95 (978-1-4669-7717-4(5)) Trafford Publishing.

Jennerich, Douglas Todd. My Little Half-Moon. Berube, Kate, illus. 2017. (ENG.). 32p. (J). (gr. k-3). 16.99 (978-0-399-16901-4(6), G.P. Putnam's Sons Books for Young Readers) Penguin Young Readers Group.

Jensen, Ivan. Mary Rode to Bethlehem on Me. 2012. (ENG.). 45p. (J). pap. 17.95 (978-1-4327-9473-6(6)) Outskirts Pr., Inc.

Jepsen, D. R. Fred's Exciting Night. 2008. 20p. pap. 24.95 (978-1-60813-547-9(0)) America Star Bks.

JibJab Bros Studios. Trucks Are Terrific! (StoryBots) JibJab Bros Studios, illus. 2017. (ENG., Illus.). 24p. (J). (— 1). bds. 7.99 (978-1-5247-1825-1(4), Random Hse. Bks. for Young Readers) Random Hse. Children's Bks.

Jiggly Giraffe Book & Soft Rattle. 2014. (Illus.). (J). (978-1-4723-3976-8(2)) Parragon Bk. Service Ltd.

Jill & the Beanstalk. 2004. (J). (ENG & FRE.). (978-1-84444-489-2(9)); (ALB & ENG.). (978-1-84444-492-2(9)); (ENG & URD.). (978-1-84444-485-4(6)); (ENG & TAM.). (978-1-84444-484-7(8)); (ENG & SPA.). (978-1-84444-490-8(2)); (ENG & SOM.). (978-1-84444-487-8(2)); (ENG & RUS.). (978-1-84444-482-3(1)); (ENG & POR.). (978-1-84444-481-6(3)); (ENG & PAN.). (978-1-84444-494-6(5)); (ENG & ITA.). (978-1-84444-480-9(5)); (ENG & GUJ.). (978-1-84444-479-3(1)); (ENG & VIE.). (978-1-84444-496-0(1)); (ENG & PER.). (978-1-84444-491-5(0)); (SBC & ENG.). (978-1-84444-483-0(X)); (CHI & ENG.). (978-1-84444-488-5(0)); (BEN & ENG.). (978-1-84444-478-6(3)); (ARA & ENG.). (978-1-84444-486-1(4)); E-Book incl. cd-rom (978-1-84444-463-2(5)) Mantra Lingua.

Jobling, Curtis. The Sheep Won't Sleep! McLaughlin, Tom, illus. 2016. (ENG.). 32p. (J). (— 1). pap. 9.99 (978-1-4052-6711-3(9)) Egmont Bks., Ltd. GBR. Dist: Independent Pubs. Group.

Joel, Billy. Goodnight, My Angel: A Lullabye. Gilbert, Yvonne, illus. 2004. (J). pap. (978-0-439-55378-0(4)) Scholastic, Inc.

Johanson, Rhonda. The Great Tempo Race. 2011. 32p. pap. 21.99 (978-1-4568-5363-1(5)) Xlibris Corp.

Johnson, Calvin. Buzzy the Vegetarian Vulture. Ciresi-Abremski, M. Kathleen, illus. 2012. 28p. pap. 12.95 (978-1-61493-109-6(7)) Peppertree Pr., The.

Johnson, Jay, illus. Ten Little Pumpkins. 2012. (J). (978-0-545-46862-6(0)) Scholastic, Inc.

Johnson, Kathleen A. A Voice Came to Me. 2006. lib. bdg. 17.95 (978-0-9785623-0-4(5)) Voice of Light Pubns.

Johnson, Stewart Martin. Bad News Belinda. 2017. (ENG., Illus.). 35p. (J). pap. 14.95 (978-1-78554-651-8(1), ad852607-79cc-4c4e-b283-66e3d3990d3a) Austin, Stan AUS. Dist: Bookmasters Distribution.

Johnston-Brown, A. M. The Chronicles of Pleasant Grove. 2006. (J). pap. 12.95 (978-0-9760718-5-3(1)) Retriever Pr.

Johnston, Teresa. Thanksgiving for Emily Ann. Newton, Vanessa Brantley, illus. 2014. (ENG.). 32p. (J). (gr. -1-k). 6.99 (978-0-545-43413-3(0), Cartwheel Bks.) Scholastic, Inc.

Johnston, Tony. First Grade, Here I Come! Sweet, Melissa & Walker, David, illus. 2015. (ENG.). 32p. (J). (gr. k-2). 8.99 (978-0-545-20143-8(8), Cartwheel Bks.) Scholastic, Inc.

—10 Fat Turkeys. Deas, Rich. illus. 2009. (ENG.). 28p. (J). (gr. -1-k). bds. 6.99 (978-0-545-16469-6(9), Cartwheel Bks.) Scholastic, Inc.

—10 Fat Turkeys. Deas, Richard F., illus. 2004. (ENG.). 32p. (J). (gr. -1-k). pap. 3.99 (978-0-439-45948-8(6), Cartwheel Bks.) Scholastic, Inc.

Jolley, Mike. I'll See You in the Morning. Moriuchi, Mique, illus. 2008. (ENG.). (J). (gr. -1 — 1). bds. 6.99 (978-0-8118-6543-2(6)) Chronicle Bks. LLC.

Jones, A. Responsibility. 2011. 32p. pap. 24.95 (978-1-4626-2167-5(8)) America Star Bks.

Jones, Christianne C. The Elf Boogie. Randall, Emma, illus. 2015. (Holiday Jingles Ser.). (ENG.). 20p. (gr. -1 — 1). bds. 5.99 (978-1-4795-6493-4(1)) Picture Window Bks.

—Eric No Juega, 1 vol. Ruíz, Carlos, tr. Demski, James, Jr., illus. 2006. (Read-It! Readers en Español: Story Collection).Tr. of Eric Won't Do It. (SPA.). 24p. (gr. -1-3). 21.32 (978-1-4048-1683-1(6), Easy Readers) Picture Window Bks.

—The Reindeer Dance. Randall, Emma, illus. 2015. (Holiday Jingles Ser.). (ENG.). 20p. (gr. -1 — 1). bds. 5.99 (978-1-4795-6496-5(6)) Picture Window Bks.

—The Santa Shimmy. Randall, Emma, illus. 2015. (Holiday Jingles Ser.). (ENG.). 20p. (gr. -1 — 1). bds. 5.99 (978-1-4795-6494-1(X)) Picture Window Bks.

—The Snowman Shuffle. Randall, Emma, illus. 2015. (Holiday Jingles Ser.). (ENG.). 20p. (gr. -1 — 1). bds. 5.99 (978-1-4795-6495-8(8)) Picture Window Bks.

Jones, Frankie. Bedtime: Trace the Trails with Your Finger to Get to Bed! Galloway, Fhiona, illus. 2016. (ENG.). 10p. (J). (gr. -1 — 1). bds. 7.99 (978-1-4998-0267-2(6)) Little Bee Books Inc.

Jones, Gareth. The Imaginarium. 2012. 108p. 23.49 (978-1-78035-472-9(X), Fastprint Publishing) Upfront Publishing Ltd. GBR. Dist: Printondemand-worldwide.com.

Jones, Gareth P. Are You the Pirate Captain? Parsons, Garry, illus. 2016. (ENG.). 32p. (gr. -1-3). (J). 17.99 (978-1-5124-0427-2(6)); 35.99 (978-1-5124-0446-3(2)) Lerner Publishing Group.

—The Dinosaurs Are Having a Party! Parsons, Garry, illus. 2015. (J). 17.32 (978-1-4677-6317-2(9)) Lerner Publishing Group.

Jones, Kelly. Mama. Kewley, Ken, illus. 2004. 32p. (J). (978-0-9745930-0-5(1)) Stunt Publishing.

Jones, Melanie Davis. Balls. Bronson, Linda, illus. 2011. (Rookie Ready to Learn - Numbers & Shapes Ser.). 32p. (J). (gr. -1-k). lib. bdg. 23.00 (978-0-531-26445-4(9), Children's Pr.) Scholastic Library Publishing.

—I Can Ski! 2004. (Rookie Reader Skill Set Ser.). (ENG., Illus.). 32p. (J). (gr. k-2). pap. 4.95 (978-0-516-27901-5(7), Children's Pr.) Scholastic Library Publishing.

—I Can Ski! Boles, Terry, illus. 2003. (Rookie Readers Ser.). 32p. (J). 19.50 (978-0-516-22878-5(1), Children's Pr.) Scholastic Library Publishing.

Jones, Nathan Smith. The Boy Who Ate America. Nelson, Casey, illus. 2007. 32p. (J). (gr. -1-3). 16.95 (978-1-59038-814-3(3), Shadow Mountain) Shadow Mountain Publishing.

Jones, Pip. Squishy McFluff: The Invisible Cat! 2017. (Squishy Mcfluff Ser.). (ENG., Illus.). 80p. (gr. k-2). pap. 8.95 (978-0-571-30250-5(5)) Faber & Faber, Inc.

Jones-Sorge, Jennifer Elaine. Monsters, Monsters, Monsters! The Power in Me Is Bigger Then Any Monster I've Ever Met! 2012. 48p. pap. 24.95 (978-1-4626-7555-5(7)) America Star Bks.

Joosse, Barbara M. Evermore Dragon. Cecil, Randy, illus. 2015. (ENG.). 32p. (J). (gr. -1-2). 15.99 (978-0-7636-6882-2(6)) Candlewick Pr.

Joosse, Barbara M. & Lisberg, Anneke. Better Together: A Book of Family. Schorr, Jared, illus. 2017. (ENG.). 22p. (J). (gr. -1-k). bds. 14.95 (978-1-4197-2538-8(6), Abrams Appleseed) Abrams, Inc.

Jordan, Apple. The Sweetest Spring. Matta, Gabriella & Legramandi, Francesco, illus. 2008. (Step into Reading Ser.). (ENG.). 32p. (J). (gr. k-3). pap. 3.99 (978-0-375-84810-0(X), RH/Disney) Random Hse. Children's Bks.

Jordan, Apple J. Winter Wishes. Marrucchi, Elisa, illus. 2006. (Step into Reading Ser.). (ENG.). 32p. (J). (gr. k-3). per. 3.99 (978-0-7364-2409-7(1), RH/Disney) Random Hse. Children's Bks.

Jordan, Christina. I Wish I Were a Furry Ferret, 1 vol. Utomo, Gabhor, illus. 2011. (I Wish I Were ... Ser.). (ENG.). 24p. (J). (gr. k-3). 28.50 (978-1-61641-656-0(4)) Magic Wagon.

—I Wish I Were a Howler Monkey, 1 vol. Utomo, Gabhor, illus. 2011. (I Wish I Were ... Ser.). (ENG.). 24p. (J). (gr. k-3). 28.50 (978-1-61641-657-7(2)) Magic Wagon.

—I Wish I Were a Humpback Whale, 1 vol. Utomo, Gabhor, illus. 2011. (I Wish I Were ... Ser.). (ENG.). 24p. (J). (gr. k-3). 28.50 (978-1-61641-658-4(0)) Magic Wagon.

—I Wish I Were a Komodo Dragon, 1 vol. Utomo, Gabhor, illus. 2011. (I Wish I Were ... Ser.). (ENG.). 24p. (J). (gr. k-3). 28.50 (978-1-61641-659-1(9)) Magic Wagon.

—I Wish I Were a Speedy Cheetah, 1 vol. Utomo, Gabhor, illus. 2011. (I Wish I Were ... Ser.). (ENG.). 24p. (J). (gr. k-3). 28.50 (978-1-61641-660-7(2)) Magic Wagon.

—I Wish I Were an Enormous Elephant, 1 vol. Utomo, Gabhor, illus. 2011. (I Wish I Were ... Ser.). (ENG.). 24p. (J). (gr. k-3). 28.50 (978-1-61641-661-4(0)) Magic Wagon.

Jordan, Dana Hall. Clang Went the Cymbals: An Onomatopoeia Alphabet Book. Burma, Willingham, illus. 2008. 32p. (J). 15.99 (978-0-9798664-0-1(5)) Capture Bks.

Jordan, Deloris. Did I Tell You I Love You Today? Evans, Shane W., illus. 2004. (ENG.). 32p. (J). (gr. -1-3). 18.99 (978-0-689-85271-8(1), Simon & Schuster/Paula Wiseman Bks.) Simon & Schuster/Paula Wiseman Bks.

Jordan, Mary Ellen & Weldon, Andrew. Lazy Daisy, Cranky Frankie: Bedtime on the Farm. Weldon, Andrew, illus. 2013. (ENG., Illus.). 24p. (J). (gr. -1-3). 15.99 (978-0-8075-4400-6(0)) Whitman, Albert & Co.

Jorden, Edwin W. Cookie Paws/Spreadin' the Sweetness. Waywell, Valerie J., illus. 2008. 32p. (J). 12.95 (978-0-9793483-1-0(5)) Gilded Dog Enterprises LLC.

Joy, Angelica. My Cat Merigold. Bolle, Frank, illus. 2008. 56p. pap. 19.95 (978-1-59858-591-9(6)) Dog Ear Publishing, LLC.

Joy, N. The Secret Olivia Told Me. Devard, Nancy, illus. 2007. 32p. (J). (gr. -1-3). 16.95 (978-1-933491-08-0(6)) Just Us Bks., Inc.

Joyce, Melanie. I Love You Because ... Lovsin, Polona, illus. 2016. (ENG.). 24p. (J). (gr. -1-1). 16.99 (978-1-4998-0212-2(9)) Little Bee Books Inc.

—What Pirates Really Do. Paterson, Alex, illus. 2016. (ENG.). 32p. (J). (gr. -1-3). 16.99 (978-1-4998-0257-3(9)) Little Bee Books Inc.

Jules, Jacqueline. Happy Hanukkah Lights. Shapiro, Michelle, illus. 2010. (Hanukkah Ser.). (ENG.). 12p. (J). (gr. -1 — 1). 5.95 (978-0-7613-5120-7(5), Kar-Ben Publishing) Lerner Publishing Group.

Jules, Jacqueline & Hechtkopf, Jacqueline. Going on a Hametz Hunt. Brown, Rick, illus. 2010. (Passover Ser.). (ENG.). 12p. (J). (gr. -1 — 1). 5.95 (978-0-7613-5124-5(8), Kar-Ben Publishing) Lerner Publishing Group.

—Goodnight Sh'ma. Hall, Melanie W., illus. 2008. (ENG.). 12p. (J). (gr. -1 — 1). pap. 5.95 (978-0-8225-8945-7(1), Kar-Ben Publishing) Lerner Publishing Group.

Jungle Limbo. l.t. ed. 2003. (Illus.). 31p. (J). spiral bd. 7.95 (978-0-9741074-0-0(9)) Catterfly Pr.

Kaczka, Fallon. What about Oysters. 2010. 24p. 13.00 (978-1-4520-2066-2(3)) AuthorHouse.

Kai Dotlich, Rebecca. What Can a Crane Pick Up? Lowery, Mike, illus. 2012. (ENG.). 32p. (J). (gr. k-k). 16.99 (978-0-375-86726-2(0), Knopf Bks. for Young Readers) Random Hse. Children's Bks.

—What Can a Crane Pick Up? Lowery, Mike, illus. 2014. (ENG.). 28p. (J). (-k). bds. 6.99 (978-0-385-75383-8(7), Knopf Bks. for Young Readers) Random Hse. Children's Bks.

Kaldor, Connie & Campagne, Carmen. Lullaby Berceuse: A Warm Prairie Night. Deines, Brian, illus. 2006. (ENG & FRE.). 40p. (J). (gr. -1-2). 16.95 (978-2-923163-22-2(2)) La Montagne Secrete CAN. Dist: Independent Pubs. Group.

Kalman, Bobbie. Hip-Hop Dancers. 2010. (My World Ser.). (ENG., Illus.). 16p. (J). (gr. k-2). (978-0-7787-9431-8(8)); pap. (978-0-7787-9475-2(X)) Crabtree Publishing Co.

Kander, Beth & Kenyon, Bret. Glubbery Gray, the Knight-Eating Beast, 1 vol. Labbé, Jesse, illus. 2010. (ENG.). 40p. (J). (gr. k-3). 17.99 (978-1-58980-867-6(3)) Pelican Publishing Co., Inc.

Kaputa, Christine C. Bad Kitty! 2007. 16p. per. 9.95 (978-1-59858-478-3(2)) Dog Ear Publishing, LLC.

Karp, Ken, illus. Will You Wear a Blue Hat? 2009. (Rookie Toddler: Sing along Toddler Ser.). (ENG.). 12p. (J). (gr. -1). bds. 6.95 (978-0-531-24549-1(7)) Scholastic Library Publishing.

Karr, Lily. My Easter Bunny! Johnson, Jay B., illus. 2012. (ENG.). 12p. (J). (gr. -1-k). bds. 4.99 (978-0-545-37117-9(1), Cartwheel Bks.) Scholastic, Inc.

—My Pumpkin. Marts, Doreen Mulryan, illus. 2014. (ENG.). 12p. (J). (gr. -1 — 1). bds. 4.99 (978-0-545-49332-1(3), Cartwheel Bks.) Scholastic, Inc.

Karwoski, Gail & Gootman, Marilyn E. Thank You, Trees! Balouch, Kristen, illus. 2013. (Tu B'Shevat Ser.). (ENG.). 12p. (J). (gr. -1 — 1). pap. 5.95 (978-1-58013-973-1(6), Kar-Ben Publishing) Lerner Publishing Group.

Kass, Daniele L., ed. The City Trail: A Skip-Counting Tale. 2010. 40p. pap. 18.49 (978-1-4520-1219-3(9)) AuthorHouse.

Katz, Alan. Don't Say That Word! Catrow, David, illus. 2007. (ENG.). 32p. (J). (gr. -1-3). 17.99 (978-0-689-86971-6(1), McElderry, Margaret K. Bks.) McElderry, Margaret K. Bks.

—Stalling. Smith, Elwood H., illus. 2010. (ENG.). 40p. (J). (gr. -1-2). 16.99 (978-1-4169-5567-2(4), McElderry, Margaret K. Bks.) McElderry, Margaret K. Bks.

Katz, Karen. Shake It up, Baby! Katz, Karen, illus. 2009. (ENG., Illus.). 14p. (J). (gr. -1 — 1). bds. 7.99 (978-1-4169-6737-8(0), Little Simon) Little Simon.

—Ten Tiny Babies. Katz, Karen, illus. 2011. (Classic Board Bks.). (ENG., Illus.). 32p. (J). (gr. -1-k). bds. 7.99 (978-1-4424-1394-8(8), Little Simon) Little Simon.

—Ten Tiny Babies. Katz, Karen, illus. 2008. (ENG., Illus.). 32p. (J). (gr. -1-k). 17.99 (978-1-4169-3546-9(0), McElderry, Margaret K. Bks.) McElderry, Margaret K. Bks.

Katz, Karin Jill. There's a Fly in My Soup. 2012. 16p. pap. 15.99 (978-1-4772-6331-0(4)) AuthorHouse.

Katz, Susan B. ABC School's for Me! Munsinger, Lynn, illus. 2015. (ENG.). 32p. (J). (gr. -1-k). 16.99 (978-0-545-53092-7(X), Scholastic Pr.) Scholastic, Inc.

—All Year Round. Ojala, Eiko, illus. 2016. (ENG.). 32p. (J). (gr. -1-1). 17.99 (978-0-545-74100-2(9), Orchard Bks.) Scholastic, Inc.

—My Mama Earth. Launay, Melissa, illus. 2012. (ENG.). 24p. (J). 16.99 (978-1-84686-418-6(6)) Barefoot Bks., Inc.

—My Mama Hung the World for Me. Newey, Gail, illus. 2009. (J). (978-1-84686-269-4(8)) Barefoot Bks., Inc.

Kaufman, Jeanne. Young Henry & the Dragon. Tessler, Daria, illus. 2011. (J). (978-1-934860-11-3(5)) Shenanigan Bks.

Kavanagh, Peter. I Love My Mama. Chapman, Jane, tr. Chapman, Jane, illus. 2003. 32p. (J). 12.95 (978-1-85430-806-1(8), Simon & Schuster Bks. For Young Readers) Simon & Schuster Bks. For Young Readers.

Kay, Karin. Floppy Cat. 2009. (J). 16.95 (978-0-9823818-0-9(8)) Floppy Cat Co.

Kay, Verla. Civil War Drummer Boy. Day, Larry, illus. 2012. (ENG.). 32p. (J). (gr. 1-3). 16.99 (978-0-399-23992-2(8), G.P. Putnam's Sons Books for Young Readers) Penguin Young Readers Group.

—Hornbooks & Inkwells. Schindler, S. D., illus. 2011. (ENG.). 32p. (J). (gr. -1-3). 16.99 (978-0-399-23870-3(0), G.P. Putnam's Sons Books for Young Readers) Penguin Young Readers Group.

—Whatever Happened to the Pony Express? Root, Kimberly Bulcken & Root, Barry, illus. 2010. (ENG.). 32p. (J). (gr. k-3). 16.99 (978-0-399-24483-4(2), G.P. Putnam's Sons Books for Young Readers) Penguin Young Readers Group.

Kearney, Meg. The Girl in the Mirror. 2012. (ENG.). 176p. (YA). (gr. 9-17). pap. 15.00 (978-0-89255-385-3(5), 255385) Persea Bks., Inc.

—Trouper. Lewis, E. B., illus. 2013. (ENG.). 32p. (J). (gr. -1-3). 16.99 (978-0-545-10041-0(0), Scholastic Pr.) Scholastic, Inc.

—When You Never Said Goodbye: An Adoptee's Search for Her Birth Mother. 2017. (ENG.). 224p. (YA). (gr. 9-17). 17.95 (978-0-89255-479-9(7), 255479) Persea Bks., Inc.

Keckler, Ben. From Here to There. Davis, Dick, illus. 2005. (Express Yourself Ser.). 42p. (J). (gr. 3-7). lib. bdg. 16.95 (978-0-9769093-0-9(8)) Eagle Creek Pubns., LLC.

—Incredibly Lonely, That's Me. Davis, Dick, illus. 2007. (Express Yourself Ser.). 42p. (J). (gr. 3-7). 17.95 (978-0-9769093-2-3(4)) Eagle Creek Pubns., LLC.

Keegan, Anne. A Cat for Claire. 2008. 28p. pap. 15.00 (978-1-4389-2737-4(1)) AuthorHouse.

Keep, Richard. Clatter Bash! A Day of the Dead Celebration, 1 vol. Keep, Richard, illus. (ENG., Illus.). 32p. (J). (gr. k-3). 2008. pap. 7.95 (978-1-56145-461-7(3)) 2004. 15.95 (978-1-56145-322-1(6)) Peachtree Pubs.

Kehoe, Stasia Ward. The Sound of Letting Go. 2014. (ENG.). 400p. (YA). (gr. 7). 17.99 (978-0-670-01553-5(9), Viking Books for Young Readers) Penguin Young Readers Group.

Keillor, Garrison. The Old Man Who Loved Cheese. braille ed. 2004. (Illus.). (J). (gr. k-3). spiral bd. (978-0-616-01687-9(5)) Canadian National Institute for the Blind/Institut National Canadien pour les Aveugles.

Keiser, Frances R. Annie the River Otter: The Adventures of Pelican Pete. Keiser, Hugh M., illus. l.t. ed. 2006. (ENG.). 34p. (J). 19.99 (978-0-9668845-4-8(X)) Sagaponack Bks.

Keith, Donna. I Love You All the Same, 1 vol. Edgson, Allison, illus. 2014. (ENG.). 20p. (J). bds. 9.99 (978-0-529-10204-1(8)) Nelson, Thomas Inc.

—I Love You Even When, 1 vol. Edgson, Allison, illus. 2015. (ENG.). 20p. (J). bds. 9.99 (978-0-7180-3644-7(1)) Nelson, Thomas Inc.

Keller, Elinoar & Peleg-Segal, Naama. Just Like I Wanted. Gordon-Noy, Aya, illus. 2015. (ENG.). 26p. (J). 17.00 (978-0-8028-5453-7(2), Eerdmans Bks For Young Readers) Eerdmans, William B. Publishing Co.

Keller, Holly. What I See. 2003. (Green Light Readers Level 1 Ser.). (ENG., Illus.). 24p. (J). (gr. -1-3). pap. 3.95 (978-0-15-204854-9(5)) Houghton Mifflin Harcourt Publishing Co.

Keller, Joy. Monster Trucks. Saburi, Misa, illus. 2017. (ENG.). 32p. (J). 16.99 (978-1-62779-617-0(7), 9781627796170, Holt, Henry & Co. Bks. For Young Readers) Holt, Henry & Co.

Kelley, Maria Felicia. Buz Words: Discovering Words in Pairs. Kelley, Maria Felicia, illus. 2007. (Illus.). 32p. (J). (gr. -1-3). 14.95 (978-0-9650918-1-7(3)) April Arts Press & Productions.

Kelley, Marty. Almost Everybody Farts. 2017. (ENG., Illus.). 32p. (J). (gr. -1). 12.95 (978-1-4549-1954-4(X)) Sterling Publishing Co., Inc.

—The Messiest Desk. 2009. (J). (978-1-55933-319-1(7)) Zino Pr. Children's Bks.

Kelley, Marty, illus. Spring Goes Squish: A Vibrant Volume of Vociferous Vernal Verse. 2008. (J). (gr. k-2). 14.95 (978-1-55933-315-3(4)) Zino Pr. Children's Bks.

—Winter Woes. 2003. 32p. (J). 12.95 (978-1-55933-306-1(5)) Zino Pr. Children's Bks.

Kellogg, Steven. There Was an Old Woman Who Swallowed a Fly. 2003. (ENG., Illus.). (J). 16.00 (978-0-689-81703-8(7), Simon & Schuster/Paula Wiseman Bks.) Simon & Schuster/Paula Wiseman Bks.

Kellum, Rebecca L. The Conceited Little Girl. 2007. 24p. per. 24.95 (978-1-4241-9810-8(0)) America Star Bks.

Kelly, John. The Beastly Pirates. 2015. (ENG., Illus.). 32p. (J). (gr. -1-1). 18.99 (978-1-4088-4983-5(6), 9781408849835, Bloomsbury USA Childrens) Bloomsbury Publishing USA.

—Sir Scaly Pants the Dragon Knight. Kelly, John, illus. 2015. (ENG., Illus.). 32p. (J). (gr. -1-1). 18.99 (978-1-4088-5602-4(6), 9781408856024, Bloomsbury USA Childrens) Bloomsbury Publishing USA.

Kelly, L. J. R. Sometimes It's Storks. Hilts, Brothers, illus. 2017. (ENG.). 32p. (J). (-k). 16.99 (978-0-399-25682-0(2), G.P. Putnam's Sons Books for Young Readers) Penguin Young Readers Group.

Kelly, Mij. The Bump. Allan, Nicholas, illus. 2012. (ENG.). 32p. (J). (978-1-58925-107-6(5)) Tiger Tales.

—Lion's Lullaby. Clifton-Brown, Holly, illus. 2016. (ENG.). 32p. (J). (gr. -1 — 1). 16.99 *(978-1-4847-2526-9(3))* Disney Pr.
—One More Sheep. Ayto, Russell, illus. 2006. (ENG.). 32p. (J). (gr. k-3). 16.95 *(978-1-56145-378-8(1))* Peachtree Pubs.
Kelly, Sharon L. C. M. Coco's Vineyard Vacation: Double Fun on Martha's Vineyard. Galbraith, Alison L., illus. 2005. 40p. (J). 16.95 *(978-0-9766283-0-9(9))* Secret Garden Bookworks.
Kemble, Mai S. The Moon & the Night Sweeper. Kemble, Mai S., illus. 2008. (Illus.). (J). pap. 6.95 *(978-1-60108-023-3(9))* Red Cygnet Pr.
Kemble, Mai S., illus. The Moon & the Night Sweeper. 2007. 30p. (J). (gr. -1-2). 15.95 *(978-1-60108-013-4(1))* Red Cygnet Pr.
Kemp, Anna. The Worst Princess. Ogilvie, Sara, illus. 2014. (ENG.). 32p. (J). (gr. -1-2). 16.99 *(978-0-385-37125-4(X)*, Random Hse. Bks. for Young Readers) Random Hse. Children's Bks.
Kendall, Carolyn. Phibby & Ribby. 2013. 32p. pap. *(978-1-4602-0387-3(9))* FriesenPress.
Kennedy, Anne Vittur. One Spring Lamb, 1 vol. 2016. (ENG., Illus.). 20p. (J). bds. 8.99 *(978-0-7180-8782-1(8))* Nelson, Thomas Inc.
Kenney, Cindy. Junior Asparagus. 2004. (ENG., Illus.). 100p. (J). pap. 3.99 *(978-0-310-70722-6(6))* Zonderkidz.
—Laura Carrot. 2004. (ENG., Illus.). 100p. (J). pap. 3.99 *(978-0-310-70723-3(4))* Zonderkidz.
Kenny, Cindy. Larry Cucumber: I Can. 2004. (ENG., Illus.). 100p. (J). pap. 3.99 *(978-0-310-70721-9(8))* Zonderkidz.
Kerner, Susan. Always by My Side, 1 vol. Haywood, Ian Benfold, illus. 2013. (ENG.). 32p. (J). 16.99 *(978-1-59572-336-9(6))*; pap. 6.99 *(978-1-59572-337-6(4))* Star Bright Bks., Inc.
Kerns, Kristen. Tommy Fakes the Flu. Barrett, Casey, illus. 2013. 24p. pap. 8.99 *(978-1-938768-28-6(0))* Gypsy Pubns.
Ketteman, Helen. Goodnight, Little Monster, 0 vols. Leick, Bonnie, illus. 2010. (ENG.). 32p. (J). (gr. -1-3). 16.99 *(978-0-7614-5683-4(X)*, 9780761456834, Amazon Children's Publishing) Amazon Publishing.
—If Beaver Had a Fever, 0 vols. O'Malley, Kevin, illus. 2011. (ENG.). 32p. (J). (gr. -1-3). 16.99 *(978-0-7614-5951-4(0)*, 9780761459514, Amazon Children's Publishing) Amazon Publishing.
Khamis, Johnny. Costi & the Raindrop Adventure. Belanger, Damon, illus. 2007. 32p. (J). (gr. -1-3). 6.95 *(978-1-60005-029-9(8))* Happy About.
Khan, Aliyah. The Adventures of Solomon Spider: Solomon Sees the City. 2011. 28p. (gr. -1 — 1). pap. 14.09 *(978-1-4490-1546-6(8))* AuthorHouse.
Khan, Hena. Golden Domes & Silver Lanterns: A Muslim Book of Colors. Amini, Mehrdokht, illus. 2012. (ENG.). 32p. (J). (gr. -1-2). 17.99 *(978-0-8118-7905-7(4))* Chronicle Bks. LLC.
Kilkka, Mary. Meet the Nydees, 1 vol. 2010. 28p. 24.95 *(978-1-4512-1495-6(2))* America Star Bks.
Kilpatrick, Leanne. Two by Two: Noah's Story in Rhyme. McCullough, Marilyn, illus. 2013. 28p. pap. *(978-0-906672-67-9(8))* Oleander Pr., The.
Kimaya. All the Flavours of Love. 2012. 40p. pap. 13.95 *(978-1-4525-0649-4(3))* Balboa Pr.
Kimla, Lenka J. I Love My Mommy. Golds, Alexandra Kimla, illus. 2008. 22p. pap. 24.95 *(978-1-60703-126-0(4))* America Star Bks.
Kimmelman, Leslie. Everybody Bonjours! McMenemy, Sarah, illus. 2008. (ENG.). 40p. (J). (gr. -1-2). 16.99 *(978-0-375-84443-0(0)*, Knopf Bks. for Young Readers) Random Hse. Children's Bks.
—How Do I Love You? McCue, Lisa, illus. 2005. 32p. (J). lib. bdg. 16.89 *(978-0-06-001201-4(3))* HarperCollins Pubs.
—Round the Turkey: A Grateful Thanksgiving. Cote, Nancy, illus. 2012. (J). 34.28 *(978-1-61913-130-9(7))* Weigl Pubs., Inc.
—Trick ARRR Treat: A Pirate Halloween. Monlongo, Jorge, illus. 2017. (ENG.). 32p. (J). (gr. -1-k). pap. 7.99 ***(978-0-8075-8066-0(X))*** Whitman, Albert & Co.
Kimmelman, Leslie. Trick Arrr Treat: A Pirate Halloween. Monlongo, Jorge, illus. 2015. (ENG.). 32p. (J). (gr. -1-3). 16.99 *(978-0-8075-8061-5(9))* Whitman, Albert & Co.
Kinerk, Robert. Clorinda. Kellogg, Steven, illus. 2007. (ENG.). 40p. (J). (gr. -1-3). 7.99 *(978-1-4169-3964-1(4)*, Simon & Schuster/Paula Wiseman Bks.) Simon & Schuster/Paula Wiseman Bks.
—Clorinda Plays Baseball! Kellogg, Steven, illus. 2012. (ENG.). 40p. (J). (gr. -1-3). 16.99 *(978-0-689-86865-8(0)*, Simon & Schuster/Paula Wiseman Bks.) Simon & Schuster/Paula Wiseman Bks.
—Clorinda Takes Flight. Kellogg, Steven, illus. 2007. (ENG.). 40p. (J). (gr. -1-3). 17.99 *(978-0-689-86864-1(2)*, Simon & Schuster/Paula Wiseman Bks.) Simon & Schuster/Paula Wiseman Bks.
Kinerk, Robert & Kellogg, Steven. Clorinda. Kellogg, Steven, illus. 2003. (ENG., Illus.). 40p. (J). (gr. -1-3). 17.99 *(978-0-689-86449-0(3)*, Simon & Schuster/Paula Wiseman Bks.) Simon & Schuster/Paula Wiseman Bks.
Kingsbury, Karen. Always Daddy's Princess, 1 vol. Docampo, Valeria, illus. rev. ed. 2013. (ENG.). 32p. (J). 15.99 *(978-0-310-71647-1(0))* Zonderkidz.
—Let's Go on a Mommy Date, 1 vol. Andreasen, Dan, illus. 2008. (ENG.). 32p. (J). (gr. -1-3). 15.99 *(978-0-310-71214-5(9))* Zonderkidz.
—Let's Have a Daddy Day, 1 vol. Andreasen, Dan, illus. 2010. (ENG.). 32p. (J). (gr. -1-2). 15.99 *(978-0-310-71215-2(7))* Zonderkidz.
—Whatever You Grow up to Be, 1 vol. Docampo, Valeria, illus. rev. ed. 2014. (ENG.). 32p. (J). 15.99 *(978-0-310-71646-4(2))* Zonderkidz.
Kinsman, Josephine. Ginger's New Tail. 2011. 40p. pap. 24.95 *(978-1-4626-1184-3(2))* America Star Bks.
Kirk, Bill. There's a Spider in My Sink! Brown, Suzy, illus. 2008. 16p. pap. 9.95 *(978-1-935137-25-2(5))* Guardian Angel Publishing, Inc.
Kirk, David. Truckeroo School. Kirk, David, illus. 2017. (ENG., Illus.). 40p. (J). 17.99 *(978-1-250-01690-4(8)*, 9781250016904) Feiwel & Friends.
Kirk, David & Scholastic / LeapFrog. Miss Spider's Tea Party. 2008. (J). 13.99 *(978-1-59319-934-0(1))* LeapFrog Enterprises, Inc.
Kirkham, Teresa. Tattle Tom. 2003. 27p. pap. 12.95 *(978-1-4137-0141-8(8))* America Star Bks.
Kittinger, Jo S. A Lunch with Punch. 2004. (Rookie Reader Español Ser.). (ENG., Illus.). 32p. (J). (gr. k-2). pap. 4.95 *(978-0-516-27785-1(5)*, Children's Pr.) Scholastic Library Publishing.
Kitzmiller, Brenda. Muddy Mud — an Easy to Read Beginning Reader Book. 2005. 24p. 7.85 *(978-1-4116-2937-0(X))* Lulu Pr., Inc.
Klay, Sharon Joy. Denny Grows a Giant Pumpkin. 2010. 28p. pap. 12.99 *(978-1-4520-2871-2(0))* AuthorHouse.
Kleback, Amanda. Hoo Hoo's Song. Kleback, Amanda & Kleback, Brian, illus. 2009. 24p. pap. 12.00 *(978-1-4389-1322-3(2))* AuthorHouse.
Klein-Higger, Joni. Ten Tzedakah Pennies. Leff, Tova, illus. 2005. 30p. (J). 10.95 *(978-1-929628-19-3(6))* Hachai Publishing.
Klein, Pamela. Swing! Tanis, Joel E., illus. 2006. (ENG.). (J). 15.95 *(978-1-932514-05-6(8))* College of DuPage Pr.
Kleinhenz, Sydnie Meltzer. Pleased to Eat You. 2003. (Silly Millies Ser.: 3). (Illus.). 32p. lib. bdg. 17.90 *(978-0-7613-2909-1(9)*, Millbrook Pr.) Lerner Publishing Group.
—Trabajar y Jugar. Reasor, Mick, illus. 2006. (Rookie Reader Español Ser.). (SPA.). 23p. (J). (gr. k-2). lib. bdg. 19.50 *(978-0-516-25306-0(9))* Scholastic Library Publishing.
Kleven, Elisa. Sun Bread. 2004. (gr. k-3). 17.20 *(978-0-613-83005-8(9)*, Turtleback) Turtleback Bks.
Kleven, Elisa, illus. The Horribly Hungry Gingerbread Boy: A San Francisco Story. 2016. 40p. (J). *(978-1-59714-352-3(9))* Heyday.
Klier, Kimberly Wagner & National Geographic Learning Staff. Firefly Friend. Garland, Michael, illus. 2010. (Rise & Shine Ser.). (ENG.). 32p. (C). (gr. k-2). pap. 7.95 *(978-0-516-26817-0(1))* National Geographic School Publishing, Inc.
Klug, Eric. The Monster in My Closet. Klug, Eric, illus. 2007. (Illus.). 32p. (J). (gr. -1-3). 15.95 *(978-1-60108-007-3(7))* Red Cygnet Pr.
Knaggs, Robin A. I Am a Squirmy Wormy. 2012. 16p. pap. 9.99 *(978-1-60911-969-0(X)*, Strategic Bk. Publishing) Strategic Book Publishing & Rights Agency (SBPRA).
Kneen, Maggie. The Christmas Surprise. Kneen, Maggie, illus. 2006. (Illus.). 18p. (J). (gr. k-4). reprint ed. 16.00 *(978-0-7567-9637-6(X))* DIANE Publishing Co.
Kneff, Steff F. Emlyn & the Gremlin: Emlyn & the Gremlin Series. Spooner, Luke, illus. l.t. ed. 2014. 1. (ENG.). 52p. (gr. k-3). 26.95 *(978-1-62253-399-2(2))*; pap. 10.95 *(978-1-62253-398-5(4))* Evolved Publishing.
Knights, Nancy. Gracie's Hill. Norie, Rooney, illus. 2007. 28p. per. 7.95 *(978-1-58275-192-4(7))* Black Forest Pr.
Knowles, Kent. Lucius & the Storm. Knowles, Kent, illus. 2007. (Illus.). 32p. (J). (gr. -1-3). 15.95 *(978-1-60108-005-9(0))* Red Cygnet Pr.
Knowlton, Laurie. I Know a Librarian Who Chewed on a Word, 1 vol. Leonhard, Herb, illus. 2012. (ENG.). 32p. (J). (gr. k-3). 16.99 *(978-1-58980-892-8(4))* Pelican Publishing Co., Inc.
Koertge, Ron. Shakespeare Makes the Playoffs. 2012. (ENG., Illus.). 176p. (YA). (gr. 7). pap. 6.99 *(978-0-7636-5852-6(9))* Candlewick Pr.
Kohuth, Jane. Ducks Go Vroom. Garofoli, Viviana, illus. 2011. (Step into Reading Ser.). (ENG.). 32p. (J). (gr. -1-1). pap. 3.99 *(978-0-375-86560-2(8)*, Random Hse. Bks. for Young Readers) Random Hse. Children's Bks.
Koller, Jackie French. One Monkey Too Many. Munsinger, Lynn, illus. 2003. (ENG.). 32p. (J). (gr. -1-3). pap. 7.99 *(978-0-15-204764-1(6))* Houghton Mifflin Harcourt Publishing Co.
Kondrchek, Jamie. My Favorite Time of Day (Mi Hora Preferida del Dia) Vega, Eida de la, tr. from ENG. Rasemas, Joe, illus. 2009. (Day in the Life Ser.). (SPA & ENG.). 32p. (J). (gr. -1-1). lib. bdg. 25.70 *(978-1-58415-837-0(9))* Mitchell Lane Pubs., Inc.
Kondrchek, Jamie & Rasemas, Joe. On My Way to School (De Camino a la Escuela) Vega, Eida de la, tr. Rasemas, Joe, illus. 2009. (Day in the Life Ser.). (SPA & ENG., Illus.). 32p. (J). (gr. -1-1). 25.70 *(978-1-58415-840-0(9))* Mitchell Lane Pubs., Inc.
—What Day Is It? (Que Dia Es Hoy?) Vega, Eida de la, tr. Rasemas, Joe, illus. 2009. (Day in the Life Ser.). (SPA & ENG., Illus.). 32p. (J). (gr. -1-1). 25.70 *(978-1-58415-838-7(7))* Mitchell Lane Pubs., Inc.
—What Should I Wear Today? (Que Ropa Me Pondre Hoy?) Vega, Eida de la, tr. Rasemas, Joe, illus. 2009. (Day in the Life Ser.). (ENG & SPA., Illus.). 32p. (J). (gr. -1-1). 25.70 *(978-1-58415-839-4(5))* Mitchell Lane Pubs., Inc.
Koontz, Dean. Robot Santa: The Further Adventures of Santa's Twin. Parks, Phil, illus. 2004. (Santa's Twin Ser.: Bk. 2). 72p. (J). 20.89 *(978-0-06-050944-6(9))* HarperCollins Pubs.
—Santa's Twin. Parks, Phil, illus. 2004. (Santa's Twin Ser.: Bk. 1). (ENG.). 64p. pap. 12.95 *(978-0-06-057223-5(X)*, William Morrow Paperbacks) HarperCollins Pubs.
Koster, Gloria. Mitzi's Mitzvah. Conger, Holli, illus. 2013. (ENG.). 12p. (J). (gr. -1 — 1). 5.95 *(978-1-4677-0695-7(7)*, Kar-Ben Publishing) Lerner Publishing Group.
Kovalkova-McKenna, Svetlana & McKenna, Alexandra. The Fairy Book. 2009. 52p. pap. 7.58 *(978-0-557-06160-0(1))* Lulu Pr., Inc.
Kovalkova-McKenna, Svetlana & McKenna, Konstantin. Oberon. 2009. 44p. pap. 7.26 *(978-0-557-06114-3(8))* Lulu Pr., Inc.
Kovanchak, Danielle. It's about Time. 2009. 44p. pap. 16.99 *(978-1-4389-7023-3(4))* AuthorHouse.
Kowalski, Eli. Kushka, the Dog Named Cat. 2010. (ENG.). (J). 14.95 *(978-0-9819861-4-2(5))* Sports Challenge Network.
Kowen, Dorothy. Thando Rocker. Sherrell, Craig, illus. 2012. (ENG.). 24p. (J). (gr. k-2). pap. 7.95 *(978-1-4314-0087-4(4))* Jacana Media ZAF. Dist: Independent Pubs. Group.
Kralovansky, Susan. Twelve Cowboys Ropin', 1 vol. Kralovansky, Susan, illus. 2015. (ENG., Illus.). 32p. (J). (gr. k-3). 16.99 *(978-1-4556-2081-4(5))* Pelican Publishing Co., Inc.
Kramer, Andrew. Pajama Pirates. Lammle, Leslie, illus. 2010. (ENG.). 40p. (J). (gr. k-3). 16.99 *(978-0-06-125194-8(1))* HarperCollins Pubs.
Kramer, Jennifer E. Good Luck Charlie. Moores, Jeff, illus. 2005. (Rookie Reader Skill Set Ser.). (ENG.). 32p. (J). (gr. k-2). pap. 4.95 *(978-0-516-25826-3(5)*, Children's Pr.) Scholastic Library Publishing.
Kramer, Paul. Do Not Dread Wetting the Bed. 2012. (ENG & ACE.). 32p. (J). (gr. -1-3). 15.95 *(978-0-9819745-0-7(3))* Aloha Wellness Pubs.
Krans, Kim. Whose Moon Is That? 2017. (ENG., Illus.). 48p. (J). (gr. -1-2). 17.99 *(978-1-101-93227-8(9)*, Random Hse. Bks. for Young Readers) Random Hse. Children's Bks.
Krauss, Ruth. I Can Fly. Blair, Mary, illus. 2003. (Little Golden Book Ser.). (ENG.). 24p. (J). (gr. -1-2). 4.99 *(978-0-307-00146-7(6)*, 312-12, Golden Bks.) Random Hse. Children's Bks.
Krebs, Laurie. Riding on a Caravan: A Silk Road Adventure. 2017. (ENG., Illus.). 32p. (J). (gr. -1-4). 8.99 ***(978-1-78285-344-2(8))*** Barefoot Bks., Inc.
—We're Roaming in the Rainforest. Wilson, Anne, illus. 2010. 40p. (J). (ENG.). (gr. k-5). 8.99 *(978-1-84686-545-9(X))*; (SPA.). (gr. k-5). pap. 8.99 *(978-1-84686-551-0(4))*; (ENG.). (gr. -1-5). 16.99 *(978-1-84686-331-8(7))* Barefoot Bks., Inc.
—We're Sailing down the Nile: A Journey Through Egypt. Wilson, Anne, illus. 2007. (ENG.). 40p. (J). (gr. -1-3). 16.99 *(978-1-84686-040-9(7))* Barefoot Bks., Inc.
—We're Sailing to Galapagos: A Week in the Pacific. Restelli, Grazia, illus. 2007. (ENG.). 32p. (J). (gr. k-1). pap. 8.99 *(978-1-84686-102-4(0))* Barefoot Bks., Inc.
Krebs, Laurie & Cis, Valeria. The Beeman. Cis, Valeria, illus. 2008. (ENG., Illus.). 40p. (J). (gr. -1-3). 16.99 *(978-1-84686-146-8(2))* Barefoot Bks., Inc.
Krensky, Stephen. Fraidy Cats. Lewin, Betsy, illus. 2015. (Scholastic Reader, Level 2 Ser.). (ENG.). 32p. (J). (gr. -1-3). pap. 3.99 *(978-0-545-79966-9(X)*, Cartwheel Bks.) Scholastic, Inc.
—I Know a Lot! Gillingham, Sara, illus. 2013. (Empowerment Ser.). (ENG.). 12p. (J). (gr. -1 — 1). bds. 6.95 *(978-1-4197-0938-8(0)*, Abrams Appleseed) Abrams, Inc.
—Snack Attack. Curtis, Stacy, illus. 2008. (Ready-To-Reads Ser.). (ENG.). 32p. (J). (gr. -1-1). pap. 3.99 *(978-1-4169-0238-6(4)*, Simon Spotlight) Simon Spotlight.
—What Do You See? A Lift-the-Flap Book about Endangered Animals. Schimler, Amy, illus. 2009. (Little Green Bks.). (ENG.). 16p. (J). (gr. -1-k). 6.99 *(978-1-4169-7123-8(8)*, Little Simon) Little Simon.
Krieb & Krieb. We're off to Find the Witch's House. Alley, R. W., illus. 2007. (ENG.). 32p. (J). (gr. -1-2). 6.99 *(978-0-14-240854-4(9)*, Puffin Books) Penguin Young Readers Group.
Kristina Learns about Fishing. 2007. (J). *(978-0-9792728-0-6(7))* Tracepaper Bks. Inc.
Kroll, Virginia. Mosquito, 1 vol. LePlatt, Betsy, illus. 2011. (ENG.). 32p. (J). (gr. k-3). 16.99 *(978-1-58980-883-6(5))* Pelican Publishing Co., Inc.
—On the Way to Kindergarten. Schlossberg, Elizabeth, illus. 2008. (ENG.). 32p. (J). (gr. -1-k). pap. 6.99 *(978-0-14-241144-5(2)*, Puffin Books) Penguin Young Readers Group.
Kroupa, Robert J. Just Like You. 2011. (J). *(978-0-9825503-4-2(0))* IGI Pr.
Kruckvich, Francis. The Blue Chequered Harlequin. 2004. (Illus.). (YA). pap. *(978-0-9746226-2-0(1))* Scribolin.
Kruckvich, Francis, text. A Hero & a Great Man. 2003. (Illus.). 33p. (YA). pap. 4.95 *(978-0-9746226-0-6(5))* Scribolin.
Krulik, Nancy. Dribble, Dribble, Drool! Blecha, Aaron, illus. 2016. (George Brown, Class Clown Ser.: 18). (ENG.). 128p. (J). (gr. 2-4). 14.75 *(978-0-606-39308-9(0))* Turtleback Bks.
Krull, Kathleen & Brewer, Paul. Fartiste. Kulikov, Boris, illus. 2008. (ENG.). 40p. (J). (gr. -1-3). 17.99 *(978-1-4169-2828-7(6)*, Simon & Schuster Bks. For Young Readers) Simon & Schuster Bks. For Young Readers.
Kruse, Donald W. Cluck, Cluck, Cluck Splash! Crank, Donny, illus. 2012. 48p. pap. 12.95 *(978-1-59663-856-3(7)*, Castle Keep Pr.) Rock, James A. & Co. Pubs.
—Fleas, Please. Crank, Donny, illus. 2012. 48p. pap. 12.95 *(978-1-59663-858-7(3)*, Castle Keep Pr.) Rock, James A. & Co. Pubs.
—There's a Goof on My Roof. Crank, Donny, illus. 2012. 48p. pap. 12.95 *(978-1-59663-855-6(9)*, Castle Keep Pr.) Rock, James A. & Co. Pubs.
Krystosek, Richard. Chicken Scratch. 2013. 36p. pap. 24.95 *(978-1-63000-536-8(3))* America Star Bks.
Kubler, Annie. Dingle Dangle Scarecrow. 2003. (Baby Board Bks.). (ENG., Illus.). 12p. (J). (gr. 1-1). bds. *(978-0-85953-626-4(2))* Child's Play International Ltd.
Kuczenski, Tyler & Schumacher, Dan. Twelve Little Piggies. 2011. 28p. pap. 12.03 *(978-1-4567-5313-9(4))* AuthorHouse.
Kulka, Joe. Vacation's Over! Return of the Dinosaurs. Kulka, Joe, illus. 2010. (Carolrhoda Picture Bks.). (ENG., Illus.). 32p. (J). (gr. k-3). lib. bdg. 17.95 *(978-0-7613-5212-9(0))* Lerner Publishing Group.
Kumin, Maxine. Oh, Harry! Moser, Barry, illus. 2011. (ENG.). 32p. (J). (gr. -1-3). 16.99 *(978-1-59643-439-4(2)*, 9781596434394) Roaring Brook Pr.
Kupchella, Rick. Girls Can! Make it Happen. Brown, Marilyn, illus. 2004. (ENG.). 40p. (J). 16.95 *(978-0-9726504-3-4(1))* TRISTAN Publishing, Inc.
—Tell Me What We Did Today. Hanson, Warren, illus. (ENG.). 32p. (J). 15.95 *(978-0-9726504-0-3(7))* TRISTAN Publishing, Inc.
Kurd, Tariq. Gordon the Goblin in Oh My! Is That a Pork Pie? Robertson, Laura, illus. 2012. 36p. pap. *(978-1-907762-10-9(8))* Malt Publishing.
Kurilovitch, Mike. Silly Sisters. 2012. 32p. pap. 18.48 *(978-1-4772-6011-1(0))* AuthorHouse.
Kurtz, Kevin. A Day in the Salt Marsh, 1 vol. Powell, Consie, illus. 2007. (Day in the Habitat Ser.). (ENG.). 32p. (J). (gr. -1-3). 15.95 *(978-0-9768823-5-0(3))* Arbordale Publishing.
Kuskin, Karla. A Boy Had a Mother Who Bought Him a Hat. Hawkes, Kevin, illus. 2010. (ENG.). 32p. (J). (gr. -1-3). 16.99 *(978-0-06-075330-6(7))* HarperCollins Pubs.
—So, What's It Like to Be a Cat? Lewin, Betsy, illus. (ENG.). (J). (gr. -1-3). 2008. 40p. 7.99 *(978-0-689-85930-4(9))* 2005. 32p. 17.99 *(978-0-689-84733-2(5))* Simon & Schuster Children's Publishing. (Atheneum Bks. for Young Readers).
Kutner, Merrily. Down on the Farm. Hillenbrand, Will, illus. 2016. (ENG.). 24p. (J). (gr. -1 — 1). bds. 7.99 *(978-0-8234-2177-0(5))* Holiday Hse., Inc.
—The Zombie Nite Cafe. Long, Ethan, illus. 2007. (ENG.). 32p. (J). (gr. -1-3). 16.95 *(978-0-8234-1963-0(0))* Holiday Hse., Inc.
Kyle, Tracey C. Gazpacho for Nacho, 0 vols. 2014. (ENG.). 32p. (J). (gr. 1-3). 16.99 *(978-1-4778-1727-8(1)*, 9781477817278, Amazon Children's Publishing) Amazon Publishing.
Kyrja. Learning Magick, 1 vol. Osborn, Tonia Benington, illus. 2016. (Rupert's Tales Ser.: 6). (ENG.). 48p. (J). 16.99 *(978-0-7643-4973-7(2)*, 9780764349737) Schiffer Publishing, Ltd.
—Rupert's Tales: A Book of Bedtime Stories, 1 vol. Osborn, Tonia Bennington, illus. 2014. (ENG.). 64p. (J). (gr. 5-8). 19.99 *(978-0-7643-4694-1(6)*, 9780764346941) Schiffer Publishing, Ltd.
—Rupert's Tales: The Wheel of the Year - Samhain, Yule, Imbolc, & Ostara, 1 vol. Osborn, Tonia Bennington, illus. 2012. (ENG.). 64p. (J). 19.99 *(978-0-7643-3987-5(7)*, 9780764339875) Schiffer Publishing, Ltd.
—Rupert's Tales: The Wheel of the Year Activity Book, 1 vol. Osborn, Tonia Bennington, illus. 2012. (ENG.). 40p. (J). pap. 9.99 *(978-0-7643-4020-8(4)*, 9780764340208) Schiffer Publishing, Ltd.
Kyrja, et al. Rupert's Tales: The Wheel of the Year Beltane, Litha, Lammas, & Mabon, 1 vol. 2011. (ENG., Illus.). 64p. (J). 19.99 *(978-0-7643-3689-8(4)*, 9780764336898, Schiffer Publishing Ltd) Schiffer Publishing, Ltd.
Kysiak, Penelope Ann. You Can't Steal One's Wishes, 1 vol. 2009. 35p. pap. 24.95 *(978-1-60749-149-1(4))* America Star Bks.

S

L & M Trustam. Turn Left for Christmas. 2011. (Illus.). 28p. pap. 12.19 *(978-1-4567-7084-6(5))* AuthorHouse.
La Coccinella. Little Star. 2014. (Look & See! Ser.). (ENG., Illus.). 24p. (J). (gr. -1 — 1). bds. 6.95 *(978-1-4549-0599-8(9))* Sterling Publishing Co., Inc.
—Look & See: Mommy, Where Are You? 2014. (Look & See! Ser.). (ENG., Illus.). 24p. (J). (gr. -1 — 1). bds. 6.95 *(978-1-4549-0615-5(4))* Sterling Publishing Co., Inc.
—Look & See: What Sound Do You Make? 2014. (Look & See! Ser.). (ENG., Illus.). 24p. (J). (gr. -1 — 1). bds. 6.95 *(978-1-4549-0642-1(1))* Sterling Publishing Co., Inc.
Lacasse, Monique. Good Morning to You. 2012. 24p. pap. 15.99 *(978-1-4691-8623-8(3))* Xlibris Corp.
Laconi, Kristin. Karma the Kangaroo Takes the Court. 2010. 24p. pap. 12.99 *(978-1-4490-3227-2(3))* AuthorHouse.
Ladbrooke, Sheree. Big Alien School. 2011. (Illus.). 20p. pap. 12.52 *(978-1-4567-8779-0(9))* AuthorHouse.
Laden, Nina. Grow Up! 2003. (ENG., Illus.). 26p. (J). (gr. -1-7). bds. 6.99 *(978-0-8118-3761-3(0))* Chronicle Bks. LLC.
—If I Had a Little Dream. Castrillon, Melissa, illus. 2017. (ENG.). 32p. (J). (gr. -1-3). 17.99 *(978-1-4814-3924-4(3)*, Simon & Schuster/Paula Wiseman Bks.) Simon & Schuster/Paula Wiseman Bks.
—Peek-A Boo! 2015. (ENG., Illus.). 22p. (J). (gr. -1 — 1). bds. 6.99 *(978-1-4521-3396-6(4))* Chronicle Bks. LLC.
—Peek-A Choo-Choo! 2016. (ENG., Illus.). 22p. (J). (gr. -1 — 1). bds. 6.99 *(978-1-4521-5473-2(2))* Chronicle Bks. LLC.
—Peek-A Zoo! 2014. (ENG., Illus.). 22p. (J). (gr. -1 — 1). bds. 6.99 *(978-1-4521-1175-9(8))* Chronicle Bks. LLC.
Lagonegro, Melissa. Friends for a Princess. 2004. (Disney Princess Step into Reading Ser.). (gr. -1-2). lib. bdg. 13.55 *(978-0-613-73713-5(X)*, Turtleback) Turtleback Bks.
Lagonegro, Melissa & RH Disney Staff. Just Keep Swimming. Harchy, Atelier Philippe, illus. 2005. (Step into Reading Ser.). (ENG.). 32p. (J). (gr. k-3). pap. 3.99 *(978-0-7364-2319-9(2)*, RH/Disney) Random Hse. Children's Bks.
Lagonegro, Melissa, et al. Sharing & Caring. RH Disney Staff et al, illus. 2014. (Pictureback(R) Ser.). (ENG.). 16p. (J). (gr. -1-2). 4.99 *(978-0-7364-3334-1(1)*, RH/Disney) Random Hse. Children's Bks.
Lai, Thanhhà. Inside Out & Back Again. (ENG.). (J). (gr. 3-7). 2013. 288p. pap. 8.99 *(978-0-06-196279-0(1))* 2011. 272p. 16.99 *(978-0-06-196278-3(3))* HarperCollins Pubs.
—Inside Out & Back Again. 2014. (ENG.). 288p. (J). (gr. 3-7). 12.24 *(978-1-63245-350-1(9))* Lectorum Pubns., Inc.
—Inside Out & Back Again. 2009. 9.68 *(978-0-7848-3887-7(9)*, Everbind) Marco Bk. Co.
—Inside Out & Back Again. 2013. 18.00 *(978-1-61383-970-6(7))* Perfection Learning Corp.
—Inside Out & Back Again. 2013. (J). lib. bdg. 18.40 *(978-0-606-27126-4(0)*, Turtleback) Turtleback Bks.
Laínez, René Colato. Señor Pancho Had a Rancho. Smith, Elwood, illus. 2014. (ENG & SPA.). 32p. (J). (gr. -1-1). 6.99 *(978-0-8234-3173-1(8))* Holiday Hse., Inc.
—Señor Pancho Had a Rancho. Smith, Elwood H., illus. 2013. (ENG.). 32p. (J). (gr. -1-1). 16.95 *(978-0-8234-2632-4(7))* Holiday Hse., Inc.
Lakeshore Learning Materials Staff. Is Your Mama a Llama? Big Book Theme Packet. 2008. (J). pap. 44.50 *(978-1-60666-043-0(8))* Lakeshore Learning Materials.
Lamar, Gail Renfroe. Moon of the Wishing Night. Mask, Cynthia, illus. 2004. 32p. (J). 17.95 *(978-1-57966-047-5(9)*, River City Kids) River City Publishing.
Lamba, Marie & Lamba, Baldev. Green, Green: A Community Gardening Story. Sanchez, Sonia, illus. 2017. (ENG.). 32p. (J). 17.99 *(978-0-374-32797-2(1)*, 9780374327972, Farrar, Straus & Giroux (BYR)) Farrar, Straus & Giroux.
Lambert, Patricia. The Blue Ribbon Chicken. 2005. 36p. (J). pap. 14.93 *(978-1-4116-6163-9(X))* Lulu Pr., Inc.
Laminack, Lester L. The Ultimate Read-Aloud Resource: Making Every Moment Intentional & Instructional with Best Friend Books. 2016. (ENG.). 128p. (J). (gr. k-8). pap. 34.99 *(978-1-338-10925-2(1)*, Teaching Resources) Scholastic, Inc.
Lamont, Priscilla. Nursery Rhyme Crimes: Little Bo Peep. 2012. (Illus.). 24p. (J). pap. *(978-1-84780-354-2(7)*, Frances Lincoln) Quarto Publishing Group UK.
—Tom, Tom, the Piper's Son. 2012. (ENG., Illus.). 24p. (J). (gr. k-3). 15.99 *(978-1-84780-155-5(2)*, Frances Lincoln) Quarto Publishing Group UK GBR. Dist: Hachette Bk. Group.
Lampson, Rosalie. Give Mom a Minute. 2009. 32p. pap. 13.99 *(978-1-4490-1407-0(0))* AuthorHouse.
Landgraf, James, Jr. Monsters Monsters Go Away. Warrick, Jessica, illus. 2008. 40p. (J). 8.99 *(978-0-9819283-0-2(7))* Makdan Publishing.
Lang, Suzanne. Hooray for Kids! Lang, Max, illus. 2016. (ENG.). 40p. (J). (gr. -1-2). 17.99 *(978-0-553-53783-3(0)*,

Random Hse. Bks. for Young Readers) Random Hse. Children's Bks.

Langcaon, Jeff, illus. My Grandpa's Battleship Missouri Tour. 2007. (J). 14.95 *(978-1-56647-831-1(6))* Mutual Publishing LLC.

Langham, Tony. Creepy Crawly Calypso. Harter, Debbie, illus. 2004. (ENG.). 32p. (J). 16.99 *(978-1-84148-699-4(X))* Barefoot Bks., Inc.

Langham, Tony & Harter, Debbie. Creepy Crawly Calypso. 2005. (ENG.). 32p. (J). pap. 9.99 *(978-1-902283-46-3(5))* Barefoot Bks., Inc.

Laplante, Carole. Night Noises. Byrne-Walker, Mary Ann, illus. 2012. 40p. pap. 9.95 *(978-1-62006-046-9(9))* Sunbury Press, Inc.

Lapytski, Serge & Lapytski, Kristina. The Heart of a Lion! E-Hare. 2011. 84p. pap. 12.84 *(978-1-4567-4281-2(7))* AuthorHouse.

LaRamee-Jones, Shanda & McDougall, Carol. Baby Talk, 1 vol. 2013. (Baby Steps Ser.). (ENG., Illus.). 14p. (J). (gr. -1-k). bds. 8.95 *(978-1-77108-000-2(0))* Nimbus Publishing, Ltd. CAN. Dist: Orca Bk. Pubs. USA.

Larkin, Susan. All the Ways I Love You. Trotter, Stuart, illus. 2012. 16p. (J). *(978-1-4351-3857-5(0))* Barnes & Noble, Inc.

LaRochelle, David. Monster & Son. Chou, Joey, illus. 2016. (ENG.). 32p. (J). (gr. -1 — 1). 16.99 *(978-1-4521-2937-2(1))* Chronicle Bks. LLC.

Laskin, Pamela L. Ronit & Jamil. 2017. 192p. (YA). (gr. 8). 17.99 *(978-0-06-245854-4(X)*, Tegen, Katherine Bks) HarperCollins Pubs.

Lasseter, John. Disney/Pixar a Bug's Life Read-along. 2007. (ENG., Illus.). (J). (gr. -1-3). *(978-0-7634-2180-9(4))* Walt Disney Records.

Lavender, Todd. Farmer Fred & His Hen So Red. Lavender, Todd, illus. 2012. (Illus.). 48p. pap. 9.99 *(978-0-9850410-0-7(5))* Akmaeon Publishing, LLC.

Lavin, Christine & Franco-Feeney, Betsy. Hole in the Bottom of the Sea. McHugh, Patricia & Feeney, Kathryn, eds. Franco-Feeney, Betsy, illus. 2012. (ENG., Illus.). 32p. (J). 18.95 incl. audio compact disk *(978-0-9726487-8-3(X))* Puddle Jump Pr., Ltd.

Law, Felicia. Colors. Knight, Paula, illus. 2015. (Patchwork Ser.). (ENG.). 24p. (J). (gr. k-3). lib. bdg. 22.60 *(978-1-59953-709-2(5))* Norwood Hse. Pr.

—Family. Knight, Paula, illus. 2015. (Patchwork Ser.). (ENG.). 24p. (J). (gr. k-3). lib. bdg. 22.60 *(978-1-59953-711-5(7))* Norwood Hse. Pr.

—Feelings. Knight, Paula, illus. 2015. (Patchwork Ser.). (ENG.). 24p. (J). (gr. k-3). lib. bdg. 22.60 *(978-1-59953-712-2(5))* Norwood Hse. Pr.

—Numbers. Knight, Paula, illus. 2015. (Patchwork Ser.). (ENG.). 24p. (J). (gr. k-3). lib. bdg. 22.60 *(978-1-59953-710-8(9))* Norwood Hse. Pr.

—Shapes. Knight, Paula, illus. 2015. (Patchwork Ser.). (ENG.). 24p. (J). (gr. k-3). pap. 11.94 *(978-1-60357-804-2(8))*; lib. bdg. 22.60 *(978-1-59953-714-6(1))* Norwood Hse. Pr.

—Size. Knight, Paula, illus. 2015. (Patchwork Ser.). (ENG.). 24p. (J). (gr. k-3). pap. 11.94 *(978-1-60357-803-5(X))*; lib. bdg. 22.60 *(978-1-59953-713-9(3))* Norwood Hse. Pr.

Law, Jessica. A Hole in the Bottom of the Sea. McDonald, Jill, illus. 2013. (ENG.). 24p. (J). (gr. k-3). pap. 6.99 *(978-1-84686-948-8(X))* Barefoot Bks., Inc.

Lawler, Janet. If Kisses Were Colors. Jay, Alison, illus. (ENG.). (J). (gr. -1 — 1). 2010. 22p. bds. 6.99 *(978-0-8037-3530-9(8))* 2003. 32p. 16.99 *(978-0-8037-2617-8(1))* Penguin Young Readers Group. (Dial Bks).

—The Prehistoric Games, 1 vol. Davey, Martin, illus. 2016. (ENG.). 32p. (J). (gr. k-8). 16.99 *(978-1-4556-2138-5(2))* Pelican Publishing Co., Inc.

—Snowzilla, 0 vols. Haley, Amanda, illus. 2012. (ENG.). 32p. (J). (gr. -1-3). 16.99 *(978-0-7614-6188-3(4)*, 9780761461883, Amazon Children's Publishing) Amazon Publishing.

Lawless, Mary Ann. The Proud Christmas Tree. McCool, Arlene, illus. 2006. (J). 12.95 *(978-0-9772795-0-0(2))* Tuesday's Child.

Lawrence, John. This Little Chick. Lawrence, John, illus. 2013. (ENG., Illus.). 32p. (J). (gr. -1-k). 4.99 *(978-0-7636-6350-6(6))* Candlewick Pr.

Lawson, JonArno. Leap! Bisaillon, Josée, illus. 2017. (ENG.). 32p. (J). (gr. -1-2). 16.99 ***(978-1-77138-678-4(9))*** Kids Can Pr., Ltd. CAN. Dist: Hachette Bk. Group.

Lawson, Robert, illus. Just for Fun: A Collection of Stories & Verses. 2013. (Dover Children's Classics Ser.). (ENG.). 64p. (gr. 2-5). pap. 6.99 *(978-0-486-49720-4(8))* Dover Pubns., Inc.

Layton, Roxanne A. Keep Goin' Owen! 2012. 24p. pap. 24.95 *(978-1-4626-6599-0(3))* America Star Bks.

Lebost, Diana. Mr. Kite & the Perilous Flight: Izzy & Daisy. Ersoz, Sahin, illus. 2013. 88p. pap. 18.95 *(978-0-9912023-5-5(X))* Pep & Olie Publishing.

LeBox, Annette. Peace Is an Offering. Graegin, Stephanie, illus. 2015. (ENG.). 34p. (J). (gr. -1-k). 16.99 *(978-0-8037-4091-4(3)*, Dial Bks) Penguin Young Readers Group.

LeBreton, Heather. Rhyming with the Little Ones, 1 vol. LeBreton, Zachary, illus. 2009. 31p. pap. 24.95 *(978-1-60749-114-9(1))* America Star Bks.

Lebrun, Jessica. Rainbow's Mist. 2008. 17p. pap. 24.95 *(978-1-60563-242-1(2))* America Star Bks.

LeCron, Helen Cowles. The Animal Etiquette Book of Rhymes. Day, Maurice, illus. 2014. (ENG.). 64p. (J). (gr. 1-5). pap. 4.99 *(978-0-486-78234-8(4))* Dover Pubns., Inc.

Lee, Calee M. I Love You! Tharp, Tricia, illus. 2013. 32p. pap. 9.99 *(978-1-62395-471-0(1))* Xist Publishing.

Lee, Deborah Baptiste & Atcheson-Melton, Patty. In the Shade of the Spade: This Tale in a Poetry Format Takes Us on a Journey, the Illustrations Are Bright & Whimsical. You Can Almost Hear Music. Baptiste, Annette Green, illus. 2013. 48p. pap. 14.95 *(978-0-9858839-1-1(X))* Lee, Deborah I.

Lee, George Douglas. Oppy Stops the Hopping Popper. Lee, Brenda Donaloio, ed. Lee, George Douglas, illus. 2012. (Illus.). 30p. pap. 10.95 *(978-0-9848486-1-4(4))* Electric Theatre Radio Hour.

—Twyla the Truffle Pig. Lee, Brenda Donaloio, ed. Lee, George Douglas, illus. 2012. (Illus.). 34p. pap. 10.95 *(978-0-9848486-0-7(6))* Electric Theatre Radio Hour.

Lee, Jonathan. So I Could Fly Free. 2008. (ENG., Illus.). 32p. (J). *(978-1-85345-434-9(6))* Crusade for World Revival.

Lee, Mark. Twenty Big Trucks in the Middle of the Street. Cyrus, Kurt, illus. 2013. (ENG.). 32p. (J). (gr. -1-2). 15.99 *(978-0-7636-5809-0(X))* Candlewick Pr.

Leech, Carlyle & Leech, Thirma. Ha-Ha Farm. 2009. (ENG., Illus.). 24p. (J). (gr. -1-1). 14.95 *(978-1-59583-396-9(X)*, 9781595833969, Green Tiger Pr.) Laughing Elephant.

Lees, Caroline. Silly Sea Stories. 2010. (Illus.). 48p. pap. 19.49 *(978-1-4389-0701-7(X))* AuthorHouse.

Lefranc, Karin & Parker, Tyler. I Want to Eat Your Books. 2015. (ENG., Illus.). 32p. (J). (gr. -1-k). 16.99 *(978-1-63450-172-9(1)*, Sky Pony Pr.) Skyhorse Publishing Co., Inc.

Leiter, Richard & Kober, Shahar. The Flying Hand of Marco B. 2015. (ENG., Illus.). 24p. (J). (gr. k-2). 15.99 *(978-1-58536-888-4(1)*, 203813) Sleeping Bear Pr.

Leman, Nora. The Alpha Building Crew. Hartmann, April, illus. 2005. (J). *(978-1-58967-110-6(3))* Kindermusik International.

Lemke, Donald. Book-O-Beards. Lentz, Bob, illus. 2015. (Wearable Bks.). (ENG.). 12p. (gr. -1-1). bds. 7.99 *(978-1-62370-183-3(X)*, Wear-A-Book) Capstone Young Readers of Coughlan Cos.

—Book-O-Hats. Lentz, Bob, illus. 2015. (Wearable Bks.). (ENG.). 12p. (gr. -1-1). bds. 7.99 *(978-1-62370-184-0(8)*, Wear-A-Book) Capstone Young Readers of Coughlan Cos.

Lemke, Donald B. Book-O-Teeth. Lentz, Bob, illus. 2015. (Wearable Bks.). (ENG.). 12p. (gr. -1-1). bds. 7.99 *(978-1-62370-186-4(4)*, Wear-A-Book) Capstone Young Readers of Coughlan Cos.

Lenton, Steven. Five Christmas Penguins. 2016. (ENG., Illus.). 12p. (J). (gr. -1). bds. 9.99 *(978-1-62686-822-9(0)*, Silver Dolphin Bks.) Readerlink Distribution Services, LLC.

Leon, Loni. Can you Imagine..., 1. Leon, Loni & Huston, Kyle, illus. 2006. 49p. (J). 21.95 *(978-0-9728556-0-0(2))* Sullivan, Kelley Enterprises.

Leonard, Marcia. El Hombre de Hojalata. Handelman, Dorothy, photos by. 2005. (ENG & SPA., Illus.). 32p. (J). (gr. -1-1). pap. 4.99 *(978-0-8225-3310-8(3))* Lerner Publishing Group.

—Me Gusta el Desorden. Translations.com Staff, tr. from ENG. Handelman, Dorothy, photos by. 2007. (Lecturas para niños de Verdad - Nivel 1 (Real Kids Readers - Level 1) Ser.).Tr. of I Like Mess. (SPA., Illus.). 32p. (gr. k-2). per. 5.95 *(978-0-8225-7800-0(X)*, Ediciones Lerner) Lerner Publishing Group.

—Me Gusta el Desorden; I Like Mess. 2008. pap. 34.95 *(978-0-8225-9495-6(1))* Lerner Publishing Group.

—Mi Dia de Campamento. Translations.com Staff, tr. from ENG. Handelman, Dorothy, photos by. 2007. (Lecturas para niños de Verdad - Nivel 1 (Real Kids Readers - Level 1) Ser.).Tr. of My Camp-Out. (SPA., Illus.). 32p. (gr. k-2). per. 5.95 *(978-0-8225-7798-0(4)*, Ediciones Lerner) Lerner Publishing Group.

—Mi Dia de Campamento; My Camp Out. 2008. pap. 34.95 *(978-0-8225-9496-3(X))* Lerner Publishing Group.

—Saltar, Brincar, Correr. Translations.com Staff, tr. from ENG. Handelman, Dorothy, photos by. 2007. (Lecturas para niños de Verdad - Nivel 1 (Real Kids Readers - Level 1) Ser.).Tr. of Hop, Skip, Run. (SPA., Illus.). 32p. (gr. k-2). per. 5.95 *(978-0-8225-7799-7(2)*, Ediciones Lerner) Lerner Publishing Group.

—Saltar, Brincar, Correr; Hop, Skip, Run. 2008. pap. 34.95 *(978-0-8225-9497-0(8))* Lerner Publishing Group.

—Trae la Pelota, Tito. Handelman, Dorothy, photos by. 2005.Tr. of Get the Ball, Slim. (Illus.). 32p. (J). (ENG & SPA.). (gr. -1-1). pap. 4.99 *(978-0-8225-3293-4(X))*; (SPA., (gr. 1-1). per. 5.95 *(978-0-8225-3292-7(1)*, Ediciones Lerner) Lerner Publishing Group.

Leonard, Marcia & Handelman, Dorothy. The Pet Vet. Handelman, Dorothy, illus. Leonard, Marcia, photos by. 2005. (ENG & SPA., Illus.). 32p. (J). (gr. -1-1). pap. 4.99 *(978-0-8225-3299-6(9))* Lerner Publishing Group.

Leone, Elaine H. Grandy Goose Rhymes. 2013. (ENG.). 116p. pap. 10.99 *(978-1-4675-6477-9(X))* Independent Pub.

Lessac, Frané. Island Counting 1 2 3. Lessac, Frané, illus. 2007. (ENG., Illus.). 24p. (J). (— 1). bds. 6.99 *(978-0-7636-3518-3(9))* Candlewick Pr.

Lester, Alison. Magic Beach. Lester, Alison, illus. 2006. (ENG., Illus.). 32p. (J). (gr. -1-k). pap. 11.99 *(978-1-74114-488-8(4))* Allen & Unwin AUS. Dist: Independent Pubs. Group.

—Noni the Pony. Lester, Alison, illus. 2012. (ENG., Illus.). 32p. (J). (gr. -1-k). 15.99 *(978-1-4424-5959-5(X)*, Beach Lane Bks.) Beach Lane Bks.

—Noni the Pony Goes to the Beach. Lester, Alison, illus. 2015. (ENG., Illus.). 32p. (J). (gr. -1-3). 17.99 *(978-1-4814-4625-9(8)*, Beach Lane Bks.) Beach Lane Bks.

Lettera, Janine Hamel. My First Day of School. 2012. 16p. pap. 7.31 *(978-1-4251-1614-9(0))* Trafford Publishing.

Leuck, Laura. Goodnight, Baby Monster. Date not set. 32p. (J). (gr. -1-1). pap. 4.99 *(978-0-06-443723-3(X))* HarperCollins Pubs.

—Jeepers Creepers: A Monstrous ABC. Parkins, David, illus. 2003. (ENG.). 32p. (J). (gr. -1-7). 15.95 *(978-0-8118-3509-1(X)*, 53408263) Chronicle Bks. LLC.

—My Creature Teacher. Nash, Scott, illus. 2004. (ENG.). 32p. (J). (gr. -1-1). 15.99 *(978-0-06-029694-0(1))* HarperCollins Pubs.

—Santa Claws. Grimly, Gris, illus. 2006. (ENG.). 32p. (J). (gr. -1-3). 16.95 *(978-0-8118-4992-0(9))* Chronicle Bks. LLC.

Levine, Abby. This Is the Dreidel. Billin-Frye, Paige, illus. 2012. (J). 34.28 *(978-1-61913-134-7(X))* Weigl Pubs., Inc.

Levine, Martha Peaslee. Stop That Nose!, 1 vol. White, Lee, illus. 2006. (ENG.). 32p. (J). (gr. -1-3). 14.95 *(978-0-7614-5280-5(X))* Marshall Cavendish Corp.

Levine, Rhoda. Three Ladies Beside the Sea. Gorey, Edward, illus. 2010. (ENG.). 40p. (J). (gr. k-4). 14.95 *(978-1-59017-354-1(6)*, NYR Children's Collection) New York Review of Bks., Inc., The.

Lewin, Betsy. Where Is Tippy Toes? Lewin, Betsy, illus. 2010. (ENG., Illus.). 32p. (J). (gr. -1-2). 16.99 *(978-1-4169-3808-8(7)*, Atheneum Bks. for Young Readers) Simon & Schuster Children's Publishing.

Lewis, Anne Margaret. Puddle Jumpers. Cote, Nancy, illus. 2016. (ENG.). 32p. (J). (gr. -1-k). 16.99 *(978-1-63450-185-9(3)*, Sky Pony Pr.) Skyhorse Publishing Co., Inc.

Lewis, Brandt. Fingers for Halloween. Doerrfeld, Cori, illus. 2017. (ENG.). 12p. (J). (gr. -1 — 1). bds. 7.99 ***(978-0-316-37800-0(3))*** Little, Brown Bks. for Young Readers.

Lewis, Brandt. Fingers for Lunch. Doerrfeld, Cori, illus. 2016. (ENG.). 12p. (J). (gr. -1 — 1). bds. 7.99 *(978-0-316-37799-7(6))* Little, Brown Bks. for Young Readers.

Lewis, J. Patrick. The Snowflake Sisters. Desimini, Lisa, illus. 2012. (ENG.). 32p. (J). (gr. -1-3). pap. 16.99 *(978-1-4424-6719-4(3)*, Atheneum Bks. for Young Readers) Simon & Schuster Children's Publishing.

—What's Looking at You Kid? 2012. (ENG., Illus.). 32p. (J). (gr. k-5). 14.95 *(978-1-58536-793-1(1))* Sleeping Bear Pr.

Lewis, J. Patrick & Lewis, Leigh. It's Not the Baby. Frost, Maddie, illus. 2017. (ENG.). 14p. (J). (gr. -1 — 1). bds. 9.99 ***(978-1-68152-194-7(6))*** Amicus.

Lewis, Jan. First Fairy Tales: Puss in Boots. 2015. (ENG., Illus.). 24p. bds. 6.99 *(978-1-86147-626-5(4)*, Armadillo) Anness Publishing GBR. Dist: National Bk. Network.

—First Fairy Tales Aladdin & the Lamp. 2013. (ENG., Illus.). 24p. (J). (gr. -1-12). bds. 6.99 *(978-1-86147-337-0(0)*, Armadillo) Anness Publishing GBR. Dist: National Bk. Network.

—First Fairy Tales Goldilocks & the Three Bears. 2013. (ENG., Illus.). 24p. (J). (gr. -1-12). bds. 6.99 *(978-1-86147-332-5(X)*, Armadillo) Anness Publishing GBR. Dist: National Bk. Network.

—First Fairy Tales Little Red Riding Hood. 2013. (ENG., Illus.). 24p. (J). (gr. -1-12). bds. 6.99 *(978-1-86147-336-3(2)*, Armadillo) Anness Publishing GBR. Dist: National Bk. Network.

—First Fairy Tales Snow White. 2013. (ENG., Illus.). 24p. (J). (gr. -1-12). bds. 6.99 *(978-1-86147-335-6(4)*, Armadillo) Anness Publishing GBR. Dist: National Bk. Network.

—Princess Fairy Tales: Cinderella, the Princess & the Pea, Sleeping Beauty, the Little Mermaid. Lewis, Jan, illus. 2015. (ENG., Illus.). 48p. bds. 9.99 *(978-1-86147-423-0(7)*, Armadillo) Anness Publishing GBR. Dist: National Bk. Network.

Lewis, Jan, illus. The Emperor's New Clothes. 2015. (ENG.). 24p. (J). (gr. -1-2). bds. 6.99 *(978-1-86147-413-1(X)*, Armadillo) Anness Publishing GBR. Dist: National Bk. Network.

—First Fairy Tales: Cinderella. 2013. (ENG.). 24p. (J). (gr. -1-k). bds. 6.99 *(978-1-86147-334-9(6)*, Armadillo) Anness Publishing GBR. Dist: National Bk. Network.

—First Fairy Tales: Sleeping Beauty. 2013. (ENG.). 24p. (J). (gr. -1-k). bds. 6.99 *(978-1-86147-338-7(9)*, Armadillo) Anness Publishing GBR. Dist: National Bk. Network.

—First Fairy Tales: The Ugly Duckling. 2013. (ENG.). 24p. (J). (gr. -1-k). bds. 6.99 *(978-1-86147-333-2(8)*, Armadillo) Anness Publishing GBR. Dist: National Bk. Network.

—First Fairy Tales: Three Little Pigs. 2013. (ENG.). 24p. (J). (gr. -1-k). bds. 6.99 *(978-1-86147-331-8(1)*, Armadillo) Anness Publishing GBR. Dist: National Bk. Network.

—Magical Fairy Tales: Aladdin & the Lamp; the Ugly Duckling; the Emperor's New Clothes; Puss in Boots. 2016. (ENG.). 48p. bds. 9.99 *(978-1-86147-700-2(7)*, Armadillo) Anness Publishing GBR. Dist: National Bk. Network.

—The Princess & the Pea. 2015. (ENG.). 24p. bds. 6.99 *(978-1-86147-467-4(9)*, Armadillo) Anness Publishing GBR. Dist: National Bk. Network.

Lewis, Jill & Blue Bananas. Coconut Jack. Waters, Erica-Jane, illus. 2009. (Blue Bananas Ser.). (ENG.). 48p. (J). (gr. k-2). pap. 5.99 *(978-1-4052-4132-8(2))* Egmont Bks., Ltd. GBR. Dist: Independent Pubs. Group.

Lewis, Kevin. Dinosaur, Dinosaur. Kirk, Daniel, illus. 2006. (J). *(978-0-439-78228-9(7)*, Orchard Bks.) Scholastic, Inc.

Lewis, Kevin & Kirk, Daniel. My Truck Is Stuck! Kirk, Daniel, illus. 2006. (ENG., Illus.). 30p. (J). (gr. -1 — 1). bds. 7.99 *(978-0-7868-3739-7(X))* Hyperion Pr.

Lewis, Michael G. The Great Pirate Christmas Battle, 1 vol. Jaskiel, Stan, illus. 2014. (ENG.). 32p. (J). (gr. k-3). 16.99 *(978-1-4556-1934-4(5))* Pelican Publishing Co., Inc.

Lewis, Rose A. Sweet Dreams. Corace, Jen, illus. 2012. (ENG.). 32p. (J). (gr. -1-k). 16.95 *(978-1-4197-0189-4(4)*, Abrams Bks. for Young Readers) Abrams, Inc.

Lewison, Wendy Cheyette. Silly Milly. Westcott, Nadine Bernard, illus. 2010. (Scholastic Reader Level 1 Ser.). (ENG.). 32p. (J). (gr. -1-3). pap. 3.99 *(978-0-545-06859-8(2))* Scholastic, Inc.

—Silly Milly. 2010. (Scholastic Reader Level 1 Ser.). lib. bdg. 13.55 *(978-0-606-10556-9(5)*, Turtleback) Turtleback Bks.

—Two Is for Twins. Nakata, Hiroe, illus. 2011. (ENG.). 28p. (J). (gr. -1 — 1). 2011. bds. 11.99 *(978-0-670-01310-4(2)*, Viking Books for Young Readers) Penguin Young Readers Group.

Liberto, Lorenzo. Matt the Rat & His Magic Cloud / Raton Mateo y Su Nube Magica: A Day at School / un Dia de Escuela. Gomez, Rocio, ed. Torres, Irving, illus. 2003. (Matt the Rat Ser. / La Serie de Ratón Mateo). (ENG & SPA.). 32p. (J). lib. bdg. 20.00 *(978-0-9743668-0-7(3))* Harvest Sun Pr., LLC.

Liberts, Jennifer. Go, Go, Trucks! Yamada, Mike, illus. 2017. (Step into Reading Ser.). (ENG.). 32p. (J). (gr. -1-1). 3.99 ***(978-0-399-54951-9(X))***; lib. bdg. 12.99 ***(978-0-399-54952-6(8))*** Random Hse. Children's Bks. (Random Hse. Bks. for Young Readers).

Lichtenheld, Tom. What Mess? 2012. (ENG., Illus.). 40p. (J). (gr. -1-3). pap. 7.00 *(978-0-316-20123-0(5))* Little, Brown Bks. for Young Readers.

—What Mess? 2012. (J). lib. bdg. 17.20 *(978-0-606-26686-4(0)*, Turtleback) Turtleback Bks.

Lies, Brian. Bats at the Ballgame. 2010. (Bat Book Ser.). (ENG., Illus.). 32p. (J). (gr. -1-3). 16.99 *(978-0-547-24970-4(5))* Houghton Mifflin Harcourt Publishing Co.

—Bats at the Beach. (Bat Book Ser.). (ENG., Illus.). 32p. (J). (gr. -1 — 1). 2011. bds. 11.99 *(978-0-547-55437-2(0))* 2006. 17.99 *(978-0-618-55744-8(X))* Houghton Mifflin Harcourt Publishing Co.

—Bats at the Library. 2014. (Bat Book Ser.). (ENG., Illus.). 32p. (J). (gr. -1-3). pap. 7.99 *(978-0-544-33920-0(7)*, HMH Books For Young Readers) Houghton Mifflin Harcourt Publishing Co.

—Bats at the Library. Lies, Brian, illus. 2008. (Bat Book Ser.). (ENG., Illus.). 32p. (J). (gr. -1-3). 17.99 *(978-0-618-99923-1(X))* Houghton Mifflin Harcourt Publishing Co.

Lindahl, Ben. The World Outside My Door. 2012. 24p. pap. 15.99 *(978-1-4691-7652-9(1))* Xlibris Corp.

Lindbergh, Reeve. Homer: The Library Cat. Wilsdorf, Anne, illus. 2011. (ENG.). 32p. (J). (gr. -1-3). 16.99 *(978-0-7636-3448-3(4))* Candlewick Pr.

—My Little Grandmother Often Forgets. Brown, Kathryn, illus. 2007. (ENG.). 32p. (J). (gr. -1-1). 16.99 *(978-0-7636-1989-3(2))* Candlewick Pr.

—Nobody Owns the Sky. Paparone, Pamela, illus. 2004. 32p. (J). *(978-1-85269-344-2(4))*; *(978-1-85269-347-3(9))*; *(978-1-85269-343-5(6))*; *(978-1-85269-342-8(8))*; *(978-1-85269-345-9(2))* Mantra Lingua.

Linden, Joanne. Ben & Zip: Two Short Friends. Goldsmith, Tom, illus. 2014. (ENG.). 32p. (J). (gr. -1-k). 16.95 *(978-1-936261-28-4(6))* Flashlight Pr.

Ling, Nancy Tupper. Double Happiness. Chau, Alina, illus. 2015. (ENG.). 48p. (J). (gr. k-3). 16.99 *(978-1-4521-2918-1(5))* Chronicle Bks. LLC.

Listening with Zachary. (J). pap. 13.75 *(978-0-8136-4655-8(3))* Modern Curriculum Pr.

Lithgow, John. The Carnival of the Animals. Kulikov, Boris, illus. 2004. (ENG.). 40p. (J). (gr. -1-3). 19.99 *(978-0-689-86721-7(2)*, Simon & Schuster Bks. For Young Readers) Simon & Schuster Bks. For Young Readers.

—Carnival of the Animals. Kulikov, Boris, illus. 2007. (ENG.). 40p. (J). (gr. -1-3). 7.99 *(978-0-689-87343-0(3)*, Simon & Schuster Bks. For Young Readers) Simon & Schuster Bks. For Young Readers.

—I'm a Manatee. Hoyt, Ard, illus. 2007. (ENG.). 32p. (J). (gr. -1-3). pap. 9.99 *(978-0-689-85452-1(8)*, Little Simon) Little Simon.

—I'M a Manatee. Hoyt, Ard, illus. 2003. (ENG.). 32p. (J). (gr. -1-3). 18.99 *(978-0-689-85427-9(7)*, Simon & Schuster Bks. For Young Readers) Simon & Schuster Bks. For Young Readers.

—Mahalia Mouse Goes to College. Oleynikov, Igor, illus. 2007. (ENG.). 40p. (J). (gr. -1-3). 17.99 *(978-1-4169-2715-0(8)*, Simon & Schuster Bks. For Young Readers) Simon & Schuster Bks. For Young Readers.

little bee books, little bee. Dive into the Sea! Llewhellin, Gareth, illus. 2016. (ENG.). 12p. (J). (gr. -1 — 1). bds. 7.99 *(978-1-4998-0297-9(8))* Little Bee Books Inc.

little bee books, little bee & Llewhellin, Gareth. Jump into Fall! 2016. (ENG., Illus.). 12p. (J). (gr. -1 — 1). bds. 6.99 *(978-1-4998-0298-6(6))* Little Bee Books Inc.

Little Bee Books Staff. Our Christmas Stockings: A Touch-and-Feel Book. 2015. (ENG., Illus.). 12p. (J). (gr. -1-1). 6.99 *(978-1-4998-0144-6(0))* Little Bee Books Inc.

—Our Christmas Tree: A Touch-and-Feel Book. 2015. (ENG., Illus.). 12p. (J). (gr. -1-1). 6.99 *(978-1-4998-0145-3(9))* Little Bee Books Inc.

—Who's Hiding? Baruzzi, Agnese, illus. 2015. (ENG.). 16p. (J). (gr. -1-1). 9.99 *(978-1-4998-0168-2(8))* Little Bee Books Inc.

Little, Jean. I Know an Old Laddie. 2004. (Illus.). (J). (gr. k-3). spiral bd. *(978-0-616-01703-6(0))* Canadian National Institute for the Blind/Institut National Canadien pour les Aveugles.

Litton, Jonathan. Dino. Galloway, Fhiona, illus. 2016. (My Little World Ser.). (ENG.). 24p. (J). (gr. -1-k). mass mkt. 3.99 *(978-1-58925-485-5(6))* Tiger Tales.

—Moo. Galloway, Fhiona, illus. 2016. (My Little World Ser.). (ENG.). 24p. (J). (gr. -1-k). mass mkt. 3.99 *(978-1-58925-484-8(8))* Tiger Tales.

—Peek-Through Forest. Nowowiejska, Kasia, illus. 2015. (Little Snappers Ser.). (ENG.). 12p. (J). (gr. -1-2). bds. 9.99 *(978-1-68010-508-7(6))* Tiger Tales.

—Planet Pop-Up: Monkey on the Moon. Anderson, Nicola, illus. 2015. (Planet Pop-Up Ser.). (ENG.). 12p. (J). (gr. -1). 12.95 *(978-1-62686-372-9(5)*, Silver Dolphin Bks.) Readerlink Distribution Services, LLC.

—Planet Pop-Up: Sheep Rules the Roost! Anderson, Nicola, illus. 2015. (Planet Pop-Up Ser.). (ENG.). 12p. (J). (gr. -1). 12.95 *(978-1-62686-354-5(7)*, Silver Dolphin Bks.) Readerlink Distribution Services, LLC.

—Planet Pop-Up: Tiger Takes Off. Anderson, Nicola, illus. 2015. (Planet Pop-Up Ser.). (ENG.). 12p. (J). (gr. -1). 12.95 *(978-1-62686-373-6(3)*, Silver Dolphin Bks.) Readerlink Distribution Services, LLC.

—Roar: A Big-Mouthed Book of Sounds! Galloway, Fhiona, illus. 2014. (ENG.). 16p. (J). bds. 7.99 *(978-1-58925-593-7(3))* Tiger Tales.

—Snap: A Peek-Through Book of Shapes. Galloway, Fhiona, illus. 2014. (My Little World Ser.). (ENG.). 16p. (J). (gr. -1-k). bds. 7.99 *(978-1-58925-566-1(6))* Tiger Tales.

—Splish Splash: Pop-Up Fun. Galloway, Fhiona, illus. 2016. (Little Snappers Ser.). (ENG.). 10p. (J). (gr. -1-k). 9.99 *(978-1-58925-259-2(4))* Tiger Tales.

—Surprise: A Book of Christmas Shapes. Galloway, Fhiona, illus. 2014. (ENG.). 16p. (J). (gr. -1-k). bds. 7.99 *(978-1-58925-567-8(4))* Tiger Tales.

Litwin, Eric. Ice Cream & Dinosaurs. Lichtenheld, Tom, illus. 2016. (Groovy Joe Ser.: 1). (ENG.). 40p. (J). (gr. -1-k). 17.99 *(978-0-545-88378-8(4)*, Orchard Bks.) Scholastic, Inc.

—The Nuts: Bedtime at the Nut House. Magoon, Scott, illus. 2014. (ENG.). 32p. (J). (gr. -1-3). 18.00 *(978-0-316-32244-7(X))* Little, Brown Bks. for Young Readers.

—The Nuts: Sing & Dance in Your Polka Dot Pants. Magoon, Scott, illus. 2015. (ENG.). 32p. (J). (gr. -1-3). 18.00 *(978-0-316-32250-8(4))* Little Brown & Co.

—The Nuts: Keep Rolling! Magoon, Scott, illus. 2017. (ENG.). 32p. (J). (gr. -1-3). 17.99 *(978-0-316-32251-5(2))* Little, Brown Bks. for Young Readers.

—Pete the Cat Saves Christmas. Dean, James, illus. (Pete the Cat Ser.). 40p. (J). (gr. -1-3). 2014. (ENG.). 17.99 *(978-0-06-211062-6(4))* 2012. lib. bdg. 18.89 *(978-0-06-211063-3(2))* HarperCollins Pubs.

—Rocking in My School Shoes. Dean, James, illus. 2011. (Pete the Cat Ser.). 40p. (J). (gr. -1-3). (ENG.). 17.99 *(978-0-06-191024-1(4))*; lib. bdg. 17.89 *(978-0-06-191025-8(2))* HarperCollins Pubs.

Litwin, Eric, ed. Rocking in My School Shoes. 2011. *(978-0-545-50106-4(7))* Scholastic, Inc.

Livermore, Edward. Phebe the Blackberry Girl. 2004. reprint ed. pap. 15.95 (978-1-4191-4126-3(0)); pap. 1.99 (978-1-4192-4126-0(5)) Kessinger Publishing, LLC.

Lloyd, Ashley. Red, 1 vol. Matkovich, Gregory, illus. 2009. 19p. pap. 24.95 (978-1-61546-913-0(3)) PublishAmerica, Inc.

Lloyd-Jones, Sally. Old MacNoah Had an Ark. Newton, Jill, illus. 2008. (HarperBlessings Ser.). 32p. (J). (gr. -1-2). 17.89 (978-0-06-055718-8(4)) HarperCollins Pubs.

—Skip to the Loo, My Darling! a Potty Book. Jeram, Anita, illus. 2016. (ENG.). 32p. (J). (-k). 11.99 (978-0-7636-7234-8(3)) Candlewick Pr.

—Time to Say Goodnight. Chapman, Jane, illus. 2006. (ENG.). 32p. (J). (gr. -1-2). 15.99 (978-0-06-054328-0(0)) HarperCollins Pubs.

—Tiny Bear's Bible, 1 vol. Oleynikov, Igor, illus. 2015. (ENG.). 22p. (J). bds. 15.99 (978-0-310-74787-1(2)) Zonderkidz.

Lobel, Arnold. On Market Street. Lobel, Anita, illus. 25th anniv. ed. 2006. (ENG.). 40p. (J). (gr. -1-3). pap. 6.99 (978-0-688-08745-6(0), Greenwillow Bks.) HarperCollins Pubs.

Lobel, Arnold & Lobel, Adrianne. The Frogs & Toads All Sang. Lobel, Arnold & Lobel, Adrianne, illus. 2009. (ENG., Illus.). 32p. (J). (gr. -1-2). 16.99 (978-0-06-180022-1(8)) HarperCollins Pubs.

Lodge, Alison & Lodge, Ali. Clever Chameleon. Lodge, Alison, illus. 2005. (Illus.). 24p. (J). 15.99 (978-1-84148-347-4(8)) Barefoot Bks., Inc.

Lomax M.Ed., L. E. A Saint Called Nicholas: The Christmas Legends Series, Vol. I. 2012. 52p. pap. 23.99 (978-1-4582-0584-1(3), Abbott Pr.) Author Solutions, Inc.

Lombardi, Elizabeth L. Jonathan's Journey. 2012. (ENG.). (J). (978-1-62148-014-3(3)) SteinerBooks, Inc.

London, Jonathan. I'm a Truck Driver. Parkins, David, illus. 2010. (ENG.). 32p. (J). (gr. -1-2). 15.99 (978-0-8050-7989-0(0), 9780805079890, Holt, Henry & Co. Bks. For Young Readers) Holt, Henry & Co.

Long, Ethan. Clara & Clem Take a Ride. 2012. (Penguin Young Readers Level 1 Ser.). lib. bdg. 13.55 (978-0-606-26639-0(9), Turtleback) Turtleback Bks.

—Clara & Clem under the Sea. Long, Ethan, illus. 2014. (Penguin Young Readers, Level 1 Ser.). (ENG., Illus.). 32p. (J). (gr. k-1). pap. 3.99 (978-0-448-47812-8(9), Penguin Young Readers) Penguin Young Readers Group.

—Hi! 2015. (Animal Sounds Ser.). (ENG., Illus.). 20p. (J). (gr. -1 — 1). bds. 7.95 (978-1-4197-1365-1(5)) Abrams, Inc.

—One Drowsy Dragon. 2010. (Illus.). (J). (978-0-545-23412-2(3), Orchard Bks.) Scholastic, Inc.

Longstreth, Galen Goodwin. Yes, Let's. Wicks, Maris, illus. 2013. (ENG.). 32p. (J). (gr. -1-3). 15.95 (978-1-933718-87-3(0)) Tanglewood Pr.

Lopez, Cece. Mini Munchkin Mania Mini Series Presents: Mini Munchkin in the Mirror. 2013. (ENG.). 25p. (J). pap. 13.95 (978-1-4327-9896-3(0)) Outskirts Pr., Inc.

Lord, Jill Roman. If Jesus Walked Beside Me. Wummer, Amy, illus. 2014. (If Jesus Ser.). 22p. (J). bds. 6.99 (978-0-8249-1920-7(3), Ideal Pubns.) Worthy Publishing.

The Lost Treasure of Skull Island. 2012. (Illus.). (J). (978-1-4351-4328-9(0)) Barnes & Noble, Inc.

Lotz, Dana R. Kids' Tales. 2008. 85p. pap. 19.95 (978-1-60672-179-7(8)) America Star Bks.

Lougheed, Cordelia. Tales of the Magpie. 2008. 36p. pap. 22.95 (978-1-4327-2032-2(5)) Outskirts Pr., Inc.

Louise, Verna & McKinney, Doris. Tales & Rhymes for Children: Cute Little Stories for Kids. 2012. 64p. pap. 20.95 (978-1-4497-3339-1(5), WestBow Pr.) Author Solutions, Inc.

Love, Maryann Cusimano. Sleep, Baby, Sleep. van Lieshout, Maria, illus. 2013. (ENG.). 30p. (J). (gr. -1-k). bds. 6.99 (978-0-399-16144-5(9), Philomel Bks.) Penguin Young Readers Group.

—You Are My I Love You. Ichikawa, Satomi, illus. (Little Letters Ser.). (ENG.). (J). (gr. -1-k). 2012. 32p. 4.99 (978-0-448-46307-0(5), Grosset & Dunlap) 2010. 30p. bds. 6.99 (978-0-399-24395-0(X), Philomel Bks.) Penguin Young Readers Group.

—You Are My I Love You / Tú Eres Mi Te Quiero. Ichikawa, Satomi, illus. 2012. (SPA & ENG.). 28p. (J). (gr. -1 — 1). bds. 6.99 (978-0-399-24396-7(8), Philomel Bks.) Penguin Young Readers Group.

—You Are My Miracle. Ichikawa, Satomi, illus. (ENG.). (J). (gr. -1 — 1). 2012. 28p. bds. 6.99 (978-0-399-25791-9(8)) 2005. 32p. 16.99 (978-0-399-24037-9(3)) Penguin Young Readers Group. (Philomel Bks.).

—You Are My Wish. Ichikawa, Satomi, illus. 2010. (ENG.). 32p. (J). (gr. -1-k). 16.99 (978-0-399-24752-1(1), Philomel Bks.) Penguin Young Readers Group.

—You Are My Wonders. Ichikawa, Satomi & Lewin, Ted, illus. 2012. (ENG.). 32p. (J). (gr. -1-2). 16.99 (978-0-399-25293-8(2), Philomel Bks.) Penguin Young Readers Group.

Love, Pamela. Two Feet up, Two Feet Down. Chapman, Lynne, illus. 2005. (Rookie Reader Español Ser.). (ENG.). 32p. (J). (gr. k-2). pap. 4.95 (978-0-516-24646-8(1), Children's Pr.) Scholastic Library Publishing.

Lovelace, Victoria. Animal Crackers & Alphabet Soup. 2014. (ENG.). 84p. pap. 19.95 (978-1-4670-3532-3(7), b9230d6d-2918-4b50-9842-302a1082f149) AuthorHouse.

Lovett, Louise Sheppa, illus. A Happy Day. Lovett, Louise Sheppa, . 2008. 32p. (J). 18.50 (978-0-9793419-0-8(6)) Tish & Co. LLC.

Low, Alice. Blueberry Mouse. Friend, David Michael, tr. Friend, David Michael, illus. 2004. (J). 15.95 (978-1-59336-111-2(4)); pap. (978-1-59336-112-9(2)) Mondo Publishing.

Low, J. H. Lost in the Gardens. Low, J. H., illus. 2015. (ENG., Illus.). 48p. 10.00 (978-981-4677-10-3(8)) Marshall Cavendish International (Asia) Private Ltd. SGP. Dist: National Bk. Network.

Lowery, Paul. Do You Know Where Sea Turtles Go? 2007. (J). 15.99 (978-0-9792379-0-4(4)) PBL Stories LLC.

Lubner, Susan. A Horse's Tale: A Colonial Williamsburg Adventure. Moore, Margie, illus. 2008. (ENG.). 32p. (J). (gr. -1-1). 17.95 (978-0-8109-9490-4(9), Abrams Bks. for Young Readers) Abrams, Inc.

Lucado, Max. One Hand, Two Hands, 1 vol. 2010. (ENG.). 32p. (gr. -1-3). 14.99 (978-1-4003-1649-6(9)) Nelson, Thomas Inc.

—The Tallest of Smalls, 1 vol. Monescillo, Maria, illus. 2009. (ENG.). 32p. (gr. -1-2). 16.99 (978-1-4003-1514-7(X)) Nelson, Thomas Inc.

Lucas, Sally. Dancing Dinos at the Beach. Lucas, Margeaux, illus. 2010. (Step into Reading Ser.). (ENG.). 32p. (J). (gr. -1-1). pap. 3.99 (978-0-375-85640-2(4), Random Hse. Bks. for Young Readers) Random Hse. Children's Bks.

Lucas, Sally & Lucas, Margeaux. Dancing Dinos Go to School. 2006. (Step into Reading Ser.: Vol. 1). (ENG., Illus.). 32p. (J). (gr. -1-1). pap. 4.99 (978-0-375-83241-3(6), Random Hse. Bks. for Young Readers) Random Hse. Children's Bks.

Luebs, Robin. Please Pick Me up, Mama! Luebs, Robin, illus. 2009. (ENG., Illus.). 40p. (J). (gr. -1-k). 15.99 (978-1-4169-7977-7(8), Beach Lane Bks.) Beach Lane Bks.

Lumley, Jemima. The Journey Home from Grandpa's. Fatus, Sophie, illus. (ENG.). 24p. (J). 2012. (gr. -1-2). 16.99 (978-1-84686-898-6(X)) 2006. pap. 6.99 (978-1-84686-029-4(6)) 2006. (gr. -1-k). 9.99 (978-1-84686-026-3(1)) 2006. (gr. -1-3). 16.99 (978-1-905236-37-4(9)) Barefoot Bks., Inc.

—The Journey Home from Grandpa's. Fatus, Sophie, illus. 2010. (ENG.). 16p. (J). (gr. -1-3). pap. 5.99 (978-1-84686-277-9(9)) Barefoot Bks., Inc.

Lumley, Jemima & Penner, Fred. The Journey Home from Grandpa's. Fatus, Sophie, illus. 2011. (ENG.). 24p. (J). (gr. -1-2). 9.99 (978-1-84686-658-6(8)) Barefoot Bks., Inc.

Luna, James, et al. The Place Where You Live / el Lugar Donde Vives. Muraida, Thelma, illus. 2015. (SPA & ENG.). 32p. (J). (gr. k-3). 17.95 (978-1-55885-813-8(X)) Arte Publico Pr.

Lund, Deb. All Aboard the Dinotrain. Fine, Howard, illus. (ENG.). (J). (gr. -1 — 1). 2011. 30p. bds. 7.99 (978-0-547-55415-0(X)) 2009. 40p. pap. 7.99 (978-0-547-24825-7(3)) Houghton Mifflin Harcourt Publishing Co.

—Dinosailors. Fine, Howard, illus. 2008. (ENG.). 36p. (J). (gr. -1-3). pap. 6.99 (978-0-15-206124-1(X)) Houghton Mifflin Harcourt Publishing Co.

—Dinosoaring. Fine, Howard, illus. 2012. (ENG.). 40p. (J). (gr. -1-3). 16.99 (978-0-15-206016-9(2)) Houghton Mifflin Harcourt Publishing Co.

—Monsters on Machines. Neubecker, Robert, illus. 2017. (ENG.). 40p. (J). (gr. -1-3). pap. 6.99 (978-0-544-92783-4(4), HMH Books For Young Readers) Houghton Mifflin Harcourt Publishing Co.

—Monsters on Machines. Neubecker, Robert, illus. 2017. (ENG.). (J). (gr. -1-3). lib. bdg. 17.20 **(978-0-606-39815-2(5))** Turtleback Bks.

Lurie, Susan. Swim, Duck, Swim! Head, Murray, photos by. (ENG., Illus.). 32p. (J). 2016. bds. 7.99 (978-1-250-07740-0(0), 9781250077400) 2014. (gr. -1-2). 16.99 (978-1-250-04642-0(4), 9781250046420) Feiwel & Friends.

—Will You Be My Friend? Head, Murray, illus. 2016. (ENG.). 32p. (J). 16.99 (978-1-250-04643-7(2), 9781250046437) Feiwel & Friends.

Lutterbach, Johanna. Little Orly & the Cricket. Polchlopek, Mary Ann, illus. 2008. 24p. pap. 11.49 (978-1-4389-0656-0(0)) AuthorHouse.

Lyford, Joan. Daisybelle & Dash, a Bedtime Story. 2012. 24p. pap. 14.93 (978-1-4669-1154-3(9)) Trafford Publishing.

Lynch, Jane, et al. Marlene, Marlene, Queen of Mean. Tusa, Tricia, illus. 2014. (ENG.). 32p. (J). (gr. -1-2). lib. bdg. 19.99 (978-0-375-97329-1(X), Random Hse. Bks. for Young Readers) Random Hse. Children's Bks.

Lynne, Kimberlee, illus. The Frog & the Mouse. 2011. (First Steps in Music Ser.). (ENG.). 32p. (J). (gr. k-2). 16.95 (978-1-57999-802-8(X)) G I A Pubns., Inc.

Lyon, George Ella. Planes Fly! Wiggins, Mick, illus. 2013. (ENG.). 40p. (J). (gr. -1-2). 17.99 (978-1-4424-5025-7(8)) Simon & Schuster Children's Publishing.

—Sleepsong. Catalanotto, Peter, illus. 2008. (ENG.). 40p. (J). (gr. -1-k). 16.99 (978-0-689-86973-0(8), Atheneum/Richard Jackson Bks.) Simon & Schuster Children's Publishing.

—Trucks Roll! Frazier, Craig, illus. 2007. (ENG.). 40p. (J). (gr. -1-2). 18.99 (978-1-4169-2435-7(3), Atheneum/Richard Jackson Bks.) Simon & Schuster Children's Publishing.

Lyon, George Ella & Lyon, Benn. Boats Float! Wiggins, Mick, illus. 2015. (ENG.). 40p. (J). (gr. -1-3). 17.99 (978-1-4814-0380-1(X)) Simon & Schuster Children's Publishing.

Lyon, Tammie Speer, illus. Hickory Dickory Dock! gif. ed. 2006. 10p. (J). (gr. -1-k). bds. 10.95 (978-1-57791-213-2(6)) Brighter Minds Children's Publishing.

—Mary Had a Little Lamb. 2006. 8p. (J). bds. 10.95 (978-1-57791-210-1(1)) Brighter Minds Children's Publishing.

Lyons, P. J. God Is Watching over You, 1 vol. Warnes, Tim, illus. 2016. (ENG.). 16p. (J). bds. 9.99 (978-0-310-74881-6(X)) Zonderkidz.

—Thank You, Lord, for Everything, 1 vol. Warnes, Tim, illus. 2015. (ENG.). 16p. (J). bds. 9.99 (978-0-310-74812-0(7)) Zonderkidz.

Maccarone, Grace. Bunny Race! Long, Ethan, illus. 2009. (J). (978-0-545-11290-1(7)) Scholastic, Inc.

—Miss Lina's Ballerinas. Davenier, Christine, illus. 2010. (ENG.). 40p. (J). (gr. -1-1). 17.99 (978-0-312-38243-8(X), 9780312382438) Feiwel & Friends.

—Miss Lina's Ballerinas & the Wicked Wish. Davenier, Christine, illus. 2012. (ENG.). 40p. (J). (gr. k-1). 16.99 (978-1-250-00580-9(9), 9781250005809) Feiwel & Friends.

—Princess Tales: Once upon a Time in Rhyme with Seek-and-Find Pictures. de Marcken, Gail, illus. 2013. (ENG.). 32p. (J). (gr. -1-1). 16.99 (978-0-312-67958-3(0), 9780312679583) Feiwel & Friends.

—Princess Tales Around the World: Once upon a Time in Rhyme with Seek-And-Find Pictures. de Marcken, Gail, illus. 2017. (ENG.). 32p. (J). 16.99 (978-1-250-06103-4(2), 9781250061034) Feiwel & Friends.

—Six Super Easy-To-Read Stories. 2009. (Scholastic Reader Ser.). (Illus.). (J). pap. (978-0-439-85277-7(3)) Scholastic, Inc.

—Turkey Day. Manders, John, illus. 2010. (Scholastic Reader Level 1 Ser.). (ENG.). 32p. (J). (gr. -1-3). pap. 3.99 (978-0-545-12001-2(2), Cartwheel Bks.) Scholastic, Inc.

MacGregor, Helen & Chadwick, Stephen. Goldilocks & the Three Bears: An Impeccable Judged Musical, 1 vol. Lowe, Harriet et al, eds. Eccles, Jane, illus. 2005. (and C Black Musicals Ser.). (ENG.). 56p. (J). (gr. 2-6). pap. 42.95 **(978-0-7136-7085-1(1))** HarperCollins Pubs. Ltd. GBR. Dist: Independent Pubs. Group.

MacHale, D. J. The Monster Princess. Boiger, Alexandra, illus. 2010. (ENG.). 40p. (J). (gr. -1-1). 17.99 (978-1-4169-4809-4(0), Aladdin) Simon & Schuster Children's Publishing.

Macht, Heather. You May Just Be a Dinosaur, 1 vol. Gillard, Jason, illus. 2015. (ENG.). 32p. (J). (gr. k-3). 16.99 (978-1-4556-2040-1(8)) Pelican Publishing Co., Inc.

MacIver, Juliette. Yak & Gnu. Chapman, Cat, illus. 2015. (ENG.). 32p. (J). (gr. -1-2). 14.99 (978-0-7636-7561-5(X)) Candlewick Pr.

Mack, Harry. The Treasure Mystery Clues. 2011. 70p. pap. 19.95 (978-1-4626-2487-4(1)) America Star Bks.

Mack, Jeff. Hush Little Polar Bear. Mack, Jeff, illus. (ENG., Illus.). (J). (gr. -1-1). 2013. 36p. bds. 7.99 (978-1-59643-945-0(9), 9781596439450) 2008. 40p. 17.99 (978-1-59643-368-7(X), 9781596433687) Roaring Brook Pr.

—The Things I Can Do. Mack, Jeff, illus. 2013. (ENG., Illus.). 32p. (J). (gr. -1-1). 16.99 (978-1-59643-675-6(1), 9781596436756) Roaring Brook Pr.

Mackall, Dandi. The Super Gifts of Spring: Easter. 2015. (Seasons Ser.). (ENG., Illus.). 32p. (J). (gr. -1-3). 9.99 (978-1-4336-8233-9(8), B&H Kids) B&H Publishing Group.

—Wonderful Gifts of Winter. Blackmore, Katherine, illus. (Seasons Ser.). (ENG.). 32p. (gr. -1-3). 2017. (J). pap. 3.99 **(978-1-4627-4524-1(5))** 2014. 9.99 (978-1-4336-8239-1(7)) B&H Publishing Group. (B&H Kids).

Mackall, Dandi Daley. God Loves Me More Than That. 2008. (Dandilion Rhymes Ser.). (ENG., Illus.). 40p. (J). (gr. -1-2). 10.99 (978-1-4000-7316-0(2), WaterBrook Pr.) Crown Publishing Group.

—The Lost Lamb & the Good Shepherd. Manuzak, Lisa, illus. 2016. (Flipside Stories Ser.). (ENG.). 48p. (J). 14.99 (978-1-4964-1121-1(8)) Tyndale Hse. Pubs.

—No, No Noah!, 1 vol. Kucharik, Elena, illus. 2007. (ENG.). 26p. (gr. -1-k). bds. 6.99 (978-1-4003-1007-4(5)) Nelson, Thomas Inc.

—One Small Donkey, 1 vol. 2016. (ENG., Illus.). 32p. (J). 14.99 (978-0-7180-8747-0(X)) Nelson, Thomas Inc.

Macken, JoAnn Early. Baby Says Moo! Walker, David, illus. 2015. (ENG.). 30p. (J). (gr. -1 — 1). bds. 8.99 (978-1-4847-2098-1(9)) Hyperion Bks. for Children.

MacLachlan, Patricia. The Moon's Almost Here. dePaola, Tomie, illus. 2016. (ENG.). 32p. (J). (gr. -1-3). 17.99 (978-1-4814-2062-4(3), McElderry, Margaret K. Bks.) McElderry, Margaret K. Bks.

—The Poet's Dog. 2016. 96p. (J). (gr. 1-5). 14.99 (978-0-06-229262-9(5), Tegen, Katherine Bks) HarperCollins Pubs.

—Snowflakes Fall. Kellogg, Steven, illus. 2013. (ENG.). 32p. (J). (gr. -1-2). 17.99 (978-0-385-37693-8(6), Random Hse. Bks. for Young Readers) Random Hse. Children's Bks.

MacLennan, Cathy. Spooky Spooky Spooky! 2012. (ENG., Illus.). 26p. (J). (gr. k — 1). bds. 6.95 (978-1-907967-15-3(X)) Boxer Bks., Ltd. GBR. Dist: Sterling Publishing Co., Inc.

MacIver, Juliette. The Frog Who Lost His Underpants. Chapman, Cat, illus. 2014. (ENG.). 32p. (J). (gr. -1-1). 14.99 (978-0-7636-6782-5(X)) Candlewick Pr.

Macmillan, Sue. Bouncy, Pouncy Puppy. Ward, Sarah, illus. 2014. (Cheery Chasers Ser.). (ENG.). 8p. (J). (gr. -1 — 1). bds. 4.99 (978-0-7641-6698-3(0)) Barron's Educational Series, Inc.

—Happy, Hoppy Bunny. Ward, Sarah, illus. 2014. (Cheery Chasers Ser.). (ENG.). 8p. (J). (gr. -1 — 1). bds. 4.99 (978-0-7641-6699-0(9)) Barron's Educational Series, Inc.

—Racing, Chasing Kitten. Ward, Sarah, illus. 2014. (Cheery Chasers Ser.). (ENG.). 8p. (J). (gr. -1 — 1). bds. 4.99 (978-0-7641-6701-0(4)) Barron's Educational Series, Inc.

Macnaughton, Tina. One Snowy Rescue. 2015. (ENG.). pap. (978-0-545-92909-7(1)) Scholastic, Inc.

MacRae, Tom. When I Woke up I Was a Hippopotamus. Collins, Ross, illus. 2011. (Andersen Press Picture Books Ser.). (J). 16.95 (978-0-7613-8099-3(X)) Andersen Pr. GBR. Dist: Lerner Publishing Group.

Macveety, Sue Maney. Singing Sea/el Mar Que Canta. Zantay, Valerie, tr. 2005. (SPA., Illus.). 33p. per. 15.99 (978-1-4134-7275-2(3)) Xlibris Corp.

Madden, Colleen, illus. Happy Birthday to You! 2017. (ENG.). 26p. (J). (gr. -1-5). 12.95 (978-1-63322-243-4(8), Moondance) Quarto Publishing Group USA.

Madison, Paul. The Purple Monkey. 2012. (Illus.). 32p. pap. 17.25 (978-1-4669-3909-7(5)) Trafford Publishing.

Madison, Ron. Ned & the General: A Lesson about Deployment. Covolo, David, illus. 2004. 26p. (J). (gr. -1-3). (978-1-887206-25-9(6)) Ned's Head Productions.

Mae, Darcie. Sammy & Robert. 2008. 24p. pap. 24.95 (978-1-60474-811-6(7)) America Star Bks.

—Sammy & Robert's Animal Adventures. 2008. 32p. pap. 24.95 (978-1-60703-987-7(7)) America Star Bks.

Magliaro, Elaine. Things to Do. Chien, Catia, illus. 2017. (ENG.). 40p. (J). (gr. -1-k). 16.99 (978-1-4521-1124-7(3)) Chronicle Bks. LLC.

Magnayon, Megan Coy. PuzzlePal Books: Pretty Pig. Cohen, Melissa, illus. 2013. (PuzzlePal Bks.). (ENG.). 10p. (J). (gr. -1). bds. 14.95 (978-1-60710-698-2(1), Silver Dolphin Bks.) Readerlink Distribution Services, LLC.

Magnus, Kellie. Little Lion Goes to School. Robinson, Michael, illus. l.t. ed. 2003. 16p. (J). 9.99 (978-0-9744211-0-0(3)) Media Magic New York.

Magoo, Flossy. Upside down & Backwards. 2011. 24p. pap. 11.32 (978-1-4520-6789-6(9)) AuthorHouse.

Magsamen, Sandra. Baa, Moo, I Love You! A Book of Animal Sounds. 2014. (I Love Learning Ser.). (ENG., Illus.). 14p. (J). (gr. -1 — 1). bds. 7.99 (978-0-316-13358-6(2)) Little, Brown Bks. for Young Readers.

—Bedtime Bunny. 2009. (Board Books with Plush Toy Ser.). (ENG., Illus.). 20p. (J). (gr. -1 — 1). bds. 7.99 (978-0-316-00390-2(5)) Little, Brown Bks. for Young Readers.

—I Love Shapes! 2014. (I Love Learning Ser.). (ENG., Illus.). 14p. (J). (gr. -1 — 1). bds. 7.99 (978-0-316-13357-9(4)) Little, Brown Bks. for Young Readers.

—I Love You, Honey Bunny. Magsamen, Sandra, illus. 2016. (ENG., Illus.). 12p. (J). (— 1). bds. 7.99 (978-1-338-11084-5(5), Cartwheel Bks.) Scholastic, Inc.

—I Ruff You (Made with Love) Magsamen, Sandra, illus. 2016. (ENG., Illus.). 12p. (J). (gr. -1-k). bds. 7.99 (978-1-338-11082-1(9), Cartwheel Bks.) Scholastic, Inc.

—Love Bug. rev. ed. 2007. (Board Books with Plush Toys Ser.). (ENG., Illus.). 20p. (J). (gr. -1 — 1). 8.99 (978-0-316-06596-2(X)) Little, Brown Bks. for Young Readers.

—Twinkle, Twinkle, You're My Star. 2010. (ENG., Illus.). 10p. (J). (gr. -1 — 1). bds. 7.99 (978-0-316-04142-3(4)) Little, Brown Bks. for Young Readers.

Mahoney, Liana. Forest Green: A Walk Through the Adirondack Seasons. Henry, Maggie, illus. 2014. (J). (978-1-59531-047-7(9)) North Country Bks., Inc.

Mahy, Margaret. Bubble Trouble. Dunbar, Polly, illus. (ENG.). (J). (gr. -1-3). 2013. 40p. pap. 6.99 (978-0-547-99483-3(4)) 2011. 32p. bds. 7.99 (978-0-547-50725-5(9)) 2009. 40p. 16.00 (978-0-547-07421-4(2)) Houghton Mifflin Harcourt Publishing Co.

—The Man from the Land of Fandango. Dunbar, Polly, illus. 2012. (ENG.). 32p. (J). (gr. -1-3). 16.99 (978-0-547-81988-4(9)) Houghton Mifflin Harcourt Publishing Co.

Make Believe Ideas. Cuddle Buddies Cat. 2014. (ENG.). 8p. (J). 12.99 (978-1-78235-959-3(1)) Make Believe Ideas GBR. Dist: Nelson, Thomas Inc.

—Fairies Scratch & Sniff Camilla the Cupcake Fairy. 2014. (ENG.). 12p. (J). bds. 6.99 (978-1-78393-041-8(1)) Make Believe Ideas GBR. Dist: Nelson, Thomas Inc.

—Fairies Scratch & Sniff Lola the Lollipop Fairy. 2014. (ENG.). 12p. (J). bds. 6.99 (978-1-78393-040-1(3)) Make Believe Ideas GBR. Dist: Nelson, Thomas Inc.

—Incy Wincy Spider. 2015. (ENG.). 12p. (J). bds. 8.99 (978-1-78393-533-8(2)) Make Believe Ideas GBR. Dist: Nelson, Thomas Inc.

—Little Red Riding Hood. 2015. (ENG.). 24p. (J). bds. 7.99 (978-1-78393-536-9(7)) Make Believe Ideas GBR. Dist: Nelson, Thomas Inc.

—Molly the Muffin Fairy. 2015. (ENG.). 32p. (J). pap. 6.99 (978-1-78393-441-6(7)) Make Believe Ideas GBR. Dist: Nelson, Thomas Inc.

Make Believe Ideas, creator. Twinkle Book & Mouse Plush. 2007. (Illus.). (J). (gr. -1-3). (978-1-84610-694-1(X)) Make Believe Ideas.

Mamakas, Stavroula & Lagoutaris, Maria Mamakas. Mama Lagoo: Bath Time Battle. 2011. 28p. pap. 14.95 (978-1-4634-1524-2(9)) AuthorHouse.

Mamma Macs. Australian Animal Walkabout. 2013. 32p. pap. (978-0-9923379-0-2(9)) Serenity Press.

—Mick Mac Adoo's Australian Zoo. 2013. 30p. pap. (978-0-9923379-9-5(2)) Serenity Press.

Manalang, Dan. Ambrosia. Wong, Nichole, illus. 2006. (ENG.). 32p. (J). (gr. k-2). 14.99 (978-0-9769342-0-2(5)) Flip Publishing.

Mandel, Peter. Bun, Onion, Burger. Eliopoulos, Chris, illus. 2010. (ENG.). 40p. (J). (gr. -1-1). 12.99 (978-1-4169-2466-1(3), Simon & Schuster Bks. For Young Readers) Simon & Schuster Bks. For Young Readers.

—Jackhammer Sam. Catrow, David, illus. 2011. (ENG.). 40p. (J). (gr. -1-2). 16.99 (978-1-59643-034-1(6), 9781596430341) Roaring Brook Pr.

Mankita, Jay. Elar. 2013. (Illus.). 38p. (J). pap. 9.95 (978-1-935734-49-9(0)) Kitanie Bks.

Manlove, FionaCarding. The Cat Sat on the Mat. Carding, Hannah, illus. 2011. (ENG.). 32p. (J). (gr. -1-k). pap. 9.99 **(978-1-85714-373-7(6))** Ragged Bears USA.

Manolessou, Katherina. Mummy & Me. 2017. (ENG., Illus.). 24p. (J). (— 1). bds. 10.99 **(978-1-4472-8877-0(7))** Pan Macmillan GBR. Dist: Independent Pubs. Group.

Manolessou, Katherina. Zoom Zoom Zoom. (ENG., Illus.). (J). (gr. -1-k). 2016. 30p. bds. 10.99 (978-1-4472-8871-8(8)) 2014. 32p. 19.99 (978-0-230-76378-4(2)) Pan Macmillan GBR. Dist: Independent Pubs. Group.

Mansbach, Adam. Seriously, Just Go to Sleep. Cortés, Ricardo, illus. 2012. (ENG.). 36p. (gr. k-5). 15.95 (978-1-61775-078-6(6)) Akashic Bks.

Mansfield, Andy. Journey to the Moon. 2015. (ENG., Illus.). 14p. (J). (gr. -1-2). 12.99 (978-1-4998-0072-2(X)) Little Bee Books Inc.

Manushkin, Fran. The Tushy Book. Dockray, Tracy, illus. (ENG.). (J). (gr. -1-k). 2011. 20p. bds. 6.99 (978-0-312-65913-4(X), 9780312659134) 2009. 32p. 14.99 (978-0-312-36926-2(3), 9780312369262) Feiwel & Friends.

Manwiller, S. A. The Adventures of Jack & Max the Truliest Meaning of Christmas. Manwiller, S. A. & Overly, Kristen V., illus. 2013. (ACH & ENG.). 38p. 24.99 (978-0-9838427-7-4(9)) SevenHorns Publishing.

Marchese, Stephen, illus. The Flights of Marceau: Week Two. 2007. (ENG.). 60p. (J). 16.95 (978-0-9797495-1-3(4)) Majestic Eagle Publishing.

Marchus, Linda. The Gorilla Who Wanted to Dance. Marchus, Linda, illus. 2003. (Illus.). 32p. (J). lib. bdg. 15.95 (978-0-9723122-1-9(8)) Wee Read Publishing.

Marciano, John Bemelmans. Madeline & Her Dog. 2011. (Madeline Ser.). (ENG.). 32p. (J). (gr. 1-2). pap. 3.99 (978-0-448-45438-2(6), Penguin Young Readers) Penguin Young Readers Group.

—Madeline & the Cats of Rome. 2008. (Madeline Ser.). (ENG.). 48p. (J). (gr. 1-3). 17.99 (978-0-670-06297-3(9), Viking Books for Young Readers) Penguin Young Readers Group.

—Madeline & the Old House in Paris. 2013. (Madeline Ser.). (ENG.). 48p. (J). (gr. -1-2). 17.99 (978-0-670-78485-1(0), Viking Books for Young Readers) Penguin Young Readers Group.

—Madeline at the White House. (Madeline Ser.). (ENG., (J). (gr. -1-2). 2016. Illus.). 48p. 8.99 (978-1-101-99780-2(X), Puffin Books) 2011. 45p. 17.99 (978-0-670-01228-2(9), Viking Books for Young Readers) Penguin Young Readers Group.

—Madeline at the White House. 2016. (Madeline Ser.). lib. bdg. 19.65 (978-0-606-38845-0(1)) Turtleback Bks.

—Madeline's Tea Party. 2012. (Madeline Ser.). (ENG.). 32p. (J). (gr. 1-2). pap. 3.99 (978-0-448-45439-9(4), Penguin Young Readers) Penguin Young Readers Group.

Marcus, Kimberly. Exposed. 2012. (ENG.). 272p. (YA). (gr. 9). pap. 8.99 (978-0-375-86591-6(8), Ember) Random Hse. Children's Bks.

Mariconda, Barbara. ¡Clasifícalo! Rogers, Sherry, illus. 2008.Tr. of Sort it Out! (SPA.). 32p. (J). (gr. k-4). 17.95 (978-1-60718-695-3(0)) Arbordale Publishing.

—Sort It Out!, 1 vol. Rogers, Sherry, illus. 2008. (ENG.). 32p. (J). (gr. k-4). 16.95 (978-1-934359-11-2(4)); pap. 8.95 (978-1-934359-32-7(7)) Arbordale Publishing.

Marinaro, Stacy. Carter the Acorn Collecting Cutie. 2008. 20p. pap. 10.50 (978-0-615-20807-7(X)) Marinaro, Stacy.

Markell, Denis. Hush, Little Monster. Iwai, Melissa, illus. 2012. (ENG.). 32p. (J). (gr. -1-1). 9.99 (978-1-4424-4195-8(X), Little Simon) Little Simon.

Markes, Julie. Shhhhh! Everybody's Sleeping. Parkins, David, illus. 32p. (J). (gr. -1-1). 2005. lib. bdg. 16.89 (978-0-06-053791-3(4)) 2004. (ENG.). 16.99 (978-0-06-053790-6(6)) HarperCollins Pubs.

—Thanks for Thanksgiving. Barrette, Doris, illus. (ENG.). 32p. (J). (gr. -1-3). 2008. pap. 6.99 (978-0-06-051098-5(6)) 2004. 12.99 (978-0-06-051096-1(X)) HarperCollins Pubs.

Markes, Julie. Thanks for Thanksgiving Board Book. Barrette, Doris, illus. 2017. 32p. (J). (gr. -1 — 1). bds. 7.99 **(978-0-06-264331-5(2)**, HarperFestival) HarperCollins Pubs.

Markey, Neil. Woof! Spremulli, Pam, illus. 2011. (ENG.). 34p. (J). (gr. k-k). 14.00 (978-1-935557-77-7(7)) Purple Bear Bks., Inc.

Marks, Darrell. Down on the Farm. 2013. 12p. pap. 15.99 (978-1-4817-0969-9(0)) AuthorHouse.

Marks, Nancy Freeman. Just As You Are: The Story of Leon & Sam. Buchheim, Su Jen, illus. 2003. 32p. (J). 15.00 (978-0-9722430-1-8(1)) Wave Publishing.

Markun, Alan F. New Revolution. (J). 8.95 (978-0-8022-1062-3(7)) Philosophical Library, Inc.

Marquis, Michelle. Mikey & the Mysterious Door. 2008. 32p. pap. 14.99 (978-1-4343-4823-4(7)) AuthorHouse.

Marsaw, Roy. Swim, Swam, Swum. Harris, Phyllis, illus. 2007. 32p. (J). pap. 14.95 (978-0-9744446-8-0(5)) All About Kids Publishing.

Marshall, Judy. Morning. Annelli, Nikki, illus. l.t. ed. 2005. 21p. (J). per. 9.99 (978-1-59879-050-4(1)) Lifevest Publishing, Inc.

Marshall, Linda Elovitz. Kindergarten Is Cool! Chatterton, Chris, illus. 2016. (ENG.). 32p. (J). (gr. -1-1). 8.99 (978-0-545-65266-7(9), Cartwheel Bks.) Scholastic, Inc.

—Shh... Shh... Shabbat. Golubeva, Evgenia, illus. 2016. (ENG.). 12p. (gr. -1 — 1). 5.99 (978-1-4677-5873-4(6)); 23.99 (978-1-4677-9615-6(8)) Lerner Publishing Group. (Kar-Ben Publishing).

Marshall, Natalie. Five Little Ducks. 2017. (Fingers & Toes Nursery Rhymes Ser.). (ENG.). 12p. (J). (— 1). bds. 6.99 (978-1-338-09116-8(6), Cartwheel Bks.) Scholastic, Inc.

Marshall, Natalie. Five Little Pumpkins. 2017. (Fingers & Toes Nursery Rhymes Ser.). (ENG.). 12p. (J). (gr. -1 — 1). bds. 6.99 **(978-1-338-09117-5(4)**, Cartwheel Bks.) Scholastic, Inc.

Martin, Bill, Jr. Baby Bear, Baby Bear, What Do You See? Carle, Eric, illus. (My First Reader Ser.). (ENG.). (J). (gr. -1-2). 2011. 40p. 8.99 (978-0-8050-9291-2(9), 9780805092912) 2009. 28p. bds. 7.99 (978-0-8050-8990-5(X), 9780805089905) 2007. 32p. 17.99 (978-0-8050-8336-1(7), 9780805083361) Holt, Henry & Co. (Holt, Henry & Co. Bks. For Young Readers).

—Baby Bear, Baby Bear, What Do You See? 10th Anniversary Edition with Audio CD. Carle, Eric, illus. 2016. (Brown Bear & Friends Ser.). (ENG.). 32p. (J). 19.99 (978-1-62779-731-3(9), 9781627797313, Holt, Henry & Co. Bks. For Young Readers) Holt, Henry & Co.

—Baby Bear, Baby Bear, What Do You See? Big Book. Carle, Eric, illus. 2011. (Brown Bear & Friends Ser.). (ENG.). 32p. (J). (gr. -1-k). pap. 27.99 (978-0-8050-9345-2(1), 9780805093452, Holt, Henry & Co. Bks. For Young Readers) Holt, Henry & Co.

—Brown Bear, Brown Bear, What Do You See? Carle, Eric, illus. (Brown Bear & Friends Ser.). (J). 2012. (ENG.). 28p. (gr. -1-k). bds. 12.99 (978-0-8050-9577-7(2), 9780805095777) 2010. (ENG.). 40p. (gr. -1-2). 8.99 (978-0-8050-9244-8(7), 9780805092448) 2007. 32p. pap. 7.95 (978-0-8050-8797-0(4)) 3rd anniv. ed. 2008. (ENG.). 32p. (gr. -1-k). pap. 27.95 (978-0-8050-8718-5(4), 9780805087185) 50th anniv. ed. 2016. (ENG.). 28p. bds. 9.99 (978-1-62779-722-1(X), 9781627797221) Holt, Henry & Co. (Holt, Henry & Co. Bks. For Young Readers).

—Oso Panda, Oso Panda, ¿Qué Ves Ahí? Mlawer, Teresa, tr. Carle, Eric, illus. 2008. (Brown Bear & Friends Ser.).Tr. of Brown Bear, Brown Bear, What Do You See? (SPA & ENG.). 32p. (J). (gr. -1-k). 17.95 (978-0-8050-8348-4(0), 9780805083484, Holt, Henry & Co. Bks. For Young Readers) Holt, Henry & Co.

—Oso Panda, Oso Panda, ¿Qué Ves Ahí? Mlawer, Teresa, tr. Carle, Eric, illus. 2009. (Brown Bear & Friends Ser.).Tr. of Brown Bear, Brown Bear, What Do You See? (SPA & ENG.). 26p. (J). (gr. -1-k). 9.99 (978-0-8050-8756-7(7), 9780805087567, Holt, Henry & Co. Bks. For Young Readers) Holt, Henry & Co.

—Panda Bear, Panda Bear, What Do You See? Carle, Eric, illus. (Brown Bear & Friends Ser.). (J). 2014. (ENG.). 28p. (gr. -1-k). bds. 12.99 (978-0-8050-9950-8(6), 9780805099508) 2011. (ENG.). 40p. (gr. -1-2). 8.99 (978-0-8050-9292-9(7), 9780805092929) 2007. 32p. 7.95 (978-0-8050-8799-4(0)) 2007. (ENG.). 32p. (gr. -1-k). pap. 27.99 (978-0-8050-8102-2(X), 9780805081022) 2006. (ENG.). 28p. (gr. -1-k). bds. 7.95 (978-0-8050-8078-0(3), 9780805080780) Holt, Henry & Co. (Holt, Henry & Co. Bks. For Young Readers).

—Panda Bear, Panda Bear, What Do You See?, 1 vol. Carle, Eric, illus. unabr. ed. 2011. (Brown Bear & Friends Ser.). (ENG.). (J). (gr. -1-k). 9.99 (978-1-4272-1254-2(6), 9781427212542) Macmillan Audio.

—Panda Bear, Panda Bear, What Do You See? Carle, Eric, illus. 2013. (Slide & Find Ser.). (ENG.). 22p. (J). (gr. -1 — 1). bds. 12.99 (978-0-312-51581-2(2), 9780312515812, Priddy Bks.) St. Martin's Pr.

—Panda Bear, Panda Bear, What Do You See? 10th Anniversary Edition. Carle, Eric, illus. 2013. (ENG.). 28p. (J). (gr. -1-k). 19.99 (978-0-8050-9778-8(3), 9780805097788, Holt, Henry & Co. Bks. For Young Readers) Holt, Henry & Co.

—Polar Bear, Polar Bear, What Do You Hear? Carle, Eric, illus. (Brown Bear & Friends Ser.). (J). 2012. (ENG.). 28p. (gr. -1-k). bds. 12.99 (978-0-8050-9095-6(9), 9780805090956) 2010. (ENG.). 40p. (gr. -1-2). 8.99 (978-0-8050-9245-5(5), 9780805092455) 2007. 32p. 7.95 (978-0-8050-8798-7(2)) 20th anniv. ed. 2011. (ENG.). 32p. (gr. -1-k). 19.99 (978-0-8050-9066-6(5), 9780805090666) Holt, Henry & Co. (Holt, Henry & Co. Bks. For Young Readers).

—Ten Little Caterpillars. Ehlert, Lois, illus. 2011. (ENG.). 40p. (J). (gr. -1-3). 17.99 (978-1-4424-3385-4(X), Beach Lane Bks.) Beach Lane Bks.

—The Turning of the Year. Shed, Greg, illus. 2007. (ENG.). 28p. (J). (gr. -1-3). pap. 6.99 (978-0-15-204555-5(4)) Houghton Mifflin Harcourt Publishing Co.

Martin, Bill, Jr. & Archambault, John. Chica Chica Bum Bum ABC. Ehlert, Lois, illus. 2011. (SPA.). 16p. (J). (gr. -1-1). bds. 7.99 (978-1-4424-2292-6(0), Libros Para Ninos) Libros Para Ninos.

—Chicka Chicka Boom Boom. Ehlert, Lois, illus. anniv. ed. 2009. (Chicka Chicka Book Ser.). (ENG.). 40p. (J). (gr. -1-3). 17.99 (978-1-4169-9091-8(7), Beach Lane Bks.) Beach Lane Bks.

—Chicka Chicka Boom Boom. Ehlert, Lois, illus. (Classic Board Bks.). (ENG.). (J). (gr. -1 — 1). 2012. 36p. bds. 7.99 (978-1-4424-5070-7(3)) 2010. 36p. bds. 12.99 (978-1-4169-9999-7(X)) 2006. 40p. 10.99 (978-1-4169-2718-1(2)) Little Simon. (Little Simon).

Martin, Bill, Jr. & Priddy, Roger. Polar Bear, Polar Bear, What Do You Hear? Carle, Eric, illus. 2011. (ENG.). 14p. (J). (gr. -1-k). bds. 14.95 (978-0-312-51346-7(1), 9780312513467, Priddy Bks.) St. Martin's Pr.

Martin, Bill, Jr. & Sampson, Michael. Chicka Chicka 1, 2, 3. Ehlert, Lois, illus. 2014. (Chicka Chicka Book Ser.). (ENG.). 36p. (J). (gr. -1 — 1). bds. 7.99 (978-1-4814-0056-5(8), Little Simon) Little Simon.

—Chicka Chicka 1, 2, 3. Ehlert, Lois, illus. 2004. (Chicka Chicka Book Ser.). (ENG.). 40p. (J). (gr. -1-2). 17.99 (978-0-689-85881-9(7), Simon & Schuster Bks. For Young Readers) Simon & Schuster Bks. For Young Readers.

—Chicka Chicka 1, 2, 3. Ehlert, Lois, illus. 2005. (J). (gr. -1-3). 29.95 (978-0-439-76677-7(X), WHCD669) Weston Woods Studios, Inc.

—Chicka Chicka 1, 2, 3: Lap Edition. Ehlert, Lois, illus. 2013. (Chicka Chicka Book Ser.). (ENG.). 36p. (J). (gr. -1-1). bds. 12.99 (978-1-4424-6613-5(8), Little Simon) Little Simon.

—Kitty Cat, Kitty Cat, Are You Going to Sleep?, 0 vols. Bryant, Laura J., illus. 2011. (ENG.). 24p. (J). (gr. -1-3). 15.99 (978-0-7614-5946-0(4), 9780761459460, Amazon Children's Publishing) Amazon Publishing.

—Kitty Cat, Kitty Cat, Are You Waking Up?, 0 vols. Bryant, Laura J., illus. 2011. (ENG.). 26p. (J). (gr. -1-1). pap. 6.99 (978-0-7614-5841-8(7), 9780761458418, Amazon Children's Publishing) Amazon Publishing.

Martin, Bill & Sampson, Michael R. Spunky Little Monkey. Won, Brian, illus. 2017. (ENG.). 32p. (J). (gr. -1-k). 17.99 (978-0-545-77643-1(0), Scholastic Pr.) Scholastic, Inc.

Martin, Bill, Jr., et al. Chicka Chicka Boom Boom. Ehlert, Lois, illus. 2008. (J). 13.99 (978-1-59319-935-7(X)) LeapFrog Enterprises, Inc.

—Chicka Chicka Box Box! Chicka Chicka Boom Boom; Chicka Chicka 1, 2, 3. Ehlert, Lois, illus. 2013. (Chicka Chicka Book Ser.). (ENG.). 80p. (J). (gr. -1-3). 35.99 (978-1-4814-0223-1(4), Beach Lane Bks.) Beach Lane Bks.

Martin, David. Peep & Ducky. Walker, David, illus. (ENG.). (J). (— 1). 2015. 24p. bds. 6.99 (978-0-7636-7243-0(2)) 2013. 32p. 14.99 (978-0-7636-5039-1(0)) Candlewick Pr.

—Peep & Ducky Rainy Day. Walker, David, illus. 2015. (ENG.). 32p. (J). (— 1). 14.99 (978-0-7636-6884-6(2)) Candlewick Pr.

—Shh! Bears Sleeping. Johnson, Steve & Fancher, Lou, illus. 2016. (ENG.). 32p. (J). (gr. -1-2). 16.99 (978-0-670-01718-8(3), Viking Books for Young Readers) Penguin Young Readers Group.

Martin-Duttmann, Robin. Zoo on the Moon. 2013. 24p. pap. 12.97 (978-1-62212-735-1(8), Strategic Bk. Publishing) Strategic Book Publishing & Rights Agency (SBPRA).

Martin, Emily Winfield. Day Dreamers: A Journey of Imagination. (ENG., Illus.). 32p. (J). 2016. (— 1). bds. 8.99 (978-1-101-93522-4(7)) 2014. (gr. -1-2). 17.99 (978-0-385-37670-9(7)) 2014. (gr. -1-2). lib. bdg. 20.99 (978-0-375-97326-0(5)) Random Hse. Children's Bks. (Random Hse. Bks. for Young Readers).

—Dream Animals: A Bedtime Journey. 2013. (ENG., Illus.). 32p. (J). (gr. -1-k). 17.99 (978-0-449-81080-4(1)); lib. bdg. 20.99 (978-0-375-97149-5(1)) Random Hse. Children's Bks. (Random Hse. Bks. for Young Readers).

—The Wonderful Things You Will Be. Martin, Emily Winfield, illus. 2015. (ENG., Illus.). 36p. (J). (gr. -1-2). 17.99 (978-0-385-37671-6(5), Random Hse. Bks. for Young Readers) Random Hse. Children's Bks.

—The Wonderful Things You Will Be. 2015. (ENG., Illus.). 36p. (J). (gr. -1-2). lib. bdg. 20.99 (978-0-375-97327-7(3), Random Hse. Bks. for Young Readers) Random Hse. Children's Bks.

Martin, John, et al. Aesop's Fables in Rhyme for Little Philosophers. 2014. (ENG., Illus.). 96p. (J). (gr. 1-5). pap. 12.99 (978-0-486-78180-8(1)) Dover Pubns., Inc.

Martin, Mike. 365 Stories & Rhymes for Girls. (365 Stories Treasuries Ser.). 384p. (J). 9.98 (978-1-4054-1959-8(8)) Parragon, Inc.

Martin, Steve & Chast, Roz. The Alphabet from A to Y with Bonus Letter Z! 2007. (ENG., Illus.). 64p. (J). (gr. k-k). 17.95 (978-0-385-51662-4(2), Flying Dolphin Pr.) Knopf Doubleday Publishing Group.

Marzollo, Jean. I Spy Animals. 2012. (I Spy — Scholastic Ser.). lib. bdg. 13.55 (978-0-606-23968-4(5), Turtleback) Turtleback Bks.

—I Spy Little Toys. Wick, Walter, illus. Wick, Walter, photos by. 2011. (I Spy Ser.). (ENG.). 26p. (J). (gr. -1-k). bds. 6.99 (978-0-545-22096-5(3)) Scholastic, Inc.

—Shanna's Lost Shoe. 2004. (ENG., Illus.). 24p. (gr. -1-1). pap. 3.99 (978-0-7868-1832-7(8), Jump at the Sun) Hyperion Bks. for Children.

Masessa, Ed. Scarecrow Magic. Myers, Matt, illus. 2015. (ENG.). 32p. (J). (gr. -1-k). 16.99 (978-0-545-69109-3(5)) Scholastic, Inc.

Maslyn, Stacie K. B. & Maslyn, Stacie K. Mad Maddie Maxwell, 1 vol. Schettle, Jane, illus. 2007. (I Can Read! Ser.). (ENG.). 32p. (J). (gr. -1-1). pap. 3.99 (978-0-310-71467-5(2)) Zonderkidz.

Mason, Margaret. Inside All, 1 vol. Welch, Holly, illus. 2008. (ENG.). 32p. (J). (gr. -1-2). 16.95 (978-1-58469-111-2(5)); pap. 8.95 (978-1-58469-112-9(3)) Dawn Pubns.

Massie, Felix. Terry Perkins & His Upside down Frown. 2018. (ENG., Illus.). 32p. (J). 17.99 (978-1-84780-620-8(1), Frances Lincoln Children's Bks.) Quarto Publishing Group UK GBR. Dist: Littlehampton Bk Services, Ltd.

Massie, Rosemary. Rhymen the Rabbit: Meeting the Forest Ranger, 2011. 28p. pap. 13.95 (978-1-4634-2572-2(4)) AuthorHouse.

—Rhymen the Rabbit: Save the Forest. 2011. 28p. pap. 13.95 (978-1-4634-1597-6(4)) AuthorHouse.

Massini, Sarah, illus. Love Always Everywhere. 2014. (ENG.). 32p. (J). (gr. -1-2). 16.99 (978-0-385-37552-8(2), Random Hse. Bks. for Young Readers) Random Hse. Children's Bks.

—Love Always Everywhere. 2014. (J). (978-0-385-37553-5(0)) Random Hse., Inc.

Mathes, Charles. In Every Moon There Is a Face. Graston, Arlene, illus. 2003. 32p. 15.95 (978-0-9701907-4-1(3)) Illumination Arts Publishing Co., Inc.

Matheson, Christie. Tap the Magic Tree. Matheson, Christie, illus. 2013. (ENG., Illus.). 40p. (J). (gr. -1-3). 16.99 (978-0-06-227445-8(7), Greenwillow Bks.) HarperCollins Pubs.

Matthies, Janna. Two Is Enough. Liddiard, Merrilee & Mourning, Tuesday, illus. 2015. (ENG.). 40p. (J). (gr. -1-17). 15.95 (978-0-7624-5561-4(6), Running Pr. Kids) Running Pr. Bk. Pubs.

Mau, Connie. Catch me if you Can. Lemus, Kristina, illus. l.t. ed. 2006. 28p. (J). 14.95 (978-0-9778843-0-8(9)) Mau, C. Publishing Co.

Maurer, Amy J. A Purple Hippopotamus Pillow & Pink Penguin Sheets. Smith, Rachel, illus. 2006. 52p. (J). 19.99 (978-1-59879-239-3(3)); per. 15.99 (978-1-59879-167-9(2)) Lifevest Publishing, Inc.

Maurer, Ashley, illus. Jennie Jenkins. 2015. (First Steps in Music Ser.). (ENG.). 32p. (J). (— 1). 16.95 (978-1-62277-139-4(7)) G I A Pubns., Inc.

Mauzy, Barbara. Don't Be a Schwoe: Embracing Differences, 1 vol. 2011. (ENG., Illus.). 80p. (J). 16.99 (978-0-7643-3566-2(9), 9780764335662) Schiffer Publishing, Ltd.

Maxwell, John C. Sometimes You Win — Sometimes You Learn for Kids. Björkman, Steve, illus. 2016. (ENG.). 32p. (J). (gr. -1-3). 18.00 (978-0-316-28408-0(4)) Little Brown & Co.

May, Robert L. Rudolph Shines Again. Caparo, Antonio Javier, illus. 2015. (ENG.). 40p. (J). (gr. -1-1). 17.99 (978-1-4424-7498-7(X), Little Simon) Little Simon.

Mayfield, Dan. Jasper & the Magpie: Enjoying Special Interests Together. Merry, Alex, illus. 2014. (ENG.). 36p. (J). 15.95 (978-1-84905-579-6(3), 6080) Kingsley, Jessica Pubs. GBR. Dist: Macmillan Distribution Ltd.

Mayhew, James. Starlight Sailor. Morris, Jackie, illus. (ENG.). 24p. (J). 2013. (gr. -1-1). 14.99 (978-1-84686-936-5(6)) 2012. pap. 6.99 (978-1-84686-750-7(9)) 2009. (gr. -1-3). 16.99 (978-1-84686-185-7(3)) Barefoot Bks., Inc.

Mayo, Margaret. Emergency! Ayliffe, Alex, illus. 2003. 32p. (J). (gr. -1-1). 14.95 (978-0-87614-922-5(0), Carolrhoda Bks.) Lerner Publishing Group.

McAllen, Bob. Dirtiest Hair in the World. McClure, Tom, illus. 2008. (ENG.). 44p. (J). (gr. k-3). lib. bdg. 17.99 (978-1-934277-24-9(X)) Mam Green Publishing, Inc.

McBride, Martha J. Avery Finds Five Dollars. l.t. ed. 2004. 36p. (J). per. 19.99 (978-1-59196-434-6(2)) Instant Pub.

McCabe, Lauren A. How Many Spots Have I Got? Foulke, Nancy, illus. 2005. (J). 16.00 (978-1-893516-02-1(4)) Our Child Pr.

McCanna, Tim. Barnyard Boogie! Black, Allison, illus. 2017. (ENG.). 24p. (gr. -1-k). 12.95 (978-1-4197-2346-9(4), Abrams Appleseed) Abrams, Inc.

—Bitty Bot. Carpenter, Tad, illus. 2016. (Bitty Bot Ser.). (ENG.). 32p. (J). (gr. -1-3). 16.99 (978-1-4814-4929-8(X), Simon & Schuster Bks. For Young Readers) Simon & Schuster Bks. For Young Readers.

—Water Song. Smythe, Richard, illus. 2017. (ENG.). 32p. (J). (gr. -1-3). 17.99 (978-1-4814-6881-7(2), Simon & Schuster/Paula Wiseman Bks.) Simon & Schuster/Paula Wiseman Bks.

McCardell, Ken. BibleRhymes' Christmas Story, bk. 3. Chirco, Antonella, illus. ed. 2008. (BibleRhymes Ser.: 3). 28p. (J). 17.95 (978-0-9790605-2-6(4), BibleRhymes) BibleRhymes Publishing, L.L.C.

—BibleRhymes' Creation. Chirco, Antonella, illus. 2007. (BibleRhymes Ser.). 32p. (J). 17.95 (978-0-9790605-0-2(8), BibleRhymes) BibleRhymes Publishing, L.L.C.

—BibleRhymes' Noah & the Ark, bk. 2. Chirco, Antonella, illus. 2007. (BibleRhymes Ser.: 2). 28p. (J). 17.95 (978-0-9790605-1-9(6), BibleRhymes) BibleRhymes Publishing, L.L.C.

McCarthy, Michael. The Story of Daniel in the Lions' Den. Ferri, Giuliano, illus. 2003. 32p. (J). (gr. 1-3). 16.99 (978-1-84148-209-5(9)) Barefoot Bks., Inc.

McCarty, Bryan. Devyn's Gold. 2008. pap. 17.00 (978-0-8059-8640-2(5)) Dorrance Publishing Co., Inc.

McClure, Brian D. The Ants. Plumlee, Buddy, illus. 2009. (Brian D. Mcclure Childrens Book Collection). 57p. (J). (gr. -1-3). 16.95 (978-1-933426-10-5(1)) Universal Flag Publishing.

—The Birds & the Frogs. Plumlee, Buddy, illus. 2009. (Brian D. Mcclure Childrens Book Collection). 37p. (J). (gr. -1-3). 16.95 (978-1-933426-13-6(6)) Universal Flag Publishing.

—The Up down Day. Plumlee, Buddy, illus. 2009. (Brian D. Mcclure Childrens Book Collection). 47p. (J). (gr. -1-3). 14.95 (978-1-933426-07-5(1)) Universal Flag Publishing.

—Who Am I? 2006. (Illus.). 52p. (J). 12.95 (978-1-933426-03-7(9)) Universal Flag Publishing.

McConduit, Alexander Brian. Snoballs for All, 1 vol. Ganucheau, Paulina, illus. 2015. (ENG.). 32p. (J). (gr. k-3). pap. 8.99 (978-1-4556-2002-9(5)) Pelican Publishing Co., Inc.

McCormick, Patricia. Sold. 2008. 263p. (J). (gr. 7-12). 19.65 (978-1-4178-1810-5(7), Turtleback) Turtleback Bks.

McCowan, Linda. Cancer Rhymes with Dancer. 2007. (Illus.). 24p. (J). (gr. -1-3). pap. 12.95 (978-0-9814596-0-8(9)) McCowan, Linda.

McCue, Lisa. HideAway Hedgehog & the Magical Rainbow. 2015. (HideAway Pets Bks.). (ENG., Illus.). 26p. (J). (gr. -1-2). 9.95 (978-1-4549-1602-4(8)) Sterling Publishing Co., Inc.

—My First Mother Goose. 2009. (Carry along Bks.). (ENG., Illus.). 20p. (J). (gr. -1-k). bds. 14.99 (978-0-7944-1931-8(3), Reader's Digest Children's Bks.) Studio Fun International.

McCue, Lisa, illus. Time for Bed! A Cozy Counting Bedtime Book. 2015. (ENG.). 20p. (J). (gr. -1 — 1). bds. 12.99 (978-0-7944-3337-6(5)) Reader's Digest Assn., Inc., The.

McCully, Emily Arnold. Late Nate in a Race. McCully, Emily Arnold, illus. 2013. (I Like to Read(r) Ser.). (ENG., Illus.). 24p. (J). (gr. -1-3). pap. 6.99 (978-0-8234-2755-0(2)) Holiday Hse., Inc.

McDaniel Rockstad, Jean. Eric Jay, Eric Jay, What Are You Gonna Do All Day? 2011. (Illus.). 24p. 16.95 (978-1-60844-941-5(6)) Dog Ear Publishing, LLC.

McDermid, Val. My Granny Is a Pirate. Robins, Arthur, illus. 2012. (ENG.). 32p. (J). (gr. -1-k). pap. 9.99 (978-1-4083-0927-8(0)) Hodder & Stoughton GBR. Dist: Hachette Bk. Group.

McDermott, Tom. Otis Steele & the Taileebone: A Southern Tall Tale, 1 vol. Crosby, Jeff, illus. 2013. (ENG.). 32p. (J). (gr. k-2). 16.99 (978-1-4556-1736-4(9)) Pelican Publishing Co., Inc.

McDonald, Jill. Over in the Meadow. McDonald, Jill & Reed, Susan, illus. 2011. (ENG.). 24p. (J). (gr. 1-4). 16.99 (978-1-84686-543-5(3)) Barefoot Bks., Inc.

McDonald, Lisa. The Adventures of Penelope the Tea Cup Pig. 2012. 36p. pap. 32.70 (978-1-4771-3182-4(5)) Xlibris Corp.

McDonald, Rae A. A Fishing Surprise. Kemly, Kathleen, illus. 2007. (ENG.). 32p. (J). (gr. -1-3). 16.95 (978-1-55971-977-3(X)) Cooper Square Publishing Llc.

McDonnell, Patrick. Art. 2006. (ENG., Illus.). 48p. (J). (gr. -1-3). 17.99 (978-0-316-11491-2(X)) Little, Brown Bks. for Young Readers.

—Art. 2011. (J). (gr. -1-3). 29.95 (978-0-545-10697-9(4)) Weston Woods Studios, Inc.

—Hug Time. 2007. (ENG., Illus.). 48p. (J). (gr. -1-3). 14.99 (978-0-316-11494-3(4)) Little, Brown Bks. for Young Readers.

McDonough, Kelly. Things I Don't Like. 2012. 32p. pap. 24.95 (978-1-4626-8177-8(8)) America Star Bks.

Mcghee, Alison. Only a Witch Can Fly. Yoo, Taeeun, illus. movie tie-in ed. 2009. (ENG.). 32p. (J). (gr. -1-3). 16.99 (978-0-312-37503-4(4), 9780312375034) Feiwel & Friends.

McGinnis, Bsn. Call My Mom!! 2013. 24p. pap. 14.99 (978-1-4669-5595-0(3)) Trafford Publishing.

McGovern, Ann. Little Wolf. 2011. 48p. (gr. 2-4). pap. 8.95 (978-1-4620-2711-8(3)) iUniverse, Inc.

McGranaghan, John. Saturn for My Birthday, 1 vol. Edelson, Wendy, illus. 2008. (ENG.). 32p. (J). (gr. -1-4). 16.95 (978-1-934359-13-6(0)); pap. 8.95 (978-1-934359-27-3(0)) Arbordale Publishing.

McGrath, Barbara Barbieri. Teddy Bear Counting. Nihoff, Tim, illus. 2010. (McGrath Math Ser.). (ENG.). 32p. (J). (gr. -1-2). 16.95 (978-1-58089-215-5(9)); pap. 7.95 (978-1-58089-216-2(7)) Charlesbridge Publishing, Inc.

McGrath, Brenda. Ding Bat Audio Book. 2006. (Illus.). 16p. (J). 13.99 (978-0-9799050-0-1(1)) All Around Our World Publishing Co., Inc.

McGraw, Jason. Beating the Odds. 2007. 30p. 47.88 (978-0-615-13681-3(8)) McGraw, Jason A.

McGregor, Janet C. Happy for a Honk & a Wave. Craft, Donna, illus. 2010. 20p. pap. 12.95 (978-1-936343-04-1(5)) Peppertree Pr., The.

McGuckin, Mitchelle. Bullfrog Henry. 2010. 60p. pap. 23.99 (978-1-4490-9547-5(X)) AuthorHouse.

McGuiness, Elle J. & Brown, Heather. Bee & Me: A Mini-Motion Book. 2010. (ENG., Illus.). 12p. (J). 9.99 (978-0-7407-9362-2(4)) Andrews McMeel Publishing.

McGuinness, Elle J. Bee & Me. 2014. (ENG.). 14p. (J). (gr. -1-k). bds. 5.99 (978-1-4494-4371-9(0)) Andrews McMeel Publishing.

—Bee & Me. Brown, Heather, illus. 2008. (ENG.). 28p. (J). (gr. -1). 16.99 (978-0-7407-7734-9(3)) Andrews McMeel Publishing.

McHenry, E. B. Poodlena. 2004. (Illus.). (J). (978-1-58234-962-6(2)) Bloomsbury Publishing USA.

—Poodlena. McHenry, E. B., illus. 2004. (ENG., Illus.). 32p. (J). (gr. -1-3). 16.95 (978-1-58234-824-7(3), 9781582348247, Bloomsbury USA Childrens) Bloomsbury Publishing USA.

Mcintosh, Sharon. Grandma S Donut Hat. 2013. 22p. pap. 9.99 (978-1-62697-407-4(1)) Salem Author Services.

McIntyre, Sarah & O'Connell, David. Jampires. 2015. (ENG., Illus.). 32p. (J). (gr. -1-k). 16.99 (978-0-545-81663-2(7)) Scholastic, Inc.

McKay, Sindy. We Both Read-My Day (Picture Book) Johnson, Meredith, illus. 2007. (We Both Read Ser.). 44p. (J). (gr. -1-2). lib. bdg. 14.95 (978-1-60115-005-9(9)) Treasure Bay, Inc.

McKee, Brett. Monsters Don't Cry! Burfoot, Ella, illus. 2012. (ENG.). 32p. (J). (gr. -1-k). 19.99 (978-1-84939-291-4(9)) Andersen Pr. GBR. Dist: Independent Pubs. Group.

—The Tickle Ghost. McKee, David, illus. 2011. (ENG.). 32p. (J). (gr. k-2). 19.99 (978-1-84939-246-4(3)) Andersen Pr. GBR. Dist: Independent Pubs. Group.

McKellar, Danica. Goodnight, Numbers! Padrón, Alicia, illus. 2017. (ENG.). 40p. (J). (-k). 16.99 (978-1-101-93378-7(X), Crown Books For Young Readers) Random Hse. Children's Bks.

McKendry, Sam. Are You Ticklish? Mitchell, Melanie, illus. 2008. (ENG.). 12p. (J). bds. 5.95 (978-1-58117-706-0(2), Intervisual/Piggy Toes) Bendon, Inc.

McKenna, Mark, et al, illus. Banana Tail. 2003. 32p. (J). 12.95 (978-0-9727681-3-9(0)) Active Media Publishing, LLC.

McKernan, Wendy. The Thing I Say I Saw Last Night: A Christmas Story. Bzymek, Izabela, illus. 2011. 32p. (J). (978-0-9866204-0-9(8)); pap. (978-0-9866204-1-6(6)) Little Dragon Publishing.

McKissack, Patricia C. Where Crocodiles Have Wings. Barner, Bob, illus. 2005. (ENG.). 32p. (J). (gr. -1-3). 16.95 (978-0-8234-1748-3(4)) Holiday Hse., Inc.

McKittrick, Erin. My Coyote Nose & Ptarmigan Toes: An Almost-True Alaskan Adventure. Higman, Valisa, illus. 2016. (Paws IV Ser.). (ENG.). 32p. (J). (gr. -1-2). pap. 10.99 *(978-1-63217-031-6(0),* Little Bigfoot) Sasquatch Bks.
McLaughlin, Julie. Hungry Mr. Gator. McKay, Ann Marie, illus. 2005. (J). 15.99 *(978-0-933101-24-1(4))* Legacy Pubns.
McLaughlin, Lauren. Wonderful You: An Adoption Story. So, Meilo, illus. 2017. (ENG.). 32p. (J). (gr. -1-2). 17.99 *(978-0-553-51001-0(0),* Random Hse. Bks. for Young Readers) Random Hse. Children's Bks.
McLelland, Michael J. Beating the Bully. Kirk, Andrea Cope, illus. 2007. 16p. (J). 15.99 *(978-1-59955-006-0(7))* Cedar Fort, Inc./CFI Distribution.
McLeod, Kimberly. Little Mitchell Tried to Be Good, but Most of the Time He Was Misunderstood. 2012. 42p. 25.00 *(978-0-9829825-5-6(0))* Creative Energy, LLC.
McLeod, Kris Aro. Hush-a-Bye Counting: A Bedtime Book. Allyn, Virginia, illus. 2008. (ENG.). 20p. (J). (gr. -1). 14.95 *(978-1-58117-785-5(2),* Intervisual/Piggy Toes) Bendon, Inc.
McLoughlin Brothers, creator. Snowflake Stories. 2011. (American Antiquarian Society Ser.). (ENG., Illus.). 16p. (gr. 1). 24.95 *(978-1-4290-9735-2(3))* Applewood Bks.
McManis, Margaret. Olé! Cinco de Mayo!, 1 vol. Harrington, David, illus. 2013. (ENG.). 32p. (J). (gr. k-3). 16.99 *(978-1-4556-1754-8(7))* Pelican Publishing Co., Inc.
McMasters, Anne. Anne's Stories for Children of All Ages. 2008. 24p. pap. 12.50 *(978-1-4343-9204-6(X))* AuthorHouse.
McMillan, Ernest. Psalms of Passion. 2006. 48p. pap. 8.95 *(978-1-59800-224-9(4))* Outskirts Pr., Inc.
McMullan, Kate. Mamas' Kisses. Nyeu, Tao, illus. 2017. (ENG.). 40p. (J). (-k). 16.99 *(978-0-525-42832-9(1),* Dial Bks) Penguin Young Readers Group.
McMurtrie, Kevin. The Day I Was Invisible. 2013. 28p. pap. 13.55 *(978-1-4669-7976-5(3))* Trafford Publishing.
—Have You Seen My Duck? 2012. 20p. pap. 13.77 *(978-1-4669-4847-1(7))* Trafford Publishing.
McNair, Don J. Who Wants to Play?, 1 vol. 2009. 28p. pap. 24.95 *(978-1-60836-315-5(5))* America Star Bks.
McNally, Jeanne. The Girl Who Wore Many Hats. 2010. 40p. pap. 16.99 *(978-1-4490-5735-0(7))* AuthorHouse.
McNamee, Kevin. Just for Today. Movshina, Marina, illus. 2012. 16p. pap. 9.95 *(978-1-61633-314-0(6))* Guardian Angel Publishing, Inc.
—The Soggy Town of Hilltop. Ruble, Eugene, illus. 2010. 20p. pap. 10.95 *(978-1-61633-041-5(4))* Guardian Angel Publishing, Inc.
McNease, Mitzy. Chester's Presents. Cox, Kim, illus. 2006. 28p. (J). 10.95 *(978-0-9779488-0-2(3))* Blancmange Publishing LLC.
McNeely Schultz, Geri. Kristie's Excellent Adventures: A Visit to the Fridge. Bertolami, Vince, illus. 2013. (ENG.). 40p. (J). pap. 9.99 *(978-1-935766-88-9(0))* Windy City Pubs.
McPhail, David. Big Brown Bear/El Gran Oso Pardo. Flor Ada, Alma & Campoy, F. Isabel, trs. 2007. (Green Light Readers Level 1 Ser.). (ENG & SPA., Illus.). 28p. (J). (gr. -1-3). pap. 3.95 *(978-0-15-205970-5(9))* Houghton Mifflin Harcourt Publishing Co.
McPike, Elizabeth. Little Bitty Friends. Barton, Patrice, illus. 2016. (ENG.). 32p. (J). (— 1). 16.99 *(978-0-399-17255-7(6),* G.P. Putnam's Sons Books for Young Readers) Penguin Young Readers Group.
—Little Sleepyhead. Barton, Patrice, illus. 2015. (ENG.). 26p. (J). (— 1). 16.99 *(978-0-399-16240-4(2),* G.P. Putnam's Sons Books for Young Readers) Penguin Young Readers Group.
McRae, G. c. Pretty Ballerina. Anderson, David, illus. 2013. 44p. pap. *(978-0-9876845-3-0(1))* Warne, MacDonald Media.
McVoy, Terra Elan. After the Kiss. 2010. (ENG.). 400p. (YA). (gr. 9-18). 16.99 *(978-1-4424-0211-9(3),* Simon Pulse) Simon Pulse.
McWilliams, Amanda & Moore, Clement C. Ozark Night Before Christmas, 1 vol. Rice, James, illus. 2004. (Night Before Christmas Ser.). (ENG.). 32p. (J). (gr. k-3). 16.99 *(978-1-58980-056-4(7))* Pelican Publishing Co., Inc.
Me & Dog. 2014. (ENG., Illus.). 48p. (J). (gr. -1-3). 17.99 *(978-1-4424-9413-8(1),* Simon & Schuster Bks. For Young Readers) Simon & Schuster Bks. For Young Readers.
Meachen Rau, Dana. My Special Space. Kim, Julie J., illus. 2003. (Rookie Readers Ser.). 32p. (J). 19.50 *(978-0-516-22881-5(1),* Children's Pr.) Scholastic Library Publishing.
—Stickers, Shells, & Snowglobes. 2004. (Compass Point Early Reader Ser.). (J). 18.60 *(978-0-7565-0574-5(7))* Compass Point Bks.
Mead, David & Berry, Ron. Who's at the Door? 2010. (Illus.). 12p. (J). (gr. -1-1). 10.99 *(978-0-8249-1431-8(7),* Ideal Pubns.) Worthy Publishing.
Meade, Holly. If I Never Forever Endeavor. Meade, Holly, illus. 2011. (ENG., Illus.). 32p. (J). (gr. -1-3). 16.99 *(978-0-7636-4071-2(9))* Candlewick Pr.
Meadows, Michelle. Hibernation Station. Cyrus, Kurt, illus. 2010. (ENG.). 40p. (J). (gr. -1-3). 17.99 *(978-1-4169-3788-3(9),* Simon & Schuster Bks. For Young Readers) Simon & Schuster Bks. For Young Readers.
—Itsy-Bitsy Baby Mouse. Cordell, Matthew, illus. 2012. (ENG.). 40p. (J). (gr. -1-2). 15.99 *(978-1-4169-3786-9(2),* Simon & Schuster Bks. For Young Readers) Simon & Schuster Bks. For Young Readers.
—Piggies in Pajamas. Hoyt, Ard, illus. 2013. (ENG.). 32p. (J). (gr. -1-2). 15.99 *(978-1-4169-4982-4(8),* Simon & Schuster Bks. For Young Readers) Simon & Schuster Bks. For Young Readers.
—Piggies in the Kitchen. Hoyt, Ard, illus. 2011. (ENG.). 32p. (J). (gr. -1-2). 14.99 *(978-1-4169-3787-6(0),* Simon & Schuster Bks. For Young Readers) Simon & Schuster Bks. For Young Readers.
—Super Bugs. Mayer, Bill, illus. 2016. (ENG.). 40p. (J). (gr. -1-k). 16.99 *(978-0-545-68756-0(X))* Scholastic, Inc.
—Traffic Pups. Andreasen, Dan, illus. 2011. (ENG.). 32p. (J). (gr. -1-3). 15.99 *(978-1-4169-2485-2(X),* Simon & Schuster Bks. For Young Readers) Simon & Schuster Bks. For Young Readers.
Meddour, Wendy. The Glump & the Peeble. Ashdown, Rebecca, illus. 2016. (ENG.). 28p. (J). (gr. -1-3). 17.99 *(978-1-84780-709-0(7),* Frances Lincoln Children's Bks.) Quarto Publishing Group UK GBR. Dist: Hachette Bk. Group.
Medlock-Adams, Michelle. Counting Cows. Meyers, Mark, illus. 2010. 26p. (J). (gr. -1-k). 7.99 *(978-0-8249-1636-1(3),* Ideal Pubns.) Worthy Publishing.
Meister, Cari. I Love Trees. Sirrell, Terry, illus. 2011. (Rookie Ready to Learn Ser.). 40p. (J). pap. 5.95 *(978-0-531-26733-2(4));* (gr. -1-k). lib. bdg. 23.00 *(978-0-531-26501-7(3))* Scholastic Library Publishing. (Children's Pr.).
—What Can I Be? Phillips, Matt, illus. 2003. (Rookie Readers Ser.). 24p. (J). 19.50 *(978-0-516-22876-1(5),* Children's Pr.) Scholastic Library Publishing.
Meister, Cari & Sirrell, Terry. Me Fascinan los árboles. Sirrell, Terry, illus. 2011. (Rookie Ready to Learn Español Ser.). (SPA., Illus.). 40p. (J). lib. bdg. 23.00 *(978-0-531-26118-7(2),* Children's Pr.) Scholastic Library Publishing.
—Me Fascinan los Árboles. Sirrell, Terry, illus. 2011. (Rookie Ready to Learn Español Ser.). (SPA., Illus.). 40p. (J). pap. 5.95 *(978-0-531-26786-8(5),* Children's Pr.) Scholastic Library Publishing.
Meister, Victoria Buhlig. Our Playtime Friend. 2011. 28p. 13.59 *(978-1-4567-2883-0(0))* AuthorHouse.
Melcher, Mary, illus. Puppies Count. 2010. (J). *(978-1-58865-596-7(2))* Kidsbooks, LLC.
Melling, David. Colour with Splosh! 2017. (Splosh Ser.). (ENG., Illus.). 32p. (J). (gr. -1-k). pap. 7.99 ***(978-1-4449-3181-5(4))*** Hachette Children's Group GBR. Dist: Hachette Bk. Group.
Melmed, Laura Krauss. Before We Met. Tsong, Jing Jing, illus. 2016. (ENG.). 32p. (J). (gr. -1-3). 17.99 *(978-1-4424-4156-9(9),* Beach Lane Bks.) Beach Lane Bks.
—I Love You As Much... Board Book & Picture Frame. 2003. (Illus.). 22p. (J). (gr. -1-2). 12.99 *(978-0-06-008659-6(9),* HarperFestival) HarperCollins Pubs.
—My Love Will Be with You. Sorensen, Henri, illus. 2009. (ENG.). 24p. (J). (gr. -1-2). 17.99 *(978-0-06-155260-1(7))* HarperCollins Pubs.
Meltzer Kleinhenz, Sydnie. Work & Play. Reasor, Mick, illus. 2011. (Rookie Ready to Learn — Out & about: In My Community Ser.). 32p. (J). (gr. -1-k). lib. bdg. 25.00 *(978-0-531-27179-7(X));* (ENG.). pap. 5.95 *(978-0-531-26829-2(2))* Scholastic Library Publishing. (Children's Pr.).
Meltzer, Lynn. The Construction Crew. Eko-Burgess, Carrie, illus. (ENG.). (J). 2017. 32p. bds. 7.99 *(978-1-250-11267-5(2),* 9781250112675) 2011. 40p. (gr. -1-k). 15.99 *(978-0-8050-8884-7(9),* 9780805088847) Holt, Henry & Co. (Holt, Henry & Co. Bks. For Young Readers).
Melvin, Alice. The High Street. 2011. (ENG., Illus.). 52p. (J). (gr. -1-3). 15.95 *(978-1-85437-943-6(7))* Tate Publishing, Ltd. GBR. Dist: Abrams, Inc.
Merberg, Julie & Bober, Suzanne. Dreaming with Rousseau. 2007. (Mini Masters Ser.: MINI). (ENG., Illus.). 22p. (J). (gr. -1 — 1). bds. 6.99 *(978-0-8118-5712-3(3))* Chronicle Bks. LLC.
—Mini Masters: 4 Board Books Inside! Degas, Matisse, Monet, Van Gogh, 4 vols. 2006. (Mini Masters Ser.: MINI). (ENG., Illus.). (J). (gr. -1 — 1). bds. 19.99 *(978-0-8118-5518-1(X))* Chronicle Bks. LLC.
—Painting with Picasso. 2006. (Mini Masters Ser.: MINI). (ENG., Illus.). 22p. (J). (gr. -1 — 1). bds. 6.99 *(978-0-8118-5505-1(8))* Chronicle Bks. LLC.
—Sharing with Renoir. 2005. (Mini Masters Ser.: MINI). (ENG., Illus.). 22p. (J). (gr. -1 — 1). bds. 6.99 *(978-0-8118-4757-5(8))* Chronicle Bks. LLC.
—Sunday with Seurat. 2005. (Mini Masters Ser.: MINI). (ENG., Illus.). 16p. (J). (gr. -1 — 1). bds. 6.95 *(978-0-8118-4758-2(6))* Chronicle Bks. LLC.
Mercer, Graham. The Secret Cave. 2009. 52p. pap. 10.50 *(978-1-4092-9055-1(7))* Lulu Pr., Inc.
Meredith, Samantha. Flip & Find Builders. 2016. (Flip & Find Ser.). (ENG., Illus.). 10p. (J). (— 1). bds. 7.99 *(978-1-4472-7714-9(7))* Pan Macmillan GBR. Dist: Independent Pubs. Group.
—Flip & Find Farmers Board Book. 2016. (Flip & Find Ser.). (ENG., Illus.). 10p. (J). (— 1). bds. 7.99 *(978-1-4472-7715-6(5))* Pan Macmillan GBR. Dist: Independent Pubs. Group.
—Flip & Find Pilots: A Guess Who/Where Flap Book about a Pilot. Meredith, Samantha, illus. 2016. (Flip & Find Ser.). (ENG., Illus.). 12p. (J). (— 1). bds. 7.99 *(978-1-4472-7717-0(1))* Pan Macmillan GBR. Dist: Independent Pubs. Group.
Mermelstein, Yael. A Car That Goes Far. Rosenfeld, Dina, ed. Romanenko, Vitaliy & Romanenko, Vasilisa, illus. 2009. 30p. (J). (gr. 1-3). 12.95 *(978-1-929628-47-6(1))* Hachai Publishing.
—Izzy the Whiz & Passover McClean. Hartman, Carrie, illus. 2012. (Passover Ser.). (ENG.). 32p. (J). (gr. -1-2). lib. bdg. 17.95 *(978-0-7613-5653-0(3),* Kar-Ben Publishing) Lerner Publishing Group.
—Izzy the Whiz & Passover Mcclean. Hartman, Carrie, illus. 2012. (Passover Ser.). (ENG.). 32p. (J). (gr. -1-2). pap. 7.95 *(978-0-7613-5654-7(1),* Kar-Ben Publishing) Lerner Publishing Group.
Merz, Jennifer. Playground Day. 2007. 32p. 16.00 *(978-978-061-896-4(1),* Clarion Bks.) Houghton Mifflin Harcourt Trade & Reference Pubs.
Messinger, Midge. Freddie Q. Freckle. Messinger, Robert, ed. Ferraro-Oster, Margaret, illus. unabr. ed. 2003. 40p. (gr. -1-2). 12.95 *(978-1-893237-00-1(1))* Little Mai Pr.
Messinger, Robert. I've Got Mail! Salerno, John, illus. 2003. 40p. (J). 12.95 *(978-1-893237-01-8(X))* Little Mai Pr.
Messner, Kate. Rolling Thunder. Ruth, Greg, illus. 2017. (ENG.). 32p. (J). (gr. -1-3). 17.99 *(978-0-545-47012-4(9),* Scholastic Pr.) Scholastic, Inc.
Metcalf, Paula. My Mummy. Barnard, Lucy, illus. 2015. (ENG.). 24p. (J). (-1). bds. 9.99 *(978-1-4472-7699-9(X))* Pan Macmillan GBR. Dist: Independent Pubs. Group.
Metlen, Ryan W. & Metlen, Ryan. Ewe. 2009. (J). *(978-1-58768-054-0(8),* HiddenSpring) Paulist Pr.
Metzger, Steve. Dancing Clock. Nez, John Abbott, illus. 2011. (ENG.). 32p. 12.95 *(978-1-58925-100-7(8));* (J). pap. 7.95 *(978-1-58925-429-9(5))* Tiger Tales.
—Five Little Bunnies Hopping on a Hill. 2006. (J). *(978-0-439-80382-3(9))* Scholastic, Inc.
—Five Spooky Ghosts Playing Tricks at School. Harrald-Pilz, Marilee, illus. 2005. (J). *(978-0-439-80381-6(0))* Scholastic, Inc.
—I Love You All Year Long. Keay, Claire, illus. 2009. 20p. (J). (gr. -1-k). 8.95 *(978-1-58925-847-1(9))* Tiger Tales.
—Ice Cream King. Downing, Julie, illus. 2011. (ENG.). 32p. (J). (gr. -1-2). 15.95 *(978-1-58925-096-3(6));* pap. 7.95 *(978-1-58925-427-5(9))* Tiger Tales.
—This Is the House That Monsters Built. Lee, Jared D., illus. 2016. (ENG.). 32p. (J). (gr. -1-k). 9.99 *(978-0-545-61112-1(1))* Scholastic, Inc.
—The Tooth Fairy Loses a Tooth! Busby, Ailie, illus. 2011. (ENG.). 16p. (J). (gr. -1-1). pap. 5.99 *(978-1-4424-1259-0(3),* Little Simon) Little Simon.
—The Turkey Train. Paillot, Jim, illus. 2013. (ENG.). 32p. (J). (gr. -1-k). 6.99 *(978-0-545-49229-4(7),* Cartwheel Bks.) Scholastic, Inc.
—Under the Apple Tree. Girasole, Alessia, illus. 2009. (J). *(978-0-545-14200-7(8))* Scholastic, Inc.
—We're Going on a Leaf Hunt. Sakamoto, Miki, illus. 2008. (ENG.). 32p. (J). (gr. -1-3). pap. 6.99 *(978-0-439-87377-2(0),* Cartwheel Bks.) Scholastic, Inc.
Meyers, Susan. Bear in the Air. Bates, Amy, illus. 2010. (ENG.). 32p. (J). (gr. k-2). 15.95 *(978-0-8109-8398-4(2),* Abrams Bks. for Young Readers) Abrams, Inc.
—Everywhere Babies. Frazee, Marla, illus. 2011. (ENG.). 30p. (J). (gr. -1 — 1). bds. 11.99 *(978-0-547-51074-3(8))* Houghton Mifflin Harcourt Publishing Co.
—Everywhere Babies. Frazee, Marla, illus. 2004. (ENG.). 30p. (J). (gr. k — 1). bds. 6.95 *(978-0-15-205315-4(8))* Houghton Mifflin Harcourt Publishing Co.
—Rock-A-Bye Room. Bates, Amy June, illus. 2013. (ENG.). 32p. (J). (gr. -1-k). 17.95 *(978-1-4197-0537-3(7),* Abrams Bks. for Young Readers) Abrams, Inc.
—This Is the Way a Baby Rides. Nakata, Hiroe, illus. 2005. (ENG.). 32p. (J). (gr. -1-1). 15.95 *(978-0-8109-5763-3(9),* Abrams Bks. for Young Readers) Abrams, Inc.
Michalak, Jamie. The Coziest Place. Davis, Jon, illus. 2013. (ENG.). 32p. (J). (gr. -1-k). 14.99 *(978-1-58925-121-2(0))* Tiger Tales.
Micklos, John. One Leaf, Two Leaves, Count with Me! McFarland, Clive, illus. 2017. (ENG.). 32p. (J). (— 1). 16.99 ***(978-0-399-54471-2(2),*** Nancy Paulsen Books) Penguin Young Readers Group.
Mike. New Pet. Mike, illus. l.t. ed. 2005. (ENG., Illus.). 32p. (J). lib. bdg. 14.95 *(978-0-9658365-8-6(4))* Beetle Bug Bks.
Milam, Mary Kay. The Zooming Star Babies. Date not set. (J). pap. *(978-1-890622-65-7(6))* Leathers Publishing.
Mileto, Richard. Superbird. 2005. per. 15.50 *(978-0-8059-9658-6(3))* Dorrance Publishing Co., Inc.
Mill, Lynda. Let's Climb the Apple Tree. 2012. 44p. pap. 17.45 *(978-1-4669-6871-4(0))* Trafford Publishing.
Millen, C. M. The Ink Garden of Brother Theophane. Wisnewski, Andrea, illus. 2010. (ENG.). 32p. (J). (gr. k-3). 17.95 *(978-1-58089-179-0(9))* Charlesbridge Publishing, Inc.
Miller, Deborah U. & Ostrove, Karen. Fins & Scales: A Kosher Tale. Ostrove, Karen, illus. 2004. (Israel Ser.). (Illus.). 32p. (J). (gr. 1-3). pap. 4.95 *(978-0-929371-25-2(9),* Kar-Ben Publishing) Lerner Publishing Group.
Miller, Janet. DuckDumB. 2010. 32p. pap. 21.95 *(978-0-557-57669-2(5))* Lulu Pr., Inc.
Miller, Joanne Fairchild & Logsdon, Clara Isabel. What If It Were Possible? 2016. (ENG., Illus.). 40p. (J). pap. 9.95 *(978-1-63047-638-0(2))* Morgan James Publishing.
Miller, Jules. Ellie & the Truth about the Tooth Fairy. Miller, Jules, illus. 2014. (ENG., Illus.). 36p. (J). (gr. -1-k). 16.95 *(978-1-62873-590-1(2),* Sky Pony Pr.) Skyhorse Publishing Co., Inc.
Miller, Pam. Wrinkles. Ostrom, Bob, illus. 2005. (Rookie Readers Ser.). (ENG.). 32p. (J). (gr. k-2). lib. bdg. 19.50 *(978-0-516-24860-8(X),* Children's Pr.) Scholastic Library Publishing.
—Wrinkles. Ostrom, Bob, illus. 2006. (Rookie Reader Skill Set Ser.). (ENG.). 32p. (J). (gr. k-2). per. 4.95 *(978-0-516-25021-2(3),* Children's Pr.) Scholastic Library Publishing.
Miller, Pat. We're Going on a Book Hunt. Bernard Westcott, Nadine, illus. 2008. (J). (gr. -1). 17.95 *(978-1-60213-034-0(5),* Upstart Bks.) Highsmith Inc.
Miller, Pat Zietlow. Sharing the Bread: An Old-Fashioned Thanksgiving Story. McElmurry, Jill, illus. 2015. (ENG.). 32p. (J). (gr. -1-3). 17.99 *(978-0-307-98182-0(7),* Schwartz & Wade Bks.) Random Hse. Children's Bks.
Millsaps, Grace & Murphy, Ryan. You Wouldn't Like Me Without My Coffee. Marin, Danny, illus. 2014. (ENG.). 40p. (J). (gr. k-2). 17.95 *(978-0-9904093-0-4(9))* Millfree Mursaps Media.
Minor, Florence F. If You Were a Panda Bear. Minor, Wendell, illus. 2013. (ENG.). 32p. (J). (gr. -1-3). 17.99 *(978-0-06-195090-2(4),* Tegen, Katherine Bks) HarperCollins Pubs.
—If You Were a Penguin. Minor, Wendell, illus. 2009. 32p. (J). (gr. -1-2). lib. bdg. 18.89 *(978-0-06-113098-4(2))* HarperCollins Pubs.
Minor, Wendell. My Farm Friends. Bodett, Tom, illus. 2012. 29.95 *(978-1-4301-1096-5(1))* Live Oak Media.
—My Farm Friends. Minor, Wendell, illus. (ENG., Illus.). (J). (gr. -1-k). 2013. 26p. bds. 7.99 *(978-0-399-25799-5(3),* Nancy Paulsen Books) 2011. 28p. 17.99 *(978-0-399-24477-3(8),* G.P. Putnam's Sons Books for Young Readers) Penguin Young Readers Group.
Minor, Wendell & Minor, Florence F. If You Were a Penguin. Minor, Wendell, illus. 2008. (ENG., Illus.). 32p. (J). (gr. -1-2). 17.99 *(978-0-06-113097-7(4),* Tegen, Katherine Bks) HarperCollins Pubs.
Mitchell, Colleen. A Dinosaur under My Bed. Daly, Karen Anne, illus. 2013. 24p. (J). pap. 7.49 *(978-0-9853600-2-3(X))* Thistlewood Publishing.
Mitchell, Sheena. Out of the Ark. 2012. 48p. pap. 18.41 *(978-1-4669-1489-6(0))* Trafford Publishing.
Mitton, Tony. All Afloat on Noah's Boat. Parker-Rees, Guy, illus. 2017. (ENG.). 32p. (J). (gr. -1-k). pap. 7.99 *(978-1-84616-242-8(4),* Orchard Bks.) Hachette Children's Group GBR. Dist: Hachette Bk. Group.
—Dinosaurumpus! Parker-Rees, Guy, illus. (ENG.). (J). (gr. -1-k). 2014. 30p. bds. 6.99 *(978-0-545-69480-3(9),* Cartwheel Bks.) 2003. 32p. 16.99 *(978-0-439-39514-4(3),* Orchard Bks.) Scholastic, Inc.
—Snowy Bear. Brown, Alison, illus. (ENG.). (J). 2016. 26p. bds. 7.99 *(978-1-68119-084-6(2),* 9781681190846) 2015. 32p. (gr. -1-1). 16.99 *(978-1-61963-905-8(X),* 9781619639058) Bloomsbury Publishing USA. (Bloomsbury USA Childrens).
—The Somethingosaur. Ayto, Russell, illus. 2014. (ENG.). 32p. (J). 17.99 *(978-0-00-758395-9(8),* HarperCollins Children's Bks.) HarperCollins Pubs. Ltd. GBR. Dist: HarperCollins Pubs.
—Truckload of Fun, 10 bks., Set. Parker, Ant, illus. 2007. (Amazing Machines Ser.). (ENG.). 24p. (J). (gr. -1-k). 24.99 *(978-0-7534-6154-9(4),* 9780753461549, Kingfisher) Roaring Brook Pr.
—Twist & Hop, Minibeast Bop. Parker-Rees, Guy, illus. 2017. (ENG.). 32p. (J). (gr. -1-k). pap. 7.99 *(978-1-4083-3687-8(1),* Orchard Bks.) Hachette Children's Group GBR. Dist: Hachette Bk. Group.
Mitton, Tony & Parker, Ant. Super Submarines. 2014. (Amazing Machines Ser.). (ENG., Illus.). 24p. (J). (gr. -1-k). 4.99 *(978-0-7534-7208-8(2),* 9780753472088, Kingfisher) Roaring Brook Pr.
—Super Submarines. 2014. (Amazing Machines Ser.). (J). lib. bdg. 14.75 *(978-0-606-36133-0(2))* Turtleback Bks.
Mockford, Caroline & Blackstone, Stella. Cleo's Color Book. Mockford, Caroline, illus. 2007. (Cleo Ser.). (ENG., Illus.). 24p. (J). (gr. -1-k). bds. 6.99 *(978-1-84686-060-7(1))* Barefoot Bks., Inc.
Modarressi, Mitra. Owlet's First Flight. Modarressi, Mitra, illus. 2012. (ENG., Illus.). 32p. (J). (gr. -1-k). 16.99 *(978-0-399-25526-7(5),* G.P. Putnam's Sons Books for Young Readers) Penguin Young Readers Group.
Moerder, Lynne. Things That Go Burp! in the Night. Moerder, Lynne, illus. 2015. (ENG., Illus.). 32p. (J). (gr. -1-k). 16.99 *(978-1-4847-1669-4(8))* Hyperion Bks. for Children.
Mogk, Matt. That's Not Your Mommy Anymore: A Zombie Tale. Wells, Aja, illus. 2011. (ENG.). 32p. pap. 10.00 *(978-1-56975-926-4(X))* Ulysses Pr.
Mohler, Marie. Leonard's Song. 2008. 32p. 18.95 *(978-1-4357-1372-7(9))* Lulu Pr., Inc.
Molokie, Tom. Introducing Willy Mcspry. 2011. 36p. pap. 15.65 *(978-1-4634-3697-1(1))* AuthorHouse.
Moncure, Jane Belk. Here We Go 'Round the Year: A Book about the Months. Billin-Frye, Paige, illus. 2013. (Magic Castle Readers Ser.). (ENG.). 32p. (J). (gr. -1-2). 25.64 *(978-1-62323-582-6(0),* 206318) Child's World, Inc., The.
—Hop-Skip-Jump-a-Roo Zoo: A Book about Imitating. Girouard, Patrick, illus. 2013. (Magic Castle Readers Ser.). (ENG.). 32p. (J). (gr. -1-2). 25.64 *(978-1-62323-566-6(9),* 206300) Child's World, Inc., The.
—Nanny Goat's Boat: A Book of Rhyming. Girouard, Patrick, illus. 2013. (Magic Castle Readers Ser.). (ENG.). 32p. (J). (gr. -1-2). 25.64 *(978-1-62323-567-3(7),* 206301) Child's World, Inc., The.
—One Tricky Monkey up on Top: A Counting Adventure. Rooney, Ronnie, illus. 2013. (Magic Castle Readers Ser.). (ENG.). 32p. (J). (gr. -1-2). 25.64 *(978-1-62323-581-9(2),* 206314) Child's World, Inc., The.
—'Smile,' Says Little Crocodile: A Book about Good Habits. DeSantis, Susan, illus. 2013. (Magic Castle Readers Ser.). (ENG.). 32p. (J). (gr. -1-2). 25.64 *(978-1-62323-570-3(7),* 206305) Child's World, Inc., The.
Monroe, Chris. Bug on a Bike. Monroe, Chris, illus. 2014. (ENG., Illus.). 32p. (J). (gr. -1-2). 16.95 *(978-1-4677-2154-7(9),* Carolrhoda Bks.) Lerner Publishing Group.
Monroe, Colleen. A Is for Ark: Noah's Journey. Monroe, Michael Glenn, illus. 2004. 38p. (gr. -1-1). pap. 17.95 *(978-0-9754942-0-2(1))* Storytime Pr., Inc.
—A Wish to Be a Christmas Tree. Monroe, Michael Glenn, illus. 2005. (Holiday Ser.). (ENG.). 20p. (J). (gr. -1-1). bds. 8.99 *(978-1-58536-269-1(7),* 202284) Sleeping Bear Pr.
Montag, Aileen. All I Ever Wanted to Be. 2012. 28p. pap. 24.95 *(978-1-4626-8832-6(2))* America Star Bks.
Montes, Marisa. Los Gatos Black on Halloween. Morales, Yuyi, illus. rev. ed. 2006. (ENG.). 32p. (J). (gr. -1-3). 18.99 *(978-0-8050-7429-1(5),* 9780805074291, Holt, Henry & Co. Bks. For Young Readers) Holt, Henry & Co.
—Los Gatos Black on Halloween. 2011. (SPA.). (J). (gr. -1-3). 29.95 *(978-0-545-19701-4(5))* Weston Woods Studios, Inc.
Montgomery, Margaret, illus. The Adventures of Anna Banana Shoeshine: Anna Banana Takes a Bath. 2006. 40p. (J). *(978-1-930401-49-5(3))* Central Coast Bks./Pr.
Moore, Ann C. The Colors Join Hands for A Surprise. 2010. 24p. pap. 12.79 *(978-1-4520-7572-3(7))* AuthorHouse.
Moore, Clement C. C'Etait la Veille de Noel. Santore, Charles, illus. 2012. (FRE.). 48p. (J). 18.95 *(978-1-60433-300-8(6),* Applesauce Pr.) Cider Mill Pr. Bk. Pubs., LLC.
—Grumpy Santa. Spiridellis, Gregg & Spiridellis, Evan, illus. 2003. (ENG.). (J). *(978-0-439-53039-2(3),* Orchard Bks.) Scholastic, Inc.
Moore, Clement C., ed. & illus. The Night Before Christmas. Moore, Clement C., illus. Price, Margaret Evans, illus. 2004. (Shape Bks.). (ENG.). 16p. (J). (gr. -1-3). pap. 9.95 *(978-1-59583-009-8(X),* 9781595830098, Green Tiger Pr.) Laughing Elephant.
Moore, Johnny Ray. But Still, We Dream: (a novel in Verse), 1 vol. 2009. 60p. pap. 16.95 *(978-1-60813-491-5(1))* America Star Bks.
Moore, Julianne. My Mom Is a Foreigner, but Not to Me. So, Meilo, illus. 2013. (ENG.). 40p. (J). (gr. k-3). 16.99 *(978-1-4521-0792-9(0))* Chronicle Bks. LLC.
Moore, Karen. Everybody Counts. Reed, Lisa, illus. 2012. (Roma Downey's Little Angels Ser.). 24p. (J). bds. 7.99 *(978-0-8249-5643-1(5),* Ideal Pubns.) Worthy Publishing.
Moorthy, Anita. Monkey's Drum. Sarkar, Soumitro, illus. 2003. (ENG.). 24p. pap. 3.99 *(978-81-86211-15-1(2))* Penguin Publishing Group.
Morales, Melita. Jam & Honey. Bryant, Laura J., illus. 2011. (ENG.). 32p. (J). (gr. -1-2). 15.99 *(978-1-58246-299-8(2),* Tricycle Pr.) Random Hse. Children's Bks.
Moree, Katie. Jesse's Peekaboo Safari. 2008. 20p. pap. 24.95 *(978-1-60672-473-6(8))* America Star Bks.
Moreillon, Judi. Read to Me, 1 vol. Teis, Kyra, illus. (J). 2004. (ENG.). 32p. (gr. -1). bds. 6.95 *(978-1-59572-014-6(6))*

S

2003. 24p. 6.95 *(978-1-932065-49-7(0)*, 1-718-784-9112) Star Bright Bks., Inc.

Morgan, Kerry. Smile Rhymes. 2011. (Illus.). 32p. (gr. 1-2). pap. 13.99 *(978-1-4567-6339-8(3))* AuthorHouse.

Morgan, Michaela. Never Shake a Rattlesnake. Sharratt, Nick, illus. (ENG.). 32p. (J). (gr. -1-k). 2016. pap. 8.99 *(978-1-5098-1704-7(2))*1. 2012. pap. 8.99 *(978-0-330-51229-9(3))* Pan Macmillan GBR. Dist: Independent Pubs. Group.

Morgenstern, Susie Hoch & Morgenstern, Susie. I Will Make Miracles. Chen, Jiang Hong, illus. 2008. (ENG.). 32p. (J). (gr. -1-3). 18.99 *(978-1-59990-189-3(7)*, 9781599901893, Bloomsbury USA Childrens) Bloomsbury Publishing USA.

Moritz, S. Dianne & Mitchell, Hazel. 1, 2, 3 ... by the Sea. 2013. (ENG., Illus.). 36p. (J). pap. 6.99 *(978-1-935279-94-5(7))* Kane Miller.

Morris, Ashara. Let's Find Lucy! 2008. (Illus.). 32p. pap. 17.95 *(978-1-4327-3221-9(8))* Outskirts Pr., Inc.

Morrison, Cathy. I Want a Pet. 2012. (ENG.). 32p. (J). *(978-1-58925-113-7(X))* Tiger Tales.

Morrison, Kevin. I Can Speak Bully. Kemble, Mai S., illus. 2009. 32p. (J). 14.95 *(978-0-8091-6744-9(1)*, Ambassador Bks.) Paulist Pr.

Morrison, Toni & Morrison, Slade. Peeny Butter Fudge. Cepeda, Joe, illus. 2009. (ENG.). 32p. (J). (gr. -1-3). 17.99 *(978-1-4169-8332-3(5)*, Simon & Schuster/Paula Wiseman Bks.) Simon & Schuster/Paula Wiseman Bks.

Morrow, Barbara Olenyik. Mr. Mosquito Put on His Tuxedo. Goembel, Ponder, illus. 2009. (ENG.). 32p. (J). (gr. -1-3). 16.95 *(978-0-8234-2072-8(8))* Holiday Hse., Inc.

Morrow, Tara Jaye. Just Mommy & Me. Bratun, Katy, illus. 2004. 32p. (J). 13.89 *(978-0-06-000725-6(7))* HarperCollins Pubs.

Mortensen, Denise Dowling. Bug Patrol. Bell, Cece, illus. 2013. (ENG.). 32p. (J). (gr. -1-3). 16.99 *(978-0-618-79024-1(1))* Houghton Mifflin Harcourt Publishing Co.

Mortensen, Lori. Cindy Moo. Mack, Jeff, illus. 2012. (ENG.). 32p. (J). (gr. -1-2). 16.99 *(978-0-06-204393-1(5))* HarperCollins Pubs.

—Cowpoke Clyde & Dirty Dawg. Austin, Michael Allen, illus. 2013. (ENG.). 32p. (J). (gr. -1-3). 16.99 *(978-0-547-23993-4(9))* Houghton Mifflin Harcourt Publishing Co.

—Cowpoke Clyde Rides the Range. Austin, Michael Allen, illus. 2016. (ENG.). 32p. (J). (gr. -1-3). 16.99 *(978-0-544-37030-2(9))* Houghton Mifflin Harcourt Publishing Co.

—Mousequerade Ball: A Counting Tale. Lewin, Betsy, illus. 2016. (ENG.). 32p. (J). 16.99 *(978-1-61963-422-0(8)*, 9781619634220, Bloomsbury USA Childrens) Bloomsbury Publishing USA.

Mortimer, Anne. Christmas Mouse. Mortimer, Anne, illus. 2013. (ENG., Illus.). 24p. (J). (gr. -1-3). 12.99 *(978-0-06-208928-1(5)*, Tegen, Katherine Bks) HarperCollins Pubs.

Morton, Jane & Dreier, Ted. Moozie's Cow Wisdom for Loving to the "Uddermost" Royse, Jane, illus. 2003. (J). pap. 4.95 *(978-0-9662268-3-6(6))* Children's Kindness Network.

Moses, Brian. The Frog Olympics. Husband, Amy, illus. 2017. (ENG.). 32p. (J). (gr. -1-k). pap. 9.99 ***(978-0-7502-9683-0(6)***, Wayland) Hachette Children's Group GBR. Dist: Hachette Bk. Group.

Moss, Lloyd. Zin! Zin! Zin! A Violin. Priceman, Marjorie, illus. 2004. (gr. -1-3). 18.00 *(978-0-7569-1919-1(3))* Perfection Learning Corp.

—Zin! Zin! Zin! A Violin. Priceman, Marjorie, illus. 2005. (Stories to Go! Ser.). (ENG.). 32p. (J). (gr. -1-3). 4.99 *(978-1-4169-0838-8(2)*, Simon & Schuster/Paula Wiseman Bks.) Simon & Schuster/Paula Wiseman Bks.

Moss, Miriam. Bare Bear. McQuillan, Mary, illus. 2005. (ENG.). 32p. (J). 16.95 *(978-0-8234-1934-0(7))* Holiday Hse., Inc.

Mother Goose. The Three Little Kittens. Winter, Milo, illus. 2009. (Shape Bks.). (ENG.). 16p. (J). (gr. -1-1). pap. 9.95 *(978-1-59583-374-7(9)*, 9781595833747, Green Tiger Pr.) Laughing Elephant.

Mother Goose Staff & Studio Mouse Staff. Let's Learn. 2011. (ENG.). 10p. (J). *(978-1-59069-898-3(3))* Studio Mouse LLC.

Mother Goose Staff & Studiomouse Staff. Let's Laugh. 2011. (ENG.). 10p. (J). *(978-1-59069-897-6(5))* Studio Mouse LLC.

Moulton, Mark. Miss Fiona's Stupendous Pumpkin Pies. Good, Karen Hillard, illus. 2011. 32p. (J). pap. 7.99 *(978-0-8249-5635-6(4)*, Ideal Pubns.) Worthy Publishing.

Moulton, Mark K. A Royal Wedding. Good, Karen H., illus. 2007. (ENG.). 32p. (J). (gr. k-3). 14.99 *(978-0-8249-8677-3(6)*, Ideal Pubns.) Worthy Publishing.

—The Visit. Winget, Susan, illus. 2003. 56p. (J). 14.95 *(978-0-8249-5475-8(0)*, Ideal Pubns.) Worthy Publishing.

Moulton, Mark Kimball. The Annual Snowman's Ball. Good, Karen Hillard, illus. 2007. (ENG.). 32p. (J). (gr. -1-3). 14.99 *(978-0-8249-5564-9(1)*, Ideal Pubns.) Worthy Publishing.

—A Cricket's Carol. Blowers, Lisa, illus. 2004. 32p. (J). 14.95 *(978-0-8249-5488-8(2)*, Ideal Pubns.) Worthy Publishing.

—Everyday Angels. Winget, Susan, illus. 2003. (ENG.). 32p. (J). 14.95 *(978-0-8249-5479-6(3)*, Ideal Pubns.) Worthy Publishing.

—Miss Fiona's Stupendous Pumpkin Pies. Crouch, Karen Hillard, illus. 2008. (ENG.). 28p. (J). 14.95 *(978-0-8249-5489-5(0)*, Ideal Pubns.) Worthy Publishing.

—Miss Sadie Mcgee Who Lived in a Tree. Good, Karen H., illus. 2008. (ENG.). 32p. (J). (gr. k-3). 16.95 *(978-0-8249-5152-8(2)*, Ideal Pubns.) Worthy Publishing.

—One Enchanted Evening. Crouch, Karen Hillard, illus. 2003. 32p. (J). 14.95 *(978-0-8249-5480-2(7)*, Ideal Pubns.) Worthy Publishing.

—Reindeer Christmas. Good, Karen Hillard, illus. 2008. (ENG.). 40p. (J). (gr. -1-3). 15.99 *(978-1-4169-6108-6(9)*, Simon & Schuster/Paula Wiseman Bks.) Simon & Schuster/Paula Wiseman Bks.

—Scarecrow Pete & His Suitcase of Dreams. Crouch, Karen Hillard, illus. 2005. (ENG.). 36p. (J). (gr. -1-3). 14.95 *(978-0-8249-5151-1(4)*, Ideal Pubns.) Worthy Publishing.

—A Snowgirl Named Just Sue. Good, Karen Hillard, illus. 2008. (ENG.). 36p. (J). (gr. -1-3). 14.95 *(978-0-8249-5150-4(6)*, Ideal Pubns.) Worthy Publishing.

—A Snowman Named Just Bob. Hillard Good, Karen, illus. 2006. (ENG.). 16p. (J). (gr. k-3). 14.95 *(978-0-8249-1707-4(3)*, Ideal Pubns.) Worthy Publishing.

—A Snowman Named Just Bob. Crouch, Karen Hillard, illus. 2003. (ENG.). 36p. (J). 14.95 *(978-0-8249-5860-2(8)*, 53876801, Ideal Pubns.) Worthy Publishing.

—The Visit. Winget, Susan, tr. Winget, Susan, illus. 2003. (ENG.). 56p. (J). 14.95 *(978-0-8249-5859-6(4)*, Ideal Pubns.) Worthy Publishing.

—The Visit: The Origin of the Night Before Christmas, 1 vol. Winget, Susan, illus. 2013. (ENG.). 54p. (J). 16.99 *(978-0-7643-4575-3(3)*, 9780764345753) Schiffer Publishing, Ltd.

Moulton, Mark Kimball & Chalmers, Josh. Change the World Before Bedtime, 1 vol. Good, Karen, illus. 2012. (ENG.). 32p. (J). 16.99 *(978-0-7643-4238-7(X)*, 9780764342387) Schiffer Publishing, Ltd.

Moulton, Mark Kimball & Good, Karen Hillard. A Snowman Named Just Bob. Good, Karen Hillard, illus. 2009. (Illus.). 32p. (J). (gr. -1-3). 18.99 *(978-0-8249-5596-0(X)*, Ideal Pubns.) Worthy Publishing.

Mucha, Mark. Adventures with Edison & His Friends Vol. 1: "Crab in a Bucket" 2008. 58p. pap. 11.95 *(978-1-934449-29-5(6))* Legacy Publishing Services, Inc.

Muecke, Anne & Moore, Clement C. The Dinosaurs' Night Before Christmas. Hale, Nathan, illus. 2008. (ENG.). 36p. (J). (gr. -1-3). 18.99 *(978-0-8118-6322-3(0))* Chronicle Bks. LLC.

Mueller, Kirk Jay. Harriet Can Carry It, 1 vol. Vonthron-Laver, Sarah, illus. 2014. (ENG.). 32p. (J). 16.99 *(978-1-59572-675-9(6))* Star Bright Bks., Inc.

Muldrow, Diane & Golden Books Staff. Where Do Giggles Come From? Kennedy, Anne, illus. 2011. (Little Golden Book Ser.). (ENG.). 24p. (J). (gr. -1-2). 4.99 *(978-0-375-86133-8(5)*, Golden Bks.) Random Hse. Children's Bks.

Muñoz, Mercedes. Boogie the Booger. 2008. 20p. pap. 12.95 *(978-1-4327-2211-1(5))* Outskirts Pr., Inc.

Munshey, Sana. We're off to Make 'Umrah. 2011. (ENG., Illus.). 32p. (J). (gr. -1-k). 10.95 *(978-0-86037-458-9(0))* Kube Publishing Ltd. GBR. Dist: Consortium Bk. Sales & Distribution.

Munshey, Sana & Salem, Eman. We're off to Pray. 2016. (ENG., Illus.). 32p. (J). (gr. -1). 10.95 *(978-0-86037-529-6(3))* Kube Publishing Ltd. GBR. Dist: Consortium Bk. Sales & Distribution.

Munton, Gill. Who Ate All the Lettuce? Top That Publishing Staff, ed. Elliott, Rebecca, illus. 2007. 12p. (gr. -1-k). bds. *(978-1-84666-177-8(3)*, Tide Mill Pr.) Top That! Publishing PLC.

Murakami, Jon & BeachHouse Publishing. Geckos Surf. 2007. (ENG.). 16p. (J). (gr. -1-5). bds. 7.95 *(978-1-933067-22-3(5))* Beachhouse Publishing, LLC.

Murguia, Bethanie Deeney. Cockatoo, Too. 2016. (ENG., Illus.). 40p. (J). (gr. -1-1). 17.99 *(978-1-4998-0102-6(5))* Little Bee Books Inc.

Murguia, Bethanie Deeney. Toucans, Too. 2017. (ENG.). 40p. (J). (gr. -1-2). 17.99 ***(978-1-4998-0421-8(0))*** Little Bee Books Inc.

Murphy, Patricia J. I Need You. Bryant, Laura J., illus. 2003. (Rookie Readers Ser.). 31p. (J). (gr. 1-2). 12.60 *(978-0-7569-2065-4(5))* Perfection Learning Corp.

Murray, Alison. Fairy Felicity's Moonlight Adventure. Murray, Alison, illus. 2016. (ENG., Illus.). 24p. (J). (gr. -1-2). 15.99 *(978-0-7636-8945-2(9)*, Nosy Crow) Candlewick Pr.

—Hickory Dickory Dog. Murray, Alison, illus. 2014. (ENG., Illus.). 32p. (J). (-k). 16.99 *(978-0-7636-6826-6(5))* Candlewick Pr.

—The House That Zack Built. Murray, Alison, illus. 2016. (ENG., Illus.). 32p. (J). (-k). 16.99 *(978-0-7636-7844-9(9))* Candlewick Pr.

—One Two That's My Shoe! Murray, Alison, illus. 2012. (ENG., Illus.). 32p. (J). (gr. -1-1). 16.99 *(978-1-4231-4329-1(9))* Hyperion Pr.

Murray, Carol. Hurry Up! Garbot, Dave, illus. 2003. (Rookie Readers Ser.). (ENG.). 32p. (J). 19.50 *(978-0-516-22585-2(5)*, Children's Pr.) Scholastic Library Publishing.

Murray, Diana. City Shapes. Collier, Bryan, illus. 2016. (ENG.). 40p. (J). (gr. -1-3). 17.99 *(978-0-316-37092-9(4))* Little Brown & Co.

—Grimelda & the Spooktacular Pet Show. Ross, Heather, illus. 2017. 40p. (J). (gr. -1-3). 16.99 ***(978-0-06-226449-7(4)***, Tegen, Katherine Bks) HarperCollins Pubs.

Murray, Diana. Ned the Knitting Pirate. Lammle, Leslie, illus. 2016. (ENG.). 40p. (J). 16.99 *(978-1-59643-890-3(8)*, 9781596438903) Roaring Brook Pr.

Murray, Laura. The Gingerbread Man Loose at the Zoo. Lowery, Mike, illus. 2016. (ENG.). 32p. (J). (gr. k-3). 16.99 *(978-0-399-16867-3(2)*, G.P. Putnam's Sons Books for Young Readers) Penguin Young Readers Group.

—The Gingerbread Man Loose in the School. Lowery, Mike, illus. 2011. (ENG.). 32p. (J). (gr. k-3). 16.99 *(978-0-399-25052-1(2)*, G.P. Putnam's Sons Books for Young Readers) Penguin Young Readers Group.

—The Gingerbread Man Loose on the Fire Truck. Lowery, Mike, illus. 2013. (ENG.). 32p. (J). (gr. k-3). 16.99 *(978-0-399-25779-7(9)*, G.P. Putnam's Sons Books for Young Readers) Penguin Young Readers Group.

Murray, Laura & McPike, Elizabeth. The Gingerbread Man Loose at Christmas. Lowery, Mike, illus. 2015. (ENG.). 32p. (J). (gr. k-k). 16.99 *(978-0-399-16866-6(4)*, G.P. Putnam's Sons Books for Young Readers) Penguin Young Readers Group.

Murray, Marjorie Dennis. Halloween Night. Dorman, Brandon, illus. (ENG.). 40p. (J). (gr. k-4). 2013. pap. 6.99 *(978-0-06-185773-7(4))* 2010. 9.99 *(978-0-06-201293-7(2))* HarperCollins Pubs. (Greenwillow Bks.).

Murray, Tamsyn. Snug as a Bug. Abbot, Judi, illus. 2013. (ENG.). 32p. (J). *(978-0-85707-108-8(4))* Barnes & Noble, Inc.

—Snug as a Bug. Abbot, Judi, illus. 2014. (ENG.). 32p. (J). (gr. -1). pap. 8.99 *(978-0-85707-109-5(2))* Simon & Schuster, Ltd. GBR. Dist: Simon & Schuster, Inc.

—Snug As a Bug. Abbot, Judi & Gaviraghi, Giuditta, illus. 2013. 30p. (J). *(978-1-4351-4731-7(6))* Barnes & Noble, Inc.

Musgrave, Susan. Love You More, 1 vol. Melo, Esperança, illus. 2014. (ENG.). 24p. (J). (gr. -1-k). bds. 9.95 *(978-1-4598-0240-7(3))* Orca Bk. Pubs. USA.

—More Blueberries!, 1 vol. Melo, Esperança, illus. 2017. (ENG.). 28p. (J). (gr. -1-k). 6.95 *(978-1-4598-1505-6(X))* Orca Bk. Pubs. USA.

Musical Robot. If You're a Robot & You Know It. Carter, David A., illus. 2015. (ENG.). 14p. (J). (gr. -1-k). bds. 16.99 *(978-0-545-81980-0(6)*, Cartwheel Bks.) Scholastic, Inc.

Muten, Burleigh. Miss Emily. Phelan, Matt, illus. 2014. (ENG.). 144p. (J). (gr. 2-5). 15.99 *(978-0-7636-5734-5(4))* Candlewick Pr.

My Amazing Pet Snail. 2013. (Illus.). (J). *(978-1-4351-4755-3(3))* Barnes & Noble, Inc.

My Crazy Christmas Catastrophe Cat. 2003. (Illus.). 22p. (J). 9.95 *(978-0-9744751-1-0(4))* Timothy Lane Pr.

My First Book of Bedtime Stories. 2003. (J). 8.99 *(978-1-59384-013-6(6))* Parklane Publishing.

Myers, Lily. This Impossible Light. 2017. (ENG.). 352p. (YA). (gr. 7). 17.99 *(978-0-399-17372-1(2)*, Philomel Bks.) Penguin Young Readers Group.

Myers, Tim & Myers, Tim J. Looking for Luna, 0 vols. Reed, Mike, illus. 2009. (ENG.). 32p. (J). (gr. -1-3). 17.99 *(978-0-7614-5564-6(7)*, 9780761455646, Amazon Children's Publishing) Amazon Publishing.

Myers, Walter Dean. Street Love. (ENG.). 2007. 160p. (YA). (gr. 8-18). pap. 9.99 *(978-0-06-440732-8(2))* 2006. 144p. (J). (gr. 7-18). 15.99 *(978-0-06-028079-6(4))* HarperCollins Pubs. (Amistad).

Myers, Walter Dean & Myers, Christopher. Jazz. Myers, Christopher, illus. 2006. (ENG., Illus.). 48p. (J). (gr. -1-3). 18.95 *(978-0-8234-1545-8(7))* Holiday Hse., Inc.

Nagy, Jennifer. Goats in Coats. Broughton, Ilona & Szijgyarto, Cynthia, illus. 2009. 20p. pap. 12.99 *(978-1-4389-6586-4(9))* AuthorHouse.

Namm, Diane. Guess Who? Sheldon, David, illus. 2004. (My First Reader Ser.). (ENG.). 32p. (J). (gr. k-1). pap. 3.95 *(978-0-516-25503-3(7)*, Children's Pr.) Scholastic Library Publishing.

—Little Bear. McCue, Lisa, illus. 2003. (My First Reader Ser.). (ENG.). 32p. (J). 18.50 *(978-0-516-22931-7(1)*, Children's Pr.) Scholastic Library Publishing.

—My Best Friend. Gordon, Mike, illus. 2004. (My First Reader Ser.). (ENG.). 32p. (J). (gr. k-1). pap. 3.95 *(978-0-516-25504-0(5)*, Children's Pr.) Scholastic Library Publishing.

—My Best Friend. Gordon, Mike, tr. Gordon, Mike, illus. 2004. (My First Reader Ser.). (ENG.). 31p. (J). 18.50 *(978-0-516-24416-7(7)*, Children's Pr.) Scholastic Library Publishing.

—Pick a Pet. Suarez, Maribel, tr. Suarez, Maribel, illus. 2004. (My First Reader Ser.). (ENG.). 31p. (J). 18.50 *(978-0-516-24417-4(5)*, Children's Pr.) Scholastic Library Publishing.

Nash, Linda. The Legend of the Lilies. 2013. (ENG.). 64p. (J). 17.95 *(978-1-4497-8378-5(3)*, WestBow Pr.) Author Solutions, Inc.

Nash, Margaret. My Big, New Bed. Blake, Beccy, illus. 2008. (Tadpoles Ser.). (ENG.). 24p. (J). (gr. -1-2). lib. bdg. *(978-0-7787-3859-6(0))*; pap. *(978-0-7787-3890-9(6))* Crabtree Publishing Co.

Needham, T. L. Kitty Claus. 2012. (ENG.). 27p. (J). (-18). pap. 19.95 *(978-1-4787-1788-1(2))* Outskirts Pr., Inc.

Neff, Fred. The Memory Tree. Montmeat, Jack, illus. 2008. 36p. pap. 14.99 *(978-1-59858-854-5(0))* Dog Ear Publishing, LLC.

Negroni, Jay. Emerald's Flight, 1 vol. 2008. (ENG.). 29p. pap. 24.95 *(978-1-60672-863-5(6))* America Star Bks.

Neimark, Jill. The Hugging Tree: A Story about Resilience. Wong, Nicole, illus. 2015. (J). *(978-1-4338-1907-0(4)*, Magination Pr.) American Psychological Assn.

Neitzel, Shirley. Who Will I Be? A Halloween Rebus Story. Parker, Nancy Winslow, illus. 2005. 32p. (J). lib. bdg. 13.89 *(978-0-06-056068-3(1))* HarperCollins Pubs.

Nelsen, Donald. Sam & Emma. Gorey, Edward, illus. 2016. (ENG.). 48p. 14.99 *(978-0-486-80590-0(5))* Dover Pubns., Inc.

Nelsen, Sissy. Wiggly & Giggly. 2012. 24p. pap. 17.99 *(978-1-4772-6721-9(2))* AuthorHouse.

Nelson, Joanne. When It Snows. Moore, Cyd, illus. 2012. (Discovery Phonics Ser.). (ENG.). 16p. (J). (gr. -1-3). pap. 10.47 *(978-0-8136-1087-0(7))* Modern Curriculum Pr.

Nelson, Kadir. He's Got the Whole World in His Hands. Nelson, Kadir, illus. 2005. (ENG., Illus.). 32p. (J). (gr. -1-3). 17.99 *(978-0-8037-2850-9(6)*, Dial Bks) Penguin Young Readers Group.

Nelson-Schmidt, Michelle. Cats, Cats! Nelson-Schmidt, Michelle, illus. 2011. (ENG., Illus.). 32p. (J). pap. 5.99 *(978-1-61067-042-5(6))* Kane Miller.

—Dogs, Dogs! Nelson-Schmidt, Michelle, illus. 2011. (ENG., Illus.). 32p. (J). pap. 5.99 *(978-1-61067-041-8(8))* Kane Miller.

NeonSeon. Life of Shouty: Food & Fitness, bk. 2. NeonSeon, illus. 2011. (Life of Shouty Ser.: 2). (ENG., Illus.). 32p. (J). 14.95 *(978-0-9842069-1-9(4))* RIXKIN.

Nesbitt, Kenn. Believe It or Not, My Brother Has a Monster! Slonim, David, illus. 2015. (ENG.). 32p. (J). (gr. k-2). 16.99 *(978-0-545-65059-5(3)*, Cartwheel Bks.) Scholastic, Inc.

Nethaway, Misty. I Know My Mommy Loves Me. 2008. 17p. pap. 24.95 *(978-1-60672-475-0(4))* America Star Bks.

Neubecker, Robert. Fall Is for School. Neubecker, Robert, illus. 2017. (ENG., Illus.). 32p. (J). (gr. -1-k). 17.99 ***(978-1-4847-3254-0(5))*** Disney Pr.

Neubecker, Robert. What Little Boys Are Made Of. Neubecker, Robert, illus. 2012. (ENG., Illus.). 32p. (J). (gr. -1-3). 14.99 *(978-0-06-202355-1(1))* HarperCollins Pubs.

Neutzling, Laura. Grandpa Hugs, 1 vol. 2017. (ENG., Illus.). 20p. (J). bds. 9.99 *(978-0-7180-8940-5(5))* Nelson, Thomas Inc.

Nevius, Carol. Building with Dad, 0 vols. Thomson, Bill, illus. 2012. (ENG.). 32p. (J). (gr. k-3). pap. 9.99 *(978-0-7614-5984-2(7)*, 9780761459842, Amazon Children's Publishing) Amazon Publishing.

—Karate Hour, 0 vols. Thomson, Bill, illus. 2011. (ENG.). 34p. (J). (gr. -1-2). pap. 7.99 *(978-0-7614-5840-1(9)*, 9780761458401, Amazon Children's Publishing) Amazon Publishing.

New Burlington Books, creator. The Great Big Book of Bedtime Stories & Rhyme. 2008. (Illus.). 304p. (J). *(978-1-84538-882-9(8))* New Burlington Bks.

New Players Club LLC Staff, New Players Club L. L. C. Coco Boom Boom. 2006. 32p. 12.99 *(978-1-4116-8191-0(6))* Lulu Pr., Inc.

New, William. Sam Swallow & the Riddleworld League, 1 vol. Yayo, illus. 2013. (ENG.). 144p. (J). (gr. 3-5). pap. 12.95 *(978-1-896580-98-2(X))* Tradewind Bks. CAN. Dist: Orca Bk. Pubs. USA.

Newbery, Linda. Posy. Rayner, Catherine, illus. 2008. (ENG.). 32p. (J). (gr. -1-k). 16.99 *(978-1-4169-7112-2(2)*, Atheneum Bks. for Young Readers) Simon & Schuster Children's Publishing.

Newman, Jeff. Hand Book. Newman, Jeff, illus. 2011. (ENG., Illus.). 40p. (J). (gr. -1-3). 15.99 *(978-1-4169-5013-4(3)*, Simon & Schuster Bks. For Young Readers) Simon & Schuster Bks. For Young Readers.

Newman, Lesléa. The Boy Who Cried Fabulous. Ferguson, Peter, illus. 2007. (ENG.). 32p. (J). (gr. -1-2). pap. 7.99 *(978-1-58246-224-0(0)*, Tricycle Pr.) Random Hse. Children's Bks.

—Cats, Cats, Cats! Oller, Erika, illus. 2004. (ENG.). 32p. (J). (gr. -1-3). reprint ed. 7.99 *(978-0-689-86697-5(6)*, Simon & Schuster Bks. For Young Readers) Simon & Schuster Bks. For Young Readers.

—Dogs, Dogs, Dogs! Oller, Erika, illus. 2011. (ENG.). 30p. (J). (gr. -1-3). pap. 16.99 *(978-1-4424-5228-2(5)*, Simon & Schuster Bks. For Young Readers) Simon & Schuster Bks. For Young Readers.

—Donovan's Big Day. Dutton, Mike, illus. 2011. (ENG.). 32p. (J). (gr. -1-2). 15.99 *(978-1-58246-332-2(8)*, Tricycle Pr.) Random Hse. Children's Bks.

—Just Like Mama. Gorton, Julia, illus. 2010. (ENG.). 32p. (J). (gr. k-2). 15.95 *(978-0-8109-8393-9(1)*, Abrams Bks. for Young Readers) Abrams, Inc.

—A Kiss on the Keppie, 0 vols. Blackmore, Katherine & Wiltse, Kris, illus. 2012. (ENG.). 24p. (J). (gr. -1-2). 12.99 *(978-0-7614-6241-5(4)*, 9780761462415, Amazon Children's Publishing) Amazon Publishing.

—Where Is Bear? Gorbachev, Valeri, illus. 2006. (ENG.). 44p. (J). (gr. -1 — 1). pap. 6.99 *(978-0-15-205918-7(0))* Houghton Mifflin Harcourt Publishing Co.

Newman, Tracy. Hanukkah Is Coming! Garofoli, Viviana, illus. 2015. (ENG.). 12p. (J). (gr. -1 — 1). pap. 5.99 *(978-1-4677-5241-1(X)*, Kar-Ben Publishing) Lerner Publishing Group.

—Passover Is Coming! Garófoli, Viviana, illus. 2016. (ENG.). 12p. (J). (gr. -1 — 1). 5.99 *(978-1-4677-5242-8(8)*, Kar-Ben Publishing) Lerner Publishing Group.

—Passover Is Coming! Garofoli, Viviana, illus. 2016. (ENG.). 12p. (gr. -1 — 1). 23.99 *(978-1-4677-9610-1(7)*, Kar-Ben Publishing) Lerner Publishing Group.

—Purim Is Coming! Garófoli, Viviana, illus. 2017. (ENG.). 12p. (gr. -1 — 1). 5.99 *(978-1-5124-0827-0(1)*, Kar-Ben Publishing) Lerner Publishing Group.

—Rosh Hashanah Is Coming! Garofoli, Viviana, illus. 2016. (ENG.). 12p. (gr. -1 — 1). 23.99 *(978-1-5124-0945-1(6)*, Kar-Ben Publishing) Lerner Publishing Group.

—Sukkot Is Coming! Garófoli, Viviana, illus. 2017. (ENG.). 12p. (gr. -1 — 1). bds. 5.99 *(978-1-5124-0828-7(X)*, Kar-Ben Publishing) Lerner Publishing Group.

Nguyen, Vincent, illus. The Crabfish. 2010. (First Steps in Music Ser.). (ENG.). 24p. (J). (gr. -1-k). 16.95 *(978-1-57999-772-4(4))* G I A Pubns., Inc.

Nicholls, Paul, illus. I Want to Be A... Pirate. 2014. (J). *(978-1-4351-5500-8(9))* Barnes & Noble, Inc.

Nicola, Robbin. Fighter Joe: The Fish of Which Dreams Are Made. Wolf, Claudia, illus. 2006. 24p. (J). per. 2.99 *(978-1-59958-001-2(2))* Journey Stone Creations, LLC.

Niemann, Christoph. Subway. Niemann, Christoph, illus. 2010. (Illus.). 40p. (J). (gr. -1-k). (ENG.). 16.99 *(978-0-06-157779-6(0))*; lib. bdg. 17.89 *(978-0-06-157780-2(4))* HarperCollins Pubs. (Greenwillow Bks.).

The Night Before Kindergarten. 2014. (Night Before Ser.). (ENG.). 32p. (J). (gr. 7-12). 8.24 *(978-1-63245-263-4(4))* Lectorum Pubns., Inc.

Nikola-Lisa, W. My Teacher Can Teach... Anyone! Galindo, Felipe, illus. 2004. (ENG.). 32p. (J). (gr. -1-2). 16.95 *(978-1-58430-163-9(5))*; pap. 9.95 *(978-1-60060-276-4(2))* Lee & Low Bks., Inc.

Nister, Ernest, illus. Merry Magic-Go-Round: An Antique Book of Changing Pictures. 2005. 14p. (J). (gr. k-4). reprint ed. 19.00 *(978-0-7567-9156-8(1))* DIANE Publishing Co.

Nobisso, Josephine. Hot Cha-Cha! Holub, Joan, illus. 2009. (ENG.). 32p. (J). (gr. k-2). 16.95 *(978-0-940112-18-6(3))* Gingerbread Hse.

—The Numbers Dance: A Counting Comedy. Ziborova, Dasha, illus. 2005. (ENG.). 32p. (J). (gr. k-2). 16.95 *(978-0-940112-11-7(6))*; pap. 8.95 *(978-0-940112-12-4(4))* Gingerbread Hse.

Nolan, Allia Zobel. Animal Parade. Maddocks, Maria, illus. 2011. (ENG.). 10p. (J). (gr. -1 — 1). 12.99 *(978-0-547-55867-7(8))* Houghton Mifflin Harcourt Publishing Co.

—God's Oak Tree. Chung, Chi, illus. 2007. 16p. (J). (gr. -1). 12.99 *(978-0-8254-5536-0(7))* Kregel Pubns.

Noonan, Julia. My Pumpkin. Lawson, Peter, illus. 2005. (My First Reader Ser.). (ENG.). 32p. (J). (gr. k-1). lib. bdg. 18.50 *(978-0-516-24876-9(6)*, Children's Pr.) Scholastic Library Publishing.

Norman, Kim. I Know a Wee Piggy. Cole, Henry, illus. 2012. (ENG.). 32p. (J). (gr. -1-k). 16.99 *(978-0-8037-3735-8(1)*, Dial Bks) Penguin Young Readers Group.

—She'll Be Coming up the Mountain. Woodruff, Liza, illus. 2016. (ENG.). 32p. (J). (gr. -1). 14.95 *(978-1-4549-1610-9(9))* Sterling Publishing Co., Inc.

—Still a Gorilla! Geran, Chad, illus. 2016. (ENG.). 32p. (J). (gr. -1-k). 16.99 *(978-0-545-75791-1(6))* Scholastic, Inc.

—This Old Van. Conahan, Carolyn Digby, illus. 2015. (ENG.). 30p. (J). (gr. -1-2). 14.95 *(978-1-4549-1063-3(1))* Sterling Publishing Co., Inc.

Norman, Kimberly. If It's Snowy & You Know It, Clap Your Paws! Woodruff, Liza, illus. 2013. (ENG.). 26p. (J). (gr. -1). 14.95 *(978-1-4549-0384-0(8))* Sterling Publishing Co., Inc.

—Ten on the Sled. Woodruff, Liza, illus. 2010. (ENG.). 26p. (J). (gr. -1). 14.95 *(978-1-4027-7076-0(6))* Sterling Publishing Co., Inc.

Norris, Eryl. What's That in the Water? Mansfield, Andy, illus. 2015. (ENG.). 18p. (J). (gr. -1-1). 9.99 (978-1-4998-0139-2(4)) Little Bee Books Inc.
North, Sherry. Because I Am Your Daddy. Hall, Marcellus, illus. 2010. (ENG.). 32p. (J). (gr. -1-1). 16.95 (978-0-8109-8392-2(3), Abrams Bks. for Young Readers) Abrams, Inc.
—Because You Are My Baby. Hall, Marcellus, illus. 2008. (ENG.). 32p. (J). (gr. -1-1). 16.95 (978-0-8109-9482-9(8), Abrams Bks. for Young Readers) Abrams, Inc.
Northcutt, Allen. The Legend of Chris Moose: The Most Beautiful Moose in the World. 2012. (ENG.). 48p. (J). 17.95 (978-1-938462-01-6(7)) Old Stone Pr.
Nosy Crow Staff. Bizzy Bear: Fun on the Farm. Davies, Benji, illus. 2011. (Bizzy Bear Ser.). (ENG.). 8p. (J). (gr. k — 1). bds. 6.99 (978-0-7636-5879-3(0), Nosy Crow) Candlewick Pr.
—Bizzy Bear: Let's Get to Work! Davies, Benji, illus. 2012. (Bizzy Bear Ser.). (ENG.). 8p. (J). (gr. k — 1). bds. 6.99 (978-0-7636-5899-1(5), Nosy Crow) Candlewick Pr.
—Bizzy Bear: off We Go! Davies, Benji, illus. 2012. (Bizzy Bear Ser.). (ENG.). 8p. (J). (gr. k — 1). bds. 6.99 (978-0-7636-5900-4(2), Nosy Crow) Candlewick Pr.
—Bizzy Bear: Zookeeper. Davies, Benji, illus. 2015. (Bizzy Bear Ser.). (ENG.). 8p. (J). (— 1). bds. 6.99 (978-0-7636-7603-2(9), Nosy Crow) Candlewick Pr.
—Fire Rescue! Davies, Benji, illus. 2013. (Bizzy Bear Ser.). (ENG.). 8p. (J). (— 1). bds. 6.99 (978-0-7636-6518-0(5), Nosy Crow) Candlewick Pr.
—Flip Flap Safari. Scheffler, Axel, illus. 2015. (ENG.). 28p. (J). (gr. -1-2). 11.99 (978-0-7636-7605-6(5), Nosy Crow) Candlewick Pr.
—Pirate Adventure. Davies, Benji, illus. 2013. (Bizzy Bear Ser.). (ENG.). 8p. (J). (— 1). bds. 6.99 (978-0-7636-6519-7(3), Nosy Crow) Candlewick Pr.
Novak, Matt. A Wish for You. Novak, Matt, illus. 2010. (Illus.). 32p. (J). 16.99 (978-0-06-155202-1(X), Greenwillow Bks.) HarperCollins Pubs.
Noyes, Diana. The Tickle Bug. Noyes, Diana, illus. l.t. ed. 2005. (Illus.). 20p. (J). per. 9.99 (978-1-59879-080-1(3)) Lifevest Publishing, Inc.
Numeroff, Laura Joffe. Dogs Don't Wear Sneakers. Mathieu, Joe, illus. 2014. 40p. pap. 8.00 (978-1-61003-344-2(2)) Center for the Collaborative Classroom.
—Lots of Lambs. Munsinger, Lynn, illus. 2012. (ENG.). 20p. (J). (gr. k — 1). 9.99 (978-0-547-40206-2(6)) Houghton Mifflin Harcourt Publishing Co.
Nutt, Robert. Amy's Light. Nutt, Robert, illus. 2010. (Illus.). 44p. (J). (gr. -1-3). 16.95 (978-1-58469-128-0(X)); (ENG., pap. 8.95 (978-1-58469-129-7(8)) Dawn Pubns.
O'Brien, Anne Sibley. Abracadabra, It's Spring! Gal, Susan, illus. 2016. (Seasonal Magic Ser.). (ENG.). 24p. (J). (gr. -1-k). 14.95 (978-1-4197-1891-5(6), Abrams Appleseed) Abrams, Inc.
—Hocus Pocus, It's Fall! Gal, Susan, illus. 2016. (ENG.). 24p. (J). (gr. -1-k). 12.95 (978-1-4197-2125-0(9), Abrams Appleseed) Abrams, Inc.
Ocker, Christ Holder. A Mouse Without a House. 2006. (J). per. (978-1-59872-711-1(7)) Instant Pub.
O'Connell, Jennifer Barrett. It's Halloween Night! 2012. lib. bdg. 17.20 (978-0-606-26206-4(7), Turtleback) Turtleback Bks.
O'Connor, Frankie. The Ants Go Marching One by One. Paiva, Johannah Gilman, ed. Groot, Nicole, illus. 2014. (ENG.). 32p. (J). (gr. -1-3). 7.99 (978-1-4867-0004-2(7)) Flowerpot Children's Pr. Inc. CAN. Dist: Cardinal Pubs. Group.
October the Octopus: A Huggable Concept Book about the Months of the Year. 2014. (ENG., Illus.). 28p. (J). (gr. -1-k). 24.99 (978-1-4814-2047-1(X), Simon & Schuster/Paula Wiseman Bks.) Simon & Schuster/Paula Wiseman Bks.
Odanaka, Barbara. Smash! Mash! Crash! There Goes the Trash! Hillenbrand, Will, illus. 2006. (ENG.). 32p. (J). (gr. -1-3). 18.99 (978-0-689-85160-5(X), McElderry, Margaret K. Bks.) McElderry, Margaret K. Bks.
O'Dare, Helen. Love. O'Byrne, Nicola, illus. 2016. (ENG.). 26p. (J). bds. 6.99 (978-1-62686-677-5(5), Silver Dolphin Bks.) Readerlink Distribution Services, LLC.
Ode, Eric. Bigfoot Does Not Like Birthday Parties. Temairik, Jaime, illus. 2015. (ENG.). 40p. (J). (gr. -1-3). 16.99 (978-1-63217-004-0(3), Little Bigfoot) Sasquatch Bks.
Odgers, Sally. Good Night, Truck. McKenzie, Heath, illus. 2016. (ENG.). 32p. (J). 16.99 (978-1-250-07019-7(8), 9781250070197) Feiwel & Friends.
Odhiambo, Tori. Close to Home: The African Savannah. 2012. 32p. pap. 21.99 (978-1-4691-9510-0(0)) Xlibris Corp.
O'donnell, Tamara J. Grand Mommy's Dress up Box. 2006. (J). (978-0-9790337-1-1(3)) Crosam Pr.
Oelschlager, Vanita. My Grampy Can't Walk. Hegan, Robin & Blackwood, Kristin, illus. 2008. (ENG.). 36p. (J). (gr. -1-3). 9.95 (978-0-9800162-0-8(7)) VanitaBooks.
O'Garden, Irene. The Scrubbly-Bubbly Car Wash. Jabar, Cynthia, illus. 2003. (ENG.). 32p. (J). (gr. -1-1). 15.99 (978-0-694-00871-1(0)) HarperCollins Pubs.
O'Hair, Margaret. Twin to Twin. Courtin, Thierry, illus. 2003. (ENG.). 32p. (J). (gr. -1-3). 17.99 (978-0-689-84494-2(8), McElderry, Margaret K. Bks.) McElderry, Margaret K. Bks.
Ohanesian, Diane. The ABCs of Thanks & Please. Chamberlain, Margaret, illus. 2011. (J). (978-0-545-37962-5(8)) Scholastic, Inc.
Oldfield, Rachel. Up up Up. Reed, Susan, illus. 2011. (ENG.). 24p. (J). (gr. -1-2). 9.99 (978-1-84686-550-3(6)) Barefoot Bks., Inc.
Olin, Marilyn. Mom, Mac & Cheese, Please! Pantic, Dunja, illus. 2013. (ENG.). 28p. (J). (gr. -1-k). 16.95 (978-1-62087-995-5(6), 620995, Sky Pony Pr.) Skyhorse Publishing Co., Inc.
Oliver, Ilanit. Ten Flying Brooms. Poling, Kyle, illus. 2015. (ENG.). 24p. (J). (gr. -1-k). 3.99 (978-0-545-81336-5(0), Cartwheel Bks.) Scholastic, Inc.
Olsen, Bevan. Bethlehem's Star. 2008. 16p. pap. 2.99 (978-1-59955-181-4(0)) Cedar Fort, Inc./CFI Distribution.
—The Innkeeper's Christmas. 2010. (Illus.). 12p. (J). pap. 2.99 (978-1-59955-433-4(X)) Cedar Fort, Inc./CFI Distribution.
—The Magi. 2011. (Illus.). 12p. (J). pap. 2.99 (978-1-59955-924-7(2), Bonneville Bks.) Cedar Fort, Inc./CFI Distribution.
Olsen, Jan Z. Mat Man Hats. Delaney, Molly, illus. 2008. (ENG.). 36p. stu. ed. 13.75 (978-1-891627-93-4(7)) Handwriting Without Tears.
Olson, Julie, illus. Already Asleep. 2006. (ENG.). 32p. (J). (gr. -1-3). 12.95 (978-0-9766805-6-7(4)) Keene Publishing.
Olson, Nancy. Thanksgiving at Grandma's. Marino, Michael F., illus. 2009. 24p. pap. 10.95 (978-1-4251-8909-9(1)) Trafford Publishing.
One Big Pair of Underwear. 2014. (ENG., Illus.). 40p. (J). (gr. -1-3). 17.99 (978-1-4424-5336-4(2), Beach Lane Bks.) Beach Lane Bks.
Opie, David, illus. Monkey & the Engineer. 2007. 24p. (J). 14.95 (978-0-9793972-6-4(X)) JD Publishing.
Oppenheim, Joanne F. The Prince's Bedtime. Latimer, Miriam, illus. (ENG.). 32p. (J). (gr. -1-3). 2007. pap. 7.99 (978-1-84686-106-2(3)) 2006. 16.99 (978-1-84148-597-3(7)) Barefoot Bks., Inc.
Oppenheim, Joanne F. & Barefoot Books Staff. The Prince's Breakfast. Latimer, Miriam, illus. 2014. 32p. (J). (gr. -1-2). 9.99 (978-1-78285-075-5(9)); 16.99 (978-1-78285-074-8(0)) Barefoot Bks., Inc.
—El Principe No Duerme. Latimer, Miriam, illus. 2014. (SPA.). 32p. (J). (gr. -1-1). pap. 7.99 (978-1-78285-077-9(5)) Barefoot Bks., Inc.
Oppenheim, Joanne F. & Latimer, Muriam. The Prince's Bedtime. Latimer, Miriam, illus. 2007. (ENG., Illus.). 32p. (J). (gr. -1-2). 9.99 (978-1-84686-096-6(2)) Barefoot Bks., Inc.
Oppenheim, Shulamith. Where Do I End & You Begin? Felix, Monique, illus. 2015. (ENG.). 32p. (J). (gr. 1-3). 17.99 (978-1-56846-274-5(3), Creative Editions) Creative Co., The.
Orbach, Ruth. Apple Pigs. 2016. (ENG., Illus.). 32p. (J). (gr. k-2). 15.99 (978-1-84365-302-8(8)) National Trust, Aylesbury GBR. Dist: Independent Pubs. Group.
Organ, Betty. Peter's Christmas Eve Adventure, 1 vol. Martin, Shawn, illus. 2010. (ENG.). 32p. (J). (gr. k-3). 10.95 (978-1-897174-68-5(3), Tuckamore Bks) Creative Bk. Publishing CAN. Dist: Orca Bk. Pubs. USA.
Orgel, Doris. Sarah's Room. Sendak, Maurice, illus. 2005. 47p. (J). (gr. k-4). reprint ed. 15.00 (978-0-7567-9683-9(0)) DIANE Publishing Co.
Ormerod, Jan. The Animal Bop Won't Stop! Gardiner, Lindsey, illus. 2011. (J). (978-1-4380-8419-0(6)) Barron's Educational Series, Inc.
—If You're Happy & You Know It! Gardiner, Lindsey, illus. 2003. 32p. (J). (gr. -1-3). 15.95 (978-1-932605-07-7(5)); pap. 5.95 (978-1-932605-10-7(5)) Star Bright Bks., Inc.
Ormerod, Jan, et al. Doing the Animal Bop. 2005. (Illus.). (J). (978-0-7641-8299-0(4)) Barron's Educational Series, Inc.
Orshoski, Paul. We Both Read-My Sitter Is a T-Rex! (Level 1-2) Ebbeler, Jeffrey, illus. 2011. (ENG.). 44p. (J). 9.95 (978-1-60115-253-4(1)); pap. 4.99 (978-1-60115-254-1(X)) Treasure Bay, Inc.
—We Both Read-The Mouse in My House. Ebbeler, Jeffrey, illus. 2012. 44p. (J). 9.95 (978-1-60115-257-2(4)); pap. 4.99 (978-1-60115-258-9(2)) Treasure Bay, Inc.
Orshoski, Paul & Max, Dave. We Both Read-The Ant & the Pancake. 2015. (ENG., Illus.). 44p. (J). (gr. k-1). pap. 4.99 (978-1-60115-272-5(8)) Treasure Bay, Inc.
Osmond, Jimmy. The Awesome Possum Family Band. 2014. (ENG., Illus.). 40p. (J). (gr. -1-3). 16.99 (978-1-62157-211-4(0), Regnery Kids) Regnery Publishing, Inc., An Eagle Publishing Co.
Oso Se Va de Viaje. 2014. (ENG & SPA., Illus.). (J). (978-1-78285-088-5(0)) Barefoot Bks., Inc.
Osteen, Victoria. Gifts from the Heart. Palmisciano, Diane, illus. 2010. (ENG.). 32p. (J). (gr. -1-2). 17.99 (978-1-4169-5551-1(8), Little Simon Inspirations) Little Simon Inspirations.
Ostrove, Karen. Rise & Shine: A Challah-Day Tale. Scott, Kimberley, illus. 2013. (Shabbat Ser.). (ENG.). 24p. (J). (gr. -1-3). 7.95 (978-0-7613-7500-5(7)); lib. bdg. 17.95 (978-0-7613-7499-2(X)) Lerner Publishing Group. (Kar-Ben Publishing).
OSullivan, Michaeleen, tr. A Monarch Universe: Children's Picture Book. 2007. (Illus.). 34p. (J). pap. 22.95 (978-0-9800222-0-9(7)) UPfirst.com Bks.
O'Toole-Freel, Judy. Aardvark, Aardvark, How Do You Do!, 1 vol. 2008. (ENG.). 31p. 24.95 (978-1-4241-6618-3(7)) America Star Bks.
Ovadia, Ron. Hank. 2013. 30p. 16.95 (978-1-60844-834-0(7)) Dog Ear Publishing, LLC.
Owen, Karen. I Could Be- Barroux, illus. 2009. (J). (978-1-84686-289-2(2)) Barefoot Bks., Inc.
—I Could Be, You Could Be. Barroux, illus. 2010. (ENG.). 32p. (J). (gr. 1-3). 16.99 (978-1-84686-405-6(4)) Barefoot Bks., Inc.
Owen, Karen & Barroux. I Could Be, You Could Be. 2012. (ENG., Illus.). 32p. (J). (gr. -1-1). pap. 7.99 (978-1-84686-763-7(0)) Barefoot Bks., Inc.
Owen, Linda. Robin's Song, 1 vol. 2009. (ENG.). 28p. (J). pap. (978-1-85345-495-0(8)) Crusade for World Revival.
Owens, Lucy. My Lime Green Butterfly. 2011. 40p. pap. 22.65 (978-1-4568-7103-1(X)) Xlibris Corp.
Oxenbury, Helen. Pig Tale. Oxenbury, Helen, illus. 2010. (ENG., Illus.). 32p. (J). (gr. -1-1). 16.99 (978-1-4424-2153-0(3), McElderry, Margaret K. Bks.) McElderry, Margaret K. Bks.
Pace, Dianne. Odel's Diner. 2007. (J). per. 12.95 (978-0-89315-419-6(9)) Lambert Bk. Hse., Inc.
Packard, Mary. The New Baby. Haley, Amanda, illus. 2004. (My First Reader Ser.). (ENG.). 32p. (J). (gr. k-1). pap. 3.95 (978-0-516-25506-4(1), Children's Pr.) Scholastic Library Publishing.
Page, Nick & Page, Claire. The Winter Prince. Shimmen, Cathy, illus. 2006. (Read with Me (Make Believe Ideas) Ser.). 31p. (J). (gr. k-2). (978-1-84610-172-4(7)) Make Believe Ideas.
Page, Nick & Claire. Elves & the Shoemaker. 2006. (Read with Me (Make Believe Ideas) Ser.). (Illus.). 32p. (J). (gr. k-2). (978-1-84610-161-8(1)) Make Believe Ideas.
Page, Stefan. We're Going to the Farmers' Market. 2014. (ENG., Illus.). 16p. (J). (gr. -1 — 1). bds. 7.99 (978-1-4521-1834-5(5)) Chronicle Bks. LLC.
Palfreman-Bunker, Claire. Can Kittens Take a Catnap? Relf, Adam, illus. 2007. (J). pap. (978-0-545-02595-9(8)) Scholastic, Inc.
Paluch, Beily. Braid the Challah: A Playful Action Rhyme. Argoff, Patti, illus. 2014. 12p. (J). bds. 6.95 (978-1-929628-83-4(8)) Hachai Publishing.
—Braid the Challah: A Playful Action Rhyme. Argoff, Beily, illus. 2004. 12p. (J). bds. 6.95 (978-1-929628-17-9(X)) Hachai Publishing.
Pandya, Mamata. The Hare Scare: Based on the Original Gujarati Story by Gijubhai Badheka. 2004. (Illus.). 24p. (J). (978-81-291-0441-0(5)) Rupa & Co.
Pankiw, Dr Mary & Pankiw, Mary. Misilla Mouse. 2011. 32p. pap. (978-1-4269-5476-4(X)) Trafford Publishing (UK) Ltd.
Pantin, Yolanda. Splash! Faria, Rosana, illus. 2003. (SPA.). 16p. (J). (gr. -1-1). (978-980-6437-19-7(5)) Playco Editores, C.A.
Paquette, Ammi-Joan. Bunny Bus. Withrow, Lesley Breen, illus. 2017. (ENG.). 32p. (J). 16.99 (978-0-374-30225-2(1), 9780374302252, Farrar, Straus & Giroux (BYR)) Farrar, Straus & Giroux.
—Ghost in the House. Record, Adam, illus. 2015. (ENG.). 20p. (J). (gr. -1-2). 9.99 (978-0-7636-7622-3(5)) Candlewick Pr.
Paraskevas, Betty. Peter Pepper's Pet Spectacular. Paraskevas, Michael, illus. 2007. 32p. (J). (gr. 2-6). pap. 14.95 (978-1-60095-257-9(7)) Carson-Dellosa Publishing, LLC.
Parenteau, Shirley. Bears in Beds. Walker, David, illus. 2012. (ENG.). 32p. (J). (gr. k-k). 15.99 (978-0-7636-5338-5(1)) Candlewick Pr.
—Bears in the Bath. Walker, David, illus. (ENG.). (J). (— 1). 2016. 30p. bds. 6.99 (978-0-7636-7946-0(1)) 2014. 32p. 15.99 (978-0-7636-6418-3(9)) Candlewick Pr.
—Bears on Chairs. Walker, David, illus. 2011. (ENG.). 32p. (J). (gr. -1 — 1). bds. 6.99 (978-0-7636-5092-6(7)) Candlewick Pr.
Park, Barbara. Ma! There's Nothing to Do Here! A Word from Your Baby-in-Waiting. Garofoli, Viviana, illus. 2008. (Picture Book Ser.). (ENG.). 40p. (J). (gr. -1-2). 15.99 (978-0-375-83852-1(X), Random Hse. Bks. for Young Readers) Random Hse. Children's Bks.
Park, Linda Sue. Bee-Bim Bop! Lee, Ho Baek, illus. (ENG.). 32p. (J). (gr. -1-3). 2008. pap. 7.99 (978-0-547-07671-3(1)) 2005. 17.99 (978-0-618-26511-4(2)) Houghton Mifflin Harcourt Publishing Co.
—Xander's Panda Party. Phelan, Matt, illus. 2013. (ENG.). 40p. (J). (gr. -1-3). 16.99 (978-0-547-55865-3(1)) Houghton Mifflin Harcourt Publishing Co.
Parker, Amy. Night Night, Daddy, 1 vol. 2016. (Night Night Ser.). (ENG., Illus.). 20p. (J). bds. 9.99 (978-0-7180-4230-1(1)) Nelson, Thomas Inc.
—A Night Night Prayer, 1 vol. Pedler, Caroline, illus. 2015. (Night Night Ser.). (ENG.). 24p. (J). pap. 3.99 (978-0-7180-3652-2(2)) Nelson, Thomas Inc.
—The Plans I Have for You, 1 vol. Newton, Vanessa & Brantley-Newton, Vanessa, illus. 2015. (ENG.). 32p. (J). 16.99 (978-0-310-72410-0(4)) Zonderkidz.
Parker, Emma. At the Circus. 2010. (Illus.). 20p. pap. (978-1-877561-52-8(5)) First Edition Ltd.
—Blah the Bacteria. 2010. (Illus.). pap. (978-1-877547-46-1(8)) First Edition Ltd.
—Dancing Class. 2010. (Illus.). pap. (978-1-877561-05-4(3)) First Edition Ltd.
—Davey Dory. 2010. (Illus.). 20p. pap. (978-1-877561-58-0(4)) First Edition Ltd.
—The Fluffiest Chicken. 2010. (Illus.). pap. (978-1-877561-13-9(4)) First Edition Ltd.
—Granny Odd Legs. 2010. (Illus.). pap. (978-1-877547-86-7(7)) First Edition Ltd.
—Groat & the Coat. 2010. (Illus.). pap. (978-1-877547-99-7(9)) First Edition Ltd.
—How Many Fish? 2010. (Illus.). pap. (978-1-877561-10-8(X)) First Edition Ltd.
—How Shall I Get to School Today? 2010. (Illus.). pap. (978-1-877547-84-3(0)) First Edition Ltd.
—Karaoke Colin. 2010. (Illus.). 20p. pap. (978-1-877561-34-4(7)) First Edition Ltd.
—The Magic Show. 2010. (Illus.). pap. (978-1-877561-23-8(1)) First Edition Ltd.
—The Magic Snow Globe. 2010. (Illus.). pap. (978-1-877561-30-6(4)) First Edition Ltd.
—Missy Hip Hoppo. 2010. (Illus.). 16p. pap. (978-1-877561-56-6(8)) First Edition Ltd.
—The Monkey in the Tree. 2010. (Illus.). pap. (978-1-877547-91-1(3)) First Edition Ltd.
—Mr Grumpy Bunny. 2010. (Illus.). pap. (978-1-877561-22-1(3)) First Edition Ltd.
—Pet Day. 2010. (Illus.). pap. (978-1-877561-28-3(2)) First Edition Ltd.
—Safari Adventure. 2010. (Illus.). pap. (978-1-877561-29-0(0)) First Edition Ltd.
—Sam the Traveling Snail. 2010. (Illus.). pap. (978-1-877561-19-1(3)) First Edition Ltd.
—Skipping Sally. 2010. (Illus.). pap. (978-1-877561-24-5(X)) First Edition Ltd.
—Snafu & the Shoes. 2010. (Illus.). pap. (978-1-877561-00-9(2)) First Edition Ltd.
—The Snowman Olympics. 2010. (Illus.). 20p. pap. (978-1-877561-36-8(3)) First Edition Ltd.
—Sooty the Stink Bomb. 2010. (Illus.). pap. (978-1-877561-15-3(0)) First Edition Ltd.
—The Space Rocket. 2010. (Illus.). pap. (978-1-877547-87-4(5)) First Edition Ltd.
—The Spaghetti Tree. 2010. (Illus.). pap. (978-1-877561-02-3(9)) First Edition Ltd.
—Splat & the Hat. 2010. (Illus.). pap. (978-1-877561-04-7(5)) First Edition Ltd.
—Summer Camp. 2010. (Illus.). pap. (978-1-877561-27-6(4)) First Edition Ltd.
—There's a Bear in My Bed. 2010. (Illus.). pap. (978-1-877547-97-3(2)) First Edition Ltd.
—The Wedding Day. 2010. (Illus.). 16p. pap. (978-1-877561-51-1(7)) First Edition Ltd.
—The Wickedest Witch. 2010. (Illus.). pap. (978-1-877561-17-7(7)) First Edition Ltd.
Parker, Emma & Renaud, Marguerite. Aliens from Zen. 2010. (Illus.). 16p. pap. (978-1-877561-79-5(7)) First Edition Ltd.
—Chatterbox Caz. 2010. (Illus.). 16p. pap. (978-1-877561-77-1(0)) First Edition Ltd.
Parker, Laurie. It Really Said Christmas. Parker, Laurie, illus. 2003. (Illus.). (J). (978-0-9729615-0-9(X)) Parker, Laurie.
Parker, Marjorie Blain. I Love You near & Far. Henry, Jed, illus. 2015. (Snuggle Time Stories Ser.). (ENG.). 24p. (J). (gr. -1-1). 9.95 (978-1-4549-0507-3(7)) Sterling Publishing Co., Inc.
—Psst! I Love You. Hanson, Sydney, illus. 2017. (Snuggle Time Stories Ser.). (ENG.). 32p. (J). (gr. -1-k). 9.95 (978-1-4549-1721-2(0)) Sterling Publishing Co., Inc.
Parkins, Rebecca Katherine. Lilly the Little Lava Mouse. 2009. 180p. pap. 43.49 (978-1-4389-4330-5(X)) AuthorHouse.
Parkinson, Helen. How Well Can Wombats Bat? 2012. 28p. pap. 32.70 (978-1-4797-2235-8(9)) Xlibris Corp.
Parry, Rosanne. Daddy's Home! Leonard, David, illus. 2009. (ENG.). 20p. (J). bds. 6.99 (978-0-8249-1823-1(1), Ideal Pubns.) Worthy Publishing.
Pastor Wil. It's Good, Okay, & Alright, 1 vol. 2010. 28p. pap. 24.95 (978-1-4489-7065-0(2)) PublishAmerica, Inc.
A Path of Clouds: The Book off Rhymes. 2013. 50p. pap. (978-965-550-241-1(4)) Contento De Semrik.
Patricelli, Leslie. Be Quiet, Mike! 2011. (ENG., Illus.). 40p. (J). (gr. -1-2). 14.99 (978-0-7636-4477-2(3)) Candlewick Pr.
Pattou, Edith. Ghosting, 0 vols. 2014. (ENG.). 432p. (YA). (gr. 7-12). 16.99 (978-1-4778-4774-9(X), 9781477847749, Skyscape) Amazon Publishing.
Paul, Ann Whitford. If Animals Kissed Good Night. Walker, David, illus. 2014. (ENG.). 34p. (J). (gr. -1-1). bds. 7.99 (978-0-374-30021-0(6), 9780374300210, Farrar, Straus & Giroux (BYR)) Farrar, Straus & Giroux.
Paul, Miranda. Trainbots. McG, Shane, illus. 2016. (ENG.). 32p. (J). (gr. -1-3). 16.99 (978-1-4998-0167-5(X)) Little Bee Books Inc.
—10 Little Ninjas. Wragg, Nate, illus. 2016. (ENG.). 32p. (J). (-k). 14.99 (978-0-553-53497-9(1), Knopf Bks. for Young Readers) Random Hse. Children's Bks.
Paul, Ruth. Stomp! 2013. pap. (978-0-545-52940-2(9)) Scholastic, Inc.
Paul, Ruth & Lombana, J. P. Stomp! Ia Marchar! 2013. (SPA & ENG., Illus.). (978-0-545-52795-8(3)) Scholastic, Inc.
Pauline Wall & Shelley Smith. What the Owl Saw: (a Christmas Story) 2012. 20p. pap. 15.19 (978-1-4669-2813-8(1)) Trafford Publishing.
Paulus, Kristin Harkison. There's a Lion on the Dance Floor. 2010. (Illus.). 28p. pap. 12.98 (978-1-4490-2692-9(3)) AuthorHouse.
Pavey, Peter. One Dragon's Dream. Pavey, Peter, illus. 2009. (ENG., Illus.). 40p. (J). (gr. -1-2). 17.99 (978-0-7636-4470-3(6)) Candlewick Pr.
Paxton, Tom. The Marvelous Toy. Cox, Steve, illus. 2014. (ENG.). 22p. (J). (gr. -1-2). bds. 7.95 (978-1-62354-043-2(7)) Charlesbridge Publishing, Inc.
Pearce, Clemency. Frangoline & the Midnight Dream. Elliott, Rebecca, illus. 2011. (ENG.). 32p. (J). (gr. -1-k). 16.99 (978-0-545-31426-8(7), Chicken Hse., The) Scholastic, Inc.
Pearson, Debora. Big City Song. Reed, Lynn Rowe, illus. 2006. (ENG.). 32p. (J). (gr. -1-3). 16.95 (978-0-8234-1988-3(6)) Holiday Hse., Inc.
Pearson, Mary E. Fast Dan. Doty, Eldon C., illus. 2003. (Rookie Reader Skill Set Ser.). (ENG.). 32p. (J). (gr. k-2). pap. 4.95 (978-0-516-27494-2(5), Children's Pr.) Scholastic Library Publishing.
—Generous Me. Krejca, Gary, illus. 2011. (Rookie Ready to Learn — All about Me! Ser.). 40p. (J). (gr. -1-k). lib. bdg. 25.00 (978-0-531-26427-0(0)); (ENG.). pap. 5.95 (978-0-531-26652-6(4)) Scholastic Library Publishing. (Children's Pr.).
—I Can Do It All. Shelley, Jeff, illus. 2011. (Rookie Ready to Learn Ser.). (J). (gr. -1-k). (ENG.). 40p. pap. 5.95 (978-0-531-26654-0(0)); 32p. lib. bdg. 23.00 (978-0-531-26429-4(7), Children's Pr.) Scholastic Library Publishing.
Pearson, Mary E. & Shelly, Jeff. Puedo Hacer de Todo. Shelly, Jeff, illus. 2011. (Rookie Ready to Learn Español Ser.).Tr. of I Can Do It All. (SPA., Illus.). 40p. (J). pap. 5.95 (978-0-531-26787-5(3)); lib. bdg. 23.00 (978-0-531-26119-4(0)) Scholastic Library Publishing. (Children's Pr.).
Peck, Jan. Way down Deep in the Deep Blue Sea. Petrone, Valeria, illus. 2004. (ENG.). 32p. (J). (gr. -1-3). 17.99 (978-0-689-85110-0(3), Simon & Schuster Bks. For Young Readers) Simon & Schuster Bks. For Young Readers.
—Way Out West on My Little Pony, 1 vol. Leonhard, Herb, illus. 2010. (ENG.). 32p. (J). (gr. k-3). 16.99 (978-1-58980-697-9(2)) Pelican Publishing Co., Inc.
—Way up High in a Tall Green Tree. Petrone, Valeria, illus. 2005. (ENG.). 32p. (J). (gr. -1-3). 18.99 (978-1-4169-0071-9(3), Simon & Schuster Bks. For Young Readers) Simon & Schuster Bks. For Young Readers.
Peck, Judith. The Bright Blue Button & the Button-Hole. Stasolla, Mario, illus. 2004. 28p. (J). 18.95 (978-0-9746119-5-2(6)) Imagination Arts Pubns.
Pedlar, David Stewart. The Emu Who Knew He Could Fly! 2013. 32p. pap. 16.95 (978-1-4525-7612-1(2), Balboa Pr.) Author Solutions, Inc.
Peet, Bill. The Caboose Who Got Loose, 1 vol. Peet, Bill, illus. 2008. (Read along Book & CD Ser.). (ENG., Illus.). 48p. (J). (gr. -1-3). audio compact disk 10.99 (978-0-618-95979-2(3)) Houghton Mifflin Harcourt Publishing Co.
Pelham, David. Sam's Sandwich. Pelham, David, illus. 2015. (ENG., Illus.). 24p. (J). (gr. -1-2). 9.99 (978-0-7636-7808-1(2)) Candlewick Pr.
Penecale Jr., Richard P. The Luckiest Frog. 2009. 33p. (J). pap. 24.95 (978-1-4327-3023-9(1)) Outskirts Pr., Inc.
Penn, M. W. Sidney the Silly Who Only Eats 6. Tommer, Sarah, illus. 2007. 32p. (J). (978-0-9784047-2-7(6)) Pays et Terroirs.
Pepin, Rebecca. Bobby Dog & the Flying Frog. Fuller, Cari, illus. 2004. (J). (gr. 4-18). 16.99 (978-0-9760684-0-2(0)); pap. 11.99 (978-0-9760684-1-9(9)) FulloPep Pubns.
Pepper, Lily. In the Garden at Granddad's. 2012. (Illus.). 24p. pap. 19.82 (978-1-4772-2642-1(7)) AuthorHouse.
Pereira, Chritine M. Madilynn Rose Rhyming Fairy: Volume 1, 1 vol. 2010. 44p. pap. 24.95 (978-1-61546-591-0(X)) PublishAmerica, Inc.
Perez, Irene. Rain or Shine. 2008. 16p. pap. 12.50 (978-1-4389-0873-1(3)) AuthorHouse.
Pérez-Mercado, Mary Margaret. Splat! Torrey, Rich, illus. 2011. (Rookie Ready to Learn Ser.). 40p. (J). pap. 5.95 (978-0-531-26678-6(8)); (gr. -1-k). lib. bdg. 23.00 (978-0-531-26373-0(8)) Scholastic Library Publishing. (Children's Pr.).

S

Perez, Olga. Sitting on Cloud 9 at the 50-Yard Line. 2012. (Illus.). 28p. pap. 19.99 *(978-1-4772-9225-9(X))* AuthorHouse.

Perkins, Al. The Ear Book. Payne, Henry, illus. 2007. (Bright & Early Books(R) Ser.). (ENG.). 36p. (J). (gr. k-k). 9.99 *(978-0-375-84251-1(9)*, Random Hse. Bks. for Young Readers) Random Hse. Children's Bks.

Perl, Erica S. Chicken Butt! Cole, Henry, illus. 2009. (ENG.). 32p. (J). (gr. -1-k). 13.95 *(978-0-8109-8325-0(7)*, Abrams Bks. for Young Readers) Abrams, Inc.

—Chicken Butt's Back! Cole, Henry, illus. 2011. (ENG.). 32p. (J). (gr. -1-k). 13.95 *(978-0-8109-9729-5(0)*, Abrams Bks. for Young Readers) Abrams, Inc.

—Ferocious Fluffity: A Mighty Bite-Y Class Pet. Cole, Henry, illus. 2016. (ENG.). 32p. (J). (gr. k-2). 16.95 *(978-1-4197-2182-3(8)*, Abrams Bks. for Young Readers) Abrams, Inc.

Perlman, Willa. Good Night, World. Fisher, Carolyn, illus. 2011. (ENG.). 40p. (J). (gr. -1-k). 16.99 *(978-1-4424-0197-6(4)*, Beach Lane Bks.) Beach Lane Bks.

Perrin, Martine. Cock-a-Doodle Who? 2012. (ENG., Illus.). 40p. (J). (gr. -1-3). 12.99 *(978-0-8075-1107-7(2))* Whitman, Albert & Co.

Perry, Andrea. The Bicklebys' Birdbath. Angaramo, Roberta, illus. 2010. (ENG.). 40p. (J). (gr. -1-1). 16.99 *(978-1-4169-0624-7(X)*, Atheneum Bks. for Young Readers) Simon & Schuster Children's Publishing.

Perry, Laurie. Brown Bear, 1 vol. Mackay, Hugh, illus. 2010. 22p. pap. 24.95 *(978-1-4489-5702-6(8))* PublishAmerica, Inc.

Perry, Rex, illus. All Things Bright & Beautiful. 2004. 24p. (J). lib. bdg. 8.00 *(978-1-4242-0638-4(3))* Fitzgerald Bks.

Pesca, Jodi. Angels Angels Everywhere. 2013. 20p. pap. 24.95 *(978-1-63000-001-1(9))* America Star Bks.

Petit, Denice. Twenty-Two Turtles. 2013. (ENG.). 34p. (J). pap. 15.95 *(978-1-4327-9875-8(8))* Outskirts Pr., Inc.

Petty, Dini. The Queen, the Bear & the Bumblebee. Cowles, Rose, illus. 32p. (J). 19.95 *(978-1-55285-151-7(6))* Whitecap Bks., Ltd. CAN. Dist: Graphic Arts Ctr. Publishing Co.

Pfeiffer, Kathleen. Spartacus Sprout, Please Watch Out! 2011. 32p. pap. 15.99 *(978-1-257-50163-2(1))* Lulu Pr., Inc.

Pfister, Marcus. Questions, Questions. 2011. (ENG & GER., Illus.). 32p. (J). (gr. -1-2). 16.95 *(978-0-7358-4000-3(8))* North-South Bks., Inc.

Pfundstein, Valerie. Veterans: Heroes in Our Neighborhood. Chernesky, Felicia, ed. Anderson, Aaron, illus. 2012. (ENG.). 32p. (J). 18.95 *(978-0-9837186-1-(X))* Novanglus Publishing, LLC.

Pham, LeUyen. Big Sister, Little Sister. Pham, LeUyen, illus. 2005. (ENG., Illus.). 40p. (J). (gr. -1-k). 15.99 *(978-0-7868-5182-9(1))* Hyperion Pr.

Phelan, Anne. Skydive to Hive. Rottinger, Amy, illus. 2012. 24p. pap. 11.95 *(978-1-61244-098-9(3))* Halo Publishing International.

Phifer, Larry & Phifer. World on a String. 2013. (ENG.). 17.95 *(978-0-9886984-0-6(4))* Storytime Works.

Philips, Lyn D. Curiosity. Gadeselli, Natalie, illus. 2013. 32p. pap. *(978-1-904928-27-0(7))* Copeland & Wickson.

Phillips, Dee. What Can I Be? 2010. (Look at Me! Ser.). (ENG.). 5p. (J). (gr. -1-k). bds. 6.95 *(978-1-84696-199-1(8)*, TickTock Books) Octopus Publishing Group GBR. Dist: Independent Pubs. Group.

Phillips, Dixie & Snider, K. C. Stilts the Stork. 2011. 20p. pap. 10.95 *(978-1-61633-143-6(7))* Guardian Angel Publishing, Inc.

Phillips, Jan. Just for Today. Shapiro, Alison Bonds, illus. 2005. (ENG.). 32p. (J). (gr. -1-5). 15.95 *(978-1-932073-07-2(8))* Kramer, H.J. Inc.

Phillips, Jean. The Meaning of Christmas: A Children's Story in Picture & Verse. 2005. (ENG., Illus.). 24p. pap. 7.95 *(978-0-929292-67-0(7)*, 800-747-0738) Hannibal Bks.

Phillips, Leigh Hope. Birthday Wishes. Fountain, John, illus. 2005. (J). pap. *(978-1-933156-10-1(4))*; per. *(978-1-933156-03-3(1))* GSVQ Publishing. (VisionQuest Kids).

Phillips, Terrie. The Ski Trip. 2006. (Illus.). 38p. (J). lib. bdg. 12.95 *(978-0-9789449-0-2(9))* Tbooks Publishing Co.

Phyllarry (Rittmueller), Kathryn. Beauregart the Bear. 2009. (ENG., Illus.). 64p. (J). 12.95 *(978-0-943972-80-0(9))* Homestead Publishing.

Piantedosi, John J. The Cat That Purred. Maglio-Macullar, Andrea, illus. 2014. (ENG.). (J). pap. 11.95 *(978-1-56548-540-2(8))* New City Press of the Focolare.

Picayo, Mario. Fun, Fun, One Crab on the Run. Byer, Stacey, illus. 2012. (J). *(978-1-934370-27-8(4))* Editorial Campana.

Pick Me up, Mama! 2014. (ENG., Illus.). 34p. (J). (gr. -1-k). bds. 5.99 *(978-1-4814-1633-7(2)*, Little Simon) Little Simon.

Pierce, Christa. Did You Know That I Love You? Pierce, Christa, illus. 2014. (ENG., Illus.). 32p. (J). (gr. -1-3). 17.99 *(978-0-06-229744-0(9))* HarperCollins Pubs.

Pierce, Craig. A Greyhound's Tale: Running for Glory, Walking for Home. Santiago, Tony, illus. 2004. (J). per. 15.00 *(978-0-9762564-0-3(1)*, American Dog) Ideate Prairie.

Pierce, Terry. Tae Kwon Do! Bonita, Todd, illus. 2006. (Step into Reading Ser.). (ENG.). 32p. (J). (gr. -1-1). per. 3.99 *(978-0-375-83448-6(6)*, Random Hse. Bks. for Young Readers) Random Hse. Children's Bks.

Piernas-Davenport, Gail. Shante Keys & the New Year's Peas. Eldridge, Marion, illus. (ENG.). 32p. (J). (gr. k-2). 2017. pap. 7.99 ***(978-0-8075-7331-0(0))*** 2007. lib. bdg. 16.99 *(978-0-8075-7330-3(2))* Whitman, Albert & Co.

Pignataro, Anna. Our Love Grows. 2016. (ENG.). 24p. (J). (-4). 16.99 *(978-1-4926-3418-8(2)*, 9781492634188, Sourcebooks Jabberwocky) Sourcebooks, Inc.

Pigott, Louise. Squirrel Me Timbers. 2016. (Fiction Picture Bks.). (ENG., Illus.). 24p. (gr. k-1). lib. bdg. 24.65 *(978-1-4795-9177-0(7)*, Fiction Picture Bks.) Picture Window Bks.

Pilkey, Dav. God Bless the Gargoyles. 2016. (ENG., Illus.). 40p. (J). (gr. -1-3). 17.99 *(978-0-545-93514-2(8))* Scholastic, Inc.

Pinczes, Elinor J. Inchworm & a Half. Enos, Randall, illus. 2003. (ENG.). 32p. (J). pap. 6.99 *(978-0-618-31101-9(7))* Houghton Mifflin Harcourt Publishing Co.

Pinder, Eric. I'd Rather Be Riding My Bike. Cardinal, John, illus. l.t. ed. 2013. 42p. (gr. k-1). pap. 10.95 *(978-1-62253-401-2(8))* Evolved Publishing.

—If All the Animals Came Inside. Brown, Marc, illus. 2012. (ENG.). 40p. (J). (gr. -1-3). 17.99 *(978-0-316-09883-0(3))* Little Brown & Co.

Pingry, Patricia A. Noses & Toes. Rose, Drew, illus. 2005. (J). *(978-0-8249-6594-5(9)*, Ideal Pubns.) Worthy Publishing.

—On Christmas Morning. Barretta, Gene, illus. 2007. (ENG.). 26p. (J). (gr. -1-3). bds. 6.99 *(978-0-8249-6713-0(5)*, Ideal Pubns.) Worthy Publishing.

—One Baby Jesus. Edleson, Wendy, illus. 2008. (Ideals Christmas Classic Ser.). (ENG.). 30p. (J). (gr. -1-k). pap. 3.95 *(978-0-8249-5511-3(0)*, Ideal Pubns.) Worthy Publishing.

—Sounds. Rose, Drew, illus. 2005. (J). *(978-0-8249-6596-9(5)*, Ideal Pubns.) Worthy Publishing.

Pinkney, Andrea Davis. The Red Pencil. Evans, Shane W., illus. 2014. (ENG.). 336p. (J). (gr. 4-17). 17.99 *(978-0-316-24780-1(4))* Little, Brown Bks. for Young Readers.

Pitman, Gayle E. This Day in June. Litten, Kristyna, illus. 2013. (J). *(978-1-4338-1658-1(X))*; pap. *(978-1-4338-1659-8(8))* American Psychological Assn. (Magination Pr.).

Pixton, Amy. Mary Had a Little Lamb. 2010. (Indestructibles Ser.). (ENG., Illus.). 12p. (J). (gr. k — 1). pap. 5.95 *(978-0-7611-5860-8(X)*, 15860) Workman Publishing Co., Inc.

Pixton, Kaaren & Sickler, Jonas. Humpty Dumpty: Hey, Bay Look at the Humpty Dumpty - On the Great Wall of China! 2010. (Indestructibles Ser.). (ENG., Illus.). 12p. (J). (gr. k — 1). pap. 5.95 *(978-0-7611-5861-5(8)*, 15861) Workman Publishing Co., Inc.

Plawner, Michael A. Then & Now. 2009. 60p. pap. 10.99 *(978-0-557-08595-8(0))* Lulu Pr., Inc.

Plourde, Lynn. Only Cows Allowed!, 1 vol. Sollers, Jim & Reed, Rebecca Harrison, illus. 2011. (ENG.). 32p. (gr. -1-3). 16.95 *(978-0-89272-790-2(X))* Down East Bks.

Plourde, Paulette. My Magic Pillow. 2005. (Illus.). 40p. (J). per. 8.99 *(978-1-932338-76-8(4))* Lifevest Publishing, Inc.

Plume, Ilse. The Twelve Days of Christmas. 2005. (ENG., Illus.). 32p. (J). (gr. -1). 17.95 *(978-1-56792-300-1(3))* Godine, David R. Pub.

Plume, Ilse, illus. & adapted by. The Farmer in the Dell. Plume, Ilse, adapted by. 2010. (ENG.). 32p. pap. 8.95 *(978-1-56792-390-2(9))* Godine, David R. Pub.

Plunkett, Windyann. Fiddle Me a Riddle & Bring Me the Moon. Davidson, Mary, illus. 2011. 24p. pap. 24.95 *(978-1-4626-3920-5(8))* America Star Bks.

Poer, Karla R. The Busy-Body Book of Fun-Atomy Tunes. 2008. (ENG.). 56p. pap. 21.99 *(978-1-4389-3296-5(0))* AuthorHouse.

Polacco, Patricia. G Is for Goat. Polacco, Patricia, illus. 2006. (ENG., Illus.). 32p. (J). (gr. -1-k). reprint ed. pap. 7.99 *(978-0-14-240550-5(7)*, Puffin Books) Penguin Young Readers Group.

Polette, Nancy. Flying with Mother Goose. 2003. pap. 7.95 *(978-1-931334-19-8(6)*, CLC0285) Pieces of Learning.

Pollock, Hal. Monster at the Bat. 2009. (ENG.). 32p. (J). (gr. 4-7). 15.95 *(978-1-59687-884-6(3))* IBks., Inc.

Poltarnees, Welleran & Laughing Elephant Staff, compiled by. The Laughing Elephant's Book of Christmas. 2013. (ENG., Illus.). 96p. 12.95 *(978-1-59583-626-7(8))* Laughing Elephant.

Poole, Bud. Little Miss Muffet Gets Saved: A Christian Nursery Rhyme. 2012. 20p. pap. 7.95 *(978-1-4497-4170-9(3)*, WestBow Pr.) Author Solutions, Inc.

Poole, Helen. Clara's Crazy Curls, 1 vol. Poole, Helen, illus. 2014. (ENG., Illus.). 40p. (J). (-1-3). 14.95 *(978-1-62370-043-0(4))* Capstone Young Readers of Coughlan Cos.

Pop the Bubbles 1,2,3. 2011. (ENG., Illus.). 46p. (J). 15.95 *(978-0-9834645-0-1(2))* FUNdamentals/Leap In Faith.

Porter, Annaliese & Bancroft, Bronwyn. The Outback. 2005. (Illus.). 28p. (J). *(978-1-875641-86-4(6))* Magabala Bks.

Porter, Pamela. Yellow Moon, Apple Moon, 1 vol. James, Matt, illus. 2008. (ENG.). 32p. (J). (gr. k — 1). 17.95 *(978-0-88899-809-5(0))* Groundwood Bks. CAN. Dist: Publishers Group West (PGW).

Post, Jim. Frog in the Kitchen Sink. Vasconcellos, Daniel, illus. 2015. (ENG.). 26p. (J). bds. 9.99 *(978-1-4494-6709-8(1))* Andrews McMeel Publishing.

Postgate, Daniel. Love Stinks. 2012. (J). *(978-1-61913-132-3(3))* Weigl Pubs., Inc.

Potter, Beatrix. Tickle, Tickle, Peter! 2012. (Peter Rabbit Ser.). (ENG.). 10p. (J). (gr. -1-k). bds. 9.99 *(978-0-7232-6750-8(2)*, Warne) Penguin Young Readers Group.

Powell, Amy. Hope Music. Farley, Katherine, illus. 2006. 32p. (J). (gr. -1-3). per. 12.00 *(978-0-9773608-4-0(9))* Shiny Red Ball Publishing.

Prasadam-halls, Smriti. I'll Never Let You Go. Brown, Alison, illus. 2015. (ENG.). 32p. (J). 16.99 *(978-1-61963-922-5(X)*, 9781619639225, Bloomsbury USA Childrens) Bloomsbury Publishing USA.

Prasadam-Halls, Smriti. T. Veg: The Story of a Carrot-Crunching Dinosaur. Manolessou, Katherina, illus. 2017. (ENG.). 32p. (J). (gr. -1-3). 16.95 *(978-1-4197-2494-7(0)*, Abrams Bks. for Young Readers) Abrams, Inc.

Precious Moments, Precious. Precious Moments: Happy Harvest, 1 vol. 2016. (ENG., Illus.). 32p. (J). bds. 9.99 *(978-0-7180-3241-8(1))* Nelson, Thomas Inc.

Prendergast, Gabrielle. Audacious, 1 vol. 2015. (ENG.). 336p. (YA). (gr. 8-12). pap. 12.95 *(978-1-4598-0264-3(0))* Orca Bk. Pubs. USA.

—Capricious, 1 vol. 2014. (ENG.). 352p. (YA). (gr. 8-12). 19.95 *(978-1-4598-0267-4(5))* Orca Bk. Pubs. USA.

Prescott, Brian. Chloe Knows Her Alphabet. 2013. 20p. pap. *(978-1-909192-51-5(1))* Beaten Track Publishing.

Preston-Gannon, Frann. What a Hoot! 2015. (ENG., Illus.). 20p. (J). (-k). bds. 12.95 *(978-1-57687-758-6(2)*, powerHouse Bks.) powerHouse Cultural Entertainment, Inc.

Price, Mary Elizabeth. Wallbaby Bumblebees. 2004. (Illus.). 40p. (J). per. 15.75 *(978-0-9715402-2-4(5)*, 410-707-6686) Barnhardt & Ashe Publishing, Inc.

Price, Olivia. All Aboard Noah's Ark: A Touch & Feel Book. Mitchell, Melanie, illus. 2008. (ENG.). 12p. (J). (gr. -1). 12.95 *(978-1-58117-778-7(X)*, Intervisual/Piggy Toes) Bendon, Inc.

—Bible Stories: A Touch & Feel Book. Mitchell, Melanie, illus. 2008. (ENG.). 12p. (J). (gr. -1). 12.95 *(978-1-58117-802-9(6)*, Intervisual/Piggy Toes) Bendon, Inc.

Price, Roxanne M. Buckeyes Bow Ties & Sweater Vests. 2010. (Illus.). 20p. pap. *(978-1-4251-8537-4(1))* Trafford Publishing (UK) Ltd.

Priddy, Roger. Alphaprints Fun in the Sun! 2017. (Alphaprints Ser.). (ENG., Illus.). 10p. (J). bds. 7.99 *(978-0-312-52518-7(4)*, 9780312525187, Priddy Bks.) St. Martin's Pr.

—Alphaprints: Sweet Heart. 2015. (Alphaprints Ser.). (ENG., Illus.). 12p. (J). (gr. -1 — 1). bds. 7.99 *(978-0-312-51913-1(3)*, 9780312519131, Priddy Bks.) St. Martin's Pr.

—Bedtime Lullaby. 2013. (Baby Boxsets Ser.). (ENG.). 32p. (J). (gr. -1-1). 14.99 *(978-0-312-51564-5(2)*, 9780312515645, Priddy Bks.) St. Martin's Pr.

—Best Friends: We Are Best Friends. 2015. (Best Friends Ser.). (ENG.). 20p. (J). (gr. -1-1). bds. 9.99 *(978-0-312-51922-3(2)*, 9780312519223, Priddy Bks.) St. Martin's Pr.

—Cow - Animal Buddies. 2015. (Animal Buddies Ser.). (ENG.). 8p. (J). (gr. -1 — 1). bds. 5.99 *(978-0-312-51854-7(4)*, 9780312518547, Priddy Bks.) St. Martin's Pr.

—Easter Surprise. 2011. (ENG., Illus.). (J). (gr. -1-k). bds. 9.99 *(978-0-312-51002-2(0)*, 9780312510022, Priddy Bks.) St. Martin's Pr.

—I Love You. 2015. (Mini Tab Ser.). (ENG.). 16p. (J). (gr. -1 — 1). bds. 5.99 *(978-0-312-51919-3(2)*, 9780312519193, Priddy Bks.) St. Martin's Pr.

—Lift the Tab: Christmas. 2016. (Lift-The-Flap Tab Bks.). (ENG.). 16p. (J). bds. 8.99 *(978-0-312-52071-7(9)*, 9780312520717, Priddy Bks.) St. Martin's Pr.

—Little Friends: Big Adventure. 2015. (Little Friends Ser.). (ENG., Illus.). 12p. (J). (gr. -1 — 1). bds. 14.99 *(978-0-312-51869-1(2)*, 9780312518691, Priddy Bks.) St. Martin's Pr.

—Little Friends: Let's Play. 2014. (Little Friends Ser.). (ENG., Illus.). 8p. (J). (gr. -1 — 1). bds. 8.99 *(978-0-312-51683-3(5)*, 9780312516833, Priddy Bks.) St. Martin's Pr.

—My World. 2015. (Hello Kitty Ser.). (ENG.). 16p. (J). (gr. -1-1). bds. 12.99 *(978-0-312-51817-2(X)*, 9780312518172, Priddy Bks.) St. Martin's Pr.

—Puppy. 2015. (Animal Buddies Ser.). (ENG., Illus.). 8p. (J). (gr. -1 — 1). bds. 5.99 *(978-0-312-51867-7(6)*, 9780312518677, Priddy Bks.) St. Martin's Pr.

—Santa Claus. 2012. (Funny Faces Ser.). (ENG., Illus.). 10p. (J). (gr. -1-1). bds. 8.99 *(978-0-312-51558-4(8)*, 9780312515584, Priddy Bks.) St. Martin's Pr.

—Spooky Bus. 2013. (Shaped Board Bks.). (ENG., Illus.). 6p. (J). (gr. -1-k). bds. 6.99 *(978-0-312-51618-5(5)*, 9780312516185, Priddy Bks.) St. Martin's Pr.

—Tiger - Animal Buddies. 2015. (Animal Buddies Ser.). (ENG., Illus.). 8p. (J). (gr. -1 — 1). bds. 5.99 *(978-0-312-51865-3(X)*, 9780312518653, Priddy Bks.) St. Martin's Pr.

Prince, April Jones. Dig In! Berg, Michelle, illus. 2013. (ENG.). 14p. (J). (gr. -1 — 1). bds. 7.95 *(978-1-4197-0522-9(9))* Abrams, Inc.

—Dive In! Berg, Michelle, illus. 2013. (ENG.). 14p. (J). (gr. -1 — 1). bds. 7.95 *(978-1-4197-0523-6(7))* Abrams, Inc.

Prince, Joshua. I Saw an Ant on the Railroad Track. Pamintuan, Macky, illus. 2006. (ENG.). 24p. (J). (gr. -1-k). 14.95 *(978-1-4027-2183-0(8)*, 1252268) Sterling Publishing Co., Inc.

Pritchard, Alicia Michele. Critter Pics. 2008. 53p. pap. 22.50 *(978-1-4357-1134-1(3))* Lulu Pr., Inc.

Prochovnic, Dawn Babb. A to Z Sign with Me: Sign Language for the Alphabet, 1 vol. Bauer, Stephanie, illus. 2012. (ENG.). 32p. 28.50 *(978-1-61641-835-9(4)*, Looking Glass Library) Magic Wagon.

—The Best Day in Room A: Sign Language for School Activities, 1 vol. Bauer, Stephanie, illus. 2009. (Story Time with Signs & Rhymes Ser.). (ENG.). 32p. (gr. -1-3). 28.50 *(978-1-60270-667-5(0)*, Looking Glass Library) ABDO Publishing Co.

—The Big Blue Bowl: Sign Language for Food, 1 vol. Bauer, Stephanie, illus. 2009. (Story Time with Signs & Rhymes Ser.). (ENG.). 32p. (gr. -1-3). 28.50 *(978-1-60270-668-2(9)*, Looking Glass Library) ABDO Publishing Co.

—Famous Fenton Has a Farm: Sign Language for Farm Animals, 1 vol. Bauer, Stephanie, illus. 2009. (Story Time with Signs & Rhymes Ser.). (ENG.). 32p. (gr. -1-3). 28.50 *(978-1-60270-669-9(7)*, Looking Glass Library) ABDO Publishing Co.

—Four Seasons! Five Senses! Sign Language for the Seasons & Senses, 1 vol. Bauer, Stephanie, illus. 2012. (ENG.). 32p. 28.50 *(978-1-61641-836-6(2)*, Looking Glass Library) Magic Wagon.

—Hip Hip Hooray! It's Family Day! Sign Language for Family, 1 vol. Bauer, Stephanie, illus. 2012. (ENG.). 32p. 28.50 *(978-1-61641-837-3(0)*, Looking Glass Library) Magic Wagon.

—The Nest Where I Like to Rest: Sign Language for Animals, 1 vol. 2009. (Story Time with Signs & Rhymes Ser.). (ENG., Illus.). 32p. (gr. -1-3). 28.50 *(978-1-60270-670-5(0)*, Looking Glass Library) ABDO Publishing Co.

—One Trick for One Treat: Sign Language for Numbers, 1 vol. Bauer, Stephanie, illus. 2012. (ENG.). 32p. 28.50 *(978-1-61641-838-0(9)*, Looking Glass Library) Magic Wagon.

—Opposites Everywhere: Sign Language for Opposites, 1 vol. Bauer, Stephanie, illus. 2012. (ENG.). 32p. 28.50 *(978-1-61641-839-7(7)*, Looking Glass Library) Magic Wagon.

—See the Colors: Sign Language for Colors, 1 vol. Bauer, Stephanie, illus. 2009. (Story Time with Signs & Rhymes Ser.). (ENG.). 32p. (gr. -1-3). 28.50 *(978-1-60270-671-2(9)*, Looking Glass Library) ABDO Publishing Co.

—Shape Detective: Sign Language for Shapes, 1 vol. Bauer, Stephanie, illus. 2012. (ENG.). 32p. 28.50 *(978-1-61641-840-3(0)*, Looking Glass Library) Magic Wagon.

—Silly Sue: Sign Language for Actions, 1 vol. Bauer, Stephanie, illus. 2009. (Story Time with Signs & Rhymes Ser.). (ENG.). 32p. (gr. -1-3). 28.50 *(978-1-60270-672-9(7)*, Looking Glass Library) ABDO Publishing Co.

—So Many Feelings: Sign Language for Feelings & Emotions, 1 vol. Bauer, Stephanie, illus. 2012. (ENG.). 32p. (J). 28.50 *(978-1-61641-841-0(9)*, Looking Glass Library) Magic Wagon.

—Story Time with Signs & Rhymes, 8 vols., Set. Incl. Best Day in Room A: Sign Language for School Activities. Bauer, Stephanie, illus. 28.50 *(978-1-60270-667-5(0))*; Big Blue Bowl: Sign Language for Food. Bauer, Stephanie, illus. 28.50 *(978-1-60270-668-2(9))*; Famous Fenton Has a Farm: Sign Language for Farm Animals. Bauer, Stephanie, illus. 28.50 *(978-1-60270-669-9(7))*; Nest Where I Like to Rest: Sign Language for Animals. 28.50 *(978-1-60270-670-5(0))*; See the Colors: Sign Language for Colors. Bauer, Stephanie, illus. 28.50 *(978-1-60270-671-2(9))*; Silly Sue: Sign Language for Actions. Bauer, Stephanie, illus. 28.50 *(978-1-60270-672-9(7))*; Watch Me Go! Sign Language for Vehicles. Bauer, Stephanie, illus. 28.50 *(978-1-60270-673-6(5))*; Wear a Silly Hat: Sign Language for Clothing. Bauer, Stephanie, illus. 28.50 *(978-1-60270-674-3(3))*; (gr. -1-3). (Story Time with Signs & Rhymes Ser.). 32p. 2009. 228.00 *(978-1-60270-666-8(2)*, Looking Glass Library) ABDO Publishing Co.

—There's a Story in My Head: Sign Language for Body Parts, 1 vol. Bauer, Stephanie, illus. 2012. (ENG.). 32p. 28.50 *(978-1-61641-842-7(7)*, Looking Glass Library) Magic Wagon.

—Watch Me Go! Sign Language for Vehicles, 1 vol. Bauer, Stephanie, illus. 2009. (Story Time with Signs & Rhymes Ser.). (ENG.). 32p. (gr. -1-3). 28.50 *(978-1-60270-673-6(5)*, Looking Glass Library) ABDO Publishing Co.

—Wear a Silly Hat: Sign Language for Clothing, 1 vol. Bauer, Stephanie, illus. 2009. (Story Time with Signs & Rhymes Ser.). (ENG.). 32p. (gr. -1-3). 28.50 *(978-1-60270-674-3(3)*, Looking Glass Library) ABDO Publishing Co.

Prose, Francine. Rhino, Rhino, Sweet Potato. Armstrong, Matthew S., illus. 2009. 32p. (J). (gr. -1-k). lib. bdg. 18.89 *(978-0-06-008079-2(5))* HarperCollins Pubs.

Provencher, Rose-Marie. Slithery Jake. Carter, Abby, illus. 2004. (ENG.). 32p. (J). 15.99 *(978-0-06-623820-3(X))* HarperCollins Pubs.

Publications International Ltd. Staff. BK & Plush Mickey Mouse Club House. 2010. (J). 12.98 *(978-1-4127-8864-9(1))* Phoenix International Publications, Inc.

—Mother Goose Treasury. 2007. (ENG., Illus.). 320p. (J). (gr. -1-3). bds. *(978-1-4127-6334-9(7)*, 1412763347) Phoenix International Publications, Inc.

—Mother Goose Treasury. 2007. (Illus.). 316p. 15.98 *(978-1-4127-8734-5(3))* Publications International, Ltd.

Publications International Ltd. Staff, creator. Mother Goose. 2007. (Pop-up Treasury Ser.). (Illus.). 16p. (J). (gr. -1-3). 12.98 *(978-1-4127-8833-5(1))* Publications International, Ltd.

Publications International Ltd. Staff, ed. Baby Einstein. 2007. (J). 5.98 *(978-1-4127-8481-8(6))* Phoenix International Publications, Inc.

—Baby Einstein: Look, Listen, & Discover. 2010. 14p. (J). bds. 22.98 *(978-1-4127-4517-8(9)*, 1412745179) Phoenix International Publications, Inc.

—Thomas & Friends: Ding! Dong! A Visit from Thomas. 2011. 12p. (J). bds. 9.98 *(978-1-60553-985-0(6))* Phoenix International Publications, Inc.

Pulchinski, Erin. Ethan Is Caught Blue Faced! Werrun, Anna, illus. 2013. 32p. pap. *(978-1-4602-2416-8(7))* FriesenPress.

Pulley, Kelly. The Cycling Wangdoos. Pulley, Kelly, illus. 2011. (Illus.). 32p. (J). (gr. -1-3). 16.95 *(978-0-9820812-1-1(9)*, Frog Legs Ink) Gauthier Pubns. Inc.

—The Cycling Wangdoos, 1 vol. 2017. (ENG.). 32p. (J). 16.99 ***(978-0-7643-5406-9(X)**, 9780764354069)* Schiffer Publishing, Ltd.

Pulley, Kelly. Ten Unusual Features of Lulu McDunn. Pulley, Kelly, illus. 2010. (Illus.). 32p. (J). (gr. -1). 16.95 *(978-0-9820812-7-3(8)*, Frog Legs Ink) Gauthier Pubns. Inc.

Pumphrey, W. Jerome. Creepy Things Are Scaring Me! (Illus.). 32p. (J). (gr. -1-3). 5.99 *(978-0-06-443680-9(2))* HarperCollins Pubs.

Punter, Russell. There Was a Crooked Man. Semple, David, illus. 2010. (First Reading Level 2 Ser.). 32p. (J). 6.99 *(978-0-7945-2682-5(9)*, Usborne) EDC Publishing.

Punter, Russell & MacKinnon, Mairi. Snail Brings the Mail. Blunt, Fred, illus. 2014. (Usborne Phonics Readers Ser.). (ENG.). (J). pap. 6.99 *(978-0-7945-3369-4(8)*, Usborne) EDC Publishing.

Quaal, Jean. If Roosters Crow? 2009. 32p. pap. 14.95 *(978-1-4327-3671-2(X))* Outskirts Pr., Inc.

Quattlebaum, Mary. Jo MacDonald Saw a Pond. Bryant, Laura J., illus. 2013. (ENG.). 26p. (J). (gr. -1 — 1). bds. 7.95 *(978-1-58469-224-9(3))* Dawn Pubns.

Queen Latifah. Queen of the Scene. Morrison, Frank, illus. 2006. 32p. (J). (gr. -1-3). 17.89 incl. audio compact disk *(978-0-06-077857-6(1)*, Geringer, Laura Book) HarperCollins Pubs.

Rabbett, Martin. Forever Buster: What a Name! What a Dog, We Exclaim! Burns, Donna, illus. 2007. (J). 13.95 *(978-0-9794649-0-4(0))* Hula Moon Pr.

Rabe, Tish. Cooking with the Grinch (Dr. Seuss) Brannon, Tom, illus. 2017. (Step into Reading Ser.). (ENG.). 32p. (J). (gr. -1-1). pap. 4.99 ***(978-1-5247-1462-8(3))**;* lib. bdg. 12.99 ***(978-1-5247-1463-5(1))*** Random Hse. Children's Bks. (Random Hse. Bks. for Young Readers).

—Huff & Puff. Guile, Gill, illus. 2014. (My First I Can Read Ser.). (ENG.). 24p. (J). (gr. -1-3). 16.99 *(978-0-06-230502-2(6))*; pap. 3.99 *(978-0-06-230501-5(8))* HarperCollins Pubs.

—Huff & Puff & the New Train. Guile, Gill, illus. 2014. (My First I Can Read Ser.). (ENG.). 24p. (J). (gr. -1-3). pap. 3.99 *(978-0-06-230503-9(4))* HarperCollins Pubs.

—Huff & Puff Have Too Much Stuff! Guile, Gill, illus. 2014. (My First I Can Read Ser.). (ENG.). 24p. (J). (gr. -1-3). pap. 3.99 *(978-0-06-230505-3(0))* HarperCollins Pubs.

—I Love You, Grandma! Hitch, David, illus. 2016. (Little Golden Book Ser.). (J). (-k). (ENG.). 24p. 4.99 *(978-1-101-93455-5(7))*; ***(978-1-5182-1618-3(8))*** Random Hse. Children's Bks. (Golden Bks.).

—Look for the Lorax. 2012. (Step into Reading Level 1 Ser.). lib. bdg. 13.55 *(978-0-606-23720-8(8)*, Turtleback) Turtleback Bks.

—Love You, Hug You, Read to You! Endersby, Frank, illus. 2015. (ENG.). 32p. (J). (gr. -1 — 1). bds. 7.99 *(978-1-101-93655-9(X)*, Random Hse. Bks. for Young Readers) Random Hse. Children's Bks.

—Oh, Baby, the Places You'll Go! Seuss, Dr., illus. 2015. (ENG.). 32p. (J). (gr. k-12). 9.99 *(978-0-553-52057-6(1)*,

Random Hse. Bks. for Young Readers) Random Hse. Children's Bks.
—The Thinga-Ma-Jigger Is Coming Today! Moroney, Christopher, illus. 2010. (Little Golden Book Ser.). (ENG.). 24p. (J). (gr. -1-2). 4.99 *(978-0-375-85927-4(6)*, Golden Bks.) Random Hse. Children's Bks.
—Thump!/The Lost Egg (Cat in the Hat/Seuss) Ruiz, Aristides & Mathieu, Joe, illus. 2013. (Pictureback(R) Ser.). (ENG.). 32p. (J). (gr. -1-2). pap. 4.99 *(978-0-307-98063-2(4)*, Random Hse. Bks. for Young Readers) Random Hse. Children's Bks.
Rabe, Tish & Seuss, Dr. Look for the Lorax. Ruiz, Aristides et al, illus. 2012. (Step into Reading Ser.). (ENG.). 32p. (J). (gr. -1-1). pap. 3.99 *(978-0-375-86999-0(9)*, Random Hse. Bks. for Young Readers) Random Hse. Children's Bks.
Raczka, Bob. Fall Mixed Up. Cameron, Chad, illus. 2011. (Carolrhoda Picture Books Ser.). (ENG.). 40p. (J). (gr. -1-3). lib. bdg. 17.95 *(978-0-7613-4606-7(6)*, Carolrhoda Bks.) Lerner Publishing Group.
—Joy in Mudville. Dibley, Glin, illus. 2014. (ENG.). 32p. (J). (gr. -1-3). 17.95 *(978-0-7613-6015-5(8)*, Carolrhoda Bks.) Lerner Publishing Group.
—Summer Wonders. Stead, Judy, illus. 2012. (J). 34.28 *(978-1-61913-125-5(0))* Weigl Pubs., Inc.
Raden, Tammy. My Dog Blue. 2009. 24p. pap. 11.49 *(978-1-4490-3228-9(1))* AuthorHouse.
Radzinski, Kandy. What Cats Want for Christmas. Radzinski, Kandy, illus. rev. ed. 2007. (ENG., Illus.). 32p. (J). (gr. k-6). 16.95 *(978-1-58536-340-7(5))* Sleeping Bear Pr.
—Where to Sleep. 2010. (ENG.). 22p. (J). 9.95 *(978-1-58536-535-7(1))* Sleeping Bear Pr.
—Where to Sleep. Radzinski, Kandy, illus. 2009. (ENG., Illus.). 32p. (J). (gr. k-6). 15.95 *(978-1-58536-436-7(3))* Sleeping Bear Pr.
Rae, Jennifer. Gilbert de la Frogponde: A Swamp Story. braille ed. 2004. (Illus.). (J). (gr. k-3). spiral bd. *(978-0-616-04561-9(1))*; spiral bd. *(978-0-616-03054-7(1))* Canadian National Institute for the Blind/Institut National Canadien pour les Aveugles.
Rae, Philippa. Count the Sheep to Sleep. Röhr, Stéphanie, illus. 2012. (ENG.). 28p. (J). (gr. -1-k). 12.95 *(978-1-61608-660-2(2)*, 608660, Sky Pony Pr.) Skyhorse Publishing Co., Inc.
Rainey. School Is Cool. Huggens, Karin, illus. 2004. (J). *(978-0-9666199-9-7(4))* DreamDog Pr.
Rainforth, Hannah. Barnaby Bennett, 1 vol. Teo, Ali, illus. 2008. (ENG.). 32p. (J). (gr. -1-3). pap. 5.95 *(978-1-59572-156-3(8))* Star Bright Bks., Inc.
—Barnaby Bennett. Teo, Ali, illus. 2007. 32p. (J). (gr. -1-3). pap. 10.00 *(978-1-86969-232-2(2))* Univ. of Hawaii Pr.
Raisner Glass, Beth. Blue-Ribbon Dad. Moore, Margie, illus. 2011. (ENG.). 32p. (J). (gr. k-2). 15.95 *(978-0-8109-9727-1(4)*, Abrams Bks. for Young Readers) Abrams, Inc.
Rand, Paul & Rand, Ann. Listen! Listen! 2016. (ENG., Illus.). 32p. (J). (gr. -1-1). 17.95 *(978-1-61689-494-8(6))* Princeton Architectural Pr.
Randall, Marilyn. Elmer the Christmas Elf. 2009. 32p. 18.95 *(978-0-557-15333-6(6))* Lulu Pr., Inc.
—A Hard Nut to Crack. 2009. 36p. pap. 18.95 *(978-0-557-15891-1(5))* Lulu Pr., Inc.
—Inside Out. 2009. 26p. 18.95 *(978-0-557-15699-3(8))* Lulu Pr., Inc.
Randles, Slim & Montoya, Jerry, illus. Ol' Jimmy Dollar. 2015. 42p. (J). *(978-1-936744-40-4(6))* LPD Pr.
Ransom, Candice. Apple Picking Day! Meza, Erika, illus. 2016. (Step into Reading Ser.). (ENG.). 32p. (J). (gr. -1-1). pap. 3.99 *(978-0-553-53858-8(6)*, Random Hse. Bks. for Young Readers) Random Hse. Children's Bks.
—Pumpkin Day! Meza, Erika, illus. 2015. (Step into Reading Ser.). (ENG.). 32p. (J). (gr. -1-1). 12.99 *(978-0-375-97466-3(0)*, Random Hse. Bks. for Young Readers) Random Hse. Children's Bks.
—Tooth Fairy's Night. 2017. (Step into Reading Ser.). (ENG., Illus.). 32p. (J). (gr. -1-1). 3.99 *(978-0-399-55364-6(9)*, Random Hse. Bks. for Young Readers) Random Hse. Children's Bks.
Ransome, Arthur. Aladdin & His Wonderful Lamp in Rhyme. Mackenzie, Thomas, illus. 2011. (Calla Editions Ser.). (ENG.). 160p. (gr. 5). 30.00 *(978-1-60660-002-3(8))* Dover Pubns., Inc.
Raschka, Chris. Farmy Farm. Raschka, Chris, illus. 2011. (ENG., Illus.). 8p. (J). (gr. -1 — 1). bds. 8.99 *(978-0-545-21981-5(7)*, Orchard Bks.) Scholastic, Inc.
—Five for a Little One. Raschka, Chris, illus. 2006. (ENG., Illus.). 48p. (J). (gr. -1-2). 17.99 *(978-0-689-84599-4(5)*, Atheneum/Richard Jackson Bks.) Simon & Schuster Children's Publishing.
—Hip Hop Dog. Radunsky, Vladimir, illus. 2010. (ENG.). 32p. (J). (gr. -1-3). 16.99 *(978-0-06-123963-2(1))* HarperCollins Pubs.
—Little Black Crow. Raschka, Chris, illus. 2010. (ENG., Illus.). 40p. (J). (gr. -1-2). 16.99 *(978-0-689-84601-4(0)*, Atheneum/Richard Jackson Bks.) Simon & Schuster Children's Publishing.
Rash, Andy. Agent A to Agent Z. 2004. (Illus.). (J). *(978-0-439-36883-4(9)*, Levine, Arthur A. Bks.) Scholastic, Inc.
Rasmussen, Halfdan. The Ladder. Nelson, Marilyn, tr. from DAN. Pratt, Pierre, illus. 2006. (ENG.). 62p. (J). (gr. -1-3). 17.99 *(978-0-7636-2282-4(6))* Candlewick Pr.
Rathmann, Peggy. The Day the Babies Crawled Away. Rathmann, Peggy, illus. 2003. (ENG., Illus.). 40p. (J). (gr. -1-k). 17.99 *(978-0-399-23196-4(X)*, G.P. Putnam's Sons Books for Young Readers) Penguin Young Readers Group.
Ratnett, Michael. Dracula Steps Out. Goulding, June & Smyth, Iain, illus. 2005. 12p. (J). (gr. k-4). reprint ed. 16.00 *(978-0-7567-8585-7(5))* DIANE Publishing Co.
Ratzlaff, Aaron J. Quills. 2011. (ENG.). 40p. (J). pap. 13.99 *(978-0-8361-9509-5(4))* Herald Pr.
Rauchwerger, Diane Levin. Dinosaur Goes to Israel. Wolff, Jason, illus. 2012. (Israel Ser.). (ENG.). 24p. (J). (gr. -1-1). pap. 7.95 *(978-0-7613-5134-4(5))*; lib. bdg. 16.95 *(978-0-7613-5133-7(7))* Lerner Publishing Group. (Kar-Ben Publishing).
—Dinosaur on Hanukkah. Wolff, Jason, illus. 2005. (ENG.). 24p. (J). (gr. -1-1). 15.95 *(978-1-58013-145-2(X))*; per. 7.95 *(978-1-58013-143-8(3))* Lerner Publishing Group. (Kar-Ben Publishing).
Rauchwerger, Diane Levin & Levin, Diane. Dinosaur on Shabbat. Wolff, Jason, illus. 2006. (ENG.). 24p. (J). (gr. -1-1). lib. bdg. 15.95 *(978-1-58013-159-9(X)*, Kar-Ben Publishing) Lerner Publishing Group.
Rauss, Ron. Can I Just Take a Nap? Shepperson, Rob, illus. 2012. (ENG.). 32p. (J). (gr. -1-1). 15.99 *(978-1-4424-3497-4(X)*, Simon & Schuster/Paula Wiseman Bks.) Simon & Schuster/Paula Wiseman Bks.
Ravishankar, Anushka. Excuse Me, Is This India? Leutwiler, Anita, illus. 2003. 24p. (J). 14.95 *(978-81-86211-56-4(X))* Tara Publishing IND. Dist: Consortium Bk. Sales & Distribution.
Ray, Christie Jones & Ray, Christie Jones. Pick-A-Pick-a-Pumpkin. 2012. (Illus.). 36p. pap. 12.00 *(978-0-9853223-4-2(9))* Rose Water Cottage Pr.
Ray, J. Hamilton. Squirrels on Skis. Lemaître, Pascal, illus. 2013. (Beginner Books Ser.). (ENG.). 64p. (J). (gr. k-3). 9.99 *(978-0-449-81081-1(X)*, Random Hse. Bks. for Young Readers) Random Hse. Children's Bks.
Ray, Mary Lyn. Go to Sleep, Little Farm. Neal, Christopher Silas, illus. (ENG.). (J). 2015. 38p. (— 1). bds. 8.99 *(978-0-544-57916-3(X))* 2014. 40p. (gr. -1-3). 16.99 *(978-0-544-15014-0(7))* Houghton Mifflin Harcourt Publishing Co. (HMH Books For Young Readers).
Reade, O. K. The Little Girl & Her Shadow. 2015. (Illus.). (J). 12.99 *(978-1-4621-1618-8(3))* Cedar Fort, Inc./CFI Distribution.
Reader's Digest Staff & Mitter, Matt. We Love Cookies! Brannon, Tom, illus. 2010. (Hugs Book Ser.). (ENG.). 12p. (J). (— 1). bds. 10.99 *(978-0-7944-2176-2(8))* Reader's Digest Assn., Inc., The.
Reader's Digest Staff & Shepherd, Jodie. Guess Who Baby Animals. Ovresat, Laura, illus. 2011. (Guess Who Ser.). (ENG.). 10p. (J). (gr. -1-k). bds. 7.99 *(978-0-7944-2196-0(2))* Reader's Digest Assn., Inc., The.
Reasoner, Charles. Charles Reasoner's Little Cuddles. Llewhellin, Gareth, illus. 2015. (Charles Reasoner's Little Cuddles Ser.). (ENG.). 10p. (gr. -1 — 1). bds. 17.97 *(978-1-4795-8061-3(9)*, Charles Reasoners Little Cuddles) Picture Window Bks.
—Color Crunch! 2009. (Bite Bks.). (Illus.). (J). bds. 7.99 *(978-1-934650-15-8(3))* Just For Kids Pr., LLC.
—Halloween Ghost, 1 vol. 2014. (Charles Reasoner Halloween Bks.). (ENG.). 12p. (gr. -1 — 1). bds. 5.99 *(978-1-4795-5971-8(7))* Picture Window Bks.
—I'm Just a Bird. 2008. *(978-1-84666-153-2(6))* Top That! Publishing PLC.
—I'm Just a Fish. 2008. (Googley-Eye Bks.). (ENG.). 12p. (J). (gr. -1). 7.99 *(978-1-84666-155-6(2))* Top That! Publishing PLC GBR. Dist: Independent Pubs. Group.
—I'm Just a Frog. 2008. *(978-1-84666-159-4(5))* Top That! Publishing PLC.
—Inside Jolly Rodger's Pirate Ship. 2014. (Illus.). (J). *(978-1-4351-5466-7(5))* Barnes & Noble, Inc.
—Let It Snow. Jones, Anna, illus. 2013. (Charles Reasoner Holiday Bks.). (ENG.). 10p. (gr. -1 — 1). bds. 9.99 *(978-1-4048-8147-1(6))* Picture Window Bks.
—Peek-A-Boo Ghosts. Le Ray, Marina & Jones, Anna, illus. 2013. (Charles Reasoner Peek-A-Boo Bks.). (ENG.). 10p. (gr. -1 — 1). bds. 9.99 *(978-1-4795-2359-7(3))*; bds. 4.99 *(978-1-4795-2360-3(7))* Picture Window Bks.
—Winter Friends, 1 vol. Reasoner, Charles & Jones, Anna, illus. 2013. (Charles Reasoner Holiday Bks.). (ENG.). 10p. (gr. -1 — 1). bds. 4.99 *(978-1-4048-8156-3(5))* Picture Window Bks.
Reasoner, Charles, illus. Bear Hugs. 2015. (J). *(978-1-4795-5944-2(X))* Picture Window Bks.
—Honey Bunny. 2015. (J). *(978-1-4795-5945-9(8))* Picture Window Bks.
—Peep! Peep! 2015. (J). *(978-1-4795-5943-5(1))* Picture Window Bks.
—Puppy Love. 2015. (J). *(978-1-4795-5946-6(6))* Picture Window Bks.
Reasoner, Charles & Wood, Hannah. Peek-A-Boo Reindeer, 1 vol. Reasoner, Charles, illus. 2014. (Charles Reasoner Peek-A-Boo Bks.). (ENG.). 10p. (gr. -1 — 1). bds. 12.99 *(978-1-4795-5179-8(1))* Picture Window Bks.
—Peek-A-Boo Snowman, 1 vol. Reasoner, Charles, illus. 2014. (Charles Reasoner Peek-A-Boo Bks.). (ENG., Illus.). 10p. (gr. -1 — 1). bds. 12.99 *(978-1-4795-5181-1(3))* Picture Window Bks.
Reasoner, Charles & Wood, Steven. Little Monster. 2015. (Charles Reasoner Halloween Bks.). (ENG., Illus.). 12p. (gr. -1 — 1). bds. 5.99 *(978-1-4795-8502-1(5))* Picture Window Bks.
—Owl's Halloween. 2015. (Charles Reasoner Halloween Bks.). (ENG., Illus.). 12p. (gr. -1 — 1). bds. 5.99 *(978-1-4795-8500-7(9))* Picture Window Bks.
—Scaredy Cat. 2015. (Charles Reasoner Halloween Bks.). (ENG., Illus.). 12p. (gr. -1 — 1). bds. 5.99 *(978-1-4795-8501-4(7))* Picture Window Bks.
Rebecca, Rebecca. The Turtle Who Did His Best. 2016. (ENG., Illus.). 26p. pap. 5.99 *(978-1-61984-471-1(0))* Price World Publishing.
Redmond, E. S. The Unruly Queen. Redmond, E. S., illus. 2012. (ENG., Illus.). 32p. (J). (gr. -1-2). 15.99 *(978-0-7636-3445-2(X))* Candlewick Pr.
Reed, Susan. Up, up, Up! Oldfield, Rachel, illus. 2010. (ENG.). 24p. (J). (gr. -1-2). 16.99 *(978-1-84686-369-1(4))* Barefoot Bks., Inc.
Reeder, Kim Cooley. Runaway Tomato. Agnew, Lincoln, illus. 2014. (ENG.). 34p. (J). (gr. -1-k). 16.99 *(978-0-8037-3694-8(0)*, Dial Bks) Penguin Young Readers Group.
Refrolo, C. T. Grandchild of Mine: You & I. 2006. (J). 12.00 *(978-0-8059-6845-3(8))* Dorrance Publishing Co., Inc.
Regan, Patrick. The Marvelous Monsters Talent Show. Bonson, Tom, illus. 2014. (J). *(978-1-4351-5617-3(X)*, Blackbirch Pr., Inc.) Barnes & Noble, Inc.
Reich, Ashley. Izzy Lizzy. Reich, Ashley, illus. 2005. (Illus.). 32p. (J). per. 16.00 *(978-0-9754298-3-9(3)*, Ithaca Pr.) Authors & Artists Publishers of New York, Inc.
Reichert, Amy. While Mama Had a Quick Little Chat. Boiger, Alexandra, illus. 2005. (ENG.). 40p. (J). (gr. -1-2). 16.99 *(978-0-689-85170-4(7)*, Atheneum/Richard Jackson Bks.) Simon & Schuster Children's Publishing.
Reid, Carol. Spook-Ee Wook-Ee Halloween. 2012. 24p. pap. 17.99 *(978-1-4772-5845-3(0))* AuthorHouse.
Reid, Rob. Comin' down to Storytime. Bernard Westcott, Nadine, illus. 2009. (J). (gr. -1-3). 17.95 *(978-1-60213-039-5(6)*, Upstart Bks.) Highsmith Inc.
—Wave Goodbye, 1 vol. Williams, Lorraine, illus. 2013. (ENG.). 24p. (J). pap. 9.95 *(978-1-60060-341-9(6))* Lee & Low Bks., Inc.
Reid, Robin L. Rhyming Ricky Rutherford. Lipp, Tony, illus. 2012. 24p. pap. 24.95 *(978-1-4626-8896-8(9))* America Star Bks.
Reidy, Jean. All Through My Town. Timmers, Leo, illus. (ENG.). (J). (gr. -1-k). 2015. 26p. bds. 7.99 *(978-1-61963-562-3(3)*, 9781619635623) 2013. 32p. 14.99 *(978-1-59990-785-7(2)*, 9781599907857) 2013. 32p. lib. bdg. 15.89 *(978-1-61963-029-1(X)*, 9781619630291) Bloomsbury Publishing USA. (Bloomsbury USA Childrens).
—Busy Builders, Busy Week! Timmers, Leo, illus. 2016. (ENG.). 32p. (J). 16.99 *(978-1-61963-556-2(9)*, 9781619635562, Bloomsbury USA Childrens) Bloomsbury Publishing USA.
—Too Pickley! Leloup, Geneviève, illus. (Too! Bks.). (ENG.). (J). (gr. -1 — 1). 2012. 26p. bds. 7.99 *(978-1-59990-680-5(5)*, 9781599906805) 2010. 32p. 11.99 *(978-1-59990-309-5(1)*, 9781599903095) Bloomsbury Publishing USA. (Bloomsbury USA Childrens).
—Too Princessy! Leloup, Geneviève, illus. (Too! Bks.). (ENG.). (J). (gr. -1 — 1). 2013. 26p. bds. 7.99 *(978-1-59990-955-4(3)*, 9781599909554) 2012. 32p. 12.99 *(978-1-59990-722-2(4)*, 9781599907222) Bloomsbury Publishing USA. (Bloomsbury USA Childrens).
—Too Purpley! Leloup, Geneviève, illus. (Too! Bks.). (ENG.). (J). (gr. -1 — 1). 2011. 26p. bds. 7.99 *(978-1-59990-679-9(1)*, 9781599906799) 2010. 32p. 11.99 *(978-1-59990-307-1(5)*, 9781599903071) Bloomsbury Publishing USA. (Bloomsbury USA Childrens).
Reiser, Lynn. You & Me, Baby. Gentieu, Penny, photos by. 2008. (ENG., Illus.). 32p. (J). (— 1). bds. 6.99 *(978-0-375-84420-1(1)*, Knopf Bks. for Young Readers) Random Hse. Children's Bks.
Reiss, Mike. Santa's Eleven Months Off, 1 vol. Montgomery, Michael G., illus. (ENG.). (J). 2016. 28p. (gr. -1-3). pap. 7.95 *(978-1-56145-962-9(3))* 2007. 32p. (gr. k-3). 16.95 *(978-1-56145-421-1(4))* Peachtree Pubs.
Reiss, Mike & Reiss, Mike. The Boy Who Wouldn't Share. Catrow, David, illus. 2008. (ENG.). 32p. (J). (gr. 1-3). 16.99 *(978-0-06-059132-8(3))* HarperCollins Pubs.
—Late for School, 1 vol. Austin, Michael, illus. 2003. (ENG.). 32p. (J). (gr. k-3). 16.95 *(978-1-56145-286-6(6)*, Q35957) Peachtree Pubs.
Rena, Regina. Where Do Cows Moo? 2010. 20p. pap. 12.99 *(978-1-4490-8204-8(1))* AuthorHouse.
Rescek, Sanja. Buggy Buddies Fairy Moonbeam. Rescek, Sanja, illus. 2015. (Buggy Buddies Ser.). (ENG., Illus.). 8p. (J). (-k). bds. 8.99 *(978-1-4472-7614-2(0))* Pan Macmillan GBR. Dist: Independent Pubs. Group.
—Buggy Buddies Fairy Sunshine. Rescek, Sanja, illus. 2015. (Buggy Buddies Ser.). (ENG., Illus.). 8p. (J). (-k). bds. 8.99 *(978-1-4472-7612-8(4))* Pan Macmillan GBR. Dist: Independent Pubs. Group.
Resnicoff, Stan. Stanley, the Seal of Approval. 2012. (ENG.). (J). pap. *(978-1-4675-1535-1(3))* Independent Pub.
Rex, Michael. Goodnight Goon: A Petrifying Parody. Rex, Michael, illus. 2012. (ENG., Illus.). 30p. (J). (gr. -1 — 1). bds. 6.99 *(978-0-399-26011-7(0)*, G.P. Putnam's Sons Books for Young Readers) Penguin Publishing Group.
—Goodnight Goon: A Petrifying Parody. Rex, Michael, illus. 2008. (ENG., Illus.). 32p. (J). (gr. -1-k). 15.99 *(978-0-399-24534-3(0)*, G.P. Putnam's Sons Books for Young Readers) Penguin Young Readers Group.
—Truck Duck. Rex, Michael, illus. 2008. (ENG., Illus.). 26p. (J). (gr. -1 — 1). bds. 7.99 *(978-0-399-25092-7(1)*, G.P. Putnam's Sons Books for Young Readers) Penguin Young Readers Group.
Rexroth, Sharon. America from the Sky. 2006. (J). 9.95 *(978-1-57166-429-7(7))*; per. 22.95 *(978-1-57166-430-3(0))* Quixote Pr.
—Ohio. 2006. (ENG., Illus.). (J). per. 19.95 *(978-1-57166-421-1(1))* Quixote Pr.
Rey, H. A. Curious George Pat-A-Cake. 2011. (Curious George Ser.). (ENG., Illus.). 8p. (J). (gr. k — 1). bds. 9.99 *(978-0-547-51689-9(4))* Houghton Mifflin Harcourt Publishing Co.
—Happy Birthday, Curious George! 2016. (Curious George Ser.). (ENG., Illus.). 14p. (J). (— 1). bds. 7.99 *(978-0-544-75050-0(0)*, HMH Books For Young Readers) Houghton Mifflin Harcourt Publishing Co.
—Happy Halloween. 2008. (Curious George Ser.). (ENG., Illus.). 14p. (J). (gr. -1 — 1). bds. 7.99 *(978-0-618-91952-9(X))* Houghton Mifflin Harcourt Publishing Co.
—Happy St. Patrick's Day. 2014. (Curious George Ser.). (ENG., Illus.). 14p. (J). (— 1). bds. 7.99 *(978-0-544-08888-7(3))* Houghton Mifflin Harcourt Publishing Co.
—Whose House? 2017. (ENG., Illus.). 24p. (J). (gr. -1-3). 8.99 *(978-0-544-94975-1(7)*, HMH Books For Young Readers) Houghton Mifflin Harcourt Publishing Co.
Rey, H. A. & Rey, Margret. The H. A. Rey Treasury of Stories. 2015. (Dover Children's Classics Ser.). (ENG., Illus.). 112p. (J). (gr. 2-4). pap. 14.99 *(978-0-486-78468-7(1))* Dover Pubns., Inc.
Reyes, Cameron. In Your Heart. DeBroech, Sarah, illus. 2011. 28p. pap. 24.95 *(978-1-4560-1009-6(3))* America Star Bks.
Reynolds, Luke. If My Love Were a Fire Truck. Mack, Jeff, illus. 2017. (ENG.). 32p. (J). (gr. -1-2). 16.99 *(978-1-101-93740-2(8)*, Doubleday Bks. for Young Readers) Random Hse. Children's Bks.
Rhodes, Julie & Quarto Generic Staff. The Very Noisy House. Paul, Korky, illus. 2014. (ENG.). 32p. (J). (gr. -1-k). 17.99 *(978-1-84507-983-3(3)*, Frances Lincoln) Quarto Publishing Group UK GBR. Dist: Hachette Bk. Group.
Rhodes, Lou. The Phlunk's Worldwide Symphony. Elliott, Tori, illus. 2014. (ENG.). 32p. (J). pap. *(978-0-9573690-2-3(6))* Strata Bks.
Rhodes, Tiffany. What I Learned This Christmas. 2013. (Illus.). 42p. pap. 15.99 *(978-0-9899099-1-4(3))* Bee Creative, LLC.
Rhymes, Wriggly. No Place Like Home. 2013. (Illus.). 40p. pap. 11.00 *(978-1-78035-602-0(1)*, Fastprint Publishing) Upfront Publishing Ltd. GBR. Dist: Printondemand-worldwide.com.
Ricci, Christine. Dora's Nursery Rhyme Adventure. Fruchter, Jason, illus. 2005. (Dora the Explorer Ser.). (J). *(978-0-7172-9819-8(1))* Scholastic, Inc.
Riccobono, Michael P. Billy Balonie & the Belly Buttonie. 2010. (Illus.). 28p. pap. 19.00 *(978-1-4490-3119-0(6))* AuthorHouse.
Rice, Dona Herweck & Aucoin, Lee. All about Me, 1 vol. 2009. (Early Childhood Themes Ser.). (ENG., Illus.). 16p. (J). (gr. -1-2). pap. 19.99 *(978-1-4333-1468-1(1))* Shell Educational Publishing.
Rice, James. Gaston(r) Goes to Texas, 1 vol. Rice, James, illus. 2007. (Gaston(r) Ser.). (ENG., Illus.). 32p. (J). (gr. 1-3). 16.99 *(978-1-58980-531-6(3))* Pelican Publishing Co., Inc.
—Gaston(r) Lays an Offshore Pipeline, 1 vol. Rice, James, illus. 2007. (Gaston(r) Ser.). (ENG., Illus.). 32p. (J). (gr. k-3). 16.99 *(978-1-58980-510-1(0))* Pelican Publishing Co., Inc.
Rice, James, illus. Gaston Joins the Circus, 1 vol. 2015. (ENG.). 32p. (J). (gr. k-3). pap. 9.95 *(978-1-4556-2092-0(0))* Pelican Publishing Co., Inc.
—Gaston(r) Joins the Circus, 1 vol. 2015. (ENG.). 32p. (J). (gr. k-3). 16.99 *(978-1-4556-2129-3(3))* Pelican Publishing Co., Inc.
Richards, Arlene. That's Bingzy! Busy Building Self-Esteem. 2007. (J). per. 15.95 *(978-0-9794323-2-3(4))* Bing Note, Inc.
Richards, Dawn. My Mommy Is Magic. Massey, Jane, illus. 2015. (ENG.). 32p. (J). (gr. -1-k). 8.99 *(978-0-7641-6757-7(X))* Barron's Educational Series, Inc.
Richards, Kitty & RH Disney Staff. Run, Remy, Run! Disney Storybook Artists Staff, illus. 2007. (Step into Reading Ser.). (ENG.). 32p. (J). (gr. k-3). pap. 3.99 *(978-0-7364-2476-9(8)*, RH/Disney) Random Hse. Children's Bks.
Richmond, Marianne. Hooray for You! A Celebration Of "You-Ness" 2015. (Marianne Richmond Ser.: 0). (ENG.). 24p. (J). (-2). bds. 7.99 *(978-1-4926-1555-2(2))* Sourcebooks, Inc.
—I Love You So... 2013. (ENG.). 24p. (J). bds. 7.99 *(978-1-4022-7953-9(1)*, Sourcebooks Jabberwocky) Sourcebooks, Inc.
—The Night Night Book. Richmond, Marianne, illus. 2011. (Marianne Richmond Ser.: 0). (ENG., Illus.). 24p. (J). (gr. -1-3). bds. 7.95 *(978-1-934082-90-4(2)*, Sourcebooks Jabberwocky) Sourcebooks, Inc.
—Oh, the Things My Mom Will Do. 2013. (ENG., Illus.). 32p. (J). (-2). 9.99 *(978-1-4022-8215-7(X)*, 9781402282157); 16.99 *(978-1-4022-8233-1(8))* Sourcebooks, Inc. (Sourcebooks Jabberwocky).
—Si Pudiera Conservarte Pequeño... 2014. (SPA & ENG., Illus.). 24p. (J). bds. 6.99 *(978-1-4926-0369-6(4)*, Sourcebooks Jabberwocky) Sourcebooks, Inc.
—You Are My Heart. 2015. (ENG., Illus.). 32p. (J). (-2). 16.99 *(978-1-4926-1542-2(0)*, Sourcebooks Jabberwocky) Sourcebooks, Inc.
—You Are My Merry. 2015. (ENG.). 32p. (J). (-2). 16.99 *(978-1-4926-2894-1(8)*, Sourcebooks Jabberwocky) Sourcebooks, Inc.
Riddle, Waide Aaron. The Chocolate Man A Children's Horror Tale. Aragon Art Studio, illus. ed. 2010. (ENG.). 44p. pap. 15.00 *(978-0-615-38560-0(5))* Green Ghost Pr.
Ridley, Sharon, illus. My Wildflower Friends. Phillips, Marilyn, photos by. 2006. (J). *(978-0-9786168-0-9(4))* Rio Wildflower Pubns.
Rigg, Jo. Millie Moo. 2007. (Illus.). 10p. (J). *(978-1-84332-473-7(3))* Priddy Bks.
—Rocky Dog. 2007. (Illus.). 10p. (J). *(978-1-84332-474-4(1))* Priddy Bks.
Riley, Kellee, illus. Tolee's Rhyme Time. 2009. (Ni Hao, Kai-Lan Ser.). (ENG.). 24p. (J). pap. 3.99 *(978-1-4169-9024-6(0)*, Simon Spotlight/Nickelodeon) Simon Spotlight/Nickelodeon.
Ringler, Matt. It's Fall! Shearing, Leonie, illus. 2006. 28p. (J). pap. *(978-0-439-87146-4(8))* Scholastic, Inc.
—One Little, Two Little, Three Little Apples. Kennedy, Anne, illus. 2005. (J). pap. *(978-0-439-77500-7(0))* Scholastic, Inc.
Rink, Cynthia A. Where Does the Wind Blow? Rink, Cynthia A., illus. 2004. (Sharing Nature with Children Book Ser.). (Illus.). 32p. (J). (gr. k-5). 16.95 *(978-1-58469-041-2(0))* Dawn Pubns.
Rink, Cynthia A., illus. Where Does the Wind Blow? 2004. (Sharing Nature with Children Book Ser.). 32p. (J). pap. 7.95 *(978-1-58469-040-5(2))* Dawn Pubns.
Rinker, Sherri Duskey. Goodnight, Goodnight, Construction Site. Lichtenheld, Tom, illus. (ENG.). (J). 2017. 30p. bds. 7.99 *(978-1-4521-1173-5(1))* 2016. 32p. (gr. -1 — 1). 18.99 *(978-1-4521-5215-8(2))* 2016. 20p. (gr. -1-7). 12.99 *(978-1-4521-5463-3(5))* 2015. 66p. (gr. -1 — 1). 15.99 *(978-1-4521-4698-0(5))* 2011. 32p. (gr. -1-1). 16.99 *(978-0-8118-7782-4(5))* Chronicle Bks. LLC.
—Goodnight, Goodnight, Construction Site: Let's Go! Lichtenheld, Tom, illus. 2017. (ENG.). 10p. (J). (gr. -1 — 1). bds. 8.99 ***(978-1-4521-6476-2(2))*** Chronicle Bks. LLC.
—Mighty, Mighty Construction Site. Lichtenheld, Tom, illus. 2017. (ENG.). 40p. (J). 16.99 *(978-1-4521-5216-5(0))* Chronicle Bks. LLC.
—Steam Train, Dream Train. Lichtenheld, Tom, illus. 2013. (ENG.). 40p. (J). (gr. -1-1). 16.99 *(978-1-4521-0920-6(6))* Chronicle Bks. LLC.
—Steam Train, Dream Train Sound Book. Lichtenheld, Tom, illus. 2015. (ENG.). 12p. (J). (gr. -1-k). 12.99 *(978-1-4521-2825-2(1))* Chronicle Bks. LLC.
Rinker, Sherri Duskey & Lichtenheld, Tom. Goodnight, Goodnight, Construction Site. 2012. 12.95 *(978-0-545-50222-1(5))* Scholastic, Inc.
Risco, Elle D. Dora Had a Little Lamb. Savitsky, Steve, illus. 2007. (Dora the Explorer Ser.). (J). (gr. -1-2). 11.65 *(978-0-7569-8294-2(4))* Perfection Learning Corp.
Ritchie, Alison. Me & My Dad! Edgson, Alison, illus. 2007. (J). pap. *(978-0-545-02064-0(6))* Scholastic, Inc.
Ritchie, Joseph R. Baby Looney Tunes Visit a Haunted House. Halverson, Lydia, illus. 2005. (Baby Looney Tunes Ser.). 14p. (J). (gr. -1-3). bds. 9.95 *(978-0-8249-6609-6(0)*, Ideal Pubns.) Worthy Publishing.

S

—Frosty the Snowman Returns. Rose, Drew, illus. 2006. 14p. (J). (gr. -1-k). bds. 9.95 (978-0-8249-6670-6(8), Ideal Pubns.) Worthy Publishing.
—Peek-a-Boo! Halverson, Lydia, illus. 2004. (ENG.). 14p. (J). bds. 7.95 (978-0-8249-6550-1(7), Ideal Pubns.) Worthy Publishing.
—Peter Cottontail's Busy Day. Halverson, Lydia, illus. (J). 2009. 14p. (gr. -1-k). bds. 6.99 (978-0-8249-1842-2(8)) 2006. (ENG.). 26p. (gr. -1-k). 12.95 (978-0-8249-6652-2(X)) 2005. (ENG.). 16p. bds. 9.95 (978-0-8249-6571-6(X)) Worthy Publishing. (Ideal Pubns.).
—Peter Cottontail's Easter Egg Hunt. Thornburgh, Rebecca McKillip, illus. (J). 2012. 14p. bds. 6.99 (978-0-8249-1880-4(0)) 2004. (ENG.). 12p. (gr. -1-k). bds. 9.95 (978-0-8249-6522-8(1)) Worthy Publishing. (Ideal Pubns.).
—Peter Cottontaol's Easter Egg Hunt. Thornburgh, Rebecca, illus. 2006. (ENG.). 26p. (J). (gr. -1-k). 12.95 (978-0-8249-6653-9(8), Ideal Pubns.) Worthy Publishing.
—Where's Santa? Halverson, Lydia, illus. 2006. (ENG.). 14p. (J). (gr. -1-k). bds. 7.95 (978-0-8249-6673-7(2), Ideal Pubns.) Worthy Publishing.
Ritter, Philip. Tales in Rhyme from Three Little Mischief Maker's Country Time: The Escapades of Three Little Mischief Makers. 2005. (J). pap. 10.00 (978-0-8059-6928-3(4)) Dorrance Publishing Co., Inc.
Rizzi, Kathleen. What's in My Dresser?, 1 vol. Riggs, Jenna, illus. 2013. (ENG.). 32p. (J). bds. 7.99 (978-1-59572-165-5(7)) Star Bright Bks., Inc.
Rml. An Interesting Crew. 2012. 16p. (-18). pap. 15.99 (978-1-4772-8699-9(3)) AuthorHouse.
Roadhouse, Patricia. Gah Reen Galoshes. 2009. 28p. pap. 16.99 (978-1-4389-7318-0(7)) AuthorHouse.
Roaring Fork Conservancy (Basalt, Colo.) Staff, contrib. by. Dee Dee the Fryingpan River Dipper. 2017. (J). **(978-1-883551-90-2(0)**, Maple Corners Press) Attic Studio Publishing Hse.
Robbins, Becky. Creature Teacher. 2016. (ENG., Illus.). 25p. (J). pap. 10.95 (978-1-78612-354-1(1), 9b9495a8-cc78-438c-ac17-3ade2a4a0aac) Austin, Stan AUS. Dist: Bookmasters Distribution.
Robbins, Karen. Care for Our World Play Set. 2012. (ENG.). (J). 34.95 (978-1-935414-63-6(1)) Casemate Pubs. & Bk. Distributors, LLC.
Roberts, Bethany. Thanksgiving Mice! Cushman, Doug, illus. 2005. (ENG.). 32p. (J). (gr. -1 — 1). 5.95 (978-0-618-60486-9(3)) Houghton Mifflin Harcourt Publishing Co.
Roberts, Deborah. Mr Otagiri's Promise. Ju-Young Im, Joy & Da-Young Im, Linda, illus. 2012. 40p. pap. (978-1-77067-719-7(4)) FriesenPress.
Roberts, Justin. The Smallest Girl in the Smallest Grade. Robinson, Christian, illus. 2014. (ENG.). 32p. (J). (gr. -1-k). 16.99 (978-0-399-25743-8(8), G.P. Putnam's Sons Books for Young Readers) Penguin Young Readers Group.
Robertson, Si & Nelson, Ashley Howard. Uncle Si, the Christmas Elf: Work Hard, Nap Hard. Gilpin, Stephen, illus. 2014. (ENG.). 48p. (J). (gr. -1-3). 29.99 (978-1-4814-1821-8(1), Simon & Schuster Bks. For Young Readers) Simon & Schuster Bks. For Young Readers.
Robertson, Si, et al. Everything's Better with a Beard. 2014. (ENG., Illus.). 48p. (J). (gr. -1-3). 14.99 (978-1-4814-1817-1(3), Simon & Schuster Bks. For Young Readers) Simon & Schuster Bks. For Young Readers.
Robinson, David. The Mushroom Picker. 2013. (ENG., Illus.). 48p. 25.00 (978-1-900828-41-3(3)) Violette Editions GBR. Dist: D.A.P./Distributed Art Pubs.
Robinson, Dierdre. I Don't Look Like You & That's Ok. 2011. 12p. (gr. 1-2). pap. 8.32 (978-1-4567-4466-3(6)) AuthorHouse.
Robinson, Hilary. Beauty & the Pea. Sanfilippo, Simona, illus. 2013. (ENG.). 32p. (J). (978-0-7787-1155-1(2)) Crabtree Publishing Co.
—Cinderella & the Beanstalk. Sanfilippo, Simona, illus. 2013. (ENG.). 32p. (J). (978-0-7787-1156-8(0)); pap. (978-0-7787-1161-2(7)) Crabtree Publishing Co.
—Croc by the Rock. Gordon, Mike, illus. 2005. 32p. (J). lib. bdg. 9.00 (978-1-4242-0885-2(8)) Fitzgerald Bks.
—A Croc Shock! Gordon, Mike, illus. 2009. (Get Set Readers Ser.). 32p. (J). (gr. -1-2). lib. bdg. 22.60 (978-1-60754-265-0(X)) Windmill Bks.
—The Elves & the Emperor. Sanfilippo, Simona, illus. 2012. (ENG.). 32p. (J). (978-0-7787-8025-0(2)); pap. (978-0-7787-8036-6(8)) Crabtree Publishing Co.
—Goldilocks & the Wolf. Sanfilippo, Simona, illus. 2012. (ENG.). 32p. (J). (978-0-7787-8023-6(6)); pap. (978-0-7787-8034-2(1)) Crabtree Publishing Co.
—Hansel, Gretel, & the Ugly Duckling. Sanfilippo, Simona, illus. 2013. (ENG.). 32p. (J). (978-0-7787-1157-5(9)); pap. (978-0-7787-1166-7(8)) Crabtree Publishing Co.
—Rapunzel & the Billy Goats. Sanfilippo, Simona, illus. 2013. (ENG.). 32p. (J). pap. (978-0-7787-1158-2(7)) Crabtree Publishing Co.
—Snow White & the Enormous Turnip. Sanfilippo, Simona, illus. 2012. (ENG.). 32p. (J). pap. (978-0-7787-8035-9(X)) Crabtree Publishing Co.
—Three Pigs & a Gingerbread Man. Sanfilippo, Simona, illus. 2012. (ENG.). 32p. (J). (978-0-7787-8026-7(0)); pap. (978-0-7787-8037-3(6)) Crabtree Publishing Co.
Robinson, Michelle. And the Robot Went ... Ruzzier, Sergio, illus. 2017. (ENG.). 32p. (J). (gr. -1-3). 16.99 (978-0-544-58652-9(2), Clarion Bks.) Houghton Mifflin Harcourt Trade & Reference Pubs.
—The Forgetful Knight. Blunt, Fred, illus. 2016. (ENG.). 40p. (J). (gr. -1-3). 16.99 (978-0-8037-4067-9(0), Dial Bks) Penguin Young Readers Group.
—Goodnight Digger: The Perfect Bedtime Book! 2015. (Goodnight Ser.). (ENG., Illus.). 32p. (J). (gr. -1 — 1). pap. 7.99 (978-1-4380-0661-1(6)) Barron's Educational Series, Inc.
—Goodnight Pirate: The Perfect Bedtime Book! 2015. (Goodnight Ser.). (ENG., Illus.). 32p. (J). (gr. -1 — 1). pap. 7.99 (978-1-4380-0662-8(4)) Barron's Educational Series, Inc.
—Goodnight Princess: The Perfect Bedtime Book! 2015. (Goodnight Ser.). (ENG., Illus.). 32p. (J). (gr. -1 — 1). pap. 7.99 (978-1-4380-0663-5(2)) Barron's Educational Series, Inc.
Robleda, Margarita. Ramon y Su Raton. Suarez, Maribel, illus. (Rana, Rema, Rimas Ser.). (SPA.). 16p. (J). (gr. k-3). 7.95 (978-1-59437-818-8(5)) Santillana USA Publishing Co., Inc.
Rodgers, Phillip W. When Was God Born?, 1 vol. 2008. (Discovering God Ser.). 32p. (J). 12.99 (978-0-8254-3608-6(7)) Kregel Pubns.
Rodriguez, Antonio Orlando. Mi Bicicleta es un Hada y Otros Secretos Por el Estilo. (SPA.). 68p. (J). (gr. k-2). (978-958-30-0797-2(8)) Panamericana Editorial COL. Dist: Lectorum Pubns., Inc.
Rogers, Anne. CAPTAIN DAN & SAILOR SAM. 2008. 37p. pap. 24.95 (978-1-4092-1029-0(4)) Lulu Pr., Inc.
—Sooty Wooty Is a Cat. 2008. 32p. pap. 23.95 (978-1-4092-2565-2(8)) Lulu Pr., Inc.
Rollins, Jack & Nelson, Steve. Frosty the Snowman. Thornburgh, Rebecca McKillip, illus. 2003. (ENG.). 24p. (J). bds. 6.95 (978-0-8249-6500-6(0), Ideal Pubns.) Worthy Publishing.
—Frosty the Snowman Sticker Book. Thornburgh, Rebecca, illus. 2012. 24p. (J). 5.99 (978-0-8249-5646-2(X), Ideal Pubns.) Worthy Publishing.
Romagnoli, L. M. Memories of Me, 1 vol. 2009. 22p. pap. 24.95 (978-1-60836-084-0(9)) America Star Bks.
Roman, Lisa. Boots. Steckler, Megan, illus. 2009. 24p. pap. 24.95 (978-1-60749-329-7(2)) America Star Bks.
Rooney, Rachel. A Patch of Black, 8. Allwright, Deborah, illus. 2014. (ENG.). 32p. (J). (-k). pap. 9.99 (978-0-230-71443-4(9)) Pan Macmillan GBR. Dist: Independent Pubs. Group.
Root, Phyllis. Flip, Flap, Fly! A Book for Babies Everywhere. Walker, David, illus. 2011. (ENG.). 32p. (J). (gr. -1 — 1). bds. 6.99 (978-0-7636-5325-5(X)) Candlewick Pr.
—Looking for a Moose. Cecil, Randy, illus. 2008. (ENG.). 40p. (J). (gr. -1-2). pap. 6.99 (978-0-7636-3885-6(4)) Candlewick Pr.
—One Duck Stuck. 2003. (gr. k-3). 17.20 (978-0-613-60361-4(3), Turtleback) Turtleback Bks.
—One Duck Stuck: A Mucky Ducky Counting Book. Chapman, Jane, illus. 2003. (ENG.). 40p. (J). (gr. k-k). pap. 6.99 (978-0-7636-1566-6(8)) Candlewick Pr.
—One Duck Stuck: A Mucky Ducky Counting Book. Chapman, Jane, illus. 2008. (Candlewick Press Big Book Ser.). (ENG.). 40p. (J). (gr. k-k). pap. 24.99 (978-0-7636-3817-7(X)) Candlewick Pr.
—Ten Sleepy Sheep. Gaber, Susan, illus. 2009. (ENG.). 12p. (J). (-k). bds. 7.99 (978-0-7636-4142-9(1)) Candlewick Pr.
Rosario, Joann. Swiggly Swiggly Do! Rosario, Joann, illus. 2004. (Illus.). 5p. (J). (gr. -1-5). pap. 10.00 (978-0-9758746-6-0(7), 1246169) J.G.R. Enterprises.
Roscoe, Lily. The Night Parade. Walker, David, illus. 2014. (ENG.). 32p. (J). (— 1). 16.99 (978-0-545-39623-3(9), Orchard Bks.) Scholastic, Inc.
Rose, Caroline Starr. Blue Birds. 2016. (ENG.). 400p. (J). (gr. 5). 8.99 (978-0-14-751187-4(9), Puffin Books) Penguin Young Readers Group.
Rose, Caroline Starr & McPike, Elizabeth. Blue Birds. 2015. (ENG., Illus.). 400p. (J). (gr. 5). bds. 16.99 (978-0-399-16810-9(9), G.P. Putnam's Sons Books for Young Readers) Penguin Young Readers Group.
Rose, Deborah Lee. Someone's Sleepy. Andreasen, Dan, illus. 2013. (ENG.). 32p. (J). (gr. -1-k). 16.95 (978-1-4197-0539-7(3), Abrams Bks. for Young Readers) Abrams, Inc.
Rose, Dorothy. The Haunted House. Oechsli, Kelly, illus. 2014. (ENG.). 24p. (J). (gr. -1-k). pap. 13.99 (978-1-4814-2646-6(X), Little Simon) Little Simon.
Roseman-Mendoza, Natalie. Maritza's Garden Path. 2009. 32p. pap. 24.95 (978-1-60749-386-0(1)) America Star Bks.
Rosen, Michael. The Bus Is for Us. Tyler, Gillian, illus. 2015. (ENG.). 32p. (J). (-k). 16.99 (978-0-7636-6983-6(0)) Candlewick Pr.
—Running with Trains: A Novel in Poetry & Two Voices. 2012. (ENG.). 112p. (J). (gr. 5). 15.95 (978-1-59078-863-9(X), Wordsong) Boyds Mills Pr.
Rosen, Wendy & End, Jackie. Chicken Fingers, Mac & Cheese... Why Do You Always Have to Say Please? Tuck-Bernstein, Cheryl, illus. 2005. 32p. (J). 14.99 (978-0-7666-1986-9(9)) Modern Publishing.
Rosenbaum, Andria Warmflash. A Grandma Like Yours: A Grandpa Like Yours. Björnson, Barbara, illus. 2006. 32p. (J). 16.95 (978-1-58013-167-4(0), Kar-Ben Publishing) Lerner Publishing Group.
Rosenbaum, Andria Warmflash & Gill, Deirdre. Trains Don't Sleep. Rosenbaum, Andria Warmflash & Gill, Deirdre, illus. 2017. (ENG., Illus.). 40p. (J). (gr. -1-3). 16.99 (978-0-544-38074-5(6), HMH Books For Young Readers) Houghton Mifflin Harcourt Publishing Co.
Rosenthal, Amy Krouse. It's Not Fair! Lichtenheld, Tom, illus. 2008. (ENG.). 40p. (J). (gr. -1-3). 16.99 (978-0-06-115257-3(9)) HarperCollins Pubs.
—Little Miss, Big Sis. Reynolds, Peter H., illus. 2015. (ENG.). 40p. (J). (gr. -1-3). 17.99 (978-0-06-230203-8(5)) HarperCollins Pubs.
—Plant a Kiss. Reynolds, Peter H., illus. 2011. (ENG.). 40p. (J). (gr. -1-3). 14.99 (978-0-06-198675-8(5)) HarperCollins Pubs.
Rosenthal, Amy Krouse & Redmond, Lea. On the Spot. te Loo, Sanne, illus. 2017. (ENG.). 32p. (J). (gr. -1-2). 16.99 (978-1-101-93230-8(9), Random Hse. Bks. for Young Readers) Random Hse. Children's Bks.
Ross, Barbara & Beatty, Nicholas. The Goops Circus: A Whimsical Telling of Do-Good Tales. Camille, Diana, illus. 2010. (Goops Ser.). 58p. (J). 19.95 incl. audio compact disk (978-0-9712368-4-4(4)) Goops Unlimited.
Ross, Michael Elsohn. Mama Me Alimenta. Wolff, Ashley, illus. 2008.Tr. of Mama's Milk. (ENG & SPA.). 32p. (J). (gr. -1-2). pap. 6.99 (978-1-58246-245-5(3), Tricycle Pr.) Random Hse. Children's Bks.
Rossetti-Shustak, Bernadette. I Love You Through & Through. Church, Caroline Jayne, illus. 2005. (ENG.). 24p. (J). (gr. k — 1). bds. 8.95 (978-0-439-67363-1(1), Cartwheel Bks.) Scholastic, Inc.
—I Love You Through & Through: Board Book & Plush. Church, Caroline Jayne, illus. 2014. (ENG.). 24p. (J). (— 1). 14.99 (978-0-545-64792-2(4), Cartwheel Bks.) Scholastic, Inc.
Roth, Anthony H. Little Anthony Doesn't Want to Eat His Dinner. 2012. 26p. 24.95 (978-1-4626-5776-6(1)) America Star Bks.
Roth, Carol. Here Comes the Choo Choo! Cushman, Doug, illus. 2007. (J). (978-0-15-205582-0(7)) Harcourt Trade Pubs.
—The Little School Bus. Paparone, Pamela, illus. 2004. (ENG.). 32p. (J). (gr. k-1). pap. 7.95 (978-0-7358-1905-4(X)) North-South Bks., Inc.
—Will You Still Love Me? Howarth, Daniel, illus. 2011. (ENG.). 16p. (J). (gr. -1 — 1). bds. 7.99 (978-0-8075-9116-1(5)) Whitman, Albert & Co.
Roth, Carol & Julian, Sean. Five Little Ducklings Go to Bed. 2013. (Illus.). 32p. (J). pap. (978-0-7358-4153-6(5)) North-South Bks., Inc.
Roth-Fisch, Marla. Sensitive Sam: Sam's Sensory Adventure Has a Happy Ending! 2009. (ENG., Illus.). 29p. (J). pap. 9.95 (978-1-932565-86-7(8)) Future Horizons, Inc.
Roth, Megan. I Love You More. Vincent, Kay, illus. 2016. (ENG.). 12p. (J). 8.99 (978-1-62686-763-5(1), Silver Dolphin Bks.) Readerlink Distribution Services, LLC.
Rothstein, Gloria L. Sheep Asleep. Date not set. 224p. (J). (gr. -1-1). pap. 4.99 (978-0-06-443717-2(5)) HarperCollins Pubs.
Rouss, Sylvia A. The Littlest Pair. Hannon, Holly, illus. 2005. 32p. (J). (gr. -1-1). 14.95 (978-1-930143-17-3(6), Devora Publishing) Simcha Media Group.
Rovetch, L. Bob. I Need a Kazoot! Castillon, Carly, illus. 2006. (J). (978-1-58987-055-0(7)) Kindermusik International.
—1,2,3 Octopus & Me. Gévry, Claudine, illus. 2006. (J). (978-1-58987-011-6(5)) Kindermusik International.
Rowe, Ben. Can an Alligator Drive a Nail with His Tail? 2008. 18p. pap. 24.95 (978-1-60610-625-9(2)) America Star Bks.
Rowland, Lucy. Pirate Pete & His Smelly Feet. Chambers, Mark, illus. 2017. (ENG.). 32p. (J). (gr. -1-1). 16.99 **(978-1-5098-1776-4(X))** Pan Macmillan GBR. Dist: Independent Pubs. Group.
Roy, Keri Anne & Holt, K. A. Brains for Lunch: A Zombie Novel in Haiku?! Wilson, Gahan, illus. 2010. (ENG.). 96p. (J). (gr. 4-9). 22.99 (978-1-59643-629-9(8), 9781596436299) Roaring Brook Pr.
Rubin, Susan Goldman. Jacob Lawrence in the City. 2009. (ENG., Illus.). 24p. (J). (gr. -1 — 1). bds. 7.99 (978-0-8118-6582-1(7)) Chronicle Bks. LLC.
Rubinger, Ami. Big Cat, Small Cat. Baitner, Ray, tr. from HEB. Rubinger, Ami, illus. 2009. (ENG., Illus.). 28p. (J). (gr. -1-k). 13.95 (978-0-7892-1029-6(0), Abbeville Kids) Abbeville Pr., Inc.
—I Dream of an Elephant. Rubinger, Ami, illus. 2010. (ENG., Illus.). 28p. (J). (gr. k-k). 13.95 (978-0-7892-1058-6(4), Abbeville Kids) Abbeville Pr., Inc.
Ruble, Kam. Princess Annado Tandy's Versery Rhymes. McMullen, T. C., illus. l.t. ed. 2007. 88p. (J). per. (978-0-9779680-4-6(9)) Global Authors Pubns.
Rudi, Julie A. That's How Much I Love You. Beeke, Tiphanie, illus. 2013. (ENG.). 20p. (gr. -1). bds. 8.95 (978-1-58925-644-6(1)) Tiger Tales.
Rudolph the Red-Nosed Reindeer. 2014. (ENG., Illus.). 40p. (J). (gr. -1-1). 17.99 (978-1-4424-7495-6(5), Little Simon) Little Simon.
Rudy, Maggie & Abrams, Pam. The House That Mouse Built. Wolf, Bruce, photos by. 2011. (ENG., Illus.). 32p. (J). (gr. -1). 14.99 (978-1-935703-25-9(0)) Downtown Bookworks.
Rueda, Claudia, illus. I Know an Old Lady Who Swallowed a Fly. 2005. 14p. (J). 12.95 (978-1-58117-267-6(2), Intervisual/Piggy Toes) Bendon, Inc.
Ruelle, Karen Gray. Bark Park, 1 vol. Ruelle, Karen Gray, illus. (ENG., Illus.). 32p. (J). (gr. -1-1). 2014. pap. 7.95 (978-1-56145-773-1(6)) 2008. 15.95 (978-1-56145-434-1(6)) Peachtree Pubs.
Rumbaugh, Melinda. Somebunny Loves You! Biscoe, Cee, illus. 2015. (ENG.). 16p. (J). 12.99 (978-0-8249-1950-4(5), Ideal Pubns.) Worthy Publishing.
Rumble. 2014. (ENG., Illus.). 560p. (YA). (gr. 9). 19.99 (978-1-4424-8284-5(2), McElderry, Margaret K. Bks.) McElderry, Margaret K. Bks.
Rundstrom, Teressa. The Adventures of Tommy Toad. Marshall, Setsu, illus. 2004. 40p. (J). per. (978-1-932062-41-0(6)) Hability Solution Services, Inc.
Russell, James. The Dragon Hunters. Choi, Link, illus. 2017. (Dragon Brothers Ser.: 1). (ENG.). 32p. (J). (-4). 16.99 (978-1-4926-4861-1(2), 9781492648611, Sourcebooks Jabberwocky) Sourcebooks, Inc.
Russell, James. The Dragon Riders. Choi, Link, illus. 2017. (Dragon Brothers Ser.: 3). (ENG.). 32p. (J). (-4). 16.99 **(978-1-4926-4867-3(1)**, Sourcebooks Jabberwocky) Sourcebooks, Inc.
Ryan, Pam Muñoz. Hello Ocean. Astrella, Mark, illus. 2014. 32p. pap. 8.00 (978-1-61003-319-0(1)) Center for the Collaborative Classroom.
—Hello, Ocean / Hola Mar. Canetti, Yanitzia, tr. from ENG. Astrella, Mark, illus. 2003. (ENG & SPA.). 32p. (J). (gr. -1-2). pap. 7.95 (978-1-57091-372-3(2)) Charlesbridge Publishing, Inc.
Ryder, Joanne. Bear of My Heart. Moore, Margie, illus. 2009. (ENG.). 32p. (J). (gr. -1 — 1). bds. 9.99 (978-1-4169-5472-9(4), Little Simon) Little Simon.
—Won't You Be My Kissaroo? Sweet, Melissa, illus. (ENG.). (J). (gr. -1 — 1). 2015. 40p. pap. 6.99 (978-0-15-205820-3(6), HMH Books For Young Readers) 2008. 15p. bds. 6.95 (978-0-15-206060-2(X)) Houghton Mifflin Harcourt Publishing Co.
Rylant, Cynthia. All in a Day. McClure, Nikki, illus. (ENG.). (J). 2017. 30p. bds. 8.95 (978-1-4197-2612-5(9), Abrams Appleseed) 2009. 32p. (gr. -1-k). 18.95 (978-0-8109-8321-2(4), Abrams Bks. for Young Readers) Abrams, Inc.
—If You'll Be My Valentine. Kosaka, Fumi, illus. 2005. (ENG.). 32p. (J). (gr. -1-3). pap. 6.99 (978-0-06-009271-9(8)) HarperCollins Pubs.
—The Stars Will Still Shine. Beeke, Tiphanie, illus. 2005. 40p. (J). lib. bdg. 17.89 (978-0-06-054640-3(9)); (ENG.). (gr. -1-3). 17.99 (978-0-06-054639-7(5)) HarperCollins Pubs.
Sadler, Marilyn & Bollen, Roger. Money, Money, Honey Bunny! 2006. (Bright & Early Books(R) Ser.). (ENG., Illus.). 36p. (J). (gr. -1-k). 9.99 (978-0-375-83370-0(6), Random Hse. Bks. for Young Readers) Random Hse. Children's Bks.
Sáenz, Benjamin Alire. Aristotle & Dante Discover the Secrets of the Universe. 2014. lib. bdg. 23.30 (978-0-606-35117-1(5)) Turtleback Bks.
Sagendorph, Jean. Starry Night, Hold Me Tight. Siebold, Kim, illus. 2015. (ENG.). 18p. (J). (gr. -1-17). bds. 6.95 (978-0-7624-5853-0(4), Running Pr. Kids) Running Pr. Bk. Pubs.
Salas, Laura Purdie. A Leaf Can Be- Dabija, Violeta, illus. 2012. (Millbrook Picture Bks). (ENG.). 32p. (J). (gr. k-2). lib. bdg. 17.95 (978-0-7613-6203-6(7), Millbrook Pr.) Lerner Publishing Group.
Salom, Andree. When the Anger Ogre Visits. Salom, Ivette, illus. 2015. (ENG.). 40p. (J). 18.95 (978-1-61429-166-4(7)) Wisdom Pubns.
Salomon, Bob & Young, Rick. Beyond the Laces. 2015. (ENG., Illus.). (J). pap. 12.95 (978-1-4951-5694-6(X)) Independent Pub.
Saltzberg, Barney. Redbird: Friends Come in Different Sizes. 2015. (ENG., Illus.). 22p. (J). bds. 5.95 (978-0-7611-8190-3(3)) Workman Publishing Co., Inc.
—Redbird: Colors, Colors, Everywhere! 2015. (ENG., Illus.). 22p. (J). bds. 5.95 (978-0-7611-8185-9(7)) Workman Publishing Co., Inc.
—Would You Rather Be a Princess or a Dragon? 2016. (ENG., Illus.). 32p. (J). 16.99 (978-1-62672-358-0(3), 9781626723580) Roaring Brook Pr.
Salzano, Tammi. I Love You Just the Way You Are. Grey, Ada, illus. 2014. (ENG.). 32p. (J). (gr. -1-3). 16.99 (978-1-58925-161-8(X)) Tiger Tales.
San Souci, Robert D. Cinderella Skeleton. Catrow, David, illus. 2004. (ENG.). 32p. (J). (gr. -1-3). reprint ed. pap. 6.99 (978-0-15-205069-6(8)) Houghton Mifflin Harcourt Publishing Co.
Sanchez, Jenny Torres. Death, Dickinson, & the Demented Life of Frenchie Garcia. 2013. (ENG.). 272p. (YA). (gr. 2-17). pap. 10.95 (978-0-7624-4680-3(3), Running Pr. Kids) Running Pr. Bk. Pubs.
Sandage, Charley. ALL AROUND ARKANSAS student Edition. 2005. (Illus.). (J). pap. (978-0-9638956-5-3(6)) Archeological Assessments, Inc.
Sandall, Ellie. Everybunny Dance! 2017. (ENG., Illus.). 32p. (J). (gr. -1-3). 17.99 (978-1-4814-9822-7(3), McElderry, Margaret K. Bks.) McElderry, Margaret K. Bks.
Sandburg, Carl. Rootabaga Stories. 2009. 128p. (gr. 3-18). pap. 10.95 (978-1-60664-425-6(4)) Rodgers, Alan Bks.
Sanders, Karen Nordberg. Ruth & Naomi. Rooney, Ronnie, illus. 2007. 16p. (J). (gr. k-4). 1.99 (978-0-7586-1283-0(4)) Concordia Publishing Hse.
Sanderson, Ruth. A Castle Full of Cats. 2015. (ENG., Illus.). 40p. (J). (gr. -1-2). lib. bdg. 19.99 (978-0-375-97154-9(8), Random Hse. Bks. for Young Readers) Random Hse. Children's Bks.
Sandoval, Anna. Tickle a Daisy. 2007. 28p. per. 24.95 (978-1-4241-8470-5(3)) America Star Bks.
Sandra De Mos. Cleo's Playground Adventure. 2009. 40p. pap. 16.99 (978-1-4389-2049-8(0)) AuthorHouse.
Sanger, Amy Wilson. Yum Yum Dim Sum. Sanger, Amy Wilson, illus. 2003. (ENG., Illus.). 22p. (J). (gr. k — 1). bds. 6.99 (978-1-58246-108-3(2), Knopf Bks. for Young Readers) Random Hse. Children's Bks.
Sanger, Amy Wilson & Wilson Sanger, Amy. A Little Bit of Soul Food. Wilson Sanger, Amy, illus. 2004. (World Snacks Ser.). (ENG., Illus.). 20p. (J). (— 1). bds. 6.99 (978-1-58246-109-0(0), Tricycle Pr.) Random Hse. Children's Bks.
Sanrio Company, LTD. Hello Kitty Presents the Storybook Collection: Thumbelina. 2017. (Hello Kitty Storybook Ser.). (ENG., Illus.). 32p. (J). (gr. -1-k). pap. 6.95 (978-1-4197-2489-3(4), Abrams Appleseed) Abrams, Inc.
Santa's Busy Christmas Eve. 2003. (J). 4.99 (978-1-59384-011-2(X)) Parklane Publishing.
Santore, Charles. Cuento de Nochebuena: Una Visita de San Nicolas. 2012. (ENG & SPA.). 48p. (J). 18.95 (978-1-60433-299-5(9), Applesauce Pr.) Cider Mill Pr. Bk. Pubs., LLC.
Santoro, Scott. Which Way to Witch School? Santoro, Scott, illus. (ENG., Illus.). 32p. (J). (gr. -1-2). 2012. pap. 5.99 (978-0-06-078183-5(1)) 2010. 16.99 (978-0-06-078181-1(5)) HarperCollins Pubs.
Sapp, Karen. Who Is Sleeping? 2009. (Rookie Preschool-NEW Ser.). (ENG.). 24p. (J). pap. 6.95 (978-0-531-24586-6(1)); (gr. -1). lib. bdg. 23.00 (978-0-531-24411-1(3)) Scholastic Library Publishing. (Children's Pr.).
Sargent, Dave M., Jr. Vicious Vera, 9 vols. Huff, Jeane Lirley, illus. 2004. (Doggie Tails Ser.: 9). (J). pap. 10.95 (978-1-56763-854-7(6)) Ozark Publishing.
Sarno-Doyle, Christine. Your Inside Shape. 2012. (ENG., Illus.). 32p. (J). 17.95 (978-0-9824461-0-2(1)) SDP Publishing.
Saroyan, William & Tinkelman, Murray. Me. 2016. (ENG., Illus.). 64p. (gr. 1-3). pap. 9.99 (978-0-486-81066-9(6)) Dover Pubns., Inc.
Sarta, Jon. Your Adoption Story. 2005. 20p. 9.99 (978-1-4116-6439-5(6)) Lulu Pr., Inc.
Sartell, Debra. Time for Bed, Baby Ted. Chorao, Kay, illus. 2010. (ENG.). 32p. (J). (gr. -1). 16.95 (978-0-8234-1968-5(1)) Holiday Hse., Inc.
Sassi, Laura. Goodnight, Ark, 1 vol. Chapman, Jane, illus. 2014. (ENG.). 32p. (J). 16.99 (978-0-310-73784-1(2)) Zonderkidz.
—Goodnight, Manger, 1 vol. Chapman, Jane, illus. 2015. (ENG.). 32p. (J). 16.99 (978-0-310-74556-3(X)) Zonderkidz.
Sauer, Abe. Goodnight Loon. Davauer, Nathaniel, illus. 2014. (ENG.). 28p. (J). 9.95 (978-0-8166-9703-8(5)) Univ. of Minnesota Pr.
Saupé, Rick. Moses P Rose Has Broken His Nose. DeBroeck, Sarah, illus. 2012. 28p. pap. 24.95 (978-1-4626-0547-7(8)) America Star Bks.
Sauro, Joan. Does God Ever Sleep? 2005. (ENG., Illus.). 32p. (J). (gr. -1-3). 8.99 (978-1-59473-110-5(1), 9781594731105, Skylight Paths Publishing) LongHill Partners, Inc.
Sauvageau-Smestad, Sheila. Rain, Rain, What a Pain! 2006. (Illus.). 37p. (J). per. 17.95 (978-0-9771971-6-3(6)) Brass Frog Bookworks.
Savage, Stephen. Ten Orange Pumpkins: A Counting Book. 2013. (ENG., Illus.). 48p. (J). (gr. -1-k). 16.99

(978-0-8037-3938-3(9), Dial Bks) Penguin Young Readers Group.

Sayre, April Pulley. If You're Hoppy. Urbanovic, Jackie, illus. 2011. (ENG.). 40p. (J). (gr. -1-k). 16.99 (978-0-06-156634-9(9), Greenwillow Bks.) HarperCollins Pubs.

Sayres, Brianna Caplan. Tiara Saurus Rex. Boldt, Mike, illus. 2015. (ENG.). 32p. (J). (gr. -1-1). 16.99 (978-1-61963-263-9(2), 9781619632639, Bloomsbury USA Childrens) Bloomsbury Publishing USA.

—Where Do Diggers Sleep at Night? Slade, Christian, illus. (ENG.). (J). (-k). 2014. 26p. bds. 7.99 (978-0-385-37415-6(1)) 2012. 32p. 16.99 (978-0-375-86848-1(8)) Random Hse. Children's Bks. (Random Hse. Bks. for Young Readers).

—Where Do Jet Planes Sleep at Night? Slade, Christian, illus. 2017. (ENG.). 32p. (J). (gr. -1-2). 16.99 (978-0-399-55448-3(3)); lib. bdg. 19.99 **(978-0-399-55449-0(1))** Random Hse. Children's Bks. (Random Hse. Bks. for Young Readers).

Sayres, Brianna Caplan. Where Do Steam Trains Sleep at Night? Slade, Christian, illus. (ENG.). (J). (gr. -1 — 1). 2017. 26p. bds. 7.99 **(978-0-553-52100-9(4))** 2016. 32p. 19.99 (978-0-375-97471-7(7)) Random Hse. Children's Bks. (Random Hse. Bks. for Young Readers).

Scaglione, Joanne & Small, Gail. The Big Squeal: A Wild, True, & Twisted Tail, Vol. Endelman, David, illus. 2005. (ENG.). 56p. pap. 35.00 (978-1-57886-256-6(6)) Rowman & Littlefield Education.

Scanlon, Cara. Where Did Grandma Go? Mattes-Ruggiero, Lynn, illus. 2008. (J). (978-1-930596-85-6(5)) Amherst Pr.

—Where Did Grandpa Go? Mattes-Ruggiero, Lynn, illus. 2008. (J). (978-1-930596-86-3(3)) Amherst Pr.

Scanlon, Liz Garton. Happy Birthday, Bunny! Graegin, Stephanie, illus. 2013. (ENG.). 32p. (J). (gr. -1-3). 16.99 (978-1-4424-0287-4(3), Beach Lane Bks.) Beach Lane Bks.

—In the Canyon. Wolff, Ashley, illus. 2015. (ENG.). 40p. (J). (gr. -1-3). 17.99 (978-1-4814-0348-1(6), Beach Lane Bks.) Beach Lane Bks.

—Think Big. Newton, Vanessa & Magnette, Paul, illus. 2012. (ENG.). 32p. (J). (gr. -1-6). 16.99 (978-1-59990-611-9(2), 9781599906119, Bloomsbury USA Childrens) Bloomsbury Publishing USA.

Scelsa, Greg & Debney, John. Friends Forever. Faulkner, Stacey, ed. Mahan, Benton, illus. 2006. (J). pap. 2.99 (978-1-59198-322-4(3)) Creative Teaching Pr., Inc.

Schade, Susan. Riff Raff Sails the High Cheese. Kennedy, Anne, illus. 2014. (I Can Read Level 2 Ser.). (ENG.). 24p. (J). (gr. -1-3). pap. 3.99 (978-0-06-230509-1(3)) HarperCollins Pubs.

Schaefer, Lola M. An Island Grows. Felstead, Cathie, illus. 2006. (ENG.). 40p. (J). (gr. -1-3). 17.99 (978-0-06-623930-9(3), Greenwillow Bks.) HarperCollins Pubs.

—Loose Tooth. Wickstrom, Sylvie K., tr. Wickstrom, Sylvie K., illus. 2004. (My First I Can Read Bks.). 32p. (J). (gr. -1-18). 14.99 (978-0-06-052776-1(5)) HarperCollins Pubs.

Schaefer, Peggy. Trick or Treat! Halverson, Lydia, illus. 2009. (ENG.). 16p. (J). (gr. -1-k). bds. 12.99 (978-0-8249-1828-6(2), Ideal Pubns.) Worthy Publishing.

Schafer, Milton. I'm Big! Lew-Vriethoff, Joanne, illus. 2006. (J). (978-1-4156-8150-3(3), Dial) Penguin Publishing Group.

Schamerhorn, Ronna. Dreamy Navy Boy. 2007. 44p. per. 24.95 (978-1-4241-8372-2(3)) America Star Bks.

Scharer, Niko. Emily's House, 1 vol. Fitzgerald, Joanne, illus. 2010. (ENG.). 22p. (J). (gr. k — 1). bds. 7.95 (978-0-88899-831-6(7)) Groundwood Bks. CAN. Dist: Publishers Group West (PGW).

Schaumberg, Rose Mary & Schaumberg, Emily Rose. I'll Miss My Grandma, Wouldn't You? 2008. (Illus.). 40p. pap. 16.99 (978-1-4389-1335-3(4)) AuthorHouse.

Scheffler, Axel. Treasury of Rhyming Stories. Scheffler, Axel, illus. 2015. (ENG., Illus.). 22p. (J). (-k). bds. 13.99 (978-1-4472-7725-5(2)) Pan Macmillan GBR. Dist: Independent Pubs. Group.

Scheffler, Axel, illus. Freddy the Frog. 2015. (Buggy Buddies Ser.). (ENG.). 12p. (J). (— 1). bds. 7.99 (978-0-230-75614-4(X)) Pan Macmillan GBR. Dist: Independent Pubs. Group.

—Katie the Kitten. (Buggy Buddies Ser.). (ENG.). 12p. (J). (— 1). 2015. bds. 7.99 (978-0-230-75615-1(8)) 2014. 13.99 (978-1-4472-6805-5(9)) Pan Macmillan GBR. Dist: Independent Pubs. Group.

—Rhyming Stories: Pip the Dog & Freddy the Frog. 2015. (ENG.). 20p. (J). (— 1). bds. 9.99 (978-1-4472-6824-6(5)) Pan Macmillan GBR. Dist: Independent Pubs. Group.

—Rhyming Stories Bk. 2: Katie the Kitten; Lizzy the Lamb. 2015. (ENG.). 20p. (J). (— 1). bds. 9.99 (978-1-4472-6828-4(8)) Pan Macmillan GBR. Dist: Independent Pubs. Group.

Schertle, Alice. The Adventures of Old Bo Bear. Parkins, David, illus. 2005. (J). 16.95 (978-978-081-183-9(4)) Chronicle Bks. LLC.

—El Camioncito Azul. McElmurry, Jill, illus. 2013. (Little Blue Truck Ser.).Tr. of Little Blue Truck. (SPA & ENG.). 30p. (J). (— 1). bds. 7.99 (978-0-547-98397-4(2)) Houghton Mifflin Harcourt Publishing Co.

—Little Blue Truck. McElmurry, Jill, illus. 2015. (Little Blue Truck Ser.). (ENG.). 30p. (J). (— 1). bds. 12.99 (978-0-544-05685-5(X)); bds. 7.99 (978-0-544-56803-7(6)) Houghton Mifflin Harcourt Publishing Co. (HMH Books For Young Readers).

—Little Blue Truck Leads the Way. McElmurry, Jill, illus. (Little Blue Truck Ser.). (ENG.). (J). 2016. 38p. (— 1). bds. 12.99 (978-0-544-70899-0(7), HMH Books For Young Readers) 2012. 40p. (gr. -1-3). 26.99 (978-0-547-85060-3(3)) Houghton Mifflin Harcourt Publishing Co.

—Little Blue Truck's Christmas. McElmurry, Jill, illus. 2014. (Little Blue Truck Ser.). (ENG.). 24p. (J). (— 1). 14.99 (978-0-544-32041-3(7), HMH Books For Young Readers) Houghton Mifflin Harcourt Publishing Co.

—The Skeleton in the Closet. Jobling, Curtis, illus. 2003. (ENG.). 32p. (J). (gr. 1-18). 15.99 (978-0-688-17738-6(7)) HarperCollins Pubs.

Schick-Jacobowitz, Jeannie, et al. A Bit of Applause for Mrs. Claus. 2012. (ENG.). 32p. (J). (-3). 15.99 (978-1-4022-7085-7(2), Sourcebooks Jabberwocky) Sourcebooks, Inc.

Schiller, Pam. Five Little Ducks. Newsom, Carol, illus. 2014. 19p. (J). **(978-1-60128-879-0(4))** Frog Street Pr.

Schindel, John. Busy Barnyard. Holt, Steven, illus. photos by. 2006. (Busy Book Ser.). (ENG., Illus.). 20p. (J). (— 1). bds. 7.99 (978-1-58246-168-7(6), Tricycle Pr.) Random Hse. Children's Bks.

—Busy Elephants. Harvey, Martin, photos by. 2011. (Busy Book Ser.). (ENG., Illus.). 20p. (J). (— 1). bds. 6.99 (978-1-58246-383-4(2), Tricycle Pr.) Random Hse. Children's Bks.

—Busy Kitties. Franzen, Sean, photos by. 2004. (Busy Book Ser.). (ENG., Illus.). 20p. (J). (— 1). bds. 6.99 (978-1-58246-130-4(9), Knopf Bks. for Young Readers) Random Hse. Children's Bks.

—Busy Piggies. Holt, Steven, illus. Holt, Steven, photos by. 2006. (Busy Book Ser.). (ENG.). 20p. (J). (gr. k — 1). bds. 6.99 (978-1-58246-169-4(4), Tricycle Pr.) Random Hse. Children's Bks.

Schmatjen, Marc. My Giraffe Makes Me Laugh. 2010. 24p. 12.95 (978-1-4520-0941-4(4)) AuthorHouse.

Schmidt, Hans-Christian. Are You Sleeping Little One. Lindgren, Laura, tr. from GER. Nemet, Andrea, illus. 2012. (ENG.). 18p. (J). (gr. k-k). bds. 6.95 (978-0-7892-1120-0(3), Abbeville Kids) Abbeville Pr., Inc.

Schneider, Josh. Everybody Sleeps (but Not Fred) 2015. (ENG., Illus.). 32p. (J). (gr. -1-3). 16.99 (978-0-544-33924-8(X)) Houghton Mifflin Harcourt Publishing Co.

Schnell, David. The Night Before Baseball at the Park by the Bay. Pamintuan, Macky, illus. 2013. (ENG.). 32p. 0.00 (978-0-9891043-0-2(3)) Prospect Palo Alto Publishing.

Schnitzlein, Danny. The Monster Who Ate My Peas, 1 vol. Faulkner, Matt, illus. 2010. (ENG.). 32p. (J). pap. 7.95 (978-1-56145-533-1(4)) Peachtree Pubs.

—The Monster Who Did My Math, 1 vol. Mayer, Bill, illus. (ENG.). 32p. (J). 2012. pap. 7.95 (978-1-56145-668-0(3)) 2007. 16.95 (978-1-56145-420-4(6)) Peachtree Pubs.

—Trick or Treat on Monster Street, 1 vol. Faulkner, Matt, illus. 2008. (ENG.). 32p. (J). (gr. k-3). 16.95 (978-1-56145-465-5(6)) Peachtree Pubs.

Schoen, Sarah. Omar the Smiling Labrador, 1 vol. 2010. 26p. pap. 24.95 (978-1-4489-6231-0(5)) PublishAmerica, Inc.

Schoenherr, Ian. Cat & Mouse. Schoenherr, Ian, illus. 2008. (Illus.). 40p. (J). (gr. -1). lib. bdg. 17.89 (978-0-06-136314-6(6), Greenwillow Bks.) HarperCollins Pubs.

—Don't Spill the Beans! Schoenherr, Ian, illus. 2010. (Illus.). 32p. (J). (gr. -1 — 1). (ENG.). 16.99 (978-0-06-172457-2(2)); lib. bdg. 17.89 (978-0-06-172458-9(0)) HarperCollins Pubs. (Greenwillow Bks.).

—Read It, Don't Eat It! Schoenherr, Ian, illus. 2009. (Illus.). 32p. (J). (gr. -1 — 1). (ENG.). 17.99 (978-0-06-172455-8(6)); lib. bdg. 18.89 (978-0-06-178034-9(0)) HarperCollins Pubs. (Greenwillow Bks.).

Scholastic, Inc. Staff & Barnes, Derrick D. Low-Down Bad-Day Blues. Boyd, Aaron, illus. 2004. (Just for You Ser.). (ENG.). 32p. (gr. k-1). pap. 3.99 (978-0-439-56867-8(6), Teaching Resources) Scholastic, Inc.

Scholastic, Inc. Staff & Bermiss, Aamir Lee. I Hate to Be Sick! Wilson-Max, Ken, illus. 2004. (Just for You Ser.). (ENG.). 32p. (gr. k-3). pap. 3.99 (978-0-439-56877-7(3), Teaching Resources) Scholastic, Inc.

Scholastic, Inc. Staff & Roberson, Karla. My Shoelaces Are Hard to Tie! Holley, Vanessa, illus. 2004. (Just for You Ser.). (ENG.). 32p. pap. 3.99 (978-0-439-56869-2(2), Teaching Resources) Scholastic, Inc.

Scholastic, Inc. Staff, et al. Don't Hit Me! Grier, Gary, illus. 2004. (Just for You Ser.). (ENG.). 32p. (gr. k-1). pap. 3.99 (978-0-439-56860-9(9), Teaching Resources) Scholastic, Inc.

Scholastic Library Publishing. The Three Little Kittens Get Dressed. 2009. (Rookie Preschool Ser.). 24p. (J). (gr. -1). lib. bdg. 23.00 (978-0-531-24404-3(0), Children's Pr.) Scholastic Library Publishing.

Schomer-Wendel, Gretchen & Schomer, Adam Anthony. All Around Town. 2009. (Becka & the Big Bubble Ser.). (Illus.). 32p. (J). (gr. -1-3). pap. 10.55 (978-1-60754-105-9(X)) Windmill Bks.

—Becka Goes to Chicago. 2009. (Becka & the Big Bubble Ser.). (Illus.). 32p. (J). (gr. -1-2). 22.60 (978-1-60754-119-6(X)); pap. 10.55 (978-1-60754-120-2(3)) Windmill Bks.

—Becka Goes to India. 2009. (Becka & the Big Bubble Ser.). (Illus.). 32p. (J). (gr. -1-3). pap. 10.55 (978-1-60754-111-0(4)) Windmill Bks.

—Becka Goes to San Diego. 2009. (Becka & the Big Bubble Ser.). (Illus.). 32p. (J). (gr. -1-2). 22.60 (978-1-60754-113-4(0)); pap. 10.55 (978-1-60754-114-1(9)) Windmill Bks.

—Becka Goes to San Francisco. 2009. (Becka & the Big Bubble Ser.). (Illus.). 32p. (J). (gr. -1-2). 22.60 (978-1-60754-107-3(6)); pap. 10.55 (978-1-60754-108-0(4)) Windmill Bks.

—Becka Goes to the North Pole. 2009. (Becka & the Big Bubble Ser.). (Illus.). 32p. (J). (gr. -1-3). pap. 10.55 (978-1-60754-117-2(3)) Windmill Bks.

Schotter, Roni. All about Grandmas. Nadeau, Janice, illus. 2012. (ENG.). 32p. (J). (gr. -1-k). 16.99 (978-0-8037-3714-3(9), Dial Bks) Penguin Young Readers Group.

—Hanukkah! Hafner, Marylin, illus. 2014. (ENG.). 32p. (J). (gr. -1-3). pap. 7.99 (978-0-316-37028-8(2)) Little, Brown Bks. for Young Readers.

Schrader, Missy Wolgemuth & Schrader, Missy W. Hooray! I Obeyed!, 1 vol. Nuffer, Bruce, ed. 2008. (ENG., Illus.). 12p. (J). (gr. -1). bds. 3.99 (978-0-310-71396-8(X)) Zondervan.

Schroeder, Lisa. Chasing Brooklyn. 2011. (ENG.). 432p. (YA). (gr. 9). pap. 11.99 (978-1-4169-9174-8(3), Simon Pulse) Simon Pulse.

—Far from You. 2008. (ENG.). 368p. (YA). (gr. 8-18). 15.99 (978-1-4169-7506-9(3), Simon Pulse) Simon Pulse.

Schuepbach, Lynnette. Cat Time. 2006. 28p. pap. 12.95 (978-0-9759613-2-2(2)) Creative Sources.

Schulman, Janet. 10 Easter Egg Hunters. 2015. lib. bdg. 14.75 (978-0-606-36379-2(3)) Turtleback Bks.

—10 Easter Egg Hunters: A Holiday Counting Book. Davick, Linda, illus. (ENG.). (J). (gr. -1 — 1). 2012. 26p. bds. 6.99 (978-0-375-86637-1(X)) 2011. 32p. 8.99 (978-0-375-86787-3(2)) Random Hse. Children's Bks. (Knopf Bks. for Young Readers).

—10 Trick-or-Treaters: A Halloween Counting Book. Davick, Linda, illus. (ENG.). (J). (gr. -1-2). 2009. 26p. bds. 6.99 (978-0-375-85347-0(2), Knopf Bks. for Young Readers) 2008. 32p. pap. 7.99 (978-0-385-73614-5(2), Dragonfly Bks.) Random Hse. Children's Bks.

—10 Valentine Friends. Davick, Linda, illus. 2012. (ENG.). 26p. (J). (gr. -1 — 1). bds. 6.99 (978-0-375-87130-6(6), Knopf Bks. for Young Readers) Random Hse. Children's Bks.

Schultz, Doreen. The Days of Noah. 2013. 26p. pap. 9.99 (978-1-62697-228-5(1)) Salem Author Services.

Schulz, Kathy. I Do Not Want To. Rescek, Sanja, illus. 2011. (Rookie Ready to Learn Ser.). 40p. (J). pap. 5.95 (978-0-531-26707-3(5)); (gr. -1-k). lib. bdg. 23.00 (978-0-531-26525-3(0)) Scholastic Library Publishing. (Children's Pr.).

—I Need a Little Help. Iosa, Ann, illus. 2011. (Rookie Ready to Learn — All about Me! Ser.). 32p. (J). (gr. -1-k). lib. bdg. 25.00 (978-0-531-26526-0(9), Children's Pr.) Scholastic Library Publishing.

—Necesito una Ayudita. Iosa, Ann, illus. 2011. (Rookie Ready to Learn Español Ser.). (SPA.). 32p. (J). pap. 5.95 (978-0-531-26782-0(2)); lib. bdg. 23.00 (978-0-531-26114-9(X)) Scholastic Library Publishing. (Children's Pr.).

Schwartz, Amy, illus. 100 Things That Make Me Happy. 2014. (ENG.). 40p. (J). (gr. -1-k). 16.95 (978-1-4197-0518-2(0), Abrams Appleseed) Abrams, Inc.

Schwartz, Betty & Seresin, Lynn. Puppies, Puppies, Everywhere! A Back-And-Forth Opposites Book. Powell, Luciana Navarro, illus. 2015. (J). (978-1-62370-236-6(4)) Capstone Young Readers of Coughlan Cos.

—Ten Playful Tigers: A Touch-And-Feel Counting Book. Powell, Luciana Navarro, illus. 2015. (Back-And-Forth Bks.). (ENG.). 22p. (gr. -1 — 1). bds. 9.99 (978-1-62370-233-5(X)) Capstone Young Readers of Coughlan Cos.

—You're It, Little Red Fish! A Back-And-Forth Color Book. Powell, Luciana Navarro, illus. 2015. (J). (978-1-62370-235-9(6)) Capstone Young Readers of Coughlan Cos.

Schwartz, Corey Rosen. Ninja Red Riding Hood. Santat, Dan, illus. 2014. (ENG.). 40p. (J). (gr. k-3). 16.99 (978-0-399-16354-8(9), G.P. Putnam's Sons Books for Young Readers) Penguin Young Readers Group.

—The Three Ninja Pigs. Santat, Dan, illus. 2012. (ENG.). 40p. (J). (gr. k-3). 16.99 (978-0-399-25514-4(1), G.P. Putnam's Sons Books for Young Readers) Penguin Young Readers Group.

Schwartz, Corey Rosen. Twinderella, a Fractioned Fairy Tale. Marcero, Deborah, illus. 2017. (ENG.). 32p. (J). (gr. -1-3). 17.99 **(978-0-399-17633-3(0)**, G.P. Putnam's Sons Books for Young Readers) Penguin Young Readers Group.

Schwartz, Corey Rosen & Coulton, Beth. Goldi Rocks & the Three Bears. Wragg, Nate, illus. 2014. (ENG.). 32p. (J). (gr. k-3). 17.99 (978-0-399-25685-1(7), G.P. Putnam's Sons Books for Young Readers) Penguin Young Readers Group.

Schwartz, Corey Rosen & Gomez, Rebecca J. Hensel & Gretel, Ninja Chicks. Santat, Dan, illus. 2016. (ENG.). 40p. (J). (gr. k-3). 17.99 (978-0-399-17626-5(8), G.P. Putnam's Sons Books for Young Readers) Penguin Young Readers Group.

—What about Moose? Yamaguchi, Keika, illus. 2015. (ENG.). 40p. (J). (gr. -1-3). 17.99 (978-1-4814-0496-9(2), Atheneum Bks. for Young Readers) Simon & Schuster Children's Publishing.

Scieszka, Jon. Dizzy Izzy. Shannon, David et al, illus. 2014. (Jon Scieszka's Trucktown Ser.). (ENG.). 24p. (J). (gr. -1-1). 16.99 (978-1-4814-1460-9(7), Simon Spotlight) Simon Spotlight.

Scillian, Devin. Brewster the Rooster. White, Lee, illus. rev. ed. 2007. (ENG.). 32p. (J). (gr. 3-7). 16.95 (978-1-58536-311-7(1)) Sleeping Bear Pr.

—Johnny Kaw: A Tall Tale. Sneed, Brad, illus. 2013. (ENG.). 32p. (J). (gr. 1-4). 15.95 (978-1-58536-791-7(5), 202353) Sleeping Bear Pr.

Scotford, Groenewald & Scotford, Tina. A Bush Buffet in the Land of Kachoo. 2014. (Land of Kachoo Ser.). (ENG.). 32p. (J). (gr. k-2). pap. 10.95 (978-1-4314-0761-3(5)) Jacana Media ZAF. Dist: Independent Pubs. Group.

Scott, Janine. Café Cosmos. Wood, Hannah, illus. 2009. (Treasure Chest Readers Ser.). 24p. (J). (gr. -1-2). pap. 8.15 (978-1-60754-674-0(4)); lib. bdg. 22.60 (978-1-60754-673-3(6)) Windmill Bks.

—Mars Mouse. Wood, Hannah, illus. 2009. (Treasure Chest Readers Ser.). 24p. (J). (gr. -1-2). pap. 8.15 (978-1-60754-677-1(9)); lib. bdg. 22.60 (978-1-60754-676-4(0)) Windmill Bks.

Scott, Joanna I. Stanley the Moose: Book One of the Woodsie Tails Series. 2009. (Illus.). 40p. (J). 19.95 net. (978-0-9796678-1-0(5)) Cherakota Publishing.

Sears, Gale. The Missing Christmas Treasure. Johnson, Meredith, illus. 2012. (J). (978-1-60861-283-3(X)) Covenant Communications, Inc.

Seaworthy, Oscar. Port Side Pirates. 2008. (ENG., Illus.). 32p. (J). 6.99 (978-1-84686-205-2(1)); 9.99 (978-1-84686-153-6(5)) Barefoot Bks., Inc.

Seder, Rufus Butler. ¡Al Galope! Un Libro de Scanimation. 2009. (Scanimation Ser.). (SPA., Illus.). 12p. (J). (gr. -1-3). 12.95 (978-0-7611-5415-0(9), 15415) Workman Publishing Co., Inc.

—Waddle! 2009. (Scanimation Ser.). (ENG., Illus.). 12p. (gr. -1-2). 13.95 (978-0-7611-5112-8(5), 15112) Workman Publishing Co., Inc.

Seeger, Laura Vaccaro. Green. 2014. (KOR.). 36p. (J). (978-89-7938-085-9(2)) Dasan Publishing Hse.

—Green. Seeger, Laura Vaccaro, illus. 2012. (ENG., Illus.). 36p. (J). (gr. -1-1). 16.99 (978-1-59643-397-7(3), 9781596433977) Roaring Brook Pr.

Seigerman, Michelle. A Christmastime Book of Rhymes. 2005. 35p. pap. 13.08 (978-1-4116-4960-6(5)) Lulu Pr., Inc.

Self, Timothy. Davy the Dolphin. l.t. ed. 2003. (Illus.). 22p. (J). per. 8.99 (978-1-932338-30-0(6)) Lifevest Publishing, Inc.

Selig, Josh. Ride the Potato Train. Gibbons, Cassandra, illus. 2013. 30p. (J). (978-1-4844-0420-1(3), Planet Dexter) Penguin Publishing Group.

Seltzer, Eric. Bake, Mice, Bake! Rosenberg, Natascha, illus. 2012. (Penguin Young Readers, Level 1 Ser.). (ENG.). 32p. (J). (gr. k-1). mass mkt. 3.99 (978-0-448-45763-5(6), Penguin Young Readers) Penguin Young Readers Group.

—Bake, Mice, Bake! 2012. (Penguin Young Readers Level 1 Ser.). lib. bdg. 13.55 (978-0-606-23625-6(2), Turtleback) Turtleback Bks.

—Doodle Dog. Seltzer, Eric, illus. 2005. (Doodle Dog Ser.). (ENG., Illus.). 32p. (J). (gr. -1-1). pap. 3.99 (978-0-689-85910-6(4), Simon Spotlight) Simon Spotlight.

—Granny Doodle Day. Seltzer, Eric, illus. 2006. (Doodle Dog Ser.). (ENG., Illus.). 32p. (J). (gr. -1-1). pap. 3.99 (978-0-689-85911-3(2), Simon & Schuster/Paula Wiseman Bks.) Simon & Schuster/Paula Wiseman Bks.

Seltzer, Eric & Hall, Kirsten. Dog on His Bus. Braun, Sebastien, illus. 2012. (Penguin Young Readers, Level 2 Ser.). (ENG.). 32p. (J). (gr. 1-2). pap. 3.99 (978-0-448-45904-2(3), Penguin Young Readers) Penguin Young Readers Group.

—Dog on His Bus. Braun, Sebastien, illus. 2012. (Penguin Young Readers Level 2 Ser.). lib. bdg. 13.55 (978-0-606-25815-9(9), Turtleback) Turtleback Bks.

Sendak, Maurice. Bumble-Ardy. Sendak, Maurice, illus. 2011. (ENG., Illus.). 40p. (J). 17.95 (978-0-06-205198-1(9)) HarperCollins Pubs.

—One Was Johnny Board Book: A Counting Book. Sendak, Maurice, illus. 2017. (Illus.). 46p. (J). (gr. -1-3). bds. 7.95 (978-0-06-266809-7(9)) HarperCollins Pubs.

Senior, Suzy. Teddy Bear Says Goodnight. Mitchell, Melanie, illus. 2014. (Teddy Bear Says Ser.). (ENG.). 12p. (J). (— 1). bds. 7.99 (978-0-7459-6436-2(2)) Lion Hudson PLC GBR. Dist: Independent Pubs. Group.

Senir, Mirik & Shubow, Mary Jane. When I First Held You: A Lullaby from Israel. 2009. (J). lib. bdg. 17.95 (978-0-7613-5096-5(9), Kar-Ben Publishing) Lerner Publishing Group.

Sensel, Joni. Bears Barge In. Bivins, Christopher, illus. 2003. 32p. (J). (gr. -1-18). 14.95 (978-0-9701195-0-6(X)) Dream Factory Bks.

Serfozo, Mary. Plumply, Dumply Pumpkin. Petrone, Valeria, illus. 2006. (Classic Board Bks.). (ENG.). 28p. (J). (gr. -1-1). bds. 6.99 (978-0-689-86277-9(6), Little Simon) Little Simon.

Serfozo, Mary & Petrone, Valeria. Plumply, Dumply Pumpkin. 2004. (ENG., Illus.). 32p. (J). (gr. -1-3). 7.99 (978-0-689-87135-1(X), Aladdin) Simon & Schuster Children's Publishing.

Sesame Street Staff. Fairly Furry 2 bk Rhyming Rapunzel Rosita & Beanstalk. 2007. 15.99 (978-1-59069-624-8(7)) Studio Mouse LLC.

Sesame Workshop. Just One You! 2015. (Sesame Street Scribbles Elmo Ser.: 0). (ENG.). 32p. (J). (-3). 10.99 (978-1-4022-9735-9(1), Sourcebooks Jabberwocky) Sourcebooks, Inc.

Seskin, Steve & Shamblin, Allen. A Chance to Shine. Christie, R. & Christie, Gregory, illus. 2006. (ENG.). 30p. (J). (gr. -1-2). 16.99 (978-1-58246-167-0(8), Tricycle Pr.) Random Hse. Children's Bks.

Seuss, Dr. The Big Orange Book of Beginner Books. 2015. (Beginner Books(R) Ser.). (ENG., Illus.). 240p. (J). (gr. -1-2). 16.99 (978-0-553-52425-3(9), Random Hse. Bks. for Young Readers) Random Hse. Children's Bks.

—The Bippolo Seed & Other Lost Stories. 2011. (Classic Seuss Ser.). (ENG., Illus.). 72p. (J). (gr. k-4). 15.00 (978-0-375-86435-3(0), Random Hse. Bks. for Young Readers) Random Hse. Children's Bks.

—The Cat in the Hat. 2010. (ENG., Illus.). 64p. pap. (978-0-00-734869-5(X), HarperCollins Children's Bks.) HarperCollins Pubs. Ltd.

—The Cat in the Hat. 2012. (Beginner Books(R) Ser.). (ENG.). 72p. (J). (gr. k-3). 17.99 (978-0-449-81086-6(0), Random Hse. Bks. for Young Readers) Random Hse. Children's Bks.

—The Cat in the Hat Book & Hat. 2012. (Beginner Books Ser.). (ENG.). 72p. (J). (gr. k-3). 24.99 (978-0-307-93044-6(0), Random Hse. Bks. for Young Readers) Random Hse. Children's Bks.

—The Cat in the Hat/el Gato Ensombrerado: Bilingual Edition. 2015. (Classic Seuss Ser.). (ENG & SPA.). 72p. (J). (gr. -1-2). 15.00 (978-0-553-52443-7(7), Random Hse. Bks. for Young Readers) Random Hse. Children's Bks.

—The Cat in the Hat's. Ruiz, Aristides, illus. 2014. (Great Big Board Book Ser.). (ENG.). 12p. (J). (gr. k — 1). bds. 12.99 (978-0-679-89360-8(1), Random Hse. Bks. for Young Readers) Random Hse. Children's Bks.

—Come over to My House. Kath, Katie, illus. 2016. (Beginner Books(R) Ser.). (ENG.). 64p. (J). (gr. k-4). 9.99 (978-0-553-53665-2(6), Random Hse. Bks. for Young Readers) Random Hse. Children's Bks.

—Comment le Grinch a Volé Noël! 2013. (FRE & ENG., Illus.). 64p. (J). (gr. -1-3). 12.95 (978-1-61243-244-1(1)) Ulysses Pr.

—Daisy-Head Mayzie. 2016. (Classic Seuss Ser.). (ENG., Illus.). 64p. (J). (gr. k-4). 17.99 (978-0-553-53900-4(0)); lib. bdg. 20.99 (978-0-553-53906-6(X)) Random Hse. Children's Bks. (Random Hse. Bks. for Young Readers).

—Fox in Socks. 2015. (Big Bright & Early Board Book Ser.). (ENG., Illus.). 24p. (J). (— 1). bds. 6.99 (978-0-553-51336-3(2), Random Hse. Bks. for Young Readers) Random Hse. Children's Bks.

—Fox in Socks: Dr. Seuss's Book of Tongue Tanglers. 2011. (Bright & Early Board Books Ser.). (ENG., Illus.). 24p. (J). (gr. k-1). bds. 4.99 (978-0-307-93180-1(3), Random Hse. Bks. for Young Readers) Random Hse. Children's Bks.

—Fox in Socks & Socks in Box. 2015. (ENG., Illus.). 24p. (J). (— 1). 11.99 (978-0-553-52424-6(0), Random Hse. Bks. for Young Readers) Random Hse. Children's Bks.

—El Gato Ensombrerado. 2015. (Beginner Books(R) Ser.). (ENG & SPA., Illus.). 72p. (J). (gr. -1-2). lib. bdg. 13.99 (978-0-553-50980-9(2), Random Hse. Bks. for Young Readers) Random Hse. Children's Bks.

—Hay un Molillo en Mi Bolsillo! Canetti, Yanitzia, tr. from ENG. 2007.Tr. of There's a Wocket in my Pocket! (SPA., Illus.). 26p. (J). (gr. k-3). 8.99 (978-1-933032-25-2(1)) Lectorum Pubns., Inc.

—Hop on Pop. 2015. (Big Bright & Early Board Book Ser.). (ENG., Illus.). 24p. (J). (— 1). bds. 6.99

S

(978-0-553-49679-6(4), Random Hse. Bks. for Young Readers) Random Hse. Children's Bks.
—Horton & the Kwuggerbug & More Lost Stories. 2014. (ENG., Illus.). 56p. (J). (gr. -1-3). 16.99 *(978-0-385-38298-4(7),* Random Hse. Bks. for Young Readers) Random Hse. Children's Bks.
—Horton Hears a Who Pop-Up! 2008. (ENG., Illus.). 22p. (J). (gr. k-12). 25.99 *(978-0-375-84194-1(6),* Robin Corey Bks.) Random Hse. Children's Bks.
—How the Grinch Stole Christmas! Jonaitis, Alice, ed. Seuss, Dr., illus. deluxe ed. 2014. (Classic Seuss Ser.). (ENG., Illus.). 64p. (J). (gr. k-4). 25.99 *(978-0-679-89153-6(6),* Random Hse. Bks. for Young Readers) Random Hse. Children's Bks.
—How the Grinch Stole Christmas! Book & Grinch. 2015. (Classic Seuss Ser.). (ENG.). 64p. (J). (gr. k-4). 26.99 *(978-0-553-52445-1(3),* Random Hse. Bks. for Young Readers) Random Hse. Children's Bks.
—The Lorax. Seuss, Dr., illus. 2010. (ENG., Illus.). 24p. bds. *(978-0-00-732618-1(1),* HarperCollins Children's Bks.) HarperCollins Pubs. Ltd.
—McElligot's Pool. 2014. (Classic Seuss Ser.). (ENG., Illus.). 64p. (J). (gr. k-4). 17.99 *(978-0-385-37906-9(4),* Random Hse. Bks. for Young Readers) Random Hse. Children's Bks.
—Mr. Brown Can Moo! Can You? 2014. (Big Bright & Early Board Book Ser.). (ENG., Illus.). 24p. (J). (-k). bds. 6.99 *(978-0-385-38712-5(1),* Random Hse. Bks. for Young Readers) Random Hse. Children's Bks.
—Oh, Baby! Go, Baby! Gerardi, Jan, illus. 2010. (Dr. Seuss Nursery Collection). (ENG.). 14p. (J). (gr. k — 1). 11.99 *(978-0-375-85738-6(9),* Random Hse. Bks. for Young Readers) Random Hse. Children's Bks.
—Oh, the Places You'll Go! Seuss, Dr., illus. 2003. (Dr Seuss - Yellow Back Book Ser.). (ENG., Illus.). 48p. pap. *(978-0-00-715852-2(1),* HarperCollins Children's Bks.) HarperCollins Pubs. Ltd.
—Oh, the Places You'll Go! 2003. 7.95 *(978-1-56890-373-6(1))* Peaceable Kingdom Pr.
—Oh, the Thinks You Can Think! (Big Bright & Early Board Book Ser.). (ENG., Illus.). 24p. (J). (-k). 2014. bds. 6.99 *(978-0-385-38713-2(X))* 2009. bds. 4.99 *(978-0-375-85794-2(X))* Random Hse. Children's Bks. (Random Hse. Bks. for Young Readers).
—Un Pez, Dos Peces, Pez Rojo. Canetti, Yanitzia, tr. from ENG. 2005. 64p. (J). 8.99 *(978-1-930332-83-6(1))* Lectorum Pubns., Inc.
—Virent Ova! Viret Perna! Tunberg, Jennifer Morrish & Tunberg, Terence O., trs. from ENG. 2003.Tr. of Green Eggs & Ham. (LAT., Illus.). 72p. (J). 50.00 *(978-0-86516-555-7(6))* Bolchazy-Carducci Pubs.
—What Pet Should I Get? 2015. (Classic Seuss Ser.). (ENG., Illus.). 48p. (J). (gr. -1-2). 17.99 *(978-0-553-52426-0(7));* lib. bdg. 20.99 *(978-0-553-52427-7(5))* Random Hse. Children's Bks. (Random Hse. Bks. for Young Readers).
—What Pet Should I Get? 2015. 48p. (J). lib. bdg. 30.60 *(978-0-606-37381-4(0))* Turtleback Bks.
—What Was I Scared Of? A Glow-in-the-Dark Encounter. 2009. (Classic Seuss Ser.). (ENG., Illus.). 32p. (J). (gr. k-4). 12.99 *(978-0-375-85342-5(1),* Random Hse. Bks. for Young Readers) Random Hse. Children's Bks.
—Y Pensar Que lo Vi Por la Calle Porvenir, 1. Canetti, Yanitza James, tr. from ENG. 2006.Tr. of And to Think That I Saw It on Mulberry Street. (SPA., Illus.). (J). (gr. -1-3). 14.99 *(978-1-933032-07-8(3))* Lectorum Pubns., Inc.
—Yoruga la Tortuga y Otros Cuentos, 1. Canetti, Yanitzia, tr. from ENG. 2008.Tr. of Yertle the Turtle & Other Stories. (SPA., Illus.). 76p. (J). (gr. 2-3). 15.99 *(978-1-933032-41-2(3))* Lectorum Pubns., Inc.
—Your Favorite Seuss: A Baker's Dozen by the One & Only Dr. Seuss. 2004. (Classic Seuss Ser.). (ENG., Illus.). 368p. (J). (gr. k-4). 34.99 *(978-0-375-81061-9(7),* Random Hse. Bks. for Young Readers) Random Hse. Children's Bks.
Seuss, Dr., illus. Poisson Un - Poisson Deux - Poisson Rouge - Poisson Bleu. 2011. (FRE & ENG.). 64p. (J). (gr. -1-3). 12.95 *(978-1-61243-029-4(5))* Ulysses Pr.
Seuss, Dr. & Berger, Sholem. (Eyn Fish, Tsvey Fish, Royter Fish, Bloyer Fish. 2007. (YID., Illus.). 62p. (J). *(978-0-9726939-3-6(9))* Twenty-fourth Street Bks, LLC.
Seuss, Dr. & Seuss. The Eye Book. abr. ed. 2016. (Big Bright & Early Board Book Ser.). (ENG., Illus.). 24p. (J). (gr. -1 — 1). bds. 6.99 *(978-0-553-53631-7(1),* Random Hse. Bks. for Young Readers) Random Hse. Children's Bks.
—The Foot Book. abr. ed. 2016. (Big Bright & Early Board Book Ser.). (ENG., Illus.). 24p. (J). (gr. -1 — 1). bds. 6.99 *(978-0-553-53630-0(3),* Random Hse. Bks. for Young Readers) Random Hse. Children's Bks.
Shaber, Mark. Animals & Stuff. LaGrange, Tiffany, illus. 2008. 32p. pap. 12.95 *(978-1-934246-10-8(7))* Peppertree Pr., The.
Shamberger, Lindsey. I, I, I for Iguan. 2012. 44p. pap. 24.95 *(978-1-4626-7536-4(0))* America Star Bks.
Shamblin, Seskin & National Geographic Learning Staff. A Chance to Shine. Christie, R. Gregory, illus. 2008. (ENG.). 32p. (C). (gr. -1-2). pap. 12.95 *(978-0-58246-304-9(2))* National Geographic School Publishing, Inc.
Shanker, Myrna Gelman. Lazar, the Good Deed Dog. Robinson, Linda, illus. 2010. (J). *(978-0-9829273-0-4(4))* IGI Pr.
Shankman, Ed. I Met a Moose in Maine One Day. O'Neill, Dave, illus. 2008. (Shankman & O'Neill Ser.). (ENG.). 32p. (J). (gr. -1-3). 14.95 *(978-1-933212-77-7(2),* Commonwealth Editions) Applewood Bks.
shapouri, naiyer. Sweet Dreams Buggy. 2009. 32p. pap. 13.60 *(978-0-557-04866-3(4))* Lulu Pr., Inc.
Sharp, Michael. Captain Tristan Am I. Van Tine, Laura, illus. 2009. 20p. (J). pap. *(978-1-897455-10-4(0))* Avatar Pubns., Inc.
—Vayda Jane Bean. 2007. (J). *(978-1-897455-68-5(2))* Avatar Pubns., Inc.
Sharp, Paul. Pablo el Lanzador. Sharp, Paul, illus. 2011. (Rookie Ready to Learn Español Ser.). (SPA., Illus.). 40p. (J). pap. 5.95 *(978-0-531-26781-3(4));* lib. bdg. 23.00 *(978-0-531-26113-2(1))* Scholastic Library Publishing. (Children's Pr.).
Sharp, Paul, illus. Paul the Pitcher. 2011. (Rookie Ready to Learn — All about Me! Ser.). 40p. (J). (gr. -1-k). lib. bdg. 25.00 *(978-0-531-26426-3(2));* (ENG.). pap. 5.95 *(978-0-531-26651-9(6))* Scholastic Library Publishing. (Children's Pr.).
Sharratt, Nick. What's in the Witch's Kitchen? Sharratt, Nick, illus. 2011. (ENG., Illus.). 20p. (J). (gr. -1-2). 12.99 *(978-0-7636-5224-1(5))* Candlewick Pr.
Sharratt, Nick & Tucker, Stephen. The Three Billy Goats Gruff, 2 vols. Sharratt, Nick, illus. 2017. (Lift-The-Flap Fairy Tales Ser.). (ENG., Illus.). 24p. (J). (gr. -1-k). 10.99 ***(978-1-5098-2978-1(4))*** Pan Macmillan GBR. Dist: Independent Pubs. Group.
Sharratt, Nick & Tucker, Stephen. The Three Little Pigs, 2 vols. Sharratt, Nick, illus. 2016. (Lift-The-Flap Fairy Tales Ser.). (ENG., Illus.). 24p. (J). (gr. -1-k). bds. 11.99 *(978-1-5098-1713-9(1))* Pan Macmillan GBR. Dist: Independent Pubs. Group.
Shaskan, Stephen. A Dog Is a Dog. 2011. (ENG., Illus.). 40p. (J). (gr. -1-1). 14.99 *(978-0-8118-7896-8(1))* Chronicle Bks. LLC.
—Toad on the Road: A Cautionary Tale. Shaskan, Stephen, illus. 2017. (Illus.). 32p. (J). (gr. -1-3). 17.99 *(978-0-06-239347-0(2))* HarperCollins Pubs.
Shattil, Wendy, et al, photos by. Sierra Babies. 2013. (Illus.). 26p. (J). 8.95 *(978-1-56037-557-9(4))* Farcountry Pr.
Shaw, Nancy. Sheep Go to Sleep. Apple, Margot, illus. 2015. (ENG.). 32p. (J). (gr. -1-3). 16.99 *(978-0-544-30989-0(8),* HMH Books For Young Readers) Houghton Mifflin Harcourt Publishing Co.
Shaw, Nancy E. Sheep Blast Off! Apple, Margot, illus. 2011. (ENG.). 32p. (J). (gr. -1-3). pap. 5.99 *(978-0-547-52025-4(5))* Houghton Mifflin Harcourt Publishing Co.
—Sheep Go to Sleep (board Book) Apple, Margot, illus. 2016. (Sheep in a Jeep Ser.). (ENG.). 30p. (J). (gr. -1-3). bds. 7.99 *(978-0-544-64053-5(5),* HMH Books For Young Readers) Houghton Mifflin Harcourt Publishing Co.
—Sheep in a Jeep. Apple, Margot, illus. (ENG.). 32p. (J). (gr. -1-3). 2013. 26.99 *(978-0-547-99383-6(8))* 2006. audio compact disk 10.99 *(978-0-618-69522-5(2))* Houghton Mifflin Harcourt Publishing Co.
—Sheep in a Shop, 1 vol. Apple, Margot, illus. 2009. (ENG.). 32p. (J). (gr. -1-3). audio compact disk 10.99 *(978-0-547-23767-1(7))* Houghton Mifflin Harcourt Publishing Co.
—Sheep in a Shop (board Book) Apple, Margot, illus. 2017. (ENG.). 28p. (J). (— 1). bds. 7.99 ***(978-1-328-70286-9(3),*** HMH Books For Young Readers) Houghton Mifflin Harcourt Publishing Co.
Shaw, Nancy E. Sheep Out to Eat. Apple, Margot, illus. 2005. (ENG.). 28p. (J). (gr. k — 1). bds. 5.95 *(978-0-618-58339-3(4))* Houghton Mifflin Harcourt Publishing Co.
Shaw, Stephanie. A Cookie for Santa. Robert, Bruno, illus. 2014. (ENG.). 32p. (J). (gr. 1-4). 15.99 *(978-1-58536-883-9(0),* 203675) Sleeping Bear Pr.
Shea, Bob. Race You to Bed. Shea, Bob, illus. 2010. (ENG., Illus.). 40p. (J). (gr. -1-2). 16.99 *(978-0-06-170417-8(2),* Tegen, Katherine Bks) HarperCollins Pubs.
Shear, Dani. The Foodie Club. Weinstein, Holly, illus. 2013. (ENG.). 50p. (J). 16.99 *(978-1-61053-027-9(6))* Blackbird Bks.
Sheehan, Monica. Love Is You & Me. Sheehan, Monica, illus. 2013. (ENG., Illus.). 48p. (J). (gr. -1-3). 14.99 *(978-1-4424-3607-7(7),* Little Simon) Little Simon.
Shelton, Jayne C. In Grandma's Arms. Katz, Karen, illus. 2008. (ENG.). 24p. (J). (gr. -1-k). bds. 6.99 *(978-0-545-06868-0(1))* Scholastic, Inc.
Shepherd, Donna J. Bradybug. Grady, Kit, illus. 2010. 20p. pap. 10.95 *(978-1-61633-071-2(6))* Guardian Angel Publishing, Inc.
—Chizzy's Topsy Tale. Collier, Kevin Scott, illus. 2008. 20p. pap. 10.95 *(978-1-935137-10-8(7))* Guardian Angel Publishing, Inc.
Shepherd, Donna J. & Foster, Jack. Where Is Salami. 2011. (Illus.). 16p. pap. 9.95 *(978-1-61633-147-4(X))* Guardian Angel Publishing, Inc.
Sherwood, Lance. Grandpa Tales. 2012. 54p. pap. 14.95 *(978-0-615-72525-3(2))* Spitzer, Lance.
Shields, Carol Diggory. Saturday Night at the Dinosaur Stomp. Nash, Scott, illus. 2008. (ENG.). 32p. (J). (gr. -1-3). pap. 6.99 *(978-0-7636-3887-0(0))* Candlewick Pr.
—Wombat Walkabout. Blackall, Sophie, illus. 2009. (ENG.). 32p. (J). (gr. -1-k). 16.99 *(978-0-525-47865-2(5),* Dutton Books for Young Readers) Penguin Young Readers Group.
Shields, Gillian. When the World Is Ready for Bed. Currey, Anna, illus. (ENG.) (J). (gr. -1 — 1). 2010. 26p. bds. 7.99 *(978-1-59990-533-4(7),* 9781599905334) 2009. 32p. 14.99 *(978-1-59990-339-2(3),* 9781599903392) Bloomsbury Publishing USA. (Bloomsbury USA Childrens).
—When the World Was Waiting for You. Currey, Anna, illus. (ENG.) (J). (gr. -1 — 1). 2012. 26p. bds. 7.99 *(978-1-59990-849-6(2),* 9781599908496) 2011. 32p. 14.99 *(978-1-59990-531-0(0),* 9781599905310) Bloomsbury Publishing USA. (Bloomsbury USA Childrens).
—When the World Was Waiting for You Baby Book. Currey, Anna, illus. 2013. (ENG.). 32p. (J). (gr. -1-1). 22.99 *(978-1-4088-4213-3(0),* 9781408842133, Bloomsbury USA Childrens) Bloomsbury Publishing USA.
Shirtliffe, Leanne. The Change Your Name Store. Kügler, Tina, illus. 2014. (ENG.). 32p. (J). (gr. -1-k). 16.95 *(978-1-62873-608-3(9),* Sky Pony Pr.) Skyhorse Publishing Co., Inc.
—No More Beige Food. Kugler, Tina, illus. 2016. (ENG.). 32p. (J). (gr. -1-k). 16.99 *(978-1-63450-180-4(2),* Sky Pony Pr.) Skyhorse Publishing Co., Inc.
Shively, Julie. What Belongs? Kurtz, John, illus. 2004. (Baby Looney Toons Ser.). (ENG.). 16p. (J). 6.95 *(978-0-8249-6561-7(2),* Ideal Pubns.) Worthy Publishing.
Shoopman, Jim. Zachary Hamm in the Land of Eggs. 2012. 82p. pap. 14.95 *(978-0-9846558-1-6(6))* Taylor and Seale Publishing, LLC.
Shovan, Laura. The Last Fifth Grade of Emerson Elementary. 2016. (ENG.). 256p. (J). (gr. 3-7). 15.99 *(978-0-553-52137-5(3),* Lamb, Wendy Bks.) Random Hse. Children's Bks.
Shukla, Umesh. Love You Back Grandma. Balogh, Andras, illus. 2018. 32p. (J). 15.95 *(978-0-9963756-5-8(1))* All About Kids Publishing.
Shulman, Lisa. Old MacDonald Had a Woodshop. Wolff, Ashley, illus. 2004. (ENG.). 32p. (J). (gr. -1-k). reprint ed. pap. 6.99 *(978-0-14-240186-6(2),* Puffin Books) Penguin Young Readers Group.
Shulman, Mark. Gorilla Garage, 0 vols. Nguyen, Vincent, illus. 2013. (ENG.). 42p. (J). (gr. -1-3). pap. 9.99 *(978-1-4778-1663-9(1),* 9781477816639, Amazon Children's Publishing) Amazon Publishing.
Sickler, Jonas, illus. Hey Diddle Diddle: Hey Baby Look at the Cat & His Fiddle - in New Orleans! 2010. (Indestructibles Ser.). (ENG.). 12p. (J). (gr. k — 1). pap. 5.95 *(978-0-7611-5862-2(6),* 15862) Workman Publishing Co., Inc.
Siddals, Mary McKenna. Bringing the Outside In. Barton, Patrice, illus. 2016. (ENG.). 32p. (J). (gr. -1-2). 20.99 *(978-0-375-97165-5(3),* Random Hse. Bks. for Young Readers) Random Hse. Children's Bks.
—Compost Stew: An A to Z Recipe for the Earth. Wolff, Ashley, illus. 2010. (ENG.). 40p. (J). (gr. -1-2). 15.99 *(978-1-58246-316-2(6),* Tricycle Pr.) Random Hse. Children's Bks.
Sidman, Joyce. Before Morning. Krommes, Beth, illus. 2016. (ENG.). 48p. (J). (gr. -1-3). 17.99 *(978-0-547-97917-5(7),* HMH Books For Young Readers) Houghton Mifflin Harcourt Publishing Co.
Sierra, Judy. Ballyhoo Bay. Anderson, Derek, illus. 2009. (ENG.). 40p. (J). (gr. -1-3). 16.99 *(978-1-4169-5888-8(6),* Simon & Schuster/Paula Wiseman Bks.) Simon & Schuster/Paula Wiseman Bks.
—Born to Read. Brown, Marc, illus. 2008. (ENG.). 40p. (J). (gr. -1-2). 16.99 *(978-0-375-84687-8(5),* Knopf Bks. for Young Readers) Random Hse. Children's Bks.
—Make Way for Readers. Karas, G. Brian, illus. 2016. (ENG.). 32p. (J). (gr. -1-3). 17.99 *(978-1-4814-1851-5(3),* Simon & Schuster Bks. For Young Readers) Simon & Schuster Bks. For Young Readers.
—The Secret Science Project That Almost Ate the School. Gammell, Stephen, illus. 2006. (ENG.). 32p. (J). (gr. 1-4). 17.99 *(978-1-4169-1175-3(8),* Simon & Schuster/Paula Wiseman Bks.) Simon & Schuster/Paula Wiseman Bks.
—Sleepy Little Alphabet: A Bedtime Story from Alphabet Town. Sweet, Melissa, illus. 2009. (ENG.). 40p. (J). (gr. -1 — 1). 16.99 *(978-0-375-84002-9(8),* Knopf Bks. for Young Readers) Random Hse. Children's Bks.
—The Sleepy Little Alphabet: A Bedtime Story from Alphabet Town. Sweet, Melissa, illus. 2014. (ENG.). 34p. (J). (— 1). bds. 6.99 *(978-0-385-75400-2(0),* Knopf Bks. for Young Readers) Random Hse. Children's Bks.
—Suppose You Meet a Dinosaur: a First Book of Manners. Bowers, Tim, illus. 2016. (ENG.). 40p. (J). (gr. -1-2). 7.99 *(978-1-101-93250-6(3),* Dragonfly Bks.) Random Hse. Children's Bks.
—Thelonius Monster's Sky-High Fly Pie. 2010. (ENG.). 40p. (J). (gr. -1-3). pap. 7.99 *(978-0-375-85949-6(7),* Dragonfly Bks.) Random Hse. Children's Bks.
—We Love Our School! Davick, Linda, illus. 2016. (ENG.). 24p. (J). (gr. -1-2). 6.99 *(978-1-101-94025-9(5),* Dragonfly Bks.) Random Hse. Children's Bks.
—We Love Our School! A Read-Together Rebus Story. Davick, Linda, illus. 2011. (ENG.). 24p. (J). (gr. -1-2). 7.99 *(978-0-375-86728-6(7),* Knopf Bks. for Young Readers) Random Hse. Children's Bks.
—What Time Is It, Mr. Crocodile? Cushman, Doug, illus. 2007. (ENG.). 32p. (J). (gr. -1-3). pap. 7.99 *(978-0-15-205850-0(8))* Houghton Mifflin Harcourt Publishing Co.
—Wild about Books. Brown, Marc, tr. Brown, Marc, illus. 2004. (ENG.). 40p. (J). (gr. -1-2). 16.95 *(978-0-375-82538-5(X),* Knopf Bks. for Young Readers) Random Hse. Children's Bks.
—Wild about You! Brown, Marc, illus. 2012. (ENG.). 40p. (J). (gr. -1-3). 17.99 *(978-0-307-93178-8(1),* Knopf Bks. for Young Readers) Random Hse. Children's Bks.
—ZooZical. Brown, Marc, illus. 2011. (ENG.). 40p. (J). (gr. -1-2). 17.99 *(978-0-375-86847-4(X),* Knopf Bks. for Young Readers) Random Hse. Children's Bks.
Signorino, Slug, illus. I Know an Old Lady Who Swallowed a Fly: A Traditional Rhyme. 2004. 16p. (J). (gr. k-4). reprint ed. pap. 10.00 *(978-0-7567-9066-0(2))* DIANE Publishing Co.
Sileo, Frank J. Did You Hear? A Story about Gossip. Zivoin, Jennifer, illus. 2017. (J). ***(978-1-4338-2720-4(4),*** Magination Pr.) American Psychological Assn.
Sileo, Frank J. A World of Pausabilities: An Exercise in Mindfulness. Zivoin, Jennifer, illus. 2017. (J). *(978-1-4338-2323-7(3),* Magination Pr.) American Psychological Assn.
Sill, Cathryn. About Mollusks: A Guide for Children, 1 vol. Sill, John, illus. 2008. (About... Ser.). (ENG.). 40p. (J). (gr. k-3). pap. 7.95 *(978-1-56145-406-8(0))* Peachtree Pubs.
Silverman, Erica. The Hanukkah Hop! D'Amico, Steven, illus. 2011. (ENG.). 32p. (J). (gr. -1-3). 12.99 *(978-1-4424-0604-9(6),* Simon & Schuster Bks. For Young Readers) Simon & Schuster Bks. For Young Readers.
—On the Morn of Mayfest. Frazee, Marla, illus. 2011. (ENG.). 32p. (J). (gr. -1-2). pap. 13.99 *(978-1-4424-4341-9(3),* Simon & Schuster Bks. For Young Readers) Simon & Schuster Bks. For Young Readers.
—Wake up, City! Fournier, Laure, illus. 2016. (ENG.). 32p. (J). (gr. -1-3). 16.99 *(978-1-4998-0173-6(4))* Little Bee Books Inc.
Silverstein, Shel. A Giraffe & a Half. Silverstein, Shel, illus. 40th anniv. ed. 2014. (ENG., Illus.). 48p. (J). (gr. -1-3). 17.99 *(978-0-06-025655-5(9))* HarperCollins Pubs.
Silvestri, Linda. Clementina & the Hooey-Phooey Circus Troupe. 2007. (ESP., Illus.). (YA). 12.95 *(978-0-9710696-8-8(9))* Jorlan Publishing, Inc.
Simmons, Andra. What Anna Loves. Capaldi, Gina, illus. 2006. 24p. (J). (gr. -1-3). 15.95 *(978-1-59714-044-7(9))* Heyday.
Simon, Chaman. Lodo! Handelman, Dorothy, photos by. 2005.Tr. of Mud! (ENG & SPA., Illus.). 32p. (J). (gr. -1-1). pap. 4.99 *(978-0-8225-3295-8(6))* Lerner Publishing Group.
—Lodo! Nivel 1. Handelman, Dorothy, photos by. 2005. (Lecturas para Niños de Verdad (Real Kids Readers) Ser.).Tr. of Mud! (SPA., Illus.). 32p. (J). (gr. 1-1). per. 5.95 *(978-0-8225-3294-1(8),* Ediciones Lerner) Lerner Publishing Group.
—Me Gusta Ganar! Translations.com Staff, tr. from ENG. Handelman, Dorothy, photos by. 2007. (Lecturas para niños de Verdad - Nivel 1 (Real Kids Readers - Level 1) Ser.).Tr. of I Like to Win! (SPA., Illus.). 32p. (gr. k-2). per. 5.95 *(978-0-8225-7801-7(8),* Ediciones Lerner) Lerner Publishing Group.
—Me Gusta Ganar; I Like to Win. 2008. pap. 34.95 *(978-0-8225-9499-4(4))* Lerner Publishing Group.
Simon, Mary Manz. God Made the Moon. Walkley, Lizzie, illus. 2016. (J). *(978-0-8249-1981-8(5),* Ideal Pubns.) Worthy Publishing.
—God Made the Sun. Walkley, Lizzie, illus. 2016. (J). *(978-0-8249-1980-1(7),* Ideal Pubns.) Worthy Publishing.
Sing to Baby Jesus. 2013. (Illus.). 32p. (J). 14.99 *(978-1-62108-071-8(4))* Covenant Communications, Inc.
Singer, Marilyn. City Lullaby. Cneut, Carll, illus. 2007. (ENG.). 32p. (J). (gr. -1-3). 16.99 *(978-0-618-60703-7(X))* Houghton Mifflin Harcourt Publishing Co.
—I'm Gonna Climb a Mountain in My Patent Leather Shoes. Avril, Lynne, illus. 2014. (ENG.). 40p. (J). (gr. k-2). 16.95 *(978-1-4197-0336-2(6),* Abrams Bks. for Young Readers) Abrams, Inc.
—Miss Muffet, or What Came After. Litchfield, David, illus. 2016. (ENG.). 40p. (J). (gr. 1-4). 16.99 *(978-0-547-90566-2(1))* Houghton Mifflin Harcourt Publishing Co.
—What Is Your Dog Doing? Habbley, Kathleen, illus. 2011. (ENG.). 32p. (J). (gr. -1-2). 12.99 *(978-1-4169-7931-9(X),* Atheneum Bks. for Young Readers) Simon & Schuster Children's Publishing.
—What's a Banana? Pizzoli, Greg, illus. 2016. (ENG.). 24p. (J). (gr. -1-k). 12.95 *(978-1-4197-2139-7(9),* Abrams Appleseed) Abrams, Inc.
—What's an Apple? Pizzoli, Greg, illus. 2016. (ENG.). 24p. (J). (gr. -1-k). 12.95 *(978-1-4197-2140-3(2),* Abrams Appleseed) Abrams, Inc.
Singlehurst, Naomi. Grandpa, What's That Sound in the Middle of the Night? Ellen Koski, Rachel, ed. Jamieson, Victoria, illus. 2008. (ENG.). 32p. (J). (gr. k-2). 14.95 *(978-1-930650-24-4(8))* mTrellis Publishing, Inc.
Sinke, Grandma Janet Mary. Grandma's Christmas Tree. Pennington, Craig, illus. l.t. ed. 2004. (Grandma Janet Mary Ser.). 50p. (J). *(978-0-9742732-1-1(X))* My Grandma & Me Pubs.
Siomades, Lorianne. Cuckoo Can't Find You. Siomades, Lorianne, illus. 2003. (ENG., Illus.). 32p. (J). (gr. -1-18). 12.95 *(978-1-56397-778-7(8))* Boyds Mills Pr.
Sipe, Kelly. What It Takes to Be a Hero. 2012. 24p. pap. 12.45 *(978-1-4624-0326-4(3),* Inspiring Voices) Author Solutions, Inc.
Sirotich, Erica & Sirotich, Erica. Found Dogs. 2017. (ENG., Illus.). 32p. (J). (-k). 16.99 ***(978-0-399-18641-7(7),*** Dial Bks) Penguin Young Readers Group.
Siwak, Brenda S. Counting on the Bay. Dodge, Barbara A., illus. 2006. (J). per. 14.95 *(978-0-9790906-0-8(1))* Pleasant Plains Pr.
Siy, Alexandra. One Tractor. Rogers, Jacqueline, illus. 2009. (ENG.). 32p. (J). (gr. -1-k). pap. 6.95 *(978-0-8234-2188-6(0))* Holiday Hse., Inc.
Skalak, Daniel. All Summer's Fun. Skalak, Daniel, illus. 2006. (Illus.). 32p. (J). (gr. -1-3). 15.95 *(978-1-60108-000-4(X))* Red Cygnet Pr.
Skene, Pat. Monster Lunch, 1 vol. Ross, Graham T., illus. 2008. (Orca Echoes Ser.). (ENG.). 64p. (J). (gr. 2-3). pap. 6.95 *(978-1-55143-941-9(7))* Orca Bk. Pubs. USA.
Skillen, Roy. The Three Wise Men. 2010. 24p. pap. 11.50 *(978-1-60911-107-6(9),* Eloquent Bks.) Strategic Book Publishing & Rights Agency (SBPRA).
Sklansky, Amy E. You Are My Little Pumpkin Pie. 2013. (ENG., Illus.). 16p. (J). (gr. -1 — 1). bds. 6.99 *(978-0-316-20714-0(4))* Little, Brown Bks. for Young Readers.
Skotnicki, Jill. Ham & Beans: Have You Seen the Color Green? 2010. 28p. pap. 12.49 *(978-1-4520-6452-9(0))* AuthorHouse.
Slack, Michael. Elecopter. Slack, Michael, illus. 2013. (ENG., Illus.). 32p. (J). (gr. -1 — 1). 15.99 *(978-0-8050-9304-9(4),* 9780805093049, Holt, Henry & Co. Bks. For Young Readers) Holt, Henry & Co.
—Turtle Tug to the Rescue. Slack, Michael, illus. 2017. (ENG., Illus.). 40p. (J). 16.99 *(978-1-62779-194-6(9),* 9781627791946, Holt, Henry & Co. Bks. For Young Readers) Holt, Henry & Co.
Slack, Michael H. & Slack, Mike. Monkey Truck. Slack, Michael H. & Slack, Mike, illus. 2011. (ENG., Illus.). 32p. (J). (gr. -1 — 1). 12.99 *(978-0-8050-8878-6(4),* 9780805088786, Holt, Henry & Co. Bks. For Young Readers) Holt, Henry & Co.
Slade, Suzanne. The House That George Built. Bond, Rebecca, illus. 2015. (ENG.). 32p. (J). (gr. 1-4). pap. 7.95 *(978-1-58089-263-6(9))* Charlesbridge Publishing, Inc.
Slate, Joseph. Miss Bindergarten Has a Wild Day in Kindergarten. Wolff, Ashley, illus. 2006. (ENG.). 40p. (J). (gr. -1-k). reprint ed. pap. 6.99 *(978-0-14-240709-7(7),* Puffin Books) Penguin Young Readers Group.
Slater, David Michael. The Boy & the Book. Kolar, Bob, illus. 2015. (ENG.). 32p. (J). (-k). lib. bdg. 16.95 *(978-1-58089-562-0(X))* Charlesbridge Publishing, Inc.
Slater, Teddy. The Luckiest St. Patrick's Day Ever! Long, Ethan, illus. 2007. (J). *(978-0-439-86648-4(0))* Scholastic, Inc.
—Tim Feels Scared. Rescek, Sanja, illus. 2011. (J). *(978-0-545-35179-9(0))* Scholastic, Inc.
SLAY, Jenette. ABBY, the Easter Chicken. 2008. 29p. 13.96 *(978-1-4357-1062-7(2))* Lulu Pr., Inc.
Sloat, Teri. There Was an Old Man Who Painted the Sky. Vitale, Stefano, illus. 2009. (ENG.). 32p. (J). (gr. -1-2). 16.95 *(978-0-8050-6751-4(5),* 9780805067514, Holt, Henry & Co. Bks. For Young Readers) Holt, Henry & Co.
Sloat, Teri. Zip! Zoom! on a Broom. Bonnet, Rosalinde, illus. 2017. (ENG.). 40p. (J). (gr. -1-3). 16.99 ***(978-0-316-25673-5(0))*** Little Brown & Co.
Slonim, David. I Loathe You. Slonim, David, illus. 2012. (ENG., Illus.). 24p. (J). (gr. -1-2). 15.99 *(978-1-4424-2244-5(0),* Aladdin) Simon & Schuster Children's Publishing.
Smallman, Steve. Bear's Big Bottom, 1 vol. Yarlett, Emma, illus. 2014. (ENG.). 32p. (gr. -1-2). 14.95 *(978-1-62370-118-5(X))* Capstone Young Readers of Coughlan Cos.

—Smelly Peter: The Great Pea Eater. Dreidemy, Joëlle, illus. 2008. 32p. (J). (gr. 4-7). 15.95 *(978-1-58925-076-5(1))* Tiger Tales.
—Spot a Lot Animal Escape. Slater, Nicola, illus. 2014. (ENG.). (J). (gr. -1-3). *(978-1-4723-5096-1(0))* Parragon Bk. Service Ltd.
Smalls, Irene. I Can't Take a Bath! Boyd, Aaron, illus. 2004. (Just for You Ser.). (ENG.). 32p. (J). (gr. 1-1). pap. 3.99 *(978-0-439-56852-4(8))* Scholastic, Inc.
Smart Kidz, creator. The ABC's of How I Love You: You're My Alphabet of Love! 2013. (Parent Love Letters Ser.). (ENG., Illus.). 12p. (gr. -1). bds. 12.99 *(978-1-891100-30-7(0)*, Smart Kids) Penton Overseas, Inc.
Smart Kidz Media, creator. O Christmas Tree! 2013. (ENG., Illus.). 12p. (J). bds. 12.99 *(978-1-939658-05-0(5)*, Smart Kids) Penton Overseas, Inc.
—Silent Night. 2013. (ENG., Illus.). 12p. (J). bds. 12.99 *(978-1-939658-01-2(2)*, Smart Kids) Penton Overseas, Inc.
Smart Kidz Media Studios Staff, ed. It's Bedtime! 2011. 16p. 7.99 *(978-1-891100-78-9(5)*, Smart Kids) Penton Overseas, Inc.
Smeltzer, Jennifer. Scrolls & Coals. 2004. (J). 14.95 *(978-0-9754804-3-4(X)*, Rockhill Bks.) Kansas City Star Bks.
Smerek, Kim. What Is Zazu?, 1 bk. Smerek, Kim, illus. 2003. (Illus.). 24p. (J). bds. 7.95 *(978-0-9745116-0-3(9))* Sunshine Bks. for Children.
Smethurst, Julia. Finclucky from Kentucky: A Picture Book. 2013. (J). *(978-1-938905-36-0(9))* Acclaim Pr., Inc.
Smith, Bill O. Chickadees At Night. Murphy, Charles R., illus. 2012. 32p. *(978-0-615-56972-7(2))* Smith, Bill O.
Smith, C. Michelle. Skeeter Sneeter Doodlebop. Foreman, A., illus. 2009. 24p. pap. 15.63 *(978-1-934840-54-2(8))* Nimble Bks. LLC.
Smith, Charles R., Jr. I Am the World. 2013. (ENG., Illus.). 48p. (J). (gr. -1-2). 17.99 *(978-1-4424-2302-2(1))* Simon & Schuster Children's Publishing.
Smith, Danna. Dos en el Zoológico: Un Libro para Contar. Petrone, Valeria, illus. 2011.Tr. of Two at the Zoo - A Counting Book. (ENG & SPA.). 30p. (J). (gr. k — 1). bds. 4.99 *(978-0-547-58137-8(8))* Houghton Mifflin Harcourt Publishing Co.
—The Hawk of the Castle: A Story of Medieval Falconry. Ibatoulline, Bagram, illus. 2017. (ENG.). 40p. (J). (gr. -1-3). 16.99 *(978-0-7636-7992-7(5))* Candlewick Pr.
—Pirate Nap: A Book of Colors. Petrone, Valeria, illus. 2011. (ENG.). 40p. (J). lib. bdg. 14.99 *(978-0-547-57531-5(9))* Houghton Mifflin Harcourt Publishing Co.
—Swallow the Leader. Sherry, Kevin, illus. 2016. (ENG.). 32p. (J). (gr. -1-3). 16.99 *(978-0-544-10518-8(4)*, Clarion Bks.) Houghton Mifflin Harcourt Trade & Reference Pubs.
Smith, Hope Anita. Keeping the Night Watch. Lewis, E. B., illus. 2014. (ENG.). 80p. (J). (gr. 5-8). pap. 9.99 *(978-0-312-65936-3(9)*, 9780312659363) Square Fish.
Smith, Ian & Julian, Sean. Rooster's Alarm. Smith, Ian, illus. 2009. (Tadpoles Ser.). (ENG., Illus.). 24p. (J). (gr. -1-2). pap. *(978-0-7787-3905-0(8))*; (gr. k-2). lib. bdg. *(978-0-7787-3874-9(4))* Crabtree Publishing Co.
Smith, Icy. Daddy, My Favorite Guy. 2013. 28p. 16.95 *(978-0-9856237-9-1(9))* East West Discovery Pr.
Smith, Jennifer Lynne. Things I Wonder. Perez, Angela J., ed. Gray, Angela M., illus. 2007. 36p. (J). 14.95 *(978-0-9778328-5-9(6))* His Work Christian Publishing.
Smith, Loretta. Bela & the Gold Medallion. Marconi, Gloria, illus. Preston, James, photos by. 2012. 32p. pap. 13.00 *(978-1-930357-27-3(3))* Do The Write Thing Foundation of DC.
Smith, Maggie. One Naked Baby. 2015. (ENG., Illus.). 34p. (J). (— 1). bds. 6.99 *(978-0-553-49889-9(4)*, Knopf Bks. for Young Readers) Random Hse. Children's Bks.
Smith, Michael. My Ducky Buddy. Oliva, Octavio, illus. 2011. 23p. (J). *(978-0-9821675-4-0(7))* East West Discovery Pr.
Smith, Michael & Oliva, Octavio. Grasshopper Buddy. Oliva, Octavio, illus. 2012. (SPA & ENG., Illus.). (J). *(978-0-9856237-0-8(5))* East West Discovery Pr.
Smith, Richard G. When the Moon Fell Down. Date not set. 32p. (J). (gr. -1-18). pap. 4.99 *(978-0-06-443550-5(4))* HarperCollins Pubs.
Smith, Shoham. An after Bedtime Story. Tsarfati, Einat, illus. 2016. (ENG.). 48p. (J). (gr. k-2). 16.95 *(978-1-4197-1873-1(8)*, Abrams Bks. for Young Readers) Abrams, Inc.
Sneed, Dani & Fisher, Doris. My Half Day, 1 vol. Lee, Karen, illus. 2008. (Basic Math Numbers Ser.). (ENG.). 32p. (J). (gr. -1-3). 16.95 *(978-1-934359-14-3(9))*; pap. 8.95 *(978-1-934359-29-7(7))* Arbordale Publishing.
Snelson, Doug. Who's Got the Face? 2007. (Illus.). 48p. (J). 16.95 *(978-0-9777811-0-2(0))* Petalous Publishing, LLC.
Snow, Pegeen. Eat Your Peas, Louise! Venezia, Mike, illus. 2011. (Rookie Ready to Learn Ser.). 40p. (J). (ENG.). pap. 5.95 *(978-0-531-26709-7(1))*; (gr. -1-k). lib. bdg. 23.00 *(978-0-531-26527-7(7))* Scholastic Library Publishing. (Children's Pr.).
Snow, Peggy. My Favorite Places from a to Z. Barber, Brian, illus. 2007. (My Favorites Ser.). (ENG.). 32p. (J). (gr. -1). lib. bdg. 15.99 *(978-1-934277-03-4(7))* Mam Green Publishing, Inc.
—My Favorite Sounds from a to Z. 2007. (ENG.). 32p. (J). lib. bdg. 15.99 *(978-1-934277-02-7(9))* Mam Green Publishing, Inc.
Snowden, Gary. Hank & Kale Visit the Aquarium. Smith, William E., illus. 2012. 24p. pap. 8.99 *(978-1-938768-05-7(1))* Gypsy Pubns.
Snyder, Betsy E. Haiku Night. 2017. (ENG., Illus.). 14p. (J). (— 1). bds. 6.99 ***(978-0-375-84397-6(3)***, Random Hse. Bks. for Young Readers) Random Hse. Children's Bks.
Snyder, Betsy E. Sweet Dreams Lullaby. 2012. (ENG., Illus.). 32p. (J). (— 1). bds. 6.99 *(978-0-307-98060-1(X)*, Random Hse. Bks. for Young Readers) Random Hse. Children's Bks.
Snyder, Betsy E., illus. I Can Dance. 2015. (ENG.). 14p. (J). (gr. -1 — 1). bds. 8.99 *(978-1-4521-2929-7(0))* Chronicle Bks. LLC.
—I Can Play. 2015. (ENG.). 14p. (J). (gr. -1 — 1). bds. 8.99 *(978-1-4521-2905-1(3))* Chronicle Bks. LLC.
—Lily's Potty. 2010. 16p. (J). bds. *(978-1-60906-001-5(6))* Begin Smart LLC.
Snyder, Laurel. The Longest Night: A Passover Story. Chien, Catia, illus. 2013. (ENG.). 40p. (J). (gr. -1-3). 17.99 *(978-0-375-86942-6(5)*, Schwartz & Wade Bks.) Random Hse. Children's Bks.
Snyder, Robert. Itsy Bitsy Spider. Snyder, Robert, illus. 2009. (ENG., Illus.). 20p. (J). 12.99 *(978-0-8249-1821-7(5)*, Ideal Pubns.) Worthy Publishing.
Snyder, Sally. If It's to Be, It's up to Me! The ABC's of Character Building. Snyder, Sally, illus. 2008. (ENG., Illus.). 59p. (J). (gr. -1-3). 22.50 *(978-1-933197-57-9(9))* Orange Frazer Pr.
Snyder, Susan. There's a Frog Trapped in the Bathroom. Johanson, Anna, illus. 2005. 23p. (J). (gr. 1-3). 9.95 *(978-0-9715411-0-8(8))* Kotzig Publishing, Inc.
—The Very Stubborn Centipede. Johanson, Anna, illus. 2005. 24p. (J). (gr. 2-4). 9.95 *(978-0-9767163-0-3(5))* Kotzig Publishing, Inc.
Snyder, Susan E. Shivers & Shakes. 2006. (Illus.). 31p. (J). (gr. k-2). 9.95 *(978-0-9767163-5-8(6))* Kotzig Publishing, Inc.
Sobel, June. B Is for Bulldozer: A Construction ABC. Iwai, Melissa, illus. 2006. 28p. (gr. -1-k). 17.00 *(978-0-7569-7037-6(7))* Perfection Learning Corp.
—B Is for Bulldozer: A Construction ABC. Iwai, Melissa, illus. 2006. (ENG.). 32p. (J). (gr. -1-3). pap. 7.99 *(978-0-15-205774-9(9))* Houghton Mifflin Harcourt Publishing Co.
—The Goodnight Train. Huliska-Beith, Laura, illus. 2006. (ENG.). 32p. (J). (gr. -1-3). 16.99 *(978-0-15-205436-6(7))* Houghton Mifflin Harcourt Publishing Co.
—Shiver Me Letters: A Pirate ABC. Cole, Henry, illus. (ENG.). 32p. (J). (gr. -1-3). 2009. pap. 7.99 *(978-0-15-206679-6(9))* 2006. 16.99 *(978-0-15-216732-5(3))* Houghton Mifflin Harcourt Publishing Co.
Sobel, June & Iwai, Melissa. B Is for Bulldozer: A Construction ABC. Iwai, Melissa, illus. 2013. (ENG., Illus.). 32p. (J). (— 1). bds. 7.99 *(978-0-544-10808-0(6))* Houghton Mifflin Harcourt Publishing Co.
Sones, Sonya. What My Girlfriend Doesn't Know. 2013. (ENG., Illus.). 320p. (YA). (gr. 7). pap. 9.99 *(978-1-4424-9384-1(4)*, Simon & Schuster Bks. For Young Readers) Simon & Schuster Bks. For Young Readers.
—What My Mother Doesn't Know. 2004. 259p. (gr. 7-12). 19.00 *(978-0-7569-4268-7(3))* Perfection Learning Corp.
—What My Mother Doesn't Know. 2013. (ENG., Illus.). 288p. (YA). (gr. 7). pap. 11.99 *(978-1-4424-9385-8(2)*, Simon & Schuster Bks. For Young Readers) Simon & Schuster Bks. For Young Readers.
Sonnichsen, A. L. Red Butterfly. Bates, Amy June, illus. 2015. (ENG.). 400p. (J). (gr. 3-7). 17.99 *(978-1-4814-1109-7(8))* Simon & Schuster, Inc.
Soprano, Sophie, illus. Laughing All the Way. 2008. (J). *(978-1-59811-642-7(8))* Covenant Communications.
Soule, Jean Conder. Never Tease a Weasel. Booth, George, illus. 2011. (ENG.). 40p. (J). (gr. -1-2). pap. 6.99 *(978-0-375-87285-3(X)*, Dragonfly Bks.) Random Hse. Children's Bks.
Spangler, Lois. The Fort on Fourth Street, 1 vol. Wald, Christina, illus. 2013. (ENG.). 32p. (J). (gr. 1-4). 17.95 *(978-1-60718-620-5(9))*; pap. 9.95 *(978-1-60718-632-8(2))* Arbordale Publishing.
Sparkes, Amy. Ellie's Magical Wellies. East, Nick, illus. 2017. (ENG.). 32p. (J). (gr. -1-k). pap. 10.99 ***(978-1-4052-7379-4(8))*** Egmont Bks., Ltd. GBR. Dist: Independent Pubs. Group.
Sparks, Evan. Freddy's Tale. 2006. 44p. pap. 14.88 *(978-1-4116-7427-1(8))* Lulu Pr., Inc.
Sparrow, Leilani. My First Day. Taylor, Dan, illus. 2015. (ENG.). 32p. (J). (gr. -1-k). 16.99 *(978-1-4998-0111-8(4))* Little Bee Books Inc.
—My New Shoes. Taylor, Dan, illus. 2016. (ENG.). 32p. (J). (gr. -1-k). 16.99 *(978-1-4998-0363-1(X))* Little Bee Books Inc.
Spencer, Jamie. The Train to Maine. Reed, Rebecca, illus. 2008. (ENG.). 32p. (J). (gr. -1-3). 15.95 *(978-0-89272-767-4(5))* Down East Bks.
Sperring, Mark. Dino-Daddy. Lloyd, Sam, illus. 2015. (ENG.). 32p. (J). (gr. -1-1). 18.99 *(978-1-4088-4969-9(0)*, 9781408849699, Bloomsbury USA Childrens) Bloomsbury Publishing USA.
—The Shape of My Heart. Paterson, Alys, illus. (ENG.). 32p. (J). 2015. (gr. -1-1). bds. 7.99 *(978-1-68119-017-4(6)*, 9781681190174) 2012. lib. bdg. 15.89 *(978-1-59990-963-9(4)*, 9781599909639) 2012. (gr. -1-k). 16.99 *(978-1-59990-962-2(6)*, 9781599909622) Bloomsbury Publishing USA. (Bloomsbury USA Childrens).
Sperring, Mark & Teckentrup, Britta. Your Hand in My Hand. 2015. (ENG.). 32p. (J). (gr. -1-k). 15.99 *(978-0-545-80642-8(9)*, Scholastic Pr.) Scholastic, Inc.
Spinelli, Eileen. Another Day As Emily. Lew-Vriethoff, Joanne, illus. (ENG.). 240p. (J). (gr. 3-7). 2015. 6.99 *(978-0-449-80989-1(7)*, Yearling) 2014. 12.99 *(978-0-449-80987-7(0)*, Knopf Bks. for Young Readers) 2014. lib. bdg. 15.99 *(978-0-449-80988-4(9)*, Knopf Bks. for Young Readers) Random Hse. Children's Bks.
—Do You Have a Cat? Valério, Geraldo, illus. 2010. (ENG.). 32p. (J). (gr. -1-3). 16.00 *(978-0-8028-5351-6(X)*, Eerdmans Bks For Young Readers) Eerdmans, William B. Publishing Co.
—Do You Have a Dog? Valério, Geraldo, illus. 2011. (ENG.). 26p. (J). 16.00 *(978-0-8028-5387-5(0)*, Eerdmans Bks For Young Readers) Eerdmans, William B. Publishing Co.
—Hug a Bug. Andreasen, Dan, illus. 2009. 32p. (J). (gr. -1-3). lib. bdg. 17.89 *(978-0-06-051833-2(2))* HarperCollins Pubs.
—I Know It's Autumn. Hayashi, Nancy, tr. Hayashi, Nancy, illus. 2004. 32p. (J). (gr. -1-2). lib. bdg. 17.89 *(978-0-06-029423-6(X))* HarperCollins Pubs.
—Love My Shoes! 2011. 18p. (J). (gr. -1-k). bds. 7.99 *(978-0-8249-1853-8(3)*, Ideal Pubns.) Worthy Publishing.
—The Perfect Thanksgiving. Adinolfi, JoAnn, illus. 2007. (ENG.). 32p. (J). (gr. -1-2). 7.99 *(978-0-312-37505-8(0)*, 9780312375058) Square Fish.
—Silly Tilly, 0 vols. Slonim, David, illus. 2012. (ENG.). 32p. (J). (gr. -1-2). pap. 9.99 *(978-0-7614-5990-3(1)*, 9780761459903, Amazon Children's Publishing) Amazon Publishing.
—Thankful, 1 vol. Preston, Archie, illus. (ENG.). (J). 2017. 20p. bds. 8.99 ***(978-0-310-76140-2(9))*** 2015. 32p. 16.99 *(978-0-310-00088-4(2))* Zonderkidz.
—Together at Christmas. Lee, Bin, illus. 2012. (ENG.). 24p. (J). (gr. -1-3). 15.99 *(978-0-8075-8010-3(4))* Whitman, Albert & Co.
—When No One Is Watching. Johnson, David, illus. 2013. (ENG.). 26p. (J). 16.00 *(978-0-8028-5303-5(X)*, Eerdmans Bks For Young Readers) Eerdmans, William B. Publishing Co.
—When Papa Comes Home Tonight. McPhail, David, illus. 2009. (ENG.). 32p. (J). (gr. -1-k). 16.99 *(978-1-4169-1028-2(X)*, Simon & Schuster Bks. For Young Readers) Simon & Schuster Bks. For Young Readers.
Spinelli, Eileen & Spinelli. Bath Time, 1 vol. Pedersen, Janet, illus. 2003. (ENG.). 32p. (J). 14.95 *(978-0-7614-5117-4(X))* Marshall Cavendish Corp.
—I Know It's Autumn. Hayashi, Nancy, tr. Hayashi, Nancy, illus. 2004. (ENG.). 32p. (J). (gr. -1-2). 16.99 *(978-0-06-029422-9(1))* HarperCollins Pubs.
Spinelli, Jerry. I Can Be Anything! 2010. (ENG., Illus.). 32p. (J). (gr. -1-3). 17.99 *(978-0-316-16226-5(4))* Little, Brown Bks. for Young Readers.
Spink, Matt. Some Birds. 2016. (ENG., Illus.). 32p. (J). (gr. -1-k). 15.95 *(978-1-4197-2070-3(8)*, Abrams Appleseed) Abrams, Inc.
Sprenkle, Connie L. My Shining Star. 2011. 24p. pap. 15.99 *(978-1-4568-2168-5(7))* Xlibris Corp.
Springfield, Pepper. Meet the Bobs & Tweets. Caldwell, Kristy, illus. 2016. (Bobs & Tweets Ser.: No. 1). (ENG.). 80p. (J). (gr. -1-3). 9.99 *(978-0-545-87072-6(0))* Scholastic, Inc.
Springfield, Pepper. Perfecto Pet Show. Caldwell, Kristy, illus. 2017. (Bobs & Tweets Ser.: 2). (ENG.). 80p. (J). (gr. -1-3). 9.99 ***(978-0-545-87073-3(9))*** Scholastic, Inc.
Spruill, Edward L. & Spruill, Sonya. Jordan's Hair. Peringer, Stephen Mercer, illus. 2005. 16p. (J). (gr. -1-3). 8.00 *(978-0-8170-1484-1(5))* Judson Pr.
Spurr, Elizabeth. At the Beach, 1 vol. Oliphant, Manelle, illus. 2013. (ENG.). 22p. (J). (gr. -1 — 1). bds. 6.95 *(978-1-56145-583-6(0))* Peachtree Pubs.
—Halloween Sky Ride. Long, Ethan, illus. 2005. (ENG.). 32p. (J). (gr. -1-3). 16.95 *(978-0-8234-1870-1(7))* Holiday Hse., Inc.
—Happy Sparkling Hanukkah. Madden, Colleen, illus. 2011. (J). *(978-1-4027-9660-9(9))* Sterling Publishing Co., Inc.
—In the Garden, 1 vol. Oliphant, Manelle, illus. 2012. (ENG.). 22p. (J). bds. 6.95 *(978-1-56145-581-2(4))* Peachtree Pubs.
—In the Wind, 1 vol. Oliphant, Manelle, illus. 2016. (In the Weather Ser.). (ENG.). 22p. (J). (gr. -1-k). bds. 6.95 *(978-1-56145-854-7(6))* Peachtree Pubs.
—In the Woods, 1 vol. Oliphant, Manelle, illus. 2012. (ENG.). 22p. (J). bds. 6.95 *(978-1-56145-582-9(2))* Peachtree Pubs.
—Monsters, Mind Your Manners! Scales, Simon, illus. 2012. (J). 34.28 *(978-1-61913-124-8(2))* Weigl Pubs., Inc.
Squillace, Elisa, illus. Down in the Jungle. 2005. (Classic Books with Holes Board Book Ser.). (ENG.). 14p. (J). (gr. -1-1). bds. *(978-1-904550-61-7(4))* Child's Play International Ltd.
Staake, Bob. Beachy & Me. 2016. (ENG., Illus.). 40p. (J). (gr. -1-2). 16.99 *(978-0-385-37314-2(7))*; lib. bdg. 19.99 *(978-0-375-97198-3(X))* Random Hse. Children's Bks. (Random Hse. Bks. for Young Readers).
—Look! Another Book! 2012. (Look! a Book! Ser.). (ENG., Illus.). 48p. (J). (gr. -1-3). 16.99 *(978-0-316-20459-0(5))* Little Brown & Co.
—My Pet Book. 2014. (ENG., Illus.). 40p. (J). (gr. -1-2). lib. bdg. 20.99 *(978-0-375-97195-2(5)*, Random Hse. Bks. for Young Readers) Random Hse. Children's Bks.
—The Red Lemon. Staake, Bob, illus. 2012. (ENG., Illus.). 32p. (J). (gr. -1-3). pap. 7.99 *(978-0-307-97846-2(X)*, Dragonfly Bks.) Random Hse. Children's Bks.
—The Red Lemon. 2012. lib. bdg. 18.40 *(978-0-606-26785-4(9)*, Turtleback) Turtleback Bks.
Stainton, Sue. I Love Dogs. Truesdell, Sue, illus. 2010. (J). lib. bdg. 15.89 *(978-0-06-117058-4(5))* HarperCollins Pubs.
—I Love Dogs! Truesdell, Sue & Staake, Bob, illus. 2014. (ENG.). 32p. (J). (gr. -1-3). 14.99 *(978-0-06-117057-7(7))* HarperCollins Pubs.
Stair, Karen Smith. Glasses, Glasses Oh What Do I See. 2004. (Illus.). 32p. 14.95 *(978-0-9755407-1-8(8))* Book Pubs. Network.
Stanley, Robert. Nelly Goes Out to Sea, 1 vol. 2010. 46p. pap. 24.95 *(978-1-4489-8828-0(4))* PublishAmerica, Inc.
Stanton, Andy. Danny Mcgee Drinks the Sea. Layton, Neal, illus. 2017. (ENG.). 32p. (J). (gr. -1-3). 17.99 ***(978-1-5247-1736-0(3))***; lib. bdg. 20.99 ***(978-1-5247-1737-7(1))*** Random Hse. Children's Bks. (Schwartz & Wade Bks.).
Stead, Judy, illus. Mister Sun. 2006. (J). *(978-1-58987-097-0(2))* Kindermusik International.
Steer, Dugald A. Snappy Little Halloween. Matthews, Derek, illus. 2004. 20p. (J). (gr. k-4). reprint ed. 13.00 *(978-0-7567-7403-5(9))* DIANE Publishing Co.
Steig, Jeanne. Tales from Gizzard's Grill. Turner, Sandy, illus. 2004. 80p. (J). 17.89 *(978-0-06-000960-1(8)*, Cotler, Joanna Books) HarperCollins Pubs.
Stein, Gertrude. To Do: A Book of Alphabets & Birthdays. 2011. (ENG., Illus.). 128p. 30.00 *(978-0-300-17097-9(1))* Yale Univ. Pr.
Stein, Kristen. The Vegetarian Lion. 2006. 36p. (J). pap. 13.28 *(978-1-4116-6459-3(0))* Lulu Pr., Inc.
Stein, Mathilde. Monstersong. Van Der Linden, Gerdien, illus. 2007. (ENG.). 32p. (J). (gr. -1-3). 15.95 *(978-1-932425-90-1(X))* Lemniscaat USA.
Stein, Peter. Bugs Galore. Staake, Bob, illus. 2013. (ENG.). 32p. (J). (— 1). bds. 6.99 *(978-0-7636-6220-2(8))* Candlewick Pr.
—Cars Galore. Staake, Bob, illus. (ENG.). (J). (gr. -1-3). 2012. 30p. bds. 6.99 *(978-0-7636-6148-9(1))* 2011. 32p. 15.99 *(978-0-7636-4743-8(8))* Candlewick Pr.
Steinberg, D. J. Kindergarten, Here I Come! Chambers, Mark, illus. 2012. (ENG.). 32p. (J). (gr. -1-k). pap. 3.99 *(978-0-448-45624-9(9)*, Grosset & Dunlap) Penguin Young Readers Group.
Steinberg, Laya. All Around Me, I See. Arbo, Cris, illus. 2005. (Sharing Nature with Children Book Ser.). 32p. (J). 16.95 *(978-1-58469-068-9(2))*; pap. 8.95 *(978-1-58469-069-6(0))* Dawn Pubns.
—Thesaurus Rex Finds a Friend. Harter, Debbie, illus. 2006. (J). *(978-1-905236-48-0(4))* Barefoot Bks., Inc.
Steiner, Nancy. On This Night: The Steps of the Seder in Rhyme. Leff, Tova, illus. 2013. 32p. (J). 10.95 *(978-1-929628-51-3(X))* Hachai Publishing.
Stenton, Murray, illus. My Brother Is Special: A Sibling with Cerebral Palsy. 2016. (J). pap. ***(978-1-61599-309-3(6))*** Loving Healing Pr., Inc.
Stephenson, Midji. Whose Tail on the Trail at Grand Canyon. Spengler, Kenneth, illus. 2012. (J). *(978-1-934656-55-6(0))* Grand Canyon Assn.
Sterling Children's, Sterling. Builders. Finn, Rebecca, illus. 2015. (Busy Bks.). (ENG.). 10p. (J). (— 1). bds. 8.95 *(978-1-4549-1733-5(4))* Sterling Publishing Co., Inc.
—Railway. Finn, Rebecca, illus. 2015. (Busy Bks.). (ENG.). 10p. (J). (— 1). bds. 8.95 *(978-1-4549-1735-9(0))* Sterling Publishing Co., Inc.
Sterling Publishing Co., Inc. Staff. Garage. Finn, Rebecca, illus. 2015. (Busy Bks.). (ENG.). 10p. (J). (— 1). bds. 8.95 *(978-1-4549-1734-2(2))* Sterling Publishing Co., Inc.
Sternberg, Julie. Like Bug Juice on a Burger. Cordell, Matthew, illus. (Eleanor Ser.). (ENG.). (J). (gr. 1-4). 2016. 192p. pap. 6.95 *(978-1-4197-2049-9(X))* 2013. 176p. 15.95 *(978-1-4197-0190-0(8))* Abrams, Inc. (Amulet Bks.).
—Like Carrot Juice on a Cupcake. Cordell, Matthew, illus. (Eleanor Ser.). (ENG.). (J). (gr. 1-4). 2017. 200p. pap. 6.95 *(978-1-4197-2384-1(7))* 2014. 192p. 15.95 *(978-1-4197-1033-9(8))* Abrams, Inc. (Amulet Bks.).
—Like Pickle Juice on a Cookie. Cordell, Matthew, illus. (Eleanor Ser.). (ENG.). (J). 2016. 144p. (gr. 1-4). pap. 6.95 *(978-1-4197-2050-5(3))* 2011. 128p. (gr. 3-7). 15.95 *(978-0-8109-8424-0(5))* Abrams, Inc. (Amulet Bks.).
Sterner, Wendy L. Seymore Monster. 2008. 32p. pap. 24.95 *(978-1-60441-748-7(X))* America Star Bks.
Stevens, Gary J. If I Called You a Hippopotamus! Stead, April-Nicole, illus. 2010. 24p. pap. 11.50 *(978-1-60911-280-6(6)*, Eloquent Bks.) Strategic Book Publishing & Rights Agency (SBPRA).
Stevens, K. T. Stories for Children. 2012. 22p. pap. 16.95 *(978-1-4626-9031-2(9))* America Star Bks.
Stewart, Sarah. The Library. Small, David, illus. pap. 35.95 incl. audio compact disk *(978-1-59519-010-9(4))*; 2004. (J). (gr. -1-2). 28.95 incl. audio compact disk *(978-1-59519-011-6(2))* Live Oak Media.
Stewart, Wilson N. Cock-a-Doodle-Who? 2007. (ENG., Illus.). 6p. (J). 15.99 *(978-0-7868-0826-7(8))* Hyperion Bks. for Children.
Stiegemeyer, Julie. Cheep! Cheep! Baicker-McKee, Carol, illus. 2006. (ENG.). 24p. (J). (gr. k-k). 9.95 *(978-1-58234-682-3(8)*, 9781582346823, Bloomsbury USA Childrens) Bloomsbury Publishing USA.
—Seven Little Bunnies, 0 vols. Bryant, Laura J., illus. 2010. (ENG.). 24p. (J). (gr. -1-3). 15.99 *(978-0-7614-5600-1(7)*, 9780761456001, Amazon Children's Publishing) Amazon Publishing.
Stihler, Cherie B. Polar Polka: Counting Polar Bears in Alaska. Brooks, Erik, illus. 2008. (Paws IV Ser.). (ENG.). 32p. (J). (gr. -1-2). pap. 10.95 *(978-1-57061-520-7(9)*, Little Bigfoot) Sasquatch Bks.
Stofko, Michael D. The Tale of Taylor the Tailor. 2012. 30p. pap. 19.99 *(978-1-4772-0238-8(2))* AuthorHouse.
—A Visit from the Zoo. 2011. 32p. pap. 12.77 *(978-1-4567-2968-4(3))* AuthorHouse.
Stohs, Anita Reith. Oh, Come, Little Children. Huang, Benrei, illus. 2006. 22p. (J). (gr. -1-3). 14.99 *(978-0-7586-1215-1(X))* Concordia Publishing Hse.
Stolz, Donald R. Classroom Times: Charactoons & Rhymes. Thornton, Barbara, illus. 2011. 266p. 76.95 *(978-1-60976-951-2(1)*, Strategic Bk. Publishing) Strategic Book Publishing & Rights Agency (SBPRA).
Stone, Kate & Accord Publishing Staff. Bunnies for Tea. 2013. (ENG., Illus.). 10p. (J). bds. 7.99 *(978-1-4494-2887-7(8))* Andrews McMeel Publishing.
Stone, Tanya Lee. T Is for Turkey: A True Thanksgiving Story. Kelley, Gerald, illus. 2009. (ENG.). 24p. (J). (gr. -1-k). mass mkt. 4.99 *(978-0-8431-2570-2(5)*, Price Stern Sloan) Penguin Young Readers Group.
Storm, Raen. God's Palette. 2007. 16p. per. 24.95 *(978-1-4137-1793-8(4))* America Star Bks.
Story Time Book: Rhyme Time & Story Time. 2004. reprint ed. pap. 15.95 *(978-1-4191-1380-2(1))* Kessinger Publishing, LLC.
Straker, Bethany, illus. The Funny Bunny Fly. 2014. (ENG.). 32p. (J). (gr. -1-k). 14.95 *(978-1-62914-610-2(2)*, Sky Pony Pr.) Skyhorse Publishing Co., Inc.
Stranaghan, Crystal. The 13th Floor: Colouring Outside the Lines. Bzymek, Izabela, illus. 2012. 34p. (-18). *(978-1-926691-25-1(3))* Gumboot Bks.
Stranaghan, Crystal J. Then It Rained. Espadaler, Rosa, illus. 2007. 24p. (J). *(978-0-9784047-8-9(5))* Pays et Terroirs.
Stratford, Anne Margaret. My Daddy Is A Soldier. 2008. (Illus.). 40p. (J). 17.99 *(978-0-9817938-0-1(0))* Diamond Fly Publishing, Inc.
Strong, Cynda. Where Do Angels Sleep? Denos, Julia, illus. 2007. 24p. (J). (gr. -1-3). 14.99 *(978-0-7586-1298-4(2))* Concordia Publishing Hse.
Strouss, Jessica & Strouss, Stephen. There's a Dog at My Feet when I Eat. 2010. 36p. 15.49 *(978-1-4269-4342-3(3))* Trafford Publishing.
Stuart, Pamela Haught. Just like my Papa. 2008. 40p. per. 16.99 *(978-1-4343-5369-6(9))* AuthorHouse.
Stubbs, Tommy, illus. A Crack in the Track. 2004. (Bright & Early Board Books(TM) Ser.). (ENG.). 24p. (J). (— 1). bds. 4.99 *(978-0-375-82755-6(2)*, Random Hse. Bks. for Young Readers) Random Hse. Children's Bks.
Studio Mouse, creator. Rhymes on the Go! rev. ed. 2008. (ENG., Illus.). 36p. (J). 12.99 *(978-1-59069-614-9(X))* Studio Mouse LLC.
Sturges, Philemon. I Love Bugs! Halpern, Shari, illus. 2005. (ENG.). 32p. (J). (gr. -1-3). 17.99 *(978-0-06-056168-0(8))* HarperCollins Pubs.
—I Love School! Halpern, Shari, illus. 2014. 32p. pap. 7.00 *(978-1-61003-329-9(9))* Center for the Collaborative Classroom.
—I Love School! Halpern, Shari, illus. 32p. (J). (gr. -1-1). 2004. lib. bdg. 14.89 *(978-0-06-009285-6(8))* 2006. (ENG.). reprint ed. pap. 6.99 *(978-0-06-009286-3(6))* HarperCollins Pubs.
—I Love Tools! Halpern, Shari, illus. 2006. 24p. (J). (gr. -1-1). 14.89 *(978-0-06-009288-7(2))* HarperCollins Pubs.

S

—I Love Trains! Halpern, Shari, illus. (ENG.). (J). (gr. -1-1). 2006. 28p. bds. 6.99 *(978-0-06-083774-7(8),* HarperFestival) 2003. 32p. pap. 6.99 *(978-0-06-443667-0(5))* HarperCollins Pubs.

Sturgis, Brenda Reeves. 10 Turkeys in the Road, 0 vols. Slonim, David, illus. 2011. (ENG.). 32p. (J). (gr. -1-1). 16.99 *(978-0-7614-5847-0(6),* 9780761458470, Amazon Children's Publishing) Amazon Publishing.

Sturtevant, Karen. The Adventures of Gert & Stu & Zippy Too. 2012. 36p. pap. 18.99 *(978-1-4772-9360-7(4))* AuthorHouse.

Stutson, Caroline. Blue Corn Soup. Weidner, Teri, illus. 2017. (ENG.). 32p. (J). (gr. k-2). 16.99 ***(978-1-58536-967-6(5),*** 204325) Sleeping Bear Pr.

—By the Light of the Halloween Moon, 0 vols. Hawkes, Kevin, illus. 2012. (ENG.). 32p. (J). (gr. k-4). pap. 7.99 *(978-0-7614-6244-6(9),* 9780761462446, Amazon Children's Publishing) Amazon Publishing.

—Prairie Primer: A to Z. Lamb, Susan Condie, illus. 2006. 29p. (J). (gr. -1-2). reprint ed. 16.00 *(978-1-4223-5585-5(3))* DIANE Publishing Co.

StVil, Lola. Girls Like Me. 2016. (ENG.). 320p. (YA). (gr. 7). 17.99 *(978-0-544-70674-3(9),* HMH Books For Young Readers) Houghton Mifflin Harcourt Publishing Co.

Suarez, Maribel, illus. Rebecca. (Rowing Frog's Rhymes Ser.). 16p. (J). (gr. k-3). 7.95 *(978-1-59437-840-9(1))* Santillana USA Publishing Co., Inc.

Suen, Anastasia. Subway. Katz, Karen, illus. 2008. (ENG.). 24p. (J). (gr. -1-k). bds. 6.99 *(978-0-670-01109-4(6),* Viking Books for Young Readers) Penguin Young Readers Group.

Sullivan, Kevin. The Best Hawaiian Style Mother Goose Ever! Aoki, Deb, illus. 2006. 40p. 16.95 incl. cd-rom *(978-0-9644149-6-9(1))* Hawaya, Inc.

Sullivan, Licsw. Mindfully Me! 2012. 12p. pap. 10.99 *(978-1-105-46639-7(6))* Lulu Pr., Inc.

Sully, Katherine. Where, Oh Where Is Huggle Buggle Bear? Samuel, Janet, illus. 2013. (J). *(978-1-4351-4776-8(6))* Barnes & Noble, Inc.

Sunita, Sunita. Gobble You Up! 2013. (ENG & RAJ., Illus.). 40p. (J). (gr. -1). 34.95 *(978-81-923171-4-4(5))* Tara Books Agency IND. Dist: Publishers Group West (PGW).

Surgal, Jon. Have You Seen My Dinosaur? Mathieu, Joe, illus. 2010. (Beginner Books(R) Ser.). (ENG.). 48p. (J). (gr. -1-1). 9.99 *(978-0-375-85639-6(0),* Random Hse. Bks. for Young Readers) Random Hse. Children's Bks.

Surplice, Holly. Guinea Pig Party. Surplice, Holly, illus. 2015. (ENG., Illus.). 24p. (J). (— 1). bds. 7.99 *(978-0-7636-7604-9(7),* Nosy Crow) Candlewick Pr.

—Peek-a-Boo Bunny. Surplice, Holly, illus. 2014. (ENG., Illus.). 32p. (J). (gr. -1-3). 9.99 *(978-0-06-224265-5(2))* HarperCollins Pubs.

Sutcliffe, Mandy. Hop along Boo, Time for Bed. 2016. (ENG., Illus.). 40p. (J). (gr. -1-2). 17.99 *(978-0-399-54947-2(1),* Random Hse. Bks. for Young Readers) Random Hse. Children's Bks.

Suter, Janine. Noah's Floating Animal Park. Gunther, Richard, illus. 2009. 32p. (J). 10.99 *(978-0-89051-576-1(X))* Master Bks.

Sutherland, Marc. The Waiting Place. Sutherland, Marc, illus. 2004. (Illus.). 24p. (J). (gr. k-4). reprint ed. 15.00 *(978-0-7567-8382-2(8))* DIANE Publishing Co.

Sutton, Kay. Nan & Grandad's Book of Short Stories. 2009. (Illus.). 52p. pap. 20.49 *(978-1-4490-0575-7(6))* AuthorHouse.

Sutton, Sally. Construction Board Book Boxed Set. Lovelock, Brian, illus. 2016. (ENG.). (J). (-k). bds. 19.99 *(978-0-7636-9260-5(3))* Candlewick Pr.

—Construir una Carretera (Roadwork) Lovelock, Brian, illus. 2013. (SPA.). 28p. (J). (-k). bds. 6.99 *(978-0-7636-6494-7(4))* Candlewick Pr.

—Demolicion. Lovelock, Brian, illus. 2014. (SPA.). 22p. (J). (-k). bds. 6.99 *(978-0-7636-7031-3(6))* Candlewick Pr.

—Demolition. Lovelock, Brian, illus. (ENG.). (J). 2014. 22p. (-k). bds. 6.99 *(978-0-7636-6493-0(6))* 2012. 32p. (gr. -1-2). 16.99 *(978-0-7636-5830-4(8))* Candlewick Pr.

—Farmer John's Tractor. Belton, Robyn, illus. 2013. (ENG.). 32p. (J). (gr. -1-2). 15.99 *(978-0-7636-6430-5(8))* Candlewick Pr.

Sweeney, Linda Booth. When the Wind Blows. Christy, Jana, illus. 2015. (ENG.). 32p. (J). (gr. -1-k). 16.99 *(978-0-399-16015-8(9),* G.P. Putnam's Sons Books for Young Readers) Penguin Young Readers Group.

Sweet Dreams, Pout-Pout Fish. 2015. (Pout-Pout Fish Mini Adventure Ser.). (ENG., Illus.). 12p. (J). (gr. -1 — 1). bds. 5.99 *(978-0-374-38010-6(4),* 9780374380106, Farrar, Straus & Giroux (BYR)) Farrar, Straus & Giroux.

Sweetland, Nancy & Sweetland, Robert. If I Could/Si Yo Pudiera. 2008. (ENG & SPA.). 32p. (J). (gr. 4-7). pap. 7.95 *(978-0-9794462-2-1(8));* 16.95 *(978-0-9770906-9-3(8))* Continental Sales, Inc. (Raven Tree Pr.,Csi).

Swenson, Jamie A. Boom! Boom! Boom! Walker, David, illus. 2013. (ENG.). 32p. (J). (gr. -1-1). 16.99 *(978-0-374-30868-1(3),* 9780374308681, Farrar, Straus & Giroux (BYR)) Farrar, Straus & Giroux.

Swerling, Lisa & Lazar, Ralph. We Without You. 2013. (ENG., Illus.). 96p. 9.95 *(978-1-4521-2232-8(6))* Chronicle Bks. LLC.

Swift, Ginger. Little Blue Boat. Persico, Zoe, illus. 2016. (ENG.). 10p. (J). bds. 0.00 *(978-1-68052-077-4(6))* Cottage Door Pr.

Swinburne, Stephen R. Safe in a Storm. Bell, Jennifer, illus. 2016. (J). *(978-0-545-66987-0(1));* (ENG.). 32p. (gr. -1-k). 10.99 *(978-0-545-86792-4(4))* Scholastic, Inc.

Symes, Sally. Funny Face, Sunny Face. Beardshaw, Rosalind, illus. 2015. (ENG.). 32p. (J). (-k). 14.99 *(978-0-7636-7606-3(3),* Nosy Crow) Candlewick Pr.

Tabby, Abigail. Monsters Munch Lunch! 2013. (Step into Reading Level 1 Ser.). lib. bdg. 13.55 *(978-0-606-26983-4(5),* Turtleback) Turtleback Bks.

Tafolla, Carmen. Fiesta Babies. Córdova, Amy, illus. 2010. (ENG & SPA.). 24p. (J). (gr. k — 1). 12.99 *(978-1-58246-319-3(0),* Tricycle Pr.) Random Hse. Children's Bks.

—What Can You Do with a Rebozo? ?Qué Puedes Hacer con un Rebozo? Córdova, Amy & Cordova, Amy, illus. 2009. (SPA & ENG.). 32p. (J). (gr. -1-2). pap. 7.99 *(978-1-58246-271-4(2),* Tricycle Pr.) Random Hse. Children's Bks.

—What Can You Do with a Rebozo? (¿Qué Puedes Hacer Con un Rebozo?) Córdova, Amy & Córdova, Amy, illus. 2009. (SPA & ENG.). 30p. (J). (gr. -1-2). 14.99 *(978-1-58246-270-7(4),* Tricycle Pr.) Random Hse. Children's Bks.

Taft, Jean & dePaola, Tomie. Worm Weather. Hunt, Matt, illus. 2015. (ENG.). 32p. (J). (-k). bds. 3.99 *(978-0-448-48740-3(3),* Grosset & Dunlap) Penguin Young Readers Group.

Tango-Hampton, Doreen. I Like Gum. Pfleegor, Gina, illus. 2007. (ENG.). 32p. (J). (gr. -1-3). 15.95 *(978-0-9726614-2-3(5))* Shenanigan Bks.

Tara, Stephanie L. Gwynne, Fair & Shining. Fodi, Lee Edward, illus. 2006. (J). (gr. -1-3). 16.95 *(978-1-933285-62-7(1))* Brown Books Publishing Group.

Tarpley, Todd. Ten Tiny Toes. 2012. (ENG., Illus.). 32p. (J). (gr. -1 — 1). 16.99 *(978-0-316-12921-3(6))* Little Brown & Co.

Tarter, Mildred. Alexis Sets up Search Groups. 2013. 26p. pap. 16.49 *(978-1-4389-6881-0(7))* AuthorHouse.

—Rexis! Where Are You! 2010. 24p. pap. 16.49 *(978-1-4389-6874-2(4))* AuthorHouse.

Taxali, Gary. This Is Silly! 2010. (J). *(978-0-439-71837-0(6),* Scholastic Pr.) Scholastic, Inc.

Taylor, Bonnie Highsmith. Simon Can't Say Hippopotamus. Hornung, Phyllis, tr. Hornung, Phyllis, illus. 2003. 24p. (J). 14.95 *(978-1-59336-017-7(7));* pap. *(978-1-59336-018-4(5))* Mondo Publishing.

Taylor-Butler, Christine. Ah-Choo. Koeller, Carol, illus. 2005. (My First Reader Ser.). (ENG.). 32p. (J). (gr. k-1). 18.50 *(978-0-516-25175-2(9),* Children's Pr.) Scholastic Library Publishing.

Taylor, C. Brian. Atop the Tree Top: A Christmas Story. Butler, Sharon, illus. 2003. (J). 15.95 *(978-0-9747054-0-8(3))* Rilly Silly Bk. Co., The.

Taylor, Dorothea. There's a Dragon in My Closet. Palmer, Charly, illus. 2017. (Denene Millner Bks.). (ENG.). 32p. (J). (gr. -1-3). 17.95 ***(978-1-57284-227-4(X))*** Agate Publishing, Inc.

Taylor, Martin. The Lost Treasure of the Sunken City. Catling, Andy, illus. 2012. (J). *(978-1-4351-4330-2(2))* Barnes & Noble, Inc.

Taylor, Thomas. The Pets You Get. Reynolds, Adrian, illus. 2013. 32p. (gr. -1-3). 16.95 *(978-1-4677-1143-2(8))* Andersen Pr. GBR. Dist: Lerner Publishing Group.

Taylor, Yvonne. Hartlie: The Streak. Taylor, Yvonne, ed. (Hartlie: Vol. 1). (Illus.). 32p. (J). 10.99 *(978-0-9709187-0-3(4))* Peaceable Productions.

Teague, Mark. The Pirate Jamboree. 2016. (ENG., Illus.). 40p. (J). (gr. -1-k). 17.99 *(978-0-545-63221-8(8))* Scholastic, Inc.

Tedesco, Tina. The Stork Dropped Your Here for a Reason. 2006. (J). pap. 8.00 *(978-0-8059-7233-7(1))* Dorrance Publishing Co., Inc.

Templeton, Donna L. Mother's Surprise. Berlinger, Nancy A., illus. 2009. (ENG.). 32p. (J). pap. 9.99 *(978-0-9764336-6-8(4))* MJS Publishing Group LLC.

Tenney, Yevet. I Never Got to Say Goodbye. 2013. 24p. pap. 9.99 *(978-0-9889595-1-4(8))* Mindstir Media.

Testa, Joseph Anthony. Are Cat Ears Made of Chocolate? A Children's Rhyme. 2012. 28p. pap. 17.99 *(978-1-4772-7977-9(6))* AuthorHouse.

Testa, Maria. Becoming Joe Dimaggio. Hunt, Scott, illus. 2005. (ENG.). 64p. (J). (gr. 5-9). reprint ed. pap. 6.99 *(978-0-7636-2444-6(6))* Candlewick Pr.

Themerson, Franciszka & Themerson, Franciszka. My First Nursery Book. 2009. (ENG., Illus.). 72p. (J). (gr. k-2). 16.95 *(978-0-8109-7978-9(0),* Abrams Bks. for Young Readers) Abrams, Inc.

Thimble The Fairy. Thimble the Fairy's Acorns & Tea. Patch, Sebastion, illus. 2011. (ENG.). 48p. (J). 8.99 *(978-0-9827304-0-9(3))* Eleve Publishing.

Thomas, Deborah Kadiar. Cemetery Jamboree, 1 vol. Thomas, Deborah Kadiar, illus. 2016. (ENG., Illus.). 32p. (J). (gr. k-5). pap. 9.95 *(978-1-4556-2239-9(7))* Pelican Publishing Co., Inc.

Thomas, Jan. Rhyming Dust Bunnies. Thomas, Jan, illus. 2009. (ENG., Illus.). 40p. (J). (gr. -1-3). 14.99 *(978-1-4169-7976-0(X),* Beach Lane Bks.) Beach Lane Bks.

Thomas Nelson. God Loves You Little One, 1 vol. 2016. (God's Little Ones Ser.). (ENG., Illus.). 12p. (J). (gr. -1). bds. 8.99 *(978-0-7180-8756-2(9))* Nelson, Thomas Inc.

—Little Mermaid. 2015. (ENG., Illus.). 12p. (J). (gr. -1-k). bds. *(978-1-78393-499-7(9))* Make Believe Ideas.

Thomas Nelson Community College Staff. God's Love in My Heart, 1 vol. 2014. (ENG.). 24p. bds. 9.99 *(978-0-529-11141-8(1))* Nelson, Thomas Inc.

Thomas Nelson Publishing Staff & Hall, Hannah. God Bless You & Good Night, 1 vol. 2013. (God Bless Book Ser.). (ENG.). 20p. (J). bds. 9.99 *(978-1-4003-2294-7(4))* Nelson, Thomas Inc.

Thomas, Patricia. Red Sled. Demarest, Chris L., illus. 2008. (ENG.). 32p. (J). (gr. -1-1). 16.95 *(978-1-59078-559-1(2))* Boyds Mills Pr.

Thompson, Chad. Yankee Doodle, 1 vol. 2011. (Early Childhood Themes Ser.). (ENG.). 16p. (J). (gr. -1-2). pap. 19.99 *(978-1-4333-2365-2(6));* pap. 6.99 *(978-1-4333-2364-5(8))* Teacher Created Materials, Inc.

Thompson, Chad J. Rhymes with Doug. Thompson, Chad J., illus. 2016. (ENG., Illus.). 40p. (J). (gr. -1-3). 16.99 *(978-1-4814-7095-7(7),* Aladdin) Simon & Schuster Children's Publishing.

Thompson, Kim Mitzo. Five Little Monkeys Jumping on the Bed. Girouard, Patrick, illus. 2010. (Padded Board Book W/CD Ser.). 8p. (J). (gr. k-2). bds. 10.99 incl. audio compact disk *(978-1-59922-581-4(6))* Twin Sisters IP, LLC.

—The Wheels on the Bus. Holm, Sharon Lane, illus. 2010. (Padded Board Book W/CD Ser.). 8p. (J). (gr. k-2). bds. 10.99 incl. audio compact disk *(978-1-59922-580-7(8))* Twin Sisters IP, LLC.

Thompson, Lauren. Chew, Chew, Gulp! Krosoczka, Jarrett J., illus. 2011. (ENG.). 32p. (J). (gr. -1-k). 14.99 *(978-1-4169-9744-3(X),* McElderry, Margaret K. Bks.) McElderry, Margaret K. Bks.

—Hop, Hop, Jump! Krosoczka, Jarrett J., illus. 2012. (ENG.). 32p. (J). (gr. -1-3). 15.99 *(978-1-4169-9745-0(8),* McElderry, Margaret K. Bks.) McElderry, Margaret K. Bks.

—Leap Back Home to Me. Cordell, Matthew, illus. 2011. (ENG.). 32p. (J). (gr. -1-1). 17.99 *(978-1-4169-0664-3(9),* McElderry, Margaret K. Bks.) McElderry, Margaret K. Bks.

—One Starry Night. Bean, Jonathan, illus. (ENG.). 32p. (J). 2011. (gr. -1-3). lib. bdg. 17.99 *(978-0-689-82851-5(9))* 2003. 6.99 *(978-0-689-84215-3(5))* McElderry, Margaret K. Bks. (McElderry, Margaret K. Bks.).

Thompson, Shannon Raines. Mad about Miller. Stone, Kathrine Thompson, ed. Shehan, Terece, illus. 2006. 24p. (YA). 12.95 *(978-1-59971-853-8(7))* Aardvark Global Publishing.

—Nuts about Neal. Stone, Kathrine Thompson, ed. Shehan, Terece, illus. 2006. 24p. (YA). 12.95 *(978-1-59971-852-1(9))* Aardvark Global Publishing.

Thomson, Sarah L. Pirates, Ho!, 0 vols. Gilpin, Stephen, illus. 2012. (ENG.). 32p. (J). (gr. k-3). pap. 7.99 *(978-0-7614-6247-7(3),* 9780761462477, Amazon Children's Publishing) Amazon Publishing.

Thong, Roseanne Greenfield. Gai See: What You Can See in Chinatown. Choi, Yangsook, illus. 2007. (ENG.). 40p. (J). (gr. 1-4). 16.95 *(978-0-8109-9337-2(6),* Abrams Bks. for Young Readers) Abrams, Inc.

—Green Is a Chile Pepper: A Book of Colors. 2014. (Multicultural Shapes & Colors Ser.). (Illus.). 40p. (J). lib. bdg. 28.50 *(978-1-60753-707-6(9))* Amicus Publishing.

—Green Is a Chile Pepper: A Book of Colors. Parra, John, illus. (ENG.). 40p. (J). (gr. -1-k). 2016. 7.99 *(978-1-4521-5645-3(X))* 2014. 16.99 *(978-1-4521-0203-0(1))* Chronicle Bks. LLC.

—One Is a Drummer: A Book of Numbers. 2014. (Multicultural Shapes & Colors Ser.). (Illus.). 40p. (J). lib. bdg. 28.50 *(978-1-60753-567-6(X))* Amicus Publishing.

—Red Is a Dragon. Lin, Grace, illus. 2014. 40p. pap. 7.00 *(978-1-61003-333-6(7))* Center for the Collaborative Classroom.

—Red Is a Dragon: A Book of Colors. 2014. (Multicultural Shapes & Colors Ser.). (Illus.). 40p. (J). lib. bdg. 28.50 *(978-1-60753-565-2(3))* Amicus Publishing.

—Red Is a Dragon: A Book of Colors. Lin, Grace, illus. 2008. (ENG.). 40p. (J). (gr. -1-17). pap. 7.99 *(978-0-8118-6481-7(2))* Chronicle Bks. LLC.

—Round Is a Mooncake: A Book of Shapes. 2014. (Multicultural Shapes & Colors Ser.). (Illus.). 40p. (J). lib. bdg. 28.50 *(978-1-60753-564-5(5))* Amicus Publishing.

—Round Is a Tortilla. Parra, John, illus. 2015. (ENG.). 40p. (J). (gr. -1-k). 7.99 *(978-1-4521-4568-6(7))* Chronicle Bks. LLC.

—Round Is a Tortilla: A Book of Shapes. 2014. (Multicultural Shapes & Colors Ser.). (Illus.). 40p. (J). lib. bdg. 28.50 *(978-1-60753-566-9(1))* Amicus Publishing.

—Round Is a Tortilla: A Book of Shapes. Parra, John, illus. 2013. (ENG.). 40p. (J). (gr. -1-k). 16.99 *(978-1-4521-0616-8(9))* Chronicle Bks. LLC.

Thornton, E. J. I Have a Secret: Do I Keep It? 2004. (Illus.). 24p. per. 8.95 *(978-1-932344-66-0(7))* Thornton Publishing, Inc.

Thrasher, Grady. Tim & Sally's Beach Adventure. Rabon, Elaine Hearn, illus. 2008. 48p. (J). (gr. -1-3). 18.95 *(978-1-58818-161-9(8))* Hill Street Pr., LLC.

Ticktock Media, Ltd. Staff. At the Beach with the Snappy Little Crab. 2009. (Touch & Feel Fun Ser.). (ENG.). 10p. (J). (gr. k — 1). bds. 5.95 *(978-1-84696-809-9(7),* TickTock Books) Octopus Publishing Group GBR. Dist: Independent Pubs. Group.

—In the Garden with the Hungry Little Snail. 2009. (Touch & Feel Fun Ser.). (ENG.). 10p. (J). (gr. k — 1). bds. 5.95 *(978-1-84696-810-5(0),* TickTock Books) Octopus Publishing Group GBR. Dist: Independent Pubs. Group.

—Under the Ocean with the Little Yellow Submarine. 2009. (Touch & Feel Fun Ser.). (ENG.). 10p. (J). (gr. k — 1). bds. 5.95 *(978-1-84696-811-2(9),* TickTock Books) Octopus Publishing Group GBR. Dist: Independent Pubs. Group.

—Zoom into Space with the Shiny Red Rocket. 2009. (Touch & Feel Fun Ser.). (ENG.). 10p. (J). (gr. k — 1). bds. 5.95 *(978-1-84696-812-9(7),* TickTock Books) Octopus Publishing Group GBR. Dist: Independent Pubs. Group.

Tietz, Heather. Yes, Jesus Loves You. Miller, Nancy, illus. 2009. 20p. (J). (gr. k-4). 14.95 *(978-0-8091-6743-2(3),* Ambassador Bks.) Paulist Pr.

Tiger Tales, ed. Baby's First Bunny. Ward, Sarah, illus. 2016. (To Baby with Love Ser.). (ENG.). 10p. (J). (gr. -1 — 1). 14.99 *(978-1-58925-213-4(6))* Tiger Tales.

—Ten Tiny Gingerbread Men. Galloway, Ruth, illus. 2015. (ENG.). 24p. (J). (gr. -1-2). pap. 4.99 *(978-1-58925-470-1(8))* Tiger Tales.

Tiger Tales Staff. Hug! Mantle, Ben, illus. 2013. (ENG.). 16p. (J). bds. *(978-1-58925-637-8(9))* Tiger Tales.

Tiger Tales Staff & Mantle, Ben. Five Little Pumpkins. Tiger Tales Staff, ed. 2010. (ENG., Illus.). 24p. (J). (gr. -1-k). bds. 8.95 *(978-1-58925-856-3(8))* Tiger Tales.

Tiger Tales, Tiger, ed. Twinkle, Twinkle, Little Baby. Ward, Sarah, illus. 2017. (To Baby with Love Ser.). (ENG.). 12p. (J). (gr. -1 — 1). bds. 9.99 ***(978-1-68010-515-5(9))*** Tiger Tales.

Tilby, Ginny. You Should, You Should. 2013. (ENG.). 32p. (J). (gr. k-3). 16.95 *(978-1-938301-70-4(6))* Familius LLC.

Tillis, Dionne. Willameana Whitney White & the Magical Butterfly. 2012. 24p. pap. 17.99 *(978-1-4685-7286-5(5))* AuthorHouse.

Tillman, Nancy. On the Night You Were Born. 2010. (ENG., Illus.). 32p. (J). (— 1). bds. 7.99 *(978-0-312-60155-3(7),* 9780312601553) Feiwel & Friends.

—On the Night You Were Born. Tillman, Nancy, illus. 2006. (ENG., Illus.). 32p. (J). (gr. -1 — 1). 16.95 *(978-0-312-34606-5(9),* 9780312346065) Feiwel & Friends.

—On the Night You Were Born, 1 vol., Set. unabr. ed. 2012. (ENG., Illus.). 32p. (J). (— 1). 12.99 *(978-1-4272-2646-4(6),* 9781427226464) Macmillan Audio.

—The Spirit of Christmas. Tillman, Nancy, illus. 2009. (ENG., Illus.). 32p. (J). (gr. -1-3). 17.99 *(978-0-312-54965-7(2),* 9780312549657) Feiwel & Friends.

—Tumford the Terrible. Tillman, Nancy, illus. 2011. (Tumford Ser.). (ENG., Illus.). 32p. (J). (gr. -1-1). 16.99 *(978-0-312-36840-1(2),* 9780312368401) Feiwel & Friends.

—Wherever You Are: My Love Will Find You. Tillman, Nancy, illus. (ENG., Illus.). 32p. (J). (gr. -1-3). 2012. bds. 7.99 *(978-1-250-01797-0(1),* 9781250017970) 2010. 16.99 *(978-0-312-54966-4(0),* 9780312549664) Feiwel & Friends.

—You're Here for a Reason. 2015. (ENG., Illus.). 32p. (J). (gr. -1-3). 17.99 *(978-1-250-05626-9(8),* 9781250056269) Feiwel & Friends.

Tillman, Nancy & Metaxas, Eric. It's Time to Sleep, My Love. Tillman, Nancy, illus. 2011. (ENG., Illus.). 34p. (J). (— 1). bds. 7.99 *(978-0-312-67336-9(1),* 9780312673369) Feiwel & Friends.

Timbaland & Myers, Christopher. Nighttime Symphony. Myers, Christopher, illus. 2014. (ENG., Illus.). 32p. (J). 16.99 *(978-1-4424-1208-8(9),* Atheneum Bks. for Young Readers) Simon & Schuster Children's Publishing.

Timmers, Leo. Gus's Garage. Timmers, Leo, illus. 2017. (ENG., Illus.). 32p. (J). (gr. -1-k). 16.99 ***(978-1-77657-092-8(8));*** 9.99 ***(978-1-77657-094-2(4))*** Gecko Pr. NZL. Dist: Lerner Publishing Group.

Tinsley, Jillian. Wally the Warthog. Wood, Douglas, illus. 2012. 24p. (J). pap. 10.99 *(978-1-61254-782-4(6))* Small Pr., The.

Tischler, Tracey. Heroes in the Sandbox. 2009. 28p. pap. 13.95 *(978-1-4490-5502-8(8))* AuthorHouse.

To Be Perfectly Honest: A Novel Based on an Untrue Story. 2014. (ENG., Illus.). 496p. (YA). (gr. 7). pap. 11.99 *(978-0-689-87605-9(X),* Simon & Schuster Bks. For Young Readers) Simon & Schuster Bks. For Young Readers.

Todd, Mark. Food Trucks! 2014. (ENG., Illus.). 32p. (J). (gr. -1-3). 16.99 *(978-0-544-15784-2(2),* HMH Books For Young Readers) Houghton Mifflin Harcourt Publishing Co.

Todd, Traci N. Wiggle, Waggle, Loop-De-Loo! Barner, Bob, illus. 2006. (J). *(978-1-58987-009-3(3))* Kindermusik International.

Tolstoy, Aleksei, et al. The Gigantic Turnip. 2009. (ENG., Illus.). (J). 16.99 *(978-1-84686-298-4(1))* Barefoot Bks., Inc.

Tomlin, Chris & Barrett, Pat. Good Good Father for Little Ones, 1 vol. 2017. (ENG., Illus.). 24p. (J). bds. 9.99 *(978-0-7180-8697-8(X))* Nelson, Thomas Inc.

Tomlinson, Jill. The Gorilla Who Wanted to Grow Up. Howard, Paul, illus. 2014. (ENG.). 112p. (J). (gr. -1-2). pap. 9.99 *(978-1-4052-7195-0(7))* Egmont Bks., Ltd. GBR. Dist: Independent Pubs. Group.

Toms, Kate. The Bear Who Dares. 2008. (Kate Toms Ser.). (Illus.). 26p. (gr. -1-k). bds. 7.99 *(978-1-84610-819-8(5))* Make Believe Ideas GBR. Dist: Nelson, Thomas Inc.

—I Udderly Love You! 2007. (Kate Toms Ser.). (Illus.). 26p. (gr. -1). bds. 7.95 *(978-1-84610-460-2(2))* Make Believe Ideas GBR. Dist: Nelson, Thomas Inc.

—Twinkle Twinkle Box Set. 2007. (Illus.). 26p. (gr. -1). per. *(978-1-84610-672-9(9))* Make Believe Ideas.

—Twinkle, Twinkle, Little Star. 2007. (Kate Toms Ser.). (Illus.). 26p. (gr. -1). bds. 7.99 *(978-1-84610-485-5(8))* Make Believe Ideas GBR. Dist: Nelson, Thomas Inc.

Toms, Kate & Make Believe Ideas Staff. Itsy Bitsy Spider. 2009. (Kate Toms Ser.). (Illus.). 26p. (gr. -1-k). bds. 7.99 *(978-1-84610-974-4(4))* Make Believe Ideas GBR. Dist: Nelson, Thomas Inc.

Top That Publishing Staff, ed. The Midnight Fairies. Atkins, Alison, illus. 2007. (Sparkling Jigsaw Book Ser.). 10p. (J). (gr. -1). bds. *(978-1-84666-278-2(8),* Tide Mill Pr.) Top That! Publishing PLC.

—There Were Ten Bears in a Bed: A Count-and-Feel Book. Atkins, Alison, illus. 2007. (Story Book Ser.). 22p. (J). (gr. -1). bds. *(978-1-84666-130-3(7),* Tide Mill Pr.) Top That! Publishing PLC.

Toral, Miguel A. Babu Goes Back to the Zoo. 2009. 32p. pap. 15.70 *(978-1-4389-6330-3(0))* AuthorHouse.

Torres, J. Checkers & Dot at the Beach. Lum, J., illus. 2013. (J). E-Book *(978-1-77049-448-0(0))* Tundra Bks.

—Checkers & Dot at the Beach. Lum, J., illus. 2013. (Checkers & Dot Ser.). (ENG.). 16p. (J). (— 1). bds. 7.95 *(978-1-77049-444-2(8),* Tundra Bks.) Tundra Bks. CAN. Dist: Penguin Random Hse. LLC.

—Checkers & Dot at the Zoo. Lum, J., illus. 2012. (Checkers & Dot Ser.). (ENG.). 16p. (J). (gr. k — 1). bds. 7.95 *(978-1-77049-442-8(1),* Tundra Bks.) Tundra Bks. CAN. Dist: Penguin Random Hse. LLC.

—Checkers & Dot on the Farm. Lum, J., illus. 2013. (Checkers & Dot Ser.). (ENG.). 16p. (J). (— 1). bds. 7.95 *(978-1-77049-443-5(X),* Tundra Bks.) Tundra Bks. CAN. Dist: Penguin Random Hse. LLC.

Tougas, Chris. Dojo Daycare. 2014. (Dojo Ser.: 1). (ENG., Illus.). 32p. (J). (gr. -1-3). 16.95 *(978-1-77147-057-5(7),* Owlkids) Owlkids Bks. Inc. CAN. Dist: Publishers Group West (PGW).

Tran-Davies, N. Daddy Is a Conundrum! 2012. 40p. (-18). pap. *(978-1-4602-0043-8(8))* FriesenPress.

Trapani, Iza. Gabe & Goon. Trapani, Iza, illus. 2016. (ENG., Illus.). 32p. (J). (gr. -1-1). lib. bdg. 16.95 *(978-1-58089-640-5(5))* Charlesbridge Publishing, Inc.

—Haunted Party. Trapani, Iza, illus. 2010. (ENG., Illus.). 28p. (J). (gr. -1-2). pap. 7.95 *(978-1-58089-247-6(7))* Charlesbridge Publishing, Inc.

Trasler, Janee. Bathtime for Chickies. Trasler, Janee, illus. 2015. (Chickies Ser.). (ENG., Illus.). 24p. (J). (gr. -1 — 1). bds. 8.99 *(978-0-06-234229-4(0),* HarperFestival) HarperCollins Pubs.

—Big Chickie, Little Chickie. Trasler, Janee, illus. 2016. (Illus.). 24p. (J). (gr. -1 — 1). bds. 8.99 *(978-0-06-234231-7(2),* HarperFestival) HarperCollins Pubs.

—A New Chick for Chickies. Trasler, Janee, illus. 2014. (Chickies Ser.). (ENG., Illus.). 24p. (J). (gr. -1 — 1). bds. 8.99 *(978-0-06-227471-7(6),* HarperFestival) HarperCollins Pubs.

Tregay, Sarah. Love & Leftovers. 2011. (ENG.). 448p. (YA). (gr. 8). 17.99 *(978-0-06-202358-2(6),* Tegen, Katherine Bks) HarperCollins Pubs.

Trent, Shanda. Farmers' Market Day. Dippold, Jane, illus. 2013. (ENG.). 32p. (J). (gr. -1-1). 12.95 *(978-1-58925-115-1(6))* Tiger Tales.

Treyes, Jill. Brooke & Brandon Welcome Brandon. 2010. 28p. pap. 12.99 *(978-1-4389-1939-3(5))* AuthorHouse.

Trinco, Trish. The Leaf That Wouldn't Leave. Langdo, Bryan, illus. 2008. (ENG.). 32p. (J). 16.95 *(978-0-931674-90-7(5),* Waldman House Pr.) TRISTAN Publishing, Inc.

Trumbauer, Lisa. The Great Reindeer Rebellion. Ho, Jannie, illus. 2014. (ENG.). 32p. (J). (gr. -1). pap. 6.95 *(978-1-4549-1356-6(8))* Sterling Publishing Co., Inc.

—A Tooth Is Loose. Gray, Steve, illus. (Rookie Ready to Learn Ser.). (J). 2011. 32p. pap. 5.95 *(978-0-531-26735-6(0))* 2011. 32p. (gr. -1-k). lib. bdg. 23.00 *(978-0-531-26503-1(X))* 2005.

(ENG.). 24p. (gr. k-2). pap. 4.95 *(978-0-516-25841-6(9))* Scholastic Library Publishing. (Children's Pr.).
Trumbauer, Lisa & Gray, Steve. Un Diente Está Flojo. Gray, Steve, illus. 2011. (Rookie Ready to Learn Español Ser.). (SPA., Illus.). 32p. (J). pap. 5.95 *(978-0-531-26785-1(7))*; lib. bdg. 23.00 *(978-0-531-26117-0(4))* Scholastic Library Publishing. (Children's Pr.).
Tsitoukis, Kristen L. The Tooth Song. 2008. 16p. pap. 8.50 *(978-1-4343-9539-9(1))* AuthorHouse.
Tucker, Kathy. Do Pirates Take Baths? 2015. (Illus.). 27p. (J). *(978-1-4896-3861-8(X))* Weigl Pubs., Inc.
Tucker, Lindy. Oddvark & the Yellow Kazoo. 2013. 94p. pap. 12.95 *(978-1-4575-2083-9(4))* Dog Ear Publishing, LLC.
Tucker Slingsby Ltd., Staff. My Big Book of Fairy Tales in Rhyme! Lewis, Jan, illus. 2004. 224p. (J). *(978-1-902272-31-3(5))* Tucker Slingsby, Ltd.
Tudor, Tasha. Around the Year. Tudor, Tasha, illus. 2004. (ENG., Illus.). 64p. (J). (gr. -1-3). 7.99 *(978-0-689-87350-8(6))*, Aladdin) Simon & Schuster Children's Publishing.
Tuell, Todd. Ninja, Ninja, Never Stop! Carpenter, Tad, illus. 2014. (ENG.). 32p. (J). (gr. -1-k). 14.95 *(978-1-4197-1027-8(3))*, Abrams Appleseed) Abrams, Inc.
Tugwood, Wendy. I Love You Three. 2016. (ENG., Illus.). 24p. (J). (gr. -1-1). 14.95 *(978-1-77085-784-1(2))*, 9781770857841) Firefly Bks., Ltd.
Turnbull, Elizabeth. Bonnwit Kabrit. Vaganos, Erin, illus. 2013. 36p. 17.95 *(978-1-61153-073-5(3))* Light Messages Publishing.
Turner, Jennifer. My Name Is Jake. Bell, Susan, illus. 2012. 32p. (J). 14.99 *(978-1-938032-04-2(7))*; pap. 7.99 *(978-1-938032-05-9(5))* Peaks Pr. LLC.
Turner, Marie B. God Made the Animals. Romero, Naomi, illus. 2017. (J). 6.99 ***(978-1-5064-2185-8(7))***, Sparkhouse Family) Augsburg Fortress, Pubs.
Tutu Nene - Hawaiian Mother Goose Rhymes. 2004. (J). audio compact disk 14.99 *(978-0-931548-60-4(8))* Island Heritage Publishing.
Tuzee, John & Tuzee, Diane. Charlie Canoe & Other Boats, Too. Kasun, Mike, illus. 2006. (J). *(978-0-9755348-2-3(3))* Kids Life Pr.
Twin Sister Produtions. Sesame Street What Did Elmo Say? 2008. (ENG.). 20p. (J). (gr. -1-3). 9.99 *(978-1-59069-657-6(3))* Studio Mouse LLC.
Twin Sisters(r) Staff. Five Little Skunks. 2010. (J). (gr. k-2). pap. 4.99 *(978-1-59922-509-8(3))* Twin Sisters IP, LLC.
Twinn, A. Down by the Station. Stockham, Jess, illus. 2007. (Classic Books with Holes 8x8 with CD Ser.). (ENG.). 16p. (J). (gr. -1-1). pap. incl. audio compact disk *(978-1-904550-68-6(1))* Child's Play International Ltd.
—Ten Little Monkeys: Jumping on the Bed. Freeman, Tina, illus. 2007. (Classic Books with Holes 8x8 with CD Ser.). (ENG.). 16p. (J). (gr. -1-1). pap. incl. audio compact disk *(978-1-904550-67-9(3))* Child's Play International Ltd.
Tyler, Jenny & Hawthorn, Phillip. Who's Making That Noise? 2008. (Luxury Flap Bks). 16p. (J). 9.99 *(978-0-7945-1695-6(5))*, Usborne) EDC Publishing.
—Who's Making That Smell? Cartwright, Stephen, illus. 2007. (Luxury Flap Bks). 16p. (J). (gr. -1-3). 9.99 *(978-0-7945-1696-3(3))*, Usborne) EDC Publishing.
Uhlig, Elizabeth. I Want to Be. Uhlig, Elizabeth, illus. 2008. (ENG., Illus.). (J). pap. 12.95 *(978-0-9815345-1-0(1))* Marble Hse. Editions.
Ulz, Ivan. Fire Truck! Kaida, Garrett, illus. 2013. 36p. 19.00 *(978-0-9896231-0-0(6))* Temple Street Pr.
Underwood, Deborah. Bad Bye, Good Bye. Bean, Jonathan, illus. 2014. (ENG.). 32p. (J). (gr. -1-3). 16.99 *(978-0-547-92852-4(1))*, HMH Books For Young Readers) Houghton Mifflin Harcourt Publishing Co.
Unser, Virginia. The Night Before Cat-Mas. Anagost, Karen, illus. 2007. (Petite Plush Kit Ser.). 64p. (J). (gr. -1-3). 9.95 *(978-1-59359-882-2(3))* Peter Pauper Pr. Inc.
Up above & down Below. 2008. (Illus.). 42p. (J). lib. bdg. 14.95 *(978-0-9795400-1-1(1))* NANUQ Publishing.
Upton, Elizabeth. Maxi the Little Taxi. Cole, Henry, illus. 2016. (ENG.). 32p. (J). (gr. -1-k). 17.99 *(978-0-545-79860-0(4))*, Scholastic Pr.) Scholastic, Inc.
Urbigkit, Cat. Puppies, Puppies Everywhere! 2006. (ENG., Illus.). 24p. (J). (gr. -1-1). 12.95 *(978-1-59078-363-4(8))* Boyds Mills Pr.
Valko, Danna. Dee & Maya Are Best Friends. 2013. (Illus.). *(978-1-62510-726-8(9))*; *(978-1-62563-112-1(X))* Tate Publishing, Ltd.
Vamos, Samantha R. Alphabet Trains. O'Rourke, Ryan, illus. 2015. (ENG.). 32p. (J). (gr. -1-2). lib. bdg. 14.95 *(978-1-58089-592-7(1))* Charlesbridge Publishing, Inc.
Van Buren, David. I Love You As Big As the World. Warnes, Tim, illus. 2013. (ENG.). 22p. (J). bds. *(978-1-58925-603-3(4))* Tiger Tales.
Van Dusen, Chris. A Camping Spree with Mr. Magee. 2003. (Mr. Mcgee Ser.: MCGE). (ENG., Illus.). 36p. (J). (gr. -1-7). 15.99 *(978-0-8118-3603-6(7))* Chronicle Bks. LLC.
—The Circus Ship. Van Dusen, Chris, illus. 2015. (ENG., Illus.). 40p. (J). (gr. -1-3). 6.99 *(978-0-7636-5592-1(9))* Candlewick Pr.
—The Circus Ship Big Book. 2011. (ENG., Illus.). 40p. (J). (gr. -1-3). pap. 24.99 *(978-0-7636-5593-8(7))* Candlewick Pr.
—Down to the Sea with Mr. Magee. 2006. (ENG., Illus.). 36p. (J). (gr. -1-7). pap. 6.99 *(978-0-8118-5225-8(3))* Chronicle Bks. LLC.
—If I Built a Car. Van Dusen, Chris, illus. (ENG., Illus.). (J). 2007. 40p. (gr. k-k). pap. 7.99 *(978-0-14-240825-4(5))*, Puffin Books) 2005. 32p. (gr. -1-k). 17.99 *(978-0-525-47400-5(5))*, Dutton Books for Young Readers) Penguin Young Readers Group.
—If I Built a Car. Van Dusen, Chris, illus. 2007. (Illus.). (gr. -1-3). lib. bdg. 17.00 *(978-0-7569-8149-5(2))* Perfection Learning Corp.
—If I Built a House. 2012. (ENG.). 32p. (J). (-k). 17.99 *(978-0-8037-3751-8(3))*, Dial Bks) Penguin Young Readers Group.
—King Hugo's Huge Ego. 2011. (ENG., Illus.). 40p. (J). (gr. -1-2). 16.99 *(978-0-7636-5004-9(8))* Candlewick Pr.
—Learning to Ski with Mr. Magee. 2010. (ENG., Illus.). 36p. (J). (gr. -1-3). 15.99 *(978-0-8118-7495-3(8))* Chronicle Bks. LLC.
—Randy Riley's Really Big Hit. Van Dusen, Chris, illus. 2012. (ENG., Illus.). 32p. (J). (gr. -1-3). 15.99 *(978-0-7636-4946-3(5))* Candlewick Pr.
Van Dusen, Ross, illus. Crocka Dog in the Evil Forest. 2015. (J). *(978-1-936744-54-1(6))*, Rio Grande Bks.) LPD Pr.
—How Crocka Dog Came to Be. 2015. (J). *(978-1-936744-39-8(2))* LPD Pr.
—Lyle Got Stuck in a Tree & Became an Honorary Fireman. 2015. (J). *(978-1-936744-45-9(7))*, Rio Grande Bks.) LPD Pr.
—What Makes a Rainbow? 2015. (J). *(978-1-936744-32-9(5))*, Rio Grande Bks.) LPD Pr.
—What Makes a Snowflake? 2015. (J). *(978-1-936744-48-0(1))*, Rio Grande Bks.) LPD Pr.
—What Makes the Lightning? 2016. (J). *(978-1-943681-03-7(1))*, Rio Grande Bks.) LPD Pr.
Van Fleet, Mara. Little Color Fairies. Van Fleet, Mara, illus. 2012. (ENG., Illus.). 16p. (J). (gr. -1-1). 14.99 *(978-1-4424-3434-9(1))*, Simon & Schuster/Paula Wiseman Bks.) Simon & Schuster/Paula Wiseman Bks.
—Night-Night, Princess. Van Fleet, Mara, illus. 2014. (ENG., Illus.). 16p. (J). (gr. -1-1). 14.99 *(978-1-4424-8646-1(5))*, Simon & Schuster/Paula Wiseman Bks.) Simon & Schuster/Paula Wiseman Bks.
—Three Little Mermaids. Van Fleet, Mara, illus. 2011. (ENG., Illus.). 16p. (J). (gr. -1-k). 15.99 *(978-1-4424-1286-6(0))*, Simon & Schuster/Paula Wiseman Bks.) Simon & Schuster/Paula Wiseman Bks.
Van Fleet, Matthew. Color Dog. Stanton, Brian, illus. Stanton, Brian, photos by. 2015. (ENG.). 22p. (J). (gr. -1-k). 19.99 *(978-1-4814-4986-1(9))*, Simon & Schuster Bks. For Young Readers) Simon & Schuster Bks. For Young Readers.
—Lick! Van Fleet, Matthew, illus. 2013. (ENG., Illus.). 14p. (J). (gr. -1-1). 9.99 *(978-1-4424-6049-2(0))*, Simon & Schuster/Paula Wiseman Bks.) Simon & Schuster/Paula Wiseman Bks.
Van Fleet, Matthew. Tails. 2017. (ENG., Illus.). 20p. (J). (— 1). 14.99 ***(978-1-328-88685-9(9))***, HMH Books For Young Readers) Houghton Mifflin Harcourt Publishing Co.
Van Laan, Nancy. Scrubba Dub. Pons, Bernadette, illus. 2008. (ENG.). 32p. (J). (gr. -1-1). 8.99 *(978-1-4169-7859-6(3))*, Simon & Schuster/Paula Wiseman Bks.) Simon & Schuster/Paula Wiseman Bks.
—Teeny Tiny Tingly Tales. Chess, Victoria, illus. 2008. (ENG.). 32p. (J). (gr. -1-2). 8.99 *(978-1-4169-7572-4(1))*, Simon & Schuster/Paula Wiseman Bks.) Simon & Schuster/Paula Wiseman Bks.
Van Lemon, M. Champions of the Garden Games: Winter Fun for Everyone. 2009. 48p. pap. 20.95 *(978-1-4490-3580-8(9))* AuthorHouse.
Vandever, Daniel W. Fall in Line, Holden. Frank, LaFrenda, ed. Vandever, Daniel W., illus. 2017. (Illus.). 32p. (J). ***(978-1-893354-50-0(4))*** Salina Bookshelf Inc.
Vantrease, Norma. Ants in My Pants. Cox, Steve, illus. 2004. (Rookie Readers Ser.). 31p. (J). 12.60 *(978-0-7569-4280-9(2))* Perfection Learning Corp.
Vassallo, Rebecca. Listen to Luther. 2006. 24p. (J). 10.87 *(978-1-4116-8169-9(X))* Lulu Pr., Inc.
Vaughn, C. L. I See Aliens. 2007. 15p. 10.95 *(978-1-4357-0117-5(8))* Lulu Pr., Inc.
Vazov, George D. The Other Side of the Mushroom. 2006. 12.00 *(978-0-8059-9018-8(6))* Dorrance Publishing Co., Inc.
Velazquez, Catherine. Dirty Birdie. 2012. 32p. pap. 18.48 *(978-0-578-10152-1(1))* Jiovanie.
Velde, Marie. Laundry Day. 2007. (Illus.). (J). bds. 22.95 *(978-1-933156-17-0(1))*, Visikid Bks.) GSVQ Publishing.
Venkatraman, Padma. A Time to Dance. 2014. (ENG.). 320p. (YA). (gr. 7). 17.99 *(978-0-399-25710-0(1))*, Nancy Paulsen Books) Penguin Young Readers Group.
Verburg, Bonnie. The Tree House That Jack Built. Teague, Mark, illus. 2014. (ENG.). 40p. (J). (gr. -1-k). 17.99 *(978-0-439-85336-5(9))*, Orchard Bks.) Scholastic, Inc.
Verde, Susan. The Museum. Reynolds, Peter H., illus. 2013. (ENG.). 32p. (J). (gr. k-2). 16.95 *(978-1-4197-0594-6(6))*, Abrams Bks. for Young Readers) Abrams, Inc.
—You & Me. Reynolds, Peter H., illus. 2015. (ENG.). 32p. (J). (gr. k-2). 14.95 *(978-1-4197-1197-8(0))*, Abrams Bks. for Young Readers) Abrams, Inc.
Verdick, Elizabeth. Peep Leap, 0 vols. Bendall-Brunello, John, illus. 2013. (ENG.). 32p. (J). (gr. -1-2). 16.99 *(978-1-4778-1640-0(2))*, 9781477816400, Amazon Children's Publishing) Amazon Publishing.
Verdick, Elizabeth & Lisovskis, Marjorie. Cuddle. 2013. (Happy Healthy Baby Ser.). (ENG., Illus.). 22p. (J). bds. 6.99 *(978-1-57542-423-1(1))* Free Spirit Publishing, Inc.
—Move. 2013. (Happy Healthy Baby Ser.). (ENG., Illus.). 22p. (J). bds. 6.99 *(978-1-57542-422-4(3))* Free Spirit Publishing, Inc.
Viau, Nancy. City Street Beat. 2015. (Illus.). 32p. (J). *(978-1-4896-3855-7(5))* Weigl Pubs., Inc.
—City Street Beat. Bakos, Barbara, illus. 2014. (ENG.). 32p. (J). (gr. -1-3). 16.99 *(978-0-8075-1164-0(1))* Whitman, Albert & Co.
—Storm Song. Gynux, illus. 2013. 24p. pap. 12.99 *(978-1-4778-6646-7(9))* Amazon Publishing.
Viau, Nancy & Bolinao, Mela. Storm Song, 0 vols. Gynux, illus. 2013. (ENG.). 24p. (J). (gr. k-3). 12.99 *(978-1-4778-1646-2(1))*, 9781477816462, Amazon Children's Publishing) Amazon Publishing.
Vigneault, Gilles. A Gift for Sophie. Jorisch, Stéphane, illus. 2013. (ENG.). 44p. (J). (gr. k-2). 16.95 *(978-2-923163-98-7(2))* La Montagne Secrete CAN. Dist: Independent Pubs. Group.
Virján, Emma J. What This Story Needs Is a Pig in a Wig. Virján, Emma J., illus. 2015. (Pig in a Wig Book Ser.). (ENG., Illus.). 40p. (J). (gr. -1-3). 9.99 *(978-0-06-232724-6(0))* HarperCollins Pubs.
Viscardi, Dolly. All Around Cats. Brooks, David, illus. 2004. (ENG.). 32p. (J). (gr. k-3). 15.95 *(978-1-55971-072-5(1))* Cooper Square Publishing Llc.
Vischer, Phil. I Thank God for This Day! Reed, Lisa, illus. 2016. (J). *(978-0-8249-1966-5(1))*, Ideal Pubns.) Worthy Publishing.
Vision, Mutiya Sahar. Disabilities. Alcantara, Ignacio, illus. 2009. 32p. 17.00 *(978-0-9659538-9-4(0))* Von Curtis Publishing.
Viswanath, Shobha. The Blue Jackal. Joshi, Dileep, illus. 2016. (ENG.). 34p. (J). 15.00 *(978-0-8028-5466-7(4))*, Eerdmans Bks For Young Readers) Eerdmans, William B. Publishing Co.
von Olfers, Sibylle. Mother Earth & Her Children: A Quilted Fairy Tale. Zipes, Jack, tr. from GER. Schoen-Smith, Sieglinde, illus. 2015. (ENG.). 32p. (J). (— 1). 12.95 *(978-1-933308-50-0(8))* Breckling Pr.
—Mother Earth & Her Children Coloring Book: Color the Wonderful World of Nature As You See It! 24 Magical, Mythical Coloring Scenes. Zipes, Jack, tr. Schoen-Smith, Sieglinde, illus. 2015. (ENG.). 24p. (J). (gr. 2-4). pap. 6.95 *(978-1-933308-54-8(0))* Breckling Pr.
von Rosenberg, Byron. Dale the Uniclyde: An adventure in Friendship. Parrott, Heather, illus. 2007. 22p. (J). 11.95 *(978-0-9759858-6-1(8))* Red Mountain Creations.
Wagenbach, Debbie. The Grouchies. Mack, Steve, illus. 2009. 32p. (J). (gr. -1-3). 14.95 *(978-1-4338-0543-1(X))*; pap. 9.95 *(978-1-4338-0553-0(7))* American Psychological Assn. (Magination Pr.).
Wagner, Linda. Lady Flatterley. 2008. 44p. pap. 22.95 *(978-1-4327-3233-2(1))* Outskirts Pr., Inc.
Wahl, Jan. Elf Night. Weevers, Peter, illus. 2005. (Picture Bks.). 32p. (gr. k-2). 15.25 *(978-1-57505-512-1(0))* Lerner Publishing Group.
—I Met a Dinosaur. Sheban, Chris, illus. 2015. (ENG.). 32p. (J). (gr. 1-3). 17.99 *(978-1-56846-233-2(6))*, Creative Editions) Creative Co., The.
Wahman, Joe. Snowboy 1, 2, 3. Wahman, Wendy, illus. 2012. (ENG.). 32p. (J). (gr. -1-1). 14.99 *(978-0-8050-8732-1(X))*, 9780805087321, Holt, Henry & Co. Bks. For Young Readers) Holt, Henry & Co.
Walden, Libby. Bear Hugs. Riley, Vicky, illus. 2017. (ENG.). 18p. (J). (gr. -1-1). bds. 7.99 ***(978-1-68010-519-3(1))*** Tiger Tales.
Walker, Anna. I Love My Mom. Walker, Anna, illus. 2010. (ENG., Illus.). 32p. (J). (gr. -1-1). 9.99 *(978-1-4169-8318-7(X))*, Simon & Schuster Bks. For Young Readers) Simon & Schuster Bks. For Young Readers.
—I Love to Dance. Walker, Anna, illus. 2011. (ENG., Illus.). 32p. (J). (gr. -1-1). 9.99 *(978-1-4169-8323-1(6))*, Simon & Schuster Bks. For Young Readers) Simon & Schuster Bks. For Young Readers.
—I Love to Sing. Walker, Anna, illus. 2011. (ENG., Illus.). 32p. (J). (gr. -1-1). 9.99 *(978-1-4169-8322-4(8))*, Simon & Schuster Bks. For Young Readers) Simon & Schuster Bks. For Young Readers.
—I Love Vacations. Walker, Anna, illus. 2011. (ENG., Illus.). 32p. (J). (gr. -1-1). 9.99 *(978-1-4169-8321-7(X))*, Simon & Schuster Bks. For Young Readers) Simon & Schuster Bks. For Young Readers.
Walker, Joni. Tell Me What God Made. Walker, Joni, illus. 2007. (Illus.). 20p. (J). (gr. -1-3). bds. 6.49 *(978-0-7586-1247-2(8))* Concordia Publishing Hse.
Walker, Joni, illus. Jesus Hears Me. 2008. 20p. (J). (gr. -1). bds. 6.49 *(978-0-7586-1508-4(6))* Concordia Publishing Hse.
Wallace, Adam. How to Catch a Leprechaun. Elkerton, Andy, illus. 2016. (ENG.). 32p. (J). (-6). 10.99 *(978-1-4926-3291-7(0))*, 9781492632917, Sourcebooks Jabberwocky) Sourcebooks, Inc.
—How to Catch a Monster. Elkerton, Andy, illus. 2017. (ENG.). 40p. (J). (-3). 10.99 ***(978-1-4926-4894-9(9))***, Sourcebooks Jabberwocky) Sourcebooks, Inc.
—How to Catch an Elf. Elkerton, Andy, illus. 2016. (ENG.). 32p. (J). (-3). 10.99 *(978-1-4926-4631-0(8))*, 9781492646310, Sourcebooks Jabberwocky) Sourcebooks, Inc.
—How to Catch the Tooth Fairy. Elkerton, Andy, illus. 2016. (ENG.). 32p. (J). (-6). 10.99 *(978-1-4926-3733-2(5))*, 9781492637332, Sourcebooks Jabberwocky) Sourcebooks, Inc.
Wallace, Nancy K. The Christmas Cats, 1 vol. Housley, Cathren, illus. 2011. (ENG.). 32p. (J). (gr. k-3). 16.99 *(978-1-58980-979-6(3))* Pelican Publishing Co., Inc.
Wallace, Rhea. If You Re Happy & You Know It. 2016. (Nursery Rhymes Ser.). (ENG., Illus.). (J). (gr. -1). bds. 5.96 ***(978-1-68342-045-3(4))*** Rourke Educational Media.
Wallingford, Stephanie & Rynders, Dawn. A Day at the Lake. Villnave, Erica Pelton, illus. 2013. (ENG.). 32p. (-k). pap. 10.95 *(978-1-938063-03-9(1))*, Mighty Media Kids) Mighty Media Pr.
Walsh, Joanna. The Biggest Kiss. Abbot, Judi, illus. 2011. (ENG.). 32p. (J). (gr. -1-3). 14.99 *(978-1-4424-2769-3(8))*, Simon & Schuster/Paula Wiseman Bks.) Simon & Schuster/Paula Wiseman Bks.
—I Love Mom. Abbot, Judi, illus. 2014. (ENG.). 32p. (J). (gr. -1-3). 16.99 *(978-1-4814-2808-8(X))*, Simon & Schuster/Paula Wiseman Bks.) Simon & Schuster/Paula Wiseman Bks.
—The Perfect Hug. Abbot, Judi, illus. 2012. (ENG.). 32p. (J). (gr. -1-3). 14.99 *(978-1-4424-6606-7(5))*, Simon & Schuster/Paula Wiseman Bks.) Simon & Schuster/Paula Wiseman Bks.
Walters, Virginia. Are We There Yet, Daddy? Schindler, S. D., illus. 2005. 27p. (J). (gr. k-4). reprint ed. 16.00 *(978-0-7567-9708-9(X))* DIANE Publishing Co.
Walton, A. E. What Should I Do with My Love for You? 2009. 24p. pap. 11.49 *(978-1-4389-8532-9(0))* AuthorHouse.
Walton, Ann. Something to Do. Hinrichsen, Natalie, illus. 2010. (ENG.). 24p. (J). (gr. k-2). pap. 6.00 *(978-1-77009-706-3(6))* Jacana Media ZAF. Dist: Independent Pubs. Group.
Walton, Mildred D. Spring Reborn. 2012. 28p. pap. 21.99 *(978-1-4691-2556-5(0))* Xlibris Corp.
Walton, Rick. Bunny Christmas: A Family Celebration. Miglio, Paige, illus. 2004. 32p. (J). (ENG.). 15.99 *(978-0-06-008415-8(4))*; lib. bdg. 16.89 *(978-0-06-008416-5(2))* HarperCollins Pubs.
—Frankenstein. Hale, Nathan, illus. 2012. (ENG.). 48p. (J). (gr. -1-3). 14.99 *(978-0-312-55366-1(8))*, 9780312553661) Feiwel & Friends.
—Frankenstein's Fright Before Christmas. Hale, Nathan, illus. 2014. (ENG.). 32p. (J). (gr. -1-3). 16.99 *(978-0-312-55367-8(6))*, 9780312553678) Feiwel & Friends.
—10 Little Monsters Go to San Fransisco. Smiley, Jess Smart, illus. 2015. (ENG.). 32p. (J). 16.95 *(978-1-942672-99-9(3))* Familius LLC.
—10 Little Monsters Visit Oregon. Smiley, Jess Smart, illus. 2014. (ENG.). 32p. (J). 16.95 *(978-1-939629-29-6(2))*, 9781939629296) Familius LLC.
—10 Little Monsters Visit Washington. Smiley, Jess Smart, illus. 2015. (ENG.). 32p. (J). 16.95 *(978-1-942672-98-2(5))* Familius LLC.
Walvoord, Linda. Razzamadaddy, 1 vol. Yoshikawa, Sachiko, tr. Yoshikawa, Sachiko, illus. 2004. (ENG.). 32p. (J). 14.95 *(978-0-7614-5158-7(7))* Marshall Cavendish Corp.
Walz, Susan. Balloons to the Moon. 2008. 29p. pap. 24.95 *(978-1-60474-586-3(X))* America Star Bks.
Wang, Margaret. Eency Weency Spider. Rueda, Claudia, illus. 2006. (ENG.). 22p. (J). (gr. -1-3). bds. 10.95 *(978-1-58117-418-2(7))*, Intervisual/Piggy Toes) Bendon, Inc.
—Who Stole the Cookie from the Cookie Jar? Schneider, Christine, illus. 2006. (ENG.). 12p. (J). (gr. -1-3). 4.95 *(978-1-58117-429-8(2))*, Intervisual/Piggy Toes) Bendon, Inc.
Ward, B. J. Farty Marty. Kellogg, Steven, illus. 2013. (ENG.). 32p. (J). (gr. -1-3). 16.99 *(978-1-4424-3901-6(7))*, Simon & Schuster Bks. For Young Readers) Simon & Schuster Bks. For Young Readers.
Ward, Helen. Spots in a Box. Ward, Helen, illus. 2015. (ENG., Illus.). 40p. (J). (gr. -1-2). 16.99 *(978-0-7636-7597-4(0))*, Templar) Candlewick Pr.
Ward, Jennifer. Because You Are My Baby. Long, Sylvia, illus. 2007. (ENG.). 32p. (J). (gr. -1-1). 15.95 *(978-0-87358-911-6(4))* Cooper Square Publishing Llc.
—The Busy Tree, 0 vols. Falkenstern, Lisa, illus. 2009. (ENG.). 32p. (J). (gr. k-3). 17.99 *(978-0-7614-5550-9(7))*, 9780761455509, Amazon Children's Publishing) Amazon Publishing.
—The Seed & the Giant Saguaro. Rangner, Mike K., illus. 2003. (ENG.). 32p. (J). (gr. -1-3). 15.95 *(978-0-87358-845-4(2))* Cooper Square Publishing Llc.
—The Sunhat. Sisson, Stéphanie Roth, illus. 2013. (ENG.). (J). 15.95 *(978-1-933855-78-3(9))*, Rio Nuevo Pubs.) Rio Nuevo Pubs.
—Way up in the Arctic. Spengler, Kenneth J., illus. 2007. (SPA & ENG.). 32p. (J). (gr. -1-3). 15.95 *(978-0-87358-928-4(9))* Cooper Square Publishing Llc.
Ward, Lindsay. The Importance of Being 3. 2016. (ENG., Illus.). 32p. (J). (— 1). 16.99 *(978-0-525-42869-5(0))*, Dial Bks) Penguin Young Readers Group.
Wardlaw, Lee. Red, White, & Boom! Lee, Huy Voun, illus. 2012. (ENG.). 32p. (J). (gr. -1-2). 16.99 *(978-0-8050-9065-9(7))*, 9780805090659, Holt, Henry & Co. Bks. For Young Readers) Holt, Henry & Co.
Wargin, Kathy-jo. F Is for Fireflies: God's Summertime Alphabet, 1 vol. Bronson, Linda, illus. 2011. (ENG.). 40p. (J). (gr. -1-2). 15.99 *(978-0-310-71663-1(2))* Zonderkidz.
—Moose on the Loose. Bendall-Brunello, John, illus. 2009. (ENG.). 32p. (J). (gr. k-6). 15.95 *(978-1-58536-427-5(4))* Sleeping Bear Pr.
—P Is for Pumpkin: God's Harvest Alphabet, 1 vol. Pang, YaWen Ariel, illus. 2008. (ENG.). 40p. (J). (gr. -1-3). 15.99 *(978-0-310-71180-3(0))* Zonderkidz.
Wargin, Kathy-jo & Bendall-Brunello, John, illus. Scare a Bear. 2010. (ENG.). 32p. (J). (gr. -1-3). 15.95 *(978-1-58536-430-5(4))* Sleeping Bear Pr.
Warner, Carl. A World of Food: Discover Magical Lands Made of Things You Can Eat! 2012. (ENG., Illus.). 32p. (J). (gr. k-2). 18.95 *(978-1-4197-0162-7(2))*, Abrams Bks. for Young Readers) Abrams, Inc.
Warner, Michael N. Tales to Make You Scream for Your Momma. Warner, Robert, illus. 2015. 208p. (J). pap. 11.95 *(978-0-9963756-1-0(9))* All About Kids Publishing.
Warnes, Tim. Daddy Hug. Chapman, Jane, illus. 2008. (ENG.). 32p. (J). (gr. -1-k). 17.99 *(978-0-06-058950-9(7))* HarperCollins Pubs.
Warnes, Tim, illus. Sweet Dreams, Little Bear. 2013. (ENG.). 18p. (gr. -1). bds. 8.95 *(978-1-58925-604-0(2))* Tiger Tales.
Warnes, Tim, et al. My Little Box of Bedtime Stories: Can't You Sleep, Puppy?/Time to Sleep, Little Bear!/What Are You Doing in My Bed?/Sleep Tight, Giner Kitten/Good Night, Emily!/Don't Be Afraid, Little Ones. Pedler, Caroline & Massey, Jane, illus. 2013. (ENG.). (J). (gr. -1-1). pap. 8.95 *(978-1-58925-442-8(2))* Tiger Tales.
Warnock, Chris. Toys Overboard!, 1 vol. 2009. (ENG.). 48p. 24.95 *(978-1-60672-197-1(6))* America Star Bks.
Wassmann, Marilyn B. & Wassman, Paul A., illus. What the Wind Blew In: 6 Stories to Read with Children. 2010. 29p. (J). *(978-1-4535-6303-8(2))* Xlibris Corp.
Watson, Clyde. Midnight Moon. Natti, Susanna, illus. 2006. (ENG.). 24p. (J). (gr. -1-k). *(978-1-59692-162-7(5))* MacAdam/Cage Publishing, Inc.
Watson, Richard A. & National Geographic Learning Staff. In the Dark Cave. Norman, Dean, illus. 2010. (Rise & Shine Ser.). (ENG.). 40p. (C). (gr. -1-2). 9.95 *(978-1-59572-038-2(3))* National Geographic School Publishing, Inc.
Wax, Wendy. City Witch, Country Switch, 0 vols. Gibala-Broxholm, Scott, illus. 2013. (ENG.). 42p. (J). (gr. -1-3). pap. 9.99 *(978-1-4778-1676-9(3))*, 9781477816769, Amazon Children's Publishing) Amazon Publishing.
—What Do You Say? Please & Thank You. Dillard, Sarah, illus. 2005. (J). *(978-1-58987-108-3(1))* Kindermusik International.
Wax, Wendy & Kwiat, Ernie. Guess Who, Elmo! 2007. (Guess Who Ser.). (ENG., Illus.). 10p. (J). (gr. -1-k). bds. 10.99 *(978-0-7944-1211-4(X))*, Reader's Digest Children's Bks.) Studio Fun International.
Weale, David. Doors in the Air, 1 vol. Pratt, Pierre, illus. 2012. (ENG.). 32p. (J). (gr. -1-3). 19.95 *(978-1-55469-250-7(4))* Orca Bk. Pubs. USA.
Weatherford, Carole Boston. Freedom in Congo Square. Christie, R. Gregory, illus. 2016. (ENG.). 40p. (J). (gr. -1-3). 17.99 *(978-1-4998-0103-3(3))* Little Bee Books Inc.
—Sugar Hill: Harlem's Historic Neighborhood. Christie, R. Gregory, illus. 2014. (ENG.). 32p. (J). (gr. k-3). 16.99 *(978-0-8075-7650-2(6))* Whitman, Albert & Co.
Weathers, R. F. Jill's Joyful Surprise. 2005. 32p. pap. 18.00 *(978-1-4208-5263-9(9))* AuthorHouse.
Webb, Steve. City Kitty Cat. Le Huche, Magali, illus. 2015. (ENG.). 32p. (J). (gr. -1-3). 17.99 *(978-1-4814-4331-9(3))*, Simon & Schuster Bks. For Young Readers) Simon & Schuster Bks. For Young Readers.
—Happy Zappa Cat. Le Huche, Magali, illus. 2014. (ENG.). 32p. 15.99 *(978-0-85707-620-5(5))*, Simon & Schuster Children's) Simon & Schuster, Ltd. GBR. Dist: Simon & Schuster, Inc.

Webster, Kyle T. Please Say Please! Webster, Kyle T., illus. 2016. (ENG., Illus.). 32p. (J). (gr. -1-k). 17.99 *(978-0-545-84485-7(1)*, Scholastic Pr.) Scholastic, Inc.

Weeks, Sarah. Catfish Kate & the Sweet Swamp Band. Smith, Elwood H., illus. 2009. (ENG.). 32p. (J). (gr. -1-3). 17.99 *(978-1-4169-4026-5(X)*, Atheneum Bks. for Young Readers) Simon & Schuster Children's Publishing.

—If I Were a Lion. Solomon, Heather M., illus. 2004. (ENG.). 40p. (J). (gr. -1-3). 17.99 *(978-0-689-84836-0(6)*, Atheneum Bks. for Young Readers) Simon & Schuster Children's Publishing.

—Mac & Cheese. Manning, Jane K., illus. 2010. (I Can Read Level 1 Ser.). (ENG.). 32p. (J). (gr. -1-3). 16.99 *(978-0-06-117079-9(8))*; pap. 3.99 *(978-0-06-117081-2(X))* HarperCollins Pubs.

—Mac & Cheese & the Perfect Plan. Manning, Jane, illus. 2012. 32p. (J). lib. bdg. 17.89 *(978-0-06-117083-6(6))*; (ENG.). 16.99 *(978-0-06-117082-9(8))*; (ENG.). pap. 3.99 *(978-0-06-117084-3(4))* HarperCollins Pubs.

—Pip Squeak. Manning, Jane K., illus. (I Can Read Level 1 Ser.). 32p. (J). 2008. (ENG.). (gr. k-3). pap. 3.99 *(978-0-06-075638-3(1))* 2007. (gr. -1-3). lib. bdg. 16.89 *(978-0-06-075637-6(3)*, Geringer, Laura Book) HarperCollins Pubs.

Weeks, Sarah & Weeks. Baa-Choo! Manning, Jane K., illus. 2006. (I Can Read Level 1 Ser.). (ENG.). 32p. (J). (gr. k-3). pap. 3.99 *(978-0-06-443740-0(X))* HarperCollins Pubs.

Wegwerth, A. L. Little Bo Peep & Her Bad, Bad Sheep: A Mother Goose Hullabaloo. Flowers, Luke, illus. 2016. (Fiction Picture Bks.). (ENG.). 40p. (gr. -1-2). lib. bdg. 22.65 *(978-1-4795-6483-5(4)*, Fiction Picture Bks.) Picture Window Bks.

Weidknecht, Lisa. E Is for Emotions. 2009. 56p. pap. 21.99 *(978-1-4343-9260-2(0))* AuthorHouse.

Weigel, Jeff. Atomic Ace & the Robot Rampage. Weigel, Jeff, illus. 2006. (ENG., Illus.). 32p. (J). (gr. 1-5). 6.95 *(978-0-8075-0485-7(8))*; 15.95 *(978-0-8075-0484-0(X))* Whitman, Albert & Co.

Weimer, Heidi. You're My Little Love Bug! 2013. (ENG., Illus.). 12p. (gr. -1). bds. 12.99 *(978-1-891100-29-1(7)*, Smart Kids) Penton Overseas, Inc.

Weimer, Heidi R. Happy Birthday to You! 2007. (ENG., Illus.). 14p. (gr. -1-k). bds. 12.99 *(978-0-8249-6699-7(6)*, Ideal Pubns.) Worthy Publishing.

—How Do I Kiss You? Sharp, Chris, illus. 2008. (ENG.). 18p. (J). (gr. -1-k). bds. 12.99 *(978-0-8249-1814-9(2)*, Ideal Pubns.) Worthy Publishing.

—Love from My Heart: To a Precious Sweet Little Girl. 2005. (ENG., Illus.). 14p. (J). (gr. -1-3). bds. 12.99 *(978-0-8249-6655-3(4)*, Ideal Pubns.) Worthy Publishing.

—Love from My Heart: To a Snuggly Cuddly Little Boy. 2005. (Parent Love Letters Ser.). (ENG., Illus.). 14p. (J). (gr. -1-3). bds. 12.99 *(978-0-8249-6654-6(6)*, Ideal Pubns.) Worthy Publishing.

Weinberger, Kimberly. Dolphin's Big Leap. Ziss, Debra, illus. 2003. (Hello Reader! Ser.). 30p. (J). *(978-0-439-44159-9(5))* Scholastic, Inc.

Weinshall Liberman, Judith. Ice Cream Snow. 2012. (Illus.). 34p. 18.99 *(978-1-4575-1578-1(4))* Dog Ear Publishing, LLC.

Weinstone, David. All My Friends Are Fast Asleep. Le Huche, Magali, illus. 2017. (ENG.). 40p. (J). 17.99 ***(978-0-374-30535-2(8)***, 9780374305352, Farrar, Straus & Giroux (BYR)) Farrar, Straus & Giroux.

Weinstone, David. Music Class Today! Vogel, Vin, illus. 2015. (ENG.). 40p. (J). (gr. -1 — 1). 17.99 *(978-0-374-35131-1(7)*, 9780374351311, Farrar, Straus & Giroux (BYR)) Farrar, Straus & Giroux.

Weiss, Ellen. Twins in the Park. Williams, Sam, illus. 2003. (Ready-To-Reads Ser.). (ENG.). 24p. (J). (gr. -1-k). pap. 3.99 *(978-0-689-85742-3(X)*, Simon Spotlight) Simon Spotlight.

—Whatever You Do, I Love You. Williams, Sam, illus. 2010. (ENG.). 16p. (J). (gr. -1 — 1). bds. 7.99 *(978-1-4424-0809-8(X)*, Little Simon) Little Simon.

Wekelo, Kerry. Audrey's Journey: Round & Round Yoga. 2012. 16p. pap. 15.99 *(978-1-4685-9645-8(4))* AuthorHouse.

Welch, Willy. Grumbly Bunnies. Lyon, Tammie Speer, illus. 2004. 32p. (J). 15.95 *(978-1-58089-086-1(5))* Charlesbridge Publishing, Inc.

Wells, Philip. Daddy Island. Daly, Niki, illus. 2015. 24p. (J). (gr. -1-k). 7.99 *(978-1-84148-198-2(X))* Barefoot Bks., Inc.

Wells, Rosemary. Hand in Hand. Wells, Rosemary, illus. 2016. (ENG., Illus.). 32p. (J). 17.99 *(978-1-62779-434-3(4)*, 9781627794343, Holt, Henry & Co. Bks. For Young Readers) Holt, Henry & Co.

—Love Waves. Wells, Rosemary, illus. 2011. (ENG., Illus.). 32p. (J). (gr. -1-2). 15.99 *(978-0-7636-4989-0(9))* Candlewick Pr.

—Love Waves: Midi Edition. Wells, Rosemary, illus. 2012. (ENG., Illus.). 32p. (J). (gr. k — 1). 8.99 *(978-0-7636-6224-0(0))* Candlewick Pr.

—Noisy Nora. Wells, Rosemary, illus. 2007. (Illus.). 28p. (gr. -1-2). 17.00 *(978-0-7569-7870-9(X))* Perfection Learning Corp.

—Read to Your Bunny. Wells, Rosemary, illus. 2003. (ENG., Illus.). 6p. (J). bds. 7.99 *(978-0-439-54337-8(1)*, Cartwheel Bks.) Scholastic, Inc.

Wells, Zachariah, et al. Anything but Hank! Orchard, Eric, illus. 2008. (ENG.). 50p. (J). (gr. k-3). 19.95 *(978-1-897231-36-4(9))* Biblioasis CAN. Dist: Consortium Bk. Sales & Distribution.

Welsh, Karen Leis. Frolicking Friends. 2012. (Illus.). 44p. pap. 21.99 *(978-1-4685-6422-8(6))* AuthorHouse.

Welton, Jude. Tomas Loves... A Rhyming Book about Fun, Friendship - & Autism. Telford, Jane, illus. 2015. (ENG.). 32p. 15.95 *(978-1-84905-544-4(0)*, 7155) Kingsley, Jessica Pubs. GBR. Dist: Macmillan Distribution Ltd.

Wendel, Gretchen Schomel, et al. All Around Town. Renthrope, Damon, illus. 2007. (ENG.). 32p. (J). (gr. -1-3). 11.99 *(978-1-933754-10-9(9))* Waterside Publishing.

—Becka Goes to India. Renthrope, Damon, illus. 2007. (ENG.). 32p. (J). 11.99 *(978-1-933754-13-0(3))* Waterside Publishing.

—Becka Goes to San Francisco. Renthrope, Damon, illus. 2007. (ENG.). 32p. (J). 11.99 *(978-1-933754-12-3(5))* Waterside Publishing.

—Becka Goes to the North Pole. Renthrope, Damon, illus. 2007. (ENG.). 28p. (J). 11.99 *(978-1-933754-11-6(7))* Waterside Publishing.

Wendel, Gretchen Schomer & Schomer, Adam Anthomy. Becka Goes to San Diego. Renthrope, Damon, illus. 2008. (ENG.). 32p. (J). (gr. -1-3). 11.99 *(978-1-933754-51-2(6))* Waterside Publishing.

Wendel, Gretchen Schomer & Schomer, Adam Anthony. All Around Town. Renthrope, Damon, illus. 2009. (Becka & the Big Bubble Ser.). 32p. (J). (gr. -1-2). lib. bdg. 22.60 *(978-1-60754-104-2(1))* Windmill Bks.

—Becka Goes to Chicago. Renthrope, Damon, illus. 2008. (ENG.). 36p. (J). (gr. -1-3). 11.99 *(978-1-933754-52-9(4))* Waterside Publishing.

—Becka Goes to India. Renthrope, Damon, illus. 2009. (Becka & the Big Bubble Ser.). 32p. (J). (gr. -1-2). lib. bdg. 22.60 *(978-1-60754-110-3(6))* Windmill Bks.

—Becka Goes to the North Pole. Renthrope, Damon, illus. 2009. (Becka & the Big Bubble Ser.). 32p. (J). (gr. -1-2). lib. bdg. 22.60 *(978-1-60754-116-5(5))* Windmill Bks.

Wenz, Graham D. The Day a Cockroach Crawled under My Door: This Book Won't Be a Bore! 2012. 44p. pap. 21.99 *(978-1-4797-0761-4(9))* Xlibris Corp.

Western, Colleen. Why Elephants Don't Ride School Buses. 2011. 16p. (gr. 1-2). pap. 10.67 *(978-1-4269-6865-5(5))* Trafford Publishing.

Westheimer, Ruth K. Leopold. (ENG., Illus.). 2017. 36p. pap. 11.99 ***(978-1-68336-709-3(X))*** 2015. 34p. (J). 23.99 *(978-1-63026-918-0(2))* Turner Publishing Co.

Weston, Robert Paul. Prince Puggly of Spud & the Kingdom of Spiff. 2013. (ENG., Illus.). 224p. (J). (gr. 3-7). 15.99 *(978-1-59514-567-3(2)*, Razorbill) Penguin Young Readers Group.

Weston Woods Staff, creator. Each Peach Pear Plum. 2011. 38.75 *(978-0-439-77214-3(1))*; 18.95 *(978-0-439-77212-9(5))*; 29.95 *(978-0-439-77213-6(3))* Weston Woods Studios, Inc.

—Goodnight Moon. 2011. 29.95 *(978-0-439-73472-1(X))*; 38.75 *(978-0-439-72686-3(7))*; 18.95 *(978-0-439-72684-9(0))* Weston Woods Studios, Inc.

—How Do Dinosaurs Eat Their Food? 2011. 18.95 *(978-0-439-02748-9(9))*; 38.75 *(978-0-439-02740-3(3))* Weston Woods Studios, Inc.

—How Do Dinosaurs Get Well Soon? 2011. 38.75 *(978-0-439-84622-6(6))*; 18.95 *(978-0-439-84621-9(8))*; 29.95 *(978-0-439-76689-0(3))* Weston Woods Studios, Inc.

—How Do Dinosaurs Go to School? 2011. 38.75 *(978-0-545-19712-0(0))* Weston Woods Studios, Inc.

—In the Small, Small Pond. 2011. 38.75 *(978-0-439-84578-6(5))* Weston Woods Studios, Inc.

—Johnny Appleseed. 2011. 38.75 *(978-0-439-72733-4(2))*; 18.95 *(978-0-439-72731-0(6))* Weston Woods Studios, Inc.

—Madeline's Rescue. 2011. 38.75 *(978-0-439-72772-3(3))*; 18.95 *(978-0-439-72770-9(7))*; 29.95 *(978-0-439-73488-2(6))* Weston Woods Studios, Inc.

—May I Bring a Friend? 2011. 29.95 *(978-0-439-73490-5(8))*; 38.75 *(978-0-439-72836-2(3))*; 18.95 *(978-0-439-72783-9(9))* Weston Woods Studios, Inc.

Whatley, Bruce. That Magnetic Dog. 2015. (ENG., Illus.). 32p. (J). (gr. -1-3). pap. 9.99 *(978-0-207-18420-8(8))* HarperCollins Pubs. Australia AUS. Dist: HarperCollins Pubs.

Wheeler, Lisa. Boogie Knights. Siegel, Mark, illus. 2008. (ENG.). 40p. (J). (gr. -1-3). 16.99 *(978-0-689-87639-4(4)*, Atheneum/Richard Jackson Bks.) Simon & Schuster Children's Publishing.

—Castaway Cats. Goembel, Ponder, illus. 2006. (ENG.). 32p. (J). (gr. -1-2). 17.99 *(978-0-689-86232-8(6)*, Atheneum/Richard Jackson Bks.) Simon & Schuster Children's Publishing.

—Dino-Baseball. Gott, Barry, illus. 2010. (ENG.). 32p. (J). (gr. k-3). lib. bdg. 16.95 *(978-0-7613-4429-2(2)*, Carolrhoda Bks.) Lerner Publishing Group.

—Dino-Basketball. Gott, Barry, illus. 2011. (Carolrhoda Picture Bks.). (ENG.). 32p. (J). (gr. k-3). 16.95 *(978-0-7613-6393-4(9))* Lerner Publishing Group.

—Dino-Boarding. Gott, Barry, illus. 2014. (ENG.). 32p. (J). (gr. k-3). lib. bdg. 16.95 *(978-1-4677-0213-3(7)*, Carolrhoda Bks.) Lerner Publishing Group.

—Dino-Dancing. Gott, Barry, illus. 2017. (ENG.). 32p. (J). (gr. k-3). lib. bdg. 17.99 ***(978-1-5124-0316-9(4)***, Carolrhoda Bks.) Lerner Publishing Group.

—Dino-Football. Gott, Barry, illus. 2012. (Carolrhoda Picture Bks.). (ENG.). 32p. (J). (gr. k-3). lib. bdg. 16.95 *(978-0-7613-6394-1(7))* Lerner Publishing Group.

—Dino-Hockey. Gott, Barry, illus. 2007. (Carolrhoda Picture Bks.). (ENG.). 32p. (J). (gr. k-3). 16.95 *(978-0-8225-6191-0(3)*, Carolrhoda Bks.) Lerner Publishing Group.

—Dino-Racing. Gott, Barry, illus. 2016. (ENG.). 32p. (gr. k-3). (J). lib. bdg. 17.99 *(978-1-5124-0314-5(8))*; 35.99 *(978-1-5124-0886-7(7))* Lerner Publishing Group. (Carolrhoda Bks.).

—Dino-Soccer. Gott, Barry, illus. 2009. (Carolrhoda Picture Bks.). (ENG.). 32p. (J). (gr. k-3). 16.95 *(978-0-8225-9028-6(X))* Lerner Publishing Group.

—Dino-Swimming. Gott, Barry, illus. 2015. (ENG.). 32p. (J). (gr. k-3). lib. bdg. 16.99 *(978-1-4677-0214-0(5)*, Carolrhoda Bks.) Lerner Publishing Group.

—Farmer Dale's Red Pickup Truck. Bates, Ivan, illus. 2014. (ENG.). 32p. (J). (— 1). bds. 7.99 *(978-0-544-24765-9(5)*, HMH Books For Young Readers) Houghton Mifflin Harcourt Publishing Co.

—Jazz Baby. Christie, R. Gregory, illus. 2007. (ENG.). 40p. (J). (gr. -1-3). 17.99 *(978-0-15-202522-9(7))* Houghton Mifflin Harcourt Publishing Co.

—One Dark Night. Bates, Ivan, illus. 2006. (ENG.). 32p. (J). (gr. -1-3). reprint ed. pap. 6.99 *(978-0-15-205888-3(5))* Houghton Mifflin Harcourt Publishing Co.

—The Pet Project: Cute & Cuddly Vicious Verses. OHora, Zachariah, illus. 2013. (ENG.). 40p. (J). (gr. -1-3). 16.99 *(978-1-4169-7595-3(0)*, Atheneum Bks. for Young Readers) Simon & Schuster Children's Publishing.

—Seadogs: An Epic Ocean Operetta. Siegel, Mark, illus. 2006. (ENG.). 40p. (J). (gr. 2-5). reprint ed. 7.99 *(978-1-4169-4103-3(7)*, Atheneum Bks. for Young Readers) Simon & Schuster Children's Publishing.

—Uncles & Antlers. Floca, Brian, illus. 2014. (ENG.). 40p. (J). (gr. -1-3). 17.99 *(978-1-4814-3018-0(1)*, Atheneum Bks. for Young Readers) Simon & Schuster Children's Publishing.

Where Does the Sun Go? 2006. (Illus.). 40p. (J). (gr. -1-3). 14.95 *(978-0-9786813-0-2(4))* Elora Pr.

Whincup, Sara. The St John's Cross Spider. Yapsangco, Kenn, illus. 2015. (ENG.). 28p. (J). pap. 28.22 *(978-1-5035-0985-6(0))* Xlibris Corp.

Whitaker, Kent. Big Mo's Tennis Ball Hunt. 2007. (Illus.). (J). *(978-0-9779053-8-6(1))* Great American Pubs.

White, Dianne. Blue on Blue. Krommes, Beth, illus. 2014. (ENG.). 48p. (J). (gr. k-3). 17.99 *(978-1-4424-1267-5(4)*, Beach Lane Bks.) Beach Lane Bks.

White, Kathryn. El Hermanito de Ruby. Latimer, Miriam, illus. 2013. (SPA.). 32p. (J). pap. 7.99 *(978-1-78285-026-7(0))* Barefoot Bks., Inc.

—Ruby's Baby Brother. Latimer, Miriam, illus. 2013. (ENG.). 32p. (J). 16.99 *(978-1-84686-864-1(5))*; (gr. -1-2). pap. 7.99 *(978-1-84686-950-1(1))* Barefoot Bks., Inc.

—Ruby's School Walk. Latimer, Miriam, illus. 2010. (ENG.). 32p. (J). (gr. -1-2). 16.99 *(978-1-84686-275-5(2))* Barefoot Bks., Inc.

—Ruby's Sleepover. Latimer, Miriam, illus. 2012. (ENG.). 32p. (J). 16.99 *(978-1-84686-593-0(X))* Barefoot Bks., Inc.

White, Kimberly. Mood Music: Musical Colors Series Axford, Elizabeth C., ed. 2003. (Musical Colors Rhyming Story Coloring Book Ser.). (ENG., Illus.). 16p. (J). spiral bd. 10.95 *(978-1-931844-06-2(2)*, PP1018) Piano Pr.

White, Loricia. Little Tail's Rhyming Roots. 2012. 74p. pap. 19.95 *(978-1-4626-6885-4(2))* America Star Bks.

White, Matthew & Sanderson, Ana. Little Red Riding Hood & the Wolf: A Howling Hilarious Musical, 1 vol. Baiton, Janice, ed. Eccles, Jane, illus. 2005. (and C Black Musicals Ser.). (ENG.). 56p. (J). (gr. 2-6). pap. 42.95 incl. cd-rom ***(978-0-7136-6958-9(6))*** HarperCollins Pubs. Ltd. GBR. Dist: Independent Pubs. Group.

Whiteside, Andy. Valentino Finds a Home, 1 vol. Hnatov, Catherine, illus. 2012. (ENG.). (J). 32p. 15.95 *(978-1-59572-284-3(X))*; 24p. pap. 5.95 *(978-1-59572-286-7(6))* Star Bright Bks., Inc.

Whybrow, Ian. The Christmas Bear. Scheffler, Axel, illus. 2016. (ENG.). 10p. (J). (gr. -1-2). bds. 8.99 *(978-1-5098-0696-6(2))* Pan Macmillan GBR. Dist: Independent Pubs. Group.

—Faraway Farm. Ayliffe, Alex, illus. 2006. (ENG.). 32p. (J). (gr. -1-2). lib. bdg. 15.95 *(978-1-57505-938-9(X)*, Carolrhoda Bks.) Lerner Publishing Group.

—Say Hello to the Snowy Animals! Eaves, Edward, illus. 2012. (J). *(978-0-7607-9675-7(0))* Barnes & Noble, Inc.

—Where's Tim's Ted? It's Time for Bed! Ayto, Russell, illus. 2014. (ENG.). 32p. (J). 17.99 *(978-0-00-755929-9(1)*, HarperCollins Children's Bks.) HarperCollins Pubs. Ltd. GBR. Dist: HarperCollins Pubs.

Whyte, Hugh, illus. Rock Steady: A Story of Noah's Ark. 2006. 28p. (J). (gr. k-4). reprint ed. 17.00 *(978-1-4223-5556-5(X))* DIANE Publishing Co.

Widgen, Susan. A Caring Deed for Becky. Novak, Steven, illus. 2012. 36p. pap. 8.99 *(978-1-60820-579-0(7))* MLR Pr., LLC.

Wiersum, Gale. The Animals' Christmas Eve. 2007. (Little Golden Book Ser.). (ENG., Illus.). 24p. (J). (gr. -1-k). 4.99 *(978-0-375-83923-8(2)*, Golden Bks.) Random Hse. Children's Bks.

Wigden, Susan. I Want to Learn to Dance. Franzese, Nora Tapp, illus. 2012. 36p. pap. 11.99 *(978-1-60820-725-1(0))* MLR Pr., LLC.

Wiggins, Leah Holder. My Neighbor Is Gone. Wiggins, Margaret W., illus. 2006. 28p. (J). per. 17.99 *(978-0-9768579-5-2(2))* eVision, LLC.

Wilcox, Leah. Falling for Rapunzel. Monks, Lydia, illus. 2003. (ENG.). 32p. (J). (gr. -1-3). 15.99 *(978-0-399-23794-2(1)*, G.P. Putnam's Sons Books for Young Readers) Penguin Young Readers Group.

—Waking Beauty. Monks, Lydia, illus. 2011. (ENG.). 32p. (J). (gr. -1-k). pap. 6.99 *(978-0-14-241538-2(3)*, Puffin Books) Penguin Young Readers Group.

Wild, Margaret. This Little Piggy Went Dancing. Niland, Deborah, illus. 2014. (ENG.). 24p. (J). (-k). 15.99 *(978-1-74331-511-8(2))* Allen & Unwin AUS. Dist: Independent Pubs. Group.

Wilde, Gloria. Lucifer: Good Angel Gone Bad. Bauer, John, illus. 2007. 36p. 14.95 *(978-1-57258-462-4(9)*, 945-6323) TEACH Services, Inc.

Wilden, Beverley. Who Said Monsters Don't Exist? 2010. (Illus.). 32p. pap. 12.99 *(978-1-4490-7313-8(1))* AuthorHouse.

Wilder, Beth. Bugs in Shoes, 1 vol. 2012. (ENG., Illus.). 64p. (J). 14.99 *(978-0-7643-3967-7(2)*, 9780764339677) Schiffer Publishing, Ltd.

Wildman, Dale. Do You Know the Way to Find an A? A Rhyming ABC Book. Sisung, Peter, illus. 2006. 24p. (J). per. 2.99 *(978-1-59958-002-9(0))* Journey Stone Creations, LLC.

Wilkinson, Thomas M. A Forest Through the Trees. 2009. 87p. pap. 12.99 *(978-0-557-17693-9(X))* Lulu Pr., Inc.

Wilkinson, William L. Glorious Praise. Blackmon, Kim, illus. 2012. 32p. pap. 10.00 *(978-1-62050-019-4(1))* Angels of Agape.

Wilks, Mike. The Weather Works. Wilks, Mike, illus. 2016. (ENG., Illus.). 32p. (J). 17.95 *(978-0-7649-7538-7(2))* Pomegranate Communications, Inc.

Willard, Nancy. A Starlit Snowfall. Pinkney, Jerry, illus. 2011. (ENG.). 32p. (J). (gr. -1-3). 6.99 *(978-0-316-18366-6(0))* Little Brown & Co.

Willems, Mo, illus. Nanette's Baguette. 2016. (ENG.). 40p. (J). (gr. -1-k). 17.99 *(978-1-4847-2286-2(8))* Disney Pr.

Williams, Becky. Ten Little Mermaids. East, Jacqueline, illus. 2007. (Story Book Ser.). 22p. (J). (gr. -1). bds. *(978-1-84666-375-8(X)*, Tide Mill Pr.) Top That! Publishing PLC.

Williams, Brenda. Millie's Chickens. Cis, Valeria, illus. 40p. (J). (gr. k-4). 2015. pap. 8.99 *(978-1-78285-083-0(X))* 2014. 16.99 *(978-1-78285-082-3(1))* Barefoot Bks., Inc.

—Outdoor Opposites. Oldfield, Rachel, illus. 2015. 32p. (J). (gr. -1-2). 9.99 *(978-1-78285-095-3(3))* Barefoot Bks., Inc.

Williams, Carol Lynch. Glimpse. 2010. (ENG.). 496p. (YA). (gr. 9-18). 16.99 *(978-1-4169-9730-6(X)*, Simon & Schuster/Paula Wiseman Bks.) Simon & Schuster/Paula Wiseman Bks.

Williams, Carol Lynch & Gregg, L. B. Glimpse. Gregg, Anna, photos by. 2012. (ENG., Illus.). 512p. (YA). (gr. 9). pap. 12.99 *(978-1-4169-9731-3(8)*, Simon & Schuster/Paula Wiseman Bks.) Simon & Schuster/Paula Wiseman Bks.

Williams, David K. The Picnic. Ovresat, Laura, illus. 2006. (Green Light Readers Level 1 Ser.). (gr. -1-1). 13.95 *(978-0-7569-7209-7(4))* Perfection Learning Corp.

Williams, David K. & Williams, David. The Picnic. Ovresat, Laura, illus. 2006. (Green Light Readers Level 1 Ser.). (ENG.). 24p. (J). (gr. -1-3). pap. 3.95 *(978-0-15-205782-4(X))* Houghton Mifflin Harcourt Publishing Co.

—Tick Tock. Ovresat, Laura, illus. 2006. (Green Light Readers Level 1 Ser.). (ENG.). 24p. (J). (gr. -1-3). pap. 3.95 *(978-0-15-205605-6(X))* Houghton Mifflin Harcourt Publishing Co.

Williams, Dawn. Very Little Venus & the Very Friendly Fly. Chou, Joey, illus. 2007. 48p. (J). 15.00 *(978-0-9770783-2-5(9))* SunriseHouse Pubs.

Williams, Delphine. Freckles with All the Speckles. 2008. 36p. pap. 24.95 *(978-1-60703-402-5(6))* America Star Bks.

Williams, Harland, illus. The Kid with Too Many Nightmares. 2004. (J). *(978-0-8431-1582-6(3)*, Price Stern Sloan) Penguin Publishing Group.

Williams, Lisa E. The Christmas Hippo. 2012. (Illus.). 28p. pap. 16.95 *(978-1-4497-2474-0(4)*, WestBow Pr.) Author Solutions, Inc.

Williams, Nate & Snow, Virginia Brimhall. Spring Walk, 1 vol. 2015. (ENG., Illus.). 32p. (J). (gr. 2-3). 16.99 *(978-1-4236-3879-7(4))* Gibbs Smith, Publisher.

Williams, Rozanne Lanczak. Purple Snerd. 2003. (Green Light Readers — Level 2 Ser.). (gr. k-3). lib. bdg. 13.50 *(978-0-613-66373-1(X)*, Turtleback) Turtleback Bks.

Williams, Sam. That's Love. Moriuchi, Mique, illus. 2006. 24p. (J). (gr. -1-3). 16.95 *(978-0-8234-2028-5(0))* Holiday Hse., Inc.

Williams, Sandra. Look with Me. 2012. (Illus.). 40p. pap. 20.99 *(978-1-4772-1318-6(X))* AuthorHouse.

Williams, Sue. I Went Walking. Vivas, Julie, illus. 2014. 32p. pap. 27.00 *(978-1-61003-230-8(6))* Center for the Collaborative Classroom.

—I Went Walking. Vivas, Julie, illus. 2004. (J). (gr. -1-2). audio compact disk 28.95 *(978-1-59112-720-8(3))* 2003. pap. 39.95 incl. audio compact disk *(978-1-59112-721-5(1))* 2003. pap. 39.95 incl. audio compact disk *(978-1-59112-721-5(1))* Live Oak Media.

—Let's Go Visiting. Vivas, Julie, illus. 2003. (ENG.). 32p. (J). (gr. k — 1). bds. 6.95 *(978-0-15-204638-5(0))* Houghton Mifflin Harcourt Publishing Co.

Williams, Vera B. Amber Was Brave, Essie Was Smart. Williams, Vera B., illus. 2004. (ENG., Illus.). 72p. (J). (gr. 2-7). reprint ed. pap. 7.99 *(978-0-06-057182-5(9)*, Greenwillow Bks.) HarperCollins Pubs.

Willis, Jeanne. The Cow Tripped over the Moon: a Nursery Rhyme Emergency. Stewart, Joel, illus. 2015. (ENG.). 32p. (J). (gr. -1-2). 15.99 *(978-0-7636-7402-1(8))* Candlewick Pr.

—Hippospotamus. Ross, Tony, illus. 2012. (Andersen Press Picture Bks). (ENG.). 32p. (J). (gr. -1-3). 16.95 *(978-1-4677-0316-1(8))* Lerner Publishing Group.

—I'M Sure I Saw a Dinosaur. Reynolds, Adrian, illus. 2011. (Andersen Press Picture Books Ser.). 16.95 *(978-0-7613-8093-1(0))* Andersen Pr. GBR. Dist: Lerner Publishing Group.

—Slug Needs a Hug! Ross, Tony, illus. 2015. (ENG.). 32p. (J). (gr. -1-3). 17.99 *(978-1-4677-9317-9(5))*; 17.99 *(978-1-4677-9309-4(4))* Lerner Publishing Group.

—Upside down Babies. Reynolds, Adrian, illus. 2014. (ENG.). 32p. (J). (gr. -1-3). 16.95 *(978-1-4677-3424-0(1))* Lerner Publishing Group.

—We're Going to a Party! Ross, Tony, illus. (ENG.). 16p. (J). 2015. (-k). pap. 14.99 *(978-1-84939-456-7(3))* 2013. (gr. -1-k). 12.99 *(978-1-84939-122-1(X))* Andersen Pr. GBR. Dist: Independent Pubs. Group.

—Who's in the Loo? Reynolds, Adrian, illus. 10th ed. 2016. (ENG.). 16p. (J). (— 1). bds. 9.99 *(978-1-78344-420-5(7))* Andersen Pr. GBR. Dist: Independent Pubs. Group.

—The Wind in the Wallows. Ross, Tony, illus. 2013. (ENG.). 32p. (J). (gr. -1-k). pap. 9.99 *(978-1-84939-453-6(9))* Andersen Pr. GBR. Dist: Independent Pubs. Group.

Wilson, Sarah. Do Not Wake Jake. Johnson, Meredith, illus. 2006. (Step-By-Step Readers Ser.). (J). *(978-1-59939-059-8(0)*, Reader's Digest Young Families, Inc.) Studio Fun International.

Wilson, Bob. Stanley Bagshaw & the Twenty Two Ton Whale. 2006. (Stanley Bagshaw Ser.). (Illus.). 32p. (J). (gr. k-2). pap. 6.95 *(978-1-903015-50-6(2))* Barn Owl Bks, London GBR. Dist: Independent Pubs. Group.

Wilson, Karma. Animal Strike at the Zoo - It's True! Spengler, Margaret, illus. 2006. (ENG.). 32p. (J). (gr. -1-1). 16.99 *(978-0-06-057502-1(6))* HarperCollins Pubs.

—Bear Counts. Chapman, Jane, illus. 2015. (Bear Bks.). (ENG.). 32p. (J). (gr. -1-2). 16.99 *(978-1-4424-8092-6(0)*, McElderry, Margaret K. Bks.) McElderry, Margaret K. Bks.

—Bear Feels Scared. Chapman, Jane, illus. 2011. (Bear Bks.). (ENG.). 34p. (J). (gr. -1 — 1). bds. 7.99 *(978-1-4424-2755-6(8)*, Little Simon) Little Simon.

—Bear Feels Scared. Chapman, Jane, illus. 2008. (Bear Bks.). (ENG.). 40p. (J). (gr. -1-3). 17.99 *(978-0-689-85986-1(4)*, McElderry, Margaret K. Bks.) McElderry, Margaret K. Bks.

—Bear Feels Sick. Chapman, Jane, illus. 2012. (Bear Bks.). (ENG.). 34p. (J). (gr. -1-2). bds. 7.99 *(978-1-4424-4093-7(7)*, Little Simon) Little Simon.

—Bear Feels Sick. Chapman, Jane, illus. 2007. (Bear Bks.). (ENG.). 40p. (J). (gr. -1-3). 17.99 *(978-0-689-85985-4(6)*, McElderry, Margaret K. Bks.) McElderry, Margaret K. Bks.

—Bear Sees Colors. Chapman, Jane, illus. 2014. (Bear Bks.). (ENG.). 32p. (J). (gr. -1-2). 16.99 *(978-1-4424-6536-7(0)*, McElderry, Margaret K. Bks.) McElderry, Margaret K. Bks.

—Bear Snores On. Chapman, Jane, illus. 2005. (Bear Bks.). (ENG.). 34p. (J). (gr. -1-k). bds. 7.99 *(978-1-4169-0272-0(4)*, Little Simon) Little Simon.

—Bear Stays up for Christmas. Chapman, Jane, illus. 2011. (Bear Bks.). (ENG.). 34p. (J). (gr. -1 — 1). bds. 7.99 *(978-1-4424-2790-7(6)*, Little Simon) Little Simon.

—Bear Stays up for Christmas. Chapman, Jane, illus. 2004. (Bear Bks.). (ENG.). 40p. (J). (gr. -1-3). 17.99 *(978-0-689-85278-7(9)*, McElderry, Margaret K. Bks.) McElderry, Margaret K. Bks.

—Bear Wants More. Chapman, Jane, illus. 2008. (Bear Bks.). (ENG.). 34p. (J). (gr. -1-2). bds. 7.99 (978-1-4169-4922-0(4), Little Simon) Little Simon.
—Bear Wants More. Chapman, Jane, illus. 2003. (Bear Bks.). (ENG.). 40p. (J). (gr. -1-3). 17.99 (978-0-689-84509-3(X), McElderry, Margaret K. Bks.) McElderry, Margaret K. Bks.
—Bear's Loose Tooth. Chapman, Jane, illus. 2014. (Bear Bks.). (ENG.). 34p. (J). (gr. -1-k). bds. 7.99 (978-1-4424-8936-3(7), Little Simon) Little Simon.
—Bear's Loose Tooth. Chapman, Jane, illus. 2011. (Bear Bks.). (ENG.). 40p. (J). (gr. -1-3). 17.99 (978-1-4169-5855-0(X), McElderry, Margaret K. Bks.) McElderry, Margaret K. Bks.
—Bear's New Friend. Chapman, Jane, illus. 2009. (Bear Bks.). (ENG.). 34p. (J). (gr. -1-2). bds. 7.99 (978-1-4169-5438-5(4), Little Simon) Little Simon.
—Bear's New Friend. Chapman, Jane, illus. 2006. (Bear Bks.). (ENG.). 40p. (J). (gr. -1-3). 17.99 (978-0-689-85984-7(8), McElderry, Margaret K. Bks.) McElderry, Margaret K. Bks.
—Big Bear, Small Mouse. Chapman, Jane, illus. 2016. (Bear Bks.). (ENG.). 32p. (J). (gr. -1-2). 16.99 (978-1-4814-5971-6(6), McElderry, Margaret K. Bks.) McElderry, Margaret K. Bks.
—The Cow Loves Cookies. Hall, Marcellus, illus. 2010. (ENG.). 40p. (J). (gr. -1-3). 17.99 (978-1-4169-4206-1(8), McElderry, Margaret K. Bks.) McElderry, Margaret K. Bks.
—Dormouse Dreams. Liwska, Renata, illus. 2017. (ENG.). 40p. (J). (gr. -1-k). 16.99 (978-1-4231-7874-3(2)) Disney Pr.
—Duddle Puck: The Puddle Duck. Hall, Marcellus, illus. 2015. (ENG.). 40p. (J). (gr. -1-3). 17.99 (978-1-4424-4927-5(6), McElderry, Margaret K. Bks.) McElderry, Margaret K. Bks.
—A Frog in the Bog. Rankin, Joan, illus. (ENG.). 32p. (J). (gr. -1-3). 2007. 7.99 (978-1-4169-2727-3(1)) 2003. 17.99 (978-0-689-84081-4(0)) McElderry, Margaret K. Bks. (McElderry, Margaret K. Bks.).
—Hilda Must Be Dancing. Watts, Suzanne, illus. (ENG.). 32p. (J). (gr. -1-3). 2008. 7.99 (978-1-4169-5083-7(4)) 2004. 17.99 (978-0-689-84788-2(2)) McElderry, Margaret K. Bks. (McElderry, Margaret K. Bks.).
—Hogwash! McMullan, Jim, illus. 2011. (ENG.). 40p. (J). (gr. -1-3). 17.99 (978-0-316-98840-7(5)) Little, Brown Bks. for Young Readers.
—Horseplay! McMullan, Jim, illus. 2012. (ENG.). 40p. (gr. -1-3). 16.99 (978-0-316-93842-6(4)) Little Brown & Co.
—How to Bake an American Pie. Colón, Raúl, illus. 2007. (ENG.). 40p. (J). (gr. -1-3). 18.99 (978-0-689-86506-0(6), McElderry, Margaret K. Bks.) McElderry, Margaret K. Bks.
—Mama Always Comes Home. Dyer, Brooke, illus. 32p. (J). (gr. -1-1). 2007. (ENG.). pap. 6.99 (978-0-06-057507-6(7), Harper Trophy) 2005. 15.99 (978-0-06-057505-2(0)) HarperCollins Pubs.
—Mama, Why? Mendez, Simon, illus. 2011. (ENG.). 40p. (J). (gr. -1-2). 16.99 (978-1-4169-4205-4(X), McElderry, Margaret K. Bks.) McElderry, Margaret K. Bks.
—Moose Tracks! Davis, Jack E., illus. 2006. (ENG.). 32p. (J). (gr. -1-2). 17.99 (978-0-689-83437-0(3), McElderry, Margaret K. Bks.) McElderry, Margaret K. Bks.
—Never, Ever Shout in a Zoo. Cushman, Douglas, illus. 2004. (ENG.). 32p. (J). (gr. -1-3). 16.99 (978-0-316-98564-2(3)) Little, Brown Bks. for Young Readers.
—Princess Me. Unzner, Christa, illus. 2007. (ENG.). 32p. (J). (gr. -1-3). 16.99 (978-1-4169-4098-2(7), McElderry, Margaret K. Bks.) McElderry, Margaret K. Bks.
—Sleepyhead. Segal, John, illus. 2012. (Classic Board Bks.). (ENG.). 32p. (J). (gr. -1 — 1). bds. 7.99 (978-1-4424-3433-2(3), Little Simon) Little Simon.
—Sleepyhead. Segal, John, illus. 2006. (ENG.). 32p. (J). (gr. -1-2). 16.99 (978-1-4169-1241-5(X), McElderry, Margaret K. Bks.) McElderry, Margaret K. Bks.
—Whopper Cake. Hillenbrand, Will, illus. 2007. (ENG.). 32p. (J). (gr. -1-3). 17.99 (978-0-689-83844-6(1), McElderry, Margaret K. Bks.) McElderry, Margaret K. Bks.
Wilson, Kris E. & Maurer, Toby. How Putter Learned His ABC's: An alphabet Book for Your Littlest Golfer. 2010. 17.00 (978-0-578-05153-6(2)) Sandy Putter Pr.
Wilson, Land. Sofia's Dream. O'Malley, Judy, ed. Cornelison, Sue, illus. 2010. (ENG.). 40p. (J). (gr. -1-2). 18.95 (978-0-9829938-1-1(1)) March 4th, Inc.
Wilson, Porcia D. My Pink Friend: A Rhyming Love Story. 2012. 44p. pap. 18.99 (978-1-4685-6852-3(3)) AuthorHouse.
Wilson, Sarah. Love & Kisses. Sweet, Melissa, illus. 2014. (ENG.). 24p. (J). (— 1). bds. 6.99 (978-0-7636-7391-8(9)) Candlewick Pr.
Wilson, Zachary. A Circle in the Sky. Adinolfi, JoAnn, illus. (Rookie Ready to Learn Ser.). (J). 2011. (ENG.). 40p. pap. 5.95 (978-0-531-26746-2(6)) 2011. 40p. (gr. -1-k). lib. bdg. 23.00 (978-0-531-26446-1(7)) 2006. (ENG.). 32p. (gr. k-2). lib. bdg. 19.50 (978-0-531-12570-0(X)) Scholastic Library Publishing. (Children's Pr.).
—Un Circulo en el Cielo. Adinolfi, JoAnn, illus. 2011. (Rookie Ready to Learn Español Ser.). (SPA.). 40p. (J). pap. 5.95 (978-0-531-26791-2(1), Children's Pr.) Scholastic Library Publishing.
Wilson, Zachary & Adinolfi, JoAnn. Un Circulo en el Cielo. Adinolfi, JoAnn, illus. 2011. (Rookie Ready to Learn Español Ser.). (SPA., Illus.). 40p. (J). lib. bdg. 23.00 (978-0-531-26123-1(9), Children's Pr.) Scholastic Library Publishing.
Winburn, William B. Hide-And-Peek. 2010. (J). (978-85-312-5235-8(0)) Children's Pr., Ltd.
Windolph, Maria Theresa. Sugar Bear. 2008. 16p. pap. 24.95 (978-1-60474-813-0(3)) America Star Bks.
Wing, Natasha. The Night Before Class Picture Day. 2016. (Night Before Ser.). lib. bdg. 14.75 (978-0-606-38834-4(6)) Turtleback Bks.
—The Night Before First Grade. Zemke, Deborah, illus. (Night Before Ser.). (ENG.). 32p. (J). (gr. k-1). 2014. 12.99 (978-0-448-48256-9(8)) 2005. pap. 4.99 (978-0-448-43747-7(3)) Penguin Young Readers Group. (Grosset & Dunlap).
—The Night Before Hanukkah. Wummer, Amy, illus. 2014. (Night Before Ser.). (ENG.). 32p. (J). (gr. -1-k). 4.99 (978-0-448-48140-1(5), Grosset & Dunlap) Penguin Young Readers Group.
—The Night Before Hanukkah. 2014. (Night Before Ser.). lib. bdg. 13.55 (978-0-606-36160-6(X)) Turtleback Bks.
—The Night Before Kindergarten. Durrell, Julie, illus. 2014. (Night Before Ser.). (ENG.). 32p. (J). (gr. -1-k). 12.99 (978-0-448-48255-2(X), Grosset & Dunlap) Penguin Young Readers Group.
—The Night Before My Birthday. Wummer, Amy, illus. 2014. (Night Before Ser.). (ENG.). 32p. (J). (gr. -1-k). 4.99 (978-0-448-48000-8(X), Grosset & Dunlap) Penguin Young Readers Group.
—The Night Before My Birthday. 2014. (Night Before Ser.). lib. bdg. 14.75 (978-0-606-34133-2(1), Turtleback) Turtleback Bks.
—The Night Before Preschool. Wummer, Amy, illus. 2011. (Night Before Ser.). (ENG.). 32p. (J). (gr. -1-k). pap. 4.99 (978-0-448-45451-1(3), Grosset & Dunlap) Penguin Young Readers Group.
—The Night Before St. Patrick's Day. Wummer, Amy, illus. 2009. (Night Before Ser.). (ENG.). 32p. (J). (gr. -1-3). pap. 4.99 (978-0-448-44852-7(1), Grosset & Dunlap) Penguin Young Readers Group.
—The Night Before the Snow Day. Wummer, Amy, illus. 2016. (Night Before Ser.). (ENG.). 32p. (J). (-k). pap. 4.99 (978-0-399-53942-8(5), Grosset & Dunlap) Penguin Young Readers Group.
—The Night Before the Tooth Fairy. Newman, Barbara Johansen, illus. 2003. (Night Before Ser.). (ENG.). 32p. (J). (gr. -1-3). pap. 4.99 (978-0-448-43252-6(8), Grosset & Dunlap) Penguin Young Readers Group.
Wing, Natasha & dePaola, Tomie. The Night Before the Fourth of July. Wummer, Amy, illus. 2015. (Night Before Ser.). (ENG.). 32p. (J). (gr. -1-k). bds. 4.99 (978-0-448-48712-0(8), Grosset & Dunlap) Penguin Young Readers Group.
Winn, L. B. Butterpod Jerome & the Planet of Gabool. Winn, L. B., illus. 2007. (Illus.). (J). pap. 18.95 (978-0-9791884-0-4(7)) Winn, Lynnette.
Winnette, Sandy. A Snow Angel Story Book: Little Beth & the Snow Angel. 2008. 108p. pap. 11.99 (978-1-4343-8133-0(1)) AuthorHouse.
Winslow, Tim, illus. The Kingdom of Avalon. 2005. 48p. (J). (978-0-9748505-0-4(0)) Winslow's Art.
Winters, Ben H. Literally Disturbed No. 1: Tales to Keep You up at Night. Watkins, Adam F., illus. 2013. (ENG.). 64p. (J). (gr. 3-7). 9.99 (978-0-8431-7194-5(4), Price Stern Sloan) Penguin Young Readers Group.
Winters, Kari-Lynn. No-Matter-What Friend, 1 vol. Pratt, Pierre, illus. 2014. (ENG.). 32p. (J). (gr. k-2). 16.95 (978-1-896580-83-8(1)) Tradewind Bks. CAN. Dist: Orca Bk. Pubs. USA.
Winters, Kari-Lynn, et al. Stinky Skunk Mel. George, Kallie, ed. 2014. (ENG., Illus.). 32p. (J). (gr. -1-3). 15.95 (978-1-897476-83-3(3)) Simply Read Bks. CAN. Dist: Ingram Publisher Services.
Winters, Kay. Voices from the Oregon Trail. Day, Larry, illus. 2014. (ENG.). 48p. (J). (gr. 2-4). 17.99 (978-0-8037-3775-4(0), Dial Bks) Penguin Young Readers Group.
Winthrop, Elizabeth. Dumpy la Rue. Lewin, Betsy, illus. rev. ed. 2004. (ENG.). 40p. (J). (gr. -1-3). reprint ed. pap. 8.99 (978-0-8050-7535-9(6), 9780805075359, Holt, Henry & Co. Bks. For Young Readers) Holt, Henry & Co.
Winthrop, Elizabeth & Winthrop. Dancing Granny, 1 vol. Murdocca, Sal, illus. 2003. (ENG.). 32p. (J). 16.95 (978-0-7614-5141-9(2)) Marshall Cavendish Corp.
Wise, William. Ten Sly Piranhas: A Counting Story in Reverse (A Tale of Wickedness - And Worse!) Chess, Victoria, illus. 2004. (ENG.). 32p. (J). (gr. -1-k). pap. 5.99 (978-0-14-240074-6(2), Puffin Books) Penguin Young Readers Group.
Wishinsky, Frieda. Jennifer Jones Won't Leave Me Alone. Layton, Neal, illus. 2005. (Carolrhoda Picture Bks.). 32p. (J). (gr. -1-3). per. 6.95 (978-1-57505-921-1(5)); (gr. k-2). 15.95 (978-0-87614-921-8(2)) Lerner Publishing Group.
Wissinger, Tamera Will. Gone Camping: A Novel in Verse. Cordell, Matthew, illus. 2017. (ENG.). 112p. (J). (gr. 1-4). 15.99 (978-0-544-63873-0(5), HMH Books For Young Readers) Houghton Mifflin Harcourt Publishing Co.
—This Old Band. Loveridge, Matt, illus. 2014. (ENG.). 32p. (J). (gr. -1-k). 16.95 (978-1-62873-595-6(3), Sky Pony Pr.) Skyhorse Publishing Co., Inc.
Wissinger, Tamera Will & Long, Earlene R. Gone Fishing: A Novel. Cordell, Matthew & Brown, Richard, illus. (ENG.). 128p. (J). 2015. (gr. 5-7). pap. 6.99 (978-0-544-43931-3(7), HMH Books For Young Readers) 2013. (gr. 1-4). 15.99 (978-0-547-82011-8(9)) Houghton Mifflin Harcourt Publishing Co.
Witte, Anna. El Loro Tico Tango. Witte, Anna, illus. 2011. (SPA., Illus.). 24p. (J). (gr. -1-1). 9.99 (978-1-84686-670-8(7)) Barefoot Bks., Inc.
—The Parrot Tico Tango. 2005. (ENG., Illus.). 24p. (J). (gr. -1-3). 6.99 (978-1-905236-11-4(5)) Barefoot Bks., Inc.
—The Parrot Tico Tango. Witte, Anna, illus. 2005. (Illus.). 24p. (J). (gr. k-3). 15.99 (978-1-84148-243-9(9)) Barefoot Bks., Inc.
Witte, Anna & Amador, Brian. The Parrot Tico Tango. Witte, Anna, illus. 2011. (ENG., Illus.). 24p. (J). (gr. -1-2). 9.99 (978-1-84686-669-2(3)) Barefoot Bks., Inc.
Wojtusik, Elizabeth. Kitty Up! Yoshikawa, Sachiko, illus. 2008. (J). (978-0-8037-3045-8(4), Dial) Penguin Publishing Group.
Wolf, Allan. New Found Land: Lewis & Clark's Voyage of Discovery. 2007. (ENG., Illus.). 512p. (YA). (gr. 7-9). per. 14.99 (978-0-7636-3288-5(0)) Candlewick Pr.
Wolf, Linda. Cozy Kitty, 1 vol. 2009. 43p. pap. 24.95 (978-1-61546-636-8(3)) America Star Bks.
Wolf, Mária. Maggy Cans. 2012. 52p. (gr. 4-6). pap. 11.95 (978-1-4772-8093-5(6)) AuthorHouse.
Wolf, Sallie. Truck Stuck. Davies, Andy Robert, illus. (ENG.). (J). (— 1). 2017. 28p. bds. 7.99 (978-1-58089-781-5(9)) 2009. 32p. pap. 7.95 (978-1-58089-257-5(4)) Charlesbridge Publishing, Inc.
Wolfe, Greg. Shmelf the Hanukkah Elf. McWilliam, Howard, illus. 2016. (ENG.). 32p. (J). 16.99 (978-1-61963-521-0(6), 9781619635210, Bloomsbury USA Childrens) Bloomsbury Publishing USA.
Wolff, Ashley. The Baby Chicks Are Singing: Sing along in English & Spanish! Wolff, Ashley, illus. 2005. (ENG., Illus.). 22p. (J). (gr. -1 — 1). bds. 7.99 (978-0-316-06732-4(6)) Little, Brown Bks. for Young Readers.
Wolff, Virginia Euwer. This Full House. 2009. (Make Lemonade Trilogy: No. 3). (ENG.). 496p. (YA). (gr. 9-18). 17.99 (978-0-06-158304-9(9), HarperTeen) HarperCollins Pubs.
—True Believer. 2004. (Make Lemonade Trilogy: No. 2). 272p. (J). (gr. 7-18). pap. 38.00 incl. audio (978-0-8072-2283-6(6), Listening Library) Random Hse. Audio Publishing Group.
Wood, Audrey. A Dog Needs a Bone! 2007. (J). pap. (978-0-545-00006-2(8)) Blue Sky Pr.
—Piggy Pie Po. Wood, Don, illus. (ENG.). (J). 2016. 30p. (— 1). bds. 7.99 (978-0-544-79113-8(4), HMH Books For Young Readers) 2010. 32p. (gr. -1-3). 17.99 (978-0-15-202494-9(8)) Houghton Mifflin Harcourt Publishing Co.
—Silly Sally. braille ed. 2004. (J). (gr. 1). spiral bd., bds. (978-0-616-01864-4(9)) Canadian National Institute for the Blind/Institut National Canadien pour les Aveugles.
—Silly Sally: Lap-Sized Board Book. 2007. (ENG., Illus.). 30p. (J). (gr. -1-3). bds. 11.99 (978-0-15-205902-6(4)) Houghton Mifflin Harcourt Publishing Co.
—Ten Little Fish. Wood, Bruce, illus. 2004. (ENG.). 40p. (J). (gr. -1-k). 17.99 (978-0-439-63569-1(1), Blue Sky Pr., The) Scholastic, Inc.
Wood, Carol. Grandma Carol's Book of Stories in Rhyme. 2009. (Illus.). 48p. pap. 19.49 (978-1-4389-5413-4(1)) AuthorHouse.
Woodend, Rosetta. Sammy Salmon's Big Adventure: The lifecycle of a Salmon, 1. 2005. (Illus.). 12p. (J). per. 9.95 (978-0-9760342-0-9(4)) Animal Tracks Pr.
Woodruff, Liza, illus. What Time Is It? 2005. (My First Reader Ser.). (ENG.). 32p. (J). (gr. k-4). per. 3.95 (978-0-516-25279-7(8), Children's Pr.) Scholastic Library Publishing.
Woodruff, Liza & Demar, Regier. What Time Is It? Woodruff, Liza, illus. 2005. (My First Reader Ser.). (ENG., Illus.). 32p. (J). (gr. k-1). 18.50 (978-0-516-25180-6(5), Children's Pr.) Scholastic Library Publishing.
Woodward, Caroline. Singing Away the Dark. Morstad, Julie, illus. 2011. (ENG.). 36p. (J). (gr. -1-3). 16.95 (978-1-897476-41-3(8)) Simply Read Bks. CAN. Dist: Ingram Publisher Services.
Woolf, Julia. Jack's Room. 2009. (Rookie Preschool Ser.). (ENG.). 24p. (J). (gr. -1). 23.00 (978-0-531-24400-5(8)); pap. 6.95 (978-0-531-24575-0(6)) Scholastic Library Publishing. (Children's Pr.).
Worth, Bonnie. The Cat in the Hat - Cooking with the Cat. Moroney, Christopher, illus. 2003. (Step into Reading Ser.). (ENG.). 32p. (J). (gr. -1-1). pap. 3.99 (978-0-375-82494-4(4), 53560581, Random Hse. Bks. for Young Readers) Random Hse. Children's Bks.
Worthen, Diane. Oliver's Wish: A Tale from the Garden. 2012. 36p. pap. 20.99 (978-1-4685-4005-5(X)) AuthorHouse.
Wreggelsworth, Irene. The Funny, Naughty Bunny: A Bilingual Book in English & German. Piccione, Dana, illus. 2010. (ENG.). 102p. pap. 26.99 (978-1-4537-2122-3(3)) CreateSpace Independent Publishing Platform.
Wright, Blanche Fisher, illus. The Real Mother Goose. 2017. (First Avenue Classics Ser.). (ENG.). 214p. (gr. -1-4). 19.99 **(978-1-5124-6673-7(5)**, First Avenue Editions) Lerner Publishing Group.
Wright, Maureen. Barnyard Fun, 0 vols. De Tagyos, Paul Ratz, illus. 2013. (ENG.). 24p. (J). (gr. -1-3). 16.99 (978-1-4778-1643-1(7), 9781477816431, Amazon Children's Publishing) Amazon Publishing.
—Earth Day, Birthday!, 0 vols. Kim, Violet, illus. 2012. (ENG.). 32p. (J). (gr. k-3). 17.99 (978-0-7614-6109-8(4), 9780761461098, Amazon Children's Publishing) Amazon Publishing.
—Sleep, Big Bear, Sleep!, 0 vols. Hillenbrand, Will, illus. 2009. (ENG.). 32p. (J). (gr. -1-3). 16.99 (978-0-7614-5560-8(4), 9780761455608, Amazon Children's Publishing) Amazon Publishing.
—Sneeze, Big Bear, Sneeze!, 0 vols. Hillenbrand, Will, illus. 2011. (ENG.). 32p. (J). (gr. -1-3). 16.99 (978-0-7614-5959-0(6), 9780761459590, Amazon Children's Publishing) Amazon Publishing.
Wuehr, Tina L. Field Dance. Brown, Mari, illus. 2005. 18p. (J). (gr. -1-3). (978-0-9739962-0-3(X)) Wuehr, Tina.
—Neela Potts Has Lots of Knots. Brown, Mari, illus. 2008. 30p. (J). (gr. -1-3). (978-0-9739962-3-4(4)) Wuehr, Tina.
Wundram, Bill. Finnius: The Tale of a Lost Little Elephant. Tucker, Eric, illus. 2003. (J). (978-1-59152-011-5(8), Sweetgrass Bks.) Farcountry Pr.
Xinran, Xinran & Mother's Bridge of Love Staff. Motherbridge of Love. Masse, Josée, illus. 2013. (ENG.). 32p. (J). (gr. k-3). 7.99 (978-1-78285-040-3(6)) Barefoot Bks., Inc.
Xiong, Kim, illus. Paper Horse. 2008. (ENG & CHI.). 37p. (J). 18.95 (978-1-60603-003-5(5)) Better Chinese LLC.
Yackle, Deanne. Jenny & Me. 2005. (J). lib. bdg. (978-0-9725485-4-0(8)) Waterfall Ridge.
Yankovic, Al, pseud. My New Teacher & Me! Hargis, Wes, illus. 2013. (ENG.). 40p. (J). (gr. -1-3). 17.99 (978-0-06-219203-5(5)) HarperCollins Pubs.
—When I Grow Up. Hargis, Wes, illus. 2011. (ENG.). 32p. (J). (gr. -1-3). 17.99 (978-0-06-192691-4(4)) HarperCollins Pubs.
Yarrow, Peter & Lipton, Lenny. Puff, the Magic Dragon. Puybaret, Eric, illus. 2007. (ENG.). 24p. (J). 16.95 (978-1-4027-5279-7(2)); 16.95 (978-1-4027-5219-3(9)) Sterling Publishing Co., Inc.
Yates, Gene. The Dragon Opposites Book. 2005. (Illus.). 14p. (J). (978-1-58865-283-6(1)) Kidsbooks, LLC.
Yates, Gene, illus. The Chameleon Colors Book. 2006. (J). (978-1-58865-361-1(7)) Kidsbooks, LLC.
—The Dragon Opposites Book. 2006. (J). (978-1-58865-362-8(5)) Kidsbooks, LLC.
—The Giraffe Numbers Book. 2006. (J). (978-1-58865-364-2(1)) Kidsbooks, LLC.
Yates, Gene & Frank, Thomas. What Can Simon Be? Yates, Gene, illus. 2006. (Illus.). (J). (978-1-58865-366-6(8)) Kidsbooks, LLC.
Yates, Philip. A Pirate's Twelve Days of Christmas. Serra, Sebastià, illus. 2015. (ENG.). 32p. (J). (gr. -1-1). pap. 6.95 (978-1-4549-1682-6(6)) Sterling Publishing Co., Inc.
Yee, Wong Herbert. Eek! There's a Mouse in the House, 1 vol. 2013. (ENG., Illus.). 24p. (J). (gr. -1-3). audio compact disk 10.99 (978-0-544-02282-9(3)) Houghton Mifflin Harcourt Publishing Co.
—Hamburger Heaven. 2005. (ENG., Illus.). 32p. (J). (gr. -1-3). reprint ed. 5.95 (978-0-618-54885-9(8)) Houghton Mifflin Harcourt Publishing Co.
—My Autumn Book. Yee, Wong Herbert, illus. 2015. (ENG., Illus.). 32p. (J). (gr. -1-1). 14.99 (978-0-8050-9922-5(0), 9780805099225, Holt, Henry & Co. Bks. For Young Readers) Holt, Henry & Co.
—Summer Days & Nights. Yee, Wong Herbert, illus. 2012. (ENG., Illus.). 32p. (J). (gr. -1-1). 16.99 (978-0-8050-9078-9(9), 9780805090789, Holt, Henry & Co. Bks. For Young Readers) Holt, Henry & Co.
—Tracks in the Snow. Yee, Wong Herbert, illus. 2007. (ENG., Illus.). 32p. (J). (gr. -1-1). per. 7.99 (978-0-312-37134-0(9), 9780312371340) Square Fish.
Ying, Jonathan. Not Quite Black & White. Ying, Victoria, illus. 2016. 32p. (J). (gr. -1-3). 14.99 (978-0-06-238066-1(4)) HarperCollins Pubs.
Yolen, Jane. Come to the Fairies' Ball. Lippincott, Gary, illus. 2009. (ENG.). 32p. (J). (gr. 2-4). 17.95 (978-1-59078-464-8(2), Wordsong) Boyds Mills Pr.
—¿Cómo Aprenden los Colores los Dinosaurios? Teague, Mark, illus. 2006. (How Do Dinosaurs... Ser.).Tr. of How Do Dinosaurs Learn Their Colors? (SPA.). 12p. (J). (gr. -1-k). bds. 6.99 (978-0-439-87192-1(1), Scholastic en Espanol) Scholastic, Inc.
—Como Dicen Estoy Enojado los Dinosaurios? Teague, Mark, illus. 2014. (SPA.). 40p. (J). (gr. -1-k). pap. 6.99 (978-0-545-62780-1(X), Scholastic en Espanol) Scholastic, Inc.
—Creepy Monsters, Sleepy Monsters. Murphy, Kelly, illus. 2013. (ENG.). 32p. (J). (gr. -1-2). 5.99 (978-0-7636-6283-7(6)) Candlewick Pr.
—How Do Dinosaurs Choose Their Pets? Teague, Mark, illus. 2016. (ENG.). 40p. (J). (gr. -1-k). 16.99 (978-1-338-03278-9(X), Blue Sky Pr., The) Scholastic, Inc.
—How Do Dinosaurs Clean Their Rooms? Teague, Mark, illus. 2004. (How Do Dinosaurs... Ser.). (ENG.). 12p. (J). (gr. -1-k). bds. 6.99 (978-0-439-64950-6(1), Blue Sky Pr., The) Scholastic, Inc.
—How Do Dinosaurs Count to Ten? Teague, Mark, illus. 2004. (How Do Dinosaurs... Ser.). (ENG.). 12p. (J). (gr. -1-k). bds. 6.99 (978-0-439-64949-0(8), Blue Sky Pr., The) Scholastic, Inc.
—How Do Dinosaurs Eat Their Food? Teague, Mark, illus. 2005. (How Do Dinosaurs... ? Ser.). (ENG.). 40p. (J). (gr. -1-k). 16.99 (978-0-439-24102-1(2), Blue Sky Pr., The) Scholastic, Inc.
—How Do Dinosaurs Get Well Soon? Teague, Mark, illus. 2003. (How Do Dinosaurs... Ser.). (ENG.). 40p. (J). (gr. -1-3). 16.99 (978-0-439-24100-7(6), Blue Sky Pr., The) Scholastic, Inc.
—How Do Dinosaurs Go to School? Teague, Mark, illus. 2007. (How Do Dinosaurs... Ser.). (ENG.). 40p. (J). (gr. -1-k). 16.99 (978-0-439-02081-7(6)) Scholastic, Inc.
—How Do Dinosaurs Go to School? Teague, Mark, illus. 2011. (J). (gr. -1-3). 18.95 (978-0-545-19707-6(4)); 29.95 (978-0-545-19700-7(7)) Weston Woods Studios, Inc.
—How Do Dinosaurs Go to Sleep? Teague, Mark, illus. 2016. (How Do Dinosaurs... ? Ser.). (ENG.). 12p. (J). (— 1). bds. 6.99 (978-0-545-94120-4(2), Blue Sky Pr., The) Scholastic, Inc.
—How Do Dinosaurs Learn Their Colors? Teague, Mark, illus. 2006. (How Do Dinosaurs... Ser.). (ENG.). 12p. (J). (gr. -1-k). bds. 6.99 (978-0-439-85653-9(1), Blue Sky Pr., The) Scholastic, Inc.
—How Do Dinosaurs Love Their Cats? Teague, Mark, illus. 2010. (How Do Dinosaurs... ? Ser.). (ENG.). 6p. (J). (gr. -1-k). bds. 6.99 (978-0-545-15354-6(9)) Scholastic, Inc.
—How Do Dinosaurs Love Their Dogs? Teague, Mark, illus. 2010. (How Do Dinosaurs... Ser.). (ENG.). 6p. (J). (gr. -1-k). bds. 6.99 (978-0-545-15352-2(2)) Scholastic, Inc.
—How Do Dinosaurs Play with Their Friends? Teague, Mark, illus. 2006. (How Do Dinosaurs... Ser.). (ENG.). 12p. (J). (gr. -1-k). bds. 6.99 (978-0-439-85654-6(X), Blue Sky Pr., The) Scholastic, Inc.
—How Do Dinosaurs Say Good Night? Teague, Mark, illus. 2008. (How Do Dinosaurs... Ser.). (ENG.). (J). (gr. -1-3). 9.99 (978-0-545-09319-4(8)) Scholastic, Inc.
—How Do Dinosaurs Say Happy Birthday? Teague, Mark, illus. 2011. (How Do Dinosaurs... Ser.). (ENG.). 12p. (J). (gr. -1-k). bds. 6.99 (978-0-545-15353-9(0), Blue Sky Pr., The) Scholastic, Inc.
—How Do Dinosaurs Say Happy Chanukah? Teague, Mark, illus. 2012. (How Do Dinosaurs... ? Ser.). (ENG.). 40p. (J). (— 1). 16.99 (978-0-545-41677-1(9), Blue Sky Pr., The) Scholastic, Inc.
—How Do Dinosaurs Say I Love You? Teague, Mark, illus. (J). 2011. pap. (978-0-545-33076-3(9)) 2009. (ENG.). 40p. 16.99 (978-0-545-14314-1(4), Blue Sky Pr., The) Scholastic, Inc.
—How Do Dinosaurs Say I'm Mad? Teague, Mark, illus. 2013. (How Do Dinosaurs... ? Ser.). (ENG.). 40p. (J). (gr. -1-k). 16.99 (978-0-545-14315-8(2), Blue Sky Pr., The) Scholastic, Inc.
—How Do Dinosaurs Say Merry Christmas? Teague, Mark, illus. 2012. (How Do Dinosaurs... ? Ser.). (ENG.). 40p. (J). (gr. -1-k). 16.99 (978-0-545-41678-8(7), Blue Sky Pr., The) Scholastic, Inc.
—How Do Dinosaurs Stay Friends? Teague, Mark, illus. 2016. (ENG.). 40p. (J). (gr. -1-k). 16.99 (978-0-545-82934-2(8), Exhibit A) Scholastic, Inc.
—How Do Dinosaurs Stay Safe? Teague, Mark, illus. 2015. (ENG.). 40p. (J). (gr. -1-k). 16.99 (978-0-439-24104-5(9), Blue Sky Pr., The) Scholastic, Inc.
—My Father Knows the Names of Things. Jorisch, Stéphane, illus. 2010. (ENG.). 32p. (J). (gr. -1-3). 17.99 (978-1-4169-4895-7(3), Simon & Schuster Bks. For Young Readers) Simon & Schuster Bks. For Young Readers.
—The Scarecrow's Dance. Ibatoulline, Bagram, illus. 2009. (ENG.). 32p. (J). (gr. -1-3). 16.99 (978-1-4169-3770-8(6), Simon & Schuster Bks. For Young Readers) Simon & Schuster Bks. For Young Readers.
—Sing a Season Song. Ashlock, Lisel Jane, illus. 2015. (ENG.). 48p. (J). (gr. 1-3). 19.99 (978-1-56846-255-4(7), Creative Editions) Creative Co., The.
—Waking Dragons. Anderson, Derek, illus. 2012. (ENG.). 32p. (J). (gr. -1-3). 16.99 (978-1-4169-9032-1(1), Simon &

Schuster Bks. For Young Readers) Simon & Schuster Bks. For Young Readers.
—What to Do with a Box. Sheban, Chris, illus. 2016. (ENG.). 32p. (J). (gr. 1-3). 18.99 *(978-1-56846-289-9(1),* Creative Editions) Creative Co., The.
—Where Have the Unicorns Gone? Sanderson, Ruth, illus. 2003. (ENG.). 32p. (J). (gr. -1-3). 9.99 *(978-0-689-86359-2(4),* Simon & Schuster/Paula Wiseman Bks.) Simon & Schuster Bks. For Young Readers.
Yolen, Jane, narrated by. How Do Dinosaurs Eat Their Food? 2011. (J). (gr. -1-2). 29.95 *(978-0-439-02746-5(2))* Weston Woods Studios, Inc.
Yolen, Jane & Stemple, Heidi E. Y. Not All Princesses Dress in Pink. Lanquetin, Anne-Sophie, illus. 2010. (ENG.). 32p. (J). (gr. -1-3). 17.99 *(978-1-4169-8018-6(0),* Simon & Schuster Bks. For Young Readers) Simon & Schuster Bks. For Young Readers.
—Sleep, Black Bear, Sleep. Dyer, Brooke, illus. 2007. 32p. (J). (gr. -1-1). (ENG.). 15.99 *(978-0-06-081560-8(4));* lib. bdg. 16.89 *(978-0-06-081561-5(2))* HarperCollins Pubs.
Yoon, Salina. Humpty Dumpty. Yoon, Salina, illus. 2012. (ENG., Illus.). 18p. (J). (gr. -1 — 1). bds. 5.99 *(978-1-4424-1411-2(1),* Little Simon) Little Simon.
—Jack & Jill: A Halloween Nursery Rhyme. Yoon, Salina, illus. 2012. (ENG., Illus.). 18p. (J). (gr. -1 — 1). bds. 5.99 *(978-1-4424-1410-5(3),* Little Simon) Little Simon.
—Old MacDonald Had a Farm. 2008. (Salina Yoon Bks.). (ENG., Illus.). 12p. (J). (gr. -1-k). bds. 6.99 *(978-0-8431-2817-8(8),* Price Stern Sloan) Penguin Young Readers Group.
York Lumbard, Alexis. Angels. Weedn, Flavia, illus. 2013. (ENG.). 28p. (J). (gr. -1-1). 14.95 *(978-1-937786-15-1(3),* Wisdom Tales) World Wisdom, Inc.
You Can Be Anything! 2006. (Illus.). 32p. (J). 14.95 *(978-0-9786813-1-9(2))* Elora Pr.
Young, Ed. Seven Blind Mice. Young, Ed, illus. 2007. (Illus.). pap. 14.95 incl. audio *(978-0-439-02784-7(5));* (J). 24.95 incl. audio *(978-0-439-02782-3(9))* Scholastic, Inc.
—Seven Blind Mice. Young, Ed, illus. 2011. (Illus.). 18.95 *(978-0-439-02785-4(3));* (J). 29.95 *(978-0-439-02783-0(7))* Weston Woods Studios, Inc.
Young, Karen. A Chimpanzee Tale. 2009. (Illus.). 36p. pap. 16.99 *(978-1-4389-2448-9(8))* AuthorHouse.
Young, Samantha. I Can't Wait. 2012. 12p. pap. 15.99 *(978-1-4772-6013-5(7))* AuthorHouse.
Young, Shelley. Doc Broc's Cave Adventure. Young, Shelley, illus. 2005. (Illus.). 44p. 19.95 *(978-1-58054-406-1(1))* Woodland Publishing, Inc.
Zabel, Alanna. A Chair in the Air. 2006. 35p. pap. 16.00 *(978-1-4116-7436-3(7))* Lulu Pr., Inc.
Zabini, Eleni & Livanios, Eleni. Best Grandma in the World! Lütje, Susanne, illus. 2015. (ENG.). 16p. (J). bds. 7.95 *(978-0-7358-4225-0(6))* North-South Bks., Inc.
—Best Grandpa in the World! Lütje, Susanne, illus. 2015. (ENG.). 16p. (J). bds. 7.95 *(978-0-7358-4237-3(X))* North-South Bks., Inc.
Zaglada, Vladimir. Gymmy the Owl & His Friends. 2012. 52p. pap. 24.99 *(978-1-4772-0226-5(9))* AuthorHouse.
—Gymmy the Owl & His Friends: Tales in Rhyme about the Animal Kingdom's Natural Gymnasts. 2012. 52p. pap. 24.99 *(978-1-4685-6011-4(5))* AuthorHouse.
Zaibak, Bushra. I am Not Afraid. 2007. (Illus.). 37p. (J). mass mkt. *(978-0-9787849-7-3(9))* Lucent Interpretations, LLC.
Zalesny, Michele. The Elves' Surprise. 2008. (ENG., Illus.). 20p. (J). pap. 9.25 *(978-1-935125-06-8(0))* Robertson Publishing.
The Zany Zanimal Zoo. 2005. (Illus.). 40p. (J). 14.95 *(978-0-9769738-0-5(4))* Redel, Nicole.
Zaring, Laurie. Who Could You Be at the Zoo? Barlup, Jessica, illus. 2013. 24p. pap. 12.95 *(978-1-61244-175-7(0))* Halo Publishing International.
Zarins, Kim. The Helpful Puppy. McCully, Emily Arnold, illus. 2013. (ENG.). 32p. (J). pap. 6.99 *(978-0-8234-2919-6(9))* Holiday Hse., Inc.
Zeeh, Shawn. Tucker Farm: Under the Big Top. 2012. 36p. pap. 21.99 *(978-1-4771-2685-1(6))* Xlibris Corp.
Zelaya, Carol. Caring for Emily's Family. 2008. (Illus.). 24p. (J). (gr. 2-3). 14.95 *(978-0-9796265-1-7(X))* Richlee Publishing.
—Emily Waits for Her Family. Metcalf, Kristin, illus. 2007. (Emily the Chickadee Ser.). 32p. (J). (gr. 2-3). 14.95 *(978-0-9796265-0-0(1))* Richlee Publishing.
—Emily's New Home: Emily the Chickadee. 2008. (Illus.). 36p. (J). (gr. 2-3). 14.95 *(978-0-9796265-2-4(8))* Richlee Publishing.
Zenz, Aaron. The Hiccupotamus, 0 vols. 2009. (ENG.). 32p. (J). (gr. -1-2). 12.99 *(978-0-7614-5622-3(8),* 9780761456223, Amazon Children's Publishing) Amazon Publishing.
Zettler, Andrew. The Teeniest Tiniest Yawn. Zettler, Andrew, illus. Lt. ed. 2014. (ENG., Illus.). 36p. (J). 17.99 *(978-0-9912370-0-5(5))* Royal Penny Pr., The.
Ziefert, Harriet. Messy Bessie: Where's My Homework? De Muth, Roger, illus. 2007. (J). *(978-1-4287-4707-4(9))* Handprint Bks.
Zimmerman, Kwanza A. What Day Is It? 2008. 16p. per. 24.95 *(978-1-4241-9954-9(9))* America Star Bks.
Zinner, Gennieve. The UFB's of Bugsville, Florida USA, 1 vol. Ballinger, Carolyn, illus. 2010. 48p. pap. 24.95 *(978-1-4489-7977-6(3))* PublishAmerica, Inc.
Zinsmeister, Elke, illus. Ten Fat Sausages. 2005. (Classic Books with Holes Board Book Ser.). (ENG.). 14p. (J). (gr. -1-1). bds. *(978-1-904550-59-4(2))* Child's Play International Ltd.
Zobel-Nolan, Allia. Mrs. McGee's Coconut. Cottrill, Peter, illus. 2009. 32p. (J). (gr. -1-2). 15.95 *(978-1-58925-079-6(6));* pap. 6.95 *(978-1-58925-414-5(7))* Tiger Tales.
Zoellick, Todd. Daniel Harrington Fairbanks the Third & a Day on the Farm. 2012. 40p. pap. 18.58 *(978-1-4772-8408-7(7))* AuthorHouse.
—Daniel Harrington Fairbanks the Third & the Dog That Wouldn't Bark. 2009. 52p. pap. 20.49 *(978-1-4490-1047-8(4))* AuthorHouse.
Zolan, Donald, illus. My Favorite Farm Animal Friends. 2010. (ENG.). 5p. (J). bds. 5.99 *(978-0-7369-2663-8(1))* Harvest Hse. Pubs.
Zolkower, Edie Stoltz. When It's Purim. Bjomson, Barb, illus. 2009. (Very First Board Bks.). (ENG.). 12p. (J). (gr. -1 — 1). 5.95 *(978-0-8225-8947-1(8),* Kar-Ben Publishing) Lerner Publishing Group.
Zoss, Lori. A Bed for Fred. 2013. 24p. 15.95 *(978-1-936449-52-1(8))* Roberts & Ross Publishing.
Zschock, Martha Day. Hello, Rockies! 2014. (Hello! Ser.). (ENG., Illus.). 16p. (J). (gr. -1-k). bds. 9.95 *(978-1-938700-21-7(X),* 9781938700217, Commonwealth Editions) Applewood Bks.
Zuckerman, Linda. The Day Is Waiting, 1 vol. Freeman, Don, illus. 2015. (ENG.). 32p. (J). 9.99 *(978-0-310-74054-4(1))* Zonderkidz.
Zvetkoff, Kathleen Charnes. The Adventures of Willy the Monkey. 2008. 40p. pap. *(978-0-9784909-5-9(9))* Soul Asylum Poetry.
365 Stories & Rhymes for Boys. (365 Stories Treasuries Ser.). 384p. (J). 9.98 *(978-1-4054-1958-1(X))* Parragon, Inc.

STORIES WITHOUT WORDS

Andersen, Hans Christian. Los Cisnes Salvajes.Tr. of Wild Swans. (SPA., Illus.). 48p. (J). (gr. 3-5). 9.56 *(978-84-241-5524-7(6))* Everest Editora ESP. Dist: Lectorum Pubns., Inc.
Andersen, Hans Christian & Maguire, Thomas Aquinas. The Wild Swans. 2012. (ENG., Illus.). 104p. (J). (gr. k). 24.95 *(978-1-897476-36-9(1))* Simply Read Bks. CAN. Dist: Ingram Publisher Services.
Ardizzone, Edward. The Wrong Side of the Bed. 2017. (ENG., Illus.). 32p. (J). (gr. -1-1). 13.99 ***(978-0-14-137027-9(0))*** Penguin Bks., Ltd. GBR. Dist: Independent Pubs. Group.
Atak, illus. Topsy Turvy World. 2013. (ENG.). 30p. (J). (gr. -1). 18.95 *(978-1-909263-04-8(4))* Flying Eye Bks. GBR. Dist: Consortium Bk. Sales & Distribution.
Baker, Jeannie. Mirror. Baker, Jeannie, illus. 2010. (ENG., Illus.). 48p. (J). (gr. k-4). 18.99 *(978-0-7636-4848-0(5))* Candlewick Pr.
Baker, Liza. Harold & the Purple Crayon: Under the Sea. 2003. (Festival Reader Ser.). (ENG., Illus.). 32p. (J). (gr. -1-2). pap. 3.99 *(978-0-06-000178-0(X),* HarperFestival) HarperCollins Pubs.
Bartlett, T. C. Tuba Lessons. Felix, Monique, illus. (ENG.). 32p. (J). (gr. 1-17). 2011. pap. 9.95 *(978-0-89812-522-1(7),* Creative Paperbacks) 2009. 17.95 *(978-1-56846-209-7(3))* Creative Co., The.
Becker, Aaron. Journey. Becker, Aaron, illus. 2013. (ENG., Illus.). 40p. (J). (gr. -1-3). 15.99 *(978-0-7636-6053-6(1))* Candlewick Pr.
—Quest. 2014. (ENG., Illus.). 40p. (J). (gr. -1-3). 15.99 *(978-0-7636-6595-1(9))* Candlewick Pr.
—Quest. 2015. (CHI.). 40p. (J). *(978-7-5133-1677-4(5))* New Star Publishing Hse.
—Return. Becker, Aaron, illus. 2016. (ENG., Illus.). 40p. (J). (gr. -1-3). 15.99 *(978-0-7636-7730-5(2))* Candlewick Pr.
Boyd, Lizi. Flashlight. 2014. (ENG., Illus.). 40p. (J). (gr. -1-1). 16.99 *(978-1-4521-1894-9(9))* Chronicle Bks. LLC.
—Inside Outside. Boyd, Lizi, illus. 2013. (ENG., Illus.). 40p. (J). (gr. -1-1). 15.99 *(978-1-4521-0644-1(4))* Chronicle Bks. LLC.
Camcam, Princesse, creator. Fox's Garden. 2014. (Stories Without Words Ser.). (ENG., Illus.). 32p. (J). (gr. -1-3). 14.95 *(978-1-59270-167-4(1))* Enchanted Lion Bks., LLC.
Capstone Press Staff. Flood, 1 vol. Vila, Alvaro F., illus. 2013. (Fiction Picture Bks.). (ENG.). 32p. (gr. 1-3). 22.60 *(978-1-4048-8006-1(2),* Fiction Picture Bks.) Picture Window Bks.
Carmi, Giora. A Circle of Friends, 1 vol. Carmi, Giora, illus. 2003. (ENG., Illus.). 32p. (J). 15.95 *(978-1-932065-00-8(8))* Star Bright Bks., Inc.
Carmi, Giora, illus. A Circle of Friends, 1 vol. 2006. (ENG.). 32p. (J). (gr. k-9). pap. 5.95 *(978-1-59572-060-3(X))* Star Bright Bks., Inc.
Cole, Henry. Spot, the Cat. Cole, Henry, illus. 2016. (ENG., Illus.). 32p. (J). (gr. -1-3). 17.99 *(978-1-4814-4225-1(2),* Little Simon) Little Simon.
Colón, Raúl. Draw! Colón, Raúl, illus. 2014. (ENG., Illus.). 40p. (J). (gr. -1-3). 17.99 *(978-1-4424-9492-3(1),* Simon & Schuster/Paula Wiseman Bks.) Simon & Schuster/Paula Wiseman Bks.
Dahl, Michael. Alien Snow, 1 vol. Glass House Graphics Staff, illus. 2011. (Good vs Evil Ser.). (ENG.). 48p. (gr. 1-2). pap. 6.29 *(978-1-4342-3444-5(4),* Good vs Evil) Stone Arch Bks.
Dematons, Charlotte. Holland. 2013. (ENG., Illus.). 56p. (J). (gr. -1). 19.95 *(978-1-935954-28-6(8),* 9781935954286) Lemniscaat USA.
—Yellow Balloon. 2004. (ENG., Illus.). 32p. (J). 15.95 *(978-1-932425-01-7(2),* Lemniscaat) Boyds Mills Pr.
Diamond, Donna. The Shadow. Diamond, Donna, illus. 2010. (ENG., Illus.). 32p. (J). (gr. k-3). 15.99 *(978-0-7636-4678-7(7))* Candlewick Pr.
Donovan, Jane Monroe. Small, Medium & Large. Donovan, Jane Monroe, illus. 2010. (ENG., Illus.). 32p. (J). (gr. 1-4). 15.95 *(978-1-58536-447-3(9),* 202172) Sleeping Bear Pr.
Dorémus, Gaëtan, creator. Bear Despair. 2012. (Stories Without Words Ser.). (ENG., Illus.). 32p. (J). (gr. -1-2). 14.95 *(978-1-59270-125-4(6))* Enchanted Lion Bks., LLC.
Drummond, Sarah, illus. Raven & the Red Ball. 2013. (ENG.). 28p. (J). 9.95 *(978-0-7649-6609-5(X))* Pomegranate Communications, Inc.
Dudley, Rebecca. Hank Finds an Egg. Dudley, Rebecca, photos by. 2013. (ENG., Illus.). 40p. (J). 16.99 *(978-1-4413-1158-0(0))* Peter Pauper Pr. Inc.
The Farmer & the Clown. 2014. (ENG., Illus.). 32p. (J). (gr. -1-3). 17.99 *(978-1-4424-9744-3(0),* Beach Lane Bks.) Beach Lane Bks.
Felix, Monique. The Alphabet. Felix, Monique, illus. 2012. (Mouse Book Ser.). (ENG., Illus.). 32p. (J). (gr. -1-k). 12.99 *(978-1-56846-226-4(3),* Creative Editions) Creative Co., The.
Félix, Monique. The Alphabet. 2015. (J). pap. *(978-1-62832-262-0(4),* Creative Paperbacks) Creative Co., The.
Felix, Monique. The Colors. Felix, Monique, illus. 2013. (ENG., Illus.). 32p. (J). (gr. -1-k). 12.99 *(978-1-56846-234-9(4),* Creative Editions) Creative Co., The.
—Mouse Book: the Valentine. Felix, Monique, illus. 2013. (Mouse Book Ser.). (ENG., Illus.). 32p. (J). (gr. -1-k). 12.99 *(978-1-56846-247-9(6),* Creative Editions) Creative Co., The.
—The Numbers. Felix, Monique, illus. 2013. (ENG., Illus.). 32p. (J). (gr. -1-k). 12.99 *(978-1-56846-235-6(2),* Creative Editions) Creative Co., The.
—The Wind. 2012. (Mouse Book Ser.). (ENG.). 32p. (J). (gr. -1-k). 12.99 *(978-1-56846-227-1(1),* Creative Editions) Creative Co., The.
Furie, Matt, illus. The Night Riders. 2013. (ENG.). 48p. (J). (gr. -1-3). 8.95 *(978-1-938073-72-4(X))* McSweeney's Publishing.
Garoche, Camille. Snow Rabbit. 2015. (ENG., Illus.). 56p. (J). (gr. -1-3). 16.95 *(978-1-59270-181-0(7))* Enchanted Lion Bks., LLC.
Geisert, Arthur, creator. Thunderstorm. (ENG., Illus.). (J). 2015. 34p. (gr. k). 60.00 *(978-1-59270-170-4(1))* 2013. 32p. (gr. -1). 17.95 *(978-1-59270-133-9(7))* Enchanted Lion Bks., LLC.
Genhart, Michael. I See You. Lew-Vriethoff, Joanne, illus. 2017. 40p. (J). 15.95 ***(978-1-4338-2758-7(1),*** Magination Pr.) American Psychological Assn.
Goldstyn, Jacques. Letters to a Prisoner. Li, Karen, tr. from FRE. 2017. Orig. Title: Le Prisonnier Sans Frontières. (ENG., Illus.). 48p. (J). (gr. 4). 18.95 ***(978-1-77147-251-7(0))*** Owlkids Bks. Inc. CAN. Dist: Publishers Group West (PGW).
Gordon, Domenica More. Archie. 2012. (ENG., Illus.). 48p. (J). (gr. -1-1). 17.99 *(978-1-59990-936-3(7),* 9781599909363, Bloomsbury USA Childrens) Bloomsbury Publishing USA.
—Archie's Vacation. 2014. (ENG., Illus.). 32p. (J). (gr. -1-1). 17.99 *(978-1-61963-190-8(3),* 9781619631908, Bloomsbury USA Childrens) Bloomsbury Publishing USA.
Gorey, Edward. The West Wing. 2009. (ENG., Illus.). 64p. 12.00 *(978-1-60819-064-5(1),* 9781608190645) Bloomsbury Publishing USA.
Griesmer, Russell. My Hometown. Wong, Priscilla, illus. 2015. (ENG.). 40p. (gr. 1-4). 15.95 *(978-1-62370-174-1(0))* Capstone Young Readers of Coughlan Cos.
Guojing. The Only Child. 2015. (ENG., Illus.). 112p. (J). (gr. k-4). 22.99 *(978-0-553-49705-2(7),* Schwartz & Wade Bks.) Random Hse. Children's Bks.
Himler, Ronald. Dancing Boy, 1 vol. Himler, Ronald, illus. 2005. (ENG., Illus.). 32p. (J). (gr. -1-k). 15.95 *(978-1-59572-020-7(0))* Star Bright Bks., Inc.
Hussenot, Victor. The Land of Lines. 2015. (ENG., Illus.). 44p. (J). (gr. 1-4). 12.99 *(978-1-4521-4282-1(3))* Chronicle Bks. LLC.
Idle, Molly. Flora & the Peacocks. 2016. (ENG., Illus.). 40p. (J). (gr. -1-k). 17.99 *(978-1-4521-3816-9(8))* Chronicle Bks. LLC.
Idle, Molly, illus. Flora & the Flamingo. 2013. (ENG.). 44p. (J). (gr. -1-1). 17.99 *(978-1-4521-1006-6(9))* Chronicle Bks. LLC.
Kuhlmann, Torben. Moletown. Kuhlmann, Torben, illus. 2015. (ENG., Illus.). 32p. (J). 17.95 *(978-0-7358-4208-3(6))* North-South Bks., Inc.
Kumon. What Does Baby See? 2008. (Illus.). 12p. (J). bds. *(978-1-934618-27-1(6))* Begin Smart LLC.
Lawson, JonArno & Smith, Sydney. Sidewalk Flowers, 1 vol. 2015. (ENG., Illus.). 32p. (J). (gr. -1-2). 16.95 *(978-1-55498-431-2(9))* Groundwood Bks. CAN. Dist: Publishers Group West (PGW).
Lee, Jihyeon. Pool. 2015. (ENG., Illus.). 56p. (J). (gr. -1-k). 16.99 *(978-1-4521-4294-4(7))* Chronicle Bks. LLC.
Lee, Suzy. Lines. Lee, Suzy, illus. 2017. (ENG., Illus.). 40p. (J). (gr. -1-k). 17.99 ***(978-1-4521-5665-1(4))*** Chronicle Bks. LLC.
—Mirror. 2010. (ENG., Illus.). 48p. (J). (gr. -1). 15.95 *(978-1-934734-39-1(X))* Seven Footer Pr.
—Wave. 2008. (ENG., Illus.). 40p. (J). (gr. -1-17). 15.99 *(978-0-8118-5924-0(X))* Chronicle Bks. LLC.
Lehman, Barbara. Museum Trip. 2006. (ENG., Illus.). 40p. (J). (gr. -1-3). 16.99 *(978-0-618-58125-2(1))* Houghton Mifflin Harcourt Publishing Co.
—Rainstorm. 2007. (ENG., Illus.). 32p. (J). (gr. -1-3). 17.99 *(978-0-618-75639-1(6))* Houghton Mifflin Harcourt Publishing Co.
—The Secret Box. 2011. (ENG., Illus.). 48p. (J). (gr. -1-3). 16.99 *(978-0-547-23868-5(1))* Houghton Mifflin Harcourt Publishing Co.
—Trainstop. 2008. (ENG., Illus.). 32p. (J). (gr. -1-3). 16.99 *(978-0-618-75640-7(X))* Houghton Mifflin Harcourt Publishing Co.
Lehrer, Damon, illus. Rocket Boy. 2016. (J). ***(978-1-56792-587-6(1))*** Godine, David R. Pub.
Lemke, Donald. Diver Down, 1 vol. Glass House Graphics Staff, illus. 2011. (Good vs Evil Ser.). (ENG.). 48p. (gr. 1-2). pap. 6.29 *(978-1-4342-3446-9(0),* Good vs Evil) Stone Arch Bks.
Lemke, Donald B. The Awakening, 1 vol. 2011. (Good vs Evil Ser.). (ENG.). 48p. (gr. 1-2). lib. bdg. 23.99 *(978-1-4342-2089-9(3),* Good vs Evil) Stone Arch Bks.
—Diver Down, 1 vol. 2011. (Good vs Evil Ser.). (ENG.). 48p. (gr. 1-2). lib. bdg. 23.99 *(978-1-4342-2092-9(3),* Good vs Evil) Stone Arch Bks.
Logan, Laura. Little Butterfly. Logan, Laura, illus. 2016. (Illus.). 32p. (J). (gr. -1-3). 14.99 *(978-0-06-228126-5(7))* HarperCollins Pubs.
Luthardt, Kevin. Peep!, 1 vol. Luthardt, Kevin, illus. (ENG., Illus.). 36p. (J). 2013. (gr. -1-1). 7.95 *(978-1-56145-682-6(9))* 2003. (gr. k-1). 15.95 *(978-1-56145-046-6(4))* Peachtree Pubs.
Mayer, Mercer. Frog Goes to Dinner. Mayer, Mercer, illus. 2003. (Boy, a Dog, & a Frog Ser.). (ENG., Illus.). 32p. (J). (gr. -1-k). 6.99 *(978-0-8037-2884-4(0),* Dial Bks) Penguin Young Readers Group.
—Octopus Soup, 0 vols. Mayer, Mercer, illus. 2011. (ENG., Illus.). 24p. (J). (gr. k-3). 16.99 *(978-0-7614-5812-8(3),* 9780761458128, Amazon Children's Publishing) Amazon Publishing.
McCully, Emily Arnold. Picnic. McCully, Emily Arnold, illus. 2003. (Illus.). 32p. (J). (gr. -1-k). 16.89 *(978-0-06-623855-5(2));* (ENG., 17.99 *(978-0-06-623854-8(4))* HarperCollins Pubs.
—School. McCully, Emily Arnold, illus. 2005. (Illus.). 32p. (J). lib. bdg. 16.89 *(978-0-06-623857-9(9))* HarperCollins Pubs.
Merveille, David. Mr Hulot on the Beach. 2016. (ENG., Illus.). 32p. (J). 18.95 *(978-0-7358-4254-0(X))* North-South Bks., Inc.
Miyares, Daniel. Float. Miyares, Daniel, illus. 2015. (ENG., Illus.). 48p. (J). (gr. -1-3). 17.99 *(978-1-4814-1524-8(7),* Simon & Schuster Bks. For Young Readers) Simon & Schuster Bks. For Young Readers.
More Gordon, Domenica. Archie. More Gordon, Domenica, illus. 2012. (ENG., Illus.). 48p. (J). (gr. -1-1). 18.89 *(978-1-59990-947-9(2),* 9781599909479, Bloomsbury USA Childrens) Bloomsbury Publishing USA.
Muggenthaler, Eva, creator. Fish on a Walk. 2012. (ENG., Illus.). 32p. (J). (gr. -1-2). 16.95 *(978-1-59270-116-2(7))* Enchanted Lion Bks., LLC.
Newman, Jeff. The Boys. Newman, Jeff, illus. 2010. (ENG., Illus.). 40p. (J). (gr. -1-2). 17.99 *(978-1-4169-5012-7(5),* Simon & Schuster Bks. For Young Readers) Simon & Schuster Bks. For Young Readers.
Nolan, Dennis. Hunters of the Great Forest. Nolan, Dennis, illus. 2014. (ENG., Illus.). 40p. (J). (gr. -1-2). 17.99 *(978-1-59643-896-5(7),* 9781596438965) Roaring Brook Pr.
—Sea of Dreams. Nolan, Dennis, illus. 2011. (ENG., Illus.). 40p. (J). (gr. -1-2). 17.99 *(978-1-59643-470-7(8),* 9781596434707) Roaring Brook Pr.
Nordling, Lee. Andrew the Seeker. Roberts, Scott, illus. 2017. (Game for Adventure Ser.). (ENG.). 32p. (J). (gr. k-3). 25.32 *(978-1-5124-1330-4(5),* Graphic Universe™) Lerner Publishing Group.
—BirdCatDog. Bosch, Meritxell, illus. 2014. (J). lib. bdg. 25.32 *(978-1-4677-4522-2(7),* Graphic Universe™) Lerner Publishing Group.
—BirdCatDog. 2014. (ENG.). 32p. pap. 6.95 *(978-1-4677-4523-9(5))* Lerner Publishing Group.
—Fishfishfish. Bosch, Meritxell, illus. 2015. (Three-Story Bks.). (ENG.). 32p. (J). (gr. k-3). lib. bdg. 25.26 *(978-1-4677-4575-8(8),* Graphic Universe™) Lerner Publishing Group.
—SheHeWe. Bosch, Meritxell, illus. 2015. (ENG.). 32p. (J). (gr. k-3). pap. 6.95 *(978-1-4677-4578-9(2));* lib. bdg. 25.26 *(978-1-4677-4574-1(X))* Lerner Publishing Group. (Graphic Universe™).
Pett, Mark. The Boy & the Airplane. Pett, Mark, illus. 2013. (ENG., Illus.). 40p. (J). 15.99 *(978-1-4424-5123-0(8),* Simon & Schuster Bks. For Young Readers) Simon & Schuster Bks. For Young Readers.
—The Girl & the Bicycle. Pett, Mark, illus. 2014. (ENG., Illus.). 40p. (J). 17.99 *(978-1-4424-8319-4(9),* Simon & Schuster Bks. For Young Readers) Simon & Schuster Bks. For Young Readers.
Pham, LeUyen. The Bear Who Wasn't There. Pham, LeUyen, illus. 2016. (ENG., Illus.). 40p. (J). 16.99 *(978-1-59643-970-2(X),* 9781596439702) Roaring Brook Pr.
Pinkney, Jerry. The Lion & the Mouse. 2009. (ENG., Illus.). 40p. (J). (gr. -1-3). 18.00 *(978-0-316-01356-7(0))* Little, Brown Bks. for Young Readers.
—The Lion & the Mouse. 2011. 29.95 *(978-0-545-29677-9(3))* Weston Woods Studios, Inc.
Polhemus, Coleman. The Crocodile Blues. Polhemus, Coleman, illus. 2007. (ENG., Illus.). 48p. (J). (gr. -1-2). 16.99 *(978-0-7636-3543-5(X))* Candlewick Pr.
Raschka, Chris. A Ball for Daisy. Raschka, Chris, illus. (ENG., Illus.). (J). (gr. -1-2). 2015. 36p. bds. 8.99 *(978-0-553-53723-9(7))* 2011. 32p. 17.99 *(978-0-375-85861-1(X))* Random Hse. Children's Bks. (Schwartz & Wade Bks.).
—A Ball for Daisy. 2013. (CHI.). 48p. (J). (gr. -1-2). *(978-7-5414-5730-2(2))* Yunnan Juvenile and Children's Bks. Pr.
—Daisy Gets Lost. Raschka, Chris, illus. 2013. (ENG., Illus.). 32p. (J). (gr. -1-2). 17.99 *(978-0-449-81741-4(5),* Schwartz & Wade Bks.) Random Hse. Children's Bks.
Ray, Lynn E. Hallelujah. 2010. (ENG., Illus.). 32p. (J). (gr. k-3). 12.95 *(978-1-897476-07-9(8))* Simply Read Bks. CAN. Dist: Ingram Publisher Services.
Reed, Adolph, ed. Ice. 2011. (Stories Without Words Ser.). (ENG., Illus.). 32p. (J). (gr. -1-2). 14.95 *(978-1-59270-098-1(5))* Enchanted Lion Bks., LLC.
Rey, H. A. & Rey, Margret. The H. A. Rey Treasury of Stories. 2015. (Dover Children's Classics Ser.). (ENG., Illus.). 112p. (J). (gr. 2-4). pap. 14.99 *(978-0-486-78468-7(1))* Dover Pubns., Inc.
Riphagen, Loes, illus. Animals Home Alone. 2011. (ENG.). 32p. (J). (gr. -1-3). 15.95 *(978-1-934734-55-1(1))* Seven Footer Pr.
Rogers, Gregory. The Hero of Little Street. Rogers, Gregory, illus. 2012. (ENG., Illus.). 32p. (J). (gr. k-3). 17.99 *(978-1-59643-729-6(4),* 9781596437296) Roaring Brook Pr.
Runton, Andy. Owly & Wormy, Bright Lights & Starry Nights. Runton, Andy, illus. 2012. (ENG., Illus.). 40p. (J). (gr. -1-3). 17.99 *(978-1-4169-5775-1(8),* Atheneum Bks. for Young Readers) Simon & Schuster Children's Publishing.
—Owly & Wormy, Friends All Aflutter! Runton, Andy, illus. 2011. (ENG., Illus.). 40p. (J). (gr. -1-2). 16.99 *(978-1-4169-5774-4(X),* Atheneum Bks. for Young Readers) Simon & Schuster Children's Publishing.
Schories, Pat. Breakfast for Jack. 2004. (Jacks Ser.). (ENG., Illus.). 32p. (J). 13.95 *(978-1-932425-16-1(0),* Lemniscaat) Boyds Mills Pr.
—Jack & the Night Visitors. 2006. (Jack's Bks.). (ENG., Illus.). 32p. (J). (gr. -1-1). 14.95 *(978-1-932425-33-8(0),* Lemniscaat) Boyds Mills Pr.
—Jack Wants a Snack. 2008. (Jacks Ser.). (ENG.). 32p. (J). (gr. -1-1). 13.95 *(978-1-59078-546-1(0),* Front Street) Boyds Mills Pr.
—When Jack Goes Out. 2010. (Jacks Ser.). (ENG., Illus.). 32p. (J). (gr. -1-1). 14.95 *(978-1-59078-652-9(1),* Front Street) Boyds Mills Pr.
Sickler, Jonas. Frere Jacques: Hey Baby! Look Where Jacques is Sleeping — and Dreaming — in Paris! Sickler, Jonas & Pixton, Kaaren, illus. 2011. (Indestructibles Ser.). (ENG.). 12p. (J). (gr. k — 1). pap. 5.95 *(978-0-7611-5923-0(1),* 15923) Workman Publishing Co., Inc.
Sickler, Jonas & Pixton, Kaaren, illus. Hickory Dickory Dock: Hey Baby! Look at the Mouse that Went up the Clock — Big Ben in London! 2011. (Indestructibles Ser.). (ENG.). 12p. (J). (gr. k — 1). pap. 5.95 *(978-0-7611-5921-6(5),* 15921) Workman Publishing Co., Inc.
Sim, Stephanie. Copycat. 2016. (ENG., Illus.). 32p. (J). (gr. -1-2). 16.95 *(978-1-927018-76-7(5))* Simply Read Bks. CAN. Dist: Ingram Publisher Services.
Sís, Peter. Dinosaur! Sís, Peter, illus. 2005. (ENG., Illus.). 28p. (J). (gr. -1-1). bds. 7.99 *(978-0-06-075967-4(4),* Greenwillow Bks.) HarperCollins Pubs.

Staake, Bob. Bluebird. Staake, Bob, illus. 2013. (ENG., Illus.). 40p. (J). (gr. -1-3). 17.99 *(978-0-375-87037-8(7),* Schwartz & Wade Bks.) Random Hse. Children's Bks.
Sturm, James, illus. Birdsong: a Story in Pictures: TOON Level 1. 2016. (ENG.). 60p. (J). (gr. k). 12.95 *(978-1-935179-94-8(2))* TOON Books / RAW Junior, LLC.
Tan, Shaun. The Arrival. Tan, Shaun, illus. 2007. (ENG., Illus.). 128p. (J). (gr. 7-12). 21.99 *(978-0-439-89529-3(4),* Levine, Arthur A. Bks.) Scholastic, Inc.
—The Arrival. 2007. (J). *(978-0-439-89530-9(8),* Levine, Arthur A. Bks.) Scholastic, Inc.
Tanaka, Shinsuke, illus. Wings. 2006. (ENG.). 80p. (J). (gr. -1). 14.95 *(978-1-933327-19-8(7))* Purple Bear Bks., Inc.
Thomson, Bill. Chalk, 0 vols. Thomson, Bill, illus. 2010. (ENG., Illus.). 40p. (J). (gr. -1-3). 15.99 *(978-0-7614-5526-4(4),* 9780761455264, Amazon Children's Publishing) Amazon Publishing.
Tolman, Marije & Tolman, Ronald. The Island. 2012. (ENG., Illus.). 32p. (J). (gr. -1). 17.95 *(978-1-935954-19-4(9),* 9781935954194) Lemniscaat USA.
—The Tree House. 2010. (ENG., Illus.). 32p. (J). (gr. -1-1). 17.95 *(978-1-59078-806-6(0),* Lemniscaat) Boyds Mills Pr.
Turkowski, Einar, illus. Houses Floating Home. 2016. (ENG.). 32p. (J). (gr. -1-3). 16.95 *(978-1-59270-183-4(3))* Enchanted Lion Bks., LLC.
Varon, Sara. Robot Dreams. Varon, Sara, illus. 2016. (ENG., Illus.). 224p. (J). pap. 9.99 *(978-1-250-07350-1(2),* 9781250073501) Square Fish.
Vidal, Beatriz Martin, illus. Bird. 2015. (ENG.). 32p. (J). 16.95 *(978-1-927018-64-4(1))* Simply Read Bks. CAN. Dist: Ingram Publisher Services.
Villeneuve, Anne. The Red Scarf. 2010. (ENG., Illus.). 40p. (J). (gr. k-3). 17.95 *(978-0-88776-989-4(6),* Tundra Bks.) Tundra Bks. CAN. Dist: Penguin Random Hse. LLC.
Wiesner, David. Free Fall. Wiesner, David, illus. 2008. (ENG., Illus.). 32p. (J). (gr. -1-3). 17.99 *(978-0-06-156741-4(8))* HarperCollins Pubs.
Young, Cybèle. Out the Window, 1 vol. 2014. (ENG., Illus.). 30p. (J). (-k). bds. 12.95 *(978-1-55498-370-4(3))* Groundwood Bks. CAN. Dist: Publishers Group West (PGW).
Zoboli, Giovanna. Professional Crocodile. Di Giorgio, Mariachiara, illus. 2017. (ENG.). 32p. (J). (gr. k-3). 17.99 ***(978-1-4521-6506-6(8))*** Chronicle Bks. LLC.

STORKS

Gish, Melissa. Storks. 2015. (Illus.). 46p. (J). *(978-1-60818-571-9(0),* Creative Education) Creative Co., The.
—Storks: Living Wild. 2016. (Living Wild Ser.). (ENG.). 48p. (J). (gr. 5-9). pap. 12.00 *(978-1-62832-172-2(5),* Creative Paperbacks) Creative Co., The.
Otfinoski, Steven. Storks & Cranes. 2009. (Animals Animals 10 Ser.). 48p. (gr. 3). 29.93 *(978-0-7614-3973-8(0))* Marshall Cavendish Corp.
Riggs, Kate. Amazing Animals: Storks. 2017. (Amazing Animals Ser.). (ENG., Illus.). 24p. (J). (gr. 1-3). pap. 8.99 ***(978-1-62832-366-5(3),*** Creative Paperbacks) Creative Co., The.
Riggs, Kate. Storks. 2017. (Illus.). 24p. (J). *(978-1-60818-758-4(6),* Creative Education) Creative Co., The.
World Book, Inc. Staff, contrib. by. Storks & Other Large Wading Birds. 2005. (World Book's Animals of the World Ser.). (Illus.). 64p. (J). *(978-0-7166-1267-4(4))* World Bk., Inc.
—World Book's Animals of the World Set 4. 2005. (World Book's Animals of the World Ser.). (Illus.). 64p. (gr. 2-8). 189.00 *(978-0-7166-1261-2(5))* World Bk., Inc.

STORKS—FICTION

Award, Anna, et al. The Fox & the Stork & the Man, His Son & the Donkey. 2014. (ENG.). 24p. (J). pap. 6.95 *(978-1-84135-955-7(6))* Award Pubns. Ltd. GBR. Dist: Parkwest Pubns., Inc.
Drescher, Henrik. The Strange Appearance of Howard Cranebill. 2006. (ENG., Illus.). 32p. (J). (gr. -1-1). *(978-1-59692-134-4(X))* MacAdam/Cage Publishing, Inc.
Frisch, Wilhelmine. The Storks of Lillegaard. Jauss, Anne Marie, illus. 2011. 230p. 46.95 *(978-1-258-08105-8(9))* Literary Licensing, LLC.
Lehman-Wilzig, Tami. Stork's Landing. Shuttlewood, Anna, illus. 2014. (ENG.). 32p. (J). (gr. -1-2). 17.95 *(978-1-4677-1395-5(3),* Kar-Ben Publishing) Lerner Publishing Group.
McDermott, Gerald. The Fox & the Stork. 2003. (Green Light Readers Level 2 Ser.). (ENG., Illus.). 24p. (J). (gr. -1-3). pap. 3.95 *(978-0-15-204837-2(5))* Houghton Mifflin Harcourt Publishing Co.
Penovi, Celina. The Clumsy Stork - la Cigüeña Despistad. 2009. 32p. pap. 17.50 *(978-1-4490-2746-9(6))* AuthorHouse.
Percy, Graham. The Fox & the Stork. 2009. (Aesop's Fables Ser.). (ENG., Illus.). 32p. (J). (gr. k-3). 28.50 *(978-1-60253-200-7(1),* 200036) Child's World, Inc., The.
Phillips, Dixie & Snider, K. C. Stilts the Stork. 2011. 20p. pap. 10.95 *(978-1-61633-143-6(7))* Guardian Angel Publishing, Inc.
Postgate, Oliver. Noggin & the Storks. Firmin, Peter, illus. 2017. (Noggin the Nog Ser.: 8). (ENG.). 48p. (J). (gr. 1-3). 8.99 ***(978-1-4052-8144-7(8))*** Egmont Bks., Ltd. GBR. Dist: Independent Pubs. Group.
Tedesco, Tina. The Stork Dropped Your Here for a Reason. 2006. (J). pap. 8.00 *(978-0-8059-7233-7(1))* Dorrance Publishing Co., Inc.

STORMALONG, ALFRED BULLTOP

Metaxas, Eric. Stormalong, 1 vol. Vanderbeek, Don, illus. 2004. (Rabbit Ears-A Classic Tale Ser.). (ENG.). 36p. (gr. k-5). 25.65 *(978-1-59197-772-8(X))* Spotlight.

STORMS

see also Hurricanes; Meteorology; Rain and Rainfall; Snow; Thunderstorms; Tornadoes; Winds
also other kinds of storms

Aarons, Jacob. Stormy Weather. 2005. (Illus.). 20p. (J). *(978-0-328-13452-6(X),* Scott Foresman) Addison-Wesley Educational Pubs., Inc.
Aboff, Marcie. Tornadoes!, 1 vol. Sotirovski, Aleksandar, illus. 2012. (First Graphics: Wild Earth Ser.). (ENG.). 24p. (gr. 1-2). lib. bdg. 23.99 *(978-1-4296-7608-3(6))* Capstone Press of Coughlan Cos.
Ahearn, Dan & Ahearn, Janet. Storm Chasers. 2011. (Navigators Ser.). (J). pap. *(978-1-61672-961-5(9))* Benchmark Education Co.
Appleby, Alex. It's Stormy! 2013. (What's the Weather? Ser.). (Illus.). 24p. (J). (gr. k-2). pap. 48.90 *(978-1-4339-9406-7(2));* pap. 8.15 *(978-1-4339-9405-0(4));* (ENG., lib. bdg. 22.60 *(978-1-4339-9404-3(6))* Stevens, Gareth Publishing LLLP.
—It's Stormy!/Es una Tormenta! 2013. (What's the Weather? / Qu Tiempo Hace? Ser.). (ENG & SPA., Illus.). 24p. (J). (gr. k-2). lib. bdg. 22.60 *(978-1-4339-9456-2(9))* Stevens, Gareth Publishing LLLP.
Ball, Jacqueline A. Blizzard! The 1888 Whiteout. 2005. (X-Treme Disasters That Changed America Ser.). (Illus.). 32p. (J). (gr. 2-5). lib. bdg. 25.27 *(978-1-59716-006-3(7))* Bearport Publishing Co., Inc.
Benchmark Education Company. The Power of Storms (Teacher Guide) 2005. *(978-1-4108-4636-5(9))* Benchmark Education Co.
Benchmark Education Company, LLC Staff, compiled by. Storms: Theme Set. 2006. (J). 109.00 *(978-1-4108-7080-3(4))* Benchmark Education Co.
Berger, Melvin & Berger, Gilda. Hurricanes Have Eyes but Can't See: And Other Amazing Facts about Wild Weather. 2003. (Illus.). 48p. (J). *(978-0-439-54980-6(9))* Scholastic, Inc.
Bowman, Chris. Survive a Blizzard. 2016. (Survival Zone Ser.). (ENG., Illus.). 24p. (J). (gr. 3-7). 25.95 *(978-1-62617-441-2(5),* Torque Bks.) Bellwether Media.
—Survive a Tornado. 2016. (Survival Zone Ser.). (ENG., Illus.). 24p. (J). (gr. 3-7). 25.95 *(978-1-62617-444-3(X),* Torque Bks.) Bellwether Media.
Brannon, Barbara. Discover Storms. 2005. (J). pap. *(978-1-4108-5124-6(9))* Benchmark Education Co.
Bryan, Dale-Marie. Tornadoes. 2013. (Illus.). 48p. (J). pap. 15.64 *(978-1-62403-005-5(X),* Core Library); (ENG., (gr. 3-6). lib. bdg. 32.79 *(978-1-61783-940-5(X))* ABDO Publishing Co.
Bullard, Lisa. Blizzards. (Pull Ahead Books-Forces of Nature Ser.). (ENG., 32p. (gr. k-3). 2015. Illus.). 22.65 *(978-1-5124-1047-1(0))* 2008. 22.60 *(978-0-8225-8828-3(5))* Lerner Publishing Group. (Lerner Pubns.).
Bundey, Nikki. Storms & People. 2005. (Science of Weather Ser.). (Illus.). 32p. (gr. 4-6). lib. bdg. 21.27 *(978-1-57505-499-5(X))* Lerner Publishing Group.
Cain, Marie Mowery. Storm Watch. 2013. (Big Books, Red Ser.). (ENG & SPA., Illus.). 16p. pap. 33.00 *(978-1-59246-214-8(6))* Big Books, by George!
Canavan, Roger. You Wouldn't Want to Live Without Extreme Weather! Bergin, Mark, illus. 2015. (You Wouldn't Want to Live Without... Ser.). (ENG.). (J). 40p. pap. 9.95 *(978-0-531-21408-4(7));* 32p. lib. bdg. 29.00 *(978-0-531-21365-0(X))* Scholastic Library Publishing. (Watts, Franklin).
—You Wouldn't Want to Live Without Extreme Weather! 2015. (You Wouldn't Want to Live Without Ser.). lib. bdg. 20.80 *(978-0-606-36711-0(X))* Turtleback Bks.
Canizares, Susan & Chessen, Betsey. Storms: Tormentas. 2004. (Science Emergent Readers Ser.). (ENG & SPA., Illus.). (J). *(978-0-439-66392-2(X))* Scholastic, Inc.
Cernak, Linda. The Science of a Tornado. 2015. (21st Century Skills Library: Disaster Science Ser.). (ENG., Illus.). 32p. (J). (gr. 4-8). 29.93 *(978-1-63362-482-5(X),* 206836) Cherry Lake Publishing.
Challen, Paul. Hurricane & Typhoon Alert! 3rd rev. ed. 2011. (Disaster Alert! Ser.: No. 17). (ENG., Illus.). 32p. (J). (gr. 3-6). pap. *(978-0-7787-1626-6(0))* Crabtree Publishing Co.
Challoner, Jack. DK Eyewitness Books: Hurricane & Tornado: Hurricane & Tornado. 2014. (DK Eyewitness Bks.). (ENG., Illus.). 72p. (J). (gr. 3-7). pap. 9.99 *(978-1-4654-2053-4(3),* DK Children) Dorling Kindersley Publishing, Inc.
Connell, Kate. Hoping for Rain: The Dust Bowl Adventures of Patty & Earl Buckler. 2004. (I Am American Ser.). (ENG., Illus.). 40p. (J). (gr. 3-7). pap. 6.99 *(978-0-7922-6903-8(9),* National Geographic Children's Bks.) National Geographic Society.
Davies, Jon. Storm Chasers! on the Trail of Twisters. Rath, Robert, illus. Davies, Jon & Reed, Jim, photos by. 2007. 48p. (J). (gr. 3-7). pap. 12.95 *(978-1-56037-407-7(1))* Farcountry Pr.
Donnelly, Karen. Storms of the Past & the Future. 2009. (Earth's Changing Weather & Climate Ser.). 24p. (gr. 4-4). 42.50 *(978-1-61512-250-9(8),* PowerKids Pr.) Rosen Publishing Group, Inc., The.
Donnelly, Karen J. Storms of the Past & the Future. 2003. (Earth's Changing Weather & Climate Ser.). (Illus.). 24p. (J). lib. bdg. 22.60 *(978-0-8239-6216-7(4),* PowerKids Pr.) Rosen Publishing Group, Inc., The.
Doudna, Kelly. It Is Stormy, 1 vol. 2003. (Weather Ser.). (ENG., Illus.). 24p. (J). (gr. k-3). lib. bdg. 24.21 *(978-1-57765-776-7(4),* SandCastle) ABDO Publishing Co.
Doudna, Kelly & Craig, Diane. Winter Storm or Blizzard?, 1 vol. 2016. (This or That? Weather Ser.). (ENG., Illus.). 24p. (J). (gr. k-4). 25.65 *(978-1-62403-958-4(8))* ABDO Publishing Co.
Dougherty, Terri. The Worst Tornadoes of All Time, 1 vol. 2012. (Epic Disasters Ser.). (ENG.). 32p. (gr. 3-4). pap. 8.29 *(978-1-4296-8015-8(6));* lib. bdg. 27.99 *(978-1-4296-7660-1(4))* Capstone Press of Coughlan Cos. (Edge Bks.).
Dreier, David. Be a Storm Chaser. 2008. (Scienceworks! Ser.). (Illus.). 32p. (gr. 3-5). lib. bdg. 26.00 *(978-0-8368-8929-1(0))* Stevens, Gareth Publishing LLLP.
Dreier, David Louis. Be a Storm Chaser. 2008. (Scienceworks! Ser.). 32p. pap. 8.95 *(978-0-8368-8936-9(3))* Stevens, Gareth Publishing LLLP.
Faidley, Warren, Jr. How to Survive Any Storm: Severe Weather Handbook. 2003. (Illus.). 213p. spiral bd. 17.95 *(978-0-9728107-0-8(6))* Weatherstock, Inc.
Fleisher, Paul. Lightning, Hurricanes, & Blizzards: The Science of Storms. 2010. (Weatherwise Ser.). (ENG.). 48p. (gr. 4-8). lib. bdg. 29.27 *(978-0-8225-7536-8(1))* Lerner Publishing Group.
Furgang, Adam. Adapting to Intense Storms. 2012. (Science to the Rescue: Adapting to Climate Change Ser.). (ENG.). 64p. (YA). (gr. 5-8). lib. bdg. 31.95 *(978-1-4488-6848-3(3),* Rosen Reference) Rosen Publishing Group, Inc., The.
Garbe, Suzanne. Threatening Skies: History's Most Dangerous Weather, 1 vol. 2013. (Dangerous History Ser.). (ENG.). 32p. (gr. 3-4). 27.99 *(978-1-4765-0128-4(9),* Edge Bks.) Capstone Press of Coughlan Cos.
Garland, Sherry. Voices of the Dust Bowl, 1 vol. Hierstein, Judith, illus. 2012. (Voices of History Ser.). (ENG.). 40p. (J). (gr. 3-3). 17.99 *(978-1-58980-964-2(5))* Pelican Publishing Co., Inc.
Gifford, Clive. Chasing the World's Most Dangerous Storms. 2010. (Extreme! Ser.). (ENG.). 32p. (gr. 3-4). pap. 47.70 *(978-1-4296-5123-3(7),* Fact Finders) Capstone Press of Coughlan Cos.
Gleason, Carrie. Ocean Storm Alert! 2004. (Disaster Alert! Ser.). (ENG., Illus.). 32p. (J). pap. *(978-0-7787-1611-2(2))* Crabtree Publishing Co.
Goin, Miriam. National Geographic Readers - Storms! 2009. (Readers Ser.). (ENG., Illus.). 32p. (J). (gr. -1-1). lib. bdg. 13.90 *(978-1-4263-0395-1(5),* National Geographic Children's Bks.) National Geographic Society.
—Storms. 2009. (Readers Ser.). (ENG., Illus.). 32p. (J). (gr. -1-1). 3.99 *(978-1-4263-0394-4(7),* National Geographic Children's Bks.) National Geographic Society.
Goin, Miriam Busch. Storms (1 Hardcover/1 CD) 2016. (National Geographic Readers: Pre-Reader Ser.). (ENG.). (J). *(978-1-4301-2125-1(4))* Live Oak Media.
—Storms (1 Paperback/1 CD) 2016. (National Geographic Readers: Pre-Reader Ser.). (ENG.). (J). pap. *(978-1-4301-2124-4(6))* Live Oak Media.
Gray, Susan H. Storm Chaser. 2015. (21st Century Skills Library: Cool STEAM Careers Ser.). (ENG., Illus.). 32p. (J). (gr. 4-7). 29.93 *(978-1-63362-565-5(6),* 206444) Cherry Lake Publishing.
Group/McGraw-Hill, Wright. Savage Storms: Tornadoes & Hurricanes, 6 vols. (Book2WebTM Ser.). (gr. 4-8). 36.50 *(978-0-322-04424-1(3))* Wright Group/McGraw-Hill.
Harcourt School Publishers Staff. When Storm Library Book Grade K: Harcourt School Publishers Storytown. 2009. pap. 8.75 *(978-0-15-352482-0(0))* Harcourt Schl. Pubs.
Hardyman, Robyn. Snow & Blizzards. 2010. (Weatherwise Ser.). 32p. (ENG.). (J). pap. 10.60 *(978-1-61532-276-3(0),* PowerKids Pr.); (Illus.). (YA). (gr. 3-6). lib. bdg. 26.50 *(978-1-61532-264-0(7))* Rosen Publishing Group, Inc., The.
—Wind & Storms. 2010. (Weatherwise Ser.). 32p. (ENG.). (J). pap. 10.60 *(978-1-61532-282-4(5),* PowerKids Pr.); (Illus.). (YA). (gr. 3-6). lib. bdg. 26.50 *(978-1-61532-267-1(1))* Rosen Publishing Group, Inc., The.
Hiscock, Bruce. Big Storm. 2008. (ENG.). 32p. (J). (gr. 1-4). pap. 7.95 *(978-1-59078-600-0(9))* Boyds Mills Pr.
Homer, Katie. Brainstorming Creative Guide to Help Parents & Children Through Severe Weather. 2008. 32p. 19.95 *(978-1-933466-73-6(1))* Kansas City Star Bks.
Hurricanes, Typhoons, & Other Tropical Cyclones. 2nd ed. 2009. (Illus.). 47p. (J). *(978-0-7166-9824-1(2))* World Bk., Inc.
Jeffrey, Gary. Hurricane Hunters & Tornado Chasers. 2009. (Graphic Careers Ser.). (ENG.). 48p. (YA). (gr. 5-5). 58.50 *(978-1-61512-885-3(9),* Rosen Reference) Rosen Publishing Group, Inc., The.
—Hurricane Hunters & Tornado Chasers. Garofalo, Gianluca, illus. 2008. (Graphic Careers Ser.). (ENG.). 48p. (gr. 5-8). per. 14.05 *(978-1-4042-1459-0(3));* (YA). lib. bdg. 31.95 *(978-1-4042-1458-3(5))* Rosen Publishing Group, Inc., The.
—Tornadoes & Superstorms. 2007. (Graphic Natural Disasters Ser.). (ENG.). 48p. (YA). 58.50 *(978-1-4488-1667-5(X),* Rosen Reference) Rosen Publishing Group, Inc., The.
—Tornadoes & Superstorms. Riley, Terry, illus. 2007. (Graphic Natural Disasters Ser.). (ENG.). 48p. (gr. 5-8). pap. 14.05 *(978-1-4042-1985-4(4));* (J). lib. bdg. 31.95 *(978-1-4042-1993-9(5))* Rosen Publishing Group, Inc., The.
Jensen, Belinda. A Snowstorm Shows Off: Blizzards. Kurilla, Renee, illus. 2016. (Bel the Weather Girl Ser.). (ENG.). 24p. (J). (gr. -1-3). 25.32 *(978-1-4677-7961-6(X),* Millbrook Pr.) Lerner Publishing Group.
—Spinning Wind & Water: Hurricanes. Kurilla, Renee, illus. 2016. (Bel the Weather Girl Ser.). (ENG.). 24p. (J). (gr. -1-3). 25.32 *(978-1-4677-7962-3(8),* Millbrook Pr.) Lerner Publishing Group.
Joanne, O'Sullivan. Bizarre Weather: Howling winds, pouring rain, blazing heat, freezing cold, huge hurricanes, violent earthquakes, tsunami's, tornadoes & more of nature's Fury. 2013. (ENG., Illus.). 160p. (J). pap. 7.95 *(978-1-936140-72-5(1),* Imagine Publishing) Charlesbridge Publishing, Inc.
Johnson, Robin. What Is a Blizzard? 2016. (ENG., Illus.). 24p. (J). *(978-0-7787-2395-0(X))* Crabtree Publishing Co.
Kallio, Jamie. 12 Things to Know about Wild Weather. 2015. (ENG., Illus.). 32p. (J). *(978-1-63235-035-0(1))* Pr. Room Editions LLC.
Kliman, Gilbert, et al. My Personal Story about Tropical Storm Stan: A Guided Activity Workbook for Children, Adolescents & Families. 2006. (Illus.). spiral bd. 19.00 *(978-0-9790846-8-3(7))* Children's Psychological Health Ctr., Inc., The.
KociendaGenevieve. BLIZZARDS: KILLER SNOWSTORM BEGINNING BOOK WITH ONLINE ACCESS. 2014. (ENG.). 24p. pap. 9.50 *(978-1-107-62164-0(X))* Cambridge Univ. Pr.
Koontz, Robin. The Science of a Tsunami. 2015. (21st Century Skills Library: Disaster Science Ser.). (ENG., Illus.). 32p. (J). (gr. 4-8). 29.93 *(978-1-63362-483-2(8),* 206840) Cherry Lake Publishing.
Kosara, Tori. Wild Weather Around the World. 2010. (Illus.). 46p. (J). pap. *(978-0-545-32147-1(6))* Scholastic, Inc.
Kostigen, Thomas M. Extreme Weather: Surviving Tornadoes, Tsunamis, Hailstorms, Thunder Snow, Hurricanes, & More! 2014. (ENG., Illus.). 112p. (J). (gr. 3-7). pap. 12.99 *(978-1-4263-1811-5(1),* National Geographic Children's Bks.) National Geographic Society.
Lay, Kathryn. Hail to the King!, 1 vol., Vol. 4. Wolff, Jason, illus. 2011. (Wendy's Weather Warriors Ser.). (ENG.). 80p. (gr. 2-5). 27.07 *(978-1-60270-757-3(X),* Calico Chapter Bks) Magic Wagon.
Leavitt, Amie Jane. A Daredevil's Guide to Storm Chasing, 1 vol. 2013. (Daredevils' Guides). (ENG.). 48p. (gr. 3-4). lib. bdg. 31.99 *(978-1-4296-9984-6(1))* Capstone Press of Coughlan Cos.
Levey, Richard H. Dust Bowl! The 1930s Black Blizzards. 2005. (X-Treme Disasters That Changed America Ser.). 32p. (J). lib. bdg. 25.27 *(978-1-59716-007-0(5))* Bearport Publishing Co., Inc.
Levy, Janey. World's Worst Hurricanes. 2009. (Deadly Disasters Ser.). (Illus.). 24p. (J). lib. bdg. 22.60 *(978-1-4042-4511-2(1),* PowerKids Pr.) Rosen Publishing Group, Inc., The.
Linde, Barbara M. The Power of Storms. 2005. (J). pap. *(978-1-4108-4588-7(5))* Benchmark Education Co.
—When Floods Flow. 2015. (Eye on the Sky Ser.). (ENG., Illus.). 32p. (J). (gr. 3-4). pap. 10.50 *(978-1-4824-2880-3(6))* Stevens, Gareth Publishing LLLP.
Lindeen, Mary & Kesselring, Susan. Being Safe with Weather. McGeehan, Dan & Moore, David, illus. 2011. (Be Safe Ser.). (ENG.). 24p. (J). (gr. k-3). lib. bdg. 27.07 *(978-1-60954-374-7(2),* 200085) Child's World, Inc., The.
MacAulay, Kelley & Kalman, Bobbie. Cambios del Estado del Tiempo: Las Tormentas. 2006. (Libro de Bobbie Kalman Ser.). (SPA & ENG., Illus.). 32p. (J). (gr. 3-7). pap. *(978-0-7787-8390-9(1));* lib. bdg. *(978-0-7787-8376-3(6))* Crabtree Publishing Co.
—Changing Weather: Storms. 2006. (Nature's Changes Ser.). (ENG., Illus.). 32p. (J). (gr. 4-7). pap. *(978-0-7787-2314-1(3))* Crabtree Publishing Co.
—Les Tempêtes. Briere, Marie-Josee, tr. from ENG. 2007. (Petit Monde Vivant Ser.). (FRE., Illus.). 32p. (J). (gr. 4-7). pap. 9.95 *(978-2-89579-166-9(X))* Bayard Canada Livres CAN. Dist: Crabtree Publishing Co.
Maloof, Torrey. Extreme Weather, 1 vol. 2015. (Science Readers: Content & Literacy Ser.). (ENG., Illus.). 32p. (J). (gr. 3-3). pap. 8.99 *(978-1-4807-4647-3(9))* Teacher Created Materials, Inc.
Manolis, Kay. Blizzards. 2008. (Extreme Weather Ser.). (ENG., Illus.). 24p. (J). (gr. 2-5). lib. bdg. 25.95 *(978-1-60014-183-6(8))* Bellwether Media.
Markovics, Joyce. Blizzard. 2014. (It's a Disaster! Ser.). 24p. (J). (gr. -1-3). lib. bdg. 23.93 *(978-1-62724-125-0(6))* Bearport Publishing Co., Inc.
Markovics, Joyce L. Blitzed by a Blizzard! 2010. (Disaster Survivors Ser.). (Illus.). 32p. (YA). (gr. 4-7). lib. bdg. 25.27 *(978-1-936087-54-9(5))* Bearport Publishing Co., Inc.
—Tormenta de Nieve. 2014. (Pedacitos Primeros Lectores: Que Desastre! Ser.). (SPA., Illus.). 24p. (J). (gr. -1-2). lib. bdg. 23.93 *(978-1-62724-245-5(7))* Bearport Publishing Co., Inc.
Marquardt, Meg. The Science of a Flood. 2015. (21st Century Skills Library: Disaster Science Ser.). (ENG., Illus.). 32p. (J). (gr. 4-8). 29.93 *(978-1-63362-479-5(X),* 206824) Cherry Lake Publishing.
Marrin, Albert. Years of Dust: The Story of the Dust Bowl. 2009. (ENG., Illus.). 128p. (J). (gr. 5-18). 22.99 *(978-0-525-42077-4(0),* Dutton Books for Young Readers) Penguin Young Readers Group.
Maurer, Daniel D. Do You Really Want to Drive in a Blizzard? A Book about Predicting Weather. Alberini, Teresa, illus. 2016. (Adventures in Science Ser.). (ENG.). 24p. (J). (gr. k-3). 20.95 *(978-1-60753-959-9(4))* Amicus Publishing.
McElligott, Matthew. Mad Scientist Academy: the Weather Disaster. 2016. (Mad Scientist Academy Ser.: 2). (ENG., Illus.). 40p. (J). (gr. k-3). 17.99 *(978-0-553-52376-8(7),* Crown Books For Young Readers) Random Hse. Children's Bks.
Meister, Cari. Blizzards. 2015. (Illus.). 24p. (J). lib. bdg. 25.65 *(978-1-62031-223-0(9))* Jump! Inc.
Mezzanotte, Jim. Dust Storms. (Wild Weather Ser.). 24p. 2009. (ENG.). (J). (gr. k-3). pap. 8.15 *(978-1-4339-2360-9(2))* 2009. (ENG.). (J). (gr. k-3). lib. bdg. 22.00 *(978-1-4339-2346-3(7))* 2007. (Illus.). (gr. 1-4). pap. 8.15 *(978-0-8368-7918-6(X))* 2007. (Illus.). (gr. 1-4). lib. bdg. 22.00 *(978-0-8368-7911-7(2))* Stevens, Gareth Publishing LLLP. (Weekly Reader Leveled Readers).
—Granizadas (Hailstorms) 2009. (Tiempo extremo Ser.). (SPA.). 24p. (J). (gr. k-3). pap. 8.15 *(978-1-4339-2367-8(X));* lib. bdg. 22.00 *(978-1-4339-2353-1(X))* Stevens, Gareth Publishing LLLP. (Weekly Reader Leveled Readers).
—Hailstorms. (Wild Weather Ser.). 24p. 2009. (ENG.). (J). (gr. k-3). pap. 8.15 *(978-1-4339-2361-6(0))* 2009. (ENG.). (J). (gr. k-3). lib. bdg. 22.00 *(978-1-4339-2347-0(5))* 2007. (Illus.). (gr. 1-4). pap. 8.15 *(978-0-8368-7919-3(8))* 2007. (Illus.). (gr. 1-4). lib. bdg. 22.00 *(978-0-8368-7912-4(0))* Stevens, Gareth Publishing LLLP. (Weekly Reader Leveled Readers).
—Snowstorms. (Wild Weather Ser.). 24p. 2009. (ENG.). (J). (gr. k-3). pap. 8.15 *(978-1-4339-2363-0(7))* 2009. (ENG.). (J). (gr. k-3). lib. bdg. 22.00 *(978-1-4339-2349-4(1))* 2007. (Illus.). (gr. 1-4). pap. 8.15 *(978-0-8368-7921-6(X))* 2007. (Illus.). (gr. 1-4). lib. bdg. 22.00 *(978-0-8368-7914-8(7))* Stevens, Gareth Publishing LLLP. (Weekly Reader Leveled Readers).
—Tormentas de Nieve. 2007. (Tormentas (Storms) Ser.). (SPA., Illus.). 24p. (gr. 1-4). pap. 8.15 *(978-0-8368-8079-3(X));* lib. bdg. 22.00 *(978-0-8368-8072-4(2))* Stevens, Gareth Publishing LLLP. (Weekly Reader Leveled Readers).
—Tormentas de Nieve (Snowstorms) 2009. (Tiempo extremo Ser.). (SPA.). 24p. (J). (gr. k-3). pap. 8.15 *(978-1-4339-2369-2(6));* lib. bdg. 22.00 *(978-1-4339-2355-5(6))* Stevens, Gareth Publishing LLLP. (Weekly Reader Leveled Readers).
—Tormentas de Polvo. 2007. (Tormentas (Storms) Ser.). (ENG & SPA., Illus.). 24p. (gr. 1-4). pap. 8.15 *(978-0-8368-8080-9(3));* lib. bdg. 22.00 *(978-0-8368-8073-1(0))* Stevens, Gareth Publishing LLLP. (Weekly Reader Leveled Readers).
—Tormentas de polvo (Dust Storms) 2009. (Tiempo extremo Ser.). (SPA.). 24p. (J). (gr. k-3). pap. 8.15 *(978-1-4339-2370-8(X));* lib. bdg. 22.00 *(978-1-4339-2356-2(4))* Stevens, Gareth Publishing LLLP. (Weekly Reader Leveled Readers).
Morris, Neil & Steele, Philip. Inside Hurricanes & Tornadoes. 2006. (Inside Nature's Disasters Ser.). (Illus.). 36p. (gr. 3-7). lib. bdg. 26.00 *(978-0-8368-7249-1(5),* Gareth Stevens Learning Library) Stevens, Gareth Publishing LLLP.
Osborne, Mary Pope. Twisters & Other Terrible Storms: A Nonfiction Companion to Twister on Tuesday. Osborne, Will & Murdocca, Sal, illus. 2003. (Magic Tree House - Fact

S

Tracker Ser.: 8). (ENG.). 128p. (J). (gr. 2-5). 6.99 (978-0-375-81358-0(6), Random Hse. Bks. for Young Readers) Random Hse. Children's Bks.
Pattison, Darcy. Prairie Storms, 1 vol. Rietz, Kathleen, illus. 2011. (ENG.). 32p. (J). (gr. -1-4). 16.95 (978-1-60718-129-3(0)); pap. 8.95 (978-1-60718-139-2(8)) Arbordale Publishing.
Peppas, Lynn. Severe Storm & Blizzard Alert! 2004. (Disaster Alert! Ser.). (ENG., Illus.). 32p. (J). pap. (978-0-7787-1605-1(8)); lib. bdg. (978-0-7787-1573-3(6)) Crabtree Publishing Co.
Perish, Patrick. Survive a Hurricane. 2016. (Survival Zone Ser.). (ENG., Illus.). 24p. (J). (gr. 3-7). 25.95 (978-1-62617-443-6(1), Torque Bks.) Bellwether Media.
—Survive a Tsunami. 2016. (Survival Zone Ser.). (ENG., Illus.). 24p. (J). (gr. 3-7). 25.95 (978-1-62617-445-0(8), Torque Bks.) Bellwether Media.
Phelan, Glen. Extreme Weather. 2007. (Reading Expeditions Ser.). (ENG., Illus.). 32p. (J). pap. 17.95 (978-0-7922-4575-9(X)) CENGAGE Learning.
Portman, Michael. Blinding Blizzards. 2012. (Angry Earth Ser.). (ENG.). 32p. (gr. 3-6). (J). pap. 10.50 (978-1-4339-6531-9(3), Gareth Stevens Learning Library); (YA). lib. bdg. 26.60 (978-1-4339-6529-6(1)) Stevens, Gareth Publishing LLLP.
Probst, Jeff. Extreme Weather. 2017. (Challenge Yourself Ser.: 4). (ENG., Illus.). 176p. (J). (gr. 3-7). 8.99 (978-0-14-751810-1(5), Puffin Books) Penguin Young Readers Group.
Rajczak, Michael. Deadly Droughts. 2016. (Where's the Water? Ser.). (Illus.). 24p. (J). (gr. 3-2). pap. 8.15 (978-1-4824-4680-7(4)); lib. bdg. 22.60 (978-1-4824-4682-1(0)) Stevens, Gareth Publishing LLLP.
Ransom, Candice. The Day of the Black Blizzard. Harden, Laurie, illus. 2016. (On My Own History Ser.). (ENG.). 48p. (J). (gr. 2-4). pap. 6.95 (978-1-5124-1152-2(3), First Avenue Editions) Lerner Publishing Group.
Raum, Elizabeth. Blizzard! 2016. (Natural Disasters Ser.). (ENG., Illus.). 32p. (J). (gr. 1-4). 20.95 (978-1-60753-988-9(8)) Amicus Publishing.
—Can You Survive Storm Chasing? An Interactive Survival Adventure, 1 vol. 2011. (You Choose: Survival Ser.). (ENG.). 112p. (gr. 3-4). pap. 6.95 (978-1-4296-7347-1(8)); lib. bdg. 31.99 (978-1-4296-6587-2(4)) Capstone Press of Coughlan Cos. (You Choose Bks.).
Rea, Amy C. Perspectives on the Dust Bowl. 2018. (ENG.). 32p. (gr. 3-6). **(978-1-63235-399-3(7)**, 12-Story Library) Pr. Room Editions LLC.
Rice, William B. Las Inundaciones y las Ventiscas, 1 vol. rev. ed. 2010. (Science Readers: a Closer Look Ser.).Tr. of Floods & Blizzards. (SPA., Illus.). 32p. (J). (gr. 2-3). pap. 8.99 (978-1-4333-2157-3(2)) Shell Educational Publishing.
—Los Tornados, 1 vol. rev. ed. 2010. (Science Readers: a Closer Look Ser.). (SPA., Illus.). 32p. (J). (gr. 2-3). pap. 8.99 (978-1-4333-2155-9(6)) Shell Educational Publishing.
Rigby. When Day Turned to Night. 2014. (Rigby Literacy Ser.). (ENG.). 32p. (gr. 4-4). pap. 11.10 (978-0-7578-2002-1(6)) Rigby Education.
Roker, Al. Al Roker's Extreme Weather. 2017. 48p. (J). (gr. 3-7). 16.99 **(978-0-06-248499-4(0))** HarperCollins Pubs.
Royston, Angela. Storms! 2010. (Eyewitness Disaster Ser.). 32p. (J). (gr. 2-5). 28.50 (978-1-60870-004-2(6)) Marshall Cavendish GBR. Dist: Marshall Cavendish Corp.
Roza, Greg. Severe Storms: Measuring Velocity. (Math for the Real World Ser.). 32p. 2009. (ENG., Illus.). (gr. 6-7). pap. 10.00 (978-1-4042-6085-6(4)) 2009. (gr. 5-5). 47.90 (978-1-60851-365-9(3), PowerKids Pr.) 2006. (Illus.). (YA). (gr. 5-9). lib. bdg. 25.25 (978-1-4042-3366-9(0)) Rosen Publishing Group, Inc., The.
Rudolph, Jessica. Erased by a Tornado! 2010. (Disaster Survivors Ser.). (Illus.). 32p. (YA). (gr. 4-7). lib. bdg. 25.27 (978-1-936087-52-5(9)) Bearport Publishing Co., Inc.
Salzmann, Mary Elizabeth. Biggest, Baddest Book of Storms, 1 vol. 2014. (Biggest, Baddest Books Set 2 Ser.). (ENG.). 24p. (gr. k-4). 25.65 (978-1-62403-519-7(1)) ABDO Publishing Co.
Sandler, Michael. Catastrophic Storms: Set Of 6. 2011. (Navigators Ser.). (J). pap. 48.00 net. (978-1-4108-5082-9(X)) Benchmark Education Co.
Schuetz, Kristin. Severe Weather. 2015. (Understanding Weather Ser.). (ENG., Illus.). 24p. (J). (gr. k-3). lib. bdg. 25.95 (978-1-62617-254-8(4), Blastoff! Readers) Bellwether Media.
Schuh, Mari C. Tsunamis [Scholastic]. 2010. (Earth in Action Ser.). (ENG.). 24p. pap. 0.49 (978-1-4296-5802-7(9), Pebble Plus) Capstone Press of Coughlan Cos.
Shea, Therese. When Blizzards Blow. 2015. (Eye on the Sky Ser.). (ENG., Illus.). 32p. (J). (gr. 3-4). pap. 10.50 (978-1-4824-2876-6(8)) Stevens, Gareth Publishing LLLP.
Shores, Lori. How to Build a Tornado in a Bottle, 1 vol. 2010. (Hands-On Science Fun Ser.). (ENG., 24p. (gr. k-1). Illus.). pap. 7.29 (978-1-4296-5577-4(1)); lib. bdg. 26.65 (978-1-4296-4493-8(1)) Capstone Press of Coughlan Cos. (Pebble Plus).
Shulman, Mark & Meredith Books Staff. Super Storms That Rocked the World: Hurricanes, Tsunamis, & Other Disasters. 2008. (Illus.). 40p. (J). (gr. 4-7). per. 6.99 (978-0-696-23978-6(7)) Meredith Bks.
Stein, Paul. Storms of the Future. 2009. (Library of Future Weather & Climate Ser.). 64p. (gr. 5-5). 58.50 (978-1-60853-651-1(3)) Rosen Publishing Group, Inc., The.
Stewart, Mark. Blizzards & Winter Storms. 2008. (Ultimate 10 Ser.). 48p. (YA). (gr. 5-9). lib. bdg. 31.00 (978-0-8368-9150-8(3)) Stevens, Gareth Publishing LLLP.
Storm: Level Q, 6 vols. (Wonder Worldtm Ser.). 48p. 39.95 (978-0-7802-2953-2(3)) Wright Group/McGraw-Hill.
Storm Trackers: Six-Pack. (Greetings Ser.: Vol. 3). (gr. 3-5). 31.00 (978-0-7635-2076-2(4)) Rigby Education.
Temple, Bob. Ice Storm! The 1998 Freeze. 2006. (X-Treme Disasters That Changed America Ser.). (Illus.). 32p. (YA). (gr. 2-5). lib. bdg. 25.27 (978-1-59716-275-3(2)) Bearport Publishing Co., Inc.
Thomas, Rick & Picture Window Books Staff. Eye of the Storm: A Book about Hurricanes, 1 vol. Shea, Denise, illus. 2005. (Amazing Science: Weather Ser.). (ENG.). 24p. (gr. -1-3). per. 8.95 (978-1-4048-1845-3(6)) Picture Window Bks.
Thompson, Tamara. Solar Storms. 2012. (At Issue Ser.). (ENG.). 128p. (gr. 10-12). pap. 27.80 (978-0-7377-6206-8(3), Greenhaven Pr., Inc.) Cengage Gale.
Thompson, Tamara, ed. Solar Storms. 2012. (At Issue Ser.). (ENG.). 128p. (gr. 10-12). lib. bdg. 34.45 (978-0-7377-6205-1(5), Greenhaven Pr., Inc.) Cengage Gale.
Tieck, Sarah. Storm Chasers, 1 vol. 2011. (Extreme Jobs Ser.). (ENG., Illus.). 32p. (J). (gr. 2-5). 28.50 (978-1-61783-028-0(3)) ABDO Publishing Co.
Time for Kids Magazine Staff, ed. Storms! 2006. (Time for Kids Science Scoops Ser.). (Illus.). 32p. (gr. 1-3). 14.00 (978-0-7569-6674-4(4)) Perfection Learning Corp.
Tras las Tormentas: 6 Small Books. (Saludos Ser.: Vol. 3). (SPA.). (gr. 3-5). 31.00 (978-0-7635-2082-3(9)) Rigby Education.
Trueit, Trudi Strain. Stormy Days. 2009. (Benchmark Rebus: Weather Watch Ser.). 24p. (gr. k-1). 15.95 (978-0-7614-4016-1(X)) Marshall Cavendish Corp.
Way, Jennifer L. & Gaffney, Timothy R. Severe-Storm Scientists: Chasing Tornadoes & Hurricanes. 2015. (Extreme Science Careers Ser.). (ENG., Illus.). 128p. (J). (gr. 7-7). 37.27 (978-0-7660-6968-8(0)) Enslow Pubs., Inc.
Webster, Christine. Storms. (Illus.). 24p. (J). 2013. (978-1-61913-542-0(6)) 2012. (ENG., (gr. 4-7). lib. bdg. 27.13 (978-1-61913-540-6(X), AV2 by Weigl) 2006. (gr. 3-7). lib. bdg. 24.45 (978-1-59036-412-3(0)) 2006. pap. 8.95 (978-1-59036-418-5(X)) Weigl Pubs., Inc.
Weil, Ann. Deadly Storms, 1 vol. unabr. ed. 2012. (Disasters Ser.). (ENG.). 92p. (YA). (gr. 9-12). 8.95 (978-1-61651-935-3(5)) Saddleback Educational Publishing, Inc.
Wendorff, Anne. Ice Storms. 2008. (Extreme Weather Ser.). (ENG., Illus.). 24p. (J). (gr. 2-5). lib. bdg. 25.95 (978-1-60014-186-7(2)) Bellwether Media.
Wetterer, Margaret K. & Wetterer, Charles M. Caminando Bajo la Nieve. Young, Mary O'Keefe, illus. 2007. (Yo Solo Historia Ser.). 48p. (J). (gr. 4-7). per. 6.95 (978-0-8225-7789-8(5)) Lerner Publishing Group.
—The Snow Walker. Young, Mary, illus. 2010. (ENG.). 48p. (C). (gr. 2-4). pap. 10.95 (978-0-87614-959-1(X)) National Geographic School Publishing, Inc.
Winchester, Simon. When the Sky Breaks: Hurricanes, Tornadoes, & the Worst Weather in the World. 2017. (Smithsonian Ser.). (ENG., Illus.). 96p. (J). (gr. 5). 22.99 (978-0-451-47635-7(2), Viking Books for Young Readers) Penguin Young Readers Group.
Wind & Storms: 6 Each of 1 Student Book, 6 vols. (Sunshinetm Science Ser.). 24p. (gr. 1-2). 41.95 (978-0-7802-1376-0(9)) Wright Group/McGraw-Hill.
Wind & Storms: Big Book. (Sunshinetm Science Ser.). 24p. (gr. 1-2). 37.50 (978-0-7802-1377-7(7)) Wright Group/McGraw-Hill.
Woods, Michael & Woods, Mary B. Blizzards. 2008. (Disasters up Close Ser.). (ENG., Illus.). 64p. (gr. 4-8). lib. bdg. 27.93 (978-0-8225-6575-8(7), Lerner Pubns.) Lerner Publishing Group.
—Hurricanes. 2006. (Disasters up Close Ser.). (Illus.). 64p. (J). (gr. 3-7). lib. bdg. 27.93 (978-0-8225-4710-5(4), Lerner Pubns.) Lerner Publishing Group.
World Book, Inc Staff, contrib. by. Blizzards. (J). 2007. (978-0-7166-9802-9(1)) 2nd ed. 2009. (Illus.). 47p. (978-0-7166-9818-0(8)) World Bk., Inc.
—Ice Storms. 2nd ed. 2009. (Illus.). 47p. (J). (978-0-7166-9825-8(0)) World Bk., Inc.
Yomtov, Nel. The Children's Blizzard Of 1888: A Cause-And-Effect Investigation. 2016. (Cause-And-Effect Disasters Ser.). (ENG., Illus.). 40p. (J). (gr. 4-6). 46.65 (978-1-5124-1129-4(9), Lerner Pubns.) Lerner Publishing Group.
Zoehfeld, Kathleen Weidner. School of Dragons #3: Storm Approaching! (DreamWorks Dragons) Random House, illus. 2017. (ENG.). 80p. (J). (gr. 2-5). pap. 7.99 (978-1-101-93343-5(7), Random Hse. Bks. for Young Readers) Random Hse. Children's Bks.

STORMS—FICTION

ABDO Publishing Company Staff. Storm Cliff Stables, 1 vol. 2014. (Storm Cliff Stables Ser.: 4). (ENG.). 112p. (J). (gr. 7-11). lib. bdg. 108.28 (978-1-62402-048-3(8), Calico Chapter Bks) Magic Wagon.
Albert, Burton. Windsongs & Rainbows. 2008. (ENG.). 28p. (J). 11.99 (978-1-4169-7122-1(X), Simon & Schuster/Paula Wiseman Bks.) Simon & Schuster/Paula Wiseman Bks.
Asare, Meshack. Sosu's Call. Asare, Meshack, illus. 2006. (ENG., Illus.). 40p. (J). (gr. k-4). 11.99 (978-1-929132-21-8(2)) Kane Miller.
Bailey, David J. The Storm. 2016. (ENG.). 190p. (J). pap. 11.95 (978-1-78554-826-0(3), 5b2b8f35-3768-4ec6-b355-c37d9c3384a8) Austin, Stan AUS. Dist: Bookmasters Distribution.
Banks, Kate. El Pajaro, el Mono y la Serpiente en la Selva. Bogacki, Tomek, illus. (SPA.). 24p. (J). (gr. k-2). (978-84-261-3129-4(8), JV2823) Juventud, Editorial ESP. Dist: Lectorum Pubns., Inc.
Bates, Sonya. Thunder Creek Ranch, 1 vol. Charko, Kasia, illus. 2013. (Orca Echoes Ser.). (ENG.). 64p. (J). (gr. 2-3). pap. 6.95 (978-1-4598-0112-7(1)) Orca Bk. Pubs. USA.
Benson, Donna. Ghost Finds 100ct Diamond in Little Rock. 2012. 36p. 19.95 (978-1-4626-6892-2(5)) America Star Bks.
Bentley, Sue. Sunshine Shimmers. 2014. (Magic Puppy Ser.: 12). lib. bdg. 14.75 (978-0-606-34141-7(2), Turtleback) Turtleback Bks.
Beveridge, Cathy. Stormstruck. 2006. (ENG., Illus.). 214p. (J). pap. (978-1-55380-041-5(9)) Ronsdale Pr.
Bodett, Tom. Williwaw! unabr. ed. 2004. 208p. (J). (gr. 5-9). pap. 38.00 incl. audio (978-0-8072-8226-7(X), LL0169, Listening Library) Random Hse. Audio Publishing Group.
Bolme, Edward Sarah. Jesus Stops a Storm. Gillette, Tim, illus. l.t. ed. 2003. 20p. (J). bds. 6.99 (978-0-9725546-3-3(7)) CREST Pubns.
Bos, Samone & Dorling Kindersley Publishing Staff. Twister! A Terrifying Tale of Superstorms. 2014. (DK Adventures Ser.). (ENG.). 128p. (J). (gr. 3-7). pap. 5.99 (978-1-4654-1973-6(X), DK Children) Dorling Kindersley Publishing, Inc.
Bridwell, Norman. Clifford the Big Red Dog. Bridwell, Norman, illus. 2010. (Clifford 8x8 Ser.). (ENG., Illus.). 32p. (J). (gr. -1-3). pap. 3.99 (978-0-545-21578-7(1), Cartwheel Bks.) Scholastic, Inc.
Caban, Connie. Don't Be Afraid of the Storm. Page, illus. 2011. 32p. pap. 12.95 (978-1-936343-97-3(5)) Peppertree Pr., The.
Caine, Rachel, pseud. Lord of Misrule. 2009. (Morganville Vampires Ser.: Bk. 5). 352p. (YA). lib. bdg. 20.00 (978-1-4242-4704-2(7)) Fitzgerald Bks.
—Lord of Misrule. 2009. (Morganville Vampires Ser.: 5). (ENG.). 256p. (YA). (gr. 9-18). mass mkt. 7.99 (978-0-451-22572-6(4), Berkley) Penguin Publishing Group.
Carroll, Mona. Jacob's Storm, 1 vol. 2010. 22p. 24.95 (978-1-4489-8069-7(0)) PublishAmerica, Inc.
Caught in the Storm: Individual Title Six-Packs. (gr. k-1). 23.00 (978-0-7635-9046-8(0)) Rigby Education.
Chriscoe, Sharon. Scary Weather, Scaredy Cat, 1 vol. 2008. (ENG.). 48p. 24.95 (978-1-60474-143-8(0)) America Star Bks.
Churchill, Ginger. Wild Rose's Weaving. Wong, Nicole, illus. 2011. (ENG.). 32p. (J). (gr. -1-3). 15.95 (978-1-933718-56-9(0)) Tanglewood Pr.
Clegg, Maryanne & Bester, Maryanne. Why Dog Is Afraid of Storms. Bester, Shayle, illus. 2012. (ENG.). 32p. (J). (gr. -1-k). pap. 12.95 (978-1-4314-0219-9(2)) Jacana Media ZAF. Dist: Independent Pubs. Group.
Corpus, Terrizita. The Grumpy Lighthouse Keeper. Prewett, Maggie, illus. 2017. (ENG.). 32p. (J). (gr. k-3). pap. 13.99 **(978-1-925360-18-9(0))** Magabala Bks. AUS. Dist: Independent Pubs. Group.
Crawford, Ruth. Squirrel Boy & Brad: The Storm. 2010. 24p. pap. 12.99 (978-1-4490-1611-1(1)) AuthorHouse.
Crossley-Holland, Kevin. Storm. Marks, Alan, illus. 2013. (Red Bananas Ser.). (ENG.). 48p. (J). (gr. k-2). pap. 5.99 (978-1-4052-6264-4(8)) Egmont Bks., Ltd. GBR. Dist: Independent Pubs. Group.
Crummel, Susan Stevens. Ten-Gallon Bart Beats the Heat, 0 vols. Donohue, Dorothy, illus. 2010. (ENG.). 40p. (J). (gr. k-3). 17.99 (978-0-7614-5634-6(1), 9780761456346, Amazon Children's Publishing) Amazon Publishing.
Dahl, Michael. Claws in the Snow, 1 vol. Vue, Tou, illus. 2010. (Dragonblood Ser.). (ENG.). 40p. (gr. 1-3). pap. 6.25 (978-1-4342-2308-1(6), Zone Bks.) Stone Arch Bks.
—Claws in the Snow, 1 vol. Evans, Mark & Vue, Tou, illus. 2009. (Dragonblood Ser.). (ENG.). 40p. (gr. 1-3). 23.99 (978-1-4342-1262-7(9), Zone Bks.) Stone Arch Bks.
D'Amico, Carmela & D'Amico, Steven. Ella Sets Sail. 2008. (J). (978-0-439-83156-7(3), Levine, Arthur A. Bks.) Scholastic, Inc.
Davies, Benji. The Winter Whale. Davies, Benji, illus. 2017. (ENG., Illus.). 32p. (J). 16.99 (978-1-250-11186-9(2), 9781250111869, Holt, Henry & Co. Bks. For Young Readers) Holt, Henry & Co.
Davis, Ashley. The Big Storm. 2006. (Neighborhood Readers Ser.). (ENG.). 16p. (gr. 1-3). pap. 6.50 (978-1-4042-7192-0(9), Rosen Classroom) Rosen Publishing Group, Inc., The.
Dearen, Patrick. When the Sky Rained Dust. 2004. 132p. (J). pap. 14.95 (978-1-57168-830-9(7), Eakin Pr.) Eakin Pr.
Disney Book Group Staff & Hapka, Catherine. Me & Our Mom. Disney Storybook Art Team, illus. 2015. (ENG.). 24p. (J). (gr. -1-k). pap. 4.99 (978-1-4847-0688-6(9)) Disney Pr.
Draper, Penny. Ice Storm!, 1 vol. 2011. (Disaster Strikes! Ser.: 6). (ENG.). 192p. (J). (gr. 4-8). pap. 8.95 (978-1-55050-451-4(7)) Coteau Bks. CAN. Dist: Orca Bk. Pubs. USA.
Dudgeon and Oxenham, Dudgeon and Oxenham. Cyclones & Shadows. 2017. (ENG.). 168p. (J). (gr. 1-5). 9.95 **(978-1-925164-76-3(4))** Fremantle Pr. AUS. Dist: Independent Pubs. Group.
Edwards, Carol. Jacy Meets Betsy: Jacy's Search for Jesus Book 2. Frey, Daniel, illus. 2006. 32p. (J). 15.95 (978-0-9755314-1-9(7)) Majestic Publishing, LLC.
Erickson, Mary Ellen. Snowstorm. 2005. (J). (978-0-9765453-3-0(0)) Dr. Mary's Bks.
Erin, Bethany. The Wind & the Blows. 2010. 24p. pap. 11.99 (978-1-4490-7569-9(X)) AuthorHouse.
Ering, Timothy Basil. The Unexpected Love Story of Alfred Fiddleduckling. Ering, Timothy Basil, illus. 2017. (ENG., Illus.). 48p. (J). (-k). 15.99 (978-0-7636-6432-9(4)) Candlewick Pr.
Fane, Judy B. Paddy the Pelican Survives the Storm. Alden, Carol, illus. 2010. 48p. pap. 16.50 (978-1-60911-448-0(5), Eloquent Bks.) Strategic Book Publishing & Rights Agency (SBPRA).
Fernandez, Joy C. Rockman. 2010. 36p. pap. 16.45 (978-1-4520-6751-3(1)) AuthorHouse.
Fisher, Pam. Pammy the Pig. 2011. 20p. 13.99 (978-1-4567-1796-4(0)) AuthorHouse.
The Fisherman. 2013. (Illus.). 16p. pap. 9.95 (978-1-61633-446-8(0)) Guardian Angel Publishing, Inc.
Friedman, Laurie. Ruby Valentine Saves the Day. Avril, Lynne, illus. 2010. (Carolrhoda Picture Bks.). (ENG.). 32p. (J). (gr. k-3). lib. bdg. 16.95 (978-0-7613-4213-7(3)) Lerner Publishing Group.
Fudge, Keith. The Rainy Day Discovery. 2006. (J). per. 11.95 (978-1-889743-37-0(2)) Robbie Dean Pr.
Gaskins, Terry & Treigle, Jimmy. The Very Big Storm: Created by Terry Gaskins Inspired by Jimmy Treigle. 2009. 28p. pap. 13.99 (978-1-4389-4220-9(6)) AuthorHouse.
Geisert, Arthur, creator. Thunderstorm. (ENG., Illus.). (J). 2015. 34p. (gr. k). 60.00 (978-1-59270-170-4(1)) 2013. 32p. (gr. -1). 17.95 (978-1-59270-133-9(7)) Enchanted Lion Bks., LLC.
Gillespie, Gary Franklin. Storytime with Grandp. 2011. 60p. pap. 31.99 (978-1-4653-3598-2(6)) Xlibris Corp.
Gonzales Betrand, Diane. The Story Circle / el Circulo de Cuentos. Martin, Wendy, illus. 2016. (ENG, MUL & SPA.). 32p. (J). (gr. k-3). 17.95 (978-1-55885-826-8(1), Piñata Books) Arte Publico Pr.
Gramatky, Hardie. Little Toot. Gramatky, Hardie, illus. 2007. (ENG., Illus.). 104p. (J). (gr. -1-2). 17.99 (978-0-399-24713-2(0), G.P. Putnam's Sons Books for Young Readers) Penguin Young Readers Group.
Graves, Susan Elaine. Lily the Lucky Ducky, 1 vol. 2010. 44p. 24.95 (978-1-4489-4433-0(3)) PublishAmerica, Inc.
Gray, P. J. The Lab Book 3, 1 vol. 2015. (Trippin' Ser.). (ENG.). 64p. (YA). (gr. 9-12). pap. 8.95 (978-1-62250-933-1(1)) Saddleback Educational Publishing, Inc.
Green, John, et al. Let It Snow: Three Holiday Romances. (ENG.). 368p. (YA). (gr. 7). 2014. mass mkt. 7.99 (978-0-14-751501-8(7)) 2008. pap. 10.99 (978-0-14-241214-5(7)) Penguin Young Readers Group. (Speak).
Hall, Rose. After the Storm. Jazvic, Beryl, illus. 2005. (J). bds. 19.95 (978-0-9770503-0-7(0)) Institute For Behavior Change Incorporated The.
Hatfield, Ruth. The Book of Storms. Call, Greg, illus. 2015. (Book of Storms Trilogy Ser.: 1). (ENG.). 368p. (J). (gr. 5-9). 16.99 (978-0-8050-9998-0(0), 9780805099980, Holt, Henry & Co. Bks. For Young Readers) Holt, Henry & Co.
—The Book of Storms. Call, Greg, illus. 2016. (Book of Storms Trilogy Ser.). (ENG.). 384p. (J). (gr. 5-9). 18.40 (978-0-606-39364-5(1)) Turtleback Bks.
Haughton, Emma. Rainy Day. Rinaldi, Angelo, illus. (Carolrhoda Picture Books Ser.). 32p. (J). 2004. pap. 6.95 (978-1-57505-668-5(2)) 2003. (gr. -1-3). 6.95 (978-1-57505-452-0(3), Carolrhoda Bks.) Lerner Publishing Group.
Horácek, Petr. Puffin Peter. Horácek, Petr, illus. 2013. (ENG., Illus.). 40p. (J). (gr. -1-2). 16.99 (978-0-7636-6572-2(X)) Candlewick Pr.
Iwamura, Kazuo. Hooray for Summer! 2010. (ENG., Illus.). 32p. (J). (gr. -1-k). 16.95 (978-0-7358-2285-6(9)) North-South Bks., Inc.
Jax, T. L. Fraidy-Frieda's Light Show. Jax, T. L., illus. l.t. ed. 2004. (Illus.). 30p. (J). 9.95 (978-0-9743890-2-8(1)) Flaxenfluff Pr., LLC.
Jennings, Arleen Nalsh. God Is in the Rain. 2012. 64p. (gr. 1-2). pap. 8.95 (978-1-4759-3292-8(8)) iUniverse, Inc.
Jennings, Sharon. Bearcub & Mama. Watt, Mélanie, illus. 2007. (ENG.). 32p. (J). (gr. -1-2). 6.95 (978-1-55453-162-2(4)) Kids Can Pr., Ltd. CAN. Dist: Hachette Bk. Group.
Johnson, Amy Crane. Cinnamon & the April Shower. Mommaerts, Robb, illus. 2009. (ENG.). 32p. (J). (gr. -1-3). 16.95 (978-1-934960-54-7(3), Raven Tree Pr.,Csi) Continental Sales, Inc.
Johnson, D. B. Henry Works. 2004. 32p. (J). (gr. k-3). 15.00 (978-0-618-55204-7(9)) Houghton Mifflin Harcourt Trade & Reference Pubs.
Johnson, Kristin F. Black Blizzard. 2017. (Day of Disaster Ser.). (ENG.). 112p. (gr. 6-12). (J). 26.65 (978-1-5124-2774-5(8)); (YA). 12.99 **(978-1-5124-3507-8(4)**, Darby Creek); (YA). 39.99 **(978-1-5124-2781-3(0)**, Darby Creek); (YA). 39.99 **(978-1-5124-3506-1(6)**, Darby Creek) Lerner Publishing Group.
K/H (Pathways). Kindergarten Stepping Stones: Kindergarten the Bravest Dog Ever - The True Story of Balto Trade Book. rev. ed. 2010. (ENG.). 48p. pap. 9.00 (978-0-7575-8646-0(5)) Kendall Hunt Publishing Co.
Kapica, Dan. Mangrove Seed Chronicles: Learning to Trust. 2007. (Illus.). 64p. 24.95 (978-0-9797158-0-8(6), Mangrove Seed Expressions) Mangrove Seed, Inc.
Kehret, Peg. Flood Disaster. 2008. (ENG.). 160p. (J). (gr. 3-7). pap. 8.99 (978-1-4169-9109-0(3), Simon & Schuster/Paula Wiseman Bks.) Simon & Schuster/Paula Wiseman Bks.
King-Cargile, Gillian. The Toy & the Twister. Krull, Kevin, illus. 2015. (Stuffed Bunny Science Adventure Ser.). (ENG.). 36p. (J). (gr. k-3). 18.99 (978-0-87580-496-5(9)) Northern Illinois Univ. Pr.
Klise, Kate. Grammy Lamby & the Secret Handshake. Klise, Kate & Klise, M. Sarah, illus. 2012. (ENG.). 32p. (J). (gr. -1-3). 17.99 (978-0-8050-9313-1(3), 9780805093131, Holt, Henry & Co. Bks. For Young Readers) Holt, Henry & Co.
Lake, Julie. Galveston's Summer of the Storm. 2003. (Chaparral Bks.). (ENG.). 158p. pap. 17.95 (978-0-87565-272-6(7)) Texas Christian Univ. Pr.
Lance, Scott. Pourman's Library. 2003. 108p. (YA). pap. 10.95 (978-0-595-30148-5(7)) iUniverse, Inc.
Lasser, Jessica. Stormy the Cloud. 2012. 24p. pap. 17.99 (978-1-4685-6214-9(2)) AuthorHouse.
Leeson, Christine. Molly & the Storm. Hansen, Gaby, illus. 2003. 32p. (J). (gr. k-2). tchr. ed. 15.95 (978-1-58925-027-7(3)) Tiger Tales.
Little, Judy. Yody & Bippy the Boo: Friends for Life. 2010. 28p. pap. 12.49 (978-1-4389-7145-2(1)) AuthorHouse.
London, Lewis. Wesley Owl. 2010. (Illus.). 36p. (J). pap. 16.99 (978-1-4490-6122-7(2)) AuthorHouse.
Lyon, Nathan W. & Ellis, Kevin L. Sam the Clam. 2010. 28p. pap. 14.95 (978-1-4520-7784-0(3)) AuthorHouse.
MacFarlane, John. Stormstruck! 2015. (ENG.). 160p. (J). (gr. 3-7). 16.95 (978-0-8234-3394-0(3)) Holiday Hse., Inc.
Maguire, Gregory. What-the-Dickens: The Story of a Rogue Tooth Fairy. 2007. (ENG., Illus.). 304p. (J). (gr. 4-7). 15.99 (978-0-7636-2961-8(8)) Candlewick Pr.
—What-the-Dickens: The Story of a Rogue Tooth Fairy. 2007. (ENG.). 304p. (J). (gr. 4-8). 24.80 (978-1-4287-6555-9(7), Follettbound) Follett School Solutions.
Maria, Miss Yvonne. Beautiful Black Mermaids of the Bayou, 1 vol. 2009. 48p. pap. 16.95 (978-1-60836-236-3(1)) America Star Bks.
Matsakis, Cynthia. Sister Sun, Brother Storm. Silver, Jane, illus. 2012. 32p. 24.95 (978-1-4575-0768-7(4)) Dog Ear Publishing, LLC.
Maurer, Tracy Nelson. Storm Codes. Rodriguez, Christina, illus. 2007. 40p. (J). pap. 8.95 (978-0-89317-064-6(X), WW-064X); (gr. 1-7). lib. bdg. 17.95 (978-0-89317-063-9(1), WW-0631) Finney Co., Inc. (Windward Publishing).
May, Maggie. Pilot, Swaydy & Friends. Larade, April, illus. 2011. 30p. pap. 24.95 (978-1-4560-8499-8(2)) America Star Bks.
Mayer, Mercer. Just a Big Storm. Mayer, Mercer, illus. 2013. (Little Critter Ser.). (ENG., Illus.). 24p. (J). (gr. -1-2). pap. 3.99 (978-0-06-147804-8(0), HarperFestival) HarperCollins Pubs.
—Just a Big Storm. 2013. (Little Critter Ser.). (J). lib. bdg. 13.55 (978-0-606-27153-0(8), Turtleback) Turtleback Bks.
—Little Critter Fall Storybook Collection. Mayer, Mercer, illus. 2015. (Little Critter Ser.). (ENG., Illus.). 192p. (J). (gr. -1-3). 11.99 (978-0-06-238032-6(X)) HarperCollins Pubs.
Maylin, Grace B. There Will Come Another: A Lesson from the Trees. Maylin, Grace B., photos by. 2007. (Illus.). per. (978-0-9792384-0-6(4)) Maylin, Grace.

McPhail, David. The Searcher & Old Tree. McPhail, David, illus. 2011. (ENG., Illus.). 32p. (J). (gr. -1-2). pap. 7.95 (978-1-58089-224-7(8)) Charlesbridge Publishing, Inc.
Messenger, Shannon. Let the Storm Break. 2014. (Sky Fall Ser.: 2). (ENG., Illus.). 400p. (YA). (gr. 7). 17.99 (978-1-4424-5044-8(4), Simon Pulse) Simon Pulse.
Messier, Mireille. The Branch. Pratt, Pierre, illus. 2016. (ENG.). 32p. (J). (gr. -1-2). 16.95 (978-1-77138-564-0(2)) Kids Can Pr., Ltd. CAN. Dist: Hachette Bk. Group.
Milway, Alex. Operation Robot Storm: The Mythical 9th Division. Milway, Alex, illus. 2013. (ENG., Illus.). 224p. (J). pap. 5.99 (978-1-61067-074-6(4)) Kane Miller.
Monninger, Joseph. Stay Alive #4: Flood. 2014. (Stay Alive Ser.: 4). (ENG.). 208p. (J). (gr. 3-7). pap. 5.99 (978-0-545-56359-8(3), Scholastic Paperbacks) Scholastic, Inc.
Montes, Hugo & Montes, Michelle. Young Eagles Armor Academy: Caught in the Storm, V02. 2010. 76p. (J). pap. 5.99 (978-1-60683-022-2(8)) Harrison House Pubs.
Montgomery, R. A. Island of Time. Louie, Wes & Cannella, Marco, illus. 2008. 144p. (J). (gr. 2-7). pap. 6.99 (978-1-933390-28-4(X)) Chooseco LLC.
Moss, Marissa. Rose's Journal: The Story of a Girl in the Great Depression. 2004. (Young American Voice Bks.). (Illus.). (gr. 3-7). 17.00 (978-0-7569-4230-4(6)) Perfection Learning Corp.
Munoz, Norma. Los Cuentos de la Casa del Arbol. Olson, John & Olson, Johan, illus. rev. ed. 2005. (Castillo de la Lectura Blanca Ser.). (SPA & ENG.). 72p. (J). (gr. -1-3). pap. 6.95 (978-970-20-0124-9(2)) Castillo, Ediciones, S. A. de C. V. MEX. Dist: Macmillan.
Murray, Eva & Hogan, Jamie. Island Birthday, 1 vol. 2015. (ENG., Illus.). 32p. (gr. 1-7). 16.95 (978-0-88448-425-7(4), 884425) Tilbury Hse. Pubs.
Nevis, Lance. Animal Rain. Laible MBA, Steve William, ed. Piper, Tom, illus. 2012. 36p. pap. 10.99 (978-0-9850142-7-8(X)) Kodel Group, LLC, The.
Oldfield, Jenny. Midnight Snow. Bright, Alasdair, illus. 2006. (ENG.). 144p. (J). (gr. 2-4). pap. 6.95 (978-0-340-91076-4(3)) Hachette Children's Group GBR. Dist: Hachette Bk. Group.
Parker, Emma. The Lightning Game. 2010. (Illus.). 24p. pap. (978-1-877561-55-9(X)) First Edition Ltd.
Pearson, Iris & Merrill, Mike. The Adventures of Lady: The Big Storm. Pearson, Iris, ed. Project Firefly Animation Studios, illus. rev. ed. 2007. 34p. (J). 11.99 (978-0-9789984-2-4(1)) Adventures of Lady LLC, The.
—The Adventures of Lady: The Big Storm Coloring Book. Pearson, Iris, ed. Project Firefly Animation Studios, illus. 2007. 34p. (J). pap. 5.49 (978-0-9789984-3-1(X)) Adventures of Lady LLC, The.
Pfister, Marcus. Rainbow Fish Finds His Way. James, J. Alison, tr. from GER. Pfister, Marcus, illus. 2006. (Rainbow Fish Ser.). (ENG., Illus.). 32p. (J). (gr. k-3). 18.95 (978-0-7358-2084-5(8)) North-South Bks., Inc.
Polacco, Patricia. The Mermaid's Purse. Polacco, Patricia, illus. 2016. (ENG., Illus.). 48p. (J). (gr. k-3). 17.99 (978-0-399-16692-1(0), G.P. Putnam's Sons Books for Young Readers) Penguin Young Readers Group.
Preus, Margi. Storm's Coming! Geister, David, illus. 2016. (ENG.). 32p. (J). 16.95 (978-1-68134-018-0(6)) Minnesota Historical Society Pr.
Priestley, Chris. Tales of Terror from the Black Ship. Roberts, David, illus. 2008. (Tales of Terror Ser.: 1). (ENG.). 256p. (YA). (gr. 3-6). 12.99 (978-1-59990-290-6(7), 9781599902906, Bloomsbury USA Childrens) Bloomsbury Publishing USA.
Randall, Alison L. The Wheat Doll, 1 vol. Farnsworth, Bill, illus. 2008. (ENG.). 32p. (J). (gr. k-3). 16.95 (978-1-56145-456-3(7)) Peachtree Pubs.
Randolph, Joanne. Stormy: A Storm Cloud's Story. 2009. (Nature Stories Ser.). (Illus.). 24p. (J). (gr. -1-2). pap. 8.15 (978-1-60754-093-9(2)); lib. bdg. 22.60 (978-1-60754-092-2(4)) Windmill Bks.
Ransom, Candice. The Night of the Hurricane's Fury. Tong, Paul, illus. 2009. (On My Own History Ser.). (ENG.). 48p. (gr. 2-4). 25.26 (978-0-8225-7893-2(X)) Lerner Publishing Group.
Regan, Dian. The Snow Blew Inn. Cushman, Doug, illus. 2011. (ENG.). 32p. (J). 16.95 (978-0-8234-2351-4(4)) Holiday Hse., Inc.
Reinoso, Carlos. Little Ducky Jr. & the Whirlwind Storm: A Tale of Loss, Hope,and Renewal. Reinoso, Carlos, illus. l.t. ed. 2005. (Illus.). 50p. (J). 8.99 (978-0-9777672-0-5(5)) Behavioral Health & Human Development Ctr.
Rivers, Phoebe. A Perfect Storm. 2013. (Saranormal Ser.: 10). (ENG., Illus.). 160p. (J). (gr. 3-7). 15.99 (978-1-4424-8959-2(6)); pap. 5.99 (978-1-4424-8958-5(8)) Simon Spotlight. (Simon Spotlight).
Rixon, Denise. The Owl That Barked: Tammy, 1 vol. 2009. 203p. pap. 24.95 (978-1-4489-8472-5(6)) America Star Bks.
Robertson, Charmaine. The Worst Storm. 2016. (Rosen REAL Readers: STEM & STEAM Collection). 12p. (gr. 1-k). pap. 6.33 (978-1-5081-2640-9(2), Rosen Classroom) Rosen Publishing Group, Inc., The.
Rocco, John. Blizzard. Rocco, John, illus. 2014. (ENG., Illus.). 40p. (J). (gr. -1-k). 17.99 (978-1-4231-7865-1(3)) Disney Pr.
Rossi, Joyce. The Gullywasher: El Chaparron Torrencial. 2004. (ENG, SPA & MUL., Illus.). 32p. (J). (gr. k-3). pap. 7.95 (978-0-87358-728-0(6)) Cooper Square Publishing Llc.
Rylant, Cynthia. Annie & Snowball & the Wintry Freeze. Stevenson, Suçie, illus. (Annie & Snowball Ser.: 8). (ENG.). 40p. (J). (gr. k-2). 2011. pap. 3.99 (978-1-4169-7206-8(4)) 2010. 16.99 (978-1-4169-7205-1(6)) Simon Spotlight. (Simon Spotlight).
—The Storm. McDaniels, Preston, illus. 2003. (Lighthouse Family Ser.: 1). (ENG.). 80p. (J). (gr. 1-5). pap. 5.99 (978-0-689-84882-7(X), Simon & Schuster Bks. For Young Readers) Simon & Schuster Bks. For Young Readers.
—The Storm. 2003. (Lighthouse Family Ser.: 1). (gr. 3-6). 16.00 (978-0-613-87052-8(2), Turtleback) Turtleback Bks.
Saddleback Educational Publishing Staff, ed. Crash, 1 vol. unabr. ed. 2011. (Heights Ser.). (ENG.). 49p. (gr. 5-8). pap. 7.95 (978-1-61651-283-5(0)) Saddleback Educational Publishing, Inc.
Sargent, Dave & Sargent, Pat. The Chuck Wagon: Don't Be Stubborn, 10 vols., Vol. 7. Lenoir, Jane, illus. 2005. (Colorado Cowboys Ser.: 10). 32p. (J). pap. 10.95 (978-1-59381-099-3(7)); lib. bdg. 23.60 (978-1-59381-098-6(9)) Ozark Publishing.
—The Colorado Blizzard: Be Determined, 10 vols., Vol. 8. Lenoir, Jane, illus. 2005. (Colorado Cowboys Ser.: 10). 32p. (J). pap. 10.95 (978-1-59381-027-6(X)) Ozark Publishing.
—The Drought: Have Faith, 10 vols., Vol. 9. Lenoir, Jane, illus. 2005. (Colorado Cowboys Ser.: 10). 32p. (J). pap. 10.95 (978-1-59381-103-7(9)); lib. bdg. 23.60 (978-1-59381-102-0(0)) Ozark Publishing.
Scholastic, Inc. Staff & Kaplan, Arie. The Official Stormtrooper Training Manual. 2016. (Lego Star Wars Ser.). (ENG.). 48p. (J). (gr. 2-5). 10.99 (978-0-545-92542-6(8)) Scholastic, Inc.
Seaman, Kathleen. Annycole, 1 vol. 2009. 49p. pap. 16.95 (978-1-4489-1970-3(3)) America Star Bks.
Shields, Gillian. Sophie Makes a Splash. Turner, Helen, illus. 2008. (Mermaid S. O. S. Ser.: 3). (ENG.). 96p. (J). (gr. 1-4). pap. 4.50 (978-1-59990-212-8(5), 9781599902128, Bloomsbury USA Childrens) Bloomsbury Publishing USA.
Simmons, Derek. Flash of Life. 2006. 85p. pap. 16.95 (978-1-4241-3890-6(6)) PublishAmerica, Inc.
Sniegoski, Thomas E. Monstrous. 2017. (Savage Ser.). (ENG., Illus.). 448p. (YA). (gr. 9). 18.99 **(978-1-4814-7718-5(8)**, Simon Pulse) Simon Pulse.
Sniegoski, Tom. Monstrous. 2017. (YA). pap. **(978-1-4814-7719-2(6)**, Simon Pulse) Simon Pulse.
Snyder, Maria V. Storm Watcher. 2013. 228p. (gr. 4-8). pap. 9.99 (978-1-61603-033-9(X)) Leap Bks.
Steig, William. Brave Irene. Steig, William, illus. unabr. ed. 2013. (ENG., Illus.). (J). (gr. -1-3). 12.99 (978-1-4272-3780-4(8), 9781427237804) Macmillan Audio.
A Stormy Adventure: Facing the Fear of Storms. 2004. (J). 6.99 (978-0-9753870-3-0(0)) Write On!
Sweeney, Linda Booth. When the Wind Blows. Christy, Jana, illus. 2015. (ENG.). 32p. (J). (gr. -1-k). 16.99 (978-0-399-16015-8(9), G.P. Putnam's Sons Books for Young Readers) Penguin Young Readers Group.
Swenson, Jamie A. Boom! Boom! Boom! Walker, David, illus. 2013. (ENG.). 32p. (J). (gr. -1-1). 16.99 (978-0-374-30868-1(3), 9780374308681, Farrar, Straus & Giroux (BYR)) Farrar, Straus & Giroux.
Swinburne, Stephen R. Safe in a Storm. Bell, Jennifer, illus. 2016. (J). (978-0-545-66987-0(1)); (ENG.). 32p. (gr. -1-k). 10.99 (978-0-545-86792-4(4)) Scholastic, Inc.
Swinney, Kay. Marty Moose & the Mystical Reunion, 1 vol. 2009. 73p. pap. 19.95 (978-1-61546-867-6(6)) America Star Bks.
Tafuri, Nancy. The Big Storm: A Very Soggy Counting Book. Tafuri, Nancy, illus. 2013. (Classic Board Bks.). (ENG., Illus.). 34p. (J). (gr. -1 — 1). bds. 7.99 (978-1-4424-8179-4(X), Little Simon) Little Simon.
—The Big Storm: A Very Soggy Counting Book. Tafuri, Nancy, illus. 2009. (ENG., Illus.). 32p. (J). (gr. -1-2). 18.99 (978-1-4169-6795-8(8), Simon & Schuster Bks. For Young Readers) Simon & Schuster Bks. For Young Readers.
Tate, Elizabeth Dawn. There's a Storm Brewing Outside. 2009. 24p. pap. 15.50 (978-1-60693-239-1(X), Eloquent Bks.) Strategic Book Publishing & Rights Agency (SBPRA).
Tekavec, Heather. Storm Is Coming! Spengler, Margaret, illus. 2004. (ENG.). 32p. (J). (gr. -1-3). reprint ed. pap. 6.99 (978-0-14-240070-8(X), Puffin Books) Penguin Young Readers Group.
Ungerer, Tomi. Fog Island. 2013. (ENG., Illus.). 48p. 16.95 (978-0-7148-6535-5(4)) Phaidon Pr., Inc.
Viau, Nancy. Storm Song. Gynux, illus. 2013. 24p. pap. 12.99 (978-1-4778-6646-7(9)) Amazon Publishing.
Viau, Nancy & Bolinao, Mela. Storm Song, 0 vols. Gynux, illus. 2013. (ENG.). 24p. (J). (gr. k-3). 12.99 (978-1-4778-1646-2(1), 9781477816462, Amazon Children's Publishing) Amazon Publishing.
Voorhees, Coert. Storm Wrangler. 2011. (ENG., Illus.). 24p. 16.95 (978-1-936474-07-3(7), 4f038b6a-35ac-432d-8e8e-7dfdecea85de) Bright Sky Pr.
Ward, Jennifer. The Sunhat. Sisson, Stéphanie Roth, illus. 2013. (ENG.). (J). 15.95 (978-1-933855-78-3(9), Rio Nuevo Pubs.) Rio Nuevo Pubs.
Welsh, Karen Leis. Frolicking Friends. 2012. (Illus.). 44p. pap. 21.99 (978-1-4685-6422-8(6)) AuthorHouse.
Weston Woods Staff, creator. Brave Irene. 2011. 29.95 (978-0-439-73468-4(1)); 18.95 (978-0-439-72665-8(4)); 38.75 (978-0-439-72666-5(2)) Weston Woods Studios, Inc.
Wetterer, Margaret K. & Wetterer, Charles M. The Snowshoeing Adventure of Milton Daub, Blizzard Trekker. Trover, Zachary, illus. 2010. (History's Kid Heroes Ser.). (ENG.). 32p. (gr. 3-5). pap. 8.95 (978-0-7613-6194-7(4), Graphic Universe™) Lerner Publishing Group.
White, Dianne. Blue on Blue. Krommes, Beth, illus. 2014. (ENG.). 48p. (J). (gr. k-3). 17.99 (978-1-4424-1267-5(4), Beach Lane Bks.) Beach Lane Bks.
Williams, Teresa Ann. Friends of Wildwood, 1 vol. 2009. 48p. pap. 16.95 (978-1-4489-9419-9(5)) America Star Bks.
Willis, Jeanne. La Tormenta Monstruosa. (Cotton Cloud Ser.). (SPA.). (J). (gr. 1-3). pap. (978-84-480-0180-3(X)) Timun Mas, Editorial S.A. ESP. Dist: Lectorum Pubns., Inc.
Wozniak, Paul. Stranded in a Snowstorm! Webber, Mike, illus. 2014. (ENG.). 82p. pap. 11.95 (978-1-63047-173-6(9)) Morgan James Publishing.
Xiong, Kim, illus. Paper Horse. 2008. (ENG & CHI.). 37p. (J). 18.95 (978-1-60603-003-5(5)) Better Chinese LLC.
Yoon, Salina. Stormy Night. (ENG., Illus.). (J). 2016. 32p. bds. 7.99 (978-1-68119-165-2(2), 9781681191652) 2015. 40p. (gr. -1-1). 14.99 (978-0-8027-3780-9(3), 9780802737809) Bloomsbury Publishing USA. (Bloomsbury USA Childrens).

STORYTELLING

Bicknell, Joanna. Build a Story Book. 2007. (Illus.). 20p. (J). (gr. k-5). pap. (978-1-84610-426-8(2)) Make Believe Ideas.
Boston, David, illus. Wonder Tales from Around the World. 2006. (World Storytelling from August House Ser.). (ENG.). 158p. (J). (gr. 3-7). pap. 19.95 (978-0-87483-422-2(8), AH228) August Hse. Pubs., Inc.
Braun, Eric, et al. Encounter: Narrative Nonfiction Picture Books. 2017. (Encounter: Narrative Nonfiction Picture Bks.). (ENG.). 40p. (gr. 3-5). pap. 47.70 (978-1-4914-8051-9(3)) Encounter Bks.
Brown, Roberta Simpson. Queen of the Cold-Blooded Tales. Hall, Wendell E., illus. 2005. (American Storytelling Ser.). (ENG.). 175p. (J). (gr. 5-17). pap. 9.95 (978-0-87483-408-6(2)) August Hse. Pubs., Inc.
Career Building Through Using Digital Story Tools. 2013. (Digital Career Building Ser.). 64p. (YA). (gr. 7-12). pap. 77.70 (978-1-4777-1736-3(6)) Rosen Publishing Group, Inc., The.
Charlesworth, Liza. Punctuation Tales: A Motivating Collection of Super-Funny Storybooks That Help Kids Master the Mechanics of Writing. 2009. (ENG.). 32.99 (978-0-545-11401-1(2), Teaching Resources) Scholastic, Inc.
Doyle, Alfreda C. Story Time Literacy Coach: Literacy, Storytelling & Rhyme. unabr. ed. 2005. (Alfreda's Radio Ser.: Vol. 1). (gr. 5-9). spiral bd. 39.95 (978-1-56820-305-8(5)) Story Time Stories That Rhyme.
Edupress, creator. My Story Book: Primary. 2009. 32p. pap. 1.99 (978-1-56472-944-6(3)) Edupress, Inc.
Glaser, Jason. Career Building Through Using Digital Story Tools. 2013. (Digital Career Building Ser.). 64p. (YA). (gr. 7-12). 31.95 (978-1-4777-1722-6(6)); pap. 12.95 (978-1-4777-1735-6(8)) Rosen Publishing Group, Inc., The.
Hamilton, Martha & Weiss, Mitch. Through the Grapevine: World Tales Kids Can Read & Tell. Lyon, Carol, illus. (ENG.). 128p. (J). (gr. 1-6). 2006. pap. 15.95 (978-0-87483-624-0(7)) 2005. 24.95 (978-0-87483-625-7(5)) August Hse. Pubs., Inc.
How Rabbit Caught the Sun: Individual Title Six-Packs. (Story Steps Ser.). (gr. k-2). 32.00 (978-0-7635-9811-2(9)) Rigby Education.
How the Geese Saved Rome: Individual Title Six-Packs. (Story Steps Ser.). (gr. k-2). 32.00 (978-0-7635-9801-3(1)) Rigby Education.
Jones, James Lucas & Torres, J., eds. Yo Gabba Gabba: Comic Book Time. 2011. (Illus.). 128p. (J). 24.99 (978-1-934964-49-1(2)) Oni Pr., Inc.
K/H (Pathways). Pathways: Grade 6 Dr. Rabbit Trade Book. rev. ed. 2011. (ENG.). 30p. pap. 11.00 (978-0-7575-4840-6(7)) Kendall Hunt Publishing Co.
LaFosse, Michael G. & Alexander, Richard L. Story-Gami Kit: Creating Origami Using Folding Stories. 2010. (ENG., Illus.). 1p. (gr. 1-4). 16.95 (978-0-8048-4134-4(9)) Tuttle Publishing.
Langston-George, Rebecca, et al. Encounter: Narrative Nonfiction Stories. 2017. (Encounter: Narrative Nonfiction Stories Ser.). (ENG.). (gr. 3-5). 187.92 **(978-1-5157-7347-4(7))** Encounter Bks.
Madden-Lunsford, Kerry. Nothing Fancy about Kathryn & Charlie. Madden-Lunsford, Lucy, illus. 2013. (ENG.). 36p. (J). pap. 14.95 (978-0-9828528-0-4(0)) Mockingbird Publishing.
Matthews, Caitlín & Matthews, John. Legends of the Sea: Create-A-Story Kit. 2011. (Storyworld Ser.). (ENG., Illus.). 22p. (J). (gr. 4-7). 9.99 (978-0-7636-5320-0(9), Templar) Candlewick Pr.
Matthews, John & Matthews, Caitlín. Storyworld: Create a Story Kit. 2010. (Illus.). (978-0-7636-5319-4(5)) Templar Publishing.
McFarlane, Marilyn. Sacred Stories: Wisdom from World Religions. Berg, Caroline O., illus. 2012. (ENG.). 192p. (J). (gr. 4-9). 17.99 (978-1-58270-334-3(5)) Aladdin/Beyond Words.
Nayeri, Daniel, How to Tell a Story: Read the Book, Roll the Blocks, Build Adventures! Won, Brian, illus. 2015. (ENG.). 144p. (J). (gr. 3-7). pap. 19.95 (978-0-7611-8457-7(0)) Workman Publishing Co., Inc.
Neuburger, Emily K. Show Me a Story: 40 Craft Projects & Activities to Spark Children's Storytelling. 2012. (ENG.). 144p. 26.95 (978-1-61212-148-2(9), 622148); (Illus.). (J). pap. 16.95 (978-1-60342-988-7(3), 62988) Storey Publishing, LLC.
Otfinoski, Steven & Braun, Eric. Encounter: Narrative Nonfiction Stories. 2016. (Encounter: Narrative Nonfiction Stories Ser.). (ENG.). 66.64 (978-1-4914-8046-5(7)) Encounter Bks.
Otfinoski, Steven & Langston-George, Rebecca. Encounter: Narrative Nonfiction Stories. 2017. (Encounter: Narrative Nonfiction Stories Ser.). (ENG.). (gr. 3-5). pap. 40.75 (978-1-5157-7349-8(3)) Encounter Bks.
Packard, Mary. The Storyteller. Land Eagle, illus. 2009. 196p. (J). (978-1-4351-1557-6(0)) Metro Bks.
Reid, Rob. Storytime Slam: 15 Lesson Plans for Preschool & Primary Story Programs. 2006. (Illus.). 85p. per. 16.95 (978-1-932146-52-3(0), Upstart Bks.) Highsmith Inc.
Rustad, Martha E. H. Learning about Folktales, Fables, & Fairy Tales, 1 vol. 2014. (Language Arts Ser.). (ENG.). 24p. (gr. k-1). 26.65 (978-1-4914-0577-2(5), Pebble Plus) Capstone Press of Coughlan Cos.
Set of 7 StoryTellers. (Classic Storytellers Ser.). (Illus.). (gr. 4-8). lib. bdg. (978-1-58415-321-4(0)) Mitchell Lane Pubs., Inc.
Snedeker, Gus. Tell Me a Story: Family Folklore. 2013. (Illus.). 48p. (J). pap. (978-1-4222-2499-1(6)) Mason Crest.
—Tell Me a Story: Family Folklore. Jabbour, Alan, ed. 2012. (North American Folklore for Youth Ser.). (Illus.). 48p. (J). (gr. 4). 19.95 (978-1-4222-2488-5(0)) Mason Crest.
A Storyteller's Journey, 6 Pack. (Bookweb Ser.). 32p. (gr. 4-18). 34.00 (978-0-7635-3738-8(1)) Rigby Education.
Stotter, Ruth. A Loop of String: String Stories & String Stunts: Traditional & Original String Figures & Stories. Coffey, Kevin, illus. 2009. 110p. (J). pap. 22.95 (978-1-58790-170-6(6)) Regent Pr.
The Tug of War: Individual Title Six-Pack. (Story Steps Ser.). (gr. k-2). 23.00 (978-0-7635-9620-0(5)) Rigby Education.
Watts, Eleanor. Storytelling. 2006. (Oxford Applied Linguistics Ser.). (ENG., Illus.). 88p. 12.50 (978-0-19-441976-5(2)) Oxford Univ. Pr., Inc.
Welsh, Anne Marie & Tuchman, Laura. A World of Girls. Garcia, Helena, illus. 2010. 40p. (J). (978-0-88441-750-7(6)) Girl Scouts of the USA.
Whelon, Chuck. Word Play: Write Your Own Crazy Comics, No. 1. 2011. (Dover Children's Activity Bks.). (ENG., Illus.). 64p. (J). (gr. 3-5). pap. 5.99 (978-0-486-48165-4(4)) Dover Pubns., Inc.
—Word Play! - Write Your Own Crazy Comics, No. 2. 2011. (Dover Children's Activity Bks.). (ENG., Illus.). 64p. (J). (gr. 3-5). pap. 5.99 (978-0-486-48166-1(2)) Dover Pubns., Inc.

STORYTELLING—COLLECTIONS

DeSpain, Pleasant. Sweet Land of Story: Thirty-Six American Tales to Tell. (ENG., Illus.). 176p. (J). (gr. 3-7). 2006. 19.95 (978-0-87483-569-4(0)) 2005. pap. 12.95 (978-0-87483-600-4(X)) August Hse. Pubs., Inc.
Hamilton, Martha, et al. Noodlehead Stories: World Tales Kids Can Read & Tell. 2006. (ENG., Illus.). 96p. (J). (gr. 1-6). pap. 14.95 (978-0-87483-585-4(2)) August Hse. Pubs., Inc.
Lil Gems & Black, Magenta. Tutu's Lil Gems. 2012. 60p. pap. 8.95 (978-0-9885632-3-0(1)) Pink Kiss Publishing Co.
Young, Richard & Young, Judy D. African-American Folktales. 2006. (American Storytelling Ser.). (ENG.). 176p. (J). (gr. 3-7). pap. 12.95 (978-0-87483-309-6(4)) August Hse. Pubs., Inc.

STORYTELLING—FICTION

Abbott, Jacob. Stories Told to Rollo's Cousin Lucy. 2005. pap. 22.95 (978-1-4179-5651-7(8)) Kessinger Publishing, LLC.
Adams, W. Royce. Raid on Rairarubi. 2008. 148p. (gr. 4-7). pap. 10.95 (978-0-9712206-8-3(9)) Rairarubia Bks.
Akbarpour, Ahmad. That Night's Train, 1 vol. Saghafi, Majid, tr. from PER. Arsenault, Isabelle, illus. 2012. (ENG.). 96p. (J). (gr. 3). 14.95 (978-1-55498-169-4(7)) Groundwood Bks. CAN. Dist: Publishers Group West (PGW).
Alary, Laura. Mira & the Big Story. Todd, Sue, illus. 2012. (ENG.). 36p. (J). 12.00 (978-1-55896-693-2(5), Skinner Hse. Bks.) Unitarian Universalist Assn.
Auxier, Jonathan. The Night Gardener. (ENG.). (YA). (gr. 3-7). 2015. 384p. pap. 8.95 (978-1-4197-1531-0(3)) 2014. 368p. 16.95 (978-1-4197-1144-2(X)) Abrams, Inc. (Amulet Bks.).
—The Night Gardener. 2015. (J). lib. bdg. 19.60 (978-0-606-36891-9(4)) Turtleback Bks.
BAtey, Kathey. Exaggeration Aggravation. 2006. (J). per. 15.00 (978-0-9790017-1-0(4)) Spirited Presentations.
—Exaggeration Aggravation. GEbhard, Andy, illus. 2006. (J). 8.00 (978-0-9790017-0-3(6)) Spirited Presentations.
Beck, Ian. The Secret History of Tom Trueheart. 2007. (Illus.). 352p. (J). (gr. 3-7). 16.99 (978-0-06-115210-8(2)); lib. bdg. 17.89 (978-0-06-115211-5(0)) HarperCollins Pubs.
Beharrell, Gayle. The Adventures of Charlie. 2008. 36p. pap. 16.99 (978-1-4389-2546-2(8)) AuthorHouse.
Benton, Jim. The End (Almost) Benton, Jim, illus. 2014. (ENG., Illus.). 40p. (J). (gr. -1-k). 16.99 (978-0-545-17731-3(6), Scholastic Pr.) Scholastic, Inc.
—The End (Almost) 2014. (Illus.). (J). (978-0-545-67536-9(7), Scholastic Pr.) Scholastic, Inc.
Blubaugh, Penny. Serendipity Market. 2011. (ENG.). 304p. (YA). (gr. 8). pap. 8.99 (978-0-06-146877-3(0), HarperTeen) HarperCollins Pubs.
Blume, Lesley M. M. Cornelia & the Audacious Escapades of the Somerset Sisters. (ENG.). 272p. (J). (gr. 3-7). 2008. 7.99 (978-0-440-42110-8(1), Yearling) 2006. 15.95 (978-0-375-83523-0(7), Knopf Bks. for Young Readers) Random Hse. Children's Bks.
Bottner, Barbara. Miss Brooks' Story Nook (where Tales Are Told & Ogres Are Welcome) Emberley, Michael, illus. 2014. (ENG.). 40p. (J). (gr. k-4). 16.99 (978-0-449-81328-7(2), Knopf Bks. for Young Readers) Random Hse. Children's Bks.
Bowling, Joyce E. & Sester, Richard. A Path of Stitches, 1 vol. 2010. 22p. pap. 24.95 (978-1-4489-6426-0(1)) PublishAmerica, Inc.
Brown, Sharon. Nana, Tell Me a Story. 2009. 58p. pap. 15.99 (978-1-4415-4478-0(X)) Xlibris Corp.
Broyles, Beverly Ashley, illus. Grandmother's Alligator/Burukenge Wa Nyanya Activity Guide. 2005. (ENG & SWA.). (J). 12.95 (978-0-9703632-7-5(3)) Wakefield Connection, The.
Burford, Lorrimer. A Jamaican Storyteller's Tale. 2005. (ENG., Illus.). 197p. pap. 7.99 (978-976-8184-84-9(1)) Penguin Publishing Group.
Cahill, Byron. The Legend of Skywoman. 2005. (J). pap. (978-1-4108-4232-9(0)) Benchmark Education Co.
Cardno, Anthony R. The Firflake: A Christmas Story. Cornue, Don, illus. 2008. 56p. pap. 8.95 (978-0-595-52468-6(0)) iUniverse, Inc.
Catalanotto, Peter. Ivan the Terrier. Catalanotto, Peter, illus. 2007. (ENG., Illus.). 32p. (J). (gr. -1-3). 17.99 (978-1-4169-1247-7(9), Atheneum/Richard Jackson Bks.) Simon & Schuster Children's Publishing.
Cazet, Denys. Grandpa Spanielson's Chicken Pox Stories No. 1: The Octopus. Cazet, Denys, illus. 2005. (I Can Read Bks.). (Illus.). 48p. (J). (gr. -1-3). lib. bdg. 16.89 (978-0-06-051089-3(7)) HarperCollins Pubs.
—The Octopus. Cazet, Denys, illus. 2008. (Grandpa Spanielson's Chicken Pox Stories Ser.). (Illus.). (J). (gr. -1-3). pap. 16.95 incl. audio (978-1-4301-0455-1(4));Set. pap. 31.95 incl. audio compact disk (978-1-4301-0460-5(0));Set. pap. 29.95 incl. audio (978-1-4301-0457-5(0)) Live Oak Media.
—The Shrunken Head. 2007. (I Can Read Bks.: No. 3). (Illus.). 48p. (J). (gr. -1-3). lib. bdg. 16.89 (978-0-06-073014-7(5)) HarperCollins Pubs.
—A Snout for Chocolate. 2006. (I Can Read Bks.). (Illus.). (J). (gr. -1-3). (ENG.). 48p. 15.99 (978-0-06-051093-0(5)); 47p. lib. bdg. 16.89 (978-0-06-051094-7(3)) HarperCollins Pubs.
—A Snout for Chocolate. Cazet, Denys, illus. 2008. (Grandpa Spanielson's Chicken Pox Stories Ser.). (Illus.). (J). (gr. -1-3). pap. 16.95 incl. audio (978-1-4301-0463-6(5));Set. pap. 31.95 incl. audio compact disk (978-1-4301-0468-1(6));Set. pap. 29.95 incl. audio (978-1-4301-0465-0(1)) Live Oak Media.
—A Snout for Chocolate. 2007. (I Can Read Bks.). (Illus.). 48p. (gr. -1-3). 15.00 (978-0-7569-8056-6(9)) Perfection Learning Corp.
Church, Alfred J. Three Greek Children. 2008. (Illus.). 160p. pap. 9.95 (978-1-59915-081-9(6)) Yesterday's Classics.
Clark, Simon P. Tell the Story to Its End. 2015. (ENG., Illus.). 208p. (YA). (gr. 7). 18.99 (978-1-250-06675-6(1), 9781250066756, St. Martin's Griffin) St. Martin's Pr.
Clayton, Colleen. What Happens Next. 2013. (ENG.). 320p. (YA). (gr. 10-17). pap. 10.00 (978-0-316-19869-1(2), Poppy) Little, Brown Bks. for Young Readers.
Connelly, Valerie. Goosh Gosh from the Lilac Kitchen & Other Childhood Stories. 2013. (Illus.). 42p. pap. 14.95 (978-1-935993-49-0(6)) Nightengale Pr.
Connolly, Brian A. Hawk. 2007. 156p. 20.95 (978-1-60264-030-6(0)); 160p. per. 13.95 (978-1-60264-029-0(7)) Virtualbookworm.com Publishing, Inc.

Contreras, Kathleen. Braids - Trencitas. Lindmark, Margaret, illus. 2009. (ENG & SPA.). 32p. (J). (gr. -1-3). 14.99 (978-1-933032-27-6(8)) Lectorum Pubns., Inc.

Cooke, Trish. Look Back! Binch, Caroline, illus. 2017. (ENG.). 32p. (J). pap. 8.95 **(978-1-56656-099-3(3)**, Crocodile Bks.) Interlink Publishing Group, Inc.

Cooper, Bernice Soroka. The Little Elf-Frog. 2012. 24p. pap. 17.99 (978-1-4772-9525-0(9)) AuthorHouse.

Cowley, Joy. Big Bear & Little Bear: Story. Lam, Amy, illus. 2013. (ENG.). 8p. pap. (978-1-927186-23-7(4), Joy Cowley Club) Flying Start Bks.

Dadey, Debbie. Treasure in Trident City. Avakyan, Tatevik, illus. 2014. (Mermaid Tales Ser.: 8). (ENG.). 128p. (J). (gr. 1-4). pap. 5.99 (978-1-4424-8266-1(4), Aladdin) Simon & Schuster Children's Publishing.

Dadey, Debby & Dadey, Debbie. Treasure in Trident City, 1 vol., Bk. 8. 2015. (Mermaid Tales Ser.). (ENG.). 120p. (J). (gr. 2-4). 24.21 (978-1-61479-329-8(8), Spotlight) ABDO Publishing Co.

Derubertis, Barbara. Eddie Elephant's Exciting Egg-Sitting. 2010. pap. 45.32 (978-0-7613-6507-5(9)) Kane Press, Inc.

deRubertis, Barbara. Eddie Elephant's Exciting Egg-Sitting. Alley, R. W., illus. 2010. (Animal Antics A to Z Ser.). 32p. (J). (gr. -1-3). pap. 7.95 (978-1-57565-309-9(5)); lib. bdg. 22.60 (978-1-57565-316-7(8)) Kane Press, Inc.

—Maxwell Moose's Mountain Monster. Alley, R. W., illus. 2011. (Animal Antics A to Z Ser.). 32p. (J). pap. 45.32 (978-0-7613-7659-0(3)); (ENG.). lib. bdg. 22.60 (978-1-57565-334-1(6)); (ENG.). (gr. -1-3). pap. 7.95 (978-1-57565-325-9(7)) Kane Press, Inc.

deRubertis, Barbara & DeRubertis, Barbara. Eddie Elephant's Exciting Egg-Sitting. Alley, R. W., illus. 2012. (Animal Antics A to Z Ser.). 32p. (J). (gr. 2 — 1). cd-rom 7.95 (978-1-57565-398-3(2)) Kane Press, Inc.

—Maxwell Moose's Mountain Monster. Alley, R. W., illus. 2012. (Animal Antics A to Z Ser.). 32p. (J). (gr. 2 — 1). cd-rom 7.95 (978-1-57565-406-5(7)) Kane Press, Inc.

DiSalvo-Ryan, DyAnne. The Sloppy Copy Slipup. 2005. (ENG., Illus.). 128p. (J). (gr. 2-6). 16.95 (978-0-8234-1947-0(9)) Holiday Hse., Inc.

Dokey, Cameron. The Storyteller's Daughter: A Retelling of the Arabian Nights. 2007. (Once upon a Time Ser.). (ENG.). 240p. (YA). (gr. 9). mass mkt. 7.99 (978-1-4169-3776-0(5), Simon Pulse) Simon Pulse.

Donaldson, Julia. The Fish Who Cried Wolf. Scheffler, Axel, illus. (J). 2017. (ENG.). 40p. (gr. -1-k). 17.99 (978-0-439-92825-0(7)) 2008. pap. (978-0-545-03454-8(X)) Scholastic, Inc. (Levine, Arthur A. Bks.).

Dubison, Valentine. Willington Woods. 2008. 52p. pap. 7.95 (978-1-4327-2153-4(4)) Outskirts Pr., Inc.

Eagar, Lindsay. Hour of the Bees. (ENG.). 368p. (J). (gr. 5-9). 2017. pap. 8.99 **(978-0-7636-9120-2(8))** 2016. 16.99 (978-0-7636-7922-4(4)) Candlewick Pr.

Falatko, Julie. Snappsy the Alligator (Did Not Ask to Be in This Book) Miller, Tim J., illus. 2016. (ENG.). 40p. (J). (gr. -1-3). 16.99 (978-0-451-46945-8(3), Viking Books for Young Readers) Penguin Young Readers Group.

Farber, Erica. Kooky Campout. Scarry, Huck, illus. 2015. (Richard Scarry's Great Big Schoolhouse Ser.). (ENG.). 24p. (J). (gr. 1-2). 12.95 (978-1-4027-9914-3(4)) Sterling Publishing Co., Inc.

Fox, Mem. This & That. Horacek, Judy, illus. 2017. (ENG.). 32p. (J). (gr. -1-k). 17.99 (978-1-338-03780-7(3), Scholastic Pr.) Scholastic, Inc.

Fraillon, Zana. The Bone Sparrow. 2016. (ENG.). 240p. (J). (gr. 4-7). 16.99 (978-1-4847-8151-7(1)) Hyperion Bks. for Children.

Funke, Cornelia. CORAZÓN DE TINTA. 2006. (SPA., Illus.). 598p. (J). (978-84-7844-235-5(9)) Siruela, Ediciones S.A.

Gamble, Adam & Jasper, Mark. Good Night Books. Chan, Suwin, illus. 2017. (Good Night Our World Ser.). (ENG.). 20p. (J). (— 1). bds. 9.95 **(978-1-60219-470-0(X))** Good Night Bks.

Gonzales Betrand, Diane. The Story Circle / el Circulo de Cuentos. Martin, Wendy, illus. 2016. (ENG, MUL & SPA.). 32p. (J). (gr. k-3). 17.95 (978-1-55885-826-8(1), Piñata Books) Arte Publico Pr.

Grey, Mini. Toys in Space. 2013. (ENG.). 32p. (J). (gr. k-3). 16.99 (978-0-307-97812-7(5), Knopf Bks. for Young Readers) Random Hse. Children's Bks.

Griffiths, Andy. The 39-Story Treehouse. Denton, Terry, illus. 2015. (Treehouse Bks.). (ENG.). 352p. (J). (gr. 1-5). 13.99 (978-1-250-02692-7(X), 9781250026927) Feiwel & Friends.

—The 39-Story Treehouse. Barcellona, Christine, ed. Denton, Terry, illus. 2016. (Treehouse Bks.: 3). (ENG.). 368p. (J). pap. 6.99 (978-1-250-07511-6(4), 9781250075116) Square Fish.

Gutsche, Brigitte. The Intruder. 2006. (J). pap. (978-0-88092-743-7(7)) Royal Fireworks Publishing Co.

Hadley, Caroline. Woodside; or, Look, Listen & Learn. 2007. (ENG., Illus.). 80p. per. (978-1-4065-1557-2(4)) Dodo Pr.

Hanson, Mary. How to Save Your Tail: If You Are a Rat Nabbed by Cats Who Really Like Stories about Magic Spoons, Wolves with Snout-Warts, Big, Hairy Chimney Trolls ... & Cookies, Too. 2008. (ENG., Illus.). 112p. (J). (gr. 1-4). 5.99 (978-0-440-42228-0(0), Yearling) Random Hse. Children's Bks.

Hartley, Steve. Oliver Fibbs & the Giant Boy-Munching Bugs. Lum, Bernice, illus. unabr. ed. 2015. (Oliver Fibbs Ser.: 2). (ENG.). 192p. (J). (gr. 2-5). pap. 8.99 (978-1-4472-2024-4(2)) Pan Macmillan GBR. Dist: Independent Pubs. Group.

Hartnett, Sonya. The Silver Donkey. Powers, Don, illus. 2014. (ENG.). 272p. (J). (gr. 5). 16.99 (978-0-7636-7211-9(4)) Candlewick Pr.

—The Silver Donkey. Spudvilas, Anne, illus. 2004. viii, 193p. (J). (978-0-670-04240-1(4), Viking Adult) Penguin Publishing Group.

Hedman, Jack. The Gift of Gab: A Collection of Recollections. 2012. 48p. pap. 21.88 (978-1-4669-1021-8(6)) Trafford Publishing.

Hughes, V. I. Aziz the Story Teller. Czernecki, Stefan, illus. 2006. 29p. (J). (gr. k-4). reprint ed. 17.00 (978-1-4223-5298-4(6)) DIANE Publishing Co.

Hunter, Todd H. Elf Night: A Christmas Story. Gavrilovskiy, Olga, illus. 2006. 52p. (J). (gr. -1-7). 16.95 (978-0-9788085-0-1(9)) Tetoca Pr.

Isabel, Delgado Maria. Chave's Memories / Los Recuerdos de Chave. Yvonne, Symank, illus. 2008. 32p. (J). pap. 7.95 (978-1-55885-244-0(1), Piñata Books) Arte Publico Pr.

Johnston, Tony. My Abuelita. Morales, Yuyi, illus. 2009. (ENG.). 32p. (J). (gr. -1-3). 17.99 (978-0-15-216330-3(1)) Houghton Mifflin Harcourt Publishing Co.

Jones, Lloyd. Mister Pip. 2010. 256p. 21.85 (978-0-7569-9114-2(5)) Perfection Learning Corp.

Kasza, Keiko. Silly Goose's Big Story. Kasza, Keiko, illus. 2012. (ENG., Illus.). 32p. (J). (gr. -1-k). 16.99 (978-0-399-25542-7(7), G.P. Putnam's Sons Books for Young Readers) Penguin Young Readers Group.

Kinelski, Marilyn D. Am I Important? 2011. 28p. pap. 13.59 (978-1-4634-1965-3(1)) AuthorHouse.

Kirby, Matthew J. Icefall. (ENG.). 336p. (J). (gr. 3-7). 2013. pap. 6.99 (978-0-545-27425-8(7), Scholastic Paperbacks) 2011. 17.99 (978-0-545-27424-1(9), Scholastic Pr.) Scholastic, Inc.

Koksal, Erin. Bedtime for Abbie. 2010. 23p. (J). pap. 11.95 (978-1-4327-5693-2(1)) Outskirts Pr., Inc.

Kroll, Steven. The Tyrannosaurus Game, 0 vols. Schindler, S. D., illus. 2010. (ENG.). 32p. (J). (gr. -1-3). 17.99 (978-0-7614-5603-2(1), 9780761456032, Amazon Children's Publishing) Amazon Publishing.

Kurtz, Jane. In the Small, Small Night. Isadora, Rachel, illus. 2005. (Amistad Ser.). (ENG.). 32p. (J). (gr. k-5). 17.99 (978-0-06-623814-2(5), Greenwillow Bks.) HarperCollins Pubs.

LaRochelle, David. It's a Tiger! Tankard, Jeremy, illus. 2012. (ENG.). 36p. (J). (gr. -1-k). 16.99 (978-0-8118-6925-6(3)) Chronicle Bks. LLC.

Lehrhaupt, Adam. This Is a Good Story. Le Huche, Magali, illus. 2017. (ENG.). 40p. (J). (gr. k-3). 17.99 **(978-1-4814-2935-1(3)**, Simon & Schuster/Paula Wiseman Bks.) Simon & Schuster/Paula Wiseman Bks.

Lin, Grace. Starry River of the Sky. (ENG., Illus.). (J). (gr. 3-7). 2014. 320p. pap. 10.99 (978-0-316-12597-0(0)) 2012. 304p. 17.99 (978-0-316-12595-6(4)) Little, Brown Bks. for Young Readers.

—Starry River of the Sky. 2014. (J). lib. bdg. 20.85 (978-0-606-32277-5(9), Turtleback) Turtleback Bks.

Lin, Grace. When the Sea Turned to Silver. (ENG.). (J). (gr. 3-7). 2017. 400p. pap. 9.99 **(978-0-316-12594-9(6))** 2016. (Illus.). 384p. 18.99 (978-0-316-12592-5(X)) Little, Brown Bks. for Young Readers.

—When the Sea Turned to Silver. 2017. (J). lib. bdg. 20.85 **(978-0-606-40629-1(8))** Turtleback Bks.

Little, Jean & de Vries, Maggie. Once upon a Golden Apple: 25th Anniversary Edition. Gilman, Phoebe, illus. 25th ed. 2016. (ENG.). 26p. (J). (— 1). bds. 7.99 (978-0-670-07007-7(6), Puffin Canada) Penguin Random House Canada Young Readers CAN. Dist: Penguin Random Hse. LLC.

Lobel, Arnold. Historias de Ratones. 2003. (SPA.). 64p. (978-84-95123-95-4(9), KA7695) Kalandraka Editora, S.L. ESP. Dist: Lectorum Pubns., Inc.

Lodding, Linda Ravin. Little Red Riding Sheep. Atkinson, Cale, illus. 2017. (ENG.). 40p. (J). (gr. -1-3). 17.99 (978-1-4814-5748-4(9)) Simon & Schuster Children's Publishing.

Lois, Lowry. Gooney Bird Greene. Middy Chilman, Thomas, illus. 2004. (Gooney Bird Ser.: No. 1). 88p. (gr. 2-5). 16.00 (978-0-7569-2583-3(5)) Perfection Learning Corp.

Lyon, George Ella. My Friend, the Starfinder. Gammell, Stephen, illus. 2008. (ENG.). 40p. (J). (gr. -1-2). 17.99 (978-1-4169-2738-9(7), Atheneum/Richard Jackson Bks.) Simon & Schuster Children's Publishing.

Lyons, Kelly Starling. Tea Cakes for Tosh. Lewis, E. B., illus. 2012. (ENG.). 32p. (J). (gr. k-3). 16.99 (978-0-399-25213-6(4), G.P. Putnam's Sons Books for Young Readers) Penguin Young Readers Group.

Maguire, Gregory. What-the-Dickens: The Story of a Rogue Tooth Fairy. (ENG., Illus.). 304p. (gr. 4-7). 2008. pap. 8.99 (978-0-7636-4147-4(2)) 2007. (J). 15.99 (978-0-7636-2961-8(8)) Candlewick Pr.

—What-the-Dickens: The Story of a Rogue Tooth Fairy. 2007. (ENG.). 304p. (J). (gr. 4-8). 24.80 (978-1-4287-6555-9(7), Follettbound) Follett School Solutions.

Manley, Craig. The Rammarg Files. 2006. (J). lib. bdg. (978-0-88092-742-0(9)) Royal Fireworks Publishing Co.

Manushkin, Fran. Katie's Spooky Sleepover. Lyon, Tammie, illus. 2016. (Katie Woo Ser.). (ENG.). 32p. (gr. k-2). lib. bdg. 21.32 (978-1-4795-9640-9(X)) Picture Window Bks.

Martins, E. V. Cookie Nana's Story Book: Featuring " Grumpy Granddad " 2009. (Illus.). 40p. pap. 16.99 (978-1-4389-2325-3(2)) AuthorHouse.

Matthews, John and Caitlin. StoryWorld: Christmas Tales: Create-A-Story Kit. 2011. (Storyworld Ser.). (ENG., Illus.). (J). (gr. 4-7). 9.99 (978-0-7636-5573-0(2), Templar) Candlewick Pr.

—StoryWorld: Tales from the Haunted House: Create-A-Story Kit. 2011. (Storyworld Ser.). (ENG., Illus.). (J). (gr. 4-7). 9.99 (978-0-7636-5568-6(6), Templar) Candlewick Pr.

McCleery, William. Wolf Story. Chappell, Warren, illus. 2012. (ENG.). 88p. (J). (gr. k-4). 15.95 (978-1-59017-589-7(1), NYR Children's Collection) New York Review of Bks., Inc., The.

McLaughlin, Tom. The Story Machine. 2015. (ENG., Illus.). 32p. (J). (gr. -1-1). 12.99 (978-1-4088-3934-8(2), 9781408839348, Bloomsbury USA Childrens) Bloomsbury Publishing USA.

Michaelis, Antonia. Tiger Moon. 2009. (ENG.). 480p. (YA). (gr. 7-11). pap. 9.95 (978-0-8109-4499-2(5), Amulet Bks.) Abrams, Inc.

Moore Thomas, Shelley & Thomas, Shelley Moore. The Seven Tales of Trinket, 1 vol. 2012. (ENG., Illus.). 384p. (J). (gr. 3-7). 16.99 (978-0-374-36745-9(0), 9780374367459, Farrar, Straus & Giroux (BYR)) Farrar, Straus & Giroux.

Muggenthaler, Eva, creator. Fish on a Walk. 2012. (ENG., Illus.). 32p. (J). (gr. -1-2). 16.95 (978-1-59270-116-2(7)) Enchanted Lion Bks., LLC.

Mullarkey, Lisa. The Campfire Capers, 1 vol. 2014. (Storm Cliff Stables Ser.). (ENG., Illus.). 112p. (J). (gr. 7-11). 27.07 (978-1-62402-049-0(6)) Magic Wagon.

Murguia, Bethanie Deeney. The Too-Scary Story. 2017. (ENG., Illus.). 40p. (J). (gr. -1-k). 16.99 (978-0-545-73242-0(5)) Scholastic, Inc.

Muth, Jon J. Zen Ghosts. 2010. (ENG.). 40p. (J). (gr. -1-3). 17.99 (978-0-439-63430-4(X), Scholastic Pr.) Scholastic, Inc.

—Zen Shorts. 2010. (ENG.). (J). (gr. -1-3). 18.99 (978-0-545-22760-5(7)) Scholastic, Inc.

—Zen Shorts. Muth, Jon J., illus. 2005. (ENG., Illus.). 40p. (J). (gr. -1-3). 17.99 (978-0-439-33911-7(1)) Scholastic, Inc.

—Zen Shorts. collector's ed. 2008. (ENG., Illus.). 40p. (J). (gr. -1-3). 25.00 (978-0-545-04087-7(6), Scholastic) Scholastic, Inc.

—Zen Socks. 2015. (ENG., Illus.). 40p. (J). (gr. -1-3). 17.99 (978-0-545-16669-0(1), Scholastic Pr.) Scholastic, Inc.

Nance, Andrew. Return to Daemon Hall: Evil Roots. Polhemus, Coleman, illus. 2011. (ENG.). 256p. (YA). (gr. 7-12). 18.99 (978-0-8050-8748-2(6), Holt, Henry & Co. Bks. For Young Readers) Holt, Henry & Co.

Nash, Scott. Tuff Fluff: The Case of Duckie's Missing Brain. Nash, Scott, illus. 2004. (Illus.). (J). 101.94 (978-0-7636-2503-0(5)); (ENG., 40p. (gr. 1-4). 16.99 (978-0-7636-1882-7(9)) Candlewick Pr.

Niemi, Renee. Because Gage Believed. 2013. 20p. pap. 24.95 (978-1-62709-730-7(9)) America Star Bks.

Nimmo, Jenny. The Beasties. Millward, Gwen, illus. 2012. (ENG.). 32p. (J). (gr. -1-k). pap. 8.99 (978-1-4052-4335-3(X)) Egmont Bks., Ltd. GBR. Dist: Independent Pubs. Group.

Oppenheim, Joanne F. The Prince's Bedtime. Latimer, Miriam, illus. 2007. (ENG.). 32p. (J). (gr. -1-3). pap. 7.99 (978-1-84686-106-2(3)) Barefoot Bks., Inc.

Paulsen, Gary. Fishbone's Song. 2016. (ENG., Illus.). 160p. (J). (gr. 5). 16.99 (978-1-4814-5226-7(6), Simon & Schuster Bks. For Young Readers) Simon & Schuster Bks. For Young Readers.

Pellowski. The Story Vine. 2008. (ENG.). 132p. (J). (gr. -1-3). 7.99 (978-1-4169-7578-6(0), Simon & Schuster/Paula Wiseman Bks.) Simon & Schuster/Paula Wiseman Bks.

Porte, Barbara Ann. Beauty & the Serpent: Thirteen Tales of Unnatural Animals. Covey, Rosemary Feit, illus. 2008. (ENG.). 128p. (YA). (gr. 7). pap. 7.99 (978-1-4169-7579-3(9), Simon & Schuster/Paula Wiseman Bks.) Simon & Schuster/Paula Wiseman Bks.

Porter, Rhonda. Brody Meets a Bully. 2008. 16p. pap. 24.95 (978-1-60610-311-1(3)) America Star Bks.

Priestley, Chris. Tales of Terror from the Black Ship. Roberts, David, illus. 2008. (Tales of Terror Ser.: 1). (ENG.). 256p. (YA). (gr. 3-6). 12.99 (978-1-59990-290-6(7), 9781599902906, Bloomsbury USA Childrens) Bloomsbury Publishing USA.

Prineas, Sarah. Ash & Bramble. 2015. (ENG.). 464p. (YA). (gr. 8). 17.99 (978-0-06-233794-8(7)) HarperCollins Pubs.

Resman, Michael. The Villagers. Senelwa, Fred, tr. Gathigo, Cyrus Ngatia, illus. 2012. 40p. pap. (978-976-8142-41-2(3)) Producciones de la Hamaca.

Revell, Mike. Stonebird. 2016. (ENG.). 288p. (J). (gr. 5-9). pap. 9.99 (978-1-68144-514-4(X)) Quercus NA.

Rivard, Émilie & Quinn, Sarah. Really & Truly. Delisle, Anne-Claire & Owlkids Books Inc. Staff, illus. 2012. (ENG.). 24p. (J). (gr. -1-3). 15.95 (978-1-926973-40-1(2)) Owlkids Bks. Inc. CAN. Dist: Publishers Group West (PGW).

Rosenthal, Eileen. I'll Save You Bobo! Rosenthal, Marc, illus. 2012. (ENG.). 40p. (J). (gr. -1-1). 14.99 (978-1-4424-0378-9(0), Atheneum Bks. for Young Readers) Simon & Schuster Children's Publishing.

Russo, Marisabina. I Will Come Back for You. 2014. (ENG.). 40p. (J). (gr. k-4). 7.99 (978-0-385-39149-8(8), Dragonfly Bks.) Random Hse. Children's Bks.

Say, Allen. Kamishibai Man. 2005. (ENG., Illus.). 32p. (J). (gr. -1-3). 17.99 (978-0-618-47954-2(6)) Houghton Mifflin Harcourt Publishing Co.

Schmidt, Gary D. Mara's Stories: Glimmers in the Darkness. 2008. (ENG.). 160p. (YA). (gr. 5-9). per. 14.99 (978-0-312-37388-7(0), 9780312373887) Square Fish.

Shannon, David. Jangles: A Big Fish Story. Shannon, David, illus. 2012. (ENG., Illus.). 32p. (J). (gr. -1-3). 17.99 (978-0-545-14312-7(8), Blue Sky Pr., The) Scholastic, Inc.

Shelton, Dave. Thirteen Chairs. (ENG.). 256p. (J). (gr. 7). 2016. pap. 9.99 (978-1-338-03248-2(8)) 2015. (Illus.). 17.99 (978-0-545-81665-6(3)) Scholastic, Inc.

Sidney, Margaret. Polly Pepper's Book. 2011. 316p. 50.95 (978-1-258-10539-6(X)) Literary Licensing, LLC.

Slater, David Michael. Milo & the Monster, 1 vol. Ebbeler, Jeff, illus. 2009. (David Michael Slater Set 2 Ser.). (ENG.). 32p. (gr. -1-4). 28.50 (978-1-60270-656-9(5), Looking Glass Library) ABDO Publishing Co.

Small, Lily. Mia the Mouse. 2015. (Fairy Animals of Misty Wood Ser.: 4). (ENG., Illus.). 144p. (J). (gr. k-3). pap. 5.99 (978-1-62779-144-1(2), 9781627791441, Holt, Henry & Co. Bks. For Young Readers) Holt, Henry & Co.

Spinner, Stephanie. It's a Miracle! A Hanukkah Storybook. McElmurry, Jill, illus. 2007. (ENG.). 48p. (J). (gr. -1-3). 6.99 (978-1-4169-5001-1(X), Aladdin) Simon & Schuster Children's Publishing.

Stead, Philip C. Bear Has a Story to Tell. Stead, Erin E., illus. 2012. (ENG.). 32p. (J). (gr. -1-1). 16.99 (978-1-59643-745-6(6), 9781596437456) Roaring Brook Pr.

Stein, David Ezra. Interrupting Chicken. Stein, David Ezra, illus. (ENG., Illus.). 40p. (J). (gr. -1-3). 2016. 7.99 (978-0-7636-8903-2(3)) 2010. 16.99 (978-0-7636-4168-9(5)) Candlewick Pr.

—Interrupting Chicken. (J). 1.25 (978-1-4498-6832-1(0)); 2011. 37.75 (978-1-4498-6828-4(2)); 2011. 39.75 (978-1-4498-6829-1(0)); 2011. 37.75 (978-1-4498-6831-4(2)) Recorded Bks., Inc.

—Interrupting Chicken. Stein, David Ezra, illus. 2016. (ENG., Illus.). 40p. (J). (gr. -1-3). 18.40 (978-0-606-39099-6(5)) Turtleback Bks.

Stewart, Paul. Far-Flung Adventures: Hugo Pepper. 2012. (Far-Flung Adventures Ser.). (ENG.). 272p. (J). (gr. 3-7). 7.99 (978-0-385-75223-7(7), Yearling) Random Hse. Children's Bks.

Swindells, Robert. Shrapnel. 2009. (ENG., Illus.). 224p. (YA). (gr. 7-18). pap. 14.99 (978-0-552-55930-0(X)) Transworld Publishers Ltd. GBR. Dist: Independent Pubs. Group.

Tanner, Lian. Battlesong. Szabla, Liz, ed. 2017. (Icebreaker Trilogy Ser.: 3). (ENG.). 304p. (J). 16.99 (978-1-250-05218-6(1), 9781250052186) Feiwel & Friends.

Theroux, Phyllis. Serefina under the Circumstances. Priceman, Marjorie, illus. 2004. 30p. (J). (gr. k-4). reprint ed. (978-0-7567-7756-2(9)) DIANE Publishing Co.

Tompert, Ann. Grandfather Tang's Story. Parker, Robert A., illus. 2015. (ENG.). 32p. (J). (gr. -1-2). 16.99 (978-0-517-57487-4(X), Knopf Bks. for Young Readers) Random Hse. Children's Bks.

Turk, Evan. The Storyteller. Turk, Evan, illus. 2016. (ENG., Illus.). 48p. (J). (gr. -1-3). 18.99 (978-1-4814-3518-5(3)) Simon & Schuster Children's Publishing.

Vincent, Harris T. & Brewer, Mary. When Grandmother Was A Little Girl. 2010. 40p. 23.99 (978-1-4520-7728-4(2)) AuthorHouse.

Virján, Emma J. What This Story Needs Is a Pig in a Wig. Virján, Emma J., illus. 2015. (Pig in a Wig Book Ser.). (ENG., Illus.). 40p. (J). (gr. -1-3). 9.99 (978-0-06-232724-6(0)) HarperCollins Pubs.

Wade, Maryam. Bently & the Silver Wings. 2011. 24p. pap. 24.95 (978-1-4560-7503-3(9)) America Star Bks.

Walde, Christine. The Candy Darlings. 2006. (ENG.). 310p. (YA). (gr. 9-12). per. 18.95 (978-0-618-58969-2(4)) Houghton Mifflin Harcourt Publishing Co.

Wallace-Brodeur, Ruth. Stories from the Big Chair. 2010. (ENG.). 48p. (J). (gr. -1-3). 6.99 (978-1-4424-1439-6(1), McElderry, Margaret K. Bks.) McElderry, Margaret K. Bks.

Watt, Mélanie. Chester's Back! Watt, Mélanie, illus. (Chester Ser.). (ENG., Illus.). 32p. (J). (gr. -1-3). 2013. 8.95 (978-1-55453-461-6(5)) 2008. 18.95 (978-1-55453-287-2(6)) Kids Can Pr., Ltd. CAN. Dist: Hachette Bk. Group.

Weston Woods Staff, creator. A Story-A Story. 2011. 29.95 (978-0-439-73521-6(1)); 18.95 (978-0-439-72891-1(6)) Weston Woods Studios, Inc.

—A Story-Astory. 2011. 38.75 (978-0-439-72892-8(4)) Weston Woods Studios, Inc.

Wiggin, Kate Douglas. Polly Oliver's Problem. 2007. 108p. per. 9.95 (978-1-60312-369-3(5)); 22.95 (978-1-60312-707-3(0)) Aegypan.

Willems, Mo. I Broke My Trunk! Willems, Mo, illus. 2011. (Elephant & Piggie Book Ser.). (ENG., Illus.). 64p. (J). (gr. -1-k). 9.99 (978-1-4231-3309-4(9)) Hyperion Pr.

Wolfson, Jill. What I Call Life. 2008. (ENG.). 288p. (J). (gr. 5-9). pap. 19.99 (978-0-312-37752-6(5), 9780312377526) Square Fish.

Wooding, Chris. Poison. 2006. 1.00 (978-1-4237-9048-8(0)) Recorded Bks., Inc.

Wyeth, Sharon Dennis. The Granddaughter Necklace. Ibatoulline, Bagram, illus. (J). 2013. (ENG.). 32p. (gr. -1-3). 18.99 (978-0-545-08125-2(4)) 2012. pap. (978-0-545-23983-7(4)) Scholastic, Inc. (Levine, Arthur A. Bks.).

Yaccarino, Dan. I Am a Story. Yaccarino, Dan, illus. 2016. (Illus.). 40p. (J). (gr. -1-3). 17.99 (978-0-06-241106-8(3)) HarperCollins Pubs.

Zarins, Kim. Sometimes We Tell the Truth. 2016. **(978-1-4814-7554-9(1))** Simon & Schuster, Inc.

—Sometimes We Tell the Truth. 2016. (ENG., Illus.). 448p. (YA). (gr. 9). 17.99 (978-1-4814-6499-4(X), Simon Pulse) Simon Pulse.

Zusak, Markus. The Book Thief. 2014. (ENG.). 576p. (YA). 17.24 (978-1-63245-052-4(6)) Lectorum Pubns., Inc.

—The Book Thief. 2009. 12.64 (978-0-7848-1941-8(6), Everbind) Marco Bk. Co.

—The Book Thief. 2008. 552p. (gr. 7-12). 23.00 (978-0-7569-8440-3(8)) Perfection Learning Corp.

—The Book Thief. (ENG., Illus.). (YA). (gr. 7). 2016. 592p. lib. bdg. 22.99 (978-0-399-55652-4(4)) 2007. 592p. pap. 12.99 (978-0-375-84220-7(9)) 2013. 576p. pap. 12.99 (978-0-385-75472-9(8)) 2016. 592p. 19.99 (978-1-101-93418-0(2)) Random Hse. Children's Bks. (Knopf Bks. for Young Readers).

—The Book Thief. l.t. ed. 2006. (ENG.). 552p. 23.99 (978-1-4104-6806-2(2)); 757p. (YA). (gr. 7-12). 24.95 (978-0-7862-9021-5(8)) Thorndike Pr.

—The Book Thief. 2008. (ENG., Illus.). 560p. pap. (978-0-552-77389-8(1), Black Swan) Transworld Publishers Ltd.

—The Book Thief. 2007. 552p. lib. bdg. 24.50 (978-1-4177-9738-7(X)) 2013. lib. bdg. 24.50 (978-0-606-34656-6(2)) Turtleback Bks. (Turtleback).

—La Ladrona de Libros. 2010. (Vintage Espanol Ser.).Tr. of Book Thief. (SPA.). 544p. (YA). (gr. 7). pap. 12.99 (978-0-307-47573-2(5), Vintage Espanol) Knopf Doubleday Publishing Group.

STOVES—FICTION

Fussell, Bonnie. More Than a Stove. Sadler, Dale, illus. l.t. ed. 2004. 32p. (J). pap. 7.99 (978-0-615-12702-6(9)) Blackberry Pubs.

STOWE, HARRIET BEECHER, 1811-1896

Adler, David A. A Picture Book of Harriet Beecher Stowe. Bootman, Colin, illus. 2003. (ENG.). 32p. (J). (gr. k-3). tchr. ed. 17.95 (978-0-8234-1646-2(1)) Holiday Hse., Inc.

Elliot, Henry. Harriet Beecher Stowe: The Voice of Humanity in White America. 2009. (Voices for Freedom Ser.). (ENG., Illus.). 64p. (J). (gr. 5-8). pap. (978-0-7787-4837-3(5)); lib. bdg. (978-0-7787-4821-2(9)) Crabtree Publishing Co.

Griffiths, Katie. Harriet Beecher Stowe. 2016. (Great American Thinkers Ser.). (ENG.). 128p. (J). (gr. 9-9). 45.64 (978-1-5026-1930-3(X)) Cavendish Square Publishing.

Griskey, Michele. Harriet Beecher Stowe. 2005. (Classic Storytellers Ser.). (Illus.). 48p. (J). (gr. 4-8). lib. bdg. 29.95 (978-1-58415-375-7(X)) Mitchell Lane Pubs., Inc.

Haugen, Brenda. Harriet Beecher Stowe: The Inspiring Life Story of the Abolition Advocate. 2016. (Inspiring Stories Ser.). (ENG., Illus.). 112p. (gr. 5-7). lib. bdg. 35.99 (978-0-7565-5164-3(1), CPB Grades 4-8) Compass Point Bks.

Marsh, Carole. Harriet Beecher Stowe. 2003. 12p. (gr. k-4). 2.95 (978-0-635-02356-8(3)) Gallopade International.

Rau, Dana Meachen. Who Was Harriet Beecher Stowe? 2015. (Who Was... ? Ser.). lib. bdg. 16.00 (978-0-606-36598-7(2)) Turtleback Bks.

Rau, Dana Meachen & dePaola, Tomie. Who Was Harriet Beecher Stowe? Harrison, Nancy & Copeland, Gregory, illus. 2015. (Who Was? Ser.). (ENG.). 112p. (J). (gr. 3-7). 5.99 (978-0-448-48301-6(7), Grosset & Dunlap) Penguin Young Readers Group.

Sonneborn, Liz. Harriet Beecher Stowe. 2009. (Leaders of the Civil War Era Ser.). (Illus.). 120p. (gr. 6-12). 35.00 (978-1-60413-302-8(3), Chelsea Hse.) Facts On File, Inc.

STRATEGIC MATERIALS
see Materials
STRATIGRAPHIC GEOLOGY
see Geology, Stratigraphic
STRATOSPHERE
Jakubiak, David J. What Can We Do about Ozone Loss? 2012. (Illus.). 24p. (J). 49.50 *(978-1-4488-5379-3(6),* PowerKids Pr.); (J). pap. 8.25 *(978-1-4488-5118-8(1),* PowerKids Pr.); (YA). (gr. 2-5). lib. bdg. 22.60 *(978-1-4488-4985-7(3))* Rosen Publishing Group, Inc., The.
STRAVINSKY, IGOR, 1882-1971
Whiting, Jim. The Life & Times of Igor Stravinsky. 2004. (Masters of Music Ser.). (Illus.). 48p. (gr. 4-8). lib. bdg. 20.95 *(978-1-58415-277-4(X))* Mitchell Lane Pubs., Inc.
STRAWBERRY SHORTCAKE (FICTITIOUS CHARACTER)—FICTION
Ackelsberg, Amy. Easter Surprise. Thomas, Laura, illus. 2011. (Strawberry Shortcake Ser.). (ENG.). 24p. (J). (gr. -1-k). mass mkt. 4.99 *(978-0-448-45547-1(1),* Grosset & Dunlap) Penguin Young Readers Group.
—Happy New Year! 2014. (Strawberry Shortcake Ser.). (ENG., Illus.). 24p. (J). (gr. -1-k). 4.99 *(978-0-448-48248-4(7),* Grosset & Dunlap) Penguin Young Readers Group.
—Puppy Love! Artful Doodlers Limited Staff, illus. 2014. (Strawberry Shortcake Ser.). (ENG.). 24p. (J). (gr. -1-k). 4.99 *(978-0-448-48150-0(2),* Grosset & Dunlap) Penguin Young Readers Group.
Ball, Georgia & Mebberson, Amy. Strawberry Shortcake, Vol. 1. 2013. (ENG., Illus.). 104p. (J). (gr. 4-8). pap. 14.99 *(978-1-937676-61-2(7),* 9781937676612) Ape Entertainment.
Bryant, Megan E. Rapunzel. Huxtable, Tonja & Huxtable, John, illus. 2007. (Berry Fairy Tales Ser.). (J). *(978-1-4287-4159-1(3),* Grosset & Dunlap) Penguin Publishing Group.
Grosset & Dunlap. Berry Merry Holiday Treasury. 2014. (Strawberry Shortcake Ser.). (ENG.). 160p. (J). (gr. -1-k). 9.99 *(978-0-448-48360-3(2),* Grosset & Dunlap) Penguin Young Readers Group.
Grosset and Dunlap Staff. Welcome to Berry Bitty City. Thomas, Laura, illus. 2009. (Strawberry Shortcake Ser.). (ENG.). 16p. (J). (gr. -1-k). pap. 5.99 *(978-0-448-45254-8(5),* Grosset & Dunlap) Penguin Young Readers Group.
Harimann, Sierra. We Love You, Strawberry Shortcake! Beighley, Marci, illus. 2009. (Strawberry Shortcake Ser.). (ENG.). 32p. (J). (gr. 1-2). pap. 3.99 *(978-0-448-45252-4(9),* Penguin Young Readers) Penguin Young Readers Group.
Jacobs, Lana. A Brand-New Look. 2013. (Penguin Young Readers Level 2 Ser.). lib. bdg. 13.55 *(978-0-606-29293-1(4),* Turtleback) Turtleback Bks.
—Lost & Found. 2012. (Penguin Young Readers Level 2 Ser.). lib. bdg. 13.55 *(978-0-606-23626-3(0),* Turtleback) Turtleback Bks.
—Show-And-Tell. 2013. (Penguin Young Readers Level 2 Ser.). lib. bdg. 13.55 *(978-0-606-31694-1(9),* Turtleback) Turtleback Bks.
Matheis, Mickie. Berryella & Prince Berry Charming. Thomas, Laura, illus. 2015. (Strawberry Shortcake Ser.). (ENG.). 24p. (J). (gr. -1-k). 4.99 *(978-0-448-48706-9(3),* Grosset & Dunlap) Penguin Young Readers Group.
—The Butterfly Parade. 2016. (Penguin Young Readers Level 2 Ser.). lib. bdg. 13.55 *(978-0-606-38429-2(4))* Turtleback Bks.
—Camp Berry. Thomas, Laura, illus. 2014. (Strawberry Shortcake Ser.). (ENG.). 32p. (J). (gr. 1-3). pap. 3.99 *(978-0-448-48153-1(7),* Penguin Young Readers) Penguin Young Readers Group.
Okaty, Nicole. Orange Blossom's Fruity Fun Book: A Juicy Orange Adventure. 2004. (Illus.). 39p. *(978-0-439-70466-3(9))* Scholastic, Inc.
Running Press Staff. Berry Best Friends. 2009. (Miniature Editions Ser.). (ENG.). 128p. 5.95 *(978-0-7624-3589-0(5),* Running Pr.) Running Pr. Bk. Pubs.
Strawberry Shortcake Activity Book Collection. 2005. (J). *(978-1-59487-137-5(X))* Artist Studios, Ltd.
Strawberry Shortcake Berry Loveable Diary. 2005. 7.95 *(978-1-59487-083-5(7))* Artist Studios, Ltd.
STREAMLINING
see Aerodynamics
STREET TRAFFIC
see Traffic Regulations
STREETS
see also Roads
Mara, Wil. What Should I Do? Near a Busy Street. 2011. (Community Connections: What Should I Do? Ser.). (ENG., Illus.). 24p. (J). (gr. 2-5). lib. bdg. 25.64 *(978-1-61080-051-8(6),* 1330910) Cherry Lake Publishing.
Our Street: Big Book: Level D. Group 1. (Sunshine Ser.). 8p. 20.95 *(978-0-7802-5732-0(4))* Wright Group/McGraw-Hill.
Riggs, Sandy. Safe Streets. 2006. (Reader's Clubhouse Level 2 Reader Ser.). (ENG., Illus.). 24p. (J). (gr. 1-4). pap. 3.99 *(978-0-7641-3300-8(4))* Barron's Educational Series, Inc.
Stewart, Kara. A City Street. 2009. (Real Life Readers Ser.). 8p. (gr. k-1). pap. 5.15 *(978-1-4042-7961-2(X),* Rosen Classroom) Rosen Publishing Group, Inc., The.
STRINGED INSTRUMENTS
see also names of stringed instruments, e.g. Guitar; etc.
Dick, William & Scott, Laurie. Mastery for Strings, 3 vols. 2004. 109p. spiral bd. 15.95 *(978-0-9753919-0-7(9))* Mastery For Strings Pubns.
Ganeri, Anita. Stringed Instruments. 2011. (ENG., Illus.). 32p. (J). pap. 10.95 *(978-1-77092-032-3(3))* Saunders Bk. Co. CAN. Dist: RiverStream Publishing.
Kreutzer, Rudolph. Forty-Two Studies for Violin. Singer, Edmund, ed. (Carl Fischer Music Library: No. 120). 73p. (J). pap. 10.95 *(978-0-8258-0025-2(0))* Fischer, Carl LLC.
Lillywhite, Rosalind & Marshall, Andrew. Abracadabra Double Bass: The Way to Learn Through Songs & Tunes, 1 vol. 2005. (Abracadabra Ser.). (ENG., Illus.). 64p. (J). pap. 24.95 incl. audio compact disk ***(978-0-7136-7097-4(5))*** HarperCollins Pubs. Ltd. GBR. Dist: Independent Pubs. Group.
Nunn, Daniel. Strings, 1 vol. 2011. (Instruments & Music Ser.). (ENG.). 24p. (gr. -1-1). pap. 6.29 *(978-1-4329-5069-9(X),* Acorn) Heinemann-Raintree.
Shaskan, Trisha Speed. The String Family in Harmony!, 1 vol. Meganck, Robert & Communication Design (Firm) Staff, illus. 2010. (Musical Families Ser.). (ENG.). 24p. (gr. 2-3). lib. bdg. 25.32 *(978-1-4048-6043-8(6))* Picture Window Bks.
Smith, Erica. Making Music with Stringed Instruments. 2009. (Reading Room Collection 2 Ser.). 24p. (gr. 3-4). 42.50 *(978-1-60851-979-8(1),* PowerKids Pr.) Rosen Publishing Group, Inc., The.
Storey, Rita. The Violin & Other Stringed Instruments. 2010. (J). 28.50 *(978-1-59920-212-9(3))* Black Rabbit Bks.
Wearing, Katie & Scott, Elaine. Abracadabra Viola Beginner, 1 vol. rev. ed. 2007. (Abracadabra Ser.). (ENG., Illus.). 32p. (J). pap. 11.95 incl. audio compact disk ***(978-0-7136-7839-0(9))*** HarperCollins Pubs. Ltd. GBR. Dist: Independent Pubs. Group.
STRINGED INSTRUMENTS—FICTION
Baker, Keith. Just How Long Can a Long String Be? 2009. (J). pap. *(978-0-545-08662-2(0),* Levine, Arthur A. Bks.) Scholastic, Inc.
Meadows, Daisy. Victoria the Violin Fairy #6. 2010. (ENG.). 80p. (J). lib. bdg. 15.39 *(978-1-4242-4735-6(7))* Fitzgerald Bks.
STRUCTURAL BOTANY
see Plant Anatomy
STRUCTURAL DRAFTING
see Mechanical Drawing
STUDENT ACTIVITIES
see also College and School Journalism; School Sports
Abbott, John A. Press-Out & Play Autoshop Fun. 2013. (ENG.). 18p. (J). pap. 4.99 *(978-1-78235-569-4(3))* Make Believe Ideas GBR. Dist: Nelson, Thomas Inc.
—Press-Out & Play Construction Crew. 2013. (ENG.). 18p. (J). pap. 4.99 *(978-1-78235-568-7(5))* Make Believe Ideas GBR. Dist: Nelson, Thomas Inc.
—Press-Out & Play Dino Park. 2013. (ENG.). 18p. (J). pap. 4.99 *(978-1-78235-566-3(9))* Make Believe Ideas GBR. Dist: Nelson, Thomas Inc.
Abrams, Pam. Finger Fun. 2011. (PACKtivities Ser.: 2). (ENG.). 48p. (J). (gr. -1-3). 9.99 *(978-1-935703-37-2(4))* Downtown Bookworks.
Accord Publishing Staff. Go Fun! Doodle: Summer Fun. 2012. (ENG.). 72p. (J). pap. 4.99 *(978-1-4494-1735-2(3))* Andrews McMeel Publishing.
—Go Fun! Dot-to-Dot: Summer Fun. 2012. (ENG.). 72p. (J). pap. 4.99 *(978-1-4494-1814-4(7))* Andrews McMeel Publishing.
—Zoo Babies. 2010. (ENG., Illus.). 12p. (J). (gr. -1). 9.99 *(978-0-7407-9201-4(6))* Andrews McMeel Publishing.
Ackland, Nick. Little Giraffe at the Beach. Walshaw, Sam, illus. 2017. (Little Explorers Ser.). (ENG.). 10p. (J). (gr. -1 — 1). bds. 6.99 *(978-0-7641-6894-9(0))* Barron's Educational Series, Inc.
—Out & About. Bradley, Jennie, illus. 2017. (Busy Baby Ser.). (ENG.). 10p. (J). (gr. -1 — 1). bds. 6.99 *(978-0-7641-6893-2(2))* Barron's Educational Series, Inc.
Activities & Events. 48p. *(978-0-86388-508-2(X),* 001-1541, Routledge) Taylor & Francis Group.
Adam, Sarah E., illus. Abby in Vermont Coloring & Activity Book. 2008. 32p. (J). 4.95 *(978-0-9793790-1-7(6))* Howard Printing, Inc.
Adatto, Miryam. Creative Haven Dreamscapes Coloring Book. 2013. (Adult Coloring Ser.). (ENG.). 64p. (gr. 3). pap. 5.99 *(978-0-486-49422-7(5))* Dover Pubns., Inc.
Adventure 1001 Stickers. 2016. (ENG., Illus.). 48p. (J). (gr. k-2). pap. 9.99 *(978-1-4052-7729-7(7))* Egmont Bks., Ltd. GBR. Dist: Independent Pubs. Group.
Adventure Doodle Book. 2016. (ENG., Illus.). 128p. (J). (gr. k-2). pap. 9.99 *(978-1-4052-7730-3(0))* Egmont Bks., Ltd. GBR. Dist: Independent Pubs. Group.
Adventures in Suburbia-Boston. 2nd ed. 2003. (J). per. 19.95 *(978-0-9743319-1-1(0))* Kiwi Media Group, Inc.
After a Death: An Activity Book for Children. 2007.Tr. of Despues de un Fallecimiento: un Cuaderno de Actividado para Ninos. (EST., Illus.). 65p. pap. 12.95 *(978-1-890534-10-3(2))* Dougy Ctr.
Aguinaco, Carmen F. Amigos de Jesús 2009: A Bilingual Catechetical Program. un Programa Catequético BilingüE. Advent 2008 - November 2009. Petersen, William, illus. 2008.Tr. of Friends of Jesus 2009. (ENG & SPA.). 408p. (J). pap. 99.00 *(978-0-89570-503-7(6))* Claretian Pubns.
Ahearn, Dan. Time for Kids Readers. 2003. (Time for Kids Readers Ser.). (ENG.). pap. 84.96 *(978-0-15-340566-2(X))* Harcourt Schl. Pubs.
Akhila Rajan And Ananya Rajan. Crafabets Adventure. 2011. 56p. pap. 31.99 *(978-1-4568-3197-4(6))* Xlibris Corp.
Al-Muzher, Engineer Khalid Mohammed. Smart Boy Diary: How smartly can you keep your innovative ideas? 2011. 32p. pap. 19.67 *(978-1-4567-8299-3(1))* AuthorHouse.
Alderson, Phil. Busy Kids Dinosaurs Magnetic Playbook. 2007. (Busy Kids Ser.). (Illus.). 10p. (J). (gr. -1-3). bds. *(978-1-84610-552-4(8))* Make Believe Ideas.
Allain, Moose. Fill-Me-In. Allain, Moose, illus. 2016. (ENG., Illus.). 96p. (J). (gr. 1-4). 16.99 *(978-0-7636-8532-4(1),* Big Picture Press) Candlewick Pr.
Allen, Heather. BOOST Earth Day Is Every Day! Activity Book. 2013. (BOOST Educational Ser.). (ENG.). 48p. (J). (gr. 3-5). pap. 5.99 *(978-0-486-49433-3(0))* Dover Pubns., Inc.
Altmann, Scott. Guitar Rock Star Sticker Activity Book. 2008. (Dover Little Activity Bks.). (ENG.). 4p. (J). (gr. -1-5). pap. 1.50 *(978-0-486-46790-0(2))* Dover Pubns., Inc.
—Sugar Skulls Stickers. 2016. (Dover Little Activity Books Stickers Ser.). (ENG., Illus.). 4p. (J). (gr. 1-4). 1.99 *(978-0-486-80884-0(X))* Dover Pubns., Inc.
Altmann, Scott & Whelon, Chuck. 3-D Mazes — Vampires. 2012. (Dover 3-D Mazes Ser.). (ENG.). 32p. (J). (gr. 1-6). 5.99 *(978-0-486-49019-9(X))* Dover Pubns., Inc.
Ameet Studio, Ameet. I'm Batman! 2016. (LEGO Batman Movie Ser.). (ENG.). 96p. (J). (gr. 1-3). pap. 12.99 *(978-1-338-11223-8(6))* Scholastic, Inc.
—The Otherworldly League! 2016. (LEGO DC Super Heroes Ser.: Bk. 1). (ENG.). 32p. (J). (gr. 2-5). pap., act. bk. ed. 8.99 *(978-1-338-04744-8(2))* Scholastic, Inc.
—Quest for the Kyber Saber. 2016. (LEGO Star Wars Ser.). (ENG.). 32p. (J). (gr. 2-5). pap. 8.99 *(978-1-338-04743-1(4))* Scholastic, Inc.
Ameet Studio Staff. Doodle Activity Book. Ameet Studio Staff, illus. 2016. (Lego Star Wars Ser.). (ENG., Illus.). 96p. (J). (gr. 2-5). pap. 8.99 *(978-1-338-11229-0(5))* Scholastic, Inc.
—Epic Space Adventures. Ameet Studio Staff, illus. 2016. (Lego Star Wars Ser.). (ENG., Illus.). 32p. (J). (gr. 1-3). pap. 8.99 *(978-0-545-91727-8(1))* Scholastic, Inc.
—Quest for the Keys. 2015. (LEGO Elves Ser.). (ENG.). 32p. (J). (gr. 2-5). pap., act. bk. ed. 8.99 *(978-0-545-87253-9(7))* Scholastic, Inc.
—Space Adventures! Ameet Studio Staff, illus. 2016. (Lego City Ser.). (ENG., Illus.). 32p. (J). (gr. 1-3). pap. 8.99 *(978-0-545-92731-4(5))* Scholastic, Inc.
—Way of the Ghost. 2015. (Lego Ninjago Ser.). (ENG.). 32p. (J). (gr. 2-5). pap., act. bk. ed. 8.99 *(978-0-545-82554-2(7))* Scholastic, Inc.
American Girl Editors & Anton, Carrie, eds. Poster Pack: 60 Cute, Fun, & Inspiring Posters from American Girl! 2010. (ENG.). 64p. (YA). (gr. 3-18). pap. 9.95 *(978-1-59369-795-2(3))* American Girl Publishing, Inc.
American Girl Editors & Magruder, Trula, eds. Oodles of Ocean Fun: A Collection of Posters, Puzzles, Doodles, Cards, Crafts, Stickers, Frames. 2011. (ENG.). 80p. (YA). (gr. 3-18). spiral bd. 12.95 *(978-1-59369-771-6(6))* American Girl Publishing, Inc.
American Girl Editors & Richards, Mary, eds. Oodles of Sweet Stuff. 2011. (ENG.). 80p. (J). spiral bd. 12.95 *(978-1-59369-826-3(7))* American Girl Publishing, Inc.
Amery, Heather. Cinderella Kid Kit with Pop Out Coach. Cartwright, Stephen, illus. 2006. (Usborne First Stories Ser.). 16p. (J). (gr. -1-3). pap. 8.99 *(978-1-58086-877-8(0),* Usborne) EDC Publishing.
Anastasio, Dina. Mask Making Around the World. 2011. (Early Connections Ser.). (J). *(978-1-61672-588-4(5))* Benchmark Education Co.
Anderson, Airlie. What to Doodle? Jr. — Princesses, Fairies, Mermaids & More! 2013. (Dover Doodle Bks.). (ENG.). 128p. (J). (gr. k-3). pap. 4.99 *(978-0-486-49951-2(0))* Dover Pubns., Inc.
Anderson, Dee. Reading Is Funny! Motivating Kids to Read with Riddles. 2008. (Illus.). 216p. 40.00 *(978-0-8389-0957-7(4))* American Library Assn.
Andreae, Giles. Missing Treasure! Ayto, Russell, illus. 2008. (Captain Flinn & the Pirate Dinosaurs Ser.). (ENG.). 32p. (J). (gr. -1-3). 17.99 *(978-1-4169-6745-3(1),* McElderry, Margaret K. Bks.) McElderry, Margaret K. Bks.
Andrew, Edwards & Fleur, Thornton. Footsteps of the Past: William Booth. 2005. (Footsteps of the Past Ser.). pap. 5.00 *(978-1-903087-83-1(X))* DayOne Pubns. GBR. Dist: Send The Light Distribution LLC.
Andrews, Jackie. On the Farm. 2012. (ENG., Illus.). 24p. (J). pap. 6.50 *(978-1-84135-354-8(X))* Award Pubns. Ltd. GBR. Dist: Parkwest Pubns., Inc.
Anholt, Laurence. Anholt's Artists Activity Book. 2012. (ENG.). 48p. (J). (gr. -1-3). pap. 11.99 *(978-1-4380-0114-2(2))* Barron's Educational Series, Inc.
Annie's. My Can-Do Book. 2016. (ENG.). 4p. 6.99 *(978-1-59012-498-7(7),* Annie's) Annie's Publishing, LLC.
Anorak Press Staff & Olmedillas, Cathy, compiled by. Anorak: The Happy Mag For Kids. 2012. (ENG., Illus.). 64p. (J). pap. 9.99 *(978-1-4236-3317-4(2),* Anorak Pr.) Gibbs Smith, Publisher.
Anton, Carrie, ed. Doll Tees Felt Fashions (Revised) 2013. (ENG.). 32p. (J). 24.99 *(978-1-60958-214-2(4))* American Girl Publishing, Inc.
—Go for It! Start Smart, Have Fun, & Stay Inspired in Any Activity. Laskey, Shannon, illus. 2008. (American Girl Library). (ENG.). 64p. (YA). (gr. 3-18). pap. 9.95 *(978-1-59369-423-4(7))* American Girl Publishing, Inc.
Applesauce Press, Applesauce. The Dinosaur Lover's Cookie Kit. 2016. (ENG.). 48p. (J). (gr. k). 16.95 *(978-1-60433-654-2(4),* Applesauce Pr.) Cider Mill Pr. Bk. Pubs., LLC.
Applesauce Press, Applesauce, et al. Message in a Bottle. 2016. (ENG.). 80p. (J). 19.95 *(978-1-60433-636-8(6),* Applesauce Pr.) Cider Mill Pr. Bk. Pubs., LLC.
Archer, Mandy. Ballet. 2015. (Little Hands Creative Sticker Play Ser.). (ENG.). 64p. (J). (gr. -1-2). pap. 9.99 *(978-1-4380-0566-9(0))* Barron's Educational Series, Inc.
—Christmas: With 200 Stickers, Puzzles & Games, Fold-Out Pages, & Creative Play. 2013. (My First Creativity Bks.). (ENG.). 66p. (J). (gr. -1-2). pap. 9.99 *(978-1-4380-0322-1(6))* Barron's Educational Series, Inc.
—Fluffy Animals. 2015. (Little Hands Creative Sticker Play Ser.). (ENG.). 64p. (J). (gr. -1-2). pap. 9.99 *(978-1-4380-0567-6(9))* Barron's Educational Series, Inc.
—Mermaid Kingdom: Over 1000 Reusable Stickers! 2014. (Little Hands Creative Sticker Play Ser.). (ENG.). 64p. (J). (gr. -1-2). pap. 9.99 *(978-1-4380-0535-5(0))* Barron's Educational Series, Inc.
—Pets: Creative Play, Fold-Out Pages, Puzzles & Games, over 200 Stickers! 2014. (My First Creativity Bks.). (ENG.). 66p. (J). (gr. -1-2). pap. 9.99 *(978-1-4380-0443-3(5))* Barron's Educational Series, Inc.
Archie Superstars Staff. Archie's Fun 'n' Games Activity Book. 2013. (ENG., Illus.). 192p. (J). (gr. 4-7). 6.99 *(978-1-936975-51-8(3))* Archie Comic Pubns., Inc.
Arciniega Bailey, Yvette. Squiggly Wiggly Lines. 2013. 34p. pap. 7.99 *(978-1-4575-2390-8(6))* Dog Ear Publishing, LLC.
Arcturus Publishing Staff. Lots to Spot: Farm. 2017. (ENG., Illus.). 48p. (J). (gr. k-5). 9.99 ***(978-1-78428-476-3(9),*** 9781784284763) Arcturus Publishing GBR. Dist: Bookmasters Distribution.
—The Magical Fairy Activity Book. 2014. (ENG.). 96p. (J). pap. 9.95 *(978-1-78212-597-6(3))* Arcturus Publishing GBR. Dist: Bookmasters Distribution.
—Paper Planes. 2013. (ENG.). 96p. (J). pap. 12.95 *(978-1-78212-289-0(3))* Arcturus Publishing GBR. Dist: Bookmasters Distribution.
Armadillo. Superstickers Fun! Numbers, Colours, Sizes, Opposites. 2017. (ENG., Illus.). 64p. (J). (gr. -1-12). pap. 8.99 *(978-1-86147-773-6(2),* Armadillo) Anness Publishing GBR. Dist: National Bk. Network.
Armadillo Publishing Staff & Armadillo Press Saff. 200 Stickers! Playtime, Dressing up, Party, Food & Drink: An Entertaining Play & Learn Book. 2017. (ENG., Illus.). 64p. (J). (gr. -1-12). pap. 8.99 *(978-1-86147-772-9(4),* Armadillo) Anness Publishing GBR. Dist: National Bk. Network.
Aronnax, Pierre. The Oceanology Handbook: A Course for Underwater Explorers. Hawkins, Emily & Twist, Clint, eds. 2010. (Ologies Ser.). (ENG., Illus.). 80p. (J). (gr. 4-7). 14.99 *(978-0-7636-4874-9(4))* Candlewick Pr.
Arsenal Football Club PLC & Arsenal Football Club PLC. The Official Arsenal Sticker Activity Book. 2014. (ENG.). 16p. (J). (gr. -1-3). pap. 9.99 *(978-1-78097-327-2(6))* Carlton Bks., Ltd. GBR. Dist: Independent Pubs. Group.
Artz, Tracy. The Sneaky Leprechaun. 2011. 41p. pap. 10.95 *(978-1-4327-6324-4(5))* Outskirts Pr., Inc.
Aryal, Naren. Hello, Beaker! Morehead State University. Schartup, Adam, illus. 2013. (ENG.). (J). 14.95 *(978-1-62086-151-6(8))* Mascot Bks., Inc.
Attansia, Fabiana, illus. Alice in Wonderland Coloring Book. 2016. (ENG.). 80p. (J). (gr. k). pap. 9.95 *(978-1-4549-2089-2(0))* Sterling Publishing Co., Inc.
—Peter Pan Coloring Book. 2016. (ENG.). 80p. (J). (gr. k). pap. 9.95 *(978-1-4549-2090-8(4))* Sterling Publishing Co., Inc.
Auerbach, Annie & Disney Book Group Staff. P Is for Princess. Disney Storybook Artists Staff, illus. 2013. (ENG.). 26p. (J). (gr. -1-k). bds. 12.99 *(978-1-4231-6471-5(7))* Disney Pr.
AWARD & Award, Anna. Dot to Dot Count & Colour Fun. 2015. (ENG.). 16p. (J). pap. 3.99 *(978-1-78270-122-4(2))* Award Pubns. Ltd. GBR. Dist: Parkwest Pubns., Inc.
Award, Anna. English. Burton, Terry, illus. 2012. (ENG.). 36p. (J). pap. 8.25 *(978-1-84135-801-7(0))* Award Pubns. Ltd. GBR. Dist: Parkwest Pubns., Inc.
—English/French. Burton, Terry, illus. 2012. (ENG.). 36p. (J). pap. 8.25 *(978-1-84135-802-4(9))* Award Pubns. Ltd. GBR. Dist: Parkwest Pubns., Inc.
Award Publications Staff. ABC. 2012. (ENG., Illus.). 24p. (J). 6.50 *(978-1-84135-552-8(6))* Award Pubns. Ltd. GBR. Dist: Parkwest Pubns., Inc.
—Ballerina Lisa: Glitter Paper Doll. 2012. (ENG.). 12p. (J). pap. 6.50 *(978-1-84135-629-7(8))* Award Pubns. Ltd. GBR. Dist: Parkwest Pubns., Inc.
—Fairy Belle. 2012. (ENG., Illus.). 12p. (J). pap. 6.50 *(978-1-84135-631-0(X))* Award Pubns. Ltd. GBR. Dist: Parkwest Pubns., Inc.
—Little Stars: My First Words. 2012. (ENG., Illus.). 24p. (J). pap. 4.95 *(978-1-84135-574-0(7))* Award Pubns. Ltd. GBR. Dist: Parkwest Pubns., Inc.
—My First Alphabet: Activities in Key Skills, Parent Tips. 2012. (ENG., Illus.). 24p. (J). pap. 4.95 *(978-1-84135-573-3(9))* Award Pubns. Ltd. GBR. Dist: Parkwest Pubns., Inc.
—My First Writing. 2012. (ENG., Illus.). 24p. (J). pap. 4.95 *(978-1-84135-572-6(0))* Award Pubns. Ltd. GBR. Dist: Parkwest Pubns., Inc.
—Princess Sophia: Glitter Paper Doll. 2012. (ENG.). 12p. (J). pap. 6.50 *(978-1-84135-630-3(1))* Award Pubns. Ltd. GBR. Dist: Parkwest Pubns., Inc.
—123. 2012. (ENG., Illus.). 24p. (J). 6.50 *(978-1-84135-553-5(4))* Award Pubns. Ltd. GBR. Dist: Parkwest Pubns., Inc.
Award Staff & Award, Anna. Yoohoo & Friends. 2015. (ENG.). 48p. (J). pap. 7.99 *(978-1-78270-013-5(7))* Award Pubns. Ltd. GBR. Dist: Parkwest Pubns., Inc.
Ayers, Chris. My Daily Zoo: A Drawing Activity Book for All Ages. 2011. (ENG., Illus.). 96p. pap. 9.95 *(978-1-933492-63-6(5))* Design Studio Pr.
AZ Books. Bright Colors. 2013. (Matching Pictures Ser.). (ENG.). 20p. (J). (gr. -1-k). bds. 5.95 *(978-1-61889-310-9(6))* AZ Bks. LLC.
AZ Books, creator. Lion & His Kingdom. 2013. (Amusing Stories Ser.). (ENG., Illus.). 10p. (J). (gr. -1-k). bds. 7.95 *(978-1-61889-306-2(8))* AZ Bks. LLC.
—Meeting Friends. 2013. (Velvet Fantasy Ser.). (ENG., Illus.). 16p. (J). (gr. 1-3). pap. 4.95 *(978-1-61889-295-9(9))* AZ Bks. LLC.
—Sea Adventures. 2013. (Spot In! Ser.). (ENG., Illus.). 10p. (J). (gr. 1-3). 15.95 *(978-1-61889-314-7(9))* AZ Bks. LLC.
—Space Adventures. 2013. (Spot In! Ser.). (ENG., Illus.). 10p. (J). (gr. 1-3). 15.95 *(978-1-61889-313-0(0))* AZ Bks. LLC.
—Stylish Gifts. 2013. (Velvet Fantasy Ser.). (ENG., Illus.). 16p. (J). (gr. 1-3). pap. 4.95 *(978-1-61889-296-6(7))* AZ Bks. LLC.
AZ Books Staff. Fast Cars. Tulup, Natasha, ed. 2012. (Workshop Ser.). (ENG.). 10p. (J). (gr. -1-k). bds. 10.95 *(978-1-61889-161-7(8))* AZ Bks. LLC.
—Flying Planes. Tulup, Natasha, ed. 2012. (Workshop Ser.). (ENG.). 10p. (J). (gr. -1-k). 10.95 *(978-1-61889-159-4(6))* AZ Bks. LLC.
—Happy Holidays. 2013. (Velvet Fantasy Ser.). (ENG., Illus.). 16p. (J). (gr. 1-3). pap. 4.95 *(978-1-61889-294-2(0))* AZ Bks. LLC.
—Making Machines. Sisoj, Natalja, ed. 2012. (Modeling Clay Bks.). (ENG.). 12p. (J). (gr. -1-2). bds. 10.95 *(978-1-61889-198-3(7))* AZ Bks. LLC.
—Making the Farm. Sisoj, Natalja, ed. 2012. (Modeling Clay Bks.). (ENG.). 12p. (J). (gr. -1-2). bds. 10.95 *(978-1-61889-197-6(9))* AZ Bks. LLC.
—Making the Forest. Sisoj, Natalja, ed. 2012. (Modeling Clay Bks.). (ENG.). 12p. (J). (gr. -1-2). bds. 10.95 *(978-1-61889-199-0(5))* AZ Bks. LLC.
—Sailing Ships. Tulup, Natasha, ed. 2012. (Workshop Ser.). (ENG.). 10p. (J). (gr. -1-k). bds. 10.95 *(978-1-61889-162-4(6))* AZ Bks. LLC.
—Shapes. Slusar, Julia, ed. 2012. (Pull It Out Ser.). (ENG.). 10p. (J). (— 1). 7.95 *(978-1-61889-194-5(4))* AZ Bks. LLC.
—Stylish Girls. 2013. (Velvet Fantasy Ser.). (ENG., Illus.). 16p. (J). (gr. 1-3). pap. 4.95 *(978-1-61889-292-8(4))* AZ Bks. LLC.
AZ Books Staff & Evans, Olivia. Making the Zoo. Sisoj, Natalja, ed. 2012. (Modeling Clay Bk Ser.). (ENG., Illus.). 12p. (J). (gr. -1-2). bds. 10.95 *(978-1-61889-196-9(0))* AZ Bks. LLC.
B&H Kids Editorial Staff. Mix & Match: Fun with God's Animals. 2017. (ENG.). 32p. (J). (gr. -1 — 1). 12.99 *(978-1-4336-4315-6(4),* B&H Kids) B&H Publishing Group.
Babsky, Irene. Let's Play with Words: Fun Activities, Games & Write-In Word Puzzles. 2015. (ENG., Illus.). 64p. (J). (gr. k-3). 7.99 *(978-1-86147-294-6(3))* Anness Publishing GBR. Dist: National Bk. Network.
Baby Einstein: Let's Learn! 12 Book Block. 2013. 10p. (J). bds. 9.98 *(978-1-4508-3093-5(5),* 1450830935) Phoenix International Publications, Inc.
Backshall, Steve. Steve Backshall Annual 2017. 2016. (Steve Backshall Ser.). (ENG.). 64p. (J). (gr. 4-6). 10.99

S

(978-1-5101-0156-2(X), Orion Children's Bks.) Hachette Children's Group GBR. Dist: Hachette Bk. Group.

Bailey, Ellen & Mosedale, Julian. The London Activity Book: With Palaces, Puzzles & Pictures to Colour. Pinder, Andrew, illus. 2013. (ENG.). 64p. (J). (gr. 2-4). pap. 8.99 *(978-1-78055-095-4(2))* O'Mara, Michael Bks., Ltd. GBR. Dist: Independent Pubs. Group.

Baines, Becky. National Geographic Kids Funny Fill-In: My Backyard Adventure. 2014. (NG Kids Funny Fill In Ser.). (ENG.). 48p. (J). (gr. 3-7). pap. 4.99 *(978-1-4263-1738-5(7)*, National Geographic Children's Bks.) National Geographic Society.

Baines, Becky & National Geographic Staff. Action Journal: Talk Like a Pirate, Analyze Your Dreams, Fingerprint Your Friends, Rule Your Own Country, & Other Wild Things to Do to Be Yourself. 2010. (ENG.). 176p. (J). (gr. 5-9). pap. 12.95 *(978-1-4263-0748-5(9)*, National Geographic Children's Bks.) National Geographic Society.

Baker, Sandy. Colorea Mi Jardin: Un Libro para Colorear Pájaros, Abejas, Mariposas y Bichos. Thiessen, Carolyn, tr. 2013. 32p. pap. 7.00 *(978-0-9832383-8-6(3))* Black Garnet Pr.

Baker, Yaba. Princess Briana. 2004. (Illus.). 72p. (J). 17.99 *(978-1-928889-05-2(0)*, 262-002) Just Like Me, Inc.

Balcom, Katherine. Waterpark. 2014. pap. 11.66 *(978-1-4896-2243-3(8))* Weigl Pubs., Inc.

Balkan, Gabrielle. The 50 States. Linero, Sol, illus. 2016. (50 States Ser.). (ENG.). 32p. (J). (gr. 3-6). pap., act. bk. ed. 9.99 *(978-1-84780-862-2(X)*, Wide Eyed Editions) Quarto Publishing Group UK GBR. Dist: Hachette Bk. Group.

Ball, Liz, illus. A Standardbred Star: Learn about Harness Racing with Star & Friends. 2007. (YA). 3.95 *(978-0-9793891-0-8(0))* United States Trotting Association.

Banks, Rosie. Secret Kingdom. 2017. (Secret Kingdom Ser.). (ENG.). 12p. (J). (gr. k-2). pap., act. bk. ed. 5.99 ***(978-1-4083-2948-1(4)***, Orchard Bks.) Hachette Children's Group GBR. Dist: Hachette Bk. Group.

Barbaresi, Nina. Glitter Rubber Duckies Stickers. 2008. (ENG., Illus.). 4p. (J). (gr. -1-5). 1.50 *(978-0-486-46842-6(9))* Dover Pubns., Inc.

Barchers, Suzanne. The Big Book of Holidays & Cultural Celebrations. rev. ed. 2013. (Classroom Resources Ser.). (ENG., Illus.). 296p. (gr. k-2). pap. 19.99 *(978-1-4258-1046-7(2))*; 280p. (gr. 3-5). pap. 19.99 *(978-1-4258-1048-1(9))* Shell Educational Publishing.

Barefoot Books, et al. Dotty Spotty Doodles. 2008. (ENG., Illus.). 24p. (J). pap. 6.99 *(978-1-84686-232-8(9))* Barefoot Bks., Inc.

—Pirates Fun Activities. 2008. (ENG., Illus.). 16p. (J). pap. 4.99 *(978-1-84686-217-5(5))* Barefoot Bks., Inc.

Barefoot Books Staff, et al. Zig Zag Zebra. 2008. (ENG., Illus.). 24p. (J). pap., act. bk. ed. 6.99 *(978-1-84686-233-5(7))* Barefoot Bks., Inc.

Barkan, Joanne. A Western Activity Book: Set Of 6. 2011. (Navigators Ser.). (J). pap. 50.00 net. *(978-1-4108-2579-7(5))* Benchmark Education Co.

Barker, Cicely Mary & Warne. Flower Fairies. 2010. (Flower Fairies Ser.). (ENG.). 24p. (J). (gr. -1-2). pap., act. bk. ed. 6.99 *(978-0-7232-6495-8(3)*, Warne) Penguin Young Readers Group.

Barnabas Fund. Brothers & Sisters: Loving Our Persecuted Family. 2012. (ENG., Illus.). 38p. pap. 10.00 *(978-0-9853109-7-4(9))* Isaac Publishing.

Barner, Bob. Animals! Matching Game. 2011. (ENG.). 72p. (J). (gr. -1-17). bds. 14.99 *(978-1-4521-0055-5(1))* Chronicle Bks. LLC.

—Dinosaurs! Matching Game. 2009. (ENG.). 72p. (J). (gr. -1-17). bds. 14.99 *(978-0-8118-6980-5(6))* Chronicle Bks. LLC.

Barnhart, Norm, et al. My First Guides. 2017. (My First Guides). (ENG.). 24p. (gr. 1-2). 151.92 *(978-1-5157-3595-3(8)*, First Facts) Capstone Press of Coughlan Cos.

Barry, Ron & Fitzgerald, Paula. Me 'n Mom: A Keepsake Scrapbook Journal. Sharp, Chris, illus. 2009. (ENG.). 33p. pap. 14.99 *(978-0-8249-1435-6(X)*, Ideal Pubns.) Worthy Publishing.

Bartfeld, Martha & Hutchinson, Alberta. Infinite Coloring Mandala Designs. 2009. (Dover Design Coloring Bks.). (ENG., Illus.). 96p. (gr. 3-5). pap. 9.99 incl. cd-rom *(978-0-486-46949-2(2))* Dover Pubns., Inc.

Basaluzzo, Constanza & Stanford, Elisa. The Baby Bible 1,2,3, 1 vol. 2009. (Baby Bible Ser.). (ENG.). 48p. (J). bds. 12.99 *(978-1-4347-6540-6(7))* Cook, David C.

Battaglioli, Peter. What to Doodle? Crazy Faces. 2013. (Dover Doodle Bks.). (ENG.). 48p. (J). (gr. 2-5). pap. 4.99 *(978-0-486-49100-4(5))* Dover Pubns., Inc.

Baur, Becky. Dotty's First Book. 2017. (ENG., Illus.). 14p. (gr. -1-k). 12.95 *(978-0-500-65107-0(8)*, 565107) Thames & Hudson.

Bear, Magdalen. Walking Automata: A Collection of Self-Moving Models to Cut Out & Make. 2004. (Illus.). 32p. 10.00 *(978-1-899618-50-7(3))* Tarquin Pubns. GBR. Dist: Parkwest Pubns., Inc.

Beathard, Patricia. Schools of Yesteryear: History of the One-Room School. 2012. 68p. (gr. 4-6). pap. 27.68 *(978-1-4669-7024-3(3))* Trafford Publishing.

Beaton, Clare. Make Your Own Theatre Cinderella. 2014. (Make Your Own Ser.). (ENG.). 20p. (J). (gr. k-2). pap. 7.99 *(978-1-905710-18-8(6))* B Small Publishing GBR. Dist: Independent Pubs. Group.

—Noah's Ark. 2014. (Make Your Own Ser.). (ENG.). 20p. (J). (gr. k-2). pap. 7.99 *(978-1-905710-25-6(9))* B Small Publishing GBR. Dist: Independent Pubs. Group.

—Snow White. 2014. (Make Your Own Ser.). (ENG.). 20p. (J). (gr. k-2). pap. 7.99 *(978-1-905710-32-4(1))* B Small Publishing GBR. Dist: Independent Pubs. Group.

Beaty, Andrea. Iggy Peck's Big Project Book for Amazing Architects. Roberts, David, illus. 2017. (ENG.). 96p. (J). (gr. k-2). pap. 14.99 ***(978-1-4197-1892-2(4)***, Abrams Bks. for Young Readers) Abrams, Inc.

Beaumont, Chris. Amazing Cubeecraft Paper Models: 16 Never-Before-Seen Paper Models. 2013. (ENG., Illus.). 32p. (J). (gr. 3-6). pap. 9.99 *(978-0-486-49272-8(9))* Dover Pubns., Inc.

Beausoliel, Loyan & Wells, Leah. Games That Sing: 25 Activities to Keep Children on Their Toes. 2011. (Illus.). 52p. pap. 16.95 incl. audio compact disk *(978-1-4291-2116-3(5))* Heritage Music Pr.

Beecroft, Simon & Harvey, Guy. The Tintin & Snowy Big Activity Book. 2011. (ENG., Illus.). 96p. pap. 19.95 *(978-0-86719-761-7(7))* Last Gasp of San Francisco.

Behrens, Janice & Butler, Marybeth. I'm Not Ready! A Morning Routine Book. 2017. (Rookie Toddler(tm) Ser.). (ENG., Illus.). 12p. (J). bds. 6.95 *(978-0-531-22977-4(7)*, Children's Pr.) Scholastic Library Publishing.

Beilenson, Suzanne. Quiz Book: Who R U? 2008. (Activity Book Ser.). 160p. (J). (gr. k-5). spiral bd. 12.99 *(978-1-59359-807-5(6))* Peter Pauper Pr. Inc.

Beirut, Michael. Designing with Pixar: 45 Activities to Create Your Own Characters, Worlds, & Stories. 2016. (ENG., Illus.). 80p. (J). (gr. 1-7). pap. 14.99 *(978-1-4521-5505-0(4))* Chronicle Bks. LLC.

Bell, Robin. My Adventure with Pirates: Advanced My Adventure. 2009. (ENG.). 44p. (J). 8.99 *(978-1-59092-462-4(2))* Blue Forge Pr.

Belle, Magnolia. Teen Titans Go! - Power Moves Doodle Book. 2016. (ENG., Illus.). 128p. (J). (gr. 3-7). pap. 6.99 *(978-0-316-33339-9(5))* Little, Brown Bks. for Young Readers.

Benchmark Education Company, LLC Staff, compiled by. Sort & Classify. 2006. (J). 204.00 *(978-1-4108-7051-3(0))* Benchmark Education Co.

Bender, Albert C. More 'Kids in the Alley' Tales. 2011. (Illus.). 200p. pap. 16.95 *(978-1-4327-7174-4(4))* Outskirts Pr., Inc.

Bentley, Linda M. & Bentley, Linda. The Big Book of Quick & Easy Art Activities: More Than 75 Creative Activities with Curriculum Connections That Keep Kids Creating & Learning All Year Long! 2007. (ENG., Illus.). 208p. pap. 26.99 *(978-0-439-58060-1(9)*, Teaching Resources) Scholastic, Inc.

Berenstain, Jan & Berenstain, Stan. The Berenstain Bears' Christmas Coloring & Activity Book. 2014. (ENG.). 256p. (J). (gr. k-3). pap. 8.99 *(978-0-486-79209-5(9))* Dover Pubns., Inc.

—The Berenstain Bears(r)' First Time Do-It! Book. 2014. (ENG., Illus.). 112p. (J). (gr. k-3). pap. 12.99 *(978-0-486-78179-2(8))* Dover Pubns., Inc.

—The Berenstain Bears Giant Coloring & Activity Book. 2013. (ENG.). 272p. (J). (gr. -1-2). pap. 7.99 *(978-0-486-49341-1(5))* Dover Pubns., Inc.

Bernard, Stephanie. Using Cursive Today, 1 vol. 2015. (Classroom Resources Ser.). (ENG., Illus.). 80p. (gr. 2-5). mass mkt. 9.99 *(978-1-4258-1544-8(8))* Shell Educational Publishing.

Bernd & Richter, Susan. I See You Through My Heart. 2008. bds. 8.95 *(978-1-931353-44-1(1))* Saddle Pal Creations, Inc.

Berrios, Frank. Justice for All! (DC Super Friends) Golden Books, illus. 2016. (Color Plus 1,000 Stickers Ser.). (ENG.). 64p. (J). (gr. -1-2). pap. 9.99 *(978-1-101-93151-6(5)*, Golden Bks.) Random Hse. Children's Bks.

Berrow, G. M. My Little Pony: Applejack & the Honest-To-Goodness Switcheroo. 2014. (ENG.). 160p. (J). (gr. 3-7). pap. 5.99 *(978-0-316-24825-9(8))* Little, Brown Bks. for Young Readers.

Beston, Clare. Make Your Own Roman Arena. 2014. (Make Your Own Ser.). (ENG.). 20p. (J). (gr. k-2). pap. 7.99 *(978-1-905710-17-1(8))* B Small Publishing GBR. Dist: Independent Pubs. Group.

Beylon, Cathy. Shiny Dinosaurs Stickers. 2004. (Dover Little Activity Books Stickers Ser.). (ENG., Illus.). 2p. (J). (gr. -1-5). 1.50 *(978-0-486-43536-7(9))* Dover Pubns., Inc.

Big Blue Bubble Inc., Big Blue. My Singing Monsters Downloaded. 2015. (My Singing Monsters Ser.). (ENG., Illus.). 48p. (J). (gr. 1). pap. 12.99 *(978-1-4052-7683-2(5))* Egmont Bks., Ltd. GBR. Dist: Independent Pubs. Group.

Big Picture Press, Big Picture. Animalium Activity Book. Scott, Katie, illus. 2016. (ENG.). 72p. (J). (gr. 2-5). 14.99 *(978-0-7636-8919-3(X)*, Big Picture Press) Candlewick Pr.

—Where Did They Go? Bomoff, Emily, illus. 2016. (ENG.). 32p. (J). (-k). 14.99 *(978-0-7636-8920-9(3)*, Big Picture Press) Candlewick Pr.

Big Tent Entertainment LLC Staff. Things to Do with Domo. 2013. (ENG., Illus.). 34p. bds., act. bk. ed. 12.95 *(978-1-4197-0691-2(8)*, Abrams Image) Abrams, Inc.

Biggs, Kathy. Dragonflies of North America: A Color & learn Book for All Ages, with Activities. Manolis, Tim, illus. l.t. ed. 2007. (ENG.). 48p. (J). *(978-0-9677934-4-3(0))* Azalea Creek Publishing.

—Dragonflies of North America: A Color & Learn Book for All Ages, with Activities. Manolis, Tim, illus. l.t. ed. 2007. 48p. (J). cd-rom *(978-0-9677934-5-0(9))* Azalea Creek Publishing.

Billet, Marion. My Big London Play Set, 2 vols. Billet, Marion, illus. 2017. (ENG., Illus.). 1p. (J). (gr. -1-1). pap. 26.99 *(978-1-5098-1548-7(1))* Pan Macmillan GBR. Dist: Independent Pubs. Group.

Billet, Marion, illus. I Love Music: My First Sound Book. 2016. (ENG.). 16p. (J). (gr. -1 — 1). 9.99 *(978-1-338-03261-1(5)*, Cartwheel Bks.) Scholastic, Inc.

Bird, Grace. Beetles Ahoy! 2009. 48p. pap. *(978-1-84923-423-8(X))* YouWriteOn.

Birney, Betty G. Humphrey's Book of Fun Fun Fun. 2013. (Humphrey Ser.). (ENG.). 240p. (J). (gr. 3-7). pap. 6.99 *(978-0-14-750951-2(3)*, Puffin Books) Penguin Young Readers Group.

Blackbird Publishing Staff. Mr. HookWorm Coloring Book. 2007. (Illus.). 32p. (J). per. 1.50 *(978-0-9789798-7-4(7))* Blackbird's World Publishing Co.

Bloomenstein, Susan. Allover Patterns Stained Glass Coloring Book. 2012. (Dover Stained Glass Coloring Book Ser.). (ENG., Illus.). 32p. (gr. 3-5). pap. 6.99 *(978-0-486-49784-6(4))* Dover Pubns., Inc.

—Make Your Own Flower Bouquet Sticker Activity Book. 2016. (Dover Little Activity Books Stickers Ser.). (ENG.). 8p. (J). (gr. -1-2). pap. 1.99 *(978-0-486-80589-4(1))* Dover Pubns., Inc.

Bloomsbury USA. My Activity Books for Boys. 2014. (Sticker Activity Bks.). (ENG.). 192p. (J). (gr. -1-3). pap. 10.99 *(978-1-61963-639-2(5)*, 9781619636392, Bloomsbury USA Childrens) Bloomsbury Publishing USA.

—My Amazing Adventure Activity & Sticker Book. 2015. (ENG.). 112p. (J). (gr. k-3). pap. 12.99 *(978-1-61963-760-3(X)*, 9781619637603, Bloomsbury USA Childrens) Bloomsbury Publishing USA.

—My Animals Activity & Sticker Book. 2015. (ENG.). 112p. (J). (gr. k-3). pap. 12.99 *(978-1-61963-762-7(6)*, 9781619637627, Bloomsbury USA Childrens) Bloomsbury Publishing USA.

—My Christmas Activity & Sticker Book. 2014. (ENG., Illus.). 32p. (J). (gr. -1-1). pap. 4.99 *(978-1-61963-311-7(6)*, 9781619633117, Bloomsbury USA Childrens) Bloomsbury Publishing USA.

—My Halloween Activity & Sticker Book. 2016. (ENG., Illus.). 112p. (J). pap. 12.99 *(978-1-61963-996-6(3)*, 9781619639966, Bloomsbury Activity Bks.) Bloomsbury Publishing USA.

—My Jolly Red Santa Activity & Sticker Book. 2015. (ENG., Illus.). 32p. (J). (gr. -1-3). pap. 4.99 *(978-1-61963-791-7(X)*, 9781619637917, Bloomsbury USA Childrens) Bloomsbury Publishing USA.

—My Pink Princess Activity & Sticker Book: Bloomsbury Activity Books. 2014. (ENG., Illus.). 32p. (J). (gr. -1-1). pap. 4.99 *(978-1-61963-307-0(8)*, 9781619633070, Bloomsbury USA Childrens) Bloomsbury Publishing USA.

—My Pirate Activity & Sticker Book: Bloomsbury Activity Books. 2014. (ENG., Illus.). 32p. (J). (gr. -1-1). pap. 4.99 *(978-1-61963-306-3(X)*, 9781619633063, Bloomsbury USA Childrens) Bloomsbury Publishing USA.

—My Snowman Activity & Sticker Book. 2014. (ENG., Illus.). 32p. (J). (gr. -1-1). pap. 4.99 *(978-1-61963-312-4(4)*, 9781619633124, Bloomsbury USA Childrens) Bloomsbury Publishing USA.

Boam, Jon, illus. Colour Me Menagerie. 2012. (Colour Me Ser.). (ENG.). 24p. (J). (gr. -1-k). 6.00 *(978-1-907704-09-3(4))* Nobrow Ltd. GBR. Dist: Consortium Bk. Sales & Distribution.

Boardworks Learning Centers: I've Got It! 2006. (J). bds. *(978-0-9755252-8-9(X))* Evergreen Pr. of Brainerd, LLC.

Bohn, Kendall. Abstract Adventure. 2009. (Kaleidoscopia Coloring Book Ser.). (Illus.). (J). 8.95 *(978-0-929636-98-6(8))* Itasca Bks.

Bohn, Kendall, creator. Prehistoric Adventure: A Kaleidoscopia Coloring Book. 2005. (Illus.). 56p. pap. 8.95 *(978-0-929636-37-5(6))* Syren Bk. Co.

Bokor, Dina. Alphabet: In the World of Things. 2013. (ENG.). 18p. (J). pap. 11.95 *(978-1-4787-0031-9(9))* Outskirts Pr., Inc.

Bolte, Mari. My First Sketchbook, 1 vol. Makuc, Lucy & Dynamo Limited Staff, illus. 2014. (My First Sketchbook Ser.). (ENG.). 24p. (gr. 1-2). 101.28 *(978-1-4914-0285-6(7)*, First Facts) Capstone Press of Coughlan Cos.

—Sleepover Girls Crafts, 1 vol. Franco, Paula, illus. 2014. (Sleepover Girls Crafts Ser.). (ENG.). 32p. (gr. 3-4). 111.96 *(978-1-4914-1737-9(4)*, Snap Bks.) Capstone Press of Coughlan Cos.

Bone, Emily & Pratt, Leonie. Recycling Things to Make & Do. 2010. (Activity Book Ser.). 32p. (J). pap. 6.99 *(978-0-7945-2675-7(6)*, Usborne) EDC Publishing.

Boodey, Erin. Work Your Body Grow Your Brain. Konecny, John, illus. 2012. 26p. 13.99 *(978-1-937165-23-9(X))* Orange Hat Publishing.

Bordessa, Kris. Great Medieval Projects. Braley, Shawn, illus. 2008. (Build It Yourself Ser.). (ENG.). 128p. (J). (gr. 3-7). 21.95 *(978-1-934670-26-2(X))* Octavio Publishing.

—Great Medieval Projects: You Can Build Yourself. Braley, Shawn, illus. 2008. (Build It Yourself Ser.). (ENG.). 128p. (J). (gr. 3-7). pap. 15.95 *(978-0-9792268-0-9(5))* Octavio Publishing.

Boréal, Carole. I Love Paris, Rome, Berlin, London. 2015. (ENG., Illus.). 152p. (J). (gr. 7-12). pap. 14.99 *(978-1-4521-3516-8(9))* Chronicle Bks. LLC.

Boredom Busters. 2008. (Best Friends Club Ser.). 64p. *(978-1-4075-1611-0(6))* Parragon, Inc.

Borja, Richard. Flash! Alphabet Enigma. 2009. 48p. pap. 14.92 *(978-1-84728-659-8(3))* Lulu Pr., Inc.

Bork, Rhoda. Pioneering: Activities to Live History. 2007. (J). *(978-0-9786018-6-7(6))* Sparrow Media Group, Inc.

Boutan, Mila. Rousseau: Art Activity Pack. 2005. (Illus.). 22p. (J). (gr. 4-8). pap. 10.00 *(978-0-7567-9413-2(7))* DIANE Publishing Co.

Bowles, Anna. The Cars, Trains, & Planes Creativity Book: Games, Cut-Outs, Art Paper, Stickers, & Stencils. 2016. (Creativity Bks.). (ENG.). 80p. (J). (gr. k-4). pap. 12.99 *(978-1-4380-0779-3(5))* Barron's Educational Series, Inc.

Bowman, Crystal. Our Daily Bread for Kids. 2015. (Our Daily Bread for Kids Ser.). (ENG.). 48p. (-3). 3.99 *(978-1-62707-482-7(1))* Discovery Hse. Pubs.

Bowman, Lucy. Drawing, Doodling & Coloring Book Girls. 2012. (Activity Cards Ser.). 128p. (J). pap. 13.99 *(978-0-7945-3297-0(7)*, Usborne) EDC Publishing.

—Girl's Activity Book. 2013. (Doodle Bks). 96p. (J). pap. 12.99 *(978-0-7945-3172-0(5)*, Usborne) EDC Publishing.

Bowman, Lucy & MacLaine, James. The Usborne Little Girls' Activity Book. Watt, Fiona, ed. Harrison, Erica et al, illus. 2014. (ENG.). 64p. (J). pap. 9.99 *(978-0-7945-2790-7(6)*, Usborne) EDC Publishing.

Boyds Mills Press Staff. Drawing Activities. 2008. (Highlights Hidden Pictures Ser.). (ENG., Illus.). 32p. (J). (gr. -1-3). pap. 5.49 *(978-1-59078-579-9(7))* Highlights for Children.

—Highlights Hidden Pictures 2009, Vol. 4. Highlights for Children Editorial Staff, ed. 2008. (ENG., Illus.). 48p. (J). (gr. -1-9). pap. 5.95 *(978-1-59078-682-6(3))* Boyds Mills Pr.

—Sticker Fun. 2007. (Highlights Hidden Pictures#174; Sticker Fun Ser.: Vol. 3). (ENG., Illus.). 16p. (J). (gr. k-2). pap. 5.95 *(978-0-87534-233-7(7))* Boyds Mills Pr.

Brack, Amanda. Sticker Your Bricks: Decorate Your Building Block Creations with Reusable Stickers. 2016. (ENG., Illus.). 96p. (J). (gr. k). 12.99 *(978-1-5107-0722-1(0)*, Sky Pony Pr.) Skyhorse Publishing Co., Inc.

Brack, Susan. Horsing Around! Stickers. 2011. (Dover Little Activity Books Stickers Ser.). (ENG.). 8p. (J). (gr. k-3). pap. 1.50 *(978-0-486-48186-9(7))* Dover Pubns., Inc.

—Mommy & Me Stickers. 2011. (Dover Little Activity Books Stickers Ser.). (ENG.). 8p. (J). (gr. k-3). pap. 1.50 *(978-0-486-48233-0(2))* Dover Pubns., Inc.

Bradford, Valerie Ann. Activites Makes Learning Fun. 2011. 54p. 24.99 *(978-1-4653-3771-9(7))*; pap. 15.99 *(978-1-4653-3770-2(9))* Xlibris Corp.

—Activities Makes Learning Fun: Volume II. 2011. 52p. 24.99 *(978-1-4653-4707-7(0))*; pap. 15.99 *(978-1-4653-4706-0(2))* Xlibris Corp.

Brain Quest Editors. Brain Quest America: 850 Questions 850 Answers Celebrating Our Nation's History People & Culture. rev. ed. 2013. (ENG.). 152p. (J). (gr. 3-6). 11.95 *(978-0-7611-7239-0(4)*, 17239) Workman Publishing Co., Inc.

—Brain Quest for the Car: 1100 Questions, 1100 Answers, All about America. rev. ed. 2013. (ENG.). 152p. (J). (gr. 2-6). 11.95 *(978-0-7611-7401-1(X)*, 17401) Workman Publishing Co., Inc.

—Brain Quest Presidents. 3rd rev. ed. 2013. (ENG.). 152p. (J). (gr. 3-6). 11.95 *(978-0-7611-7238-3(6)*, 17238) Workman Publishing Co., Inc.

Brandt, DeAnna & Brandt, Daniel. Bug Log Kids. 2017. (Nature Journals). (ENG., Illus.). 88p. (J). (gr. k-7). spiral bd. 9.95 *(978-1-59193-727-2(2))* Adventure Pubns.

Bravest Warriors: Things to Doodle & Do! 2015. (ENG.). 128p. (J). pap. 12.99 *(978-1-4215-7984-9(7))* Viz Media.

Bree, Loris & Bree, Marlin. Kid's Travel Fun Book: Draw. Make Stuff. Play Games. Have Fun for Hours! 2nd ed. 2007. (Kid's Travel Ser.). (ENG., Illus.). 96p. (J). (gr. 2-4). per. 7.95 *(978-1-892147-13-4(0))* Marlor Pr., Inc.

Brett, Anna. Ballerina Theater: Color & Create Your Own Beautiful 3D Scenes. 2017. (3D Colorscapes Ser.). (ENG.). 48p. (J). (gr. 3-7). bds. 10.99 *(978-0-7641-6882-6(7))* Barron's Educational Series, Inc.

—The Fairy Creativity Book: Games, Cut-Outs, Art Paper, Stickers, & Stencils. 2017. (Creativity Bks.). (ENG.). 80p. (J). (gr. 1-6). pap. 12.99 *(978-1-4380-0967-4(4))* Barron's Educational Series, Inc.

—Koob - The Backwards Book. Ward, Elle, illus. 2016. (ENG.). 144p. (J). (gr. 2-5). pap. 11.99 *(978-0-545-90662-3(8)*, Scholastic Nonfiction) Scholastic, Inc.

—Nature: Creative Play, Fold-Out Pages, Puzzles & Games, over 200 Stickers! 2015. (My First Creativity Bks.). (ENG.). 66p. (J). (gr. -1-2). pap. 9.99 *(978-1-4380-0756-4(6))* Barron's Educational Series, Inc.

—Pirates: Creative Play, Fold-Out Pages, Puzzles & Games, over 200 Stickers! 2015. (My First Creativity Bks.). (ENG.). 66p. (J). (gr. -1-2). pap. 9.99 *(978-1-4380-0757-1(4))* Barron's Educational Series, Inc.

Briant, Monta Z. & Z, Susan. Songs for Little Hands: Activity Guide & CD. 2008. (ENG., Illus.). 80p. 12.95 *(978-1-4019-1797-5(6))* Hay Hse., Inc.

Bright & Beyond - 1 Ano. 2007. (J). 9.95 *(978-0-9763648-3-2(2))* Pal Toys, LLC.

Bright & Beyond - 2 Anos. 2007. (SPA.). (J). 9.95 *(978-0-9763648-4-9(0))* Pal Toys, LLC.

Bright & Beyond - Preescolar: Anos 3 To 5. 2007. Orig. Title: Bright & Beyond - Preschool. (SPA.). (J). 9.95 *(978-0-9763648-5-6(9))* Pal Toys, LLC.

Briley, Randy William. Sketchboy. 2013. 104p. pap. 23.00 *(978-0-9896269-1-0(1))* Raven Mad Studios.

Broadbent, Paul. Being A Cartoonist. 2007. (Trackers-Math Ser.). (gr. 2-5). pap. 5.00 *(978-1-59055-937-6(1))* Pacific Learning, Inc.

—Beneath Our Feet. 2007. (Trackers-Math Ser.). (gr. 2-5). pap. 5.00 *(978-1-59055-929-1(0))* Pacific Learning, Inc.

Brooks, Felicity. Getting Dressed Magnet Book. Widdowson, Kay, illus. 2009. (Magnet Bks). 10p. (J). bds. 19.99 *(978-0-7945-2356-5(0)*, Usborne) EDC Publishing.

Brooks, Felicity & Fearn, Katrina. First Dot-To-Dot Animals. 2013. (First Dot-To-Dot Ser.). 16p. (J). pap. 5.99 *(978-0-7945-3198-0(9)*, Usborne) EDC Publishing.

—First Dot-To-Dot Things That Go. 2013. (First Dot-To-Dot Ser.). 16p. (J). pap. 5.99 *(978-0-7945-3162-1(8)*, Usborne) EDC Publishing.

Brooks, Susie. Get into Art Places: Discover Great Art & Create Your Own! 2016. (Get into Art Ser.). (ENG., Illus.). 32p. pap. 8.99 *(978-0-7534-7237-8(6)*, 9780753472378, Kingfisher) Roaring Brook Pr.

—Get into Art Telling Stories: Discover Great Art & Create Your Own! 2016. (Get into Art Ser.). (ENG., Illus.). 32p. pap. 8.99 *(978-0-7534-7238-5(4)*, 9780753472385, Kingfisher) Roaring Brook Pr.

—People: Discover Great Art & Create Your Own! 2013. (Get into Art Ser.). (ENG., Illus.). 32p. (J). (gr. 2-9). 14.99 *(978-0-7534-7059-6(4)*, 9780753470596, Kingfisher) Roaring Brook Pr.

Broom, Jenny. ArtCards: Accessorize. Haworth, Hennie, illus. 2013. (ENG.). 72p. (J). (gr. 1-4). pap. 17.99 *(978-0-7636-6892-1(3)*, Big Picture Press) Candlewick Pr.

—Artcards: Fashion. Haworth, Hennie, illus. 2014. (ENG.). 72p. (J). (gr. 1-4). pap. 17.99 *(978-0-7636-7519-6(9)*, Big Picture Press) Candlewick Pr.

—Color Create: Animals. Nój, Nahta, illus. 2012. (ENG.). 32p. (J). (gr. k). 16.95 *(978-1-60710-493-3(8)*, Silver Dolphin Bks.) Readerlink Distribution Services, LLC.

Brothers Grimm & Sweeney, Monica. Loom Magic Creatures! 25 Awesome Animals & Mythical Beings for a Rainbow of Critters. 2014. (ENG., Illus.). 128p. (J). (gr. k). 12.95 *(978-1-62914-795-6(8)*, Sky Pony Pr.) Skyhorse Publishing Co., Inc.

Brown, Cynthia Light. Amazing Kitchen Chemistry Projects. Shedd, Blair, illus. 2008. (Build It Yourself Ser.). (ENG.). 128p. (J). (gr. 3-7). 21.95 *(978-1-934670-06-4(5))* Octavio Publishing.

Brown, Kyle. My Wedding Activity Book. 2009. 48p. pap. 9.95 *(978-0-557-06217-1(9))* Lulu Pr., Inc.

Brumage, Katherine. The Super Silly Yosemite Sticker & Activity Book: Puzzles, Games, Mazes & More! Hansen, Doug, illus. 2011. (ENG.). 24p. (J). (gr. -1-5). pap. 7.95 *(978-1-59714-155-0(0))* Yosemite Assn.

Bryan, Sarah Jane & Beilenson, Suzanne. Mega Magna Forms Princess. McGregor, Barbara, illus. 2008. (Activity Book Ser.). 48p. (J). (gr. -1-3). spiral bd. 19.95 *(978-1-59359-808-2(4))* Peter Pauper Pr. Inc.

—Mega Magna Forms Safari Adventure. Klug, David, illus. 2008. (Activity Book Ser.). 48p. (J). (gr. -1-3). spiral bd. 19.95 *(978-1-59359-809-9(2))* Peter Pauper Pr. Inc.

Buckingham, Faye. The Calm Coloring Book for Creative Kids. 2016. (ENG.). 96p. (J). pap. 9.95 *(978-1-78599-091-5(8)*, f30044e7-0cb9-4f77-b14a-f44baa13183d) Arcturus Publishing GBR. Dist: Bookmasters Distribution.

Buffolano, Sandra. Coping with Tourette Syndrome: A Workbook for Kids with Tic Disorders. 2008. (Instant Help Ser.). (ENG.). 136p. (J). (gr. k-5). pap. 24.95

(978-1-57224-673-7(1), Instant Help Books) New Harbinger Pubns.

Bugbird, T. Bff Fashion Boutique Designer. 2009. 48p. pap. (978-1-84610-967-6(1)) Make Believe Ideas.

Build It Yourself. 2011. (Build It Yourself Ser.). (ENG.). 32p. (gr. 3-4). pap. 190.80 (978-1-4296-6432-5(0), Edge Bks.) Capstone Press of Coughlan Cos.

Build Your Own Superheroes Sticker Book. 2017. (Build Your Own Sticker Bks.). (ENG.). (J). pap. 8.99 **(978-0-7945-3877-4(0)**, Usborne) EDC Publishing.

Bumpers, Katrina. Alphabet Fun, Book 2: Coloring & Activity Book. 2008. (Illus.). 64p. (gr. -1-3). pap. 10.95 (978-0-9797208-1-9(8)) K's Kids Publishing.

Bunnell, Jacinta. Sometimes the Spoon Runs Away with Another Spoon Coloring Book. Kusinitz, Nat, illus. 2010. (Reach & Teach Ser.). (ENG.). 32p. pap. 10.00 (978-1-60486-329-1(3)) PM Pr.

Bunton, M. Catherine. The Little Maestro: A Forest Club Activity Book. 2010. 90p. pap. 9.95 (978-1-60594-392-3(4), Llumina Pr.) Aeon Publishing Inc.

Burgerman, Jon, illus. Jon Burgerman's Daily Doodle. 2017. (ENG.). 112p. (J). (gr. 3-7). pap. 19.99 **(978-1-78627-041-2(2))** King, Laurence Publishing GBR. Dist: Hachette Bk. Group.

Burke, Fatti & Burke, John. Irelandopedia Activity Book: With Colouring Pages, a Huge Pull-Out Map of Ireland & Lots of Things to See & Do. 2016. (ENG., Illus.). 32p. (J). pap. 16.00 (978-0-7171-7149-1(3)) M.H. Gill & Co. U. C. IRL. Dist: Dufour Editions, Inc.

Burlew, Rich, creator. The Order of the Stick Coloring Book. 2012. (Illus.). 32p. (YA). pap. 4.99 (978-0-9854139-0-3(5)) Giant in the Playground.

Burnett, Gretel. The A-B-C Smarts: Book 2. 2009. 84p. pap. 28.99 (978-1-4490-4575-3(8)) AuthorHouse.

Bush-Retherford, Dody & Clark, Paul. Lil Witches Wheel of the Year Coloring Book. 2009. 69p. pap. 9.00 (978-0-557-09779-1(7)) Lulu Pr., Inc.

Busy Kids Horses & Ponies Sticker Activity Book. 2008. (Busy Kids Ser.). (Illus.). 12p. (J). (gr. -1-3). pap. (978-1-84610-722-1(9)) Make Believe Ideas.

But I Don't Know: Women's Ministry. 2005. mass mkt. 6.50 (978-1-59317-001-1(7)) Warner Pr., Inc.

Butler, Megan, et al. Summer Brain Quest: Between Grades 1 And 2. Dukes, Rachel & Yan, Edison, illus. 2017. (Summer Brain Quest Ser.). (ENG.). 160p. (J). (gr. 1-2). pap. 12.95 (978-0-7611-8917-6(3)) Workman Publishing Co., Inc.

—Summer Brain Quest: Between Grades K And 1. Wicks, Maris & Yan, Edison, illus. 2017. (Summer Brain Quest Ser.). (ENG.). 160p. (J). (gr. k-1). pap. 12.95 (978-0-7611-8916-9(5)) Workman Publishing Co., Inc.

Butterfield, M. & Edom, H. Science with Air. rev. ed. 2008. (Science Activities Ser.). 24p. (J). pap. 5.99 (978-0-7945-2331-2(5), Usborne) EDC Publishing.

Butterfield, Moira. Bible Stories Creativity Book. 2013. (Creativity Bks.). (ENG.). 80p. (J). (gr. 1-6). pap. 12.99 (978-1-4380-0319-1(6)) Barron's Educational Series, Inc.

—The Underwater Creativity Book: Games, Cut-Outs, Art Paper, Stickers, & Stencils! 2014. (Creativity Bks.). (ENG.). 80p. (J). (gr. k-5). pap. 12.99 (978-1-4380-0546-1(6)) Barron's Educational Series, Inc.

—The Wildlife Adventure Creativity Book. 2013. (Creativity Bks.). (ENG.). 88p. (J). (gr. 1-6). pap. 12.99 (978-1-4380-0241-5(6)) Barron's Educational Series, Inc.

Butterfield, Moira & Potter, William. Halloween Pocket Activity Fun & Games: Games, Puzzles, Fold-Out Scenes, Patterned Paper, Stickers! 2014. (Pocket Activity Fun & Games Ser.). (ENG.). 96p. (J). (gr. 1-5). pap. 7.99 (978-1-4380-0516-4(4)) Barron's Educational Series, Inc.

Butz, Steve. Year Round Project-Based Activities for STEM Grd 2-3. 2013. (ENG.). 112p. pap. 14.99 (978-1-4206-3027-5(X)) Teacher Created Resources, Inc.

Buzz. (Disney Fun Shaped Coloring Ser.). 64p. pap. (978-1-4054-9381-9(X)) Parragon, Inc.

Cabanillas, Laura Sabin. The Abc's of Character. Sebastian, illus. 2009. 60p. pap. 12.95 (978-0-9818488-2-2(6)) Ajoyin Publishing, Inc.

The California Mission Activity Book. 2003. (Missions of California Ser.). (Illus.). 144p. (gr. 4-6). pap. 19.95 (978-0-404-28506-7(6), Rosen Classroom) Rosen Publishing Group, Inc., The.

Callella, Trisha. I Have, Who Has? Language Arts, Grades 3-4: 38 Interactive Card Games, Vol. 2206. Hamaguchi, Carla, ed. Hillam, Corbin, illus. 2006. (I Have, Who Has? Ser.). 204p. (J). (gr. 3-4). per. 19.99 (978-1-59198-228-9(6), 2206) Creative Teaching Pr., Inc.

—I Have, Who Has? Language Arts, Grades 5-6: 38 Interactive Card Games. Hamaguchi, Carla, ed. Hillam, Corbin, illus. 2006. (I Have, Who Has? Ser.). 204p. (J). (gr. 5-6). per. 19.99 (978-1-59198-229-6(4)) Creative Teaching Pr., Inc.

Calma, Jocelyn. Little Malia's Big Poi Idea. Robinson, Don, illus. 2009. 28p. (J). 12.99 (978-1-59524-328-7(3)) Giddy Up, LLC.

Calver, Paul & Award, Anna. My Favourite Rescuers Sticker Book. 2015. (ENG., Illus.). 20p. (J). pap. 7.99 (978-1-907604-21-8(9)) Award Pubns. Ltd. GBR. Dist: Parkwest Pubns., Inc.

Calver, Paul & Gunzi, Christiane. Aircraft: Play & Learn with Stickers. 2012. (My Sticker Activity Bks.). (ENG.). 12p. (J). pap. 3.99 (978-1-4380-0085-5(5)) Barron's Educational Series, Inc.

—Farm: Play & Learn with Stickers. 2012. (My Sticker Activity Bks.). (ENG.). 12p. (J). pap. 3.99 (978-1-4380-0086-2(3)) Barron's Educational Series, Inc.

—Farm Babies: Play & Learn with Stickers. 2012. (My Sticker Activity Bks.). (ENG.). 12p. (J). pap. 4.99 (978-1-4380-0087-9(1)) Barron's Educational Series, Inc.

—Pets: Play & Learn with Stickers. 2012. (My Sticker Activity Bks.). (ENG.). 12p. (J). pap. 3.99 (978-1-4380-0088-6(X)) Barron's Educational Series, Inc.

Campoy, F. Isabel. My Day from A to Z. 2009. 32p. (gr. -1-2). pap. 14.95 (978-1-60396-324-4(3), Alfaguara) Santillana USA Publishing Co., Inc.

Candle Books, creator. More 365 Activities for Kids, 1 vol. 2005. (Illus.). 366p. (J). (gr. -1-3). spiral bd. 13.99 (978-0-8254-7292-3(X), Candle Bks.) Lion Hudson PLC GBR. Dist: Kregel Pubns.

Candlewick Press Staff. Winter at Hogwarts, Set. 2016. (ENG.). 48p. (J). (gr. 3-7). 15.99 (978-0-7636-9589-7(0)) Candlewick Pr.

Carbone, Courtney. Amazing Animals (the World of Eric Carle) 2014. (Deluxe Reusable Sticker Book Ser.). (ENG.). 24p. (J). (gr. -1-2). pap. 6.99 (978-0-385-38787-3(3), Golden Bks.) Random Hse. Children's Bks.

—Half-Shell Heroes! (Teenage Mutant Ninja Turtles) Golden Books Staff & Sciarrone, Claudio, illus. 2013. (Color Plus Chunky Crayons Ser.). (ENG.). 48p. (J). (gr. -1-2). pap. 3.99 (978-0-307-98233-9(5), Golden Bks.) Random Hse. Children's Bks.

—Heart of a Hero (DC Super Friends) Golden Books, illus. 2014. (Color Plus Card Stock Ser.). (ENG.). 48p. (J). (gr. -1-2). pap. 3.99 (978-0-553-50886-4(5), Golden Bks.) Random Hse. Children's Bks.

—Power-Packed! (DC Super Friends) Golden Books, illus. 2014. (Deluxe Stickerific Ser.). (ENG.). 64p. (J). (gr. -1-2). pap. 5.99 (978-0-385-38720-0(2), Golden Bks.) Random Hse. Children's Bks.

Carle, Eric & Chronicle Books Staff. The Very Hungry Caterpillar Lacing Cards. 2012. (ENG., Illus.). 10p. (J). (gr. -1-17). 15.99 (978-1-4521-0819-3(6)) Chronicle Bks. LLC.

Carlton Books, ed. Kate & Pippa Dress-Up Sticker Book: Create Stylish Outfits & Design Your Own Accessories! 2013. (ENG., Illus.). 24p. (J). (gr. 1). pap. 7.95 (978-1-78097-147-6(8)) Carlton Bks., Ltd. GBR. Dist: Sterling Publishing Co., Inc.

—Vacation Doodles: Doodle Your Way to Vacation Heaven! 2010. (ENG., Illus.). 96p. (J). (gr. 2). pap. 7.95 (978-1-84732-652-2(8)) Carlton Bks., Ltd. GBR. Dist: Sterling Publishing Co., Inc.

Carlton Books UK. Science Museum. 2013. (ENG.). 24p. (J). (gr. k-2). pap., act. bk. ed. 8.99 (978-1-78097-347-0(0)) Carlton Bks., Ltd. GBR. Dist: Independent Pubs. Group.

Carlton Publishing Group. My Mandalas. 2016. (Cool & Calm Coloring for Kids Ser.). (ENG.). 48p. (J). (gr. 2-6). pap. 6.99 (978-1-4380-0884-4(8)) Barron's Educational Series, Inc.

Carluccio, Maria. The Sounds Around Town. 2016. (ENG.). 32p. (J). (gr. -1-k). bds. 14.99 (978-1-78285-281-0(6)) Barefoot Bks., Inc.

Carole Marsh. Los Angeles Coloring & Activity Book. 2004. (City Bks.). 24p. (gr. k-5). pap. 3.95 (978-0-635-02229-5(X)) Gallopade International.

—San Francisco Coloring & Activity Book. 2004. (City Bks.). 24p. (J). (gr. k-5). pap., act. bk. ed. 3.95 (978-0-635-02228-8(1)) Gallopade International.

Carousel Party Time Sticker 'n' Style. 2008. (Bratz Sticker Activity Ser.). 12p. pap. (978-1-4075-3043-7(7)) Parragon, Inc.

Carson-Dellosa Publishing Staff. Add & Subtract, Grade 1. 2010. (Home Workbooks Ser.). (ENG.). 64p. (gr. 1-1). pap. 4.49 (978-1-60418-792-2(1)) Carson-Dellosa Publishing, LLC.

—Add & Subtract, Grade 2. 2010. (Home Workbooks Ser.). (ENG.). 64p. (gr. 2-2). pap. 4.49 (978-1-60418-797-7(2)) Carson-Dellosa Publishing, LLC.

—All about Me, Grades Pk - 1. 2010. (Home Workbooks Ser.). (ENG.). 64p. (gr. -1-1). pap. 4.49 (978-1-60418-767-0(0)) Carson-Dellosa Publishing, LLC.

—Alphabet Animals, Grades PK - K. 2010. (Home Workbooks Ser.). (ENG.). 64p. (gr. -1-k). pap. 4.49 (978-1-60418-760-1(3)) Carson-Dellosa Publishing, LLC.

—Alphabet, Grades PK - K: Dot-to-Dot. 2010. (Home Workbooks Ser.). (ENG.). 64p. (gr. -1-k). pap. 4.49 (978-1-60418-759-5(X)) Carson-Dellosa Publishing, LLC.

—Alphabet, Grades PK - K: Sounds & Pictures. 2010. (Home Workbooks Ser.). (ENG.). 64p. (gr. -1-k). pap. 4.49 (978-1-60418-758-8(1)) Carson-Dellosa Publishing, LLC.

—Beginning Math, Grade K. 2010. (Home Workbooks Ser.). (ENG.). 64p. (gr. k-k). pap. 4.49 (978-1-60418-776-2(X)) Carson-Dellosa Publishing, LLC.

—Beginning Reading, Grade 1. 2010. (Home Workbooks Ser.). (ENG.). 64p. (gr. 1-1). pap. 4.49 (978-1-60418-786-1(7)) Carson-Dellosa Publishing, LLC.

—Beginning Reading, Grades K. 2010. (Home Workbooks Ser.). (ENG.). 64p. (gr. k-k). pap. 4.49 (978-1-60418-773-1(5)) Carson-Dellosa Publishing, LLC.

—Beginning Vocabulary, Grade K. 2010. (Home Workbooks Ser.). (ENG.). 64p. (gr. k-k). pap. 4.49 (978-1-60418-775-5(1)) Carson-Dellosa Publishing, LLC.

—Colors, Grades PK - K. 2010. (Home Workbooks Ser.). (ENG.). 64p. (gr. -1-k). pap. 4.49 (978-1-60418-765-6(4)) Carson-Dellosa Publishing, LLC.

—Cursive Practice, Grade 2-3. 2010. (Home Workbooks Ser.). (ENG.). 64p. (gr. 2-3). pap. 4.49 (978-1-60418-801-1(4)) Carson-Dellosa Publishing, LLC.

—Everyday Words in Spanish: Photographic. 2004. (ENG.). 104p. (gr. -1-8). 7.49 (978-1-936022-83-0(4)) Carson-Dellosa Publishing, LLC.

—First Grade Skills. 2010. (Home Workbooks Ser.). (ENG.). 64p. (gr. 1-1). pap. 4.49 (978-1-60418-784-7(0)) Carson-Dellosa Publishing, LLC.

—Get Ready for Kindergarten. 2010. (Home Workbooks Ser.). (ENG.). 64p. (gr. k-k). pap. 4.49 (978-1-60418-771-7(9)) Carson-Dellosa Publishing, LLC.

—Hidden Pictures, Grades PK - 1. 2010. (Home Workbooks Ser.). (ENG.). 64p. (gr. -1-1). pap. 4.49 (978-1-60418-770-0(0)) Carson-Dellosa Publishing, LLC.

—Kindergarten Skills. 2010. (Home Workbooks Ser.). (ENG.). 64p. (gr. k-k). pap. 4.49 (978-1-60418-772-4(7)) Carson-Dellosa Publishing, LLC.

—Letters & Sounds, Grades K - 1. 2010. (Home Workbooks Ser.). (ENG.). 64p. (gr. k-1). pap. 4.49 (978-1-60418-779-3(4)) Carson-Dellosa Publishing, LLC.

—Letters, Grades PK - K: Uppercase & Lowercase. 2010. (Home Workbooks Ser.). (ENG.). 64p. (gr. -1-k). pap. 4.49 (978-1-60418-757-1(3)) Carson-Dellosa Publishing, LLC.

—Mailboxes & Letters. 2009. (ENG.). 34p. (gr. -1-8). 6.99 (978-1-60418-612-3(7)) Carson-Dellosa Publishing, LLC.

—Mazes,Grades PK - 1. 2010. (Home Workbooks Ser.). (ENG.). 64p. (gr. -1-1). pap. 4.49 (978-1-60418-769-4(7)) Carson-Dellosa Publishing, LLC.

—Multiplication, Grade 3. 2010. (Home Workbooks Ser.). (ENG.). 64p. (gr. 3-3). pap. 4.49 (978-1-60418-802-8(2)) Carson-Dellosa Publishing, LLC.

—Number Play, Grade K. 2010. (Home Workbooks Ser.). (ENG.). 64p. (gr. k-k). pap. 4.49 (978-1-60418-777-9(8)) Carson-Dellosa Publishing, LLC.

—Numbers 0-20, Grades PK - K. 2010. (Home Workbooks Ser.). (ENG.). 64p. (gr. -1-k). pap. 4.49 (978-1-60418-762-5(X)) Carson-Dellosa Publishing, LLC.

—Numbers 0-30, Grades K - 1. 2010. (Home Workbooks Ser.). (ENG.). 64p. (gr. k-1). pap. 4.49 (978-1-60418-783-0(2)) Carson-Dellosa Publishing, LLC.

—Numbers 0-30, Grades Pk - K: Dot-to-Dot. 2010. (Home Workbooks Ser.). (ENG.). 64p. (gr. -1-k). pap. 4.49 (978-1-60418-763-2(8)) Carson-Dellosa Publishing, LLC.

—Phonics for First Grade. 2010. (Home Workbooks Ser.). (ENG.). 64p. (gr. 1-1). pap. 4.49 (978-1-60418-785-4(9)) Carson-Dellosa Publishing, LLC.

—Phonics for Kindergarten, Grade K. 2010. (Home Workbooks Ser.). (ENG.). 64p. (gr. k-k). pap. 4.49 (978-1-60418-774-8(3)) Carson-Dellosa Publishing, LLC.

—Printing Practice for Beginners. 2010. (Home Workbooks Ser.). (ENG.). 64p. (gr. k-1). pap. 4.49 (978-1-60418-780-9(8)) Carson-Dellosa Publishing, LLC.

—Printing Practice, Grade 2. 2010. (Home Workbooks Ser.). (ENG.). 64p. (gr. 2-2). pap. 4.49 (978-1-60418-795-3(6)) Carson-Dellosa Publishing, LLC.

—Puzzles & Games: Word Play. 2010. (Home Workbooks Ser.). (ENG.). 64p. (gr. k-1). pap. 4.49 (978-1-60418-782-3(4)) Carson-Dellosa Publishing, LLC.

—Puzzles & Games for Math, Grade 1. 2010. (Home Workbooks Ser.). (ENG.). 64p. (gr. 1-1). pap. 4.49 (978-1-60418-791-5(3)) Carson-Dellosa Publishing, LLC.

—Puzzles & Games for Math, Grade 3. 2010. (Home Workbooks Ser.). (ENG.). 64p. (gr. 3-3). pap. 4.49 (978-1-60418-803-5(0)) Carson-Dellosa Publishing, LLC.

—Puzzles & Games, Grade 1. 2010. (Home Workbooks Ser.). (ENG.). 64p. (gr. 1-1). pap. 4.49 (978-1-60418-793-9(X)) Carson-Dellosa Publishing, LLC.

—Same & Different, Grades Pk - K. 2010. (Home Workbooks Ser.). (ENG.). 64p. (gr. -1-k). pap. 4.49 (978-1-60418-768-7(9)) Carson-Dellosa Publishing, LLC.

—Scissors Skills, Grades PK - 1. 2010. (Home Workbooks Ser.). (ENG.). 64p. (gr. -1-1). pap. 4.49 (978-1-60418-766-3(2)) Carson-Dellosa Publishing, LLC.

—Spelling & Writing for Beginners, Grade 1. 2010. (Home Workbooks Ser.). (ENG.). 64p. (gr. 1-1). pap. 4.49 (978-1-60418-788-5(3)) Carson-Dellosa Publishing, LLC.

—Word Play, Grades K - 1: Rhyming. 2010. (Home Workbooks Ser.). (ENG.). 64p. (gr. k-1). pap. 4.49 (978-1-60418-781-6(6)) Carson-Dellosa Publishing, LLC.

Carson-Dellosa Publishing Staff, compiled by. Beginning Vocabulary, Grade 1. 2010. (Home Workbooks Ser.). (ENG.). 64p. (gr. 1-1). pap. 4.49 (978-1-60418-789-2(1)) Carson-Dellosa Publishing, LLC.

—Numbers 0-10, Grades PK - K. 2010. (Home Workbooks Ser.). (ENG.). 64p. (gr. -1-k). pap. 4.49 (978-1-60418-761-8(1)) Carson-Dellosa Publishing, LLC.

—Preschool Skills. 2010. (Home Workbooks Ser.). (ENG.). 64p. (gr. -1 — 1). pap. 4.49 (978-1-936022-11-3(7)) Carson-Dellosa Publishing, LLC.

—Puzzles & Games for Beginners, Grade K. 2010. (Home Workbooks Ser.). (ENG.). 64p. (gr. k-k). pap. 4.49 (978-1-60418-778-6(6)) Carson-Dellosa Publishing, LLC.

—Puzzles & Games for Math, Grade 2. 2010. (Home Workbooks Ser.). (ENG.). 64p. (gr. 2-2). pap. 4.49 (978-1-60418-798-4(0)) Carson-Dellosa Publishing, LLC.

—Puzzles & Games, Grade 2. 2010. (Home Workbooks Ser.). (ENG.). 64p. (gr. 2-2). pap. 4.49 (978-1-60418-799-1(9)) Carson-Dellosa Publishing, LLC.

—Puzzles & Games, Grade 2: Word Play. 2010. (Home Workbooks Ser.). (ENG.). 64p. (gr. 2-2). pap. 4.49 (978-1-60418-796-0(4)) Carson-Dellosa Publishing, LLC.

Cedar Fort. Hooray for Mom! Drawing My Favorite Moments with Mom. 2017. (ENG.). (J). 14.99 **(978-1-4621-1990-5(5))** Cedar Fort, Inc./CFI Distribution.

Ceol, Cheryl. Can You Picture This? You Draw It / You Say It / You Find It / You Write It. 2012. 44p. pap. 20.99 (978-1-4525-6422-7(1)) Balboa Pr.

Cerasi, Christopher. Star Wars: Fandex Deluxe Edition. deluxe ed. 2008. (ENG., Illus.). 75p. (J). (gr. 4-12). 13.95 (978-0-7611-5230-9(X), 15230) Workman Publishing Co., Inc.

Cerato, Mattia, illus. On the Site Activity Book. 2017. (Just Imagine & Play! Ser.). (ENG.). 48p. (J). (gr. -1-1). pap. 9.95 (978-1-63322-245-8(4), Walter Foster Jr) Quarto Publishing Group USA.

Cernek, Kim. Preschool Songs & Fingerplays: Building Language Experience Through Rhythm & Movement. 2006. (Early Learning Ser.). (Illus.). 128p. (J). (gr. -1-1). per. 13.99 (978-1-59198-223-4(5)) Creative Teaching Pr., Inc.

Chakrabarti, Nina. Hello Nature: Draw, Collect, Make & Grow. 2016. (ENG.). 224p. (J). (gr. 2-6). 17.95 (978-1-78067-735-4(9)) King, Laurence Publishing GBR. Dist: Hachette Bk. Group.

Chambers, Jo. Caring for Wild Animals. 2007. (Trackers-Math Ser.). (gr. 2-5). pap. 5.00 (978-1-59055-933-8(9)) Pacific Learning, Inc.

Chaney, Scott. Christian Warriors: Games, Gear, Gospel - Especially for Christian Youth. 2009. (Illus.). 144p. (J). 49.95 (978-1-58117-938-5(3), Intervisual/Piggy Toes) Bendon, Inc.

Charles, Emmanuel. Punch-Out Dragons: Mix & Match! Sturdy & Easy to Make! 2015. (ENG.). 32p. (J). (gr. 1-4). 9.99 (978-0-486-79613-0(2)) Dover Pubns., Inc.

Charlesbridge, ed. Sir Cumference Classroom Activities. 2015. (ENG.). 32p. (J). (gr. 3-7). pap. 9.95 (978-1-58089-724-2(X)) Charlesbridge Publishing, Inc.

Charlesworth, Eric. Solve & Match Math Practice Pages: 50+ Motivating, Self-Checking Activities That Help Kids Review & Master Essential Math Skills. 2011. (ENG.). 64p. (gr. 2-3). pap. 11.99 (978-0-545-28815-6(0)); (gr. 4-6). pap. 11.99 (978-0-545-28816-3(9)) Scholastic, Inc. (Teaching Resources).

Charlesworth, Liza. Introduction to Nonfiction Write-On - Wipe-Off Flip Chart: An Interactive Learning Tool That Teaches Young Learners How to Navigate Nonfiction Text Features for Reading Success. 2009. (ENG.). 22p. (gr. k-3). pap. 24.99 (978-0-545-15660-8(2), Teaching Resources) Scholastic, Inc.

—My 100th Day, Set. 2011. (ENG., Illus.). 30p. (gr. -1-2). pap. 15.99 (978-0-545-29295-5(6), Teaching Resources) Scholastic, Inc.

—Personal Poster Set: My Name: 30 Fill-In Personal Posters for Students to Display with Pride. 2013. (ENG.). (gr. -1-2). 15.99 (978-0-545-53562-5(X), Teaching Resources) Scholastic, Inc.

—Punctuation Tales: A Motivating Collection of Super-Funny Storybooks That Help Kids Master the Mechanics of Writing. 2009. (ENG.). 32.99 (978-0-545-11401-1(2), Teaching Resources) Scholastic, Inc.

Charlesworth, Liza, ed. Sight Word Tales: 25 Read-Aloud Storybooks That Target & Teach the Top 100 Sight Words. 2008. (ENG.). (gr. k-2). 77.99 (978-0-545-01642-1(8)) Scholastic, Inc.

Chihuly Art Kit. 2006. (Chihuly Ser.). (J). (gr. -1). 28.00 (978-1-57684-157-0(X)) Chihuly Workshop, Inc.

Chilek, Laurie. ¡Qué miedo! ¡un tobogán! (the Scary Slide) 2007. (Lecturas del barrio (Neighborhood Readers) Ser.). (SPA.). 8p. 29.95 (978-1-4042-7291-0(7), Rosen Classroom) Rosen Publishing Group, Inc., The.

Chlebowski, Rachel. Better Together! (Shimmer & Shine) Golden Books, illus. 2017. (Color & Paint Plus Stickers Ser.). (ENG.). 128p. (J). (gr. -1-2). pap. 9.99 (978-0-399-55793-4(8), Golden Bks.) Random Hse. Children's Bks.

Chorba, April. Dot Jewelry: Make Pretty Paper Bracelets & Necklaces. 2013. (ENG.). 56p. (J). (gr. 3). 19.99 (978-0-545-49278-2(5)) Klutz.

—Thumb Doodles: The Epic Saga at Your Fingertips. Klutz Editors, ed. 2013. (ENG.). 40p. (J). (gr. 3). 16.99 (978-0-545-49284-3(X)) Klutz.

Chorba, April & Kane, Barbara. Potholders & Other Loopy Projects. 2013. (ENG.). 40p. (J). (gr. 2-5). 19.99 (978-0-545-44943-4(X)) Klutz.

Chorba, April & Murphy, Pat. The Book of Impossible Objects: 25 Eye-Popping Projects to Make, See & Do. 2013. (ENG.). 48p. (J). (gr. 3). 19.99 (978-0-545-49647-6(0)) Klutz.

Chorba, April & Phillips, Karen. It's All about Us (... Especially Me!) A Journal of Totally Personal Questions for You & Your Friends. 2013. (ENG.). 126p. (J). (gr. 3). 16.99 (978-0-545-49280-5(7)) Klutz.

Chouette Publishing Staff. Caillou - The Little Artist. Sevigny, Eric, illus. 2011. (Coloring & Activity Book Ser.). (ENG.). 96p. (J). (gr. -1-1). 7.95 (978-2-89450-809-1(3)) Caillouet, Gerry.

Chronicle Books Staff & Estellon, Pascale. The Giant Play & Learn Book. 2008. (ENG., Illus.). 124p. (J). (gr. -1-7). pap. 19.99 (978-0-8118-6254-7(2)) Chronicle Bks. LLC.

Chronicle Books Staff & Frank, Paul. Julius!, Kit. 2009. (ENG.). 48p. (J). (gr. -1-2). act. bk. ed. 14.95 (978-0-8118-6095-6(7)) Chronicle Bks. LLC.

Cider Mill Press Staff. Mashmallow Launcher: Make Your Own... Awesome... - Everything You Need to Build Your Owns Blaster! 2010. (ENG.). 64p. (J). 19.95 (978-1-60433-151-6(8), Applesauce Pr.) Cider Mill Pr. Bk. Pubs., LLC.

Ciminera, Siobhan. Stuck on Christmas! Collection/Jupiterimages Unlimited, illus. 2008. (ENG.). 48p. (J). (gr. -1-2). 12.99 (978-1-4169-6784-2(2), Simon Scribbles) Simon Scribbles.

Citylit Kids. Write On! 2012. 68p. pap. 10.00 (978-1-936328-10-9(0)) CityLit Pr.

Civardi, Anne. Moving House Sticker Book. 2009. (First Experiences Sticker Bks). 18p. (J). pap. 6.99 (978-0-7945-2430-2(3), Usborne) EDC Publishing.

—New Baby Sticker Book. 2008. (First Experiences Sticker Bks). (Illus.). 16p. (J). pap. 6.99 (978-0-7945-2181-3(9), Usborne) EDC Publishing.

Clarence, S. M. Beat Bugs Activity Book with Stickers. 2017. (Beat Bugs Ser.). 160p. (J). (gr. -1-3). pap. 12.99 (978-0-06-264075-8(5), HarperFestival) HarperCollins Pubs.

Clark, Isabel. Sticker & Color-In Playbook: At Home. Tulip, Jenny, illus. 2016. (ENG.). 16p. (J). (gr. -1-12). pap. 4.99 (978-1-86147-720-0(1), Armadillo) Anness Publishing GBR. Dist: National Bk. Network.

Clark, Ruth E. Airport Mouse Activity Fun Book 1. Jones, Phil, illus. 2010. 16p. (J). pap. 5.99 (978-0-9792963-6-9(6)) Huntington Ludlow Media Group.

—Airport Mouse Becomes a VIP/VIM World Traveler Activity Fun Book 4. Jones, Phil, illus. 2010. 16p. (J). pap. 5.99 (978-0-9792963-9-0(0)) Huntington Ludlow Media Group.

—Airport Mouse Explores on Opening Day Activity Fun Book 3. Jones, Phil, illus. 2010. 16p. (J). pap. 5.99 (978-0-9792963-8-3(2)) Kimball, Jane A.

—Airport Mouse Works the Night Shift Activity Fun Book 2. Jones, Phil, illus. 2010. 16p. (J). pap. 5.99 (978-0-9792963-7-6(4)) Huntington Ludlow Media Group.

Clarke, Catriona. 50 Things to Do on Vacation. Meredith, Samantha, illus. 2007. (Activity Cards Ser.). 50p. (J). (gr. 4-7). 9.99 (978-0-7945-1704-5(8), Usborne) EDC Publishing.

Clarke, Isabel. Sticker & Color-In Playbook: At the Shops. Tulip, Jenny, illus. 2016. (ENG.). 16p. (J). (gr. -1-12). pap. 4.99 (978-1-86147-732-3(5), Armadillo) Anness Publishing GBR. Dist: National Bk. Network.

—Sticker & Color-In Playbook: With over 50 Reusable Stickers: Playtime. Tulip, Jenny, illus. 2016. (ENG.). 16p. (J). (gr. -1-12). pap. 4.99 (978-1-86147-733-0(3), Armadillo) Anness Publishing GBR. Dist: National Bk. Network.

Classroom Complete Press, creator. High Frequency Picture Words, Grades PK-2. 2011. (Literacy Skills Ser.). (ENG.). 39.95 (978-1-55319-514-6(0), Classroom Complete Pr.) Rainbow Horizons Publishing, Inc.

—High Frequency Sight Words, Grades PK-2. 2011. (Literacy Skills Ser.). (ENG.). 39.95 (978-1-55319-513-9(2), Classroom Complete Pr.) Rainbow Horizons Publishing, Inc.

—Sight & Picture Words, Grades PK-2. 2011. (Literacy Skills Ser.). (ENG.). 54.95 (978-1-55319-515-3(9), Classroom Complete Pr.) Rainbow Horizons Publishing, Inc.

Claybourne, Anna & McCullough, Missy. Fashion Stylist Spring/Summer Collection. 2016. (ENG.). 52p. (J). pap. 12.95 (978-1-78067-693-7(X)) King, Laurence Publishing GBR. Dist: Hachette Bk. Group.

Clibbon, Meg. Imagine You're a Princess! Princess Megerella & Princess Lulubelle. Clibbon, Lucy, illus. 2005. (ENG.). 32p. (J). (gr. -1-4). pap. 7.95 (978-1-55037-920-4(8), 9781550379204) Annick Pr., Ltd. CAN. Dist: Publishers Group West (PGW).

S

Cline, Mike & Yi-Cline, Nancy. Franky Fox's Fun with English Activity Book, Level A1. Yi-Cline, Nancy, ed. Cline, Mike, illus. 2007. (Illus.). 62p. pap. 7.99 (978-0-9777419-1-5(5), SIAB) Lingo Pr. LLC.

—Franky Fox's Fun with English Level A1. Yi-Cline, Nancy, ed. Cline, Mike, illus. 2007. (Illus.). 65p. 14.99 (978-0-9777419-0-8(7), SITB) Lingo Pr. LLC.

Clineff, Jeff. Too Many Kitties. Movshina, Marina, illus. 2007. (ESK.). 24p. (J). 9.95 (978-1-933090-10-8(3)) Guardian Angel Publishing, Inc.

Clover, Forever & Bell, Holly. Forever Clover: Forever Friends Sticker & Activity Book. 2015. (Forever Clover Ser.). (ENG., Illus.). 64p. (J). (gr. k-4). pap. 7.99 (978-1-921894-42-8(3)) Hardie Grant Egmont Pty, Ltd. AUS. Dist: Independent Pubs. Group.

Cloyd, Nancy J. & Wach, Delia Bowman. Teddy Bear's Favorite Pictures: A Quiet Time Sharing Book. Wach, Delia Bowman, illus. 2007. (Illus.). 32p. (J). (gr. -1). 15.95 (978-0-929915-75-3(5)) Headline Bks., Inc.

Coan, Sharon. Special Me, 1 vol. 2009. (Early Childhood Themes Ser.). (ENG., Illus.). 16p. (J). (gr. -1-2). pap. 6.99 (978-1-4333-1469-8(X)) Shell Educational Publishing.

—Yo Soy Especial, 1 vol. rev. ed. 2010. (Early Childhood Themes Ser.).Tr. of Special Me. (SPA., Illus.). 16p. (J). (gr. -1-2). pap. 19.99 (978-1-4333-1945-7(4)); pap. 6.99 (978-1-4333-1944-0(6)) Shell Educational Publishing.

Cohen, Liz Zoller & Dicillo, Mike. My Interactive Point-And-Play 10-Book Library, 10 vols. 2011. (Illus.). (J). (978-1-60553-886-0(8)) Publications International, Ltd.

Colich, Abby, et al. Go-To Guides. 2017. (Go-To Guides). (ENG.). 32p. (gr. 3-4). 111.96 (978-1-5157-3670-7(9), Snap Bks.) Capstone Press of Coughlan Cos.

Colleen, Marcie. Love, Triangle. Shea, Bob, illus. 2017. 32p. (J). (gr. -1-3). 17.99 **(978-0-06-241084-9(9))** HarperCollins Pubs.

Collins Easy Learning, Collins Easy. First Words - Wipe Clean: Bed Six Cat. 2017. (Collins Easy Learning Preschool Ser.). (ENG.). 24p. (J). (gr. -1-k). 7.95 **(978-0-00-821293-3(7))** HarperCollins Pubs. Ltd. GBR. Dist: Independent Pubs. Group.

Collins, Elaine Banks. See What I Can Do. Floyd, John, Jr., illus. 2006. 10p. (J). (gr. -1). bds. 5.95 (978-0-9752860-4-3(8)) OurRainbow Pr., LLC.

Coloring Fun: Coloring/Activity Book (English/Spanish) Low Price Point. 2006. (Illus.). (J). 2.99 (978-0-9770455-9-4(5)) Mighty Kids Media.

Compendium Inc, creator. My Artwork. 2011. 64p. (J). pap. 5.95 (978-1-932319-98-9(0)) Compendium, Inc., Publishing & Communications.

—My Writing. 2011. (ENG.). 64p. (J). pap. 5.95 (978-1-932319-97-2(2)) Compendium, Inc., Publishing & Communications.

Conlon, Mara. Brainiac's Go Green! Activity Book. Klug, David, illus. 2008. (Activity Book Ser.). 127p. (J). (gr. k-5). 12.99 (978-1-59359-806-8(8)) Peter Pauper Pr. Inc.

—Butterflies & Friends: An Art Activity Book for Adventurous Artists of All Ages. Zschock, Martha, illus. 2009. (Scratch & Sketch Ser.). 64p. (J). (gr. 1). spiral bd., act. bk. ed. 12.99 (978-1-59359-841-9(6)) Peter Pauper Pr. Inc.

—Ready, Set, Draw... under the Sea! Steckler, Kerren Barbas, illus. 2009. (Activity Bks). 40p. (J). spiral bd. 15.99 (978-1-59359-837-2(8)) Peter Pauper Pr. Inc.

Connery-Boyd, Peg. Atlanta Braves. 2016. (Hawk's Nest Activity Bks.: 0). (ENG.). 64p. (J). (gr. k-3). pap., act. bk. ed. 8.99 (978-1-4926-3566-6(9)) Sourcebooks, Inc.

—Baltimore Orioles. 2016. (Hawk's Nest Activity Bks.: 0). (ENG.). 64p. (J). (gr. k-3). pap., act. bk. ed. 8.99 (978-1-4926-3361-7(5)) Sourcebooks, Inc.

—Big Book of Major League Baseball Activities. 2016. (Hawk's Nest Activity Bks.: 0). (ENG.). 176p. (J). (gr. k-3). pap. 12.99 (978-1-4926-3380-8(1)) Sourcebooks, Inc.

—Boston Red Sox. 2016. (Hawk's Nest Activity Bks.: 0). (ENG.). 64p. (J). (gr. k-3). pap., act. bk. ed. 8.99 (978-1-4926-3362-4(3)) Sourcebooks, Inc.

—Chicago Cubs. 2016. (Hawk's Nest Activity Bks.: 0). (ENG.). 64p. (J). (gr. k-3). pap., act. bk. ed. 8.99 (978-1-4926-3364-8(X), 9781492633648) Sourcebooks, Inc.

—Cleveland Indians. 2016. (Hawk's Nest Activity Bks.: 0). (ENG.). 64p. (J). (gr. k-3). pap., act. bk. ed. 8.99 (978-1-4926-3562-8(6)) Sourcebooks, Inc.

—Los Angeles Dodgers. 2016. (Hawk's Nest Activity Bks.: 0). (ENG.). 64p. (J). (gr. k-3). pap., act. bk. ed. 8.99 (978-1-4926-3365-5(8)) Sourcebooks, Inc.

—Milwaukee Brewers. 2016. (Hawk's Nest Activity Bks.: 0). (ENG.). 64p. (J). (gr. k-3). pap., act. bk. ed. 8.99 (978-1-4926-3366-2(6)) Sourcebooks, Inc.

—Minnesota Twins. 2016. (Hawk's Nest Activity Bks.: 0). (ENG.). 64p. (J). (gr. k-3). pap., act. bk. ed. 8.99 (978-1-4926-3374-7(7)) Sourcebooks, Inc.

—New England. 2016. (Hawk's Nest Activity Bks.: 0). (ENG.). 64p. (J). pap. 8.99 (978-1-4926-3379-2(8), 9781492633792, Sourcebooks Jabberwocky) Sourcebooks, Inc.

—New York Mets. 2016. (Hawk's Nest Activity Bks.: 0). (ENG.). 64p. (J). (gr. k-3). pap., act. bk. ed. 8.99 (978-1-4926-3367-9(4)) Sourcebooks, Inc.

—New York Yankees. 2016. (Hawk's Nest Activity Bks.: 0). (ENG.). 64p. (J). (gr. k-3). pap., act. bk. ed. 8.99 (978-1-4926-3373-0(9)) Sourcebooks, Inc.

—Philadelphia Phillies. 2016. (Hawk's Nest Activity Bks.: 0). (ENG.). 64p. (J). (gr. k-3). pap., act. bk. ed. 8.99 (978-1-4926-3368-6(2)) Sourcebooks, Inc.

—Pittsburgh Pirates. 2016. (Hawk's Nest Activity Bks.: 0). (ENG.). 64p. (J). (gr. k-3). pap., act. bk. ed. 8.99 (978-1-4926-3369-3(0)) Sourcebooks, Inc.

—San Francisco Giants. 2016. (Hawk's Nest Activity Bks.: 0). (ENG.). 64p. (J). (gr. k-3). pap., act. bk. ed. 8.99 (978-1-4926-3370-9(4)) Sourcebooks, Inc.

—St. Louis Cardinals. 2016. (Hawk's Nest Activity Bks.: 0). (ENG.). 64p. (J). (gr. k-3). pap., act. bk. ed. 8.99 (978-1-4926-3371-6(2)) Sourcebooks, Inc.

—Tampa Bay Rays. 2016. (Hawk's Nest Activity Bks.: 0). (ENG.). 64p. (J). (gr. k-3). pap., act. bk. ed. 8.99 (978-1-4926-3375-4(5)) Sourcebooks, Inc.

—Texas. 2016. (Hawk's Nest Activity Bks.: 0). (ENG.). 64p. (J). (-3). pap. 8.99 (978-1-4926-3967-1(2), 9781492639671, Sourcebooks Jabberwocky) Sourcebooks, Inc.

—Texas Rangers. 2016. (Hawk's Nest Activity Bks.: 0). (ENG.). 64p. (J). (gr. k-3). pap., act. bk. ed. 8.99 (978-1-4926-3565-9(0)) Sourcebooks, Inc.

—Toronto Blue Jays Activity Book. 2016. (Hawk's Nest Activity Bks.: 0). (ENG.). 64p. (J). (gr. k-3). pap. 8.99 (978-1-4926-3376-1(3)) Sourcebooks, Inc.

—Totally Michigan! 2016. (Hawk's Nest Activity Bks.: 0). (ENG.). 64p. (J). (-3). pap. 8.99 (978-1-4926-4191-9(X), 9781492641919, Sourcebooks Jabberwocky) Sourcebooks, Inc.

—Totally Pacific Northwest! 2016. (Hawk's Nest Activity Bks.: 0). (ENG.). 64p. (J). (-3). pap. 8.99 (978-1-4926-3969-5(9), 9781492639695, Sourcebooks Jabberwocky) Sourcebooks, Inc.

—Totally Toronto! 2016. (Hawk's Nest Activity Bks.: 0). (ENG.). 64p. (J). (-3). pap. 8.99 (978-1-4926-3968-8(0), 9781492639688, Sourcebooks Jabberwocky) Sourcebooks, Inc.

—Washington Nationals. 2016. (Hawk's Nest Activity Bks.: 0). (ENG.). 64p. (J). (gr. k-3). pap., act. bk. ed. 8.99 (978-1-4926-3372-3(0)) Sourcebooks, Inc.

Conway, Laurence. Sing & Learn! 2009. 92p. pap. 30.00 (978-1-60693-543-9(7), Eloquent Bks.) Strategic Book Publishing & Rights Agency (SBPRA).

Cook, David C., 3rd. Mary & Martha. 2008. (Pencil Fun Bks). 16p. (J). pap. 9.90 (978-1-4347-6816-2(3)) Cook, David C.

Cook, Deanna F. Let's Play Farmers Market: 100 Stickers + Games, Crafts, & Fun! 2016. (ENG., Illus.). 96p. (J). (gr. -1). spiral bd., act. bk. ed. 14.95 (978-1-61212-650-0(2)) Storey Publishing, LLC.

Cook, Deanna F. & Craig, Katie. Horse Play! 25 Crafts, Parties, & Activities for Horse-Crazy Kids. 2016. (ENG., Illus.). 68p. (J). (gr. 3-8). spiral bd., act. bk. ed. 12.95 (978-1-61212-759-0(2)) Storey Publishing, LLC.

Cookie Jar Entertainment Inc Staff. ABC Doodlebops. 2007. 32p. mass mkt. 4.99 (978-1-60095-270-8(4), Doodlebops) Cookie Jar.

—Doodlebops Count to Ten. 2007. 32p. mass mkt. 4.99 (978-1-60095-356-9(5), Doodlebops) Cookie Jar.

—Doodlebops Rock. 2007. 32p. (J). mass mkt. 4.99 (978-1-60095-269-2(0), Doodlebops) Cookie Jar.

Cool Things Press. 75 Cool Things to Color. 2008. 80p. pap. 12.95 (978-0-615-20795-7(2)) Cool Things Pr.

—75 Cool Things to Cut Out. 2008. 152p. pap. 15.95 (978-0-615-20796-4(0)) Cool Things Pr.

Coon, Cyndi, illus. Art That Pops! How to Make Wacky 3-D Creations That Jump, Spin, & Spring! 2006. 48p. (J). pap. (978-0-439-81337-2(9)) Scholastic, Inc.

Copeland, Cynthia L. Family Fun Night: Second Edition. 2016. (ENG., Illus.). 224p. pap. 16.95 (978-1-60433-611-5(0)) Cider Mill Pr. Bk. Pubs., LLC.

Copeland, Peter F. Scenes of Olde New York Coloring Book. 2009. (Dover History Coloring Book Ser.). (ENG.). 48p. (gr. 3-8). pap. 4.99 (978-0-486-47494-6(1)) Dover Pubns., Inc.

Corr, Christopher. Whole World: Fun Eco Activities. 2008. (ENG., Illus.). 24p. (J). pap. 4.99 (978-1-84686-220-5(5)) Barefoot Bks., Inc.

Cosmic City Blast off! Preschool Guide. 2007. (Vacation Bible School Ser.). 112p. (J). (gr. 3-5). pap. 9.99 (978-1-4347-9963-0(8)) Cook, David C.

Cosneau, Géraldine. All Around the World: Sports & Games. 2016. (ENG., Illus.). 48p. (J). (gr. -1-2). pap. 16.95 (978-1-84976-410-0(7)) Tate Publishing, Ltd. GBR. Dist: Abrams, Inc.

Cosneau, Olivia. At the Seashore: My Nature Sticker Activity Book. 2016. (ENG., Illus.). 24p. (J). (gr. k-3). pap. 7.99 (978-1-61689-461-0(X)) Princeton Architectural Pr.

—Butterflies of the World: My Nature Sticker Activity Book. 2016. (ENG., Illus.). 24p. (J). (gr. k-3). pap. 7.99 (978-1-61689-465-8(2)) Princeton Architectural Pr.

Costanzo, Beth. A Day at the Beach. 2009. 28p. pap. 12.49 (978-1-4389-8180-2(5)) AuthorHouse.

Cousins, Lucy. Doodle with Maisy. 2013. (Maisy Ser.). (ENG.). 80p. (J). (gr. -1-2). pap. 8.99 (978-0-7636-6490-9(1)) Candlewick Pr.

Cowling, Dan. Color Yourself Smart: Geography. Franklin, Mark, illus. 2012. (Color Yourself Smart Ser.). (ENG.). 128p. 19.95 (978-1-60710-216-8(1), Thunder Bay Pr.) Readerlink Distribution Services, LLC.

Crabtree Publishing, creator. Green Team, Set. 2008. (ENG.). 32p. (J). (978-0-7787-4094-0(3)) Crabtree Publishing Co.

Crane, Cheryl L. Facing Lions, Giants & Other Big Dudes: A Bible Study Workbook on Courage for Ages 6-12. 2008. 112p. pap. 17.95 (978-1-4401-0609-5(6)) iUniverse, Inc.

—Pressing on When the Pressure's On: A Bible Study Workbook on Perseverance for Ages 6-12. 2009. 112p. pap. 10.95 (978-1-4401-5830-8(4)) iUniverse, Inc.

Creative Kids. 2016. (Creative Kids Ser.). 32p. (gr. 3-3). 171.00 (978-1-4994-8097-9(0)); pap. 70.50 (978-1-4994-8117-4(9)) Rosen Publishing Group, Inc., The. (Windmill Bks.).

Creative Writing Book IR. 2017. (Write Your Own Bks.). (ENG.). (J). spiral bd. 14.99 **(978-0-7945-3874-3(6)**, Usborne) EDC Publishing.

Crimi-Trent, Ellen & Priddy, Roger. Schoolies - My Fun Activity Box. 2014. (Schoolies Ser.). (ENG.). (J). (gr. -1-1). act. bk. ed. 14.99 (978-0-312-51725-0(4), 9780312517250, Priddy Bks.) St. Martin's Pr.

—Super Sticker Book. 2014. (Schoolies Ser.). (ENG.). 130p. (J). (gr. -1-1). pap. 12.99 (978-0-312-51724-3(6), 9780312517243, Priddy Bks.) St. Martin's Pr.

Crook, Lydia. Paper Play. Running Press Staff, ed. 2013. (ENG., Illus.). 112p. (J). (gr. -1-17). pap. 12.95 (978-0-7624-4957-6(8), Running Pr. Kids) Running Pr. Bk. Pubs.

Crossling, Nick & Creative Haven. Creative Haven Alhambra Designs. 2013. (Adult Coloring Ser.). (ENG., Illus.). 64p. (gr. 3). pap. 5.99 (978-0-486-49316-9(4)) Dover Pubns., Inc.

CrossStaff Publishing, creator. The Ten Commandments Movie Coloring Book: Part 1. 2007. (Epic Stories of the Bible Ser.). (Illus.). 32p. (J). (gr. -1-3). 5.99 (978-0-9743876-1-1(4)) CrossStaff Publishing.

Cryan, Mary Beth. BFF - Farm: Easy-to-Make Models for You & a Friend! 2013. (Dover Children's Activity Bks.). (ENG.). 16p. (J). (gr. 1-5). pap. 9.99 (978-0-486-49112-7(9)) Dover Pubns., Inc.

—BFF - Pets: Easy-to-Make Models to Share with Your Best Friend! 2013. (Dover Children's Activity Bks.). (ENG.). 16p. (J). (gr. 1-5). pap. 9.99 (978-0-486-49113-4(7)) Dover Pubns., Inc.

—My Christmas Tree. 2014. (ENG.). 24p. (J). (gr. 2-5). pap. 9.99 (978-0-486-77775-7(8)) Dover Pubns., Inc.

—Standups! at Work: 8 Easy-To-Make Models! 2013. (ENG.). 16p. (J). (gr. 2-5). pap. 9.99 (978-0-486-49132-5(3)) Dover Pubns., Inc.

—Standups! Presidents: 8 Easy-To-Make Models! 2013. (ENG.). 16p. (J). (gr. 2-5). pap. 9.99 (978-0-486-49131-8(5)) Dover Pubns., Inc.

Cuban, Mark. Let's Go Mavs! 2007. (978-1-932888-72-0(1)) Mascot Bks., Inc.

Culham, Ruth. Daily Trait Warm-Ups: 180 Revision & Editing Activities to Kick off Writing Time. 2009. (ENG.). 208p. 27.99 (978-0-545-09599-0(9), Teaching Resources) Scholastic, Inc.

Currie, Lisa. Me, You, Us: A Book to Fill Out Together. 2014. (ENG., Illus.). 186p. (gr. k-12). pap. 15.00 (978-0-399-16794-2(3), TarcherPerigee) Penguin Publishing Group.

Currie, Robin. The Baby Bible ABCs, 1 vol. Basaluzzo, Constanza, illus. 2009. (Baby Bible Ser.). (ENG.). 48p. (J). bds. 12.99 (978-1-4347-6542-0(3)) Cook, David C.

Curry, Don, ed. Madagascar, Kit, Bk. 2. 2008. 32p. (J). act. bk. ed. 14.99 (978-0-696-23489-7(0)) Meredith Bks.

Cutting, David. Toy Doctor Sticker Paper Doll. 2015. (ENG.). 4p. (J). (gr. k-3). pap. 1.50 (978-0-486-79098-5(3)) Dover Pubns., Inc.

Cuxart, Bernadette. Modeling Clay Animals: Easy-to-Follow Projects in Simple Steps. 2010. (ENG.). 96p. (J). (gr. 2-7). pap. 11.99 (978-0-7641-4579-7(7)) Barron's Educational Series, Inc.

—Spooky Characters: Easy-To-Follow Clay-Making Projects in Simple Steps. 2013. (Modeling Clay Bks.). (ENG.). 36p. (J). (gr. k-4). pap. 6.99 (978-1-4380-0358-0(7)) Barron's Educational Series, Inc.

Dahl, Michael. Hello Genius. Vidal, Oriol, illus. 2015. (Hello Genius Ser.). (ENG.). 20p. (gr. 1-2). bds. 31.96 (978-1-4795-8062-0(7)) Picture Window Bks.

Dahl, Michael. Hello Genius Milestone Box. Vidal, Oriol, illus. 2016. (Hello Genius Ser.). (ENG.). 24p. pap. 11.99 **(978-1-4795-9838-0(0))** Picture Window Bks.

Dahlen, Noelle. Owls Coloring Book. 2014. (Dover Coloring Bks.). (ENG.). 32p. (J). (gr. k). pap. 3.99 (978-0-486-78033-7(3)) Dover Pubns., Inc.

Dailey, Joanna. The Catholic Children's Bible Activity Booklet. 2013. (ENG.). (J). (gr. 1-4). spiral bd. 29.95 (978-1-59982-181-8(8)) St. Mary's Pr. of MN.

Danescary, Pollygeist. Monster High - Happy Howlidays! 2014. (ENG., Illus.). 32p. (J). (gr. 1-4). pap. 7.99 (978-0-316-27709-9(6)) Little, Brown Bks. for Young Readers.

—Summer Scarecation: An Activity Journal for Ghouls. 2013. (ENG.). 208p. (J). (gr. 3-7). pap. 10.00 (978-0-316-24652-1(2)) Little, Brown Bks. for Young Readers.

Daniels, Marilyn, et al. Toddlers at Play. 2011. (Sign to Speak Ser.). (ENG.). 240p. (J). (gr. -1-k). pap. 19.95 (978-1-887120-91-3(2)) Production Assocs., Inc.

Danks, Fiona, et al. Nature's Playground: Activities, Crafts, & Games to Encourage Children to Get Outdoors. 2007. (ENG., Illus.). 192p. (J). (gr. 2-4). pap. 19.95 (978-1-55652-723-4(3)) Chicago Review Pr., Inc.

David C. Cook Publishing Company Staff. Blast off! Preschool Student Book. 2007. (Vacation Bible School Ser.). 24p. (J). (gr. 3-5). pap. 2.99 (978-1-4347-9956-2(5)) Cook, David C.

—Bread or Stone, 10, Pack. 2008. (Pencil Fun Bks.). (ENG.). 16p. (J). pap. 9.90 (978-1-4347-6823-0(6)) Cook, David C.

—Cc Crafts, Red Book. 2007. (Childrens Church Kit Ser.). pap. 14.99 (978-0-7814-4492-7(6)) Cook, David C.

—Cc Leader's Guide, Red Book. 2007. (Childrens Church Kit Ser.). pap. 49.99 (978-0-7814-4494-1(2)) Cook, David C.

—CC Snacks & Games, Red Book. 2007. (Childrens Church Kit Ser.). pap. 14.99 (978-0-7814-4491-0(8)) Cook, David C.

—Cosmic City Elementary Student Book. 2007. (Vacation Bible School Ser.). 24p. (J). (gr. 6-12). pap. 2.99 (978-1-4347-9955-5(7)) Cook, David C.

—Jesus & Me: BOZ's Big Book of Bible Fun. 2008. (Boz the Bear Ser.). 236p. (J). pap. 14.99 (978-1-4347-6789-9(2)) Cook, David C.

—Jesus Feeds 5000. 2008. (Pencil Fun Bks). 16p. (J). pap. 9.90 (978-0-7814-4900-7(6)) Cook, David C.

—Lazarus Lives, 10, Pack. 2008. (Pencil Fun Bks). 16p. (J). pap. 9.90 (978-1-4347-6820-9(1)) Cook, David C.

—Let the Children Come 2009. (Pencil Fun Bks). 16p. (J). pap. 9.90 (978-1-4347-6815-5(5)) Cook, David C.

—The Lord's Prayer. 2008. (Pencil Fun Bks). 16p. (J). pap. 9.90 (978-0-7814-4901-4(4)) Cook, David C.

—Outer Limits Mission Log Upper Elementary Student Book. 2007. (Vacation Bible School Ser.). 24p. (YA). (gr. 9-12). pap. 2.99 (978-1-4347-9954-8(9)) Cook, David C.

—Pencil Fun Book: Jesus Is Alive. 2007. (Pencil Fun Books Ser.). 16p. (J). (gr. 3-7). 9.90 (978-0-7814-4521-4(3)) Cook, David C.

—Pencil Fun Book: Joeseph Saves His Family. 2007. (Pencil Fun Books Ser.). 16p. (J). (gr. 3-7). 9.90 (978-0-7814-4522-1(1)) Cook, David C.

—Pencil Fun Book: Noah Builds an Ark. 2007. (Pencil Fun Books Ser.). 16p. (J). (gr. 3-7). 9.90 (978-0-7814-4523-8(X)) Cook, David C.

—Ring, Robe & Shoes, 10, Pack. 2008. (Pencil Fun Bks). 16p. (J). pap. 9.90 (978-1-4347-6822-3(8)) Cook, David C.

—Scripture Pictures - Miracles & Parables of Jesus. 2005. 106p. 29.99 (978-0-7814-4201-5(X), 078144201X) Cook, David C.

David C. Cook Publishing Company Staff, creator. Classy, Flashy Bible Dramas. 2008. (Bible Fun Stuff for Tweens Ser.). (Illus.). 112p. (J). (gr. 4-5). pap. 16.99 (978-1-4347-6858-2(9)) Cook, David C.

—Full Tilt Wacky Games. 2008. (Bible Fun Stuff for Middle School Ser.). (Illus.). 112p. (J). (gr. 6-8). pap. 19.99 (978-1-4347-6855-1(4)) Cook, David C.

—Game-a-Thon. 2008. (Bible Funstuff Ser.). (ENG., Illus.). 112p. (YA). (gr. 4-5). pap. 19.99 (978-1-4347-6857-5(0)) Cook, David C.

—Memory Maker Bible Crafts. 2008. (Bible Fun Stuff for 2nd-3rd Grades Ser.). (Illus.). 112p. (J). (gr. 2-3). pap. 19.99 (978-1-4347-6859-9(7)) Cook, David C.

—Score with Scripture Games. 2008. (Bible Fun Stuff for K-1 Ser.). (Illus.). 112p. (J). (gr. k-1). pap. 19.99 (978-1-4347-6861-2(9)) Cook, David C.

—Stick'em up Bible Crafts. 2008. (Bible Fun Stuff for Preschool Ser.). (Illus.). 112p. (J). (gr. -1-k). pap. 19.99 (978-1-4347-6864-3(3)) Cook, David C.

—Through-the-Bible Crafts. 2008. (Bible Fun Stuff for K-1 Ser.). (Illus.). 112p. (J). (gr. k-1). pap. 19.99 (978-1-4347-6862-9(7)) Cook, David C.

David C. Cook Publishing Company Staff & Cook, David C. Ooze & Awes in God's Creations, 1 vol. 2009. (Bible Funstuff Ser.). (ENG.). 112p. (J). pap. 19.99 (978-1-4347-6720-2(5)) Cook, David C.

David, Juliet. Dot to Dot Coloring & Stickers Bk. 1, 1 vol., 1. Smith, Jan, illus. 2008. (Candle Activity Fun Ser.). 24p. (J). (gr. 4-7). pap. 6.99 (978-0-8254-7360-9(8), Candle Bks.) Lion Hudson PLC GBR. Dist: Kregel Pubns.

Davidson, Susanna. Animalium Poster Book. Scott, Katie, illus. 2017. (ENG.). 56p. (J). (gr. 2-4). pap. 22.00 (978-0-7636-9318-3(9), Big Picture Press) Candlewick Pr.

Davies, Hannah. The Big Fabulous Colouring Book. 2017. (ENG.). 48p. (J). (gr. 3). pap. 14.99 **(978-1-78055-452-5(4))** O'Mara, Michael Bks., Ltd. GBR. Dist: Independent Pubs. Group.

Davis, Jenny. The U. S. Lawyer-Presidents Coloring & Activity Book. 2008. (ENG.). 32p. (J). (gr. -1-3). pap. 5.95 (978-1-59031-976-5(1)) American Bar Assn.

Davis, Jenny B. The U. S. Supreme Court Coloring & Activity Book. 2007. (ENG., Illus.). 32p. (J). (gr. 1-17). pap. 5.95 (978-1-59031-924-6(9)) American Bar Assn.

—The U. S. Supreme Court Coloring Book. 3rd ed. 2014. (ENG., Illus.). 32p. (J). (gr. 1-12). pap. 5.95 (978-1-62722-399-7(1)) American Bar Assn.

Dawnay, Gabby. London Calls Sticker Book. Barrow, Alex, illus. 2017. (ENG.). 20p. (J). (gr. k-17). pap. 11.95 (978-1-84976-384-4(4)) Tate Publishing, Ltd. GBR. Dist: Abrams, Inc.

Daynes, Katie & Watt, Fiona, eds. Baby Scrapbook. 2008. (Baby Scrapbook Ser.). (Illus.). 32p. (J). bds. 19.99 (978-0-7945-1957-5(1), Usborne) EDC Publishing.

DC Comics. DC Superheroes Papercraft. 2016. (ENG., Illus.). 96p. (J). (gr. 1-5). pap. 12.99 (978-0-316-35640-4(9)) Little, Brown Bks. for Young Readers.

DC Comics Staff. DC Super Friends Wipe Clean Activity Book. 2017. (ENG.). 56p. (J). spiral bd. 12.99 (978-0-374-30398-3(3), 9780374303983, Farrar, Straus & Giroux (BYR)) Farrar, Straus & Giroux.

de Klerk, Roger, illus. Foxy Learns Colors. 2009. (Foxy Learns Ser.). 16p. (J). pap. 4.95 (978-1-59496-181-6(6)) Teora USA LLC.

—Foxy Learns Shapes. 2009. (Foxy Learns Ser.). 16p. (J). pap. 4.95 (978-1-59496-179-3(4)) Teora USA LLC.

—Foxy Learns to Add. 2009. (Foxy Learns Ser.). 16p. (J). pap. 4.95 (978-1-59496-178-6(6)) Teora USA LLC.

—Foxy Learns to Tell Time. 2009. (Foxy Learns Ser.). 16p. (J). pap. 4.95 (978-1-59496-180-9(8)) Teora USA LLC.

De Lopez, Jacqueline Salazar. Little Hands, Busy Minds. 2012. 162p. pap. 39.95 (978-0-9853094-8-0(2)) Warren Publishing, Inc.

de Sturtz, Maria Ester H. Milagros en la Biblia. Fernandez, Lucia, illus. 2007. (Manos a la Obra Ser.). 32p. (J). (gr. -1-4). per. 7.99 (978-0-7586-1458-2(6)) Concordia Publishing Hse.

de Sturtz, Marie Ester H. Por Las Aguas De la Biblia (God & Water in the Bible) 2011. 32p. pap. 1.99 (978-0-7586-2677-6(0)) Concordia Publishing Hse.

—Por Las Aguas De La Biblia (God & Water in the Bible) - Bilingual. 2011. 32p. pap. 1.99 (978-0-7586-2679-0(7)) Concordia Publishing Hse.

—Reyes y Profetas (Kings & Prophets) 2011. 32p. pap. 1.99 (978-0-7586-2676-9(2)) Concordia Publishing Hse.

—Reyes y profetas (Kings & Prophets) - Bilingual. 2011. 32p. pap. 1.99 (978-0-7586-2678-3(9)) Concordia Publishing Hse.

Dean, James. Pete the Cat: My First I Can Draw. Dean, James, illus. 2016. (Pete the Cat Ser.). (Illus.). 160p. (J). (gr. -1-3). pap. 9.99 (978-0-06-230443-8(7), HarperFestival) HarperCollins Pubs.

—Pete the Cat's Big Doodle & Draw Book. Dean, James, illus. 2015. (Pete the Cat Ser.). (ENG., Illus.). 128p. (J). (gr. -1-3). pap. 12.99 (978-0-06-230442-1(9), HarperFestival) HarperCollins Pubs.

DeNinno, Joanne & Gill, Kim. The Question Challenge Card Game Fun Sheets. 2012. 34.95 net. (978-1-60723-023-6(2)) Super Duper Pubns.

Denmark-Allen, Eva. I Was, I Am, I Will Be! - Yo Fui! Yo soy! Yo Sere! 2007. (ENG & SPA., Illus.). 56p. (J). per. 12.00 (978-0-9792016-8-4(3)) Professional Publishing Hse. LLC.

Dent, Sabrina. Proverbs Kids Fun Activity Book. 2006. (Illus.). 40p. (J). 5.99 (978-0-9796148-0-4(5)) Joint Heir Multimedia.

deRubertis, Barbara & Roser, Nancy. Let's Read Together: Resource Guide. 2005. (Let's Read Together Ser.). (Illus.). 56p. pap. 12.95 (978-1-57565-139-2(4)) Kane Press, Inc.

Desalle, Nicole. Safe at Play. 2011. pap. 39.95 (978-0-7664-3752-4(3)) Abrams & Co. Pubs., Inc.

DeShazer, Dennis & Green, Jon, creators. Music Is for Children: Kit B Advanced, Level 6. 2007. (Boz: the Green Bear Next Door Ser.). (J). (gr. -1-3). pap., stu. ed. 5.95 (978-0-7814-4973-1(1), 83725) Cook, David C.

DeShong, Molly, et al. Which One Doesn't Belong? Fd163. 2012. 34.95 net. (978-1-60723-049-6(6)) Super Duper Pubns.

Desjardins, Margaret M. Murky, Quirky, Beserky Math. Bohart, Lisa, illus. 2013. 24p. pap. 13.95 (978-1-61493-210-9(7)) Peppertree Pr., The.

Desso, Karen. Early Learning Reading Games: Levels A-D. 2007. 119p. spiral bd. 15.99 (978-0-9793576-8-8(3)) New Learning Publishing.

Deuchars, Marion. Draw Paint Print Like the Great Artists. 2014. (ENG., Illus.). 224p. (J). (gr. 3-7). pap. 19.95 (978-1-78067-281-6(0)) King, Laurence Publishing GBR. Dist: Hachette Bk. Group.

—Let's Make More Great Placemat Art. 2013. (ENG., Illus.). 72p. (J). (gr. k-5). 12.95 (978-1-85669-935-8(8)) King, Laurence Publishing GBR. Dist: Hachette Bk. Group.

Deuchars, Marion, illus. Art Play. 2016. (ENG.). 224p. (J). (gr. 2-6). pap. 19.95 *(978-1-78067-877-1(0))* King, Laurence Publishing GBR. Dist: Hachette Bk. Group.
Deveny, Mary Alice. Pockets: Book: Nonfiction_Juvenile, The Molly Brave Preschool Series Vol. 1. Sweetman, Gary W., photos by. 2011. (Illus.). 40p. (J). pap. 14.95 *(978-1-61245-000-1(8))* Molly Brave.
Deyes, Alfie. The Pointless Book Bk. 2: Continued by Alfie Deyes Finished by You. 2015. (ENG., Illus.). 192p. (gr. 3-17). pap. 12.95 *(978-0-7624-5920-9(4))*, Running Pr.) Running Pr. Bk. Pubs.
Dickason, Chris. The Clever Kids' Dickason, Chris, illus. 2015. (ENG., Illus.). 32p. (J). (gr. 1). pap., act. bk. ed. 6.99 ***(978-1-78055-319-1(6))*** O'Mara, Michael Bks., Ltd. GBR. Dist: Independent Pubs. Group.
—The Clever Kids' Colouring Book: Genius. Dickason, Chris, illus. 2015. (ENG., Illus.). 32p. (J). (gr. 1). pap. 6.99 ***(978-1-78055-318-4(8))*** O'Mara, Michael Bks., Ltd. GBR. Dist: Independent Pubs. Group.
Dickason, Chris & Buster Books Staff. The Planes, Trains & Cars Colouring Book. Dickason, Chris, illus. 2017. (ENG., Illus.). 64p. (J). (gr. k-2). pap. 6.99 ***(978-1-78055-251-4(3))*** O'Mara, Michael Bks., Ltd. GBR. Dist: Independent Pubs. Group.
Dickinson, Gill & Lowe, Jason. Crafts for Kids: Birthdays - Easter - Halloween - Christmas - Mother's Day - Thanksgiving - And More... 2008. (ENG., Illus.). 128p. (gr. -1-17). pap. 12.95 *(978-0-600-61506-4(5))*, Hamlyn) Octopus Publishing Group GBR. Dist: Hachette Bk. Group.
Diehn, Andi. Explore Poetry! With 25 Great Projects. Stone, Bryan, illus. 2015. (Explore Your World Ser.). (ENG.). 96p. (gr. 1-5). 19.95 *(978-1-61930-279-2(9))* Open City Bks.
Diesen, Deborah. The Pout-Pout Fish Giant Sticker Book. Hanna, Dan, illus. 2016. (Pout-Pout Fish Novelty Ser.). (ENG.). 128p. (J). pap. 12.99 *(978-1-250-06394-6(9))*, 9781250063946, Farrar, Straus & Giroux (BYR)) Farrar, Straus & Giroux.
Dinosaurs. 2007. (Velvet Art Activity Book Ser.). 8p. pap. *(978-1-4075-0360-8(X))* Parragon, Inc.
Dischler, Patricia. Tea Party Celebrations! 2012. (ENG.). pap. 19.95 *(978-1-4675-3709-4(8))* Independent Pub.
Disney. Disney Pixar Inside Out Funbook. 2015. (ENG.). 240p. (J). pap. 10.99 *(978-1-4434-4873-4(7))* HarperCollins Pubs.
Disney Book Group Staff. Minnie's Fashion & Fun. Disney Storybook Artists Staff, illus. 2013. (Book & Magnetic Play Set Ser.). (ENG.). 32p. (J). (gr. -1-k). 14.99 *(978-1-4231-8443-0(2))* Disney Pr.
—Ready to Be a Princess. Disney Storybook Art Team, illus. 2013. (Book & Magnetic Play Set Ser.). (ENG.). 32p. (J). (gr. -1-k). 14.99 *(978-1-4231-8445-4(9))* Disney Pr.
Disney Book Group Staff, illus. The Avengers: a Mighty Sticker Book. 2013. (Sticker-Activity Storybook Ser.). (ENG.). 88p. (J). (gr. 3-7). pap. 12.99 *(978-1-4231-8508-6(0))* Marvel Worldwide, Inc.
Disney Enterprises Inc. Staff, creator. Disney's Lilo & Stitch Time for Fun! Bath Time Bubble Book. 2007. (Disney Bath Time Bubble Bks.). (Illus.). (J). (gr. -1-k). 4.99 *(978-0-7666-2553-2(2))* Modern Publishing.
Disney Mickey Mouse Clubhouse, Disney Mickey. Disney Mickey Mouse Clubhouse: Schoolhouse Fun: A,B,Cs And 1, 2, 3s. 2015. (ENG.). 40p. (J). (gr. -1-1). 12.99 *(978-0-7944-3388-8(X))* Studio Fun International.
Disney Modern Publishing & Greenwald, Todd J., creators. Wizards of Waverly Place: A Day in the Life. 2009. (Illus.). (J). pap. 4.99 *(978-0-7666-3301-8(2))* Modern Publishing.
Divas. 2007. (Velvet Art Activity Book Ser.). 8p. pap. *(978-1-4075-0361-5(8))* Parragon, Inc.
Do It Yourself Set Of 15. 2014. (ENG.). pap. 134.85 *(978-1-4846-2352-7(5))*, NA-h) Heinemann-Raintree.
Dodd, Emma. A Spoonful for Bunny: A Book to Melt Your Heart. 2017. (Sprinkle with Kisses Ser.). (ENG., Illus.). 10p. (J). (gr. -1 — 1). bds. 6.99 *(978-0-7641-6884-0(3))* Barron's Educational Series, Inc.
Doherty, Gillian. 1001 Animals to Spot. 2010. (1001 Things to Spot Ser.). 32p. (J). 9.99 *(978-0-7945-2704-4(3))*, Usborne) EDC Publishing.
—1001 Things to Spot Long Ago. Gower, Teri, illus. rev. ed. 2006. (1001 Things to Spot Ser.). 32p. (J). (gr. -1-3). pap. 6.99 *(978-0-7945-0716-9(6))*, Usborne) EDC Publishing.
Donahue, Peter. Cool Cars & Trucks Stained Glass Jr. Coloring Book. 2012. (Dover Stained Glass Coloring Book Ser.). (ENG.). 32p. (J). (gr. -1-3). pap. 3.99 *(978-0-486-49874-4(3))* Dover Pubns., Inc.
—Not-Your-Average Superhero Mazes. 2009. (Dover Children's Activity Bks.). (ENG.). 48p. (J). (gr. 1-4). pap. 4.99 *(978-0-486-47039-9(3))* Dover Pubns., Inc.
—Not-Your-Average Superhero Stickers. 2009. (Dover Little Activity Books Stickers Ser.). (ENG., Illus.). 4p. (J). (gr. -1-2). 1.50 *(978-0-486-47040-5(7))* Dover Pubns., Inc.
—What to Doodle? Jr. - Superheroes & Robots! 2013. (Dover Doodle Bks.). (ENG.). 128p. (J). (gr. 1-5). pap. 4.99 *(978-0-486-49954-3(5))* Dover Pubns., Inc.
Donaldson, Julia. My First Animal Fun Sticker Book. Sharratt, Nick, illus. 2016. (ENG.). 30p. (J). (gr. -1-2). pap. 8.99 *(978-1-5098-1622-4(4))* Pan Macmillan GBR. Dist: Independent Pubs. Group.
—Room on the Broom Big Activity Book. Scheffler, Axel, illus. 2015. (ENG.). 48p. (J). (gr. -1-3). pap. 10.99 *(978-0-448-48944-5(9))*, Grosset & Dunlap) Penguin Young Readers Group.
Donner, Candie. Easter Activity Book. Kinney, Cyndi, ed. 2013. (J). pap. 22.99 *(978-1-61625-617-3(6))*; cd-rom 12.99 *(978-1-61625-616-6(8))* Knowledge Box Central.
Dorling Kindersley Publishing Staff. ABC Games. 2016. (Skills for Starting School Ser.). (ENG.). 52p. (J). (gr. -1-k). 9.99 *(978-1-4654-4455-4(6))*, DK Children) Dorling Kindersley Publishing, Inc.
—American Girl Dress Up. 2017. (Ultimate Sticker Collections). (ENG.). 96p. (J). (gr. 1-4). pap. 12.99 *(978-1-4654-5690-8(2))*, DK Children) Dorling Kindersley Publishing, Inc.
—American Girl: the Story of America. 2017. (ENG., Illus.). 64p. (J). (gr. 2-5). 12.99 *(978-1-4654-5689-2(9))*, DK Children) Dorling Kindersley Publishing, Inc.
—Animals. 2012. (Ultimate Sticker Collections). (ENG.). 96p. (J). (gr. 1-4). pap. 12.99 *(978-0-7566-9287-2(3))*, DK Children) Dorling Kindersley Publishing, Inc.
—Baby Touch Your Nose. 2016. (ENG., Illus.). 14p. (J). (— 1). bds. 5.99 *(978-1-4654-5071-5(8))*, DK Children) Dorling Kindersley Publishing, Inc.
—Bedtime. 2014. (ENG.). 12p. (J). (gr. -1 — 1). bds. 9.99 *(978-1-4654-2035-0(5))*, DK Children) Dorling Kindersley Publishing, Inc.
—Big Red Barn. 2017. (ENG.). 12p. (J). (— 1). bds. 14.99 ***(978-1-4654-6313-5(5))***, DK Children) Dorling Kindersley Publishing, Inc.
—Build Your Own Adventure. 2015. (ENG.). 80p. (J). (gr. 2-5). 24.99 *(978-1-4654-3590-3(5))*, DK Children) Dorling Kindersley Publishing, Inc.
—Deadly Battles. 2016. (Ultimate Sticker Collections). (ENG.). 96p. (J). (gr. 1-4). pap. 12.99 *(978-1-4654-5110-1(2))*, DK Children) Dorling Kindersley Publishing, Inc.
—Disney Frozen. 2014. (ENG.). 96p. (J). (gr. 2-4). pap. 12.99 *(978-1-4654-3435-7(6))*, DK Children) Dorling Kindersley Publishing, Inc.
—Disney Frozen: Ultimate Sticker Collection. 2015. (Ultimate Sticker Collections). (ENG.). 96p. (J). (gr. 1-4). pap. 12.99 *(978-1-4654-4080-8(1))*, DK Children) Dorling Kindersley Publishing, Inc.
—Disney Frozen Factivity Fun READERLINK. 2015. (ENG.). 96p. (J). (gr. 1-4). pap. 16.99 *(978-1-4654-4200-0(6))* Dorling Kindersley Publishing, Inc.
—Disney Infinity. 2014. (Ultimate Sticker Collections). (ENG.). 96p. (J). (gr. 1-4). pap. 12.99 *(978-1-4654-1669-8(2))*, DK Children) Dorling Kindersley Publishing, Inc.
—Disney Moana. 2016. (Ultimate Sticker Bks.). (ENG.). 16p. (J). (gr. k-4). pap. 6.99 *(978-1-4654-5260-3(5))*, DK Children) Dorling Kindersley Publishing, Inc.
—Disney Moana: the Essential Guide. 2016. (ENG., Illus.). 64p. (J). (gr. 1-4). 12.99 *(978-1-4654-5259-7(1))*, DK Children) Dorling Kindersley Publishing, Inc.
—Disney Pixar Finding Dory. 2016. (ENG.). 96p. (J). (gr. -1-1). pap. 12.99 *(978-1-4654-4979-5(5))*, DK Children) Dorling Kindersley Publishing, Inc.
—Disney Pixar Finding Dory: the Essential Collection. 2016. (ENG.). 88p. (J). (gr. k-4). 19.99 *(978-1-4654-5273-3(7))*, DK Children) Dorling Kindersley Publishing, Inc.
—Disney Pixar Finding Dory: the Essential Guide. 2016. (ENG., Illus.). 64p. (J). (gr. k-4). 12.99 *(978-1-4654-4978-8(7))*, DK Children) Dorling Kindersley Publishing, Inc.
—Factivity Fun: LEGO(r) NEXO KNIGHTS. 2017. (ENG.). 96p. (J). (gr. 1-4). pap. 12.99 *(978-1-4654-5854-4(9))*, DK Children) Dorling Kindersley Publishing, Inc.
—Fashion. 2014. (ENG.). 96p. (J). (gr. 2-4). pap. 12.99 *(978-1-4654-1653-7(6))*, DK Children) Dorling Kindersley Publishing, Inc.
—The Good Dinosaur. 2015. (Ultimate Sticker Bks.). (ENG.). 16p. (J). (gr. k-4). pap. 6.99 *(978-1-4654-1571-4(8))*, DK Children) Dorling Kindersley Publishing, Inc.
—Good Night Sophie - A Touch & Feel Book. 2017. (ENG.). 12p. (J). (— 1). bds. 5.99 *(978-1-4654-5625-0(2))*, DK Children) Dorling Kindersley Publishing, Inc.
—Heroes Unite! 2014. (Ultimate Sticker Collections). (ENG.). 96p. (J). (gr. 1-4). pap. 12.99 *(978-1-4654-1684-1(6))*, DK Children) Dorling Kindersley Publishing, Inc.
—Leaf it to Cubs. 2008. 16p. (J). (gr. k-5). 2.49 *(978-0-7566-3324-0(9))* Dorling Kindersley Publishing, Inc.
—The Lego(r) Batman Movie: The Essential Collection. 2017. (ENG.). 88p. (J). (gr. 1-4). 19.99 ***(978-1-4654-6358-6(5))***, DK Children) Dorling Kindersley Publishing, Inc.
—LEGO Ninja, Go! 2015. (DK Readers Ser.). (ENG., Illus.). 48p. (J). (gr. 1-3). pap. 3.99 *(978-1-4654-2948-3(4))*, DK Children) Dorling Kindersley Publishing, Inc.
—Marvel the Avengers Factivity Fun READERLINK. 2015. (ENG.). 96p. (J). (gr. 1-4). pap. 16.99 *(978-1-4654-4201-7(4))* Dorling Kindersley Publishing, Inc.
—My Encyclopedia of Very Important Things. 2016. (ENG., Illus.). 224p. (J). (gr. k-4). 16.99 *(978-1-4654-4968-9(X))*, DK Children) Dorling Kindersley Publishing, Inc.
—My First Out & About. 2017. (My First Bks.). (ENG.). 36p. (J). (— 1). bds. 5.99 ***(978-1-4654-6083-7(7))***, DK Children) Dorling Kindersley Publishing, Inc.
—My World: Disney Lion Guard. 2017. (ENG.). 40p. (J). (gr. k-3). 9.99 *(978-1-4654-5553-6(1))*, DK Children) Dorling Kindersley Publishing, Inc.
—The Ninjago Movie. 2017. (Ultimate Sticker Collections). (ENG.). 96p. (J). (gr. 1-4). pap. 12.99 ***(978-1-4654-6115-5(9))***, DK Children) Dorling Kindersley Publishing, Inc.
—On the Move. 2016. (DK Braille Ser.). (ENG.). 32p. (J). (gr. 2-4). 22.99 *(978-1-4654-3610-8(3))*, DK Children) Dorling Kindersley Publishing, Inc.
—Playtime. 2017. (My First Bks.). (ENG.). 36p. (J). (— 1). bds. 5.99 *(978-1-4654-5677-9(5))*, DK Children) Dorling Kindersley Publishing, Inc.
—Please & Thank You. 2017. (Skills for Starting School Ser.). (ENG.). 18p. (J). (— 1). bds. 5.99 *(978-1-4654-5679-3(1))*, DK Children) Dorling Kindersley Publishing, Inc.
—Rogue One. 2016. (Ultimate Sticker Collections). (ENG.). 96p. (J). (gr. 1-4). pap. 12.99 *(978-1-4654-5266-5(4))*, DK Children) Dorling Kindersley Publishing, Inc.
—Skills for Starting School My Sticker Reward Chart Book. 2017. (Skills for Starting School Ser.). (ENG.). 60p. (J). (-k). pap. 12.99 ***(978-1-4654-6137-7(X))***, DK Children) Dorling Kindersley Publishing, Inc.
—Skills for Starting School Ready to Read. 2017. (Skills for Starting School Ser.). (ENG.). 40p. (J). (-k). pap. 6.99 *(978-1-4654-6012-7(8))*, DK Children) Dorling Kindersley Publishing, Inc.
—Sleepover Party. 2016. (ENG., Illus.). 80p. (J). (gr. 2-4). 14.99 *(978-1-4654-5097-5(1))*, DK Children) Dorling Kindersley Publishing, Inc.
—Sophie la Girafe: ABC Flashcards. 2017. (ENG.). 26p. (J). (— 1). bds. 9.99 *(978-1-4654-5702-8(X))*, DK Children) Dorling Kindersley Publishing, Inc.
—Spider-Man. 2014. (ENG.). 96p. (J). (gr. 2-4). pap. 12.99 *(978-1-4654-1661-2(7))*, DK Children) Dorling Kindersley Publishing, Inc.
—Spot the Difference: Building Site. 2017. (Spot the Difference Ser.). (ENG.). 16p. (J). (-k). bds. 6.99 ***(978-1-4654-5493-5(4))***, DK Children) Dorling Kindersley Publishing, Inc.
—Spot the Difference: Out & About. 2017. (Spot the Difference Ser.). (ENG.). 16p. (J). (-k). bds. 6.99 ***(978-1-4654-5599-4(X))***, DK Children) Dorling Kindersley Publishing, Inc.
—Star Wars Factivity Fun READERLINK. 2015. (ENG.). 96p. (J). (gr. 1-4). pap. 16.99 *(978-1-4654-4202-4(2))* Dorling Kindersley Publishing, Inc.
—Star Wars Rebels. 2015. (ENG.). 96p. (J). (gr. 3-7). pap. 12.99 *(978-1-4654-2943-8(3))*, DK Children) Dorling Kindersley Publishing, Inc.
—Stop the Stone Monsters! 2017. (DK Readers Ser.). (ENG.). 24p. (J). (-k). pap. 3.99 *(978-1-4654-5576-5(0))*, DK Children) Dorling Kindersley Publishing, Inc.
—Tractor. 2014. (ENG., Illus.). 12p. (J). (gr. -1 — 1). bds. 9.99 *(978-1-4654-1665-0(X))*, DK Children) Dorling Kindersley Publishing, Inc.
—Ultimate Factivity Collection: LEGO City: LEGO City. 2014. (ENG.). 96p. (J). (gr. 2-4). pap. 12.99 *(978-1-4654-1667-4(6))*, DK Children) Dorling Kindersley Publishing, Inc.
—Ultimate Factivity Collection: Star Wars: Star Wars. 2014. (ENG.). 96p. (J). (gr. 2-4). pap. 12.99 *(978-1-4654-1660-5(9))*, DK Children) Dorling Kindersley Publishing, Inc.
—Ultimate Sticker Book: Princess. 2016. (Ultimate Sticker Bks.). (ENG.). 32p. (J). (gr. k-3). pap. 6.99 *(978-1-4654-5073-9(4))*, DK Children) Dorling Kindersley Publishing, Inc.
—Ultimate Sticker Collection: American Girl. 2016. (Ultimate Sticker Collections). (ENG.). 96p. (J). (gr. k-3). pap. 12.99 *(978-1-4654-4922-1(1))*, DK Children) Dorling Kindersley Publishing, Inc.
—Ultimate Sticker Collection: DC Comics Super Heroes. 2016. (Ultimate Sticker Collections). (ENG.). 96p. (J). (gr. 1-4). pap. 12.99 *(978-1-4654-4549-0(8))*, DK Children) Dorling Kindersley Publishing, Inc.
—Ultimate Sticker Collection: Disney Tsum Tsum. 2016. (Ultimate Sticker Collections). (ENG.). 96p. (J). (gr. 1-4). pap. 12.99 *(978-1-4654-4422-6(X))*, DK Children) Dorling Kindersley Publishing, Inc.
—Ultimate Sticker Collection: LEGO Minifigure: Mash-Up! 2016. (Ultimate Sticker Collections). (ENG.). 96p. (J). (gr. 1-4). pap. 12.99 *(978-1-4654-4464-6(5))*, DK Children) Dorling Kindersley Publishing, Inc.
—Ultimate Sticker Collection: LEGO NEXO KNIGHTS. 2016. (ENG.). 96p. (J). (gr. 1-4). pap. 12.99 *(978-1-4654-4594-0(3))*, DK Children) Dorling Kindersley Publishing, Inc.
—Ultimate Sticker Collection: LEGO Winter Wonderland. 2016. (Ultimate Sticker Collections). (ENG.). 96p. (J). (gr. 1-4). pap. 12.99 *(978-1-4654-5475-1(6))*, DK Children) Dorling Kindersley Publishing, Inc.
—Ultimate Sticker Collection: Star Wars: the Force Awakens. 2015. (Ultimate Sticker Collections). (ENG.). 96p. (J). (gr. 1-4). pap. 12.99 *(978-1-4654-3817-1(3))*, DK Children) Dorling Kindersley Publishing, Inc.
—100 First Words. 2017. (ENG.). 16p. (J). (— 1). bds. 9.99 *(978-1-4654-5700-4(3))*, DK Children) Dorling Kindersley Publishing, Inc.
Dorling Kindersley Publishing Staff & Davies, Beth. Rise of the Rogues. 2016. (DK Readers Ser.). (ENG.). 48p. (J). (gr. k-2). pap. 3.99 *(978-1-4654-5861-2(1))*, DK Children) Dorling Kindersley Publishing, Inc.
—Team Batman. 2016. (DK Readers Ser.). (ENG.). 24p. (J). (-k). pap. 3.99 *(978-1-4654-5859-9(X))*, DK Children) Dorling Kindersley Publishing, Inc.
Dorling Kindersley Publishing Staff & March, Julia. Heroes into Battle. 2014. (Ultimate Sticker Collections). (ENG.). 96p. (J). (gr. 1-4). pap. 12.99 *(978-1-4654-2846-2(1))*, DK Children) Dorling Kindersley Publishing, Inc.
Dorling Kindersley Publishing Staff, et al. Disney Elena of Avalor. 2017. (ENG.). 64p. (J). (gr. k-2). 12.99 *(978-1-4654-5554-3(X))*, DK Children) Dorling Kindersley Publishing, Inc.
Dot-to-Dot 1-100+ Spanish Version. 2007. (J). per. *(978-1-58232-163-9(9))* ECS Learning Systems, Inc.
Doughty, Sarah. Flippin' Awesome: Water Bottle Flip Games, Tricks & Stunts for Everyone! 2016. (ENG., Illus.). 64p. (J). (gr. 4-9). pap. 14.99 ***(978-1-63158-169-4(4))***, Racehorse Publishing) Skyhorse Publishing Co., Inc.
Dover. Animals Activities Dover Chunky Book. 2009. (Dover Little Activity Bks.). (ENG., Illus.). 320p. (J). (gr. -1-5). pap. 6.99 *(978-0-486-47424-3(0))* Dover Pubns., Inc.
—Bugs Activities Dover Chunky Book. 2009. (Dover Little Activity Bks.). (ENG., Illus.). 320p. (J). (gr. -1-5). 6.99 *(978-0-486-47425-0(9))* Dover Pubns., Inc.
—Cool Construction Site Stickers. 2016. (Dover Little Activity Books Stickers Ser.). (ENG.). 4p. (J). (gr. -1-3). pap. 1.99 *(978-0-486-80316-6(3))* Dover Pubns., Inc.
—Dinosaurs Activities Dover Chunky Book. 2009. (Dover Little Activity Bks.). (ENG., Illus.). 320p. (J). (gr. -1-5). pap. 6.99 *(978-0-486-47426-7(7))* Dover Pubns., Inc.
—Emoji Stickers. 2016. (Dover Little Activity Books Stickers Ser.). (ENG.). 8p. (J). (gr. -1-3). pap. 1.99 *(978-0-486-80442-2(9))* Dover Pubns., Inc.
—Friendly Lion Tattoos. 2014. (ENG.). 2p. (J). (gr. 1-4). pap. 1.99 *(978-0-486-49495-1(0))* Dover Pubns., Inc.
—Friendly Monkey Tattoos. 2014. (ENG.). 2p. (J). (gr. 1-4). pap. 1.99 *(978-0-486-49494-4(2))* Dover Pubns., Inc.
—Moustache Stickers. 2014. (ENG.). 4p. (J). (gr. k-3). pap. 1.50 *(978-0-486-78036-8(8))* Dover Pubns., Inc.
—On the Go Activities Dover Chunky Book. 2009. (Dover Little Activity Bks.). (ENG., Illus.). 320p. (J). (gr. -1-5). pap. 6.99 *(978-0-486-47430-4(5))* Dover Pubns., Inc.
—Spot the Differences, Bk. 4. 2012. (Dover Children's Activity Bks.). (ENG.). 64p. (J). (gr. 3-5). pap. 9.99 *(978-0-486-48085-5(2))* Dover Pubns., Inc.
—Spot the Differences Bk. 4: Art Masterpiece Mysteries. 2013. (Dover Children's Activity Bks.). (ENG.). 64p. (J). (gr. 3-5). pap. 9.99 *(978-0-486-48086-2(0))* Dover Pubns., Inc.
Dover & Printworks KMG Staff. Sea Life Field Guide. 2013. (ENG.). 48p. (J). (gr. 3-8). pap. 5.99 *(978-0-486-49157-8(9))* Dover Pubns., Inc.
Dover & Tattoos. Moustache Tattoos: For Your Face or Finger! 2013. (Dover Tattoos Ser.). (ENG., Illus.). 2p. (J). (gr. 3-4). pap. 1.99 *(978-0-486-49329-9(6))* Dover Pubns., Inc.
Dover Publications Inc. Staff, ed. Revolutionary War, Kit. 2009. (ENG.). 4p. (J). (gr. 5). 19.99 *(978-0-486-47356-7(2))* Dover Pubns., Inc.
Dover Staff. Spectacular Scales & Nifty Notes Tattoos. 2011. (Dover Tattoos Ser.). (ENG.). 4p. (J). (gr. 1-4). pap. 1.99 *(978-0-486-48191-3(3))* Dover Pubns., Inc.
Dover Staff & Printworks KMG Staff. Dinosaurs Field Guide. 2013. (ENG.). 48p. (J). (gr. 3-8). pap. 5.99 *(978-0-486-49156-1(0))* Dover Pubns., Inc.
Dowley, Tim. Bible Adventures, 1 vol. 2017. (Activity Fun Ser.). (ENG.). 64p. (J). pap. 4.99 ***(978-1-78128-337-0(0))***, Candle Bks.) Lion Hudson PLC GBR. Dist: Kregel Pubns.
—Bible Children, 1 vol. 2017. (Activity Fun Ser.). (ENG.). 64p. (J). pap. 4.99 ***(978-1-78128-329-5(X))***, Candle Bks.) Lion Hudson PLC GBR. Dist: Kregel Pubns.
—Bible People, 1 vol. 2017. (Activity Fun Ser.). (ENG.). 64p. (J). pap. 4.99 ***(978-1-78128-328-8(1))***, Candle Bks.) Lion Hudson PLC GBR. Dist: Kregel Pubns.
Down, Heather. Postcards from Space: The Chris Hadfield Story. 2013. 50p. pap. *(978-1-894813-65-5(0))* Wintertickle Pr.
Downtown Bookworks Inc. Staff & Wolf, Laurie Goldrich. Boy-Made: Green & Groovy. 2012. (Green & Groovy Ser.: 3). (ENG.). 64p. (J). (gr. 1). 16.99 *(978-1-935703-28-0(5))* Downtown Bookworks.
Dowsett, Elizabeth & Bazaldua, Barbara. La Guia Esencial. 2017. (ENG & SPA.). 64p. (J). (gr. k-2). 12.99 *(978-1-4654-6133-9(7))*, DK Children) Dorling Kindersley Publishing, Inc.
Doyle, James. The Superhero Handbook: 20 Super Activities to Help You Save the World! Ford, Jason, illus. 2017. (ENG.). 144p. (J). (gr. 2-6). pap. 12.99 *(978-1-78067-974-7(2))* King, Laurence Publishing GBR. Dist: Hachette Bk. Group.
Draught Associates. Visual Aid Doodling Book for Creative Kids. 2012. (ENG.). 96p. (J). (gr. k-6). pap. 11.95 *(978-1-907317-70-5(8))* Black Dog Publishing Ltd. GBR. Dist: Two Rivers Distribution.
Dream Rooms. 2008. (Cool Creations CD Rom Activity Books Ser.). 32p. *(978-1-4054-9586-8(3))* Parragon, Inc.
Dreamworks Animation Publishing, LLC. Olivia Stickers. Kurtz, John, illus. 2015. (Dover Little Activity Books Stickers Ser.). (ENG.). 4p. (J). (gr. k-3). 1.99 *(978-0-486-80276-3(0))* Dover Pubns., Inc.
Duke, Nell K., et al. Engaging Families in Children's Literacy Development: A Guide for Leading Successful Workshops, Including - Ready-to-Show Videos * Step-by-Step Plans & Schedules * Easy-to-Prepare Workshop Activities * Read-Aloud Trade Book Pack. 2014. (ENG., Illus.). 48p. pap. 149.99 *(978-0-545-56148-8(5))*, Teaching Resources) Scholastic, Inc.
Dunn, Justine. Hey! There's Science in My Literature! Grades 1-2. Radtke, Becky, illus. 2007. (Rigby Best Teachers Press Ser.). 96p. per. 13.99 *(978-1-4190-2848-9(0))* Houghton Mifflin Harcourt Supplemental Pubs.
Dunn, Mary. My Adventure in the Southeast: Advanced My Adventure. 2007. 44p. (J). pap. 8.99 *(978-1-59092-436-5(3))* Blue Forge Pr.
—My Adventure on a Dinosaur Dig. 2006. 44p. (J). 8.99 *(978-1-59092-281-1(6))* Blue Forge Pr.
—My Adventure with Mozart. 2006. 44p. (J). 8.99 *(978-1-59092-459-4(2))* Blue Forge Pr.
—My Adventure with Rembrandt. 2006. 44p. (J). 8.99 *(978-1-59092-463-1(0))* Blue Forge Pr.
Dutton, Michael. Amusement Park Science Activity Book. 2015. (ENG.). 48p. (J). (gr. 3). pap. 4.99 *(978-0-486-78035-1(X))* Dover Pubns., Inc.
Dworkin, Motoko. A Year in Japan: Folktales, Songs & Art for the Classroom. 2nd ed. 2012. (Illus.). 151p. pap. 26.95 *(978-0-9836716-1-9(3))* Paradise Copies, Inc.
Dyan, Penelope. Sticks — the for Boys Only Version — Because Sticks Are Also People. Dyan, Penelope, illus. 2008. (Illus.). 52p. pap. 11.95 *(978-1-935118-13-8(7))* Bellissima Publishing, LLC.
Early Concepts. 2017. (Early Concepts Ser.). 24p. (gr. 4-6). 118.00 ***(978-1-5081-6249-0(2))***; pap. 41.25 ***(978-1-5081-6252-0(2))*** Rosen Publishing Group, Inc., The. (PowerKids Pr.).
The Easter Activity Book. 2013. (ENG.). 144p. (J). pap. 9.95 *(978-1-78212-147-3(1))* Arcturus Publishing GBR. Dist: Bookmasters Distribution.
Eckel, Jessie. The Boys' Coloring Book. 2013. (ENG.). 128p. (J). (gr. -1-2). pap. 8.95 *(978-1-4549-0716-9(9))* Sterling Publishing Co., Inc.
—The Girls' Coloring Book. 2013. (ENG.). 128p. (J). (gr. -1-2). pap. 8.95 *(978-1-4549-0717-6(7))* Sterling Publishing Co., Inc.
Ede, Lara. Press-Out & Play Busy Farm. 2013. (ENG.). 18p. (J). pap. 4.99 *(978-1-78235-565-6(0))* Make Believe Ideas GBR. Dist: Nelson, Thomas Inc.
—Press-Out & Play Fairy Land. 2013. (ENG.). 18p. (J). pap. 4.99 *(978-1-78235-567-0(7))* Make Believe Ideas GBR. Dist: Nelson, Thomas Inc.
—Press-Out & Play Pampered Pets. 2013. (ENG.). 18p. (J). pap. 4.99 *(978-1-78235-564-9(2))* Make Believe Ideas GBR. Dist: Nelson, Thomas Inc.
Edison, Erin. Destruction. 2013. (Destruction Ser.). (ENG.). 12p. (gr. k-1). bds. 119.88 *(978-1-4914-1517-7(7))*, Pebble Plus) Capstone Press of Coughlan Cos.
The Education of Little Tree: Activity Pack. 2003. 118p. (YA). pap. *(978-1-58049-627-8(X))*, PA0127) Prestwick Hse., Inc.
Educational Adventures, creator. Blazin' Hot: Coloring/Activity Book (Spanish) w/ Snipe. 2006. (SPA., Illus.). (J). 2.99 *(978-0-9770455-5-6(2))* Mighty Kids Media.
Edupress, creator. My Story Book: Primary. 2009. 32p. pap. 1.99 *(978-1-56472-944-6(3))* Edupress, Inc.
Edwards, Andrew & Thornton, Fleur. Wilberforce: an Activity Book: 24 Ready to Use Lesson Plans. 2007. (Illus.). 32p. (J). (gr. 3-7). pap. 6.99 *(978-0-89221-672-7(7))* New Leaf Pub. Group.
Einhorn, Kama. All about Me: 40 Fun Reproducible Activities That Guide Children to Share about Themselves in Pictures. 2012. (Follow-The-Directions Ser.). (ENG.). 48p. (gr. k-1). pap. 10.99 *(978-0-545-32959-0(0))*, Teaching Resources) Scholastic, Inc.
—Letter of the Week Flip Chart: Write-On/Wipe-Off Activity Pages That Introduce Each Letter from A to Z. 2010. (ENG.). 26p. (gr. -1-1). pap. 24.99 *(978-0-545-22417-8(9))*, Teaching Resources) Scholastic, Inc.

S

—Number of the Week Flip Chart: Lively, Interactive Acvtive Pages That Teaches Each Number from 0 to 30. 2013. (ENG.). 28p. (gr. -1-2). pap. 25.99 *(978-0-545-45709-5(2),* Teaching Resources) Scholastic, Inc.

Eisbruch, Emily. Curious Kids Activity Guide to Michigan. 2007. pap. 9.95 *(978-0-9789140-0-4(7))* Curious Kids Guides.

Eisenberg, Rebecca & Kjesbo, Rynette. Cool in School Communication Game: Gb362. Lefebvre, Patrick, photos by. 2011. (Illus.). (J). 64.95 net. *(978-1-58650-994-1(2))* Super Duper Pubns.

Elder, Jeremy. Animal Kaleidoscope Designs Coloring Book. 2017. (Dover Coloring Bks.). (ENG., Illus.). 32p. (J). (gr. 3-6). pap. 3.99 *(978-0-486-80883-3(1))* Dover Pubns., Inc.

—ComicQuest ZOMBIES UNLEASHED. 2013. (Dover Children's Activity Bks.). (ENG.). 48p. (J). (gr. 3-8). pap. 4.99 *(978-0-486-49943-7(X))* Dover Pubns., Inc.

—Graffiti Tattoos. 2016. (Dover Little Activity Bks.). (ENG.). 4p. (J). (gr. 3-6). pap. 1.99 *(978-0-486-80697-6(9))* Dover Pubns., Inc.

—Japanese Tattoo Art Stained Glass Coloring Book. 2010. (Dover Design Stained Glass Coloring Book Ser.). (ENG., Illus.). 32p. (J). (gr. 1-5). pap. 7.99 *(978-0-486-47533-2(6))* Dover Pubns., Inc.

—Monsters Destroyed My City! Sticker Activity Book. 2012. (Dover Little Activity Books Stickers Ser.). (ENG.). 4p. (J). (gr. 1-5). pap. 1.50 *(978-0-486-48878-3(0))* Dover Pubns., Inc.

—Pinball Mazes Activity Book: Can You Top the High Score? 2012. (Dover Children's Activity Bks.). (ENG.). 48p. (J). (gr. 3-8). 4.99 *(978-0-486-49003-8(3))* Dover Pubns., Inc.

Ellcock, Stephen & Froese, Tom. Stickyscapes: New York. 2016. (Magma for Laurence King Ser.). (ENG., Illus.). (gr. 1-3). pap. 14.95 *(978-1-85669-984-6(6))* King, Laurence Publishing GBR. Dist: Hachette Bk. Group.

Elliot, Rachel. Seek & Find Fairy: Find a Charm Book. Regan, Lisa, illus. 2014. (Seek & Find Ser.). (ENG.). 32p. (J). (gr. -1-1). 9.99 *(978-0-7641-6696-9(4))* Barron's Educational Series, Inc.

—Seek & Find Princess: Find a Charm Book. Regan, Lisa, illus. 2014. (Seek & Find Ser.). (ENG.). 32p. (J). (gr. -1-1). 9.99 *(978-0-7641-6697-6(2))* Barron's Educational Series, Inc.

Ellis, Colette. Credo: I Believe. Avakoff, Caroline, ed. Pelicano, Christopher J., illus. 2009. (Faith & Life Ser.). 121p. (J). pap. 7.95 *(978-0-89870-898-1(2))* Ignatius Pr.

Ellis, Paula. Arizona Activity Book, 1 vol. Nitzsche, Shane, illus. 2012. (Color & Learn Ser.). (ENG.). 64p. (J). (gr. 2-3). pap. 5.95 *(978-1-59193-288-8(2))* Adventure Pubns.

—Great Lakes Activity Book, 1 vol. Kaiser, Anna et al, illus. 2015. (Color & Learn Ser.). (ENG.). (J). pap. 5.95 *(978-1-59193-526-1(1))* Adventure Pubns.

—Great Smoky Mountains Activity Book, 1 vol. Nitzsche, Shane, illus. 2015. (Color & Learn Ser.). (ENG.). 64p. (J). (gr. 2-3). pap. 5.95 *(978-1-59193-455-4(9))* Adventure Pubns.

—Minnesota Activity Book, 1 vol. Nitzsche, Shane, illus. 2013. (Color & Learn Ser.). (ENG.). 64p. (J). (gr. k-2). pap. 5.95 *(978-1-59193-377-9(3))* Adventure Pubns.

—Texas Activity Book, 1 vol. Nitzsche, Shane, illus. 2012. (Color & Learn Ser.). (ENG.). 64p. (J). (gr. 2-3). pap. 5.95 *(978-1-59193-376-2(5))* Adventure Pubns.

—Yosemite Activity Book, 1 vol. Nitzsche, Shane, illus. 2013. (Color & Learn Ser.). (ENG.). 64p. (J). (gr. 2-3). pap. 5.95 *(978-1-59193-299-4(8))* Adventure Pubns.

Elrod, Julie. Splitting Hares. 2008. 36p. pap. 16.50 *(978-1-60693-484-5(8),* Eloquent Bks.) Strategic Book Publishing & Rights Agency (SBPRA).

Encarnacion, Elizabeth. 3-D Doodle Book & Kit: Where Your Imagination Can Really Jump off the Page! 2012. (ENG.). 80p. (J). (gr. 5). 12.95 *(978-1-60433-095-3(3),* Applesauce Pr.) Cider Mill Pr. Bk. Pubs., LLC.

Engelbreit, Mary. Mary Engelbreit's Color ME Christmas. Engelbreit, Mary, illus. 2016. (Illus.). 96p. (J). (gr. -1-3). pap. 15.99 *(978-0-06-256260-9(6))* HarperCollins Pubs.

Engelbreit, Mary. Mary Engelbreit's Color ME Christmas Book of Postcards. Engelbreit, Mary, illus. 2017. (Illus.). 20p. (J). (gr. -1). pap. 9.99 ***(978-0-06-266327-6(5))*** HarperCollins Pubs.

Enyancha. Legends of the Garden: Faeries & Herbs: A Child's Activity Book for Exploring the Worlds of Faeries & Herbs. 2013. (ENG.). 56p. pap. 24.95 *(978-1-4327-9080-6(3))* Outskirts Pr., Inc.

Enz, Tammy. Build It Yourself, 4 vols., Set. Incl. Build Your Own Car, Rocket, & Other Things That Go. lib. bdg. 27.99 *(978-1-4296-5437-1(6));* Build Your Own Fort, Igloo, & Other Hangouts. Haus, Estudio, illus. lib. bdg. 27.99 *(978-1-4296-5436-4(8));* Build Your Own Mini Golf Course, Lemonade Stand, & Other Things to Do. lib. bdg. 27.99 *(978-1-4296-5438-8(4));* (gr. 3-4). (Build It Yourself Ser.). (ENG.). 32p. 2010. Set lib. bdg. 83.97 *(978-1-4296-5440-1(6),* Edge Bks.) Capstone Press of Coughlan Cos.

Epstein, Len. Presidents Facts & Fun Activity Book. 2012. (Dover Children's Activity Bks.). (ENG.). 48p. (J). (gr. 3-5). pap. 4.99 *(978-0-486-48277-4(4))* Dover Pubns., Inc.

Estellon, Pascale. The Color-Play Coloring Book. 2012. (ENG.). 24p. (J). (gr. -1-3). 16.99 *(978-1-4521-0545-1(6))* Chronicle Bks. LLC.

—Photo Finish. 2010. (ENG., Illus.). 64p. (J). (gr. k). pap. 10.95 *(978-1-934734-54-4(3))* Seven Footer Pr.

—Picture This. 2010. (ENG., Illus.). 64p. (J). (gr. k). pap. 10.95 *(978-1-934734-53-7(5))* Seven Footer Pr.

Etringer, Kathy. Mrs. E's Extraordinary Number Activities. Mitchell, Judy & Sussman, Ellen, eds. Rojas, Mary Galan, illus. 2006. 128p. (J). pap. 13.95 *(978-1-57310-506-4(6))* Teaching & Learning Co.

Evan-Moor. The Never-Bored Kid Book 2, Ages 6-7, Vol. 2. 2006. (Never-Bored Kid Book Ser.). (ENG., Illus.). 144p. (J). pap. 9.99 *(978-1-59673-158-5(3),* EMC 6309) Evan-Moor Educational Pubs.

—The Never-Bored Kid Book 2, Ages 7-8, Vol. 2. 2006. (Never-Bored Kid Book Ser.). (ENG., Illus.). 144p. (J). pap. 9.99 *(978-1-59673-159-2(1),* EMC6310) Evan-Moor Educational Pubs.

—The Never-Bored Kid Book 2, Ages 8-9, Vol. 2. 2006. (Never-Bored Kid Book Ser.). (ENG., Illus.). 144p. (J). pap. 9.99 *(978-1-59673-160-8(5),* EMC 6311) Evan-Moor Educational Pubs.

—The Never-Bored Kid Book, Ages 5-6. 2006. (Never-Bored Kid Book Ser.). (ENG., Illus.). 160p. (J). pap. 9.99 *(978-1-59673-154-7(0),* EMC 6303) Evan-Moor Educational Pubs.

Extreme Borders. 2008. (Cool Creations CD Rom Activity Books Ser.). 32p. *(978-1-4054-9585-1(5))* Parragon, Inc.

Fairley, Melissa. Superstar Pocket Activity Fun & Games: Games & Puzzles, Fold-Out Scenes, Patterned Paper, Stickers! 2014. (Pocket Activity Fun & Games Ser.). (ENG.). 96p. (J). (gr. 1-5). pap. 7.99 *(978-1-4380-0448-8(6))* Barron's Educational Series, Inc.

Falligant, Erin, ed. 3-D Studio. Laskey, Shannon, illus. 2008. 48p. (J). 17.95 *(978-1-59369-414-2(8))* American Girl Publishing, Inc.

Fanelli, Sara. The Onion's Great Escape. 2012. (ENG., Illus.). 68p. (gr. k-5). pap. 24.95 *(978-0-7148-5703-9(3))* Phaidon Pr., Inc.

Farquhar, Jackie, et al. Try This at Home: Planet-Friendly Projects for Kids. 2008. (ENG., Illus.). 96p. (J). (gr. 3-4). pap. 10.95 *(978-2-89579-192-8(9))* Owlkids Bks. Inc. CAN. Dist: Publishers Group West (PGW).

Fearns, Georgie. Dress up 5 Seconds of Summer. Fearns, Georgie, illus. 2016. (ENG., Illus.). 34p. (J). (gr. 1-3). pap. 9.99 *(978-1-78055-367-2(6))* O'Mara, Michael Bks., Ltd. GBR. Dist: Independent Pubs. Group.

Fearns, Georgie & Buster Books Staff. Dress up One Direction. Fearns, Georgie, illus. 2013. (ENG., Illus.). 34p. (J). (gr. 1-3). pap. 7.99 *(978-1-78055-162-3(2))* O'Mara, Michael Bks., Ltd. GBR. Dist: Independent Pubs. Group.

Feelings Garden Coloring & Activity Book. 2005. (J). *(978-0-9768827-2-5(8))* Prevention Through Puppetry, Inc.

Feldman, Jean. Dr Jean Variety Pack. 2007. (J). (gr. -1-3). pap. 56.87 incl. audio compact disk *(978-1-59198-719-2(9))* Creative Teaching Pr., Inc.

—Highway Letters, Numbers & Shapes: PreK-1. 2010. 80p. pap. 22.99 *(978-1-61601-036-2(3))* Creative Teaching Pr., Inc.

—Sing along & Read along with Dr. Jean All-in-One Pack (with Lap Books) 2009. pap. 58.86 incl. audio compact disk *(978-1-60689-163-6(4))* Youngheart Music.

Felix, Rebecca. Cool Toys & Games. 2016. (Cool Toys & Games Ser.: 6). (ENG.). 32p. (J). (gr. 3-6). lib. bdg. 171.00 *(978-1-68078-044-4(1),* Checkerboard Library) ABDO Publishing Co.

Fingerprint Fabulous: Create Sweet & Sparkly Thumbprint Art. 2010. (ENG.). 40p. (J). (gr. 1). spiral bd. 14.95 *(978-1-59174-748-2(1))* Klutz.

First Look & Find: Scooby Doo. 2013. 18p. (J). bds. 9.98 *(978-1-4508-6369-8(8),* 1450863698) Phoenix International Publications, Inc.

First Look & Find: Sofia the First. 2013. 12p. (J). bds. 9.98 *(978-1-4127-7211-2(7),* 1412772117) Phoenix International Publications, Inc.

First Sticker Learning Book. 2008. (Photographic Sticker Fun Learning Ser.). 48p. pap. *(978-1-4054-9555-4(3))* Parragon, Inc.

Fish, Sandra Palmer. Peace by Piece. 2012. (ENG.). pap. 19.05 *(978-1-4675-2679-1(7))* Independent Pub.

Fisher, Verna & Stone, Bryan. Explore Colonial America! 25 Great Projects, Activities, Experiments. 2009. (Explore Your World Ser.). (ENG., Illus.). 96p. (J). (gr. k-4). pap. 12.95 *(978-1-934670-37-8(5))* Octavio Publishing.

Fitchett, Jilda, 4th. Aunt Molly's Transition — Seeing Death in A New Light. 2006. (Illus.). 91p. (J). per. 15.95 *(978-0-9773244-0-8(0))* Light Line.

Fitzsimmons, Christy. Krissy & the Indians, 1 vol. Steckler, Megan, illus. 2009. 28p. pap. 24.95 *(978-1-61546-206-3(6))* America Star Bks.

Flad, Antje, illus. Hey, Who Did That? 2016. (Mini Movers Ser.). (ENG.). 12p. (J). (gr. -1 — 1). bds. 4.99 *(978-0-7641-6868-0(1))* Barron's Educational Series, Inc.

—Knock, Knock, Who's There? 2016. (Mini Movers Ser.). (ENG.). 12p. (J). (gr. -1 — 1). bds. 4.99 *(978-0-7641-6866-6(5))* Barron's Educational Series, Inc.

Flinn, Lisa & Younger, Barbara. Sharing God's Love in Children's Church: A Year's Worth of Programs for Children Ages 3-7. 2008. (Illus.). 136p. pap. 21.99 *(978-0-687-49165-0(7))* Abingdon Pr.

Florence, Debbi Michiko. Japan. Caputo, James, illus. 2009. (Kaleidoscope Kids Ser.). (ENG.). 96p. (J). (gr. 3-8). 19.99 *(978-0-8249-6828-1(X));* pap. 12.99 *(978-0-8249-6829-8(8))* Worthy Publishing. (Ideal Pubns.).

Flynn, Riley. Asking Questions & Finding Solutions. 2016. (Science & Engineering Practices Ser.). (ENG., Illus.). 24p. (gr. k-1). lib. bdg. 26.65 *(978-1-5157-0947-3(7),* Pebble Plus) Capstone Press of Coughlan Cos.

Fodor's Travel Publications, Inc. Staff. Get Outside Creativity Book. 2016. (ENG.). 80p. (J). (gr. 1-4). pap. 12.99 *(978-1-4263-2326-3(3),* National Geographic Children's Bks.) National Geographic Society.

Fogle, Robin. A Christmas Story. 2006. (J). pap. 1.79 *(978-1-59317-159-9(5))* Warner Pr., Inc.

Ford, Jason. The Superhero Comic Kit. 2015. (ENG., Illus.). 60p. (J). (gr. 2-6). pap. 19.95 *(978-1-78067-622-7(0))* King, Laurence Publishing GBR. Dist: Hachette Bk. Group.

Formaro, Amanda, et al. 101 Things to Do While You Poo: Activities, Puzzles, Games, Jokes, & Toilet-Paper Crafts to Keep You Busy While You Do Your Business! 2016. (101 Things Ser.). (ENG.). 176p. (J). (gr. 3-7). pap. 12.95 *(978-1-63322-081-2(8))* Quarto Publishing Group USA.

Forthun, Angela. Joozu! Activities for Beginners. 2004. (JPN.). 80p. (J). 49.95 *(978-1-86366-717-3(2))* Education Services Australia Ltd. AUS. Dist: Cheng & Tsui Co.

Foundotos, Zoe. Activities & Games. 2009. (ENG., Illus.). 240p. (J). (gr. -1-k). 17.95 *(978-1-57912-796-1(7),* 81796, Black Dog & Leventhal Pubs. Inc.) Hachette Bks.

Four, Melissa. Snowflake Friends: A Magnetic Playbook. 2008. (ENG., Illus.). 12p. (J). (gr. -1-k). bds. 14.95 *(978-1-4052-3039-1(8))* Egmont Bks., Ltd. GBR. Dist: Independent Pubs. Group.

Fowler, Eleri. Easter to Color. Fowler, Eleri, illus. 2017. (Illus.). 96p. (J). (gr. -1). pap. 15.99 *(978-0-06-256996-7(1))* HarperCollins Pubs.

Franceschelli, Christopher. Cityblock. Peskimo, illus. 2016. (Alphablock Ser.). (ENG.). 96p. (J). (gr. -1-k). bds. 16.95 *(978-1-4197-2189-2(5),* Abrams Appleseed) Abrams, Inc.

Frank, Lisa. A Magical World! Giant Coloring & Activity Book. 2010. (Lisa Frank Ser.). (Illus.). 96p. (J). 2.49 *(978-0-7666-3777-1(8))* Modern Publishing.

Free Spirit Publishing. Classroom Warm-Ups: Quick & Meaningful Activities for All Grades. 2014. (In a Jar(r) Ser.). (ENG.). (gr. -1-12). 9.99 *(978-1-57542-465-1(7))* Free Spirit Publishing, Inc.

—Icebreakers in a Jar(r). 2016. (In a Jar(r) Ser.). (ENG.). (J). (gr. 3-7). 9.99 *(978-1-63198-128-9(5))* Free Spirit Publishing, Inc.

French, Cathy. Make a Necklace. 2011. (Early Connections Ser.). (J). *(978-1-61672-235-7(5))* Benchmark Education Co.

—Make an Animal Mobile. 2011. (Early Connections Ser.). (J). *(978-1-61672-559-4(1))* Benchmark Education Co.

—Make an Island. 2011. (Early Connections Ser.). (J). *(978-1-61672-560-0(5))* Benchmark Education Co.

French, Felicity. Colour & Frame? Patterns. 2016. (ENG.). 64p. pap. 12.95 *(978-1-78243-585-3(9))* O'Mara, Michael Bks., Ltd. GBR. Dist: Independent Pubs. Group.

—Kids Unplugged Animal Adventures Activity Book. 2016. (ENG.). 64p. (J). 7.99 *(978-1-4413-1996-8(4))* Peter Pauper Pr. Inc.

Friedman, Pamela & Bauer, Larry. Activites de Fin d'Annee Scolaire. (FRE.). pap. *(978-0-439-98519-2(6))* Scholastic Canada, Ltd.

Friel, Helen, des. Midnight Creatures: A Pop-Up Shadow Search Book. 2016. (ENG., Illus.). 10p. (J). (gr. -1-1). 24.95 *(978-1-78067-822-1(3))* King, Laurence Publishing GBR. Dist: Hachette Bk. Group.

From Trash to Treasure. 2013. (From Trash to Treasure Ser.). 32p. (J). (gr. 3-6). 159.00 *(978-1-4777-1539-0(8));* pap. 423.00 *(978-1-4777-2704-1(3));* pap. 70.50 *(978-1-4777-2703-4(5))* Rosen Publishing Group, Inc., The. (PowerKids Pr.).

Fulcher, Roz. Science Around the House: Simple Projects Using Household Recyclables. 2010. (Dover Children's Science Bks.). (ENG., Illus.). 80p. (J). (gr. 3-5). pap. 6.99 *(978-0-486-47645-2(6))* Dover Pubns., Inc.

Fun to Learn Activity Book - Blue. 2005. (J). per. *(978-1-933581-50-7(6))* Byeway Bks.

Fun to Learn Activity Book - Red. 2005. (J). per. *(978-1-933581-49-1(2))* Byeway Bks.

Gaffney, Sean Kevin & Activity Books. AREA 51 UFO Maintenance & Repair Manual Activity Book. 2012. (Dover Children's Activity Bks.). (ENG., Illus.). 48p. (J). (gr. 3-5). pap. 7.99 *(978-0-486-49035-9(1))* Dover Pubns., Inc.

Galloway, Fhiona, illus. Busy Day Sticker Book. 2014. (My Little World Ser.). (ENG.). 14p. (J). pap. 3.99 *(978-1-58925-446-6(5))* Tiger Tales.

Galvin, Laura. The Big Wide World. 2006. (ENG., Illus.). 48p. (J). (gr. -1-2). pap., act. bk. ed. 3.99 *(978-1-59249-469-9(2),* 1C100) Soundprints.

Galvin, Laura Gates & Studio Mouse Editorial. Animals & Nature. 2006. (Peep & the Big Wide Worldtm Ser.). (ENG., Illus.). 48p. (J). (gr. -1-2). pap. 3.99 *(978-1-59249-470-5(6),* 1C101) Soundprints.

Gandolfi, Claudine. Scratch & Sketch Vikings: An Art Activity Book for Legendary Artists & Explorers of All Ages. Zschock, Martha Day, illus. 2015. (ENG.). 64p. (J). 12.99 *(978-1-4413-1813-8(5),* 9781441318138) Peter Pauper Pr. Inc.

Gaspas, Diane & Creative Haven Staff. Creative Haven Chinese Designs Coloring Book. 2013. (Adult Coloring Ser.). (ENG., Illus.). 64p. (gr. 3). pap. 5.99 *(978-0-486-49313-8(X))* Dover Pubns., Inc.

George, Joshua. Ancient Egyptians Sticker Book: Create Extraordinary Egyptian Sticker Scenes! Myer, Ed, illus. 2017. (Sticker History Ser.). (ENG.). 38p. (J). (gr. k-6). pap. 8.99 *(978-1-78445-873-7(2))* Top That! Publishing PLC GBR. Dist: Independent Pubs. Group.

—Ancient Romans Sticker Book: Create Riotous Roman Sticker Scenes! Myer, Ed, illus. 2017. (Sticker History Ser.). (ENG.). 38p. (J). (gr. k-6). pap. 8.99 *(978-1-78445-872-0(4))* Top That! Publishing PLC GBR. Dist: Independent Pubs. Group.

—Ice Age. Myer, Ed, illus. 2016. (Sticker History Ser.). (ENG.). 38p. (J). (gr. 2-6). pap. 8.99 *(978-1-78445-860-7(0))* Top That! Publishing PLC GBR. Dist: Independent Pubs. Group.

—Opposites with Animals. 2016. (ENG.). 10p. (J). (gr. -1-k). 9.99 *(978-1-78445-648-1(9))* Top That! Publishing PLC GBR. Dist: Independent Pubs. Group.

—Tracing: Early Learning Through Art. Stanley, Mandy, illus. 2017. (Arty Mouse Creativity Bks.). (ENG.). 48p. (J). (gr. -1-k). pap. 6.99 ***(978-1-78445-624-5(1))*** Top That! Publishing PLC GBR. Dist: Independent Pubs. Group.

—Vehicles. Crisp, Dan, illus. 2017. (Search & Find Ser.). (ENG.). 48p. (J). (gr. k-2). pap. 6.99 ***(978-1-78700-030-8(3))*** Top That! Publishing PLC GBR. Dist: Independent Pubs. Group.

George, Joshua. Vikings Sticker Book: Create Action-Packed Viking Sticker Scenes! Myer, Ed, illus. 2017. (Sticker History Ser.). (ENG.). 38p. (J). (gr. k-6). pap. 8.99 *(978-1-78445-866-9(X))* Top That! Publishing PLC GBR. Dist: Independent Pubs. Group.

Gibeau, Claire Janvier. Active Alphabet. 2009. 16p. pap. 8.49 *(978-1-4490-3828-1(X))* AuthorHouse.

Gibson, Karen Bush. Native American History for Kids: With 21 Activities. 2010. (For Kids Ser.). (ENG., Illus.). 144p. (J). (gr. 4-18). pap. 17.95 *(978-1-56976-280-6(5))* Chicago Review Pr., Inc.

Giddy Up Staff. Littlest Pet Shop Color N Carry II. 2009. act. bk. ed. 5.99 *(978-1-59524-267-9(8))* Giddy Up, LLC.

—Littlest Pet Shop ColorBlast. 2009. act. bk. ed. 7.99 *(978-1-59524-268-6(6))* Giddy Up, LLC.

—Transformers Color N Carry II. 2009. (J). act. bk. ed. 6.99 *(978-1-59524-269-3(4))* Giddy Up, LLC.

Giddy Up Staff, contrib. by. Blendy Pen Small Blister Kit. 2009. 6.99 *(978-0-9770652-8-8(6))* Giddy Up, LLC.

—Hannah Montana Surprize Ink Book. 2009. (J). 6.99 *(978-1-59524-430-7(1))* Giddy Up, LLC.

—High School Musical Surprize Ink Book. 2009. (J). 6.99 *(978-1-59524-435-2(2))* Giddy Up, LLC.

—Littlest Pet Shop Rub N Color Mini Book. 2009. 4.99 *(978-1-59524-322-5(4))* Giddy Up, LLC.

—Littlest Pet Shop Surprize Ink Book. 2009. (J). 6.99 *(978-1-59524-222-8(8))* Giddy Up, LLC.

—Littlest Pet Shop Surprize Ink Book 2. 2009. (J). 6.99 *(978-1-59524-287-7(2))* Giddy Up, LLC.

—Littlest Pet Shop Water Wow Book. 2009. 6.99 *(978-1-59524-223-5(6))* Giddy Up, LLC.

—Littlests Pet Shop Color Blast Mini. 2009. 4.99 *(978-1-59524-280-8(5))* Giddy Up, LLC.

—Mickey Color Blast Mini. 2009. 4.99 *(978-1-59524-317-1(8))* Giddy Up, LLC.

—Mickey Surprize Ink Book. 2009. 6.99 *(978-1-59524-293-8(7))* Giddy Up, LLC.

—Mickey Water Wow Book. 2009. 6.99 *(978-1-59524-304-1(6))* Giddy Up, LLC.

—My Little Pony Color Blast Mini. 2009. 4.99 *(978-1-59524-120-7(5))* Giddy Up, LLC.

—My Little Pony Surprize Ink Book 3. 2009. 6.99 *(978-1-59524-101-6(9))* Giddy Up, LLC.

—Princess Pop Beads How to Book. 2009. (J). 15.99 *(978-1-59524-407-9(7))* Giddy Up, LLC.

—Princess Water Wow Book. 2009. 14.14 *(978-1-159-52429-6(7))* General Bks. LLC.

—Sesame Street Surprize Ink Book 2. 2009. 6.99 *(978-1-59524-072-9(1))* Giddy Up, LLC.

—Spiderman Blendy Pen Poster Book. 2009. (J). 12.99 *(978-1-59524-457-4(3))* Giddy Up, LLC.

—Spiderman Color Blast Mini. 2009. 4.99 *(978-1-59524-488-8(3))* Giddy Up, LLC.

—Spiderman Surprize Ink Book. 2009. (J). 6.99 *(978-1-59524-036-1(5))* Giddy Up, LLC.

—Spiderman Surprize Ink Book2. 2009. 6.99 *(978-1-59524-100-9(0))* Giddy Up, LLC.

—Spiderman Water Wow Book. 2009. 6.99 *(978-1-59524-273-0(2))* Giddy Up, LLC.

—Sponge Bob Rub N Color Mini. 2009. 4.99 *(978-1-59524-443-7(3))* Giddy Up, LLC.

—SpongeBob Surprize Ink Book 4. 2009. 6.99 *(978-1-59524-205-1(8))* Giddy Up, LLC.

—Thomas Tank Rub N Color Mini Book. 2009. 4.99 *(978-1-59524-321-8(6))* Giddy Up, LLC.

—Thomas Tank Surprize Ink Book. 2009. 6.99 *(978-1-59524-288-4(0))* Giddy Up, LLC.

—Thomas Tank Water Wow Book. 2009. 6.99 *(978-1-59524-290-7(2))* Giddy Up, LLC.

—Tigger & Pooh Surprize Ink Book. 2009. (J). 6.99 *(978-1-59524-289-1(9))* Giddy Up, LLC.

—Transformers Animated Water Wow Book. 2009. 6.99 *(978-1-59524-434-5(4))* Giddy Up, LLC.

Giglio, Judy. Third Grade Scholar. Boyer, Robin, illus. 2005. (ENG.). 32p. (J). pap. 2.99 *(978-1-58947-458-1(9))* School Zone Publishing Co.

Gilkerson, Patricia. My Adventure in the Desert. 2006. 44p. (J). 8.99 *(978-1-59092-278-1(6))* Blue Forge Pr.

—My Adventure Inside a Volcano. 2006. 44p. (J). 8.99 *(978-1-59092-443-3(6))* Blue Forge Pr.

—My Adventure on a Ranch. 2006. 44p. (J). 8.99 *(978-1-59092-282-8(4))* Blue Forge Pr.

—My Adventure Scuba Diving. 2006. (My Adventure Ser.). 44p. (J). (gr. -1-3). pap. 8.99 *(978-1-59092-286-6(7))* Blue Forge Pr.

—My Adventure with Dogs. 2009. (ENG.). 44p. (J). 8.99 *(978-1-59092-451-8(7))* Blue Forge Pr.

—My Adventure with Eagles. 2009. (ENG.). 44p. (J). 8.99 *(978-1-59092-453-2(3))* Blue Forge Pr.

—My Adventure with Owls. 2009. (ENG.). 44p. (J). 8.99 *(978-1-59092-460-0(6))* Blue Forge Pr.

—My Adventure with Sea Horses. 2009. (ENG.). 44p. (J). 8.99 *(978-1-59092-465-5(7))* Blue Forge Pr.

—My Adventure with Sea Turtles. 2009. (ENG.). 44p. (J). 8.99 *(978-1-59092-466-2(5))* Blue Forge Pr.

—My Adventure with Sharks. 2009. (ENG.). 44p. (J). 8.99 *(978-1-59092-468-6(1))* Blue Forge Pr.

—My Adventure with Squirrels. 2009. (ENG.). 44p. (J). 8.99 *(978-1-59092-470-9(3))* Blue Forge Pr.

—My Adventure with Whales. 2009. (ENG.). 44p. (J). 8.99 *(978-1-59092-475-4(4))* Blue Forge Pr.

—My Adventure with Wild Horses. 2006. 44p. (J). 8.99 *(978-1-59092-312-2(X))* Blue Forge Pr.

—My Adventure with Wolves. 2009. (ENG.). 44p. (J). 8.99 *(978-1-59092-476-1(2))* Blue Forge Pr.

Gill, Mickey & Gill, Cheryl. Dude Diary 2. 2011. (ENG., Illus.). (J). (gr. 4-7). 10.99 *(978-1-892951-53-3(3))* Fine Print Publishing Co.

—Dude Diary 4: Write Stuff, Draw Randomly, Destroy If Needed! 2013. (ENG., Illus.). (J). pap. 10.99 *(978-1-892951-65-6(7))* Fine Print Publishing Co.

—New! Girl Diary: Your Days, Your Way! 2013. (ENG., Illus.). (J). 10.99 *(978-1-892951-68-7(1))* Fine Print Publishing Co.

Gillespie, L. Sticker Dressing Warriors. Ordas, Emi, illus. 2013. (Sticker Dressing Ser.). 34p. (J). pap. 8.99 *(978-0-7945-3353-3(1),* Usborne) EDC Publishing.

Gillespie, Lisa Jane. Sticker Dressing Extreme Sports. Ordas, Emi, illus. 2014. (Usborne Activities Ser.). (ENG.). 24p. (J). (gr. -1-3). 8.99 *(978-0-7945-3164-5(4),* Usborne) EDC Publishing.

Gilpen, Rebecca. Boy's Activity Book. 2013. (Doodle Bks). 96p. (J). pap. 12.99 *(978-0-7945-3171-3(7),* Usborne) EDC Publishing.

—Christmas Activity Book. 2012. (Activity Bks). 100p. (J). pap. 12.99 *(978-0-7945-3321-2(3),* Usborne) EDC Publishing.

Gilpin, Rebecca. Amazing Activity Book (formerly Boys' Activity Book) 2015. (Doodle Bks.). (ENG.). 96+ 4p. (J). (gr. k-5). pap. 12.99 *(978-0-7945-3527-8(5),* Usborne) EDC Publishing.

—Cosas de Hadas. 2005. (Titles in Spanish Ser.). (SPA.). 32p. (J). pap. 8.95 *(978-0-7460-6393-4(8),* Usborne) EDC Publishing.

—Travel Activity Book. 2013. (Doodle Bks). 96p. (J). pap. 12.99 *(978-0-7945-3287-1(X),* Usborne) EDC Publishing.

Gingold, Janet. My Adventure on a Lake: Advanced My Adventure. 2009. (ENG.). 72p. (J). pap. 9.99 *(978-1-59092-442-6(8))* Blue Forge Pr.

—My Adventure with Arthropods: Advanced My Adventure. 2007. 44p. (J). pap. 8.99 *(978-1-59092-447-1(9))* Blue Forge Pr.

—My Adventure with Reptiles: Advanced My Adventure. 2009. (ENG.). 72p. (J). pap. 9.99 *(978-1-59092-464-8(9))* Blue Forge Pr.

Gleisner, Jenna Lee. A Trip to the Pumpkin Patch. 2017. (Welcome, Fall! Ser.). (ENG.). 24p. (J). (gr. -1-2). lib. bdg. 27.07 *(978-1-5038-1664-0(8),* 211494) Child's World, Inc., The.

Goebel, Jenny. Foreman Farley Has a Backhoe. Van Doninck, Sebastiaan, illus. 2014. (Penguin Core Concepts Ser.). (ENG.). 32p. (J). (gr. -1-k). 3.99 *(978-0-448-46398-8(9),* Grosset & Dunlap) Penguin Young Readers Group.

Golden Books. Barbie Loves Parties (Barbie) Duarte, Pamela & Musselman, Christian, illus. 2014. (Full-Color Activity Book with Stickers Ser.). (ENG.). 32p. (J). (gr. -1-2). pap. 5.99 *(978-0-385-38495-7(5),* Golden Bks.) Random Hse. Children's Bks.

—Fry Cook Freak-Out! (SpongeBob SquarePants) Petrossi, Fabrizio, illus. 2014. (Color Plus Chunky Crayons Ser.). (ENG.). 48p. (J). (gr. -1-2). pap. 3.99 *(978-0-385-37430-9(5),* Golden Bks.) Random Hse. Children's Bks.

—Living the Dream Life (Barbie: Life in the Dream House) 2014. (Full-Color Activity Book with Stickers Ser.). (ENG., Illus.). 32p. (J). (gr. -1-2). pap. 4.99 *(978-0-385-37911-3(0),* Golden Bks.) Random Hse. Children's Bks.

—Mega-Mutations! (Teenage Mutant Ninja Turtles) Golden Books, illus. 2014. (Jumbo Coloring Book Ser.). (ENG., Illus.). 224p. (J). (gr. -1-2). pap. 5.99 *(978-0-385-38504-6(8),* Golden Bks.) Random Hse. Children's Bks.

—Numbers, Letters, & More! (PAW Patrol) Golden Books, illus. 2017. (Full-Color Activity Book with Stickers Ser.). (ENG., Illus.). 64p. (J). (gr. -1-2). pap. 6.99 ***(978-1-5247-6930-7(4),*** Golden Bks.) Random Hse. Children's Bks.

—On the Ball! Golden Books, illus. 2016. (Deluxe Paint Box Book Ser.). (ENG., Illus.). 128p. (J). (gr. -1-2). pap. 7.99 *(978-0-399-55494-0(7),* Golden Bks.) Random Hse. Children's Bks.

—Pat the Zoo (Pat the Bunny) LV Studio, illus. 2012. (Touch-And-Feel Ser.). (ENG.). 16p. (J). (gr. k — 1). 14.99 *(978-0-307-97797-7(8),* Golden Bks.) Random Hse. Children's Bks.

—Peeps Full-Color Activity Book (Peeps) Golden Books, illus. 2017. (Full-Color Activity Book with Stickers Ser.). (ENG., Illus.). 48p. (J). (gr. -1-2). pap. 5.99 *(978-1-5247-1909-8(9),* Golden Bks.) Random Hse. Children's Bks.

—Pet in the City. Golden Books, illus. 2016. (Color Plus Crayons & Sticker Ser.). (ENG., Illus.). 48p. (J). (gr. -1-2). pap. 4.99 *(978-0-399-55489-6(0),* Golden Bks.) Random Hse. Children's Bks.

—Puppy Love! (Bubble Guppies) Golden Books, illus. 2012. (Full-Color Activity Book with Stickers Ser.). (ENG., Illus.). 32p. (J). (gr. -1-2). pap. 3.99 *(978-0-307-98197-4(5),* Golden Bks.) Random Hse. Children's Bks.

—Ruff-Ruff Rescues! (Paw Patrol) Golden Books, illus. 2015. (Color & Paint Plus Stickers Ser.). (ENG., Illus.). 128p. (J). (gr. -1-2). pap. 9.99 *(978-0-553-52080-4(6),* Golden Bks.) Random Hse. Children's Bks.

—Secret Life of Pets. Golden Books, illus. 2016. (4 Color Plus 1,000 Stickers Ser.). (ENG., Illus.). 64p. (J). (gr. -1-2). pap. 12.99 *(978-0-399-55852-8(7),* Golden Bks.) Random Hse. Children's Bks.

—Secret Life of Pets Deluxe Stickerific (Secret Life of Pets) Golden Books, illus. 2016. (Deluxe Stickerific Ser.). (ENG., Illus.). 64p. (J). (gr. -1-2). pap. 5.99 *(978-0-399-55488-9(2),* Golden Bks.) Random Hse. Children's Bks.

—Sticker Celebration! (Nickelodeon) Golden Books, illus. 2015. (Color Plus 1,000 Stickers Ser.). (ENG., Illus.). 64p. (J). (gr. -1-2). pap. 9.99 *(978-0-553-52271-6(X),* Golden Bks.) Random Hse. Children's Bks.

—Trolls Paper Doll Playset. Golden Books, illus. 2017. (Reusable Sticker & Paper Doll Ser.). (ENG., Illus.). 24p. (J). (gr. 1-4). pap. 9.99 ***(978-1-5247-6396-1(9),*** Golden Bks.) Random Hse. Children's Bks.

Golden Books. Umi Egg Hunt (Team Umizoomi) Golden Books & Aikins, David, illus. 2013. (Full-Color Activity Book with Stickers Ser.). (ENG.). 32p. (J). (gr. -1-2). pap. 3.99 *(978-0-307-98211-7(4),* Golden Bks.) Random Hse. Children's Bks.

Golden Books Staff. Jumbo Coloring Party. Golden Books Staff, illus. 2010. (Jumbo Coloring Book Ser.). (ENG., Illus.). 224p. (J). (gr. -1-2). pap. 5.99 *(978-0-375-86352-3(4),* Golden Bks.) Random Hse. Children's Bks.

—The Lorax Deluxe Doodle Book. Gerardi, Jan, illus. 2013. (Super Coloring Book Ser.). (ENG.). 256p. (J). (gr. -1-2). pap. 9.99 *(978-0-449-81061-3(5),* Golden Bks.) Random Hse. Children's Bks.

—Mutants & Monsters! (Teenage Mutant Ninja Turtles) Golden Books Staff & Johnson, Shane, illus. 2016. (Hologramatic Sticker Book Ser.). (ENG.). 64p. (J). (gr. -1-2). pap. 4.99 *(978-1-101-93701-3(7),* Golden Bks.) Random Hse. Children's Bks.

—My Heart Is Happy! Fruchter, Jason, illus. 2009. (Hologramatic Sticker Book Ser.). (ENG.). 48p. (J). (gr. -1-2). pap. 3.99 *(978-0-375-85723-2(0),* Golden Bks.) Random Hse. Children's Bks.

—Rubble on the Double! (Paw Patrol) Golden Books Staff & Lovett, Nathaniel, illus. 2016. (Color Plus Crayons & Sticker Ser.). (ENG.). 48p. (J). (gr. -1-2). pap. 4.99 *(978-1-101-93699-3(1),* Golden Bks.) Random Hse. Children's Bks.

—Tree's Company. Mathieu, Joe & Ruiz, Aristides, illus. 2011. (Reusable Sticker Book Ser.). (ENG.). 12p. (J). (gr. -1-2). 6.99 *(978-0-375-86559-6(4),* Golden Bks.) Random Hse. Children's Bks.

—Wedding Bells. Sarl Aky-Aka Creations & Golden Books Staff, illus. 2008. (Hologramatic Sticker Book Ser.). (ENG.). 48p. (J). (gr. -1-2). pap. 3.99 *(978-0-375-84285-6(3),* Golden Bks.) Random Hse. Children's Bks.

Golden Books Staff & Artful Doodlers Limited Staff. Blue's Quilt. 2005. (Illus.). 32p. (J). (gr. -1-2). pap. 0.48 *(978-0-375-87512-0(3),* Golden Bks.) Random Hse. Children's Bks.

Golden Twomey, Emily, illus. Creative Copycat Coloring Book: Cool Pictures to Copy & Complete. 2016. (Copycat Coloring Bks.). (ENG.). 48p. (J). (gr. 1-5). pap. 6.99 *(978-1-4380-0840-0(6))* Barron's Educational Series, Inc.

Golding, Elizabeth. Challenging Coloring: Millions of Animals: Over 90 Awesome Coloring Pages. Mallet, Lisa et al, illus. 2017. (Challenging... Bks.). (ENG.). 96p. (J). (gr. 3-7). pap. 7.99 *(978-1-4380-0978-0(X))* Barron's Educational Series, Inc.

—Forty-Eight Funny Faces: Use the Cling-On Stickers to Make Funny Faces! Mallett, Lisa, illus. 2015. (ENG.). 56p. (J). (gr. -1-2). pap. 8.99 *(978-1-4380-0599-7(7))* Barron's Educational Series, Inc.

—Rainy Day Activity Fun & Games: Drawing, Searching, Numbers, More! Dot to Dot, Mazes, Puzzles Galore! Neradova, Maria, illus. 2016. (What Shall I Do? Bks.). (ENG.). 64p. (J). (gr. -1-2). bds. 8.99 *(978-0-7641-6863-5(0))* Barron's Educational Series, Inc.

—Sticker Stencil House. Skaltsas, Christos, illus. 2015. (ENG.). 31p. (J). (gr. k-4). 9.99 *(978-0-7641-6793-5(6))* Barron's Educational Series, Inc.

—Sunny Day Activity Fun & Games: Drawing, Searching, Numbers, More! Dot to Dot, Mazes, Puzzles Galore! Neradova, Maria, illus. 2016. (What Shall I Do? Bks.). (ENG.). 64p. (J). (gr. -1-2). bds. 8.99 *(978-0-7641-6864-2(9))* Barron's Educational Series, Inc.

Golding, Elizabeth & Gray, Dean. A Moonlight Book - Christmas Hide-and-Seek. 2016. (ENG., Illus.). 12p. (J). (gr. -1-17). 10.95 *(978-0-7624-5965-0(4),* Running Pr. Kids) Running Pr. Bk. Pubs.

Golliher, Bill & Vaughan, Jack, illus. Webber Interactive WH Questions Level 2: Whcd22. 2006. (J). cd-rom 49.99 *(978-1-58650-647-6(1))* Super Duper Pubns.

Gomi, Taro. Story Doodles Place Mats. 2012. (ENG., Illus.). 104p. (J). (gr. -1-17). 12.99 *(978-1-4521-0739-4(4))* Chronicle Bks. LLC.

Gonzales, Sharon, illus. Airport Explorers: 2008 Activity Book. 2008. 32p. (J). 6.95 *(978-0-9745294-2-4(7))* San Diego County Regional Airport Authority.

Good Attitudes Make You SHine. 2007. (Illus.). 48p. (J). pap. 15.00 *(978-0-9799440-0-0(7))* Artists On Video, LLC / (d/b/a) MN Productions.

Goodings, Christina. My Look & Point Story of Jesus Stick-A-Story Book. Hudson, Annabel, illus. 2015. (ENG.). 16p. (J). (gr. -1-k). 6.99 *(978-0-7459-6539-0(3))* Lion Hudson PLC GBR. Dist: Independent Pubs. Group.

Goodridge, Teresa. Glitter Girls Stickers. 2017. (Dover Little Activity Books Stickers Ser.). (ENG.). 4p. (J). (gr. 1-4). pap. 1.99 *(978-0-486-81561-9(7))* Dover Pubns., Inc.

—Happy Christmas Stickers. 2016. (Dover Little Activity Books Stickers Ser.). (ENG., Illus.). 4p. (J). (gr. k-3). pap. 1.99 *(978-0-486-80774-4(6))* Dover Pubns., Inc.

Goodwin, Brenda L., concept. The Mangoes & the Kids: Teach A Child, Change the World. 2007. (Illus.). 37p. 10.00 *(978-0-9745861-2-0(9))* Science & God, Inc.

Gordon, Lynn. 52 Fun Things to Do in the Car. Johnson, Karen & Synarski, Susan, illus. rev. ed. 2009. (ENG.). 54p. (J). (gr. -1-17). 6.95 *(978-0-8118-6371-1(9))* Chronicle Bks. LLC.

—52 Fun Things to Do on the Plane. Johnson, Karen & Synarski, Susan, illus. rev. ed. 2009. (ENG.). 54p. (J). (gr. -1-17). 6.95 *(978-0-8118-6372-8(7))* Chronicle Bks. LLC.

Gordon, Lynn & Chronicle Books Staff. Cool Tricks for Kids. Synarski, Susan & Johnson, Karen, illus. 2008. (ENG.). 54p. (gr. 8-17). 6.95 *(978-0-8118-6374-2(3))* Chronicle Bks. LLC.

Goren, Ada. Shoe Box Learning Centers - Sight Words: 30 Instant Centers with Reproducible Templates & Activities That Help Kids Learn 200+ Sight Words-Independently! 2012. (ENG.). 80p. (gr. k-2). pap. 12.99 *(978-0-545-24871-6(X),* Teaching Resources) Scholastic, Inc.

Graham, Ian. Build Your Own Cool Cars. 2004. (Illus.). 48p. *(978-0-439-67662-5(2))* Scholastic, Inc.

Granhold, Adriana. Mattie Knowsmath & the Great Shape Hunt. 2012. 32p. pap. 24.95 *(978-1-4626-7202-8(7))* America Star Bks.

Gravois, Michael. Reading Response Scrapbooking Activities: Reproducible Fonts, Clip Art, & Templates with Easy Step-by-Step Directions & Presentation Tips to Help All Students Showcase Their Learning. 2007. (ENG., Illus.). 80p. pap. 12.99 *(978-0-439-54893-9(4),* Teaching Resources) Scholastic, Inc.

Greaves, Helen & Greaves, Simon. Doodle Yourself Smart ... Math. 2012. (Doodle Bks.). (ENG., Illus.). 128p. pap. 12.95 *(978-1-60710-441-4(5),* Thunder Bay Pr.) Readerlink Distribution Services, LLC.

Green, John. Great Scenes from Horror Stories. 2012. (Dover Classic Stories Coloring Book Ser.). (ENG.). 32p. (gr. 3-5). pap. 3.99 *(978-0-486-48840-0(3))* Dover Pubns., Inc.

Green, John & Appelbaum, Stanley. Life in Old Japan Coloring Book. 2008. (Dover History Coloring Book Ser.). (ENG.). 48p. (J). (gr. 1-5). pap. 4.99 *(978-0-486-46883-9(6))* Dover Pubns., Inc.

Green, John & Blaisdell, Bob. Great Scenes from Dickens' Novels. 2005. (Dover Classic Stories Coloring Book Ser.). (ENG., Illus.). 32p. (J). (gr. 3-8). pap. 3.95 *(978-0-486-43985-3(2))* Dover Pubns., Inc.

Green, John & Drawing Staff. How to Draw Horses. 2009. (Dover How to Draw Ser.). (ENG., Illus.). 64p. (J). (gr. 1-4). pap. 4.99 *(978-0-486-46759-7(7))* Dover Pubns., Inc.

Green, John, et al. Merry Christmas! Stained Glass Coloring Book. 2008. (Holiday Stained Glass Coloring Book Ser.). (ENG., Illus.). 96p. (gr. 1-5). pap. 12.99 *(978-0-486-46944-7(1))* Dover Pubns., Inc.

Greenwald, Todd J., contrib. by. Wizards of Waverly Place Sticker Activity Book. 2009. (Wizards of Waverly Place Ser.). (Illus.). (J). pap. 4.99 *(978-0-7666-3308-7(X))* Modern Publishing.

Groeneweg, Nicole. Interactive Projects & Displays: Ideas for a Student-Created Learning Environment. F, Stacey, ed. Yamada, Jane, illus. 2006. (J). pap. 13.99 *(978-1-59198-315-6(0))* Creative Teaching Pr., Inc.

Grosset & Dunlap. Starry Sticker & Activity Book. 2013. (Magic Kitten Ser.). (ENG., Illus.). 32p. (J). (gr. k-3). 6.99 *(978-0-448-46581-4(7),* Grosset & Dunlap) Penguin Young Readers Group.

Guckian, Mara Ellen & Teacher Created Resources Staff. Alphabet Mystery Pictures, PreK-1. 2012. (Start to Finish (Teacher Created Resources) Ser.). (ENG., Illus.). 64p. pap. 6.99 *(978-1-4206-2787-9(2))* Teacher Created Resources, Inc.

—Number Mystery Pictures, Prek-1. 2012. (Start to Finish (Teacher Created Resources) Ser.). (ENG., Illus.). 64p. pap. 6.99 *(978-1-4206-2788-6(0))* Teacher Created Resources, Inc.

Gul, Hasibe, et al. My Wonderful Body. 2011. (ENG.). 16p. (J). (gr. -1 — 1). pap. 3.95 *(978-1-59784-241-9(9))* Tughra Bks.

—Nutritious Vegetables. 2011. (ENG.). 16p. (J). (gr. -1 — 1). pap. 3.95 *(978-1-59784-239-6(7))* Tughra Bks.

Gunes, Aysenur. Makkah & Madinah Activity Book. Polat, Ercan, illus. 2015. (Discover Islam Sticker Activity Bks.). (ENG.). 32p. (J). 5.95 *(978-0-86037-544-9(7))* Kube Publishing Ltd. GBR. Dist: Consortium Bk. Sales & Distribution.

—Mosques of the World Activity Book. Polat, Ercan, illus. 2015. (Discover Islam Sticker Activity Bks.). (ENG.). 32p. (J). 5.95 *(978-0-86037-539-5(0))* Kube Publishing Ltd. GBR. Dist: Consortium Bk. Sales & Distribution.

Gunnell, Beth, et al. Girls' Gorgeous World: Doodling & Colouring. Jackson, Katy et al, illus. 2015. (ENG.). 128p. (J). (gr. 2). pap. 12.99 *(978-1-78055-151-7(7))* O'Mara, Michael Bks., Ltd. GBR. Dist: Independent Pubs. Group.

—Summer Fun Doodles: Sunny Full-Color Pictures to Complete & Create. 2013. (ENG., Illus.). 128p. (J). (gr. -1-17). pap. 12.95 *(978-0-7624-4901-9(2),* Running Pr. Kids) Running Pr. Bk. Pubs.

Haas, Jessie. Horse Crazy! 1,001 Fun Facts, Craft Projects, Games, Activities, & Know-How for Horse-Loving Kids. 2009. (ENG., Illus.). 376p. (J). (gr. 3-8). pap. 16.95 *(978-1-60342-154-6(8),* 62154) Storey Publishing, LLC.

Hadley, Suzanne. Faithgirlz Handbook: How to Let Your Faith Shine Through. 2009. (Faithgirlz! Ser.). (ENG.). 96p. (J). (gr. 4-7). pap. 9.99 *(978-0-310-71966-3(6))* Zonderkidz.

Hagen, E. Happiness. 2012. 32p. pap. 17.25 *(978-1-4669-6450-1(2))* Trafford Publishing.

Hamaguchi, Carla. Letters, Numbers, Color & Shape Learning Centers. 2006. (Early Learning Ser.). (Illus.). 96p. (J). (gr. -1-1). pap. 20.99 *(978-1-59198-214-2(6),* 2228) Creative Teaching Pr., Inc.

—Letters, Numbers, Colors & Shapes Activity Pages. 2006. (Illus.). 144p. (J). (gr. -1-1). per. 15.99 *(978-1-59198-225-8(1),* 2227) Creative Teaching Pr., Inc.

Hamlet: Activity Pack. 2003. 133p. (YA). pap. *(978-1-58049-622-3(9),* PA0121) Prestwick Hse., Inc.

Hammah, Aisha. The Image Game. Stubblefield, Linda, ed. Hammah, Aisha, illus. 2013. (Illus.). 192p. pap. *(978-0-9810759-8-3(3));* pap. *(978-0-9810759-3-8(2))* WTL International.

Handford, Martin. Where's Waldo? the Treasure Hunt: Activity Book. Handford, Martin, illus. 2016. (Where's Waldo? Ser.). (ENG., Illus.). 96p. (J). (gr. 2-5). pap. 12.99 *(978-0-7636-8811-0(8))* Candlewick Pr.

Hannah, Waldron & Magma Books Staff. Magic & Fairy-Tale Dice. 2012. (ENG., Illus.). 14.95 *(978-1-85669-919-8(6))* King, Laurence Publishing GBR. Dist: Hachette Bk. Group.

Hansen Moench, Megan. Know Your State Activity Book Utah, 1 vol. Padavick, Nate, illus. 2015. (ENG.). 272p. (J). pap. 14.99 *(978-1-4236-4056-1(X))* Gibbs Smith, Publisher.

—Know Your State Activity Book Washington, 1 vol. Padavick, Nate, illus. 2015. (ENG.). 272p. (J). pap. 14.99 *(978-1-4236-4059-2(4))* Gibbs Smith, Publisher.

Hanson, Anders & Mann, Elissa. Cool String Art: Creative Activities That Make Math & Science Fun for Kids!, 1 vol. 2013. (Cool Art with Math & Science Ser.). (ENG.). 32p. (J). (gr. 3-6). lib. bdg. 28.50 *(978-1-61783-824-8(1),* Checkerboard Library) ABDO Publishing Co.

—Cool Structures: Creative Activities That Make Math & Science Fun for Kids!, 1 vol. 2013. (Cool Art with Math & Science Ser.). (ENG.). 32p. (J). (gr. 3-6). lib. bdg. 28.50 *(978-1-61783-825-5(X),* Checkerboard Library) ABDO Publishing Co.

—Cool Tessellations: Creative Activities That Make Math & Science Fun for Kids!, 1 vol. 2013. (Cool Art with Math & Science Ser.). (ENG.). 32p. (J). (gr. 3-6). lib. bdg. 28.50 *(978-1-61783-826-2(8),* Checkerboard Library) ABDO Publishing Co.

Hanson, P. H. My Mommy's Tote. 2013. (ENG.). 16p. (J). (gr. -1-1). 14.95 *(978-0-7611-7740-1(X),* 17740) Workman Publishing Co., Inc.

Harding, James. From Wibbleton to Wobbleton: Adventures with the Elements of Music & Movement. Noyes, Eli, illus. 2014. (Pentatonic Press Integrated Learning Ser.: 3). (ENG.). 201p. pap. 32.00 *(978-0-9773712-5-9(5))* Pentatonic Pr.

Hargrove, Julia. Tomb of the Unknowns. 2003. (Historic Monuments Ser.). (Illus.). 48p. (J). pap. 6.95 *(978-1-57310-405-0(1))* Teaching & Learning Co.

Haring, Keith. Nina's Book of Little Things. Haring, Keith, illus. 2013. (ENG., Illus.). 80p. (J). (gr. 1-4). pap. 19.99 *(978-0-7636-6893-8(1),* Big Picture Press) Candlewick Pr.

Harper, Valentina. Creative Coloring Animals: Art Activity Pages to Relax & Enjoy! 2014. (ENG., Illus.). 72p. pap. 9.99 *(978-1-57421-971-5(5),* Design Originals) Fox Chapel Publishing Co., Inc.

Harvest House Publishers. The Jesus Bible for Kids Coloring Book. International Publishing Services Pty Ltd, illus. 2017. (ENG.). 160p. (J). 9.99 *(978-0-7369-6999-4(3))* Harvest Hse. Pubs.

Hasibe, Gul & Balci. Delicious Fruits. 2011. (ENG.). 16p. (J). (gr. -1 — 1). pap. 3.95 *(978-1-59784-240-2(0))* Tughra Bks.

Hattenhauer, Ina, illus. Dollhouse Sticker Book. 2012. (Sticker Activity Book Ser.). 24p. (J). pap. 8.99 *(978-0-7945-2944-4(5),* Usborne) EDC Publishing.

Haugen-McLane, Janie. Real-World Picture Words Software - Household Words. 2004. (J). cd-rom 69.95 *(978-1-58804-374-0(6))* P C I Education.

—Real-World Picture Words Software - Kitchen/Bathroom Words. 2004. (J). cd-rom 69.95 *(978-1-58804-375-7(4))* P C I Education.

Hauser, Jill Frankel. Kindergarten Success: Helping Children Excel Right from the Start. Hauser, Savlan, illus. (ENG.). 128p. (J). (gr. 3-7). 2008. per. 14.25 *(978-0-8249-6758-1(5))* 2005. 14.95 *(978-0-8249-6777-2(1))* Worthy Publishing. (Ideal Pubns.).

Haws, Ileen. Nothin' 2 Do. 2008. 67p. pap. 9.90 *(978-1-4357-3654-2(0))* Lulu Pr., Inc.

Hay, Sam. The Nutcracker. Dudziuk, Kasia, illus. 2017. (3D Colouring & Activity Ser.). (ENG.). 24p. (J). (gr. 1-4). pap. 11.99 ***(978-1-4052-7912-3(5))*** Egmont Bks., Ltd. GBR. Dist: Independent Pubs. Group.

Hayes, Susan. Read It Build It - Skyscraper. Abbott, Simon, illus. 2016. (Read It Build It Ser.). (ENG.). 16p. (J). (gr. -1-k). 15.99 *(978-1-4052-7164-6(7))* Egmont Bks., Ltd. GBR. Dist: Independent Pubs. Group.

Haynes, Betsy. My Adventure Panning for Gold. 2007. 44p. (J). 8.99 *(978-1-59092-444-0(4))* Blue Forge Pr.

Haynes-Mayes, Ingrid. A Recipe of Ideas for Phonemic Awareness & Phonics: Hands-on Activities for Primary Grades. 2006. (J). per. *(978-1-59872-635-0(8))* Instant Pub.

Headway Level A Thinking Book. (J). *(978-0-89688-280-5(2),* 88-280) Open Court Publishing Co.

Hecht, Kristina. A Bird & a Bee, 1 vol. 2009. 16p. pap. 24.95 *(978-1-60836-408-4(9))* America Star Bks.

Hedde, Rebecca. Science with Magnets. rev. ed. 2008. (Science Activities Ser.). 24p. (J). pap. 5.99 *(978-0-7945-1406-8(5),* Usborne) EDC Publishing.

Heimberg, Justin. The Spirit Glass: A Book of Magically Hidden Images. 2011. (ENG., Illus.). 32p. (J). (gr. 2). 16.95 *(978-1-934734-49-0(7))* Seven Footer Pr.

Heller, Ruth, illus. Wildflowers. 2011. (Designs for Coloring Ser.). (ENG.). 64p. (J). (gr. 1-4). 6.99 *(978-0-448-45462-7(9),* Grosset & Dunlap) Penguin Young Readers Group.

Hendrickson Publishers, creator. The Explorer Bible. 2006. (Illus.). 190p. (J). (gr. -1-3). pap. 12.95 *(978-1-59856-042-8(5))* Hendrickson Pubs. Marketing, LLC.

Henig, Sherry. Group Rules! The Social Skills & Ground Rules for Children's Groups. 2008. (Illus.). 32p. (J). pap. *(978-0-9777203-5-4(7))* Brenner Publishing, LLC.

Heos, Bridget. Brain Quest Workbook: Grade 5. Rockefeller, Matt, illus. 2015. (ENG.). 320p. (J). (gr. 5-5). pap. 12.95 *(978-0-7611-8278-8(0))* Workman Publishing Co., Inc.

Heos, Bridget, et al. Summer Brain Quest: Between Grades 4 And 5. Thomas, Chad & Yan, Edison, illus. 2017. (Summer Brain Quest Ser.). (ENG.). 160p. (J). (gr. 4-5). pap. 12.95 *(978-0-7611-8920-6(3))* Workman Publishing Co., Inc.

Herbert, Janis. Abraham Lincoln for Kids: His Life & Times with 21 Activities. 2007. (For Kids Ser.). (ENG., Illus.). 160p. (J). (gr. 4-7). pap. 16.95 *(978-1-55652-656-5(3))* Chicago Review Pr., Inc.

Hewitt, Angie. First Numbers: Touch-And-Trace Early Learning Fun! 2017. (Little Groovers Ser.). (ENG., Illus.). 12p. (J). (— 1). bds. 7.99 *(978-1-5107-0838-9(3),* Sky Pony Pr.) Skyhorse Publishing Co., Inc.

Hibbard, Derrick. College Fast Track: Essential Habits for Less Stress & More Success. 2011. (ENG.). 123p. pap. 12.95 *(978-1-888960-23-5(X))* Fine Print Pr., The.

Hickerson, Brandy. My Brother & Me. 2008. 60p. pap. 31.99 *(978-1-4363-1635-4(9))* Xlibris Corp.

Highlights, creator. The Jumbo Book of Things to Find & Color. 2017. (Highlights(tm) Jumbo Books & Pads Ser.). (ENG.). 256p. (J). (gr. -1-k). pap. 12.99 *(978-1-62979-779-3(0),* Highlights) Boyds Mills Pr.

Highlights for Children, compiled by. Fun at School. 2009. (Hidden Pictures Playground Ser.). (ENG., Illus.). 32p. (J). (gr. -1-1). pap. 5.49 *(978-0-87534-319-8(8))* Highlights for Children.

—Good Sports. 2009. (Hidden Pictures Playground Ser.). (ENG., Illus.). 32p. (J). (gr. -1-1). pap. 5.49 *(978-0-87534-320-4(1))* Highlights for Children.

—Highlights Hidden Picture Playground: on Vacation. 2009. (Highlights Hidden Pictures Ser.). (ENG., Illus.). 32p. (J). (gr. -1-1). pap. 5.49 *(978-0-87534-321-1(X))* Highlights for Children.

Highlights for Children Editorial Staff. The Big Fun Book of Kindergarten Activities. 2017. (Highlights(tm) Big Fun Activity Workbooks Ser.). (ENG.). 256p. (J). (gr. -1-k). pap. 12.99 *(978-1-62979-763-2(4),* Highlights) Boyds Mills Pr.

—The Big Fun Book of Preschool Activities. 2017. (Highlights(tm) Big Fun Activity Workbooks Ser.). (ENG.). 256p. (J). (gr. -1-k). pap. 12.99 *(978-1-62979-762-5(6),* Highlights) Boyds Mills Pr.

Highlights for Children Editorial Staff, compiled by. All about Fall. 2016. (Highlights(tm) All about Activity Bks.). (ENG.). 32p. (J). (gr. -1-k). pap. 4.99 *(978-1-62979-539-3(9),* Highlights) Boyds Mills Pr.

—All about Summer. 2016. (All about Activity Bks.). (ENG.). 32p. (J). (gr. -1-k). pap. 4.99 *(978-1-62979-538-6(0),* Highlights) Boyds Mills Pr.

—Animal Antics. 2016. (Hidden Pictures#174; Silly Fill-In Stories Ser.). (ENG.). 64p. (J). (gr. k-4). pap. 4.99 *(978-1-62979-550-8(X),* Highlights) Boyds Mills Pr.

Highlights for Children Editorial Staff, creator. All about Spring. 2017. (All about Activity Bks.). (ENG.). 32p. (J). (gr. -1-k). pap. 4.99 *(978-1-62979-696-3(4),* Highlights) Boyds Mills Pr.

—Christmas Fun. 2016. (Highlights(tm) Carry-And-Play Board Bks.). (ENG.). 24p. (J). (gr. -1-k). bds. 8.99 *(978-1-62979-711-3(1),* Highlights) Boyds Mills Pr.

—Find It! Animals. 2016. (Highlights(tm) Find It! Lift-The-Flap Board Bks.). (ENG.). 14p. (J). (— 1). 7.99 *(978-1-62979-537-9(2),* Highlights) Boyds Mills Pr.

—Halloween Fun. 2016. (Highlights(tm) Carry-And-Play Board Bks.). (ENG.). 24p. (J). (gr. -1-k). bds. 8.99 *(978-1-62979-710-6(3),* Highlights) Boyds Mills Pr.

—Imagine & Draw. 2016. (Highlights(tm) Write-On Wipe-off Activity Bks.). (ENG.). 28p. (J). (gr. k-3). pap. 8.99 *(978-1-62979-699-4(9),* Highlights) Boyds Mills Pr.

—Jumbo Pad of Puzzling Fun. 2016. (Highlights(tm) Jumbo Books & Pads Ser.). (ENG.). 256p. (J). (gr. k-4). pap. 12.99 *(978-1-62979-617-8(4),* Highlights) Boyds Mills Pr.

—That's Silly! 2016. (Highlights(tm) Write-On Wipe-off Activity Bks.). (ENG.). 28p. (J). (gr. -1-k). pap. 8.99 *(978-1-62979-544-7(5),* Highlights) Boyds Mills Pr.

Highlights for Children Editorial Staff & Boyds Mills Press Staff. Highlights Hidden Pictures Sticker Fun, Vol. 2. 2007. (Highlights Hidden Pictures#174; Sticker Fun Ser.). (ENG., Illus.). 16p. (J). (gr. k-2). pap. 5.95 *(978-0-87534-232-0(9))* Boyds Mills Pr.

Highlights Staff, compiled by. Find It! First Words. 2016. (Find It! Lift-The-Flap Board Bks.). (ENG.). 14p. (J). (— 1). 7.99 *(978-1-62979-536-2(4),* Highlights) Boyds Mills Pr.

—Silly School. 2016. (Hidden Pictures#174; Silly Fill-In Stories Ser.). (ENG.). 64p. (J). (gr. k-4). pap. 4.99 *(978-1-62979-551-5(8),* Highlights) Boyds Mills Pr.

Hill, Kevin. A - Z Animal Coloring & Activity Book: English & Spanish. 2012. 60p. (gr. -1). pap. 12.95 *(978-1-4772-0407-8(5))* AuthorHouse.

Hinkler Books, creator. Pop Diva Make-Up Kit. 2014. (Glamour Girl Ser.). (ENG., Illus.). (J). (gr. 4-7). *(978-1-74352-899-0(X))* Hinkler Bks. Pty, Ltd.

S

—Princess Make-Up Kit. 2014. (Glamour Girl Ser.). (ENG., Illus.). (J). (gr. 4-7). *(978-1-74352-898-3(1))* Hinkler Bks. Pty, Ltd.

Hinkler Books, ed. My Amazing Sticker Activity Book. 2012. 48p. (J). 10.99 *(978-1-74308-633-9(4))* Hinkler Bks. Pty, Ltd. AUS. Dist: Ideals Pubns.

—My Pretty Pink Tea Party. 2012. 40p. (J). 19.99 *(978-1-74308-981-1(3))* Hinkler Bks. Pty, Ltd. AUS. Dist: Ideals Pubns.

Hodgson, Julie. Fun with Number Rhymes for the Early Years. 2005. (Illus.). 96p. pap. *(978-1-903853-72-6(9))* Brilliant Pubns.

Hoerner, L. Cat & Dog Dress up Sticker Paper Dolls. 2015. (Dover Little Activity Books Paper Dolls Ser.). (ENG.). 4p. (J). (gr. k-3). 1.50 *(978-0-486-79371-9(0))* Dover Pubns., Inc.

—Fanciful Fairies & Dazzling Dragons Coloring Book. 2013. (ENG.). 32p. (gr. 3-6). pap. 3.99 *(978-0-486-49979-6(0))* Dover Pubns., Inc.

Hoffman, Joan. Tracing Trails Pre-Writing Skills. 2008. (ENG.). 32p. (J). pap. 3.99 *(978-1-60159-117-3(9))* School Zone Publishing Co.

Holdaway, Chelsea. The Sabbath Is a Special Day: A Sacrament Meeting Activity Book. 2017. (ENG.). (J). (gr. -1-k). pap. 5.99 ***(978-1-4621-2105-2(5))*** Cedar Fort, Inc./CFI Distribution.

Holden, Pam. Make a Scarecrow. Storey, Jim, illus. 2015. (ENG.). 16p. (-1). pap. *(978-1-77654-133-1(2)*, Red Rocket Readers) Flying Start Bks.

Holland, Beth. Webber HearBuilder Following Directions Fun Sheets: Hbbk55. Ink, Bruce & Golliher, Bill, illus. 2011. 216p. (J). spiral bd. 34.95 net. *(978-1-58650-992-7(6))* Super Duper Pubns.

Hollihan, Kerrie Logan. Theodore Roosevelt for Kids: His Life & Times, 21 Activities. 2010. (For Kids Ser.). (ENG., Illus.). 144p. (J). (gr. 4-18). pap. 16.95 *(978-1-55652-955-9(4))* Chicago Review Pr., Inc.

Holmqvist, Lisa. Paint with the Masters Coloring Book. 2008. (ENG., Illus.). 48p. pap. 9.95 *(978-91-85639-13-7(3))* Dokument forlag, Fotograf Malcolm Jacobsson SWE. Dist: SCB Distributors.

Holt, William T. Brand New Shoes Coloring & Activity Book. 2013. (Illus.). 66p. pap. 5.75 *(978-0-9895062-1-2(5))* SearlStudio Publishing.

Honig, Bruce. In Pursuit of the Aha! & Ha! Ha! Ha!: Games & Activities for Kids & Their Parents. 2009. 97p. pap. 12.90 *(978-1-4116-2959-2(0))* Lulu Pr., Inc.

—The Pursuit of the Aha & Ha! Ha! Ha!: Games & Activities That Support, Challenge & Use Creative Thinking (Divergent) in the Classroom. 2009. 97p. pap. 12.92 *(978-1-4116-3052-9(1))* Lulu Pr., Inc.

Hopscotch Set C Add-On Package. 2013. pap. 85.50 *(978-1-61391-264-5(1))* Pacific Learning, Inc.

Hourglass Press, Hourglass & Sauza, Saul. The Super-Deluxe, Epic Journal of Awesomeness. 2015. (ENG.). 64p. (J). (gr. 1-7). pap. 5.99 *(978-0-486-78328-4(6))* Dover Pubns., Inc.

House, Katherine L. Lighthouses for Kids: History, Science, & Lore with 21 Activities. 2008. (For Kids Ser.). (ENG., Illus.). 128p. (J). (gr. 4-7). pap. 16.95 *(978-1-55652-720-3(9))* Chicago Review Pr., Inc.

Hruby, Patrick. Natural Wonders: A Patrick Hruby Coloring Book. 2011. (ENG.). 32p. pap. 9.95 *(978-1-934429-71-6(6))* AMMO Bks., LLC.

Huffman, Julie. 101 Ways to Gross Out Your Friends: Science Experiments, Jokes, Activities & Recipes for Loads of Gross, Gooey Fun. 2016. (101 Series for Kids Ser.). (ENG., Illus.). 144p. (J). (gr. 3-7). pap. 12.95 *(978-1-63322-168-0(7)*, Walter Foster Jr) Quarto Publishing Group USA.

Hughes, Mónica. Stripes. 2005. (Big Cat Ser.). (gr. k-2). pap. 6.50 *(978-0-60457-021-2(0))* Pacific Learning, Inc.

Hunter, Hannah Klaus. Be Happy & Color! Mindful Activities & Coloring Pages for Kids. 2016. (ENG.). 96p. (J). (gr. k-6). pap. 12.95 *(978-1-63322-101-7(6)*, Walter Foster Jr) Quarto Publishing Group USA.

Ikids. Fashion Girls Around the World. 2010. (ENG., Illus.). 10p. (J). (gr. -1-1). 19.99 *(978-1-58476-960-6(2))* Innovative Kids.

I'm a Flower Girl! Activity & Sticker Book. 2016. (ENG., Illus.). 32p. (J). pap. 4.99 *(978-1-61963-993-5(9)*, 9781619639935, Bloomsbury Activity Bks.) Bloomsbury Publishing USA.

In the Garden. 2012. (Collins Big Cat Ser.). (ENG., Illus.). 16p. (J). pap., wbk. ed. 4.99 *(978-0-00-747489-9(X))* HarperCollins Pubs. Ltd. GBR. Dist: Independent Pubs. Group.

Information Explorer, 16 vols., Set. Incl. Super Smart Information Strategies: Creating a Digital Portfolio. Rabbat, Suzy. 2011. lib. bdg. 28.50 *(978-1-61080-121-8(0)*, 201128); Super Smart Information Strategies: Find the Right Site. Truesdell, Ann. 2010. lib. bdg. 28.50 *(978-1-60279-638-6(6)*, 200341); Super Smart Information Strategies: Find Your Way Online. Rabbat, Suzy. 2010. lib. bdg. 28.50 *(978-1-60279-639-3(4)*, 200342); Super Smart Information Strategies: Get Ready for a Winning Science Project. Buczynski, Sandra. 2011. lib. bdg. 28.50 *(978-1-61080-124-9(5)*, 201134); Super Smart Information Strategies: Go Straight to the Source. Fontichiaro, Kristin. 2010. lib. bdg. 28.50 *(978-1-60279-640-9(8)*, 200343); Super Smart Information Strategies: Hit the Books. Rabbat, Suzy. 2010. lib. bdg. 28.50 *(978-1-60279-641-6(6)*, 200344); Super Smart Information Strategies: Make the Grade. Gordon, Carol. 2010. lib. bdg. 28.50 *(978-1-60279-642-3(4)*, 200345); Super Smart Information Strategies: Online Etiquette & Safety. Cornwall, Phyllis. 2010. lib. bdg. 28.50 *(978-1-60279-956-1(3)*, 200637); Super Smart Information Strategies: Podcasting 101. Fontichiaro, Kristin. 2010. lib. bdg. 28.50 *(978-1-60279-953-0(9)*, 200631); Super Smart Information Strategies: Put It All Together. Cornwall, Phyllis. 2010. lib. bdg. 28.50 *(978-1-60279-643-0(2)*, 200346); Super Smart Information Strategies: Shooting Video to Make Learning Fun. Green, Julie. 2010. lib. bdg. 28.50 *(978-1-60279-955-4(5)*, 200635); Super Smart Information Strategies: Social Studies Projects That Shine. Wilkie, Sara. 2011. lib. bdg. 28.50 *(978-1-61080-123-2(7)*, 201132); Super Smart Information Strategies: Team up Online. Pascaretti, Vicki & Wilkie, Sara. 2010. lib. bdg. 28.50 *(978-1-60279-644-7(0)*, 200347); Super Smart Information Strategies: Using Digital Images. Rabbat, Suzy. 2010. lib. bdg. 28.50 *(978-1-60279-954-7(7)*, 200633); Super Smart Information Strategies: Write It Down. Green, Julie. 2010. lib. bdg. 28.50 *(978-1-60279-645-4(9)*, 200348); Super Smart Information Strategies: Your Fascinating Family History. Johnson, Mary J. 2011. lib. bdg. 28.50 *(978-1-61080-122-5(9)*, 201130); 32p. (gr. 4-8). 2011. Set lib. bdg. 456.00 *(978-1-61080-149-2(0))* Cherry Lake Publishing.

Ingram, Zoe. America the Beautiful to Color: A Road Trip to Color By. Ingram, Zoe, illus. 2017. (Illus.). 96p. (J). (gr. -1). pap. 15.99 *(978-0-06-256990-5(2))* HarperCollins Pubs.

Inkpen, Mick. Kipper's, Bk. 1. 2004. (ENG., Illus.). 24p. (J). (gr. -1-k). pap., act. bk. ed. 4.99 *(978-0-340-85525-6(8))* Hodder & Stoughton GBR. Dist: Hachette Bk. Group.

J., Mary & Davis, Wayne R. Spur of the Moment Preschool. 2005. (Godprints Bible Funstuff Ser.). 112p. pap., pap. 16.99 *(978-0-7814-4230-5(3)*, 0781442303) Cook, David C.

Jacobson, John, et al. Say Hello Wherever You Go: Music Strategies, Songs & Activities for Grades K-2. 2010. (ENG.). 40p. pap. 19.99 incl. audio compact disk *(978-1-4234-8824-8(5)*, 1423488245) Leonard, Hal Corp.

Jacobson, Ryan. Constellations Activity Book, 1 vol. Nitzsche, Shane, illus. 2012. (Color & Learn Ser.). (ENG.). 64p. (J). (gr. k-5). pap. 6.95 *(978-1-59193-325-0(0))* Adventure Pubns.

Jan, Young. The Orange Slipknot Curriculum Unit. 2008. 138p. spiral bd. *(978-0-9772525-6-5(6))* Raven Publishing Inc. of Montana.

Jaramillo, Gloria. Busy Kids' Colors, Shapes & Sizes. Poirier, Nadine, illus. 2008. (Busy Kids Ser.). 36p. (J). (gr. -1-k). bds. 12.99 *(978-2-7641-1677-7(2))* Gardner Pubns.

Jensen, Pamela. Reverently, Quietly: Sacrament Meeting Activity Book. 2014. pap. 5.99 *(978-1-4621-1215-9(3)*, Horizon Pubs.) Cedar Fort, Inc./CFI Distribution.

Jerome, Kate B. Lucky to Live in Texas. 2017. (Arcadia Kids Ser.). (ENG., Illus.). 32p. (J). 16.99 ***(978-0-7385-2769-7(6))*** Arcadia Publishing.

Jiang, Helga. Clay Charm Magic! 25 Amazing, Teeny-Tiny Projects to Make with Polymer Clay. 2014. (ENG.). 128p. (J). (gr. k). 12.95 *(978-1-63220-398-4(7)*, Sky Pony Pr.) Skyhorse Publishing Co., Inc.

Joel's Library Jam, 1 VHS cassette. 2005. (J). VHS, cd-rom *(978-0-9744419-1-7(0)*, CET) Greater Cincinnati TV Educational Foundation.

Johnson, Dirk, illus. Purdue University Coloring & Activity Adventure Book. 2007. 52p. (J). pap. *(978-0-9790923-0-5(2))* DirkDesigns, LLC.

Johnson, Robin. Toys & Games in Different Places. 2017. 24p. (J). ***(978-0-7787-3662-2(8))*** Crabtree Publishing Co.

Johnstone, Michael. Fun Time Teddy Bear Stickers: Sticker & Colour-In Playbook with over 200 Reusable Stickers. Tulip, Jenny, illus. 2017. (ENG.). 72p. (J). (gr. -1-12). pap. 8.99 *(978-1-86147-771-2(6)*, Armadillo) Anness Publishing GBR. Dist: National Bk. Network.

Jones, Karl & Price, Stern. Thanksgiving Activity Book. Chou, Joey, illus. 2015. (ENG.). 16p. (J). (gr. 3-7). bds. 9.99 *(978-0-8431-8296-5(2)*, Price Stern Sloan) Penguin Young Readers Group.

Joseph, Patricia L. This Is Bb. 2008. 20p. pap. 24.95 *(978-1-60672-351-7(0))* PublishAmerica, Inc.

K 1001 Learning Activities. 2013. (gr. k-k). spiral bd. 12.99 *(978-1-4508-5666-9(7)*, 1450856667) Phoenix International Publications, Inc.

Kagan, Miguel. Match Mine: Language Builder. 2008. per. 19.00 *(978-1-879097-21-6(4))* Kagan Publishing.

Kalman, Bobbie. I Can Do It! 2011. (ENG.). 16p. (J). *(978-1-4271-1015-2(8))* Crabtree Publishing Co.

Kampia, Judy. God's Great Book: A Complete Collection of Bible Stories & Activities for All Ages. 2007. 596p. 36.99 *(978-1-4257-4890-6(2))* Xlibris Corp.

Kann, Victoria. Goldidoodles. Kann, Victoria, illus. 2013. (Pinkalicious Ser.). (ENG., Illus.). 128p. (J). (gr. -1-3). pap. 12.99 *(978-0-06-223334-9(3)*, HarperFestival) HarperCollins Pubs.

—Pinkadoodles. Kann, Victoria, illus. 2011. (Pinkalicious Ser.). (ENG., Illus.). 128p. (J). (gr. -1-7). pap. 12.99 *(978-0-06-202265-3(2)*, HarperFestival) HarperCollins Pubs.

—Pinkafy Your World. Kann, Victoria, illus. 2013. (Pinkalicious Ser.). (ENG., Illus.). 12p. (J). (gr. -1-3). pap. 6.99 *(978-0-06-223333-2(5)*, HarperFestival) HarperCollins Pubs.

Kavanagh, James. Mammals Nature Activity Book. Leung, Raymond, illus. 2nd ed. 2011. (Nature Activity Book Ser.). (ENG.). 32p. (J). (gr. 4-7). 6.95 *(978-1-58355-581-1(1))* Western National Parks Assn.

—My First Arctic Nature. Leung, Raymond, illus. 2011. (Nature Activity Book Ser.). (ENG.). 32p. (J). (gr. 2-4). act. bk. ed. 6.95 *(978-1-58355-586-6(2))* Western National Parks Assn.

—My First Forests Nature. Leung, Raymond, illus. 2011. (Nature Activity Book Ser.). (ENG.). 32p. (J). (gr. 2-4). act. bk. ed. 6.95 *(978-1-58355-588-0(9))* Western National Parks Assn.

—My First Grasslands Nature. Leung, Raymond, illus. 2011. (Nature Activity Book Ser.). (ENG.). 32p. (J). (gr. 2-4). act. bk. ed. 6.95 *(978-1-58355-589-7(7))* Western National Parks Assn.

—My First Seashores Nature. Leung, Raymond, illus. 2011. (Nature Activity Book Ser.). (ENG.). 32p. (J). (gr. 2-4). act. bk. ed. 6.95 *(978-1-58355-590-3(0))* Western National Parks Assn.

—My First Wetlands Nature. Leung, Raymond, illus. 2011. (Nature Activity Book Ser.). (ENG.). 32p. (J). (gr. 2-4). act. bk. ed. 6.95 *(978-1-58355-591-0(9))* Western National Parks Assn.

—Seashore Wildlife. Leung, Raymond, illus. 2nd ed. 2011. (Nature Activity Book Ser.). (ENG.). 32p. (J). (gr. 4-7). act. bk. ed. 6.95 *(978-1-58355-584-2(6))* Western National Parks Assn.

—Southwest Desert Wildlife Nature. Leung, Raymond, illus. 2nd ed. 2011. (Nature Activity Book Ser.). (ENG.). 32p. (J). (gr. 4-7). act. bk. ed. 6.95 *(978-1-58355-585-9(4))* Western National Parks Assn.

Kavanagh, James & Waterford Press Staff. Pond Life Nature Activity Book. Leung, Raymond, illus. 2nd ed. 2011. (Nature Activity Book Ser.). (ENG.). 32p. (J). (gr. 4-7). 6.95 *(978-1-58355-582-8(X))* Western National Parks Assn.

Kaye, Megan. Do You Know Who You Are? Singer, Allison, ed. 2014. (ENG., Illus.). 192p. (YA). (gr. 8-12). pap. 15.99 *(978-1-4654-1649-0(8)*, DK Children) Dorling Kindersley Publishing, Inc.

Kelleher, Damian. Planes. Robson, Matthew, illus. 2008. (ENG.). 30p. (J). (gr. 3-7). pap., act. bk. ed. 8.95 *(978-1-84425-465-1(8)*, 1844254658) Haynes Publishing PLC GBR. Dist: Hachette Bk. Group.

Keller, Sunny. Life Hacks for Kids. 2017. (ENG., Illus.). 208p. (J). (gr. 5-7). 14.99 ***(978-1-328-74213-1(X)***, HMH Books For Young Readers) Houghton Mifflin Harcourt Publishing Co.

Kemp, Henry Lucia. Now I Know My Numbers, Colors, Shapes & More. 2014. (Now I Know My Ser.). (ENG.). 224p. (gr. -1-1). pap. 8.99 *(978-0-545-77682-0(1)*, Teaching Resources) Scholastic, Inc.

Kenney, Sean. Cool Creations in 101 Pieces. Kenney, Sean, illus. 2014. (ENG., Illus.). 32p. (J). (gr. -1-4). 14.99 *(978-1-62779-017-8(9)*, 9781627790178, Holt, Henry & Co. Bks. For Young Readers) Holt, Henry & Co.

—Cool Creations in 35 Pieces. Kenney, Sean, illus. 2013. (ENG., Illus.). 32p. (J). (gr. -1-3). 14.99 *(978-0-8050-9692-7(2)*, 9780805096927, Holt, Henry & Co. Bks. For Young Readers) Holt, Henry & Co.

—Totally Cool Creations. Kenney, Sean, illus. 2013. (ENG., Illus.). 128p. (J). (gr. -1-3). pap. 19.99 *(978-1-250-03110-5(9)*, 9781250031105) Square Fish.

Key Porter Books, creator. Face Painting: Enchanting Designs for Faces & Bodies. rev. ed. 2007. (Gymboree Play & Music Ser.). (ENG., Illus.). 36p. (J). (gr. -1-2). bds. *(978-1-55263-962-7(2))* Magma.

—Music Play: Inspired Ways to Explore Music. rev. ed. 2007. (Gymboree Play & Music Ser.). (ENG., Illus.). 36p. (J). (gr. -1-2). bds. *(978-1-55263-964-1(9))* Magma.

Key Porter Books Staff. Gymboree in a Princess Castle. rev. ed. 2007. (ENG., Illus.). 1p. (J). *(978-1-55263-923-8(1))* Magma.

—Gymboree on a Pirate Ship. rev. ed. 2007. (ENG., Illus.). 1p. (J). *(978-1-55263-921-4(5))* Magma.

Khan, Sarah. Dinosaur Quiz Cards. 2012. (Activity Cards Ser.). 50p. (J). 9.99 *(978-0-7945-3262-8(4)*, Usborne) EDC Publishing.

Kids: Watershed Protection. 2003. (J). *(978-1-888631-29-6(5))* Project WET Foundation.

Kids Can Do It! 2017. (Kids Can Do It! Ser.). 32p. (gr. 8-8). 171.00 ***(978-1-4994-8268-3(X))***; pap. 70.50 ***(978-1-4994-8378-9(3))*** Rosen Publishing Group, Inc., The. (Windmill Bks.).

Killam, Catherine D. The Sweeet Old Lady Coloring & Activity Book. Svensson, Richard, illus. 2013. 62p. pap. 6.99 *(978-0-9910700-4-6(5))* Enchanted Forest Publishing.

—The Sweeet Old Lady down the Street. Svensson, Richard, illus. 2013. 42p. pap. 9.99 *(978-0-9910700-2-2(X))* Enchanted Forest Publishing.

King, Sharon. Junior Alien Zone: Creative Experiences for Hands of All Ages! 2009. (Illus.). 51p. pap. 14.95 *(978-1-4327-1162-7(8))* Outskirts Pr., Inc.

King, Trey. Star Wars: a Very Vader Valentine's Day. Cook, Katie, illus. 2013. (ENG.). 16p. (J). (gr. 3-7). pap. 6.99 *(978-0-545-51560-3(2))* Scholastic, Inc.

Kings, Gary & Ginger, Richard. Funky Junk: Recycle Rubbish into Art! Green, Barry, illus. 2012. (Dover Children's Activity Bks.). (ENG.). 64p. (J). (gr. 3-5). pap. 9.99 *(978-0-486-49022-9(X))* Dover Pubns., Inc.

Kirkby, Joanne & Cooper, Sharon, illus. Mosaic Picture Sticker Book. 2015. (Mosaic Sticker Bks.). (ENG.). 24+12p. (J). (gr. k-5). pap. 10.99 *(978-0-7945-3015-0(X)*, Usborne) EDC Publishing.

Klawitter, Pamela Amick. Centers on the Go: Fun, Creative Activity Folders to Take to Your Seat. VanBlaricum, Pam, ed. Armstrong, Bev & Baker, Don, illus. 2005. 192p. pap. 19.99 *(978-0-88160-378-1(3)*, LW435, Learning Works, The) Creative Teaching Pr., Inc.

Kliman, Gilbert. My Personal Story about Hurricanes Katrina & Rita: A Guided Activity Workbook for Middle & High School Students. 2005. (YA). spiral bd. 19.00 *(978-0-9790846-9-0(5))* Children's Psychological Health Ctr., Inc., The.

Kliman, Gilbert, et al. My Personal Story about Tropical Storm Stan: A Guided Activity Workbook for Children, Adolescents & Families. 2006. (Illus.). spiral bd. 19.00 *(978-0-9790846-8-3(7))* Children's Psychological Health Ctr., Inc., The.

Kline, Trish & Donev, Mary. The Busy Preschooler's Guide to Learning. 2007. (Illus.). 128p. (J). per. 60.00 *(978-1-934307-17-5(3))* Ghost Hunter Productions.

—Celebration of Letters A & B: Busy Preschoolers. 2007. (Illus.). 16p. (J). per. 20.00 *(978-1-934307-04-5(1))* Ghost Hunter Productions.

—Celebration of Letters C & D: Busy Preschoolers. 2007. (Illus.). 16p. (J). per. 20.00 *(978-1-934307-05-2(X))* Ghost Hunter Productions.

—Celebration of Letters E & F: Busy Preschoolers. 2007. (Illus.). 16p. (J). per. 20.00 *(978-1-934307-06-9(8))* Ghost Hunter Productions.

—Celebration of Letters G & H: Busy Preschoolers. 2007. (Illus.). 16p. (J). per. 20.00 *(978-1-934307-07-6(6))* Ghost Hunter Productions.

—Celebration of Letters I & J: Busy Preschoolers. 2007. (Illus.). 16p. (J). per. 20.00 *(978-1-934307-08-3(4))* Ghost Hunter Productions.

—Celebration of Letters K & L: Busy Preschoolers. 2007. (Illus.). 16p. (J). per. 20.00 *(978-1-934307-09-0(2))* Ghost Hunter Productions.

—Celebration of Letters M & N: Busy Preschoolers. 2007. (Illus.). 16p. (J). per. 20.00 *(978-1-934307-10-6(6))* Ghost Hunter Productions.

—Celebration of Letters O & Q: Busy Preschoolers. 2007. (Illus.). 16p. (J). per. 20.00 *(978-1-934307-11-3(4))* Ghost Hunter Productions.

—Celebration of Letters P & R: Busy Preschoolers. 2007. (Illus.). 16p. (J). per. 20.00 *(978-1-934307-12-0(2))* Ghost Hunter Productions.

—Celebration of Letters S & T: Busy Preschoolers. 2007. (Illus.). 16p. (J). per. 20.00 *(978-1-934307-13-7(0))* Ghost Hunter Productions.

—Celebration of Letters U & V: Busy Preschoolers. 2007. (Illus.). 16p. (J). per. 20.00 *(978-1-934307-14-4(9))* Ghost Hunter Productions.

—Celebration of Letters W & X: Busy Preschoolers. 2007. (Illus.). 16p. (J). per. 20.00 *(978-1-934307-15-1(7))* Ghost Hunter Productions.

—Celebration of Letters Y & Z: Busy Preschoolers. 2007. (Illus.). 16p. (J). per. 20.00 *(978-1-934307-16-8(5))* Ghost Hunter Productions.

Klug, Kirsten. Oregon Is Fun! Rain or Sun! Skorpen, Neal, illus. 2011. 20p. (J). pap. 7.95 *(978-0-9798173-3-5(1))* Bamboo River Pr.

Klutz Editors. Create Your Own Quote Art. 2016. (ENG.). 10p. (J). (gr. 3-7). 19.99 *(978-0-545-90651-7(2))* Klutz.

—Doodlewire. 2010. (ENG.). 40p. (J). (gr. 3). 14.99 *(978-1-59174-843-4(7))* Klutz.

—The Encyclopedia of My Immaturity: Your Own Personal Stinky Diary Ah. 2011. (ENG.). 60p. (J). (gr. 3-7). 16.99 *(978-1-59174-923-3(9))* Klutz.

—El libro del body Crayon. 2004. (SPA., Illus.). 42p. (J). spiral bd. 17.95 *(978-968-5528-02-3(0))* Klutz Latino MEX. Dist: Independent Pubs. Group.

—Make Your Own Mini Erasers. 2016. (ENG.). 48p. (J). (gr. 3-7). 21.99 *(978-1-338-03750-0(1))* Klutz.

—The Many Moods of Me Journal. 2015. (ENG.). 76p. (J). (gr. 3-7). 16.99 *(978-0-545-80546-9(5))* Klutz.

—Marker Everything. 2016. (ENG.). 48p. (J). (gr. 3-7). 19.99 *(978-0-545-85851-9(8))* Klutz.

—Neon Chalk Lettering. 2016. (ENG.). 76p. (J). (gr. 3-7). 18.99 *(978-1-338-03754-8(4))* Scholastic, Inc.

—Sew Mini Treats. 2016. (ENG.). 48p. (J). (gr. 3-7). 21.99 *(978-0-545-90652-4(0))* Klutz.

—Shimmer Art. 2016. (ENG.). 48p. (J). (gr. 7). 21.99 *(978-0-545-90650-0(4))* Klutz.

Klutz Editors, contrib. by. Paper Fashions Fancy. 2008. (ENG., Illus.). 58p. (J). (gr. 3-18). 21.95 *(978-1-59174-519-8(5))* Klutz.

Klutz Editors, ed. Glossy Bands: Stretchy Bracelets to Share with Your Friends. 2010. (ENG.). 40p. (J). (gr. 3-18). 19.95 *(978-1-59174-730-7(9))* Klutz.

Klutz Editors & Boyle, Brendan. The Klutz Book of Inventions. Cassidy, John, ed. 2010. (ENG.). 200p. (J). (gr. 3-18). 19.99 *(978-1-59174-879-3(8))* Klutz.

Klutz Editors & Dzwonik, Cristian. De las 1000 y una Actividades. 2005. (SPA., Illus.). 120p. (J). spiral bd. 15.95 *(978-968-5528-17-7(9))* Klutz Latino MEX. Dist: Independent Pubs. Group.

Klutz Editors & Scholastic Editors. My Egg-Carton Animals. 2017. (Klutz Jr Ser.). (ENG.). 28p. (J). 12.99 *(978-0-545-93244-8(0))* Scholastic, Inc.

—My Hand Art. 2017. (Klutz Jr Ser.). (ENG.). 28p. (J). 12.99 *(978-0-545-93246-2(7))* Scholastic, Inc.

—My Twinkly Tiaras. 2017. (Klutz Jr Ser.). (ENG.). 28p. (J). 14.99 *(978-0-545-93249-3(1))* Scholastic, Inc.

Knighton, Kate. 50 Easter Things to Make & Do. 2009. (50 Easter Things to Make & Do Ser.). 104p. (J). (gr. 1). spiral bd. 9.99 *(978-0-7945-2206-3(8)*, Usborne) EDC Publishing.

Koerner, Sandy, et al. Water Adventures Around the World, 10 vols. 2008. (ENG.). 30p. (J). (gr. 3-5). pap. 25.00 *(978-1-58321-558-6(1))* American Water Works Assn.

Kozlowski, Bryan. Cook Me a Story: A Treasury of Stories & Recipes Inspired by Your Favourite Fairy Tales. 2016. (ENG.). 80p. (J). (gr. k-6). 16.95 *(978-1-63322-066-9(4)*, Walter Foster Jr) Quarto Publishing Group USA.

Kraft, Ellen Christiansen. Design Your Own Sneakers Sticker Activity Book. 2016. (Dover Little Activity Bks.). (ENG.). 4p. (J). (gr. k-3). 1.99 *(978-0-486-80881-9(5))* Dover Pubns., Inc.

—Graduation Day Stickers. 2009. (Dover Little Activity Books Stickers Ser.). (ENG., Illus.). 4p. (J). (gr. -1-5). 1.50 *(978-0-486-47130-3(6))* Dover Pubns., Inc.

—Thank You Stickers. 2011. (Dover Little Activity Books Stickers Ser.). (ENG.). 4p. (J). (gr. k-3). pap. 1.50 *(978-0-486-48192-0(1))* Dover Pubns., Inc.

Kramer, Lance. Great Ancient China Projects: You Can Build Yourself. Weinberg, Steven, illus. 2008. (Build It Yourself Ser.). (ENG.). 128p. (J). (gr. 3-7). pap. 21.95 *(978-1-934670-02-6(2))* Octavio Publishing.

Kratt, Chris & Kratt, Martin. Wild Tech! (Wild Kratts) Random House, illus. 2017. (Pictureback(R) Ser.). (ENG.). 24p. (J). (gr. -1-2). 4.99 ***(978-1-101-93904-8(4))***, Random Hse. Bks. for Young Readers) Random Hse. Children's Bks.

Krause, Maria. Alhambra: Create Your Own Castle! — Sticker Book. 2015. (ENG.). 16p. (J). (gr. 1-4). pap. 9.95 *(978-3-7913-7220-4(3))* Prestel Verlag GmbH & Co KG. DEU. Dist: Penguin Random Hse. LLC.

—Hokusai Coloring Book. 2015. (ENG.). 32p. (J). (gr. 1-4). pap. 8.95 *(978-3-7913-7215-0(7))* Prestel Verlag GmbH & Co KG. DEU. Dist: Penguin Random Hse. LLC.

Krech, Bob & Grabell, Jeff. Algebra Readiness: Mini-Lessons, Games, & Activities to Review & Reinforce Essential Math Concepts & Skills. 2008. (Reteaching Math Ser.). (ENG.). 96p. pap. 14.99 *(978-0-439-52966-2(2)*, Teaching Resources) Scholastic, Inc.

Krech, Bob & Kennan, Audrey. Multiplication & Division: Mini-Lessons, Games, & Activities to Review & Reinforce Essential Math Concepts & Skills. 2008. (Reteaching Math Ser.). (ENG.). 96p. (gr. 4-6). pap. 14.99 *(978-0-439-52967-9(0)*, Teaching Resources) Scholastic, Inc.

Krech, Bob, et al. Addition & Subtraction: Mini-Lessons, Games, & Activities to Review & Reinforce Essential Math Concepts & Skills. 2008. (Reteaching Math Ser.). (ENG.). 96p. pap. 14.99 *(978-0-439-52964-8(6)*, Teaching Resources) Scholastic, Inc.

Krezel, Cindy. Kids' Container Gardening: Year-Round Projects for Inside & Out. Curtis, Bruce, photos by. 2nd ed. 2010. (ENG., Illus.). 88p. (J). (gr. 1-6). pap. 14.95 *(978-1-883052-75-1(0))* Ball Publishing.

Kronheimer, Ann. The Peter Pan Colouring Book. 2017. (ENG.). 32p. (J). (gr. 1-4). pap. 6.99 ***(978-1-78055-435-8(4))*** O'Mara, Michael Bks., Ltd. GBR. Dist: Independent Pubs. Group.

—The Wonderful Wizard of Oz Colouring Book. 2017. (ENG.). 32p. (J). (gr. 1-4). pap. 8.99 ***(978-1-78055-436-5(2))*** O'Mara, Michael Bks., Ltd. GBR. Dist: Independent Pubs. Group.

Kurowski, Kathryn. Year Round Project-Based Activities for STEM PreK-K. 2013. (ENG.). 112p. pap. 14.99 *(978-1-4206-3024-4(5))* Teacher Created Resources, Inc.

Kurtz, John. FLIP OUTS — Bird Bash: Color Your Own Cartoon! 2015. (ENG., Illus.). 64p. (J). (gr. k-3). pap. 1.99 *(978-0-486-79485-3(7))* Dover Pubns., Inc.
—FLIP OUTS — Funny Farm: Color Your Own Cartoon! 2015. (ENG., Illus.). 64p. (J). (gr. k-3). pap. 1.99 *(978-0-486-79483-9(0))* Dover Pubns., Inc.
—Ice Palace Sticker Activity Book. 2016. (Dover Little Activity Books Stickers Ser.). (ENG.). 4p. (J). (gr. k-2). pap. 1.99 *(978-0-486-80528-3(X))* Dover Pubns., Inc.
—Santa Claus Christmas Paper Dolls. 2013. (Dover Paper Dolls Ser.). (ENG.). 32p. (J). (gr. 1-5). pap. 9.99 *(978-0-486-49424-1(1))* Dover Pubns., Inc.
—What to Doodle? at School. 2013. (ENG.). 64p. (J). (gr. k-3). pap. 1.50 *(978-0-486-49229-2(X))* Dover Pubns., Inc.
LAIKA. The Boxtrolls: Make Your Own Boxtroll Punch-Out Activity Book. 2014. (ENG., Illus.). 12p. (J). (gr. 3-7). pap. 7.99 *(978-0-316-33268-2(2))* Little, Brown Bks. for Young Readers.
Laliberte, Mario, illus. Match, Sort & Play. 2007. (Hands-on Bks.). 48p. (J). (gr. -1-k). spiral bd. *(978-2-7641-1936-5(4))* Tormont Pubns.
Lamb, Stacey, et al, illus. My First Christmas Activity Book. 2013. (ENG.). 50p. (J). pap. 11.99 *(978-0-7945-3182-9(2))*, Usborne) EDC Publishing.
Lamb, Stacey, illus. Wipe-Clean Dot-To-Dot. 2013. (Wipe-Clean Bks). 20p. (J). pap. 7.99 *(978-0-7945-3278-9(0))*, Usborne) EDC Publishing.
Lambert, Lydia. Scrub-A-Dub Elf: Splash & Play with Elf. Jones, Anna, illus. 2016. (Scrub-A-Dub Bath Mitt & Bath Book Sets Ser.). (ENG.). 8p. (J). (gr. -1 — 1). 9.99 *(978-1-4380-7740-6(8))* Barron's Educational Series, Inc.
Lambert, Nat. Magnetic Silly Animals. 2007. (ENG., Illus.). 10p. (J). (gr. -1-k). 9.99 *(978-1-84666-346-8(6))* Top That! Publishing PLC GBR. Dist: Independent Pubs. Group.
—Rainy Day Activity Book. 2017. (ENG.). 96p. (J). (gr. 2-4). pap. 9.99 ***(978-1-78445-695-5(0))*** Top That! Publishing PLC GBR. Dist: Independent Pubs. Group.
Lambert, Nat. 3D Shark Attack! Make a Hungry Shark Smash Through Your Wall. Smith, Mark, illus. 2015. (Press Out & Build Wall Model Ser.). (ENG.). 24p. (J). (gr. 2). 19.99 *(978-1-78244-973-7(6))* Top That! Publishing PLC GBR. Dist: Independent Pubs. Group.
Lane, Leena. Christmas Fun: Bible Activity Book. Bishop, Roma, illus. 2015. (J). pap. 9.95 *(978-0-8198-1651-1(5))* Pauline Bks. & Media.
—Easter Days: My First Bible Activity Book. 2008. (Illus.). 31p. (J). pap. 6.95 *(978-1-59325-123-9(8))* Word Among Us Pr.
Langeler, Gerard. Let's Make Faces. Grindell, Joan & Grindell, Mark, illus. 2009. (ENG.). 24p. (J). (gr. -1-3). spiral bd. 14.95 *(978-1-932565-63-8(9))* Future Horizons, Inc.
Language Arts Explorer, 26 vols., Set. Incl. Save the Planet: Compost It. Barker, David. 32p. 2010. lib. bdg. 28.50 *(978-1-60279-656-0(4)*, 200349); Save the Planet: Growing Your Own Garden. Hirsch, Rebecca. 32p. 2010. lib. bdg. 28.50 *(978-1-60279-657-7(2)*, 200350); Save the Planet: Helping Endangered Animals. Hirsch, Rebecca. 32p. 2010. lib. bdg. 28.50 *(978-1-60279-658-4(0)*, 200351); Save the Planet: Keeping Water Clean. Farrell, Courtney. 32p. 2010. lib. bdg. 28.50 *(978-1-60279-659-1(9)*, 200352); Save the Planet: Local Farms & Sustainable Foods. Vogel, Julia. 32p. 2010. lib. bdg. 28.50 *(978-1-60279-660-7(2)*, 200353); Save the Planet: Protecting Our Natural Resources. Hirsch, Rebecca. 32p. 2010. lib. bdg. 28.50 *(978-1-60279-661-4(0)*, 200354); Save the Planet: Reduce, Reuse, & Recycle. Minden, Cecilia. 32p. 2010. lib. bdg. 28.50 *(978-1-60279-662-1(9)*, 200355); Save the Planet: Using Alternative Energies. Farrell, Courtney. 32p. 2010. lib. bdg. 28.50 *(978-1-60279-663-8(7)*, 200356); Set. Language Arts Explorer: History Digs. Cherry Lake Publishing Staff. (J). 2011. lib. bdg. 285.00 *(978-1-61080-243-7(8))*; Set. Language Arts Explorer: Science Lab. Cherry Lake Publishing Staff. (J). 2011. lib. bdg. 228.00 *(978-1-61080-245-1(4))*; (gr. 4-8). 2011. Set lib. bdg. 741.00 *(978-1-61080-239-0(X))* Cherry Lake Publishing.
Larranaga, Ana Martin. Noisy Town. 2014. (Rattle Buggy Buddies Ser.). (ENG., Illus.). 10p. (J). (— 1). bds. 7.99 *(978-1-4472-6799-7(0))* Pan Macmillan GBR. Dist: Independent Pubs. Group.
Larson, Jennifer. Category Cut-Ups Workbook with CD-ROM: Bk335. Prince, Audrey & Webber, Thomas, eds. 2006. (J). 26.95 *(978-1-58650-635-3(8))* Super Duper Pubns.
Last, Shari. DK Readers L3: Star Wars: Rebel Heroes. 2017. (DK Readers Ser.). (ENG.). 64p. (J). (gr. 2-4). pap. 3.99 *(978-1-4654-5582-6(5)*, DK Children) Dorling Kindersley Publishing, Inc.
Latham, Donna. Garbage: Investigate What Happens When You Throw It Out with 25 Projects. Hetland, Beth, illus. 2011. (Build It Yourself Ser.). (ENG.). 128p. (J). (gr. 3-7). 21.95 *(978-1-936313-47-1(2))* Open City Bks.
Lazoo Publishing Staff. Imagine That! A Coloring Book for Growing Young Minds. Miyakoshi, Junko, tr. 2009. (King of Play Ser.). (ENG.). 200p. (gr. -1). pap. 14.95 *(978-1-934734-05-6(5))* Seven Footer Pr.
—Stickers! An Activity Book with Stickers. Miyakoshi, Junko, tr. 2010. (King of Play Ser.). (ENG., Illus.). 52p. (J). (gr. -1). pap. 7.95 *(978-1-934734-37-7(3))* Seven Footer Pr.
Lazoo Publishing Staff & ZOO, La. Let's Color! A Coloring Book Like No Other. Miyakoshi, Junko, tr. 2009. (King of Play Ser.). (ENG.). 128p. (gr. -1). pap. 12.95 *(978-1-934734-02-5(0))* Seven Footer Pr.
—Squiggles! A Drawing Book. Oku, Makiko, tr. 2009. (King of Play Ser.). (ENG., Illus.). 64p. (J). (gr. -1). pap. 7.95 *(978-1-934734-13-1(6))* Seven Footer Pr.
Le Quere, Ashley. Modern Art Activity Book. 2017. (ENG., Illus.). 64p. (J). (gr. 1-7). pap. 12.95 ***(978-1-4549-2563-7(9))*** Sterling Publishing Co., Inc.
Learning Company Books Staff. Learning with Curious George Pre-K Reading. 2012. (Learning with Curious George Ser.). (ENG., Illus.). 64p. (J). (gr. -1-3). pap. 4.99 *(978-0-547-79054-1(6))* Houghton Mifflin Harcourt Publishing Co.
Learning Company, Inc. Staff. Achieve!: First Grade: Building Skills for School Success. 2012. (Achieve! Ser.). (ENG., Illus.). 320p. (J). (gr. -1-3). pap. 12.99 *(978-0-547-79112-8(7))* Houghton Mifflin Harcourt Publishing Co.
—Achieve!: Pre-Kindergarten: Building Skills for School Success. 2012. (Achieve! Ser.). (ENG., Illus.). 320p. (J). (gr. -1-3). pap. 12.99 *(978-0-547-79107-4(0))* Houghton Mifflin Harcourt Publishing Co.
—Learning with Curious George Kindergarten Math. 2012. (Learning with Curious George Ser.). (ENG., Illus.). 64p. (J). (gr. -1-3). pap. 4.99 *(978-0-547-79097-8(X))* Houghton Mifflin Harcourt Publishing Co.
—Pre-K Math. 2012. (Learning with Curious George Ser.). (ENG., Illus.). 64p. (J). (gr. -1-3). pap. 4.99 *(978-0-547-79055-8(4))* Houghton Mifflin Harcourt Publishing Co.
Learning Company, Inc. Staff & Houghton Mifflin Harcourt Children's Group Staff, creators. Learning with Curious George Kindergarten Reading. 2012. (Learning with Curious George Ser.). (ENG., Illus.). 64p. (J). (gr. -1-3). pap. 4.99 *(978-0-547-79096-1(1))* Houghton Mifflin Harcourt Publishing Co.
Learning Company Staff. Achieve!: Kindergarten: Building Skills for School Success. 2012. (Achieve! Ser.). (ENG., Illus.). 320p. (J). (gr. -1-3). pap. 12.99 *(978-0-547-79108-1(9))* Houghton Mifflin Harcourt Publishing Co.
LeCompte, David & Padrick, Kendell. Eugene Stillwell Wants to Know! Part III. 2009. (Eugene Stillwell Wants to Know! Ser.). (ENG.). 96p. (J). (gr. 4-6). pap. 4.95 *(978-1-929945-91-7(4))* Big Guy Bks., Inc.
Lecreux, Michele & Gallais, Celia. The Boy's Book of Adventure: The Little Guidebook for Smart & Resourceful Boys. Millet, Esao & Millet, Jocelyn, illus. 2013. (ENG.). 128p. (J). (gr. 3-7). 14.99 *(978-0-7641-6611-2(5))* Barron's Educational Series, Inc.
—The Girl's Book of Adventure: The Little Guidebook for Smart & Resourceful Girls. Millet, Esao & Millet, Jocelyn, illus. 2013. (ENG.). 128p. (J). (gr. 3-7). 14.99 *(978-0-7641-6610-5(7))* Barron's Educational Series, Inc.
Lee, Amy. The Magical World of Amy Lee. 2016. (ENG.). 112p. (J). (gr. 3-7). 11.99 *(978-1-338-12016-5(6))* Scholastic, Inc.
Lee, J. H., creator. Boo Paper Doll Set. 2013. (ENG.). 18p. (J). (gr. -1-17). pap. 14.99 *(978-1-4521-1065-3(4))* Chronicle Bks. LLC.
Lee, Martin, et al. 40 Elaboration Activities That Take Writing from Bland to Brilliant! Lee, Martin, illus. 2007. (40 Elaboration Activities That Take Writing from Bland to Brilliant! Ser.). (ENG., Illus.). 80p. pap. 12.99 *(978-0-439-55434-3(9)*, Teaching Resources) Scholastic, Inc.
—40 Elaboration Activities That Take Writing from Bland to Brilliant! 2007. (40 Elaboration Activities That Take Writing from Bland to Brilliant! Ser.). (ENG., Illus.). 80p. pap. 12.99 *(978-0-439-55433-6(0)*, Teaching Resources) Scholastic, Inc.
Leisure Arts, creator. Scrapbooking with Your Kids: The Ultimate Guide to Kid-Friendly Crafting. 2008. (ENG., Illus.). 196p. pap. 22.95 *(978-1-60140-525-8(1))* Leisure Arts, Inc.
Lesson in a Bag-Reconciliation Lesson 6. 2012. (ENG.). 24.99 *(978-1-59982-403-1(5))* St. Mary's Pr. of MN.
Lesson in a Bag-Reconciliation Lesson 7. 2012. (ENG.). 24.99 *(978-1-59982-404-8(3))* St. Mary's Pr. of MN.
Lesson in a Bag-Reconciliation Lesson 8. 2012. (ENG.). 24.99 *(978-1-59982-405-5(1))* St. Mary's Pr. of MN.
Lester, Stephanie. Year Round Project-Based Activities for STEM Grd 1-2. 2013. (ENG.). 112p. pap. 14.99 *(978-1-4206-3025-1(3))* Teacher Created Resources, Inc.
Levin, Freddie. ABC Fun Stained Glass Jr. Coloring Book. 2012. (Dover Stained Glass Coloring Book Ser.). (ENG.). 32p. (J). (gr. -1-1). pap. 3.99 *(978-0-486-49875-1(1))* Dover Pubns., Inc.
—Glitter Hanukkah Stickers. 2009. (Dover Little Activity Books Stickers Ser.). (ENG., Illus.). 2p. (J). (gr. 1-4). 1.99 *(978-0-486-47018-4(0))* Dover Pubns., Inc.
—Outer Space Activity Book. 2009. (Dover Little Activity Bks.). (ENG.). 64p. (J). (gr. k-3). pap. 1.99 *(978-0-486-47389-5(9))* Dover Pubns., Inc.
Levin, Michael. Start to Finish: Word Searches. 2006. (ENG.). 64p. pap. 6.99 *(978-1-4206-5994-8(4))* Teacher Created Resources, Inc.
Levin, Michael H. Start to Finish - Word Searches, Grades 3-4. 2006. (Start to Finish (Lerner) Ser.). (ENG., Illus.). 64p. (gr. 3-5). per. 6.99 *(978-1-4206-5995-5(2))* Teacher Created Resources, Inc.
Levy, Talia. Scratch & Sketch Trace-Along Doodle Mania: An Art Activity Book for Imaginative Artists of All Ages. Zschock, Martha Day, illus. 2014. (ENG.). (J). (gr. k). 14.99 *(978-1-4413-1727-8(9)*, 9781441317278) Peter Pauper Pr. Inc.
Lew-McCabe, Minette, illus. Make Your Own Hawaii Landmarks. 2007. *(978-1-59700-381-0(6))* Island Heritage Publishing.
Li, Maggie. Big City Sticker Book: an Activity Book of the World for Busy Hands. 2016. (ENG.). 64p. (J). (gr. -1-3). pap. 14.99 *(978-1-84365-301-1(X)*, Pavilion) Pavilion Bks. GBR. Dist: Independent Pubs. Group.
Lickens, Alice. Castle Explorer: Sticker & Activity Book. 2016. (ENG., Illus.). 20p. (J). (gr. -1-1). pap. 7.99 *(978-1-909881-62-4(7))* National Trust, Aylesbury GBR. Dist: Independent Pubs. Group.
—Flower Explorer. Lickens, Alice, illus. 2016. (ENG., Illus.). 20p. (J). (gr. -1-1). pap., act. bk. ed. 7.99 *(978-1-909881-63-1(5))* National Trust, Aylesbury GBR. Dist: Independent Pubs. Group.
—Pond Explorer: Nature Sticker & Activity Book. 2015. (ENG.). 20p. (J). (gr. -1-1). pap. 7.99 *(978-1-909881-50-1(3))* National Trust, Aylesbury GBR. Dist: Independent Pubs. Group.
Lierman, Jane. Cursive Writing Practice - Inspiring Quotes: Reproducible Activity Pages with Motivational & Character-Building Quotes That Make Handwriting Practice Meaningful. 2009. (ENG.). 48p. pap. 10.99 *(978-0-545-09437-5(2)*, Teaching Resources) Scholastic, Inc.
Life Changing Miracles: 30+ Powerful Fun Hands-on Learning Activities for Kids for Remarkable Improvement in Life Choices & Actions. 2006. (J). ring bd. 19.95 *(978-0-9786034-0-3(0)*, LCMRingbound); cd-rom 19.95 *(978-0-9786034-1-0(9))* Insight Services, Inc. (Children's Insight).
Light Brown, Cynthia. Amazing Kitchen Chemistry Projects. Shedd, Blair D., illus. 2008. (Build It Yourself Ser.). (ENG.). 128p. (J). (gr. 3-7). pap. 15.95 *(978-0-9792268-2-3(1))* Octavio Publishing.
Light, Steve. Cars Go. 2016. (ENG., Illus.). 16p. (J). (gr. -1 — 1). bds. 9.99 *(978-1-4521-5067-3(2))* Chronicle Bks. LLC.
Liguori Publications, creator. Every Day of Advent & Christmas, Year C: A Book of Activities for Children. 2006. (Illus.). 31p. pap. 2.95 *(978-0-7648-1541-6(5))* Liguori Pubns.
Lil' Bratz 5 in 1 Superly Duperly. 2005. 52p. pap. 3.99 *(978-0-7666-2251-7(7))* Modern Publishing.
Limon, Daniel, illus. The Colossal Creature Count: Add up All of the Animals to Solve Each Scene. 2017. (ENG.). 48p. (J). (gr. 1-4). pap. 9.99 *(978-1-4380-0992-6(5))* Barron's Educational Series, Inc.
Linn, Susie. Coloring: Early Learning Through Art. 2017. (Arty Mouse Creativity Bks.). (ENG.). 48p. (J). (gr. -1-k). pap. 6.99 *(978-1-78445-625-2(X))* Top That! Publishing PLC GBR. Dist: Independent Pubs. Group.
—Pasting: Early Learning Through Art. 2017. (Arty Mouse Creativity Bks.). (ENG.). 48p. (J). (gr. -1-k). pap. 6.99 ***(978-1-78700-039-1(7))*** Top That! Publishing PLC GBR. Dist: Independent Pubs. Group.
Linn, Susie. Trace, Copy, Color & Cut. Stanley, Mandy, illus. 2016. (Arty Mouse Creativity Bks.). (ENG.). 192p. (J). (gr. -1-1). pap. 16.99 *(978-1-78445-694-8(2))* Top That! Publishing PLC GBR. Dist: Independent Pubs. Group.
Litchfield, Jo, illus. Baby Brother Look & Say. 2008. (Look & Say Board Bks). 12p. (J). bds. 7.99 *(978-0-7945-2101-1(0)*, Usborne) EDC Publishing.
Little & Large Sticker Activity Bk - Monster Machines. 2008. 24p. pap. *(978-1-84810-059-6(0))* Miles Kelly Publishing, Ltd.
Little & Large Sticker Activity Bugs. 2008. 24p. pap. *(978-1-84810-057-2(4))* Miles Kelly Publishing, Ltd.
Little & Large Sticker Activity Dinosaurs. 2008. 24p. pap. *(978-1-84810-058-9(2))* Miles Kelly Publishing, Ltd.
Little & Large Sticker Activity on the Farm. 2008. 24p. pap. *(978-1-84810-060-2(4))* Miles Kelly Publishing, Ltd.
Little & Large Sticker Activity Pirates. 2008. 24p. pap. *(978-1-84810-061-9(2))* Miles Kelly Publishing, Ltd.
Little & Large Sticker Activity Sharks. 2008. 24p. pap. *(978-1-84810-062-6(0))* Miles Kelly Publishing, Ltd.
Little & Large Sticker Activity Space. 2008. 24p. pap. *(978-1-84810-063-3(9))* Miles Kelly Publishing, Ltd.
Little & Large Sticker Activity Whales & Dolphins. 2008. 24p. pap. *(978-1-84810-064-0(7))* Miles Kelly Publishing, Ltd.
Little Children's Dinosaur Activity Book. 2017. (Activity Books for Little Children Ser.). (ENG.). (J). pap. 9.99 ***(978-0-7945-3796-8(0)***, Usborne) EDC Publishing.
Littlefield, Cindy A. Pop-Out & Paint Farm Animals. 2013. (ENG.). 48p. (J). (gr. 3-8). pap. 12.95 *(978-1-61212-139-0(X))* Storey Publishing, LLC.
Litton, Jonathan. Dinosaurs Sticker Activity Fun. 2015. (ENG., Illus.). 96p. (J). (gr. -1-3). 9.99 *(978-1-58925-316-2(7))* Tiger Tales.
—I Spy Learn & Go Sticker Activity. Galloway, Fhiona, illus. 2015. (My Little World Ser.). (ENG.). 48p. (J). (gr. -1-3). 9.99 *(978-1-58925-313-1(2))* Tiger Tales.
—I Spy on the Farm Sticker Activity. Galloway, Fhiona, illus. 2015. (My Little World Ser.). (ENG.). 48p. (J). (gr. -1-2). 9.99 *(978-1-58925-312-4(4))* Tiger Tales.
, Liverpool Football Club, Liverpool Football Club. The Official Liverpool FC Sticker Colouring Book. 2014. (ENG.). 24p. (J). (gr. -1-3). pap. 8.99 *(978-1-78097-326-5(8))* Carlton Bks., Ltd. GBR. Dist: Independent Pubs. Group.
Liverpool Football Club Staff. The Official Liverpool FC Sticker Activity Book. 2014. (ENG.). 16p. (J). (gr. -1-3). pap. 8.99 *(978-1-78097-325-8(X))* Carlton Bks., Ltd. GBR. Dist: Independent Pubs. Group.
Ljungkvist, Laura. Search & Spot: Go! 2016. (Search & Spot Book Ser.). (ENG., Illus.). 40p. (J). (gr. -1-3). 16.99 *(978-0-544-57042-9(1)*, HMH Books For Young Readers) Houghton Mifflin Harcourt Publishing Co.
Lluch, Alex A. Let's Leap Ahead - Pre-K Fun Pad! 2013. (ENG.). 80p. (J). (gr. -1). pap. 3.95 *(978-1-61351-020-9(9))* WS Publishing.
—Let's Leap Ahead Kindergarten. 2013. (ENG.). 250p. (J). (gr. -1). spiral bd. 9.95 *(978-1-936061-84-6(8))* WS Publishing.
—Let's Leap Ahead Kindergarten School Games. 2014. (ENG., Illus.). 50p. (J). (gr. -1-k). spiral bd. 9.95 *(978-1-61351-081-0(0))* WS Publishing.
—Let's Leap Ahead Kindergarten Wipe-Off. 2013. (ENG.). 80p. (J). (gr. k). bds. 12.95 *(978-1-61351-013-1(6))* WS Publishing.
—Let's Leap Ahead Pre-K. 2013. (ENG.). 250p. (J). (gr. -1). spiral bd. 9.95 *(978-1-936061-83-9(X))* WS Publishing.
—Let's Leap Ahead Pre-K School Games. 2014. (ENG.). 50p. (J). (gr. -1-k). spiral bd. 9.95 *(978-1-61351-080-3(2))* WS Publishing.
—Let's Leap Ahead Pre-K Wipe-Off. 2013. (ENG.). 80p. (J). (gr. -1). bds. 12.95 *(978-1-61351-012-4(8))* WS Publishing.
Lluch, Isabel B. & Lluch, Emily. B. F. F. Quizzes. 2013. (ENG.). 128p. (J). (gr. 6). pap. 7.95 *(978-1-61351-030-8(6))* WS Publishing.
Lobdell-Bulson, Jodi. The Toddler Room: Free Play. 2013. 16p. pap. 7.95 *(978-1-4582-1256-6(4)*, Abbott Pr.) Author Solutions, Inc.
Lohmann, Raychelle Cassada. The Anger Workbook for Teens: Activities to Help You Deal with Anger & Frustration. 2009. (Instant Help Ser.). (ENG.). 144p. (YA). (gr. 6-12). pap. 16.95 *(978-1-57224-699-7(5)*, Instant Help Books) New Harbinger Pubns.
Lombardo, Michelle. The OrganWise Guys Pepto's Place Activity Book. Herron, Mark, illus. 2003. (J). pap., act. bk. ed. 4.95 *(978-1-931212-52-6(X))* OrganWise Guys Inc., The.
London Science Museum Staff. This Book Thinks You're a Scientist: Experiment, Imagine, Create. Russell, Harriet, illus. 2016. (ENG.). 96p. (J). (gr. 2-5). pap. 14.95 *(978-0-500-65081-3(0)*, 565081) Thames & Hudson.
Lonely Planet Publications Staff. Family Height Chart, 1 vol. 2017. (Lonely Planet Kids Ser.). (ENG.). (J). pap. 14.99 ***(978-1-78657-689-7(9)***, 5512) Lonely Planet Pubns.
—Lonely Planet Backyard Explorer, 1 vol. 2017. (Lonely Planet Kids Ser.). (ENG., Illus.). 72p. (J). 12.99 ***(978-1-78657-319-3(9)***, 5405) Lonely Planet Pubns.
Longhi, Phoebe. The Steampunk Coloring & Activity Book: Containing Illustrations, Recipes, Formulas & Other Activities to Entertain & Entice Creativity for the Prevention of Ennui & General Malaise among the Youth of Today & Their Progenitors. 2012. (ENG., Illus.). 64p. pap. 11.95 *(978-1-933149-63-9(9))* Manic D Pr.
Longoria, Dora. Beans a la Charr. 2009. 28p. pap. 15.49 *(978-1-4389-4028-1(9))* AuthorHouse.
Lorini, Andrea. The Christmas Stocking. Pagnoni, Roberta & Rigo, Laura, illus. 2016. (Little People Shape Bks.). (ENG.). 10p. (J). (gr. -1-k). bds. 7.99 *(978-0-7641-6850-5(9))* Barron's Educational Series, Inc.
Lu, Nick, illus. Bumper-To-Bumper Stroller Cars. 2017. (ENG.). 10p. (J). 9.99 *(978-1-4521-5504-3(6))* Chronicle Bks. LLC.
Lublin, Nancy, et al. Do Something! A Handbook for Young Activists. 2010. (ENG., Illus.). 280p. (J). (gr. 4-7). pap. 13.95 *(978-0-7611-5747-2(6)*, 15747) Workman Publishing Co., Inc.
Lucas Film Book Group. Star Wars Color by Number. 2017. (ENG.). 128p. (YA). (gr. 7-12). pap. 14.99 ***(978-1-368-00568-5(3)***, Disney Lucasfilm Press) Disney Publishing Worldwide.
Lucero, Jaime. Bilingual Bingo: Easy-to-Make Reproducible Games-in English & Spanish-That Reinforce Key Vocabulary for Emergent Readers & English Language Learners. 2008. (ENG.). 80p. (gr. k-3). pap. 12.99 *(978-0-439-70067-2(1)*, Teaching Resources) Scholastic, Inc.
Lumsden, Colin, illus. Apostles. 2003. (Bible Colour & Learn Ser.). 32p. pap. 2.50 *(978-1-903087-51-0(1))* DayOne Pubns. GBR. Dist: Send The Light Distribution LLC.
Lunis, Natalie. Making a Weather Station. 2011. (Early Connections Ser.). (J). *(978-1-61672-613-3(X))* Benchmark Education Co.
Luthringer, Melisande, illus. On the Farm. 2017. (Just Imagine & Play! Ser.). (ENG.). 48p. (J). (gr. -1-1). pap. 9.95 *(978-1-63322-244-1(6)*, Walter Foster Jr) Quarto Publishing Group USA.
Mac a'Bháird, Natasha. Cliffs of Moher & the Burren: My Ireland Activity Book. Nolan, Alan, illus. 2015. (ENG.). 24p. (J). pap. 12.00 *(978-1-84717-770-4(0))* O'Brien Pr., Ltd., The IRL. Dist: Dufour Editions, Inc.
Mac a'Bháird, Natasha. Dublin: My Ireland Activity Book. Nolan, Alan, illus. 2017. (ENG.). 24p. (J). pap. 12.00 ***(978-1-84717-892-3(8))*** O'Brien Pr., Ltd., The IRL. Dist: Dufour Editions, Inc.
Machell, Dawn, illus. Super Sticker Activity: Baby Animals. 2016. (ENG.). 32p. (J). (gr. -1). 5.99 *(978-1-62686-648-5(1)*, Silver Dolphin Bks.) Readerlink Distribution Services, LLC.
—Super Sticker Activity: Christmas. 2016. (Super Sticker Activity Ser.). (ENG.). 32p. (J). (gr. -1). pap. 5.99 *(978-1-62686-665-2(1)*, Silver Dolphin Bks.) Readerlink Distribution Services, LLC.
—Super Sticker Activity: Dinos. 2016. (ENG.). 32p. (J). (gr. -1). 5.99 *(978-1-62686-649-2(X)*, Silver Dolphin Bks.) Readerlink Distribution Services, LLC.
—Super Sticker Activity: Things That Go. 2016. (ENG.). 32p. (J). (gr. -1). 5.99 *(978-1-62686-650-8(3)*, Silver Dolphin Bks.) Readerlink Distribution Services, LLC.
—Super Sticker Activity: Tricks & Treats. 2016. (Super Sticker Activity Ser.). (ENG.). 32p. (J). (gr. -1). 5.99 *(978-1-62686-705-5(4)*, Silver Dolphin Bks.) Readerlink Distribution Services, LLC.
MacKenzie, Carine. Bible Heroes Elijah. 2005. (Bible Art Ser.). (ENG.). 16p. (J). act. bk. ed. 1.99 *(978-1-84550-089-4(X)*, 7336c626-8c11-4b07-8c54-3f395d9c105e) Christian Focus Pubns. GBR. Dist: Bookmasters Distribution.
MacKinnon, Mairi. The Usborne Animal Alphabet Activity Book. Home, Sarah & Barker, Vicky, illus. 2014. (ENG.). (J). pap. 9.99 *(978-0-7945-3274-1(8)*, Usborne) EDC Publishing.
Maclaine, James. Drawing, Doodling & Coloring Book Boys. 2012. (Activity Cards Ser.). 128p. (J). pap. 13.99 *(978-0-7945-3296-3(9)*, Usborne) EDC Publishing.
MacLaine, James & Bowman, Lucy. The Usborne Little Boys' Activity Book. Watt, Fiona, ed. Harrison, Erica et al, illus. 2014. (ENG.). 64p. (J). pap. 9.99 *(978-0-7945-2888-1(0)*, Usborne) EDC Publishing.
Macmillan Children's Books Staff. Party Time Sticker Book: Over 250 Stickers. 2014. (Star Paws Animal Dress-Up Ser.). (ENG.). 24p. (J). (gr. -1-2). pap. 5.99 *(978-1-4380-0432-7(X))* Barron's Educational Series, Inc.
—Pirates Sticker Book: Over 250 Stickers. 2014. (Star Paws Animal Dress-Up Ser.). (ENG.). 24p. (J). (gr. -1-2). pap. 5.99 *(978-1-4380-0433-4(8))* Barron's Educational Series, Inc.
—Princesses Sticker Book: Over 250 Stickers. 2014. (Star Paws Animal Dress-Up Ser.). (ENG.). 24p. (J). (gr. -1-2). pap. 5.99 *(978-1-4380-0434-1(6))* Barron's Educational Series, Inc.
—Super Heroes Sticker Book: Over 250 Stickers. 2014. (Star Paws Animal Dress-Up Ser.). (ENG.). 24p. (J). (gr. -1-2). pap. 5.99 *(978-1-4380-0435-8(4))* Barron's Educational Series, Inc.
Mad Libs Staff. Mad about Mad Libs. 2013. (Mad Libs Ser.). (ENG.). 240p. (J). (gr. 3-7). mass mkt. 6.99 *(978-0-8431-7604-9(0)*, Mad Libs) Penguin Young Readers Group.
Maderna, Victoria. Bacon Stickers. 2016. (Dover Little Activity Books Stickers Ser.). (ENG.). 8p. (J). (gr. k-3). pap. 1.99 *(978-0-486-80443-9(7))* Dover Pubns., Inc.
—Look & Find Letters to Color. 2013. (Dover Coloring Bks.). (ENG., Illus.). 32p. (J). (gr. -1-2). pap. 3.99 *(978-0-486-48702-1(4))* Dover Pubns., Inc.
—Look & Find Numbers to Color. 2014. (ENG.). 48p. (J). (gr. k-5). pap. 4.99 *(978-0-486-49464-7(0))* Dover Pubns., Inc.
—Look & Find Opposites to Color. 2014. (ENG.). 48p. (J). (gr. k-5). pap. 4.99 *(978-0-486-49463-0(2))* Dover Pubns., Inc.
—Playful Pictures — Animals. 2013. (ENG., Illus.). 32p. (J). (gr. -1-8). pap. 3.99 *(978-0-486-49268-1(0))* Dover Pubns., Inc.
—Strawberry Stickers. 2016. (Dover Little Activity Books Stickers Ser.). (ENG.). 8p. (J). (gr. k-3). pap. 1.99 *(978-0-486-80317-3(1))* Dover Pubns., Inc.
Magruder, Trula, ed. Doll School (Revised) 2013. (ENG.). 32p. (J). 21.99 *(978-1-60958-212-8(8))* American Girl Publishing, Inc.
—The Poster Puzzle Book: Puzzles to Solve & Posters to Share. 2009. (ENG.). 64p. (YA). (gr. 3-18). spiral bd. 9.95 *(978-1-59369-591-0(8))* American Girl Publishing, Inc.

S

Mahon, Elaine. Preparing for First Reconciliation: A Guide for Families. 2013. (ENG., Illus.). 32p. (J). pap. 8.95 (978-1-84730-400-1(1)) Veritas Pubns. IRL. Dist: Dufour Editions, Inc.
Mai. Many Hands. 2012. 24p. pap. 15.99 (978-1-4771-4246-2(0)) Xlibris Corp.
Make Believe Ideas. The Best Book in the World Because I Made It. 2014. (ENG.). 70p. (J). pap. 14.99 (978-1-78235-926-5(5)) Make Believe Ideas GBR. Dist: Nelson, Thomas Inc.
—Dot Art. 2013. (ENG.). 80p. (J). pap. 9.99 (978-1-78235-523-6(5)) Make Believe Ideas GBR. Dist: Nelson, Thomas Inc.
—First 100 Pretty Pink Words. 2014. (ENG.). 26p. (J). bds. 8.99 (978-1-78393-232-0(5)) Make Believe Ideas GBR. Dist: Nelson, Thomas Inc.
—Guess What. 2015. (ENG.). 40p. (J). pap. 6.99 (978-1-78393-467-6(0)) Make Believe Ideas GBR. Dist: Nelson, Thomas Inc.
—I Love Felt ABC. 2015. (ENG.). 24p. (J). pap. 6.99 (978-1-78393-527-7(8)) Make Believe Ideas GBR. Dist: Nelson, Thomas Inc.
—I Love to Learn Math Games. 2013. (ENG.). 40p. (J). pap. 4.99 (978-1-78235-201-3(5)) Make Believe Ideas GBR. Dist: Nelson, Thomas Inc.
—I Love to Learn Phonics Letter Sounds. 2013. (ENG.). 40p. (J). pap. 4.99 (978-1-78235-204-4(X)) Make Believe Ideas GBR. Dist: Nelson, Thomas Inc.
—I Love to Learn Phonics Read & Spell. 2013. (ENG.). 40p. (J). pap. 4.99 (978-1-78235-205-1(8)) Make Believe Ideas GBR. Dist: Nelson, Thomas Inc.
—Make This Book. 2015. (ENG.). 70p. (J). spiral bd. 14.99 (978-1-78393-459-1(X)) Make Believe Ideas GBR. Dist: Nelson, Thomas Inc.
—My Best Ever: Things That Go. 2013. (ENG.). 16p. (J). bds. 12.99 (978-1-78235-609-7(6)) Make Believe Ideas GBR. Dist: Nelson, Thomas Inc.
—Paulette's Sticker Salon. 2014. (ENG.). 40p. (J). pap. 6.99 (978-1-78393-444-7(1)) Make Believe Ideas GBR. Dist: Nelson, Thomas Inc.
—Quack-A-doodle-moo. 2015. (ENG.). 28p. (J). spiral bd. 9.99 (978-1-78393-526-0(X)) Make Believe Ideas GBR. Dist: Nelson, Thomas Inc.
—Secret Message Cards. 2015. (ENG.). (J). pap. 9.99 (978-1-78393-456-0(5)) Make Believe Ideas GBR. Dist: Nelson, Thomas Inc.
—Strictly Pink Sticker Activity Fun. 2014. (ENG.). 68p. (J). spiral bd. 14.99 (978-1-78235-970-8(2)) Make Believe Ideas GBR. Dist: Nelson, Thomas Inc.
—Talk to the Door. 2015. (ENG.). 42p. (J). pap. 9.99 (978-1-78393-460-7(3)) Make Believe Ideas GBR. Dist: Nelson, Thomas Inc.
—Think Bubbles. 2013. (ENG.). 80p. (J). pap. 12.99 (978-1-78235-711-7(4)) Make Believe Ideas GBR. Dist: Nelson, Thomas Inc.
—Ultimate Sticker File: Dinosaurs. 2014. (ENG.). 96p. (J). pap. 6.99 (978-1-78393-115-6(9)) Make Believe Ideas GBR. Dist: Nelson, Thomas Inc.
—Under the Sea. 2015. (ENG.). 24p. (J). pap. 6.99 (978-1-78393-471-3(9)) Make Believe Ideas GBR. Dist: Nelson, Thomas Inc.
—1000 Hootiful Stickers. 2014. (ENG.). 56p. (J). pap. 6.99 (978-1-78393-140-8(X)) Make Believe Ideas GBR. Dist: Nelson, Thomas Inc.
—1000 Stickers: Christmas. 2013. (ENG.). 56p. (J). pap. 6.99 (978-1-78235-572-4(3)) Make Believe Ideas GBR. Dist: Nelson, Thomas Inc.
Make Believe Ideas, creator. Busy Baby: First 100 Things That Go. 2008. (Busy Baby Ser.). (Illus.). 26p. (J). (gr. -1-k). bds. (978-1-84610-774-0(1)) Make Believe Ideas.
—The Great Fairy Candy Store Sticker Activity Book. 2014. (ENG., Illus.). 46p. (J). (gr. -1-3). 7.99 (978-1-78235-967-8(2)) Make Believe Ideas GBR. Dist: Nelson, Thomas Inc.
—Lots of Love. 2014. (ENG., Illus.). (J). (978-1-78235-933-3(8)) Make Believe Ideas.
—Mouseton Abbey Sticker Activity Book. 2014. (ENG., Illus.). (J). (gr. -1-3). pap. (978-1-78235-887-9(0)) Make Believe Ideas.
—My Fairy Dress up Book. 2007. (Illus.). 12p. (J). (gr. -1-3). (978-1-84610-530-2(7)) Make Believe Ideas.
—My Princess Dress up Book. 2007. (Illus.). 12p. (J). (gr. -1-3). (978-1-84610-529-6(3)) Make Believe Ideas.
—My Scrapbook about Me. 2007. (Illus.). 20p. (J). (gr. k-2). (978-1-84610-424-4(6)) Make Believe Ideas.
—Pink Puppy Sticker Activity Book. 2014. (ENG., Illus.). 96p. (J). (gr. -1-3). 9.99 (978-1-78235-947-0(8)) Make Believe Ideas GBR. Dist: Nelson, Thomas Inc.
Man-Kong, Mary. Code Racers. 2017. (Pictureback(R) Ser.). (ENG., Illus.). 24p. (J). (gr. -1-2). pap. 4.99 (978-0-399-55932-7(9), Random Hse. Bks. for Young Readers) Random Hse. Children's Bks.
—Dream Dancer. Golden Books, illus. 2013. (Color Plus Chunky Crayons Ser.). (ENG.). 48p. (J). (gr. -1-2). pap. 3.99 (978-0-307-98103-5(7), Golden Bks.) Random Hse. Children's Bks.
—Easter Stencil Fun! (Peter Cottontail) Karl, Linda, illus. 2014. (Color Plus Stencil Ser.). (ENG.). 64p. (J). (gr. -1-2). pap. 5.99 (978-0-385-37442-2(9), Golden Bks.) Random Hse. Children's Bks.
—Hoppy Easter! (Peter Cottontail) Karl, Linda, illus. 2013. (Full-Color Activity Book with Stickers Ser.). (ENG.). 32p. (J). (gr. -1-2). pap. 3.99 (978-0-307-98230-8(0), Golden Bks.) Random Hse. Children's Bks.
—Mermaid Style. 2014. (Color Plus Chunky Crayons Ser.). (ENG., Illus.). 48p. (J). (gr. -1-2). pap. 3.99 (978-0-385-37306-7(6), Golden Bks.) Random Hse. Children's Bks.
—Pink-Tastic! (Barbie) Duarte, Pamela, illus. 2016. (Coloring Book Ser.). (ENG.). 128p. (J). (gr. -1-2). pap. 5.99 (978-1-101-93248-3(1), Golden Bks.) Random Hse. Children's Bks.
—Pop Star Dreams (Barbie) Golden Books Staff & Duarte, Pamela, illus. 2013. (Color Plus Tattoos Ser.). (ENG.). 48p. (J). (gr. -1-2). pap. 3.99 (978-0-449-81611-0(7), Golden Bks.) Random Hse. Children's Bks.
—Purr-Fect Valentine! (Barbie) Golden Books, illus. 2012. (Deluxe Paint Box Book Ser.). (ENG.). 128p. (J). (gr. -1-2). pap. 7.99 (978-0-307-98210-0(6), Golden Bks.) Random Hse. Children's Bks.
—Spy Style. 2016. (Color Plus Crayons & Sticker Ser.). (ENG.). 48p. (J). (gr. -1-2). pap. 4.99 (978-0-553-53916-5(7), Golden Bks.) Random Hse. Children's Bks.
Mancini, Joan. 25 Super Sight Word Songs & Mini-Books: Fun Songs Set to Favorite Tunes with Companion Read & Write Mini-Books That Teach Essential Sight Words. 2009. (ENG.). 112p. (gr. k-2). 20.99 (978-0-545-10582-8(X), Teaching Resources) Scholastic, Inc.
Mancini-Wilson, Debbie. Color My World: An Interactive Poetry Book for Kids of All Ages. 2007. (Illus.). 80p. (J). 19.99 (978-0-9787586-0-8(9)) Harmony Pubns., LLC.
Manualidades y Otro Actividades. 2006. 32p. (J). pap. 8.99 (978-0-7460-6647-8(3), Usborne) EDC Publishing.
Manushkin, Fran. Katie Woo's Super Stylish Activity Book, 1 vol. Alder, Charlie, illus. 2013. (Katie Woo Ser.). (ENG.). 64p. (gr. k-2). pap. 4.95 (978-1-4795-2047-3(0)) Picture Window Bks.
Marie-France, Marcie & Lebuis, Peter. Divisions Chansons et Activités, 1 vol. 2013. (ENG & FRE.). 64p. 19.95 (978-1-55386-235-2(X), 9781553862352) Jordan, Sara Publishing.
—Multiplications Chansons et Activités, 2 vols. 2013. (ENG & FRE.). 64p. 19.95 (978-1-55386-229-1(5), 9781553862291) Jordan, Sara Publishing.
—Soustractions Chansons et Activités, 2 vols. 2013. (ENG & FRE.). 64p. 19.95 (978-1-55386-232-1(5), 9781553862321) Jordan, Sara Publishing.
Marinaro, Stacy. If I Became a U. S. Marine. 2009. 46p. 24.95 (978-0-615-21988-2(8)) Marinaro, Stacy.
Marrero, Alba. Diego's Busy Week: Learn the days of the week as you tag along with a boy named Diego. 2009. 20p. pap. 10.99 (978-1-4389-5201-7(5)) AuthorHouse.
Marsh, Carole. America's National Parks Coloring & Activity Book. 2016. (Non-State Ser.). (ENG., Illus.). (J). pap. 5.99 (978-0-635-12460-9(2)) Gallopade International.
—The Big Florida Reproducible Activity Book! 2004. (Florida Experience Ser.). (Illus.). 96p. pap. 12.95 (978-0-635-06408-0(1)) Gallopade International.
—The Big New Hampshire Reproducible Activity Book-New Version. 2015. (New Hampshire Experience Ser.). (ENG.). (J). pap. 12.95 (978-0-635-06491-2(X)) Gallopade International.
—The Big Oklahoma Reproducible Activity Book! 2008. (Oklahoma Experience Ser.). (Illus.). 96p. pap. 12.95 (978-0-635-06402-8(2)) Gallopade International.
—Electricity: Common Core Lessons & Activities. 2013. (Common Core Ser.). (ENG., Illus.). 24p. (J). (gr. 4-7). pap. 4.99 (978-0-635-10614-8(0)) Gallopade International.
—Quit Bossing Us Around! The Declaration of Independence. 2004. (American Milestones Ser.). (Illus.). 28p. (J). (gr. 4-12). pap. 5.95 (978-0-635-02680-4(5)) Gallopade International.
Martin, Jorge. Fingerprint Fun. Martin, Jorge, illus. 2016. (ENG., Illus.). 32p. (J). (gr. -1-1). pap. 7.99 (978-1-78055-304-7(8)) O'Mara, Michael Bks., Ltd. GBR. Dist: Independent Pubs. Group.
Martinez, Kathleen & Edwards, Sue. Colossal Clubs: Activities-Based Curriculum for School-Age Programs. Edwards, Mark, illus. 2006. per. 29.95 (978-0-917505-39-3(5), School Age Notes) Gryphon Hse., Inc.
Marvel Book Group, et al. My Ultimate Super Hero Manual. 2016. (ENG.). 176p. (J). (gr. 3-7). 13.99 (978-1-4847-5075-9(6), Marvel Pr.) Disney Publishing Worldwide.
Marvel Comics. Color Your Own Marvel Masters. 2017. (ENG., Illus.). 120p. (J). (gr. -1-17). pap. 9.99 **(978-1-302-90273-5(3))** Marvel Worldwide, Inc.
—Color Your Own Thor. 2017. (ENG., Illus.). 120p. (J). (gr. -1-17). 9.99 **(978-1-302-90378-7(0))** Marvel Worldwide, Inc.
Masters, Neil. Butterflies Coloring Book. 2013. (ENG.). 34p. 12.07 (978-1-62884-656-0(9), Baby Professor (Education Kids)) Speedy Publishing LLC.
Masterson, Josephine. A Nest for Robin. 2015. (Rosen REAL Readers: STEM & STEAM Collection). (ENG.). 12p. (gr. 1-2). pap. 6.33 (978-1-4994-9511-9(0), Rosen Classroom) Rosen Publishing Group, Inc., The.
Math Puzzle Pad (was Math Games Pad) 2017. (Tear-Off Pads Ser.). (ENG.). (J). pap. 5.99 **(978-0-7945-3805-7(3)**, Usborne) EDC Publishing.
Matheis, Mickie. Peanuts Mad Libs. 2015. (Mad Libs Ser.). (ENG.). 48p. (J). (gr. 3-7). pap. 4.99 (978-0-8431-8331-3(4), Mad Libs) Penguin Young Readers Group.
Matthews, Caitlín & Matthews, John. Legends of the Sea: Create-A-Story Kit. 2011. (Storyworld Ser.). (ENG., Illus.). 22p. (J). (gr. 4-7). 9.99 (978-0-7636-5320-0(9), Templar) Candlewick Pr.
Matthews, John & Matthews, Caitlin. Storyworld: Create a Story Kit. 2010. (Illus.). (978-0-7636-5319-4(5)) Templar Publishing.
Matz, Rita T. What Can I Do Today? 2013. 118p. (gr. -1-6). pap. 12.19 (978-1-4669-8324-3(8)) Trafford Publishing.
May, Darcy. Glitter Christmas Fairy Sticker Paper Doll. 2008. (Dover Little Activity Books Paper Dolls Ser.). (ENG., Illus.). 2p. (J). (gr. 1-4). 1.99 (978-0-486-46536-4(5)) Dover Pubns., Inc.
Mayer, Kirsten. Make a Minion. 2013. (ENG., Illus.). 12p. (J). (gr. -1-1). pap. 6.99 (978-0-316-24031-4(1)) Little, Brown Bks. for Young Readers.
—Monster High. 2015. (ENG., Illus.). 128p. (J). (gr. 1-17). pap. 12.99 (978-0-316-28721-0(0)) Little, Brown Bks. for Young Readers.
—Monster High: Create-A-Monster Design Lab Sticker Book. 2015. (ENG., Illus.). 96p. (J). (gr. k-17). pap. 12.99 (978-0-316-33746-5(3)) Little, Brown Bks. for Young Readers.
Mazurkiewicz, Jessica. Butterfly Fun Activity Book. 2009. (Dover Little Activity Bks.). (ENG., Illus.). 64p. (J). (gr. k-3). pap. 1.99 (978-0-486-47198-3(5)) Dover Pubns., Inc.
—Forever Inspired Coloring Book - Unicorns & Mystical Creatures. 2016. (ENG., Illus.). 96p. (J). (gr. 3-7). pap. 7.99 (978-1-944686-22-2(3), Racehorse Publishing) Skyhorse Publishing Co., Inc.
—Forever Inspired Coloring Book: Fairyworld. 2016. (ENG., Illus.). 96p. (J). (gr. 3-7). pap. 7.99 (978-1-944686-23-9(1), Racehorse Publishing) Skyhorse Publishing Co., Inc.
—Haunted House Activity Book. 2010. (Dover Little Activity Bks.). (ENG., Illus.). 64p. (J). (gr. k-3). pap. 1.50 (978-0-486-47522-6(0)) Dover Pubns., Inc.
—Psalms Stained Glass Coloring Book. 2011. (Dover Stained Glass Coloring Book Ser.). (ENG., Illus.). 32p. (J). (gr. 2-5). pap. 7.99 (978-0-486-47834-0(3)) Dover Pubns., Inc.
—Santa's Workshop Stained Glass Coloring Book. 2008. (Holiday Stained Glass Coloring Book Ser.). (ENG., Illus.). 32p. (J). (gr. 3-5). pap. 6.99 (978-0-486-46937-9(9)) Dover Pubns., Inc.
—Treasure Hunt. 2009. (Dover Little Activity Bks.). (ENG.). 64p. (J). (gr. k-3). pap., act. bk. ed. 1.99 (978-0-486-47042-9(3)) Dover Pubns., Inc.
—3-D Coloring Book — Abstractions. 2014. (Dover 3-D Coloring Book Ser.). (ENG., Illus.). 32p. (J). (gr. 3-5). pap. 5.99 (978-0-486-48416-7(5)) Dover Pubns., Inc.
Mazurkiewicz, Jessica & Noble, Marty. 3-D Coloring Book - Christmas Designs. 2013. (Dover 3-D Coloring Book Ser.). (ENG.). 128p. (J). (gr. 3-12). pap. 9.99 (978-0-486-49343-5(1)) Dover Pubns., Inc.
McCann, Emily. Animal Doodles. McCann, Emily, illus. 2011. (Doodle On! Ser.). (ENG., Illus.). 160p. (J). (gr. k-4). 15.99 (978-0-230-74485-1(0)) Pan Macmillan GBR. Dist: Independent Pubs. Group.
McCarthy, Pat. Heading West: Life with the Pioneers, 21 Activities. 2009. (For Kids Ser.). (ENG., Illus.). 144p. (J). (gr. 4-7). pap. 16.95 (978-1-55652-809-5(4)) Chicago Review Pr., Inc.
McCumbee, Stephie. The Garden in My Mind Activity Guide: Lessons for Social Skill & Common Core Development. Griffin, Lisa M., illus. 2014. (ENG.). 48p. pap. 20.95 (978-1-934490-55-6(5)) Boys Town Pr.
McKay, Jodi. Where Are the Words? Holmes, Denise, illus. 2016. (ENG.). 32p. (J). (gr. -1-3). 16.99 (978-0-8075-8733-1(8)) Whitman, Albert & Co.
McLaughlin, Kari Massie. My Adventure with Dragonflies. 2009. 44p. (J). 8.99 (978-1-59092-452-5(5)) Blue Forge Pr.
—My Adventure with Flamingos. 2009. 44p. (J). 8.99 (978-1-59092-454-9(1)) Blue Forge Pr.
—My Adventure with Ladybugs. 2009. (ENG.). 44p. (J). 8.99 (978-1-59092-457-0(6)) Blue Forge Pr.
—My Adventure with Penguins. 2009. (ENG.). 44p. (J). 8.99 (978-1-59092-461-7(4)) Blue Forge Pr.
—My Adventure with the Cherokee. 2007. 44p. (J). 8.99 (978-1-59092-446-4(0)) Blue Forge Pr.
—My Adventure with the Wright Brothers. 2007. 44p. (J). 8.99 (978-1-59092-471-6(1)) Blue Forge Pr.
—My Adventure with Thomas Edison. 2007. 44p. (J). 8.99 (978-1-59092-472-3(X)) Blue Forge Pr.
McManaman, Yelena & Droujkova, Maria. Moebius Noodles: Adventurous Math for the Playground Crowd. 2015. (Natural Math Ser.: 3). (Illus.). 88p. pap. 15.00 (978-0-9776939-5-5(3)) Delta Stream Media.
McNab, Laura. Glitter Art. 2013. (ENG.). 80p. (J). pap. 9.99 (978-1-78235-522-9(7)) Make Believe Ideas GBR. Dist: Nelson, Thomas Inc.
McNamara, Margaret. The Pumpkin Patch. Gordon, Mike, illus. 2008. (Robin Hill School Ser.). (J). (gr. -1-1). pap. 16.95 (978-1-4301-0622-7(0)) Live Oak Media.
McNeil, Niki, et al. HOCPP 1053 Narnia. 2005. spiral bd. 15.50 (978-1-60308-053-8(8)) In the Hands of a Child.
—HOCPP 1072 Katy's Big Snow Day. 2006. spiral bd. 15.50 (978-1-60308-072-9(4)) In the Hands of a Child.
—HOCPP 1073 Charlotte & Wilbur. 2006. spiral bd. 24.50 (978-1-60308-073-6(2)) In the Hands of a Child.
McNutt, Nan. The Spindle Whorl. Fernandes, Roger & Point, Susan, illus. 2nd ed. 2011. (Native American Art Activity Book Ser.). (ENG.). 56p. (J). (gr. 3-5). pap. 9.95 (978-0-88240-762-3(7), West Winds Pr.) Graphic Arts Ctr. Publishing Co.
—The Twined Basket. Youso, Justin & Kaino, Kim, illus. 2011. (Native American Art Activity Book Ser.). (ENG.). 56p. (J). (gr. 5-7). pap. 9.95 (978-0-88240-760-9(0), West Winds Pr.) Graphic Arts Ctr. Publishing Co.
McSweeney's. The Goods: Volume 1. 2013. (ENG., Illus.). 96p. (J). pap. 22.99 (978-0-7636-6894-5(X), Big Picture Press) Candlewick Pr.
Meekins, Katrina L. Deep Blue Year of Festivals: Intergenerational Celebrations. 2016. (Deep Blue Ser.). 48p. pap. 12.99 (978-1-5018-2033-5(8)) Abingdon Pr.
Meloche, Renee Taft. Heroes for Young Readers Activity Guide for Books 1-4: Educational & Character-Building Lessons for Children. 2006. (Heroes for Young Readers Ser.). (Illus.). 90p. per. 12.99 (978-1-57658-367-8(8)) YWAM Publishing.
—Heroes for Young Readers Activity Guide for Books 13-16: Educational & Character-Building Lessons for Children. 2006. (ENG., Illus.). 85p. pap. 12.99 (978-1-57658-370-8(8)) YWAM Publishing.
Menten, Ted. Steampunk Vixens Paper Dolls. 2014. (ENG.). 32p. (gr. 6-12). pap. 9.99 (978-0-486-78340-6(5)) Dover Pubns., Inc.
Meredith, Samantha & Wyk, Hanri van, illus. Weddings Sticker Color Book. 2011. (First Sticker Coloring Bks). 20p. (J). pap. 5.99 (978-0-7945-3108-9(3), Usborne) EDC Publishing.
Merrill, Yvonne Y. America Vol. 3: Art Activities about Lewis & Clark, Pioneers, & Plains Indians. Simpson, Mary, illus. 2009. (Hands-on Ser.: 3). (ENG.). 82p. (gr. k-10). pap. 25.00 (978-0-9778797-1-7(2)) KK.
Metropolitan Museum of Art Staff, contrib. by. Color Magic Sticker Play Book. 2008. (ENG., Illus.). 16p. (J). (gr. k-2). spiral bd. 25.95 (978-0-8109-7126-4(7), Abrams Bks. for Young Readers) Abrams, Inc.
Metsola, Aino-Maija, illus. My First Words. 2017. (ENG.). 14p. (J). bds. 12.99 (978-1-62686-968-4(5), Silver Dolphin Bks.) Readerlink Distribution Services, LLC.
Meyer, Jan. Brain Quest, Grade 3: A Whole Year of Curriculum-Based Exercises & Activities in One Fun Book! Shults, Anna, ed. 2008. (ENG., Illus.). 320p. (J). (gr. 3-3). wbk. ed. 12.95 (978-0-7611-4916-3(3), 14916) Workman Publishing Co., Inc.
Michael O'Mara. Dress up Taylor Swift. Fearns, Georgie, illus. 2016. (ENG.). 34p. (J). (gr. 1-3). pap. 9.99 (978-1-78055-387-0(0)) O'Mara, Michael Bks., Ltd. GBR. Dist: Independent Pubs. Group.
Michael O'Mara Books. I Heart Lists. 2017. (I Heart Ser.). (ENG.). 128p. (J). (gr. 2). pap. 8.99 **(978-1-78055-450-1(8))** O'Mara, Michael Bks., Ltd. GBR. Dist: Independent Pubs. Group.
Michaels, Sarah, et al. Extra Ring Bling Rings: Rb67. 2013. 9.95 (978-1-60723-093-9(3)) Super Duper Pubns.
—Ring Bling Extra Hands: Rb69. 2013. pap. 14.95 (978-1-60723-092-2(5)) Super Duper Pubns.
Michele, Tracey. Make a String Phone. 2011. (Learn-Abouts Ser.). (Illus.). 16p. (J). pap. 7.95 (978-1-59920-607-3(2)) Black Rabbit Bks.
—Make a Treasure Map. 2011. (Illus.). 16p. (J). pap. 7.95 (978-1-59920-606-6(4)) Black Rabbit Bks.
Micheletti, Judy. Snibbles: Really Creative Problem Solving Lessons & Mind-Stimulating Exercises for Gifted Students & Their Teachers, Ages 5 through Really Old! 2005. (Illus.). 70p. (978-0-910609-50-0(0)) Gifted Education Pr.
Micronations: Invent Your Own Country & Culture with 25 Projects. 2014. (Build It Yourself Ser.). (ENG., Illus.). 128p. (J). (gr. 3-7). 21.95 (978-1-61930-218-1(7)) Open City Bks.
Midgley, Elizabeth Cole. Daily Discoveries for August. Mitchell, Judith, ed. Guymon, Jennette King, illus. 2005. 192p. (J). pap. 12.95 (978-1-57310-452-4(3)) Teaching & Learning Co.
—Daily Discoveries for October. Mitchell, Judith, ed. Guymon, Jennette King, illus. 2005. 192p. (J). pap. 12.95 (978-1-57310-454-8(X)) Teaching & Learning Co.
—Daily Discoveries for September. Mitchess, Judith, ed. Guymon, Jennette King, illus. 2005. 192p. (J). pap. 12.95 (978-1-57310-453-1(1)) Teaching & Learning Co.
Miles, David, illus. Wild about the Bible Sticker & Activity Book, 1 vol. 2016. (Adventure Bible Ser.). (ENG.). 32p. (J). pap. 6.99 (978-0-310-75405-3(4)) Zonderkidz.
Miles, Lisa. Best Friends: Over 1000 Reusable Stickers! 2014. (Little Hands Creative Sticker Play Ser.). (ENG.). 64p. (J). (gr. -1-2). pap. 9.99 (978-1-4380-0390-0(0)) Barron's Educational Series, Inc.
—The Fairy Tale Creativity Book: Games, Cut-Outs, Art Paper, Stickers, & Stencils! 2014. (Creativity Bks.). (ENG.). 88p. (J). (gr. 1-5). pap. 12.99 (978-1-4380-0385-6(4)) Barron's Educational Series, Inc.
—The Girls' Super Activity Book. 2013. (ENG.). 144p. (J). pap. 8.95 (978-1-78212-060-5(2)) Arcturus Publishing GBR. Dist: Bookmasters Distribution.
Miller, Eileen Rudisill. Fashion Models Paper Dolls. 2013. (Dover Paper Dolls Ser.). (ENG.). 32p. (J). (gr. 2-5). pap. 7.99 (978-0-486-48877-6(2)) Dover Pubns., Inc.
—Glitter Princess Stickers. 2008. (Dover Little Activity Books Stickers Ser.). (ENG., Illus.). 2p. (J). (gr. 1-4). 1.99 (978-0-486-46577-7(2)) Dover Pubns., Inc.
—Glitter Snow Princess Sticker Paper Doll. 2009. (Dover Little Activity Books Paper Dolls Ser.). (ENG.). 2p. (J). (gr. 1-4). pap. 1.99 (978-0-486-47138-9(1)) Dover Pubns., Inc.
—Happy Easter Stained Glass Coloring Book. 2010. (Holiday Stained Glass Coloring Book Ser.). (ENG., Illus.). 32p. (J). (gr. -1-8). pap. 6.99 (978-0-486-47296-6(5)) Dover Pubns., Inc.
—Nutcracker Ballet Paper Dolls with Glitter! 2011. (Dover Paper Dolls Ser.). (ENG.). 32p. (J). (gr. 1-4). pap. 12.99 (978-0-486-48390-0(8)) Dover Pubns., Inc.
—Teen Pop Stars Paper Dolls. 2011. (Dover Celebrity Paper Dolls Ser.). (ENG., Illus.). 32p. (J). (gr. 1-5). pap. 7.99 (978-0-486-48096-1(8)) Dover Pubns., Inc.
Miller, Mona. A Very Busy Coloring Book. Golden Books, illus. 2013. (Jumbo Coloring Book Ser.). (ENG.). 224p. (J). (gr. -1-2). pap. 5.99 (978-0-449-81609-7(5), Golden Bks.) Random Hse. Children's Bks.
Milton, Elizabeth. Dinotrux: Build It Up: A Dinotrux Sticker Book. 2016. (ENG., Illus.). 12p. (J). (gr. -1-1). pap. 6.99 (978-0-316-26079-4(7)) Little, Brown Bks. for Young Readers.
Minden, Cecilia & Roth, Kate. Language Arts Explorer Junior, 10 vols., Set. Incl. How to Write a Journal. lib. bdg. 25.64 (978-1-60279-994-3(6), 200988); How to Write a Letter. lib. bdg. 25.64 (978-1-60279-991-2(1), 200982); How to Write a Poem. lib. bdg. 25.64 (978-1-60279-995-0(4), 200990); How to Write a Report. lib. bdg. 25.64 (978-1-61080-105-8(9), 201112); How to Write about Your Adventure. lib. bdg. 25.64 (978-1-61080-106-5(7), 201114); How to Write an Ad. lib. bdg. 25.64 (978-1-61080-107-2(5), 201116); How to Write an E-Mail. lib. bdg. 25.64 (978-1-60279-993-6(8), 200986); How to Write an Interview. lib. bdg. 25.64 (978-1-60279-996-7(2), 200992); How to Write & Give a Speech. lib. bdg. 25.64 (978-1-61080-108-9(3), 201118); 24p. (gr. 1-4). 2011. Set lib. bdg. 256.40 (978-1-61080-153-9(9)) Cherry Lake Publishing.
Miner, Julie Dobson. EEK! Mini Monsters Tattoos. 2016. (Dover Little Activity Bks.). (ENG.). 4p. (J). (gr. -1-2). pap. 1.99 (978-0-486-80586-3(7)) Dover Pubns., Inc.
—EEK! Monsters Coloring Book. 2017. (Dover Coloring Bks.). (ENG., Illus.). 32p. (J). (gr. -1-2). pap. 3.99 (978-0-486-81441-4(6)) Dover Pubns., Inc.
Mitchell, Cindi. Connect-the-Dot Math: 35 Reproducible Dot-to-Dot Activities That Help Kids Practice Multi-Digit Addition & Subtraction & Basic Multiplication & Division Facts. 2009. (ENG.). 80p. pap. 12.99 (978-0-439-44993-9(6), Teaching Resources) Scholastic, Inc.
Mitton, Tony. Flashing Fire Engines. Parker, Ant, illus. 2016. (Amazing Machines Ser.). (ENG.). 24p. pap., act. bk. ed. 4.99 (978-0-7534-7256-9(2), 9780753472569, Kingfisher) Roaring Brook Pr.
—My Amazing Machines Cool Cars Activity Book. Parker, Ant, illus. 2017. (Amazing Machines Ser.). (ENG.). 24p. pap. 5.99 (978-0-7534-7296-5(1), 9780753472965, Kingfisher) Roaring Brook Pr.
—My Amazing Machines Terrific Trains Activity Book. Parker, Ant, illus. 2017. (Amazing Machines Ser.). (ENG.). 24p. (J). pap. 5.99 (978-0-7534-7295-8(3), 9780753472958, Kingfisher) Roaring Brook Pr.
Mitzo Thompson, Kim, et al. Coloring Journal for Girls. 2017. (ENG.). 64p. (J). spiral bd. 9.99 **(978-1-68322-195-1(8))** Barbour Publishing, Inc.
—Make Your Own Sticker Crafts, Gifts, & More. 2017. (ENG.). 12p. (J). pap. 4.99 **(978-1-68322-198-2(2))** Barbour Publishing, Inc.

Modern Publishing, creator. Smurfs & Smiles! Giant Coloring & Activity Book. 2010. (Smurf Ser.). (Illus.). 96p. (J). 2.49 *(978-0-7666-3746-7(8))* Modern Publishing.
—The Smurfs Super Coloring & Activity Bk. 2010. (Smurf Ser.). (Illus.). (J). 3.99 *(978-0-7666-3774-0(3))* Modern Publishing.
—A Smurfy Day! Giant Coloring & Activity Book. 2010. (Smurf Ser.). (Illus.). 96p. (J). 2.49 *(978-0-7666-3745-0(X))* Modern Publishing.
—Way to Go, Wildcats! 2009. (Disney High School Musical 3: Senior Year Ser.). (Illus.). (J). (gr. 4-7). pap. 2.99 *(978-0-7666-3233-2(4))* Modern Publishing.
Modern Publishing Staff. Angry Birds Giant Coloring & Activity Book-Big Surprise! 2013. pap. *(978-1-55993-451-0(4))* PSI & Assocs.
—Ariel's World! 2007. (Disney Bath Time Bubble Bks.). (J). (gr. -1-k). 4.99 *(978-0-7666-2554-9(0))* Modern Publishing.
—Colors! 2007. (Disney Bath Time Bubble Bks.). (Illus.). (J). (gr. -1-k). 4.99 *(978-0-7666-2552-5(4))* Modern Publishing.
—Feelings! 2007. (Disney Bath Time Bubble Bks.). (Illus.). (J). (gr. -1-k). 4.99 *(978-0-7666-2550-1(8))* Modern Publishing.
—Fisher-Price Laugh, Smile & Learn. 2009. 96p. (J). (gr. -1). pap. 2.99 *(978-0-7666-3488-6(4))* Modern Publishing.
—Fisher Price Little People Kindergarten, Vol. 1. 2013. pap., wbk. ed. *(978-0-7666-2817-5(5))* Modern Publishing.
—Fisher-Price Precious Planet. 2010. (Color by Number Bks.). (J). 64p. pap. 2.99 *(978-0-7666-3727-6(1))*; 112p. (gr. -1). pap. 4.99 *(978-0-7666-3755-9(7))* Modern Publishing.
—Fisher-Price Spike. 2010. (Super Coloring & Activity Bks.). 112p. (J). (gr. -1). pap. 4.99 *(978-0-7666-3756-6(5))* Modern Publishing.
—Fisher-Price Spike the Ultra Dinosaur. 2009. (Giant Coloring & Activity Bks.). 96p. (J). (gr. -1). pap. 2.99 *(978-0-7666-3491-6(4))* Modern Publishing.
—Lisa Frank Super Coloring & Activity Book with Handle: A Colorful World! 2010. 96p. pap. 5.99 *(978-0-7666-3807-5(3))* Modern Publishing.
—Opposites! 2007. (Disney Bath Time Bubble Bks.). (Illus.). (J). (gr. -1-k). 4.99 *(978-0-7666-2556-3(7))* Modern Publishing.
—Toys! 2007. (Disney Bath Time Bubble Bks.). (Illus.). (J). (gr. -1-k). 4.99 *(978-0-7666-2549-5(4))* Modern Publishing.
—Zhu Zhu Pets Giant Coloring & Activity Book: Furry Friends! 2010. 96p. (J). pap. 2.99 *(978-0-7666-3764-1(6))* Modern Publishing.
—Zhu Zhu Pets Giant Coloring & Activity Book: Happy Hamsters! 2010. 96p. (J). pap. 2.99 *(978-0-7666-3765-8(4))* Modern Publishing.
Modern Publishing Staff, ed. Lots of Fun in Care a Lot. 2005. 12p. pap. 3.99 *(978-0-7666-1868-8(4))* Modern Publishing.
—Record Breaking Racers. 2005. 32p. pap. 2.99 *(978-0-7666-1909-8(5))* Modern Publishing.
—Sun & Fun in Care a Lot. 2005. 12p. pap. 3.99 *(978-0-7666-1869-5(2))* Modern Publishing.
—Tuned up Challengers. 2005. 12p. pap. 2.99 *(978-0-7666-1908-1(7))* Modern Publishing.
Modern Publishing Staff & Disney Staff, contrib. by. A Day in the Life. 2007. 39p. pap. 4.99 *(978-0-7666-2811-3(6))* Modern Publishing.
Moerbeek, Kees, illus. & des. Jungle Explorers. Moerbeek, Kees, des. 2008. (Roly Poly Box Bks.). (ENG.). 24p. (J). (gr. -1-1). *(978-1-84643-243-9(X))* Child's Play International Ltd.
—Ocean Explorers. Moerbeek, Kees, des. 2008. (Roly Poly Box Bks.). (ENG.). 24p. (J). (gr. -1-1). *(978-1-84643-245-3(6))* Child's Play International Ltd.
—Snow Explorers. Moerbeek, Kees, des. 2008. (Roly Poly Box Bks.). (ENG.). 24p. (J). (gr. -1-1). *(978-1-84643-244-6(8))* Child's Play International Ltd.
—Space Explorers. Moerbeek, Kees, des. 2008. (Roly Poly Box Bks.). (ENG.). 24p. (J). (gr. -1-1). *(978-1-84643-246-0(4))* Child's Play International Ltd.
Moffatt, Frances. My Fashion Doodles & Designs: 200 Activities to Sketch, Color & Create. 2015. (ENG., Illus.). 208p. (gr. 2). pap. 16.95 *(978-1-61243-434-6(7))* Ulysses Pr.
Molnar, Ilona, et al. Fingerprint Princesses & Fairies. 2016. (Fingerprint Art Ser.). (ENG., Illus.). 160p. (J). (gr. 3-7). pap. 14.99 *(978-1-63159-142-6(8))*, Quarry Bks.) Quarto Publishing Group USA.
Monet, Claude & Noble, Marty. Colorier Vos Propres Tableaux de Monet. 2013. (Dover Children's Bilingual Coloring Book Ser.). (FRE & ENG.). 64p. (gr. 3-12). pap. 5.99 *(978-0-486-49328-2(8))* Dover Pubns., Inc.
Monsen, John, et al. Pirate's Log: A Handbook for Aspiring Swashbucklers. Ford, Gilbert, illus. 2008. (ENG.). 172p. (J). (gr. 3-5). 15.95 *(978-0-8118-6435-0(9))* Chronicle Bks. LLC.
MoonRattles. Heritage Holiday Activity Guide: Chinese New Year 2007, 1 vol. 2006. (Illus.). 52p. (J). spiral bd. *(978-0-9790920-0-8(0))* MoonRattles.
—Heritage Holiday Activity Guide: Seventh Lunar Month. 2007. (Illus.). 52p. (J). spiral bd. *(978-0-9790920-5-3(1))* MoonRattles.
Morris, Linda Loper. No Yellow Horse, If You Please. 2011. 28p. pap. 15.99 *(978-1-4628-4628-3(9))* Xlibris Corp.
Mother Goose Programs, prod. What's the BIG Idea? Shapes & Spaces Librarian Manual. 2008. 70p. pap. *(978-0-9753985-9-3(8))* Mother Goose Programs.
Mucklow, Lacy. Color Me Fearless: Nearly 100 Coloring Templates to Boost Strength & Courage. Porter, Angela, illus. 2016. (Zen Coloring Book Ser.). (ENG.). 208p. pap. 16.99 *(978-1-63106-195-0(X))*, Race Point Publishing) Quarto Publishing Group USA.
Mucklow, Lacy & Porter, Angela. Color Me to Sleep: Nearly 100 Coloring Templates to Promote Relaxation & Restful Sleep. 2016. (Zen Coloring Book Ser.). (ENG., Illus.). 208p. pap. 16.99 *(978-1-63106-237-7(9))*, Race Point Publishing) Quarto Publishing Group USA.
Multicultural Activities Blackline Masters. (Greetings Ser.). (gr. 3-5). 21.00 *(978-0-7635-2230-8(9))*; 21.00 *(978-0-7635-2231-5(7))* Rigby Education.
Mummakay. Flying Free: Meditations for Kids in Star Language. 2013. (Illus.). 36p. pap. 16.95 *(978-1-4525-0905-1(0))*, Balboa Pr.) Author Solutions, Inc.
Munro, Fiona. Princesses: With 200 Stickers, Puzzles & Games, Fold-Out Pages, & Creative Play. 2013. (My First Creativity Bks.). (ENG.). 66p. (J). (gr. -1-2). pap. 9.99 *(978-1-4380-0323-8(4))* Barron's Educational Series, Inc.
—Under the Sea. 2013. (My First Creativity Activity Bks.). (ENG.). 66p. (J). (gr. -1-2). pap. 9.99 *(978-1-4380-0240-8(8))* Barron's Educational Series, Inc.
Music. ABCs & Much More Activity & Coloring Book. 2008. (Illus.). 177p. (J). pap. 14.95 *(978-0-9818635-1-1(5))* Music, Movement & Magination Bks.
Mussler-Wright, Richard & Baran, Laura. PCS Edventures! Bricklab Grade 3. 2007. (Illus.). spiral bd. *(978-0-9753193-5-2(3))* PCS Edventures, Inc.
—PCS Edventures! Bricklab Grade 4. 2006. spiral bd. *(978-0-9753193-6-9(1))* PCS Edventures, Inc.
My Activity Books for Girls. 2014. (Sticker Activity Bks.). (ENG.). 192p. (J). (gr. -1-3). pap. 10.99 *(978-1-61963-638-5(7))*, 9781619636385, Bloomsbury USA Childrens) Bloomsbury Publishing USA.
My Colours Sticker Activity Book. 2014. (ENG.). 16p. (J). pap. *(978-1-4088-4730-5(2))*, 238775) Bloomsbury Publishing Plc.
My Pretty Pink Ballet Activity & Sticker Book. 2014. (ENG.). 32p. (J). pap. *(978-1-4088-4732-9(9))*, 238789) Bloomsbury Publishing Plc.
My Puptatl Book. 2006. (J). spiral bd. 8.00 *(978-0-9786947-0-8(8))* Puptattle Pr., Inc.
My Puptatl Youth Book. 2006. (J). spiral bd. 8.00 *(978-0-9786947-1-5(6))* Puptattle Pr., Inc.
My Snowman Activity Book. 2007. (Shaped Christmas Activity Ser.). 64p. pap. *(978-1-4075-0358-5(8))* Parragon, Inc.
My Space Activity & Sticker Book. 2014. (ENG.). 32p. (J). pap. *(978-1-4088-4731-2(0))*, 238784) Bloomsbury Publishing Plc.
My Sparkletastic Sticker Activity Book. 2015. (ENG.). 72p. (J). pap. *(978-1-78393-747-9(5))* Make Believe Ideas.
My Spooky Halloween Activity & Sticker Book. 2014. (Sticker Activity Bks.). (ENG.). 32p. (J). (gr. -1-1). pap. 4.99 *(978-1-61963-332-2(9))*, 9781619633322, Bloomsbury USA Childrens) Bloomsbury Publishing USA.
My Utterly Fluttery Sticker Activity Book. 2015. (ENG.). 56p. (J). (gr. -1-7). pap. *(978-1-78393-753-0(X))* Make Believe Ideas.
My Very Own Activity Pages: Summer 2004. 2004. (J). pap. 1.79 *(978-1-59317-067-7(X))* Warner Pr., Inc.
My Weird School Classroom Activity Sheet. (J). *(978-0-06-072730-7(6))* HarperCollins Pubs.
Nance, Andrew Jordan. Puppy Mind. Durk, Jim, illus. 2016. (ENG.). (J). (gr. -1-2). 16.95 *(978-1-941529-44-7(5))*, Plum Blossom Bks.) Parallax Pr.
Nancy Giorgio-Kupiec. Nanje's Imagination or Is It ? 2009. 20p. pap. 10.49 *(978-1-4389-7068-4(4))* AuthorHouse.
Narayan, Jasmine. Color with Me, Grandma! Color, Create, & Connect with Your Grandchild. Davies, Hannah, illus. 2017. (Side-By-Side Book Ser.). (ENG.). 128p. (J). (gr. -1-2). pap. 12.99 *(978-1-63106-306-0(5))*, Race Point Publishing) Quarto Publishing Group USA.
National Geographic. National Geographic Kids Weird but True! 2014. lib. bdg. 24.50 *(978-0-606-35578-0(2))* Turtleback Bks.
National Geographic Kids. National Geographic - Look Up! 2016. (Look & Learn Ser.). (ENG., Illus.). 24p. (J). (-k). bds. 6.99 *(978-1-4263-2454-3(5))*, National Geographic Children's Bks.) National Geographic Society.
—National Geographic Kids in the Jungle Sticker Activity Book: Over 1,000 Stickers! 2015. (NG Sticker Activity Bks.). (ENG.). 56p. (J). (gr. -1-3). pap. 6.99 *(978-1-4263-2056-9(6))*, National Geographic Children's Bks.) National Geographic Society.
National Geographic Kids Staff. Colors! 2012. (ENG., Illus.). 24p. (J). (gr. k-k). bds. 6.99 *(978-1-4263-0929-8(5))*, National Geographic Children's Bks.) National Geographic Society.
—Creepy Crawly. 2016. (NG Sticker Activity Bks.). (ENG.). 56p. (J). (gr. -1-3). pap., act. bk. ed. 6.99 *(978-1-4263-2425-3(1))*, National Geographic Children's Bks.) National Geographic Society.
—Dinos! 2014. (NG Sticker Activity Bks.). (ENG.). 56p. (J). (gr. -1-3). pap. 6.99 *(978-1-4263-1773-6(5))*, National Geographic Children's Bks.) National Geographic Society.
—In My Backyard: Over 1,000 Stickers! 2016. (NG Sticker Activity Bks.). (ENG.). 56p. (J). (gr. -1-3). pap., act. bk. ed. 6.99 *(978-1-4263-2403-1(0))*, National Geographic Children's Bks.) National Geographic Society.
—Junior Ranger: Puzzles, Games, Facts, & Tons More Fun Inspired by the U. S. National Parks! 2016. (ENG.). 160p. (J). (gr. 3-7). pap., act. bk. ed. 14.99 *(978-1-4263-2304-1(2))*, National Geographic Children's Bks.) National Geographic Society.
—National Geographic Kids Amazing Pets Sticker Activity Book: Over 1,000 Stickers! 2014. (ENG., Illus.). 56p. (J). (gr. -1-3). pap. 6.99 *(978-1-4263-1555-8(4))*, National Geographic Children's Bks.) National Geographic Society.
—National Geographic Kids: Animal Creativity Book: Cut-Outs, Games, Stencils, Stickers. 2013. (ENG.). 80p. (J). (gr. 1-4). pap. 12.99 *(978-1-4263-1402-5(7))*, National Geographic Children's Bks.) National Geographic Society.
—National Geographic Kids Cool Animals Sticker Activity Book: Over 1,000 Stickers! 2013. (ENG., Illus.). 56p. (J). (gr. -1-3). pap. 6.99 *(978-1-4263-1113-0(3))*, National Geographic Children's Bks.) National Geographic Society.
—National Geographic Kids Cutest Animals Sticker Activity Book: Over 1,000 Stickers! 2013. (ENG., Illus.). 56p. (J). (gr. -1-3). pap. 6.99 *(978-1-4263-1112-3(5))*, National Geographic Children's Bks.) National Geographic Society.
—National Geographic Kids Super Space Sticker Activity Book: Over 1,000 Stickers! 2014. (ENG., Illus.). 56p. (J). (gr. -1-3). pap. 6.99 *(978-1-4263-1556-5(2))*, National Geographic Children's Bks.) National Geographic Society.
—On Safari: Over 1,000 Stickers! 2016. (NG Sticker Activity Bks.). (ENG.). 56p. (J). (gr. -1-3). pap. 6.99 *(978-1-4263-2402-4(2))*, National Geographic Children's Bks.) National Geographic Society.
—Opposites! 2012. (Look & Learn Ser.). (ENG., Illus.). 24p. (J). (gr. k-k). bds. 6.99 *(978-1-4263-1043-0(9))*, National Geographic Children's Bks.) National Geographic Society.
—Outrageous Facts, Awesome Activities, Plus Cool Stickers for Tons of Wacky Fun! 2016. (Weird but True Ser.). (ENG., Illus.). 160p. (J). (gr. 3-7). pap. 12.99 *(978-1-4263-2456-7(1))*, National Geographic Children's Bks.) National Geographic Society.
—Patterns! 2013. (Look & Learn Ser.). (ENG.). 24p. (J). (-k). bds. 6.99 *(978-1-4263-1123-9(0))*, National Geographic Children's Bks.) National Geographic Society.
—People! 2013. (Look & Learn Ser.). (ENG.). 24p. (J). (-k). bds. 6.99 *(978-1-4263-1122-2(2))*, National Geographic Children's Bks.) National Geographic Society.
—Same & Different. 2012. (ENG., Illus.). 24p. (J). (gr. k-k). bds. 6.99 *(978-1-4263-0928-1(7))*, National Geographic Children's Bks.) National Geographic Society.
—Shapes! 2012. (Look & Learn Ser.). (ENG., Illus.). 24p. (J). (gr. k-k). bds. 6.99 *(978-1-4263-1042-3(0))*, National Geographic Children's Bks.) National Geographic Society.
—Stuck Inside Creativity Book. 2016. (ENG.). 80p. (J). (gr. 1-4). pap. 12.99 *(978-1-4263-2552-6(5))*, National Geographic Children's Bks.) National Geographic Society.
National Geographic Staff. Xtreme Illusions. 2012. (ENG., Illus.). 48p. (J). (gr. 3-7). 16.95 *(978-1-4263-1011-9(0))*, National Geographic Children's Bks.) National Geographic Society.
National Marine Fisheries Service (U.S.), ed. Understanding Marine Debris: Games & Activities for Kids of All Ages. 2009. (ENG., Illus.). 22p. 2.50 *(978-0-16-083974-0(2))*, National Marine Fisheries Service) United States Government Printing Office.
National Oceanic and Atmospheric Administration (U.S.) & National Marine Fisheries Service (U.S.), compiled by. Chesapeake Bay Activity Book. 2008. (ENG., Illus.). 24p. (gr. 3-6). pap. 3.50 *(978-0-16-081321-4(2))*, National Marine Fisheries Service) United States Government Printing Office.
National Park Service Staff, ed. Junior Paleontologist Activity Book: Ages 5 to 12: Explore, Learn, Protect. Wood, Ethan, illus. rev. ed. 2012. (ENG.). 22p. (gr. k-6). 6.00 *(978-0-16-090846-0(9))* National Park Service Div. of Pubns.
Natural History Museum. The Bumper Dinosaur Activity Book: Stickers, Games & Dino-Doodling Fun! 2016. (ENG.). 96p. (J). (gr. -1-1). pap. 16.99 *(978-0-565-09358-7(4))* Natural History Museum Pubns. GBR. Dist: Independent Pubs. Group.
Natural History Museum, London. Butterfly Activity Book. 2017. (ENG., Illus.). 32p. (J). (gr. k-2). pap. 7.99 ***(978-0-565-09408-9(4))*** Natural History Museum Pubns. GBR. Dist: Independent Pubs. Group.
Naylor, Amy. Whoosh! Easy Paper Airplanes for Kids: Color, Fold & Fly! 2013. (ENG.). 48p. (J). (gr. -1-3). pap. 6.99 *(978-0-486-49231-5(1))* Dover Pubns., Inc.
Neal, Angie & Kjesbo, Rynette. Simply Social 7 at School. Bristol, Mark, illus. 2011. 216p. (J). spiral bd. 34.95 net. *(978-1-60723-005-2(4))* Super Duper Pubns.
Nemmers, Lee. Monsters: An Art Activity Book for Creative Kids of All Ages. Zschock, Martha Day, illus. 2013. (Scratch & Sketch Ser.). (ENG.). 64p. (J). (gr. k). spiral bd. 12.99 *(978-1-4413-1154-2(8))* Peter Pauper Pr. Inc.
—Scratch & Sketch Trace-Along Constellations: An Art Activity Book for Artistic Stargazers of All Ages. Zschock, Martha Day, illus. 2014. (ENG.). (J). (gr. k). 14.99 *(978-1-4413-1726-1(0))*, 9781441317261) Peter Pauper Pr. Inc.
—Scratch & Sketch Trace-Along Robots: An Art Activity Book for Artistic Inventors of All Ages. Wheeler, David Cole, illus. 2015. (ENG.). 64p. (J). 14.99 *(978-1-4413-1812-1(7))*, 9781441318121) Peter Pauper Pr. Inc.
Nemmers, Tom. Knights Scratch & Sketch: For Brave Artists & Loyal Subjects of All Ages. Barbas Steckler, Kerren, illus. 2007. (Scratch & Sketch sER.). 80p. (J). 12.99 *(978-1-59359-877-8(7))* Peter Pauper Pr. Inc.
Nesworthy, Lauren. Darth Vader, Rebel Hunter! 2016. (Star Wars DK Readers Level 2 Ser.). lib. bdg. 13.55 *(978-0-606-38713-2(7))* Turtleback Bks.
The Never-Bored Kid Book, Ages 7-8. 2006. (J). 14.99 *(978-1-59673-155-4(9))*, EMC 6304) Evan-Moor Educational Pubs.
Newland, Sonya. Doodle Yourself Smart... Geometry. 2012. (Doodle Bks.). (ENG., Illus.). 128p. pap. 12.95 *(978-1-60710-440-7(7))*, Thunder Bay Pr.) Readerlink Distribution Services, LLC.
—Doodle Yourself Smart... Physics. 2012. (Doodle Bks.). (ENG., Illus.). 128p. pap. 12.95 *(978-1-60710-439-1(3))*, Thunder Bay Pr.) Readerlink Distribution Services, LLC.
Newman-D'Amico, Fran. Birthday Activity Book. 2006. (Dover Little Activity Bks.). (ENG., Illus.). 64p. (J). (gr. k-3). per., act. bk. ed. 1.99 *(978-0-486-44441-3(4))* Dover Pubns., Inc.
—Christmas Fun Activity Book. 2015. (Dover Children's Activity Bks.). (ENG.). 48p. (J). (gr. -1-2). pap. 4.99 *(978-0-486-79183-8(1))* Dover Pubns., Inc.
—Design Your Own Ugly Christmas Sweater Sticker Activity Book. 2015. (Dover Little Activity Bks.). (ENG., Illus.). 4p. (J). (gr. k-3). 1.99 *(978-0-486-80104-9(7))* Dover Pubns., Inc.
—Fun on the Go. 2005. (Dover Little Activity Bks.). (ENG., Illus.). 64p. (J). (gr. k-3). per., act. bk. ed. 1.99 *(978-0-486-44456-7(2))* Dover Pubns., Inc.
—Glitter Decorate a Christmas Tree Sticker Activity Book. 2009. (Dover Little Activity Books Stickers Ser.). (ENG., Illus.). 2p. (J). (gr. 1-4). pap. 1.99 *(978-0-486-47127-3(6))* Dover Pubns., Inc.
—Make Your Own Pizza:Sticker Activity Book. 2006. (Dover Little Activity Books Stickers Ser.). (ENG., Illus.). 4p. (J). (gr. k-3). act. bk. ed. 1.99 *(978-0-486-45224-1(7))* Dover Pubns., Inc.
—My Busy Backyard Activity Book. 2016. (Dover Little Activity Bks.). (ENG.). 64p. (J). (gr. k-3). pap. 1.99 *(978-0-486-81034-8(8))* Dover Pubns., Inc.
—Vacation Fun Activity Book. 2007. (Dover Children's Activity Bks.). (ENG., Illus.). 64p. (J). (gr. -1-2). per. 4.99 *(978-0-486-45896-0(2))* Dover Pubns., Inc.
Nextoy Staff, et al. I Can Kenken! Vol. 1: 75 Puzzles for Having Fun with Math. 2008. (ENG.). 112p. (J). pap. 7.99 *(978-0-312-54641-0(6))*, 9780312546410, St. Martin's Griffin) St. Martin's Pr.
—I Can Kenken! Vol. 2: 75 Puzzles for Having Fun with Math. 2008. (ENG.). 112p. (J). pap. 17.99 *(978-0-312-54642-7(4))*, 9780312546427, St. Martin's Griffin) St. Martin's Pr.
—I Can Kenken! Vol. 3: 75 Puzzles for Having Fun with Math. 2008. (ENG.). 112p. (J). pap. 17.99 *(978-0-312-54643-4(2))*, 9780312546434, St. Martin's Griffin) St. Martin's Pr.
Nicholls, Paul. Wind-up Race Cars. 2010. (Wind-up Bks). 14p. (J). bds. 29.99 *(978-0-7945-2657-3(8))*, Usborne) EDC Publishing.
Nichols, Kaitlyn. Make Clay Charms. 2013. (ENG.). 56p. (J). (gr. 3). 21.99 *(978-0-545-49856-2(2))* Klutz.
—Safety Pin Bracelets: Turn Ordinary Safety Pins into Extraordinary Bracelets. 2011. (ENG.). 48p. (J). (gr. 3-7). 19.99 *(978-1-59174-932-5(8))* Klutz.
—Toolbox Jewelry. 2013. (ENG.). 60p. (J). (gr. 3). 21.99 *(978-0-545-56134-1(5))* Klutz.
Nicholson, Sue & Robins, Deri. The Great Big Art Activity Book. 2008. (Illus.). 240p. (J). *(978-1-84538-618-4(3))* New Burlington Bks.
Nixon, Caroline. Kid's Box Level 3 Activity Book with Online Resources. 2nd ed. 2014. (ENG.). 88p. pap. 29.50 *(978-1-107-64400-7(3))* Cambridge Univ. Pr.
Noble, Marty. Famous Fairy Tales Coloring Book. 2013. (Dover Coloring Bks.). (ENG.). 32p. (gr. -1-8). pap. 3.99 *(978-0-486-49707-5(0))* Dover Pubns., Inc.
—Fanciful Butterflies Stained Glass Coloring Book. 2012. (Dover Nature Stained Glass Coloring Book Ser.). (ENG., Illus.). 32p. (gr. 3-5). pap. 7.99 *(978-0-486-48649-9(4))* Dover Pubns., Inc.
—Impressionist Art. 2009. (Dover Stained Glass Coloring Book Ser.). (ENG., Illus.). 32p. (gr. 6-8). pap. 6.99 *(978-0-486-46538-8(1))* Dover Pubns., Inc.
—Mandalas GemGlow Stained Glass Coloring Book. 2010. (Dover Design Stained Glass Coloring Book Ser.). (ENG., Illus.). 32p. (J). (gr. 1-5). pap. 7.99 *(978-0-486-47478-6(X))* Dover Pubns., Inc.
Noble, Marty & Creative Haven. Creative Haven African Designs Coloring Book. 2013. (Adult Coloring Ser.). (ENG., Illus.). 64p. (gr. 3). pap. 5.99 *(978-0-486-49309-1(1))* Dover Pubns., Inc.
Noble, Marty & Creative Haven Staff. Creative Haven Day of the Dead Coloring Book. 2013. (Adult Coloring Ser.). (ENG., Illus.). 64p. (gr. 3). pap. 5.99 *(978-0-486-49213-1(3))* Dover Pubns., Inc.
Nola, Lisa. My Listography: My Amazing Life in Lists. Russell, Nathaniel, illus. 2008. (ENG.). 120p. (gr. 3-7). 12.95 *(978-0-8118-6399-5(9))* Chronicle Bks. LLC.
Northcott, Richard. In the Mountains. Geatches, Hazel, ed. 2013. (ENG.). 40p. pap. 9.38 *(978-0-19-464687-1(4))* Oxford Univ. Pr., Inc.
Nosy Crow Staff. The Coloring Book of Cards & Envelopes: a Year of Celebrations. Jones, Rebecca, illus. 2017. (ENG.). 74p. (J). (gr. k-12). pap. 15.99 *(978-0-7636-9529-3(7))*, Nosy Crow) Candlewick Pr.
—The Coloring Book of Cards & Envelopes: Summertime. Jones, Rebecca, illus. 2017. (ENG.). 74p. (J). (gr. k-12). pap. 10.99 *(978-0-7636-9340-4(5))*, Nosy Crow) Candlewick Pr.
—Press-Out & Color: Butterflies. Ingram, Zoe, illus. 2017. (ENG.). 20p. (J). (gr. 5). 15.99 *(978-0-7636-9506-4(8))*, Nosy Crow) Candlewick Pr.
O'Brien, Jeanne. Finding Shapes in Nature: Parks, Forests & Backyards. 2010. 28p. pap. 15.99 *(978-1-4500-5772-1(1))* Xlibris Corp.
O'Connon, Jane & Harper Collins/Leap Frog. LeapReader Book, Fancy Nancy Explorer Extraordinaire! Glasser, Robin Preiss, illus. 2017. (J). (gr. -1-7). pap. ***(978-1-60685-272-9(8))*** LeapFrog Enterprises, Inc.
O'Dowd, Chris & Murphy, Nick Vincent. Moone Boy & the Marvellous Activity Manual. 2017. (ENG., Illus.). 144p. (J). (gr. 3-7). 9.99 ***(978-1-5098-3259-0(9))*** Pan Macmillan GBR. Dist: Independent Pubs. Group.
The OH Book. 2007. (Illus.). 12p. (J). 14.99 *(978-0-9793506-1-0(1))* Sportime International.
Okido Staff. Color Me In! An Activity Book. 2013. (ENG., Illus.). 128p. (J). (gr. k-3). pap. 14.95 *(978-0-500-65017-2(9))*, 565017) Thames & Hudson.
—What's Inside? See-Through Pages & Magic Surprises! 2013. (ENG., Illus.). 96p. (J). (gr. -1-3). 19.95 *(978-0-500-65019-6(5))*, 565019) Thames & Hudson.
Olabi, Adriana. Fine Motor Activities. 2012. 84p. pap. 26.50 *(978-1-61897-712-0(1))*, Strategic Bk. Publishing) Strategic Book Publishing & Rights Agency (SBPRA).
Olmedillas, Cathy, compiled by. Anorak. 2013. (ENG., Illus.). 64p. (J). pap. 9.99 *(978-1-4236-3340-2(7))*, Anorak Pr.) Gibbs Smith, Publisher.
Olsen, Jan Z., creator. Color Print & Number Wall Cards. 2013. (ENG.). tchr. ed. 18.95 *(978-1-934825-11-2(5))* Handwriting Without Tears.
Omoth, Tyler. Busting Boredom with Technology. 2017. (Boredom Busters Ser.). (ENG., Illus.). 32p. (gr. 3-4). lib. bdg. 27.99 *(978-1-5157-4705-5(0))* Capstone Press of Coughlan Cos.
Omoth, Tyler & Swanson, Jennifer. Boredom Busters. 2017. (Boredom Busters Ser.). (ENG.). 32p. (gr. 3-4). 111.96 *(978-1-5157-4718-5(2))*, Edge Bks.) Capstone Press of Coughlan Cos.
One of a Kind. 2015. (ENG., Illus.). 26p. (gr. -1). bds. *(978-1-78393-804-9(8))* Make Believe Ideas.
O'Neal, Claire. Washington, D. C. 2009. (Class Trip Ser.). (Illus.). 48p. (J). (gr. 2-5). lib. bdg. 29.95 *(978-1-58415-809-7(3))* Mitchell Lane Pubs., Inc.
Onish, Liane. Brain Quest, Grade 2: A Whole Year of Curriculum-Based Exercises & Activities in One Fun Book! Swann, Jill, ed. 2008. (ENG., Illus.). 320p. (J). (gr. 2-2). wbk. ed. 12.95 *(978-0-7611-4915-6(5))*, 14915) Workman Publishing Co., Inc.
—Brain Quest, Pre-K: A Whole Year of Curriculum-Based Exercises & Activities in One Fun Book! Fung, Jane, ed. 2008. (ENG., Illus.). 320p. (J). (gr. -1 — 1). wbk. ed. 12.95 *(978-0-7611-4961-3(9))*, 14961) Workman Publishing Co., Inc.
Onish, Liane B. Mr. Potato Head: the Busy Day. Durk, Jim, illus. 2008. (Storytime Stickers Ser.). (ENG.). 16p. (J). (gr. -1-k). pap. 5.95 *(978-1-4027-5354-1(3))* Sterling Publishing Co., Inc.
—Solve-the-Riddle Math Practice: 50+ Reproducible Activity Sheets That Help Students Master Key Math Skills - And Solve Rib - Tickling Riddles. 2009. (ENG.). 64p. pap. 11.99 *(978-0-545-10102-8(6))*, Teaching Resources) Scholastic, Inc.
O'Reilly, Wenda. Art Ditto. 2007. 24.95 *(978-1-889613-56-7(8))* Birdcage Pr.
Orloff, Karen Kaufman. Mystery at the Aquarium (a Nightlight Detective Book) Smith, Jamie, illus. 2014. (ENG.). 26p. (J). 12.99 *(978-1-4413-1615-8(9))*, 9781441316158) Peter Pauper Pr. Inc.

S

Ortac, Arda. Sharp Kids Activity. Ortac, Feride, illus. 2009. 80p. Bk. 1. pap. 9.00 *(978-1-60743-151-0(3))*Bk. 02. pap. 9.00 *(978-1-60743-152-7(1))* Independent Pub.

Ortiz, Associate Professor Enrique. Ten Elephants & a Spider's Web: A Traditional Latin American Counting Rhyme & Other Activities: Spanish/English. 2009. 20p. 10.80 *(978-0-615-26124-9(8))* Ortiz, Enrique Publishing.

Ortler, Brett. Animal Tracks Activity Book, 1 vol. 2015. (Color & Learn Ser.). (ENG.). 64p. (J). (gr. k-5). pap. 5.95 *(978-1-59193-538-4(5))* Adventure Pubns.

—Outer Space Activity Book. Juliano, Phil, illus. 2017. (Color & Learn Ser.). (ENG.). 64p. (J). (gr. k-5). pap. 6.95 *(978-1-59193-708-1(6))* Adventure Pubns.

Osborne, Mary Pope & Boyce, Natalie Pope. Games & Puzzles from the Tree House. Murdocca, Sal, illus. 2010. (Magic Tree House Ser.). (ENG.). 256p. (J). (gr. 1-4). act. bk. ed. 6.99 *(978-0-375-86216-8(1)*, Random Hse. Bks. for Young Readers) Random Hse. Children's Bks.

Osborne, Nancy. Rhyming Words: Cut & Paste. l.t. ed. 2007. (Illus.). 52p. ring bd. 9.95 *(978-1-928856-07-8(1))* Osborne Pr.

O'Shay, Alex. Ten Acts of Kindess: An Alex Story. 2011. 44p. pap. 16.59 *(978-1-4634-2027-7(7))* AuthorHouse.

Osteen, Victoria. My Happy Heart Books, Set. Day, Betsy, illus. 2009. (ENG.). 66p. (J). (gr. -1-k). bds. 19.99 *(978-1-4169-5549-8(6)*, Little Simon Inspirations) Little Simon Inspirations.

Over 100 Things to Do on a Plane. 2017. (Activity Puzzle Bks.). (ENG.). (J). pap. 5.99 ***(978-0-7945-3966-5(1)***, Usborne) EDC Publishing.

Pacheco, Luis Gabriel & Pacheco, Alma Rosa, illus. Juegos Recreativos para Ninos. 2003. (SPA.). 182p. (J). pap. *(978-970-651-625-1(5))* Editorial Oceano De Mexico, S.A. DE C.V.

Page, Claire. Fashion Show Sticker Book. 2007. (Illus.). 12p. (J). (gr. -1-3). pap. *(978-1-84610-643-9(5))* Make Believe Ideas.

Pal Toys, creator. Bright & Beyond - Age 1 English. 2007. (J). 9.95 *(978-0-9763648-7-0(5))* Pal Toys, LLC.

—Bright & Beyond - Age 2 English. 2007. (J). 9.95 *(978-0-9763648-8-7(3))* Pal Toys, LLC.

—Bright & Beyond - Baby English. 2007. (J). 9.95 *(978-0-9763648-6-3(7))* Pal Toys, LLC.

—Bright & Beyond - Bebes. 2007. (J). 9.95 *(978-0-9763648-2-5(4))* Pal Toys, LLC.

—Bright & Beyond - Preschool English. 2007. (J). 9.95 *(978-0-9763648-9-4(1))* Pal Toys, LLC.

Palomares, Susanna, et al. Hearts & Minds: An Afterschool Program for Developing Reading Literacy & Emotional Intelligence. 2012. 158p. pap. 28.95 *(978-1-56499-084-6(2))* Innerchoice Publishing.

Pan Macmillan Limited Staff. Bin Weevils - The Official Annual 2014. unabr. ed. 2013. (ENG.). 64p. (J). (gr. 2). 12.99 *(978-1-4472-2579-9(1))* Pan Macmillan GBR. Dist: Independent Pubs. Group.

Panaccione, Nancy. Mine! Diary: My Ideas Need Expressing. 2013. (ENG., Illus.). (J). (gr. 4-7). 12.95 *(978-1-892951-67-0(3))* Fine Print Publishing Co.

Panchyk, Richard. Franklin Delano Roosevelt for Kids: His Life & Times with 21 Activities. 2007. (For Kids Ser.). (ENG., Illus.). 160p. (J). (gr. 4-8). pap. 14.95 *(978-1-55652-657-2(1))* Chicago Review Pr., Inc.

Pantone. Pantone: Sticker Book with Posters. 2015. (Pantone Ser.). (ENG., Illus.). 54p. (J). (gr. -1-17). pap. 12.95 *(978-1-4197-1628-7(X)*, Abrams Appleseed) Abrams, Inc.

Parkes, Lois. Paper Sport: Activities, Games & Puzzles for Sporty Kids. 2012. 44p. pap. 21.99 *(978-1-4771-2582-3(5))* Xlibris Corp.

Parr, Todd & Chronicle Books Staff. Save the Blue. 2009. (ENG.). 160p. (J). (gr. -1-3). 9.99 *(978-0-8118-7153-2(3))* Chronicle Bks. LLC.

Parsons, Sandra J. What Could a Kid Do? 2011. 24p. pap. 15.99 *(978-1-4628-8733-0(3))* Xlibris Corp.

Paul Frank Industries. Julius! Dress up! Lacing Cards. 2011. (ENG.). 10p. (J). (gr. -1-12). 14.99 *(978-0-8118-7951-4(8))* Chronicle Bks. LLC.

Paul Frank Industries Staff. Julius! School Planner. 2009. (ENG.). 88p. (YA). (gr. 4-9). 14.99 *(978-0-8118-6553-1(3))* Chronicle Bks. LLC.

Paulding, Barbara. Circus Scratch & Sketch: An Art Activity Book. Zschock, Martha, illus. 2009. (Scratch & Sketch Ser.). 64p. (J). (gr. -1). spiral bd. 14.99 *(978-1-59359-832-7(7))* Peter Pauper Pr. Inc.

—Water Magic. Steckler, Kerren Barbas, illus. 2009. (Young Artist Ser.). 24p. (J). (gr. -1). 15.99 *(978-1-59359-842-6(4))* Peter Pauper Pr. Inc.

PC Treasures Staff, ed. Barney's Giant Coloring & Activity Book. 2009. (ENG., Illus.). 384p. (J). pap. 3.99 *(978-1-60072-220-2(2))* PC Treasures, Inc.

Pearlstein, Don. Make Your Own Laptop: Color & Build Your Own Computer! Stillerman, Robbie, illus. 2011. (Dover Children's Activity Bks.). (ENG.). 24p. (J). (gr. k-3). pap. 9.99 *(978-0-486-48532-4(3))* Dover Pubns., Inc.

Pedigree Books. Angry Birds Star Wars Super Interactive Annual 2014. 2013. 80p. (J). 12.99 *(978-1-908152-05-3(2))* Pedigree Bks., Ltd. GBR. Dist: Diamond Bk. Distributors.

—Angry Birds Super Interactive Annual 2014. 2013. 80p. (J). 12.99 *(978-1-908152-04-6(4))* Pedigree Bks., Ltd. GBR. Dist: Diamond Bk. Distributors.

—Annoying Orange Super Interactive Annual 2014. 2013. 80p. (J). 12.99 *(978-1-908152-06-0(0))* Pedigree Bks., Ltd. GBR. Dist: Diamond Bk. Distributors.

—Barbie Annual 2014. 2013. 80p. (J). 12.99 *(978-1-907602-72-6(0))* Pedigree Bks., Ltd. GBR. Dist: Diamond Bk. Distributors.

—Cut the Rope Super Interactive Annual 2014. 2013. 80p. (J). 12.99 *(978-1-908152-08-4(7))* Pedigree Bks., Ltd. GBR. Dist: Diamond Bk. Distributors.

—Dreamworks Heroes Annual 2014. 2013. (Illus.). 80p. (J). 12.99 *(978-1-907602-99-3(2))* Pedigree Bks., Ltd. GBR. Dist: Diamond Bk. Distributors.

—Family Guy Annual 2014. 2013. 80p. (J). 12.99 *(978-1-907602-73-3(9))* Pedigree Bks., Ltd. GBR. Dist: Diamond Bk. Distributors.

—Olly Murs Special by Smash Hits Annual 2014. 2013. 80p. (J). 12.99 *(978-1-907602-90-0(9))* Pedigree Bks., Ltd. GBR. Dist: Diamond Bk. Distributors.

—One Direction Special by Smash Hits Annual 2014. 2013. 80p. (J). 12.99 *(978-1-907602-89-4(5))* Pedigree Bks., Ltd. GBR. Dist: Diamond Bk. Distributors.

—Pokemon Annual 2014. 2013. 80p. (J). 12.99 *(978-1-907602-74-0(7))* Pedigree Bks., Ltd. GBR. Dist: Diamond Bk. Distributors.

—Shoot Annual 2014. 2013. 80p. (J). 12.99 *(978-1-907602-75-7(5))* Pedigree Bks., Ltd. GBR. Dist: Diamond Bk. Distributors.

—Smurfs 2 Annual 2014. 2013. 80p. (J). 12.99 *(978-1-907602-91-7(7))* Pedigree Bks., Ltd. GBR. Dist: Diamond Bk. Distributors.

—Sonic the Hedgehog Super Interactive Annual 2014. 2013. 80p. (J). 12.99 *(978-1-908152-07-7(9))* Pedigree Bks., Ltd. GBR. Dist: Diamond Bk. Distributors.

—South Park Annual 2014. 2013. 80p. (J). 12.99 *(978-1-907602-94-8(1))* Pedigree Bks., Ltd. GBR. Dist: Diamond Bk. Distributors.

—Star Wars Annual 2014. 2013. 80p. (J). 12.99 *(978-1-907602-84-9(4))* Pedigree Bks., Ltd. GBR. Dist: Diamond Bk. Distributors.

—Star Wars: the Clone Wars Annual 2014: The Clone Wars Annual 2014. 2013. 80p. (J). 12.99 *(978-1-907602-95-5(X))* Pedigree Bks., Ltd. GBR. Dist: Diamond Bk. Distributors.

—Tatty Teddy & Blue Nose Friends Annual 2014. 2013. 80p. (J). 12.99 *(978-1-907602-92-4(5))* Pedigree Bks., Ltd. GBR. Dist: Diamond Bk. Distributors.

—Turbo Annual 2014. 2013. 80p. (J). 12.99 *(978-1-907602-93-1(3))* Pedigree Bks., Ltd. GBR. Dist: Diamond Bk. Distributors.

Peek Inside the Jungle. 2017. (Peek Inside BDs Ser.). (ENG.). (J). bds. 11.99 ***(978-0-7945-3920-7(3)***, Usborne) EDC Publishing.

Peek, Patsy. Reading Comprehension Practice: Grades 2-8 Practice Worksheets Featuring Story Webs, Newspaper Ads, Fliers. 2012. 64p. (gr. 2-4). pap. 13.95 *(978-1-4772-4933-8(8))* AuthorHouse.

Peirce, Lincoln. Big Nate - Fun Blaster. Peirce, Lincoln, illus. 2015. (Big Nate Activity Book Ser.: 2). (ENG., Illus.). 224p. (J). (gr. 3-7). pap. 6.99 *(978-0-06-234951-4(1))* HarperCollins Pubs.

—Big Nate Super Scribbler. Peirce, Lincoln, illus. 2015. (Big Nate Activity Book Ser.: 5). (ENG., Illus.). 224p. (J). (gr. 3-7). pap. 6.99 *(978-0-06-234922-4(8))* HarperCollins Pubs.

Pencil Fun Book: Jesus Is Born. 2007. (Pencil Fun Books Ser.). 16p. (J). (gr. 3-7). 9.90 *(978-0-7814-4520-7(5))* Cook, David C.

Penovi, Celina. Guess It If You Can! — ¿Adivinarás Quizás? Volume I - School Time! — Volumen I - Hora de ir a la Escuela! 2009. 24p. pap. 15.99 *(978-1-4490-2744-5(X))* AuthorHouse.

Perchyonok, Tamara. Chemistry & Fun for Kids of All Ages: Billingual Book. 2007. pap. 9.00 *(978-0-8059-8606-8(5))* Dorrance Publishing Co., Inc.

Percy, Tasha. The Official IRB Rugby World Cup 2015 Activity Book. 2015. (ENG., Illus.). 56p. (J). (gr. 2). spiral bd. 9.95 *(978-1-78312-123-6(8))* Carlton Kids GBR. Dist: Sterling Publishing Co., Inc.

Pereira, Diego Jourdan. Animal Antics Hidden Pictures. 2013. (ENG., Illus.). 48p. (J). (gr. 3). pap. 4.99 *(978-0-486-49210-0(9))* Dover Pubns., Inc.

—FLIP OUTS — Fairy Fun: Color Your Own Cartoon! 2015. (ENG., Illus.). 64p. (J). (gr. k-3). pap. 1.99 *(978-0-486-79487-7(3))* Dover Pubns., Inc.

—Pink Party Coloring Book. 2014. (ENG., Illus.). 32p. (J). (gr. k-6). pap. 3.99 *(978-0-486-78124-2(0))* Dover Pubns., Inc.

Perkins, Miss Quinn. I Know When the Rainbow Comes. Perkins, Terrell D., illus. 2013. 28p. pap. 9.95 *(978-0-9851628-0-1(5))* Soulful Storytellers, Inc.

Perry, Phyllis J. Colorado Fun: Activities for on the Road & at Home. Tarr, Lisa M., illus. 2007. 80p. (J). (gr. 1-7). pap. 12.95 *(978-1-55566-402-2(4)*, Johnson Bks.) Bower Hse.

Peter Pauper Press, Inc., creator. Kids Unplugged Fashion Activity Book. 2017. (ENG.). (J). pap. 7.99 ***(978-1-4413-2278-4(7))*** Peter Pauper Pr. Inc.

—Scratch & Sketch Horses (Trace-Along) An Art Activity Book for Artistic Horse Lovers of All Ages. 2016. (ENG.). (J). 14.99 ***(978-1-4413-2251-7(5))*** Peter Pauper Pr. Inc.

—Scratch & Sketch National Parks (Trace-Along) An Art Activity Book for Artistic Rangers of All Ages. 2017. (ENG., Illus.). (J). 14.99 ***(978-1-4413-2271-5(X))*** Peter Pauper Pr. Inc.

—Scratch & Sketch Take Flight (Trace-Along) An Art Activity Book for Artistic Aviators of All Ages. 2016. (ENG.). (J). 14.99 ***(978-1-4413-2250-0(7))*** Peter Pauper Pr. Inc.

Peter Pauper Press Staff, creator. America: An Art Activity Book for Patriotic Artists & Explorers of All Ages. 2008. (Activity Book Ser.). (Illus.). 64p. (J). (gr. k-5). 12.99 *(978-1-59359-802-0(5))* Peter Pauper Pr. Inc.

—Garden Fairies: Scratch & Sketch: an Art Activity Book. 2007. (Activity Book Ser.). (Illus.). 64p. (J). (gr. 3-7). 12.99 *(978-1-59359-870-9(X))* Peter Pauper Pr. Inc.

Petruccio, Steven James. Create Your Own Dream Car Sticker Activity Book. 2006. (Dover Little Activity Books Stickers Ser.). (ENG., Illus.). 4p. (J). (gr. k-3). pap. 1.50 *(978-0-486-44737-7(5))* Dover Pubns., Inc.

—Create Your Own Fire Truck. 2010. (Dover Little Activity Books Stickers Ser.). (ENG., Illus.). 4p. (J). (gr. 1-4). pap. 1.50 *(978-0-486-47548-6(4))* Dover Pubns., Inc.

—Create Your Own Robot. 2006. (Dover Little Activity Books Stickers Ser.). (ENG., Illus.). 4p. (J). (gr. k-3). pap., act. bk. ed. 1.99 *(978-0-486-44878-7(9))* Dover Pubns., Inc.

—Let's Build a House! Coloring Book. 2017. (Dover Coloring Bks.). (ENG.). 32p. (J). (gr. 1-4). pap. 3.99 *(978-0-486-81213-7(8))* Dover Pubns., Inc.

Pfister, Marcus. Rainbow Fish Classroom Companion. 2017. (ENG., Illus.). 48p. (J). (gr. -1-3). pap., tchr. ed. 14.95 ***(978-0-7358-4290-8(6))*** North-South Bks., Inc.

Phillips, Dee. Big Zoo. 2009. (Flip Flap Fun Bks.). (ENG.). 5p. (J). (gr. -1-k). bds. 5.95 *(978-1-84696-086-4(X)*, TickTock Books) Octopus Publishing Group GBR. Dist: Independent Pubs. Group.

Phillips, Jillian. The World Around Us! Seeing. 2010. (Dover Coloring Bks.). (ENG., Illus.). 32p. (J). (gr. k-3). pap. 4.99 *(978-0-486-47731-2(2))* Dover Pubns., Inc.

Phillips, Karen. Doodle Journal: My Life in Scribbles. 2010. (ENG., Illus.). 76p. (J). (gr. 3-18). 16.95 *(978-1-59174-736-9(8))* Klutz.

—Fashionably Me: A Journal That's Just My Style. Higgins, Anne Keenan, illus. 2013. (ENG.). 100p. (J). (gr. 3). 16.99 *(978-0-545-56165-5(5))* Klutz.

—The Truth about My Name: And What It Reveals about Me! 2010. (ENG.). 50p. (J). (gr. 3-18). 16.99 *(978-1-59174-855-7(0))* Klutz.

Phillips, Karen, ed. My All-Time Top 5: Make the Lists of Your Life. 2008. (ENG., Illus.). 60p. (J). (gr. 3-18). 16.95 *(978-1-59174-516-7(0))* Klutz.

Phillips, Karen & Klutz Editors. Friendship Pixies: Charmed Little Dolls to Make & Share. 2011. (ENG.). 40p. (J). (gr. 3-3). 16.99 *(978-1-59174-917-2(4))* Klutz.

—Sticker Design Studio: Create Your Own Custom Stickers. 2011. (ENG.). 54p. (J). (gr. 3-7). 16.99 *(978-1-59174-935-6(2))* Klutz.

Phillips, S. & Parker, H. First 100 Box of Books Words,Animals,Things That Go. 2009. 26p. pap. *(978-1-84879-200-5(X))* Make Believe Ideas.

Phillips, Sarah. Wipe Clean Giant. 2008. (Trace, Stick & Learn Ser.). (Illus.). 72p. (J). (gr. -1-3). pap., act. bk. ed. *(978-1-84610-419-0(X))* Make Believe Ideas.

Phillipson, Fiona. Fairies. 2012. (My First Creativity Bks.). (ENG.). 66p. (J). (gr. -1-2). pap. 9.99 *(978-1-4380-0177-7(0))* Barron's Educational Series, Inc.

Phoenix Books Staff, illus. Sofia the First Royal Picnic - Little Sound Book. 2014. 12p. (J). bds. 9.98 *(978-1-4508-7487-8(8)*, 0b73a7ef-ea68-4afb-b340-9a4f6fc740c0) Phoenix International Publications, Inc.

—Thomas' Piano Book. 2014. 14p. (J). bds. 12.98 *(978-1-4508-6584-5(4)*, 1450865844) Phoenix International Publications, Inc.

Phoenix International Staff, illus. Disney Jr. Look & Find. 2014. 24p. (J). 7.98 *(978-1-4508-8491-4(1)*, 1450884911) Phoenix International Publications, Inc.

—Doc Mcstuffins the Doc Is in. 2014. 10p. (J). bds. 17.98 *(978-1-4508-8186-9(6)*, 1450881866) Phoenix International Publications, Inc.

—Sesame at the Zoo Look & Find. 2014. 24p. (J). 7.98 *(978-1-4508-8417-4(2)*, 1450884172) Phoenix International Publications, Inc.

—Sesame Street(r) Big Fire Truck. 2014. 10p. (J). bds. *(978-1-4508-7442-7(8)*, 88c653bc-7055-470d-ae38-8642c9dd9e9d) Phoenix International Publications, Inc.

—Thomas & the Telescope. 2014. 12p. (J). bds. 17.98 *(978-1-4508-7993-4(4)*, 1450879934) Phoenix International Publications, Inc.

Piano, Maureen. My Adventure to the Wonders of the World. 2006. 44p. (J). 8.99 *(978-1-59092-445-7(2))* Blue Forge Pr.

—My Adventure with Tidepools. 2009. (ENG.). 44p. (J). 8.99 *(978-1-59092-473-0(8))* Blue Forge Pr.

Pickett, Cheryl. Creation Inspirations: A New View of Your Neighborhood. 2013. 126p. pap. 14.95 *(978-0-9841855-1-1(8))* Brighter Day Publishing.

Picthall, Chez. My Bike. Gunzi, Christiane, ed. 2015. (ENG., Illus.). 20p. (J). pap. 6.50 *(978-1-906572-54-9(2))* Award Pubns. Ltd. GBR. Dist: Parkwest Pubns., Inc.

—My Favourite Racers Sticker Book. Rayner, Katy, ed. 2015. (ENG., Illus.). 20p. (J). pap. 7.99 *(978-1-906572-65-5(8))* Award Pubns. Ltd. GBR. Dist: Parkwest Pubns., Inc.

Pikachu Press, . Pokémon Super Activity Book: Do You Know Unova? 2012. (Pokemon Pikachu Press Ser.). (ENG.). 200p. (J). (gr. 3-6). act. bk. ed. 12.99 *(978-1-60438-156-6(6))* Pokemon, USA, Inc.

Pincock, Amy. Quiet Book Patterns. 2013. 14.99 *(978-1-4621-1245-6(5)*, Horizon Pubs.) Cedar Fort, Inc./CFI Distribution.

Pinder, Andrew, illus. The Boys' Doodle Book: Amazing Pictures to Complete & Create. 2008. (ENG.). 128p. (J). (gr. -1-17). pap. 12.95 *(978-0-7624-3506-7(2))* Running Pr. Bk. Pubs.

—The Girls' Doodle Book: Amazing Pictures to Complete & Create. 2008. (ENG.). 128p. (J). (gr. -1-17). pap. 12.95 *(978-0-7624-3505-0(4))* Running Pr. Bk. Pubs.

Pinestein Press. Abcs of Language & Literacy. Carroll, Raymond, illus. 2007. 180p. per. 19.99 *(978-0-9795364-4-1(8))* Chowder Bay Bks.

—Pre-K Prep! Carroll, Raymond, illus. 2007. 180p. per. 19.99 *(978-0-9795364-3-4(X))* Chowder Bay Bks.

Pinnington, Andrea. The Christmas Creativity Book: Includes Games, Cut-Outs, Fold-Out Scenes, Textures, Stickers, & Stencils. 2011. (Creativity Bks.). (ENG.). 80p. (J). (gr. 1-4). pap. 12.99 *(978-1-4380-0037-4(5))* Barron's Educational Series, Inc.

—Christmas Pocket Activity Fun & Games: Games, Puzzles, Fold-Out Scenes, Patterned Paper, Stickers! 2014. (Pocket Activity Fun & Games Ser.). (ENG.). 96p. (J). (gr. 1-5). pap. 7.99 *(978-1-4380-0517-1(2))* Barron's Educational Series, Inc.

—The Horse & Pony Creativity Book. 2013. (Creativity Bks.). (ENG., Illus.). 80p. (J). (gr. 1-6). pap. 12.99 *(978-1-4380-0127-2(4))* Barron's Educational Series, Inc.

—Princess Pocket Activity Fun & Games: Includes Games, Cutouts, Foldout Scenes, Textures, Stickers, & Stencils. 2013. (Pocket Activity Fun & Games Ser.). (ENG.). 96p. (J). (gr. 1-4). pap. 7.99 *(978-1-4380-0313-9(7))* Barron's Educational Series, Inc.

Pipe, Jim. Castle Sticker Book: Complete Your Own Mighty, Medieval Fortress! Taylor, Maria, illus. 2014. (ENG.). 40p. (J). (gr. 1). pap. 9.95 *(978-1-78312-013-0(4))* Carlton Bks., Ltd. GBR. Dist: Sterling Publishing Co., Inc.

—Doll's House Sticker Book: Decorate Your Very Own Victorian Home! Taylor, Maria, illus. 2014. (ENG.). 40p. (J). (gr. 1). pap. 9.95 *(978-1-78097-293-0(8))* Carlton Bks., Ltd. GBR. Dist: Sterling Publishing Co., Inc.

Pitamic, Maja & Laidlaw, Jill A. Fine Art Adventures: Over 35 Fun & Creative Art Projects Inspired by Classic Masterpieces from Around the World. 2017. (Art Adventures Ser.). (ENG.). 144p. (J). (gr. 1). pap. 19.99 ***(978-0-912777-04-7(4))*** Chicago Review Pr., Inc.

Pitches, Neale & Hollingsworth, Toni. CSI Comprehensive Strategies Instruction Kit: Grade 6. 2008. (CSI). (gr. 6). 895.00 *(978-1-60457-111-0(X))* Pacific Learning, Inc.

Pivard, Gilles. Where Is Turold. 2012. (ENG & FRE., Illus.). 20p. *(978-2-8151-0107-3(6))* OREP Edition & Communication.

Pixton, Amy. Indestructibles: Things That Go! Lomp, Stephan, illus. 2017. (Indestructibles Ser.). (ENG.). 12p. (J). pap. 5.95 *(978-0-7611-9362-3(6))* Workman Publishing Co., Inc.

Play Pen Books Staff. Animals: Easy Instructions Make Bringing Your Origami to Life Fun from Start to Finish! 2010. (ENG.). 24p. (J). pap. 12.95 *(978-1-60433-153-0(4)*, Applesauce Pr.) Cider Mill Pr. Bk. Pubs., LLC.

Playmobil & Buster Books Staff. The Official Playmobil Activity Book. 2014. (ENG.). 64p. (J). (gr. k-2). pap. 8.99 *(978-1-78055-302-3(1))* O'Mara, Michael Bks., Ltd. GBR. Dist: Independent Pubs. Group.

Pledger, Maurice, illus. Dinosaurs & Bugs. 2014. (ENG.). 120p. (J). (gr. -1). act. bk. ed. 12.95 *(978-1-62686-106-0(4)*, Silver Dolphin Bks.) Readerlink Distribution Services, LLC.

—Into the Wild. 2014. (ENG.). 120p. (J). (gr. -1). act. bk. ed. 12.95 *(978-1-62686-107-7(2)*, Silver Dolphin Bks.) Readerlink Distribution Services, LLC.

Plum, Joan Ensor & Plum, Paul S. I Am Special: Jesus Is Our Friend. Most, Andee, illus. 5th ed. 2007. 112p. (J). (gr. k-1). per. 11.95 *(978-1-59276-296-5(4))* Our Sunday Visitor, Publishing Div.

Poitier, Anton. Design & Doodle: A Book of Astonishing Invention - Amazing Things to Imagine, Draw, & Discover. Running Press Staff, ed. 2013. (ENG., Illus.). 128p. (gr. k). pap. 12.95 *(978-0-7624-5047-3(9)*, Running Pr. Kids) Running Pr. Bk. Pubs.

Poitier, Anton, illus. Opposites: Twist & Find the Opposite. 2014. (Twisters Ser.). (ENG.). 10p. (J). (gr. -1 — 1). bds. 7.99 *(978-0-7641-6688-4(3))* Barron's Educational Series, Inc.

Polette, Nancy. A-Z Activities for the K-2 Student. 2005. (J). pap. 19.95 *(978-1-931334-71-6(4))* Pieces of Learning.

Polsky, Cheryl. Libby & Her Friends Explore Los Angeles, Californi. 2012. 28p. pap. 17.99 *(978-1-4772-2125-9(5))* AuthorHouse.

Popescu, Anna Ildiko. Stamps & Doodles: Animals. 2013. (Stamps & Doodles Ser.). (ENG., Illus.). 64p. (J). (gr. k). 14.95 *(978-1-60710-458-2(X)*, Silver Dolphin Bks.) Readerlink Distribution Services, LLC.

Posner-Sanchez, Andrea. Peeps Guide to Life (Peeps) Random House, illus. 2017. (Official Guide Ser.). (ENG.). 80p. (J). (gr. k-12). 9.99 *(978-1-5247-1910-4(2)*, Random Hse. Bks. for Young Readers) Random Hse. Children's Bks.

Poston, Valerie Williams, illus. ArbeZ ZebrA Teaches A to Z, 3 vols., Vol. 1. 2007. 33p. (J). spiral bd. 39.99 *(978-0-9779063-0-7(2))* Gain Literacy Skills / Lynette Gain Williams.

Powell, Richard. Seal. Gardner, Louise, illus. 2014. (Bathing Beauties Ser.). (ENG.). 8p. (J). (gr. -1 — 1). 7.99 *(978-1-4380-7444-3(1))* Barron's Educational Series, Inc.

Pratt, Leonie. Mermaid Things to Make & Do Kid Kit. 2005. 32p. (J). 15.99 *(978-1-58086-842-6(8)*, Usborne) EDC Publishing.

Press, Judy & Trezzo-Braren, Loretta. Big Fun Craft Book: Creative Fun for 2 to 6 Year Olds. Trezzo-Braren, Loretta, illus. 2008. (ENG., Illus.). (J). (gr. -1-1). 160p. 16.99 *(978-0-8249-6826-7(3))*; 142p. pap. 12.99 *(978-0-8249-6827-4(1))* Worthy Publishing. (Ideal Pubns.).

Press, Pikachu. Pokemon Fefties: How to Make 16 of Your Favorite Pokemon. 2013. (ENG.). 80p. (J). (gr. 3-6). 14.99 *(978-1-60438-177-1(9))* Pokemon, USA, Inc.

Prestel. Botticelli: Coloring Book, 1 vol. 2016. (ENG.). 32p. (J). (gr. 1-4). pap. 8.95 *(978-3-7913-7227-3(0))* Prestel Verlag GmbH & Co KG. DEU. Dist: Penguin Random Hse. LLC.

Prestel, ed. Coloring Book: Turner. 2012. (ENG.). 32p. (J). (gr. 1-4). pap. 8.95 *(978-3-7913-7090-3(1))* Prestel Verlag GmbH & Co KG. DEU. Dist: Penguin Random Hse. LLC.

Price, Roger & Stern, Leonard. Happily Ever Mad Libs. 2010. (Mad Libs Ser.). (ENG.). 48p. (J). (gr. 3-7). 4.99 *(978-0-8431-9962-8(8)*, Mad Libs) Penguin Young Readers Group.

—Holly, Jolly Mad Libs. 2009. (Mad Libs Ser.). (ENG.). 224p. (J). (gr. 3-7). 6.99 *(978-0-8431-8950-6(9)*, Mad Libs) Penguin Young Readers Group.

—Mad Libs Forever. 2013. (Mad Libs Ser.). (ENG.). 240p. (J). (gr. 3-7). pap. 6.99 *(978-0-8431-7667-4(9)*, Mad Libs) Penguin Young Readers Group.

—The Wizard of Oz Mad Libs. 2013. (Mad Libs Ser.). (ENG.). 48p. (J). (gr. 3-7). 4.99 *(978-0-8431-8017-6(X)*, Mad Libs) Penguin Young Readers Group.

Price, Roger, et al. All I Want for Christmas Is Mad Libs. 2013. (Mad Libs Ser.). (ENG.). 240p. (J). (gr. 3-7). pap. 6.99 *(978-0-8431-7666-7(0)*, Mad Libs) Penguin Young Readers Group.

Price, Sean Stewart, et al. Kids' Guides. 2011. (Kids' Guides). (ENG.). 32p. (gr. 3-4). lib. bdg. 111.96 *(978-1-4296-6535-3(1)*, Edge Bks.) Capstone Press of Coughlan Cos.

Priddy, Roger. ABC 123. 2014. (Hello Kitty Ser.). (ENG.). 60p. (J). (gr. -1-1). pap., wbk. ed. 12.99 *(978-0-312-51764-9(5)*, 9780312517649, Priddy Bks.) St. Martin's Pr.

—Braid It! 2015. (Make It! Ser.). (ENG.). 64p. (J). (gr. k-3). pap. 12.99 *(978-0-312-51848-6(X)*, 9780312518486, Priddy Bks.) St. Martin's Pr.

—Busy Babies Words. 2010. 8p. (J). bds. 4.99 *(978-0-312-50854-8(9))*, Priddy Bks.) St. Martin's Pr.

—Doll's House. 2013. (Lift-The-Flap Tab Bks.). (ENG.). 16p. (J). (gr. -1 — 1). bds. 8.99 *(978-0-312-51657-4(6)*, 9780312516574, Priddy Bks.) St. Martin's Pr.

—Dot-to-Dot for Tiny Tots. 2014. (Dot to Dot Ser.). (ENG.). 64p. (J). (gr. -1 — 1). pap. 6.99 *(978-0-312-51716-8(5)*, 9780312517168, Priddy Bks.) St. Martin's Pr.

—Dot to Dot for Tiny Tots. 2014. (Dot to Dot Ser.). (ENG.). 64p. (J). (gr. -1 — 1). spiral bd. 12.99 *(978-0-312-51772-4(6)*, 9780312517724, Priddy Bks.) St. Martin's Pr.

—Dot-to-Dot Puzzles & Mazes. 2014. (Dot to Dot Ser.). (ENG.). 64p. (J). (gr. -1 — 1). pap. 6.99 *(978-0-312-51717-5(3)*, 9780312517175, Priddy Bks.) St. Martin's Pr.

—First 100 Stickers: First Numbers, Colors, Shapes. 2017. (First 100 Ser.). (ENG.). 80p. (J). pap. 9.99 *(978-0-312-52063-2(8)*, 9780312520632, Priddy Bks.) St. Martin's Pr.

—First 100 Trucks & Things That Go. 2016. (First 100 Ser.). (ENG.). 80p. (J). pap. 9.99 *(978-0-312-52145-5(6),* 9780312521455, Priddy Bks.) St. Martin's Pr.
—Hello Kitty: Playtime. 2016. (Hello Kitty Ser.). (ENG.). 10p. (J). bds. 12.99 *(978-0-312-51954-4(0),* 9780312519544, Priddy Bks.) St. Martin's Pr.
—It's Time to Play. 2013. (Bright Baby Ser.). (ENG.). 8p. (J). (gr. -1 — 1). bds. 4.99 *(978-0-312-51636-9(3),* 9780312516369, Priddy Bks.) St. Martin's Pr.
—Kitty's Color Activity Book. Crimi-Trent, Ellen, illus. 2014. (Schoolies Ser.). (ENG.). 76p. (J). (gr. -1-1). pap. 6.99 *(978-0-312-51675-8(4),* 9780312516758, Priddy Bks.) St. Martin's Pr.
—Let's Go Learning: I Love Animals. 2013. (Let's Go Learning Ser.). (ENG.). 104p. (J). (gr. -1-1). pap. 6.99 *(978-0-312-51069-5(1),* 9780312510695, Priddy Bks.) St. Martin's Pr.
—Let's Go Learning: I Love Trucks. 2013. (Let's Go Learning Ser.). (ENG.). 104p. (J). (gr. -1-1). pap. 6.99 *(978-0-312-51071-8(3),* 9780312510718, Priddy Bks.) St. Martin's Pr.
—Lift-The-tab: I Love You. 2015. (ENG., Illus.). 16p. (J). bds. 8.99 *(978-0-312-52032-8(8),* 9780312520328, Priddy Bks.) St. Martin's Pr.
—Little Friends Gift Set. 2014. (Little Friends Ser.). (ENG.). (J). (gr. -1 — 1). 19.99 *(978-0-312-51777-9(7),* 9780312517779, Priddy Bks.) St. Martin's Pr.
—Mo Chéad Focóir. Ó' Murchadha, Niall, tr. 2013. (GLE & IRL.). 10p. (J). 19.00 *(978-0-7171-5807-2(1))* M.H. Gill & Co. U. C. IRL. Dist: Dufour Editions, Inc.
—My Big Activity Workbook. 2008. (My Big Step by Step Ser.). (ENG., Illus.). 56p. (J). (gr. -1-k). spiral bd., wbk. ed. 12.95 *(978-0-312-50214-0(1),* 9780312502140, Priddy Bks.) St. Martin's Pr.
—My Giant Seek-And-Find Activity Book. 2016. (ENG., Illus.). 200p. (J). pap. 9.99 *(978-0-312-52065-6(4),* 9780312520656, Priddy Bks.) St. Martin's Pr.
—My Pretty Princess. 2013. (Princess World Ser.). (ENG.). 134p. (J). (gr. k-2). pap., act. bk. ed. 12.99 *(978-0-312-51640-6(1),* 9780312516406, Priddy Bks.) St. Martin's Pr.
—My Super Duper Coloring Activity Book. 2015. (ENG.). 308p. (J). (gr. -1-1). pap. 12.99 *(978-0-312-51818-9(8),* 9780312518189, Priddy Bks.) St. Martin's Pr.
—Noisy Playtown. 2016. (Playtown Ser.). (ENG.). 12p. (J). bds. 14.99 *(978-0-312-51958-2(3),* 9780312519582, Priddy Bks.) St. Martin's Pr.
—Nursery Rhymes. 2013. (Baby Boxsets Ser.). (ENG.). 32p. (J). (gr. -1-1). 14.99 *(978-0-312-51563-8(4),* 9780312515638, Priddy Bks.) St. Martin's Pr.
—Play & Learn with Wallace: Giant Sticker Book. 2014. (Play & Learn with Wallace Ser.). (ENG.). 130p. (J). (gr. -1-1). pap., act. bk. ed. 12.99 *(978-0-312-51726-7(2),* 9780312517267, Priddy Bks.) St. Martin's Pr.
—Sticker Doodle Boo! 2013. (Sticker Doodle Ser.). (ENG.). 128p. (J). (gr. k-3). pap. 6.99 *(978-0-312-51614-7(2),* 9780312516147, Priddy Bks.) St. Martin's Pr.
—Sticker Doodle Do. 2013. (Sticker Doodle Ser.). (ENG., Illus.). 128p. (J). (gr. -1-3). pap. 6.99 *(978-0-312-51591-1(X),* 9780312515911, Priddy Bks.) St. Martin's Pr.
—Sticker Doodle I Love You! 2013. (Sticker Doodle Ser.). (ENG.). 128p. (J). (gr. k-3). pap. 6.99 *(978-0-312-51647-5(9),* 9780312516475, Priddy Bks.) St. Martin's Pr.
—Sticker Doodle You. 2013. (Sticker Doodle Ser.). (ENG., Illus.). 128p. (J). (gr. -1-3). pap. 6.99 *(978-0-312-51589-8(8),* 9780312515898, Priddy Bks.) St. Martin's Pr.
—Sticker Early Learning: Activity Book. 2016. (ENG., Illus.). 96p. (J). pap. 9.99 *(978-0-312-52066-3(2),* 9780312520663, Priddy Bks.) St. Martin's Pr.
—Sticker Early Learning: Sorting. 2016. (ENG., Illus.). 24p. (J). pap. 4.99 *(978-0-312-52018-2(2),* 9780312520182, Priddy Bks.) St. Martin's Pr.
—Sticker Friends: Bear. 2016. (Sticker Friends Ser.). (ENG.). 24p. (J). pap. 4.99 *(978-0-312-51968-1(0),* 9780312519681, Priddy Bks.) St. Martin's Pr.
—Sticker Friends: Chick. 2016. (Sticker Friends Ser.). (ENG.). 24p. (J). pap. 4.99 *(978-0-312-51967-4(2),* 9780312519674, Priddy Bks.) St. Martin's Pr.
—Sticker Friends: Christmas. 2016. (Sticker Friends Ser.). (ENG.). 24p. (J). pap. 4.99 *(978-0-312-52050-2(6),* 9780312520502, Priddy Bks.) St. Martin's Pr.
—Sticker Friends: Kitten. 2016. (Sticker Friends Ser.). (ENG.). 24p. (J). pap. 4.99 *(978-0-312-51965-0(6),* 9780312519650, Priddy Bks.) St. Martin's Pr.
—Sticker Friends: Puppy. 2016. (Sticker Friends Ser.). (ENG.). 24p. (J). pap. 4.99 *(978-0-312-51966-7(4),* 9780312519667, Priddy Bks.) St. Martin's Pr.
—Stickerpedia. 2015. (ENG.). 148p. (J). (gr. k-3). pap. 12.99 *(978-0-312-51911-7(7),* 9780312519117, Priddy Bks.) St. Martin's Pr.
—Super Dinky Doodles. 2014. (Dinky Doodles Ser.). (ENG.). 128p. (J). (gr. k-3). pap. 4.99 *(978-0-312-51665-9(7),* 9780312516659, Priddy Bks.) St. Martin's Pr.
—Tracing & Pen Control. 2010. (ENG.). 28p. (J). (gr. -1-1). spiral bd., wbk. ed. 6.99 *(978-0-312-50870-8(0),* 9780312508708, Priddy Bks.) St. Martin's Pr.
—Treasure Hunt for Boys. 2010. (ENG.). 22p. (J). (gr. k-3). bds. 9.99 *(978-0-312-50818-0(2),* 9780312508180, Priddy Bks.) St. Martin's Pr.
—Treasure Hunt for Girls. 2010. (ENG.). 22p. (J). (gr. k-3). bds. 9.99 *(978-0-312-50817-3(4),* 9780312508173, Priddy Bks.) St. Martin's Pr.
—Uppercase Alphabet. 2010. (ENG.). 28p. (J). (gr. -1-1). spiral bd., wbk. ed. 7.99 *(978-0-312-50867-8(0),* 9780312508678, Priddy Bks.) St. Martin's Pr.
—Wipe Clean - Early Learning. 2007. (Wipe Clean Early Learning Activity Bks.). (ENG., Illus.). 56p. (J). (— 1). spiral bd. 12.95 *(978-0-312-49922-8(1),* 9780312499228, Priddy Bks.) St. Martin's Pr.
—Wipe Clean Workbook Numbers 1-20. 2010. (ENG.). 28p. (J). (gr. -1-1). spiral bd., wbk. ed. 6.99 *(978-0-312-50869-2(7),* 9780312508692, Priddy Bks.) St. Martin's Pr.
—1000 Activities. 2009. (ENG.). 246p. (J). (gr. -1-2). pap. 9.95 *(978-0-312-50650-6(3),* 9780312506506, Priddy Bks.) St. Martin's Pr.
Priddy, Roger & Powell, Sarah. The Cardboard Box Book. Sido, Barbi, illus. 2014. (ENG.). 48p. (J). (gr. k-3). 12.99 *(978-0-312-51738-0(6),* 9780312517380, Priddy Bks.) St. Martin's Pr.
Priddy, Roger & Priddy Books Staff. Preschool Color & Activity Book. 2011. (ENG., Illus.). 84p. (J). (gr. -1-k). pap. 6.99 *(978-0-312-51317-7(8),* 9780312513177, Priddy Bks.) St. Martin's Pr.
Priestley, Michael. Writing: 25 Reproducible Mini-Tests That Help Students Prepare for & Succeed on Standardized Tests. 2008. (Standardized Test Practice Ser.). (ENG.). 64p. pap. 11.99 *(978-0-545-06402-6(3),* Teaching Resources) Scholastic, Inc.
Princess 1001 Stickers. 2016. (ENG., Illus.). 48p. (J). (gr. k-2). pap. 9.99 *(978-1-4052-7731-0(9))* Egmont Bks., Ltd. GBR. Dist: Independent Pubs. Group.
Prothero, Tiffany. Let's Go Green! An Earth-Friendly Coloring Book. 2009. (Dover Nature Coloring Book Ser.). (ENG., Illus.). 32p. (J). (gr. -1-2). pap. 3.99 *(978-0-486-46817-4(8))* Dover Pubns., Inc.
Pruett, Jason. Seek & Find: Book of Mormon Stories (Board Book) 2017. (ENG., Illus.). (gr. -1). bds. 12.99 ***(978-1-4621-2099-4(7))*** Cedar Fort, Inc./CFI Distribution.
Pruett, Mary, illus. Color the Western Birds. 2010. (Pruett Ser.). (ENG.). 32p. (J). pap. 4.99 *(978-0-87108-957-1(2))* Pruett Publishing Co.
Publications International Ltd. Staff. Marvel Heroes Extreme Look & Find. 2014. 24p. (J). 9.98 *(978-1-4508-7263-8(8),* 1450872638) Phoenix International Publications, Inc.
—Sesame Street: Say Cheese Elmo: Play-A-Sound Camera Book. 2013. 12p. (J). (gr. k-3). bds. 16.99 *(978-1-4508-3228-1(8),* 72cb51f4-311b-45cb-87a5-a5d14e7b6c62) Phoenix International Publications, Inc.
—1St Look & Find Spiderman. 2009. 16p. (J). bds. 9.98 *(978-1-4127-7770-4(4))* Phoenix International Publications, Inc.
—1St Look & Find What's Different Tigger & Pooh. 2013. 12p. (J). (gr. -1-1). bds. 7.98 *(978-1-4127-1880-6(5),* b9d2cf07-a5f4-4865-8cf4-66ad1cd9b1bf) Phoenix International Publications, Inc.
Publications International Ltd. Staff, creator. Disney Princess: the Little Mermaid: Play-A-Sound Book. 2013. 12p. (J). (gr. k-4). bds. 10.99 *(978-1-4508-6773-3(1),* 18a3bf8b-49b6-41ec-8af3-9adb0da6460f) Phoenix International Publications, Inc.
—Look & Find: Disney Princess: the Little Mermaid. 2013. 24p. (J). (gr. 1-3). 7.98 *(978-1-4508-6996-6(3),* 23104826-4b2a-459d-8edc-2f0362eaf16d) Phoenix International Publications, Inc.
—Sesame Street ABCs & 123s Wipe-off Activity Kit. 2007. (Wipe off Activity Kit Ser.). 14.98 *(978-1-4127-7442-0(X))* Publications International, Ltd.
—Tonka Wipe-off Activity Kit: ABCs And 123s. 2007. (Wipe off Activity Kit Ser.). 14.98 *(978-1-4127-7443-7(8))* Publications International, Ltd.
Publications International Ltd. Staff, ed. Abby Cadabby Fairy Tale Fun. 2009. 16p. (J). bds. 9.98 *(978-1-4127-1720-5(5),* PIL Kids) Publications International, Ltd.
—Baby Einstein. 2007. (J). 9.98 *(978-1-4127-6695-1(8))* Phoenix International Publications, Inc.
—Baby Einstein(r) Baby's First Stories & Songs: Look, Listen, Laugh. 2014. 24p. (J). bds. *(978-1-4508-8586-7(1),* 1450885861) Publications International, Ltd.
—Baby Einstein (tm) My First Smart Pad(tm) Library: Electronic Activity Pad & 8-Book Library. 2015. (J). 29.98 *(978-1-4508-7609-4(9),* 1450876099) Publications International, Ltd.
—Dena Designs: My Doodles. 2011. 100p. (J). spiral bd. 13.98 *(978-1-4508-0990-0(1))* Publications International, Ltd.
—Disney Big Hero 6 Look & Find. 2014. 24p. (J). 7.98 *(978-1-4508-8381-8(8),* 1450883818) Publications International, Ltd.
—Disney Classics Shaped Books. 2011. 8p. (J). bds. 4.98 *(978-1-4508-0909-2(X))* Publications International, Ltd.
—Disney Fairies: Best Friends Forever Scrapbook. 2011. 48p. (J). spiral bd. 11.98 *(978-1-60553-468-8(4))* Publications International, Ltd.
—Disney Jr.: Doc Mcstuffins: 12 Board Book Block Set. 2014. 10p. (J). bds. 9.98 *(978-1-4508-7395-6(2),* 1450873952) Phoenix International Publications, Inc.
—Disney Jr. Sound Storybook Treasury. 2014. 36p. (J). 24.95 *(978-1-4508-7597-4(1),* 8d42104c-490f-432d-ba43-f7132a0f97e8) Phoenix International Publications, Inc.
—Disney(r) Junior Look & Find(r) Treasury: 4 Look & Find Books & 1 Big Volume. 2014. 72p. (J). *(978-1-4508-8355-9(9),* 1450883559) Phoenix International Publications, Inc.
—Disney(r) JuniorLots & Lots of Look & Find(r): So Much to Find! More Than 900 Find'ems! Hours & Hours of Fun! 2015. 192p. (J). pap. *(978-1-4508-9408-1(9),* 1450894089) Publications International, Ltd.
—Disney(r) Little First Look & Find(tm) Minnie Best Friends. 2014. 18p. (J). bds. *(978-1-4508-8351-1(6),* 1450883516) Phoenix International Publications, Inc.
—Disney(r) Mickey Mouse Clubhouse Let's Explore: Take a Closer Look! a Magnifying Glass & Sound Book. 2014. 14p. (J). *(978-1-4508-7599-8(8),* 1450875998) Phoenix International Publications, Inc.
—Disney(r) Mickey Mouse Clubhouse Silly Sing-Along: Sing High! Sing Low! Sing with an Echo! 2014. 14p. (J). *(978-1-4508-7604-9(8),* ae256d2e-eb06-4361-9ac8-2e21277a9d86) Phoenix International Publications, Inc.
—Disney(r) Mickey Mouse Clubhouse Super Look & Find(r) Activity Pad: Look, Find, & Match! Search for What's Different! Use Stickers on the Play Scene- or Anywhere! 2014. 64p. (J). *(978-1-4508-8556-0(X),* 145088556X) Phoenix International Publications, Inc.
—Disney Minnie Let's Have a Tea Party: Play-A-Sound Book & Cuddly Minnie. 2014. 6p. (J). bds. 19.98 *(978-1-4508-7453-3(3),* 3ed17924-bf5b-4c7a-b781-4089274af8c) Phoenix International Publications, Inc.
—Disney(r) Minnie My First Look & Find(r) Best Friends. 2014. 18p. (J). bds. 9.98 *(978-1-4508-7919-4(5),* 1450879195) Phoenix International Publications, Inc.
—Disney Pixar. 2010. 64p. (J). pap. 10.98 *(978-1-60553-357-5(2),* PIL Kids) Publications International, Ltd.
—Disney Pixar:Planes: 12 Board Book Block Set. 2014. 10p. (J). bds. 9.98 *(978-1-4508-7362-8(6),* 1450873626) Phoenix International Publications, Inc.
—Disney Princess Me Reader Electronic Reader & 8-Book Library 3 Inch. 2013. (gr. k-4). 25.98 *(978-1-4508-6873-0(8),* 1450868738) Phoenix International Publications, Inc.
—Disney Princess My Charming Life Deluxe Scrapbook. 2011. 48p. (J). spiral bd. 11.98 *(978-1-60553-469-5(2))* Publications International, Ltd.
—Disney(r) Princess Super Look & Find(r) Activity Pad. 2014. 64p. (J). *(978-1-4508-8557-7(8),* 1450885578) Phoenix International Publications, Inc.
—Disney Princess Write & Erase Look & Find. 2012. 28p. (J). bds. 9.98 *(978-1-4508-4079-8(5),* 3a875535-bfb4-4654-9a9d-1ef47a7a8d3b) Phoenix International Publications, Inc.
—Disney(r) Sofia the First the Perfect Party: A Flashlight Adventure Sound Book. 2014. 14p. (J). 16.98 *(978-1-4508-7476-2(2),* 31bc99fe-fde1-4d89-9e76-09c40bd0ccb5) Phoenix International Publications, Inc.
—Disney(r) Super Look & Find(r) Activity Pad: 100's of Find 'ems, Best-Loved Characters! Hidden Pictures! More Than 50 Stickers! 2014. 64p. (J). *(978-1-4508-8558-4(6),* 1450885586) Publications International, Ltd.
—Dora the Explorer Ballerina Songs: Play-A-Sound Book & Huggable Dora. 2014. 6p. (J). bds. 19.98 *(978-1-4508-7449-6(5),* 8127d4c1-9e76-4d4f-80b8-6c35da23c50a) Phoenix International Publications, Inc.
—Electronic Time for Learning: States. 2010. 120p. 18.98 *(978-1-4127-9853-2(1),* PIL Kids) Publications International, Ltd.
—Hello Kitty(r); Hello Kitty's Guitar. 2014. 12p. (J). bds. 17.98 *(978-1-4508-7603-2(X),* 145087603X) Phoenix International Publications, Inc.
—I Can Be a Princess: Picture Book. 2014. 22p. (J). bds. 4.98 *(978-1-4508-8582-9(9),* 1450885829) Publications International, Ltd.
—Jake & the Neverland Pirates. 2014. 8p. (J). bds. *(978-1-4508-7763-3(X),* e168afdc-4d1e-411f-b3c5-d4e40b1ae222) Phoenix International Publications, Inc.
—Little First Look & Find Disney Best Friends. 2008. (J). bds. 3.98 *(978-1-4127-8437-5(9))* Phoenix International Publications, Inc.
—Look & Find: Disney Princess: Winter Dreams. 2013. 24p. (J). (gr. 1-3). 7.99 *(978-1-4127-7695-0(3),* 6d2a82ab-c0bb-4992-b098-a59561ffbf42) Phoenix International Publications, Inc.
—Marvel: Spider-Man: Spectacular Spider Powers! 2014. 12p. (J). bds. *(978-1-4508-6830-3(4),* 4081a6bc-7da7-4aa0-ac34-16d92600c8f0) Phoenix International Publications, Inc.
—Mickey & Friends Look & Find Extreme. 2014. 24p. (J). 9.98 *(978-1-4508-8775-5(9),* 1450887759) Publications International, Ltd.
—Mickey Mouse Clubhouse, What's Different? 2009. 24p. (J). 7.98 *(978-1-4127-1876-9(7),* PIL Kids) Publications International, Ltd.
—Minnie Mouse: Surprise, Surprise! Play-A-Sound Book. 2012. 10p. (J). (gr. k-3). bds. 7.99 *(978-1-4508-6848-8(7),* 0897e306-d7d1-4df0-a08f-afd88e1cfa82) Phoenix International Publications, Inc.
—My First Wipe-off: A to Z Animals Dictionary. 2010. 28p. (J). spiral bd. 7.98 *(978-1-4127-9386-5(6))* Phoenix International Publications, Inc.
—My Little Treasury Cuddle up Stories. 2014. 160p. (J). bds. *(978-1-4508-7282-9(4),* 1450872824) Phoenix International Publications, Inc.
—My Little Treasury My First Bible Stories. 2014. 160p. (J). bds. *(978-1-4508-7298-0(0),* 1450872980) Phoenix International Publications, Inc.
—Nickelodeon Dora the Explorer: Follow the Music: Piano Book. 2013. 14p. (J). bds. 16.98 *(978-1-4508-6380-3(9),* 355bc6ba-2b76-413c-bb3d-3975072deb9b) Phoenix International Publications, Inc.
—Nickelodeon Dora the Explorer Little Piano Book. 2014. 12p. (J). bds. *(978-1-4508-7593-6(9),* 1450875939) Publications International, Ltd.
—Nickelodeon(tm) Little First Look & Find(tm) Bubble Guppies. 2014. 18p. (J). bds. *(978-1-4508-8347-4(8),* 1450883478) Phoenix International Publications, Inc.
—Out & About. 2010. 18p. (J). bds. 12.98 *(978-1-4127-4466-9(0),* PIL Kids) Publications International, Ltd.
—Planes 2 Look & Find. 2014. 24p. (J). 7.98 *(978-1-4508-8350-4(8),* 1450883508) Phoenix International Publications, Inc.
—Sesame I Can Do It. 2009. 16p. (J). bds. 9.98 *(978-1-4127-1706-9(X))* Phoenix International Publications, Inc.
—Sesame Street: Trick or Treat with Elmo. 2009. 12p. (J). bds. *(978-1-4127-7896-1(4),* 1412778964) Phoenix International Publications, Inc.
—Sesame Write & Erase Board Book. 2014. 28p. (J). bds. 9.98 *(978-1-4508-8130-2(0),* 1450881300) Phoenix International Publications, Inc.
—Sketch This: Hundreds of Ways to Express Yourself! 2014. 160p. spiral bd. *(978-1-4508-8107-4(6),* 1450881076) Publications International, Ltd.
—Spongebob Squarepants. 2007. (J). 9.98 *(978-1-4127-6481-0(5))* Phoenix International Publications, Inc.
—Spongebob Squarepants Sea Mail. 2014. 6p. (J). bds. 19.98 *(978-1-4508-7454-0(1),* dcd91ed2-9e34-4ce7-b781-6a9ed2ae624a) Phoenix International Publications, Inc.
—Sunshine Doodle Book. Designs, Dena, illus. 2016. 80p. (J). spiral bd. *(978-1-68022-410-8(7),* 1680224107, PIL Kids) Publications International, Ltd.
—Super Cute & Happy Doodle Activity Book. Designs, Dena, illus. 2016. 80p. (J). spiral bd. *(978-1-68022-411-5(5),* 1680224115, PIL Kids) Publications International, Ltd.
—Super Fun Sticker Activities: More Than 1,000 Stickers! 2014. 64p. (J). pap. *(978-1-4508-3188-8(5),* 1450831885) Publications International, Ltd.
—Thomas Celebration Pop Up Sound. 2010. 14p. 19.98 *(978-1-4127-4513-0(6))* Publications International, Ltd.
—Write-And-Erase Look & Find(r) Disney Minnie: Packed with 'find 'ems & Picture Puzzles! Look, Circle, Wipe Clean, & Play Again! 2014. 28p. (J). bds. 9.98 *(978-1-4508-7918-7(7),* 1450879187) Phoenix International Publications, Inc.
Publishing, Autumn. I Want to Color BIG Pictures. 2009. 80p. pap. 12.99 *(978-1-60095-389-7(1))* Carson-Dellosa Publishing, LLC.
Publishing Group, Carlton. Doodle & Activity Advent Placemats: With 36 Tear-Out Doodle Placemats! 2014. (Doodle Mats Ser.). (ENG.). 72p. (J). (gr. 1-4). pap. 10.99 *(978-1-4380-0586-7(5))* Barron's Educational Series, Inc.
Puzzle Society Staff. Mom's Pocket Posh: 100 Puzzles & Games to Play with Your Kids Ages 7 to 12. 2012. (ENG.). 128p. pap. 7.99 *(978-1-4494-1823-6(6))* Andrews McMeel Publishing.
Racknor & Morrow. Wordszart. 2011. 92p. pap. 29.99 *(978-0-557-55589-5(2))* Lulu Pr., Inc.
Radford, Megan. Canada Doodles, 1 vol. Cook, Peter, illus. 2014. (ENG.). 240p. pap. 9.99 *(978-1-4236-3621-2(X))* Gibbs Smith, Publisher.
Radtke, Becky. Fairy Tales. 2004. (Dover Little Activity Bks.). (ENG., Illus.). 64p. (J). (gr. 3-5). pap., act. bk. ed. 1.50 *(978-0-486-43854-2(6))* Dover Pubns., Inc.
—Going Green! Activity Book. 2009. (Dover Little Activity Bks.). (ENG.). 64p. (J). (gr. 3-5). pap. 1.99 *(978-0-486-46810-5(0))* Dover Pubns., Inc.
—Keep the Scene Green! Earth-Friendly Activities. 2010. (Dover Children's Activity Bks.). (ENG., Illus.). 30p. (J). (gr. 1-5). pap. 3.99 *(978-0-486-47534-9(4))* Dover Pubns., Inc.
—Little Cars & Trucks. 2007. (Dover Little Activity Bks.). (ENG., Illus.). 64p. (J). (gr. 3-5). per., act. bk. ed. 1.99 *(978-0-486-45685-0(4))* Dover Pubns., Inc.
—Trains Activity Book. 2007. (Dover Little Activity Bks.). (ENG., Illus.). 64p. (J). (gr. k-3). per. 1.99 *(978-0-486-45683-6(8))* Dover Pubns., Inc.
Radtke, Becky J. All about Marvelous Me! A Draw & Write Journal. 2014. (ENG.). 64p. (J). (gr. 1-4). pap. 5.99 *(978-0-486-78626-1(9))* Dover Pubns., Inc.
—BOOST Keep the Scene Green! Earth-Friendly Activities. 2013. (BOOST Educational Ser.). (ENG.). 32p. (J). (gr. 1-2). pap. 4.99 *(978-0-486-49417-3(9))* Dover Pubns., Inc.
—Christmas Color by Number. 2015. (Dover Children's Activity Bks.). (ENG.). 32p. (J). (gr. -1-2). pap. 3.99 *(978-0-486-80051-6(2))* Dover Pubns., Inc.
—Four Seasons of Fun Activity Book. 2013. (ENG.). 48p. (J). (gr. 1-4). pap. 4.99 *(978-0-486-49894-2(8))* Dover Pubns., Inc.
—Hooray for the USA! Activity Book. 2016. (Dover Little Activity Bks.). (ENG.). 64p. (J). (gr. -1-3). pap. 1.99 *(978-0-486-80780-5(0))* Dover Pubns., Inc.
Rand McNally, creator. Kids' Backseat Travel Kit. 2015. (ENG.). (J). (gr. 4-7). pap. 19.99 *(978-0-528-01327-0(0))* Rand McNally.
Random House. It's All about Me! 2017. (ENG.). 128p. (J). (gr. -1-2). 12.99 *(978-1-5247-1405-5(4),* Random Hse. Bks. for Young Readers) Random Hse. Children's Bks.
Rankie, Barbara. Subtraction Unplugged, 2 vols. 2nd ed. 2013. (ENG.). 64p. 19.95 *(978-1-55386-217-8(1),* 1553862171) Jordan, Sara Publishing.
Ransom, Sharon L., ed. Cocurricular Activities: Their Values & Benefits, 11 vols. 2005. (Illus.). 64p. (YA). lib. bdg. 219.45 *(978-1-59084-888-3(8))* Mason Crest.
Ranson, Erin. Under the Sea. Green, Barry, illus. 2007. (Magnetic Story & Play Scene Ser.). (ENG.). 10p. (J). (gr. -1-1). 9.99 *(978-1-84666-089-4(0))* Top That! Publishing PLC GBR. Dist: Independent Pubs. Group.
Rasinski, Timothy V. Daily Word Ladders: 150+ Reproducible Word Study Lessons That Help Kids Boost Reading, Vocabulary, Spelling & Phonics Skills! 2008. (Daily Word Ladders Ser.). (ENG.). 176p. (gr. 1-2). pap. 19.99 *(978-0-545-07476-6(2),* Teaching Resources) Scholastic, Inc.
Rasmussen, R. Kent. World War I for Kids: A History with 21 Activities. 2014. (For Kids Ser.). (ENG., Illus.). 192p. (J). (gr. 4). pap. 17.95 *(978-1-61374-556-4(7))* Chicago Review Pr., Inc.
Reader, Jenny. Girl 2 Girl: The Swap Book You Share with Your Friends. Martin, Caroline & Davies, Nic, illus. 2003. 96p. (J). pap. *(978-0-439-56743-5(2))* Scholastic, Inc.
Regan, Lisa. Monsters: Over 1000 Reusable Stickers! 2014. (Little Hands Creative Sticker Play Ser.). (ENG.). 64p. (J). (gr. -1-2). pap. 9.99 *(978-1-4380-0389-4(7))* Barron's Educational Series, Inc.
Reilly, Kathleen M. Cities: Discover How They Work. Casteel, Tom, illus. 2014. (Build It Yourself Ser.). (ENG.). 128p. (J). (gr. 3-7). 21.95 *(978-1-61930-213-6(6))* Open City Bks.
—The Human Body: 25 Fantastic Projects Illuminate How the Body Works. Braley, Shawn, illus. 2008. (Build It Yourself Ser.). (ENG.). 128p. (J). (gr. 3-7). pap. 15.95 *(978-1-934670-24-8(3))* Octavio Publishing.
—Planet Earth: 25 Environmental Projects You Can Build Yourself. Rizvi, Farah, illus. 2008. (Build It Yourself Ser.). (ENG.). 128p. (J). (gr. 3-7). 21.95 *(978-1-934670-05-7(7));* pap. 15.95 *(978-1-934670-04-0(9))* Octavio Publishing.
Resort Day Time Sticker 'n' Style. 2008. (Bratz Sticker Activity Ser.). 12p. pap. *(978-1-4075-3044-4(5))* Parragon, Inc.
Rettore. Duck & Friends: A Soft & Fuzzy Book Just for Baby! 2017. (Friends Cloth Bks.). (ENG.). 8p. (J). (gr. -1 — 1). 9.99 *(978-1-4380-0975-9(5))* Barron's Educational Series, Inc.
Rey, H. A. Curious George Super Sticker Activity Book. 2009. (Curious George Ser.). (ENG., Illus.). 124p. (J). (gr. -1-3). act. bk. ed. 12.99 *(978-0-547-23896-8(7))* Houghton Mifflin Harcourt Publishing Co.
Reynolds, Peter H. Big Screen Books: For Big Fans of Story Sharing: the Dot Download: the Dot - Download. 2011. (J). cd-rom 29.95 *(978-1-891405-71-6(3))* FableVision Pr.
—The Dot: Make Your Mark Kit. Reynolds, Peter H., illus. 2013. (Creatrilogy Ser.). (ENG., Illus.). (J). (gr. k-4). 24.99 *(978-0-7636-6978-2(4))* Candlewick Pr.

Rhatigan, Joe. American Presidents. Owsley, Anthony, illus. 2016. (Just a Pencil Gets You Many Days of Fun Ser.). (ENG.). 144p. (J). (gr. 3-7). pap. 7.95 *(978-1-63322-111-6(3),* Moondance) Quarto Publishing Group USA.

—Doodle Games. Owsley, Anthony, illus. 2016. (Just a Pencil Gets You Many Days of Fun Ser.). (ENG.). 144p. (J). (gr. 3-7). pap. 7.95 *(978-1-63322-112-3(1),* Moondance) Quarto Publishing Group USA.

—The Totally Hilarious All about America Activity Book. Owsley, Anthony, illus. 2016. (All You Need Is a Pencil Ser.: 3). (ENG.). 144p. (J). (gr. 2-5). pap. 7.95 *(978-1-62354-076-0(3))* Charlesbridge Publishing, Inc.

—Weird Quizzes, Wacky Games, & Disturbing Doodles. Owsley, Anthony, illus. 2016. (All You Need Is a Pencil Ser.: 4). (ENG.). 144p. (J). (gr. 2-5). pap. 7.95 *(978-1-62354-077-7(1))* Charlesbridge Publishing, Inc.

Rhodes, Karen. Do You Know Jesus? 2005. (J). pap. 1.79 *(978-1-59317-111-7(0))* Warner Pr., Inc.

Rhodes, Lisa. Animals of Africa. 2010. (Pruett Ser.). (ENG.). 32p. (J). pap. 3.95 *(978-0-87108-953-3(X))* Pruett Publishing Co.

—Animals of Mountain West Region. 2010. (Pruett Ser.). (ENG.). 32p. (J). pap. 3.95 *(978-0-87108-956-4(4))* Pruett Publishing Co.

Richards, Mary & American Girl Editors, eds. Lists! A Year of Stuff about Me. 2011. (ENG.). 96p. (J). spiral bd. 10.95 *(978-1-59369-903-1(4))* American Girl Publishing, Inc.

Richardson, Sarah. Art in a Box. 2011. (ENG., Illus.). 20p. (J). (gr. k-6). 21.95 *(978-1-85437-927-6(5))* Tate Publishing, Ltd. GBR. Dist: Abrams, Inc.

richmond, keli. Literacy Speaks 2. 2008. (J). pap. 197.00 *(978-0-9799245-5-2(3))* Northern Speech Services.

Riley, Margaret. Crafty Parties for Kids: Creative Ideas, Invitations, Games, Favors, & More. 2013. (ENG., Illus.). 32p. pap. 9.99 *(978-1-57421-353-9(9),* 9781574213539, Design Originals) Fox Chapel Publishing Co., Inc.

Rising Moon, creator. The Great Colorado Activity Book. 2007. (ENG., Illus.). 56p. (J). (gr. 1-5). pap. 7.95 *(978-0-87358-921-5(1))* Cooper Square Publishing Llc.

Rivera, Mirabelle. What Is your favorite Color? 2008. 20p. pap. 24.95 *(978-1-4241-8454-5(1))* America Star Bks.

Rivers-Moore, Debbie. Chinese New Year. Davis, Caroline, illus. 2015. (Create & Celebrate Ser.). (ENG.). 48p. (J). (gr. -1-2). pap. 6.99 *(978-1-4380-0703-8(5))* Barron's Educational Series, Inc.

—The First Christmas. 2014. (Create & Celebrate! Ser.). (ENG.). 48p. (J). (gr. -1-2). pap. 6.99 *(978-1-4380-0542-3(3))* Barron's Educational Series, Inc.

—In the Ocean. 2017. (My First Noisy Bath Bks.). (ENG.). 8p. (J). (gr. -1 — 1). 4.99 *(978-1-4380-7828-1(5))* Barron's Educational Series, Inc.

RiverStream Readers - Level 1. 2013. (RiverStream Readers Ser.: 1). 124p. (gr. -1-2). 11.49 *(978-1-62588-901-0(1))* Black Rabbit Bks.

RiverStream Readers - Level 2. 2013. (RiverStream Readers Ser.: 2). 124p. (gr. -1-2). 11.49 *(978-1-62588-902-7(X))* Black Rabbit Bks.

RiverStream Readers - Level 3. 2013. (RiverStream Readers Ser.: 3). 124p. (gr. -1-2). 11.49 *(978-1-62588-903-4(8))* Black Rabbit Bks.

RiverStream Readers - Pre-1. 2013. (RiverStream Readers Ser.: PK). 124p. (gr. -1-2). 11.49 *(978-1-62588-900-3(3))* Black Rabbit Bks.

Robertson, Robbin Davis. The Sneaky Shoe Bug. Sexton, Jessa R., ed. Keaggy, Sarah, illus. 2012. 44p. 16.00 *(978-0-9860150-4-5(0))* O'More Publishing.

Robles Echeverria, Maria De Jesus & ALONSO CURIEL, Jorge David. Paisaje de Risas. DIVINCENZO, Yoselem G., illus. 2013. 72p. pap. 14.99 *(978-1-61196-924-5(7))* Pintos, Yoselem G.

Robson, Kirsteen. Aliens Sticker Book. Burnett, Seb, illus. 2014. (Usborne Activities Ser.). (ENG.). 22p. (J). 8.99 *(978-0-7945-3101-0(6),* Usborne) EDC Publishing.

—Wipe-Clean Pirate Activities. 2015. (Wipe-Clean Bks.). (ENG.). 22p. (J). (gr. k-5). pap. 7.99 *(978-0-7945-3543-8(7),* Usborne) EDC Publishing.

—Wipe-Clean Vacation Activities. 2015. (Wipe-Clean Bks.). (ENG.). 22p. (J). (gr. k-5). pap. 7.99 *(978-0-7945-3480-6(5),* Usborne) EDC Publishing.

Robson, Kirsten. Big Maze Book. 2013. (Doodle Bks). 64p. (J). pap. 9.99 *(978-0-7945-3345-8(0),* Usborne) EDC Publishing.

Rock Spring Elementary. Roadrunner Writing Rocks! 2013. 210p. pap. 15.00 *(978-0-9859367-2-3(X))* Pen & Publish Inc.

Roeder, Annette. The Art Coloring Book. 2012. (ENG.). 128p. (J). (gr. 1-4). pap. 12.95 *(978-3-7913-7108-5(8))* Prestel Verlag GmbH & Co KG. DEU. Dist: Penguin Random Hse. LLC.

—Vincent Van Gogh. Prestel, ed. 2009. (ENG.). 32p. (J). (gr. 1-4). pap. 8.95 *(978-3-7913-4331-0(9))* Prestel Verlag GmbH & Co KG. DEU. Dist: Penguin Random Hse. LLC.

Rogers, Kirsteen. Haunted House Sticker Book. 2012. (Sticker Activity Book Ser.). 24p. (J). pap. 8.99 *(978-0-7945-3163-8(6),* Usborne) EDC Publishing.

—Monsters Sticker Book. 2012. (Sticker Activity Book Ser.). 34p. (J). pap. 8.99 *(978-0-7945-3325-0(6),* Usborne) EDC Publishing.

Rogge, Robie. Peekaboo! Stroller Cards: in the Forest. White, Teagan, illus. 2017. (ENG.). 10p. (J). (gr. -1 — 1). 9.99 ***(978-1-4521-5384-1(1))*** Chronicle Bks. LLC.

Romeo & Juliet: Activity Pack. 2003. 130p. (YA). pap. *(978-1-58049-621-6(0),* PA0126) Prestwick Hse., Inc.

Romero, Kyle & Padron, Maria Lorena. Herbert Hoover Junior Ranger Activity Book. National Park Service Staff & Herbert Hoover National Historic Site (U.S), eds. 2013. (ENG., Illus.). 15p. (J). 6.00 *(978-0-16-092067-7(1))* National Park Service Div. of Pubns.

Rookie Ready to Learn - All about Me!, 5 vols., Set. Incl. Being Me. Broski, Julie. Vigla, Vincent, illus. 40p. lib. bdg. 23.00 *(978-0-531-26428-7(9));* Generous Me. Pearson, Mary E. Krejca, Gary, illus. 40p. lib. bdg. 25.00 *(978-0-531-26427-0(0));* I Need a Little Help. Schulz, Kathy. Iosa, Ann, illus. 32p. lib. bdg. 25.00 *(978-0-531-26526-0(9));* Just Like Me. Neasi, Barbara J. Hantel, Johanna, illus. 40p. lib. bdg. 25.00 *(978-0-531-26371-6(1));* Paul the Pitcher. Sharp, Paul, illus. 40p. lib. bdg. 25.00 *(978-0-531-26426-3(2));* (J). (gr. -1-k). (Rookie Ready to Learn Ser.). 2011. Set lib. bdg. 115.00 *(978-0-531-28350-9(X),* Children's Pr.) Scholastic Library Publishing.

Ross, Suzanne. BOOST Rain Forest Activity Book. 2013. (BOOST Educational Ser.). (ENG.). 48p. (J). (gr. 1-2). pap. 5.99 *(978-0-486-49413-5(6))* Dover Pubns., Inc.

Rouss, Sylvia A. Sammy Spider's Shabbat Fun Book. Kahn, Katherine Janus, illus. 2006. (Sammy Spider Set Ser.). (ENG.). 24p. (J). (gr. -1-3). pap. 4.95 *(978-1-58013-147-6(6),* Kar-Ben Publishing) Lerner Publishing Group.

Rowe, Thereza. Sticker Shape Create. 2016. (ENG.). 64p. (J). (gr. 1-3). pap. 14.95 *(978-1-61689-521-1(7))* Princeton Architectural Pr.

Rowlands, Caroline. The Ballet Creativity Book: With Games, Cut-Outs, Art Paper, Stickers, & Stencils. 2015. (Creativity Bks.). (ENG.). 80p. (J). (gr. k-5). pap. 12.99 *(978-1-4380-0555-3(5))* Barron's Educational Series, Inc.

—The Halloween Tattoo Book: With 24 Spooky Play Tattoos to Wear & Share! 2013. (ENG.). 48p. (J). (gr. 1-5). pap. 6.99 *(978-1-4380-0325-2(0))* Barron's Educational Series, Inc.

Roytman, Arkady. Secret Agent Sticker Activity. 2009. (Dover Little Activity Books Stickers Ser.). (ENG., Illus.). 4p. (J). (gr. k-3). 1.50 *(978-0-486-47136-5(5))* Dover Pubns., Inc.

—Treasures of King Tut's Tomb Stained Glass Coloring Book. 2009. (Dover Stained Glass Coloring Book Ser.). (ENG., Illus.). 32p. (J). (gr. -1-5). pap. 6.99 *(978-0-486-46996-6(4))* Dover Pubns., Inc.

Roytman, Arkady, et al. Build a 3-D Poster Coloring Book — Outer Space. 2012. (Dover 3-D Coloring Book Ser.). (ENG.). 32p. (J). (gr. 3-5). 5.99 *(978-0-486-49831-7(X))* Dover Pubns., Inc.

Running Press. Smurfs the Lost Village: Dress Me up Smurfette & Friends: A Magnetic Kit. 2017. (Miniature Editions Ser.). (ENG., Illus.). 32p. pap. 9.95 *(978-0-7624-6153-0(5),* Running Pr. Minature Editions) Running Pr. Bk. Pubs.

Running Press, Running. Mighty Morphin Power Rangers Dragon Dagger & Sticker Book: With Sound! 2016. (Miniature Editions Ser.). (ENG., Illus.). 16p. pap. 12.95 *(978-0-7624-6074-8(1),* Running Pr. Minature Editions) Running Pr. Bk. Pubs.

Running Press Staff, ed. CreARTivity: Chunky Chalk. 2014. (ENG., Illus.). 64p. (J). (gr. -1-17). pap. 14.95 *(978-0-7624-5624-6(8),* Running Pr. Kids) Running Pr. Bk. Pubs.

—CreARTivity: Perfect Pattern Art. 2014. (ENG., Illus.). 64p. (J). (gr. -1-17). pap. 14.95 *(978-0-7624-5626-0(4),* Running Pr. Kids) Running Pr. Bk. Pubs.

—Frozen: Melting Olaf the Snowman Kit. 2015. (Miniature Editions Ser.). (ENG., Illus.). 32p. pap. 12.95 *(978-0-7624-5740-3(6),* Running Pr. Minature Editions) Running Pr. Bk. Pubs.

—Hello Kitty Fun, Friendly Doodles: Supercute Full-Color Pictures to Create & Complete. 2013. (ENG., Illus.). 160p. (J). (gr. -1-17). pap. 12.95 *(978-0-7624-5092-3(4),* Running Pr. Kids) Running Pr. Bk. Pubs.

—Outer Space. 2013. (ENG.). 24p. (J). (gr. -1-17). pap. 12.95 *(978-0-7624-5216-3(1),* Running Pr. Kids) Running Pr. Bk. Pubs.

—Scratch & Stencil: Ponies. 2013. (ENG.). 24p. (J). (gr. -1-17). pap. 12.95 *(978-0-7624-5215-6(3),* Running Pr. Kids) Running Pr. Bk. Pubs.

—Trolls: Poppy & Branch Finger Puppets. 2016. (Miniature Editions Ser.). (ENG., Illus.). 9.95 *(978-0-7624-5980-3(8),* Running Pr. Minature Editions) Running Pr. Bk. Pubs.

Running Press Staff, et al. Hello Kitty, Dress Me Up Kit: A Magnetic Kit. 2009. (Miniature Editions Ser.). (ENG.). 16p. pap. 6.95 *(978-0-7624-3595-1(X))* Running Pr. Bk. Pubs.

Rupp, Cecelia, ed. How to Be #1 Kid at Table Manners: Activity Book. 2012. (ENG.). pap. 44.95 *(978-1-4675-3185-6(5))* Independent Pub.

Ruth, Angie. My Adventure Bug Collecting. 2006. 44p. (J). 8.99 *(978-1-59092-448-8(7))* Blue Forge Pr.

—My Adventure in the Snow. 2006. 44p. (J). 8.99 *(978-1-59092-435-8(5))* Blue Forge Pr.

Ryals, Lexi & Hargreaves, Roger. Mr. Men Little Miss All Year Round. 2014. (Mr. Men & Little Miss Ser.). (ENG., Illus.). 80p. (J). (gr. -1-2). 9.99 *(978-0-8431-8065-7(X),* Price Stern Sloan) Penguin Young Readers Group.

Ryan, Nellie, et al. Girls' World of Doodles: Over 100 Pictures to Complete & Create. 2011. (ENG.). 128p. (J). (gr. -1-17). pap. 12.95 *(978-0-7624-4287-4(5))* Running Pr. Bk. Pubs.

Sabatino, Chris. City Doodles - Boston. 2013. (ENG., Illus.). 240p. (J). pap. 9.99 *(978-1-4236-3207-8(9))* Gibbs Smith, Publisher.

—Monster Doodles for Kids, 1 vol. 2011. (ENG., Illus.). 240p. (J). pap., pap. 9.99 *(978-1-4236-2020-4(8))* Gibbs Smith, Publisher.

—Pocketdoodles for Boys, 1 vol. 2010. (ENG.). 272p. (J). (gr. 1). 9.99 *(978-1-4236-0756-4(2))* Gibbs Smith, Publisher.

—Superhero Doodles for Kids, 1 vol. 2012. (ENG., Illus.). 272p. (J). pap. 9.99 *(978-1-4236-2483-7(1))* Gibbs Smith, Publisher.

Sach, Jacqueline. The Wham-O Hacky Sack Handbook: The Tips & Tricks for Becoming an Expert Shredder! 2008. (ENG.). 78p. (J). (gr. 5-18). pap. 14.95 *(978-1-60433-002-1(3),* Applesauce Pr.) Cider Mill Pr. Bk. Pubs., LLC.

Sachse, Dina, illus. My Body: 12 Lift-N-Learn Flashcards about the Human Body, 12 vols. 2013. (Early Start Singles Ser.). (ENG.). 12p. (J). *(978-1-77132-070-2(2))* SpiceBox Products Ltd.

—My Clothes: 12 Lift-N-Learn Flashcards about Clothes, 26 vols. 2013. (Early Start Singles Ser.). (ENG.). 12p. (J). *(978-1-77132-101-3(6))* SpiceBox Products Ltd.

—My Food: 12 Lift-N-Learn Flashcards about Food!, 26 vols. 2013. (Early Start Singles Ser.). (ENG.). 12p. (J). *(978-1-77132-102-0(4))* SpiceBox Products Ltd.

Saddleback Educational Publishing Staff, ed. A Very Good Year. 2011. (Carter High Senior Year Ser.). (ENG.). 16p. (YA). (gr. 9-12). cd-rom 7.95 *(978-1-61651-342-9(X))* Saddleback Educational Publishing, Inc.

Sage, Alison. Stop That Robot! Band 00/Lilac. Dunn, Gary, illus. 2007. (Collins Big Cat Ser.). (ENG.). 16p. (J). (gr. -1-k). pap. 5.99 *(978-0-00-718678-5(9))* HarperCollins Pubs. Ltd. GBR. Dist: Independent Pubs. Group.

Salch, Megan. 100+ Activities for Houston Kids 2006. 2005. (Illus.). 40p. pap. 19.95 *(978-0-9776154-0-7(5))* Salch, Megan F.

Salzmann, Mary Elizabeth. Money for School, 1 vol. 2010. (Your Piggy Bank: A Guide to Spending & Saving for Kids! Ser.). (ENG.). 24p. (J). (gr. k-3). 27.07 *(978-1-61641-031-5(0))* Magic Wagon.

Sanchez, John Joseph P. Illuminating the Legacy: A Coloring & Activity Book of the CNMI's History. Ogo, Luis S., illus. 2006. 106p. (J). (gr. 4-5). pap. *(978-1-878453-89-1(0))* Univ. of Guam, Micronesian Area Research Ctr.

Sanders, Nancy I. Cut & Paste Mini-Books: Math: 15 Fun, Interactive Mini-Books That Reinforce Key Math Concepts & Boost Reading Skills. 2010. (ENG.). 128p. (gr. k-1). pap. 16.99 *(978-0-439-60630-1(6),* Teaching Resources) Scholastic, Inc.

Santa Activity Book. 2007. (Shaped Christmas Activity Ser.). 64p. pap. *(978-1-4075-0776-7(1))* Parragon, Inc.

Santoro. My Secret Place. Santoro, illus. 2014. (Gorjuss Ser.). (ENG., Illus.). 128p. (J). (gr. 2-4). 12.99 *(978-0-7636-7453-3(2),* Candlewick Entertainment) Candlewick Pr.

Samat, Marjorie. Creative Cats Stickers. 2016. (Dover Little Activity Bks.). (ENG., Illus.). 4p. pap. 1.99 *(978-0-486-80703-4(7))* Dover Pubns., Inc.

Sateren, Shelley Swanson. Max & Zoe: the Very Best Art Project, 1 vol. Sullivan, Mary, illus. 2013. (Max & Zoe Ser.). (ENG.). 32p. (gr. k-2). pap. 5.19 *(978-1-4795-2329-0(1),* Max & Zoe) Picture Window Bks.

Saunders, Katie. Preschool Days Treasury: Preschool Learning Friendships & Fun. 2013. (Toddler Bks.). (ENG., Illus.). 48p. (J). (gr. -1 — 1). 9.99 *(978-0-7641-6625-9(5))* Barron's Educational Series, Inc.

—Toddler Christmas: Activities, Games, & Stories for Excited Toddlers. 2013. (Toddler Bks.). (ENG.). 48p. (J). (gr. -1 — 1). 9.99 *(978-0-7641-6631-0(X))* Barron's Educational Series, Inc.

Sayre, April Pulley. The Slowest Book Ever. Murphy, Kelly, illus. 2016. (ENG.). 176p. (J). (gr. 2-7). 16.95 *(978-1-62091-783-1(1))* Boyds Mills Pr.

Sazaklis, John. Design & Draw. 2012. (Dark Knight Rises Ser.). (ENG.). 64p. (J). (gr. -1-3). pap., act. bk. ed. 6.99 *(978-0-06-213226-0(1),* HarperFestival) HarperCollins Pubs.

Scarry, Richard. Best Busytown. 2013. (ENG., Illus.). 118p. (J). (gr. -1-2). pap., act. bk. ed. 14.95 *(978-1-4027-7315-0(3))* Sterling Publishing Co., Inc.

—Richard Scarry's Best Ever Color, Shapes, & Numbers: Includes Giant Poster & 80+ Stickers! 2014. (Richard Scarry's Sticker & Poster Bks.). (ENG.). 20p. (J). (gr. -1-1). pap. 5.99 *(978-1-4380-0413-6(3))* Barron's Educational Series, Inc.

—Richard Scarry's My First School Journal. 2013. (ENG.). 32p. (J). (gr. -1 — 1). 7.99 *(978-0-7641-6621-1(2))* Barron's Educational Series, Inc.

—Richard Scarry's Welcome to Busytown! Includes Giant Poster & 80+ Stickers! 2014. (Richard Scarry's Sticker & Poster Bks.). (ENG.). 20p. (J). (gr. -1-1). pap. 5.99 *(978-1-4380-0414-3(1))* Barron's Educational Series, Inc.

Schab, Lisa M. Cool, Calm, & Confident: A Workbook to Help Kids Learn Assertiveness Skills. 2009. (Instant Help Ser.). (ENG.). 184p. (J). (gr. k-5). pap. 18.95 *(978-1-57224-630-0(8),* Instant Help Books) New Harbinger Pubns.

Schachner, Judy. Get Busy with Skippyjon Jones! Schachner, Judy, illus. 2013. (Skippyjon Jones Ser.). (ENG., Illus.). 16p. (J). (gr. -1-k). 6.99 *(978-0-448-47783-1(1),* Grosset & Dunlap) Penguin Young Readers Group.

Scheunemann, Pam. Cool Stuff for Bath & Beauty: Creative Projects for Kids, 1 vol. 2012. (Cool Stuff Ser.). (ENG., Illus.). 32p. (J). (gr. 3-6). 28.50 *(978-1-61714-980-1(2))* ABDO Publishing Co.

—Cool Stuff for Your Garden: Creative Projects for Kids, 1 vol. 2012. (Cool Stuff Ser.). (ENG., Illus.). 32p. (J). (gr. 3-6). 28.50 *(978-1-61714-984-9(5))* ABDO Publishing Co.

Schmitt, Conrad. ¡Así Se Dice! 2009. (Glencoe Spanish Ser.). (ENG & SPA.). 160p. (gr. 6-12). pap., wbk. ed. 21.84 *(978-0-07-892935-9(0),* 0078929350) McGraw-Hill Education.

—Así Se Dice 2009, Level 1A. 2009. (Glencoe Spanish Ser.). (ENG & SPA.). 160p. (gr. 6-12). pap., wbk. ed. 21.84 *(978-0-07-892934-2(2),* 0078929342) McGraw-Hill Education.

Scholastic. Essential Handbook (Yo-Kai Watch) 2016. (Yo-Kai Watch Ser.). (ENG.). 192p. (J). (gr. 2-5). pap. 9.99 *(978-1-338-05831-4(2))* Scholastic, Inc.

—Harry Potter Magical Places & Characters Poster Coloring Book. 2016. (Harry Potter Ser.). (ENG.). 40p. (J). (gr. 3). pap. 24.99 *(978-1-338-13292-2(X))* Scholastic, Inc.

—Stone Monsters Attack! 2016. (LEGO NEXO Knights Ser.). (ENG.). 32p. (J). (gr. 2-5). pap. 8.99 *(978-1-338-05560-3(7))* Scholastic, Inc.

Scholastic & Klutz Editors. 101 Outrageously Fun Things to Do. 2017. (ENG.). 80p. (J). (gr. 3-7). 19.99 *(978-1-338-10640-4(6))* Klutz.

Scholastic & Marsham, Liz. Fantastic Beasts & Where to Find Them: Coloring & Creativity Book. 2016. (ENG.). 80p. (J). (gr. 3-7). pap. 8.99 *(978-1-338-11608-9(0))* Scholastic, Inc.

Scholastic, Inc. Staff. Clifford Forever Friends. 2008. 29.99 *(978-0-439-93520-3(2))* Scholastic, Inc.

—Early Learning Sticker Workbook. 2015. (Scholastic Early Learners Ser.). (ENG.). 104p. (J). (gr. -1-k). bds. 9.99 *(978-0-545-90335-6(1),* Cartwheel Bks.) Scholastic, Inc.

—Harry Potter Postcard Coloring Book. 2016. (ENG.). 40p. (J). (gr. 3). pap. 9.99 *(978-1-338-04575-8(X))* Scholastic, Inc.

—Kindergarten. 2015. (Scholastic Early Learners Ser.). (ENG.). 56p. (J). (gr. -1 — 1). bds., wbk. ed. 9.99 *(978-0-545-90326-4(2),* Cartwheel Bks.) Scholastic, Inc.

—Pre-K. 2015. (Scholastic Early Learners Ser.). (ENG.). 56p. (J). (gr. -1 — 1). bds., wbk. ed. 9.99 *(978-0-545-90324-0(6),* Cartwheel Bks.) Scholastic, Inc.

—Sketch Surprise! Scholastic, Inc. Staff, illus. 2016. (Shopkins Ser.). (ENG., Illus.). 64p. (J). (gr. 3-3). 12.99 *(978-0-545-90498-8(6))* Scholastic, Inc.

—Vowel Sounds. 2010. (ENG.). (gr. k-2). 14.99 *(978-0-545-21376-9(2))* Teacher's Friend Pubns., Inc.

—Wipe-Clean Workbook, Grade 1. 2015. (Scholastic Early Learners Ser.). (ENG.). 56p. (J). (gr. k-2). bds. 9.99 *(978-0-545-90327-1(0),* Cartwheel Bks.) Scholastic, Inc.

—Write & Wipe ABC 123. 2015. (Scholastic Early Learners Ser.). (ENG.). 28p. (J). (gr. -1-k). bds. 8.99 *(978-0-545-90640-1(7),* Cartwheel Bks.) Scholastic, Inc.

Scholastic, Inc. Staff, contrib. by. Accents. 2017. (Tape It Up! Ser.). (ENG.). (gr. -1-6). 5.99 ***(978-1-338-12795-9(0))*** Teacher's Friend Pubns., Inc.

—Accents: Color Your Classroom! 2017. (Color Your Classroom Ser.). (ENG.). (gr. -1-6). 5.99 ***(978-1-338-12796-6(9))*** Teacher's Friend Pubns., Inc.

—Color Your Classroom! Birthdays. 2017. (Color Your Classroom Ser.). (ENG.). (gr. -1-6). 2.49 ***(978-1-338-12800-0(0))*** Teacher's Friend Pubns., Inc.

—Color Your Classroom! Welcome. 2017. (Color Your Classroom Ser.). (ENG.). (gr. -1-6). 2.49 ***(978-1-338-12799-7(3))*** Teacher's Friend Pubns., Inc.

—Early Math: 25 Ready-to-Go Manipulative Wheels That Help Children Practice & Master Key Early Math Skills. 2010. (ENG.). 112p. (gr. -1-1). 20.99 *(978-0-545-22376-8(8),* Teaching Resources) Scholastic, Inc.

—Grocery Games! 2016. (Shopkins Ser.). (ENG.). 96p. (J). (gr. -1-3). pap. 12.99 *(978-1-338-03805-7(2))* Scholastic, Inc.

—Harry Potter: Magical Creatures Postcard Coloring Book. 2016. (Harry Potter Ser.). (ENG.). 40p. (J). (gr. 3). pap. 9.99 *(978-1-338-05459-0(7))* Scholastic, Inc.

—Harry Potter Poster Coloring Book. 2016. (Harry Potter Ser.). (ENG.). 40p. (J). (gr. 3). pap. 24.99 *(978-1-338-05460-6(0))* Scholastic, Inc.

—Name Plates. 2017. (Tape It Up! Ser.). (ENG.). (gr. -1-6). 5.99 ***(978-1-338-12805-5(1))*** Teacher's Friend Pubns., Inc.

—Name Plates: Color Your Classroom! 2017. (Color Your Classroom Ser.). (ENG.). (gr. -1-6). 5.99 ***(978-1-338-12806-2(X))*** Teacher's Friend Pubns., Inc.

—Trace, Play, & Learn: ABC 123 (Scholastic Early Learners) 2015. (Scholastic Early Learners Ser.). (ENG.). 12p. (J). (— 1). bds. 12.99 *(978-0-545-90313-4(0),* Cartwheel Bks.) Scholastic, Inc.

—Traditional Manuscript, Grades K-1. 2010. (Scholastic Success with Ser.). (ENG.). 48p. (gr. k-1). pap. 5.99 *(978-0-545-20073-8(3),* Teaching Resources) Scholastic, Inc.

—Turn-to-Learn Wheels in Color - Phonics: 25 Ready-to-Go Manipulative Wheels That Help Children Practice & Master Key Phonics Skills to Become Successful Readers. 2010. (ENG.). 112p. (gr. k-2). 20.99 *(978-0-545-22400-0(4),* Teaching Resources) Scholastic, Inc.

Scholastic, Inc. Staff & Klutz Editors. Coloring Crush. 2015. (ENG.). 78p. (J). (gr. 3-7). 16.99 *(978-0-545-93097-0(9))* Klutz.

Scholastic, Inc. Staff & Malone, Sydney. For Me & U! Fun for BFFs. 2014. (ENG.). 112p. (J). (gr. 1-3). pap. 8.99 *(978-0-545-73297-0(2),* Scholastic Paperbacks) Scholastic, Inc.

Scholastic, Inc. Staff & Sevaly, Karen. Bulletin Board Wild West Ranch, Set. 2007. (ENG.). (J). (gr. -1-5). 10.99 *(978-0-439-92012-4(4))* Scholastic, Inc.

Scholastic Library Publishing. Rookie Ready to Learn, 30 vols., Set. Incl. Set. Rookie Ready to Learn - All about Me! (gr. -1-k). lib. bdg. 115.00 *(978-0-531-28350-9(X));* Set. Rookie Ready to Learn - Animals. (gr. k-3). lib. bdg. 115.00 *(978-0-531-27450-7(0));* Set. Rookie Ready to Learn - First Science: Me & My World. (gr. -1-k). lib. bdg. 115.00 *(978-0-531-23850-9(4));* Set. Rookie Ready to Learn - I Can! (gr. -1-k). lib. bdg. 115.00 *(978-0-531-25150-8(0));* Set. Rookie Ready to Learn - My Family & Friends. (gr. -1-k). lib. bdg. 115.00 *(978-0-531-24450-0(4));* Set. Rookie Ready to Learn - Numbers & Shapes. (gr. -1-k). lib. bdg. 115.00 *(978-0-531-24300-8(1));* Set. Rookie Ready to Learn - Out & About: In My Community. (gr. -1-k). lib. bdg. 115.00 *(978-0-531-25905-4(6));* Set. Rookie Ready to Learn - Seasons & Weather. (gr. -1-k). lib. bdg. 115.00 *(978-0-531-26724-0(5));* (J). 2011, 2011. Set lib. bdg. 920.00 *(978-0-531-29149-8(9),* Children's Pr.) Scholastic Library Publishing.

—A True Book-Experiments. 2011. (True Book-Experiments Ser.). (J). 174.00 *(978-0-531-20912-7(1),* Children's Pr.) Scholastic Library Publishing.

—A True Book-Physical Science. 2011. (True Book-Physical Science Ser.). (J). 174.00 *(978-0-531-25935-1(8),* Children's Pr.) Scholastic Library Publishing.

Scholastic Magazines, inc Staff, contrib. by. Harry Potter: Magical Artifacts Coloring Book. 2016. (ENG.). 96p. (J). (gr. 3-7). pap. 15.99 *(978-1-338-03002-0(7))* Scholastic, Inc.

—Harry Potter Magical Places & Characters Coloring Book. 2016. (ENG.). 96p. (J). (gr. 3). pap. 15.99 *(978-1-338-03001-3(9))* Scholastic, Inc.

Scholastic Teaching Resources, Scholastic Teaching. Weekly Reader - Summer Express. 2017. (Weekly Reader: Summer Express Ser.). (ENG., Illus.). 144p. (gr. -1 — 1). pap. 10.99 *(978-1-338-10888-0(3))* Scholastic, Inc.

Scholastic Teaching Resources Staff. Fantastic Beasts & Where to Find Them: The Beasts Poster Book. 2016. (ENG.). 24p. (J). (gr. 3-7). pap. 7.99 *(978-1-338-11852-0(8))* Scholastic, Inc.

—Kindergarten Basic Skills: Alphabet & Fine-Motor Skills. 2012. (Kindergarten Basic Skills Ser.). (ENG.). 48p. pap. 6.99 *(978-0-545-42964-1(1))* Teacher's Friend Pubns., Inc.

—Kindergarten Basic Skills: Numbers & Counting. 2012. (Kindergarten Basic Skills Ser.). (ENG.). 48p. pap. 6.99 *(978-0-545-42965-8(X))* Teacher's Friend Pubns., Inc.

—Kindergarten Basic Skills: Visual Perception, Classifying & More. 2012. (Kindergarten Basic Skills Ser.). (ENG.). 48p. pap. 6.99 *(978-0-545-42963-4(3))* Teacher's Friend Pubns., Inc.

—Preschool Basic Skills: Colors, Shapes & More. 2012. (Preschool Basic Skills Ser.). (ENG.). 48p. pap. 6.99 *(978-0-545-42969-6(2))* Teacher's Friend Pubns., Inc.

—Preschool Basic Skills: Fine-Motor & Scissor Skills. 2012. (Preschool Basic Skills Ser.). (ENG., Illus.). 48p. pap. 6.99 *(978-0-545-42966-5(8))* Teacher's Friend Pubns., Inc.

—Preschool Basic Skills: Visual Perception & Drawing. 2012. (Preschool Basic Skills Ser.). (ENG.). 48p. pap. 6.99 *(978-0-545-42967-2(6))* Teacher's Friend Pubns., Inc.

—Weekly Reader - Summer Express. 2017. (Weekly Reader: Summer Express Ser.). (ENG.). 144p. (gr. 3-4). pap. 10.99 (978-1-338-10892-7(1)) Scholastic, Inc.

—Weekly Reader - Summer Express, Between Grades 1 & 2. 2017. (Weekly Reader: Summer Express Ser.). (ENG., Illus.). 144p. (gr. 1-2). pap. 10.99 (978-1-338-10890-3(5)) Scholastic, Inc.

—Weekly Reader - Summer Express, Between Grades 2 & 3. 2017. (Weekly Reader: Summer Express Ser.). (ENG., Illus.). 144p. (gr. 2-3). pap. 10.99 (978-1-338-10891-0(3)) Scholastic, Inc.

—Weekly Reader - Summer Express (Between Grades K & 1) 2017. (Weekly Reader: Summer Express Ser.). (ENG., Illus.). 144p. (gr. k-1). pap. 10.99 (978-1-338-10889-7(1)) Scholastic, Inc.

School, Blue Mountain. Colored Pencils. 2013. 26p. pap. 6.99 (978-1-61720-891-1(4)) Wilder Pubns., Corp.

School Zone. Animal Alphabet. 2008. (ENG.). 26p. (J). 5.99 (978-1-58947-932-6(7)) School Zone Publishing Co.

School Zone Interactive Staff. Dot-to-Dots. Boyer, Robin, illus. 2006. (ENG.). 64p. (J). (gr. 1-2). 7.99 (978-1-58947-302-7(7)) School Zone Publishing Co.

—Hidden Pictures. Sullivan, Mary, illus. rev. ed. 2006. (ENG.). 64p. (J). (gr. 1-2). 7.99 (978-1-58947-301-0(9)) School Zone Publishing Co.

School Zone Staff. Big Hidden Pictures & More. 2009. 320p. (J). pap. 12.99 (978-1-60159-258-3(2)) School Zone Publishing Co.

Schuette, Sarah L. Spot It, Learn It!, 1 vol. 2014. (Spot It, Learn It! Ser.). (ENG.). 32p. (gr. 1-2). lib. bdg. 109.28 (978-1-4765-7920-7(2), Aplus Bks.) Capstone Press of Coughlan Cos.

Schuette, Sarah L. & Marks, Jennifer L. Spot It. 2016. (Spot It Ser.). (ENG.). 32p. lib. bdg. 327.84 (978-1-5157-4015-5(3), Aplus Bks.) Capstone Press of Coughlan Cos.

Schuler, Kimberly B. I Will Remember You: My Catholic Guide Through Grief. 2011. 144p. (J). (gr. 2-6). pap. 10.95 (978-0-8198-3704-2(0)) Pauline Bks. & Media.

Schulz, Charles M. Good Grief! Charlie Brown Doodles: Create & Complete Pictures with the Peanuts Gang. 2012. (ENG.). 64p. (J). (gr. 1-17). pap. 7.95 (978-0-7624-4448-9(7)) Running Pr. Bk. Pubs.

Schulz, Charles M., creator. Snoopy Loves to Doodle: Create & Complete Pictures with the Peanuts Gang. 2011. (ENG.). 64p. (J). (gr. -1-17). pap. 7.95 (978-0-7624-4378-9(2)) Running Pr. Bk. Pubs.

Science Explorer Junior, 20 vols., Set. Incl. Experiment with Bugs. Gray, Susan H. 32p. (gr. 3-6). 2010. lib. bdg. 28.50 (978-1-60279-842-7(7), 200550); Experiment with Heat. Lockwood, Sophie. 32p. (gr. 3-6). 2010. lib. bdg. 28.50 (978-1-60279-843-4(5), 200552); Experiment with Liquids. Mullins, Matt. 32p. (gr. 3-6). 2010. lib. bdg. 28.50 (978-1-60279-846-5(X), 200558); Experiment with Magnets. Taylor-Butler, Christine. 32p. (gr. 3-6). 2010. lib. bdg. 28.50 (978-1-60279-844-1(3), 200554); Experiment with Plants. Gray, Susan H. 32p. (gr. 3-6). 2010. lib. bdg. 28.50 (978-1-60279-839-7(7), 200544); Experiment with Rocks. Lockwood, Sophie. 32p. (gr. 3-6). 2010. lib. bdg. 28.50 (978-1-60279-836-6(2), 200538); Experiment with Seeds. Gray, Susan H. 32p. (gr. 3-6). 2010. lib. bdg. 28.50 (978-1-60279-835-9(4), 200536); Experiment with Soil. Franchino, Vicky. 32p. (gr. 3-6). 2010. lib. bdg. 28.50 (978-1-60279-837-3(0), 200540); Experiment with Solar Energy. Taylor-Butler, Christine. 32p. (gr. 3-6). 2010. lib. bdg. 28.50 (978-1-60279-840-3(0), 200546); Experiment with Solids. Gregory, Josh. 32p. (gr. 3-6). 2010. lib. bdg. 28.50 (978-1-60279-845-8(1), 200556); Experiment with Water. Simon, Charnan & Kazunis, Ariel. 32p. (gr. 3-6). 2010. lib. bdg. 28.50 (978-1-60279-838-0(9), 200542); Experiment with Weather. Orr, Tamra. 32p. (gr. 3-6). 2010. lib. bdg. 28.50 (978-1-60279-841-0(9), 200548); Set. Science Explorer Junior: Think Like a Scientist. Cherry Lake Publishing Staff. (J). (gr. 4-8). 2011. lib. bdg. 228.00 (978-1-61080-249-9(7)); 2011. Set lib. bdg. 570.00 (978-1-61080-247-5(0)) Cherry Lake Publishing.

Science Explorer Junior: Think Like a Scientist, 8 vols., Set. Incl. Think Like a Scientist at the Beach. Rau, Dana Meachen. lib. bdg. 28.50 (978-1-61080-168-3(7), 201106); Think Like a Scientist in the Backyard. Mullins, Matt. lib. bdg. 28.50 (978-1-61080-167-6(9), 201104); Think Like a Scientist in the Car. Mullins, Matt. lib. bdg. 28.50 (978-1-61080-164-5(4), 201098); Think Like a Scientist in the Classroom. Hindman, Susan. lib. bdg. 28.50 (978-1-61080-170-6(9), 201110); Think Like a Scientist in the Garden. Mullins, Matt. lib. bdg. 28.50 (978-1-61080-166-9(0), 201102); Think Like a Scientist in the Gym. Taylor-Butler, Christine. lib. bdg. 28.50 (978-1-61080-163-8(6), 201096); Think Like a Scientist in the Kitchen. Mullins, Matt. lib. bdg. 28.50 (978-1-61080-165-2(2), 201100); Think Like a Scientist on the Playground. Rau, Dana Meachen. lib. bdg. 28.50 (978-1-61080-169-0(5), 201108); 32p. (gr. 4-8). (Science Explorer Junior Ser.). 2011. Set lib. bdg. 228.00 (978-1-61080-249-9(7)) Cherry Lake Publishing.

Scollen, Chris. Busy Kids Baby Animals Sticker Activity Book. 2008. (Busy Kids Ser.). (Illus.). 12p. (J). (gr. -1-3). pap. (978-1-84610-636-1(2)) Make Believe Ideas.

—Busy Kids Farm Animals Sticker Activity Book. 2008. (Busy Kids Ser.). (Illus.). 12p. (gr. -1-3). 4.99 (978-1-84610-638-5(9)) Make Believe Ideas GBR. Dist: Nelson, Thomas Inc.

—Busy Kids Kittens & Puppies Sb. 2008. (Busy Kids Ser.). (Illus.). 20p. (J). (gr. -1-3). 4.99 (978-1-84610-632-3(X)) Make Believe Ideas GBR. Dist: Nelson, Thomas Inc.

—Busy Kids Sticker Storybook Sleeping Beauty. 2008. (Illus.). 12p. (J). (gr. -1-3). pap. (978-1-84610-807-5(1)) Make Believe Ideas.

—Busy Kids Tractors & Trucks Sticker Activity Book. 2008. (Busy Kids Ser.). (Illus.). 20p. (J). (gr. -1-3). 4.99 (978-1-84610-634-7(6)) Make Believe Ideas GBR. Dist: Nelson, Thomas Inc.

—1000 Stickers Sweet Treats. 2013. (ENG.). 56p. (J). pap. 6.99 (978-1-78235-485-7(9)) Make Believe Ideas GBR. Dist: Nelson, Thomas Inc.

Scollen, Chris, et al. Diggers & Dumpers. 2008. (Busy Kids Ser.). (Illus.). 12p. (gr. -1-3). 4.99 (978-1-84610-723-8(7)) Make Believe Ideas GBR. Dist: Nelson, Thomas Inc.

Scott, Ellen. Design Your Own Teddy Bears Sticker Activity Book. 2017. (Dover Little Activity Bks.). (ENG., Illus.). 4p. (gr. k-3). 1.99 **(978-0-486-81866-5(7))** Dover Pubns., Inc.

Scott, James. The Indian in the Cupboard: Activity Pack. 2003. 138p. (YA). pap. (978-1-58049-625-4(3), PA0124) Prestwick Hse., Inc.

Scott, Xavier. Great Diary Planner for Teens: Diary. 2013. (ENG.). 50p. 14.77 (978-1-62884-694-2(1), Speedy Kids (Children's Fiction)) Speedy Publishing LLC.

Scotton, Rob. Doodle & Draw. Scotton, Rob, illus. 2013. (Splat the Cat Ser.). (ENG., Illus.). 64p. (J). (gr. -1-3). pap. 6.99 (978-0-06-211607-9(X), HarperFestival) HarperCollins Pubs.

Scraper, Katherine, et al. Boredom Busters! Try This! Free & Inexpensive Things to Make & Do. 2011. (J). pap. (978-1-4509-5325-2(5)) Benchmark Education Co.

Seddon, Wayne & Seddon, Leigh. Scribbles: Using your eyes to see with your Mind. 2008. 44p. pap. 20.00 (978-1-59858-559-9(2)) Dog Ear Publishing, LLC.

Seek-and-Find Fun. 2010. (Spot It Ser.). 32p. 77.97 (978-1-4296-5198-1(9), Aplus Bks.) Capstone Press of Coughlan Cos.

Seifert, Sheila & Naylor, Beth. Stepping up, Stepping Out. 2008. (DSJ Ser.). (Illus.). 112p. (J). (gr. 1-6). pap. 16.99 (978-0-7814-4562-7(0)) Cook, David C.

Seifert, Sheila, et al. Lead the Way, Jesus. 2008. (DSJ Ser.). (Illus.). 112p. (J). (gr. 1-6). pap. 16.99 (978-0-7814-4560-3(4)) Cook, David C.

Selber, Danielle. Pope Francis Bobblehead. 2015. (Miniature Editions Ser.). (ENG., Illus.). 32p. pap. 9.95 (978-0-7624-5692-5(2), Running Pr. Minature Editions) Running Pr. Bk. Pubs.

Serrano, Shea. Bun B's Rapper Coloring & Activity Book. 2013. (ENG.). 48p. pap., act. bk. ed. 12.95 (978-1-4197-1041-4(9), Abrams Image) Abrams, Inc.

Sesame Workshop. I Am a Friend. 2011. (J). (gr. k-1). pap. 3.99 (978-1-59922-884-6(X)) Twin Sisters IP, LLC.

—I Like School. 2011. (J). (gr. k-1). pap. 3.99 (978-1-59922-885-3(8)) Twin Sisters IP, LLC.

—Sesame Play-N-Learn 123S. 2011. (J). (gr. k-1). bds. 3.99 (978-1-59545-896-4(4)) Twin Sisters IP, LLC.

—Sesame Play-N-Learn Abcs. 2011. (J). (gr. k-1). bds. 3.99 (978-1-59545-895-7(6)) Twin Sisters IP, LLC.

—Sesame Play-N-Learn Dot to Dots. 2011. (J). (gr. k-1). bds. 3.99 (978-1-59545-897-1(2)) Twin Sisters IP, LLC.

—Sesame Play-N-Learn Mazes. 2011. (J). (gr. k-1). bds. 3.99 (978-1-59545-898-8(0)) Twin Sisters IP, LLC.

Sesame Workshop, ed. ABC Sesame Street Flash Cards. 2009. (ENG.). 30p. 9.95 (978-1-74185-997-3(2), Ideal Pubns.) Worthy Publishing.

—Pets Elmos World Flash Cards. 2009. (ENG.). 30p. 9.95 (978-1-74185-995-9(6), Ideal Pubns.) Worthy Publishing.

—Your Body Elmos World Flash Cards. 2009. (ENG.). 15p. 9.95 (978-1-74185-994-2(8), Ideal Pubns.) Worthy Publishing.

Seuss, Dr. The Little Blue Box of Bright & Early Board Books by Dr. Seuss. 2012. (Bright & Early Board Books(TM) Ser.). (ENG., Illus.). 24p. (J). (— 1). bds. 19.96 (978-0-307-97586-7(X), Random Hse. Bks. for Young Readers) Random Hse. Children's Bks.

—My Book about Christmas by ME, Myself: With Some Help from the Grinch & Dr. Seuss. 2016. (ENG., Illus.). 64p. (J). (gr. -1-3). 16.99 (978-0-553-52446-8(1), Random Hse. Bks. for Young Readers) Random Hse. Children's Bks.

—Oh, the Places You'll Go! the Read It! Write It! Collection, 2 vols. 2016. (ENG., Illus.). 120p. (J). (gr. -1-3). 32.99 (978-0-553-53872-4(1), Random Hse. Bks. for Young Readers) Random Hse. Children's Bks.

Sevaly, Karen & Scholastic, Inc. Staff. Counting Money Puzzles. 2007. (ENG.). (J). (gr. k-2). pap. 12.99 (978-0-439-91217-4(2)) Scholastic, Inc.

Sévigny, Éric, illus. Caillou: My First Sticker Book: Includes 400 Fun Stickers. 2015. (Coloring & Activity Book Ser.). (ENG.). 64p. (J). (gr. -1-1). 9.99 (978-2-89718-179-6(6)) Caillouet, Gerry.

Sexton, Brenda & Sloan, Price Stern. Have a Crazy Christmas! Sexton, Brenda, illus. 2016. (Mad Libs Junior Ser.). (ENG., Illus.). 32p. (J). (gr. -1-k). bds., act. bk. ed. 7.99 (978-0-8431-8939-1(8), Mad Libs) Penguin Young Readers Group.

Shaffer, Christy. Glow-In-the-Dark Snowflakes Stickers. 2009. (Dover Little Activity Books Stickers Ser.). (ENG., Illus.). 2p. (J). (gr. 1-4). 1.50 (978-0-486-47062-7(8)) Dover Pubns., Inc.

—Learning about Mythical Creatures. 2005. (Dover Little Activity Bks.). (ENG., Illus.). 16p. (J). (gr. 3-5). pap. 1.50 (978-0-486-44047-7(8)) Dover Pubns., Inc.

Shanddaramon. A Pagan Book of ABCs. 2009. 60p. pap. 24.95 (978-0-557-09532-2(8)) Lulu Pr., Inc.

—The 12 Days of Yule. 2008. 33p. 16.95 (978-0-615-26465-3(4)) Astor Pr.

Share Time with Me. 2004. (J). per. 5.95 (978-0-9760282-0-8(4)) RAPC - Sparkle & Shine Project.

Shaw-Russell, Susan. Coral Reef Fish Friends Sticker Activity Book. 2016. (Dover Little Activity Books Stickers Ser.). (ENG.). 8p. (J). (gr. -1-3). pap. 1.99 (978-0-486-80775-1(4)) Dover Pubns., Inc.

—Deep Sea Diner Sticker Activity Book. 2012. (Dover Little Activity Books Stickers Ser.). (ENG., Illus.). 4p. (J). (gr. k-3). pap. 1.50 (978-0-486-48674-1(5)) Dover Pubns., Inc.

—Make Your Own Bookmark Sticker Activity Book: Monsters, Robots & More! 2014. (ENG.). 8p. (J). (gr. k-3). pap. 1.50 (978-0-486-78142-6(9)) Dover Pubns., Inc.

—Make Your Own Bookmark Sticker Activity Book: Princesses, Mermaids & More! 2014. (ENG.). 8p. (J). (gr. k-3). pap. 1.50 (978-0-486-78141-9(0)) Dover Pubns., Inc.

—Moustache Sticker Activity Book. 2015. (Dover Little Activity Bks.). (ENG.). 4p. (J). (gr. 2-5). pap. 1.50 (978-0-486-80108-7(X)) Dover Pubns., Inc.

—Pampered Pooches Sticker Activity Book. 2012. (Dover Little Activity Books Stickers Ser.). (ENG.). 4p. (J). (gr. k-3). pap. 1.50 (978-0-486-48940-7(X)) Dover Pubns., Inc.

—Robots Activity Book. 2009. (Dover Little Activity Bks.). (ENG., Illus.). 64p. (J). (gr. k-3). pap. 1.99 (978-0-486-47227-0(2)) Dover Pubns., Inc.

—Seek, Sketch & Color — Alphabet. 2013. (Dover Children's Activity Bks.). (ENG.). 64p. (J). (gr. 1-3). pap. 5.99 (978-0-486-49772-3(0)) Dover Pubns., Inc.

—Seek, Sketch & Color — Animals. 2013. (Dover Children's Activity Bks.). (ENG.). 64p. (J). (gr. 1-3). pap. 5.99 (978-0-486-49773-0(9)) Dover Pubns., Inc.

—Smiley Robot Tattoos. 2011. (Dover Tattoos Ser.). (ENG., Illus.). 4p. (J). (gr. 1-4). pap. 1.50 (978-0-486-48190-6(5)) Dover Pubns., Inc.

—The Three Bears Activity Book. 2009. (Dover Little Activity Bks.). (ENG., Illus.). 64p. (J). (gr. -1-5). pap. 1.99 (978-0-486-47059-7(8)) Dover Pubns., Inc.

Shaw-Russell, Susan, et al. Animals on Parade Find & Color. 2012. (Dover Children's Activity Bks.). (ENG.). 48p. (J). (gr. k-6). pap. 4.99 (978-0-486-48938-4(8)) Dover Pubns., Inc.

Shealy, Dennis. Joker's Joyride - Built for Speed. Random House Editors, illus. 2010. (Pictureback(R) Ser.). (ENG.). 32p. (J). (gr. -1-2). pap. 4.99 (978-0-375-85967-0(5), Random Hse. Bks. for Young Readers) Random Hse. Children's Bks.

Sheets, Bethany Pease. Doodle Designs. 2013. (ENG.). 40p. pap. 6.95 (978-1-60705-774-1(3)) C & T Publishing.

Sheldon, Ken. Sing-Along & Learn - Science: 12 Lively Learning Songs & Instant Activities That Teach Key Science Concepts. 2010. (ENG., Illus.). 32p. (gr. k-2). 13.99 (978-0-545-09438-2(0), Teaching Resources) Scholastic, Inc.

Shepherd-Guenette, C. Lost & Found. 2005. pap. (978-1-84401-531-3(9)) Athena Pr.

Sherman, Michael & Klutz Editors. Me vs. You: Head to Head Pencil Puzzles! 2011. (ENG.). 50p. (J). (gr. 3-7). 10.99 (978-1-59174-929-5(8)) Klutz.

Shulman, Mark & National Geographic Kids Staff. Are You "Normal"? More Than 100 Questions That Will Test Your Weirdness. 2011. (ENG., Illus.). 176p. (J). (gr. 3-7). pap. 12.95 (978-1-4263-0837-6(X), National Geographic Children's Bks.) National Geographic Society.

Signoretti, Brenda. Freddie the Frog & Friends. REVILLE, TONI-ANN, illus. 2011. 32p. pap. 12.99 (978-1-4634-4633-8(0)) AuthorHouse.

Silver, Donald & Wynne, Patricia J. Geographic Terms: 15 Engaging Mini-Books That Students Read-And Interact With-To Really Learn about Key Landforms. 2009. (ENG.). 72p. pap. 13.99 (978-0-439-35527-8(3), Teaching Resources) Scholastic, Inc.

Simon and Schuster UK Staff. Colour in 5 SOS! 2014. (ENG.). 32p. (J). 5.99 (978-1-4711-2469-3(X), Simon & Schuster Children's) Simon & Schuster, Ltd. GBR. Dist: Simon & Schuster, Inc.

—Colour in One Direction! 2014. (ENG.). 32p. (J). pap. 5.99 (978-1-4711-1867-8(3), Simon & Schuster Children's) Simon & Schuster, Ltd. GBR. Dist: Simon & Schuster, Inc.

—Ultimate Boy Band Pack! 2014. (ENG.). 48p. (J). 8.99 (978-1-4711-2473-0(8), Simon & Schuster Children's) Simon & Schuster, Ltd. GBR. Dist: Simon & Schuster, Inc.

Simon, M. Ed. Parrots 2 Peacocks Pattern Book. 2005. pap. 34.65 (978-1-4010-6134-0(6)) Xlibris Corp.

Sinclair, Donna. The Family Story Bible Colouring Book. 2013. (ENG., Illus.). 28p. (J). (gr. 10-10). 5.95 (978-1-77064-570-7(5)) Wood Lake Publishing, Inc. CAN. Dist: Westminster John Knox Pr.

Singer, Allison & Kempster-Barry, Rachel. This Book Is about You. 2017. (ENG.). 192p. (YA). (gr. 8-12). pap. 15.99 **(978-1-4654-5657-1(0)**, DK Children) Dorling Kindersley Publishing, Inc.

Sisler, Celeste. Legend of the NeverBeast - Fawn's Field Guide: A Reusable Sticker Book. 2015. (ENG., Illus.). 12p. (J). (gr. -1-3). pap. 6.99 (978-0-316-28355-7(X)) Little, Brown Bks. for Young Readers.

Sitomer, Alan Lawrence. Teaching Teens & Reaping Results in a Wi-Fi, Hip-Hop,Where-Has-All-the-Sanity-Gone World: Stories, Strategies, Tools, & Tips from a Three-Time Teacher of the Year Award Winner. 2009. (ENG.). 208p. pap. 25.99 (978-0-545-03603-0(8), Teaching Resources) Scholastic, Inc.

Siuda, Erik & Creative Haven. Creative Haven Modern Tattoo Designs Coloring Book. 2013. (Adult Coloring Ser.). (ENG., Illus.). 64p. (gr. 6). pap. 5.99 (978-0-486-49326-8(1)) Dover Pubns., Inc.

Skiles, Janet. Happy Birthday! Tattoos. 2016. (Dover Little Activity Bks.). (ENG., Illus.). 2p. (J). (gr. k-3). 1.99 (978-0-486-81070-6(4)) Dover Pubns., Inc.

—Silly Sea Animals Tattoos. 2016. (Dover Little Activity Bks.). (ENG.). 2p. (J). (gr. k-3). 1.99 (978-0-486-81093-5(3)) Dover Pubns., Inc.

Skinner. Forbidden Activities for Neglected Children. 2014. (ENG., Illus.). 36p. pap. 9.95 (978-0-86719-798-3(6)) Last Gasp of San Francisco.

Skylanders TRU Feature Shop, 42 vols. 2014. (ENG.). (J). pap., pap., pap. 353.58 (978-0-448-48793-9(4), Grosset & Dunlap) Penguin Young Readers Group.

Slam! Activity Pack. 2003. 172p. (YA). pap. (978-1-58049-624-7(5), PA0123) Prestwick Hse., Inc.

Small Object Staff. I Like to Draw/I Like to Write. 2013. (ENG., Illus.). 144p. 14.95 (978-1-4521-0903-9(6)) Chronicle Bks. LLC.

Small World Creations. Chalkboard Princesses. 2016. (Chalkboard Bks.). (ENG.). 10p. (J). (gr. -1-2). bds. 7.99 (978-0-7641-6871-0(1)) Barron's Educational Series, Inc.

Smart Kids Publishing Staff. My Snuggle up Bedtime Book. Smart Kids Publishing Staff, illus. 2007. (Illus.). 16p. 14.99 (978-0-8249-6695-9(3), Ideal Pubns.) Worthy Publishing.

SmartInk Books Staff. CityBLOCKS Stacking Blocks. Crisp, Dan, illus. 2011. (ENG.). 10p. (J). (gr. -1-17). 21.99 (978-1-4521-0275-7(9)) Chronicle Bks. LLC.

SmartLab, creator. Custom Car Design Shop. 2011. (SmartLAB Ser.). (J). 7.99 (978-1-60380-123-2(5), SmartLab) becker&mayer! books.

—Fashion Designer. 2011. (SmartLAB Ser.). (J). 7.99 (978-1-60380-122-5(7), SmartLab) becker&mayer! books.

—Fashion Studio. 2011. (SmartLAB Ser.). (J). (gr. 2). 24.99 (978-1-60380-127-0(8), SmartLab) becker&mayer! books.

—Glitter Spa Lab. 2011. (SmartLAB Ser.). (J). 7.99 (978-1-60380-118-8(9), SmartLab) becker&mayer! books.

—It's Alive! T. Rex. 2011. (SmartLAB Ser.). (J). (gr. 1). 14.99 (978-1-60380-066-2(2), SmartLab) becker&mayer! books.

—Secret Formula Lab. 2011. (SmartLAB Ser.). (J). 7.99 (978-1-60380-120-1(0), SmartLab) becker&mayer! books.

SMARTLAB Creative Team. Indoor Outdoor Science Lab. 2010. 12p. mass mkt. 39.99 (978-1-60380-051-8(4)) becker&mayer! books.

—Inside Out! the Human Body. 2010. 12p. mass mkt. 39.99 (978-1-60380-052-5(2)) becker&mayer! books.

Smiley, Jess Smart. Rumpus on the Run: A Monster Look-N-Find Book. 2013. (ENG., Illus.). 22p. (J). (gr. -1-3). 14.95 (978-1-62086-444-9(4)) Mascot Bks., Inc.

Smith, A. G. FRENCH EDITION of Gargoyles & Medieval Monsters Coloring Book. 2013. (Dover Children's Bilingual Coloring Book Ser.). (FRE & ENG.). 48p. (J). (gr. 3-12). pap. 4.99 (978-0-486-49327-5(X)) Dover Pubns., Inc.

—Tallest Building in the World - Burj Khalifa: Cut & Assemble. 2011. (Dover Children's Activity Bks.). (ENG., Illus.). 20p. (gr. 3-6). pap. 9.99 (978-0-486-48235-4(9)) Dover Pubns., Inc.

Smith, A. g. & Smith, A. G. The White House Cut & Assemble. 2010. (Dover Children's Activity Bks.). (ENG., Illus.). 20p. (J). (gr. 3-6). pap. 9.99 (978-0-486-47681-0(2)) Dover Pubns., Inc.

Smith, Kimberly. Monkeying Around: Meet Chippey & His Friends. Goris, Laura, illus. 2012. 44p. (J). pap. 14.98 (978-0-9843166-6-3(3)) Artists' Orchard, LLC, The.

Smith, Naniloa. The Children Are Happy Activity Book with Animals from the Southwest. 2003. (J). 11.00 (978-0-9744005-0-1(5)) In the Desert.

Smith, Nikki. Five Little Speckled Frogs Activity Guide. 2010. 66p. pap. 10.00 (978-0-557-36823-5(5)) Lulu Pr., Inc.

Smith, Sherri Graves. Bully's Game Day Rules. Danielson, Damon, illus. 2013. (ENG.). (J). 14.95 (978-1-62086-334-3(0)) Mascot Bks., Inc.

—Cimarron's Game Day Rules. Danielson, Damon, illus. 2013. (ENG.). (J). 14.95 (978-1-62086-230-8(1)) Mascot Bks., Inc.

—Cocky's Game Day Rules. Danielson, Damon, illus. 2013. (ENG.). (J). 14.95 (978-1-62086-085-4(6)) Mascot Bks., Inc.

—Nittany Lion's Game Day Rules. Danielson, Damon, illus. 2013. (ENG.). (J). 14.95 (978-1-62086-233-9(6)) Mascot Bks., Inc.

—Reveille's Game Day Rules. Danielson, Damon, illus. 2013. (ENG.). (J). (gr. -1-3). 14.95 (978-1-62086-350-3(2)) Mascot Bks., Inc.

—Tiger's Game Day Rules. Danielson, Damon, illus. 2013. (ENG.). (J). (gr. -1-3). 14.95 (978-1-62086-086-1(4)) Mascot Bks., Inc.

Snape, Charles & Snape, Juliet. Brain Busters: Games, Puzzles & More! 2012. (Dover Children's Activity Bks.). (ENG., Illus.). 64p. (J). (gr. 3-5). pap. 9.99 (978-0-486-48779-3(2)) Dover Pubns., Inc.

Snellenberger, Earl & Snellenberger, Bonita. Noah's Ark Pre-School Activity Book. Snellenberger, Earl & Snellenberger, Bonita, illus. 2014. (ENG., Illus.). 98p. (J). (gr. -1-3). pap. 8.99 (978-0-89051-832-8(7)) Master Bks.

—The Wonders of God's World Dinosaur Activity Book. Snellenberger, Earl & Snellenberger, Bonita, illus. 2008. (Illus.). 128p. (J). (gr. -1). per. 8.99 (978-0-89051-515-0(8)) Master Bks.

Snider, Brandon T. Brain Food. 2013. (Plants vs. Zombies Ser.). (ENG.). 224p. (J). (gr. 1-5). 10.99 (978-0-06-229492-0(X), HarperFestival) HarperCollins Pubs.

Snow, Philip. Animals of the Bible. Snow, Philip, illus. 2005. (Bible Discover & Colour Ser.). (Illus.). 32p. (J). (gr. -1-7). 4.00 (978-1-903087-88-6(0)) DayOne Pubns. GBR. Dist: Send The Light Distribution LLC.

—Birds of the Bible. Snow, Philip, illus. 2005. (Bible Discover & Colour Ser.). (Illus.). 32p. (J). (gr. -1-7). 4.00 (978-1-903087-89-3(9)) DayOne Pubns. GBR. Dist: Send The Light Distribution LLC.

Snozek, Lee Anne & Coloring Books for Adults. Outrageous Octagons. 2009. (Dover Design Coloring Bks.). (ENG., Illus.). 32p. (gr. 3-8). pap. 3.99 (978-0-486-47301-7(5)) Dover Pubns., Inc.

So, Patty. So Simple at-Home A Month of Ideas: 31 Fun & Simple Activities to Reinforce Your Child's Reading Success! 2007. 36p. (J). spiral bd. (978-0-9772158-5-0(7)) So Simple Learning.

Social Studies Explorer, 21 vols., Set. Incl. Bangladesh. Orr, Tamra. 48p. 2010. lib. bdg. 31.36 (978-1-60279-829-8(X), 200524); Brazil. Franchino, Vicky. 48p. 2010. lib. bdg. 31.36 (978-1-60279-827-4(3), 200520); China. Raatma, Lucia. 48p. 2010. lib. bdg. 31.36 (978-1-60279-823-6(0), 200512); India. Raatma, Lucia. 48p. 2010. lib. bdg. 31.36 (978-1-60279-824-3(9), 200514); Indonesia. Orr, Tamra. 48p. 2010. lib. bdg. 31.36 (978-1-60279-826-7(5), 200518); Japan. Somervill, Barbara. 48p. 2010. lib. bdg. 31.36 (978-1-60279-832-8(X), 200530); Mexico. Somervill, Barbara. 48p. 2010. lib. bdg. 31.36 (978-1-60279-833-5(8), 200532); Nigeria. Rau, Dana Meachen. 48p. 2010. lib. bdg. 31.36 (978-1-60279-830-4(3), 200526); Pakistan. Labrecque, Ellen. 48p. 2010. lib. bdg. 31.36 (978-1-60279-828-1(1), 200522); Philippines. Franchino, Vicky. 48p. 2010. lib. bdg. 31.36 (978-1-60279-834-2(6), 200534); Russia. Marsico, Katie. 48p. 2010. lib. bdg. 31.36 (978-1-60279-831-1(1), 200528); United States. Marsico, Katie. 48p. 2010. lib. bdg. 31.36 (978-1-60279-825-0(7), 200516); Set. Social Studies Explorer: It's Cool to Learn about Countries. Cherry Lake Publishing Staff. (J). 2011. lib. bdg. 125.44 (978-1-61080-148-5(2)); Set. Social Studies Explorer: It's Cool to Learn about the United States. Cherry Lake Publishing Staff. (J). 2011. lib. bdg. 156.80 (978-1-61080-191-1(1)); (gr. 4-8). 2011. Set lib. bdg. 658.56 (978-1-61080-253-6(5)) Cherry Lake Publishing.

Social Studies Explorer: It's Cool to Learn about Countries, 4 vols., Set. Incl. Egypt. Marsico, Katie. lib. bdg. 31.36 (978-1-61080-100-3(8), 201094); Ethiopia. Somervill, Barbara. lib. bdg. 31.36 (978-1-61080-099-0(0), 201092); Germany. Franchino, Vicky. lib. bdg. 31.36 (978-1-61080-098-3(2), 201090); Vietnam. Rau, Dana Meachen. lib. bdg. 31.36 (978-1-61080-097-6(4), 201088); 48p. (gr. 4-8). (Social Studies Explorer Ser.). 2011. Set lib. bdg. 125.44 (978-1-61080-148-5(2)) Cherry Lake Publishing.

Soffer, Ruth. Animal Illustrations to Paint or Color. 2007. (Dover Art Coloring Book Ser.). (ENG., Illus.). 48p. (J). (gr. 3-8). 5.99 (978-0-486-45696-6(X)) Dover Pubns., Inc.

Sokol, Dawn DeVries. The Doodle Circle: A Fill-In Journal for BFFs to Share. 2013. (ENG.). 160p. (J). (gr. 3-7). pap. 12.95 (978-1-61769-053-2(8), Amulet Bks.) Abrams, Inc.

S

Sood, Sana Hoda. Diwali: A Cultural Adventure. Hoda, Rubina, illus. 2013. (ENG.). (J). (gr. -1-3). 14.95 *(978-1-62086-396-1(0))* Mascot Bks., Inc.

Sosa, Carlos. Celebrations. 2007. (Familia Banderas Ser.). (Illus.). 48p. (J). (gr. 3-7). per. 9.95 *(978-1-933669-11-3(X))* Literary Architects, LLC.

—Cultures. 2007. (Familia Banderas Ser.). (Illus.). 48p. (J). (gr. 3-7). per. 9.95 *(978-1-933669-12-0(8))* Literary Architects, LLC.

Southall, Margo. Differentiated Small-Group Reading Lessons: Scaffolded & Engaging Lessons for Word Recognition, Fluency, & Comprehension That Help Every Reader Grow. 2009. (ENG.). 160p. pap. 20.99 *(978-0-439-83920-4(3)*, Teaching Resources) Scholastic, Inc.

—Ready-To-Go Differentiated Literacy Centers: Grade 1: Engaging Centers Designed to Help Every Student Meet the Common Core. 2014. (ENG.). 160p. (gr. 1-1). 199.99 *(978-0-545-54997-4(3)*, Teaching Resources) Scholastic, Inc.

Sovak, Jan. Build a Giant Poster Coloring Book — Under the Sea. 2013. (Dover Build a Poster Coloring Book Ser.). (ENG., Illus.). 48p. (J). (gr. 2-6). pap. 4.99 *(978-0-486-49139-4(0))* Dover Pubns., Inc.

Sovak, Jan, et al. Build a 3-D Poster Coloring Book — Fairies. 2012. (Dover 3-D Coloring Book Ser.). (ENG.). 16p. (J). (gr. 3-5). pap. 5.99 *(978-0-486-49830-0(1))* Dover Pubns., Inc.

Spear, Kevin. My Very Own Activity Pages: Spring 2004. 2004. (Illus.). (J). pap. 1.79 *(978-1-59317-077-6(7))* Warner Pr., Inc.

Spine-Tingling 1001 Stickers. 2016. (ENG., Illus.). 48p. (J). (gr. k-2). pap. 9.99 *(978-1-4052-7812-6(9))* Egmont Bks., Ltd. GBR. Dist: Independent Pubs. Group.

Spohn, Rebecca. Ready, Set, Create! A Kid's Guide to Crafting. 2012. (ENG., Illus.). 92p. pap. 19.95 *(978-1-59647-425-3(4))* Good Year Bks.

Squires, Patricia. Enter Here. 2008. 62p. (J). 41.99 *(978-1-4257-7867-5(4))* Xlibris Corp.

Stadler, Charlotte. Making Patterns. 2011. (Early Connections Ser.). (J). *(978-1-61672-640-9(7))* Benchmark Education Co.

Stampy (Joseph Garrett), Stampy (Joseph. Stick with Stampy! Sticker Book. 2017. (ENG., Illus.). 24p. (J). (gr. 2-5). pap. 6.99 *(978-0-399-55633-3(8)*, Random Hse. Bks. for Young Readers) Random Hse. Children's Bks.

Stanley, Mandy, illus. Arty Words. 2016. (Arty Mouse Wipe Clean with Pen Ser.). (ENG.). 24p. (J). (gr. -1-2). pap. 7.99 *(978-1-78445-858-4(9))* Top That! Publishing PLC GBR. Dist: Independent Pubs. Group.

Stansbie, Stephanie. Dinosaurs: A Busy Sticker Activity Book. Nowowiejska, Kasia, illus. 2016. (Little Snappers Ser.). (ENG.). 96p. (J). (gr. -1-1). 9.99 *(978-1-58925-319-3(1))* Tiger Tales.

The Star-Spangled Workbook. 2006. per. 34.95 *(978-0-9787820-1-6(1))* King, Joel.

Stardoll. Stardoll: Sticker Red Carpet Dress Up. 2013. (Stardoll Ser.). (ENG.). 24p. (J). (gr. 2-4). pap. 6.99 *(978-0-85751-178-2(5))* Transworld Publishers Ltd. GBR. Dist: Independent Pubs. Group.

—Sticker Catwalk Dress Up. 2013. (Stardoll Ser.). (ENG.). 24p. (J). (gr. 2-4). pap. 6.99 *(978-0-85751-176-8(9))* Transworld Publishers Ltd. GBR. Dist: Independent Pubs. Group.

—Sticker Holiday Dress Up. 2013. (Stardoll Ser.). (ENG.). 24p. (J). (gr. 2-4). pap. 6.99 *(978-0-85751-177-5(7))* Transworld Publishers Ltd. GBR. Dist: Independent Pubs. Group.

Staying Focused. 2007. (J). per. 10.00 *(978-0-9788937-2-9(7))* Amani Publishing, LLC.

Stead, Emily. On the Farm. 2013. (My First Creativity Activity Bks.). (ENG.). 66p. (J). (gr. -1-2). pap. 9.99 *(978-1-4380-0239-2(4))* Barron's Educational Series, Inc.

—Things That Go! With 200 Stickers, Puzzles & Games, Fold-Out Pages, & Creative Play. 2013. (My First Creativity Bks.). (ENG.). 66p. (J). (gr. -1-2). pap. 9.99 *(978-1-4380-0324-5(2))* Barron's Educational Series, Inc.

Steck, Jim. Cartoon Kids Sticker Book. 2016. (Dover Little Activity Books Stickers Ser.). (ENG.). 4p. (J). (gr. 1-4). 1.99 *(978-0-486-80880-2(7))* Dover Pubns., Inc.

Steck-Vaughn Staff. Three Cheers for November. 2004. (Three Cheers For... ! Ser.). (ENG., Illus.). 96p. (gr. -1 — 1). pap. 12.99 *(978-0-7398-9310-4(6))* Houghton Mifflin Harcourt Publishing Co.

Steck-Vaughn Staff, creator. Sensational Seasons: Spring. 2007. (Sensational Seasons Ser.). (Illus.). 96p. per. 13.99 *(978-1-4190-3393-3(X))* Steck-Vaughn.

Steele-Saccio, Eva. Headbands & Hairstyles: Make & Wear Super Stylish Headbands. 2010. (ENG.). 60p. (J). (gr. 3-18). 19.99 *(978-1-59174-864-9(X))* Klutz.

—The Marvelous Book of Magical Mermaids. 2014. (ENG.). 50p. (J). (gr. 1). 19.99 *(978-0-545-69214-4(8))* Klutz.

Steele-Staccio, Eva & Klutz Editors. The Marvelous Book of Magical Horses: Dress up Paper Horses & Their Fairy Friends. 2011. (ENG.). 56p. (J). (gr. 1-1). spiral bd. 19.99 *(978-1-59174-926-4(3))* Klutz.

Steers, Billy. Tractor Mac. 2016. (Tractor Mac Ser.: 2). (ENG., Illus.). 128p. (J). pap., act. bk. ed. 12.99 *(978-0-374-30118-7(2)*, 9780374301187, Farrar, Straus & Giroux (BYR)) Farrar, Straus & Giroux.

Stella, Heather. Get Ready for Kindergarten: Numbers, Time & Opposites - 251 Fun Exercises for Mastering Skills for Success in School. 2013. (Get Ready for School Ser.). (ENG.). 128p. (J). (gr. -1-2). pap. 7.95 *(978-1-57912-938-5(2)*, 81938, Black Dog & Leventhal Pubs. Inc.) Hachette Bks.

—Get Ready for Kindergarten - Letters & Sight Words: 247 Fun Exercises for Mastering Skills for Success in School. 2013. (Get Ready for School Ser.). (ENG.). 128p. (J). (gr. -1-2). pap. 7.95 *(978-1-57912-937-8(4)*, 81937, Black Dog & Leventhal Pubs. Inc.) Hachette Bks.

—Get Ready for Pre-K: Letters & Sight Words - 245 Fun Exercises for Mastering Basic Skills. 2013. (Get Ready for School Ser.). (ENG.). 128p. (J). (gr. -1-k). pap. 7.99 *(978-1-57912-935-4(8)*, 81935, Black Dog & Leventhal Pubs. Inc.) Hachette Bks.

—Get Ready for Pre-K: Numbers, Shapes & Colors - 249 Fun Exercises for Mastering Basic Skills. 2013. (Get Ready for School Ser.). (ENG.). 128p. (J). (gr. -1-17). pap. 7.95 *(978-1-57912-936-1(6)*, 81936, Black Dog & Leventhal Pubs. Inc.) Hachette Bks.

—Get Ready for School First Grade Laptop Workbook: Sight Words, Beginning Reading, Handwriting, Vowels & Consonants, Word Families. 2014. (Get Ready for School Ser.). (ENG.). 193p. (J). (gr. -1-17). spiral bd. 13.95 *(978-1-57912-975-0(7)*, 81975, Black Dog & Leventhal Pubs. Inc.) Hachette Bks.

—Get Ready for School Pre-Kindergarten Laptop Workbook: Uppercase Letters, Tracing, Beginning Sounds, Writing, Patterns. 2014. (Get Ready for School Ser.). (ENG.). 194p. (J). (gr. -1-17). spiral bd. 13.95 *(978-1-57912-973-6(0)*, 81973, Black Dog & Leventhal Pubs. Inc.) Hachette Bks.

Stella, Heather & Lima, Athena Anna. Get Ready for First Grade: Spelling, Writing & Reading. 2012. (Get Ready for School Ser.). (ENG., Illus.). 320p. (J). (gr. -1-17). 17.95 *(978-1-57912-896-8(3)*, 81896, Black Dog & Leventhal Pubs. Inc.) Hachette Bks.

Stelzer, Roberto. Robots: 6 Robots to Make & Decorate. Stelzer, Roberto, illus. 2016. (ENG., Illus.). 6p. (J). (gr. 1-5). bds. 16.99 *(978-1-84365-310-3(9)*, Pavilion) Pavilion Bks. GBR. Dist: Independent Pubs. Group.

Stephens, Edna Cucksey. Core Democratic Values with Rock U. S. A. Herrick, Mark J., illus. 2004. (Connect-It Ser.). 62p. (J). (gr. -1-3). pap. 24.95 *(978-0-9749412-0-2(4))* EDCO Publishing, Inc.

Stephens, Jay. Freaky Fun Activities. 2014. (Kids DIY Ser.). (ENG.). 64p. (J). pap. 12.99 *(978-1-4403-2214-3(7)*, Impact) F&W Media, Inc.

Stephens, Sarah Hines & Mann, Bethany. Do It Now! Tricks: Rad Stunts & Sneaky Pranks. 2012. (ENG.). 80p. (J). pap. 6.99 *(978-1-61628-391-9(2))* Weldon Owen, Inc.

Sterling Children's, Sterling. Color Your Own Doll's House. 2016. (ENG., Illus.). 32p. (J). (gr. 2). pap. 7.95 *(978-1-4549-2222-3(2))* Sterling Publishing Co., Inc.

—Make a Yellow Dot the Sun. 2017. (ENG., Illus.). 96p. (J). (gr. k-6). pap. 12.95 *(978-1-4549-2288-9(5))* Sterling Publishing Co., Inc.

Sterling Publishing Co., Inc. Begin Smart(tm) Play Colors/Colores Juego. 2016. (Begin Smart(tm) Ser.). (ENG & SPA., Illus.). 16p. (J). (— 1). bds. 8.95 *(978-1-4549-1757-1(1))* Sterling Publishing Co., Inc.

Stern, Leonard & Price, Roger. Dance Mania Mad Libs. 2009. (Mad Libs Ser.). (ENG.). 48p. (J). (gr. 3-7). 4.99 *(978-0-8431-3712-5(6)*, Mad Libs) Penguin Young Readers Group.

—Hello Kitty Loves Mad Libs. 2013. (Hello Kitty Ser.). (ENG.). 48p. (J). (gr. 3-7). 3.99 *(978-0-8431-7609-4(1)*, Mad Libs) Penguin Young Readers Group.

—Peace, Love, & Mad Libs. 2009. (Mad Libs Ser.). (ENG.). 48p. (J). (gr. 3-7). 4.99 *(978-0-8431-8930-8(4)*, Mad Libs) Penguin Young Readers Group.

Stevenson, May. Brilliant Activities for Reading Non-Fiction: Comprehension Activities for 7-11 Year Olds. 2006. (Illus.). 128p. pap. *(978-1-903853-46-7(X))* Brilliant Pubns.

Stevenson-Spurgon, Barbara J. Old Silent One & Fresh Water Fishing: This Is a Bitty Book. 2008. 40p. pap. 17.99 *(978-1-4343-7790-6(3))* AuthorHouse.

Stewart, Whitney. Mindful Kids: 50 Activities for Calm, Focus & Peace. Braun, Mina, illus. 2017. (ENG.). 50p. (J). (gr. -1-4). 14.99 ***(978-1-78285-327-5(8))*** Barefoot Bks., Inc.

Sticker Activity Book. 2008. (Bratz Activity with Buttons Ser.). 32p. pap. *(978-1-4075-2058-2(X))* Parragon, Inc.

Sticker It Up! 2013. (Imagine It! Ser.). (ENG., Illus.). 40p. (J). (gr. 3-7). *(978-1-77132-069-6(9))* SpiceBox Products Ltd.

Stillerman, Robbie. Glitter Jewelry Sticker Activity Book. 2008. (Dover Little Activity Books Stickers Ser.). (ENG., Illus.). 2p. (J). (gr. 1-4). 1.50 *(978-0-486-46576-0(4))* Dover Pubns., Inc.

—Mix & Match Jewelry Sticker Activity Book. 2006. (Dover Little Activity Bks.). (ENG., Illus.). 4p. (J). (gr. -1-5). pap. 1.50 *(978-0-486-44880-0(0))* Dover Pubns., Inc.

—Monster Mix & Match Sticker Activity Book. 2007. (Dover Little Activity Bks.). (ENG., Illus.). 4p. (J). (gr. -1-5). pap. 1.50 *(978-0-486-45663-8(3))* Dover Pubns., Inc.

Stilson, Linda J. Sew Easy Felt Puppets. 2005. (Illus.). 118p. 23.25 *(978-0-9770043-8-6(4))* New Global Publishing.

Stohs, Anita Reith. Praise God with Paper Cups: 45 Easy Bible Crafts; Grades 1-5. Koehler, Ed, illus. 2005. (CPH Teaching Resource Ser.). 64p. pap. 10.99 *(978-0-7586-0842-0(X))* Concordia Publishing Hse.

Stone, Sandra J. Playing: A Kid's Curriculum. Kizer, Fran, illus. 2nd ed. 2005. 234p. (Orig.). per. 18.95 *(978-1-59647-003-3(8))* Good Year Bks.

Storey Publishing Staff & Danks, Hugh. The Bug Book & Bug Bottle. rev. ed. 2009. (ENG., Illus.). 112p. (gr. k-6). pap., act. bk. ed. 18.95 *(978-0-7611-4889-0(2)*, 14889) Workman Publishing Co., Inc.

Strait, Mark, et al, creators. Webber Interactive WH Questions Level 1: Whcd11. 2006. (J). cd-rom 49.95 *(978-1-58650-642-1(0))* Super Duper Pubns.

Strauss, Elizabeth. Beginning Reading 1-2. 2008. (ENG.). 32p. (J). pap. 2.99 *(978-0-88743-756-4(7))* School Zone Publishing Co.

Strickland, Tessa & DePalma, Kate. The Barefoot Book of Children. Dean, David, illus. 2016. (ENG.). 64p. (J). (gr. k-5). 19.99 *(978-1-78285-296-4(4))* Barefoot Bks., Inc.

Studio Mouse. Sesame Street Celebrates School: Learn & Carry 4 Books with CD. rev. ed. 2007. (ENG.). 4x20p. 14.99 *(978-1-59069-565-4(8))* Studio Mouse LLC.

Studio Rarekwai Staff. Stickerbomb 3. 2016. (ENG., Illus.). 108p. pap. 24.95 *(978-1-78067-759-0(6))* King, Laurence Publishing GBR. Dist: Hachette Bk. Group.

Sun, Ming-Ju. Creative Haven Japanese Kimono Designs Coloring Book. 2013. (Adult Coloring Ser.). (ENG., Illus.). 64p. (gr. 3). pap. 5.99 *(978-0-486-49344-2(X))* Dover Pubns., Inc.

Sunflower Education Staff. A Golden Thread. 2012. 54p. pap. 11.95 *(978-1-937166-13-7(9))* Sunflower Education.

Super Duper Publications Staff. Electronic Spinner 1-6: Spin267. 2007. (J). 10.95 *(978-1-58650-744-2(3))* Super Duper Pubns.

Suzuki, Genevieve A. & Murakami, Jon J. The Original Poi Cats on Oahu. 2005. 24p. (J). pap. 5.95 *(978-1-56647-731-4(X))* Mutual Publishing LLC.

Swanson, Maggie. Floral Fantasies Stained Glass Coloring Book. 2013. (Dover Stained Glass Coloring Book Ser.). (ENG., Illus.). 32p. (gr. 3-8). pap. 7.99 *(978-0-486-49807-2(7))* Dover Pubns., Inc.

—Lucky Cats Stickers. 2015. (Dover Little Activity Books Stickers Ser.). (ENG.). 4p. (J). (gr. k-3). pap. 1.99 *(978-0-486-79982-7(4))* Dover Pubns., Inc.

—My Backyard Color by Number. 2017. (ENG.). 32p. (J). (gr. -1-2). pap. 3.99 *(978-0-486-81461-2(0))* Dover Pubns., Inc.

—My Storybook Paper Dolls. 2013. (Dover Paper Dolls Ser.). (ENG., Illus.). 32p. (J). (gr. 1). pap. 9.99 *(978-0-486-48989-6(2))* Dover Pubns., Inc.

—Spark - Sun, Moon & Stars Coloring Book. 2015. (Dover Coloring Bks.). (ENG., Illus.). 64p. (J). (gr. 1-4). pap. 5.99 *(978-0-486-80216-9(7))* Dover Pubns., Inc.

Swanson, Tom, illus. Twas the Night Before Christmas. 2011. (Recordable Bks). 12p. (J). ring bd. 24.99 *(978-1-60130-261-8(4)*, Usborne) EDC Publishing.

Sykes, Andy. The Hexjibber Colouring & Activity Book. 2007. 84p. pap. 14.95 *(978-1-4303-2817-9(7))* Lulu Pr., Inc.

Sylvan Learning Staff. Kindergarten Word Games (Sylvan Fun on the Run Series) 2012. (Sylvan Fun on the Run Series, Language Arts Ser.). (ENG.). 32p. (J). (gr. -1-2). pap. 3.99 *(978-0-307-47947-1(1)*, Sylvan Learning Publishing) Random Hse. Children's Bks.

—Pre-K Page per Day: Letters. 2012. (Sylvan Page per Day Series, Language Arts Ser.). (ENG.). 64p. (J). (gr. -1-2). pap. 6.99 *(978-0-307-94455-9(7)*, Sylvan Learning Publishing) Random Hse. Children's Bks.

—Pre-K Page per Day: Numbers. 2012. (Sylvan Page per Day Series, Math Ser.). (ENG.). 64p. (J). (gr. -1-2). pap. 6.99 *(978-0-307-94456-6(5)*, Sylvan Learning Publishing) Random Hse. Children's Bks.

Szpirglas, Jeff. Train Your Brain: How Your Brain Learns Best. 2017. 48p. (J). ***(978-0-7787-3498-7(6))*** Crabtree Publishing Co.

Tai, Elise See. Write & Draw Dinosaurs. 2014. (Wipe-Clean Stencil Bks.). (ENG., Illus.). 24p. (J). (gr. -1-1). bds. 9.99 *(978-0-7641-6710-2(3))* Barron's Educational Series, Inc.

Tainsh, Robert & Priddy, Roger. Zoo's Who? 2005. (Baby Touch & Feel Ser.). (ENG., Illus.). 12p. (J). (gr. -1 — 1). bds. 9.99 *(978-0-312-49431-5(9)*, 9780312494315, Priddy Bks.) St. Martin's Pr.

Talhamy, Sarah. Children's Workbook. 2005. (J). ring bd. *(978-0-615-12907-5(2))* SLG.

Tallarico, Tony, Sr. Little Hidden Pictures. 2008. (Dover Little Activity Bks.). (ENG., Illus.). 64p. (J). (gr. 3-5). pap. 1.99 *(978-0-486-46581-4(0))* Dover Pubns., Inc.

Tallarico, Tony, Sr. & Activity Books Staff. More Little Hidden Pictures. 2013. (Dover Little Activity Bks.). (ENG., Illus.). 64p. (J). (gr. k-3). 1.99 *(978-0-486-49337-4(7))* Dover Pubns., Inc.

Tallarico, Tony, Sr. & Tallarico, Tony J., Jr. Cars & Trucks Mazes. 2013. (ENG., Illus.). 48p. (J). (gr. 2-5). pap. 4.99 *(978-0-486-49890-4(5))* Dover Pubns., Inc.

Tallarico, Tony J., Jr. Baseball Facts & Fun Activity Book. 2017. (Dover Children's Activity Bks.). (ENG.). 48p. (J). (gr. 1-4). pap. 4.99 *(978-0-486-81442-1(4))* Dover Pubns., Inc.

—Famous Firsts Activity Book. 2013. (Dover Children's Activity Bks.). (ENG.). 48p. (J). (gr. 3-8). pap. 4.99 *(978-0-486-48839-4(X))* Dover Pubns., Inc.

—Presidents Activity Book. 2009. (Dover Little Activity Bks.). (ENG., Illus.). 64p. (J). (gr. k-3). pap. 1.99 *(978-0-486-47388-8(0))* Dover Pubns., Inc.

Tangerine Designs Ltd. Who Am I? Moo, I Am a Cow! Peep Through the Eyes. Who Are You Today? 2014. (Bathtime Faces Ser.). (ENG.). 8p. (J). (gr. -1 — 1). 5.99 *(978-1-4380-7531-0(6))* Barron's Educational Series, Inc.

—Who Am I? Roar, I Am a Tiger! Peep Through the Eyes. Who Are You Today? 2014. (Bathtime Faces Ser.). (ENG.). 8p. (J). (gr. -1 — 1). 5.99 *(978-1-4380-7532-7(4))* Barron's Educational Series, Inc.

Taplin, Sam. Diggers Sticker Book. 2008. (Sticker Bks). (Illus.). 16p. (J). pap. 6.99 *(978-0-7945-2109-7(6)*, Usborne) EDC Publishing.

—Farm Sticker Book. 2008. (Sticker Bks). (Illus.). 16p. (J). pap. 6.99 *(978-0-7945-2110-3(X)*, Usborne) EDC Publishing.

—Zoo (First Sticker Book) Johansson, Cecilia, illus. 2011. (First Sticker Book Ser.). 24p. (J). pap. 6.99 *(978-0-7945-2927-7(5)*, Usborne) EDC Publishing.

Tauber, Sabine. Architecture: Create Your Own City! — Sticker Book. 2015. (ENG.). 16p. (J). (gr. 1-4). pap. 9.95 *(978-3-7913-7221-1(1))* Prestel Verlag GmbH & Co KG. DEU. Dist: Penguin Random Hse. LLC.

—Hieronymus Bosch: Coloring Book. 2014. (ENG., Illus.). 32p. (J). (gr. 1-4). pap. 8.95 *(978-3-7913-7176-4(2))* Prestel Verlag GmbH & Co KG. DEU. Dist: Penguin Random Hse. LLC.

—Medieval Creatures Sticker Book. 2016. (ENG., Illus.). 16p. (J). (gr. 1-4). pap. 9.95 *(978-3-7913-7281-5(5))* Prestel Verlag GmbH & Co KG. DEU. Dist: Penguin Random Hse. LLC.

Taylor, Adam. George in the UK: The Unknown Kingdom. Taylor, Adam & West, Jeannette, eds. 2011. (Illus.). 28p. (J). 8.99 *(978-0-9766062-9-1(1))* Higher Ground Pr.

Taylor, Jeremy. Strength of Love. 2012. 32p. pap. 24.95 *(978-1-4626-7083-3(0))* America Star Bks.

Taylor, Jo. Back to School Sticker Paper Dolls. 2014. (ENG.). 4p. (J). (gr. k-3). pap. 1.50 *(978-0-486-78140-2(2))* Dover Pubns., Inc.

—Sneaker Designs Coloring Book. 2017. (Dover Coloring Bks.). (ENG.). 32p. (J). (gr. 1-4). pap. 3.99 *(978-0-486-80935-9(8))* Dover Pubns., Inc.

Taylor, Lee. Which Is Worse? 2016. (ENG.). 192p. (J). (gr. 2-5). pap. 7.99 *(978-1-338-04304-4(8)*, Scholastic Reference) Scholastic, Inc.

Taylor Trade Publish. Meet Ranger Rick Jr. Critter Crafts & Recipes. 2016. (Ranger Rick: Animal Fun for Young Children Ser.). (ENG., Illus.). 32p. (J). (gr. -1-1). pap. 5.99 *(978-1-63076-210-0(5))* Taylor Trade Publishing.

Teaching Resources Staff. Phonics Tales! Interactive E-Storybooks: 25 e-Books with Engaging Interactive Whiteboard Activities That Teach Key Phonics Skills. 2013. (ENG., Illus.). 136p. (gr. k-2). 129.99 *(978-0-545-54447-4(5)*, Teaching Resources) Scholastic, Inc.

Terada, Junzo. Magical Menagerie: 20 Punch-Out Animals for Play & Display. 2009. (ENG.). 20p. (gr. 13-17). 24.95 *(978-0-8118-7003-0(0))* Chronicle Bks. LLC.

The Broons. The Broons Colouring Book. 2016. (ENG., Illus.). 64p. (J). pap. 11.99 ***(978-1-910230-36-7(7))*** Black and White Publishing Ltd. GBR. Dist: Independent Pubs. Group.

The Editors at Michael O'Mara. Big Book of Amazing Activities. 2017. (ENG., Illus.). 128p. (J). (gr. k). pap. 12.99 *(978-1-62686-733-8(X)*, Silver Dolphin Bks.) Readerlink Distribution Services, LLC.

The Learning Company, The Learning. Achieve! Grade 1: Think. Play. Achieve! 2014. (Achieve! Ser.). (ENG., Illus.). 320p. (J). (gr. -1-3). pap. 12.99 *(978-0-544-37261-0(1)*, HMH Books For Young Readers) Houghton Mifflin Harcourt Publishing Co.

—Achieve! Grade 2: Think. Play. Achieve! 2014. (Achieve! Ser.). (ENG., Illus.). 320p. (J). (gr. -1-3). pap. 12.99 *(978-0-544-37251-1(4)*, HMH Books For Young Readers) Houghton Mifflin Harcourt Publishing Co.

—Achieve! Grade 3: Think. Play. Achieve! 2014. (Achieve! Ser.). (ENG., Illus.). 320p. (J). (gr. 2-5). pap. 12.99 *(978-0-544-37241-2(7)*, HMH Books For Young Readers) Houghton Mifflin Harcourt Publishing Co.

The Museum of Modern Art, contrib. by. MoMA Art While You Eat Place Mats. 2013. (ENG., Illus.). 104p. (J). (gr. -1-17). 12.99 *(978-1-4521-0635-9(5))* Chronicle Bks. LLC.

The Topps Company & Lucasfilm Ltd Staff. Star Wars Topps Classic Sticker Book. 2017. (ENG., Illus.). 76p. (J). (gr. 1-17). pap. 12.95 ***(978-1-4197-2711-5(7)***, Abrams Bks. for Young Readers) Abrams, Inc.

Thenen, Peter Von & Creative Haven Staff. Creative Haven Prismatic Designs Coloring Book. 2013. (Adult Coloring Ser.). (ENG., Illus.). 64p. (gr. 3). pap. 5.99 *(978-0-486-49312-1(1))* Dover Pubns., Inc.

Theodore, Elizabeth. Lily's Lollipop Moments. 2006. (Illus.). 60p. (J). ring bd. 22.50 *(978-0-9792472-2-4(5))* Lily Wish Factory.

Things That Go! Activity Book. 2007. (Stamper Activity Ser.). 32p. pap. *(978-1-4054-9297-3(X))* Parragon, Inc.

Thinking Kids & Carson-Dellosa Publishing. All Set for Kindergarten Kit. 2017. (ENG.). 87p. (gr. k-k). 24.99 ***(978-1-4838-3988-2(5)***, Thinking Kids) Carson-Dellosa Publishing, LLC.

—All Set for Prekindergarten Kit. 2017. (ENG.). 87p. (gr. -1 — 1). 24.99 ***(978-1-4838-3987-5(7)***, Thinking Kids) Carson-Dellosa Publishing, LLC.

Thinking Kids & Carson-Dellosa Publishing, compiled by. Kindergarten Essentials. 2017. (ENG.). 256p. (gr. k-k). pap. 5.99 ***(978-1-4838-3817-5(X)***, Thinking Kids) Carson-Dellosa Publishing, LLC.

—Prekindergarten Essentials. 2017. (ENG.). 256p. (gr. -1 — 1). pap. 5.99 ***(978-1-4838-3816-8(1)***, Thinking Kids) Carson-Dellosa Publishing, LLC.

Thomas, Danita & Thomas, John E. Inventos y Experimentos para Ninos: Una Nueva Coleccion de Inventos y Experimentos un Poco Locos y Chiflados. 2007. (Kid Concoctions - Spanish Ser.). (Illus.). 80p. (J). per. 9.99 *(978-0-8054-4498-8(X)*, B&H Bks.) B&H Publishing Group.

Thomas Nelson. B Is for Breakdancing Bear 123 Wipe Clean. 2015. (ENG.). 50p. (J). (gr. -1-2). *(978-1-78393-658-8(4))* Make Believe Ideas.

—B Is for Breakdancing Bear ABC Wipe Clean. 2015. (ENG.). 54p. (J). (gr. -1-2). *(978-1-78393-657-1(6))* Make Believe Ideas.

—Beat the Book. 2016. (ENG.). 70p. (J). (gr. 1-5). spiral bd. *(978-1-78598-074-9(2))* Make Believe Ideas.

—Build-A-Bakerina! 2015. (ENG.). 28p. (gr. -1). *(978-1-78393-549-9(9))* Make Believe Ideas.

—Designer Diva. 2016. (ENG.). 86p. (J). (gr. -1-6). pap. *(978-1-78598-145-6(5))* Make Believe Ideas.

—Dress-Up Princess. 2016. (ENG.). (J). (gr. -1-7). *(978-1-78598-070-1(X))* Make Believe Ideas.

—Everyone Is Entitled to My Opinion. 2016. (ENG.). 128p. (J). (gr. -1-7). *(978-1-78598-685-7(6))* Make Believe Ideas.

—Farmyard Fun. 2016. (ENG.). 86p. (J). (gr. -1-6). pap. *(978-1-78598-146-3(3))* Make Believe Ideas.

—A Hole Lot of Fun. 2016. (ENG., Illus.). 64p. (J). (gr. k-4). pap. *(978-1-78598-150-0(1))* Make Believe Ideas.

—Maze Activity Books Halloween. 2016. (ENG.). 38p. (J). (gr. -1-7). pap. *(978-1-78598-399-3(7))* Make Believe Ideas.

—My Pirate Activity Book. 2016. (ENG.). 64p. (J). (gr. k-4). spiral bd. *(978-1-78393-862-9(5))* Make Believe Ideas.

—My Princess Activity Book. 2016. (ENG.). 64p. (J). (gr. k-4). spiral bd. *(978-1-78393-861-2(7))* Make Believe Ideas.

—Pug Sticker Activity Book. 2016. (ENG.). 48p. (J). (gr. -1-7). pap. *(978-1-78598-655-0(4))* Make Believe Ideas.

—Shut up! I'm Coloring. 2016. (ENG.). 128p. (J). (gr. -1-7). *(978-1-78598-683-3(X))* Make Believe Ideas.

—Sticker Books My First ABC Activity Book. 2016. (ENG., Illus.). 56p. (J). (gr. -1-7). pap. *(978-1-78598-349-8(0))* Make Believe Ideas.

—Totally Glitz. 2015. (ENG.). 80p. (J). pap. *(978-1-78393-746-2(7))* Make Believe Ideas.

Thomas, Vernada. Pre-Handwriting Book. 2008. 200p. 29.99 *(978-1-4363-8001-0(4))*; pap. 19.99 *(978-1-4363-8000-3(6))* Xlibris Corp.

Thompson, Becki & Reinke, Missy. Building Math Vocabulary: 70 Engaging Reproducible Activities That Go Beyond the Textbook to Help Students Practice & Really Learn the Math Terms They Need to Know. 2009. (ENG.). 80p. pap. 14.99 *(978-0-545-04875-0(3)*, Teaching Resources) Scholastic, Inc.

Thompson, Gabrielle. My First Sticker Art. 2016. (ENG.). 56p. (J). (gr. -1-7). pap. *(978-1-78598-148-7(X))* Make Believe Ideas.

—My Super Sparkly Sticker Purse. 2016. (ENG.). 96p. (J). (gr. -1-7). pap. *(978-1-78598-147-0(1))* Make Believe Ideas.

Thomson, Ruth. Art Pocket Activity Fun & Games: Games & Puzzles, Fold-Out Scenes, Patterned Paper, Stickers! 2014. (Pocket Activity Fun & Games Ser.). (ENG.). 96p. (J). (gr. 1-5). pap. 7.99 *(978-1-4380-0445-7(1))* Barron's Educational Series, Inc.

—The Science & Inventions Creativity Book: Games, Models to Make, High-Tech Craft Paper, Stickers, & Stencils. 2013. (Creativity Bks.). (ENG., Illus.). 80p. (J). (gr. 1-6). pap. 12.99 *(978-1-4380-0251-4(3))* Barron's Educational Series, Inc.

—Science & Inventions Pocket Activity Fun & Games: Games & Puzzles, Fold-Out Scenes, Patterned Paper, Stickers! 2014. (Pocket Activity Fun & Games Ser.). (ENG.). 96p. (J). (gr. 1-5). pap. 7.99 *(978-1-4380-0447-1(8))* Barron's Educational Series, Inc.

Ticktock Media, Ltd. Staff. Birthday Party. 2009. (Busy Tots Ser.). (ENG.). 10p. (J). (gr. -1-k). bds. 6.95 *(978-1-84696-801-3(1)*, TickTock Books) Octopus Publishing Group GBR. Dist: Independent Pubs. Group.

—Guess What? Everyday Things. 2008. (Mini Flap Ser.). (ENG.). 10p. (J). (gr. k — 1). bds. 5.95

(978-1-84696-818-1(6), TickTock Books) Octopus Publishing Group GBR. Dist: Independent Pubs. Group.
—Little Helper. 2009. (Busy Tots Ser.). (ENG.). 10p. (J). (gr. -1-k). bds. 6.95 (978-1-84696-798-6(8), TickTock Books) Octopus Publishing Group GBR. Dist: Independent Pubs. Group.
—My Fairy Garden. 2008. (Sparkle Bks.). (ENG.). 10p. (J). (gr. -1-k). bds. 6.95 (978-1-84696-802-0(X), TickTock Books) Octopus Publishing Group GBR. Dist: Independent Pubs. Group.
—My Night-Time Animals. 2008. (Sparkle Bks.). (ENG.). 10p. (J). (gr. -1-k). bds. 6.95 (978-1-84696-803-7(8), TickTock Books) Octopus Publishing Group GBR. Dist: Independent Pubs. Group.
—My Ocean Creatures. 2008. (Sparkle Bks.). (ENG.). 10p. (J). (gr. -1-k). bds. 6.95 (978-1-84696-804-4(6), TickTock Books) Octopus Publishing Group GBR. Dist: Independent Pubs. Group.
—My Space Adventure. 2008. (Sparkle Bks.). (ENG.). 10p. (J). (gr. -1-k). bds. 6.95 (978-1-84696-805-1(4), TickTock Books) Octopus Publishing Group GBR. Dist: Independent Pubs. Group.
—My World: Opposites. 2008. (Tab Bks.). (ENG.). 10p. (J). (gr. -1-k). bds. 4.95 (978-1-84696-823-5(2), TickTock Books) Octopus Publishing Group GBR. Dist: Independent Pubs. Group.
—Shopping Day. 2009. (Busy Tots Ser.). (ENG.). 10p. (J). (gr. -1-k). bds. 6.95 (978-1-84696-799-3(6), TickTock Books) Octopus Publishing Group GBR. Dist: Independent Pubs. Group.
—Summer Vacation. 2009. (Busy Tots Ser.). (ENG.). 10p. (J). (gr. -1-k). bds. 6.95 (978-1-84696-800-6(3), TickTock Books) Octopus Publishing Group GBR. Dist: Independent Pubs. Group.
—What Am I? Animal Moms & Babies. 2008. (Mini Flap Ser.). (ENG.). 10p. (J). (gr. k — 1). bds. 5.95 (978-1-84696-817-4(8), TickTock Books) Octopus Publishing Group GBR. Dist: Independent Pubs. Group.
Tierney, Tom. Fashions of the Roaring Twenties Coloring Book. 2013. (Dover Coloring Bks.). (ENG., Illus.). 32p. (gr. 3-12). pap. 3.99 (978-0-486-49950-5(2)) Dover Pubns., Inc.
—Pin-Up Girls of World War II. 2009. (Dover Celebrity Paper Dolls Ser.). (ENG., Illus.). 32p. (gr. 6). pap. 9.99 (978-0-486-47033-7(4)) Dover Pubns., Inc.
Tiger Tales, ed. Funny Faces (Boys) 2014. (ENG.). 14p. (J). (gr. -1-k). 3.99 (978-1-58925-304-9(3)) Tiger Tales.
—Funny Faces (Girls) 2014. (ENG.). 14p. (J). (gr. -1-k). 3.99 (978-1-58925-305-6(1)) Tiger Tales.
—Nursery Rhymes Sticker Book. Galloway, Fhiona, illus. 2015. (My Little World Ser.). (ENG.). 14p. (J). (gr. -1-3). 3.99 (978-1-58925-452-7(X)) Tiger Tales.
Tiger Tales Staff. Christmas Sticker Activities. 2014. (My First Sticker Activity Book Ser.). (ENG.). 40p. (J). (gr. -1-3). 6.99 (978-1-58925-307-0(8)) Tiger Tales.
—Halloween Sticker Activities. 2014. (My First Sticker Activity Book Ser.). (ENG.). 40p. (J). (gr. -1-3). 6.99 (978-1-58925-306-3(X)) Tiger Tales.
Tigger. (Disney Fun Shaped Coloring Ser.). 64p. pap. (978-1-4054-9264-5(3)) Parragon, Inc.
Tillworth, Mary. Rock & Rule. Golden Books, illus. 2012. (Color Plus Chunky Crayons Ser.). (ENG.). 48p. (J). (gr. -1-2). pap. 3.99 (978-0-307-97620-8(3), Golden Bks.) Random Hse. Children's Bks.
Tincknell, Cathy. Amazing Things for Boys to Make & Do. Kelly, John, illus. 2013. (Dover Children's Activity Bks.). (ENG.). 32p. (J). (gr. 3-5). 6.99 (978-0-486-49723-5(2)) Dover Pubns., Inc.
—Amazing Things for Girls to Make & Do. Kelly, John, illus. 2013. (Dover Children's Activity Bks.). (ENG.). 32p. (J). (gr. 3-5). 6.99 (978-0-486-49722-8(4)) Dover Pubns., Inc.
TNT Ministries Staff. God's Miracle Maker: Elisha. 2007. (King of Clubs Ser.). (ENG.). 96p. (J). pap. 17.99 (978-1-84550-291-1(4), 9781845502911) Christian Focus Pubns. GBR. Dist: Bookmasters Distribution.
Todd, Richard E. Baptism: A Bible Study Wordbook for Kids. 2009. (Children's Wordbooks Ser.). (ENG., Illus.). 32p. (gr. 4-7). pap. 5.99 (978-1-60066-194-5(7)) WingSpread Publishers.
—Church: A Bible Study Wordbook for Kids. 2009. (Children's Wordbooks Ser.). (ENG., Illus.). 32p. (gr. 4-7). pap. 5.99 (978-1-60066-196-9(3)) WingSpread Publishers.
—Communion: A Bible Study Wordbook for Kids. 2009. (Children's Wordbooks Ser.). (ENG., Illus.). 32p. (gr. 4-7). pap. 5.99 (978-1-60066-195-2(5)) WingSpread Publishers.
—Giving: A Bible Study Wordbook for Kids. 2009. (Children's Wordbooks Ser.). (ENG., Illus.). 32p. (gr. 4-7). pap. 5.99 (978-1-60066-197-6(1)) WingSpread Publishers.
The Toddler Room: Free Play. 2013. 16p. pap. 7.95 (978-1-4582-1259-7(9), Abbott Pr.) Author Solutions, Inc.
Toms, Kate. Sticky Little Fingers Rainy Day Activity Book. 2007. (Illus.). 48p. (J). (gr. -1-3). (978-1-84610-483-1(1)) Make Believe Ideas.
Tonges Wilshire, et al. Slurping Soup & Other Confusions. 2nd ed. 2013. (Illus.). 82p. pap. (978-1-909193-22-2(4)) Summertime Publishing.
Tonka 5 in 1 Superly Duperly. 2005. 52p. pap. 3.99 (978-0-7666-2249-4(5)) Modern Publishing.
Top That. Let's Stencil Things That Go. 2008. (978-1-84666-584-4(1)) Top That! Publishing PLC.
Top That Publishing Staff, ed. Funny Monsters. 2005. 12p. (978-1-84510-734-5(9)) Top That! Publishing PLC.
Top That!, creator. Roald Dahl Build Your Own Willy Wonka's Chocolate Factory. 2005. (Press Out & Build Ser.). (Illus.). 12p. (J). pap. (978-1-905359-58-5(6)) Top That! Publishing PLC.
Top That! Kids, creator. Magnetic Silly Faces. 2007. (Illus.). 10p. (J). (978-1-84666-345-1(8)) Top That! Publishing PLC.
Torres, Laura & Sherman, Michael. Limpiapipas de Locura. 2004. (SPA., Illus.). 46p. (J). spiral bd. 15.95 (978-968-5528-09-2(8)) Klutz Latino MEX. Dist: Independent Pubs. Group.
Toufexis, George. Big Apple Brain Busters Activity Book. 2016. (Dover Children's Activity Bks.). (ENG.). 48p. (J). (gr. 2-5). pap. 4.99 (978-0-486-79926-1(3)) Dover Pubns., Inc.
—Chicago Challenge Activity Book. 2016. (Dover Children's Activity Bks.). (ENG.). 48p. (J). (gr. 2-5). pap. 4.99 (978-0-486-79927-8(1)) Dover Pubns., Inc.
—Glitter Tattoos Day of the Dead. 2014. (ENG.). 2p. (J). (gr. 1-4). pap. 1.99 (978-0-486-78014-6(7)) Dover Pubns., Inc.
—Monster Mall Activity Book. 2013. (Dover Children's Activity Bks.). (ENG.). 48p. (J). (gr. 3-8). pap. 4.99 (978-0-486-49962-8(6)) Dover Pubns., Inc.
—Monster Matrix Activity Book. 2013. (Dover Children's Activity Bks.). (ENG.). 48p. (J). (gr. 3-8). pap. 4.99 (978-0-486-49963-5(4)) Dover Pubns., Inc.
—The Outrageous Human Body Activity Book. 2013. (Dover Children's Science Bks.). (ENG.). 48p. (J). (gr. 3-8). pap. 4.99 (978-0-486-49116-5(1)) Dover Pubns., Inc.
—U. S. A. Facts & Fun Activity Book. 2017. (Dover Children's Activity Bks.). (ENG.). 48p. (J). (gr. 3-6). pap. 4.99 (978-0-486-81379-0(7)) Dover Pubns., Inc.
—Ultimate Horse-Athon Facts & Activity Book. 2013. (ENG.). 48p. (J). (gr. 3-8). pap. 4.99 (978-0-486-49184-4(6)) Dover Pubns., Inc.
Tracey, Andrée. Marvelous Me! a Personalized Coloring Book. 2016. (Dover Coloring Bks.). (ENG.). 32p. (J). (gr. -1-3). pap. 4.99 (978-0-486-80758-4(4)) Dover Pubns., Inc.
Traditional. Jolly Old Santa's Workshop Activity Book. Pulley, Kelly & Reed, Lisa, illus. 2014. 16p. (J). 4.99 (978-0-8249-5665-3(6), Ideal Pubns.) Worthy Publishing.
Trafford, Adrienne. Cat & Dog See the World Coloring Book. 2014. (ENG., Illus.). 32p. (J). (gr. -1-5). pap. 3.99 (978-0-486-49468-5(3)) Dover Pubns., Inc.
—Tarot Designs Coloring Book. 2014. (ENG., Illus.). 32p. (J). (gr. 6-8). pap. 3.99 (978-0-486-49460-9(8)) Dover Pubns., Inc.
Tredick, Kim, et al. Summer Brain Quest: Between Grades 5 And 6. Pietch, Carey & Yan, Edison, illus. 2017. (Summer Brain Quest Ser.). (ENG.). 160p. (J). (gr. 5-6). pap. 12.95 (978-0-7611-9328-9(6)) Workman Publishing Co., Inc.
Trembinsky, Laverne Gray. A Friend Sent from Heaven for Andrew: A Little Boy Finds His Self Experencing Loneliness Because His Family Had to Move Because of Financial Hardsh. 2009. 45p. (J). pap. 10.95 (978-1-4327-3458-9(X)) Outskirts Pr., Inc.
Troupe, Thomas Kingsley. I Want to Be... Rodriguez, Christina Ann et al, illus. 2015. (I Want to Be... Ser.). (ENG.). 24p. (gr. k-3). 106.60 (978-1-4795-8006-4(6)) Picture Window Bks.
Troupe, Thomas Kingsley, et al. Making a Jack-O'-Lantern. 2011. (Step-By-Step Stories Ser.). (ENG.). 32p. (gr. 1-2). lib. bdg. 109.28 (978-1-4296-6027-3(9), Aplus Bks.) Capstone Press of Coughlan Cos.
Trumbauer, Lisa. Brain Quest, Grade 1: A Whole Year of Curriculum-Based Exercises & Activities in One Fun Book! Rogers, Betsy, ed. 2008. (ENG., Illus.). 320p. (J). (gr. 1-1). wbk. ed. 12.95 (978-0-7611-4914-9(7), 14914) Workman Publishing Co., Inc.
—Brain Quest, Kindergarten: A Whole Year of Curriculum-Based Exercises & Activities in One Fun Book! Oliver, Kimberly, ed. 2008. (ENG., Illus.). 320p. (J). (gr. k-k). wbk. ed. 12.95 (978-0-7611-4912-5(0), 14912) Workman Publishing Co., Inc.
Tsukamoto, Allen. Somethin Fishy for the Small Fry. 2006. 28p. (J). pap. 5.95 (978-0-944462-50-8(2)) Hawaii Fishing News.
Tuchman, Gail & Gray, Margaret. AddUps Fun for All Seasons! Griego, Tony, illus. 2012. (Dover Little Activity Bks.). (ENG.). 32p. (J). (gr. k-3). pap. 1.50 (978-0-486-49860-7(3)) Dover Pubns., Inc.
—AddUps Going Places! Griego, Tony, illus. 2012. (Dover Little Activity Bks.). (ENG.). 32p. (J). (gr. k-3). pap. 1.50 (978-0-486-49861-4(1)) Dover Pubns., Inc.
—AddUps My Day! Griego, Tony, illus. 2012. (Dover Little Activity Bks.). (ENG.). 32p. (J). (gr. k-3). pap. 1.50 (978-0-486-49862-1(X)) Dover Pubns., Inc.
Tucker, Angel. Four Pals on a Field Trip: An Adventure with Friends Who Are Different. Pileggi, Steve, illus. 2013. (Four Pals Ser.). (ENG.). 34p. (J). (gr. -1-3). pap. 8.95 (978-1-62086-487-6(8)) Mascot Bks., Inc.
Tudhope, Simon. Build Your Own Motorcycles Sticker Book. 2015. (Build Your Own Sticker Bks.). (ENG.). 24+10p. (J). (gr. k-5). pap. 8.99 (978-0-7945-3546-9(1), Usborne) EDC Publishing.
Tullet, Hervé. The Giant Game of Sculpture. 2014. (ENG., Illus.). 16p. (gr. k-3). 29.95 (978-0-7148-6800-4(0)) Phaidon Pr., Inc.
Tunnell, Amber. The Night Sky: Stories of the Stars (Bedtime Shadow Book) Zschock, Martha Day, illus. 2014. (ENG.). 7p. (J). 12.99 (978-1-4413-1581-6(0), 9781441315816) Peter Pauper Pr. Inc.
Tupera, Tupera. Make Faces. 2015. (ENG., Illus.). 52p. (J). (gr. 1-4). pap. 12.95 (978-1-4521-3930-2(X)) Chronicle Bks. LLC.
—Make More Faces: Doodle & Sticker Book with 52 Faces + 6 Sticker Sheets. 2015. (ENG., Illus.). 52p. (J). (gr. -1-2). pap. 12.95 (978-1-4521-3983-8(0)) Chronicle Bks. LLC.
Turrell, Linda. Complete Library Skills, Grade 5. rev. ed. 2004. (ENG., Illus.). 128p. (gr. 5-5). pap. 13.99 (978-0-7424-1955-1(X), IFG99136, Instructional Fair) Carson-Dellosa Publishing, LLC.
Twin Sisters(r), et al. Celebrate Easter! Prayer & Activity Book. 2017. (I'm Learning the Bible Activity Book Ser.). (ENG.). 32p. (J). pap. 4.99 (978-1-68322-073-2(0)) Barbour Publishing, Inc.
—He Is Risen! Activity Book & Free Album Download. 2017. (I'm Learning the Bible Activity Book Ser.). (ENG.). 32p. (J). (-5). pap. 4.99 (978-1-68322-076-3(5)) Barbour Publishing, Inc.
—Year-Round Crafts for Kids. 2017. (I'm Learning the Bible Activity Book Ser.). (ENG.). 32p. (J). pap. 4.99 (978-1-68322-078-7(1)) Barbour Publishing, Inc.
Twin Sisters(r) Staff. Learning with Elmo: Animals. 2010. (J). (gr. k-2). 9.99 (978-1-59922-402-2(X)) Twin Sisters IP, LLC.
Twin Sisters(r) Staff, creator. Gross & Annoying Songs. 2005. (Illus.). 95p. (J). pap. 12.99 incl. audio compact disk (978-1-57583-821-2(4)) Twin Sisters IP, LLC.
Twin Sisters(r) Staff, et al. Glitter Scripture Art. 2016. (ENG.). 8p. (J). spiral bd. 6.99 (978-1-63409-093-3(4)) Barbour Publishing, Inc.
Tyndale, prod. Big Bible Fun Color & Learn, Vol. 1. 2014. (Happy Day Ser.). (ENG.). 96p. (J). pap. 2.49 (978-1-4143-9500-5(0)) Tyndale Hse. Pubs.
Tyrtania, Joachim & Hemrich-Skomer, Denise. Together Time: Cycle A. 2007. (Illus.). 80p. per. 10.95 (978-0-9787087-2-6(5)) Bound by Grace Pr., LLC.
U. S. National Geographic Society Staff. Xtreme Illusions. 2012. (ENG.). 48p. (J). (gr. 3-7). lib. bdg. 25.95 (978-1-4263-1084-3(6), National Geographic Children's Bks.) National Geographic Society.
Underwater Activity Book. 2007. (Stamper Activity Ser.). 32p. pap. (978-1-4054-9298-0(8)) Parragon, Inc.
Usborne Books Staff, creator. Usborne Doodle Pad for Boys. 2014. (ENG., Illus.). (J). pap. 5.99 (978-0-7945-3291-8(8), Usborne) EDC Publishing.
—Usborne Doodle Pad for Girls. 2014. (ENG., Illus.). (J). pap. 5.99 (978-0-7945-3189-8(X), Usborne) EDC Publishing.
—50 Travel Games & Activities. 2006. (Activity Cards Ser.). 50p. (J). 9.99 (978-0-7945-1319-1(0), Usborne) EDC Publishing.
Valencia, Vanessa. Mamma's Planet Earth. 2011. 24p. pap. 10.95 (978-1-4525-3921-8(9)) Balboa Pr.
Valois, Rob. Intergalactic Adventure. 2008. (Star Wars). (ENG.). 32p. (J). (gr. 1-3). pap., act. bk. ed. 4.99 (978-0-448-44997-5(8)) Penguin Publishing Group.
Van Leeuwen, Michele D., creator. Summer Bridge Activities: Grades PK to K. 2012. (Summer Bridge Activities Ser.). (ENG., Illus.). 150p. pap. 14.95 (978-1-60996-440-5(3)) Carson-Dellosa Publishing, LLC.
Van Leeuwen, Wendy. The Ten Commandments Activity Book. 2007. (Illus.). 16p. (J). pap. 1.89 (978-1-59317-210-7(9)) Warner Pr., Inc.
Van Vleet, Carmella. Explore Ancient Egypt! 25 Great Projects, Activities, Experiments. Kim, Alex, illus. 2006. (Explore Your World Ser.). (ENG.). 96p. (J). (gr. k-4). pap. 12.95 (978-0-9792268-3-0(X)) Octavio Publishing.
—Explore Ancient Rome! 25 Great Projects, Activities, Experiments. Kim, Alex, illus. 2008. (Explore Your World Ser.). (ENG.). 96p. (J). (gr. k-4). pap. 12.95 (978-0-9792268-4-7(8)) Octavio Publishing.
Various Experts, compiled by. The Very Merry Christmas Activity Pad: Festive Puzzles, Amazing Mazes, Cool Doodles, Fantastic Fun! 2012. (ENG.). 64p. (J). pap. 10.95 (978-1-84858-819-6(4)) Arcturus Publishing GBR. Dist: Bookmasters Distribution.
Verma, Dinesh, et al. Hindi Alphabet Activity Book International Edition. 2009. 112p. pap. 25.00 (978-0-557-10678-3(8)) Lulu Pr., Inc.
Virden, William & Borg, Mary. My Colorado Teacher Guide. 2010. 43p. pap. 3.95 (978-1-59363-656-2(3)) Prufrock Pr.
Virges, Audrey M. A Day in Kindergarten. 2012. 60p. pap. 24.99 (978-1-4772-8168-0(1)) AuthorHouse.
Vision, David & Vision, Mutiya. What Makes Me Beautiful? ¿Qué Es lo Que Me Hace Hermoso? 2013.Tr. of ¿Qué Es lo Que Me Hace Hermoso? (Illus.). 24p. (J). 17.00 (978-0-9816254-1-6(X), Vision Works Publishing) Soul Vision Works Publishing.
Vogt, Janet. Music Brain Teasers. 2006. pap. 19.95 (978-0-89328-248-6(0)) Lorenz Corp., The.
Volke, Gordon. Big World Activity Sticker Book, Vol. 2. 2004. (Illus.). 16p. 7.25 (978-1-84161-130-3(1)) Ravette Publishing, Ltd. GBR. Dist: Parkwest Pubns., Inc.
Vous, Nous. Show + Tell: Animal Activities: With 3 Posters, 40 Stickers & Coloring + Activity Book. 2017. (ENG.). 18p. (J). (gr. -1-k). pap. 9.99 (978-1-84780-775-5(5), Wide Eyed Editions) Quarto Publishing Group UK GBR. Dist: Hachette Bk. Group.
Walden, Libby. Construction Sticker Activity Fun. 2015. (ENG., Illus.). 96p. (J). (gr. -1-3). 9.99 (978-1-58925-315-5(9)) Tiger Tales.
—Emergency Services Sticker Activity Fun. 2015. (ENG., Illus.). 96p. (J). 9.99 (978-1-58925-314-8(0)) Tiger Tales.
Waldron, Hannah, illus. Pirate Adventure Dice. 2014. (ENG.). 16p. (J). (gr. 1-4). 14.95 (978-1-85669-938-9(2)) King, Laurence Publishing GBR. Dist: Hachette Bk. Group.
Walker, Gloria. Stop & Go Safety. 2008. 24p. (J). pap. 14.95 (978-1-883589-91-2(6)) Clark Publishing, Inc.
Walker, Persephone. Brain Quest Workbook: Grade 6. Thornborrow, Nick, illus. 2015. (ENG.). 320p. (J). (gr. 6-6). pap. 12.95 (978-0-7611-8243-6(8)) Workman Publishing Co., Inc.
Walker, Persephone, et al. Summer Brain Quest: Between Grades 2 And 3. Cummings, Matt & Yan, Edison, illus. 2017. (Summer Brain Quest Ser.). (ENG.). 160p. (J). (gr. 2-3). pap. 12.95 (978-0-7611-8918-3(1)) Workman Publishing Co., Inc.
—Summer Brain Quest: Between Grades 3 And 4. Yan, Edison, illus. 2017. (Summer Brain Quest Ser.). (ENG.). 160p. (J). (gr. 4-5). pap. 12.95 (978-0-7611-8919-0(X)) Workman Publishing Co., Inc.
Walker, Sylvia. My Sleepover Coloring Book. 2010. (Dover Coloring Bks.). (ENG., Illus.). 32p. (J). (gr. -1-4). pap. 3.99 (978-0-486-47656-8(1)) Dover Pubns., Inc.
—Our New Baby Coloring Book. 2014. (Dover Coloring Bks.). (ENG.). 32p. (J). (gr. -1-2). pap. 3.99 (978-0-486-49462-3(4)) Dover Pubns., Inc.
Wallace, Melissa. It's Great to Be a Baton Rouge Kid: An a-Z Coloring Book, 1 vol. 2017. (ENG., Illus.). 32p. pap. 4.95 **(978-1-4556-2373-0(3))** Pelican Publishing Co., Inc.
Walter Foster Creative Team. Marvel's Avengers Chalkboard 123: Learn Numbers with Reusable Chalkboard Pages! 2017. (ENG., Illus.). 14p. (J). (gr. -1-1). bds. 12.95 **(978-1-63322-254-0(3)**, Walter Foster Jr) Quarto Publishing Group USA.
—My Big, Crazy Drawing & Doodle Book: An Interactive Adventure with More Than 100 Creative Ideas for Tons of Doodling Fun. 2015. (ENG., Illus.). 128p. (J). (gr. 1-3). pap. 14.95 (978-1-60058-475-6(6)) Quarto Publishing Group USA.
—My Learning Adventures: USA. 2013. (My Learning Adventures Ser.). (ENG., Illus.). 80p. (J). (gr. -1). spiral bd. 12.95 (978-1-60710-629-6(9), Silver Dolphin Bks.) Readerlink Distribution Services, LLC.
—Sticker Pictures - Animals. 2017. (Sticker & Color-By-Number Ser.). (ENG., Illus.). 48p. (J). (gr. k-3). pap. 9.95 (978-1-63322-279-3(9), Walter Foster Jr) Quarto Publishing Group USA.
Warner Press, creator. The Best Christmas Gift Ever: Coloring & Activity Book. 2008. (J). (gr. -1-3). pap. 11.34 (978-1-59317-324-1(5)) Warner Pr., Inc.
—Bible Sports Heroes: Great Lessons You Can Learn from God's Favorite Athletes Activity Book. 2008. (J). (gr. -1-3). pap. 11.34 (978-1-59317-325-8(3)) Warner Pr., Inc.
—Don't You Wonder about This World? 2008. (Illus.). (J). pap. 11.34 (978-1-59317-321-0(0)) Warner Pr., Inc.
—Learning the Lord's Prayer: Coloring & Activity Book. 2008. (J). (gr. -1-3). pap. 11.34 (978-1-59317-323-4(7)) Warner Pr., Inc.
—Zacchaeus Climbs a Tree Coloring Book. 2009. (ENG., Illus.). 16p. (J). (gr. -1-k). pap. 11.34 (978-1-59317-337-1(7)) Warner Pr., Inc.
Warner Press Kids, creator. The First Christmas. 2008. (Illus.). 16p. (J). (gr. 1-5). pap. 11.34 (978-1-59317-326-5(1)) Warner Pr., Inc.
—The Jelly Bean Prayer Coloring & Activity Book. 2009. (Illus.). (J). (gr. -1-2). 11.34 (978-1-59317-348-7(2)) Warner Pr., Inc.
—The Jelly Bean Witness. 2009. 16p. (J). (gr. 1-5). pap. 11.34 (978-1-59317-350-0(4)) Warner Pr., Inc.
—Jesus Is Born: Coloring Book. 2008. 16p. (J). (gr. -1-3). pap. 11.34 (978-1-59317-322-7(9)) Warner Pr., Inc.
—Paul, a Servant of Jesus: Activity Book. 2008. 16p. (J). (gr. -1-3). pap. 11.34 (978-1-59317-327-2(X)) Warner Pr., Inc.
—Queen Esther. 2008. (Illus.). 16p. (J). (gr. -1-2). pap. 11.34 (978-1-59317-220-6(6)) Warner Pr., Inc.
Wasikhongo, Odalo Magruder. My First Book of Numbers. Wasikhongo, Odalo Magruder, illus. 2012. (Illus.). 24p. pap. 5.00 (978-0-9845203-2-9(5)) WasiWorks Studio LLC.
Watkins, Courtney. Dream It! Draw It! Think It! Do It! Activities to Spark Creative Adventures. 2016. (ENG., Illus.). 96p. (J). pap. 9.99 (978-1-4494-8034-9(9)) Andrews McMeel Publishing.
Watt, Fiona. Big Dinosaur Sticker Book. 2013. (Sticker Activity Bks). 34p. (J). pap. 8.99 (978-0-7945-3373-1(6), Usborne) EDC Publishing.
—Big Doodling Book. 2012. (Activity Bks). 96p. (J). bds. 11.99 (978-0-7945-3269-7(1), Usborne) EDC Publishing.
—Big Drawing Book. Thompson, Josephine & Day, Caroline, illus. 2013. (Doodle Bks). 95p. (J). pap. 11.99 (978-0-7945-3365-6(5), Usborne) EDC Publishing.
—Lots of Things to Find & Color. 2011. 96p. pap. 12.99 (978-0-7945-2963-5(1), Usborne) EDC Publishing.
—Monster Doodles. 2010. (Doodle Cards Ser.). 50p. (J). 9.99 (978-0-7945-2550-7(4), Usborne) EDC Publishing.
—Rubber Stamp Activities. 2017. (Stamp Activities* Ser.). (ENG.). 64p. (J). 19.99 **(978-0-7945-4007-4(4)**, Usborne) EDC Publishing.
—Spooky Sticker Book. 2008. (Sticker Bks). (Illus.). 32p. (J). pap. 8.99 (978-0-7945-2342-8(0), Usborne) EDC Publishing.
—Sticker Dolly Dressing Costumes Around the World. 2013. (Sticker Dolly Dressing Ser.). 34p. (J). pap. 8.99 (978-0-7945-3382-3(5), Usborne) EDC Publishing.
—Sticker Dolly Dressing Parties. Moore, Jo, illus. 2013. (Sticker Dolly Dressing Ser.). 34p. (J). pap. 8.99 (978-0-7945-3370-0(1), Usborne) EDC Publishing.
—Sticker Dressing Explorers. 2013. (Sticker Dressing Ser.). 34p. (J). pap. 8.99 (978-0-7945-3374-8(4), Usborne) EDC Publishing.
—Winter Wonderland Sticker Book. 2012. (Sticker Activity Bks). 34p. (J). pap. 8.99 (978-0-7945-3320-5(5), Usborne) EDC Publishing.
Weakland, Mark. SI Kids Rookie Books. 2013. (SI Kids Rookie Bks.). (ENG.). 20p. (gr. 1-2). bds. 143.10 (978-1-4914-1518-4(5)) Capstone Press of Coughlan Cos.
Weber, Amy & Creative Haven Staff. Creative Haven Curious Creatures Coloring Book. 2013. (Adult Coloring Ser.). (ENG., Illus.). 64p. (gr. 3). pap. 5.99 (978-0-486-49269-8(9)) Dover Pubns., Inc.
Weber, Belinda. I Wonder Why Animals Are Amazing Sticker Activity Book. 2013. (I Wonder Why Ser.). (ENG., Illus.). 24p. (J). (gr. k-3). 6.99 (978-0-7534-6830-2(1), 9780753468302, Kingfisher) Roaring Brook Pr.
—I Wonder Why Dinosaurs Ruled Sticker Activity Book. 2013. (I Wonder Why Ser.). (ENG., Illus.). 24p. (J). (gr. k-3). 6.99 (978-0-7534-6806-7(9), 9780753468067, Kingfisher) Roaring Brook Pr.
Weber, Belinda & Butterfield, Moira. I Wonder Why Cars Go Fast. 2014. (I Wonder Why Ser.). (ENG., Illus.). 24p. (J). (gr. k-3). act. bk. ed. 6.99 (978-0-7534-7141-8(8), 9780753471418, Kingfisher) Roaring Brook Pr.
Wehrmeijer, Annelien. Ruby & Molly. van de Liegraaf, Deborah, illus. 2014. (My Best Friend & Me Ser.). (ENG.). 10p. (J). (gr. -1 — 1). bds. 6.99 (978-0-7641-6661-7(1)) Barron's Educational Series, Inc.
Weidemann, Christiane. A Year in Art: The Activity Book. 2015. (ENG.). 376p. (J). (gr. 3-7). 24.95 (978-3-7913-7194-8(0)) Prestel Verlag GmbH & Co KG. DEU. Dist: Penguin Random Hse. LLC.
Weisburd, Claudia & Sniad, Tamara. Afterschool Style Guide: Graffitiwall. 2006. 79p. spiral bd. 29.95 incl. cd-rom (978-0-9797125-2-4(1)) Foundation, Inc.
—Global GraffitiWall. 2008. (Illus.). 76p. spiral bd. 24.95 (978-0-9797125-3-1(X)) Foundation, Inc.
Weisburd, Claudia, et al. Afterschool Style in Practice: 25 Skill-Building Meetngs for Staff. 2007. (Illus.). 182p. spiral bd. 59.95 (978-0-9797125-0-0(5)) Foundation, Inc.
Wellington, Monica. Color & Cook CHRISTMAS COOKIES. 2009. (Dover Coloring Bks.). (ENG., Illus.). 32p. (J). (gr. -1-3). pap. 4.99 (978-0-486-47448-9(8)) Dover Pubns., Inc.
—My Garden. 2011. (Dover Sticker Bks.). (ENG., Illus.). 6p. (J). (gr. k-5). 7.99 (978-0-486-48381-8(9)) Dover Pubns., Inc.
—My Garden Stickers. 2011. (Dover Sticker Bks.). (ENG., Illus.). 4p. (J). (gr. k-3). pap. 5.99 (978-0-486-48374-0(6)) Dover Pubns., Inc.
—Night House Bright House Find & Color. 2013. (ENG.). 32p. (J). (gr. -1-2). pap. 3.99 (978-0-486-49162-2(5)) Dover Pubns., Inc.
Wells, Jason & Wells, Jeff. Albert Is Our Mascot. Carlson, Patrick, illus. 2013. (That's Not Our Mascot Ser.). (ENG.). (J). 14.95 (978-1-62086-283-4(2)) Mascot Bks., Inc.
—Aubie Is Our Mascot. Carlson, Patrick, illus. 2013. (That's Not Our Mascot Ser.). (ENG.). (J). 14.95 (978-1-62086-292-6(1)) Mascot Bks., Inc.
—Big Al Is Our Mascot. Carlson, Patrick, illus. 2013. (That's Not Our Mascot Ser.). (ENG.). (J). 14.95 (978-1-62086-290-2(5)) Mascot Bks., Inc.
—Big Red Is Our Mascot. Carlson, Patrick, illus. 2013. (That's Not Our Mascot Ser.). (ENG.). (J). 14.95 (978-1-62086-291-9(3)) Mascot Bks., Inc.

S

—Bully Is Our Mascot. Carlson, Patrick, illus. 2013. (That's Not Our Mascot Ser.). (ENG.). (J). 14.95 (978-1-62086-294-0(8)) Mascot Bks., Inc.

—Cocky Is Our Mascot. Carlson, Patrick, illus. 2013. (That's Not Our Mascot Ser.). (ENG.). (J). 14.95 (978-1-62086-287-2(5)) Mascot Bks., Inc.

—Hairy Dawg Is Our Mascot. Carlson, Patrick, illus. 2013. (That's Not Our Mascot Ser.). (ENG.). (J). 14.95 (978-1-62086-284-1(0)) Mascot Bks., Inc.

—Mike the Tiger Is Our Mascot. Carlson, Patrick, illus. 2013. (That's Not Our Mascot Ser.). (ENG.). (J). 14.95 (978-1-62086-293-3(X)) Mascot Bks., Inc.

—Rebel Is Our Mascot. 2013. (ENG., Illus.). (J). (gr. -1-3). 14.95 (978-1-62086-295-7(6)) Mascot Bks., Inc.

—Reveille Is Our Mascot. Carlson, Patrick, illus. 2013. (That's Not Our Mascot Ser.). (ENG.). (J). 14.95 (978-1-62086-296-4(4)) Mascot Bks., Inc.

—Scratch Is Our Mascot. Carlson, Patrick, illus. 2013. (That's Not Our Mascot Ser.). (ENG.). (J). 14.95 (978-1-62086-285-8(9)) Mascot Bks., Inc.

—Smokey Is Our Mascot. Carlson, Patrick, illus. 2013. (That's Not Our Mascot Ser.). (ENG.). (J). 14.95 (978-1-62086-288-9(3)) Mascot Bks., Inc.

—Truman Is Our Mascot. Carlson, Patrick, illus. 2013. (That's Not Our Mascot Ser.). (ENG.). (J). 14.95 (978-1-62086-286-5(7)) Mascot Bks., Inc.

Wells, Rachel, illus. That's Not My Sticker Book Christmas. rev. ed. 2012. (That's Not My . . Sticker Bks). 28p. (J). pap. 4.99 (978-0-7945-3318-2(3), Usborne) EDC Publishing.

Wesleyan Publishing House, creator. Knowing God's Truth: 52 Reproducible in-Class Activities & Family Devotionals. 2006. (Building Kids Faith Ser.). (Illus.). 100p. per. 15.99 (978-0-89827-342-7(0)) Wesleyan Publishing Hse.

The Western Hemisphere Through the Five Themes of Geography Map Activities Book plus 5 Transparencies. 2005. (Western Hemisphere Through the Five Themes of Geography Ser.). 16p. 55.95 (978-1-4042-5159-5(6), Rosen Classroom) Rosen Publishing Group, Inc., The.

Westing, Jemma. Out of the Box. 2017. (ENG., Illus.). 144p. (J). (gr. 2-5). 19.99 (978-1-4654-5896-4(4), DK Children) Dorling Kindersley Publishing, Inc.

What Is a Tangaroo. 2007. (Illus.). 32p. (J). pap. 24.99 (978-0-9793506-2-7(X)) Sportime International.

What Would You Choose? 2016. (What Would You Choose? Ser.). 00032p. (J). lib. bdg. 106.40 **(978-1-4824-6073-5(4))** Stevens, Gareth Publishing LLLP.

Whelon, Chuck. Create Your Own Dinosaurs Sticker Activity Book. 2015. (ENG.). 4p. (J). (gr. k-3). pap. 1.99 (978-0-486-78957-6(8)) Dover Pubns., Inc.

—FLIP OUTS — Dinosaurs: Color Your Own Cartoon! 2015. (ENG., Illus.). 64p. (J). (gr. k-3). pap. 1.99 (978-0-486-79486-0(5)) Dover Pubns., Inc.

—Sea Animals Finger Tattoos. 2014. (ENG.). 2p. (J). (gr. 1-4). 1.50 (978-0-486-78440-3(1)) Dover Pubns., Inc.

—Smiley Things That Go Sticker Activity Book. 2014. (ENG., Illus.). 4p. (J). (gr. 1-4). pap. 1.99 (978-0-486-78021-4(X)) Dover Pubns., Inc.

—What to Doodle? Fantastic Fantasy! 2009. (Dover Doodle Bks.). (ENG., Illus.). 64p. (J). (gr. 2-5). pap. 5.99 (978-0-486-47044-3(X)) Dover Pubns., Inc.

—What to Doodle? Things That Go! 2009. (Dover Doodle Bks.). (ENG., Illus.). 64p. (J). (gr. -1-2). pap. 5.99 (978-0-486-47045-0(8)) Dover Pubns., Inc.

—Word Play - Write Your Own Crazy Comics, No. 1. 2013. (BOOST Educational Ser.). (ENG.). 64p. (J). (gr. 3-5). pap. 5.99 (978-0-486-49441-8(1)) Dover Pubns., Inc.

—Zoo Animals Finger Tattoos. 2014. (ENG.). 2p. (J). (gr. 1-4). 1.50 (978-0-486-78439-7(8)) Dover Pubns., Inc.

White, Mia. CAREFUL, YOU Could HURT the DOLPHINS - Zoe's World Dr. Mia White. White, Mia, illus. 2007. (Illus.). per. 24.00 (978-1-60361-710-9(8)) Belle Media International, Inc. Div of True News.

Wick, Walter. Once upon a Time: Picture Puzzles to Search & Solve. Wick, Walter, photos by. 2006. (Can You See What I See? Ser.). (ENG., Illus.). 40p. (J). (gr. -1-3). 13.99 (978-0-439-61777-2(4), Cartwheel Bks.) Scholastic, Inc.

Wiemeier, Aaron. My Feelings Workbook. Trapp, Karla, illus. 2011. 104p. (J). pap. 19.95 (978-1-59850-095-0(3)) Youthlight, Inc.

Wiggles 5 in 1 Superly Duperly. 2005. 52p. pap. 3.99 (978-0-7666-2252-4(5)) Modern Publishing.

Wik, John & Creative Haven Staff. Creative Haven Tessellation Patterns Coloring Book. 2013. (Adult Coloring Ser.). (ENG., Illus.). 64p. (J). (gr. 3). pap. 5.99 (978-0-486-49165-3(X)) Dover Pubns., Inc.

Wilde, Cindy, et al, illus. Color with Me. 2016. (ENG.). 96p. (J). (gr. 1-6). spiral bd. 12.95 (978-1-4549-1930-8(2)) Sterling Publishing Co., Inc.

—Color with Mom. 2016. (ENG.). 96p. (J). (gr. 1-6). spiral bd. 12.95 (978-1-4549-1931-5(0)) Sterling Publishing Co., Inc.

Wilde, Cindy, illus. Fabulous Copycat Coloring Book: Pretty Pictures to Copy & Complete. 2016. (Copycat Coloring Bks.). (ENG.). 48p. (J). (gr. 1-5). pap. 6.99 (978-1-4380-0841-7(4)) Barron's Educational Series, Inc.

Wilde, Cindy & French, Felicity, illus. Beautiful Coloring. 2016. (ENG.). 128p. (J). (gr. 2-6). pap. 12.95 (978-1-4549-1885-1(3)) Sterling Publishing Co., Inc.

Wildot Press. Jacob's Back Yard. 2006. (Illus.). 42p. (J). spiral bd. 14.95 (978-0-9789043-9-5(7)) Wildot Pr.

—Jacob's Front Yard. 2006. (Illus.). 39p. (J). spiral bd. 15.95 (978-0-9789043-8-8(9)) Wildot Pr.

Wildwood Forest Customizable Outdoor Banner. 2009. (Vacation Bible School Ser.). (J). 35.00 (978-2-608-00908-1(5)) Cook, David C.

Wilkinson, Naomi. One Hundred Things to Spot. 2017. (Learn with Little Mouse Ser.). (ENG.). 80p. (J). (gr. -1-k). 16.99 **(978-1-78603-033-7(0)**, Wide Eyed Editions) Quarto Publishing Group UK GBR. Dist: Hachette Bk. Group.

Williams, Christine M. Building a Sight Vocabulary with Comprehension: The It Family. 2012. 24p. pap. 17.99 (978-1-4772-8498-8(2)) AuthorHouse.

Williams, Colleen Madonna Flood. My Adventure in the Mesozoic Period: Advanced My Adventure. 2009. (ENG.). 44p. (J). pap. 8.99 (978-1-59092-437-2(1)) Blue Forge Pr.

—My Adventure in the Wild West. 2007. 44p. (J). 8.99 (978-1-59092-439-6(8)) Blue Forge Pr.

—My Adventure on April Fool's Day. 2009. (ENG.). 44p. (J). 8.99 (978-1-59092-544-7(0)) Blue Forge Pr.

—My Adventure on Christmas. 2006. 44p. (J). 8.99 (978-1-59092-545-4(9)) Blue Forge Pr.

—My Adventure on Easter. 2007. 44p. (J). 8.99 (978-1-59092-546-1(7)) Blue Forge Pr.

—My Adventure on Father's Day. 2007. 44p. (J). 8.99 (978-1-59092-547-8(5)) Blue Forge Pr.

—My Adventure on Groundhog Day. 2009. (ENG.). 44p. (J). 8.99 (978-1-59092-548-5(3)) Blue Forge Pr.

—My Adventure on Halloween. 2006. 44p. (J). 8.99 (978-1-59092-549-2(1)) Blue Forge Pr.

—My Adventure on Martin Luther King Jr. Day. 2009. (ENG.). 44p. (J). 8.99 (978-1-59092-551-5(3)) Blue Forge Pr.

—My Adventure on Mother's Day. 2007. 44p. (J). 8.99 (978-1-59092-552-2(1)) Blue Forge Pr.

—My Adventure on My Birthday. 2009. 44p. (J). 8.99 (978-1-59092-553-9(X)) Blue Forge Pr.

—My Adventure on New Year's Day. 2006. 44p. (J). 8.99 (978-1-59092-554-6(8)) Blue Forge Pr.

—My Adventure on President's Day. 2007. 44p. (J). 8.99 (978-1-59092-555-3(6)) Blue Forge Pr.

—My Adventure on St. Patrick's Day. 2007. 44p. (J). 8.99 (978-1-59092-556-0(4)) Blue Forge Pr.

—My Adventure on Thanksgiving Day. 2006. 44p. (J). 8.99 (978-1-59092-557-7(2)) Blue Forge Pr.

—My Adventure on the Fourth of July. 2009. (ENG.). 44p. (J). 8.99 (978-1-59092-560-7(2)) Blue Forge Pr.

—My Adventure on Valentine's Day. 2009. (ENG.). 44p. (J). 8.99 (978-1-59092-558-4(0)) Blue Forge Pr.

—My Adventure on Veteran's Day. 2006. 44p. (J). 8.99 (978-1-59092-559-1(9)) Blue Forge Pr.

—My Adventure with Knights. 2009. (ENG.). 44p. (J). 8.99 (978-1-59092-456-3(8)) Blue Forge Pr.

—My Adventure with Leonardo da Vinci. 2009. (ENG.). 44p. (J). 8.99 (978-1-59092-458-7(4)) Blue Forge Pr.

—My Adventure with Shakespeare. 2009. (ENG.). 44p. (J). 8.99 (978-1-59092-467-9(3)) Blue Forge Pr.

—My Adventure with Vikings. 2009. (ENG.). 44p. (J). 8.99 (978-1-59092-474-7(6)) Blue Forge Pr.

—Schooling Day-by-day in May. 2007. 44p. (J). 8.99 (978-1-59092-521-8(1)) Blue Forge Pr.

Williams, Lynette Gain. Handwriting Begins with Art: The Partner Book to ArbeZ ZebrA Teaches A to Z. 2007. 165p. (J). spiral bd. 19.99 (978-0-9779063-1-4(0)) Gain Literacy Skills / Lynette Gain Williams.

Willians, Rozanne Lanczak. Sing & Read with Greg & Steve All-in-One Pack. 2009. pap. 58.86 (978-1-60689-164-3(2)) Youngheart Music.

Wilson, CeCe. The Thunder Cloud Cookies. 2015. (Rosen REAL Readers: STEM & STEAM Collection). (ENG.). 12p. (gr. 1-2). pap. 6.33 (978-1-4994-9523-2(4), Rosen Classroom) Rosen Publishing Group, Inc., The.

Winslow, Jeremy. Hours of Coloring Fun with Shapes & Patterns. 2011. 182p. 30.99 (978-1-4568-8227-3(9)); pap. 20.99 (978-1-4568-8226-6(0)) Xlibris Corp.

Wipe-Clean Action Words to Copy. 2017. (Wipe-Clean Bks.). (ENG.). (J). pap. 7.99 **(978-0-7945-3938-2(6)**, Usborne) EDC Publishing.

Wipe-Clean Dinosaur Activities. 2017. (Wipe-Clean Activity Books* Ser.). (ENG.). (J). pap. 7.99 **(978-0-7945-3987-0(4)**, Usborne) EDC Publishing.

Withers, Margaret. Welcome to the Lord's Table: A Practical Course for Preparing Children to Receive Holy Communion. 3rd rev. ed. 2013. (ENG., Illus.). 96p. pap. (978-1-84101-734-1(5), Barnabas for Children) Bible Reading Fellowship.

Wojciechowska, Maia. Shadow of a Bull. 2007. 151p. (gr. 3-7). 17.00 (978-0-7569-7999-7(4)) Perfection Learning Corp.

Wood, Anita. The BFF Journal, 1 vol. Kalis, Jennifer, illus. 2011. (ENG.). 144p. (J). (gr. 1). spiral bd. 12.99 (978-1-4236-1814-0(9)) Gibbs Smith, Publisher.

—City Doodles San Francisco, 1 vol. 2013. (ENG., Illus.). 240p. (J). pap., pap. 9.99 (978-1-4236-3286-3(9)) Gibbs Smith, Publisher.

—Doodle Your Day, 1 vol. Kalis, Jennifer, illus. 2013. (ENG.). 224p. (J). pap. 16.99 (978-1-4236-2368-7(1)) Gibbs Smith, Publisher.

—Pocketdoodles for Girls, 1 vol. Kalis, Jennifer, illus. 2010. (ENG.). 272p. (J). (gr. 1). 9.99 (978-1-4236-0755-7(4)) Gibbs Smith, Publisher.

—Pocketdoodles for Princesses, 1 vol. Kalis, Jennifer, illus. 2011. (ENG.). 272p. (J). (gr. 3). 9.99 (978-1-4236-1877-5(7)) Gibbs Smith, Publisher.

—Travel Doodles for Kids, 1 vol. 2012. (ENG., Illus.). 272p. (J). pap. 9.99 (978-1-4236-2454-7(8)) Gibbs Smith, Publisher.

Wood, Anita & Sabatino, Chris. Camping Doodles, 1 vol. 2013. (ENG., Illus.). 240p. (J). pap., pap. 9.99 (978-1-4236-3168-2(4)) Gibbs Smith, Publisher.

Wood, Kristen. Find Albert Alberta Too. 2009. 36p. 19.95 (978-1-935159-11-7(9)) My Campus Adventure, Inc.

—Find Big Al. 2009. 36p. 19.95 (978-1-935159-10-0(0)) My Campus Adventure, Inc.

—Find Reveille. 2009. 36p. 19.95 (978-1-935159-08-7(9)) My Campus Adventure, Inc.

—Find Uga Hairy Dawg Too. 2009. 36p. 19.95 (978-1-935159-09-4(7)) My Campus Adventure, Inc.

Wood, Mark. Beyond Classroom Enrichment: Creative Units for Gifted Students. 2004. (Illus.). 80p. (978-0-910609-48-7(9)) Gifted Education Pr.

Woodworth, Viki. United States Maze Craze. 2009. (Dover Children's Activity Bks.). (ENG., Illus.). 64p. (J). (gr. 3-4). pap. 4.99 (978-0-486-46831-0(3)) Dover Pubns., Inc.

—The 50 States: Facts & Fun. 2010. (Dover Little Activity Bks.). (ENG., Illus.). 64p. (J). (gr. 1-5). 1.99 (978-0-486-47524-0(7)) Dover Pubns., Inc.

Woram, Catherine & Youngs, Clare. Rainy Day Book of Things to Make & Do. 2012. (ENG., Illus.). 160p. pap. (978-1-84975-272-5(9)) Ryland Peters & Small.

Workman Publishing Company Staff. Space. 2014. (Eyelike Stickers Ser.). (ENG.). 12p. (J). pap. 6.95 (978-0-7611-7965-8(8), 17965) Workman Publishing Co., Inc.

Workman Publishing, Workman. Paint by Sticker Kids: Create 10 Pictures One Sticker at a Time. 2016. (Paint by Sticker Ser.). (ENG., Illus.). 34p. (J). (gr. k-5). 9.95 (978-0-7611-8941-1(6)) Workman Publishing Co., Inc.

—Paint by Sticker Kids: under the Sea. 2017. (Paint by Sticker Ser.). (ENG., Illus.). 34p. (J). (gr. 1-4). 9.95 (978-1-5235-0038-3(7)) Workman Publishing Co., Inc.

—Zoo Animals. 2016. (Paint by Sticker Ser.). (ENG., Illus.). 34p. (J). (gr. k-6). 9.95 (978-0-7611-8960-2(2)) Workman Publishing Co., Inc.

World Book, Inc Staff, contrib. by. Fun with Painting & Sculpture. 2011. (J). (978-0-7166-0226-2(1)) World Bk., Inc.

The World of Eric Carle My Alphabet Activity Kit. 2007. (J). 16.99 (978-0-9794445-0-0(0)) Loew-Cornell, Inc.

The World of Eric Carle My Animals Activity Kit. 2007. (J). 16.99 (978-0-9794445-4-8(3)) Loew-Cornell, Inc.

The World of Eric Carle My Numbers Activity Kit. 2007. (J). 16.99 (978-0-9794445-1-7(9)) Loew-Cornell, Inc.

The World of Eric Carle My Shapes Activity Kit. 2007. (J). 16.99 (978-0-9794445-3-1(5)) Loew-Cornell, Inc.

World of Football. 2012. (Collins Big Cat Ser.). (ENG.). 16p. (J). pap., wbk. ed. 4.99 (978-0-00-747286-4(2)) HarperCollins Pubs. Ltd. GBR. Dist: Independent Pubs. Group.

Worms, Penny. Creativity Book: Alice in Wonderland. 2016. (ENG., Illus.). 88p. (J). (gr. 1). spiral bd. 16.95 (978-1-78312-045-1(2)) Carlton Bks., Ltd. GBR. Dist: Sterling Publishing Co., Inc.

—The Dinosaur Creativity Book. 2015. (Creativity Bks.). (ENG.). 80p. (J). (gr. 1-5). pap. 12.99 (978-1-4380-0717-5(5)) Barron's Educational Series, Inc.

—Dinosaurs. 2012. (My First Creativity Bks.). (ENG.). 66p. (J). (gr. -1-2). pap. 9.99 (978-1-4380-0178-4(9)) Barron's Educational Series, Inc.

—The Monster Creativity Book: Games, Cut-Outs, Art Paper, Stickers, & Stencils. 2016. (Creativity Bks.). (ENG.). 80p. (J). (gr. k-4). pap. 12.99 (978-1-4380-0781-6(7)) Barron's Educational Series, Inc.

Wrecks, Billy. Here Come the Heroes! Golden Books, illus. 2013. (Jumbo Coloring Book Ser.). (ENG.). 224p. (J). (gr. -1-2). pap. 5.99 (978-0-449-81610-3(9), Golden Bks.) Random Hse. Children's Bks.

Wright, Natalie. Slime 101: How to Make Stretchy, Fluffy, Glittery & Colorful Slime! 2017. (ENG., Illus.). 48p. (gr. 1-6). pap. 6.99 **(978-0-486-82091-0(2))** Dover Pubns., Inc.

Wynne, Patricia J. BOOST Seashore Activity Book. 2013. (BOOST Educational Ser.). (ENG.). 48p. (J). (gr. 1-2). pap. 5.99 (978-0-486-49408-1(X)) Dover Pubns., Inc.

—Butterfly Activity Book. 2007. (Dover Children's Activity Bks.). (ENG., Illus.). 48p. (J). (gr. -1-2). per. 4.95 (978-0-486-45692-8(7)) Dover Pubns., Inc.

—Creative Haven SeaScapes Coloring Book. 2013. (Adult Coloring Ser.). (ENG.). 64p. (gr. 3). pap. 5.99 (978-0-486-49423-4(3)) Dover Pubns., Inc.

—Glow-in-the-Dark Skeleton Stickers. 2009. (Dover Little Activity Books Stickers Ser.). (ENG., Illus.). 2p. (J). (gr. 1-4). pap. 1.99 (978-0-486-47129-7(2)) Dover Pubns., Inc.

—Wild Animals Activity Book. 2008. (Dover Children's Activity Bks.). (ENG., Illus.). 48p. (J). (gr. k-3). pap. 4.95 (978-0-486-46564-7(0)) Dover Pubns., Inc.

Wynne, Patricia J. & Whelon, Chuck. 3-D Mazes — Dinosaurs. 2012. (Dover 3-D Mazes Ser.). (ENG.). 32p. (J). (gr. 1-6). 5.99 (978-0-486-49015-1(7)) Dover Pubns., Inc.

Yasuda, Anita. Explore Simple Machines! With 25 Great Projects. 2011. (Explore Your World Ser.). (ENG., Illus.). 96p. (J). (gr. k-4). pap. 12.95 (978-1-936313-82-2(0)) Open City Bks.

—Explore Water! 25 Great Projects, Activities, Experiments. Stone, Bryan, illus. 2011. (Explore Your World Ser.). (ENG.). 96p. (J). (gr. k-4). pap. 12.95 (978-1-936313-42-6(1)) Open City Bks.

Yasuda, Anita & Stone, Bryan. Explore the Solar System! 25 Great Projects, Activities, Experiments. Stone, Bryan, illus. 2009. (Explore Your World Ser.). (ENG., Illus.). 96p. (J). (gr. k-4). pap. 12.95 (978-1-934670-36-1(7)) Octavio Publishing.

Yates, Irene. Christmas Activities for ks1 Maths. 2005. pap. (978-1-903853-68-9(0)) Brilliant Pubns.

—Christmas Activities for Ks2 Maths. 2005. (Illus.). 64p. pap. (978-1-903853-69-6(9)) Brilliant Pubns.

—Christmas Activities for Language & L. 2007. (978-1-903853-67-2(2)) Brilliant Pubns.

Yo-Kai Watch. It's Yo-Kai Watch Time: Puzzle & Friends. 2016. (ENG., Illus.). 128p. (J). (gr. 3-7). pap. 6.99 (978-0-316-36107-1(0)) Little, Brown Bks. for Young Readers.

Yoon, Salina, illus. At the Beach Mad Art. 2009. (Mad Art Ser.). (ENG.). 12p. (J). (gr. -1-k). 6.99 (978-0-8431-3527-5(1), Price Stern Sloan) Penguin Young Readers Group.

Young, Helen Ann. Your World Discovery Scrapbook. Young, Tim Blair, illus. 2013. 40p. pap. (978-1-908353-03-0(1)) Young Editions.

Young, Jeanna & Johnson, Jacqueline Kinney. Princess Charity Sticker & Activity Book, 1 vol. Aranda, Omar, illus. 2015. (Princess Parables Ser.). (ENG.). 16p. (J). pap. 3.99 (978-0-310-74644-7(2)) Zonderkidz.

Young, Karen Romano & dePaola, Tomie. Oceans Doodle Book. 2015. (Smithsonian Ser.). (ENG., Illus.). 128p. (J). (gr. 3-7). bds. 12.99 (978-0-448-48688-8(1), Grosset & Dunlap) Penguin Young Readers Group.

Young, Karen Romano, et al. Blast off! Doodle Book. Morgan, Pau, illus. 2015. (Smithsonian Ser.). (ENG.). 128p. (J). (gr. 3-7). bds. 12.99 (978-0-448-48210-1(X), Grosset & Dunlap) Penguin Young Readers Group.

Ytearie Milliona Devalt. Princess Million: All about Me & Activity Book. 2009. 32p. pap. 12.99 (978-1-4389-2526-4(3)) AuthorHouse.

Zelinski, E. J. Pensar a lo Grande: Ejercicios Simples y Divertidos para Potenciar la Creatividad. (SPA.). 212p. (978-84-95456-79-3(6), 87420) Ediciones Oniro S.A.

Zimmerman, Bill. City Doodles New York, 1 vol. 2013. (ENG., Illus.). 240p. (J). pap., pap. 9.99 (978-1-4236-3227-6(3)) Gibbs Smith, Publisher.

—Pocketdoodles for Young Artists, 1 vol. Bloom, Tom, illus. 2010. (ENG.). 272p. (J). (gr. 1). 9.99 (978-1-4236-0466-2(0)) Gibbs Smith, Publisher.

Zondervan. The Beginner's Bible Super Girls of the Bible Sticker & Activity Book, 1 vol. 2015. (Beginner's Bible Ser.). (ENG.). 16p. (J). pap. 3.99 (978-0-310-75118-2(7)) Zonderkidz.

—Faithgirlz Promises for You Coloring Devotional: 60 Days Discovering God's Hope & Love, 1 vol. 2017. (Faithgirlz Ser.). (ENG.). 128p. (J). 12.99 (978-0-310-76119-8(0)) Zonderkidz.

Zondervan Staff. The Beginner's Bible a Christmas Celebration Sticker & Activity Book, 1 vol. 2015. (Beginner's Bible Ser.). (ENG.). 16p. (J). pap. 3.99 (978-0-310-74670-6(1)) Zonderkidz.

—The Beginner's Bible Super Heroes of the Bible Sticker & Activity Book, 1 vol. Pulley, Kelly, illus. 2015. (Beginner's Bible Ser.). (ENG.). 16p. (J). pap. 3.99 (978-0-310-74751-2(1)) Zonderkidz.

ZOO, La. Incredible Stickers! An Activity Book with Stickers. Miyakoshi, Junko, tr. 2010. (King of Play Ser.). (ENG., Illus.). 52p. (J). (gr. -1). pap. 7.95 (978-1-934734-38-4(1)) Seven Footer Pr.

Zook, Melinda. L-E-t-t-e-r-s. 2012. 24p. pap. 24.95 (978-1-4626-7175-5(6)) America Star Bks.

Zourelias, Diana. Build a Giant Poster Coloring Book — United States Map. 2013. (Dover Build a Poster Coloring Book Ser.). (ENG., Illus.). 48p. (J). (gr. 3-5). pap. 4.99 (978-0-486-49152-3(8)) Dover Pubns., Inc.

—Fun Facts about Everyday Inventions. 2013. (Dover Coloring Bks.). (ENG.). 32p. (J). (gr. 3-8). pap. 3.99 (978-0-486-49778-5(X)) Dover Pubns., Inc.

—SPARK Garden Daze Find It! Color It! 2017. (Dover Coloring Bks.). (ENG.). 64p. (gr. 1-4). pap. 5.99 (978-0-486-81384-4(3)) Dover Pubns., Inc.

—SPARK Silly Sea Life Find It! Color It! 2016. (Dover Coloring Bks.). (ENG.). 64p. (J). (gr. 1-4). pap. 5.99 (978-0-486-81095-9(X)) Dover Pubns., Inc.

Zschock, Martha & Zschock, Martha Day, illus. Spooky Scratch & Sketch: For Spooky Artists & Trick-or-Treaters of All Ages. 2007. (Scratch & Sketch sER.). 80p. (J). 12.99 (978-1-59359-881-5(5)) Peter Pauper Pr. Inc.

STUDENT AID

see Scholarships; Student Loan Funds

STUDENT GUIDANCE

see Educational Counseling; Vocational Guidance

STUDENT LIFE AND CUSTOMS

see Students

STUDENT LOAN FUNDS

see also Scholarships

Aresty, Reecy. Getting into College & Paying for It: Solutions for High School & College Families Guaranteed to Cut the Cost! l.t. ed. 2003.Tr. of Sueno Americano: Como Ingresar a la Universidad Y Pagar Los Mas Bajos Costos! (SPA., Illus.). 258p. (YA). per. 27.95 (978-0-9760251-1-5(6)) College Assistance, Inc.

Bryfonski, Dedria. Student Loans. Greenhaven Press Editors, ed. 2011. (At Issue Ser.). (ENG.). 128p. (gr. 10-12). 39.40 (978-0-7377-5600-5(4)); pap. 27.80 (978-0-7377-5601-2(2), Greenhaven Pr., Inc.) Cengage Gale.

Merino, Noël. Student Loans. 2016. (At Issue Ser.). (ENG.). 128p. (J). (gr. 10-12). 39.40 (978-0-7377-7410-8(X), Greenhaven Pr., Inc.) Cengage Gale.

Rugg, Frederick E. Financial Aid in Less Than 3000 Words. 6p. (YA). 9th rev. ed. 2003. pap. 6.95 (978-1-883062-51-4(9)) 10th rev. ed. 2004. pap. 6.95 (978-1-883062-57-6(8)) Rugg's Recommendations.

—Thirty Questions & Answers on the Colleges. (YA). 9th rev. ed. 2003. 20p. pap. 9.95 (978-1-883062-52-1(7)) 10th rev. ed. 2004. 20p. pap. 9.95 (978-1-883062-56-9(X)) 11th rev. ed. 2005. 21p. pap. 9.95 (978-1-883062-61-3(6)) Rugg's Recommendations.

A Student's Guide to Financial Empowerment. 2013. (Student's Guide to Financial Empowerment Ser.). 64p. (YA). (gr. 7-12). 191.70 (978-1-4488-9362-1(3)); pap. 77.70 (978-1-4777-2693-8(4)); pap. 466.20 (978-1-4777-2694-5(2)) Rosen Publishing Group, Inc., The.

STUDENT MOVEMENTS

see Youth Movement

STUDENT PROTESTS

see Youth Movement

STUDENT REVOLT

see Youth Movement

STUDENTS

Ahlberg, Janet & Ahlberg, Allan. Starting School. 2004. (J). (gr. k-3). spiral bd. (978-0-616-11861-0(9)) Canadian National Institute for the Blind/Institut National Canadien pour les Aveugles.

Aillaud, Cindy. Recess at 20 Below. 2015. (ENG., Illus.). 32p. (J). (gr. k-5). 19.99 (978-1-943328-23-9(4), Alaska Northwest Bks.) Graphic Arts Ctr. Publishing Co.

Bily, Cynthia A. Dress Codes in Schools. Gale, ed. 2014. (Issues That Concern You Ser.). (ENG., Illus.). 144p. (gr. 7-10). lib. bdg. 42.00 (978-0-7377-6930-2(0), Greenhaven Pr., Inc.) Cengage Gale.

Bullard, Lisa. Who Works at Hannah's School? Becker, Paula J., illus. 2017. (Cloverleaf Books (tm) — off to School Ser.). (ENG.). 24p. (J). (gr. k-2). 25.32 **(978-1-5124-3940-3(1)**, Millbrook Pr.) Lerner Publishing Group.

—Who Works at Hannah's School? Becker, Paula, illus. 2017. (Cloverleaf Books (tm) — off to School Ser.). (ENG.). (J). (gr. k-2). pap. 7.99 **(978-1-5124-5581-6(4)**, Millbrook Pr.) Lerner Publishing Group.

Cider Mill Press Staff & Copeland, Cynthia L. Secrets of Middle School: Everything You Need to Succeed. 2010. (ENG.). 144p. (J). pap. 12.95 (978-1-60433-195-0(X), Applesauce Pr.) Cider Mill Pr. Bk. Pubs., LLC.

Crockett, Kyle A. Nutrition for Achievement in Sports & Academics. Borus, Joshua, ed. 2013. (Understanding Nutrition: a Gateway to Physical & Mental Health Ser.). (Illus.). 48p. (J). (gr. 5-18). pap. 9.95 (978-1-4222-2990-3(4)); 19.95 (978-1-4222-2884-5(3)) Mason Crest.

Doudna, Kelly. School Around the World, 1 vol. 2004. (Around the World Ser.). (ENG., Illus.). 24p. (J). (gr. k-3). lib. bdg. 24.21 (978-1-59197-569-4(7), SandCastle) ABDO Publishing Co.

Elliott, Tommy. I Don't Want To: Go to School. 2009. 24p. pap. 13.49 (978-1-4389-5123-2(X)) AuthorHouse.

Fastje, Shanaya B. Mystery School. 2009. 28p. pap. 13.99 (978-1-4490-0115-5(7)) AuthorHouse.

Fradin, Dennis Brindell. Turning Points in History, 6 vols., Group 4. Incl. First Lunar Landing. 31.36 (978-0-7614-4256-1(1)); Hurricane Katrina. Fradin, Judith Bloom. 31.36 (978-0-7614-4261-5(8)); Louisiana Purchase.

31.36 *(978-0-7614-4257-8(X))*; Montgomery Bus Boycott. 31.36 *(978-0-7614-4258-5(8))*; September 11, 2001. 31.36 *(978-0-7614-4259-2(6))*; Stamp Act of 1765. (Illus.). (J). 31.36 *(978-0-7614-4260-8(X))*; 48p. (gr. 3-18). (Turning Points in U. S. History 4 Ser.). 2009. Set lib. bdg. 188.16 o.p. *(978-0-7614-4255-4(3))* Marshall Cavendish Corp.

Fry, Ron. Surefire Tips to Improve Your Memory Skills, 01 vols., 1. 2016. (Surefire Study Success Ser.). (ENG.). 128p. (YA). 35.60 *(978-1-5081-7089-1(4)*, Rosen Young Adult) Rosen Publishing Group, Inc., The.

—Surefire Tips to Improve Your Reading Skills, 01 vols., 1. 2016. (Surefire Study Success Ser.). (ENG.). 128p. (YA). 35.60 *(978-1-5081-7094-5(0)*, Rosen Young Adult) Rosen Publishing Group, Inc., The.

Gagliardi, Tina. School Survival: Keeping Your Cool at School, 1 vol. 2008. (Essential Health: Strong Beautiful Girls Set 1 Ser.). (ENG.). 112p. (J). (gr. 6-12). lib. bdg. 35.64 *(978-1-60453-104-6(5))* ABDO Publishing Co.

Glasser, Debbie & Schenck, Emily. New Kid, New Scene: A Guide to Moving & Switching Schools. 2011. (Illus.). 112p. (J). 14.95 *(978-1-4338-1039-8(5))*; pap. 9.95 *(978-1-4338-1038-1(7))* American Psychological Assn. (Magination Pr.).

Gold, Susan Dudley. Tinker V. des Moines: Free Speech for Students. 2006. (Supreme Court Milestones Ser.). (Illus.). 128p. (gr. 7-7). lib. bdg. 42.79 *(978-0-7614-2142-9(4)*, Benchmark Bks.) Marshall Cavendish Corp.

Hartzler, Aaron. Rapture Practice: A True Story about Growing up Gay in an Evangelical Family. 2014. (ENG.). 416p. (YA). (gr. 10-17). pap. 11.99 *(978-0-316-09464-1(1))* Little, Brown Bks. for Young Readers.

Haugen, David M. Discipline & Punishment. 2012. (Teen Rights & Freedoms Ser.). (ENG., Illus.). 176p. (gr. 10-12). lib. bdg. 42.00 *(978-0-7377-6401-7(5)*, Greenhaven Pr., Inc.) Cengage Gale.

Hudson, David L. Rights of Students. 2nd rev. ed. 2010. (Point/Counterpoint Ser.). 112p. (C). (gr. 9). 35.00 *(978-1-60413-692-0(8)*, Chelsea Hse.) Facts On File, Inc.

Hughes, Susan & Owlkids Books Inc. Staff. Off to Class: Incredible & Unusual Schools Around the World. 2011. (ENG., Illus.). 64p. (J). (gr. 3-7). 22.95 *(978-1-926818-85-6(7))*; pap. 14.95 *(978-1-926818-86-3(5))* Owlkids Bks. Inc. CAN. Dist: Publishers Group West (PGW).

Jeffrey, Gary. The Little Rock Nine & the Fight for Equal Education. 2012. (Graphic History of the Civil Rights Movement Ser.). (Illus.). 24p. (J). (gr. 3-8). lib. bdg. 23.95 *(978-1-4339-7483-0(5))* Stevens, Gareth Publishing LLLP.

Johnston, Kurt, et al. My School, 1 vol. 2007. (Middle School Survival Ser.). (ENG., Illus.). 192p. (YA). (gr. 7-9). pap. 9.99 *(978-0-310-27882-5(1))* Zondervan.

Kenney, Karen Latchana. Cool School Clubs: Fun Ideas & Activities to Build School Spirit, 1 vol. 2011. (Cool School Spirit Ser.). (ENG., Illus.). 32p. (J). (gr. 3-6). 28.50 *(978-1-61714-666-4(8)*, Checkerboard Library) ABDO Publishing Co.

Lewis, Jan, illus. School Trip. 2012. (First Time Ser.). (ENG.). 24p. (J). *(978-1-84643-489-1(0))* Child's Play International Ltd.

Lucas, Eileen. The Little Rock Nine Stand up for Their Rights. Gustavson, Adam, illus. 2011. (History Speaks: Picture Books Plus Reader's Theater Ser.). 48p. pap. 56.72 *(978-0-7613-7634-7(8))* Lerner Publishing Group.

Lusted, Marcia Amidon & Thain, Gerald J. Tinker v. Des Moines: The Right to Protest in Schools, 1 vol. 2012. (Landmark Supreme Court Cases Ser.). (ENG., Illus.). 160p. (J). (gr. 6-12). 37.07 *(978-1-61783-477-6(7))* ABDO Publishing Co.

Marcovitz, Hal. Teens & Career Choices. Developed in Association with the Gallup Organization Staff, ed. 2013. (Gallup Youth Survey: Major Issues & Trends Ser.: 14). 112p. (J). (gr. 7-18). 24.95 *(978-1-4222-2950-7(5))* Mason Crest.

Mattern, Joanne. After School (Después de la Escuela) 2006. (My Day at School/ Mi dia en la escuela Ser.). (ENG & SPA., Illus.). 24p. (gr. k-3). pap. 8.15 *(978-0-8368-7364-1(5)*, Weekly Reader Leveled Readers) Stevens, Gareth Publishing LLLP.

—Despues de la Escuela (After School) 2006. (My Day at School/ Mi dia en la escuela Ser.). (ENG & SPA., Illus.). 24p. (gr. k-3). lib. bdg. 22.00 *(978-0-8368-7357-3(2)*, Weekly Reader Leveled Readers) Stevens, Gareth Publishing LLLP.

McCarney, Rosemary. The Way to School, 1 vol. 2015. (ENG., Illus.). 32p. (J). (gr. 1-4). 18.95 *(978-1-927583-78-4(0))* Second Story Pr. CAN. Dist: Orca Bk. Pubs. USA.

McPherson, Stephanie Sammartino. Stressed Out in School? Learning to Deal with Academic Pressure. 2009. (Issues in Focus Today Ser.). (Illus.). 112p. (J). (gr. 6-18). lib. bdg. 33.27 *(978-0-7660-3069-5(5))* Enslow Pubs., Inc.

Meet Our New Student, 8 vols., Set. Incl. Meet Our New Student from Australia. Weil, Ann. (Illus.). 47p. (J). (gr. 3-7). 2008. lib. bdg. 29.95 *(978-1-58415-652-9(X))*; Meet Our New Student from China. Orr, Tamra. (Illus.). 48p. (YA). (gr. 2-5). 2008. lib. bdg. 29.95 *(978-1-58415-647-5(3))*; Meet Our New Student from Colombia. Murcia, Rebecca Thatcher. (Illus.). 48p. (J). (gr. 1-5). 2008. lib. bdg. 29.95 *(978-1-58415-650-5(3))*; Meet Our New Student from Great Britain. Orr, Tamra. (Illus.). 48p. (J). (gr. 4-7). 2008. lib. bdg. 29.95 *(978-1-58415-648-2(1))*; Meet Our New Student from Haiti. Torres, John A. (Illus.). 48p. (YA). (gr. 2-5). 2008. lib. bdg. 29.95 *(978-1-58415-653-6(8))*; Meet Our New Student from India. Ejaz, Khadija. (Illus.). 48p. (J). (gr. 2-5). 2009. lib. bdg. 25.70 *(978-1-58415-779-3(8))*; Meet Our New Student from Israel. Saul, Laya. (Illus.). 48p. (J). (gr. 3-7). 2008. lib. bdg. 29.95 *(978-1-58415-651-2(1))*; Meet Our New Student from Japan. McManus, Lori. 48p. (J). (gr. 2-5). 2009. 29.95 *(978-1-58415-780-9(1))*; Meet Our New Student from Korea. Kjelle, Marylou Morano. (Illus.). 48p. (YA). (gr. 2-5). 2008. lib. bdg. 29.95 *(978-1-58415-649-9(X))*; Meet Our New Student from Malaysia. Weil, Ann. (Illus.). 48p. (J). (gr. 1-5). 2008. lib. bdg. 29.95 *(978-1-58415-654-3(6))*; Meet Our New Student from Mali. Ogunnaike, Oludamini. (Illus.). 48p. (J). (gr. 2-5). 2009. lib. bdg. 25.70 *(978-1-58415-734-2(8))*; Meet Our New Student from Mexico. Orr, Tamra. (Illus.). 48p. (YA). (gr. 2-5). 2008. lib. bdg. 29.95 *(978-1-58415-646-8(5))*; Meet Our New Student from New Zealand. Weil, Ann. (Illus.). 48p. (J). (gr. 2-5). 2008. lib. bdg. 29.95 *(978-1-58415-657-4(0))*; Meet Our New Student from Nicaragua. Torres, John Albert. 48p. (J). (gr. 2-5). 2009. 29.95 *(978-1-58415-834-9(4))*; Meet Our New Student from Nigeria. Ogunnaike, Anna M. (Illus.). 47p. (YA). (gr. 2-5). 2008. lib. bdg. 29.95 *(978-1-58415-655-0(4))*; Meet Our New Student from Quebec. Weil, Ann. 48p. (J). (gr. 2-5). 2009. 29.95 *(978-1-58415-778-6(X))*; Meet Our New Student from South Africa. Koosman, Melissa. (Illus.). 47p. (J). (gr. 2-5). 2009. lib. bdg. 29.95 *(978-1-58415-781-6(X))*; Meet Our New Student from Tanzania. Weil, Ann. 48p. (YA). (gr. 2-5). 2008. lib. bdg. 29.95 *(978-1-58415-656-7(2))*; Meet Our New Student from Zambia. Torres, John Albert. 48p. (J). (gr. 2-5). 2010. 29.95 *(978-1-58415-735-9(6))*; 2010. Set lib. bdg. 599.00 *(978-1-58415-783-0(6))* Mitchell Lane Pubs., Inc.

Messina, Noreen E. Teenwork: Four Teens Tell All: A Guide for Finding Jobs. 2005. (Illus.). 126p. (gr. 6-12). per. 12.75 *(978-1-59070-598-8(X))* Goodheart-Willcox Pub.

Meyer, Terry. Navigating a New School. 2012. (Middle School Survival Handbook Ser.). (ENG., Illus.). 64p. (YA). (gr. 5-8). lib. bdg. 31.95 *(978-1-4488-8312-7(1)*, Rosen Reference) Rosen Publishing Group, Inc., The.

Meyer, Terry Teague. Navigating a New School. 2012. (Middle School Survival Handbook Ser.). (ENG., Illus.). 64p. (YA). (gr. 5-8). pap. 12.95 *(978-1-4488-8319-6(9)*, Rosen Reference) Rosen Publishing Group, Inc., The.

Miller, Jake. Who's Who in a School Community. 2005. (Communities at Work Ser.). (ENG., Illus.). 24p. (gr. 2-3). pap. 8.25 *(978-1-4042-5030-7(1)*, PowerKids Pr.) Rosen Publishing Group, Inc., The.

—Who's Who in School Community. 2005. (Communities at Work Ser.). (Illus.). 24p. (J). (gr. 2-4). lib. bdg. 22.60 *(978-1-4042-2788-0(1)*, PowerKids Pr.) Rosen Publishing Group, Inc., The.

Miller, Karen. Student Life. 2011. (Opposing Viewpoints Ser.). (ENG.). 240p. pap. 29.45 *(978-0-7377-4991-5(1))*; 224p. (gr. 12-12). 48.80 *(978-0-7377-4990-8(3))* Cengage Gale. (Greenhaven Pr., Inc.).

Newsom, Tony. High School Student Safety Tips. 2007. (ENG., Illus.). 95p. (YA). pap. 8.99 *(978-0-9787143-5-2(0))* Carrington Bks.

—Middle School Student Safety Tips. 2007. (ENG., Illus.). 43p. (YA). pap. 8.99 *(978-0-9787143-4-5(2))* Carrington Bks.

—Student Safety Tips: 45 that Every 3rd - 5th Grader Must Know!, 2 vols., Spanish Edition. 2nd ed. 2007. (ENG., Illus.). 52p. pap. 6.99 *(978-0-9787143-2-1(6))* Carrington Bks.

Palmer, Erin. School Dances, Yes or No. 2016. (Seeing Both Sides Ser.). (ENG.). 32p. (gr. 3-6). 32.79 *(978-1-68191-384-1(4))* Rourke Educational Media.

Pearsall, Shelley. All of the Above. Steptoe, Javaka, illus. 2007. 234p. (gr. 3-7). 18.00 *(978-0-7569-8144-0(1))* Perfection Learning Corp.

Reid, Stephanie. School, 1 vol. 2011. (Early Childhood Themes Ser.). (ENG.). 16p. (J). (gr. -1-2). pap. 6.99 *(978-1-4333-2353-9(2))*; pap. 19.99 *(978-1-4333-2354-6(0))* Teacher Created Materials, Inc.

Rice, Dona Herweck. Big Kid School, 1 vol. 2011. (Early Childhood Themes Ser.). (ENG.). 16p. (J). (gr. -1-2). pap. 6.99 *(978-1-4333-2355-3(9))*; pap. 19.99 *(978-1-4333-2356-0(7))* Teacher Created Materials, Inc.

Ross, Michael & Johnson, Greg. 10 Reasons to Stay Christian in High School: A Guide to Staying Sane When Everyone Else Has Jumped off the Deep End. 2015. (ENG.). 192p. (YA). pap. 7.99 *(978-1-63058-375-0(8)*, GoTandem) Barbour Publishing, Inc.

Ruurs, Margriet. My School in the Rain Forest: How Children Attend School Around the World. 2009. (ENG., Illus.). 32p. (J). (gr. 2-4). 17.95 *(978-1-59078-601-7(7))* Boyds Mills Pr.

Shea, John M. Self-Injury & Cutting: Stopping the Pain. 2013. (Helpline: Teen Issues & Answers Ser.). (ENG., Illus.). 80p. (YA). (gr. 7-12). lib. bdg. 33.25 *(978-1-4488-9448-2(4)*, Rosen Classroom) Rosen Publishing Group, Inc., The.

Swim, Luann. Cracking the System. 2012. 60p. pap. 29.95 *(978-1-937065-00-3(6))* B & B Educational Advancement & Pubns., Inc.

Twin Talk: Advice from a TV Talk Show. 2005. (Illus.). 37p. *(978-0-439-12406-5(9))* Scholastic, Inc.

Vizzini, Ned. Teen Angst? Naaah... A Quasi-Autobiography. 2010. (ENG.). 272p. (YA). (gr. 7). pap. 9.99 *(978-0-385-73945-0(1)*, Ember) Random Hse. Children's Bks.

Whyte, Donna. What Makes a Good Teacher? Here's What the Kids Say! Garamella, Joyce Orchard, illus. 2003. 32p. (J). 6.95 *(978-1-884548-59-8(8)*, Crystal Springs Bks.) Staff Development for Educators.

Words for All Time: Students Letters to Holocaust Survivors. 2008. (YA). mass mkt. 19.95 *(978-0-9793771-6-7(1))* ComteQ Publishing.

Wright, Pamela. Rant Room. 2011. 82p. pap. 19.95 *(978-1-4560-9428-7(9))* America Star Bks.

STUDENTS—EMPLOYMENT

Messina, Noreen E. Now Hiring: A Story of Four Teens Finding Their First Jobs. 3rd ed. 2009. (ENG.). 126p. (gr. 6-14). 26.64 *(978-1-60525-177-6(1))* Goodheart-Willcox Pub.

—Teenwork: Four Teens Tell All: A Guide for Finding Jobs. 2005. (Illus.). 126p. (gr. 6-12). per. 12.75 *(978-1-59070-598-8(X))* Goodheart-Willcox Pub.

Troutman, Kathryn K. Creating Your High School Resume, Second Edition: A Step-by-Step Guide to Preparing an Effective Resume for Jobs, College & Training Programs. 2nd ed. 2003. (Illus.). 160p. pap. 10.95 *(978-1-56370-902-9(3)*, JIST Works) JIST Publishing.

STUDENTS—FICTION

Abrams, Amir. Diva Rules. 2015. (Mcpherson High Ser.). (ENG., Illus.). 300p. (YA). (gr. 9). pap. 9.95 *(978-0-7582-9480-7(8)*, Dafina) Kensington Publishing Corp.

Abramsen, Ruth M. Akeelah's Spider. 2008. 36p. per. 13.95 *(978-1-59800-440-3(9))* Outskirts Pr., Inc.

Achi, Taro. Mamoru the Shadow Protector Volume 1. 2008. (ENG., Illus.). 176p. (YA). pap. 9.95 *(978-1-59796-183-7(3))* DrMaster Pubns. Inc.

Alegria, Malin. Cruzar el Limite (Crossing the Boundary) 2012. (Border Town (Spanish) Ser.: 1). (SPA.). lib. bdg. 16.00 *(978-0-606-26239-2(3)*, Turtleback) Turtleback Bks.

Alexander, Shannon Lee. Life after Juliet. 2016. (ENG.). 304p. (J). 16.99 *(978-1-63375-323-5(9)*, 9781633753235) Entangled Publishing, LLC.

Alfonsi, Alice. Freaked Out. 2004. 148p. (J). lib. bdg. 16.92 *(978-1-4242-0687-2(1))* Fitzgerald Bks.

Allen-Vath, Ami. Prom Bitch. 2016. (ENG.). 240p. (J). (gr. 8). 16.99 *(978-1-63450-184-2(5)*, Sky Pony Pr.) Skyhorse Publishing Co., Inc.

Alpine, Rachele. Operation Pucker Up. 2015. (Mix Ser.). (ENG., Illus.). 256p. (J). (gr. 4-8). 17.99 *(978-1-4814-3236-8(2)*, Aladdin) Simon & Schuster Children's Publishing.

Anderson, Jeff. Zack Delacruz 2 (working Title) 2016. (Zack Delacruz Ser.). (ENG., Illus.). 192p. (J). (gr. 5-8). 12.95 *(978-1-4549-2067-0(X))* Sterling Publishing Co., Inc.

Anna, Jennifer. Yen Shei & the American Bonsai. 2009. (ENG., Illus.). 88p. (YA). pap. 14.99 *(978-1-59092-153-1(4))* Blue Forge Pr.

Anonymous. The Book of David. 2014. (ENG., Illus.). 288p. (YA). (gr. 9). pap. 9.99 *(978-1-4424-8985-1(5)*, Simon Pulse) Simon Pulse.

Baker, Mary. Christmas Annie. 2009. 70p. pap. 7.96 *(978-0-557-17289-4(6))* Lulu Pr., Inc.

Banim, Lisa. Hands off My Crush-Boy! 2004. 125p. (J). lib. bdg. 16.92 *(978-1-4242-0684-1(7))* Fitzgerald Bks.

Banks, Anna. Joyride. 2015. (ENG.). 288p. (YA). (gr. 7). 17.99 *(978-1-250-03961-3(4)*, 9781250039613) Feiwel & Friends.

Bargiel, Nina G. & Amsterdam, Shane. Fintastic Friends Forever. 2016. (Illus.). 32p. (J). ***(978-1-5182-1661-9(7))*** Little Brown & Co.

Barnholdt, Lauren. Heat of the Moment. 2015. (Moment of Truth Ser.: 1). (ENG.). 304p. (YA). (gr. 8). pap. 9.99 *(978-0-06-232139-8(0)*, HarperTeen) HarperCollins Pubs.

—One Moment in Time. 2015. (Moment of Truth Ser.: 2). (ENG.). 304p. (YA). (gr. 8). pap. 9.99 *(978-0-06-232141-1(2)*, HarperTeen) HarperCollins Pubs.

Bean, Raymond. Blown Away, 0 vols. unabr. ed. 2012. (Sweet Farts Ser.: 3). (ENG.). 172p. (J). (gr. 4-6). pap. 9.95 *(978-1-61218-251-3(8)*, 9781612182513, Amazon Children's Publishing) Amazon Publishing.

—Rippin' It Old School, 0 vols. unabr. ed. 2010. (Sweet Farts Ser.: 2). (ENG.). 184p. (J). (gr. 4-6). pap. 9.95 *(978-1-935597-08-7(6)*, 9781935597087, Two Lions) Amazon Publishing.

—Sweet Farts, 0 vols. unabr. ed. 2012. (Sweet Farts Ser.: 1). (ENG.). 138p. (J). (gr. 4-6). pap. 9.95 *(978-1-61218-250-6(X)*, 9781612182506, Amazon Children's Publishing) Amazon Publishing.

Beck, Ricky. A Puzzled Heart. 2008. 85p. pap. 19.95 *(978-1-60441-385-4(9))* America Star Bks.

Bennett, W. J., Jr. Sydney & Garrett's Great Arkansas Adventury. 2005. (J). pap. *(978-0-9794044-6-7(0))* Archeological Assessments, Inc.

Benoit, Charles. You. 2012. (ENG.). 256p. (YA). (gr. 8). pap. 8.99 *(978-0-06-194706-3(7)*, HarperTeen) HarperCollins Pubs.

Benton, Jim. Nobody's Perfect. I'm As Close As It Gets. Benton, Jim, illus. 2013. (Dear Dumb Diary Year Two Ser.: 3). (ENG., Illus.). 144p. (J). (gr. 3-7). pap. 5.99 *(978-0-545-37764-5(1)*, Scholastic Paperbacks) Scholastic, Inc.

—Nobody's Perfect. I'm As Close As It Gets. 2013. (Dear Dumb Diary: Year Two Ser.: 3). lib. bdg. 16.00 *(978-0-606-31535-7(7)*, Turtleback) Turtleback Bks.

—You Can Bet on That. Benton, Jim, illus. 2014. (Dear Dumb Diary Year Two Ser.: 5). (ENG., Illus.). 160p. (J). (gr. 3-7). pap. 5.99 *(978-0-545-64257-6(4)*, Scholastic Paperbacks) Scholastic, Inc.

Binder, John. The Girl Who Applied Everywhere. 2011. 160p. (YA). 17.99 *(978-1-936679-02-7(7))* Wicker Park Pr., Ltd.

Bittmann, Suzy. Life with Molly Mcgee - Sports Chick: Caught in a Pickle. 2010. 211p. pap. 15.99 *(978-0-557-46339-8(4))* Lulu Pr., Inc.

Blanda, Dominick. The Super Duper Kid Fantastic. 2009. 32p. pap. 14.99 *(978-1-4389-4566-8(3))* AuthorHouse.

Bow, James. The Young City: The Unwritten Books. 2008. (Unwritten Bks.: 3). (ENG.). 264p. (YA). (gr. 7). pap. 12.99 *(978-1-55002-846-1(4))* Dundurn CAN. Dist: Ingram Publisher Services.

Brian, Kate, pseud. Cruel Love. 2011. (Privilege Ser.). (ENG.). 224p. (YA). (gr. 9). pap. 9.99 *(978-1-4424-0788-6(3)*, Simon & Schuster Bks. For Young Readers) Simon & Schuster Bks. For Young Readers.

—Sweet Deceit. 2010. (Privilege Ser.: Bk. 4). (ENG.). 224p. (YA). (gr. 9-18). pap. 9.99 *(978-1-4169-6762-0(1)*, Simon & Schuster Bks. For Young Readers) Simon & Schuster Bks. For Young Readers.

Bristow, Catherine. My Strange & Terrible Malady. 2008. (YA). pap. 15.95 *(978-1-934575-19-2(4))* Autism Asperger Publishing Co.

Brown, Teri. Read My Lips. 2008. (ENG.). 256p. (YA). (gr. 9-12). pap. 8.99 *(978-1-4169-5868-0(1)*, Simon Pulse) Simon Pulse.

Bryant, Ann. School Friends - Drama at Silver Spires. 2013. pap. 5.99 *(978-0-7945-3147-8(4)*, Usborne) EDC Publishing.

—School Friends - Welcome to Silver Spires. 2013. pap. 5.99 *(978-0-7945-3146-1(6)*, Usborne) EDC Publishing.

Bryant, Jen. Ringside 1925: Views from the Scopes Trial. 2009. (ENG.). 240p. (J). (gr. 5). 7.99 *(978-0-440-42189-4(6)*, Yearling) Random Hse. Children's Bks.

Buckley, Kate. Choices: A Novel. 2009. 208p. (J). pap. 14.95 *(978-1-935359-12-8(6))* Book Pubs. Network.

Burke, Morgan. Get It Started. 2010. (Party Room Ser.: 1). (ENG.). 272p. (J). (gr. 11). pap. 12.99 *(978-1-4424-1420-4(0)*, Simon Pulse) Simon Pulse.

Burleigh, Cyril. The Hilltop Boys on the River. 2005. 26.95 *(978-1-4218-0327-2(5)*, 1st World Library - Literary Society) 1st World Publishing, Inc.

Cabot, Meg. Party Princess, Vol. VII. 2008. (Princess Diaries: 7). (ENG.). 320p. (YA). (gr. 8). pap. 9.99 *(978-0-06-154374-6(8)*, HarperTeen) HarperCollins Pubs.

Caine, Rachel, pseud. Fall of Night. 2013. (Morganville Vampires Ser.: 14). (ENG.). 368p. (YA). (gr. 9). pap. 9.99 *(978-0-451-41426-7(8)*, Berkley) Penguin Publishing Group.

Calame, Don. Call the Shots. 2013. (ENG.). 464p. (YA). (gr. 9). pap. 7.99 *(978-0-7636-6454-1(5))* Candlewick Pr.

—Swim the Fly. 2010. (ENG., Illus.). 352p. (YA). (gr. 9). pap. 7.99 *(978-0-7636-4776-6(4))* Candlewick Pr.

Cannon, Chris. Blackmail Boyfriend. 2015. (ENG., Illus.). 260p. (J). pap. 16.99 *(978-1-943892-03-7(2))* Entangled Publishing, LLC.

Carolina Esquivel Rael. Anthony P the Talker. 2009. 44p. pap. 16.99 *(978-1-4389-5861-3(7))* AuthorHouse.

Carter, Aimée. The Goddess Test. 2011. (Goddess Test Ser.: 1). lib. bdg. 20.85 *(978-0-606-26943-8(6)*, Turtleback) Turtleback Bks.

Carter, Nikki & Elliott, Kevin. The Break-Up Diaries, Vol. 2. 2011. (ENG.). 288p. (YA). (gr. 9). pap. 9.95 *(978-0-7582-6888-4(2)*, K-Teen/Dafina) Kensington Publishing Corp.

Chapman, Allen. Frank Roscoes Secret or the Darewell Chu. 2007. pap. *(978-1-4065-1431-5(4))* Dodo Pr.

Charbonneau, Joelle. Need. 2017. (ENG.). 352p. (YA). (gr. 7). pap. 9.99 *(978-0-544-93883-0(6)*, HMH Books For Young Readers) Houghton Mifflin Harcourt Publishing Co.

Cheng, Haw. Sixth Grade Was a Nightmare, & Seventh Is Worse: A 12-Year Old Speaks Out. Thurman, Joann M., ed. Costner, Howard, illus. Date not set. 128p. (J). (gr. 3-9). 11.95 *(978-0-89896-335-9(4))* Larksdale.

Clark-Elliott, Mary. The Day Ms. Qualbaum Came to Visit. 2013. 44p. pap. 20.72 *(978-1-4907-0921-5(5))* Trafford Publishing.

Clements, Andrew. Frindle. Selznick, Brian, illus. 105p. (J). (gr. 3-5). pap. 4.50 *(978-0-8072-1522-7(8)*, Listening Library) Random Hse. Audio Publishing Group.

—Frindle. unabr. ed. 2004. (Middle Grade Cassette Librariestm Ser.). 105p. (J). (gr. 3-7). pap. 29.00 incl. audio *(978-0-8072-7994-6(3)*, S YA 961 SP, Listening Library) Random Hse. Audio Publishing Group.

—Jake Drake, Class Clown. Pedersen, Janet, illus. 2007. (Jake Drake Ser.: Bk. 4). (ENG.). 96p. (J). (gr. 2-5). pap. 5.99 *(978-1-4169-4912-1(7)*, Atheneum Bks. for Young Readers) Simon & Schuster Children's Publishing.

—Jake Drake, Teacher's Pet. Pedersen, Janet, illus. 2007. (Jake Drake Ser.: 3). (ENG.). 96p. (J). (gr. 2-5). pap. 5.99 *(978-1-4169-3932-0(6)*, Atheneum Bks. for Young Readers) Simon & Schuster Children's Publishing.

Cleveland, Marie. Jason's Giant Dilemma: A Storybook Land Adventure. 2007. 76p. per. 19.95 *(978-1-4241-7811-7(8))* America Star Bks.

Cole, Cathy. The Trouble with Love. 2015. 200p. (J). ***(978-0-545-87877-7(2))*** Scholastic, Inc.

Colfer, Chris. Struck by Lightning: The Carson Phillips Journal. (ENG.). 272p. (YA). (gr. 10-17). 2013. pap. 10.00 *(978-0-316-23293-7(9))* 2012. 17.99 *(978-0-316-23295-1(5))* Little, Brown Bks. for Young Readers.

Constantine, Robin. The Promise of Amazing. 2015. (ENG.). 400p. (YA). (gr. 9). pap. 9.99 *(978-0-06-227949-1(1))* HarperCollins Pubs.

Cook, Eileen. Getting Revenge on Lauren Wood. 2010. (ENG.). (YA). (gr. 9). 288p. pap. 9.99 *(978-1-4424-0976-7(2))*; 272p. 15.99 *(978-1-4169-7433-8(4))* Simon Pulse. (Simon Pulse).

Cooper, T. & Glock-Cooper, Allison. Changers Book Two: Oryon. 2015. (Changers Ser.). (ENG., Illus.). 288p. (J). (gr. 6). pap. 11.95 *(978-1-61775-307-7(6)*, Black Sheep) Akashic Bks.

—Drew. 2014. (Changers Ser.). (ENG., Illus.). 288p. (gr. 6). pap. 11.95 *(978-1-61775-195-0(2)*, Black Sheep) Akashic Bks.

Crane, Cheri J. Moment of Truth: A Novel. 2005. 238p. (YA). *(978-1-59156-727-1(0))* Covenant Communications.

Craw, Gloria. Atlantis Quest. 2016. (Atlantis Rising Ser.: 2). (ENG.). 356p. (YA). 16.99 *(978-1-63375-283-2(6)*, 9781633752832) Entangled Publishing, LLC.

Crilley, Mark. Autumn. Crilley, Mark, illus. 2007. (Miki Falls Ser.: 3). (ENG., Illus.). 176p. (YA). (gr. 8-12). pap. 8.99 *(978-0-06-084618-3(6))* HarperCollins Pubs.

Cummings, C. R. The Cadet Under-Officer: The Army Cadets. 2nd ed. 2013. 368p. pap. *(978-0-9875975-5-7(8))* DoctorZed Publishing.

Daniels, Babygirl. Glitter. 2009. (ENG., Illus.). 208p. (YA). (gr. 9). pap. 9.95 *(978-1-60162-198-6(1)*, Urban Renaissance) Kensington Publishing Corp.

Danziger, Paula. It's a Fair Day, Amber Brown. Ross, Tony, illus. 2003. (Readalongs for Beginning Readers Ser.). (J). 25.95 incl. audio *(978-1-59112-246-3(5))*; pap. 29.95 incl. audio *(978-1-59112-247-0(3))* Live Oak Media.

Danzinger, Paula. Get Ready for Second Grade, Amber Brown. Ross, Tony, illus. 2003. (Readalongs for Beginning Readers Ser.). (J). 25.95 incl. audio *(978-1-59112-234-0(1))*; pap. 29.95 incl. audio *(978-1-59112-235-7(X))* Live Oak Media.

David, Christopher. Denholme & the Skeleton Mystery. 2006. 274p. pap. 22.52 *(978-1-4120-8014-9(2))* Trafford Publishing.

de Campi, Alex. Kat & Mouse. 2017. (ENG., Illus.). 96p. pap. 5.99 *(978-1-59816-549-4(6)*, 9781598165494) TOKYOPOP, Inc.

De Pauw, Linda Grant. In Search of Molly Pitcher. 164p. 2008. pap. 12.00 *(978-1-4357-0607-1(2))* 2007. 30.00 *(978-1-4303-1345-8(5))* Lulu Pr., Inc.

Delsol, Wendy. Flock. 2013. (ENG.). 400p. (YA). (gr. 7). pap. 8.99 *(978-0-7636-6467-1(7))* Candlewick Pr.

Divine, L. Hustlin' 2009. (Drama High Ser.: 7). lib. bdg. 26.95 *(978-0-606-00156-4(5)*, Turtleback) Turtleback Bks.

—Keep It Movin' 2009. (Drama High Ser.: 8). lib. bdg. 20.80 *(978-0-606-00157-1(3)*, Turtleback) Turtleback Bks.

Donovan, Rebecca. Out of Breath, 0 vols. unabr. ed. 2013. (Breathing Ser.: 3). (ENG.). 432p. (YA). (gr. 10-12). pap. 9.99 *(978-1-4778-1718-6(2)*, 9781477817186, Amazon Children's Publishing) Amazon Publishing.

Duffield, W. J. The Radio Boys in the Thousand Islands. 2006. (ENG.). 150p. pap. 18.99 *(978-1-4264-6513-0(0))*; 166p. pap. 21.99 *(978-1-4264-6572-7(6))* Creative Media Partners, LLC.

Duncan, Lois. Killing Mr. Griffin. 2010. (ENG.). 272p. (YA). (gr. 7-17). pap. 10.99 *(978-0-316-09900-4(7))* Little, Brown Bks. for Young Readers.

—Killing Mr. Griffin. 223p. (YA). (gr. 7-18). pap. 4.50 *(978-0-8072-1373-5(X)*, Listening Library) Random Hse. Audio Publishing Group.

Eggleston, Edward. The Hoosier Schoolboy. 2013. (Collected Works of Edward Eggleston). 425p. reprint ed. lthr. 79.00 *(978-0-7812-1178-9(6))* Reprint Services Corp.

—The Schoolmaster's Stories for Boys & Girls. 2013. (Collected Works of Edward Eggleston). 279p. reprint ed. lthr. 79.00 *(978-0-7812-1176-5(X))* Reprint Services Corp.

Ennis, Ryan R. The Thursday Surprise: A Story about Kids & Autism. Stroud, Brenda, illus. 2011. 86p. pap. 9.95 (978-0-9843426-7-9(2)) G Publishing LLC.
Esham, Barbara. Last to Finish: A Story about the Smartest Boy in Math Class. Gordon, Mike, illus. 2008. 32p. (J). (gr. k-18). 16.95 (978-1-60336-456-0(0), Adventures of Everyday Geniuses, The) Mainstream Connections Publishing.
Fairchild Hawks, Lyn. How Wendy Redbird Dancing Survived the Dark Ages of Nought. 2013. (ENG.). 286p. (C). pap. 16.99 (978-0-9888837-2-7(4)) Hawks, Lyn.
Faris, Stephanie. Piper Morgan in Charge. 2016. (Piper Morgan Ser.: 2). (ENG., Illus.). 112p. (J). (gr. 1-4). pap. 5.99 (978-1-4814-5711-8(X), Aladdin) Simon & Schuster Children's Publishing.
Farley, Robin. Mia & the Girl with a Twirl. 2013. (Mia I Can Read Bks.). (J). lib. bdg. 13.55 (978-0-606-31811-2(9), Turtleback) Turtleback Bks.
Feder, Aliza & Sofer, Rochel. We Need to Talk. 2008. 250p. 18.95 (978-1-934440-30-8(2), Devora Publishing) Simcha Media Group.
Fergus, Maureen. Recipe for Disaster. 2009. (ENG.). 256p. (J). (gr. 5-9). 8.95 (978-1-55453-320-6(1)); 18.95 (978-1-55453-319-0(8)) Kids Can Pr., Ltd. CAN. Dist: Hachette Bk. Group.
Ferguson, Donald. The Chums of Scranton High at Ice Hockey. 2007. 124p. per. (978-1-4065-2361-4(5)) Dodo Pr.
—Chums of Scranton High at Ice Hockey. 2006. 25.95 (978-1-4218-2936-4(3)); pap. 10.95 (978-1-4218-3036-0(1)) 1st World Publishing, Inc.
—Chums of Scranton High on the Cinder Pat. 2006. 25.95 (978-1-4218-2937-1(1)); pap. 10.95 (978-1-4218-3037-7(X)) 1st World Publishing, Inc.
—The Chums of Scranton High on the Cinder Path. 2007. 124p. per. (978-1-4065-2363-8(1)) Dodo Pr.
—The Chums of Scranton High, or, Hugh Morgan's Uphill Fight. 2007. 136p. per. (978-1-4065-2362-1(3)) Dodo Pr.
—Chums of Scranton High Out for the Penna. 2006. 25.95 (978-1-4218-2938-8(X)); pap. 10.95 (978-1-4218-3038-4(8)) 1st World Publishing, Inc.
—The Chums of Scranton High Out for the Pennant, or, in the Three Town League. 2007. 124p. per. (978-1-4065-2364-5(X)) Dodo Pr.
Ferguson, Jo Ann. The Cabinet of Souls. 2016. lib. bdg. 17.20 (978-0-606-38787-3(0)) Turtleback Bks.
Ferguson, John B. Cindy Before. 2003. (YA). per. 10.95 (978-0-9728144-4-7(2)) Casion Pr.
Figueroa, Acton. So Not the Drama. 2005. (Illus.). 79p. (J). (978-1-4156-3929-0(9)) Disney Pr.
Finn, Perdita. Stealing the Show. Moran, Mike, illus. 2006. (Time Flyers Ser.: Vol. 1). 109p. (J). pap. (978-0-439-74433-1(4)) Scholastic, Inc.
Fischer, JoAnn. Our Teacher Is A Fish! 2008. (ENG.). 34p. pap. 10.00 (978-1-4196-7477-8(3)) CreateSpace Independent Publishing Platform.
Fitzpatrick, Huntley. The Boy Most Likely To. 2015. (ENG.). 432p. (YA). (gr. 9). 17.99 (978-0-8037-4142-3(1), Dial Bks) Penguin Young Readers Group.
Flower, Graham Jessie. Grace Harlowe's Return to Overton Campus. l.t. ed. 2007. (ENG.). 154p. pap. 19.99 (978-1-4264-3783-0(8)); 146p. pap. 19.99 (978-1-4264-3853-0(2)) Creative Media Partners, LLC.
—Grace Harlowe's Return to Overton Campus. 2004. reprint ed. 1.99 (978-1-4192-2222-1(8)); pap. 20.95 (978-1-4191-2222-4(3)) Kessinger Publishing, LLC.
—Grace Harlowe's Second Year at Overton College. 2004. reprint ed. pap. 1.99 (978-1-4192-2223-8(6)); pap. 20.95 (978-1-4191-2223-1(1)) Kessinger Publishing, LLC.
Flower, Jessie Graham. Grace Harlowe's Return to Overton Campus. 2007. 260p. 29.95 (978-1-4344-9674-4(0)); per. 19.95 (978-1-4344-9673-7(2)) Wildside Pr., LLC.
—Grace Harlowe's Second Year at Overton Campus. 2007. 252p. 29.95 (978-1-4344-9676-8(7)); per. 19.95 (978-1-4344-9675-1(9)) Wildside Pr., LLC.
—Grace Harlowe's Sophomore Year at High School. 2007. 256p. 29.95 (978-1-4344-9678-2(3)); per. 19.95 (978-1-4344-9677-5(5)) Wildside Pr., LLC.
—Grace Harlowe's Third Year at Overton College. 2007. 252p. 29.95 (978-1-4344-9680-5(5)); per. 19.95 (978-1-4344-9679-9(1)) Wildside Pr., LLC.
Foglia, Auttem. The Big Picture. 2010. 48p. pap. 10.59 (978-1-4520-6681-3(7)) AuthorHouse.
Foglio, Kaja & Foglio, Phil. Agatha Heterodyne & the Clockwork Princess: A Gaslamp Fantasy with Adventure, Romance & Mad Science. Foglio, Kaja & Foglio, Phil, eds. 2013. (ENG., Illus.). 112p. (YA). pap. 25.00 (978-1-890856-39-7(8), 9781890856397) Studio Foglio, LLC.
Frank, E. R. Friction. 2004. (ENG.). 208p. (YA). (gr. 7). reprint ed. pap. 10.99 (978-0-689-85385-2(8), Simon Pulse) Simon Pulse.
Freeman, Hilary. The Boy from France. 2012. (ENG.). 192p. (YA). (gr. 8). pap. 11.99 (978-1-84812-301-4(9)) Bonnier Publishing GBR. Dist: Independent Pubs. Group.
Froley, Margaux. Escape Theory. 2014. (ENG., Illus.). 288p. (YA). (gr. 9). pap. 9.99 (978-1-61695-342-3(X), Soho Teen) Soho Pr., Inc.
Fujinari, Yuuki. Ugly Duckling's Love Revolution, Vol. 3. 2011. (Ugly Duckling's Love Revolution Ser.: 3). (ENG., Illus.). 192p. (gr. 8-17). pap. 11.99 (978-0-7595-3177-2(3), Yen Pr.) Orbit.
Fujishima, Kosuke. Oh My Goddess!, Vol. 25. Fujishima, Kosuke, illus. 2007. (Oh My Goddess! Ser.). (ENG., Illus.). 176p. pap. 10.95 (978-1-59307-644-3(4)) Dark Horse Comics.
Gallardo, Adam J. Zombified. 2015. (Zombie Apocalypse Ser.). (ENG.). 352p. (YA). (gr. 13). pap. 9.95 (978-1-61773-100-6(5), K-Teen) Kensington Publishing Corp.
Gardner, Hunter. School. 2014. (ENG.). 250p. (YA). (gr. 7-12). pap. 16.99 (978-1-938463-14-3(5)) Bitingduck Pr.
Gayle, Emi. Night & Day. 2014. 132p. (YA). (978-1-937744-55-7(8)) J. Taylor Publishing.
Gibsen, Cole. Life Unaware. 2015. 284p. (YA). (978-1-62844-152-9(6)) Entangled Publishing, LLC.
Glass, George. Black-Tie Spy. 2013. 94p. (J). pap. (978-0-545-47271-5(7)) Scholastic, Inc.
Goode, John. End of the Innocence. 2016. (ENG., Illus.). (J). 29.99 (978-1-63533-008-3(4), Harmony Ink Pr.) Dreamspinner Pr.
Goodwin, Vincent. Body-Snatcher, 1 vol. 2014. (Graphic Horror Set 3 Ser.). (ENG.). 32p. (J). (gr. 5-8). lib. bdg. 28.50 (978-1-62402-013-1(5), Graphic Planet) Magic Wagon.
Gottesfeld, Jeff. Choices. 2014. (Campus Confessions Ser.: 3). (YA). lib. bdg. 20.80 (978-0-606-34000-7(9), Turtleback) Turtleback Bks.
—Frenemies. 2014. (Campus Confessions Ser.: 2). (YA). lib. bdg. 20.80 (978-0-606-33999-5(X), Turtleback) Turtleback Bks.
Grabenstein, Chris. I Funny: A Middle School Story. Patterson, James, ed. Park, Laura, illus. 2012. 303p. (J). 11.99 (978-0-316-22638-7(6), 1351607) Little Brown & Co.
Grant, Robert. Jack in the Bush or A Summer on a Salmon River. 2005. pap. 33.95 (978-1-4179-5573-2(2)) Kessinger Publishing, LLC.
Gray, Laurie. Maybe I Will. 2013. 212p. pap. 14.95 (978-1-935462-72-9(5)) Luminis Bks., Inc.
Greene, Janice. The 75-Cent Son, 1 vol. unabr. ed. 2010. (Q Reads Ser.). (ENG.). 32p. (YA). (gr. 9-12). pap. 6.95 (978-1-61651-186-9(9)) Saddleback Educational Publishing, Inc.
Greer, Hannah. The Gift of Re, the Adventures of the Whiz Kids. 2009. 200p. 24.50 (978-1-60860-466-1(7), Eloquent Bks.) Strategic Book Publishing & Rights Agency (SBPRA).
Gregorio, I. W. None of the Above. 2015. (ENG.). 352p. (YA). (gr. 9). 17.99 (978-0-06-233531-9(6)) HarperCollins Pubs.
Gutman, Dan. Mayor Hubble Is in Trouble! 2012. (My Weirder School Ser.: 6). (J). lib. bdg. 14.75 (978-0-606-26525-6(2), Turtleback) Turtleback Bks.
Hancock, H. Irving. The High School Captain of the Team. rev. ed. 2006. 212p. 27.95 (978-1-4218-1740-8(3)); pap. 12.95 (978-1-4218-1840-5(X)) 1st World Publishing, Inc. (1st World Library - Literary Society).
—The High School Captain of the Team. 2007. 176p. per. (978-1-4065-1987-7(1)) Dodo Pr.
—The High School Freshmen. rev. ed. 2006. 212p. 27.95 (978-1-4218-1741-5(1)); pap. 12.95 (978-1-4218-1841-2(8)) 1st World Publishing, Inc. (1st World Library - Literary Society).
—The High School Freshmen. 2007. 180p. per. (978-1-4065-1988-4(X)) Dodo Pr.
—The High School Left End. rev. ed. 2006. 212p. 27.95 (978-1-4218-1742-2(X)); pap. 12.95 (978-1-4218-1842-9(6)) 1st World Publishing, Inc. (1st World Library - Literary Society).
—The High School Left End. 2007. 176p. per. (978-1-4065-1989-1(8)) Dodo Pr.
—The High School Pitcher. 2007. 176p. per. (978-1-4065-1990-7(1)) Dodo Pr.
Hapka, Catherine, pseud. Friends 4 Ever? 2008. (High School Musical Stories from East High Ser.). 124p. (J). (gr. 3-7). 12.65 (978-0-7569-8820-3(9)) Perfection Learning Corp.
Hautman, Pete. What Boys Really Want. 2012. (ENG.). 304p. (J). (gr. 7). 17.99 (978-0-545-11315-1(6), Scholastic Pr.) Scholastic, Inc.
Hawkins, Rachel. Hex Hall, Bk. 1. 2010. (ENG.). 336p. (J). (gr. 7-17). 16.99 (978-1-4231-2130-5(9)) Hyperion Pr.
Hawthorne, Mike, illus. Machine Teen: History 101001. 2012. (ENG.). 120p. (J). (gr. 4-17). pap. 14.99 (978-0-7851-6486-9(3)) Marvel Worldwide, Inc.
Heydt, Scott. Mice Don't Taste Like Chicken. Aaron, Rich, illus. 2011. 188p. pap. 13.00 (978-0-9830109-2-0(7)) Helm Publishing.
Hoena, Blake A. Raw, 1 vol. Cano, Fernando, illus. 2013. (Tony Hawk: Live2Skate Ser.). (ENG.). 72p. (gr. 4-5). pap. 5.95 (978-1-4342-6188-5(3)); lib. bdg. 25.32 (978-1-4342-4086-6(X)) Stone Arch Bks.
Holder, Nancy & Viguié, Debbie. Legacy & Spellbound. 2008. (Wicked Ser.). (ENG.). 672p. (YA). (gr. 9). pap. 8.99 (978-1-4169-7117-7(3), Simon Pulse) Simon Pulse.
Holm, Jennifer L. Middle School Is Worse Than Meatloaf: A Year Told Through Stuff. Castaldi, Elicia, illus. 2011. (ENG.). 128p. (J). (gr. 3-7). pap. 8.99 (978-1-4424-3663-3(8), Atheneum Bks. for Young Readers) Simon & Schuster Children's Publishing.
Hunt, Leo. Eight Rivers of Shadow. 2017. (ENG.). 368p. (YA). (gr. 9). pap. 9.99 (978-0-7636-9457-9(6)) Candlewick Pr.
Hurwitz, Kathleen A. Timothy's Tic. Mc Kelvey, Shawn, illus. 2008. 40p. (gr. -1 — 1). 16.99 (978-1-4389-1924-9(7)) AuthorHouse.
Ignatow, Amy. The Long-Distance Dispatch Between Lydia Goldblatt & Julie Graham-Chang. 2011. (Popularity Papers). (ENG., Illus.). 208p. (J). (gr. 3-7). 16.95 (978-0-8109-9724-0(X), Amulet Bks.) Abrams, Inc.
—The Popularity Papers. 2012. (Popularity Papers). (ENG., Illus.). 208p. (J). (gr. 3-7). 16.95 (978-1-4197-0182-5(7), Amulet Bks.) Abrams, Inc.
Ignatow, Amy & Allen, Rinne. The Popularity Papers Bk. 2: The Long-Distance Dispatch Between Lydia Goldblatt & Julie Graham-Chang. 2012. (Popularity Papers). (ENG., Illus.). 208p. (J). (gr. 3-7). pap. 8.95 (978-1-4197-0183-2(5), Amulet Bks.) Abrams, Inc.
Immenschuh, Marilyn Y. Samantha & the Kids of Room 220. 2007. 148p. per. 11.95 (978-0-595-46842-3(X)) iUniverse, Inc.
Inches, Alison. School Gyrls POW Scrapbook. 2010. (School Gyrls Ser.). (ENG.). 64p. (J). pap. 7.99 (978-1-4424-0865-4(0), Simon Spotlight) Simon Spotlight.
Izumi, Kaneyoshi. Seiho Boys' High School!, Vol. 3. Izumi, Kaneyoshi, illus. 2010. (ENG., Illus.). 200p. pap. 9.99 (978-1-4215-3733-7(8)) Viz Media.
Jager, Hartmut. The Secret of the Green Paint: Annette Vetter Adventure #2. 2007. (Illus.). 196p. (YA). pap. 9.95 (978-0-944851-28-9(2)) Earth Star Pubns.
James, Steven. Blur, 0 vols. 2014. (Blur Trilogy Ser.: 1). (ENG.). 368p. (YA). (gr. 7-12). pap. 9.99 (978-1-4778-4727-5(8), 9781477847275, Amazon Children's Publishing) Amazon Publishing.
Jeremiah, Omari. Paper Boy Four: L. O. E. P. S. Worst Nightmare. Rollins, Berni, illus. 2007. 96p. (YA). (gr. 7-12). pap. 12.99 (978-1-929188-15-4(3)) Morton Bks.
Jones, Carrie. Flying. 2016. (Flying Ser.: 1). (ENG.). 256p. (YA). 17.99 (978-0-7653-3657-6(X), 9780765336576, Tor Teen) Doherty, Tom Assocs., LLC.
Jones, Jasmine, adapted by. Just Like Lizzie. 2003. (Lizzie Mcguire Ser.). (Illus.). 153p. (J). 12.65 (978-0-7569-2720-2(X)) Perfection Learning Corp.
—Lizzie Loves Ethan. 2003. (Lizzie Mcguire Ser.). (Illus.). 152p. (J). 12.65 (978-0-7569-2721-9(8)) Perfection Learning Corp.
—Oh, Brother! 2005. 146p. (J). lib. bdg. 16.92 (978-1-4242-0682-7(0)) Fitzgerald Bks.
Kadence, Sam. Unicorns & Rainbow Poop. (J). 2016. (ENG., Illus.). 27.99 (978-1-63477-988-3(6), Harmony Ink Pr.) 2014. 246p. pap. (978-1-63216-417-9(5)) Dreamspinner Pr.
Katcher, Brian. The Improbable Theory of Ana & Zak. 2015. (ENG.). 336p. (YA). (gr. 8). 17.99 (978-0-06-227277-5(2), Tegen, Katherine Bks) HarperCollins Pubs.
Kate, Lauren. Passion. (Fallen Ser.: Bk. 3). (ENG.). (YA). (gr. 7). 2012. 448p. pap. 10.99 (978-0-385-73917-7(6), Ember) 2011. 432p. 17.99 (978-0-385-73916-0(6), Delacorte Pr.) Random Hse. Children's Bks.
—Passion. 2012. (Fallen Ser.: 3). lib. bdg. 22.10 (978-0-606-26410-5(8), Turtleback) Turtleback Bks.
Katschke, Judy. First Grade Feast!/By Judy Katschke; Illustrated by Clare Elsom. Elsom, Clare, illus. 2014. 32p. (J). pap. (978-0-545-75844-4(0)) Scholastic, Inc.
Kelly, Jamie & Benton, Jim. Never Underestimate Your Dumbness. 2008. (Dear Dumb Diary Ser.). (Illus.). 150p. (gr. 4-7). 16.00 (978-0-7569-8814-2(4)) Perfection Learning Corp.
Kelm, Tracy Martin. Light. 2011. 116p. pap. 11.95 (978-1-4327-6308-4(3)) Outskirts Pr., Inc.
Kenneally, Miranda. Catching Jordan. 2011. (Hundred Oaks Ser.: Bk. 1). (ENG.). 288p. (YA). (gr. 7-12). pap. 9.99 (978-1-4022-6227-2(2)) Sourcebooks, Inc.
—Stealing Parker. 2012. (Hundred Oaks Ser.: Bk. 2). (ENG.). 256p. (YA). (gr. 7-12). pap. 10.99 (978-1-4022-7187-8(5)) Sourcebooks, Inc.
Kerick, Mia. Not Broken, Just Bent [Library Edition]. 2014. 180p. pap. 14.99 (978-1-62798-529-1(8), Harmony Ink Pr.) Dreamspinner Pr.
Kern, Peggy. The Test. 2011. (Bluford Ser.: 18). (J). (gr. k-12). pap. 4.95 (978-1-59194-234-4(9)) Townsend Pr.
King, A. S. I Crawl Through It. 2015. (ENG.). 336p. (YA). (gr. 10-17). 18.00 (978-0-316-33409-9(X)) Little, Brown Bks. for Young Readers.
—I Crawl Through It. 2016. (YA). lib. bdg. 22.10 (978-0-606-38333-2(6)) Turtleback Bks.
Komura, Ayumi. Mixed Vegetables, Vol. 8. Komura, Ayumi, illus. 2010. (Mixed Vegetables Ser.: 8). (ENG., Illus.). 208p. pap. 9.99 (978-1-4215-3235-6(2)) Viz Media.
Korman, Gordon. Born to Rock (repackage) 2017. (ENG.). 240p. (J). (gr. 5-9). pap. 8.99 (978-1-4847-9841-6(4)) Hyperion Bks. for Children.
Koss, Amy Goldman. The Not-So-Great Depression. 2010. (ENG.). 272p. (YA). (gr. 7-18). pap. 19.99 (978-1-59643-613-8(1)) Roaring Brook Pr.
Kravetz, Stacy. The Fosters: Keep Your Frenemies Close. 2015. (ENG.). 224p. (YA). (gr. 7-12). pap. 9.99 (978-1-4847-1620-5(5)) Hyperion Bks. for Children.
Krossing, Karen. Cut the Lights, 1 vol. 2013. (Orca Limelights Ser.). (ENG.). 136p. (J). (gr. 6-9). pap. 9.95 (978-1-4598-0413-5(9)) Orca Bk. Pubs. USA.
Krulik, Nancy. How I Survived Middle School: Madame President. 2006. 104p. pap. (978-0-439-90090-4(5)) Scholastic, Inc.
LaCour, Nina. We Are Okay. 2017. (ENG.). 240p. (YA). (gr. 9). 17.99 (978-0-525-42589-2(6), Dutton Books for Young Readers) Penguin Young Readers Group.
Langan, John. Search for Safety. 2012. (Bluford High — Scholastic Ser.: 13). lib. bdg. 16.00 (978-0-606-26204-0(0), Turtleback) Turtleback Bks.
Langan, Paul. Promises to Keep, 19. 2013. (Bluford Ser.: 19). pap. 5.95 (978-1-59194-303-7(5)) Townsend Pr.
—Survivor, 20. 2013. (Bluford Ser.: 20). pap. 5.95 (978-1-59194-304-4(3)) Townsend Pr.
Langhorne Folan, Karyn & Langan, Paul. Breaking Point. 2011. (Bluford Ser.: 16). (J). (gr. k-12). pap. 4.95 (978-1-59194-232-0(2)) Townsend Pr.
Laughton, Geoff. By the Creek. 2016. (ENG., Illus.). (J). 24.99 (978-1-63477-945-6(2), Harmony Ink Pr.) Dreamspinner Pr.
Lay, Kathryn. Book 4: Time under the Sea. 2016. (Time Twisters Ser.). (ENG.). (J). (gr. 2-6). lib. bdg. 27.07 (978-1-62402-180-0(8)) ABDO Publishing Co.
Leach, Sara. Warm Up, 1 vol. 2014. (Orca Limelights Ser.). (ENG.). 128p. (J). (gr. 6-9). pap. 9.95 (978-1-4598-0428-9(7)) Orca Bk. Pubs. USA.
Lewis, Corey & Ko, Erik. Rival Schools. 2007. (Illus.). 200p. (YA). pap. 12.95 (978-0-9738652-2-6(9)) URON Entertainment Corp. CAN. Dist: Diamond Bk. Distributors.
Lewman, David. The Case of the Plagued Play. 2013. (Club CSI Ser.: 6). (ENG., Illus.). 160p. (J). (gr. 3-7). 15.99 (978-1-4424-7261-7(8)); pap. 6.99 (978-1-4424-7260-0(X)) Simon Spotlight. (Simon Spotlight).
Lezin, Katya. Knight Swam. 2010. 138p. pap. 14.99 (978-0-557-20384-0(8)) Lulu Pr., Inc.
Li, August. Fox-Hat & Neko. 2016. (ENG., Illus.). (YA). 29.99 (978-1-63533-018-2(1), Harmony Ink Pr.) Dreamspinner Pr.
Liang, Kuan & Yung, Kao. Magic Lover's Tower, Vol. 1. 2008. (ENG., Illus.). 176p. (YA). pap. 9.95 (978-1-59796-153-0(1)) DrMaster Pubns. Inc.
Lockwood, Cara. The Scarlet Letterman. 2007. (Bard Academy Ser.: 2). (ENG.). 272p. (gr. 7-12). pap. 17.99 (978-1-4165-2490-8(8)) Pocket Books.
Lorimer, Janet. The Bad-Luck Play, 1 vol. unabr. ed. 2010. (Q Reads Ser.). (ENG.). 32p. (YA). (gr. 9-12). pap. 6.95 (978-1-61651-198-2(2)) Saddleback Educational Publishing, Inc.
—Student Bodies, 1 vol. unabr. ed. 2010. (Q Reads Ser.). (ENG.). 32p. (YA). (gr. 9-12). pap. 6.95 (978-1-61651-219-4(9)) Saddleback Educational Publishing, Inc.
Lynne, Zoe. That Witch! 2016. (ENG., Illus.). (J). 24.99 (978-1-63477-959-3(2)) 2013. 204p. pap. 14.99 (978-1-62380-692-7(5)) Dreamspinner Pr. (Harmony Ink Pr.).
Lynne, Zoe. That Witch! [Library Edition]. 2013. 204p. pap. 14.99 (978-1-62380-927-0(4), Harmony Ink Pr.) Dreamspinner Pr.
Mackler, Carolyn. Infinite in Between. 2015. (ENG.). 480p. (YA). (gr. 8). 17.99 (978-0-06-173107-5(2), HarperTeen) HarperCollins Pubs.
Madigan, L. K. Flash Burnout. 2010. (ENG.). 336p. (YA). (gr. 9). pap. 7.99 (978-0-547-40493-6(X)) Houghton Mifflin Harcourt Publishing Co.
Madonna, pseud. A Rose by Any Other Name. Fulvimari, Jeffrey, illus. 2007. (English Roses Ser.: 4). (ENG.). 144p. (J). (gr. 3-7). 10.99 (978-0-14-240885-8(9), Puffin Books) Penguin Young Readers Group.
Mariotte, Jeff. Dark Vengeance Vol. 2: Winter, Spring. 2012. (ENG.). 448p. (YA). (gr. 9). pap. 10.99 (978-1-4424-2976-5(3), Simon Pulse) Simon Pulse.
Marrs, Christie, creator. The Perfect Gift: I B Hoofinit's Horse Tales. l.t. ed. 2004. (Illus.). 57p. (J). mass mkt. 5.99 (978-1-928890-19-5(9)) I. B. Hoofinit Co.
Marsh, Carole. Adventure to the Planet Mars! 2007. (Field Trips (Gallopade International) Ser.). (Illus.). 114p. (J). (gr. 2-9). 14.95 (978-0-635-06392-2(1)) Gallopade International.
Martin, Maggie Ann. The Big F. 2017. (ENG.). 304p. (YA). pap. 10.99 (978-1-250-12321-3(6), 9781250123213) Feiwel & Friends.
Maschari, Jennifer. Things That Surprise You. 2017. 288p. (J). (gr. 3-7). 16.99 (978-0-06-243892-8(1)) HarperCollins Pubs.
Mathews, Temple. The Sword of Armaggeddon. 2010. ix, 291p. (978-1-935618-17-1(2)) BenBella Bks.
Mattel. Monster High: Great Scarrier Reef 8x8. 2016. (ENG., Illus.). 24p. (J). (gr. -1-3). pap. 3.99 (978-0-316-30127-5(2)) Little, Brown Bks. for Young Readers.
—Monster High: Great Scarrier Reef Reader. 2016. (Passport to Reading Level 3 Ser.). (ENG., Illus.). 32p. (J). (gr. -1-3). pap. 3.99 (978-0-316-30130-5(2)) Little, Brown Bks. for Young Readers.
—Monster High: Great Scarrier Reef: the Deluxe Junior Novel. 2016. (ENG.). 144p. (J). (gr. 3-7). 9.99 (978-0-316-27046-5(6)) Little, Brown Bks. for Young Readers.
Mayfield, Jamie. A Broken Kind of Life. 2016. (ENG., Illus.). (YA). (gr. 9-12). 24.99 (978-1-63477-926-5(6), Harmony Ink Pr.) Dreamspinner Pr.
McCormick, Wilfred. Quick Kick: A Bronc Burnett Story. 2011. 192p. 42.95 (978-1-258-10149-7(1)) Literary Licensing, LLC.
McDaniel, Lurlene. Losing Gabriel: a Love Story. 2017. (ENG.). 336p. (YA). (gr. 7). pap. 9.99 (978-0-385-74422-5(6), Ember) Random Hse. Children's Bks.
McEwan, Jamie. Rufus the Scrub Does Not Wear a Tutu. Margeson, John, illus. 2006. 64p. (J). (gr. 2-3). 14.95 (978-1-58196-060-0(3), Darby Creek) Lerner Publishing Group.
—Scrubs Forever! Margeson, John, illus. 2008. (Darby Creek Exceptional Titles Ser.). (ENG.). 64p. (J). (gr. 2-5). lib. bdg. 14.95 (978-1-58196-069-3(7), Darby Creek) Lerner Publishing Group.
Mcgill, Leslie. Fighter. 2014. (Cap Central Ser.: 1). (YA). lib. bdg. 20.80 (978-0-606-35737-1(8)) Turtleback Bks.
—Hacker. 2014. (Cap Central Ser.: 3). (YA). lib. bdg. 20.80 (978-0-606-35739-5(4)) Turtleback Bks.
—Running Scared. 2014. (Cap Central Ser.: 2). (YA). lib. bdg. 20.80 (978-0-606-35738-8(6)) Turtleback Bks.
McGinnis, Mindy. The Female of the Species. (YA). (gr. 9). 2017. 368p. pap. 9.99 (978-0-06-232090-2(4)) 2016. 352p. 17.99 (978-0-06-232089-6(0)) HarperCollins Pubs. (Tegen, Katherine Bks).
McGovern, Cammie. A Step Toward Falling. (YA). (gr. 9). 2016. 384p. pap. 9.99 (978-0-06-227114-3(8)) 2015. (ENG.). 368p. 17.99 (978-0-06-227113-6(X)) HarperCollins Pubs. (HarperTeen).
—A Step Toward Falling. 2016. (YA). lib. bdg. 20.85 (978-0-606-39483-3(4)) Turtleback Bks.
Meade, L. T. The Rebel of the School. 2007. (ENG.). 272p. pap. 21.99 (978-1-4346-4869-3(9)); 302p. pap. 24.99 (978-1-4346-4870-9(2)) Creative Media Partners, LLC.
Michaels, Robbie. Caught in the Middle. 2016. (Caught in the ACT Ser.: Vol. 2). (ENG., Illus.). (YA). 24.99 (978-1-63477-951-7(7), Harmony Ink Pr.) Dreamspinner Pr.
Miglis, Jenny. New Student Starfish. Martinez, Heather, illus. 2003. (SpongeBob SquarePants Ser.). (ENG.). 64p. (J). pap. 3.99 (978-0-689-86164-2(8), Simon Spotlight/Nickelodeon) Simon Spotlight/Nickelodeon.
Millman, Selena. Anyone Can Make A Difference. 2006. 109p. (YA). per. (978-0-9793058-6-3(1)) Millman, Selena.
Money, Mo. Little Sister. 2011. (School Gyrls Ser.). (ENG.). 112p. (J). pap. 5.99 (978-1-4424-0879-1(0), Simon & Schuster/Paula Wiseman Bks.) Simon & Schuster/Paula Wiseman Bks.
Moore, Stephanie Perry. Always Upbeat/All That. 2012. (Lockwood Lions Ser.). (YA). lib. bdg. 26.90 (978-0-606-26492-1(2), Turtleback) Turtleback Bks.
Mori, Kotaro. Stray Little Devil. (Stray Little Devil Ser.). (ENG., Illus.). (YA). Vol. 1. 2006. 200p. pap. 9.95 (978-1-59796-043-4(8)) Vol. 2. 2006. 200p. pap. 9.95 (978-1-59796-044-1(6)) Vol. 3. 2006. 200p. pap. 9.95 (978-1-59796-045-8(4)) Vol. 4. 2007. 208p. pap. 9.95 (978-1-59796-046-5(2)) DrMaster Pubns. Inc.
Morpurgo, Michael. The War of Jenkins' Ear. 2nd ed. 2017. (ENG.). 192p. (J). (gr. 5-7). pap. 9.99 (978-1-4052-2672-1(2)) Egmont Bks., Ltd. GBR. Dist: Independent Pubs. Group.
Morrison, Gertrude W. The Girls of Central High Aiding the Red Cross. l.t. ed. 2007. (ENG.). 150p. pap. 19.99 (978-1-4264-2244-7(X)) Creative Media Partners, LLC.
Morton, Scott. An Encyclopedia for My Son, 1 vol. 2010. 46p. 24.95 (978-1-4489-4748-5(0)) PublishAmerica, Inc.
Moses, Jennifer Anne. Tales from My Closet. 2014. 298p. (J). pap. (978-0-545-66811-8(5), Scholastic Pr.) Scholastic, Inc.
Noël, Alyson. Shadowland. 2010. (Immortals Ser.: 3). (ENG.). 368p. (YA). (gr. 7-12). pap. 9.99 (978-0-312-65005-6(1), 9780312650056, St. Martin's Griffin) St. Martin's Pr.
Norton, Tamra. Comfortable in My Own Genes: A Novel. 2004. 175p. pap. 15.95 (978-1-55517-772-0(7)) Cedar Fort, Inc./CFI Distribution.
Now I'll Tell You Everything. 2014. (Alice Ser.: 25). (ENG., Illus.). 544p. (YA). (gr. 9). pap. 12.99 (978-1-4424-4591-8(2), Atheneum Bks. for Young Readers) Simon & Schuster Children's Publishing.
Nurse, Holly. Meridian Brown Goes to School. 2009. (Illus.). 60p. pap. (978-1-84748-535-9(9)) Athena Pr.

Oboh, Rolic. Treasure Hunt. 2006. 108p. pap. 7.99 *(978-1-84426-318-9(5))* Upfront Publishing Ltd. GBR. Dist: Printondemand-worldwide.com.
Offit, Sidney. Adventures of Homer Fink. Galdone, Paul, illus. 2016. (ENG.). 192p. pap. 11.99 *(978-1-5040-3621-4(2))* Open Road Integrated Media, Inc.
O'Keeffe, Frank. Harry Flammable: A Novel (Large Print 16pt) 2013. 240p. pap. *(978-1-4596-6316-9(0))* ReadHowYouWant.com, Ltd.
Optic, Oliver, pseud. Outward Bound. 2007. 180p. (gr. 4-7). per. *(978-1-4068-4343-9(1))* Echo Library.
—Outward Bound: Or Young America Afloat. l.t. ed. 2007. (ENG.). 274p. pap. 23.99 *(978-1-4264-9153-5(0))* Creative Media Partners, LLC.
Padian, Maria. Wrecked. 2016. (ENG.). 368p. (YA). (gr. 9-12). 17.95 *(978-1-61620-624-6(1))* Algonquin Bks. of Chapel Hill.
Park, Barbara. Cheater Pants. 2004. (Junie B. Jones Ser.: 21). (gr. k-3). lib. bdg. 14.75 *(978-0-613-85713-0(5)*, Turtleback) Turtleback Bks.
—Junie B.'s Essential Survival Guide to School. Brunkus, Denise, illus. 2013. (Junie B. Jones Ser.). (ENG.). 144p. (J). (gr. 1-4). 12.99 *(978-0-449-81783-4(0)*, Random Hse. Bks. for Young Readers) Random Hse. Children's Bks.
Pascal, Francine. Una Larga Noche.Tr. of All Night Long. (SPA.). 128p. (J). 7.95 *(978-84-272-3875-6(4))* Molino, Editorial ESP. Dist: AIMS International Bks., Inc.
—Peligrosa Tentacion.Tr. of Dangerous Love. (SPA., Illus.). 136p. (J). 7.95 *(978-84-272-3876-3(2))* Molino, Editorial ESP. Dist: AIMS International Bks., Inc.
—Querida Hermana.Tr. of Dear Sister. (SPA., Illus.). 168p. (J). 7.95 *(978-84-272-3877-0(0))* Molino, Editorial ESP. Dist: AIMS International Bks., Inc.
Paterson, Katherine. Marvin One Too Many. Clark Brown, Jane, illus. 2003. (Readalongs for Beginning Readers Ser.). (J). pap. 29.95 incl. audio *(978-1-59112-255-5(4))* Live Oak Media.
Patterson, James & Grabenstein, Chris. I Funny: A Middle School Story. Park, Laura, illus. (I Funny Ser.: 1). (ENG.). 320p. (J). (gr. 3-7). 2015. pap. 8.00 *(978-0-316-20692-1(X))* 2013. 13.99 *(978-0-316-32200-3(8))* Little Brown & Co. (Jimmy Patterson).
Patterson, Matthew. Shake Them up, Mrs Nut. 2008. 104p. per. 9.95 *(978-1-4327-2008-7(2))* Outskirts Pr., Inc.
Paul, Naomi. Code Name Komiko. 2014. (Illus.). 288p. (YA). (gr. 6-12). pap. 10.95 *(978-1-62324-024-0(7))* Enslow Pubs., Inc.
Pavey, Stephen. Free RollinApos. 2005. pap. 24.95 *(978-1-4137-0890-5(0))* PublishAmerica, Inc.
Payne, K. E. Because of Her. 2014. (ENG.). 264p. (J). (gr. 7). pap. 11.95 *(978-1-62639-049-2(5))* Bold Strokes Bks.
—365 Days. 2011. (ENG.). 280p. (J). (gr. 7). pap. 13.95 *(978-1-60282-540-6(8))* Bold Strokes Bks.
Peirce, Lincoln. Big Nate: I Can't Take It! 2013. (ENG., Illus.). 224p. pap. 9.99 *(978-1-4494-2937-9(8))* Andrews McMeel Publishing.
—Big Nate: Mr. Popularity. Peirce, Lincoln, illus. 2014. (Big Nate Ser.). (ENG., Illus.). 224p. (J). (gr. 3-7). pap. 9.99 *(978-0-06-208700-3(2))* HarperCollins Pubs.
—Big Nate — Mr. Popularity. 2014. (Big Nate Graphic Novels Ser.: 4). (J). lib. bdg. 20.85 *(978-0-606-35482-0(4))* Turtleback Bks.
—Big Nate Goes for Broke. Peirce, Lincoln, illus. (Big Nate Ser.: 4). (Illus.). 224p. (J). (gr. 3-7). 2016. pap. 6.99 *(978-0-06-236753-2(6))* 2012. (ENG., 12.99 *(978-0-06-199661-0(0))* 2012. lib. bdg. 14.89 *(978-0-06-199662-7(9))* HarperCollins Pubs.
—Big Nate Goes for Broke. 2016. (Big Nate Ser.: 4). 224p. (J). lib. bdg. 17.20 *(978-0-606-38137-6(6))* Turtleback Bks.
Pennypacker, Sara. Clementine's Letter. Frazee, Marla, illus. 2009. (Clementine Book Ser.). (ENG.). 160p. (J). (gr. 1-3). pap. 5.99 *(978-0-7868-3885-1(X))* Hyperion Pr.
Perry, Ellyse;Clark. Winning Touch. 2017. (Ellyse Perry Ser.: 3). (ENG.). 160p. (J). (gr. 4-7). 12.99 *(978-0-14-378128-8(6))* Random Hse. Australia AUS. Dist: Independent Pubs. Group.
Perry, Fred. Grossery Games. 2012. (ENG., Illus.). 128p. (J). (gr. 4-7). pap. 10.99 *(978-0-9850925-5-9(6)*, 9780985092559) Antarctic Pr., Inc.
—Playing Dead. 2012. (ENG., Illus.). 128p. (J). pap. 10.99 *(978-0-9850925-4-2(8)*, 9780985092542) Antarctic Pr., Inc.
Perry, Hailey. On the Move. 2010. 188p. pap. 12.00 *(978-1-60844-428-1(7))* Dog Ear Publishing, LLC.
Philips, Fleur. Crumble. 2013. 168p. (YA). pap. 8.99 *(978-0-9889299-0-6(2))* Philips, Fleur.
Phillips, Lyda. Mr Touchdown. 2008. 184p. 23.95 *(978-1-4401-0976-8(1))*; pap. 13.95 *(978-1-60528-029-5(1))* iUniverse, Inc. (iUniverse Star).
Phillips, Rebecca. These Things I've Done. 2017. 352p. (YA). (gr. 9). 17.99 ***(978-0-06-257090-1(0)***, HarperTeen) HarperCollins Pubs.
Pilumeli, Tanya. The Dragonfly Keeper. 2008. 264p. (J). per. 12.95 *(978-0-9801396-0-0(0))* FAVA Pr.
Polak, Monique. Straight Punch, 1 vol. 2014. (ENG.). 256p. (YA). (gr. 8-12). pap. 12.95 *(978-1-4598-0391-6(4))* Orca Bk. Pubs. USA.
Potter, Ryan. Perennial, 0 vols. 2014. (ENG.). 296p. (YA). (gr. 7-9). pap. 9.99 *(978-1-4778-1818-3(9)*, 9781477818183, Amazon Children's Publishing) Amazon Publishing.
Poulsen, David A. Blind Date. 2nd rev. ed. 2008. (Lawrence High Yearbook Ser.). (ENG.). 96p. (J). (gr. 2-7). pap. *(978-1-55263-933-7(9))* Me to We.
—Wild Thing. 2008. (Lawrence High Yearbook Ser.). (ENG.). 96p. (gr. 2-7). pap. *(978-1-55263-931-3(2))* Me to We.
Prendergast, Gabrielle. Capricious, 1 vol. 2014. (ENG.). 352p. (YA). (gr. 8-12). 19.95 *(978-1-4598-0267-4(5))* Orca Bk. Pubs. USA.
Pugin-Rodas, M. C. The Eight Ball Club: Ocean of Fire. 2007. (ENG., Illus.). 144p. pap. 15.95 *(978-0-9793761-2-2(2))* ESOL Publishing.
Rain, Mandy. Rock 'n' Roll. 2011. (School Gyrls Ser.). (ENG.). 128p. (J). pap. 5.99 *(978-1-4424-0878-4(2)*, Simon & Schuster/Paula Wiseman Bks.) Simon & Schuster/Paula Wiseman Bks.
Ramirez, D. a. & Ramirez, D. A. Kingdom of Glass. 2012. 336p. pap. 12.99 *(978-0-9834198-8-4(4))* Vinspire Publishing LLC.
Ramos, Dania. Who's Ju? 2015. (ENG.). 174p. (J). pap. 9.95 *(978-1-937997-61-8(8))* Northampton Hse.
Ramsey, Jo. Blue Jeans & Sweatshirts. 2016. (ENG., Illus.). (J). 24.99 ***(978-1-63477-942-5(8)***, Harmony Ink Pr.) Dreamspinner Pr.
Ramsey, R. M. The Browser Bunch: The Browser Files Presents... the Big Lie. 2006. (J). pap. 8.00 *(978-0-8059-7172-9(6))* Dorrance Publishing Co., Inc.
Redgate, Riley. Seven Ways We Lie. 2017. (ENG.). 368p. (YA). pap. 9.95 *(978-1-4197-2348-3(0)*, Amulet Bks.) Abrams, Inc.
Regan, Dian. Cyberpals According to Kaley. 2006. (Illus.). 128p. (J). (gr. 3-7). 15.95 *(978-1-58196-051-8(4)*, Darby Creek) Lerner Publishing Group.
Richards, Justin. Sorted! 2009. (Agent Alfie Ser.: 2). (ENG., Illus.). 176p. (J). (gr. 2-4). pap. 6.99 *(978-0-00-727358-4(4)*, HarperCollins Children's Bks.) HarperCollins Pubs. Ltd. GBR. Dist: HarperCollins Pubs.
Robbins, Maureen & Steinkraus, Kyla. Ready, Set, Race! Reese, Bob, illus. 2011. (ENG.). 24p. (gr. 2-3). pap. 8.95 *(978-1-61236-033-1(5))* Rourke Educational Media.
Roberts, Dw. Pep Squad Mysteries Book: Trouble on Avalance Mountain. 2010. (Illus.). 86p. pap. 8.99 *(978-0-557-16575-9(X))* Lulu Pr., Inc.
Robins, Eleanor. Art Show Mystery, 1 vol. unabr. ed. 2011. (Carter High Mysteries Ser.). (ENG.). 46p. (YA). (gr. 9-12). 7.95 *(978-1-61651-560-7(0))* Saddleback Educational Publishing, Inc.
—Aztec Ring Mystery, 1 vol. unabr. ed. 2011. (Carter High Mysteries Ser.). (ENG.). 46p. (YA). (gr. 9-12). 7.95 *(978-1-61651-561-4(9))* Saddleback Educational Publishing, Inc.
—Boy of Their Dreams, 1 vol. unabr. ed. 2011. (Carter High Chronicles Ser.). (ENG.). 51p. (YA). (gr. 9-12). pap. 7.95 *(978-1-61651-305-4(5))* Saddleback Educational Publishing, Inc.
—Break All Rules, 1 vol. unabr. ed. 2011. (Choices Ser.). (ENG.). 48p. (YA). (gr. 9-12). 7.95 *(978-1-61651-590-4(2))* Saddleback Educational Publishing, Inc.
—Broken Promise, 1 vol. unabr. ed. 2011. (Choices Ser.). (ENG.). 50p. (YA). (gr. 9-12). 7.95 *(978-1-61651-591-1(0))* Saddleback Educational Publishing, Inc.
—Don't Get Caught, 1 vol. unabr. ed. 2011. (Choices Ser.). (ENG.). 52p. (YA). (gr. 9-12). 7.95 *(978-1-61651-592-8(9))* Saddleback Educational Publishing, Inc.
—Easy Pass, 1 vol. unabr. ed. 2011. (Choices Ser.). (ENG.). 51p. (YA). (gr. 9-12). 7.95 *(978-1-61651-596-6(1))* Saddleback Educational Publishing, Inc.
—Friend or Foe?, 1 vol. unabr. ed. 2011. (Choices Ser.). (ENG.). 52p. (YA). (gr. 9-12). 7.95 *(978-1-61651-593-5(7))* Saddleback Educational Publishing, Inc.
—It Does Matter, 1 vol. unabr. ed. 2011. (Carter High Senior Year Ser.). (ENG.). 49p. (YA). (gr. 9-12). pap. 7.95 *(978-1-61651-324-5(1))* Saddleback Educational Publishing, Inc.
—It Is Not a Date, 1 vol. unabr. ed. 2011. (Carter High Chronicles Ser.). (ENG.). 51p. (YA). (gr. 9-12). pap. 7.95 *(978-1-61651-309-2(8))* Saddleback Educational Publishing, Inc.
—Just Be Yourself, 1 vol. unabr. ed. 2011. (Carter High Senior Year Ser.). (ENG.). 50p. (YA). (gr. 9-12). pap. 7.95 *(978-1-61651-325-2(X))* Saddleback Educational Publishing, Inc.
—The Last Time, 1 vol. unabr. ed. 2011. (Carter High Senior Year Ser.). (ENG.). 49p. (YA). (gr. 9-12). pap. 7.95 *(978-1-61651-326-9(8))* Saddleback Educational Publishing, Inc.
—Library Book Mystery, 1 vol. unabr. ed. 2011. (Carter High Mysteries Ser.). (ENG.). 48p. (YA). (gr. 9-12). 7.95 *(978-1-61651-564-5(3))* Saddleback Educational Publishing, Inc.
—One Date Too Many, 1 vol. unabr. ed. 2011. (Carter High Chronicles Ser.). (ENG.). 50p. (YA). (gr. 9-12). pap. 7.95 *(978-1-61651-310-8(1))* Saddleback Educational Publishing, Inc.
—One More Chance, 1 vol. unabr. ed. 2011. (Carter High Senior Year Ser.). (ENG.). 51p. (YA). (gr. 9-12). pap. 7.95 *(978-1-61651-327-6(6))* Saddleback Educational Publishing, Inc.
—Pay Back, 1 vol. unabr. ed. 2011. (Choices Ser.). (ENG.). 52p. (YA). (gr. 9-12). 7.95 *(978-1-61651-594-2(5))* Saddleback Educational Publishing, Inc.
—Someone to Count, 1 vol. unabr. ed. 2011. (Carter High Senior Year Ser.). (ENG.). 50p. (YA). (gr. 9-12). pap. 7.95 *(978-1-61651-328-3(4))* Saddleback Educational Publishing, Inc.
—Time to Move On, 1 vol. unabr. ed. 2011. (Carter High Senior Year Ser.). (ENG.). 50p. (YA). (gr. 9-12). pap. 7.95 *(978-1-61651-329-0(2))* Saddleback Educational Publishing, Inc.
—Too Late, 1 vol. unabr. ed. 2011. (Carter High Chronicles Ser.). (ENG.). 52p. (YA). (gr. 9-12). pap. 7.95 *(978-1-61651-312-2(8))* Saddleback Educational Publishing, Inc.
—Trust Me, 1 vol. unabr. ed. 2011. (Choices Ser.). (ENG.). 52p. (YA). (gr. 9-12). 7.95 *(978-1-61651-599-7(6))* Saddleback Educational Publishing, Inc.
—The Worst Year Ever, 1 vol. unabr. ed. 2011. (Carter High Senior Year Ser.). (ENG.). 50p. (YA). (gr. 9-12). pap. 7.95 *(978-1-61651-330-6(6))* Saddleback Educational Publishing, Inc.
Rose, Deborah Lee. The Spelling Bee Before Recess. Armstrong-Ellis, Carey F., illus. 2013. (ENG.). 32p. (J). (gr. 1-4). 16.95 *(978-1-4197-0847-3(3)*, Abrams Bks. for Young Readers) Abrams, Inc.
Rose, Sue. Jinxed! 2006. (Unfabulous! Ser.). (Illus.). 118p. (J). *(978-1-4156-5170-4(1))* Scholastic, Inc.
Ryan, Hugh. Spy Academy: Mission Twinpossible. 2012. 93p. (J). pap. *(978-0-545-37173-5(2))* Scholastic, Inc.
Ryan, Patrick. Gemini Bites. 2011. (ENG.). 240p. (J). (gr. 7-8). 17.99 *(978-0-545-22128-3(5)*, Scholastic Pr.) Scholastic, Inc.
Rylander, Chris. Crisis Zero. 2016. (Codename Conspiracy Ser.: 3). 400p. (J). (gr. 3-7). 16.99 *(978-0-06-232747-5(X)*, Waldon Pond Pr.) HarperCollins Pubs.
Sachar, Louis. Sideways Stories from Wayside School. McCauley, Adam, illus. rev. ed. 2004. (Wayside School Ser.). (ENG.). 128p. (J). (gr. 3-7). pap. 6.99 *(978-0-380-73148-0(7))* HarperCollins Pubs.
Saddleback Educational Publishing Staff, ed. Boy of Their Dreams. 2011. (Carter High Chronicles Ser.). (ENG.). 16p. (YA). (gr. 9-12). tchr. ed. 7.95 incl. cd-rom *(978-1-61651-315-3(2))* Saddleback Educational Publishing, Inc.
—The Easy Way. 2011. (Carter High Chronicles Ser.). (ENG.). 16p. (YA). (gr. 9-12). tchr. ed. 7.95 incl. cd-rom *(978-1-61651-316-0(0))* Saddleback Educational Publishing, Inc.
—The Fastest Runner. 2011. (Carter High Chronicles Ser.). (ENG.). 16p. (YA). (gr. 9-12). cd-rom 7.95 *(978-1-61651-318-4(7))* Saddleback Educational Publishing, Inc.
—It Does Matter. 2011. (Carter High Senior Year Ser.). (ENG.). 16p. (YA). (gr. 9-12). tchr. ed. 7.95 incl. cd-rom *(978-1-61651-334-4(9))* Saddleback Educational Publishing, Inc.
—It Is Not a Date. 2011. (Carter High Chronicles Ser.). (ENG.). 16p. (YA). (gr. 9-12). cd-rom 7.95 *(978-1-61651-319-1(5))* Saddleback Educational Publishing, Inc.
—Just Be Yourself. 2011. (Carter High Senior Year Ser.). (ENG.). 16p. (YA). (gr. 9-12). cd-rom 7.95 *(978-1-61651-335-1(7))* Saddleback Educational Publishing, Inc.
—One Date Too Many. 2011. (Carter High Chronicles Ser.). (ENG.). 16p. (YA). (gr. 9-12). tchr. ed. 7.95 incl. cd-rom *(978-1-61651-320-7(9))* Saddleback Educational Publishing, Inc.
—One More Chance. 2011. (Carter High Senior Year Ser.). (ENG.). 16p. (YA). (gr. 9-12). cd-rom 7.95 *(978-1-61651-337-5(3))* Saddleback Educational Publishing, Inc.
—Right Kind of Win. 2011. (Carter High Chronicles Ser.). (ENG.). 16p. (YA). (gr. 9-12). cd-rom 7.95 *(978-1-61651-321-4(7))* Saddleback Educational Publishing, Inc.
—Someone to Count On. 2011. (Carter High Senior Year Ser.). (ENG.). 16p. (YA). (gr. 9-12). cd-rom 7.95 *(978-1-61651-338-2(1))* Saddleback Educational Publishing, Inc.
—Time to Move. 2011. (Carter High Senior Year Ser.). (ENG.). 16p. (YA). (gr. 9-12). tchr. ed. 7.95 incl. cd-rom *(978-1-61651-339-9(X))* Saddleback Educational Publishing, Inc.
—Too Late. 2011. (Carter High Chronicles Ser.). (ENG.). 16p. (YA). (gr. 9-12). cd-rom 7.95 *(978-1-61651-322-1(5))* Saddleback Educational Publishing, Inc.
Sáenz, Benjamin Alire. Sammy & Juliana in Hollywood. 2004. (ENG.). 240p. (J). (gr. 10-12). 19.95 *(978-0-938317-81-4(4))* Cinco Puntos Pr.
Schoon, Christian. Zenn Scarlett. 2013. (ENG.). 304p. (J). (gr. 7). pap. 9.99 *(978-1-908844-55-2(8)*, Strange Chemistry) Watkins Media Limited GBR. Dist: Penguin Random Hse. LLC.
Schraff, Anne. A Boy Called Twister, 1 vol. unabr. ed. 2010. (Urban Underground Ser.). (ENG.). 180p. (YA). (gr. 9-12). pap. 9.95 *(978-1-61651-002-2(1))* Saddleback Educational Publishing, Inc.
—The Experiment, 1 vol. unabr. ed. 2010. (Q Reads Ser.). (ENG.). 32p. (YA). (gr. 9-12). pap. 6.95 *(978-1-61651-181-4(8))* Saddleback Educational Publishing, Inc.
—If You Were Mine, 1 vol. 2013. (Urban Underground Ser.). (ENG.). 195p. (YA). (gr. 9-12). pap. 9.95 *(978-1-62250-041-3(5))* Saddleback Educational Publishing, Inc.
—Leap of Faith, 1 vol. unabr. ed. 2011. (Urban Underground Ser.). (ENG.). 201p. (YA). (gr. 9-12). pap. 9.95 *(978-1-61651-588-1(0))* Saddleback Educational Publishing, Inc.
—One of Us, 1 vol. unabr. ed. 2010. (Urban Underground Ser.). (ENG.). 180p. (YA). (gr. 9-12). pap. 9.95 *(978-1-61651-004-6(8))* Saddleback Educational Publishing, Inc.
—Outrunning the Darkness, 1 vol. unabr. ed. 2010. (Urban Underground Ser.). (ENG.). 191p. (YA). (gr. 9-12). pap. 9.95 *(978-1-61651-000-8(5))* Saddleback Educational Publishing, Inc.
—Shadows of Guilt, 1 vol. unabr. ed. 2010. (Urban Underground Ser.). (ENG.). 179p. (YA). (gr. 9-12). pap. 9.95 *(978-1-61651-001-5(3))* Saddleback Educational Publishing, Inc.
—Waters Edge, 1 vol. unabr. ed. 2011. (Urban Underground Ser.). (ENG.). 197p. (YA). (gr. 9-12). pap. 9.95 *(978-1-61651-589-8(9))* Saddleback Educational Publishing, Inc.
Schraff, Anne E. Don't Think about Tomorrow. 2012. (Urban Underground — Harriet Tubman High School Ser.: 23). (YA). lib. bdg. 20.80 *(978-0-606-23796-3(8)*, Turtleback) Turtleback Bks.
—Hurting Time. 2012. (Urban Underground — Cesar Chavez High School Ser.: 27). (YA). lib. bdg. 20.80 *(978-0-606-26597-3(X)*, Turtleback) Turtleback Bks.
—If You Were Mine. 2013. (Urban Underground — Harriet Tubman High School Ser.). (YA). lib. bdg. 20.80 *(978-0-606-31581-4(0)*, Turtleback) Turtleback Bks.
—The One for Me. 2013. (Urban Underground — Harriet Tubman High School Ser.). lib. bdg. 20.80 *(978-0-606-31582-1(9)*, Turtleback) Turtleback Bks.
—Out of Love for You. 2012. (Urban Underground — Harriet Tubman High School Ser.: 24). (YA). lib. bdg. 20.80 *(978-0-606-23797-0(6)*, Turtleback) Turtleback Bks.
—The Outcasts. 2012. (Urban Underground — Harriet Tubman High School Ser.: 21). (YA). lib. bdg. 20.80 *(978-0-606-23794-9(1)*, Turtleback) Turtleback Bks.
—The Rescuers. 2012. (Urban Underground — Harriet Tubman High School Ser.: 25). (YA). lib. bdg. 20.80 *(978-0-606-23798-7(4)*, Turtleback) Turtleback Bks.
—See No Evil. 2012. (Urban Underground — Harriet Tubman High School Ser.: 22). (YA). lib. bdg. 20.80 *(978-0-606-23795-6(X)*, Turtleback) Turtleback Bks.
Schuck, Philip. A Ricochet from Circumstance. 2005. (YA). 19.95 *(978-0-9764670-0-7(3))* Smithfield Capital Corp.
Schweizer, Chris. The Creeps: Book 1: Night of the Frankenfrogs. 2015. (ENG., Illus.). 128p. (J). (gr. 3-7). 17.95 *(978-1-4197-1379-8(5)*, Amulet Bks.) Abrams, Inc.
—The Trolls Will Feast! 2016. (Creeps Ser.). (ENG., Illus.). 128p. (J). (gr. 3-7). 17.95 *(978-1-4197-1882-3(7)*, Amulet Bks.) Abrams, Inc.
Scott, Elizabeth. Something, Maybe. 2010. (ENG.). 240p. (YA). (gr. 9). pap. 9.99 *(978-1-4169-5356-2(6)*, Simon Pulse) Simon Pulse.
Shen, Prudence. Nothing Can Possibly Go Wrong. Hicks, Faith Erin, illus. 2013. (ENG.). 288p. (YA). (gr. 7). pap. 17.99 *(978-1-59643-659-6(X)*, 9781596436596, First Second Bks.) Roaring Brook Pr.
The Shoe Grabber: Individual Title Six-Pack. (Story Steps Ser.). (gr. k-2). 23.00 *(978-0-7635-9832-7(1))* Rigby Education.
Simon, Coco. Alexis: The Icing on the Cupcake. 2014. (Cupcake Diaries: 20). lib. bdg. 17.20 *(978-0-606-35786-9(6))* Turtleback Bks.
—Alexis & the Perfect Recipe. 2013. (Cupcake Diaries: 4). (ENG., Illus.). 160p. (J). (gr. 3-7). 15.99 *(978-1-4424-7493-2(9)*, Simon Spotlight) Simon Spotlight.
—Alexis the Icing on the Cupcake. 2014. (Cupcake Diaries: 20). (ENG., Illus.). 160p. (J). (gr. 3-7). pap. 6.99 *(978-1-4814-0468-6(7)*, Simon Spotlight) Simon Spotlight.
—Katie & the Cupcake Cure. 2011. (Cupcake Diaries: 1). (ENG.). 160p. (J). (gr. 3-7). pap. 6.99 *(978-1-4424-2275-9(0)*, Simon Spotlight) Simon Spotlight.
—Katie & the Cupcake War. 2014. (Cupcake Diaries: 9). (ENG., Illus.). 160p. (J). (gr. 3-7). 17.99 *(978-1-4424-9609-5(6)*, Simon Spotlight) Simon Spotlight.
—Katie & the Cupcake War. 2012. (Cupcake Diaries: 9). lib. bdg. 17.20 *(978-0-606-26335-1(7)*, Turtleback) Turtleback Bks.
—Katie Sprinkled Secrets. 2015. (Cupcake Diaries: 25). (ENG., Illus.). 160p. (J). (gr. 3-7). pap. 6.99 *(978-1-4814-2919-1(1)*, Simon Spotlight) Simon Spotlight.
Simone, Ni-Ni & London, Kelli. The Break-Up Diaries. 2011. (ENG.). 272p. (YA). (gr. 9-18). 9.95 *(978-0-7582-6316-2(3)*, K-Teen/Dafina) Kensington Publishing Corp.
Skogen, Jennifer. Burning #1, 1 vol. 2015. (Haunting of Grey Hills Ser.). (ENG.). 216p. (YA). (gr. 9-12). lib. bdg. 27.13 *(978-1-68076-029-3(7)*, Epic Pr.) ABDO Publishing Co.
—Distant Deep #5. 2015. (Haunting of Grey Hills Ser.). (ENG.). 200-216p. (YA). (gr. 9-12). lib. bdg. 27.13 *(978-1-68076-033-0(5)*, Epic Pr.) ABDO Publishing Co.
—Sinews of Thy Heart #4. 2015. (Haunting of Grey Hills Ser.). (ENG.). 200-216p. (J). (gr. 9-12). lib. bdg. 27.13 *(978-1-68076-032-3(7)*, 1391657, Epic Pr.) ABDO Publishing Co.
Slater, Calvin. Game On. 2015. 332p. (YA). *(978-1-4806-9396-8(0))* Kensington Publishing Corp.
St. Mark Kindergarten. Kindergarten Goes to Outer Space for the Day. 2009. 28p. pap. 12.49 *(978-1-4490-0587-0(X))* AuthorHouse.
Standiford, Natalie. The Boy on the Bridge. 2013. (ENG.). 256p. (J). (gr. 9). 17.99 *(978-0-545-33481-5(0)*, Scholastic Pr.) Scholastic, Inc.
Standish, Burt L. Frank Merriwell's Pupils. Rudman, Jack, ed. 2003. (Frank Merriwell Ser.). pap. 9.95 *(978-0-8373-9133-5(4))* Merriwell, Frank Inc.
Stapleton, Rhonda. Flirting with Disaster. 2010. (ENG.). 256p. (YA). (gr. 7-18). pap. 9.99 *(978-1-4169-7465-9(2)*, Simon Pulse) Simon Pulse.
Starmer, Aaron. Spontaneous. 2016. (ENG.). 368p. (YA). (gr. 9). 17.99 *(978-0-525-42974-6(3)*, Dutton Books for Young Readers) Penguin Young Readers Group.
Step up 2: the Streets. 2008. 160p. pap. 4.99 *(978-1-4231-1319-5(5))* Disney Pr.
Stephens, Sarah Hines. Spring Break-Up. 2006. (Zoey 101 Ser.). 103p. (J). *(978-1-4156-8963-9(6))* Scholastic, Inc.
Stilton, Thea. Thea Stilton & the Blue Scarab Hunt. 2012. (Thea Stilton Ser.: 11). lib. bdg. 19.65 *(978-0-606-26183-8(4)*, Turtleback) Turtleback Bks.
Stine, R. L. The Lost Girl: A Fear Street Novel. 2015. (Fear Street Ser.). (ENG.). 272p. (YA). 17.99 *(978-1-250-05163-9(0)*, 9781250051639, St. Martin's Griffin) St. Martin's Pr.
—The Rottenest Angel. Park, Trip, illus. (Rotten School Ser.: Bk. 10). 4.99 *(978-0-06-078829-2(1))* HarperCollins Pubs.
—The Rottenest Angel, 1 vol. Park, Trip, illus. 2011. (Rotten School Ser.: No. 10). (ENG.). 128p. (gr. 2-5). 24.21 *(978-1-59961-834-0(6))* Spotlight.
Stratemeyer, Edward. The Rover Boys at College or the Right R. 2004. reprint ed. pap. 22.95 *(978-1-4191-8114-6(9))* Kessinger Publishing, LLC.
—The Rover Boys at College or the Right Road & the Wrong. 2004. reprint ed. pap. 1.99 *(978-1-4192-8114-3(3))* Kessinger Publishing, LLC.
Strohmeyer, Sarah. The Secrets of Lily Graves. 2014. (ENG.). 304p. (YA). (gr. 8). pap. 9.99 *(978-0-06-225960-8(1))* HarperCollins Pubs.
Sullivan, Michael. Escapade Johnson & the Witches of Belknap County. Kolitsky, Joy, illus. 2008. (Escapade Johnson Ser.). (ENG.). 99p. (J). (gr. 2-4). pap. 3.95 *(978-1-929945-90-0(6))* Big Guy Bks., Inc.
Tackett, Wendy. The Snow Wish. 2011. 100p. (gr. 4-6). 19.95 *(978-1-4620-2608-1(7))*; pap. 9.95 *(978-1-4620-2606-7(0))* iUniverse, Inc.
Taddonio, Lea. Book 3: First Fight. 2016. (Head over Heels Ser.). (ENG., Illus.). 46p. (J). (gr. 2-8). lib. bdg. 28.50 ***(978-1-62402-194-7(8))*** ABDO Publishing Co.
Taylor, Chloë. Cute As a Button. Zhang, Nancy, illus. 2014. (Sew Zoey Ser.: 5). (ENG.). 176p. (J). (gr. 3-7). pap. 5.99 *(978-1-4814-0248-4(X)*, Simon Spotlight) Simon Spotlight.
—Dressed to Frill. Zhang, Nancy, illus. 2015. (Sew Zoey Ser.: 12). (ENG.). 160p. (J). (gr. 3-7). pap. 6.99 *(978-1-4814-2930-6(2)*, Simon Spotlight) Simon Spotlight.
Taylor, Chloe. On Pins & Needles. Christy, Jana & Zhang, Nancy, illus. 2013. (Sew Zoey Ser.: 2). (ENG.). 160p. (J). (gr. 3-7). 15.99 *(978-1-4424-7937-1(X))*; pap. 6.99 *(978-1-4424-7936-4(1))* Simon Spotlight. (Simon Spotlight).
—Ready to Wear. Christy, Jana & Zhang, Nancy, illus. 2013. (Sew Zoey Ser.: 1). (ENG.). 176p. (J). (gr. 3-7). pap. 6.99 *(978-1-4424-7933-3(7)*, Simon Spotlight) Simon Spotlight.
Tennant, Kim. Thin Club. 2007. 52p. per. 10.00 *(978-1-4257-2619-5(4))* Xlibris Corp.

S

Thaler, Mike. The Class Picture Day from the Black Lagoon. Lee, Jared D., illus. 2012. 64p. (J). pap. (978-0-545-47666-9(6)) Scholastic, Inc.

There's No Room for You, Maddie Morrison. 2006. (J). per. 6.99 (978-0-9786117-0-5(5)) Neal Morgan Publishing.

Thomas, Debbie. Class Act. 2015. (ENG.). 224p. (J). pap. 13.00 (978-1-78117-262-9(5)) Mercier Pr., Ltd., The IRL. Dist: Dufour Editions, Inc.

Thomas, Erin. Haze, 1 vol. 2012. (Orca Sports Ser.). (ENG.). 192p. (YA). (gr. 6-10). pap. 9.95 (978-1-4598-0070-0(2)) Orca Bk. Pubs. USA.

Thomas, Paul R., reader. The Reeve's Tale. 2006. pap. 10.00 (978-0-8425-2667-8(6)) Brigham Young Univ.

Thomas, Terri. The Barge Ghost, 1 vol. unabr. ed. 2010. (Q Reads Ser.). (ENG.). 32p. (YA). (gr. 9-12). pap. 6.95 (978-1-61651-211-8(3)) Saddleback Educational Publishing, Inc.

Thompson, Brian. Reject High. 2013. 270p. pap. 11.95 (978-0-9891056-0-6(1)) Great Nation Publishing.

Tomlinson, Everett T. Winning His W. 2006. pap. (978-1-4068-1194-0(7)) Echo Library.

Umezu, Kazuo. The Drifting Classroom. Roman, Annette, ed. Umezu, Kazuo, illus. 2007. (Drifting Classroom Ser.: 8). (ENG., Illus.). 192p. pap. 9.99 (978-1-4215-0960-0(1)) Viz Media.

Uncle Tom's Cabin: Response Journal. 2003. 48p. (YA). (978-1-58049-983-5(X), RJ83) Prestwick Hse., Inc.

Walters, Eric. Stuffed, 1 vol. 2006. (Orca Soundings Ser.). (ENG.). 136p. (YA). (gr. 8-12). per. 9.95 (978-1-55143-500-8(4)) Orca Bk. Pubs. USA.

Warner, Susan & Wetherell, Elizabeth. Daisy in the Field. 2011. 272p. 29.95 (978-1-4638-9964-6(5)); pap. 16.95 (978-1-4638-0163-2(7)) Rodgers, Alan Bks.

Watson, Paul. The Robot. 2011. (ENG.). 272p. (YA). (gr. 7). E-Book (978-1-101-54326-9(4), Razorbill) Penguin Young Readers Group.

Weatherly, L. A. Them. 2013. (ENG.). 80p. (YA). (gr. 6-12). pap. 6.95 (978-1-78112-185-6(0)); lib. bdg. 22.60 (978-1-78112-184-9(2)) Lerner Publishing Group.

Webster, Jean. Daddy-Long-Legs. 2004. reprint ed. pap. 1.99 (978-1-4192-1490-5(X)); pap. 19.95 (978-1-4191-1490-8(5)) Kessinger Publishing, LLC.

Wells, Robison. Dark Energy. 2016. 288p. (YA). (gr. 8). 17.99 (978-0-06-227505-9(4), HarperTeen) HarperCollins Pubs.

Weston, Alan & Gempko, Gloria. The Girl from Keelonia. 2003. (J). pap. 7.95 (978-0-9742808-0-6(1)) Lill-Till Pr.

White, Sarah. Our Broken Pieces. 2017. 288p. (YA). (gr. 9). pap. 9.99 (**978-0-06-247313-4(1)**, HarperTeen) HarperCollins Pubs.

Whitesides, Tyler. Curse of the Broomstaff. 2013. (Janitors Ser.: 3). (ENG., Illus.). 384p. (J). (gr. 5). 18.99 (978-1-60907-605-4(2), Shadow Mountain) Shadow Mountain Publishing.

—Janitors. 2011. (Janitors Ser.: Bk. 1). pap. 34.99 (978-1-60908-075-4(0)); (J). 17.99 (978-1-60908-056-3(4)) Deseret Bk. Co.

—Janitors. 2012. (Janitors Ser.: 1). (ENG., Illus.). 320p. (J). (gr. 5). pap. 7.99 (978-1-60907-065-6(8), Shadow Mountain) Shadow Mountain Publishing.

—Secrets of New Forest Academy. 2013. (Janitors Ser.: 2). (ENG., Illus.). 368p. (J). (gr. 5). pap. 8.99 (978-1-60907-546-0(3), Shadow Mountain) Shadow Mountain Publishing.

Whittemore, Jo. Confidentially Yours #3: Heather's Crush Catastrophe. 2016. (Confidentially Yours Ser.: 3). 288p. (J). (gr. 3-7). 6.99 (**978-0-06-235897-4(9)**) HarperCollins Pubs.

Wilkes, Nita. Stalking Bailey. 2010. 185p. pap. 10.95 (978-1-4327-4862-3(9)) Outskirts Pr., Inc.

Williams, Nicole. Clash. 2012. (Crash Ser.: 2). (ENG.). 288p. (YA). (gr. 11). pap. 9.99 (978-0-06-226715-3(9)) HarperCollins Pubs.

—Crash. 2012. (Crash Ser.: 1). (ENG.). 384p. (YA). (gr. 11). pap. 9.99 (978-0-06-226714-6(0)) HarperCollins Pubs.

—Crush. 2013. (Crash Ser.: 3). (ENG.). 400p. (YA). (gr. 11). pap. 9.99 (978-0-06-226717-7(5)) HarperCollins Pubs.

Winfield, Arthur M. The Mystery at Putnam Hall. 2007. 272p. 26.95 (978-1-4218-4130-4(4)); per. 11.95 (978-1-4218-4228-8(9)) 1st World Publishing, Inc. (1st World Library - Literary Society).

—Rover Boys at College or the Right Road. 2006. pap. 30.95 (978-1-4286-4106-8(8)) Kessinger Publishing, LLC.

—Rover Boys at School. 2006. pap. (978-1-4068-3129-0(8)) Echo Library.

—The Rover Boys down East or the Struggle for the Stanhope Fortune. 2006. (ENG.). 316p. per. 30.95 (978-1-4286-4113-6(0)) Kessinger Publishing, LLC.

—Rover Boys in Alaska or Lost in the Fiel. 2006. pap. 30.95 (978-1-4286-4107-5(6)) Kessinger Publishing, LLC.

—The Rover Boys in Business or the Search for the Missing Bonds. 2006. (ENG.). 316p. per. 30.95 (978-1-4286-4098-6(3)) Kessinger Publishing, LLC.

—The Rover Boys in the Air or from College Campus to the Clouds. 2006. (ENG.). 316p. per. 30.95 (978-1-4286-4103-7(3)) Kessinger Publishing, LLC.

—Rover Boys on A Tour or Last Days at Bri. 2006. pap. 31.95 (978-1-4286-4389-5(3)) Kessinger Publishing, LLC.

Wolf, Sara. Forget Me Always. 2016. (Lovely Vicious Ser.: 2). (ENG.). 250p. (YA). pap. 9.99 (978-1-63375-317-4(4), 9781633753174) Entangled Publishing, LLC.

Yang, Gene Luen. Animal Crackers: A Gene Luen Yang Collection. 2012. (ENG., Illus.). 216p. (YA). pap. 14.95 (978-1-59362-183-4(3), 9781593621834) Slave Labor Bks.

Young, Karen Romano. Doodlebug: A Novel in Doodles. 2012. (ENG., Illus.). 128p. (J). (gr. 3-7). pap. 7.99 (978-1-250-01020-9(9), 9781250010209) Square Fish.

Yung, Kao & Liang, Kuan. Magic Lover's Tower, Vol. 2. 2008. (Magic Lover's Tower Ser.). (ENG., Illus.). 176p. (YA). (gr. 8). pap. 9.95 (978-1-59796-154-7(X)) DrMaster Pubns. Inc.

Yunisa. Schoolaholic Princess 1: the Miracle Boys. 2008. 242p. pap. 15.88 (978-1-4357-6026-4(3)) Lulu Pr., Inc.

—Schoolaholic Princess 3: Simfoni Cinta. 2008. 220p. pap. 14.88 (978-1-4357-6045-5(X)) Lulu Pr., Inc.

Ziegesar, Cecily von. I Will Always Love You. 2010. (Gossip Girl Ser.: 12). (ENG.). 400p. (YA). (gr. 10-17). pap. 10.99 (978-0-316-04359-5(1), Poppy) Little, Brown Bks. for Young Readers.

Zielinski, Valerie & Skaletski, Roslyn. The Adventures of Bella. 2011. 48p. pap. 14.00 (978-1-4634-2018-5(8)) AuthorHouse.

Zurchin, Cynthia, et al. The Whale Done School: Transforming a School's Culture by Catching Students Doing Things Right. 2012. 124p. pap. 14.95 (978-1-4685-9536-9(9)) AuthorHouse.

STUDENTS—PERSONNEL WORK

see Educational Counseling

STUDY, METHOD OF

see Study Skills

STUDY SKILLS

see also Self-Culture

also subjects with the subdivision Study and Teaching, e.g. Art—Study and Teaching, etc.

Anhalt, Edward. Raise Your GPA 1 Full Grade. 2003. 265p. (YA). pap. 19.95 (978-0-595-24645-8(1), Writers Club Pr.) iUniverse, Inc.

Beck, Isabel. Questioning the Author: An Approach for Enhancing Student Engagement with Text. 122p. 84.95 incl. DVD (978-0-322-04355-8(7)) Wright Group/McGraw-Hill.

Berry, Joy. A Fun & Easy Way to Do Your Homework. Bartholomew, illus. 2010. (Fun & Easy Way Ser.). (ENG.). 48p. (J). (gr. 1-5). pap. 7.95 (978-1-60577-320-9(4)) Berry, Joy Enterprises.

—A Fun & Easy Way to Get Good Grades. Bartholomew, illus. 2010. (Fun & Easy Way Ser.). (ENG.). 48p. (J). (gr. 1-5). pap. 7.95 (978-1-60577-321-6(2)) Berry, Joy Enterprises.

—Get Good Grades. 2009. (Fun & Easy Way Ser.). (ENG.). 52p. (J). (gr. 2-5). pap. 7.95 (978-1-60577-311-7(5)) Berry, Joy Enterprises.

Bidaisee, Sharlini. Toddler's Basic Knowledge. 2006. 13p. (J). 10.30 (978-1-4116-6849-2(9)) Lulu Pr., Inc.

Black, Howard, et al. Learning on Purpose: A Self-Management Approach to Study Skills. 2006. (Learning on Purpose Ser.). 320p. (gr. 7-12). pap. 14.99 (978-0-89455-753-8(X)) Critical Thinking Co., The.

Boothroyd, Jennifer. How I Do My Homework. 2014. (First Step Nonfiction - Responsibility in Action Ser.). (ENG., Illus.). 24p. (gr. k-2). pap. 6.95 (978-1-4677-3650-3(3)); lib. bdg. 23.93 (978-1-4677-3633-6(3), Lerner Pubns.) Lerner Publishing Group.

Burling, Alexis. Strengthening Test Preparation Skills. 2017. (Skills for Success Ser.). 64p. (J). (gr. 12-12). 34.45 (**978-1-5081-7574-2(8)**, Rosen Young Adult) Rosen Publishing Group, Inc., The.

Caillou: Thinking Skills. 2003. 32p. pap., wbk. ed. 14.95 incl. cd-rom (978-1-57791-030-5(3)) Brighter Minds Children's Publishing.

Cali, Charlene C. The Nature of Study Skills: Hardworking Helen K Honeybee Study Skills 3. Norcross, Harry, illus. 56p. (J). (gr. 8-9). 14.95 (978-1-57543-101-7(7)) MAR*CO Products, Inc.

Cassel, Katrina L. The Middle School Survival Manual. 2010. 128p. (J). (gr. 6-18). pap. 8.99 (978-0-7586-1790-3(9)) Concordia Publishing Hse.

Chapman, Sherill, et al, adapted by. Dot-to-Dot Stories. 2004. (Kids Can Learn with Franklin Ser.). (ENG., Illus.). 32p. (J). (gr. 1-3). 3.95 (978-1-55337-600-2(5)) Kids Can Pr., Ltd. CAN. Dist: Hachette Bk. Group.

Childs, Mattie S. Lesson Helpers. 2004. 74p. (YA). per. 19.99 (978-1-4116-0948-8(4)) Lulu Pr., Inc.

Creative Imaging. 2nd ed. 2004. 116p. (YA). pap. (978-0-938465-01-0(5)) Zo Publishing.

Doherty, Edith J. S. Primary Independent. 60p. (J). pap., stu. ed. 14.95 (978-0-945984-06-1(5), Zephyr Pr.) Chicago Review Pr., Inc.

DynaNotes Test Taking Tips. 2006. (J). pap. (978-1-933854-37-3(5)) DynaStudy, Inc.

DynaNotes Test Taking Tips Transparency Set. 2006. (J). trans. (978-1-933854-38-0(3)) DynaStudy, Inc.

Everett, Reese. Homework, Yes or No. 2016. (Seeing Both Sides Ser.). (ENG.). 32p. (gr. 3-6). 32.79 (978-1-68191-380-3(1)) Rourke Educational Media.

Fetty, Margaret, ed. The Ultimate Book of Second Grade Skills: Grade 2. Hierstein, Judy & Boyer, Lyn, illus. 2009. (Ultimate Book of Skills Ser.). 224p. pap. 16.99 (978-1-4190-9953-3(1)) Steck-Vaughn.

Fry, Ron. Surefire Tips to Improve Your Memory Skills, 01 vols., 1. 2016. (Surefire Study Success Ser.). (ENG.). 128p. (YA). 35.60 (978-1-5081-7089-1(4), Rosen Young Adult) Rosen Publishing Group, Inc., The.

—Surefire Tips to Improve Your Reading Skills, 01 vols., 1. 2016. (Surefire Study Success Ser.). (ENG.). 128p. (YA). 35.60 (978-1-5081-7094-5(0), Rosen Young Adult) Rosen Publishing Group, Inc., The.

—Surefire Tips to Improve Your Study Skills, 01 vols., 1. 2016. (Surefire Study Success Ser.). (ENG.). 128p. (J). 35.60 (978-1-5081-7098-3(3), Rosen Young Adult) Rosen Publishing Group, Inc., The.

Future Ready Project Skills. 2017. (Future Ready Project Skills Ser.). 48p. (gr. 3-4). pap. 70.20 (**978-0-7660-8809-2(X)**) Enslow Pubs., Inc.

Gehret, Jeanne. The Don't-Give-Up Kid: And Learning Differences. DePauw, Sandra A., illus. 2nd rev. ed. 2003. 40p. (J). (gr. 1-5). 13.95 (978-0-9625136-3-3(6)) Verbal Images Pr.

Girard, Vanessa P. High School Survival Guide: United in Diversity. 2008. (Illus.). 72p. (YA). pap. 11.95 (978-0-939479-33-7(8), Backintyme) Backintyme Publishing.

Goldhammer, Richard. Gotta Do Homework! Elephant Notes - Study Tips You'll Never Forget. 2003. (Elephant Notes Ser.). (YA). (gr. 6-8). spiral bd. (978-0-9716873-0-1(7)) ElephantSide Pr.

Greve, Meg. Taking Notes & Close Reading. 2014. (ENG.). 24p. (gr. 3-5). 28.50 (978-1-62717-689-7(6)) Rourke Educational Media.

Hands-On Literacy Center - Farm Set. (J). (gr. -1-1). pap. 149.00 (978-0-9673268-9-4(3)) Learning Fasten-Ations, Inc.

Heiderer, Conrad. Alpha-Blocke: Alpha-Blocke.com Learning Forum Animals, Art & the Alphabet Series with Case & Talking CD. 2004. (Illus.). 32p. spiral bd. 39.95 incl. audio compact disk (978-0-9746699-0-8(3)) Heiderer, Conrad.

Holt, Rinehart and Winston Staff. Holt Science & Technology: Directed Reading Answer Key. 4th ed. 2004. (Illus.). pap. 11.20 (978-0-03-037018-2(3)) Holt McDougal.

—Holt Science & Technology: Directed Reading Worksheets. 4th ed. 2004. pap. 15.00 (978-0-03-036994-0(0)); pap. 15.00 (978-0-03-036993-3(2)); pap. 15.00 (978-0-03-036992-6(4)) Holt McDougal.

HOP, LLC. Hooked on Kindergarten. 2006. 99.99 (978-1-933863-88-7(9)) HOP, LLC.

—Hooked on Pre-K. 2006. 99.99 (978-1-933863-89-4(7)) HOP, LLC.

—Sylvan School Success. 2006. 199.99 (978-1-931020-76-3(0)) HOP, LLC.

Jensen, Eric. Student Success Secrets. 5th ed. 2003. (ENG., Illus.). 256p. pap. 10.99 (978-0-7641-2007-7(7)) Barron's Educational Series, Inc.

Kids Can Press Staff. Measurement. 2003. (Kids Can Learn with Franklin Ser.). (ENG., Illus.). 32p. (J). (gr. k-1). 3.95 (978-1-55337-595-1(5)) Kids Can Pr., Ltd. CAN. Dist: Hachette Bk. Group.

Lambert, Monica & Algozzine, Bob. Strategies That Make Learning Fun. 2nd ed. 2003. (Illus.). 184p. (gr. k-12). 36.95 (978-1-57035-915-6(6), 211LEARN) Cambium Education, Inc.

Learning Company Books Staff, ed. Reader Rabbit 1st Grade Workbook. 2003. (Illus.). 320p. (J). (gr. 1-18). pap., wbk. ed. (978-0-7630-7543-9(4)) Magma.

—Reader Rabbit Kindergarten Workbook. 2003. (Illus.). 320p. (J). (gr. k-18). pap., wbk. ed. (978-0-7630-7542-2(6)) Magma.

—Reader Rabbit Preschool Workbook. 2003. (Illus.). 320p. (J). (gr. -1-18). pap., wbk. ed. (978-0-7630-7541-5(8)) Magma.

Moore, Gary W. Becoming a Master Student: Keys to Student Success. 2004. 305p. 38.00 (978-0-9760939-0-9(1), 0-9760939-0-1) Tudor Assocs. Pr.

Morris, Daphne. Trevor Romain's How to Do Homework Without Throwing up DVD Educator Kit. 2007. (J). 69.99 (978-1-934365-00-7(9)) Romain, Trevor Co., The.

—Trevor Romain's How to Do Homework Without Throwing up VHS Educator Kit. 2007. (J). 69.99 (978-1-934365-01-4(7)) Romain, Trevor Co., The.

Mosley, Nina Simone. Studying & Test Taking. 2014. (ENG.). 24p. (gr. 3-5). 28.50 (978-1-62717-688-0(8)) Rourke Educational Media.

Moss, Marissa. Amelia's Book of Notes & Note Passing. Moss, Marissa, illus. 2006. (Amelia Ser.). (ENG., Illus.). 80p. (J). (gr. 4-7). 9.95 (978-0-689-87446-8(4), Simon & Schuster/Paula Wiseman Bks.) Simon & Schuster/Paula Wiseman Bks.

Moss, Wendy. School Made Easier: A Kid's Guide to Study Strategies & Anxiety-Busting Tools. 2014. (Illus.). vii, 128p. pap. (978-1-4338-1336-8(X), Magination Pr.) American Psychological Assn.

Moss, Wendy L. & DeLuca-Acconi, Robin. School Made Easier: A Kid's Guide to Study Strategies & Anxiety-Busting Tools. 2013. (Illus.). 128p. 14.95 (978-1-4338-1335-1(1), Magination Pr.) American Psychological Assn.

Newsom, Mary T. & Jones, Joy. The Homework Survival Kit. (J). (978-0-9637644-2-3(X)) Spoken Word, The.

Osborne, Corinne. Picture Book Learning, Vol. 1. 2004. (ENG & AFA.). 60p. per. 11.99 (978-0-9760725-0-8(5), PBLSSV1P) Picture Bk. Learning, Inc.

Percival, Simon. The Practical Guide to Revision Techniques. 2005. (Practical Guides). (ENG., Illus.). 72p. per. (978-1-85539-201-4(1), Network Continuum Education) Bloomsbury Publishing Plc.

Rosenberg, Gary, et al. Jon & Jayne's Guide to Getting Through School. 2009. (Jon & Jayne Doe Ser.: No. 3). (ENG., Illus.). 128p. (YA). (gr. 7-11). pap. 9.95 (978-0-7573-0735-5(3), HCI Teens) Health Communications, Inc.

Royston, Angela. Tips for Better Planning. 2017. (Student's Toolbox Ser.). (ENG., Illus.). 32p. (J). (gr. 4-6). 17.99 (978-0-7502-9097-5(8), Wayland) Hachette Children's Group GBR. Dist: Hachette Bk. Group.

Rozakis, Laurie. Get Test Smart! The Ultimate Guide to Middle School Standardized Tests. 2007. 144p. (J). (978-1-4287-1884-5(2), Scholastic Reference) Scholastic, Inc.

Scholastic, Inc. Staff & Stevens, Chris. Thirty Days Has September: Cool Ways to Remember Stuff. Home, Sarah, illus. 2008. (Best at Everything Ser.). (ENG.). 128p. (J). (gr. 3-7). 12.99 (978-0-545-10740-2(7), Scholastic Nonfiction) Scholastic, Inc.

School Zone Publishing Company Staff. Following Directions. (Illus.). (J). 19.99 incl. audio compact disk (978-0-88743-930-8(6)) School Zone Publishing Co.

Scott, John, suppl. How to Study. 2004. (YA). 30.00 (978-1-879498-80-8(4)) SportAmerica.

Sirotowitz, Sandi, et al. Study Strategies for Early School Success: Seven Steps to Improve Your Learning. Dimatteo, Richard, illus. 2003. (Seven Steps Family Guides). (ENG.). 146p. pap. 18.00 (978-1-886941-55-7(6)) Specialty Pr., Inc.

Steck-Vaughn, creator. Using Information Resources, Grade 2. 2009. (Using Information Resources Ser.). (Illus.). 64p. pap. 9.99 (978-1-4190-9937-3(X)) Steck-Vaughn.

—Using Information Resources, Grade 3. 2009. (Using Information Resources Ser.). (Illus.). 64p. pap. 9.99 (978-1-4190-9938-0(8)) Steck-Vaughn.

—Using Information Resources, Grade 4. 2009. (Using Information Resources Ser.). (Illus.). 64p. pap. 9.99 (978-1-4190-9939-7(6)) Steck-Vaughn.

—Using Information Resources, Grade 5. 2009. (Using Information Resources Ser.). (Illus.). 64p. pap. 9.99 (978-1-4190-9940-3(X)) Steck-Vaughn.

—Using Information Resources, Grade 6. 2009. (Using Information Resources Ser.). (Illus.). 64p. pap. 9.99 (978-1-4190-9941-0(8)) Steck-Vaughn.

Stern, Judith M. & Ben-Ami, Uzi. Many Ways to Learn: A Kid's Guide to LD. Chesworth, Michael, illus. 2nd rev. ed. 2010. 96p. (J). (gr. 3-8). 14.95 (978-1-4338-0739-8(4)); pap. 9.95 (978-1-4338-0740-4(8)) American Psychological Assn. (Magination Pr.).

Study Skills & Strategies for Students in High School. 2005. spiral bd. 40.00 (978-0-9745999-4-6(8)) Mangrum-Strichart Learning Resources.

Study Skills Fun. 2003. 34.95 (978-1-57543-115-4(7)) MAR*CO Products, Inc.

Summer School Program: Grade 1 Complete Package. (gr. 1-18). 650.00 (978-0-7578-3236-9(9)) Rigby Education.

Summer School Program: Grade 2 Complete Package. (gr. 2-18). 750.00 (978-0-7578-3237-6(7)) Rigby Education.

Summer School Program: Grade 3 Complete Package. (gr. 3-18). 750.00 (978-0-7578-3238-3(5)) Rigby Education.

Summer School Program: Grade 4 Complete Package. (gr. 4-18). 750.00 (978-0-7578-3239-0(3)) Rigby Education.

Summer School Program: Grade 5 Complete Package. (gr. 5-18). 650.00 (978-0-7578-3240-6(7)) Rigby Education.

Summer School Program: Grade 6 Complete Package. (gr. 6-18). 725.00 (978-0-7578-3241-3(5)) Rigby Education.

Summer School Program: Grade 7 Complete Package. (gr. 7-18). 725.00 (978-0-7578-3242-0(3)) Rigby Education.

Summer School Program: Grade 8 Complete Package. (gr. 8-18). 725.00 (978-0-7578-3243-7(1)) Rigby Education.

Summer School Program: Grade K Complete Package. (gr. k-18). 650.00 (978-0-7578-3235-2(0)) Rigby Education.

Swim, Luann. Cracking the System. 2012. 60p. pap. 29.95 (978-1-937065-00-3(6)) B & B Educational Advancement & Pubns., Inc.

Teacher Created Resources Staff. Mastering Fifth Grade Skills. 2006. (ENG.). 240p. (gr. 5). pap. 19.99 (978-1-4206-3941-4(2)) Teacher Created Resources, Inc.

ThemeMaker Student Tool. 2005. 4.90 (978-0-9769527-9-4(3)) Mindwing Concepts, Inc.

Thinking Kids & Carson-Dellosa Publishing, compiled by. Adventures in Learning. 2017. (Adventures in Learning Ser.). (ENG.). 256p. (gr. -1 — 1). pap. 12.99 (**978-1-4838-3510-5(3)**, Thinking Kids) Carson-Dellosa Publishing, LLC.

Walsh, Brian Everard. Thinking, Reading, Remembering: Brain-Friendly Tips & Techniques for a Student's Enriched Learning. 2013. 76p. pap. (978-0-9917463-5-4(X)) Walsh Seminars, Ltd.

Watkins, Dewhite. Quick & Dirty Secrets of College Success: A Professor Tells It All. 2004. 128p. (YA). per. 14.95 (978-0-9742632-1-2(4)) Blue Boy Publishing Co.

The Weaver Curriculum. 2004. (gr. k-12). Vol. 1. 145.00 (978-1-58095-842-4(7), WV001, Weaver) Vol. 2. 145.00 (978-1-58095-843-1(5), WV002, Weaver) Vol. 3. 145.00 (978-1-58095-844-8(3), WV003, Lifepac) Vol. 4. 145.00 (978-1-58095-845-5(1), WV004, Lifepac) Vol. 5. 145.00 (978-1-58095-846-2(X), WV005, Weaver) Alpha Omega Pubns., Inc.

Whamond, Dave, illus. Superbrain: The Insider's Guide to Getting Smart. 2015. (ENG.). 72p. (J). (gr. 4-6). pap. 9.95 (978-1-55451-734-3(6), 9781554517343) Annick Pr., Ltd. CAN. Dist: Publishers Group West (PGW).

Whitney, Brooks. How to Master the School Universe: Homework, Teachers, Tests, Bullies, & Other Ways to Survive the Classroom. Kennedy, Kelly, illus. 2004. 80p. (J). pap. (978-0-439-57902-5(3)) Scholastic, Inc.

Willis, Mariaemma & Kindle Hodson, Victoria. Mid-life Crisis Begins in Kindergarten: How we learn the habit of settling for Less. 2004. spiral bd. 10.00 (978-0-9772350-0-1(9)) LearningSuccess Pr.

STUNT PERFORMERS

Cohn, Jessica. ¡Intrépidos! Dobles de Riesgo. 2016. (TIME for Kids en Español - Level 5 Ser.). (SPA.). 64p. (gr. 5-5). lib. bdg. 31.99 (978-1-5157-2946-4(X)) Time for Kids Inc AUS. Dist: Capstone Pub.

Cohn, Jessica & Kuligowski, Stephanie. Fearless! Stunt People, 1 vol. 2nd rev. ed. 2013. (Nonfiction Readers Ser.). (ENG.). 64p. (J). (gr. 5-5). pap. 10.99 (978-1-4333-4941-6(8)) Teacher Created Materials, Inc.

Cummins, Julie. Sam Patch: Daredevil Jumper. Austin, Michael Allen, illus. 2009. (ENG.). 32p. (J). (gr. -1-3). 16.95 (978-0-8234-1741-4(7)) Holiday Hse., Inc.

Goldsworthy, Steve. A Daredevil's Guide to Stunts, 1 vol. 2013. (Daredevils' Guides). (ENG.). 48p. (gr. 3-4). 31.99 (978-1-4296-9987-7(6)) Capstone Press of Coughlan Cos.

Gonzalez, Lissette. Stunt Performers & Stunt Doubles. (Dangerous Jobs Ser.). 24p. 2009. (gr. 2-3). 42.50 (978-1-61512-136-6(6)) 2007. (Illus.). (J). (gr. -1-3). lib. bdg. 22.60 (978-1-4042-3780-3(1)) Rosen Publishing Group, Inc., The. (PowerKids Pr.).

Hamilton, S. L. Daredevil. 2015. 32p. E-Book 27.07 (978-1-62403-757-3(7)) ABDO Publishing Co.

—Stunt Performer. 2015. 32p. pap. 27.07 (978-1-62403-760-3(7)) ABDO Publishing Co.

Horn, Geoffrey M. Movie Stunts & Special Effects. 2006. (Making Movies Ser.). (Illus.). 32p. (gr. 5-8). lib. bdg. 26.00 (978-0-8368-6840-1(4)) Stevens, Gareth Publishing LLLP.

Kuligowski, Stephanie & Cohn, Jessica. Fearless! Stunt People. 1 vol. 2nd rev. ed. 2013. (Nonfiction Readers Ser.). (ENG., Illus.). 64p. (J). (gr. 5-5). pap. 31.96 (978-1-4333-7440-1(4)) Teacher Created Materials, Inc.

Mello, Tara Baukus. Stunt Driving. rev. ed. 2007. (Race Car Legends Ser.). (Illus.). 71p. (YA). (gr. 5-9). lib. bdg. 25.00 (978-0-7910-8666-7(6)) Facts On File, Inc.

Monnig, Alex. Stunt Performers in Action. 2017. (Dangerous Jobs in Action Ser.). (ENG.). 32p. (J). (gr. 3-6). lib. bdg. 27.07 (978-1-5038-1633-6(8), 211149) Child's World, Inc., The.

Pipe, Jim. Stunt Crews: Death-Defying Feats. 2012. (Mission Impossible Ser.). (Illus.). 32p. (gr. 4-8). lib. bdg. 31.35 (978-1-936333-30-1(9)) Brown Bear Bks.

Richard, Stephen. Stunt Man. 2008. (321 Go! Ser.). (ENG., Illus.). 32p. pap. (978-1-84167-784-2(1)) Ransom Publishing Ltd.

Ridley, Frances. Stunt Pros. 2009. (ENG., Illus.). 32p. (J). (gr. 4-7). lib. bdg. (978-0-7787-3779-7(9)) Crabtree Publishing Co.

Thomas, Isabel. Being a Stunt Performer. 2012. (On the Radar: Awesome Jobs Ser.). (ENG., Illus.). 32p. (gr. 4-8). lib. bdg. 26.60 (978-0-7613-7776-4(X), Lerner Pubns.) Lerner Publishing Group.

Tougas, Joe. Mind-Blowing Movie Stunts. 2015. (Wild Stunts Ser.). (ENG., Illus.). 32p. (gr. 3-4). lib. bdg. 27.99 (978-1-4914-4256-2(5)) Capstone Press of Coughlan Cos.

Tougas, Joe, et al. Wild Stunts. 2015. (Wild Stunts Ser.). (ENG.). 32p. (gr. 3-4). 111.96 (978-1-4914-6666-7(9), Edge Bks.) Capstone Press of Coughlan Cos.

Turner, Cherie. Stunt Performers: Life Before the Camera. 2005. (Extreme Careers Ser.). (Illus.). 64p. (YA). (gr. 5-8). 26.50 (978-0-8239-3371-6(7)) Rosen Publishing Group, Inc., The.

Wood, Alix. Stunt Performer, 1 vol., 1. 2014. (World's Coolest Jobs Ser.). (ENG.). 32p. (J). (gr. 3-6). 26.25

(978-1-4777-5999-8(9), PowerKids Pr.) Rosen Publishing Group, Inc., The.

STUYVESANT, PETER, 1592-1672

Cody, Matt W. Peter Stuyvesant. 2010. (Leaders of the Colonial Era Ser.). 120p. (gr. 5-8). 35.00 *(978-1-60413-740-8(1),* Chelsea Hse.) Facts On File, Inc.

Krizner, L. J. Peter Stuyvesant: New Amsterdam, & the Origins of New York. 2009. (Library of American Lives & Times Ser.). 112p. (gr. 5-5). 69.20 *(978-1-60853-498-2(7))* Rosen Publishing Group, Inc., The.

Krizner, L. J. & Sita, Lisa. Peter Stuyvesant: New Amsterdam & the Origins of New York. 2005. (Library of American Lives & Times). (Illus.). 112p. (J). (gr. 4-8). lib. bdg. 34.60 *(978-0-8239-5732-3(2))* Rosen Publishing Group, Inc., The.

Whiting, Jim. Peter Stuyvesant. 2007. (Profiles in American History Ser.). (Illus.). 48p. (J). (gr. 3-7). lib. bdg. 29.95 *(978-1-58415-526-3(4))* Mitchell Lane Pubs., Inc.

STYLE, LITERARY

see also Criticism; Letter Writing; Literature—History and Criticism; Rhetoric

Bodden, Valerie. Imagery & Description. 2016. (Illus.). 80p. (J). *(978-1-60818-728-7(4),* Creative Education) Creative Co., The.

—Wording & Tone. (Odysseys in Prose Ser.). (Illus.). 80p. (J). 2017. (ENG.). (gr. 7-11). pap. 14.99 *(978-1-62832-326-9(4),* Creative Paperbacks) 2016. *(978-1-60818-730-0(6),* Creative Education) Creative Co., The.

Donovan, Sandy. Bored Bella Learns about Fiction & Nonfiction, 1 vol. Hernandez, Leeza, illus. 2010. (In the Library). (ENG.). 24p. (gr. k-4). lib. bdg. 26.65 *(978-1-4048-5758-2(3))* Picture Window Bks.

STYLE IN DRESS

see Costume; Fashion

SU DOKU

see Sudoku

SUBMARINE DIVING

see Deep Diving

SUBMARINE EXPLORATION

see Underwater Exploration

SUBMARINE GEOLOGY

Meredith, Susan. Undersea Life to Color. Cooper, Jenny, illus. 2014. (ENG.). (J). pap. 5.99 *(978-0-7945-2854-6(6),* Usborne) EDC Publishing.

SUBMARINE WARFARE

see also Submarines (Ships)

Nardo, Don. In the Water: Strategies & Tactics. 2014. (J). *(978-1-59935-464-4(0))* Reynolds, Morgan Inc.

—In the Water: Torpedoes, Missiles, & Dive-Bombs. 2014. (ENG.). (J). 27.45 *(978-1-59935-460-6(8))* Reynolds, Morgan Inc.

West, Krista. Underwater Warfare of the Future. (Library of Future Weaponry Ser.). 64p. 2009. (gr. 6-6). 58.50 *(978-1-60853-642-9(4))* 2005. (Illus.). (J). (gr. 2-7). lib. bdg. 31.95 *(978-1-4042-0522-2(5))* Rosen Publishing Group, Inc., The.

SUBMARINES (SHIPS)

Allen, Kenny. Submarines. 2012. (Monster Machines Ser.). (Illus.). 24p. (J). (gr. 1-3). pap. 8.15 *(978-1-4339-7180-8(1));* lib. bdg. 22.60 *(978-1-4339-7179-2(8))* Stevens, Gareth Publishing LLLP.

Aloian, Molly. Deep-Diving Submarines. 2011. (ENG.). 32p. (J). *(978-0-7787-2728-6(9));* (Vehicles on the Move Ser.: No. 14). pap. *(978-0-7787-2735-4(1))* Crabtree Publishing Co.

Alpert, Barbara. U. S. Military Submarines, 1 vol. 2012. (U. S. Military Technology Ser.). (ENG., Illus.). 32p. (gr. 1-2). lib. bdg. 26.65 *(978-1-4296-8440-8(2))* Capstone Press of Coughlan Cos.

Amato, William. Nuclear Submarines. 2009. (High-Tech Vehicles Ser.). 24p. (gr. 2-3). 42.50 *(978-1-61513-306-2(2),* PowerKids Pr.) Rosen Publishing Group, Inc., The.

—Submarinos nucleares (Nuclear Submarines) 2009. (Vehículos de alta tecnología (High-Tech Vehicles) Ser.). (SPA.). 24p. (gr. 2-3). 42.50 *(978-1-60854-720-3(5),* Editorial Buenas Letras) Rosen Publishing Group, Inc., The.

Boatner, Kay. Funny Fill-In - My Ocean Adventure. 2013. (ENG., Illus.). 48p. (J). (gr. 3-7). pap. 4.99 *(978-1-4263-1643-2(7),* National Geographic Children's Bks.) National Geographic Society.

Bodden, Valerie. Submarines. 2012. (Illus.). 23p. (J). 25.65 *(978-1-60818-128-5(6),* Creative Education) Creative Co., The.

Brook, Henry. True Sea Stories. 2005. (True Adventure Stories Ser.). (Illus.). 154p. (J). (gr. 5). lib. bdg. 12.95 *(978-1-58086-693-4(X))* EDC Publishing.

Cooke, Tim. Submarines. 2012. (Ultimate Military Machines Ser.). (Illus.). 32p. (gr. 4-7). lib. bdg. 31.35 *(978-1-59920-822-0(9))* Black Rabbit Bks.

Diedrick, Noah. Submarines: Use Place Value Understanding & Properties of Operations to Perform Multi-Digit Arithmetic. 2014. (Rosen Common Core Math Readers Ser.). (ENG.). 24p. (J). (gr. 3-4). pap. 8.25 *(978-1-4777-4936-4(5),* PowerKids Pr.) Rosen Publishing Group, Inc., The.

Doeden, Matt. Submarines. 2005. (Pull Ahead Books-Mighty Movers Ser.). (ENG., Illus.). 32p. (gr. k-3). lib. bdg. 22.60 *(978-0-8225-2669-8(7),* Lerner Pubns.); per. 7.95 *(978-0-8225-2900-2(9))* Lerner Publishing Group.

Doyle, Kevin. Submarines. 2004. (Military Hardware in Action Ser.). (Illus.). 48p. (J). (gr. 4-9). lib. bdg. 25.26 *(978-0-8225-4704-4(X))* Lerner Publishing Group.

Ellis, Catherine. Submarines. (Mega Military Machines Ser.). 24p. 2009. (gr. 1-1). 42.50 *(978-1-61514-638-3(5),* PowerKids Pr.) 2007. (Illus.). (J). (gr. 3-7). lib. bdg. 22.60 *(978-1-4042-3665-3(1))* Rosen Publishing Group, Inc., The.

—Submarines/Submarinos. 2009. (Mega Military Machines/Megamaquinas militares Ser.). (ENG & SPA.). 24p. (gr. 1-1). 42.50 *(978-1-61514-643-7(1),* Editorial Buenas Letras) Rosen Publishing Group, Inc., The.

—Submarines/Submarinos. Brusca, Maria Cristina, tr. from ENG. 2007. (Mega Military Machines / Megamaquinas Militares Ser.). (SPA., Illus.). 24p. (J). lib. bdg. 22.60 *(978-1-4042-7620-8(3),* PowerKids Pr.) Rosen Publishing Group, Inc., The.

Fein, Eric. The USS Greeneville Submarine Disaster: When Disaster Strikes! 2005. (When Disaster Strikes! Ser.). (Illus.). 48p. (YA). (gr. 5-8). lib. bdg. 29.25 *(978-0-8239-3676-2(7))* Rosen Publishing Group, Inc., The.

Frith, Alex. Submarines II. 2011. (Submarines Ser.). 80p. (J). pap. 8.99 *(978-0-7945-2557-6(1),* Usborne) EDC Publishing.

Garcia, Adam. Inside Submarines: Use Place Value Understanding & Properties of Operations to Perform Multi-Digit Arithmetic, 1 vol. 2015. (InfoMax Common Core Math Readers Ser.). (ENG.). 24p. (J). pap. 8.25 *(978-1-4777-4627-1(7),* Rosen Classroom) Rosen Publishing Group, Inc., The.

Gilpin, Daniel & Pang, Alex. Modern Warships & Submarines. 2010. (Machines Close-Up Ser.). 32p. (J). (gr. 4-7). 28.50 *(978-1-60870-110-0(7))* Marshall Cavendish Corp.

Hamilton, John. Submarines. 2012. (Military Ships Ser.). 32p. (J). (gr. 3-9). 27.07 *(978-1-61783-524-7(2),* A&D Xtreme) ABDO Publishing Co.

Harasymiw, Mark. Extreme Jobs in Extreme Places: Life on a Submarine. 2013. (Extreme Jobs in Extreme Places Ser.). (Illus.). 32p. (gr. 3-6). pap. 10.50 *(978-1-4339-8503-4(9));* lib. bdg. 26.60 *(978-1-4339-8502-7(0))* Stevens, Gareth Publishing LLLP.

Jackson, Kay. Navy Submarines in Action. 2009. (Amazing Military Vehicles Ser.). 24p. (gr. 3-5). (J). pap. 8.25 *(978-1-4358-3161-2(6),* PowerKids Pr.); 42.50 *(978-1-61511-324-8(X),* PowerKids Pr.); (YA). lib. bdg. 22.60 *(978-1-4358-2751-6(1))* Rosen Publishing Group, Inc., The.

Kiland, Taylor Baldwin & Teitelbaum, Michael. Military Submarines: Sea Power. 2015. (Military Engineering in Action Ser.). (ENG., Illus.). 48p. (J). (gr. 6-6). 27.93 *(978-0-7660-6918-3(4));* pap. 11.70 *(978-0-7660-7069-1(7))* Enslow Pubs., Inc.

Langley, Andrew. Submarines. 2010. (Machines on the Move Ser.). 32p. (J). 28.50 *(978-1-60753-062-6(7))* Amicus Publishing.

—Submarines. 2012. (Illus.). 32p. (gr. 1-3). pap. 8.95 *(978-1-926722-72-6(8))* Saunders Bk. Co. CAN. Dist: RiverStream Publishing.

Lock, Deborah. Submarines & Submersibles, Level 1. 2007. (DK Readers Ser.). (ENG., Illus.). 32p. (J). (gr. k-2). pap. 3.99 *(978-0-7566-2550-4(5),* DK Children) Dorling Kindersley Publishing, Inc.

Mahaney, Ian F. Extreme Submarines. 2015. (Extreme Machines Ser.). (ENG.). 32p. (J). (gr. 3-4). pap. 10.00 *(978-1-4994-1188-1(X),* PowerKids Pr.) Rosen Publishing Group, Inc., The.

Mallory, Kenneth. Adventure Beneath the Sea: Living in an Underwater Science Station. Skerry, Brian, photos by. 2010. (ENG., Illus.). 48p. (J). (gr. 4-6). 18.95 *(978-1-59078-607-9(6))* Boyds Mills Pr.

Marciniak, Kristin. Fascinating Military Submarines, 1 vol. 2014. (Ready for Military Action Ser.). (ENG.). 48p. (gr. 3-6). lib. bdg. 32.79 *(978-1-62403-651-4(1))* ABDO Publishing Co.

Matsen, Bradford. The Incredible Submersible Alvin Discovers a Strange Deep-Sea World. 2003. (Incredible Deep-Sea Adventures Ser.). (Illus.). 48p. (J). (gr. 4-10). lib. bdg. 23.93 *(978-0-7660-2189-1(0))* Enslow Pubs., Inc.

Mattern, Joanne. Submarines. 2015. (Rookie Read-About(tm) Science: How Things Work Ser.). (ENG., Illus.). 32p. (J). lib. bdg. 25.00 *(978-0-531-21374-2(9),* Children's Pr.) Scholastic Library Publishing.

Murray, Stuart. Submarines. 2014. (Illus.). 48p. (J). *(978-1-4351-5371-4(5))* Barnes & Noble, Inc.

—Submarines, 01 vols., 1. 2016. (What's Inside? Ser.). (ENG.). 48p. (J). pap. 11.75 *(978-1-5081-4615-5(2),* PowerKids Pr.) Rosen Publishing Group, Inc., The.

Nardo, Don. In the Water: Strategies & Tactics. 2014. (J). *(978-1-59935-464-4(0))* Reynolds, Morgan Inc.

—In the Water: Submarines. 2014. (J). *(978-1-59935-458-3(6))* Reynolds, Morgan Inc.

Nelson, Drew. Submarines & Submersibles. 2013. (Military Machines Ser.). (Illus.). 32p. (J). (gr. 3-6). pap. 10.50 *(978-1-4339-8478-5(4));* lib. bdg. 26.60 *(978-1-4339-8477-8(6))* Stevens, Gareth Publishing LLLP.

Oxlade, Chris. Inside Submarines. Viana, Tatio, illus. 2017. (Inside Military Machines Ser.). (ENG.). (J). (gr. 3-6). lib. bdg. 26.65 ***(978-1-5124-3224-4(5))*** Lerner Publishing Group.

Parker, Steve. Ships & Submarines. 2010. (How It Works Ser.). 40p. (J). (gr. 3-18). lib. bdg. 19.95 *(978-1-4222-1798-6(1))* Mason Crest.

Ross, David. The World's Most Powerful Submarines. 2016. (World's Most Powerful Machines Ser.). 00224p. (J). (gr. 9-9). 45.10 *(978-1-4994-6586-0(6))* Rosen Publishing Group, Inc., The.

Ruck, Colleen. Submarines. 2011. (My Favorite Machines Ser.). 24p. (gr. 2-5). 28.50 *(978-1-59920-678-3(1))* Black Rabbit Bks.

Spilsbury, Louise & Spilsbury, Richard. The Submarine, 1 vol. 2010. (Tales of Invention Ser.). (ENG.). 32p. (gr. 3-5). 30.65 *(978-1-4329-3831-4(2),* NA-h) Heinemann-Raintree.

Stefoff, Rebecca. Submarines. 2006. (Great Inventions Ser.). (Illus.). 128p. (gr. 8-7). lib. bdg. 29.95 *(978-0-7614-2229-7(3),* Benchmark Bks.) Marshall Cavendish Corp.

Stone, Lynn M. Submarines. 2005. (Fighting Forces Ser.). (Illus.). 32p. (J). (gr. 4-8). lib. bdg. 28.50 *(978-1-59515-466-8(3),* 1244408) Rourke Educational Media.

Teitelbaum, Michael. Submarines: Underwater Stealth. 2006. (Mighty Military Machines Ser.). (Illus.). 48p. (J). (gr. 4-10). lib. bdg. 25.27 *(978-0-7660-2659-9(0))* Enslow Pubs., Inc.

Walker, Sally M. Secrets of a Civil War Submarine: Solving the Mysteries of the H. L. Hunley. 2005. (ENG., Illus.). 112p. (gr. 4-12). 18.95 *(978-1-57505-830-6(8),* Carolrhoda Bks.) Lerner Publishing Group.

—Shipwreck Search: Discovery of the H. L. Hunley. Verstraete, Elaine, illus. (On My Own Science Ser.). (ENG.). 48p. (gr. 2-4). 2007. per. 6.95 *(978-0-8225-6449-2(1),* First Avenue Editions) 2006. lib. bdg. 25.26 *(978-1-57505-878-8(2),* Millbrook Pr.) Lerner Publishing Group.

Weller, George. The Story of Submarines. 2003. 210p. pap. 29.00 *(978-0-7581-4985-5(9))* Textbook Pubs.

West, David. Submarines. West, David, illus. 2017. (What's Inside? Ser.). (Illus.). 24p. (gr. k-3). 28.50 ***(978-1-62588-405-3(2),*** Smart Apple Media) Black Rabbit Bks.

—Submarines. 2015. (Mechanic Mike's Machines (continuation) Ser.). (Illus.). 24p. (J). (gr. k-3). 27.10 *(978-1-62588-068-0(5))* Black Rabbit Bks.

West, Krista. Underwater Warfare of the Future. (Library of Future Weaponry Ser.). 64p. 2009. (gr. 6-6). 58.50 *(978-1-60853-642-9(4))* 2005. (Illus.). (J). (gr. 2-7). lib. bdg. 31.95 *(978-1-4042-0522-2(5))* Rosen Publishing Group, Inc., The.

Zuehlke, Jeffrey. Indonesia in Pictures. 2nd ed. 2005. (Visual Geography Series, Second Ser.). (Illus.). 80p. (YA). (gr. 7-12). lib. bdg. 27.93 *(978-0-8225-2074-0(5))* Lerner Publishing Group.

SUBMARINES (SHIPS)—FICTION

Appleton, Victor. Into the Abyss. 2007. (Tom Swift, Young Inventor Ser.). (ENG.). 160p. (gr. 3-7). 27.07 *(978-1-59961-350-5(6))* Spotlight.

—Tom Swift & His Submarine Boat or Unde. 2006. pap. *(978-1-4065-0908-3(6))* Dodo Pr.

Bennett, Jeffrey, et al. Max Goes to Jupiter: A Science Adventure with Max the Dog. Carroll, Michael, illus. 2008. (Science Adventures with Max the Dog Ser.). (ENG.). 32p. (J). (gr. 2-4). 16.95 *(978-0-9721819-3-8(8))* Big Kid Science.

Blaine, John. The Boy Scouts on a Submarine. 2007. 112p. pap. 18.99 *(978-1-4346-3960-8(6))* Creative Media Partners, LLC.

—Boy Scouts on A Submarine. 2006. 25.95 *(978-1-4218-2969-2(X));* pap. 10.95 *(978-1-4218-3069-8(8))* 1st World Publishing, Inc.

—The Boy Scouts on a Submarine. Lt. ed. 2007. 124p. pap. 19.99 *(978-1-4346-3961-5(4))* Creative Media Partners, LLC.

Bunn, Bill. Kill Shot. 2015. (ENG.). 244p. pap. 16.99 *(978-1-938463-53-2(6))* Bitingduck Pr.

Carlson, Drew. Attack of the Turtle. Johnson, David A., illus. 2008. (ENG.). 157p. (YA). (gr. 4-9). per. 8.00 *(978-0-8028-5338-7(2))* Eerdmans, William B. Publishing Co.

Cummings, Mary. And the Baker's Boy Went to Sea. 2006. (Illus.). 195p. (YA). 16.95 *(978-0-9774855-0-5(1))* Sparkling Pr.

De Lesseps, Ferdinand Zoticus. Oceanology: The True Account of the Voyage of the Nautilus. Steer, Dugald A. & Hawkins, Emily, eds. 2009. (Ologies Ser.: 8). (ENG., Illus.). 32p. (J). (gr. 3-7). 24.99 *(978-0-7636-4290-7(8))* Candlewick Pr.

Dickinson, Peter. Emma Tupper's Diary. 2014. (ENG.). 212p. (J). (gr. 4). pap. 12.00 *(978-1-61873-063-3(0),* Big Mouth Hse.) Small Beer Pr.

Drake, Robert L. The Boy Allies under the Sea. 2005. 27.95 *(978-1-4218-1083-6(2));* 244p. pap. 12.95 *(978-1-4218-1183-3(9))* 1st World Publishing, Inc. (1st World Library - Literary Society).

Driscoll, James R. The Brighton Boys with the Submarine Fleet. 2005. 26.95 *(978-1-59540-819-8(3),* 1st World Library - Literary Society) 1st World Publishing, Inc.

Durham, Victor G. Submarine Boys & the Spies. 2006. 27.95 *(978-1-4218-3008-7(6));* pap. 12.95 *(978-1-4218-3108-4(2))* 1st World Publishing, Inc.

—The Submarine Boys & the Spies: Dodging the Sharks of the Deep. 2007. (ENG.). 160p. pap. 19.99 *(978-1-4346-2818-3(3));* 170p. pap. 21.99 *(978-1-4346-2847-3(7))* Creative Media Partners, LLC.

—Submarine Boys for the Flag. 2006. 27.95 *(978-1-4218-3009-4(4));* pap. 12.95 *(978-1-4218-3109-1(0))* 1st World Publishing, Inc.

—The Submarine Boys for the Flag: Deeding Their Lives to Uncle Sam. 2007. (ENG.). 158p. pap. 19.99 *(978-1-4346-2849-7(3));* 174p. pap. 21.99 *(978-1-4346-2884-8(1))* Creative Media Partners, LLC.

—Submarine Boys Lightning Cruise. 2006. 27.95 *(978-1-4218-3010-0(8));* pap. 12.95 *(978-1-4218-3110-7(4))* 1st World Publishing, Inc.

—The Submarine Boys' Lightning Cruise: The Young Kings of the Deep. 2007. (ENG.). 156p. pap. 19.99 *(978-1-4346-2848-0(5));* 174p. pap. 21.99 *(978-1-4346-2883-1(3))* Creative Media Partners, LLC.

—Submarine Boys on Duty. 2006. 27.95 *(978-1-4218-3011-7(6));* pap. 12.95 *(978-1-4218-3111-4(2))* 1st World Publishing, Inc.

—Submarine Boys Trial Trip. 2006. 26.95 *(978-1-4218-3012-4(4));* pap. 11.95 *(978-1-4218-3112-1(0))* 1st World Publishing, Inc.

Emmett, Jonathan. The Treasure of Captain Claw. Cox, Steve, illus. 2012. (ENG.). 32p. (J). (gr. -1-k). pap. 9.99 *(978-1-84616-741-6(8))* Hodder & Stoughton GBR. Dist: Hachette Bk. Group.

Falls, Kat. Rip Tide. 2011. (J). (Dark Life Ser.: 2). (ENG.). 320p. (gr. 3-7). 16.99 *(978-0-545-17843-3(6));* 314p. pap. *(978-0-545-43175-0(1))* Scholastic, Inc. (Scholastic Pr.).

Fleming, Candace. Papa's Mechanical Fish. Kulikov, Boris, illus. 2013. (ENG.). 40p. (J). (gr. k-3). 17.99 *(978-0-374-39908-5(5),* 9780374399085, Farrar, Straus & Giroux (BYR)) Farrar, Straus & Giroux.

Freer, Dave. Cuttlefish. 2012. (ENG.). 299p. (YA). (gr. 7). 16.95 *(978-1-61614-625-2(7))* Prometheus Bks., Pubs.

Gardner, Charlie. The Beatles Yellow Submarine. Edelmann, Heinz, illus. 2006. 37p. (J). (gr. 4-8). reprint ed. 18.00 *(978-1-4223-5184-0(X))* DIANE Publishing Co.

Gilson, Jamie. Thirteen Ways to Sink a Sub. (J). 4.50 *(978-0-8072-1387-2(X),* Listening Library) Random Hse. Audio Publishing Group.

Larry, H. I. Deep Waters. Oswald, Ash, illus. 2008. (Zac Power Ser.: 2). (ENG.). 96p. (J). (gr. 3-6). pap. 5.99 *(978-0-312-34655-3(7),* 9780312346553) Square Fish.

London, C. Alexander. Blood in the Water. 2014. (Tides of War Ser.: 1). (ENG.). 224p. (J). (gr. 5-9). pap. 5.99 *(978-0-545-66298-7(2),* Scholastic Paperbacks) Scholastic, Inc.

McOmber, Rachel B., ed. McOmber Phonics Storybooks: The Sub. rev. ed. (Illus.). (J). *(978-0-944991-22-0(X))* Swift Learning Resources.

Mitton, Tony & Parker, Ant. Super Submarines. 2014. (Amazing Machines Ser.). (ENG., Illus.). 24p. (J). (gr. -1-k). 4.99 *(978-0-7534-7208-8(2),* 9780753472088, Kingfisher) Roaring Brook Pr.

—Super Submarines. 2014. (Amazing Machines Ser.). (J). lib. bdg. 14.75 *(978-0-606-36133-0(2))* Turtleback Bks.

My Day in a Submarine. 2004. (J). ring bd. 3.25 *(978-0-9762740-3-2(5),* Flat Kids) Smart Smiles Co., The.

Osborne, Mary Pope. Das magische Baumhaus 09. Der Ruf der Delfine. 18.95 *(978-3-7855-4185-2(6))* Loewe Verlag GmbH DEU. Dist: Distribooks, Inc.

Prestwood, Donna. Center World. 2006. 120p. per. 10.95 *(978-1-59824-206-5(7))* E-BookTime LLC.

Ralphson, G. Harvey. Boy Scouts in a Submarine. 2007. 104p. per. *(978-1-4068-3726-1(1))* Echo Library.

Rockwood, Roy. Under the Ocean to the South Pole. 2007. 120p. per. *(978-1-4068-3972-2(8))* Echo Library.

—Under the Ocean to the South Pole. 2009. 152p. 24.95 *(978-1-60664-626-7(5));* pap. 12.95 *(978-1-60664-365-5(7))* Rodgers, Alan Bks.

—Under the Ocean to the South Pole or the Strange Cruise of the Submarine Wonder. 2007. 180p. 95.99 *(978-1-4280-7589-4(5));* per. 89.99 *(978-1-4280-7588-7(7))* IndyPublish.com.

Roddy, Lee. Secret of the Sunken Sub. 2006. (Ladd Family Adventure Ser.: Vol. 5). (Illus.). 132p. (Orig.). (J). (gr. 4-7). per. 7.99 *(978-0-88062-254-7(7))* Mott Media.

Roy, Philip. Journey to Atlantis. 2009. (ENG., Illus.). 224p. pap. 10.95 *(978-1-55380-076-7(1))* Ronsdale Pr. CAN. Dist: SPD-Small Pr. Distribution.

—Submarine Outlaw. 2008. (ENG., Illus.). 254p. pap. 10.95 *(978-1-55380-058-3(3))* Ronsdale Pr. CAN. Dist: SPD-Small Pr. Distribution.

Swann, Stephen. Where's Our Submarine. 2009. 58p. pap. 21.50 *(978-1-4452-3146-4(8))* Lulu Pr., Inc.

Trowell, Michelle. Pilot Your Own Deep-Sea Submarine. Dronsfield, Paul, illus. 2007. 22p. (J). (gr. -1-3). *(978-1-84666-352-9(0),* Tide Mill Pr.) Top That! Publishing PLC.

Verne, Jules. Twenty Thousand Leagues under the Sea. Lt. ed. 2006. 592p. pap. *(978-1-84702-222-6(7))* Echo Library.

—Veinte Mil Leguas de Viaje Submarino.Tr. of Twenty Thousand Leagues under the Sea. (SPA., Illus.). 160p. (YA). 11.95 *(978-84-7281-075-4(5),* AF1075) Auriga, Ediciones S.A. ESP. Dist: Continental Bk. Co., Inc.

—20,000 Leagues under the Sea. 2008. (Bring the Classics to Life Ser.). (ENG., Illus.). 72p. (gr. 4-12). pap., act. bk. ed. 10.95 *(978-1-55576-091-5(0),* EDCTR405B) EDCON Publishing Group.

—20,000 Leagues under the Sea. D'Achille, Gino, illus. 2005. (Reader's Workshop Ser.). (ENG.). 88p. (C). pap. 17.95 *(978-0-7362-2806-0(3))* CENGAGE Learning.

—20,000 Leagues under the Sea, 1 vol. Fisher, Eric Scott, illus. 2011. (Calico Illustrated Classics Ser.: No. 3). (ENG.). 112p. (YA). (gr. 3-6). 27.07 *(978-1-61641-110-7(4))* Magic Wagon.

—20,000 Leagues under the Sea: Retold from the Jules Verne Original. Andreasen, Dan, illus. 2006. (Classic Starts(tm) Ser.). (ENG.). 160p. (J). (gr. 2-4). 6.95 *(978-1-4027-2533-3(7))* Sterling Publishing Co., Inc.

Verne, Jules & Fuentes, Benny. 20,000 Leguas de Viaje Submarino, 1 vol. Smith, Tod, illus. 2010. (Classic Fiction Ser.). (SPA.). 72p. (gr. 2-3). 27.99 *(978-1-4342-2324-1(8),* Graphic Revolve en Español) Stone Arch Bks.

SUBSTANCE ABUSE

see also Alcoholism; Drug Abuse; Tobacco Habit

Abramovitz, Melissa. Understanding Addiction. 2017. (Understanding Psychology Ser.). (ENG.). 80p. (YA). (gr. 5-12). ***(978-1-68282-271-5(0))*** ReferencePoint Pr., Inc.

Ambrose, Marylou & Deisler, Veronica. Investigate Cocaine & Crack. 2014. (Investigate Drugs Ser.). (Illus.). 112p. (J). (gr. 5-12). lib. bdg. 33.27 *(978-0-7660-4255-1(3))* Enslow Pubs., Inc.

—Investigate Methamphetamines. 2014. (Investigate Drugs Ser.). (Illus.). 112p. (J). (gr. 5-12). lib. bdg. 33.27 *(978-0-7660-4254-4(5))* Enslow Pubs., Inc.

Aretha, David. Inhalants: A MyReportLinks. com Book. 2005. (Drugs Ser.). (Illus.). 48p. (J). lib. bdg. 26.60 *(978-0-7660-5280-2(X),* MyReportLinks.com Bks.) Enslow Pubs., Inc.

Bankston, John. Inhalants = Busted! 2006. (Busted! Ser.). (Illus.). 104p. (J). (gr. 6-12). lib. bdg. 33.27 *(978-0-7660-2472-4(5),* 1250497) Enslow Pubs., Inc.

Berry, Joy. Substance Abuse. 2009. (ENG.). 52p. (J). (gr. k-7). pap. 7.95 *(978-1-60577-502-9(9))* Berry, Joy Enterprises.

Bestor, Sheri Mabry. Substance Abuse: The Ultimate Teen Guide. 2015. (It Happened to Me Ser.: 36). (ENG., Illus.). 208p. pap. 30.00 *(978-1-4422-5662-0(1))* Rowman & Littlefield Publishers, Inc.

—Substance Abuse: The Ultimate Teen Guide. 2013. (It Happened to Me Ser.: 36). (ENG., Illus.). 208p. (J). 55.00 *(978-0-8108-8558-5(1))* Scarecrow Pr., Inc.

Bigelow, Barbara C. & Edgar, Kathleen J. The UXL Encyclopedia of Drugs & Addictive Substances, 5 vols. 2005. (Illus.). (J). *(978-1-4144-0448-6(4)); (978-1-4144-0449-3(2)); (978-1-4144-0447-9(6)); (978-1-4144-0446-2(8)); (978-1-4144-0445-5(X))* Cengage Gale.

Brinkerhoff, Shirley. Drug Therapy & Substance-Related Disorders. 2004. (Encyclopedia of Psychiatric Drugs & Their Disorders Ser.). (Illus.). 128p. (YA). lib. bdg. 24.95 *(978-1-59084-577-6(3))* Mason Crest.

Burlingame, Jeff. Crystal Meth. 2013. (Dangerous Drugs Ser.). 64p. (J). (gr. 6-9). pap. 15.28 *(978-1-62712-059-3(9))* Cavendish Square Publishing.

Centore, Michael. Intervention & Recovery. Vol. 13. Becker, Sara, ed. 2016. (Drug Addiction & Recovery Ser.). (Illus.). 64p. (J). (gr. 7). 23.95 *(978-1-4222-3605-5(6))* Mason Crest.

Connolly, Sean. Inhalants. 2006. (Straight Talking Ser.). (Illus.). 46p. (YA). (gr. 4-7). lib. bdg. 32.80 *(978-1-58340-648-9(4))* Black Rabbit Bks.

—Inhalants. 2009. (Straight Talking Ser.). (Illus.). 46p. (YA). (gr. 8-12). pap. *(978-1-895058-53-6(8))* Saunders Bk. Co.

Cross, Carrie L. & Iorizzo, Carrie. Crystal Meth. 2011. (ENG.). 48p. (J). pap. *(978-0-7787-5514-2(2));* (gr. 4-7). lib. bdg. *(978-0-7787-5507-4(X))* Crabtree Publishing Co.

Curriculum in a Box: Substance Abuse. 2005. (YA). 924.95 incl. DVD *(978-1-55548-256-5(2),* 377dv) Human Relations Media.

Eben Field, Jon & Field, Jon Eben. Dealing with Drugs Inhalants & Solvents. 2011. (ENG.). 48p. (J). pap. *(978-0-7787-5515-9(0));* (gr. 4-7). lib. bdg. *(978-0-7787-5508-1(8))* Crabtree Publishing Co.

Esherick, Joan. Drug - & Alcohol-Related Health Issues. McDonnell, Mary Ann & Forman, Sara, eds. 2013. (Young

S

Adult's Guide to the Science of Health Ser.: 15). 128p. (J). (gr. 7-18). 24.95 *(978-1-4222-2808-1(8))* Mason Crest.

Espejo, Roman. Chemical Dependency. 2011. (Opposing Viewpoints Ser.). (ENG.). 224p. (gr. 12-12). lib. bdg. 48.80 *(978-0-7377-5215-1(7))*; 240p. (J). pap. 29.45 *(978-0-7377-5216-8(5))* Cengage Gale. (Greenhaven Pr., Inc.).

Flath, Camden. 21st-Century Counselors: New Approaches to Mental Health & Substance Abuse. 2010. (New Careers for the 21st Century Ser.). 64p. (YA). (gr. 7-18). pap. 9.95 *(978-1-4222-2046-7(X))*; (Illus.). lib. bdg. 22.95 *(978-1-4222-1825-9(2))* Mason Crest.

Flynn, Noa. Inhalants & Solvents: Sniffing Disaster. 2009. (Illicit & Misused Drugs Ser.). (Illus.). 128p. (YA). (gr. 7-18). lib. bdg. 24.95 *(978-1-4222-0157-2(0))* Mason Crest.

Friedman, Lauri S. Addiction. Haugen, David M., ed. 2013. (Introducing Issues with Opposing Viewpoints Ser.). (ENG., Illus.). 144p. (gr. 7-10). 42.00 *(978-0-7377-4164-3(3)*, Greenhaven Pr., Inc.) Cengage Gale.

Harrow, Jeremy. Crystal Meth. 2007. (Incredibly Disgusting Drugs Ser.). (Illus.). 48p. (YA). (gr. 5-9). lib. bdg. 29.25 *(978-1-4042-1953-3(6))* Rosen Publishing Group, Inc., The.

Hasan, Heather. Caffeine & Nicotine: A Dependent Society. 2009. (Drug Abuse & Society Ser.). 64p. (gr. 6-6). 58.50 *(978-1-61512-218-9(4))* Rosen Publishing Group, Inc., The.

Henneberg, Susan. Defeating Addiction & Alcoholism, 01 vols., 1. 2016. (Effective Survival Strategies Ser.). (ENG., Illus.). 64p. (J). 32.95 *(978-1-4994-6179-4(8)*, Rosen Young Adult) Rosen Publishing Group, Inc., The.

Higgins, Melissa. Living with Substance Addiction, 1 vol. 2012. (Living with Health Challenges Set 1 Ser.). (ENG.). 112p. (J). (gr. 6-12). lib. bdg. 35.64 *(978-1-61783-129-4(8)*, Essential Library) ABDO Publishing Co.

Human Relations Media, prod. Clued in! on Addiction & Your Brain. 2005. (ENG.). (J). pap. 4.95 *(978-1-55548-050-9(0)*, 674) Human Relations Media.

Hunter, David. Thousands of Deadly Chemicals: Smoking & Health. 2008. (J). pap. 26.95 *(978-1-4222-1334-6(X))* Mason Crest.

Information Plus Alcohol & Tobacco November 2005, Vol. 2005. 2005. 49.00 *(978-1-4144-0405-9(0))* Cengage Gale.

Ingram, W. Scott. Marijuana. 2008. (Junior Drug Awareness Ser.). (Illus.). 110p. (gr. 5-8). lib. bdg. 30.00 *(978-0-7910-9695-6(5)*, Chelsea Hse.) Facts On File, Inc.

Jacobson, Robert. Illegal Drugs America's Anguish. 2005. (Information Plus Reference: Illegal Drugs Ser.). 168p. (J). per. 49.00 *(978-1-4144-0419-6(0))* Cengage Gale.

Juzwiak, Rich. Addictive Personality. 2009. (Teen Mental Health Ser.). 48p. (gr. 5-6). 53.00 *(978-1-60853-292-6(5))* Rosen Publishing Group, Inc., The.

Juzwiak, Richard. Addictive Personality. 2008. (Teen Mental Health Ser.). (Illus.). 48p. (YA). (gr. 7-12). lib. bdg. 29.25 *(978-1-4042-1802-4(5))* Rosen Publishing Group, Inc., The.

Keegan, Kyle, et al. Chasing the High: A Firsthand Account of One Young Person's Experience with Substance Abuse. 2008. (ENG., Illus.). 208p. per. 11.95 *(978-0-19-531472-4(7))* Oxford Univ. Pr., Inc.

Koellhoffer, Tara. Inhalants & Solvents. 2008. (Junior Drug Awareness Ser.). 112p. (gr. 5-8). 30.00 *(978-0-7910-9698-7(X)*, Chelsea Hse.) Facts On File, Inc.

Latta, Sara L. Investigate Steroids & Performance Drugs. 2014. (Investigate Drugs Ser.). (Illus.). 112p. (J). (gr. 5-12). lib. bdg. 33.27 *(978-0-7660-4240-7(5))* Enslow Pubs., Inc.

Leonard, Basia & Roberts, Jeremy. The Truth about Prescription Drugs. 2011. (Drugs & Consequences Ser.). (Illus.). 64p. (YA). (gr. 7-12). lib. bdg. 31.95 *(978-1-4488-4642-9(0))* Rosen Publishing Group, Inc., The.

Lessa, Nicholoas & Lessa, M. S. W. Living with Alcoholism & Drug Addiction. 2009. (Teen's Guides). 192p. (gr. 6-12). 34.95 *(978-0-8160-7326-9(0))* Facts On File, Inc.

Libal, Autumn. The FDA & Psychiatric Drugs: Drugs & Psychology for the Mind & Body, 19 vols., Set. 2004. (Psychiatric Disorders Ser.). (Illus.). 128p. (J). lib. bdg. *(978-1-59084-559-2(5))* Mason Crest.

Libal, Joyce. Drug Therapy an Substance-Related Disorders. 2003. (Psychiatric Disorders: Drugs & Psychology for the Mind & Bod Ser.). (Illus.). 124p. (YA). (gr. 8-12). pap. 14.95 *(978-1-4222-0401-6(4))* Mason Crest.

—Substance-Related Disorders. McDonnell, Mary Ann & Esherick, Donald, eds. 2013. (State of Mental Illness & Its Therapy Ser.: 19). (Illus.). 128p. (J). (gr. 7-18). 24.95 *(978-1-4222-2838-8(X))* Mason Crest.

Marcovitz, Hal. Drug Abuse. 2008. (Hot Topics Ser.). (ENG., Illus.). 128p. (gr. 7-10). lib. bdg. 39.40 *(978-1-4205-0081-3(3)*, LML02109-242085, Lucent Bks.) Cengage Gale.

Mason, Paul. Know the Facts about Drinking & Smoking. 2009. (J). 70.50 *(978-1-4358-5463-5(2)*, Rosen Reference) Rosen Publishing Group, Inc., The.

Medina, Sarah. Know the Facts about Drugs. 2009. 48p. (J). 70.50 *(978-1-4358-5459-8(4)*, Rosen Reference); (ENG.). (YA). pap. 11.75 *(978-1-4358-5458-1(6)*, Rosen Reference); (ENG., Illus.). (YA). (gr. 5-9). lib. bdg. 29.25 *(978-1-4358-5337-9(7))* Rosen Publishing Group, Inc., The.

Menhard, Francha Roffe & Salas, Laura Purdie. The Facts about Inhalants. 2009. (Benchmark Rockets Ser.). (Illus.). 32p. (J). (gr. 5-9). 28.50 *(978-0-7614-4350-6(9))* Marshall Cavendish Corp.

Merino, Noël, ed. Underage Drinking. 2007. (Issues That Concern You Ser.). (ENG., Illus.). 104p. (YA). (gr. 7-12). lib. bdg. 36.95 *(978-0-7377-3091-3(9))* Cengage Gale.

Mooney, Carla. The Dangers of Marijuana. 2016. (ENG.). 80p. (YA). (gr. 5-12). *(978-1-68282-020-9(3))* ReferencePoint Pr., Inc.

Nagle, Jeanne M. Polysubstance Abuse. 2005. (Drug Abuse Prevention Library). (Illus.). 64p. (YA). (gr. 7-12). lib. bdg. 31.95 *(978-0-8239-3154-5(4)*, DRPOLY) Rosen Publishing Group, Inc., The.

Parks, Peggy J. Smoking. rev. ed. 2014. (Matters of Opinion Ser.). (ENG.). 64p. (J). (gr. 4-6). lib. bdg. 27.93 *(978-1-59953-602-6(1))* Norwood Hse. Pr.

—Teens & Substance Abuse. 2015. (ENG., Illus.). 80p. (J). lib. bdg. *(978-1-60152-832-2(9))* ReferencePoint Pr., Inc.

Petersen, Christine. Inhalants. 2013. 64p. (J). (gr. 6-9). 34.21 *(978-1-60870-824-6(1))*; pap. 15.28 *(978-1-62712-060-9(2))* Cavendish Square Publishing.

Poole, H. W. Alcohol & Tobacco, Vol. 13. Becker, Sara, ed. 2016. (Drug Addiction & Recovery Ser.). (Illus.). 64p. (J). (gr. 7). 23.95 *(978-1-4222-3599-7(8))* Mason Crest.

Prentzas, G. S. (Scott). The Truth about Inhalants. 2013. (Drugs & Consequences Ser.). (Illus.). 64p. (J). (gr. 7-12). 31.95 *(978-1-4777-1893-3(1))* Rosen Publishing Group, Inc., The.

Rebman, Renée C. Addictions & Risky Behaviors: Cutting, Bingeing, Snorting, & Other Dangers. 2006. (Issues in Focus Today Ser.). (Illus.). 104p. (J). (gr. 6-12). lib. bdg. 33.27 *(978-0-7660-2165-5(3))* Enslow Pubs., Inc.

Rebman, Renee C. Are You Doing Risky Things? Cutting, Bingeing, Snorting, & Other Dangers. 2014. (Got Issues? Ser.). (Illus.). 112p. (YA). (gr. 6-12). lib. bdg. 33.27 *(978-0-7660-5996-2(0))* Enslow Pubs., Inc.

Robinson, Matthew. Inhalant Abuse. 2009. (Incredibly Disgusting Drugs Ser.). 48p. (gr. 5-8). 53.00 *(978-1-61513-501-1(4)*, Rosen Reference) Rosen Publishing Group, Inc., The.

Sanna, E. J. Heroin & Other Opioids: Poppies' Perilous Children. Henningfield, Jack E., ed. 2012. (Illicit & Misused Drugs Ser.). 128p. (J). (gr. 7). 24.95 *(978-1-4222-2433-5(3))*; pap. 14.95 *(978-1-4222-2452-6(X))* Mason Crest.

Schaefer, Wyatt. Addiction. 2007. (Social Issues Firsthand Ser.). (ENG., Illus.). 192p. (gr. 10-12). lib. bdg. 38.30 *(978-0-7377-2494-3(3)*, LML02109-156295, Greenhaven Pr., Inc.) Cengage Gale.

Schwartzenberger, Tina, ed. Substance Use & Abuse. 2006. (Understanding Global Issues Ser.). (Illus.). 56p. (J). (gr. 3-7). lib. bdg. 28.50 *(978-1-59036-232-7(2))* Weigl Pubs., Inc.

Sharp, Katie John. Teenagers & Tobacco: Nicotine & the Adolescent Brain. 2008. (Illus.). 112p. (J). pap. 26.95 *(978-1-4222-1333-9(1))* Mason Crest.

Sherry, Clifford J. Inhalants. 2009. (Drug Abuse Prevention Library). 64p. (gr. 5-5). 58.50 *(978-1-60853-430-2(8))* Rosen Publishing Group, Inc., The.

Sommers, Michael. Cocaine. 2009. (Incredibly Disgusting Drugs Ser.). 48p. (gr. 5-8). 53.00 *(978-1-61513-493-9(X)*, Rosen Reference) Rosen Publishing Group, Inc., The.

Steffens, Bradley. Is Marijuana Harmful? 2016. (ENG.). 80p. (J). (gr. 5-12). lib. bdg. *(978-1-68282-097-1(1))* ReferencePoint Pr., Inc.

Substance Abuse, Addiction, & Treatment. 2011. (J). *(978-0-7614-7943-7(0)*, Marshall Cavendish Reference Bks.) Marshall Cavendish Corp.

Thomas, Amy N. Burning Money: The Cost of Smoking. 2007. (Tobacco: the Deadly Drug Ser.). (Illus.). 112p. (YA). (gr. 3-7). pap. 12.95 *(978-1-4222-0808-3(7))* Mason Crest.

Tina, Schwartzenberger. Substance Use & Abuse. 2007. (Understanding Global Issues Ser.). 56p. (J). pap. 11.95 *(978-1-59036-506-9(2))* Weigl Pubs., Inc.

Uhl, Xina M. Who Is Using Opioids & Opiates? 2017. (Opioids & Opiates: the Silent Epidemic* Ser.: Vol. 5). (ENG.). (YA). (gr. 7-12). 23.95 ***(978-1-4222-3827-1(X))*** Mason Crest.

SUBSTANCE ABUSE—FICTION

Cohn, Rachel. You Know Where to Find Me. (ENG.). (YA). (gr. 7). 2009. 224p. pap. 8.99 *(978-0-689-87860-2(5))* 2008. 208p. 16.99 *(978-0-689-87859-6(1))* Simon & Schuster Bks. For Young Readers. (Simon & Schuster Bks. For Young Readers).

Gardner, Hunter. School. 2014. (ENG.). 250p. (YA). (gr. 7-12). pap. 16.99 *(978-1-938463-14-3(5))* Bitingduck Pr.

Ghent, Natale. Book of Living & Dying. 2006. (ENG.). 288p. (J). mass mkt. 6.99 *(978-0-00-639350-4(0)*, Harper Trophy) HarperCollins Pubs.

Gibson, Sylvia Scott & Gibson, James E. Latawnya the Naughty Horse Two, 1 vol. Gibson, Gregory V., illus. 2010. 22p. 24.95 *(978-1-4489-7859-5(9))* PublishAmerica, Inc.

Iversen, Jeremy. Rush. 2011. (ENG.). 272p. (YA). (gr. 9). pap. 11.99 *(978-1-4424-2400-5(1)*, Simon Pulse) Simon Pulse.

—21. 2005. (ENG.). 272p. (YA). pap. 6.99 *(978-0-689-87623-3(8)*, Simon Pulse) Simon Pulse.

Kiely, Brendan. The Gospel of Winter. 2015. (ENG., Illus.). 320p. (YA). (gr. 9). pap. 11.99 *(978-1-4424-8490-0(X)*, McElderry, Margaret K. Bks.) McElderry, Margaret K. Bks.

Lancett, Peter. Gun Dog. 2008. (Cutting Edge Ser.). (ENG.). 200p. pap. *(978-1-84167-713-2(2))* Ransom Publishing Ltd.

Marie, Jessica. Keeping Broken Promises, 1 vol. 2010. 182p. pap. 24.95 *(978-1-4489-5273-1(5))* America Star Bks.

Millar, Martin. Lonely Werewolf Girl. 2008. (ENG.). 560p. per. *(978-0-9796636-6-6(0))* CSA Telltapes, Ltd.

Nayeri, Daniel and Dina. Another Jekyll, Another Hyde. 2012. (ENG., Illus.). 400p. (YA). (gr. 9). 17.99 *(978-0-7636-5261-6(X))* Candlewick Pr.

Smith-Leckie, Nina. The Fall & Rise of Abuse-a-Saurus Rex. Gordon, Danny, illus. 2003. 28p. (YA). (gr. 5-18). pap. 6.95 *(978-0-9725382-0-6(8))* Prairie Arts, Inc.

Tharp, Tim. The Spectacular Now. (ENG.). 304p. (YA). (gr. 9). 2010. pap. 8.99 *(978-0-375-86502-2(0)*, Knopf Bks. for Young Readers) 2013. pap. 9.99 *(978-0-385-75430-9(2)*, Ember) Random Hse. Children's Bks.

SUBURBAN HOMES

see Architecture, Domestic

SUBURBAN LIFE

Bodden, Valerie. A Suburb. (My First Look At Ser.). 24p. (J). 2011. (ENG.). (gr. 1-17). pap. 7.99 *(978-1-926722-31-3(0)*, Creative Paperbacks) 2007. (Illus.). (gr. -1-3). lib. bdg. 24.25 *(978-1-58341-514-6(9)*, Creative Education) Creative Co., The.

Downer, Ann. Wild Animal Neighbors: Sharing Our Urban World. 2013. (ENG., Illus.). 64p. (gr. 5-12). 33.27 *(978-0-7613-9021-3(9)*, Twenty-First Century Bks.) Lerner Publishing Group.

Flatt, Lizann. Life in a Suburban City. 2010. (Learn about Urban Life Ser.). (ENG., Illus.). 32p. (J). (gr. 3-6). lib. bdg. *(978-0-7787-7394-8(9))*; (gr. 4-9). pap. *(978-0-7787-7404-4(X))* Crabtree Publishing Co.

Rogers, Amy B. American Communities: We Live in a Suburb, 01 vols., 1. 2016. (American Communities Ser.). (ENG.). 24p. (J). pap. 8.25 *(978-1-5081-4200-3(9)*, PowerKids Pr.) Rosen Publishing Group, Inc., The.

Sterling, Kristin. Living in Suburban Communities. 2008. pap. 34.95 *(978-0-8225-9479-6(X))*; (ENG., Illus.). 24p. lib. bdg. 23.93 *(978-0-8225-8598-5(7)*, Lerner Pubns.) Lerner Publishing Group.

Summers, Portia. My School Community. 2016. (Zoom in on Communities Ser.). 24p. (J). (gr. 2-2). pap. 9.35 *(978-0-7660-7824-6(8))* Enslow Pubs., Inc.

—My Suburban Community. 2016. (Zoom in on Communities Ser.). 24p. (gr. 2-2). pap. 9.35 *(978-0-7660-7833-8(7))* Enslow Pubs., Inc.

Thompson, Gare. A Suburban Community of the 1950s. 2007. (Reading Expeditions Ser.). (ENG., Illus.). 24p. (J). pap. 14.95 *(978-0-7922-8691-2(X))* CENGAGE Learning.

SUBWAYS

Brimner, Larry Dane. Subway: The Story of Tunnels, Tubes, & Tracks. Waldman, Neil, illus. 2004. (ENG.). 32p. (J). (gr. 2-4). 15.95 *(978-1-59078-176-0(7))* Boyds Mills Pr.

Lassieur, Allison. Subways in Action. 2012. (Transportation Zone Ser.). (ENG.). 24p. (gr. 1-2). pap. 41.70 *(978-1-4296-8395-1(3))*; (Illus.). pap. 7.29 *(978-1-4296-7967-1(0))*; (Illus.). lib. bdg. 25.32 *(978-1-4296-7690-8(6))* Capstone Press of Coughlan Cos. (First Facts).

Leighton, Christina. City Trains. 2017. (Amazing Trains Ser.). (ENG., Illus.). 24p. (J). (gr. k-3). lib. bdg. 25.95 ***(978-1-62617-669-0(8)**,* Blastoff! Readers) Bellwether Media.

Miller, Heather Lynn. Subway Ride. Rama, Sue, illus. 2011. (ENG.). 32p. (J). (gr. -1-3). pap. 7.95 *(978-1-58089-112-7(8))* Charlesbridge Publishing, Inc.

New York Transit Museum Staff. New York City Subway Trains: 12 Classic Punch-and-Build Trains, 1 vol. 2003. (ENG., Illus.). 48p. (J). (gr. 2-3). pap. 19.99 *(978-1-58685-324-2(4))* Gibbs Smith, Publisher.

Peters, Elisa. Let's Ride the Subway! 2014. (Public Transportation Ser.). 24p. (J). (gr. k-2). 23.60 *(978-1-4777-6521-0(2))*; pap. 49.50 *(978-1-4777-6516-6(6))* Rosen Publishing Group, Inc., The. (PowerKids Pr.).

Peters, Elisa & Eida, de la Vega. Let's Ride the Subway! (¡Vamos a Tomar el Metro!) de la Vega, Eida, ed. 2014. (Transporte Público / Public Transportation Ser.). (SPA & ENG.). 24p. (J). (gr. k-2). lib. bdg. 23.60 *(978-1-4777-6765-6(1)*, PowerKids Pr.) Rosen Publishing Group, Inc., The.

Reis, Ronald A. The New York City Subway System. 2009. (Building America Ser.). (Illus.). 144p. (J). (gr. 5-8). 35.00 *(978-1-60413-046-1(6)*, Chelsea Hse.) Facts On File, Inc.

Ryan, Phillip. Subways. 2010. (All Aboard! Ser.). (ENG.). 24p. (J). pap. 8.25 *(978-1-4488-1213-4(5))*; lib. bdg. 22.60 *(978-1-4488-0636-2(4))* Rosen Publishing Group, Inc., The.

Santella, Andrew. Building the New York Subway. 2007. (Cornerstones of Freedom Ser.). (ENG., Illus.). 48p. (J). (gr. 4-6). 26.00 *(978-0-516-23638-4(5)*, Children's Pr.) Scholastic Library Publishing.

Summers, Alex. Subway. 2017. (Transportation & Me! Ser.). (ENG.). (J). (gr. k-1). 28.51 ***(978-1-68342-165-8(5))*** Rourke Educational Media.

Winget, Mary. Subways. 2007. (Pull Ahead Books-Mighty Movers Ser.). (ENG., Illus.). 32p. (gr. k-3). lib. bdg. 22.60 *(978-0-8225-6418-8(1)*, Lerner Pubns.); per. 7.95 *(978-0-8225-6424-9(6)*, First Avenue Editions) Lerner Publishing Group.

SUBWAYS—FICTION

Bluemle, Elizabeth. Tap Tap Boom Boom. Karas, G. Brian, illus. 2014. (ENG.). 32p. (J). (gr. -1-2). 16.99 *(978-0-7636-5696-6(8))* Candlewick Pr.

Cohen, Miriam. Down in the Subway, 1 vol. Greenberg, Melanie Hope, illus. 2003. (ENG.). 32p. (J). (gr. k-3). pap. 6.95 *(978-1-932065-24-4(5))*; 15.95 *(978-1-932065-08-4(3))* Star Bright Bks., Inc.

Derrick, Patricia & O'Neil, Shirley. Rathbone the Rat. Martinez, J-P Loppo, illus. 2007. 32p. (J). (gr. -1-3). 18.95 incl. audio compact disk *(978-1-933818-17-7(4))* Animalations.

Holman, Felice. Slake's Limbo. unabr. ed. 2004. 117p. (J). (gr. 7-18). pap. 29.00 incl. audio *(978-0-8072-8744-6(X)*, YA254SP, Listening Library) Random Hse. Audio Publishing Group.

Jacobs, Paul DuBois & Swender, Jennifer. Count on the Subway. Yaccarino, Dan, illus. 2014. (ENG.). 32p. (J). (-k). 14.99 *(978-0-307-97923-0(7))*; lib. bdg. 17.99 *(978-0-307-97924-7(5))* Random Hse. Children's Bks. (Knopf Bks. for Young Readers).

—My Subway Ride, 1 vol. Aiko, Selina, illus. 2004. (ENG.). 32p. (J). (gr. 2-3). 15.99 *(978-1-58685-357-0(0))* Gibbs Smith, Publisher.

Niemann, Christoph. Subway. Niemann, Christoph, illus. 2010. (Illus.). 40p. (J). (gr. -1-k). (ENG.). 16.99 *(978-0-06-157779-6(0))*; lib. bdg. 17.89 *(978-0-06-157780-2(4))* HarperCollins Pubs. (Greenwillow Bks.).

Oliver, Lin. Beware! Shadows in the Night. Kallis, Samantha, illus. 2016. (Fantastic Frame Ser.: 3). (ENG.). 128p. (J). (gr. 2-4). 11.99 *(978-0-448-48091-6(3)*, Grosset & Dunlap) Penguin Young Readers Group.

Potter, Ellen. Olivia Kidney & the Secret Beneath the City. 2009. (ENG.). 336p. (J). (gr. 3-7). 9.99 *(978-0-14-241263-3(5)*, Puffin Books) Penguin Young Readers Group.

Reid, Barbara. The Subway Mouse. Reid, Barbara, illus. 2005. (Illus.). (J). *(978-0-439-77430-7(6))* Scholastic, Inc.

Sarcone-Roach, Julia. Subway Story. 2011. (ENG.). 40p. (J). (gr. k-3). 16.99 *(978-0-375-85859-8(8)*, Knopf Bks. for Young Readers) Random Hse. Children's Bks.

Shusterman, Neal. Downsiders. 2009. (ENG.). 272p. (YA). (gr. 7). pap. 10.99 *(978-1-4169-9747-4(4)*, Simon & Schuster Bks. For Young Readers) Simon & Schuster Bks. For Young Readers.

Spiegelman, Nadja. Lost in NYC: A Subway Adventure. Sánchez, Sergio García, illus. 2015. (ENG.). 52p. (J). (gr. 2-7). 16.95 *(978-1-935179-81-8(0))* TOON Books / RAW Junior, LLC.

Stilton, Geronimo. The Phantom of the Subway. Wolf, Matt, illus. 2004. (Geronimo Stilton Ser.: No. 13). 112p. (J). lib. bdg. 10.00 *(978-1-4242-0282-9(5))* Fitzgerald Bks.

Suen, Anastasia. Subway. Katz, Karen, illus. 2008. (ENG.). 24p. (J). (gr. -1-k). bds. 6.99 *(978-0-670-01109-4(6)*, Viking Books for Young Readers) Penguin Young Readers Group.

SUCCESS

see also Business; Leadership; Life Skills

The Action Principles: Armed Service Tribute Edition. 2nd ed. 2003. mass mkt. 20.00 *(978-1-884864-19-3(8))* American Success Institute, Inc.

Adler, Mia Sharon. Essential Proteen-Student Journal: A Life Skills Program for Helping Teens Succeed: Student Journal. 2006. (ENG.). 48p. (YA). pap. 5.98 *(978-0-87822-582-8(X)*, 5284) Research Pr.

Antill, Sara. Grit. 2013. (Character Strength Ser.). 24p. (J). (gr. 3-6). pap. 49.50 *(978-1-4488-9815-2(3))*; pap. 8.25 *(978-1-4488-9814-5(5))*; lib. bdg. 22.60 *(978-1-4488-9678-3(9))* Rosen Publishing Group, Inc., The. (PowerKids Pr.).

—Zest. 2013. (Character Strength Ser.). 24p. (J). (gr. 3-6). pap. 49.50 *(978-1-4488-9813-8(7))*; pap. 8.25 *(978-1-4488-9812-1(9))*; lib. bdg. 22.60 *(978-1-4488-9677-6(0))* Rosen Publishing Group, Inc., The. (PowerKids Pr.).

Berman, Ron. Who's Got Next? Future Leaders of America. 2013. (Av2 Audio Chapter Bks.). (ENG., Illus.). 92p. (J). (gr. 4-7). lib. bdg. 27.13 *(978-1-62127-998-3(7)*, AV2 by Weigl) Weigl Pubs., Inc.

Bernstein, Ben. Stressed Out! for Teens. 2014. (ENG., Illus.). xi, 254p. (J). 34.95 *(978-1-942672-54-8(3))* Familius LLC.

Berry, Joy. You Can... Work It! Being Smart, Being Creative, Being Assertive, Being in Control, Getting Organized & Attaining Goals! 2009. (ENG.). 304p. (J). (gr. 5-7). pap. 12.95 *(978-1-60577-602-6(5))* Berry, Joy Enterprises.

Bishop, John. Goal Setting for Students: Winner of three national parenting book Awards. 2003. (Illus.). (YA). pap. 11.95 *(978-0-9743700-0-2(2))* Accent On Success.

Black, Donnette. Madam C. J. Walker's Road to Success. 2010. 36p. pap. 17.50 *(978-1-4520-2443-1(X))* AuthorHouse.

Carroll, D. S. Victory over Victory: An Essay Studying our Personal & Cultural Compulsion in Pursuit of Victory, Its Costs, & Its Alternatives of Arrogance or Mo. 2011. 222p. 29.99 *(978-1-4628-4552-1(5))*; pap. 19.99 *(978-1-4628-4551-4(7))* Xlibris Corp.

Conway, Hollis. Grasshopper: The Hollis Conway Story. 2004. 30p. (J). per. *(978-1-59196-584-8(5))* Instant Pub.

Covey, Stephen R. & Covey, Sean. The 6 Most Important Decisions You'll Ever Make: A Guide for Teens. 2006. (ENG., Illus.). 336p. (gr. 8-18). pap. 16.99 *(978-0-7432-6504-1(1)*, Touchstone) Touchstone.

Crockett, Kyle A. Nutrition for Achievement in Sports & Academics. Borus, Joshua, ed. 2013. (Understanding Nutrition: a Gateway to Physical & Mental Health Ser.). (Illus.). 48p. (J). (gr. 5-18). pap. 9.95 *(978-1-4222-2990-3(4))*; 19.95 *(978-1-4222-2884-5(3))* Mason Crest.

Crow, Gary & Crow, Marissa. The Success Train. 2003. (Illus.). 73p. (J). pap. 9.95 *(978-0-9741685-5-5(6))* Koenisha Pubns.

Dugan, Christine. From Rags to Riches. 1 vol. 2nd rev. ed. 2013. (Nonfiction Readers Ser.). (ENG.). 64p. (J). (gr. 5-5). pap. 10.99 *(978-1-4333-4910-2(8))* Teacher Created Materials, Inc.

Dyer, Wayne. I Am: Why Two Little Words Mean So Much. 2012. (ENG., Illus.). 32p. 15.99 *(978-1-4019-3975-5(9))* Hay Hse., Inc.

Dyer, Wayne & Dyer, Summer. 10 Secrets for Success & Inner Peace for Teens. 2004. 12.95 *(978-1-4019-0270-4(7)*, 2707, Hay Hse. Lifestyles) Hay Hse., Inc.

Dyer, Wayne & Tracy, Kristina. ¡Eres Increible! 10 Formas de Permitir Que Tu Grandeza Brille a Traves de Ti. Siegel, Melanie, illus. 2007.Tr. of Incredible You! 10 Ways to Let Your Greatness Shine Through. (SPA & ENG.). 32p. 14.95 *(978-1-4019-1700-5(3))* Hay Hse., Inc.

Fiszer, Edward P. Thoughts to Inspire: Daily Messages for Young People. 2004. (ENG.). 176p. pap. 46.00 *(978-1-57886-124-8(1))* Scarecrow Pr., Inc.

Flemmings, Tyrone. Home Schooled Boss. 2011. 12p. pap. 12.99 *(978-1-4567-5157-9(3))* AuthorHouse.

Graham, Stedman. Move Without the Ball: Put Your Skills & Your Magic to Work for You. 2004. (ENG., Illus.). 208p. pap. 14.99 *(978-0-7432-3440-5(5)*, Touchstone) Touchstone.

Hansen, Mark & Ferber, Kevin S. Success 101 for Teens: Dollars & Sense for a Winning Financial Life. 2012. (ENG.). 176p. pap. 12.95 *(978-1-55778-901-3(0)*, 4580c8ac-14b2-4d64-ae8a-be308d9302c6) Paragon Hse. Pubs.

Harrington, Paul. The Secret to Teen Power. 2010. (JPN., Illus.). 254p. (YA). *(978-4-04-791630-2(7))* Fukuinkan Shoten.

—The Secret to Teen Power. 2009. (ENG., Illus.). 192p. (YA). (gr. 7-18). 19.99 *(978-1-4169-9498-5(X))* Simon Pulse/Beyond Words.

Harris, Laurie Lanzen. Biography for Beginners: African-American Leaders. 2007. (J). lib. bdg. 30.00 *(978-1-931360-35-7(9))* Favorable Impressions.

Hauser, Jill Frankel. The Kid's Guide to Becoming the Best You Can Be! Developing 5 Traits You Need to Achieve Your Personal Best. Kline, Michael, illus. (ENG.). 128p. (J). (gr. 3-7). 2008. pap. 14.25 *(978-0-8249-6788-8(7))* 2006. 16.95 *(978-0-8249-6789-5(5))* Worthy Publishing. (Ideal Pubns.).

Howat, Irene. Ten Boys Who Used Their Talents. 2012. (Lightkeepers Ser.). (ENG., Illus.). 160p. (J). (gr. 3-7). per. 8.99 *(978-1-84550-146-4(2)*, cd5b19a1-cb3e-4f1d-a5bc-00dec664cd78) Christian Focus Pubns. GBR. Dist: Bookmasters Distribution.

—Ten Girls Who Used Their Talents. 2014. (Lightkeepers Ser.). (ENG., Illus.). 160p. (J). (gr. 3-7). per. 8.99 *(978-1-84550-147-1(0)*, de728062-6bc3-4bf7-87b9-a97ebd0810fb) Christian Focus Pubns. GBR. Dist: Bookmasters Distribution.

Hunt, Christopher. Victory after High School: Survive or Thrive —You Choose! 2005. 144p. (YA). per. 16.95 *(978-0-9765973-4-6(9))* Adjust Communications.

Hunt, Rameck, et al. We Beat the Street: How a Friendship Pact Led to Success. 2006. (ENG., Illus.). 208p. (J). (gr. 5-18). 7.99 *(978-0-14-240627-4(9)*, Puffin Books) Penguin Young Readers Group.

Islam, Sabirul. The World at Your Feet: Three Strikes to a Successful Entrepreneurial Life. 2010. (Illus.). 120p. pap. *(978-0-462-09952-1(0))* Marshall Cavendish.

Kiefer, Jeanne. Jobs for Kids: A Smart Kid's Q & A Guide. Green, Anne Canevari, illus. 2003. (Single Titles Ser.). 112p. (gr. 5-8). lib. bdg. 25.90 *(978-0-7613-2611-3(1)*, Millbrook Pr.) Lerner Publishing Group.

Leslie, Roger. Success Express for Teens: 50 Life-Changing Activities. 2003. (Illus.). 224p. pap. 14.95 *(978-1-886298-09-5(2))* Bayou Publishing.

Lewis, Carole. Pathway to Success. 2004. (First Place Bible Studies). 240p. pap. 19.99 *(978-0-8307-2927-2(5)*, Gospel Light) Gospel Light Pubns.

Mandino, Og. Og Mandino's Great Trilogy: The Greatest Salesman in the World, the Greatest Secret in the World & the Greatest Miracle in the World. 2008. 420p. (J). *(978-0-8119-0428-5(8))* Lifetime Bks.

Marcovitz, Hal. Puerto Ricans. 2009. (Successful Americans Ser.). 64p. (YA). (gr. 9-12). 22.95 *(978-1-4222-0516-7(9))* Mason Crest.

—Russian Americans. 2007. (Successful Americans Ser.). (Illus.). 64p. (YA). (gr. 7-18). pap. 9.95 *(978-1-4222-0868-7(0))* Mason Crest.

McDuffie, Daryl L. ABC's to Unlimited Success: How to Turn All Your Dreams into Reality. 2003. (YA). per. 9.97 *(978-0-9727582-0-8(8))* G Publishing LLC.

Mitchell-Tulloss, Delores. ABCs of Character for People Around the World. Hardison, Brian, illus. 2007. 32p. (J). pap. *(978-0-9670712-6-8(7))* zReyomi Publishing.

Mr. Blue. From Underdog to Wonderdog: Top Ten Tricks to Lead Your Pack. 2012. (ENG., Illus.). 52p. (J). (gr. 1-5). pap. 14.95 *(978-1-936354-26-9(8)*, Tremendous Leadership) Tremendous Life Bks.

Norris, David A. Lasting Success: Quality Decisions, Relationships & Untamed Emotions. 2003. (Illus.). 256p. per. *(978-0-943177-12-0(X)*, 0-943177-12-x) Heartland Foundation, Inc.

Novak, Robby & Montague, Brad. Kid President's Guide to Being Awesome. (J). (gr. 3-7). 2016. 256p. pap. 12.99 *(978-0-06-243871-3(9))* 2015. (ENG., Illus.). 240p. 21.99 *(978-0-06-235868-4(5))* HarperCollins Pubs.

O'Connor, Frances. Frequently Asked Questions about Academic Anxiety. 2009. (FAQ: Teen Life Ser.). 64p. (gr. 5-6). 58.50 *(978-1-61512-560-9(4))* Rosen Publishing Group, Inc., The.

Orr, Tamra. Zest. 2013. (7 Character Strengths of Highly Successful Students Ser.). 64p. (J). (gr. 5-8). pap. 77.70 *(978-1-4488-9568-7(5))* Rosen Publishing Group, Inc., The.

Orr, Tamra B. Zest. 2013. (7 Character Strengths of Highly Successful Students Ser.). 64p. (J). (gr. 5-8). 31.95 *(978-1-4488-9541-0(3))*; pap. 12.95 *(978-1-4488-9567-0(7))* Rosen Publishing Group, Inc., The.

Ortega, Julian G. Warrior Inspiration. 2010. 152p. pap. 11.95 *(978-1-59330-659-5(8))* Aventine Pr.

Paxson, Jillip Naysinthe, told to. The First Thirty. anniv. ed. 2015. (ENG.). 96p. (YA). (gr. 5-16). pap. 10.00 *(978-0-9758794-1-2(3))* IdeaList Enterprises, Inc.

Paxson, Jillip Naysinthe & Siegman, Greg Forbes. The First Thirty. 2005. 96p. (YA). per. 10.00 *(978-0-9758794-0-5(5))* IdeaList Enterprises, Inc.

Preparing for School Success. 2017. ***(978-1-59723-348-4(X))*** Active Parenting Pubs.

Rameck, Hunt, et al. We Beat the Street: How a Friendship Pact Led to Success. 2014. (ENG.). 208p. (J). 12.24 *(978-1-63245-093-7(3))* Lectorum Pubns., Inc.

Rayel, Michael G. A 31-Day Success Principles for Kids & Teens. 2006. 64p. (J). pap. *(978-0-9737070-3-8(8))* Soar Dime, Limited/Oikos Global.

Reber, Deborah. Doable: The Girls' Guide to Accomplishing Just about Anything. 2015. (ENG., Illus.). 208p. (YA). (gr. 7). pap. 12.99 *(978-1-58270-466-1(X)*, Simon Pulse) Simon Pulse.

Richardson, Dot. Go for It: Conversations on Being You. 2004. (Girls Explore, Reach for the Stars Ser.). (Illus.). 140p. (J). 20.00 *(978-0-9749456-0-6(9)*, Girls Explore) Girls Explore LLC.

Ross, Margaret. Casey & the Amazing Good Finder: Teaching Adults & Children How to Succeed in School, Work, Life & Relationships. l.t. ed. 2005. (Illus.). 32p. (J). 9.99 *(978-0-9715713-5-8(X))* Kamaron Institute Pr.

Rossi, Debra M. No Horsing Around: Kick off to Success in School. 2004. (Illus.). 32p. (J). 5.95 *(978-0-9758982-0-8(5))* Rossi, Debra.

Scott, John, text. Juniors: How to Make the Team. 2004. (YA). 30.00 *(978-1-879498-78-5(2))* SportAmerica.

Seifert, Sheila & Naylor, Beth. And the Winner Is. 2007. (Discipleship Junction Ser.). (ENG., Illus.). 112p. (J). per. 19.99 *(978-0-7814-4512-2(4))* Cook, David C.

Shelton, C. H. & Shelton, C. H. A Kid's Guide to Being a Winner. Gillespie, Greg G., illus. 2011. 38p. (J). (gr. 2-8). 9.99 *(978-0-9841910-4-8(6))* Choice PH.

Shepherd, Jodie. Perseverance: I Have Grit! 2015. (Rookie Talk about It(tm) Ser.). (ENG., Illus.). 32p. (J). pap. 5.95 *(978-0-531-21379-7(X)*, Children's Pr.) Scholastic Library Publishing.

Siddoway, Ramona. Grit. 2013. (7 Character Strengths of Highly Successful Students Ser.). 64p. (J). (gr. 5-8). 31.95 *(978-1-4488-9540-3(5))*; pap. 77.70 *(978-1-4488-9560-1(X))*; pap. 12.95 *(978-1-4488-9559-5(6))* Rosen Publishing Group, Inc., The.

Silverman, Robin Landew. Reaching Your Goals. 2004. (Life Balance Ser.). (ENG.). 80p. (J). 20.50 *(978-0-531-12342-3(1)*, Watts, Franklin) Scholastic Library Publishing.

Skills for Success. 2017. (Skills for Success Ser.). 64p. (gr. 12-12). 172.25 ***(978-1-4994-6636-2(6)***, Rosen Young Adult) Rosen Publishing Group, Inc., The.

Smith, Charles R., Jr. 28 Days: Moments in Black History That Changed the World. Evans, Shane W., illus. 2015. (ENG.). 56p. (J). (gr. -1-5). 18.99 *(978-1-59643-820-0(7)*, 9781596438200) Roaring Brook Pr.

Tebow, Tim. Shaken: Young Reader's Edition: Fighting to Stand Strong No Matter What Comes Your Way. 2017. (ENG.). 208p. (J). (gr. 5). 17.99 ***(978-0-7352-8996-3(4)***, WaterBrook Pr.) Crown Publishing Group.

Wilson, Nolan. The Teen's Guide to Getting Ahead: How to Succeed in High School & Beyond. 2008. 192p. (YA). (gr. 8-11). pap. 15.95 *(978-1-897073-92-6(5))* Lobster Pr. CAN. Dist: Orca Bk. Pubs. USA.

The 7 Character Strengths of Highly Successful Students. 2013. (7 Character Strengths of Highly Successful Students Ser.). 64p. (J). (gr. 5-8). 223.65 *(978-1-4488-9554-0(5))*; pap. 543.90 *(978-1-4777-1242-9(9))*; pap. 90.65 *(978-1-4777-1241-2(0))* Rosen Publishing Group, Inc., The.

SUDOKU

Arcturus Publishing Staff. The Magical Fairy Activity Book. 2014. (ENG.). 96p. (J). pap. 9.95 *(978-1-78212-597-6(3))* Arcturus Publishing GBR. Dist: Bookmasters Distribution.

Bloom, Jonathan. The Must Have Sudoku Holiday Gift 480 Puzzles. 2012. 278p. pap. *(978-0-9814261-5-0(8))* Sudokids.Com.

Granny, Smith. Granny Smith's Sudoku Solver: For Beginners & Other Wise People. 2010. 100p. pap. 12.95 *(978-1-4520-0287-3(8))* AuthorHouse.

Griffiths-Jones, Sam & Moog, Bob. Sudoku for Kids. 2006. (Spinner Books for Kids Ser.). (ENG.). 158p. (J). (gr. 4-7). pap. 6.95 *(978-1-57528-963-2(6))* Univ. Games.

Highlights for Children Editorial Staff, creator. Riddle Sudoku. 2016. (Highlights(tm) Puzzlemania(r) Puzzle Pads Ser.). (ENG.). 64p. (J). (gr. k-4). pap. 4.99 *(978-1-62979-697-0(2)*, Highlights) Boyds Mills Pr.

Kattan, Peter & Kattan, Nicola. Kindergarten Sudoku: 4x4 Sudoku Puzzles for Kids. 2007. 48p. pap. 7.50 *(978-0-615-15334-6(8))* Kattan, Peter I.

Molski, Carol. Bible Word Suduko. Koehler, Ed, illus. 2007. (CPH Teaching Resource Ser.). (ENG.). 64p. pap. 10.99 *(978-0-7586-1344-8(X))* Concordia Publishing Hse.

Moog, Bob. Do You Sudoku? Spicy: Over 200 Puzzles for Experienced Sudoku Solvers. 2006. (Spinner Bks.). (ENG.). 264p. per. 9.95 *(978-1-57528-899-4(0))* Univ. Games.

Pazzelli, John. A First Sudoku Book. Zourelias, Diana, illus. 2006. (Dover Children's Activity Bks.). (ENG.). 64p. (J). (gr. 3-8). per. 3.95 *(978-0-486-45074-2(0))* Dover Pubns., Inc.

Puzzle Society Staff. Pocket Posh Girl Sudoku: 100 Puzzles. 2010. (ENG.). 128p. pap. 7.99 *(978-0-7407-9858-0(8))* Andrews McMeel Publishing.

—Pocket Posh Girl Sudoku 2 Vol. 2: 100 Puzzles. 2011. (ENG.). 128p. pap. 7.99 *(978-1-4494-0738-4(2))* Andrews McMeel Publishing.

Rios, Michael. Sudoku Puzzles for Clever Kids. 2017. (ENG.). 96p. (J). (gr. 3). pap. 6.95 ***(978-1-4549-2279-7(6)***, Puzzlewright) Sterling Publishing Co., Inc.

Shortz, Will, intro. Will Shortz Presents the Monster Book of Sudoku for Kids: 150 Fun Puzzles. 2006. (ENG., Illus.). 176p. (J). (gr. 3-7). pap. 8.99 *(978-0-312-36842-5(9)*, 9780312368425, St. Martin's Griffin) St. Martin's Pr.

Sirkis, Rafael. Wacky Facts. 2007. (Apple Paperbacks Ser.). (ENG., Illus.). 144p. (J). (gr. 4-7). pap. 4.99 *(978-0-439-02280-4(0))* Scholastic, Inc.

Stickels, Terry & Immanuvel, Anthony. Sudoku. 2010. (Go Games Ser.). (ENG.). 288p. pap. 7.95 *(978-1-936140-08-4(X)*, Imagine Publishing) Charlesbridge Publishing, Inc.

Teora, creator. Picture Sudoku. 2008. (Illus.). 12p. (J). (gr. -1-3). pap. 4.95 *(978-1-59496-166-3(2))* Teora USA LLC.

—Sudoku 1: 42 Puzzles for Kids. 2005. (Illus.). 24p. (J). pap. 3.95 *(978-1-59496-126-7(3))* Teora USA LLC.

—Sudoku 2: 42 Puzzles for Kids. 2005. (Illus.). 24p. (J). pap. 3.95 *(978-1-59496-127-4(1))* Teora USA LLC.

SUEZ CANAL (EGYPT)

Bodden, Valerie. Suez Canal. 2006. (Modern Wonders of the World Ser.). (Illus.). 32p. (J). 18.95 *(978-1-58341-441-5(X)*, Creative Education) Creative Co., The.

Fiscus, James. The Suez Crisis. 2009. (War & Conflict in the Middle East Ser.). 64p. (gr. 5-5). 58.50 *(978-1-60854-741-8(8))* Rosen Publishing Group, Inc., The.

Fiscus, James W. The Suez Crisis. 2004. (War & Conflict in the Middle East Ser.). (Illus.). 64p. (gr. 7-12). lib. bdg. 31.95 *(978-0-8239-4550-4(2))* Rosen Publishing Group, Inc., The.

Riggs, Kate. Suez Canal. 2009. (Now That's Big Ser.). 24p. (J). (gr. 1-5). lib. bdg. 24.25 *(978-1-58341-706-5(0)*, Creative Education) Creative Co., The.

SUFFRAGE

see also classes of people with the subdivision Suffrage, e.g. Women—Suffrage; etc.

Berlatsky, Noah. Voting Rights. Greenhaven Press Staff, ed. 2015. (Opposing Viewpoints Ser.). (ENG.). 224p. (gr. 10-12). pap. 33.80 *(978-0-7377-7301-9(4)*, Greenhaven Pr., Inc.) Cengage Gale.

Burgan, Michael. The Voting Rights Act of 1965: An Interactive History Adventure. 2015. (You Choose: History Ser.). (ENG.). 112p. (gr. 3-4). pap. 6.95 *(978-1-4914-1805-5(2)*, You Choose Bks.) Capstone Press of Coughlan Cos.

Durrett, Deanne. Right to Vote. 2005. (American Rights Ser.). (Illus.). 144p. (gr. 5-8). 35.00 *(978-0-8160-5661-3(7))* Facts On File, Inc.

Isler, Claudia. The Right to Vote. 2009. (Individual Rights & Civic Responsibility Ser.). 128p. (gr. 7-12). 63.90 *(978-1-61513-516-5(2))* Rosen Publishing Group, Inc., The.

Kamma, Anne. If You Lived When Women Won Their Rights. Johnson, Pamela, illus. 2008. (If You... Ser.). (ENG.). 64p. (J). (gr. 2-5). pap. 7.99 *(978-0-439-74869-8(0)*, Scholastic Reference) Scholastic, Inc.

Lansford, Tom. Political Participation & Voting Rights, Vol. 8. Lansford, Tom, ed. 2016. (Foundations of Democracy Ser.). (Illus.). 64p. (J). (gr. 7). 23.95 *(978-1-4222-3631-4(5))* Mason Crest.

Orr, Tamra. A History of Voting Rights. 2012. (J). lib. bdg. 29.95 *(978-1-61228-262-6(8))* Mitchell Lane Pubs., Inc.

Quinn, Barbara & Isler, Claudia. Understanding Your Right to Vote. 2011. (Personal Freedom & Civic Duty Ser.). (Illus.). 144p. (YA). (gr. 7-12). lib. bdg. 35.95 *(978-1-4488-4665-8(X))* Rosen Publishing Group, Inc., The.

SUFFRAGETTES

see Suffragists

SUFFRAGISTS

Adiletta, Dawn. Elizabeth Cady Stanton: Women's Suffrage & the First Vote. (Library of American Lives & Times Ser.). 112p. 2009. (gr. 5-5). 69.20 *(978-1-60853-479-1(0))* 2005. (Illus.). (J). (gr. -1-3). lib. bdg. 34.60 *(978-1-4042-2647-0(8))* Rosen Publishing Group, Inc., The.

Barnham, Kay. Emmeline Pankhurst - Votes for Women! Brilliant Biographies of the Dead Famous. 2017. (History VIPs Ser.). (ENG., Illus.). 32p. (J). (gr. 4-6). pap. 12.99 *(978-0-7502-9940-4(1)*, Wayland) Hachette Children's Group GBR. Dist: Hachette Bk. Group.

Bjornlund, Lydia D. Women of the Suffrage Movement. 2003. (Women in History Ser.). (ENG., Illus.). 112p. (J). 33.45 *(978-1-59018-173-7(5)*, Lucent Bks.) Cengage Gale.

Bohannon, Lisa Frederkisen. Failure Is Impossible: The Story of Susan B. Anthony. 2004. (Feminist Voices Ser.). (Illus.). 112p. (YA). (gr. 6-12). 23.95 *(978-1-883846-77-0(3)*, First Biographies) Reynolds, Morgan Inc.

Boothroyd, Jennifer. Susan B. Anthony: A Life of Fairness. 2006. (Pull Ahead Bks.). (Illus.). 32p. (J). (gr. 3-7). lib. bdg. 22.60 *(978-0-8225-3479-2(7)*, Lerner Pubns.) Lerner Publishing Group.

—Susan B. Anthony: Una Vida de Igualdad. Translations.com Staff, tr. 2006. (Libros para Avanzar-Biografías (Pull Ahead Books-Biographies) Ser.). (ENG & SPA., Illus.). 32p. (gr. k-3). lib. bdg. 22.60 *(978-0-8225-6234-4(0))* Lerner Publishing Group.

Brown, Don. A Voice from the Wilderness: The Story of Anna Howard Shaw. 2010. 32p. (J). (gr. k-3). pap. 5.95 *(978-0-618-58544-1(3))* Houghton Mifflin Harcourt Trade & Reference Pubs.

Carson, Mary Kay. Who Was Susan B. Anthony Vote? And Other Questions about Women's Suffrage. 2015. (Good Question! Ser.). (ENG., Illus.). 32p. (J). (gr. 2). pap. 5.95 *(978-1-4549-1242-2(1))* Sterling Publishing Co., Inc.

—Why Couldn't Susan B. Anthony Vote? And Other Questions about Women's Suffrage. 2015. (Good Question! Ser.). (ENG., Illus.). 40p. (J). (gr. 2). 12.95 *(978-1-4549-1241-5(3))* Sterling Publishing Co., Inc.

Connors, Kathleen. The Life of Susan B. Anthony, Vol. 1. 2014. (Famous Lives Ser.). (ENG.). 24p. (J). (gr. 1-2). 22.60 *(978-1-4824-0425-8(7))* Stevens, Gareth Publishing LLLP.

Cooper, Meghan. The Women's Suffrage Movement. 2017. (J). ***(978-1-5026-2711-7(6))*** Cavendish Square Publishing.

Day, Meredith & Adams, Colleen. A Primary Source Investigation of Women's Suffrage. 2015. (Uncovering American History Ser.). (ENG., Illus.). 64p. (J). (gr. 5-6). 32.95 *(978-1-4994-3519-1(3)*, Rosen Central) Rosen Publishing Group, Inc., The.

Edison, Erin. Susan B. Anthony, 1 vol. 2013. (Great Women in History Ser.). (ENG., Illus.). 24p. (gr. k-1). lib. bdg. 21.99 *(978-1-62065-075-2(4)*, Pebble Bks.) Capstone Press of Coughlan Cos.

Frey, Wendy. Citizen Heroes. 2007. (Illus.). 68p. (J). *(978-1-4105-0887-4(0))*; *(978-1-4105-0888-1(9))* Johnston, Don Inc.

Gaines, Alison. Mary Edwards Walker. 2017. (J). ***(978-1-5026-2745-2(0))*** Cavendish Square Publishing.

Goddu, Krystyna Poray. What's Your Story, Susan B. Anthony? 2016. (Cub Reporter Meets Famous Americans Ser.). (ENG.). 32p. (J). (gr. k-3). 26.65 *(978-1-4677-8785-7(X)*, Lerner Pubns.) Lerner Publishing Group.

Goldsmith, Bonnie Zucker. Dr. Mary Edwards Walker: Civil War Surgeon & Medal of Honor Recipient, 1 vol. 2010. (Military Heroes Ser.). (ENG.). 112p. (J). (gr. 6-12). lib. bdg. 35.64 *(978-1-60453-966-0(6))* ABDO Publishing Co.

Goodman, Susan E. & Smith, Michael W., Jr. Women Work for Change. 2006. (Hampton-Brown Edge: Reading, Writing, & Language (c)2009 Ser.). (ENG., Illus.). 36p. (J). pap. 18.95 *(978-0-7922-5456-0(2))* CENGAGE Learning.

Harness, Cheryl. Mary Walker Wears the Pants: The True Story of the Doctor, Reformer, & Civil War Hero. Molinari, Carlo, illus. 2013. (ENG.). 32p. (J). (gr. 1-3). 16.99 *(978-0-8075-4990-2(8))* Whitman, Albert & Co.

Havelin, Kate. Victoria Woodhull: Fearless Feminist. 2006. (Trailblazer Biographies Ser.). (ENG., Illus.). 112p. (gr. 5-9). lib. bdg. 31.93 *(978-0-8225-5986-3(2)*, Lerner Pubns.) Lerner Publishing Group.

Heroes of the Women's Suffrage Movement. 2016. (Heroes of the Women's Suffrage Movement Ser.). 128p. (gr. 6-6). lib. bdg. 223.62 *(978-0-7660-7507-8(9))* Enslow Pubs., Inc.

Herweck, Dona. Susan B. Anthony, 1 vol. 2nd rev. ed. 2014. (TIME for KIDS(r) Nonfiction Readers Ser.). (ENG., Illus.). 28p. (J). (gr. 2-2). pap. 23.96 *(978-1-4807-1063-4(6))* Shell Educational Publishing.

Hicks, Peter. Documenting Women's Suffrage. 2010. (Documenting History Ser.). (Illus.). 48p. (J). pap. 11.75 *(978-1-4358-9675-8(0)*, Rosen Reference); (YA). (gr. 5-9). lib. bdg. 29.25 *(978-1-4358-9672-7(6))* Rosen Publishing Group, Inc., The.

Hollihan, Kerrie Logan. Rightfully Ours: How Women Won the Vote, 21 Activities. 2012. (For Kids Ser.). (ENG., Illus.). 144p. (J). (gr. 4). pap. 16.95 *(978-1-883052-89-8(0))* Chicago Review Pr., Inc.

Hopkinson, Deborah. Susan B. Anthony: Fighter for Women's Rights. Bates, Amy, illus. 2005. 32p. (J). lib. bdg. 15.00 *(978-1-4242-1563-8(3))* Fitzgerald Bks.

—Susan B. Anthony: Fighter for Women's Rights. Bates, Amy June, illus. 2005. (Ready-To-read SOFA Ser.). (ENG.). 32p. (J). (gr. 1-3). pap. 3.99 *(978-0-689-86909-9(6)*, Simon Spotlight) Simon Spotlight.

Howell, Izzi. Emily Davison. 2016. (Fact Cat: History Ser.). (ENG., Illus.). 24p. (J). (gr. k-2). 14.99 *(978-0-7502-9770-7(0)*, Wayland) Hachette Children's Group GBR. Dist: Hachette Bk. Group.

Kendall, Martha E. Susan B. Anthony: Fighter for Women's Voting Rights. 2015. (Legendary American Biographies Ser.). 96p. (J). (gr. 6-12). 27.94 *(978-0-7660-6500-0(6))*; pap. 10.95 *(978-0-7660-6501-7(4))* Enslow Pubs., Inc.

Kent, Deborah. Elizabeth Cady Stanton: Founder of the Women's Suffrage Movement. 2016. (Heroes of the Women's Suffrage Movement Ser.). 128p. (J). (gr. 6-6). 37.27 *(978-0-7660-7889-5(2))* Enslow Pubs., Inc.

—Elizabeth Cady Stanton: Woman Knows the Cost of Life. 2010. (Americans—the Spirit of a Nation Ser.). (Illus.). 128p. (J). lib. bdg. 33.27 *(978-0-7660-3357-3(0))* Enslow Pubs., Inc.

Litwin, Laura Baskes. Susan. B. Anthony: Social Reformer & Feminist. 2016. (Heroes of the Women's Suffrage Movement Ser.). (Illus.). 128p. (J). (gr. 6-6). 37.27 *(978-0-7660-7888-8(4))* Enslow Pubs., Inc.

Mattern, Joanne. Elizabeth Cady Stanton & Susan B. Anthony: Fighting Together for Women's Rights. (Women Who Shaped History Ser.). 24p. 2009. (gr. 2-3). 42.50 *(978-1-60854-818-7(X))* 2003. (Illus.). (J). lib. bdg. 22.60 *(978-0-8239-6503-8(1))* Rosen Publishing Group, Inc., The. (PowerKids Pr.).

McPherson, Stephanie Sammartino. Susan B. Anthony. 2006. (History Maker Bios Ser.). (Illus.). 48p. (J). (gr. 3-7). lib. bdg. 26.60 *(978-0-8225-5938-2(2)*, Lerner Pubns.) Lerner Publishing Group.

Mosley, Shelley & Charles, John. The Suffragists in Literature for Youth: The Fight for the Vote, Vol. annot. ed. 2006. (Literature for Youth Ser.: 10). (ENG.). 342p. (gr. 3-7). per. 70.00 *(978-0-8108-5372-0(8))* Scarecrow Pr., Inc.

Orr, Tamra B. The Life & Times of Susan B. Anthony. 2006. (Profiles in American History Ser.). (Illus.). 48p. (J). (gr. 3-7). lib. bdg. 29.95 *(978-1-58415-445-7(4))* Mitchell Lane Pubs., Inc.

Penne, Barbra. Susan B. Anthony: Pioneering Leader of the Women's Rights Movement. 2015. (Britannica Beginner Bios Ser.). (ENG.). 32p. (J). 23.45 *(978-1-62275-951-4(6)*, Britannica Educational Publishing) Rosen Publishing Group, Inc., The.

Pollack, Pamela D. & Belviso, Meg. Who Was Susan B. Anthony? Lacey, Mike & Harrison, Nancy, illus. 2014. (Who Was? Ser.). (ENG.). 112p. (J). (gr. 3-7). 5.99 *(978-0-448-47963-7(X)*, Grosset & Dunlap) Penguin Young Readers Group.

Rappaport, Doreen. Elizabeth Started All the Trouble. Faulkner, Matt, illus. 2016. (ENG.). 40p. (J). (gr. 1-3). 17.99 *(978-0-7868-5142-3(2))* Disney Pr.

Rossi, Ann & National Geographic Learning Staff. Votes for Women. 2007. (Language, Literacy, & Vocabulary - Reading Expeditions Ser.). (ENG., Illus.). 40p. (J). pap. 19.95 *(978-0-7922-8626-4(X))* CENGAGE Learning.

Slade, Suzanne. Friends for Freedom: The Story of Susan B. Anthony & Frederick Douglass. Tadgell, Nicole, illus. 2014. (ENG.). 40p. (J). (gr. 1-4). 16.95 *(978-1-58089-568-2(9))* Charlesbridge Publishing, Inc.

—Friends for Freedom: The Story of Susan B. Anthony & Frederick Douglass. 2014. (Illus.). 39p. *(978-1-60734-651-7(6))* Charlesbridge Publishing, Inc.

Somervill, Barbara A. Votes for Women! The Story of Carrie Chapman Catt. 2004. (Feminist Voices Ser.). (Illus.). 128p. (YA). (gr. 6-12). 23.95 *(978-1-883846-96-1(X)*, First Biographies) Reynolds, Morgan Inc.

Stone, Tanya Lee. Elizabeth Leads the Way: Elizabeth Cady Stanton & the Right to Vote. Gibbon, Rebecca, illus. 2008. (ENG.). 32p. (J). (gr. 1-5). 18.99 *(978-0-8050-7903-6(3)*, 9780805079036, Holt, Henry & Co. Bks. For Young Readers) Holt, Henry & Co.

—Elizabeth Leads the Way: Elizabeth Cady Stanton & the Right to Vote. Gibbon, Rebecca, illus. 2010. (ENG.). 32p. (J). (gr. 1-5). pap. 8.99 *(978-0-312-60236-9(7)*, 9780312602369) Square Fish.

Todd, Anne M. Susan B. Anthony: Activist. 2009. (Women of Achievement Ser.). (Illus.). 128p. (gr. 6-12). 35.00 *(978-1-60413-087-4(3)*, Chelsea Hse.) Facts On File, Inc.

Van Meter, Larry A. Women Win the Vote: The Hard-Fought Battle for Women's Suffrage. 2009. (America's Living History Ser.). (Illus.). 128p. (J). (gr. 5-9). lib. bdg. 33.27 *(978-0-7660-2940-8(9))* Enslow Pubs., Inc.

Wallner, Alexandra. Susan B. Anthony. Wallner, Alexandra, illus. 2012. (ENG., Illus.). 32p. (J). 16.95 *(978-0-8234-1953-1(3))* Holiday Hse., Inc.

Weidt, Maryann N. Fighting for Equal Rights: A Story about Susan B. Anthony. Sartor, Amanda, tr. Sartor, Amanda, illus. 2003. (Creative Minds Biographies Ser.). (ENG.). 64p. (gr. 4-8). pap. 8.95 *(978-1-57505-609-8(7))* Lerner Publishing Group.

White, Linda Arms. I Could Do That! Esther Morris Gets Women the Vote. Carpenter, Nancy, illus. 2005. (ENG.). 40p. (J). (gr. 2-4). 18.99 *(978-0-374-33527-4(3)*, 9780374335274, Farrar, Straus & Giroux (BYR)) Farrar, Straus & Giroux.

—I Could Do That! Esther Morris Gets Women the Vote. unabr. ed. 2006. (J). (gr. 2-4). 29.95 *(978-0-439-90582-4(6)*, WHCD692) Weston Woods Studios, Inc.

SUGAR

Aronson, Marc & Budhos, Marina Tamar. Sugar Changed the World: A Story of Magic, Spice, Slavery, Freedom, & Science. 2010. (ENG., Illus.). 176p. (YA). (gr. 7-18). 21.99 *(978-0-618-57492-6(1))* Houghton Mifflin Harcourt Publishing Co.

Braithwaite, Jill. From Cane to Sugar. 2004. (Start to Finish Ser.). (Illus.). 24p. (J). (gr. k-2). lib. bdg. 18.60 *(978-0-8225-0940-0(7))* Lerner Publishing Group.

Eagen, Rachel. The Biography of Sugar. 2005. (How did That Get There? Ser.). (ENG., Illus.). 32p. (J). (gr. 4-5). pap. *(978-0-7787-2521-3(9))*; lib. bdg. *(978-0-7787-2485-8(9))* Crabtree Publishing Co.

Friesen, Helen Lepp. Maple Syrup. 2011. 24p. (YA). (gr. 2-4). *(978-1-77071-660-5(2))*; pap. *(978-1-77071-666-7(1))* Weigl Educational Pubs. Ltd.

Furgang, Adam. Salty & Sugary Snacks: The Incredibly Disgusting Story. 2011. (Incredibly Disgusting Food Ser.). (Illus.). 48p. (YA). pap. 11.75 *(978-1-4488-2283-6(1)*, Rosen Reference); (gr. 5-9). lib. bdg. 29.25 *(978-1-4488-1267-7(4))* Rosen Publishing Group, Inc., The.

Hayes, Amy. Turning Sap into Maple Syrup. 2015. (Step-By-Step Transformations Ser.). (ENG., Illus.). 24p. (J). (gr. 1-1). pap. 8.22 *(978-1-5026-0457-6(4))* Cavendish Square Publishing.

Murray, Julie. Cane to Sugar, 1 vol. 2006. (Beginning to End Set 1 - 8 Titles Ser.). (ENG., Illus.). 24p. (gr. k-4). 25.65 *(978-1-59679-834-2(3)*, Buddy Bks.) ABDO Publishing Co.

O'Ryan, Ellie. The Sugary Secrets Behind Candy. McClurkan, Rob, illus. 2015. (Science of Fun Stuff Ser.). (ENG.). 48p. (J). (gr. 1-3). pap. 3.99 *(978-1-4814-5626-5(1)*, Simon Spotlight) Simon Spotlight.

Owings, Lisa. From Sugar Beet to Sugar. 2015. (Start to Finish, Second Ser.). (Illus.). 24p. (J). (gr. k-3). (ENG.). lib. bdg. 23.93 *(978-1-4677-6020-1(X))*; 23.99 *(978-1-4677-6290-8(3))* Lerner Publishing Group. (Lerner Pubns.).

Oxlade, Chris. The Circulatory System: Where Do I Get My Energy?, 1 vol. 2014. (Show Me Science Ser.). (ENG., Illus.). 32p. (gr. 3-5). lib. bdg. 30.65 *(978-1-4329-8751-0(8)*, Raintree Perspectives) Heinemann-Raintree.

Perritano, John. Sugar & Sweeteners. 2017. (J). ***(978-1-4222-3744-1(3))*** Mason Crest.

Reinke, Beth Bence. Sugars & Fats. 2013. (Healthy Eating with Myplate Ser.). (ENG.). 24p. (J). (gr. 1-4). 28.50 *(978-1-62323-601-4(0)*, 206403) Child's World, Inc., The.

Schuh, Mari. Sugars & Fats. 2012. (What's on Myplate? Ser.). (ENG.). 24p. (gr. k-1). pap. 41.70 (978-1-4296-9423-0(8), Pebble Plus) Capstone Press of Coughlan Cos.

WalkerTheo. SUGAR: OUR GUILTY PLEASURE LOW INTERMEDIATE BOOK WITH ONLINE ACCESS. 2014. (ENG., Illus.). 28p. (J). pap. 9.50 (978-1-107-68146-0(4)) Cambridge Univ. Pr.

Woolf, Alex. The Story of Sugar. 2016. (Story of Food Ser.). (ENG., Illus.). 32p. (J). (gr. 4-6). 16.99 (978-0-7502-9660-1(7), Wayland) Hachette Children's Group GBR. Dist: Hachette Bk. Group.

SUGARCANE

Eagen, Rachel. The Biography of Sugar. 2005. (How Did That Get Here? Ser.). (ENG., Illus.). 32p. (J). (gr. 4-5). lib. bdg. (978-0-7787-2485-8(9)) Crabtree Publishing Co.

SUICIDE

see also Assisted Suicide; Right to Die

Bleuel, Amy & Chapman, Wesley. Project Semicolon: Your Story Isn't Over. 2017. 352p. (YA). (gr. 9). pap. 9.99 **(978-0-06-246652-5(6))** HarperCollins Pubs.

Cartlidge, Cherese. Teens & Suicide. 2017. (Teen Mental Health Ser.). (ENG.). 80p. (J). (gr. 5-12). **(978-1-68282-131-2(5))** ReferencePoint Pr., Inc.

Eagen, Rachel. Suicide. 2010. (ENG.). 48p. (J). pap. (978-0-7787-2138-3(8)); lib. bdg. (978-0-7787-2131-4(0)) Crabtree Publishing Co.

Esherick, Joan. The Silent Cry: Teen Suicide & Self-Destructive Behaviors. 2006. (Science of Health Ser.). (Illus.). 128p. (YA). lib. bdg. 24.95 (978-1-59084-851-7(9)) Mason Crest.

Galas, Judith C. & Nelson, Richard E. The Power to Prevent Suicide: A Guide for Teens Helping Teens. 2nd ed. 2006. (ENG., Illus.). 128p. (YA). (gr. 8-12). pap. 14.99 (978-1-57542-206-0(9)) Free Spirit Publishing, Inc.

Goldsmith, Connie. Understanding Suicide: A National Epidemic. 2016. (ENG.). 112p. (J). (gr. 7-12). 35.99 (978-1-4677-8570-9(9), Twenty-First Century Bks.) Lerner Publishing Group.

Huddle, Lorena & Schleifer, Jay. Teen Suicide. 2011. (Illus.). 48p. (J). 167.70 (978-1-4488-4873-7(3)); (YA). (gr. 7-12). lib. bdg. 29.25 (978-1-4488-4586-6(6)) Rosen Publishing Group, Inc., The.

Lerner, Adrienne. Suicide in Arthur Miller's Death of a Salesman. 2008. (Social Issues in Literature Ser.). (ENG., Illus.). 199p. (YA). (gr. 10-12). 28.45 (978-0-7377-4019-6(1), LML02109-239999); pap. 40.95 (978-0-7377-4018-9(3), LML02109-239993) Cengage Gale. (Greenhaven Pr., Inc.).

Libal, Joyce. Antidepressants & Suicide: When Treatment Kills. (Antidepressants Ser.). (Illus.). 112p. (YA). (gr. 7-18). 2008. lib. bdg. 24.95 (978-1-4222-0099-5(X)) 2007. pap. 14.95 (978-1-4222-0407-8(3)) Mason Crest.

Marcovitz, Hal. Suicide, 1 vol. 2010. (Essential Issues Set 1 Ser.). (ENG.). 112p. (J). (gr. 6-12). lib. bdg. 35.64 (978-1-60453-958-5(5), Essential Library) ABDO Publishing Co.

—Teens & Suicide. Developed in Association with the Gallup Organization Staff, ed. 2013. (Gallup Youth Survey: Major Issues & Trends Ser.: 14). 112p. (J). (gr. 7-18). 24.95 (978-1-4222-2958-3(0)) Mason Crest.

—Teens & Suicide. 2008. (Gallup Youth Survey, Major Issues & Trends Ser.). (Illus.). 112,128p. (YA). (gr. 7-9). lib. bdg. 22.95 (978-1-59084-724-4(5)) Mason Crest.

Parks, Peggy J. How Can Suicide Be Reduced? 2014. (In Controversy Ser.). (ENG., Illus.). 96p. (J). lib. bdg. (978-1-60152-662-5(8)) ReferencePoint Pr., Inc.

Peterson, Judy Monroe. I'm Suicidal, Now What? 2015. (Teen Life 411 Ser.). (ENG., Illus.). 112p. (J). (gr. 6-7). 35.60 (978-1-4994-6136-7(4), Rosen Young Adult) Rosen Publishing Group, Inc., The.

Powell, Jillian. Self-Harm & Suicide. 2008. (Emotional Health Issues Ser.). (Illus.). 48p. (YA). (gr. 7-12). lib. bdg. 31.00 (978-0-8368-9202-4(X)) Stevens, Gareth Publishing LLLP.

Salomon, Ron. Suicide. 2007. (Psychological Disorders Ser.). (Illus.). 109p. (YA). (gr. 7-12). lib. bdg. 37.50 (978-0-7910-9007-7(8)) Facts On File, Inc.

Smid, Emmi. Luna's Red Hat: An Illustrated Storybook to Help Children Cope with Loss & Suicide. Smid, Emmi, illus. 2015. (ENG., Illus.). 34p. (J). 19.95 (978-1-84905-629-8(3), 7723) Kingsley, Jessica Pubs. GBR. Dist: Macmillan Distribution Ltd.

Thiele, Christine. What Catholic Teens Should Know about Suicide. Larkin, Jean K., ed. 2004. (What Catholic Teens Should Know Ser.). (Illus.). 8p. (YA). 7.95 (978-0-89837-240-3(2), 441110) Pflaum Publishing Group.

Wahl, Elizabeth. Do You Have a Friend Who Is Suicidal? 2016. (Got Issues? Ser.). (ENG., Illus.). 112p. (J). (gr. 7-8). lib. bdg. 37.27 (978-0-7660-7191-9(X)) Enslow Pubs., Inc.

Wohlenhaus, Kim, ed. Suicide Information for Teens. 2nd rev. ed. 2010. (Teen Health Ser.). 376p. lib. bdg. 69.00 (978-0-7808-1088-4(0)) Omnigraphics, Inc.

SUICIDE—FICTION

Allison, Jennifer. Gilda Joyce, Psychic Investigator. 2006. (Gilda Joyce Ser.). (ENG.). 336p. (J). (gr. 5-18). reprint ed. 8.99 (978-0-14-240698-4(8), Puffin Books) Penguin Young Readers Group.

Anonymous. Jay's Journal. Sparks, Beatrice, ed. (ENG.). 240p. (YA). 2012. (gr. 9). 17.99 (978-1-4424-8094-0(7)) 2010. (gr. 7). pap. 10.99 (978-1-4424-1993-3(8)) Simon Pulse. (Simon Pulse).

Asher, Jay. Thirteen Reasons Why. 2014. (ENG.). 336p. (YA). 15.24 (978-1-63245-099-9(2)) Lectorum Pubns., Inc.

—Thirteen Reasons Why. 2009. 11.72 (978-0-7848-3782-5(1), Everbind) Marco Bk. Co.

—Thirteen Reasons Why. (ENG.). (YA). (gr. 7). 2017. 336p. pap. 10.99 **(978-0-451-47829-0(0))** 2011. 336p. pap. 10.99 (978-1-59514-188-0(X)) 2007. 320p. 18.99 (978-1-59514-171-2(5)) 10th anniv. ed. 2016. 352p. 18.99 (978-1-59514-788-2(8)) Penguin Young Readers Group. (Razorbill).

—Thirteen Reasons Why. 2011. (ENG.). (YA). (gr. 7-12). lib. bdg. 21.60 **(978-1-60686-991-8(4))** Perfection Learning Corp.

—Thirteen Reasons Why. 2011. lib. bdg. 22.10 (978-0-606-15085-9(4), Turtleback) Turtleback Bks.

Avery, Tom. My Brother's Shadow. 2014. (ENG.). 176p. (J). (gr. 4-7). 16.99 (978-0-385-38487-2(4), Schwartz & Wade Bks.) Random Hse. Children's Bks.

Banting, Celia. I only said I couldn't Cope. 2006. (Illus.). 240p. (YA). per. 14.99 (978-0-9786648-2-4(5)) Wighita Pr.

—I Only Said Yes So That They'd Like Me. 2006. (Illus.). 224p. (YA). per. 14.99 (978-0-9786648-1-7(7)) Wighita Pr.

Bernard, Romily. Remember Me. 2014. (Find Me Ser.: 2). (ENG.). 368p. (YA). (gr. 8). 17.99 (978-0-06-222906-9(0), HarperTeen) HarperCollins Pubs.

Bird, Faye. My Second Life. 2016. (ENG.). 272p. (YA). 17.99 (978-0-374-34886-1(3), 9780374348861, Farrar, Straus & Giroux (BYR)) Farrar, Straus & Giroux.

Boonen, Stefan. Totally Lisa. 2008. (ENG., Illus.). 118p. (J). (gr. 4-7). 15.95 (978-1-60537-005-7(3)) Clavis Publishing.

Borris, Albert. Crash into Me. (ENG.). 272p. (YA). (gr. 9). 2010. pap. 9.99 (978-1-4169-9827-3(6)) 2009. 16.99 (978-1-4169-7435-2(0)) Simon Pulse. (Simon Pulse).

Brewer, Zac. Madness. 2017. 304p. (YA). (gr. 9). 17.99 **(978-0-06-245785-1(3))** HarperCollins Pubs.

Butcher, Kristin. The Hemingway Tradition. 2004. 92p. 19.95 (978-0-7569-4299-1(3)) Perfection Learning Corp.

Carlson, Melody. Beyond Reach. 2007. (Secret Life of Samantha Mcgregor Ser.: No. 2). (ENG.). 256p. (J). (gr. 7-12). per. 14.99 (978-1-59052-693-4(7), Multnomah) Doubleday Religious Publishing Group, The.

Chalifour, Francis. After. 2005. (ENG.). 144p. (J). (gr. 7). pap. 7.95 (978-0-88776-705-0(2), Tundra Bks.) Tundra Bks. CAN. Dist: Penguin Random Hse. LLC.

—Le Fils du Pendu. 2006. (FRE.). 168p. (J). (gr. 7). per. 7.95 (978-0-88776-795-1(8), Livres Toundra) Tundra Bks. CAN. Dist: Penguin Random Hse. LLC.

Chapman, Erica M. Teach Me to Forget. 2016. (ENG.). 288p. (YA). 17.99 (978-1-4405-9457-1(0), Simon Pulse) Simon Pulse.

Clark, Tracy. Mirage. 2016. (ENG.). 272p. (J). (gr. 9). 17.99 (978-0-544-51790-5(3), HMH Books For Young Readers) Houghton Mifflin Harcourt Publishing Co.

Clarke, Cat. Undone. 2014. (ENG.). 384p. (YA). (gr. 8-12). 16.99 (978-1-4022-9224-8(4), 9781402292248) Sourcebooks, Inc.

Cohn, Rachel. You Know Where to Find Me. (ENG.). (YA). (gr. 7). 2009. 224p. pap. 8.99 (978-0-689-87860-2(5)) 2008. 208p. 16.99 (978-0-689-87859-6(1)) Simon & Schuster Bks. For Young Readers. (Simon & Schuster Bks. For Young Readers).

Connelly, Neil. Into the Hurricane. 2017. (ENG.). 240p. (J). (gr. 9). 17.99 **(978-0-545-85381-1(8)**, Levine, Arthur A. Bks.) Scholastic, Inc.

Cross, Mimi. Before Goodbye, 0 vols. 2016. (ENG.). 389p. (YA). (gr. 8-12). pap. 9.99 (978-1-5039-4972-0(9), 9781503949720, Skyscape) Amazon Publishing.

Crutcher, Chris. Chinese Handcuffs. 2004. (ENG.). 304p. (YA). (gr. 9). pap. 9.99 (978-0-06-059839-6(5), Greenwillow Bks.) HarperCollins Pubs.

Davis, Lane. I Swear. (ENG., Illus.). 288p. (YA). (gr. 9). 2013. pap. 10.99 (978-1-4424-3507-0(0)) 2012. 16.99 (978-1-4424-3506-3(2)) Simon & Schuster Bks. For Young Readers. (Simon & Schuster Bks. For Young Readers).

Deal, Paul. Lighting Candles. 2003. 122p. (YA). 20.95 (978-0-595-65804-6(0)); pap. 10.95 (978-0-595-28457-3(4)) iUniverse, Inc.

Deuker, Carl. High Heat. 2005. (ENG.). 352p. (J). (gr. 8-18). pap. 8.99 (978-0-06-057248-8(5), HarperTeen) HarperCollins Pubs.

Donley, Jan. The Side Door. 2010. (ENG.). 288p. (J). (gr. 9). pap. 14.95 (978-1-935226-12-3(6)) Spinsters Ink Bks.

Dunn, Pintip. The Darkest Lie. 2016. viii, 292p. (YA). **(978-1-5182-2703-5(1)**, Kensington Bks.) Kensington Publishing Corp.

Falkoff, Michelle. Playlist for the Dead. 2015. (ENG.). 288p. (YA). (gr. 8). 17.99 (978-0-06-231050-7(X), HarperTeen) HarperCollins Pubs.

Ford, Michael Thomas. Suicide Notes. 2010. (ENG.). 304p. (YA). (gr. 9). pap. 9.99 (978-0-06-073757-3(3), HarperTeen) HarperCollins Pubs.

Forman, Gayle. I Was Here. l.t. ed. 2015. (ENG.). 420p. 24.99 (978-1-4104-8255-6(3)) Cengage Gale.

—I Was Here. 2015. (ENG.). 288p. (J). (gr. 9). 18.99 (978-0-451-47147-5(4), Viking Books for Young Readers) Penguin Publishing Group.

—I Was Here. 2016. (ENG.). 304p. (YA). (gr. 9). pap. 10.99 (978-0-14-751403-5(7), Speak) Penguin Young Readers Group.

—I Was Here. 2016. lib. bdg. 22.10 (978-0-606-38404-9(9)) Turtleback Bks.

Fortunati, Karen. The Weight of Zero. 2016. (ENG.). 400p. (YA). (gr. 9). 17.99 (978-1-101-93889-8(7), Delacorte Pr.) Random Hse. Children's Bks.

Foxlee, Karen. The Anatomy of Wings. 2010. (ENG.). 384p. (Orig.). (YA). (gr. 9). pap. 9.99 (978-0-375-84761-5(8), Knopf Bks. for Young Readers) Random Hse. Children's Bks.

Freymann-Weyr, Garret. Stay with Me. 2007. (ENG.). 320p. (YA). (gr. 9-12). pap. 8.99 (978-0-618-88404-9(1)) Houghton Mifflin Harcourt Publishing Co.

Froley, Margaux. Escape Theory. 2014. (ENG., Illus.). 288p. (YA). (gr. 9). pap. 9.99 (978-1-61695-342-3(X), Soho Teen) Soho Pr., Inc.

Garsee, Jeannine. The Unquiet. 2012. (ENG.). 400p. (YA). (gr. 9). 16.99 (978-1-59990-723-9(2), 9781599907239, Bloomsbury USA Childrens) Bloomsbury Publishing USA.

Giles, Gail. What Happened to Cass McBride? 2007. (ENG.). 240p. (J). (gr. 10-17). per. 9.99 (978-0-316-16639-3(1)) Little, Brown Bks. for Young Readers.

—What Happened to Cass McBride? 2007. 211p. 18.00 (978-0-7569-8178-5(6)) Perfection Learning Corp.

—What Happened to Cass McBride? A Novel. 2006. (ENG.). 224p. pap. (978-0-00-639197-5(4), Harper Trophy) HarperCollins Pubs.

Going, K. L. Fat Kid Rules the World. 2004. (ENG.). 224p. (YA). (gr. 7-18). reprint ed. pap. 9.99 (978-0-14-240208-5(7), Speak) Penguin Young Readers Group.

Goobie, Beth. Who Owns Kelly Paddik?, 1 vol. 2003. (Orca Soundings Ser.). (ENG.). 128p. (YA). (gr. 8-12). pap. 9.95 (978-1-55143-239-7(0)) Orca Bk. Pubs. USA.

—Who Owns Kelly Paddik? 2004. (Orca Soundings Ser.). 89p. 19.95 (978-0-7569-4358-5(2)) Perfection Learning Corp.

Gormally, Eleanor. The Little Flower Bulb: Helping Children Bereaved by Suicide. Loki & Splink, illus. 2011. (ENG.). 32p. (J). (gr. -1-3). pap. 21.95 (978-1-84730-260-1(2)) Veritas Pubns. IRL. Dist: Dufour Editions, Inc.

Hand, Cynthia. The Last Time We Say Goodbye. 400p. (YA). (gr. 8). 2016. pap. 9.99 (978-0-06-231848-0(9)) 2015. (ENG.). 17.99 (978-0-06-231847-3(0)) HarperCollins Pubs. (HarperTeen).

—The Last Time We Say Goodbye. 2016. (YA). lib. bdg. 20.85 (978-0-606-38130-7(9)) Turtleback Bks.

Healey, Karen. The Shattering. 2013. (ENG.). 336p. (YA). (gr. 7-17). pap. 8.99 (978-0-316-12573-4(3)) Little, Brown Bks. for Young Readers.

Holtz-Bacha, Christina. Second Chance. 2007. 96p. 8.95 (978-0-9773082-6-2(X)) LBF Bks., LLC.

Hopkins, Ellen. Impulse. (ENG.). (YA). (gr. 9-12). 2008. 688p. pap. 12.99 (978-1-4169-0357-4(7)) 2007. 672p. 22.99 (978-1-4169-0356-7(9)) McElderry, Margaret K. Bks. (McElderry, Margaret K. Bks.).

—Rumble. 2016. lib. bdg. 24.50 (978-0-606-38277-9(1)) Turtleback Bks.

Hubbard, Jennifer. Try Not to Breathe. 2013. (ENG.). 256p. (YA). (gr. 9). pap. 8.99 (978-0-14-242387-5(4), Speak) Penguin Young Readers Group.

Hubbard, Jenny. And We Stay. 2014. (ENG.). 240p. (YA). (gr. 9). lib. bdg. 19.99 (978-0-375-98955-1(2), Delacorte Pr.) Random Hse. Children's Bks.

Jacobus, Ann. Romancing the Dark in the City of Light: A Novel. 2015. (ENG.). 288p. (YA). (gr. 7-12). 18.99 (978-1-250-06443-1(0), 9781250064431) St. Martin's Pr.

Johnston, Jeffry W. Fragments. 2007. (ENG.). 208p. (YA). (gr. 7). per. 6.99 (978-1-4169-2486-9(8), Simon Pulse) Simon Pulse.

Kaulen, Diane Bouman. In the Wake of Suicide: A Child's Journey. McAdoo, Grami & McAdoo, O'Pa, illus. 2008. (J). (gr. 3-5). 14.95 (978-0-9764026-5-7(3)) Longhorn Creek Pr.

King, A. S. Glory O'Brien's History of the Future. 2014. (ENG.). 320p. (YA). (gr. 10-17). 18.00 (978-0-316-22272-3(0)) Little, Brown Bks. for Young Readers.

Kirby, Jessi. Moonglass. (ENG.). (YA). (gr. 7). 2012. 256p. pap. 9.99 (978-1-4424-1695-6(5)) 2011. 240p. 16.99 (978-1-4424-1694-9(7)) Simon & Schuster Bks. For Young Readers. (Simon & Schuster Bks. For Young Readers).

Konen, Leah. The After Girls. 2013. (ENG.). 304p. (YA). 17.95 (978-1-4405-6108-5(7), Simon Pulse) Simon Pulse.

LaCour, Nina. Hold Still. 2010. (ENG.). 272p. (YA). (gr. 7-18). 10.99 (978-0-14-241694-5(0), Speak) Penguin Young Readers Group.

Larkin, John. The Pause. 2015. (ENG.). 336p. (YA). (gr. 8). pap. 14.99 (978-0-85798-170-7(6)) Random Hse. Australia AUS. Dist: Independent Pubs. Group.

Lecesne, James. Trevor. (ENG., Illus.). (J). (gr. 5-9). 2013. 112p. pap. 9.95 (978-1-60980-487-9(2)) 2012. 114p. 14.95 (978-1-60980-420-6(1)) Seven Stories Pr. (Triangle Square).

Leveen, Tom. Random. 2014. (ENG., Illus.). 224p. (YA). (gr. 9). 17.99 (978-1-4424-9956-0(7), Simon Pulse) Simon Pulse.

Levy, Michelle. Not after Everything. 2015. (ENG.). 336p. (YA). (gr. 9-12). 17.99 (978-0-8037-4158-4(8), Dial Bks) Penguin Publishing Group.

Lynch, Chris. Freewill. 2006. 148p. (YA). (gr. 7-10). reprint ed. 16.00 (978-0-7567-9869-7(8)) DIANE Publishing Co.

Maguire, Eden. Arizona. 2010. (Beautiful Dead Ser.: 2). (ENG.). 288p. (YA). (gr. 8-12). pap. 11.99 (978-1-4022-3945-8(9)) Sourcebooks, Inc.

Maynard, Joyce. The Cloud Chamber. 2006. (ENG.). 288p. (YA). (gr. 7-7). pap. 13.99 (978-1-4169-2699-3(2), Simon Pulse) Simon Pulse.

McDaniel, Lurlene. Breathless. 2010. (ENG.). 180p. (YA). (gr. 7). mass mkt. 7.99 (978-0-440-24016-7(6), Delacorte Bks. for Young Readers) Random Hse. Children's Bks.

—So Much to Live For. 2003. (Dawn Rochelle Ser.: No. 3). (ENG., Illus.). 160p. (YA). (gr. 7-12). reprint ed. pap. 4.99 (978-1-58196-005-1(0)) Lerner Publishing Group.

Messer, Celeste M. A Message from Teddy. Hoeffner, Deb, illus. 2004. 82-92p. 4.95 (978-0-9702171-5-8(3)) AshleyAlan Enterprises.

Mickle, Shelley Fraser. The Turning Hour. 2004. 264p. (YA). pap. 16.95 (978-1-57966-008-6(8)) River City Publishing.

Mitchell, Todd. Backwards. 2013. (ENG.). 288p. (YA). (gr. 7). 17.99 (978-0-7636-6277-6(1)) Candlewick Pr.

Moir, Louise. Rafi's Red Racing Car: Explaining Suicide & Grief to Young Children. 2016. (ENG., Illus.). 40p. 17.95 (978-1-78592-200-8(9), 8893) Kingsley, Jessica Pubs. GBR. Dist: Macmillan Distribution Ltd.

Naidoo, Vahini. Fall to Pieces, 0 vols. 2012. (ENG.). 324p. (YA). (gr. 8-12). 16.99 (978-0-7614-6217-0(1), 9780761462170, Amazon Children's Publishing) Amazon Publishing.

Niven, Jennifer. All the Bright Places. 2015. (ENG.). 400p. pap. (978-0-14-135703-4(7)) Penguin Bks., Ltd.

—All the Bright Places. (ENG.). (YA). (gr. 9). 2016. 416p. pap. 10.99 (978-0-385-75591-7(0), Ember) 2015. 400p. lib. bdg. 20.99 (978-0-385-75589-4(9), Knopf Bks. for Young Readers) 2015. 400p. 17.99 (978-0-385-75588-7(0), Knopf Bks. for Young Readers) Random Hse. Children's Bks.

—All the Bright Places. 2016. lib. bdg. 22.10 (978-0-606-38876-4(1)) Turtleback Bks.

Norriss, Andrew. Friends for Life. 2015. (ENG.). 240p. (J). (gr. 3-7). 17.99 (978-0-545-85186-2(6)) Scholastic, Inc.

Peters, Julie Anne. By the Time You Read This, I'll Be Dead. 2011. (ENG.). 240p. (J). (gr. 5-9). pap. 9.99 (978-1-4231-3021-5(9)) Hyperion Pr.

Pike, Christopher, pseud. Remember Me: Her Death Will Not Go Unpunished... 2010. (Remember Me Ser.: Vols. 1-3). (ENG., Illus.). 848p. (YA). (gr. 9). pap. 9.99 (978-1-4424-0596-7(1), Simon Pulse) Simon Pulse.

Pitcher, Chelsea. The S-Word. 2013. (ENG.). 320p. pap. 19.99 (978-1-4516-9516-8(0), Gallery Bks.) Gallery Bks.

Preller, James. The Fall. 2015. (ENG.). 208p. (J). (gr. 4-9). 16.99 (978-0-312-64301-0(2), 9780312643010) Feiwel & Friends.

Quick, Matthew. Forgive Me, Leonard Peacock. 2013. (ENG.). 288p. (YA). (gr. 10-17). 18.00 (978-0-316-22133-7(3)) Little, Brown Bks. for Young Readers.

Rivers, Karen. Before We Go Extinct: A Novel. 2016. (ENG.). 256p. (YA). 17.99 (978-0-374-30240-5(5), 9780374302405, Farrar, Straus & Giroux (BYR)) Farrar, Straus & Giroux.

Rodriguez, Cindy L. When Reason Breaks. 2015. (ENG.). 304p. (YA). (gr. 7-12). 17.99 (978-1-61963-412-1(0), 9781619634121, Bloomsbury USA Childrens) Bloomsbury Publishing USA.

Rollins, Danielle. Breaking. 2017. (ENG.). 304p. (YA). 17.99 (978-1-61963-740-5(5), 9781619637405, Bloomsbury USA Childrens) Bloomsbury Publishing USA.

Ryan, Darlene. Cuts Like a Knife, 1 vol. 2012. (Orca Soundings Ser.). (ENG.). 128p. (YA). (gr. 8-12). 16.95 (978-1-4598-0120-2(2)); pap. 9.95 (978-1-4598-0119-6(9)) Orca Bk. Pubs. USA.

—Five Minutes More, 1 vol. 2009. (ENG.). 224p. (YA). (gr. 7-12). pap. 12.95 (978-1-55469-006-0(4)) Orca Bk. Pubs. USA.

Sales, Leila. This Song Will Save Your Life. 2013. (ENG.). 288p. (YA). (gr. 7). 18.99 (978-0-374-35138-0(4), 9780374351380, Farrar, Straus & Giroux (BYR)) Farrar, Straus & Giroux.

Sanchez, Jenny Torres. Death, Dickinson, & the Demented Life of Frenchie Garcia. 2013. (ENG.). 272p. (YA). (gr. 2-17). pap. 10.95 (978-0-7624-4680-3(3), Running Pr. Kids) Running Pr. Bk. Pubs.

Sappenfield, Heather. The View from Who I Was. 2015. (ENG.). 336p. (YA). pap. 11.99 (978-0-7387-4174-1(4), Flux) North Star Editions.

Stork, Francisco X. The Memory of Light. 2016. (Arthur a Levine Novel Bks.). (ENG.). 336p. (YA). (gr. 7). 17.99 (978-0-545-47432-0(9)) Scholastic, Inc.

Summers, Courtney. Fall for Anything. 2010. (ENG.). 240p. (YA). (gr. 7-18). pap. 15.99 (978-0-312-65673-7(4), 9780312656737, St. Martin's Griffin) St. Martin's Pr.

Thompson, Holly. Orchards. 2012. (ENG.). 336p. (YA). (gr. 7). pap. 9.99 (978-0-385-73978-8(8), Ember) Random Hse. Children's Bks.

Thrash, Maggie. We Know It Was You. 2016. (Strange Ser.). (ENG., Illus.). 352p. (YA). (gr. 9). 17.99 (978-1-4814-6200-6(8), Simon Pulse) Simon Pulse.

Trueman, Terry. Inside Out. 128p. 2003. (J). lib. bdg. 16.89 (978-0-06-623963-7(X)) 2004. (ENG.). (YA). (gr. 9). reprint ed. pap. 8.99 (978-0-06-447376-7(7), HarperTeen) HarperCollins Pubs.

—No Right Turn. 2009. (ENG.). 176p. (YA). (gr. 9). pap. 8.99 (978-0-06-057493-2(3), HarperTeen) HarperCollins Pubs.

Vaught, Susan. Trigger. 2006. (ENG.). 304p. (YA). (gr. 7-12). 16.95 (978-1-58234-920-6(7), 9781582349206, Bloomsbury USA Childrens) Bloomsbury Publishing USA.

Warga, Jasmine. My Heart & Other Black Holes. 2015. (ENG.). 320p. (YA). (gr. 9). 17.99 (978-0-06-232467-2(5)) HarperCollins Pubs.

Weingarten, Lynn. Suicide Notes from Beautiful Girls. (ENG., Illus.). 336p. (YA). (gr. 9). 2016. pap. 10.99 (978-1-4814-1858-4(0)) 2015. 17.99 (978-1-4814-1853-9(X)) Simon Pulse. (Simon Pulse).

—Suicide Notes from Beautiful Girls. 2016. (ENG.). (YA). (gr. 9). lib. bdg. 22.10 **(978-0-606-39882-4(1))** Turtleback Bks.

Williams, Carol Lynch. Glimpse. 2010. (ENG.). 496p. (YA). (gr. 9-18). 16.99 (978-1-4169-9730-6(X), Simon & Schuster/Paula Wiseman Bks.) Simon & Schuster/Paula Wiseman Bks.

Williams, Carol Lynch & Gregg, L. B. Glimpse. Gregg, Anna, photos by. 2012. (ENG., Illus.). 512p. (YA). (gr. 9). pap. 12.99 (978-1-4169-9731-3(8), Simon & Schuster/Paula Wiseman Bks.) Simon & Schuster/Paula Wiseman Bks.

Williams, Katie. Absent. 2013. (ENG.). 180p. (YA). (gr. 7-12). 16.99 (978-0-8118-7150-1(9)) Chronicle Bks. LLC.

Young, Suzanne. The Epidemic. 2016. (Program Ser.: 4). (ENG., Illus.). 384p. (YA). (gr. 9). 17.99 (978-1-4814-4470-5(0), Simon Pulse) Simon Pulse.

—The Program. (Program Ser.: 1). (ENG., Illus.). (YA). (gr. 9). 2014. 432p. pap. 11.99 (978-1-4424-4581-9(5)) 2013. 416p. 17.99 (978-1-4424-4580-2(7)) Simon Pulse. (Simon Pulse).

—The Treatment. (ENG., Illus.). (YA). (gr. 9). 2015. (Program Ser.: 2). 368p. pap. 11.99 (978-1-4424-4584-0(X)) 2014. (Program Ser.). 352p. 18.99 (978-1-4424-4583-3(1)) Simon Pulse. (Simon Pulse).

SUKKOT

Fishman, Cathy Goldberg. On Sukkot & Simchat Torah. Hall, Melanie, illus. 2006. (ENG.). 32p. (J). (gr. -1-4). lib. bdg. 17.95 (978-1-58013-165-0(4), Kar-Ben Publishing) Lerner Publishing Group.

Kropf, Latifa Berry. It's Sukkah Time. Cohen, Tod, illus. Cohen, Tod, photos by. 2003. (Sukkot & Simchat Torah Ser.). 24p. (J). (gr. -1-1). 12.95 (978-1-58013-084-4(4), Kar-Ben Publishing) Lerner Publishing Group.

—It's Sukkah Time! Cohen, Tod, photos by. 2012. (Sukkot & Simchat Torah Ser.). (ENG., Illus.). 24p. (J). (gr. -1-1). 9.95 (978-1-4677-0741-1(4), Kar-Ben Publishing) Lerner Publishing Group.

Miller, Reagan. Sukkot. 2010. (ENG., Illus.). 32p. (J). pap. (978-0-7787-4784-0(0)); (gr. 1-3). (978-0-7787-4766-6(2)) Crabtree Publishing Co.

SUKKOT—FICTION

Axe-Bronk, Susan. The Vanishing Gourds: A Sukkot Mystery. Monelli, Marta, illus. 2012. (Sukkot & Simchat Torah Ser.). (ENG.). 24p. (J). (gr. -1-3). 7.95 (978-0-7613-7504-3(X)); lib. bdg. 17.95 (978-0-7613-7503-6(1)) Lerner Publishing Group. (Kar-Ben Publishing).

Cohen, Deborah Bodin. Engineer Ari & the Sukkah Express. Kober, Shahar, illus. 2010. (Sukkot & Simchat Torah Ser.). (ENG.). 32p. (J). (gr. k-3). pap. 7.95 (978-0-7613-5128-3(0)); lib. bdg. 17.95 (978-0-7613-5126-9(4)) Lerner Publishing Group. (Kar-Ben Publishing).

Kimmel, Eric A. The Mysterious Guests: A Sukkot Story. Krenina, Katya, illus. 2008. (ENG.). 32p. (J). (gr. 1-5). 16.95 (978-0-8234-1893-0(6)) Holiday Hse., Inc.

Korngold, Jamie S. Sadie's Sukkah Breakfast. Fortenberry, Julie, illus. 2011. (Sukkot & Simchat Torah Ser.). (ENG.). 24p. (J). (gr. -1-1). pap. 7.95 (978-0-7613-5648-6(7)); lib. bdg. 16.95 (978-0-7613-5647-9(9)) Lerner Publishing Group. (Kar-Ben Publishing).

Newman, Tracy. Sukkot Is Coming! Garófoli, Viviana, illus. 2017. (ENG.). 12p. (gr. -1 — 1). bds. 5.99 (978-1-5124-0828-7(X), Kar-Ben Publishing) Lerner Publishing Group.

Ofanansky, Allison. Sukkot Treasure Hunt. Alpern, Eliyahu, illus. Alpern, Eliyahu, photos by. 2009. (Sukkot & Simchat Torah Ser.). (ENG.). 32p. (J). (gr. -1-5). 15.95

(978-0-8225-8763-7(7), Kar-Ben Publishing) Lerner Publishing Group.

Rouss, Sylvia A. Sammy Spider's First Sukkot. Kahn, Katherine Janus, illus. 2004. (ENG.). 32p. (J). (gr. -1-3). 17.95 (978-1-58013-142-1(5)); pap. 7.95 (978-1-58013-083-7(6)) Lerner Publishing Group. (Kar-Ben Publishing).

Steinberg, Laya. The Best Sukkot Pumpkin Ever. Madden, Colleen M., illus. 2017. (ENG.). 32p. (gr. -1-3). 17.99 **(978-1-5124-0863-8(8)**, Kar-Ben Publishing) Lerner Publishing Group.

Terwilliger, Kelly. Bubbe Isabella & the Sukkot Cake. Hornung, Phyllis, illus. 2005. 24p. (J). (gr. 3-8). per. 6.95 (978-1-58013-128-5(X), Kar-Ben Publishing) Lerner Publishing Group.

Weilerstein, Sadie Rose. K'tonton's Sukkot Adventure. 2016. (ENG., Illus.). 32p. pap. 11.95 (978-0-8276-1268-6(0)) Jewish Pubn. Society.

SULLIVAN, ANNIE, 1866-1936

Adams, Colleen. The Courage of Helen Keller. (Reading Room Collection 2 Ser.). 24p. 2009. (gr. 3-4). 42.50 (978-1-60851-992-7(9), PowerKids Pr.) 2003. (Illus.). (J). lib. bdg. 22.60 (978-0-8239-3710-3(0)) Rosen Publishing Group, Inc., The.

Adler, David A. Helen Keller. Wallner, John, illus. 2006. (ENG.). 32p. (J). (gr. -1-3). 4.95 (978-0-8234-2042-1(6)) Holiday Hse., Inc.

—Helen Keller. Wallner, John C. & Wallner, John, illus. 2003. (ENG.). 32p. (J). (gr. k-3). tchr. ed. 14.95 (978-0-8234-1606-6(2)) Holiday Hse., Inc.

Berne, Emma Carlson & Hodge, Marie. Helen Keller: Courage in Darkness. 2009. (Sterling Biographies(r) Ser.). (ENG., Illus.). 128p. (J). (gr. 5-18). pap. 5.95 (978-1-4027-5147-9(8)) Sterling Publishing Co., Inc.

Butler, Darren J. Helen Keller: Leader Without Sight or Sound. 2012. (Illus.). 108p. (J). pap. (978-1-59421-083-9(7)) Seacoast Publishing, Inc.

Delano, Marfe Ferguson. Helen's Eyes: A Photobiography of Annie Sullivan, Helen Keller's Teacher. (Photobiographies Ser.). (ENG., Illus.). 64p. (J). (gr. 5). 2015. pap. 7.99 (978-1-4263-2222-8(4)) 2008. 17.95 (978-1-4263-0209-1(6)) 2008. 27.90 (978-1-4263-0210-7(X)) National Geographic Society. (National Geographic Children's Bks.).

Devillier, Christy. Helen Keller, 1 vol. 2004. (First Biographies Set Iv Ser.). (ENG., Illus.). 32p. (gr. k-4). 27.07 (978-1-59197-514-4(X), Buddy Bks.) ABDO Publishing Co.

Hollingsworth, Tamara. Helen Keller: A New Vision, 1 vol. 2nd rev. ed. 2013. (Nonfiction Readers Ser.). (ENG., Illus.). 48p. (J). (gr. 4-4). pap. 29.96 (978-1-4807-1115-0(2)) Shell Educational Publishing.

—Helen Keller: Una Nueva Visión. 2017. (TIME for Kids en Español - Level 4 Ser.). (SPA & ENG., Illus.). 48p. (gr. 4-4). lib. bdg. 31.99 (978-1-5157-5144-1(9)) Time for Kids Inc AUS. Dist: Capstone Pub.

Hopkinson, Deborah. Annie & Helen. Colón, Raúl, illus. 2012. (ENG.). 48p. (J). (gr. -1-3). 17.99 (978-0-375-85706-5(0), Schwartz & Wade Bks.) Random Hse. Children's Bks.

MacLeod, Elizabeth. Helen Keller. Krystoforski, Andrej, illus. 2007. (Kids Can Read Ser.). (ENG.). 32p. (J). (gr. 1-3). 3.95 (978-1-55453-000-7(8)); 14.95 (978-1-55337-999-7(3)) Kids Can Pr., Ltd. CAN. Dist: Hachette Bk. Group.

—Helen Keller: A Determined Life. 2004. (Snapshots: Images of People & Places in History Ser.). (ENG., Illus.). 32p. (J). (gr. 3-7). 7.95 (978-1-55337-509-8(2)) Kids Can Pr., Ltd. CAN. Dist: Hachette Bk. Group.

Mattern, Joanne. Helen Keller. 2015. (Rookie Biographies(r) Ser.). (ENG., Illus.). 32p. (J). pap. 5.95 (978-0-531-20995-0(4)) Scholastic Library Publishing.

O'Brien, John A. Who Was Helen Keller? Harrison, Nancy, illus. 2003. (Who Was... ? Ser.). 107p. (J). (gr. 3-7). 12.65 (978-0-7569-1596-4(1)) Perfection Learning Corp.

Rappaport, Doreen. Helen's Big World: The Life of Helen Keller. Tavares, Matt, illus. 2012. (Big Words Ser.). (ENG.). 48p. (J). (gr. 1-3). 17.99 (978-0-7868-0890-8(X)) Hyperion Pr.

SUMER

see also Babylonia

Howell, Izzi & Minay, Rachel. Ancient Sumer. 2017. (Explore! Ser.). (ENG., Illus.). 32p. (J). (gr. 4-6). 16.99 (978-1-5263-0088-1(5), Wayland) Hachette Children's Group GBR. Dist: Hachette Bk. Group.

SUMERIANS

Fine, Jil. Writing in Ancient Mesopotamia. 2003. (Writing in the Ancient World Ser.). (Illus.). 24p. (J). lib. bdg. 22.60 (978-0-8239-6509-0(0), PowerKids Pr.) Rosen Publishing Group, Inc., The.

Hunter, Nick. Daily Life in Ancient Sumer. 2015. (Daily Life in Ancient Civilizations Ser.). (ENG., Illus.). 48p. (gr. 3-6). pap. 8.99 (978-1-4846-2583-5(8)) Heinemann-Raintree.

SUMMER

Aloian, Molly. How Do We Know It Is Summer? 2013. (ENG., Illus.). 24p. (J). (978-0-7787-0960-2(4)); pap. (978-0-7787-0964-0(7)) Crabtree Publishing Co.

Amoroso, Cynthia & Noyed, Robert B. Summer. 2014. (Seasons of the Year Ser.). (ENG.). 24p. (J). (gr. -1-2). 25.64 (978-1-62687-026-0(8), 206825) Child's World, Inc., The.

Anderson, Sheila. Are You Ready for Summer? 2010. (Lightning Bolt Books (tm) — Our Four Seasons Ser.). (ENG.). 32p. (gr. k-2). pap. 7.95 (978-0-7613-5671-4(1)); lib. bdg. 26.60 (978-0-7613-4585-5(X)) Lerner Publishing Group.

Appleby, Alex. Qu Sucede en Verano? / What Happens in Summer?, Vol. 1. 2014. (Cuatro Estaciones Estupendas / Four Super Seasons Ser.). (SPA & BYN.). 24p. (J). (gr. k-k). 22.60 (978-1-4824-0128-8(2)) Stevens, Gareth Publishing LLLP.

—What Happens in Summer?, Vol. 1. 2014. (Four Super Seasons Ser.). (ENG.). 24p. (J). (gr. k-k). 22.60 (978-1-4824-0109-7(6)) Stevens, Gareth Publishing LLLP.

Barklem, Jill. Cuento de Verano.Tr. of Summer Story. (J). pap. 8.95 (978-84-233-2619-8(5)) Ediciones Destino ESP. Dist: Planeta Publishing Corp.

Barnham, Kay. Summer. 2010. (Seasons Ser.). (ENG.). 24p. (J). lib. bdg. 22.60 (978-1-61532-570-2(0), PowerKids Pr.) Rosen Publishing Group, Inc., The.

Baxter, Nicola. Summer. 2009. (J). 24.25 (978-1-59771-122-7(5)) Sea-To-Sea Pubns.

Brush, Jim. Extreme Summer Sports. 2013. (Illus.). 46p. (J). 35.65 (978-1-59771-407-5(0)) Sea-To-Sea Pubns.

Butterworth Moira. Summer. James, Helen, illus. 2005. (Seasons (Smart Apple Media) Ser.). 32p. (YA). (gr. 2-4). lib. bdg. 27.10 (978-1-58340-615-1(8)) Black Rabbit Bks.

Carole, Bonnie. Blue & Yellow in Summer. 2015. (ENG.). 24p. (gr. -1-1). pap. 8.95 (978-1-63430-079-7(3)) Rourke Educational Media.

Carr, Aaron. Summer. 2013. 25.00 (978-1-62127-494-0(2)) Weigl Pubs., Inc.

Casado, Dami & Casado, Alicia. El Verano. 2005. (Brujita Mo y las Cuatro Estaciones Ser.). (SPA & ESP., Illus.). 14p. (J). (gr. k-4). per., bds. 7.99 (978-84-272-6235-5(3)) Molino, Editorial ESP. Dist: Santillana USA Publishing Co., Inc.

Collinson, Clare. Summer. 2010. (Thinking about the Seasons Ser.). 32p. 28.50 (978-1-59771-261-3(2)) Sea-To-Sea Pubns.

Davis, Rebecca F. Playas y Bicicletas: Un Libro para Contar en el Verano. 2012. (Vamos a Contar / Counting Bks.).Tr. of Beaches & Bicycles - A Summer Counting Book. (ENG, SPA & MUL.). 32p. (gr. 1-2). lib. bdg. 27.32 (978-1-4296-8250-3(7), A+ Bilingue/Bilingual) Capstone Press of Coughlan Cos.

DeGezelle, Terri. Exploring Summer, 1 vol. 2012. (Exploring the Seasons Ser.). (ENG.). 24p. (gr. k-1). pap. 7.29 (978-1-4296-7912-1(3)); pap. 41.70 (978-1-4296-8352-4(X)); lib. bdg. 26.65 (978-1-4296-7698-4(1)) Capstone Press of Coughlan Cos. (Pebble Plus).

Dolphin, Colleen. Signs of Summer, 1 vol. 2012. (Signs of the Seasons Ser.). (ENG.). 24p. (J). (gr. k-3). lib. bdg. 24.21 (978-1-61783-394-6(0), SandCastle) ABDO Publishing Co.

Endres, Hollie J. The Letter Ss Set: Spring & Summer, 6 vols. 2004. (Letter Bks.). (ENG.). 8p. (gr. k-1). pap. 29.70 (978-0-7368-4118-4(0), Letter Bks.) Capstone Press of Coughlan Cos.

Enslow, Brian. Summer Colors. 2011. (All about Colors of the Seasons Ser.). (Illus.). 24p. (J). (gr. -1-18). pap. 7.95 (978-1-59845-266-2(5), Enslow Elementary) Enslow Pubs., Inc.

Eystad, Janet Lynn. What I Got into Last Summer. 2012. 28p. 24.95 (978-1-4626-5316-4(2)) America Star Bks.

Felix, Rebecca. How's the Weather in Summer? 2014. (21st Century Basic Skills Library: Let's Look at Summer Ser.). (ENG.). 24p. (J). (gr. k-3). 22.79 (978-1-63137-596-5(2), 205167) Cherry Lake Publishing.

—Keeping Cool in Summer. 2014. (21st Century Basic Skills Library: Let's Look at Summer Ser.). (ENG.). 24p. (J). (gr. k-3). 22.79 (978-1-63137-597-2(0), 205171) Cherry Lake Publishing.

—Visiting the Beach in Summer. 2014. (21st Century Basic Skills Library: Let's Look at Summer Ser.). (ENG., Illus.). 24p. (J). (gr. k-3). 22.79 (978-1-63137-598-9(9), 205175) Cherry Lake Publishing.

—What Do Bees Do in Summer? 2014. (21st Century Basic Skills Library: Let's Look at Summer Ser.). (ENG., Illus.). 24p. (J). (gr. k-3). pap. 12.79 (978-1-63137-646-7(2), 205188) Cherry Lake Publishing.

—What Do People Do in Summer? 2014. (21st Century Basic Skills Library: Let's Look at Summer Ser.). (ENG., Illus.). 24p. (J). (gr. k-3). 22.79 (978-1-63137-602-3(0), 205191) Cherry Lake Publishing.

—What Happens to Plants in Summer? 2014. (21st Century Basic Skills Library: Let's Look at Summer Ser.). (ENG.). 24p. (J). (gr. k-3). 22.79 (978-1-63137-603-0(9), 205195) Cherry Lake Publishing.

Flatt, Lizann. Shaping up Summer. Barron, Ashley, illus. 2014. (Math in Nature Ser.: 4). (ENG.). 32p. (J). (gr. k-4). 14.95 (978-1-926973-87-6(9), Owlkids) Owlkids Bks. Inc. CAN. Dist: Publishers Group West (PGW).

Gamble, Adam & Jasper, Mark. Good Night Summer. Blackmore, Katherine, illus. 2017. (Good Night Our World Ser.). (ENG.). 20p. (J). (— 1). bds. 9.95 (978-1-60219-440-3(8)) Good Night Bks.

George, Jean Craighead. Summer Moon. 2003. (J). (gr. 3-7). 20.75 (978-0-8446-7243-4(2)) Smith, Peter Pub., Inc.

Glaser, Rebecca. Summer. 2012. (ENG., Illus.). 24p. (J). lib. bdg. 25.65 (978-1-62031-015-1(5)) Jump! Inc.

Hedlund, Stephanie. Summer. Bauer, Stephanie, illus. 2013. (Seasons Ser.). 24p. (J). (gr. k-4). lib. bdg. 27.07 (978-1-61641-994-3(6), Looking Glass Library- Nonfiction) Magic Wagon.

Here Comes Summer! 2003. (J). per. (978-1-57657-969-5(7)) Paradise Pr., Inc.

Herriges, Ann. Summer. 2006. (Seasons Ser.). (ENG., Illus.). 24p. (J). (gr. k-3). lib. bdg. 25.95 (978-1-60014-032-7(7)) Bellwether Media.

—Summer. 2011. (Blastoff! Readers Ser.). 24p. (J). pap. 5.95 (978-0-531-26248-1(0), Children's Pr.) Scholastic Library Publishing.

Herrington, Lisa M. How Do You Know It's Summer? 2013. (ENG.). 32p. (J). 23.00 (978-0-531-29948-7(1)); pap. 5.95 (978-0-531-22577-6(1)) Scholastic Library Publishing.

Jackson, Ellen B. The Summer Solstice. 2003. (Illus.). 32p. (J). (gr. 3-6). pap. 7.95 (978-0-7613-1985-6(9), Millbrook Pr.) Lerner Publishing Group.

Jeffries, Joyce. Dinosaurs in the Summer. 2014. (Dinosaur School Ser.). 24p. (J). (gr. -1-1). 22.60 (978-1-4824-0714-3(0)) Stevens, Gareth Publishing LLLP.

Kalz, Jill. Summer. 2005. (My First Look at Seasons Ser.). (Illus.). 24p. (J). (gr. k-3). lib. bdg. 15.95 (978-1-58341-364-7(2), Creative Education) Creative Co., The.

Latham, Irene. When the Sun Shines on Antarctica: And Other Poems about the Frozen Continent. Wadham, Anna, illus. 2016. (ENG.). 32p. (gr. 3-6). (J). 19.99 (978-1-4677-5216-9(9)); 30.65 (978-1-4677-9729-0(4), Millbrook Pr.) Lerner Publishing Group.

Latta, Sara L. ¿Qué Pasa en el Verano? What Happens in Summer? 2010. (SPA.). (J). 23.94 (978-0-7660-3243-9(4), Enslow Elementary) Enslow Pubs., Inc.

—What Happens in Summer? 2006. (I Like the Seasons! Ser.). (Illus.). 24p. (J). (gr. 1-3). lib. bdg. 22.60 (978-0-7660-2416-8(4), Enslow Elementary) Enslow Pubs., Inc.

—Why Is It Summer? 2012. (Why Do We Have Seasons? Ser.). (Illus.). 24p. (J). (gr. k-18). pap. 7.95 (978-1-59845-390-4(4), Enslow Elementary) Enslow Pubs., Inc.

Lim, Annalees. 10-Minute Seasonal Crafts for Summer. 2014. (10-Minute Seasonal Crafts Ser.). (Illus.). 24p. (J). (gr. k-3). lib. bdg. 26.25 (978-1-4777-9210-0(4)) Windmill Bks.

Lindeen, Mary. Summer! 2015. (BeginningtoRead Ser.). (ENG., Illus.). 32p. (J). (gr. k-2). lib. bdg. 22.60 (978-1-59953-680-4(3)) Norwood Hse. Pr.

—Summer. 2015. (BeginningtoRead Ser.). (ENG., Illus.). 32p. (J). (gr. k-2). pap. 11.94 (978-1-60357-740-3(8)) Norwood Hse. Pr.

Mackall, Dandi. The Special Gifts of Summer: Celebrations. 2015. (Seasons Ser.). (ENG., Illus.). 32p. (J). (gr. -1-3). 9.99 (978-1-4336-8235-3(4), B&H Kids) B&H Publishing Group.

Macken, JoAnn Early. Summer. 2006. (Seasons of the Year Ser.). (Illus.). 16p. (gr. -1-2). pap. 5.30 (978-0-8368-6360-4(7)); lib. bdg. 19.00 (978-0-8368-6355-0(0)) Stevens, Gareth Publishing LLLP. (Weekly Reader Leveled Readers).

—Summer (Verano) 2006. (Seasons of the Year/ Las estaciones del ano Ser.). (SPA., Illus.). 16p. (gr. -1-2). pap. 5.30 (978-0-8368-6539-4(1), Weekly Reader Leveled Readers) Stevens, Gareth Publishing LLLP.

Macken, JoAnn Early & Early Macken, JoAnn. Summer/Verano. 2006. (Seasons of the Year/Las Estaciones del Ano Ser.). (ENG & SPA., Illus.). 16p. (gr. -1-2). lib. bdg. 19.00 (978-0-8368-6534-9(0), Weekly Reader Leveled Readers) Stevens, Gareth Publishing LLLP.

McGee, Randel. Fun & Festive Summer Crafts: Tie-Dyed Shirts, Bug Cages, & Sand Castles. 2014. (Fun & Festive Crafts for the Seasons Ser.). (Illus.). 48p. (J). (gr. 3-4). lib. bdg. 25.27 (978-0-7660-4319-0(3), Enslow Elementary) Enslow Pubs., Inc.

Meister, Cari. Summer Is Super. Lingenfelter, Jim, illus. 2010. (First Graphics: Seasons Ser.). (ENG.). 24p. (gr. 1-2). pap. 35.70 (978-1-4296-5694-8(8)); lib. bdg. 23.99 (978-1-4296-4730-4(2)) Capstone Press of Coughlan Cos.

Mercado, Nancy E. Boredom Busters! Activities to Do for Kids Like You! 2003. (Illus.). 38p. (J). (978-0-439-52312-7(5)) Scholastic, Inc.

Moon, Walt K. ¡El Verano Es Divertido! 2017. (Bumba Books (tm) en Español — Diviértete con Las Estaciones (Season Fun) Ser.). (SPA., Illus.). 24p. (J). (gr. -1-1). 25.32 (978-1-5124-2862-9(0)) Lerner Publishing Group.

—Summer Is Fun! 2016. (Bumba Books (tm) — Season Fun Ser.). (ENG., Illus.). 24p. (J). (gr. -1-1). 25.32 (978-1-5124-1412-7(3)) Lerner Publishing Group.

Murray, Julie. Summer, 1 vol. 2016. (ENG., Illus.). 24p. **(978-1-62970-921-5(2)**, 1391201) ABDO Publishing Co.

Murray, Julie. El Verano. 2016. (Las Estaciones Ser.). (SPA.). 24p. (J). (gr. k-5). pap. 7.95 (978-1-4966-0711-9(2)) Capstone Classroom.

Owen, Ruth. How Do You Know It's Summer? (Signs of the Seasons Ser.). 24p. (J). 2016. (ENG.). (gr. k-3). pap. 7.95 (978-1-944998-50-9(0)) 2012. (gr. -1-3). lib. bdg. 23.93 (978-1-61772-399-5(1)) Bearport Publishing Co., Inc.

Pfeffer, Wendy. The Longest Day: Celebrating the Summer Solstice. Bleck, Linda, illus. 2015. (ENG.). 40p. (J). (gr. 2-4). pap. 8.99 (978-0-14-751556-8(4), Puffin Books) Penguin Young Readers Group.

Publications International Ltd. Staff, ed. Staying Smart in Summer: Entering 1st Grade. 2011. 128p. (J). 7.98 (978-1-4508-1421-8(2)) Phoenix International Publications, Inc.

—Staying Smart in Summer: Entering 2nd Grade. 2011. 128p. (J). 7.98 (978-1-4508-1420-1(4)) Phoenix International Publications, Inc.

—Staying Smart in Summer: Entering Kindergarten. 2011. 128p. (J). 7.98 (978-1-4508-1422-5(0)) Phoenix International Publications, Inc.

Ross, Kathy. Crafts to Make in the Summer. Enright, Vicky, illus. 2003. (Crafts for All Seasons Ser.: 3). (ENG.). 64p. (gr. k-3). pap. 9.95 (978-0-7613-0334-3(0), First Avenue Editions) Lerner Publishing Group.

Rustad, Martha E. H. Today Is a Sunny Day. 2017. (What Is the Weather Today? Ser.). (ENG., Illus.). 24p. (gr. k-2). pap. 6.29 (978-1-4966-0943-4(3), Pebble Bks.) Capstone Press of Coughlan Cos.

Schuh, Mari C. Crayola Summer Colors. 2017. (Crayola (r) Seasons Ser.). (ENG.). 24p. (J). (gr. -1-3). 26.65 **(978-1-5124-3290-9(3))** Lerner Publishing Group.

Smith, Kim. Sunny Summer Lapbook. Kinney, Cyndi, ed. 2013. (J). pap. 25.99 (978-1-61625-542-8(0)); cd-rom 19.99 (978-1-61625-541-1(2)) Knowledge Box Central.

—Sunny Summer Lapbook: Assembled. Kinney, Cyndi, ed. 2013. (J). pap. 35.99 (978-1-61625-544-2(7)) Knowledge Box Central.

Smith, Sian. What Can You See in Summer?, 1 vol. 2014. (Seasons Ser.). (ENG.). 24p. (gr. -1-1). pap. 5.99 (978-1-4846-0355-0(9), Acorn) Heinemann-Raintree.

Sterling, Kristin. It's Sunny Today. 2009. (Lightning Bolt Books — What's the Weather Like? Ser.). (ENG., Illus.). 32p. (gr. k-2). 26.60 (978-0-7613-4259-5(1), Lerner Pubns.); pap. 7.95 (978-0-7613-5022-4(5)) Lerner Publishing Group.

Thayer, Tanya. Summer. 2005. (First Step Nonfiction Ser.). (Illus.). 24p. (gr. k-2). lib. bdg. 17.27 (978-0-8225-1984-3(4)) Lerner Publishing Group.

Ticktock Media, Ltd. Staff. Summer Vacation. 2009. (Busy Tots Ser.). (ENG.). 10p. (J). (gr. -1-k). bds. 6.95 (978-1-84696-800-6(3), TickTock Books) Octopus Publishing Group GBR. Dist: Independent Pubs. Group.

Turnbull, Stephanie. Summer. 2013. (Seasons Ser.). (Illus.). 24p. (J). (gr. 1-4). 25.65 (978-1-59920-848-0(2)) Black Rabbit Bks.

Ventura, Marne & Peschke, Marci. Kylie Jean Summer Camp Craft Queen, 1 vol. Mourning, Tuesday, illus. 2014. (Kylie Jean Craft Queen Ser.). (ENG.). 32p. (gr. 2-3). lib. bdg. 26.65 (978-1-4795-2193-7(0)) Picture Window Bks.

Winnick, Nick. Summer. 2010. (World of Wonder Ser.). 24p. (J). (gr. 2-4). lib. bdg. 25.70 (978-1-61690-047-2(4)) Weigl Pubs., Inc.

—Summer: Wow Study of Day & Seasons. 2010. (J). pap. 9.95 (978-1-61690-051-9(2)); (978-1-61690-055-7(5)) Weigl Pubs., Inc.

SUMMER—FICTION

Abbott, Hailey. Next Summer. 2005. (Summer Boys Ser.: 2). (ENG.). 240p. (J). (gr. 7-12). pap. 9.99 (978-0-439-75540-5(9)) Scholastic, Inc.

—Summer Boys. 2004. (Summer Boys Ser.: 1). (ENG.). 224p. (J). (gr. 7). pap. 9.99 (978-0-439-54020-9(8)) Scholastic, Inc.

Ackerman, Jill. Welcome Summer. Davis, Nancy, illus. 2010. (Little Scholastic Ser.). (ENG.). 10p. (J). (gr. k — 1). bds. 5.99 (978-0-545-15164-1(3), Cartwheel Bks.) Scholastic, Inc.

Acosta, Margarita. Summer at Grandma's. 2013. 36p. pap. 14.95 (978-1-60594-983-3(3), Llumina Pr.) Aeon Publishing Inc.

Alley, R. W. Gretchen over the Beach. 2016. (ENG., Illus.). 32p. (J). (gr. -1-3). 14.99 (978-0-547-90708-6(7)) Houghton Mifflin Harcourt Publishing Co.

Alvarez, Julia. De Como Tia Lola Salvo el Verano. 2012. (Tia Lola Stories Ser.). (ENG & SPA.). 192p. (J). (gr. 3-7). 6.99 (978-0-307-93023-1(8), Yearling) Random Hse. Children's Bks.

Anderson, D. M. Killer Cows. 2010. 274p. (YA). pap. 13.99 (978-1-59080-686-9(7), Quake) Echelon Press Publishing.

Anne, Paula. Sultry Smith. 2009. 80p. pap. 9.99 (978-1-60860-970-3(7), Eloquent Bks.) Strategic Book Publishing & Rights Agency (SBPRA).

Applegate, Katherine. Sun-Kissed Christmas. 2010. (Summer Ser.). (ENG.). 208p. (YA). (gr. 9-18). pap. 8.99 (978-1-4169-9397-1(5), Simon Pulse) Simon Pulse.

Aronskind, Ofer. That Same Summer. 2008. 156p. pap. 12.95 (978-0-595-50605-7(4)) iUniverse, Inc.

Austin, Heather. Boatyard Ducklings. Austin, Heather, illus. 2008. (ENG., Illus.). 32p. (J). (gr. -1-3). 15.95 (978-0-89272-663-9(6)) Down East Bks.

Baier, Hiltrud. Greta in Schweden. 2009. 114p. pap. (978-3-8391-2523-6(5)) Books on Demand GmbH.

Bailey, Mary. Vhan Zeely & the Time Prevaricators. 2009. 192p. 25.50 (978-1-60693-477-7(5), Eloquent Bks.) Strategic Book Publishing & Rights Agency (SBPRA).

Baker, Mary. Amy's Apple Butter Granny. 2009. 48p. pap. 16.95 (978-1-61582-032-0(9)) America Star Bks.

Barbour, Ralph Henry. The Lilac Girl. 2006. (Illus.). pap. (978-1-4065-0778-2(4)) Dodo Pr.

Barclay, Jane. How Hot Was It? Cole, Kathryn, ed. Donato, Janice, illus. (ENG.). 24p. (J). 14.95 (978-1-894222-70-9(9)) Lobster Pr. CAN. Dist: Univ. of Toronto Pr.

Becker, Laura. The Wonder of a Summer Day. Steffen, Jennifer, illus. 2008. (ENG.). 40p. (J). (gr. -1-3). lib. bdg. (978-1-934363-25-6(1)) Zoe Life Publishing.

Beckford, Lois. The Interesting Pen Pal. 2010. 44p. pap. 21.99 (978-1-4415-0878-2(3)) Xlibris Corp.

Bee, Clair. No Hitter: A Chip Hilton Sports Story. 2011. 192p. (gr. 3-8). 42.95 (978-1-258-09702-8(8)) Literary Licensing, LLC.

Beil, Michael D. Summer at Forsaken Lake. Kneen, Maggie, illus. 2013. (ENG.). 336p. (J). (gr. 5). pap. 8.99 (978-0-375-86496-4(2), Yearling) Random Hse. Children's Bks.

Benson, Donna. Spotlight on the Cupcakes: The Cupcakes Club #3. 2008. (ENG.). 115p. (J). pap. 7.95 (978-0-9799159-2-5(9)) Pink Lemonade, LLC.

Bentley, Marla. Summer Sounds Level 1 Beginner/Elementary. 2010. (ENG.). 46p. pap. 11.00 (978-84-8323-995-7(7)) Cambridge Univ. Pr.

Benton, Jim. The Super-Nice Are Super-Annoying. Benton, Jim, illus. 2012. (Dear Dumb Diary Year Two Ser.). (ENG., Illus.). 144p. (J). (gr. 3-7). pap. 5.99 (978-0-545-37763-8(3), Scholastic Paperbacks) Scholastic, Inc.

—The Worst Things in Life Are Also Free. Benton, Jim, illus. 2010. (Dear Dumb Diary Ser.: 10). (ENG., Illus.). 160p. (J). (gr. 3-7). pap. 6.99 (978-0-545-11614-5(7), Scholastic Paperbacks) Scholastic, Inc.

Bice, Charles. What Lies Beneath. 2009. 208p. pap. 16.50 (978-0-578-03340-2(2)) Wimabi Pr.

Black, Allyson. Crushed, Bk. 5. Spaziante, Patrick & Riley, Kellee, illus. 2011. (Scarlett & Crimson Ser.). (ENG.). 112p. (J). pap. 6.99 (978-1-4169-9648-4(6), Simon Spotlight) Simon Spotlight.

Blackwell-Burke, Melissa & Kunkel, Kristen. Summertime Surprise. 2003. (J). spiral bd. 14.95 (978-1-58605-956-9(4), LeapFrog Schl. Hse.) LeapFrog Enterprises, Inc.

Blume, Judy. Otherwise Known as Sheila the Great. 2004. (ENG.). 160p. (J). (gr. 3-7). 7.99 (978-0-425-19380-8(2), Berkley) Penguin Publishing Group.

Bracken- Murphy, Julie. Sammy's Summer Vacation. 2007. 52p. per. 13.95 (978-1-4327-0615-9(2)) Outskirts Pr., Inc.

Bradford, Michael. Button Hill, 1 vol. 2015. (ENG.). 264p. (J). (gr. 4-7). pap. 9.95 (978-1-4598-0755-6(3)) Orca Bk. Pubs. USA.

Branch, Dianne. Summer Fun. 2012. 12p. pap. 15.99 (978-1-4772-1108-3(X)) AuthorHouse.

Brenner, Tom. And Then Comes Summer. Kim, Jaime, illus. 2017. (ENG.). 32p. (J). (gr. -1-3). 16.99 (978-0-7636-6071-0(X)) Candlewick Pr.

Brimhall Snow, Virginia. Summer Walk, 1 vol. 2016. (ENG., Illus.). 32p. (J). 16.99 (978-1-4236-4215-2(5)) Gibbs Smith, Publisher.

Brody, Jessica. Boys of Summer. 2016. (ENG., Illus.). 352p. (YA). (gr. 9). 17.99 (978-1-4814-6349-2(7), Simon Pulse) Simon Pulse.

Brogle, Jennifer. The Adventures of Jennifer & Sherry: Summertime. 2013. 60p. pap. 25.36 (978-1-4669-7560-6(1)) Trafford Publishing.

Buffie, Margaret. Who Is Frances Rain? 20th ed. 2007. (ENG.). 184p. (J). (gr. 7-9). 7.95 (978-1-55453-209-4(4)) Kids Can Pr., Ltd. CAN. Dist: Hachette Bk. Group.

Bunting, Eve. Frog & Friends: The Best Summer Ever. 2012. (I Am A Reader!, Frog & Friends Ser.). (ENG., Illus.). 48p. (J). (gr. k-3). pap. 3.99 (978-1-58536-691-0(9)); lib. bdg. 9.95 (978-1-58536-550-0(5)) Sleeping Bear Pr.

Burk, Josh. The Summer of Saint Nick. 2007. (ENG.). 152p. (YA). per. 12.95 (978-0-9768042-2-2(0)) Maven Of Memory Publishing.

Burningham, John. Picnic. Burningham, John, illus. 2014. (ENG., Illus.). 32p. (J). (-k). 16.99 (978-0-7636-6945-4(8)) Candlewick Pr.

Burns, A. M. & Ricci, Caitlin. Running with the Pack. 2016. (ENG., Illus.). (YA). pap. 14.99 **(978-1-63477-063-7(3)**, Harmony Ink Pr.) Dreamspinner Pr.

Bush, Laura & Hager, Jenna Bush. Our Great Big Backyard. Rogers, Jacqueline, illus. 40p. (J). (gr. -1-3). 2018. pap. 7.99 **(978-0-06-246841-3(3))** 2016. (ENG.). 18.99 (978-0-06-246835-2(9)) 2016. lib. bdg. 19.89 (978-0-06-246836-9(7)) HarperCollins Pubs.

Butcher, Kristin. Zach & Zoe: Bully & the Beagle, 1 vol. 2009. (Lorimer Streetlights Ser.). (ENG.). 120p. (J). (gr. 2-4). 8.95 (978-1-55277-427-4(9), 9781552774274) Lorimer, James & Co., Ltd., Pubs. CAN. Dist: Casemate Pubs. & Bk. Distributors, LLC.

Buyea, Rob. Mr. Terupt Falls Again. 2013. (ENG.). 384p. (J). (gr. 4-7). 7.99 (978-0-307-93046-0(7), Yearling) Random Hse. Children's Bks.

—Mr. Terupt Falls Again. 2013. lib. bdg. 18.40 (978-0-606-32236-2(1), Turtleback) Turtleback Bks.

Calame, Don. Swim the Fly. 2010. (ENG., Illus.). 352p. (YA). (gr. 9). pap. 7.99 (978-0-7636-4776-6(4)) Candlewick Pr.

Castanga, Felicity. The Incredible Here & Now. l.t. ed. 2013. 212p. pap. (978-1-4596-7083-9(3)) ReadHowYouWant.com, Ltd.

Chapman, Brenda. Where Trouble Leads. 2007. (Jennifer Bannon Mystery Ser.: 3). (ENG., Illus.). 136p. (YA). (gr. 5-18). per. 9.95 (978-1-894917-44-5(8), Napoleon & Co.) Dundurn CAN. Dist: Ingram Publisher Services.

Cheney, Cora. The Doll of Lilac Valley. Cassidy, Nancy White, illus. 2003. 128p. 11.95 (978-0-9714612-5-3(2)) Green Mansion Pr. LLC.

Chiew, Suzanne. That's What Friends Are For. Pedler, Caroline, illus. 2017. (ENG.). 32p. (J). (gr. -1-2). 16.99 **(978-1-68010-040-2(8))** Tiger Tales.

Child's Play Staff. Summer. Busby, Ailie, illus. 2015. (Seasons Ser.: 4). (ENG.). 12p. (J). (gr. 1-1). bds. (978-1-84643-742-7(3)) Child's Play International Ltd.

Christensen, Gerda. Troll Peter Discovers the Bog-Woman's Secret & Other Stories. 2010. 40p. pap. 18.27 (978-1-4251-8822-1(2)) Trafford Publishing.

Clark, Catherine. The Summer of Everything. 2016. 448p. (J). (gr. 8). pap. 9.99 (978-0-06-235922-3(3), HarperTeen) HarperCollins Pubs.

Combs, Sarah. Breakfast Served Anytime. 2014. (ENG.). 272p. (J). (gr. 7). 16.99 (978-0-7636-6791-7(9)) Candlewick Pr.

Compagnucci, Veronica M. Emily Finds Her Voice. 2013. 40p. pap. 24.95 (978-1-63004-288-2(9)) America Star Bks.

Creech, Sharon. Absolutely Normal Chaos. 2012. 230p. (J). (gr. 4-7). lib. bdg. 17.20 (978-0-613-02936-0(4), Turtleback) Turtleback Bks.

Crowley, Kieran Mark. Colm & the Lazarus Key. 2009. (ENG., Illus.). 224p. (J). pap. 14.95 (978-1-85635-646-6(9)) Mercier Pr., Ltd., The IRL. Dist: Dufour Editions, Inc.

Cruea, Kim. Summer Falls Junior Rangers: The First Adventures. 2008. 73p. pap. 19.95 (978-1-60474-552-8(5)) America Star Bks.

Dagostino, Argus. Belcher Bomb. 2008. 53p. pap. 16.95 (978-1-60441-596-4(7)) America Star Bks.

Dalton, Michelle. Sixteenth Summer. 2011. (Sixteenth Summer Ser.). (ENG.). 304p. (YA). (gr. 7-18). pap. 9.99 (978-1-4424-2344-2(7), Simon Pulse) Simon Pulse.

—Swept Away. 2015. (Sixteenth Summer Ser.). (ENG., Illus.). 320p. (YA). (gr. 7). pap. 10.99 (978-1-4814-3608-3(2), Simon Pulse) Simon Pulse.

Dangerous Summer 2. 2006. (J). (978-1-933343-19-8(2)) Stabenfeldt Inc.

Daniels, Darla. Carrie Goes Camping. 2011. 24p. pap. 16.95 (978-1-4626-0642-9(3)) America Star Bks.

Darling, Angela. Maddie's Camp Crush. 2013. (Crush Ser.: 2). (ENG.). 160p. (J). (gr. 3-7). pap. 5.99 (978-1-4424-8334-7(2), Simon Spotlight) Simon Spotlight.

D'Ath, Justin. Pool. 2009. (ENG.). 288p. (Orig.). (YA). 13.95 (978-1-876462-51-2(5), Ford Street Publishing) Hybrid Pubs. AUS. Dist: International Publishers Marketing.

Davidson, Thomas A. Penny Found in Willowbrooke. 2009. 40p. pap. 14.75 (978-1-60693-774-7(X), Strategic Bk. Publishing) Strategic Book Publishing & Rights Agency (SBPRA).

Day, Karen. A Million Miles from Boston. 2012. (ENG.). 224p. (J). (gr. 3-7). pap. 6.99 (978-0-375-85974-8(8), Yearling) Random Hse. Children's Bks.

Dearie, Anne Crofton. Ginger Cat. 2011. (Illus.). 92p. pap. 12.10 (978-1-4567-7484-4(0)) AuthorHouse.

DeFelice, Cynthia. Fort. 2015. (ENG.). 208p. (J). (gr. 3-7). 16.99 (978-0-374-32427-8(1), 9780374324278, Farrar, Straus & Giroux (BYR)) Farrar, Straus & Giroux.

—Fort. 2016. (ENG.). 224p. (J). pap. 6.99 (978-1-250-07973-2(X), 9781250079732) Square Fish.

—Fort. 2016. (J). lib. bdg. 17.20 (978-0-606-38552-7(5)) Turtleback Bks.

dePaola, Tomie. Four Friends in Summer. dePaola, Tomie, illus. 2003. (ENG., Illus.). 32p. (J). (gr. -1-3). reprint ed. 17.99 (978-0-689-85693-8(8), Simon & Schuster Bks. For Young Readers) Simon & Schuster Bks. For Young Readers.

Dessen, Sarah. That Summer. (ENG.). (YA). (gr. 7-18). 2006. 208p. 17.99 (978-0-670-06110-5(7), Viking Books for Young Readers) 2004. 224p. 10.99 (978-0-14-240172-9(2), Speak) Penguin Young Readers Group.

Disney Book Group Staff. Palace Pets: Summer the Kitten for Rapunzel. 2014. (ENG.). 10p. (J). (gr. -1-k). bds. 9.99 (978-1-4847-1184-2(X)) Disney Pr.

Doisingh, Kanisha. Once upon a Time: In London Town with Minnie Drew. 2011. 28p. pap. 16.99 (978-1-4567-5731-1(8)) AuthorHouse.

Dorling Kindersley Publishing Staff. Summer Adventures. 2013. (DK Reader Level 3 Ser.). lib. bdg. 13.55 (978-0-606-31476-3(8), Turtleback) Turtleback Bks.

Dorling Kindersley Publishing Staff & Saunders, Catherine. Let's Explore! 2015. (DK Adventures Ser.). (ENG.). 128p. (J). (gr. 3-7). pap. 5.99 (978-1-4654-3533-0(6), DK Children) Dorling Kindersley Publishing, Inc.

—Summer Adventures, Level 3. 2013. (DK Readers Ser.). (ENG.). 48p. (J). (gr. 2-4). pap. 3.99 (978-1-4654-0259-2(4), DK Children) Dorling Kindersley Publishing, Inc.

Doyle, Patrick H. T. Edgar Font's Hunt for a House to Haunt: Adventure One: the Castle Tower Lighthouse. 2006. (Illus.). 213p. (J). (gr. -1). per. 6.99 (978-0-9786132-0-4(1)) Armadillo Bks.

—Edgar Font's Hunt for a House to Haunt: Adventure Two: the Fakersville Power Station. Doyle, Patrick H. T., illus. 2007. (Edgar Font's Hunt for a House to Haunt Ser.). (Illus.). 303p. (J). (gr. 4-7). per. 7.99 (978-0-9786132-1-1(X)) Armadillo Bks.

DuVall, Nell. Summer Day. Weltner, Dave, illus. l.t. ed. 2003. 13p. 7.95 (978-0-9706654-6-1(6)) Sprite Pr.

Edwards, Marnie. Magical Mix-Ups: Spells & Surprises. Hodgkinson, Leigh, illus. 2014. (Magical Mix-Ups Ser.). (ENG.). (J). (gr. 2-5). pap. 6.99 (978-0-7636-6610-1(6), Nosy Crow) Candlewick Pr.

Ellis, Amanda & Block, Maggie. Jwenlapaix in the Bateyes. 2009. 52p. pap. 24.00 (978-1-4389-4391-6(1)) AuthorHouse.

Emzer, Counselor. The Day Before Summer Vacation. 2004. 31p. pap. 24.95 (978-1-4137-2680-0(1)) PublishAmerica, Inc.

Engle, Dawn A. Ella's Golden Heart Goes to Camp. 2011. 40p. pap. 14.95 (978-1-60911-392-6(6), Eloquent Bks.) Strategic Book Publishing & Rights Agency (SBPRA).

Enright, Elizabeth. Thimble Summer. unabr. ed. 2004. 136p. (J). (gr. 3-7). pap. 36.00 incl. audio (978-0-8072-0671-3(7), Listening Library) Random Hse. Audio Publishing Group.

—Thimble Summer. Enright, Elizabeth, illus. 2008. (ENG., Illus.). 144p. (J). (gr. 3-7). pap. 6.99 (978-0-312-38002-1(X), 9780312380021) Square Fish.

Everett, Clare. Henrietta - a Rabbit's Tale of Summer Time Fun. 2012. 116p. pap. (978-1-84914-296-0(3)) CompletelyNovel.com.

Faris, Stephanie. Piper Morgan Summer of Fun Collection Books 1-4: Piper Morgan Joins the Circus; Piper Morgan in Charge!; Piper Morgan to the Rescue; Piper Morgan Makes a Splash. Fleming, Lucy, illus. 2017. (Piper Morgan Ser.). (ENG.). 432p. (J). (gr. 1-4). pap. 23.99 **(978-1-4814-9978-1(5)**, Aladdin) Simon & Schuster Children's Publishing.

Ferrer, Caridad. When the Stars Go Blue. 2010. (ENG.). 336p. (YA). (gr. 9-18). pap. 22.99 (978-0-312-65004-9(3), 9780312650049, St. Martin's Griffin) St. Martin's Pr.

Finn, Katie. Revenge, Ice Cream, & Other Things Best Served Cold. 2015. (Broken Hearts & Revenge Novel Ser.: 2). (ENG.). 400p. (YA). (gr. 8). 17.99 (978-1-250-04525-6(8), 9781250045256) Feiwel & Friends.

Firestone, Carrie. The Unlikelies. 2017. (ENG.). 336p. (YA). (gr. 9-17). 17.99 **(978-0-316-38286-1(8))** Little, Brown Bks. for Young Readers.

Fischer, Debbie Reed. This Is Not the Abby Show. 2016. (ENG.). 320p. (J). (gr. 4-7). 16.99 (978-0-553-53634-8(6), Delacorte Bks. for Young Readers) Random Hse. Children's Bks.

Fisher, Rick. Unknown Heroes. 2007. (ENG., Illus.). 32p. (J). per. 14.95 (978-1-59800-899-9(4)) Outskirts Pr., Inc.

Fitzhugh, Percy K. Pee-Wee Harris. 2004. reprint ed. pap. 1.99 (978-1-4192-4057-7(9)); pap. 15.95 (978-1-4191-4057-0(4)) Kessinger Publishing, LLC.

Flaggert, Candy. Ok, Said Carrie Katherine, 1 vol. Chipka, Sandy, illus. 2008. (ENG.). 25p. 24.95 (978-1-60563-502-6(2)) America Star Bks.

Franco, Betsy. Summer Beat. Middleton, Charlotte, illus. 2011. (ENG.). 36p. (J). (gr. -1-1). 14.99 (978-1-4424-4339-6(1), McElderry, Margaret K. Bks.) McElderry, Margaret K. Bks.

Furgang, Kathy. A Happy Summer Day & un día feliz de Verano: 6 English, 6 Spanish Adaptations. 2011. (ENG & SPA.). (J). 75.00 net. (978-1-4108-5656-2(9)) Benchmark Education Co.

Galante, Cecilia. The Summer of May. Carpenter, Tad, illus. (ENG.). 256p. (J). (gr. 4-8). 2012. pap. 6.99 (978-1-4169-8304-0(X)) 2011. 16.99 (978-1-4169-8023-0(7)) Simon & Schuster/Paula Wiseman Bks. (Simon & Schuster/Paula Wiseman Bks.).

Gale, Emily. The Other Side of Summer. 2017. 336p. (J). (gr. 3-7). 16.99 (978-0-06-265674-2(0)) HarperCollins Pubs.

Gallo, Tina. OLIVIA in the Park. Rose, Drew, illus. 2010. (Olivia TV Tie-In Ser.). (ENG.). 48p. (J). (gr. -1-1). 5.99 (978-1-4169-9887-7(X), Simon Scribbles) Simon Scribbles.

Garcia, Cristina. Dreams of Significant Girls. 2011. (ENG.). 256p. (YA). (gr. 9-18). 16.99 (978-1-4169-7920-3(4), Simon & Schuster Bks. For Young Readers) Simon & Schuster Bks. For Young Readers.

Garcia, Cristina. Dreams of Significant Girls. 2012. (ENG.). 256p. (J). (gr. 9). pap. 8.99 (978-1-4169-7930-2(1), Simon & Schuster Bks. For Young Readers) Simon & Schuster Bks. For Young Readers.

The Gauntlet. (J). 14.00 (978-1-931555-16-6(8)) Our Lady of Victory Schl.

George, J. A. Camp Aconyte. 2008. 65p. pap. 19.95 (978-1-60610-631-0(7)) America Star Bks.

Geras, Adèle. Happy Endings. 2016. (ENG.). 180p. (J). (gr. 6). pap. 9.95 (978-1-58988-115-0(X)) Dry, Paul Bks., Inc.

Germain, Kerry. Kimo's Summer Vacation. Montes, Keoni, illus. 2003. 52p. (J). 12.95 (978-0-9705889-4-4(1)) Island Paradise Publishing.

Ghigna, Charles. I See Summer, 1 vol. Jatkowska, Ag, illus. 2011. (I See Ser.). (ENG.). 24p. (gr. -1 — 1). pap. 6.10 (978-1-4048-6852-6(6), I See) Picture Window Bks.

Gifford, Peggy. Moxy Maxwell Does Not Love Stuart Little. Fisher, Valorie, photos by. 2008. (Moxy Maxwell Ser.). (ENG., Illus.). 112p. (J). (gr. 2-5). 5.99 (978-0-440-42230-3(2), Yearling) Random Hse. Children's Bks.

Gill, Amber. Joseph's Summer. 2006. 71p. pap. 16.95 (978-1-4241-0122-1(0)) PublishAmerica, Inc.

Giordano, Anthony. Another Boring Summer... Again! 2009. 154p. (YA). pap. 11.25 (978-1-60695-077-7(0)) Callanish Pr.

Goode, Suzi. The Lost Wizard Series Bk 1. 2007. pap. 11.95 (978-1-59374-817-3(5)) Whiskey Creek Pr., LLC.

Gow, Kailin. Loving Summer. 2012. 250p. (-18). pap. 9.99 (978-1-59748-044-4(4), The Edge) Sparklesoup LLC.

Grant, Katy. Tug-of-War. 2010. (Summer Camp Secrets Ser.). (ENG.). 256p. (J). (gr. 3-7). pap. 7.99 (978-1-4169-9161-8(1), Aladdin) Simon & Schuster Children's Publishing.

Greeley, David. Seven Friends, 1 vol. Marquis, KariAnn, illus. 2010. 38p. 24.95 (978-1-4489-4101-8(6)) PublishAmerica, Inc.

Green, Holly G. Don't Slam the Door. Scott, Sarah Chamberlin, illus. 2005. (ENG.). 39p. (J). (gr. 2-7). 19.95 (978-0-9744803-7-4(1)) PublishingWorks.

Greenwald, Lisa. Dog Beach Unleashed. (Seagate Summers Ser.). (ENG.). (YA). 2016. 256p. (gr. 3-7). pap. 7.95 (978-1-4197-2056-7(2)) 2015. (Illus.). 240p. (gr. 5-9). 15.95 (978-1-4197-1481-8(3)) Abrams, Inc. (Amulet Bks.).

—Welcome to Dog Beach. (Seagate Summers Ser.). (ENG.). (YA). (gr. 3-7). 2015. 288p. pap. 6.95 (978-1-4197-1497-9(X)) 2014. 272p. 15.95 (978-1-4197-1018-6(4)) Abrams, Inc. (Amulet Bks.).

Greer, Hannah. The Castle Ivengless: The Velvet Bag Memoirs, Bk. 3. 2009. 145p. pap. 24.95 (978-1-60749-105-7(2)) America Star Bks.

Grund, Carol A. Anna Mei, Escape Artist. 2011. 168p. (J). (gr. 4-7). pap. 8.95 (978-0-8198-0794-6(X)) Pauline Bks. & Media.

Gundel, Jean. The Mystery Key at Camp Green Meadow. Robertson, R. H., illus. 2011. (J). pap. 14.95 (978-1-59571-730-6(7)) Word Association Pubs.

Gutman, Dan. Back to School, Weird Kids Rule! 2014. (My Weird School Ser.). (J). lib. bdg. 16.00 (978-0-606-35502-5(2)) Turtleback Bks.

Hall, Donald. Lucy's Summer. McCurdy, Michael, illus. 2008. (ENG.). 40p. (J). (gr. 1-18). pap. 10.95 (978-1-56792-348-3(8)) Godine, David R. Pub.

Han, Jenny. The Complete Summer I Turned Pretty Trilogy: The Summer I Turned Pretty; It's Not Summer Without You; We'll Always Have Summer. 2013. (Summer I Turned Pretty Ser.). (ENG., Illus.). 928p. (YA). (gr. 7). pap. 32.99 (978-1-4424-9832-7(3), Simon & Schuster Bks. For Young Readers) Simon & Schuster Bks. For Young Readers.

—It's Not Summer Without You, 6 vols. 2010. (Summer I Turned Pretty Ser.: 2). (YA). 90.75 (978-1-4498-2018-3(2)); 88.75 (978-1-4498-2020-6(4)); 230.75 (978-1-4498-2015-2(8)); 1.25 (978-1-4498-2022-0(0)); 73.75 (978-1-4498-2016-9(6)) Recorded Bks., Inc.

—It's Not Summer Without You. (Summer I Turned Pretty Ser.). (ENG.). (YA). (gr. 7). 2011. 320p. pap. 10.99 (978-1-4169-9556-2(0)) 2010. 288p. 18.99 (978-1-4169-9555-5(2)) Simon & Schuster Bks. For Young Readers. (Simon & Schuster Bks. For Young Readers).

—The Summer I Turned Pretty. (Summer I Turned Pretty Ser.). (ENG.). (YA). (gr. 7). 2010. 304p. pap. 10.99 (978-1-4169-6829-0(6)) 2009. 288p. 19.99 (978-1-4169-6823-8(7)) Simon & Schuster Bks. For Young Readers. (Simon & Schuster Bks. For Young Readers).

—The Summer I Turned Pretty. 2010. lib. bdg. 22.10 (978-0-606-14529-9(X), Turtleback) Turtleback Bks.

Hartgraves, Richard. Little Cedar. 2006. 130p. pap. 24.95 (978-1-4241-4603-1(8)) PublishAmerica, Inc.

Hawthorne, Rachel. Island Girls & Boys. 2005. (ENG.). 336p. (YA). (gr. 9). pap. 8.99 (978-0-06-075546-1(6), HarperTeen) HarperCollins Pubs.

Hayes, Karel. The Summer Visitors, 10 vols. Hayes, Karel, illus. 2011. (ENG., Illus.). 32p. (J). (gr. -1-3). 17.95 (978-0-89272-918-0(X)) Down East Bks.

Hearst, Allyson. White Pajamas: A Karate Story. 2011. 68p. pap. 19.95 (978-1-4626-3871-0(6)) America Star Bks.

Heflin, Ronald. Caddo Lake. 2011. 156p. pap. 24.95 (978-1-4626-0093-9(X)) America Star Bks.

Heidtke, John. A Summer's Passage on Sutter's Bay. 2005. (J). per. (978-0-9748426-6-0(4), Accent Pubns.) Ajoyin Publishing, Inc.

Hemmerle, Jamie. The Lost & Found Summer. 2010. (Illus.). 312p. pap. 15.95 (978-1-4327-6268-1(0)) Outskirts Pr., Inc.

Hesse, Karen. Come on, Rain! 2004. (J). (gr. k-3). 29.95 (978-1-55592-500-0(6)) Weston Woods Studios, Inc.

Hillert, Margaret. It's Summer, Dear Dragon. Schimmell, David, illus. 2009. (BeginningtoRead Ser.). 32p. (J). (gr. k-2). lib. bdg. 22.60 (978-1-59953-313-1(8)) Norwood Hse. Pr.

Hobbs, Olivia. The Summer of Violet. 2011. 56p. pap. 15.99 (978-1-4653-3539-5(0)) Xlibris Corp.

Hogan, Jamie. Seven Days of Daisy, 1 vol. Hogan, Jamie, illus. 2011. (ENG., Illus.). 32p. (J). (gr. -1-3). 14.95 (978-0-89272-919-7(8)) Down East Bks.

Hopkinson, Deborah. Pioneer Summer. Fancy, Patrick, illus. 2005. 74p. (J). lib. bdg. 15.00 (978-1-59054-911-7(2)) Fitzgerald Bks.

Hordos, Sandra. Marissa Plans a Princess Tea Party. Allen, Joshua, illus. 2010. 28p. pap. 12.49 (978-1-4520-2557-5(6)) AuthorHouse.

Horsfall, S. J. Jodie & Lilly... & the Fake Mansion. 2009. 58p. pap. 7.50 (978-0-557-12474-9(3)) Lulu Pr., Inc.

Horvath, Polly. My One Hundred Adventures. 2010. (My One Hundred Adventures Ser.). (ENG., Illus.). 272p. (J). (gr. 3-7). 7.99 (978-0-375-85526-9(2), Yearling) Random Hse. Children's Bks.

Howell, Hayley L. Sammy's Two Left Feet: Groovin' with Mr. Smooth: Discovering How to Believe in Yourself. 2010. 32p. pap. 15.95 (978-1-4520-5733-0(8)) AuthorHouse.

Howington, C. D. Aunt Cindy's House. 2011. 96p. pap. 19.95 (978-1-4626-1113-3(3)) America Star Bks.

Howland, Leila. The Brightest Stars of Summer: A Silver Sisters Story. 2016. (Silver Sisters Ser.: 2). (Illus.). 368p. (J). (gr. 3-7). 16.99 (978-0-06-231872-5(1)) HarperCollins Pubs.

—The Forget-Me-Not Summer. Kim, Ji-Hyuk, illus. 2016. (Silver Sisters Ser.: 1). 368p. (J). (gr. 3-7). pap. 6.99 (978-0-06-231870-1(5)) HarperCollins Pubs.

Hughes, Susan. Earth to Audrey. Poulin, Stéphane, illus. 2007. (ENG.). 32p. (J). (gr. k-3). 6.95 (978-1-55453-165-3(9)) Kids Can Pr., Ltd. CAN. Dist: Hachette Bk. Group.

Hurst, Elva. Summer on the Farm. 2014. (Farm Life Ser.). 80p. pap. 6.99 (978-0-7369-6091-5(0)) Harvest Hse. Pubs.

—Summer on the Farm: A True Story. 2014. (Farm Life Ser.). (ENG., Illus.). 80p. (J). pap. 6.99 (978-0-7369-6090-8(2)) Harvest Hse. Pubs.

Innocenti, Jane. Aunt Jane's Summer Garden. 2012. 20p. pap. 24.95 (978-1-62709-103-9(3)) America Star Bks.

Irvine, Kitty. Mysterious Moorings with Mouse. 2017. (ENG.). 96p. (J). pap. 11.95 **(978-1-78693-220-4(2)**, 2bcedaac-1c94-4640-ab5f-7088dc6903a6) Austin, Stan AUS. Dist: Bookmasters Distribution.

Irwin, Inez Haynes. Maida's Little House. 2004. reprint ed. pap. 27.95 (978-1-4179-4236-7(3)) Kessinger Publishing, LLC.

Irwin, Ms. Judy. What Did You Say? 2012. 78p. pap. (978-0-9877088-5-4(6)) Irwin, Judy.

Iwamura, Kazuo. Hooray for Summer! 2010. (ENG., Illus.). 32p. (J). (gr. -1-k). 16.95 (978-0-7358-2285-6(9)) North-South Bks., Inc.

Jackson, Byron & Jackson, Kathryn. A Day at the Seashore. 2010. (Little Golden Book Ser.). (ENG., Illus.). 24p. (J). (gr. -1-2). 4.99 (978-0-375-85425-5(8), Golden Bks.) Random Hse. Children's Bks.

Jacobs, Caroline E. The S. W. F. Club. 2007. (ENG.). 120p. pap. 18.99 (978-1-4346-2899-2(X)); 134p. pap. 19.99 (978-1-4346-2900-5(7)) Creative Media Partners, LLC.

Jain, Rohan. Summertime for Me. 2017. (Text Connections Guided Close Reading Ser.). (J). (gr. k). (978-1-4900-1765-5(8)) Benchmark Education Co.

Jakubowski, Michele. Secrets in Somerville. Pinelli, Amerigo, illus. 2016. (Sleuths of Somerville Ser.). (ENG.). 144p. (gr. 4-6). lib. bdg. 25.99 (978-1-4965-3175-9(2)) Stone Arch Bks.

Jennings, Patrick. Lucky Cap. 2012. (ENG.). 224p. (J). (gr. 4-7). 6.99 (978-1-60684-306-2(0), Carolrhoda Bks.) Lerner Publishing Group.

Jocelyn, Marthe. Mayfly. 2004. (ENG., Illus.). 32p. (J). (gr. -1-k). 14.95 (978-0-88776-676-3(5), Tundra Bks.) Tundra Bks. CAN. Dist: Penguin Random Hse. LLC.

—Ready for Summer. 2008. (ENG., Illus.). 16p. (J). (gr. -1-k). bds. 7.95 (978-0-88776-860-6(1), Tundra Bks.) Tundra Bks. CAN. Dist: Penguin Random Hse. LLC.

—Would You. 2008. (ENG.). 176p. (YA). (gr. 4-7). 19.99 (978-0-88776-816-3(4), Tundra Bks.) Tundra Bks. CAN. Dist: Penguin Random Hse. LLC.

Johnson, Amy Crane. Mason Moves Away/Mason se Muda: A Solomon Raven Story: un cuento del cuervo Salomon, 4 vols. de la Vega, Eida, tr. Mommaerts, Robb, illus. 2004. (Solomon Raven Ser.: 4).Tr. of Mason se Muda. (SPA & ENG.). 32p. (J). (gr. -1-3). 16.95 (978-0-9720192-3-1(5), 626999, Raven Tree Pr.,Csi) Continental Sales, Inc.

Johnson, James Ray. Timmy Wee Pee & Castle Friends. 2009. 28p. pap. 24.95 (978-1-60836-886-0(6)) America Star Bks.

Johnston, E. K. Exit, Pursued by a Bear. 2017. lib. bdg. 22.10 **(978-0-606-39797-1(3))** Turtleback Bks.

Joseph, Curtis M. Max Baxter. 2008. 57p. pap. 16.95 (978-1-60610-206-0(0)) America Star Bks.

—Order of Godalming: Max Baxter, 1 vol. 2009. 64p. pap. 19.95 (978-1-60836-525-8(5)) America Star Bks.

Katz, Karen. Baby Loves Summer! Katz, Karen, illus. 2012. (ENG., Illus.). 14p. (J). (gr. -1 — 1). bds. 6.99 (978-1-4424-2746-4(9), Little Simon) Little Simon.

—Where Is Baby's Beach Ball? Katz, Karen, illus. 2009. (ENG., Illus.). 14p. (J). (gr. -1 — 1). bds. 6.99 (978-1-4169-4962-6(3), Little Simon) Little Simon.

Kaur, K. S. The Horncastles & the Magnopeus Medicine. Kaur, Bal, illus. 2012. 154p. pap. (978-1-78148-023-6(0)) Grosvenor Hse. Publishing Ltd.

Keefer, Nick T. Pear-A-Dise. Bowser, Sean T., illus. 2013. 28p. pap. 12.95 (978-0-9894814-6-5(8)) Warren Publishing, Inc.

Kelly, Katy. Melonhead & the Big Stink. 2011. (Melonhead Ser.). (ENG.). 224p. (J). (gr. 3-7). 6.99 (978-0-375-84527-7(5), Yearling) Random Hse. Children's Bks.

Kinney, Jeff. Dog Days. 2009. (Diary of a Wimpy Kid Ser.: 4). (ENG., Illus.). 224p. (J). (gr. 3-7). 13.95 (978-0-8109-8391-5(5), Amulet Bks.) Abrams, Inc.

—Dog Days. (Diary of a Wimpy Kid Ser.: 4). (J). 2011. 75.75 (978-1-4407-7756-1(X)) 2010. (SPA.). 181.75 (978-1-4407-7748-6(9)) 2010. 54.75 (978-1-4407-7747-9(0)) 2010. 44.75 (978-1-4407-7753-0(5)) 2010. 46.75 (978-1-4407-7751-6(9)) 2009. 52.75 (978-1-4407-7749-3(7)) 2009. 1.25 (978-1-4407-7755-4(1)) Recorded Bks., Inc.

—Dog Days. 2009. (Diary of a Wimpy Kid Ser.: 4). (J). lib. bdg. 25.70 (978-0-606-23665-2(1), Turtleback) Turtleback Bks.

Kinton, P. D. Wishing for Wizards & Chips for Te. 2010. 28p. pap. (978-1-907211-26-3(8)) Grosvenor Hse. Publishing Ltd.

Kirby, Stan. Captain Awesome Takes a Dive. O'Connor, George, illus. 2012. (Captain Awesome Ser.: 4). (ENG.). 128p. (J). (gr. k-4). 16.99 (978-1-4424-4203-0(4)); pap. 5.99 (978-1-4424-4202-3(6)) Little Simon. (Little Simon).

—Captain Awesome Takes a Dive. 2012. (Captain Awesome Ser.: 4). lib. bdg. 14.75 (978-0-606-26325-2(X), Turtleback) Turtleback Bks.

Koraido, Beth S. Summers with Grampa Gus. 2008. 63p. pap. 19.95 (978-1-60703-384-4(4)) America Star Bks.

Korda, Lerryn. It's Vacation Time. Korda, Lerryn, illus. 2010. (Playtime with Little Nye Ser.). (ENG., Illus.). 26p. (J). (— 1). 8.99 (978-0-7636-4813-8(2)) Candlewick Pr.

Kraft, Erik P. Lenny & Mel's Summer Vacation. Kraft, Erik P., illus. 2012. (Ready-For-Chapters Ser.). (ENG., Illus.). 64p. (J). (gr. 2-5). pap. 6.99 (978-0-689-86874-0(X), Simon & Schuster/Paula Wiseman Bks.) Simon & Schuster/Paula Wiseman Bks.

Kreitzer, Dora. Summer in Connecticut. 2012. 18p. pap. 16.95 (978-1-4626-8665-0(6)) America Star Bks.

LaBree Stute, Lela. Summer Pugs. 2010. 44p. pap. 19.99 (978-0-557-41763-6(5)) Lulu Pr., Inc.

Lacy, Sandy Allbee. Pepe & Lupita & the Great Yawn Jar. Schrom, Garren, illus. 2013. 36p. pap. 10.95 (978-1-60494-923-0(6)) Wheatmark, Inc.

Larry Sweitzer. The Ghost, the Eggheads, & Babe Ruth's Piano: A Novel. 2009. 180p. 23.95 (978-1-4401-7103-1(3)); pap. 13.95 (978-1-4401-7104-8(1)) iUniverse, Inc.

Le Blanc, Lennie. The Minnesota Summer. 2011. 116p. (gr. 4-6). pap. 10.95 (978-1-4620-3887-9(5)) iUniverse, Inc.

Leoni, Nancy. Toby Goes to Camp, 1 vol. Leoni, Nancy, illus. 2009. (Illus.). 28p. pap. 24.95 (978-1-61546-417-3(4)) America Star Bks.

Levy, Dana Alison. The Family Fletcher Takes Rock Island. (ENG.). 272p. (J). (gr. 4-7). 2017. 6.99 **(978-0-553-52133-7(0)**, Yearling) 2016. 16.99 (978-0-553-52130-6(6), Delacorte Bks. for Young Readers) Random Hse. Children's Bks.

Lewis, Kevin. Kj's Adventures. 2011. 28p. pap. 15.99 (978-1-4653-3573-9(0)) Xlibris Corp.

Lewis, Linda. Loving Two Is Hard to Do. 2008. (ENG.). 160p. (YA). (gr. 7). pap. 8.95 (978-1-4169-7534-2(9), Simon Pulse) Simon Pulse.

Lowery, Rae. Charlie & the Case of the Big Bully: The Adventures of Charlie #4, 1 vol. 2010. 108p. pap. 19.95 (978-1-4489-5558-9(0)) America Star Bks.

Lowry, Brigid. Things You Either Hate or Love. 2006. (ENG.). 179p. (YA). (gr. 7-12). 16.95 (978-0-8234-2004-9(3)) Holiday Hse., Inc.

—Things You Either Hate or Love. 2007. (ENG.). 192p. (YA). (gr. 8-12). pap. 18.99 *(978-0-312-36308-6(7)*, 9780312363086, St. Martin's Griffin) St. Martin's Pr.

Lubar, David. Dog Days. (Exceptional Reading & Language Arts Titles for Intermediate Grades Ser.). 80p. (J). (gr. 4-8). 2011. (ENG.). per. 6.95 *(978-1-58196-025-9(5))* 2004. 15.95 *(978-1-58196-013-6(1))* Lerner Publishing Group. (Darby Creek).

Luciani, Brigitte. How Will We Get to the Beach? Tharlet, Eve, illus. 2003. (ENG.). 36p. (J). (gr. -1). pap. 7.95 *(978-0-7358-1783-8(9))* North-South Bks., Inc.

Luper, Eric. Gumball's Summer Journal That He Definitely Finished All on His Own. Reed, Stephen, illus. 2015. (Amazing World of Gumball Ser.). (ENG.). 112p. (J). (gr. 3-7). 8.99 *(978-0-8431-8282-8(2)*, Cartoon Network Books) Penguin Young Readers Group.

Luxa, Sue. One Golden Summer. 2004. (Illus.). 80p. (J). pap. 8.95 *(978-1-890437-99-2(9)*, 1234248) Western Reflections Publishing Co.

Mack, Winnie. After All, You're Callie Boone. 2013. (ENG.). 192p. (J). (gr. 4-7). pap. 14.99 *(978-1-250-02735-1(7)*, 9781250027351) Square Fish.

MacKay, Elly. Shadow Chasers. 2014. (ENG., Illus.). 32p. (J). (gr. -1-17). 16.95 *(978-0-7624-4720-6(6)*, Running Pr. Kids) Running Pr. Bk. Pubs.

MacPherson, Lorry. Lynne Woke Up! Alexander, Yvonne Rabdau, illus. 2007. 20p. per. 24.95 *(978-1-4137-2536-0(8))* America Star Bks.

Malik, Katherine. Giselle's Magical World, 1 vol. 2009. 150p. pap. 24.95 *(978-1-4489-1902-4(9))* America Star Bks.

Maloney, Peter. Here Comes Summer! 2004. (Illus.). 32p. pap. *(978-0-439-55363-6(6))* Scholastic, Inc.

Marder, Larry. Beanworld: Tales of the Beanworld. Schutz, Diana, ed. Marder, Larry, illus. 2012. (ENG., Illus.). 64p. 14.99 *(978-1-59582-897-2(4))* Dark Horse Comics.

Marino Walters, Jennifer. Sweet Summer. Nez, John, illus. 2016. (Seasons Ser.). (ENG.). 24p. (J). (gr. -1-1). lib. bdg. 25.32 *(978-1-63440-048-0(8))* Red Chair Pr.

The Marsh Runners. 2004. (J). per. 14.95 *(978-0-9761178-0-3(0))* Maritime Kids Quest Pr.

Martin, Amy. As You Wake. 2013. 294p. pap. 10.93 *(978-0-9882051-2-3(2))* Martin, Amy.

Martin, Ann M. Ten Good & Bad Things about My Life (So Far) 2013. (ENG.). 288p. (J). (gr. 4-7). pap. 7.99 *(978-1-250-03413-7(2)*, 9781250034137) Square Fish.

Martin-Fluet, Marie T. The Fairies' Century Celebration. 2011. 40p. pap. 18.62 *(978-1-4567-2477-1(0))* AuthorHouse.

Maskame, Estelle. Did I Mention I Need You? 2016. (Did I Mention I Love You (DIMILY) Ser.: 2). (ENG.). 384p. (YA). (gr. 8-12). pap. 10.99 *(978-1-4926-3218-4(X)*, 9781492632184) Sourcebooks, Inc.

Maunder, Roger. Mundy Pond. 2006. (ENG.). 195p. per. *(978-1-897174-09-8(8)*, Tuckamore Bks) Creative Bk. Publishing.

Mayfield, Holly. Melvin: A True Story with a Happy Ending. Gilman, Sara, illus. 2013. 38p. pap. 9.99 *(978-0-9892711-9-6(6))* Mindstir Media.

Mazer, Anne. The Best Is Yet to Come. 2004. (Amazing Days of Abby Hayes Ser.: No. 1). 109p. (J). lib. bdg. 16.92 *(978-1-4242-1197-5(2))* Fitzgerald Bks.

—That's the Way the Cookie Crumbles. 2005. (Amazing Days of Abby Hayes Ser.: Bk. 16). (Illus.). 119p. (J). (gr. 3-7). 12.65 *(978-0-7569-6480-1(6))* Perfection Learning Corp.

McBroom, Jill D. Here Comes Bobbyblob! 2008. 16p. pap. 7.76 *(978-1-4251-7174-2(5))* Trafford Publishing.

McCahan, Erin. The Lake Effect. 2017. (ENG.). 400p. (YA). (gr. 7). 17.99 ***(978-0-8037-4052-5(2)***, Dial Bks) Penguin Young Readers Group.

McCoy, Mary. Camp So-And-So. 2017. (ENG.). 424p. (YA). (gr. 8-12). 18.99 *(978-1-5124-1597-1(9))*; 9.99 ***(978-1-5124-3428-6(0)***, Carolrhoda Lab™); 38.65 ***(978-1-5124-3429-3(9)***, Carolrhoda Lab™); 38.65 ***(978-1-5124-2693-9(8)***, Carolrhoda Lab™) Lerner Publishing Group.

McDonald, Megan. Judy Moody & the Not Bummer Summer. Reynolds, Peter H., illus. movie tie-in ed. (Judy Moody Ser.: Bk. 10). (ENG.). (J). (gr. 1-4). 2011. 128p. pap. 5.99 *(978-0-7636-5351-4(9))*Bk. 10. 2012. 208p. 15.99 *(978-0-7636-5711-6(5))*Bk. 10. 2012. 208p. pap. 5.99 *(978-0-7636-5710-9(7))* Candlewick Pr.

—Judy Moody & the Not Bummer Summer. 2012. (Judy Moody Ser.: 10). lib. bdg. 16.00 *(978-0-606-23800-7(X)*, Turtleback) Turtleback Bks.

McDonald, Megan & Michalak, Jamie. The Poop Picnic. Reynolds, Peter H. & Candlewick Press Staff, illus. 2011. (Judy Moody Ser.). (ENG.). 48p. (J). (gr. k-3). pap. 3.99 *(978-0-7636-5553-2(8))* Candlewick Pr.

McKnight, Gillian. To Catch a Prince: To Catch a Prince; the Frog Prince. 2011. (ENG., Illus.). 432p. (YA). (gr. 7). pap. 9.99 *(978-1-4424-3139-3(3)*, Simon & Schuster Bks. For Young Readers) Simon & Schuster Bks. For Young Readers.

McLachlan, Jenny. Sunkissed. 2017. (Ladybirds Ser.: 3). (ENG.). 224p. (YA). 16.99 *(978-1-250-06150-8(4)*, 9781250061508) Feiwel & Friends.

McLean, Matthew. A Bewitching Summer, 1 vol. 2009. 100p. pap. 19.95 *(978-1-60836-686-6(3))* America Star Bks.

McMullan, Kate. Five Days till Summer. Alley, R. W., illus. 2014. (Pearl & Wagner Ser.: 5). (ENG.). 48p. (J). (gr. 1-3). pap. 3.99 *(978-0-448-48137-1(5)*, Penguin Young Readers) Penguin Young Readers Group.

McPhail, J. A. Dawn of Day. Battis, Gwen, illus. 2012. 200p. 17.99 *(978-0-9851196-2-1(4))* Rowe Publishing and Design.

Mead, Purnima. Bibia Tells Her Story! 2010. 24p. 14.50 *(978-1-4490-4753-5(X))* AuthorHouse.

Meadows, Daisy. Cara the Camp Fairy. 2011. (Rainbow Magic Ser.). (ENG., Illus.). 176p. (J). (gr. 2-5). pap. 6.99 *(978-0-545-30877-9(1)*, Scholastic Paperbacks) Scholastic, Inc.

—Joy the Summer Vacation Fairy. Ripper, Georgie, illus. 2007. (Rainbow Magic Ser.). (ENG.). 192p. (J). (gr. -1-3). 6.99 *(978-0-439-93442-8(7)*, Scholastic Paperbacks) Scholastic, Inc.

—Joy the Summer Vacation Fairy. Ripper, Georgie, illus. 2007. (Rainbow Magic — Special Edition Ser.). 177p. (gr. -1-3). lib. bdg. 17.20 *(978-1-4177-7081-6(3)*, Turtleback) Turtleback Bks.

—Kylie the Carnival Fairy. Ripper, Georgie, illus. 2008. (Rainbow Magic Ser.). (ENG.). 192p. (J). (gr. -1-3). pap. 6.99 *(978-0-545-05475-1(3)*, Scholastic Paperbacks) Scholastic, Inc.

Meddaugh, Susan. Pool Party. 2011. (Martha Speaks Ser.). (ENG., Illus.). 24p. (J). (gr. -1-3). pap. 3.99 *(978-0-547-43882-5(6))* Houghton Mifflin Harcourt Publishing Co.

Meister, Cari. Tiny Goes to the Movies. 2016. (Penguin Young Readers Level 2 Ser.). lib. bdg. 13.55 *(978-0-606-38851-1(6))* Turtleback Bks.

Menefee, Angelo K. Billy's First Summer Vacation. 2007. (Illus.). (J). per. 16.95 *(978-1-60002-249-4(9))* Mountain Valley Publishing, LLC.

Meredith, Susan Markowitz. A Happy Summer Day: Set Of 6. 2010. (Early Connections Ser.). (J). 37.00 net. *(978-1-4108-1371-8(1))* Benchmark Education Co.

Meyer, C. The Very First Unicorn. 2013. 24p. pap. 24.95 *(978-1-63004-317-9(6))* America Star Bks.

Michalak, Jamie. Judy Moody & the Thrill Points Race. Candlewick Press Staff, illus. 2011. (Judy Moody Ser.). (ENG.). 48p. (J). (gr. k-3). pap. 3.99 *(978-0-7636-5552-5(X))* Candlewick Pr.

Michels, Anna. 26 Kisses. 2016. (ENG.). (YA). (gr. 9). pap. 12.99 *(978-1-4814-8515-9(6))* Simon & Schuster.

Miller, Leah Rae. The Summer I Became a Nerd. 2013. (ENG.). 352p. (YA). (gr. 9). pap. 9.99 *(978-1-62061-238-5(0)*, 9781620612385) Entangled Publishing, LLC.

Montague, Chester. Timmy's Vacation. 2008. 40p. pap. 24.95 *(978-1-60441-225-3(9))* America Star Bks.

Montgomery, E. j. Hailey Walker & the Mystery of the Absent Professor. 2013. 180p. pap. 13.95 *(978-1-4575-2068-6(0))* Dog Ear Publishing, LLC.

Morah, Chizoba. The Anderson Twins. 2007. 76p. per. 19.95 *(978-1-60441-015-0(9))* America Star Bks.

Morgan, Melissa J. Suddenly Last Summer. 2008. (Camp Confidential Ser.: 20). (ENG.). 160p. (J). (gr. 3-7). pap. 4.99 *(978-0-448-44881-7(5)*, Grosset & Dunlap) Penguin Young Readers Group.

Morgan, Retta & Morgan, Kris. Love Hates. 2011. 152p. pap. 11.99 *(978-1-4567-1448-2(1))* AuthorHouse.

Morris, Susan. Fritha's Summer. 2009. (Illus.). 251p. (J). pap. *(978-0-9551886-6-4(0))* M Pr.

Mostoller, Marcia. Emma's Summer Camp Dilemm. 2011. 64p. pap. 19.95 *(978-1-4626-2814-8(1))* America Star Bks.

Mun-Ensor, Michelle. Aloh. 2011. 32p. pap. 24.95 *(978-1-4560-9848-3(9))* America Star Bks.

Mutrie, Matthew. Brady O'Brian Saves the Day. Morales, Andrew, illus. 2007. 37p. pap. 24.95 *(978-1-4241-9009-6(6))* America Star Bks.

Naylor, Phyllis Reynolds. Boys Rock! 2007. (Boy/Girl Battle Ser.). (ENG.). 144p. (J). (gr. 3-7). 5.99 *(978-0-440-41990-7(5)*, Yearling) Random Hse. Children's Bks.

—The Grooming of Alice. 2012. (Alice Ser.: 12). (ENG., Illus.). 240p. (J). (gr. 5-9). pap. 6.99 *(978-1-4424-3496-7(1)*, Atheneum Bks. for Young Readers) Simon & Schuster Children's Publishing.

—Intensely Alice. 2009. (Alice Ser.: 21). (ENG.). 288p. (YA). (gr. 9-18). 16.99 *(978-1-4169-7551-9(9)*, Atheneum Bks. for Young Readers) Simon & Schuster Children's Publishing.

—Intensely Alice. 2010. (Alice Ser.: 21). (ENG.). 288p. (YA). (gr. 9). mass mkt. 6.99 *(978-1-4169-7554-0(3)*, Simon Pulse) Simon Pulse.

Neel, Julien. The Perfect Summer. Neel, Julien, illus. 2012. (Lou! Ser.: 4). (ENG., Illus.). 48p. (J). (gr. 6-9). pap. 8.95 *(978-0-8225-9169-6(3)*, Graphic Universe™) Lerner Publishing Group.

Neel, Julien & Burrell, Carol klio. The Perfect Summer. Neel, Julien, illus. 2012. (Lou! Ser.: 4). (ENG., Illus.). 48p. (J). (gr. 6-9). lib. bdg. 27.93 *(978-0-7613-8780-0(3)*, Graphic Universe™) Lerner Publishing Group.

Neely, Judith. And Even More. 2009. 24p. pap. 11.49 *(978-1-4389-5649-7(5))* AuthorHouse.

Nicholas, Nicki. Peter & Lil's Summer Day Adventure. 2011. 24p. pap. 15.50 *(978-1-4269-5358-3(5))* Trafford Publishing.

Nickelodeon. Surf's Up, SpongeBob! 2013. (SpongeBob Squarepants 8X8 Ser.). lib. bdg. 14.75 *(978-0-606-31934-8(4)*, Turtleback) Turtleback Bks.

Night, P. J. Home, Sweet Haunt. 2013. (Creepover Ser.: 15). lib. bdg. 16.00 *(978-0-606-32047-4(4)*, Turtleback) Turtleback Bks.

Noël, Alyson. Cruel Summer. 2008. (ENG.). 240p. (YA). (gr. 8-12). pap. 9.99 *(978-0-312-35511-1(4)*, 9780312355111, St. Martin's Griffin) St. Martin's Pr.

—Forever Summer. 2011. (ENG.). 464p. (YA). (gr. 8-12). pap. 9.99 *(978-0-312-60439-4(4)*, 9780312604394, St. Martin's Griffin) St. Martin's Pr.

Nolan, Allia Zobel. God's Light, Shining Bright. Bryant, Laura J., illus. 2006. 8p. (J). 12.99 *(978-0-8254-5527-8(8))* Kregel Pubns.

Nosy Crow Staff. Violet Rose & the Summer Campout. Ho, Jannie, illus. 2017. (ENG.). 52p. (J). (gr. -1-3). 8.99 *(978-0-7636-9333-6(2)*, Nosy Crow) Candlewick Pr.

Ockler, Sarah. Twenty Boy Summer. 2010. (ENG.). 320p. (YA). (gr. 7-17). pap. 10.99 *(978-0-316-05158-3(6))* Little, Brown Bks. for Young Readers.

O'Connell, Jenny. Local Girls: An Island Summer Novel. 2008. (ENG.). 320p. pap. 19.99 *(978-1-4165-6335-8(0))* Pocket Books.

—Rich Boys: An Island Summer Novel. 2008. (ENG.). 288p. pap. 18.99 *(978-1-4165-6336-5(9)*, MTV Bks.) MTV Books.

O'Connor, Sheila. Sparrow Road. 2012. (ENG.). 272p. (J). (gr. 5-18). pap. 6.99 *(978-0-14-242136-9(7)*, Puffin Books) Penguin Young Readers Group.

Older, Daniel José. Shadowshaper. 2016. (ENG.). 297p. (YA). (gr. 9). 20.85 *(978-0-606-39124-5(X))* Turtleback Bks.

Olsen, Alana. It's Summer. 2016. (Four Seasons Ser.). (ENG., Illus.). 24p. (gr. 1-1). pap. 8.25 *(978-1-5081-5187-6(3)*, PowerKids Pr.) Rosen Publishing Group, Inc., The.

Ormondroyd, Edward. Castaways on Long Ago. 2003. (Illus.). 188p. (gr. 5-18). 12.95 *(978-0-9714612-8-4(7))* Green Mansion Pr. LLC.

Packard, Diane. Batina & Croakus. 2013. 36p. pap. 20.99 *(978-1-4817-0420-5(6))* AuthorHouse.

Pak, Kenard. Goodbye Summer, Hello Autumn. Pak, Kenard, illus. 2016. (ENG., Illus.). 32p. (J). 17.99 *(978-1-62779-415-2(8)*, 9781627794152, Holt, Henry & Co. Bks. For Young Readers) Holt, Henry & Co.

Panini Publishing, creator. Scooby Doo! Summer Annual. 2011. (Illus.). 63p. (J). (gr. 4-7). pap. *(978-1-84653-145-3(4))* Panini Publishing.

Pantelo, Amber. The Totally Meaningless Summer. 2004. 75p. (YA). pap. 12.95 *(978-0-7414-1914-9(9))* Infinity Publishing.

Papademetriou, Lisa & Minsky, Terri. A Very Lizzie Summer. 2005. (Lizzie Mcguire Super Special Ser.). (Illus.). 265p. (J). *(978-1-4155-9625-8(5))* Disney Pr.

Parish, Herman. Amelia Bedelia Digs In. 2017. (Amelia Bedelia Chapter Book Ser.: 12). lib. bdg. 14.75 ***(978-0-606-40061-9(3))*** Turtleback Bks.

Parr, Letitia. When Sea & Sky Are Blue. Watts, John, illus. 32p. (J). (gr. -1-3). 13.95 *(978-0-87592-059-7(4))* Scroll Pr., Inc.

Patterson, C. Marie. Little Dinky's Love for Basketball. 2009. 24p. pap. 15.99 *(978-1-4415-1255-0(1))* Xlibris Corp.

Patterson, James & Tebbetts, Chris. How I Survived Bullies, Broccoli, & Snake Hill. Park, Laura, illus. 2013. (Middle School Ser.: 4). (ENG.). 336p. (J). (gr. 3-7). 14.00 *(978-0-316-23175-6(4)*, Jimmy Patterson) Little Brown & Co.

Pearson, Harry. Alicia. 2008. (Clique Ser.). (ENG., Illus.). 144p. (YA). (gr. 7-17). pap. 6.99 *(978-0-316-02753-3(7)*, Poppy) Little, Brown Bks. for Young Readers.

Perez, Angela J. Zack Attack! Hazard, Andrea, illus. 2007. 36p. (J). 17.95 *(978-0-9778328-9-7(9))* His Work Christian Publishing.

Perkins, Stephanie, ed. Summer Days & Summer Nights: Twelve Summer Romances. 2016. (ENG., Illus.). 400p. (YA). 19.99 *(978-1-250-07912-1(8)*, 9781250079121, St. Martin's Griffin) St. Martin's Pr.

Phelan, Matt. Bluffton: My Summers with Buster. Phelan, Matt, illus. 2017. (ENG., Illus.). 232p. (J). (gr. 4-7). pap. 12.99 *(978-0-7636-8706-9(5))* Candlewick Pr.

—Bluffton: My Summers with Buster. Phelan, Matt, illus. 2017. (ENG., Illus.). (J). (gr. 4-7). lib. bdg. 24.50 ***(978-0-606-39837-4(6))*** Turtleback Bks.

Philbin, Joanna. Rules of Summer. 2014. (Rules of Summer Ser.: 1). (ENG.). 368p. (YA). (gr. 10-17). pap. 10.99 *(978-0-316-21204-5(0)*, Poppy) Little, Brown Bks. for Young Readers.

Pier, Stanwood. The Jester of St. Timothy's. 2007. (ENG.). 116p. pap. 18.99 *(978-1-4346-1157-4(4))*; 128p. pap. 19.99 *(978-1-4346-1228-1(7))* Creative Media Partners, LLC.

Pittar, Gill. Milly, Molly & Special Friends (book W/dolls) 2006. 28p. pap. *(978-1-86972-104-6(7))* Milly Molly Bks.

Polak, Monique. Forensics Squad Unleashed, 1 vol. 2016. (ENG.). 208p. (J). (gr. 3-6). pap. 9.95 *(978-1-4598-0979-6(3))* Orca Bk. Pubs. USA.

Posner, Renee & Quinton, Sasha. Suzy Season Loves Summer. D'Argo, Laura, illus. (Be Mine Bears Ser.). (J). bds. 4.99 *(978-1-58209-351-2(2))* Bks. Are Fun, Ltd.

Posner-Sanchez, Andrea & Julius, Jessica. Olaf's Perfect Day (Disney Frozen) RH Disney Staff & Disney Storybook Art Team Staff, illus. 2015. (Little Golden Book Ser.). (ENG.). 24p. (J). (-k). 4.99 *(978-0-7364-3356-3(2)*, Golden/Disney) Random Hse. Children's Bks.

Poydar, Nancy. Cool Ali. Poydar, Nancy, illus. 2014. (ENG., Illus.). 32p. (J). (gr. -1-2). 16.99 *(978-1-4814-2531-5(5)*, McElderry, Margaret K. Bks.) McElderry, Margaret K. Bks.

Price, Jennifer L. Half Moon: Phases of the Moon: Book 2, 1 vol. 2009. 252p. pap. 27.95 *(978-1-4489-2193-5(7))* PublishAmerica, Inc.

Priddy, Roger. Alphaprints Fun in the Sun! 2017. (Alphaprints Ser.). (ENG., Illus.). 10p. (J). bds. 7.99 *(978-0-312-52518-7(4)*, 9780312525187, Priddy Bks.) St. Martin's Pr.

Pyne, Jane. Tommy's Secret. 2009. 86p. pap. 10.49 *(978-1-4389-9102-3(9))* AuthorHouse.

Raczka, Bob. Summer Wonders. Stead, Judy, illus. 2012. (J). 34.28 *(978-1-61913-125-5(0))* Weigl Pubs., Inc.

Rad, Charles J. The Boy they called a Snowball. 2007. 140p. pap. 20.95 *(978-1-84753-461-3(9))* Lulu Pr., Inc.

Ramirez, Terry. Growing up with Olivi: The Beguiling Blue-Haired Beauty of Boysenberry Lane. 2009. 96p. pap. 9.95 *(978-0-595-47668-8(6))* iUniverse, Inc.

Ramos, Ramona J. A Summer with Kaitlyn & Lexi. 2011. 48p. pap. 16.95 *(978-1-4626-1890-3(1))* America Star Bks.

Random House. Barbie Summer 2016 Chapter Book (Barbie) 2016. (Barbie Chapters Ser.). (ENG., Illus.). 64p. (J). (gr. 1-4). lib. bdg. 12.99 *(978-1-101-94021-1(2)*, Random Hse. Bks. for Young Readers) Random Hse. Children's Bks.

—Barbie Summer 2016 Movie Pictureback (Barbie) 2016. (Pictureback(R) Ser.). (ENG., Illus.). 24p. (J). (gr. -1-2). 4.99 *(978-1-101-93750-1(5)*, Random Hse. Bks. for Young Readers) Random Hse. Children's Bks.

Rayner, Shoo. Dead Heat. 2016. (History of Britain In 12... Ser.). (ENG., Illus.). 64p. (J). (gr. k-2). pap. 7.99 *(978-1-4083-3463-8(1)*, Orchard Bks.) Hachette Children's Group GBR. Dist: Hachette Bk. Group.

Rebello, Kevin. Julia & Mckinley's Day at the Beach. 2009. 32p. pap. 12.99 *(978-1-4389-7330-2(6))* AuthorHouse.

Reimiller, Diane L. A Duck Named Quackers, 1 vol. Jastrzebski, Brandy, illus. 2009. 12p. pap. 24.95 *(978-1-60836-771-9(1))* America Star Bks.

Rey, H. A. Curious George & the Ice Cream Surprise. 2011. (Curious George Ser.). (ENG., Illus.). 24p. (J). (gr. -1-3). 13.99 *(978-0-547-24284-2(0))*; pap. 4.99 *(978-0-547-24285-9(9))* Houghton Mifflin Harcourt Publishing Co.

Richardson, Bernard. Freddy Weller's Holiday. 2011. 50p. 24.99 *(978-1-4628-9548-9(4))*; pap. 15.99 *(978-1-4628-9547-2(6))* Xlibris Corp.

Richens, Carol & Smith, Lori. Lori's Summer Fun with Tamara! 2009. 33p. 16.40 *(978-1-4357-1113-6(0))* Lulu Pr., Inc.

Ritchie, Polly. A Pocket Full of Frogs. 2007. 124p. pap. 10.00 *(978-0-9795103-2-8(5))* Ascended Ideas.

Roberts, Johanna Lonsdorf. Summer at the Cabin. Shaggy Dog Press, ed. Challoner, Audrey, illus. 2007. 32p. (J). per. *(978-0-9722007-2-1(X))* Shaggy Dog Pr.

Robinson, Stephen. The Duke of Cork. 2011. 86p. pap. 19.95 *(978-1-4560-3340-8(9))* America Star Bks.

Rodgers, Mary. Summer Switch. 224p. (J). (gr. 4-6). pap. 4.95 *(978-0-8072-1550-0(3)*, Listening Library) Random Hse. Audio Publishing Group.

Romer, Ruth. The Great Lemonade Standoff. 2005. (J). pap. *(978-1-4108-4200-8(2))* Benchmark Education Co.

Rue, Nancy N. Lucy's Perfect Summer, 1 vol. 2016. (Faithgirlz / a Lucy Novel Ser.). (ENG.). 192p. (J). pap. 7.99 *(978-0-310-75504-3(2))* Zonderkidz.

Ryan, Tom. Way to Go, 1 vol. 2012. (ENG.). 224p. (YA). (gr. 8-12). pap. 12.95 *(978-1-4598-0077-9(X))* Orca Bk. Pubs. USA.

Rylant, Cynthia. Annie & Snowball & the Book Bugs Club. Stevenson, Suçie, illus. (Annie & Snowball Ser.: 9). (ENG.). 40p. (J). (gr. k-2). 2012. pap. 3.99 *(978-1-4169-7201-3(3))* 2011. 16.99 *(978-1-4169-7199-3(8))* Simon Spotlight. (Simon Spotlight).

—Annie & Snowball & the Book Bugs Club. 2012. (Annie & Snowball Ready-To-Read Ser.). lib. bdg. 13.55 *(978-0-606-23692-8(9)*, Turtleback) Turtleback Bks.

—Mr. Putter & Tabby Clear the Decks. Howard, Arthur, illus. alt. ed. 2011. (Mr. Putter & Tabby Ser.). (ENG.). 44p. (J). (gr. 1-4). pap. 5.99 *(978-0-547-57695-4(1))* Houghton Mifflin Harcourt Publishing Co.

Sadd, Kenn. Crazy Cracked Pots. 2009. 144p. pap. 24.95 *(978-1-61546-673-3(8))* America Star Bks.

Sam's Last Summer. 2006. (J). per. 5.95 *(978-0-9790796-3-4(2))* PJR Assocs., Ltd.

Sanrio Company, Ltd. Staff. Hello Kitty, Hello Summer! Hirashima, Jean, illus. 2013. (ENG.). 14p. (J). (gr. -1 — 1). bds. 7.95 *(978-1-4197-0687-5(X)*, Abrams Appleseed) Abrams, Inc.

Schraff, Anne. One Amazing Summer. 2017. (Red Rhino Ser.). lib. bdg. 18.40 ***(978-0-606-40324-5(8))*** Turtleback Bks.

Schronk, Julie. The Grass Grows Green. 2007. 208p. per. 24.95 *(978-1-60441-057-0(4))* America Star Bks.

Schwartz, Joanne. Pinny in Summer, 1 vol. Malenfant, Isabelle, illus. 2016. (ENG.). 32p. (J). (gr. -1-2). 16.95 *(978-1-55498-782-5(2))* Groundwood Bks. CAN. Dist: Publishers Group West (PGW).

Sheckels, Astrid, illus. Nic & Nellie, 1 vol. 2013. (ENG.). 32p. (J). (gr. 1-4). 17.95 *(978-1-934031-52-0(6)*, 9781934031520) Islandport Pr., Inc.

Simms, Abigail & Gabrielle. Let's Turn Our World Upside Down. 2013. 28p. pap. 16.09 *(978-1-4669-8156-0(3))* Trafford Publishing.

Simon, Coco. Emma All Stirred Up! (Cupcake Diaries: 7). (ENG., 160p. (J). (gr. 3-7). 2013. Illus.). 17.99 *(978-1-4424-8567-9(1))* 2012. pap. 6.99 *(978-1-4424-5078-3(9))* Simon Spotlight. (Simon Spotlight).

—Emma All Stirred Up! 2012. (Cupcake Diaries: 7). lib. bdg. 17.20 *(978-0-606-26309-2(8)*, Turtleback) Turtleback Bks.

Simoneau, Shelly. The Cows Came Running & the Horses Did Too! 2011. 28p. pap. 14.99 *(978-1-4567-3107-6(6))* AuthorHouse.

Sinclair, Gardine. Stageschool by the Sea. 2013. 176p. (J). pap. *(978-1-78299-389-6(4))* FeedARead.com.

Sioux Rose. Cassandra's Tale: Invitation to the Circle. 2010. 200p. pap. 16.95 *(978-1-4401-9510-5(2))* iUniverse, Inc.

Sís, Peter. Ice Cream Summer. 2015. (ENG., Illus.). 40p. (J). (gr. k-3). 17.99 *(978-0-545-73161-4(5)*, Scholastic Pr.) Scholastic, Inc.

Skalak, Daniel. All Summer's Fun. Skalak, Daniel, illus. 2006. (Illus.). 32p. (J). (gr. -1-3). 15.95 *(978-1-60108-000-4(X))* Red Cygnet Pr.

Sloan, L. Bridges. 2005. 164p. 22.99 *(978-1-58832-123-7(1))*; per. 12.99 *(978-1-58832-122-0(3))* Unlimited Publishing LLC.

Smith, Charles R., Jr. Chameleon. 2010. (ENG., Illus.). 384p. (YA). (gr. 7). pap. 7.99 *(978-0-7636-4660-8(1))* Candlewick Pr.

Smoot, Madeline, compiled by. Summer Shorts: A Short Story Collection. 2005. (ENG., Illus.). 360p. (J). (gr. 2-7). pap. 8.95 *(978-0-9769417-5-0(9))* Blooming Tree Pr.

Smythe, Katie. The Summer Picnic. 2015. (Rosen REAL Readers: STEM & STEAM Collection). (ENG.). 8p. pap. 5.46 *(978-1-4994-9557-7(9)*, Rosen Classroom) Rosen Publishing Group, Inc., The.

Sommer, Sharon. The Adventures of Summer Hills: Rowdy Red's Lesson. 2008. 28p. per. 24.95 *(978-1-4241-9374-5(5))* America Star Bks.

Spinelli, Eileen. Now It Is Summer. DePalma, Mary Newell, illus. 2011. (ENG.). 36p. (YA). (gr. -1-3). 16.00 *(978-0-8028-5340-0(4)*, Eerdmans Bks For Young Readers) Eerdmans, William B. Publishing Co.

—Summerhouse Time. Lew-Vriethoff, Joanne, illus. 2009. (ENG.). 224p. (J). (gr. 3-7). 6.99 *(978-0-440-42224-2(8)*, Yearling) Random Hse. Children's Bks.

Sprenger, Luke. Sommer in Canvas Bay. 2008. 92p. pap. 13.95 *(978-1-4092-3213-1(1))* Lulu Pr., Inc.

Spruill, Beverle. The Dream Box. 2009. 24p. pap. 13.50 *(978-1-4490-3783-3(6))* AuthorHouse.

Staffen, Julie. Krista Kay Summer Adventures. 2010. 156p. pap. 10.95 *(978-1-60920-005-3(5))* Ajoyin Publishing, Inc.

Stanek, Robert, pseud. Bugville Critters Start Summer Vacation. 2011. (Illus.). 32p. pap. 4.99 *(978-1-57545-257-9(X)*, Reagent Pr. Bks. for Young Readers) RP Media.

—Start Summer Vacation. 2010. (Illus.). 32p. pap. 8.99 *(978-1-57545-174-9(3)*, Reagent Pr. Bks. for Young Readers) RP Media.

Stevens, Michael J. Silver Spitfire. 2010. 164p. pap. *(978-1-907652-13-4(2))* Grosvenor Hse. Publishing Ltd.

Stewart, A. W. Rooktime. 2010. 284p. pap. 15.49 *(978-1-4520-1460-9(4))* AuthorHouse.

Stewart, Dianne C. Longitude - Zero Degrees. 2009. (ENG.). 200p. pap. 8.95 *(978-0-9667359-4-9(3)*, BeanPole Bks.) Harren Communications, LLC.

Stewart, Kiera. The Summer of Bad Ideas. 2017. 304p. (J). (gr. 3-7). 16.99 *(978-0-06-236021-2(3))* HarperCollins Pubs.

Stine, R. L. Attack of the Jack. 2017. (Goosebumps SlappyWorld Ser.: 2). lib. bdg. 17.20 ***(978-0-606-40169-2(5))*** Turtleback Bks.

Stine, R. L. Temptation. 2012. (ENG.). 416p. (YA). (gr. 7). pap. 10.99 *(978-1-4424-5068-4(1)*, Simon Pulse) Simon Pulse.

Stoddart, Heidi Jardine. East to the Sea, 1 vol. 2007. (ENG., Illus.). 32p. (J). (gr. -1-2). pap. 10.95 *(978-1-55109-577-6(7))* Nimbus Publishing, Ltd. CAN. Dist: Orca Bk. Pubs. USA.

Strasser, Todd & Thacker, Nola. The Shore: Shirt & Shoes Not Required; LB (Laguna Beach) 2011. (ENG.). 480p. (YA). (gr. 9). pap. 9.99 *(978-1-4424-1970-4(9)*, Simon Pulse) Simon Pulse.

Stratton, Erin. There's Nothing Wrong with Boys. Gregeory, Vicki, illus. 2010. 26p. pap. 12.00 *(978-1-60911-021-5(8)*,

S

Eloquent Bks.) Strategic Book Publishing & Rights Agency (SBPRA).

Summer Fun: Individual Title Six-Packs. (Literatura 2000 Ser.). (gr. -1-1). 28.00 (978-0-7635-0064-1(X)) Rigby Education.

Swayne Tidwell, Deborah. Magic Eraser & Camp Real. 2009. 16p. pap. 8.50 (978-1-4343-8916-9(2)) AuthorHouse.

Tamaki, Mariko. This One Summer. Tamaki, Jillian, illus. 2014. (ENG.). 320p. (YA). (gr. 7). 21.99 (978-1-62672-094-7(0), 9781626720947); pap. 18.99 (978-1-59643-774-6(X), 9781596437746) Roaring Brook Pr. (First Second Bks.).

Tan, Shaun. Rules of Summer. 2014. (ENG.). 48p. (J). (gr. 3-7). 18.99 (978-0-545-63912-5(3), Levine, Arthur A. Bks.) Scholastic, Inc.

Tashjian, Janet. My Life As a Book. Tashjian, Jake, illus. 2010. (My Life Ser.: 1). (ENG.). 224p. (J). (gr. 4-7). 17.99 (978-0-8050-8903-5(9), 9780805089035, Holt, Henry & Co. Bks. For Young Readers) Holt, Henry & Co.

—My Life As a Book. Tashjian, Jake, illus. 2011. (My Life Ser.: 1). (ENG.). 240p. (J). (gr. 4-7). pap. 7.99 (978-0-312-67289-8(6), 9780312672898) Square Fish.

Taylor, Chloe. Knot Too Shabby! Zhang, Nancy, illus. 2014. (Sew Zoey Ser.: 7). (ENG.). 176p. (J). (gr. 3-7). pap. 5.99 (978-1-4814-1398-5(8), Simon Spotlight) Simon Spotlight.

—Swatch Out! Zhang, Nancy, illus. 2014. (Sew Zoey Ser.: 8). (ENG.). 176p. (J). (gr. 3-7). pap. 5.99 (978-1-4814-1535-4(2), Simon Spotlight) Simon Spotlight.

Thaler, Mike. The Summer Vacation from the Black Lagoon. Lee, Jared D., illus. 2010. 62p. (J). (978-0-545-07224-3(7)) Scholastic, Inc.

Thomas, Patricia. Firefly Mountain, 1 vol. Sylvada, Peter, illus. 2007. (ENG.). 32p. (J). (gr. 1-5). 16.95 (978-1-56145-360-3(9)) Peachtree Pubs.

Thompson, Kay. Eloise at the Wedding, Pack. 2012. (Eloise Ser.). (ENG.). 192p. (J). (gr. -1-1). pap. 15.96 (978-1-4424-4949-7(7), Simon Spotlight) Simon Spotlight.

Thompson, Lauren. Mouse's First Summer. Erdogan, Buket, illus. 2013. (Classic Board Bks.). (ENG.). 34p. (J). (gr. -1 — 1). bds. 7.99 (978-1-4424-5842-0(9), Little Simon) Little Simon.

—Mouse's First Summer. Erdogan, Buket, illus. 2014. (J). (978-1-4351-5506-0(8)) Simon & Schuster.

Thomson, Sarah L. Feel the Summer. Yamada, Kana, illus. 2006. (ENG.). 32p. (J). (gr. -1-3). 14.95 (978-1-59687-174-8(1)) IBks., Inc.

Toska, Mary Lou. Ernest's Dream: A Young Boy Wanting to Spend the Summer in the High Alps. 2012. 20p. pap. 24.95 (978-1-4626-8662-9(1)) America Star Bks.

Treanor, H. T. The Sun Stone. Tarnowski, Mark, illus. 2012. 16p. pap. 10.00 (978-1-60976-125-7(1), Strategic Bk. Publishing) Strategic Book Publishing & Rights Agency (SBPRA).

Turner, Julie Anne. A Tale of Summerland. 2007. (Illus.). 72p. pap. (978-1-84401-902-1(0)) Athena Pr.

Ulrich, Paulina. Flightless Bird. 2011. (ENG.). 424p. pap. 11.99 (978-1-4565-3438-7(6)) CreateSpace Independent Publishing Platform.

Vail, Rachel. Shells, Smells, & the Horrible Flip-Flops of Doom. Cordell, Matthew, illus. 2012. (Justin Case Ser.: 2). (ENG.). 192p. (J). (gr. 2-4). 16.99 (978-1-250-00081-1(5), 9781250000811) Feiwel & Friends.

—Shells, Smells, & the Horrible Flip-Flops of Doom. Cordell, Matthew, illus. 2013. (Justin Case Ser.: 2). (ENG.). 208p. (J). (gr. 2-4). pap. 6.99 (978-1-250-02723-8(3), 9781250027238) Square Fish.

Valentin, Karen. Block Party. 2009. 32p. (J). (gr. -1-3). 6.95 (978-1-60349-017-7(5), Marimba Bks.) Hudson Publishing Group, The.

Velez, Edia L. Jessica's Summer Vacation - Las Vacaciones de Verano de Jéssic. 2011. 44p. pap. 18.49 (978-1-4490-2301-0(0)) AuthorHouse.

Viva, Frank. Sea Change. Viva, Frank, illus. 2016. (ENG., Illus.). 120p. (J). (gr. 2-7). 18.95 (978-1-935179-92-4(6)) TOON Books / RAW Junior, LLC.

Voake, Steve. Daisy Dawson on the Farm. Meserve, Jessica, illus. 2013. (Daisy Dawson Ser.). (ENG.). 96p. (J). (gr. 1-4). pap. 5.99 (978-0-7636-6340-7(9)) Candlewick Pr.

Vogel, Vin. The Thing about Yetis. 2015. (ENG., Illus.). 32p. (J). (gr. -1-k). 16.99 (978-0-8037-4170-6(7), Dial Bks) Penguin Young Readers Group.

Walker, Melissa. Lovestruck Summer. 2009. (ENG.). 272p. (J). (gr. 9-18). pap. 5.99 (978-0-06-171586-0(7), HarperTeen) HarperCollins Pubs.

Wallace, Bonny. The Raymond Wikins' Adventures, Children of Straw. 2009. 70p. pap. 9.95 (978-1-60860-699-3(6), Eloquent Bks.) Strategic Book Publishing & Rights Agency (SBPRA).

Wargin, Kathy-jo. F Is for Fireflies: God's Summertime Alphabet, 1 vol. Bronson, Linda, illus. 2011. (ENG.). 40p. (J). (gr. -1-2). 15.99 (978-0-310-71663-1(2)) Zonderkidz.

Waters, Cassie. Cool Down. 2012. (Pool Girls Ser.: 3). (ENG.). 160p. (J). (gr. 3-7). 15.99 (978-1-4424-5377-7(X)); pap. 5.99 (978-1-4424-4709-7(5)) Simon Spotlight. (Simon Spotlight).

—Heat Wave. 2012. (Pool Girls Ser.: 2). (ENG.). 160p. (J). (gr. 3-7). pap. 5.99 (978-1-4424-4146-0(1), Simon Spotlight) Simon Spotlight.

Weetman, Nova. A Hot Cold Summer: Choose Your Own Ever After. 2016. (ENG.). 256p. (J). pap. 5.99 (978-1-61067-354-9(9)) Kane Miller.

Weihrich, Carroll. On Jim Street. 2003. 144p. 24.50 (978-1-932621-19-8(9)); per. 15.00 (978-1-932621-18-1(0)) Open Bk. Publishing.

Welles, Lee. Enter the Earth. Hameister, Ann, illus. 2006. (Gaia Girls Ser.: 1). (ENG.). 336p. (YA). (gr. 4-7). 18.95 (978-1-933609-00-3(1)) Chelsea Green Publishing.

Wells, Carolyn. Patty's Butterfly Days. 2005. 28.95 (978-1-4218-0309-8(7), 1st World Library - Literary Society) 1st World Publishing, Inc.

Wells, Rosemary. Ivy Takes Care. LaMarche, Jim, illus. (ENG.). 208p. (J). (gr. 3-7). 2015. pap. 6.99 (978-0-7636-7660-5(8)) 2013. 15.99 (978-0-7636-5352-1(7)) Candlewick Pr.

White, Alexis. Three Peas in a Pod. 2008. 56p. pap. 11.95 (978-1-4327-1869-5(X)) Outskirts Pr., Inc.

Wiebe, Kathleen. Willow Creek Summer. 2005. 217p. (J). (gr. 7-12). 7.95 (978-1-55050-169-8(0)) Coteau Bks. CAN. Dist: Fitzhenry & Whiteside, Ltd.

Wiersbitzky, Shannon. What Flowers Remember. 2014. 158p. (J). 18.95 (978-1-60898-166-3(5)) namelos llc.

Wiggin, Kate Douglas. A Summer in a Canyon. 2007. 140p. 24.95 (978-1-60312-626-7(0)) Aegypan.

Wilkins, Phil Cole. Dragog & the Seven Weeks of Summer. 2012. 164p. (gr. -1). pap. 15.60 (978-1-4567-8998-5(8)) AuthorHouse.

Williams, Alan. Archy the Flying Dolphin & the Vampire's Curse. 2007. pap. 15.38 (978-1-4251-3151-7(4)) Trafford Publishing.

Williams, Billie A. Fourteen Is Too Many: The Survivors. 2013. 24p. pap. 24.95 (978-1-63004-179-3(3)) America Star Bks.

Wines, Michael P. Stupid Alabama: A Laugh-So-Hard-You-Will-Snot about Growing up to Discover Not All Things Are Stupid but a Lot of Them Are. Gierhart, Steve, ed. Floyd, Claire, illus. 2013. (ENG.). 244p. (YA). pap. 17.95 (978-1-938667-13-8(1)) Ardent Writer Pr., LLC, The.

Winkler, Henry & Oliver, Lin. Summer School! What Genius Thought That Up? 2006. (Hank Zipzer Ser.: No. 8). (Illus.). 157p. (J). (gr. 3-9). lib. bdg. 24.21 (978-1-59961-107-5(4)) Spotlight.

Wishinsky, Frieda. Camp Disaster, 1 vol. 2016. (Orca Currents Ser.). (ENG.). 144p. (J). (gr. 5-9). pap. 9.95 (978-1-4598-1114-0(3)) Orca Bk. Pubs. USA.

Wittman, Kathy A. Raina's Vision Quest, 1 vol. 2010. 78p. pap. 19.95 (978-1-61582-656-8(4)) America Star Bks.

Wittman, Patricia. Scrabble Creek. 2013. (ENG., Illus.). 32p. (J). (gr. -1-3). 16.99 (978-1-4814-2145-4(X), Simon & Schuster Bks. For Young Readers) Simon & Schuster Bks. For Young Readers.

Wolf, Mária. Maggy Cans. 2012. 52p. (gr. 4-6). pap. 11.95 (978-1-4772-8093-5(6)) AuthorHouse.

Wong, Janet S. Minn & Jake's Almost Terrible Summer. Côté, Geneviève, illus. 2008. (ENG.). 112p. (J). (gr. 2-5). 15.99 (978-0-374-34977-6(0), 9780374349776, Farrar, Straus & Giroux (BYR)) Farrar, Straus & Giroux.

Woodbury, Mary. The Ghost in the Machine. 2005. 222p. (J). (gr. 6-9). pap. 7.95 (978-1-55050-227-5(1)) Coteau Bks. CAN. Dist: Fitzhenry & Whiteside, Ltd.

Yang, Belle. Summertime Rainbow: A Mandarin Chinese-English Bilingual Book of Colors. Yang, Belle, illus. 2012. (ENG & CHI., Illus.). 22p. (J). (gr. k — 1). bds. 6.99 (978-0-7636-5280-7(6)) Candlewick Pr.

Yee, Wong Herbert. Summer Days & Nights. Yee, Wong Herbert, illus. 2012. (ENG., Illus.). 32p. (J). (gr. -1-1). 16.99 (978-0-8050-9078-9(9), 9780805090789, Holt, Henry & Co. Bks. For Young Readers) Holt, Henry & Co.

Young, Marlene Lauster. Before Summer's End. 2012. 36p. (-18). pap. 20.99 (978-1-4772-6810-0(3)) AuthorHouse.

Zappone, Melanie Lippincott. The Sounds of Summer Sank in the Sea. 2011. 24p. (gr. -1). 12.68 (978-1-4567-3856-3(9)) AuthorHouse.

SUMMER—POETRY

Carpenter, Stephen, illus. What I Did on My Summer Vacation: Kids' Favorite Funny Summer Vacation Poems. 2009. (Giggle Poetry Ser.). (ENG.). 80p. (J). (gr. 1-8). pap. 8.95 (978-1-4169-7047-7(9)) Meadowbrook Pr.

Forman, Ruth. Young Cornrows Callin Out the Moon. Bayoc, Cbabi, illus. 2007. (ENG.). 24p. (J). (gr. -1-3). lib. bdg. 16.95 (978-0-89239-218-6(5)) Lee & Low Bks., Inc.

Lansky, Bruce. What I Did on My Summer Vacation: Kids' Favorite Funny Poems about Summer Vacation. Carpenter, Stephen, illus. 2009. (978-0-88166-539-0(8)) Meadowbrook Pr.

SUMMER HOMES

see Architecture, Domestic; Houses

SUMMER RESORTS—FICTION

Doktorski, Jennifer Salvato. The Summer after You & Me. 2015. (ENG.). 304p. (YA). (gr. 8-12). pap. 10.99 (978-1-4926-1903-1(5)) Sourcebooks, Inc.

SUMMER THEATER—FICTION

Knudsen, Michelle. Revenge of the Evil Librarian. 2017. (ENG.). (YA). (gr. 9). 16.99 (978-0-7636-8828-8(2)) Candlewick Pr.

SUN

see also Solar Energy; Solar System

Adamson, Thomas K. The Sun [Scholastic]. 2011. (Exploring the Galaxy Ser.). 24p. pap. 0.50 (978-1-4296-6290-1(5), Pebble Plus) Capstone Press of Coughlan Cos.

Anderson, Michael. The Sun, Stars, & Galaxies. 2011. (Illus.). 96p. (J). lib. bdg. 31.70 (978-1-61530-519-3(X)) Rosen Publishing Group, Inc., The.

Appleby, Alex. It's Sunny! 2013. (What's the Weather? Ser.). 24p. (J). (gr. k-2). pap. 48.90 (978-1-4339-9410-4(0)); pap. 8.15 (978-1-4339-9409-8(7)); (ENG., Illus.). lib. bdg. 22.60 (978-1-4339-9408-1(9)) Stevens, Gareth Publishing LLLP.

—It's Sunny! / Est Soleado! 2013. (What's the Weather? / Qu Tiempo Hace? Ser.). (SPA & ENG., Illus.). 24p. (J). (gr. k-2). 22.60 (978-1-4339-9454-8(2)) Stevens, Gareth Publishing LLLP.

Asch, Frank. The Sun Is My Favorite Star. 2008. (ENG., Illus.). 32p. (J). (gr. -1-3). pap. 7.99 (978-0-15-206397-9(8)) Houghton Mifflin Harcourt Publishing Co.

Asimov, Isaac & Hantula, Richard. El Sol. Porras, Carlos & D'Andrea, Patricia, trs. from ENG. 2003. (Isaac Asimov's Biblioteca del Universo del Siglo XXI).Tr. of Sun. (SPA., Illus.). 32p. (gr. 2-6). lib. bdg. 26.00 (978-0-8368-3861-9(0), Gareth Stevens Learning Library) Stevens, Gareth Publishing LLLP.

Aspen-Baxter, Linda & Kissock, Heather. El Sol. 2012. (Mirando Al Cielo Ser.). (SPA., Illus.). 24p. (J). (gr. k-2). 27.13 (978-1-61913-219-1(2), AV2 by Weigl) Weigl Pubs., Inc.

Asselin, Kristine Carlson. Our Sun, 1 vol. (Solar System & Beyond Ser.). (ENG., 32p. (gr. 3-4). 2011. Illus.). pap. 8.10 (978-1-4296-6238-3(7)) 2011. pap. 47.70 (978-1-4296-6409-7(6)) 2010. lib. bdg. 27.32 (978-1-4296-5393-0(0)) Capstone Press of Coughlan Cos. (Fact Finders).

Bang, Molly & Chisholm, Penny. Living Sunlight: How Plants Bring the Earth to Life. Bang, Molly, illus. 2009. (ENG., Illus.). 40p. (J). (gr. -1-3). 18.99 (978-0-545-04422-6(7), Blue Sky Pr., The) Scholastic, Inc.

—Rivers of Sunlight: How the Sun Moves Water Around the Earth. 2017. (ENG., Illus.). 48p. (J). (gr. -1-3). 18.99 (978-0-545-80541-4(4), Blue Sky Pr., The) Scholastic, Inc.

Bartlett, Melissa. What Makes the Sun So Hot? 2013. (Rosen Readers Ser.). (ENG.). 24p. (J). (gr. 3-4). pap. 49.50 (978-1-4777-2543-6(1)); pap. 8.25 (978-1-4777-2542-9(3)) Rosen Publishing Group, Inc., The. (Rosen Classroom).

Bath, Louella. Mysteries of the Sun. 2013. (InfoMax Readers Ser.). (ENG.). 24p. (J). (gr. 3-4). pap. 49.50 (978-1-4777-2595-5(4)); (Illus.). pap. 8.25 (978-1-4777-2593-1(8)) Rosen Publishing Group, Inc., The. (Rosen Classroom).

Bauer, Marion Dane. Sun. Wallace, John, illus. 2016. (Weather Ready-To-Reads Ser.). (ENG.). 32p. (J). (gr. -1-1). pap. 3.99 (978-1-4814-6339-3(X), Simon Spotlight) Simon Spotlight.

Bell, Cassie. The Hot Sun. 2016. (Spring Forward Ser.). (J). (gr. k). (978-1-4900-3734-9(9)) Benchmark Education Co.

Bell, Trudy E. The Sun: Our Nearest Star. 2003. (New Solar System Ser.). (J). lib. bdg. 28.50 (978-1-58340-286-3(1)) Black Rabbit Bks.

Benchmark Education Co., LLC. Fun in the Sun Big Book. 2014. (Shared Reading Foundations Ser.). (J). (gr. -1). (978-1-4509-9439-2(3)) Benchmark Education Co.

Blaisdell, Molly. Our Sun. 2008. (Discovering & Exploring Science Ser.). (Illus.). 16p. (J). (gr. -1-3). 12.95 (978-0-7569-8257-7(X)) Perfection Learning Corp.

Boothroyd, Jennifer. What Does Sunlight Do? 2014. (First Step Nonfiction - Let's Watch the Weather Ser.). 24p. (gr. k-2). (Illus.). pap. 6.95 (978-1-4677-4496-6(4)); (ENG.). lib. bdg. 23.93 (978-1-4677-3921-4(9), Lerner Pubns.) Lerner Publishing Group.

Branley, Franklyn M. Sunshine Makes the Seasons. Rex, Michael, illus. 2005. (Let's-Read-And-Find-Out Science 2 Ser.). (ENG.). 40p. (J). (gr. k-4). pap. 5.99 (978-0-06-059205-9(2), Collins) HarperCollins Pubs.

Branley, Franklyn Mansfield. Sunshine Makes the Seasons. Rex, Michael, illus. 2005. (Let's-Read-and-Find-Out-Science Ser.). (ENG.). 40p. (J). (gr. -1 — 1). 15.99 (978-0-06-059203-5(6)) HarperCollins Pubs.

Bredeson, Carmen. What Do You Know about the Sun? 2008. (I Like Space! Ser.). (Illus.). 32p. (J). (gr. 1-3). lib. bdg. 23.94 (978-0-7660-2941-5(7), Enslow Elementary) Enslow Pubs., Inc.

Bredeson, Carmen & Dyson, Marianne. Exploring the Sun. 2015. (Launch into Space! Ser.). (ENG.). 32p. (J). (gr. 3-4). pap. 10.52 (978-0-7660-6833-9(1)) Enslow Pubs., Inc.

Bredeson, Carmen, et al. Exploring the Sun. 2015. (Launch into Space! Ser.). (ENG., Illus.). 32p. (J). (gr. 3-4). 25.27 (978-0-7660-6835-3(8)) Enslow Pubs., Inc.

Brennan, Linda Crotta. There Is Day & Night. 2014. (Tell Me Why Library). (ENG., Illus.). 24p. (J). (gr. 2-5). 25.64 (978-1-63188-007-0(1), 205435) Cherry Lake Publishing.

Brinkman, Patricia. Discover the Sun. 2006. (J). pap. (978-1-4108-6477-2(4)) Benchmark Education Co.

—The Sun. 2006. (J). pap. (978-1-4108-6474-1(X)) Benchmark Education Co.

Budd Josselin. The Sun Is Not a Yellow Balloon: Fun with the Sun for Kids. 2013. 28p. pap. 9.74 (978-1-63022-159-1(7), Baby Professor (Education Kids)) Speedy Publishing LLC.

Burton, Margie, et al. Our Sun. 2011. (Early Connections Ser.). (J). (978-1-61672-532-7(X)) Benchmark Education Co.

Capaccio, George. The Sun. 2009. (Space!). 64p. (gr. 5-18). lib. bdg. 32.79 (978-0-7614-4242-4(1)) Marshall Cavendish Corp.

Carson, Mary Kay. Far-Out Guide to the Sun. 2010. (Far-Out Guide to the Solar System Ser.). (Illus.). 48p. (J). pap. 8.95 (978-1-59845-180-1(4), Enslow Elementary); (gr. 2-5). 25.27 (978-0-7660-3179-1(9)) Enslow Pubs., Inc.

Chrismer, Melanie. The Sun. 2008. (Scholastic News Nonfiction Readers Ser.). (ENG., Illus.). 24p. (J). (gr. 1-2). pap. 6.95 (978-0-531-14768-9(1)) Scholastic Library Publishing.

Coan, Sharon. Lo Que Puede Hacer el Sol. 2016. (TIME for KIDS(r) Nonfiction Readers Ser.). (SPA.). 12p. (J). (gr. k-k). 4.99 (978-1-4938-2962-0(2)) Teacher Created Materials, Inc.

—What the Sun Can Do. 2015. (TIME for KIDS(r) Nonfiction Readers Ser.). (ENG., Illus.). 12p. (gr. k-k). 4.99 (978-1-4938-2053-5(2)) Teacher Created Materials, Inc.

Crabtree Editor & Miller, Reagan. The Sun. 2012. (Journey Through Space Ser.). (ENG.). 24p. (J). (gr. 3-6). lib. bdg. (978-0-7787-5309-4(3)) Crabtree Publishing Co.

DeCristofano, Carolyn Cinami. The Sun & the Moon. Morley, Taia, illus. 2016. (Let's-Read-And-Find-Out Science 1 Ser.). 40p. (J). (gr. -1-3). pap. 6.99 (978-0-06-233803-7(X)) HarperCollins Pubs.

Demuth, Patricia Brennan. The Sun: Our Amazing Star. 2016. (Penguin Core Concepts Ser.). (ENG., Illus.). 32p. (J). (gr. -1-1). pap. 3.99 (978-0-448-48828-8(0), Grosset & Dunlap) Penguin Young Readers Group.

Dickmann, Nancy. Exploring the Sun. 2015. (Spectacular Space Science Ser.). (ENG., Illus.). 48p. (J). (gr. 5-6). 30.25 (978-1-4994-3621-1(1), Rosen Central) Rosen Publishing Group, Inc., The.

Dobeck, Maryann. Circling the Sun. 2004. (Reading PowerWorks Ser.). (Illus.). 16p. (gr. 1-3). pap. 6.10 (978-0-7608-8917-6(1)) Sundance/Newbridge Educational Publishing.

Doudna, Kelly. It Is Sunny, 1 vol. 2003. (Weather Ser.). (ENG., Illus.). 24p. (J). (gr. k-3). lib. bdg. 24.21 (978-1-57765-777-4(2), SandCastle) ABDO Publishing Co.

Duffey, Gary. Windows. 2012. 16p. pap. 7.95 (978-1-4582-0512-4(6), Abbott Pr.) Author Solutions, Inc.

Eckart, Edana. Watching the Sun. 2004. (Welcome Bks.). (ENG., Illus.). 24p. (J). (gr. -1-2). pap. 4.95 (978-0-516-25939-0(3), Children's Pr.) Scholastic Library Publishing.

Edison, Erin. Sunlight, 1 vol. 2011. (Weather Basics Ser.). (ENG.). 24p. (gr. k-1). pap. 7.29 (978-1-4296-7081-4(9)); pap. 41.70 (978-1-4296-7087-6(8)); lib. bdg. 26.65 (978-1-4296-6056-3(2)) Capstone Press of Coughlan Cos. (Pebble Plus).

Edison, Erin & Saunders-Smith, Gail. Luz del Sol. Strictly Spanish LLC. Staff, tr. from ENG. 2013. (Lo Básico Sobre el Tiempo/Weather Basics Ser.).Tr. of Sunlight. (SPA, ENG & MUL.). 24p. (gr. k-1). lib. bdg. 26.65 (978-1-62065-166-7(1)) Capstone Press of Coughlan Cos.

Elish, Dan. The Sun. 2006. (Kaleidoscope Space Ser.). (Illus.). 48p. (gr. 3-7). lib. bdg. 20.95 (978-0-7614-2048-4(7), Benchmark Bks.) Marshall Cavendish Corp.

Feinstein, Stephen. The Sun: A Myreportlinks. com Book. 2005. (Solar System Ser.). (Illus.). 48p. (J). (gr. 4-10). lib. bdg. 25.26 (978-0-7660-5305-2(9), MyReportLinks.com Bks.) Enslow Pubs., Inc.

Flynn, Claire E. A Trip to the Sun. 2015. (Fantastic Science Journeys Ser.). (ENG.). 32p. (J). (gr. 2-3). pap. 10.50 (978-1-4824-2014-2(7)) Stevens, Gareth Publishing LLLP.

Ganeri, Anita. Sunshine. 2004. (Weather Around You Ser.). (Illus.). 24p. (gr. 1-4). lib. bdg. 22.00 (978-0-8368-4301-9(0), Weekly Reader Leveled Readers) Stevens, Gareth Publishing LLLP.

Garbe, Suzanne. The Science Behind Wonders of the Sun: Sun Dogs, Lunar Eclipses, & Green Flash. 2016. (Science Behind Natural Phenomena Ser.). (ENG., Illus.). 32p. (gr. 3-4). lib. bdg. 27.99 (978-1-5157-0778-3(4), Edge Bks.) Capstone Press of Coughlan Cos.

Gardener, Ryan. Thank You God for Making the Sun. 2008. 28p. pap. 12.95 (978-1-4389-1488-6(1)) AuthorHouse.

Gardner, Robert. Far-Out Science Projects about Earth's Sun & Moon. LaBaff, Tom, illus. 2007. (Rockin' Earth Science Experiments Ser.). 48p. (J). (gr. 3-4). lib. bdg. 25.27 (978-0-7660-2736-7(8), Enslow Elementary) Enslow Pubs., Inc.

—Science Fair Projects about the Sun & the Moon. 2016. (Hands-On Science Ser.). 48p. (J). pap. 11.70 (978-0-7660-8215-1(6)) Enslow Pubs., Inc.

Gendell, Megan & Connolly, Rachel. Your Home in Space: Everything You Wanted to Know about Earth, the Sun, & the Moon. 2008. (Illus.). 32p. (J). (978-0-545-04457-8(X)) Scholastic, Inc.

Gifford, Clive. Stars, Galaxies, & the Milky Way. 2015. (Watch This Space! Ser.). (ENG., Illus.). 32p. (J). (gr. 3-7). lib. bdg. (978-0-7787-2022-5(5)) Crabtree Publishing Co.

Glaser, Chaya. El Sol: Una Superestrella. 2015. (Fuera de Este Mundo Ser.). (SPA., Illus.). 24p. (J). (gr. -1-3). lib. bdg. 23.93 (978-1-62724-597-5(9)) Bearport Publishing Co., Inc.

—The Sun: A Super Star. 2015. (Out of This World Ser.). (ENG.). 24p. (J). (gr. -1-3). lib. bdg. 23.93 (978-1-62724-569-2(3)) Bearport Publishing Co., Inc.

Goldstein, Margaret. The Sun. 2009. pap. 6.95 (978-0-8225-4760-0(0)) Lerner Publishing Group.

Goldstein, Margaret J. The Sun. 2003. (Our Universe Ser.). (ENG., Illus.). 32p. (gr. 2-4). lib. bdg. 22.60 (978-0-8225-4647-4(7)) Lerner Publishing Group.

Graham, Ian. Our Sun. 2015. (Space Ser.). (Illus.). 24p. (gr. 3-6). lib. bdg. 28.50 (978-1-62588-210-3(6)) Black Rabbit Bks.

Gregoire, Maryellen. Our Sun, 1 vol. 2011. (Wonder Readers Emergent Level Ser.). (ENG & ACE.). (gr. -1-1). 32p. pap. 5.99 (978-1-4296-7868-1(2)); 16p. pap. 35.94 (978-1-4296-8136-0(5)) Capstone Press of Coughlan Cos. (Wonder Readers).

Hansen, Rosanna. Seven Wonders of the Sun & Other Stars. 2011. (Seven Wonders Ser.). (ENG.). 80p. (gr. 5-8). 33.26 (978-0-7613-5450-5(6)) Lerner Publishing Group.

Harman, Alice. Sun, 01 vols., 1. 2016. (Fact Finders: Space Ser.). (ENG., Illus.). 24p. (J). pap. 8.25 (978-1-5081-9137-7(9), Windmill Bks.) Rosen Publishing Group, Inc., The.

Hicks, Terry Allan. Why Does the Sun Set? 2009. (Tell Me Why, Tell Me How Ser.). 32p. (gr. 3-18). 29.93 (978-0-7614-3993-6(5)) Marshall Cavendish Corp.

Howard, Fran. The Sun, 1 vol. 2008. (Universe Ser.). (ENG.). 32p. (gr. k-4). 27.07 (978-1-59928-932-8(6), Buddy Bks.) ABDO Publishing Co.

Hunter, Nick. Stars & Constellations, 1 vol. 2013. (Night Sky: & Other Amazing Sights in Space Ser.). (ENG.). 32p. (gr. 1-3). 27.32 (978-1-4329-7517-3(X)); pap. 8.95 (978-1-4329-7522-7(6)) Heinemann-Raintree. (Heinemann First Library).

—The Sun, 1 vol. 2012. (Astronaut Travel Guides). (ENG.). 48p. (gr. 3-6). pap. 9.95 (978-1-4109-4583-9(9)); lib. bdg. 32.65 (978-1-4109-4574-7(X)) Heinemann-Raintree. (NA-r).

Hutson, Matt. The Inside Story of the Sun. 2006. (J). 7.80 (978-1-933798-06-6(8)) Sally Ride Science.

James, Lincoln. The Sun: Star of the Solar System. 2010. (Our Solar System Ser.). 24p. (J). (gr. k-3). (ENG.). pap. 8.15 (978-1-4339-3849-8(9)); (Illus.). lib. bdg. 22.60 (978-1-4339-3848-1(0)) Stevens, Gareth Publishing LLLP.

Jefferis, David. The Sun: Our Local Star. 2008. (Exploring Our Solar System Ser.). (ENG., Illus.). 32p. (J). (gr. 3-7). pap. (978-0-7787-3749-0(7)) Crabtree Publishing Co.

Jemison, Mae & Rau, Dana Meachen. Exploring Our Sun. 2013. (True Book™—Dr. Mae Jemison & 100 Year Starship™ Ser.). (ENG., Illus.). 48p. (J). pap. 6.95 (978-0-531-24062-5(2)); lib. bdg. 29.00 (978-0-531-25502-5(6)) Scholastic Library Publishing.

Kalman, Bobbie. La Tierra y el Sol. 2009. (SPA.). 32p. (J). (978-0-7787-8241-4(7)); pap. (978-0-7787-8258-2(1)) Crabtree Publishing Co.

Kalman, Bobbie & MacAulay, Kelley. Earth & the Sun. 2008. (Looking at Earth Ser.). (ENG., Illus.). 32p. (J). (gr. 3-7). pap. (978-0-7787-3212-9(6)); lib. bdg. (978-0-7787-3202-0(9)) Crabtree Publishing Co.

Kaner, Etta. Who Likes the Sun? Lafrance, Marie, illus. 2007. (Exploring the Elements Ser.). (ENG.). 32p. (J). (gr. -1-2). 14.95 (978-1-55337-840-2(7)) Kids Can Pr., Ltd. CAN. Dist: Hachette Bk. Group.

Kelly, Harold G. Inside the Sun. 2009. (Reading Room Collection 2 Ser.). 24p. (gr. 3-4). 42.50 (978-1-60851-974-3(0), PowerKids Pr.) Rosen Publishing Group, Inc., The.

—El Sol por dentro (Inside the Sun) 2009. (Reading Room Collection: Spanish Ser.). (SPA.). 24p. (gr. 3-4). 42.50 (978-1-60854-177-5(0), Editorial Buenas Letras) Rosen Publishing Group, Inc., The.

Kerrod, Robin & Posada, Mia. Dandelions: Stars in the Grass. 2003. (Illus.). 32p. (J). pap. 6.95 (978-1-57505-399-8(3)) Lerner Publishing Group.

Kissock, Heather. Sun. 2011. (J). (978-1-61690-953-6(6)); (978-1-61690-599-6(9)) Weigl Pubs., Inc.

Koehler, Max. Journey to the Sun, 1 vol. 2014. (Spotlight on Space Science Ser.). (ENG., Illus.). 32p. (J). (gr. 5-5). pap. 11.75 (978-1-4994-0378-7(X), 1384639, PowerKids Pr.) Rosen Publishing Group, Inc., The.

Lawrence, Ellen. The Sun: The Star of Our Solar System. 2013. (Zoom into Space Ser.). (Illus.). 24p. (J). (gr. -1-3). lib. bdg. 23.93 (978-1-909673-00-7(5)) Ruby Tuesday Books Limited GBR. Dist: Bearport Publishing Co., Inc.

Lilly, Melinda. Sun & Moon. Thompson, Scott M., photos by. 2005. (Rourke Discovery Library). (Illus.). 24p. (J). (gr. 1-4). lib. bdg. 14.95 *(978-1-59515-405-7(1),* 1244276) Rourke Educational Media.
Lindeen, Mary. Sun & Shade. 2017. (BeginningtoRead Ser.). (ENG.). 32p. (J). (-2). 22.60 ***(978-1-59953-872-3(5))***; pap. 11.94 ***(978-1-68404-091-9(4))*** Norwood Hse. Pr.
Lundgren, Julie K. Sun: Energy for Our Solar System. 2014. (ENG.). 24p. (gr. k-3). 28.50 *(978-1-62717-726-9(4))* Rourke Educational Media.
MacDonald, Margaret. Energy from the Sun. 2011. (Learn-Abouts Ser.). (Illus.). 16p. (J). pap. 7.95 *(978-1-59920-634-9(X))* Black Rabbit Bks.
Martin, Justin McCory. The Sun. 2007. (Illus.). 16p. (J). 3.95 *(978-0-545-00730-6(5))* Scholastic, Inc.
Mason Crest. Sun, Vol. 7. 2016. (Solar System Ser.: Vol. 7). (ENG., Illus.). 48p. (J). (gr. 5-8). 20.95 *(978-1-4222-3553-9(X))* Mason Crest.
McNeil, Niki, et al. HOCPP 1124 the Sun. 2006. spiral bd. 16.00 *(978-1-60308-124-5(0))* In the Hands of a Child.
Miller, Reagan. The Sun. 2012. (ENG.). 24p. (J). pap. *(978-0-7787-5314-8(X))* Crabtree Publishing Co.
Miller, Violet. Why Does the Sun Set? 2013. (Nature's Super Secrets Ser.). (Illus.). 24p. (J). (gr. 1-3). 22.60 *(978-1-4339-8180-7(7))*; pap. 8.15 *(978-1-4339-8181-4(5))* Stevens, Gareth Publishing LLLP.
Mitchell, Melanie. Sun. 2004. (First Step Nonfiction). (J). lib. bdg. 17.76 *(978-0-8225-0187-9(2),* Lerner Pubns.); (ENG., Illus.). 24p. lib. bdg. 23.93 *(978-0-8225-5139-3(X))* Lerner Publishing Group.
Mitchell, Melanie S. The Sun. 2003. (First Step Nonfiction Ser.). (Illus.). 22p. (J). pap. 5.95 *(978-0-8225-3593-5(9),* Lerner Pubns.) Lerner Publishing Group.
Moon, Walt K. Let's Explore the Sun. 2017. (Bumba Books (tm) — a First Look at Space Ser.). (ENG.). 24p. (J). (gr. -1-1). 25.32 ***(978-1-5124-3348-7(9))*** Lerner Publishing Group.
Moore, David. Expl on Your Own the Sun Shines. 2009. (Explore on Your Own Ser.). (ENG.). (C). pap. 7.95 *(978-0-7362-5591-2(5))* National Geographic School Publishing, Inc.
Morgan, Emily R. Next Time You See a Sunset. 2012. (Next Time You See Ser.). (ENG., Illus.). 32p. (J). (gr. k-5). pap. 12.95 *(978-1-936959-16-7(X))* National Science Teachers Assn.
—La Próxima Vez Que Veas la Puesta del Sol. 2016. (Next Time You See Ser.). (SPA., Illus.). 32p. (J). (gr. 2-4). pap. 12.95 *(978-1-68140-282-6(3))* National Science Teachers Assn.
Moskal, Greg. Our Sun. 2003. (Real Readers Series: Level Blue Ser.). (ENG., Illus.). 12p. (gr. 1-2). pap. 5.90 *(978-0-8239-6354-6(3))* Rosen Publishing Group, Inc., The.
Murphy, Patricia J. Why Is the Sun So Hot? (Library of Why Ser.). 24p. 2009. (gr. 3-4). 42.50 *(978-1-60853-966-6(0),* PowerKids Pr.) 2004. (Illus.). (J). lib. bdg. 22.60 *(978-0-8239-6235-8(0))* Rosen Publishing Group, Inc., The.
Nadeau, Isaac. Learning about the Movement of the Sun & Other Stars with Graphic Organizers. 2006. (Graphic Organizers in Science Ser.). (ENG., Illus.). 24p. (gr. 4-6). pap. 8.25 *(978-1-4042-5040-6(9),* PowerKids Pr.) Rosen Publishing Group, Inc., The.
Nations, Susan. Hace Sol. 2007. (Que tiempo hace? (Let's Read about Weather) Ser.). (ENG & SPA., Illus.). 12p. (J). (gr. -1-2). lib. bdg. 15.00 *(978-0-8368-8111-0(7),* Weekly Reader Leveled Readers) Stevens, Gareth Publishing LLLP.
—Let's Read about Sun. 2007. (Let's Read about Weather Ser.). (Illus.). 12p. (gr. -1-2). lib. bdg. 15.00 *(978-0-8368-7807-3(8),* Weekly Reader Leveled Readers) Stevens, Gareth Publishing LLLP.
Nations, Susan & Boyett, Suzi. Hace Sol. 2007. (Que tiempo hace? (Let's Read about Weather) Ser.). (ENG & SPA., Illus.). 12p. (J). (gr. -1-2). pap. 4.10 *(978-0-8368-8116-5(8),* Weekly Reader Leveled Readers) Stevens, Gareth Publishing LLLP.
Nelson, Robin. Un Día Soleado. Translations.com Staff, tr. from ENG. 2006. (Mi Primer Paso Al Mundo Real - el Estado Del Tiempo (First Step Nonfiction - Weather) Ser.). Tr. of Sunny Day. (SPA., Illus.). 24p. (gr. k-2). lib. bdg. 23.93 *(978-0-8225-6213-9(8),* Ediciones Lerner) Lerner Publishing Group.
—Un Día Soleado (A Sunny Day) 2006. (Mi Primer Paso al Mundo Real Ser.). (Illus.). 23p. (J). (gr. -1-3). per. 5.95 *(978-0-8225-6552-9(8),* Ediciones Lerner) Lerner Publishing Group.
—Sunny. (First Step Nonfiction - Kinds of Weather Ser.). (ENG., 8p. (gr. -1-1). 2015. Illus.). 11.99 *(978-1-5124-1039-6(X))* 2005. pap. 4.95 *(978-0-8225-5367-0(8),* Lerner Pubns.) Lerner Publishing Group.
—A Sunny Day. 2005. (First Step Nonfiction Ser.). (Illus.). 24p. (gr. k-2). lib. bdg. 17.27 *(978-0-8225-0176-3(7))* Lerner Publishing Group.
Nuestra Estrella: El Sol. (SPA.). (J). 10.00 *(978-84-342-1470-5(9))* Parramon Ediciones S.A. ESP. Dist: Distribuidora Norma, Inc.
Olien, Rebecca. Exploring the Sun. (Objects in the Sky Ser.). 24p. (gr. 3-3). 2009. 42.50 *(978-1-60851-142-6(1))* 2007. (Illus.). (J). lib. bdg. 22.60 *(978-1-4042-3464-2(0))* Rosen Publishing Group, Inc., The. (PowerKids Pr.).
Orme, Helen & Orme, David. Let's Explore the Sun. 2007. (Space Launch! Ser.). (Illus.). 24p. (gr. 1-4). pap. 8.15 *(978-0-8368-8133-2(8))*; lib. bdg. 23.00 *(978-0-8368-7948-3(1))* Stevens, Gareth Publishing LLLP. (Gareth Stevens Learning Library).
Orr, Tamra. I Spy in the Sky the Sun. 2011. (Randy's Corner Ser.). (Illus.). 32p. (J). (gr. k-3). lib. bdg. 25.70 *(978-1-58415-972-8(3))* Mitchell Lane Pubs., Inc.
Our Friend the Sun. 2004. (J). pap. 14.95 *(978-1-932762-07-5(8))* Elderberry Press, Inc.
Owen, Ruth. The Sun. 2013. (Explore Outer Space Ser.). 32p. (J). (gr. 3-6). pap. 10.00 *(978-1-61533-757-6(1))*; pap. 60.00 *(978-1-61533-758-3(X))*; lib. bdg. 25.25 *(978-1-61533-720-0(2))* Windmill Bks.
Owens, L. L. The Sun. McGeehan, Dan, illus. 2011. (Space Neighbors Ser.). (ENG.). 24p. (J). (gr. 1-4). lib. bdg. 27.07 *(978-1-60954-388-4(2),* 200882) Child's World, Inc., The.
Oxlade, Chris. Space Watch: The Sun. 2010. (Eye on Space Ser.). 24p. (J). pap. 8.25 *(978-1-61532-550-4(6),* PowerKids Pr.); (ENG.). lib. bdg. 22.60 *(978-1-61532-543-6(3))* Rosen Publishing Group, Inc., The.
Parker, Steve. The Sun. 2007. (Earth & Space Ser.). (Illus.). 48p. (YA). (gr. 5-9). lib. bdg. 29.25 *(978-1-4042-3737-7(2))* Rosen Publishing Group, Inc., The.
Peters, Elisa. The Sun. 2012. (PowerKids Readers: the Universe Ser.). (ENG., Illus.). 24p. (J). (gr. k-2). pap. 8.25 *(978-1-4488-7465-1(3))*; lib. bdg. 22.60 *(978-1-4488-7385-2(1))* Rosen Publishing Group, Inc., The. (PowerKids Pr.).
—The Sun: El Sol. 2012. (PowerKids Readers: the Universe / el universo Ser.). (SPA & ENG., Illus.). 24p. (J). (gr. k-2). lib. bdg. 22.60 *(978-1-4488-7821-5(7),* PowerKids Pr.) Rosen Publishing Group, Inc., The.
Peterson, Cris. Seed, Soil, Sun: Earth's Recipe for Food. Lundquist, David R., photos by. (ENG., Illus.). 32p. (J). (gr. k-4). 2012. pap. 7.95 *(978-1-59078-947-6(4))* 2010. 17.95 *(978-1-59078-713-7(7))* Boyds Mills Pr.
Phelan, Glen. Earth, Sun, Moon. 2007. (Reading Expeditions Ser.). (ENG., Illus.). 32p. (J). pap. 17.95 *(978-0-7922-4573-5(3))* CENGAGE Learning.
Phelan, Glen & National Geographic Learning Staff. Stars. 2007. (Language, Literacy, & Vocabulary - Reading Expeditions Ser.). (ENG., Illus.). 36p. (J). pap. 18.95 *(978-0-7922-5433-1(3))* CENGAGE Learning.
Picray, Michael E. The Sun with Code. 2012. (Sky Science Ser.). (ENG., Illus.). 24p. (J). (gr. 4-7). lib. bdg. 27.13 *(978-1-61913-097-5(1),* AV2 by Weigl) Weigl Pubs., Inc.
Ponka, Katherine. Math on the Sun. 2016. (Solve It! Math in Space Ser.). (Illus.). 24p. (J). (gr. 3-2). 22.60 *(978-1-4824-4936-5(6))* Stevens, Gareth Publishing LLLP.
Portillo, Athena Yvette. Sun & Moon. 2007. (Illus.). 32p. (J). pap. 8.00 *(978-0-8059-7278-8(1))* Dorrance Publishing Co., Inc.
Reilly, Carmel. The Sun. 2011. (Sky Watching Ser.). 32p. (gr. 2-4). 28.50 *(978-1-60870-584-9(6))* Marshall Cavendish GBR. Dist: Marshall Cavendish Corp.
Rhythms of the Sun. 2004. lib. bdg. 30.00 net. *(978-0-9749364-0-6(5))* Chuttani, Kabir.
Rice, Dona. Here Comes the Sun, 1 vol. (Science Readers: Content & Literacy Ser.). (ENG., Illus.). 24p. (gr. k-k). 2015. (J). 22.96 *(978-1-4938-1139-7(8))* 2014. pap. 8.99 *(978-1-4807-4529-2(4))* Teacher Created Materials, Inc.
Rice, William. Our Sun, 1 vol. (Science Readers: Content & Literacy Ser.). (ENG., Illus.). 24p. (gr. 1-1). 2015. (J). 22.96 *(978-1-4938-1157-1(6))* 2014. pap. 8.99 *(978-1-4807-4570-4(7))* Teacher Created Materials, Inc.
Riggs, Kate. Across the Universe: the Sun. 2015. (Across the Universe Ser.). (ENG.). 24p. (J). (gr. 1-3). pap. 9.99 *(978-1-62832-085-5(0),* Creative Paperbacks) Creative Co., The.
—The Sun. 2015. (J). *(978-1-60818-485-9(4),* Creative Education) Creative Co., The.
Roberts, Jeremy. Benito Mussolini. 2005. (First Step Nonfiction Ser.). (Illus.). 112p. (J). (gr. 3-7). lib. bdg. 29.27 *(978-0-8225-2648-3(4),* Lerner Pubns.) Lerner Publishing Group.
Robertson, Charmaine. All about Sunlight. 2016. (Rosen REAL Readers: STEM & STEAM Collection). 8p. (gr. 1-k). pap. 5.46 *(978-1-5081-2410-8(8),* Rosen Classroom) Rosen Publishing Group, Inc., The.
Roca, Núria, et al. The Sun. 2014. (Solar System Ser.). (ENG., Illus.). 36p. (J). (gr. -1-2). pap. 7.99 *(978-1-4380-0478-5(8))* Barron's Educational Series, Inc.
Rogers, Kate. Exploring the Sun. 2017. (J). ***(978-1-5345-2250-3(6),*** KidHaven Publishing) Greenhaven Publishing LLC.
Rosenberg, Pam. Sunny Weather Days. 2006. (Scholastic News Nonfiction Readers Ser.). (ENG., Illus.). 24p. (J). (gr. 1-2). lib. bdg. 22.00 *(978-0-531-16770-0(4))* Scholastic Library Publishing.
Roumanis, Alexis. The Sun. 2016. (Illus.). 24p. (J). *(978-1-5105-0983-2(6))* SmartBook Media, Inc.
Rushworth, Gary. Our Solar System the Sun: Set Of 6. 2011. (Navigators Ser.). (J). pap. 44.00 net. *(978-1-4108-6220-4(8))* Benchmark Education Co.
—Our Solar System: the Sun: Text Pairs. 2008. (Bridges/Navigators Ser.). (J). (gr. 3). 89.00 *(978-1-4108-8371-1(X))* Benchmark Education Co.
Rustad, Martha E. H. Does the Sun Sleep? Noticing Sun, Moon, & Star Patterns. Conger, Holli, illus. 2015. (ENG.). 24p. (J). (gr. k-2). 25.32 *(978-1-4677-8560-0(1),* Millbrook Pr.) Lerner Publishing Group.
—El Sol/the Sun. 2012. (En el Espacio/Out in Space Ser.). (MUL.). 24p. (gr. k-1). pap. 35.70 *(978-1-4296-8557-3(3))*; pap. 5.95 *(978-1-4296-8556-6(5))* Capstone Press of Coughlan Cos.
—The Sun. (Space Ser.). (ENG., Illus.). 24p. (gr. k-1). 2016. lib. bdg. 21.99 *(978-1-4914-8324-4(5))* 2008. pap. 6.29 *(978-1-4296-2837-2(5),* 1284184) Capstone Press of Coughlan Cos. (Pebble Bks.).
—The Sun [Scholastic]. 2009. (Out in Space Ser.). 24p. (gr. k-1). pap. 2.50 *(978-1-4296-4052-7(9),* Pebble Bks.) Capstone Press of Coughlan Cos.
—Today Is a Sunny Day. 2017. (What Is the Weather Today? Ser.). (ENG., Illus.). 24p. (gr. k-1). lib. bdg. 21.99 *(978-1-5157-4920-2(7),* Pebble Bks.) Capstone Press of Coughlan Cos.
Ryback, Carol. The Sun. 2006. (In the Sky Ser.). (Illus.). 24p. (gr. 1-4). pap. 8.15 *(978-0-8368-6351-2(8))*; lib. bdg. 22.00 *(978-0-8368-6346-8(1))* Stevens, Gareth Publishing LLLP. (Weekly Reader Leveled Readers).
Sabatino, Michael. How Long Will the Sun Last? 2013. 32p. (J). (gr. 2-5). 25.25 *(978-1-4339-9223-0(X))*; pap. 10.50 *(978-1-4339-9224-7(8))*; pap. 63.00 *(978-1-4339-9225-4(6))* Stevens, Gareth Publishing LLLP.
Sasso, Sandy Eisenberg. Adam & Eve's New Day. Rothenberg, Joani Keller, illus. 2006. (ENG.). 24p. (gr. -1). bds. 7.99 *(978-1-59473-205-8(1),* 9781594732058, Skylight Paths Publishing) LongHill Partners, Inc.
Schatz, Dennis & Fraknoi, Andrew. Solar Science: Exploring Sunspots, Seasons, Eclipses, & More. 2015. (ENG., Illus.). 360p. (J). pap. 39.95 *(978-1-941316-07-8(7))* National Science Teachers Assn.
Sexton, Colleen. The Sun. 2010. (Exploring Space Ser.). (ENG., Illus.). 24p. (J). (gr. k-3). lib. bdg. 25.95 *(978-1-60014-400-4(4),* Blastoff! Readers) Bellwether Media.
Shepherd, Jodie. Journey to the Sun. Becker, Paula J., illus. 2017. (Cloverleaf Books (tm) — Space Adventures Ser.). (ENG.). 24p. (J). (gr. k-2). 25.32 *(978-1-5124-2538-3(9),* Millbrook Pr.) Lerner Publishing Group.
Shepherd, Jodie. To the Sun! Becker, Paula J., illus. 2017. (Cloverleaf Books (tm) — Space Adventures Ser.). (ENG.). 24p. (J). (gr. k-2). 6.99 ***(978-1-5124-3900-7(2))***; 38.65 ***(978-1-5124-3899-4(5))***; 38.65 ***(978-1-5124-2835-3(3))*** Lerner Publishing Group. (Millbrook Pr.).
Simon, Seymour. The Sun. rev. ed. 2015. (ENG., Illus.). 32p. (J). (gr. 1-5). pap. 6.99 *(978-0-06-234505-9(2))* HarperCollins Pubs.
—The Sun. 2015. (J). lib. bdg. 17.20 *(978-0-606-37729-4(8))* Turtleback Bks.
Sohn, Emily & Harter, Adam. Sun, Moon, & Stars: A Cosmic Case. 2011. (IScience Readers Ser.). 32p. (J). (gr. 3-4). lib. bdg. 22.60 *(978-1-59953-421-3(5))* Norwood Hse. Pr.
Sohn, Emily & Ohlenroth, Patricia. Solar Energy: Saving the School Budget. 2011. (IScience Readers Ser.). 48p. (J). (gr. 5-6). lib. bdg. 23.94 *(978-1-59953-430-5(4))* Norwood Hse. Pr.
Sparrow, Giles. Destination the Sun. (Illus.). 32p. (J). 2010. pap. 10.00 *(978-1-4358-3467-5(4))* 2009. (ENG., lib. bdg. 25.25 *(978-1-4358-3448-4(8))* Rosen Publishing Group, Inc., The. (PowerKids Pr.).
Stefoff, Rebecca. The Sun & the Earth. 2014. 48p. pap. 29.93 *(978-1-62712-521-5(3))* Cavendish Square Publishing.
Sterling, Kristin. It's Sunny Today. 2009. (Lightning Bolt Books — What's the Weather Like? Ser.). (ENG., Illus.). 32p. (gr. k-2). 26.60 *(978-0-7613-4259-5(1),* Lerner Pubns.); pap. 7.95 *(978-0-7613-5022-4(5))* Lerner Publishing Group.
Stewart, Melissa. Beneath the Sun, 1 vol. Bergum, Constance R., illus. 2014. (ENG.). 32p. (J). (gr. -1-3). 16.95 *(978-1-56145-733-5(7))* Peachtree Pubs.
Stewart, Tobi Stanton. Solar Storms. (Reading Room Collection 2 Ser.). 24p. 2009. (gr. 3-4). 42.50 *(978-1-60851-987-3(2),* PowerKids Pr.) 2003. (ENG.). (gr. 3-4). pap. 7.05 *(978-0-8239-6398-0(5),* Rosen Classroom) 2003. (Illus.). (J). lib. bdg. 22.60 *(978-0-8239-3709-7(7))* Rosen Publishing Group, Inc., The.
Storad, Conrad J. Day & Night. 2011. (ENG., Illus.). 24p. (gr. k-1). pap. 8.95 *(978-1-61741-926-3(5))* Rourke Educational Media.
—Our Sun Brings Life. 2011. (ENG., Illus.). 24p. (gr. k-1). pap. 8.95 *(978-1-61741-925-6(7))* Rourke Educational Media.
Stott, Carole. Mission: Space: Explore the Galaxy. 2016. (Illus.). 128p. (J). *(978-1-4654-5376-1(8))* Dorling Kindersley Publishing, Inc.
The Sun. 2nd ed. 2008. (New Solar System Ser.). 32p. (YA). (gr. 3-6). 23.00 *(978-1-60413-205-2(1))* Facts On File, Inc.
The Sun: Level L, 6 vols. (Wonder Worldtm Ser.). 16p. 34.95 *(978-0-7802-4607-2(1))* Wright Group/McGraw-Hill.
The Sun & Other Stars Instructional Guide. 2009. (Grade 8: Science Exit Project Kits Ser.). spiral bd. *(978-1-4042-4026-1(8),* Rosen Classroom) Rosen Publishing Group, Inc., The.
Sundance/Newbridge LLC Staff. Circling the Sun. 2004. (Reading PowerWorks Ser.). (gr. 1-3). 37.50 *(978-0-7608-8916-9(3))* Sundance/Newbridge Educational Publishing.
—Our Sun, Our Weather. 2007. (Early Science Ser.). (gr. k-3). 18.95 *(978-1-4007-6531-7(5))*; pap. 6.10 *(978-1-4007-6527-0(7))* Sundance/Newbridge Educational Publishing.
Taylor-Butler, Christine. The Sun. 2014. (True Book(tm), A — Space Ser.). (ENG.). 48p. (J). lib. bdg. 31.00 *(978-0-531-21157-1(6))* Scholastic Library Publishing.
Tomecek, Steve. Sun. 2016. (Jump into Science Ser.). (ENG., Illus.). 32p. (J). (gr. -1-3). pap. 7.99 *(978-1-4263-2368-3(9),* National Geographic Children's Bks.) National Geographic Society.
—Sun. Golembe, Carla, illus. 2006. (Jump into Science Ser.). (ENG.). 32p. (J). (gr. -1-3). per. 6.95 *(978-0-7922-5582-6(8),* National Geographic Children's Bks.) National Geographic Society.
Trueit, Trudi Strain. Sunny Days. 2009. (Benchmark Rebus: Weather Watch Ser.). 24p. (gr. k-1). 15.95 *(978-0-7614-4017-8(8))* Marshall Cavendish Corp.
Turnbull, Stephanie. Sun, Moon & Stars. Chen, Kuo Kang & Mayer, Uwe, illus. 2006. (Beginners Nature: Level 2 Ser.). 32p. (J). (gr. 1-3). 4.99 *(978-0-7945-1399-3(9),* Usborne) EDC Publishing.
Waldendorf, Kurt. How Far Is the Sun? 2017. (Comparison Fun Ser.). (ENG.). 24p. (J). (gr. -1-2). lib. bdg. 27.07 *(978-1-5038-1677-0(X),* 211512) Child's World, Inc., The.
Waxman, Laura Hamilton. The Sun. 2010. (Early Bird Astronomy Ser.). (ENG.). 48p. (gr. 2-5). lib. bdg. 26.60 *(978-0-7613-3871-0(3))* Lerner Publishing Group.
Wells, Robert E. Why Do Elephants Need the Sun? 2012. (J). 34.28 *(978-1-61913-142-2(0))* Weigl Pubs., Inc.
—Why Do Elephants Need the Sun? Wells, Robert E., illus. 2012. (Wells of Knowledge Science Ser.). (ENG., Illus.). 32p. (J). (gr. -1-3). pap. 7.99 *(978-0-8075-9082-9(7))* Whitman, Albert & Co.
What Is a Sun? 2014. (Let's Find Out! Ser.). 32p. (J). (gr. 3-6). 23.45 *(978-1-62275-461-8(1))* Rosen Publishing Group, Inc., The.
Wilkins, Mary-Jane. The Sun. 2017. (Fast Track: Our Solar System Ser.). (Illus.). 24p. (gr. k-3). 28.50 ***(978-1-78121-363-6(1))*** Brown Bear Bks.
World Book, contrib. by. The Sun & Other Stars. 2nd ed. 2006. (Illus.). 64p. (J). *(978-0-7166-9521-9(9))* World Bk., Inc.
World Book, Inc Staff, contrib. by. The Sun & Other Stars. (J). 2010. *(978-0-7166-9539-4(1))* 2006. 63p. *(978-0-7166-9501-1(4))* World Bk., Inc.

SUN—FICTION

Aesop. The Wind & the Sun. 2012. (J). 29.99 *(978-1-61913-108-8(0))* Weigl Pubs., Inc.
Arrington, Linda. Purple Time. 2012. 36p. pap. 24.95 *(978-1-4626-9613-0(9))* America Star Bks.
Asch, Frank. Moonbear's Sunrise. Asch, Frank, illus. 2014. (Moonbear Ser.). (ENG., Illus.). 32p. (J). (gr. -1-3). 16.99 *(978-1-4424-6647-0(2),* Aladdin) Simon & Schuster Children's Publishing.
Bailey, Jacqui. Sun up, Sun Down: The Story of Day & Night, 1 vol. Lilly, Matthew, illus. 2004. (Science Works). (ENG.). 32p. (gr. 3-6). per. 7.95 *(978-1-4048-1128-7(1))* Picture Window Bks.
Bell, Cassie. The Boy & the Sun. 2016. (Spring Forward Ser.). (J). (gr. k). *(978-1-4900-6011-8(1))* Benchmark Education Co.
Bell-Martin, Janelle. Oh, Mr. Sun, 1 vol. 2012. (Early Childhood Themes Ser.). (ENG.). 16p. (J). (gr. -1-2). pap. 19.99 *(978-1-4333-3472-6(0))*; pap. 6.99 *(978-1-4333-3471-9(2))* Teacher Created Materials, Inc.
Belle, Deborah A. The Day the Sun Called Out Sick!!! Collenberger, Chris, illus. 2013. 30p. pap. 12.99 *(978-0-9853406-0-5(6))* Scribez, Scarebz & Vibez.
Boles, Rhonda G. Why Does the Sun Set, Mommy? 2009. 24p. pap. 10.99 *(978-1-4389-8112-3(0))* AuthorHouse.
Brewer, Michelle. Sunrise in My Cup. 2011. 28p. (gr. -1). pap. 13.99 *(978-1-4567-3995-9(6))* AuthorHouse.
Brinkley, Inez. Rainbows & Promises. 2006. 43p. (J). 15.98 *(978-1-4116-9579-5(8))* Lulu Pr., Inc.
Bronn, Charles Heil. The Sun, the Moon, & the Gardener's Son. Kami, Y. Z., illus. 2006. 30p. (J). (gr. 4-12). reprint ed. 16.00 *(978-1-4223-5222-9(6))* DIANE Publishing Co.
Brown, Betisa Garagozlu. Sister Sun & Sister Moon. 2012. 28p. pap. 13.95 *(978-1-4525-4635-3(5))* Balboa Pr.
Bruchac, Joseph. How Chipmunk Got His Stripes. 2003. (gr. k-3). lib. bdg. 17.20 *(978-0-613-61631-7(6),* Turtleback) Turtleback Bks.
Butler, Andrea. El Senor Sol y el Senor Mar, Level 3. Flor Ada, Alma, tr. Hong, Lily T., illus. 2003. (Dejame Leer Ser.). (SPA.). 16p. (J). (gr. -1-3). 6.50 *(978-0-673-36302-2(3),* Good Year Bks.) Celebration Pr.
Carrington, Samala. Sally Sunshine Mandy Moon. 2011. 20p. (gr. -1). pap. 12.99 *(978-1-4567-6708-2(9))* AuthorHouse.
Clifford, Kathryn & Renn, Chantal. George the Sun Safe Superstar. 2012. (Illus.). 26p. pap. 11.00 *(978-1-78035-317-3(0),* Fastprint Publishing) Upfront Publishing Ltd. GBR. Dist: Printondemand-worldwide.com.
Climent, Elena. Triste Historia del Sol con Final Feliz. (SPA.). (J). (gr. k-3). pap. 4.76 net. *(978-0-8136-1521-9(6),* TR4081) Modern Curriculum Pr.
Dalton, Kippy. Groundhog & the Sun. Czernichowska, Joanna, illus. 2016. (Spring Forward Ser.). (J). (gr. 1). *(978-1-4900-9369-7(9))* Benchmark Education Co.
Davis, Darren. Atlas Gt Planets. 2006. (ENG.). 16p. (J). (gr. -1-12). bds. 5.99 *(978-1-59559-103-6(6))* Left Field,Angel Gate.
Denver, John. John Denver's Sunshine on My Shoulders, 1 vol. Canyon, Christopher, illus. 2004. (ENG.). 32p. pap. 8.95 *(978-1-58469-050-4(X))* Dawn Pubns.
Dewdney, Anna. Llama Llama Sand & Sun. 2015. (Llama Llama Ser.). (ENG., Illus.). 10p. (J). (gr. -1-k). bds. 12.99 *(978-0-448-49639-9(9),* Grosset & Dunlap) Penguin Young Readers Group.
di Chiara, Francesca, illus. The Sun & the Wind. 2007. (First Reading Level 1 Ser.). 32p. (J). (gr. -1-3). 8.99 *(978-0-7945-1811-0(7),* Usborne) EDC Publishing.
Eagle, Golden. Father Sun & Luis the Lizard. l.t. ed. 2005. (Illus.). 22p. (J). per. 12.99 *(978-1-59879-026-9(9))* Lifevest Publishing, Inc.
Esteban, Angel. Pablo, Pablo en Busca del Sol. 2003. (SPA.). 48p. *(978-84-263-1408-6(2),* LV1312) Vives, Luis Editorial (Edelvives) ESP. Dist: Lectorum Pubns., Inc.
Fischer, Kelly. The Moon Throws a Birthday Party. Duckworth, Michelle, illus. 2011. (ENG.). 32p. (J). 19.50 *(978-1-58385-237-8(9))* ktf-writers-studio.
Gerstein, Mordicai. The Night World. 2015. (ENG., Illus.). 40p. (J). (gr. -1-3). 18.00 *(978-0-316-18822-7(0))* Little Brown & Co.
Gill, David Macinnis. Shadow on the Sun. 2075. (ENG.). 352p. (J). (gr. 9). 9.99 *(978-0-06-207336-5(2),* Greenwillow Bks.) HarperCollins Pubs.
Glickman, Claudia. Skin Sense. 2007. (Illus.). 16p. (J). *(978-0-615-16242-3(8))* L.G. Publishing.
Goins, Debra Lynn. One Day I Tried to Catch the Sun. 2011. 24p. (gr. 1-2). pap. 11.32 *(978-1-4634-1872-4(8))* AuthorHouse.
Graham, Bob. How the Sun Got to Coco's House. Graham, Bob, illus. 2015. (ENG., Illus.). 40p. (J). (gr. -1-1). 17.99 *(978-0-7636-8109-8(1))* Candlewick Pr.
Guess What the Sun Saw? Individual Title Six-Packs. (gr. -1-2). 23.00 *(978-0-7635-8808-3(3))* Rigby Education.
Handa, Nimret. Good Night Stories. 2004. (Illus.). 20p. (J). *(978-81-291-0373-4(7))* Rupa & Co.
Hardesty, Michael. Who Made the Sun, Mommy? 2011. 28p. 15.95 *(978-1-4520-7721-5(5))* AuthorHouse.
Heo, Yumi, illus. Sun & Moon Have a Tea Party. 2016. (J). *(978-0-385-39033-0(5),* Schwartz & Wade Bks.) Random Hse. Children's Bks.
Hija del Sol y de Luna (Daughter of Sun & Moon) (SPA.). 24p. (J). 4.95 *(978-84-246-1610-6(3))* La Galera, S.A. Editorial ESP. Dist: AIMS International Bks., Inc.
Hofmeister, Alan, et al. Mat in the Sun. (Reading for All Learners Ser.). (Illus.). (J). pap. *(978-1-56861-094-8(7))* Swift Learning Resources.
Holm, Jennifer L. I'm Sunny! (My First Comics) Holm, Matthew, illus. 2016. (ENG.). 24p. (J). (— 1). 7.99 *(978-0-553-53346-0(0),* Random Hse. Bks. for Young Readers) Random Hse. Children's Bks.
Hooten, K. J. The Egg Nanny Tales. 2008. 98p. pap. 19.95 *(978-1-60563-722-8(X))* America Star Bks.
Hopkins, Leslie. A World Apart. 2012. 20p. pap. 17.99 *(978-1-4772-6783-7(2))* AuthorHouse.
Hougasian, Amy. The Big Foot Sun. 2008. 36p. pap. 16.99 *(978-1-4343-3920-1(3))* AuthorHouse.
Inkpen, Mick. Ploo & the Terrible Gnobbler. 2003. (ENG., Illus.). 32p. (J). (gr. -1-k). 17.99 *(978-0-340-85573-7(8))* Hodder & Stoughton GBR. Dist: Hachette Bk. Group.
Jasmine, Jean-Pierre. It's Raining Uber. 2013. 166p. (J). pap. 13.99 *(978-1-4808-0122-6(4))* Archway Publishing.
Jefferson, Patti Brassard. How Long Will You Love Me? Jefferson, Patti Brassard, illus. 2013. (Illus.). 28p. pap. 12.95 *(978-1-61244-178-8(5))* Halo Publishing International.
Johnson, Angela. A Cool Moonlight. 2005. (ENG.). 144p. (J). (gr. 3-7). reprint ed. 6.99 *(978-0-14-240284-9(2),* Puffin Books) Penguin Young Readers Group.

S

Johnson, Anne & Mortenson. Catch the Sun. 2013. 11.50 *(978-1-59298-983-6(7))* Beaver's Pond Pr., Inc.

Kleven, Elisa. Sun Bread. 2004. (gr. k-3). 17.20 *(978-0-613-83005-8(9),* Turtleback) Turtleback Bks.

Kuracka, Vicki. When the Sun Sleeps. 2010. 16p. pap. 9.99 *(978-1-60911-509-8(0),* Eloquent Bks.) Strategic Book Publishing & Rights Agency (SBPRA).

Lawrence, Maggie. An Element of Fun. 2008. 76p. pap. 27.95 *(978-1-4092-4969-6(7))* Lulu Pr., Inc.

Layman, John S. Armageddon & Son. 2005. (ENG., Illus.). 96p. (YA). pap. 9.95 *(978-1-932664-33-1(5),* 9781932664331) Oni Pr., Inc.

Lee, Zaina. Sun Takes a Holiday. 2009. 28p. pap. 13.99 *(978-1-4389-9992-0(5))* AuthorHouse.

Lenhardt, Lisa M. Good Morning Son. 2012. 16p. pap. 15.99 *(978-1-4772-1647-7(2))* AuthorHouse.

—Good Morning Sun. 2012. 16p. pap. 15.99 *(978-1-4772-1651-4(0))* AuthorHouse.

Lewis, Kelly. Where Is the Sun? 2016. (Spring Forward Ser.). (J). (gr. 1). *(978-1-4900-3726-4(8))* Benchmark Education Co.

Llewellyn, Claire. The Sun Is up Pink a Band. Lopez, Ayesha, illus. 2016. (Cambridge Reading Adventures Ser.). (ENG.). 16p. pap. 6.56 *(978-1-107-54987-6(6))* Cambridge Univ. Pr.

Luna, Pilar P. Hello, Sunny Day! 2012. 40p. pap. 20.99 *(978-1-4490-0244-2(7))* AuthorHouse.

Mack, Karen. The Magical Adventures of Sun Beams. 2009. 42p. 31.99 *(978-1-4415-3636-5(1))* Xlibris Corp.

Matsakis, Cynthia. Sister Sun, Brother Storm. Silver, Jane, illus. 2012. 32p. 24.95 *(978-1-4575-0768-7(4))* Dog Ear Publishing, LLC.

McClure, Brian D. The Sun & the Moon. 2006. (Illus.). 36p. (J). 14.95 *(978-1-933426-09-9(8))* Universal Flag Publishing.

Mill, Fran. Harriet's Hunt for the Sun. 2010. 28p. pap. 12.49 *(978-1-4520-1491-3(4))* AuthorHouse.

Miller, Jules, illus. When Night Became Day. 2015. (ENG.). 32p. (J). (gr. -1-k). 16.95 *(978-1-62914-632-4(3),* Sky Pony Pr.) Skyhorse Publishing Co., Inc.

Mutuku, E. M. When the Sun Challenged the Moon. 2012. 20p. pap. 15.50 *(978-1-4634-4718-2(3))* AuthorHouse.

Neher, Anna-Luise. A Tale from the Trunk No. 2: With Words! Words! Words! 2009. 56p. pap. 10.82 *(978-1-4251-8284-7(4))* Trafford Publishing.

Newton, Maria. Sol the Sun. 2011. 24p. pap. 28.03 *(978-1-4568-5420-1(8))* Xlibris Corp.

Nieto, Terry. Sun Go Away. 2010. 24p. pap. 15.99 *(978-1-4535-3543-1(8))* Xlibris Corp.

Nix, Pamela. Tummel the Tumbleweed. Barnes, Trisha, ed. Paulson, Arlie & Nix, Pamela, illus. 2011. 26p. (J). pap. 7.99 *(978-0-9815914-9-0(3))* River Canyon Pr.

Nolan, Allia Zobel. When God Tucks in the Day. Chung, Chi, illus. 2005. 16p. (J). 12.99 *(978-0-8254-5524-7(3))* Kregel Pubns.

O'Day, Joseph E. I Like Sunshine! Foster, Ron, illus. 2007. (J). *(978-1-929039-41-8(7))* Ambassador Bks., Inc.

Paratore, Coleen Murtagh. Catching the Sun. 2010. (J). *(978-0-618-45780-9(1))* Houghton Mifflin Harcourt Publishing Co.

Pittis, Arthur M. Sun So Hot I Froze to Death: A Waldorf Reader for Advanced Fourth Grade. Mitchell, David S., ed. Peacock, Ausa M., illus. 2005. (ENG.). (J). bds. 12.00 *(978-1-888365-65-8(X))* Waldorf Publications.

Pugliano-Martin, Carol. How Davy Crockett Moved the Sun: An American Tall Tale. 2006. (J). pap. *(978-1-4108-6168-9(6))* Benchmark Education Co.

Rihani, Ina. Song to the Sun. 2012. 56p. pap. 31.99 *(978-1-4653-1123-8(8))* Xlibris Corp.

Ritz, Lee F. The Sun & the Wind. Hale, Randy, illus. 2013. 62p. 23.99 *(978-1-940840-00-0(7))* Ritz, Lee Pubns.

Rodenbur, Susan. The Boy Who Captured the Sun. Kirkpatrick, Karen, illus. 2007. 32p. per. 12.95 *(978-1-59858-515-5(0))* Dog Ear Publishing, LLC.

Rodricks, Marie. Razzle the Sunbeam. 2008. 68p. pap. 10.49 *(978-1-4343-9651-8(7))* AuthorHouse.

Rosario, Joann. Where Did Sabrina Go? Rosario, Joann, illus. 2004. (Illus.). 13p. (J). (gr. -1-5). pap. 10.00 *(978-0-9758746-1-5(6))* J.G.R. Enterprises.

Salwi, Dilip. Meet the Four Elements (Marathi) 2nd ed. 2013. (ENG.). 64p. pap. 6.95 *(978-93-5036-121-4(3))* Ratna, Sagar Pvt. Ltd. IND. Dist: Midpoint Trade Bks., Inc.

Santillo, LuAnn. The Sun. Santillo, LuAnn, ed. 2003. (Half-Pint Kids Readers Ser.). (Illus.). 7p. (J). (gr. -1-1). pap. 1.00 *(978-1-59256-047-9(4))* Half-Pint Kids, Inc.

Seda, Gus. Prohex the Cat. 2012. 44p. pap. 24.95 *(978-1-4626-7704-7(5))* America Star Bks.

Shaposhnik, Alina. A Warm Yellow Pancake, 1 vol. 2010. 22p. 24.95 *(978-1-4489-7067-4(9))* PublishAmerica, Inc.

Sharpe, Katie & Sharpe, Tony. Wake up Sun. 2008. (ENG.). 28p. 14.99 *(978-1-4389-2897-5(1))* AuthorHouse.

Sijercic, Hedina. An Unusual Family: A Romani Folktale. Greven, Doris, illus. 2009. 28p. pap. *(978-0-9781707-7-6(6))* Magoria Bks.

Sinois, Latrice J. You Are My Sunshine. 2012. 20p. pap. 17.99 *(978-1-4772-5731-9(4))* AuthorHouse.

Smale, Denise L. What If the Sun Didn't Rise. Smale, Denise L. & Blowars, Ryan, illus. 2011. 32p. pap. 24.95 *(978-1-4560-5032-0(X))* America Star Bks.

Sparks, Shanti. Honey & the Sunset. 2008. (Illus.). 38p. (J). pap. 9.00 *(978-0-8059-7553-6(5))* Dorrance Publishing Co., Inc.

Stead, Judy, illus. Mister Sun. 2006. (J). *(978-1-58987-097-0(2))* Kindermusik International.

The Sun in the Sky. 2003. lib. bdg. 12.99 *(978-0-9740997-0-5(8))* Lisa The Weather Wonder Inc.

The Sun's Story. 2013. (Illus.). 36p. pap. 14.99 *(978-1-940426-01-3(4))* Love Ink LLC.

Swarbrick, David E. Peggy's Play House. 2011. 24p. pap. 24.95 *(978-1-4626-1989-4(4))* America Star Bks.

Sweeney, Monica. How the Crayons Saved the Rainbow. Parker-Thomas, Feronia, illus. 2016. (ENG.). 32p. (J). (gr. -1-k). 16.99 *(978-1-5107-0583-8(X),* Sky Pony Pr.) Skyhorse Publishing Co., Inc.

Thompson, Carol. Sun! 2014. (Whatever the Weather Ser.). (ENG., Illus.). 12p. (J). (gr. k-k). bds. *(978-1-84643-680-2(X))* Child's Play International Ltd.

Tomos, Angharad. Diffodd Yr Haul. 2005. (WEL., Illus.). 48p. pap. *(978-0-86243-080-1(1))* Y Lolfa.

Tsinajinnie, Veronica. Johonaa'ei: Bringer of Dawn. Thomas, Peter A., tr. from NAV. Singer, Ryan, illus. 2007. (ENG & NAV.). 32p. (J). (gr. -1-3). 17.95 *(978-1-893354-54-8(7))* Salina Bookshelf Inc.

Veil, Karney. Sun & Moon Play Hide & Seek: A Children's Story. 2012. 24p. (-18). pap. 24.95 *(978-1-4626-9401-3(2))* America Star Bks.

Waller, C. L. Lady Sun & the Man in the Moon. 2008. 16p. per. 24.95 *(978-1-4241-8670-9(6))* America Star Bks.

Walton, Ann. The Tale of Sun & Moon. Hinrichsen, Tamsin, illus. 2010. (ENG.). 32p. (J). (gr. k-2). 11.95 *(978-1-77009-705-6(8))* Jacana Media ZAF. Dist: Independent Pubs. Group.

Where Does the Sun Go? 2006. (Illus.). 40p. (J). (gr. -1-3). 14.95 *(978-0-9786813-0-2(4))* Elora Pr.

Wilhelm, Hans. Hello, Sun! Wilhelm, Hans, illus. 2005. (Illus.). 32p. (gr. k-2). 15.25 *(978-1-57505-348-6(9))* Lerner Publishing Group.

Yankey, Lindsey. Sun & Moon. 2015. (ENG., Illus.). 32p. (J). (gr. -1-3). 16.95 *(978-1-927018-60-6(9))* Simply Read Bks. CAN. Dist: Ingram Publisher Services.

Young, Justin. A Most Vivid Day! 2010. (ENG., Illus.). 40p. (J). (gr. k-2). 16.95 *(978-0-9785418-1-1(2))* Dream Character, Inc.

SUN—RADIATION

see Solar Radiation

SUN-DIALS

see Sundials

SUN GLASSES

see Eyeglasses

SUNDAY

see Sabbath

SUNDIALS

Bryson, Theresa. Make a Sundial. 2011. (Early Connections Ser.). (J). *(978-1-61672-558-7(3))* Benchmark Education Co.

SUNFLOWERS

Barry, Frances. Big Yellow Sunflower. Barry, Frances, illus. 2008. (Fold Out & Find Out Ser.). (ENG., Illus.). 22p. (J). (-k). 8.99 *(978-0-7636-3724-8(6))* Candlewick Pr.

Bellavia, Rebecca. Planting Sunflowers: Represent & Interpret Data. 2014. (Math Masters: Measurement & Data Ser.). 24p. (J). (gr. 2-3). 23.60 *(978-1-4777-6408-4(9));* (ENG.). pap. 8.25 *(978-1-4777-4825-1(3))* Rosen Publishing Group, Inc., The. (Rosen Classroom).

Berger, Melvin & Berger, Gilda. A Sunflower Grows Up. 2008. (Illus.). 32p. (J). *(978-0-439-02530-0(3))* Scholastic, Inc.

Cooper, Jason. Sunflower. 2003. (Life Cycles II Ser.). (Illus.). 24p. (J). lib. bdg. 27.07 *(978-1-58952-708-9(9))* Rourke Educational Media.

De la Bédoyère, Camilla. Seed to Sunflower. 2012. (Illus.). 24p. (gr. 1-3). pap. 7.95 *(978-1-926853-40-6(7))* Saunders Bk. Co. CAN. Dist: RiverStream Publishing.

—Seed to Sunflower. 2013. (Illus.). 24p. (J). *(978-1-4351-4710-2(3))* Barnes & Noble, Inc.

Diary of a Sunflower: Individual Title Six-Packs. (Story Steps Ser.). (gr. k-2). 32.00 *(978-0-7635-9839-6(9))* Rigby Education.

Dickmann, Nancy. A Sunflower's Life, 1 vol. 2010. (Watch It Grow Ser.). (ENG., Illus.). 24p. (gr. -1-1). 22.65 *(978-1-4329-4144-4(5));* pap. 6.29 *(978-1-4329-4153-6(4))* Heinemann-Raintree. (Acorn).

—La Vida del Girasol. 2011. (¡Mira Cómo Crece! Ser.). 24p. (gr. -1-1). (SPA & ENG.). 22.65 *(978-1-4329-5277-8(3));* (ENG & SPA.). pap. 6.29 *(978-1-4329-5289-1(7))* Heinemann-Raintree. (Bellota).

Ferrero, Mar, illus. My Sunflower: A Pop-Up Book from Seed to Sunflower. 2016. (Grow with Me! Ser.). (ENG.). 16p. (J). (gr. -1-3). 16.95 *(978-1-63322-084-3(2))* Quarto Publishing Group USA.

Franks, Katie. Sunflowers up Close. (Nature up Close Ser.). 24p. 2009. (gr. k-1). 42.50 *(978-1-61514-829-5(9))* 2008. (Illus.). (J). (gr. 3-7). lib. bdg. 22.60 *(978-1-4042-4141-1(8))* Rosen Publishing Group, Inc., The. (PowerKids Pr.).

—Sunflowers up Close / Los Girasoles. 2009. (Nature up Close / la naturaleza de cerca Ser.). (ENG & SPA.). 24p. (gr. k-1). 42.50 *(978-1-61514-835-6(3),* Editorial Buenas Letras) Rosen Publishing Group, Inc., The.

—Sunflowers up Close/Los Girasoles. Sanz, Pilar, tr. from ENG. 2008. (Nature up Close / la Naturaleza de Cerca Ser.). (Illus.). 24p. (J). (gr. -1-3). lib. bdg. 22.60 *(978-1-4042-7680-2(7),* Editorial Buenas Letras) Rosen Publishing Group, Inc., The.

Hipp, Andrew. El Girasol: Por Dentro y Por Fuera. Brusca, Maria Cristina, tr. di Gaudesi, Andrea Ricciardi, illus. 2004. (Explora la Naturaleza (Getting into Nature) Ser.). (SPA.). 27p. (J). (gr. 3-7). lib. bdg. 25.25 *(978-1-4042-2868-9(3))* Rosen Publishing Group, Inc., The.

—El Girasol: Por dentro y por fuera (Sunflower:Inside & Out) 2009. (Explora la Naturaleza (Getting into Nature) Ser.). (SPA.). 32p. (gr. 3-4). 47.90 *(978-1-61512-336-0(9),* Editorial Buenas Letras) Rosen Publishing Group, Inc., The.

—Sunflower. 2004. (Getting into Nature Ser.). (Illus.). 32p. (J). lib. bdg. 25.25 *(978-0-8239-4210-7(4))* Rosen Publishing Group, Inc., The.

—Sunflowers: Inside & Out. 2009. (Getting into Nature Ser.). 32p. (gr. 3-4). 47.90 *(978-1-61512-726-9(7),* PowerKids Pr.) Rosen Publishing Group, Inc., The.

Life Cycles - from Seed to Sunflower. 2005. (J). per. 8.95 *(978-1-59566-145-6(X))* QEB Publishing Inc.

Markovics, Joyce L. Sunflower. 2015. (See It Grow Ser.). (ENG.). 24p. (J). (gr. -1-3). lib. bdg. 23.93 *(978-1-62724-843-3(9))* Bearport Publishing Co., Inc.

Massie, Elizabeth. Looking at a Sunflower. 2016. (Spring Forward Ser.). (J). (gr. 1). *(978-1-4900-2234-5(1))* Benchmark Education Co.

Nelson, Robin. Sunflowers. 2009. pap. 34.95 *(978-0-7613-4122-2(6))* Lerner Publishing Group.

Peters, Elisa. It's a Sunflower! 2009. (Everyday Wonders Ser.). 24p. (gr. 1-1). 42.50 *(978-1-61512-324-7(5));* (Illus.). (J). lib. bdg. 22.60 *(978-1-4042-4458-0(1))* Rosen Publishing Group, Inc., The. (PowerKids Pr.).

—It's a Sunflower! Es un Girasol! 2009. (Everyday Wonders / Maravillas de Todos Los días Ser.). (SPA & ENG.). 24p. (J). lib. bdg. 22.60 *(978-1-4358-2523-9(3),* PowerKids Pr.) Rosen Publishing Group, Inc., The.

—It's a Sunflower! / ¡Es un Girasol! 2009. (Everyday Wonders / Maravillas de todos los días Ser.). (ENG & SPA.). 24p. (gr. 1-1). 42.50 *(978-1-61512-330-8(X),* Editorial Buenas Letras) Rosen Publishing Group, Inc., The.

Phelps, Bonnie. The Life Cycle of a Sunflower. 2015. (Watch Them Grow! Ser.). (ENG.). 24p. (J). (gr. 1-1). pap. 8.25 *(978-1-4994-0684-9(3),* PowerKids Pr.) Rosen Publishing Group, Inc., The.

Reid, Barbara. Seed to Sunflower: A First Look Board Book. Crysler, Ian, photos by. 2004. (Illus.). 12p. (J). (gr. k-2). reprint ed. 10.00 *(978-0-7567-7853-8(0))* DIANE Publishing Co.

Riggs, Kate. Grow with Me: Sunflower. 2013. (Grow with Me Ser.). (ENG.). 32p. (J). (gr. 1-3). pap. 9.99 *(978-0-89812-771-3(8),* Creative Paperbacks) Creative Co., The.

—Sunflower. 2012. (Grow with Me Ser.). (Illus.). 32p. (J). (gr. 3-8). 19.95 *(978-1-60818-218-3(5),* Creative Education) Creative Co., The.

Schuh, Mari C. From Seed to Sunflower. 2016. (Start to Finish, Second Ser.). (ENG.). 24p. (J). (gr. k-3). 23.99 *(978-1-5124-0914-7(6))* Lerner Publishing Group.

Smith, Ian. How Does it Grow? From Seed to Sunflower. 2004. (Illus.). 24p. (J). lib. bdg. 15.95 *(978-1-59566-016-9(X))* QEB Publishing Inc.

Stewart, David. How a Seed Grows into a Sunflower. Franklin, Carolyn, illus. 2008. (Amaze Ser.). (ENG.). 32p. (J). (gr. k-3). 27.00 *(978-0-531-20442-9(1),* Children's Pr.) Scholastic Library Publishing.

Sunflowers. 2009. (First Step Nonfiction - Plant Life Cycles Ser.). (gr. k-2). 21.27 *(978-0-7613-4072-0(6),* Lerner Pubns.) Lerner Publishing Group.

Thomson, Ruth. A Sunflower's Life Cycle. 2010. (Let's Look at Life Cycles Ser.). 24p. (J). (ENG.). pap. 8.25 *(978-1-61532-230-5(2),* PowerKids Pr.); lib. bdg., E-Book 42.50 *(978-1-4488-0360-6(8));* (Illus.). lib. bdg. 22.60 *(978-1-61532-219-0(1),* PowerKids Pr.) Rosen Publishing Group, Inc., The.

Watts, Barrie. Sunflower. 2003. 32p. (J). lib. bdg. 24.25 *(978-1-58340-232-0(2))* Black Rabbit Bks.

SUNFLOWERS—FICTION

Brown, Ruth. Ten Seeds. 2013. (ENG., Illus.). 24p. (J). (gr. -1-k). 10.99 *(978-1-84939-251-8(X))* Andersen Pr. GBR. Dist: Independent Pubs. Group.

Harris, Mary Beth. Susie Sunflower. Pederson, Gunda, illus. 2010. 24p. 16.49 *(978-1-4520-5171-0(2))* AuthorHouse.

Higgs, Liz Curtis. The Sunflower Parable, 1 vol. Munger, Nancy, illus. 10th anniv. ed. 2007. (Parable Ser.). (ENG.). 32p. (gr. -1-2). 7.99 *(978-1-4003-0845-3(3))* Nelson, Thomas Inc.

I Am a Wish. 2013. 36p. pap. 16.99 *(978-1-4808-0094-6(5))* Archway Publishing.

Kaider, Azi Sabi. Angela's Sunflower. 2012. 24p. pap. 16.95 *(978-1-4772-9703-2(0))* AuthorHouse.

Kosinski, Colleen Rowan, illus. Lilla's Sunflowers. 2016. (ENG.). 32p. (J). (gr. -1-k). 16.99 *(978-1-5107-0464-0(7),* Sky Pony Pr.) Skyhorse Publishing Co., Inc.

Maile's Sunflower. 2nd ed. 2006. (J). *(978-0-9787864-0-3(8))* MJ Brooks Co.

Mockford, Caroline. What's This? A Seed's Story. Mockford, Caroline, illus. 2007. (ENG., Illus.). 32p. (J). (gr. -1-2). pap. 7.99 *(978-1-84686-071-3(7))* Barefoot Bks., Inc.

Monroe, Darrell. Sammy Sunflower. 2012. 32p. pap. 19.99 *(978-1-4772-6891-9(X))* AuthorHouse.

My Sunflowers. 2003. (J). per. *(978-1-57657-897-1(6))* Paradise Pr., Inc.

Ochiltree, Dianne. Sunflowers Measure Up! 2003. (Hello Math Reader Ser.). (Illus.). (J). *(978-0-439-24228-8(2))* Scholastic, Inc.

Parton, Paula. I Always Wondered. Parton, Paula, illus. 2009. (Illus.). 44p. pap. 11.95 *(978-1-935118-48-0(X))* Bellissima Publishing, LLC.

Post, Cynthia W. Carrie Flower: Goes to Camp. 2011. pap. 15.95 *(978-0-7414-6462-0(4))* Infinity Publishing.

—Carrie Flower: Goes to the Hospital. 2011. pap. 12.95 *(978-0-7414-6461-3(6))* Infinity Publishing.

—Carrie Flower: Meet Carrie Flower. 2011. pap. 10.95 *(978-0-7414-6463-7(2))* Infinity Publishing.

Powell, Jillian. Sam's Sunflower. Boccardo, Johanna, illus. 2008. (Tadpoles Ser.). (ENG.). 24p. (J). (gr. -1-3). pap. *(978-0-7787-3895-4(7));* lib. bdg. *(978-0-7787-3864-0(7))* Crabtree Publishing Co.

Rochester, Andre, illus. The Sunflower & Rose. 2010. (ENG.). 36p. (J). 22.95 *(978-0-9817291-1-4(8))* Metaphors 4 Life.

Tazewell, Lora A. Jelly Bread & Water Juice. 2009. 48p. pap. 17.49 *(978-1-4389-1973-7(5))* AuthorHouse.

Vojtech, Anna. Surprise in the Meadow. Vojtech, Anna, illus. 2016. (ENG., Illus.). 32p. (J). 16.95 *(978-0-8234-3556-2(3))* Holiday Hse., Inc.

Wagner, Larry. The Adventures of Sally Sunflower. 2004. 23p. pap. 24.95 *(978-1-4137-4009-7(X))* PublishAmerica, Inc.

SUNKEN CITIES

see Extinct Cities

SUNKEN TREASURE

see Buried Treasure

SUPERIOR, LAKE—FICTION

Brown, Anne Greenwood. Deep Betrayal. 2013. (ENG.). 352p. (YA). (gr. 7). pap. 9.99 *(978-0-385-74204-7(5),* Ember) Random Hse. Children's Bks.

—Lies Beneath. 2013. (ENG.). 320p. (YA). (gr. 7). pap. 8.99 *(978-0-385-74202-3(9),* Ember) Random Hse. Children's Bks.

Erdrich, Louise. Chickadee. Erdrich, Louise, illus. 2012. (Birchbark House Ser.: 4). (Illus.). 208p. (J). (gr. 3-7). (ENG.). 16.99 *(978-0-06-057790-2(8));* lib. bdg. 17.89 *(978-0-06-057791-9(6))* HarperCollins Pubs.

Ernst, Kathleen. Trouble at Fort la Pointe. 2009. (Mysteries Through Time Ser.). 144 - 176p. (YA). (gr. 4-8). 31.95 *(978-1-60754-426-5(1));* pap. 15.25 *(978-1-60754-427-2(X))* Windmill Bks.

Wargin, Kathy-jo. The Voyageur's Paddle. Geister, David & Van Frankenhuyzen, Gijsbert, illus. rev. ed. 2007. (Myths, Legends, Fairy & Folktales Ser.). (ENG.). 40p. (J). (gr. 1-4). 19.99 *(978-1-58536-007-9(4),* 201942) Sleeping Bear Pr.

SUPERMAN (FICTITIOUS CHARACTER)—FICTION

Aptekar, Devan. Darkseid's Revenge. Gordon, Eric A. & Gordon, Steven E., illus. 2012. (ENG.). 24p. (J). (gr. -1-3). pap. 3.99 *(978-0-06-188533-4(9),* HarperFestival) HarperCollins Pubs.

—Darkseid's Revenge. Gordon, Eric A. & Gordon, Steven E., illus. 2012. (Justice League Classic 8X8 Ser.). (J). lib. bdg. 13.55 *(978-0-606-23566-2(3),* Turtleback) Turtleback Bks.

Baltazar, Art & Aureliani, Franco. Adventures Begin! Baltazar, Art, illus. 2013. (Superman Family Adventures Ser.). (ENG., Illus.). 32p. (gr. 1-2). 22.60 *(978-1-4342-4786-5(4))* Stone Arch Bks.

—And Now... Braniac!, 1 vol. 2014. (Superman Family Adventures Ser.). (ENG., Illus.). 32p. (gr. 1-2). 22.60 *(978-1-4342-6478-7(5))* Stone Arch Bks.

—And Now... Ma Kent!, 1 vol. 2014. (Superman Family Adventures Ser.). (ENG., Illus.). 32p. (gr. 1-2). 22.60 *(978-1-4342-9006-9(9))* Stone Arch Bks.

—Attack of the Toyman!, 1 vol. 2014. (Superman Family Adventures Ser.). (ENG., Illus.). 32p. (gr. 1-2). 22.60 *(978-1-4342-6476-3(9))* Stone Arch Bks.

—Because You Demanded It... Darkseid!, 1 vol. 2014. (Superman Family Adventures Ser.). (ENG., Illus.). 32p. (gr. 1-2). 22.60 *(978-1-4342-9005-2(0))* Stone Arch Bks.

—Enter Bizarro!, 1 vol. 2013. (Superman Family Adventures Ser.). (ENG., Illus.). 32p. (gr. 1-2). 22.60 *(978-1-4342-4790-2(2))* Stone Arch Bks.

—General Zod Dogs!, 1 vol. 2014. (Superman Family Adventures Ser.). (ENG., Illus.). 32p. (gr. 1-2). 22.60 *(978-1-4342-6479-4(3))* Stone Arch Bks.

—Menace of Metallo! Baltazar, Art, illus. 2013. (Superman Family Adventures Ser.). (ENG., Illus.). 32p. (gr. 1-2). 22.60 *(978-1-4342-4794-0(5))* Stone Arch Bks.

—The Mysterious Alien Menace!, 1 vol. 2014. (Superman Family Adventures Ser.). (ENG., Illus.). 32p. (gr. 1-2). 22.60 *(978-1-4342-6477-0(7))* Stone Arch Bks.

—Superman Family Adventures, 1 vol. (Superman Family Adventures Ser.). (ENG.). 32p. (gr. 1-2). 2014. 271.20 *(978-1-4342-8766-3(1))* 2013. 135.60 *(978-1-4342-8829-5(3))* Stone Arch Bks.

—Who Is the Purple Superman?, 1 vol. Baltazar, Art, illus. 2013. (Superman Family Adventures Ser.). (ENG., Illus.). 32p. (gr. 1-2). 22.60 *(978-1-4342-4793-3(7))* Stone Arch Bks.

Batman vs. Superman: Their Greatest Battles. 2015. lib. bdg. 20.85 *(978-0-606-37886-4(3))* Turtleback Bks.

Bird, Benjamin. The Amazing Adventures of Superman!, 4 vols. Levins, Tim, illus. 2015. (Amazing Adventures of Superman! Ser.). (ENG.). 32p. (gr. k-2). 101.28 *(978-1-4795-8002-6(3))* Picture Window Bks.

—Bubble Trouble! Levins, Tim, illus. 2015. (Amazing Adventures of Superman! Ser.). (ENG.). 32p. (gr. k-2). pap. 3.95 *(978-1-4795-6524-5(5),* DC Super Heroes) Stone Arch Bks.

—Magic Monsters! Levins, Tim, illus. 2015. (Amazing Adventures of Superman! Ser.). (ENG.). 32p. (gr. k-2). pap. 3.95 *(978-1-4795-6525-2(3),* DC Super Heroes) Stone Arch Bks.

—Supergirl's Pet Problem! Levins, Tim, illus. 2015. (Amazing Adventures of Superman! Ser.). (ENG.). 32p. (gr. k-2). pap. 3.95 *(978-1-4795-6523-8(7),* DC Super Heroes) Stone Arch Bks.

—Superman Colors, 1 vol. Beavers, Ethen, illus. 2014. (DC Board Bks.). (ENG.). 20p. (gr. -1 — 1). bds. 5.99 *(978-1-4795-5890-2(7))* Picture Window Bks.

Bird, Benjamin & Siegel, Jerry. Day of the Bizarros! Levins, Tim, illus. 2015. (Amazing Adventures of Superman! Ser.). (ENG.). 32p. (gr. k-2). pap. 3.95 *(978-1-4795-6522-1(9),* DC Super Heroes) Stone Arch Bks.

Black, Jake & Meredith Books Staff. Robo Monster. Stewart, Scott, illus. 2008. 22p. (J). pap. 3.99 *(978-0-696-23957-1(4))* Meredith Bks.

Bond, Gwenda. Double Down. 2016. (Lois Lane Ser.). (ENG.). 384p. (gr. 9-12). 16.95 *(978-1-63079-038-7(9))* Switch Pr.

—Fallout. (Lois Lane Ser.). (ENG.). 304p. (gr. 9-12). 2016. pap. 9.95 *(978-1-63079-006-6(0))* 2015. 16.95 *(978-1-63079-005-9(2))* Switch Pr.

Bookworks, Downtown & Katz, David Bar. My First Superman Book: Touch & Feel. 2011. (DC Super Heroes Ser.). (ENG.). 12p. (J). bds. 11.99 *(978-1-935703-00-6(5))* Downtown Bookworks.

Bright, J. E. Cyborg Superman. Levins, Tim, illus. 2013. (Man of Steel Ser.). (ENG.). 88p. (gr. 2-3). pap. 5.95 *(978-1-4342-4219-8(6))* Stone Arch Bks.

—Cyborg Superman, 1 vol. Levins, Tim & DC Comics Staff, illus. 2013. (Man of Steel Ser.). (ENG.). 88p. (gr. 2-3). 26.65 *(978-1-4342-4089-7(4))* Stone Arch Bks.

—Lex Luthor & the Kryptonite Caverns, 1 vol. Vecchio, Luciano, illus. 2012. (DC Super-Villains Ser.). (ENG.). 56p. (gr. 2-3). pap. 5.95 *(978-1-4342-3896-2(2),* DC Super-villains) Stone Arch Bks.

Cosentino, Ralph. Superman: The Story of the Man of Steel. 2010. (ENG., Illus.). 40p. (J). (gr. -1-2). 16.99 *(978-0-670-06285-0(5),* Viking Books for Young Readers) Penguin Young Readers Group.

Dahl, Michael. A Buried Starship. Levins, Tim & Vecchio, Luciano, illus. 2017. (Superman Tales of the Fortress of Solitude Ser.). (ENG.). 40p. (gr. 1-3). lib. bdg. 24.65 *(978-1-4965-4395-0(5),* DC Super Heroes) Stone Arch Bks.

—Good Morning, Superman! Lozano, Omar, illus. 2017. (DC Super Heroes Ser.). (ENG.). 32p. (gr. -1-2). lib. bdg. 22.65 *(978-1-5158-0970-8(6),* DC Super Heroes) Stone Arch Bks.

—The Museum Monsters. Schoening, Dan, illus. (Superman Ser.). (ENG.). 56p. (gr. 2-3). 2013. pap. 4.95 *(978-1-4342-1372-3(2))* 2009. lib. bdg. 26.65 *(978-1-4342-1157-6(6))* Stone Arch Bks. (DC Super Heroes).

—Rays of Doom. Levins, Tim & Vecchio, Luciano, illus. 2017. (Superman Tales of the Fortress of Solitude Ser.). (ENG.). 40p. (gr. 1-3). lib. bdg. 24.65 *(978-1-4965-4396-7(3),* DC Super Heroes) Stone Arch Bks.

—Superman Tales of the Fortress of Solitude. 2017. (Superman Tales of the Fortress of Solitude Ser.). (ENG.). 40p. (gr. 1-3). 98.60 *(978-1-4965-4414-8(5),* DC Super Heroes) Stone Arch Bks.

Dahl, Michael, et al. The Last Son of Krypton. 2009. (Superman Ser.). (ENG., Illus.). 56p. (gr. 2-3). lib. bdg. 26.65 *(978-1-4342-1155-2(X),* DC Super Heroes) Stone Arch Bks.

—Last Son of Krypton. 2013. (Superman Ser.). (ENG., Illus.). 56p. (gr. 2-3). pap. 4.95 *(978-1-4342-1370-9(6),* DC Super Heroes) Stone Arch Bks.

DC Comics Staff. Superman. 2013. (Stand-Up Mover Ser.: 1). (ENG.). 10p. (J). bds. 8.99 *(978-0-7944-2839-6(8))* Reader's Digest Assn., Inc., The.
DC Comics Staff, et al. Death of Superman. Kahan, Bob, ed. rev. ed. 2011. (Superman Ser.). (ENG., Illus.). 168p. (YA). pap. 12.99 *(978-1-56389-097-0(6))* DC Comics.
Dorling Kindersley Publishing Staff. Amazing Battles! 2015. (DK Readers Ser.). (ENG., Illus.). 48p. (J). (gr. 1-3). pap. 3.99 *(978-1-4654-3011-3(3),* DK Children) Dorling Kindersley Publishing, Inc.
Fisch, Sholly & Age, Heroic. Happy Birthday, Superman!, 1 vol. Bone, J., illus. 2014. (DC Super Friends Ser.). (ENG.). 32p. (gr. 1-2). 22.60 *(978-1-4342-9222-3(3))* Stone Arch Bks.
Fisch, Sholly, et al. Bottle of the Planets. 2015. (All-New Batman: the Brave & the Bold Ser.). (ENG., Illus.). 32p. (gr. 2-3). lib. bdg. 22.60 *(978-1-4342-9658-0(X))* Stone Arch Bks.
Hoena, Blake A. Under the Red Sun, 1 vol. Schoening, Dan, illus. (Superman Ser.). (ENG.). 56p. (gr. 2-3). 2013. pap. 4.95 *(978-1-4342-1375-4(7))* 2009. lib. bdg. 26.65 *(978-1-4342-1159-0(2))* Stone Arch Bks. (DC Super Heroes).
Kiernan, Kenny, illus. Save the Day! 2013. (J). *(978-1-4844-0146-0(8))* Scholastic, Inc.
King, Trey. Friends & Foes! Wang, Sean, illus. 2015. (LEGO DC Super Heroes Ser.: 1). (ENG.). 24p. (J). (gr. -1-3). pap. 3.99 *(978-0-545-78504-4(9))* Scholastic, Inc.
—Race Around the World! Wang, Sean, illus. 2016. (LEGO DC Super Heroes Ser.). (ENG.). 24p. (J). (gr. -1-3). pap. 3.99 *(978-0-545-86797-9(5))* Scholastic, Inc.
Korte, Steve. Mxy's Magical Mayhem. Levins, Tim, illus. 2013. (Man of Steel Ser.). (ENG.). 88p. (gr. 2-3). pap. 5.95 *(978-1-4342-4826-8(7));* 26.65 *(978-1-4342-4488-8(1))* Stone Arch Bks.
Lemke, Donald. Bizarro's Last Laugh. 2017. (Justice League Classic: I Can Read! Ser.). (J). lib. bdg. 13.55 ***(978-0-606-39632-5(2))*** Turtleback Bks.
—Glowing Kryptonite & Illustrated Book. 2013. (Miniature Editions Ser.). (ENG., Illus.). 48p. pap. 9.95 *(978-0-7624-4909-5(8),* Running Pr. Minature Editions) Running Pr. Bk. Pubs.
—Superman: A Giant Attack. 2015. (Justice League Classic: I Can Read! Ser.). (J). lib. bdg. 13.55 *(978-0-606-36955-8(4))* Turtleback Bks.
—Superman - A Giant Attack. Ferguson, Lee, illus. 2015. (I Can Read Level 2 Ser.). (ENG.). 32p. (J). (gr. -1-3). pap. 3.99 *(978-0-06-234488-5(9))* HarperCollins Pubs.
—Superman Classic: Bizarro's Last Laugh. Spaziante, Patrick, illus. 2017. (I Can Read Level 2 Ser.). 32p. (J). (gr. -1-3). pap. 3.99 *(978-0-06-236089-2(2))* HarperCollins Pubs.
—Superman Classic: Pranking News. Spaziante, Patrick, illus. 2016. (I Can Read Level 2 Ser.). 32p. (J). (gr. -1-3). pap. 3.99 *(978-0-06-236085-4(X))* HarperCollins Pubs.
—Superman Versus the Silver Banshee. 2013. (Justice League Classic: I Can Read! Ser.). (J). lib. bdg. 13.55 *(978-0-606-27156-1(2),* Turtleback) Turtleback Bks.
—Superman vs. the Silver Banshee. Smith, Andy, illus. 2013. (I Can Read Level 2 Ser.). (ENG.). 32p. (J). (gr. -1-3). pap. 3.99 *(978-0-06-188524-2(X))* HarperCollins Pubs.
Lemke, Donald B. Superman. Ku, Min Sung, illus. 2014. (DC Super Friends Word Adventures Ser.). (ENG.). 12p. (gr. -1 — 1). bds. 6.99 *(978-1-4795-5243-6(7))* Picture Window Bks.
The Man of Steel. 2013. (Man of Steel Ser.). (ENG.). 88p. (gr. 2-3). 213.20 *(978-1-4342-4811-4(9));* 106.60 *(978-1-4342-4812-1(7));* pap. 47.60 *(978-1-4342-4863-3(1));* pap. 23.80 *(978-1-4342-4864-0(X))* Stone Arch Bks. (DC Super Heroes).
Manning, Matthew K. The Poisoned Planet, 1 vol. Vecchio, Luciano, illus. 2012. (Man of Steel Ser.). (ENG.). 88p. (gr. 2-3). lib. bdg. 26.65 *(978-1-4342-4091-0(6))* Stone Arch Bks.
—Superman: An Origin Story. Baltazar, Art & Vecchio, Luciano, illus. 2015. (DC Super Heroes Origins Ser.). (ENG.). 48p. (gr. k-2). lib. bdg. 23.99 *(978-1-4342-9728-0(4))* Stone Arch Bks.
—Superman & the Poisoned Planet. Vecchio, Luciano, illus. 2012. (Man of Steel Ser.). (ENG.). 88p. (gr. 2-3). pap. 5.95 *(978-1-4342-4224-2(2))* Stone Arch Bks.
—Superman Battles the Billionaire Bully. Beavers, Ethen, illus. 2017. (DC Super Hero Stories Ser.). (ENG.). 56p. (gr. 1-3). lib. bdg. 25.32 *(978-1-4965-4634-0(2),* DC Super Heroes) Stone Arch Bks.
McCLOUD, Scott. Be Careful What You Wish For... Burchett, Rick & Austin, Terry, illus. 2012. (Superman Adventures Ser.). (ENG.). 32p. (gr. 2-3). lib. bdg. 22.60 *(978-1-4342-4550-2(0))* Stone Arch Bks.
—Distant Thunder, 1 vol. Burchett, Rick & Austin, Terry, illus. 2012. (Superman Adventures Ser.). (ENG.). 32p. (gr. 2-3). 22.60 *(978-1-4342-4551-9(9))* Stone Arch Bks.
—Eye to Eye, 1 vol. Burchett, Rick & Austin, Terry, illus. 2012. (Superman Adventures Ser.). (ENG.). 32p. (gr. 2-3). lib. bdg. 22.60 *(978-1-4342-4552-6(7))* Stone Arch Bks.
—Seonimod, 1 vol. Austin, Terry & Burchett, Rick, illus. 2013. (Superman Adventures Ser.). (ENG.). 32p. (gr. 2-3). lib. bdg. 22.60 *(978-1-4342-4711-7(2))* Stone Arch Bks.
—Superman Adventures. 2013. (Superman Adventures Ser.). (ENG.). 32p. (gr. 1-2). 90.40 *(978-1-4342-4859-6(3))* Stone Arch Bks.
—Tiny Problems!, 1 vol. Austin, Terry & Burchett, Rick, illus. 2013. (Superman Adventures Ser.). (ENG.). 32p. (gr. 2-3). lib. bdg. 22.60 *(978-1-4342-4712-4(0))* Stone Arch Bks.
Miller, Bryan Q. The Guardian, Vol. 1. 2013. (ENG., Illus.). 144p. pap. 14.99 *(978-1-4012-3824-7(6))* DC Comics.
Peterson, Scott. Parasite's Feeding Frenzy, 1 vol. Cavallaro, Mike, illus. 2012. (Man of Steel Ser.). (ENG.). 88p. (gr. 2-3). lib. bdg. 26.65 *(978-1-4342-4099-6(1));* pap. 5.95 *(978-1-4342-4221-1(8))* Stone Arch Bks.
Rau, Zachary. The Incredible Shrinking Super Hero! With Wonder Woman. Gordon, Steven E., illus. 2009. (ENG.). 24p. (J). (gr. -1-3). pap. 3.99 *(978-0-06-187855-8(3),* HarperFestival) HarperCollins Pubs.
Rosen, Lucy. Friends & Foes. Gordon, Steven E. & Gordon, Eric A., illus. 2013. (I Can Read Level 2 Ser.). (ENG.). 32p. (J). (gr. -1-3). pap. 3.99 *(978-0-06-223595-4(8))* HarperCollins Pubs.
—Parasite City. Gordon, Steven E. & Gordon, Eric A., illus. 2011. (ENG.). 24p. (J). (gr. -1-3). pap. 3.99 *(978-0-06-188532-7(0),* HarperFestival) HarperCollins Pubs.
—Superman Phonics Fun. 2012. (My First I Can Read Ser.). (ENG., Illus.). 12p. (J). (gr. -1-3). pap. 12.99 *(978-0-06-188541-9(X))* HarperCollins Pubs.
—Superman's Superpowers. Tong, Andie, illus. 2013. (I Can Read Level 2 Ser.). (ENG.). 32p. (J). (gr. -1-3). pap. 3.99 *(978-0-06-223597-8(4))* HarperCollins Pubs.
Sazaklis, John. Battle - Battle in Metropolis. Smith, Andy & Vancata, Brad, illus. 2013. (ENG.). 24p. (J). (gr. -1-3). pap. 3.99 *(978-0-06-188537-2(1),* HarperFestival) HarperCollins Pubs.
—Battle in Metropolis. 2013. (Justice League Classic 8X8 Ser.). lib. bdg. 13.55 *(978-0-606-31827-3(5),* Turtleback) Turtleback Bks.
—Day of Doom. 2013. (Justice League Classic: I Can Read! Ser.). (J). lib. bdg. 13.55 *(978-0-606-32162-4(4),* Turtleback) Turtleback Bks.
—The Fate of Krypton. Roberts, Jeremy, illus. 2013. (Man of Steel Ser.). (ENG.). 24p. (J). (gr. -1-3). pap. 3.99 *(978-0-06-223593-0(1),* HarperFestival) HarperCollins Pubs.
—Man of Steel. 2013. (Man of Steel Ser.). (ENG.). 12p. (J). (gr. -1-3). pap. 6.99 *(978-0-06-223605-0(9),* HarperFestival) HarperCollins Pubs.
—Superman: Escape from the Phantom Zone. Gordon, Steven E., illus. 2011. (I Can Read Level 2 Ser.). (ENG.). 32p. (J). (gr. -1-3). pap. 3.99 *(978-0-06-188519-8(3))* HarperCollins Pubs.
—Superman Classic - Day of Doom. Smith, Andy & Vancata, Brad, illus. 2013. (I Can Read Level 2 Ser.). (ENG.). 32p. (J). (gr. -1-3). pap. 3.99 *(978-0-06-221001-2(7))* HarperCollins Pubs.
—Superman Saves Smallville. Roberts, Jeremy, illus. 2013. (Man of Steel Ser.). (ENG.). 24p. (J). (gr. -1-3). pap. 3.99 *(978-0-06-223603-6(2),* HarperFestival) HarperCollins Pubs.
—Superman vs. Bizarro, 1 vol. Vecchio, Luciano, illus. 2013. (DC Super Heroes Ser.). (ENG.). 56p. (gr. 2-3). lib. bdg. 26.65 *(978-1-4342-6012-3(7))* Stone Arch Bks.
Sazaklis, John & Farley, John. Attack of the Toyman. Smith, Andy, illus. 2012. (ENG.). 24p. (J). (gr. -1-3). pap. 3.99 *(978-0-06-188535-8(5),* HarperFestival) HarperCollins Pubs.
—Attack of the Toyman. 2012. (Justice League Classic 8X8 Ser.). (J). lib. bdg. 13.55 *(978-0-606-26859-2(6),* Turtleback) Turtleback Bks.
Sazaklis, John & Vancata, Brad. Superman: Day of Doom. Smith, Andy, illus. 2013. 29p. (YA). *(978-1-4844-0620-5(6))* Harper & Row Ltd.
Scholastic, Inc. Staff & Kogge, Michael. Cross Fire. 2016. (Batman vs. Superman: Dawn of Justice Ser.). (ENG.). 144p. (J). (gr. 2-5). pap. 5.99 *(978-0-545-91630-1(5))* Scholastic, Inc.
—Cross Fire. 2016. (Batman vs. Superman: Dawn of Justice Ser.). (ENG.). 144p. (J). (gr. 2-5). lib. bdg. 16.00 *(978-0-606-38097-3(3))* Turtleback Bks.
Schwartz, Alvin. The Atomic Age Superman, Vol. 2. Boring, Wayne, illus. 2016. (Superman Ser.). (ENG.). 180p. 49.99 *(978-1-63140-537-2(3),* 9781631405372) Idea & Design Works, LLC.
Shealy, Dennis & Random House Staff. Heroes United! - Attack of the Robot! Doescher, Erik et al, illus. 2008. (Pictureback(R) Ser.). (ENG.). 32p. (J). (gr. -1-2). pap. 4.99 *(978-0-375-84409-6(0),* Random Hse. Bks. for Young Readers) Random Hse. Children's Bks.
Siegel, Jerry, et al. Adventures of Superman. Gordon, Steven E. et al, illus. 2013. 125p. (J). *(978-1-4351-5063-8(5))* Barnes & Noble, Inc.
Simonson, Louise. Lex Luthor's Power Grab! Vecchio, Luciano, illus. 2015. (Superman: Comic Chapter Bks.). (ENG.). 88p. (gr. 3-7). lib. bdg. 21.32 *(978-1-4965-0508-8(5))* Stone Arch Bks.
Simonson, Louise & Sutton, Laurie S. Superman: Comic Chapter Books, 2 vols. Vecchio, Luciano, illus. 2015. (Superman: Comic Chapter Bks.). (ENG.). 88p. (gr. 3-7). 42.64 *(978-1-4965-1999-3(X))* Stone Arch Bks.
Slott, Dan, et al. Masquerade in Red!, 1 vol. 2013. (Batman Adventures Ser.). (ENG.). 32p. (gr. 2-3). 22.60 *(978-1-4342-6036-9(4))* Stone Arch Bks.
Sonneborn, Scott. Moon Bandits. Cavallaro, Mike & DC Comics Staff, illus. 2013. (Man of Steel Ser.). (ENG.). 88p. (gr. 2-3). 26.65 *(978-1-4342-4093-4(2))* Stone Arch Bks.
—The Moon Bandits. Cavallaro, Mike, illus. 2013. (Man of Steel Ser.). (ENG.). 88p. (gr. 2-3). pap. 5.95 *(978-1-4342-4223-5(4))* Stone Arch Bks.
—Partners in Peril. Smith, Andy & Vancata, Brad, illus. 2013. (ENG.). 24p. (J). (gr. -1-3). pap. 3.99 *(978-0-06-221007-4(6),* HarperFestival) HarperCollins Pubs.
Stephens, Sarah Hines. Superman Classic: Superman & the Mayhem of Metallo. Mada Design Staff, illus. 2010. (Superman Classics). (ENG.). 24p. (J). (gr. -1-3). pap. 3.99 *(978-0-06-188529-7(0),* HarperFestival) HarperCollins Pubs.
Stevens, Eric, et al. The Menace of Metallo, 1 vol. 2013. (Superman Ser.). (ENG., Illus.). 56p. (gr. 2-3). pap. 4.95 *(978-1-4342-1371-6(4),* DC Super Heroes) Stone Arch Bks.
Stewart, Yale. Alien Superman!, 1 vol. Stewart, Yale, illus. 2014. (Amazing Adventures of Superman! Ser.). (ENG., Illus.). 32p. (gr. k-2). lib. bdg. 25.32 *(978-1-4795-5733-2(1),* DC Super Heroes) Stone Arch Bks.
—The Amazing Adventures of Superman! Stewart, Yale, illus. 2014. (Amazing Adventures of Superman! Ser.). (ENG., Illus.). 32p. (gr. k-2). 101.28 *(978-1-4795-5816-2(8),* DC Super Heroes) Stone Arch Bks.
—Battle of the Super Heroes!, 1 vol. Stewart, Yale, illus. 2014. (Amazing Adventures of Superman! Ser.). (ENG., Illus.). 32p. (gr. k-2). 25.32 *(978-1-4795-5731-8(5),* DC Super Heroes) Stone Arch Bks.
—Creatures from Planet X!, 1 vol. Stewart, Yale, illus. 2014. (Amazing Adventures of Superman! Ser.). (ENG., Illus.). 32p. (gr. k-2). lib. bdg. 25.32 *(978-1-4795-5734-9(X),* DC Super Heroes) Stone Arch Bks.
—Escape from Future World!, 1 vol. Stewart, Yale, illus. 2014. (Amazing Adventures of Superman! Ser.). (ENG., Illus.). 32p. (gr. k-2). lib. bdg. 25.32 *(978-1-4795-5732-5(3),* DC Super Heroes) Stone Arch Bks.
Stone Arch Books & Fisch, Sholly. DC Super Friends, 1 vol. 2014. (DC Super Friends Ser.). (ENG.). 32p. (gr. 1-2). 90.40 *(978-1-4342-9526-2(5))* Stone Arch Bks.
Stone Arch Books Staff & Sutton, Laurie S. Superman: Comic Chapter Books, 1 vol. Vecchio, Luciano, illus. 2014. (Superman: Comic Chapter Bks.). (ENG.). 88p. (gr. 3-7). 42.64 *(978-1-4342-9378-7(5),* DC Super Heroes) Stone Arch Bks.
Sudduth, Brent. I Am Superman! Edwards, Tommy Lee, illus. 2006. (Superman Returns Ser.). 24p. (J). (gr. 4-7). pap. 3.99 *(978-0-696-22905-3(6))* Meredith Bks.
Sudduth, Brent & Meredith Books Staff. Doom in a Box. Panosian, Dan, illus. 2008. 22p. (J). pap. 3.99 *(978-0-696-23956-4(6))* Meredith Bks.
Sudeith, Alaina. Superman Classic: The Superman Reusable Sticker Book. 2011. (ENG.). 12p. (J). (gr. -1-3). pap. 6.99 *(978-0-06-188538-9(X),* HarperFestival) HarperCollins Pubs.
Superman Adventures. 2013. (Superman Adventures Ser.). (ENG.). 32p. (gr. 1-2). 180.80 *(978-1-4342-4860-2(7))* Stone Arch Bks.
Superman: Comic Chapter Books, 1 vol. 2014. (Superman: Comic Chapter Bks.). (ENG.). 88p. (gr. 3-7). pap. 11.90 *(978-1-4342-9535-4(4),* DC Super Heroes) Stone Arch Bks.
Sutton, Laurie S. The Dark Side of the Apokolips. Vecchio, Luciano, illus. 2015. (Superman: Comic Chapter Bks.). (ENG.). 88p. (gr. 3-7). lib. bdg. 21.32 *(978-1-4965-0509-5(3))* Stone Arch Bks.
—Demons of Deep Space. Vecchio, Luciano, illus. 2012. (Man of Steel Ser.). (ENG.). 88p. (gr. 2-3). lib. bdg. 26.65 *(978-1-4342-4098-9(3));* pap. 5.95 *(978-1-4342-4220-4(X))* Stone Arch Bks.
—Going Ape. Gordon, Eric A. & Gordon, Steven E., illus. 2012. (I Can Read Level 2 Ser.). (ENG.). 32p. (J). (gr. -1-3). pap. 3.99 *(978-0-06-188522-8(3))* HarperCollins Pubs.
—Going Ape. 2012. (Justice League Classic: I Can Read! Ser.). (J). lib. bdg. 13.55 *(978-0-606-26260-6(1),* Turtleback) Turtleback Bks.
—Night of a Thousand Doomsdays, 1 vol. Vecchio, Luciano, illus. 2013. (Man of Steel Ser.). (ENG.). 88p. (gr. 2-3). 26.65 *(978-1-4342-4487-1(3))* Stone Arch Bks.
—Night of a Thousand Doomsdays. Vecchio, Luciano, illus. 2013. (Man of Steel Ser.). (ENG.). 88p. (gr. 2-3). pap. 5.95 *(978-1-4342-4827-5(5))* Stone Arch Bks.
—The Planet Collector, 1 vol. Vecchio, Luciano, illus. 2014. (Superman: Comic Chapter Bks.). (ENG.). 88p. (gr. 3-7). 21.32 *(978-1-4342-9133-2(2))* Stone Arch Bks.
—The Real Man of Steel, 1 vol. Vecchio, Luciano, illus. 2014. (Superman: Comic Chapter Bks.). (ENG.). 88p. (gr. 3-7). 21.32 *(978-1-4342-9134-9(0))* Stone Arch Bks.
Teitelbaum, Michael. I Am Superman. Farley, Rick, illus. 2009. (I Can Read Level 2 Ser.). (ENG.). 32p. (J). (gr. -1-3). pap. 3.99 *(978-0-06-187857-2(X))* HarperCollins Pubs.
—I Am Superman. 2009. (Justice League Classic: I Can Read! Ser.). (J). lib. bdg. 13.55 *(978-0-606-06951-9(8),* Turtleback) Turtleback Bks.
—Meet the Super Heroes. 2009. (Justice League Classic: I Can Read! Ser.). (J). lib. bdg. 13.55 *(978-0-606-06941-0(0),* Turtleback) Turtleback Bks.
—Superman Versus Mongul. Mada Design Staff, illus. 2011. (I Can Read Level 2 Ser.). (ENG.). 32p. (J). (gr. -1-3). pap. 3.99 *(978-0-06-188518-1(5))* HarperCollins Pubs.
Vivinetto, Gina. With Superman & Wonder Woman. Farley, Rick & Tripp, Kanila, illus. 2011. (ENG.). 24p. (J). (gr. -1-3). pap. 3.99 *(978-0-06-188531-0(2),* HarperFestival) HarperCollins Pubs.
Wallace, Daniel. The Man of Tomorrow. 2016. (Backstories Ser.). (ENG.). 128p. (J). (gr. 3-7). pap. 5.99 *(978-0-545-86818-1(1))* Scholastic, Inc.
Weissburg, Paul. The Man of Gold, 1 vol. Cavallaro, Mike & Levins, Tim, illus. 2012. (Man of Steel Ser.). (ENG.). 88p. (gr. 2-3). lib. bdg. 26.65 *(978-1-4342-4095-8(9));* pap. 5.95 *(978-1-4342-4222-8(6))* Stone Arch Bks.
Wrecks, Billy. Batman's Hero Files (DC Super Friends) Random House Editors et al, illus. 2015. (Step into Reading Ser.). (ENG.). 24p. (J). (gr. -1-1). 4.99 *(978-0-553-50808-6(3),* Random Hse. Bks. for Young Readers) Random Hse. Children's Bks.
—Bizarro Day! 2013. (Step into Reading Level 2 Ser.). lib. bdg. 13.55 *(978-0-606-26971-1(1),* Turtleback) Turtleback Bks.
—Bizarro Day! (DC Super Friends) Legramandi, Francesco, illus. 2013. (Step into Reading Ser.). (ENG.). 32p. (J). (gr. k-3). pap. 3.99 *(978-0-307-98119-6(3),* Random Hse. Bks. for Young Readers) Random Hse. Children's Bks.
—Green Lantern vs. the Meteor Monster! Random House Staff, illus. 2011. (Pictureback Ser.). (ENG.). 24p. (J). (gr. -1-2). pap. 3.99 *(978-0-375-87297-6(3),* Random Hse. Bks. for Young Readers) Random Hse. Children's Bks.
—Heroes! Golden Books Staff, illus. 2011. (Holographic Sticker Book Ser.). (ENG.). 48p. (J). (gr. -1-2). pap. 3.99 *(978-0-375-85331-9(6),* Golden Bks.) Random Hse. Children's Bks.
—Superman! (DC Super Friends) Beavers, Ethen, illus. 2013. (Little Golden Book Ser.). (ENG.). 24p. (J). (-k). 4.99 *(978-0-307-93195-5(1),* Golden Bks.) Random Hse. Children's Bks.
—X-Ray Vision! (DC Super Friends) Borkowski, Michael, illus. 2014. (Pictureback Ser.). (ENG.). 16p. (J). (gr. -1-2). 4.99 *(978-0-385-38718-7(0),* Random Hse. Bks. for Young Readers) Random Hse. Children's Bks.
Yang, Gene Luen. Superman, Volume 1: Before Truth. 2016. lib. bdg. 29.40 *(978-0-606-39485-7(0))* Turtleback Bks.

SUPERMARKETS

Allan, Jasper. Let's Go to the Supermarket. 2008. (Real Readers - Upper Emergent Ser.). (ENG., Illus.). 12p. (gr. 1-2). pap. 5.90 *(978-0-8239-8125-0(8))* Rosen Publishing Group, Inc., The.
Cohen, Marina. 3-D Shapes. 2010. (My Path to Math Ser.). (ENG.). 24p. (J). (gr. k-3). *(978-0-7787-6779-4(5));* pap. *(978-0-7787-6788-6(4))* Crabtree Publishing Co.
Colby, Jennifer. Grocery Store. 2016. (21st Century Junior Library: Explore a Workplace Ser.). (ENG., Illus.). 24p. (J). (gr. 2-5). 27.07 *(978-1-63471-073-2(8),* 208371) Cherry Lake Publishing.
Craats, Rennay. Le Magasin Général: Le Début de la Colonie. Karvonen, Tanjah, tr. from ENG. 2011. (FRE., Illus.). 24p. (gr. 3-6). *(978-1-77071-420-5(0))* Weigl Educational Pubs. Ltd.
Hutchings, Amy. What Happens at a Supermarket? 2009. (Where People Work Ser.). 24p. (J). (gr. -1-3). lib. bdg. 22.00 *(978-1-4339-0069-3(6),* Weekly Reader Leveled Readers) Stevens, Gareth Publishing LLLP.
—What Happens at a Supermarket?/Qué Pasa en un Supermercado? 2009. (Where People Work Ser.). 24p. (gr. -1-3). pap. 8.15 *(978-1-4339-0133-1(1),* Weekly Reader Leveled Readers) Stevens, Gareth Publishing LLLP.
Hutchings, Amy & Nations, Susan. What Happens at a Supermarket?/Qué Pasa en un Supermercado? 2009. (Where People Work/Dónde Trabaja la Gente? Ser.). (SPA & ENG.). 24p. (gr. -1-3). (J). lib. bdg. 22.00 *(978-1-4339-0077-8(7));* pap. 8.15 *(978-1-4339-0141-6(2))* Stevens, Gareth Publishing LLLP. (Weekly Reader Leveled Readers).
Keogh, Josie. A Trip to the Grocery Store. 2012. (PowerKids Readers: My Community Ser.). (ENG., Illus.). 24p. (J). (gr. k-2). 22.60 *(978-1-4488-7403-3(3));* pap. 8.25 *(978-1-4488-7482-8(3))* Rosen Publishing Group, Inc., The. (PowerKids Pr.).
—A Trip to the Grocery Store: De Visita en la Tienda. 2012. (PowerKids Readers: My Community / Mi comunidad Ser.). (SPA & ENG., Illus.). 24p. (J). (gr. k-2). lib. bdg. 22.60 *(978-1-4488-7827-7(6),* PowerKids Pr.) Rosen Publishing Group, Inc., The.
Marsico, Katie. Working at a Grocery Store. 2008. (21st Century Junior Library: Careers Ser.). (ENG., Illus.). 24p. (gr. 2-5). lib. bdg. 25.64 *(978-1-60279-265-4(8),* 200170) Cherry Lake Publishing.
Mattern, Joanne. I Use Math at the Store. 2005. (I Use Math Ser.). (Illus.). 24p. (gr. k-3). pap. 8.15 *(978-0-8368-4863-2(2));* lib. bdg. 22.00 *(978-0-8368-4856-4(X))* Stevens, Gareth Publishing LLLP. (Weekly Reader Leveled Readers).
Mattern, Joanne, et al. I Use Math at the Store (USO las Matematicas en la Tienda) 2005. (I Use Math/ Uso las matematicas Ser.). (ENG & SPA., Illus.). 24p. (gr. k-3). lib. bdg. 22.00 *(978-0-8368-6001-6(2),* Weekly Reader Leveled Readers) Stevens, Gareth Publishing LLLP.
The Super Supermarket Plan: Individual Title Six-Packs. (gr. k-1). 23.00 *(978-0-7635-8844-1(X))* Rigby Education.

S

SUPERMARKETS—FICTION

Benavides, Desiree. Little Henry's Adventures: Henry's Trip to the Supermarket. 2008. 24p. pap. 24.95 *(978-1-60563-011-3(X))* America Star Bks.
Elya, Susan Middleton. Bebé Goes Shopping. Salerno, Steven, illus. 2008. (ENG.). 36p. (J). (gr. -1-3). pap. 7.99 *(978-0-15-206142-5(8))* Houghton Mifflin Harcourt Publishing Co.
Food from the Farm: Individual Title Six-Packs. (gr. -1-2). 23.00 *(978-0-7635-8994-3(2))* Rigby Education.
Gutman, Dan. Rappy Goes to the Supermarket. Bowers, Tim, illus. 2017. (I Can Read Level 2 Ser.). 32p. (J). (gr. -1-3). 3.99 *(978-0-06-225262-3(3))* HarperCollins Pubs.
Herman, Alison & Grossman, Lynne. Dolly Goes to the Supermarket. Eve, Lealand, illus. 2007. 22p. (J). 24.96 *(978-0-9746153-0-1(7))* DMH Pr., Inc.
In the Supermarket: Individual Title, 6 Packs. (Chiquilibros Ser.). (gr. k-1). 23.00 *(978-0-7635-0453-3(X))* Rigby Education.
Meredith Books Staff. Foodfight! Curry, Don, ed. 2008. (I Can Find It Ser.). 22p. (J). 7.99 *(978-0-696-23425-5(4))* Meredith Bks.
—Foodfight! Deluxe Sound Storybook. Curry, Don, ed. 2008. 22p. (J). 15.95 *(978-0-696-23424-8(6))* Meredith Bks.
Neill, Joan Walmer. The Amazing Tale of Bub the Trier. 2012. 36p. pap. 20.00 *(978-1-4772-6240-5(7))* AuthorHouse.
Rockwell, Anne. At the Supermarket. Rockwell, Anne, illus. 2015. (ENG., Illus.). 30p. (J). (gr. -1-k). bds. 7.99 *(978-1-62779-315-5(1),* 9781627793155, Holt, Henry & Co. Bks. For Young Readers) Holt, Henry & Co.
Scarry, Richard. Richard Scarry's the Supermarket Mystery. 2014. (ENG., Illus.). 34p. (J). (gr. 1-2). 4.95 *(978-1-4549-1011-4(9))* Sterling Publishing Co., Inc.
Scholastic Inc, contrib. by. Supermarket Surprises. 2015. (Shopkins Ser.). (ENG., Illus.). 16p. (J). (gr. -1-3). pap. 6.99 *(978-0-545-90500-8(1))* Scholastic, Inc.
Snell, Gordon & Askin, Corrina. The Supermarket Ghost. Byrne, Bob, illus. 2007. (ENG.). 80p. (J). pap. 10.95 *(978-1-84717-049-1(8))* O'Brien Pr., Ltd., The IRL. Dist: Dufour Editions, Inc.
Spitzer, Linda & Myers, Sarah. Tales of the Paper Bag Fairies/Color Version. 2005. 54p. (J). pap. 14.95 *(978-1-4116-4095-5(0))* Lulu Pr., Inc.
When Dad Got Lost: Individual Title, 6 packs. (gr. -1-2). 27.00 *(978-0-7635-9484-8(9))* Rigby Education.

SUPERNATURAL

see also Spirits

Chmielewski, Gary. The Ghost Zone: Jokes, Riddles, Tongue Twisters & Daffynitions. Caputo, Jim, illus. rev. ed. 2009. (Funny Zone Ser.). (ENG.). 24p. (J). (gr. 2-4). lib. bdg. 22.60 *(978-1-59953-297-4(2))* Norwood Hse. Pr.
Cox, Barbara & Forbes, Scott. Beyond the Grave, Vol. 1. 2014. (Creepy Chronicles Ser.). (ENG., Illus.). 32p. (J). (gr. 5-6). 26.60 *(978-1-4824-0226-1(2))* Stevens, Gareth Publishing LLLP.
—Maniacal Monsters & Bizarre Beasts, Vol. 1. 2014. (Creepy Chronicles Ser.). (ENG., Illus.). 32p. (J). (gr. 5-6). 26.60 *(978-1-4824-0236-0(X))* Stevens, Gareth Publishing LLLP.
Day, Jon. Arswyd Mawr! Yr Anhygoel A'r Anesboniadwy. 2005. (WEL., Illus.). 32p. pap. *(978-0-86381-415-0(8))* Gwasg Carreg Gwalch.
—Supernatural. 2004. (Illus.). 32p. pap. *(978-1-904516-01-9(7),* Pavilion Children's Books) Pavilion Bks.
Ganeri, Anita & West, David. Supernatural Creatures. 2012. (Illus.). 32p. 70.50 *(978-1-4488-5233-8(1));* pap. 11.75 *(978-1-4488-5232-1(3));* lib. bdg. 26.50 *(978-1-4488-5197-3(1))* Rosen Publishing Group, Inc., The. (PowerKids Pr.).
Howard, Ian T. One Love, Two Worlds. Bishop, Tracey, illus. 2010. 36p. pap. 14.75 *(978-1-60911-771-9(9),* Eloquent Bks.) Strategic Book Publishing & Rights Agency (SBPRA).
Kroll, Jennifer. The Science of Superpowers. 2016. (Time for Kids Nonfiction Readers Ser.). (ENG.). (J). (gr. 5-8). lib. bdg. 22.10 ***(978-0-606-39544-1(X))*** Turtleback Bks.
Kuligowski, Stephanie. Unsolved! Mysterious Events, 1 vol. 2nd rev. ed. 2013. (Nonfiction Readers Ser.). (ENG., Illus.). 48p. (J). (gr. 4-4). pap. 29.96 *(978-1-4807-1103-7(9))* Shell Educational Publishing.
—Unsolved! Mysterious Places, 1 vol. 2nd rev. ed. 2013. (Nonfiction Readers Ser.). (ENG., Illus.). 48p. (J). (gr. 4-4).

pap. 29.96 (978-1-4807-1104-4(7)) Shell Educational Publishing.

Mariolle, Mathieu. Even for A Dreamer Like Me. 3rd rev. ed. 2010. pap. 56.72 (978-0-7613-6960-8(0)) Lerner Publishing Group.

Miles, Liz. Terrifying Tales: Ghosts, Ghouls, & Other Things That Go Bump in the Night. 2010. (Culture in Action Ser.). (ENG., Illus.). 32p. (gr. 3-6). 30.65 (978-1-4109-3926-5(X), NA-r) Heinemann-Raintree.

Omoth, Tyler & McCollum, Sean. Paranormal Handbooks. 2016. (Paranormal Handbooks Ser.). (ENG.). 32p. (gr. 3-4). 111.96 (978-1-5157-1325-8(3), Edge Bks.) Capstone Press of Coughlan Cos.

Steinberg, Lewis M. Investigating Miracles. 2016. (Understanding the Paranormal Ser.). 48p. (J). (gr. 5-5). lib. bdg. 26.85 (978-1-5081-0223-6(6), Britannica Educational Publishing) Rosen Publishing Group, Inc., The.

Stevens, C. J. The Supernatural Side of Maine. 2003. (YA). 12.00 (978-1-882425-16-7(2)) Wade, John Pub.

Walker, Kathryn. Mysterious Healing. 2009. (Unsolved! Ser.). (ENG., Illus.). 32p. (J). (gr. 3-5). pap. (978-0-7787-4163-3(X)); (gr. 4-6). lib. bdg. (978-0-7787-4150-3(8)) Crabtree Publishing Co.

World Book, Inc Staff, contrib. by. Tales of Mystery & the Unknown: A Supplement to Childcraft — the How & Why Library. 2006. (Illus.). 208p. (J). (978-0-7166-0616-1(X)) World Bk., Inc.

SUPERNATURAL—FICTION

Acioli, Socorro. The Head of the Saint. Hahn, Daniel, tr. from POR. Snell, Alexis, illus. 2016. (ENG.). 192p. (YA). (gr. 7). 16.99 (978-0-553-53792-5(X), Delacorte Pr.) Random Hse. Children's Bks.

Acosta, Marta. Dark Companion. 2013. (ENG.). 368p. (YA). (gr. 8-12). pap. 10.99 (978-0-7653-2965-3(4), 9780765329653, Tor Teen) Doherty, Tom Assocs., LLC.

Adamchuk, Rachelle G. Disappearance: The First Part of Trickery & Honest Deception. 2006. 169p. pap. 16.99 (978-1-4120-8991-3(3)) Trafford Publishing.

Afterglow. 2014. (ENG., Illus.). 336p. (YA). (gr. 9). pap. 11.99 (978-1-4424-5038-7(X), Simon & Schuster Bks. For Young Readers) Simon & Schuster Bks. For Young Readers.

Aguirre, Ann. Public Enemies. 2015. (Immortal Game Ser.: 2). (ENG.). 384p. (YA). (gr. 7). 17.99 (978-1-250-02466-4(8), 9781250024664) Feiwel & Friends.

Ainley, Christian. The Enchanted Amulet: The Chronicles of Peralucia (Book One) 2009. (Illus.). 272p. pap. 15.49 (978-1-4389-5903-0(6)) AuthorHouse.

Alender, Katie. As Dead as It Gets. 2013. (Bad Girls Don't Die Ser.). (ENG.). 448p. (J). (gr. 7-17). pap. 9.99 (978-1-4231-3778-8(7)) Hyperion Pr.

—Famous Last Words. 2014. (ENG.). 320p. (J). (gr. 7). 18.99 (978-0-545-63997-2(2)) Scholastic, Inc.

—From Bad to Cursed. 2012. (ENG.). 448p. (YA). (gr. 7-17). pap. 9.99 (978-1-4231-3777-1(9)) Hyperion Pr.

Alexander, William. A Properly Unhaunted Place. Murphy, Kelly, illus. 2017. (ENG.). 192p. (J). (gr. 3-7). 16.99 **(978-1-4814-6915-9(0)**, McElderry, Margaret K. Bks.) McElderry, Margaret K. Bks.

Allende, Isabel. City of the Beasts. 2009. (P. S. Ser.: Bk. 1). (ENG.). 448p. pap. 14.99 (978-0-06-182511-8(5), Harper Perennial) HarperCollins Pubs.

—City of the Beasts. Peden, Margaret Sayers, tr. from SPA. 2004. (City of the Beasts Ser.: Bk. 1). (ENG.). 432p. (J). (gr. 5-18). reprint ed. pap. 7.99 (978-0-06-053503-2(2), Rayo) HarperCollins Pubs.

Almond, David. Clay. 2008. (ENG.). 272p. (YA). (gr. 7-12). pap. 8.99 (978-0-440-42013-2(X), Delacorte Bks. for Young Readers) Random Hse. Children's Bks.

Andersen, Hans Christian. The Wild Swans. 2014. (Little Golden Book Ser.). (ENG., Illus.). 24p. (J). (-k). 3.99 (978-0-375-86430-8(X), Golden Bks.) Random Hse. Children's Bks.

Anderson, Jodi Lynn. My Diary from the Edge of the World. 2015. (ENG., Illus.). 432p. (J). (gr. 3-7). 16.99 (978-1-4424-8387-3(3), Aladdin) Simon & Schuster Children's Publishing.

—My Diary from the Edge of the World. 2017. (ENG., Illus.). 448p. (J). (gr. 3-7). pap. 7.99 (978-1-4424-8388-0(1), Simon & Schuster/Paula Wiseman Bks.) Simon & Schuster/Paula Wiseman Bks.

Anderson, Maree. Freaks in the City, Bk.2. 2015. (ENG., Illus.). 290p. pap. (978-0-9941160-2-4(0)) Anderson, Maree.

Anderson, R. J. Spell Hunter. 2009. (Faery Rebels Ser.). (ENG.). 336p. (J). (gr. 8-18). 16.99 (978-0-06-155474-2(X)) HarperCollins Pubs.

—Wayfarer. 2010. (ENG.). 304p. (J). (gr. 8-18). 16.99 (978-0-06-155477-3(4), HarperTeen) HarperCollins Pubs.

Angelini, Josephine. Dreamless. 2013. (Starcrossed Trilogy Ser.: 2). (ENG.). 512p. (YA). (gr. 8). pap. 9.99 (978-0-06-201202-9(9), HarperTeen) HarperCollins Pubs.

—Goddess. 2013. (Starcrossed Trilogy Ser.: 3). (ENG.). 432p. (YA). (gr. 8). 17.99 (978-0-06-201203-6(7), HarperTeen) HarperCollins Pubs.

—Starcrossed. (Starcrossed Trilogy Ser.: 1). (ENG.). (YA). (gr. 8). 2012. 512p. pap. 9.99 (978-0-06-201200-5(2)) 2011. 496p. 17.99 (978-0-06-201199-2(5)) HarperCollins Pubs. (HarperTeen).

Appelbaum, Susannah. Divah. 2016. (ENG.). 400p. (YA). (gr. 6). 17.99 (978-1-63450-674-8(X), Sky Pony Pr.) Skyhorse Publishing Co., Inc.

Appelt, Kathi & Mcghee, Alison. Maybe a Fox. 2016. (ENG., Illus.). 272p. (J). (gr. 5-9). 17.99 (978-1-4424-8242-5(7), Atheneum/Caitlyn Dlouhy Books) Simon & Schuster Children's Publishing.

Applegate, Katherine. The Capture. 2012. (Animorphs Ser.: 6). lib. bdg. 17.20 (978-0-606-26194-4(X), Turtleback) Turtleback Bks.

Archer, Jennifer. The Shadow Girl. 2013. (ENG.). 336p. (YA). (gr. 8). pap. 9.99 (978-0-06-183460-8(2), HarperTeen) HarperCollins Pubs.

—Through Her Eyes. 2012. (ENG.). 400p. (YA). (gr. 8). pap. 9.99 (978-0-06-183459-2(9), HarperTeen) HarperCollins Pubs.

Armstrong, K. L. & Marr, M. A. Loki's Wolves. (Blackwell Pages Ser.: 1). (ENG.). (J). (gr. 3-7). 2014. 374p. pap. 8.99 (978-0-316-20497-2(8)) 2013. (Illus.). 358p. 17.00 (978-0-316-20496-5(X)) Little, Brown Bks. for Young Readers.

—Odin's Ravens. 2014. (Blackwell Pages Ser.: 2). (ENG., Illus.). 342p. (J). (gr. 3-7). 17.00 (978-0-316-20498-9(6)) Little, Brown Bks. for Young Readers.

Armstrong, Kelley. The Awakening. (Darkest Powers Ser.: 2). (YA). (gr. 8). 2010. 384p. pap. 9.99 (978-0-06-145055-6(3)) 2009. 368p. 17.99 (978-0-06-166276-8(3)) HarperCollins Pubs.

—The Awakening, 7 vols. 2009. (Darkest Powers Ser.: 2). (YA). 103.75 (978-1-4407-3099-3(7)); 133.75 (978-1-4407-3103-7(9)) Recorded Bks., Inc.

—The Calling. 2012. (Darkness Rising Ser.: Bk. 2). 336p. pap. (978-1-907410-47-5(3)) Atom Pr.

—The Calling. (Darkness Rising Ser.: 2). (YA). (gr. 8). 2013. 352p. pap. 9.99 (978-0-06-179706-4(5)) 2012. 336p. 17.99 (978-0-06-179705-7(7)) HarperCollins Pubs.

—Empire of Night. 2015. (Age of Legends Trilogy Ser.: 2). 432p. (YA). (gr. 8). 17.99 (978-0-06-207127-9(0)) HarperCollins Pubs.

—The Gathering. (Darkness Rising Ser.: 1). (YA). (gr. 8). 2012. 384p. pap. 9.99 (978-0-06-179703-3(0)) 2011. 368p. 17.99 (978-0-06-179702-6(2)) HarperCollins Pubs.

—The Gathering, 7 vols. (Darkness Rising Ser.: Bk. 1). (YA). 100.75 (978-1-4498-6186-5(5)); 1.25 (978-1-4498-6189-6(X)); 2013. 102.75 (978-1-4498-6184-1(9)) Recorded Bks., Inc.

—The Reckoning. (Darkest Powers Ser.: 3). (YA). (gr. 8). 2011. 416p. pap. 9.99 (978-0-06-145056-3(1)) 2010. 400p. 17.99 (978-0-06-166283-6(6)) HarperCollins Pubs.

—The Rising. 2013. (Darkness Rising Ser.: 3). 416p. (YA). (gr. 8). 17.99 (978-0-06-179708-8(1)) HarperCollins Pubs.

—Sea of Shadows. (gr. 8). 2015. (Age of Legends Trilogy Ser.: 1). 432p. (YA). pap. 9.99 (978-0-06-207125-5(4)) 2014. (Age of Legends Trilogy: Bk. 1). 416p. (J). 17.99 (978-0-06-207124-8(6)) HarperCollins Pubs.

—Sea of Shadows. 2015. (Age of Legends Ser.: 1). (YA). lib. bdg. 20.85 (978-0-606-36511-6(7)) Turtleback Bks.

—The Summoning. (Darkest Powers Ser.: 1). (YA). (gr. 8). 2009. 416p. pap. 9.99 (978-0-06-145054-9(5)) 2008. 400p. 17.99 (978-0-06-166269-0(0)) HarperCollins Pubs.

—The Summoning, 7 vols. 2009. (Darkest Powers Ser.: 1). (J). 81.75 (978-1-4361-9717-5(1)); 243.75 (978-1-4361-9718-2(X)) Recorded Bks., Inc.

Arnett, Dee. Gifted. 2008. 240p. pap. 18.95 (978-1-4092-0442-8(1)) Lulu Pr., Inc.

Arnett, Mindee. The Nightmare Affair. (Arkwell Academy Ser.: 1). (ENG.). (YA). (gr. 9-12). 2014. 400p. pap. 12.99 (978-0-7653-3336-0(8), 9780765333360) 2013. 368p. 17.99 (978-0-7653-3333-9(3), 9780765333339) Doherty, Tom Assocs., LLC. (Tor Teen).

—The Nightmare Dilemma. (Arkwell Academy Ser.: 2). (ENG.). (YA). 2015. 400p. (gr. 8-12). pap. 10.99 (978-0-7653-3337-7(6), 9780765333377) 2014. 384p. (gr. 9-12). 17.99 (978-0-7653-3334-6(1), 9780765333346) Doherty, Tom Assocs., LLC. (Tor Teen).

Arnold, Shari. Mystique. 2012. (YA). (978-1-4521-0363-1(1)) Chronicle Bks. LLC.

Arroyo, Raymond. The Lost Staff of Wonders. 2017. (Will Wilder Ser.). (ENG.). 352p. (J). (gr. 3-7). 16.99 (978-0-553-53967-7(1), Crown Books For Young Readers) Random Hse. Children's Bks.

—The Relic of Perilous Falls. 2016. (Will Wilder Ser.). (ENG.). 336p. (J). (gr. 3-7). lib. bdg. 19.99 (978-0-553-53960-8(4)); 16.99 (978-0-553-53959-2(0)) Random Hse. Children's Bks. (Crown Books For Young Readers).

Arsenault, Emily. The Leaf Reader. 2017. (ENG.). 240p. (YA). (gr. 9). 18.99 (978-1-61695-782-7(4), Soho Teen) Soho Pr., Inc.

Ashton, Brodi. Everbound. 2013. (Everneath Ser.: 2). (ENG.). (YA). (gr. 8). 384p. pap. 9.99 (978-0-06-207117-0(3)); 368p. 17.99 (978-0-06-207116-3(5)) HarperCollins Pubs.

—Everneath. 2012. (Everneath Ser.: 1). (ENG.). (YA). (gr. 9). 400p. pap. 9.99 (978-0-06-207114-9(9)); 384p. 17.99 (978-0-06-207113-2(0)) HarperCollins Pubs.

—Evertrue. 2014. (Everneath Ser.: 3). (ENG.). 368p. (YA). (gr. 9). 17.99 (978-0-06-207119-4(X)) HarperCollins Pubs.

Atwater-Rhodes, Amelia. Bloodwitch (Book 1) 2015. (Maeve'ra Ser.). (ENG.). 304p. (YA). (gr. 7). pap. 9.99 (978-0-385-74304-4(1), Ember) Random Hse. Children's Bks.

—Persistence of Memory. 2010. (Den of Shadows Ser.: Bk. 4). (ENG.). 224p. (YA). (gr. 7). pap. 8.99 (978-0-440-24004-4(2), Delacorte Pr.) Random Hse. Children's Bks.

—Poison Tree. 2013. (ENG.). 240p. (YA). (gr. 7). pap. 8.99 (978-0-385-73755-5(6), Ember) Random Hse. Children's Bks.

—Promises to Keep. 2014. (ENG.). 256p. (YA). (gr. 7). pap. 8.99 (978-0-385-74193-4(6), Ember) Random Hse. Children's Bks.

—Token of Darkness. 2011. (ENG.). 208p. (YA). (gr. 7). pap. 8.99 (978-0-385-73751-7(3), Ember) Random Hse. Children's Bks.

Atwood, Megan. The Bridge of Death. 2012. (Paranormalists Ser.: 4). (ENG.). 104p. (YA). (gr. 6-12). pap. 7.95 (978-0-8225-9090-3(5), Darby Creek); lib. bdg. 27.93 (978-0-7613-8335-2(2)) Lerner Publishing Group.

—The Cursed Ballet. 2013. (Dario Quincy Academy of Dance Ser.: 3). (ENG.). 104p. (gr. 6-12). (J). lib. bdg. 27.93 (978-1-4677-0932-3(8)); (YA). pap. 7.95 (978-1-4677-1485-3(2)) Lerner Publishing Group. (Darby Creek).

—The Haunting of Apartment 101. 2012. (Paranormalists Ser.: 1). (ENG.). 112p. (YA). (gr. 6-12). pap. 7.95 (978-0-8225-9077-4(8), Darby Creek) Lerner Publishing Group.

—Leaping at Shadows. 2013. (Dario Quincy Academy of Dance Ser.: 1). (ENG.). 112p. (YA). (gr. 6-12). pap. 7.95 (978-1-4677-1483-9(6)); lib. bdg. 27.93 (978-1-4677-0930-9(1)) Lerner Publishing Group. (Darby Creek).

—The Mayhem on Mohawk Avenue. 2012. (Paranormalists Ser.: 3). (ENG.). 104p. (YA). (gr. 6-12). pap. 7.95 (978-0-8225-9088-0(3), Darby Creek); lib. bdg. 27.93 (978-0-7613-8334-5(4)) Lerner Publishing Group.

—Stolen Luck. 2013. (Dario Quincy Academy of Dance Ser.: 2). (ENG.). 112p. (gr. 6-12). (J). lib. bdg. 27.93 (978-1-4677-0931-6(X)); (YA). pap. 7.95 (978-1-4677-1484-6(4)) Lerner Publishing Group. (Darby Creek).

—The Terror of Black Eagle Tavern. 2012. (Paranormalists Ser.: 2). (ENG.). 104p. (YA). (gr. 6-12). pap. 7.95 (978-0-8225-9078-1(6), Darby Creek); lib. bdg. 27.93 (978-0-7613-8333-8(6)) Lerner Publishing Group.

—Twin Dangers. 2013. (Dario Quincy Academy of Dance Ser.: 4). (ENG.). 112p. (gr. 6-12). (J). lib. bdg. 27.93 (978-1-4677-0933-0(6)); (YA). pap. 7.95 (978-1-4677-1486-0(0)) Lerner Publishing Group. (Darby Creek).

Baer, Marianna. The Inconceivable Life of Quinn. 2017. (ENG.). 384p. (YA). 18.95 (978-1-4197-2302-5(2), Amulet Bks.) Abrams, Inc.

Baggott, Julianna. The Prince of Fenway Park. 2011. (ENG.). 352p. (J). (gr. 3-7). pap. 6.99 (978-0-06-087244-1(6)) HarperCollins Pubs.

Barnes, Jennifer Lynn. Every Other Day. 2013. (ENG.). 352p. (J). (gr. 7). pap. 9.99 (978-1-60684-415-1(6), Carolrhoda Lab™) Lerner Publishing Group.

—Fate. 2009. (ENG.). 368p. (YA). (gr. 7-18). pap. 8.99 (978-0-385-73537-7(5), Delacorte Bks. for Young Readers) Random Hse. Children's Bks.

—Tattoo. 2007. (ENG.). 272p. (YA). (gr. 7-12). pap. 7.99 (978-0-385-73347-2(X), Delacorte Bks. for Young Readers) Random Hse. Children's Bks.

Barnes, Vivi. Paper or Plastic. 2015. (Entangled Teen Ser.). (ENG.). 352p. (YA). pap. 9.99 (978-1-62266-521-1(X), 9781622665211) Entangled Publishing, LLC.

Bast, Michael. Death's Academy. 2014. (J). pap. 14.99 (978-1-4621-1380-4(X), Horizon Pubs.) Cedar Fort, Inc./CFI Distribution.

Bastian, Kimberlee Ann. The Orphan, the Soulcatcher, & the Black Blizzard. 2012. 258p. pap. 22.50 (978-1-105-06633-7(9)) Lulu.com GBR. Dist: Lulu Pr., Inc.

Bauer, Marion Dane. The Red Ghost. Ferguson, Peter, illus. 2009. (Stepping Stone Book Ser.). (ENG.). 96p. (J). (gr. 1-4). 4.99 (978-0-375-84082-1(6), Random Hse. Bks. for Young Readers) Random Hse. Children's Bks.

Beatty, Robert. Serafina & the Black Cloak. (Serafina Ser.). (ENG.). (J). (gr. 3-7). 2016. 320p. pap. 7.99 (978-1-4847-1187-3(4)) 2015. 304p. 16.99 (978-1-4847-0901-6(2)) Hyperion Bks. for Children.

—Serafina & the Black Cloak. 2016. (J). lib. bdg. 18.40 (978-0-606-38336-3(0)) Turtleback Bks.

—Serafina & the Splintered Heart. 2017. (Serafina Ser.: bk.3). (ENG.). 368p. (J). (gr. 3-7). 16.99 **(978-1-4847-7504-2(X))** Hyperion Bks. for Children.

—Serafina & the Twisted Staff. (Serafina Ser.). (ENG.). (J). (gr. 3-7). 2017. 400p. pap. 7.99 **(978-1-4847-7806-7(5))** 2016. 384p. 16.99 (978-1-4847-7503-5(1)) Hyperion Bks. for Children.

—Serafina & the Twisted Staff. 2017. (J). lib. bdg. 18.40 **(978-0-606-39977-7(1))** Turtleback Bks.

The Beautiful & the Damned. 2014. (ENG., Illus.). 288p. (YA). (gr. 7). pap. 11.99 (978-1-4424-8836-6(0), Simon Pulse) Simon Pulse.

Becker, Tom. Lifeblood. 2010. (Darkside Ser.: 2). (ENG.). 288p. (J). (gr. 7). 7.99 (978-0-545-03746-4(8), Orchard Bks.) Scholastic, Inc.

Bedard, Michael. The Green Man. 2014. (ENG., Illus.). 306p. (YA). (gr. 5). pap. 9.99 (978-1-77049-511-1(8), Tundra Bks.) Tundra Bks. CAN. Dist: Penguin Random Hse. LLC.

Bedford, Martyn. The Flip. 2012. (ENG.). 272p. (YA). (gr. 7). pap. 8.99 (978-0-375-86552-7(7), Ember) Random Hse. Children's Bks.

Beherns, Kathryn J. Breakdown. 2016. (Atlas of Cursed Places Ser.). (ENG.). 96p. (YA). (gr. 6-12). lib. bdg. 26.65 (978-1-5124-1323-6(2), Darby Creek) Lerner Publishing Group.

Bellairs, John. The Revenge of the Wizard's Ghost (A Johnny Dixon Mystery: Book Four) 2011. 108p. pap. 14.95 (978-1-61756-336-2(6)) Open Road Integrated Media, Inc.

Benson, Amber. Among the Ghosts. Grace, Sina, illus. 2011. (ENG.). 256p. (J). (gr. 3-7). pap. 6.99 (978-1-4169-9426-8(2), Aladdin) Simon & Schuster Children's Publishing.

Benz, Derek & Lewis, J. S. The Brimstone Key. 2011. (Grey Griffins: the Clockwork Chronicles Ser.: 1). (ENG.). 400p. (J). (gr. 3-7). pap. 22.99 (978-0-316-04521-6(7)) Little, Brown Bks. for Young Readers.

Betterton, Jerry W. The Adventures of Hot Rolls. 2013. 44p. pap. 24.99 (978-1-4797-8184-3(3)) Xlibris Corp.

Bick, Ilsa J. Draw the Dark. (Carolrhoda YA Ser.). (ENG.). 344p. (YA). (gr. 9-12). 2011. pap. 9.95 (978-0-7613-8131-0(7)) 2010. 16.95 (978-0-7613-5686-8(X)) Lerner Publishing Group. (Carolrhoda Lab™).

—Shadows. 2012. (Ashes Trilogy Ser.: Bk. 2). (ENG.). 528p. (gr. 9). 17.99 (978-1-60684-176-1(9), Carolrhoda Lab™) Lerner Publishing Group.

Billingsley, Franny. Chime. 2011. (Playaway Young Adult Ser.). (YA). 59.99 (978-1-61707-143-0(9)) Findaway World, LLC.

—Chime. 2012. (ENG.). 384p. (YA). (gr. 7-18). 8.99 (978-0-14-242092-8(1), Speak) Penguin Young Readers Group.

Bisognin, Marzia. Dream House: A Novel by CutiePieMarzia. 2016. (ENG.). 224p. (gr. 7). 17.99 (978-1-5011-3526-2(0), Atria Bks.) Simon & Schuster.

Black, Holly. Ironside: A Modern Faery's Tale. (ENG.). 336p. (YA). (gr. 9). 2008. pap. 10.99 (978-0-689-86821-4(9)) 2007. 17.99 (978-0-689-86820-7(0)) McElderry, Margaret K. Bks. (McElderry, Margaret K. Bks.).

—Kin. Naifeh, Ted, illus. (Good Neighbors Ser.: 1). (ENG.). 144p. (J). (gr. 7). 2009. pap. 12.99 (978-0-439-85565-5(9)) 2008. 16.99 (978-0-439-85562-4(4)) Scholastic, Inc. (Graphix).

—Kith. Naifeh, Ted, illus. 2010. (Good Neighbors Ser.: 2). (ENG.). 128p. (J). (gr. 3-7). pap. 12.99 (978-0-439-85566-2(7), Graphix) Scholastic, Inc.

—Modern Faerie Tales: Tithe; Valiant; Ironside. 2010. (ENG.). 1040p. (YA). (gr. 9). pap. 24.99 (978-1-4424-2020-5(0), McElderry, Margaret K. Bks.) McElderry, Margaret K. Bks.

—Valiant: A Modern Faerie Tale. 2006. (ENG.). 320p. (YA). (gr. 8-12). pap. 10.99 (978-0-689-86823-8(5), McElderry, Margaret K. Bks.) McElderry, Margaret K. Bks.

Black, Holly & DiTerlizzi, Tony. Lucinda's Secret. DiTerlizzi, Tony, illus. 2013. (Spiderwick Chronicles Ser.: 3). (ENG., Illus.). (J). (gr. 1-5). 128p. 15.99 (978-1-4424-8700-0(3)); 144p. pap. 7.99 (978-1-4424-8697-3(X)) Simon & Schuster Bks. For Young Readers. (Simon & Schuster Bks. For Young Readers).

Blackwell, Paul E. Undercurrent. 2013. 320p. (YA). (gr. 9). 17.99 (978-0-06-212350-3(5), HarperTeen) HarperCollins Pubs.

Block, Francesca Lia. Blood Roses. 2008. 144p. (J). (gr. 9-18). 15.99 (978-0-06-076384-8(1), Cotler, Joanna Books) HarperCollins Pubs.

—Pretty Dead. (ENG.). (YA). (gr. 9). 2010. 224p. pap. 8.99 (978-0-06-154787-4(5)) 2009. 208p. 16.99 (978-0-06-154785-0(9)) HarperCollins Pubs. (HarperTeen).

—Teen Spirit. 2014. (ENG.). 240p. (YA). (gr. 9). 17.99 (978-0-06-200809-1(9), HarperTeen) HarperCollins Pubs.

Blomfield, Alan. The Pendant of Epoch. 2008. 128p. (978-1-86950-714-5(2)) HarperCollins Pubs. Australia.

Blubaugh, Penny. Blood & Flowers. 2011. (ENG.). 352p. (YA). (gr. 8-18). 16.99 (978-0-06-172862-4(4), HarperTeen) HarperCollins Pubs.

Blue Moon. 2014. (Dead City Ser.: 2). (ENG., Illus.). 336p. (J). (gr. 4-8). pap. 7.99 (978-1-4424-4132-3(1), Aladdin) Simon & Schuster Children's Publishing.

Blumenthal, Deborah. The Lifeguard. (ENG.). 288p. (YA). (gr. 8-12). 2013. 9.99 (978-0-8075-4536-2(8)) 2012. 16.99 (978-0-8075-4535-5(X)) Whitman, Albert & Co.

Blythe, Daniel. Shadow Breakers. 2013. (J). (978-0-545-47980-6(0)); (ENG.). 256p. (gr. 5-9). 16.99 (978-0-545-47979-0(7)) Scholastic, Inc. (Chicken Hse., The).

Boles, Jim. Ivan the Invacar & the Cave. Cunningham, Bob, illus. 2013. 52p. pap. 19.95 (978-0-9858052-2-7(6)) People Ink Pr.

Bond, Gwenda & Rowe, Chistopher. The Lost Legacy. Thomas, Glenn, illus. 2017. (Supernormal Sleuthing Service Ser.: 1). 416p. (J). (gr. 3-7). 16.99 (978-0-06-245994-7(5), Greenwillow Bks.) HarperCollins Pubs.

Boone, Martina. Illusion. 2016. (Heirs of Watson Island Ser.). (ENG., Illus.). 480p. (YA). (gr. 9). 17.99 (978-1-4814-1128-8(4), Simon Pulse) Simon Pulse.

—Persuasion. 2015. (Heirs of Watson Island Ser.). (ENG., Illus.). 464p. (YA). (gr. 9). 17.99 (978-1-4814-1125-7(X), Simon Pulse) Simon Pulse.

Booraem, Ellen. Texting the Underworld. 2013. (ENG.). 320p. (J). (gr. 5). 16.99 (978-0-8037-3704-4(1), Dial Bks) Penguin Young Readers Group.

Bostick, B. k. Huber Hill & the Dead Man's Treasure. 2011. (J). (978-1-59955-911-7(0), Bonneville Bks.) Cedar Fort, Inc./CFI Distribution.

Bosworth, Jennifer. The Killing Jar. 2016. (ENG.). 352p. (YA). 17.99 (978-0-374-34137-4(0), 9780374341374, Farrar, Straus & Giroux (BYR)) Farrar, Straus & Giroux.

Bourbeau, Julie. The Wednesdays. Beene, Jason, illus. (ENG.). 256p. (J). (gr. 2-5). 2013. pap. 7.99 (978-0-375-87286-0(8), Yearling) 2012. 16.99 (978-0-375-86890-0(9), Knopf Bks. for Young Readers) Random Hse. Children's Bks.

Bourne, Tracey. Not Just a Dream! 2009. (Illus.). 52p. pap. 11.49 (978-1-4389-4819-5(0)) AuthorHouse.

Bouton, Warren Hussey. The Captain's Return: A Spooky Tale from Nantucket. Locke, Barbara Kauffmann, illus. 2004. (J). per. 5.95 (978-0-9700555-4-5(4)) Hither Creek Pr.

Bowler, Tim. Buried Thunder. 2011. (ENG.). 224p. (J). 16.95 (978-0-8234-2397-2(2)) Holiday Hse., Inc.

Bowvayne. A Spell Behind Bars. Snow, Alan, illus. 2006. (Misadventures of Danny Cloke Ser.). 208p. (J). (gr. 6). lib. bdg. 12.99 (978-1-58086-926-3(2), Usborne) EDC Publishing.

Bracegirdle, P. J. Sinister Scenes. (Joy of Spooking Ser.). (ENG.). 320p. (J). (gr. 3-7). 2012. pap. 6.99 (978-1-4169-3421-9(9)) 2011. 15.99 (978-1-4169-3420-2(0)) McElderry, Margaret K. Bks. (McElderry, Margaret K. Bks.).

—Unearthly Asylum. (Joy of Spooking Ser.). (ENG.). (J). (gr. 3-7). 2011. 320p. pap. 5.99 (978-1-4169-3419-6(7)) 2010. 304p. 15.99 (978-1-4169-3418-9(9)) McElderry, Margaret K. Bks. (McElderry, Margaret K. Bks.).

Braswell, Liz. The Fallen. movie tie-in ed. 2011. (Nine Lives of Chloe King Ser.: 1). (ENG.). 256p. (YA). (gr. 9). pap. 8.99 (978-1-4424-4134-7(8), Simon Pulse) Simon Pulse.

Bray, Libba. A Great & Terrible Beauty. 2005. (Gemma Doyle Trilogy Ser.: Bk. 1). (ENG.). 432p. (YA). (gr. 7). reprint ed. pap. 9.99 (978-0-385-73231-4(7), Ember) Random Hse. Children's Bks.

—Lair of Dreams. 2015. (Diviners Ser.: 2). (ENG.). 624p. (YA). (gr. 10-17). 19.00 (978-0-316-12604-5(7)); (gr. 7-17). E-Book (978-0-316-36488-1(6)) Little, Brown Bks. for Young Readers.

—Rebel Angels. 2006. (Gemma Doyle Trilogy Ser.: Bk. 2). (ENG.). 576p. (YA). (gr. 7-12). pap. 10.99 (978-0-385-73341-0(0), Ember) Random Hse. Children's Bks.

—The Sweet Far Thing. 2009. (Gemma Doyle Trilogy Ser.: Bk. 3). (ENG.). 848p. (YA). (gr. 7). pap. 10.99 (978-0-440-23777-8(7), Ember) Random Hse. Children's Bks.

Bredeson, Michelle. Legends. 2012. 220p. pap. (978-1-61706-158-5(1)) Roxby Media Ltd.

Breese, K. Ryer. Past Continuous. 2011. (ENG.). 304p. (YA). (gr. 9-13). pap. 20.99 (978-0-312-54772-1(2), 9780312547721, St. Martin's Griffin) St. Martin's Pr.

Brennan, Herbie. The Faeman Quest. (Faerie Wars Chronicles Ser.). (ENG.). 368p. (YA). (gr. 7). 2012. pap. 9.99 (978-1-59990-833-5(6), 9781599908335) 2011. 18.99 (978-1-59990-476-4(4), 9781599904764) Bloomsbury Publishing USA. (Bloomsbury USA Childrens).

—Faerie Lord. (Faerie Wars Chronicles Ser.). (ENG.). 432p. (YA). (gr. 7). 2009. pap. 8.99 (978-1-59990-330-9(X), 9781599903309) 2008. 18.95 (978-1-59990-120-6(X), 9781599901206) Bloomsbury Publishing USA. (Bloomsbury USA Childrens).

—Faerie Lord. 2009. 1.00 (978-1-4074-4311-9(9)) Recorded Bks., Inc.

—Faerie Wars. 2003. (Faerie Wars Chronicles Ser.). (ENG., Illus.). 368p. (YA). (gr. 7). 17.95 (978-1-58234-810-0(3), 9781582348100, Bloomsbury USA Childrens) Bloomsbury Publishing USA.

—Faerie Wars. 2007. (ENG.). 384p. (gr. 7-12). per. 6.99 *(978-0-7653-5674-1(0)*, 9780765356741, Tor Bks.) Doherty, Tom Assocs., LLC.
—Faerie Wars. 1.00 *(978-1-4074-5906-6(6))* Recorded Bks., Inc.
—Ruler of the Realm. (Faerie Wars Chronicles Ser.). (ENG.). (YA). (gr. 7). 2007. 448p. pap. 9.99 *(978-1-59990-149-7(8)*, 9781599901497) 2006. (Illus.). 432p. 18.95 *(978-1-58234-881-0(2)*, 9781582348810) Bloomsbury Publishing USA. (Bloomsbury USA Childrens).
Brewer, Heather. The Cemetery Boys. 2015. (ENG.). 288p. (YA). (gr. 8). 17.99 *(978-0-06-230788-0(6)*, HarperTeen) HarperCollins Pubs.
—The Cemetery Boys. 2016. (YA). lib. bdg. 20.85 *(978-0-606-38741-5(2))* Turtleback Bks.
Brezenoff, Steve. Alley of Shadows, 1 vol. Martin, Cynthia, illus. 2008. (Vortex Bks.). (ENG.). 112p. (gr. 2-3). pap. 7.19 *(978-1-59889-922-1(8)*, Vortex Bks.) Stone Arch Bks.
—Burning Secrets, 1 vol. Vue, Tou, illus. (Vortex Bks.). (ENG.). 112p. (gr. 2-3). 2008. pap. 7.19 *(978-1-59889-920-7(1))* 2007. 26.65 *(978-1-59889-854-5(X))* Stone Arch Bks. (Vortex Bks.).
—Curses for Sale, 1 vol. Percival, Tom, illus. 2012. (Ravens Pass Ser.). (ENG.). 96p. (gr. 2-3). pap. 6.15 *(978-1-4342-4209-9(9))*; lib. bdg. 25.32 *(978-1-4342-3763-7(X))* Stone Arch Bks.
—New in Town, 1 vol. Percival, Tom, illus. 2012. (Ravens Pass Ser.). (ENG.). 96p. (gr. 2-3). pap. 6.15 *(978-1-4342-4210-5(2))*; lib. bdg. 25.32 *(978-1-4342-3793-4(1))* Stone Arch Bks.
Brockmann, Suzanne & Brockmann, Melanie. Night Sky. 2014. (Night Sky Ser.: 1). (ENG.). 496p. (YA). (gr. 8-12). 16.99 *(978-1-4926-0144-9(6))* Sourcebooks, Inc.
—Wild Sky: A Night Sky Novel. 2015. (Night Sky Ser.: 2). (ENG.). 448p. (YA). (gr. 8-12). 16.99 *(978-1-4926-0484-6(4))*; pap. 9.99 *(978-1-4926-2314-4(8))* Sourcebooks, Inc.
Brodey, Lisette. Mystical High. 2013. (ENG.). 264p. (YA). pap. 13.95 *(978-0-9815836-8-6(7))* Saberlee Bks.
Brodien-Jones, Chris. The Glass Puzzle. 2013. (Illus.). 319p. (J). *(978-0-385-74298-6(3)*, Delacorte Pr) Random House Publishing Group.
Brodien-Jones, Christine. The Dreamkeepers. 2009. (ENG.). 148p. (YA). (gr. 7). pap. 8.99 *(978-1-4424-0221-8(0)*, Simon & Schuster Bks. For Young Readers) Simon & Schuster Bks. For Young Readers.
—The Glass Puzzle. 2013. (ENG., Illus.). 336p. (J). (gr. 4-7). 16.99 *(978-0-385-74297-9(5)*, Delacorte Bks. for Young Readers) Random Hse. Children's Bks.
Brody, Jessica. A Week of Mondays. 2016. (ENG.). 464p. (YA). 17.99 *(978-0-374-38270-4(0)*, 9780374382704, Farrar, Straus & Giroux (BYR)) Farrar, Straus & Giroux.
Brooks, Martha. Bone Dance, 1 vol. 2005. (ENG.). 184p. (J). (gr. 6-16). pap. 8.95 *(978-0-88899-336-6(6))* Groundwood Bks. CAN. Dist: Publishers Group West (PGW).
Bross, Lanie. Fates. (ENG.). (YA). (gr. 7). 2015. 354p. pap. 9.99 *(978-0-385-74283-2(5)*, Ember) 2014. 336p. 17.99 *(978-0-385-74282-5(7)*, Delacorte Pr.) Random Hse. Children's Bks.
Brown, Anne Greenwood. Promise Bound. 2014. (ENG.). 368p. (YA). (gr. 7). 17.99 *(978-0-385-74383-9(1)*, Delacorte Pr.) Random Hse. Children's Bks.
Brown, Merry. Gold Manor Ghost House. 2013. 328p. pap. 13.99 *(978-0-615-79766-3(0))* YA Bks.
Brown, Roberta Simpson. The Walking Trees & Other Scary Stories. 2006. (ENG.). 140p. (J). (gr. 6-9). pap. 11.95 *(978-0-87483-143-6(1))* August Hse. Pubs., Inc.
Bruchac, Joseph. Wolf Mark, 1 vol. 2013. (ENG.). 392p. (J). 17.95 *(978-1-60060-661-8(X)*, Tu Bks.) Lee & Low Bks., Inc.
Buckingham, Royce. The Dead Boys. 2010. (ENG.). 208p. (J). (gr. 5-18). 16.99 *(978-0-399-25222-8(3)*, G.P. Putnam's Sons Books for Young Readers) Penguin Young Readers Group.
—Demonkeeper. 2007. 216p. (J). *(978-1-4287-4608-4(0))* Penguin Publishing Group.
Buckley-Archer, Linda. The Many Lives of John Stone. 2015. (ENG., Illus.). 544p. (YA). (gr. 7). 17.99 *(978-1-4814-2637-4(0))* Simon & Schuster Children's Publishing.
Bunting, Eve. Forbidden. 2015. (ENG.). 224p. (YA). (gr. 7). 17.99 *(978-0-544-39092-8(X))* Houghton Mifflin Harcourt Publishing Co.
Burne, Cristy. Takeshita Demons: Monster Matsuri. 2012. (Illus.). 128p. (J). pap. *(978-1-84780-137-1(4)*, Frances Lincoln) Quarto Publishing Group UK.
Burnham, Erik. Ghostbusters, Vol. 2. Schoening, Dan, illus. 2012. (Ghostbusters Ser.). (ENG.). 104p. pap. 17.99 *(978-1-61377-279-9(3)*, 9781613772799) Idea & Design Works, LLC.
—The New Ghostbusters. 2016. lib. bdg. 30.60 *(978-0-606-38722-4(6))* Turtleback Bks.
Burns, Laura J. & Metz, Melinda. Sacrifice. 2011. (ENG.). 272p. (YA). (gr. 9). 17.99 *(978-1-4424-3900-9(9))*; pap. 9.99 *(978-1-4424-0818-0(9))* Simon & Schuster Bks. For Young Readers. (Simon & Schuster Bks. For Young Readers).
Butler, Erin. Blood Hex. 2013. 260p. pap. *(978-1-77130-351-4(4))* Evernight Publishing.
Cabot, Meg. Abandon. 2011. (ENG.). 320p. (J). (gr. 9-18). 17.99 *(978-0-545-28410-3(4))* Scholastic, Inc.
—Awaken. 2013. (ENG.). 336p. (J). (gr. 9). 17.99 *(978-0-545-28412-7(0))* Scholastic, Inc.
—Haunted. 2007. (Mediator Ser.: No. 5). 263p. 18.00 *(978-0-7569-7831-0(9))* Perfection Learning Corp.
—Underworld. 2012. (Abandon Ser.). (ENG.). 336p. (J). (gr. 9). 17.99 *(978-0-545-28411-0(2))* Scholastic, Inc.
Cabot, Meg, et al. Prom Nights from Hell. 2010. (ENG.). 336p. (YA). (gr. 9). pap. 9.99 *(978-0-06-197600-1(8)*, HarperTeen) HarperCollins Pubs.
Cach, Lisa. Wake unto Me. 2011. (ENG.). 320p. (YA). (gr. 7-18). 8.99 *(978-0-14-241436-1(0)*, Speak) Penguin Young Readers Group.
Caine, Rachel, pseud. Bite Club, 10 vols. 2011. (Morganville Vampires Ser.: 10). (ENG.). 368p. (YA). (gr. 9). pap. 9.99 *(978-0-451-23468-1(5)*, Berkley) Penguin Publishing Group.
—Bitter Blood. 2013. (Morganville Vampires Ser.: 13). (ENG.). 432p. (YA). (gr. 9). pap. 9.99 *(978-0-451-41424-3(1)*, Berkley) Penguin Publishing Group.
—Black Dawn. 2012. (Morganville Vampires Ser.: 12). (ENG.). 400p. (YA). (gr. 9). pap. 9.99 *(978-0-451-23793-4(5)*, Berkley) Penguin Publishing Group.
—Daylighters. 2013. (Morganville Vampires Ser.: 15). (ENG.). 368p. (YA). (gr. 9). 17.99 *(978-0-451-41427-4(6)*, Berkley) Penguin Publishing Group.
—Ghost Town, 9 vols. 2011. (Morganville Vampires Ser.: 9). (ENG.). 368p. (YA). (gr. 9-18). 9.99 *(978-0-451-23291-5(7)*, Berkley) Penguin Publishing Group.
—Last Breath, 11 vols. 2012. (Morganville Vampires Ser.: 11). (ENG.). 368p. (YA). (gr. 9). 9.99 *(978-0-451-23580-0(0)*, Berkley) Penguin Publishing Group.
—Lord of Misrule. 2009. (Morganville Vampires Ser.: Bk. 5). 352p. (YA). lib. bdg. 20.00 *(978-1-4242-4704-2(7))* Fitzgerald Bks.
—Lord of Misrule. 2009. (Morganville Vampires Ser.: 5). (ENG.). 256p. (YA). (gr. 9-18). mass mkt. 7.99 *(978-0-451-22572-6(4)*, Berkley) Penguin Publishing Group.
—Midnight Alley. 2007. (Morganville Vampires Ser.: Bk. 3). 256p. (YA). lib. bdg. 20.00 *(978-1-4242-4705-9(5))* Fitzgerald Bks.
—Midnight Alley. 2007. (Morganville Vampires Ser.: 3). (ENG.). 256p. (YA). (gr. 9-18). mass mkt. 7.99 *(978-0-451-22238-1(5)*, Berkley) Penguin Publishing Group.
—Midnight Bites: Stories of the Morganville Vampires. 2016. (Morganville Vampires Ser.). (ENG.). 512p. (YA). (gr. 9). pap. 9.99 *(978-1-101-98978-4(5)*, Berkley) Penguin Publishing Group.
Caine, Rachel, pseud. Paper & Fire. (Great Library: 2). (ENG.). (YA). (gr. 9). 2017. 400p. pap. 9.99 ***(978-0-451-47314-1(0))*** 2016. 368p. 17.99 *(978-0-451-47240-3(3))* Penguin Publishing Group. (Berkley).
—Paper & Fire. 2017. (Great Library: 2). lib. bdg. 20.85 ***(978-0-606-40361-0(2))*** Turtleback Bks.
Cameron, Erica. Sing Sweet Nightingale. 2014. (Dream War Saga Ser.: 1). (ENG.). 376p. (YA). (gr. 7-9). pap. 9.95 *(978-1-937053-96-3(2))* Spencer Hill Pr.
Campbell, D. Andrew. Catharsis. 2013. 340p. pap. 12.50 *(978-0-9897522-0-6(8))* Broviak Publishing.
Campi, Alex de. Valentine Volume 1: Ice of Death TP: Ice of Death TP. 2012. (ENG., Illus.). 352p. (YA). pap. 24.99 *(978-1-60706-624-8(6)*, 9781607066248) Image Comics.
Cann, Kate. Consumed. (ENG.). 336p. (J). (gr. 9). 2012. pap. 9.99 *(978-0-545-26387-0(5))* 2011. 16.99 *(978-0-545-26388-7(3))* Scholastic, Inc.
—Possessed. (ENG.). 336p. (J). (gr. 9-9). 2011. pap. 9.99 *(978-0-545-12813-1(7))* 2010. 16.99 *(978-0-545-12812-4(9))* Scholastic, Inc.
Carman, Patrick. Thirteen Days to Midnight. 2011. (ENG.). 304p. (J). (gr. 7-17). pap. 10.99 *(978-0-316-00404-6(9))* Little, Brown Bks. for Young Readers.
Carr, Elias & Karre, Andrew. The Combination. 2011. (Night Fall Ser.). (ENG.). 120p. (YA). (gr. 6-12). pap. 7.95 *(978-0-7613-7810-5(3))* Lerner Publishing Group.
Carroll, Jenny, pseud & Cabot, Meg. Shadowland, 5 vols. unabr. ed. 2005. (Mediator Ser.: 1). (YA). (gr. 3-7). 69.75 *(978-1-4193-4144-1(8)*, 42055) Recorded Bks., Inc.
Casella, Jody. Thin Space. 2013. (ENG.). 256p. (YA). (gr. 7). 16.99 *(978-1-58270-435-7(X))*; pap. 10.99 *(978-1-58270-392-3(2))* Simon Pulse. (Simon Pulse).
Cashore, Kristin. Jane, Unlimited. 2017. (ENG.). 464p. (YA). (gr. 9). 18.99 ***(978-0-8037-4149-2(9)***, Kathy Dawson Books) Penguin Young Readers Group.
Cast, P. C. & Cast, Kristin. Awakened. 2013. (House of Night Novels Ser.: 8). (ENG.). 304p. (YA). (gr. 7-12). mass mkt. 9.99 *(978-1-250-04692-5(0)*, 9781250046925, St. Martin's Paperbacks) St. Martin's Pr.
—Betrayed. 2013. (House of Night Novels Ser.: 2). (ENG.). 320p. (YA). (gr. 7-12). mass mkt. 9.99 *(978-1-250-04693-2(9)*, 9781250046932, St. Martin's Paperbacks) St. Martin's Pr.
—Burned. (House of Night Novels Ser.: 7). (ENG.). 336p. (YA). (gr. 7-12). 2011. pap. 10.99 *(978-0-312-38796-9(2)*, 9780312387969) 2010. 17.99 *(978-0-312-60616-9(8)*, 9780312606169) St. Martin's Pr. (St. Martin's Griffin).
—Destined. 2013. (House of Night Novels Ser.: 9). (ENG.). 336p. (YA). (gr. 7-12). pap. 10.99 *(978-0-312-38798-3(9)*, 9780312387983, St. Martin's Griffin) St. Martin's Pr.
—Neferet's Curse. 2013. (House of Night Novellas Ser.: 3). (ENG., Illus.). 160p. (YA). (gr. 7). 12.99 *(978-1-250-00025-5(4)*, 9781250000255, St. Martin's Griffin) St. Martin's Pr.
—Tempted. 2013. (House of Night Novels Ser.: 6). (ENG.). 352p. (YA). (gr. 7-12). mass mkt. 9.99 *(978-1-250-04698-7(X)*, 9781250046987, St. Martin's Paperbacks) St. Martin's Pr.
—Untamed. 2008. (House of Night Novels Ser.: 4). (ENG.). 352p. (YA). (gr. 8-12). pap. 10.99 *(978-0-312-37983-4(8)*, 9780312379834, St. Martin's Griffin) St. Martin's Pr.
—Untamed. l.t. ed. 2009. (House of Night Ser.: Bk. 4). (ENG.). 510p. (YA). 23.95 *(978-1-4104-1965-1(7))* Thorndike Pr.
Castro, Adam-Troy. Gustav Gloom & the Four Terrors. Margiotta, Kristen, illus. 2013. (Gustav Gloom Ser.: 3). (ENG.). 248p. (J). (gr. 3-7). 12.99 *(978-0-448-45835-9(7)*, Grosset & Dunlap) Penguin Young Readers Group.
—Gustav Gloom & the Nightmare Vault, No. 2. Margiotta, Kristen, illus. 2013. (Gustav Gloom Ser.: 2). (ENG.). 248p. (J). (gr. 3-7). 12.99 *(978-0-448-45834-2(9)*, Grosset & Dunlap) Penguin Young Readers Group.
—Gustav Gloom & the Nightmare Vault #2. Margiotta, Kristen, illus. 2014. (Gustav Gloom Ser.: 2). (ENG.). 248p. (J). (gr. 3-7). 7.99 *(978-0-448-48329-0(7)*, Grosset & Dunlap) Penguin Young Readers Group.
—Gustav Gloom & the People Taker. Margiotta, Kristen, illus. 2012. (Gustav Gloom Ser.: 1). (ENG.). 232p. (J). (gr. 3-7). 12.99 *(978-0-448-45833-5(0)*, Grosset & Dunlap) Penguin Young Readers Group.
—Gustav Gloom & the People Taker #1. Margiotta, Kristen, illus. 2014. (Gustav Gloom Ser.: 1). (ENG.). 248p. (J). (gr. 3-7). 7.99 *(978-0-448-48328-3(9)*, Grosset & Dunlap) Penguin Young Readers Group.
Castro, Adam-Troy & dePaola, Tomie. Gustav Gloom & the Cryptic Carousel #4. Margiotta, Kristen, illus. 2015. (Gustav Gloom Ser.: 4). (ENG.). 248p. (J). (gr. 3-7). 7.99 *(978-0-448-48719-9(5)*, Grosset & Dunlap) Penguin Young Readers Group.
—Gustav Gloom & the Inn of Shadows #5. Margiotta, Kristen, illus. 2015. (Gustav Gloom Ser.: 5). (ENG.). 248p. (J). (gr. 3-7). bds. 12.99 *(978-0-448-46458-9(6)*, Grosset & Dunlap) Penguin Young Readers Group.
Chadda, Sarwat. The City of Death. 2013. (J). pap. *(978-0-545-38519-0(9))*; (ENG.). 336p. (gr. 4-7). 16.99 *(978-0-545-38518-3(0)*, Levine, Arthur A. Bks.) Scholastic, Inc.
—The Savage Fortress. 2012. (ENG.). 304p. (J). (gr. 4-7). 16.99 *(978-0-545-38516-9(4)*, Levine, Arthur A. Bks.) Scholastic, Inc.
Chandler, Elizabeth. The Back Door of Midnight. 2010. (Dark Secrets Ser.: Vol. 5). (ENG.). 320p. (YA). (gr. 7-18). pap. 9.99 *(978-1-4424-0626-1(7)*, Simon Pulse) Simon Pulse.
Childs, Tera Lynn & Childs, Tera. Oh. My. Gods. 2009. (ENG.). 288p. (YA). (gr. 7-18). 7.99 *(978-0-14-241420-0(4)*, Speak) Penguin Young Readers Group.
Christopher, Neil. The Hidden: A Compendium of Arctic Giants, Dwarves, Gnomes, Trolls, Faeries & Other Strange Beings from Inuit Oral History, 1 vol. Austin, Mike, illus. 2014. (ENG.). 256p. (YA). (gr. 7). 29.95 *(978-1-927095-59-1(X))* Inhabit Media Inc. CAN. Dist: Independent Pubs. Group.
Clare, Cassandra. City of Ashes. 2008. (Mortal Instruments Ser.: Bk. 2). (YA). (gr. 9). 64.99 *(978-1-60640-964-0(6))* Findaway World, LLC.
—City of Ashes. 2008. (Mortal Instruments Ser.: 2). (ENG.). 464p. (YA). (gr. 9-12). 24.99 *(978-1-4169-1429-7(3)*, McElderry, Margaret K. Bks.) McElderry, Margaret K. Bks.
—City of Bones. (Mortal Instruments Ser.: Bk. 1). (ENG., Illus.). (YA). (gr. 9). 2015. 544p. pap. 13.99 *(978-1-4814-5592-3(3))* 2007. 496p. 21.99 *(978-1-4169-1428-0(5))* 2015. 544p. pap. 13.99 *(978-1-4814-7030-8(2))* McElderry, Margaret K. Bks. (McElderry, Margaret K. Bks.).
—City of Bones. 2008. (Mortal Instruments Ser.: Bk. 1). 485p. (gr. 9-12). 23.00 *(978-1-60686-361-9(4))* Perfection Learning Corp.
—City of Bones, 12 vols. 2007. (Mortal Instruments Ser.: 1). (YA). 131.75 *(978-1-4281-5454-4(X))*; 120.75 *(978-1-4281-5450-6(7))*; 1.25 *(978-1-4281-5445-2(0))*; 286.75 *(978-1-4281-5449-0(3))*; 122.75 *(978-1-4281-5448-3(5))*; 133.75 *(978-1-4281-5452-0(3))* Recorded Bks., Inc.
—City of Bones. 2013. (The Mortal Instruments Ser.: Bk. 1). pap. *(978-1-4424-9306-3(2))* Simon & Schuster, Inc.
—City of Bones. l.t. ed. 2008. (Mortal Instruments Ser.: 1). 629p. (YA). 31.95 *(978-1-4104-0958-4(9))* Thorndike Pr.
—City of Bones. 2015. (Mortal Instruments Ser.: Bk. 1). 544p. (YA). lib. bdg. 25.75 *(978-0-606-37731-7(X))* Turtleback Bks.
—City of Fallen Angels. 2011. (Mortal Instruments Ser.: 4). (ENG.). 432p. (YA). (gr. 9-18). 24.99 *(978-1-4424-0354-3(3)*, McElderry, Margaret K. Bks.) McElderry, Margaret K. Bks.
—City of Fallen Angels, 11 vols. (Mortal Instruments Ser.: 4). (YA). 2012. 133.75 *(978-1-4618-0638-7(0))* 2011. 135.75 *(978-1-4618-0637-0(2))* 2011. 133.75 *(978-1-4618-0641-7(0))* 2011. 317.75 *(978-1-4618-0642-4(9))* 2011. 1.25 *(978-1-4640-2483-2(9))* Recorded Bks., Inc.
—City of Glass. (Mortal Instruments Ser.: Bk. 3). (ENG., (YA). (gr. 9). 2015. Illus.). 592p. pap. 13.99 *(978-1-4814-5598-5(2))* 2009. 560p. 24.99 *(978-1-4169-1430-3(7))* McElderry, Margaret K. Bks. (McElderry, Margaret K. Bks.).
—City of Glass. 2010. 23.00 *(978-1-60686-827-0(6))* Perfection Learning Corp.
—City of Glass. 2009. pap. *(978-1-4424-9308-7(9))* Simon & Schuster.
—City of Glass. 2015. (Mortal Instruments Ser.: Bk. 3). 592p. (YA). lib. bdg. 25.75 *(978-0-606-37733-1(6))* Turtleback Bks.
—City of Heavenly Fire. 2014. (Mortal Instruments Ser.: No. 6). (ENG., Illus.). 752p. (YA). (gr. 9). 24.99 *(978-1-4424-1689-5(0)*, McElderry, Margaret K. Bks.) McElderry, Margaret K. Bks.
—City of Lost Souls. (Mortal Instruments Ser.: Bk. 5). (ENG., (YA). (gr. 9). 2015. Illus.). 592p. pap. 13.99 *(978-1-4814-5600-5(8))* 2012. 544p. 21.99 *(978-1-4424-1686-4(6))* McElderry, Margaret K. Bks. (McElderry, Margaret K. Bks.).
—City of Lost Souls, 16 vols. 2012. (Mortal Instruments Ser.: Bk. 5). (YA). 135.75 *(978-1-4640-3948-5(8))*; 133.75 *(978-1-4640-3951-5(8))*; 317.75 *(978-1-4640-3949-2(6))*; 133.75 *(978-1-4640-3952-2(6))* Recorded Bks., Inc.
—City of Lost Souls. 2015. (Mortal Instruments Ser.: Bk. 5). 592p. (YA). lib. bdg. 25.75 *(978-0-606-37736-2(0))* Turtleback Bks.
—City of Lost Souls. 2012. 512p. pap. *(978-1-4063-3760-0(9))* Walker Bks., Ltd.
—Clockwork Angel. (Infernal Devices Ser.: Bk. 1). (ENG., Illus.). (YA). (gr. 9). 2015. 544p. pap. 13.99 *(978-1-4814-5602-9(4))* 2010. 496p. 24.99 *(978-1-4169-7586-1(1))* McElderry, Margaret K. Bks. (McElderry, Margaret K. Bks.).
—Clockwork Angel. 2012. (Infernal Devices Ser.: 1). (ENG.). 240p. (gr. 8-17). pap. 13.00 *(978-0-316-20098-1(0)*, Yen Pr.) Orbit.
—Clockwork Angel. 2015. (Infernal Devices Ser.: Bk. 1). 544p. (YA). lib. bdg. 25.75 *(978-0-606-37737-9(9))* 2012. (Infernal Devices Graphic Novel Ser.: 1). lib. bdg. 24.55 *(978-0-606-32257-7(4)*, Turtleback) Turtleback Bks.
—Clockwork Prince. (Infernal Devices Ser.: Bk. 2). (YA). 2015. (ENG., Illus.). 560p. (gr. 9). pap. 13.99 *(978-1-4814-5601-2(6))* 2011. (ENG., Illus.). 528p. (gr. 9-18). 24.99 *(978-1-4169-7588-5(8))* 2011. 502p. *(978-1-4424-5174-2(2))* McElderry, Margaret K. Bks. (McElderry, Margaret K. Bks.).
—Clockwork Prince. 2013. (Infernal Devices Ser.: 2). (ENG., Illus.). 256p. (gr. 8-17). pap. 13.00 *(978-0-316-20096-7(4)*, Yen Pr.) Orbit.
—Clockwork Prince. 2015. (Infernal Devices Ser.: Bk. 2). 560p. (YA). lib. bdg. 25.75 *(978-0-606-37895-6(2))* 2013. (Infernal Devices Graphic Novel Ser.: 2). lib. bdg. 24.55 *(978-0-606-32258-4(2)*, Turtleback) Turtleback Bks.
—Clockwork Princess. 2013. (YA). (Infernal Devices Ser.: 3). (ENG., Illus.). 592p. (gr. 9). 24.99 *(978-1-4169-7590-8(X))*; 570p. *(978-1-4424-8541-9(8))* McElderry, Margaret K. Bks. (McElderry, Margaret K. Bks.).
—The Infernal Devices: Clockwork Angel; Clockwork Prince; Clockwork Princess. 2013. (Infernal Devices Ser.: Bks. 1-3). (ENG.). 1520p. (YA). (gr. 9). 74.99 *(978-1-4424-8372-9(5)*, McElderry, Margaret K. Bks.) McElderry, Margaret K. Bks.
—Lady Midnight. 2016. (Dark Artifices Ser.: 1). (ENG., Illus.). 720p. (YA). (gr. 9-12). 24.99 *(978-1-4424-6835-1(1)*, McElderry, Margaret K. Bks.) McElderry, Margaret K. Bks.
—Lady Midnight. 2017. lib. bdg. 26.95 ***(978-0-606-40535-5(6))*** Turtleback Bks.
Clare, Cassandra & Lewis, Joshua. The Shadowhunter's Codex. 2013. (Mortal Instruments Ser.). (ENG., Illus.). 288p. (YA). (gr. 9). 24.99 *(978-1-4424-1692-5(0))*; 49.99 *(978-1-4424-9682-8(7))* McElderry, Margaret K. Bks. (McElderry, Margaret K. Bks.).
Clare, Cassandra, et al. The Bane Chronicles. Clare, Cassandra, ed. 2014. (Bane Chronicles Ser.). (ENG., Illus.). 528p. (YA). (gr. 9). 22.99 *(978-1-4424-9599-9(5)*, McElderry, Margaret K. Bks.) McElderry, Margaret K. Bks.
Clare, Cassandra, et al. Tales from the Shadowhunter Academy. (Tales from the Shadowhunter Academy Ser.). (ENG.). (YA). (gr. 9). 2017. 704p. pap. 14.99 ***(978-1-4814-4326-5(7))*** 2016. (Illus.). 672p. 23.99 *(978-1-4814-4325-8(9))* McElderry, Margaret K. Bks. (McElderry, Margaret K. Bks.).
Clark, Tracy. Deviate. 2015. (Light Key Trilogy Ser.: 2). (ENG.). 356p. (YA). pap. 9.99 *(978-1-62266-523-5(6)*, 9781622665235) Entangled Publishing, LLC.
Clewarth, John. Firestorm Rising. 2012. (Illus.). 200p. pap. *(978-1-4710-3681-1(2))* Lulu.com.
Climer, Steven Lee. Young of Heart. 2006. (YA). pap. *(978-0-9790649-5-1(3))* Mardi Gras Publishing, LLC.
Cochran, Molly. Legacy. (Legacy Ser.). (ENG.). (YA). (gr. 9). 2012. 448p. pap. 9.99 *(978-1-4424-1740-3(4))* 2011. 432p. 17.99 *(978-1-4424-1739-7(0))* Simon & Schuster/Paula Wiseman Bks. (Simon & Schuster/Paula Wiseman Bks.).
—Poison. (Legacy Ser.). (ENG., 368p. (YA). (gr. 9). 2014. Illus.). pap. 9.99 *(978-1-4424-5051-6(7))* 2012. 17.99 *(978-1-4424-5050-9(9))* Simon & Schuster/Paula Wiseman Bks. (Simon & Schuster/Paula Wiseman Bks.).
Cody, Matthew. The Dead Gentleman. 2012. (ENG.). 288p. (J). (gr. 5). 6.99 *(978-0-375-84490-4(2)*, Yearling) Random Hse. Children's Bks.
—Powerless. 2011. (Supers of Noble's Green Ser.). (ENG.). 288p. (J). (gr. 3-7). 7.99 *(978-0-375-84489-8(9)*, Yearling) Random Hse. Children's Bks.
—Super. (Supers of Noble's Green Ser.). (ENG.). 304p. (J). (gr. 3-7). 2014. 7.99 *(978-0-375-87291-4(4)*, Yearling) 2012. 16.99 *(978-0-375-86894-8(1)*, Knopf Bks. for Young Readers) Random Hse. Children's Bks.
—Villainous. 2015. (Supers of Noble's Green Ser.). (ENG.). 320p. (J). (gr. 3-7). 6.99 *(978-0-385-75492-7(2)*, Yearling) Random Hse. Children's Bks.
Cole, Kresley. Dead of Winter. 2015. (Arcana Chronicles Ser.). (ENG.). 320p. (YA). (gr. 9). pap. 11.99 *(978-1-4814-2346-5(0))*; (Illus.). 18.99 *(978-1-4814-2345-8(2))* Simon & Schuster Bks. For Young Readers. (Simon & Schuster Bks. For Young Readers).
—Endless Knight. 2013. (Arcana Chronicles Ser.: 2). (YA). 116.75 *(978-1-4703-8987-1(8))*; 246.75 *(978-1-4703-8090-8(0))*; 116.75 *(978-1-4703-8957-4(6))*; 118.75 *(978-1-4703-8997-0(5))*; 1.25 *(978-1-4703-8070-0(6))* Recorded Bks., Inc.
—Endless Knight: The Arcana Chronicles Book 2. 2013. (Arcana Chronicles Ser.). (ENG., Illus.). 336p. (YA). (gr. 9). 18.99 *(978-1-4424-3667-1(0)*, Simon & Schuster Bks. For Young Readers) Simon & Schuster Bks. For Young Readers.
—Poison Princess. 2013. (Arcana Chronicles Ser.: 1). (YA). 1.25 *(978-1-4703-8731-0(X))* Recorded Bks., Inc.
—Poison Princess. (Arcana Chronicles Ser.). (ENG., (YA). (gr. 9). 2013. Illus.). 400p. pap. 10.99 *(978-1-4424-3665-7(4))* 2012. 384p. 18.99 *(978-1-4424-3664-0(6))* Simon & Schuster Bks. For Young Readers. (Simon & Schuster Bks. For Young Readers).
Columbus, Chris & Vizzini, Ned. Battle of the Beasts. 2014. (House of Secrets Ser.: 2). (ENG.). 480p. (J). (gr. 3-7). 17.99 *(978-0-06-219249-3(3))* HarperCollins Pubs.
—House of Secrets. 2015. (House of Secrets Ser.: Vol. 1). (KOR.). 580p. (J). *(978-89-491-7127-2(9))* Biryongso Publishing Co.
—House of Secrets. Call, Greg, illus. (House of Secrets Ser.: 1). (J). 2014. (ENG.). 512p. (gr. 3-7). pap. 7.99 *(978-0-06-219247-9(7))* 2013. (ENG.). 496p. (gr. 3-7). 17.99 *(978-0-06-219246-2(9))* 2013. 490p. *(978-0-06-225964-6(4))* HarperCollins Pubs.
—House of Secrets. 2014. (House of Secrets Ser.: 1). (J). lib. bdg. 18.40 *(978-0-606-35070-9(5)*, Turtleback) Turtleback Bks.
Connolly, Tina. Seriously Shifted. 2016. (Seriously Wicked Ser.). (ENG.). 240p. (YA). 17.99 *(978-0-7653-8375-4(6)*, 9780765383754, Tor Teen) Doherty, Tom Assocs., LLC.
Conway, K. R. Stormfront, vol. 2. 2014. (The Undertow Ser.). 428p. (YA). (gr. 7-17). pap. 15.95 *(978-0-9897763-4-9(4))* Conway, Kathleen R.
Cook, Kristi. Haven. 2012. (ENG.). 448p. (YA). (gr. 9). pap. 9.99 *(978-1-4424-0761-9(1)*, Simon Pulse) Simon Pulse.
—Mirage. (ENG., (YA). (gr. 9). 2013. Illus.). 416p. pap. 9.99 *(978-1-4424-4300-6(6))* 2012. 384p. 16.99 *(978-1-4424-4299-3(9))* Simon Pulse. (Simon Pulse).
Coppel, Alfred Jr. & Coppel, Alfred. The Peacemaker. 2011. 24p. pap. 6.95 *(978-1-4638-0006-2(1))* Rodgers, Alan Bks.
Córdova, Zoraida. Labyrinth Lost. (Brooklyn Brujas Ser.: 1). (ENG.). (YA). (gr. 8-12). 2017. 352p. pap. 10.99 *(978-1-4926-2316-8(4))* 2016. 336p. 17.99 *(978-1-4926-2094-5(7)*, 9781492620945) Sourcebooks, Inc.
—The Savage Blue. 2014. (Vicious Deep Ser.: 2). (ENG.). 416p. (YA). (gr. 7-12). pap. 14.99 *(978-1-4926-0124-1(1))* Sourcebooks, Inc.
—The Vast & Brutal Sea. (Vicious Deep Ser.: 3). (ENG.). 336p. (YA). 2015. (gr. 8-12). pap. 9.99 *(978-1-4926-0867-7(X))* 2014. (gr. 7-12). 16.99 *(978-1-4022-9620-8(7)*, 9781402296208) Sourcebooks, Inc.
—The Vicious Deep. 2012. (Vicious Deep Ser.: 1). (ENG.). 384p. (YA). (gr. 7-12). pap. 9.99 *(978-1-4022-7441-1(6))* Sourcebooks, Inc.
Cormier, Robert. Fade. 2004. (ENG.). 320p. (YA). (gr. 9-17). pap. 7.99 *(978-0-385-73134-8(5)*, Delacorte Bks. for Young Readers) Random Hse. Children's Bks.

Corriveau, Art. 13 Hangmen. 2012. (ENG.). 352p. (J). (gr. 3-7). 17.95 *(978-1-4197-0159-7(2)*, Amulet Bks.) Abrams, Inc.

Cosimano, Elle. The Suffering Tree. 2017. (ENG.). 368p. (YA). (gr. 9-17). 17.99 ***(978-1-4847-2659-4(6))*** Hyperion Bks. for Children.

Cosper, Andy. The Adventures of Drew Kreeger: Book 1. 2008. 56p. pap. 14.95 *(978-1-4327-3320-9(6))* Outskirts Pr., Inc.

Coville, Bruce. Always October. 2012. (ENG.). 384p. (J). (gr. 3-7). 16.99 *(978-0-06-089095-7(9))* HarperCollins Pubs.

Cowing, Sue. Call Me Drog. 2014. (ENG.). 320p. (J). 13.99 *(978-0-00-757804-7(0))* HarperCollins Pubs. Ltd. GBR. Dist: Independent Pubs. Group.

—You Will Call Me Drog. 2011. (Exceptional Reading & Language Arts Titles for Intermediate Grades Ser.). (ENG.). 288p. (J). (gr. 4-7). 16.95 *(978-0-7613-6076-6(X)*, Carolrhoda Bks.) Lerner Publishing Group.

Craddock, Erik. Dragon Boogie. Craddock, Erik, illus. 2012. (Stone Rabbit Ser.: Vol. 7). (ENG., Illus.). 96p. (J). (gr. 2-5). pap. 6.99 *(978-0-375-86912-9(3)*, Random Hse. Bks. for Young Readers) Random Hse. Children's Bks.

—Dragon Boogie. 2012. (Stone Rabbit Ser.: 7). lib. bdg. 17.20 *(978-0-606-23868-7(9)*, Turtleback) Turtleback Bks.

Cremer, Andrea. Bloodrose. 2012. (Nightshade Ser.: 3). (ENG.). 448p. (YA). (gr. 9). pap. 10.99 *(978-0-14-242370-7(X)*, Speak) Penguin Young Readers Group.

—Bloodrose. 2012. (Nightshade Ser.: 3). lib. bdg. 22.10 *(978-0-606-26635-2(6)*, Turtleback) Turtleback Bks.

—Nightshade. (Nightshade Ser.: 1). (ENG.). (YA). (gr. 9-18). 2011. 496p. pap. 9.99 *(978-0-14-241980-9(X)*, Speak) 2010. 464p. 17.99 *(978-0-399-25482-6(X)*, Philomel Bks.) Penguin Young Readers Group.

—Rift. 2013. (Nightshade Ser.). (ENG.). 480p. (YA). (gr. 9). pap. 9.99 *(978-0-14-242493-3(5)*, Speak) Penguin Young Readers Group.

—Snakeroot. 2014. (Nightshade Ser.: 4). (ENG.). 352p. (YA). (gr. 9). pap. 9.99 *(978-0-14-750860-7(6)*, Speak) Penguin Young Readers Group.

—Wolfsbane. (Nightshade Ser.: 2). (ENG.). (YA). (gr. 9-18). 2012. 432p. 9.99 *(978-0-14-242098-0(0)*, Speak) 2011. 400p. 17.99 *(978-0-399-25483-3(8)*, Philomel Bks.) Penguin Young Readers Group.

Cross, Mimi. Shining Sea, 0 vols. 2016. (ENG.). 432p. (YA). (gr. 9-12). pap. 9.99 *(978-1-5039-3553-2(1)*, 9781503935532, Skyscape) Amazon Publishing.

Crowe, Sara. Bone Jack. 2017. (ENG.). 256p. (J). (gr. 5). 16.99 *(978-0-399-17651-7(9)*, Philomel Bks.) Penguin Young Readers Group.

Crowl, M. Tara. Eden's Wish. 2015. (Eden of the Lamp Ser.). (ENG., Illus.). 268p. (J). (gr. 3-7). 16.99 *(978-1-4847-1185-9(8))* Hyperion Bks. for Children.

Crowley, Kieran Mark. Colm & the Ghost's Revenge. 2012. (ENG.). 320p. (J). pap. 13.95 *(978-1-85635-997-9(2))* Mercier Pr., Ltd., The IRL. Dist: Dufour Editions, Inc.

Curham, Siobhan. Dark of the Moon. 2014. (Shipwrecked Ser.: 2). (ENG.). 288p. (J). (gr. 7). pap. 12.99 *(978-1-4052-6458-7(6))* Egmont Bks., Ltd. GBR. Dist: Independent Pubs. Group.

Cusick, Richie Tankersley. Blood Brothers: The Unseen #3. 2006. (Unseen Ser.: 3). (ENG.). 272p. (YA). (gr. 7-18). 8.99 *(978-0-14-240583-3(3)*, Speak) Penguin Young Readers Group.

—It Begins - Rest in Peace, Vol. 1. 2012. (Unseen Ser.: 1). (ENG.). 576p. (YA). (gr. 7). pap. 7.99 *(978-0-14-242336-3(X)*, Speak) Penguin Young Readers Group.

—The Unseen 1 It Begins. 2005. (Unseen Ser.: 1). (ENG.). 304p. (YA). (gr. 7-7). 8.99 *(978-0-14-240463-8(2)*, Speak) Penguin Young Readers Group.

—The Unseen Volume 2: Blood Brothers/Sin & Salvation. 2012. (Unseen Ser.: 2). (ENG.). 640p. (YA). (gr. 7). pap. 7.99 *(978-0-14-242337-0(8)*, Speak) Penguin Young Readers Group.

Dahl, Michael. Dark Tower Rising, 1 vol. Kovar, Ben, illus. 2012. (Troll Hunters Ser.). (ENG.). 112p. (gr. 2-3). lib. bdg. 25.32 *(978-1-4342-3308-0(1)*, Troll Hunters) Stone Arch Bks.

—Fallen Star, 1 vol. Kovar, Ben, illus. 2012. (Troll Hunters Ser.). (ENG.). 112p. (gr. 2-3). lib. bdg. 25.32 *(978-1-4342-3310-3(3)*, Troll Hunters) Stone Arch Bks.

—The Lava Crown, 1 vol. Kovar, Ben, illus. 2012. (Troll Hunters Ser.). (ENG.). 112p. (gr. 2-3). lib. bdg. 25.32 *(978-1-4342-3309-7(X)*, Troll Hunters) Stone Arch Bks.

—Skyfall, 1 vol. Kovar, Ben, illus. 2012. (Troll Hunters Ser.). (ENG.). 112p. (gr. 2-3). lib. bdg. 25.32 *(978-1-4342-3307-3(3)*, Troll Hunters) Stone Arch Bks.

—Troll Hunters, 1 vol. Kovar, Ben, illus. 2012. (Troll Hunters Ser.). (ENG.). 320p. (gr. 4-4). 12.95 *(978-1-4342-4590-8(X))* Stone Arch Bks.

Damico, Gina. Wax. (ENG.). (gr. 7). 2017. 384p. (YA). pap. 9.99 *(978-0-544-93718-5(X))* 2016. 368p. (J). 17.99 *(978-0-544-63315-5(6))* Houghton Mifflin Harcourt Publishing Co. (HMH Books For Young Readers).

Darke, J. A. Spine Shivers. Evans, Neil, illus. 2016. (Spine Shivers Ser.). (ENG.). 128p. (gr. 3-4). 159.90 *(978-1-4965-3080-6(2))* Stone Arch Bks.

Darrows, Eva. The Awesome. 2015. (ENG.). 352p. (YA). (gr. 10). pap. 9.99 *(978-1-78108-324-6(X)*, Ravenstone) Rebellion GBR. Dist: Simon & Schuster, Inc.

Davies, Anna. Wrecked. (ENG., Illus.). 336p. (YA). (gr. 9). 2013. pap. 9.99 *(978-1-4424-3279-6(9))* 2012. 16.99 *(978-1-4424-3278-9(0))* Simon & Schuster Bks. For Young Readers. (Simon & Schuster Bks. For Young Readers).

Davies, Jocelyn. A Beautiful Dark. 2012. (ENG.). 416p. (YA). (gr. 8). pap. 9.99 *(978-0-06-199066-3(3)*, HarperTeen) HarperCollins Pubs.

—A Fractured Light. 2013. (ENG.). 368p. (YA). (gr. 8). pap. 9.99 *(978-0-06-199068-7(X)*, HarperTeen) HarperCollins Pubs.

—A Radiant Sky. 2014. (ENG.). 384p. (YA). (gr. 8). pap. 9.99 *(978-0-06-199070-0(1)*, HarperTeen) HarperCollins Pubs.

Davis, Bryan. Beyond the Gateway (Reapers Trilogy V2) 2015. (ENG.). 384p. (YA). pap. 12.99 *(978-0-9898122-4-5(3))* Scrub Jay Journeys.

Dawson, Delilah S. Servants of the Storm. 2014. (ENG., Illus.). 384p. (YA). (gr. 9). 17.99 *(978-1-4424-8378-1(4)*, Simon Pulse) Simon Pulse.

De Haven, Tom. The Orphan's Tent. 2005. (Illus.). 192p. mass mkt. 5.99 *(978-0-7434-9772-5(4))* ibooks, Inc.

De la Cruz, Melissa. Triple Moon: Summer on East End. 2015. (Summer on East End Ser.). (ENG.). 368p. (YA). (gr. 7). 17.99 *(978-0-399-17355-4(2)*, G.P. Putnam's Sons Books for Young Readers) Penguin Young Readers Group.

de Lint, Charles. The Blue Girl. 2006. (ENG.). 384p. (YA). (gr. 7-18). reprint ed. 7.99 *(978-0-14-240545-1(0)*, Firebird) Penguin Young Readers Group.

—Waifs & Strays. 2004. (ENG.). 416p. (YA). (gr. 7-18). 8.99 *(978-0-14-240158-3(7)*, Firebird) Penguin Young Readers Group.

Degrado, Louis Paul. The Questors' Adventures: The Round House & the Moaning Walls. 2012. 326p. 29.95 *(978-1-4759-4469-3(1))*; pap. 19.95 *(978-1-4759-4470-9(5))* iUniverse, Inc.

DeGreeff, Davy. Tommy Bomani: Badru Rising, 1 vol. Brookins, Sam, illus. 2010. (Tommy Bomani: Teen Warrior Ser.: Bk. 3). (ENG.). 112p. (gr. 3-8). 27.07 *(978-1-60270-699-6(9)*, Calico Chapter Bks) Magic Wagon.

—Tommy Bomani: Land of Legend, 1 vol. Brookins, Sam, illus. 2010. (Tommy Bomani: Teen Warrior Ser.: Bk. 2). (ENG.). 112p. (gr. 3-8). 27.07 *(978-1-60270-698-9(0)*, Calico Chapter Bks) Magic Wagon.

—Tommy Bomani: Prophecy Fulfilled, 1 vol. Brookins, Sam, illus. 2010. (Tommy Bomani: Teen Warrior Ser.: Bk. 4). (ENG.). 112p. (gr. 3-8). 27.07 *(978-1-60270-700-9(6)*, Calico Chapter Bks) Magic Wagon.

—Tommy Bomani: Shape-Shifter, 1 vol. Brookins, Sam, illus. 2010. (Tommy Bomani: Teen Warrior Ser.: Bk. 1). (ENG.). 112p. (gr. 3-8). 27.07 *(978-1-60270-697-2(2)*, Calico Chapter Bks) Magic Wagon.

Del Negro, Janice M. Passion & Poison: Tales of Shape-Shifters, Ghosts, & Spirited Women, 0 vols. Natale, Vince, illus. 2013. (ENG.). 64p. (J). (gr. 5-7). pap. 9.99 *(978-1-4778-1685-1(2)*, 9781477816851, Amazon Children's Publishing) Amazon Publishing.

Delaney, Joseph. Attack of the Fiend. Arrasmith, Patrick, illus. 2009. (Last Apprentice Ser.: 4). (ENG.). 576p. (YA). (gr. 8-18). pap. 9.99 *(978-0-06-089129-9(7)*, Greenwillow Bks.) HarperCollins Pubs.

—Clash of the Demons. Arrasmith, Patrick, illus. (Last Apprentice Ser.: 6). (YA). (gr. 8). 2009. 416p. lib. bdg. 18.89 *(978-0-06-134463-3(X))* 2009. (ENG.). 416p. 17.99 *(978-0-06-134462-6(1))*Bk. 6. 2010. (ENG.). 432p. pap. 9.99 *(978-0-06-134464-0(8))* HarperCollins Pubs. (Greenwillow Bks.).

—A Coven of Witches. Arrasmith, Patrick, illus. (Last Apprentice Short Fiction Ser.: 2). 240p. (YA). (gr. 8). 2011. (ENG.). pap. 9.99 *(978-0-06-196040-6(3))* 2010. lib. bdg. 17.89 *(978-0-06-196039-0(X))* 2010. (ENG.). 16.99 *(978-0-06-196038-3(1))* HarperCollins Pubs. (Greenwillow Bks.).

—Curse of the Bane. Arrasmith, Patrick, illus. (Last Apprentice Ser.: 2). (YA). (gr. 8-9). 2007. (ENG.). 496p. pap. 9.99 *(978-0-06-076623-8(9))* 2006. (ENG.). 480p. 17.99 *(978-0-06-076621-4(2))*Bk. 2. 2006. 480p. lib. bdg. 19.89 *(978-0-06-076622-1(0))* HarperCollins Pubs. (Greenwillow Bks.).

—Fury of the Seventh Son, Bk. 13. Arrasmith, Patrick, illus. (Last Apprentice Ser.: 13). (ENG.). 480p. (YA). (gr. 8). 2015. pap. 9.99 *(978-0-06-219232-5(9))* 2014. 17.99 *(978-0-06-219231-8(0))* HarperCollins Pubs. (Greenwillow Bks.).

—Ghost Prison. (ENG.). 112p. (YA). (gr. 6-12). 2014. pap. 5.99 *(978-1-4926-0174-6(8))* 2013. 12.99 *(978-1-4022-9318-4(6)*, 9781402293184) Sourcebooks, Inc.

—Grimalkin the Witch Assassin Bk. 9, Bk. 9. Arrasmith, Patrick, illus. 2012. (Last Apprentice Ser.: 9). (ENG.). 400p. (YA). (gr. 8). 17.99 *(978-0-06-208207-7(8)*, Greenwillow Bks.) HarperCollins Pubs.

—The Last Apprentice Bk. 8: Rage of the Fallen. Arrasmith, Patrick, illus. 2012. (Last Apprentice Ser.: 8). (ENG.). 416p. (YA). (gr. 8). pap. 9.99 *(978-0-06-202758-0(1)*, Greenwillow Bks.) HarperCollins Pubs.

—The Last Apprentice - Revenge of the Witch, Bk. 1. Arrasmith, Patrick, illus. 2006. (Last Apprentice Ser.: 1). (ENG.). 384p. (YA). (gr. 8). reprint ed. pap. 9.99 *(978-0-06-076620-7(4)*, Greenwillow Bks.) HarperCollins Pubs.

—A New Darkness. 2014. (ENG.). 352p. (YA). (gr. 8). 17.99 *(978-0-06-233453-4(0)*, Greenwillow Bks.) HarperCollins Pubs.

—Night of the Soul Stealer, Bk. 3. 2008. (Last Apprentice Ser.: 3). (ENG.). 528p. (YA). (gr. 8-18). pap. 9.99 *(978-0-06-076626-9(3)*, Greenwillow Bks.) HarperCollins Pubs.

—Night of the Soul Stealer Bk. 3. Arrasmith, Patrick, illus. 2007. (Last Apprentice Ser.: 3). (ENG.). 512p. (YA). (gr. 8-9). 17.99 *(978-0-06-076624-5(7)*, Greenwillow Bks.) HarperCollins Pubs.

—Rage of the Fallen, Bk. 8. Arrasmith, Patrick, illus. 2011. (Last Apprentice Ser.: 8). (ENG.). 416p. (YA). (gr. 8-18). 17.99 *(978-0-06-202756-6(5)*, Greenwillow Bks.) HarperCollins Pubs.

—Revenge of the Witch, Bk. 1. Arrasmith, Patrick, illus. 2005. (Last Apprentice Ser.: 1). (ENG.). 368p. (YA). (gr. 8). 17.99 *(978-0-06-076618-4(2)*, Greenwillow Bks.) HarperCollins Pubs.

—Rise of the Huntress, Bk. 7. Arrasmith, Patrick, illus. 2010. (Last Apprentice Ser.: 7). (ENG.). 448p. (YA). (gr. 8-18). 17.99 *(978-0-06-171510-5(7)*, Greenwillow Bks.) HarperCollins Pubs.

—Rise of the Huntress Bk. 7, Bk. 7. Arrasmith, Patrick, illus. 2011. (Last Apprentice Ser.: 7). (ENG.). 464p. (YA). (gr. 8). pap. 9.99 *(978-0-06-171512-9(3)*, Greenwillow Bks.) HarperCollins Pubs.

—Slither, Bk. 11. 2013. (Last Apprentice Ser.: 11). (ENG.). 416p. (YA). (gr. 8). 17.99 *(978-0-06-219234-9(5)*, Greenwillow Bks.) HarperCollins Pubs.

—The Spook's Bestiary: The Guide to Creatures of the Dark. Heller, Julek, illus. 2011. (Last Apprentice Short Fiction Ser.: 3). (ENG.). 240p. (YA). (gr. 8). 16.99 *(978-0-06-208114-8(4)*, Greenwillow Bks.) HarperCollins Pubs.

—The Spook's Tale - And Other Horrors. 2010. (Last Apprentice Short Fiction Ser.: 1). (ENG.). 176p. (YA). (gr. 8-18). pap. 8.99 *(978-0-06-173031-3(9)*, Greenwillow Bks.) HarperCollins Pubs.

—The Spook's Tale: And Other Horrors. 2009. (Last Apprentice Short Fiction Ser.: 1). (ENG.). 176p. (YA). (gr. 8-18). 16.99 *(978-0-06-173028-3(9)*, Greenwillow Bks.) HarperCollins Pubs.

—The Spook's Tale-And Other Horrors. 2009. (Last Apprentice Short Fiction Ser.: 1). 176p. (YA). (gr. 8). lib. bdg. 14.89 *(978-0-06-173030-6(0)*, Greenwillow Bks.) HarperCollins Pubs.

—Wrath of the Bloodeye. (Last Apprentice Ser.: 5). (ENG.). (YA). (gr. 8-18). 2009. 544p. pap. 9.99 *(978-0-06-134461-9(3))*Bk. 5. 2008. 528p. 17.99 *(978-0-06-134459-6(1))* HarperCollins Pubs. (Greenwillow Bks.).

Delany, Shannon. Destiny & Deception: A 13 to Life Novel. 2012. (13 to Life Ser.: 4). (ENG.). 304p. (YA). (gr. 7). pap. 17.99 *(978-0-312-62446-0(8)*, 9780312624460, St. Martin's Griffin) St. Martin's Pr.

—Rivals & Retribution: A 13 to Life Novel. 2012. (13 to Life Ser.: 5). (ENG.). 320p. (YA). (gr. 8-12). pap. 17.99 *(978-0-312-62518-4(9)*, 9780312625184, St. Martin's Griffin) St. Martin's Pr.

Delany, Shannon & Redgrave, Saoirse. Secrets & Shadows: A 13 to Life Novel. 2011. (13 to Life Ser.: 2). (ENG.). 320p. (YA). (gr. 7-18). pap. 9.99 *(978-0-312-60915-3(9)*, 9780312609153, St. Martin's Griffin) St. Martin's Pr.

Delsol, Wendy. Flock. 2013. (ENG.). 400p. (YA). (gr. 7). pap. 8.99 *(978-0-7636-6467-1(7))* Candlewick Pr.

—Frost. (ENG., Illus.). (YA). (gr. 7). 2012. 384p. pap. 8.99 *(978-0-7636-6249-3(6))* 2011. 376p. 15.99 *(978-0-7636-5386-6(1))* Candlewick Pr.

—Stork. (ENG., Illus.). (YA). (gr. 7). 2011. 368p. pap. 8.99 *(978-0-7636-5687-4(9))* 2010. 357p. 15.99 *(978-0-7636-4844-2(2))* Candlewick Pr.

Demetrios, Heather. Exquisite Captive. 2014. (Dark Caravan Cycle Ser.: 1). (ENG., Illus.). 480p. (YA). (gr. 8). 17.99 *(978-0-06-231856-5(X))* HarperCollins Pubs.

Derek the Ghost Staff. Monsters on the March. Fischer, Scott M., illus. 2013. (Scary School Ser.: 2). (ENG.). 272p. (J). (gr. 3-7). pap. 6.99 *(978-0-06-196097-0(7))* HarperCollins Pubs.

—The Northern Frights. Fischer, Scott M., illus. 2013. (Scary School Ser.: 3). (ENG.). 272p. (J). (gr. 3-7). 16.99 *(978-0-06-196098-7(5))* HarperCollins Pubs.

—Scary School. Fischer, Scott M., illus. (Scary School Ser.: 1). (ENG.). (J). (gr. 3-7). 2012. 272p. pap. 6.99 *(978-0-06-196094-9(2))* 2011. 256p. 16.99 *(978-0-06-196092-5(6))* HarperCollins Pubs.

Despain, Bree. The Dark Divine. 2010. (ENG.). 384p. (gr. 7). pap. 9.99 *(978-1-60684-154-9(8)*, Carolrhoda Lab™) Lerner Publishing Group.

—The Lost Saint. 2011. (ENG.). 416p. (J). (gr. 7). pap. 9.99 *(978-1-60684-235-5(8)*, Carolrhoda Lab™) Lerner Publishing Group.

—The Savage Grace. 2013. (ENG.). 496p. (J). (gr. 7). pap. 9.99 *(978-1-60684-416-8(4)*, Carolrhoda Lab™) Lerner Publishing Group.

Desrochers, Lisa. Original Sin. 2011. (Personal Demons Ser.: 2). (ENG.). 400p. (YA). (gr. 9-18). pap. 25.99 *(978-0-7653-2809-0(7)*, 9780765328090, Tor Teen) Doherty, Tom Assocs., LLC.

Diamand, Emily. Ways to See a Ghost. 2013. (ENG.). 400p. (YA). (gr. 8). pap. 11.99 *(978-1-84877-554-1(7))* Bonnier Publishing GBR. Dist: Independent Pubs. Group.

DiTerlizzi, Tony & Black, Holly. Lucinda's Secret. l.t. ed. 2006. (Spiderwick Chronicles: Bk. 3). (Illus.). 142p. (J). (gr. 4-7). 23.95 *(978-0-7862-8585-3(0))* Thorndike Pr.

d'Lacey, Chris. Alexander's Army. 2015. (UFiles Ser.: 2). (ENG.). 304p. (J). (gr. 3-7). 16.99 *(978-0-545-60880-0(5)*, Scholastic Pr.) Scholastic, Inc.

—Dark Fire. (Last Dragon Chronicles Ser.: 5). (ENG.). 576p. (J). (gr. 3-7). 2011. pap. 8.99 *(978-0-545-10273-5(1))* 2010. 17.99 *(978-0-545-10272-8(3)*, Orchard Bks.) Scholastic, Inc.

—A Dark Inheritance. 2014. (UFiles Ser.). (ENG.). 304p. (J). (gr. 3-7). 16.99 *(978-0-545-60876-3(7)*, Scholastic Pr.) Scholastic, Inc.

—The Fire Eternal. 2008. (Last Dragon Chronicles Ser.: 4). (ENG.). 512p. (J). (gr. 3-7). 17.99 *(978-0-545-05163-7(0)*, Orchard Bks.) Scholastic, Inc.

—The Fire Eternal. 2010. (Last Dragon Chronicles Ser.: 4). lib. bdg. 19.65 *(978-0-606-12558-1(2)*, Turtleback) Turtleback Bks.

—Fire Star. 2008. (Last Dragon Chronicles Ser.: 3). (ENG.). 560p. (J). (gr. 3-7). 8.99 *(978-0-439-90185-7(5)*, Orchard Bks.) Scholastic, Inc.

—The Fire Within. 2007. (Last Dragon Chronicles Ser.: 1). (ENG.). 352p. (J). (gr. 3-7). pap. 8.99 *(978-0-439-67244-3(9)*, Orchard Bks.) Scholastic, Inc.

—Fire World. 2012. (Last Dragon Chronicles Ser.: 6). lib. bdg. 19.65 *(978-0-606-23967-7(7)*, Turtleback) Turtleback Bks.

—Icefire. 2007. (Last Dragon Chronicles Ser.: 2). (ENG.). 432p. (J). (gr. 3-7). pap. 8.99 *(978-0-439-67246-7(5)*, Orchard Bks.) Scholastic, Inc.

d'Lacey, Jay & d'Lacey, Chris. Rain & Fire. 2012. (Last Dragon Chronicles Ser.). (ENG.). 304p. (J). (gr. 3-7). 16.99 *(978-0-545-41453-1(9)*, Orchard Bks.) Scholastic, Inc.

Donnelly, Jennifer. Dark Tide. 2015. (Waterfire Saga Ser.: Bk. 3). (ENG.). 400p. (YA). (gr. 7-12). 17.99 *(978-1-4231-8201-6(4))* Hyperion Bks. for Children.

—Deep Blue. 2014. (Waterfire Saga Novel Ser.: Bk. 1). (ENG., Illus.). 352p. (YA). (gr. 7-12). 17.99 *(978-1-4231-3316-2(1))* Disney Pr.

—Deep Blue. 2015. (Waterfire Saga Ser.: Bk. 1). (ENG.). 368p. (YA). (gr. 7-12). pap. 9.99 *(978-1-4847-1310-5(9))* Hyperion Bks. for Children.

—Rogue Wave. 2015. (Waterfire Saga Novel Ser.: Bk. 2). (ENG.). 320p. (YA). (gr. 7-12). 17.99 *(978-1-4231-8200-9(6))* Disney Pr.

—Rogue Wave. 2016. (Waterfire Saga Ser.: Bk. 2). (ENG.). 336p. (YA). (gr. 7-12). pap. 9.99 *(978-1-4847-1301-3(X))* Hyperion Bks. for Children.

—Waterfire Saga, Book Four: Sea Spell. 2016. (Waterfire Saga Novel Ser.). (ENG.). 368p. (YA). (gr. 7-12). 17.99 *(978-1-4847-1290-0(0))* Hyperion Bks. for Children.

Dorset, Skylar. The Boy with the Hidden Name. 2014. (Otherworld Ser.: 2). (ENG.). 320p. (YA). (gr. 7-12). pap. 9.99 *(978-1-4022-9256-9(2)*, 9781402292569) Sourcebooks, Inc.

—The Girl Who Never Was. 2014. (Otherworld Ser.: 1). (ENG.). 304p. (YA). (gr. 7-12). pap. 9.99 *(978-1-4022-9253-8(8)*, 9781402292538) Sourcebooks, Inc.

Duff, Hilary. Devoted: An Elixir Novel. 2012. (Elixir Ser.). (ENG.). 368p. (YA). (gr. 9). pap. 9.99 *(978-1-4424-0856-2(1)*, Simon & Schuster Bks. For Young Readers) Simon & Schuster Bks. For Young Readers.

—Elixir. 2011. (Playaway Young Adult Ser.). (YA). 59.99 *(978-1-4417-7416-3(5))* Findaway World, LLC.

—Elixir. 2011. (Elixir Ser.). (ENG.). 336p. (YA). (gr. 9). pap. 9.99 *(978-1-4424-0854-8(5)*, Simon & Schuster Bks. For Young Readers) Simon & Schuster Bks. For Young Readers.

—True: An Elixir Novel. (Elixir Ser.). (ENG.). 304p. (YA). (gr. 7). 2014. Illus.). pap. 9.99 *(978-1-4424-0858-6(8))* 2013. 17.99 *(978-1-4424-0857-9(X))* Simon & Schuster Bks. For Young Readers. (Simon & Schuster Bks. For Young Readers).

Duff, Hilary & Allen, Elise. Elixir. 2010. (Elixir Ser.). (ENG.). 336p. (YA). (gr. 9-18). 17.99 *(978-1-4424-0853-1(7)*, Simon & Schuster Bks. For Young Readers) Simon & Schuster Bks. For Young Readers.

Duncan, Lois. Down a Dark Hall. 2011. (ENG.). 240p. (YA). (gr. 7-17). pap., pap. 10.99 *(978-0-316-09898-4(1))* Little, Brown Bks. for Young Readers.

—Down a Dark Hall. 181p. (YA). (gr. 7-18). pap. 4.99 *(978-0-8072-1370-4(5)*, Listening Library) Random Hse. Audio Publishing Group.

Duncan, S. L. The Salvation of Gabriel Adam. 2015. (Revelation Saga Ser.: 2). (ENG.). 400p. (gr. 6). pap. 9.99 *(978-1-60542-602-0(4))* Nodin Pr.

Dunning, John Harris & Singh, Nikhil. Salem Brownstone: All along the Watchtowers. Singh, Nikhil, illus. 2010. (ENG., Illus.). 96p. (YA). (gr. 7-18). 18.99 *(978-0-7636-4735-3(7))* Candlewick Pr.

Durst, Sarah Beth. Conjured. 2014. (ENG.). 384p. (YA). (gr. 9). pap. 9.99 *(978-0-8027-3749-6(8)*, 9780802737496, Bloomsbury USA Childrens) Bloomsbury Publishing USA.

—Ice. (ENG.). (YA). (gr. 7). 2010. 336p. pap. 8.99 *(978-1-4169-8644-7(8))* 2009. 320p. 16.99 *(978-1-4169-8643-0(X))* McElderry, Margaret K. Bks. (McElderry, Margaret K. Bks.).

Edge, Christopher. The Black Crow Conspiracy. 2015. (Penelope Tredwell Mysteries Ser.: 3). (ENG.). 272p. (J). (gr. 3-7). 16.99 *(978-0-8075-0780-3(6))* Whitman, Albert & Co.

—Shadows of the Silver Screen. 2014. (Penelope Tredwell Mysteries Ser.: 2). (ENG.). 256p. (J). (gr. 3-7). 16.99 *(978-0-8075-7319-8(1))* Whitman, Albert & Co.

—Twelve Minutes to Midnight. 2014. (Penelope Tredwell Mysteries Ser.: Book 1). (ENG.). 256p. (J). (gr. 3-7). 16.99 *(978-0-8075-8133-9(X))* Whitman, Albert & Co.

Elfgren, Sara B. & Strandberg, Mats. Fire: The Engelsfors Trilogy Book II. 2014. (Engelsfors Trilogy Ser.: 2). (ENG.). 704p. (gr. 9-13). 18.99 *(978-1-4683-0672-9(3)*, 460672) Overlook Pr., The.

Eliopulos, Nick. The Book of Shane. 2015. (Spirit Animals Special Edition Ser.). (ENG.). 192p. (J). (gr. 3-7). 12.99 *(978-0-545-91098-9(6))* Scholastic, Inc.

Enderle, Dotti. Ghost Detectors Volume 1: Let the Specter-Detecting Begin, Books 1-3. McWilliam, Howard, illus. 2013. (Ghost Detectors Ser.: 1). (ENG.). 192p. (gr. 2-7). pap. 8.95 *(978-1-938063-28-2(7)*, Mighty Media Junior Readers) Mighty Media Pr.

Endless Knight. 2014. (Arcana Chronicles Ser.). (ENG., Illus.). 336p. (YA). (gr. 9). pap. 11.99 *(978-1-4424-3668-8(9)*, Simon & Schuster Bks. For Young Readers) Simon & Schuster Bks. For Young Readers.

Estep, Jennifer. Killer Frost. 2014. (ENG.). 368p. (YA). (gr. 9). pap. 9.95 *(978-0-7582-8152-4(8)*, K-Teen) Kensington Publishing Corp.

—Touch of Frost. 2011. (ENG.). 336p. (YA). (gr. 9). 9.95 *(978-0-7582-6692-7(8)*, K-Teen) Kensington Publishing Corp.

Evangelista, Kate. Til Death. 2014. (Fractured Souls Ser.). (ENG.). (YA). (gr. 7-12). pap. 9.99 *(978-1-62266-232-6(6)*, 9781622662326) Entangled Publishing, LLC.

Evans, Neil, illus. Spine Shivers. 2016. (Spine Shivers Ser.). (ENG.). 128p. (gr. 3-4). pap. 13.90 *(978-1-4965-3083-7(7))* Stone Arch Bks.

Ewing, Lynne. Daughters of the Moon, Vol. 1. 2010. (ENG.). 848p. (J). (gr. 7-17). pap. 9.99 *(978-1-4231-3450-3(8))* Disney Pr.

Fallon, Leigh. Carrier of the Mark. 2011. (Carrier of the Mark Ser.: 1). (ENG.). 352p. (YA). (gr. 8). pap. 8.99 *(978-0-06-202787-0(5)*, HarperTeen) HarperCollins Pubs.

—Shadow of the Mark. 2013. (Carrier of the Mark Ser.: 2). (ENG.). 320p. (YA). (gr. 8). pap. 9.99 *(978-0-06-212600-3(0)*, HarperTeen) HarperCollins Pubs.

Fama, Elizabeth. Monstrous Beauty. 2013. (ENG.). 352p. (YA). (gr. 7-12). pap. 9.99 *(978-1-250-03425-0(6))* Square Fish.

Fantaskey, Beth. Jekel Loves Hyde. 2011. (ENG.). 288p. (YA). (gr. 9). pap. 8.99 *(978-0-547-55027-5(8))* Houghton Mifflin Harcourt Publishing Co.

Farley, Christina. Gilded, 0 vols. 2014. (Gilded Ser.: 1). (ENG.). 352p. (YA). (gr. 7-13). pap. 9.99 *(978-1-4778-1097-2(8)*, 9781477810972) Amazon Publishing.

Farley, Steven. The Black Stallion & the Shape-Shifter. 2010. (Black Stallion Ser.). (ENG.). 272p. (J). (gr. 3-7). 8.99 *(978-0-375-84532-1(1)*, Yearling) Random Hse. Children's Bks.

Feil, Hila. Blue Moon. 2007. (ENG., Illus.). 272p. (YA). (gr. 7). pap. 17.99 *(978-0-15-205933-0(4))* Houghton Mifflin Harcourt Publishing Co.

Ferguson, Jo Ann. The Cabinet of Souls. 2016. lib. bdg. 17.20 *(978-0-606-38787-3(0))* Turtleback Bks.

Fewer, Patrick W. Sammy the Snow Snake: A Halloween Haunting Yukon Style. 2009. 24p. pap. 11.49 *(978-1-4490-2075-0(5))* AuthorHouse.

Fields, Jan. The Emerald Dragon. 2015. (Creative Girls Enchanted Adventures Ser.). (ENG.). 104p. (J). (gr. 2-5). pap. 5.99 *(978-1-57367-467-6(2)*, Annie's) Annie's Publishing, LLC.

—Wellspring of Magic. 2015. (Creative Girls Enchanted Adventures Ser.). (ENG.). 128p. (J). (gr. 2-5). pap. 5.99 *(978-1-57367-463-8(X)*, Annie's) Annie's Publishing, LLC.

Fischer, Rusty. Vampire Book of the Month Club. 2016. (ENG.). 312p. (YA). (gr. 6). pap. 9.99 *(978-1-942546-38-2(6))* Nodin Pr.

—Zombies Don't Cry. 2011. (Living Dead Love Story Ser.: 1). (ENG.). 371p. (YA). (gr. 6-18). pap. 9.95 (978-1-60542-382-1(3), Gold Medallion) Medallion Pr., Inc.
Fisher, Catherine. Darkwater. 2012. (ENG.). 240p. (YA). (gr. 7). 16.99 (978-0-8037-3818-8(8), Dial Bks) Penguin Young Readers Group.
Fitzpatrick, Becca. The Complete Hush, Hush Saga: Hush, Hush; Crescendo; Silence; Finale. 2012. (Hush, Hush Saga Ser.: Bks. 1-4). (ENG.). 1744p. (YA). (gr. 9). 74.99 (978-1-4424-7372-0(X), Simon & Schuster Bks. For Young Readers) Simon & Schuster Bks. For Young Readers.
—Crescendo. 2011. (Hush, Hush Saga: Bk. 2). (SPA.). 408p. (YA). pap. 20.95 (978-84-666-4639-0(6)) Ediciones B ESP. Dist: Spanish Pubs., LLC.
—Crescendo. (Hush, Hush Saga Ser.: Bk. 2). (ENG.). (YA). (gr. 9). 2012. 464p. pap. 12.99 (978-1-4169-8944-8(7)) 2010. 432p. 18.99 (978-1-4169-8943-1(9)) Simon & Schuster Bks. For Young Readers. (Simon & Schuster Bks. For Young Readers).
—Finale. (Hush, Hush Saga Ser.). (ENG., (YA). (gr. 9). 2013. Illus.). 480p. pap. 12.99 (978-1-4424-2668-9(3)) 2012. 464p. 19.99 (978-1-4424-2667-2(5)) Simon & Schuster Bks. For Young Readers. (Simon & Schuster Bks. For Young Readers).
—Hush, Hush. (SPA.). 368p. 2010. (Hush, Hush Saga: Bk. 1). (YA). pap. 20.95 (978-84-666-4417-4(2)) pap. 13.95 (978-84-9872-932-0(7)) Ediciones B ESP. Dist: Spanish Pubs., LLC.
—Hush, Hush, 3 vols. Ruiz, Derek, ed. 2012. (Hush, Hush Saga: Bk. 1). (Illus.). 120p. (YA). 19.95 (978-0-9836131-1-4(7)) Sea Lion Bks.
—Hush, Hush. (Hush, Hush Saga Ser.: Bk. 1). (ENG.). (YA). (gr. 9-18). 2010. 432p. pap. 11.99 (978-1-4169-8942-4(0)) 2009. 400p. 21.99 (978-1-4169-8941-7(2)) Simon & Schuster Bks. For Young Readers. (Simon & Schuster Bks. For Young Readers).
—Silence. (Hush, Hush Saga Ser.: Bk. 3). (ENG.). (YA). (gr. 9). 2013. 464p. pap. 12.99 (978-1-4424-2665-8(9)) 2011. 448p. 18.99 (978-1-4424-2664-1(0)) Simon & Schuster Bks. For Young Readers. (Simon & Schuster Bks. For Young Readers).
Fletcher, Brenden. Yearbook. 2016. (Gotham Academy Ser.: 3). lib. bdg. 29.40 (978-0-606-39222-8(X)) Turtleback Bks.
Fowley-Doyle, Moira. The Accident Season. 2015. (ENG.). 304p. (YA). (gr. 9). 17.99 (978-0-525-42948-7(4), Kathy Dawson Books) Penguin Young Readers Group.
France, Emily. Signs of You. 2016. (ENG.). 240p. (YA). (gr. 9). 18.99 (978-1-61695-657-8(7), Soho Teen) Soho Pr., Inc.
Fraustino, Lisa Rowe. The Hole in the Wall. 2011. (ENG.). 232p. (J). (gr. 2-8). pap. 8.00 (978-1-57131-698-1(1)) Milkweed Editions.
Frazier, Angie. The Eternal Sea. 2011. (ENG.). 368p. (J). (gr. 7-7). 17.99 (978-0-545-11475-2(6), Scholastic Pr.) Scholastic, Inc.
—Everlasting. 2010. (ENG.). 336p. (J). (gr. 7-18). 17.99 (978-0-545-11473-8(X), Scholastic Pr.) Scholastic, Inc.
Frenette, Bethany. Burn Bright. 2014. (Dark Star Ser.). (ENG.). 352p. (YA). (gr. 7-12). 17.99 (978-1-4231-4666-7(2)) Hyperion Bks. for Children.
—Dark Star. 2013. (Dark Star Ser.). (ENG.). 384p. (YA). (gr. 7-12). pap. 9.99 (978-1-4231-4853-1(3)) Hyperion Pr.
Friesner, Esther M. Spirit's Princess. 2012. (Princesses of Myth Ser.). (ENG.). 464p. (YA). (gr. 7). 17.99 (978-0-375-86907-5(7), Random Hse. Bks. for Young Readers) Random Hse. Children's Bks.
Frost, Heather. Guardians. 2013. (Seers - Trilogy Ser.: Vol. 3). (ENG.). 424p. (J). (gr. 8-12). pap. 17.99 (978-1-4621-1035-3(5), Sweetwater Bks.) Cedar Fort, Inc./CFI Distribution.
Frost, Mark. Rogue: The Paladin Prophecy Book 3. 2015. (Paladin Prophecy Ser.). (ENG.). 368p. (YA). (gr. 7). 17.99 (978-0-375-87047-7(4), Random Hse. Bks. for Young Readers) Random Hse. Children's Bks.
Fujishima, Kosuke. Oh My Goddess!, Vol. 34. Fujishima, Kosuke, illus. 2010. (ENG., Illus.). 144p. pap. 10.99 (978-1-59582-448-6(0)) Dark Horse Comics.
G. Nadel, H. Eternal. l.t. ed. 2013. 194p. pap. (978-1-4596-6748-8(4)) ReadHowYouWant.com, Ltd.
Gaiman, NEil. Coraline. 2003. (FRE.). (J). (gr. 5-8). pap. **(978-2-226-14019-7(0))** Albin-Michel, Editions.
—Coraline. McKean, Dave, illus. (P. S. Ser.). (ENG.). 2006. 192p. (gr. 6-8). pap. 12.99 (978-0-06-113937-6(8), William Morrow Paperbacks) 2004. 224p. (J). (gr. 3-7). pap. 8.99 (978-0-06-057591-5(3)) HarperCollins Pubs.
—Coraline, 12 Copies. 2003. (J). pap. 71.88 (978-0-06-056895-5(X)); pap. 71.88 (978-0-06-057152-8(7)) HarperCollins Pubs.
—Coraline. 2003. 162p. (gr. 7-9). 17.00 (978-0-7569-1568-1(6)) Perfection Learning Corp.
—Coraline. McKean, Dave, illus. 2007. 151p. (J). (gr. 6-8). 60.00 (978-1-59606-147-7(2)) Subterranean Pr.
—CORALINE. 2009. (SPA.). 160p. (YA). pap. 12.95 (978-84-9838-237-2(8)) Publicaciones y Ediciones Salamandra, S.A. ESP. Dist: Spanish Pubs., LLC.
—CORALINE. 2009. (SPA.). 188p. (YA). 20.95 (978-84-92429-74-5(7)) Roca Editorial ESP. Dist: Spanish Pubs., LLC.
—Coraline. 3rd ed. 2003. (SPA., Illus.). 160p. (978-84-7888-579-4(X), 1952) Emece Editores.
—Coraline. McKean, Dave, illus. movie tie-in ed. 2008. (ENG.). 176p. (J). (gr. 3). pap. 6.99 (978-0-06-164969-1(4), HarperFestival) HarperCollins Pubs.
—Coraline. 2012. (J). (gr. 5-8). lib. bdg. 18.40 (978-0-613-67322-8(0), Turtleback) Turtleback Bks.
—Coraline. McKean, Dave, illus. 10th anniv. ed. 2012. (HarperClassics Ser.). (ENG.). 208p. (J). (gr. 3-7). pap. 7.99 (978-0-380-80734-5(3)) HarperCollins Pubs.
—Coraline: Reading Group Guide. McKean, Dave, illus. (978-0-06-056878-8(X)) HarperCollins Pubs.
—The Graveyard Book. McKean, Dave, illus. (J). 2014. (ENG.). 352p. (gr. 5-7). pap. 9.99 (978-0-06-234918-7(X)) 2010. (ENG.). 352p. (gr. 5). pap. 8.99 (978-0-06-053094-5(4)) 2008. 552p. pap. 17.99 (978-0-06-170912-8(3)) 2008. (ENG.). 320p. (gr. 5-7). 17.99 (978-0-06-053092-1(8)) 2008. 320p. (gr. 5-7). lib. bdg. 18.89 (978-0-06-053093-8(6)) HarperCollins Pubs.
—The Graveyard Book. 2009. 19.00 (978-1-60686-823-2(3)) Perfection Learning Corp.
—The Graveyard Book. 2011. (Literature Kit Ser.). (ENG., Illus.). 55p. pap. 12.95 (978-1-55319-559-7(0), Classroom Complete Pr.) Rainbow Horizons Publishing, Inc.
—The Graveyard Book, 7 vols. 2008. (J). 256.75 (978-1-4361-5882-4(6)); 100.75 (978-1-4361-5887-9(7)) Recorded Bks., Inc.
—The Graveyard Book. l.t. ed. 2009. (ENG.). 373p. (YA). 23.95 (978-1-4104-1441-0(8)) Thorndike Pr.
—The Graveyard Book. 2010. (J). lib. bdg. 19.65 (978-0-606-14883-2(3), Turtleback) Turtleback Bks.
Gaiman, NEil & Russell, P. Craig. The Graveyard Book Graphic Novel. Russell, P. Craig, illus. 2014. (ENG., Illus.). (J). (gr. 3-7). Vol. 1. 192p. 19.99 (978-0-06-219481-7(X)) Vol. 2. 176p. 19.99 (978-0-06-219483-1(6)) HarperCollins Pubs.
Gallicano, Todd Calgi. Guardians of the Gryphon's Claw. 2017. (Sam London Adventure Ser.: 1). (ENG.). 384p. (J). (gr. 5). 16.99 **(978-1-5247-1365-2(1))**; lib. bdg. 19.99 **(978-1-5247-1366-9(X))** Random Hse. Children's Bks. (Delacorte Bks. for Young Readers).
Garcia, Kami. Unbreakable. (Legion Ser.: 1). (ENG.). (YA). (gr. 7-17). 2014. 336p. pap. 10.00 (978-0-316-21018-8(8)) 2013. 320p. 18.00 (978-0-316-21017-1(X)) Little, Brown Bks. for Young Readers.
Garcia, Kami & Stohl, Margaret. Beautiful Chaos. (Beautiful Creatures Ser.: 3). (ENG.). 528p. (YA). (gr. 7-17). 2012. pap. 13.99 (978-0-316-12351-8(X)) 2011. 18.99 (978-0-316-12352-5(8)) Little, Brown Bks. for Young Readers.
—Beautiful Creatures. 2009. (Beautiful Creatures Ser.: 1). (ENG.). 576p. (YA). (gr. 7-17). 17.99 (978-0-316-04267-3(6)) Little Brown & Co.
—Beautiful Creatures. (Beautiful Creatures Ser.: 1). (ENG.). 592p. (YA). (gr. 7-17). 2010. pap. 12.99 (978-0-316-07703-3(8)) 2012. mass mkt. 7.99 (978-0-316-23165-7(7)) 2012. pap. 10.99 (978-0-316-23167-1(3)) Little, Brown Bks. for Young Readers.
—Beautiful Creatures. 2013. (ENG., Illus.). 240p. (gr. 8-17). 20.00 (978-0-316-18271-3(0), Yen Pr.) Orbit.
—Beautiful Creatures. 2010. (Beautiful Creatures Ser.: 1). (YA). lib. bdg. 23.30 (978-0-606-26699-4(2), Turtleback) Turtleback Bks.
—The Beautiful Creatures Complete Paperback Collection: Beautiful Creatures; Beautiful Darkness; Beautiful Chaos; Beautiful Redemption. 2013. (Beautiful Creatures Ser.: Bks. 1-4). (ENG.). 2272p. (YA). (gr. 7-17). pap. 50.00 (978-0-316-25090-0(2)) Little, Brown Bks. for Young Readers.
—Beautiful Darkness. 2010. (Beautiful Creatures Ser.: Bk. 2). (YA). 59.99 (978-1-60941-036-0(X)) Findaway World, LLC.
—Beautiful Darkness. (Beautiful Creatures Ser.: 2). 2011. (ENG.). 528p. (YA). (gr. 7-17). pap. 12.99 (978-0-316-07704-0(6)) 2010. (ENG.). 512p. (YA). (gr. 7-17). 17.99 (978-0-316-07705-7(4)) 2010. 512p. pap. 17.99 (978-0-316-09861-8(2)) Little, Brown Bks. for Young Readers.
—Beautiful Darkness. 2011. (Beautiful Creatures Ser.: 2). (YA). lib. bdg. 24.50 (978-0-606-26700-7(X), Turtleback) Turtleback Bks.
—Beautiful Redemption. (Beautiful Creatures Ser.: 4). (ENG.). (YA). (gr. 7-17). 2013. 496p. pap. 13.99 (978-0-316-12356-3(0)) 2012. 464p. 18.99 (978-0-316-12353-2(6)) 2012. 576p. pap. 9.99 (978-0-316-22519-9(3)) Little, Brown Bks. for Young Readers.
—Beautiful Redemption. 2013. (Beautiful Creatures Ser.: 4). (YA). lib. bdg. 24.50 (978-0-606-32282-9(5), Turtleback) Turtleback Bks.
—Dangerous Creatures. 2015. (ENG.). 400p. (J). (gr. 7-17). pap. 12.99 (978-0-316-37032-5(0)) 2014. 327p. (YA). (978-0-316-37626-6(4)) 2014. (Dangerous Creatures Ser.: Bk. 1). (ENG.). 384p. (YA). (gr. 7-17). 19.00 (978-0-316-37031-8(2)) Little, Brown Bks. for Young Readers.
Gardner, Matt. Alabaster Shadows. 2015. (ENG., Illus.). 184p. (J). pap. 12.99 (978-1-62010-264-0(1), 9781620102640) Oni Pr., Inc.
Garsee, Jeannine. The Unquiet. 2012. (ENG.). 400p. (YA). (gr. 9). 16.99 (978-1-59990-723-9(2), 9781599907239, Bloomsbury USA Childrens) Bloomsbury Publishing USA.
Gates, J. Gabriel & Keel, Charlene. Ghost Crown. 2012. (Tracks Ser.). (ENG.). 456p. (YA). (gr. 6-12). pap. 9.95 (978-0-7573-1594-7(1), HCI Teens) Health Communications, Inc.
Gensler, Sonia. The Dark Between. 2015. (ENG.). 352p. (YA). (gr. 7). pap. 9.99 (978-0-375-86140-6(8), Ember) Random Hse. Children's Bks.
George, Jessica Day. Silver in the Blood. (ENG.). 368p. (YA). 2016. pap. 9.99 (978-1-68119-024-2(9), 9781681190242) 2015. (gr. 7). 17.99 (978-1-61963-431-2(7), 9781619634312) Bloomsbury Publishing USA. (Bloomsbury USA Childrens).
Geragotelis, Brittany. Life's a Witch. 2013. (Life's a Witch Ser.). (ENG., Illus.). 320p. (YA). (gr. 9). 16.99 (978-1-4424-6655-5(3), Simon & Schuster Bks. For Young Readers) Simon & Schuster Bks. For Young Readers.
Germano, Yveta. Bring Me Back. 2013. 298p. 27.99 (978-1-938516-75-7(3)); 318p. pap. 13.99 (978-1-938516-17-7(6)) Midnight Hologram, LLC.
Gibsen, Cole. Katana. 2012. (Katana Novel Ser.: 1). (ENG.). 384p. (YA). pap. 9.95 (978-0-7387-3040-0(8), Flux) North Star Editions.
—Senshi. 2013. (Katana Novel Ser.: 2). (ENG.). 384p. (YA). pap. 9.99 (978-0-7387-3261-9(3), Flux) North Star Editions.
—Shinobi. 2014. (Katana Novel Ser.: 3). (ENG.). 288p. (YA). pap. 9.99 (978-0-7387-3911-3(1), Flux) North Star Editions.
Gibson, Jo. Afraid. 2014. (ENG.). 336p. (YA). (gr. 13). pap. 9.95 (978-1-61773-242-3(7), K-Teen) Kensington Publishing Corp.
Gier, Kerstin. Dream On. Bell, Anthea, tr. from GER. 2016. (Silver Trilogy Ser.: 2). (ENG.). 336p. (YA). 17.99 (978-1-62779-079-6(9), 9781627790796, Holt, Henry & Co. Bks. For Young Readers) Holt, Henry & Co.
—Just Dreaming. Bell, Anthea, tr. from GER. 2017. (Silver Trilogy Ser.). (ENG.). 368p. (YA). 18.99 (978-1-62779-080-2(2), 9781627790802, Holt, Henry & Co. Bks. For Young Readers) Holt, Henry & Co.
Gilman, Charles. Professor Gargoyle. 2012. (Tales from Lovecraft Middle School Ser.: 1). (ENG., Illus.). 160p. (J). (gr. 4-7). 13.99 (978-1-59474-591-1(9)) Quirk Bks.
—The Slither Sisters. 2013. (Tales from Lovecraft Middle School Ser.: 2). (ENG., Illus.). 160p. (J). (gr. 4-7). 13.99 (978-1-59474-593-5(5)) Quirk Bks.
Gleason, Colleen. The Clockwork Scarab. 2014. (Stoker & Holmes Ser.: 1). (ENG.). 384p. (YA). (gr. 7-12). pap. 11.99 (978-1-4521-2873-3(1)) Chronicle Bks. LLC.
—The Spiritglass Charade. 2014. (Stoker & Holmes Ser.: 2). (ENG., Illus.). 360p. (YA). (gr. 7-12). 17.99 (978-1-4521-1071-4(9)) Chronicle Bks. LLC.
Golden, Christopher & Lebbon, Tim. The Sea Wolves Bk. 2, Bk. 2. Ruth, Greg, illus. 2012. (Secret Journeys of Jack London Ser.: 2). (ENG.). 400p. (YA). (gr. 8). 16.99 (978-0-06-186320-2(3), HarperTeen) HarperCollins Pubs.
—The Wild. Ruth, Greg, illus. 2011. (Secret Journeys of Jack London Ser.: 1). (ENG.). 368p. (YA). (gr. 5-18). 15.99 (978-0-06-186317-2(3), HarperTeen) HarperCollins Pubs.
Golding, Julia. The Chimera's Curse, 0 vols. 2010. (Companions Quartet Ser.: 4). (ENG.). 320p. (J). (gr. 4-7). pap. 9.99 (978-0-7614-5726-8(7), 9780761457268, Amazon Children's Publishing) Amazon Publishing.
—The Gorgon's Gaze, 0 vols., Bk. 2. 2010. (Companions Quartet Ser.: 2). (ENG.). 320p. (J). (gr. 4-7). pap. 9.99 (978-0-7614-5653-7(8), 9780761456537, Amazon Children's Publishing) Amazon Publishing.
—Mines of the Minotaur, 0 vols., Bk. 3. unabr. ed. 2010. (Companions Quartet Ser.: 3). (ENG.). 288p. (gr. 5-9). pap. 9.99 (978-0-7614-5796-1(8), 9780761457961, Amazon Children's Publishing) Amazon Publishing.
—Secret of the Sirens, 0 vols. 2009. (Companions Quartet Ser.: 1). (ENG.). 368p. (J). (gr. 4-7). pap. 9.99 (978-0-7614-5617-9(1), 9780761456179, Amazon Children's Publishing) Amazon Publishing.
Goldstein, Lori A. Becoming Jinn. 2015. (Becoming Jinn Ser.: 1). (ENG.). 384p. (YA). (gr. 7). 17.99 (978-1-250-05539-2(3), 9781250055392) Feiwel & Friends.
Goodman, Alison. The Dark Days Club. 2016. (Lady Helen Novel Ser.: Bk. 1). (ENG.). 496p. (YA). (gr. 9). 18.99 (978-0-670-78547-6(4), Viking Books for Young Readers) Penguin Young Readers Group.
—The Dark Days Pact. 2017. (Lady Helen Novel Ser.: 2). (ENG.). 496p. (YA). (gr. 9). 18.99 (978-0-670-78548-3(2), Viking Books for Young Readers) Penguin Young Readers Group.
Goodman, Carol. Blythewood. 2014. (Blythewood Novel Ser.). (ENG.). 512p. (YA). (gr. 7). pap. 9.99 (978-0-14-242251-9(7), Speak) Penguin Young Readers Group.
—Ravencliffe. 2015. (Blythewood Novel Ser.). (ENG.). 432p. (YA). (gr. 7). pap. 10.99 (978-0-14-242252-6(5), Speak) Penguin Young Readers Group.
Goodman, Carol & Wells, Rosemary. Hawthorn. 2015. (Blythewood Novel Ser.). (ENG.). 416p. (YA). (gr. 7). bds. 17.99 (978-0-670-78478-3(8), Viking Books for Young Readers) Penguin Young Readers Group.
Grant, Donna. Hungrige Begierde. 2014.Tr. of The Hunger. (GER.). pap. 5.99 (978-1-942017-15-8(4)) DL Grant, LLC.
Grant, Michael. Fear. 2012. (Gone Ser.: 5). (ENG.). 528p. (YA). (gr. 9). 17.99 (978-0-06-144915-4(6), Tegen, Katherine Bks) HarperCollins Pubs.
—Gone. (Gone Ser.: 1). 576p. 2014. (ENG.). (YA). (gr. 8). pap. 9.99 (978-0-06-144878-2(8), Tegen, Katherine Bks) 2008. (Illus.). (J). (gr. 7-18). lib. bdg. 18.89 (978-0-06-144877-5(X), HarperTeen) 2008. (ENG., Illus.). (YA). (gr. 8-18). 17.99 (978-0-06-144876-8(1), Tegen, Katherine Bks) HarperCollins Pubs.
—Hunger. (Gone Ser.: 2). (ENG.). 608p. (YA). (gr. 8-18). 2014. pap. 9.99 (978-0-06-144908-6(3)) 2009. (Illus.). 17.99 (978-0-06-144906-2(7)) HarperCollins Pubs. (Tegen, Katherine Bks).
—Lies. (Gone Ser.: 3). 464p. (YA). (gr. 8). 2014. (ENG.). pap. 9.99 (978-0-06-144911-6(3)) 2010. lib. bdg. 18.89 (978-0-06-144910-9(5)) 2010. (ENG.). 17.99 (978-0-06-144909-3(1)) HarperCollins Pubs. (Tegen, Katherine Bks).
—Light. 2013. (Gone Ser.: 6). 432p. (YA). (gr. 9). (ENG.). 18.99 (978-0-06-144918-5(0)); lib. bdg. 19.89 (978-0-06-144919-2(9)) HarperCollins Pubs. (Tegen, Katherine Bks).
—Messenger of Fear. 2014. (Messenger of Fear Ser.: 1). (ENG.). 272p. (YA). (gr. 9). 17.99 (978-0-06-220740-1(7), Tegen, Katherine Bks) HarperCollins Pubs.
—Plague. (Gone Ser.: 4). (ENG.). (YA). (gr. 8). 2014. 528p. pap. 9.99 (978-0-06-144914-7(8)) 2011. 512p. 17.99 (978-0-06-144912-3(1)) HarperCollins Pubs. (Tegen, Katherine Bks).
—The Tattooed Heart. 2015. (Messenger of Fear Ser.: 2). (ENG.). 400p. (YA). (gr. 9). 17.99 (978-0-06-220743-2(1)) HarperCollins Pubs.
Gratton, Tessa. Blood Magic. (Blood Journals). (YA). 2012. (ENG.). 432p. (gr. 9). pap. 9.99 (978-0-375-86485-8(7), Bluefire) 2011. pap. (978-0-375-86486-5(5)) Random Hse. Children's Bks.
Gratton, Tessa, et al. Storybook: A Collection of Stories. 2012. (Carolrhoda YA Ser.). (ENG., Illus.). 304p. (YA). (gr. 7-12). 17.95 (978-0-7613-7527-2(9)) Lerner Publishing Group.
Gray, Claudia. Fateful. (ENG.). (YA). (gr. 9). 2012. 352p. pap. 9.99 (978-0-06-200621-9(5)) 2011. 336p. 17.99 (978-0-06-200620-2(7)) HarperCollins Pubs. (HarperTeen).
—Sorceress. 2016. (Spellcaster Ser.: 3). 368p. (YA). (gr. 8). pap. 9.99 (978-0-06-196125-0(6), HarperTeen) HarperCollins Pubs.
Green, Dawn A. Marianne Wellman's School for Girls. 2011. 236p. pap. 24.95 (978-1-4626-0715-0(2)) America Star Bks.
Greenfield, Amy Butler. Chantress Alchemy. 2015. (Chantress Ser.). (ENG., Illus.). 368p. (YA). (gr. 7). pap. 10.99 (978-1-4424-5708-9(2), McElderry, Margaret K. Bks.) McElderry, Margaret K. Bks.
Gregory, Philippa. Changeling, 10 vols. 2012. (Order of Darkness Ser.). (YA). 92.75 (978-1-4640-4583-7(6)); 90.75 (978-1-4640-4586-8(0)); 90.75 (978-1-4640-4587-5(9)); 265.75 (978-1-4640-4584-4(4)) Recorded Bks., Inc.
—Changeling. van Deelen, Fred & Taylor, Sally, illus. 2013. (Order of Darkness Ser.: 1). (ENG.). 352p. (YA). (gr. 9). pap. 9.99 (978-1-4424-5345-6(1), Simon Pulse) Simon Pulse.
—Changeling. Taylor, Sally & van Deelen, Fred, illus. 2012. (Order of Darkness Ser.: 1). (ENG.). 272p. (YA). (gr. 9). 18.99 (978-1-4424-5344-9(3), Simon Pulse) Simon Pulse.
—Fools' Gold. van Deelen, Fred, illus. 2014. (Order of Darkness Ser.: 3). (ENG.). 384p. (YA). (gr. 9). pap. 9.99 (978-1-4424-7691-2(5)); 19.99 (978-1-4424-7690-5(7)) Simon Pulse. (Simon Pulse).
—Stormbringers. van Deelen, Fred, illus. 2013. (Order of Darkness Ser.: 2). (ENG.). 336p. (YA). (gr. 9). pap. 9.99 (978-1-4424-7688-2(5)); 17.99 (978-1-4424-7687-5(7)) Simon Pulse. (Simon Pulse).
Griffo, Michael. Unwelcome. 2011. (ENG.). 352p. (YA). (gr. 9). pap. 9.95 (978-0-7582-5339-2(7), K-Teen) Kensington Publishing Corp.
Griswold-Ford, Valerie. Last Rites. 2013. 322p. pap. (978-1-897492-66-6(9)) Dragon Moon Pr.
Hammond, Andrew. Blood Eagle Tortures. 2013. (ENG.). 336p. (YA). (gr. 7). pap. 8.99 (978-0-7553-7824-1(5)) Headline Publishing Group GBR. Dist: Hachette Bk. Group.
—Guardians' Reckoning. 2014. (ENG.). 368p. (YA). (gr. 7). pap. 8.99 (978-0-7553-7825-8(3)) Headline Publishing Group GBR. Dist: Hachette Bk. Group.
—Mask of Death. 2012. (ENG.). 336p. (YA). (gr. 7-17). pap. 8.99 (978-0-7553-7823-4(7)) Headline Publishing Group GBR. Dist: Hachette Bk. Group.
—Traitor's Revenge. 2012. (ENG.). 352p. (YA). (gr. 7-17). pap. 8.99 (978-0-7553-7822-7(9)) Headline Publishing Group GBR. Dist: Hachette Bk. Group.
Hand, Cynthia. Boundless. 2013. (Unearthly Ser.: 3). (ENG.). 448p. (YA). (gr. 8). pap. 9.99 (978-0-06-199621-4(1)); 17.99 (978-0-06-199620-7(3)) HarperCollins Pubs. (HarperTeen).
—Hallowed. 2012. (Unearthly Ser.: 2). (ENG.). (YA). (gr. 8). 432p. pap. 9.99 (978-0-06-199619-1(X)); 416p. 17.99 (978-0-06-199618-4(1)) HarperCollins Pubs. (HarperTeen).
—Unearthly. 2011. (Unearthly Ser.: 1). (ENG.). 464p. (YA). (gr. 8). pap. 9.99 (978-0-06-199617-7(3), HarperTeen) HarperCollins Pubs.
Hanlon, Jennifer. A Shadow's Tale. 2014. (ENG.). 274p. (J). (gr. -1-12). pap. 12.95 (978-1-78279-136-2(1), Our Street Bks.) Hunt, John Publishing Ltd. GBR. Dist: National Bk. Network.
Hansen, Justin LaRocca. Brothers Unite. 2016. (Secondhand Heroes Ser.). (ENG., Illus.). 160p. (J). (gr. 3-7). pap. 10.99 (978-0-8037-4094-5(8), Dial Bks) Penguin Young Readers Group.
—In the Trenches. 2017. (Secondhand Heroes Ser.). (ENG., Illus.). 160p. (J). (gr. 3-7). pap. 10.99 (978-0-8037-4095-2(6), Dial Bks) Penguin Young Readers Group.
Hardinge, Frances. Cuckoo Song. (ENG.). (YA). (gr. 7-12). 2016. 432p. pap. 9.95 (978-1-4197-1939-4(4)) 2015. 416p. 17.95 (978-1-4197-1480-1(5)) Abrams, Inc. (Amulet Bks.).
—Cuckoo Song. 2016. lib. bdg. 20.80 (978-0-606-38211-3(9)) Turtleback Bks.
Harold & I. 2007. (ENG., Illus.). 291p. (J). (gr. 3-8). per. 13.99 (978-0-7684-2432-4(1)) Send The Light Distribution LLC.
Harrison, Kim, pseud. Early to Death, Early to Rise. 2011. (Madison Avery Ser.: 2). (ENG., Illus.). 256p. (YA). (gr. 9). pap. 8.99 (978-0-06-144169-1(4)) HarperCollins Pubs.
—Once Dead, Twice Shy. (Madison Avery Ser.: 1). 2010. (ENG.). 256p. (YA). (gr. 8). pap. 8.99 (978-0-06-144168-4(6)) 2009. 240p. (J). lib. bdg. 17.89 (978-0-06-171820-5(3), HarperTeen) 2009. 240p. (J). (gr. 9-18). 16.99 (978-0-06-171816-8(5), HarperTeen) HarperCollins Pubs.
—Something Deadly This Way Comes. 2011. (Madison Avery Ser.: 3). (ENG.). 256p. (YA). (gr. 9-18). 16.99 (978-0-06-171819-9(X)) HarperCollins Pubs.
Harrold, A. F. The Imaginary. Gravett, Emily, illus. 2015. (ENG.). 240p. (YA). (gr. 3-6). 16.99 (978-0-8027-3811-0(7), 9780802738110, Bloomsbury USA Childrens) Bloomsbury Publishing USA.
—The Song from Somewhere Else. Pinfold, Levi, illus. 2017. (ENG.). 240p. (J). 16.99 (978-1-68119-401-1(5), 9781681194011, Bloomsbury USA Childrens) Bloomsbury Publishing USA.
Hashway, Kelly. Stalked by Death. 2013. (Touch of Death Ser.: 2). (ENG.). 320p. (YA). (gr. 10-12). pap. 9.95 (978-1-937053-51-2(2)) Spencer Hill Pr.
Hastings, Rook. Nearly Departed. 2010. (ENG.). 272p. (J). (gr. 6-9). 8.99 (978-0-00-725810-9(0), HarperCollins Children's Bks.) HarperCollins Pubs. Ltd. GBR. Dist: HarperCollins Pubs.
Hatfield, Ruth. The Book of Shadows. 2017. (Book of Storms Trilogy Ser.: 3). (ENG., Illus.). 288p. (J). 16.99 (978-1-62779-003-1(9), 9781627790031, Holt, Henry & Co. Bks. For Young Readers) Holt, Henry & Co.
—The Book of Storms. Call, Greg, illus. 2015. (Book of Storms Trilogy Ser.: 1). (ENG.). 368p. (J). (gr. 5-9). 16.99 (978-0-8050-9998-0(0), 9780805099980, Holt, Henry & Co. Bks. For Young Readers) Holt, Henry & Co.
—The Color of Darkness. 2016. (Book of Storms Trilogy Ser.: 2). (ENG., Illus.). 336p. (J). 16.99 (978-1-62779-001-7(2), 9781627790017, Holt, Henry & Co. Bks. For Young Readers) Holt, Henry & Co.
Hautman, Pete. The Cydonian Pyramid. 2014. (Klaatu Diskos Ser.). (ENG.). 368p. (YA). (gr. 7). pap. 8.99 (978-0-7636-6933-1(4)) Candlewick Pr.
—The Obsidian Blade. 2012. (Klaatu Diskos Ser.). (ENG., Illus.). 320p. (YA). (gr. 7). 16.99 (978-0-7636-5403-0(5)) Candlewick Pr.
Havard, Amanda. The Survivors. 2011. (ENG.). (YA). 294p. 21.99 (978-0-9833190-0-9(6)); 300p. pap. 11.99 (978-0-9833190-2-3(2)) Chafie Pr., LLC.
Hawken, Eleanor. The Grey Girl, Bk. 2. 2014. (ENG.). 272p. (J). (gr. 4-7). 9.99 (978-1-4714-0195-4(2)) Bonnier Publishing GBR. Dist: Independent Pubs. Group.
Hawkins, Rachel. Demonglass. 2012. (ENG.). 384p. (YA). (gr. 6-17). pap. 8.99 (978-1-4231-2844-1(3)) Hyperion Pr.
—Hex Hall, Bk. 1. 2010. (ENG.). 336p. (J). (gr. 7-17). 16.99 (978-1-4231-2130-5(9)) Hyperion Pr.
—Journey's End. 2016. (ENG.). 304p. (J). (gr. 3-7). 16.99 (978-0-399-16960-1(1), G.P. Putnam's Sons Books for Young Readers) Penguin Young Readers Group.
—Lady Renegades: A Rebel Belle Novel. 2016. (Rebel Belle Ser.: 3). (ENG.). 272p. (YA). (gr. 7). 17.99

S

(978-0-399-25695-0(4), G.P. Putnam's Sons Books for Young Readers) Penguin Young Readers Group.

—Miss Mayhem. 2015. (Rebel Belle Ser.: 2). (ENG.). 288p. (YA). (gr. 7). 17.99 (978-0-399-25694-3(6), G.P. Putnam's Sons Books for Young Readers) Penguin Young Readers Group.

—Rebel Belle. 2015. (Rebel Belle Ser.: 1). (ENG.). 368p. (YA). (gr. 7). pap. 9.99 (978-0-14-751435-6(5), Speak) Penguin Young Readers Group.

—School Spirits. 2014. (Hex Hall Novel Ser.). (ENG.). 304p. (YA). (gr. 7-12). pap. 9.99 (978-1-4231-4850-0(9)) Hyperion Bks. for Children.

—School Spirits. 2013. (Hex Hall Novel Ser.). (ENG.). 304p. (YA). (gr. 7-12). 17.99 (978-1-4231-4849-4(5)) Hyperion Pr.

—Spell Bound (a Hex Hall Novel) 2013. (ENG.). 352p. (YA). (gr. 7-17). pap. 9.99 (978-1-4231-2140-4(6)) Hyperion Pr.

Hawthorne, Nathaniel. Nathaniel Hawthorne. McConnell, James, illus. 2004. (Great American Short Stories Ser.). 80p. (gr. 4-7). lib. bdg. 24.00 (978-0-8368-4252-4(9), Gareth Stevens Learning Library) Stevens, Gareth Publishing LLLP.

Hawthorne, Rachel. Shadow of the Moon. 2010. (Dark Guardian Ser.: 4). (ENG.). 256p. (YA). (gr. 9-18). pap. 8.99 (978-0-06-196290-5(2), HarperTeen) HarperCollins Pubs.

Hay, Sam. Night of the Howling Hound, No. 3. Cooper, Simon, illus. 2014. (Undead Pets Ser.: 3). (ENG.). 112p. (J). (gr. 1-3). 5.99 (978-0-448-47797-8(1), Grosset & Dunlap) Penguin Young Readers Group.

Hayes, Christine. The Mothman's Curse. Hindle, James K., illus. 2015. (ENG.). 320p. (J). (gr. 3-7). 15.99 (978-1-62672-027-5(4), 9781626720275) Roaring Brook Pr.

Hayes, Gwen. Dreaming Awake. 2012. (ENG.). 332p. (YA). (gr. 7-18). 9.99 (978-0-451-23554-1(1), Berkley) Penguin Publishing Group.

—Falling Under. 2011. (ENG.). 336p. (YA). (gr. 7-18). 9.99 (978-0-451-23268-7(2), Berkley) Penguin Publishing Group.

Healey, Karen. The Shattering. 2013. (ENG.). 336p. (YA). (gr. 7-17). pap. 8.99 (978-0-316-12573-4(3)) Little, Brown Bks. for Young Readers.

Hearn, Julie. The Minister's Daughter. 2006. (ENG.). 272p. (YA). (gr. 7-12). pap. 7.99 (978-0-689-87691-2(2), Atheneum Bks. for Young Readers) Simon & Schuster Children's Publishing.

Helget, Nicole. Wonder at the Edge of the World. 2015. (ENG., Illus.). 384p. (J). (gr. 3-7). 17.00 (978-0-316-24510-4(0)) Little, Brown Bks. for Young Readers.

Henderson, Jason. The Triumph of Death. 2012. (Alex Van Helsing Ser.: 3). (ENG.). 320p. (YA). (gr. 8). 17.99 (978-0-06-195103-9(X), HarperTeen) HarperCollins Pubs.

—Vampire Rising. (Alex Van Helsing Ser.: 1). (ENG.). (YA). (gr. 8). 2011. 272p. pap. 8.99 (978-0-06-195100-8(5)) 2010. 256p. 16.99 (978-0-06-195099-5(8)) HarperCollins Pubs. (HarperTeen).

—Voice of the Undead. 2011. (Alex Van Helsing Ser.: 2). (ENG.). 304p. (YA). (gr. 8). 16.99 (978-0-06-195101-5(3), HarperTeen) HarperCollins Pubs.

Henry, Pam. Cold Call. 2011. 200p. pap. (978-1-84903-065-6(0)) Schiel & Denver Publishing Ltd.

Hensley, Nathaniel. The Strange Tale of Hector & Hannah Crowe. 2015. (ENG.). 222p. (J). (gr. 8-18). 13.95 (978-1-937240-49-3(5)) Casa de Snapdragon LLC.

Hibbs, Sasha. Black Amaranth. 2013. 286p. pap. (978-1-77130-526-6(6)) Evernight Publishing.

Higgins, Simon. Moonshadow #2: the Nightmare Ninja. 2012. (Moonshadow Ser.: 2). (ENG.). 384p. (J). (gr. 3-7). pap. 6.99 (978-0-316-05534-5(4)) Little, Brown Bks. for Young Readers.

Hightman, J. P. Spirit. 2008. 224p. (gr. 7-18). (ENG.). (J). 16.99 (978-0-06-085063-0(9)); (YA). lib. bdg. 17.89 (978-0-06-085064-7(7)) HarperCollins Pubs. (HarperTeen).

Hill, C. J. Slayers. 2013. (Slayers Ser.: 1). (ENG.). 400p. (YA). (gr. 7). pap. 9.99 (978-0-312-67514-1(3)) Square Fish.

—Slayers: Friends & Traitors. 2014. (Slayers Ser.: 2). (ENG.). 416p. (YA). (gr. 7). pap. 10.99 (978-1-250-05079-3(0), 9781250050793) Square Fish.

Hill, William. Department Nineteen. 2012. (Department Nineteen Ser.: 1). (ENG.). 544p. (YA). (gr. 9). 9.99 (978-1-59514-485-0(4), Razorbill) Penguin Young Readers Group.

Hite, Kenneth. Where the Deep Ones Are. 2009. 32p. 19.95 (978-1-58978-103-0(1), Atlas Games) Trident, Inc.

Hoban, Russell. A Birthday for Frances. Hoban, Lillian, illus. 2012. (I Can Read Level 2 Ser.). (ENG.). 48p. (J). (gr. k-3). pap. 3.99 (978-0-06-083797-6(7)) HarperCollins Pubs.

Hocking, Amanda. Ascend. 2012. (Trylle Novel Ser.: 3). (ENG.). 336p. (YA). (gr. 7). pap. 8.99 (978-1-250-00633-2(3), 9781250006332, St. Martin's Griffin) St. Martin's Pr.

—Ascend. l.t. ed. 2012. (Trylle Trilogy: Bk. 3). (ENG.). 412p. (J). (gr. 8-12). 23.99 (978-1-4104-5014-2(7)) Thorndike Pr.

—Elegy. (Watersong Novel Ser.: 4). (ENG.). 560p. (YA). (gr. 7). 2014. mass mkt. 9.99 (978-1-250-05654-2(3), 9781250056542, St. Martin's Paperbacks) 2013. 17.99 (978-1-250-00567-0(1), 9781250005670, St. Martin's Griffin) St. Martin's Pr.

—Lullaby. 2013. (Watersong Novel Ser.: 2). (ENG.). 368p. (YA). (gr. 7). mass mkt. 9.99 (978-1-250-04675-8(0), 9781250046758, St. Martin's Paperbacks) St. Martin's Pr.

—Switched. 2012. (Trylle Novel Ser.: 1). (ENG.). 336p. (YA). (gr. 7). pap. 8.99 (978-1-250-00631-8(7), 9781250006318, St. Martin's Griffin) St. Martin's Pr.

—Switched. l.t. ed. 2012. (Trylle Trilogy: Bk. 1). (ENG.). 408p. (gr. 7-12). 23.99 (978-1-4104-4865-1(7)) Thorndike Pr.

—Tidal. (Watersong Novel Ser.: 3). (ENG.). 352p. (YA). (gr. 7). 2014. pap. 11.99 (978-1-250-00566-3(3), 9781250005663, St. Martin's Griffin) 2014. mass mkt. 9.99 (978-1-250-05657-3(8), 9781250056573, St. Martin's Paperbacks) 2013. 17.99 (978-1-250-00811-4(5), 9781250008114, St. Martin's Griffin) St. Martin's Pr.

—Torn. 2012. (Trylle Novel Ser.: 2). (ENG.). 336p. (YA). (gr. 7-12). pap. 8.99 (978-1-250-00632-5(5), 9781250006325, St. Martin's Griffin) St. Martin's Pr.

—Torn. l.t. ed. 2012. (Trylle Trilogy: Bk. 2). (ENG.). 450p. (J). (gr. 7-12). 23.99 (978-1-4104-5013-5(9)) Thorndike Pr.

—Wake. 2013. (Watersong Novel Ser.: 1). (ENG.). 320p. (YA). (gr. 7). pap. 10.99 (978-1-250-00564-9(7), 9781250005649, St. Martin's Griffin) St. Martin's Pr.

Hodkin, Michelle. The Evolution of Mara Dyer. (Mara Dyer Trilogy Ser.: 2). (ENG., Illus.). (YA). (gr. 9). 2013. 560p. pap. 12.99 (978-1-4424-2180-6(0)) 2012. 544p. 19.99 (978-1-4424-2179-0(7)) Simon & Schuster Bks. For Young Readers. (Simon & Schuster Bks. For Young Readers).

—The Retribution of Mara Dyer. 2014. (Mara Dyer Trilogy: Vol. 3). (ENG., Illus.). 480p. (YA). (gr. 9). 18.99 (978-1-4424-8423-8(3), Simon & Schuster Bks. For Young Readers) Simon & Schuster Bks. For Young Readers.

—The Unbecoming of Mara Dyer. (Mara Dyer Trilogy Ser.: 1). (ENG., Illus.). (YA). (gr. 9). 2012. 480p. pap. 12.99 (978-1-4424-2177-6(0)) 2011. 464p. 21.99 (978-1-4424-2176-9(2)) Simon & Schuster Bks. For Young Readers. (Simon & Schuster Bks. For Young Readers).

Hoffman, Alice. Nightbird. 2016. lib. bdg. 18.40 (978-0-606-38451-3(0)) Turtleback Bks.

Hoffman, Nina Kiriki. Spirits That Walk in Shadow. 2008. (ENG.). 320p. (YA). (gr. 7-18). 9.99 (978-0-14-241158-2(2), Firebird) Penguin Young Readers Group.

Hogan, Edward. Daylight Saving. 2012. (ENG., Illus.). 224p. (YA). (gr. 7). 16.99 (978-0-7636-5913-4(4)) Candlewick Pr.

Holder, Nancy. The Screaming Season. 3rd ed. 2011. (Possessions Ser.). (ENG.). 336p. (YA). (gr. 7-18). 9.99 (978-1-59514-333-4(5), Razorbill) Penguin Young Readers Group.

Holder, Nancy & Viguié, Debbie. Crusade. (Crusade Ser.). (ENG.). (YA). (gr. 9). 2011. 496p. pap. 9.99 (978-1-4169-9803-7(9)) 2010. 480p. 16.99 (978-1-4169-9802-0(0)) Simon Pulse. (Simon Pulse).

—Damned. 2011. (Crusade Ser.). (ENG.). 544p. (YA). (gr. 9). pap. 9.99 (978-1-4169-9805-1(5), Simon Pulse) Simon Pulse.

—Vanquished. 2012. (Crusade Ser.). (ENG.). 496p. (YA). (gr. 9). 16.99 (978-1-4169-9806-8(3)); pap. 9.99 (978-1-4169-9807-5(1)) Simon Pulse. (Simon Pulse).

Holt, Simon. The Devouring #2: Soulstice. 2010. (Devouring: Book 2 Ser.). (ENG.). 288p. (YA). (gr. 7-17). pap. 19.99 (978-0-316-03574-3(2)) Little, Brown Bks. for Young Readers.

Holub, Joan & Williams, Suzanne. Cassandra the Lucky. 2013. (Goddess Girls Ser.: 12). (ENG., Illus.). 256p. (J). (gr. 3-7). 16.99 (978-1-4424-8818-2(2)); pap. 7.99 (978-1-4424-8817-5(4)) Simon & Schuster Children's Publishing. (Aladdin).

Hopkinson, Nalo. The Chaos. (ENG., 256p. (YA). (gr. 9). 2013. Illus.). pap. 9.99 (978-1-4424-5926-7(3)) 2012. 16.99 (978-1-4169-5488-0(0)) McElderry, Margaret K. Bks. (McElderry, Margaret K. Bks.).

Horning, Mandy Cha'rae. The Defenders: Rise of the Perfected. 2012. 118p. (gr. 10-12). 23.99 (978-1-4772-5327-4(0)); pap. 14.95 (978-1-4772-5328-1(9)) AuthorHouse.

Horowitz, Anthony. Evil Star. 2007. (Gatekeepers Ser.: 2). 318p. lib. bdg. 19.65 (978-1-4177-7663-4(3), Turtleback) Turtleback Bks.

—Necropolis, 9 vols. 2009. (Gatekeepers Ser.: 4). (J). 92.75 (978-1-4407-0430-7(9)); 120.75 (978-1-4407-0436-9(8)); 122.75 (978-1-4407-0434-5(1)); 254.75 (978-1-4407-0431-4(7)); 1.25 (978-1-4407-0439-0(2)); 90.75 (978-1-4407-0432-1(5)) Recorded Bks., Inc.

—Necropolis. (Gatekeepers Ser.: 4). (ENG.). 400p. (J). (gr. 3-7). 2011. pap. 8.99 (978-0-439-68006-6(9), Scholastic Paperbacks) 2009. 17.99 (978-0-439-68003-5(4), Scholastic Pr.) Scholastic, Inc.

—Necropolis. 2009. 400p. pap. (978-1-4063-2108-1(7)) Walker Bks., Ltd.

—Nightrise. 2008. (Gatekeepers Ser.: 3). (ENG.). 368p. (J). (gr. 3-7). pap. 8.99 (978-0-439-68007-3(7), Scholastic Paperbacks) Scholastic, Inc.

—Oblivion. 2014. (Gatekeepers Ser.: 5). (ENG.). 592p. (J). (gr. 3-7). pap. 9.99 (978-0-439-68005-9(0), Scholastic Paperbacks) Scholastic, Inc.

—Oblivion. 2014. (Gatekeepers Ser.: 5). lib. bdg. 20.85 (978-0-606-36035-7(2)) Turtleback Bks.

—Raven's Gate. 2006. (Gatekeepers Ser.: 1). (ENG.). 272p. (J). (gr. 3-7). pap. 8.99 (978-0-439-68009-7(3), Scholastic Paperbacks) Scholastic, Inc.

—Raven's Gate. 2005. 288p. pap. (978-1-84428-619-5(3)) Walker Bks., Ltd.

—Return to Groosham Grange: The Unholy Grail. 2010. (ENG.). 224p. (J). (gr. 5-18). 7.99 (978-0-14-241571-9(5), Puffin Books) Penguin Young Readers Group.

—The Switch. 2010. (ENG.). 192p. (J). (gr. 5-18). 7.99 (978-0-14-241547-4(2), Puffin Books) Penguin Young Readers Group.

Houck, Colleen. Reawakened. 2015. (Reawakened Ser.: Bk. 1). (ENG.). 400p. (YA). (gr. 9-12). 17.99 (978-0-385-37656-3(1), Delacorte Pr.) Random Hse. Children's Bks.

—Recreated. (Reawakened Ser.: 2). (ENG.). 416p. (YA). (gr. 9). 2017. pap. 10.99 **(978-0-385-37663-1(4)**, Ember) 2016. 17.99 (978-0-385-37660-0(X), Delacorte Pr.) Random Hse. Children's Bks.

—Reunited. 2017. (ENG.). 464p. (YA). (gr. 9). 17.99 **(978-0-399-55568-8(4)**, Delacorte Pr.) Random Hse. Children's Bks.

Houck, Colleen. Tiger's Quest. (Tiger's Curse Ser.: Bk. 2). (ENG.). (J). (gr. 7). 2013. 512p. pap. 9.95 (978-1-4549-0358-1(9)) 2011. 496p. 17.95 (978-1-4027-8404-0(X)) Sterling Publishing Co., Inc.

Howard, A. G. Ensnared. 2015. (Splintered Ser.). (ENG.). 416p. (YA). (gr. 9-17). pap. 9.99 (978-1-4197-1675-1(1)); 17.95 (978-1-4197-1229-6(2)) Abrams, Inc. (Amulet Bks.).

—Splintered. 2013. (Splintered Ser.). (ENG., Illus.). 384p. (YA). (gr. 9-17). 17.95 (978-1-4197-0428-4(1), Amulet Bks.) Abrams, Inc.

—Splintered. 2014. (Splintered Ser.: 1). (J). lib. bdg. 19.60 (978-0-606-35235-2(X)) Turtleback Bks.

—Unhinged. (Splintered Ser.). (ENG.). (YA). (gr. 9-17). 2015. 416p. pap. 9.99 (978-1-4197-1373-6(6)) 2014. 400p. 17.95 (978-1-4197-0971-5(2)) Abrams, Inc. (Amulet Bks.).

—Unhinged. 2015. (Splintered Ser.: 2). (J). lib. bdg. 19.60 (978-0-606-36565-9(6)) Turtleback Bks.

Howe, James. Howie Monroe & the Doghouse of Doom. Helquist, Brett, illus. 2003. (Tales from the House of Bunnicula Ser.: 3). (ENG.). 112p. (J). (gr. 2-4). pap. 5.99 (978-0-689-83952-8(9), Atheneum Bks. for Young Readers) Simon & Schuster Children's Publishing.

Hulme-Cross, Benjamin. The House of Memories. Evergreen, Nelson, illus. 2015. (Dark Hunter Ser.). (ENG.). 64p. (J). (gr. 4-8). pap. 4.99 (978-1-4677-8085-8(5)) Lerner Publishing Group.

—The Marsh Demon. Evergreen, Nelson, illus. 2015. (Dark Hunter Ser.). (ENG.). 64p. (J). (gr. 4-8). 17.32 (978-1-4677-8658-4(6)) Lerner Publishing Group.

—The Red Thirst. Evergreen, Nelson, illus. 2015. (Dark Hunter Ser.). (ENG.). 64p. (J). (gr. 4-8). pap. 4.99 (978-1-4677-8088-9(X)) Lerner Publishing Group.

—Ship of Death. Evergreen, Nelson, illus. 2015. (Dark Hunter Ser.). (ENG.). 64p. (J). (gr. 4-8). pap. 4.99 (978-1-4677-8090-2(1)) Lerner Publishing Group.

—The Stone Witch. Evergreen, Nelson, illus. 2015. (Dark Hunter Ser.). (ENG.). 64p. (J). (gr. 4-8). pap. 4.99 (978-1-4677-8089-6(8)) Lerner Publishing Group.

—Wolf Trap. Evergreen, Nelson, illus. 2015. (Dark Hunter Ser.). (ENG.). 64p. (J). (gr. 4-8). pap. 4.99 (978-1-4677-8086-5(3)) Lerner Publishing Group.

Hunter, C. C. Almost Midnight. 2016. (Shadow Falls: after Dark Ser.). (ENG.). 416p. (YA). pap. 10.99 (978-1-250-08100-1(9), 9781250081001, St. Martin's Griffin) St. Martin's Pr.

—Awake at Dawn. (Shadow Falls Novel Ser.: 2). (ENG.). 400p. (YA). (gr. 7-12). 2013. mass mkt. 9.99 (978-1-250-04679-6(3), 9781250046796, St. Martin's Paperbacks) 2011. pap. 10.99 (978-0-312-62468-2(9), 9780312624682, St. Martin's Griffin) St. Martin's Pr.

—Born at Midnight. (Shadow Falls Novel Ser.: 1). (ENG.). 416p. (YA). (gr. 7-12). 2013. mass mkt. 9.99 (978-1-250-04680-2(7), 9781250046802, St. Martin's Paperbacks) 2011. pap. 10.99 (978-0-312-62467-5(0), 9780312624675, St. Martin's Griffin) St. Martin's Pr.

—Chosen at Nightfall. 2013. (Shadow Falls Novel Ser.: 5). (ENG.). (YA). (gr. 7). 432p. mass mkt. 9.99 (978-1-250-04765-6(X), 9781250047656, St. Martin's Paperbacks); 416p. pap. 10.99 (978-1-250-01289-0(9), 9781250012890, St. Martin's Griffin) St. Martin's Pr.

—Eternal. 2014. (Shadow Falls: after Dark Ser.: 2). (ENG.). 400p. (YA). mass mkt. 9.99 (978-1-250-07016-6(3), 9781250070166, St. Martin's Paperbacks); (gr. 7-12). 19.99 (978-1-250-05630-6(6), St. Martin's Griffin) St. Martin's Pr.

—Eternal: Shadow Falls: After Dark. 2014. (Shadow Falls: after Dark Ser.: 2). (ENG.). 400p. (YA). (gr. 7-12). pap. 9.99 (978-1-250-04461-7(8), 9781250044617, St. Martin's Griffin) St. Martin's Pr.

—Next Chapter: Taken at Dusk - Whispers at Moonrise, 2 bks. in 1. 2014. (Shadow Falls Novel Ser.). (ENG.). 784p. (YA). (gr. 8-12). pap. 13.99 (978-1-250-06695-4(6), 9781250066954, St. Martin's Griffin) St. Martin's Pr.

—Reborn. 2014. (Shadow Falls: after Dark Ser.: 1). (ENG.). 400p. (YA). (gr. 7). pap. 10.99 (978-1-250-03591-2(0), 9781250035912, St. Martin's Griffin) St. Martin's Pr.

—Taken at Dusk. 2012. (Shadow Falls Novel Ser.: 3). (ENG.). 400p. (YA). (gr. 7-12). pap. 10.99 (978-0-312-62469-9(7), 9780312624699, St. Martin's Griffin) St. Martin's Pr.

—Taken at Dusk: A Shadow Falls Novel. 2013. (Shadow Falls Novel Ser.: 3). (ENG.). 400p. (YA). (gr. 7-12). mass mkt. 9.99 (978-1-250-04681-9(5), 9781250046819, St. Martin's Paperbacks) St. Martin's Pr.

—Whispers at Moonrise. (Shadow Falls Novel Ser.: 4). (ENG.). 400p. (YA). (gr. 7-12). 2013. mass mkt. 9.99 (978-1-250-04682-6(3), 9781250046826, St. Martin's Paperbacks) 2012. pap. 10.99 (978-1-250-01191-6(4), 9781250011916, St. Martin's Griffin) St. Martin's Pr.

Hunter, Erin. Moonrise. 2015. (Warriors — the New Prophecy Ser.: 2). (J). lib. bdg. 18.40 (978-0-606-36501-7(X)) Turtleback Bks.

Hutchins, Hazel. TJ & the Haunted House, 1 vol. 2003. (Orca Young Readers Ser.). (ENG., Illus.). 112p. (J). (gr. 3-6). pap. 4.99 (978-1-55143-262-5(5)) Orca Bk. Pubs. USA.

In a World Just Right. 2015. (ENG., Illus.). 432p. (YA). (gr. 7). 18.99 (978-1-4814-1660-3(X)) Simon & Schuster Children's Publishing.

Inglis, Lucy. City of Halves. 2015. (ENG.). 368p. (J). (gr. 7). 17.99 (978-0-545-82958-8(5), Chicken Hse., The) Scholastic, Inc.

Inzana, Ryan. Ichiro. (ENG., Illus.). 288p. (YA). (gr. 7). 2014. pap. 12.99 (978-0-547-61789-3(5), HMH Books For Young Readers) 2012. 24.99 (978-0-547-25269-8(2)) Houghton Mifflin Harcourt Publishing Co.

Irving, Washington. Washington Irving. Hall, Tracy, illus. 2004. (Great American Short Stories Ser.). 80p. (gr. 4-7). lib. bdg. 24.00 (978-0-8368-4253-1(7), Gareth Stevens Learning Library) Stevens, Gareth Publishing LLLP.

Jacobs, John Hornor. The Conformity. 2015. (YA). 18.65 (978-1-4677-6182-6(6)) Lerner Publishing Group.

—The Shibboleth. 2014. (Twelve-Fingered Boy Trilogy: Bk. 2). 408p. (YA). (gr. 9-12). 17.95 (978-0-7613-9008-4(1), Carolrhoda Lab™) Lerner Publishing Group.

—The Twelve-Fingered Boy. (Twelve-Fingered Boy Trilogy Ser.: Bk. 1). (ENG.). 280p. (YA). (gr. 9-12). 2014. pap. 9.95 (978-1-4677-3706-7(2)) 2013. 17.95 (978-0-7613-9007-7(3)) Lerner Publishing Group.

James, J. Alison. Runa. 2012. (ENG.). 144p. (YA). (gr. 7). pap. 8.99 (978-1-4424-7482-6(3), Atheneum Bks. for Young Readers) Simon & Schuster Children's Publishing.

James, Syrie & James, Ryan M. Forbidden. 2012. (ENG.). 416p. (YA). (gr. 8). pap. 9.99 (978-0-06-202789-4(1), HarperTeen) HarperCollins Pubs.

Jarvis, Robin. Dancing Jax. 2012. (ENG., Illus.). 576p. (YA). 8.99 (978-0-00-745341-2(8), HarperCollins Children's Bks.) HarperCollins Pubs. Ltd. GBR. Dist: HarperCollins Pubs.

—Freax & Rejex. 2013. (Dancing Jax Ser.: 2). (ENG., Illus.). 544p. (YA). 8.99 (978-0-00-745343-6(4), HarperCollins Children's Bks.) HarperCollins Pubs. Ltd. GBR. Dist: HarperCollins Pubs.

Jay, Stacey. Juliet Immortal. 2012. (ENG.). 324p. (YA). (gr. 9). pap. 9.99 (978-0-385-74017-3(4), Ember) Random Hse. Children's Bks.

—Romeo Redeemed. 2013. (ENG.). 384p. (YA). (gr. 9). pap. 9.99 (978-0-385-74019-7(0), Ember) Random Hse. Children's Bks.

Jinadasa, Devin. The Silver Moon: The War Begins. 2015. (ENG.). 78p. pap. 8.95 (978-1-78455-431-6(6), a4a0f8fb-73ae-4ffc-8746-8885291558dc) Austin, Stan AUS. Dist: Bookmasters Distribution.

Jinks, Catherine. How to Catch a Bogle. Watts, Sarah, illus. 2014. (How to Catch a Bogle Ser.: 1). (ENG.). 336p. (J). (gr. 5-7). pap. 7.99 (978-0-544-33627-8(5), HMH Books For Young Readers) Houghton Mifflin Harcourt Publishing Co.

—The Last Bogler. (How to Catch a Bogle Ser.: 3). (ENG.). 336p. (J). (gr. 5-7). 2017. pap. 7.99 (978-0-544-81309-0(X)) 2016. (Illus.). 16.99 (978-0-544-08696-8(1)) Houghton Mifflin Harcourt Publishing Co. (HMH Books For Young Readers).

Johnson, Christine. Nocturne. (ENG.). (YA). (gr. 7). 2012. 384p. pap. 9.99 (978-1-4424-0777-0(8)) 2011. 368p. 16.99 (978-1-4424-0776-3(X)) Simon Pulse. (Simon Pulse).

Johnson, Maureen. Devilish. 2013. (ENG.). 304p. (YA). (gr. 7). pap. 9.99 (978-0-14-750855-3(X), Speak) Penguin Young Readers Group.

Johnson, Varian. The Return. 2016. (Spirit Animals: Fall of the Beasts Ser.: 3). (ENG.). 192p. (J). (gr. 3-7). 16.99 (978-0-545-87696-4(6)) Scholastic, Inc.

Jolley, Dan. Five Elements #1: the Emerald Tablet. 2017. (Five Elements Ser.: 1). (Illus.). 320p. (J). (gr. 3-7). pap. 6.99 **(978-0-06-241166-2(7))** HarperCollins Pubs.

Jones, Carrie. Captivate. 2010. (Need Ser.). (ENG.). (YA). (gr. 7-12). 304p. pap. 9.99 (978-1-59990-523-5(X), 9781599905235); 288p. 16.99 (978-1-59990-342-2(3), 9781599903422) Bloomsbury Publishing USA. (Bloomsbury USA Childrens).

—Endure. 2012. (Need Ser.). (ENG.). 272p. (YA). 17.99 (978-1-59990-554-9(X), 9781599905549, Bloomsbury USA Childrens) Bloomsbury Publishing USA.

—Entice. (Need Ser.). (ENG.). (YA). 2011. 288p. pap. 9.99 (978-1-59990-693-5(7), 9781599906935) 2010. 272p. (gr. 7-12). 17.99 (978-1-59990-553-2(1), 9781599905532) Bloomsbury Publishing USA. (Bloomsbury USA Childrens).

—Need. 2009. (Need Ser.). (ENG.). 336p. (YA). (gr. 7). pap. 9.99 (978-1-59990-453-5(5), 9781599904535, Bloomsbury USA Childrens) Bloomsbury Publishing USA.

Jones, Carrie, et al. After Obsession. 2012. (ENG.). 336p. (YA). (gr. 7-12). pap. 9.99 (978-1-59990-913-4(8), 9781599909134, Bloomsbury USA Childrens) Bloomsbury Publishing USA.

Jones, Kelly. Unusual Chickens for the Exceptional Poultry Farmer. Kath, Katie, illus. 2015. (ENG.). 224p. (J). (gr. 3-7). 16.99 (978-0-385-75552-8(X), Knopf Bks. for Young Readers) Random Hse. Children's Bks.

Jordan, Devin. The Dragon's Pearl. Di Bartolo, Jim, illus. 2010. (ENG.). 352p. (YA). (gr. 5-9). pap. 8.99 (978-1-4169-6411-7(8), Simon & Schuster Bks. For Young Readers) Simon & Schuster Bks. For Young Readers.

Jordan, Sophie. Hidden. 2012. (Firelight Ser.: 3). (ENG.). 272p. (YA). (gr. 8). 17.99 (978-0-06-193512-1(3)) HarperCollins Pubs.

Karchut, Darby. Griffin Rising. 2011. 176p. (YA). pap. 15.95 (978-1-60619-210-8(8)) Twilight Times Bks.

Kate, Lauren. Fallen. (Fallen Ser.: Bk. 1). (ENG.). (YA). (gr. 7). 2010. 480p. pap. 10.99 (978-0-385-73913-9(3), Ember) 2009. 464p. 17.99 (978-0-385-73893-4(5), Delacorte Pr.) Random Hse. Children's Bks.

—Fallen. 2010. (Fallen Ser.: 1). lib. bdg. 22.10 (978-0-606-15168-9(0), Turtleback) Turtleback Bks.

—Fallen in Love. 2012. (Fallen Ser.). (ENG.). (YA). (gr. 7). 224p. pap. 8.99 (978-0-385-74262-7(2), Ember); 256p. 15.99 (978-0-385-74261-0(4), Delacorte Pr.) Random Hse. Children's Bks.

—Oscuros. 2011. (Vintage Espanol Ser.: Bk. 1).Tr. of Fallen. (SPA.). 416p. (YA). (gr. 5). pap. 9.95 (978-0-307-74500-2(7), Vintage Espanol) Knopf Doubleday Publishing Group.

—Pasión. 2011. (Vintage Espanol Ser.: Bk. 3).Tr. of Passion. (SPA.). 384p. (YA). (gr. 7). pap. 9.95 (978-0-307-74523-1(6), Vintage Espanol) Knopf Doubleday Publishing Group.

—Passion. (Fallen Ser.: Bk. 3). (ENG.). (YA). (gr. 7). 2012. 448p. pap. 10.99 (978-0-385-73917-7(6), Ember) 2011. 432p. 17.99 (978-0-385-73916-0(8), Delacorte Pr.) Random Hse. Children's Bks.

—Passion. 2012. (Fallen Ser.: 3). lib. bdg. 22.10 (978-0-606-26410-5(8), Turtleback) Turtleback Bks.

—Rapture. (Fallen Ser.). (ENG.). (YA). (gr. 7). 2014. 480p. pap. 10.99 (978-0-385-73919-1(2), Ember) 2012. 464p. 17.99 (978-0-385-73918-4(4), Delacorte Pr.) Random Hse. Children's Bks.

—Torment. (Fallen Ser.: Bk. 2). (ENG.). (YA). (gr. 7). 2011. 480p. pap. 10.99 (978-0-385-73915-3(X), Ember) 2010. 464p. 17.99 (978-0-385-73914-6(1), Delacorte Pr.) Random Hse. Children's Bks.

—Torment. 2011. (Fallen Ser.: 2). lib. bdg. 22.10 (978-0-606-22247-1(2), Turtleback) Turtleback Bks.

—Tormento. 2011. (Vintage Espanol Ser.: Bk. 2).Tr. of Torment. (SPA.). 416p. (YA). (gr. 7). pap. 9.95 (978-0-307-74512-5(0), Vintage Espanol) Knopf Doubleday Publishing Group.

—Unforgiven. (Fallen Ser.). (ENG.). 368p. (YA). (gr. 7). 2016. pap. 10.99 (978-0-385-74264-1(9), Ember) 2015. 18.99 (978-0-385-74263-4(0), Delacorte Pr.) 2015. lib. bdg. 21.99 (978-0-375-99068-7(2), Delacorte Pr.) Random Hse. Children's Bks.

Kavanagh, Herminie Templeton. Darby O'Gill & the Crocks of Gold: And Other Irish Tales. Schluenderfritz, Ted, illus. 2003. ix, 155p. (J). pap. 14.95 (978-1-928832-85-0(7)) Sophia Institute Pr.

Kaymer, Lin. Who Is Mackie Spence? 2015. (ENG.). 208p. (YA). 17.99 (978-1-4405-8460-2(5), Simon Pulse) Simon Pulse.

Keaton, Kelly. A Beautiful Evil. (ENG.). (YA). (gr. 9). 2013. 320p. pap. 11.99 (978-1-4424-0928-6(2)) 2012. 304p. 17.99 (978-1-4424-0927-9(4)) Simon Pulse. (Simon Pulse).

—Darkness Becomes Her. (ENG.). (YA). (gr. 9). 2012. 320p. pap. 9.99 (978-1-4424-0925-5(8)) 2011. 288p. 16.99 (978-1-4424-0924-8(X)) Simon Pulse. (Simon Pulse).

—The Wicked Within. (ENG., Illus.). 288p. (YA). (gr. 9). 2014. pap. 9.99 (978-1-4424-9316-2(X)) 2013. 17.99 (978-1-4424-9315-5(1)) Simon Pulse. (Simon Pulse).

Keeble, Helen. Fang Girl. 2012. (ENG.). 352p. (YA). (gr. 8). pap. 9.99 (978-0-06-208225-1(6), HarperTeen) HarperCollins Pubs.

Kemmerer, Brigid. Sacrifice. 2014. (Elemental Ser.). (ENG.). 336p. (YA). (gr. 13). pap. 9.95 (978-0-7582-9439-5(5), K-Teen) Kensington Publishing Corp.

Kenyon, Sherrilyn. Infamous, 4 vols. (Chronicles of Nick Ser.: 3). (ENG.). 480p. (YA). (gr. 7). 2013. pap. 11.99

(978-1-250-00285-3(0), 9781250002853) 2012. 19.99 *(978-1-250-00282-2(6)*, 9781250002822) St. Martin's Pr. (St. Martin's Griffin).

—Inferno. 2014. (Chronicles of Nick Ser.: 4). (ENG.). 464p. (YA). (gr. 7). pap. 11.99 *(978-1-250-00286-0(9)*, 9781250002860, St. Martin's Griffin) St. Martin's Pr.

—Infinity, Vol. 1. Ahn, JiYoung, illus. 2013. (Dark-Hunters Ser.: 1). (ENG.). 240p. (gr. 11-17). 13.00 *(978-0-316-19053-4(5)*, Yen Pr.) Orbit.

—Infinity. (Chronicles of Nick Ser.: 1). (ENG.). 480p. (YA). (gr. 7-18). 2011. pap. 11.99 *(978-0-312-60304-5(5)*, 9780312603045) 2010. 19.99 *(978-0-312-59907-2(2)*, 9780312599072) St. Martin's Pr. (St. Martin's Griffin).

—Invincible. (Chronicles of Nick Ser.: 2). (ENG.). 432p. (YA). (gr. 7). 2012. pap. 11.99 *(978-0-312-60327-4(4)*, 9780312603274) 2011. 27.99 *(978-0-312-59906-5(4)*, 9780312599065) St. Martin's Pr. (St. Martin's Griffin).

Keswick, Kitty. Freaksville. Cox, Val, illus. 2010. 328p. (YA). (gr. 8-12). pap. 16.99 *(978-1-61603-001-8(1))* Leap Bks.

Kibuishi, Kazu. Escape from Lucien. 2015. (Amulet Ser.: 6). (ENG., Illus.). 224p. (J). (gr. 3-7). 24.99 *(978-0-545-84899-2(7)*, Graphix) Scholastic, Inc.

—Firelight. 2016. (Amulet Ser.: 7). (ENG., Illus.). 208p. (J). (gr. 3-7). 24.99 *(978-0-545-83966-2(1))*; pap. 12.99 *(978-0-545-43316-7(9))* Scholastic, Inc. (Graphix).

—Firelight. 2016. (Amulet Ser.: 7). (ENG., Illus.). 224p. (J). (gr. 3-7). lib. bdg. 24.50 *(978-0-606-38070-6(1))* Turtleback Bks.

—The Last Council. 2015. (Amulet Ser.: 4). (ENG.). 224p. (J). (gr. 3-7). 24.99 *(978-0-545-20886-4(6)*, Graphix) Scholastic, Inc.

Kibuishi, Kazu, illus. Firelight. 2016. 197p. (J). *(978-1-4806-9909-0(8))* Baker & Taylor, CATS.

Kimmel, Elizabeth Cody. ParaNorman: A Novel. 2013. (ENG., Illus.). 256p. (J). (gr. 3-7). pap. 6.99 *(978-0-316-20987-8(2))* Little, Brown Bks. for Young Readers.

—Suddenly Supernatural 4: Crossing Over. 2011. (Suddenly Supernatural Ser.: 4). (ENG.). 256p. (J). (gr. 3-7). pap. 5.99 *(978-0-316-13345-6(0))* Little, Brown Bks. for Young Readers.

—Suddenly Supernatural: Scaredy Kat. 2010. (Suddenly Supernatural Ser.: 2). (ENG.). 272p. (J). (gr. 3-7). pap. 5.99 *(978-0-316-08745-2(9))* Little, Brown Bks. for Young Readers.

—Suddenly Supernatural: School Spirit. 2010. (Suddenly Supernatural Ser.: 1). (ENG.). 336p. (J). (gr. 3-7). pap. 7.99 *(978-0-316-07821-4(2))* Little, Brown Bks. for Young Readers.

Kindl, Patrice. Owl in Love. 2004. (ENG.). 224p. (YA). (gr. 7-18). pap. 14.95 *(978-0-618-43910-2(2))* Houghton Mifflin Harcourt Publishing Co.

Kingfisher, Rupert. Madame Pamplemousse & Her Incredible Edibles. Hellard, Sue, illus. 2008. (ENG.). 144p. (YA). (gr. 3-6). 15.99 *(978-1-59990-306-4(7)*, 9781599903064, Bloomsbury USA Childrens) Bloomsbury Publishing USA.

Klause, Annette Curtis. Freaks: Alive, on the Inside! (ENG.). 336p. (YA). 2007. (gr. 9). pap. 9.99 *(978-0-689-87038-5(8))* 2006. (Illus.). (gr. 8-18). 16.95 *(978-0-689-87037-8(X))* McElderry, Margaret K. Bks. (McElderry, Margaret K. Bks.).

Knight, Karsten. Afterglow. 2013. (ENG., Illus.). 336p. (YA). (gr. 9). 17.99 *(978-1-4424-5037-0(1)*, Simon & Schuster Bks. For Young Readers) Simon & Schuster Bks. For Young Readers.

—Embers & Echoes. (ENG., (YA). (gr. 9). 2013. Illus.). 496p. pap. 9.99 *(978-1-4424-5035-6(5))* 2012. 480p. 16.99 *(978-1-4424-5030-1(4))* Simon & Schuster Bks. For Young Readers. (Simon & Schuster Bks. For Young Readers).

—Wildefire. 2011. (ENG.). 400p. (YA). (gr. 9-18). 16.99 *(978-1-4424-2117-2(7)*, Simon & Schuster Bks. For Young Readers) Simon & Schuster Bks. For Young Readers.

Kogler, Jennifer. The Otherworldlies. 2008. 400p. (J). lib. bdg. 17.89 *(978-0-06-073960-7(6))*; (ENG.). (gr. 5-18). 16.99 *(978-0-06-073959-1(2))* HarperCollins Pubs. (Eos).

Kogler, Jennifer Anne. The Siren's Cry. 2011. (ENG.). 384p. (YA). (gr. 8). 16.99 *(978-0-06-199443-2(X)*, HarperTeen) HarperCollins Pubs.

Kogler, Jennifer Anne & Kogler, Jennifer A. The Otherworldlies. 2009. (ENG.). 400p. (YA). (gr. 8). pap. 8.99 *(978-0-06-073961-4(4)*, HarperTeen) HarperCollins Pubs.

Konen, Leah. The After Girls. 2013. (ENG.). 304p. (YA). 17.95 *(978-1-4405-6108-5(7)*, Simon Pulse) Simon Pulse.

Korman, Gordon. The Dragonfly Effect. 2016. (Hypnotists Ser.: 3). lib. bdg. 17.20 *(978-0-606-38813-9(3))* Turtleback Bks.

—The Hypnotists. (ENG.). 240p. (J). (gr. 3-7). 2013. (Hypnotists Ser.: 1). 16.99 *(978-0-545-50322-8(1)*, Scholastic Pr.)Bk. 1. 2014. pap. 6.99 *(978-0-545-50325-9(6)*, Scholastic Paperbacks) Scholastic, Inc.

—The Hypnotists. 2014. (Hypnotists Ser.: 1). lib. bdg. 17.20 *(978-0-606-35808-8(0))* Turtleback Bks.

—Memory Maze. 2014. (Hypnotists Ser.: 2). (ENG.). 240p. (J). (gr. 3-7). 16.99 *(978-0-545-50329-7(9)*, Scholastic Pr.) Scholastic, Inc.

—Memory Maze. 2015. (Hypnotists Ser.: 2). lib. bdg. 17.20 *(978-0-606-37016-5(1))* Turtleback Bks.

Kotecki, Nathan. The Suburban Strange. (Suburban Strange Ser.). (ENG.). (YA). (gr. 9). 2013. 384p. pap. 8.99 *(978-0-544-10479-2(X))* 2012. 368p. 16.99 *(978-0-547-72996-1(0))* Houghton Mifflin Harcourt Publishing Co.

Kozlowsky, M. P. The Dyerville Tales. Thompson, Brian, illus. 2014. (ENG.). 336p. (J). (gr. 3-7). 16.99 *(978-0-06-199871-3(0)*, Waldon Pond Pr.) HarperCollins Pubs.

—Juniper Berry. Madrid, Erwin, illus. 2012. (ENG.). 240p. (J). (gr. 3-7). pap. 5.99 *(978-0-06-199870-6(2)*, Waldon Pond Pr.) HarperCollins Pubs.

Kreie, Chris. Blood Moon. 2017. (Midnight Ser.). (ENG.). 96p. (YA). (gr. 6-12). 26.65 *(978-1-5124-2772-1(1))*; 12.99 ***(978-1-5124-3483-5(3)***, Darby Creek); 39.99 ***(978-1-5124-3482-8(5)***, Darby Creek); 39.99 ***(978-1-5124-2792-9(6)***, Darby Creek) Lerner Publishing Group.

Krovatin, Christopher. Mountain of Bones. (Gravediggers Ser.: 1). (ENG.). (J). (gr. 3-7). 2013. 352p. pap. 6.99 *(978-0-06-207741-7(4))* 2012. 336p. 16.99 *(978-0-06-207740-0(6))* HarperCollins Pubs. (Tegen, Katherine Bks).

—Terror Cove. 2013. (Gravediggers Ser.: 2). (ENG.). 368p. (J). (gr. 3-7). 16.99 *(978-0-06-207743-1(0)*, Tegen, Katherine Bks) HarperCollins Pubs.

Krys, Michelle. Hexed. 2014. (ENG.). 384p. (YA). (gr. 7). 17.99 *(978-0-385-74337-2(8)*, Delacorte Pr.) Random Hse. Children's Bks.

Kurtagich, Dawn. And the Trees Crept In. (ENG.). (gr. 10-17). 2017. 368p. (J). pap. 9.99 ***(978-0-316-29871-1(9))*** 2016. 352p. (YA). 17.99 *(978-0-316-29870-4(0))* Little, Brown Bks. for Young Readers.

Laar-Yond C.T. Six Fingers & the Blue Warrior. Playcrib, illus. 2013. 36p. pap. 14.00 *(978-1-62212-177-9(5)*, Strategic Bk. Publishing) Strategic Book Publishing & Rights Agency (SBPRA).

Lackey, Mercedes & Edghill, Rosemary. Conspiracies. 2011. (Shadow Grail Ser.: 2). (ENG.). 352p. (YA). (gr. 8-12). pap. 19.99 *(978-0-7653-1762-9(1)*, 9780765317629, Tor Teen) Doherty, Tom Assocs., LLC.

—Shadow Grail #3: Sacrifices. 2013. (Shadow Grail Ser.: 3). (ENG.). 304p. (YA). (gr. 8-12). pap. 14.99 *(978-0-7653-1763-6(X)*, 9780765317636, Tor Teen) Doherty, Tom Assocs., LLC.

—Shadow Grail #4: Victories. 2014. (Shadow Grail Ser.: 4). (ENG.). 256p. (YA). (gr. 8-12). pap. 11.99 *(978-0-7653-1764-3(8)*, 9780765317643, Tor Teen) Doherty, Tom Assocs., LLC.

LaFleur, Suzanne. Listening for Lucca. 2015. (ENG.). 240p. (J). (gr. 4-7). pap. 7.99 *(978-0-307-98030-4(8)*, Yearling) Random Hse. Children's Bks.

Lanagan, Margo. Red Spikes. 2009. (ENG.). 192p. (YA). (gr. 9). pap. 7.99 *(978-0-375-84304-4(3)*, Knopf Bks. for Young Readers) Random Hse. Children's Bks.

Langer, Dana. Siren Sisters. 2017. (ENG., Illus.). 256p. (J). (gr. 4-8). 16.99 *(978-1-4814-6686-8(0)*, Simon & Schuster/Paula Wiseman Bks.) Simon & Schuster/Paula Wiseman Bks.

Langrish, Katherine. The Shadow Hunt. 2010. 322p. lib. bdg. *(978-0-06-111678-0(5))* HarperCollins Pubs.

—Troll Blood. Stevens, Tim & Wyatt, David, illus. 2008. 352p. (gr. 5-8). (ENG.). (J). 16.99 *(978-0-06-111674-2(2))*; (YA). lib. bdg. 17.89 *(978-0-06-111675-9(0)*, Eos) HarperCollins Pubs.

—Troll Mill. 2008. (ENG., Illus.). 336p. (YA). (gr. 7). pap. 7.99 *(978-0-06-058309-5(6)*, Eos) HarperCollins Pubs.

Latta, Ruth. The Revenant & Other Stories for Hallowe'en. 2004. 54p. *(978-0-9683382-8-5(3))* Latta, Roger K.

Lauren, Christina. The House. 2015. (ENG., Illus.). 384p. (YA). (gr. 9). 18.99 *(978-1-4814-1371-8(6))* Simon & Schuster Children's Publishing.

Lawrence, Theo. Mystic City. (Mystic City Trilogy Ser.). (ENG.). 416p. (YA). (gr. 7). 2014. pap. 9.99 *(978-0-385-74161-3(8)*, Ember) 2012. 17.99 *(978-0-385-74160-6(X)*, Delacorte Pr.) Random Hse. Children's Bks.

—Toxic Heart: a Mystic City Novel. 2015. (Mystic City Trilogy Ser.). (ENG.). 368p. (YA). (gr. 7). pap. 9.99 *(978-0-385-74163-7(4)*, Ember) Random Hse. Children's Bks.

Lee, Kathy. The Runaway Train. 2011. 144p. pap. *(978-1-84427-505-2(1))* Scripture Union.

Lee, Mackenzi. This Monstrous Thing. 2015. (ENG.). 384p. (YA). (gr. 8). 17.99 *(978-0-06-238277-1(2))* HarperCollins Pubs.

Lee, Stan. The Dragon's Return. Tong, Andie, illus. 2017. (Zodiac Ser.). (ENG.). 448p. (J). (gr. 3-7). pap. 9.99 *(978-1-4847-5255-5(4))* Disney Pr.

—The Dragon's Return. 2017. (Zodiac Legacy Ser.: 2). (J). lib. bdg. 20.85 *(978-0-606-39500-7(8))* Turtleback Bks.

Lee, Stan & Moore, Stuart. The Dragon's Return. Tong, Andie, illus. 2016. (Zodiac Ser.: Bk. 2). (ENG.). 432p. (J). (gr. 3-7). 16.99 *(978-1-4847-1352-5(4))* Disney Pr.

Lemke, Donald B. The Awakening, 1 vol. 2011. (Good vs Evil Ser.). (ENG.). 48p. (gr. 1-2). lib. bdg. 23.99 *(978-1-4342-2089-9(3)*, Good vs Evil) Stone Arch Bks.

Lewis, Richard. The Demon Queen. 2012. (ENG.). 240p. (YA). (gr. 7). pap. 11.99 *(978-1-4169-3590-2(8)*, Simon & Schuster Bks. For Young Readers) Simon & Schuster Bks. For Young Readers.

—Monster's Proof. (ENG.). 288p. (YA). (gr. 7). 2010. pap. 7.99 *(978-1-4169-3592-6(4))* 2009. 15.99 *(978-1-4169-3591-9(6))* Simon & Schuster Bks. For Young Readers. (Simon & Schuster Bks. For Young Readers).

Lewis, Sylvia. Beautiful Decay. 2013. (ENG.). 304p. (YA). (gr. 2-17). pap. 9.95 *(978-0-7624-4611-7(0)*, Running Pr. Kids) Running Pr. Bk. Pubs.

Liggett, Kim. Blood & Salt. 2015. (ENG.). 352p. (YA). (gr. 9-12). 17.99 *(978-0-399-16648-8(3)*, G.P. Putnam's Sons Books for Young Readers) Penguin Young Readers Group.

Lim, Rebecca. Afterlight. 2016. (ENG., Illus.). 240p. (gr. 8). 11.95 *(978-1-925240-49-8(5))* Text Publishing Co. AUS. Dist: Consortium Bk. Sales & Distribution.

—Exile (Mercy, Book 2) 2016. (Mercy Ser.: 2). (ENG.). 304p. (J). pap. 9.99 *(978-0-00-816904-6(7)*, HarperCollins Children's Bks.) HarperCollins Pubs. Ltd. GBR. Dist: HarperCollins Pubs.

Lindsey, Mary. Fragile Spirits. 2014. (ENG.). 320p. (YA). (gr. 7). 17.99 *(978-0-399-16186-5(4)*, Philomel Bks.) Penguin Young Readers Group.

—Shattered Souls. 2012. (ENG.). 356p. (YA). (gr. 9). pap. 8.99 *(978-0-14-242190-1(1)*, Speak) Penguin Young Readers Group.

Liparulo, Robert. Gatekeepers, 1 vol. 2009. (Dreamhouse Kings Ser.: 3). (ENG.). 320p. pap. 9.99 *(978-1-59554-729-3(0))* Nelson, Thomas Inc.

—House of Dark Shadows, 1 vol. 2009. (Dreamhouse Kings Ser.: 1). (ENG.). 304p. pap. 9.99 *(978-1-59554-727-9(4))* Nelson, Thomas Inc.

—Whirlwind, 1 vol. 2010. (Dreamhouse Kings Ser.: 5). (ENG.). 320p. pap. 9.99 *(978-1-59554-892-4(0))* Nelson, Thomas Inc.

Lipinski, Maureen. Cleopatra Ascending. 2013. (Shadow's Edge Novel Ser.: 2). (ENG.). 240p. (YA). pap. 9.99 *(978-0-7387-3193-3(5)*, Flux) North Star Editions.

Livingston, Lesley. Descendant. 2013. (Starling Trilogy Ser.: 2). (ENG.). 336p. (YA). (gr. 8). 17.99 *(978-0-06-206310-6(3)*, HarperTeen) HarperCollins Pubs.

Lloyd-Jones, Emily. The Hearts We Sold. 2017. (ENG.). 400p. (YA). (gr. 10-17). 17.99 ***(978-0-316-31459-6(5))*** Little Brown & Co.

London, J. A. After Daybreak. 2013. (Darkness Before Dawn Ser.: 3). (ENG., Illus.). 336p. (YA). (gr. 9). pap. 9.99 *(978-0-06-202067-3(6)*, HarperTeen) HarperCollins Pubs.

Long, Loren & Bildner, Phil. Blastin' the Blues. Long, Loren, illus. 2011. (Sluggers Ser.: 5). (ENG., Illus.). 448p. (J). (gr. 3-7). pap. 8.99 *(978-1-4169-1891-2(4)*, Simon & Schuster Bks. For Young Readers) Simon & Schuster Bks. For Young Readers.

—Home of the Brave. Long, Loren, illus. (Sluggers Ser.: 6). (ENG., Illus.). (J). (gr. 3-7). 2011. pap. 8.99 *(978-1-4169-1892-9(2))* 2010. 15.99 *(978-1-4169-1868-4(X))* Simon & Schuster Bks. For Young Readers. (Simon & Schuster Bks. For Young Readers).

—Magic in the Outfield. Long, Loren, illus. 2009. (Sluggers Ser.: 1). (ENG., Illus.). 160p. (J). (gr. 3-7). pap. 8.99 *(978-1-4169-1884-4(1)*, Simon & Schuster Bks. For Young Readers) Simon & Schuster Bks. For Young Readers.

—Water, Water Everywhere. Long, Loren, illus. (Sluggers Ser.: 4). (ENG., Illus.). (J). (gr. 3-7). 2010. 288p. pap. 7.99 *(978-1-4169-1890-5(6))* 2009. 272p. 14.99 *(978-1-4169-1866-0(3))* Simon & Schuster Bks. For Young Readers. (Simon & Schuster Bks. For Young Readers).

Loyd, Todd. Dark Ride. 2012. (ENG.). 320p. (YA). (gr. 7-9). pap. 15.00 *(978-1-936487-22-6(5)*, 1936487225) Franklin Green Publishing.

Lu, Marie. The Midnight Star. 2016. (Young Elites Novel Ser.: 3). (ENG., Illus.). 336p. (YA). (gr. 7). 18.99 *(978-0-399-16785-0(4)*, G.P. Putnam's Sons Books for Young Readers) Penguin Young Readers Group.

—The Rose Society. 2015. (Young Elites Ser.: 2). (ENG., Illus.). 416p. (YA). (gr. 7). 18.99 *(978-0-399-16784-3(6)*, G.P. Putnam's Sons Books for Young Readers) Penguin Publishing Group.

—The Rose Society. 2016. (Young Elites Novel Ser.). (ENG.). 432p. (YA). (gr. 7). pap. 10.99 *(978-0-14-751169-0(0)*, Speak) Penguin Young Readers Group.

—The Rose Society. l.t. ed. 2015. (Young Elites Ser.). (ENG.). 24.99 *(978-1-4104-8465-9(3))* Thorndike Pr.

—The Rose Society. 2016. (Young Elites Ser.: 2). (ENG.). 432p. (YA). (gr. 7). 22.10 *(978-0-606-39314-0(5))* Turtleback Bks.

—The Young Elites. 2014. (ENG., Illus.). 368p. (YA). (gr. 7). 18.99 *(978-0-399-16783-6(8)*, G.P. Putnam's Sons Books for Young Readers) Penguin Publishing Group.

—The Young Elites. 2015. (Young Elites Novel Ser.). (ENG.). 384p. (YA). (gr. 7). pap. 10.99 *(978-0-14-751168-3(2)*, Speak) Penguin Young Readers Group.

—The Young Elites. 2015. (ENG.). (YA). (gr. 7). lib. bdg. 21.60 ***(978-1-68065-052-5(1))*** Perfection Learning Corp.

—The Young Elites. 2015. (Young Elites Ser.: 1). lib. bdg. 22.10 *(978-0-606-37575-7(9))* Turtleback Bks.

Lubar, David. The Vanishing Vampire: A Monsterrific Tale. 2013. (Monsterrific Tales Ser.). (ENG., Illus.). 144p. (J). (gr. 3-7). 15.99 *(978-0-7653-3077-2(6)*, 9780765330772, Starscape) Doherty, Tom Assocs., LLC.

—The Wavering Werewolf: A Monsterrific Tale. 2014. (Monsterrific Tales Ser.). (ENG.). 144p. (J). (gr. 3-7). 15.99 *(978-0-7653-3079-6(2)*, 9780765330796, Starscape) Doherty, Tom Assocs., LLC.

Lynne, Zoe. Carnival - Decatur. 2016. (ENG., Illus.). (J). 24.99 ***(978-1-63477-948-7(7)***, Harmony Ink Pr.) Dreamspinner Pr.

Maberry, Jonathan. The Orphan Army. 2015. (Nightsiders Ser.: 1). (ENG., Illus.). 400p. (J). (gr. 3-7). 16.99 *(978-1-4814-1575-0(1)*, Simon & Schuster Bks. For Young Readers) Simon & Schuster Bks. For Young Readers.

—The Orphan Army. 2016. (Nightsiders Ser.: 1). lib. bdg. 18.40 *(978-0-606-38959-4(8))* Turtleback Bks.

—Vault of Shadows. (Nightsiders Ser.: 2). (ENG.). 464p. (J). (gr. 3-7). 2017. pap. 8.99 *(978-1-4814-1579-8(4))* 2016. (Illus.). 16.99 *(978-1-4814-1578-1(6))* Simon & Schuster Bks. For Young Readers. (Simon & Schuster Bks. For Young Readers).

Mabry, Samantha. A Fierce & Subtle Poison. 2016. (ENG.). 288p. (YA). (gr. 8-12). 17.95 *(978-1-61620-521-8(0))* Algonquin Bks. of Chapel Hill.

MacHale, D. J. The Black. (Morpheus Road Ser.: 2). (ENG.). (J). (gr. 5-9). 2012. 432p. pap. 9.99 *(978-1-4169-6520-6(3))* 2011. 416p. 18.99 *(978-1-4169-6517-6(3))* Simon & Schuster Children's Publishing. (Aladdin).

—The Blood. (Morpheus Road Ser.: 3). (ENG.). 384p. (J). (gr. 5-9). 2013. pap. 8.99 *(978-1-4169-6521-3(1))* 2012. 17.99 *(978-1-4169-6518-3(1))* Simon & Schuster Children's Publishing. (Aladdin).

—The Light. 2010. (Morpheus Road Ser.: 1). (ENG.). 352p. (J). (gr. 5-9). pap. 9.99 *(978-1-4169-6519-0(X)*, Aladdin) Simon & Schuster Children's Publishing.

—The Light. 2010. (Morpheus Road Ser.: 1). (ENG.). 352p. (J). (gr. 5-18). 17.99 *(978-1-4169-6516-9(5)*, Simon & Schuster/Paula Wiseman Bks.) Simon & Schuster/Paula Wiseman Bks.

MacHale, D.j. Black Moon Rising. 2017. (J). pap. ***(978-1-101-93260-5(0))*** Random Hse., Inc.

Machale, D.j. The Library: Mysterious Messenger (Book 1) 2016. (Library: 1). (ENG.). 256p. (J). (gr. 3-7). 16.99 *(978-1-101-93253-7(8)*, Random Hse. Bks. for Young Readers) Random Hse. Children's Bks.

MacKey, Cindy. Hannah's Day of Revelations. 2013. 46p. pap. 13.99 *(978-0-9892699-4-0(9))* Cyrano Bks.

Mackey, Heather. Dreamwood. 2014. (ENG.). 352p. (J). (gr. 5). 16.99 *(978-0-399-25067-5(0)*, G.P. Putnam's Sons Books for Young Readers) Penguin Young Readers Group.

Maguire, Eden. Arizona. 2010. (Beautiful Dead Ser.: 2). (ENG.). 288p. (YA). (gr. 8-12). pap. 11.99 *(978-1-4022-3945-8(9))* Sourcebooks, Inc.

Mahoney, Karen. Falling to Ash. 2014. (ENG.). 346p. (YA). (gr. 8). pap. 9.99 *(978-0-552-56526-4(1))* Transworld Publishers Ltd. GBR. Dist: Independent Pubs. Group.

Maizel, Rebecca. Stolen Nights. 2013. (Vampire Queen Ser.: 2). (ENG.). 320p. (YA). (gr. 7-18). pap. 9.99 *(978-0-312-64992-0(4)*, 9780312649920, St. Martin's Griffin) St. Martin's Pr.

Malkin, Nina. Swear. (ENG.). 480p. (YA). (gr. 11). 2012. pap. 9.99 *(978-1-4424-2111-0(8))* 2011. 17.99 *(978-1-4424-2110-3(X))* Simon Pulse. (Simon Pulse).

—Swoon. 2010. (ENG.). 432p. (YA). (gr. 11). pap. 9.99 *(978-1-4169-9801-3(2)*, Simon Pulse) Simon Pulse.

Maloney, Andrew. The Master Song. 2014. (Illus.). 352p. (YA). *(978-1-62911-176-6(7))* Whitaker Hse.

—Verse of Valor. 2015. 285p. (YA). *(978-1-62911-357-9(3))* Whitaker Hse.

Mancusi, Mari. Scorched. (Scorched Ser.: 1). (ENG.). (YA). (gr. 6-12). 2014. 368p. pap. 9.99 *(978-1-4022-9227-9(9))* 2013. 352p. 16.99 *(978-1-4022-8458-8(6)*, 9781402284588) Sourcebooks, Inc.

—Shattered. (Scorched Ser.: 2). (ENG.). (YA). 2015. 416p. (gr. 8-12). pap. 9.99 *(978-1-4926-0869-1(6))* 2014. 400p. (gr. 7-12). 16.99 *(978-1-4022-8461-8(6)*, 9781402284618) Sourcebooks, Inc.

Mankell, Henning. Shadows in the Twilight. 2010. (Joel Gustafson Stories Ser.: No. 2). (ENG.). 208p. (YA). (gr. 7). pap. 7.99 *(978-0-440-24043-3(3)*, Delacorte Bks. for Young Readers) Random Hse. Children's Bks.

Marillier, Juliet. Cybele's Secret. 2011. (ENG.). 444p. (YA). (gr. 7). pap. 9.99 *(978-0-553-49486-0(4)*, Knopf Bks. for Young Readers) Random Hse. Children's Bks.

—Wildwood Dancing. 2008. (ENG.). 432p. (YA). (gr. 7). pap. 10.99 *(978-0-375-84474-4(0)*, Knopf Bks. for Young Readers) Random Hse. Children's Bks.

Mariolle, Mathieu. Changing Moon. MiniKim et al, illus. 2010. (Nola's Worlds Ser.: 1). (ENG.). 136p. (J). (gr. 6-9). 30.60 *(978-0-7613-6502-0(8))* Lerner Publishing Group.

—Changing Moon. Jeffrey, Erica Olson, tr. from FRE. MiniKim et al, illus. 2010. (Nola's Worlds Ser.: 1). (ENG.). 136p. (J). (gr. 6-9). pap. 9.95 *(978-0-7613-6538-9(9)*, Graphic Universe™) Lerner Publishing Group.

—Changing Moon. rev. ed. 2010. pap. 56.72 *(978-0-7613-6953-0(8))* Lerner Publishing Group.

—Even for a Dreamer Like Me. MiniKim et al, illus. 2010. (Nola's Worlds Ser.: 3). (ENG.). 128p. (J). (gr. 6-9). 30.60 *(978-0-7613-6505-1(2))* Lerner Publishing Group.

—Even for a Dreamer Like Me. Jeffrey, Erica Olson, tr. from FRE. MiniKim et al, illus. 2010. (Nola's Worlds Ser.: 3). (ENG.). 136p. (J). (gr. 6-9). pap. 9.95 *(978-0-7613-6541-9(9)*, Graphic Universe™) Lerner Publishing Group.

—Ferrets & Ferreting Out. Buffiere, Mélanie & Lajic, Maïté, illus. 2010. (Nola's Worlds Ser.: 2). (ENG.). 136p. (J). (gr. 6-9). pap. 9.95 *(978-0-7613-6542-6(7)*, Graphic Universe™) Lerner Publishing Group.

—Ferrets & Ferreting Out. MiniKim et al, illus. 2010. (Nola's Worlds Ser.: 2). (ENG.). 136p. (J). (gr. 6-9). 30.60 *(978-0-7613-6504-4(4))* Lerner Publishing Group.

—Nola's Worlds, 3 vols., Set. MiniKim et al, illus. Incl. Changing Moon. 136p. 30.60 *(978-0-7613-6502-0(8))*; Even for a Dreamer Like Me. 128p. 30.60 *(978-0-7613-6505-1(2))*; Ferrets & Ferreting Out. 136p. 30.60 *(978-0-7613-6504-4(4))*; (Illus.). (J). (gr. 6-9). 2010. Set lib. bdg. 91.80 *(978-0-7613-6500-6(1)*, Graphic Universe™) Lerner Publishing Group.

Marr, Melissa & Pratt, Tim, eds. Rags & Bones: New Twists on Timeless Tales. 2015. (ENG.). 368p. (YA). (gr. 10-17). pap. 12.99 *(978-0-316-21293-9(8))* Little, Brown Bks. for Young Readers.

Marr, Melissa, et al. Enthralled: Paranormal Diversions. 2011. (ENG.). 464p. (YA). (gr. 8). pap. 9.99 *(978-0-06-201578-5(8))* HarperCollins Pubs.

—Love Is Hell. 2008. (ENG.). 272p. (YA). (gr. 9-18). pap. 9.99 *(978-0-06-144304-6(2)*, HarperTeen) HarperCollins Pubs.

Marr Osb, Andrew. From Beyond to Here: Merendael's Gift & Other Stories. 2012. 320p. (gr. 4-6). 29.95 *(978-1-4759-3460-1(2))*; pap. 19.95 *(978-1-4759-3458-8(0))* iUniverse, Inc.

Martin, Benjamin. Samurai Awakening. 2012. (ENG.). 320p. (J). (gr. 7-12). 17.99 *(978-4-8053-1228-5(9))* Tuttle Publishing.

Martin, R. T. Dark Star. 2017. (Midnight Ser.). (ENG.). 96p. (YA). (gr. 6-12). 26.65 *(978-1-5124-2769-1(1))*; 12.99 ***(978-1-5124-3486-6(8)***, Darby Creek); 39.99 ***(978-1-5124-3485-9(X)***, Darby Creek); 39.99 ***(978-1-5124-2789-9(6)***, Darby Creek) Lerner Publishing Group.

Marz, Ron. Witchblade Redemption, Vol. 4. 2012. (ENG., Illus.). 160p. pap. 19.99 *(978-1-60706-424-4(3)*, 9781607064244) Image Comics.

Mass, Wendy. The Last Present. (ENG.). 256p. (J). (gr. 3-7). 2015. pap. 6.99 *(978-0-545-31017-8(2))* 2013. 16.99 *(978-0-545-31016-1(4)*, Scholastic Pr.) Scholastic, Inc.

—13 Gifts. 2013. (ENG.). 352p. (J). (gr. 3-7). pap. 6.99 *(978-0-545-31004-8(0))* Scholastic, Inc.

—13 Gifts. 2013. (Willow Falls Ser.: 3). lib. bdg. 17.20 *(978-0-606-31957-7(3)*, Turtleback) Turtleback Bks.

Matas, Carol. The Freak. rev. ed. 2008. (Freak (Key Porter Books) Ser.). (ENG.). 128p. (J). (gr. 5-18). pap. *(978-1-55263-930-6(4))* Magma.

—Tales of a Reluctant Psychic: The Freak, Visions, & Far. 2009. (ENG.). 424p. (YA). (gr. 7-18). pap. *(978-1-55470-203-9(8))* Me to We.

Mather, Adriana. How to Hang a Witch. 2016. (ENG.). 368p. (YA). (gr. 7). 17.99 *(978-0-553-53947-9(7)*, Knopf Bks. for Young Readers) Random Hse. Children's Bks.

McBride, Lish. Hold Me Closer, Necromancer. 2010. (Necromancer Ser.: 1). (ENG.). 352p. (YA). (gr. 9-13). 16.99 *(978-0-8050-9098-7(3)*, 9780805090987, Holt, Henry & Co. Bks. For Young Readers) Holt, Henry & Co.

—Necromancing the Stone. 2013. (Necromancer Ser.: 2). (ENG.). 368p. (YA). (gr. 9-13). pap. 9.99 *(978-1-250-03415-1(9)*, 9781250034151) Square Fish.

McCall, Guadalupe Garcia. Summer of the Mariposas. 2012. (ENG.). 352p. (YA). 19.95 *(978-1-60060-900-8(7)*, Tu Bks.) Lee & Low Bks., Inc.

McCarry, Sarah. All Our Pretty Songs. 2013. (Metamorphoses Trilogy Ser.: 1). (ENG.). 240p. (YA). (gr. 8-12). pap. 9.99 *(978-1-250-02708-5(X)*, 9781250027085, St. Martin's Griffin) St. Martin's Pr.

—Dirty Wings. 2014. (Metamorphoses Trilogy Ser.: 2). (ENG.). 288p. (YA). (gr. 8-12). 19.99 *(978-1-250-04938-4(5)*, 9781250049384, St. Martin's Griffin) St. Martin's Pr.

McCaughan, Timothy. Crimson Soul. 2005. 200p. per. 12.95 *(978-1-58961-438-3(0))* PageFree Publishing, Inc.

McClellan, Rachel. Fractured Truth. 2014. 16.99 *(978-1-4621-1392-7(3)*, Horizon Pubs.) Cedar Fort, Inc./CFI Distribution.

S

McCormack, Devon. Hideous. 2016. (ENG., Illus.). (J). 24.99 (978-1-63533-028-1(9), Harmony Ink Pr.) Dreamspinner Pr.

McCracken, Connie. Indigo Boy & Crystalline Girl. Craig, Chris, illus. 2009. 24p. pap. 10.95 (978-1-4269-0423-3(1)) Trafford Publishing.

McCune, D. J. Death & Co. 2013. (Death & Co Ser.: 1). (ENG.). 288p. (YA). (gr. 8). pap. 11.99 (978-1-4714-0092-6(1)) Bonnier Publishing GBR. Dist: Independent Pubs. Group.

—Death & Co Mortal Knife Book 2. 2014. (Death & Co Ser.: 2). (ENG.). 304p. (YA). (gr. 8). 11.99 (978-1-4714-0231-9(2)) Bonnier Publishing GBR. Dist: Independent Pubs. Group.

McDonald, Megan. Judy Moody Advina el Futuro. Reynolds, Peter H., illus. 2004. (SPA.). 74p. (J). (gr. 3-5). pap. 7.95 (978-1-59437-837-9(1)) Ediciones Alfaguara ESP. Dist: Two Rivers Distribution.

McEntire, K. D. Lightbringer. 2011. (ENG.). 319p. (YA). (gr. 7). 16.99 (978-1-61614-539-2(0)) Prometheus Bks., Pubs.

—Never. 2013. (Lightbringer Ser.). (ENG.). 311p. (J). (gr. 7). 17.99 (978-1-61614-771-6(7)) Prometheus Bks., Pubs.

—Reaper. 2012. (ENG.). 342p. (YA). (gr. 7). 16.95 (978-1-61614-632-0(X)) Prometheus Bks., Pubs.

McGann, Oisín. Under Fragile Stone, Vol. 2. 2005. (ENG., Illus.). 384p. (J). pap. 12.95 (978-0-86278-835-3(8)) O'Brien Pr., Ltd., The IRL. Dist: Dufour Editions, Inc.

McKenzie, Paige. The Haunting of Sunshine Girl. (ENG.). 2016. 320p. (gr. 7-10). pap. 9.99 (978-1-60286-302-6(4)) 2015. (Haunting of Sunshine Girl Ser.: Bk. 1). 304p. (YA). 16.00 (978-1-60286-272-2(9)) Perseus Bks. Group. (Weinstein Bks.).

McMann, Lisa. Bang. (Visions Ser.: 2). (ENG., (YA). (gr. 9). 2014. Illus.). 272p. pap. 9.99 (978-1-4424-6628-9(6)) 2013. 256p. 16.99 (978-1-4424-6625-8(1)) Simon Pulse. (Simon Pulse).

—Crash. 2013. (Visions Ser.: 1). (ENG.). 256p. (YA). (gr. 9). 16.99 (978-1-4424-0391-8(8), Simon Pulse) Simon Pulse.

—Cryer's Cross. 2011. (ENG.). (YA). (gr. 9). 256p. pap. 9.99 (978-1-4169-9482-4(3)); (Illus.). 240p. 16.99 (978-1-4169-9481-7(5)) Simon Pulse. (Simon Pulse).

—Gasp. 2014. (Visions Ser.: 3). (ENG., Illus.). 288p. (YA). (gr. 9). 17.99 (978-1-4424-6630-2(8), Simon Pulse) Simon Pulse.

McNamee, Graham. Bonechiller. 2012. (ENG.). 304p. (YA). (gr. 7). pap. 9.99 (978-0-307-97593-5(2), Ember) Random Hse. Children's Bks.

McNeal, Tom. Far Far Away. (ENG.). (YA). (gr. 7). 2014. 400p. pap. 9.99 (978-0-375-84329-7(9), Ember) 2013. 384p. 17.99 (978-0-375-84972-5(6), Knopf Bks. for Young Readers) Random Hse. Children's Bks.

McNish, Cliff. Savannah Grey. (ENG.). 272p. (YA). (gr. 7-12). 2013. pap. 9.95 (978-1-4677-0913-2(1)) 2011. 17.95 (978-0-7613-7025-3(0)) Lerner Publishing Group. (Carolrhoda Lab™).

McTiernan, Deborah. Lilly Noble & Actual Magic. 2013. (ENG.). 318p. (YA). pap. 14.99 (978-0-9891807-0-2(0)) Actual Magic Enterprises, LLC.

Mead, Richelle. Blood Promise. 2010. (Vampire Academy Ser.: 4). (ENG.). 528p. (YA). (gr. 7-18). 9.99 (978-1-59514-310-5(6), Razorbill) Penguin Young Readers Group.

—Blood Promise. 2010. (Vampire Academy Ser.: 4). lib. bdg. 20.85 (978-0-606-14565-7(6), Turtleback) Turtleback Bks.

—The Golden Lily. (Bloodlines Ser.: 2). (ENG.). (YA). (gr. 7). 2013. 448p. pap. 10.99 (978-1-59514-602-1(4)) 2012. 432p. 18.99 (978-1-59514-318-1(1)) Penguin Young Readers Group. (Razorbill).

—Last Sacrifice. 2011. (Vampire Academy Ser.: 6). (ENG.). 608p. (YA). (gr. 7-18). 10.99 (978-1-59514-440-9(4), Razorbill) Penguin Young Readers Group.

—Midnight Jewel. 2017. (Glittering Court Ser.: 2). (ENG.). 416p. (YA). (gr. 7). 19.99 (978-1-59514-843-8(4), Razorbill) Penguin Young Readers Group.

—Spirit Bound. 2011. (Vampire Academy Ser.: 5). (ENG.). 512p. (YA). (gr. 7-18). 9.99 (978-1-59514-366-2(1), Razorbill) Penguin Young Readers Group.

Mebus, Scott. Spirits in the Park, Vol. 2. 2010. (ENG.). 400p. (J). (gr. 3-7). 8.99 (978-0-14-241645-7(2), Puffin Books) Penguin Young Readers Group.

Meldrum, Christina. Madapple. 2010. (ENG.). 416p. (YA). (gr. 9-18). pap. 10.99 (978-0-375-85177-3(1), Knopf Bks. for Young Readers) Random Hse. Children's Bks.

Melissa Strangway. Abigail's Mirror. 2010. 316p. pap. 18.95 (978-1-4401-6176-6(3)) iUniverse, Inc.

Melo, Filipe. The Incredible Adventures of Dog Mendonca & Pizzaboy Vol. 2: Apocalypse. Simon, Philip, ed. 2014. (ENG., Illus.). 152p. pap. 14.99 (978-1-61655-267-1(0)) Dark Horse Comics.

Mercer, Sienna. Howl-Oween! 2014. (My Brother the Werewolf Ser.: 3). (ENG.). 240p. (J). (gr. 4-6). pap. 6.99 (978-1-4052-6797-7(6)) Egmont Bks., Ltd. GBR. Dist: Independent Pubs. Group.

—My Brother the Werewolf - Tail Spin Vol. 4. 2014. (My Brother the Werewolf Ser.: 4). (ENG.). 240p. (J). (gr. 4-6). pap. 9.99 (978-1-4052-6798-4(4)) Egmont Bks., Ltd. GBR. Dist: Independent Pubs. Group.

Messenger, Shannon. Let the Sky Fall. 2013. (Sky Fall Ser.: 1). (ENG., (YA). (gr. 7). Illus.). 432p. pap. 10.99 (978-1-4424-5042-4(8)); 416p. 17.99 (978-1-4424-5041-7(X)) Simon Pulse. (Simon Pulse).

—Let the Storm Break. 2014. (Sky Fall Ser.: 2). (ENG., Illus.). 400p. (YA). (gr. 7). 17.99 (978-1-4424-5044-8(4), Simon Pulse) Simon Pulse.

—Let the Wind Rise. (Sky Fall Ser.: 3). (ENG., Illus.). (YA). (gr. 7). 2017. 432p. pap. 10.99 (978-1-4814-4655-6(X)) 2016. 416p. 17.99 (978-1-4814-4654-9(1)) Simon Pulse. (Simon Pulse).

Messer, Celeste M. Andi's Choice. Hoeffner, Deb, illus. 2004. 82-92p. 4.95 (978-0-9702171-6-5(1)) AshleyAlan Enterprises.

—The Boy Who Cried Wolf. Hoeffner, Deb, illus. 2004. 82-92p. 4.95 (978-0-9702171-9-6(6)) AshleyAlan Enterprises.

Messner, Kate. All the Answers. (ENG.). 2016. 272p. (J). pap. 7.99 (978-1-68119-020-4(6), 9781681190204) 2015. 256p. (YA). (gr. 3-6). 16.99 (978-1-61963-374-2(4), 9781619633742) Bloomsbury Publishing USA. (Bloomsbury USA Childrens).

Metz, Melinda. Raven's Point. 2005. pap. (978-0-06-052373-2(5)) HarperCollins Canada, Ltd.

Meyer, Kai. Arcadia Awakens. (Arcadia Ser.: 1). (ENG.). (YA). (gr. 9). 2013. 480p. pap. 9.99 (978-0-06-200607-3(X)) 2012. 464p. 17.99 (978-0-06-200606-6(1)) HarperCollins Pubs.

—Arcadia Falls. 2014. (Arcadia Ser.: 3). (ENG.). 480p. (YA). (gr. 9). 17.99 (978-0-06-200610-3(X)) HarperCollins Pubs.

Meyer, Stephenie. Breaking Dawn. (Twilight Saga Ser.: 4). (ENG.). 768p. (YA). (gr. 7-17). 2012. mass mkt. 7.99 (978-0-316-22613-4(0)) 2010. pap. 16.99 (978-0-316-06793-5(8)) 2008. 22.99 (978-0-316-06792-8(X), Tingley, Megan Bks.)Pt. II. 2012. pap. 14.99 (978-0-316-22642-4(4)) Little, Brown Bks. for Young Readers.

—Breaking Dawn. 2010. (Twilight Saga Ser.: 4). (YA). lib. bdg. 29.40 (978-0-606-23108-4(0), Turtleback) Turtleback Bks.

—Life & Death: Twilight Reimagined. 2016. (ENG.). 400p. (YA). (gr. 7-17). pap. 9.99 (978-0-316-50545-1(5)) Little, Brown Bks. for Young Readers.

Michaelis, Antonia. The Secret Room. 2012. (ENG., Illus.). 208p. (J). (gr. 2-7). 14.95 (978-1-61608-960-3(1), 608960, Sky Pony Pr.) Skyhorse Publishing Co., Inc.

Miles, Elizabeth. Envy. (Fury Ser.: 2). (ENG., (YA). (gr. 9). 2013. Illus.). 416p. pap. 9.99 (978-1-4424-2222-3(X)) 2012. 400p. 17.99 (978-1-4424-2221-6(1)) Simon Pulse. (Simon Pulse).

—Eternity. 2013. (Fury Ser.: 3). (ENG., Illus.). 336p. (YA). (gr. 9). 17.99 (978-1-4424-2227-8(0)); pap. 9.99 (978-1-4424-2228-5(9)) Simon Pulse. (Simon Pulse).

—Fury, 11 vols. 2012. (YA). 271.75 (978-1-4640-3955-3(0)); 126.75 (978-1-4640-3958-4(5)); 110.75 (978-1-4640-3957-7(7)); 112.75 (978-1-4640-3954-6(2)) Recorded Bks., Inc.

—Fury. (Fury Ser.). (ENG.). (YA). (gr. 9). 2012. 400p. pap. 9.99 (978-1-4424-2225-4(4)) 2011. 384p. 17.99 (978-1-4424-2224-7(6)) Simon Pulse. (Simon Pulse).

Milford, Kate. The Boneshaker. Offermann, Andrea, illus. 2011. (ENG.). 384p. (J). (gr. 5-7). pap. 7.99 (978-0-547-55004-6(9)) Houghton Mifflin Harcourt Publishing Co.

—The Broken Lands. Offermann, Andrea, illus. 2012. (ENG.). 464p. (YA). (gr. 7). 16.99 (978-0-547-73966-3(4)) Houghton Mifflin Harcourt Publishing Co.

Miller, Kirsten. The Eternal Ones: What If Love Refused to Die? 2011. (ENG.). 432p. (YA). (gr. 7-18). 9.99 (978-1-59514-375-4(0), Razorbill) Penguin Young Readers Group.

Miller, Whitney A. The Crimson Gate. 2015. (ENG.). 312p. (YA). pap. 9.99 (978-0-7387-4204-5(X), Flux) North Star Editions.

—The Violet Hour. 2014. (ENG.). 312p. (YA). pap. 9.99 (978-0-7387-3721-8(6), Flux) North Star Editions.

Mitchell, Briar Lee & Keely, Jack. The Whistlebrass Storm Watcher. 2016. (Whistlebrass Mysteries Ser.: 2). (ENG.). 272p. (YA). pap. 12.95 (978-1-68261-268-2(6)) Simon & Schuster.

Mitchell, Saundra. The Elementals. 2014. (ENG.). 304p. (YA). (gr. 7). pap. 8.99 (978-0-544-30239-6(7), HMH Books For Young Readers) Houghton Mifflin Harcourt Publishing Co.

—The Springsweet. 2013. (ENG.). 304p. (YA). (gr. 7). pap. 8.99 (978-0-544-00327-9(6)) Houghton Mifflin Harcourt Publishing Co.

Monahan, Hillary. Bloody Mary, Book 2 Mary: Unleashed. 2015. (Bloody Mary Ser.). (ENG.). 256p. (YA). (gr. 7-12). 17.99 (978-1-4231-8539-0(0)) Hyperion Bks. for Children.

—Mary: The Summoning. 2014. (Bloody Mary Ser.). (ENG.). 256p. (YA). (gr. 7-12). 16.99 (978-1-4231-8519-2(6)) Hyperion Bks. for Children.

—Summoning. 2015. (Bloody Mary Ser.). (ENG.). 272p. (YA). (gr. 7-12). pap. 9.99 (978-1-4231-8693-9(1)) Hyperion Bks. for Children.

Montgomery, R. A. Return to Haunted House. 2010. (Illus.). 80p. (J). pap. 7.99 (978-1-933390-40-6(9)) Chooseco LLC.

Moore, Alice. Touched by Darkness. 2011. 208p. 24.95 (978-1-4502-9095-1(7)); pap. 14.95 (978-1-4502-9096-8(5)) iUniverse, Inc.

Moore, Kelly, et al. Neverwas. 2014. (YA). pap. (978-0-545-43419-5(X)); (Amber House Ser.: 2). (ENG.). 320p. (J). (gr. 9). 17.99 (978-0-545-43418-8(1), Levine, Arthur A. Bks.) Scholastic, Inc.

Moore, Stuart, et al. The Dragon's Return. 2016. (978-1-4847-7415-1(9)) Disney Publishing Worldwide.

Moreci, Michael & Seeley, Steve. Murder, Death, & the Devil, Vol. 1. 2012. (ENG., Illus.). 160p. (YA). pap. 14.99 (978-1-60706-657-6(2), 9781607066576) Image Comics.

Morgan, Melissa J. Charmed Forces. 2008. (Camp Confidential Ser.: 19). (ENG.). 256p. (J). (gr. 3-7). pap. 5.99 (978-0-448-44722-3(3), Grosset & Dunlap) Penguin Young Readers Group.

Morgan, Page. The Beautiful & the Cursed. (Dispossessed Ser.). (ENG.). 352p. (YA). (gr. 7). 2014. pap. 9.99 (978-0-385-74312-9(2), Ember) 2013. 18.99 (978-0-385-74311-2(4), Delacorte Pr.) Random Hse. Children's Bks.

Morin, James F. Rothshield Chasing Shadows. 2006. pap. 14.95 (978-1-59330-422-5(6)) Aventine Pr.

Morris, Paula. Unbroken. 2014. (ENG.). 304p. (J). (gr. 7). pap. 9.99 (978-0-545-41642-9(6)) Scholastic, Inc.

Moskowitz, Hannah. Teeth. 2013. (ENG.). 288p. (YA). (gr. 9). 17.99 (978-1-4424-6532-9(8)); pap. 9.99 (978-1-4424-4946-6(2)) Simon Pulse. (Simon Pulse).

—Zombie Tag. 2011. (ENG.). 240p. (J). (gr. 4-7). 15.99 (978-1-59643-720-3(0), 9781596437203) Roaring Brook Pr.

Mosley, Walter. When the Thrill Is Gone, 3 vols. 2012. (Leonid McGill Mystery Ser.: Bk. 3). (ENG.). 384p. (gr. 12). 16.00 (978-0-451-23565-7(7), Berkley) Penguin Publishing Group.

Moss, Marissa. The Pharaoh's Secret. 2009. (ENG., Illus.). 320p. (J). (gr. 3-7). 16.95 (978-0-8109-8378-6(8), Amulet Bks.) Abrams, Inc.

Mould, Chris. The Icy Hand. Mould, Chris, illus. 2008. (Something Wickedly Weird Ser.: 2). (ENG., Illus.). 176p. (J). (gr. 5-9). 9.95 (978-1-59643-385-4(X), 9781596433854) Roaring Brook Pr.

Moulton, Courtney Allison. Shadows in the Silence. 2014. (Angelfire Ser.: 3). (ENG.). 480p. (YA). (gr. 9). pap. 9.99 (978-0-06-200241-9(4), Tegen, Katherine Bks) HarperCollins Pubs.

Mull, Brandon. Grip of the Shadow Plague. Dorman, Brandon, illus. 2009. (Fablehaven Ser.: 3). (ENG.). 512p. (J). (gr. 3-8). pap. 8.99 (978-1-4169-8603-4(0), Aladdin) Simon & Schuster Children's Publishing.

Murdock, Catherine Gilbert. Wisdom's Kiss. 2013. (ENG.). 320p. (YA). (gr. 7). pap. 8.99 (978-0-547-85540-0(0)) Houghton Mifflin Harcourt Publishing Co.

—Wisdom's Kiss: A Thrilling & Romantic Adventure, Incorporating Magic, Villany, & a Cat. 2011. (ENG.). 304p. (YA). (gr. 7). 16.99 (978-0-547-56687-0(5)) Houghton Mifflin Harcourt Publishing Co.

Murgia, Jennifer. Forest of Whispers. 2014. (Hedge Witch Ser.: 1). (ENG., Illus.). 328p. (gr. 9-12). pap. 9.95 (978-1-937053-56-7(3)) Spencer Hill Pr.

Murphy, Emily Bain. The Disappearances. 2017. (ENG.). 400p. (YA). (gr. 7). 17.99 (978-0-544-87936-2(8), HMH Books For Young Readers) Houghton Mifflin Harcourt Publishing Co.

Murphy, Jill. A Bad Spell for the Worst Witch. Murphy, Jill, illus. 2014. (Worst Witch Ser.). (ENG., Illus.). 128p. (J). (gr. 3-7). pap. 5.99 (978-0-7636-7252-2(1)) Candlewick Pr.

Myers, Bill. The Chamber of Lies, 1 vol. 2009. (Elijah Project Ser.). (ENG.). 128p. (J). (gr. 4-7). pap. 6.99 (978-0-310-71196-4(7)) Zonderkidz.

—The Enemy Closes In, 1 vol. 2009. (Elijah Project Ser.). (ENG.). 128p. (J). (gr. 4-7). pap. 6.99 (978-0-310-71194-0(0)) Zonderkidz.

Myers, Bill & Riordan, James. On the Run, 1 vol. 2009. (Elijah Project Ser.). (ENG.). 128p. (J). (gr. 4-7). pap. 4.99 (978-0-310-71193-3(2)) Zonderkidz.

Myers, Kate Kae. The Vanishing Game. (ENG.). (YA). (gr. 7). 2014. 384p. pap. 9.99 (978-1-61963-127-4(X), 9781619631274) 2012. 368p. 17.99 (978-1-59990-694-2(5), 9781599906942) Bloomsbury Publishing USA. (Bloomsbury USA Childrens).

Myers, Walter Dean. Dope Sick. (ENG.). 208p. (YA). (gr. 9). 2010. pap. 9.99 (978-0-06-121479-0(5)) 2009. 17.99 (978-0-06-121477-6(9)) HarperCollins Pubs. (Amistad).

Naifeh, Ted. The League of Ordinary Gentleman. 2011. (Courtney Crumrin Tales Ser.). (Illus.). 56p. (J). (gr. 2). pap. 5.99 (978-1-934964-68-2(9)) Oni Pr., Inc.

Naughton, Sarah. The Blood List. 2014. (ENG.). 304p. (YA). pap. 9.99 (978-0-85707-866-7(6), Simon & Schuster Children's) Simon & Schuster, Ltd. GBR. Dist: Simon & Schuster, Inc.

—The Hanged Man Rises. 2013. (ENG., Illus.). 240p. (J). pap. 6.99 (978-0-85707-864-3(X), Simon & Schuster Children's) Simon & Schuster, Ltd. GBR. Dist: Simon & Schuster, Inc.

Nayeri, Daniel and Dina. Another Faust. 2010. (ENG., Illus.). 400p. (YA). (gr. 9). pap. 8.99 (978-0-7636-4834-3(5)) Candlewick Pr.

—Another Jekyll, Another Hyde. 2012. (ENG., Illus.). 400p. (YA). (gr. 9). 17.99 (978-0-7636-5261-6(X)) Candlewick Pr.

Neill, Chloe. Charmfall. 2012. (Dark Elite Ser.: 3). (ENG.). 288p. (YA). (gr. 9). 9.99 (978-0-451-23080-5(9), Berkley) Penguin Publishing Group.

Neilsen, David. Beyond the Doors. 2017. (ENG.). 368p. (J). (gr. 3-7). 16.99 **(978-1-101-93582-8(0)**, Crown Books For Young Readers) Random Hse. Children's Bks.

—Dr. Fell & the Playground of Doom. (ENG.). (J). (gr. 3-7). 2017. 256p. 6.99 **(978-1-101-93581-1(2)**, Yearling) 2016. (Illus.). 240p. 16.99 (978-1-101-93578-1(2), Crown Books For Young Readers) Random Hse. Children's Bks.

Newsome, Richard. The Emerald Casket. Duddle, Jonny, illus. (Archer Legacy Ser.). (J). (gr. 3-7). 2012. 384p. pap. 6.99 (978-0-06-194493-2(9)) 2011. 368p. 16.99 (978-0-06-194492-5(0)) HarperCollins Pubs. (Waldon Pond Pr.).

—The Mask of Destiny. Duddle, Jonny, illus. 2013. 384p. (J). (gr. 3-7). pap. 6.99 (978-0-06-194495-6(5), Waldon Pond Pr.) HarperCollins Pubs.

Nichols, Lee. Deception. 2010. (Haunting Emma Ser.). (ENG.). 336p. (YA). (gr. 9-12). 16.99 (978-1-59990-308-8(3), 9781599903088); pap. 9.99 (978-1-59990-421-4(7), 9781599904214) Bloomsbury Publishing USA. (Bloomsbury USA Childrens).

—Surrender. 2011. (Haunting Emma Ser.). (ENG.). 272p. (YA). (gr. 9-12). pap. 9.99 (978-1-59990-423-8(3), 9781599904238, Bloomsbury USA Childrens) Bloomsbury Publishing USA.

Nickerson, Jane. The Mirk & Midnight Hour. 2014. (ENG.). 384p. (YA). (gr. 9). 16.99 (978-0-385-75286-2(5), Knopf Bks. for Young Readers) Random Hse. Children's Bks.

Night, P. J. You Can't Come in Here!, 1 vol. 2013. (You're Invited to a Creepover Ser.). (ENG.). 160p. (J). (gr. 3-6). lib. bdg. 24.21 (978-1-61479-066-2(3), Essential Library) ABDO Publishing Co.

—You Can't Come in Here! 2011. (You're Invited to a Creepover Ser.: 2). (ENG.). 160p. (J). (gr. 3-7). pap. 6.99 (978-1-4424-2095-3(2), Simon Spotlight) Simon Spotlight.

Nishi, Yoshiyuki. Muhyo & Roji's Bureau of Supernatural Investigation, Vol. 18. Nishi, Yoshiyuki, illus. 2010. (ENG., Illus.). 192p. pap. 9.99 (978-1-4215-2840-3(1)) Viz Media.

Noël, Alyson. The Beginning: Evermore + Blue Moon. 2013. (Immortals Ser.). (ENG.). 608p. (YA). (gr. 7-12). pap. 9.99 (978-1-250-03728-2(X), 9781250037282, St. Martin's Griffin) St. Martin's Pr.

—Blue Moon. 2009. (Immortals Ser.: 2). (ENG.). 304p. (YA). (gr. 7-12). pap. 11.99 (978-0-312-53276-5(8), 9780312532765, St. Martin's Griffin) St. Martin's Pr.

—Blue Moon. 2009. (Immortals Ser.: 2). (YA). lib. bdg. 20.85 (978-0-606-07221-2(7), Turtleback) Turtleback Bks.

—Blue Moon: The Immortals. 2013. (Immortals Ser.: 2). (ENG.). 304p. (YA). (gr. 7-12). mass mkt. 9.99 (978-1-250-04684-0(X), 9781250046840, St. Martin's Paperbacks) St. Martin's Pr.

—Dark Flame. (Immortals Ser.: 4). (ENG.). 336p. (YA). (gr. 7-12). 2013. mass mkt. 9.99 (978-1-250-04687-1(4), 9781250046871, St. Martin's Paperbacks) 2012. pap. 10.99 (978-0-312-58375-0(3), 9780312583750, St. Martin's Griffin) 2010. 17.99 (978-0-312-59097-0(0), 9780312590970, St. Martin's Griffin) St. Martin's Pr.

—Desafío: Quinto Libro de la Serie de Los Inmortales. 2012. (Vintage Espanol Ser.). (SPA.). 336p. (YA). (gr. 7). pap. 10.95 (978-0-307-95147-2(2), Vintage Espanol) Knopf Doubleday Publishing Group.

—Echo. 2013. (Soul Seekers Ser.: 2). (ENG.). 352p. (YA). (gr. 7). mass mkt. 9.99 (978-1-250-04689-5(0), 9781250046895, St. Martin's Paperbacks) St. Martin's Pr.

—Eternidad: Libro Primero de la Serie de Los Inmortales. 2010. (Vintage Espanol Ser.).Tr. of Evermore. (SPA.). 384p. (YA). (gr. 7). pap. 13.95 (978-0-307-74115-8(X), Vintage Espanol) Knopf Doubleday Publishing Group.

—Everlasting. 2013. (Immortals Ser.: 6). (ENG.). 352p. (YA). (gr. 7-12). pap. 10.99 (978-1-250-02517-3(6), 9781250025173, St. Martin's Griffin) St. Martin's Pr.

—Evermore. 2009. (Immortals Ser.: 1). (ENG.). 320p. (YA). (gr. 7-12). pap. 10.99 (978-0-312-53275-8(X), 9780312532758, St. Martin's Griffin) St. Martin's Pr.

—Evermore. 2009. (Immortals Ser.: 1). (YA). lib. bdg. 22.10 (978-0-606-10569-9(7), Turtleback) Turtleback Bks.

—Evermore: The Immortals. 2013. (Immortals Ser.: 1). (ENG.). 320p. (YA). (gr. 7-12). mass mkt. 9.95 (978-1-250-04683-3(1), 9781250046833, St. Martin's Paperbacks) St. Martin's Pr.

—Fated. 2012. (Soul Seekers Ser.: 1). (ENG.). 368p. (YA). (gr. 7). 18.99 (978-0-312-66485-5(0), 9780312664855, St. Martin's Griffin) St. Martin's Pr.

—Luna Azul. 2010. (Vintage Espanol Ser.).Tr. of Blue Moon. (SPA.). 368p. (YA). (gr. 7). pap. 13.95 (978-0-307-74116-5(8), Vintage Espanol) Knopf Doubleday Publishing Group.

—Mystic. 2013. (Soul Seekers Ser.: 3). (ENG.). 320p. (YA). (gr. 7). mass mkt. 9.99 (978-1-250-04818-9(4), 9781250048189, St. Martin's Paperbacks); 18.99 (978-0-312-66488-6(5), 9780312664886, St. Martin's Griffin); pap. 9.99 (978-0-312-57567-0(X), 9780312575670, St. Martin's Griffin) St. Martin's Pr.

—Night Star. 2013. (Immortals Ser.: 5). (ENG.). 320p. (YA). (gr. 7-12). mass mkt. 9.99 (978-1-250-04688-8(2), 9781250046888, St. Martin's Paperbacks) St. Martin's Pr.

—Shadowland. (Immortals Ser.: 3). (ENG.). 368p. (YA). 2010. (gr. 7-12). pap. 9.99 (978-0-312-65005-6(1), 9780312650056) 2009. (gr. 8-12). 17.99 (978-0-312-59044-4(X), 9780312590444) St. Martin's Pr. (St. Martin's Griffin).

—Shadowland: The Immortals. 2013. (Immortals Ser.: 3). (ENG.). 368p. (YA). (gr. 7-12). mass mkt. 9.99 (978-1-250-04686-4(6), 9781250046864, St. Martin's Paperbacks) St. Martin's Pr.

Nolan, Han. Dancing on the Edge. 2007. (ENG., Illus.). 272p. (YA). (gr. 7-12). pap. 7.99 (978-0-15-205884-5(2)) Houghton Mifflin Harcourt Publishing Co.

Nomura, Mizuki. Book Girl & the Corrupted Angel. 2012. (Book Girl Ser.: 4). (ENG., Illus.). 240p. (YA). (gr. 8-17). pap. 13.00 (978-0-316-07694-4(5), Yen Pr.) Orbit.

—Book Girl & the Wayfarer's Lamentation, Vol. 5. 2012. (Book Girl Ser.: 5). (ENG., Illus.). 272p. (YA). (gr. 8-17). pap. 11.99 (978-0-316-07695-1(3), Yen Pr.) Orbit.

—The Scribe Who Faced God. (Book Girl Ser.: 7). (ENG.). (YA). (gr. 8-17). Pt. 1. 2013. 224p. 13.00 (978-0-316-07697-5(X))Pt. 2. 2014. (Illus.). 256p. pap. 11.99 (978-0-316-07698-2(8)) Orbit. (Yen Pr.).

Noyes, Deborah. The Ghosts of Kerfol. 2010. (ENG., Illus.). 176p. (YA). (gr. 9). pap. 7.99 (978-0-7636-4825-1(6)) Candlewick Pr.

—Plague in the Mirror. 2013. (ENG.). 272p. (YA). (gr. 9). 16.99 (978-0-7636-5980-6(0)) Candlewick Pr.

Ogburn, Jacqueline. The Unicorn in the Barn. Green, Rebecca, illus. 2017. (ENG.). 304p. (J). (gr. 5-7). 16.99 (978-0-544-76112-4(X), HMH Books For Young Readers) Houghton Mifflin Harcourt Publishing Co.

O'Hara, Mo. My Big Fat Zombie Goldfish. 2013. (My Big Fat Zombie Goldfish Ser.: Bk. 1). (ENG., Illus.). 192p. (J). (gr. 2-5). 12.99 (978-1-250-02919-5(8), 9781250029195) Feiwel & Friends.

O'Hart, Sinead. Eye of the North. 2017. (ENG.). 352p. (J). (gr. 3-7). 16.99 (978-1-101-93503-3(0), Knopf Bks. for Young Readers) Random Hse. Children's Bks.

Okorafor, Nnedi. Akata Witch. (ENG.). (YA). (gr. 7). 2017. 384p. pap. 10.99 **(978-0-14-242091-1(3)**, Speak) 2011. 368p. 17.99 (978-0-670-01196-4(7), Viking Books for Young Readers) Penguin Young Readers Group.

Older, Daniel José. Shadowshaper. (ENG.). (J). 2016. 320p. (gr. 7). pap. 9.99 (978-1-338-03247-5(X)) 2015. 304p. (gr. 9). 17.99 (978-0-545-59161-4(9)) Scholastic, Inc.

Oliver, Jana. The Demon Trapper's Daughter. 2011. (Demon Trappers Ser.: 1). (ENG.). 368p. (YA). (gr. 7-18). pap. 9.99 (978-0-312-61478-2(0), 9780312614782, St. Martin's Griffin) St. Martin's Pr.

—Forgiven. 2012. (Demon Trappers Ser.: 3). (ENG.). 368p. (YA). (gr. 7). pap. 9.99 (978-0-312-61480-5(2), 9780312614805, St. Martin's Griffin) St. Martin's Pr.

Oppel, Kenneth. The Nest. Klassen, Jon, illus. (ENG.). (J). (gr. 5). 2016. 272p. pap. 7.99 (978-1-4814-3233-7(8)) 2015. 256p. 16.99 (978-1-4814-3232-0(X)) Simon & Schuster Bks. For Young Readers. (Simon & Schuster Bks. For Young Readers).

—Such Wicked Intent. (ENG., 320p. (YA). (gr. 7). 2012. Illus.). 16.99 (978-1-4424-0318-5(7))Bk. 2. 2013. pap. 9.99 (978-1-4424-0319-2(5)) Simon & Schuster Bks. For Young Readers. (Simon & Schuster Bks. For Young Readers).

Osbourne, Ozzy, pseud & Zink, Michelle. Guardian of the Gate. 2011. (Prophecy of the Sisters Trilogy Ser.: 2). (ENG.). 368p. (YA). (gr. 7-17). pap. 8.99 (978-0-316-02740-3(5)) Little, Brown Bks. for Young Readers.

Ostow, Micol. Amity. 2014. (ENG.). 362p. (J). (gr. 9). 18.99 (978-1-60684-156-3(4), Carolrhoda Lab™) Lerner Publishing Group.

Ostow, Micol & Ostow, David. The Devil & Winnie Flynn. 2016. (ENG., Illus.). 336p. (YA). (gr. 9). pap. 10.99 (978-1-61695-703-2(4), Soho Teen) Soho Pr., Inc.

Owens, Jeanette. The Nature Spirits. 2012. (Illus.). 44p. pap. 24.40 (978-1-4772-4283-4(X)) AuthorHouse.

Parker, Daniel. April. 2014. (Countdown Ser.: 4). (ENG.). 144p. (YA). (gr. 7). pap. 13.99 (978-1-4814-2589-6(7), Simon Pulse) Simon Pulse.

—August. 2014. (Countdown Ser.: 8). (ENG.). 144p. (YA). (gr. 7). pap. 13.99 (978-1-4814-2593-3(5), Simon Pulse) Simon Pulse.

—February. 2014. (Countdown Ser.: 2). (ENG.). 144p. (J). (gr. 7). pap. 13.99 (978-1-4814-2587-2(0), Simon Pulse) Simon Pulse.

—January. 2014. (Countdown Ser.: 1). (ENG.). 144p. (YA). (gr. 7). pap. 13.99 *(978-1-4814-2586-5(2),* Simon Pulse) Simon Pulse.
—July. 2014. (Countdown Ser.: 7). (ENG.). 144p. (YA). (gr. 7). pap. 13.99 *(978-1-4814-2592-6(7),* Simon Pulse) Simon Pulse.
—June. 2014. (Countdown Ser.: 6). (ENG.). 144p. (YA). (gr. 7). pap. 13.99 *(978-1-4814-2591-9(9),* Simon Pulse) Simon Pulse.
—March. 2014. (Countdown Ser.: 3). (ENG.). 144p. (YA). (gr. 7). pap. 13.99 *(978-1-4814-2588-9(9),* Simon Pulse) Simon Pulse.
—May. 2014. (Countdown Ser.: 5). (ENG.). 144p. (YA). (gr. 7). pap. 13.99 *(978-1-4814-2590-2(0),* Simon Pulse) Simon Pulse.
—November. 2014. (Countdown Ser.: 11). (ENG.). 144p. (YA). (gr. 7). pap. 13.99 *(978-1-4814-2596-4(X),* Simon Pulse) Simon Pulse.
—October. 2014. (Countdown Ser.: 10). (ENG.). 144p. (YA). (gr. 7). pap. 13.99 *(978-1-4814-2595-7(1),* Simon Pulse) Simon Pulse.
—September. 2014. (Countdown Ser.: 9). (ENG.). 144p. (YA). (gr. 7). pap. 13.99 *(978-1-4814-2594-0(3),* Simon Pulse) Simon Pulse.
Parker, Natalie C. Behold the Bones. 2016. (Beware the Wild Ser.: 2). 368p. (YA). (gr. 8). 17.99 *(978-0-06-224155-9(9),* HarperTeen) HarperCollins Pubs.
Patten, E. J. The Legend Thief. Rocco, John, illus. 2013. (Hunter Chronicles Ser.: 2). (ENG.). 384p. (J). (gr. 3-7). 16.99 *(978-1-4424-2035-9(9),* Simon & Schuster Bks. For Young Readers) Simon & Schuster Bks. For Young Readers.
—Return to Exile. Rocco, John, illus. (Hunter Chronicles Ser.: 1). (ENG.). 512p. (J). (gr. 3-7). 2013. pap. 7.99 *(978-1-4424-2033-5(2))* 2011. 16.99 *(978-1-4424-2032-8(4))* Simon & Schuster Bks. For Young Readers. (Simon & Schuster Bks. For Young Readers).
Paulson, Ingrid. Valkyrie Rising. 2012. (Valkyrie Rising Ser.). (ENG.). 352p. (YA). (gr. 8). 17.99 *(978-0-06-202572-2(4),* HarperTeen) HarperCollins Pubs.
Peacock, Kathleen. Willowgrove. 2016. (Hemlock Trilogy Ser.: 3). 384p. (YA). (gr. 9). pap. 9.99 *(978-0-06-204872-1(4),* Tegen, Katherine Bks) HarperCollins Pubs.
Pearce, Jackson. Fathomless. 2013. (Fairy Tale Retelling Ser.). (ENG.). 320p. (YA). (gr. 10-17). pap. 8.99 *(978-0-316-20777-5(2))* Little, Brown Bks. for Young Readers.
—Sisters Red. 2011. (Fairy Tale Retelling Ser.). (ENG.). 352p. (YA). (gr. 10-17). pap. 10.99 *(978-0-316-06867-3(5))* Little, Brown Bks. for Young Readers.
—Sweetly. 2012. (Fairy Tale Retelling Ser.). (ENG.). 336p. (YA). (gr. 10-17). pap. 8.99 *(978-0-316-06866-6(7))* Little, Brown Bks. for Young Readers.
Penn, Mw. The Pe'lerin of the Orb. 2013. 228p. pap. 11.95 *(978-0-9840425-4-8(7))* MathWord Pr., LLC.
Perales, Alonso M. Brujas, Lechuzas y Espantos/Witches, Owls & Spooks. Pluecker, John, tr. from SPA. 2008. (ENG & SPA., Illus.). 96p. (J). (gr. 3-7). pap. 9.95 *(978-1-55885-512-0(2),* Piñata Books) Arte Publico Pr.
Peretti, Frank E. The Deadly Curse of Toco-Rey. Life Publishers International Staff, tr. from ENG. 2005. (RUS., Illus.). 156p. (J). *(978-0-7361-0347-3(3))* Life Pubs. International.
Peretti, Frank E. & Thomas Nelson & Sons Staff. The Secret of the Desert Stone, 1 vol. 2005. (Cooper Kids Adventure Ser.: 5). (ENG.). 160p. pap. 6.99 *(978-1-4003-0574-2(8))* Nelson, Thomas Inc.
Perez, Marlene. Dead Is a Battlefield. 2012. (Dead Is Ser.: 6). (ENG.). 240p. (YA). (gr. 7). pap. 7.99 *(978-0-547-60734-4(2))* Houghton Mifflin Harcourt Publishing Co.
—Dead Is a Battlefield. 2012. (Dead Is Ser.: 6). lib. bdg. 18.40 *(978-0-606-24759-7(9),* Turtleback) Turtleback Bks.
—Dead Is a Killer Tune. 2012. (Dead Is Ser.: 7). lib. bdg. 18.40 *(978-0-606-26623-9(2),* Turtleback) Turtleback Bks.
—Dead Is a State of Mind. 2009. (Dead Is Ser.: 2). (ENG., Illus.). 192p. (YA). (gr. 7-18). pap. 7.99 *(978-0-15-206210-1(6))* Houghton Mifflin Harcourt Publishing Co.
—Dead Is Just a Dream. (Dead Is Ser.: 8). (ENG.). 176p. (YA). (gr. 7). 2014. pap. 7.99 *(978-0-544-33634-6(8),* HMH Books For Young Readers) 2013. 16.99 *(978-0-544-10262-0(2))* Houghton Mifflin Harcourt Publishing Co.
—Dead Is Just a Dream. 2014. (Dead Is Ser.: 8). lib. bdg. 18.40 *(978-0-606-35990-0(7))* Turtleback Bks.
—Dead Is Just a Rumor. 2010. (Dead Is Ser.: 4). (ENG., Illus.). 224p. (YA). (gr. 7-18). pap. 7.99 *(978-0-547-34592-5(5))* Houghton Mifflin Harcourt Publishing Co.
—Dead Is Not an Option. 2011. (Dead Is Ser.: 5). (ENG.). 256p. (YA). (gr. 7-18). pap. 7.99 *(978-0-547-34593-2(3))* Houghton Mifflin Harcourt Publishing Co.
—Dead Is So Last Year. 2009. (Dead Is Ser.: 3). (ENG., Illus.). 208p. (J). (gr. 7-18). pap. 7.99 *(978-0-15-206216-3(5))* Houghton Mifflin Harcourt Publishing Co.
—Dead Is the New Black. 2008. (Dead Is Ser.: 1). (ENG., Illus.). 208p. (YA). (gr. 7-18). pap. 8.99 *(978-0-15-206408-2(7))* Houghton Mifflin Harcourt Publishing Co.
Peterfreund, Diana. Ascendant. (ENG.). (YA). (gr. 9). 2012. 416p. pap. 8.99 *(978-0-06-149005-7(9))* 2010. 400p. 17.99 *(978-0-06-149002-6(4))* HarperCollins Pubs. (HarperTeen).
—Rampant. 2010. (ENG.). 432p. (YA). (gr. 9). pap. 8.99 *(978-0-06-149004-0(0),* HarperTeen) HarperCollins Pubs.
Peterson, Shelley. Sundancer: The Saddle Creek Series. 2017. (Saddle Creek Ser.: 2). (ENG.). 408p. (YA). pap. 12.99 ***(978-1-4597-3948-2(5))*** Dundurn CAN. Dist: Ingram Publisher Services.
Peterson, Will. The Gathering. 2010. (Triskellion Ser.: 3). (ENG., Illus.). 384p. (YA). (gr. 9-18). 16.99 *(978-0-7636-4847-3(7))* Candlewick Pr.
Pierce, Tamora. Emperor Mage. 2015. (Immortals Ser.: 3). (ENG., Illus.). 368p. (YA). (gr. 7). pap. 10.99 *(978-1-4814-4026-4(8))* Simon & Schuster Children's Publishing.
—Emperor Mage. 2005. (Immortals Ser.: 3). (ENG.). 384p. (YA). (gr. 7). pap. 7.99 *(978-1-4169-0337-6(2),* Simon Pulse) Simon Pulse.
—The Realms of the Gods. 2005. (Immortals Ser.: No. 4). 347p. (gr. 7-12). 18.00 *(978-0-7569-5775-9(3))* Perfection Learning Corp.
—The Realms of the Gods. 2015. (Immortals Ser.: 4). (ENG., Illus.). 352p. (YA). (gr. 7). pap. 10.99 *(978-1-4814-4028-8(4))* Simon & Schuster Children's Publishing.
—Wild Magic. 2005. (Immortals Ser.: No. 1). (Illus.). 362p. (gr. 7-12). 18.00 *(978-0-7569-5508-3(4))* Perfection Learning Corp.
—Wild Magic. 2015. (Immortals Ser.: 1). (ENG., Illus.). 368p. (YA). (gr. 7). pap. 10.99 *(978-1-4814-4022-6(5))* Simon & Schuster Children's Publishing.
Pietron, Barbara. Thunderstone. 2013. (ENG.). 262p. (YA). pap. 12.99 *(978-1-940368-91-7(X))* Scribe Publishing Co.
Pike, Christopher, pseud. Black Knight. 2014. (Witch World Ser.: 2). (ENG., Illus.). 464p. (YA). (gr. 9). 19.99 *(978-1-4424-6733-0(9));* pap. 11.99 *(978-1-4424-6734-7(7))* Simon Pulse. (Simon Pulse).
—Deepest Desires, Instant Remorse No. 2, Bk. 2. 2010. (Thirst Ser.: 2). (ENG.). 608p. (YA). (gr. 9). pap. 11.99 *(978-1-4169-8309-5(0),* Simon Pulse) Simon Pulse.
—The Eternal Dawn. 2010. (Thirst Ser.: 3). (ENG.). 512p. (YA). (gr. 9-18). pap. 11.99 *(978-1-4424-1317-7(4),* Simon Pulse) Simon Pulse.
—Human Urges, Fatal Consequences. 2009. (Thirst Ser.: 1). (ENG., Illus.). 624p. (YA). (gr. 9). pap. 12.99 *(978-1-4169-8308-8(2),* Simon Pulse) Simon Pulse.
—Red Queen. 2014. (Witch World Ser.: 1). (ENG., Illus.). 560p. (YA). (gr. 9). pap. 9.99 *(978-1-4424-3029-7(X),* Simon Pulse) Simon Pulse.
—The Sacred Veil. 2013. (Thirst Ser.: 5). (ENG., Illus.). 512p. (YA). (gr. 7). pap. 12.99 *(978-1-4424-6731-6(2),* Simon Pulse) Simon Pulse.
—The Shadow of Death. 2011. (Thirst Ser.: 4). (ENG., Illus.). 528p. (YA). (gr. 9). pap. 10.99 *(978-1-4424-1319-1(0),* Simon Pulse) Simon Pulse.
—Strange Girl. 2015. (ENG., Illus.). 432p. (YA). (gr. 9). pap. 12.99 *(978-1-4814-5058-4(1),* Simon Pulse) Simon Pulse.
—Thirst, 3 vols. 2013. (Thirst Ser.). (ENG.). 1744p. (YA). (gr. 9). pap. 30.99 *(978-1-4424-8375-0(X),* Simon Pulse) Simon Pulse.
—Witch World. 2012. (Witch World Ser.: 1). (ENG.). 528p. (YA). (gr. 9). 17.99 *(978-1-4424-3028-0(1),* Simon Pulse) Simon Pulse.
Pitcher, Chelsea. The Last Faerie Queen. 2015. (ENG.). 408p. (YA). pap. 11.99 *(978-0-7387-4349-3(6),* Flux) North Star Editions.
Plum, Amy. Die for Me. (Die for Me Ser.: 1). (ENG.). (YA). (gr. 9). 2012. 368p. pap. 8.99 *(978-0-06-200402-4(6))* 2011. 352p. 17.99 *(978-0-06-200401-7(8))* HarperCollins Pubs. (HarperTeen).
—Until I Die. 2013. (Die for Me Ser.: 2). (ENG.). 384p. (YA). (gr. 9). pap. 9.99 *(978-0-06-200405-5(0),* HarperTeen) HarperCollins Pubs.
Plum-Ucci, Carol. Fire Will Fall. 2011. (ENG.). 492p. (YA). (gr. 9). pap. 25.99 *(978-0-547-55007-7(3))* Houghton Mifflin Harcourt Publishing Co.
Poblocki, Dan. The Nightmarys. 2011. (ENG.). 336p. (J). (gr. 3-7). pap. 7.99 *(978-0-375-84257-3(8),* Yearling) Random Hse. Children's Bks.
—The Stone Child. 2010. (ENG.). 288p. (J). (gr. 3-7). pap. 7.99 *(978-0-375-84255-9(1),* Yearling) Random Hse. Children's Bks.
Poe, Edgar Allen. Edgar Allan Poe. McConnell, James, illus. 2004. (Great American Short Stories Ser.). 80p. (gr. 4-7). lib. bdg. 24.00 *(978-0-8368-4254-8(5),* Gareth Stevens Learning Library) Stevens, Gareth Publishing LLLP.
Pollock, Tom. Our Lady of the Streets. 2017. (Skyscraper Throne Ser.: 3). (ENG.). 464p. (YA). (gr. 7-9). pap. 14.99 *(978-1-68144-381-2(3),* Jo Fletcher Books) Quercus NA.
Pon, Cindy. Silver Phoenix. (Silver Phoenix Ser.: 1). (ENG.). (YA). (gr. 9). 2011. 368p. pap. 8.99 *(978-0-06-173024-5(6))* 2009. 352p. 17.99 *(978-0-06-173021-4(1))* HarperCollins Pubs. (Greenwillow Bks.).
Ponti, James. Dark Days. 2015. (Dead City Ser.: 3). (ENG., Illus.). 304p. (J). (gr. 3-7). 17.99 *(978-1-4814-3636-6(8),* Aladdin) Simon & Schuster Children's Publishing.
—Dead City. (Dead City Ser.: 1). (ENG., Illus.). (J). (gr. 4-8). 2013. 304p. pap. 7.99 *(978-1-4424-4130-9(5))* 2012. 288p. 17.99 *(978-1-4424-4129-3(1))* Simon & Schuster Children's Publishing. (Aladdin).
Poole, Gabriella. Blood Ties. 2010. (ENG.). 304p. (YA). (gr. 7-17). pap. 9.99 *(978-0-340-98925-8(4))* Hodder & Stoughton GBR. Dist: Hachette Bk. Group.
Popescu, Petru. Birth of the Pack. rev. ed. 2007. (ENG.). 352p. (YA). (gr. 8-12). pap. 20.99 *(978-0-7653-1641-7(2),* 9780765316417, Tor Teen) Doherty, Tom Assocs., LLC.
Porte, Barbara Ann. Beauty & the Serpent: Thirteen Tales of Unnatural Animals. Covey, Rosemary Feit, illus. 2008. (ENG.). 128p. (YA). (gr. 7). pap. 7.99 *(978-1-4169-7579-3(9),* Simon & Schuster/Paula Wiseman Bks.) Simon & Schuster/Paula Wiseman Bks.
Porter, Sarah. Lost Voices. 2011. (Lost Voices Trilogy Ser.: 1). (ENG.). 304p. (YA). (gr. 7-18). 16.99 *(978-0-547-48250-7(7))* Houghton Mifflin Harcourt Publishing Co.
—The Twice Lost. (Lost Voices Trilogy Ser.: 3). (ENG.). 480p. (YA). (gr. 7). 2014. pap. 8.99 *(978-0-547-48255-2(8),* HMH Books For Young Readers) 2013. 16.99 *(978-0-547-48252-1(3))* Houghton Mifflin Harcourt Publishing Co.
—Waking Storms. (Lost Voices Trilogy Ser.: 2). (ENG.). (YA). (gr. 7). 2013. 416p. pap. 8.99 *(978-0-547-48254-5(X))* 2012. 400p. 16.99 *(978-0-547-48251-4(5))* Houghton Mifflin Harcourt Publishing Co.
Porter, Tracey. Lark. 2011. (ENG.). 192p. (YA). (gr. 8-18). 15.99 *(978-0-06-112287-3(4),* HarperTeen) HarperCollins Pubs.
Priestley, Chris. Through Dead Eyes. 2014. (ENG.). 240p. (YA). (gr. 7). pap. 13.99 *(978-1-4088-1107-8(3),* 9781408811078, Bloomsbury USA Childrens) Bloomsbury Publishing USA.
Prm, Katherine & Dee, Stacy. The Veil. 2010. 233p. (YA). pap. 15.95 *(978-1-59705-540-6(9))* Wings ePress, Inc.
Promitzer, Rebecca. The Pickle King. 2010. (ENG.). 416p. (J). (gr. 3-7). 17.99 *(978-0-545-17087-1(7),* Chicken Hse., The) Scholastic, Inc.
Quinn, Kate Karyus. Another Little Piece. 2013. (ENG.). 432p. (YA). (gr. 9). 17.99 *(978-0-06-213595-7(3),* HarperTeen) HarperCollins Pubs.
Raabe, Emily. Lost Children of the Far Islands. 2014. (ENG.). 288p. (J). (gr. 3-7). 16.99 *(978-0-375-87091-0(1),* Knopf Bks. for Young Readers) Random Hse. Children's Bks.
Randall, Thomas. The Waking: A Winter of Ghosts. 2011. (YA). pap. 9.99 *(978-1-59990-252-4(4),* Bloomsbury USA Childrens) Bloomsbury Publishing USA.
—The Waking: Dreams of the Dead. 2nd ed. 2010. (ENG., Illus.). 304p. (YA). (gr. 7-18). pap. 8.99 *(978-1-59990-585-3(X),* 9781599905853, Bloomsbury USA Childrens) Bloomsbury Publishing USA.
Randall, Thomas & Golden, Christopher. Spirits of the Noh. 2011. (ENG.). 272p. (YA). (gr. 7-18). pap. 9.99 *(978-1-59990-251-7(6),* 9781599902517, Bloomsbury USA Childrens) Bloomsbury Publishing USA.
Raymond, Roger & Savoy, Darryl. Ralph Filmore: Paranormal Investigator. O'Reilly, Sean Patrick, ed. 2012. (Illus.). 78p. (J). pap. 14.95 *(978-1-926914-31-2(7))* Arcana Studio, Inc.
Reber, Kelseyleigh. If I Fall: The Circle & Cross: Book One. 2013. (ENG.). 238p. (J). pap. 14.99 *(978-0-9889351-3-6(9))* Aperture Pr., LLC.
Reed, Bliss & Reed, Sinclair. This Summer I Plan to Rule the World. rev. ed. 2009. (ENG., Illus.). 100p. (J). (gr. k-7). pap. *(978-0-9822200-2-3(2))* Temmen, Edition, Horst Temmen.
Reeves, Dia. Bleeding Violet. 2010. (ENG.). 480p. (YA). (gr. 9). pap. 20.99 *(978-1-4169-8619-5(7),* Simon Pulse) Simon Pulse.
—Slice of Cherry. 2011. (ENG.). (YA). (gr. 9). 528p. pap. 9.99 *(978-1-4169-8621-8(9));* 512p. 16.99 *(978-1-4169-8620-1(0))* Simon Pulse. (Simon Pulse).
Reger, Rob & Gruner, Jessica. Dark Times. Reger, Rob & Parker, Buzz, illus. 2011. (Emily the Strange Ser.: 3). (ENG.). 248p. (YA). (gr. 8). pap. 8.99 *(978-0-06-145237-6(8))* HarperCollins Pubs.
Regin, Andrew. Guardians: Volume 1. 2012. 286p. pap. 27.95 *(978-1-4626-8856-2(X))* America Star Bks.
Reichs, Kathy. Virals. 2014. lthr. 79.00 *(978-1-62715-582-3(1))* Leatherbound Bestsellers.
—Virals. (Virals Ser.: 1). (ENG.). (J). (gr. 5-18). 2011. 480p. 10.99 *(978-1-59514-426-3(9),* Puffin Books) 2010. 464p. 17.99 *(978-1-59514-342-6(4),* Razorbill) Penguin Young Readers Group.
—Virals. 2011. 20.00 *(978-1-61383-226-4(5))* Perfection Learning Corp.
Reichs, Kathy & Reichs, Brendan. Terminal. 2015. (Virals Ser.: 5). (ENG.). 432p. (J). (gr. 5). 17.99 *(978-1-59514-528-4(1),* G.P. Putnam's Sons Books for Young Readers) Penguin Young Readers Group.
—Trace Evidence. 2016. (Virals Ser.). lib. bdg. 20.85 *(978-0-606-38400-1(6))* Turtleback Bks.
—Virals. 2011. (Virals Ser.: 1). lib. bdg. 20.85 *(978-0-606-23069-8(6),* Turtleback) Turtleback Bks.
—Virals Short Stories Omnibus. 2016. (Virals Ser.). (ENG.). 304p. (J). (gr. 5). 9.99 *(978-0-14-751920-7(9),* Puffin Books) Penguin Young Readers Group.
Reiss, Kathryn. Pale Phoenix. 2003. (ENG., Illus.). 336p. (J). (gr. 5-7). pap. 15.95 *(978-0-15-204927-0(4))* Houghton Mifflin Harcourt Publishing Co.
—Sweet Miss Honeywell's Revenge: A Ghost Story. 2005. (ENG.). 444p. (YA). (gr. 7-12). pap. 22.95 *(978-0-15-205471-7(5))* Houghton Mifflin Harcourt Publishing Co.
Renae, Cameo. Hidden Wings. 2013. 270p. pap. 13.99 *(978-1-939769-21-3(3))* Crushing Hearts and Black Butterfly Publishing.
Rhodes, Jewell Parker. Ninth Ward. 2010. (ENG.). 224p. (J). (gr. 5-17). 15.99 *(978-0-316-04307-6(9))* Little, Brown Bks. for Young Readers.
Ribar, Lindsay. Rocks Fall Everyone Dies. 2016. (ENG.). 336p. (YA). (gr. 7). 17.99 *(978-0-525-42868-8(2),* Kathy Dawson Books) Penguin Young Readers Group.
Richards, Justin. The Chaos Code. 2007. (ENG.). 400p. (YA). (gr. 7-12). 17.95 *(978-1-59990-124-4(2),* 9781599901244, Bloomsbury USA Childrens) Bloomsbury Publishing USA.
Richardson, Tracy. The Field. unabr. ed. 2013. (ENG.). 200p. (YA). (gr. 7-12). pap. 11.95 *(978-1-935462-82-8(2))* Luminis Bks., Inc.
Riggs, Ransom. Hollow City. 2015. (Miss Peregrine's Peculiar Children Ser.: Bk. 2). (ENG., Illus.). 416p. (YA). pap. 10.99 *(978-1-59474-735-9(0))* Quirk Bks.
—Hollow City. Riggs, Ransom, illus. 2014. (ENG., Illus.). 352p. (YA). (gr. 9). 18.99 *(978-1-59474-612-3(5))* Quirk Bks.
—Hollow City. Riggs, Ransom, illus. 2015. (Miss Peregrine's Peculiar Children Ser.: 2). (Illus.). lib. bdg. 22.10 *(978-0-606-36394-5(7))* Turtleback Bks.
—Library of Souls. 2015. (Miss Peregrine's Peculiar Children Ser.: Bk. 3). (ENG., Illus.). 464p. (YA). (gr. 9). 18.99 *(978-1-59474-758-8(X))* Quirk Bks.
—Library of Souls. 2017. (Miss Peregrine's Peculiar Children Ser.: 3). (ENG.). (YA). (gr. 9). lib. bdg. 23.30 ***(978-0-606-39808-4(2))*** Turtleback Bks.
Riggs, Ransom. Miss Peregrine's Home for Peculiar Children. (ENG., Illus.). (YA). (gr. 9). 2013. 368p. pap. 10.99 *(978-1-59474-603-1(6))* 2011. (Miss Peregrine's Peculiar Children Ser.: 1). 352p. 18.99 *(978-1-59474-476-1(9))* 2016. (Miss Peregrine's Peculiar Children Ser.: 1). 392p. pap. 11.99 *(978-1-59474-902-5(7))* Quirk Bks.
—Miss Peregrine's Home for Peculiar Children. l.t. ed. 2012. (ENG.). 484p. (J). (gr. 8-12). 23.99 *(978-1-4104-5023-4(6))* Thorndike Pr.
—Miss Peregrine's Home for Peculiar Children. 2013. (Miss Peregrine's Peculiar Children Ser.: 1). lib. bdg. 22.10 *(978-0-606-32081-8(4),* Turtleback) Turtleback Bks.
Riggs, Ransom & Jean, Cassandra. Hollow City: the Graphic Novel. 2016. (Miss Peregrine's Peculiar Children: the Graphic Novel Ser.: 2). (ENG., Illus.). 272p. (J). (gr. 8-17). 20.00 *(978-0-316-30679-9(7),* Yen Pr.) Orbit.
Riggs, Ransom, et al. Miss Peregrine's Home for Peculiar Children. 2011. pap. *(978-1-59474-574-4(9))* Quirk Bks.
Ritter, William. Beastly Bones. (Jackaby Ser.: 2). (ENG.). (YA). (gr. 8-12). 2016. 320p. pap. 9.95 *(978-1-61620-636-9(5))* 2015. 304p. 17.95 *(978-1-61620-354-2(4))* Algonquin Bks. of Chapel Hill.
—Beastly Bones. 2016. (Jackaby Ser.: 2). lib. bdg. 20.80 *(978-0-606-39017-0(0))* Turtleback Bks.
—Ghostly Echoes: A Jackaby Novel. 2016. (Jackaby Ser.: 3). (ENG.). 352p. (YA). (gr. 8-12). 17.95 *(978-1-61620-579-9(2))* Algonquin Bks. of Chapel Hill.
—Jackaby. (Jackaby Ser.: 1). (ENG.). 304p. (YA). (gr. 9-12). 2015. pap. 9.95 *(978-1-61620-546-1(6))* 2014. 16.95 *(978-1-61620-353-5(6),* 73353) Algonquin Bks. of Chapel Hill.
Rivers, Phoebe. Moment of Truth. 2012. (Saranormal Ser.: 5). (ENG.). 160p. (J). (gr. 3-7). 15.99 *(978-1-4424-6127-7(6));* pap. 5.99 *(978-1-4424-6125-3(X))* Simon Spotlight. (Simon Spotlight).
—Spirits of the Season. 2012. (Saranormal Ser.: 4). (ENG.). 160p. (J). (gr. 3-7). 15.99 *(978-1-4424-5379-1(6));* pap. 6.99 *(978-1-4424-5223-7(4))* Simon Spotlight. (Simon Spotlight).
—Yesterday & Today. 2013. (Saranormal Ser.: 11). (ENG., Illus.). 160p. (J). (gr. 3-7). 15.99 *(978-1-4424-8962-2(6));* pap. 5.99 *(978-1-4424-8961-5(8))* Simon Spotlight. (Simon Spotlight).
Rivers, Rae. Declan. 2014. (ENG.). 336p. pap. 11.99 ***(978-0-00-810443-6(3),*** HarperImpulse) HarperCollins Pubs. Ltd. GBR. Dist: HarperCollins Pubs.
Robinson, Gary. Paranormal: A Billy Buckhorn Supernatural Adventure. 2014. (PathFinders Ser.). (ENG.). 147p. (J). pap. *(978-1-939053-08-4(0))* Book Publishing Co.
—Supranormal. 2015. (ENG.). 128p. (J). pap. *(978-1-939053-12-1(9))* Book Publishing Co.
Robinson, Jimmie. Evil & Malice - Save the World! 2009. (ENG., Illus.). 128p. (J). pap. 14.99 *(978-1-60706-091-8(4),* 9781607060918) Image Comics.
Robison, Dan. Death Chant: Kimo's Battle with the Shamanic Forces. 2006. 194p. (J). pap. *(978-0-922993-52-9(1))* Marquette Bks., LLC.
Röder, Marlene. In the River Darkness. Reichel, Tammi, tr. 2014. 224p. 18.95 *(978-1-62324-010-3(7))* Enslow Pubs., Inc.
Rollins, Danielle. Burning. (ENG.). (YA). 2017. 368p. pap. 9.99 *(978-1-68119-205-5(5),* 9781681192055) 2016. 352p. 17.99 *(978-1-61963-738-2(3),* 9781619637382) Bloomsbury Publishing USA. (Bloomsbury USA Childrens).
Romney, J. P. The Monster on the Road Is Me. 2016. (ENG.). 336p. (YA). 17.99 *(978-0-374-31654-9(6),* 9780374316549, Farrar, Straus & Giroux (BYR)) Farrar, Straus & Giroux.
Rosati, Gina. Auracle. 2014. (ENG.). 304p. (YA). (gr. 7-12). pap. 16.99 *(978-1-250-04006-0(X),* 9781250040060) Square Fish.
Rose, Imogen. Initiation: Japanese Language Edition. Galeano, Tomomi, tr. 2013. 482p. pap. 16.99 *(978-1-940015-04-0(9))* Imogen Rose.
Rosenberg, Madelyn & Crockett, Mary. Dream Boy. 2014. (ENG.). 336p. (YA). (gr. 7-12). pap. 9.99 *(978-1-4022-9583-6(9),* 9781402295836) Sourcebooks, Inc.
Rosoff, Meg. There Is No Dog. 2012. (ENG.). 288p. (YA). (gr. 7-18). 17.99 *(978-0-399-25764-3(0),* G.P. Putnam's Sons Books for Young Readers) Penguin Young Readers Group.
—There Is No Dog. l.t. ed. 2012. (ENG.). 392p. (J). (gr. 7-12). 23.99 *(978-1-4104-4707-4(3))* Thorndike Pr.
Rossetti, Rinsai. The Girl with Borrowed Wings. 2012. (ENG.). 304p. (YA). (gr. 7). 17.99 *(978-0-8037-3566-8(9),* Dial Bks) Penguin Young Readers Group.
Rossi, Veronica. Riders. 2016. (ENG.). 368p. (YA). 17.99 *(978-0-7653-8254-2(7),* 9780765382542, Tor Teen) Doherty, Tom Assocs., LLC.
Roux, Madeleine. Asylum. (ENG.). (gr. 9). 2014. 336p. (J). pap. 9.99 *(978-0-06-222097-4(7))* 2013. (Illus.). 320p. (YA). 17.99 *(978-0-06-222096-7(9))* HarperCollins Pubs.
—Asylum. 2015. (SPA.). 320p. (YA). (gr. 9-12). pap. 20.99 *(978-987-612-778-3(0))* V&R Editoras.
—Catacomb. 2015. (Asylum Ser.: 3). (ENG.). 336p. (YA). (gr. 9). 17.99 *(978-0-06-236405-0(7))* HarperCollins Pubs.
—Sanctum. 2014. (Illus.). 343p. (YA). *(978-0-06-235182-1(6))* Harper & Row Ltd.
—Sanctum. 2014. (Asylum Ser.: 2). (ENG., Illus.). 352p. (YA). (gr. 9). 17.99 *(978-0-06-222099-8(3))* HarperCollins Pubs.
Ruiz Zafón, Carlos. The Prince of Mist. 2011. (ENG.). 256p. (YA). (gr. 7-17). pap., pap. 10.99 *(978-0-316-04480-6(6))* Little, Brown Bks. for Young Readers.
Russell, Randy. Dead Rules. 2011. (ENG.). 384p. (YA). (gr. 8-18). 16.99 *(978-0-06-198670-3(4),* HarperTeen) HarperCollins Pubs.
Sabatini, Kimberly. Touching the Surface. 2013. (ENG., Illus.). 352p. (YA). (gr. 9). pap. 9.99 *(978-1-4424-4003-6(1),* Simon Pulse) Simon Pulse.
Sacerdoti, Daniela. Spirit Bk. 3: The Sarah Midnight Trilogy. 2014. (Sarah Midnight Trilogy Ser.). (ENG.). 416p. (YA). (gr. 7). pap. 12.99 *(978-1-84502-540-3(7))* Black and White Publishing Ltd. GBR. Dist: Independent Pubs. Group.
Sak., M. J. The Stone Summons. 2007. 141p. pap. 15.95 *(978-1-84799-791-3(0))* Lulu Pr., Inc.
Samms, Olivia. Sketchy. 2013. pap. *(978-1-4778-6650-4(7))* Amazon Publishing.
Sands, Kevin. The Blackthorn Key. (Blackthorn Key Ser.: 1). (ENG., Illus.). (J). (gr. 5-9). 2016. 400p. pap. 7.99 *(978-1-4814-4652-5(5))* 2015. 384p. 18.99 *(978-1-4814-4651-8(7))* Simon & Schuster Children's Publishing. (Aladdin).
—The Blackthorn Key. 2016. lib. bdg. 18.40 *(978-0-606-38966-2(0))* Turtleback Bks.
Sands, Kevin. Mark of the Plague. (Blackthorn Key Ser.: 2). (ENG.). (J). (gr. 5-9). 2017. 560p. pap. 7.99 ***(978-1-4814-4675-4(4))*** 2016. (Illus.). 544p. 17.99 *(978-1-4814-4674-7(6))* Simon & Schuster Children's Publishing. (Aladdin).
Savage, J. Scott. Making the Team. Holgate, Doug, illus. 2013. (Case File 13 Ser.: 2). (ENG.). 272p. (J). (gr. 3-7). 14.99 *(978-0-06-213331-1(4))* HarperCollins Pubs.
—Zombie Kid. Holgate, Doug, illus. 2013. (Case File 13 Ser.: 1). (ENG.). 304p. (J). (gr. 3-7). pap. 6.99 *(978-0-06-213327-4(6))* HarperCollins Pubs.
Schaenen, Inda. All the Cats of Cairo. 2007. 225p. (J). (gr. -1-10). per. 8.95 *(978-0-9768126-5-4(7))* Brown Barn Bks.
Schreiber, Ellen. Full Moon Kisses. 2013. (Full Moon Ser.: 3). (ENG.). 224p. (YA). (gr. 8). pap. 9.99 *(978-0-06-198654-3(2),* Tegen, Katherine Bks) HarperCollins Pubs.
—Immortal Hearts. 2013. (Vampire Kisses Ser.: 9). (ENG.). 272p. (YA). (gr. 8). pap. 9.99 *(978-0-06-207009-8(6),* Tegen, Katherine Bks) HarperCollins Pubs.

S

—Magic of the Moonlight. (Full Moon Ser.: 2). (ENG.). (YA). (gr. 8). 2012. 256p. pap. 9.99 *(978-0-06-198656-7(9))* 2011. 240p. 17.99 *(978-0-06-198657-4(7))* HarperCollins Pubs. (Tegen, Katherine Bks).

—Once in a Full Moon. 2011. (Full Moon Ser.: 1). (ENG.). 320p. (YA). (gr. 8). pap. 8.99 *(978-0-06-198652-9(6)*, Tegen, Katherine Bks) HarperCollins Pubs.

Schwab, Victoria. The Archived. 2014. (Archived Ser.). (ENG., Illus.). 352p. (YA). (gr. 7-12). pap. 9.99 *(978-1-4231-7108-9(X))* Hyperion Bks. for Children.

—The Unbound. (Archived Ser.). (ENG., Illus.). (YA). (gr. 7-12). 2015. 360p. pap. 9.99 *(978-1-4231-9464-4(0))* 2014. 362p. 16.99 *(978-1-4231-7820-0(3))* Hyperion Bks. for Children.

Scott, Michael. The Alchemyst. 2009. (ENG., Illus.). 375p. (gr. 6-10). 19.00 *(978-1-60686-514-9(5))* Perfection Learning Corp.

—The Alchemyst. (Secrets of the Immortal Nicholas Flamel Ser.: Bk. 1). (ENG.). 400p. (YA). (gr. 7). 2008. pap. 10.99 *(978-0-385-73600-8(2)*, Ember) 2007. (Illus.). 16.99 *(978-0-385-73357-1(7)*, Delacorte Bks. for Young Readers) Random Hse. Children's Bks.

—The Enchantress. 2012. (Secrets of the Immortal Nicholas Flamel Ser.). (ENG.). 528p. (YA). (gr. 7). 18.99 *(978-0-385-73535-3(9)*, Delacorte Bks. for Young Readers) Random Hse. Children's Bks.

—The Enchantress. 2013. (Secrets of the Immortal Nicholas Flamel Ser.: 6). (ENG.). 528p. (YA). (gr. 7). pap. 10.99 *(978-0-385-73536-0(7)*, Ember) Random Hse. Children's Bks.

—The Enchantress. 2013. (Secrets of the Immortal Nicholas Flamel Ser.: 6). lib. bdg. 22.10 *(978-0-606-31947-8(6)*, Turtleback) Turtleback Bks.

—The Magician. 2009. (Secrets of the Immortal Nicholas Flamel Ser.: Bk. 2). (ENG.). 496p. (YA). (gr. 7). pap. 10.99 *(978-0-385-73728-9(9)*, Ember) Random Hse. Children's Bks.

—The Necromancer. 2011. (Secrets of the Immortal Nicholas Flamel Ser.). (ENG.). 416p. (YA). (gr. 7). pap. 10.99 *(978-0-385-73532-2(4)*, Ember) Random Hse. Children's Bks.

—The Necromancer the Secrets of the Immortal Nicholas Flamel. l.t. ed. 2010. (Secrets of the Immortal Nicholas Flamel Ser.). (ENG.). 492p. 23.99 *(978-1-4104-2851-6(6))* Thorndike Pr.

—The Sorceress. (Secrets of the Immortal Nicholas Flamel Ser.: 3). (ENG.). 512p. (YA). (gr. 7-18). 2010. pap. 10.99 *(978-0-385-73530-8(8)*, Ember) 2009. 17.99 *(978-0-385-73529-2(4)*, Delacorte Bks. for Young Readers) Random Hse. Children's Bks.

—The Sorceress. 2010. (Secrets of the Immortal Nicholas Flamel Ser.: 3). lib. bdg. 22.10 *(978-0-606-14133-8(2)*, Turtleback) Turtleback Bks.

—The Sorceress the Secrets of the Immortal Nicholas Flamel. l.t. ed. 2009. (Secrets of the Immortal Nicholas Flamel Ser.). (ENG.). 614p. (YA). 23.95 *(978-1-4104-2092-3(2))* Thorndike Pr.

—The Warlock. (Secrets of the Immortal Nicholas Flamel Ser.: 5). (ENG.). 400p. (YA). (gr. 7). 2012. pap. 10.99 *(978-0-385-73534-6(0)*, Ember) 2011. 18.99 *(978-0-385-73533-9(2)*, Delacorte Bks. for Young Readers) Random Hse. Children's Bks.

—The Warlock. 2012. (Secrets of the Immortal Nicholas Flamel Ser.: 5). lib. bdg. 22.10 *(978-0-606-26411-2(6)*, Turtleback) Turtleback Bks.

—The Warlock the Secrets of the Immortal Nicholas Flamel. l.t. ed. 2011. (Secrets of the Immortal Nicholas Flamel Ser.). (ENG.). 486p. 23.99 *(978-1-4104-4157-7(1))* Thorndike Pr.

Seabrooke, Brenda. Cemetery Street. 2008. 144p. (J). (gr. 3-7). 16.95 *(978-0-8234-2115-2(5))* Holiday Hse., Inc.

Sedgwick, Marcus. Midwinterblood. 2013. (ENG.). 272p. (YA). (gr. 7). 17.99 *(978-1-59643-800-2(2)*, 9781596438002) Roaring Brook Pr.

Seduction. 2014. (Legacy Ser.). (ENG., Illus.). 416p. (YA). (gr. 9). 17.99 *(978-1-4814-0023-7(1)*, Simon & Schuster/Paula Wiseman Bks.) Simon & Schuster/Paula Wiseman Bks.

Seeley, Tim. Rebirth, Vol. 2. 2012. (ENG., Illus.). 160p. (YA). pap. 16.99 *(978-1-60706-637-8(8)*, 9781607066378) Image Comics.

Selzer, Adam. I Kissed a Zombie, & I Liked It. 2010. (ENG.). 192p. (YA). (gr. 7-18). pap. 7.99 *(978-0-385-73503-2(0)*, Delacorte Bks. for Young Readers) Random Hse. Children's Bks.

Shadowboxer. 2014. (ENG.). 288p. (J). (gr. 8). pap. 9.99 *(978-1-78108-282-9(0)*, Ravenstone) Rebellion GBR. Dist: Simon & Schuster, Inc.

Shanker, Tarun & Zekas, Kelly. These Vicious Masks. 2016. (These Vicious Masks Ser.). (ENG.). 320p. (YA). pap. 9.99 *(978-1-250-07389-1(8)*, 9781250073891) Feiwel & Friends.

Sheff, Nic. Harmony House. 2016. 304p. (J). (gr. 9). 17.99 *(978-0-06-233709-2(2)*, HarperTeen) HarperCollins Pubs.

Shields, Gillian. Eternal. (Immortal Ser.: 3). (ENG.). (YA). (gr. 8). 2012. 384p. pap. 9.99 *(978-0-06-200040-8(3))* 2011. 368p. 16.99 *(978-0-06-200039-2(X))* HarperCollins Pubs. (Tegen, Katherine Bks).

—Immortal. 2010. (Immortal Ser.: 1). (ENG.). 384p. (YA). (gr. 8). pap. 8.99 *(978-0-06-137583-5(7)*, Tegen, Katherine Bks) HarperCollins Pubs.

Shirvington, Jessica. Corruption. 2017. (Disruption Ser.: 02). 448p. 9.99 *(978-1-4607-5219-7(8))* HarperCollins Pubs. Australia AUS. Dist: HarperCollins Pubs.

—Emblaze. 2013. (Embrace Ser.: 3). (ENG.). 464p. (YA). (gr. 7-12). pap. 14.99 *(978-1-4022-7131-1(X))*; 16.99 *(978-1-4022-6846-5(7))* Sourcebooks, Inc.

—Empower. 2014. (Embrace Ser.: 5). (ENG.). 496p. (YA). (gr. 7-12). 16.99 *(978-1-4022-9460-0(3))* Sourcebooks, Inc.

—Endless. 2014. (Embrace Ser.: 4). (ENG.). 480p. (YA). (gr. 7-12). pap. 9.99 *(978-1-4022-8945-3(6))* Sourcebooks, Inc.

—Entice. 2013. (Embrace Ser.: 2). (ENG.). 464p. (YA). (gr. 7-12). pap. 10.99 *(978-1-4022-7128-1(X))* Sourcebooks, Inc.

—One Past Midnight. (ENG.). 352p. (YA). (gr. 9). 2015. pap. 9.99 *(978-0-8027-3707-6(2)*, 9780802737076) 2014. 17.99 *(978-0-8027-3702-1(1)*, 9780802737021) Bloomsbury Publishing USA. (Bloomsbury USA Childrens).

Showalter, Gena. Alice in Zombieland. 2013. lib. bdg. 20.85 *(978-0-606-31712-2(0)*, Turtleback) Turtleback Bks.

Shull, Megan. The Swap. 400p. (J). (gr. 5-9). 2016. pap. 7.99 *(978-0-06-231170-2(0))* 2014. (ENG.). 16.99 *(978-0-06-231169-6(7))* HarperCollins Pubs. (Tegen, Katherine Bks).

Shulman, Polly & Airgood, Ellen. The Poe Annex. 2015. (ENG.). 272p. (J). (gr. 5). 16.99 *(978-0-399-16614-3(9)*, Nancy Paulsen Books) Penguin Young Readers Group.

Shusterman, Neal. Bruiser. 2010. (ENG.). 336p. (YA). (gr. 9-18). 17.99 *(978-0-06-113408-1(2)*, HarperTeen) HarperCollins Pubs.

—Dread Locks. 2006. (Dark Fusion Ser.: 1). (ENG.). 176p. (YA). (gr. 7-18). 7.99 *(978-0-14-240599-4(X)*, Speak) Penguin Young Readers Group.

—Duckling Ugly. 2007. (Dark Fusion Ser.: 2). (ENG.). 224p. (YA). (gr. 7-18). 7.99 *(978-0-14-240684-7(8)*, Speak) Penguin Young Readers Group.

—Red Rider's Hood. 2006. (Dark Fusion Ser.: 3). (ENG.). 192p. (YA). (gr. 7-18). 6.99 *(978-0-14-240678-6(3)*, Speak) Penguin Young Readers Group.

—Scorpion Shards. 2013. (Star Shards Chronicles Ser.: 1). (ENG., Illus.). (YA). (gr. 7). 240p. 17.99 *(978-1-4424-5836-9(4))*; 256p. pap. 9.99 *(978-1-4424-5114-8(9))* Simon & Schuster Bks. For Young Readers. (Simon & Schuster Bks. For Young Readers).

—Shattered Sky. 2013. (Star Shards Chronicles Ser.: 3). (ENG., Illus.). 544p. (YA). (gr. 7). 17.99 *(978-1-4424-5835-2(6))*; pap. 9.99 *(978-1-4424-5117-9(3))* Simon & Schuster Bks. For Young Readers. (Simon & Schuster Bks. For Young Readers).

—Thief of Souls. 2013. (Star Shards Chronicles Ser.: 2). (ENG., Illus.). (YA). (gr. 7). 304p. 17.99 *(978-1-4424-5837-6(2))*; 320p. pap. 9.99 *(978-1-4424-5112-4(2))* Simon & Schuster Bks. For Young Readers. (Simon & Schuster Bks. For Young Readers).

Shutter. 2015. (ENG.). 384p. (YA). (gr. 8-12). 17.99 *(978-1-250-04467-9(7))* Feiwel & Friends.

Sierra, Judy. Never Kick a Ghost & Other Silly Chillers. Constantin, Pascale, illus. 2011. (I Can Read Level 2 Ser.). (ENG.). 32p. (J). (gr. k-3). pap. 3.99 *(978-0-06-143521-8(X))* HarperCollins Pubs.

Silver Phoenix Staff & Pon, Cindy. Fury of the Phoenix. 2011. (Silver Phoenix Ser.: 2). (ENG.). 368p. (YA). (gr. 9-18). 17.99 *(978-0-06-173025-2(4)*, Greenwillow Bks.) HarperCollins Pubs.

Simmons, Derek. Flash of Life. 2006. 85p. pap. 16.95 *(978-1-4241-3890-6(6))* PublishAmerica, Inc.

Sinclair, Alison. Lightborn. 2011. (Darkborn Trilogy Ser.: 2). (ENG., Illus.). 312p. (gr. 12). 7.99 *(978-0-451-46358-6(7)*, Ace Bks.) Penguin Publishing Group.

Singleton, Linda Joy. Don't Die, Dragonfly. Karre, Andrew, ed. 2004. (Seer Ser.: 1). (ENG.). 288p. (YA). pap. 9.95 *(978-0-7387-0526-2(8))* Llewellyn Pubns.

—Last Dance. 2005. (Seer Ser.: 2). (ENG.). 264p. (YA). pap. 9.95 *(978-0-7387-0638-2(8)*, Flux) Llewellyn Pubns.

Skogen, Jennifer. Burning #1, 1 vol. 2015. (Haunting of Grey Hills Ser.). (ENG.). 216p. (YA). (gr. 9-12). lib. bdg. 27.13 *(978-1-68076-029-3(7)*, Epic Pr.) ABDO Publishing Co.

—Forests of the Night #2. 2015. (Haunting of Grey Hills Ser.). (ENG.). 200-216p. (YA). (gr. 9-12). lib. bdg. 27.13 *(978-1-68076-030-9(0)*, Epic Pr.) ABDO Publishing Co.

Skovron, Jon. Misfit. 2011. (ENG.). 384p. (YA). (gr. 9-17). 16.95 *(978-1-4197-0021-7(9)*, Amulet Bks.) Abrams, Inc.

Slade, Arthur G. The Dark Deeps. 2011. (Hunchback Assignments Ser.: Vol. 2). (ENG.). 320p. (YA). (gr. 7). pap. 9.99 *(978-0-375-85404-0(5)*, Ember) Random Hse. Children's Bks.

—The Hunchback Assignments. 2010. (Hunchback Assignments Ser.). (ENG.). 288p. (YA). (gr. 7). pap. 8.99 *(978-0-375-85403-3(7)*, Ember) Random Hse. Children's Bks.

Slater, Adam. The Shadowing - Hunted. 2011. (ENG.). 208p. (gr. 7). 16.99 *(978-1-60684-261-4(7)*, Carolrhoda Lab™) Lerner Publishing Group.

—The Shadowing #2: Skinned. 2012. (ENG.). 256p. (J). (gr. 7-7). 16.99 *(978-1-60684-262-1(5)*, Carolrhoda Lab™) Lerner Publishing Group.

Sleator, William & Monticone, Ann. The Phantom Limb. 2011. (ENG.). 224p. (YA). (gr. 9-17). 16.95 *(978-0-8109-8428-8(8)*, Amulet Bks.) Abrams, Inc.

Smeltzer, Jennifer. Scrolls & Coals. 2004. (J). 14.95 *(978-0-9754804-3-4(X)*, Rockhill Bks.) Kansas City Star Bks.

Smith, Alexander Gordon. The Fury. 2013. (ENG.). 688p. (YA). (gr. 7). 19.99 *(978-0-374-32495-7(6)*, 9780374324957, Farrar, Straus & Giroux (BYR)) Farrar, Straus & Giroux.

Smith, Cynthia Leitich. Blessed. (Tantalize Ser.). (ENG., Illus.). (YA). (gr. 9). 2012. 464p. pap. 8.99 *(978-0-7636-5479-5(5))* 2011. 480p. 17.99 *(978-0-7636-4326-3(2))* Candlewick Pr.

—Diabolical. 2012. (Tantalize Ser.). (ENG., Illus.). 368p. (YA). (gr. 9). 17.99 *(978-0-7636-5118-3(4))* Candlewick Pr.

—Feral Curse. 2014. (Feral Ser.). (ENG., Illus.). 272p. (YA). (gr. 9). 17.99 *(978-0-7636-5910-3(X))* Candlewick Pr.

—Tantalize. 2007. (Tantalize Ser.). (ENG., Illus.). 336p. (YA). (gr. 9-12). 16.99 *(978-0-7636-2791-1(7))* Candlewick Pr.

Smith, Jennifer E. The Storm Makers. Helquist, Brett, illus. 2013. (ENG.). 384p. (J). (gr. 3-7). pap. 8.00 *(978-0-316-17959-1(0))* Little, Brown Bks. for Young Readers.

Smith, L. J. Dark Visions: The Strange Power - The Possessed - The Passion. 2009. (Dark Visions Ser.: Bks 1-3). (ENG.). 752p. (YA). (gr. 7). pap. 9.99 *(978-1-4169-8956-1(0)*, Simon Pulse) Simon Pulse.

—Destiny Rising. 2012. (Vampire Diaries: the Hunters Ser.: 3). (ENG.). 400p. (YA). (gr. 9). 17.99 *(978-0-06-201773-4(X)*, HarperTeen) HarperCollins Pubs.

—The Fury & Dark Reunion, 2 vols. 2007. (Vampire Diaries: Nos. 3-4). (ENG.). 528p. (YA). (gr. 8-12). pap. 9.99 *(978-0-06-114098-3(8)*, HarperTeen) HarperCollins Pubs.

—The Fury & Dark Reunion. 2007. (Vampire Diaries: 3). (YA). lib. bdg. 20.85 *(978-0-606-07135-2(0)*, Turtleback) Turtleback Bks.

—Midnight. (Vampire Diaries: the Return Ser.: 3). (ENG.). (YA). (gr. 8). 2012. 592p. pap. 9.99 *(978-0-06-172086-4(0))* 2011. 576p. 17.99 *(978-0-06-172085-7(2))* HarperCollins Pubs. (HarperTeen).

—Moonsong Vol. 9. 2013. (Vampire Diaries: the Hunters Ser.: 2). (ENG.). 416p. (YA). (gr. 9). pap. 10.99 *(978-0-06-201771-0(3)*, HarperTeen) HarperCollins Pubs.

—Nightfall. (Vampire Diaries: the Return Ser.: 1). (ENG.). (YA). (gr. 8). 2010. 608p. pap. 9.99 *(978-0-06-172080-2(1))* 2009. 592p. 17.99 *(978-0-06-172077-2(1))* HarperCollins Pubs. (HarperTeen).

—Phantom. (Vampire Diaries: the Hunters Ser.: 1). (ENG.). (YA). (gr. 9). 2012. 432p. pap. 9.99 *(978-0-06-201769-7(1))* 2011. 416p. 17.99 *(978-0-06-201768-0(3))* HarperCollins Pubs. (HarperTeen).

—Shadow Souls. (Vampire Diaries: the Return Ser.: 2). (ENG.). (YA). (gr. 8). 2011. 624p. pap. 9.99 *(978-0-06-172083-3(6))* 2010. (Illus.). 608p. 17.99 *(978-0-06-172081-9(X))* HarperCollins Pubs. (HarperTeen).

—The Temptation. 2014. (Secret Circle Ser.: 6). (ENG.). 304p. (YA). (gr. 8). pap. 9.99 *(978-0-06-213045-7(5)*, HarperTeen) HarperCollins Pubs.

Smith, L. J. & Clark, Aubrey. Unseen, 0 vols. 2013. (Vampire Diaries: the Salvation Ser.: 1). (ENG.). 306p. (YA). (gr. 7-9). pap. 9.99 *(978-1-4778-0967-9(8)*, 9781477809679, 47North) Amazon Publishing.

Smith, L. J. & Williamson, Kevin. The Asylum. 2012. (Vampire Diaries: Stefan's Diaries: 5). (ENG.). 256p. (YA). (gr. 9). pap. 9.99 *(978-0-06-211395-5(X)*, HarperTeen) HarperCollins Pubs.

Smith, L. J., et al. The Ripper. 2011. (Vampire Diaries: Stefan's Diaries: 4). (ENG.). 256p. (YA). (gr. 9). pap. 10.99 *(978-0-06-211393-1(3)*, HarperTeen) HarperCollins Pubs.

Smith, Lane. Return to Augie Hobble. 2015. (ENG., Illus.). 288p. (J). (gr. 3-7). 16.99 *(978-1-62672-054-1(1)*, 9781626720541) Roaring Brook Pr.

—Return to Augie Hobble. 2017. (J). lib. bdg. 18.40 *(978-0-606-38550-3(9))* Turtleback Bks.

Smith-Ready, Jeri. Shade. (ENG.). (YA). (gr. 9). 2011. 336p. pap. 9.99 *(978-1-4169-9407-7(6))* 2010. 320p. 17.99 *(978-1-4169-9406-0(8))* Simon Pulse. (Simon Pulse).

—Shift. (ENG.). (YA). (gr. 9). 2012. 400p. pap. 9.99 *(978-1-4169-9409-1(2))* 2011. 384p. 17.99 *(978-1-4169-9408-4(4))* Simon Pulse. (Simon Pulse).

—Shine. 2012. (ENG.). 416p. (YA). (gr. 9). pap. 9.99 *(978-1-4424-3946-7(7)*, Simon Pulse) Simon Pulse.

Smith, Ronald L. The Mesmerist. 2017. (ENG.). 272p. (J). (gr. 5-7). 16.99 *(978-0-544-44528-4(7)*, Clarion Bks.) Houghton Mifflin Harcourt Trade & Reference Pubs.

Smith, Sarah. The Other Side of Dark. (ENG., 320p. (YA). (gr. 7). 2011. Illus.). pap. 11.99 *(978-1-4424-0281-2(4))* 2010. 16.99 *(978-1-4424-0280-5(6))* Simon & Schuster Children's Publishing. (Atheneum Bks. for Young Readers).

Sniegoski, Thomas E. Aerie & Reckoning. 2010. (Fallen Ser.: 2). (ENG.). 576p. (YA). (gr. 11-18). pap. 9.99 *(978-1-4424-0863-0(4)*, Simon Pulse) Simon Pulse.

—End of Days Vol. 3. 2011. (Fallen Ser.: 3). (ENG.). 384p. (YA). (gr. 9). pap. 9.99 *(978-1-4424-2349-7(8)*, Simon Pulse) Simon Pulse.

—The Fallen 5: Armageddon. 2013. (Fallen Ser.: 5). (ENG., Illus.). 592p. (YA). (gr. 9). pap. 9.99 *(978-1-4424-6005-8(9)*, Simon Pulse) Simon Pulse.

—The Fallen & Leviathan. 2010. (Fallen Ser.: 1). (ENG.). 544p. (YA). (gr. 11). pap. 11.99 *(978-1-4424-0862-3(6)*, Simon Pulse) Simon Pulse.

—Forsaken. 2012. (Fallen Ser.: 4). (ENG.). 416p. (YA). (gr. 9). pap. 9.99 *(978-1-4424-4699-1(4)*, Simon Pulse) Simon Pulse.

Snow, Carol. Snap. 2009. (ENG.). 224p. (YA). (gr. 8-18). 16.99 *(978-0-06-145211-6(4)*, HarperTeen) HarperCollins Pubs.

—Switch. 2009. (ENG.). 240p. (YA). (gr. 8). pap. 8.99 *(978-0-06-145210-9(6)*, HarperTeen) HarperCollins Pubs.

Snyder, Zilpha Keatley. The Egypt Game. Raible, Alton, illus. 2009. (ENG.). 240p. (J). (gr. 3-7). pap. 8.99 *(978-1-4169-9051-2(8)*, Atheneum Bks. for Young Readers) Simon & Schuster Children's Publishing.

—The Unseen. 2005. 199p. 16.00 *(978-0-7569-5670-7(6))* Perfection Learning Corp.

Somers, Ian. The Secret Gift. 2015. (ENG.). 368p. (J). pap. 13.00 *(978-1-84717-647-9(X))* O'Brien Pr., Ltd., The IRL. Dist: Dufour Editions, Inc.

Spooky Stories Treasury Lenticular Cover. 2007. 80p. *(978-1-4075-0127-7(5))* Parragon, Inc.

Spradlin, Michael P. Live & Let Shop. 2005. (Spy Goddess Ser.: Bk. 1). (ENG., Illus.). 224p. (gr. 7-18). 15.99 *(978-0-06-059407-7(1))* HarperCollins Pubs.

Springer, Nancy. Possessing Jessie. 2010. (ENG.). 128p. (YA). (gr. 7-18). pap. 16.95 *(978-0-8234-2259-3(3))* Holiday Hse., Inc.

St. Crow, Lili. Betrayals. 2009. (Strange Angels Ser.: 2). (ENG., Illus.). 304p. (YA). (gr. 7-18). 9.99 *(978-1-59514-252-8(5)*, Razorbill) Penguin Young Readers Group.

—Betrayals, 10 vols. 2010. (Strange Angels Ser.: 2). (YA). 95.75 *(978-1-4407-7156-9(1))* Recorded Bks., Inc.

—Betrayals. 2009. (Strange Angels Ser.: 2). lib. bdg. 20.85 *(978-0-606-09020-9(7)*, Turtleback) Turtleback Bks.

—Jealousy. 2010. (Strange Angels Ser.: 3). (ENG.). 320p. (YA). (gr. 7-18). 9.99 *(978-1-59514-290-0(8)*, Razorbill) Penguin Young Readers Group.

—Jealousy, 10 vols. 2010. (Strange Angels Ser.: 3). (J). 86.75 *(978-1-4498-2774-8(8))*; 68.75 *(978-1-4498-2773-1(X))*; 83.75 *(978-1-4498-2776-2(4))*; 1.25 *(978-1-4498-2777-9(2))*; 209.75 *(978-1-4498-2772-4(1))* Recorded Bks., Inc.

—Jealousy. 2010. (Strange Angels Ser.: 3). lib. bdg. 20.85 *(978-0-606-14566-4(4)*, Turtleback) Turtleback Bks.

—Reckoning. 2011. (Strange Angels Ser.: 5). (ENG.). 320p. (YA). (gr. 7-18). 9.99 *(978-1-59514-395-2(5)*, Razorbill) Penguin Young Readers Group.

—Strange Angels. 2009. (Strange Angels Ser.: 1). (ENG., Illus.). 304p. (YA). (gr. 7-18). pap. 9.99 *(978-1-59514-251-1(7)*, Razorbill) Penguin Young Readers Group.

—Strange Angels, 9 vols. 2009. (Strange Angels Ser.: 1). (J). 114.75 *(978-1-4407-6199-7(X))*; 84.75 *(978-1-4407-6195-9(7))*; 117.75 *(978-1-4407-6197-3(3))*; 87.75 *(978-1-4407-6193-5(0))*; 181.75 *(978-1-4407-6194-2(9))* Recorded Bks., Inc.

—Strange Angels. 2009. (Strange Angels Ser.: 1). lib. bdg. 20.85 *(978-0-606-08957-9(8)*, Turtleback) Turtleback Bks.

Stahler, David, Jr. Doppelganger. (YA). 2008. (ENG.). 272p. (gr. 8). pap. 8.99 *(978-0-06-087234-2(9)*, HarperTeen) 2006. (Illus.). 272p. (gr. 7-12). 16.99 *(978-0-06-087232-8(2))* 2006. (Illus.). 258p. (gr. 7-12). lib. bdg. 17.89 *(978-0-06-087233-5(0))* HarperCollins Pubs.

Staniszewski, Anna. Finders Reapers. 2016. (Switched at First Kiss Ser.: 2). (ENG.). 272p. (J). (gr. 5-8). pap. 7.99 *(978-1-4926-1549-1(8)*, Sourcebooks Jabberwocky) Sourcebooks, Inc.

—I'm with Cupid. 2015. (Switched at First Kiss Ser.: 1). (ENG.). 240p. (J). (gr. 5-8). pap. 7.99 *(978-1-4926-1546-0(3)*, 9781492615460, Sourcebooks Jabberwocky) Sourcebooks, Inc.

—Match Me If You Can. 2017. (Switched at First Kiss Ser.: 3). (ENG.). 240p. (J). (gr. 5-8). pap. 7.99 *(978-1-4926-1552-1(8)*, 9781492615521, Sourcebooks Jabberwocky) Sourcebooks, Inc.

Stayer, Elizabeth. Santa's Magic Stardust. 2009. 40p. pap. 18.49 *(978-1-4490-2884-8(5))* AuthorHouse.

Stegmaier, Laura J. Ling-Ling Turner, Ppi: Mystery of the Rising Island. 2013. 92p. pap. 10.95 *(978-1-4575-2363-2(9))* Dog Ear Publishing, LLC.

Stein, Tammar. Kindred. 2012. (ENG.). 276p. (YA). (gr. 7). pap. 8.99 *(978-0-375-85349-4(9)*, Ember) Random Hse. Children's Bks.

Stentiford, Tyler Michael. A Darker Secret. 2009. (ENG.). 128p. (YA). pap. 9.99 *(978-1-60138-315-0(0))* Atlantic Publishing Group, Inc.

Stevenson, Robert Louis. Dr. Jekyll & Mr. Hyde. 2008. (Bring the Classics to Life Ser.). (ENG., Illus.). 72p. (gr. 4-12). pap., act. bk. ed. 10.95 *(978-0-931334-50-4(0)*, EDCTR-402B) EDCON Publishing Group.

Stevenson, Sarah Jamila. The Truth Against the World. 2014. (ENG.). 360p. (YA). pap. 9.99 *(978-0-7387-4058-4(6)*, Flux) North Star Editions.

Stevermer, Caroline & Wrede, Patricia C. The Grand Tour: Being a Revelation of Matters of High Confidentiality & Greatest Importance, Including Extracts from the Intimate Diary of a Noblewoman & the Sworn Testimony of a Lady of Quality. 2006. (ENG., Illus.). 480p. (YA). (gr. 7-12). pap. 21.95 *(978-0-15-205556-1(8))* Houghton Mifflin Harcourt Publishing Co.

Stiefvater, Maggie. Blue Lily, Lily Blue. 2014. (Raven Cycle Ser.: 3). (ENG.). 400p. (J). (gr. 9). 18.99 *(978-0-545-42496-7(8)*, Scholastic Pr.) Scholastic, Inc.

—The Dream Thieves. (Raven Cycle Ser.: 2). (ENG.). 448p. (J). (gr. 9). 2014. pap. 9.99 *(978-0-545-42495-0(X)*, Scholastic Paperbacks) 2013. 18.99 *(978-0-545-42494-3(1)*, Scholastic Pr.) Scholastic, Inc.

—The Dream Thieves. 2014. (Raven Cycle Ser.: 2). lib. bdg. 20.85 *(978-0-606-36029-6(8))* Turtleback Bks.

—Forever. (Shiver Ser.: 3). (ENG.). (J). (gr. 9). 2014. 416p. pap. 9.99 *(978-0-545-68280-0(0))* 2011. 400p. 17.99 *(978-0-545-25908-8(8)*, Scholastic Pr.) Scholastic, Inc.

—Forever. l.t. ed. 2011. (Shiver Trilogy: Bk. 3). (ENG.). 598p. 23.99 *(978-1-4104-3606-1(3))* Thorndike Pr.

—Forever. 2014. (Wolves of Mercy Falls Ser.: 3). lib. bdg. 20.85 *(978-0-606-36649-6(0))* Turtleback Bks.

—Hunted, Bk. 2. 2014. (Spirit Animals Ser.: 2). (ENG., Illus.). 192p. (J). (gr. 3-7). 12.99 *(978-0-545-52244-1(7))* Scholastic, Inc.

—Lament: The Faerie Queen's Deception. 2008. (Lament Novel Ser.: 1). (ENG., Illus.). 336p. (YA). (gr. 8-18). pap. 9.95 *(978-0-7387-1370-0(8)*, 1286181, Flux) North Star Editions.

—Linger. 2014. (Shiver Ser.). (ENG.). (YA). (gr. 9). lib. bdg. 20.60 ***(978-1-68065-091-4(2))*** Perfection Learning Corp.

—Linger. (Shiver Ser.: 2). (ENG.). (J). (gr. 9). 2014. 384p. pap. 9.99 *(978-0-545-68279-4(7))* 2010. 368p. 17.99 *(978-0-545-12328-0(3)*, Scholastic Pr.) Scholastic, Inc.

—Linger. l.t. ed. 2011. (Shiver Trilogy: Bk. 2). (ENG.). 488p. 23.99 *(978-1-4104-3447-0(8))* Thorndike Pr.

—The Raven King. 2016. (Raven Cycle Ser.: 4). (ENG.). 400p. (YA). (gr. 9). 18.99 *(978-0-545-42498-1(4)*, Scholastic Pr.) Scholastic, Inc.

—Shiver. 2011. (Shiver Trilogy: Bk. 1). 9.64 *(978-0-7848-3572-2(1)*, Everbind) Marco Bk. Co.

—Shiver. (ENG.). (gr. 9). 2014. (Shiver Ser.). (YA). lib. bdg. 20.60 ***(978-1-68065-090-7(4))*** 2010. (Shiver Trilogy: Bk. 1). 392p. 20.00 *(978-1-60686-750-1(4))* Perfection Learning Corp.

—Shiver. (Shiver Ser.: 1). (ENG.). (J). 2014. 416p. (gr. 9). pap. 9.99 *(978-0-545-68278-7(9))* 2009. 400p. (gr. 7-18). 17.99 *(978-0-545-12326-6(7)*, Scholastic Pr.) Scholastic, Inc.

—Shiver. l.t. ed. 2010. (Shiver Trilogy: Bk. 1). (ENG.). 506p. 23.95 *(978-1-4104-2667-3(X))* Thorndike Pr.

—Shiver. 2014. (Wolves of Mercy Falls Ser.: 1). lib. bdg. 20.85 *(978-0-606-36647-2(4))* Turtleback Bks.

—Sinner. 2015. (Shiver Ser.). (ENG.). 368p. (J). (gr. 9). pap. 10.99 *(978-0-545-65459-3(9))* Scholastic, Inc.

Stiefvater, Maggie & Scholastic, Inc. Staff. Shiver; Linger; Forever. 2011. (Shiver Ser.). (ENG.). (J). (gr. 9-9). 52.97 *(978-0-545-32686-5(9)*, Scholastic Pr.) Scholastic, Inc.

Stine, R. L. The Horror at Chiller House. 2011. (Goosebumps Horrorland Ser.: 19). (ENG.). 160p. (J). (gr. 3-7). pap. 6.99 *(978-0-545-16200-5(9)*, Scholastic Paperbacks) Scholastic, Inc.

—Night of the Giant Everything. 2011. (Goosebumps Hall of Horrors Ser.: 2). (ENG.). 160p. (J). (gr. 3-7). pap. 6.99 *(978-0-545-28935-1(1)*, Scholastic Paperbacks) Scholastic, Inc.

—Revenge of the Lawn Gnomes. 2011. (Classic Goosebumps Ser.: 19). (ENG.). 160p. (J). (gr. 3-7). pap. 6.99 *(978-0-545-29835-3(0)*, Scholastic Paperbacks) Scholastic, Inc.

—The Taste of Night. (Dangerous Girls Ser.: 2). (ENG.). 2005. 288p. (YA). (gr. 8-18). pap. 8.99 *(978-0-06-059618-7(X)*, HarperTeen) 2004. 240p. (J). (gr. 7-18). 14.99 *(978-0-06-059616-3(3))* HarperCollins Pubs.

—Temptation. 2012. (ENG.). 416p. (YA). (gr. 7). pap. 10.99 *(978-1-4424-5068-4(1)*, Simon Pulse) Simon Pulse.

Stone, Jeff. Five Ancestors Out of the Ashes: Phoenix. 2013. (Five Ancestors Out of the Ashes Ser.: 1). (ENG.). 304p. (J). (gr. 4-7). 6.99 *(978-0-375-87097-2(0)*, Yearling) Random Hse. Children's Bks.

—Five Ancestors Out of the Ashes #1: Phoenix. 2012. (Five Ancestors Out of the Ashes Ser.). (ENG.). 288p. (J). (gr. 4-7). 16.99 *(978-0-375-87018-7(0)*, Random Hse. Bks. for Young Readers) Random Hse. Children's Bks.

—Lion. 2013. (Five Ancestors Out of the Ashes Ser.). (ENG.). 240p. (J). (gr. 4-7). 16.99 *(978-0-375-87019-4(9)*, Random Hse. Bks. for Young Readers) Random Hse. Children's Bks.

Strange, Jason. The Demon Card, 1 vol. Evergreen, Nelson & Kendall, Bradford, illus. 2012. (Jason Strange Ser.). (ENG.).

72p. (gr. 2-3). pap. 6.25 *(978-1-4342-3884-9(9))*; lib. bdg. 25.32 *(978-1-4342-3296-0(4))* Stone Arch Bks.

—The Graveyard Plot, 1 vol. Evergreen, Nelson & Kendall, Bradford, illus. 2012. (Jason Strange Ser.). (ENG.). 72p. (gr. 2-3). pap. 6.25 *(978-1-4342-3886-3(5))* Stone Arch Bks.

Strickland, Brad. The House Where Nobody Lived. 2006. (Lewis Barnavelt Ser.). (ENG.). 176p. (J). (gr. 3-7). 16.99 *(978-0-8037-3148-6(5)*, Dial Bks) Penguin Young Readers Group.

Strom, Yale. The Wedding That Saved a Town. Prosmitsky, Jenya, illus. 2008. (J). (gr. -1). 17.95 *(978-0-8225-7376-0(8)*, Kar-Ben Publishing) Lerner Publishing Group.

Stroud, Jonathan. Buried Fire. 2004. 332p. (J). pap. *(978-0-7818-5794-9(5))* Hippocrene Bks., Inc.

—The Creeping Shadow. 2016. (Lockwood & Co Ser.). (ENG., Illus.). 464p. (J). (gr. 3-7). 16.99 *(978-1-4847-0967-2(5))* Hyperion Bks. for Children.

—The Hollow Boy. 2015. (Lockwood & Co Ser.). (ENG.). 400p. (J). (gr. 3-7). 16.99 *(978-1-4847-0968-9(3))* Hyperion Bks. for Children.

—Lockwood & Co. Book Three the Hollow Boy. 2016. (Lockwood & Co Ser.). (ENG.). 416p. (J). (gr. 3-7). pap. 7.99 *(978-1-4847-1189-7(0))* Hyperion Bks. for Children.

—Lockwood & Co. the Screaming Staircase. 2014. (Lockwood & Co Ser.). (ENG., Illus.). 416p. (J). (gr. 3-7). pap. 7.99 *(978-1-4231-8692-2(3))* Hyperion Bks. for Children.

—The Screaming Staircase. 2013. (Lockwood & Co Ser.: Bk. 1). (ENG.). 400p. (J). (gr. 3-7). 16.99 *(978-1-4231-6491-3(1))* Hyperion Pr.

—The Whispering Skull. (ENG.). (J). (gr. 3-7). 2015. (Lockwood & Co Ser.). 464p. pap. 7.99 *(978-1-4231-9462-0(4))* 2014. (Lockwood & Co. Ser.: 2). 448p. 17.99 *(978-1-4231-6492-0(X))* Hyperion Bks. for Children.

Sublime. 2014. (ENG., Illus.). 336p. (YA). (gr. 9). 17.99 *(978-1-4814-1368-8(6)*, Simon & Schuster Bks. For Young Readers) Simon & Schuster Bks. For Young Readers.

Sullivan, Laura L. Under the Green Hill. 2011. (ENG.). 336p. (J). (gr. 4-8). pap. 17.99 *(978-0-312-55149-0(5)*, 9780312551490) Square Fish.

Suma, Nova Ren. Imaginary Girls. 2012. (ENG.). 352p. (YA). (gr. 9-18). pap. 8.99 *(978-0-14-242143-7(X)*, Speak) Penguin Young Readers Group.

—The Walls Around Us. (ENG.). 336p. (YA). (gr. 9-12). 2016. pap. 9.95 *(978-1-61620-590-4(3))* 2015. 17.95 *(978-1-61620-372-6(2))* Algonquin Bks. of Chapel Hill.

—The Walls Around Us. 2016. lib. bdg. 20.80 *(978-0-606-37957-1(6))* Turtleback Bks.

Summy, Barrie. The Disappearance of Emily H. 2015. (ENG.). 256p. (J). (gr. 5). 16.99 *(978-0-385-73943-6(5)*, Delacorte Bks. for Young Readers) Random Hse. Children's Bks.

Sundell, Joanne. Arctic Shadow. 2015. (Watch Eyes Trilogy Ser.: 2). (ENG.). 278p. (YA). 25.95 *(978-1-4328-3008-3(2)*, Five Star Trade) Cengage Gale.

—Arctic Will. 2016. (ENG.). 326p. (YA). 25.95 *(978-1-4328-3175-2(5)*, Five Star) Cengage Gale.

Sunseri, Heather. Mindsiege. 2013. (ENG.). 374p. (YA). pap. 14.00 *(978-0-9887153-5-6(X))* Sunseri, Heather.

Talkington, Amy. Liv, Forever. (ENG., Illus.). (YA). (gr. 9). 2015. 280p. pap. 10.99 *(978-1-61695-479-6(5))* 2014. 284p. 17.99 *(978-1-61695-322-5(5))* Soho Pr., Inc. (Soho Teen).

Tanigawa, Nagaru. The Boredom of Haruhi Suzumiya. 2010. (Haruhi Suzumiya Ser.: 3). (ENG., Illus.). 224p. (YA). (gr. 10-17). 24.00 *(978-0-316-03886-7(5))*; pap. 18.00 *(978-0-316-03887-4(3))* Little, Brown Bks. for Young Readers.

—The Disappearance of Haruhi Suzumiya. 2010. (Haruhi Suzumiya Ser.: 4). (ENG., Illus.). 192p. (YA). (gr. 10-17). pap. 18.00 *(978-0-316-03889-8(X))* Little, Brown Bks. for Young Readers.

—The Dissociation of Haruhi Suzumiya. 2013. (Haruhi Suzumiya Ser.: 9). (ENG., Illus.). 192p. (YA). (gr. 10-17). pap. 8.99 *(978-0-316-03894-2(6))* Little, Brown Bks. for Young Readers.

—The Intrigues of Haruhi Suzumiya. 2012. (Haruhi Suzumiya Ser.: 7). (ENG.). 288p. (YA). (gr. 10-17). 15.99 *(978-0-316-03895-9(4))*; pap. 18.00 *(978-0-316-03896-6(2))* Little, Brown Bks. for Young Readers.

—The Rampage of Haruhi Suzumiya. 2011. (Haruhi Suzumiya Ser.: 4). (ENG.). 240p. (YA). (gr. 10-17). pap. 18.00 *(978-0-316-03884-3(9))* Little, Brown Bks. for Young Readers.

—The Sigh of Haruhi Suzumiya. 2009. (Haruhi Suzumiya Ser.: Bk. 1). (Illus.). 208p. (YA). (gr. 10-18). 14.99 *(978-0-316-03881-2(4))* Hachette Bk. Group.

—The Sigh of Haruhi Suzumiya, Bk. 1. 2009. (Haruhi Suzumiya Ser.: 2). (ENG., Illus.). 208p. (YA). (gr. 10-17). pap. 18.00 *(978-0-316-03879-9(2))* Little, Brown Bks. for Young Readers.

—The Surprise of Haruhi Suzumiya. 2013. (Haruhi Suzumiya Ser.: 10). (ENG., Illus.). 368p. (YA). (gr. 10-17). 24.00 *(978-0-316-03898-0(9))*; pap. 10.99 *(978-0-316-03897-3(0))* Little, Brown Bks. for Young Readers.

—The Wavering of Haruhi Suzumiya. 2011. (Haruhi Suzumiya Ser.: 6). (ENG & JPN.). 208p. (YA). (gr. 10-17). pap. 18.00 *(978-0-316-03892-8(X))* Little, Brown Bks. for Young Readers.

Tanigawa, Nagaru, et al. The Melancholy of Suzumiya Haruhi-Chan. 2012. (Melancholy of Suzumiya Haruhi-Chan Ser.: 6). (ENG., Illus.). 160p. (gr. 11-17). pap. 11.99 *(978-0-316-22914-2(8)*, Yen Pr.) Orbit.

Tanquary, Kathryn. The Night Parade. 2016. (ENG.). 336p. (J). (gr. 5-8). 16.99 *(978-1-4926-2324-3(5)*, 9781492623243, Sourcebooks Jabberwocky) Sourcebooks, Inc.

Taylor, G. P. The First Escape. 2008. (Dopple Ganger Chronicles Ser.: 1). (ENG., Illus.). 288p. (J). (gr. 3-7). 19.99 *(978-1-4143-1947-6(9)*, SaltRiver) Tyndale Hse. Pubs.

—The Great Mogul Diamond. 2011. (Dopple Ganger Chronicles Ser.: 3). (ENG.). 304p. (J). (gr. 3-7). 19.99 *(978-1-4143-1949-0(5)*, SaltRiver) Tyndale Hse. Pubs.

—The Shadowmancer Returns: The Curse of Salamander Street. 2007. (Shadowmancer; 04 Ser.). 240p. (J). *(978-1-4287-4670-1(6)*, Putnam Juvenile) Penguin Publishing Group.

Taylor, Laini. Daughter of Smoke & Bone. 2011. (ENG.). 432p. (YA). (gr. 10-17). 20.00 *(978-0-316-13402-6(3))* Little Brown & Co.

—Daughter of Smoke & Bone. 2012. (ENG.). (YA). (gr. 10-17). 448p. pap. 12.99 *(978-0-316-13399-9(X))*; 624p. pap. 28.99 *(978-0-316-22435-2(9))* Little, Brown Bks. for Young Readers.

—Daughter of Smoke & Bone. 2012. (Daughter of Smoke & Bone Ser.: 1). (YA). lib. bdg. 24.50 *(978-0-606-26704-5(2)*, Turtleback) Turtleback Bks.

—Days of Blood & Starlight. (ENG.). (YA). (gr. 10-17). 2014. 544p. pap. 12.99 *(978-0-316-13398-2(1))* 2012. (Illus.). 528p. 18.99 *(978-0-316-13397-5(3))* 2012. 688p. 39.99 *(978-0-316-22433-8(2))* Little, Brown Bks. for Young Readers.

—Lips Touch: Three Times. Di Bartolo, Jim, illus. (ENG.). 288p. (J). (gr. 7-7). 2011. pap. 14.99 *(978-0-545-05586-4(5))* 2009. 17.99 *(978-0-545-05585-7(7))* Scholastic, Inc. (Levine, Arthur A. Bks.).

Teitelbaum, Michael. The Phantom Pharaoh. 2015. (Cold Whispers Ser.). (ENG., Illus.). 32p. (J). (gr. 2-6). lib. bdg. 26.60 *(978-1-62724-810-5(2))* Bearport Publishing Co., Inc.

Terrell, Heather. Eternity. 2011. (Fallen Angel Ser.: 2). (ENG.). 304p. (YA). (gr. 8). pap. 8.99 *(978-0-06-196571-5(5)*, HarperTeen) HarperCollins Pubs.

Thomas, Novene. The Enchanted Opera: Supernaturally Enchanting & Spiritually Enlightening. 2013. 192p. pap. 13.95 *(978-1-62212-986-7(5)*, Strategic Bk. Publishing) Strategic Book Publishing & Rights Agency (SBPRA).

Thompson, Kate. Midnight's Choice. unabr. ed. 2004. (Switchers Ser.: Vol. 2). 240p. (J). (gr. 5-9). pap. 38.00 incl. audio *(978-0-8072-8769-9(5)*, Listening Library) Random Hse. Audio Publishing Group.

Thomson, Celia & Braswell, Liz. The Nine Lives of Chloe King: The Fallen; the Stolen; the Chosen. 2011. (Nine Lives of Chloe King Ser.). (ENG.). 784p. (YA). (gr. 9). pap. 13.99 *(978-1-4424-3570-4(4)*, Simon Pulse) Simon Pulse.

Thomson, Sarah L. Mercy: The Last New England Vampire, 1 vol. 2011. (ENG.). 178p. (J). pap. 16.95 *(978-1-934031-36-0(4)*, 9caae975-eeb4-4b56-8673-b3abbf16fc2f) Islandport Pr., Inc.

Ticktock Media, Ltd. Staff. The Unexplained: Encounters with Ghosts, Monsters, & Aliens. 2008. (ENG.). 96p. (J). (gr. 2-4). pap. 9.95 *(978-1-84696-807-5(0)*, TickTock Books) Octopus Publishing Group GBR. Dist: Independent Pubs. Group.

Tieman, Cate. Darkest Fear. 2014. (Birthright Ser.: 1). (ENG., Illus.). 368p. (YA). (gr. 9). pap. 9.99 *(978-1-4424-8245-6(1)*, Simon Pulse) Simon Pulse.

Toft, Di. The Twilight Circus. 2011. (Wolven Ser.: 2). (ENG.). 384p. (J). (gr. 3-7). 17.99 *(978-0-545-29492-8(4)*, Chicken Hse., The) Scholastic, Inc.

—Wolven, Bk. 1. 2011. (Wolven Ser.: 1). (ENG.). 352p. (J). (gr. 3-7). pap. 7.99 *(978-0-545-17110-6(5)*, Chicken Hse., The) Scholastic, Inc.

Towell, Katy. Skary Childrin & the Carousel of Sorrow. 2013. (ENG.). 272p. (J). (gr. 3-7). pap. 8.99 *(978-0-375-87240-2(X)*, Knopf Bks. for Young Readers) Random Hse. Children's Bks.

Trapani, Iza. Haunted Party. Trapani, Iza, illus. 2010. (ENG., Illus.). 28p. (J). (gr. -1-2). pap. 7.95 *(978-1-58089-247-6(7))* Charlesbridge Publishing, Inc.

Trivas, Tracy. The Wish Stealers. 2011. (ENG.). 288p. (J). (gr. 3-7). pap. 7.99 *(978-1-4169-8726-0(6)*, Aladdin) Simon & Schuster Children's Publishing.

Troupe, Thomas Kingsley. Darling Doll. Faber, Rudy, illus. 2016. (Hauntiques Ser.). (ENG.). 128p. (gr. 4-6). lib. bdg. 25.32 *(978-1-4965-3548-1(0))* Stone Arch Bks.

—Ghostly Goalie. Faber, Rudy, illus. 2016. (Hauntiques Ser.). (ENG.). 128p. (gr. 4-6). lib. bdg. 25.32 *(978-1-4965-3544-3(8))* Stone Arch Bks.

—Hauntiques, 4 vols. Faber, Rudy, illus. 2016. (Hauntiques Ser.). (ENG.). 128p. (gr. 4-6). 101.28 *(978-1-4965-3561-0(8))* Stone Arch Bks.

—Phantom's Favorite. Faber, Rudy, illus. 2016. (Hauntiques Ser.). (ENG.). 128p. (gr. 4-6). lib. bdg. 25.32 *(978-1-4965-3546-7(4))* Stone Arch Bks.

—Wandering Wagon. Faber, Rudy, illus. 2016. (Hauntiques Ser.). (ENG.). 128p. (gr. 4-6). lib. bdg. 25.32 *(978-1-4965-3547-4(2))* Stone Arch Bks.

Tubb, Kristin O'Donnell. The 13th Sign. 2013. (ENG.). 272p. (J). (gr. 5-9). 16.99 *(978-0-312-58352-1(4)*, 9780312583521) Feiwel & Friends.

—The 13th Sign. 2014. (ENG.). 288p. (J). (gr. 5-9). pap. 9.99 *(978-1-250-05059-5(6)*, 9781250050595) Square Fish.

Turner, Suzy. The Ghost of Josiah Grimshaw: A Morgan Sisters Novel. 2013. 286p. pap. *(978-989-97348-6-9(1))* Turner, Suzanne.

—The Temporal Stone: A Morgan Sisters Novel. 2013. 288p. pap. *(978-989-98351-0-8(2))* Turner, Suzanne.

Turnquist, Myrtle Moose. How Do Dandelions Grow. 2011. 48p. pap. 20.50 *(978-1-4634-3776-3(5))* AuthorHouse.

van Arsdale, Peternelle. The Beast Is an Animal. 2017. (ENG., Illus.). 352p. (YA). (gr. 9). 17.99 *(978-1-4814-8841-9(4)*, McElderry, Margaret K. Bks.) McElderry, Margaret K. Bks.

Vance, Talia. Silver. 2012. (Bandia Novel Ser.: 1). (ENG.). 384p. (YA). pap. 9.99 *(978-0-7387-3303-6(2)*, Flux) North Star Editions.

Vande Velde, Vivian. All Hallows' Eve: 13 Stories. 2010. (ENG., Illus.). 240p. (YA). (gr. 7). pap. 8.99 *(978-0-15-206473-0(7))* Houghton Mifflin Harcourt Publishing Co.

Verano, M. Diary of a Haunting. (Diary of a Haunting Ser.). (ENG., Illus.). (YA). (gr. 9). 2016. 336p. pap. 10.99 *(978-1-4814-3068-5(8))* 2015. 320p. 17.99 *(978-1-4814-3069-2(6))* Simon Pulse. (Simon Pulse).

—Possession. 2016. (Diary of a Haunting Ser.). (ENG., Illus.). 352p. (YA). (gr. 9). 17.99 *(978-1-4814-6441-3(8)*, Simon Pulse) Simon Pulse.

Verday, Jessica. The Beautiful & the Damned. 2013. (ENG., Illus.). 272p. (YA). (gr. 7). 17.99 *(978-1-4424-8835-9(2)*, Simon Pulse) Simon Pulse.

—The Hidden. (ENG.). 400p. (YA). (gr. 9). 2012. pap. 12.99 *(978-1-4169-7898-5(4))* 2011. 17.99 *(978-1-4169-7897-8(6))* Simon Pulse. (Simon Pulse).

—The Hollow. (ENG.). (YA). (gr. 7). 2010. 528p. pap. 11.99 *(978-1-4169-7894-7(1))*No. 1. 2009. 544p. 17.99 *(978-1-4169-7893-0(3))* Simon Pulse. (Simon Pulse).

Vernick, Shirley Reva. The Black Butterfly. 2014. (ENG.). 226p. (J). 19.95 *(978-1-935955-79-5(9))* Cinco Puntos Pr.

Verstraete, Majanka. The Doll Maker: Weirdville. l.t. ed. 2013. 1. (ENG.). 86p. (gr. 2-6). pap. 9.95 *(978-1-62253-065-6(9))* Evolved Publishing.

Viguie, Debbie & Holder, Nancy. Unleashed. 2012. (Wolf Spring Chronicles Ser.). (ENG.). 400p. (YA). (gr. 7). pap. 9.99 *(978-0-385-74099-9(9)*, Ember) Random Hse. Children's Bks.

Voelkel, Jon & Voelkel, Pamela. The River of No Return, Bk. 3. 2012. (Jaguar Stones Ser.: Bk. 3). (ENG.). 352p. (J). (gr. 5). 16.99 *(978-1-60684-073-3(8)*, Darby Creek) Lerner Publishing Group.

Volk, Gretchen. The Amazing Adventures of Tristy Ruth, Raisin Girl. 2012. 258p. pap. *(978-1-105-51531-6(1))* Lulu.com.

Wade, Rebecca. The Theft & the Miracle. 2007. 351p. (J). (gr. 4-7). lib. bdg. 17.89 *(978-0-06-077495-0(9))* HarperCollins Pubs.

Walker, Melissa. Ashes to Ashes. 2013. (ENG.). 336p. (YA). (gr. 8). 17.99 *(978-0-06-207734-9(1)*, Tegen, Katherine Bks) HarperCollins Pubs.

—Dust to Dust. 2016. 320p. (YA). (gr. 8). pap. 9.99 *(978-0-06-207738-7(4)*, Tegen, Katherine Bks) HarperCollins Pubs.

Wallace, Kali. Shallow Graves. (YA). (gr. 9). 2017. 384p. pap. 9.99 ***(978-0-06-236621-4(1))*** 2016. 368p. 17.99 *(978-0-06-236620-7(3))* HarperCollins Pubs. (Tegen, Katherine Bks).

Wallace, Rich. Wicked Cruel. 2015. (ENG.). 208p. (J). (gr. 5). pap. 6.99 *(978-0-375-86514-5(4)*, Yearling) Random Hse. Children's Bks.

Walsh, Sara. The Dark Light. (ENG., (YA). (gr. 9). 2013. Illus.). 512p. pap. 9.99 *(978-1-4424-3458-5(9))* 2012. 496p. 16.99 *(978-1-4424-3455-4(4))* Simon Pulse. (Simon Pulse).

Walters, Ednah. Awakened: Book One of the Guardian Legacy. 2010. 272p. (YA). pap. 12.99 *(978-1-61706-038-0(0))* Pill Hill Pr.

Warburton, Ruth. A Witch Alone. 2013. (ENG.). 432p. (YA). (gr. 7). pap. 10.99 *(978-1-4449-0471-0(X))* Hodder & Stoughton GBR. Dist: Hachette Bk. Group.

—Witch Finder. 2014. (ENG.). 384p. (J). (gr. 7). pap. 10.99 *(978-1-4449-1446-7(4))* Hodder & Stoughton GBR. Dist: Hachette Bk. Group.

—Witch Hunt. 2014. (ENG.). 400p. (J). (gr. 7-12). pap. 10.99 *(978-1-4449-1448-1(0))* Hodder & Stoughton GBR. Dist: Hachette Bk. Group.

Wasserman, Robin. The Book of Blood & Shadow. 2012. (ENG.). 448p. (YA). (gr. 7). 17.99 *(978-0-375-86876-4(3))*; lib. bdg. 20.99 *(978-0-375-96876-1(8))* Random Hse. Children's Bks. (Knopf Bks. for Young Readers).

Waters, Daniel. Break My Heart 1,000 Times. 2013. (ENG., Illus.). 352p. (YA). (gr. 7-17). pap. 9.99 *(978-1-4231-2228-9(3))* Hyperion Pr.

Watson, Andi. Princess Decomposia & Count Spatula. 2015. (ENG., Illus.). 176p. (YA). (gr. 8). 19.99 *(978-1-62672-275-0(7)*, 9781626722750, First Second Bks.) Roaring Brook Pr.

Watson, Jude. Sting. 2016. (ENG.). 272p. (J). (gr. 3-7). 16.99 *(978-0-545-86346-9(5)*, Scholastic Pr.) Scholastic, Inc.

Watts, Julia. Free Spirits. 2009. (ENG.). 176p. (J). (gr. 1). pap. 8.95 *(978-0-9667359-2-5(7)*, BeanPole Bks.) Harren Communications, LLC.

Watts, Leander. Beautiful City of the Dead. 2007. (ENG.). 256p. (YA). (gr. 7-12). pap. 14.99 *(978-0-618-59499-3(X))* Houghton Mifflin Harcourt Publishing Co.

Weatherly, L. A. Angel Burn. 2011. (Angel Ser.: 1). (ENG., Illus.). 464p. (YA). (gr. 9). pap. 9.99 *(978-0-7636-5846-5(4))*; 17.99 *(978-0-7636-5652-2(6))* Candlewick Pr.

—Angel Fire. 2012. (Angel Ser.: 2). (ENG., Illus.). (YA). (gr. 9). pap. 8.99 *(978-0-7636-6064-2(7))*; 17.99 *(978-0-7636-5679-9(8))* Candlewick Pr.

Weiss, Sonya. Reckoning. 2016. (ENG., Illus.). 210p. (J). pap. 15.00 *(978-1-60183-730-1(5))* Kensington Publishing Corp.

Wells, Charity. The Trouble with the Supernatural, 1 vol. 2010. 84p. pap. 19.95 *(978-1-4489-2117-1(1))* America Star Bks.

Wells, Robison. Blackout. (Blackout Ser.: 1). (ENG.). (YA). (gr. 8). 2014. 448p. pap. 9.99 *(978-0-06-202613-2(5))* 2013. 432p. 17.99 *(978-0-06-202612-5(7))* HarperCollins Pubs. (HarperTeen).

—Dead Zone. (Blackout Ser.: 2). (ENG.). (YA). (gr. 8). 2015. 400p. pap. 9.99 *(978-0-06-227503-5(8))* 2014. 384p. 17.99 *(978-0-06-227502-8(X))* HarperCollins Pubs. (HarperTeen).

Welvaert, Scott R. The Mosquito King: An Agate & Buck Adventure, 1 vol. Garvey, Brann, illus. (Vortex Bks.). (ENG.). 112p. (gr. 2-3). 2008. pap. 6.95 *(978-1-59889-923-8(6))* 2007. 26.65 *(978-1-59889-857-6(4))* Stone Arch Bks. (Vortex Bks.).

West, Carly Anne. The Bargaining. 2015. (ENG., Illus.). 416p. (YA). (gr. 9). 17.99 *(978-1-4424-4182-8(8)*, Simon Pulse) Simon Pulse.

—The Murmurings. (ENG., 384p. (YA). (gr. 9). 2014. Illus.). pap. 11.99 *(978-1-4424-4180-4(1))* 2013. 16.99 *(978-1-4424-4179-8(8))* Simon Pulse. (Simon Pulse).

West, Kasie. Pivot Point. 2013. (Pivot Point Ser.: Bk. 1). (ENG.). 384p. (YA). (gr. 8). pap. 9.99 *(978-0-06-211736-6(X)*, HarperTeen) HarperCollins Pubs.

—Split Second. 2014. (Pivot Point Ser.: Bk. 2). (ENG.). 368p. (YA). (gr. 8). 17.99 *(978-0-06-211738-0(6)*, HarperTeen) HarperCollins Pubs.

West, Temple. Velvet. 2015. (ENG.). 416p. (YA). (gr. 8). pap. 9.99 *(978-1-250-05708-2(6)*, 9781250057082) Feiwel & Friends.

Westerfeld, Scott. Horizon. 2017. (Horizon Ser.: 1). (ENG.). 256p. (J). (gr. 4-7). 14.99 *(978-0-545-91677-6(1))* Scholastic, Inc.

Westover, Steve. Crater Lake: Battle for Wizard Island. 2012. pap. 14.99 *(978-1-59955-960-5(9))* Cedar Fort, Inc./CFI Distribution.

—Return of the Mystic Gray. 2013. 15.99 *(978-1-4621-1187-9(4))* Cedar Fort, Inc./CFI Distribution.

Weyn, Suzanne. The Invisible World. 2012. (ENG.). 240p. (J). (gr. 9-9). 17.99 *(978-0-545-33486-0(1)*, Scholastic Pr.) Scholastic, Inc.

White, Kiersten. Endlessly. (Paranormalcy Ser.: 3). (ENG.). (YA). (gr. 8). 2013. 416p. pap. 9.99 *(978-0-06-198589-8(9))* 2012. 400p. 17.99 *(978-0-06-198588-1(0))* HarperCollins Pubs. (HarperTeen).

—Paranormalcy. (Paranormalcy Ser.: 1). (ENG.). (YA). (gr. 8). 2011. 368p. pap. 9.99 *(978-0-06-198585-0(6))* 2010. 352p. 16.99 *(978-0-06-198584-3(8))* HarperCollins Pubs. (HarperTeen).

—Supernaturally. (Paranormalcy Ser.: 2). (ENG.). (YA). (gr. 8). 2012. 368p. pap. 9.99 *(978-0-06-198587-4(2))* 2011. 352p. 17.99 *(978-0-06-198586-7(4))* HarperCollins Pubs. (HarperTeen).

Whitten, A. J. The Cellar. 2011. (ENG.). 288p. (YA). (gr. 7-18). pap. 16.99 *(978-0-547-23253-9(5))* Houghton Mifflin Harcourt Publishing Co.

—The Well. 2009. (ENG., Illus.). 336p. (YA). (gr. 7-18). pap. 18.95 *(978-0-547-23229-4(2))* Houghton Mifflin Harcourt Publishing Co.

Whyte, Elana. My Gift: A Book about a Child Who Sees Spirit. 2013. 32p. pap. 13.95 *(978-1-4525-8724-0(8)*, Balboa Pr.) Author Solutions, Inc.

Wiebe, Joanna. The Wicked Awakening of Anne Merchant. 2015. (V Trilogy Ser.: Bk. 2). (ENG.). 320p. (gr. 7). pap. 12.95 *(978-1-940363-29-5(2))* BenBella Bks.

Wignall, K. J. Death. 2014. (Mercian Trilogy Ser.: 3). (ENG.). 298p. (YA). (gr. 7). pap. 10.99 *(978-1-4052-5862-3(4))* Egmont Bks., Ltd. GBR. Dist: Independent Pubs. Group.

Wilde, Oscar & Fisher, Eric Scott. The Picture of Dorian Gray, 1 vol. 2012. (Calico Illustrated Classics Ser.: No. 4). (ENG., Illus.). 112p. (J). (gr. 3-6). 27.07 *(978-1-61641-618-8(1))* Magic Wagon.

Williams, Carol Lynch. Messenger. 2016. (ENG., Illus.). 288p. (YA). (gr. 7). 17.99 *(978-1-4814-5776-7(4)*, Simon & Schuster/Paula Wiseman Bks.) Simon & Schuster/Paula Wiseman Bks.

Williams, Tad & Beale, Deborah. The Dragons of Ordinary Farm. Swearingen, Greg, illus. 2009. (ENG.). 416p. (J). (gr. 4-7). 16.99 *(978-0-06-154345-6(4))* HarperCollins Pubs.

Willocks, Tim. Doglands. 2012. (ENG.). 324p. (YA). (gr. 7). pap. 9.99 *(978-0-375-85818-5(0)*, Ember) Random Hse. Children's Bks.

Wilson, N. D. The Drowned Vault. 2013. (Ashtown Burials Ser.: Bk. 2). (ENG.). 464p. (J). (gr. 3-7). 8.99 *(978-0-375-86397-4(4)*, Yearling) Random Hse. Children's Bks.

Wilson, Norah & Doherty, Heather. Embrace the Night. 2013. 226p. pap. *(978-1-927651-09-4(3)*, Something Shiny Pr.) Wilson, Norah.

Winter, Isobelle. Weather. Odgers, Sally, ed. Kelsey, Amanda, illus. 2013. 236p. (J). pap. 23.25 *(978-1-61572-946-3(1))* Damnation Bks.

Winters, Cat. The Cure for Dreaming. (ENG., Illus.). (YA). 2016. 384p. (gr. 8-17). pap. 9.95 *(978-1-4197-1941-7(6))* 2014. 368p. (gr. 7-17). 17.95 *(978-1-4197-1216-6(0))* Abrams, Inc. (Amulet Bks.).

Wrede, Patricia C. & Stevermer, Caroline. The Mislaid Magician or Ten Years After: Being the Private Correspondence Between Two Prominent Families Regarding a Scandal Touching the Highest Levels of Government & Thesecurity of the Realm. 2009. (ENG., Illus.). 336p. (J). (gr. 7). pap. 18.95 *(978-0-15-206209-5(2))* Houghton Mifflin Harcourt Publishing Co.

Yancey, Rick. The Curse of the Wendigo. 2011. (Monstrumologist Ser.: 2). (ENG.). 464p. (YA). (gr. 9). pap. 12.99 *(978-1-4169-8451-1(8)*, Simon & Schuster Bks. For Young Readers) Simon & Schuster Bks. For Young Readers.

—The Final Descent. 2013. (Monstrumologist Ser.: 4). (ENG., Illus.). 320p. (YA). (gr. 9). 18.99 *(978-1-4424-5153-7(X)*, Simon & Schuster Bks. For Young Readers) Simon & Schuster Bks. For Young Readers.

—The Isle of Blood. (Monstrumologist Ser.: 3). (ENG.). 560p. (YA). (gr. 9). 2012. pap. 12.99 *(978-1-4169-8453-5(4))* 2011. (Illus.). 18.99 *(978-1-4169-8452-8(6))* Simon & Schuster Bks. For Young Readers. (Simon & Schuster Bks. For Young Readers).

—The Monstrumologist. (Monstrumologist Ser.: 1). (ENG.). (YA). (gr. 9). 2010. 464p. pap. 11.99 *(978-1-4169-8449-8(6))* 2009. 448p. 21.99 *(978-1-4169-8448-1(8))* Simon & Schuster Bks. For Young Readers. (Simon & Schuster Bks. For Young Readers).

Yates, Alexander. The Winter Place. 2015. (ENG., Illus.). 448p. (YA). (gr. 9). 17.99 *(978-1-4814-1981-9(1))* Simon & Schuster Children's Publishing.

Yo-Kai Watch. How to Draw Yo-Kai. 2016. (ENG., Illus.). 64p. (J). (gr. 3-7). pap. 9.99 *(978-0-316-36292-4(1))* Little, Brown Bks. for Young Readers.

—Yo-Kai Watch. 2016. (ENG., Illus.). 12p. (J). (gr. -1-1). pap. 6.99 *(978-0-316-36106-4(2))* Little, Brown Bks. for Young Readers.

Yolen, Jane. Foiled. Cavallaro, Mike, illus. 2010. (ENG.). 160p. (J). (gr. 6-9). pap. 17.99 *(978-1-59643-279-6(9)*, 9781596432796, First Second Bks.) Roaring Brook Pr.

Yolen, Jane & Stemple, Adam. Stone Cold. Zangara, Orion, illus. 2016. (Stone Man Mysteries Ser.: 1). (ENG.). 80p. (J). (gr. 7-12). pap. 8.99 *(978-1-5124-1155-3(8))*; lib. bdg. 29.32 *(978-1-4677-4196-5(5))* Lerner Publishing Group. (Graphic Universe™).

Yorinks, Arthur. The Invisible Man. Cushman, Doug, illus. 2011. (ENG.). 32p. (J). (gr. -1-3). 16.99 *(978-0-06-156148-1(7))* HarperCollins Pubs.

Young, Suzanne. Hotel for the Lost. 2016. (ENG., Illus.). 304p. (YA). (gr. 9). pap. 10.99 *(978-1-4814-2301-4(0)*, Simon Pulse) Simon Pulse.

—Hotel Ruby. 2015. (ENG., Illus.). 288p. (YA). (gr. 9). 17.99 *(978-1-4814-2300-7(2)*, Simon Pulse) Simon Pulse.

—A Need So Beautiful. 2012. (Need So Beautiful Ser.: No. 1). (ENG.). 288p. (YA). (gr. 9). pap. 8.99 *(978-0-06-200825-1(0))* HarperCollins Pubs.

Yovanoff, Brenna. The Replacement. 2011. (ENG.). 368p. (YA). (gr. 7-18). 8.99 *(978-1-59514-381-5(5)*, Razorbill) Penguin Young Readers Group.

Yovanoff, Brenna, et al. The Curiosities: A Collection of Stories. 2014. (ENG.). 304p. (YA). (gr. 7-12). pap. *(978-1-4677-1623-9(5)*, Carolrhoda Lab™) Lerner Publishing Group.

Zafón, Carlos Ruiz. Marina. 2014. (ENG.). 336p. (YA). (gr. 7-17). 19.00 *(978-0-316-04471-4(7))* Little, Brown Bks. for Young Readers.

—The Watcher in the Shadows. (ENG.). (YA). (gr. 7-17). 2014. 288p. pap. 10.99 *(978-0-316-04475-2(X))* 2013. 272p. 18.00 *(978-0-316-04476-9(8))* Little, Brown Bks. for Young Readers.

Zink, Michelle. Circle of Fire. 2012. (Prophecy of the Sisters Trilogy Ser.: 3). (ENG.). 368p. (YA). (gr. 7-17). pap. 22.99 (978-0-316-03446-3(0)) Little, Brown Bks. for Young Readers.

—Prophecy of the Sisters. 2010. (Prophecy of the Sisters Trilogy Ser.: 1). (ENG.). 368p. (YA). (gr. 7-17). pap. 8.99 (978-0-316-02741-0(3)) Little, Brown Bks. for Young Readers.

—A Temptation of Angels. 2013. (ENG.). 448p. (YA). (gr. 7). pap. 9.99 (978-0-14-242423-0(4), Speak) Penguin Young Readers Group.

Zuravicky, Orli. Dear Diary: Monster House. 2006. (Illus.). 32p. (J). lib. bdg. 15.00 (978-1-4242-1561-4(7)) Fitzgerald Bks.

SUPERSONIC AERODYNAMICS

see Aerodynamics, Supersonic

SUPERSONIC WAVES

see Ultrasonic Waves

SUPERSTITION

see also Alchemy; Apparitions; Astrology; Charms; Divination; Dreams; Fairies; Folklore; Fortune-Telling; Ghosts; Occultism; Vampires; Witchcraft

Rigby Education Staff. Keep Tradition. (Greetings Ser.). (Illus.). (gr. 3-5). 21.00 (978-0-7635-2229-2(5)) Rigby Education.

Sanna, Ellyn. Folk Customs. 2004. (North American Folklore Ser.). (Illus.). 112p. (YA). (gr. 7-18). lib. bdg. 22.95 (978-1-59084-336-9(3)) Mason Crest.

Stewart, Sheila. The Psychology of Our Dark Side: Humans' Love Affair with Vampires & Werewolves. 2010. (Making of a Monster Ser.). (Illus.). 64p. (YA). (gr. 7-18). pap. 9.95 (978-1-4222-1960-7(7)); lib. bdg. 22.95 (978-1-4222-1807-5(4)) Mason Crest.

SUPERSTITION—FICTION

Applegate, Katherine. Never Race a Runaway Pumpkin. Biggs, Brian, illus. 2009. (Roscoe Riley Rules Ser.: 7). (ENG.). 96p. (J). (gr. 1-5). 15.99 (978-0-06-178372-2(2)); pap. 4.99 (978-0-06-178370-8(6)) HarperCollins Pubs.

—Never Race a Runaway Pumpkin. 2009. (Roscoe Riley Rules Ser.: 7). (J). lib. bdg. 14.75 (978-0-606-06090-5(1), Turtleback) Turtleback Bks.

The Bad Luck of King Fred: Individual Title Six-Packs. (Action Packs Ser.). 104p. (gr. 3-5). 44.00 (978-0-7635-8408-5(8)) Rigby Education.

Belgue, Nancy. Colette & the Silver Samovar, 1 vol. 2010. (Orca Young Readers Ser.). (ENG., Illus.). 152p. (J). (gr. 3-6). pap. 7.95 (978-1-55469-321-4(7)) Orca Bk. Pubs. USA.

Brodeur, Tom. Regina Silsby's Secret War. 2004. 248p. (J). 7.49 (978-1-59166-235-8(4)) BJU Pr.

Brown, Marc. Arthur & the Bad-Luck Brain. 2003. (Marc Brown Arthur Chapter Bks.). (Illus.). 55p. (gr. 2-4). 14.25 (978-0-7569-1701-2(8)) Perfection Learning Corp.

Bunting, Eve. The Banshee. McCully, Emily Arnold, illus. 2009. (ENG.). 32p. (J). (gr. -1-3). 16.00 (978-0-618-82162-4(7)) Houghton Mifflin Harcourt Publishing Co.

Chan, Crystal. Bird. (ENG.). (J). (gr. 3-7). 2015. 320p. pap. 8.99 (978-1-4424-5091-2(6)) 2014. (Illus.). 304p. 16.99 (978-1-4424-5089-9(4), Atheneum Bks. for Young Readers) Simon & Schuster Children's Publishing.

Christopher, Matt. Shadow over Second. Dewdney, Anna, illus. 2009. (New Peach Street Mudders Sports Library). 64p. (J). (gr. 2-4). lib. bdg. 23.93 (978-1-59953-320-9(0)) Norwood Hse. Pr.

Goebel, Jenny. Fortune Falls. (ENG.). 208p. (J). (gr. 3-7). 2017. pap. 6.99 **(978-1-338-13470-4(1))** 2016. 16.99 (978-0-545-81190-3(2), Scholastic Pr.) Scholastic, Inc.

Hairston, Lisa Lee & Graham, Joanne. The Luckiest Girl in Luckyville. 2013. 36p. pap. 15.50 (978-1-4669-8192-8(X)) Trafford Publishing.

Haven, Paul. Two Hot Dogs with Everything. Jessell, Tim, illus. 2007. (ENG.). 320p. (J). (gr. 3-7). per. 7.99 (978-0-375-83349-6(8), Yearling) Random Hse. Children's Bks.

McMullan, Kate. Beware! It's Friday the 13th, 1 vol. Basso, Bill, illus. 2006. (Dragon Slayers' Academy Ser.: No. 13). (ENG.). 112p. (gr. 1-7). 24.21 (978-1-59961-122-8(8)) Spotlight.

Nelson, Suzanne. Dead in the Water. 2013. 171p. (J). pap. (978-0-545-54302-6(9)) Scholastic, Inc.

Nervelle, Rosemarie. The Witch of Beaver Creek Mine. 2007. (ENG.). 160p. (J). (gr. 3-7). 14.95 (978-0-89272-741-4(1)); 2nd ed. pap. 9.95 (978-0-89272-763-6(2)) Down East Bks.

O'Connor, Jane. Just My Luck! 2013. (Fancy Nancy - I Can Read! Ser.). (J). lib. bdg. 13.55 (978-0-606-35044-0(6), Turtleback) Turtleback Bks.

Parish, Herman. Amelia Bedelia Tries Her Luck. 2013. (Amelia Bedelia: I Can Read! Ser.). (J). lib. bdg. 13.55 (978-0-606-32445-8(3), Turtleback) Turtleback Bks.

Scaletta, Kurtis. A Topps League Story: Book Three: Zip It! Wight, Eric, illus. 2012. (Topps Ser.). (ENG.). 112p. (J). (gr. 1-4). pap. 5.95 (978-1-4197-0437-6(0), Amulet Bks.) Abrams, Inc.

Sullivan, Laura L. Under the Green Hill. 2011. (ENG.). 336p. (J). (gr. 4-8). pap. 17.99 (978-0-312-55149-0(5), 9780312551490) Square Fish.

Westergard, Tim. The Jesus Box, 1 vol. 2009. 16p. pap. 24.95 (978-1-60749-694-6(1)) America Star Bks.

SURF

see Ocean Waves

SURFING

Bass, Scott. Surf! Your Guide to Longboarding, Shortboarding, Tubing, Aerials, Hanging Ten & More. 2003. (Extreme Sports Ser.). (ENG., Illus.). 64p. (J). (gr. 4-7). pap. 8.95 (978-0-7922-5108-8(3), National Geographic Children's Bks.) National Geographic Society.

Buckley Jr, Jim. Big Wave Surfing. 2015. (ENG.). 48p. (gr. 3-6). 35.64 (978-1-63430-438-2(1)) Rourke Educational Media.

Carr, Aaron. Surf. 2013. (ENG & SPA.). (J). (978-1-62127-637-1(6)) Weigl Pubs., Inc.

—Surfing. (Illus.). (J). 2013. 32p. 27.13 (978-1-61913-515-4(9)) 2012. (ENG., 24p. pap. 12.95 (978-1-61913-521-5(3), AV2 by Weigl) Weigl Pubs., Inc.

Cassriel, Betsy R. Kiteboarding. 2015. (ENG.). 48p. (gr. 3-6). 35.64 (978-1-63430-439-9(X)) Rourke Educational Media.

Crossingham, John & Kalman, Bobbie. Extreme Surfing. 2003. (Extreme Sports - No Limits Ser.). (ENG., Illus.). 32p. (J). (gr. 3). pap. (978-0-7787-1715-7(1)); lib. bdg. (978-0-7787-1669-3(4)) Crabtree Publishing Co.

De Macedo, Joao. How to Be a Surfer. 2007. (Illus.). 176p. (J). pap. 24.95 (978-1-84126-201-7(3)) Meyer & Meyer Sport, Ltd. GBR. Dist: Cardinal Pubs. Group.

DeLa Vega, Timothy T., et al. 200 Years of Surfing Literature: An Annotated Bibliography. 2004. (Illus.). 108p. per. 19.95 (978-0-9754328-0-8(X)) DeLaVega, T.

Dugan, Christine. ¡Hang Ten! Surfin. 2017. (TIME for Kids en Español - Level 4 Ser.). (SPA., Illus.). 48p. (gr. 4-4). lib. bdg. 31.99 (978-1-5157-5136-6(8)) Time for Kids Inc AUS. Dist: Capstone Pub.

—Hang Ten! Surfing, 1 vol. 2nd rev. ed. 2013. (Nonfiction Readers Ser.). (ENG., Illus.). 48p. (J). (gr. 4-4). pap. 29.96 (978-1-4807-1107-5(1)) Shell Educational Publishing.

—Hang Ten! Surfing, 1 vol. 2nd rev. ed. 2012. (TIME for KIDS(r) Nonfiction Readers Ser.). (ENG.). 48p. (J). (gr. 4-4). pap. 9.99 (978-1-4333-4831-0(4)) Teacher Created Materials, Inc.

Fanning, Mick & Baker, Tim. Surf for Your Life: Grommets' Edition. 2011. (ENG., Illus.). 128p. (J). (gr. 7-18). pap. 14.99 (978-1-86471-823-2(4)) Random Hse. Australia AUS. Dist: Independent Pubs. Group.

Fitzpatrick, Jim. Surfing. 2007. (21st Century Skills Library: Healthy for Life Ser.). (ENG.). 32p. (gr. 4-8). lib. bdg. 28.50 (978-1-60279-019-3(1), 200036) Cherry Lake Publishing.

Goldish, Meish. Surf Dog Miracles. 2012. (Dog Heroes Ser.). 32p. (J). (gr. 2-7). lib. bdg. 25.27 (978-1-61772-577-7(3)) Bearport Publishing Co., Inc.

Goranson, Christopher D. Danny Harf: Wakeboarding Superstar. 2009. (Extreme Sports Biographies Ser.). 64p. (gr. 3-4). 58.50 (978-1-61512-461-9(6), Rosen Reference) Rosen Publishing Group, Inc., The.

Hamilton, Bethany. Ask Bethany, 1 vol. rev. ed. 2014. (Faithgirlz / Soul Surfer Ser.). (ENG., Illus.). 192p. (J). pap. 9.99 (978-0-310-74572-3(1)) Zonderkidz.

Hamilton, Bethany & Bundschuh, Rick. Soul Surfer: A True Story of Faith, Family, & Fighting to Get Back on the Board. 2006. (ENG., Illus.). 240p. pap. 15.00 (978-1-4165-0346-0(3), MTV Bks.) MTV Books.

Hamilton, S. L. Surfing. 2010. (Xtreme Sports Ser.). 32p. (gr. 3-9). 27.07 (978-1-61613-005-3(9), A&D Xtreme) ABDO Publishing Co.

Kelley, K. C. Stand-up Paddleboarding. 2011. (Extreme Sports Ser.). (ENG., Illus.). 32p. (J). (gr. 2-5). lib. bdg. 28.50 (978-1-60973-179-3(4), 201134) Child's World, Inc., The.

—Surfing. 2011. (Extreme Sports Ser.). (ENG., Illus.). 32p. (J). (gr. 2-5). lib. bdg. 28.50 (978-1-60973-185-4(9), 201135) Child's World, Inc., The.

—Surf's Up! 2008. (Reading Rocks! Ser.). (ENG., Illus.). 32p. (J). (gr. 2-5). 28.50 (978-1-60253-103-1(X), 200764) Child's World, Inc., The.

KociendaGenevieve. CATCH A WAVE: THE STORY OF SURFING BEGINNING BOOK WITH ONLINE ACCESS. 2014. (ENG.). 24p. (J). pap. 9.50 (978-1-107-65191-3(3)) Cambridge Univ. Pr.

Labrecque, Ellen. Sky Surfing. 2012. (Extreme Sports Ser.). (ENG., Illus.). 32p. (J). (gr. 2-5). lib. bdg. 28.50 (978-1-60973-212-7(X), 201133) Child's World, Inc., The.

—Windsurfing. 2011. (Extreme Sports Ser.). (ENG., Illus.). 32p. (J). (gr. 2-5). lib. bdg. 28.50 (978-1-60973-188-5(3), 201139) Child's World, Inc., The.

Laval, Anne-Marie. Windsurfing & Kite Surfing. 2012. (Adrenaline Rush Ser.). 32p. (gr. 4-7). lib. bdg. 31.35 (978-1-59920-683-7(8)) Black Rabbit Bks.

Mahaney, Ian F. Danny Harf: Wakeboarding Champion. 2009. (Extreme Sports Biographies Ser.). 24p. (gr. 3-4). 42.50 (978-1-61512-462-6(4), PowerKids Pr.) Rosen Publishing Group, Inc., The.

Mason, Paul. Surfing. 2012. (To the Limit Ser.). (ENG., Illus.). 32p. (J). (gr. 5-8). pap. 10.00 (978-1-4488-7070-7(4)); lib. bdg. 25.25 (978-1-4488-7030-1(5)) Rosen Publishing Group, Inc., The. (PowerKids Pr.).

—Surfing: The World's Most Fantastic Surf Spots & Techniques, 1 vol. 2011. (Passport to World Sports Ser.). (ENG.). 32p. (gr. 3-4). lib. bdg. 27.99 (978-1-4296-6879-8(2), Edge Bks.) Capstone Press of Coughlan Cos.

Mattern, Joanne. Kiteboarding. 2008. (Illus.). 24p. (J). lib. bdg. (978-1-60472-396-0(3)) Rourke Educational Media.

McClellan, Ray. Surfing. 2008. (Action Sports Ser.). (ENG., Illus.). 24p. (J). (gr. 3-7). lib. bdg. 25.95 (978-1-60014-145-4(5)) Bellwether Media.

McFee, Shane. Surfing. 2008. (Living on the Edge Ser.). (Illus.). 24p. (J). (gr. 2-5). lib. bdg. 22.60 (978-1-4042-4219-7(6)) Rosen Publishing Group, Inc., The.

Merlin, Hope & Green, Naima. An Insider's Guide to Surfing, 1 vol. 2015. (ENG.). 48p. (YA). 30.25 (978-1-4777-8081-7(5), Rosen Reference) Rosen Publishing Group, Inc., The.

Nardo, Don. Surfing. Gale, ed. 2014. (Science Behind Sports Ser.). (ENG., Illus.). 128p. (gr. 7-10). lib. bdg. 39.40 (978-1-4205-1156-7(4), Lucent Bks.) Cengage Gale.

Orr, Tamra B. Extreme Skysurfing. 2013. 48p. (J). (gr. 4-8). 29.93 (978-1-60870-232-9(4)) Cavendish Square Publishing.

Otfinoski, Steven. Extreme Surfing. 2011. (Sports on the Edge Ser.). (Illus.). 48p. (J). (gr. 6). 29.93 (978-1-60870-231-2(6)) Marshall Cavendish GBR. Dist: Marshall Cavendish Corp.

Pierce, Terry. Surfing A to Z Coloring Book. Kofsky, Kristen, illus. 2004. 24p. pap. 4.95 (978-1-57306-178-0(6)) Bess Pr., Inc.

Poolos, Jamie. Surfing & Wind Surfing. 2015. (Sports to the Extreme Ser.). (ENG., Illus.). 48p. (J). (gr. 5-6). 30.25 (978-1-4994-3573-3(8), Rosen Central) Rosen Publishing Group, Inc., The.

Reed, Kevin. The Dog's Guide to Surfing: Hanging Ten with Man's Best Friend. Crump, A. K., ed. 2005. (ENG., Illus.). 128p. (gr. 5-18). pap. (978-0-9674898-7-2(3)) Temmen, Edition, Horst Temmen.

Sandler, Michael. Super Surfers. 2009. (X-Moves Ser.). (Illus.). 24p. (YA). (gr. 2-5). lib. bdg. 22.61 (978-1-59716-953-0(6)) Bearport Publishing Co., Inc.

Scherer, Randy. Kelly Slater. Greenhaven Press Staff, ed. 2012. (People in the News Ser.). (ENG., Illus.). 128p. (gr. 7-10). lib. bdg. 39.40 (978-1-4205-0757-7(5), Lucent Bks.) Cengage Gale.

Smalley, Carol Parenzan. Ride the Giant Waves with Garrett Mcnamara. 2006. (Extreme Sports Ser.). (Illus.). 32p. (J). (gr. 1-4). lib. bdg. 25.70 (978-1-58415-486-0(1)) Mitchell Lane Pubs., Inc.

Smith, Ryan A. Surfboards. 2006. 32p. (gr. 3-5). 22.45 (978-1-4103-0719-4(0), Blackbirch Pr., Inc.) Cengage Gale.

—Surfboards: From Start to Finish. Howard, Devon, photos by. 2006. (Made in the U. S. A. Ser.). (ENG., Illus.). 32p. (J). (gr. 3-7). lib. bdg. 25.65 (978-1-4103-0728-6(X), Blackbirch Pr., Inc.) Cengage Gale.

Surfing. 2004. (I-Quest Ser.). (J). (978-1-84229-743-6(0)) Top That! Publishing PLC.

Timblin, Stephen. Kitesurfing. 2012. (Extreme Sports Ser.). (ENG., Illus.). 32p. (J). (gr. 2-5). lib. bdg. 28.50 (978-1-60973-183-0(2), 201127) Child's World, Inc., The.

Wiseman, Blaine. Surfing. 2015. (J). (978-1-4896-4299-8(4)) Weigl Pubs., Inc.

—Surfing: X Games. 2008. (Extreme Ser.). (Illus.). 32p. (J). (gr. 4-6). pap. 9.95 (978-1-59036-917-3(3)); lib. bdg. 26.00 (978-1-59036-916-6(5)) Weigl Pubs., Inc.

Yomtov, Nel. The Science of a Cutback. 2015. (21st Century Skills Library: Full-Speed Sports Ser.). (ENG., Illus.). 32p. (J). (gr. 4-7). 29.93 (978-1-63362-581-5(8), 206508) Cherry Lake Publishing.

Young, Jeff C. Shooting the Curl: Surfing, 1 vol. 2011. (Adrenaline Adventure Ser.). (ENG., Illus.). 32p. (YA). (gr. 3-6). 27.07 (978-1-61613-552-2(2)) ABDO Publishing Co.

SURFING—FICTION

Alexander, Kwame. Surf's Up. Miyares, Daniel, illus. 2016. (ENG.). 32p. (J). 17.95 (978-0-7358-4220-5(5)) North-South Bks., Inc.

Allen, J. Kent. Embritt Waters & the Mark of the Rattlesnake. 2006. 229p. (J). pap. 14.95 (978-0-7414-2769-4(9)) Infinity Publishing.

Apte, Sunita. Ride the Whale: A Surfer Tall Tale. Reed, Kyle, illus. 2006. 16p. (J). pap. (978-0-439-74638-0(8)) Scholastic, Inc.

The Beach by the Bay: Tanner & Kai Go Surfing. 2007. (Illus.). 24p. (J). 15.95 (978-0-9796039-0-7(0)) Sandbridge Sons Publishing.

Bo, Ben. Skullcrack. (ENG.). 207p. (J). pap. (978-0-7475-4220-9(1)) Bloomsbury Publishing Plc GBR. Dist: Penguin Canada.

—Skullcrack. 2003. (ENG.). 168p. (YA). (gr. 5-12). pap. 6.95 (978-0-8225-3311-5(1)) Lerner Publishing Group.

Bundschuh, Rick. Burned, 1 vol. 2014. (Faithgirlz / Soul Surfer Ser.). (ENG.). 128p. (J). pap. 7.99 (978-0-310-74555-6(1)) Zonderkidz.

—Clash, 1 vol. 2014. (Faithgirlz / Soul Surfer Ser.). (ENG.). 128p. (J). pap. 7.99 (978-0-310-74582-2(9)) Zonderkidz.

Choyce, Lesley. Wave Warrior, 1 vol. 2007. (Orca Soundings Ser.). (ENG.). (YA). (gr. 8-12). 112p. 14.95 (978-1-55143-649-4(3)); 128p. per. 9.95 (978-1-55143-647-0(7)) Orca Bk. Pubs. USA.

Christopher, Matt. Catching Waves. 2006. (ENG.). 128p. (J). (gr. 3-7). per. 15.99 (978-0-316-05848-3(3)) Little, Brown Bks. for Young Readers.

Condon, Bill. Pipeline News, 1 vol. rev. ed. 2013. (Fiction Readers Ser.). (ENG., Illus.). 32p. (J). (gr. 3-3). pap. 8.99 (978-1-4333-5635-3(X)) Shell Educational Publishing.

Connor, James. Surfing Summer. 2011. 138p. 22.99 (978-1-4568-8368-3(2)); pap. 15.99 (978-1-4568-8367-6(4)) Xlibris Corp.

—Surfing Summers. 2011. 138p. 22.99 (978-1-4568-9545-7(1)); pap. 15.99 (978-1-4568-9544-0(3)) Xlibris Corp.

Dalton, Michelle. Pulled Under. 2014. (Sixteenth Summer Ser.). (ENG., Illus.). 288p. (YA). (gr. 7). pap. 9.99 (978-1-4814-0700-7(7), Simon Pulse) Simon Pulse.

Dean, James. Pete at the Beach. Dean, James, illus. 2013. (My First I Can Read Ser.). (ENG., Illus.). 32p. (J). (gr. -1-3). 16.99 (978-0-06-211073-2(X)) HarperCollins Pubs.

deGroat, Diane. Gilbert, the Surfer Dude. deGroat, Diane, illus. 2010. (I Can Read Level 2 Ser.). (ENG., Illus.). 32p. (J). (gr. k-3). pap. 3.99 (978-0-06-125213-6(1)) HarperCollins Pubs.

—Gilbert, the Surfer Dude. 2009. (Illus.). 31p. (J). lib. bdg. 18.89 (978-0-06-125212-9(3)) HarperCollins Pubs.

Dempsey, Kristy. Surfer Chick. Cole, Henry, illus. 2012. (ENG.). 32p. (J). (gr. -1-k). 16.95 (978-1-4197-0188-7(6), Abrams Bks. for Young Readers) Abrams, Inc.

Denton, Terry. The Obelisk of Eeeno. 2004. (Storymaze Ser.). (ENG., Illus.). 144p. (J). (gr. 4-8). pap. 11.99 (978-1-74114-089-7(7)) Allen & Unwin AUS. Dist: Independent Pubs. Group.

Garcia, Jeffrey. Santa Claus & the Molokai Mules. 2009. 32p. 17.95 (978-0-9840942-0-2(2)) Garcia, Jeffrey.

Germain, Kerry. Kimo's Surfing Lesson. Moore, Nicolette, illus. 2007. 48p. (gr. k-5). (J). 12.95 (978-0-9705889-5-1(X)); pap. 12.95 (978-0-9705889-3-7(3)) Island Paradise Publishing.

Glass, Lisa. Air. 2016. (Blue Ser.: 2). (ENG.). 320p. 16.99 (978-1-68144-512-0(3)) Quercus NA.

—Blue. 2015. (Blue Ser.: 1). (ENG.). 352p. (J). (gr. 7-17). 16.99 (978-1-62365-414-6(9), Quercus) Quercus NA.

Gorman, Chris. Indi Surfs. 2015. (ENG., Illus.). 40p. (J). (gr. -1-3). 16.95 (978-1-57687-765-4(5), powerHouse Bks.) powerHouse Cultural Entertainment, Inc.

Hall, Susan & Hall, Susan, illus. Surf That Wave! 2006. (Backyardigans Ser.). (ENG.). 24p. (J). (gr. -1-3). pap. 3.99 (978-1-4169-1482-2(X), Simon Spotlight/Nickelodeon) Simon Spotlight/Nickelodeon.

Harvey, Paul & Pearson Education Staff. Surfer! 2nd ed. 2008. (ENG.). 32p. pap. 11.99 (978-1-4058-6969-0(0)) Pearson Education.

Hemphill, Rick, illus. The Adventures of Kirra & Rincon: Li'l Kids, Big Waves. 2005. 32p. (J). 17.99 (978-0-9766408-0-6(5)) Kerr, Justin & Shelley.

Hoeffner, Karol Ann. Surf Ed. 2010. (ENG.). 288p. (YA). (gr. 9). pap. 13.99 (978-1-4424-1418-1(9), Simon Pulse) Simon Pulse.

Irwin, Bindi, et al. Surfing with Turtles: Bindi Wildlife Adventures. 2013. (Bindi's Wildlife Adventures Ser.: 8). (ENG.). 112p. (J). (gr. 3-6). pap. 4.99 (978-1-4022-8094-8(7), Sourcebooks Jabberwocky) Sourcebooks, Inc.

Kearins, Krit. Surf's up Penny. 2009. (978-1-61658-332-3(0)) Independent Pub.

Kuperman, Marina. Turtle Feet, Surfer's Beat. 2007. 164p. (J). pap. 9.99 (978-0-9801109-0-6(4)) Kuperman, Marina.

Larose, Melinda. Surfin' Turf. 2014. (World of Reading Ser.). (J). lib. bdg. 13.55 (978-0-606-34108-0(0), Turtleback) Turtleback Bks.

Leblanc, A. J. Donnie & His First Surf Lesson. 2012. 20p. pap. 24.95 (978-1-4626-8646-9(X)) PublishAmerica, Inc.

MacPherson, D. R. The First Wave. 2009. 68p. pap. 21.00 (978-1-60860-456-2(X), Eloquent Bks.) Strategic Book Publishing & Rights Agency (SBPRA).

—The Sport of Kings. 2011. 92p. pap. 25.00 (978-1-60911-294-3(6), Strategic Bk. Publishing) Strategic Book Publishing & Rights Agency (SBPRA).

Maddox, Jake. Beach Bully, 1 vol. Aburtov, illus. 2013. (Jake Maddox Sports Stories Ser.). (ENG.). 72p. (gr. 2-3). pap. 5.95 (978-1-4342-6206-6(5)) Stone Arch Bks.

—Beach Bully. 2013. (Jake Maddox Sports Stories Ser.). (ENG.). 72p. (gr. 2-3). pap. 35.70 (978-1-4342-6234-9(0)) Stone Arch Bks.

—Beach Bully, 1 vol. Aburtov, Jesus, illus. 2013. (Jake Maddox Sports Stories Ser.). (ENG.). 72p. (gr. 2-3). lib. bdg. 25.32 (978-1-4342-5973-8(0)) Stone Arch Bks.

—Shark Attack! Tiffany, Sean, illus. 2009. (Jake Maddox Sports Stories Ser.). (ENG.). 72p. (gr. 2-3). 25.32 (978-1-4342-1210-8(6)) Stone Arch Bks.

—Storm Surfer, 1 vol. Mourning, Tuesday, illus. 2008. (Jake Maddox Girl Sports Stories Ser.). (ENG.). 72p. (gr. 2-3). lib. bdg. 25.32 (978-1-4342-0471-4(5)); per. 5.95 (978-1-4342-0521-6(5)) Stone Arch Bks.

—Windsurfing Winner, 1 vol. Tiffany, Sean, illus. 2011. (Jake Maddox Sports Stories Ser.). (ENG.). 72p. (gr. 2-3). lib. bdg. 25.32 (978-1-4342-2535-1(6)) Stone Arch Bks.

Man-Kong, Mary. Barbie in a Mermaid Tale. Golden Books Staff, illus. 2010. (Pictureback(R) Ser.). (ENG.). 16p. (J). (gr. -1-2). pap. 3.99 (978-0-375-85735-5(4), Random Hse. Bks. for Young Readers) Random Hse. Children's Bks.

Marie, Cynthia. Sister Aggie Goes Surfing. 2012. 50p. pap. 20.95 (978-1-4497-5404-4(X), WestBow Pr.) Author Solutions, Inc.

McIntosh, Kenneth. Close-Up: Forensic Photography. 2009. (J). pap. 24.95 (978-1-4222-1455-8(9)) Mason Crest.

—Close-Up: Forensic Photography, 5 vols. Sanborn, Casey, illus. 2007. (Crime Scene Club Ser.: Bk. 5). 144p. (YA). (gr. 9-12). lib. bdg. 24.95 (978-1-4222-0251-7(8)) Mason Crest.

McKinley, Ryan. The Pirate Bride. 2010. 105p. 21.95 (978-1-4327-5546-1(3)); (Illus.). pap. 14.95 (978-1-4327-5545-4(5)) Outskirts Pr., Inc.

Mindes, Erin. Missy Moo, Where Are You off to? Surfing Adventure. Harston, David, illus. 2011. (J). 14.95 (978-0-9841558-8-0(0)) Tasty Minstrel Games.

Morecroft, Judith. Malu Kangaroo. Bancroft, Bronwyn, illus. 2008. (ENG.). 40p. (J). (gr. k-2). pap. 11.95 (978-1-921272-51-6(1)) Little Hare Bks. AUS. Dist: Independent Pubs. Group.

Morgan, Melissa J. Sunrise. 2009. (Summer Confidential Ser.: 1). (ENG.). 240p. (J). (gr. 5-6). pap. 7.99 (978-0-448-44988-3(9), Grosset & Dunlap) Penguin Young Readers Group.

—Twilight. 2009. (Summer Confidential Ser.: 3). (ENG.). 240p. (J). (gr. 5-18). pap. 7.99 (978-0-448-44990-6(0), Grosset & Dunlap) Penguin Young Readers Group.

Murakami, Jon & BeachHouse Publishing. Geckos Surf. 2007. (ENG.). 16p. (J). (gr. -1-5). bds. 7.95 (978-1-933067-22-3(5)) Beachhouse Publishing, LLC.

Neri, Greg. Surf Mules. 2104. (ENG.). 288p. (YA). pap. (978-1-4677-4238-2(4)) Lerner Publishing Group.

Noël, Alyson. Forever Summer. 2011. (ENG.). 464p. (YA). (gr. 8-12). pap. 9.99 (978-0-312-60439-4(4), 9780312604394, St. Martin's Griffin) St. Martin's Pr.

—Laguna Cove. 2006. (ENG.). 224p. (YA). (gr. 8-13). pap. 9.99 (978-0-312-34869-4(X), 9780312348694, St. Martin's Griffin) St. Martin's Pr.

Priebe, Val. I Only Surf Online, 1 vol. Santillan, Jorge H., illus. 2011. (Sports Illustrated Kids Victory School Superstars Ser.). (ENG.). 56p. (gr. 1-3). pap. 5.95 (978-1-4342-3394-3(4)); lib. bdg. 26.65 (978-1-4342-2233-6(0)) Stone Arch Bks.

Publications International Ltd. Staff. Interactive Sound Surfs Up. 2007. 24p. (J). 16.98 (978-1-4127-6829-0(2), PIL Kids) Publications International, Ltd.

Renaud, Andrea. Sammy the Surfing Pelican Meets Steve the Surf Guru. l.t. ed. 2003. (Illus.). 32p. (J). per. (978-0-9717041-3-8(9)) A Happy Friend, Inc.

Roddy, Lee. The Mystery of the Wild Surfer. 2006. (Ladd Family Adventure Ser.: Vol. 6). (Illus.). 135p. (J). (gr. 4-7). per. 7.99 (978-0-88062-255-4(5)) Mott Media.

Ross, Jeff. Dawn Patrol, 1 vol. 2012. (Orca Sports Ser.). (ENG.). 160p. (YA). (gr. 6-10). pap. 9.95 (978-1-4598-0062-5(1)) Orca Bk. Pubs. USA.

Sattler, Jennifer. Pig Kahuna. (Pig Kahuna Ser.). (ENG., Illus.). (J). (gr. -1-1). 2014. 30p. bds. 7.99 (978-1-61963-196-0(2), 9781619631960) 2011. 32p. 16.99 (978-1-59990-635-5(X), 9781599906355) Bloomsbury Publishing USA. (Bloomsbury USA Childrens).

Spaziante, Patrick, illus. OLIVIA Learns to Surf. 2010. (Olivia TV Tie-In Ser.). (ENG.). 12p. (J). (gr. -1-1). bds. 6.99 (978-1-4424-0330-7(6), Simon Spotlight) Simon Spotlight.

Starfall Education. Surfer Girl. Starfall Education, ed. 2004. (ENG., Illus.). 8p. (J). pap. (978-1-59577-014-1(3)) Starfall Education.

Stilton, Geronimo. Surfing for Secrets. 2015. (Geronimo Stilton Cavemice Ser.: 8). lib. bdg. 17.20 (978-0-606-37058-5(7)) Turtleback Bks.

Terrell, Brandon, et al. Riptide Pride, 1 vol. 2011. (Sports Illustrated Kids Graphic Novels Ser.). (ENG., Illus.). 56p. (gr. 2-3). pap. 7.19 (978-1-4342-3399-8(5)); lib. bdg. 26.65 (978-1-4342-2238-1(1)) Stone Arch Bks.

Tsong, Jing Jing. Sam Surfs. 2010. 20p. (J). pap. 7.95 (978-1-933067-33-9(0)) Beachhouse Publishing, LLC.

Vermeulen, Mariska. Kaila & Kahuna Finger Puppet Book. van de Liejgraaf, Deborah, illus. 2016. (My Best Friend & Me Ser.). (ENG.). 10p. (J). (gr. -1-k). bds. 6.99 (978-0-7641-6832-1(0)) Barron's Educational Series, Inc.

Wahn, Udo. Cabo & Coral Go Surfing! Lyn, Jami, illus. 2007. 48p. (J). pap. 17.95 (978-0-615-17598-0(8)) Caboandcoral.com.

SURGEONS

Bankston, John. Joseph Lister & the Story of Antiseptics. 2004. (Uncharted, Unexplored, & Unexplained Ser.). (Illus.). 48p. (J). (gr. 4-8). lib. bdg. 29.95 (978-1-58415-262-0(1)) Mitchell Lane Pubs., Inc.

Benge, Janet & Benge, Geoff. Ben Carson: A Chance at Life. 2014. (ENG., Illus.). 192p. (YA). pap. 9.99 *(978-1-62486-034-8(6))* Emerald Bks.

—Paul Brand: Helping Hands. 2011. (ENG.). (YA). pap. 9.99 *(978-1-57658-536-8(0))* YWAM Publishing.

Hooks, Gwendolyn. Tiny Stitches: The Life of Medical Pioneer Vivien Thomas. Bootman, Colin, illus. 2016. (ENG.). 32p. (J). (gr. 2-6). 17.95 *(978-1-62014-156-4(6))* Lee & Low Bks., Inc.

Lewis, Gregg & Lewis, Deborah Shaw. Gifted Hands: The Ben Carson Story, 1 vol. rev. ed. 2014. (ZonderKidz Biography Ser.). (ENG., Illus.). 176p. (J). pap. 7.99 *(978-0-310-73830-5(X))* Zonderkidz.

Lim, Bridget & Ramen, Fred. Albucasis: The Father of Modern Surgery. 2016. (Physicians, Scientists, & Mathematicians of the Islamic World Ser.). 112p. (gr. 6-6). 37.10 *(978-1-5081-7140-9(8))* Rosen Publishing Group, Inc., The.

Marsh, Carole. Antonia C. Novello: First Female U. S. Surgeon General: First Female U. S. Surgeon General. 2003. 12p. (gr. k-4). 2.95 *(978-0-635-02139-7(0))* Gallopade International.

—Charles Drew: Dedicated Doctor. 2004. (1000 Readers Ser.). (Illus.). 12p. (J). (gr. k-4). per. 2.95 *(978-0-635-02528-9(0))* Gallopade International.

Murphy, Jim. Breakthrough! How Three People Saved Blue Babies & Changed Medicine Forever. 2015. (ENG., Illus.). 144p. (J). (gr. 5-7). 18.99 *(978-0-547-82183-2(2)*, Clarion Bks.) Houghton Mifflin Harcourt Trade & Reference Pubs.

Ramen, Fred. Albucasis (Abu al-Qasim Al-Zahrawi) Renowned Muslim Surgeon of the Tenth Century. 2009. (Great Muslim Philosophers & Scientists of the Middle Ages Ser.). 112p. (gr. 6-6). 66.50 *(978-1-61513-178-5(7)*, Rosen Reference) Rosen Publishing Group, Inc., The.

Saxby, Claire. Meet Weary Dunlop. Lord, Jeremy, illus. (ENG.). 32p. (J). 2016. (gr. k-2). 14.99 *(978-0-85798-587-3(6))* 2015. (gr. -1-k). 21.99 *(978-0-85798-536-1(1))* Random Hse. Australia AUS. Dist: Independent Pubs. Group.

Schraff, Anne. Charles Drew: Pioneer in Medicine. 2003. (Famous Inventors Ser.). (Illus.). 32p. (J). (gr. 1-4). lib. bdg. 22.60 *(978-0-7660-2008-5(8))* Enslow Pubs., Inc.

—Dr. Charles Drew: Blood Bank Innovator. 2003. (African-American Biographies Ser.). (Illus.). 112p. (J). (gr. 6-12). lib. bdg. 27.94 *(978-0-7660-2117-4(3))* Enslow Pubs., Inc.

—The Life of Dr. Charles Drew: Blood Bank Innovator. 2015. (Legendary African Americans Ser.). 96p. (J). (gr. 6-12). pap. 10.95 *(978-0-7660-6266-5(X))* Enslow Pubs., Inc.

Schraff, Anne E. The Life of Dr. Charles Drew: Blood Bank Innovator. 2015. (Legendary African Americans Ser.). 96p. (J). (gr. 6-12). 27.94 *(978-0-7660-6265-8(1))* Enslow Pubs., Inc.

Stoltman, Joan. Gareth's Guide to Becoming a Brain Surgeon. 2017. (Gareth Guides to an Extraordinary Life Ser.). 32p. (J). (gr. 4-5). pap. 63.00 ***(978-1-5382-0334-7(0))*** Stevens, Gareth Publishing LLLP.

Venezia, Mike. Charles Drew: Doctor Who Got the World Pumped up to Donate Blood. Venezia, Mike, illus. 2009. (Getting to Know the World's Greatest Inventors & Scientists Ser.). (ENG., Illus.). 32p. (J). (gr. 3-4). pap. 6.95 *(978-0-531-21334-6(X)*, Children's Pr.); (gr. 2-5). 28.00 *(978-0-531-23725-0(7))* Scholastic Library Publishing.

Wyckoff, Edwin Brit. The African-American Heart Surgery Pioneer: The Genius of Vivien Thomas. 2013. (Genius Inventors & Their Great Ideas Ser.). 48p. (J). (gr. 3-4). pap. 8.95 *(978-1-4644-0210-4(8))*; (Illus.). 25.27 *(978-0-7660-4140-0(9))* Enslow Pubs., Inc. (Enslow Elementary).

—Heart Man: Vivien Thomas, African-American Heart Surgery Pioneer. 2007. (Genius at Work! Great Inventor Biographies Ser.). (Illus.). 32p. (J). (gr. 3-7). lib. bdg. 23.94 *(978-0-7660-2849-4(6)*, Enslow Elementary) Enslow Pubs., Inc.

SURGERY

Alagna, Magdalena. Everything You Need to Know about the Dangers of Cosmetic Surgery. (Need to Know Library). 64p. 2009. (gr. 5-5). 58.50 *(978-1-60854-093-8(6))* 2005. (Illus.). (YA). (gr. 4-6). lib. bdg. 31.95 *(978-0-8239-3552-9(3))* Rosen Publishing Group, Inc., The.

Alter, Judy. Surgery. 2008. (21st Century Skills Innovation Library: Innovation in Medicine Ser.). (ENG., Illus.). 32p. (gr. 4-8). lib. bdg. 28.50 *(978-1-60279-224-1(0)*, 200155) Cherry Lake Publishing.

Apel, Melanie Ann. Let's Talk about When You Have to Get Stitches. 2009. (Let's Talk Library). 24p. (gr. 2-3). 42.50 *(978-1-60853-447-0(2)*, PowerKids Pr.) Rosen Publishing Group, Inc., The.

Bankston, John. Joseph Lister & the Story of Antiseptics. 2004. (Uncharted, Unexplored, & Unexplained Ser.). (Illus.). 48p. (J). (gr. 4-8). lib. bdg. 29.95 *(978-1-58415-262-0(1))* Mitchell Lane Pubs., Inc.

Cobb, Allan B. The Bionic Human. 2009. (Library of Future Medicine Ser.). 64p. (gr. 5-5). 58.50 *(978-1-60853-631-3(9))* Rosen Publishing Group, Inc., The.

Galliker, Leslie. Joint Replacements, 1 vol. 2013. (Medical Marvels Ser.). (ENG.). 112p. (J). (gr. 6-12). lib. bdg. 35.64 *(978-1-61783-903-0(5)*, Essential Library) ABDO Publishing Co.

Giddens, Sandra. Future Techniques in Surgery. 2009. (Library of Future Medicine Ser.). 64p. (gr. 5-5). 58.50 *(978-1-60853-630-6(0))* Rosen Publishing Group, Inc., The.

Harris, Michael C. Spare Parts for People. 2010. (Cool Science Ser.). 48p. (J). (gr. 3-6). 28.50 *(978-1-60870-080-6(1))* Marshall Cavendish GBR. Dist: Marshall Cavendish Corp.

Hatkoff, Juliana, et al. Winter's Tail: How One Little Dolphin Learned to Swim Again. 2009. (Winter's Tail Ser.). (ENG.). 40p. (J). (gr. -1-3). 16.99 *(978-0-545-12335-8(6)*, Scholastic Pr.) Scholastic, Inc.

Herrington, Lisa M. I Need Stitches. 2015. (Rookie Read-About(tm) Health Ser.). (ENG., Illus.). 32p. (J). lib. bdg. 25.00 *(978-0-531-21039-0(1))* Scholastic Library Publishing.

Knight, Geof. Cosmetic Procedures, 1 vol. 2011. (Hot Topics Ser.). (ENG.). 56p. (gr. 7-8). 34.65 *(978-1-4329-4868-9(7)*, NA-h) Heinemann-Raintree.

Libal, Autumn. Can I Change the Way I Look? A Teen's Guide to the Health Implications of Cosmetic Surgery, Makeovers, & Beyond. 2006. (Science of Health Ser.). (Illus.). 128p. (YA). 24.95 *(978-1-59084-843-2(8))* Mason Crest.

Lusted, Marcia Amidon. Cosmetic Surgery, 1 vol. 2009. (Essential Viewpoints Set 4 Ser.). (ENG., Illus.). 112p. (J). (gr. 6-12). lib. bdg. 35.64 *(978-1-60453-530-3(X))* ABDO Publishing Co.

May, Erica. Emerson Learns about Surgery. Millward, Hayley, illus. 2013. (ENG.). (J). (gr. -1-3). 14.95 *(978-1-62086-279-7(4))* Mascot Bks., Inc.

Murphy, Jim. Breakthrough! How Three People Saved Blue Babies & Changed Medicine Forever. 2015. (ENG., Illus.). 144p. (J). (gr. 5-7). 18.99 *(978-0-547-82183-2(2)*, Clarion Bks.) Houghton Mifflin Harcourt Trade & Reference Pubs.

Silverstein, Virginia. Handy Health Guide to Bites & Stings. 2013. (Handy Health Guides). 48p. (J). (gr. 5-12). pap. 8.95 *(978-1-4644-0485-6(2))* Enslow Pubs., Inc.

—Handy Health Guide to Burns & Blisters. 2013. (Handy Health Guides). 48p. (J). (gr. 5-12). pap. 8.95 *(978-1-4644-0487-0(9))* Enslow Pubs., Inc.

Stearman, Kaye. The Debate about Cosmetic Surgery. 2010. (Ethical Debates Ser.). (ENG.). 48p. (YA). lib. bdg. 29.25 *(978-1-4358-9650-5(5)*, Rosen Reference) Rosen Publishing Group, Inc., The.

Winkler, Kathleen. Cosmetic Surgery for Teens: Choices & Consequences. 2003. (Teen Issues Ser.). (Illus.). 64p. (J). lib. bdg. 22.60 *(978-0-7660-1957-7(8))* Enslow Pubs., Inc.

SURGERY—VOCATIONAL GUIDANCE

Bailey, Diane. Brain Surgeons. 2008. (Extreme Careers Ser.). (Illus.). 62p. (YA). (gr. 5-9). lib. bdg. 31.95 *(978-1-4042-1787-4(8))* Rosen Publishing Group, Inc., The.

Ellis, Catherine. Planes. 2007. (Mega Military Machines Ser.). (Illus.). 24p. (J). (gr. 3-7). lib. bdg. 22.60 *(978-1-4042-3667-7(8))* Rosen Publishing Group, Inc., The.

Giddens, Sandra & Giddens, Owen. Future Techniques in Surgery. 2005. (Library of Future Medicine Ser.). (Illus.). 64p. (YA). (gr. 7-12). lib. bdg. 31.95 *(978-0-8239-3667-0(8))* Rosen Publishing Group, Inc., The.

SURINAME

Streissguth, Thomas. Suriname in Pictures. 2009. (Visual Geography Series, Second Ser.). (ENG.). 80p. (gr. 5-12). 31.93 *(978-1-57505-964-8(9))* Lerner Publishing Group.

Williams, Colleen Madonna Flood & Flood Williams, Colleen Madonna. Suriname. 2009. (South America Today Ser.). (Illus.). 63p. (J). (gr. 4-7). 21.95 *(978-1-4222-0641-6(6))* Mason Crest.

SURVEYING

see also Geodesy

Marsico, Katie. Levels. 2013. (21st Century Junior Library: Basic Tools Ser.). (ENG.). 24p. (J). (gr. 2-5). 25.64 *(978-1-62431-172-7(5)*, 203008); pap. 12.79 *(978-1-62431-304-2(3)*, 203010) Cherry Lake Publishing.

Merrill, Amy French. A Day in the Life of a Colonial Surveyor. 2009. (Library of Living & Working in Colonial Times Ser.). 24p. (gr. 3-3). 42.50 *(978-1-60853-740-2(4)*, PowerKids Pr.) Rosen Publishing Group, Inc., The.

Nelson, Robin. What Does a Level Do? 2012. (First Step Nonfiction - Tools at Work Ser.). (ENG., Illus.). 24p. (gr. k-2). lib. bdg. 23.93 *(978-0-7613-8981-1(4)*, Lerner Pubns.) Lerner Publishing Group.

Petersen, Christine. The Surveyor. 2010. (Colonial People Ser.). 48p. (gr. 3-18). 29.93 *(978-0-7614-4805-1(5))* Marshall Cavendish Corp.

SURVIVAL

see also Wilderness Survival

Adams, Simon. Titanic. 2014. (DK Eyewitness Bks.). (ENG.). 72p. (J). (gr. 3-7). pap. 9.99 *(978-1-4654-2057-2(6)*, DK Children) Dorling Kindersley Publishing, Inc.

Ashcraft, Tami Oldham & McGearhart, Susea. Red Sky in Mourning: A True Story of Love, Loss, & Survival at Sea. 2003. (ENG.). 240p. (gr. 8-17). pap. 18.99 *(978-0-7868-8676-0(5))* Hyperion Pr.

Bailey, Diane. Survival Skills, Vol. 10. 2016. (Great Outdoors! Ser.). (Illus.). 48p. (J). (gr. 5). 20.95 *(978-1-4222-3574-4(2))* Mason Crest.

Bell, Samantha. How to Survive Being Lost at Sea. 2015. (Survival Guides). (ENG.). 24p. (J). (gr. 2-5). 27.07 *(978-1-60973-159-5(X)*, 208795) Child's World, Inc., The.

Benge, Janet & Benge, Geoff. Louis Zamperini: Redemption. 2014. (ENG.). 218p. (YA). pap. 9.99 *(978-1-62486-049-2(4))* Emerald Bks.

Blake, Kevin. Lost in the Antarctic. 2014. (Stranded! Ser.). (ENG.). 32p. (J). (gr. 2-7). lib. bdg. 26.60 *(978-1-62724-289-9(9))* Bearport Publishing Co., Inc.

Bond, Rebecca. Out of the Woods: A True Story of an Unforgettable Event. 2015. (ENG., Illus.). 40p. (J). (gr. k-4). 17.99 *(978-0-374-38077-9(5)*, 9780374380779, Farrar, Straus & Giroux (BYR)) Farrar, Straus & Giroux.

Borgenicht, David & Heimberg, Justin. The Worst-Case Scenario Survival Handbook. 2014. (Worst Case Scenario Survival Handbook Ser.). 128p. (gr. 4-7). 41.35 *(978-1-59920-974-6(8))* Black Rabbit Bks.

Brown, Alex. Secret Missions. 2009. (Difficult & Dangerous Ser.). (J). 28.50 *(978-1-59920-159-7(3))* Black Rabbit Bks.

Brush, Jim & Scarborough, Kate. Extreme Survival. 2012. (Fast Facts Ser.). (Illus.). 32p. (gr. 4-6). pap. 28.50 *(978-1-59771-325-2(2))* Sea-To-Sea Pubns.

Butterfield, Moira. Survive & Thrive: A Pocket Guide to Wilderness Safety Skills. 2016. (ENG.). 112p. (J). (gr. 3-7). pap. 11.99 *(978-1-4380-0842-4(2))* Barron's Educational Series, Inc.

Catel, Patrick. Surviving Stunts & Other Amazing Feats. 2011. (Extreme Survival Ser.). (ENG.). 56p. (gr. 5-5). pap. 9.49 *(978-1-4109-3976-0(6)*, Raintree Freestyle) Heinemann-Raintree.

Champion, Neil. Finding Food & Water. 2012. (Illus.). 32p. (gr. 3-7). pap. 8.95 *(978-1-926722-55-9(8))* Saunders Bk. Co. CAN. Dist: RiverStream Publishing.

—Fire & Cooking. 2012. (Illus.). 32p. (gr. 3-7). pap. 8.95 *(978-1-926722-57-3(4))* Saunders Bk. Co. CAN. Dist: RiverStream Publishing.

—In an Emergency. 2012. (Illus.). 32p. (gr. 3-7). pap. 8.95 *(978-1-926722-58-0(2))* Saunders Bk. Co. CAN. Dist: RiverStream Publishing.

Colson, Rob. Ultimate Survivor Guide for Kids. 2015. (ENG., Illus.). 96p. (J). (gr. 5-8). pap. 9.95 *(978-1-77085-619-6(6)*, 9781770856196) Firefly Bks., Ltd.

Conklin, Wendy. Surviving the Wild Backyard. 2015. (Building Fluency Through Reader's Theater Ser.). (ENG., Illus.). 32p. (gr. 4-4). pap. 7.99 *(978-1-4938-1290-5(4))* Teacher Created Materials, Inc.

Cook, Peter & Salariya, David. Sail on a 19th-Century Whaling Ship! Grisly Tasks You'd Rather Not Do. Antram, David, illus. 2004. (You Wouldn't Want to Ser.). (ENG.). (J). 29.00 *(978-0-531-12356-0(1))* Scholastic Library Publishing.

Currie, Stephen. Escapes from Man-Made Disasters. 2003. (Great Escapes Ser.). (ENG., Illus.). 112p. (J). pap. 30.85 *(978-1-59018-277-2(4))* Cengage Gale.

—Escapes from Natural Disasters. 2004. (Great Escapes Ser.). (ENG., Illus.). 112p. (J). 30.85 *(978-1-59018-278-9(2)*, Lucent Bks.) Cengage Gale.

Dakota, Heather. Jurassic Survival Guide. 2014. (Illus.). 96p. (J). *(978-0-545-80815-6(4))* Scholastic, Inc.

Doeden, Matt. Can You Survive a Virus Outbreak? An Interactive Doomsday Adventure. 2015. (You Choose: Doomsday Ser.). (ENG., Illus.). 112p. (gr. 3-4). lib. bdg. 31.99 *(978-1-4914-5851-8(8)*, You Choose Bks.) Capstone Press of Coughlan Cos.

—Can You Survive Extreme Mountain Climbing? An Interactive Survival Adventure, 1 vol. 2012. (You Choose: Survival Ser.). (ENG., 112p. (gr. 3-4). Illus.). pap. 6.95 *(978-1-4296-9478-0(5))*; pap. 41.70 *(978-1-4296-9479-7(3))*; (Illus.). lib. bdg. 31.99 *(978-1-4296-8583-2(2))* Capstone Press of Coughlan Cos. (You Choose Bks.).

—Can You Survive the Desert? An Interactive Survival Adventure, 1 vol. 2012. (You Choose: Survival Ser.). (ENG.). 112p. (gr. 3-4). pap. 6.95 *(978-1-4296-7995-4(6))*; 31.99 *(978-1-4296-7543-7(8))*; pap. 41.70 *(978-1-4296-8479-8(8))* Capstone Press of Coughlan Cos. (You Choose Bks.).

—You Choose: Survival. 2012. (You Choose: Survival Ser.). (ENG.). 112p. (gr. 3-4). 63.98 *(978-1-4296-9185-7(9))*; pap. 13.90 *(978-1-4296-9491-9(2))*; pap. 333.60 *(978-1-4296-9483-4(1))*; pap. 55.60 *(978-1-4296-9482-7(3))*; 191.94 *(978-1-4296-8181-0(0))*; 63.98 *(978-1-4296-8180-3(2))*; pap. 250.20 *(978-1-4296-8482-8(8))*; pap. 41.70 *(978-1-4296-8481-1(X))*; pap. 13.90 *(978-1-4296-9514-5(5))* Capstone Press of Coughlan Cos. (You Choose Bks.).

Doeden, Matt & Penn, Jim. Can You Survive the Jungle? An Interactive Survival Adventure, 1 vol. 2011. (You Choose: Survival Ser.). (ENG.). 112p. (gr. 3-4). pap. 6.95 *(978-1-4296-7349-5(4))*; lib. bdg. 31.99 *(978-1-4296-6588-9(2))* Capstone Press of Coughlan Cos. (You Choose Bks.).

Dowswell, P. True Survival Stories. 2004. (True Adventure Stories Ser.). 144p. (J). lib. bdg. 12.95 *(978-1-58086-457-2(0))* EDC Publishing.

Dowswell, Paul. Survival. rev. ed. 2012. (Usborne True Stories Ser.). (Illus.). 144p. (J). (gr. 4-7). per. 4.99 *(978-0-7945-1843-1(5)*, Usborne) EDC Publishing.

Dugan, Christine. Struggle for Survival. 2016. (TIME for KIDS(r) Nonfiction Readers Ser.). 48p. (gr. 6-6). pap. 9.99 *(978-1-4938-3605-5(6))* Teacher Created Materials, Inc.

Earl, C. F. & Vanderhoof, Gabrielle. Army Rangers. 2010. (Special Forces Ser.). (Illus.). 64p. (YA). (gr. 7-18). lib. bdg. 22.95 *(978-1-4222-1838-9(4))* Mason Crest.

Eggleton, Jill. Living to Tell the Tale. 2007. (Connectors Ser.). (gr. 2-5). pap. *(978-1-877453-15-1(3))* Global Education Systems Ltd.

Extreme Survival, 6 vols., Set. Incl. Animal Survival. Hile, Lori. pap. 9.49 *(978-1-4109-3980-7(4))*; Surviving Stunts & Other Amazing Feats. Catel, Patrick. pap. 9.49 *(978-1-4109-3976-0(6))*; (gr. 5-5). (Extreme Survival Ser.). (ENG.). 56p. 2011. Set pap. 18.98 *(978-1-4109-3981-4(2))*; Set lib. bdg. 103.95 *(978-1-4109-3974-6(X))* Heinemann-Raintree. (Raintree Freestyle).

Felix, Rebecca. Duct Tape Survival Gear. 2017. (Create with Duct Tape Ser.). (ENG.). 32p. (J). (gr. 2-5). 12.99 ***(978-1-5124-3855-0(3)***, Lerner Pubns.); 39.99 ***(978-1-5124-3854-3(5)***, Lerner Pubns.); 39.99 ***(978-1-5124-2763-9(2)***, Lerner Pubns.); (Illus.). 26.65 *(978-1-5124-2666-3(0))* Lerner Publishing Group.

Fink, Courtney. Wings, Shells, & Fur: Surviving in the Wild. 2013. (InfoMax Readers Ser.). (ENG.). 24p. (J). (gr. 3-4). pap. 49.50 *(978-1-4777-2520-7(2))*; pap. 8.25 *(978-1-4777-2519-1(9))* Rosen Publishing Group, Inc., The. (Rosen Classroom).

Goldish, Meish. Lost in a Desert. 2015. (Illus.). 32p. (J). lib. bdg. *(978-1-62724-285-1(6))* Bearport Publishing Co., Inc.

—Lost on a Mountain. 2015. (Illus.). 32p. (J). lib. bdg. *(978-1-62724-292-9(9))* Bearport Publishing Co., Inc.

Hanel, Rachael. Can You Survive Antarctica? An Interactive Survival Adventure, 1 vol. 2011. (You Choose: Survival Ser.). (ENG.). 112p. (gr. 3-4). pap. 6.95 *(978-1-4296-7345-7(1))*; pap. 41.70 *(978-1-4296-7346-4(X))*; lib. bdg. 31.99 *(978-1-4296-6589-6(0))* Capstone Press of Coughlan Cos. (You Choose Bks.).

Hanel, Rachael & Lassieur, Allison. You Choose: Survival. 2013. (You Choose: Survival Ser.). (ENG.). 112p. (gr. 3-4). 63.98 *(978-1-4296-9971-6(X))*; pap. 13.90 *(978-1-62065-713-3(9))* Capstone Press of Coughlan Cos. (You Choose Bks.).

Hanel, Rachael, et al. You Choose: Can You Survive Collection. 2017. (You Choose: Survival Ser.). (ENG.). 328p. (gr. 3-4). pap. 9.99 ***(978-1-5157-6198-3(3)***, You Choose Bks.) Capstone Press of Coughlan Cos.

Hanel, Rachael, et al. You Choose: Survival. 2013. (You Choose: Survival Ser.). (ENG.). 112p. (gr. 3-4). 319.90 *(978-1-4296-9963-1(9))*; pap. 417.00 *(978-1-62065-715-7(5))*; pap. 69.50 *(978-1-62065-714-0(7))* Capstone Press of Coughlan Cos. (You Choose Bks.).

Hoena, B. A. Can You Survive an Alien Invasion? An Interactive Doomsday Adventure. Fisher-Johnson, Paul, illus. 2015. (You Choose: Doomsday Ser.). (ENG.). 112p. (gr. 3-4). lib. bdg. 31.99 *(978-1-4914-5853-2(4)*, You Choose Bks.) Capstone Press of Coughlan Cos.

Howell, John. The Life & Adventures of Alexander Selkirk, the Real Robinson Crusoe: A Narrative Founded on Facts. unabr. ed. 2012. (Illus.). 94p. 39.99 *(978-1-4622-8912-7(6))* Repressed Publishing LLC.

Hubbard, Ben. Tornado: Perspectives on Tornado Disasters, 1 vol. 2014. (Disaster Dossiers Ser.). (ENG., Illus.). 56p. (gr. 7-8). pap. 9.49 *(978-1-4846-0189-1(0)*, NA-h) Heinemann-Raintree.

Hunter, Nick. Military Survival, 1 vol. 2011. (Extreme Survival Ser.). (ENG.). 56p. (gr. 5-5). lib. bdg. 34.65 *(978-1-4109-3970-8(7)*, Raintree Freestyle) Heinemann-Raintree.

Jeffrey, Gary. Defying Death at Sea. Riley, Terry, illus. 2010. (Graphic Survival Stories Ser.). 48p. (YA). 58.50 *(978-1-61532-897-0(1))*; (ENG.). pap. 14.05 *(978-1-61532-863-5(7))*; (gr. 5-8). 31.95 *(978-1-4358-3530-6(1))* Rosen Publishing Group, Inc., The. (Rosen Reference).

Kras, Sara Louise. The Hunted: Polar Prey. 2014. 64p. (J). 15.95 *(978-1-62285-080-8(7))* Enslow Pubs., Inc.

Kyi, Tanya Lloyd. When the Worst Happens: Extraordinary Stories of Survival. Parkins, David, illus. 2014. (ENG.). 128p. (J). (gr. 5-8). pap. 14.95 *(978-1-55451-682-7(X)*, 9781554516827) Annick Pr., Ltd. CAN. Dist: Publishers Group West (PGW).

Lacey, Saskia. Hidden by Time. 2015. (Building Fluency Through Reader's Theater Ser.). (ENG., Illus.). 32p. (J). (gr. 4-4). pap. 7.99 *(978-1-4938-1292-9(0))* Teacher Created Materials, Inc.

Lake, G. G. Take Your Pick of Survival Situations. 2017. (Take Your (Equally Horrible) Pick! Ser.). (ENG., Illus.). 32p. (gr. 1-2). lib. bdg. 26.65 *(978-1-5157-4473-3(6)*, Blazers) Capstone Press of Coughlan Cos.

Lassieur, Allison. Can You Survive Being Lost at Sea? An Interactive Survival Adventure. 2013. (You Choose: Survival Ser.). (ENG.). 112p. (gr. 3-4). pap. 41.70 *(978-1-62065-712-6(0)*, You Choose Bks.) Capstone Press of Coughlan Cos.

—Can You Survive the Titanic? An Interactive Survival Adventure, 1 vol. 2011. (You Choose: Survival Ser.). (ENG.). 112p. (gr. 3-4). pap. 6.95 *(978-1-4296-7351-8(6))*; lib. bdg. 31.99 *(978-1-4296-6586-5(6))* Capstone Press of Coughlan Cos. (You Choose Bks.).

Law, Felicia. Caught in the Rapids. 2015. (Science to the Rescue Ser.). (ENG., Illus.). 32p. (J). (gr. 3-6). *(978-0-7787-1674-7(0))* Crabtree Publishing Co.

Lee, Sungju & McClelland, Susan Elizabeth. Every Falling Star: The True Story of How I Survived & Escaped North Korea. 2016. (ENG.). 336p. (J). (gr. 8-17). 16.95 *(978-1-4197-2132-8(1)*, Amulet Bks.) Abrams, Inc.

Lewis, Brenda Ralph. Wilderness Rescue with the U. S. Search & Rescue Task Force. 2004. (Rescue & Prevention Ser.). (Illus.). 96p. (YA). (gr. 7-18). lib. bdg. 22.95 *(978-1-59084-404-5(1))* Mason Crest.

Lewis, Simon. Survival at Sea. 2009. (Difficult & Dangerous Ser.). (J). 28.50 *(978-1-59920-160-3(7))* Black Rabbit Bks.

—Survival at Sea. 2009. (Difficult & Dangerous Ser.). (Illus.). 32p. (J). (gr. 3-7). pap. *(978-1-897563-27-4(2))* Saunders Bk. Co.

Long, David. Survivors: Extraordinary Tales from the Wild & Beyond. Hyndman, Kerry, illus. 2017. (ENG.). 192p. 19.95 ***(978-0-571-31601-4(8))*** Faber & Faber, Inc.

Lusted, Marcia. Surviving Accidents & Crashes. 2014. (Shockzone: True Survival Stories Ser.). (ENG., Illus.). 32p. (gr. 5-8). lib. bdg. 26.60 *(978-1-4677-1439-6(9)*, Lerner Pubns.) Lerner Publishing Group.

Lusted, Marcia Amidon. Surviving Natural Disasters. 2014. (Shockzone: True Survival Stories Ser.). (ENG., Illus.). 32p. (gr. 5-8). lib. bdg. 26.60 *(978-1-4677-1438-9(0)*, Lerner Pubns.) Lerner Publishing Group.

Mack, Molly. Finding Food in the Wild, 01 vols., 1. 2016. (Wilderness Survival Skills Ser.). (ENG., Illus.). 24p. (J). pap. 8.25 *(978-1-5081-4307-9(2)*, PowerKids Pr.) Rosen Publishing Group, Inc., The.

Makerspace Survival. 2017. (Makerspace Survival Ser.). 48p. (gr. 9-10). 181.50 ***(978-1-4994-3405-7(7))***; pap. 70.50 ***(978-1-4994-3410-1(3))*** Rosen Publishing Group, Inc., The. (PowerKids Pr.).

Markle, Sandra. Rescues! 2006. (ENG., Illus.). 88p. (gr. 3-8). lib. bdg. 25.26 *(978-0-8225-3413-6(4))* Lerner Publishing Group.

McCarthy, Tom. Survival: True Stories. 2016. (Mystery & Mayhem Ser.). (ENG.). 128p. (gr. 3). 19.95 *(978-1-61930-476-5(7))* Open City Bks.

McCumiskey, Gavin. Shackleton: A Graphic Account: the Voyage of the James Caird. Butler, David, illus. 2016. (ENG.). 96p. (J). pap. 16.00 *(978-1-84889-281-1(0))* Collins Pr., The IRL. Dist: Dufour Editions, Inc.

McGee, Brenda Holt & Keiser, Debbie Triska. High-Interest Nonfiction: Survivors 3-5. Hoelscher, Wolfgang, ed. 2003. (Skills for Success Ser.). 128p. (gr. 3-5). pap. 16.99 *(978-0-88724-950-1(7)*, CD-4320) Carson-Dellosa Publishing, LLC.

McNab, Chris. Survival at Sea. Carney, John, ed. 2014. (Extreme Survival in the Military Ser.: 12). 64p. (J). (gr. 7-18). lib. bdg. 23.95 *(978-1-4222-3084-8(8))* Mason Crest.

—Surviving Captivity. Carney, John, ed. 2014. (Extreme Survival in the Military Ser.: 12). 64p. (J). (gr. 7-18). lib. bdg. 23.95 *(978-1-4222-3089-3(9))* Mason Crest.

—Surviving the World's Extreme Regions: Desert, Arctic, Mountains, & Jungle. Carney, John, ed. 2014. (Extreme Survival in the Military Ser.: 12). (Illus.). 64p. (J). (gr. 7-18). lib. bdg. 23.95 *(978-1-4222-3092-3(9))* Mason Crest.

Mooney, Carla. Surviving in Cold Places. 2014. (Shockzone: True Survival Stories Ser.). (ENG., Illus.). 32p. (gr. 5-8). lib. bdg. 26.60 *(978-1-4677-1434-1(8)*, Lerner Pubns.) Lerner Publishing Group.

—Surviving in Wild Waters. 2014. (Shockzone: True Survival Stories Ser.). (ENG., Illus.). 32p. (gr. 5-8). lib. bdg. 26.60 *(978-1-4677-1436-5(4)*, Lerner Pubns.) Lerner Publishing Group.

Moss, Wendy & Campbell, Denise. The Survival Guide for Kids in Special Education (and Their Parents) Understanding What Special Ed Is & How It Can Help You. 2017. (ENG., Illus.). 152p. (J). (gr. 3-8). pap. 14.99 ***(978-1-63198-167-8(6))*** Free Spirit Publishing, Inc.

Oliver, Martin. Boys Only: How to Survive Anything! Ecob, Simon, illus. 2012. (Best at Everything Ser.). (ENG.). 64p. (J). (gr. 3-7). pap. 6.99 *(978-0-545-43096-8(8)*, Scholastic Paperbacks) Scholastic, Inc.

Olson, Tod. Lost in the Pacific, 1942: Not a Drop to Drink. 2016. (J). *(978-0-545-92808-3(7))* Scholastic, Inc.

Osborne, Mary Pope & Boyce, Natalie Pope. Magic Tree House Survival Guide. Murdocca, Sal, illus. 2014. (Magic Tree House Ser.). (ENG.). 144p. (J). (gr. 2-5). 12.99 *(978-0-553-49737-3(5)*, Random Hse. Bks. for Young Readers) Random Hse. Children's Bks.

S

Owen, Ruth. Jungle Survival Guide. 2010. (ENG., Illus.). 32p. (J). pap. *(978-0-7787-7555-3(0))*; lib. bdg. *(978-0-7787-7533-1(X))* Crabtree Publishing Co.

Oxlade, Chris. Be a Survivor. Sassin, Eva, illus. 2015. (Go Wild Ser.). (ENG.). 32p. (J). (gr. 3-6). 26.65 *(978-1-4677-6356-1(X))* Lerner Publishing Group.

—Be an Explorer. Sassin, Eva, illus. 2015. (Go Wild Ser.). (ENG.). 32p. (gr. 3-6). (J). lib. bdg. 26.65 *(978-1-4677-6358-5(6))*; 26.65 *(978-1-4677-7223-5(2))* Lerner Publishing Group.

Perish, Patric. Survive an Earthquake. 2017. (Survival Zone Ser.). (ENG., Illus.). 24p. (J). (gr. 3-7). lib. bdg. 25.95 *(978-1-62617-584-6(5)*, Torque Bks.) Bellwether Media.

Perish, Patrick. Survive a Fire. 2017. (Survival Zone Ser.). (ENG., Illus.). 24p. (J). (gr. 3-7). lib. bdg. 25.95 *(978-1-62617-581-5(0)*, Torque Bks.) Bellwether Media.

—Survive a Plane Crash. 2017. (Survival Zone Ser.). (ENG., Illus.). 24p. (J). (gr. 3-7). lib. bdg. 25.95 *(978-1-62617-582-2(9)*, Torque Bks.) Bellwether Media.

—Survive an Avalanche. 2017. (Survival Zone Ser.). (ENG., Illus.). 24p. (J). (gr. 3-7). lib. bdg. 25.95 *(978-1-62617-583-9(7)*, Torque Bks.) Bellwether Media.

—Survive on a Desert Island. 2016. (Survival Zone Ser.). (ENG., Illus.). 24p. (J). (gr. 3-7). 25.95 *(978-1-62617-448-1(2)*, Torque Bks.) Bellwether Media.

Philbrick, Nathaniel. In the Heart of the Sea (Young Readers Edition) 2015. (ENG., Illus.). 208p. (J). (gr. 3-7). 8.99 *(978-1-101-99776-5(1)*, Puffin Books) Penguin Young Readers Group.

Porterfield, Jason. Shipwreck: True Stories of Survival. (Survivor Stories Ser.). 48p. (gr. 5-5). 2009. 53.00 *(978-1-60853-256-8(9)*, Rosen Reference) 2006. (Illus.). (YA). lib. bdg. 29.25 *(978-1-4042-1000-4(8))* Rosen Publishing Group, Inc., The.

Prentzas, G. S. Lost at Sea. 2015. (Illus.). 32p. (J). lib. bdg. *(978-1-62724-290-5(2))* Bearport Publishing Co., Inc.

Prins, Marcel & Steenhuis, Peter Henk. Hidden Like Anne Frank. Watkinson, Laura, tr. from DUT. 2014. (ENG., Illus.). 240p. (J). (gr. 7). 18.99 *(978-0-545-54362-0(2)*, Levine, Arthur A. Bks.) Scholastic, Inc.

Rice, William. ¡Supervivencia! Desierto. 2017. (TIME for Kids en Español - Level 4 Ser.). (SPA., Illus.). 48p. (gr. 4-4). lib. bdg. 31.99 *(978-1-5157-5123-6(6))* Time for Kids Inc AUS. Dist: Capstone Pub.

—¡Supervivencia! Océano. 2017. (TIME for Kids en Español - Level 4 Ser.). (SPA., Illus.). 48p. (gr. 4-4). lib. bdg. 31.99 *(978-1-5157-5124-3(4))* Time for Kids Inc AUS. Dist: Capstone Pub.

Rice, William B. Struggle for Survival. 2016. (TIME for KIDS(r) Nonfiction Readers Ser.). 48p. (gr. 6-6). pap. 9.99 *(978-1-4938-3603-1(X))* Teacher Created Materials, Inc.

Rice, William B. Struggle for Survival: Shelter. 2016. (Time for Kids Nonfiction Readers Ser.). (ENG.). (J). (gr. 5-8). lib. bdg. 20.85 ***(978-0-606-39540-3(7))*** Turtleback Bks.

Ridley, Frances. Lost at Sea. 2008. (Crabtree Contact Ser.). (ENG., Illus.). 32p. (J). (gr. 3-7). lib. bdg. *(978-0-7787-3809-1(4))* Crabtree Publishing Co.

Searl, Duncan. Trapped! 2005. (Illus.). 48p. (J). *(978-0-669-51413-1(6))* Great Source Education Group, Inc.

Spalding, Frank. Plane Crash: True Stories of Survival. (Survivor Stories Ser.). 48p. (gr. 5-5). 2009. 53.00 *(978-1-60853-255-1(0)*, Rosen Reference) 2006. (Illus.). (YA). lib. bdg. 29.25 *(978-1-4042-0999-2(9)*, 1267009) Rosen Publishing Group, Inc., The.

Spilsbury, Richard & Spilsbury, Louise. The Cave of Shadows. 2015. (Science Adventures Ser.). (ENG., Illus.). 32p. (J). (gr. 3-7). 31.35 *(978-1-62588-147-2(9))* Black Rabbit Bks.

—Crushed! 2015. (Science Adventures Ser.). (ENG., Illus.). 32p. (J). (gr. 3-7). 31.35 *(978-1-62588-145-8(2))* Black Rabbit Bks.

—A Cry in the Dark. 2015. (Science Adventures Ser.). (ENG., Illus.). 32p. (J). (gr. 3-7). 31.35 *(978-1-62588-144-1(4))* Black Rabbit Bks.

—Escape the Volcano. 2015. (Science Adventures Ser.). (ENG., Illus.). 32p. (J). (gr. 3-7). 31.35 *(978-1-62588-146-5(0))* Black Rabbit Bks.

—Shipwrecked. 2015. (Science Adventures Ser.). (ENG., Illus.). 32p. (J). (gr. 3-7). 31.35 *(978-1-62588-149-6(5))* Black Rabbit Bks.

—Shipwrecked: Explore Floating & Sinking & Use Science to Survive. 2016. (Illus.). 30p. (J). pap. *(978-1-62588-399-5(4))* Black Rabbit Bks.

—Sparks, Shocks, & Secrets: Explore Electricity & Use Science to Survive. 2016. (Illus.). 30p. (J). pap. *(978-1-62588-400-8(1))* Black Rabbit Bks.

Stride, Lottie & Oliver, Martin. Girls Only: How to Survive Anything! Geremia, Daniela & Ecob, Simon, illus. 2012. (Best at Everything Ser.). (ENG.). 64p. (J). (gr. 3-7). pap. 6.99 *(978-0-545-43095-1(X)*, Scholastic Paperbacks) Scholastic, Inc.

Surviving Disaster. 2015. (Surviving Disaster Ser.). (ENG.). 48p. (J). (gr. 5-6). pap., pap., pap. 423.00 *(978-1-4777-8627-7(9)*, Rosen Central) Rosen Publishing Group, Inc., The.

Survivors: Ordinary People, Extraordinary Circumstances, 13 vols., Set. Incl. Danger in the Deep: Surviving Shark Attacks. Zoldak, Joyce. (YA). 24.95 *(978-1-4222-0451-1(2))*; Enemy Within: Overcoming Cancer & Other Life-Threatening Diseases. Therrien, Patricia. (YA). 24.95 *(978-1-4222-0450-4(2))*; In Defense of Our Country: Survivors of Military Conflict. Nelson, Sheila. (YA). 24.95 *(978-1-4222-0452-8(9))*; Nature's Wrath: Surviving Natural Disasters. Sanna, Ellyn. (YA). 24.95 *(978-1-4222-0454-2(5))*; Never Again: Survivors of the Holocaust. Nelson, Sheila. (J). 24.95 *(978-1-4222-0459-7(6))*; Those Who Remain: What It Means to Be a Survivor. Sanna, Ellyn. (Illus.). (J). 24.95 *(978-1-4222-0457-3(X))*; When Danger Hits Home: Survivors of Domestic Violence. Zoldak, Joyce. (YA). 24.95 *(978-1-4222-0460-3(X))*; 128p. (gr. 7-12). 2010. 2009. Set lib. bdg. 324.35 *(978-1-4222-0449-8(9))* Mason Crest.

Tarshis, Lauren. I Survived Collection, Bks. 1-4. 2016. (*I Survived* Ser.). (ENG.). 432p. (J). (gr. 2-5). pap. 9.99 *(978-1-338-10249-9(4)*, Scholastic Paperbacks) Scholastic, Inc.

—I Survived Collector's Toolbox (I Survived) 2015. (I Survived Ser.). (ENG.). (J). (gr. 3-7). 49.90 *(978-0-545-86101-4(2))* Scholastic, Inc.

—Nature Attacks! 2015. (Illus.). (J). (I Survived True Stories Ser.: 2). (ENG.). 176p. (gr. 2-5). 12.99 *(978-0-545-85231-9(5)*, Scholastic Paperbacks); 157p. *(978-0-545-90802-3(7)*, Scholastic Pr.) Scholastic, Inc.

Vale, Janice. True Life Survival. Wademan, Spike, illus. 2007. (Collins Big Cat Ser.). (ENG.). 32p. (J). (gr. 2-4). pap. 7.99 *(978-0-00-723078-5(8))* HarperCollins Pubs. Ltd. GBR. Dist: Independent Pubs. Group.

Ventura, Marne. How to Survive a Flood. 2015. (Survival Guides). (ENG.). 24p. (J). (gr. 2-5). 27.07 *(978-1-60973-158-8(1)*, 208791) Child's World, Inc., The.

—How to Survive a Tornado. 2015. (Survival Guides). (ENG.). 24p. (J). (gr. 2-5). 27.07 *(978-1-60973-161-8(1)*, 208792) Child's World, Inc., The.

—How to Survive a Tsunami. 2015. (Survival Guides). (ENG.). 24p. (J). (gr. 2-5). 27.07 *(978-1-60973-164-9(6)*, 208793) Child's World, Inc., The.

—How to Survive an Animal Attack. 2015. (Survival Guides). (ENG.). 24p. (J). (gr. 2-5). 27.07 *(978-1-60973-163-2(8)*, 208794) Child's World, Inc., The.

Verstraete, Larry. Surviving the Hindenburg. 2012. (ENG., Illus.). 40p. (J). (gr. k-5). 16.95 *(978-1-58536-787-0(7))* Sleeping Bear Pr.

Wacholtz, Anthony. Can You Survive a Zombie Apocalypse? Nathan, James, illus. 2015. (You Choose: Doomsday Ser.). (ENG.). 112p. (gr. 3-4). pap. 6.95 *(978-1-4914-5925-6(5)*, You Choose Bks.) Capstone Press of Coughlan Cos.

Werther, Scott P. Alive! Airplane Crash in the Andes Mountains. 2003. (Survivor Ser.). (Illus.). 48p. (J). 24.50 *(978-0-516-24329-0(2)*, Children's Pr.) Scholastic Library Publishing.

Wilson, Patrick. Surviving by Trapping, Fishing, & Eating Plants. Carney, John, ed. 2014. (Extreme Survival in the Military Ser.: 12). (Illus.). 64p. (J). (gr. 7-18). lib. bdg. 23.95 *(978-1-4222-3088-6(0))* Mason Crest.

—Surviving Natural Disasters. Carney, John, ed. 2014. (Extreme Survival in the Military Ser.: 12). 64p. (J). (gr. 7-18). lib. bdg. 23.95 *(978-1-4222-3091-6(0))* Mason Crest.

Wulffson, Don L. The Upside-Down Voyage. Lyall, Dennis, illus. 2005. (J). *(978-1-59336-334-5(6))*; pap. *(978-1-59336-335-2(4))* Mondo Publishing.

Yomtov, Nel. True Stories of Survival. Chater, Mack et al, illus. 2015. (True Stories of Survival Ser.). (ENG.). 32p. (gr. 3-4). 122.60 *(978-1-4914-6915-6(3)*, Graphic Library) Capstone Press of Coughlan Cos.

Yomtov, Nelson. Terrors from the Deep: True Tales of Surviving Shark Attacks. 2015. (True Stories of Survival Ser.). (ENG., Illus.). 32p. (gr. 3-4). lib. bdg. 30.65 *(978-1-4914-6573-8(5))* Capstone Press of Coughlan Cos.

You Choose: Survival. 2011. (You Choose: Survival Ser.). (ENG.). 112p. (gr. 3-4). 127.96 *(978-1-4296-6590-2(4))*; pap. 166.80 *(978-1-4296-7354-9(0))*; pap. 27.80 *(978-1-4296-7353-2(2))* Capstone Press of Coughlan Cos. (You Choose Bks.).

Zullo, Allan. Miracle Pets: True Tales of Courage & Survival. 2011. 122p. *(978-0-545-25507-3(4))* Scholastic, Inc.

SURVIVAL—FICTION

Aaron, Chester. An American Ghost. 2011. (YA). pap. *(978-1-936144-28-0(X))* Zumaya Pubns. LLC.

—Gideon. 2009. (ENG., Illus.). 190p. (YA). pap. 12.99 *(978-1-934841-62-4(5)*, Zumaya Thresholds) Zumaya Pubns. LLC.

Acton, Vanessa. Aftershock. 2017. (Day of Disaster Ser.). (ENG.). 112p. (gr. 6-12). (J). 26.65 *(978-1-5124-2777-6(2))*; (YA). 12.99 ***(978-1-5124-3502-3(3)***, Darby Creek); (YA). 39.99 ***(978-1-5124-2785-1(3)***, Darby Creek); (YA). 39.99 ***(978-1-5124-3500-9(7)***, Darby Creek) Lerner Publishing Group.

—Backfire. 2017. (Day of Disaster Ser.). (ENG.). 112p. (gr. 6-12). (J). 26.65 *(978-1-5124-2775-2(6))*; (YA). 12.99 ***(978-1-5124-3504-7(X)***, Darby Creek); (YA). 39.99 ***(978-1-5124-2782-0(9)***, Darby Creek); (YA). 39.99 ***(978-1-5124-3503-0(1)***, Darby Creek) Lerner Publishing Group.

Acton, Vanessa. Vortex. 2017. (Day of Disaster Ser.). (ENG.). 104p. (YA). (gr. 6-12). 26.65 *(978-1-5124-2773-8(X))*; 12.99 ***(978-1-5124-3513-9(9)***, Darby Creek); 39.99 ***(978-1-5124-2780-6(2)***, Darby Creek); 39.99 ***(978-1-5124-3512-2(0)***, Darby Creek) Lerner Publishing Group.

Adams, Carolyn Lee. Ruthless. 2015. (ENG., Illus.). 256p. (YA). (gr. 9). 17.99 *(978-1-4814-2262-8(6)*, Simon Pulse) Simon Pulse.

Adams, Michael. The Last Girl. 2017. (Last Trilogy Ser.: 1). (ENG.). 400p. (YA). (gr. 9). pap. 12.99 ***(978-1-76029-340-6(7))*** Allen & Unwin AUS. Dist: Independent Pubs. Group.

Aguirre, Ann. Enclave. 2011. (Razorland Trilogy Ser.: 1). (ENG.). 272p. (YA). (gr. 7-18). 18.99 *(978-0-312-65008-7(6)*, 9780312650087) Feiwel & Friends.

—Enclave. 2012. (Razorland Trilogy Ser.: 1). (ENG.). 288p. (YA). (gr. 7). pap. 9.99 *(978-0-312-55137-7(1)*, 9780312551377) Square Fish.

—Horde. 2013. (Razorland Trilogy Ser.: 3). (ENG.). 432p. (YA). (gr. 7). 17.99 *(978-1-250-02463-3(3)*, 9781250024633) Feiwel & Friends.

—Horde. 2014. (Razorland Trilogy Ser.: 3). (ENG.). 464p. (YA). (gr. 7). pap. 10.99 *(978-1-250-05077-9(4)*, 9781250050779) Square Fish.

—Outpost. 2013. (Razorland Trilogy Ser.: 2). (ENG.). 352p. (YA). (gr. 7). pap. 10.99 *(978-1-250-03418-2(3)*, 9781250034182) Square Fish.

Alderson, Sarah. Losing Lila. 2013. (ENG.). 352p. (J). pap. 10.00 *(978-0-85707-197-2(1)*, Simon & Schuster Children's) Simon & Schuster, Ltd. GBR. Dist: Simon & Schuster, Inc.

Allison, Samuel B. An American Robinson Crusoe. 2005. 136p. pap. 10.95 *(978-1-4218-0186-5(8))*; 26.95 *(978-1-4218-0086-8(1))* 1st World Publishing, Inc. (1st World Library - Literary Society).

—*An American Robinson Crusoe.* 2004. reprint ed. pap. 15.95 *(978-1-4191-0613-2(9))*; pap. 1.99 *(978-1-4192-0613-9(3))* Kessinger Publishing, LLC.

Anderson, Laurie Halse. Fever 1793. 2014. (ENG.). 272p. (J). 12.24 *(978-1-63245-124-8(7))* Lectorum Pubns., Inc.

Anderson, T. Neill. City of the Dead: Galveston Hurricane 1900. 2013. (J). pap. 16.95 *(978-1-58089-515-6(8))*; (ENG., Illus.). 144p. (YA). (gr. 7). 16.95 *(978-1-58089-514-9(X))* Charlesbridge Publishing, Inc.

Appelfeld, Aharon. Adam & Thomas. Green, Jeffrey M., tr. from HEB. Dumas, Philippe, illus. 2017. (ENG.). 160p. (J). (gr. 3-7). pap. 14.95 *(978-1-60980-744-3(8)*, Triangle Square) Seven Stories Pr.

Appelt, Kathi. The Underneath. Small, David, illus. 2010. (KOR.). 395p. (YA). pap. *(978-89-527-5767-8(X))* Sigongsa Co., Ltd.

—The Underneath. Small, David, illus. (ENG.). (J). (gr. 5-9). 2010. 336p. pap. 8.99 *(978-1-4169-5059-2(1))* 2008. 320p. 17.99 *(978-1-4169-5058-5(3))* Simon & Schuster Children's Publishing. (Atheneum Bks. for Young Readers).

—The Underneath. 2010. lib. bdg. 19.65 *(978-0-606-14504-6(4)*, Turtleback) Turtleback Bks.

Appleton, Victor. Tom Swift & his Wireless Message. 2005. 26.95 *(978-1-4218-1506-0(0))*; 196p. pap. 11.95 *(978-1-4218-1606-7(7))* 1st World Publishing, Inc. (1st World Library - Literary Society).

—Tom Swift & His Wireless Message or Th. 2006. pap. *(978-1-4065-0911-3(6))* Dodo Pr.

Armentrout, Jennifer L. Opposition. (ENG.). 2013. (Lux Ser.: Bk. 5). (J). pap. 9.99 *(978-1-62266-026-1(9)*, Entangled Teen) 2014. (Lux Novel Ser.: 5). 500p. (YA). 19.99 *(978-1-62266-733-8(6)*, 9781622667338) 2014. (Lux Novel Ser.: 5). 500p. (YA). (gr. 7-12). pap. 11.99 *(978-1-62266-264-7(4)*, 9781622662647) Entangled Publishing, LLC.

—Origin. 2013. (ENG.). (Lux Ser.: Bk. 4). (J). pap. 9.99 *(978-1-62061-280-4(1))*; (Lux Novel Ser.: 4). 400p. (YA). (gr. 7-12). pap. 9.99 *(978-1-62266-075-9(7)*, 9781622660759) Entangled Publishing, LLC.

Armstrong, Kelley. The Calling. 2012. (Darkness Rising Ser.: Bk. 2). 336p. pap. *(978-1-907410-47-5(3))* Atom Pr.

—The Calling. (Darkness Rising Ser.: 2). (YA). (gr. 8). 2013. 352p. pap. 9.99 *(978-0-06-179706-4(5))* 2012. 336p. 17.99 *(978-0-06-179705-7(7))* HarperCollins Pubs.

—The Rising. 2013. (Darkness Rising Ser.: 3). 416p. (YA). (gr. 8). 17.99 *(978-0-06-179708-8(1))* HarperCollins Pubs.

Aronson, Sarah. Believe. 2013. (ENG.). 296p. (YA). (gr. 7-12). 17.95 *(978-1-4677-0697-1(3)*, Carolrhoda Lab™) Lerner Publishing Group.

Arvidson, Douglas. Brothers of the Fire Star. Scarborough, Rob, illus. 2012. 207p. (YA). pap. 15.95 *(978-1-890109-91-2(6)*, Cross Time) Crossquarter Publishing Group.

Asai, Carrie. The Book of the Shadow. Alarcao, Renato, illus. 2013. (Samurai Girl Ser.: 2). (ENG.). 224p. (YA). (gr. 11). pap. 13.99 *(978-1-4814-1540-8(9)*, Simon Pulse) Simon Pulse.

Asch, Frank. Survival School. Kanzler, John, illus. 2014. (Class Pets Ser.). (ENG.). 96p. (J). (gr. 2-6). pap. 13.99 *(978-1-4814-3627-4(9)*, Simon & Schuster/Paula Wiseman Bks.) Simon & Schuster/Paula Wiseman Bks.

Ashley, Bernard. Solitaire. 2012. (Fiction Ser.). 338p. (J). pap. 6.99 *(978-0-7945-3031-0(1)*, Usborne) EDC Publishing.

Avalos, Francisco. Amazon Tale. 2013. 124p. 29.99 *(978-1-4797-6689-5(5))*; pap. 19.99 *(978-1-4797-6688-8(7))* Xlibris Corp.

Ayder, Earl. The Longest Shortcut. McGrellis, Cynthia, illus. 2005. 40p. pap. 8.53 *(978-0-7578-9857-0(2))* Rigby Education.

Bacigalupi, Paolo. The Drowned Cities. 2013. (ENG.). 464p. (J). (gr. 10-17). pap. 10.99 *(978-0-316-05622-9(7))* 2012. 448p. (YA). 17.99 *(978-0-316-20037-0(9))* Little, Brown Bks. for Young Readers.

—The Drowned Cities. 2012. 352p. *(978-1-59606-506-2(0))* Subterranean Pr.

—The Drowned Cities. 2013. (J). lib. bdg. 22.10 *(978-0-606-31749-8(X)*, Turtleback) Turtleback Bks.

Bailey, Em. The Special Ones. 2017. (ENG.). 304p. (YA). (gr. 7). 17.99 *(978-0-544-91229-8(2)*, HMH Books For Young Readers) Houghton Mifflin Harcourt Publishing Co.

Ballantyne, Robert Michael. Jarwin & Cuffy. l.t. ed. 2007. (ENG.). 102p. pap. 19.99 *(978-1-4346-3724-6(7))* Creative Media Partners, LLC.

Bassoff, Leah & DeLuca, Laura. Lost Girl Found, 1 vol. 2014. (ENG., Illus.). 192p. (J). (gr. 7). 16.95 *(978-1-55498-416-9(5))* Groundwood Bks. CAN. Dist: Publishers Group West (PGW).

Bauer, Joan. Backwater. 2005. 185p. 18.00 *(978-0-7569-5779-7(6))* Perfection Learning Corp.

Beaudoin, Sean. The Infects. 2014. (ENG.). 384p. (YA). (gr. 9). pap. 8.99 *(978-0-7636-7160-0(6))* Candlewick Pr.

Beckhorn, Susan Williams. The Wolf's Boy. 2016. (ENG., Illus.). 236p. (J). (gr. 3-7). 16.99 *(978-1-4847-2553-5(0))* Disney Pr.

Beha, Eileen. Tango: The Tale of an Island Dog. 2010. (ENG.). 256p. (YA). (gr. 3-6). pap. 7.99 *(978-1-59990-485-6(3)*, 9781599904856, Bloomsbury USA Childrens) Bloomsbury Publishing USA.

Bell, Joanne. Juggling Fire, 1 vol. 2009. (ENG.). 184p. (YA). (gr. 7-12). pap. 12.95 *(978-1-55469-094-7(3))* Orca Bk. Pubs. USA.

Beveridge, Cathy. Stormstruck. 2006. (ENG., Illus.). 214p. (J). pap. *(978-1-55380-041-5(9))* Ronsdale Pr.

Bick, Ilsa J. Ashes. (Ashes Trilogy Ser.: Bk. 1). (ENG.). 480p. (gr. 9). 2012. (J). pap. 9.99 *(978-1-60684-385-7(0))* 2011. 17.99 *(978-1-60684-175-4(0))* Lerner Publishing Group. (Carolrhoda Lab™).

—Monsters. (ENG.). 688p. (J). (gr. 9). 2014. pap. 9.99 *(978-1-60684-544-8(6))* 2013. (Ashes Trilogy Ser.: Bk. 3). 18.99 *(978-1-60684-177-8(7))* Lerner Publishing Group. (Carolrhoda Lab™).

—Shadows. (Ashes Trilogy Ser.: Bk. 2). (ENG.). 528p. (gr. 9). 2013. (J). pap. 9.99 *(978-1-60684-445-8(8))* 2012. 17.99 *(978-1-60684-176-1(9))* Lerner Publishing Group. (Carolrhoda Lab™).

—White Space, Bk. 1. 2014. (Dark Passages Ser.: Bk. 1). (ENG.). 560p. (J). (gr. 9). 18.99 *(978-1-60684-419-9(9))* Lerner Publishing Group.

Birdseye, Tom. Storm Mountain. 2010. (ENG.). 256p. (J). (gr. 3-7). 16.95 *(978-0-8234-2130-5(9))* Holiday Hse., Inc.

Black, Deirdre. River Run. 2012. (After the Dust Settled Ser.). (ENG.). 120p. (YA). (gr. 6-12). pap. 7.95 *(978-0-8225-7274-9(5)*, Darby Creek); lib. bdg. 27.93 *(978-0-7613-8326-0(3))* Lerner Publishing Group.

Black Ice. 2014. (ENG., Illus.). 400p. (YA). (gr. 9). 19.99 *(978-1-4424-7426-0(2)*, Simon & Schuster Bks. For Young Readers) Simon & Schuster Bks. For Young Readers.

Blizzard: Colorado 1886. 2014. (Survivors Ser.). (ENG., Illus.). 160p. (J). (gr. 3-7). pap. 6.99 *(978-1-4814-0969-8(7)*, Aladdin) Simon & Schuster Children's Publishing.

Block, Francesca Lia. The Island of Excess Love. 2014. (ENG.). 224p. (YA). (gr. 9). 16.99 *(978-0-8050-9631-6(0)*, 9780805096316, Holt, Henry & Co. Bks. For Young Readers) Holt, Henry & Co.

—Love in the Time of Global Warming. 2013. (ENG.). 240p. (YA). (gr. 9-13). 16.99 *(978-0-8050-9627-9(2)*, 9780805096279, Holt, Henry & Co. Bks. For Young Readers) Holt, Henry & Co.

Bodeen, S. A. The Compound. 2011. 9.46 *(978-0-7848-3490-9(3)*, Everbind) Marco Bk. Co.

—The Compound. 2009. (Compound Ser.: 1). (ENG.). 272p. (YA). (gr. 7-12). pap. 9.99 *(978-0-312-57860-2(1)*, 9780312578602) Square Fish.

—The Fallout. 2013. (Compound Ser.: 2). (ENG.). 336p. (YA). (gr. 7). 18.99 *(978-0-312-65011-7(6)*, 9780312650117) Feiwel & Friends.

—Found. 2017. (Shipwreck Island Ser.: 4). (ENG.). 160p. (J). 16.99 *(978-1-250-02783-2(7)*, 9781250027832) Feiwel & Friends.

—Lost. 2015. (Shipwreck Island Ser.: 2). (ENG.). 144p. (J). (gr. 5-8). 16.99 *(978-1-250-02779-5(9)*, 9781250027795) Feiwel & Friends.

—The Raft. 2013. (ENG.). 256p. (YA). (gr. 7-12). pap. 9.99 *(978-1-250-02739-9(X)*, 9781250027399) Square Fish.

—Trapped. 2016. (Shipwreck Island Ser.: 3). (ENG.). 160p. (J). 16.99 *(978-1-250-02781-8(0)*, 9781250027818) Feiwel & Friends.

Bondoux, Anne-Laure. A Time of Miracles. Maudet, Y., tr. from FRE. 2012. (ENG., Illus.). 192p. (YA). (gr. 7). pap. 7.99 *(978-0-375-86036-2(3)*, Ember) Random Hse. Children's Bks.

Boorman, Kate A. Darkthaw: A Winterkill Novel. 2015. (Winterkill Ser.). (ENG.). 336p. (YA). (gr. 7-17). 17.95 *(978-1-4197-1663-8(8)*, Amulet Bks.) Abrams, Inc.

—Heartfire: A Winterkill Novel. 2016. (Winterkill Ser.: 3). (ENG.). 336p. (YA). (gr. 7-17). 17.95 *(978-1-4197-2124-3(0)*, Amulet Bks.) Abrams, Inc.

Borgenicht, David & Khan, Hena. Amazon: You Decide How to Survive! 2015. (WorstCase Scenario Ultimate Adventure Ser.). (ENG., Illus.). 204p. (gr. 3-8). 47.10 *(978-1-59920-980-7(2)*, 1389530) Black Rabbit Bks.

—Mars: You Decide How to Survive! Labat, Yancey, illus. 2011. (Worst Case Scenario Ser.: WORS). (ENG.). 208p. (J). (gr. 4-7). 12.99 *(978-0-8118-7124-2(X))* Chronicle Bks. LLC.

Borgenicht, David & Lurie, Alexander. Deadly Seas: You Decide How to Survive! 2015. (WorstCase Scenario Ultimate Adventure Ser.). (ENG., Illus.). 204p. (gr. 3-8). 47.10 *(978-1-59920-981-4(0))* Black Rabbit Bks.

Borgenicht, David, et al. The Worst-Case Scenario: Everest - You Decide How to Survive! Labat, Yancey, illus. 2011. (Worst Case Scenario Ser.). (ENG.). 208p. (J). (gr. 4-5). 12.99 *(978-0-8118-7123-5(1))* Chronicle Bks. LLC.

Bowen, Carl. Bone Yard. Lee, Marc, illus. 2016. (Firestormers Ser.). (ENG.). 112p. (gr. 4-8). lib. bdg. 26.65 *(978-1-4965-3306-7(2))* Stone Arch Bks.

Bradman, Tony. Alien. 2012. (Stoke Books Titles Ser.). 64p. (J). (gr. 5-8). pap. 45.32 *(978-0-7613-9214-9(9))* Stoke Bks.

Brallier, Max. The Last Kids on Earth. Holgate, Douglas, illus. (J). 2017. pap. ***(978-0-425-28872-6(2))*** 2016. (Last Kids on Earth Ser.: Vol. 2). (ENG.). 304p. (gr. 3-7). 13.99 *(978-0-670-01662-4(4))* 2015. (Last Kids on Earth Ser.: 1). (ENG.). 240p. (gr. 3-7). 13.99 *(978-0-670-01661-7(6))* Penguin Young Readers Group. (Viking Books for Young Readers).

Braun, Melinda. Avalanche. 2016. (ENG., Illus.). 272p. (YA). (gr. 9). 17.99 *(978-1-4814-3822-3(0)*, Simon Pulse) Simon Pulse.

—Stranded. 2015. (ENG., Illus.). 272p. (YA). (gr. 9). 17.99 *(978-1-4814-3819-3(0)*, Simon Pulse) Simon Pulse.

Bray, Libba. Beauty Queens. (ENG.). 400p. (J). (gr. 7). 2012. pap. 10.99 *(978-0-439-89598-9(7)*, Scholastic Paperbacks) 2011. 18.99 *(978-0-439-89597-2(9)*, Scholastic Pr.) Scholastic, Inc.

Brown, Frank. Among the Pandemoniumous Mismaides: A Fantasy. 2008. 148p. 22.95 *(978-0-595-71458-2(7))* iUniverse, Inc.

Brown, Peter. The Wild Robot. 2016. (ENG., Illus.). 288p. (J). (gr. 3-7). 16.99 *(978-0-316-38199-4(3))* Little, Brown Bks. for Young Readers.

Bruchac, Joseph. Arrow of Lightning. 2017. (Killer of Enemies Ser.). (ENG.). 400p. (YA). 19.95 ***(978-1-62014-330-8(5)***, Tu Bks.) Lee & Low Bks., Inc.

—Killer of Enemies. (Killer of Enemies Ser.). (ENG.). 400p. (YA). 2016. pap. 11.99 *(978-1-62014-276-9(7))* 2013. 19.95 *(978-1-62014-143-4(4))* Lee & Low Bks., Inc. (Tu Bks.).

—Trail of the Dead, 1 vol. 2015. (Killer of Enemies Ser.). (ENG.). 400p. (YA). 19.95 *(978-1-62014-261-5(9))* Lee & Low Bks., Inc.

Brunson, Emma. Survivor Spirit Book: Megan's Ark. 2010. 204p. pap. 13.50 *(978-1-60911-834-1(2)*, Eloquent Bks.) Strategic Book Publishing & Rights Agency (SBPRA).

Buckley, Michael. Raging Sea. 2016. (Undertow Trilogy Ser.: 2). (ENG.). 368p. (YA). (gr. 7). 18.99 *(978-0-544-34844-8(3)*, HMH Books For Young Readers) Houghton Mifflin Harcourt Publishing Co.

—Undertow. (Undertow Trilogy Ser.). (ENG.). (gr. 7). 2016. 400p. (YA). pap. 10.99 *(978-0-544-81319-9(7))* 2015. 384p. (J). 18.99 *(978-0-544-34825-7(7))* Houghton Mifflin Harcourt Publishing Co. (HMH Books For Young Readers).

Burgess, Thornton W. Whitefoot the Woodmouse. 2011. 118p. 23.95 *(978-1-4638-9567-9(4))* Rodgers, Alan Bks.

Cantor, Jillian. Searching for Sky. 2014. (ENG.). 288p. (YA). (gr. 7-12). 17.99 *(978-1-61963-351-3(5)*, 9781619633513, Bloomsbury USA Childrens) Bloomsbury Publishing USA.

Capetta, Amy Rose. Unmade. (ENG.). 384p. (YA). (gr. 9). 2016. pap. 9.99 *(978-0-544-54258-7(4))* 2015. 17.99 *(978-0-544-08737-8(2))* Houghton Mifflin Harcourt Publishing Co. (HMH Books For Young Readers).

Carey, Anna. Eve. (Eve Ser.: 1). (ENG.). (YA). (gr. 8). 2012. 352p. pap. 9.99 *(978-0-06-204851-6(1))* 2011. 336p. 17.99 *(978-0-06-204850-9(3))* HarperCollins Pubs.
—Eve. 2012. (SPA.). 224p. (YA). pap. 20.95 *(978-84-9918-434-0(0))* Roca Editorial ESP. Dist: Spanish Pubs., LLC.
Carnesi, Mônica. Little Dog Lost: The True Story of a Brave Dog Named Baltic. Carnesi, Mônica, illus. 2012. (ENG., Illus.). 32p. (J). (gr. -1-k). 16.99 *(978-0-399-25666-0(0),* Nancy Paulsen Books) Penguin Young Readers Group.
Carr, Elias & Karre, Andrew. Fight the Wind. 2012. (After the Dust Settled Ser.). (ENG.). 104p. (YA). (gr. 6-12). pap. 7.95 *(978-0-8225-9034-7(4),* Darby Creek); lib. bdg. 27.93 *(978-0-7613-8331-4(X))* Lerner Publishing Group.
Casanova, Mary. When Eagles Fall. 2014. (Fesler-Lampert Minnesota Heritage Ser.). (ENG.). 160p. pap. 9.95 *(978-0-8166-9211-8(4))* Univ. of Minnesota Pr.
Cawthon, Scott & Breed-Wrisley, Kira. The Silver Eyes. 2016. (Five Nights at Freddy's Ser.: 1). (ENG.). 400p. (J). (gr. 7-7). pap. 9.99 *(978-1-338-13437-7(X))* Scholastic, Inc.
Cawthon, Scott & Breed-Wrisley, Kira. The Silver Eyes. 2016. (Five Nights at Freddy's Ser.: bk.1). (YA). lib. bdg. 20.85 ***(978-0-606-39982-1(8))*** Turtleback Bks.
Chabert, Jack. Mystery of the Map. Merritt, Kory, illus. 2016. (Poptropica Ser.: bk.1). (ENG.). 112p. (J). (gr. 1-4). 9.95 *(978-1-4197-2067-3(8),* Amulet Bks.) Abrams, Inc.
Chabot, Jason. Below. 2016. (Broken Sky Chronicles Ser.: 1). (ENG.). 308p. (J). 29.95 *(978-1-68162-602-4(0));* (YA). pap. 16.95 *(978-1-68162-601-7(2))* Turner Publishing Co.
Chabot, Jason. Beyond: Broken Sky Chronicles, Book 3. 2017. (Broken Sky Chronicles Ser.: 3). (ENG.). 432p. (J). 35.99 ***(978-1-68162-608-6(X));*** (YA). pap. 19.99 *(978-1-68162-607-9(1))* Turner Publishing Co.
Chapman, Elsie. Divided (Dualed Sequel) 2015. (ENG.). 336p. (YA). (gr. 7). pap. 9.99 *(978-0-449-81298-3(7),* Ember) Random Hse. Children's Bks.
Charbonneau, Joelle. Graduation Day. (ENG.). 304p. (gr. 7). 2015. (Testing Ser.: 3). (YA). pap. 9.99 *(978-0-544-54120-7(0))* 2014. (Testing Trilogy: Bk. 3). (J). 17.99 *(978-0-547-95921-4(4))* Houghton Mifflin Harcourt Publishing Co. (HMH Books For Young Readers).
—Independent Study. (ENG.). (YA). (gr. 7). 2015. (Testing Ser.: 2). 336p. pap. 9.99 *(978-0-544-43945-0(7),* HMH Books For Young Readers) 2014. (Testing Trilogy: Bk. 2). 320p. 17.99 *(978-0-547-95920-7(6))* Houghton Mifflin Harcourt Publishing Co.
—Independent Study. 2015. (Testing Ser.: 2). lib. bdg. 20.85 *(978-0-606-36832-2(9))* Turtleback Bks.
Choyce, Lesley. Breaking Point, 1 vol. 2012. (Orca Soundings Ser.). (ENG.). 128p. (YA). (gr. 8-12). 16.95 *(978-1-4598-0129-5(6));* pap. 9.95 *(978-1-4598-0128-8(8))* Orca Bk. Pubs. USA.
Christopher, John. Empty World. 2015. (ENG., Illus.). 256p. (J). (gr. 5-9). pap. 7.99 *(978-1-4814-2000-6(3),* Aladdin) Simon & Schuster Children's Publishing.
Clark, Georgia. Parched. Garns, Allen, illus. 2014. (ENG.). 256p. (YA). (gr. 7). 17.95 *(978-0-8234-2949-3(0))* Holiday Hse., Inc.
Cole, Brock. The Goats. Cole, Brock, illus. 2010. (ENG., Illus.). 192p. (YA). (gr. 7-10). pap. 9.99 *(978-0-312-61191-0(9),* 9780312611910) Square Fish.
Collins, Suzanne. Catching Fire. 2009. (Hunger Games Trilogy: Bk. 2). (YA). 74.99 *(978-1-61574-572-2(6))* Findaway World, LLC.
—Catching Fire. 2009. 12.04 *(978-0-7848-3842-6(9),* Everbind) Marco Bk. Co.
—Catching Fire. 2011. 480p. pap. *(978-1-4071-3209-9(1))* Scholastic.
—Catching Fire. (Hunger Games Ser.: 2). (ENG.). (gr. 7). 2014. 448p. (YA). pap. 12.99 *(978-0-545-79188-5(X),* Tangerine Pr.) 2013. 400p. (YA). pap. 12.99 *(978-0-545-58617-7(8),* Scholastic Pr.) 2010. (Illus.). 400p. (J). lib. bdg. 22.99 *(978-0-545-31059-8(8),* Scholastic Pr.) 2009. 400p. (J). 18.99 *(978-0-439-02349-8(1),* Scholastic Pr.) 2013. 400p. (J). pap. 12.99 *(978-0-545-60368-3(4),* Scholastic Paperbacks) Scholastic, Inc.
—Catching Fire. l.t. ed. (Hunger Games Trilogy: 2). (ENG.). (YA). 2012. 498p. (gr. 7-12). pap. 14.99 *(978-1-59413-585-9(1),* Large Print Pr.) 2009. 500p. 23.95 *(978-1-4104-2044-2(2))* Thorndike Pr.
—Catching Fire. 2013. (Hunger Games Trilogy Ser.: 2). lib. bdg. 24.50 *(978-0-606-32025-2(3),* Turtleback) Turtleback Bks.
—Catching Fire. 2011. (Hunger Games Trilogy: Bk. 2). (CHI.). 344p. (YA). (gr. 7-12). pap. *(978-7-5063-5566-7(3))* Writers' Publishing Hse.
—EN LLAMAS. 2012. (Hunger Games Trilogy: Bk. 2). (SPA.). 416p. (J). pap. 19.99 *(978-84-272-0213-9(X))* Molino, Editorial ESP. Dist: Lectorum Pubns., Inc.
—En Llamas, Bk. 2. 2010. (Hunger Games Trilogy: Bk. 2).Tr. of Catching Fire. (SPA.). 416p. (J). (gr. 8-12). pap. 19.99 *(978-84-272-0000-5(5))* Lectorum Pubns., Inc.
—The Hunger Games. 2009. (Hunger Games Trilogy: Bk. 1). 10.85 *(978-0-7848-3801-3(1),* Everbind) Marco Bk. Co.
—The Hunger Games. 2010. (Hunger Games Trilogy: Bk. 1). (ENG.). 374p. (gr. 7-12). 21.00 *(978-1-60686-581-1(1))* Perfection Learning Corp.
—The Hunger Games. Fournier, Guillaume, tr. 2011. (Hunger Games Trilogy: Bk. 1). (FRE.). 398p. (YA). (gr. 7-12). pap. *(978-2-266-18269-0(2))* Presses Pocket.
—The Hunger Games. 2011. (Hunger Games Trilogy: 1). (YA). 69.75 *(978-1-4561-3196-8(6))* Recorded Bks., Inc.
—The Hunger Games. 2010. (Hunger Games Ser.: 1). (ENG.). 384p. (J). (gr. 7-18). pap. 10.99 *(978-0-439-02352-8(1),* Scholastic Pr.) Scholastic, Inc.
—The Hunger Games. O'Brien, Tim, illus. 2009. 448p. pap. *(978-1-4071-0908-4(1),* Scholastic) Scholastic, Inc.
—The Hunger Games. (Hunger Games Ser.: 1). (ENG.). (gr. 7). 2008. 384p. (J). 18.99 *(978-0-439-02348-1(3),* Scholastic Pr.) 2012. 384p. (J). pap. 12.99 *(978-0-545-42511-7(5))*Set. 2014. (YA). pap. 38.97 *(978-0-545-79191-5(X),* Scholastic Pr.) Scholastic, Inc.
—The Hunger Games. l.t. ed. (Hunger Games Trilogy: Bk. 1). (ENG.). (YA). 2012. 484p. (gr. 7-12). pap. 14.99 *(978-1-59413-587-3(8),* Large Print Pr.) 2009. 486p. 23.95 *(978-1-4104-1986-6(X))* Thorndike Pr.
—The Hunger Games. 2010. (Hunger Games Trilogy Ser.: 1). lib. bdg. 22.10 *(978-1-4178-3173-9(1),* Turtleback) Turtleback Bks.
—The Hunger Games. 2010. (Hunger Games Trilogy: Bk. 1). (CHI.). 324p. (YA). (gr. 7-12). pap. *(978-7-5063-5153-9(6))* Writers' Publishing Hse.
—The Hunger Games: Foil Edition. 2014. (Hunger Games Ser.: 1). (ENG.). 448p. (YA). (gr. 7). pap. 12.99 *(978-0-545-79187-8(1),* Scholastic Pr.) Scholastic, Inc.
—The Hunger Games Trilogy Set: The Hunger Games; Catching Fire; Mockingjay. 2010. (Hunger Games Ser.: 1). (ENG.). (J). (gr. 7-18). 53.97 *(978-0-545-26535-5(5),* Scholastic Pr.) Scholastic, Inc.
—The Hunger Games Trilogy Collection. 2014. (Hunger Games Ser.). (ENG.). (J). (gr. 9). pap. 36.97 *(978-0-545-67031-9(4),* Scholastic Pr.) Scholastic, Inc.
—Los Juegos del Hambre. 2009. (Hunger Games Trilogy: Bk. 1).Tr. of Hunger Games. (SPA.). pap. 19.99 *(978-84-9867-539-9(1))* RBA Libros, S.A. ESP. Dist: Lectorum Pubns., Inc.
—Los Juegos del Hambre. 2012. (Hunger Games Trilogy Spanish Ser.: 1).Tr. of Hunger Games. (SPA.). lib. bdg. 33.05 *(978-0-606-26447-1(7),* Turtleback) Turtleback Bks.
—LOS JUEGOS DEL HAMBRE. 2012. (Hunger Games Trilogy: Bk. 1). (SPA.). 400p. (J). pap. 19.99 *(978-84-272-0212-2(1))* Molino, Editorial ESP. Dist: Lectorum Pubns., Inc.
—Mockingjay. 2011. (Hunger Games Trilogy: Bk. 3). (CHI.). 435p. (YA). (gr. 7-12). pap. *(978-986-213-216-6(7))* Locus Publishing Co.
—Mockingjay. (Hunger Games Trilogy: 3). (YA). 2011. 77.75 *(978-1-4561-3203-3(2))* 2010. 1.25 *(978-1-4640-2636-2(X))* 2010. 75.75 *(978-1-4561-3205-7(9))* Recorded Bks., Inc.
—Mockingjay. 2011. (Hunger Games Ser.: Vol. 3). (ENG.). 448p. (YA). (gr. 8-12). pap. *(978-1-4071-3210-5(5))* Scholastic Canada, Ltd.
—Mockingjay. 2014. (Hunger Games Ser.: 3). (ENG.). 448p. (YA). (gr. 7). pap. 12.99 *(978-0-545-79190-8(1),* Scholastic Pr.) 2014. (Hunger Games Ser.: 3). (ENG.). 400p. (YA). (gr. 7). pap. 12.99 *(978-0-545-78829-8(3),* Scholastic Paperbacks) 2014. (Hunger Games Ser.: 3). (ENG.). 400p. (J). (gr. 7). pap. 12.99 *(978-0-545-66326-7(1),* Scholastic Pr.) 2010. (Hunger Games Ser.: 3). (ENG.). 400p. (J). (gr. 7-7). lib. bdg. 22.99 *(978-0-545-31060-4(1),* Scholastic Pr.) 2010. (Hunger Games Ser.: 3). (ENG.). 400p. (J). (gr. 7-18). 18.99 *(978-0-439-02351-1(3),* Scholastic Pr.) 2010. pap. *(978-0-439-02354-2(8),* Scholastic Pr.) Scholastic, Inc.
—Mockingjay. l.t. ed. (Hunger Games Trilogy: Bk. 3). (ENG.). (YA). 2012. 502p. (gr. 7-12). pap. 14.99 *(978-1-59413-586-6(X),* Large Print Pr.) 2010. 503p. 23.99 *(978-1-4104-2841-7(9))* Thorndike Pr.
—Mockingjay. 2014. (Hunger Games Trilogy Ser.: 3). lib. bdg. 24.50 *(978-0-606-36328-0(9));* lib. bdg. 24.50 *(978-0-606-35133-1(7))* Turtleback Bks.
—Sinsajo. 2010. (Hunger Games Trilogy: Bk. 3).Tr. of Mockingjay. (SPA.). 424p. (J). (gr. 8-12). pap. 19.99 *(978-84-272-0038-8(2))* Molino, Editorial ESP. Dist: Lectorum Pubns., Inc.
—SINSAJO. 2012. (Hunger Games Trilogy: Bk. 3). (SPA.). 424p. (J). pap. 19.99 *(978-84-272-0214-6(8))* Molino, Editorial ESP. Dist: Lectorum Pubns., Inc.
—Sinsajo. 2012. (Hunger Games Trilogy Spanish Ser.: 3).Tr. of Mockingjay. (SPA.). lib. bdg. 33.05 *(978-0-606-26449-5(3),* Turtleback) Turtleback Bks.
Condon, Bill. How to Survive in the Jungle by the Person Who Knows, 1 vol. rev. ed. 2013. (Fiction Readers Ser.). (ENG., Illus.). 28p. (J). (gr. 3-3). pap. 8.99 *(978-1-4333-5599-8(X))* Shell Educational Publishing.
—How to Survive in the Jungle by the Person Who Knows. rev. ed. 2013. (Fiction Readers Ser.). (ENG., Illus.). 28p. (gr. 3-3). pap. 19.96 *(978-1-4807-1721-3(5))* Teacher Created Materials, Inc.
Connell, Richard Edward. The Most Dangerous Game. 2010. (Creative Short Stories Ser.). (Illus.). 48p. (J). (gr. 5-18). 19.95 *(978-1-58341-920-5(9),* Creative Education) Creative Co., The.
Connelly, Neil. Into the Hurricane. 2017. (ENG.). 240p. (J). (gr. 9). 17.99 ***(978-0-545-85381-1(8),*** Levine, Arthur A. Bks.) Scholastic, Inc.
Cooper, Susan. Ghost Hawk. 2013. (ENG.). 336p. (J). (gr. 5-9). 16.99 *(978-1-4424-8141-1(2),* McElderry, Margaret K. Bks.) McElderry, Margaret K. Bks.
Cremer, Andrea. The Inventor's Secret. (Inventor's Secret Ser.). (ENG.). (YA). (gr. 7). 2015. 416p. pap. 10.99 *(978-0-14-751436-7(X),* Speak) 2014. 336p. 18.99 *(978-0-399-15962-6(2),* Philomel Bks.) Penguin Young Readers Group.
Crewe, Megan. The Lives We Lost. 2014. (Fallen World Trilogy Ser.). (ENG.). 304p. (YA). (gr. 7-12). pap. 9.99 *(978-1-4231-4632-2(8))* Hyperion Bks. for Children.
—The Worlds We Make. 2014. (Fallen World Trilogy Ser.). (ENG.). 288p. (J). (gr. 5-9). 16.99 *(978-1-4231-4618-6(2))* Hyperion Bks. for Children.
Crockett, S. D. After the Snow. 2012. (After the Snow Ser.: 1). (ENG.). 304p. (YA). (gr. 7-12). 16.99 *(978-0-312-64169-6(9))* Feiwel & Friends.
—After the Snow. 2013. (After the Snow Ser.: 1). (ENG.). 320p. (YA). (gr. 7-12). pap. 9.99 *(978-1-250-01676-8(2))* Square Fish.
Crossan, Sarah. Breathe. (Breathe Ser.: 1). (ENG.). (YA). (gr. 9). 2013. 400p. pap. 9.99 *(978-0-06-211870-7(6))* 2012. 384p. 17.99 *(978-0-06-211869-1(2))* HarperCollins Pubs. (Greenwillow Bks.).
Crowder, Melanie. Parched. (ENG.). 160p. (J). (gr. 5-7). 2014. pap. 7.99 *(978-0-544-33631-5(3),* HMH Books For Young Readers) 2013. 15.99 *(978-0-547-97651-8(8))* Houghton Mifflin Harcourt Publishing Co.
Cummings, Lindsay. The Death Code. (Murder Complex Ser.: 2). 512p. (YA). (gr. 9). 2016. pap. 9.99 *(978-0-06-222004-2(7))* 2015. (ENG.). 17.99 *(978-0-06-222003-5(9))* HarperCollins Pubs. (Greenwillow Bks.).
—The Murder Complex. 2014. (Murder Complex Ser.: 1). (ENG.). 416p. (YA). (gr. 9). 17.99 *(978-0-06-222000-4(4),* Greenwillow Bks.) HarperCollins Pubs.
Curtis, Simon. Boy Robot. 2016. (ENG., Illus.). 432p. (YA). (gr. 9). 17.99 *(978-1-4814-5929-7(5),* Simon Pulse) Simon Pulse.
Cushman, Karen. Rodzina. 2016.Tr. of Rodzina. (ENG.). 224p. (J). (gr. 5-7). pap. 6.99 *(978-0-544-54029-3(8),* HMH Books For Young Readers) Houghton Mifflin Harcourt Publishing Co.
Dando-Collins, Stephen. Caesar the War Dog - Operation Black Shark. 2016. (Caesar the War Dog Ser.: 5). (ENG.). 288p. (J). (gr. 4-6). pap. 11.99 *(978-0-85798-863-8(8))* Random Hse. Australia AUS. Dist: Independent Pubs. Group.
Dashner, James. The Death Cure. (Maze Runner Ser.: Bk. 3). (ENG.). 352p. (YA). (gr. 7). 2013. pap. 9.99 *(978-0-385-73878-1(1))* 2011. 18.99 *(978-0-385-73877-4(3))* Random Hse. Children's Bks. (Delacorte Pr.).
—The Death Cure. 2013. (Maze Runner Ser.: 3). lib. bdg. 20.85 *(978-0-606-27005-2(1),* Turtleback) Turtleback Bks.
—The Fever Code. 2016. (Maze Runner Ser.). (ENG.). 384p. (YA). (gr. 7). 18.99 *(978-0-553-51309-7(5));* lib. bdg. 21.99 *(978-0-553-51310-3(9))* Random Hse. Children's Bks. (Delacorte Pr.).
—The Kill Order. 2014. (Maze Runner Ser.: 4). (ENG.). 384p. (YA). (gr. 7). pap. 9.99 *(978-0-385-74289-4(4),* Delacorte Pr.) Random Hse. Children's Bks.
—The Kill Order. 2014. (Maze Runner Ser.: 0). lib. bdg. 20.85 *(978-0-606-35572-8(3))* Turtleback Bks.
—The Maze Runner: Virus Letal. 2013. 362p. (YA). pap. 15.99 *(978-987-612-565-9(6))* V&R Editoras.
—The Maze Runner & the Scorch Trials, Bks. 1 & 2. collector's ed. 2015. (Maze Runner Ser.). (ENG.). 816p. (YA). (gr. 7). pap. 19.99 *(978-0-553-53824-3(1),* Delacorte Pr.) Random Hse. Children's Bks.
—The Scorch Trials. (Maze Runner Ser.: 2). (ENG.). (YA). (gr. 7). 2011. 400p. pap. 9.99 *(978-0-385-73876-7(5))* 2010. 384p. 18.99 *(978-0-385-73875-0(7))* 2015. (Illus.). 384p. 18.99 *(978-0-553-53822-9(5))* 2015. 384p. pap. 10.99 *(978-0-553-53841-0(1))* Random Hse. Children's Bks. (Delacorte Pr.).
—The Scorch Trials. 2011. (Maze Runner Ser.: 2). lib. bdg. 20.85 *(978-0-606-23430-6(6),* Turtleback) Turtleback Bks.
Davenport, Roger. Wanderer. (ENG.). 2016. 268p. (J). (gr. 6). pap. 8.99 *(978-1-5107-0389-6(6))* 2013. 288p. (YA). (gr. 8-12). 16.95 *(978-1-62087-541-4(1),* 620541) Skyhorse Publishing Co., Inc. (Sky Pony Pr.).
Davies, Stephen. Outlaw. 2011. (ENG.). 304p. (YA). (gr. 7). 16.99 *(978-0-547-39017-8(3))* Houghton Mifflin Harcourt Publishing Co.
Dawson, Delilah S. Strike. 2016. (ENG., Illus.). 480p. (YA). (gr. 9). 17.99 *(978-1-4814-2342-7(8),* Simon Pulse) Simon Pulse.
De la Peña, Matt. The Hunted. 2015. (ENG.). 384p. (YA). (gr. 9). lib. bdg. 20.99 *(978-0-375-98992-6(7),* Delacorte Pr.) Random Hse. Children's Bks.
—The Living. (ENG.). (YA). (gr. 9). 2015. 336p. pap. 9.99 *(978-0-385-74121-7(9),* Ember) 2013. 320p. lib. bdg. 20.99 *(978-0-375-98991-9(9),* Delacorte Pr.) Random Hse. Children's Bks.
Deborah, Ellis. The Breadwinner. 2014. (ENG.). 176p. (J). 13.20 *(978-1-63245-145-3(X))* Lectorum Pubns., Inc.
Defoe, Daniel. Aventuras de Robinson Crusoe. 2003. (Advanced Reading Ser.: Vol. 73).Tr. of Adventures of Robinson Crusoe. (SPA., Illus.). 118p. (J). (gr. 4-7). *(978-84-239-9043-6(5))* Espasa Calpe, S.A.
—Robinson Crusoe. 2012. 338p. pap. 10.99 *(978-1-61382-256-2(1))* Simon & Brown.
—Robinson Crusoe. Akib, Jamel, illus. 2006. (Classic Starts(tm) Ser.). (ENG.). 160p. (J). (gr. 2-4). 6.95 *(978-1-4027-2664-4(3))* Sterling Publishing Co., Inc.
—Robinson Crusoe: With a Discussion of Resourcefulness. Landgraf, Kenneth, illus. 2003. (Values in Action Illustrated Classics Ser.). 190p. (J). *(978-1-59203-035-4(1))* Learning Challenge, Inc.
—Robinson Crusoe, Level 4. 2009. (ENG.). 96p. pap. 12.75 *(978-84-8323-553-9(6))* Cambridge Univ. Pr.
—ROBINSON CRUSOE LEVEL 4 INTERMEDIATE BOOK WITH CD-ROM AND AUDIO CD, 1 vol. 2009. (ENG.). 96p. pap. 16.50 incl. cd-rom, audio compact disk *(978-84-8323-550-8(1))* Cambridge Univ. Pr.
Defoe, Daniel, et al. Robinson Crusoe: The Complete Story of Robinson Crusoe. (Classics Illustrated Ser.). (Illus.). 52p. (YA). pap. 4.95 *(978-1-57209-021-7(9))* Classics International Entertainment, Inc.
DeStefano, Lauren. Sever. 2013. (Chemical Garden Trilogy Ser.: 3). (ENG.). 400p. (YA). (gr. 9). pap. 9.99 *(978-1-4424-0910-1(X))* Simon & Schuster.
—Sever. 2013. (Chemical Garden Trilogy Ser.: 3). (ENG.). 384p. (YA). (gr. 9). 17.99 *(978-1-4424-0909-5(6),* Simon & Schuster Bks. For Young Readers) Simon & Schuster Bks. For Young Readers.
Diaz, Stephanie. Evolution. 2015. (Extraction Ser.: 3). (ENG.). 320p. (YA). (gr. 7). 21.99 *(978-1-250-04126-5(0),* 9781250041265, St. Martin's Griffin) St. Martin's Pr.
—Extraction. 2014. (Extraction Ser.: 1). (ENG.). 416p. (YA). (gr. 7-12). 18.99 *(978-1-250-04117-3(1),* 9781250041173, St. Martin's Griffin) St. Martin's Pr.
—Rebellion. 2015. (Extraction Ser.: 2). (ENG.). 336p. (YA). (gr. 7). 19.99 *(978-1-250-04125-8(2),* 9781250041258, St. Martin's Griffin) St. Martin's Pr.
Dixon, John. Phoenix Island. 2014. (ENG.). 320p. pap. 11.99 *(978-1-4767-3865-9(3),* Gallery Bks.) Gallery Bks.
Doeden, Matt. Can You Survive a Global Blackout? An Interactive Doomsday Adventure. Nathan, James, illus. 2015. (You Choose: Doomsday Ser.). (ENG.). 112p. (gr. 3-4). lib. bdg. 31.99 *(978-1-4914-5850-1(X),* You Choose Bks.) Capstone Press of Coughlan Cos.
—Can You Survive an Artificial Intelligence Uprising? An Interactive Doomsday Adventure. Fisher-Johnson, Paul, illus. 2016. (You Choose: Doomsday Ser.). (ENG.). 112p. (gr. 3-4). lib. bdg. 31.99 *(978-1-4914-8107-3(2),* You Choose Bks.) Capstone Press of Coughlan Cos.
—Can You Survive an Asteroid Strike? An Interactive Doomsday Adventure. Davidson, Paul, illus. 2016. (You Choose: Doomsday Ser.). (ENG.). 112p. (gr. 3-4). lib. bdg. 31.99 *(978-1-4914-8109-7(9),* You Choose Bks.) Capstone Press of Coughlan Cos.
dos Santos, Steven. The Culling. 2013. (Torch Keeper Ser.: 1). (ENG.). 432p. (YA). pap. 9.99 *(978-0-7387-3537-5(X),* Flux) North Star Editions.
Doyle, Bill & Borgenicht, David. Everest: You Decide How to Survive! 2015. (WorstCase Scenario Ultimate Adventure Ser.). (ENG., Illus.). 204p. (gr. 3-8). 47.10 *(978-1-59920-978-4(0))* Black Rabbit Bks.
Dragon, Laura. Hurricane Boy, 1 vol. 2014. (ENG., Illus.). 160p. (J). (gr. 3-7). pap. 8.95 *(978-1-4556-1916-0(7))* Pelican Publishing Co., Inc.
Duey, Kathleen & Bale, Karen A. Earthquake: San Francisco 1906. 2014. (Survivors Ser.). (ENG., Illus.). 160p. (J). (gr. 3-7). pap. 6.99 *(978-1-4814-0079-4(7),* Aladdin) Simon & Schuster Children's Publishing.
—Fire: Chicago 1871. 2014. (Survivors Ser.). (ENG., Illus.). 176p. (J). (gr. 3-7). pap. 6.99 *(978-1-4424-9054-3(3),* Aladdin) Simon & Schuster Children's Publishing.
—Fire: Chicago 1871. 2014. (Survivors Ser.). (ENG., Illus.). 176p. (J). (gr. 3-7). 16.99 *(978-1-4424-9055-0(1),* Simon & Schuster/Paula Wiseman Bks.) Simon & Schuster/Paula Wiseman Bks.
—Flood: Mississippi 1927. 2015. (Survivors Ser.). (ENG., Illus.). 176p. (J). (gr. 3-7). pap. 6.99 *(978-1-4814-1642-9(1),* Aladdin) Simon & Schuster Children's Publishing.
—Titanic: April 1912. 2014. (Survivors Ser.). (ENG., Illus.). 192p. (J). (gr. 3-7). 15.99 *(978-1-4424-9052-9(7),* Simon & Schuster/Paula Wiseman Bks.) Simon & Schuster/Paula Wiseman Bks.
Duncan, Alexandra. Blight. 2017. 400p. (YA). (gr. 8). 17.99 *(978-0-06-239699-0(4),* Greenwillow Bks.) HarperCollins Pubs.
Dunivan, Dennis W. Escape from Communist Heaven. 2013. (ENG., Illus.). 392p. 17.99 *(978-1-59181-229-6(1))* Sentient Pubns.
DuPrau, Jeanne. Voyagers: Escape the Vortex (Book 5) 2016. (Voyager Ser.). (ENG.). 208p. (J). (gr. 3-7). 12.99 *(978-0-385-38670-8(2),* Random Hse. Bks. for Young Readers) Random Hse. Children's Bks.
Durst, Sarah Beth. Vessel. (ENG., Illus.). 432p. (YA). (gr. 7). 2013. pap. 9.99 *(978-1-4424-2377-0(3))* 2012. 16.99 *(978-1-4424-2376-3(5))* McElderry, Margaret K. Bks. (McElderry, Margaret K. Bks.).
Duyvis, Corinne. On the Edge of Gone. 2016. (ENG.). 464p. (J). (gr. 8-17). 17.95 *(978-1-4197-1903-5(3),* Amulet Bks.) Abrams, Inc.
Eames, Brian. The Dagger X. 2013. (Dagger Chronicles Ser.). (ENG.). 368p. (J). (gr. 3-7). 15.99 *(978-1-4424-6855-9(6),* Simon & Schuster Bks. For Young Readers) Simon & Schuster Bks. For Young Readers.
—The Dagger X. 2013. (Dagger Chronicles Ser.). (ENG., Illus.). 368p. (J). (gr. 3-7). pap. 6.99 *(978-1-4424-6856-6(4),* Simon & Schuster/Paula Wiseman Bks.) Simon & Schuster/Paula Wiseman Bks.
Egan, Kate. The Hunger Games - Catching Fire. 2013. (ENG., Illus.). 160p. (J). (gr. 7-12). pap. 18.99 *(978-0-545-59933-7(4))* Scholastic, Inc.
Ellis, Deborah. The Breadwinner. 2013. 164p. pap. *(978-1-4596-6483-8(3))* ReadHowYouWant.com, Ltd.
—The Breadwinner. 2015. (Breadwinner Ser.: 1). lib. bdg. 20.80 *(978-0-606-37232-9(6))* Turtleback Bks.
—Parvana's Journey, 1 vol. 2015. (Breadwinner Ser.). (ENG., Illus.). 200p. (J). (gr. 4-9). pap. 9.95 *(978-1-55498-770-2(9))* Groundwood Bks. CAN. Dist: Publishers Group West (PGW).
Eshbaugh, Julie. Obsidian & Stars. 2017. 368p. (YA). (gr. 9). 17.99 *(978-0-06-239928-1(4),* HarperTeen) HarperCollins Pubs.
Etienne, Sara Wilson. Lotus & Thorn. 2016. (ENG., Illus.). 464p. (YA). (gr. 9). 17.99 *(978-0-399-25669-1(5),* G.P. Putnam's Sons Books for Young Readers) Penguin Young Readers Group.
Everett, Mikaela. The Unquiet. 2015. (ENG.). 464p. (YA). (gr. 9). 17.99 *(978-0-06-238127-9(X),* Greenwillow Bks.) HarperCollins Pubs.
Falls, Kat. Inhuman. 2015. (ENG.). 384p. (J). (gr. 7). pap. 9.99 *(978-0-545-37101-8(5),* Scholastic Pr.) Scholastic, Inc.
Fane, Judy B. Paddy the Pelican Survives the Storm. Alden, Carol, illus. 2010. 48p. pap. 16.50 *(978-1-60911-448-0(5),* Eloquent Bks.) Strategic Book Publishing & Rights Agency (SBPRA).
Finke, M. e. Taconi & Claude: Double Trouble. 2011. 102p. pap. 8.95 *(978-1-61633-130-6(5))* Guardian Angel Publishing, Inc.
Fiona Fox Staff, ed. The Swiss Family Robinson. 2012. (ENG., Illus.). 224p. (J). 15.00 *(978-1-84135-839-0(8))* Award Pubns. Ltd. GBR. Dist: Parkwest Pubns., Inc.
Fleming, Bryn. Cassie & Jasper: Cattle Drive Danger. 2016. (Range Riders Ser.). (ENG.). 147p. (J). pap. 10.99 *(978-1-941821-95-4(2),* West Winds Pr.) Graphic Arts Ctr. Publishing Co.
—Cassie & Jasper: Kidnapped Cattle. 2016. (Range Riders Ser.). (ENG.). 147p. (J). 24.99 *(978-1-943328-66-6(8),* West Winds Pr.) Graphic Arts Ctr. Publishing Co.
Flood, Nancy Bo. Warriors in the Crossfire. 2013. (ENG.). 144p. (J). (gr. 6-9). pap. 7.95 *(978-1-62091-026-9(8))* Boyds Mills Pr.
Frey, James & Johnson-Shelton, Nils. The Calling. (Endgame Ser.: 1). (ENG.). (gr. 9). 2015. 496p. (YA). pap. 10.99 *(978-0-06-233259-2(7))* 2014. 464p. (J). 19.99 *(978-0-06-233258-5(9),* HarperTeen) HarperCollins Pubs.
—The Complete Training Diaries. 2015. (Endgame: the Training Diaries: Nos. 1-3). (ENG.). 416p. (YA). (gr. 9). pap. 9.99 *(978-0-06-233276-9(7))* HarperCollins Pubs.
—Sky Key. 2015. (Endgame Ser.: 2). (ENG.). 512p. (YA). (gr. 9). 19.99 *(978-0-06-233261-5(9))* HarperCollins Pubs.
Fukuda, Andrew. The Hunt. 2012. (Hunt Trilogy Ser.: 1). (ENG.). 304p. (YA). (gr. 7). pap. 11.99 *(978-1-250-00529-8(9),* 9781250005298); 17.99 *(978-1-250-00514-4(0),* 9781250005144) St. Martin's Pr. (St. Martin's Griffin).
—The Prey. 2013. (Hunt Trilogy Ser.: 2). (ENG.). 336p. (YA). (gr. 7-12). pap. 10.99 *(978-1-250-00530-4(2),* 9781250005304); 18.99 *(978-1-250-00511-3(6),* 9781250005113) St. Martin's Pr. (St. Martin's Griffin).
Garner, Em. Contaminated 2 - Mercy Mode. 2014. (ENG.). 341p. (J). (gr. 7). 17.99 *(978-1-60684-356-7(7),* Carolrhoda Lab™) Lerner Publishing Group.

S

Garretson, Dee. Wildfire Run. 2011. (ENG.). 288p. (J). (gr. 3-7). pap. 6.99 (978-0-06-195350-7(4)) HarperCollins Pubs.

Gary, Paulsen. Hatchet. 2014. (ENG.). 192p. (J). (gr. 3-3). 12.24 (978-1-63245-105-7(0)) Lectorum Pubns., Inc.

Gemeinhart, Dan. Scar Island. 2017. (ENG.). 256p. (J). (gr. 3-7). 16.99 (978-1-338-05384-5(1), Scholastic Pr.) Scholastic, Inc.

George, Jean Craighead. Julie of the Wolves. Schoenherr, John, illus. (Julie of the Wolves Ser.: 1). (ENG.). (J). (gr. 8-18). 2016. 224p. pap. 6.99 (978-0-06-440058-9(1)) 2003. 208p. pap. 8.99 (978-0-06-054095-1(8), HarperTeen) HarperCollins Pubs.

—Julie of the Wolves. l.t. ed. 2004. (Beeler Mystery Ser.). 32.95 (978-1-58118-121-0(3)) LRS.

Gessner, Marina, pseud. The Distance from Me to You. 2015. (ENG.). 352p. (YA). (gr. 7). 16.99 (978-0-399-17323-3(4), G.P. Putnam's Sons Books for Young Readers) Penguin Young Readers Group.

Gibbs, Stuart. Spy Camp. (Spy School Ser.). (ENG., Illus.). (J). (gr. 3-7). 2014. 352p. pap. 7.99 (978-1-4424-5754-6(6)) 2013. 336p. 17.99 (978-1-4424-5753-9(8)) Simon & Schuster Bks. For Young Readers. (Simon & Schuster Bks. For Young Readers).

Gillespie, Hollis. We Will Be Crashing Shortly. 2015. (ENG.). 240p. (YA). 17.99 (978-1-4405-6770-4(0), Simon Pulse) Simon Pulse.

Gilman, David. Blood Sun. 2012. (Danger Zone Ser.). (ENG.). 432p. (YA). (gr. 7). pap. 10.99 (978-0-440-42241-9(8), Ember) Random Hse. Children's Bks.

Gilmore, Grace. Lost in the Blizzard. Brown, Petra, illus. 2015. (Tales from Maple Ridge Ser.: 5). (ENG.). 128p. (J). (gr. k-4). pap. 5.99 (978-1-4814-4749-2(1), Little Simon) Little Simon.

Glasgow, Kathleen. Girl in Pieces. 2016. (ENG.). 416p. (YA). (gr. 9). lib. bdg. 21.99 (978-1-101-93473-9(5), Delacorte Pr.) Random House Publishing Group.

—Girl in Pieces. 2016. (ENG.). 416p. (YA). (gr. 9). 18.99 (978-1-101-93471-5(9), Delacorte Pr.) Random Hse. Children's Bks.

Gleitzman, Morris. Then. 2013. (Once Ser.: 2). (ENG.). 224p. (YA). (gr. 7). pap. 9.99 (978-1-250-00341-6(5), 9781250003416) Square Fish.

Golden, Christopher & Lebbon, Tim. The Wild. Ruth, Greg, illus. 2011. (Secret Journeys of Jack London Ser.: 1). (ENG.). 368p. (YA). (gr. 5-18). 15.99 (978-0-06-186317-2(3), HarperTeen) HarperCollins Pubs.

Goodman, Gabriel. Plague Riders. 2012. (After the Dust Settled Ser.). (ENG.). 112p. (YA). (gr. 6-12). pap. 7.95 (978-0-8225-9033-0(6), Darby Creek); lib. bdg. 27.93 (978-0-7613-8330-7(1)) Lerner Publishing Group.

Gott, Robert. Jinxed. 2007. 96p. (YA). pap. (978-1-4207-0732-8(9)) Sundance/Newbridge Educational Publishing.

Grant, Donna. Hungrige Begierde. 2014.Tr. of The Hunger. (GER.). pap. 5.99 (978-1-942017-15-8(4)) DL Grant, LLC.

Grant, Katy. Hide & Seek, 1 vol. (ENG.). 240p. (J). 2012. pap. 7.95 (978-1-56145-669-7(1)) 2010. (gr. 3-7). 15.95 (978-1-56145-542-3(3)) Peachtree Pubs.

Grant, Michael. Fear. 2012. (Gone Ser.: 5). (ENG.). 528p. (YA). (gr. 9). 17.99 (978-0-06-144915-4(6), Tegen, Katherine Bks) HarperCollins Pubs.

—Gone. (Gone Ser.: 1). 576p. 2014. (ENG.). (YA). (gr. 8). pap. 9.99 (978-0-06-144878-2(8), Tegen, Katherine Bks) 2008. (Illus.). (J). (gr. 7-18). lib. bdg. 18.89 (978-0-06-144877-5(X), HarperTeen) 2008. (ENG., Illus.). (YA). (gr. 8-18). 17.99 (978-0-06-144876-8(1), Tegen, Katherine Bks) HarperCollins Pubs.

—Hunger. (Gone Ser.: 2). (ENG.). 608p. (YA). (gr. 8-18). 2014. pap. 9.99 (978-0-06-144908-6(3)) 2009. (Illus.). 17.99 (978-0-06-144906-2(7)) HarperCollins Pubs. (Tegen, Katherine Bks).

—Lies. (Gone Ser.: 3). 464p. (YA). (gr. 8). 2014. (ENG.). pap. 9.99 (978-0-06-144911-6(3)) 2010. lib. bdg. 18.89 (978-0-06-144910-9(5)) 2010. (ENG.). 17.99 (978-0-06-144909-3(1)) HarperCollins Pubs. (Tegen, Katherine Bks).

—Light. 2013. (Gone Ser.: 6). 432p. (YA). (gr. 9). (ENG.). 18.99 (978-0-06-144918-5(0)); lib. bdg. 19.89 (978-0-06-144919-2(9)) HarperCollins Pubs. (Tegen, Katherine Bks).

—Plague. (Gone Ser.: 4). (ENG.). (YA). (gr. 8). 2014. 528p. pap. 9.99 (978-0-06-144914-7(8)) 2011. 512p. 17.99 (978-0-06-144912-3(1)) HarperCollins Pubs. (Tegen, Katherine Bks).

Griffin, Paul. Adrift. 2015. (ENG.). 240p. (J). (gr. 7). 17.99 (978-0-545-70939-2(3), Scholastic Pr.) Scholastic, Inc.

Gunderson, Jessica. Passage to Fortune: Searching for Saguenay. Kurtz, Rory, illus. 2016. (Discovering the New World Ser.). (ENG.). 96p. (gr. 3-4). lib. bdg. 26.65 (978-1-4965-3481-1(6), Connect) Stone Arch Bks.

—Passage to Fortune: Searching for Saguenay. Kurtz, Rory, illus. 2016. (Discovering the New World Ser.). (ENG.). 96p. (gr. 3-4). pap. 7.95 (978-1-4965-3482-8(4), Connect) Stone Arch Bks.

Gutman, Dan. Getting Air. 2008. (ENG.). 240p. (J). (gr. 3-7). pap. 5.99 (978-0-689-87681-3(5), Simon & Schuster Bks. For Young Readers) Simon & Schuster Bks. For Young Readers.

Hall, Teri. Away. 2011. (ENG.). 240p. (YA). (gr. 7-18). 16.99 (978-0-8037-3502-6(2), Dial Bks) Penguin Young Readers Group.

Halpern, Jake & Kujawinski, Peter. Nightfall. 2015. (ENG., Illus.). 368p. (YA). (gr. 7). 17.99 (978-0-399-17580-0(6), G.P. Putnam's Sons Books for Young Readers) Penguin Young Readers Group.

Hannon, Rose. Finding Agate: An Epic Story of a Poodle's Heart & His Will to Survive. 2010. 268p. pap. 16.99 (978-1-4490-8986-3(0)) AuthorHouse.

Harrison, Margot. The Killer in Me. 2016. (ENG., Illus.). 364p. (YA). (gr. 9-17). 17.99 (978-1-4847-2799-7(1)) Hyperion Bks. for Children.

Hart, Alison. Emma's River, 1 vol. Bachem, Paul, illus. 2010. (ENG.). 160p. (J). (gr. 2-5). 12.95 (978-1-56145-524-9(5), Peachtree Junior) Peachtree Pubs.

Havard, Amanda. The Survivors. 2011. (ENG.). (YA). 294p. 21.99 (978-0-9833190-0-9(6)); 300p. pap. 11.99 (978-0-9833190-2-3(2)) Chafie Pr., LLC.

Heard, Margaret. It's Water Time. 2013. 42p. pap. 16.99 (978-1-105-86035-5(3)) Lulu Pr., Inc.

Heltzel, Anne. Circle Nine. 2011. (ENG.). 272p. (YA). (gr. 9). 16.99 (978-0-7636-5333-0(0)) Candlewick Pr.

Helvig, Kristi. Burn Out. 2015. (ENG., Illus.). 272p. (gr. 9). pap. 9.99 (978-1-60684-569-1(1), Carolrhoda Lab™) Lerner Publishing Group.

—Strange Skies, Bk. 2. 2015. (ENG.). 272p. (gr. 9). 17.99 (978-1-60684-481-6(4), Carolrhoda Lab™) Lerner Publishing Group.

Hicks, Faith Erin. The Nameless City. 2016. (Nameless City Ser.: 1). (ENG., Illus.). 240p. (J). pap. 14.99 (978-1-62672-156-2(4), 9781626721562, First Second Bks.) Roaring Brook Pr.

Higson, Charlie. The End (an Enemy Novel) (Enemy Novel Ser.). (ENG.). 512p. (YA). (gr. 9-17). 2017. pap. 9.99 **(978-1-4847-3291-5(X))** 2016. 17.99 (978-1-4847-1695-3(7)) Hyperion Bks. for Children.

—The Fallen (an Enemy Novel) 2014. (Enemy Novel Ser.). (ENG.). 544p. (YA). (gr. 9-17). 17.99 (978-1-4231-6566-8(7)) Disney Pr.

—The Fallen (an Enemy Novel) 2015. (Enemy Novel Ser.). (ENG.). 560p. (YA). (gr. 9-17). pap. 9.99 (978-1-4231-6636-8(1)) Hyperion Bks. for Children.

—The Fear (new Cover) (an Enemy Novel) 2014. (Enemy Novel Ser.). (ENG.). 496p. (YA). (gr. 9-17). pap. 9.99 (978-1-4847-2144-5(6)) Hyperion Bks. for Children.

—The Hunted (an Enemy Novel) 2015. (Enemy Novel Ser.: 6). (ENG.). 464p. (YA). (gr. 9-17). 17.99 (978-1-4231-6567-5(5)) Hyperion Bks. for Children.

—The Sacrifice. 2013. (Enemy Novel Ser.). (ENG.). 496p. (YA). (gr. 9-17). 17.99 (978-1-4231-6565-1(9)) Hyperion Pr.

—The Sacrifice (an Enemy Novel) 2014. (Enemy Novel Ser.). (ENG.). 512p. (YA). (gr. 9-17). pap. 9.99 (978-1-4231-6635-1(3)) Hyperion Bks. for Children.

Hirsch, Jeff. Black River Falls. 2016. (ENG.). 336p. (YA). (gr. 7). 17.99 (978-0-544-39099-7(7)) Houghton Mifflin Harcourt Publishing Co.

—The Darkest Path. 2013. (YA). pap. (978-0-545-51224-4(7), Scholastic Pr.) Scholastic, Inc.

—The Eleventh Plague. (ENG.). 288p. (J). (gr. 7). 2012. pap. 9.99 (978-0-545-29015-9(5)) 2011. 17.99 (978-0-545-29014-2(7)) Scholastic, Inc. (Scholastic Pr.).

Ho & Ho, Minfong. The Stone Goddess. 2006. (Reader's Workshop Ser.). (ENG., Illus.). 200p. (C). pap. 19.95 (978-0-7362-3160-2(9)) CENGAGE Learning.

Hobbs, Will. Crossing the Wire. 2007. (Illus.). 216p. (gr. 5-9). 17.00 (978-0-7569-8053-5(4)) Perfection Learning Corp.

—Downriver. 2012. (ENG., Illus.). 208p. (J). (gr. 5-9). pap. 7.99 (978-1-4424-4547-5(5), Atheneum Bks. for Young Readers) Simon & Schuster Children's Publishing.

Hobbs, Will & Hobbs, William. Wild Man Island. 2003. (ENG.). 192p. (J). (gr. 5-18). pap. 5.99 (978-0-380-73310-1(2)) HarperCollins Pubs.

Hoena, Blake. Can You Survive a Supervolcano Eruption? An Interactive Doomsday Adventure. Vanzo, Filippo, illus. 2016. (You Choose: Doomsday Ser.). (ENG.). 112p. (gr. 3-4). lib. bdg. 31.99 (978-1-4914-8108-0(0), You Choose Bks.) Capstone Press of Coughlan Cos.

Holmes, Kathryn. The Distance Between Lost & Found. 2015. (ENG.). 304p. (YA). (gr. 8). 17.99 (978-0-06-231726-1(1)) HarperCollins Pubs.

Holyoke, Polly. The Neptune Challenge. (ENG.). 352p. (J). 2016. (gr. 5-9). pap. 7.99 (978-1-4847-1571-0(3)) 2015. (gr. 3-7). 16.99 (978-1-4847-1345-7(1)) Hyperion Bks. for Children.

Hoyle, Tom. Thirteen. 2015. (ENG.). 224p. (J). (gr. 7-12). 16.95 (978-0-8234-3294-3(7)) Holiday Hse., Inc.

Hughes, Alison. Lost in the Backyard, 1 vol. 2015. (ENG.). 144p. (J). (gr. 4-7). pap. 9.95 (978-1-4598-0794-5(4)) Orca Bk. Pubs. USA.

Hughes, Mark Peter. A Crack in the Sky. 2011. (Greenhouse Chronicles Ser.). (ENG.). 416p. (J). (gr. 3-7). 9.99 (978-0-385-73709-8(2), Yearling) Random Hse. Children's Bks.

Hunter, Erin. The Blazing Star. 2014. (Warriors Ser.: Bk. 4). (ENG., Illus.). 320p. (J). 16.99 (978-0-06-206358-8(8)) HarperCollins Pubs.

—The Broken Path. 2014. (Survivors Ser.: 4). 320p. (J). (gr. 3-7). lib. bdg. 17.89 (978-0-06-210269-0(9)) HarperCollins Pubs.

—Darkness Falls. 2014. (Survivors Ser.: 3). (ENG.). 320p. (J). (gr. 3-7). pap. 7.99 (978-0-06-210266-9(4)) HarperCollins Pubs.

—Darkness Falls. 2014. (Survivors Ser.: 3). (J). lib. bdg. 18.40 (978-0-606-35496-7(4)) Turtleback Bks.

—Dead of Night. 2017. (Survivors Gathering Darkness Ser.: 2). (J). lib. bdg. 18.40 **(978-0-606-39621-9(7))** Turtleback Bks.

—The Empty City. (Survivors Ser.: 1). (J). (gr. 3-7). 2013. (ENG.). 304p. pap. 7.99 (978-0-06-210258-4(3)) 2012. (ENG.). 288p. 16.99 (978-0-06-210256-0(7)) 2012. 288p. lib. bdg. 17.89 (978-0-06-210257-7(5)) HarperCollins Pubs.

—The Empty City. 2013. (Survivors Ser.: 1). (J). lib. bdg. 18.40 (978-0-606-31803-7(8), Turtleback) Turtleback Bks.

—The Empty City & a Hidden Enemy. 2014. (Survivors Ser.). (ENG.). 592p. (J). (gr. 3-7). pap. 7.99 (978-0-06-232146-6(3)) HarperCollins Pubs.

—The Endless Lake. 2014. (Survivors Ser.: 5). 320p. (J). (gr. 3-7). (ENG.). 16.99 (978-0-06-210272-0(9)); lib. bdg. 17.89 (978-0-06-210273-7(7)) HarperCollins Pubs.

—A Hidden Enemy. (Survivors Ser.: 2). (J). (gr. 3-7). 2014. (ENG.). 304p. pap. 7.99 (978-0-06-210262-1(1)) 2013. 288p. lib. bdg. 17.89 (978-0-06-210261-4(3)) 2013. (ENG.). 288p. 16.99 (978-0-06-210260-7(5)) HarperCollins Pubs.

—A Hidden Enemy. 2014. (Survivors Ser.: 2). (J). lib. bdg. 18.40 (978-0-606-35056-3(X), Turtleback) Turtleback Bks.

—Storm of Dogs. 2015. (Survivors Ser.: 6). (J). (gr. 3-7). (ENG.). 304p. pap. 7.99 (978-0-06-210278-2(8)); (ENG.). 288p. 16.99 (978-0-06-210276-8(1)); 288p. lib. bdg. 17.89 (978-0-06-210277-5(X)) HarperCollins Pubs.

—Survivors: the Gathering Darkness #1: a Pack Divided. Kubinyi, Laszlo & Green, Julia, illus. 2015. (Survivors: the Gathering Darkness Ser.: 1). (ENG.). 304p. (J). (gr. 3-7). 16.99 (978-0-06-234333-8(5)) HarperCollins Pubs.

—Survivors: the Gathering Darkness #2: Dead of Night. Kubinyi, Laszlo & Green, Julia, illus. 2016. (Survivors: the Gathering Darkness Ser.: 2). 304p. (J). (gr. 3-7). 16.99 (978-0-06-234337-6(8)) HarperCollins Pubs.

—Tales from the Packs. 2015. (Survivors Ser.). (ENG.). 320p. (J). (gr. 3-7). pap. 6.99 (978-0-06-229154-7(8)) HarperCollins Pubs.

Hurwitz, Gregg. The Rains. 2016. (Rains Brothers Ser.). (ENG.). 352p. (YA). 17.99 (978-0-7653-8267-2(9), 9780765382672, Tor Teen) Doherty, Tom Assocs., LLC.

Isbell, Tom. The Capture. 2016. (Prey Trilogy Ser.: 2). 448p. (YA). (gr. 8). 17.99 (978-0-06-221605-2(8), HarperTeen) HarperCollins Pubs.

—The Prey. 2015. (Prey Trilogy Ser.: 1). (ENG.). 416p. (YA). (gr. 8). 17.99 (978-0-06-221601-4(5), HarperTeen) HarperCollins Pubs.

Island of the Blue Dolphins. 2011. 9.00 (978-0-7848-3655-2(8), Everbind) Marco Bk. Co.

Jacobson, Jennifer Richard. Small as an Elephant. 2011. (ENG., Illus.). 288p. (J). (gr. 4-7). 15.99 (978-0-7636-4155-9(3)) Candlewick Pr.

Jenkins, Jerry B. Crash at Cannibal Valley, 1 vol. 2006. (AirQuest Adventures Ser.). (ENG.). 160p. (J). (gr. 3-7). pap. 6.99 (978-0-310-71347-0(1)) Zonderkidz.

Jinks, Catherine. Living Hell. 2011. (ENG.). 264p. (YA). (gr. 7). pap. 14.99 (978-0-547-54998-9(9)) Houghton Mifflin Harcourt Publishing Co.

Johnson, Kristin F. Black Blizzard. 2017. (Day of Disaster Ser.). (ENG.). 112p. (gr. 6-12). (J). 26.65 (978-1-5124-2774-5(8)); (YA). 12.99 **(978-1-5124-3507-8(4)**, Darby Creek); (YA). 39.99 **(978-1-5124-3506-1(6)**, Darby Creek); (YA). 39.99 **(978-1-5124-2781-3(0)**, Darby Creek) Lerner Publishing Group.

—Deep Freeze. 2017. (Day of Disaster Ser.). (ENG.). 104p. (gr. 6-12). (J). 26.65 (978-1-5124-2776-9(4)); (YA). 12.99 **(978-1-5124-3510-8(4)**, Darby Creek); (YA). 39.99 **(978-1-5124-3509-2(0)**, Darby Creek); (YA). 39.99 **(978-1-5124-2783-7(7)**, Darby Creek) Lerner Publishing Group.

Johnson, Kristin F. Wall of Water. 2017. (Day of Disaster Ser.). (ENG.). 112p. (gr. 6-12). (J). 26.65 (978-1-5124-2778-3(0)); (YA). 12.99 **(978-1-5124-3516-0(3)**, Darby Creek); (YA). 39.99 **(978-1-5124-3515-3(5)**, Darby Creek); (YA). 39.99 **(978-1-5124-2786-8(1)**, Darby Creek) Lerner Publishing Group.

Johnson, Terry Lynn. Falcon Wild. 2017. (ENG.). 176p. (J). (gr. 5). lib. bdg. 16.99 **(978-1-58089-788-4(6))** Charlesbridge Publishing, Inc.

Johnson, Terry Lynn. Overboard! Ukropina, Jovan & Orban, Jani, illus. 2017. (Survivor Diaries). (ENG.). 112p. (J). (gr. 2-5). 9.99 (978-0-544-97010-6(1), HMH Books For Young Readers) Houghton Mifflin Harcourt Publishing Co.

Joiner, Sara K. After the Ashes. 2015. (ENG., Illus.). 352p. (J). (gr. 5-10). 17.95 (978-0-8234-3441-1(9)) Holiday Hse., Inc.

Jonsberg, Barry. Reckoning. 2016. (Pandora Jones Ser.). (ENG.). 336p. (YA). (gr. 8). pap. 12.99 (978-1-74331-813-3(8)) Allen & Unwin AUS. Dist: Independent Pubs. Group.

Kadohata, Cynthia. A Million Shades of Gray. 2011. (ENG., Illus.). 240p. (J). (gr. 5-9). pap. 7.99 (978-1-4424-2919-2(4), Atheneum Bks. for Young Readers) Simon & Schuster Children's Publishing.

Kang, Lydia & Carey, Janet Lee. Catalyst. 2015. (Control Duology Ser.). (ENG.). 400p. (YA). (gr. 7). 17.99 (978-0-8037-4093-8(X), Kathy Dawson Books) Penguin Young Readers Group.

Karr, Kathleen. Worlds Apart, 0 vols. unabr. ed. 2013. (ENG.). 208p. (J). (gr. 5-7). pap. 9.99 (978-1-4778-1710-0(7), 9781477817100, Amazon Children's Publishing) Amazon Publishing.

Karwoski, Gail Langer. When Hurricane Katrina Hit Home. Marshall, Julia, illus. 2013. Orig. Title: When Hurricane Katrina Hit Home. (ENG.). 192p. (gr. 4-7). 15.99 (978-1-62619-083-2(6), History Pr., The) Arcadia Publishing.

Kaufman, Amie & Spooner, Meagan. Their Fractured Light. 2016. (Starbound Ser.). (ENG.). 432p. (YA). (gr. 7-12). pap. 9.99 (978-1-4847-4783-4(6)) Hyperion Pr.

—This Shattered World. 2014. (Starbound Trilogy). (ENG.). 400p. (YA). (gr. 7-12). 17.99 (978-1-4231-7103-4(9)) Hyperion Bks. for Children.

Kehret, Peg. Secret Journey. 2008. (ENG.). 144p. (J). (gr. 3-7). pap. 8.99 (978-1-4169-9112-0(3), Simon & Schuster/Paula Wiseman Bks.) Simon & Schuster/Paula Wiseman Bks.

Kelley, Jane. Nature Girl. 2011. (ENG., Illus.). 256p. (J). (gr. 3-7). pap. 6.99 (978-0-375-85635-8(8), Yearling) Random Hse. Children's Bks.

Kennedy, Katie. Learning to Swear in America. (ENG.). (YA). 2017. 368p. pap. 9.99 (978-1-61963-911-9(4), 9781619639119) 2016. 352p. 17.99 (978-1-61963-909-6(2), 9781619639096) Bloomsbury Publishing USA. (Bloomsbury USA Childrens).

—What Goes Up. 2017. (ENG.). 336p. (YA). 17.99 (978-1-61963-912-6(2), 9781619639126, Bloomsbury USA Childrens) Bloomsbury Publishing USA.

Kennedy, Marlane. Disaster Strikes #3: Blizzard Night. 2014. (Disaster Strikes Ser.: 3). (ENG.). 128p. (J). (gr. 2-5). pap. 4.99 (978-0-545-53048-4(2), Scholastic Paperbacks) Scholastic, Inc.

—Earthquake Shock. 2014. (Disaster Strikes Ser.: 1). lib. bdg. 14.75 (978-0-606-35827-9(7)) Turtleback Bks.

—Tornado Alley. 2014. (Disaster Strikes Ser.: 2). lib. bdg. 14.75 (978-0-606-35828-6(5)) Turtleback Bks.

—Volcano Blast. 2015. (Disaster Strikes Ser.: 4). (ENG.). 128p. (J). (gr. 2-5). pap. 4.99 (978-0-545-53047-7(4), Scholastic Paperbacks) Scholastic, Inc.

Kephart, Beth. This Is the Story of You. 2016. (ENG., Illus.). 264p. (YA). (gr. 7-12). 17.99 (978-1-4521-4284-5(X)) Chronicle Bks. LLC.

Kerr, Gordon. Story of Robinson Crusoe. 2006. 100p. per. (978-1-4067-2131-7(X), Hesperides Pr.) Read Bks.

Key, Watt. Terror at Bottle Creek. 2016. (ENG.). 224p. (J). 16.99 (978-0-374-37430-3(9), 9780374374303, Farrar, Straus & Giroux (BYR)) Farrar, Straus & Giroux.

Keyser, Amber J. The Way Back from Broken. 2015. (ENG.). 216p. (YA). (gr. 6-12). 18.99 (978-1-4677-8817-5(1), Carolrhoda Lab™); 18.99 (978-1-4677-7590-8(8)) Lerner Publishing Group.

Khoury, Jessica. Kalahari. 2015. (ENG.). 368p. (YA). (gr. 7). 17.99 (978-1-59514-765-3(9), Razorbill) Penguin Young Readers Group.

Kimmel, Eric A. & Trueman, Matthew. Simon & the Bear: A Hanukkah Tale. 2014. (ENG., Illus.). 40p. (J). (gr. -1-k). 16.99 (978-1-4231-4355-0(8)) Hyperion Bks. for Children.

Kinch, Michael. The Fires of New Sun. 2012. (Blending Time Ser.: 2). (ENG.). 288p. (YA). pap. 9.95 (978-0-7387-3076-9(9), Flux) North Star Editions.

—The Rebels of New SUN. 2013. (Blending Time Ser.: 3). (ENG.). 288p. (YA). pap. 9.99 (978-0-7387-3151-3(X), Flux) North Star Editions.

King, Emily R. The Hundredth Queen. 2017. (Hundredth Queen Ser.: 1). (YA). (ENG.). 300p. pap. 9.99 **(978-1-5039-4365-0(8)**, 9781503943650, Amazon Children's Publishing); **(978-1-5039-9865-0(7))** Amazon Publishing.

Kizer, Amber. A Matter of Days. 2016. (ENG.). 288p. (YA). (gr. 7). pap. 9.99 (978-0-385-73974-0(5), Ember) Random Hse. Children's Bks.

—A Matter of Days. 2016. lib. bdg. 20.85 (978-0-606-38875-7(3)) Turtleback Bks.

Kloepfer, John. Nothing Left to Ooze. DeGrand, David, illus. 2014. (Zombie Chasers Ser.: 5). (ENG.). (J). (gr. 3-7). 240p. pap. 6.99 (978-0-06-223099-7(9)); 224p. 16.99 (978-0-06-223098-0(0)) HarperCollins Pubs.

—Sludgment Day. Wolfhard, Steve, illus. 2012. (Zombie Chasers Ser.: 3). (ENG.). 224p. (J). (gr. 3-7). pap. 5.99 (978-0-06-185311-1(9)); 16.99 (978-0-06-185310-4(0)) HarperCollins Pubs.

—Sludgment Day. 2012. (Zombie Chasers Ser.: 3). (J). lib. bdg. 16.00 (978-0-606-26867-7(7), Turtleback) Turtleback Bks.

—Undead Ahead. Wolfhard, Steve, illus. 2011. (Zombie Chasers Ser.: 2). (ENG.). 224p. (J). (gr. 3-7). pap. 6.99 (978-0-06-185308-1(9)); 16.99 (978-0-06-185307-4(0)) HarperCollins Pubs.

—The Zombie Chasers #7: World Zombination. DeGrand, David, illus. 2015. (Zombie Chasers Ser.: 7). (ENG.). 240p. (J). (gr. 3-7). 16.99 (978-0-06-229027-4(4)) HarperCollins Pubs.

Korman, Gordon. Escape. 2008. (Island (Playaway Audio) Ser.). (J). 34.99 (978-1-60514-854-0(7)) Findaway World, LLC.

Kras, Sara Louise. The Hunted: Polar Prey. 2014. 64p. (J). (gr. 3-4). pap. 9.95 (978-1-62285-081-5(5)) Enslow Pubs., Inc.

Krys, Michelle. Dead Girls Society. 2016. (ENG.). 304p. (YA). (gr. 7). 17.99 (978-0-553-50802-4(4), Delacorte Pr.) Random Hse. Children's Bks.

Kuehn, Stephanie. When I Am Through with You. 2017. (ENG.). 304p. (YA). (gr. 9). 17.99 **(978-1-101-99473-3(8)**, Dutton Books for Young Readers) Penguin Young Readers Group.

Kurtz, Jane. River Friendly, River Wild. Brennan, Neil, illus. 2007. (ENG.). 40p. (J). (gr. -1-3). 7.99 (978-1-4169-3487-5(1), Simon & Schuster/Paula Wiseman Bks.) Simon & Schuster/Paula Wiseman Bks.

LaFleur, Suzanne. Beautiful Blue World. (ENG., Illus.). (J). (gr. 3-7). 2017. 240p. pap. 6.99 (978-0-307-98032-8(4), Yearling) 2016. 224p. lib. bdg. 19.99 (978-0-375-99089-2(5), Lamb, Wendy Bks.) Random Hse. Children's Bks.

Lake, Nick. Hostage Three. 2014. (ENG.). 400p. (YA). (gr. 7). pap. 9.99 (978-1-61963-438-1(4), 9781619634381, Bloomsbury USA Childrens) 2013. (ENG.). 384p. (YA). (gr. 7). 17.99 (978-1-61963-123-6(7), 9781619631236, Bloomsbury USA Childrens) 2013. 368p. 17.99 (978-1-61963-149-6(0)) Bloomsbury Publishing USA.

—In Darkness. (ENG.). (YA). (gr. 9). 2014. 368p. pap. 10.99 (978-1-61963-122-9(9), 9781619631229) 2012. 352p. 17.99 (978-1-59990-743-7(7), 9781599907437) Bloomsbury Publishing USA. (Bloomsbury USA Childrens).

Lamana, Julie T. Upside down in the Middle of Nowhere. (ENG.). (J). 2015. 328p. (gr. 4-7). pap. 7.99 (978-1-4521-2880-1(4)) 2014. 320p. (gr. 3-7). 16.99 (978-1-4521-2456-8(6)) Chronicle Bks. LLC.

Lamb, Charles, et al. Tales from Shakespeare: "Twelfth Night" Strang, Kay, ed. rev. ed. 2005. (Illus.). 40p. pap. 4.95 (978-0-9542905-7-3(7)) Capercaillie Bks., Ltd GBR. Dist: Wilson & Assocs.

Lasky, Kathryn. Star Wolf. 2014. (Wolves of the Beyond Ser.: 6). (ENG.). 256p. (J). (gr. 3-7). pap. 6.99 (978-0-545-27972-7(0), Scholastic Paperbacks) Scholastic, Inc.

Law, Felicia & Way, Steve. A Storm at Sea: Sorting, Mapping, & Grids in Action. Spoor, Mike & Mostyn, David, illus. 2010. (Mandrill Mountain Math Mysteries Ser.). 32p. (J). (gr. 2-6). 22.60 (978-1-60754-815-7(1)); pap. 10.55 (978-1-60754-820-1(8)) Windmill Bks.

Lawrence, Iain. The Skeleton Tree. 2016. (ENG.). 288p. (J). (gr. 3-7). 16.99 (978-0-385-73378-6(X), Delacorte Bks. for Young Readers) Random Hse. Children's Bks.

Laybourne, Emmy. Monument 14. 2012. (Monument 14 Ser.: 1). (ENG.). 304p. (YA). (gr. 8-13). 17.99 (978-0-312-56903-7(3), 9780312569037) Feiwel & Friends.

—Monument 14. 2013. (Monument 14 Ser.: 1). (ENG.). 352p. (YA). (gr. 8-13). pap. 10.99 (978-1-250-02738-2(1), 9781250027382) Square Fish.

—Savage Drift. 2014. (Monument 14 Ser.: 3). (ENG.). 320p. (YA). (gr. 8). 17.99 (978-1-250-03642-1(9), 9781250036421) Feiwel & Friends.

—Sky on Fire. 2013. (Monument 14 Ser.: 2). (YA). (ENG.). 224p. (gr. 8-13). 18.99 (978-0-312-56904-4(1), 9780312569044); vi, 217p. (978-1-4449-1765-9(X)) Feiwel & Friends.

—Sky on Fire. 2014. (Monument 14 Ser.: 2). (ENG.). 272p. (YA). (gr. 8-13). pap. 9.99 (978-1-250-04432-7(4), 9781250044327) Square Fish.

—Sweet. 2015. (ENG.). 288p. (YA). (gr. 8). 17.99 (978-1-250-05519-4(9)) Feiwel & Friends.

Leavitt, Martine. Blue Mountain. 2014. (ENG.). 176p. (J). (gr. 3-7). 15.99 (978-0-374-37864-6(9), 9780374378646, Farrar, Straus & Giroux (BYR)) Farrar, Straus & Giroux.

Lee, Stacey. Outrun the Moon. 2017. lib. bdg. 22.10 **(978-0-606-40097-8(4))** Turtleback Bks.

Lehman, Theodore H. Defying Odds. 2014. (YA). pap. (978-1-935604-63-1(5)) Gaon Bks.

Leveen, Tom. Sick. 2013. (ENG.). 288p. (YA). (gr. 9-17). 18.95 *(978-1-4197-0805-3(8),* Amulet Bks.) Abrams, Inc.
Little, Kimberley Griffiths. Banished. 2016. (Forbidden Ser.: 2). 416p. (YA). (gr. 9). 17.99 *(978-0-06-219501-2(8))* HarperCollins Pubs.
Locke, Elsie. A Canoe in the Mist. 2005. 224p. *(978-1-86950-568-4(9))* HarperCollins Pubs. Australia.
Lorentz, Dayna. No Safety in Numbers. 2013. (No Safety in Numbers Ser.: 1). (ENG.). 288p. (YA). (gr. 7). pap. 8.99 *(978-0-14-242597-8(4),* Speak) Penguin Young Readers Group.
Lowden, Stephanie. Time of the Eagle: A Story of an Ojibwe Winter. 2004. 128p. (J). pap. 12.00 *(978-1-883953-34-8(0))* Great Lakes Literary, LLC.
Lunetta, Demitria. In the After. 2013. (In the After Ser.: 1). (ENG.). 464p. (YA). (gr. 8). 17.99 *(978-0-06-210545-5(0),* HarperTeen) HarperCollins Pubs.
Maberry, Jonathan. Bits & Pieces. 2015. (Rot & Ruin Ser.: 5). (ENG., Illus.). 592p. (YA). (gr. 7). 19.99 *(978-1-4814-4418-7(2))* Simon & Schuster Children's Publishing.
—Dust & Decay. (Rot & Ruin Ser.: 2). (ENG.). (YA). (gr. 7). 2012. 544p. pap. 11.99 *(978-1-4424-0236-2(9))* 2011. 528p. 17.99 *(978-1-4424-0235-5(0))* Simon & Schuster Bks. For Young Readers. (Simon & Schuster Bks. For Young Readers).
—Fire & Ash. (Rot & Ruin Ser.: 4). (ENG., Illus.). 544p. (YA). (gr. 7). 2014. pap. 11.99 *(978-1-4424-3993-1(9))* 2013. 18.99 *(978-1-4424-3992-4(0))* Simon & Schuster Bks. For Young Readers. (Simon & Schuster Bks. For Young Readers).
—Flesh & Bone. (Rot & Ruin Ser.: 3). (ENG., (YA). (gr. 7). 2013. Illus.). 496p. pap. 11.99 *(978-1-4424-3990-0(4))* 2012. 480p. 17.99 *(978-1-4424-3989-4(0))* Simon & Schuster Bks. For Young Readers. (Simon & Schuster Bks. For Young Readers).
—Rot & Ruin, 11 vols. 2010. (Rot & Ruin Ser.: 1). (J). 122.75 *(978-1-4498-3356-5(X));* 120.75 *(978-1-4498-3358-9(6));* 1.25 *(978-1-4498-3360-2(8));* 256.75 *(978-1-4498-3353-4(5));* 90.75 *(978-1-4498-3354-1(3))* Recorded Bks., Inc.
—Rot & Ruin. (Rot & Ruin Ser.: 1). (ENG.). (YA). (gr. 7). 2011. 480p. pap. 11.99 *(978-1-4424-0233-1(4))* 2010. 464p. 17.99 *(978-1-4424-0232-4(6))* Simon & Schuster Bks. For Young Readers. (Simon & Schuster Bks. For Young Readers).
—Rot & Ruin. 2011. (Rot & Ruin Ser.: 1). lib. bdg. 23.30 *(978-0-606-23292-0(3),* Turtleback) Turtleback Bks.
MacFarlane, John. Stormstruck! 2015. (ENG.). 160p. (J). (gr. 3-7). 16.95 *(978-0-8234-3394-0(3))* Holiday Hse., Inc.
MacHale, D. J. Storm. 2014. (SYLO Chronicles Ser.: 2). (ENG.). (J). (gr. 3-7). 512p. pap. 9.99 *(978-1-59514-668-7(7));* 2nd ed. 496p. 17.99 *(978-1-59514-667-0(9))* Penguin Young Readers Group. (Razorbill).
Manale, Shizumi Shigeto & Marshall, Richard. Running with Cosmos Flowers: The Children of Hiroshima, 1 vol. 2014. (ENG., Illus.). 152p. (YA). (gr. 8-8). 16.99 *(978-1-4556-1966-5(3))* Pelican Publishing Co., Inc.
Markle, Sandra. Family Pack. Marks, Alan, illus. 2011. (ENG.). 32p. (J). (gr. -1-3). 15.95 *(978-1-58089-217-9(5))* Charlesbridge Publishing, Inc.
Marman, Richard. Mcalister's Spark. Marman, Richard, illus. 2013. (Illus.). 364p. pap. *(978-1-909302-21-1(X))* Abela Publishing.
Marryat, Frederick. Masterman Ready. l.t. ed. 2006. 276p. pap. 23.99 *(978-1-4264-0573-0(1))* Creative Media Partners, LLC.
Marsden, John. Tomorrow, When the War Began. 2006. (Tomorrow Ser.: 1). (ENG.). 288p. (J). (gr. 7-12). 9.99 *(978-0-439-82910-6(0),* Scholastic Paperbacks) Scholastic, Inc.
Martin, Laura. The Ark Plan. DesChamps, Eric, illus. 2017. (Edge of Extinction Ser.: 1). (ENG.). (J). (gr. 3-7). lib. bdg. 17.20 ***(978-0-606-40046-6(X))*** Turtleback Bks.
Martin, R. Safe Zone. 2017. (Level Up Ser.). (ENG.). (YA). (gr. 6-12). 112p. pap. 7.99 ***(978-1-5124-5360-7(9));*** lib. bdg. 26.65 ***(978-1-5124-3986-1(X))*** Lerner Publishing Group. (Darby Creek).
Martin, T. Michael. The End Games. 2013. (ENG.). 384p. (YA). (gr. 9). 17.99 *(978-0-06-220180-5(8))* HarperCollins Pubs.
Mary-Todd, Jonathan. Pig City. 2012. (After the Dust Settled Ser.). (ENG.). 112p. (YA). (gr. 6-12). pap. 7.95 *(978-0-8225-8746-0(7),* Darby Creek); lib. bdg. 27.93 *(978-0-7613-8328-4(X))* Lerner Publishing Group.
—Shot Down. 2012. (After the Dust Settled Ser.). (ENG.). 104p. (YA). (gr. 6-12). pap. 7.95 *(978-0-7613-9399-3(4),* Darby Creek); lib. bdg. 27.93 *(978-0-7613-8329-1(8))* Lerner Publishing Group.
—Snakebite. 2012. (After the Dust Settled Ser.). (ENG.). 120p. (YA). (gr. 6-12). pap. 7.95 *(978-0-8225-8745-3(9),* Darby Creek); lib. bdg. 27.93 *(978-0-7613-8327-7(1))* Lerner Publishing Group.
Mason, Prue. Camel Rider. 2011. 9.49 *(978-0-7848-3618-7(3),* Everbind) Marco Bk. Co.
Mass, Wendy. Voyagers: the Seventh Element (Book 6) 2016. (Voyager Ser.). (ENG.). 208p. (J). (gr. 3-7). 12.99 *(978-0-385-38673-9(7),* Random Hse. Bks. for Young Readers) Random Hse. Children's Bks.
Massey, David. Taken. 2014. 311p. (YA). *(978-0-545-66129-4(3));* (ENG.). 320p. (J). (gr. 9). 18.99 *(978-0-545-66128-7(5),* Chicken Hse., The) Scholastic, Inc.
Matson, Lynne. Nil. 2014. (Nil Ser.: 1). (ENG.). 384p. (YA). (gr. 9-13). 18.99 *(978-0-8050-9771-9(6),* 9780805097719, Holt, Henry & Co. Bks. For Young Readers) Holt, Henry & Co.
—Nil Unlocked. 2015. (Nil Ser.: 2). (ENG.). 432p. (YA). (gr. 9). 17.99 *(978-1-62779-293-6(7),* 9781627792936, Holt, Henry & Co. Bks. For Young Readers) Holt, Henry & Co.
Matthews, L. S. Fish. 2006. 183p. (gr. 5-9). 16.50 *(978-0-7569-6626-3(4))* Perfection Learning Corp.
McCaffrey, Laura Williams. Marked. 2017. (ENG.). 368p. (YA). (gr. 7). pap. 9.99 *(978-0-544-93884-7(4),* HMH Books For Young Readers) Houghton Mifflin Harcourt Publishing Co.
McCaughrean, Geraldine. The Death-Defying Pepper Roux. 2010. 336p. (J). (gr. 5-18). 16.99 *(978-0-06-183665-7(6))* HarperCollins Pubs.
—The White Darkness. (YA). 2008. (ENG.). 400p. (gr. 8). pap. 9.99 *(978-0-06-089037-7(1))* 2007. 373p. (gr. 7-12). 18.89 *(978-0-06-089036-0(3))* HarperCollins Pubs. (HarperTeen).
McClintock, Norah. Taken, 1 vol. 2009. (ENG.). 176p. (YA). (gr. 7-12). pap. 14.95 *(978-1-55469-152-4(4))* Orca Bk. Pubs. USA.
McCredie, Elise. Nowhere Boys. 2016. (ENG.). 314p. (YA). (gr. 7). pap. 12.99 *(978-1-76012-016-0(2))* Hardie Grant Egmont Pty, Ltd. AUS. Dist: Independent Pubs. Group.
McDougall, Sophia. Mars Evacuees. (J). (gr. 3-7). 2016. 432p. pap. 7.99 *(978-0-06-229400-5(8))* 2015. 416p. 16.99 *(978-0-06-229399-2(0))* HarperCollins Pubs.
McGinnis, Mindy. In a Handful of Dust. 2014. (ENG.). 384p. (YA). (gr. 9). 17.99 *(978-0-06-219853-2(X),* Tegen, Katherine Bks) HarperCollins Pubs.
—Not a Drop to Drink. 2013. (ENG.). 320p. (YA). (gr. 9). 17.99 *(978-0-06-219850-1(5),* Tegen, Katherine Bks) HarperCollins Pubs.
McKay, Kirsty. Undead. 2013. (ENG.). 288p. (J). (gr. 7). pap. 9.99 *(978-0-545-38189-5(4),* Chicken Hse., The) Scholastic, Inc.
Mead, Richelle. Silver Shadows. 2014. (Bloodlines Ser.: Bk. 5). (ENG.). 416p. (YA). (gr. 7). 18.99 *(978-1-59514-321-1(1),* Razorbill) Penguin Publishing Group.
Mikaelsen, Ben. Jungle of Bones. 2014. (ENG.). 224p. (J). (gr. 3-7). 16.99 *(978-0-545-44287-9(7))* Scholastic, Inc.
—Red Midnight. 2003. (ENG.). 224p. (J). (gr. 5-18). pap. 6.99 *(978-0-380-80561-7(8),* Rayo) HarperCollins Pubs.
—Red Midnight. 2003. 212p. (gr. 5-9). 17.00 *(978-0-7569-1550-6(3))* Perfection Learning Corp.
Millard, Glenda. A Small Free Kiss in the Dark. 2010. (ENG.). 192p. (YA). (gr. 7-18). pap. 16.95 *(978-0-8234-2264-7(X))* Holiday Hse., Inc.
Monninger, Joseph. Crash. 2014. (Stay Alive Ser.: 1). lib. bdg. 16.00 *(978-0-606-35392-2(5))* Turtleback Bks.
—Flood. 2014. (Stay Alive Ser.: 4). lib. bdg. 16.00 *(978-0-606-36065-4(4))* Turtleback Bks.
—Stay Alive #4: Flood. 2014. (Stay Alive Ser.: 4). (ENG.). 208p. (J). (gr. 3-7). pap. 5.99 *(978-0-545-56359-8(3),* Scholastic Paperbacks) Scholastic, Inc.
More Than This. 2014. (ENG.). 480p. (YA). (gr. 9). pap. 10.99 *(978-0-7636-7620-9(9))* Candlewick Pr.
Morgan, Kass. Day 21. (100 Ser.: 2). (ENG.). 320p. (YA). (gr. 10-17). 2015. pap. 12.99 *(978-0-316-23457-3(5))* 2014. 18.00 *(978-0-316-23455-9(9))* Little, Brown Bks. for Young Readers.
—Homecoming. 2015. (100 Ser.: 3). (ENG.). 352p. (J). (gr. 10-17). pap. 12.99 *(978-0-316-38196-3(9))* Little, Brown Bks. for Young Readers.
Mullin, Mike. Ashen Winter. (Ashfall Trilogy Ser.). (ENG.). (J). 2013. 580p. (gr. 6). pap. 10.99 *(978-1-933718-98-9(6))* 2012. 594p. (gr. 8). 17.95 *(978-1-933718-75-0(7))* Tanglewood Pr.
—Ashfall. (Ashfall Trilogy Ser.). (ENG.). 476p. (J). 2012. (gr. 8). pap. 10.95 *(978-1-933718-74-3(9))* 2011. (gr. 6). 17.95 *(978-1-933718-55-2(2))* Tanglewood Pr.
—Sunrise. 2014. (Ashfall Trilogy Ser.). (ENG.). 466p. (J). (gr. 8). 17.99 *(978-1-939100-01-6(1))* Tanglewood Pr.
Murray, Kirsty. Vulture's Wake. 2010. (ENG.). 256p. (YA). (gr. 7-18). pap. 17.95 *(978-0-8234-2282-1(8))* Holiday Hse., Inc.
Myers, Edward. Climb or Die. 2nd ed. 2016. 154p. (J). pap. *(978-1-932727-12-8(4))* Montemayor Pr.
—Solos en la Montaña. 2016. (SPA.). 157p. (J). pap. *(978-1-932727-18-0(3))* Montemayor Pr.
Napoli, Donna Jo. Storm. 2014. (ENG., Illus.). 368p. (YA). (gr. 9). 17.99 *(978-1-4814-0302-3(8),* Simon & Schuster/Paula Wiseman Bks.) Simon & Schuster/Paula Wiseman Bks.
Naylor, Phyllis Reynolds. Roxie & the Hooligans. Boiger, Alexandra, illus. 2007. 115p. (gr. 2-5). 16.00 *(978-0-7569-8284-3(7))* Perfection Learning Corp.
Nelson, O. T. The Girl Who Owned a City. 2012. (Exceptional Reading & Language Arts Titles for Intermediate Grades Ser.). (ENG.). 208p. (YA). (gr. 5-12). pap. 9.95 *(978-0-7613-5086-6(1))* Lerner Publishing Group.
—The Girl Who Owned a City: Graphic Novel. Delk, Chrissy, illus. 2012. (Single Titles Ser.). (ENG.). 128p. (YA). (gr. 5-12). lib. bdg. 29.27 *(978-0-7613-4903-7(0),* Graphic Universe™) Lerner Publishing Group.
Northrop, Michael. Trapped. (ENG.). 240p. (J). 2012. (gr. 7). pap. 9.99 *(978-0-545-21013-3(5))* 2011. (gr. 9-10). 17.99 *(978-0-545-21012-6(7))* Scholastic, Inc. (Scholastic Pr.).
Nuri, Alya & Nuri, Alya. Amr's Adventure in Europe. 2013. 68p. pap. *(978-1-935948-29-2(6))* Roxby Media Ltd.
O'Brien, Caragh M. Birthmarked. 2010. (Birthmarked Trilogy Ser.: 1). (ENG., Illus.). 368p. (YA). (gr. 7-18). 18.99 *(978-1-59643-569-8(0),* 9781596435698) Roaring Brook Pr.
—Prized. 2011. (Birthmarked Trilogy Ser.: 2). (ENG., Illus.). 368p. (YA). (gr. 7). 16.99 *(978-1-59643-570-4(4),* 9781596435704) Roaring Brook Pr.
—Prized. 2012. (Birthmarked Trilogy Ser.: 2). (ENG.). 400p. (YA). (gr. 7). pap. 12.99 *(978-1-250-01031-5(4),* 9781250010315) Square Fish.
—Promised. 2012. (Birthmarked Trilogy Ser.: 3). (ENG.). 304p. (YA). (gr. 7). 17.99 *(978-1-59643-571-1(2),* 9781596435711) Roaring Brook Pr.
—Promised. 2013. (Birthmarked Trilogy Ser.: 3). (ENG.). 336p. (YA). (gr. 7-12). pap. 9.99 *(978-1-250-03428-1(0),* 9781250034281) Square Fish.
O'Dell, Scott. Island of the Blue Dolphins. 184p. (J). (gr. 3-5). pap. 5.99 *(978-0-8072-8327-1(4));* 2004. (gr. 5-9). pap. 36.00 incl. audio *(978-0-8072-8326-4(6),* YA163SP) Random Hse. Audio Publishing Group. (Listening Library).
—Island of the Blue Dolphins. l.t. ed. 2005. (ENG.). 223p. pap. 10.95 *(978-0-7862-7254-9(6),* Large Print Pr.) Thorndike Pr.
—Island of the Blue Dolphins. 2010. lib. bdg. 18.40 *(978-0-606-10724-2(X),* Turtleback) Turtleback Bks.
—Island of the Blue Dolphins. Schwebel, Sara L., ed. 2016. (ENG., Illus.). 256p. 29.95 *(978-0-520-28937-6(4))* Univ. of California Pr.
—Island of the Blue Dolphins: And Related Readings. 2006. (McDougal Littell Literature Connections Ser.). (ENG., Illus.). 208p. (gr. 6-8). 18.50 *(978-0-395-87473-8(4),* 2-70833) Great Source Education Group, Inc.
O'Donnell, Liam. Wild Ride: A Graphic Guide Adventure, 1 vol. Deas, Mike, illus. 2007. (Graphic Guides). (ENG.). 64p. (J). (gr. 3-7). pap. 9.95 *(978-1-55143-756-9(2))* Orca Bk. Pubs. USA.
Oelschlager, Vanita. I Came from the Water: One Haitian Boy's Incredible Tale of Survival. Blanc, Mike, illus. 2012. (ENG.). 40p. (J). (gr. -1-3). 15.95 *(978-0-9832904-4-5(X))* VanitaBooks.
Oelschlager, Vanita & Blanc, Mike. I Came from the Water: One Haitian Boy's Incredible Tale of Survival. 2012. (ENG., Illus.). 40p. (J). (gr. -1-3). pap. 8.95 *(978-0-9832904-5-2(8))* VanitaBooks.
O'Guilin, Peadar. The Call. 2016. (ENG.). 320p. (YA). (gr. 9). 18.99 *(978-1-338-04561-1(X))* Scholastic, Inc.
Olsen, Erik. Cobble Cavern. 2012. (J). pap. 16.99 *(978-1-4621-1009-4(6))* Cedar Fort, Inc./CFI Distribution.
Ormand, Kate & Louise, Kate. Dark Days. 2014. (ENG.). 256p. (J). (gr. 6). 16.95 *(978-1-62873-594-9(5),* Sky Pony Pr.) Skyhorse Publishing Co., Inc.
Osa, Nancy. The Battle of Zombie Hill: Defenders of the Overworld #1. 2015. (Defenders of the Overworld Ser.). (ENG.). 272p. (J). (gr. 6). pap. 9.99 *(978-1-63450-996-1(X),* Sky Pony Pr.) Skyhorse Publishing Co., Inc.
Paley, Jane. Hooper Finds a Family: A Hurricane Katrina Dog's Survival Tale. 2011. (ENG.). 144p. (J). (gr. 3-7). 16.99 *(978-0-06-201103-9(0))* HarperCollins Pubs.
Paquette, Ammi-Joan. Paradox. 2014. (ENG.). 240p. (YA). (gr. 7). pap. 9.99 *(978-0-375-87163-4(2),* Ember) Random Hse. Children's Bks.
Park, Linda Sue. A Long Walk to Water: Based on a True Story. (ENG., 128p. (J). (gr. 5-7). 2011. Illus.). pap. 7.99 *(978-0-547-57731-9(1))* 2010. 17.99 *(978-0-547-25127-1(0))* Houghton Mifflin Harcourt Publishing Co.
—A Long Walk to Water: Based on a True Story. 2009. 8.32 *(978-0-7848-3885-3(2),* Everbind) Marco Bk. Co.
—A Long Walk to Water: Based on a True Story. 2011. 18.00 *(978-1-61383-124-3(2))* Perfection Learning Corp.
—A Long Walk to Water: Based on a True Story. 2011. lib. bdg. 18.40 *(978-0-606-23406-1(3),* Turtleback) Turtleback Bks.
Parker, Amy Christine. Astray (Gated Sequel) 2014. (ENG.). 352p. (YA). (gr. 9). 17.99 *(978-0-449-81602-8(8),* Random Hse. Bks. for Young Readers) Random Hse. Children's Bks.
—Gated. 2013. (ENG.). 352p. (YA). (gr. 9). 17.99 *(978-0-449-81597-7(8),* Random Hse. Bks. for Young Readers) Random Hse. Children's Bks.
Parks, Kathy. The Lifeboat Clique. 2016. 336p. (YA). (gr. 8). 17.99 *(978-0-06-239396-8(0),* Tegen, Katherine Bks) HarperCollins Pubs.
Paterson, Katherine. Bread & Roses, Too. 2008. (ENG.). 288p. (J). (gr. 5-7). pap. 7.99 *(978-0-547-07651-5(7))* Houghton Mifflin Harcourt Publishing Co.
Patterson, James. Crazy House. 2017. (Crazy House Ser.: 1). (ENG.). 368p. (YA). (gr. 9-17). 17.99 ***(978-0-316-43131-6(1),*** Jimmy Patterson) Little Brown & Co.
Patterson, James & Tebbetts, Chris. Save Rafe! Park, Laura, illus. 2014. (Middle School Ser.: 6). (ENG.). 288p. (J). (gr. 3-7). 13.99 *(978-0-316-32212-6(1),* Jimmy Patterson) Little Brown & Co.
Patterson, James & Tebbetts, Christopher. Save Rafe! Park, Laura, illus. 2014. 269p. (J). *(978-0-316-28629-9(X))* Little Brown & Co.
Paulsen, Gary. Brian's Return. 2012. (Hatchet Adventure Ser.). (ENG.). 160p. (YA). (gr. 5). pap. 9.99 *(978-0-307-92960-0(4),* Ember) Random Hse. Children's Bks.
—Brian's Winter. 2012. (Hatchet Adventure Ser.). (ENG.). 176p. (YA). (gr. 5). pap. 9.99 *(978-0-307-92958-7(2),* Ember) Random Hse. Children's Bks.
—Brian's Winter. 2012. lib. bdg. 20.85 *(978-0-606-23879-3(4),* Turtleback) Turtleback Bks.
—Hatchet. 2003. (ENG.). 160p. (J). mass mkt. 9.99 *(978-0-330-31045-1(3),* Pan) Pan Macmillan GBR. Dist: Trafalgar Square Publishing.
—Hatchet. Willis, Drew, illus. 20th anniv. ed. 2007. (ENG.). 192p. (J). (gr. 5-9). 19.99 *(978-1-4169-2508-8(2),* Simon & Schuster Bks. For Young Readers) Simon & Schuster Bks. For Young Readers.
—Hatchet. 2006. 18.40 *(978-1-4177-6883-7(5),* Turtleback) Turtleback Bks.
—The River. 2012. (Hatchet Adventure Ser.). (ENG.). 176p. (YA). (gr. 5). pap. 9.99 *(978-0-307-92961-7(2),* Ember) Random Hse. Children's Bks.
—The River. 2012. lib. bdg. 20.85 *(978-0-606-23880-9(8),* Turtleback) Turtleback Bks.
Paulson, Gary. Hatchet. unabr. ed. 2004. 195p. (J). (gr. 5-9). pap. 36.00 incl. audio *(978-0-8072-8319-6(3),* YA161SP, Listening Library) Random Hse. Audio Publishing Group.
Pearson, Mary E. The Beauty of Darkness. 2016. (Remnant Chronicles Ser.: 3). (ENG., Illus.). 688p. (YA). (gr. 9-12). 18.99 *(978-0-8050-9925-6(5),* 9780805099256, Holt, Henry & Co. Bks. For Young Readers) Holt, Henry & Co.
—The Beauty of Darkness. 2017. (Remnant Chronicles Ser.: Bk. 3). (ENG.). 688p. (YA). pap. 10.99 *(978-1-250-11531-7(0),* 9781250115317) Square Fish.
—The Fox Inheritance. 2011. (Jenna Fox Chronicles Ser.: 2). (ENG.). 304p. (YA). (gr. 7-12). 16.99 *(978-0-8050-8829-8(6),* Holt, Henry & Co. Bks. For Young Readers) Holt, Henry & Co.
—The Fox Inheritance. 2013. (Jenna Fox Chronicles Ser.: 2). (ENG.). 320p. (YA). (gr. 7-12). pap. 11.99 *(978-1-250-01032-2(2),* 9781250010322) Square Fish.
Peretti, Frank E. Trapped at the Bottom of the Sea. 2004. (Cooper Kids Adventure Ser.: No. 4). 144p. (gr. 4-7). 5.99 *(978-0-89107-594-3(1));* Vol. 4. (J). (gr. 3-6). pap. 6.99 *(978-1-58134-621-3(2))* Crossway.
Peretti, Frank E. & Thomas Nelson & Sons Staff. Mayday at Two Thousand Five Hundred, 1 vol. 2005. (Cooper Kids Adventure Ser.: 8). (ENG.). 160p. pap. 6.99 *(978-1-4003-0577-3(2))* Nelson, Thomas Inc.
Perkins, Lynne Rae. Nuts to You. Perkins, Lynne Rae, illus. 2014. (ENG., Illus.). 272p. (J). (gr. 3-7). 16.99 *(978-0-06-009275-7(0),* Greenwillow Bks.) HarperCollins Pubs.
Perkins, Mitali. Bamboo People. 2010. (ENG.). 288p. (J). (gr. 5-9). 17.95 *(978-1-58089-328-2(7))* Charlesbridge Publishing, Inc.
Perry, Michael. The Scavengers. (ENG.). 336p. (J). (gr. 3-7). 2015. pap. 6.99 *(978-0-06-202617-0(8))* 2014. 16.99 *(978-0-06-202616-3(X))* HarperCollins Pubs.
Pfeffer, Susan Beth. The Dead & the Gone. 2010. (Life As We Knew It Ser.: 2). (ENG.). 336p. (YA). (gr. 7-12). pap. 8.99 *(978-0-547-25855-3(0))* Houghton Mifflin Harcourt Publishing Co.
—The Dead & the Gone. 2010. (Last Survivors Ser.: 2). 321p. lib. bdg. 19.65 *(978-0-606-14464-3(1),* Turtleback) Turtleback Bks.
—This World We Live In, Bk. 3. 2011. (Life As We Knew It Ser.: 3). (ENG.). 256p. (YA). (gr. 7). pap. 8.99 *(978-0-547-55028-2(6))* Houghton Mifflin Harcourt Publishing Co.
Philbrick, Rodman. The Big Dark. (ENG.). 192p. (J). (gr. 3-7). 2017. pap. 6.99 ***(978-0-545-78976-9(1))*** 2016. 17.99 *(978-0-545-78975-2(3))* Scholastic, Inc. (Blue Sky Pr., The).
Philbrick, Rodman. Zane & the Hurricane: A Story of Katrina. (ENG.). 192p. (J). (gr. 5-9). 2015. pap. 6.99 *(978-0-545-34239-1(2))* 2014. (Illus.). 16.99 *(978-0-545-34238-4(4))* Scholastic, Inc. (Blue Sky Pr., The).
Phillips, Dee. Titanic. 2014. (Yesterday's Voices Ser.). (YA). lib. bdg. 19.60 *(978-0-606-35583-4(9))* Turtleback Bks.
Pipe, Jim. How to Survive on a Desert Island. 2012. (Tough Guides). (ENG., Illus.). 32p. (J). (gr. 4-6). pap. 10.00 *(978-1-4488-7935-9(3),* PowerKids Pr.) Rosen Publishing Group, Inc., The.
Pon, Cindy. Want. 2017. (ENG., Illus.). 336p. (YA). (gr. 9). 18.99 ***(978-1-4814-8922-5(4),*** Simon Pulse) Simon Pulse.
Pratchett, Terry. Nation. 2008. 504p. (J). pap. 16.99 *(978-0-06-170913-5(1));* 384p. (YA). (gr. 8-18). 17.99 *(978-0-06-143301-6(2))* HarperCollins Pubs.
Prendergast, G. S. Zero Repeat Forever. 2017. (Nahx Invasions Ser.: 1). (ENG., Illus.). 496p. (YA). (gr. 9). 17.99 ***(978-1-4814-8184-7(3),*** Simon & Schuster Bks. For Young Readers) Simon & Schuster Bks. For Young Readers.
Prendergast, Gabrielle. Zero Repeat Forever. 2017. (YA). pap. ***(978-1-4814-8185-4(1),*** Simon & Schuster Bks. For Young Readers) Simon & Schuster Bks. For Young Readers.
Pressler, Mirjam. Malka. 2005. (ENG.). 288p. (YA). (gr. 7-6). reprint ed. 8.99 *(978-0-14-240269-6(9),* Speak) Penguin Young Readers Group.
—Malka. Murdoch, Brian, tr. 2005. 280p. (YA). (gr. 7-12). 13.65 *(978-0-7569-5217-4(4))* Perfection Learning Corp.
Probst, Jeff & Tebbetts, Chris. Stranded. 2013. (Stranded Ser.: 1). (ENG.). 208p. (J). (gr. 3-7). pap. 6.99 *(978-0-14-242424-7(2),* Puffin Books) Penguin Young Readers Group.
—Stranded. 2013. (Stranded Ser.: 1). lib. bdg. 17.20 *(978-0-606-36788-2(8))* Turtleback Bks.
—Trial by Fire. 2013. (Stranded Ser.: 2). (ENG.). 192p. (J). (gr. 3). pap. 6.99 *(978-0-14-242425-4(0),* Puffin Books) Penguin Publishing Group.
Probst, Jeff & Tebbetts, Christopher. Desperate Measures. 2016. (Stranded, Shadow Island Ser.: 3). lib. bdg. 17.20 *(978-0-606-37562-7(7))* Turtleback Bks.
—The Sabotage. 2015. (Stranded Ser.: 5). (ENG.). 224p. (J). (gr. 3-7). 6.99 *(978-0-14-751389-2(8),* Puffin Books) Penguin Young Readers Group.
—Trial by Fire. 2013. 174p. (J). *(978-0-14-751195-9(X))* Penguin Publishing Group.
Proimos, James, Jr. Apocalypse Meow Meow. Proimos, James, Jr., illus. 2015. (ENG., Illus.). 224p. (J). (gr. 3-6). 13.99 *(978-1-61963-472-5(4),* 9781619634725, Bloomsbury USA Childrens) Bloomsbury Publishing USA.
Proimos, James, III & Proimos, James, Jr. Apocalypse Bow Wow. Proimos, James, Jr., illus. 2015. (ENG., Illus.). 224p. (J). (gr. 3-6). 13.99 *(978-1-61963-442-8(2),* 9781619634428, Bloomsbury USA Childrens) Bloomsbury Publishing USA.
Pyron, Bobbie. A Dog's Way Home. 2012. (ENG.). 336p. (J). (gr. 3-7). pap. 6.99 *(978-0-06-198672-7(0),* Tegen, Katherine Bks) HarperCollins Pubs.
—A Dog's Way Home. Jessell, Tim, illus. 2011. (ENG.). 336p. (J). (gr. 3-7). 16.99 *(978-0-06-198674-1(7),* Tegen, Katherine Bks) HarperCollins Pubs.
R. M. Ballantyne. The Coral Island. 2007. 316p. per. 14.95 *(978-1-4218-4004-8(9),* 1st World Library - Literary Society) 1st World Publishing, Inc.
Rainfield, Cheryl. Stained. 2013. (ENG.). 304p. (YA). (gr. 9). 16.99 *(978-0-547-94208-7(7))* Houghton Mifflin Harcourt Publishing Co.
Raver-Lampman, Greg. Adrift: Lost in Life, Marooned at Sea. 2006. 132p. 14.95 *(978-1-888842-32-6(6))* Absey & Co.
Redwine, C. J. Deliverance. 2014. (Defiance Trilogy Ser.: 3). (ENG.). 480p. (YA). (gr. 8). 17.99 *(978-0-06-211723-6(8))* HarperCollins Pubs.
Reese, Jenn. Mirage. 2014. (Above World Ser.). (ENG.). 368p. (J). (gr. 5). pap. 7.99 *(978-0-7636-6929-4(6))* Candlewick Pr.
Reichs, Brendan. Nemesis. 2017. (Project Nemesis Ser.). (ENG.). 464p. (YA). (gr. 7). 17.99 *(978-0-399-54493-4(3),* G.P. Putnam's Sons Books for Young Readers) Penguin Young Readers Group.
Revis, Beth. Shades of Earth. 2013. (Across the Universe Ser.: 3). (ENG.). 448p. (YA). (gr. 9). pap. 9.99 *(978-1-59514-615-1(6),* Razorbill) Penguin Young Readers Group.
—Shades of Earth. 2013. (Across the Universe Trilogy: 3). lib. bdg. 20.85 *(978-0-606-32117-4(9),* Turtleback) Turtleback Bks.
Reyes, Laurisa White. The Rock of Ivanore. 2013. (Celestine Chronicles Ser.). (ENG.). 349p. (J). (gr. 2-7). pap. 9.95 *(978-1-933718-92-7(7))* Tanglewood Pr.
Rhodes, Jewell Parker. Ninth Ward. 2010. (ENG.). 224p. (J). (gr. 5-17). 15.99 *(978-0-316-04307-6(9))* Little, Brown Bks. for Young Readers.
—Ninth Ward. 2012. (J). lib. bdg. 18.40 *(978-0-606-26158-6(3),* Turtleback) Turtleback Bks.
Richards, Natalie D. One Was Lost. (ENG.). (YA). (gr. 7-12). 2017. Illus.). 23.99 ***(978-1-4926-6232-7(1))*** 2016. 320p. pap. 10.99 *(978-1-4926-1574-3(9),* 9781492615743) Sourcebooks, Inc.
Roberts, Jeyn. Dark Inside. (ENG.). (YA). (gr. 9). 2012. 352p. pap. 10.99 *(978-1-4424-2352-7(8))* 2011. 336p. 17.99 *(978-1-4424-2351-0(X))* Simon & Schuster Bks. For Young Readers. (Simon & Schuster Bks. For Young Readers).
—Rage Within. (ENG., 368p. (YA). (gr. 9). 2013. Illus.). pap. 9.99 *(978-1-4424-2355-8(2))* 2012. 17.99 *(978-1-4424-2354-1(4))* Simon & Schuster Bks. For Young Readers. (Simon & Schuster Bks. For Young Readers).
Rock, Peter. Klickitat. 2016. (ENG.). 240p. (YA). (gr. 8-17). 17.95 *(978-1-4197-1894-6(0),* Amulet Bks.) Abrams, Inc.
Rorby, Ginny. Lost in the River of Grass. (Carolrhoda YA Ser.). (ENG.). 264p. (YA). (gr. 7-12). 2012. pap. 9.95

S

(978-0-7613-8498-4(7)) 2011. 17.95 (978-0-7613-5685-1(1)) Lerner Publishing Group. (Carolrhoda Lab™).

Rosenblum, Gregg. City 1. 2015. (Revolution 19 Ser.: 3). (ENG.). 288p. (YA). (gr. 8). 17.99 (978-0-06-212601-6(6), HarperTeen) HarperCollins Pubs.

—Fugitive X. 2014. (Revolution 19 Ser.: 2). (ENG.). 272p. (YA). (gr. 8). 17.99 (978-0-06-212597-2(4), HarperTeen) HarperCollins Pubs.

—Revolution 19. 2013. (Revolution 19 Ser.: 1). (ENG.). 272p. (YA). (gr. 8). 17.99 (978-0-06-212595-8(8), HarperTeen) HarperCollins Pubs.

Ross, Joel. The Fog Diver. (Fog Diver Ser.: 1). (J). (gr. 3-7). 2016. 352p. pap. 6.99 (978-0-06-235294-1(6)) 2015. (ENG.). 336p. 16.99 (978-0-06-235293-4(8)) HarperCollins Pubs.

—The Fog Diver. 2016. (J). lib. bdg. 17.20 (978-0-606-38745-3(5)) Turtleback Bks.

Ross, Joel. The Lost Compass. (Fog Diver Ser.: 2). (J). (gr. 3-7). 2017. 368p. pap. 6.99 **(978-0-06-235309-2(8))** 2016. 352p. 16.99 (978-0-06-235297-2(0)) HarperCollins Pubs.

—The Lost Compass. 2017. (Fog Diver Ser.: Vol. 2). (ENG.). (J). (gr. 3-7). lib. bdg. 17.20 **(978-0-606-40052-7(4))** Turtleback Bks.

Roth, Veronica. Carve the Mark. 2017. (YA). (gr. 9). 512p. pap. 12.99 **(978-0-06-234864-7(7))**; (ENG.). 480p. 22.99 (978-0-06-234863-0(9)) HarperCollins Pubs. (Tegen, Katherine Bks).

Ryan, Carrie. Daughter of Deep Silence. 2015. (ENG.). 384p. (YA). (gr. 9). 17.99 (978-0-525-42650-9(7), Dutton Books for Young Readers) Penguin Young Readers Group.

Saddleback Educational Publishing Staff, ed. River, 1 vol. unabr. ed. 2011. (Heights Ser.). (ENG.). 49p. (gr. 5-8). pap. 7.95 (978-1-61651-281-1(4)) Saddleback Educational Publishing, Inc.

Salamon, Julie. Mutt's Promise. Weber, Jill, illus. 2016. (ENG.). 256p. (J). (gr. 3-7). 16.99 (978-0-525-42778-0(3), Dial Bks) Penguin Young Readers Group.

Salisbury, Graham. Hunt for the Bamboo Rat. 2014. (ENG., Illus.). 336p. (YA). (gr. 7). 16.99 (978-0-375-84266-5(7), Lamb, Wendy Bks.) Random Hse. Children's Bks.

Salote, Ana. Oy Yew. 2013. 276p. pap. (978-1-78299-659-0(1)) FeedARead.com.

Saltzwedel, Hans H. Hans' Journal: A Young German's Memories of His Family's Survival During Germany's Darkest Days. 2003. (Illus.). 234p. per. 19.95 net. (978-1-931934-17-6(7)) Back Yard Pub.

Savit, Gavriel. Anna & the Swallow Man. 2016. (CHI.). 272p. (YA). (gr. 7). pap. **(978-957-33-3251-0(5))** Crown Publishing Co., Ltd.

—Anna & the Swallow Man. (ENG.). (YA). (gr. 7). 2017. 256p. pap. 9.99 **(978-0-553-52208-2(6)**, Ember) 2016. 240p. 17.99 (978-0-553-51334-9(6), Knopf Bks. for Young Readers) Random Hse. Children's Bks.

—Anna & the Swallow Man. 2017. lib. bdg. 20.85 **(978-0-606-39876-3(7))** Turtleback Bks.

Schaaf, Ron. BearClaw: Finding Courage Within. 2007. (J). (978-0-9787555-1-5(0)) Hickory Tales Publishing.

Schroeder, Lisa. Far from You. 2010. (ENG.). 384p. (YA). (gr. 9). pap. 10.99 (978-1-4169-7507-6(1), Simon Pulse) Simon Pulse.

Schwarz, S. L. Treasure at Lure Lake. 2016. (Illus.). 185p. (J). pap. 12.99 (978-1-4621-1790-1(2)); **(978-1-4621-2600-2(6))** Cedar Fort, Inc./CFI Distribution.

Scott, Elizabeth. Miracle. (ENG., Illus.). (YA). (gr. 9). 2013. 240p. pap. 9.99 (978-1-4424-1707-6(2)) 2012. 220p. 16.99 (978-1-4424-1706-9(4)) Simon Pulse. (Simon Pulse).

Scott, Victoria. Fire & Flood. 2014. (ENG.). 320p. (J). (gr. 9). 17.99 (978-0-545-53746-9(0), Scholastic Pr.) Scholastic, Inc.

—Salt & Stone. 2015. (ENG.). 320p. (J). (gr. 7). 17.99 (978-0-545-53748-3(7), Scholastic Pr.) Scholastic, Inc.

Semionov, Vladimir, illus. Silver Wings. 2007. (Choose Your Own Adventure Ser.: No. 23). 107p. (J). (gr. 4-7). pap. 6.99 (978-1-933390-23-9(9)) Chooseco LLC.

Sepetys, Ruta. Between Shades of Gray. 2009. 10.36 (978-0-7848-3779-5(1), Everbind) Marco Bk. Co.

—Between Shades of Gray. (ENG., (YA). (gr. 7-18). 2012. Illus.). 384p. pap. 9.99 (978-0-14-242059-1(X), Speak) 2011. 352p. 17.99 (978-0-399-25412-3(9), Philomel Bks.) Penguin Young Readers Group.

—Between Shades of Gray. l.t. ed. 2011. (ENG.). 420p. (YA). 23.99 (978-1-4104-4083-9(4)) Thorndike Pr.

—Between Shades of Gray. 2012. lib. bdg. 20.85 (978-0-606-26089-3(7), Turtleback) Turtleback Bks.

Shakespeare, William. Twelfth Night Paperback Book. 2006. (Shakespeare Classics Ser.). (Illus.). 94p. (J). (gr. 4-7). per. 7.95 (978-1-56254-858-2(1)) Saddleback Educational Publishing, Inc.

—Twelfth Night Study Guide. 2006. (Shakespeare Classics Ser.). (Illus.). 48p. (J). (gr. 4-7). per. 17.95 (978-1-56254-859-9(X)) Saddleback Educational Publishing, Inc.

Sharp, Lydia. Whenever I'm with You. 2017. (ENG.). 304p. (J). (gr. 7). 17.99 (978-1-338-04749-3(3), Scholastic Pr.) Scholastic, Inc.

Sherman, M. Zachary & Iligan, Marlon. Damage Control, 1 vol. Cage, Josef, illus. 2012. (Bloodlines Ser.). (ENG.). 88p. (gr. 4-8). pap. 6.95 (978-1-4342-3875-7(X)); lib. bdg. 26.65 (978-1-4342-3765-1(6)) Stone Arch Bks.

Shusterman, Neal. UnSouled. (Unwind Dystology Ser.: 3). (ENG., Illus.). (YA). (gr. 7). 2014. 432p. pap. 11.99 (978-1-4424-2370-1(6)) 2013. 416p. 17.99 (978-1-4424-2369-5(2)) Simon & Schuster Bks. For Young Readers. (Simon & Schuster Bks. For Young Readers).

—Unsouled. 2014. (Unwind Dystology Ser.: 3). lib. bdg. 23.30 (978-0-606-36107-1(3)) Turtleback Bks.

—UnWholly. (Unwind Dystology Ser.: 2). (ENG.). 416p. (YA). (gr. 7). 2013. pap. 11.99 (978-1-4424-2367-1(6), Simon & Schuster Bks. For Young Readers) 2012. 19.99 (978-1-4424-2366-4(8)) Simon & Schuster Bks. For Young Readers.

—UnWholly. 2013. (Unwind Dystology Ser.: 2). lib. bdg. 23.30 (978-0-606-32336-9(8), Turtleback) Turtleback Bks.

—Unwind. 2011. 10.36 (978-0-7848-3496-1(2), Everbind) Marco Bk. Co.

—Unwind. (Unwind Dystology Ser.: 1). (ENG., Illus.). (YA). 2009. 384p. (gr. 8). pap. 11.99 (978-1-4169-1205-7(3)) 2007. 352p. (gr. 7-12). 19.99 (978-1-4169-1204-0(5)) Simon & Schuster Bks. For Young Readers. (Simon & Schuster Bks. For Young Readers).

—Unwind. 2009. (Unwind Dystology Ser.: 1). lib. bdg. 23.30 (978-0-606-10700-6(2), Turtleback) Turtleback Bks.

Sigler, Scott. Alight. 2016. (Generations Trilogy Ser.: 2). (ENG.). 464p. (gr. 9). pap. 10.00 (978-0-553-39317-0(0), Del Rey) Random House Publishing Group.

—Alive. 2016. (Generations Trilogy Ser.: 1). (ENG.). 384p. (gr. 9). pap. 12.00 (978-0-553-39312-5(X), Del Rey) Random House Publishing Group.

Smelcer, John. Edge of Nowhere. 2014. (ENG.). 194p. (J). (gr. 6). pap. 9.99 (978-1-935248-57-6(X)) Leapfrog Pr.

—The Trap. 2007. (ENG.). 176p. (YA). (gr. 7-9). per. 9.99 (978-0-312-37755-7(X), 9780312377557) Square Fish.

Smith, Alexander Gordon. The Fury. 2013. (ENG.). 688p. (YA). (gr. 7). 19.99 (978-0-374-32495-7(6), 9780374324957, Farrar, Straus & Giroux (BYR)) Farrar, Straus & Giroux.

Smith, Andrew. Grasshopper Jungle. 2015. (ENG.). 416p. (YA). (gr. 9). pap. 10.99 (978-0-14-242500-8(1), Speak) Penguin Young Readers Group.

—In the Path of Falling Objects. 2010. (ENG.). 352p. (YA). (gr. 8-12). pap. 12.99 (978-0-312-65929-5(6), 9780312659295) Square Fish.

Smith, Anne & Smith, Owen. Safari Survivor. Rayas, Rubén, illus. 2012. (Twisted Journeys (r) Ser.: 21). (ENG.). 112p. (J). (gr. 4-7). pap. 7.95 (978-1-57505-943-3(6), Graphic Universe™) Lerner Publishing Group.

Smith, Caighlan. Children of Icarus. 2016. (ENG.). 312p. (gr. 9-10). 16.95 (978-1-63079-057-8(5)) Switch Pr.

Smith, Dan. Boy X. 2017. (J). **(978-1-338-17150-1(X))**; (ENG.). 288p. (gr. 3-7). 16.99 (978-1-338-06564-0(5), Chicken Hse., The) Scholastic, Inc.

Smith, Duane. Heritage Revealed Series, 3. (J). (gr. 2-9). pap. 13.95 (978-1-886218-00-0(5)) Azimuth Pr.

Smith, Greg Leitich. Borrowed Time. 2015. (ENG., Illus.). 192p. (J). (gr. 5-7). 16.99 (978-0-544-23711-7(0)) Houghton Mifflin Harcourt Publishing Co.

Smith, Roland. The Edge. 2015. (Peak Marcello Adventure Ser.). (ENG.). 240p. (YA). (gr. 7). 17.99 (978-0-544-34122-7(8), HMH Books For Young Readers) Houghton Mifflin Harcourt Publishing Co.

—The Edge. 2016. (Peak Marcello Adventure Ser.). (ENG.). 240p. (YA). (gr. 7). pap. 7.99 (978-0-544-81354-0(5), HMH Books For Young Readers) Houghton Mifflin Harcourt Publishing Co.

—Eruption. 2012. (Storm Runners Ser.: 3). (ENG.). 160p. (J). (gr. 3-7). 16.99 (978-0-545-08174-0(2), Scholastic Pr.) Scholastic, Inc.

—The Surge. 2011. (Storm Runners Ser.: 2). (J). (ENG.). 144p. (gr. 3-7). 16.99 (978-0-545-08179-5(3)); 133p. pap. (978-0-545-39462-8(7)) Scholastic, Inc. (Scholastic Pr.).

Smith, Roland, et al. Peak. 2008. (Peak Marcello Adventure Ser.). (ENG., Illus.). 256p. (YA). (gr. 7). pap. 7.99 (978-0-15-206268-2(8)) Houghton Mifflin Harcourt Publishing Co.

Smith, Tamara Ellis. Another Kind of Hurricane. 2015. (ENG.). 336p. (J). (gr. 4-7). 16.99 (978-0-553-51193-2(9)); 19.99 (978-0-553-51194-9(7)) Random Hse. Children's Bks. (Schwartz & Wade Bks.).

Sniegoski, Thomas E. Monstrous. 2017. (Savage Ser.). (ENG., Illus.). 448p. (YA). (gr. 9). 18.99 **(978-1-4814-7718-5(8)**, Simon Pulse) Simon Pulse.

Sniegoski, Thomas E. Savage. (Savage Ser.). (ENG.). (YA). (gr. 9). 2017. 432p. pap. 9.99 (978-1-4814-4374-6(7)) 2016. (Illus.). 416p. 17.99 (978-1-4814-4373-9(9)) Simon Pulse. (Simon Pulse).

Sniegoski, Tom. Monstrous. 2017. (YA). pap. **(978-1-4814-7719-2(6)**, Simon Pulse) Simon Pulse.

Snow, Carol. The Last Place on Earth. 2016. (ENG.). 304p. (YA). (gr. 7). 16.99 (978-1-62779-039-0(X), 9781627790390, Holt, Henry & Co. Bks. For Young Readers) Holt, Henry & Co.

Sorrells/Sorrells. Scratch. 2006. 222p. (J). lib. bdg. 23.08 (978-1-4242-2214-8(1)) Fitzgerald Bks.

Speare, Elizabeth George. The Sign of the Beaver. 2011. (ENG.). 144p. (J). (gr. 5-7). pap. 7.99 (978-0-547-57711-1(7)) Houghton Mifflin Harcourt Publishing Co.

—The Sign of the Beaver. 135p. (J). (gr. 4-6). pap. 4.99 (978-0-8072-1517-3(1), Listening Library) Random Hse. Audio Publishing Group.

Sperry, Armstrong. Call It Courage. 2008. 17.20 (978-1-4178-1178-6(1), Turtleback) Turtleback Bks.

Spinale, Wendy. Everland. 2016. (ENG.). 320p. (J). (gr. 7). 17.99 (978-0-545-83694-4(8), Scholastic Pr.) Scholastic, Inc.

Spinale, Wendy. Umberland. 2017. (Everland Ser.: 2). (ENG.). 288p. (J). (gr. 7). 17.99 **(978-0-545-95318-4(9)**, Scholastic Pr.) Scholastic, Inc.

Spooner, Meagan. Lark Ascending. 2014. (ENG.). 328p. (YA). 17.95 (978-0-7613-8867-8(2)) Lerner Publishing Group.

—Shadowlark. 2013. 327p. pap. 17.95 (978-1-4677-1664-2(2)); (ENG.). 336p. (YA). (gr. 7-12). 17.95 (978-0-7613-8866-1(4), Carolrhoda Lab™) Lerner Publishing Group.

—Skylark. 2012. (Skylark Trilogy Ser.). (ENG.). 344p. (YA). (gr. 7-12). 17.95 (978-0-7613-8865-4(6)) Lerner Publishing Group.

Spradlin, Michael P. Into the Killing Seas. 2015. (J). (ENG.). 224p. (gr. 3-7). 16.99 (978-0-545-72602-3(6), Scholastic Pr.); 185p. (978-0-545-83764-4(2)) Scholastic, Inc.

Stasse, Lisa M. The Defiant. 2015. (ENG., Illus.). 352p. (YA). (gr. 7). pap. 10.99 (978-1-4424-3272-7(1)) Simon & Schuster Children's Publishing.

—The Defiant: The Forsaken Trilogy. 2014. (ENG., Illus.). 352p. (YA). (gr. 7). 17.99 (978-1-4424-3271-0(3), Simon & Schuster Bks. For Young Readers) Simon & Schuster Bks. For Young Readers.

—The Forsaken. (ENG., (YA). (gr. 7). 2013. Illus.). 400p. pap. 9.99 (978-1-4424-3266-6(7)) 2012. 384p. 16.99 (978-1-4424-3265-9(9)) Simon & Schuster Bks. For Young Readers. (Simon & Schuster Bks. For Young Readers).

—The Uprising: The Forsaken Trilogy. (ENG., (YA). (gr. 7). 2014. Illus.). 400p. pap. 9.99 (978-1-4424-3269-7(1)) 2013. 384p. 16.99 (978-1-4424-3268-0(3)) Simon & Schuster Bks. For Young Readers. (Simon & Schuster Bks. For Young Readers).

Steele, Philip. The Holocaust: the Origins, Events, & Remarkable Tales of Survival. 2016. (ENG.). 96p. (J). (gr. 7-7). 14.99 (978-1-338-03040-2(X), Scholastic Nonfiction) Scholastic, Inc.

Steig, William. Abel's Island. 2007. (Newbery Award & Honor Bks.). (Illus.). 117p. (gr. 3-7). 17.00 (978-0-7569-8290-4(1)) Perfection Learning Corp.

—Abel's Island. 2007. (Illus.). 117p. (J). (gr. 4-7). 17.20 (978-1-4177-9383-9(X), Turtleback) Turtleback Bks.

Stohl, Margaret. Icons. (ENG.). (YA). (gr. 7-17). 2014. (Icons Ser.: 1). 464p. pap. 24.99 (978-0-316-20519-1(2)) 2013. 448p. 18.00 (978-0-316-20518-4(4)) Little, Brown Bks. for Young Readers.

Sullivan, Tara. Golden Boy. (ENG.). 384p. (J). (gr. 5). 2014. pap. 8.99 (978-0-14-242450-6(1), Puffin Books) 2013. 16.99 (978-0-399-16112-4(0), G.P. Putnam's Sons Books for Young Readers) Penguin Young Readers Group.

Summers, Courtney. This Is Not a Test. 2012. (ENG.). 336p. (YA). (gr. 8). pap. 10.99 (978-0-312-65674-4(2), 9780312656744, St. Martin's Griffin) St. Martin's Pr.

Sundell, Joanne. Arctic Shadow. 2015. (Watch Eyes Trilogy Ser.: 2). (ENG.). 278p. (YA). 25.95 (978-1-4328-3008-3(2), Five Star Trade) Cengage Gale.

—Arctic Will. 2016. (ENG.). 326p. (YA). 25.95 (978-1-4328-3175-2(5), Five Star) Cengage Gale.

Sutton, Laurie. Stranded. Nathan, James, illus. 2017. (J). lib. bdg. **(978-1-4965-5185-6(0))** Stone Arch Bks.

Sylvester, Kevin. Miners. 2016. (MiNRS Ser.: 1). (ENG., Illus.). 352p. (J). (gr. 3-7). pap. 8.99 (978-1-4814-4040-0(3), McElderry, Margaret K. Bks.) McElderry, Margaret K. Bks.

—MiNRS. (MiNRS Ser.: 2). (ENG., Illus.). (J). (gr. 3-7). 2016. 352p. 17.99 (978-1-4814-4042-4(X)) 2015. 336p. 16.99 (978-1-4814-4039-4(X)) McElderry, Margaret K. Bks. (McElderry, Margaret K. Bks.).

Tait, Chris & Wyss, Johann David. The Swiss Family Robinson. Akib, Jamel, illus. 2007. 151p. (J). (978-1-4287-4213-0(1)) Sterling Publishing Co., Inc.

Tanen, Sloane. Are You Going to Kiss Me Now? 2011. (ENG.). 368p. (YA). (gr. 8-12). pap. 8.99 (978-1-4022-5461-1(X)) Sourcebooks, Inc.

Tarshis, Lauren. I Survived Hurricane Katrina 2005. 2011. (I Survived Ser.: 3). (ENG.). 112p. (J). (gr. 3-7). pap. 4.99 (978-0-545-20696-9(0), Scholastic Paperbacks) Scholastic, Inc.

—I Survived Hurricane Katrina 2005. 2011. (I Survived ... Ser.: No. 3). lib. bdg. 14.75 (978-0-606-23743-7(7), Turtleback) Turtleback Bks.

—I Survived the Attacks of September 11, 2001. 2012. (I Survived Ser.: 6). (ENG.). 112p. (J). (gr. 2-5). pap. 4.99 (978-0-545-20700-3(2), Scholastic Paperbacks) Scholastic, Inc.

—I Survived the Attacks of September 11, 2001. 2012. (I Survived . Ser.: No. 6). lib. bdg. 14.75 (978-0-606-26205-7(9), Turtleback) Turtleback Bks.

—I Survived the Battle of Gettysburg 1863. 2013. (I Survived Ser.: 7). (ENG.). 112p. (J). (gr. 2-5). pap. 4.99 (978-0-545-45936-5(2), Scholastic Pr.) Scholastic, Inc.

—I Survived the Battle of Gettysburg 1863. 2013. (I Survived ... Ser.: No. 7). lib. bdg. 14.75 (978-0-606-31530-2(6), Turtleback) Turtleback Bks.

—I Survived the Bombing of Pearl Harbor 1941. 2011. (I Survived Ser.: 4). (ENG.). 112p. (J). (gr. 2-5). pap. 4.99 (978-0-545-20698-3(7), Scholastic Paperbacks) Scholastic, Inc.

—I Survived the Bombing of Pearl Harbor 1941. 2011. (I Survived ... Ser.: No. 4). lib. bdg. 14.75 (978-0-606-23744-4(5), Turtleback) Turtleback Bks.

—I Survived the Destruction of Pompeii, 79 A. D. 2014. (I Survived Ser.: No. 10). (ENG.). 112p. (J). (gr. 2-5). pap. 4.99 (978-0-545-45939-6(7)) Scholastic, Inc.

—I Survived the Destruction of Pompeii, 79 A. D. 2014. (I Survived . Ser.: No. 10). (Illus.). 95p. (J). lib. bdg. 14.75 (978-0-606-36067-8(0)) Turtleback Bks.

—I Survived the Destruction of Pompeii, AD 79. Dawson, Scott, illus. 2014. 95p. (J). **(978-0-545-77568-7(X)**, Scholastic Pr.) Scholastic, Inc.

—I Survived the Eruption of Mount St. Helens, 1980. 2016. (I Survived Ser.: 14). (ENG.). 112p. (J). (gr. 2-5). pap. 4.99 (978-0-545-65852-2(7), Scholastic Paperbacks) Scholastic, Inc.

—I Survived the Hindenburg Disaster 1937. 2016. (I Survived Ser.: 13). (ENG.). 112p. (J). (gr. 2-5). pap. 4.99 (978-0-545-65850-8(0), Scholastic Paperbacks) Scholastic, Inc.

—I Survived the Japanese Tsunami 2011. 2013. (I Survived Ser.: No. 8). (ENG., Illus.). 112p. (J). (gr. 2-5). pap. 4.99 (978-0-545-45937-2(0)) Scholastic, Inc.

—I Survived the Japanese Tsunami 2011. 2013. (I Survived . Ser.: No. 8). lib. bdg. 14.75 (978-0-606-32390-1(2), Turtleback) Turtleback Bks.

—I Survived the Joplin Tornado 2011. 2015. (I Survived Ser.: 12). (ENG.). 112p. (J). (gr. 2-5). pap. 4.99 (978-0-545-65848-5(9), Scholastic Paperbacks) Scholastic, Inc.

—I Survived the Nazi Invasion 1944. 2014. (I Survived Ser.: 9). (ENG.). 112p. (J). (gr. 2-5). pap. 4.99 (978-0-545-45938-9(9)) Scholastic, Inc.

—I Survived the Nazi Invasion 1944. 2014. (I Survived . Ser.: No. 9). lib. bdg. 14.75 (978-0-606-35397-7(6)) Turtleback Bks.

—I Survived the San Francisco Earthquake 1906. 2012. (I Survived Ser.: 5). (ENG.). 112p. (J). (gr. 2-5). pap. 4.99 (978-0-545-20699-0(5), Scholastic Paperbacks) Scholastic, Inc.

—I Survived the San Francisco Earthquake 1906. 2012. (I Survived . Ser.: No. 5). lib. bdg. 14.75 (978-0-606-23936-3(7), Turtleback) Turtleback Bks.

—I Survived the Shark Attacks of 1916. 2010. (I Survived Ser.: 2). (ENG.). 112p. (J). (gr. 3-7). pap. 4.99 (978-0-545-20695-2(2), Scholastic Paperbacks) Scholastic, Inc.

—I Survived the Shark Attacks of 1916. 2010. (I Survived . Ser.: No. 2). lib. bdg. 14.75 (978-0-606-23742-0(9), Turtleback) Turtleback Bks.

—I Survived the Sinking of the Titanic 1912. 2010. (I Survived Ser.: 1). (ENG., Illus.). 112p. (J). (gr. 2-5). 4.99 (978-0-545-20694-5(4), Scholastic Paperbacks) Scholastic, Inc.

—I Survived the Sinking of the Titanic 1912. 2010. (I Survived . Ser.: No. 1). lib. bdg. 14.75 (978-0-606-23741-3(0), Turtleback) Turtleback Bks.

Taylor, Jessica. A Map for Wrecked Girls. 2017. (ENG.). 368p. (YA). (gr. 9). 17.99 **(978-0-7352-2811-5(6)**, Dial Bks) Penguin Young Readers Group.

Taylor, Theodore. The Cay. 2003. (ENG.). 160p. (J). (gr. 5-7). mass mkt. 6.99 (978-0-440-22912-4(X), Laurel Leaf) Random Hse. Children's Bks.

Taylor, Theodore & Taylor, Theodore. The Cay. 2003. (gr. 5-8). lib. bdg. 17.20 (978-0-613-72282-7(5), Turtleback) Turtleback Bks.

Thomas, Lex. The Burnouts. (Quarantine Ser.: 3). (ENG.). 400p. (gr. 9-12). 2016. pap. 9.99 (978-1-5124-0419-7(5), Carolrhoda Bks.) 2014. (J). 17.99 (978-1-60684-338-3(9), Carolrhoda Lab™) Lerner Publishing Group.

—The Giant. 2016. (Quarantine Ser.: 4). (ENG.). 352p. (gr. 9-12). 17.99 (978-1-5124-0103-5(X), Carolrhoda Bks.); (YA). 35.99 (978-1-5124-0159-2(5), Carolrhoda Lab™) Lerner Publishing Group.

—The Loners. (Quarantine Ser.: No. 1). (ENG.). 416p. (gr. 9). 2013. (J). pap. 9.99 (978-1-60684-438-0(5)) 2012. 17.99 (978-1-60684-329-1(X)) Lerner Publishing Group. (Carolrhoda Lab™).

—Quarantine: The Saints Book 2. 2014. (Quarantine Ser.: No. 2). (ENG.). 400p. (J). (gr. 9). pap. 9.99 (978-1-60684-540-0(3)) Lerner Publishing Group.

Thompson, Gare. Mount St. Helens 1980: Fiery Eruption! Inspiring Tales of Courage & Friendship. 2017. (Great Escapes Ser.). (ENG.). 240p. (J). (gr. 3-7). pap. 7.99 **(978-1-4380-0972-8(0))** Barron's Educational Series, Inc.

Thompson, Paul B. Lost Republic. 2014. 256p. (YA). (gr. 6-12). 19.95 (978-1-62324-000-4(X)) Enslow Pubs., Inc.

Treggiari, Jo. Ashes, Ashes. (ENG.). 352p. (J). (gr. 7). 2013. pap. 9.99 (978-0-545-25564-6(3), Scholastic Paperbacks) 2011. 17.99 (978-0-545-25563-9(5), Scholastic Pr.) Scholastic, Inc.

Troupe, Thomas Kingsley. Blizzard: a Tale of Snow-Blind Survival. Fagan, Kirbi, illus. 2016. (Survive! Ser.). (ENG.). 56p. (gr. 4-6). lib. bdg. 25.32 (978-1-4965-2554-3(X)) Stone Arch Bks.

—Lost: a Wild Tale of Survival. Fagan, Kirbi, illus. 2016. (Survive! Ser.). (ENG.). 56p. (gr. 4-6). lib. bdg. 25.32 (978-1-4965-2557-4(4)) Stone Arch Bks.

—Survive! 2016. (Survive! Ser.). (ENG.). 56p. (gr. 4-6). 101.28 (978-1-4965-2575-8(2)) Stone Arch Bks.

—Tornado: a Twisting Tale of Survival. Fagan, Kirbi, illus. 2016. (Survive! Ser.). (ENG.). 56p. (gr. 4-6). lib. bdg. 25.32 (978-1-4965-2556-7(6)) Stone Arch Bks.

—Volcano: a Fiery Tale of Survival. Fagan, Kirbi, illus. 2016. (Survive! Ser.). (ENG.). 56p. (gr. 4-6). lib. bdg. 25.32 (978-1-4965-2555-0(8)) Stone Arch Bks.

Tullson, Diane. The Darwin Expedition, 1 vol. 2007. (Orca Soundings Ser.). (ENG.). 128p. (YA). (gr. 8-12). per. 9.95 (978-1-55143-676-0(0)) Orca Bk. Pubs. USA.

Turner, Tracey. Lost in the Desert of Dread. 2014. (ENG., Illus.). 128p. (J). (978-0-7787-0725-7(3)) Crabtree Publishing Co.

—Lost in the Jungle of Doom. 2014. (ENG., Illus.). 128p. (J). (978-0-7787-0727-1(X)) Crabtree Publishing Co.

Uhlberg, Myron. A Storm Called Katrina, 1 vol. Bootman, Colin, illus. (ENG.). 40p. (J). (gr. 2-4). 2015. pap. 8.95 (978-1-56145-887-5(2)) 2011. 17.95 (978-1-56145-591-1(1)) Peachtree Pubs.

—A Storm Called Katrina. 2015. lib. bdg. 19.60 (978-0-606-37467-5(1)) Turtleback Bks.

Unsworth, Tania. Brightwood. 2016. (ENG.). 272p. (J). (gr. 4-7). 16.95 (978-1-61620-330-6(7)) Algonquin Bks. of Chapel Hill.

—The One Safe Place. 2014. (ENG.). 304p. (J). (gr. 5-8). 15.95 (978-1-61620-329-0(3), 73329) Algonquin Bks. of Chapel Hill.

Van Draanen, Wendelin. Runaway. 2012. (ENG.). 272p. (YA). (gr. 5). pap. 9.99 (978-0-307-97597-3(5), Ember) Random Hse. Children's Bks.

Van Dusen, Chris. The Circus Ship. Van Dusen, Chris, illus. 2015. (ENG., Illus.). 40p. (J). (gr. -1-3). 6.99 (978-0-7636-5592-1(9)) Candlewick Pr.

—The Circus Ship Big Book. 2011. (ENG., Illus.). 40p. (J). (gr. -1-3). pap. 24.99 (978-0-7636-5593-8(7)) Candlewick Pr.

Van Eekhout, Greg. The Boy at the End of the World. 2012. (ENG.). 240p. (YA). (gr. 5-8). pap. 8.99 (978-1-59990-918-9(9), 9781599909189, Bloomsbury USA Childrens) Bloomsbury Publishing USA.

Van Tol, Alex. Knifepoint, 1 vol. 2010. (Orca Soundings Ser.). (ENG.). 128p. (YA). (gr. 8-12). pap. 9.95 (978-1-55469-305-4(5)) Orca Bk. Pubs. USA.

—A Punta de Cuchillo, 1 vol. 2011. (Spanish Soundings Ser.). (SPA & ENG.). 136p. (YA). (gr. 8-12). pap. 9.95 (978-1-55469-863-9(4)) Orca Bk. Pubs. USA.

Vanasse, Patricia. Resilient. Shalaby, Asharaf, illus. 2013. (ENG.). 328p. (YA). pap. 13.99 (978-0-9860373-2-0(X)) Pants On Fire Pr.

Voorhees, Coert. On the Free. 2017. (ENG.). 280p. (YA). (gr. 9-12). 17.99 **(978-1-5124-2913-8(9))** Lerner Publishing Group.

Wacholtz, Anthony. Can You Survive in a Dystopia? An Interactive Doomsday Adventure. Nathan, James, illus. 2016. (You Choose: Doomsday Ser.). (ENG.). 112p. (gr. 3-4). lib. bdg. 31.99 (978-1-4914-8110-3(2), You Choose Bks.) Capstone Press of Coughlan Cos.

Walden, Mark. Aftershock. 2014. (H. I. V. E. Ser.: 7). (ENG., Illus.). 304p. (J). (gr. 3-7). 17.99 (978-1-4424-9467-1(0), Simon & Schuster Bks. For Young Readers) Simon & Schuster Bks. For Young Readers.

—Deadlock. 2015. (H. I. V. E. Ser.: 8). (ENG., Illus.). 304p. (J). (gr. 3-7). 16.99 (978-1-4424-9470-1(0), Simon & Schuster Bks. For Young Readers) Simon & Schuster Bks. For Young Readers.

—Earthfall. 2013. (Earthfall Trilogy Ser.: 1). (ENG., Illus.). 272p. (J). (gr. 3-7). 16.99 (978-1-4424-9415-2(8), Simon & Schuster Bks. For Young Readers) Simon & Schuster Bks. For Young Readers.

—Retribution. 2015. (Earthfall Trilogy Ser.: 2). (ENG., Illus.). 272p. (J). (gr. 3-7). 17.99 (978-1-4424-9418-3(2), Simon & Schuster Bks. For Young Readers) Simon & Schuster Bks. For Young Readers.

Wallace, Brandon. The Journey Home. (Wilder Boys Ser.). (ENG.). 208p. (J). 2017. (gr. 4-8). pap. 7.99 ***(978-1-4814-3266-5(4))*** 2016. (Illus.). (gr. 3-7). 16.99 *(978-1-4814-3267-2(2))* Simon & Schuster Children's Publishing. (Aladdin).

Wallace, Brandon. Wilder Boys. 2017. (Wilder Boys Ser.). (ENG.). 256p. (J). (gr. 4-8). pap. 7.99 *(978-1-4814-3263-4(X)*, Simon & Schuster/Paula Wiseman Bks.) Simon & Schuster/Paula Wiseman Bks.

Wallenfels, Stephen. Pod. 2012. (ENG.). 304p. (gr. 12). 7.99 *(978-1-937007-43-0(X)*, Ace Bks.) Penguin Publishing Group.

Walters, Eric. Fight for Power. 2015. (Rule of Three Ser.: 2). (ENG.). 352p. (YA). (gr. 7). 17.99 *(978-0-374-30179-8(4)*, 9780374301798, Farrar, Straus & Giroux (BYR)) Farrar, Straus & Giroux.

—The Rule of Three. 2014. (Rule of Three Ser.: 1). (ENG.). 416p. (YA). (gr. 7). 18.99 *(978-0-374-35502-9(9)*, 9780374355029, Farrar, Straus & Giroux (BYR)) Farrar, Straus & Giroux.

—Will to Survive. 2016. (Rule of Three Ser.: 3). (ENG.). 320p. (YA). 17.99 *(978-0-374-30181-1(6)*, 9780374301811, Farrar, Straus & Giroux (BYR)) Farrar, Straus & Giroux.

Waters, Rachel. Wanamea: A Choctaw Princess. 2007. 88p. per. 10.00 *(978-1-4257-5976-6(9))* Xlibris Corp.

Weitz, Chris. The New Order. 2015. (Young World Ser.: 2). (ENG.). 320p. (YA). (gr. 10-17). 19.00 *(978-0-316-22630-1(0))* Little, Brown Bks. for Young Readers.

—The Revival. 2016. (Young World Ser.: 3). (ENG.). 272p. (YA). (gr. 10-17). 18.99 *(978-0-316-22634-9(3))* Little, Brown Bks. for Young Readers.

—The Young World. (Young World Ser.: 1). (ENG.). (YA). (gr. 10-17). 2015. 400p. pap. 10.99 *(978-0-316-22628-8(9))* 2014. 384p. 19.00 *(978-0-316-22629-5(7))* Little, Brown Bks. for Young Readers.

Wells, Dan. Fragments. 2013. (Partials Sequence Ser.: 2). (ENG.). 576p. (YA). (gr. 9). 17.99 *(978-0-06-207107-1(6))* HarperCollins Pubs.

—Partials. (ENG.). (YA). 2013. (Partials Sequence Ser.: 1). 528p. (gr. 9). pap. 9.99 *(978-0-06-207105-7(X))* 2012. (Partials Sequence Ser.: 1). 480p. (gr. 9). 17.99 *(978-0-06-207104-0(1))* 2012. 496p. pap. 9.99 *(978-0-06-213569-8(4))* HarperCollins Pubs.

Wells, Robison. Feedback. (ENG.). (YA). 2013. (Variant Ser.: 2). 336p. (gr. 8). pap. 9.99 *(978-0-06-202611-8(9))* 2012. (Variant Ser.: 2). 320p. (gr. 8). 17.99 *(978-0-06-202610-1(0))* 2012. 320p. pap. 9.99 *(978-0-06-222830-7(7))* HarperCollins Pubs. (HarperTeen).

Westerfeld, Scott. Horizon. 2017. (Horizon Ser.: 1). (ENG.). 256p. (J). (gr. 4-7). 16.99 ***(978-1-338-19658-0(8))*** Scholastic, Inc.

Westerfeld, Scott & Lanagan, Margo. Swarm. 2018. (Zeroes Ser.: 2). lib. bdg. 24.50 ***(978-0-606-40832-5(0))*** Turtleback Bks.

Westerfeld, Scott, et al. Swarm. 2016. (Zeroes Ser.: 2). (ENG., Illus.). 464p. (YA). (gr. 9). 19.99 *(978-1-4814-4339-5(9)*, Simon Pulse) Simon Pulse.

White, Ellen Emerson. Voyage on the Great Titanic. 2010. (Dear America Ser.). (ENG., Illus.). 208p. (J). (gr. 3-7). 12.99 *(978-0-545-23834-2(X)*, Scholastic Pr.) Scholastic, Inc.

White, Jennifer. Survival Strategies of the Almost Brave. 2015. (ENG.). 320p. (J). (gr. 3-7). 16.99 *(978-0-374-30084-5(4)*, 9780374300845, Farrar, Straus & Giroux (BYR)) Farrar, Straus & Giroux.

Wiggins, Bethany. Stung. 2014. (ENG.). 320p. (YA). (gr. 9). pap. 9.99 *(978-0-8027-3589-8(4)*, 9780802735898, Bloomsbury USA Childrens) Bloomsbury Publishing USA.

Wilkinson, Kerry. Renegade. 2015. (Silver Blackthorn Trilogy Ser.: 2). (ENG.). 368p. (YA). (gr. 8-12). 18.99 *(978-1-250-06133-1(4)*, 9781250061331, St. Martin's Griffin) St. Martin's Pr.

Williams, M. C. No where to be Found: Time Is Short. l.t. ed. 2006. 38p. per. 3.65 *(978-1-59879-099-3(4))* Lifevest Publishing, Inc.

Williams, Michael. Diamond Boy. 2014. (Illus.). 384p. (YA). *(978-0-316-32067-2(6))* Little Brown & Co.

—Diamond Boy. 2014. (ENG., Illus.). 400p. (YA). (gr. 7-17). 18.00 *(978-0-316-32069-6(2))* Little, Brown Bks. for Young Readers.

—Now Is the Time for Running. 2013. (ENG.). 240p. (YA). (gr. 7-17). pap. 10.99 *(978-0-316-07788-0(7))* Little, Brown Bks. for Young Readers.

Wilson, Diane Lee. Raven Speak. (ENG.). 256p. (YA). (gr. 7). 2011. pap. 8.99 *(978-1-4169-8654-6(5))* 2010. 16.99 *(978-1-4169-8653-9(7))* McElderry, Margaret K. Bks. (McElderry, Margaret K. Bks.).

Windover, Liz. Blood Island. Utomo, Gabhor, illus. 2014. (ENG.). 144p. (J). mass mkt. 6.99 *(978-1-937133-46-7(X))* Chooseco LLC.

Winfield, Arthur M. The Rover Boys on Land & Sea or the Crusoes of Seven Islands. 2006. (ENG.). 284p. per. 28.95 *(978-1-4286-4097-9(5))* Kessinger Publishing, LLC.

The Winter Horses. 2014. (ENG., Illus.). 288p. (YA). (gr. 7). 16.99 *(978-0-385-75543-6(0)*, Knopf Bks. for Young Readers) Random Hse. Children's Bks.

Wolff, Tracy. Book 4: Arrival. 2016. (Mars Bound Ser.). (ENG.). (J). (gr. 2-8). lib. bdg. 28.50 ***(978-1-62402-200-5(6))*** ABDO Publishing Co.

Wood, Gail. Lizzie, Light Feather & the Quarry Bluff Storm. 2015. (Illus.). viii, 88p. (J). pap. *(978-1-57249-415-2(8)*, White Mane Kids) White Mane Publishing Co., Inc.

Wooding, Chris. Silver. 2014. (ENG.). 320p. (J). (gr. 7). 17.99 *(978-0-545-60392-8(7)*, Scholastic Pr.) Scholastic, Inc.

Woods, Brenda. Saint Louis Armstrong Beach. 2012. lib. bdg. 16.00 *(978-0-606-26661-1(5)*, Turtleback) Turtleback Bks.

Wyss, Johann. The Swiss Family Robinson. 2009. (Puffin Classics Ser.). (ENG.). 496p. (J). (gr. 5-7). pap. 5.99 *(978-0-14-132530-9(5)*, Puffin Books) Penguin Young Readers Group.

—Swiss Family Robinson Study Guide. 2003. (Saddleback Classics Ser.). (Illus.). 48p. (J). (gr. 4-7). per. 17.95 *(978-1-56254-532-1(9)*, SP5329) Saddleback Educational Publishing, Inc.

Wyss, Johann David. The Swiss Family Robinson. Tayal, Amit, illus. 2011. (Campfire Graphic Novels Ser.). (ENG.). 88p. (YA). (gr. 3-7). pap. 11.99 *(978-93-80028-47-7(4)*, Campfire) Steerforth Pr.

—The Swiss Family Robinson: Critical Reading Series. (Young Collector's Illustrated Classics Ser.). (Illus.). 192p. (J). (gr. 3-7). 9.95 *(978-1-56156-459-0(1))* Kidsbooks, LLC.

—Swiss Family Robinson: With a Discussion of Teamwork. Butterfield, Ned, illus. 2003. (Values in Action Illustrated Classics Ser.). 191p. (J). *(978-1-59203-036-1(X))* Learning Challenge, Inc.

Wyss, Johann David, illus. The Swiss Family Robinson. 2004. reprint ed. pap. 1.99 *(978-1-4192-5012-5(4))*; pap. 30.95 *(978-1-4191-5012-8(X))* Kessinger Publishing, LLC.

Wyss, Johann David & Kingston, William Henry Giles. The Swiss Family Robinson: A Translation from the Original German. 2016. (J). pap. *(978-1-5124-2612-0(1))* Lerner Publishing Group.

Yancey, Rick. The Infinite Sea. (5th Wave Ser.: 2). (ENG.). (YA). (gr. 9-12). 2015. 336p. pap. 10.99 *(978-1-101-99698-0(6)*, Speak) 2014. 320p. 18.99 *(978-0-399-16242-8(9)*, G.P. Putnam's Sons Books for Young Readers) Penguin Publishing Group.

—The Infinite Sea. 2015. (5th Wave Ser.: 2). lib. bdg. 22.10 *(978-0-606-38204-5(6))* Turtleback Bks.

—The Last Star. 2016. (5th Wave Ser.: 3). (ENG.). 352p. (YA). (gr. 9). 18.99 *(978-0-399-16243-5(7)*, G.P. Putnam's Sons Books for Young Readers) Penguin Young Readers Group.

—The Last Star. 2017. (5th Wave Ser.: 3). lib. bdg. 22.10 ***(978-0-606-40098-5(2))*** Turtleback Bks.

—The 5th Wave. (5th Wave Ser.: Bk. 1). (ENG.). (YA). (gr. 9). 2015. 512p. pap. 10.99 *(978-0-14-242583-1(4)*, Speak) 2013. 480p. 18.99 *(978-0-399-16241-1(0)*, G.P. Putnam's Sons Books for Young Readers) Penguin Publishing Group.

—The 5th Wave. movie tie-in ed. 2015. (ENG.). (YA). (gr. 9-12). (5th Wave Ser.: 1). 512p. pap. 10.99 *(978-0-14-751908-5(X)*, Speak); (5th Wave Ser.: Bk. 1). 480p. 18.99 *(978-1-101-99651-5(X)*, G.P. Putnam's Sons Books for Young Readers);Set. pap., pap., pap. 21.98 *(978-1-101-99998-1(5)*, Speak) Penguin Young Readers Group.

—The 5th Wave. 2015. (5th Wave Ser.: Vol. 1). (ENG.). (YA). (gr. 9). lib. bdg. 21.60 ***(978-1-62765-623-8(5))*** Perfection Learning Corp.

—The 5th Wave. 2015. (5th Wave Ser.: 1). lib. bdg. 22.10 *(978-0-606-36640-3(7))*; lib. bdg. 22.10 *(978-0-606-37680-8(1))* Turtleback Bks.

Yolen, Jane. Trash Mountain. Monroe, Chris, illus. 2015. (J). 17.32 *(978-1-4677-7170-2(8))*; (ENG.). 184p. (gr. 3-6). 16.99 *(978-1-4677-1234-7(5))* Lerner Publishing Group. (Carolrhoda Bks.).

Zeiss, Joyce Burns. Out of the Dragon's Mouth. 2015. (ENG., Illus.). 240p. (YA). pap. 11.99 *(978-0-7387-4196-3(5)*, Flux) North Star Editions.

SURVIVAL AFTER AIRPLANE ACCIDENTS, SHIPWRECKS, ETC.

see Survival

SURVIVAL OF THE FITTEST

see Natural Selection

SUSPENSION BRIDGES

see Bridges

SUTTER, JOHN AUGUSTUS, 1803-1880

Doeden, Matt. John Sutter & the California Gold Rush, 1 vol. Barnett, Charles, III et al, illus. 2005. (Graphic History Ser.). (ENG.). 32p. (gr. 3-4). 30.65 *(978-0-7368-4370-6(1)*, Graphic Library) Capstone Press of Coughlan Cos.

Hayhurst, Chris. John Sutter: California Pioneer. (Primary Sources of Famous People in American History Ser.). 32p. 2009. (gr. 2-3). 47.90 *(978-1-60851-696-4(2))* 2004. (ENG., Illus.). (gr. 4-8). pap. 10.00 *(978-0-8239-4186-5(8))* Rosen Publishing Group, Inc., The.

—John Sutter: California Pioneer / Pionero de California. 2009. (Famous People in American History/Grandes personajes en la historia de los Estados Unidos Ser.). (ENG & SPA.). 32p. (gr. 2-3). 47.90 *(978-1-61512-549-4(3)*, Editorial Buenas Letras) Rosen Publishing Group, Inc., The.

—John Sutter: Pionero de California (John Sutter: California Pioneer) 2009. (Grandes personajes en la historia de los Estados Unidos (Famous People in American History) Ser.). (SPA.). 32p. (gr. 2-3). 47.90 *(978-1-61512-803-7(4)*, Editorial Buenas Letras) Rosen Publishing Group, Inc., The.

Mattern, Joanne. America's Gold Rush: John Sutter & the Discovery of Gold in California. 2009. (Great Moments in American History Ser.). 32p. (gr. 3-3). 47.90 *(978-1-61513-139-6(6))* Rosen Publishing Group, Inc., The.

SUTTER'S FORT (SACRAMENTO, CALIF.)

Mattern, Joanne. America's Gold Rush: John Sutter & the Discovery of Gold in California. 2009. (Great Moments in American History Ser.). 32p. (gr. 3-3). 47.90 *(978-1-61513-139-6(6))* Rosen Publishing Group, Inc., The.

SWALLOWS

Savage, Stephen. Swallow. 2009. (Animal Neighbors Ser.). 32p. (gr. k-5). pap. 10.60 *(978-1-4042-4576-1(6)*, Rosen Classroom); (Illus.). (J). lib. bdg. 25.25 *(978-1-4358-4999-0(X)*, PowerKids Pr.) Rosen Publishing Group, Inc., The.

SWALLOWS—FICTION

Collins, Rachel. Sidney Swallow Sings. 2010. 32p. pap. 15.95 *(978-0-557-44696-4(1))* Lulu Pr., Inc.

Donaldson, Julia. Follow the Swallow. Smy, Pam, illus. 2008. (ENG.). 32p. (J). (gr. -1-2). pap. 9.95 *(978-1-4052-1788-0(X))* Egmont Bks., Ltd. GBR. Dist: Independent Pubs. Group.

Howie, Vicki. The Easter Swallows. Grudina, Paola Bertolini, illus. 2007. 32p. (J). 10.95 *(978-0-8198-2360-1(0))* Pauline Bks. & Media.

Morpurgo, Michael. Dear Olly. Birmingham, Christian, illus. 2007. (ENG.). 128p. (J). (gr. 4-7). mass mkt. 7.99 *(978-0-00-675333-9(7)*, HarperCollins Children's Bks.) HarperCollins Pubs. Ltd. GBR. Dist: HarperCollins Pubs.

Politi, Leo. Song of the Swallows. 2009. (ENG., Illus.). 32p. 16.95 *(978-0-89236-989-8(2))* Oxford Univ. Pr., Inc.

Rouss, Sylvia & Avalone, C. The Littlest Fish. 2008. 32p. 12.95 *(978-1-934440-53-7(1)*, Pitspopany Pr.) Simcha Media Group.

Wilde, Oscar. Le Prince Hereux. (FRE.). (J). pap. 15.95 *(978-2-07-051629-2(6))* Gallimard, Editions FRA. Dist: Distribooks, Inc.

SWAMPS

see Marshes

SWANS

Bodden, Valerie. Amazing Animals: Swans. 2011. (Amazing Animals Ser.). (ENG.). 24p. (J). (gr. 1-3). pap. 8.99 *(978-0-89812-748-5(3)*, Creative Paperbacks) Creative Co., The.

—Swans. 2009. (Amazing Animals Ser.). 24p. (J). (gr. 1-5). 24.25 *(978-1-58341-719-5(2)*, Creative Education) Creative Co., The.

Gray, Leon. Trumpeter Swan: The World's Largest Waterbird. 2013. (Even More SuperSized! Ser.). 24p. (J). (gr. k-3). lib. bdg. 23.93 *(978-1-61772-734-4(2))* Bearport Publishing Co., Inc.

Helget, Nicole Lea. Swans. 2008. (Living Wild Ser.). (Illus.). 46p. (J). (gr. 4-7). 22.95 *(978-1-58341-659-4(5)*, Creative Education) Creative Co., The.

Hoff, Mary King. Swans. 2005. (Wild World of Animals (Creative Education) Ser.). (Illus.). 32p. (J). (gr. 2-5). lib. bdg. 18.95 *(978-1-58341-354-8(5)*, Creative Education) Creative Co., The.

Meister, Cari. Do You Really Want to Meet a Swan? Fabbri, Daniele, illus. 2014. (Do You Really Want to Meet... ? Ser.). (ENG.). 24p. (J). (gr. 1-4). 27.10 *(978-1-60753-458-7(4))* Amicus Publishing.

Meyer, Therese. The Little Ballerina & Her Friends the Swans. 2004. (Illus.). 52p. *(978-0-9750325-0-3(X))* Baby Swan.

—La Petite Ballerine et Ses Amis les Cygnes (The Little Ballerina & Her Friends the Swans) Meyer, Therese, illus. 2004. (FRE., Illus.). 52p. *(978-0-9750325-1-0(8))* Baby Swan.

Stewart, Melissa. Swans. 2007. (Animals Animals Ser.). (Illus.). 48p. (gr. 3-7). lib. bdg. 29.93 *(978-0-7614-2530-4(6))* Marshall Cavendish Corp.

SWANS—FICTION

Andersen, Hans Christian. The Wild Swans. Lewis, Naomi, tr. from DAN. Gilbert, Yvonne, illus. 2005. 48p. (J). 17.99 *(978-1-84148-164-7(5))* Barefoot Bks., Inc.

—The Wild Swans: A Tale of Persistence. Lohmann, Renate, illus. 2006. (J). *(978-1-59939-093-2(0)*, Reader's Digest Young Families, Inc.) Studio Fun International.

Antony, Steve. The Queen's Handbag. 2017. (ENG.). 32p. (J). (gr. -1-k). 17.99 ***(978-1-338-03293-2(3)***, Scholastic Pr.) Scholastic, Inc.

Bradman, Tony. The Ugly Duckling Returns, 1 vol. Warburton, Sarah, illus. 2014. (After Happily Ever After Ser.). (ENG.). 56p. (gr. 2-3). lib. bdg. 25.32 *(978-1-4342-7953-8(7)*, After Happily Ever After) Stone Arch Bks.

Christopher, Lucy. Flyaway. 2011. (ENG.). 336p. (J). (gr. 5-9). 16.99 *(978-0-545-31771-9(1)*, Chicken Hse., The) Scholastic, Inc.

Consugar, Beth. Swanee Day. Rottinger, Amy, illus. 2013. 24p. pap. 12.95 *(978-1-61244-176-4(9))* Halo Publishing International.

Duncan Edwards, Pamela. Honk! Cole, Henry, illus. 2014. 32p. pap. 8.00 *(978-1-61003-226-1(8))* Center for the Collaborative Classroom.

Dunn, Lynette. The Swans of Spindrift Lake. 2016. (ENG.). 117p. (J). pap. 10.95 *(978-1-78455-580-1(0)*, 3729255b-e7f5-4b16-bd98-44a8d762371b) Austin, Stan AUS. Dist: Bookmasters Distribution.

Furukawa, Masumi, illus. The Ugly Duckling. 2007. (Flip-Up Fairy Tales Ser.). (ENG.). 24p. (J). (gr. -1-2). audio compact disk *(978-1-84643-095-4(X))* Child's Play International Ltd.

Grant, Cj. The Princess & the Swan. 2012. 48p. pap. 21.88 *(978-1-4669-1594-7(3))* Trafford Publishing.

Gulla, Rosemarie. On the Wings of the Swan. Undercuffler, Gary, illus. 2008. (Treasury of the Lost Scrolls Ser.). (ENG.). 32p. (J). (gr. 1-4). 17.99 *(978-0-9793000-0-4(2)*, Alazar Pr.) Royal Swan Enterprises, Inc.

Harvey, Tom. Guido, the Swan with an Attitude. 2011. 44p. (gr. -1). pap. 17.99 *(978-1-4269-6855-6(8))* Trafford Publishing.

Hofer, Ernst & Hofer, Nelly, illus. The Wild Swans. 2003. (ENG.). 40p. (J). (gr. 2-5). 17.95 *(978-0-88776-615-2(3)*, Tundra Bks.) Tundra Bks. CAN. Dist: Penguin Random Hse. LLC.

Kent, Allegra. Ballerina Swan. McCully, Emily Arnold, illus. 2012. (ENG.). 32p. (J). (gr. -1-3). 16.95 *(978-0-8234-2373-6(5))* Holiday Hse., Inc.

—Ballerina Swan. McCully, Emily Arnold, illus. 2013. (ENG.). 32p. (J). (gr. -1-3). pap. 6.99 *(978-0-8234-2906-6(7))* Holiday Hse., Inc.

Lane, Jessica E. The Secret of the Swans. 2009. 52p. pap. 31.99 *(978-1-4415-5517-5(X))* Xlibris Corp.

Leonard, Barry, ed. The Ugly Duckling. 2003. (Illus.). 12p. (J). (gr. k-4). reprint ed. 17.00 *(978-0-7567-6858-4(6))* DIANE Publishing Co.

Lewis, Karlanna. Gladyus & the Voodoo Priestess. 2012. 24p. pap. 15.99 *(978-1-300-00528-5(9))* Lulu Pr., Inc.

London, Jonathan. Little Swan, 0 vols. Rodanas, Kristina, illus. 2009. (ENG.). 32p. (J). (gr. -1-3). 17.99 *(978-0-7614-5523-3(X)*, 9780761455233, Amazon Children's Publishing) Amazon Publishing.

Martin, Rafe. Birdwing. 2007. (ENG.). 384p. (J). (gr. 7-12). pap. 7.99 *(978-0-439-21168-0(9)*, Levine, Arthur A. Bks.) Scholastic, Inc.

McNamee, Barbara Oakley. Kelsey & Seattle. 2007. (J). pap. 15.00 *(978-0-8059-7428-7(8))* Dorrance Publishing Co., Inc.

Meadows, Daisy. Sophia the Snow Swan Fairy. 2012. (Illus.). 65p. (J). *(978-0-545-42600-8(6))* Scholastic, Inc.

Mini Cuentos: Atletas se Entrenan, Zorro y la Ciguena.Tr. of Mini Fairy Tales: Fox & the Swan. (SPA.). (J). (gr. k-4). 4.98 *(978-970-607-621-2(2))* Larousse, Ediciones, S. A. de C. V. MEX. Dist: Continental Bk. Co., Inc.

Olsen, Kaki. Swan & Shadow: A Swan Lake Story. 2016. (ENG.). 299p. (YA). pap. 18.99 *(978-1-4621-1814-4(3)*, Sweetwater Bks.) Cedar Fort, Inc./CFI Distribution.

Parrish, Edith E. Sara the Purple Goose & Susan the Black Swan. 2010. 24p. pap. 17.99 *(978-1-4490-8879-8(1))* AuthorHouse.

Phillips, Vivian A. Swan. Date not set. (Illus.). 20p. (Orig.). (J). pap. *(978-1-888413-02-1(6))* Seasoning Quilting (Arts & Crafts).

Sarfatti, Esther, tr. El Patito Feo. Bordoy, Irene, illus. 2006. (Bilingual Tales Ser.). (SPA.). 24p. (J). (gr. -1-3). pap. 3.99 *(978-0-439-77376-8(8)*, Scholastic en Espanol) Scholastic, Inc.

Tafuri, Nancy. Whose Chick Are You? Tafuri, Nancy, illus. 2007. (ENG., Illus.). 40p. (J). (gr. -1-k). 16.99 *(978-0-06-082514-0(6)*, Greenwillow Bks.) HarperCollins Pubs.

Weis, Ms. Jane. Silas the Special Swan. 2010. 28p. pap. 12.99 *(978-1-4500-3494-4(2))* Xlibris Corp.

Welsh, Lisa. Sammy Swan: The Big Storm. 2010. 24p. pap. 14.49 *(978-1-4490-7234-6(8))* AuthorHouse.

White, E. B. The Trumpet of the Swan. unabr. ed. 2004. 210p. (J). (gr. 4-7). pap. 38.00 incl. audio *(978-0-8072-8710-1(5)*, YA243SP, Listening Library) Random Hse. Audio Publishing Group.

Wood, David & Wood, Aimee. The Beautiful Swan. 2008. 24p. pap. 14.95 *(978-1-59858-624-4(6))* Dog Ear Publishing, LLC.

Zahler, Diane. Princess of the Wild Swans. Gilbert, Yvonne, illus. 2013. (ENG.). 240p. (J). (gr. 3-7). pap. 6.99 *(978-0-06-200495-6(6))* HarperCollins Pubs.

SWEDEN

Anderson, Margaret J. Carl Linnaeus: Genius of Classification. 2015. (Genius Scientists & Their Genius Ideas Ser.). 96p. (J). (gr. 5-12). 27.94 *(978-0-7660-6540-6(5))*; pap. 10.95 *(978-0-7660-6541-3(3))* Enslow Pubs., Inc.

Anderson, Margaret Jean. Carl Linnaeus: Father of Classification. 2009. (Great Minds of Science Ser.). (Illus.). 128p. (J). (gr. 5). lib. bdg. 33.27 *(978-0-7660-3009-1(1))* Enslow Pubs., Inc.

Barber, Nicola. Focus on Sweden. 2007. (World in Focus Ser.). (Illus.). 64p. (gr. 5-12). pap. 14.05 *(978-0-8368-6746-6(7))*; lib. bdg. 34.00 *(978-0-8368-6739-8(4))* Stevens, Gareth Publishing LLLP. (Gareth Stevens Secondary Library).

Blomquist, Christopher. A Primary Source Guide to Sweden. (Countries of the World). 24p. 2009. (gr. 2-3). 42.50 *(978-1-61512-046-8(7))* 2005. (Illus.). (J). (gr. k-5). lib. bdg. 22.60 *(978-1-4042-2758-3(X))* Rosen Publishing Group, Inc., The. (PowerKids Pr.).

Docalavich, Heather. Sweden. 2007. (European Union Ser.). (Illus.). 88p. (YA). (gr. 3-7). lib. bdg. 21.95 *(978-1-4222-0063-6(9))* Mason Crest.

Docalavich, Heather & Indovino, Shaina C. Sweden. Bruton, John, ed. 2012. (Major European Union Nations Ser.). 64p. (J). (gr. 7). 22.95 *(978-1-4222-2260-7(8))* Mason Crest.

Docalavich, Heather & Indovino, Shaina Carmel. Sweden. 2012. (J). pap. *(978-1-4222-2291-1(8))* Mason Crest.

Dyan, Penelope. This Is Sweden — -A Kid's Guide to Stockholm, Swedem. Weigand, John D., photos by. 2011. (Illus.). 34p. pap. 11.95 *(978-1-61477-003-9(4))* Bellissima Publishing, LLC.

Enderlein, Cheryl L. Christmas in Sweden, 1 vol. 2013. (Christmas Around the World Ser.). (ENG., Illus.). 24p. (gr. 1-2). lib. bdg. 25.32 *(978-1-62065-140-7(8))* Capstone Press of Coughlan Cos.

Gan & Kohen, Elizabeth. Spain. 3rd ed. 2013. 144p. (J). (gr. 6-9). 47.07 *(978-1-60870-871-0(3))* Cavendish Square Publishing.

Gofen, Ethel, et al. Sweden. 2015. (J). lib. bdg. *(978-1-62713-363-0(1))*; (ENG., Illus.). 144p. (gr. 6-6). lib. bdg. 47.07 *(978-1-5026-0074-5(9))* Cavendish Square Publishing.

Grahame, Deborah A. Sweden. 2006. (Discovering Cultures Ser.). (Illus.). 48p. (J). (gr. 3-7). lib. bdg. 28.50 *(978-0-7614-1985-3(3)*, Benchmark Bks.) Marshall Cavendish Corp.

Heinrichs, Ann. Sweden. 2014. (Enchantment of the World Ser.: 2). (ENG.). 144p. (J). lib. bdg. 40.00 *(978-0-531-22017-7(6))* Scholastic Library Publishing.

Hogan, Edward Patrick, et al. Sweden. 2nd rev. ed. 2011. (Modern World Nations Ser.). (Illus.). 128p. (gr. 6-12). 35.00 *(978-1-61753-048-7(4)*, Chelsea Hse.) Facts On File, Inc.

Hyde, Natalie. Cultural Traditions in Sweden. 2015. (ENG., Illus.). 32p. (J). *(978-0-7787-8064-9(3))* Crabtree Publishing Co.

Johnson, Allen LeRoy. Sweden through the Eyes of a Six-year-old: Adventures with Grandchildren 2005. (Illus.). 180p. 15.00 *(978-1-880675-06-9(4))* Creative Enterprises.

Kemper, Bitsy. Sweden. 2015. (One World, Many Countries Ser.). (ENG.). 32p. (J). (gr. 1-4). 28.50 *(978-1-63407-057-7(7)*, 208892) Child's World, Inc., The.

Larsson, Carl. A Family: Paintings from a Bygone Age. 2007. (Illus.). 30p. (J). (gr. 1). *(978-0-86315-583-3(9))* Floris Bks.

McKenna, Amy, ed. Denmark, Finland, & Sweden. 2013. (Britannica Guide to Countries of the European Union Ser.). (ENG., Illus.). 256p. (YA). (gr. 9-12). lib. bdg. 53.00 *(978-1-61530-969-6(1))* Rosen Publishing Group, Inc., The.

Miles, Liz. Linnaeus: Organising Nature. 2017. (ENG., Illus.). 80p. (J). pap. 9.99 ***(978-0-00-820897-4(2))*** HarperCollins Pubs. Ltd. GBR. Dist: Independent Pubs. Group.

Murray, Julie. Sweden, 1 vol. 2014. (Explore the Countries Set 2 Ser.). (ENG.). 40p. (J). (gr. 7-11). lib. bdg. 29.93 *(978-1-62403-347-6(4)*, Big Buddy Bks.) ABDO Publishing Co.

Porterfield, Jason. Niklas Zennstrom & Skype. 2013. (Internet Biographies Ser.). (ENG., Illus.). 128p. (YA). (gr. 7-12). lib. bdg. 34.60 *(978-1-4488-9527-4(8)*, Rosen Classroom) Rosen Publishing Group, Inc., The.

Rydaker, Ewa. Lucia Morning in Sweden. Lewis, Anne Gillespie, ed. Stahlberg, Carina, illus. 2014. (ENG.). 35p. (J). (gr. -1-3). pap. 8.99 *(978-1-935666-65-3(7))* Nodin Pr.

Sexton, Colleen. Sweden. 2010. (Exploring Countries Ser.). (ENG., Illus.). 32p. (J). (gr. 3-7). lib. bdg. 26.95 *(978-1-60014-490-5(X)*, Blastoff! Readers) Bellwether Media.

Zocchi, Judy. In Sweden. Brodie, Neale, illus. 2005. (Global Adventures II Ser.). 32p. (J). pap. 10.95 *(978-1-59646-176-5(4))*; lib. bdg. 21.65 *(978-1-59646-087-4(3))*; per. 10.95 *(978-1-59646-177-2(2))* Dingles & Co.

—In Sweden/en Suecia. Brodie, Neale, illus. 2005. (Global Adventures I Ser.).Tr. of En Japón. (ENG & SPA.). 32p. (J). pap. 10.95 *(978-1-59646-178-9(0))*; lib. bdg. 21.65 *(978-1-59646-088-1(1))*; per. 10.95 *(978-1-59646-179-6(9))* Dingles & Co.

SWEDEN—FICTION

Andersen, Hans Christian. Pictures of Sweden. 2006. pap. *(978-1-4065-0860-4(8))* Dodo Pr.

Baier, Hiltrud. Greta in Schweden. 2009. 114p. pap. *(978-3-8391-2523-6(5))* Books on Demand GmbH.

Dines, Carol. The Queen's Soprano. 2007. (ENG., Illus.). 336p. (YA). (gr. 9). pap. 18.95 (978-0-15-206102-9(9)) Houghton Mifflin Harcourt Publishing Co.

Howard, Velma Swanston, tr. Wonderful Adventures of Nils. 2013. 354p. pap. (978-1-78139-369-7(9)) Benediction Classics.

James, J. Alison. Runa. 2012. (ENG.). 144p. (YA). (gr. 7). pap. 8.99 (978-1-4424-7482-6(3), Atheneum Bks. for Young Readers) Simon & Schuster Children's Publishing.

Lagerlöf, Selma. The Further Adventures of Nils. 2005. pap. 31.95 (978-1-4179-9042-9(2)) Kessinger Publishing, LLC.

—The Further Adventures of Nils. Howard, Velma Swanston, tr. 2003. 284p. pap. 14.95 (978-1-59224-320-4(7)); 32.95 (978-1-59224-541-3(2)) Wildside Pr., LLC.

—The Wonderful Adventures of Nils. Howard, Velma Swanston, tr. 2007. 440p. per. (978-1-4065-2572-4(3)) Dodo Pr.

—The Wonderful Adventures of Nils. 2004. reprint ed. pap. 1.99 (978-1-4192-8845-6(8)); pap. 34.95 (978-1-4191-8845-9(3)) Kessinger Publishing, LLC.

—The Wonderful Adventures of Nils. 2009. 360p. (gr. 4-7). pap. 10.99 (978-1-60459-624-3(4)) Wilder Pubns., Corp.

—The Wonderful Adventures of Nils. Howard, Velma Swanston, tr. 2003. 284p. pap. 14.95 (978-1-59224-322-8(3)) Wildside Pr., LLC.

—The Wonderful Adventures of Nils. 2003. 32.95 (978-1-59224-745-5(8)) Wildside Pr., LLC.

Lewis, Beverly & Querin, Pamela. Annika's Secret Wish. 2006. (Illus.). 32p. (J). (gr. k-4). reprint ed. 15.00 (978-0-7567-9876-5(0)) DIANE Publishing Co.

Lindgren, Astrid. Pippi Longstocking. 2013. (Puffin Chalk Ser.). (ENG.). 160p. (J). (gr. 3-7). pap. 7.99 (978-0-14-242752-1(7), Puffin Books) Penguin Young Readers Group.

—Pippi Longstocking. Nunally, Tina, tr. Child, Lauren, illus. 2011. (Pippi Longstocking Ser.). (ENG.). 208p. (J). (gr. 2-5). pap. 15.99 (978-0-670-01404-0(4), Viking Books for Young Readers) Penguin Young Readers Group.

—Seacrow Island. Ramsden, Evelyn, tr. from SWE. 2015. (ENG.). 256p. (J). (gr. 3-7). 17.95 (978-1-59017-868-3(8), NYR Children's Collection) New York Review of Bks., Inc., The.

Lindgren, Astrid & Crampton, Patricia. The Red Bird. Tomqvist, Marit, illus. 2005. (J). 5.99 (978-0-439-62797-9(4), Levine, Arthur A. Bks.) Scholastic, Inc.

Lindman. Flicka, Ricka, Dicka & the Little Dog. Lindman, illus. 2013. (Flicka, Ricka, Dicka Ser.). (ENG., Illus.). 32p. (J). (gr. k-3). 9.99 (978-0-8075-2509-8(X)) Whitman, Albert & Co.

—Flicka, Ricka, Dicka & the Strawberries. Lindman, illus. 2013. (Flicka, Ricka, Dicka Ser.). (ENG., Illus.). 32p. (J). (gr. k-3). 9.99 (978-0-8075-2512-8(X)) Whitman, Albert & Co.

—Flicka, Ricka, Dicka & the Three Kittens. Lindman, illus. 2013. (Flicka, Ricka, Dicka Ser.). (ENG., Illus.). 32p. (J). (gr. k-3). 9.99 (978-0-8075-2515-9(4)) Whitman, Albert & Co.

—Flicka, Ricka, Dicka & Their New Skates: Updated Edition with Paperdolls. Lindman, illus. 2011. (Flicka, Ricka, Dicka Ser.). (ENG., Illus.). 32p. (J). (gr. k-3). 9.99 (978-0-8075-2496-1(4)) Whitman, Albert & Co.

—Flicka, Ricka, Dicka Bake a Cake. Lindman, illus. 2013. (Flicka, Ricka, Dicka Ser.). (ENG., Illus.). 32p. (J). (gr. k-3). 9.99 (978-0-8075-2506-7(5)) Whitman, Albert & Co.

Lindman, Maj. Flicka, Ricka, Dicka & the New Dotted Dresses. 2012. (J). (978-0-8075-2495-4(6)) Whitman, Albert & Co.

—Flicka, Ricka, Dicka & the New Dotted Dresses. Lindman, Maj, illus. 2012. (Flicka, Ricka, Dicka Ser.). (ENG., Illus.). 32p. (J). (gr. k-3). 9.99 (978-0-8075-2484-8(0)) Whitman, Albert & Co.

—Flicka, Ricka, Dicka & Their New Skates. Lindman, Maj, illus. 2011. (ENG., Illus.). 32p. (J). (gr. k-3). 9.99 (978-0-8075-2491-6(3)) Whitman, Albert & Co.

—Flicka, Ricka, Dicka Go to Market. Lindman, Maj, illus. 2012. (ENG., Illus.). 32p. (J). (gr. -1-3). 9.99 (978-0-8075-2478-7(6)); (gr. k-3). 9.99 (978-0-8075-2479-4(4)) Whitman, Albert & Co.

Lindren, Astrid. Rasmus & the Vagabond. Bothmer, Gerry, tr. from SWE. Palmquist, Eric, illus. 2014. (ENG.). 180p. pap. 9.95 (978-0-87486-597-4(2)) Plough Publishing Hse.

Lois, Lowry. Number the Stars: And Related Readings. 2006. (Literature Connections Ser.). 172p. (gr. 6-12). (978-0-395-88457-7(8), 2-70863) Holt McDougal.

Mankell, Henning. A Bridge to the Stars. 2009. (Joel Gustafson Stories Ser.: No. 1). (ENG.). 180p. (YA). (gr. 7). pap. 7.99 (978-0-440-24042-6(5), Delacorte Bks. for Young Readers) Random Hse. Children's Bks.

—Journey to the End of the World. 2011. (Joel Gustafson Stories Ser.: No. 4). (ENG.). 208p. (YA). (gr. 7). pap. 7.99 (978-0-385-73498-1(0), Delacorte Bks. for Young Readers) Random Hse. Children's Bks.

—Shadows in the Twilight. 2010. (Joel Gustafson Stories Ser.: No. 2). (ENG.). 208p. (YA). (gr. 7). pap. 7.99 (978-0-440-24043-3(3), Delacorte Bks. for Young Readers) Random Hse. Children's Bks.

—When the Snow Fell. 2011. (Joel Gustafson Stories Ser.: No. 3). (ENG.). 256p. (YA). (gr. 7). pap. 8.99 (978-0-440-24044-0(1), Delacorte Bks. for Young Readers) Random Hse. Children's Bks.

McLachlan, Jenny. Sunkissed. 2017. (Ladybirds Ser.: 3). (ENG.). 224p. (YA). 16.99 (978-1-250-06150-8(4), 9781250061508) Feiwel & Friends.

Popper, Carol. David, Mormor, Horno & the Yak: An Alphabet Mystery. 2008. 24p. pap. 24.95 (978-1-4241-8772-0(9)) America Star Bks.

Thor, Annika. A Faraway Island. Schenck, Linda, tr. 2011. (ENG.). 256p. (J). (gr. 3-7). 6.99 (978-0-375-84495-9(3), Yearling) Random Hse. Children's Bks.

—The Lily Pond. Schenck, Linda, tr. 2012. (ENG.). 224p. (J). (gr. 4-7). 7.99 (978-0-385-74040-1(9), Yearling) Random Hse. Children's Bks.

Thor, Annika & Schenck, Linda. Deep Sea. 2015. (ENG.). 240p. (YA). (gr. 9). 20.99 (978-0-375-99132-5(8), Delacorte Pr.) Random Hse. Children's Bks.

Uncle Markie. Pigletté & Bobo Have Visitors. 2003. (YA). ring bd. 9.95 (978-1-933129-12-9(3)) Studio 403.

SWEDES—UNITED STATES

Gunderson, Cory Gideon. Swedish Americans. 2003. (Immigrants in America Ser.). (Illus.). 112p. (gr. 6-12). 30.00 (978-0-7910-7131-1(6), Chelsea Hse.) Facts On File, Inc.

SWEDES—UNITED STATES—FICTION

Shaw, Janet. Kirsten's Short Story Collection. Lewis, Kim & Graef, Renee, illus. 2006. (American Girls Collection). 213p. (J). (gr. 3-8). 12.95 (978-1-59369-323-7(0)) American Girl Publishing, Inc.

SWEDISH LANGUAGE

Modéré, Armelle & Hokenson, Linda. My First English/Swedish Dictionary of Sentences. 2008. (SWE & ENG.). 128p. (978-1-57534-049-4(6)) Skandisk, Inc.

SWIFT, JONATHAN, 1667-1745

Aykroyd, Clarissa. Savage Satire: The Story of Jonathan Swift. 2006. (World Writers Ser.). (Illus.). 160p. (J). (gr. 3-7). lib. bdg. 27.95 (978-1-59935-027-1(0)) Reynolds, Morgan Inc.

Saddleback Educational Publishing Staff, ed. Gulliver's Travels. 2011. (Timeless Classics Ser.). (ENG.). 48p. (YA). (gr. 9-12). pupil's gde. ed. 19.95 incl. cd-rom (978-1-61651-136-4(2)) Saddleback Educational Publishing, Inc.

SWIFT, TOM (FICTITIOUS CHARACTER)—FICTION

ABDO Publishing Company Staff. Tom Swift, Young Inventor - 4 Titles. 2007. (Tom Swift, Young Inventor Ser.). (ENG.). 165p. 108.28 (978-1-59961-349-9(2)) Spotlight.

Appleton, Victor. The Adventures of Tom Swift. 2007. 456p. per. 19.95 (978-1-4344-9982-0(0)) Wildside Pr., LLC.

—The Alien Probe. (Tom Swift Ser.). (J). (gr. 3-7). 20.95 (978-0-88411-464-2(3)) Amereon Ltd.

—The City in the Stars. (Tom Swift Ser.). (J). (gr. 3-7). 20.95 (978-0-88411-463-5(5)) Amereon Ltd.

—Into the Abyss. 2007. (Tom Swift, Young Inventor Ser.). (ENG.). 160p. (gr. 3-7). 27.07 (978-1-59961-350-5(6)) Spotlight.

—The Rescue Mission. (Tom Swift Ser.). (J). (gr. 3-7). 20.95 (978-0-88411-458-1(9)) Amereon Ltd.

—The Robot Olympics. 2006. (Tom Swift, Young Inventor Ser.: 2). (ENG.). 176p. (J). (gr. 3-7). pap. 4.99 (978-1-4169-1361-0(0), Aladdin) Simon & Schuster Children's Publishing.

—The Robot Olympics. 2007. (Tom Swift, Young Inventor Ser.). (ENG.). 160p. (gr. 4-7). 27.07 (978-1-59961-351-2(4)) Spotlight.

—Rocket Racers. 2007. (Tom Swift, Young Inventor Ser.: 4). (ENG.). 160p. (J). (gr. 3-7). pap. 8.99 (978-1-4169-3488-2(X), Aladdin) Simon & Schuster Children's Publishing.

—The Space Hotel. 2006. (Tom Swift, Young Inventor Ser.: 3). (ENG.). 160p. (J). (gr. 3-7). pap. 8.99 (978-1-4169-1751-9(9), Aladdin) Simon & Schuster Children's Publishing.

—The Space Hotel. 2007. (Tom Swift, Young Inventor Ser.). (ENG.). 160p. (gr. 4-7). 27.07 (978-1-59961-353-6(0)) Spotlight.

—Terror on the Moons of Jupiter. (Tom Swift Ser.). (J). (gr. 3-7). 20.95 (978-0-88411-460-4(0)) Amereon Ltd.

—Tom Swift among the Diamond Makers. 2005. 26.95 (978-1-4218-1086-7(7)); 196p. pap. 11.95 (978-1-4218-1186-4(3)) 1st World Publishing, Inc. (1st World Library - Literary Society).

—Tom Swift among the Diamond Makers. 2007. 224p. 29.95 (978-1-4344-9458-0(6)); per. 19.95 (978-1-4344-9457-3(8)) Wildside Pr., LLC.

—Tom Swift among the Diamond Makers or Th. 2006. pap. (978-1-4065-0892-5(6)) Dodo Pr.

—Tom Swift among the Fire Fighters. 2005. 27.95 (978-1-4218-1088-1(3)); 204p. pap. 12.95 (978-1-4218-1188-8(X)) 1st World Publishing, Inc. (1st World Library - Literary Society).

—Tom Swift among the Fire Fighters. 2006. (ENG.). pap. (978-1-4068-0726-4(5)) Echo Library.

—Tom Swift among the Fire Fighters. 2004. reprint ed. pap. 20.95 (978-1-4191-9047-6(4)); pap. 1.99 (978-1-4192-9047-3(9)) Kessinger Publishing, LLC.

—Tom Swift among the Fire Fighters: Or Battling with Flames from the Air. l.t. ed. 2007. (ENG.). 154p. pap. 21.99 (978-1-4346-1583-1(9)) Creative Media Partners, LLC.

—Tom Swift among the Fire Fighters or Bat. 2006. pap. (978-1-4065-0893-2(4)) Dodo Pr.

—Tom Swift & His Aerial Warship. 2005. 27.95 (978-1-4218-1092-8(1)); 212p. pap. 12.95 (978-1-4218-1192-5(8)) 1st World Publishing, Inc. (1st World Library - Literary Society).

—Tom Swift & His Aerial Warship. 2004. reprint ed. pap. 1.99 (978-1-4192-8451-9(7)) Kessinger Publishing, LLC.

—Tom Swift & His Aerial Warship: Or the Naval Terror of the Seas. l.t. ed. 2007. (ENG.). 156p. pap. 21.99 (978-1-4346-1578-7(2)) Creative Media Partners, LLC.

—Tom Swift & His Aerial Warship or the. 2006. pap. (978-1-4065-0894-9(2)) Dodo Pr.

—Tom Swift & his Air Glider. 2005. 26.95 (978-1-4218-1500-8(1), 1st World Library - Literary Society) 1st World Publishing, Inc.

—Tom Swift & His Air Glider. 2004. reprint ed. pap. 1.99 (978-1-4192-8452-6(5)); pap. 20.95 (978-1-4191-8452-9(0)) Kessinger Publishing, LLC.

—Tom Swift & His Air Glider or Seeking. 2006. pap. (978-1-4065-0895-6(0)) Dodo Pr.

—Tom Swift & His Air Scout. 2005. 27.95 (978-1-4218-1091-1(3)); 208p. pap. 12.95 (978-1-4218-1191-8(X)) 1st World Publishing, Inc. (1st World Library - Literary Society).

—Tom Swift & His Air Scout. 2004. reprint ed. pap. 1.99 (978-1-4192-9048-0(7)); pap. 20.95 (978-1-4191-9048-3(2)) Kessinger Publishing, LLC.

—Tom Swift & His Air Scout: Or Uncle Sam's Mastery of the Sky. l.t. ed. 2007. (ENG.). 158p. pap. 21.99 (978-1-4346-1580-0(4)) Creative Media Partners, LLC.

—Tom Swift & His Air Scout or Uncle Sam. 2006. pap. (978-1-4065-0896-3(9)) Dodo Pr.

—Tom Swift & His Airship. 2005. 27.95 (978-1-59540-801-3(0), 1st World Library - Literary Society) 1st World Publishing, Inc.

—Tom Swift & His Airship. 2006. pap. (978-1-4065-0897-0(7)) Dodo Pr.

—Tom Swift & His Airship. 2007. 224p. 29.95 (978-1-4344-9460-3(8)); per. 19.95 (978-1-4344-9459-7(4)) Wildside Pr., LLC.

—Tom Swift & His Big Tunnel. 2005. 27.95 (978-1-4218-1093-5(X)); 216p. pap. 12.95 (978-1-4218-1193-2(6)) 1st World Publishing, Inc. (1st World Library - Literary Society).

—Tom Swift & His Big Tunnel. 2004. reprint ed. pap. 1.99 (978-1-4192-8454-0(1)); pap. 20.95 (978-1-4191-8454-3(7)) Kessinger Publishing, LLC.

—Tom Swift & His Big Tunnel or the Hidd. 2006. pap. (978-1-4065-0898-7(5)) Dodo Pr.

—Tom Swift & His Electric Locomotive. 2005. 27.95 (978-1-4218-1087-4(5)); 200p. pap. 12.95 (978-1-4218-1187-1(1)) 1st World Publishing, Inc. (1st World Library - Literary Society).

—Tom Swift & His Electric Locomotive: Or Two Miles a Minute on the Rails. 2007. (ENG.). 136p. pap. 18.99 (978-1-4346-1490-2(5)) Creative Media Partners, LLC.

—Tom Swift & His Electric Locomotive or. 2006. pap. (978-1-4065-0899-4(3)) Dodo Pr.

—Tom Swift & His Electric Rifle. 2005. 26.95 (978-1-59540-802-0(9), 1st World Library - Literary Society) 1st World Publishing, Inc.

—Tom Swift & His Electric Rifle. 2006. pap. (978-1-4065-0900-7(0)) Dodo Pr.

—Tom Swift & His Electric Runabout. 2004. reprint ed. pap. 20.95 (978-1-4191-8455-0(5)); pap. 1.99 (978-1-4192-8455-7(X)) Kessinger Publishing, LLC.

—Tom Swift & His Electric Runabout. 2007. 224p. 29.95 (978-1-4344-9462-7(4)); per. 19.95 (978-1-4344-9461-0(6)) Wildside Pr., LLC.

—Tom Swift & His Electric Runabout or T. 2006. pap. (978-1-4065-0901-4(9)) Dodo Pr.

—Tom Swift & His Electronic Electroscope. (J). (gr. 5-6). 20.95 (978-0-88411-462-8(7)) Amereon Ltd.

—Tom Swift & His Giant Cannon. 2005. 27.95 (978-1-4218-1089-8(1)); 204p. pap. 12.95 (978-1-4218-1189-5(8)) 1st World Publishing, Inc. (1st World Library - Literary Society).

—Tom Swift & His Giant Cannon. 2004. reprint ed. pap. 20.95 (978-1-4191-8456-7(3)); pap. 1.99 (978-1-4192-8456-4(8)) Kessinger Publishing, LLC.

—Tom Swift & His Giant Cannon or the lo. 2006. pap. (978-1-4065-0902-1(7)) Dodo Pr.

—Tom Swift & His Great Searchlight. 2005. 204p. pap. 12.95 (978-1-4218-1190-1(1), 1st World Library - Literary Society) 1st World Publishing, Inc.

—Tom Swift & his Great Searchlight. 2005. 27.95 (978-1-4218-1090-4(5), 1st World Library - Literary Society) 1st World Publishing, Inc.

—Tom Swift & His Great Searchlight. 2004. reprint ed. pap. 20.95 (978-1-4191-8457-4(1)); pap. 1.99 (978-1-4192-8457-1(6)) Kessinger Publishing, LLC.

—Tom Swift & His Great Searchlight or O. 2006. pap. (978-1-4065-0903-8(5)) Dodo Pr.

—Tom Swift & his Motor-Boat. 2005. 26.95 (978-1-4218-1501-5(X)); 196p. pap. 11.95 (978-1-4218-1600-5(8)); 192p. pap. 11.95 (978-1-4218-1601-2(6)) 1st World Publishing, Inc. (1st World Library - Literary Society).

—Tom Swift & His Motor-Boat: Or the Rivals of Lake Carlopa. l.t. ed. 2007. (ENG.). 148p. pap. 19.99 (978-1-4346-1907-5(9)) Creative Media Partners, LLC.

—Tom Swift & his Motor-Cycle. 2005. 26.95 (978-1-4218-1502-2(8)); 192p. pap. 11.95 (978-1-4218-1602-9(4)) 1st World Publishing, Inc. (1st World Library - Literary Society).

—Tom Swift & His Motor Cycle. 2004. reprint ed. pap. 1.99 (978-1-4192-8459-5(2)) Kessinger Publishing, LLC.

—Tom Swift & His Motor-Cycle, Tom Swift & His Motor-Boat, Tom Swift & His Airship. 2007. 292p. per. 12.99 (978-1-60459-097-5(1)) Wilder Pubns., Corp.

—Tom Swift & His MotorBoat or the Rival. 2006. pap. (978-1-4065-0904-5(3)) Dodo Pr.

—Tom Swift & his Photo Telephone. 2005. 27.95 (978-1-4218-1503-9(6)); 204p. pap. 12.95 (978-1-4218-1603-6(2)) 1st World Publishing, Inc. (1st World Library - Literary Society).

—Tom Swift & His Photo Telephone or the. 2006. pap. (978-1-4065-0906-9(X)) Dodo Pr.

—Tom Swift & his Sky Racer. 2005. 26.95 (978-1-4218-1504-6(4)); 192p. pap. 11.95 (978-1-4218-1604-3(0)) 1st World Publishing, Inc. (1st World Library - Literary Society).

—Tom Swift & His Sky Racer. 2004. reprint ed. pap. 1.99 (978-1-4192-8461-8(4)) Kessinger Publishing, LLC.

—Tom Swift & His Sky Racer or the Quick. 2006. pap. (978-1-4065-0907-6(8)) Dodo Pr.

—Tom Swift & His Submarine Boat. 2004. reprint ed. pap. 20.95 (978-1-4191-8462-8(8)); pap. 1.99 (978-1-4192-8462-5(2)) Kessinger Publishing, LLC.

—Tom Swift & His Submarine Boat or Unde. 2006. pap. (978-1-4065-0908-3(6)) Dodo Pr.

—Tom Swift & His Triphibian Atomicar. (Tom Swift Ser.). (J). (gr. 5-6). 20.95 (978-0-88411-459-8(7)) Amereon Ltd.

—Tom Swift & His Undersea Search. 2007. 228p. 29.95 (978-1-4344-8363-8(0)); per. 17.95 (978-1-4344-8362-1(2)) Wildside Pr., LLC.

—Tom Swift & His Undersea Search: Or the Treasure on the Floor of the Atlantic. l.t. ed. 2007. 160p. pap. 21.99 (978-1-4346-1582-4(0)) Creative Media Partners, LLC.

—Tom Swift & His Undersea Search or the. 2006. pap. (978-1-4065-0909-0(4)) Dodo Pr.

—Tom Swift & his War Tank. 2005. 27.95 (978-1-4218-1505-3(2)); 212p. pap. 12.95 (978-1-4218-1605-0(9)) 1st World Publishing, Inc. (1st World Library - Literary Society).

—Tom Swift & His War Tank. 2004. reprint ed. pap. 20.95 (978-1-4191-9054-4(7)); pap. 1.99 (978-1-4192-9054-1(1)) Kessinger Publishing, LLC.

—Tom Swift & His War Tank or Doing His. 2006. pap. (978-1-4065-0910-6(8)) Dodo Pr.

—Tom Swift & His Wireless Message. 2007. 220p. 24.95 (978-1-4344-9231-9(1)); per. 14.95 (978-1-4344-9137-4(4)) Wildside Pr., LLC.

—Tom Swift & his Wireless Message. 2005. 26.95 (978-1-4218-1506-0(0)); 196p. pap. 11.95 (978-1-4218-1606-7(7)) 1st World Publishing, Inc. (1st World Library - Literary Society).

—Tom Swift & His Wireless Message or Th. 2006. pap. (978-1-4065-0911-3(6)) Dodo Pr.

—Tom Swift & his Wizard Camera. 2005. 26.95 (978-1-4218-1507-7(9)); 196p. pap. 11.95 (978-1-4218-1607-4(5)) 1st World Publishing, Inc. (1st World Library - Literary Society).

—Tom Swift & His Wizard Camera: Or Thrilling Adventures While Taking Moving Pictu. l.t. ed. 2007. (ENG.). 148p. pap. 19.99 (978-1-4346-1579-4(0)) Creative Media Partners, LLC.

—Tom Swift & His Wizard Camera or Thril. 2006. pap. (978-1-4065-0912-0(4)) Dodo Pr.

—Tom Swift & the Electronic Hydrolung. 2007. (ENG.). 120p. pap. 18.99 (978-1-4346-3059-9(5)); 132p. pap. 19.99 (978-1-4346-3073-5(0)) Creative Media Partners, LLC.

—Tom Swift & the Visitor from Planet X. 2006. pap. (978-1-4065-0913-7(2)) Dodo Pr.

—Tom Swift Circling the Globe. 2007. 224p. 29.95 (978-1-4344-9464-1(0)); per. 19.95 (978-1-4344-9463-4(2)) Wildside Pr., LLC.

—Tom Swift in Captivity. 2005. 27.95 (978-1-4218-1508-4(7)); 200p. pap. 12.95 (978-1-4218-1608-1(3)) 1st World Publishing, Inc. (1st World Library - Literary Society).

—Tom Swift in Captivity. 2004. reprint ed. pap. 20.95 (978-1-4191-9056-8(3)); pap. 1.99 (978-1-4192-9056-5(8)) Kessinger Publishing, LLC.

—Tom Swift in Captivity or A Daring Escap. 2006. pap. (978-1-4065-0914-4(0)) Dodo Pr.

—Tom Swift in the Caves of Ice. 2005. 27.95 (978-1-4218-1509-1(5)); 204p. pap. 12.95 (978-1-4218-1609-8(1)) 1st World Publishing, Inc. (1st World Library - Literary Society).

—Tom Swift in the Caves of Ice or the Wre. 2006. pap. (978-1-4065-0915-1(9)) Dodo Pr.

—Tom Swift in the City of Gold. 2005. 27.95 (978-1-4218-1510-7(9)); 204p. pap. 12.95 (978-1-4218-1610-4(5)) 1st World Publishing, Inc. (1st World Library - Literary Society).

—Tom Swift in the City of Gold or Marvelo. 2006. pap. (978-1-4065-0916-8(7)) Dodo Pr.

—Tom Swift in the Land of Wonders. 2005. 27.95 (978-1-4218-1511-4(7)); 204p. pap. 12.95 (978-1-4218-1611-1(3)) 1st World Publishing, Inc. (1st World Library - Literary Society).

—Tom Swift in the Land of Wonders. 2004. reprint ed. pap. 20.95 (978-1-4191-9057-5(1)); pap. 1.99 (978-1-4192-9057-2(6)) Kessinger Publishing, LLC.

—Tom Swift in the Land of Wonders or the. 2006. pap. (978-1-4065-0917-5(5)) Dodo Pr.

—The Tom Swift Omnibus #1: Tom Swift & his Motor-Cycle, Tom Swift & His Motor-Boat, Tom Swift & His Airship. 2007. 292p. 24.95 (978-1-60459-098-2(X)) Wilder Pubns., Corp.

—The Tom Swift Omnibus #2: Tom Swift & His Submarine Boat, Tom Swift & His Electric Runabout, Tom Swift & His Wireless Message. 2007. 296p. per. 12.99 (978-1-60459-099-9(8)) Wilder Pubns., Corp.

—Tom Swift Omnibus #3: Tom Swift among the Diamond Makers, Tom Swift in the Caves of Ice, Tom Swift & His Sky Racer. 2007. 296p. per. 12.99 (978-1-60459-101-9(3)); per. 12.99 (978-1-60459-102-6(1)) Wilder Pubns., Corp.

—Tom Swift Omnibus #4: Tom Swift & His Electric Rifle, Tom Swift in the City of Gold, Tom Swift & His Air Glider. 2007. 304p. 24.95 (978-1-60459-103-3(X)); per. 12.99 (978-1-60459-104-0(8)) Wilder Pubns., Corp.

—Tom Swift Omnibus #5: Tom Swift in Captivity, Tom Swift & His Wizard Camera, Tom Swift & His Great Searchlight. 2007. 312p. 24.95 (978-1-60459-106-4(4)); per. 12.99 (978-1-60459-105-7(6)) Wilder Pubns., Corp.

—The Tom Swift Omnibus #6: Tom Swift & His Giant Cannon, Tom Swift & His Photo Telephone, Tom Swift & His Aerial Warship. 2007. 296p. 24.95 (978-1-60459-109-5(9)); per. 12.99 (978-1-60459-108-8(0)) Wilder Pubns., Corp.

—The Tom Swift Omnibus #7: Tom Swift & His Big Tunnel, Tom Swift in the Land of Wonders, Tom Swift & His War Tank. 2007. 312p. 24.99 (978-1-60459-111-8(0)); per. 12.99 (978-1-60459-110-1(2)) Wilder Pubns., Corp.

—The Tom Swift Omnibus #8: Tom Swift & His Air Scout, Tom Swift & His Undersea Search, Tom Swift among the Fire Fighters, Tom Swift & His Electri. 2007. 420p. per. 14.99 (978-1-60459-112-5(9)) Wilder Pubns., Corp.

—The Tom Swift Omnibus #8: Tom Swift & His Air Scout, Tom Swift & His Undersea Search, Tom Swift among the Fire Fighters,Tom Swift & His Electric. 2007. 420p. 29.99 (978-1-60459-113-2(7)) Wilder Pubns., Corp.

—The Tom Swift Treasury. 2007. 540p. per. 29.99 (978-1-934451-09-0(6)); 600p. per. 29.99 (978-1-934451-10-6(X)) Wilder Pubns., Corp.

Appleton, Victor & Appleton, Victor, II. Under the Radar. 2007. (Tom Swift, Young Inventor Ser.: 6). (ENG.). 160p. (J). (gr. 3-7). pap. 8.99 (978-1-4169-3644-2(0), Simon & Schuster/Paula Wiseman Bks.) Simon & Schuster/Paula Wiseman Bks.

Victor, Appleton. Tom Swift among the Fire Fighters: Or Battling with Flames from the Air. 2007. (ENG.). 136p. pap. 18.99 (978-1-4346-1489-6(1)) Creative Media Partners, LLC.

—Tom Swift & His Aerial Warship: Or the Naval Terror of the Seas. 2007. (ENG.). 144p. pap. 18.99 (978-1-4346-1484-1(0)) Creative Media Partners, LLC.

—Tom Swift & His Air Scout: Or Uncle Sam's Mastery of the Sky. 2007. (ENG.). 144p. pap. 18.99 (978-1-4346-1486-5(7)) Creative Media Partners, LLC.

—Tom Swift & His Undersea Search: Or the Treasure on the Floor of the Atlantic. 2007. 142p. pap. 18.99 (978-1-4346-1488-9(3)) Creative Media Partners, LLC.

—Tom Swift & His Wizard Camera: Or Thrilling Adventures While Taking Moving Pictu. 2007. (ENG.). 132p. pap. 18.99 (978-1-4346-1485-8(9)) Creative Media Partners, LLC.

SWIMMING

see also Diving

Adler, David A. America's Champion Swimmer: Gertrude Ederle. Widener, Terry, illus. 2005. (ENG.). 32p. (J). (gr. -1-3). reprint ed. pap. 7.99 (978-0-15-205251-5(8)) Houghton Mifflin Harcourt Publishing Co.

Barr, Linda. The Water Patrol: Saving Surfers' Lives in Big Waves. 2005. (High Five Reading - Blue Ser.). (ENG., Illus.).

48p. (gr. 3-4). per. 9.00 *(978-0-7368-5749-9(4),* High Five Reading (RBL)) Capstone Press of Coughlan Cos.
Barth, Katrin & Dietze, Jurgen. Swimming: Training. 2004. (Illus.). 152p. pap. 14.95 *(978-1-84126-145-4(9))* Meyer & Meyer Sport, Ltd. GBR. Dist: Lewis International, Inc.
Boudreau, Hélène. Swimming Science. 2008. (Sports Science Ser.). (ENG., Illus.). 32p. (J). (gr. 4-6). pap. *(978-0-7787-4555-6(4));* lib. bdg. *(978-0-7787-4538-9(4))* Crabtree Publishing Co.
Buckley, James. Katie Ledecky. 2017. (Amazing Americans: Olympians Ser.). (ENG.). 24p. (J). (gr. -1-3). 17.95 ***(978-1-68402-240-3(1))*** Bearport Publishing Co., Inc.
Bussiere, Desireé. Swimming by the Numbers, 1 vol. 2013. (Sports by the Numbers Ser.). (ENG.). 24p. (J). (gr. k-3). lib. bdg. 24.21 *(978-1-61783-846-0(2),* SandCastle) ABDO Publishing Co.
Carr, Annaleise. Annaleise Carr: How I Conquered Lake Ontario to Help Kids Battling Cancer, 1 vol. 2014. (Lorimer Recordbooks Ser.). (ENG., Illus.). 144p. (YA). (gr. 7-12). 16.95 *(978-1-4594-0632-2(X),* 9781459406322); pap. 9.95 *(978-1-4594-0631-5(1),* 9781459406315) Lorimer, James & Co., Ltd., Pubs. CAN. Dist: Casemate Pubs. & Bk. Distributors, LLC.
Crossingham, John. La Natation. 2009. (Sans Limites Ser.). (FRE., Illus.). 32p. (J). pap. 9.95 *(978-2-89579-231-4(3))* Bayard Canada Livres CAN. Dist: Crabtree Publishing Co.
Davis, Marcia. Teach Your Child to Swim the Gentle Way: With Positive Reinforcement. 2011. 84p. pap. 19.95 *(978-1-4626-0268-1(1))* America Star Bks.
Flynn, Brendan. ¡Hora de Natación! 2017. (Bumba Books (tm) en Español — ¡Hora de Deportes! (Sports Time!) Ser.). (SPA., Illus.). 24p. (J). (gr. -1-1). 25.32 *(978-1-5124-2875-9(2))* Lerner Publishing Group.
—Swimming Time! 2016. (Bumba Books (tm) — Sports Time! Ser.). (ENG., Illus.). 24p. (J). (gr. -1-1). lib. bdg. 25.32 *(978-1-5124-1435-6(2))* Lerner Publishing Group.
Fox, Martha Capwell. Swimming. 2003. (History of Sports Ser.). (ENG., Illus.). 104p. (J). 30.85 *(978-1-59018-073-0(9),* Lucent Bks.) Cengage Gale.
Giff, Patricia Reilly. Horas de Sol.Tr. of Sunny Side Up. (SPA.). (J). 3.95 *(978-0-922852-52-9(9))* AIMS International Bks., Inc.
Gifford, Clive. Swimming. 2009. (Tell Me about Sports Ser.). (Illus.). 32p. (J). (gr. 3-5). 28.50 *(978-0-7614-4462-6(9))* Marshall Cavendish Corp.
—Swimming. 2008. (Personal Best Ser.). (Illus.). 32p. (YA). (gr. 3-6). lib. bdg. 26.50 *(978-1-4042-4443-6(3))* Rosen Publishing Group, Inc., The.
—Swimming & Diving. 2011. (Olympic Sports Ser.). 32p. (YA). (gr. 4-7). 19.95 *(978-1-60753-192-0(5))* Amicus Publishing.
—Swimming & Diving. 2011. (ENG., Illus.). 32p. (J). pap. 10.95 *(978-1-77092-039-2(0))* Saunders Bk. Co. CAN. Dist: RiverStream Publishing.
Goldish, Meish. Michael Phelps: Anything Is Possible! 2009. (Defining Moments Ser.). (Illus.). 32p. (YA). (gr. 2-5). lib. bdg. 25.27 *(978-1-59716-855-7(6))* Bearport Publishing Co., Inc.
Grudzina, Rebecca. Tim's Swim. Piwowarski, Marcin, illus. 2017. (Text Connections Guided Close Reading Ser.). (J). (gr. k). *(978-1-4900-1766-2(6))* Benchmark Education Co.
Guillain, Charlotte. Natación, 1 vol. 2010. (Deporte y Mi Cuerpo Ser.). (SPA., Illus.). 24p. (gr. k-2). 23.32 *(978-1-4329-4344-8(8));* pap. 6.79 *(978-1-4329-4350-9(2))* Heinemann-Raintree.
Hachette Children's Group. Swimming. 2016. (ENG., Illus.). 32p. (J). (gr. 4-6). pap. 11.99 *(978-0-7502-9460-7(4),* Wayland) Hachette Children's Group GBR. Dist: Hachette Bk. Group.
Hamilton, S. L. Swimming in the Wild. 2015. (Illus.). 32p. (J). 27.07 *(978-1-62403-752-8(6),* 1391382) ABDO Publishing Co.
Heos, Bridget. Be Safe Around Water. Baroncelli, Silvia, illus. 2015. (Be Safe! Ser.). 24p. (J). 25.65 *(978-1-60753-448-8(7))* Amicus Publishing.
Herman, Gail. Make-a-Splash Writing Rules. 2009. (Grammar All-Stars: Writing Tools Ser.). 32p. (J). (gr. 2-5). (ENG.). pap. 10.50 *(978-1-4339-2136-0(7));* lib. bdg. 26.00 *(978-1-4339-1943-5(5))* Stevens, Gareth Publishing LLLP. (Gareth Stevens Learning Library).
Hoblin, Paul. Girls Play to Win Swimming & Diving. 2011. (Girls Play to Win Ser.). 64p. (J). (gr. 3-6). lib. bdg. 27.93 *(978-1-59953-466-4(5))* Norwood Hse. Pr.
Hoena, Blake. Swimming. 2015. (J). lib. bdg. 25.65 *(978-1-62031-182-0(8),* Bullfrog Bks.) Jump! Inc.
Holden, Pam. Learning to Swim. 2015. (ENG., Illus.). 16p. (-1). pap. *(978-1-77654-081-5(6),* Red Rocket Readers) Flying Start Bks.
—Watch Me Swim, 6 pack. Hansen, Christine, illus. 2009. (Red Rocket Readers Ser.). (ENG.). 16p. (gr. -1-1). pap. *(978-1-877363-31-3(6),* Red Rocket Readers) Flying Start Bks.
Kear, Angela A. Mommy & Me Go to Swimming Lessons. 2012. 30p. pap. 15.95 *(978-1-60594-929-1(9))* Aeon Publishing Inc.
Kehm, Greg. Olympic Swimming & Diving. (Great Moments in Olympic History Ser.). 48p. (gr. 5-6). 2009. 53.00 *(978-1-61513-162-4(0),* Rosen Reference) 2007. (Illus.). (YA). lib. bdg. 29.25 *(978-1-4042-0970-1(0))* Rosen Publishing Group, Inc., The.
Kennedy, Mike. Michael Phelps. 2009. (People We Should Know Ser.). (ENG.). 48p. (J). (gr. 3-5). pap. 10.50 *(978-1-4339-2151-3(0));* lib. bdg. 31.00 *(978-1-4339-1950-3(8))* Stevens, Gareth Publishing LLLP. (Gareth Stevens Learning Library).
Knowlton, MaryLee. Safety Around Water. 2008. (Staying Safe Ser.). (ENG.). 32p. (J). (gr. -1-3). lib. bdg. *(978-0-7787-4315-6(2))* Crabtree Publishing Co.
Lanser, Amanda. The Science Behind Swimming, Diving, & Other Water Sports. 2016. (Illus.). 32p. (J). *(978-1-4914-8169-1(2))* Capstone Press of Coughlan Cos.
LeBoutillier, Nate. Swimming. 2012. (J). 35.65 *(978-1-60818-211-4(8),* Creative Education) Creative Co., The.
Lindeen, Mary & Kesselring, Susan. Being Safe around Water. McGeehan, Dan & Moore, David, Jr., illus. 2011. (Be Safe Ser.). (ENG.). 24p. (J). (gr. k-3). lib. bdg. 27.07 *(978-1-60954-298-6(3),* 200078) Child's World, Inc., The.
MacCallum, Jess. Swimming with the Fishes. 5th rev. ed. 2004. per. 5.95 *(978-0-9749673-0-1(0))* In Ardua Tendit Pr.
Macken, JoAnn Early. Swimming. 2005. (After-School Fun Ser.). (Illus.). 24p. (gr. k-3). lib. bdg. 21.00 *(978-0-8368-4516-7(1),* Weekly Reader Leveled Readers) Stevens, Gareth Publishing LLLP.
Macy, Sue. Trudy's Big Swim: How Gertrude Ederle Swam the English Channel & Took the World by Storm. Collins, Matt, illus. 2017. (ENG.). 40p. (J). (gr. 1-5). 16.95 *(978-0-8234-3665-1(9))* Holiday Hse., Inc.
Manley, Claudia B. Ultra Swimming. 2009. (Ultra Sports Ser.). 64p. (gr. 5-8). 58.50 *(978-1-60854-610-7(1),* Rosen Reference) Rosen Publishing Group, Inc., The.
Mara, Wil. What Should I Do? At the Pool. 2011. (Community Connections: What Should I Do? Ser.). (ENG.). 24p. (gr. 2-5). lib. bdg. 25.64 *(978-1-61080-056-3(7),* 201054) Cherry Lake Publishing.
Markovics, Joyce L. Michael Phelps. 2017. (Amazing Americans: Olympians Ser.). (ENG.). 24p. (J). (gr. -1-3). 17.95 ***(978-1-68402-239-7(8))*** Bearport Publishing Co., Inc.
Mason, Paul. How to Improve at Swimming. 2007. (How to Improve At- Ser.). (ENG., Illus.). 48p. (J). (gr. 3-7). pap. *(978-0-7787-3592-2(3));* lib. bdg. *(978-0-7787-3570-0(2))* Crabtree Publishing Co.
Mattern, Joanne. Swimming. Hardman, Lizabeth, ed. 2011. (Science Behind Sports Ser.). (ENG., Illus.). 128p. (YA). (gr. 7-12). 34.45 *(978-1-4205-0273-2(5))* Cengage Gale.
Miller, Amanda. Let's Talk Soccer. 2008. (Scholastic News Nonfiction Readers Ser.). (ENG.). 24p. (J). (gr. 1-2). pap. 6.95 *(978-0-531-20430-6(8))* Scholastic Library Publishing.
Minden, Cecilia. Swimming. 2008. (21st Century Skills Library: Real World Math Ser.). (ENG., Illus.). 32p. (gr. 4-8). lib. bdg. 28.50 *(978-1-60279-246-3(1),* 200197) Cherry Lake Publishing.
Morey, Allan. Swimming & Diving. 2015. (Summer Olympic Sports Ser.). (ENG., Illus.). 32p. (J). (gr. 2-4). 19.95 *(978-1-60753-809-7(1))* Amicus Publishing.
Nagle, Jeanne. What Happens to Your Body When You Swim. 2009. (How & Why of Exercise Ser.). (Illus.). 48p. (YA). (gr. 5-9). 29.25 *(978-1-4358-5309-6(1))* Rosen Publishing Group, Inc., The.
Nelson, Robin. Swimming Is Fun! 2013. (First Step Nonfiction - Sports Are Fun! Ser.). (ENG.). 24p. (gr. k-2). lib. bdg. 23.93 *(978-1-4677-1106-7(3),* Lerner Pubns.); (Illus.). pap. 6.95 *(978-1-4677-1539-3(5))* Lerner Publishing Group.
Orr, Tamra B. The Science of a Flip Turn. 2015. (21st Century Skills Library: Full-Speed Sports Ser.). (ENG., Illus.). 32p. (J). (gr. 4-7). 29.93 *(978-1-63362-583-9(4),* 206516) Cherry Lake Publishing.
Page, Jason. Swimming, Diving, & Other Water Sports. 2008. (Olympic Sports Ser.). (ENG., Illus.). 32p. (J). (gr. 3-7). pap. *(978-0-7787-4036-0(6));* lib. bdg. *(978-0-7787-4019-3(6))* Crabtree Publishing Co.
Peterson, Christine. The Science Behind Swimming, Diving, & Other Water Sports. 2016. (Science of the Summer Olympics Ser.). (ENG.). 32p. (gr. 3-4). pap. 7.95 *(978-1-4914-8161-5(7));* (Illus.). lib. bdg. 27.99 *(978-1-4914-8157-8(9))* Capstone Press of Coughlan Cos. (Edge Bks.).
Rodomista, Kim. 101 Cool Pool Games for Children: Fun & Fitness for Swimmers of All Levels. Patterson, Robin, illus. 2006. (SmartFun Activity Bks.). (ENG.). 160p. spiral bd. 19.95 *(978-0-89793-484-8(9));* (gr. -1). per. 14.95 *(978-0-89793-483-1(0))* Turner Publishing Co. (Hunter Hse.).
Romanek, Trudee. Splash It Swimming. 2012. (ENG., Illus.). 32p. (J). pap. *(978-0-7787-3163-4(4))* Crabtree Publishing Co.
Rosen, Karen. Great Moments in Olympic Swimming & Diving, 1 vol. 2014. (Great Moments in Olympic Sports Ser.). (ENG.). 64p. (gr. 10-14). lib. bdg. 32.79 *(978-1-62403-399-5(7),* SportsZone) ABDO Publishing Co.
Ryan, Emma. Surprising Swimmers. 2013. (Scholastic Reader Level 2 Ser.). (ENG.). 32p. (J). (gr. k-2). pap. 3.99 *(978-0-545-55266-0(4),* Scholastic Paperbacks) Scholastic, Inc.
Sévigny, Eric, illus. Caillou Learns to Swim. 2013. (Playtime Ser.). (ENG.). 24p. (J). (gr. -1-1). 4.99 *(978-2-89718-036-2(6))* Caillouet, Gerry.
Sheen, Barbara, ed. Michael Phelps. 2010. (People in the News Ser.). (ENG.). 96p. (YA). (gr. 7-12). 33.95 *(978-1-4205-0282-4(4))* Cengage Gale.
—Natalie Coughlin. 2013. (People in the News Ser.). (ENG., Illus.). 128p. (gr. 7-10). lib. bdg. 39.40 *(978-1-4205-0998-4(5),* Lucent Bks.) Cengage Gale.
Skinner, Tina. Hot Tubs & Spas: An Inspirational Design Guide, 1 vol. 2003. (ENG., Illus.). 144p. (gr. 10-13). pap. 24.95 *(978-0-7643-1841-2(1),* 9780764318412) Schiffer Publishing, Ltd.
Thomas, Isabel. Animal Swimming & Diving. 2016. (Animalympics Ser.). (ENG., Illus.). 32p. (gr. 1-3). lib. bdg. 29.99 *(978-1-4109-8092-2(8),* Read Me!) Heinemann-Raintree.
Tieck, Sarah. Swimming, 1 vol. 2013. (Move Your Body Ser.). (ENG.). 32p. (J). (gr. 2-5). 27.07 *(978-1-61783-564-3(1))* ABDO Publishing Co.
Timblin, Stephen. Swimming. 2008. (21st Century Skills Innovation Library: Innovation in Sports Ser.). (ENG., Illus.). 32p. (gr. 4-8). lib. bdg. 28.50 *(978-1-60279-258-6(5),* 200125) Cherry Lake Publishing.
Torsiello, David P. Michael Phelps: Swimming for Olympic Gold. 2009. (Hot Celebrity Biographies Ser.). (Illus.). 48p. (J). (gr. 5-9). lib. bdg. 25.27 *(978-0-7660-3591-1(3))* Enslow Pubs., Inc.
Way, Edward. Swimming. 2017. (Get Sporty Ser.). (ENG., Illus.). 32p. (J). (gr. 2-4). pap. 11.99 *(978-0-7502-9487-4(6),* Wayland) Hachette Children's Group GBR. Dist: Hachette Bk. Group.
Wendorff, Anne. Swimming. 2009. (My First Sports Ser.). (ENG., Illus.). 24p. (J). (gr. 2-5). lib. bdg. 25.95 *(978-1-60014-326-7(1),* Blastoff! Readers) Bellwether Media.
Wilson, CeCe. Baby Seal Learns to Swim. 2015. (Rosen REAL Readers: STEM & STEAM Collection). (ENG.). 8p. pap. 5.46 *(978-1-4994-9580-5(3),* Rosen Classroom) Rosen Publishing Group, Inc., The.
Wood, Alix. You Can Be a Swimmer, Vol. 1. 2014. (Let's Get Moving! Ser.). 32p. (J). (gr. 3-4). (ENG.). pap. 10.50 *(978-1-4824-0288-9(2));* 26.60 *(978-1-4824-0287-2(4))* Stevens, Gareth Publishing LLLP.
Zuehlke, Jeffrey. Michael Phelps (Revised Edition) 2009. pap. 40.95 *(978-0-7613-4777-4(1))* Lerner Publishing Group.

SWIMMING—FICTION

Applegate, Katherine. Never Swim in Applesauce. Biggs, Brian, illus. 2016. (Roscoe Riley Rules Ser.: 4). 128p. (J). (gr. 1-5). pap. 4.99 *(978-0-06-239251-0(4))* HarperCollins Pubs.
Ashby, Gaylene. STORY TIME A Collection of Three Children's Stories. 2008. 28p. 14.95 *(978-1-4357-1929-3(8))* Lulu Pr., Inc.
Atkins, Jeannine. Preparadas... Listas... Ya! 2004. (SPA., Illus.). (J). (gr. k-3). spiral bd. *(978-0-616-07274-5(0))* Canadian National Institute for the Blind/Institut National Canadien pour les Aveugles.
Atkins, Jill. Toad Swims for his Life! Mostyn, David, illus. 2004. (ENG.). 24p. (J). lib. bdg. 23.65 *(978-1-59646-712-5(6))* Dingles & Co.
Battiste, Alyse. Super Sally's Fantastic Fun Day. 2007. (Illus.). 68p. (J). pap. 15.97 *(978-0-9798217-1-4(1))* Candalyse Publishing.
Beinstein, Phoebe. ¡A nadar, Boots! (Swim, Boots, Swim!) Roper, Robert, illus. 2009. (Dora la Exploradora Ser.). (SPA.). 24p. (J). pap. 3.99 *(978-1-4169-7939-5(5),* Libros Para Ninos) Libros Para Ninos.
—Swim, Boots, Swim! Roper, Robert, illus. 2009. (Dora the Explorer Ser.: 29). (ENG.). 24p. (J). (gr. -1-2). pap. 3.99 *(978-1-4169-7195-5(5),* Simon Spotlight/Nickelodeon) Simon Spotlight/Nickelodeon.
Bentley, Sue. A Splash of Forever. 2014. (Magic Kitten Ser.: 14). lib. bdg. 16.00 *(978-0-606-35684-8(3))* Turtleback Bks.
—A Splash of Forever #14. Swan, Angela & Farley, Andrew, illus. 2014. (Magic Kitten Ser.: 14). (ENG.). 128p. (J). (gr. 1-3). 5.99 *(978-0-448-46797-9(6),* Grosset & Dunlap) Penguin Young Readers Group.
Braun, Sebastien. Who Can Swim? Braun, Sebastien, illus. 2014. (ENG., Illus.). 14p. (J). (— 1). bds. 6.99 *(978-0-7636-6752-8(8))* Candlewick Pr.
Brigham, Marilyn. Swim!, 0 vols. Velasquez, Eric, illus. 2012. (ENG.). 24p. (J). (gr. -1-k). 7.99 *(978-0-7614-6253-8(8),* 9780761462538, Amazon Children's Publishing) Amazon Publishing.
Bringsvaerd, Tor Age. Ruffen: The Escape to Loch Ness. Hansen, Thore, illus. 2009. (Ruffen Ser.). 72p. (J). (gr. 1-4). 16.95 *(978-0-98157661-2-1(5))* Mackenzie Smiles, LLC.
—Ruffen: The Sea Serpent Who Couldn't Swim. Hansen, Thore, illus. 2008. (Ruffen Ser.). 64p. (J). (gr. -1-3). 16.95 *(978-0-9790347-9-4(5))* Mackenzie Smiles, LLC.
Brown, Kathryn. Freddy the Brave. 2010. 43p. pap. 12.50 *(978-1-4461-2959-3(4))* Lulu Pr., Inc.
Bruna, Dick. Miffy Goes Swimming. 2004. (Illus.). 12p. bds. 5.99 *(978-1-59226-204-5(X))* Big Tent Entertainment, Inc.
—Miffy va a Nadar/Miffy Goes Swimming. 2004. (SPA., Illus.). 12p. (J). bds. 5.99 *(978-1-59226-209-0(0))* Big Tent Entertainment, Inc.
Bullion, Leslie. Uncharted Waters, 1 vol. (ENG.). 192p. (J). (gr. 3-7). 2009. pap. 7.95 *(978-1-56145-485-3(0))* 2006. 14.95 *(978-1-56145-365-8(X))* Peachtree Pubs.
Butler, Dori Hillestad. Trading Places with Tank Talbott. 2003. (ENG.). 144p. (J). (gr. 3-7). 15.99 *(978-0-8075-1708-5(9))* Whitman, Albert & Co.
Calame, Don. Swim the Fly. 2010. (ENG., Illus.). 352p. (YA). (gr. 9). pap. 7.99 *(978-0-7636-4776-6(4))* Candlewick Pr.
Capdevila, Roser & Vendrell, Maria Martinez. El Agua Inquieta. 2003.Tr. of Rough Water. (SPA.). 24p. (J). 7.95 *(978-84-233-1742-4(0))* Ediciones Destino ESP. Dist: Planeta Publishing Corp.
Carpenter, Nancy, illus. Queen Victoria's Bathing Machine. 2014. (ENG.). 40p. (J). (gr. k-3). 17.99 *(978-1-4169-2753-2(0),* Simon & Schuster/Paula Wiseman Bks.) Simon & Schuster/Paula Wiseman Bks.
Caruso, D. A. Cool by the Pool. 2005. pap. 19.99 *(978-0-9765953-0-4(3))* Mighty Kids Media.
Cassano, Carol E. A Journey to the Bottom of the Ocean: Heavenly Adventures Volume 2. 2011. 20p. pap. *(978-1-4269-7335-2(7))* Trafford Publishing (UK) Ltd.
Casteel, Seth. Puppy Pool Party! An Underwater Dogs Adventure. 2016. (ENG., Illus.). 40p. (J). (gr. -1-3). 16.99 *(978-0-316-37633-4(7))* Little Brown & Co.
Chaconas, Dori. Swimming Lesson, 7 vols. McCue, Lisa, illus. 2011. (Cork & Fuzz Ser.: 7). (ENG.). 32p. (J). (gr. 1-3). 13.99 *(978-0-670-01281-7(5),* Viking Books for Young Readers) Penguin Young Readers Group.
—The Swimming Lesson. McCue, Lisa, illus. 2014. (Cork & Fuzz Ser.: 7). (ENG.). 32p. (J). (gr. 1-3). pap. 3.99 *(978-0-448-48051-0(4),* Penguin Young Readers) Penguin Young Readers Group.
Clement, Gary, illus. Swimming, Swimming, 1 vol. 2015. (ENG.). 48p. (J). (gr. -1-2). 18.95 *(978-1-55498-449-7(1))* Groundwood Bks. CAN. Dist: Publishers Group West (PGW).
Cohen, Deborah Bodin. Nachshon, Who Was Afraid to Swim: A Passover Story. Jago, illus. 2009. (Passover Ser.). (ENG.). 32p. (J). (gr. -1-2). pap. 8.95 *(978-0-8225-8765-1(3),* Kar-Ben Publishing) Lerner Publishing Group.
Cornwall, Gaia. Jabari Jumps. Cornwall, Gaia, illus. 2017. (ENG., Illus.). 32p. (J). (gr. -1-3). 15.99 *(978-0-7636-7838-8(4))* Candlewick Pr.
Cousins, Lucy. Maisy Goes Swimming. Cousins, Lucy, illus. 2017. (Maisy Ser.). (ENG., Illus.). 16p. (J). (-k). 14.99 *(978-0-7636-9461-6(4))* Candlewick Pr.
—Maisy Learns to Swim. Cousins, Lucy, illus. (Maisy Ser.). (ENG., Illus.). 32p. (J). 2015. (-k). 6.99 *(978-0-7636-7749-7(3))* 2013. (gr. -1-k). 12.99 *(978-0-7636-6480-0(4))* Candlewick Pr.
Craig, Deborah Anne. Paddle, the Extraordinary Duck. Glueck, Michael Wells, ed. Karcz, Katherine, illus. 2011. 42p. pap. 19.95 *(978-1-4583-6916-1(1))* Lulu Pr., Inc.
Crays, Lettie L. Timmy the Turtle Learns to Swim. Rollins, Joe, illus. 2011. 44p. (J). pap. 11.95 *(978-1-937089-06-1(1))* Truth Bk. Pubs.
Crouse, Donna J. The Ruby Ring: The Whispering Cove Kids Club. 2005. 114p. pap. 12.99 *(978-0-9765339-0-0(1))* Crouse, Donna J.
Crutcher, Chris. Whale Talk. 2009. (ENG.). 304p. (YA). (gr. 8). pap. 9.99 *(978-0-06-177131-6(7),* Greenwillow Bks.) HarperCollins Pubs.
—Whale Talk. 2004. 224p. (J). (gr. 7-18). pap. 38.00 incl. audio *(978-0-8072-2289-8(5),* Listening Library) Random Hse. Audio Publishing Group.
Curr, Martin. Sharp Claws Learns to Swim. 2010. 26p. pap. 21.99 *(978-1-4535-1414-8(7))* Xlibris Corp.
Dale, Jay. Our Special Rock Pool, 1 vol. Everitt-Stewart, Andrew, illus. 2012. (Engage Literacy Green Ser.). (ENG.). 32p. (gr. k-2). pap. 5.99 *(978-1-4296-9009-6(7),* Engage Literacy) Capstone Press of Coughlan Cos.
D'Ath, Justin. Pool. 2009. (ENG.). 288p. (Orig.). (YA). 13.95 *(978-1-876462-51-2(5),* Ford Street Publishing) Hybrid Pubs. AUS. Dist: International Publishers Marketing.
Degman, Lori. Norbert's Big Dream. Bucci, Marco, illus. 2016. (ENG.). 32p. (J). (gr. k-3). 16.99 *(978-1-58536-959-1(4),* 204108) Sleeping Bear Pr.
Depken, Kristen L. Wisdom to Remember: Life Advice from a Forgetful Fish. Random House Disney Staff, illus. 2016. (Official Guide Ser.). (ENG.). 80p. (J). (gr. -1-2). 9.99 *(978-0-7364-3710-3(X),* RH/Disney) Random Hse. Children's Bks.
Devoles, Margaret. My Aunt Calls Me Saree. 2007. 88p. per. 19.95 *(978-1-4241-7579-6(8))* America Star Bks.
Diersch, Sandra. False Start, 1 vol. 2005. (Lorimer Sports Stories Ser.: 78). (ENG.). 104p. (J). (gr. 4-8). 16.95 *(978-1-55028-873-5(3),* 9781550288735); 8.95 *(978-1-55028-872-8(5),* 9781550288728) Lorimer, James & Co., Ltd., Pubs. CAN. Dist: Casemate Pubs. & Bk. Distributors, LLC.
Dipinto, Michael J. The Princess Mermaid & the Missing Sea Shells. Marsh, Bobbie, illus. 2013. 36p. pap. 15.95 *(978-1-61493-151-5(8))* Peppertree Pr., The.
Doty, M. Surviving High School. 2012. (Surviving High School Ser.: 1). (ENG.). 224p. (YA). (gr. 7-17). pap. 10.00 *(978-0-316-22015-6(9),* Poppy) Little, Brown Bks. for Young Readers.
Dubose, Sarah. Uncharted Waters. 2013. 440p. pap. *(978-1-4596-6282-7(2))* ReadHowYouWant.com, Ltd.
Dubovoy, Silvia. Turquesita. (SPA.). (J). pap. *(978-968-6465-18-1(9))* Casa de Estudios de Literatura y Talleres Artisticos Amaquemecan A.C. MEX. Dist: Lectorum Pubns., Inc.
Dyan, Penelope. Courtney's Beach. Dyan, Penelope, illus. 2008. (Illus.). 44p. pap. 11.95 *(978-1-935118-35-0(8))* Bellissima Publishing, LLC.
—Summer Surfs the Olympic Trials. 2008. 168p. pap. 11.95 *(978-1-935118-06-0(4))* Bellissima Publishing, LLC.
East, Vastine. I Swam with an Angel. 2011. 52p. pap. 31.99 *(978-1-4653-0059-6(4))* Xlibris Corp.
Elliott, Wade. What Will You Do Today? 2010. 32p. pap. 21.99 *(978-1-4535-4044-2(X))* Xlibris Corp.
Feinstein, John. Rush for the Gold: Mystery at the Olympics. 2013. (Sports Beat Ser.). (ENG.). 336p. (J). (gr. 5). pap. 7.99 *(978-0-375-87168-9(3),* Yearling) Random Hse. Children's Bks.
Fenn, G. Manville. Brownsmith's Boy. 2008. 260p. pap. 15.95 *(978-1-60664-154-5(9))* Aegypan.
Figiel, Lisa. Swimming Is Fun! 2010. 24p. pap. 11.49 *(978-1-4490-5520-2(6))* AuthorHouse.
Gallagher, Diana G. Pool Problem: The Complicated Life of Claudia Cristina Cortez, 1 vol. Garvey, Brann, illus. 2009. (Claudia Cristina Cortez Ser.). (ENG.). 88p. (gr. 2-3). 26.65 *(978-1-4342-1577-2(6),* Claudia Cristina Cortez) Stone Arch Bks.
Galvin, Laura Gates. Baby Polar Bear Learns to Swim. 2008. (Smithsonian Baby Animals Ser.). (ENG., Illus.). 16p. (gr. -1-k). 13.95 *(978-1-59249-786-7(1));* (J). 6.95 *(978-1-59249-785-0(3))* Soundprints.
Garis, Howard Roger. Sammie & Susie Littletail. 2005. 26.95 *(978-1-4218-1465-0(X),* 1st World Library - Literary Society) 1st World Publishing, Inc.
Garratt, Irene Joyce. Andrew's Activities: Two in One Stories. 2009. (Illus.). 20p. pap. 10.49 *(978-1-4389-4235-3(4))* AuthorHouse.
Garton, Sam. Otter: Let's Go Swimming! Garton, Sam, illus. 2017. (My First I Can Read Ser.). (Illus.). 32p. (J). (gr. -1-3). pap. 3.99 *(978-0-06-236663-4(7))* HarperCollins Pubs.
Glover, Darryl. The Pirate Kitty. Austin, Britta, ed. Kosir, Ana, illus. 2008. 24p. (J). 16.95 *(978-0-9821387-0-0(9))* MagicStar Inc.
Going Swimming: KinderConcepts Individual Title Six-Packs. (Kinderstarters Ser.). 8p. (gr. -1-1). 21.00 *(978-0-7635-8731-4(1))* Rigby Education.
Gottschalk, Bre. The Lucky Necklace. 2011. 24p. pap. 11.99 *(978-1-4389-8725-5(0))* AuthorHouse.
Gough, Simon. I Can'T Fly & I Can'T Swim. 2011. (Illus.). 24p. pap. 11.44 *(978-1-4567-8063-0(8))* AuthorHouse.
Green, Poppy. Forget-Me-Not Lake. Bell, Jennifer A., illus. 2015. (Adventures of Sophie Mouse Ser.: 3). (ENG.). 128p. (J). (gr. k-4). 16.99 *(978-1-4814-3000-5(9),* Little Simon) Little Simon.
Gunderson, Jessica. There's a Hurricane in the Pool!, 1 vol. Santillan, Jorge H., illus. 2011. (Sports Illustrated Kids Victory School Superstars Ser.). (ENG.). 56p. (gr. 1-3). 26.65 *(978-1-4342-2230-5(6))* Stone Arch Bks.
Hambleton, Laura. Chameleon Swims, 13 vols. 2005. (Chameleon Ser.). (ENG, URD & MUL., Illus.). 16p. (J). (gr. -1). 8.95 *(978-1-84059-446-1(2))* Milet Publishing.
—Chameleon Swims, 13 vols. Choudhury, Dorbesh, tr. from ENG. 2005. (Chameleon Ser.). (BEN, ENG & MUL., Illus.). 16p. (J). (gr. -1). 8.95 *(978-1-84059-437-9(3))* Milet Publishing.
Hancock, H. Irving. The Grammar School Boys in Summer Athletics. rev. ed. 2006. 216p. 27.95 *(978-1-4218-1748-4(9));* pap. 12.95 *(978-1-4218-1848-1(5))* 1st World Publishing, Inc. (1st World Library - Literary Society).
—The Grammar School Boys in Summer Athletics. 2007. 184p. per. *(978-1-4065-1982-2(0))* Dodo Pr.
Harvey, Pam & Panckridge, Michael. In the Deep End. 2007. 224p. *(978-0-207-20064-9(5))* HarperCollins Pubs. Australia.
Haslett, Katherine A. The Day Amy Met the Prime Minister & Mrs. Blair. 2007. (Illus.). 32p. (J). pap. 8.00 *(978-0-8059-7353-2(2))* Dorrance Publishing Co., Inc.
Herbertson, Lisa. Swimming Along. Kennedy, Catherine, illus. 2011. 26p. pap. 12.00 *(978-1-60976-293-3(2),* Eloquent Bks.) Strategic Book Publishing & Rights Agency (SBPRA).
Hicks, Betty. Swimming with Sharks / Track Attack. McCauley, Adam, illus. 2010. (Gym Shorts Ser.). (ENG.). 128p. (J). (gr.

S

2-5). pap. 16.99 *(978-0-312-60237-6(5)*, 9780312602376) Square Fish.

Higginson, Sheila Sweeny & Disney Book Group Staff. The Mermaid Dives In. Disney Storybook Art Team, illus. 2013. (ENG.). 24p. (J). (gr. -1-k). pap. 4.99 *(978-1-4231-7132-4(2))* Disney Pr.

Hofmeister, Alan, et al. Swim with Us. (Reading for All Learners Ser.). (Illus.). (J). pap. *(978-1-56861-140-2(4))* Swift Learning Resources.

Holm, Jennifer L. & Holm, Matthew. Babymouse Goes for the Gold. Holm, Jennifer L. & Holm, Matthew, illus. 2016. (Babymouse Ser.: 20). (ENG., Illus.). 96p. (J). (gr. 2-5). pap. 6.99 *(978-0-307-93163-4(3)*, Random Hse. Bks. for Young Readers) Random Hse. Children's Bks.

—The Power of the Parasite. Holm, Jennifer L. & Holm, Matthew, illus. 2012. (Squish Ser.: No. 3). (ENG., Illus.). 96p. (J). (gr. 2-5). pap. 6.99 *(978-0-375-84391-4(4))*; lib. bdg. 12.99 *(978-0-375-93785-9(4))* Random Hse. Children's Bks. (Random Hse. Bks. for Young Readers).

—The Power of the Parasite. 2012. (Squish Ser.: 3). lib. bdg. 17.20 *(978-0-606-26405-1(1)*, Turtleback) Turtleback Bks.

Howells, Amanda. The Summer of Skinny Dipping. 2010. (ENG.). 304p. (YA). (gr. 7-12). pap. 9.99 *(978-1-4022-3862-8(2)*, Sourcebooks Jabberwocky) Sourcebooks, Inc.

I love to Swim. 2004. (J). per. *(978-1-57657-473-7(3))* Paradise Pr., Inc.

Isabel, Michelle. Murtle the Sea Turtle. Isabel, Michelle & Thomas, Franselica, illus. 2011. 24p. pap. 24.95 *(978-1-4626-0114-1(6))* America Star Bks.

James, Simon. Querido Salvatierra. de la Vega, Eida, tr. from ENG. 2003.Tr. of Dear Mr. Blueberry. (SPA.). (J). (gr. k-2). pap. 7.99 *(978-1-930332-45-4(9))* Lectorum Pubns., Inc.

Jansson, Tove. Moomin's Winter Follies. 2012. (Moomin Ser.). (ENG., Illus.). 48p. (J). (gr. 4-7). pap. 9.95 *(978-1-77046-098-0(5)*, 9781770460980) Drawn & Quarterly Pubns. CAN. Dist: Macmillan.

Jennie Lyon Wood. Bath Time Bears Have So Much Fun. Kristie Kryssing, illus. 2009. 24p. pap. 12.99 *(978-1-4389-4420-3(9))* AuthorHouse.

Jentsch, R. D. Froggy & Friends Go to the Creek, 1 vol. Jentsch, Joyce Harp, illus. 2009. 41p. pap. 24.95 *(978-1-60836-966-9(8))* America Star Bks.

Johnson, Grace. The Little Fish Who Was Afraid to Swim. 2008. 36p. pap. 15.49 *(978-1-4389-2262-1(0))* AuthorHouse.

Just One More Swim. 2008. (Picture Books... Ser.). 32p. *(978-1-4075-1842-8(9))* Parragon, Inc.

Kang, Anna. Can I Tell You a Secret? Weyant, Christopher, illus. 2016. 40p. (J). (gr. -1-3). 17.99 *(978-0-06-239684-6(6))* HarperCollins Pubs.

Kemp, Dane. Imaginary Tales. 2011. 186p. pap. 24.95 *(978-1-4560-4686-6(1))* America Star Bks.

Kessler, Liz. The Tail of Emily Windsnap. Gibb, Sarah, illus. 2012. (Emily Windsnap Ser.: 1). (ENG.). 224p. (J). (gr. 3-7). pap. 5.99 *(978-0-7636-6020-8(5))* Candlewick Pr.

—The Tail of Emily Windsnap. 2012. (Emily Windsnap Ser.: 1). lib. bdg. 16.00 *(978-0-606-25544-8(3)*, Turtleback) Turtleback Bks.

Kim, YunYeong. Brown Bear's Dream. Kim, KyeMahn, illus. rev. ed. 2014. (MySELF Bookshelf Ser.). (ENG.). 32p. (J). (gr. k-2). pap. 11.94 *(978-1-60357-655-0(X))*; lib. bdg. 25.27 *(978-1-59953-646-0(3))* Norwood Hse. Pr.

Kirby, Stan. Captain Awesome Takes a Dive. O'Connor, George, illus. 2012. (Captain Awesome Ser.: 4). (ENG.). 128p. (J). (gr. k-4). 16.99 *(978-1-4424-4203-0(4))*; pap. 5.99 *(978-1-4424-4202-3(6))* Little Simon. (Little Simon).

—Captain Awesome Takes a Dive. 2012. (Captain Awesome Ser.: 4). lib. bdg. 14.75 *(978-0-606-26325-2(X)*, Turtleback) Turtleback Bks.

Knudsen, Michelle. Fish & Frog Big Book: Brand New Readers. Petrone, Valeria, illus. 2010. (Brand New Readers Ser.). (ENG.). 48p. (J). (gr. -1-3). pap. 24.99 *(978-0-7636-4810-7(8))* Candlewick Pr.

Koerner, Miranda Pike. Blue Mermaid. 2013. 210p. pap. 12.99 *(978-1-62237-202-7(6))* Turquoise Morning Pr.

Koffsky, Ann D. Noah's Swim-A-Thon. 2010. (J). *(978-0-8074-1168-1(X))* URJ Pr.

Lagonegro, Melissa & RH Disney Staff. Just Keep Swimming. Harchy, Atelier Philippe, illus. 2005. (Step into Reading Ser.). (ENG.). 32p. (J). (gr. k-3). pap. 3.99 *(978-0-7364-2319-9(2)*, RH/Disney) Random Hse. Children's Bks.

Larsen, Alison. Thomas the Turtle. 2006. (Illus.). 21p. (J). per. 14.95 *(978-1-60002-097-1(6)*, 3961) Mountain Valley Publishing, LLC.

Leaf, Autumn. Coto, Child of the Ocean. 2008. 122p. pap. 19.95 *(978-1-60703-843-6(9))* America Star Bks.

Lewis, Edwina. Who Swims? Parker, Ant, illus. 2003. (Who... Ser.). 16p. (YA). *(978-1-85602-448-8(2)*, Pavilion Children's Books) Pavilion Bks.

The Long Legged Turtle. 2013. 44p. pap. 16.99 *(978-1-4808-0460-9(6))* Archway Publishing.

Long, Tammy J. Like a Fish. 2010. (J). pap. 7.95 *(978-1-932715-81-1(9))* UMI (Urban Ministries, Inc.).

Lurie, Susan. Swim, Duck, Swim! Head, Murray, photos by. 2016. (ENG., Illus.). 32p. (J). bds. 7.99 *(978-1-250-07740-0(0)*, 9781250077400) Feiwel & Friends.

Lyles, Tanya. The Frog That Needed an Umbrella. 2006. 17.00 *(978-0-8059-9906-8(X))* Dorrance Publishing Co., Inc.

Maccarone, Grace. The Cowboy. Müller, Hildegard, illus. 2015. (I Like to Read(r) Ser.). (ENG.). 24p. (J). (gr. -1-3). 14.95 *(978-0-8234-3202-8(5))* Holiday Hse., Inc.

MacGregor, Jill. Swim Safe Little Seals. 2006. (Illus.). 31p. (J). 14.95 *(978-0-9774062-0-3(2))* Seal Publishing, LLC.

Mack, Winnie. After All, You're Callie Boone. 2013. (ENG.). 192p. (J). (gr. 4-7). pap. 14.99 *(978-1-250-02735-1(7)*, 9781250027351) Square Fish.

MacLeod, Doug. Heather Fell in the Water. Smith, Craig, illus. 2013. (ENG.). 32p. (J). (gr. -1-k). 19.99 *(978-1-74237-648-6(7))* Allen & Unwin AUS. Dist: Independent Pubs. Group.

Maddox, Jake. Diving off the Edge, 1 vol. Tiffany, Sean, illus. 2009. (Jake Maddox Sports Stories Ser.). (ENG.). 72p. (gr. 2-3). lib. bdg. 25.32 *(978-1-4342-1205-4(X))* Stone Arch Bks.

—Gold Medal Swim, 1 vol. Garcia, Eduardo, illus. 2012. (Jake Maddox Sports Stories Ser.). (ENG.). 72p. (gr. 2-3). pap. 5.95 *(978-1-4342-3902-0(0))*; lib. bdg. 25.32 *(978-1-4342-3288-5(3))* Stone Arch Bks.

—Pool Panic. Wood, Katie, illus. 2016. (Jake Maddox Girl Sports Stories Ser.). (ENG.). 72p. (gr. 2-3). lib. bdg. 25.32 *(978-1-4965-2618-2(X))* Stone Arch Bks.

—Swimming the Distance. 2015. (Jake Maddox JV Ser.). (ENG.). 96p. (gr. 3-4). lib. bdg. 25.99 *(978-1-4342-9637-5(7))* Stone Arch Bks.

Mayer, Mercer. Just a Day at the Pond. Mayer, Mercer, illus. 2008. (Little Critter Ser.). (ENG., Illus.). 24p. (J). (gr. -1-2). pap. 3.99 *(978-0-06-053961-0(5)*, HarperFestival) HarperCollins Pubs.

McBride, Anthony. The Fish That Was Afraid to Swim. 2013. 52p. pap. 21.88 *(978-1-4669-9388-4(X))* Trafford Publishing.

McCarthy, Jenna & Evans, Carolyn. Maggie Malone Makes a Splash. 2015. (Maggie Malone Ser.: 3). (ENG.). 192p. (J). (gr. 4-7). pap. 8.99 *(978-1-4022-9312-2(7)*, Sourcebooks Jabberwocky) Sourcebooks, Inc.

McDonald, Megan. Stink & the Freaky Frog Freakout. Reynolds, Peter H., illus. 2013. (Stink Ser.: 8). (ENG.). 160p. (J). (gr. 1-4). 12.99 *(978-0-7636-6140-3(6))* Candlewick Pr.

—Stink & the Freaky Frog Freakout. 2014. (Stink Ser.: 8). lib. bdg. 14.75 *(978-0-606-35164-5(7))* Turtleback Bks.

McGhee, Patti Gray. Ducky Bill's Great Race. Vermillion, Danny, illus. 2013. 46p. 24.95 *(978-1-63000-424-8(3))*; 48p. pap. 24.95 *(978-1-62709-522-8(5))* America Star Bks.

McQuinn, Anna. Leo Can Swim. Hearson, Ruth, illus. 2016. (ENG.). 24p. (J). (— 1). lib. bdg. 9.95 *(978-1-58089-725-9(8))* Charlesbridge Publishing, Inc.

McVoy, Terra Elan. In Deep. 2014. (ENG., Illus.). 304p. (YA). (gr. 9). 17.99 *(978-1-4814-0136-4(X)*, Simon Pulse) Simon Pulse.

Meadows, Daisy. Samantha the Swimming Fairy. 2010. (Sports Fairies Ser.: 5). (ENG.). 80p. (J). (gr. 2-5). 4.99 *(978-0-545-20256-5(6)*, Scholastic Paperbacks) Scholastic, Inc.

Metzger, Steve. Five Little Sharks Swimming in the Sea. Bryant, Laura, illus. 2004. (J). *(978-0-439-66139-3(0))*; pap. *(978-0-439-59228-4(3))* Scholastic, Inc.

Molski, Carol. Swimming Sal. DePalma, Mary Newell, illus. 2009. 36p. (J). (gr. -1-3). 17.00 *(978-0-8028-5327-1(7)*, Eerdmans Bks For Young Readers) Eerdmans, William B. Publishing Co.

Montgomery, Lewis B. The Case of the Purple Pool. Wummer, Amy, illus. 2011. (Milo & Jazz Mysteries Ser.). (ENG.). 96p. (J). pap. 6.95 *(978-1-57565-342-6(7))*; pap. 39.62 *(978-0-7613-8358-1(1))*;No. 7. 96p. (J). lib. bdg. 22.60 *(978-1-57565-343-3(5))* Kane Press, Inc.

Morpurgo, Michael. Main's Mermaid. 2006. (Blue Bananas Ser.). (ENG., Illus.). 48p. (J). (gr. -1-3). lib. bdg. *(978-0-7787-0851-3(9))* Crabtree Publishing Co.

Ms. T. A Chincoteague Pony Finds a Friend. 2009. 28p. pap. 12.49 *(978-1-4389-7981-6(9))* AuthorHouse.

Müller, Hildegard. The Cowboy. Müller, Hildegard, illus. 2015. (I Like to Read(r) Ser.). (ENG., Illus.). 24p. (J). (gr. -1-3). 6.99 *(978-0-8234-3316-2(1))* Holiday Hse., Inc.

Naylor, Phyllis Reynolds. Alice the Brave. (Alice Ser.: 7). (ENG., (J). 2011. Illus.). 176p. (gr. 5-9). pap. 7.99 *(978-1-4424-2851-5(1)*, Atheneum Bks. for Young Readers) 2009. 160p. (gr. 4-8). pap. 7.99 *(978-1-4169-7542-7(X)*, Aladdin) Simon & Schuster Children's Publishing.

Nickelodeon. Swim, Boots, Swim! 2013. (Dora the Explorer 8X8 Ser.). lib. bdg. 13.55 *(978-0-606-31933-1(6)*, Turtleback) Turtleback Bks.

Northrop, Michael. Surrounded by Sharks. 2014. (ENG.). 224p. (J). (gr. 4-7). 17.99 *(978-0-545-61545-7(3)*, Scholastic Pr.) Scholastic, Inc.

Nthemuka, Patty Froese. Hyacinth Doesn't Grow Up: And Hyacinth Doesn't Drown. 2010. (J). pap. 10.99 *(978-0-8163-2366-9(0))* Pacific Pr. Publishing Assn.

Oliver, Helen. Ellen's First Swim. 2009. 32p. pap. 16.49 *(978-1-4389-9828-2(7))* AuthorHouse.

O'Ryan, Ray. Drake Makes a Splash! Jack, Colin, illus. 2014. (Galaxy Zack Ser.: 8). (ENG.). 128p. (J). (gr. k-2). pap. 5.99 *(978-1-4424-9360-5(7)*, Little Simon) Little Simon.

Pants Makes the Swim Team. 2004. (J). per. 7.99 *(978-0-9755959-2-3(X))* Girl Named Pants, Inc., A.

Patenaude, Jeremy, et al. Little Dolphin. 2014. (DK Readers Ser.). (ENG.). 32p. (J). (gr. k-4). pap. 3.99 *(978-1-4654-1997-2(7)*, DK Children) Dorling Kindersley Publishing, Inc.

PeachMoon Publishing. The Adventures of Lucky the Lizard Las aventuras del lagarto Lucky. 2008. (ENG & SPA., Illus.). 100p. (J). pap. 19.95 *(978-0-9795831-4-8(4))* PeachMoon Publishing.

Petersen, Pat. The Turtle Who Couldn't Swim. Pham, Xuan, illus. 2012. 28p. 24.95 *(978-1-4626-8615-5(X))*; pap. 24.95 *(978-1-4626-4847-4(9))* America Star Bks.

Polak, Monique. Flip Turn, 1 vol. 2004. (Lorimer Sports Stories Ser.: 67). (ENG.). 104p. (J). (gr. 4-8). 16.95 *(978-1-55028-819-3(9)*, 9781550288193) Lorimer, James & Co., Ltd., Pubs. CAN. Dist: Casemate Pubs. & Bk. Distributors, LLC.

Priddy, Roger. Little Friends: Splish Splash. 2014. (Little Friends Ser.). (ENG.). 6p. (J). (gr. -1 — 1). 7.99 *(978-0-312-51682-6(7)*, 9780312516826, Priddy Bks.) St. Martin's Pr.

Random House. Hide-And-Go-Swim! (Bubble Guppies) MJ Illustrations, illus. 2014. (Nifty Lift-And-Look Ser.). (ENG.). 12p. (J). (— 1). bds. 5.99 *(978-0-385-38515-2(3)*, Random Hse. Bks. for Young Readers) Random Hse. Children's Bks.

Random House Staff. Swim, Boots, Swim! (Dora the Explorer) Random House Staff, illus. 2013. (Pictureback(R) Ser.). (ENG., Illus.). 24p. (J). (gr. -1-2). 3.99 *(978-0-449-81850-3(0)*, Random Hse. Bks. for Young Readers) Random Hse. Children's Bks.

Ratto, Linda Lee. Perfection. 2004. (YA). per. 16.95 *(978-0-9748508-3-2(7))* Power Pr.

Reed, Lynn Rowe. Swim to the Moon. 2009. 32p. pap. 12.99 *(978-1-4389-4980-2(4))* AuthorHouse.

Reh, Rusalka. The Secret of the Water Knight, 0 vols. Derbyshire, Katy, tr. unabr. ed. 2011. (ENG.). 100p. (J). (gr. 4-7). pap. 9.95 *(978-1-61109-006-2(7)*, 9781611090062) Amazon Publishing.

Reis, Jason & Hurley, Meagan. The Adventures of Burt: Burt & the Big Race. 2012. 28p. pap. 19.99 *(978-1-4634-4126-5(6))* AuthorHouse.

Rocco, John & Primiano, Jay. Swim That Rock. Rocco, John, illus. 2017. (ENG., Illus.). 304p. (J). (gr. 7). pap. 7.99 *(978-0-7636-9447-0(9))* Candlewick Pr.

Rockwell, Anne F. Katie Catz Makes a Splash. Meisel, Paul, illus. 2003. (Good Sports Ser.). 40p. (J). (gr. -1-1). 15.99 *(978-0-06-028441-1(2))* HarperCollins Pubs.

Rottman, S. L. Head above Water, 1 vol. 2003. (ENG.). 192p. (YA). (gr. 7-18). pap. 6.95 *(978-1-56145-238-5(6)*, Q21186) Peachtree Pubs.

Rushing, John Alan. A. J. Puppy Learns to Swim. Fay, David, illus. 2009. 48p. (J). pap. *(978-0-9776958-9-8(1))* CyPress Pubns.

Rylant, Cynthia. Brownie & Pearl Take a Dip. Biggs, Brian, illus. 2011. (Brownie & Pearl Ser.). (ENG.). 24p. (J). (gr. -1-3). 14.99 *(978-1-4169-8638-6(3)*, Beach Lane Bks.) Beach Lane Bks.

Scheunemann, Pam. Crocodile Tears, 1 vol. Chawla, Neena, illus. 2007. (Critter Chronicles Ser.). (ENG.). 24p. (J). (gr. k-3). lib. bdg. 24.21 *(978-1-59928-436-1(7)*, SandCastle) ABDO Publishing Co.

Scholastic, Inc. Staff. Peppa Goes Swimming. 2015. (Peppa Pig 8X8 Ser.). lib. bdg. 13.55 *(978-0-606-37082-0(X))* Turtleback Bks.

Schuurmans, Hilde. Sidney Won't Swim. Schuurmans, Hilde, illus. (Illus.). pap. 6.95 *(978-1-57091-515-4(6))* Charlesbridge Publishing, Inc.

Scotton, Rob. Splish, Splash, Splat! Scotton, Rob, illus. 2011. (Splat the Cat Ser.). (ENG., Illus.). 40p. (J). (gr. -1-3). 16.99 *(978-0-06-197868-5(X))* HarperCollins Pubs.

Seuling, Barbara. Robert Goes to Camp. Brewer, Paul, illus. 2007. (Robert Bks.). (ENG.). 160p. (J). (gr. k-4). 16.95 *(978-0-8126-2753-4(9))* Cricket Bks.

Shum, Benson. Holly's Day at the Pool: A Walt Disney Animation Studios Artist Showcase. Shum, Benson, illus. 2017. (Walt Disney Animation Studios Artist Showcase Ser.). (ENG., Illus.). 40p. (J). (gr. -1-k). 16.99 *(978-1-4847-0938-2(1))* Disney Pr.

Smith Dinbergs, Holly. Pool Pals. Maddock, Monika, illus. 2005. (Girlz Rock! Ser.). (J). pap. *(978-1-59336-705-3(8))* Mondo Publishing.

Snider, Ann. The Giant Sea & Me. 2008. (Illus.). 24p. pap. 14.99 *(978-1-4389-1720-7(1))* AuthorHouse.

Spalding, Andrea. Seal Song, 1 vol. Milelli, Pascal, illus. 2011. (ENG.). 32p. (J). (gr. -1-3). 19.95 *(978-1-55469-242-2(3))* Orca Bk. Pubs. USA.

Starin, Liz. Splashdance. Starin, Liz, illus. 2016. (ENG., Illus.). 32p. (J). 16.99 *(978-0-374-30098-2(4)*, 9780374300982, Farrar, Straus & Giroux (BYR)) Farrar, Straus & Giroux.

Stroke of Luck (Swimming) 64p. (YA). (gr. 6-12). pap. 10.95 *(978-0-8224-6482-2(9))* Globe Fearon Educational Publishing.

Sue-A-Quan, Goomatie. A Seal Fascination at Sea: A Fascinating Seal. 2008. (Illus.). 38p. (J). pap. 19.00 *(978-0-8059-7517-8(9))* Dorrance Publishing Co., Inc.

Swimming Lessons with Stewie the Duck. 2005. (J). 9.95 *(978-0-9668611-3-6(2))* Kimberly Pr., LLC.

Terada, Junzo. Animal Friends: Swimming Hole Party! 2017. (ENG., Illus.). 10p. (J). bds. 9.99 *(978-1-4521-4983-7(6))* Chronicle Bks. LLC.

Thomas, Cameron. Mystery of the Lake. Krystoforski, Andrej, illus. 2004. (Jungle of Utt Ser.). 40p. (J). 16.95 *(978-0-921800-02-6(9))* MGT Developments, Ltd. CAN. Dist: Independent Pubs. Group.

Trueit, Trudi. Mom, There's a Dinosaur in Beeson's Lake. Paillot, Jim, illus. 2011. (Secrets of a Lab Rat Ser.). (ENG.). 160p. (J). (gr. 3-7). pap. 5.99 *(978-1-4169-6112-3(7)*, Aladdin) Simon & Schuster Children's Publishing.

Trueit, Trudi Strain. Mom, There's a Dinosaur in Beeson's Lake. Paillot, Jim, illus. 2010. (Secrets of a Lab Rat Ser.). (ENG.). 160p. (J). (gr. 3-7). 14.99 *(978-1-4169-7593-9(4)*, Simon & Schuster/Paula Wiseman Bks.) Simon & Schuster/Paula Wiseman Bks.

Wan, Joyce. The Whale in My Swimming Pool. (ENG., Illus.). (J). 2016. 32p. bds. 7.99 *(978-0-374-30188-0(3)*, 9780374301880) 2015. 40p. (gr. -1-1). 17.99 *(978-0-374-30037-1(2)*, 9780374300371) Farrar, Straus & Giroux. (Farrar, Straus & Giroux (BYR)).

Ward, M. The Evergreens Get Wet: The Evergreens. 2009. (Illus.). 28p. pap. 12.49 *(978-1-4389-8960-0(1))* AuthorHouse.

Waters, Cassie. Heat Wave. 2012. (Pool Girls Ser.: 2). (ENG.). 160p. (J). (gr. 3-7). pap. 5.99 *(978-1-4424-4146-0(1)*, Simon Spotlight) Simon Spotlight.

Wells, Rosemary. Eduardo: Cumpleanos en la Piscina. 2003. Orig. Title: Edward's Big Splash. (SPA., Illus.). 22p. (J). (gr. -1-k). 12.95 *(978-1-56014-664-3(8))* Santillana USA Publishing Co., Inc.

Wheeler, Lisa. Dino-Swimming. Gott, Barry, illus. 2015. (ENG.). 32p. (J). (gr. k-3). 17.32 *(978-1-4677-8809-0(0))*; lib. bdg. 16.99 *(978-1-4677-0214-0(5))* Lerner Publishing Group. (Carolrhoda Bks.).

Wildsmith, Brian. The Little Wood Duck, 1 vol. 2007. (ENG., Illus.). 32p. (J). (gr. -1-3). 16.95 *(978-1-59572-042-9(1))* Star Bright Bks., Inc.

—The Little Wood Duck, 1 vol. Wildsmith, Brian, illus. 2006. (ENG., Illus.). 32p. (J). pap. 6.95 *(978-1-59572-049-8(9))* Star Bright Bks., Inc.

Williams, Carol Lynch. Signed, Skye Harper. 2014. (ENG., Illus.). 304p. (YA). (gr. 7). 17.99 *(978-1-4814-0032-9(0)*, Simon & Schuster/Paula Wiseman Bks.) Simon & Schuster/Paula Wiseman Bks.

Wilson, Karma. Don't Be Afraid, Little Pip. Chapman, Jane, illus. 2009. (ENG.). 40p. (J). (gr. -1-2). 16.99 *(978-0-689-85987-8(2)*, McElderry, Margaret K. Bks.) McElderry, Margaret K. Bks.

Winton, Tim. The Deep. Louise, Karen, illus. 32p. (YA). pap. 13.95 *(978-1-86368-210-7(4))* Fremantle Pr. AUS. Dist: Independent Pubs. Group.

Yasuda, Anita. The Swim Race, 1 vol. Harpster, Steve, illus. 2012. (My First Graphic Novel Ser.). (ENG.). 32p. (gr. k-2). pap. 6.25 *(978-1-4342-3864-1(4))*; lib. bdg. 24.65 *(978-1-4342-3280-9(8))* Stone Arch Bks. (My First Graphic Novel).

SWINE

see Pigs

SWITZERLAND

Carr, Simonetta. John Calvin. Taglietti, Emanuele, illus. 2008. (ENG.). 63p. (J). 18.00 *(978-1-60178-055-3(9))* Reformation Heritage Bks.

Delessert, Etienne. Night Circus. Delessert, Etienne, illus. 2015. (ENG., Illus.). 32p. (J). (gr. 2-4). 19.99 *(978-1-56846-277-6(8)*, Creative Editions) Creative Co., The.

Gale Editor & Greenhaven Press Editors, eds. Roger Federer. 2011. (People in the News Ser.). (Illus.). 128p. (YA). (gr. 9-12). lib. bdg. 33.95 *(978-1-4205-0611-2(0))* Cengage Gale.

Glaser, Jason. Roger Federer. 2011. (Today's Sports Greats Ser.). (Illus.). 32p. (gr. 4-6). (J). pap. 10.50 *(978-1-4339-5872-4(4)*, Gareth Stevens Learning Library); (YA). lib. bdg. 26.60 *(978-1-4339-5870-0(8))* Stevens, Gareth Publishing LLLP.

Hammond, Paula. Italy & Switzerland. 2004. (Cultures & Costumes Ser.). (Illus.). 64p. (YA). (gr. 7-18). lib. bdg. 19.95 *(978-1-59084-438-0(6))* Mason Crest.

Juettner Fernandes, Bonnie. The Large Hadron Collider. 2014. (Great Idea Ser.). (ENG., Illus.). 48p. (J). (gr. 4-6). lib. bdg. 26.60 *(978-1-59953-600-2(5))* Norwood Hse. Pr.

Larson, Lyn. Switzerland. 2011. (Country Explorers Ser.). (ENG., Illus.). 48p. (J). (gr. 2-4). lib. bdg. 29.27 *(978-0-7613-6418-4(8))* Lerner Publishing Group.

Levy, Patricia, et al. Switzerland. 2015. (Cultures of the World (r) Ser.). (ENG., Illus.). 144p. (J). (gr. 5-5). lib. bdg. 47.07 *(978-1-5026-0344-9(6))* Cavendish Square Publishing.

Rogers Seavey, Lura. Switzerland. 2016. (Enchantment of the World(tm) Ser.). (ENG., Illus.). 144p. (J). lib. bdg. 40.00 *(978-0-531-21887-7(2)*, Children's Pr.) Scholastic Library Publishing.

Rowell, Rebecca. Switzerland, 1 vol. 2013. (Countries of the World Set 2 Ser.). (ENG., Illus.). 144p. (J). (gr. 6-12). lib. bdg. 37.07 *(978-1-61783-638-1(9)*, Essential Library) ABDO Publishing Co.

Zobel, Derek. Switzerland. 2011. (Illus.). 32p. (J). *(978-0-531-20959-2(8))*; (ENG., (gr. 3-7). lib. bdg. 26.95 *(978-1-60014-577-3(9)*, Blastoff! Readers) Bellwether Media.

Zocchi, Judy. In Switzerland. Brodie, Neale, illus. 2005. (Global Adventures I Ser.). 32p. (J). pap. 10.95 *(978-1-59646-156-7(X))*; lib. bdg. 21.65 *(978-1-59646-006-5(7))*; per. 10.95 *(978-1-59646-157-4(8))* Dingles & Co.

—In Switzerland/en Suiza. Brodie, Neale, illus. 2005. (Global Adventures I Ser.).Tr. of En Suiza. (ENG & SPA.). 32p. (J). pap. 10.95 *(978-1-59646-158-1(6))*; lib. bdg. 21.65 *(978-1-59646-007-2(5))*; per. 10.95 *(978-1-59646-159-8(4))* Dingles & Co.

SWITZERLAND—FICTION

Angel, Ido. Vipo in Switzerland: A Swiss Skiing Adventure. 2015. (AV2 Animated Storytime Ser.). (ENG.). (J). lib. bdg. 29.99 *(978-1-4896-3925-7(X)*, AV2 by Weigl) Weigl Pubs., Inc.

Berg, Jean Horton. Pierre, the Young Watchmaker. D'Adamo, Anthony, illus. 2011. 190p. 42.95 *(978-1-258-08171-3(7))* Literary Licensing, LLC.

Cage, Elizabeth. Spy Girls Are Forever. 2013. (Spy Girls Ser.: 4). (ENG., Illus.). 192p. (YA). (gr. 7). pap. 13.99 *(978-1-4814-2082-2(8)*, Simon Pulse) Simon Pulse.

Campbell, Angella. Angel & Turkish. 2011. 32p. pap. 14.99 *(978-1-4634-0372-0(0))* AuthorHouse.

—Engel und Turkish. 2012. 32p. pap. 19.99 *(978-1-4772-2556-1(0))* AuthorHouse.

Carigiet, Alois, illus. A Bell for Ursli: A Story from the Engadine in Switzerland. 2007. 44p. (J). *(978-0-86315-614-4(2))* Floris Bks.

Chatterton, Martin. Brain Full of Holes. 2008. 208p. *(978-1-921272-28-8(7))* Little Hare Bks. AUS. Dist: HarperCollins Pubs. Australia.

—The Brain Full of Holes, 1 vol. 2010. (ENG.). 256p. (J). (gr. 5-9). 16.95 *(978-1-56145-527-0(X))* Peachtree Pubs.

Creech, Sharon. Bloomability. 2012. (Illus.). 272p. (J). (gr. 3-7). pap. 6.99 *(978-0-06-440823-3(X))* HarperCollins Pubs.

—Bloomability. unabr. ed. 2004. 273p. (J). (gr. 4-7). pap. 38.00 incl. audio *(978-0-8072-8754-5(7)*, YA257SP, Listening Library) Random Hse. Audio Publishing Group.

—Bloomability. 2012. (J). (gr. 3-6). 17.20 *(978-0-613-22826-8(X)*, Turtleback) Turtleback Bks.

—The Unfinished Angel. 2013. (ENG.). 160p. (J). (gr. 3-7). pap. 6.99 *(978-0-06-143097-8(8))* HarperCollins Pubs.

Cullen, Seán. Hamish X & the Hollow Mountain. 2008. (ENG.). 288p. (J). (gr. 7-18). 9.99 *(978-0-14-305312-5(4)*, Puffin Canada) Penguin Random House Canada Young Readers CAN. Dist: Penguin Random Hse. LLC.

Dalmatian Press Staff, adapted by. Heidi. (SPA., Illus.). (YA). 11.95 *(978-84-7281-082-2(8)*, AF1082) Auriga, Ediciones S.A. ESP. Dist: Continental Bk. Co., Inc.

—Heidi. (Young Collector's Illustrated Classics Ser.). (Illus.). 192p. (J). (gr. 3-7). 9.95 *(978-1-56156-455-2(9))* Kidsbooks, LLC.

Dunseith, Peter. Bird of Heaven: The Story of a Swazi Sangoma. 2010. 257p. pap. *(978-0-624-04557-1(9))* NB Pubs. Ltd.

Evatt, Harriet. The Mystery of the Alpine Castle. 2011. 242p. 46.95 *(978-1-258-08839-2(8))* Literary Licensing, LLC.

Fisher, Leonard Everett. William Tell. Fisher, Leonard Everett, illus. 2006. (Illus.). 28p. (J). reprint ed. 16.00 *(978-0-7567-9880-2(9))* DIANE Publishing Co.

Furlong, C. T. Killer Strangelets. 2011. (Arctic6 Ser.). 208p. (J). pap. *(978-0-9562315-6-7(X))* Inside Pocket Publishing, Ltd.

Garcia, Cristina. Dreams of Significant Girls. 2011. (ENG.). 256p. (YA). (gr. 9-18). 16.99 *(978-1-4169-7920-3(4)*, Simon & Schuster Bks. For Young Readers) Simon & Schuster Bks. For Young Readers.

García, Cristina. Dreams of Significant Girls. 2012. (ENG.). 256p. (J). (gr. 9). pap. 8.99 *(978-1-4169-7930-2(1)*, Simon & Schuster Bks. For Young Readers) Simon & Schuster Bks. For Young Readers.

A Gift to Share. 2005. (J). 17.00 *(978-0-9721457-1-8(0))* Silent Moon Bks.

Goscinny, René & Uderzo, Albert. Asterix in Switzerland. Uderzo, Albert, illus. 2004. (ENG., Illus.). 48p. pap. 12.99 *(978-0-7528-6635-2(4)*, Orion) Orion Publishing Group, Ltd. GBR. Dist: Hachette Bk. Group.

Haddix, Margaret Peterson. Caught. 2012. (Missing Ser.: 5). (ENG.). 352p. (J). (gr. 3-7). 16.99 *(978-1-4169-8982-0(X)*,

Simon & Schuster Bks. For Young Readers) Simon & Schuster Bks. For Young Readers.
—Caught. 2013. (Missing Ser.: 5). lib. bdg. 18.40 *(978-0-606-27045-8(0)*, Turtleback) Turtleback Bks.
Harvey, Jacqueline. Alice-Miranda in the Alps. 2016. (Alice-Miranda Ser.: 12). (ENG.). 336p. (J). (gr. 3-7). pap. 9.99 *(978-0-85798-274-2(5))* Random Hse. Australia AUS. Dist: Independent Pubs. Group.
Hawking, Lucy & Hawking, Stephen W. George & the Big Bang. Parsons, Garry, illus. 2012. (George's Secret Key Ser.). (ENG.). 336p. (J). (gr. 3-7). 22.99 *(978-1-4424-4005-0(8)*, Simon & Schuster Bks. For Young Readers) Simon & Schuster Bks. For Young Readers.
Hawking, Stephen W. & Hawking, Lucy. George & the Big Bang. Parsons, Garry, illus. 2013. (George's Secret Key Ser.). (ENG.). 304p. (J). (gr. 3-7). pap. 11.99 *(978-1-4424-4006-7(6)*, Simon & Schuster Bks. For Young Readers) Simon & Schuster Bks. For Young Readers.
Hedji, Charles. Fields of Discovery. 2006. 220p. pap. 24.95 *(978-1-4241-0605-9(2))* PublishAmerica, Inc.
Henderson, Jason. Vampire Rising. 2010. (Alex Van Helsing Ser.: 1). (ENG.). 256p. (YA). (gr. 8-18). 16.99 *(978-0-06-195099-5(8)*, HarperTeen) HarperCollins Pubs.
—Voice of the Undead. 2011. (Alex Van Helsing Ser.: 2). (ENG.). 304p. (YA). (gr. 8). 16.99 *(978-0-06-195101-5(3)*, HarperTeen) HarperCollins Pubs.
Hergé. The Calculus Affair. (Illus.). 62p. (J). 19.95 *(978-0-8288-5014-8(3))* French & European Pubns., Inc.
Kleinman, Estelle. Bloomability. Friedland, Joyce & Kessler, Rikki, eds. 2009. (Novel-Ties Ser.). (Illus.). 41p. pap. 16.95 *(978-0-7675-4276-0(2))* Learning Links Inc.
Klimo, Kate. Barry. 2013. (Dog Diaries: 3). lib. bdg. 18.40 *(978-0-606-32455-7(0)*, Turtleback) Turtleback Bks.
Krulik, Nancy. Nice Snowing You! Braun, Sebastien, illus. 2014. (Magic Bone Ser.: 4). (ENG.). 128p. (J). (gr. 1-3). 5.99 *(978-0-448-46446-6(2)*, Grosset & Dunlap) Penguin Young Readers Group.
—Nice Snowing You! 2014. (Magic Bone Ser.: 4). lib. bdg. 14.75 *(978-0-606-34145-5(5)*, Turtleback) Turtleback Bks.
Lee, Mackenzi. This Monstrous Thing. 2015. (ENG.). 384p. (YA). (gr. 8). 17.99 *(978-0-06-238277-1(2))* HarperCollins Pubs.
Mitchell, George. The Marmots of Lenk & the Long Sleep. 2011. 66p. pap. 20.95 *(978-1-4476-2895-8(0))* Lulu Pr., Inc.
Montgomery, R. A. Behind the Wheel. 2010. 144p. pap. 6.99 *(978-1-933390-35-2(2))* Chooseco LLC.
Mullarkey, Lisa & Mullarkey, John. Mary Molds a Monster, 1 vol. Bernard, Courtney, illus. 2015. (ENG.). 128p. (J). *(978-1-62402-088-9(7))* Magic Wagon.
Oppel, Kenneth. This Dark Endeavor: The Apprenticeship of Victor Frankenstein. 2011. (Apprenticeship of Victor Frankenstein Ser.: Bk. 1). (ENG.). (YA). (gr. 7-12). 64.99 *(978-1-4558-2316-1(3))* Findaway World, LLC.
—This Dark Endeavor: The Apprenticeship of Victor Frankenstein. (ENG., (YA). (gr. 7). 2012. Illus.). 320p. pap. 10.99 *(978-1-4424-0316-1(0))* 2011. 304p. lib. bdg. 17.99 *(978-1-4424-0315-4(2))* Simon & Schuster Bks. For Young Readers. (Simon & Schuster Bks. For Young Readers).
Osborne, Mary Pope. Dogs in the Dead of Night. Murdocca, Sal, illus. 2013. (Magic Tree House (R) Merlin Mission Ser.: 18). (ENG.). 144p. (J). (gr. 2-5). 5.99 *(978-0-375-86796-5(1)*, Random Hse. Bks. for Young Readers) Random Hse. Children's Bks.
—Dogs in the Dead of Night. 2013. (Magic Tree House Merlin Missions Ser.: 18). lib. bdg. 16.00 *(978-0-606-31939-3(5)*, Turtleback) Turtleback Bks.
Perkins, Lucy Fitch. The Swiss Twins. 2004. reprint ed. pap. 15.95 *(978-1-4191-8467-3(9))*; pap. 1.99 *(978-1-4192-8467-0(3))* Kessinger Publishing, LLC.
Rose, Imogen. Initiation: Japanese Language Edition. Galeano, Tomomi, tr. 2013. 482p. pap. 16.99 *(978-1-940015-04-0(9))* Imogen Rose.
Spyri, Johanna. Heidi. (J). 24.95 *(978-0-8488-1179-2(8))* Amereon Ltd.
—Heidi. 2014. (ENG.). 345p. 17.50 *(978-1-78270-044-9(7))* Award Pubns. Ltd. GBR. Dist: Parkwest Pubns., Inc.
—Heidi. (ENG., Illus.). (J). 2016. (gr. 3-7). 26.95 ***(978-1-358-32517-5(0))*** 2015. (gr. 4-7). 26.95 ***(978-1-340-18081-2(2))*** 2015. (gr. 4-7). 26.95 ***(978-1-340-63493-3(7))*** Creative Media Partners, LLC.
—Heidi. 2008. (Bring the Classics to Life Ser.). (Illus.). 72p. (gr. 1-12). pap., act. bk. ed. 10.95 *(978-1-55576-178-3(X)*, EDCTR-107B) EDCON Publishing Group.
—Heidi. 2003. pap. *(978-1-84637-585-9(1))* Echo Library.
—Heidi. 2017. (ENG.). 372p. 12.99 ***(978-1-5098-4292-6(6)***, 9781509842926, Collector's Library, The) Pan Macmillan GBR. Dist: Macmillan.
—Heidi. 2014. (Puffin in Bloom Ser.). (ENG., Illus.). 336p. (J). (gr. 3-7). 16.00 *(978-0-14-751402-8(9)*, Puffin Books) Penguin Young Readers Group.
—Heidi. 2011. (ENG., Illus.). (J). (gr. 3-7). 14.99 ***(978-1-61382-679-9(6))***; 14.99 ***(978-1-61382-680-5(X))*** Simon & Brown.
—Heidi. 2013. (ENG., Illus.). 336p. (J). (gr. 2-7). 14.95 *(978-1-62087-686-2(8)*, 620686, Sky Pony Pr.) Skyhorse Publishing Co., Inc.
—Heidi. Akib, Jamel, illus. 2007. (Classic Starts(tm) Ser.). (ENG.). 160p. (J). (gr. 2-4). 6.95 *(978-1-4027-3691-9(6))* Sterling Publishing Co., Inc.
—Heidi. 2013. 425p. reprint ed. lthr. 69.00 *(978-0-7426-1047-7(0))* Classic Bks.
—Heidi. l.t. ed. 2004. (Large Print Ser.). 433p. 26.00 *(978-1-58287-666-5(5))* North Bks.
—Heidi: With a Discussion of Optimism. Clift, Eva, illus. 2003. (Values in Action Illustrated Classics Ser.). 190p. (J). *(978-1-59203-030-9(0))* Learning Challenge, Inc.
—What Sami Sings with the Birds. 2010. 48p. pap. *(978-1-4076-5301-3(6))* HardPr.
Spyri, Johanna & Blaisdell, Robert. Heidi: Adapted for Young Readers. Kliros, Thea, illus. 2011. (Dover Children's Thrift Classics Ser.). (ENG.). 80p. (J). (gr. 3-8). pap. 3.00 *(978-0-486-40166-9(9))* Dover Pubns., Inc.
Spyri, Johanna & Lacey, Mike. Heidi, 1 vol. 2012. (Calico Illustrated Classics Ser.: No. 4). (ENG., Illus.). 112p. (J). (gr. 3-6). 27.07 *(978-1-61641-613-3(0))* Magic Wagon.
Spyri, Johanna & Stork, Elisabeth P. Heidi. Kirk, Maria L., illus. 2014. (J). 13.32 *(978-1-4677-5846-8(9)*, First Avenue Editions) Lerner Publishing Group.
Titus, Eve. Basil & the Lost Colony. Galdone, Paul, illus. 2017. (Great Mouse Detective Ser.: 5). (ENG.). 96p. (J). (gr. 1-4). pap. 5.99 ***(978-1-4814-6413-0(2)***, Aladdin) Simon & Schuster Children's Publishing.
Wells, Helen. Cherry Ames, Ski Nurse Mystery. 2007. (Cherry Ames Nurse Stories Ser.). 224p. (J). (gr. 3-7). 14.95 *(978-0-8261-0437-3(1))* Springer Publishing Co., Inc.
Zahn, Muriel. Grimsel: The Story of A Valiant Saint Bernard & Three Boys in the Swiss Alps. Walsh, William, illus. 2011. 178p. 42.95 *(978-1-258-07805-8(8))* Literary Licensing, LLC.

SYMBIOSIS

see Plant Ecology

SYMBOLISM

see also Christian Art and Symbolism; Heraldry

Bateman, Teresa. Red, White, Blue & Uncle Who? The Story Behind Some of America's Patriotic Symbols. 2003. (ENG., Illus.). 64p. (J). (gr. 4-6). pap. 7.95 *(978-0-8234-1784-1(0))* Holiday Hse., Inc.
Baxter, Pam. A Cup of Light: All about the Flaming Chalice. 2010. (J). pap. 5.00 *(978-1-55896-575-1(0)*, Skinner Hse. Bks.) Unitarian Universalist Assn.
Doeden, Matt. Stick Out Like a Sore Thumb: And Other Expressions about Body Parts. 2012. (It's Just an Expression Ser.). (ENG., Illus.). 32p. (J). (gr. 4-6). lib. bdg. 26.60 *(978-0-7613-7887-7(1)*, Lerner Pubns.) Lerner Publishing Group.
Douglas, Lloyd G. The Bald Eagle. 2003. (Welcome Bks.). 24p. (J). 19.00 *(978-0-516-25851-5(6))*; (ENG.). (gr. -1-2). pap. 4.95 *(978-0-516-27874-2(6))* Scholastic Library Publishing. (Children's Pr.).
Heos, Bridget. At the Eleventh Hour: And Other Expressions about Money & Numbers. 2012. (It's Just an Expression Ser.). (ENG., Illus.). 32p. (J). (gr. 4-6). lib. bdg. 26.60 *(978-0-7613-8164-8(3)*, Lerner Pubns.) Lerner Publishing Group.
Herrington, Lisa M. The Bald Eagle. 2014. (Rookie Read-About(r) American Symbols Ser.). (ENG., Illus.). 32p. (J). pap. 5.95 *(978-0-531-21837-2(6))* Scholastic Library Publishing.
Love, Mary A. Learning Through Symbolism & Celebrations. Flournoy, L. Diana, illus. 2nd rev. ed. 2011. (ENG.). 168p. pap. 24.00 *(978-1-929548-00-2(1))* Love's Creative Resources.
Marcovitz, Hal. Bald Eagle: The Story of Our National Bird. Moreno, Barry, ed. 2014. (Patriotic Symbols of America Ser.: 20). 48p. (J). (gr. 4-18). 20.95 *(978-1-4222-3120-3(8))* Mason Crest.
Patrick, Joseph. Our National Symbols. 2009. (Real Life Readers Ser.). 16p. (gr. 2-3). pap. 7.05 *(978-1-4358-0049-6(4)*, Rosen Classroom) Rosen Publishing Group, Inc., The.
Rookie Read-About(r) American Symbols (Set Of 7) 2014. (Rookie Read-About(r) American Symbols Ser.). (J). *(978-0-531-24360-2(5))* Scholastic Library Publishing.

SYMMETRY

Alaina, Maria. Both Sides are the Same. 2011. (Wonder Readers Early Level Ser.). (ENG.). 16p. (gr. -1-1). pap. 35.94 *(978-1-4296-8072-1(5)*, Wonder Readers) Capstone Press of Coughlan Cos.
Bellos, Alex & Harriss, Edmund. Patterns of the Universe: A Coloring Adventure in Math & Beauty. 2015. (ENG., Illus.). 144p. pap. 14.95 *(978-1-61519-323-3(5))* Experiment LLC, The.
—Visions of the Universe: A Coloring Journey Through Math's Great Mysteries. 2016. (ENG., Illus.). 144p. pap. 14.95 *(978-1-61519-367-7(7))* Experiment LLC, The.
Canavan, Thomas. Shapes & Symmetry: 50 Math Super Puzzles. 2011. (Math Standards Workout Ser.). (ENG., Illus.). 48p. (YA). (gr. 5-8). pap. 11.75 *(978-1-4488-6683-0(9)*, Rosen Reference); lib. bdg. 29.25 *(978-1-4488-6676-2(6))* Rosen Publishing Group, Inc., The.
Feldman, Sarah. Symmetry in Our World. 2011. (Early Connections Ser.). (J). *(978-1-61672-671-3(7))* Benchmark Education Co.
Kalman, Bobbie. What Is Symmetry in Nature? 2010. (Looking at Nature Ser.). (ENG., Illus.). 24p. (J). (gr. -1-2). lib. bdg. *(978-0-7787-3327-0(0))* Crabtree Publishing Co.
Leedy, Loreen. Seeing Symmetry. Leedy, Loreen, illus. (ENG., Illus.). 32p. (J). 2013. pap. 7.99 *(978-0-8234-2762-8(5))* 2012. 17.95 *(978-0-8234-2360-6(3))* Holiday Hse., Inc.
Moskal, Greg. Modern Buildings: Identifying Bilateral & Rotational Symmetry & Transformations. 2009. (PowerMath: Proficiency Ser.). 32p. (gr. 4-5). 47.90 *(978-1-60851-397-0(1)*, PowerKids Pr.) Rosen Publishing Group, Inc., The.

SYNAGOGUES

Hoffman, Lawrence A. & Wolfson, Ron. What You Will See Inside a Synagogue. Aron, Bill, photos by. 2008. (What You Will See Inside ... Ser.). (ENG., Illus.). 32p. (J). pap. 8.99 *(978-1-59473-256-0(6)*, 9781594732560, Skylight Paths Publishing) LongHill Partners, Inc.
Person, Hara & Lewy, Faye Tillis. My Synagogue Scrapbook. Schoenberg-Lewin, Dahlia, illus. 2006. pap. 11.95 *(978-0-8074-0990-9(1)*, 164065) URJ Pr.

SYNTHETIC PRODUCTS

see also Plastics

also names of synthetic products, e.g. Rubber, Artificial; etc.

Carr, Aaron. Natural o Hecho Por el Hombre. 2013. (SPA., Illus.). 24p. (J). *(978-1-62127-607-4(4))* Weigl Pubs., Inc.
Is It Natural or Human-Made? 2014. (ENG., Illus.). 24p. (J). *(978-0-7787-0535-2(8))* Crabtree Publishing Co.
Man-Made Materials. 2010. (Experimenting with Everyday Science Ser.). (Illus.). 176p. (gr. 6-12). 35.00 *(978-1-60413-175-8(6)*, Chelsea Hse.) Facts On File, Inc.

SYRIA

Behnke, Alison. Syria in Pictures. 2005. (Visual Geography Series, Second Ser.). (ENG., Illus.). 80p. (gr. 5-12). 31.93 *(978-0-8225-2396-3(5))* Lerner Publishing Group.
Berlatsky, Noah. Syria. Greenhaven Press Staff, ed. 2014. (Opposing Viewpoints Ser.). (ENG., Illus.). 224p. (gr. 10-12). lib. bdg. 48.80 *(978-0-7377-7006-3(6)*, Greenhaven Pr., Inc.) Cengage Gale.
Capek, Michael. Understanding Syria Today. 2014. (Illus.). 63p. (J). (gr. 3-6). 33.95 *(978-1-61228-646-4(1))* Mitchell Lane Pubs., Inc.
Draper, Allison Stark. A Historical Atlas of Syria. 2009. (Historical Atlases of South Asia, Central Asia, & the Middle East Ser.). 64p. (gr. 6-6). 61.20 *(978-1-61513-329-1(1))* Rosen Publishing Group, Inc., The.
Etheredge, Laura. Syria, Lebanon, & Jordan. 2011. (Middle East: Region in Transition Ser.). (Illus.). 248p. (YA). (gr. 9-12). lib. bdg. 40.00 *(978-1-61530-329-8(4))* Rosen Publishing Group, Inc., The.
Gelfand, Dale Evva. Syria, 1 vol. 2013. (Countries of the World Set 2 Ser.). (ENG.). 144p. (J). (gr. 6-12). lib. bdg. 37.07 *(978-1-61783-639-8(7)*, Essential Library) ABDO Publishing Co.
Kummer, Patricia K. Syria. 2005. (Enchantment of the World Ser.). (ENG., Illus.). 144p. (YA). (gr. 5-9). 39.00 *(978-0-516-23677-3(6))* Scholastic Library Publishing.
Mason, Helen. A Refugee's Journey from Syria. 2017. (Leaving My Homeland Ser.). (ENG., Illus.). 32p. (J). pap. ***(978-0-7787-3184-9(7))*** Crabtree Publishing Co.
Skinner, Patricia. Syria. 2004. (Countries of the World Ser.). (Illus.). 96p. (gr. 5-12). lib. bdg. 31.00 *(978-0-8368-3118-4(7))* Stevens, Gareth Publishing LLLP.
South, Coleman & Jermyn, Leslie. Syria: Cultures of the World. 2nd rev. ed. 2005. (Cultures of the World Ser.). (Illus.). 144p. (gr. 6-10). lib. bdg. 42.79 *(978-0-7614-2054-5(1)*, Benchmark Bks.) Marshall Cavendish Corp.
South, Coleman, et al. Syria: Cultures of the World. 2016. (Cultures of the World (r) Ser.). (Illus.). 144p. (J). (gr. 5-5). lib. bdg. 47.07 *(978-1-5026-1703-3(X))* Cavendish Square Publishing.
Stark Draper, Allison. A Historical Atlas of Syria. 2004. (Historical Atlases of South Asia, Central Asia, & the Middle East Ser.). (Illus.). 64p. (gr. 7-12). lib. bdg. 31.95 *(978-0-8239-3983-1(9))* Rosen Publishing Group, Inc., The.
Sullivan, Anne Marie. Syria. (Major Muslim Nations Ser.). 2010. 126p. (YA). (gr. 5-18). lib. bdg. 25.95 *(978-1-4222-1382-7(X))* Vol. 13. 2015. (Illus.). 128p. (J). (gr. 7). lib. bdg. 25.95 *(978-1-4222-3451-8(7))* Mason Crest.
Syria. 2010. (Modern World Nations Ser.). (Illus.). 128p. (gr. 6-12). 35.00 *(978-1-60413-617-3(0)*, Chelsea Hse.) Facts On File, Inc.
Yomtov, Nel. Syria. 2013. (ENG.). 144p. (J). 40.00 *(978-0-531-23679-6(X))* Scholastic Library Publishing.
Zahler, Kathy A. The Assads' Syria. 2009. (Dictatorships Ser.). (ENG.). 160p. (gr. 9-12). 38.60 *(978-0-8225-9095-8(6))* Lerner Publishing Group.
Zurlo, Tony. Syria in the News: Past, Present, & Future. 2006. (Middle East Nations in the News Ser.). (Illus.). 128p. (J). (gr. 4-7). lib. bdg. 34.60 *(978-1-59845-025-5(5)*, MyReportLinks.com Bks.) Enslow Pubs., Inc.

SYSTEMS ENGINEERING

see also Bionics

Lerner, K. Lee, et al. U-X-L Doomed: The Science Behind Disasters. 2015. (J). *(978-1-4103-1777-3(3))* Cengage Gale.
Mara, Wil. Robotics Engineer. 2015. (21st Century Skills Library: Cool STEAM Careers Ser.). (ENG., Illus.). 32p. (J). (gr. 4-7). pap. 14.21 *(978-1-63362-045-2(X)*, 205937) Cherry Lake Publishing.
U X L, ed. UXL Man-Made Disasters, 3 vols. 2015. (ENG.). (J). 286.00 *(978-1-4103-1774-2(9)*, UXL) Cengage Gale.
Winchester, Jim. World's Worst Aircraft. 2009. (World's Worst: from Innovation to Disaster Ser.). 80p. (gr. 8-8). 61.20 *(978-1-60854-857-6(0))* Rosen Publishing Group, Inc., The.

T

TABLE

Priddy, Roger. Mealtime - A High Contrast High Chair Book. 2013. (Hello Baby Ser.). (ENG., Illus.). 8p. (J). (gr. -1 — 1). bds. 5.99 *(978-0-312-51602-4(9)*, 9780312516024, Priddy Bks.) St. Martin's Pr.

TACOMA NARROWS BRIDGE (TACOMA, WASH.)—FICTION

Hartinger, Brent. Project Sweet Life. 2009. (J). lib. bdg. 17.89 *(978-0-06-082412-9(3)*, HarperTeen) HarperCollins Pubs.

TADPOLES

Bailer, Darice. How Do Tadpoles Become Frogs? 2010. (Tell Me Why, Tell Me How 4 Ser.). 32p. (gr. 3-5). 29.93 *(978-0-7614-4824-2(1))* Marshall Cavendish Corp.
Bekkering, Annalise. Frogs. 2010. pap. 9.95 *(978-1-60596-926-8(5))*; 24p. (J). (gr. 2-4). lib. bdg. 25.70 *(978-1-60596-925-1(7))* Weigl Pubs., Inc.
Berger, Melvin & Berger, Gilda. A Tadpole Grows Up. 2008. (Illus.). 32p. (J). *(978-0-439-02528-7(1))* Scholastic, Inc.
Ganeri, Anita. Frogs & Tadpoles. Axworthy, Anni, illus. 2010. (Animal Families Ser.). (ENG.). 14p. (J). bds. 10.99 *(978-1-84089-642-8(6))* Evans Brothers, Ltd. GBR. Dist: Independent Pubs. Group.
Godwin, Sam. The Trouble with Tadpoles: A First Look at the Life Cycle of a Frog. Abel, Simone, illus. 2004. (First Look: Science Ser.). (ENG.). 32p. (gr. -1-2). 26.65 *(978-1-4048-0654-2(7))* Picture Window Bks.
Gold, Annabelle. A Tadpole Grows Up. 2012. (InfoMax Readers Ser.). (ENG., Illus.). 24p. (J). (gr. 1-2). pap. 8.25 *(978-1-4488-8983-9(9)*, Rosen Classroom) Rosen Publishing Group, Inc., The.
Hayes, Amy. A Tadpole Becomes a Frog. 2016. (Transformations in Nature Ser.). (ENG.). 24p. (J). (gr. 1-1). pap. 8.22 *(978-1-5026-0818-5(9))* Cavendish Square Publishing.
Herrington, Lisa M. Tadpole to Frog. 2014. (Rookie Read-About(tm) Science — Life Cycles Ser.). (ENG.). 32p. (J). lib. bdg. 25.00 *(978-0-531-21057-4(X))* Scholastic Library Publishing.
Ho, Cammie. Tadpole Tadpole. 2016. (Life Cycle Bks.). (ENG., Illus.). 31p. (J). (gr. k-2). pap. 7.99 *(978-1-943241-01-9(5))* Phonic Monic.
Kalman, Bobbie. Tadpoles to Frogs. 2008. (It's Fun to Learn about Baby Animals Ser.). (ENG., Illus.). 24p. (J). (gr. k-3). pap. *(978-0-7787-3975-3(9))* Crabtree Publishing Co.
Keeping Tadpoles Alive! Individual Title Six-Packs. (Discovery World Ser.). 24p. (gr. 1-2). 33.00 *(978-0-7635-8476-4(2))* Rigby Education.
Milbourne, A. Tadpoles & Frogs. 2004. (Beginners Ser.). (J). (gr. 1-18). 32p. lib. bdg. 12.95 *(978-1-58086-465-7(1))*; (ENG., Illus.). 1p. pap. 4.95 *(978-0-7945-0164-8(8)*, Usborne) EDC Publishing.
Milbourne, Anna. Tadpoles & Frogs. Donaera, Patrizia & Wray, Zoe, illus. 2007. (Usborne Beginners Ser.). 32p. (J). 4.99 *(978-0-7945-1345-0(X)*, Usborne) EDC Publishing.
Royston, Angela. Tadpole Story. 2011. (ENG., Illus.). 24p. (J). pap. *(978-0-7787-7881-3(9))*; (gr. 3-6). *(978-0-7787-7859-2(2))* Crabtree Publishing Co.
Stewart, David. How a Tadpole Grows into a Frog. Franklin, Carolyn, illus. 2008. (Amaze Ser.). (ENG.). 32p. (J). (gr. k-3). 27.00 *(978-0-531-20443-6(X))*; pap. 8.95 *(978-0-531-20454-2(5))* Scholastic Library Publishing. (Children's Pr.).
Twinn, M. Metamorphoses: Egg, Tadpole, Frog. 2006. (Metamorphoses Ser.). (ENG., Illus.). 16p. (J). (gr. 1-5). bds. *(978-1-84643-012-1(7))* Child's Play International Ltd.
Wallace, Karen. DK Readers L1: Tale of a Tadpole. 2015. (DK Readers Ser.). (ENG., Illus.). 48p. (J). (gr. k-4). pap. 3.99 *(978-1-4654-3508-8(5)*, DK Children) Dorling Kindersley Publishing, Inc.
Zoehfeld, Kathleen Weidner. From Tadpole to Frog. 2011. (Scholastic Reader Level 1 Ser.). (ENG.). 32p. (J). (gr. -1-2). pap. 3.99 *(978-0-545-27337-4(4)*, Scholastic Paperbacks) Scholastic, Inc.

TADPOLES—FICTION

Asch, Frank. Moonbear's Pet. Asch, Frank, illus. 2014. (Moonbear Ser.). (ENG., Illus.). 32p. (J). (gr. -1-3). 17.99 *(978-1-4424-9430-5(1)*, Simon & Schuster/Paula Wiseman Bks.) Simon & Schuster/Paula Wiseman Bks.
Azore, Barbara. Wanda & the Frogs. Graham, Georgia, illus. 2007. (ENG.). 32p. (J). (gr. -1-1). 18.95 *(978-0-88776-761-6(3)*, Tundra Bks.) Tundra Bks. CAN. Dist: Penguin Random Hse. LLC.
Bickta, Brenda L. Tad's Life in the Lily Pond. 2008. 74p. pap. 19.95 *(978-1-60672-647-1(1))* America Star Bks.
Bronson, Tammy Carter. Polliwog. Bronson, Tammy Carter, illus. 2006. (ENG & SPA., Illus.). (J). 7.99 *(978-0-9678167-5-3(0))* Bookaroos Publishing, Inc.
—Polliwog. Davi, Annou, tr. Bronson, Tammy Carter, illus. 2004. (SPA & ENG., Illus.). 32p. (J). lib. bdg. 17.00 *(978-0-9678167-4-6(2))* Bookaroos Publishing, Inc.
Cain, Sheridan. The Teeny Weeny Tadpole. Tickle, Jack, illus. 2005. 32p. (J). 15.95 *(978-1-58925-047-5(8))* Tiger Tales.
Carter, Denzel T. Tadpole Grows Up. 2015. (Rosen REAL Readers: STEM & STEAM Collection). (ENG.). 12p. (gr. 1-2). pap. 6.33 *(978-1-4994-9520-1(X)*, Rosen Classroom) Rosen Publishing Group, Inc., The.
Clarke, Jane. Only Tadpoles Have Tails. Gray, Jane, illus. 2003. (Flying Foxes Ser.). (ENG.). 48p. (J). lib. bdg. *(978-0-7787-1484-2(5))* Crabtree Publishing Co.
E.C., Nanci. I Just Might! Meade, Gregory S., illus. 2007. 20p. per. 9.95 *(978-1-59858-548-3(7))* Dog Ear Publishing, LLC.
Farfan, Flores & Antonio, Jose. Axolotl: El Ajolote. Celestino, Cleofas Ramirez, illus. 2003. (SPA.). 40p. (J). *(978-968-411-569-9(5))* Ediciones Era.
Hood, Susan. Leaps & Bounce. Cordell, Matthew, illus. 2016. (ENG.). 32p. (J). (gr. -1-k). 16.99 *(978-1-4231-5234-7(4))* Disney Pr.
Jefferson, E. Louis. The Little Tadpole-A Story of Friendship: Companion Coloring Book. 2012. 48p. pap. 7.00 *(978-1-105-61123-0(X))* Lulu.com GBR. Dist: Lulu Pr., Inc.
—Terry-The Little Tadpole-Making New Friends. 2013. 90p. pap. 35.00 *(978-1-300-61843-0(4))* Lulu Pr., Inc.
Kimura, ken & Murakami, Yasunari. 999 Tadpoles. 2011. (ENG., Illus.). 40p. (J). (gr. -1-3). 17.95 *(978-0-7358-4013-3(X))* North-South Bks., Inc.
La Beree, Brian, illus. Herbert the Tadpole in the Big Change: Color-Me Version. 2007. 48p. (J). 6.95 *(978-0-9800736-0-7(X))* Sophrose Entertainment Inc.
Lobel, Arnold & Lobel, Adrianne. The Frogs & Toads All Sang. Lobel, Arnold & Lobel, Adrianne, illus. 2009. (ENG., Illus.). 32p. (J). (gr. -1-2). 16.99 *(978-0-06-180022-1(8))* HarperCollins Pubs.
Mese, John R. & Kelsey, Dawn M. On the Flippy Side. Holden, Chanler, illus. 2009. 30p. (J). 10.95 *(978-0-9725853-1-6(1))* Mosscovered Gumbo Barn.
Milbourne, Anna. In the Pond. 2007. 24p. (J). 9.99 *(978-0-7945-1544-7(4)*, Usborne) EDC Publishing.
Narváez, Concha López & Salmeron, Carmelo. Tomas Es Distinto a los Demas.Tr. of Tomas Is Different from the Others. (SPA.). 64p. (J). (gr. 2-4). *(978-84-216-3432-5(1))* Bruño, Editorial ESP. Dist: Lectorum Pubns., Inc.
Rey, H. A. Tadpole Trouble. 2007. (Curious George Ser.). (ENG., Illus.). 24p. (J). (gr. -1-3). 4.99 *(978-0-618-77712-9(1))* Houghton Mifflin Harcourt Publishing Co.
Rice, Cindy & Stolarski, Jerry. Mr. Mahaffy on Wisdom Pond: The Beginning. 2007. (ENG.). 84p. per. 19.95 *(978-1-4241-3097-9(2))* America Star Bks.
Rosenthal, Michele Marie. The Frog & the Tadpole's Great Swamp Adventure, 1 vol. 2009. 22p. pap. 24.95 *(978-1-61546-178-3(7))* America Star Bks.
Sargent, Dave & Sargent, Pat. Little Tadpole. 10. Robinson, Laura, illus. 2004. (Learn to Read Ser.: 10). 18p. (J). 20. lib. bdg. 9.95 *(978-1-56763-836-3(8))* Vol. 20. lib. bdg. 20.95 *(978-1-56763-835-6(X))* Ozark Publishing.
—Little Tadpole/el Renacuajo Pequeño, 10 vols. Robinson, Laura, illus. 2004. (Learn to Read Ser.: 10). (ENG & SPA.). 18p. (J). pap. 10.95 *(978-1-56763-567-6(9))*; lib. bdg. 20.95 *(978-1-56763-999-5(2))* Ozark Publishing.
Shanghai Animation Studio Staff & Tang, Sanmu. Tadpoles Looking for Their Mother. Xiaozhen, Wu, tr. from CHI. 2010. (Favorite Children's Ser.). (ENG., Illus.). 32p. (J). (gr. -1-3). pap. 5.95 *(978-1-60220-972-5(3))* BetterLink Pr., Inc.
Shorty. Tad, the Sad Tadpole, 1 vol. Evans, Margaret, illus. 2009. 29p. pap. 19.95 *(978-1-4489-2458-5(8))* PublishAmerica, Inc.
Sommer, Carl. King of the Pond. Budwine, Greg, illus. 2014. (J). pap. *(978-1-57537-956-2(2))* Advance Publishing, Inc.

—King of the Pond(El Rey Del Estanque) Budwine, Greg, illus. 2009. (Another Sommer-Time Story Bilingual Ser.). (SPA & ENG.). 48p. (J). lib. bdg. 16.95 *(978-1-57537-156-6(1))* Advance Publishing, Inc.
Sparks, Evan. Freddy's Tale. 2006. 44p. pap. 14.88 *(978-1-4116-7427-1(8))* Lulu Pr., Inc.
Stein, David Ezra. Tad & Dad. Stein, David Ezra, illus. 2015. (ENG., Illus.). 40p. (J). (gr. -1-k). 16.99 *(978-0-399-25671-4(7),* Nancy Paulsen Books) Penguin Young Readers Group.
There's a Rainbow in the River: Individual Title Six-Packs. (gr. k-1). 23.00 *(978-0-7635-8850-2(4))* Rigby Education.
Tiny Tiny Tadpole. 2005. (J). bds. 7.99 *(978-1-933200-17-0(0))* Family Bks. at Home.
Ward, Nick. The Tadpole Prince. 2003. (Illus.). 32p. (YA). *(978-1-84365-016-4(9),* Pavilion Children's Books) Pavilion Bks.
Weston Woods Staff, creator. The Caterpillar & the Polliwog. 2011. 38.75 *(978-0-439-73154-6(2));* 18.95 *(978-0-439-73152-2(6))* Weston Woods Studios, Inc.
Willis, Jeanne. Tadpole's Promise. Ross, Tony, illus. 2005. (ENG.). 32p. (J). (gr. -1-k). pap. 12.99 *(978-1-84270-426-4(5))* Andersen Pr. GBR. Dist: Independent Pubs. Group.
Wilson, Kevin. Brown Spot. 2006. 60p. (J). pap. 12.00 *(978-1-4116-8059-3(6))* Lulu Pr., Inc.
Wrucke, Mary. Timmy the Tadpole, 1 vol. Cooke, Bev, illus. 2009. 25p. pap. 24.95 *(978-1-60813-776-3(7))* America Star Bks.

TAE KWON DO

Adamson, Thomas K. & Heather. Tae Kwon Do, 1 vol. 2014. (Inside Martial Arts Ser.). (ENG., Illus.). 48p. (J). (gr. 3-6). lib. bdg. 32.79 *(978-1-62403-606-4(6),* SportsZone) ABDO Publishing Co.
Chesterman, Barnaby. Taekwondo: Winning Ways. James, Adam, ed. 2015. (Mastering Martial Arts Ser.). (Illus.). 96p. (J). (gr. 5). lib. bdg. 24.95 *(978-1-4222-3245-3(X))* Mason Crest.
Falk, Laine. Let's Talk Tae Kwon Do. 2008. (Scholastic News Nonfiction Readers Ser.). (ENG.). 24p. (J). (gr. 1-2). pap. 6.95 *(978-0-531-20428-3(6))* Scholastic Library Publishing.
Wells, Garrison. Tae Kwon Do: Korean Foot & Fist Combat. 2012. (Martial Arts Sports Zone Ser.). (ENG., Illus.). 32p. (gr. 4-8). lib. bdg. 26.60 *(978-0-7613-8458-8(8),* Lerner Pubns.) Lerner Publishing Group.
Wood, Alix. Tae Kwon Do. 2013. (Kid's Guide to Martial Arts Ser.). (ENG., Illus.). 32p. (J). (gr. 3-6). pap. 11.75 *(978-1-4777-0354-0(3));* lib. bdg. 26.50 *(978-1-4777-0316-8(0))* Rosen Publishing Group, Inc., The. (PowerKids Pr.).

TAFT, WILLIAM H. (WILLIAM HOWARD), 1857-1930

Benson, Michael. William H. Taft. 2004. (Presidential Leaders Ser.). (ENG., Illus.). 112p. (gr. 6-12). 29.27 *(978-0-8225-0849-6(4),* Lerner Pubns.) Lerner Publishing Group.
O'Connell, Kim A. William Howard Taft: A MyReportLinks.com Book. 2003. (Presidents Ser.). (Illus.). 48p. (J). (gr. 4-10). lib. bdg. 25.26 *(978-0-7660-5078-5(5),* MyReportLinks.com Bks.) Enslow Pubs., Inc.
Randolph, Ryan P. How to Draw the Life & Times of William Howard Taft. 2007. (Kid's Guide to Drawing the Presidents of the United States of America Ser.). (Illus.). 32p. (YA). (gr. 2-5). 26.50 *(978-1-4042-3003-3(3))* Rosen Publishing Group, Inc., The.
Rumsch, BreAnn. William Taft, 1 vol. 2009. (United States Presidents Ser.). (ENG., Illus.). 40p. (YA). (gr. 3-6). 27.07 *(978-1-60453-474-0(5))* ABDO Publishing Co.
Venezia, Mike. William Howard Taft: Twenty-Seventh President. Venezia, Mike, illus. 2007. (Getting to Know the U. S. Presidents Ser.). (Illus.). 32p. (J). (gr. 3-7). pap. 7.95 *(978-0-516-25239-1(9),* Children's Pr.) Scholastic Library Publishing.
Wilson, Natashya. How to Draw the Life & Times of William Howard Taft. 2009. (Kid's Guide to Drawing the Presidents of the United States of America Ser.). 32p. (gr. 4-4). 50.50 *(978-1-61511-165-7(4),* PowerKids Pr.) Rosen Publishing Group, Inc., The.

TAHITI

NgCheong-Lum, Roseline. Tahiti. 2nd rev. ed. 2007. (Cultures of the World Ser.). 144p. (gr. 6). lib. bdg. 42.79 *(978-0-7614-2089-7(4),* Benchmark Bks.) Marshall Cavendish Corp.

TAHITI—FICTION

Jensen, Kathryn. Splash! 2012. 194p. 29.95 *(978-1-4489-6574-8(8))* America Star Bks.
Lumry, Amanda & Hurwitz, Laura. Adventures of Riley: Dolphins in Danger. McIntyre, Sarah, illus. 2005. 36p. 15.95 *(978-0-9748411-1-3(0))* Eaglemont Pr.

TAILORS

Petersen, Christine. The Tailor. 2011. (Colonial People 2 Ser.). 48p. (gr. 3). 29.93 *(978-1-60870-417-0(3))* Marshall Cavendish Corp.

TAILORS—FICTION

Andersen, Hans Christian & Starbright Foundation Staff. The Emperor's New Clothes. Burton, Virginia Lee, illus. 2014. (Folk Tale Classics Ser.). (ENG.). 48p. (J). (gr. -1-3). 8.99 *(978-0-544-15952-5(7),* HMH Books For Young Readers) Houghton Mifflin Harcourt Publishing Co.
Brown, Jason Robert. Tickety Tock. GrandPré, Mary, illus. 2008. 32p. (J). (gr. -1-3). lib. bdg. 18.89 *(978-0-06-078753-0(8),* Geringer, Laura Book) HarperCollins Pubs.
Feierabend, John M. The Tailor & the Mouse. McGann, James, illus. 2012. (First Steps in Music Ser.). (ENG.). 32p. (J). (gr. -1-k). 16.95 *(978-1-57999-903-2(4))* G I A Pubns., Inc.
Giff, Patricia Reilly. A House of Tailors. 2006. (ENG.). 160p. (J). (gr. 3-7). per. 6.99 *(978-0-440-23800-3(5),* Yearling) Random Hse. Children's Bks.
Luxbacher, Irene. Mr. Frank, 1 vol. 2014. (ENG., Illus.). 32p. (J). (gr. -1-2). 16.95 *(978-1-55498-435-0(1))* Groundwood Bks. CAN. Dist: Publishers Group West (PGW).
McGuire, Sarah. Valiant. 2015. (ENG.). 384p. (gr. 5). 16.99 *(978-1-60684-552-3(7));* (J). 16.99 *(978-1-5124-0198-1(6))* Lerner Publishing Group. (Carolrhoda Bks.).
Perez, Marlene. Princess Rock & the Royal Inches. 2004. (Shared Connections Ser.). (J). pap. 27.00 *(978-1-4108-1633-7(8));* instr.'s gde. ed. 27.00 *(978-1-4108-1609-2(5))* Benchmark Education Co.
Stofko, Michael D. The Tale of Taylor the Tailor. 2012. 30p. pap. 19.99 *(978-1-4772-0238-8(2))* AuthorHouse.

TAIWAN

Behnke, Alison. Taiwan in Pictures. 2007. (Visual Geography (Lerner) Ser.). (Illus.). 80p. (YA). (gr. 7-12). lib. bdg. 31.93 *(978-0-8225-7148-3(X))* Twenty First Century Bks.
Hsu, Yi Ling. Typhoon Holidays: Taiwan. Cowley, Joy, ed. Kwag, Jin-yeong, illus. 2015. (Global Kids Storybooks Ser.). (ENG.). 32p. (J). (gr. 1-4). pap. 7.99 *(978-1-925233-43-8(X))* Lerner Publishing Group.
King, David C. & Orr, Tamra B. Taiwan. 2006. (Enchantment of the World Ser.). (ENG., Illus.). 144p. (J). (gr. 5-9). 37.00 *(978-0-516-24856-1(1),* Children's Pr.) Scholastic Library Publishing.
Moiz, Azra & Wu, Janice. Taiwan. 2nd ed. 2006. (Cultures of the World Ser.). (Illus.). 144p. (J). (gr. 3-7). lib. bdg. 39.93 *(978-0-7614-2069-9(X),* Benchmark Bks.) Marshall Cavendish Corp.
Moiz, Azra, et al. Taiwan. 2016. (Cultures of the World (r) Ser.). (ENG., Illus.). 144p. (J). (gr. 5-5). lib. bdg. 47.07 *(978-1-5026-1846-7(X))* Cavendish Square Publishing.
Owings, Lisa. Taiwan. 2014. (Exploring Countries Ser.). (ENG., Illus.). 32p. (J). (gr. 3-7). lib. bdg. 26.95 *(978-1-62617-070-4(3),* Blastoff! Readers) Bellwether Media.
Ryan, Michaela. Taiwan. 2003. (Countries of the World Ser.). (Illus.). 96p. (gr. 5-12). lib. bdg. 31.00 *(978-0-8368-2368-4(0))* Stevens, Gareth Publishing LLLP.
Salter, Christopher L. Taiwan. 2004. (Modern World Nations Ser.). (Illus.). 144p. (gr. 6-12). lib. bdg. 35.00 *(978-0-7910-7914-0(7),* Chelsea Hse.) Facts On File, Inc.
Somervill, Barbara A. Taiwan. 2014. (Enchantment of the World Ser.: 2). (ENG.). 144p. (J). lib. bdg. 40.00 *(978-0-531-22018-4(4))* Scholastic Library Publishing.
Wan, Vanessa. Welcome to Taiwan. 2004. (Welcome to My Country Ser.). (Illus.). 48p. (gr. 2-5). lib. bdg. 27.00 *(978-0-8368-3122-1(5))* Stevens, Gareth Publishing LLLP.

TAIWAN—FICTION

Hsu, Yi Ling. Typhoon Holidays: Taiwan. Cowley, Joy, ed. Kwag, Jin-yeong, illus. 2015. (Global Kids Storybooks Ser.). (ENG.). 32p. (gr. 1-4). 7.99 *(978-1-925246-56-8(6));* 26.65 *(978-1-925246-30-8(2));* 26.65 *(978-1-925246-04-9(3))* ChoiceMaker Pty. Ltd., The AUS. (Big and SMALL). Dist: Lerner Publishing Group.
Huang, SuHua. A Faithful Reading Partner: A Story from a Hakka Village. 2012. 28p. pap. 19.99 *(978-1-4685-6267-5(3))* AuthorHouse.
Hunt for Jade Dragon. 2014. (Michael Vey Ser.: No. 4). (ENG., Illus.). 336p. (YA). (gr. 7). 19.99 *(978-1-4814-2438-7(6),* Simon Pulse/Mercury Ink) Simon Pulse/Mercury Ink.
Itoh, Shimpei. Hyper Dolls, Vol. 5. 2003. (Illus.). 208p. pap. 15.95 *(978-1-929090-67-9(6))* International Comics & Entertainment L.L.C.
Lin, Grace. Dumpling Days. 2012. (Pacy Lin Novel Ser.). (ENG.). 272p. (J). (gr. 3-7). 15.99 *(978-0-316-12590-1(3))* Little Brown & Co.
—Dumpling Days. 2013. (Pacy Lin Novel Ser.). (ENG.). 272p. (J). (gr. 3-7). pap. 7.99 *(978-0-316-12589-5(X))* Little, Brown Bks. for Young Readers.
Pon, Cindy. Want. 2017. (ENG., Illus.). 336p. (YA). (gr. 9). 18.99 ***(978-1-4814-8922-5(4),*** Simon Pulse) Simon Pulse.

TALES

see Fables; Fairy Tales; Folklore; Legends

TALISMANS

see Charms

TALKING

see Speech

TALKING PICTURES

see Motion Pictures

TALL TALES

see also American Wit and Humor; Folklore; Legends

Capstone Press Staff. Pecos Bill, Colossal Cowboy. Weber, Lisa K., illus. 2010. (Graphic Spin Ser.). (ENG.). 40p. (gr. 1-3). lib. bdg. 25.32 *(978-1-4342-1896-4(1),* Graphic Revolve) Stone Arch Bks.
Case, Maggie. A Squirrel's Tale. 2011. 24p. (gr. -1). pap. 11.32 *(978-1-4567-5118-0(2))* AuthorHouse.
Chaud, Benjamin & Cali, Davide. The Truth about My Unbelievable Summer ... 2016. (ENG., Illus.). 44p. (J). (gr. 1-4). 12.99 *(978-1-4521-4483-2(4))* Chronicle Bks. LLC.
Coyle, Carmela Lavigna. The Tumbleweed Came Back. Rechin, Kevin, illus. 2013. 32p. (J). 15.95 *(978-1-933855-83-7(5),* Rio Nuevo Pubs.) Rio Nuevo Pubs.
Crunk, Tony. Railroad John & the Red Rock Run, 1 vol. Austin, Michael, illus. 2006. (ENG.). 32p. (J). (gr. k-3). 16.95 *(978-1-56145-363-4(3))* Peachtree Pubs.
Disney Pixar Staff. Rescue Mater: And Other Tall Tales. 2013. (Fold-Out Figure Ser.: 1). (ENG.). 32p. (J). (gr. -1-2). 14.99 *(978-0-7944-2815-0(0))* Reader's Digest Assn., Inc., The.
Enderle, Dotti. The Fat Stock Stampede at the Houston Livestock Show & Rodeo, 1 vol. Galey, Chuck, illus. 2008. (ENG.). 32p. (J). (gr. 1-3). 16.99 *(978-1-58980-443-2(0))* Pelican Publishing Co., Inc.
—Gingerbread Man Superhero!, 1 vol. Kulka, Joe, illus. 2009. (ENG.). 32p. (J). (gr. k-3). 16.99 *(978-1-58980-521-7(6))* Pelican Publishing Co., Inc.
—Granny Gert & the Bunion Brothers, 1 vol. Kulka, Joe, illus. 2006. (ENG.). 32p. (J). (gr. k-3). 16.99 *(978-1-58980-373-2(6))* Pelican Publishing Co., Inc.
Enderle, Dotti & Galey, Chuck. The Cotton Candy Catastrophe at the Texas State Fair, 1 vol. 2004. (ENG., Illus.). 32p. (J). (gr. k-3). 16.99 *(978-1-58980-189-9(X))* Pelican Publishing Co., Inc.
Garretson, Jerri. Kansas Tall Tales: Tenth Anniversary Anthology. Garretson, Jerri & Dollar, Diane A., illus. 2008. 106p. (J). pap. 19.95 *(978-0-9659712-7-0(9))* Ravenstone Pr.
Gill, Shelley. Prickly Rose. Cartwright, Shannon & Love, Judy, illus. 2014. (ENG.). 32p. (J). (gr. -1-3). pap. 7.95 *(978-1-57091-357-0(9));* lib. bdg. 17.95 *(978-1-57091-356-3(0))* Charlesbridge Publishing, Inc.
—Sitka Rose. Cartwright, Shannon, illus. 2005. (ENG.). 32p. (J). (gr. -1-3). per. 7.95 *(978-1-57091-364-8(1))* Charlesbridge Publishing, Inc.
Gleeson, Brian. Paul Bunyan, 1 vol. Meyerowitz, Rick, illus. 2004. (Rabbit Ears-A Classic Tale Ser.). (ENG.). 40p. (gr. k-5). 25.65 *(978-1-59197-767-4(3))* Spotlight.
—Pecos Bill, 1 vol. Raglin, Tim, illus. 2004. (Rabbit Ears-A Classic Tale Ser.). (ENG.). 36p. (gr. k-5). 25.65 *(978-1-59197-768-1(1))* Spotlight.
Gribnau, Joe. Kick the Cowboy, 1 vol. Tans, Adrian, illus. 2009. (ENG.). 32p. (J). (gr. k-3). 16.99 *(978-1-58980-605-4(0))* Pelican Publishing Co., Inc.
Hayes, Joe. The Gum-Chewing Rattler. 2006. (ENG., Illus.). 32p. (J). (gr. k-6). 16.95 *(978-0-938317-99-9(7))* Cinco Puntos Pr.
—The Lovesick Skunk. Castro L., Antonio, illus. 2016. (ENG.). 32p. (J). 7.95 *(978-1-941026-04-5(4))* Cinco Puntos Pr.
Heller, Marcy. Loco Dog & the Dust Devil in the Railyard. Poes, Nancy, illus. 2007. 30p. (J). (gr. -1-7). 19.95 *(978-1-929115-17-4(2))* Azro Pr., Inc.
Hopkinson, Deborah. Apples to Oregon. 2014. 17.00 *(978-1-63419-642-0(2))* Perfection Learning Corp.
Hopkinson, Deborah & Carpenter, Nancy. Apples to Oregon: Being the (Slightly) True Narrative of How a Brave Pioneer Father Brought Apples, Peaches, Pears, Plums, Grapes, & Cherries (and Children) Across the Plains. 2004. (ENG., Illus.). 40p. (J). (gr. -1-3). 17.99 *(978-0-689-84769-1(6),* Atheneum Bks. for Young Readers) Simon & Schuster Children's Publishing.
Hurston, Zora Neale & Thomas, Joyce Carol. Lies & Other Tall Tales. Myers, Christopher, illus. (ENG.). 40p. (J). 2015. (gr. -1-3). pap. 6.99 *(978-0-06-000657-0(9))* 2005. (gr. 1-5). 17.99 *(978-0-06-000655-6(2))* HarperCollins Pubs.
Irving, Washington. The Devil & Tom Walker. 2007. (Tale Blazers: American Literature Ser.). 37p. (J). (gr. 4-7). pap. 3.30 *(978-0-89598-665-8(5))* Perfection Learning Corp.
Isaacs, Anne. The Ghosts of Luckless Gulch. Santat, Dan, illus. 2008. (ENG.). 48p. (J). (gr. k-3). 18.99 *(978-1-4169-0201-0(5),* Atheneum Bks. for Young Readers) Simon & Schuster Children's Publishing.
—Meanwhile, Back at the Ranch. Hawkes, Kevin, illus. 2014. (ENG.). 56p. (J). (gr. k-4). 17.99 *(978-0-375-86745-3(7),* Schwartz & Wade Bks.) Random Hse. Children's Bks.
Jenkins, Amanda. Pecos Bill & Sluefoot Sue: An American Tall Tale. 2006. (J). pap. *(978-1-4108-7158-9(4))* Benchmark Education Co.
Johnston, Tony. Levi Strauss Gets a Bright Idea: A Fairly Fabricated Story of a Pair of Pants. Innerst, Stacy, illus. 2011. (ENG.). 32p. (J). (gr. -1-3). 16.99 *(978-0-15-206145-6(2))* Houghton Mifflin Harcourt Publishing Co.
Jones, Nathan Smith. The Boy Who Ate America. Nelson, Casey, illus. 2007. 32p. (J). (gr. -1-3). 16.95 *(978-1-59038-814-3(3),* Shadow Mountain) Shadow Mountain Publishing.
Kaplan, Bruce Eric. Meaniehead. Kaplan, Bruce Eric, illus. 2014. (ENG., Illus.). 40p. (J). (gr. -1-3). 17.99 *(978-1-4424-8542-6(6),* Simon & Schuster Bks. For Young Readers) Simon & Schuster Bks. For Young Readers.
Kellogg, Steven. Paul Bunyan. 2004. (J). (gr. k-3). 17.20 *(978-0-8085-6790-5(X),* Turtleback) Turtleback Bks.
Kimmel, Eric A. Big Sam: A Rosh Hashanah Tall Tale. Starr, Jim, illus. 2017. (J). ***(978-1-68115-525-8(7))*** Behrman Hse., Inc.
Kimmel, Eric A. & Korelitz, Jean Hanff. The Great Texas Hamster Drive, 0 vols. Whatley, Bruce, illus. 2007. (ENG.). 40p. (J). (gr. k-3). 16.99 *(978-0-7614-5357-4(1),* 9780761453574, Amazon Children's Publishing) Amazon Publishing.
Krensky, Stephen. John Henry. Oldroyd, Mark, illus. 2006. (On My Own Folklore Ser.). (ENG.). 48p. (gr. 2-4). lib. bdg. 25.26 *(978-1-57505-887-0(1),* Millbrook Pr.) Lerner Publishing Group.
—Mike Fink. Reeves, Jeni, illus. 2006. (On My Own Folklore Ser.). (ENG.). 48p. (gr. 2-4). lib. bdg. 25.26 *(978-1-57505-891-7(X),* Millbrook Pr.) Lerner Publishing Group.
Manos, John. Big Ben Helps the Town. 2006. (Early Explorers Ser.). (J). pap. *(978-1-4108-6119-1(8))* Benchmark Education Co.
McClurkan, Rob. Aw, Nuts! McClurkan, Rob, illus. 2014. (ENG., Illus.). 32p. (J). (gr. -1-3). 17.99 *(978-0-06-231729-2(6))* HarperCollins Pubs.
McDermott, Tom. Otis Steele & the Taileebone: A Southern Tall Tale, 1 vol. Crosby, Jeff, illus. 2013. (ENG.). 32p. (J). (gr. k-2). 16.99 *(978-1-4556-1736-4(9))* Pelican Publishing Co., Inc.
McKissack, Patricia C. A Million Fish... More or Less. Schutzer, Dena, illus. 2016. (ENG.). 32p. (J). (gr. -1-2). 17.99 *(978-0-679-80692-9(X),* Knopf Bks. for Young Readers) Random Hse. Children's Bks.
—Porch Lies: Tales of Slicksters, Tricksters, & Other Wily Characters. Carrilho, Andre, illus. 2006. (ENG.). 160p. (J). (gr. 3-7). 19.99 *(978-0-375-83619-0(5),* Schwartz & Wade Bks.) Random Hse. Children's Bks.
Meredith, Susan Markowitz. Tall Tales of the Bunyans. 2016. (Spring Forward Ser.). (J). (gr. 2). *(978-1-4900-9430-4(X))* Benchmark Education Co.
Metaxas, Eric. Mose the Fireman, 1 vol. Peck, Everett, illus. 2004. (Rabbit Ears-A Classic Tale Ser.). (ENG.). 40p. (gr. k-5). 25.65 *(978-1-59197-766-7(5))* Spotlight.
—Stormalong, 1 vol. Vanderbeek, Don, illus. 2004. (Rabbit Ears-A Classic Tale Ser.). (ENG.). 36p. (gr. k-5). 25.65 *(978-1-59197-772-8(X))* Spotlight.
Nolen, Jerdine. Big Jabe. Nelson, Kadir, illus. 2003. (ENG.). 32p. (J). (gr. k-5). pap. 7.99 *(978-0-06-054061-6(3),* Amistad) HarperCollins Pubs.
—Thunder Rose. Nelson, Kadir, illus. 2007. (ENG.). 32p. (J). (gr. k-3). pap. 7.99 *(978-0-15-206006-0(5))* Houghton Mifflin Harcourt Publishing Co.
—Thunder Rose. Nelson, Kadir, illus. 2007. (gr. k-3). 17.00 *(978-0-7569-8199-0(9))* Perfection Learning Corp.
Oppel, Kenneth. Peg & the Whale. 2004. (Illus.). (J). (gr. k-3). spiral bd. *(978-0-616-07245-5(7))* Canadian National Institute for the Blind/Institut National Canadien pour les Aveugles.
Orback, Craig, illus. Paul Bunyan. 2006. (On My Own Folklore Ser.). 48p. (J). (gr. -1-3). lib. bdg. 25.26 *(978-1-57505-888-7(X),* Millbrook Pr.) Lerner Publishing Group.
Petruccio, Steven James. American Legends & Tall Tales. 2011. (Dover Classic Stories Coloring Book Ser.). (ENG., Illus.). 32p. (J). (gr. 3-6). pap. 3.99 *(978-0-486-47786-2(X))* Dover Pubns., Inc.
Rossi, Joyce. The Gullywasher: El Chaparron Torrencial. 2004. (ENG, SPA & MUL., Illus.). 32p. (J). (gr. k-3). pap. 7.95 *(978-0-87358-728-0(6))* Cooper Square Publishing Llc.
Rozier, Lucy Margaret. Jackrabbit McCabe & the Electric Telegraph. Espinosa, Leo, illus. 2015. (ENG.). 40p. (J). (gr. -1-3). 17.99 *(978-0-385-37843-7(2),* Schwartz & Wade Bks.) Random Hse. Children's Bks.
San Souci, Robert D. Cut from the Same Cloth: American Women of Myth, Legend, & Tall Tale. Pinkney, Brian, illus. 2005. 140p. 17.00 *(978-0-7569-6284-5(6))* Perfection Learning Corp.
Schnetzler, Pattie L. Widdermaker. Sealock, Rick, illus. 2005. 32p. (gr. k-2). 15.95 *(978-0-87614-647-7(7))* Lerner Publishing Group.
Scillian, Devin. Johnny Kaw: A Tall Tale. Sneed, Brad, illus. 2013. (ENG.). 32p. (J). (gr. 1-4). 15.95 *(978-1-58536-791-7(5),* 202353) Sleeping Bear Pr.
Smith, Andrea P. Paul Bunyan. 2012. (Illus.). 24p. (J). 63.60 *(978-1-4488-5221-5(8));* pap. 10.60 *(978-1-4488-5220-8(X));* lib. bdg. 25.25 *(978-1-4488-5191-1(2))* Rosen Publishing Group, Inc., The. (PowerKids Pr.).
Sowash, Rick. Ripsnorting Whoppers! A Book of Ohio Tall Tales. 2003. (J). 19.95 *(978-0-9762412-1-8(8));* pap. 11.95 *(978-0-9762412-0-1(X))* Sowash, Rick Publishing Co.
Stone Arch Books Staff. Pecos Bill: Colossal Cowboy. Weber, Lisa K., illus. 2010. (Graphic Spin Ser.). (ENG.). 40p. (gr. 1-3). pap. 5.95 *(978-1-4342-2267-1(5),* Graphic Revolve) Stone Arch Bks.
—The Tall Tale of Paul Bunyan. Blecha, Aaron, illus. 2010. (Graphic Spin Ser.). (ENG.). 40p. (gr. 1-3). pap. 5.95 *(978-1-4342-2268-8(3),* Graphic Revolve) Stone Arch Bks.
Strauss, Kevin. Pecos Bill Invents the Ten-Gallon Hat, 1 vol. Harrington, David, illus. 2012. (ENG.). 32p. (J). (gr. k-3). 16.99 *(978-1-4556-1502-5(1))* Pelican Publishing Co., Inc.
Tong, Paul, illus. Pecos Bill. 2006. (On My Own Folklore Ser.). 48p. (J). (gr. -1-3). lib. bdg. 25.26 *(978-1-57505-889-4(8),* Millbrook Pr.) Lerner Publishing Group.
Webb, Lois. Tall Tales. 2007. (J). per. *(978-0-9791550-4-8(5))* About Time Publishing.
Weidt, Maryann. Mama Loved to Worry. Balsaitis, Rachael, illus. 2016. (ENG.). 32p. (J). (gr. -1-1). 16.95 *(978-0-87351-994-6(9))* Minnesota Historical Society Pr.
Welling, Peter J. Darlene Halloween & the Great Chicago Fire, 1 vol. Welling, Peter J., illus. 2007. (ENG., Illus.). 32p. (J). (gr. k-3). 16.99 *(978-1-58980-479-1(1))* Pelican Publishing Co., Inc.
Willey, Margaret. Clever Beatrice & the Best Little Pony. Solomon, Heather M., illus. 2004. (ENG.). 40p. (J). (gr. -1-3). 18.99 *(978-0-689-85339-5(4),* Atheneum Bks. for Young Readers) Simon & Schuster Children's Publishing.
Willey, Margaret, et al. Clever Beatrice. Solomon, Heather M., illus. 2003. (Avenues Ser.). (ENG.). 40p. (C). (gr. -1-3). pap. 24.95 *(978-0-689-83254-3(0))* National Geographic School Publishing, Inc.
Wood, Audrey. Bunyans. 2014. 17.00 *(978-1-63419-650-5(3))* Perfection Learning Corp.
Yeager, Anne H. American Tall Tales. 2017. (Text Connections Guided Close Reading Ser.). (J). (gr. 2). *(978-1-4900-1839-3(5))* Benchmark Education Co.

TALLCHIEF, MARIA, 1925-

Gourley, Catherine. Who Is Maria Tallchief? Taylor, Val Paul, illus. 2003. (Who Was... ? Ser.). 103p. 15.00 *(978-0-7569-1592-6(9))* Perfection Learning Corp.

TAMPA BAY RAYS (BASEBALL TEAM)

Bowker, Paul. Tampa Bay Rays, 1 vol. 2011. (Inside MLB Ser.). (ENG., Illus.). 48p. (YA). (gr. 3-6). lib. bdg. 32.79 *(978-1-61714-060-0(0))* ABDO Publishing Co.
Connery-Boyd, Peg. Tampa Bay Rays. 2016. (Hawk's Nest Activity Bks.: 0). (ENG.). 64p. (J). (gr. k-3). pap., act. bk. ed. 8.99 *(978-1-4926-3375-4(5))* Sourcebooks, Inc.
Epstein, Brad. Tampa Bay Rays 101: My First Team-Board-book. 2008. (ENG., Illus.). 22p. (J). pap. *(978-1-932530-78-0(9),* 101 Bk.) Michaelson Entertainment.
Kennedy, Mike & Stewart, Mark. Meet the Rays. 2010. (Smart about Sports Ser.). 24p. (J). (gr. k-3). lib. bdg. 22.60 *(978-1-59953-374-2(X))* Norwood Hse. Pr.
LeBoutillier, Nate. The Story of the Tampa Bay Rays. 2011. (J). 35.65 *(978-1-60818-057-8(3),* Creative Education) Creative Co., The.
Shofner, Shawndra. The Story of the Tampa Bay Devil Rays. 2007. (Baseball, the Great American Game Ser.). (Illus.). 48p. (YA). (gr. 4-7). lib. bdg. 32.80 *(978-1-58341-501-6(7))* Creative Co., The.
Stewart, Mark. The Tampa Bay Rays. 2012. (Team Spirit Ser.). 48p. (J). (gr. 3-6). lib. bdg. 29.27 *(978-1-59953-498-5(3))* Norwood Hse. Pr.

TANGANYIKA—FICTION

MacLachlan, Patricia. Lala Salama: A Tanzanian Lullaby. Zunon, Elizabeth, illus. 2011. (ENG.). 32p. (J). (gr. -1-2). 16.99 *(978-0-7636-4747-6(0))* Candlewick Pr.

TANKS (MILITARY SCIENCE)

Adams, Simon. Tanks. 2009. (War Machines Ser.). (YA). (gr. 5-9). 28.50 *(978-1-59920-224-2(7))* Black Rabbit Bks.
Alvarez, Carlos. M109A6 Paladins. 2009. (Military Machines Ser.). (ENG., Illus.). 24p. (J). (gr. 3-7). lib. bdg. 25.95 *(978-1-60014-283-3(4))* Bellwether Media.
Bodden, Valerie. Built for Battle: Tanks. 2012. (Built for Battle Ser.). (ENG., Illus.). 24p. (J). (gr. 1-3). pap. 7.99 *(978-0-89812-704-1(1),* Creative Paperbacks) Creative Co., The.
—Tanks. 2012. (Illus.). 23p. (J). 25.65 *(978-1-60818-129-2(4),* Creative Education) Creative Co., The.
Brook, Henry. Tanks. 2011. (Discovery Adventures Ser.). 80p. (J). pap. 8.99 *(978-0-7945-2137-0(1),* Usborne) EDC Publishing.
Challen, Paul C. Mighty Tanks. 2010. (Vehicles on the Move Ser.). (ENG.). 32p. (J). (gr. k-3). pap. *(978-0-7787-3063-7(8));* lib. bdg. *(978-0-7787-3049-1(2))* Crabtree Publishing Co.

Colson, Rob Scott. Tanks & Military Vehicles. 2013. (Ultimate Machines Ser.). (ENG., Illus.). 24p. (J). (gr. 3-6). pap. 8.25 *(978-1-4777-0119-5(2))*; lib. bdg. 22.60 *(978-1-4777-0067-9(6))* Rosen Publishing Group, Inc., The. (PowerKids Pr.).

Cooke, Tim. Tanks. 2012. (Ultimate Military Machines Ser.). (Illus.). 32p. (gr. 4-7). lib. bdg. 31.35 *(978-1-59920-823-7(7))* Black Rabbit Bks.

Cornish, Geoff. Tanks. 2003. (Military Hardware in Action Ser.). (ENG., Illus.). 48p. (gr. 5-9). lib. bdg. 25.26 *(978-0-8225-4701-3(5))* Lerner Publishing Group.

David, Jack. Abrams Tanks. 2007. (Military Machines Ser.). (ENG., Illus.). 24p. (J). (gr. 3-7). lib. bdg. 25.95 *(978-1-60014-101-0(3))* Bellwether Media.

David West. Tank. 2006. (Illus.). 32p. (J). pap. *(978-1-4109-2566-4(8))* Steck-Vaughn.

Dougherty, Martin J. Tanks of World War II up Close, 01 vols., 1. Pearson, Colin, illus. 2016. (Military Technology: Top Secret Clearance Ser.). (ENG.). 224p. (YA). 43.60 *(978-1-5081-7086-0(X)*, Rosen Young Adult) Rosen Publishing Group, Inc., The.

Ellis, Catherine. Tanks. 2007. (Mega Military Machines Ser.). (Illus.). 24p. (J). (gr. 3-7). lib. bdg. 21.25 *(978-1-4042-3664-6(3))* Rosen Publishing Group, Inc., The.

—Tanks/Tanques. 2009. (Mega Military Machines/Megamaquinas militares Ser.). (ENG & SPA.). 24p. (gr. 1-1). 42.50 *(978-1-61514-644-4(X)*, Editorial Buenas Letras) Rosen Publishing Group, Inc., The.

—Tanks/Tanques. Brusca, Maria Cristina, tr. from ENG. 2007. (Mega Military Machines / Megamaquinas Militares Ser.). (SPA., Illus.). 24p. (J). lib. bdg. 22.60 *(978-1-4042-7619-2(X)*, PowerKids Pr.) Rosen Publishing Group, Inc., The.

Finn, Denny Von. Abrams Tanks. 2012. (Military Vehicles Ser.). (ENG., Illus.). 24p. (J). (gr. 3-7). lib. bdg. 25.95 *(978-1-60014-814-9(X)*, Epic Bks.) Bellwether Media.

Hamilton, John. Abrams Tanks. 2011. (Military Vehicles Ser.). (Illus.). 32p. (YA). (gr. 4-7). 27.07 *(978-1-61783-073-0(9))* ABDO Publishing Co.

—Bradley Fighting Vehicles. 2011. (Military Vehicles Ser.). (Illus.). 32p. (YA). (gr. 4-7). 27.07 *(978-1-61783-074-7(7))* ABDO Publishing Co.

Harvey, Ian & Chasemore, Richard. Tanks. (Illus.). 32p. (J). mass mkt. 8.99 *(978-0-590-24940-9(1))* Scholastic, Inc.

Haskew, Michael E. Tanks: Inside & Out. 2011. (Weapons of War Ser.). (ENG.). 160p. (YA). (gr. 9-12). lib. bdg. 42.60 *(978-1-4488-5980-1(8))* Rosen Publishing Group, Inc., The.

—The World's Most Powerful Tanks. 2016. (World's Most Powerful Machines Ser.). 00224p. (J). (gr. 9-9). 45.10 *(978-1-4994-6558-7(0))* Rosen Publishing Group, Inc., The.

Jackson, Kay. Military Tanks in Action. 2009. (Amazing Military Vehicles Ser.). 24p. (gr. 3-5). (Illus.). (J). pap. 8.25 *(978-1-4358-3159-9(4)*, PowerKids Pr.); 42.50 *(978-1-61511-318-7(5)*, PowerKids Pr.); (YA). lib. bdg. 22.60 *(978-1-4358-2749-3(X))* Rosen Publishing Group, Inc., The.

Jackson, Robert. 101 Great Tanks. 2010. (101 Greatest Weapons of All Times Ser.). (Illus.). 112p. (YA). (gr. 9-12). lib. bdg. 34.60 *(978-1-4358-3595-5(6))* Rosen Publishing Group, Inc., The.

Kiland, Taylor Baldwin & Souter, Gerry. Armored Tanks: Battlefield Dominance. 2015. (Military Engineering in Action Ser.). (ENG., Illus.). 48p. (J). (gr. 6-6). 27.93 *(978-0-7660-6908-4(7))*; pap. 11.70 *(978-0-7660-7059-2(X))* Enslow Pubs., Inc.

LaFontaine, Bruce. Tanks & Armored Vehicles. 2013. (Dover History Coloring Book Ser.). (ENG., Illus.). 48p. (J). (gr. 3-8). pap. 4.99 *(978-0-486-41317-4(9))* Dover Pubns., Inc.

Mavrikis, Peter. Tanks. 2014. (Illus.). 48p. (J). *(978-1-4351-5365-3(0))* Barnes & Noble, Inc.

—Tanks, 01 vols., 1. 2016. (What's Inside? Ser.). (ENG.). 48p. (J). pap. 11.75 *(978-1-5081-4619-3(5)*, PowerKids Pr.) Rosen Publishing Group, Inc., The.

Morey, Allan. Tanks. 2014. (Illus.). 24p. (J). lib. bdg. 25.65 *(978-1-62031-106-6(2)*, Bullfrog Bks.) Jump! Inc.

Murray, Laura K. Tanks. 2016. (Seedlings Ser.). (Illus.). 24p. (J). (gr. k-2). (ENG.). pap. 7.99 *(978-1-62832-250-7(0))*; 28.50 *(978-1-60818-665-5(2))* Creative Co., The. (Creative Education).

Murrell, Deborah Jane. Knights & Armor. 2008. (Medieval Warfare Ser.). 32p. (gr. 5-8). (J). lib. bdg. 26.00 *(978-0-8368-9210-9(0)*, Gareth Stevens Secondary Library); pap. 10.50 *(978-0-8368-9337-3(9))* Stevens, Gareth Publishing LLLP.

Nagelhout, Ryan. Tanks. 2015. (Mighty Military Machines Ser.). (ENG.). 32p. (J). (gr. 1-1). pap. 10.50 *(978-1-4824-2126-2(7))* Stevens, Gareth Publishing LLLP.

Sautter, Aaron. How to Draw Indestructible Tanks, 1 vol. Whigham, Rod, illus. 2008. (Drawing Cool Stuff Ser.). (ENG.). 32p. (gr. 3-4). 27.99 *(978-1-4296-1301-9(7)*, Edge Bks.) Capstone Press of Coughlan Cos.

Silverman, Buffy. How Do Tanks Work? 2016. (Lightning Bolt Books (tm) — How Vehicles Work Ser.). (ENG., Illus.). 32p. (J). (gr. 1-3). lib. bdg. 26.65 *(978-1-4677-9502-9(X))* Lerner Publishing Group.

Souter, Gerry. Battle Tanks: Power in the Field. 2006. (Mighty Military Machines Ser.). (Illus.). 48p. (J). (gr. 4-10). 25.27 *(978-0-7660-2658-2(2))* Enslow Pubs., Inc.

Tanks. 2003. (Illus.). 32p. (YA). pap. *(978-1-904516-34-7(3)*, Pavilion Children's Books) Pavilion Bks.

West, David. Tanks. West, David, illus. 2017. (What's Inside? Ser.). (Illus.). 24p. (gr. k-3). 28.50 ***(978-1-62588-406-0(0)***, Smart Apple Media) Black Rabbit Bks.

—Tanks. 2015. (Mechanic Mike's Machines (continuation) Ser.). (Illus.). 24p. (J). (gr. k-3). 27.10 *(978-1-62588-069-7(3))* Black Rabbit Bks.

West, David, illus. Tanks. 2017. (What's Inside? Ser.). 24p. (gr. k-3). lib. bdg. 28.50 *(978-1-62588-402-2(8))* Black Rabbit Bks.

Zuehlke, Jeffrey. Tanks. 2005. (Pull Ahead Books-Mighty Movers Ser.). (ENG., Illus.). 32p. (gr. k-3). lib. bdg. 22.60 *(978-0-8225-2865-4(7)*, Lerner Pubns.) Lerner Publishing Group.

TANZANIA

Here are entered works on the jurisdiction of Tanzania formed in 1964 by the merger of Tanganyika and Zanzibar for all periods and subjects. Works on the island of Zanzibar for all periods are entered under Zanzibar. Works limited in subject coverage to the historical, political or cultural aspects of Tanganyika for the period before the merger in 1964 are entered under Tanganyika. Works on other subjects relating to Tanganyika for any pre-merger period are entered under the name of the present jurisdiction, Tanzania.

Cavallo, Anna. Tanzania. 2011. (Country Explorers Ser.). 48p. pap. 51.02 *(978-0-7613-7627-9(5))*; (ENG.). (gr. 2-4). pap. 9.95 *(978-0-7613-7084-0(6))*; (ENG.). (gr. 2-4). lib. bdg. 29.27 *(978-0-7613-6411-5(0))* Lerner Publishing Group.

Doak, Robin S. Jane Goodall: Chimpanzee Protector, 1 vol. 2014. (Women in Conservation Ser.). (ENG., Illus.). 48p. (gr. 3-6). 33.32 *(978-1-4846-0469-4(5))*; pap. 8.99 *(978-1-4846-0474-8(1))* Heinemann-Raintree. (Heinemann InfoSearch).

Edwards, Roberta. Who Is Jane Goodall? 2012. (Who Is... ? Ser.). lib. bdg. 16.00 *(978-0-606-26651-2(8)*, Turtleback) Turtleback Bks.

Ferguson, Amanda. The Attack Against the U. S. Embassies in Kenya & Tanzania. (Terrorist Attacks Ser.). 64p. 2009. (gr. 5-5). 58.50 *(978-1-60853-309-1(3))* 2005. (Illus.). (J). (gr. 7-12). lib. bdg. 31.95 *(978-0-8239-3652-6(X))* Rosen Publishing Group, Inc., The.

Guidi, Victoria. Who on Earth Is Jane Goodall? Champion for the Chimpanzees. 2009. (Scientists Saving the Earth Ser.). (Illus.). 112p. (J). (gr. 5-9). lib. bdg. 33.27 *(978-1-59845-119-1(7))* Enslow Pubs., Inc.

Hand, Carol. Jane Goodall. 2014. (Great Science Writers Ser.). (Illus.). 112p. (J). (gr. 7-12). 35.60 *(978-1-4777-7685-8(0))* Rosen Publishing Group, Inc., The.

Heale, Jay & Wong, Winnie. Tanzania. 2nd rev. ed. 2008. (Cultures of the World Ser.). 144p. (gr. 6-18). lib. bdg. 42.79 *(978-0-7614-3417-7(8)*, Benchmark Bks.) Marshall Cavendish Corp.

Krebs, Laurie. We All Went on Safari: A Counting Journey Through Tanzania. Cairns, Julia, illus. 2003. (ENG & SWA.). 32p. (J). (gr. k-3). 16.99 *(978-1-84148-478-5(4))* Barefoot Bks., Inc.

Leathers, Dan. The Snows of Kilimanjaro. 2007. (On the Verge of Extinction Ser.). (Illus.). 32p. (YA). (gr. 2-5). lib. bdg. 25.70 *(978-1-58415-584-3(1))* Mitchell Lane Pubs., Inc.

MacDonald, Joan Vos. Tanzania. Rotberg, Robert I., ed. 2012. (Evolution of Africa's Major Nations Ser.). (Illus.). 88p. (J). (gr. 7). 22.95 *(978-1-4222-2186-0(5))* Mason Crest.

—Tanzania. 2011. (J). pap. *(978-1-4222-2214-0(4))* 2006. (Illus.). 85p. (YA). lib. bdg. 21.95 *(978-1-59084-813-5(6))* Mason Crest.

Mailu, David G. Julius Nyerere: Father of Ujamaa. 2005. (Lion Book Ser.). (Illus.). ix, 81p. (J). *(978-9966-951-32-8(6))* Sasa Sema Publications Ltd.

Oachs, Emily Rose. Tanzania. 2016. (Exploring Countries Ser.). (ENG., Illus.). 32p. (J). (gr. 3-7). 26.95 *(978-1-62617-405-4(9)*, Blastoff! Readers) Bellwether Media.

Pritchett, Bev. Tanzania in Pictures. 2nd ed. 2008. (Visual Geography (Lerner) Ser.). (Illus.). 80p. (YA). (gr. 7-12). lib. bdg. 30.60 *(978-0-8225-8571-8(5))* Twenty First Century Bks.

Pugliano-Martin, Carol. Cats of the Serengeti. 2011. (Early Connections Ser.). (J). *(978-1-61672-575-4(3))* Benchmark Education Co.

Wakabi, Wairagala. Tanzania. 2004. (Countries of the World Ser.). (Illus.). 96p. (gr. 5-12). lib. bdg. 31.00 *(978-0-8368-3119-1(5))* Stevens, Gareth Publishing LLLP.

Watson, Galadriel Findlay. Mount Kilimanjaro. (J). 2013. 28.55 *(978-1-62127-476-6(4))* 2013. pap. 13.95 *(978-1-62127-482-7(9))* 2008. (Illus.). 32p. (gr. 5-6). pap. 9.95 *(978-1-59036-935-7(1))* 2008. (Illus.). 32p. (gr. 5-6). lib. bdg. 26.00 *(978-1-59036-934-0(3))* Weigl Pubs., Inc.

Weil, Ann. Meet Our New Student from Tanzania. 2008. (Meet Our New Student Ser.). 48p. (YA). (gr. 2-5). lib. bdg. 29.95 *(978-1-58415-656-7(2))* Mitchell Lane Pubs., Inc.

Williams, Megan K. Maddy's Amazing African Birthday, 1 vol. Vallecchi, Alessandro et al, photos by. 2009. (ENG., Illus.). 32p. (J). (gr. 1-4). 12.95 *(978-1-897187-47-0(5))* Second Story Pr. CAN. Dist: Orca Bk. Pubs. USA.

Winter, Jeanette. The Watcher: Jane Goodall's Life with the Chimps. Winter, Jeanette, illus. 2011. (ENG., Illus.). 48p. (J). (gr. -1-3). 17.99 *(978-0-375-86774-3(0))*, Schwartz & Wade Bks.) Random Hse. Children's Bks.

TANZANIA—FICTION

Archambault, John. By the Baobab Tree. Bender, Robert, illus. 2005. (J). *(978-1-58669-164-6(3))* Childcraft Education Corp.

Burgess, Lisa Maria. Juma & Little Sungura. Gugu, Abdul M., illus. 2013. 32p. 19.95 *(978-1-939604-06-4(0))*; pap. 9.99 *(978-1-939604-02-6(8))* Barranca Pr.

—Juma Cooks Chapati. Gugu, Abdul M., illus. 2013. 32p. 19.95 *(978-1-939604-08-8(7))*; pap. 9.99 *(978-1-939604-04-0(4))* Barranca Pr.

—Juma on Safari. Gugu, Abdul M., illus. 2013. 32p. 19.95 *(978-1-939604-07-1(9))*; pap. 9.99 *(978-1-939604-03-3(6))* Barranca Pr.

—Juma's Dhow Race. Gugu, Abdul M., illus. 2013. 32p. 19.95 *(978-1-939604-09-5(5))*; pap. 9.99 *(978-1-939604-05-7(2))* Barranca Pr.

Carlson, Martin D. Rfaud Tastes Wisdom. Oketch, Alphonce Omondi, illus. 2013. 36p. pap. 11.00 *(978-0-9848791-2-0(9))* BoCook Publishing.

Krebs, Laurie. We All Went on Safari: A Counting Journey Through Tanzania. Cairns, Julia, illus. 2010. (J). 18.10 *(978-0-7569-9319-1(9))* Perfection Learning Corp.

Krebs, Laurie & Cairns, Julia. We All Went on Safari: A Counting Journey Through Tanzania. Cairns, Julia, illus. 2004. (ENG., Illus.). 32p. (J). (gr. k-5). 8.99 *(978-1-84148-119-7(X))* Barefoot Bks., Inc.

Krulik, Nancy. Magic Bone: Two Tales, One Dog. Braun, Sebastien, illus. 2016. (Magic Bone Ser.: 12). (ENG.). 192p. (J). (gr. 1-3). 6.99 *(978-0-448-48877-6(9)*, Grosset & Dunlap) Penguin Young Readers Group.

MacLachlan, Patricia. Lala Salama: A Tanzanian Lullaby. Zunon, Elizabeth, illus. 2011. (ENG.). 32p. (J). (gr. -1-2). 16.99 *(978-0-7636-4747-6(0))* Candlewick Pr.

Matthews, T. J. The Canoeing Safari. Rheburg, Judy, illus. 2004. (J). *(978-0-938978-35-0(7))* Wycliffe Bible Translators.

—The Village Safari. Rheburg, Judy, illus. 2005. (J). *(978-0-938978-36-7(5))* Wycliffe Bible Translators.

Meyrick, Rich. Jaspa's Journey 2: The Pride of London. 2016. (ENG., Illus.). (J). (gr. 4-6). pap. 15.95 ***(978-1-62815-315-6(6))*** Speaking Volumes, LLC.

Milway, Katie Smith. The Banana-Leaf Ball: How Play Can Change the World. Evans, Shane W., illus. 2017. (CitizenKid Ser.). (ENG.). 32p. (J). (gr. 3-7). 18.95 *(978-1-77138-331-8(3))* Kids Can Pr., Ltd. CAN. Dist: Hachette Bk. Group.

Mwamgwirani, Juma Mwakimatu & Mwakimatu, Juma Mwamgwirani. The Choice. 2015. (ENG., Illus.). 148p. (J). pap. *(978-9987-08-162-2(2))* Mkuki na Nyota Pubs.

Newman, Gwill York. Bingo Bear Was Here: A Toy Bear's Climb to the Top of Africa's Highest Mountain. Babcock, Jeff, illus. 2003. 48p. (J). pap. 8.95 *(978-0-86534-395-5(0))* Sunstone Pr.

Pennels, Geraldine M. The School Shenanigans of Amy & Nontand: Volume Two Fifth Grade. 2010. 144p. pap. 11.50 *(978-1-60911-848-8(0)*, Eloquent Bks.) Strategic Book Publishing & Rights Agency (SBPRA).

Popescu, Petru. Footprints in Time. 2008. 256p. (J). (gr. 5). lib. bdg. 17.89 *(978-0-06-088400-0(2)*, Geringer, Laura Book) HarperCollins Pubs.

Quirk, Katie. A Girl Called Problem. 2013. (ENG., Illus.). 256p. (J). pap. 8.50 *(978-0-8028-5404-9(4)*, Eerdmans Bks For Young Readers) Eerdmans, William B. Publishing Co.

Robinson, Sharon. Under the Same Sun. Ford, A. G., illus. 2014. (ENG.). 40p. (J). (gr. -1-3). 17.99 *(978-0-545-16672-0(1)*, Scholastic Pr.) Scholastic, Inc.

Schwalbach, Pamela. The Happiest Day for Simeon & Sula. 2011. 28p. (gr. 4-6). pap. 15.00 *(978-1-4567-5062-6(3))* AuthorHouse.

Serengeti Safari: Animal Adventures in Africa. 2010. 64p. pap. 6.00 *(978-81-7806-191-7(0))* Unicorn Bks. Pvt Ltd. IND. Dist: Mahal, Pustak Pubs., Booksellers & Order Suppliers.

Smith, Anne & Smith, Owen. Safari Survivor. Rayas, Rubén, illus. 2012. (Twisted Journeys (r) Ser.: 21). (ENG.). 112p. (J). (gr. 4-7). pap. 7.95 *(978-1-57505-943-3(6)*, Graphic Universe™) Lerner Publishing Group.

Smith, Owen & Smith, Anne. Safari Survivor. Rubine, illus. 2012. (Twisted Journeys (r) Ser.: 21). (ENG.). 112p. (J). (gr. 4-7). lib. bdg. 27.93 *(978-0-7613-6727-7(6)*, Graphic Universe™) Lerner Publishing Group.

Stuve-Bodeen, Stephanie. Babu's Song. Boyd, Aaron, illus. 2003. (ENG.). 32p. (J). 16.95 *(978-1-58430-058-8(2))* Lee & Low Bks., Inc.

—La Escuela de Elizabeti. Sarfatti, Esther, tr. from ENG. Hale, Christy, illus. 2007. (SPA.). 32p. (J). (gr. -1-2). pap. 9.95 *(978-1-60060-235-1(5))* Lee & Low Bks., Inc.

—La Muneca de Elizabeti. Sarfatti, Esther, tr. Hale, Christy, illus. braille ed. 2004. (SPA.). (J). (gr. k-3). spiral bd. *(978-0-616-08966-8(X))* Canadian National Institute for the Blind/Institut National Canadien pour les Aveugles.

Stuve-Bodeen, Stephanie & Hale, Christy. Elizabeti's Doll. 2009. (ENG., Illus.). 34p. (J). (gr. -1-3). 16.95 *(978-1-880000-70-0(9))* Lee & Low Bks., Inc.

Sullivan, Tara. Golden Boy. (ENG.). 384p. (J). (gr. 5). 2014. pap. 8.99 *(978-0-14-242450-6(1)*, Puffin Books) 2013. 16.99 *(978-0-399-16112-4(0)*, G.P. Putnam's Sons Books for Young Readers) Penguin Young Readers Group.

Weston Woods Staff, creator. Elizabeti's Doll. 2011. 18.95 *(978-0-439-73629-9(3))*; 38.75 *(978-0-439-84574-8(2))* Weston Woods Studios, Inc.

White, Paul. Jungle Doctor & the Whirlwind. 2015. (Flamingo Fiction 9-13s Ser.). (ENG., Illus.). 176p. (J). (gr. 5-7). pap. 8.99 *(978-1-84550-296-6(5)*, 635eeceb-43fd-433d-9826-6b2bf5273d01) Christian Focus Pubns. GBR. Dist: Bookmasters Distribution.

—Jungle Doctor in Slippery Places. 2011. (Flamingo Fiction 9-13s Ser.). (ENG., Illus.). 160p. (J). (gr. 4-7). pap. 8.99 *(978-1-84550-298-0(1)*, ad8bbad9-6595-4aeb-8o4f-f089b189b088) Christian Focus Pubns. GBR. Dist: Bookmasters Distribution.

—Jungle Doctor Looks for Trouble. 2009. (Flamingo Fiction 9-13s Ser.). (ENG., Illus.). 160p. (J). pap. 8.99 *(978-1-84550-499-1(2)*, 9302ad19-8b28-4030-be88-ef9afc9f3a6c) Christian Focus Pubns. GBR. Dist: Bookmasters Distribution.

—Jungle Doctor Meets a Lion. 2011. (Flamingo Fiction 9-13s Ser.). (ENG., Illus.). 176p. (J). 8.99 *(978-1-84550-392-5(9)*, 9781845503925) Christian Focus Pubns. GBR. Dist: Bookmasters Distribution.

—Jungle Doctor on the Hop. 2015. (Flamingo Fiction 9-13s Ser.). (ENG., Illus.). 160p. (J). (gr. 4-7). per. 8.99 *(978-1-84550-297-3(3)*, 941c8ee3-121e-4dda-84ae-b6809a4d4b39) Christian Focus Pubns. GBR. Dist: Bookmasters Distribution.

—Jungle Doctor Operates. 2009. (Flamingo Fiction 9-13s Ser.). (ENG., Illus.). 160p. (J). pap. 8.99 *(978-1-84550-500-4(X)*, 5b5acc8e-b6fe-4477-b9ac-b1a8ea9426ea) Christian Focus Pubns. GBR. Dist: Bookmasters Distribution.

—Jungle Doctor Pulls a Leg. 2008. (Flamingo Fiction 9-13s Ser.). (ENG., Illus.). 176p. (J). 8.99 *(978-1-84550-389-5(9)*, f2e81c42-c4a7-4d63-91eb-64573f61d40a) Christian Focus Pubns. GBR. Dist: Bookmasters Distribution.

—Jungle Doctor Spots a Leopard. 2008. (Flamingo Fiction 9-13s Ser.). (ENG., Illus.). 176p. (J). (gr. 5-7). per. 8.99 *(978-1-84550-301-7(5)*, 6c36bf51-d79e-4a21-bb4f-54dc3b30085b) Christian Focus Pubns. GBR. Dist: Bookmasters Distribution.

—Jungle Doctor Stings a Scorpion. 2008. (Flamingo Fiction 9-13s Ser.). (ENG., Illus.). 160p. (J). 8.99 *(978-1-84550-390-1(2)*, 21dc615c-019a-4cfe-b2da-d2c676461510) Christian Focus Pubns. GBR. Dist: Bookmasters Distribution.

—Jungle Doctor to the Rescue. 2009. (Flamingo Fiction 9-13s Ser.). (ENG., Illus.). 176p. (J). pap. 8.99 *(978-1-84550-516-5(6)*, 052662e3-f01a-4a40-9e4d-88634018ee06) Christian Focus Pubns. GBR. Dist: Bookmasters Distribution.

—Jungle Doctor's Crooked Dealings. 2011. (Flamingo Fiction 9-13s Ser.). (ENG., Illus.). 144p. (J). (gr. 5-7). pap. 8.99 *(978-1-84550-299-7(X)*, 9b21af6e-da89-4bc5-b0d9-5ce6419b0795) Christian Focus Pubns. GBR. Dist: Bookmasters Distribution.

—Jungle Doctor's Enemies. 2011. (Flamingo Fiction 9-13s Ser.). (ENG., Illus.). 160p. (J). (gr. 5-7). pap. 8.99 *(978-1-84550-300-0(7)*, c2552503-49be-450c-84cc-9ec522751da8) Christian Focus Pubns. GBR. Dist: Bookmasters Distribution.

TAOISM

McGinnis, Mark W. The Show-Off Monkey & Other Taoist Tales. 2017. (ENG.). 88p. (gr. k-4). 19.95 ***(978-1-61180-347-1(0))*** Shambhala Pubns., Inc.

White, Bender Richardson. Daoism. 3rd ed. 2009. (World Religions Ser.). (Illus.). 144p. (J). (gr. 6-12). 40.00 *(978-1-60413-115-4(2)*, Chelsea Hse.) Facts On File, Inc.

TAPESTRY

Burnett, Allan. The Story of Scotland: Inspired by the Great Tapestry of Scotland. 2015. (ENG., Illus.). 128p. (J). (gr. 4-7). pap. *(978-1-78027-241-2(3))* Birlinn, Ltd.

Noble, Marty. Medieval Tapestries Coloring Book. 2004. (Dover Fashion Coloring Book Ser.). (ENG., Illus.). 32p. (gr. 6-8). pap. 3.99 *(978-0-486-43686-9(1))* Dover Pubns., Inc.

TAPESTRY—FICTION

Guibord, Maurissa. Warped. 2012. (ENG.). 348p. (YA). (gr. 7). pap. 9.99 *(978-0-385-73892-7(7)*, Ember) Random Hse. Children's Bks.

Hinrichs, Alexandra S. D. Therese Makes a Tapestry. Graef, Renee, illus. 2016. (ENG.). 40p. (J). 19.95 *(978-1-60606-473-3(8)*, J. Paul Getty Museum) Getty Pubns.

Oberon, Daphne. The Ghost Tree: Tonantzin's Blessing. 2009. 50p. pap. 23.95 *(978-1-4327-3153-3(X))* Outskirts Pr., Inc.

Perkins, T. J. Image in the Tapestry: A Kim & Kelly Mystery. 2005. (Illus.). 155p. (YA). 10.99 *(978-0-9777538-3-3(2))* GumShoe Press.

Polacco, Patricia. Christmas Tapestry. 2008. (ENG.). 48p. (J). (gr. 1-4). pap. 7.99 *(978-0-14-241165-0(5)*, Puffin Books) Penguin Young Readers Group.

TARBELL, IDA M. (IDA MINERVA), 1857-1944

McCully, Emily Arnold. Ida M. Tarbell: The Woman Who Challenged Big Business-and Won! 2014. (ENG., Illus.). 288p. (YA). (gr. 7). 18.99 *(978-0-547-29092-8(6)*, Clarion Bks.) Houghton Mifflin Harcourt Trade & Reference Pubs.

Somervill, Barbara A. Ida Tarbell: Pioneer Investigative Reporter. 2004. (World Writers Ser.). (Illus.). 112p. (YA). (gr. 6-12). 23.95 *(978-1-883846-87-9(0)*, First Biographies) Reynolds, Morgan Inc.

TARZAN (FICTITIOUS CHARACTER)—FICTION

Briggs, Andy. The Jungle Warrior. 2012. (Tarzan Ser.). (ENG.). 206p. (J). (gr. 3-6). pap. 12.99 *(978-1-4532-7108-7(2)*, Open Road Media E-riginal) Open Road Integrated Media, Inc.

—The Savage Lands. 2013. (Tarzan Ser.). (ENG.). 212p. (J). (gr. 3-6). pap. 12.99 *(978-1-4804-0014-6(9)*, Open Road Media E-riginal) Open Road Integrated Media, Inc.

—Tarzan: The Greystoke Legacy. 2011. (ENG.). 304p. pap. *(978-0-571-27238-9(X))* Faber & Faber, Ltd.

Burroughs, Edgar Rice. The Tarzan Twins. Grant, Douglas, illus. 2011. 126p. 40.95 *(978-1-258-05126-6(5))* Literary Licensing, LLC.

San Souci, Robert D. & Burroughs, Edgar Rice. Tarzan. McCurdy, Michael, illus. 2004. 31p. (J). (gr. k-4). reprint ed. 16.00 *(978-0-7567-7576-6(0))* DIANE Publishing Co.

TASMANIA

Markle, Sandra. Tasmanian Devils. 2006. (Animal Scavengers Ser.). (Illus.). 39p. (J). (gr. 3-7). pap. 7.95 *(978-0-8225-3470-9(3)*, First Avenue Editions) Lerner Publishing Group.

TASMANIA—FICTION

Johnson, Gillian. Thora & the Incredible Crystals. 2007. (Illus.). 272p. *(978-0-207-20017-5(3))* HarperCollins Pubs. Australia.

Jonsberg, Barry. Ironbark. 2010. (ENG.). 210p. (YA). (gr. 8-18). 13.99 *(978-1-74114-955-5(X))* Allen & Unwin AUS. Dist: Independent Pubs. Group.

Nowra, Louis. Into That Forest, 0 vols. 2013. (ENG.). 160p. (YA). (gr. 7-9). 16.99 *(978-1-4778-1725-4(5)*, 9781477817254, Amazon Children's Publishing); 162p. 16.99 *(978-1-4778-6725-9(2))* Amazon Publishing.

Parker, Richard. Voyage to Tasmani. Seward, Prudence, illus. 2011. 128p. 40.95 *(978-1-258-08572-8(0))* Literary Licensing, LLC.

Roy, James. Billy Mack's War. 2004. 245p. (J). pap. *(978-0-7022-3479-8(6))* Univ. of Queensland Pr.

Russon, Penni. Breathe. 2007. (ENG., Illus.). 368p. (YA). (gr. 9-18). 16.99 *(978-0-06-079393-7(7))* HarperCollins Pubs.

TAVERNS (INNS)

see also Hotels, Motels, etc.; Restaurants

The Life of a Colonial Innkeeper. 2013. (Jr. Graphic Colonial America Ser.). 24p. (J). (gr. 3-6). pap. 63.60 *(978-1-4777-1436-2(7)*, PowerKids Pr.) Rosen Publishing Group, Inc., The.

Pelleschi, Andrea. The Life of a Colonial Innkeeper. 2013. (Jr. Graphic Colonial America Ser.). 24p. (J). (gr. 3-6). 25.25 *(978-1-4777-1309-9(3))*; pap. 10.60 *(978-1-4777-1435-5(9))* Rosen Publishing Group, Inc., The. (PowerKids Pr.).

TAXATION

Crayton, Lisa A. & La Bella, Laura. Taxes: What They Are & How They Work. 2016. (Economics in the 21st Century Ser.). (ENG.). 96p. (J). (gr. 8-8). 34.60 *(978-0-7660-7376-0(9))* Enslow Pubs., Inc.

Engdahl, Sylvia. Taxation. 2010. (Issues on Trial Ser.). (ENG.). 240p. (gr. 10-12). 48.30 *(978-0-7377-4492-7(8)*, Greenhaven Pr., Inc.) Cengage Gale.

Gagne, Tammy. Teen Guide to Earning Income. 2014. (ENG., Illus.). 48p. (gr. 4-6). lib. bdg. 29.95 *(978-1-61228-470-5(1))* Mitchell Lane Pubs., Inc.

Harmon, Julian. My Dad Pays Taxes. 2013. (InfoMax Readers Ser.). (ENG.). 24p. (J). (gr. 2-3). pap. 49.50 *(978-1-4777-2442-2(7))*; (Illus.). pap. 8.25 *(978-1-4777-2440-8(0))* Rosen Publishing Group, Inc., The. (Rosen Classroom).

Hiber, Amanda. Do Tax Breaks Benefit the Economy? 2009. (At Issue Ser.). (ENG.). 128p. (gr. 10-12). 39.40 *(978-0-7377-4298-5(4)*, Greenhaven Pr., Inc.) Cengage Gale.

—What Is the Future of the U. S. Economy? 2009. (At Issue Ser.). (ENG.). 128p. (gr. 10-12). pap. 27.80

T U V

(978-0-7377-4297-8(6), Greenhaven Pr., Inc.) Cengage Gale.

Lankford, Ronald D. Should the Rich Pay Higher Taxes? Greenhaven Press Editors & Gale Editors, eds. 2014. (At Issue Ser.). (ENG.). 128p. (gr. 10-12). pap. 27.80 *(978-0-7377-6859-6(2),* Greenhaven Pr., Inc.) Cengage Gale.

—Should the Rich Pay Higher Taxes? Greenhaven Press Editors, ed. 2014. (At Issue Ser.). (ENG.). 128p. (gr. 10-12). lib. bdg. 39.40 *(978-0-7377-6858-9(4),* Greenhaven Pr., Inc.) Cengage Gale.

TAXATION—UNITED STATES

Arbus, Abby. Why Do We Pay Taxes? 2013. (Rosen Readers Ser.). (ENG.). 24p. (J). (gr. 2-3). pap. 49.50 *(978-1-4777-2297-8(1));* pap. 8.25 *(978-1-4777-2296-1(3))* Rosen Publishing Group, Inc., The. (Rosen Classroom).

Barousse, Jason. The Internal Revenue Service: Why U. S. Citizens Pay Taxes. 2017. (Landmarks of Democracy: American Institutions Ser.). 24p. (J). (gr. 7-8). pap. 8.25 ***(978-1-5081-6139-4(9),*** PowerKids Pr.) Rosen Publishing Group, Inc., The.

Bedeksy, Baron & Bedesky, Baron. What Are Taxes? 2008. (ENG., Illus.). 32p. (J). (gr. 3-7). pap. *(978-0-7787-4262-3(8))* Crabtree Publishing Co.

De Capua, Sarah. Paying Taxes. 2012. (True Book(tm), A — Civics Ser.). (ENG.). 48p. (J). lib. bdg. 31.00 *(978-0-531-26040-1(2));* pap. 6.95 *(978-0-531-26212-2(X))* Scholastic Library Publishing.

Forest, Christopher. The Rebellious Colonists & the Causes of the American Revolution. 2012. (Story of the American Revolution Ser.). (ENG.). 32p. (gr. 3-4). pap. 47.70 *(978-1-4296-9291-5(X),* Fact Finders) Capstone Press of Coughlan Cos.

Fradin, Dennis Brindell. The Stamp Act of 1765. 2009. (Turning Points in U. S. History Ser.). (Illus.). 48p. (J). (gr. 3-18). 31.36 *(978-0-7614-4260-8(X))* Marshall Cavendish Corp.

Kowalski, Kathiann M. Taxes. 2005. (Open for Debate Ser.). (Illus.). 139p. (YA). (gr. 9-12). lib. bdg. *(978-0-7614-1887-0(3),* Benchmark Bks.) Marshall Cavendish Corp.

La Bella, Laura. How Taxation Works. 2010. (Real World Economics Ser.). (Illus.). 80p. (YA). (gr. 7-18). lib. bdg. 33.25 *(978-1-4358-9463-1(4))* Rosen Publishing Group, Inc., The.

Loewen, Nancy. Taxes, Taxes! Where the Money Goes. Fitzpatrick, Brad, illus. 2005. (Money Matters Ser.). (ENG.). 24p. (gr. 1-3). lib. bdg. 26.65 *(978-1-4048-1158-4(3))* Picture Window Bks.

Mapua, Jeff. Taxation: Interpreting the Constitution. 2014. (Understanding the United States Constitution Ser.). (Illus.). 112p. (J). (gr. 7-12). 35.60 *(978-1-4777-7504-2(8))* Rosen Publishing Group, Inc., The.

Mara, Wil. Taxes at Work. 2016. (21st Century Skills Library: a Citizen's Guide Ser.). (ENG., Illus.). 32p. (J). (gr. 4-7). 29.93 *(978-1-63471-067-1(3),* 208347) Cherry Lake Publishing.

Marsico, Katie. Understanding Taxes. 2015. (21st Century Skills Library: Real World Math Ser.). (ENG., Illus.). 32p. (J). (gr. 4-7). 29.93 *(978-1-63362-577-8(X),* 206492) Cherry Lake Publishing.

Merino, Noël. Tax Reform. 2011. (Opposing Viewpoints Ser.). (ENG.). 224p. (gr. 12-12). pap. 33.80 *(978-0-7377-5242-7(4));* lib. bdg. 48.80 *(978-0-7377-5241-0(6))* Cengage Gale. (Greenhaven Pr., Inc.).

Minden, Cecilia. Understanding Taxes. 2009. (21st Century Skills Library: Real World Math Ser.). (ENG.). 32p. (gr. 4-8). lib. bdg. 28.50 *(978-1-60279-311-8(5),* 200207) Cherry Lake Publishing.

Nichols, Clive & Bussing-Burks, Marie. Taxes & Government Spending. 2011. (J). pap. 12.95 *(978-1-4488-4725-9(7));* (YA). (gr. 5-9). lib. bdg. 31.95 *(978-1-4488-4714-3(1))* Rosen Publishing Group, Inc., The.

Roxburgh, Ellis. The Whiskey Rebellion. 2017. (Rebellions, Revolts, & Uprisings Ser.). 48p. (gr. 5-5). pap. 84.30 ***(978-1-5382-0757-4(5))*** Stevens, Gareth Publishing LLLP.

Steinberg, Lynnae D. What Are Taxes? 2015. (Let's Find Out! Government Ser.). (ENG.). 32p. (J). 23.45 *(978-1-62275-981-1(8),* Britannica Educational Publishing) Rosen Publishing Group, Inc., The.

TAXIDERMY

see also Zoological Specimens—Collection and Preservation

Little & Large Sticker Activity Baby Animals. 2008. 24p. pap. *(978-1-84810-055-8(8))* Miles Kelly Publishing, Ltd.

TAYLOR, SUSIE KING, 1848-1912

Dell, Pamela. Memoir of Susie King Taylor: A Civil War Nurse. 2017. (First-Person Histories Ser.). (ENG., Illus.). 32p. (gr. 3-4). lib. bdg. 27.32 *(978-1-5157-3354-6(8),* Fact Finders) Capstone Press of Coughlan Cos.

TAYLOR, ZACHARY, 1784-1850

Elston, Heidi M. D. Zachary Taylor. 1 vol. 2009. (United States Presidents Ser.). (ENG., Illus.). 40p. (YA). (gr. 3-6). 27.07 *(978-1-60453-475-7(3))* ABDO Publishing Co.

Kops, Deborah. Zachary Taylor: America's 12th President. 2004. (Encyclopedia of Presidents Ser.). (ENG., Illus.). 110p. (YA). (gr. 5-9). 34.00 *(978-0-516-23442-7(0))* Scholastic Library Publishing.

Otfinoski, Steven. Zachary Taylor. 2011. (Presidents & Their Times 5 Ser.). (Illus.). 96p. (J). (gr. 6). 34.21 *(978-1-60870-187-2(5))* Marshall Cavendish Corp.

Roberts, Jeremy. Zachary Taylor. 2005. (Presidential Leaders Ser.). (Illus.). 112p. (J). (gr. 3-7). lib. bdg. 29.27 *(978-0-8225-1397-1(8))* Lerner Publishing Group.

Schmidt, Roderic. How to Draw the Life & Times of Zachary Taylor. (Kid's Guide to Drawing the Presidents of the United States of America Ser.). 2009. 32p. (gr. 4-4). 50.50 *(978-1-61511-169-5(7),* PowerKids Pr.) 2006. (YA). (gr. 2-5). 26.50 *(978-1-4042-2989-1(2))* Rosen Publishing Group, Inc., The.

Venezia, Mike. Zachary Taylor: Twelfth President, 1849-1850. Venezia, Mike, illus. 2005. (Getting to Know the U. S. Presidents Ser.). (ENG., Illus.). 32p. (J). (gr. 3-4). 28.00 *(978-0-516-22617-0(7),* Children's Pr.) Scholastic Library Publishing.

TCHAIKOVSKY, PETER ILICH, 1840-1893

Orchid Publishing, prod. The Sleeping Beauty Ballet by Aleksandra. 2011. (ENG., Illus.). 36p. (J). 19.95 *(978-0-9831641-2-8(6))* Orchid Publishing, Inc.

Stéphane, Ollivier. PIOTR ILYCH TCHAIKOVSKI. 2010. (Descubrimos a Los Músicos Ser.). (SPA., Illus.). 24p. (J). (gr. 2-4). 15.95 *(978-84-9825-416-7(7))* Combel Editorial, S.A. ESP. Dist: Independent Pubs. Group.

TEA

Gleason, Carrie. The Biography of Tea. 2007. (How Did That Get Here? Ser.). (ENG., Illus.). 32p. (J). (gr. 3-7). lib. bdg. *(978-0-7787-2493-3(X));* (gr. 2-9). pap. *(978-0-7787-2529-9(4))* Crabtree Publishing Co.

Sato, Shozo. Tea Ceremony: Explore the Unique Japanese Tradition of Sharing Tea. 2004. (Asian Arts & Crafts for Creative Kids Ser.). (ENG., Illus.). 64p. (J). (gr. 2-6). 15.95 *(978-0-8048-3500-8(4))* Tuttle Publishing.

Woolf, Alex. The Story of Tea. 2016. (Story of Food Ser.). (ENG., Illus.). 32p. (J). (gr. 4-6). 16.99 *(978-0-7502-9661-8(5),* Wayland) Hachette Children's Group GBR. Dist: Hachette Bk. Group.

TEA ROOMS

see Restaurants

TEACH, EDWARD, -1718

Buckley, James. Who Was Blackbeard? 2015. (Who Was... ? Ser.). lib. bdg. 16.00 *(978-0-606-37556-6(2))* Turtleback Bks.

Buckley, James & dePaola, Tomie. Who Was Blackbeard? Harrison, Nancy & Qiu, Joseph J. M., illus. 2015. (Who Was? Ser.). (ENG.). 112p. (J). (gr. 3-7). 5.99 *(978-0-448-48308-5(4),* Grosset & Dunlap) Penguin Young Readers Group.

Cooke, Tim. Blackbeard: A Notorious Pirate in the Caribbean. 2016. (Wanted! Famous Outlaws Ser.). (ENG., Illus.). 48p. (J). (gr. 6-8). pap. 14.05 *(978-1-4824-4247-2(7))* Stevens, Gareth Publishing LLLP.

Hamilton, Sue L. Blackbeard. 1 vol. 2007. (Pirates! Ser.). (ENG., Illus.). 32p. (J). (gr. 4-8). 27.07 *(978-1-59928-758-4(7),* Abdo & Daughters) ABDO Publishing Co.

Sullivan, Laura L. Blackbeard. 2015. (J). lib. bdg. *(978-1-62713-525-2(1))* Cavendish Square Publishing.

Teach, William. Pirates: The Secrets of Blackbeard's World. 2015. (ENG., Illus.). 80p. (J). (gr. 3). pap. 16.95 *(978-1-78312-116-8(5))* Carlton Kids GBR. Dist: Sterling Publishing Co., Inc.

Teach, William, retold by. Blackbeard's Pirateworld: Cut-Throats of the Caribbean. 2011. (ENG., Illus.). 80p. (J). (gr. 3). 19.95 *(978-1-84732-973-8(X))* Carlton Bks., Ltd. GBR. Dist: Sterling Publishing Co., Inc.

TEACH, EDWARD, -1718—FICTION

Castroman, Nicole. Blacksouls. 2017. (ENG., Illus.). 400p. (YA). (gr. 9). 17.99 *(978-1-4814-9105-1(9),* Simon Pulse) Simon Pulse.

Marsh, Carole. The Mystery of Blackbeard the Pirate. Marsh, Carole, photos by. 2009. (Real Kids, Real Places Ser.). (Illus.). 150p. (J). 18.99 *(978-0-635-06992-4(X),* Marsh, Carole Mysteries) Gallopade International.

O'Donnell, Liam. Blackbeard's Sword: The Pirate King of the Carolinas. Spoor, Mike, illus. 2007. (Historical Fiction Ser.). (ENG.). 56p. (gr. 2-3). pap. 6.25 *(978-1-59889-404-2(8),* Graphic Flash) Stone Arch Bks.

Penn, Audrey & Miller, Joshua. Blackbeard & the Gift of Silence. 2009. (ENG.). 350p. (J). (gr. 2-7). pap. 8.95 *(978-1-933718-32-3(3))* Tanglewood Pr.

—Blackbeard & the Sandstone Pillar: When Lightning Strikes. 2009. (ENG.). 350p. (J). (gr. 2-7). pap. 8.95 *(978-1-933718-31-6(5))* Tanglewood Pr.

Pyle, Howard. The Story of Jack Ballister's Fortunes: Being the Narrative of the Adventures of a Young Gentleman of Good Family, Who Was Kidnapped in the Year 1719 & Carried to the Plantations of the Continent of Virginia, Where He Fell in with That Famous Pirate Captain Edward Teach, or Blackbeard: of His Escape from the Pirates & the Rescue of a Young Lady from Out Their Hands. unabr. ed. 2012. (Illus.). 436p. 49.99 *(978-1-4622-8858-8(8))* Repressed Publishing LLC.

TEACHER-STUDENT RELATIONSHIPS—FICTION

Adrian, Emily. Like It Never Happened. 2015. (ENG.). 368p. (J). (gr. 9). 17.99 *(978-0-525-42823-7(2),* Dial Bks) Penguin Young Readers Group.

Alcott, Jessica. Even When You Lie to Me. 2015. (ENG.). 352p. (YA). (gr. 9). 17.99 *(978-0-385-39116-0(1),* Crown Books For Young Readers) Random Hse. Children's Bks.

Alexander, Carol. Class Clown. Friedland, Joyce & Kessler, Rikki, eds. 2007. (Novel-Ties Ser.). (Illus.). 24p. pap. 16.95 *(978-0-7675-1014-1(3))* Learning Links Inc.

Anderson, John David. Ms. Bixby's Last Day. 2016. 320p. (J). (gr. 3-7). 16.99 *(978-0-06-233817-4(X),* Walden Pond Pr.) HarperCollins Pubs.

Anderson, Laurie Halse. Teacher's Pet. 2009. (Vet Volunteers Ser.: 7). (ENG.). 160p. (J). (gr. 3-7). 6.99 *(978-0-14-241252-7(X),* Puffin Books) Penguin Young Readers Group.

Avi. Don't You Know There's a War On? 2nd ed. 2003. 208p. (J). pap. *(978-0-439-53096-5(2),* HarperCollins) HarperCollins Pubs.

—Don't You Know There's a War On? 2003. 193p. (gr. 3-7). 18.00 *(978-0-7569-1383-0(7))* Perfection Learning Corp.

—Who Was That Masked Man, Anyway? 2014. (ENG.). 176p. (J). (gr. 3-7). pap. 6.99 *(978-0-439-52355-4(9),* Scholastic Paperbacks) Scholastic, Inc.

Bick, Ilsa J. Drowning Instinct. (ENG.). 352p. (YA). (gr. 9-12). 2013. pap. 9.95 *(978-1-4677-0912-5(3))* 2012. 17.95 *(978-0-7613-7752-8(2))* Lerner Publishing Group. (Carolrhoda Lab™).

Buyea, Rob. Because of Mr. Terupt. (ENG.). (J). (gr. 3-7). 2011. 304p. 7.99 *(978-0-375-85824-6(5),* Yearling) 2010. 288p. 16.99 *(978-0-385-73882-8(X),* Delacorte Bks. for Young Readers) Random Hse. Children's Bks.

—Mr. Terupt Falls Again. 2013. (ENG.). 384p. (J). (gr. 4-7). 7.99 *(978-0-307-93046-0(7),* Yearling) Random Hse. Children's Bks.

—Mr. Terupt Falls Again. 2013. lib. bdg. 18.40 *(978-0-606-32236-2(1),* Turtleback) Turtleback Bks.

Buyea, Robert W. Saving Mr. Terupt. 2015. (ENG.). 384p. (J). (gr. 4-7). lib. bdg. 19.99 *(978-0-375-99120-2(4),* Delacorte Bks. for Young Readers) Random Hse. Children's Bks.

Clements, Andrew. Frindle. 2014. (ENG.). 112p. (J). 11.24 *(978-1-63245-158-3(1))* Lectorum Pubns., Inc.

—Head of the Class: Frindle - The Landry News - The Janitor's Boy. Selznick, Brian, illus. 2007. (ENG.). 416p. (J). (gr. 3-7). pap. 20.99 *(978-1-4169-4974-9(7),* Atheneum Bks. for Young Readers) Simon & Schuster Children's Publishing.

—Jake Drake, Teacher's Pet. 2007. (Jake Drake Ser.: 3). lib. bdg. 16.00 *(978-1-4177-9035-7(0),* Turtleback) Turtleback Bks.

DeClements, Barthe & Declements, Barthe. Sixth Grade Can Really Kill You. 2008. (ENG.). 160p. (J). (gr. 3-7). 5.99 *(978-0-14-241380-7(1),* Puffin Books) Penguin Young Readers Group.

deGroat, Diane. No More Pencils, No More Books, No More Teacher's Dirty Looks! deGroat, Diane, illus. (Gilbert Ser.). (Illus.). 32p. (J). (gr. -1-3). 2009. (ENG.). pap. 6.99 *(978-0-06-079116-2(0))* 2006. 15.99 *(978-0-06-079114-8(4))* 2006. lib. bdg. 18.89 *(978-0-06-079115-5(2))* HarperCollins Pubs.

Devargas, Casey Anthony. The Kindergarten Treasure. 2012. 44p. pap. 7.00 *(978-0-9859042-0-3(8))* CD Publishing.

Donohoe, Helen. Birdy Flynn. 2017. (ENG.). 384p. pap. 11.99 *(978-1-78074-939-6(2))* Oneworld Pubns. GBR. Dist: Publishers Group West (PGW).

Dumbleton, Mike. Watch Out for Jamie Joel. 2004. (ENG.). 144p. (J). (gr. 9). pap. 16.95 *(978-1-86508-532-6(4))* Allen & Unwin AUS. Dist: Independent Pubs. Group.

Foglia, Auttem. The Big Picture. 2010. 48p. pap. 10.59 *(978-1-4520-6681-3(7))* AuthorHouse.

Freeman, Martha. Fourth-Grade Weirdo. 2004. (Illus.). 147p. (gr. 4-7). 15.50 *(978-0-7569-4117-8(2))* Perfection Learning Corp.

Gingras, Charlotte. Pieces of Me. Ouriou, Susan, tr. from FRE. 2009. (ENG.). 144p. (J). (gr. 7-9). 17.95 *(978-1-55453-242-1(6))* Kids Can Pr., Ltd. CAN. Dist: Hachette Bk. Group.

Goodman, Gabriel. The Confessional. 2015. (ENG.). 112p. (YA). (gr. 6-12). 27.99 *(978-1-4677-5712-6(8))* Lerner Publishing Group.

Grover, Lorie Ann. Hit. 1 vol. 2015. (ENG.). 224p. (YA). pap. 8.99 *(978-0-310-72938-9(6))* Blink.

Harley, Bill. Night of the Spadefoot Toads. 1 vol. 2008. (ENG.). 192p. (J). (gr. 3-7). 15.95 *(978-1-56145-459-4(1))* Peachtree Pubs.

Hrdlitschka, Shelley. Allegra. 1 vol. 2013. (ENG.). 280p. (YA). (gr. 8-12). pap. 12.95 *(978-1-4598-0197-4(0))* Orca Bk. Pubs. USA.

Jackson, Marcus. Because My Teacher Said I Can. 2011. 24p. pap. 13.86 *(978-1-4567-6492-0(6))* AuthorHouse.

Jakobitz, Marilee. Martha Lu & the Whobegots. 2008. 32p. pap. 24.95 *(978-1-60441-482-0(0))* America Star Bks.

Johnson, Sandi. My Teacher Is an Alien. Durant, Sybrina, ed. Sturgen, Bobbi, illus. 2014. (ENG.). 30p. (J). (gr. k-5). pap. 12.99 *(978-1-929063-75-8(X),* 285) Moons & Stars Publishing For Children.

Kremer, Kevin. The Year Our Teacher Won Super Bowl. Ely, Dave, illus. 2010. (ENG.). 178p. pap. 6.50 *(978-0-9824611-1-2(9))* Snow In Sarasota Publishing.

Laird, Judie. Lori Takes Piano Lessons. 2009. 20p. pap. 10.95 *(978-1-4490-1205-2(1))* AuthorHouse.

Layne, Steven L., et al. T Is for Teachers: A School Alphabet. Ettlinger, Doris, illus. 2005. (ENG.). 40p. (J). (gr. 1-4). 16.95 *(978-1-58536-159-5(3),* 202019) Sleeping Bear Pr.

McLellan, Gretchen Brandenburg. Mrs. Mcbee Leaves Room 3. 1 vol. Zong, Grace, illus. 2017. (ENG.). 32p. (J). (gr. -1-2). 16.95 *(978-1-56145-944-5(5))* Peachtree Pubs.

Morgan, Amanda K. Such a Good Girl. 2017. (ENG., Illus.). 288p. (YA). (gr. 9). 17.99 ***(978-1-4814-4957-1(5),*** Simon Pulse) Simon Pulse.

Muluka, B. Kandu & the Lake. 2004. (Illus.). 44p. pap. *(978-9966-25-165-7(0))* Heinemann Kenya, Limited (East African Educational Publishers Ltd E.A.E.P.) KEN. Dist: Michigan State Univ. Pr.

Naylor, Phyllis Reynolds. The Agony of Alice. 2011. (Alice Ser.: 1). (ENG.). 176p. (J). (gr. 5-9). pap. 6.99 *(978-1-4424-2363-3(3),* Atheneum Bks. for Young Readers) Simon & Schuster Children's Publishing.

Nelson, R. A. Teach Me. 2007. (ENG.). 272p. (YA). (gr. 9-12). 8.99 *(978-1-59514-085-2(9),* Razorbill) Penguin Young Readers Group.

Newmann, Ed, illus. Marvin Monster's Teacher Jitters. 2006. (ENG.). 48p. (J). (gr. 4-7). per. 6.95 *(978-0-9766805-3-6(X))* Keene Publishing.

Oates, Joyce Carol. Sexy. 2005. 272p. (J). (gr. 7-18). 16.99 *(978-0-06-054149-1(0),* HarperTeen) HarperCollins Pubs.

Ohlin, Nancy. Consent. 2015. (ENG., Illus.). 288p. (YA). (gr. 9). 17.99 *(978-1-4424-6490-2(9),* Simon Pulse) Simon Pulse.

Perl, Erica S. Dotty. Denos, Julia, illus. 2010. (ENG.). 32p. (J). (gr. -1-3). 16.95 *(978-0-8109-8962-7(X),* Abrams Bks. for Young Readers) Abrams, Inc.

Polacco, Patricia & McPike, Elizabeth. An A from Miss Keller. Polacco, Patricia, illus. 2015. (ENG., Illus.). 40p. (J). (gr. k-3). bds. 17.99 *(978-0-399-16691-4(2),* G.P. Putnam's Sons Books for Young Readers) Penguin Young Readers Group.

Quick, Matthew. Every Exquisite Thing. 2016. (ENG.). 272p. (YA). (gr. 10-17). 17.99 *(978-0-316-37959-5(X))* Little Brown & Co.

Rathmann, Peggy. Ruby the Copycat. 2006. (ENG., Illus.). 32p. (J). (gr. -1-3). per. 6.99 *(978-0-439-47228-9(8),* Teaching Resources) Scholastic, Inc.

Regan, Dian. The World According to Kaley. 2005. (ENG., Illus.). 112p. (J). (gr. 2-5). 14.99 *(978-1-58196-039-6(5),* Darby Creek) Lerner Publishing Group.

Reinhardt, Dana. We Are the Goldens. 2015. (ENG.). 208p. (YA). (gr. 9). pap. 9.99 *(978-0-385-74258-0(4),* Ember) Random Hse. Children's Bks.

Rentas, Donna. Leticia Goes to School. 2008. 16p. pap. 24.95 *(978-1-4241-8966-3(7))* America Star Bks.

Ruby, Laura. Bad Apple. (ENG.). (YA). (gr. 8). 2011. 272p. pap. 8.99 *(978-0-06-124333-2(7))* 2009. 256p. 16.99 *(978-0-06-124330-1(2))* HarperCollins Pubs. (HarperTeen).

Rue, Nancy N. Totally Unfair. 1 vol. 2005. ('Nama Beach High Ser.). (ENG.). 160p. (YA). pap. 6.99 *(978-0-310-25183-5(4))* Zondervan.

Sanders, Jennifer. My Student Teacher's Last Day. 2009. 32p. pap. 12.99 *(978-1-4389-4417-3(9))* AuthorHouse.

Schraff, Anne. The Petition. 2008. (Passages Ser.). 103p. (J). (gr. 4-6). lib. bdg. 13.95 *(978-0-7569-8391-8(6))* Perfection Learning Corp.

Seevers, Tim. Love, Grandp. 2009. 28p. pap. 14.99 *(978-1-4389-3507-2(2))* AuthorHouse.

Standiford, Natalie. Breaking up Is Really, Really Hard to Do. 2005. (ENG.). 224p. (YA). (gr. 7-17). pap. 18.99 *(978-0-316-11041-9(8))* Little, Brown Bks. for Young Readers.

—The Dating Game, No. 1. 2005. (ENG.). 224p. (YA). (gr. 7-17). pap. 18.99 *(978-0-316-11040-2(X))* Little, Brown Bks. for Young Readers.

Toten, Teresa. Beware That Girl. 2016. (ENG.). 336p. (YA). (gr. 9). 17.99 *(978-0-553-50790-4(7),* Delacorte Pr.) Random Hse. Children's Bks.

Williams, Lorraine. Poor Dan. Felton, Richard, illus. 2008. 36p. per. 24.95 *(978-1-60441-170-6(8))* America Star Bks.

Wright, Kiyah. Joshua's Surprise. 2010. 28p. pap. 16.95 *(978-1-4490-8234-5(3))* AuthorHouse.

TEACHER TRAINING

see Teachers—Training of

TEACHERS

see also Educators; Teaching

Alarcon, Roben. Teachers Then & Now. 1 vol. 2006. (Primary Source Readers Ser.). (ENG.). 32p. (J). (gr. 2-2). pap. 8.99 *(978-0-7439-9375-3(6))* Shell Educational Publishing.

Ames, Michelle. Teachers in Our Community. 2009. (On the Job Ser.). (Illus.). 24p. (J). (ENG.). pap. 8.25 *(978-1-4358-2456-0(3));* lib. bdg. 22.60 *(978-1-4042-8069-4(3))* Rosen Publishing Group, Inc., The. (PowerKids Pr.).

Anthony, David. Teachers on the Job. 2017. (Jobs in Our Community Ser.). 24p. (J). (gr. 1-1). lib. bdg. 24.60 ***(978-1-5345-2147-6(X),*** KidHaven Publishing) Greenhaven Publishing LLC.

Arnold, Quinn M. Teachers. 2017. (J). ***(978-1-60818-875-8(2),*** Creative Education) Creative Co., The.

Askew, Amanda & Crowson, Andrew. Teacher. 2012. (Illus.). 24p. (gr. 1-3). pap. 7.95 *(978-1-926853-50-5(4))* Saunders Bk. Co. CAN. Dist: RiverStream Publishing.

Bao, Julie. A Loving Teacher Forever: A True Story of Loving Children, Defying Fate & Achieving Teaching Excellence. 2004. (Illus.). 32p. (J). 15.00 *(978-0-9748890-0-9(8))* Dings Bks.

Barker, Stephen. I Want to Be a Teacher. 2016. (ENG., Illus.). 10p. (J). (gr. -1-k). 10.99 *(978-1-4052-7639-9(8))* Egmont Bks., Ltd. GBR. Dist: Independent Pubs. Group.

Barth, Daisy. Thank You, Teacher, Because... 2008. (ENG., Illus.). 64p. (J). (gr. 4-7). pap. 9.95 *(978-1-933176-19-2(9))* Red Rock Pr., Inc.

Brooks, Felicity. Tessa the Teacher. Litchfield, Jo, illus. 2006. 24p. (J). per. 6.99 *(978-0-7945-0937-8(1),* Usborne) EDC Publishing.

Bryant, Jen. Six Dots: A Story of Young Louis Braille. Kulikov, Boris, illus. 2016. (ENG.). 40p. (J). (gr. -1-3). 17.99 *(978-0-449-81337-9(1),* Knopf Bks. for Young Readers) Random Hse. Children's Bks.

Crane, Natalie. I Go to Work as a Teacher. 2003. (I Go to Work As Ser.). (Illus.). (J). pap. *(978-1-58417-106-5(5));* lib. bdg. *(978-1-58417-044-0(1));* lib. bdg. *(978-1-58417-043-3(3))* Lake Street Pubs.

Cunningham, Kevin. Teacher. 2008. (21st Century Skills Library: Cool Careers Ser.). (ENG., Illus.). 32p. (gr. 4-8). lib. bdg. 28.50 *(978-1-60279-298-2(4),* 200137) Cherry Lake Publishing.

de Nijs, Erika. A Teacher's Job. 2015. (Community Workers Ser.). (ENG., Illus.). 24p. (J). (gr. 1-1). lib. bdg. 24.21 *(978-1-5026-0431-6(0))* Cavendish Square Publishing.

Deedrick, Tami. Teachers Help. 1 vol. 2014. (Our Community Helpers Ser.). (ENG.). 24p. (gr. k-1). pap. 6.29 *(978-1-4765-5153-1(7));* lib. bdg. 21.99 *(978-1-4765-3949-2(9))* Capstone Press of Coughlan Cos. (Pebble Bks.).

Delano, Marfe Ferguson. Helen's Eyes: A Photobiography of Annie Sullivan, Helen Keller's Teacher. 2008. (Photobiographies Ser.). (ENG., Illus.). 64p. (J). (gr. 5). 27.90 *(978-1-4263-0210-7(X));* 17.95 *(978-1-4263-0209-1(6))* National Geographic Society. (National Geographic Children's Bks.).

Dent, Jenny. Great Teachers. 2003. (Spiritual Teachings for Children Ser.). (Illus.). 32p. (gr. k-9). 17.95 *(978-0-85487-054-7(7))* White Eagle Publishing Trust GBR. Dist: DeVorss & Co.

Donaldson, Madeline. Louis Braille. 2008. pap. 52.95 *(978-0-8225-9393-5(9))* Lerner Publishing Group.

Early Macken, JoAnn. Teachers. Andersen, Gregg, photos by. 2010. (People in My Community Ser.). (Illus.). 24p. (gr. k-3). pap. 8.15 *(978-1-4339-3348-6(9))* Stevens, Gareth Publishing LLLP.

—Teachers / Maestros. Andersen, Gregg, photos by. 2010. (People in My Community / Mi comunidad Ser.). (SPA., Illus.). 24p. (gr. k-3). pap. 8.15 *(978-1-4339-3766-8(2))* Stevens, Gareth Publishing LLLP.

Franco, Michou. I Can Be a Teacher. 2017. (I Can Be Anything! Ser.). 24p. (gr. k-k). pap. 8.15 ***(978-1-4824-6333-0(4))*** Stevens, Gareth Publishing LLLP.

Freed, Kira. Teachers Are Important. 2017. (Text Connections Guided Close Reading Ser.). (J). (gr. k). *(978-1-4900-1780-8(1))* Benchmark Education Co.

Freeman, Dallas. Mirth & Misery: Memoirs of a Midwestern Maverick. 2003. 267p. per. 14.95 net. *(978-1-931934-22-0(3))* Back Yard Pub.

Graham, Patti. And That Is Why We Teach: A Celebration of Teachers. Wellman, Megan D., illus. 2008. (ENG.). 32p. (J). (gr. 4-7). 17.95 *(978-1-933916-23-1(0))* Nelson Publishing & Marketing.

Harper, Clay & Ingram, Jas. Are You Sure That Was a Rabbit?. 1 vol. 2012. (ENG., Illus.). 32p. (J). 12.99 *(978-0-7643-4007-9(7),* 9780764340079) Schiffer Publishing, Ltd.

Heos, Bridget. Let's Meet a Teacher. Poling, Kyle, illus. 2013. (Cloverleaf Books — Community Helpers Ser.). (ENG.). 24p. (gr. k-2). pap. 6.95 *(978-1-4677-0805-0(4));* lib. bdg. 23.93 *(978-0-7613-9026-8(X))* Lerner Publishing Group. (Millbrook Pr.).

Hord, Colleen. Joe Acaba. 2013. (ENG., Illus.). 24p. (gr. k-3). pap. 8.95 *(978-1-61810-284-3(2))* Rourke Educational Media.
Jackson, Garnet N. Shirley Chisholm, Congresswoman. 2012. (ENG., Illus.). (J). (gr. 1-4). pap. 7.47 net. *(978-0-8136-5247-4(2),* Modern Curriculum Pr.) Pearson Schl.
Jeffries, Joyce. Meet the Teacher. 2012. (People Around Town Ser.). (Illus.). 24p. (gr. k-2). 69.20 *(978-1-4339-8063-3(0));* (J). 22.60 *(978-1-4339-7340-6(5));* (J). pap. 8.15 *(978-1-4339-7341-3(3))* Stevens, Gareth Publishing LLLP.
—Meet the Teacher / Te Presento A Los Maestros. 2012. (People Around Town / Gente de mi ciudad Ser.). (SPA & ENG., Illus.). 24p. (J). (gr. k-2). 22.60 *(978-1-4339-7392-5(8))* Stevens, Gareth Publishing LLLP.
Jones, Amy Robin. Mary McLeod Bethune. 2009. (Journey to Freedom Ser.). (ENG., Illus.). 32p. (J). (gr. 4-7). 29.93 *(978-1-60253-129-1(3),* 200395) Child's World, Inc., The.
Kenney, Karen L. Teachers at Work, 1 vol. Dumm, Brian Caleb, illus. 2009. (Meet Your Community Workers Ser.). (ENG.). 32p. (J). (gr. -1-2). 28.50 *(978-1-60270-653-8(0))* Magic Wagon.
Kidde, Rita. What Do Teachers Do? 2014. (Jobs in My School Ser.). 24p. (J). (gr. k-2). lib. bdg. 23.60 *(978-1-4777-6556-2(5),* PowerKids Pr.) Rosen Publishing Group, Inc., The.
—What Do Teachers Do? (¿Qué Hacen los Maestros?) de la Vega, Eida, ed. 2014. (Oficios en Mi Escuela / Jobs in My School Ser.). (SPA & ENG.). 24p. (J). (gr. k-2). lib. bdg. 23.60 *(978-1-4777-6798-6(3),* PowerKids Pr.) Rosen Publishing Group, Inc., The.
Lawson, Sabina. Taking Action to Improve Schools. 2016. (Who's Changing the World? Ser.). (ENG., Illus.). 48p. (J). (gr. 4-6). 50.65 *(978-1-4677-9666-8(2),* Lerner Pubns.) Lerner Publishing Group.
Leake, Diyan. Teachers, 1 vol. 2008. (People in the Community Ser.). (ENG., Illus.). 24p. (gr. -1-1). 21.99 *(978-1-4329-1191-1(0),* Acorn) Heinemann-Raintree.
Leigh, Autumn. My Teacher. 2009. (Real Life Readers Ser.). 8p. (gr. k-1). pap. 5.15 *(978-1-4042-7975-9(X),* Rosen Classroom) Rosen Publishing Group, Inc., The.
Lesinski, Jeanne M. Bill Gates. 2005. (First Step Nonfiction Ser.). (Illus.). 112p. (J). (gr. 3-7). lib. bdg. 27.93 *(978-0-8225-2642-1(5),* Lerner Pubns.) Lerner Publishing Group.
Levin, Daniel T. & Hammer, David. Becoming a Responsive Science Teacher: Focusing on Student Thinking in Secondary Science. 2012. (ENG.). 270p. (J). pap. *(978-1-936959-05-1(4))* National Science Teachers Assn.
Lohse, Joyce B. Emily Griffith: Opportunity's Teacher. 2005. (Now You Know Bio Ser.). (Illus.). 50p. (J). pap. 8.95 *(978-0-86541-077-0(1))* Filter Pr., LLC.
Lowenstein, Felicia. What Does a Teacher Do? 2006. (What Does a Community Helper Do? Ser.). (Illus.). 24p. (J). (gr. 1-3). lib. bdg. 22.60 *(978-0-7660-2321-5(4),* Enslow Elementary) Enslow Pubs., Inc.
Macken, JoAnn Early. Teachers. 2010. (People in My Community Ser.). (Illus.). 24p. (J). (gr. k-3). 22.60 *(978-1-4339-3347-9(0))* Stevens, Gareth Publishing LLLP.
Mara, Wil. The Schoolmaster. 2010. (Colonial People Ser.). 48p. (gr. 3-18). 29.93 *(978-0-7614-4801-3(2))* Marshall Cavendish Corp.
Markowitz, Siri. HELP with RAISING YOUR NURSERY or PRESCHOOL CHILDREN - 26 great ideas for parents & preschool Teachers. 2009. 44p. pap. 19.99 *(978-0-557-09610-7(3))* Lulu Pr., Inc.
McDonnell, Peter. Helping Others: The Story of Fanny Jackson Coppin. 2005. (Illus.). 16p. (J). *(978-0-7367-2901-7(1))* Zaner-Bloser, Inc.
McKissack, Patricia C. & McKissack, Fredrick L. Mary McLeod Bethune: Woman of Courage. 2013. (Famous African Americans Ser.). (Illus.). 24p. (J). (gr. k-18). 22.60 *(978-0-7660-4103-5(4))* Enslow Pubs., Inc.
Mellor, C. Michael. Louis Braille: A Touch of Genius. 2006. (Illus.). 144p. (J). 35.00 *(978-0-939173-70-9(0))* National Braille Pr.
Meltzer, Mirta. My Hands Mis Manos. 2013. 32p. pap. 12.99 *(978-1-61286-157-9(1))* Avid Readers Publishing Group.
Minden, Cecilia. Teachers. 2014. (People in Our Community Ser.). (ENG.). 24p. (J). (gr. k-3). 27.07 *(978-1-62687-018-5(7),* 206808) Child's World, Inc., The.
Mitchell, Melanie. Teachers. 2005. (Pull Ahead Bks.). (Illus.). 32p. (J). lib. bdg. 22.60 *(978-0-8225-1696-5(9));* (ENG., pap. 7.95 *(978-0-8225-2536-3(4))* Lerner Publishing Group.
montell, alicia. Our Friend Oso. 2008. 206p. pap. 24.95 *(978-1-4241-7732-5(4))* America Star Bks.
Murray, Aaron R. Teachers Help Us. 2012. (All about Community Helpers Ser.). (Illus.). 24p. (J). (gr. -1-1). 22.60 *(978-0-7660-4045-8(3),* Enslow Elementary) Enslow Pubs., Inc.
Murray, Julie. Maestros. 2016. (Trabajos en Mi Comunidad Ser.). (SPA.). 24p. (J). (gr. k-5). pap. 7.95 *(978-1-4966-0727-0(9))* Capstone Classroom.
—Teachers, 1 vol. (ENG.). 2015. 24p. 27.07 *(978-1-62970-917-8(4))* 2010. 32p. (J). (gr. 2-5). 27.07 *(978-1-61613-509-6(3))* ABDO Publishing Co.
Nelid, Piper. My Father Teaches Overseas, 01 vols., 1. 2016. (Rosen REAL Readers: Social Studies Nonfiction / Fiction: Family, Community, & the World Ser.). (ENG.). 12p. (J). pap. 6.33 *(978-1-5081-1734-6(9),* Rosen Classroom) Rosen Publishing Group, Inc., The.
Nicholson, Dorinda Makanaōnalani. The School the Aztec Eagles Built, 1 vol. Nicholson, Dorinda Makanaōnalani, photos by. 2016. (ENG., Illus.). 48p. (J). 18.95 *(978-1-60060-440-9(4))* Lee & Low Bks., Inc.
Paderewski, Elliot. We Respect Our Teachers. 2016. (Rosen REAL Readers: Social Studies Nonfiction / Fiction: Family, Community, & the World Ser.). 8p. (gr. 1-k). pap. 5.46 *(978-1-5081-2296-8(2),* Rosen Classroom) Rosen Publishing Group, Inc., The.
Parkes, Elle. Hooray for Teachers! 2016. (Bumba Books (tm) — Hooray for Community Helpers! Ser.). (ENG., Illus.). 24p. (J). (gr. -1-1). 25.32 *(978-1-5124-1437-0(9))* Lerner Publishing Group.
Parkes, Elle. Que Vivan los Maestros! 2017. (Bumba Books (tm) en Español — ¡Que Vivan Los Ayudantes Comunitarios! (Hooray for Community Helpers!) Ser.). (SPA.). 24p. (J). (gr. -1-1). 25.32 ***(978-1-5124-4132-1(5))*** Lerner Publishing Group.
Pressberg, Dava. A Teacher's Tools. 2015. (Community Helpers & Their Tools Ser.). (ENG., Illus.). 24p. (J). (gr. 2-3). pap. 8.25 *(978-1-4994-0855-3(2),* PowerKids Pr.) Rosen Publishing Group, Inc., The.
Raatma, Lucia. Shirley Chisholm. 2010. (Leading Women Ser.). 96p. (YA). (gr. 7-12). 39.93 *(978-0-7614-4953-9(1))* Marshall Cavendish Corp.
Randolph, Ryan P. Frontier Schools & Schoolteachers. 2009. (Library of the Westward Expansion Ser.). 24p. (gr. 3-4). 42.50 *(978-1-60853-935-2(0),* PowerKids Pr.) Rosen Publishing Group, Inc., The.
Riggs, Kate. Seedlings: Teachers. 2017. (Seedlings Ser.). (ENG.). 24p. (J). (gr. -1-1). pap. 7.99 ***(978-1-62832-490-7(2),*** Creative Paperbacks) Creative Co., The.
Rivera, Sheila. Teacher. 2005. (First Step Nonfiction - Work People Do Ser.). (ENG.). 8p. (gr. -1-1). pap. 4.95 *(978-0-8225-5361-8(9),* Lerner Pubns.) Lerner Publishing Group.
Sanna, Ellyn. Special Education Teacher. Riggs, Ernestine G. & Gholar, Cheryl, eds. 2013. (Careers with Character Ser.: 18). 96p. (J). (gr. 7-18). 22.95 *(978-1-4222-2767-1(7))* Mason Crest.
Schraff, Anne E. Jaime Escalante: Inspirational Math Teacher. 2008. (Latino Biography Library). (Illus.). 128p. (J). (gr. k-6). lib. bdg. 33.27 *(978-0-7660-2967-5(0))* Enslow Pubs., Inc.
Schwartz, Heather E. Mary McLeod Bethune: Education & Equality. 2016. (Primary Source Readers Ser.). 32p. (J). (gr. 4-4). pap. 8.99 *(978-1-4938-3545-4(9))* Teacher Created Materials, Inc.
Schwartz, Heather E. NASA Mathematician Katherine Johnson. 2017. (STEM Trailblazer Bios Ser.). (ENG.). 32p. (J). (gr. 2-5). 26.65 ***(978-1-5124-5703-2(5))*** Lerner Publishing Group.
Shava, Ryder. Mr. Ramirez Is My Teacher, 01 vols., 1. 2016. (Rosen REAL Readers: Social Studies Nonfiction / Fiction: Family, Community, & the World Ser.). (ENG.). 8p. (J). pap. 5.46 *(978-1-5081-1710-0(1),* Rosen Classroom) Rosen Publishing Group, Inc., The.
Siemens, Jared. Teachers. 2016. (J). ***(978-1-5105-2111-7(9))*** SmartBook Media, Inc.
—Teachers. 2015. 24p. (J). *(978-1-4896-3657-7(9))* Weigl Pubs., Inc.
Stewart, Tobi. Colonial Teachers. 2009. (Reading Room Collection 1 Ser.). 16p. (gr. 2-3). 37.50 *(978-1-60851-942-2(2),* PowerKids Pr.) Rosen Publishing Group, Inc., The.
Stewart, Tobi Stanton. Colonial Teachers. 2006. (Reading Room Collection: Social Studies). (Illus.). 16p. (J). (gr. 3-7). lib. bdg. 17.25 *(978-1-4042-3351-5(2),* PowerKids Pr.) Rosen Publishing Group, Inc., The.
Sunseri, Sophia Natasha. Working As a Teacher in Your Community. 2015. (Careers in Your Community Ser.). (ENG., Illus.). 80p. (J). (gr. 7-8). 34.25 *(978-1-4994-6117-6(8),* Rosen Young Adult) Rosen Publishing Group, Inc., The.
Trent, Tererai. The Girl Who Buried Her Dreams in a Can. Gilchrist, Jan Spivey, illus. 2015. (ENG.). 34p. (J). (gr. 1-3). 17.99 *(978-0-670-01654-9(3),* Viking Books for Young Readers) Penguin Young Readers Group.
Vogel, Elizabeth. Meet My Teacher. 2009. (My School Ser.). 24p. (gr. 1-2). 37.50 *(978-1-61514-704-5(7),* PowerKids Pr.) Rosen Publishing Group, Inc., The.
Walsh, Barbara. The Poppy Lady: Moina Belle Michael & Her Tribute to Veterans. Johnson, Layne, illus. 2012. (ENG.). 40p. (J). (gr. 2-4). 16.95 *(978-1-59078-754-0(4),* Calkins Creek) Boyds Mills Pr.
Watson, Stephanie & Lawson, Sabina. Taking Action to Improve Schools. 2016. (Who's Changing the World? Ser.). (ENG., Illus.). 48p. (J). (gr. 4-6). 33.32 *(978-1-4677-9393-3(0))* Lerner Publishing Group.
Whyte, Donna. What Makes a Good Teacher? Here's What the Kids Say! Garamella, Joyce Orchard, illus. 2003. 32p. (J). 6.95 *(978-1-884548-59-8(8),* Crystal Springs Bks.) Staff Development for Educators.
Wigu Publishing. When I Grow Up I Want to Be... a Teacher! Carlee Learns a Surprising Lesson! 2013. (When I Grow Up I Want To Be....Ser.). (Illus.). 62p. pap. 12.95 *(978-1-939973-08-5(2),* Wigu Publishing) Wigu Publishing.
Winter, Jeanette. Biblioburro: A True Story from Colombia. Winter, Jeanette, illus. 2010. (ENG., Illus.). 32p. (J). (gr. 1-4). 17.99 *(978-1-4169-9778-8(4),* Beach Lane Bks.) Beach Lane Bks.
Wohlrabe, Sarah C. Helping You Learn: A Book about Teachers, 1 vol. Thomas, Eric, illus. 2003. (Community Workers Ser.). (ENG.). 24p. (gr. -1-3). per. 8.95 *(978-1-4048-0478-4(1))* Picture Window Bks.
Wolfe, Helen. Terrific Women Teachers, 1 vol. 2011. (Women's Hall of Fame Ser.). (ENG., Illus.). 112p. (J). (gr. 4-8). pap. 10.95 *(978-1-897187-86-9(6))* Second Story Pr. CAN. Dist: Orca Bk. Pubs. USA.
Wyckoff, Edwin Brit & Library. Sign Language Man: Thomas H. Gallaudet & His Incredible Work. 2010. (Genius at Work! Great Inventor Biographies Ser.). (Illus.). 32p. (J). (gr. 2-5). lib. bdg. 23.94 *(978-0-7660-3447-1(X))* Enslow Pubs., Inc.

TEACHERS—FICTION

Abramsen, Ruth M. Akeelah's Spider. 2008. 36p. per. 13.95 *(978-1-59800-440-3(9))* Outskirts Pr., Inc.
Adler, David A. Danny's Doodles: the Squirting Donuts. 2014. (Danny's Doodles Ser.: 2). (ENG.). 144p. (J). (gr. 2-5). 14.99 *(978-1-4926-1401-2(7),* Sourcebooks Jabberwocky) Sourcebooks, Inc.
—School Trouble for Andy Russell. Hillenbrand, Will, illus. 2005. (Andy Russell Ser.: Bk. 3). (ENG.). 128p. (J). (gr. 1-4). pap. 9.95 *(978-0-15-205428-1(6))* Houghton Mifflin Harcourt Publishing Co.
—School Trouble for Andy Russell. Hillenbrand, Will, illus. 2007. (Andy Russell Ser.: Bk. 3). 118p. pap. 6.60 *(978-1-4189-5227-3(3))* Houghton Mifflin Harcourt Supplemental Pubs.
—School Trouble for Andy Russell. Hillenbrand, Will, illus. 2008. (Andy Russell Ser.: Bk. 3). (J). (gr. 2-5). pap. 28.95 incl. audio compact disk *(978-1-4301-0484-1(8));* pap. 24.95 incl. audio *(978-1-4301-0483-4(X))* Live Oak Media.
—Young Cam Jansen & the Substitute Mystery, No. 11. Natti, Susanna, illus. 2006. (Young Cam Jansen Ser.: 11). (ENG.). 32p. (J). (gr. 1-3). mass mkt. 3.99 *(978-0-14-240660-1(0),* Penguin Young Readers) Penguin Young Readers Group.
Aikawa, Yu. Dark Edge. 2005. (Dark Edge Ser.). (Illus.). (YA). Vol. 3. (ENG.). 200p. pap. 9.95 *(978-1-59796-030-4(6))* Vol. 4. 208p. pap. 9.95 *(978-1-59796-024-3(1))* DrMaster Pubns. Inc.
Akbarpour, Ahmad. That Night's Train, 1 vol. Saghafi, Majid, tr. from PER. Arsenault, Isabelle, illus. 2012. (ENG.). 96p. (J). (gr. 3). 14.95 *(978-1-55498-169-4(7))* Groundwood Bks. CAN. Dist: Publishers Group West (PGW).
Alexander, Shannon Lee. Love & Other Unknown Variables. 2014. (Entangled Teen Ser.). (ENG.). 352p. (YA). (gr. 7-12). 16.99 *(978-1-62266-467-2(1),* 9781622664672) Entangled Publishing, LLC.
Alfonsi, Alice, adapted by. 'Rents: Lizzie Mcguire. 2005. 134p. (J). lib. bdg. 16.92 *(978-1-4242-0689-6(8))* Fitzgerald Bks.
Alger, Horatio. Strive & Succeed. 2007. 172p. 24.95 *(978-1-4344-8359-1(2));* per. 14.95 *(978-1-4344-8358-4(4))* Wildside Pr., LLC.
Allard, Harry & Marshall, James. Miss Nelson Has a Field Day. 2015. 32p. pap. 7.00 *(978-1-61003-506-4(2))* Center for the Collaborative Classroom.
Allard, Harry G., Jr. Miss Nelson Has a Field Day, 1 vol. Marshall, James, illus. 2012. (ENG.). 32p. (J). (gr. -1-3). audio compact disk 10.99 *(978-0-547-75376-8(4))* Houghton Mifflin Harcourt Publishing Co.
—Miss Nelson Is Back, 1 vol. Marshall, James, illus. 2011. (ENG.). 32p. (J). (gr. -1-3). audio compact disk 10.99 *(978-0-547-57718-0(4))* Houghton Mifflin Harcourt Publishing Co.
Allard, Harry G., Jr. & Marshall, James. The Miss Nelson Collection. 2014. (ENG., Illus.). 112p. (J). (gr. 1-4). 16.99 *(978-0-544-08222-9(2),* HMH Books For Young Readers) Houghton Mifflin Harcourt Publishing Co.
Amato, Mary. Edgar Allan's Official Crime Investigation Notebook. (ENG.). 176p. (J). 2011. pap. 6.99 *(978-0-8234-2386-6(7))* 2010. (gr. 1-5). 16.95 *(978-0-8234-2271-5(2))* Holiday Hse., Inc.
—Our Teacher Is a Vampire & Other (Not) True Stories. Long, Ethan, illus. (ENG.). 256p. (J). (gr. 3-7). 2017. pap. 6.99 *(978-0-8234-3769-6(8))* 2016. 16.95 *(978-0-8234-3553-1(9))* Holiday Hse., Inc.
Anderson, John David. Ms. Bixby's Last Day. 2016. 320p. (J). (gr. 3-7). 16.99 *(978-0-06-233817-4(X),* Walden Pond Pr.) HarperCollins Pubs.
Andrews, Julie & Hamilton, Emma Walton. The Very Fairy Princess: Teacher's Pet. 2013. (Passport to Reading Level 1 Ser.). (J). lib. bdg. 14.75 *(978-0-606-31741-2(4),* Turtleback) Turtleback Bks.
Andrews, Julie, et al. The Very Fairy Princess - Graduation Girl! Davenier, Christine, illus. 2014. (Very Fairy Princess Ser.). (ENG.). 32p. (J). (gr. -1-3). 18.99 *(978-0-316-21960-0(6))* Little, Brown Bks. for Young Readers.
Anna, Jennifer. Yen Shei & the American Bonsai. 2009. (ENG., Illus.). 88p. (YA). pap. 14.99 *(978-1-59092-153-1(4))* Blue Forge Pr.
Avi. The Secret School. 2003. 157p. (J). (gr. 3-7). 13.60 *(978-0-7569-1625-1(9))* Perfection Learning Corp.
Ayres, Katherine. Family Tree. 2012. 116p. pap. 7.99 *(978-1-936495-21-4(X))* BookPartners, LLC.
Barnes, Phil. My Teacher's a Robot! 2015. (ENG.). 63p. (J). (gr. 1-2). mass mkt. 8.95 *(978-1-78455-935-9(0),* e0384285-e807-49f7-959d-e33332f5b2d5) Austin, Stan AUS. Dist: Bookmasters Distribution.
Barnes, Phil. My Teacher's a Spy! 2017. (ENG.). 66p. (J). pap. 10.95 ***(978-1-78629-497-5(4),*** 050057eb-4aa0-4e8e-acb5-a4c22418a979) Austin, Stan AUS. Dist: Bookmasters Distribution.
Barnholdt, Lauren. Hailey Twitch & the Great Teacher Switch. Beaky, Suzanne, illus. 2010. (Hailey Twitch Ser.: 2). (ENG.). 176p. (J). (gr. 2-4). pap. 6.99 *(978-1-4022-2445-4(1),* Sourcebooks Jabberwocky) Sourcebooks, Inc.
Barns, Crosby H. Who Programmed the Species? The Theory of Scientific Coincidence. 2008. 36p. pap. 16.99 *(978-1-4389-0727-7(3))* AuthorHouse.
Baxter, Alice L. Adam's Atomic Adventures. 2007. 76p. per. 8.95 *(978-0-595-45616-1(2))* iUniverse, Inc.
Beasley, Cheryl. Piano Paradise: My Piano Has a Big Secret. 2006. (ENG.). 52p. per. 16.95 *(978-1-4241-4590-4(2))* PublishAmerica, Inc.
Beck, Ricky. A Puzzled Heart. 2008. 85p. pap. 19.95 *(978-1-60441-385-4(9))* America Star Bks.
Becker, Bonny. The Magical Ms. Plum. Portnoy, Amy, illus. 2011. (ENG.). 112p. (J). (gr. 1-4). 6.99 *(978-0-375-84760-8(X),* Yearling) Random Hse. Children's Bks.
Beckford, Lois. The Interesting Pen Pal. 2010. 44p. pap. 21.99 *(978-1-4415-0878-2(3))* Xlibris Corp.
Bellamy, Diane. But I Will Teach You. 2004. (YA). pap. 15.00 *(978-1-56411-297-2(7))* UBUS Communications Systems.
Bellingham, Brenda. Lilly in the Middle, 1 vol. Owen, Elizabeth, illus. 2003. (Formac First Novels Ser.: 25). (ENG.). 64p. (J). (gr. 1-5). 4.95 *(978-0-88780-589-9(2),* 9780887805899); 14.95 *(978-0-88780-590-5(6),* 9780887805905) Formac Publishing Co., Ltd. CAN. Dist: Casemate Pubs. & Bk. Distributors, LLC.
Bickel, Karla. Teacher's Remarkable Secret. Bickel, Karla, illus. l.t. ed. 2004. (Illus.). 16p. (J). (gr. -1-6). pap. 5.00 *(978-1-891452-09-3(6),* 2) Heart Arbor Bks.
Bildner, Phil. A Whole New Ballgame. Probert, Tim, illus. 2015. (Rip & Red Ser.: 1). (ENG.). 256p. (J). (gr. 3-7). 16.99 *(978-0-374-30130-9(1),* 9780374301309, Farrar, Straus & Giroux (BYR)) Farrar, Straus & Giroux.
—A Whole New Ballgame. 2016. (Rip & Red Ser.: 1). (J). lib. bdg. 17.20 *(978-0-606-38553-4(3))* Turtleback Bks.
Birney, Betty G. Mysteries According to Humphrey. 2013. (According to Humphrey Ser.: 8). lib. bdg. 16.00 *(978-0-606-31699-6(X),* Turtleback) Turtleback Bks.
Biskup, Agnieszka & Sohn, Emily. Ciencia Gráfica. Martin, Cynthia & Dominguez, Richard, illus. 2013. (Ciencia Gráfica Ser.). (SPA.). 32p. (gr. 3-4). lib. bdg. 122.60 *(978-1-62065-185-8(8))* Capstone Press of Coughlan Cos.
—Ciencia Gráfica. Martin, Cynthia & Dominguez, Richard, illus. 2013. (Ciencia Gráfica Ser.). (SPA.). 32p. (gr. 3-4). lib. bdg. 245.20 *(978-1-62065-186-5(6))* Capstone Press of Coughlan Cos.
Blane, Francisco. Little Jack Horner. Price, Nick, illus. 2010. (Rising Readers Ser.). (J). 3.49 *(978-1-60719-701-0(4))* Newmark Learning LLC.
Boné, Thomas H., illus. The Teacher Who Would Not Retire Becomes a Movie Star. 2012. (J). *(978-0-9792918-6-9(0))* Blue Marlin Pubns.
—The Teacher Who Would Not Retire Discovers a New Planet. 2009. (J). 17.95 *(978-0-9792918-3-8(6))* Blue Marlin Pubns.
Boné, Thomas H., illus. The Teacher Who Would Not Retire Retires. 2017. (J). ***(978-0-9885295-7-1(2))*** Blue Marlin Pubns.
Borden, Louise. The Last Day of School. Gustavson, Adam, illus. 2006. (ENG.). 40p. (J). (gr. 2-5). 17.99 *(978-0-689-86869-6(3),* McElderry, Margaret K. Bks.) McElderry, Margaret K. Bks.
Bowen, Anne. I Know an Old Teacher. Gammell, Stephen, illus. 2008. (ENG.). 32p. (J). (gr. k-3). 16.95 *(978-0-8225-7984-7(7),* Carolrhoda Bks.) Lerner Publishing Group.
—Que Hacen los Maestros? (Despues de Que Te Vas de la Escuela) Gott, Barry, illus. 2007. (Ediciones Lerner Single Titles Ser.). (SPA.). 32p. (J). (gr. k-3). 16.95 *(978-0-8225-6264-1(2),* Ediciones Lerner) Lerner Publishing Group.
—What Do Teachers Do (After You Leave School)? Gott, Barry, illus. 2006. (ENG.). 32p. (J). (gr. k-3). 16.95 *(978-1-57505-922-8(3),* Carolrhoda Bks.) Lerner Publishing Group.
Brenner, Emily. On the First Day of Grade School. Whatley, Bruce, illus. 2004. 32p. (J). (gr. -1-1). lib. bdg. 16.89 *(978-0-06-051041-1(2))* HarperCollins Pubs.
Brezenoff, Steve. Cheaters. 2013. (Ravens Pass Ser.). (ENG.). 96p. (gr. 2-3). pap. 35.70 *(978-1-4342-6291-2(X))* Stone Arch Bks.
—Cheaters, 1 vol. Pinelli, Amerigo, illus. 2013. (Ravens Pass Ser.). (ENG.). 96p. (gr. 2-3). lib. bdg. 25.32 *(978-1-4342-4616-5(7))* Stone Arch Bks.
—Witch Mayor, 1 vol. Percival, Tom, illus. 2012. (Ravens Pass Ser.). (ENG.). 96p. (gr. 2-3). pap. 6.15 *(978-1-4342-4212-9(9));* lib. bdg. 25.32 *(978-1-4342-3791-0(5))* Stone Arch Bks.
Brink, LeeAnn. The Stuff in the Back of the Desk. Cratty, Aaron, illus. 2006. 24p. (J). per. 10.95 *(978-1-934246-05-4(0))* Peppertree Pr., The.
Broad, Michael. Hypno Hounds!, No. 3. Broad, Michael, illus. 2011. (Agent Amelia Ser.: 3). (ENG., Illus.). 144p. (J). (gr. 2-5). pap. 5.95 *(978-0-7613-8062-7(0),* Darby Creek); lib. bdg. 22.60 *(978-0-7613-8058-0(2))* Lerner Publishing Group.
—Zombie Cows! Broad, Michael, illus. 2011. (Agent Amelia Ser.: 2). (ENG., Illus.). 144p. (J). (gr. 2-5). pap. 5.95 *(978-0-7613-8066-5(3),* Darby Creek);No. 2. lib. bdg. 22.60 *(978-0-7613-8057-3(4))* Lerner Publishing Group.
—#2 Zombie Cows! 2011. (Agent Amelia Ser.). pap. 33.92 *(978-0-7613-8342-0(5),* Darby Creek) Lerner Publishing Group.
—#3 Hypno Hounds! 2011. (Agent Amelia Ser.). pap. 33.92 *(978-0-7613-8343-7(3),* Darby Creek) Lerner Publishing Group.
Brown, Marc. Arthur's Teacher Trouble. 2004. (Arthur Adventure Ser.). (J). (gr. k-3). spiral bd. *(978-0-616-01603-9(4));* spiral bd. *(978-0-616-00406-7(0))* Canadian National Institute for the Blind/Institut National Canadien pour les Aveugles.
—La Visita del Senor Rataquemada. Sarfatti, Esther, tr. from ENG. 2003.Tr. of Arthur's Teacher Moves In. (SPA.). (J). (gr. k-2). pap. 6.95 *(978-1-930332-41-6(6))* Lectorum Pubns., Inc.
Brown, Peter. My Teacher Is a Monster! (No, I Am Not.) 2014. (ENG., Illus.). 40p. (J). (gr. -1-3). 18.99 *(978-0-316-07029-4(7))* Little, Brown Bks. for Young Readers.
Burns, Jane. My Sister's My Teacher! 2017. (ENG.). 182p. (J). pap. 14.95 ***(978-1-78612-482-1(3),*** fe6f0a4c-28f1-46f4-8feb-0bca666a9e82) Austin, Stan AUS. Dist: Bookmasters Distribution.
Buyea, Rob. Because of Mr. Terupt. (ENG.). (J). (gr. 3-7). 2011. 304p. 7.99 *(978-0-375-85824-6(5),* Yearling) 2010. 288p. 16.99 *(978-0-385-73882-8(X),* Delacorte Bks. for Young Readers) Random Hse. Children's Bks.
Byler, Linda. Big Decisions: A Novel Based on True Experiences from an Amish Writer!, 1 vol. 2011. (ENG.). 345p. pap. 13.99 *(978-1-56148-700-4(7),* Good Bks.) Skyhorse Publishing Co., Inc.
—The Little Amish Matchmaker: A Christmas Romance. 2012. (ENG.). 187p. 14.95 *(978-1-56148-776-9(7),* Good Bks.) Skyhorse Publishing Co., Inc.
—When Strawberries Bloom: A Novel Based on the True Experiences from an Amish Writer! 2010. (ENG.). 297p. pap. 13.99 *(978-1-56148-699-1(X),* Good Bks.) Skyhorse Publishing Co., Inc.
Caldwell, Daisy L. Sarah the Oh So Silly, but Shy Stegosaurus, 1 vol. 2009. 24p. pap. 24.95 *(978-1-61546-319-0(4))* America Star Bks.
Calin, Marisa. Between You & Me. 2012. (ENG.). 256p. (YA). (gr. 7-12). 16.99 *(978-1-59990-758-1(5),* 9781599907581, Bloomsbury USA Childrens) Bloomsbury Publishing USA.
Callen, Sharon. Ms. Wilde & Oscar, 1 vol. rev. ed. 2013. (Fiction Readers Ser.). (ENG., Illus.). 32p. (J). (gr. 3-3). pap. 8.99 *(978-1-4333-5611-7(2))* Shell Educational Publishing.
—Ms. Wilde & Oscar. rev. ed. 2013. (Fiction Readers Ser.). (ENG., Illus.). 32p. (gr. 3-3). pap. 19.96 *(978-1-4807-1733-6(9))* Teacher Created Materials, Inc.
Calmenson, Stephanie. Oopsy, Teacher! Yoshikawa, Sachiko, illus. 2012. (Carolrhoda Picture Bks.). (ENG.). 32p. (J). (gr. -1-2). lib. bdg. 16.95 *(978-0-7613-5894-7(3))* Lerner Publishing Group.
Calmenson, Stephanie & Cole, Joanna. Teacher's Pets. Ross, Heather, illus. 2015. (Ready, Set, Dogs! Ser.: 2). (ENG.). 144p. (J). (gr. 1-4). pap. 5.99 *(978-1-250-05705-1(1),* 9781250057051) Square Fish.
Cartee, Mary. Go Forth My Angels. 2011. 82p. pap. 19.95 *(978-1-4626-4058-4(3))* America Star Bks.
Cassidy, Sara. Seeing Orange, 1 vol. Meissner, Amy, illus. 2012. (Orca Echoes Ser.). (ENG.). 64p. (J). (gr. 2-3). pap. 6.95 *(978-1-55469-991-9(6))* Orca Bk. Pubs. USA.

TUV

Chabert, Jack. Sam Battles the Machine! 2017. (Eerie Elementary — Branches Ser.: bk.6). (ENG.). (J). lib. bdg. 14.75 ***(978-0-606-40191-3(1))*** Turtleback Bks.

Chambers, Jerry. The Cat Who Became a Teacher. 2013. 40p. pap. 24.95 *(978-1-63000-040-0(X))* America Star Bks.

Chan, Marty. The Mystery of the Mad Science Teacher. 2008. (ENG.). 127p. (J). (gr. 2-7). pap. 10.95 *(978-1-897235-38-6(0))* Thistledown Pr., Ltd. CAN. Dist: Univ. of Toronto Pr.

Chatterton, Martin. The Brain Finds a Leg. 2007. 207p. *(978-1-921049-79-8(0))* Little Hare Bks. AUS. Dist: HarperCollins Pubs. Australia.

—The Brain Finds a Leg, 1 vol. 2009. (ENG.). 224p. (YA). (gr. 5-9). 16.95 *(978-1-56145-503-4(2))* Peachtree Pubs.

Chriscoe, Sharon. Scary Weather, Scaredy Cat, 1 vol. 2008. (ENG.). 48p. 24.95 *(978-1-60474-143-8(0))* America Star Bks.

Clark-Elliott, Mary. The Day Ms. Qualbaum Came to Visit. 2013. 44p. pap. 20.72 *(978-1-4907-0921-5(5))* Trafford Publishing.

Cleary, Beverly. Querido Senor Henshaw. 2003. (Ramona Quimby Ser.).Tr. of Dear Mr. Henshaw. (SPA.). 136p. (J). 9.95 *(978-84-239-9013-9(3))* Espasa Calpe, S.A. ESP. Dist: Planeta Publishing Corp.

Clements, Andrew. Frindle. Selznick, Brian, illus. 105p. (J). (gr. 3-5). pap. 4.50 *(978-0-8072-1522-7(8),* Listening Library) Random Hse. Audio Publishing Group.

—Frindle. unabr. ed. 2004. (Middle Grade Cassette Librariestm Ser.). 105p. (J). (gr. 3-7). pap. 29.00 incl. audio *(978-0-8072-7994-6(3),* S YA 961 SP, Listening Library) Random Hse. Audio Publishing Group.

—Head of the Class: Frindle - The Landry News - The Janitor's Boy. Selznick, Brian, illus. 2007. (ENG.). 416p. (J). (gr. 3-7). pap. 20.99 *(978-1-4169-4974-9(7),* Atheneum Bks. for Young Readers) Simon & Schuster Children's Publishing.

—Jake Drake, Class Clown. Pedersen, Janet, illus. 2007. (Jake Drake Ser.: Bk. 4). (ENG.). 96p. (J). (gr. 2-5). pap. 5.99 *(978-1-4169-4912-1(7),* Atheneum Bks. for Young Readers) Simon & Schuster Children's Publishing.

—Jake Drake, Teacher's Pet. Pedersen, Janet, illus. 2007. (Jake Drake Ser.: 3). (ENG.). 96p. (J). (gr. 2-5). pap. 5.99 *(978-1-4169-3932-0(6),* Atheneum Bks. for Young Readers) Simon & Schuster Children's Publishing.

—El Periodico Landry. Selznick, Brian, illus. 2004.Tr. of Landry News. (SPA.). (YA). pap. 9.99 *(978-84-241-7886-4(6))* Everest Editora ESP. Dist: Lectorum Pubns., Inc.

Collins, Paul. Lucy, the Boss. Bocquée, Christian, illus. 2015. (Legends in Their Own Lunchbox Ser.). (ENG.). 56p. (gr. 2-3). pap. 7.99 *(978-1-4966-0254-1(4),* Legends in Their Own Lunchbox) Capstone Classroom.

Cooper, Barbara. Emma Exclamation Point. Raynor, Maggie, illus. 2004. (Meet the Puncs: A Remarkable Punctuation Family Ser.). 32p. (gr. 1-4). lib. bdg. 26.00 *(978-0-8368-4225-8(1),* Gareth Stevens Learning Library) Stevens, Gareth Publishing LLLP.

Cooper, Jay. Mutant Rat Attack! 2017. (Spy Next Door Ser.: 1). (ENG.). 144p. (J). (gr. 2-5). 9.99 *(978-0-545-93297-4(1),* Scholastic Pr.) Scholastic, Inc.

Coppock, Phil & Bower's 2008-2009 4th Grade Class. Rubber Tuesday. 2010. 70p. pap. 12.95 *(978-1-4327-5751-9(2))* Outskirts Pr., Inc.

Coville, Bruce. My Teacher Is an Alien. (My Teacher Is an Alien Ser.: Bk. 1). 123p. (J). (Illus.). (gr. 4-7). pap. 4.50 *(978-0-8072-1528-9(7))*; 2004. (gr. 3-6). pap. 29.00 incl. audio *(978-0-8072-8029-4(1),* S YA 971 SP) Random Hse. Audio Publishing Group. (Listening Library).

Cox, Judy. Don't Be Silly, Mrs. Millie!, 0 vols. Mathieu, Joe, illus. 2010. (ENG.). 34p. (J). (gr. k-3). pap. 6.99 *(978-0-7614-5727-5(5),* 9780761457275, Amazon Children's Publishing) Amazon Publishing.

—Happy Birthday, Mrs. Millie!, 0 vols. Mathieu, Joe, illus. 2012. (ENG.). 32p. (J). (gr. k-3). 16.99 *(978-0-7614-6126-5(4),* 9780761461265, Amazon Children's Publishing) Amazon Publishing.

—Mrs. Millie Goes to Philly!, 0 vols. Mathieu, Joe, illus. 2013. (ENG.). 32p. (J). (gr. -1-2). pap. 9.99 *(978-1-4778-1680-6(1),* 9781477816806, Amazon Children's Publishing) Amazon Publishing.

—Pick a Pumpkin, Mrs. Millie!, 0 vols. Mathieu, Joe, illus. 2009. (ENG.). 32p. (J). (gr. -1-3). 15.99 *(978-0-7614-5573-8(6),* 9780761455738, Amazon Children's Publishing) Amazon Publishing.

Crane, Carol. Handkerchief Quilt. Palmer, Gary, illus. 2010. (ENG.). 32p. (J). (gr. k-3). 15.95 *(978-1-58536-344-5(8))* Sleeping Bear Pr.

Creech, Sharon. A Fine, Fine School. 2004. (Illus.). (J). (gr. k-3). spiral bd. *(978-0-616-11107-9(X))* Canadian National Institute for the Blind/Institut National Canadien pour les Aveugles.

—A Fine, Fine School. Bliss, Harry, illus. 2004. (J). (gr. k-3). spiral bd. *(978-0-616-11106-2(1))* Canadian National Institute for the Blind/Institut National Canadien pour les Aveugles.

—A Fine, Fine School. Bliss, Harry, illus. 2003. (ENG.). 32p. (J). (gr. -1-3). pap. 6.99 *(978-0-06-000728-7(1))* HarperCollins Pubs.

Crisanaz, Catherine M. The Best House for Molly. 2008. 36p. per. 24.95 *(978-1-4241-9093-5(2))* America Star Bks.

Crow, P. For the Love of Miss Bard. 2010. 222p. pap. 18.00 *(978-0-9802257-9-2(5))* Peddlers Group.

Cuchna, Reid. Out of Love, 1 vol. 2009. 327p. pap. 29.95 *(978-1-60836-345-2(7))* America Star Bks.

Dahl, Roald. Matilda. 2007.Tr. of Matilda. 18.40 *(978-1-4177-8613-8(2),* Turtleback) Turtleback Bks.

Danneberg, Julie. The Big Test. Love, Judy, illus. 2011. (Mrs. Hartwells Classroom Adventures Ser.). (ENG.). 32p. (J). (gr. 1-4). 16.95 *(978-1-58089-360-2(0))*; pap. 7.95 *(978-1-58089-361-9(9))* Charlesbridge Publishing, Inc.

—Field-Trip Fiasco. Love, Judy, illus. 2015. (Mrs. Hartwells Classroom Adventures Ser.). (ENG.). 32p. (J). (gr. k-3). 16.95 *(978-1-58089-671-9(5))* Charlesbridge Publishing, Inc.

—First Year Letters. Love, Judy, illus. 2014. 32p. pap. 7.00 *(978-1-61003-320-6(5))* Center for the Collaborative Classroom.

—First Year Letters. Love, Judy, illus. 2003. (Mrs. Hartwells Classroom Adventures Ser.). (ENG.). 32p. (J). (gr. 1-4). 16.95 *(978-1-58089-084-7(9))*; pap. 6.95 *(978-1-58089-085-4(7))* Charlesbridge Publishing, Inc.

—Last Day Blues. Love, Judy, illus. 2006. (Mrs. Hartwells Classroom Adventures Ser.). (ENG.). 32p. (J). (gr. k-3). 7.95 *(978-1-58089-104-2(7))* Charlesbridge Publishing, Inc.

Danziger, Paula. The Cat Ate My Gymsuit. 2006. (ENG.). 176p. (J). (gr. 5-18). 8.99 *(978-0-14-240654-0(6),* Puffin Books) Penguin Young Readers Group.

Deal, Sarah E. The Spotless Ladybug. 2008. 31p. pap. 24.95 *(978-1-60672-964-9(0))* America Star Bks.

Dean, James. Pete the Cat & the Surprise Teacher. Dean, James, illus. 2017. (My First I Can Read Ser.). (Illus.). 32p. (J). (gr. -1-3). 3.99 *(978-0-06-240428-2(8))* HarperCollins Pubs.

DeBray, Sherry. The Teacher's Gift. Cauthen, Tommy, illus. 2004. 30p. *(978-1-59421-007-5(1))* Seacoast Publishing, Inc.

Decker, Wendy. The Bedazzling Bowl. 2006. pap. 13.99 *(978-1-60034-468-8(2))* Salem Author Services.

DeClements, Barthe. Fourth Grade Wizards. 2008. (ENG.). 128p. (J). (gr. 3-7). 5.99 *(978-0-14-241348-7(8),* Puffin Books) Penguin Young Readers Group.

Depken, Kristen L. Driving School. 2013. (Cars Step into Reading Ser.). lib. bdg. 13.55 *(978-0-606-31932-4(8),* Turtleback) Turtleback Bks.

Derby, Sally. Whoosh Went the Wind!, 0 vols. 2013. (ENG.). 32p. (J). (gr. k-3). pap. 9.99 *(978-1-4778-1677-6(1),* 9781477816776, Amazon Children's Publishing) Amazon Publishing.

Diroma, Joseph. Pinuccio. Jones, Bob, illus. 2009. 24p. pap. 14.99 *(978-1-60844-036-8(2))* Dog Ear Publishing, LLC.

Disney Book Group Staff. Mickey Mouse Clubhouse Choo Choo Express. 2009. (ENG.). 16p. (J). (gr. -1-k). pap. 4.99 *(978-1-4231-2230-2(5))* Disney Pr.

Disney Book Group Staff & Ryals, Lexi. Jessie Livin' the Life. 2014. (Jessie Junior Novel Ser.). (ENG.). 128p. (J). (gr. 3-7). pap. 5.99 *(978-1-4231-8411-9(4))* Disney Pr.

du Bois, William Pène. Twenty-One Balloons. du Bois, William Pène, illus. 2005. (Illus.). 180p. (J). lib. bdg. 15.00 *(978-1-4242-2270-4(2))* Fitzgerald Bks.

Duncan, Lois. Killing Mr. Griffin. 2010. (ENG.). 272p. (YA). (gr. 7-17). pap. 10.99 *(978-0-316-09900-4(7))* Little, Brown Bks. for Young Readers.

Dyer, K. C. Ms. Zephyr's Notebook. 2007. (ENG., Illus.). 206p. (YA). (gr. 7). pap. 12.99 *(978-1-55002-691-7(7),* Boardwalk Bks.) Dundurn CAN. Dist: Ingram Publisher Services.

Earl, David G. Koala Koala, I'm Not a Bear, I'm a Koala. Gentry, T. Kyle, illus. 2009. 32p. pap. 12.95 *(978-1-936051-22-9(2))* Peppertree Pr., The.

Eaton, Kelly Toole. Kellina Makes Her Dreams Come True. 2011. 40p. pap. 21.99 *(978-1-4568-8824-4(2))* Xlibris Corp.

Ecton, Anne Massey. Passing Through Camelot. 2006. (J). *(978-0-88092-620-1(1))* Royal Fireworks Publishing Co.

Edwards, Wysteria. Bethany Bubbles Makes a Mistake. Abbott, Jason, illus. 2011. 34p. pap. 14.50 *(978-1-60911-353-7(5),* Strategic Bk. Publishing) Strategic Book Publishing & Rights Agency (SBPRA).

Elliott, Rebecca. A Woodland Wedding. Elliott, Rebecca, illus. 2016. (Owl Diaries: 3). (ENG., Illus.). 80p. (J). (gr. k-2). 15.99 *(978-0-545-82558-0(X))* Scholastic, Inc.

Enderle, Dotti. Tell No One!, 1 vol. McWilliam, Howard, illus. 2010. (Ghost Detectors Ser.: No. 1). (ENG.). 80p. (J). (gr. 2-5). 27.07 *(978-1-60270-692-7(1))* Magic Wagon.

English, Karen. Nikki & Deja: Substitute Trouble. Freeman, Laura, illus. 2014. (ENG.). 112p. (J). (gr. 1-4). pap. 5.99 *(978-0-544-22388-2(8),* HMH Books For Young Readers) Houghton Mifflin Harcourt Publishing Co.

—Wedding Drama. Freeman, Laura, illus. 2013. (ENG.). 112p. (J). (gr. 1-4). pap. 5.99 *(978-0-544-00324-8(1))* Houghton Mifflin Harcourt Publishing Co.

Esham, Barbaraa. Mrs. Gorski, I Think I Have the Wiggle Fidgets. Gordon, Mike, illus. 2008. (ENG, SPA & FRE.). 32p. (J). (gr. k-18). 16.95 *(978-1-60336-469-0(2),* Adventures of Everyday Geniuses, The) Mainstream Connections Publishing.

Evans, Stephanie. Steven James: I Just Can't Pay Attention. 2011. 28p. 12.03 *(978-1-4567-2707-9(9))* AuthorHouse.

Feder, Aliza & Sofer, Rochel. We Need to Talk. 2008. 250p. 18.95 *(978-1-934440-30-8(2),* Devora Publishing) Simcha Media Group.

Figley, Marty Rhodes. The Prairie Adventure of Sarah & Annie, Blizzard Survivors. Hammond, Ted & Carbajal, Richard Pimentel, illus. 2011. (History's Kid Heroes Set III Ser.). pap. 51.02 *(978-0-7613-8621-6(1))*; (ENG.). 32p. (gr. 3-5). pap. 8.95 *(978-0-7613-7808-2(1))* Lerner Publishing Group. (Graphic Universe™).

—The Prairie Adventure of Sarah & Annie, Blizzard Survivors. Hammond, Ted & Carbajal, Richard, illus. 2011. (History's Kid Heroes Ser.). (ENG.). 32p. (gr. 3-5). lib. bdg. 26.60 *(978-0-7613-7805-1(7))* Lerner Publishing Group.

—The Schoolchildren's Blizzard. Haas, Shelly O., illus. 2004. (On My Own History Ser.). (ENG.). 48p. (gr. 2-4). lib. bdg. 25.26 *(978-1-57505-586-2(4),* Carolrhoda Bks.) Lerner Publishing Group.

Finchler, Judy & O'Malley, Kevin. Miss Malarkey Leaves No Reader Behind. O'Malley, Kevin, illus. 2010. (Miss Malarkey Ser.). (ENG., Illus.). 32p. (J). (gr. k-3). pap. 7.99 *(978-0-8027-2098-6(6),* 9780802720986, Bloomsbury USA Childrens) Bloomsbury Publishing USA.

Finley, Leah. Ms T. 2007. 108p. (J). per. 8.95 *(978-0-9794815-1-2(1))* Bellissima Publishing, LLC.

—The One & Only Mr C. 2009. 82p. pap. 8.95 *(978-1-935118-75-6(7))* Bellissima Publishing, LLC.

Fischer, JoAnn. Our Teacher Is A Fish! 2008. (ENG.). 34p. pap. 10.00 *(978-1-4196-7477-8(3))* CreateSpace Independent Publishing Platform.

Flake, Sharon G. The Skin I'm In. 2007. (J). lib. bdg. 19.65 *(978-1-4178-0860-1(8),* Turtleback) Turtleback Bks.

Fleischman, Paul. The Dunderheads. Roberts, David, illus. 2012. (ENG.). 56p. (J). (gr. 1-4). pap. 6.99 *(978-0-7636-5239-5(3))* Candlewick Pr.

Fleming, Candace. The Fabled Fifth Graders of Aesop Elementary School. 2012. (Aesop Elementary School Ser.). (ENG.). 176p. (J). (gr. 2-5). 7.99 *(978-0-375-87187-0(X),* Yearling) Random Hse. Children's Bks.

—The Fabled Fourth Graders of Aesop Elementary School. 2009. (Aesop Elementary School Ser.). (ENG.). 192p. (J). (gr. 2-5). 6.99 *(978-0-440-42229-7(9),* Yearling) Random Hse. Children's Bks.

Fletcher, Ralph. Flying Solo. 2008. (ENG.). 144p. (J). (gr. 5-7). pap. 7.99 *(978-0-547-07652-2(5))* Houghton Mifflin Harcourt Publishing Co.

Fox, Alex. Windsock Wesley & His Wild & Wonderful Weather MacHine, Living in Cloud. Bazzoni, Lainie M. A., illus. 2010. 48p. pap. 16.50 *(978-1-60911-873-0(1),* Eloquent Bks.) Strategic Book Publishing & Rights Agency (SBPRA).

Fox, Jennifer. My Little Pony: Hearts & Hooves. 2013. (Passport to Reading Level 1 Ser.). (ENG., Illus.). 32p. (J). (gr. -1-3). 4.99 *(978-0-316-24797-9(9))* Little, Brown Bks. for Young Readers.

Francis, Pauline, retold by. The Turn of the Screw. 2010. (Essential Classics - Horror Ser.). (Illus.). 48p. pap. *(978-0-237-54110-1(6))* Evans Brothers, Ltd.

Frank, E. R. Friction. 2004. (ENG.). 208p. (YA). (gr. 7). reprint ed. pap. 10.99 *(978-0-689-85385-2(8),* Simon Pulse) Simon Pulse.

Friedrich, Joachim. The Disappearing Bio Teacher. Date not set. (Illus.). 144p. (J). (gr. 3-7). 14.99 *(978-0-7868-0700-0(8))* Hyperion Pr.

Frost, Helen. Room 214: a Year in Poems. 2014. (ENG., Illus.). 128p. (J). (gr. 5-9). pap. 8.99 *(978-1-250-04009-1(4),* 9781250040091) Square Fish.

Funny, Ania. The Power of Ania to Change the World of Bullying. 2012. 28p. pap. 15.99 *(978-1-4797-4599-9(5))* Xlibris Corp.

Galante, Cecilia. The Summer of May. Carpenter, Tad, illus. 2012. (ENG.). 256p. (J). (gr. 4-8). pap. 6.99 *(978-1-4169-8304-0(X),* Simon & Schuster/Paula Wiseman Bks.) Simon & Schuster/Paula Wiseman Bks.

Gall, Chris. Substitute Creacher. 2011. (ENG., Illus.). 40p. (J). (gr. -1-3). 16.99 *(978-0-316-08915-9(X))* Little, Brown Bks. for Young Readers.

Gao, Charlie. Children City & Teacher Town. 2009. 80p. pap. 10.49 *(978-1-4389-7547-4(3))* AuthorHouse.

Garland, Michael. Miss Smith & the Haunted Library. 2012. (ENG.). 32p. (J). (gr. -1-2). 6.99 *(978-0-14-242122-2(7),* Puffin Books) Penguin Young Readers Group.

—Miss Smith & the Haunted Library. Garland, Michael, illus. 2009. (ENG., Illus.). 32p. (J). (gr. -1-2). 16.99 *(978-0-525-42139-9(4),* Dutton Books for Young Readers) Penguin Young Readers Group.

—Miss Smith Reads Again! 2006. (Illus.). (J). *(978-1-4156-8098-8(1),* Dutton Juvenile) Penguin Publishing Group.

—Miss Smith Reads Again! Garland, Michael, illus. 2008. (ENG., Illus.). 32p. (J). (gr. -1-2). pap. 6.99 *(978-0-14-241140-7(X),* Puffin Books) Penguin Young Readers Group.

—Miss Smith's Incredible Storybook. Garland, Michael, illus. (ENG., Illus.). 32p. (J). (gr. -1-2). 2005. pap. 6.99 *(978-0-14-240282-5(6),* Puffin Books) 2003. 16.99 *(978-0-525-47133-2(2),* Dutton Books for Young Readers) Penguin Young Readers Group.

—Miss Smith's Incredible Storybook. 2007. 29.95 incl. audio compact disk *(978-0-8045-4159-6(0))*; 27.95 incl. audio *(978-0-8045-6945-3(2))* Spoken Arts, Inc.

Gelenius, Deb. My Mom, My Teacher. 2013. 28p. pap. 11.95 *(978-1-61244-135-1(1))* Halo Publishing International.

Gensler, Sonia. The Revenant. 2013. (ENG.). 354p. (YA). (gr. 7). pap. 9.99 *(978-0-375-86139-0(4),* Ember) Random Hse. Children's Bks.

Gilbert, Frances. Today the Teacher Changed Our Seats. 2012. (Illus.). 24p. pap. 17.99 *(978-1-4772-9905-0(X))* AuthorHouse.

Gilman, Charles. Professor Gargoyle. 2012. (Tales from Lovecraft Middle School Ser.: 1). (ENG., Illus.). 160p. (J). (gr. 4-7). 13.99 *(978-1-59474-591-1(9))* Quirk Bks.

—The Slither Sisters. 2013. (Tales from Lovecraft Middle School Ser.: 2). (ENG., Illus.). 160p. (J). (gr. 4-7). 13.99 *(978-1-59474-593-5(5))* Quirk Bks.

—Teacher's Pest. 2013. (Tales from Lovecraft Middle School Ser.: 3). (ENG., Illus.). 176p. (YA). (gr. 4-7). 13.99 *(978-1-59474-614-7(1))* Quirk Bks.

Glennon, Michelle. My Big Green Teacher: Don't Rock the Boat: Saving Our Oceans. Glennon, Michelle, illus. 2008. (Illus.). 32p. (J). 19.95 *(978-0-9796625-2-2(4))* GDG Publishing.

—My Big Green Teacher: Please Turn off the Lights. Glennon, Michelle, illus. 2008. (ENG., Illus.). 32p. (J). 19.95 *(978-0-9796625-3-9(2))* GDG Publishing.

—My Big Green Teacher: Seven Generations from Now. Glennon, Michelle, illus. 2008. (Illus.). (J). 19.95 *(978-0-9797952-1-3(4))* GDG Publishing.

—My Big Green Teacher: Take a Deep Breath: Saving Our Rainforests. Glennon, Michelle, illus. 2008. (ENG., Illus.). 32p. (J). 19.95 *(978-0-9797952-0-6(6))* GDG Publishing.

—My Big Green Teacher: Taking the Green Road. Glennon, Michelle, illus. 2008. (Illus.). 32p. (J). 19.95 *(978-0-9796625-7-7(5))* GDG Publishing.

—My Big Green Teacher: Recycling: It's Easy Being Green. Glennon, Michelle, illus. 2007. (Illus.). 32p. (J). 19.95 *(978-0-9796625-6-0(7))* GDG Publishing.

Grant, Vicki. Cochonnet: (Pigboy), 1 vol. 2011. (FRE.). 112p. (J). (gr. 5-9). pap. 9.95 *(978-1-4598-0006-9(0))* Orca Bk. Pubs. USA.

—Pigboy, 1 vol. 2006. (Orca Currents Ser.). (ENG.). 128p. (J). (gr. 5-9). per. 9.95 *(978-1-55143-643-2(4))* Orca Bk. Pubs. USA.

Greene, Stephanie. Princess Posey & the Monster Stew, 4 vols. Sisson, Stéphanie Roth, illus. 2012. (Princess Posey, First Grader Ser.: 4). (ENG.). 96p. (J). (gr. k-3). pap. 5.99 *(978-0-14-242105-5(7),* Puffin Books) Penguin Young Readers Group.

—Princess Posey & the Perfect Present, Bk. 2. Sisson, Stéphanie Roth, illus. 2011. (Princess Posey, First Grader Ser.: 2). (ENG.). 96p. (J). (gr. k-3). 5.99 *(978-0-14-241828-4(5),* Puffin Books); 12.99 *(978-0-399-25462-8(5),* G.P. Putnam's Sons Books for Young Readers) Penguin Young Readers Group.

—Princess Posey & the Tiny Treasure. Sisson, Stéphanie Roth, illus. 2013. (Princess Posey, First Grader Ser.: 5). (ENG.). 96p. (J). (gr. k-3). pap. 5.99 *(978-0-14-242415-5(3),* Puffin Books) Penguin Young Readers Group.

Griffiths, Andy. Treasure Fever! 2008. (Schooling Around Ser.: No. 1). 198p. (J). pap. *(978-0-545-09222-7(1))* Scholastic, Inc.

Guest, Elissa Haden. Iris & Walter & the Substitute Teacher. Davenier, Christine, illus. 2006. (Iris & Walter Ser.). 44p. (gr. 1-4). 15.95 *(978-0-7569-7122-9(5))* Perfection Learning Corp.

Gutman, Dan. Back to School, Weird Kids Rule! Paillot, Jim, illus. 2014. (My Weird School Special Ser.). (ENG.). 144p. (J). (gr. 1-5). pap. 5.99 *(978-0-06-220685-5(0))* HarperCollins Pubs.

—Miss Brown Is Upside Down! Paillot, Jim, illus. 2015. (My Weirdest School Ser.: 3). (ENG.). 112p. (J). (gr. 1-5). pap. 4.99 *(978-0-06-228427-3(4))* HarperCollins Pubs.

—Miss Daisy Is Crazy! Paillot, Jim, illus. 2004. (My Weird School Ser.: 1). (ENG.). 96p. (J). (gr. 1-5). pap. 4.99 *(978-0-06-050700-8(4))* HarperCollins Pubs.

—Miss Holly Is Too Jolly! Paillot, Jim, illus. 2006. (My Weird School Ser.: 14). (ENG.). 112p. (J). (gr. 1-5). pap. 4.99 *(978-0-06-085382-2(4))* HarperCollins Pubs.

—Miss Kraft Is Daft! Paillot, Jim, illus. 2012. (My Weirder School Ser.: 7). (J). lib. bdg. 14.75 *(978-0-606-27125-7(2),* Turtleback) Turtleback Bks.

—Miss Laney Is Zany! Paillot, Jim, illus. 2010. (My Weird School Daze Ser.: 8). 112p. (J). (gr. 1-5). (ENG.). pap. 4.99 *(978-0-06-155415-5(4))*; lib. bdg. 15.89 *(978-0-06-155417-9(0))* HarperCollins Pubs.

—Miss Laney Is Zany! 2010. (My Weird School Daze Ser.: 8). (J). lib. bdg. 14.75 *(978-0-606-10112-7(8),* Turtleback) Turtleback Bks.

—Miss Mary Is Scary! Paillot, Jim, illus. 2010. (My Weird School Daze Ser.: 10). 112p. (J). (gr. 1-5). (ENG.). pap. 4.99 *(978-0-06-170397-3(4))*; lib. bdg. 15.89 *(978-0-06-170398-0(2))* HarperCollins Pubs.

—Miss Suki Is Kooky! Paillot, Jim, illus. 2007. (My Weird School Ser.: 17). (ENG.). 112p. (J). (gr. 1-5). pap. 4.99 *(978-0-06-123473-6(7))* HarperCollins Pubs.

—Mr. Cooper Is Super! Paillot, Jim, illus. 2015. (My Weirdest School Ser.: 1). (ENG.). 112p. (J). (gr. 1-5). pap. 4.99 *(978-0-06-228421-1(5))* HarperCollins Pubs.

—Mr. Cooper Is Super! Paillot, Jim, illus. 2015. (My Weirdest School Ser.: 1). (J). lib. bdg. 14.75 *(978-0-606-36482-9(X))* Turtleback Bks.

—Mr. Docker Is off His Rocker! Paillot, Jim, illus. 2006. (My Weird School Ser.: 10). (ENG.). 112p. (J). (gr. 1-5). pap. 4.99 *(978-0-06-082227-9(9))* HarperCollins Pubs.

—Mr. Granite Is from Another Planet!, No. 3. Paillot, Jim, illus. 2008. (My Weird School Daze Ser.: 3). (ENG.). 112p. (J). (gr. 1-5). pap. 4.99 *(978-0-06-134611-8(X))* HarperCollins Pubs.

—Mr. Jack Is a Maniac! Paillot, Jim, illus. 2014. (My Weirder School Ser.: 10). 112p. (J). (gr. 1-5). (ENG.). pap. 4.99 *(978-0-06-219841-9(6))*; lib. bdg. 15.89 *(978-0-06-219842-6(4))* HarperCollins Pubs.

—Mr. Jack Is a Maniac! 2014. (My Weirder School Ser.: 10). (J). lib. bdg. 13.55 *(978-0-606-35066-2(7),* Turtleback) Turtleback Bks.

—Mr. Nick Is a Lunatic! Paillot, Jim, illus. 2016. (My Weirdest School Ser.: 6). 112p. (J). (gr. 1-5). pap. 4.99 *(978-0-06-228436-5(3))* HarperCollins Pubs.

—Mr. Sunny Is Funny! Paillot, Jim, illus. 2008. (My Weird School Daze Ser.: 2). 112p. (J). (gr. 1-5). (ENG.). pap. 4.99 *(978-0-06-134609-5(8))*;No. 2. lib. bdg. 15.89 *(978-0-06-134610-1(1))* HarperCollins Pubs.

—Mr. Tony Is Full of Baloney! Paillot, Jim, illus. 2010. (My Weird School Daze Ser.: 11). 112p. (J). (gr. 1-5). (ENG.). pap. 4.99 *(978-0-06-170399-7(0))*; lib. bdg. 15.89 *(978-0-06-170400-0(8))* HarperCollins Pubs.

—Mrs. Dole Is Out of Control! Paillot, Jim, illus. 2008. (My Weird School Daze Ser.: 1). (ENG.). 112p. (J). (gr. 1-5). pap. 4.99 *(978-0-06-134607-1(1))* HarperCollins Pubs.

—Mrs. Lizzy Is Dizzy! Paillot, Jim, illus. 2010. (My Weird School Daze Ser.: 9). 112p. (J). (gr. 1-5). (ENG.). pap. 4.99 *(978-0-06-155416-2(2))*; lib. bdg. 15.89 *(978-0-06-155418-6(9))* HarperCollins Pubs.

—Mrs. Lizzy Is Dizzy! 2010. (My Weird School Daze Ser.: 9). (J). lib. bdg. 14.75 *(978-0-606-10113-4(6),* Turtleback) Turtleback Bks.

—Mrs. Master Is a Disaster! 2017. (My Weirdest School Ser.: 8). lib. bdg. 14.75 ***(978-0-606-40078-7(8))*** Turtleback Bks.

—Mrs. Meyer Is on Fire! Paillot, Jim, illus. 2016. 105p. (J). ***(978-1-4806-9926-7(8))*** Harper & Row Ltd.

—Mrs. Yonkers Is Bonkers! Paillot, Jim, illus. 2007. (My Weird School Ser.: 18). (ENG.). 112p. (J). (gr. 1-5). pap. 4.99 *(978-0-06-123475-0(3))* HarperCollins Pubs.

—Mrs. Yonkers Is Bonkers! Paillot, Jim, illus. 2007. (My Weird School Ser.: 18). (J). 14.75 *(978-1-4177-8222-2(6),* Turtleback) Turtleback Bks.

—Ms. Beard Is Weird! Paillot, Jim, illus. 2012. (My Weirder School Ser.: 5). (ENG.). 112p. (J). (gr. 1-5). pap. 4.99 *(978-0-06-204209-5(2))* HarperCollins Pubs.

—Ms. Cuddy Is Nutty! Paillot, Jim, illus. 2015. (My Weirdest School Ser.: 2). 112p. (J). (gr. 1-5). (ENG.). pap. 4.99 *(978-0-06-228424-2(X))*; lib. bdg. 15.89 *(978-0-06-228425-9(8))* HarperCollins Pubs.

—Ms. Hannah Is Bananas! Paillot, Jim, illus. 2004. (My Weird School Ser.: 4). (ENG.). 96p. (J). (gr. 1-5). pap. 4.99 *(978-0-06-050706-0(3))* HarperCollins Pubs.

—Ms. Krup Cracks Me Up! Paillot, Jim, illus. 2008. (My Weird School Ser.: 21). (ENG.). 112p. (J). (gr. 1-5). pap. 4.99 *(978-0-06-134605-7(5))* HarperCollins Pubs.

—Ms. Leakey Is Freaky! No. 12. Paillot, Jim, illus. 2011. (My Weird School Daze Ser.: 12). (ENG.). 112p. (J). (gr. 1-5). pap. 4.99 *(978-0-06-170402-4(4))* HarperCollins Pubs.

—My Weird School Daze! Paillot, Jim, illus. 2007. (J). *(978-1-4287-4814-9(8))* HarperCollins Pubs.

—My Weird School Daze 12-Book Box Set, 12 vols. Paillot, Jim, illus. 2013. (My Weird School Daze Ser.). (ENG.). 500p. (J). (gr. 1-5). pap. 45.00 *(978-0-06-228891-2(1))* HarperCollins Pubs.

—My Weirdest School #8: Mrs. Master Is a Disaster! Paillot, Jim, illus. 2017. (My Weirdest School Ser.: 8). 112p. (J). (gr. 1-5). pap. 4.99 *(978-0-06-242933-9(7))* HarperCollins Pubs.

—Oh, Valentine, We've Lost Our Minds! Paillot, Jim, illus. 2014. (My Weird School Special Ser.). (ENG.). 144p. (J). (gr. 1-5). pap. 5.99 *(978-0-06-228403-7(7))* HarperCollins Pubs.

—Oh, Valentine, We've Lost Our Minds! 2014. (My Weird School Ser.). (J). lib. bdg. 16.00 *(978-0-606-36460-7(9))* Turtleback Bks.

Haberdasher, Violet. Knightley Academy. 2011. (ENG.). 512p. (J). (gr. 3-7). pap. 5.99 *(978-1-4169-9144-1(1),* Aladdin) Simon & Schuster Children's Publishing.

Haggard, H. Rider. Red Eve. 2007. (ENG.). 266p. pap. 21.99 *(978-1-4346-4929-4(6));* 294p. pap. 23.99 *(978-1-4346-4930-0(X))* Creative Media Partners, LLC.

Hale, Bruce. Curse of the Were-Hyena: A Monstertown Mystery. Hale, Bruce, illus. 2016. (Monstertown Mysteries Ser.). (ENG., Illus.). 220p. (J). (gr. 3-7). 14.99 *(978-1-4847-1325-9(7))* Disney Pr.

Hallinan, P. K. My Teacher's My Friend. (ENG.). 22p. (J). pap. 6.55 *(978-0-8249-5308-9(8),* Ideal Pubns.) Worthy Publishing.

Hambrick, Sharon. Brain Games. 2009. (J). 8.99 *(978-1-59166-954-8(5))* BJU Pr.

Handwerk, Marina. Hey Cool, I've Never Seen a Teacher with His Head Cut off Before! 2007. 284p. per. 11.95 *(978-1-4327-0332-5(3))* Outskirts Pr., Inc.

Harley, Bill. Charlie Bumpers vs. the Teacher of the Year, 1 vol. Gustavson, Adam, illus. (Charlie Bumpers Ser.). (ENG.). 160p. (J). 2014. pap. 6.95 *(978-1-56145-824-0(4))* 2013. (gr. 2-4). 14.95 *(978-1-56145-732-8(9))* Peachtree Pubs.

Harney, D. G. Meet Mr. Ugly, 1 vol. 2010. 133p. pap. 24.95 *(978-1-4489-5191-8(7))* America Star Bks.

Harper, Charise Mericle. Still Just Grace. (Just Grace Ser.: 2). (ENG., Illus.). 160p. (J). 2009. (gr. 1-4). pap. 5.99 *(978-0-618-93482-9(0))* 2007. (gr. 2-5). 15.99 *(978-0-618-64643-2(4))* Houghton Mifflin Harcourt Publishing Co.

Harper, Jamie. Miss Mingo & the Fire Drill. Harper, Jamie, illus. 2012. (ENG., Illus.). 40p. (J). (gr. -1-3). pap. 6.99 *(978-0-7636-6086-4(8))* Candlewick Pr.

—Miss Mingo & the First Day of School. 2006. (Illus.). 26p. (J). *(978-1-4156-9174-8(6))* Candlewick Pr.

Harper, Jamie. Miss Mingo Weathers the Storm. Harper, Jamie, illus. (ENG., Illus.). (J). (gr. -1-3). 2017. 6.99 ***(978-0-7636-9514-9(9))*** 2012. 15.99 *(978-0-7636-4931-9(7))* Candlewick Pr.

Harris, Valerie F. & Jones, Eula V. My Teacher Doesn't Like Me. Date not set. 22p. (J). (gr. k-6). pap. *(978-1-889654-00-3(0))* Enricharamics, Inc.

Harriton, Maxine. A School Trip to the Fruit Planet, 1. I.t. ed. 2006. 34p. (J). (gr. -1-1). lib. bdg. 18.95 *(978-0-9787248-0-1(1),* 00-01-851-447X) UpTree Publishing.

Hayes, Carolyn. School Starts Today: The Mccool School Series. 2011. 28p. pap. 13.59 *(978-1-4520-6747-6(3))* AuthorHouse.

Henkes, Kevin. El Gran Dia de Lily, 1 vol. Posada, Maria Candelaria, tr. from ENG. Henkes, Kevin, illus. 2008. (SPA., Illus.). 40p. (J). (gr. -1-3). 17.99 *(978-0-06-136316-0(2))* HarperCollins Pubs.

—Lilly's Big Day. Henkes, Kevin, illus. 2006. (Illus.). 40p. (J). (gr. -1-3). (ENG.). 17.99 *(978-0-06-074236-2(4));* lib. bdg. 18.89 *(978-0-06-074237-9(2))* HarperCollins Pubs. (Greenwillow Bks.).

—Lilly's Big Day. 2014. (J). lib. bdg. 17.20 *(978-0-606-35472-1(7))* Turtleback Bks.

—Lilly's Purple Plastic Purse. Henkes, Kevin, illus. 10th anniv. ed. 2006. (ENG., Illus.). 40p. (J). (gr. -1-4). 17.99 *(978-0-688-12897-5(1),* Greenwillow Bks.) HarperCollins Pubs.

—Lilly's Purple Plastic Purse. Henkes, Kevin, illus. (Illus.). pap. 18.95 incl. audio compact disk *(978-1-59112-347-7(X));* pap. incl. audio compact disk *(978-1-59112-557-0(X));* pap. incl. audio *(978-0-87499-688-3(0));* pap. 16.95 incl. audio *(978-0-87499-686-9(4))* Live Oak Media.

—Lilly's Purple Plastic Purse 20th Anniversary Edition. Henkes, Kevin, illus. 20th ed. 2016. (Illus.). 40p. (J). (gr. -1-3). 17.99 *(978-0-06-242419-8(X),* Greenwillow Bks.) HarperCollins Pubs.

Henkes, Kevin. Lilly y Su Bolso de Plastico Morado. 2017.Tr. of Lilly's Purple Plastic Purse. (SPA.). (J). pap. ***(978-1-63245-667-0(2))*** Lectorum Pubns., Inc.

Hiaasen, Carl. Scat. 2011. 10.54 *(978-0-7848-3574-6(8),* Everbind) Marco Bk. Co.

—Scat. (ENG.). (J). (gr. 5). 2012. 400p. 7.99 *(978-0-440-42104-7(7),* Yearling) 2010. 384p. pap. 8.99 *(978-0-375-83487-5(7),* Ember) 2009. 384p. 16.99 *(978-0-375-83486-8(9),* Knopf Bks. for Young Readers) Random Hse. Children's Bks.

—Scat. 2012. lib. bdg. 18.40 *(978-0-606-26532-4(5),* Turtleback) Turtleback Bks.

Higbee, Heidi. It Could Happen... on the Bus. Hezlep, Amber, illus. 2012. 32p. (J). pap. 16.95 *(978-0-9882940-0-4(1))* Bryson Taylor Publishing.

Hill, Kirkpatrick. The Year of Miss Agnes. 2003. (Aladdin Historical Fiction Ser.). 115p. (gr. 3-7). 17.00 *(978-0-7569-1407-3(8))* Perfection Learning Corp.

Hitchcock, Shannon. Ruby Lee & Me. 2016. (ENG., Illus.). 272p. (J). (gr. 3-7). 16.99 *(978-0-545-78230-2(9),* Scholastic Pr.) Scholastic, Inc.

Hobbs, Valerie. Minnie McClary Speaks Her Mind. 2013. (ENG.). 240p. (J). (gr. 4-8). pap. 9.99 *(978-1-250-03408-3(6),* 9781250034083) Square Fish.

Holmes, Sara. Operation Yes. 2009. 234p. (J). pap. *(978-0-545-20418-7(6))* Scholastic, Inc.

Holmes, Sara Lewis. Operation Yes. 2009. (ENG.). 256p. (J). (gr. 4-7). 16.99 *(978-0-545-10795-2(4),* Levine, Arthur A. Bks.) Scholastic, Inc.

Hopkinson, Deborah. A Letter to My Teacher. Carpenter, Nancy, illus. 2017. (ENG.). 40p. (J). (gr. -1-3). 17.99 *(978-0-375-86845-0(3),* Schwartz & Wade Bks.) Random Hse. Children's Bks.

Horton, Elizabeth. Pick Me, Pick Me. Kinsley, Sean, illus. 2008. (ENG.). 32p. (J). 16.95 *(978-0-9797460-0-0(0))* Lerue Pr., LLC.

Hortten, Jacqueline Faye. Pu Beach. I.t. ed. 2004. (Illus.). 27p. (J). pap. 14.95 *(978-0-9728393-0-3(5))* Children's Bookshoppe Stop, The.

Houdek, Andrea. Mice in My Tummy. Collier, Kevin Scott, illus. 2012. 16p. pap. 9.95 *(978-1-61633-219-8(0))* Guardian Angel Publishing, Inc.

Howell, Heather. Emily's Ballet Recital. 2010. 32p. pap. 12.99 *(978-1-4490-8457-8(5))* AuthorHouse.

Hrdlitschka, Shelley. Kat's Fall. 2005. 168p. 18.95 *(978-0-7569-6315-6(X))* Perfection Learning Corp.

Hubbell, Patricia. Teacher! Sharing, Helping, Caring, 0 vols. Speir, Nancy, illus. 2009. (ENG.). 32p. (J). (gr. -1-3). 16.99 *(978-0-7614-5574-5(4),* 9780761455745, Amazon Children's Publishing) Amazon Publishing.

Hudgins, Larry. My Dog Spike, 1 vol. 2009. 55p. pap. 16.95 *(978-1-60836-421-3(6))* America Star Bks.

Huelin, Jodi. Alvin & the Chipmunks: Alvin & the Substitute Teacher. Artful Doodlers Limited Staff, illus. 2013. (I Can Read Level 2 Ser.). (ENG.). 32p. (J). (gr. -1-3). pap. 3.99 *(978-0-06-225223-4(2),* HarperFestival) HarperCollins Pubs.

—Alvin & the Substitute Teacher. 2013. (I Can Read! Level 2 Ser.). (J). lib. bdg. 13.55 *(978-0-606-32462-5(3),* Turtleback) Turtleback Bks.

Hunsaker, Debbie. Reading Rug. 2012. 28p. pap. 19.99 *(978-1-4678-7018-4(8))* AuthorHouse.

Hutt, Aletha. Mama & Baba's First Chinese Words. 2011. 16p. 12.68 *(978-1-4269-5076-6(4))* Trafford Publishing.

Jane, Pamela. Milo & the Flapjack Fiasco! Johnson, Meredith, ed. Johnson, Meredith, tr. 2004. (Illus.). 32p. (J). 13.95 *(978-1-59336-113-6(0));* pap. *(978-1-59336-114-3(9))* Mondo Publishing.

Jarvis, Mary Rowles. Dick Lionheart. 2007. (Illus.). 76p. per. *(978-1-4065-2709-4(2))* Dodo Pr.

Jocelyn, Marthe. Mable Riley: A Reliable Record of Humdrum, Peril, & Romance. 2007. 279p. (gr. 4-7). 17.00 *(978-0-7569-8183-9(2))* Perfection Learning Corp.

Johns, Eric. Mindreaders. 2007. 184p. pap. 16.95 *(978-1-4357-0121-2(6))* Lulu Pr., Inc.

Jones, A. Responsibility. 2011. 32p. pap. 24.95 *(978-1-4626-2167-5(8))* America Star Bks.

Judd, Merlynne. Circle of Friendship. 2010. 76p. pap. 24.99 *(978-1-4520-6783-4(X))* AuthorHouse.

Julie, Danneberg. First Day Jitters. 2014. (Mrs. Hartwell's Class Adventures Ser.). (ENG.). 32p. (J). (gr. k-3). 11.20 *(978-1-63245-322-8(3))* Lectorum Pubns., Inc.

Katar, Al. Captain Scratch: Island of Sirmanj. 2007. (J). 21.99 *(978-1-934035-31-3(9))* Trent's Prints.

Katschke, Judy. Teacher's Pet. Geddes, Serena, illus. 2017. (Marguerite Henry's Misty Inn Ser.: 7). (ENG.). 128p. (J). (gr. 2-5). pap. 5.99 ***(978-1-4814-6991-3(6),*** Aladdin) Simon & Schuster Children's Publishing.

Katz, T. Miss L'eau. 2007. 44p. (YA). pap. 14.99 *(978-1-59092-404-4(5))* Blue Forge Pr.

Kelly, Katy. Melonhead & the Vegalicious Disaster. Johnson, Gillian, illus. 2013. (Melonhead Ser.). (ENG.). 224p. (J). (gr. 3-7). 6.99 *(978-0-307-92969-3(8),* Yearling) Random Hse. Children's Bks.

Kelm, Tracy Martin. Light. 2011. 116p. pap. 11.95 *(978-1-4327-6308-4(3))* Outskirts Pr., Inc.

Kenah, Katharine. The Best Teacher in Second Grade. Carter, Abby, illus. 2007. (I Can Read Level 2 Ser.). (ENG.). 48p. (J). (gr. k-3). pap. 3.99 *(978-0-06-053566-7(0))* HarperCollins Pubs.

—The Best Teacher in Second Grade. Carter, Abby, illus. 2007. (I Can Read Bks.). 48p. (gr. -1-3). 14.00 *(978-0-7569-8105-1(0))* Perfection Learning Corp.

—Scholastic Reader Level 1: the Saturday Triplets #3: Teacher Trouble! Lyon, Tammie, illus. 2013. (Scholastic Reader Level 1 Ser.). (ENG.). 32p. (J). (gr. -1-2). pap. 3.99 *(978-0-545-48145-8(7))* Scholastic, Inc.

Kendall, Sydney. A Turn for de Wurst. 318p. (J). (gr. 3-5). 9.99 *(978-0-88092-461-0(6))* Royal Fireworks Publishing Co.

Kim, YeShil. The Very Best Teacher. Moriuchi, Mique, illus. 2015. (ENG.). 24p. (J). (-3). 12.99 *(978-1-4926-0998-8(6))* Sourcebooks, Inc.

Kindl, Patrice. Owl in Love. 2004. (ENG.). 224p. (YA). (gr. 7-18). pap. 14.95 *(978-0-618-43910-2(2))* Houghton Mifflin Harcourt Publishing Co.

King, Seth David. The Substitute Teacher Named Mr King. Clark, Matthew Levi, illus. 2005. 24p. (gr. 2-6). 12.00 *(978-0-9640837-6-9(0))* Ascension Education.

Kingsley, Kate. Everything but the Truth. 2010. (Young, Loaded, & Fabulous Ser.: 2). (ENG.). 304p. (YA). (gr. 9-18). pap. 9.99 *(978-1-4169-9400-8(9),* Simon Pulse) Simon Pulse.

Kline, Suzy. Horrible Harry & the June Box. Wummer, Amy, illus. 2012. (Horrible Harry Ser.). (ENG.). 80p. (J). (gr. 2-4). pap. 4.99 *(978-0-14-242185-7(5),* Puffin Books) Penguin Young Readers Group.

—Horrible Harry & the Wedding Spies. Wummer, Amy, illus. 2016. (Horrible Harry Ser.: 32). (ENG.). 80p. (J). (gr. 2-5). 4.99 *(978-0-14-750968-0(8),* Puffin Books) Penguin Young Readers Group.

—Horrible Harry & the Wedding Spies. 2016. (Horrible Harry Ser.: 32). lib. bdg. 14.75 *(978-0-606-38389-9(1))* Turtleback Bks.

—Horrible Harry Takes the Cake. Remkiewicz, Frank, illus. 2007. (Horrible Harry Ser.). (ENG.). 64p. (J). (gr. 2-4). 4.99 *(978-0-14-240939-8(1),* Puffin Books) Penguin Young Readers Group.

—Horrible Harry Takes the Cake. Remkiewicz, Frank, illus. 2007. (Horrible Harry Ser.). 45p. (gr. 2-5). 14.00 *(978-0-7569-8158-7(1))* Perfection Learning Corp.

Kline, Suzy & Wells, Rosemary. Horrible Harry & the Wedding Spies. Wummer, Amy, illus. 2015. (Horrible Harry Ser.: 32). (ENG.). 80p. (J). (gr. 2-5). bds. 14.99 *(978-0-670-01552-8(0),* Viking Books for Young Readers) Penguin Young Readers Group.

Klise, Kate. Homesick. 2012. (ENG.). 192p. (J). (gr. 5-9). 16.99 *(978-1-250-00842-8(5),* 9781250008428) Feiwel & Friends.

Knowles, Jo. Read Between the Lines. 2015. (ENG.). 336p. (YA). (gr. 9). 16.99 *(978-0-7636-6387-2(5))* Candlewick Pr.

Knudsen, Shannon. Testing the Truth. 2015. (ENG.). 104p. (YA). (gr. 6-12). 27.99 *(978-1-4677-5708-9(X))* Lerner Publishing Group.

Kolczynski, Sean. The Night Before Middle School! 2012. 28p. pap. 21.99 *(978-1-4771-4794-8(2))* Xlibris Corp.

Konigsburg, E. L. The View from Saturday. 280p. (YA). (gr. 5-18). pap. 4.95 *(978-0-8072-1511-1(2),* Listening Library) Random Hse. Audio Publishing Group.

Kremer, Kevin. Santa's Our Substitute Teacher. Ely, Dave, illus. 2006. 150p. (gr. 4-7). per. 5.99 *(978-0-9663335-4-1(3),* 703-001) Snow In Sarasota Publishing.

Krosoczka, Jarrett J. Lunch Lady & the Author Visit Vendetta. 2009. (Lunch Lady Ser.). (ENG.). 96p. (J). (gr. 3-7). pap. 6.99 *(978-0-375-86094-2(0),* Knopf Bks. for Young Readers) Random Hse. Children's Bks.

Krulik, Nancy. Doggone It! John and Wendy Staff, illus. 8th ed. 2006. (Katie Kazoo, Switcheroo Ser.: 8). (ENG.). 80p. (J). (gr. 2-4). pap. 4.99 *(978-0-448-43172-7(6),* Grosset & Dunlap) Penguin Young Readers Group.

—Flower Power. John and Wendy Staff, illus. 2008. (Katie Kazoo, Switcheroo Ser.: 27). (ENG.). 80p. (J). (gr. 2-4). pap. 4.99 *(978-0-448-44674-5(X),* Grosset & Dunlap) Penguin Young Readers Group.

—No Messin' with My Lesson. John and Wendy Staff, illus. 11th ed. 2004. (Katie Kazoo, Switcheroo Ser.: 11). (ENG.). 80p. (J). (gr. 2-4). pap. 4.99 *(978-0-448-43357-8(5),* Grosset & Dunlap) Penguin Young Readers Group.

Krulik, Nancy E. Flower Power. John and Wendy Staff, illus. 2008. (Katie Kazoo, Switcheroo Ser.). 78p. (gr. 2-5). 14.00 *(978-0-7569-8806-7(3))* Perfection Learning Corp.

Kuroda, Yosuke & Hayashiya, Shizuru. Onegai Teacher, No. 2. 2003. 120p. pap. 9.95 *(978-1-58899-179-9(2))* ComicsOne Corp./DR. Masters.

Laminack, Lester L. Snow Day!, 1 vol. Gustavson, Adam, illus. 2007. (ENG.). 32p. (J). (gr. k-2). 16.95 *(978-1-56145-418-1(4))* Peachtree Pubs.

Langdale, Mark Roland. Professor Doppelganger & the Fantastical Cloud Factory. 2012. 106p. pap. *(978-1-78003-267-2(6))* Pen Pr. Pubs., Ltd.

Larsen, Angela Sage. Broken Record, Bk. 4. 2013. (Fifties Chix Ser.: 4). (ENG., Illus.). 200p. (YA). pap. 9.95 *(978-1-60746-446-4(2),* Premiere) FastPrncil, Inc.

—Keeping Secrets, Bk. 2. 2012. (Fifties Chix Ser.: 2). (ENG.). 220p. (YA). pap. 9.95 *(978-1-60746-367-2(9),* Premiere) FastPrncil, Inc.

—Till the End of Time. 2013. (Fifties Chix Ser.: 5). (ENG.). 200p. (YA). pap. 9.95 *(978-1-60746-468-6(3),* Premiere) FastPrncil, Inc.

Lauren, Whitney. Vanessa & Johnny: The Cabinets. 2011. 84p. pap. 9.99 *(978-1-4269-5827-4(7))* Trafford Publishing.

Lawrence, Michael. Rudie Dudie. 2010. (ENG.). 160p. (J). (gr. k-2). pap. 8.99 *(978-1-4083-0483-9(X))* Hodder & Stoughton GBR. Dist: Hachette Bk. Group.

Lay, Kathryn. The Substitutes: An Up2U Action Adventure, 1 vol. Calo, Marcos, illus. 2015. (ENG.). 80p. (J). *(978-1-62402-095-7(X))* Magic Wagon.

LeapFrog Staff. Ozzie & Mack. 2008. (J). pap. 49.99 *(978-1-59319-924-1(4));* pap. 39.99 *(978-1-59319-976-0(7))* LeapFrog Enterprises, Inc.

Lee, Mary Ellen. Danny & Life on Bluff Point: Blizzard of '95 revised Edition. 2009. 160p. (gr. 4-7). pap. 12.95 *(978-0-595-53308-4(6))* iUniverse, Inc.

Leppard, Lois Gladys. The Mysterious Teacher. 2003. 160p. (J). mass mkt. 4.99 *(978-1-889893-98-3(6),* Ambassador-Emerald, International) Emerald Hse. Group, Inc.

Leuck, Laura. My Creature Teacher. Nash, Scott, illus. 2004. (ENG.). 32p. (J). (gr. -1-1). 15.99 *(978-0-06-029694-0(1))* HarperCollins Pubs.

Lewman, David. The Case of the Mystery Meat Loaf. 2012. (Club CSI Ser.: 1). (ENG.). 160p. (J). (gr. 3-7). 15.99 *(978-1-4424-4646-5(3));* pap. 7.99 *(978-1-4424-3394-6(9))* Simon Spotlight. (Simon Spotlight).

Limbaugh, Rush H., III. Rush Revere & the Brave Pilgrims: Time-Travel Adventures with Exceptional Americans. 2013. (ENG., Illus.). 224p. 19.99 *(978-1-4767-5586-1(8),* Threshold Editions) Threshold Editions.

—Rush Revere & the First Patriots: Time-Travel Adventures with Exceptional Americans. 2014. (Rush Revere Ser.: 2). (ENG., Illus.). 256p. 19.99 *(978-1-4767-5588-5(4),* Threshold Editions) Threshold Editions.

Limbaugh, Rush H., III & Limbaugh, Kathryn Adams. Rush Revere & the American Revolution. 2014. (ENG.). 256p. 19.99 *(978-1-4767-8987-3(8),* Threshold Editions) Threshold Editions.

—Rush Revere & the American Revolution. Hiers, Christopher, illus. 2014. 244p. (J). pap. *(978-1-4767-8989-7(4),* Threshold Editions) Threshold Editions.

Liz Collard. Jeremiah, the Schoolhouse Dog. 2009. 28p. pap. 12.79 *(978-1-4269-0990-0(X))* Trafford Publishing.

Lockard, Lynn. Gone Batty!!! 2009. 40p. pap. 16.99 *(978-1-4389-8516-9(9))* AuthorHouse.

Loever, Charmaine. David's Big Break. Bohman, Natasha, illus. 2008. 52p. pap. 22.99 *(978-1-4389-3173-9(5))* AuthorHouse.

Love, Maryann Cusimano. You Are My Wonders. Ichikawa, Satomi & Lewin, Ted, illus. 2012. (ENG.). 32p. (J). (gr. -1-2). 16.99 *(978-0-399-25293-8(2),* Philomel Bks.) Penguin Young Readers Group.

Lubar, David. Hyde & Shriek: A Monsterrific Tale. 2013. (Monsterrific Tales Ser.). (ENG., Illus.). 144p. (J). (gr. 3-7). 14.99 *(978-0-7653-3081-9(4),* 9780765330819, Starscape) Doherty, Tom Assocs., LLC.

Luddy, Karon. Spelldown: The Big-Time Dreams of a Small-Town Word Whiz. 2008. (Mix Ser.). (ENG.). 224p. (J). (gr. 4-8). pap. 10.99 *(978-1-4169-5452-1(X),* Simon & Schuster/Paula Wiseman Bks.) Simon & Schuster/Paula Wiseman Bks.

Luning, Barbara. The Quilted Zoo. 2008. 28p. pap. 15.99 *(978-1-4363-1778-8(9))* Xlibris Corp.

Lynch, Janet Nichols. Messed Up. 2009. (ENG.). 320p. (YA). (gr. 7-18). 17.95 *(978-0-8234-2185-5(6))* Holiday Hse., Inc.

—Peace Is a Four-Letter Word. 2005. 158p. (YA). (gr. 8-12). per. 9.95 *(978-1-59714-014-0(7),* Great Valley Bks.) Heyday.

Magee, Helen. What's French for Help, George? I.t. ed. 2007. pap. *(978-1-905665-68-6(7))* Pollinger In Print.

Mahy, Margaret. The Very Wicked Headmistress. Chamberlain, Margaret, illus. 2006. 94p. (J). (gr. 2-4). pap. 6.95 *(978-1-903015-46-9(4))* Barn Owl Bks, London GBR. Dist: Independent Pubs. Group.

Maltby, Robert I. Diquan & the Book Monster, 1 vol. 2009. 39p. pap. 24.95 *(978-1-61546-964-2(8))* America Star Bks.

Man-Kong, Mary. I Can Be a Teacher (Barbie) Golden Books Staff & Riley, Kellee, illus. 2011. (Step into Reading Ser.). (ENG.). 32p. (J). (gr. -1-1). pap. 3.99 *(978-0-375-86927-3(1),* Random Hse. Bks. for Young Readers) Random Hse. Children's Bks.

Manell, Keane. Hall Pass to the Tenth Dimension. 2009. 56p. pap. 10.95 *(978-1-4389-7401-9(9))* AuthorHouse.

Mann, Jennifer K. I Will Never Get a Star on Mrs. Benson's Blackboard. Mann, Jennifer K., illus. 2015. (ENG., Illus.). 40p. (J). (gr. k-3). 16.99 *(978-0-7636-6514-2(2))* Candlewick Pr.

Manushkin, Fran. Katie & the Fancy Substitute, 1 vol. 2014. (Katie Woo Ser.). (ENG.). 32p. (gr. k-2). 21.32 *(978-1-4795-5188-0(0))* Picture Window Bks.

Manzak, Bonnie. The Big Red Cat. 2011. 32p. pap. 21.99 *(978-1-4568-6607-5(9))* Xlibris Corp.

Marcionette, Jake. Just Jake: Dog Eat Dog. Villa, Victor Rivas, illus. 2015. (Just Jake Ser.: No. 2). (ENG.). 196p. (J). (gr. 3-7). 11.99 *(978-0-448-46693-4(7),* Grosset & Dunlap) Penguin Young Readers Group.

Matsuura, Richard & Matsuura, Ruth. Angels Masquerading on Earth. Chao, Linus, illus. (J). 7.95 *(978-1-887916-07-3(5))* Orchid Isle Publishing Co.

Mayhew, James. The Magic Toyshop. 2017. (Ella Bella Ballerina Ser.). (ENG.). 32p. (J). (gr. -1-3). 14.99 ***(978-1-4380-5005-8(4))*** Barron's Educational Series, Inc.

McClintock, Norah. Hit & Run. 2014. (Mike & Riel Mysteries Ser.: 1). (ENG.). 240p. (YA). (gr. 6-12). pap. 8.95 *(978-1-4677-2611-5(7),* Darby Creek) Lerner Publishing Group.

—Shadow of Doubt. 2012. (Robyn Hunter Mysteries Ser.: 5). (ENG.). 232p. (YA). (gr. 6-12). pap. 8.95 *(978-0-7613-9397-9(8),* Darby Creek); lib. bdg. 27.93 *(978-0-7613-8315-4(8))* Lerner Publishing Group.

McDaniel, Lurlene. Prey. 2010. (ENG.). 208p. (YA). (gr. 7). mass mkt. 7.99 *(978-0-440-24015-0(8),* Laurel Leaf) Random Hse. Children's Bks.

McDonald, Megan. Judy Moody Goes to College. (Judy Moody Ser.: 8). 2010. lib. bdg. 16.00 *(978-0-606-12352-5(0))* 2009. lib. bdg. 16.00 *(978-0-606-01313-0(X))* Turtleback Bks. (Turtleback).

—Judy Moody Goes to College, Bk. 8. Reynolds, Peter H., illus. 2010. (Judy Moody Ser.: 8). (ENG.). (J). (gr. 1-4). 144p. 15.99 *(978-0-7636-4856-5(6));* 160p. pap. 5.99 *(978-0-7636-4855-8(8))* Candlewick Pr.

McGann, Erika. The Broken Spell. 2014. (Demon Notebook Ser.: 2). (ENG.). 352p. (J). (gr. 4-8). pap. 6.99 *(978-1-4926-0296-5(5),* Sourcebooks Jabberwocky) Sourcebooks, Inc.

Mcghee, Alison. Mrs. Watson Wants Your Teeth. Bliss, Harry, illus. 2007. 32p. (J). reprint ed. 16.00 *(978-1-4223-6777-3(0))* DIANE Publishing Co.

—Mrs. Watson Wants Your Teeth. Bliss, Harry, illus. 2008. (ENG.). 36p. (J). (gr. -1-3). pap. 6.00 *(978-0-15-206348-1(X))* Houghton Mifflin Harcourt Publishing Co.

—Mrs. Watson Wants Your Teeth. Bliss, Harry, illus. unabr. ed. 2007. (Picture Book Readalong Ser.). (J). (gr. -1-2). 28.95 incl. audio compact disk *(978-1-59519-902-7(0))* Live Oak Media.

McGroary, Mary Beth. My Teacher Hates Me. 2012. 24p. 24.95 *(978-1-4626-6012-4(6))* America Star Bks.

McKissack, Robert L. Try Your Best. Cepeda, Joe, illus. 2004. (Green Light Readers Level 2 Ser.). (ENG.). 24p. (J). (gr. -1-3). pap. 3.95 *(978-0-15-205090-0(6))* Houghton Mifflin Harcourt Publishing Co.

—Try Your Best. Cepeda, Joe, illus. 2005. (Green Light Readers Level 2 Ser.). (gr. k-2). 13.95 *(978-0-7569-5630-1(7))* Perfection Learning Corp.

McMullan, Kate. Pearl & Wagner: Five Days till Summer. 2014. (Penguin Young Readers Level 3 Ser.). lib. bdg. 13.55 *(978-0-606-35727-2(0))* Turtleback Bks.

McNamara, Margaret. Summer Treasure. Gordon, Mike, illus. 2012. (Robin Hill School Ser.). (ENG.). 32p. (J). (gr. -1-1). 15.99 *(978-1-4424-3646-6(8));* pap. 3.99 *(978-1-4424-3645-9(X))* Simon Spotlight. (Simon Spotlight).

McNamara, Margaret & Thompson, Kay. Eloise Has a Lesson. Mitter, Kathryn, illus. 2005. (Eloise Ser.). (ENG.). 32p. (J). (gr. -1-1). pap. 3.99 *(978-0-689-87367-6(0),* Simon Spotlight) Simon Spotlight.

Mendenhall, Gaylee. My Teacher Is Bald! 2011. 28p. pap. 14.99 *(978-1-4634-5032-8(X))* AuthorHouse.

Michie, Brandon J. Ollie the Octopus: Animal Lessons. 2011. 20p. 13.49 *(978-1-4567-4782-4(7))* AuthorHouse.

Miller, Sarah. Miss Spitfire: Reaching Helen Keller. (ENG.). (J). (gr. 5-7). 2010. 256p. pap. 7.99 *(978-1-4424-0851-7(0))* 2007. 240p. 17.99 *(978-1-4169-2542-2(2))* Simon & Schuster Children's Publishing. (Atheneum Bks. for Young Readers).

Millman, Selena. Anyone Can Make A Difference. 2006. 109p. (YA). per. *(978-0-9793058-6-3(1))* Millman, Selena.

Millsap, Ella. A Portrait of a Church in Stone: The Keeper of the Honeybees. 2013. 62p. (J). pap. 12.00 *(978-0-9891960-3-1(8))* Professional Publishing Hse. LLC.

A Monkey Ate My Homework. 2007. 32p. pap. 4.50 *(978-0-8341-2287-1(1),* 083-412-2871) Beacon Hill Pr. of Kansas City.

Montgomery, L. M. Anne of Avonlea. 2005. pap. *(978-1-905432-15-8(1))* Dodo Pr.

—Anne of Avonlea. 2011. (Oxford Children's Classics Ser.). (ENG.). 336p. (YA). (gr. 3-18). 9.95 *(978-0-19-276359-4(8))* Oxford Univ. Pr., Inc.

—Anne of Avonlea. 2011. 214p. (gr. 4-7). pap. 15.95 *(978-1-4638-0054-3(1))* Rodgers, Alan Bks.

—Anne of Avonlea. 2005. (Aladdin Classics Ser.). (ENG., Illus.). 416p. (J). (gr. 4-7). pap. 5.99 *(978-1-4169-0328-4(3),* Aladdin) Simon & Schuster Children's Publishing.

—Anne of Avonlea. Andreasen, Dan, illus. 2009. (Classic Starts(tm) Ser.). (ENG.). 160p. (J). (gr. 2-4). 6.95 *(978-1-4027-5424-1(8))* Sterling Publishing Co., Inc.

—Anne of Avonlea. McKowen, Scott, illus. 2008. (Sterling Unabridged Classics Ser.). (ENG.). 256p. (J). 9.95 *(978-1-4027-5428-9(0))* Sterling Publishing Co., Inc.

—Anne of Avonlea. 2012. (World Classics Ser.). (ENG.). 228p. pap. 19.99 *(978-1-909438-94-1(4),* Sovereign) Bollinger, Max GBR. Dist: Lightning Source UK, Ltd., Gardners Bks. Ltd.

—Anne of Avonlea. I.t. ed. 2006. (ENG.). pap. *(978-1-4068-3173-3(5))* Echo Library.

—Kilmeny of the Orchard. 2010. 146p. pap. 16.95 *(978-1-60444-108-6(9))* IndoEuropeanPublishing.com.

Morgan, Winter. Hidden in the Chest. 2017. (Unofficial Minecrafters Academy Ser.: 5). lib. bdg. 18.40 ***(978-0-606-40310-8(8))*** Turtleback Bks.

Morrison, Jaydene & Peterson, Russell. I Hate You, Miss Bliss. 2012. 36p. pap. 20.99 *(978-1-4772-9740-7(5))* AuthorHouse.

T U V

Moss, Marissa. Amelia's 6th-Grade Notebook. Moss, Marissa, illus. 2005. (Amelia Ser.). (ENG., Illus.). 80p. (J). (gr. 4-7). 12.99 (978-0-689-87040-8(X), Simon & Schuster/Paula Wiseman Bks.) Simon & Schuster/Paula Wiseman Bks.

Mrs Bold, 6 Packs. (Literatura 2000 Ser.). (gr. 1-2). 28.00 (978-0-7635-0101-3(8)) Rigby Education.

Mrs Keen: Individual Title Six-Packs. (gr. -1-2). 27.00 (978-0-7635-9462-6(8)) Rigby Education.

Mullarkey, Lisa. The Purr-Fect-O Present: Book 10, 1 vol. Harris, Phyllis, illus. 2012. (Katharine the Almost Great Ser.). (ENG.). 80p. (J). (gr. 1-4). 27.07 (978-1-61641-831-1(1)) Magic Wagon.

My Teacher Glows in the Dark. 2014. (My Teacher Bks.: 3). (ENG., Illus.). 192p. (J). (gr. 3-7). 17.99 (978-1-4814-0432-7(6), Simon & Schuster/Paula Wiseman Bks.) Simon & Schuster/Paula Wiseman Bks.

Myracle, Lauren. Oopsy Daisy. 2012. (Flower Power Ser.). (ENG.). 368p. (J). (gr. 3-7). pap. 8.95 (978-1-4197-0418-5(4), Amulet Bks.) Abrams, Inc.

Naegele, K. Z. The Chatty Hat. 2011. 36p. pap. 24.95 (978-1-4626-3652-5(7)) America Star Bks.

Nagda, Ann Whitehead. Kevin Keeps Up. 2012. (ENG.). 96p. (J). 15.95 (978-0-8234-2657-7(2)) Holiday Hse., Inc.

Nelson, R. A. Teach Me. 2007. (ENG.). 272p. (YA). (gr. 9-12). 8.99 (978-1-59514-085-2(9), Razorbill) Penguin Young Readers Group.

Newton-Perry, Linda. Eye of the Beast. 2009. 62p. pap. 7.98 (978-0-557-06333-8(7)) Lulu Pr., Inc.

Nikola-Lisa, W. My Teacher Can Teach... Anyone! Galindo, Felipe, illus. 2004. (ENG.). 32p. (J). (gr. -1-2). 16.95 (978-1-58430-163-9(5)); pap. 9.95 (978-1-60060-276-4(2)) Lee & Low Bks., Inc.

Northrop, Michael. Gentlemen. 2009. (ENG.). 256p. (J). (gr. 9-18). 17.99 (978-0-545-09749-9(5), Scholastic Pr.) Scholastic, Inc.

Nurse, Holly. Meridian Brown Goes to School. 2009. (Illus.). 60p. pap. (978-1-84748-535-9(9)) Athena Pr.

Oceanak, Karla. Dumbstruck. Spanjer, Kendra, illus. 2011. (Aldo Zelnick Comic Novel Ser.: 4). (ENG.). 160p. (J). (gr. 3-7). 12.95 (978-1-934649-16-9(3)) Bailiwick Pr.

O'Connor, Jane. Fancy Nancy at the Museum. Enik, Ted & Glasser, Robin Preiss, illus. 2008. (I Can Read Level 1 Ser.). (ENG.). 32p. (J). (gr. -1-3). 16.99 (978-0-06-123608-2(X)); pap. 3.99 (978-0-06-123607-5(1)) HarperCollins Pubs.

O'Connor, Jane & Harper Collins / LeapFrog. Fancy Nancy at the Museum. Glasser, Robin Preiss, illus. 2008. (Fancy Nancy Ser.). (J). 13.99 (978-1-59319-940-1(6)) LeapFrog Enterprises, Inc.

Oliver, Ilanit. OLIVIA & the Best Teacher Ever. Johnson, Shane L., illus. 2012. (Olivia TV Tie-In Ser.). (ENG.). 24p. (J). (gr. -1-2). pap. 3.99 (978-1-4424-3599-5(2), Simon Spotlight) Simon Spotlight.

—Olivia & the Best Teacher Ever. 2012. (Olivia 8x8 Ser.). lib. bdg. 13.55 (978-0-606-26367-2(5), Turtleback) Turtleback Bks.

O'Shaughnessy McKenna, Colleen. Third Grade Wedding Bells? Roth, Stephanie, illus. 2006. (Third Grade Ser.). (ENG.). 160p. (J). (gr. 2-5). 15.95 (978-0-8234-1943-2(6)) Holiday Hse., Inc.

Pace, Anne Marie. A Teacher for Bear. Wohnoutka, Mike, illus. 2011. (J). (978-0-545-37776-8(5)) Scholastic, Inc.

Pallotta, Jerry. What I Saw in the Teachers' Lounge. McWilliam, Howard, illus. 2012. (J). (978-0-545-38472-8(9)) Scholastic, Inc.

Papell, David. Harlem Awakenings. 2007. 48p. pap. 12.95 (978-0-615-17531-7(7)) Papell, David.

Parbi, Eunice Efiba Asare. Yum! Yum! Yum! Trust Us! We Will Blow It! Series 1. 2012. (Illus.). 28p. pap. 21.35 (978-1-4772-4719-8(X)) AuthorHouse.

Parish, Peggy. Teach Us, Amelia Bedelia. Sweat, Lynn, illus. 2005. (Amelia Bedelia Ser.). 58p. (gr. -1-3). 14.00 (978-0-7569-4804-7(5)) Perfection Learning Corp.

Parker, Robert. Edenville Owls. 2008. 194p. (gr. 4-6). 18.00 (978-0-7569-8920-0(5)) Perfection Learning Corp.

Parr, Todd. Teachers Rock! 2016. (ENG., Illus.). 32p. (J). (gr. -1-1). 16.99 (978-0-316-26512-6(8)) Little, Brown Bks. for Young Readers.

Parton, Matthew R. My Closet Monster Ate My Homework, 1 vol. 2009. (ENG.). 30p. 24.95 (978-1-60836-184-7(5)) America Star Bks.

Passen, Lisa. The Attack of the 50-Foot Teacher. 2005. (Illus.). 28p. (J). (gr. k-4). reprint ed. 16.00 (978-0-7567-9665-5(2)) DIANE Publishing Co.

Patterson, Matthew. Shake Them up, Mrs Nut. 2008. 104p. per. 9.95 (978-1-4327-2008-7(2)) Outskirts Pr., Inc.

Pattou, Edith. Mrs. Spitzer's Garden. Tusa, Tricia, illus. gif. ed. 2007. (ENG.). 32p. (J). (gr. -1-3). 12.99 (978-0-15-205802-9(8)) Houghton Mifflin Harcourt Publishing Co.

Peck, Richard. The Teacher's Funeral. 2006. (ENG.). 224p. (J). (gr. 3-7). reprint ed. 7.99 (978-0-14-240507-9(8), Puffin Books) Penguin Young Readers Group.

Pef. Belle lisse poire du prince De. pap. 16.95 (978-2-07-054806-4(6)) Gallimard, Editions FRA. Dist: Distribooks, Inc.

Peirce, Lincoln. Big Nate Strikes Again. 2015. (Big Nate Ser.: 2). (J). lib. bdg. 17.20 (978-0-606-36504-8(4)) Turtleback Bks.

Penner, Stephen. Professor Barrister's Dinosaur Mysteries #1: The Case of the Truncated Troodon. Penner, Stephen, illus. 2010. (Illus.). 44p. pap. 19.25 (978-1-60888-005-8(2)) Nimble Bks. LLC.

Pennypacker, Sara. Clementine's Letter. Frazee, Marla, illus. 2009. (Clementine Book Ser.). (ENG.). 160p. (J). (gr. 1-3). pap. 5.99 (978-0-7868-3885-1(X)) Hyperion Pr.

Perelstein, Jennifer. Who Moved the Masterpieces? A Visit to the Mcnay Art Museum. 2010. 30p. pap. 15.99 (978-1-60844-585-1(2)) Dog Ear Publishing, LLC.

Pilkey, Dav. Captain Underpants & the Attack of the Talking Toilets. 2004. (Captain Underpants Ser.: No. 2). (J). lib. bdg. 19.95 (978-0-439-68436-1(6), Scholastic, Inc.) Scholastic, Inc.

—Captain Underpants & the Perilous Plot of Professor Poopypants. 2004. (Captain Underpants Ser.: No. 4). (J). lib. bdg. 19.95 (978-0-439-68440-8(4), Scholastic, Inc.) Scholastic, Inc.

—Captain Underpants & the Wrath of the Wicked Wedgie Woman. 2004. (Captain Underpants Ser.: No. 5). (J). lib. bdg. 19.95 (978-0-439-68441-5(2), Scholastic, Inc.) Scholastic, Inc.

Polacco, Patricia. The Art of Miss Chew. Polacco, Patricia, illus. 2012. (ENG., Illus.). 40p. (J). (gr. k-3). 17.99 (978-0-399-25703-2(9), G.P. Putnam's Sons Books for Young Readers) Penguin Young Readers Group.

—Gracias, Senor Falker. 2006. (SPA., Illus.). 34p. (J). (gr. 2-3). per. 7.99 (978-1-933032-02-3(2), LC34004) Lectorum Pubns., Inc.

—The Junkyard Wonders. Polacco, Patricia, illus. 2010. (ENG., Illus.). 48p. (J). (gr. 1-4). 17.99 (978-0-399-25078-1(6), Philomel Bks.) Penguin Young Readers Group.

—The Lemonade Club. Polacco, Patricia, illus. 2007. (ENG., Illus.). 48p. (J). (gr. 1-4). 17.99 (978-0-399-24540-4(5), Philomel Bks.) Penguin Young Readers Group.

—Mr. Wayne's Masterpiece. Polacco, Patricia, illus. 2014. (ENG., Illus.). 40p. (J). (gr. k-3). 17.99 (978-0-399-16095-0(7), G.P. Putnam's Sons Books for Young Readers) Penguin Young Readers Group.

—Thank You, Mr. Falker. Polacco, Patricia, illus. 2012. (ENG., Illus.). 40p. (J). (gr. k-3). 12.99 (978-0-399-25762-9(4), Philomel Bks.) Penguin Young Readers Group.

Pollard, Mary Jean. Octrina the Octopus. 2011. 28p. pap. 15.99 (978-1-4568-4778-4(3)) Xlibris Corp.

Poulsen, David A. Numbers. 2nd ed. 2015. (ENG.). 200p. (YA). pap. 12.99 (978-1-4597-3248-3(0)) Dundurn CAN. Dist: Ingram Publisher Services.

—Numbers. 2008. (ENG.). 232p. (YA). (gr. 6-18). (978-1-55470-095-0(7)) Me to We.

Primavera, Elise. Louise the Big Cheese & the Back-To-School Smarty-Pants. Goode, Diane, illus. 2011. (ENG.). 40p. (J). (gr. k-3). 16.99 (978-1-4424-0600-1(3), Simon & Schuster/Paula Wiseman Bks.) Simon & Schuster/Paula Wiseman Bks.

—Making Mistakes on Purpose. 2016. (Ms. Rapscott's Girls Ser.). (ENG., Illus.). 160p. (J). (gr. 3-7). 16.99 (978-0-8037-3824-9(2), Dial Bks) Penguin Young Readers Group.

Prinz, Yvonne. Still There, Clare. 2005. (ENG.). 4p. (J). pap., tchr. ed. (978-1-55192-821-0(3)) Raincoast Bk. Distribution CAN. Dist: Publishers Group West (PGW).

Profilet, Cynthia. Maggie's Golden Moment. Barron, Ann, illus. 2005. (J). (978-0-9637735-1-7(8)) Sterling Pr., Inc.

Pulver, Robin. The Case of the Incapacitated Capitals. Reed, Lynn Rowe, illus. 2012. (ENG.). 32p. (J). (gr. -1-3). 16.95 (978-0-8234-2402-3(2)) Holiday Hse., Inc.

—The Case of the Incapacitated Capitals. Reed, Lynn Rowe, illus. 2013. (ENG.). 32p. (J). (gr. -1-3). pap. 7.99 (978-0-8234-2914-1(8)) Holiday Hse., Inc.

Ramesh, Serita. Jason & the Ingenious Number Trick: A Story about Patterns. 2010. 28p. pap. 15.49 (978-1-4490-4740-5(8)) AuthorHouse.

Random House. Dora Goes to School/Dora Va a la Escuela (Dora the Explorer) MJ Illustrations, illus. 2014. (Pictureback(R) Ser.). (ENG.). 24p. (J). (gr. -1-2). 3.99 (978-0-385-37496-5(8), Random Hse. Bks. for Young Readers) Random Hse. Children's Bks.

Ransom, Jeanie Franz. Don't Squeal Unless It's a Big Deal: A Tale of Tattletales. Urbanovic, Jackie, illus. 2005. (J). 32p. 14.95 (978-1-59147-239-1(3)); 28p. (gr. -1-3). pap. 9.95 (978-1-59147-240-7(7)) American Psychological Assn. (Magination Pr.).

Ray, Delia. Ghost Girl: A Blue Ridge Mountain Story. 2016. (ENG.). 272p. (J). (gr. 5-7). pap. 6.99 (978-0-544-70633-0(1), HMH Books For Young Readers) Houghton Mifflin Harcourt Publishing Co.

Reagan, Jean. How to Amaze a Teacher. Wildish, Lee, illus. 2017. (ENG.). 32p. (J). (gr. -1-3). 17.99 (978-0-553-53825-0(X), Knopf Bks. for Young Readers) Random Hse. Children's Bks.

Red & Green Choices by Green Irene: Niki's Next Grade. 2003. (J). per. 14.50 (978-0-9742280-1-3(X)) Green Irene.

Rentala, Sita Kanaka Valli. Ocean Flows: In Prose: Zcumby's Judo (on Global Warming) 2010. 44p. (J). pap. 19.99 (978-1-4490-8780-7(9)) AuthorHouse.

Rey, H. A. Race Day. 2010. (Curious George Ser.). (ENG., Illus.). 24p. (J). (gr. -1-3). pap. 3.99 (978-0-547-39361-2(X)) Houghton Mifflin Harcourt Publishing Co.

Rissi, Anica Mrose. The Teacher's Pet. OHora, Zachariah, illus. 2017. (ENG.). 40p. (J). (gr. -1-k). 17.99 (978-1-4847-4364-5(4)) Disney Pr.

Robins, Eleanor. Where Is Mr. Zane?, 1 vol. unabr. ed. 2011. (Carter High Mysteries Ser.). (ENG.). 48p. (YA). (gr. 9-12). 7.95 (978-1-61651-569-0(4)) Saddleback Educational Publishing, Inc.

Robles, Tony. Joey Gonzalez, Great American. Pryor, Jim, illus. 2008. (ENG.). (J). (gr. 2-3). 15.95 (978-0-9767269-3-7(9)) WND Bks, Inc.

Rogers, Blessing. Gabby & Ralph Meet Their New Teacher. 2010. 24p. 11.49 (978-1-4520-5447-6(9)) AuthorHouse.

Rogers, Kelly. Buyer Beware, 1 vol. Peterschmidt, Betsy, illus. 2016. (ENG.). 48p. (J). lib. bdg. 28.50 (978-1-62402-167-1(0)) Magic Wagon.

—The House Sitters, 1 vol. Peterschmidt, Betsy, illus. 2016. (ENG.). 48p. (J). lib. bdg. (978-1-62402-168-8(9)) Magic Wagon.

—The Key, 1 vol. Peterschmidt, Betsy, illus. 2016. (ENG.). 48p. (J). lib. bdg. (978-1-62402-169-5(7)) Magic Wagon.

—Study Group. Peterschmidt, Betsy, illus. 2016. (ENG.). 48p. (J). lib. bdg. (978-1-62402-170-1(0)) Magic Wagon.

Rolle Williams, Joyce. Chris's Story: A Family Voting Secret Revealed. 2008. 24p. pap. 12.99 (978-1-4389-4258-2(3)) AuthorHouse.

Roy, James. Max Quigley: Technically Not a Bully. 2009. (ENG., Illus.). 208p. (J). (gr. 2-5). 14.99 (978-0-547-15263-9(9)) Houghton Mifflin Harcourt Publishing Co.

Roy, Ron. September Sneakers. Gurney, John Steven, illus. 2013. (Calendar Mysteries Ser.: 9). (ENG.). 80p. (J). (gr. 1-4). 4.99 (978-0-375-86887-0(9), Random Hse. Bks. for Young Readers) Random Hse. Children's Bks.

—September Sneakers. 2013. (Calendar Mysteries Ser.: 9). lib. bdg. 14.75 (978-0-606-32231-7(0), Turtleback) Turtleback Bks.

Rutland, Mirium. Miss Pistachios Big Day. 2007. (Illus.). 48p. pap. (978-1-58690-063-2(3)) Mould, Paul Publishing.

Ryan, Carol. A Bridge Through Time, 1 vol. 2010. 276p. pap. 27.95 (978-1-4489-4254-1(3)) PublishAmerica, Inc.

Sawaski, James H. The Next Chess Team: A Novel. 2012. 120p. (gr. 10-12). pap. 10.95 (978-1-4759-2425-1(9)) iUniverse, Inc.

Scanlon, Rachel. Operation Reverse April Fools' 2008. 56p. pap. 16.95 (978-1-60441-649-7(1)) America Star Bks.

Schmatz, Pat. Bluefish. (ENG.). 240p. (YA). (gr. 7). 2013. pap. 6.99 (978-0-7636-6341-4(7)) 2011. (Illus.). 15.99 (978-0-7636-5334-7(9)) Candlewick Pr.

Schraff, Anne. The Haunting of Hawthorne. 2008. (Passages Ser.). 125p. (YA). (gr. 7-9). lib. bdg. 13.95 (978-0-7569-8379-6(7)) Perfection Learning Corp.

—The Hero at Crow's Crossing, 1 vol. 2015. (Red Rhino Ser.). (ENG.). 68p. (J). (gr. 4-6). pap. 7.95 (978-1-62250-943-0(9)) Saddleback Educational Publishing, Inc.

—The Petition. 2008. (Passages Ser.). 103p. (J). (gr. 4-6). lib. bdg. 13.95 (978-0-7569-8391-8(6)) Perfection Learning Corp.

—The Quality of Mercy. 2011. (Urban Underground — Harriet Tubman High School Ser.). (YA). lib. bdg. 20.80 (978-0-606-14800-9(0), Turtleback) Turtleback Bks.

Schraff, Anne E. The Hero at Crow's Crossing. 2015. (Red Rhino Ser.). (J). lib. bdg. 18.40 (978-0-606-36844-5(2)) Turtleback Bks.

Sherrard, Valerie. Speechless. 2007. (ENG.). 176p. (YA). (gr. 6). pap. 12.99 (978-1-55002-701-3(8), Boardwalk Bks.) Dundurn CAN. Dist: Ingram Publisher Services.

Shipton, Paul. Clown School. Blake, Beccy, illus. 2005. (ENG.). 24p. (J). lib. bdg. 23.65 (978-1-59646-752-1(5)) Dingles & Co.

The Shoe Grabber: Individual Title Six-Pack. (Story Steps Ser.). (gr. k-2). 23.00 (978-0-7635-9832-7(1)) Rigby Education.

Shubert Sees the Best. 2004. (J). 9.00 (978-1-889609-23-2(4)) Loving Guidance, Inc.

Skidmore, Marlene. In Trouble Again! 2010. 24p. pap. 9.99 (978-0-9845208-9-3(9)) Faithful Life Pubs.

Slate, Joseph. Miss Bindergarten Celebrates the Last Day of Kindergarten. Wolff, Ashley, illus. 2008. (ENG.). 40p. (J). (gr. -1-k). pap. 7.99 (978-0-14-241060-8(8), Puffin Books) Penguin Young Readers Group.

Snyder, Susan E. Shivers & Shakes. 2006. (Illus.). 31p. (J). (gr. k-2). 9.95 (978-0-9767163-5-8(6)) Kotzig Publishing, Inc.

Solomons, David. My Gym Teacher Is an Alien Overlord. Ferguson, Laura Ellen, illus. 2016. (ENG.). 288p. (J). (gr. 3-7). 16.99 (978-0-451-47494-0(5), Viking Books for Young Readers) Penguin Young Readers Group.

Solomons, David. My Gym Teacher Is an Alien Overlord. 2017. lib. bdg. 18.40 **(978-0-606-40090-9(7))** Turtleback Bks.

Sommerdorf, Norma. Red River Girl. 2006. (ENG., Illus.). 192p. (J). (gr. 3-7). 16.95 (978-0-8234-1903-6(7)) Holiday Hse., Inc.

Spanyol, Jessica. Clive Is a Teacher. Spanyol, Jessica, illus. 2017. (Clive's Jobs Ser.: 4). (ENG., Illus.). 14p. (J). bds. **(978-1-84643-990-2(6))** Child's Play International Ltd.

Sparks, Kerry. Jen & the Frosted Friends: Book #2 of the Get Frosted Series. 2010. 84p. pap. 10.99 (978-1-4520-5349-3(9)) AuthorHouse.

Spurling, Wesley. Books for Jacob. 2009. 24p. pap. 14.79 (978-1-4389-2231-7(0)) AuthorHouse.

—Gerry the Giraffe. 2009. 36p. pap. 16.99 (978-1-4389-4223-0(0)) AuthorHouse.

Spyri, Johanna. Rico & Stineli. 2006. 148p. (gr. 4-7). per. 11.95 (978-1-59818-873-8(9)) Aegypan.

Stamper, Judith Bauer. Rocky Road Trip. Gangloff, Hope, illus. 2004. (Magic School Bus Science Chapter Bks.). 89p. (gr. 2-5). lib. bdg. 15.00 (978-0-7569-3093-6(6)) Perfection Learning Corp.

Stanley, Malaika Rose. Miss Bubble's Troubles. Smith, Jan, illus. 2010. (ENG.). 40p. (J). (gr. 2-4). pap. 10.99 (978-1-84853-024-9(2)) Transworld Publishers Ltd. GBR. Dist: Independent Pubs. Group.

Stilton, Geronimo. Thea Stilton & the Dragon's Code. 2009. (Geronimo Stilton Special Edition Ser.: No. 1). (Illus.). 158p. 18.00 (978-1-60686-420-3(3)) Perfection Learning Corp.

—Thea Stilton & the Dragon's Code. 2009. (Thea Stilton Ser.: 1). lib. bdg. 19.65 (978-0-606-00231-8(6), Turtleback) Turtleback Bks.

Stilton, Geronimo & Stilton, Thea. Thea Stilton & the Dragon's Code. 2009. (Thea Stilton Ser.: 1). (ENG.). 176p. (J). (gr. 2-5). pap. 8.99 (978-0-545-10367-1(3), Scholastic Paperbacks) Scholastic, Inc.

—Thea Stilton & the Ghost of the Shipwreck. 2010. (Thea Stilton Ser.: 3). lib. bdg. 19.65 (978-0-606-06843-7(0), Turtleback) Turtleback Bks.

Stine, R. L. Creature Teacher: The Final Exam. 2014. (Goosebumps Most Wanted Ser.: 6). (ENG.). 160p. (J). (gr. 3-7). pap. 6.99 (978-0-545-62773-3(7), Scholastic Paperbacks) Scholastic, Inc.

—My Friends Call Me Monster. 2009. (Goosebumps Horrorland Ser.: 7). (ENG.). 160p. (J). (gr. 3-7). 6.99 (978-0-439-91875-6(8), Scholastic Paperbacks) Scholastic, Inc.

—The Teacher from Heck, 1 vol. Park, Trip, illus. 2011. (Rotten School Ser.: No. 8). (ENG.). 128p. (gr. 2-5). 24.21 (978-1-59961-832-6(X)) Spotlight.

Strand, Jeff. Elrod McBugle on the Loose. 2006. (ENG.). 136p. (YA). per. 9.25 (978-0-7599-4325-4(7)) Hard Shell Word Factory.

Tamanini, Kara T. I Promised Not to Tell. 2009. 44p. pap. 18.50 (978-1-60860-470-8(5), Eloquent Bks.) Strategic Book Publishing & Rights Agency (SBPRA).

Tashjian, Janet. For What It's Worth. 2012. (ENG.). 288p. (YA). (gr. 7-12). 16.99 (978-0-8050-9365-0(6), 9780805093650, Holt, Henry & Co. Bks. For Young Readers) Holt, Henry & Co.

Taylor, Shane. The Magic of Mortals. 2006. (YA). pap. 11.95 (978-1-58736-542-3(1), Starbound Bks.) Wheatmark, Inc.

Thaler, Mike. The Art Teacher from the Black Lagoon, 1 vol. Lee, Jared, illus. 2012. (Black Lagoon Set 2 Ser.: No. 2). (ENG.). 32p. (J). (gr. 1-4). lib. bdg. 24.21 (978-1-59961-952-1(0)) Spotlight.

—The Computer Teacher from the Black Lagoon. Lee, Jared, illus. 2007. (J). (978-0-439-87133-4(6)) Scholastic, Inc.

—The Computer Teacher from the Black Lagoon, 1 vol. Lee, Jared, illus. 2012. (Black Lagoon Set 2 Ser.: No. 2). (ENG.). 32p. (J). (gr. 1-4). lib. bdg. 24.21 (978-1-59961-955-2(5)) Spotlight.

—The Music Teacher from the Black Lagoon, 1 vol. Lee, Jared, illus. 2011. (Black Lagoon Set 1 Ser.: No. 1). (ENG.). 32p. (gr. -1-2). lib. bdg. 24.21 (978-1-59961-796-1(X)) Spotlight.

—School Play from the Black Lagoon, 1 vol. 2014. (Black Lagoon Adventures Set 3 Ser.). (ENG.). 64p. (J). (gr. 3-6). lib. bdg. 24.21 (978-1-61479-205-5(4)) Spotlight.

—The Teacher from the Black Lagoon. Lee, Jared, illus. 2008. (From the Black Lagoon Ser.). (gr. -1-3). 14.00 (978-0-7569-8779-4(2)) Perfection Learning Corp.

—The Teacher from the Black Lagoon. Lee, Jared D., illus. 2008. (Black Lagoon Adventures Ser.). (ENG.). 32p. (J). (gr. -1-3). pap. 3.99 (978-0-545-06522-1(4), Cartwheel Bks.) Scholastic, Inc.

—The Teacher from the Black Lagoon, 1 vol. Lee, Jared, illus. 2011. (Black Lagoon Set 1 Ser.: No. 1). (ENG.). 32p. (gr. -1-2). lib. bdg. 24.21 (978-1-59961-799-2(4)) Spotlight.

—The Teacher from the Black Lagoon. Lee, Jared, illus. 2004. (J). (gr. k-3). 18.95 (978-1-55592-495-9(6)) Weston Woods Studios, Inc.

Thaler, Mike, text. The Substitute Teacher from the Black Lagoon, 1 vol. 2014. (ENG., Illus.). 32p. (J). 24.21 (978-1-61479-199-7(6)) Spotlight.

Thomas, Carroll, creator. Under the Open Sky: A Matty Trescott Novel. 2005. (Illus.). 184p. (J). per. 12.95 (978-0-9762091-2-6(8)) Antrim Hse.

Thompson, Tate. Senioritis. 2nd ed. 2003. (YA). per. 13.50 (978-0-943864-47-1(X)) Davenport, May Pubs.

Tidwell, Deborah Swayne. Magic Eraser: And the Substitute Teacher. 2008. 24p. pap. 12.99 (978-1-4343-8107-1(2)) AuthorHouse.

Townsend, Lois Ritter. Our Journey Through Breast Cancer: -a story based on a teacher's journey through breast cancer with her kindergarten Class. 2005. (Illus.). 20p. (J). pap. 6.99 (978-1-933570-93-8(8)) Aardvark Global Publishing.

Trapped by a Teacher: Individual Title Six-Packs. (Action Packs Ser.). 128p. (gr. 3-5). 44.00 (978-0-7635-3309-0(2)) Rigby Education.

Underwood, Deborah. Here Comes Teacher Cat. Rueda, Claudia, illus. 2017. (ENG.). 88p. (J). (-k). 16.99 **(978-0-399-53905-3(0)**, Dial Bks) Penguin Young Readers Group.

Van Draanen, Wendelin. Sammy Keyes & the Wedding Crasher. 2011. (Sammy Keyes Ser.: Bk. 13). (ENG.). 320p. (J). (gr. 5). 7.99 (978-0-375-85456-9(8), Yearling) Random Hse. Children's Bks.

—Sinister Substitute. Gilpin, Stephen, illus. 2010. (Gecko & Sticky Ser.). (ENG.). 224p. (J). (gr. 3-7). 12.99 (978-0-375-84378-5(7), Knopf Bks. for Young Readers) Random Hse. Children's Bks.

Volk, Gretchen. The Amazing Adventures of Tristy Ruth, Raisin Girl. 2012. 258p. pap. (978-1-105-51531-6(1)) Lulu.com.

Volponi, Paul. The Hand You're Dealt. 2010. (ENG.). 192p. (YA). (gr. 7). pap. 11.99 (978-1-4169-3990-0(3), Atheneum Bks. for Young Readers) Simon & Schuster Children's Publishing.

Waddell, Martin. Class Six & the Very Big Rabbit. Ross, Tony, illus. 2005. (Collins Big Cat Ser.). (ENG.). 80p. (J). (gr. 1-3). pap. 7.99 (978-0-00-718629-7(0)) HarperCollins Pubs. Ltd. GBR. Dist: Independent Pubs. Group.

Wagstaff, Janiel. Stella & Class: Information Experts. 2015. (ENG.). pap. 7.95 (978-1-63133-024-7(1)) Staff Development for Educators.

—Stella Writes an Opinion. 2015. (ENG.). (J). (gr. -1-3). pap. 7.95 (978-1-63133-022-3(5)) Staff Development for Educators.

Walker-Renner, Christa. Santa's Magic. 2009. 20p. pap. 11.00 (978-1-4389-8206-9(2)) AuthorHouse.

Wardlaw, Lee. 101 Ways to Bug Your Teacher. 2005. (ENG.). 256p. (J). (gr. 3-7). pap. 6.99 (978-0-14-240331-0(8), Puffin Books) Penguin Young Readers Group.

Warner, Sally. EllRay Jakes Is Magic. Biggs, Brian, illus. 2014. (EllRay Jakes Ser.: 6). (ENG.). (J). (gr. 1-3). 160p. 14.99 (978-0-670-78500-1(8), Viking Books for Young Readers); 176p. pap. 5.99 (978-0-14-242360-8(2), Puffin Books) Penguin Young Readers Group.

—Ellray Jakes Is Magic. 2014. (EllRay Jakes Ser.: 6). lib. bdg. 16.00 (978-0-606-34215-5(X), Turtleback) Turtleback Bks.

—EllRay Jakes Stands Tall. Biggs, Brian, illus. 2016. (EllRay Jakes Ser.). (ENG.). (J). (gr. 1-3). 176p. 5.99 (978-0-14-751253-6(0), Puffin Books); 160p. 14.99 (978-0-451-46913-7(5), Viking Books for Young Readers) Penguin Young Readers Group.

—Ellray Jakes Stands Tall. 2016. (EllRay Jakes Ser.: 9). lib. bdg. 16.00 (978-0-606-38420-9(0)) Turtleback Bks.

Wasserman, Sand. The Sun's Special Blessing: Happens Only Once in 28 Years - French Flap. Koffsky, Ann, illus. 2009. 36p. 12.95 (978-1-934440-76-6(0), Pitspopany Pr.) Simcha Media Group.

—The Sun's Special Blessing: Happens Only Once in 28 Years - HC. Koffsky, Ann, illus. 2009. 36p. 17.95 (978-1-934440-92-6(2), Pitspopany Pr.) Simcha Media Group.

Waters, Daniel. Break My Heart 1,000 Times. 2013. (ENG., Illus.). 352p. (YA). (gr. 7-17). pap. 9.99 (978-1-4231-2228-9(3)) Hyperion Pr.

Watts, Jeri. Kizzy Ann Stamps. 2013. (ENG., Illus.). 192p. (J). (gr. 4-7). pap. 5.99 (978-0-7636-6976-8(8)) Candlewick Pr.

Weil, Zoe. Claude & Medea: The Hellburn Dogs. 2007. (ENG., Illus.). 103p. (J). (gr. 2-7). per. 12.00 (978-1-59056-105-8(8)) Lantern Bks.

Wesson, André. Mrs. Applebee & the Sunshine Band, Book 1: Meet the Class! 2007. 48p. pap. 18.50 (978-0-615-14849-6(2)) Se7enth Swan Publishing Group, LLC.

Weston, Greg. Ocean View Terrace & the Blue Pirate Eater. 2008. 232p. pap. 14.95 (978-1-4092-0278-3(X)) Lulu Pr., Inc.

Weston Woods Staff, creator. The Gym Teacher from the Black Lagoon. 2011. 38.75 (978-0-545-19711-3(2)) Weston Woods Studios, Inc.

Whisler, Barbara. Shag Finds a Home. Jackson, Kay, illus. 2008. 24p. pap. 24.95 *(978-1-60703-730-9(0))* America Star Bks.

White, Michelle A. Anthony with an A. 2011. 16p. pap. 9.50 *(978-1-4634-1641-6(5))* AuthorHouse.

White, Russ. Cat Got Your Tongue? A Book of Idioms. Cornelison, Reuel, illus. l.t. ed. 2004. 44p. (J). per. *(978-0-9742885-0-5(0),* 00) White, Russ.

Wiggin, Kate Douglas. Polly Oliver's Problem. 2007. 108p. per. 9.95 *(978-1-60312-369-3(5));* 22.95 *(978-1-60312-707-3(0))* Aegypan.

Wiggins, Rosie. Adventures at a Ray of Hope Preschool. 2007. 32p. per. 12.95 *(978-1-4327-1657-8(3))* Outskirts Pr., Inc.

Wilder, Laura Ingalls. These Happy Golden Years. 2007. (Little House Ser.). (ENG.). 304p. (J). (gr. 3-7). pap., pap. 6.99 *(978-0-06-088541-0(0),* Harper Trophy) HarperCollins Pubs.

Williams, Stanley R. Not Me. 2008. 47p. pap. 24.95 *(978-1-4241-9577-0(2))* America Star Bks.

Wimberly, Nikisha. Hair Like That. Drewes, Dan, illus. 2010. 24p. 13.00 *(978-1-4520-0177-7(4))* AuthorHouse.

Winfrey, Michelle Whitaker. It's My Birthday. . . Finally! A Leap Year Story. Turley, Joyce M., illus. 2003. 88p. (J). (gr. 3-7). per. 11.95 *(978-0-9727179-0-8(0))* Hobby Hse. Publishing Group.

Winters, Ben H. The Secret Life of Ms. Finkleman. (ENG.). (J). (gr. 3-7). 2011. 272p. pap. 5.99 *(978-0-06-196543-2(X))* 2010. 256p. 16.99 *(978-0-06-196541-8(3))* HarperCollins Pubs.

Winters, Kay. My Teacher for President. Brunkus, Denise, illus. 2008. (ENG.). 32p. (J). (gr. k-3). pap. 6.99 *(978-0-14-241170-4(1),* Puffin Books) Penguin Young Readers Group.

—My Teacher for President. Brunkus, Denise, illus. 2008. (gr. -1-k). 17.00 *(978-0-7569-8925-5(6))* Perfection Learning Corp.

Wood, Maryrose. The Mysterious Howling, Bk. I. Klassen, Jon, illus. 2010. (Incorrigible Children of Ashton Place Ser.: 1). (ENG.). 272p. (J). (gr. 3-7). 16.99 *(978-0-06-179105-5(9))* HarperCollins Pubs.

Woodard, Amy. The Day the Teacher Rode a Horse to School. 2008. 24p. pap. 24.95 *(978-1-60441-736-4(6))* America Star Bks.

Woodrow, Allan. Class Dismissed. (ENG.). 272p. (J). (gr. 3-7). 2017. pap. 6.99 ***(978-0-545-80072-3(2),*** Scholastic Paperbacks) 2015. 16.99 *(978-0-545-80071-6(4),* Scholastic Pr.) Scholastic, Inc.

Woods, Linda J. The Gift of the Jumping Goldfish (A True Story) 2011. 48p. (gr. 1-2). pap. 19.46 *(978-1-4567-5796-0(2))* AuthorHouse.

Wright, Pauline. Why Did My Dad Go to War? 2008. 48p. pap. 19.49 *(978-1-4343-4677-3(3))* AuthorHouse.

Yankovic, Al, pseud. My New Teacher & Me! Hargis, Wes, illus. 2013. (ENG.). 40p. (J). (gr. -1-3). 17.99 *(978-0-06-219203-5(5))* HarperCollins Pubs.

Zemach, Kaethe. Ms. McCaw Learns to Draw. (J). 2008. (ENG., Illus.). 32p. (gr. -1-3). 16.99 *(978-0-439-82914-4(3))* 2006. *(978-0-439-82915-1(1))* Scholastic, Inc. (Levine, Arthur A. Bks.).

Zepeda, Frank. A Wad of Gum. 2012. 40p. pap. 19.99 *(978-1-105-73944-6(9))* Lulu Pr., Inc.

TEACHERS—TRAINING OF

Here are entered works dealing with the history and methods of training teachers, including the educational functions of teachers colleges. Works on the study of education as a science are entered under Education—Study and teaching.

Calhoun, Florence. Choosing a Career in Teaching. 2009. (World of Work Ser.). 64p. (gr. 5-5). 58.50 *(978-1-60854-336-6(6))* Rosen Publishing Group, Inc., The.

Nesbitt, Shawntelle. The Kids' Power Series Teacher Resource, 1 vol. 2011. (Kids' Power Ser.). (ENG.). 125p. (J). spiral bd. 29.95 *(978-1-926920-35-1(X))* Second Story Pr. CAN. Dist: Orca Bk. Pubs. USA.

TEACHERS AND PARENTS

see Home and School

TEACHING

see also Education; Educational Psychology; Kindergarten; Project Method in Teaching; Study Skills; Teachers—Training of

also subjects with the subdivision Study and Teaching, e.g. Science—Study and Teaching

Crane, Natalie. I Go to Work as a Teacher. 2003. (I Go to Work As Ser.). (Illus.). (J). lib. bdg. *(978-1-58417-044-0(1))* Lake Street Pubs.

Culham, Ruth. Trait Crate, Grade 6: Mentor Texts, Model Lessons, & More to Teach Writing with the 6 Traits. 2011. (Trait Crate(r) Ser.). (ENG.). (gr. 6-6). 125.00 *(978-0-545-31862-4(9),* Teaching Resources) Scholastic, Inc.

—Trait Crate, Grade 7: Mentor Texts, Model Lessons, & More to Teach Writing with the 6 Traits. 2011. (Trait Crate(r) Ser.). (ENG.). (gr. 7-7). 125.00 *(978-0-545-31863-1(7),* Teaching Resources) Scholastic, Inc.

—Trait Crate Grade 8: Mentor Texts, Model Lessons, & More to Teach Writing with the 6 Traits. 2011. (Trait Crate(r) Ser.). (ENG.). (gr. 8-8). 125.00 *(978-0-545-31864-8(5),* Teaching Resources) Scholastic, Inc.

The Education of Little Tree: Activity Pack. 2003. 118p. (YA). pap. *(978-1-58049-627-8(X),* PA0127) Prestwick Hse., Inc.

Hart, Melissa. A Guide for Using Walk Two Moons in the Classroom. 2003. (ENG.). 48p. (gr. 5-8). pap. 9.99 *(978-0-7439-3160-1(2))* Teacher Created Resources, Inc.

Kindle, Karen. Using Read-Alouds to Teach Vocabulary: Research-Based Strategies & Model Lessons for Using Fiction & Nonfiction Books to Build Children's Vocabulary & Improve Their Reading, Writing, & Speaking Skills. 2011. (ENG.). 128p. (gr. k-2). pap. 18.99 *(978-0-545-16513-6(X),* Teaching Resources) Scholastic, Inc.

La Bella, Laura. Getting a Job in Education. 2016. (Job Basics: Getting the Job You Need Ser.). 80p. (J). (gr. 8-8). 35.75 *(978-1-4777-8566-9(3))* Rosen Publishing Group, Inc., The.

Macken, JoAnn Early. Teachers. 2010. (People in My Community Ser.). (Illus.). 24p. (J). (gr. k-3). 22.60 *(978-1-4339-3347-9(0))* Stevens, Gareth Publishing LLLP.

Matthews, John. Interactive Whiteboards. 2008. (21st Century Skills Library: Global Products Ser.). (ENG.). 32p. (gr. 4-8). 28.50 *(978-1-60279-254-8(2),* 200121) Cherry Lake Publishing.

Thinking Kids & Carson-Dellosa Publishing, compiled by. Kindergarten Essentials. 2017. (ENG.). 256p. (gr. k-k). pap. 5.99 ***(978-1-4838-3817-5(X),*** Thinking Kids) Carson-Dellosa Publishing, LLC.

TEACHING—VOCATIONAL GUIDANCE

Anthony, David. Teachers on the Job. 2017. (Jobs in Our Community Ser.). 24p. (J). (gr. 1-1). lib. bdg. 24.60 ***(978-1-5345-2147-6(X),*** KidHaven Publishing) Greenhaven Publishing LLC.

Calhoun, Florence. Choosing a Career in Teaching. (World of Work Ser.). 64p. 2009. (gr. 5-5). 58.50 *(978-1-60854-336-6(6))* 2005. (Illus.). (YA). (gr. 7-12). lib. bdg. 31.95 *(978-0-8239-3247-4(8))* Rosen Publishing Group, Inc., The.

Crane, Natalie. I Go to Work as a Teacher. 2003. (I Go to Work As Ser.). (Illus.). (J). pap. *(978-1-58417-106-5(5));* lib. bdg. *(978-1-58417-043-3(3))* Lake Street Pubs.

Early Macken, JoAnn. Teachers. Andersen, Gregg, photos by. 2010. (People in My Community Ser.). (Illus.). 24p. (gr. k-3). pap. 8.15 *(978-1-4339-3348-6(9))* Stevens, Gareth Publishing LLLP.

—Teachers / Maestros. Andersen, Gregg, photos by. 2010. (People in My Community / Mi comunidad Ser.). (SPA., Illus.). 24p. (gr. k-3). pap. 8.15 *(978-1-4339-3766-8(2))* Stevens, Gareth Publishing LLLP.

Education. 2010. (What Can I Do Now? Ser.). 224p. (gr. 6-12). 32.95 *(978-0-8160-8079-3(8),* Ferguson Publishing Co.) Facts On File, Inc.

Ferguson. Teaching. 2nd rev. ed. 2008. (Discovering Careers for Your Future Ser.). 92p. (gr. 4-9). 21.95 *(978-0-8160-7292-7(2),* Ferguson Publishing Co.) Facts On File, Inc.

Heaton, J. Barrett. Careers in Teaching. 2009. (Careers in the New Economy Ser.). 144p. (gr. 7-7). 63.90 *(978-1-61511-821-2(7))* Rosen Publishing Group, Inc., The.

Kampff, Joseph. What Degree Do I Need to Pursue a Career in Education?, 1 vol. 2015. (ENG., Illus.). 80p. (J). 34.60 *(978-1-4777-7873-9(X),* Rosen Young Adult) Rosen Publishing Group, Inc., The.

Kidde, Rita. What Do Teachers Do? 2014. (Jobs in My School Ser.). 24p. (J). (gr. k-2). lib. bdg. 23.60 *(978-1-4777-6556-2(5),* PowerKids Pr.) Rosen Publishing Group, Inc., The.

Lesinski, Jeanne M. Bill Gates. 2005. (First Step Nonfiction Ser.). (Illus.). 112p. (J). (gr. 3-7). lib. bdg. 27.93 *(978-0-8225-2642-1(5),* Lerner Pubns.) Lerner Publishing Group.

Lindsey Reeves, Diane. Career Ideas for Teens in Education & Training. 2nd rev. ed. 2011. (Career Ideas for Teens Ser.). (Illus.). 182p. (gr. 6-12). 45.00 *(978-0-8160-8274-2(X))* Facts On File, Inc.

Lowenstein, Felicia. What Does a Teacher Do? 2006. (What Does a Community Helper Do? Ser.). (Illus.). 24p. (J). (gr. 1-3). lib. bdg. 22.60 *(978-0-7660-2321-5(4),* Enslow Elementary) Enslow Pubs., Inc.

Matters, Print & Kirk, Amanda. Education. 2009. (Field Guides to Finding a New Career Ser.). (C). (gr. 9-18). 152p. pap. 16.95 *(978-0-8160-7621-5(9),* Checkmark Bks.); (Illus.). 134p. 39.95 *(978-0-8160-7597-3(2),* Ferguson Publishing Co.) Facts On File, Inc.

McAlpine, Margaret. Working with Children. 2004. (My Future Career Ser.). (Illus.). 64p. (gr. 3-7). lib. bdg. 27.00 *(978-0-8368-4241-8(3),* Gareth Stevens Learning Library) Stevens, Gareth Publishing LLLP.

Miller, Malinda. Tomorrow's Teachers: Urban Leadership, Empowering Students & Improving Lives. 2010. (New Careers for the 21st Century Ser.). 64p. (YA). (gr. 7-18). pap. 9.95 *(978-1-4222-2044-3(3))* Mason Crest.

—Tomorrow's Teachers: Urban Leadership, Empowering Students, & Improving Lives. 2010. (New Careers for the 21st Century Ser.). 64p. (YA). (gr. 7-18). lib. bdg. 22.95 *(978-1-4222-1823-5(6))* Mason Crest.

Mitchell, Melanie. Teachers. 2005. (Pull Ahead Bks.). (Illus.). 32p. (J). lib. bdg. 22.60 *(978-0-8225-1696-5(9));* (ENG., pap. 7.95 *(978-0-8225-2536-3(4))* Lerner Publishing Group.

Reeves, Diane Lindsey. Career Ideas for Teens in Education & Training. 2006. (Career Ideas for Teens Ser.). (Illus.). 192p. (gr. 7-12). per. 16.95 *(978-0-8160-6919-4(0),* Checkmark Bks.) Facts On File, Inc.

Reeves, Diane Lindsey & Karlitz, Gail. Career Ideas for Teens in Education & Training. 2005. (Career Ideas for Teens Ser.). (Illus.). 192p. (gr. 6-12). 40.00 *(978-0-8160-5295-0(6),* Ferguson Publishing Co.) Facts On File, Inc.

Rivera, Sheila. Teacher. 2005. (First Step Nonfiction - Work People Do Ser.). (ENG.). 8p. (gr. -1-1). pap. 4.95 *(978-0-8225-5361-8(9),* Lerner Pubns.) Lerner Publishing Group.

Sanna, Ellyn. Special Education Teacher. 2004. (Careers with Character Ser.). (Illus.). 96p. (YA). (gr. 7-18). 22.95 *(978-1-59084-325-3(8))* Mason Crest.

Sheen, Barbara. Careers in Education. 2015. (ENG., Illus.). 80p. (J). lib. bdg. *(978-1-60152-808-7(6))* ReferencePoint Pr., Inc.

Silivanch, Annalise. A Career as a Teacher. 2010. (Essential Careers Ser.). (ENG.). 80p. (YA). lib. bdg. 33.25 *(978-1-4358-9468-6(5))* Rosen Publishing Group, Inc., The.

TEACHINGS OF JESUS

see Jesus Christ—Teachings

TEAROOMS

see Restaurants

TECHNICAL EDUCATION

see also Employees—Training of

also technical subjects with the subdivision Study and Teaching, e.g. Mathematics—Study and Teaching

Bily, Cynthia A. Career & Technical Education. Greenhaven Press Editors, ed. 2013. (Issues That Concern You Ser.). (ENG., Illus.). 144p. (gr. 7-10). lib. bdg. 42.00 *(978-0-7377-6285-3(3),* Greenhaven Pr., Inc.) Cengage Gale.

Makerspaces. 2014. (Makerspaces Ser.). 64p. (YA). (gr. 6-12). pap. 77.70 *(978-1-4777-8112-8(9))* Rosen Publishing Group, Inc., The.

Tech3000. 2003. (J). cd-rom 99.00 *(978-1-932166-06-4(8))* Achieve3000.

TECHNICAL SCHOOLS

see Technical Education

TECHNICAL TERMS

see Technology—Dictionaries

TECHNOLOGY

see also Building; Chemistry, Technical; Engineering; Inventions; Machinery; Manufactures; Measurement; Technical Education

ABDO Publishing. Cutting-Edge Science & Technology. 2016. (Cutting-Edge Science & Technology Ser.: 8). (ENG.). 112p. (J). (gr. 6-12). lib. bdg. 285.12 *(978-1-62403-911-9(1),* Essential Library) ABDO Publishing Co.

ABDO Publishing Company Staff. Innovative Technologies, 1 vol. 2013. (Innovative Technologies Ser.: 8). (ENG.). 112p. (J). (gr. 6-12). lib. bdg. 285.12 *(978-1-61783-461-5(0),* Essential Library) ABDO Publishing Co.

Allen, John. What Is the Future of Artificial Intelligence? 2016. (ENG.). 80p. (J). (gr. 5-12). *(978-1-68282-060-5(2))* ReferencePoint Pr., Inc.

—What Is the Future of Nanotechnology? 2016. (ENG.). 80p. (YA). (gr. 5-12). *(978-1-60152-962-6(7))* ReferencePoint Pr., Inc.

Allen, Kathy, et al. Tech Safety Smarts. 2013. (Tech Safety Smarts Ser.). (ENG.). 32p. (gr. 3-4). lib. bdg. 109.28 *(978-1-4296-9947-1(7),* Fact Finders) Capstone Press of Coughlan Cos.

Allen, Thomas B. & Allen, Roger MacBride. Mr. Lincoln's High-Tech War: How the North Used the Telegraph, Railroads, Surveillance Balloons, Ironclads, High-Powered Weapons, & More to Win the Civil War. 2009. (ENG., Illus.). 144p. (J). (gr. 5-18). 18.95 *(978-1-4263-0379-1(3));* lib. bdg. 25.90 *(978-1-4263-0380-7(7))* National Geographic Society. (National Geographic Children's Bks.).

Amstutz, Lisa J. Discover Nanotechnology. 2016. (Searchlight Books (tm) — What's Cool about Science? Ser.). (ENG., Illus.). 40p. (J). (gr. 3-5). 30.65 *(978-1-5124-0806-5(9))* Lerner Publishing Group.

Anderson, Jenna. How It Happens at the ATV Plant. Wolfe, Bob & Wolfe, Diane, photos by. 2004. (How It Happens Ser.). (Illus.). 32p. (J). (gr. 2-5). lib. bdg. 19.95 *(978-1-881508-94-6(3))* Oliver Pr., Inc.

Anniss, Matt. The Impact of Technology in Music. 2015. (Impact of Technology Ser.). (ENG., Illus.). 56p. (gr. 6-9). 34.65 *(978-1-4846-2638-2(9))* Heinemann-Raintree.

Bailey, Gerry. Technology. 2009. (Simply Science Ser.). (Illus.). 32p. (YA). (gr. 3-6). lib. bdg. 26.00 *(978-1-4339-0034-1(3))* Stevens, Gareth Publishing LLLP.

Barnes, John, et al. Science, Maths & Technology. 2003. (ENG., Illus.). 184p. pap. *(978-0-7487-7121-9(2))* Nelson Thornes Ltd.

Barnham, Kay. Could a Robot Make My Dinner? And Other Questions about Technology, 1 vol. 2013. (Questions You Never Thought You'd Ask Ser.). (ENG.). 32p. (gr. 1-3). 29.99 *(978-1-4109-5200-4(2));* pap. 8.95 *(978-1-4109-5206-6(1))* Heinemann-Raintree. (Read Me!).

Bartos, Judeen, ed. What Is the Role of Technology in Education? 2012. (At Issue Ser.). (ENG.). 128p. (gr. 10-12). pap. 24.45 *(978-0-7377-6218-1(7));* lib. bdg. 34.45 *(978-0-7377-6217-4(9))* Cengage Gale. (Greenhaven Pr., Inc.).

Basher, Simon & Green, Dan. Basher Science - Technology: A Byte-Sized World! Basher, Simon, illus. 2012. (Basher Science Ser.). (ENG., Illus.). 128p. (J). (gr. 5-9). 14.99 *(978-0-7534-6819-7(0),* 9780753468197, Kingfisher) Roaring Brook Pr.

—Technology: A Byte-Sized World! Basher, Simon, illus. 2012. (Basher Science Ser.). (ENG., Illus.). 128p. (J). (gr. 5-9). pap. 8.99 *(978-0-7534-6820-3(4),* 9780753468203, Kingfisher) Roaring Brook Pr.

Benchmark Education Co., LLC Staff, et al. Technology at Home & School: Past & Present. 2015. (Content Connections Ser.). (J). (gr. k). *(978-1-4900-0481-5(5))* Benchmark Education Co.

—Technology at Home & School: Past & Present: Big Book Edition. 2015. (Content Connections Ser.). (J). (gr. k). *(978-1-4900-0475-4(0))* Benchmark Education Co.

—Using Technology at Work. 2015. (Content Connections Ser.). (J). (gr. 1). *(978-1-4900-0483-9(1))* Benchmark Education Co.

—Using Technology at Work: Big Book Edition. 2015. (Content Connections Ser.). (J). (gr. 1). *(978-1-4900-0477-8(7))* Benchmark Education Co.

Benchmark Education Company, LLC Staff. Disasters of Technology Teacher's Guide. 2004. *(978-1-4108-2591-9(4))* Benchmark Education Co.

Benchmark Education Company, LLC Staff, compiled by. Invention & Technology: Theme Set. 2006. (J). 158.00 *(978-1-4108-7100-8(2))* Benchmark Education Co.

—Science & Technology. 2006. spiral bd. 115.00 *(978-1-4108-6923-4(7))* 2006. spiral bd. 105.00 *(978-1-4108-6935-7(0))* 2005. spiral bd. 55.00 *(978-1-4108-3855-1(2))* 2005. spiral bd. 110.00 *(978-1-4108-3866-7(8))* 2005. spiral bd. 42.00 *(978-1-4108-3880-3(3))* 2005. spiral bd. 235.00 *(978-1-4108-4520-7(6))* 2005. spiral bd. 255.00 *(978-1-4108-5444-5(2))* 2005. spiral bd. 145.00 *(978-1-4108-5445-2(0))* 2005. spiral bd. 170.00 *(978-1-4108-5855-9(3))* 2005. spiral bd. 130.00 *(978-1-4108-5856-6(1))* 2005. spiral bd. 125.00 *(978-1-4108-3842-1(0))* 2005. spiral bd. 60.00 *(978-1-4108-3843-8(9))* 2005. spiral bd. 115.00 *(978-1-4108-3854-4(4))* Benchmark Education Co.

—Science, Technology & Society. 2005. spiral bd. 185.00 *(978-1-4108-3753-0(X))* Benchmark Education Co.

—Science, Technology, & Society. 2005. spiral bd. 80.00 *(978-1-4108-3962-6(1));* spiral bd. 145.00 *(978-1-4108-4499-6(4));* spiral bd. 110.00 *(978-1-4108-5425-4(6));* spiral bd. 70.00 *(978-1-4108-3954-1(0));* spiral bd. 74.00 *(978-1-4108-5842-9(1));* spiral bd. 80.00 *(978-1-4108-3961-9(3));* spiral bd. 115.00 *(978-1-4108-5841-2(3))* Benchmark Education Co.

—Tools & Technology. 2006. (J). 148.00 *(978-1-4108-7034-6(0))* Benchmark Education Co.

Bender, Lionel & Dorling Kindersley Publishing Staff. Invention. 2013. (DK Eyewitness Bks.). (ENG.). 72p. (J). (gr. 3-7). 16.99 *(978-1-4654-0901-0(7),* DK Children) Dorling Kindersley Publishing, Inc.

Bensinger, Henry. Ancient Greek Technology. 2013. (Spotlight on Ancient Civilizations: Greece Ser.). (ENG.). 24p. (J). (gr. 3-4). 23.60 *(978-1-4777-0774-6(3),* PowerKids Pr.) Rosen Publishing Group, Inc., The.

Biskup, Agnieszka. The Science Behind Batman's Tools. Vecchio, Luciano, illus. 2016. (Science Behind Batman Ser.). (ENG.). 24p. (gr. 1-2). lib. bdg. 25.32 *(978-1-5157-2038-6(1),* DC Super Heroes) Stone Arch Bks.

Book Steps, 6 Pack. (Bookweb Ser.). 32p. (gr. 5-18). 34.00 *(978-0-7635-3800-2(0))* Rigby Education.

Brandt, Allison & Benchmark Education Co. Staff. Careers on the Cutting Edge. 2014. (Text Connections Ser.). (J). (gr. 5). *(978-1-4900-1369-5(5))* Benchmark Education Co.

Brezina, Corona. Careers in Nanotechnology. 2009. (Cutting-Edge Careers Ser.). 64p. (gr. 7-7). 55.90 *(978-1-61512-100-7(5))* Rosen Publishing Group, Inc., The.

—The Industrial Revolution in America: A Primary Source History of America's Transformation into an Industrial Society. 2005. (Primary Sources in American History Ser.). (Illus.). 64p. (YA). (gr. 5-8). lib. bdg. 31.95 *(978-1-4042-0179-8(3))* Rosen Publishing Group, Inc., The.

Britannica, Learning Library. Technology & Inventions. 2003. (Illus.). 64p. 14.95 *(978-1-59339-034-1(3))* Encyclopaedia Britannica, Inc.

Brocket, Jane. Spiky, Slimy, Smooth: What Is Texture? Brocket, Jane, photos by. 2011. (Jane Brocket's Clever Concepts Ser.). (ENG., Illus.). 32p. (gr. -1-2). 26.60 *(978-0-7613-4614-2(7))* Lerner Publishing Group.

Brookes, Olivia. Uncover Technology. Kent, Peter, illus. 2009. (Hide-and-Seek Visual Adventures Ser.). 24p. (J). (gr. 2-5). lib. bdg. 22.60 *(978-1-60754-658-0(2))* Windmill Bks.

Brusic, Sharon A., et al. Technology: Today & Tomorrow. 5th ed. 2003. (TECHNOLOGY: TODAY & TOMORROW Ser.). (ENG., Illus.). 624p. (gr. 9-10). stu. ed. 76.80 *(978-0-07-830829-1(1),* 0078308291) McGraw-Hill Higher Education.

Bryan, Dale-Marie. Smartphone Safety & Privacy. 2013. 64p. (J). (gr. 5-8). 31.95 *(978-1-4488-9573-1(1))* Rosen Publishing Group, Inc., The.

Bryant, Jill. Technology Mysteries Revealed. 2010. (ENG., Illus.). 32p. (J). pap. *(978-0-7787-7432-7(5));* (gr. 4-7). lib. bdg. *(978-0-7787-7417-4(1))* Crabtree Publishing Co.

Buckley, Susan Washburn & National Geographic Learning Staff. The Industrial Revolution. 2006. (Nonfiction Reading & Writing Workshops Ser.). (ENG., Illus.). 40p. (J). pap. 19.95 *(978-0-7922-8685-1(5))* CENGAGE Learning.

Burns Chong, Susan. Step-By-Step Guide to Innovating at School & Work. 2014. (Winning at Work Readiness Ser.). 64p. (J). (gr. 9-12). 32.95 *(978-1-4777-7786-2(5))* Rosen Publishing Group, Inc., The.

Burton, Margie, et al. Technology Today. 2011. (Early Connections Ser.). (J). *(978-1-61672-540-2(0))* Benchmark Education Co.

Butterfield, Moira & Jacobs, Pat. Technology. 2016. (Know It All Ser.). (ENG., Illus.). 32p. (J). (gr. 5-5). pap. 10.58 *(978-1-5026-0902-1(9),* 1398916) Cavendish Square Publishing.

Byers, Ann. Strategic Inventions of the Civil War. 2016. (Tech in the Trenches Ser.). (ENG., Illus.). 112p. (J). (gr. 9-9). lib. bdg. 42.79 *(978-1-5026-1030-0(2))* Cavendish Square Publishing.

Cain, Marie Mowery. Then & Now. 2013. (Big Books, Blue Ser.). (ENG & SPA., Illus.). 16p. pap. 33.00 *(978-1-59246-007-6(0))* Big Books, by George!

Canfield, Michael. Freaky Stories about Inventions. 2016. (Freaky True Science Ser.). (Illus.). 32p. (J). (gr. 5-4). pap. 10.50 *(978-1-4824-4819-1(X))* Stevens, Gareth Publishing LLLP.

Chambers, Jo. High Tech. 2007. (Trackers-Math Ser.). (gr. 2-5). pap. 5.00 *(978-1-59055-934-5(7))* Pacific Learning, Inc.

Chase, Alex. Technology in the 20th Century. 2015. (ENG., Illus.). 100p. (gr. 7-18). pap. 9.95 *(978-0-912517-25-4(5))* Bluewood Bks.

Children's Cool Technology Encyclopedia. 2008. (1st Encyclopedia Ser.). 224p. *(978-1-4075-1316-4(8))* Parragon, Inc.

Coad, John. Green Technology, 1 vol. 2011. (Sci-Hi: Science & Technology Ser.). (ENG., Illus.). 48p. (gr. 4-4). 33.32 *(978-1-4109-4272-2(4),* Sci-Hi) Heinemann-Raintree.

Colson, Mary. Get Inventing!, 1 vol. 2014. (Dream It, Do It! Ser.). (ENG., Illus.). 32p. (gr. 1-3). pap. 8.95 *(978-1-4109-6269-0(5),* Read Me!) Heinemann-Raintree.

Crozier, A. J. Technology & the Civil War: Text Pairs. 2008. (Bridges/Navigators Ser.). (J). (gr. 5). 89.00 *(978-1-4108-8423-7(6))* Benchmark Education Co.

Culp, Jennifer. Ancient Chinese Technology. 2016. (Spotlight on the Rise & Fall of Ancient Civilizations Ser.). 48p. (J). (gr. 6-6). pap. 11.75 *(978-1-4777-8897-4(2))* Rosen Publishing Group, Inc., The.

Cutting-Edge Technology. 2016. (Cutting-Edge Technology Ser.). 48p. (gr. 8-6). pap. 84.30 *(978-1-4824-5317-1(7));* lib. bdg. 191.70 *(978-1-4824-5118-4(2))* Stevens, Gareth Publishing LLLP.

Daly, James & Zuckerman, Amy. 2030: A Day in the Life of Tomorrow's Kids. Manders, John, illus. 2009. (ENG.). 32p. (J). (gr. 1-3). 16.99 *(978-0-525-47860-7(4),* Dutton Books for Young Readers) Penguin Young Readers Group.

Daynes, Katie. Toilets, Telephones & Other Useful Inventions. 2005. (Young Reading Series 1 Ser.). 48p. (J). (gr. 2-18). pap. 5.95 *(978-0-7945-0888-3(X),* Usborne) EDC Publishing.

Diehn, Andi. Technology: Cool Women Who Code. 2015. (Girls in Science Ser.). (ENG., Illus.). 112p. (gr. 3-7). 19.95 *(978-1-61930-321-8(3))* Open City Bks.

Digital & Information Literacy: Set 6. 2013. (Digital & Information Literacy Ser.). 48p. (J). (gr. 5-8). 146.25 *(978-1-4488-9522-9(7))* Rosen Publishing Group, Inc., The.

Digital & Information Literacy: Set 7. 2014. (Digital & Information Literacy Ser.). 48p. (YA). (gr. 5-8). 181.50 *(978-1-4777-7663-6(X),* Rosen Reference) Rosen Publishing Group, Inc., The.

Digital & Information Literacy: Sets 1 - 6. 2013. (Digital & Information Literacy Ser.). 48p. (J). (gr. 5-8). 1023.75 *(978-1-4777-0617-6(8))* Rosen Publishing Group, Inc., The.

Digital & Information Literacy: Sets 1 - 7. 2014. (Digital & Information Literacy Ser.). 48p. (YA). (gr. 5-8). 1240.25 *(978-1-4777-8099-2(8)*, Rosen Reference) Rosen Publishing Group, Inc., The.

Digital & Information Literacy: Sets 1-8. 2014. (Digital & Information Literacy Ser.). 48p. (YA). (gr. 5-8). pap. 376.00 *(978-1-4777-8118-0(8)*, Rosen Reference) Rosen Publishing Group, Inc., The.

Dorling Kindersley Publishing Staff. All about Everything. 2014. (ENG., Illus.). 304p. (J). (gr. 4-7). pap. 12.99 *(978-1-4654-1746-6(X)*, DK Children) Dorling Kindersley Publishing, Inc.

—How Things Work Encyclopedia. 2009. (ENG., Illus.). 128p. (J). (gr. 2-5). 16.99 *(978-0-7566-5835-9(7)*, DK Children) Dorling Kindersley Publishing, Inc.

—Super Cool Tech. 2016. (ENG., Illus.). 192p. (J). (gr. 3-7). 24.99 *(978-1-4654-5205-4(2)*, DK Children) Dorling Kindersley Publishing, Inc.

Dramer, Kim. The Chinese. 2011. (Technology of the Ancients Ser.). 64p. (gr. 5). 32.79 *(978-1-60870-766-9(0))* Marshall Cavendish Corp.

Duke, Shirley. Enterprise Stem. 2011. (ENG., Illus.). 48p. (gr. 4-6). pap. 10.95 *(978-1-61741-983-6(4))* Rourke Educational Media.

Dunn, Karen Lewit. Saturday Night Pizza. 2008. (Discovering & Exploring Science Ser.). (Illus.). 16p. (J). (gr. -1-3). lib. bdg. 12.95 *(978-0-7569-8419-9(X))* Perfection Learning Corp.

—Technology & Natural Disasters. 2008. (Discovering & Exploring Science Ser.). (Illus.). 16p. (J). (gr. -1-3). lib. bdg. 12.95 *(978-0-7569-8435-9(1))* Perfection Learning Corp.

—What's the Solution? 2008. (Discovering & Exploring Science Ser.). (Illus.). 16p. (J). (gr. -1-3). lib. bdg. 12.95 *(978-0-7569-8433-5(5))* Perfection Learning Corp.

Editors of TIME For Kids Magazine. Stellar Space. 2014. (TIME for Kids Big Books of WHY Ser.). (ENG., Illus.). 48p. (J). (gr. 3-17). pap. 4.99 *(978-1-60320-985-4(9))* Time Inc. Bks.

Encyclopaedia Britannica, Inc. Staff. Britannica Illustrated Science Library Series (18 Title Series), 18 vols. 2010. 599.00 *(978-1-61535-423-8(9))* Encyclopaedia Britannica, Inc.

Encyclopaedia Britannica, Inc. Staff, compiled by. Britannica Illustrated Science Library: Technology. 2009. 29.95 *(978-1-59339-854-5(9))* Encyclopaedia Britannica, Inc.

Enz, Tammy & Biskup, Agnieszka. Batman Science, 1 vol. 2014. (Batman Science Ser.). (ENG.). 32p. (gr. 3-4). lib. bdg. 109.28 *(978-1-4765-6188-2(5)*, DC Super Heroes) Stone Arch Bks.

—STEM Adventures. Pop Art Properties Staff, illus. 2013. (STEM Adventures Ser.). (ENG.). 32p. (gr. 3-4). lib. bdg. 122.60 *(978-1-4765-0464-3(4)*, Graphic Library) Capstone Press of Coughlan Cos.

Esbaum, Jill & National Geographic Kids Staff. Little Kids First Big Book of How. 2016. (National Geographic Little Kids First Big Bks.). (ENG., Illus.). 128p. (J). (gr. -1-3). 14.99 *(978-1-4263-2329-4(8)*, National Geographic Children's Bks.) National Geographic Society.

Espejo, Roman. Has Technology Increased Learning? 2008. (At Issue Ser.). (ENG., Illus.). 80-128p. (gr. 10-12). 24.45 *(978-0-7377-4103-2(1)*, Greenhaven Pr., Inc.) Cengage Gale.

Faiella, Graham. The Technology of Mesopotamia. (Technology of the Ancient World Ser.). 48p. 2009. (gr. 6-6). 61.20 *(978-1-60854-243-7(2)*, Rosen Reference) 2005. (Illus.). (J). (gr. 5-8). lib. bdg. 30.60 *(978-1-4042-0560-4(8))* Rosen Publishing Group, Inc., The.

Farndon, John. Science & Technology: The Greatest Innovations in Human History. 2016. (ENG., Illus.). 64p. 12.99 *(978-1-86147-780-4(5)*, Armadillo) Anness Publishing GBR. Dist: National Bk. Network.

—Stickmen's Guide to Aircraft. Paul de Quay, John, illus. 2016. (Stickmen's Guides to How Everything Works). (ENG.). 32p. (J). (gr. 3-6). 30.65 *(978-1-4677-9592-0(5))*; 30.65 *(978-1-5124-0690-0(2))* Lerner Publishing Group.

—Stickmen's Guide to Gigantic Machines. Paul de Quay, John, illus. 2016. (Stickmen's Guides to How Everything Works). (ENG.). 32p. (J). (gr. 3-6). 30.65 *(978-1-4677-9596-8(8))* Lerner Publishing Group.

—The Story of Science & Technology. 2010. (Journey Through History Ser.). (ENG.). 64p. (YA). lib. bdg. 31.95 *(978-1-4488-0621-8(6)*, Rosen Reference) Rosen Publishing Group, Inc., The.

—Stuff You Need Know! 2015. (ENG., Illus.). 80p. (J). (gr. 4-7). pap. 12.95 *(978-1-77085-494-9(0)*, 9781770854949) Firefly Bks., Ltd.

—Stuff You Need to Know! 2015. (ENG., Illus.). 80p. (J). (gr. 4-7). 19.95 *(978-1-77085-656-1(0)*, 9781770856561) Firefly Bks., Ltd.

Faulkner, Nicholas. A Visual History of Science & Technology. 2016. (Visual History of the World Ser.). 00096p. (YA). (gr. 8-8). 37.10 *(978-1-4994-6596-9(3))* Rosen Publishing Group, Inc., The.

Faulkner, Nicholas, ed. 101 Women of STEM. 2016. (People You Should Know Ser.). 184p. (J). (gr. 8-8). lib. bdg. 36.25 *(978-1-68048-511-0(3))* Rosen Publishing Group, Inc., The.

Fourth grade Technology: 32 lessons every fourth grader should Know, 6. 2006. (Illus.). 104p. 22.99 net. *(978-0-9787800-4-3(3))* Structured Learning.

Freedman, Jeri. Strategic Inventions of the Napoleonic Wars. 2016. (Tech in the Trenches Ser.). 112p. (J). 42.79 *(978-1-5026-2351-5(X))* Cavendish Square Publishing.

—Strategic Inventions of World War II. 2016. (Tech in the Trenches Ser.). (ENG., Illus.). 112p. (J). (gr. 9-9). lib. bdg. 42.79 *(978-1-5026-1026-3(4))* Cavendish Square Publishing.

—What Is a Technical Text?, 1 vol. 2015. (ENG., Illus.). 32p. (J). 23.45 *(978-1-62275-672-8(X)*, Britannica Educational Publishing) Rosen Publishing Group, Inc., The.

Fridell, Ron. Earth-Friendly Energy. 2009. pap. 58.95 *(978-0-7613-4692-0(9))* Lerner Publishing Group.

—Military Techonology. 2008. pap. 52.95 *(978-0-8225-9328-7(9))* Lerner Publishing Group.

Friesen, Helen Lepp. Who Lives Here? 2008. (Discovering & Exploring Science Ser.). (Illus.). 16p. (J). (gr. -1-3). lib. bdg. 12.95 *(978-0-7569-8425-0(4))* Perfection Learning Corp.

Garassino, Alessandro. La Vida. (SPA.). 40p. (YA). (gr. 5-8). *(978-84-207-5697-4(0))* Grupo Anaya, S.A. ESP. Dist: Lectorum Pubns., Inc.

Gedacht, Daniel C. Technology of Ancient Rome. 2009. (Primary Sources of Ancient Civilizations Ser.). 24p. (gr. 3-3). 42.50 *(978-1-60851-564-6(8)*, PowerKids Pr.) Rosen Publishing Group, Inc., The.

Gerdes, Louise I. Robotic Technology. Greenhaven Press Editors, ed. 2014. (Opposing Viewpoints Ser.). (ENG.). 224p. (gr. 10-12). pap. 33.80 *(978-0-7377-6339-3(6))*; lib. bdg. 48.80 *(978-0-7377-6338-6(8))* Cengage Gale. (Greenhaven Pr., Inc.).

Gifford, Clive. Computing & Coding in the Real World. 2017. 32p. (J). ***(978-0-7787-3621-9(0))*** Crabtree Publishing Co.

Gifford, Clive. Technology. 2012. (J). lib. bdg. *(978-0-531-22960-6(2))* Scholastic, Inc.

Glencoe McGraw-Hill Staff, creator. Technology Student Workbook: Today & Tomorrow. 5th ed. 2003. (TECHNOLOGY: TODAY & TOMORROW Ser.). (ENG., Illus.). 238p. (gr. 9-10). stu. ed., per., wbk. ed. 32.84 *(978-0-07-830831-4(3)*, 0078308313) McGraw-Hill Education.

Graham, Ian. Machines & Inventions. Antram, David et al, illus. 2008. (World of Wonder Ser.). (ENG.). 32p. (J). (gr. 1-4). pap. 9.95 *(978-0-531-23823-3(7)*, Children's Pr.) Scholastic Library Publishing.

Green, Dan. Technology: A Byte-Sized World! 2012. (Basher Science Ser.). (J). lib. bdg. 19.65 *(978-0-606-26712-0(3)*, Turtleback) Turtleback Bks.

Greenberger, Robert. The Technology of Ancient China. (Technology of the Ancient World Ser.). 48p. 2009. (gr. 6-6). 61.20 *(978-1-60854-238-3(6)*, Rosen Reference) 2005. (Illus.). (J). (gr. 5-8). lib. bdg. 29.25 *(978-1-4042-0558-1(6))* Rosen Publishing Group, Inc., The.

Greene, Meg. The Technology of Ancient Japan. (Technology of the Ancient World Ser.). 48p. 2009. (gr. 6-6). 61.20 *(978-1-60854-241-3(6)*, Rosen Reference) 2005. (Illus.). (J). (gr. 5-8). lib. bdg. 29.25 *(978-1-4042-0559-8(4))* Rosen Publishing Group, Inc., The.

Greenling, Jason. The Technology of Ancient China. 2016. (Ancient Innovations Ser.). 64p. (J). 34.21 *(978-1-5026-2235-8(1))* Cavendish Square Publishing.

—The Technology of the Vikings. 2016. (Ancient Innovations Ser.). 64p. (J). 34.21 *(978-1-5026-2241-9(6))* Cavendish Square Publishing.

Group/McGraw-Hill, Wright. On the Move: Level H, 6 vols. (First Explorers Ser.). 24p. (gr. 1-2). 29.95 *(978-0-7699-1449-7(7))* Shortland Pubns. (U. S. A.) Inc.

Groves, Marcia, et al. Science & Technology in the Middle Ages. 2004. (Medieval World Ser.). (ENG., Illus.). 32p. (J). pap. *(978-0-7787-1386-9(5))* Crabtree Publishing Co.

Gunston, Bill Tudor & Guy, John. Battle Machines. 2009. (ENG.). 112p. (J). (gr. 4-7). pap. 12.95 *(978-1-84696-201-1(3)*, TickTock Books) Octopus Publishing Group GBR. Dist: Independent Pubs. Group.

Hagler, Gina. The Technology of Ancient India. 2016. (Spotlight on the Rise & Fall of Ancient Civilizations Ser.). 48p. (YA). (gr. 6-6). pap. 11.75 *(978-1-4777-8942-1(1))* Rosen Publishing Group, Inc., The.

Harding, Sandra & Figueroa, Robert, eds. Science & Other Cultures. 2003. (ENG.). 304p. (gr. 13-18). 48.95 *(978-0-415-93992-8(5)*, 0415939925) Routledge.

Harris, Patricia. Understanding Coding Through Simulations. 2016. (Spotlight on Kids Can Code Ser.). 00024p. (J). (gr. 4-5). pap. 11.75 *(978-1-4994-2794-3(8)*, PowerKids Pr.) Rosen Publishing Group, Inc., The.

HarrisNic. THE GREATEST INVENTION OF ALL TIME LOW INTERMEDIATE BOOK WITH ONLINE ACCESS. 2014. (ENG., Illus.). 24p. (J). pap. 9.50 *(978-1-107-62161-9(5))* Cambridge Univ. Pr.

Haugen, David. Technology & the Cloud. Greenhaven Press Staff, ed. 2012. (At Issue Ser.). (ENG.). 128p. (gr. 10-12). pap. 27.80 *(978-0-7377-6208-2(X))*; lib. bdg. 39.40 *(978-0-7377-6207-5(1))* Cengage Gale. (Greenhaven Pr., Inc.).

Heinrichs, Ann. Nanotechnologist. 2009. (21st Century Skills Library: Cool Science Careers Ser.). (ENG.). 32p. (gr. 4-8). lib. bdg. 28.50 *(978-1-60279-307-1(7)*, 200203) Cherry Lake Publishing.

Heinz, Brian J. Nathan of Yesteryear & Michael of Today. Friar, Joanne, illus. 2006. (Exceptional Social Studies Titles for Intermediate Grades). (ENG.). 32p. (J). (gr. 3-6). lib. bdg. 22.60 *(978-0-7613-2893-3(9)*, Millbrook Pr.) Lerner Publishing Group.

Heitkamp, Kristina Lyn. Fab Lab Creating with Digital Sewing Machines. 2016. (Getting Creative with Fab Lab Ser.). 00064p. (J). (gr. 6-6). 34.45 *(978-1-4994-6508-2(4))* Rosen Publishing Group, Inc., The.

Henderson, Harry. How Mobile Devices Are Changing Society. 2015. (ENG., Illus.). 80p. (J). lib. bdg. *(978-1-60152-902-2(3))* ReferencePoint Pr., Inc.

Higginson, Sheila Sweeny. Disasters of Technology: Set Of 6. 2011. (Navigators Ser.). (J). pap. 50.00 net. *(978-1-4108-2576-6(0))* Benchmark Education Co.

High-Tech DIY Projects with 3D Printing. 2014. (Maker Kids Ser.). (Illus.). 32p. (J). (gr. 3-6). pap. 70.50 *(978-1-4777-6657-6(X))*; pap. 11.75 *(978-1-4777-6676-7(6))*; lib. bdg. 27.50 *(978-1-4777-6670-5(7))* Rosen Publishing Group, Inc., The. (PowerKids Pr.).

Hinton, Kerry. Becoming a User Interface & User Experience Engineer. 2017. (Tech Track: Building Your Career in IT Ser.). 80p. (J). (gr. 12-12). 35.75 ***(978-1-5081-7564-3(0)***, Rosen Young Adult) Rosen Publishing Group, Inc., The.

Hinton, Kerry. Fab Lab Creating with 3D Scanners. 2016. (Getting Creative with Fab Lab Ser.). 00064p. (J). (gr. 6-6). 34.45 *(978-1-4994-6502-0(5))* Rosen Publishing Group, Inc., The.

Holl, Kristi. Ancient Mesopotamian Technology. 2016. (Spotlight on the Rise & Fall of Ancient Civilizations Ser.). 48p. (YA). (gr. 6-6). pap. 11.75 *(978-1-4777-8953-7(7))* Rosen Publishing Group, Inc., The.

Holper, Paul & Torok, Simon. Imagining the Future: Invisibility, Immortality & 40 Other Incredible Ideas. 2017. (ENG., Illus.). 146p. (gr. 4-10). pap. 17.95 *(978-1-4863-0272-7(6))* CSIRO Publishing AUS. Dist: Stylus Publishing, LLC.

Holt, Rinehart and Winston Staff. Harcourt Science & Technology: Strategies & Practice Answer Key. 4th ed. 2004. (Illus.). pap. 6.00 *(978-0-03-019863-2(1))* Holt McDougal.

—Holt Science & Technology. 4th annot. ed. 2004. tchr. ed. 128.80 *(978-0-03-073174-7(7))* Holt McDougal.

—Holt Science & Technology: Chapter Resources. 5th ed. 2005. pap. 87.36 *(978-0-03-030632-7(9))* Holt McDougal.

Hosein, Ann. Technology of the Ancient World, 01 vols., 1. 2016. (History of Technology Ser.). (ENG., Illus.). 112p. (J). 32.90 *(978-1-68048-273-7(4)*, Britannica Educational Publishing) Rosen Publishing Group, Inc., The.

Hubbard, Rita L. Getting the Most Out of MOOC: Massive Open Online Courses, 1 vol. 2015. (ENG.). 48p. (YA). 30.25 *(978-1-4777-7950-7(7)*, Rosen Reference) Rosen Publishing Group, Inc., The.

Hunter, Dru. How Do We Apply Science? 2015. (Illus.). 48p. (J). *(978-1-60818-592-4(3)*, Creative Education) Creative Co., The.

—How Does It Work? 2015. (Illus.). 48p. (J). *(978-1-60818-593-1(1)*, Creative Education) Creative Co., The.

—How Does It Work? Think Like a Scientist. 2016. (Think Like a Scientist Ser.). (ENG.). 48p. (J). (gr. 5-9). pap. 12.00 *(978-1-62832-198-2(9)*, Creative Paperbacks) Creative Co., The.

Hunter, Nick & Collins UK Staff. Technology in the Battle of Britain. 2016. (ENG.). 56p. (J). (gr. 5-6). pap. 9.95 *(978-0-00-816400-3(2))* HarperCollins Pubs. Ltd. GBR. Dist: Independent Pubs. Group.

Hynson, Colin. Dream Jobs in Technology. 2017. (Illus.). 32p. (J). ***(978-0-7787-2967-9(2))*** Crabtree Publishing Co.

Jedicke, Peter. Great Inventions of the 20th Century. 2007. (Scientific American Ser.). (Illus.). 72p. (YA). (gr. 5-9). lib. bdg. 30.00 *(978-0-7910-9048-0(5))* Facts On File, Inc.

Johanson, Paula. Tech Industry. 2017. (Illus.). 32p. (J). ***(978-0-7787-3604-2(0))*** Crabtree Publishing Co.

Johnson, Rebecca L. Nanotechnology. 2005. (Cool Science Ser.). (ENG., Illus.). 48p. (J). (gr. 4-8). lib. bdg. 27.93 *(978-0-8225-2111-2(3)*, Lerner Pubns.) Lerner Publishing Group.

Jones, Tammy. I Go! 2009. (Sight Word Readers Set A Ser.). (J). 3.49 net. *(978-1-60719-143-8(1))* Newmark Learning LLC.

Kallen, Stuart A. Cutting Edge Energy Technology. 2016. (ENG.). 80p. (YA). (gr. 5-12). *(978-1-68282-038-4(6))* ReferencePoint Pr., Inc.

Kamberg, Mary-Lane. Drones & Commerce. 2016. (Inside the World of Drones Ser.). 00064p. (J). (gr. 7-7). 34.45 *(978-1-5081-7341-0(9))* Rosen Publishing Group, Inc., The.

Kindergarten Technology: 32 Lessons Every Kindergartner Should Know. 2006. 18.99 net. *(978-0-9787800-0-5(0))* Structured Learning.

Kobasa, Paul A. Personal & Household Items. 2009. (J). *(978-0-7166-0390-0(X))* World Bk., Inc.

Koellhoffer, Tara, ed. Computers & Technology. 2006. (Science News for Kids Ser.). (Illus.). 144p. (gr. 4-6). lib. bdg. 30.00 *(978-0-7910-9120-3(1)*, Chelsea Clubhouse) Facts On File, Inc.

Kops, Deborah. Were Early Computers Really the Size of a School Bus? And Other Questions about Inventions. 2011. (Is That a Fact? Ser.). (ENG.). 40p. (gr. 4-6). 26.60 *(978-0-7613-6098-8(0))* Lerner Publishing Group.

Kortemeier, Todd. 12 Unsung Heroes of Technology. 2017. (Unsung Heroes Ser.). (ENG., Illus.). 32p. (J). (gr. 3-6). 21.95 *(978-1-63235-311-5(3))* Pr. Room Editions LLC.

Kroll, Jennifer. The Cutting Edge: Breakthroughs in Technology, 1 vol. 2nd rev. ed. 2013. (TIME for KIDS(r) Nonfiction Readers Ser.). (ENG.). 64p. (J). (gr. 5-5). pap. 10.99 *(978-1-4333-4947-8(7))* Teacher Created Materials, Inc.

—A la Vanguardia: Adelantos en Tecnología. 2016. (TIME for Kids en Español - Level 5 Ser.). (SPA.). 64p. (gr. 5-5). lib. bdg. 31.99 *(978-1-5157-2927-3(3))* Time for Kids Inc AUS. Dist: Capstone Pub.

Kuhtz, Russell. Physical Science. 2016. (Study of Science Ser.). 00104p. (YA). (gr. 8-8). lib. bdg. 36.25 *(978-1-5081-0425-4(5))* Rosen Publishing Group, Inc., The.

Leavitt, Amie Jane. Fab Lab Creating with 3D Printers. 2016. (Getting Creative with Fab Lab Ser.). 00064p. (J). (gr. 6-6). 34.45 *(978-1-4994-6500-6(9))* Rosen Publishing Group, Inc., The.

Lee, Dora & Palmer, Dora. Biomimicry: Inventions Inspired by Nature. Thompson, Margot, illus. 2011. (ENG.). 40p. (J). (gr. 3-7). 18.95 *(978-1-55453-467-8(4))* Kids Can Pr., Ltd. CAN. Dist: Hachette Bk. Group.

Lew, Kristi. Powering up a Career in Nanotechnology. 2015. (Preparing for Tomorrow's Careers Ser.). (ENG., Illus.). 80p. (J). (gr. 7-8). 34.25 *(978-1-4994-6087-2(2)*, Rosen Young Adult) Rosen Publishing Group, Inc., The.

Lindeen, Mary. Then & Now, 1 vol. 2011. (Wonder Readers Fluent Level Ser.). (ENG.). (gr. -1-2). 32p. pap. 5.99 *(978-1-4296-7972-5(7))*; 16p. pap. 35.94 *(978-1-4296-8177-3(2))* Capstone Press of Coughlan Cos. (Wonder Readers).

Lowery, Zoe. Technology of the Modern World, 01 vols., 1. 2016. (History of Technology Ser.). (ENG., Illus.). 112p. (J). 32.90 *(978-1-68048-276-8(9)*, Britannica Educational Publishing) Rosen Publishing Group, Inc., The.

Macaulay, David. The Way Things Work Now. 2016. (ENG., Illus.). 400p. (YA). (gr. 7). 35.00 *(978-0-544-82438-6(5)*, HMH Books For Young Readers) Houghton Mifflin Harcourt Publishing Co.

Mackay, Jennifer. Online Schools. Greenaven Press, ed. 2013. (Technology 360 Ser.). (ENG., Illus.). 128p. (gr. 7-10). lib. bdg. 39.90 *(978-1-4205-0942-7(X)*, Lucent Bks.) Cengage Gale.

MacKay, Jennifer, ed. Roller Coasters. 2012. (Technology 360 Ser.). (ENG., Illus.). 128p. (J). (gr. 7-10). lib. bdg. 34.95 *(978-1-4205-0825-3(3)*, Lucent Bks.) Cengage Gale.

Mahoney, Emily Jankowski. Ancient Aztec Technology. 2016. (Spotlight on the Maya, Aztec, & Inca Civilizations Ser.). (Illus.). 32p. (J). (gr. 6-4). pap. 11.75 *(978-1-4994-1923-8(6)*, PowerKids Pr.) Rosen Publishing Group, Inc., The.

Mara, Wil. The Mesopotamians. 2011. (Technology of the Ancients Ser.). 64p. (gr. 5). 32.79 *(978-1-60870-767-6(9))* Marshall Cavendish Corp.

—The Romans. 2011. (Technology of the Ancients Ser.). 64p. (gr. 5). 32.79 *(978-1-60870-768-3(7))* Marshall Cavendish Corp.

Marcovitz, Hal. Technology. 2008. (Gallup Major Trends & Events Ser.). (Illus.). 128p. (J). (gr. 7-18). lib. bdg. 22.95 *(978-1-59084-969-9(8))* Mason Crest.

—What Is the Future of 3D Printing? 2016. (ENG.). 80p. (YA). (gr. 5-12). *(978-1-68282-066-7(1))* ReferencePoint Pr., Inc.

—3-D Printing. 2016. (Tech Bytes Ser.). (ENG., Illus.). 48p. (J). (gr. 4-6). pap. 13.26 *(978-1-60357-867-7(6))*; lib. bdg. 26.60 *(978-1-59953-759-7(1))* Norwood Hse. Pr.

Marquardt, Meg. Incredible Technology. 2018. (ENG.). 32p. (gr. 3-6). 31.35 ***(978-1-63235-422-8(5)***, 12-Story Library) Pr. Room Editions LLC.

Mason, Conrad. See Inside How Things Work. 2010. (See Inside Board Bks). 16p. (J). bds. 12.99 *(978-0-7945-2406-7(0)*, Usborne) EDC Publishing.

Maxim, Bailey. The 100 Most Influential Technology Leaders, 1 vol., 1. 2016. (Britannica Guide to the World's Most Influential People Ser.). (ENG.). 224p. (J). (gr. 10-10). lib. bdg. 54.00 *(978-1-68048-280-5(7)*, Britannica Educational Publishing) Rosen Publishing Group, Inc., The.

Maynard, Charles W. The Technology of Ancient Greece. (Technology of the Ancient World Ser.). 48p. 2009. (gr. 6-6). 61.20 *(978-1-60854-240-6(8)*, Rosen Reference) 2005. (Illus.). (J). (gr. 5-8). lib. bdg. 29.25 *(978-1-4042-0555-0(1))* Rosen Publishing Group, Inc., The.

—The Technology of Ancient Rome. (Technology of the Ancient World Ser.). 48p. 2009. (gr. 6-6). 61.20 *(978-1-60854-242-0(4)*, Rosen Reference) 2005. (Illus.). (J). (gr. 5-8). lib. bdg. 29.25 *(978-1-4042-0556-7(X))* Rosen Publishing Group, Inc., The.

McArdle, Matthew. 19th Century Innovations: Paving the Way. 2017. (Primary Source Readers Ser.). (Illus.). 32p. (J). (gr. 4-5). pap. 8.99 *(978-1-4938-3796-0(6))* Teacher Created Materials, Inc.

McCullough, Naomi V. The Technology of the Aztecs. 2016. (Ancient Innovations Ser.). 64p. (J). 34.21 *(978-1-5026-2239-6(4))* Cavendish Square Publishing.

McGough, Roger. Until I Met Dudley: How Everyday Things Really Work. Riddell, Chris, illus. 2012. (ENG.). 32p. (J). (gr. -1-2). pap. 8.99 *(978-1-84780-350-4(4)*, Frances Lincoln) Quarto Publishing Group UK GBR. Dist: Hachette Bk. Group.

Mitchell, Melanie. From Cloth to American Flag. 2004. (Start to Finish Ser.). (J). pap. 5.95 *(978-0-8225-2142-6(3))* Lerner Publishing Group.

Mitra, Ananda. The Digital World, 6 vols., Set. 2010. (Digital World Ser.). (gr. 6-12). 240.00 *(978-0-8160-8304-6(5)*, Chelsea Hse.) Facts On File, Inc.

Mooney, Carla. What Is the Future of Virtual Reality? 2016. (ENG.). 80p. (J). (gr. 5-12). lib. bdg. *(978-1-68282-094-0(7))* ReferencePoint Pr., Inc.

Mountjoy, Shane. Technology & the Civil War. McNeese, Tim, ed. 2009. (Civil War: A Nation Divided Ser.). 136p. (gr. 6-12). 35.00 *(978-1-60413-037-9(7)*, Chelsea Hse.) Facts On File, Inc.

Murphy, Glenn. Robots & the Whole Technology Story. 2015. (Science Sorted Ser.). (ENG., Illus.). 144p. (J). (gr. 3-7). pap. 8.99 *(978-1-4472-8487-1(9))* Pan Macmillan GBR. Dist: Independent Pubs. Group.

Murray, Jacqui. Fifth grade Technology: 32 lessons every fifth grader should Know, 6. 2006. (Illus.). 104p. 22.99 net. *(978-0-9787800-5-0(1))* Structured Learning.

Nagelhout, Ryan. Ancient Inca Technology. 2016. (Spotlight on the Maya, Aztec, & Inca Civilizations Ser.). (Illus.). 32p. (J). (gr. 6-4). pap. 11.75 *(978-1-4994-1953-5(8)*, PowerKids Pr.) Rosen Publishing Group, Inc., The.

—Freaky Stories about Technology. 2016. (Freaky True Science Ser.). (Illus.). 32p. (J). (gr. 5-4). pap. 10.50 *(978-1-4824-4838-2(6))* Stevens, Gareth Publishing LLLP.

NETS Project Staff, et al. NETS*S Curriculum Series: Multidisciplinary Units for Prekindergarten Through Grade 2. 2003. (National Educational Technology Standards for Students Curriculum Ser.). 306p. (J). pap. 34.95 *(978-1-56484-200-8(2))* International Society for Technology in Education.

Nichols, Susan. For People Who Love Tech. 2016. (Cool Careers Without College Ser.). 00104p. (J). (gr. 7-7). 38.45 *(978-1-5081-7280-2(3))* Rosen Publishing Group, Inc., The.

Nsrc. Science & Technology for Children Books: Technology of Paper. 2004. (Illus.). 64p. (J). *(978-1-933008-11-0(3))* Smithsonian Science Education Ctr. (SSEC).

Oakes, Quenton. Looking Inside a 3D Printer. 2017. (21st Century Skills Innovation Library: Makers As Innovators Junior Ser.). (ENG., Illus.). 24p. (J). (gr. 2-5). pap. 12.79 *(978-1-63472-321-3(X)*, 209329); lib. bdg. 28.50 *(978-1-63472-189-9(6)*, 209328) Cherry Lake Publishing.

O'Hara, Susan & McMahon, Maureen. NETS*S Curriculum Series: Multidisciplinary Units for Grades 6-8. 2003. (National Educational Technology Standards for Students Curriculum Ser.). (Illus.). 241p. (J). pap. 34.95 *(978-1-56484-206-0(1))* International Society for Technology in Education.

Okido Staff. How Things Work: Facts & Fun, Questions & Answers, Things to Make & Do. 2015. (ENG., Illus.). 64p. (J). (gr. -1-3). 18.95 *(978-0-500-65044-8(6)*, 565044) Thames & Hudson.

O'Neill, Terence & Williams, Josh. 3D Printing. 2013. (21st Century Skills Innovation Library: Makers As Innovators Ser.). (ENG.). 32p. (J). (gr. 4-8). 28.50 *(978-1-62431-138-3(5)*, 202872); pap. 14.21 *(978-1-62431-270-0(5)*, 202874) Cherry Lake Publishing.

Otfinoski, Steven. 3D Printing: Science, Technology, & Engineering. 2016. (Calling All Innovators: a Career for You Ser.). (ENG., Illus.). 64p. (J). lib. bdg. 32.00 *(978-0-531-21865-5(1))*; pap. 8.95 *(978-0-531-21988-1(7))* Scholastic Library Publishing. (Children's Pr.).

Out & About: Level Q, 6 vols., Vol. 2. (Explorers Ser.). 32p. (gr. 3-6). 44.95 *(978-0-7699-0608-9(7))* Shortland Pubns. (U. S. A.) Inc.

Oxlade, Chris. How Things Work. 2004. (Knowledge Masters Plus Ser.). (Illus.). 32p. (YA). pap. incl. cd-rom *(978-1-903954-43-0(6)*, Pavilion Children's Books) Pavilion Bks.

—The Way Things Work: The Complete Illustrated Guide to the Amazing World of Technology. 2004. (ENG., Illus.). 512p. (J). (gr. 3-7). 24.99 (978-0-7548-1504-4(8)) Anness Publishing GBR. Dist: National Bk. Network.

Oxlade, Chris & Farndon, John. Stickmen's Guide to Aircraft. Pyke, Jerry & Quay, John Paul de, illus. 2016. (Stickmen's Guides to How Everything Works). (ENG.). 32p. (J). (gr. 3-6). lib. bdg. 26.65 (978-1-4677-9359-9(0)) Lerner Publishing Group.

—Stickmen's Guide to Gigantic Machines. Pyke, Jerry & Quay, John Paul de, illus. 2016. (Stickmen's Guides to How Everything Works). (ENG.). 32p. (J). (gr. 3-6). lib. bdg. 26.65 (978-1-4677-9361-2(2)) Lerner Publishing Group.

Paisley, Erinne. Can Your Smartphone Change the World?, 1 vol. 2017. (PopActivism Ser.). (ENG.). 144p. (YA). (gr. 7-11). pap. 14.95 **(978-1-4598-1303-8(0))** Orca Bk. Pubs. USA.

Paley, Caitlyn. Strategic Inventions of the Revolutionary War. 2016. (Tech in the Trenches Ser.). (ENG., Illus.). 112p. (J). (gr. 9-9). lib. bdg. 42.79 (978-1-5026-1028-7(0)) Cavendish Square Publishing.

Pamplona, Alberto Hernández. A Visual Guide to Technology. 2017. (Visual Exploration of Science Ser.). 96p. (J). (gr. 12-13). 37.10 **(978-1-5081-7584-1(5)**, Rosen Young Adult) Rosen Publishing Group, Inc., The.

Paris, Stephanie. Technology Feats & Failures, 1 vol. 2nd rev. ed. 2012. (Nonfiction Readers Ser.). (ENG.). 48p. (J). (gr. 4-4). pap. 9.99 (978-1-4333-4869-3(1)) Teacher Created Materials, Inc.

—Tecnología: Hazañas y Fracasos. 2017. (TIME for Kids en Español - Level 4 Ser.). (SPA.). 48p. (gr. 4-4). lib. bdg. 31.99 (978-1-5157-5150-2(3)) Time for Kids Inc AUS. Dist: Capstone Pub.

Parker, Steve. How It Works, 10 vols., Set. Incl. Aircraft. lib. bdg. 19.95 (978-1-4222-1791-7(4)); Cars Trucks & Bikes. (Illus.). lib. bdg. 19.95 (978-1-4222-1792-4(2), 1317905); Emergency Vehicles. (Illus.). lib. bdg. 19.95 (978-1-4222-1793-1(0), 1317906); Energy & Power. lib. bdg. 19.95 (978-1-4222-1794-8(9)); Gadgets. lib. bdg. 19.95 (978-1-4222-1795-5(7)); Giant Machines. lib. bdg. 19.95 (978-1-4222-1796-2(5)); Military Machines. lib. bdg. 19.95 (978-1-4222-1797-9(3)); Ships & Submarines. lib. bdg. 19.95 (978-1-4222-1798-6(1)); Space Exploration. lib. bdg. 19.95 (978-1-4222-1799-3(X)); Speed Machines. Pang, Alex, illus. lib. bdg. 19.95 (978-1-4222-1800-6(7), 1317938); (J). (gr. 3-18). 40p. 2010. Set lib. bdg. 199.50 (978-1-4222-1790-0(6)) Mason Crest.

Payne, Jan, et al. Penicillin Was Discovered by Accident: The Truth about Inventions & Discoveries. 2016. (True or False? Ser.). (Illus.). 48p. (J). (gr. 3-3). pap. 11.70 (978-0-7660-7739-3(X)) Enslow Pubs., Inc.

Pedal Power: Individual Title Six-Packs. (Bookweb Ser.). 32p. (gr. 6-18). 34.00 (978-0-7578-0913-2(8)) Rigby Education.

Perritano, John. Science & Technology, Vol. 9. van Dijk, Ruud, ed. 2016. (Making of the Modern World: 1945 to the Present Ser.). (Illus.). 64p. (J). (gr. 7). 23.95 (978-1-4222-3641-3(2)) Mason Crest.

Piddock, Charles. Future Tech: From Personal Robots to Motorized Monocycles. 2009. (National Geographic Investigates Science Ser.). (ENG., Illus.). 64p. (J). (gr. 5-18). 17.95 (978-1-4263-0468-2(4)); 27.90 (978-1-4263-0469-9(2)) National Geographic Society. (National Geographic Children's Bks.).

Pierce, Franklin. Fiberglass Ding Repair: The Art of Polyester Resin/Fiberglas & Polyurathane Foam Surfboard Repairwork. 2004. (Illus.). 64p. (gr. 7-18). per. 19.95 (978-0-9744247-0-5(6)) Impulse Surf.

Platt, Richard. The Egyptians. Lawrence, David, illus. 2011. (How They Made Things Work! Ser.). 32p. (J). (gr. 2-5). lib. bdg. 28.50 (978-1-59771-287-3(6)) Sea-To-Sea Pubns.

—The Greeks. Lawrence, David, illus. 2011. (How They Made Things Work! Ser.). 32p. (J). (gr. 2-5). lib. bdg. 28.50 (978-1-59771-288-0(4)) Sea-To-Sea Pubns.

—In the Renaissance. Lawrence, David, illus. 2011. (How They Made Things Work! Ser.). 32p. (YA). (gr. 2-5). lib. bdg. 28.50 (978-1-59771-289-7(2)) Sea-To-Sea Pubns.

Platt, Richard & Biesty, Stephen. Stephen Biesty's Incredible Cross-Sections Book. (Illus.). (J). pap. 24.95 (978-0-590-73870-5(4)) Scholastic, Inc.

Porterfield, Jason. Fab Lab Creating with Milling Machines. 2016. (Getting Creative with Fab Lab Ser.). 00064p. (J). (gr. 6-6). 34.45 (978-1-4994-6506-8(8)) Rosen Publishing Group, Inc., The.

Publishers, Chelsea House, creator. Scientific American Set, 8-Volumes. 2007. (Scientific American Ser.). (gr. 5-8). 240.00 (978-0-7910-9811-0(7), Chelsea Hse.) Facts On File, Inc.

Reher, Matt. Apples Make Juice. 2015. (1B Our Natural World Ser.). (ENG., Illus.). 28p. (J). pap. 5.99 (978-1-63437-038-7(4)) American Reading Co.

Rhatigan, Joe & Owsley, Anthony. Inventions That Could Have Changed the World... But Didn't! 2015. (ENG., Illus.). 80p. (J). (gr. 3-7). 14.95 (978-1-62354-024-1(0)) Charlesbridge Publishing, Inc.

Rich, Mari. Technology, Vol. 10. Gilmore, Malinda & Pouson, Mel, eds. 2016. (Black Achievement in Science Ser.). (Illus.). 64p. (J). (gr. 7). 23.95 (978-1-4222-3564-5(5)) Mason Crest.

Richards, Jon. The Human-Made World. 2016. (Mapographica Ser.). (ENG., Illus.). 32p. (J). (gr. 3-6). (978-0-7787-2657-9(6)) Crabtree Publishing Co.

RIGBY. Technology Matters! Fifth Grade Class Collection Books. 2003. (Rigby on Our Way to English Ser.). (ENG.). 32p. (gr. 5-5). pap. 50.70 (978-0-7578-4472-0(3)) Rigby Education.

Ring, Susan. What Is Technology? Date not set. (Early Science Big Bks.). (Illus.). 16p. (J). (gr. -1-2). pap. 16.95 (978-1-58273-119-3(5)) Sundance/Newbridge Educational Publishing.

Roby, Cynthia. Strategic Inventions of World War I. 2016. (Tech in the Trenches Ser.). (ENG., Illus.). 112p. (J). (gr. 9-9). lib. bdg. 42.79 (978-1-5026-1024-9(8)) Cavendish Square Publishing.

Rockwood, Leigh. Ancient Egyptian Technology. 2013. (Spotlight on Ancient Civilizations: Egypt Ser.). (ENG.). 24p. (J). (gr. 3-4). 23.60 (978-1-4777-0768-5(9)); pap. 10.00 (978-1-4777-0869-9(3)) Rosen Publishing Group, Inc., The. (PowerKids Pr.).

Ryles, Briony & Hall, Derek. The Ages of Steam & Electricity. 2010. (Curriculum Connections: Technology Through the Ages Ser.). 112p. 39.95 (978-1-933834-86-3(2)) Brown Bear Bks.

—The Early 20th Century. 2010. (CC: Technology Through the Ages Ser.). 112p. (gr. 6-12). 42.80 (978-1-933834-87-0(0)) Brown Bear Bks.

—Medieval Period & the Renaissance. 2010. (CC: Technology Through the Ages Ser.). 112p. (gr. 6-12). 42.80 (978-1-933834-84-9(6)) Brown Bear Bks.

—The Modern World. 2010. (CC: Technology Through the Ages Ser.). 112p. (gr. 6-12). 42.80 (978-1-933834-88-7(9)) Brown Bear Bks.

—Prehistory & the Classical Period. 2010. (CC: Technology Through the Ages Ser.). 112p. (gr. 6-12). 42.80 (978-1-933834-83-2(8)) Brown Bear Bks.

—The Scientific Revolution. 2010. (Curriculum Connections: Technology Through the Ages Ser.). 112p. 39.95 (978-1-933834-85-6(4)) Brown Bear Bks.

Samuels, Charlie. Medieval Science (500-1500) 2010. (Science Highlights: A Gareth Stevens Timeline Ser.). (ENG.). 48p. (J). (gr. 6-8). pap. 14.05 (978-1-4339-4140-5(6)); lib. bdg. 31.95 (978-1-4339-4139-9(2)) Stevens, Gareth Publishing LLLP. (Gareth Stevens Secondary Library).

Santos, Penelope. Old & New. 2015. (Rosen REAL Readers: STEM & STEAM Collection). (ENG.). 8p. pap. 5.46 (978-1-4994-9715-1(6), Rosen Classroom) Rosen Publishing Group, Inc., The.

Sarver, Amy & National Geographic Learning Staff. Science at the Mall. 2007. (Reading Expeditions Ser.). (ENG., Illus.). 24p. (J). pap. 14.95 (978-0-7922-4569-8(5)) CENGAGE Learning.

Saunders-Smith, Gail. Tiny Robots, 1 vol. 2014. (Cool Robots Ser.). (ENG.). 24p. (gr. k-1). 26.65 (978-1-4914-0587-1(2), Pebble Plus) Capstone Press of Coughlan Cos.

Schmermund, Elizabeth. Women in Technology. 2016. (Defying Convention: Women Who Changed the Rules Ser.). (Illus.). 128p. (J). 37.27 (978-0-7660-8149-9(4)) Enslow Pubs., Inc.

Schrier, Allyson Valentine, et al. Tech Safety Smarts. 2013. (Tech Safety Smarts Ser.). (ENG.). 32p. (gr. 3-4). pap. 190.80 (978-1-62065-805-5(4), Fact Finders) Capstone Press of Coughlan Cos.

Schuette, Sarah L. Science Fun: A Spot-It Challenge, 1 vol. 2011. (Spot It Ser.). (ENG.). 32p. (gr. 1-2). lib. bdg. 27.32 (978-1-4296-5986-4(6), Aplus Bks.) Capstone Press of Coughlan Cos.

Science & Technology for Children Books, Physical Sciences & Technology Library Set, 6 vols. 2004. (Illus.). 64p. (J). (978-1-933008-26-4(1)) Smithsonian Science Education Ctr. (SSEC).

Science & Technology for Children Books, Technology of Paper Set, 8 vols. 2004. (Illus.). 64p. (J). (978-1-933008-23-3(7)) Smithsonian Science Education Ctr. (SSEC).

Scientific American Staff. Extreme Engineering. 2009. (Scientific American Cutting-Edge Science Ser.). 120p. (gr. 9-9). 63.90 (978-1-60853-075-5(2)) Rosen Publishing Group, Inc., The.

—The Nanotech Revolution. 2009. (Scientific American Cutting-Edge Science Ser.). 136p. (gr. 9-9). 63.90 (978-1-60853-082-3(5)) Rosen Publishing Group, Inc., The.

Scott Foresman Reading: Technology. 2004. (Scott Foresman Reading Ser.). (gr. 1-18). cd-rom (978-0-328-04995-0(6)); (gr. 2-18). cd-rom (978-0-328-09379-3(3)); (gr. 2-18). cd-rom (978-0-328-08691-7(6)); (gr. 2-18). cd-rom (978-0-328-04996-7(4)); (gr. 2-18). cd-rom (978-0-328-08681-8(9)); (gr. 2-18). cd-rom (978-0-328-09374-8(2)); (gr. 2-6). cd-rom (978-0-328-09384-7(X)); (gr. 2-6). cd-rom (978-0-328-08680-1(0)); (gr. 3-18). cd-rom (978-0-328-09380-9(7)); (gr. 3-18). cd-rom (978-0-328-08692-4(4)); (gr. 3-18). cd-rom (978-0-328-04997-4(2)); (gr. 3-18). cd-rom (978-0-328-08682-5(7)); (gr. 3-18). cd-rom (978-0-328-09375-5(0)); (gr. 4-18). cd-rom (978-0-328-09381-6(5)); (gr. 4-18). cd-rom (978-0-328-08683-2(5)); (gr. 4-18). cd-rom (978-0-328-08693-1(2)); (gr. 4-18). cd-rom (978-0-328-04998-1(0)); (gr. 5-18). cd-rom (978-0-328-04999-8(9)); (gr. 5-18). cd-rom (978-0-328-09377-9(7)); (gr. 5-18). cd-rom (978-0-328-08684-9(3)); (gr. 5-18). cd-rom (978-0-328-08694-8(0)); (gr. 5-18). cd-rom (978-0-328-09382-3(3)); (gr. 6-18). cd-rom (978-0-328-09378-6(5)); (gr. 6-18). cd-rom (978-0-328-08685-6(1)); (gr. 6-18). cd-rom (978-0-328-08695-5(9)); (gr. 6-18). cd-rom (978-0-328-09383-0(1)); (gr. 6-18). cd-rom (978-0-328-05000-0(8)) Addison-Wesley Educational Pubs., Inc. (Scott Foresman).

Sebastian, Emily. Technology of the Medieval & Early Modern Worlds, 01 vols., 1. 2016. (History of Technology Ser.). (ENG.). 112p. (J). 32.90 (978-1-68048-274-4(2), Britannica Educational Publishing) Rosen Publishing Group, Inc., The.

Second Grade Technology: 32 Lessons Every Second Grader Should Know, 6 vols. 2006. (Illus.). 56p. 19.99 net. (978-0-9787800-2-9(7)) Structured Learning.

Shand, Jennifer. Why Do Computers Know So Much? 2015. (Why Do... ? Ser.). lib. bdg. 19.65 (978-1-4867-0622-8(3)) Turtleback Bks.

Shoup, Kate. The Technology of Ancient Greece. 2016. (Ancient Innovations Ser.). 64p. (J). 34.21 (978-1-5026-2231-0(9)) Cavendish Square Publishing.

Sirota, Lyn A. Science Lab: Technological Design. 2011. (Explorer Library: Language Arts Explorer Ser.). (ENG.). 32p. (gr. 4-8). pap. 14.21 (978-1-61080-297-0(7), 201219); lib. bdg. 28.50 (978-1-61080-208-6(X), 201192) Cherry Lake Publishing.

Small, Cathleen. Fab Lab Creating with Vinyl Cutters. 2016. (Getting Creative with Fab Lab Ser.). 00064p. (J). (gr. 6-6). 34.45 (978-1-5081-7350-2(8)) Rosen Publishing Group, Inc., The.

Smibert, Angie. Technology Myths, Busted! 2017. (Science Myths, Busted! Ser.). (ENG.). 32p. (J). (gr. 3-6). 21.95 (978-1-63235-306-1(7)) Pr. Room Editions LLC.

Snedden, Robert. Ancient China. 2009. (Technology in Times Past Ser.). 32.80 (978-1-59920-298-3(0)) Black Rabbit Bks.

—Ancient China. 2009. (Technology in Times Past Ser.). (Illus.). 46p. (J). (gr. 4-7). pap. (978-1-897563-60-1(4)) Saunders Bk. Co.

—Ancient Greece. 2009. (Technology in Times Past Ser.). 32.80 (978-1-59920-296-9(4)) Black Rabbit Bks.

—Aztec, Inca & Maya. 2009. (Technology in Times Past Ser.). (J). 32.80 (978-1-59920-299-0(9)) Black Rabbit Bks.

—Aztec, Inca, & Maya. 2009. (Technology in Times Past Ser.). (Illus.). 46p. (J). (gr. 4-7). pap. (978-1-897563-64-9(7)) Saunders Bk. Co.

—The Medieval World. 2009. (Technology in Times Past Ser.). (Illus.). 46p. (J). (gr. 4-7). pap. (978-1-897563-65-6(5)) Saunders Bk. Co.

Solodky, M. The Technology of Ancient Egypt. (Technology of the Ancient World Ser.). 48p. 2009. (gr. 6-6). 61.20 (978-1-60854-239-0(4), Rosen Reference) 2005. (Illus.). (J). (gr. 5-8). lib. bdg. 29.25 (978-1-4042-0557-4(8)) Rosen Publishing Group, Inc., The.

Spence, Kelly. Tech Living. 2017. (Illus.). 32p. (J). **(978-0-7787-3605-9(9))** Crabtree Publishing Co.

Spilsbury, Richard, et al. Anatomy of an Investigation. 2013. (Anatomy of an Investigation Ser.). (ENG.). 56p. (gr. 7-8). pap. 47.45 (978-1-4329-7611-8(7)); lib. bdg. 103.95 (978-1-4329-7605-7(2)) Heinemann-Raintree.

Step-By-Step Transformations. 2014. (Step-By-Step Transformations Ser.). 24p. (J). (gr. k-2). 145.26 (978-1-62713-142-1(6)) Cavendish Square Publishing.

Sterling Children's, Sterling. Curious Jane. 2017. (ENG., Illus.). 128p. (J). (gr. 1-6). pap. 16.95 (978-1-4549-2235-3(4)) Sterling Publishing Co., Inc.

Steve, Parker. What about Science & Technology. 2008. 40p. pap. (978-1-84810-074-9(4)) Miles Kelly Publishing, Ltd.

Sturm, Jeanne. Nuestra Huella en la Tierra. 2012. (SPA & ENG.). 48p. (gr. 4-8). pap. 10.95 (978-1-61810-473-1(X)) Rourke Educational Media.

—Our Footprint on Earth. 2009. (ENG., Illus.). 48p. (gr. 4-8). pap. 10.95 (978-1-60694-526-1(2)) Rourke Educational Media.

Sundance/Newbridge LLC Staff. For Your Information. 2007. (Early Science Ser.). (gr. k-3). 18.95 (978-1-4007-6567-6(6)); pap. 6.10 (978-1-4007-6563-8(3)) Sundance/Newbridge Educational Publishing.

—How Life Changed. 2004. (Reading PowerWorks Ser.). (gr. 1-3). 37.50 (978-0-7608-7815-6(3)); pap. 6.10 (978-0-7608-7816-3(1)) Sundance/Newbridge Educational Publishing.

—People & Technology. 2004. (Reading PowerWorks Ser.). (gr. 1-3). 37.50 (978-0-7608-9771-3(9)); pap. 6.10 (978-0-7608-9772-0(7)) Sundance/Newbridge Educational Publishing.

—What Is Technology? 2007. (Early Science Ser.). (gr. k-3). 18.95 (978-1-4007-6585-0(4)); pap. 6.10 (978-1-4007-6581-2(1)) Sundance/Newbridge Educational Publishing.

Technology: Blueprints of the Future. 2005. (Technology Ser.). (Illus.). (gr. 4-8). lib. bdg. 159.00 (978-0-8239-7192-3(9)) Rosen Publishing Group, Inc., The.

Technology Pioneers, 8 vols., Set. Incl. Craigslist: The Company & Its Founder. Freese, Susan M. lib. bdg. 35.64 (978-1-61714-806-4(7)); EBay: The Company & Its Founder. Gitlin, Martin. lib. bdg. 35.64 (978-1-61714-807-1(5)); Google: The Company & Its Founders. Hamen, Susan E. lib. bdg. 35.64 (978-1-61714-808-8(3)); Nintendo: The Company & Its Founders. Firestone, Mary. lib. bdg. 35.64 (978-1-61714-809-5(1)); Pixar: The Company & Its Founders. Buckley, A. M. lib. bdg. 35.64 (978-1-61714-810-1(5)); Social Networking: Myspace, Facebook, & Twitter. Lusted, Marcia Amidon. lib. bdg. 35.64 (978-1-61714-811-8(3)); Wikipedia: The Company & Its Founders. Anderson, Jennifer Joline. lib. bdg. 35.64 (978-1-61714-812-5(1)); YouTube: The Company & Its Founders. Rowell, Rebecca. lib. bdg. 35.64 (978-1-61714-813-2(X)); (J). (gr. 6-12). (Technology Pioneers Set 1 Ser.: 8). (ENG., Illus.). 112p. 2011. Set lib. bdg. 285.12 (978-1-61714-805-7(9), Essential Library) ABDO Publishing Co.

Technology Takes on Nature. 2016. (Technology Takes on Nature Ser.). 00032p. (J). pap. 63.00 **(978-1-4824-5846-6(2))** Stevens, Gareth Publishing LLLP.

Technology that Changed the World. (Illus.). (J). (gr. 3-6). 103.50 (978-0-8239-7287-6(9), Reading Power) Rosen Publishing Group, Inc., The.

Technology Through Time, 3 bks., Set. Incl. Communication Through Time. Oxlade, Chris. lib. bdg. 18.98 (978-0-8172-4141-4(8)); Ships Through Time. Richards, Roy. lib. bdg. 18.98 (978-0-8172-4138-4(8)); Toys Through Time. Oxlade, Chris. lib. bdg. 18.98 (978-0-8172-4139-1(6)); 48p. (J). (gr. 4-8). 1996. (Illus.). Set lib. bdg. 56.94 (978-0-7398-3299-8(9)) Heinemann-Raintree.

Technosports: Individual Title, 6 packs. (Bookweb Ser.). 32p. (gr. 4-18). 34.00 (978-0-7635-3746-3(2)) Rigby Education.

Third Grade Technology: 32 lessons every third grader should Know, 6. 2006. (Illus.). 85p. 22.99 net. (978-0-9787800-3-6(5)) Structured Learning.

Thomas, Mark. Maracana: El Estadio de Futbol Mas Grande del Mundo. 2004. (Estructuras extraordinarias (Record-Breaking Structures) Ser.). (SPA & ENG., Illus.). 24p. (J). (gr. 3-6). lib. bdg. 22.60 (978-0-8239-6863-3(4), Editorial Buenas Letras) Rosen Publishing Group, Inc., The.

—La Represa de Itaipu: La Represa Mas Grande Del Mundo. 2004. (Estructuras extraordinarias (Record-Breaking Structures) Ser.). (SPA & ENG., Illus.). 24p. (J). (gr. 3-6). lib. bdg. 22.60 (978-0-8239-6865-7(0), Editorial Buenas Letras) Rosen Publishing Group, Inc., The.

Top That Publishing Staff. Today's Technology. 2006. (Illus.). 48p. (978-1-84510-013-1(1)) Top That! Publishing PLC.

Transforming Power of Technology, 6 vols. 2005. (Transforming Power of Technology Ser.). (Illus.). 100p. (C). (gr. 9-13). 180.00 (978-0-7910-7447-3(1), Chelsea Hse.) Facts On File, Inc.

Trowbridge, J. T. Lawrence's Adventures among the Ice-Cutters, Glass-Makers, Coal-Miners, Iron-Men, & Ship-Builders by J T Trowbridge. 2006. 256p. per. 23.99 (978-1-4255-2277-3(7)) Michigan Publishing.

Trueit, Trudi Strain. The Vikings. 2011. (Technology of the Ancients Ser.). 64p. (gr. 5). 32.79 (978-1-60870-769-0(5)) Marshall Cavendish Corp.

Turney, Jon. Technology - Ethical Debates about the Application of Science. 2008. (Dilemmas in Modern Science Ser.). (ENG., Illus.). 48p. (J). 23.99 (978-0-237-53370-0(7)) Evans Brothers, Ltd. GBR. Dist: Independent Pubs. Group.

Vallencourt, Margaret. Technology of the Industrial Revolution, 01 vols., 1. 2016. (History of Technology Ser.). (ENG., Illus.). 112p. (J). lib. bdg. 32.90 (978-1-68048-275-1(0), Britannica Educational Publishing) Rosen Publishing Group, Inc., The.

Vance, Ashlee. Elon Musk & the Quest for a Fantastic Future Young Readers' Edition. 2017. 288p. (J). (gr. 3). pap. 6.99 (978-0-06-246327-2(6)); (Illus.). 16.99 (978-0-06-246328-9(4)) HarperCollins Pubs.

Verstraete, Larry. Innovations in Everyday Technologies. 2016. (Problem Solved! Your Turn to Think Big Ser.). (ENG., Illus.). 32p. (J). (gr. 3-6). (978-0-7787-2678-4(9)) Crabtree Publishing Co.

Wainewright, Max. I'm an App Developer. 2017. 32p. (J). **(978-0-7787-3514-4(1))** Crabtree Publishing Co.

Weaver, Janice. The A to Z of Everyday Things. Blake, Francis, illus. 2004. (ENG.). 128p. (J). (gr. 5). pap. 8.95 (978-0-88776-671-8(4), Tundra Bks.) Tundra Bks. CAN. Dist: Penguin Random Hse. LLC.

Welsbacher, Anne. Earth-Friendly Design. 2009. pap. 58.95 (978-0-7613-4693-7(7)) Lerner Publishing Group.

What About..., 10 vols., Set. Incl. Dinosaurs. Matthews, Rupert. lib. bdg. 19.95 (978-1-4222-1558-6(X)); History. Williams, Brian. lib. bdg. 19.95 (978-1-4222-1559-3(8)); How We Live. Williams, Brian. lib. bdg. 19.95 (978-1-4222-1560-9(1)); Human Body. Parker, Steve. lib. bdg. 19.95 (978-1-4222-1561-6(X)); Natural World. Williams, Brian. lib. bdg. 19.95 (978-1-4222-1562-3(8)); People & Places. Williams, Brian. lib. bdg. 19.95 (978-1-4222-1563-0(6)); Planet Earth. Williams, Brian. lib. bdg. 19.95 (978-1-4222-1564-7(4)); Science & Technology. Parker, Steve. lib. bdg. 19.95 (978-1-4222-1565-4(2)); Universe. Williams, Brian. lib. bdg. 19.95 (978-1-4222-1566-1(0)); World Wonders. Williams, Brian. lib. bdg. 19.95 (978-1-4222-1567-8(9)); (J). (gr. 6-8). 2010. (Question & Answer Book Ser.). (Illus.). 40p. 2009. Set lib. bdg. 199.50 (978-1-4222-1557-9(1)) Mason Crest.

Willis, Laurie. Electronic Devices in Schools. 2012. (Issues That Concern You Ser.). (ENG., Illus.). 144p. (gr. 7-10). lib. bdg. 42.00 (978-0-7377-6292-1(6)) Cengage Gale.

Wirkner, Linda. Learning about the American Revolution with Graphic Organizers. 2009. (Graphic Organizers in Social Studies). 24p. (gr. 3-4). 42.50 (978-1-61513-083-2(7), PowerKids Pr.) Rosen Publishing Group, Inc., The.

Woods, Michael & Woods, Mary B. Technology in Ancient Cultures, 8 vols., Set. Incl. Ancient Agricultural Technology: From Sickles to Plows. lib. bdg. 31.93 (978-0-7613-6526-6(5)); Ancient Communication Technology: From Hieroglyphics to Scrolls. lib. bdg. 31.93 (978-0-7613-6529-7(X)); Ancient Computing Technology: From Abacuses to Water Clocks. lib. bdg. 31.93 (978-0-7613-6528-0(1)); Ancient Construction Technology: From Pyramids to Fortresses. (Illus.). (J). lib. bdg. 31.93 (978-0-7613-6527-3(3)); Ancient Machine Technology: From Wheels to Forges. lib. bdg. 31.93 (978-0-7613-6523-5(0)); Ancient Medical Technology: From Herbs to Scalpels. lib. bdg. 31.93 (978-0-7613-6522-8(2)); Ancient Transportation Technology: From Oars to Elephants. (Illus.). (J). lib. bdg. 31.93 (978-0-7613-6524-2(9)); Ancient Warfare Technology: From Javelins to Chariots. lib. bdg. 31.93 (978-0-7613-6525-9(7)); 96p. (gr. 6-12). 2011. (Technology in Ancient Cultures Ser.). (ENG.). 2011. Set lib. bdg. 255.44 (978-0-7613-6521-1(4), Twenty-First Century Bks.) Lerner Publishing Group.

Woolf, Alex. The Impact of Technology in Art. 2015. (Impact of Technology Ser.). (ENG., Illus.). 56p. (gr. 6-9). 34.65 (978-1-4846-2635-1(4)) Heinemann-Raintree.

Woolf, Alex & Anniss, Matthew. The Impact of Technology. 2015. (Impact of Technology Ser.). (ENG.). 56p. (gr. 6-9). lib. bdg. 138.60 (978-1-4846-2639-9(7)) Heinemann-Raintree.

World Book, Inc Staff, contrib. by. Architecture & Engineering. 2009. (J). (978-0-7166-0386-3(1)) World Bk., Inc.

—Earth & Space. 2008. (J). (978-0-7166-3016-6(8)) World Bk., Inc.

—Science & Technology. 2008. (J). (978-0-7166-3018-0(4)) World Bk., Inc.

World Book, Inc. Staff, contrib. by. Smoke Signals to Smartphones: A Timeline of Long-Distance Communication. 2016. (J). (978-0-7166-3543-7(7)) World Bk., Inc.

Ye, Ting-Xing. The Chinese Thought of It: Amazing Inventions & Innovations. 2009. (Jobs in History Ser.). (ENG., Illus.). 48p. (J). (gr. 5-7). 19.95 (978-1-55451-196-9(8), 9781554511969); pap. 9.95 (978-1-55451-195-2(X), 9781554511952) Annick Pr., Ltd. CAN. Dist: Publishers Group West (PGW).

Zumbusch, Amelie von. Ancient Roman Technology. 2013. (Spotlight on Ancient Civilizations: Rome Ser.). (ENG., Illus.). 24p. (J). (gr. 3-4). pap. 10.00 (978-1-4777-0893-4(6), PowerKids Pr.) Rosen Publishing Group, Inc., The.

Zumbusch, Amelie Von & Von Zumbusch, Amelie. Ancient Roman Technology. 2013. (Spotlight on Ancient Civilizations: Rome Ser.). (ENG.). 24p. (J). (gr. 3-4). 23.60 (978-1-4777-0780-7(8), PowerKids Pr.) Rosen Publishing Group, Inc., The.

TECHNOLOGY—DICTIONARIES

Hackney Blackwell, Amy & Manar, Elizabeth P. UXL Encyclopedia of Science. 2015. (Illus.). 10p. (YA). (978-1-4144-3085-0(X)) Cengage Gale.

Holt, Rinehart and Winston Staff. Earth Science. 5th ed. 2003. (Holt Science & Technology Ser.). (ENG., Illus.). 880p. (gr. 7-7). 103.35 (978-0-03-066478-6(0)) Houghton Mifflin Harcourt Publishing Co.

—Holt Science & Technology: Online Edition Upgrade. 2nd ed. 2003. Level A. 2.60 (978-0-03-037236-0(4))Level K. 2.60 (978-0-03-037248-3(8)) Holt McDougal.

—Life Science. 5th ed. 2003. (Holt Science & Technology Ser.). (ENG., Illus.). 912p. (gr. 6-6). 103.35 (978-0-03-066476-2(4)) Houghton Mifflin Harcourt Publishing Co.

—Physical Science. 5th ed. 2003. (Holt Science & Technology Ser.). (ENG., Illus.). 848p. (gr. 8-8). 103.35 (978-0-03-066481-6(0)) Houghton Mifflin Harcourt Publishing Co.

U X L, ed. UXL Encyclopedia of Science, 10 vols. 3rd ed. 2015. (ENG., Illus.). 10p. 819.00 *(978-1-4144-3075-1(2),* UXL) Cengage Gale.

World Book, Inc Staff, contrib. by. Technology. 2014. (Illus.). 352p. (J). *(978-0-7166-7517-4(X))* World Bk., Inc.

TECHNOLOGY—FICTION

Anderson, R. J. Quicksilver. 2013. (ENG.). 328p. (YA). (gr. 7-12). 17.95 *(978-0-7613-8799-2(4),* Carolrhoda Lab™) Lerner Publishing Group.

Anderson, Taylor. Storm Surge. 2014. (Destroyermen Ser.: 8). (ENG.). 512p. (gr. 12). mass mkt. 7.99 *(978-0-451-41909-5(X),* Ace Bks.) Penguin Publishing Group.

Anne, Paula. Sultry Smith. 2009. 80p. pap. 9.99 *(978-1-60860-970-3(7),* Eloquent Bks.) Strategic Book Publishing & Rights Agency (SBPRA).

Appleton, Victor. Tom Swift & His Wireless Message. 2007. 220p. 24.95 *(978-1-4344-9231-9(1));* per. 14.95 *(978-1-4344-9137-4(4))* Wildside Pr., LLC.

Bunce, Elizabeth C. A Curse Dark as Gold. 2010. (ENG.). 400p. (J). (gr. 7). 9.99 *(978-0-439-89577-4(4),* Scholastic Paperbacks) Scholastic, Inc.

Burton, Virginia Lee. Mike Mulligan & His Steam Shovel. 2010. (ENG., Illus.). 40p. (J). (gr. k — 1). bds. 11.99 *(978-0-547-38566-2(8))* Houghton Mifflin Harcourt Publishing Co.

Cannon, Deborah. The Pirate Vortex: Elizabeth Latimer, Pirate Hunter. 2009. 260p. pap. 20.00 *(978-1-4269-0532-2(7))* Trafford Publishing.

Carman, Patrick. Pulse. 2013. (Pulse Ser.: 1). (ENG.). 384p. (YA). (gr. 8). 17.99 *(978-0-06-208576-4(X),* Tegen, Katherine Bks) HarperCollins Pubs.

—Quake: A Pulse Novel. 2016. (Pulse Ser.: 3). 288p. (YA). (gr. 8). pap. 9.99 *(978-0-06-208597-9(2),* Tegen, Katherine Bks) HarperCollins Pubs.

Darke, J. A. Tech Fury. Evergreen, Nelson, illus. 2015. (Spine Shivers Ser.). (ENG.). 128p. (gr. 3-4). lib. bdg. 26.65 *(978-1-4965-0218-6(3))* Stone Arch Bks.

Easton, Tom. Seven Second Delay. 2015. (ENG.). 240p. (J). (gr. 7-12). 16.95 *(978-0-8234-3209-7(2))* Holiday Hse., Inc.

Flores, Valeria. ¿Como Se Metieron Ahi?/How'd They Get in There? 2012. 28p. pap. 21.99 *(978-1-4653-0884-9(9))* Xlibris Corp.

Grant, Michael. BZRK. (ENG.). 400p. (gr. 9). 2013. (J). pap. 9.99 *(978-1-60684-418-2(0))* 2012. 17.99 *(978-1-60684-312-3(5))* Lerner Publishing Group. (Carolrhoda Lab™).

—BZRK Apocalypse. 2014. (ENG.). 400p. (J). (gr. 9). 18.99 *(978-1-60684-408-3(3),* Carolrhoda Lab™) Lerner Publishing Group.

—BZRK Reloaded. 2013. (ENG.). 432p. (J). (gr. 9). 18.99 *(978-1-60684-394-9(X),* Carolrhoda Lab™) Lerner Publishing Group.

Harmer, Wendy. I Lost My Mobile at the Mall. 2011. (ENG.). 272p. (YA). (gr. 7-18). 10.99 *(978-1-935279-97-6(1))* Kane Miller.

Hautman, Pete. The Flinkwater Factor: A Novel in Five Thrilling Episodes. 2015. (Flinkwater Chronicles Ser.: 1). (ENG.). 256p. (J). (gr. 4-8). 16.99 *(978-1-4814-3251-1(6),* Simon & Schuster Bks. For Young Readers) Simon & Schuster Bks. For Young Readers.

Hord, Colleen. Everyone Uses Technology. 2015. (ENG.). 24p. (gr. k-3). 28.50 *(978-1-63430-361-3(X))* Rourke Educational Media.

Hulme, John & Wexler, Michael. The Glitch in Sleep. 2007. (Seems Ser.). (ENG., Illus.). 288p. (YA). (gr. 5-18). 16.95 *(978-1-59990-129-9(3),* 9781599901299, Bloomsbury USA Childrens) Bloomsbury Publishing USA.

—The Seems: The Lost Train of Thought. 2010. (Seems Ser.). (ENG., Illus.). 304p. (YA). (gr. 3-6). pap. 7.99 *(978-1-59990-300-2(8),* 9781599903002, Bloomsbury USA Childrens) Bloomsbury Publishing USA.

Kesselring, Mari. Techie Cheater. Epelbaum, Mariano, illus. 2014. (ENG.). 64p. (J). *(978-1-63235-038-1(6))* Pr. Room Editions LLC.

Klise, Kate. The Phantom of the Post Office. Klise, M. Sarah, illus. (43 Old Cemetery Road Ser.: 4). (ENG.). 160p. (J). (gr. 2-5). 2013. pap. 6.99 *(978-0-544-02281-2(5))* 2012. 16.99 *(978-0-547-51974-6(5))* Houghton Mifflin Harcourt Publishing Co.

—The Phantom of the Post Office. 2013. (43 Old Cemetery Road Ser.: 4). lib. bdg. 17.20 *(978-0-606-31668-2(X),* Turtleback) Turtleback Bks.

Lancaster, Mike A. Dotwav. 2016. (ENG.). 448p. (J). (gr. 6). 17.99 *(978-1-5107-0404-6(3),* Sky Pony Pr.) Skyhorse Publishing Co., Inc.

Leiber, Fritz. The Creature from Cleveland Depths. 2009. 76p. pap. 7.95 *(978-1-60664-286-3(3))* Rodgers, Alan Bks.

Lynch, Chris. Cyberia. 2008. (Cyberia Ser.: 1). (ENG.). 160p. (J). (gr. 3-7). 16.99 *(978-0-545-02793-9(4),* Scholastic Pr.) Scholastic, Inc.

—Monkey See, Monkey Don't. (Cyberia Ser.: 2). (ENG.). 144p. (J). (gr. 3-7). 2011. pap. 5.99 *(978-0-545-02797-7(7),* Scholastic Paperbacks) 2009. 16.99 *(978-0-545-02794-6(2),* Scholastic Pr.) Scholastic, Inc.

Mbuyazi, Phiwayinkosi G. The Wiby Kids - How It All Began. 2011. 204p. pap. 12.99 *(978-1-61667-337-6(0))* Raider Publishing International.

Melbourne, Lois. The STEM Club Goes Exploring. 2016. (ENG.). 48p. 15.95 *(978-1-62634-303-0(9))* Greenleaf Book Group.

Nanatsuki, Kyoichi. Project Arms, Vol. 13. Nanatsuki, Kyoichi, illus. 2006. (Project Arms Ser.). (ENG., Illus.). 208p. pap. 9.99 *(978-1-4215-0502-2(9))* Viz Media.

Nye, Barry. Hannah & the Magic Blanket - Land of the Robots. 2009. 40p. pap. 18.50 *(978-0-557-06602-5(6))* Lulu Pr., Inc.

Perry, Fred & Dlin, Doug. Gold Digger Tech Manual. 2011. (ENG.). 352p. (YA). pap., pap. 19.99 *(978-0-9844879-7-4(2),* 9780984487974) Antarctic Pr., Inc.

Peterson, Lois. Disconnect, 1 vol. 2012. (Orca Currents Ser.). (ENG.). 136p. (J). (gr. 5-9). pap. 9.95 *(978-1-4598-0143-1(1));* lib. bdg. 16.95 *(978-1-4598-0144-8(X))* Orca Bk. Pubs. USA.

Poznanski, Ursula. Erebos: It's a Game. It Watches You. Pattinson, Judith, tr. from GER. 3rd ed. 2012. (ENG.). 440p. (YA). (gr. 6-18). 29.95 *(978-1-55451-373-4(1),* 9781554513734); pap. 19.95 *(978-1-55451-372-7(3),* 9781554513727) Annick Pr., Ltd. CAN. Dist: Publishers Group West (PGW).

Random House Disney Staff. Hiro to the Rescue! Random House Disney Staff, illus. 2014. (Stepping Stone Book(TM) Ser.). (ENG., Illus.). 80p. (J). (gr. 1-4). lib. bdg. 12.99 *(978-0-7364-8154-0(0),* RH/Disney) Random Hse. Children's Bks.

Reeve, Philip. Fever Crumb. 2011. (Fever Crumb Ser.). (ENG.). 336p. (J). (gr. 7-7). pap. 9.99 *(978-0-545-22215-0(X),* Scholastic Pr.) Scholastic, Inc.

—Fever Crumb: a Web of Air. 2013. (Fever Crumb Ser.). (ENG.). 304p. (J). (gr. 7-7). pap. 9.99 *(978-0-545-22217-4(6),* Scholastic Pr.) Scholastic, Inc.

—Scrivener's Moon. 2012. (ENG.). 352p. (J). (gr. 7). 17.99 *(978-0-545-22218-1(4),* Scholastic Pr.) Scholastic, Inc.

—A Web of Air. 2011. (Fever Crumb Ser.). (ENG.). 304p. (J). (gr. 7-7). 17.99 *(978-0-545-22216-7(8))* Scholastic, Inc.

Savage, J. Scott. Fires of Invention. 2015. (Mysteries of Cove Ser.: Bk. 1). 312p. (J). 17.99 *(978-1-62972-092-0(5),* Shadow Mountain) Deseret Bk. Co.

—Gears of Revolution. 2016. (Mysteries of Cove Ser.: 2). 342p. (J). 17.99 *(978-1-62972-223-8(5),* Shadow Mountain) Deseret Bk. Co.

Serwacki, Kevin & Pallace, Chris. Joey & Johnny - The Ninjas - Get Mooned. Serwacki, Kevin & Pallace, Chris, illus. 2015. (Joey & Johnny, the Ninjas Ser.: 1). (ENG., Illus.). 320p. (J). (gr. 3-7). 12.99 *(978-0-06-229933-8(6))* HarperCollins Pubs.

Snell, Roy J. Curlie Carson Listens In. 2009. 108p. 22.95 *(978-1-60664-674-8(5));* 100p. pap. 8.95 *(978-1-60664-303-7(7))* Rodgers, Alan Bks.

Stepp, Shirley. Santa Lost His Cell Phone. 2012. 24p. 24.95 *(978-1-4626-5479-6(7))* America Star Bks.

Townsend, Kari. Fused. 2010. (ENG.). 208p. (J). (gr. 5-7). pap. 7.99 *(978-1-4022-4042-3(2),* Sourcebooks Jabberwocky) Sourcebooks, Inc.

Zuckerberg, Randi. Dot. Berger, Joe, illus. 2013. (ENG.). 32p. (J). (gr. -1-3). 17.99 *(978-0-06-228751-9(6))* HarperCollins Pubs.

TECHNOLOGY—VOCATIONAL GUIDANCE

Ching, Jacqueline. Jobs in Green Travel & Tourism. 2010. (Green Careers Ser.). 80p. (YA). (gr. 7-12). E-Book 61.20 *(978-1-4488-0134-3(6))* Rosen Publishing Group, Inc., The.

Colby, Jennifer. Computer Store. 2016. (21st Century Junior Library: Explore a Workplace Ser.). (ENG., Illus.). 24p. (J). (gr. 2-5). 27.07 *(978-1-63471-078-7(9),* 208391) Cherry Lake Publishing.

Digital Career Building. 2013. (Digital Career Building Ser.). 64p. (YA). (gr. 7-12). pap. 466.20 *(978-1-4777-7806-7(3));* pap. 77.70 *(978-1-4777-7807-4(1))* Rosen Publishing Group, Inc., The.

Digital Career Building: Set 3. 2013. (Digital Career Building Ser.). 64p. (YA). (gr. 7-12). 191.70 *(978-1-4777-1734-9(X))* Rosen Publishing Group, Inc., The.

Hagler, Gina. Top STEM Careers in Engineering. 2014. (Cutting-Edge STEM Careers Ser.). 128p. (YA). (gr. 9-12). 35.60 *(978-1-4777-7672-8(9));* pap. 18.85 *(978-1-4777-7674-2(5))* Rosen Publishing Group, Inc., The.

Hand, Carol. Careers for Tech Girls in Technology. 2015. (Tech Girls Ser.). (ENG., Illus.). 80p. (J). (gr. 7-8). 34.25 *(978-1-4994-6099-5(6),* Rosen Young Adult) Rosen Publishing Group, Inc., The.

La Bella, Laura. Top STEM Careers in Technology. 2014. (Cutting-Edge STEM Careers Ser.). (Illus.). 128p. (J). (gr. 9-12). 35.60 *(978-1-4777-7668-1(0))* Rosen Publishing Group, Inc., The.

LeBoutillier, Linda. Unusual & Awesome Jobs Using Technology: Roller Coaster Designer, Space Robotics Engineer, & More. 2015. (You Get Paid for THAT? Ser.). (ENG.). 32p. (gr. 3-4). 27.99 *(978-1-4914-2029-4(4))* Capstone Press of Coughlan Cos.

Marsico, Katie. Working at a Computer Store. 2009. (21st Century Junior Library: Careers Ser.). (ENG.). 24p. (gr. 2-5). lib. bdg. 25.64 *(978-1-60279-513-6(4),* 200277) Cherry Lake Publishing.

Reeves, Diane Lindsey. Stem. 2017. (Bright Futures Press: World of Work Ser.). (ENG., Illus.). 32p. (J). (gr. 4-7). lib. bdg. 29.93 *(978-1-63472-628-3(6),* 209546) Cherry Lake Publishing.

Spencer, Jean W. Careers Inside the World of Technology. rev. ed. 2005. (Careers & Opportunities Ser.). (Illus.). 64p. (YA). (gr. 7-12). lib. bdg. 31.95 *(978-0-8239-3266-5(4),* CITECH) Rosen Publishing Group, Inc., The.

Suen, Anastasia. Top STEM Careers in Science. 2014. (Cutting-Edge STEM Careers Ser.). (Illus.). 128p. (J). (gr. 9-12). 35.60 *(978-1-4777-7664-3(8))* Rosen Publishing Group, Inc., The.

Turning Your Tech Hobbies into a Career. 2016. (Turning Your Tech Hobbies into a Career Ser.). 00080p. (J). (gr. 7-7). 250.25 *(978-1-5081-7362-5(1),* Rosen Young Adult) Rosen Publishing Group, Inc., The.

TECHNOLOGY AND CIVILIZATION

see also Machinery in the Workplace

Apel, Melanie Ann. Technology of Ancient Greece. 2004. (Primary Sources of Ancient Civilizations Ser.). (ENG., Illus.). 24p. (gr. 4-8). pap. 8.25 *(978-0-8239-8941-6(0),* PowerKids Pr.) Rosen Publishing Group, Inc., The.

Gedacht, Daniel C. Technology of Ancient Rome. 2004. (Primary Sources of Ancient Civilizations Ser.). (Illus.). 24p. (ENG.). (gr. 4-8). pap. 8.25 *(978-0-8239-8947-8(X));* (J). lib. bdg. 22.60 *(978-0-8239-6779-7(4))* Rosen Publishing Group, Inc., The. (PowerKids Pr.).

Maxim, Bailey. The 100 Most Influential Technology Leaders, 1 vol., 1. 2016. (Britannica Guide to the World's Most Influential People Ser.). (ENG.). 224p. (J). (gr. 10-10). lib. bdg. 54.00 *(978-1-68048-280-5(7),* Britannica Educational Publishing) Rosen Publishing Group, Inc., The.

Miller, Reagan & Richardson, Hazel. Technology in the Ancient World. 2011. (ENG., Illus.). 32p. (J). *(978-0-7787-1736-2(4))* Crabtree Publishing Co.

—Technology in the Ancient World. Crabtree Publishing Co. Staff, ed. 2011. (Life in the Ancient World Ser.: No. 5). (ENG., Illus.). 32p. (J). (gr. 5-8). pap. *(978-0-7787-1743-0(7))* Crabtree Publishing Co.

Senker, Cath. Ideas That Changed the World. 2017. (10 Ser.). (ENG., Illus.). 32p. (J). (gr. 4-6). pap. 12.99 ***(978-0-7502-9141-5(9),*** Wayland) Hachette Children's Group GBR. Dist: Hachette Bk. Group.

Snedden, Robert. Ancient Egypt. 2009. (Technology in Times Past Ser.). (Illus.). 46p. (J). (gr. 4-7). pap. *(978-1-897563-61-8(2))* Saunders Bk. Co.

—Ancient Rome. 2009. (Technology in Times Past Ser.). (Illus.). 46p. (J). (gr. 4-7). pap. *(978-1-897563-63-2(9))* Saunders Bk. Co.

TECUMSEH, SHAWNEE CHIEF, 1768-1813

Aller, Susan Bivin. Tecumseh. 2004. (History Maker Bios Ser.). (J). pap. 6.95 *(978-0-8225-2073-3(7));* (ENG., Illus.). 48p. (gr. 3-6). 27.93 *(978-0-8225-0699-7(8),* Carolrhoda Bks.) Lerner Publishing Group.

Collier, James Lincoln. The Tecumseh You Never Knew. Copeland, Greg, illus. 2004. (You Never Knew Ser.). (ENG.). (J). 25.50 *(978-0-516-24426-6(4),* Children's Pr.) Scholastic Library Publishing.

Gordon, Irene Ternier. Tecumseh: Diplomat & Warrior in the War of 1812. 2009. (Amazing Stories Ser.). (ENG., Illus.). 128p. (J). (gr. 6-12). pap. 9.95 *(978-1-55277-430-4(9),* 9781552774304) Lorimer, James & Co., Ltd., Pubs. CAN. Dist: Casemate Pubs. & Bk. Distributors, LLC.

Laplante, Walter. Tecumseh. 2015. (Native American Heroes Ser.). (ENG., Illus.). 24p. (J). (gr. 1-2). 22.60 *(978-1-4824-2706-6(0))* Stevens, Gareth Publishing LLLP.

TEDDY BEARS

Anholt, Laurence. We Love Bears. Anholt, Catherine, illus. 2012. (ENG.). 32p. (J). (gr. -1-k). pap. 10.99 *(978-1-4083-1169-1(0))* Hodder & Stoughton GBR. Dist: Hachette Bk. Group.

Bart, Kathleen. A Tale of Two Teddies. 2005. 32p. (J). *(978-1-932485-23-3(6))* Reverie Publishing Co.

Beck, Isabel L., et al. Trophies Kindergarten: Where's My Teddy? 2003. (Trophies Ser.). (gr. k-6). 13.80 *(978-0-15-329517-1(1))* Harcourt Schl. Pubs.

Cook, Deanna F. Teddy Bear Doctor: Fix the Boo-Boos & Heal the Ouchies of Your Favorite Stuffed Animals. 2015. (ENG., Illus.). 64p. (J). (gr. -1). pap. 10.95 *(978-1-61212-402-5(X),* 622402) Storey Publishing, LLC.

Hudson, Amanda & Nations, Susan. This Is My Bear: Éste Es Mi Oso. 2008. (Our Toys/Nuestros Juguetes Ser.). (SPA.). 16p. (gr. -1-2). pap. 5.30 *(978-0-8368-9356-4(5),* Weekly Reader Leveled Readers) Stevens, Gareth Publishing LLLP.

—This Is My Bear/Éste Es Mi Oso. 2008. (Our Toys/Nuestros Juguetes Ser.). (SPA & ENG., Illus.). 16p. (J). (gr. -1-2). lib. bdg. 19.00 *(978-0-8368-9257-4(7),* Weekly Reader Leveled Readers) Stevens, Gareth Publishing LLLP.

Innes, Stephanie & Endrulat, Harry. A Bear in War, 1 vol. Deines, Brian, illus. 2013. (ENG.). 40p. (J). (gr. k-4). 19.95 *(978-1-927485-12-5(6))* Pajama Pr. CAN. Dist: Ingram Publisher Services.

Kay, Helen. The First Teddy Bear. Detwiler, Susan, illus. 2nd enl. ed. 2005. 38p. (J). (gr. -1-3). 18.95 *(978-0-88045-154-3(8));* per. 11.95 *(978-0-88045-153-6(X))* Stemmer Hse. Pubs.

Watt, Fiona. Este No Es Mi Osito. rev. ed. 2008. (Touchy-Feely Board Bks).Tr. of That's Not My Teddy. 10p. (J). bds. 7.99 *(978-0-7460-9208-8(3),* Usborne) EDC Publishing.

TEDDY BEARS—FICTION

A Mother's Pen. The Adventures of Backwards Bear & Baby Curl. 2011. 32p. pap. 16.19 *(978-1-4634-4412-9(5))* AuthorHouse.

Abshier, Stan. Teddy's Journal: Cruise to Japan, China, & Singapore. 2012. 96p. pap. 31.99 *(978-1-4685-2319-5(8))* AuthorHouse.

Adeney, Anne. Five Teddy Bears. Shimmen, Cathy, illus. 2008. (Tadpoles Ser.). (ENG.). 24p. (J). (gr. -1-k). pap. *(978-0-7787-3884-8(1));* lib. bdg. *(978-0-7787-3853-4(1))* Crabtree Publishing Co.

Anne Paradis, Anne. Baby Caillou, Bedtime Hide & Seek: A Lift-the-Flap Book. Chouette Publishing Staff, ed. Kary, illus. 2016. (Baby Caillou Ser.). (ENG.). 10p. (J). (— 1). bds. 6.99 *(978-2-89718-351-6(9))* Caillouet, Gerry.

Arcynski, Charlene. The Adventures of Little Sugarbear Boy: The Beginning. 2010. 28p. 15.49 *(978-1-4520-5430-8(4))* AuthorHouse.

Ashby, Gaylene. STORY TIME A Collection of Three Children's Stories. 2008. 28p. 14.95 *(978-1-4357-1929-3(8))* Lulu Pr., Inc.

Austin, Rikey. Chunky & the Bone: Alice's Bear Shop. 2012. 28p. pap. *(978-1-78092-152-5(7))* MX Publishing, Ltd.

Bauman, Amy. Everyone Is Special! 2010. 12p. (J). (gr. -1). 9.95 *(978-1-60747-719-8(X),* Pickwick Pr.) Phoenix Bks., Inc.

Baxter, Nicola. The Teddy Bears' Picnic. Howarth, Daniel, illus. 2015. (ENG.). 24p. pap. 6.99 *(978-1-86147-654-8(X),* Armadillo) Anness Publishing GBR. Dist: National Bk. Network.

Beal, T. J. Wash Day: A Teddy Doonamen Adventure. 2012. 24p. pap. 11.95 *(978-1-60693-609-2(3),* Strategic Bk. Publishing) Strategic Book Publishing & Rights Agency (SBPRA).

The Bear Who Had No Name. 2006. (J). 10.00 *(978-0-9760076-1-6(4))* Juniper Berry Pr.

Beavington, Ruth. Edward Bear. 2012. (Illus.). 112p. (gr. 1-2). 19.95 *(978-1-84624-721-7(7))* Book Guild, Ltd. GBR. Dist: Trans-Atlantic Pubns., Inc.

Beecroft, Susan. Teddy Goes to Buckingham Palace. 2013. (Illus.). 24p. pap. 9.50 *(978-1-78035-606-8(4),* Fastprint Publishing) Upfront Publishing Ltd. GBR. Dist: Printondemand-worldwide.com.

Bernal, Sandra Marie. I Want a Pand. 2011. 32p. pap. 24.95 *(978-1-4626-2897-1(4))* America Star Bks.

Blackman, Malorie. Sinclair, Wonder Bear. Allwright, Deborah, illus. 2005. (Blue Go Bananas Ser.). (ENG.). 48p. (J). (gr. 1-2). lib. bdg. *(978-0-7787-2631-9(2))* Crabtree Publishing Co.

—Sinclair, Wonder Bear. Allwright, Deborah, illus. 2003. (Blue Bananas Ser.). (ENG.). 48p. (J). (gr. k-2). pap. 5.99 *(978-1-4052-0589-4(X))* Egmont Bks., Ltd. GBR. Dist: Independent Pubs. Group.

Bolton, Violet. Heidi & Huber the Adventures Begin. 2011. (Illus.). 60p. pap. *(978-1-908447-90-6(7))* Grosvenor Hse. Publishing Ltd.

Bond, Michael. Paddington & the Christmas Surprise. Alley, R. W., illus. 2008. (Paddington Ser.). (ENG.). 32p. (J). (gr. -1-3). 16.99 *(978-0-06-168740-2(5))* HarperCollins Pubs.

—Paddington at Work. Fortnum, Peggy, illus. 2017. (Paddington Ser.). 176p. (J). (gr. 3-7). 9.99 *(978-0-06-231226-6(X))* HarperCollins Pubs.

Booking, Walt. Teddy's Tale. 2006. (Neighborhood Readers Ser.). (ENG.). 12p. (gr. 1-3). pap. 5.90 *(978-1-4042-7054-1(X),* Rosen Classroom) Rosen Publishing Group, Inc., The.

Bradley, Timothy. Teddy Bear, Teddy Bear, Say Good Night, 1 vol. Medina, Conni & Stark, Kristy, eds. 2009. (Early Childhood Themes Ser.). (ENG., Illus.). 16p. (J). (gr. -1-2). pap. 19.99 *(978-1-4333-1472-8(X))* Shell Educational Publishing.

Bradley, Timothy J. Teddy Bear, Teddy Bear, Say Good Night, 1 vol. 2009. (Early Childhood Themes Ser.). (ENG., Illus.). 16p. (J). (gr. -1-2). pap. 6.99 *(978-1-4333-1471-1(1))* Teacher Created Materials, Inc.

Bragg, Jane. Teddy Bears Christmas Miracle. 2009. 49p. pap. 18.70 *(978-0-557-22087-8(4))* Lulu Pr., Inc.

Branchaud, R. Gary. Toasty Town! 2011. 64p. pap. 19.50 *(978-1-60976-039-7(5),* Eloquent Bks.) Strategic Book Publishing & Rights Agency (SBPRA).

Brannock, Martha Lee. Teddy Bear Too-Too. 2007. 28p. per. 18.65 *(978-1-4257-4143-3(6))* Xlibris Corp.

Brignaud, Pierre, illus. Caillou: Where Is Teddy? 2015. (Step by Step Ser.). (ENG.). 24p. (J). (gr. k-k). bds. 5.99 *(978-2-89718-173-4(7))* Caillouet, Gerry.

Brooks, Felicity. Dress the Teddy Bears for Christmas. 2015. (Dress the Teddy Bears Sticker Bks.). (ENG.). 16+8p. (J). pap. 6.99 *(978-0-7945-3585-8(2),* Usborne) EDC Publishing.

—Dress the Teddy Bears Going Shopping. 2015. (Dress the Teddy Bears Sticker Bks.). (ENG.). 16+8p. (J). pap. 6.99 *(978-0-7945-3530-8(5),* Usborne) EDC Publishing.

Brown, Gwen. Clifford & His Bear. 2006. (Illus.). 48p. pap. *(978-1-84401-650-1(1))* Athena Pr.

Brown, Margaret Wise. Buenas Noches Oso. 2006. (Illus.). 24p. (J). (gr. -1-k). 12.95 *(978-1-882077-61-8(X))* Sweetwater Pr.

Buckley, Charlie. How to Wash Your Hands. 2007. (Show Jo Language Development Ser.). (Illus.). 16p. (J). (gr. -1-1). per., bds. 14.95 *(978-1-933669-09-0(8))* Literary Architects, LLC.

—Show Jo How to Make a Sandwich. 2007. (Show Jo Language Development Ser.). (Illus.). 16p. (J). (gr. -1-1). per., bds. 14.95 *(978-1-933669-08-3(X))* Literary Architects, LLC.

Burfoot, Ella, illus. Bear & Me. 2013. (J). *(978-1-4351-4753-9(7))* Barnes & Noble, Inc.

Burgess, Mark. Where Teddy Bears Come From. Ayto, Russell, illus. 2009. 32p. (J). (gr. -1-3). 16.95 *(978-1-56145-487-7(7))* Peachtree Pubs.

Burke, Ellinor Rozecki. Susana Worrywart & the Magical Teddy Bear Balloon: With CD for Relaxation. Perciopelo, illus. 2003. 32p. (J). 27.00 incl. audio compact disk *(978-0-9741586-0-0(7))* Comfort Tales, LLC.

Butterworth, Nick. Albert the Bear to the Rescue. 2008. (J). 16.99 *(978-0-06-147046-2(5))* HarperCollins Pubs.

Calder, Catherine. A Teddy Tale. 2012. 24p. pap. 15.99 *(978-1-4771-0339-5(2))* Xlibris Corp.

Capucilli, Alyssa Satin. Biscuit & the Lost Teddy Bear. Schories, Pat, illus. 2011. (My First I Can Read Ser.). (ENG.). 32p. (J). (gr. -1 — 1). 16.99 *(978-0-06-117751-4(2));* pap. 3.99 *(978-0-06-117753-8(9))* HarperCollins Pubs.

Carey, Cassandra L. The Adventures of Uncle Joe: Uncle Joe & His Bear. 2012. 30p. 24.95 *(978-1-4626-5563-2(7))* America Star Bks.

Chichester Clark, Emma. Minty & Tink. Chichester Clark, Emma, illus. 2009. (ENG., Illus.). 32p. (J). (gr. k-k). pap. 13.99 *(978-1-84270-720-3(5))* Andersen Pr. GBR. Dist: Independent Pubs. Group.

Children of Appalachia. Teddy Bear Helps on the Farm. Children of Appalachia, illus. 2007. (Illus.). 64p. (J). per. 14.95 *(978-0-929915-73-9(9))* Headline Bks., Inc.

Coleman, Tamala J. Donovan's Shoes. 2010. 28p. pap. 9.95 *(978-1-4327-5801-1(2))* Outskirts Pr., Inc.

Copes, Liz Pecchi. Whompoo: The First Night. 2011. 24p. pap. 14.95 *(978-1-4634-3585-1(1))* AuthorHouse.

Cox, Phil Roxbee. Ted in a Red Bed. Tyler, Jenny, ed. Cartwright, Stephen, illus. rev. ed. 2006. (Phonics Reader, A: Easy Words to Read Ser.). 16p. (J). (gr. -1-3). 6.99 *(978-0-7945-1510-2(X),* Usborne) EDC Publishing.

—Ted's Shed. Tyler, Jenny, ed. Cartwright, Stephen, illus. rev. ed. 2006. (Phonics Readers Ser.). 16p. (J). (gr. -1-3). pap. 6.99 *(978-0-7945-1511-9(8),* Usborne) EDC Publishing.

Cox, Phil Roxbee & Cartwright, S. Ted's Shed, Toad Makes a Road, Fat Cat on a Mat & Sam Sheep Can't Sleep. 2004. (Easy Words to Read Ser.). (Illus.). 16p. (J). (gr. 1-18). pap. 9.95 *(978-0-7945-0245-4(8),* Usborne) EDC Publishing.

Cox, Phil Roxbee & Cartwright, Stephen. Ted's Shed. 2004. (Phonics Board Bks.). (Illus.). 10p. (J). 4.95 *(978-0-7945-0304-8(7),* Usborne) EDC Publishing.

Crow, Nosy. Bunny Boo Has Lost Her Teddy: A Tiny Tab Book. 2014. (Tiny Tab Ser.). (ENG.). 8p. (J). (— 1). bds. 7.99 *(978-0-7636-7274-4(2),* Nosy Crow) Candlewick Pr.

Cuddle! (Picture Books... Ser.). 28p. *(978-1-4054-9535-6(9))* Parragon, Inc.

Curtiss, A. B. & Lucarelli, Sue. T Bear's Tale. 2005. (ENG.). 40p. (J). (gr. -1-3). 18.95 *(978-0-932529-80-0(1))* Oldcastle Publishing.

Dale, Jay. Where Is Molly's Teddy?, 1 vol. Jackson, Katy, illus. 2012. (Wonder Words Ser.). (ENG.). 32p. (gr. k-2). pap. 5.99 *(978-1-4296-8914-4(5),* Engage Literacy) Capstone Press of Coughlan Cos.

De Bear, Tedrick & Rizzi, Trefoni Michael. Teddy's Travels: America's National Parks. 2006. (ENG., Illus.). 128p. (J). spiral bd. 19.95 *(978-0-9740494-0-3(9))* TdB Pr. LLC.

De Castro, Ines E. The Teddy Bear Faeries. De Castro, Ines E., illus. 2011. (Illus.). 24p. (J). (gr. -1-3). 16.95 *(978-1-935359-72-2(X))* Book Pubs. Network.

De Marco, Clare. Freddy's Teddy. 2011. (Tadpoles Ser.). (ENG., Illus.). 24p. (J). (gr. k-2). lib. bdg. *(978-0-7787-0577-2(3));* pap. *(978-0-7787-0588-8(9))* Crabtree Publishing Co.

deVet, L. J. Teddy's Christmas Wish. Zabarylo-Duma, Ewa, illus. 2013. (J). (ENG.). 48p. *(978-0-9873686-0-7(5));* 46p. pap. *(978-0-9873686-5-2(6));* (ENG.). 48p. pap. *(978-0-9873686-1-4(3))* Print-Rite Publishers.

Dietrich, Sean, creator. Industriacide. 2004. (Illus.). 120p. (YA). per. 11.99 *(978-0-9748654-0-9(0))* Rorschach Entertainment.

Disney Book Group Staff. The Easter Egg Hunt. 2010. (Read-Along Storybook & CD Ser.). (ENG.). 32p. (J). (gr. -1-2). pap. 6.99 *(978-1-4231-2087-2(6))* Disney Pr.

Disney Press Staff, ed. Mickey's New Friend. 2011. (Illus.). 32p. (J). *(978-1-4231-4585-1(2))* Disney Pr.

Disney Staff. Winnie the Pooh. (FRE.). 96p. (J). (gr. k-5). pap. 9.95 *(978-0-7859-8848-9(3))* French & European Pubns., Inc.

d'Lacey, Chris. Frankin's Bear. Taylor, Thomas, illus. 2005. (Red Go Bananas Ser.). (ENG.). 48p. (J). (gr. 2-3). lib. bdg. *(978-0-7787-2674-6(6))* Crabtree Publishing Co.

Docherty, Thomas. Wash-A-Bye Bear. Docherty, Thomas, illus. 2013. (ENG., Illus.). 32p. (J). (gr. -1-2). 14.99 *(978-0-7636-6486-2(3),* Templar) Candlewick Pr.

Don, Freeman. Corduroy. 2014. (Corduroy Ser.). (ENG.). 32p. (J). (gr. k-12). 11.24 *(978-1-63245-291-7(X))* Lectorum Pubns., Inc.

Dorémus, Gaëtan, creator. Bear Despair. 2012. (Stories Without Words Ser.). (ENG., Illus.). 32p. (J). (gr. -1-2). 14.95 *(978-1-59270-125-4(6))* Enchanted Lion Bks., LLC.

Douglas, Babette. Blue Wise. Johnson, John, illus. 2006. (Kiss a Me Teacher Creature Stories Ser.). 62p. (J). (gr. -1-3). *(978-1-890343-07-1(2))* Kiss A Me Productions, Inc.

—Larkspur: And His Wooden Nose. Johnson, John, illus. 2006. (Kiss a Me Teacher Creature Stories Ser.). (J). (gr. -1-3). 9.99 *(978-1-890343-23-1(4))* Kiss A Me Productions, Inc.

Dracker, Pune. Doll & Teddy Bear Activity Book. Bart, Kathleen & Hofmann, Ginnie, illus. 2005. 96p. (J). pap. *(978-1-932485-24-0(4))* Reverie Publishing Co.

Dray, Matt. Dougal, the Garbage Dump Bear. Dray, Matt, illus. 2005. (Illus.). 32p. (J). pap. *(978-0-14-350097-1(X))* Penguin Publishing Group.

Dyan, Penelope. Don't Wake up the Bear! Dyan, Penelope, illus. 2013. (Illus.). 34p. pap. 11.95 *(978-1-61477-094-7(8))* Bellissima Publishing, LLC.

—Ted E Bearses Most Unfortunate Experience to Date. Dyan, Penelope, illus. 2009. (Illus.). 44p. pap. 11.95 *(978-1-935118-44-2(7))* Bellissima Publishing, LLC.

—There's a Teddy Bear in My Heart! Dyan, Penelope, illus. 2012. (Illus.). 34p. pap. 11.95 *(978-1-61477-048-0(4))* Bellissima Publishing, LLC.

Earp-Bridgmon, Krista D. The Adventures of Jim-Bob: A Bearography. 2013. 24p. pap. 10.99 *(978-1-4582-1005-0(7),* Abbott Pr.) Author Solutions, Inc.

Edwards, Pamela Duncan. Teddy Bear Hide-and-Seek. Birkett, Georgie, illus. 2008. (ENG.). 20p. (J). (gr. 2-5). 14.95 *(978-0-230-01442-8(9),* Macmillan) Pan Macmillan GBR. Dist: Trans-Atlantic Pubns., Inc.

Elliot, Rachel. Teddy Bear Tales & Rhymes! 2016. (ENG., Illus.). 48p. (J). (gr. -1-12). bds. 9.99 *(978-1-86147-741-5(4),* Armadillo) Anness Publishing GBR. Dist: National Bk. Network.

Elliott, David. What the Grizzly Knows. Grafe, Max, illus. 2008. (ENG.). 32p. (J). (gr. -1-2). 16.99 *(978-0-7636-2778-2(X))* Candlewick Pr.

Faundez, Anne. Teddy's Birthday. 2004. (QEB Start Talking Ser.). (Illus.). 24p. (J). lib. bdg. 15.95 *(978-1-59566-004-6(6))* QEB Publishing Inc.

Fischel, Emma. Land of the lost Teddies. Howarth, Daniel, illus. rev. ed. 2003. 32p. (J). (gr. 2-18). pap. 4.95 *(978-0-7945-0402-1(7),* Usborne) EDC Publishing.

Fox, Nita. Captain Benjamin Dale. Wallace, Andrea, illus. 2008. 32p. (J). (gr. -1-3). pap. 5.99 *(978-0-9816107-0-2(6))* Fox's Den Publishing.

Freedman, Claire. Cuddle Bear. Scott, Gavin, illus. 2013. 28p. (J). 12.99 *(978-1-61067-081-4(7))* Kane Miller.

—Night-Night, Emily! Massey, Jane, illus. 2005. 32p. (J). 6.95 *(978-1-58925-390-2(6))* Tiger Tales.

—Night-Night, Emily! Massey, Jane, tr. Massey, Jane, illus. 2003. 32p. (J). (gr. -1-1). tchr. ed. 15.95 *(978-1-58925-032-1(X))* Tiger Tales.

Freedman, Claire & Scott, Gavin. Cuddle Bear. 2013. (ENG.). (J). 26.99 *(978-1-61067-193-4(7))* Kane Miller.

Freeman, Don. Christmas Is Here, Corduroy! 2007. (Corduroy Ser.). (ENG., Illus.). 16p. (J). (gr. -1-k). 5.99 *(978-0-448-44650-9(2),* Grosset & Dunlap) Penguin Young Readers Group.

—Corduroy. 2011. (Corduroy Ser.). (ENG.). 28p. (J). (gr. -1 — 1). bds. 11.99 *(978-0-670-01311-1(0),* Viking Books for Young Readers) Penguin Young Readers Group.

—Corduroy Book & Bear. 2008. (Corduroy Ser.). (ENG.). 32p. (J). (gr. -1-k). 17.99 *(978-0-670-06342-0(8),* Viking Books for Young Readers) Penguin Young Readers Group.

—Corduroy's Tiny Treasury, 5 bks., Set. McCue, Lisa, illus. 2010. (Corduroy Ser.). (ENG.). 10p. (J). (gr. -1 — 1). 9.99 *(978-0-670-01230-5(0),* Viking Books for Young Readers) Penguin Young Readers Group.

—A Pocket for Corduroy. 2015. (Corduroy Ser.). (ENG.). 32p. (J). (— 1). bds. 7.99 *(978-0-451-47113-0(X),* Viking Books for Young Readers) Penguin Young Readers Group.

French, Mary B. Bear-Ly There with Compass. Coffey, Kevin, illus. 2012. 122p. pap. 6.00 *(978-0-9852821-0-3(X))* Mary B./French.

Garton, Sam. I Am Otter. Garton, Sam, illus. 2014. (ENG., Illus.). 32p. (J). (gr. -1-3). 16.99 *(978-0-06-224775-9(1))* HarperCollins Pubs.

—Otter Goes to School. Garton, Sam, illus. 2016. (Illus.). 32p. (J). (gr. -1-3). 17.99 *(978-0-06-235225-5(3))* HarperCollins Pubs.

—Otter: Hello, Sea Friends! Garton, Sam, illus. 2016. (My First I Can Read Ser.). (Illus.). 32p. (J). (gr. -1-3). pap. 3.99 *(978-0-06-236660-3(2))* HarperCollins Pubs.

—Otter in Space. Garton, Sam, illus. 2015. (ENG., Illus.). 32p. (J). (gr. -1-3). 16.99 *(978-0-06-224776-6(X))* HarperCollins Pubs.

—Otter: Oh No, Bath Time! Garton, Sam, illus. 2016. (My First I Can Read Ser.). (Illus.). 32p. (J). (gr. -1-3). pap. 3.99 *(978-0-06-236657-3(2))* HarperCollins Pubs.

—Otter: the Best Job Ever! Garton, Sam, illus. 2016. (My First I Can Read Ser.). (Illus.). 32p. (J). (gr. -1-3). pap. 3.99 *(978-0-06-236654-2(8))* HarperCollins Pubs.

Gilpin, Esther. How the Bear Got Its Hair. 2008. 24p. pap. 12.99 *(978-1-4389-1584-5(5))* AuthorHouse.

Goodin, Robert. The Kurdles. 2015. (ENG., Illus.). 64p. 24.99 *(978-1-60699-832-8(3),* 699832) Fantagraphics Bks.

Goss, Matt. Bear Crimbo. 2010. (ENG., Illus.). 72p. (J). 17.95 *(978-0-9815381-3-6(4))* Hilton Publishing Co.

Graham, Crystal L. My Little Teddy Bear: Has Anybody Seen... . 2010. 16p. 8.49 *(978-1-4520-0425-9(0))* AuthorHouse.

Grams, Kimberly. Smedley & the Sprinkle Machine. 2005. 59p. pap. 16.95 *(978-1-4241-0184-9(0))* PublishAmerica, Inc.

Granger, Trudi. Always There Bear. Llewhellin, Gareth, illus. 2015. (ENG.). 32p. (J). (-k). 16.99 *(978-1-63220-434-9(7),* Sky Pony Pr.) Skyhorse Publishing Co., Inc.

Greenberg, Nicki. Teddy Took the Train. Greenberg, Nicki, illus. 2015. (ENG., Illus.). 32p. (J). (gr. -1-1). 15.99 *(978-1-76011-213-4(5))* Allen & Unwin AUS. Dist: Independent Pubs. Group.

Group/McGraw-Hill, Wright. The Humpback Tedy: Level E, 6 vols. (Take Twostm Ser.). 16p. 29.95 *(978-0-322-08952-5(2))* Wright Group/McGraw-Hill.

Guy, Ginger Foglesong & Guy, Ginger F. Siesta. Moreno, Rene King, illus. 2005. (ENG & SPA.). 32p. (J). (gr. -1-k). 17.99 *(978-0-06-056061-4(4),* Greenwillow Bks.) HarperCollins Pubs.

Hall, Caroline V. Rhett & Abby: Abby's New Home. 2011. 40p. pap. 15.95 *(978-1-4497-1887-9(6),* WestBow Pr.) Author Solutions, Inc.

Hall, Christina. Can Checkers Come Too? Hall, Lowell, illus. 2011. 36p. pap. 24.95 *(978-1-4560-7753-2(8))* America Star Bks.

Hankins, Jim. Teddy Scares Volume 3. 2008. (Illus.). 52p. (YA). pap. 6.95 *(978-0-9791050-2-9(1))* Ape Entertainment.

Hannigan, Paula. Hugs for You. Brown, Heather, illus. 2012. (ENG.). 10p. (J). (-k). bds. 7.99 *(978-1-4494-2192-2(X))* Andrews McMeel Publishing.

Hardwell, Gary D. A Boo Bears' Story: Stormy Night. 2007. (Illus.). 36p. per. 10.00 *(978-0-9792016-9-1(1))* Professional Publishing Hse. LLC.

Harris, Joe. Wars in Toyland. 2013. (ENG., Illus.). 104p. 19.99 *(978-1-934964-93-4(X),* 9781934964934) Oni Pr., Inc.

Hayes, Geoffrey. Patrick Eats His Peas & Other Stories. Hayes, Geoffrey, illus. 2013. (ENG., Illus.). 32p. (J). (gr. -1-3). 12.95 *(978-1-935179-34-4(9))* TOON Books / RAW Junior, LLC.

—Patrick in a Teddy Bear's Picnic & Other Stories. 2011. (ENG., Illus.). 32p. (J). (gr. -1-3). 12.95 *(978-1-935179-09-2(8))* TOON Books / RAW Junior, LLC.

Hayward, Jason. Teddy Bear Adventures. 2011. 40p. pap. 24.95 *(978-1-4560-4068-0(5))* America Star Bks.

Hegg, Tom & Hanson, Warren. Peef & the Baby Sister. Hegg, Tom & Hanson, Warren, illus. 2006. (ENG., Illus.). 36p. (J). (gr. -1-3). 16.95 *(978-0-931674-67-9(0),* Waldman House Pr.) TRISTAN Publishing, Inc.

Henisz, Jerzy E. SOPHIE in PARIS & other Stories. 2009. 99p. pap. 9.46 *(978-0-557-09520-9(4))* Lulu Pr., Inc.

Henisz, Jerzy E. & Henisz, Sophie, illustrator. TEDDY BEAR who went on a Trip around the World & other Stories. 2007. 88p. (J). pap. 30.40 *(978-0-615-13851-0(9))* Henisz, Jerzy E.

Hennessy, B. G. Corduroy Lost & Found. Wheeler, Jody, illus. 2006. (Corduroy Ser.). (ENG.). 32p. (J). (gr. -1-k). 15.99 *(978-0-670-06100-6(X),* Viking Books for Young Readers) Penguin Young Readers Group.

Henny, Rose. Teddy Finds His Way: A Teddy Tale. Henny, Rose, illus. l.t. ed. 2005. (Illus.). 22p. (J). per. 17.95 *(978-0-9705458-7-9(8))* Royalty Bks. International, Inc.

Herrington, Chris. Harry & Hannah: The American Adventure. Pacheco, Jorge M., illus. 2003. (Adventures of Harry & Hannah Ser.). (ENG.). 72p. (J). (gr. 1-5). 15.00 *(978-0-9722343-0-6(6))* Herrington Teddy Bears.

Hesse, Karen. Brooklyn Bridge. Sheban, Chris, illus. 2011. (ENG.). 256p. (J). (gr. 5-9). pap. 9.99 *(978-0-312-67428-1(7),* 9780312674281) Square Fish.

Higginson, Sheila Sweeny, et al. All Stuffed Up. Disney Storybook Artists Staff, illus. 2013. (World of Reading Ser.). (ENG.). 32p. (J). (gr. -1-k). pap. 3.99 *(978-1-4231-7135-5(7))* Disney Pr.

Hill, Eric. Spot's Easter Surprise. Hill, Eric, illus. 2007. (Spot Ser.). (ENG., Illus.). 10p. (J). (gr. -1-k). bds. 5.99 *(978-0-399-24743-9(2),* Warne) Penguin Young Readers Group.

Hissey, Jane. Old Bear. 2013. (ENG., Illus.). 36p. (J). (gr. -1-1). 17.95 *(978-1-77049-481-7(2),* Tundra Bks.) Tundra Bks. CAN. Dist: Penguin Random Hse. LLC.

Holl, Robert. Apúrate, Teddy: Fiction-to-Fact Big Book. Forss, Ian, illus. enl. ed. 2004. (SPA.). (J). pap. 26.00 *(978-1-4108-2362-5(8),* 23628) Benchmark Education Co.

—Teddy on the Move. 2004. (Shared Connections Ser.). (J). pap. *(978-1-4108-1629-0(X));* instr.'s gde. ed. 27.00 *(978-1-4108-1605-4(2))* Benchmark Education Co.

Hope, Laura. The Story of a Plush Bear. 2005. pap. 9.95 *(978-1-55742-463-1(2))* Wildside Pr., LLC.

Hulst, W. G. van de & Hulst, Willem G. van de, illus. Bruno the Bear. 2014. (J). *(978-1-928136-03-3(6))* Inheritance Pubns.

Inkpen, Mick. Threadbear. 2016. (ENG., Illus.). 32p. (J). (gr. -1-k). pap. 8.99 *(978-1-4449-2405-3(2))* Hachette Children's Group GBR. Dist: Hachette Bk. Group.

—Threadbear. 2007. (ENG., Illus.). 32p. (J). (gr. -1-k). pap. 9.99 *(978-0-340-93109-7(4))* Hodder & Stoughton GBR. Dist: Hachette Bk. Group.

Ira Sleeps Over. 2005. (J). *(978-1-59564-973-7(5))* Steps To Literacy, LLC.

Judd, Christopher M. Bearable Moments. 2005. (J). 16.95 *(978-0-9766666-1-5(8))* Arcadian Hse.

Kantorovitz, Sylvie. The Very Tiny Baby. Kantorovitz, Sylvie, illus. 2014. (ENG., Illus.). 32p. (J). (gr. -1-2). lib. bdg. 14.95 *(978-1-58089-445-6(3))* Charlesbridge Publishing, Inc.

—The Very Tiny Baby. 2014. (J). pap. *(978-1-58089-446-3(1))* Charlesbridge Publishing, Inc.

Karpinski, David. Sarah's Christmas Presence. 2006. 58p. pap. 8.95 *(978-0-7414-3411-1(3))* Infinity Publishing.

Kats, Jewel. Teddy Bear Princess: A Story about Sharing & Caring. Arts, Richa Kinra, illus. 2012. 24p. (-18). pap. 13.95 *(978-1-61599-163-1(8),* Marvelous Spirit Pr.) Loving Healing Pr., Inc.

Kelly, Katherine, text. Albert Bear & the Big Celebration. 2005. (J). 12.95 *(978-0-9773481-0-7(5))* Kelly, Katherine.

Kimball, Michael D. Alligator Bay: A Beary Tale. 2009. 132p. pap. 11.95 *(978-1-4401-1804-3(3))* iUniverse, Inc.

Kleback, Amanda. Hoo Hoo's Song. Kleback, Amanda & Kleback, Brian, illus. 2009. 24p. pap. 12.00 *(978-1-4389-1322-3(2))* AuthorHouse.

Kreloff, Elliot, illus. Where's Your Nose. 2010. 24p. (J). bds. *(978-1-60906-004-6(0))* Begin Smart LLC.

Landsberry, Belinda. Anzac Ted. 2016. (ENG., Illus.). 32p. (J). (gr. -1-5). 17.99 *(978-1-921966-56-9(4),* EK Bks.) Exisle Publishing Pty Ltd. AUS. Dist: Hachette Bk. Group.

Legrand, Martine & Delvaux, Nancy. ¡una nalgada por Favor! 2006. (SPA.). 28p. (J). *(978-958-30-1886-2(4))* Panamericana Editorial.

Lesley, Sharon. The Red Scarf & Other Stories. 2010. 165p. pap. 14.95 *(978-1-4457-6720-8(1))* Lulu Pr., Inc.

Little Teddy. (Bedtime Babies Ser.). (J). 6.99 *(978-1-57755-500-1(7))* Flying Frog Publishing, Inc.

Ludde & His Naughty Teddy Bear. 2003. Orig. Title: Ludde Och Busiga Nalle. (NOR, FIN, GER, FLE & DAN.). lib. bdg. 7.95 *(978-0-9740419-0-2(4))* words4u.

MacIver, Juliette. The Frog Who Lost His Underpants. Chapman, Cat, illus. 2014. (ENG.). 32p. (J). (gr. -1-1). 14.99 *(978-0-7636-6782-5(X))* Candlewick Pr.

Mahadeo Rdh, Elizabeth. Teddy Visits the Dentist. Barth, Alexandra, illus. 2012. 40p. pap. *(978-0-9569438-0-4(2))* Mahadeo Movement, The.

—Teddy Visits the Dentist: Teddy Gets a Filling. Barth, Alexandra, illus. 2012. 42p. (-18). pap. *(978-0-9569438-2-8(9))* Mahadeo Movement, The.

Mason, Bonita. T-Bear the Most Special Bear. Hendricks, Sandy, illus. 2008. 26p. (J). 19.95 *(978-0-9798718-0-1(8))* Encore Pubns.

Matsutani, Miyoko. Peek-A-Boo. Segawa, Yasuo, illus. 2006. 20p. (J). (gr. -1). 10.95 *(978-1-74126-047-2(7))* R.I.C. Pubns. AUS. Dist: SCB Distributors.

Mauldin, Mary. What a Carrot-Astrophy! 2011. 32p. pap. 14.99 *(978-1-4634-3366-6(2))* AuthorHouse.

McCue, Lisa, illus. Corduroy's Thanksgiving. 2006. (Corduroy Ser.). (ENG.). 16p. (J). (gr. -1 — 1). bds. 5.99 *(978-0-670-06108-2(5),* Viking Books for Young Readers) Penguin Young Readers Group.

McGrath, Barbara Barbieri. Teddy Bear Counting. Nihoff, Tim, illus. 2010. (McGrath Math Ser.). (ENG.). 32p. (J). (gr. -1-2). 16.95 *(978-1-58089-215-5(9));* pap. 7.95 *(978-1-58089-216-2(7))* Charlesbridge Publishing, Inc.

McKee, David. Elmer & the Lost Teddy. McKee, David, illus. 2004. (Elmer Bks.). (Illus.). 32p. (J). 9.99 *(978-0-06-075243-9(2))* HarperCollins Pubs.

—El Principe Pedro y el oso de Peluche. (SPA.). (J). 7.95 *(978-958-04-6258-3(5))* Norma S.A. COL. Dist: Distribuidora Norma, Inc.

McKennon, Tony. You're Moving Where?! 2008. 40p. pap. 18.55 *(978-1-4389-1397-1(4))* AuthorHouse.

McLean, P. J. The Bears & the Baby. Jenkins, C. S., illus. 2012. 44p. pap. 17.44 *(978-1-4669-1335-6(5))* Trafford Publishing.

McMahon, Susan. Sean O'Grady. 2009. 12p. pap. 9.50 *(978-1-4389-5149-2(3))* AuthorHouse.

McPhail, David. Ben Loves Bear. 2013. (David Mcphail's Love Ser.). (ENG., Illus.). 22p. (J). (gr. -1-k). bds. 8.95 *(978-1-4197-0386-7(2),* Abrams Appleseed) Abrams, Inc.

—The Teddy Bear. McPhail, David, illus. 2005. (ENG., Illus.). 32p. (J). (gr. -1-1). reprint ed. pap. 8.99 *(978-0-8050-7882-4(7),* 9780805078824) Square Fish.

McRitchie, Mike. Best Friends. 2009. 25p. 13.95 *(978-0-578-03644-1(4))* McRitchie, Mike.

Meserve, Jessica. Bedtime Without Arthur. Meserve, Jessica, illus. 2010. (ENG., Illus.). 32p. (J). (gr. -1-3). 16.95 *(978-0-7613-5497-0(2))* Lerner Publishing Group.

Meyers, Susan. Bear in the Air. Bates, Amy, illus. 2010. (ENG.). 32p. (J). (gr. k-2). 15.95 *(978-0-8109-8398-4(2),* Abrams Bks. for Young Readers) Abrams, Inc.

Milne, A. A. Winnie Ille Pu. Lenardo, Alexandro, tr. from ENG. 2015.Tr. of Winnie-the-Pooh. (LAT., Illus.). 170p. (J). pap. 19.95 *(978-4-87187-394-9(3))* Ishi Pr. International.

Minarik, Else Holmelund. Un Beso para Osito. 2006. (Osito / Little Bear Ser.).Tr. of Kiss for Little Bear. (SPA.). 34p. (gr. k-3). pap. 9.95 *(978-84-204-0202-4(8))* Santillana USA Publishing Co., Inc.

Moncure, Jane Belk. The Bears Upstairs: A Book of Creative Dramatics. Girouard, Patrick, illus. 2013. (Magic Castle Readers Ser.). (ENG.). 32p. (J). (gr. -1-2). 25.64 *(978-1-62323-564-2(2),* 206302) Child's World, Inc., The.

Mooney, Bel. Mr. Tubs Is Lost. 2006. (Blue Bananas Ser.). (ENG., Illus.). 48p. (J). (gr. -1-3). lib. bdg. *(978-0-7787-0858-2(6))* Crabtree Publishing Co.

Moore, Mel. Mr P's Tale or Two. 2006. (Illus.). 21p. (J). per. *(978-0-9775919-1-6(3))* Carpe Diem Publishing.

Myers, Robin. Pinky Rabbit Learns to Share. 2008. 20p. pap. 24.95 *(978-1-60703-937-2(0))* America Star Bks.

Nash, Sarah. Scaredy Bear. Everitt-Stewart, Andy, illus. 2009. (Stories to Grow with Ser.). 24p. (J). (gr. -1-2). 22.60 *(978-1-60754-472-2(5))* Windmill Bks.

Naylor, Phyllis Reynolds. Please Do Feed the Bears. Escriva, Ana Lopez, illus. 2007. (ENG.). 40p. (J). (gr. -1-2). 11.99 *(978-1-4169-6750-7(8),* Simon & Schuster/Paula Wiseman Bks.) Simon & Schuster/Paula Wiseman Bks.

Nield, Joan. Children's Story Book. 2008. (Illus.). 24p. 11.04 *(978-1-4251-2449-6(6))* Trafford Publishing.

Niland, Kilmeny. Two Tough Teddies. Niland, Kilmeny, illus. 2008. (ENG., Illus.). 24p. (J). (gr. -1-k). 14.95 *(978-1-921272-05-9(8))* Little Hare Bks. AUS. Dist: Independent Pubs. Group.

—Two Tough Teddies Boxed Set. 2008. (Illus.). *(978-1-921272-63-9(5))* Little Hare Bks. AUS. Dist: HarperCollins Pubs. Australia.

Nosy Crow Staff. Bizzy Bear: Christmas Helper. Davies, Benji, illus. 2016. (Bizzy Bear Ser.). (ENG.). 8p. (J). (— 1). bds. 6.99 *(978-0-7636-8004-6(4),* Nosy Crow) Candlewick Pr.

Outram, Evelyn. Sav & Josh O Lucky's Christmas Adventure & Magic Street. 2010. 56p. pap. 17.95 *(978-1-60911-876-1(6),* Eloquent Bks.) Strategic Book Publishing & Rights Agency (SBPRA).

Parragon Staff. Celebrate the Year with Winnie the Pooh. 2010. (Disney Diecut Classics). 72p. (J). (gr. -1-1). *(978-1-4075-8902-2(4))* Parragon, Inc.

Payne-Sylvester, Linda. Here Comes Christmas & the Teddy Bears Get Ready. 2012. (ENG.). pap. 12.95 *(978-1-4675-5249-3(6))* Independent Pub.

Peck, James E. Meet Mr. Chair Bear. 2008. 52p. pap. 16.95 *(978-1-4241-7959-6(9))* America Star Bks.

Petrovic, Svetlana. Brown Bear, White Bear. Hardy, Vincent, illus. 2009. 28p. (J). (gr. -1-3). 17.00 *(978-0-8028-5353-0(6),* Eerdmans Bks For Young Readers) Eerdmans, William B. Publishing Co.

Publications International Ltd. Staff, ed. Dora Says Good Night. 2011. 12p. (J). bds. 11.98 *(978-1-4508-0764-7(X))* Phoenix International Publications, Inc.

—Winnie the Pooh. 2005. (J). 14.98 *(978-1-4127-3470-7(3))* Publications International, Ltd.

Rack, Charlene. The Adventures of Delaware Bear & Young George Washington. 2011. 24p. (gr. 1-2). pap. 12.79 *(978-1-4567-5681-9(8))* AuthorHouse.

Randall, Chuck. Curley's Wish Comes True. 2013. 28p. pap. 24.95 *(978-1-4626-9795-3(X))* America Star Bks.

Random House Staff. Super Soap (Team Umizoomi) O'Connell, Lorraine, illus. 2013. (Step into Reading Ser.). (ENG.). 24p. (J). (gr. -1-2). pap. 3.99 *(978-0-449-81387-4(8),* Random Hse. Bks. for Young Readers) Random Hse. Children's Bks.

Richards, J. Danielle Jennson, Life Lessons of a Little Clown. 2006. 72p. per. 8.95 *(978-1-59824-187-7(7))* E-BookTime LLC.

Robaard, Jedda. Milo & Millie. Robaard, Jedda, illus. 2014. (ENG., Illus.). 32p. (J). (-k). 14.99 *(978-0-7636-6783-2(8))* Candlewick Pr.

Robinson, Joan G. The Teddy Robinson Storybook. 2015. (Macmillan Classics Ser.). (ENG., Illus.). 272p. (J). (gr. k-2). 16.99 *(978-1-4472-7305-9(2))* Pan Macmillan GBR. Dist: Independent Pubs. Group.

Robinson, Marquita E. Teddy's Bear, 1 vol. Roscoe Robinson, illus. 2009. 15p. pap. 24.95 *(978-1-60749-249-8(0))* America Star Bks.

Roman, Javier. Adventures of Tinturu & Kumachan the M. 2007. (Illus.). 48p. pap. 16.95 *(978-1-4241-1626-3(0))* PublishAmerica, Inc.

Rose, Alea. There's a Bear in my House. Witt, Rici, illus. 2009. (ENG.). 24p. (J). reprint ed. 10.59 *(978-0-9803367-1-9(6))* Buttermoth Pr. AUS. Dist: Lulu Pr., Inc.

Rose, Eya. The Magic Blanket. 2011. 24p. pap. 15.99 *(978-1-4653-4617-9(1))* Xlibris Corp.

Rosen, Michael. Red Ted & the Lost Things. Stewart, Joel, illus. 2009. (ENG.). 40p. (J). (gr. -1-2). pap. 8.99 *(978-0-7636-4624-0(5))* Candlewick Pr.

Sarah Taylor. The Teddy That Went to Iraq. Baker, David, illus. 2011. 28p. pap. 24.95 *(978-1-4560-8382-3(1))* America Star Bks.

Saunders, Katie. Toddler Time Teddy Hunt. 2014. (Toddler Bks.). (ENG.). 12p. (J). (gr. -1 — 1). bds. 10.99 *(978-0-7641-6722-5(7))* Barron's Educational Series, Inc.

Schaffer, Jacqueline. Porsha & the Great Snowmen Adventure. 2009. 36p. pap. 15.99 *(978-1-4490-5421-2(8))* AuthorHouse.

Schauer, Tosca M. J. Bear. 2013. 28p. pap. 16.99 *(978-1-4582-0783-8(8),* Abbott Pr.) Author Solutions, Inc.

Schertle, Alice. The Adventures of Old Bo Bear. Parkins, David, illus. 2005. (J). 16.95 *(978-978-081-183-9(4))* Chronicle Bks. LLC.

Schliewen, Richard. Paulina's Teddy Bear Journey. Visaya, Artemio, illus. 2012. 104p. 24.95 *(978-1-62709-055-1(X));* pap. 19.95 *(978-1-4626-9597-3(3))* America Star Bks.

Scott, MaryJo. Corduroy's Seasons. McCue, Lisa, illus. 2016. (Corduroy Ser.). (ENG.). 14p. (J). (— 1). bds. 5.99 *(978-0-451-47249-6(7),* Viking Books for Young Readers) Penguin Young Readers Group.

Seeger, Laura Vaccaro. Dog & Bear: Tricks & Treats. Seeger, Laura Vaccaro, illus. 2014. (Dog & Bear Ser.). (ENG., Illus.). 32p. (J). (gr. -1-3). 14.99 *(978-1-59643-632-9(8),* 9781596436329) Roaring Brook Pr.

Senior, Suzy. Teddy Bear Says I Love You. Mitchell, Melanie, illus. 2014. (Teddy Bear Says Ser.). (ENG.). 12p. (J). (— 1). bds. 7.99 *(978-0-7459-6437-9(0))* Lion Hudson PLC GBR. Dist: Independent Pubs. Group.

—Teddy Bear Says Let's Hug. Mitchell, Melanie, illus. 2014. (Teddy Bear Says Ser.). (ENG.). 12p. (J). (— 1). bds. 7.99 *(978-0-7459-6439-3(7))* Lion Hudson PLC GBR. Dist: Independent Pubs. Group.

—Teddy Bear Says Wake Up! Mitchell, Melanie, illus. 2014. (Teddy Bear Says Ser.). (ENG.). 12p. (J). (— 1). bds. 7.99 *(978-0-7459-6438-6(9))* Lion Hudson PLC GBR. Dist: Independent Pubs. Group.

Shanks, Ronnie. Oh Where, Oh Where Is My Teddy Bear? 2004. 22p. pap. 24.95 *(978-1-4137-2693-0(3))* PublishAmerica, Inc.

Sharp, Kevin. The Amazing Adventures of Ted Shuttle: Book One. 2012. (Illus.). 24p. pap. 19.82 *(978-1-4772-4286-5(4))* AuthorHouse.

Sovago-Royal, Sandra. Magimus. 2009. 33p. (J). pap. 19.95 *(978-1-4327-4375-8(9))* Outskirts Pr., Inc.

Stadler, John. Catilda. Stadler, John, illus. 2010. (ENG., Illus.). 32p. (J). (gr. -1-k). 16.99 *(978-1-4424-2939-0(9),* Atheneum Bks. for Young Readers) Simon & Schuster Children's Publishing.

Stead, Philip C. Jonathan & the Big Blue Boat. Stead, Philip C., illus. 2011. (ENG., Illus.). 32p. (J). (gr. -1-2). 16.99 *(978-1-59643-562-9(3),* 9781596435629) Roaring Brook Pr.

Stephens, Edna Cucksey, et al. You & Me Make Three. Drescher, Heather, illus. 2008. (Build-A-Bear Workshop Ser.). 32p. (J). (gr. -1-3). 0.00 *(978-0-9798088-0-7(4))* EDCO Publishing, Inc.

—You & Me Make Three & Accompanying Plush B. B. the Bear. Drescher, Heather, illus. 2008. 32p. (J). 35.00 *(978-0-9798088-2-1(0))* EDCO Publishing, Inc.

Stoddard, Jutta. Miss Elli. 2004. 28p. per. 18.65 *(978-1-4134-3423-1(1))* Xlibris Corp.

Sullivan, Silvia. Hip Hip Hurray We Found Teddy: A Book Series to Teach Children Practical Life Skills & Eco-Friendly Skills. 2008. 32p. pap. 15.48 *(978-1-4343-5897-4(6))* AuthorHouse.

Sully, Katherine. Where, Oh Where Is Huggle Buggle Bear? Samuel, Janet, illus. 2013. (J). *(978-1-4351-4776-8(6))* Barnes & Noble, Inc.

Sutherland, Keith. Two Tubby Teddies Have a Very Busy Week. 2013. 40p. pap. *(978-0-9545288-7-4(5))* D S Press.

Tangerine Designs Ltd. Cuddle up Teddy: A Soft & Snuggly Pillow Book. 2014. (Sleepy Cuddle Pillow Bks.). (ENG.). 8p. (J). (gr. -1 — 1). 11.99 *(978-1-4380-0439-6(7))* Barron's Educational Series, Inc.

TUV

Teddy Bear-Duck. 2003. (J). per. *(978-1-57657-160-6(2))* Paradise Pr., Inc.
Teddy Bear Frog. 2003. (J). per. *(978-1-57657-161-3(0))* Paradise Pr., Inc.
Teddy Bear-House. 2003. (J). per. *(978-1-57657-162-0(9))* Paradise Pr., Inc.
Teddy Bear-Sheep. 2003. (J). per. *(978-1-57657-163-7(7))* Paradise Pr., Inc.
Teddy in the Toyshop. Date not set. (Illus.). (J). bds. 1.98 *(978-0-7525-9841-3(4))* Parragon, Inc.
Thomas Nelson. Ten Little Teddy Bears Splashing in the Bath. 2016. (ENG.). 24p. (gr. -1). bds. *(978-1-78598-469-3(1))* Make Believe Ideas.
Toews, Sheena. Beary Fun! 2004. 48p. pap. 10.95 *(978-1-57377-189-4(9),* 0-1988-4-02506-1) Eas'l Pubns.
—Beary Snowy. 2004. 56p. pap. 10.95 *(978-1-57377-196-2(1),* 0-1988-4-02512-2) Eas'l Pubns.
Trasler, Janee. Mimi & Bear in the Snow. Trasler, Janee, illus. (Mimi & Bear Ser.). (ENG., Illus.). (J). (gr. -1-k). 2015. 26p. bds. 7.99 *(978-0-374-30093-7(3),* 9780374300937) 2014. 32p. 16.99 *(978-0-374-34971-4(1),* 9780374349714) Farrar, Straus & Giroux. (Farrar, Straus & Giroux (BYR)).
—Mimi & Bear Make a Friend. Trasler, Janee, illus. 2017. (Mimi & Bear Ser.). (ENG., Illus.). 32p. (J). 16.99 *(978-0-374-30360-0(6),* 9780374303600, Farrar, Straus & Giroux (BYR)) Farrar, Straus & Giroux.
Ungerer, Tomi. Otto: The Autobiography of a Teddy Bear. 2010. (ENG., Illus.). 36p. (gr. 7-17). 16.95 *(978-0-7148-5766-4(1))* Phaidon Pr., Inc.
Valentine, Madeline. George in the Dark. 2014. (ENG., Illus.). 40p. (J). (gr. -1-2). 16.99 *(978-0-449-81334-8(7));* lib. bdg. 19.99 *(978-0-449-81335-5(5))* Random Hse. Children's Bks. (Knopf Bks. for Young Readers).
Vaughan, Richard & Crews, Marcia. Three Bears of the Pacific Northwest. Trammell, Jeremiah, illus. 2016. (ENG.). 20p. (J). (— 1). bds. 9.99 *(978-1-63217-076-7(0),* Little Bigfoot) Sasquatch Bks.
Vaughan, Richard Lee & Vaughan, Marcia. Three Bears of the Pacific Northwest. Trammell, Jeremiah, illus. 2011. (ENG.). 32p. (J). (gr. -1-2). 17.99 *(978-1-57061-684-6(1),* Little Bigfoot) Sasquatch Bks.
Verrett, Michael. Cozmo the Elf. 2010. 86p. pap. 32.00 *(978-0-557-25717-1(4))* Lulu Pr., Inc.
Voigt, Cynthia. Teddy & Co. Zakimi, Paola, illus. 2016. (ENG.). 192p. (J). (gr. 2-5). 16.99 *(978-0-553-51160-4(2),* Knopf Bks. for Young Readers) Random Hse. Children's Bks.
Voremberg, Linda. Robbie: A Journey of Hope, 1 vol. 2009. 52p. pap. 16.95 *(978-1-60703-486-5(7))* America Star Bks.
Waber, Bernard. Quique Duerme Fuera de Casa. Mlawer, Teresa, tr. 2003. (SPA., Illus.). (J). (gr. k-2). pap. *(978-968-6579-15-4(X),* SI6510) Sistemas Tecnicos de Edicion, S.A. de C.V. MEX. Dist: Lectorum Pubns., Inc.
Wach, Martin. The Great West Virginia Snow Adventure: Teddy Bear Guardians of the Rain Forest. 2006. (Illus.). 32p. (J). 16.95 *(978-0-929915-42-5(9))* Headline Bks., Inc.
Walling, Lani. Clyde-Fred & the Color of Friendship. 2005. 23p. (J). 9.98 *(978-1-4116-6091-5(9))* Lulu Pr., Inc.
Walton, Jess. Introducing Teddy. MacPherson, Dougal, illus. 2016. (ENG.). 32p. (J). 16.99 *(978-1-68119-210-9(1),* 9781681192109, Bloomsbury USA Childrens) Bloomsbury Publishing USA.
Watt, Fiona. That's Not My Teddy... Wells, Rachel, illus. 2008. (Usborne Touchy-Feely Board Bks.). 8p. (J). (gr. -1). bds. 7.99 *(978-0-7945-2026-7(X),* Usborne) EDC Publishing.
Watt, Fiona & Wells, Rachel, eds. That's Not My Teddy: Its Paws Are Too Woolly. 2004. (Touchy-Feely Board Bks.). (SPA & ENG., Illus.). 1p. (J). (gr. -1-18). bds. 7.95 *(978-0-7460-3782-9(1))* EDC Publishing.
Webber, Barbara. Feeling Loved: A Ted E. Bear Story. 2013. 40p. pap. 15.95 *(978-1-4525-7162-1(7),* Balboa Pr.) Author Solutions, Inc.
Wells-Dunn, Mildred. Tid Bit the Teddy Bear. 2011. 36p. pap. 21.99 *(978-1-4500-5729-5(2))* Xlibris Corp.
Weston Woods Staff, creator. Corduroy. 2011. 38.75 *(978-0-545-14080-5(3));* 29.95 *(978-0-545-14916-7(9));* 18.95 *(978-0-545-14078-2(1))* Weston Woods Studios, Inc.
Wickstrom, Sylvie K. I Love You, Mister Bear. 2004. (Illus.). 40p. (J). (gr. -1-1). pap. 14.99 *(978-0-06-029331-4(4))* HarperCollins Pubs.
Wolfe, Frances. The Little Toy Shop. Wolfe, Frances, illus. 2008. (ENG., Illus.). 32p. (J). (gr. -1-2). 19.95 *(978-0-88776-865-1(2),* Tundra Bks.) Tundra Bks. CAN. Dist: Penguin Random Hse. LLC.
Young, Billy. Teddy the Bear. 2007. 27p. 19.95 *(978-1-84799-068-6(1))* Lulu Pr., Inc.

TEENAGE

see Adolescence; Youth

TEENAGE MUTANT NINJA TURTLES (FICTITIOUS CHARACTERS)—FICTION

ABDO Publishing. Teenage Mutant Ninja Turtles: New Animated Adventures. 2016. (Teenage Mutant Ninja Turtles: New Animated Adventures Ser.: 4). (ENG.). 24p. (J). lib. bdg. 96.84 *(978-1-61479-458-5(8),* Graphic Planet) Magic Wagon.
Belle, Magnolia. Teen Titans: Hot Garbage. 2016. (J). lib. bdg. 13.55 *(978-0-606-38325-7(5))* Turtleback Bks.
Byerly, Kenny Sternin & Eisinger, Justin. Teenage Mutant Ninja Turtles Animated: Never Say Xever/The Gauntlet, Vol. 2. 2013. (Illus.). 112p. (J). pap. 7.99 *(978-1-61377-753-4(1),* 9781613777534) Idea & Design Works, LLC.
Chanda, J-P. Four's a Crowd. Let's Draw Studio Staff, illus. 2005. (Teenage Mutant Ninja Turtles Ser.: No. 7). 24p. lib. bdg. 15.00 *(978-1-59054-832-5(9))* Fitzgerald Bks.
David, Peter. Out of the Shadows. Thomas, LeSean, illus. 2007. (Teenage Mutant Ninja Turtles Ser.). (ENG.). 96p. pap. 12.95 *(978-1-84576-146-2(4),* Titan Bks.) Titan Bks. Ltd. GBR. Dist: Penguin Random Hse. LLC.
Dicicco, Peter & Flynn, Ian. Teenage Mutant Ninja Turtles Amazing Adventures, Volume 2. 2016. (Teenage Mutant Ninja Turtles Amazing Adventures Ser.: 2). lib. bdg. 30.60 *(978-0-606-38731-6(5))* Turtleback Bks.
Eastman, Kevin B. & Waltz, Tom. Sins of the Fathers. Kuhn, Andy, illus. 2013. (Teenage Mutant Ninja Turtles Ser.). (ENG.). 104p. pap. 17.99 *(978-1-61377-568-4(7),* 9781613775684) Idea & Design Works, LLC.
—Teenage Mutant Ninja Turtles Volume 2: Enemies Old, Enemies New: Enemies Old, Enemies New. Duncan, Dan & Santolouco, Mateus, illus. 2016. (Teenage Mutant Ninja Turtles Ser.). (ENG.). 104p. pap. 17.99 *(978-1-61377-288-1(2),* 9781613772881) Idea & Design Works, LLC.
Eastman, Kevin B., et al. Teenage Mutant Ninja Turtles: the Works Volume 5. 2016. (Teenage Mutant Ninja Turtles Ser.). (ENG., Illus.). 176p. (gr. 11-12). 49.99 *(978-1-63140-635-5(3),* 9781631406355) Idea & Design Works, LLC.
—Teenage Mutant Ninja Turtles Volume 1: Change Is Constant: Change Is Constant. Duncan, Dan, illus. 2012. (Teenage Mutant Ninja Turtles Ser.). (ENG.). 104p. pap. 17.99 *(978-1-61377-139-6(8),* 9781613771396) Idea & Design Works, LLC.
Farago, Andrew. Teenage Mutant Ninja Turtles: The Ultimate Visual History. 2014. (ENG., Illus.). 192p. 50.00 *(978-1-60887-185-8(1))* Insight Editions.
Golden Books. Cosmic Chaos! (Teenage Mutant Ninja Turtles) Chabot, Jacob, illus. 2016. (Color Plus Crayons & Sticker Ser.). (ENG.). 48p. (J). (gr. -1-2). pap. 4.99 *(978-0-553-53908-0(6),* Golden Bks.) Random Hse. Children's Bks.
—The Official Ninja Turtle Handbook (Teenage Mutant Ninja Turtles) Golden Books, illus. 2014. (ENG., Illus.). 64p. (J). (gr. 2-4). pap. 6.99 *(978-0-553-50768-3(0),* Random Hse. Bks. for Young Readers) Random Hse. Children's Bks.
—Sewer Squad! Chabot, Jacob, illus. 2013. (Deluxe Stickerific Ser.). (ENG.). 64p. (J). (gr. -1-2). pap. 5.99 *(978-0-307-98226-1(2),* Golden Bks.) Random Hse. Children's Bks.
Golden Books, illus. Teenage Mutant Ninja Turtles Little Golden Book Library (Teenage Mutant Ninja Turtles), 5 vols. 2017. (ENG.). 120p. (J). (-k). 24.95 ***(978-1-5247-6411-1(6),*** Golden Bks.) Random Hse. Children's Bks.
Golden Books Staff. Follow the Ninja! Golden Books Staff & Lambe, Steve, illus. 2015. (Little Golden Book Ser.). (ENG.). 24p. (J). (-k). 4.99 *(978-0-553-51204-5(8),* Golden Bks.) Random Hse. Children's Bks.
Golden Books Staff & Smith, Geof. Green vs. Mean (Teenage Mutant Ninja Turtles) Golden Books Staff & Lambe, Steve, illus. 2015. (Little Golden Book Ser.). (ENG.). 24p. (J). (-k). 4.99 *(978-1-101-93465-4(4),* Golden Bks.) Random Hse. Children's Bks.
James, Hollis. Alien Attack! Random House Staff & Spaziante, Patrick, illus. 2015. (Step into Reading Ser.). (ENG.). 24p. (J). (gr. -1-1). 4.99 *(978-0-553-52286-0(8),* Random Hse. Bks. for Young Readers) Random Hse. Children's Bks.
Lewman, David. Out of the Shadows Junior Novelization. 2016. lib. bdg. 17.20 *(978-0-606-38886-3(9))* Turtleback Bks.
—The Rise of Tiger Claw. 2016. lib. bdg. 16.00 *(978-0-606-38489-6(8))* Turtleback Bks.
Mangual, Cynthia Ines. Bug Battle! (Teenage Mutant Ninja Turtles) Random House, illus. 2017. (Step into Reading Ser.). (ENG.). 24p. (J). (gr. -1-1). pap. 4.99 *(978-0-399-55882-5(9),* Random Hse. Bks. for Young Readers) Random Hse. Children's Bks.
McCollum, Rick, et al. Teenage Mutant Ninja Turtles Classics Volume 5. 2013. (Teenage Mutant Ninja Turtles Ser.). (ENG., Illus.). 132p. pap. 19.99 *(978-1-61377-639-1(X),* 9781613776391) Idea & Design Works, LLC.
Murphy, Steve, et al. Tales of the Teenage Mutant Ninja Turtles Volume 8. May, Ross et al, illus. 2016. (Teenage Mutant Ninja Turtles Ser.). (ENG.). 120p. pap. 19.99 *(978-1-63140-561-7(6),* 9781631405617) Idea & Design Works, LLC.
Nickelodeon Teenage Mutant Ninja Turtles Staff. Masked Heroes. 2013. (Dress-Up Ser.: 1). (ENG.). 24p. (J). (gr. -1-2). 11.99 *(978-0-7944-2922-5(X),* Reader's Digest Children's Bks.) Studio Fun International.
Publications International Ltd. Staff, ed. Look & Find: Nickelodeon: Teenage Mutant Ninja Turtles. 2013. 24p. (J). (gr. 1-3). 7.98 *(978-1-4508-1972-5(9),* ceaa0b59-853d-401a-91e5-5d3db3d7adab) Phoenix International Publications, Inc.
—Teenage Mutant Ninja Turtles(tm) Dojo: A Flashlight Adventure Sound Book. 2013. 12p. (J). bds. *(978-1-4508-7438-0(X),* 145087438X) Publications International, Ltd.
Random House. Beware of Bebop & Rocksteady! (Teenage Mutant Ninja Turtles) Spaziante, Patrick, illus. 2016. (Book & CD Ser.). (ENG.). 24p. (J). (gr. -1-2). pap. 6.99 *(978-0-399-55468-1(8),* Random Hse. Bks. for Young Readers) Random Hse. Children's Bks.
—Bigfoot's Spring Break (Teenage Mutant Ninja Turtles) Spaziante, Patrick, illus. 2016. (Pictureback(R) Ser.). (ENG.). 16p. (J). (gr. -1-2). 4.99 *(978-1-101-93174-5(4),* Random Hse. Bks. for Young Readers) Random Hse. Children's Bks.
—Epic Turtle Tales (Teenage Mutant Ninja Turtles) Random House, illus. 2015. (Pictureback(R) Ser.). (ENG., Illus.). 96p. (J). (gr. -1-2). 9.99 *(978-0-553-52471-0(2),* Random Hse. Bks. for Young Readers) Random Hse. Children's Bks.
—Flip the Lid! (Teenage Mutant Ninja Turtles: Half-Shell Heroes) Spaziante, Patrick, illus. 2016. (Lift-The-Flap Ser.). (ENG.). 12p. (J). (— 1). bds. 6.99 *(978-0-553-53909-7(4),* Random Hse. Bks. for Young Readers) Random Hse. Children's Bks.
—Heart of a Ninja (Teenage Mutant Ninja Turtles) Random House, illus. 2017. (ENG., Illus.). 16p. (J). (— 1). bds. 7.99 *(978-1-101-93696-2(7),* Random Hse. Bks. for Young Readers) Random Hse. Children's Bks.
—Mean Team. Random House, illus. 2016. (Step into Reading Ser.). (ENG., Illus.). 24p. (J). (gr. -1-1). pap. 4.99 *(978-1-5247-0173-4(4),* Random Hse. Bks. for Young Readers) Random Hse. Children's Bks.
—The Mutant Files (Teenage Mutant Ninja Turtles) Random House, illus. 2014. (Pictureback(R) Ser.). (ENG., Illus.). 24p. (J). (gr. -1-2). 5.99 *(978-0-385-38746-0(6),* Random Hse. Bks. for Young Readers) Random Hse. Children's Bks.
—Ninjas on Ice! (Teenage Mutant Ninja Turtles) Spaziante, Patrick, illus. 2015. (Glitter Picturebook Ser.). (ENG.). 16p. (J). (gr. -1-2). 5.99 *(978-0-553-52272-3(8),* Random Hse. Bks. for Young Readers) Random Hse. Children's Bks.
—Red Alert! (Teenage Mutant Ninja Turtles) Spaziante, Patrick, illus. 2015. (Pictureback(R) Ser.). (ENG.). 16p. (J). (gr. -1-2). 4.99 *(978-0-553-50901-4(2),* Random Hse. Bks. for Young Readers) Random Hse. Children's Bks.
—Saved by the Shell! (Teenage Mutant Ninja Turtles) Random House, illus. 2017. (Pictureback(R) Ser.). (ENG., Illus.). 24p. (J). (gr. -1-2). pap. 5.99 ***(978-1-5247-6984-0(3),*** Random Hse. Bks. for Young Readers) Random Hse. Children's Bks.
—Show Your Colors! (Teenage Mutant Ninja Turtles) Spaziante, Patrick, illus. 2015. (Board Book Ser.). (ENG.). 24p. (J). (— 1). bds. 4.99 *(978-0-553-49776-2(6),* Random Hse. Bks. for Young Readers) Random Hse. Children's Bks.
—Teenage Mutant Ninja Turtles Scratch-and-Sniff Book (Teenage Mutant Ninja Turtles) Random House & Spaziante, Patrick, illus. 2017. (Scratch-And-Sniff Book Ser.). (ENG.). 24p. (J). (gr. -1-k). 9.99 *(978-0-399-55375-2(4),* Random Hse. Bks. for Young Readers) Random Hse. Children's Bks.
Random House, illus. Teenage Mutant Ninja Collection, 4 vols. 2015. (ENG.). 512p. (J). (gr. 3-7). 20.96 *(978-1-101-93635-1(5),* Random Hse. Bks. for Young Readers) Random Hse. Children's Bks.
Random House Editors. Mean Team. Spaziante, Patrick, illus. 2016. (Step into Reading Level 2 Ser.). (ENG.). 24p. (J). (gr. -1-1). 14.75 *(978-0-606-39354-6(4))* Turtleback Bks.
—Ninja Dad! 2016. (Step into Reading Level 1 Ser.). lib. bdg. 14.75 *(978-0-606-38484-1(7))* Turtleback Bks.
—Out of the Shadows. 2016. (Step into Reading Level 2 Ser.). lib. bdg. 14.75 *(978-0-606-38896-2(6))* Turtleback Bks.
—Pizza Party! 2017. (Step into Reading Level 2 Ser.). lib. bdg. 14.75 ***(978-0-606-40253-8(5))*** Turtleback Bks.
Random House Editors. Too Much Ooze! (Teenage Mutant Ninja Turtles) Random House Editors & Spaziante, Patrick, illus. 2015. (Step into Reading Ser.). (ENG.). 24p. (J). (gr. -1-1). 4.99 *(978-0-553-50866-6(0),* Random Hse. Bks. for Young Readers) Random Hse. Children's Bks.
Random House Staff. Monkey Business (Teenage Mutant Ninja Turtles) Random House Staff & Spaziante, Patrick, illus. 2013. (Pictureback(R) Ser.). (ENG.). 16p. (J). (gr. -1-2). 3.99 *(978-0-449-81852-7(7),* Random Hse. Bks. for Young Readers) Random Hse. Children's Bks.
—Saved by the Shell! 2012. lib. bdg. 13.55 *(978-0-606-26800-4(6),* Turtleback) Turtleback Bks.
Random House Staff & Webster, Christy. Robot Rampage! (Teenage Mutant Ninja Turtles) Random House Staff & Spaziante, Patrick, illus. 2013. (Step into Reading Ser.). (ENG.). 48p. (J). (gr. k-3). pap. 3.99 *(978-0-307-98212-4(2),* Random Hse. Bks. for Young Readers) Random Hse. Children's Bks.
Spaziante, Patrick, illus. Meet Casey Jones. 2005. (Teenage Mutant Ninja Turtles Ser.: No. 1). 24p. (J). lib. bdg. 15.00 *(978-1-59054-836-3(1))* Fitzgerald Bks.
Sternin, Joshua & Ventimilia, J. R. Rise of the Turtles, Vol. 1. 2013. (Teenage Mutant Ninja Turtles Ser.). (ENG., Illus.). 112p. (J). (gr. 2-5). pap. 7.99 *(978-1-61377-613-1(6),* 9781613776131) Idea & Design Works, LLC.
—Teenage Mutant Ninja Turtles Animated Volume 3: the Showdown: The Showdown. 2014. (Teenage Mutant Ninja Turtles Ser.). (ENG., Illus.). 132p. (J). (gr. 2-5). pap. 7.99 *(978-1-61377-833-3(3),* 9781613778333) Idea & Design Works, LLC.
Teenage Mutant Ninja Turtles Sticker Activity Books. 2004. (J). act. bk. ed. 3.49 *(978-0-7666-1299-0(6),* 69645) Modern Publishing.
Teenage Mutant Ninja Turtles, Teenage Mutant. Teenage Mutant Ninja Turtles - Battle Ready! 2015. (Ultra Build It Ser.: 3). (ENG.). 24p. (J). (gr. 1-5). pap. 10.99 *(978-0-7944-3326-0(X),* Reader's Digest Children's Bks.) Studio Fun International.
Thomas, Jim. Super Slam Turtles! Spaziante, Patrick, illus. 2005. 22p. (J). lib. bdg. 15.00 *(978-1-4242-0971-2(4))* Fitzgerald Bks.
Tillworth, Mary. Skate Like a Ninja! (Teenage Mutant Ninja Turtles) Golden Books, illus. 2017. (Little Golden Book Ser.). (ENG.). 24p. (J). (-k). 4.99 *(978-0-399-55796-5(2),* Golden Bks.) Random Hse. Children's Bks.
Torres, J., et al. Teen Titans Go!: Ready for Action. 2017. (ENG., Illus.). (gr. 2-5). pap. 12.99 *(978-1-4012-6899-2(4))* DC Comics.
Walker, Landry. Teenage Mutant Ninja Turtles Amazing Adventures, Vol. 1. 2016. (Teenage Mutant Ninja Turtles Amazing Adventures Ser.: 1). lib. bdg. 30.60 *(978-0-606-37809-3(X))* Turtleback Bks.
Waltz, Tom & Eastman, Kevin B. Teenage Mutant Ninja Turtles: Enemies Old, Enemies New: Enemies Old, Enemies New. Santolouco, Mateus & Duncan, Dan, illus. 2016. (Teenage Mutant Ninja Turtles Ser.). (ENG.). 104p. pap. 17.99 *(978-1-63140-614-0(0),* 9781631406140) Idea & Design Works, LLC.
—Teenage Mutant Ninja Turtles Volume 3: Shadows of the Past: Shadows of the Past. Duncan, Dan, illus. 2016. (Teenage Mutant Ninja Turtles Ser.). (ENG.). 104p. pap. 17.99 *(978-1-61377-405-2(2),* 9781613774052) Idea & Design Works, LLC.
—Teenage Mutant Ninja Turtles Volume 5: Krang War: Krang War. Bates, Ben, illus. 2013. (Teenage Mutant Ninja Turtles Ser.). (ENG.). 104p. pap. 17.99 *(978-1-61377-640-7(3),* 9781613776407) Idea & Design Works, LLC.
Waltz, Tom, et al. Teenage Mutant Ninja Turtles Volume 1: Change Is Constant Deluxe Edition: Change Is Constant Deluxe Edition. Duncan, Dan, illus. 2012. (Teenage Mutant Ninja Turtles Ser.). (ENG.). 192p. 49.99 *(978-1-61377-233-1(5),* 9781613772331) Idea & Design Works, LLC.
Webster, Christy. Green Team! 2012. (Step into Reading Level 4 Ser.). lib. bdg. 13.55 *(978-0-606-26801-1(4),* Turtleback) Turtleback Bks.
—Green Team! (Teenage Mutant Ninja Turtles) Spaziante, Patrick, illus. 2012. (Step into Reading Ser.). (ENG.). 48p. (J). (gr. k-3). pap. 3.99 *(978-0-307-98070-0(7),* Random Hse. Bks. for Young Readers) Random Hse. Children's Bks.
—Robot Rampage! 2013. (Step into Reading Level 4 Ser.). lib. bdg. 13.55 *(978-0-606-26985-8(1),* Turtleback) Turtleback Bks.
Williamson, Joshua, et al. Allies & Enemies. 2016. (Teenage Mutant Ninja Turtles Ser.). (ENG., Illus.). 104p. pap. 17.99 *(978-1-63140-613-3(2),* 9781631406133) Idea & Design Works, LLC.

TEETH

see also Dentistry

Allsop, Marcus. Nos gustan nuestros dientes / we like our Teeth. 2011th alt. ed. 2012. (We Like To Ser.). (ENG.). 32p. pap. 10.95 *(978-1-935826-09-5(3))* Kalindi Pr.
—We Like Our Teeth. 2011th alt. ed. 2012. (We Like To Ser.). (ENG.). 32p. pap. 9.95 *(978-1-935826-06-4(9))* Kalindi Pr.
Andrus, Aubre. Gloss, Floss, & Wash: DIY Crafts & Recipes for a Fresh Face & Teeth. 2017. (DIY Day Spa Ser.). (ENG., Illus.). 48p. (gr. 4-5). lib. bdg. 31.32 *(978-1-5157-3447-5(1))* Capstone Press of Coughlan Cos.
Arnold, Quinn M. Dentists. 2017. (J). ***(978-1-60818-872-7(8),*** Creative Education) Creative Co., The.
—Seedlings: Dentists. 2017. (Seedlings Ser.). (ENG.). 24p. (J). (gr. -1-1). pap. 7.99 ***(978-1-62832-487-7(2),*** Creative Paperbacks) Creative Co., The.
Barr, Brady. Chomp! Fierce Facts about the BITE FORCE, CRUSHING JAWS, & MIGHTY TEETH of Earth's Champion Chewers. 2017. (ENG.). 96p. (J). (gr. 2-5). lib. bdg. 22.90 *(978-1-4263-2840-4(0),* National Geographic Children's Bks.) National Geographic Society.
Bernard, Jan. Toothpaste Before the Store. McGeehan, Dan, illus. 2012. (Before the Store Ser.). (ENG.). 32p. (J). (gr. 2-5). lib. bdg. 29.93 *(978-1-60973-684-2(2),* 201259) Child's World, Inc., The.
Boyd, Nicole. Let's Brush Our Teeth. 2008. (Rosen Real Readers: Upper Emergent Ser.). (ENG., Illus.). 12p. (gr. 1-2). pap. 5.90 *(978-0-8239-8133-5(9))* Rosen Publishing Group, Inc., The.
Bozzo, Linda. Amazing Animal Teeth. (Creature Features Ser.). 24p. 2009. (gr. 2-3). 42.50 *(978-1-61512-069-7(6))* 2008. (Illus.). (J). (gr. 3-7). lib. bdg. 22.60 *(978-1-4042-4170-1(1))* Rosen Publishing Group, Inc., The. (PowerKids Pr.).
Brignaud, Pierre, illus. Caillou: I Can Brush My Teeth: Healthy Toddler. 2017. (Caillou's Essentials Ser.). (ENG.). 24p. (J). (gr. -1-k). bds. 7.99 *(978-2-89718-356-1(X))* Caillouet, Gerry.
Capici, Gaetano. What Do They Do? Dentists. 2010. (Community Connections: What Do They Do? Ser.). (ENG.). 24p. (gr. 2-5). lib. bdg. 25.64 *(978-1-60279-806-9(0),* 200502) Cherry Lake Publishing.
Casado, Dami & Casado, Alicia. Los Dientes. 2005. (Sentidos y Algo Más). (SPA & ESP.). 16p. 8.99 *(978-84-272-6418-2(6))* Molino, Editorial ESP. Dist: Santillana USA Publishing Co., Inc.
Chambers, Catherine. The Tooth Fairy. Billiau, Loic, illus. 2015. (Autobiographies You Never Thought You'd Read! Ser.). (ENG.). 32p. (gr. 1-3). pap. 7.99 *(978-1-4109-7969-8(5),* Read Me!) Heinemann-Raintree.
Chandra, Deborah & Comora, Madeleine. George Washington's Teeth. Cole, Brock, illus. 2007. (ENG.). 40p. (J). (gr. -1-3). pap. 7.99 *(978-0-312-37604-8(9),* 9780312376048) Square Fish.
Cherrington, Janelle. Who Needs Teeth?, 6 vols., Set. 2003. (Phonics Readers 1-36 Ser.). (ENG.). 8p. (gr. k-1). pap. 29.70 *(978-0-7368-3211-3(4),* Phonics Readers) Capstone Press of Coughlan Cos.
Children's Press (New York, N.Y.) Staff & Scholastic, Inc. Staff, contrib. by. Brush, Brush, Brush! 2010. (Rookie Toddler: My Body Bks). (ENG.). 12p. (J). bds. 6.95 *(978-0-531-25236-9(1))* Scholastic Library Publishing.
Cobb, Vicki. Your Body Battles A Cavity. 2009. pap. 40.95 *(978-0-7613-4623-4(6))* Lerner Publishing Group.
—Your Body Battles a Cavity. Harris, Andrew, illus. Kunkel, Dennis, photos by. 2009. (Body Battles Ser.). (ENG.). 32p. (gr. 2-5). 25.26 *(978-0-8225-7469-9(1))* Lerner Publishing Group.
Collard, Sneed B., III. Teeth. Saroff, Phyllis V., illus. 2008. (ENG.). 32p. (J). (gr. k-3). per. 7.95 *(978-1-58089-121-9(7))* Charlesbridge Publishing, Inc.
Curry, Don L. Take Care of Your Teeth. 2005. (Rookie Read-About Health Ser.). (ENG., Illus.). 32p. (J). (gr. k-2). 20.50 *(978-0-516-25875-1(3),* Children's Pr.) Scholastic Library Publishing.
Dakota, Heather. Fangs! 2007. (Illus.). 96p. (J). *(978-0-545-02564-5(8),* Scholastic) Scholastic, Inc.
De Nijs, Erika. A Dentist's Job. 2015. (Community Workers Ser.). (ENG., Illus.). 24p. (J). (gr. 1-1). pap. 8.22 *(978-1-5026-0424-8(8))* Cavendish Square Publishing.
Dientes Sanos, 6 vols. 2010. (Dientes Sanos/Healthy Teeth Ser.).Tr. of Healthy Teeth. (ENG.). 24p. lib. bdg. 79.95 *(978-1-4296-4605-5(5))* Capstone Press of Coughlan Cos.
Downtown Bookworks Inc. Staff, et al. Shark-Tastic! 2011. (Science with Stuff Ser.: 1). (ENG.). 64p. (J). (gr. 1). lib. bdg. 12.99 *(978-1-935703-29-7(3))* Downtown Bookworks.
Dyan, Penelope. Teeth! Dyan, Penelope, illus. 2012. (Illus.). 34p. pap. 11.95 *(978-1-61477-060-2(3))* Bellissima Publishing, LLC.
Encyclopaedia Britannica, Inc. Staff, compiled by. How Many Teeth? 2008. 49.95 *(978-1-59339-661-9(9))* Encyclopaedia Britannica, Inc.
Gogerly, Liz. Teeth. Gordon, Mike, illus. 2008. (Looking after Me Ser.). (ENG.). 32p. (J). (gr. -1-3). pap. *(978-0-7787-4122-0(2));* lib. bdg. *(978-0-7787-4115-2(X))* Crabtree Publishing Co.
Gray, Susan H. Dinosaur Teeth. 2007. (Scholastic News Nonfiction Readers Ser.). (ENG., Illus.). 24p. (J). (gr. 1-2). 22.00 *(978-0-531-17484-5(0))* Scholastic Library Publishing.
Grigsby, Susan. Open Wide: The Ultimate Guide to Your Teeth. 2017. (Ultimate Guide To... Ser.). (ENG., Illus.). 48p. (J). (gr. 1-3). 16.95 *(978-1-63322-123-9(7),* Seagrass) Quarto Publishing Group USA.
Harrison, Emma. From Head to Toe: The Girls' Life Guide to Taking Care of You. Montagna, Frank, illus. 2004. 124p. (J). *(978-0-439-44983-0(9))* Scholastic, Inc.
Healthy Teeth. 2010. (Healthy Teeth Ser.). (ENG.). 24p. (gr. k-1). pap. 41.70 *(978-1-4296-5767-9(7),* Pebble Plus) Capstone Press of Coughlan Cos.
Herrington, Lisa M. I Have a Cavity. 2015. (Rookie Read-About(tm) Health Ser.). (ENG., Illus.). 32p. (J). lib. bdg. 25.00 *(978-0-531-21038-3(3))* Scholastic Library Publishing.
—I Lost a Tooth. 2015. (Rookie Read-About(tm) Health Ser.). (ENG., Illus.). 32p. (J). lib. bdg. 25.00 *(978-0-531-21013-0(8))* Scholastic Library Publishing.
Hoffman, Stephanie. Sharp Teeth, Flat Teeth. 2009. (Real Life Readers Ser.). 12p. (gr. 1-2). pap. 5.90 *(978-1-4042-7917-9(2),* Rosen Classroom) Rosen Publishing Group, Inc., The.

Hutmacher, Kimberly M. Your Senses at the Dentist's Office. 2011. (Out & about with Your Senses Ser.). (ENG.). 24p. (gr. k-1). lib. bdg. 26.65 *(978-1-4296-6664-0(1),* Pebble Plus) Capstone Press of Coughlan Cos.
Johanson, Sarah Margaret. Caillou - I Can Brush My Teeth. Brignaud, Pierre, illus. 2013. (Step by Step Ser.). (ENG.). 24p. (J). (gr. -1-k). bds. *(978-2-89718-032-4(3))* Filmer Ltd.
Kachlany, Scott C. Infectious Diseases of the Mouth. 2007. (Deadly Diseases & Epidemics Ser.). (Illus.). 112p. (YA). (gr. 9-12). lib. bdg. 34.95 *(978-0-7910-9242-2(9))* Facts On File, Inc.
Kenan, Tessa. Hooray for Dentists! 2017. (Bumba Books (tm) — Hooray for Community Helpers! Ser.). (ENG.). 24p. (J). (gr. -1-1). 25.32 ***(978-1-5124-3351-7(9))*** Lerner Publishing Group.
Kimmelman, Leslie. Ben Lost a Tooth. 2005. (IOpeners Ser.). (Illus.). 8p. (J). pap. 7.56 *(978-0-7652-5132-9(9))* Celebration Pr.
Kirk, Bill. My Tooth Is Loose: The Sum of Our Parts. Ruble, Eugene, illus. 2012. 20p. pap. 10.95 *(978-1-61633-258-7(1))* Guardian Angel Publishing, Inc.
Klug, Kirsten. Healthy Smiles! 2011. (Illus.). 12p. (J). pap. 6.50 *(978-0-9798173-6-6(6))* Bamboo River Pr.
Landau, Elaine. Cavities & Toothaches. 2008. (Head-to-Toe Health Ser.). 32p. (gr. 2-7). lib. bdg. 28.50 *(978-0-7614-2848-0(8),* Benchmark Bks.) Marshall Cavendish Corp.
Lee, David. My Visit to the Dentist. 2016. (Community Helpers Ser.). 00024p. (J). (gr. 1-1). pap. 8.25 *(978-1-4994-2704-2(2),* PowerKids Pr.) Rosen Publishing Group, Inc., The.
Levine, Sara. Tooth by Tooth. Spookytooth, T. S., illus. 2016. (ENG.). 32p. (J). (gr. k-4). 26.65 *(978-1-4677-5215-2(0),* Millbrook Pr.) Lerner Publishing Group.
—Tooth by Tooth: Comparing Fangs, Tusks, & Chompers. Spookytooth, T. S., illus. 2016. (ENG.). 32p. (gr. k-4). 39.99 *(978-1-4677-9727-6(8),* Millbrook Pr.) Lerner Publishing Group.
Levine, Sara C. Tooth by Tooth: Comparing Fangs, Tusks, & Chompers. Spookytooth, T. S., illus. 2016. (Millbrook Picture Bks). (ENG.). 32p. (gr. k-4). 39.99 *(978-1-5124-0732-7(1))* Lerner Publishing Group.
Libal, Autumn. Dental Care. Noyes, Nancy & Forman, Sara, eds. 2013. (Young Adult's Guide to the Science of Health Ser.: 15). 128p. (J). (gr. 7-18). 24.95 *(978-1-4222-2807-4(X))* Mason Crest.
Libal, Autumn & Hovius, Christopher. Taking Care of Your Smile: A Teen's Guide to Dental Care. 2006. (Science of Health Ser.). (Illus.). 128p. (YA). lib. bdg. 24.95 *(978-1-59084-846-3(2))* Mason Crest.
Lizb. My Clean Teeth. 2012. (Illus.). 40p. pap. 22.88 *(978-1-4772-4661-0(4))* AuthorHouse.
Llewellyn, Claire. Your Teeth. 2008. (Look after Yourself Ser.). (Illus.). 30p. (J). (gr. 1-4). lib. bdg. 28.50 *(978-1-59771-099-2(7))* Sea-To-Sea Pubns.
Machajewski, Sarah. What If I Break a Tooth? 2016. (Benched: Dealing with Sports Injuries Ser.). 24p. (J). (gr. 3-2). 22.60 *(978-1-4824-4886-3(6))* Stevens, Gareth Publishing LLLP.
Malaspina, Ann. Tooth Traditions Around the World. Chavarri, Elisa, illus. 2013. (World Traditions Ser.). (ENG.). 32p. (J). (gr. k-3). 28.50 *(978-1-61473-430-7(5),* 205135) Child's World, Inc., The.
Markle, Sandra. What If You Had Animal Teeth? McWilliam, Howard, illus. 2013. (ENG.). 32p. (J). (gr. -1-3). pap. 4.99 *(978-0-545-48438-1(3),* Scholastic Paperbacks) Scholastic, Inc.
—What If You Had Animal Teeth? 2013. (What If... ? Ser.). lib. bdg. 14.75 *(978-0-606-31504-3(7),* Turtleback) Turtleback Bks.
Miller, Edward. The Tooth Book: A Guide to Healthy Teeth & Gums. Miller, Edward, illus. (ENG., Illus.). 32p. (J). 2009. (gr. -1-3). pap. 7.99 *(978-0-8234-2206-7(2))* 2008. (gr. k-3). 17.95 *(978-0-8234-2092-6(2))* Holiday Hse., Inc.
O'hehir, Trisha. The Toothpaste Secret. O'hehir, Trisha, illus. 2003. (Illus.). 56p. (J). (gr. 2-6). 9.95 *(978-0-9659236-1-3(4))* Perio Reports.
Olberg, Henry. The Magical Tooth Fairies: The Secret of the Magic Dust. 2012. (J). pap. *(978-0-86715-567-9(1))* Quintessence Publishing Co., Inc.
Parker, Steve. How Do My Braces Work? Teeth, 1 vol. 2011. (Inside My Body Ser.). (ENG.). 32p. (gr. 3-5). lib. bdg. 30.65 *(978-1-4109-4019-3(5),* NA-r) Heinemann-Raintree.
The Perfect Prescription for Your Teeth. 2003. 29.95 *(978-0-9747253-0-7(7))* Health & Beauty Ctr., LLC.
Pirotta, Saviour. Teeth. 2003. (Starters Ser.). 24p. (J). lib. bdg. 21.35 *(978-1-58340-259-7(4))* Black Rabbit Bks.
Price, Dan. The Braces Journal. 2007. (ENG., Illus.). 72p. (J). (gr. 7-18). pap. 9.95 *(978-1-933662-72-5(7),* Applesauce Pr.) Cider Mill Pr. Bk. Pubs., LLC.
QEB Start Reading Together National Book Stores Edition: First Experiences: Going to the Dentist. 2006. (J). per. *(978-1-59566-260-6(X))* QEB Publishing Inc.
Randolph, Joanne. Whose Teeth Are These? 2009. (Animal Clues Ser.). 24p. (gr. 1-1). 42.50 *(978-1-61511-434-4(3));* (Illus.). (J). lib. bdg. 22.60 *(978-1-4042-4456-6(5))* Rosen Publishing Group, Inc., The. (PowerKids Pr.).
—Whose Teeth Are These? De Quién Son Estos Dientes? 2009. (Animal Clues / ¿Adivina de Quién Es? Ser.). (SPA & ENG., Illus.). 23p. (J). lib. bdg. 22.60 *(978-1-4358-2533-8(0),* PowerKids Pr.) Rosen Publishing Group, Inc., The.
—Whose Teeth Are These? / ¿de quién son estos Dientes? 2009. (Animal Clues / ¿Adivina de Quién Es? Ser.). (ENG & SPA.). 24p. (gr. 1-1). 42.50 *(978-1-61511-440-5(8),* Editorial Buenas Letras) Rosen Publishing Group, Inc., The.
Riehecky, Janet. Teeth, Claws, & Jaws: Animal Weapons & Defenses, 1 vol. 2012. (Animal Weapons & Defenses Ser.). (ENG.). 32p. (gr. 1-2). 26.65 *(978-1-4296-6506-3(8));* pap. 47.70 *(978-1-4296-8504-7(2));* pap. 8.10 *(978-1-4296-8012-7(1))* Capstone Press of Coughlan Cos. (Blazers).
Rissman, Rebecca. Teeth, 1 vol. 2011. (Animal Spikes & Spines Ser.). (ENG.). 24p. (gr. -1-1). pap. 6.29 *(978-1-4329-5049-1(5));* 22.65 *(978-1-4329-5042-2(8))* Heinemann-Raintree. (Acorn).
Rissman, Rebecca & Smith, Sian. Caring for Your Teeth, 1 vol. 2012. (Take Care of Yourself! Ser.). (ENG.). 24p. (gr. -1-1). 22.65 *(978-1-4329-6708-6(8));* pap. 6.29 *(978-1-4329-6715-4(0))* Heinemann-Raintree. (Acorn).
Royston, Angela. Tooth Decay. 2009. (How's Your Health? Ser.). (J). (gr. 1-4). 28.50 *(978-1-59920-221-1(2))* Black Rabbit Bks.
—Why Do I Brush My Teeth? 2012. (My Body Ser.). (ENG., Illus.). 24p. (gr. k-4). pap. 7.95 *(978-1-926853-99-4(7))* Saunders Bk. Co. CAN. Dist: RiverStream Publishing.
Rustad, Martha E. H. I Care for My Teeth. 2017. (Healthy Me Ser.). (ENG., Illus.). 24p. (gr. k-1). lib. bdg. 21.99 *(978-1-5157-3985-2(6))* Capstone Press of Coughlan Cos.
Salzmann, Mary Elizabeth. Brush Your Teeth! Healthy Dental Habits, 1 vol. 2014. (Healthy Habits Ser.). (ENG.). 24p. (J). (gr. -1-3). 24.21 *(978-1-62403-528-9(0))* ABDO Publishing Co.
—Taking Care of Your Teeth. 2004. (Healthy Habits Ser.). (ENG., Illus.). 24p. (J). (gr. k-3). lib. bdg. 24.21 *(978-1-59197-554-0(9),* SandCastle) ABDO Publishing Co.
Santillo, LuAnn. The Dentist. Santillo, LuAnn, ed. 2003. (Half-Pint Kids Readers Ser.). (Illus.). 7p. (J). (gr. -1-1). pap. 1.00 *(978-1-59256-120-9(9))* Half-Pint Kids, Inc.
Scholastic, Inc. Staff, contrib. by. Is Your Smile Like a Crocodile's? 2016. (Rookie Toddlers Ser.). (ENG.). 12p. (J). bds. 6.95 *(978-0-531-22454-0(6),* Children's Pr.) Scholastic Library Publishing.
Schuh, Mari C. All about Teeth, 1 vol. Saunders-Smith, Gail, ed. 2008. (Healthy Teeth Ser.). (ENG., Illus.). 24p. (gr. k-1). pap. 7.29 *(978-1-4296-1784-0(5),* Pebble Plus) Capstone Press of Coughlan Cos.
—At the Dentist, 1 vol. Saunders-Smith, Gail, ed. 2008. (Healthy Teeth Ser.). (ENG., Illus.). 24p. (gr. k-1). pap. 7.29 *(978-1-4296-1788-8(8),* Pebble Plus) Capstone Press of Coughlan Cos.
—Brushing Teeth, 1 vol. Saunders-Smith, Gail, ed. 2008. (Healthy Teeth Ser.). (ENG., Illus.). 24p. (gr. k-1). pap. 7.29 *(978-1-4296-1786-4(1),* Pebble Plus) Capstone Press of Coughlan Cos.
—Un Diente Está Flojo. Guzman Ferrer, Martin Luis, tr. from ENG. 2010. (Dientes Sanos/Healthy Teeth Ser.).Tr. of Loose Tooth. (SPA, ENG & MUL.). 24p. (gr. k-1). lib. bdg. 26.65 *(978-1-4296-4598-0(9))* Capstone Press of Coughlan Cos.
—Flossing Teeth, 1 vol. Saunders-Smith, Gail, ed. 2008. (Healthy Teeth Ser.). (ENG., Illus.). 24p. (gr. k-1). pap. 7.29 *(978-1-4296-1787-1(X),* Pebble Plus) Capstone Press of Coughlan Cos.
—Loose Tooth, 1 vol. Saunders-Smith, Gail, ed. 2008. (Healthy Teeth Ser.). (ENG., Illus.). 24p. (gr. k-1). pap. 7.29 *(978-1-4296-1789-5(6),* Pebble Plus) Capstone Press of Coughlan Cos.
—Snacks for Healthy Teeth, 1 vol. Saunders-Smith, Gail, ed. 2008. (Healthy Teeth Ser.). (ENG., Illus.). 24p. (gr. k-1). pap. 7.29 *(978-1-4296-1785-7(3),* Pebble Plus) Capstone Press of Coughlan Cos.
—Uso del Hilo Dental. 2010. (Dientes Sanos/Healthy Teeth Ser.).Tr. of Flossing Teeth. (SPA, ENG & MUL.). 24p. (gr. k-1). lib. bdg. 26.65 *(978-1-4296-4600-0(4))* Capstone Press of Coughlan Cos.
Schuh, Mari C. & Schuh, Mari. All about Teeth, 1 vol. Saunders-Smith, Gail, ed. 2008. (Healthy Teeth Ser.). (ENG., Illus.). 24p. (gr. k-1). 26.65 *(978-1-4296-1238-8(X),* Pebble Plus) Capstone Press of Coughlan Cos.
Silverstein, Virginia. Handy Health Guide to Your Teeth. 2013. (Handy Health Guides). 48p. (J). (gr. 5-12). pap. 8.95 *(978-1-4644-0503-7(4))* Enslow Pubs., Inc.
Silverstein, Virginia & Nunn, Laura Silverstein. Handy Health Guide to Your Teeth. 2013. (Handy Health Guides). 48p. (J). lib. bdg. 25.27 *(978-0-7660-4280-3(4))* Enslow Pubs., Inc.
Smith, Michael & Aguiler, Manny. A Smile: B una Sonrisa. Aguiler, Manny, illus. 2015. (SPA & ENG., Illus.). 36p. (J). *(978-0-9913454-5-8(2))* East West Discovery Pr.
Smith, Penny & Dorling Kindersley Publishing Staff. A Trip to the Dentist Level 1. 2006. (DK Readers Ser.). (ENG., Illus.). 32p. (J). (gr. k-2). pap. 3.99 *(978-0-7566-1914-5(9),* DK Children) Dorling Kindersley Publishing, Inc.
Somervill, Barbara. Dental Hygienist. 2010. (21st Century Skills Library: Cool Careers Ser.). (ENG.). 32p. (gr. 4-8). lib. bdg. 28.50 *(978-1-60279-938-7(5),* 200621) Cherry Lake Publishing.
Squires, Susanne. When I Lose My Tooth. 2011. 12p. (gr. 10-12). pap. 8.32 *(978-1-4567-6724-2(0))* AuthorHouse.
Steckel, Richard & Steckel, Michele, photos by. My Teeth. 2008. (Milestones Project Chewables Ser.). (ENG., Illus.). 20p. (J). (gr. k — 1). bds. 6.99 *(978-1-58246-212-7(7),* Tricycle Pr.) Random Hse. Children's Bks.
Swanson, Diane. Teeth That Stab & Grind. 2003. (Up Close Ser.). (Illus.). 32p. (J). (gr. 2-4). 5.95 *(978-1-55054-770-2(4))* Da Capo Pr., Inc.
Teeth Sets: 1 Each of 3 Big Books. (Sunshinetm Science Ser.). (gr. 1-2). 111.50 *(978-0-7802-1449-1(8))* Wright Group/McGraw-Hill.
Telgemeier, Raina. Smile. 2010. 21.00 *(978-1-60686-896-6(9))* Perfection Learning Corp.
—Smile. 2010. (ENG.). 224p. (J). (gr. 3-7). 24.99 *(978-0-545-13205-3(3));* (Illus.). pap. 10.99 *(978-0-545-13206-0(1))* Scholastic, Inc. (Graphix).
—Smile. 2010. lib. bdg. 22.10 *(978-0-606-14082-9(4),* Turtleback) Turtleback Bks.
Tourville, Amanda Doering. Cepíllate, Usa Hilo Dental y Enjuágate. Rooney, Ronnie, illus. 2011. (Cómo Mantenernos Saludables/How to Be Healthy Ser.).Tr. of Brush, Floss, & Rinse. (SPA, MUL & ENG.). 24p. (gr. k-2). 26.65 *(978-1-4048-6889-2(5))* Picture Window Bks.
Troupe, Thomas Kingsley. Kitanai & Cavity Croc Brush Their Teeth. Christoph, Jamey, illus. 2015. (Kitanai's Healthy Habits Ser.). (ENG.). 24p. (gr. k-2). lib. bdg. 26.65 *(978-1-4795-6080-6(4))* Picture Window Bks.
VanVoorst, Jenny Fretland. Take a Closer Look at Your Teeth. 2013. (Take a Closer Look Ser.). (ENG.). 24p. (J). (gr. 2-5). 28.50 *(978-1-62323-555-0(3),* 206358) Child's World, Inc., The.
Verdick, Elizabeth. Teeth Are Not for Biting. Heinlen, Marieka, illus. 2003. (Best Behavior Ser.). (ENG.). 24p. (J). 7.95 *(978-1-57542-128-5(3))* Free Spirit Publishing, Inc.
Verdick, Elizabeth. Teeth Are Not for Biting/Los Dientes No Son para Morder. Heinlen, Marieka, illus. 2017. (Best Behavior Ser.). (ENG, SPA & MUL.). 24p. (J). bds. 7.95 ***(978-1-63198-157-9(9))*** Free Spirit Publishing, Inc.
Vogel, Elizabeth. ¡A lavarse los dientes! (Brushing My Teeth) 2009. (Limpieza y salud todo el día (Clean & Healthy All Day Long) Ser.). (SPA.). 24p. (gr. 1-1). 37.50 *(978-1-61514-293-4(2),* Editorial Buenas Letras) Rosen Publishing Group, Inc., The.
Weston Woods Staff, creator. Open Wide- Tooth School Inside. 2011. 38.75 *(978-0-439-84913-5(6))* Weston Woods Studios, Inc.
Willebrandt, Isabella. Why Do My Teeth Fall Out?, Vol. 1. 2014. (My Body Does Strange Stuff! Ser.). (ENG.). 24p. (J). (gr. 1-2). 22.60 *(978-1-4824-0296-4(3))* Stevens, Gareth Publishing LLLP.

TEETH—FICTION

Alpert, Sherri. Cassandra Gets Her Smile Back: Teaching Children to Care for Their Teeth. Seroya, Tea, illus. 2010. (Let's Talk Ser.). (ENG.). 48p. (J). (gr. -1-4). pap. 8.95 *(978-0-88282-314-0(0))* New Horizon Pr. Pubs., Inc.
Andersdatter, Karla Margaret. Marissa the Tooth Fairy. Koff, Deborah, illus. 2nd ed. 2005. (J). *(978-0-9717611-2-4(4))* Depot Bks.
Arnoff, Rebecca D. The Trouble with Tooth Fairies: The Adventures of Sam & Angela. 2013. 24p. 22.99 *(978-1-4582-1028-9(6));* pap. 12.99 *(978-1-4582-1026-5(X))* Author Solutions, Inc. (Abbott Pr.).
Balzola, Asun. Munia y el Cocollo Naranja. (SPA.). 32p. (J). *(978-84-233-1335-8(2))* Ediciones Destino ESP. Dist: Lectorum Pubns., Inc.
Bancks, Tristan. Noob, Amateur Dentist. Gorissen, Dean, illus. 2015. (Legends in Their Own Lunchbox Ser.). (ENG.). 56p. (gr. 2-3). pap. 7.99 *(978-1-4966-0253-4(6),* Legends in Their Own Lunchbox) Capstone Classroom.
Baxter, Nicola. A Visit from the Tooth Fairy: Magical Stories & a Special Message from the Little Friend Who Collects Your Baby Teeth. Manson, Beverlie, illus. 2013. (ENG.). 40p. (J). (gr. k-4). 14.99 *(978-1-84322-987-2(0),* Armadillo) Anness Publishing GBR. Dist: National Bk. Network.
Bb. Matt's 1st Tooth. 2012. 28p. pap. 24.95 *(978-1-4626-6134-3(3))* America Star Bks.
Beckford, Avril. The Tooth Fairy. 2010. 28p. (J). pap. 12.49 *(978-1-4490-9060-9(5))* AuthorHouse.
Beeler, Selby B. Throw Your Tooth on the Roof. Karas, G. Brian, illus. 2015. 32p. pap. 7.00 *(978-1-61003-501-9(1))* Center for the Collaborative Classroom.
Bell-Rehwoldt, Sheri. You Think It's Easy Being the Tooth Fairy? Slonim, David, illus. 2007. (ENG.). 32p. (J). (gr. -1-3). 15.99 *(978-0-8118-5460-3(4))* Chronicle Bks. LLC.
Bernadine, Joyce. The Teeth Keepers. 2008. 73p. pap. 19.95 *(978-1-60563-848-5(X))* America Star Bks.
Bloomfield, Denise. Toby Gets the Brush Off. 2007. 28p. (J). pap. 5.95 *(978-0-9778113-3-5(6))* HeartFelt Stories LLC.
Bond, Juliana. Pixie Tales the Wobbly Tooth. 2005. 30p. spiral bd. 12.08 *(978-1-4116-6046-5(3))* Lulu Pr., Inc.
Booth-Alberstadt, Sheila. Maggie Mcnair Has Sugar Bugs in There. Hall, Norris, illus. 2013. (ENG.). 36p. (J). (gr. -1-1). 14.95 *(978-0-9711404-6-2(4))* SBA Bks., LLC.
Borden, Louise. The Lost-and-Found Tooth. Gustavson, Adam, illus. 2008. (ENG.). 40p. (J). (gr. 2-5). 16.99 *(978-1-4169-1814-1(0),* McElderry, Margaret K. Bks.) McElderry, Margaret K. Bks.
Brockenbrough, Martha. The Dinosaur Tooth Fairy. Sanchez, Israel, illus. 2013. (ENG.). 32p. (J). (gr. -1-3). 17.99 *(978-0-545-24466-4(8),* Levine, Arthur A. Bks.) Scholastic, Inc.
Brooks, Felicity. Brush Your Teeth, Max & Millie. 2011. (Toddler Bks). 24p. (J). ring bd. 7.99 *(978-0-7945-2998-7(4),* Usborne) EDC Publishing.
Brown, Marc. Arthur's Tooth. Brown, Marc, illus. 2005. (ENG., Illus.). 32p. (J). (gr. -1-3). pap. 10.99 *(978-0-316-05960-2(9))* Little, Brown Bks. for Young Readers.
Burkert, Rand. Mouse & Lion. Burkert, Nancy Ekholm, illus. 2011. (ENG.). 32p. (J). (gr. -1-3). 18.99 *(978-0-545-10147-9(6),* Di Capua, Michael) Scholastic, Inc.
Caldwell, J. Lynn. The Tooth Fairy's Guide to Lost Teeth: A Fortune for Every Day a Tooth Is Lost. Jepson, Beth, illus. 2005. (J). per. 11.95 *(978-0-9774463-0-8(1))* Caldwell, Judy.
Callahan, Charlie. Samantha Loses Her Sweet Tooth. Callahan, Charlie, illus. 2004. (Illus.). (J). *(978-0-9754019-0-3(4))* Periscope Pr.
Callen, Sharon. Safari Camp, 1 vol. rev. ed. 2013. (Fiction Readers Ser.). (ENG., Illus.). 20p. (J). (gr. 1-1). pap. 15.96 *(978-1-4807-1150-1(0));* pap. 4.99 *(978-1-4333-5494-6(2))* Shell Educational Publishing.
Capone, Deb. Tooth Fairy Tales. 2005. (J). 14.95 *(978-0-9728666-7-5(1))* As Simple As That Publishing.
Capone, Deb & compiled by. Tooth Fairy Tales Learning & Activity Guide. Capone, Deb, compiled by. 2007. (Illus.). 20p. (J). 9.95 *(978-0-9728666-8-2(X))* As Simple As That Publishing.
Chatman, Dudley D. I Brush My Teeth & I Smile, 1 vol. 2009. 48p. pap. 16.95 *(978-1-4489-2179-9(1))* America Star Bks.
Child, Lauren. My Wobbly Tooth Must Not Ever Never Fall Out. Child, Lauren, illus. 2006. (Charlie & Lola Ser.). (ENG., Illus.). 32p. (J). (gr. -1-2). mass mkt. 6.99 *(978-0-448-44255-6(8),* Grosset & Dunlap) Penguin Young Readers Group.
Civardi, Anne. Going to the Dentist. 2009. (First Experiences Sticker Bks). 18p. (J). pap. 6.99 *(978-0-7945-2429-6(X),* Usborne) EDC Publishing.
Clark, CoraMarie. Emily's Magical Journey with Toothena the Tooth Fairy. Lawton, Val, illus. 2007. (ENG.). 32p. (J). *(978-0-9783779-0-8(7))* Strategix Ltd.
Clarke, Jacqueline A. Moose's Loose Tooth. McNally, Bruce, illus. 2003. (J). *(978-0-439-41183-7(1))* Scholastic, Inc.
Clifford, Patricia. Fox Loses a Tooth. 2012. 24p. (-18). pap. 14.93 *(978-1-4669-6790-8(0))* Trafford Publishing.
Cook, E. Diann. The Andersuns: Jarrell's Sweet Tooth. 2010. 36p. pap. 16.99 *(978-1-4490-4997-3(4))* AuthorHouse.
Cook, Julia & Jana, Laura. Melvin the Magnificent Molar. Valentine, Allison, illus. 2010. (ENG.). 32p. (J). pap. 9.95 *(978-1-931636-74-2(5))* National Ctr. For Youth Issues.
Coombs, Kate. The Tooth Fairy Wars. Parker, Jake, illus. 2014. (ENG.). 40p. (J). (gr. -1-3). 17.99 *(978-1-4169-7915-9(8))* Simon & Schuster Children's Publishing.
Cooper, Mimi. Me Versus the Tooth. 2006. 17p. (J). 9.99 *(978-1-4116-6933-8(9))* Lulu Pr., Inc.
Costamagna, Beatrice, illus. Crocodile Snap! 2016. (Crunchy Board Bks.). (ENG.). 12p. (J). (gr. -1-1). bds. 6.99 *(978-1-4998-0201-6(3))* Little Bee Books Inc.
Cousins, Lucy. Maisy, Charley, & the Wobbly Tooth. Cousins, Lucy, illus. 2009. (Maisy Ser.). (ENG., Illus.). 32p. (J). (gr. k-k). pap. 6.99 *(978-0-7636-4369-0(6))* Candlewick Pr.
Coven, Wanda. Heidi Heckelbeck Says "Cheese!" Burris, Priscilla, illus. 2015. (Heidi Heckelbeck Ser.: 14). (ENG.). 128p. (J). (gr. k-4). pap. 5.99 *(978-1-4814-2327-4(4),* Little Simon) Little Simon.
Dahl, Michael. The Missing Fang, 1 vol. Piatti, Federico, illus. 2010. (Dragonblood Ser.). (ENG.). 40p. (gr. 1-3). lib. bdg. 23.99 *(978-1-4342-1923-7(2),* Zone Bks.) Stone Arch Bks.
—Pony Brushes His Teeth, 1 vol. Vidal, Oriol, illus. 2010. (Hello Genius Ser.). (ENG.). 20p. (gr. 1-2). bds. 7.99 *(978-1-4048-5727-8(3))* Picture Window Bks.
Dale, Jay. Jo & Jess Go to the Dentist, 1 vol. Chapman, Katriona, illus. 2012. (Wonder Words Ser.). (ENG.). 32p. (gr. k-2). pap. 5.99 *(978-1-4296-8912-0(9),* Engage Literacy) Capstone Press of Coughlan Cos.
Dawson, Brianog Brady & Nolan, Alan. Danny Brown & the Talking Teeth. Connor, Michael, illus. 2017. (ENG.). 64p. (J). 12.00 ***(978-1-84717-879-4(0))*** O'Brien Pr., Ltd., The IRL. Dist: Dufour Editions, Inc.
deGroat, Diane. Gilbert & the Lost Tooth. deGroat, Diane, illus. 2012. (I Can Read Level 2 Ser.). (ENG., Illus.). 32p. (J). (gr. k-3). 16.99 *(978-0-06-125214-3(X));* pap. 3.99 *(978-0-06-125216-7(6))* HarperCollins Pubs.
Dyan, Penelope. The Story of Snagatooth — -Who Is Commonly Known As the Tooth Fairy. Dyan, Penelope, illus. 2008. (Illus.). 44p. pap. 11.95 *(978-1-935118-42-8(0))* Bellissima Publishing, LLC.
—Teeth! Dyan, Penelope, illus. 2012. (Illus.). 34p. pap. 11.95 *(978-1-61477-060-2(3))* Bellissima Publishing, LLC.
Erickson, Melissa. When the Tooth Fairy Comes... Erickson, Melissa, illus. 2007. (Illus.). 15p. (J). (gr. -1-3). 10.99 *(978-1-59879-369-7(1))* Lifevest Publishing, Inc.
Friden, Chris. Toothtime with Chomper. 2008. (Illus.). 27p. (J). bds. 14.99 *(978-0-9758785-7-6(3))* Haydenburn Lane.
—Toothtime with Chomper. Rodríguez Braojos, Alberto et al, illus. 2008. (J). *(978-0-9801849-3-8(2))* Haydenburn Lane.
Ginsburg, Herbert P., et al. Two-Two the Tooth Fairy. 2003. (Illus.). 9.95 *(978-0-7690-3039-5(4))* Seymour, Dale Pubns.
Groshek, Jodie. Brush, Brush, Brush. 2011. 28p. pap. 15.99 *(978-1-4568-5871-1(8))* Xlibris Corp.
Groves, Odessa M. Playful Teeth: Login. 2008. (Illus.). 68p. pap. 21.95 *(978-0-9820002-1-2(9))* G Publishing LLC.
Gutierrez-Haley, Lisa. The Wiggly Tooth: Adventures of Hayden & Jace. 2011. 16p. pap. 24.95 *(978-1-4626-1874-3(X))* America Star Bks.
Hall, Kirsten. The Tooth Fairy. Apperley, Dawn, illus. (My First Reader Ser.). (ENG.). 32p. (J). (gr. k-1). 2004. pap. 3.95 *(978-0-516-24640-6(2))* 2003. 18.50 *(978-0-516-22938-6(9))* Scholastic Library Publishing. (Children's Pr.).
Haris, Martha & Haris, Kimberli. The Adventures of Fairyella the Tooth Fairy & Dragonfly Floyd. 2012. 24p. pap. 14.95 *(978-1-4575-1039-7(1))* Dog Ear Publishing, LLC.
Hawley, Bill. El Diente Suelto de Carlitos, Level 2. 2003. (Dejame Leer Ser.). (SPA., Illus.). (gr. 1-4). 6.50 *(978-0-673-36330-5(9),* Good Year Bks.) Celebration Pr.
Hay, Sam. Tooth Bandits. Manuzak, Lisa, illus. 2016. (Stella & the Night Sprites Ser.: 2). (ENG.). 96p. (J). (gr. 1-3). 15.99 *(978-0-545-82001-1(4))* Scholastic, Inc.
Hill, Amanda. A Brush with the Super Dentists. 2007. (Illus.). 22p. (J). 14.99 *(978-0-9798506-0-8(6))* Super Dentists, The.
Hillert, Margaret. Dear Dragon Goes to the Dentist. Schimmell, David, illus. rev. ed. 2014. (BeginningtoRead Ser.). (ENG.). 32p. (J). (gr. k-2). lib. bdg. 22.60 *(978-1-59953-577-7(7))* Norwood Hse. Pr.
Hobbie, Holly. Charming Opal. 2011. (Toot & Puddle Ser.: 7). (ENG., Illus.). 32p. (J). (gr. -1-3). pap. 7.00 *(978-0-316-12655-7(1))* Little, Brown Bks. for Young Readers.
Hodgson, Sandra. The Toof Fairies. 2011. (Illus.). 44p. (gr. -1). pap. 16.76 *(978-1-4567-7978-8(8))* AuthorHouse.
Holloway, Jamie. Beaver Works On. 2015. (Rosen REAL Readers: STEM & STEAM Collection). (ENG.). 8p. pap. 5.46 *(978-1-4994-9489-1(0),* Rosen Classroom) Rosen Publishing Group, Inc., The.
Holt, Jessica. A Night in the Life of a Tooth Fairy. 2008. 16p. pap. 10.00 *(978-1-60693-396-1(5),* Strategic Bk. Publishing) Strategic Book Publishing & Rights Agency (SBPRA).
Hood, Karen Jean Matsko. Adventures of My Dentist & the Tooth Fairy: Activity & Coloring Book, bk. 2. Whispering Pine Press International, Inc. Staff, ed. Artistic Book and Web Design, illus. 2013. (ENG & JPN.). 174p. (J). pap. 19.95 *(978-1-59649-535-7(9))* Whispering Pine Pr. International, Inc.
—My Dentist & the Tooth Fairy: Activity & Coloring Book, bk. 10. Whispering Pine Press International, Inc. Staff, ed. 2013. (Hood Activity & Coloring Book Ser.). (ENG., Illus.). 160p. (J). pap. 19.95 *(978-1-59210-596-0(3))* Whispering Pine Pr. International, Inc.
Howell, Julie Ann. The Tooth Be Told. Cotton, Sue Lynn, illus. 2011. 24p. 18.95 *(978-1-61493-061-7(9))* Peppertree Pr., The.
Jacobs, Sherry. Grampa's Teeth. 2012. (ENG.). 42p. (J). pap. 16.95 *(978-1-4327-8104-0(9))* Outskirts Pr., Inc.
Jarvis. Alan's Big, Scary Teeth. Jarvis, illus. 2016. (ENG., Illus.). 32p. (J). (-k). 16.99 *(978-0-7636-8120-3(2))* Candlewick Pr.
Kann, Victoria. Silverlicious. Kann, Victoria, illus. 2011. (Illus.). 40p. (J). (gr. k-3). (ENG.). 17.99 *(978-0-06-178123-0(1));* lib. bdg. 18.89 *(978-0-06-178124-7(X))* HarperCollins Pubs.
Kauffman, Christopher G. Faith's Star. Jenkins, Jacqueline, illus. 2011. 32p. pap. 24.95 *(978-1-4560-9584-0(6))* America Star Bks.
Klein, Abby. Tooth Trouble. 2011. (Ready, Freddy Ser.: Bk. 1). 8.32 *(978-0-7848-3613-2(2),* Everbind) Marco Bk. Co.
—Tooth Trouble. McKinley, John, illus. 2004. (Ready, Freddy! Ser.: 1). (ENG.). 96p. (J). (gr. -1-3). 5.99 *(978-0-439-55596-8(5),* Blue Sky Pr., The) Scholastic, Inc.
Krulik, Nancy. Open Wide. John and Wendy Staff, illus. 2007. (Katie Kazoo, Switcheroo Ser.: 23). (ENG.). 80p. (J). (gr. 2-4). pap. 3.99 *(978-0-448-44439-0(9),* Grosset & Dunlap) Penguin Young Readers Group.
Laínez, René Colato. The Tooth Fairy Meets el Ratón Pérez. Lintern, Tom, illus. 2010. (ENG.). 32p. (J). (gr. -1-2). 15.99 *(978-1-58246-296-7(8),* Tricycle Pr.) Random Hse. Children's Bks.

T U V

Ledger, Kate. Twin Magic: School Bully, Beware! 2013. (Scholastic Reader Level 2 Ser.). (Illus.). 32p. (J). lib. bdg. 13.55 (978-0-606-31972-0(7), Turtleback) Turtleback Bks.

Lemke, Donald B. Book-O-Teeth. Lentz, Bob, illus. 2015. (Wearable Bks.). (ENG.). 12p. (gr. -1-1). bds. 7.99 (978-1-62370-186-4(4), Wear-A-Book) Capstone Young Readers of Coughlan Cos.

Loveridge, Pamela. The Tooth Fairy Who Lost a Tooth. 2012. 24p. pap. 28.03 (978-1-4797-4928-7(1)) Xlibris Corp.

Luppens, Michel & Béha, Philippe. What Do the Fairies Do with All Those Teeth? (Illus.). (J). pap. 15.95 (978-0-590-74050-0(4)) Scholastic, Inc.

MacHado, Cj & Jones, Gareth P. Even Cowgirls Brush Their Teeth. 2012. 26p. pap. 13.99 (978-1-4624-0463-6(4), Inspiring Voices) Author Solutions, Inc.

Maconie, Robin. Alice & Her Fabulous Teeth! Fruisen, Catherine Myler, illus. 2004. 32p. (J). per. (978-1-893974-21-0(9), Design Pr. Bks.) Savannah College of Art & Design Exhibitions.

Maguire, Gregory. What-the-Dickens: The Story of a Rogue Tooth Fairy. 2007. (ENG., Illus.). 304p. (J). (gr. 4-7). 15.99 (978-0-7636-2961-8(8)) Candlewick Pr.

Mahadeo Rdh, Elizabeth. Teddy Visits the Dentist: Teddy Gets a Filling. Barth, Alexandra, illus. 2012. 42p. (-18). pap. (978-0-9569438-2-8(9)) Mahadeo Movement, The.

Maloney, Peter & Zekauskas, Felicia. Lose That Tooth! 2005. (Illus.). 32p. (J). (978-0-439-67639-7(8)) Scholastic, Inc.

Manci, Arlene. The Grumpy Troll, 1 vol. Rawcliffe, Lee, illus. 2009. 25p. pap. 19.95 (978-1-4489-2456-1(1)) PublishAmerica, Inc.

Manushkin, Fran. The Tricky Tooth, 1 vol. Lyon, Tammie, illus. 2011. (Katie Woo Ser.). (ENG.). 32p. (gr. k-2). pap. 5.95 (978-1-4048-6611-9(6)); lib. bdg. 21.32 (978-1-4048-6516-7(0)) Picture Window Bks.

Maya Z And Nadaija R. Hall. The New-Fangled Adventures of Alexia & Z: The Case of Grams' Missing Teeth. 2009. 36p. pap. 15.95 (978-1-4389-4508-8(6)) AuthorHouse.

McClaine, Jamie. Have You Ever Seen a Moose Brushing His Teeth? Willy, April, illus. 2003. (ENG.). 24p. (J). (gr. -1). 18.95 (978-0-9709533-2-2(1)) J A F S, Inc.

Mcghee, Alison. Mrs. Watson Wants Your Teeth. Bliss, Harry, illus. 2007. 32p. (J). reprint ed. 16.00 (978-1-4223-6777-3(0)) DIANE Publishing Co.

—Mrs. Watson Wants Your Teeth. Bliss, Harry, illus. 2008. (ENG.). 36p. (J). (gr. -1-3). pap. 6.00 (978-0-15-206348-1(X)) Houghton Mifflin Harcourt Publishing Co.

—Mrs. Watson Wants Your Teeth. Bliss, Harry, illus. unabr. ed. 2007. (Picture Book Readalong Ser.). (J). (gr. -1-2). 28.95 incl. audio compact disk (978-1-59519-902-7(0)) Live Oak Media.

McRae, G. c. The Tooth. Anderson, David, illus. 2012. 36p. pap. (978-0-9876845-2-3(3)) Warne, MacDonald Media.

Meadows, Daisy. Brianna the Tooth Fairy. 2013. (Rainbow Magic — Special Edition Ser.). lib. bdg. 17.20 (978-0-606-31990-4(5), Turtleback) Turtleback Bks.

—Rainbow Magic Special Edition: Brianna the Tooth Fairy. 2013. (Rainbow Magic Special Edition Ser.). (ENG.). 176p. (J). (gr. 2-5). pap. 6.99 (978-0-545-48494-7(4), Scholastic Paperbacks) Scholastic, Inc.

Medders, James. The Tooth Fairy's Quest. Hardin, Teresa, illus. 2008. 32p. pap. 24.95 (978-1-60672-549-8(1)) America Star Bks.

Metzger, Steve. The Tooth Fairy Loses a Tooth! Busby, Ailie, illus. 2011. (ENG.). 16p. (J). (gr. -1-1). pap. 5.99 (978-1-4424-1259-0(3), Little Simon) Little Simon.

Miller, Jules. Ellie & the Truth about the Tooth Fairy. Miller, Jules, illus. 2014. (ENG., Illus.). 36p. (J). (gr. -1-k). 16.95 (978-1-62873-590-1(2), Sky Pony Pr.) Skyhorse Publishing Co., Inc.

Mills, David. Wibble Wobble. Crouth, Julia, illus. 2004. (ENG & CZE.). 32p. (J). pap. (978-1-85269-946-8(9)); pap. (978-1-85269-937-6(X)); pap. (978-1-85269-932-1(9)); pap. (978-1-85269-927-7(2)); pap. (978-1-85269-922-2(1)); pap. (978-1-85269-917-8(5)); pap. (978-1-85269-912-3(4)); pap. (978-1-85269-902-4(7)); pap. (978-1-85269-926-0(4)); pap. (978-1-85269-951-2(5)); pap. (978-1-85269-961-1(2)); pap. (978-1-85269-966-6(3)); pap. (978-1-85269-971-0(X)); pap. (978-1-85269-986-4(8)); pap. (978-1-85269-991-8(4)); pap. (978-1-85269-996-3(5)); pap. (978-1-85269-976-5(0)); pap. (978-1-85269-981-9(7)); pap. (978-1-85269-907-9(8)) Mantra Lingua.

—Wibbly Wobbly Tooth. Crouth, Julia, illus. 2004. (ENG & FRE.). 32p. (J). pap. (978-1-85269-956-7(6)); pap. (978-1-85269-941-3(8)); pap. (978-1-85269-931-4(0)); pap. (978-1-85269-936-9(1)) Mantra Lingua.

Milton, Cathlene. The Wonders of Billy Sniggies. 2013. 18p. pap. 9.99 (978-1-62697-179-0(X)) Salem Author Services.

Mitter, Matt & Rudko, Che. Ready, Set, Brush! Brannon, Tom, illus. 2008. (Pop-Up Book Ser.). (ENG.). 12p. (J). (gr. -1-k). bds. 12.99 (978-0-7944-1445-0(1), Reader's Digest Children's Bks.) Studio Fun International.

Moncure, Jane Belk. 'Smile,' Says Little Crocodile: A Book about Good Habits. DeSantis, Susan, illus. 2013. (Magic Castle Readers Ser.). (ENG.). 32p. (J). (gr. -1-2). 25.64 (978-1-62323-570-3(7), 206305) Child's World, Inc., The.

Munsch, Robert. Andrew's Loose Tooth. 2004. (Illus.). (J). (gr. k-3). spiral bd. (978-0-616-01732-6(4)); spiral bd. (978-0-616-00403-6(6)) Canadian National Institute for the Blind/Institut National Canadien pour les Aveugles.

My Tooth is Loose! With a Special Tooth Tin to Put Under Your Pillow (For Girls) 2008. (My Tooth Is Loose! Ser.). 32p. (978-1-4075-2165-7(9)) Parragon, Inc.

Nelson, James Gary. Dientecito y la Placa Peligros. Bumstead, Debbie, illus. 2011. 16p. pap. 9.95 (978-1-61633-132-0(1)) Guardian Angel Publishing, Inc.

—Smileytooth & the Castle Hassle. Bumstead, Debbie, illus. 2008. 24p. pap. 10.95 (978-1-933090-95-5(2)) Guardian Angel Publishing, Inc.

—Smileytooth & the Plaque Attack. Bumstead, Debbie, illus. 2008. 20p. pap. 10.95 (978-1-935137-48-1(4)) Guardian Angel Publishing, Inc.

Nichols, Tucker & Nichols, Jon, illus. Crabtree. 2013. (ENG.). 32p. (J). (gr. -1-3). 17.95 (978-1-936365-82-1(0)) McSweeney's Publishing.

O'Connor, Jane. Fancy Nancy & the Too-Loose Tooth. Glasser, Robin Preiss & Enik, Ted, illus. 2012. (I Can Read Level 1 Ser.). (ENG.). 32p. (J). (gr. -1-3). 16.99 (978-0-06-208301-2(5)); pap. 3.99 (978-0-06-208302-9(3)) HarperCollins Pubs.

—Fancy Nancy & the Too-Loose Tooth. 2012. (Fancy Nancy - I Can Read! Ser.). (J). lib. bdg. 13.55 (978-0-606-23551-8(5), Turtleback) Turtleback Bks.

Olberg, Henry, illus. The Magical Tooth Fairies: A Surprise in Mexico. 2012. (J). (978-0-86715-568-6(X)) Edition Q, Inc.

Ostow, Micol. Louise Trapeze Will NOT Lose a Tooth. Barrager, Brigette, illus. 2017. (Louise Trapeze Ser.). (ENG.). 112p. (J). (gr. 1-4). 14.99 (978-0-553-49751-9(0), Random Hse. Bks. for Young Readers) Random Hse. Children's Bks.

Palatini, Margie. No Biting, Louise. Reinhart, Matthew, illus. 2007. 32p. (J). (gr. -1-3). 16.99 (978-0-06-052627-6(0)); lib. bdg. 17.89 (978-0-06-052628-3(9)) HarperCollins Pubs. (Tegen, Katherine Bks).

Palatini, Margie & Davis, Jack E. Sweet Tooth. Davis, Jack E., illus. 2004. (ENG., Illus.). 40p. (J). (gr. -1-3). 18.99 (978-0-689-85159-9(6), Simon & Schuster Bks. For Young Readers) Simon & Schuster Bks. For Young Readers.

Pammer, Victoria. Katelyn & the Crooked Tooth. 2011. 28p. pap. 24.95 (978-1-4560-0996-0(6)) America Star Bks.

Park, Barbara. Toothless Wonder. Brunkus, Denise, illus. 2003. (Junie B. Jones Ser.: Bk. 3). 80p. (gr. 1-4). 15.00 (978-0-7569-1621-3(6)) Perfection Learning Corp.

—Toothless Wonder. Brunkus, Denise, illus. 2003. (Junie B. Jones Ser.: No. 3). (ENG.). 96p. (J). (gr. 1-4). pap. 4.99 (978-0-375-82223-0(2), Random Hse. Bks. for Young Readers) Random Hse. Children's Bks.

—Toothless Wonder. 2003. (Junie B. Jones Ser.: 20). (gr. k-3). lib. bdg. 14.75 (978-0-613-71014-5(2), Turtleback) Turtleback Bks.

Pidgeon, Jean, illus. Brush Your Teeth, Please: A Pop-Up Book. 2013. (Pop-Up Book Ser.: 2). (ENG.). 12p. (J). (gr. -1-k). 14.99 (978-0-7944-3040-5(6), Reader's Digest Children's Bks.) Studio Fun International.

Publications International Ltd. Staff, ed. Disney(r) Doc Mcstuffins I Can Brush My Teeth! Lift-A-Flap Sound Book. 2015. 12p. (J). bds. (978-1-4508-8991-9(3), 1450889913) Publications International, Ltd.

Random House. The Loose Tooth (Barbie) 2015. (Pictureback(R) Ser.). (ENG., Illus.). 16p. (J). (gr. -1-2). 4.99 (978-0-553-51130-7(0), Random Hse. Bks. for Young Readers) Random Hse. Children's Bks.

Rankine-Van Wassenhoven, Jacqueline. Who Stole Grandpa's Teeth? 2008. 20p. 10.94 (978-1-4357-0522-7(X)) Lulu Pr., Inc.

Ransom, Candice. Tooth Fairy's Night. 2017. (Step into Reading Ser.). (ENG., Illus.). 32p. (J). (gr. -1-1). 3.99 (978-0-399-55364-6(9), Random Hse. Bks. for Young Readers) Random Hse. Children's Bks.

Remkiewicz, Frank. Gus Loses a Tooth. 2013. (Illus.). (J). (978-0-545-46911-1(2)) Scholastic, Inc.

Rissi, Anica Mrose. Anna, Banana, & the Big-Mouth Bet. Park, Meg, illus. 2016. (Anna, Banana Ser.: 3). (ENG.). 128p. (J). (gr. 1-5). pap. 5.99 (978-1-4814-1612-2(X), Simon & Schuster Bks. For Young Readers) Simon & Schuster Bks. For Young Readers.

Roberts, Tony. Turquie the Turkey. 2011. 28p. pap. 15.99 (978-1-4568-5969-5(2)) Xlibris Corp.

Rooney, Anne. No Wobbly Teeth, 1 vol. Fiorin, Fabiano, illus. 2013. (Start Reading Ser.). (ENG.). 24p. (gr. k-1). pap. 7.95 (978-1-4765-4125-9(6)) Capstone Press of Coughlan Cos.

Ruelle, Karen Gray. Dear Tooth Fairy. Ruelle, Karen Gray, illus. 2006. (Harry & Emily Adventure Ser.). (ENG., Illus.). 32p. (J). (gr. k-3). 4.95 (978-0-8234-1984-5(3)) Holiday Hse., Inc.

—Dear Tooth Fairy: A Harry & Emily Adventure. Ruelle, Karen Gray, illus. 2006. (Holiday House Readers: Level 2 Ser.). (ENG., Illus.). 32p. (J). (gr. 5-8). 14.95 (978-0-8234-1929-6(0)) Holiday Hse., Inc.

Rutledge, Mary. The Toothless Tooth Fairy. 2011. 24p. pap. 12.74 (978-1-4634-6005-1(8)) AuthorHouse.

Santa Goes to the Dentist. 2005. (J). 5.95 net. (978-0-9769321-5-4(6)) Steingart, Nathan Publishing.

Sateren, Shelley Swanson. Max & Zoe at the Dentist, 1 vol. Sullivan, Mary, illus. 2013. (Max & Zoe Ser.). (ENG.). 32p. (gr. k-2). pap. 5.19 (978-1-4048-8057-3(7), Max & Zoe) Picture Window Bks.

Saunders, Helen. So, Where do all the teeth Go? Bolick, Brian, illus. 2006. (J). (978-0-9763143-3-2(9)) Happy Heart Kids Publishing.

Schaefer, Lola M. Loose Tooth. Wickstrom, Sylvie K., tr. Wickstrom, Sylvie K., illus. 2004. (My First I Can Read Bks.). 32p. (J). (gr. -1-18). 14.99 (978-0-06-052776-1(5)) HarperCollins Pubs.

Scotto, Michael. Sweet Tooth Bun. Gabriel, Evette, illus. 2009. (J). (978-1-935193-48-7(1)) National Network of Digital Schs.

Seuss, Dr. The Tooth Book. Mathieu, Joe, illus. (Big Bright & Early Board Book Ser.). (ENG.). 24p. (J). (— 1). 2017. bds. 6.99 (978-0-553-53864-9(0)) 2003. bds. 4.99 (978-0-375-82492-0(8)) Random Hse. Children's Bks. (Random Hse. Bks. for Young Readers).

Shehane, Kristen. Chomp! 2012. 20p. pap. 24.95 (978-1-4626-7745-0(2)) America Star Bks.

Smileytooth & the Plaque Attack: The Adventures of Smileytooth. 2006. (J). 6.95 (978-0-9778456-0-6(5)) Pontrelli, Jeany.

Speakes, Leslie. The Hygiene Mystery. 2004. 31p. pap. 24.95 (978-1-4137-1860-7(4)) PublishAmerica, Inc.

Spinelle, Nancy Louise. El Diente Flojo Del Alce (6 Pack) Gedeon, Gloria, illus. 2011.Tr. of Moose's Loose Tooth. (SPA.). 16p. (gr. k-2). pap. (978-1-61181-166-7(X), Kaeden Bks.) Kaeden Corp.

—Moose's Loose Tooth. Gedeon, Gloria, illus. Lt. ed. 2005. (ENG.). 16p. (gr. k-2). pap. 7.95 (978-1-57874-032-1(0), Kaeden Bks.) Kaeden Corp.

Star the Tooth Fairy from Treasure Cloud Shares Secrets with You! 2006. (J). per. 9.99 (978-0-9792992-0-9(9)) Twinkle Bks.

Star the Tooth Fairy is Checking on You! 2004. (J). per. 9.99 (978-0-9792992-2-3(5)) Twinkle Bks.

Star the Tooth Fairy Wants to Know if You Need Braces? 2006. (J). per. 9.99 (978-0-9792992-1-6(7)) Twinkle Bks.

Steinberg, Harriet. A Tooth with a Hole. 2012. 24p. pap. 15.99 (978-1-4797-0711-9(2)) Xlibris Corp.

Stockham, Jessica, illus. Visiting the Dentist. 2011. (First Time Ser.). (ENG.). 24p. (J). (gr. 2-2). pap. (978-1-84643-335-1(5)) Child's Play International Ltd.

Suen, Anastasia. Loose Tooth. Eitzen, Allan, illus. 2004. 28p. (gr. -1-3). 14.00 (978-0-7569-1955-9(X)) Perfection Learning Corp.

—The Tooth Fairy. Myer, Ed, illus. 2012. (ENG.). 24p. (gr. k-1). pap. 8.95 (978-1-61810-307-9(5)) Rourke Educational Media.

Tagliaferri, Sara & Spada, Alberto. My Baby Teeth, 1 vol. 2011. (ENG.). 20p. pap. 9.95 (978-90-79761-20-3(6)) Tectum B.V.B.A. BEL. Dist: Innovative Logistics.

Tamaja Press & Tillman, Gloria J. Teeth for Thanksgiving. 2017. (ENG., Illus.). 36p. (J). lib. bdg. 12.99 (978-0-9841260-7-1(4)) Tamaja Pr.

Taylor, Tracy Carol. Tale of Two Teeth. 2012. 48p. pap. 25.00 (978-1-300-17956-6(2)) Lulu Pr., Inc.

Thompson, Deanna. 100 Years Old with Baby Teeth: Will Caroline Ever Lose Her Tooth? Wolf, Claudia, illus. 2006. 24p. (J). per. 2.99 (978-1-59958-000-5(4)) Journey Stone Creations, LLC.

Thorpe, Linda W. Teeny-Weeny's Two Front Teeth. 2007. (Illus.). 16p. (J). 6.95 (978-0-9799671-0-8(4)) ThunderBolt Publishing.

Tobias, Anne B. Harry's Problem First Loose Tooth. Tobias, Tom, illus. 2008. 16p. pap. 9.95 (978-0-9818683-9-4(8)) Peppertree Pr., The.

Tooth, Lucy. Star the Tooth Fairy from Treasure Cloud Shares Secrets with You! 2010. 36p. 16.95 (978-0-557-37985-9(7)) Lulu Pr., Inc.

—Star the Tooth Fairy Haunted by Mr. Jack-O-Lantern in Pumpkinland! 2009. 36p. 16.95 (978-0-557-10300-3(2)) Lulu Pr., Inc.

—Star the Tooth Fairy Is Checking on You! 36p. 2010. 16.95 (978-0-557-49450-7(8)) 2009. 16.95 (978-0-557-07500-3(9)) Lulu Pr., Inc.

—Star the Tooth Fairy Takes A Holiday to Visit Santa at the North Pole! 2010. 40p. 17.95 (978-0-557-41623-3(X)) Lulu Pr., Inc.

—Star the Tooth Fairy Wants to Know If You Need Braces? 36p. 2010. 16.95 (978-0-557-49455-2(9)) 2009. 16.95 (978-0-557-07542-3(4)) Lulu Pr., Inc.

—Tooth Fairy Loose & Lost Baby Tooth Coloring Log. 2010. 32p. pap. 15.95 (978-0-557-56268-8(6)) Lulu Pr., Inc.

—Tooth Fairy Loose & Lost Tooth Coloring Log. 2010. 32p. pap. 15.95 (978-0-557-33177-2(3)) Lulu Pr., Inc.

Trumbauer, Lisa. Un Diente esta Flojo: A Tooth Is Loose. Gray, Steve, illus. 2005. (Rookie Reader Español Ser.). (SPA & ENG.). 24p. (gr. k-2). 19.50 (978-0-516-24449-5(3), Children's Pr.) Scholastic Library Publishing.

—A Tooth Is Loose. Gray, Steve, illus. (Rookie Ready to Learn Ser.). (J). 2011. 32p. pap. 5.95 (978-0-531-26735-6(0)) 2011. 32p. (gr. -1-k). lib. bdg. 23.00 (978-0-531-26503-1(X)) 2005. (ENG.). 24p. (gr. k-2). pap. 4.95 (978-0-516-25841-6(9)) Scholastic Library Publishing. (Children's Pr.).

Trumbauer, Lisa & Gray, Steve. Un Diente Está Flojo. Gray, Steve, illus. 2011. (Rookie Ready to Learn Español Ser.). (SPA., Illus.). 32p. (J). pap. 5.95 (978-0-531-26785-1(7)); lib. bdg. 23.00 (978-0-531-26117-0(4)) Scholastic Library Publishing. (Children's Pr.).

Tsitoukis, Kristen L. The Tooth Song. 2008. 16p. pap. 8.50 (978-1-4343-9539-9(1)) AuthorHouse.

Twinkle the Tooth Fairy. 2008. (Deluxe Charm Book Ser.). 12p. (978-1-4075-3332-2(0)) Parragon, Inc.

Van Leeuwen, Jean. Amanda Pig & the Wiggly Tooth. Schweninger, Ann, illus. 2009. (Oliver & Amanda Ser.). (ENG.). 48p. (J). (gr. 1-3). mass mkt. 3.99 (978-0-14-241290-9(2), Penguin Young Readers) Penguin Young Readers Group.

Vanek, Karen & Schmidt, Sharon Vanek. Santa Claus Meets the Tooth Fairy. 2012. 44p. pap. 21.99 (978-1-4772-4535-4(9)) AuthorHouse.

Victoria's Tooth Fairy Adventure. 2007. (Illus.). 40p. (J). 19.95 (978-0-615-17773-1(5)) Created For You.

Vries, Lizzette de & Vries, Cecile de. How the Tooth Mouse Met the Tooth Fairy. Suwannakit, Tul, illus. 2010. (J). 19.95 (978-0-86715-507-5(8)) Quintessence Publishing Co., Inc.

Wallace, Jazey. Smile Bright. Fraser, Sigmund, illus. 2012. 24p. pap. 11.50 (978-1-61897-755-7(5), Strategic Bk. Publishing) Strategic Book Publishing & Rights Agency (SBPRA).

Walsh, Alice. Uncle Farley's False Teeth. 2004. (Illus.). (J). (gr. k-3). spiral bd. (978-0-616-01807-1(X)) Canadian National Institute for the Blind/Institut National Canadien pour les Aveugles.

Webb, Carla. The Magic in Believing: The Tooth Fairies. Lee, Kim, illus. (Magic in Believing Ser.). 36p. (J). (gr. k-5). (978-0-9705726-0-8(3)) Ageless Treasures.

Weinbrenner, Darlene. My Silly Willy Loose Tooth. Weinbrenner, Jacquelyn, illus. 2012. 24p. 24.95 (978-1-4626-5180-1(1)) America Star Bks.

Wells, Mark & Wells, Meagan. Tommy's Lost Tooth. Wells, Mark, illus. 2011. (Illus.). 28p. pap. 11.99 (978-1-61170-020-6(5)) Robertson Publishing.

Westen, Leah. Jack the Tooth Rat. 2009. (Illus.). 28p. pap. 12.50 (978-1-60693-558-3(5), Eloquent Bks.) Strategic Book Publishing & Rights Agency (SBPRA).

Weston Woods Staff, creator. Ready, Freddy! #1: Tooth Trouble. 2011. 20.95 (978-0-545-05008-1(1)) Weston Woods Studios, Inc.

Wilkins, Verna. Twinkle, Twinkle, Little Star. Kubler, Annie, illus. 2003. (Classic Books with Holes 8x8 Ser.). (ENG.). 16p. (J). (gr. -1-3). pap. (978-0-85953-133-7(3)) Child's Play International Ltd.

Williamson, Melanie. El magnifico plan de Lobo/ Wolf's Magnificent Plan. Williamson, Melanie, illus. 2008. (SPA., Illus.). 29p. 20.95 (978-84-263-6837-9(9)) Vives, Luis Editorial (Edelvives) ESP. Dist: Baker & Taylor Bks.

Wilson, Karma. Bear's Loose Tooth. Chapman, Jane, illus. 2014. (Bear Bks.). (ENG.). 34p. (J). (gr. -1-k). bds. 7.99 (978-1-4424-8936-3(7), Little Simon) Little Simon.

—Bear's Loose Tooth. Chapman, Jane, illus. 2011. (Bear Bks.). (ENG.). 40p. (J). (gr. -1-3). 17.99 (978-1-4169-5855-0(X), McElderry, Margaret K. Bks.) McElderry, Margaret K. Bks.

Wing, Natasha. The Night Before the Tooth Fairy. Newman, Barbara Johansen, illus. 2003. (Night Before Ser.). (ENG.). 32p. (J). (gr. -1-3). pap. 4.99 (978-0-448-43252-6(8), Grosset & Dunlap) Penguin Young Readers Group.

The Wobbly Tooth: Individual Title Six-Packs. (Literatura 2000 Ser.). (gr. 1-2). 28.00 (978-0-7635-0158-7(1)) Rigby Education.

Wood, Audrey. Presto Change-O & Tooth Fairy. (J). audio (978-0-85953-374-4(3)) Child's Play International Ltd.

—Tooth Fairy. 2003. (Child's Play Library). (ENG., Illus.). 32p. (J). (gr. 1-2). (978-0-85953-293-8(3)) Child's Play International Ltd.

—Tooth Fairy. 2003. (gr. -1-2). 18.40 (978-0-613-76960-0(0), Turtleback) Turtleback Bks.

Xavier, Imbeus & Sanders, Martin B. Super Dentist Guy: Attack of the Yukkies. Sanders, Martin B., illus. 2003. (Illus.). 64p. lib. bdg. 11.99 (978-0-9708523-2-8(0)) DeMosi Publishing.

—Super Dentist Guy: Attack of the Yukkies. Sanders, Martin B. et al, illus. 2003. 52p. 7.99 (978-0-9708523-0-4(4)) DeMosi Publishing.

TELECOMMUNICATION

see also Artificial Satellites in Telecommunication; Interstellar Communication; Radio; Telegraph; Telephone; Television

Aaseng, Nathan. Business Builders in Broadcasting. 2005. (Business Builders Ser.: Vol. 8). (Illus.). 160p. (J). (gr. 5-18). lib. bdg. 24.95 (978-1-881508-83-0(8)) Oliver Pr., Inc.

Anniss, Matthew. Create Your Own Podcast. 2016. (Media Genius Ser.). (ENG.). 48p. (gr. 5-8). lib. bdg. 33.32 (978-1-4109-8109-7(6)) Heinemann-Raintree.

—Understanding Computer Networks. 2015. (Understanding Computing Ser.). (ENG.). 48p. (gr. 3-6). 33.32 (978-1-4846-0902-6(6), Heinemann InfoSearch) Heinemann-Raintree.

Bailey, Gerry & Way, Steve. Communication. 2008. (Simply Science Ser.). (Illus.). 32p. (YA). (gr. 3-6). lib. bdg. 26.00 (978-0-8368-9226-0(7)) Stevens, Gareth Publishing LLLP.

Ball, Jacqueline A., et al. Communication Inventions: From Hieroglyphics to DVDs. 2006. (Which Came First? Ser.). (Illus.). 32p. (YA). (gr. 3-6). lib. bdg. 25.27 (978-1-59716-129-9(2)) Bearport Publishing Co., Inc.

Bozzo, Linda & Library. Staying in Touch in the Past, Present, & Future. 2010. (Imagining the Future Ser.). (Illus.). 24p. (J). lib. bdg. 22.60 (978-0-7660-3438-9(0), Enslow Elementary) Enslow Pubs., Inc.

Christensen, Laurel. LYFSGUD: If God Sent You a Text Message. 2009. (J). (978-1-60641-108-7(X)) Deseret Bk. Co.

Cleveland, Donald. Seven Wonders of Communication. 2010. (Seven Wonders Ser.). (Illus.). 80p. (J). (gr. 5-9). lib. bdg. 33.26 (978-0-7613-4240-3(0)) Twenty First Century Bks.

Currie-McGhee, Leanne K. Brittany & Robbie Bergquist: Cell Phones for Soldiers. 2007. (Young Heroes Ser.). (ENG., Illus.). 48p. (J). (gr. 4-8). lib. bdg. 30.50 (978-0-7377-3866-7(9), Kidhaven) Cengage Gale.

Duke, Shirley. Information Waves. 2016. (Let's Explore Science Ser.). (ENG., Illus.). 48p. (gr. 5-8). 35.64 (978-1-68191-391-9(7)) Rourke Educational Media.

Einspruch, Andrew. Wired World. 2012. (Discovery Education: Technology Ser.). (ENG., Illus.). 32p. (J). (gr. 3-6). pap. 10.00 (978-1-4488-7970-0(1)); lib. bdg. 25.25 (978-1-4488-7888-8(8)) Rosen Publishing Group, Inc., The. (PowerKids Pr.).

Engdahl, Sylvia. Mobile Apps. Greenhaven Press Editors & Gale Editors, eds. 2014. (Current Controversies Ser.). (ENG., Illus.). 224p. (gr. 7-12). pap. 32.00 (978-0-7377-6891-6(6)); lib. bdg. 46.40 (978-0-7377-6890-9(8)) Cengage Gale. (Greenhaven Pr., Inc.).

Espejo, Roman. Cell Phones in Schools. Greenhaven Press Editors & Gale Editors, eds. 2014. (At Issue Ser.). (ENG.). 128p. (gr. 10-12). pap. 27.80 (978-0-7377-6156-6(3), Greenhaven Pr., Inc.) Cengage Gale.

—Cell Phones in Schools. Greenhaven Press Editors, ed. 2014. (At Issue Ser.). (ENG.). 128p. (gr. 10-12). lib. bdg. 39.40 (978-0-7377-6155-9(5), Greenhaven Pr., Inc.) Cengage Gale.

Firestone, Mary. Wireless Technology. 2009. pap. 52.95 (978-0-7613-4786-6(0)) 2008. (ENG., Illus.). 48p. (J). (gr. 4-8). 27.93 (978-0-8225-7590-0(6)) Lerner Publishing Group.

Fontichiaro, Kristin. Speak Out! Creating Podcasts & Other Audio Recordings. 2013. (Explorer Junior Library: Information Explorer Junior Ser.). (ENG.). 24p. (gr. 1-4). 28.50 (978-1-62431-022-5(2), 202539); pap. 12.79 (978-1-62431-046-1(X), 202541) Cherry Lake Publishing.

—Super Smart Information Strategies: Podcasting 101. 2010. (Explorer Library: Information Explorer Ser.). (ENG.). 32p. (gr. 4-8). lib. bdg. 28.50 (978-1-60279-953-0(9), 200631) Cherry Lake Publishing.

Graham, Ian. Great Electronic Gadget Designs 1900-Today. 2015. (Iconic Designs Ser.). (ENG., Illus.). 48p. (gr. 4-6). pap. 8.99 (978-1-4846-2623-8(0), Heinemann InfoSearch) Heinemann-Raintree.

Green, Sara. Netflix. 2017. (Brands We Know Ser.). (ENG., Illus.). 24p. (J). (gr. 3-8). 25.95 **(978-1-62617-653-9(1)**, Pilot Bks.) Bellwether Media.

Grinapol, Corinne. Reed Hastings & Netflix. 2013. (Internet Biographies Ser.). (ENG., Illus.). 128p. (YA). (gr. 7-12). lib. bdg. 34.60 (978-1-4488-9525-0(1), Rosen Classroom) Rosen Publishing Group, Inc., The.

Henderson, Harry. Communications & Broadcasting: From Wired Words to Wireless Web. 2nd rev. ed. 2006. (Milestones in Discovery & Invention Ser.). (Illus.). 224p. (YA). (gr. 7-12). 35.00 (978-0-8160-5748-1(6)) Facts On File, Inc.

Internet. 3rd rev. ed. 2006. (Careers in Focus Ser.). (Illus.). 192p. (gr. 6-12). 32.95 (978-0-8160-6564-6(0), Ferguson Publishing Co.) Facts On File, Inc.

Jackson, Aurelia. Netflix: How Reed Hastings Changed the Way We Watch Movies & TV. 2014. (Wizards of Technology Ser.: 10). 64p. (J). (gr. 7-18). 23.95 (978-1-4222-3184-5(4)) Mason Crest.

Kallen, Stuart A. The Wireless Society. 2006. (At Issue Ser.). (ENG.). 128p. (gr. 10-12). pap. 27.80 (978-0-7377-2750-0(0), Greenhaven Pr., Inc.); 117p. (YA). (gr. 9-12). pap. 34.45 (978-0-7377-2749-4(7)) Cengage Gale.

Kamberg, Mary-Lane. Cybersecurity: Protecting Your Identity & Data. 2017. (J). pap. **(978-1-4994-3907-6(5)**, Rosen Reference) Rosen Publishing Group, Inc., The.

Klein, Rebecca T. Frequently Asked Questions about Texting, Sexting, & Flaming. 2012. (FAQ: Teen Life Ser.). (ENG., Illus.). 64p. (J). (gr. 7-12). lib. bdg. 31.95 *(978-1-4488-8331-8(8))* Rosen Publishing Group, Inc., The.

Kling, Andrew A. Cloud Computing. 2014. (Technology 360 Ser.). (ENG., Illus.). 128p. (gr. 7-10). lib. bdg. 39.90 *(978-1-4205-1158-1(0)*, Lucent Bks.) Cengage Gale.

Lusted, Marcia Amidon. Netflix: The Company & Its Founders, 1 vol. 2012. (Technology Pioneers Set 2 Ser.). (ENG.). 112p. (J). (gr. 6-12). lib. bdg. 35.64 *(978-1-61783-334-2(7)*, Essential Library) ABDO Publishing Co.

Lyons, Heather. Coding to Create & Communicate. Westgate, Alex, illus. 2017. (Kids Get Coding Ser.). (ENG.). 24p. (J). (gr. 1-4). 26.65 **(978-1-5124-3944-1(4))**; pap. 7.99 **(978-1-5124-5584-7(9))** Lerner Publishing Group.

Maddison, Simon. Telecoms. 2003. 48p. (J). lib. bdg. 27.10 *(978-1-58340-352-5(3))* Black Rabbit Bks.

Mapua, Jeff. Net Neutrality & What It Means to You. 2016. (Digital & Information Literacy Ser.). 00048p. (J). (gr. 6-6). pap. 11.75 *(978-1-4994-6511-2(4)*, Rosen Reference) Rosen Publishing Group, Inc., The.

Mooney, Carla. Music & Video Streaming, 01 vols., 1. 2016. (Digital & Information Literacy Ser.). (ENG.). 48p. (J). pap. 11.75 *(978-1-4994-3769-0(2)*, Rosen Central) Rosen Publishing Group, Inc., The.

Murray, Laura K. ATandT. 2015. (Illus.). 48p. (J). *(978-1-60818-556-6(7)*, Creative Education) Creative Co., The.

—At&T: Built for Success. 2016. (Built for Success Ser.). (ENG.). 48p. (J). (gr. 5-9). pap. 12.00 *(978-1-62832-157-9(1)*, Creative Paperbacks) Creative Co., The.

Naff, Clay Farris. Do Cell Phones Cause Cancer? Greenhaven Press Editors, ed. 2013. (At Issue Ser.). (ENG.). 128p. (gr. 10-12). pap. 27.80 *(978-0-7377-6168-9(7))*; lib. bdg. 39.40 *(978-0-7377-6167-2(9))* Cengage Gale. (Greenhaven Pr., Inc.).

Nakaya, Andrea C. Cell Phones. 2016. (Matters of Opinion Ser.). (ENG.). 64p. (J). (gr. 4-6). pap. 14.60 *(978-1-60357-858-5(7))* Norwood Hse. Pr.

O'Brien, Cynthia. Innovations in Communication. 2016. (Problem Solved! Your Turn to Think Big Ser.). (ENG., Illus.). 32p. (J). (gr. 3-6). *(978-0-7787-2672-2(X))* Crabtree Publishing Co.

Oxlade, Chris. The History of Telecommunications. 2017. (History of Technology Ser.). (ENG.). 32p. (gr. 2-5). pap. 8.29 **(978-1-4846-4039-5(X)**, Heinemann First Library) Heinemann-Raintree.

Parker, Janice. Communication. 2009. (Science Q & A Ser.). (Illus.). 48p. (YA). (gr. 5-8). pap. 10.95 *(978-1-60596-067-8(5))*; lib. bdg. 29.05 *(978-1-60596-066-1(7))* Weigl Pubs., Inc.

Perritano, John. Revolution in Communications. 2009. (It Works! Ser.). 32p. (gr. 3). 28.50 *(978-0-7614-4373-5(8))* Marshall Cavendish Corp.

Prentzas, Scott. Gps. 2009. (21st Century Skills Library: Global Products Ser.). (ENG.). 32p. (gr. 4-8). lib. bdg. 28.50 *(978-1-60279-506-8(1)*, 200321) Cherry Lake Publishing.

Radios, Phones & Telecommunications. 2005. (Inventions Ser.). (Illus.). 30p. (J). pap. 15.95 incl. audio *(978-0-9724983-4-0(6))* Jazwares Distribution, Inc.

Rand, Casey. Communication, 1 vol. 2012. (Science Behind Ser.). (ENG.). 32p. (gr. 3-3). lib. bdg. 30.65 *(978-1-4109-4485-6(9)*, Raintree Perspectives) Heinemann-Raintree.

Reed, Cristie. Bluetooth. 2014. (ENG.). 24p. (gr. k-3). 28.50 *(978-1-62717-645-3(4))* Rourke Educational Media.

Robinson, Tom. Media Ownership, 1 vol. 2009. (Essential Viewpoints Set 4 Ser.). (ENG., Illus.). 112p. (J). (gr. 6-12). lib. bdg. 35.64 *(978-1-60453-534-1(2))* ABDO Publishing Co.

Sawyer, Sarah. Career Building Through Podcasting. (Digital Career Building Ser.). 64p. 2009. (gr. 6-6). 58.50 *(978-1-61512-170-0(6))* 2007. (Illus.). (YA). (gr. 7-12). lib. bdg. 31.95 *(978-1-4042-1944-1(7))* Rosen Publishing Group, Inc., The.

Scott, Celicia. YouTube: How Steve Chen Changed the Way We Watch Videos. 2014. (Wizards of Technology Ser.: 10). (Illus.). 64p. (J). (gr. 7-18). 23.95 *(978-1-4222-3188-3(7))* Mason Crest.

Small, Cathleen. American Life & Communication from the Telephone to Twitter. 2016. (Pop Culture Ser.). 112p. (J). (gr. 7-7). 39.93 *(978-1-5026-1977-8(6))* Cavendish Square Publishing.

Solway, Andrew. Communication: The Impact of Science & Technology. 2009. (Pros & Cons Ser.). (ENG.). 64p. (YA). (gr. 5-9). lib. bdg. 35.00 *(978-1-4339-1986-2(9))* Stevens, Gareth Publishing LLLP.

Turner, Matt. Genius Communication Inventions: From Morse Code to the Internet. Conner, Sarah, illus. 2017. (Incredible Inventions Ser.). (ENG.). 32p. (J). (gr. 3-6). 26.65 **(978-1-5124-3210-7(5))** Lerner Publishing Group.

Whiting, Jim. John R. Pierce: Pioneer in Satellite Communication. 2003. (Unlocking the Secrets of Science Ser.). (Illus.). 56p. (J). (gr. 4-10). lib. bdg. 25.70 *(978-1-58415-205-7(2))* Mitchell Lane Pubs., Inc.

Wooster, Patricia. Youtube Founders Steve Chen, Chad Hurley, & Jawed Karim. 2014. (STEM Trailblazer Bios Ser.). (ENG., Illus.). 32p. (gr. 2-5). lib. bdg. 26.60 *(978-1-4677-2457-9(2)*, Lerner Pubns.) Lerner Publishing Group.

TELEGRAPH

Davis, Lynn. Samuel Morse, 1 vol. 2016. (ENG., Illus.). 24p. (J). *(978-1-62403-725-2(9))* ABDO Publishing Co.

Figley, Marty Rhodes. President Lincoln, Willie Kettles, & the Telegraph Machine. 2010. pap. 56.72 *(978-0-7613-6929-5(5))* Lerner Publishing Group.

Jarnow, Jesse. Telegraph & Telephone Networks: Ground Breaking Developments in American Communications. 2004. (America's Industrial Society in the 19th Century Ser.). (ENG., Illus.). 32p. (gr. 5-8). pap. 10.00 *(978-0-8239-4279-4(1))* Rosen Publishing Group, Inc., The.

—Telegraph & Telephone Networks: Groundbreaking Developments in American Communications. 2009. (America's Industrial Society in the 19th Century Ser.). 32p. (gr. 4-4). 47.90 *(978-1-61511-341-5(X))* Rosen Publishing Group, Inc., The.

Kulling, Monica. Making Contact! Marconi Goes Wireless. 2016. (Great Idea Ser.). (ENG., Illus.). 32p. (J). (gr. k-3). pap. 6.99 *(978-1-101-91842-5(X)*, Tundra Bks.) Tundra Bks. CAN. Dist: Penguin Random Hse. LLC.

—Making Contact! Marconi Goes Wireless. Rudnicki, Richard, illus. 2013. (Great Idea Ser.). (ENG.). 32p. (J). (gr. k-3). 17.95 *(978-1-77049-378-0(6)*, Tundra Bks.) Tundra Bks. CAN. Dist: Penguin Random Hse. LLC.

Kuskowski, Alex. Super Simple Telegraph Projects: Inspiring & Educational Science Activities, 1 vol. 2016. (ENG., Illus.). 32p. (J). *(978-1-62403-732-0(1))* ABDO Publishing Co.

McCormick, Anita Louise. The Invention of the Telegraph & Telephone in American History. 2004. (In American History Ser.). (Illus.). 128p. (J). lib. bdg. 26.60 *(978-0-7660-1841-9(5))* Enslow Pubs., Inc.

Salzmann, Mary Elizabeth. Telegraph, 1 vol. 2016. (ENG., Illus.). 24p. (J). *(978-1-62403-711-5(9))* ABDO Publishing Co.

Worth, Richard. The Telegraph & Telephone. 2005. (Great Inventions Ser.). (Illus.). 48p. (gr. 5-12). lib. bdg. 31.00 *(978-0-8368-5879-2(4)*, Gareth Stevens Secondary Library) Stevens, Gareth Publishing LLLP.

Zannos, Susan. Samuel Morse & the Telegraph. 2004. (Uncharted, Unexplored, & Unexplained Ser.). (Illus.). 48p. (J). (gr. 4-8). lib. bdg. 29.95 *(978-1-58415-269-9(9))* Mitchell Lane Pubs., Inc.

TELEGRAPH—FICTION

Appleton, Victor. Tom Swift & his Wireless Message. 2005. 26.95 *(978-1-4218-1506-0(0))*; 196p. pap. 11.95 *(978-1-4218-1606-7(7))* 1st World Publishing, Inc. (1st World Library - Literary Society).

Rozier, Lucy Margaret. Jackrabbit McCabe & the Electric Telegraph. Espinosa, Leo, illus. 2015. (ENG.). 40p. (J). (gr. -1-3). 17.99 *(978-0-385-37843-7(2)*, Schwartz & Wade Bks.) Random Hse. Children's Bks.

Stockton, Frank Richard. What Might Have Been Expected. 2009. 128p. 23.95 *(978-1-60664-676-2(1))*; pap. 10.95 *(978-1-60664-305-1(3))* Rodgers, Alan Bks.

TELEPATHY

see Thought Transference

TELEPHONE

Allen, Kathy. Cell Phone Safety, 6 vols. 2013. (Tech Safety Smarts Ser.). (ENG.). 32p. (gr. 3-4). 47.70 *(978-1-62065-797-3(X)*, Fact Finders); pap. 8.10 *(978-1-62065-796-6(1))*; lib. bdg. 27.32 *(978-1-4296-9945-7(0))* Capstone Press of Coughlan Cos.

Ashley, Susan. I Can Use the Telephone. 2004. (I Can Do It! Ser.). (Illus.). 24p. (gr. k-3). pap. 8.15 *(978-0-8368-4334-7(7))*; lib. bdg. 21.00 *(978-0-8368-4327-9(4))* Stevens, Gareth Publishing LLLP. (Weekly Reader Leveled Readers).

Bader, Bonnie. Who Was Alexander Graham Bell? Groff, David, illus. 2013. (Who Was? Ser.). (ENG.). 112p. (J). (gr. 3-7). 5.99 *(978-0-448-46460-2(8)*, Grosset & Dunlap) Penguin Young Readers Group.

—Who Was Alexander Graham Bell? 2013. (Who Was... ? Ser.). lib. bdg. 16.00 *(978-0-606-32132-7(2)*, Turtleback) Turtleback Bks.

Bankston, John. Alexander Graham Bell & the Story of the Telephone. 2004. (Uncharted, Unexplored, & Unexplained Ser.). (Illus.). 48p. (J). (gr. 4-8). lib. bdg. 29.95 *(978-1-58415-243-9(5))* Mitchell Lane Pubs., Inc.

Banting, Erinn. Inventing the Telephone. 2006. (Breakthrough Inventions Ser.). (ENG., Illus.). 32p. (J). (gr. 4-7). pap. *(978-0-7787-2837-5(4))*; lib. bdg. *(978-0-7787-2815-3(3))* Crabtree Publishing Co.

Berger, Melvin. Telephones, Televisions, & Toilets. (Discovery Readers Ser.). (ENG.). 48p. (J). pap. 3.95 *(978-0-8249-5311-9(8)*, Ideal Pubns.) Worthy Publishing.

Brown, Natalie. Who Was Alexander Graham Bell? 2012. (InfoMax Readers Ser.). (ENG., Illus.). 24p. (J). (gr. 1-2). pap. 8.25 *(978-1-4488-9085-9(3)*, Rosen Classroom) Rosen Publishing Group, Inc., The.

Bryan, Dale-Marie. Smartphone Safety & Privacy. 2013. 64p. (J). (gr. 5-8). 31.95 *(978-1-4488-9573-1(1))*; pap. 77.70 *(978-1-4488-9587-8(1))*; pap. 12.95 *(978-1-4488-9586-1(3))* Rosen Publishing Group, Inc., The.

Career Building Through Creating Mobile Apps. 2013. (Digital Career Building Ser.). 64p. (YA). (gr. 7-12). pap. 77.70 *(978-1-4777-1738-7(2))* Rosen Publishing Group, Inc., The.

Chambers, Catherine. Alexander Graham Bell, 1 vol. 2014. (Science Biographies Ser.). (ENG.). 32p. (gr. 2-4). lib. bdg. 30.65 *(978-1-4109-6238-6(5)*, Raintree Perspectives) Heinemann-Raintree.

Crompton, Samuel Willard. Alexander Graham Bell & the Telephone: The Invention That Changed Communication. 2008. (Milestones in American History Ser.). (Illus.). 120p. (J). (gr. 7-12). 35.00 *(978-1-60413-004-1(0))* Facts On File, Inc.

Cunningham, Kevin. Cell Phones. 2007. (21st Century Skills Library: Global Products Ser.). (ENG.). 32p. (gr. 4-8). lib. bdg. 28.50 *(978-1-60279-022-3(1)*, 200023) Cherry Lake Publishing.

Davis, Lynn. Alexander Graham Bell, 1 vol. 2016. (ENG.). 24p. (J). *(978-1-62403-721-4(6))* ABDO Publishing Co.

Einhorn, Kama. The 4-1-1 on Phones! Borgions, Mark, illus. 2015. (History of Fun Stuff Ser.). (ENG.). 48p. (J). (gr. 1-3). pap. 3.99 *(978-1-4814-4404-0(2)*, Simon Spotlight) Simon Spotlight.

Enz, Tammy. Amazing Story of Cell Phone Technology. Pop Art Properties Staff, illus. 2013. (STEM Adventures Ser.). (ENG.). 32p. (gr. 3-4). 30.65 *(978-1-4765-0137-6(8)*, Graphic Library); pap. 8.95 *(978-1-4765-3457-2(8))* Capstone Press of Coughlan Cos.

Equipo Staff & Delafosse, Claude. El Telefono y los Medios de Communicación. (Coleccion Mundo Maravilloso). (SPA., Illus.). 40p. (J). (gr. 2-4). *(978-84-348-5484-0(8)*, SM8407) SM Ediciones.

Espejo, Roman. Smartphones. 2013. (Opposing Viewpoints Ser.). (ENG., Illus.). 224p. (gr. 10-12). pap. 33.80 *(978-0-7377-6343-0(4))*; lib. bdg. 48.80 *(978-0-7377-6342-3(6))* Cengage Gale. (Greenhaven Pr., Inc.).

Everett, Reese. Smartphones in Class, Yes or No. 2016. (ENG.). 32p. (gr. 3-6). 32.79 *(978-1-68191-382-7(8))* Rourke Educational Media.

Feinstein, Stephen. Alexander Graham Bell: The Genius Behind the Phone. 2008. (Inventors Who Changed the World Ser.). (Illus.). 128p. (J). (gr. 6-18). lib. bdg. 34.60 *(978-1-59845-055-2(7)*, MyReportLinks.com Bks.) Enslow Pubs., Inc.

Fraser, Mary Ann. Alexander Graham Bell Answers the Call. Fraser, Mary Ann, illus. 2017. (ENG., Illus.). 32p. (J). (gr. 1-4). lib. bdg. 16.99 *(978-1-58089-721-1(5))* Charlesbridge Publishing, Inc.

Guard, Anara. What If You Need to Call 911?, 1 vol. Laughead, Mike, illus. 2011. (Danger Zone Ser.). (ENG.). 24p. (gr. 1-2). lib. bdg. 25.99 *(978-1-4048-6682-9(5))* Picture Window Bks.

Hantula, Richard, et al. How Do Cell Phones Work? 2009. (Science in the Real World Ser.). (Illus.). 32p. (gr. 4-6). 28.00 *(978-1-60413-475-9(5)*, Chelsea Clubhouse) Facts On File, Inc.

Henneberg, Susan. Are Mobile Devices Harmful. 2016. (ENG.). 80p. (J). (gr. 5-12). lib. bdg. *(978-1-68282-096-4(3))* ReferencePoint Pr., Inc.

Jackman, Vernon. Bunnies & Butterflies in the Backyard & the Pirates Who Know Where They Live: Stories That Help Children Learn & Remember Their Address & Telephone Number. Theagene, Jeannisse, illus. l.t. ed. 2010. (ENG.). 32p. (J). pap. 6.99 *(978-0-9829371-1-2(3))* New Kid Safety.

Jackson, Tom. Telephones & Cellphones. 2015. (Technology Timelines Ser.). (Illus.). 32p. (gr. 3-6). 31.35 *(978-1-78121-239-4(2))* Brown Bear Bks.

James, Emily. Alexander Graham Bell. 2017. (Great Scientists & Inventors Ser.). (ENG.). 24p. (gr. k-1). lib. bdg. 26.65 *(978-1-5157-3883-1(3)*, Pebble Plus) Capstone Press of Coughlan Cos.

Jarnow, Jesse. Telegraph & Telephone Networks: Ground Breaking Developments in American Communications. 2004. (America's Industrial Society in the 19th Century Ser.). (ENG., Illus.). 32p. (gr. 5-8). pap. 10.00 *(978-0-8239-4279-4(1))* Rosen Publishing Group, Inc., The.

—Telegraph & Telephone Networks: Groundbreaking Developments in American Communications. 2009. (America's Industrial Society in the 19th Century Ser.). 32p. (gr. 4-4). 47.90 *(978-1-61511-341-5(X))* Rosen Publishing Group, Inc., The.

Kramer, Barbara. Alexander Graham Bell. 2015. (Readers Bios Ser.). (ENG.). 32p. (J). (gr. k-3). pap. 3.99 *(978-1-4263-1935-8(5)*, National Geographic Children's Bks.) National Geographic Society.

Kulling, Monica. Listen Up! Alexander Graham Bell's Talking Machine. Walz, Richard, illus. 2007. (Step into Reading Ser.). (ENG.). 48p. (J). (gr. k-3). per. 3.99 *(978-0-375-83115-7(0)*, Random Hse. Bks. for Young Readers) Random Hse. Children's Bks.

Kuskowski, Alex. Super Simple Telephone Projects: Inspiring & Educational Science Activities, 1 vol. 2016. (ENG., Illus.). 32p. (J). *(978-1-62403-733-7(X))* ABDO Publishing Co.

Lin, Yoming S. Alexander Graham Bell & the Telephone. 2012. (Eureka! Ser.). (Illus.). 24p. (J). (gr. 3-6). lib. bdg. 22.60 *(978-1-4488-5034-1(7))* Rosen Publishing Group, Inc., The.

Lyons, Heather. Programming Awesome Apps. Westgate, Alex, illus. 2017. (Kids Get Coding Ser.). (ENG.). 24p. (J). (gr. 1-4). 26.65 **(978-1-5124-3942-7(8))** Lerner Publishing Group.

Marsico, Katie. Good Manners on the Phone, 1 vol. Haslam, John, illus. 2009. (Good Manners Matter! Ser.). (ENG.). 32p. (J). (gr. -1-2). 28.50 *(978-1-60270-611-8(5))* Magic Wagon.

Masters, Nancy Robinson. How Did That Get to My House? Telephone. 2009. (Community Connections: How Did That Get to My House? Ser.). (ENG.). 24p. (gr. 2-5). lib. bdg. 25.64 *(978-1-60279-480-1(4)*, 200251) Cherry Lake Publishing.

McCormick, Anita Louise. The Invention of the Telegraph & Telephone in American History. 2004. (In American History Ser.). (Illus.). 128p. (J). lib. bdg. 26.60 *(978-0-7660-1841-9(5))* Enslow Pubs., Inc.

McLeese, Don. Cell Phones. 2008. (ENG., Illus.). 48p. (gr. 4-8). pap. 10.95 *(978-1-60694-908-5(X))* Rourke Educational Media.

Meucci, Sandra. Antonio & the Electric Scream: The Man Who Invented the Telephone. 2010. 138p. (J). pap. *(978-0-8283-2197-6(3))* Branden Bks.

Nakaya, Andrea C. Cell Phones. 2016. (Matters of Opinion Ser.). (ENG., Illus.). 64p. (J). (gr. 4-6). lib. bdg. 27.93 *(978-1-59953-755-9(9))* Norwood Hse. Pr.

Netzley, Patricia. Cell Phones: Threats to Privacy & Security. 2014. (Cell Phones & Society). (ENG., Illus.). 80p. (J). lib. bdg. *(978-1-60152-668-7(7))* ReferencePoint Pr., Inc.

Netzley, Patricia D. How Do Cell Phones Affect Health? 2014. (Cell Phones & Society). (ENG., Illus.). 80p. (J). lib. bdg. *(978-1-60152-670-0(9))* ReferencePoint Pr., Inc.

Oxlade, Chris. The Mobile Continent White Band. 2016. (Cambridge Reading Adventures Ser.). (ENG.). 32p. pap. 7.81 *(978-1-316-60067-2(X))* Cambridge Univ. Pr.

Petrie, Kristin. Telephones, 1 vol. 2009. (Everyday Inventions Ser.). (ENG., Illus.). 32p. (gr. 3-6). 27.07 *(978-1-60453-088-9(X)*, Checkerboard Library) ABDO Publishing Co.

Pipe, Jim. You Wouldn't Want to Live Without Cell Phones! Walker, Rory, illus. 2014. (You Wouldn't Want to Live Without... Ser.). (ENG.). 32p. (J). lib. bdg. 29.00 *(978-0-531-21217-2(3)*, Watts, Franklin) Scholastic Library Publishing.

Radios, Phones & Telecommunications. 2005. (Inventions Ser.). (Illus.). 30p. (J). pap. 15.95 incl. audio *(978-0-9724983-4-0(6))* Jazwares Distribution, Inc.

Rivera, Sheila. Alexander Graham Bell: A Life of Helpfulness. 2007. (Pull Ahead Bks.). (Illus.). 32p. (J). (gr. 3-7). lib. bdg. 22.60 *(978-0-8225-6463-8(7)*, Lerner Pubns.) Lerner Publishing Group.

Rowe, Brooke. Making a Telephone. Bane, Jeff, illus. 2016. (My Early Library: My Science Fun Ser.). (ENG.). 24p. (J). (gr. k-1). 28.50 *(978-1-63471-029-9(0)*, 208196) Cherry Lake Publishing.

Salzmann, Mary Elizabeth. Telephone, 1 vol. 2016. (ENG., Illus.). 24p. (J). *(978-1-62403-712-2(7))* ABDO Publishing Co.

Schuman, Michael. Alexander Graham Bell: Scientist & Inventor. 2015. (Legendary American Biographies Ser.). 96p. (J). (gr. 6-12). 27.94 *(978-0-7660-6430-0(1))* Enslow Pubs., Inc.

Schuman, Michael A. Alexander Graham Bell: Scientist & Inventor. 2015. (Legendary American Biographies Ser.). 96p. (J). (gr. 6-12). pap. 10.95 *(978-0-7660-6431-7(X))* Enslow Pubs., Inc.

Sévigny, Eric, illus. The Phone Call. 2003. (Clubhouse Ser.). (ENG.). 24p. (J). (gr. -1-1). pap. 3.99 *(978-2-89450-446-8(2))* Caillouet, Gerry.

Spilsbury, Louise. Alexander Graham Bell & the Telephone, 01 vols., 1. 2016. (Inventions That Changed the World Ser.). (ENG.). 32p. (J). pap. 10.00 *(978-1-5081-4623-0(3)*, PowerKids Pr.) Rosen Publishing Group, Inc., The.

Spilsbury, Louise & Spilsbury, Richard. The Telephone, 1 vol. 2010. (Tales of Invention Ser.). (ENG., Illus.). 32p. (gr. 3-5). 30.65 *(978-1-4329-3826-0(6))*; pap. 8.95 *(978-1-4329-3833-8(9))* Heinemann-Raintree. (NA-h).

Staley, Erin. Career Building Through Creating Mobile Apps. 2013. (Digital Career Building Ser.). 64p. (YA). (gr. 7-12). 31.95 *(978-1-4777-1727-1(7))* Rosen Publishing Group, Inc., The.

Stefoff, Rebecca. The Telephone. 2005. (Great Inventions Ser.). (Illus.). 127p. (YA). (gr. 8-12). lib. bdg. *(978-0-7614-1879-5(2)*, Benchmark Bks.) Marshall Cavendish Corp.

Venezia, Mike. Alexander Graham Bell: Setting the Tone for Communication. Venezia, Mike, illus. (Getting to Know the World's Greatest Inventors & Scientists Ser.). (ENG., Illus.). 32p. (J). 2009. (gr. 3-4). pap. 6.95 *(978-0-531-22207-2(1)*, Children's Pr.) 2008. (gr. 2-5). 28.00 *(978-0-531-14976-8(5))* Scholastic Library Publishing.

Wilcox, Christine. Cell Phones & Teens. 2014. (Cell Phones & Society). (ENG., Illus.). 80p. (J). lib. bdg. *(978-1-60152-666-3(0))* ReferencePoint Pr., Inc.

Worth, Richard. The Telegraph & Telephone. 2005. (Great Inventions Ser.). (Illus.). 48p. (gr. 5-12). lib. bdg. 31.00 *(978-0-8368-5879-2(4)*, Gareth Stevens Secondary Library) Stevens, Gareth Publishing LLLP.

Zoehfeld, Kathleen Weidner. Phones Keep Us Connected. Nowowiejska, Kasia, illus. 2017. (Let's-Read-And-Find-Out Science 2 Ser.). 40p. (J). (gr. -1-3). pap. 6.99 *(978-0-06-238667-0(0))* HarperCollins Pubs.

TELEPHONE—FICTION

Ackerman, Peter. The Lonely Phone Booth. Dalton, Max, illus. 2010. (ENG.). 32p. (J). (gr. k-2). 16.95 *(978-1-56792-414-5(X))* Godine, David R. Pub.

Appleton, Victor. Tom Swift & His Photo Telephone. 2007. 100p. per. *(978-1-4068-1621-1(3))* Echo Library.

—Tom Swift & his Photo Telephone. 2005. 27.95 *(978-1-4218-1503-9(6))*; 204p. pap. 12.95 *(978-1-4218-1603-6(2))* 1st World Publishing, Inc. (1st World Library - Literary Society).

—Tom Swift & His Photo Telephone or the. 2006. pap. *(978-1-4065-0906-9(X))* Dodo Pr.

Arnold, Janet. The Special Number. 2011. 28p. pap. 15.99 *(978-1-4568-8962-1(6))* Xlibris Corp.

Bour, Daniele. Petit ours brun repond au Teleph. pap. 12.95 *(978-2-227-74805-7(2))* Bayard Editions FRA. Dist: Distribooks, Inc.

Collins, Lori & Koski, Mary. Learn to Call 911. Brown, Dan, illus. 2007. (ENG.). 16p. (J). (gr. k-2). pap. 2.95 *(978-1-930650-05-3(1))* mTrellis Publishing, Inc.

Deutsch, Stacia & Cohon, Rhody. Bell's Breakthrough. Wenzel, David, illus. 2013. (Blast to the Past Ser.: 3). (ENG.). 128p. (J). (gr. 2-5). pap. 5.99 *(978-1-4424-9536-4(7)*, Simon & Schuster/Paula Wiseman Bks.) Simon & Schuster/Paula Wiseman Bks.

Esbensen, Barbara Juster. Who Is Calling? Date not set. 15.95 *(978-0-8050-4899-5(5))* Holt, Henry & Co.

Hinton, Nigel. 2 Die 4. 2012. (Stoke Books Titles Ser.). (ENG.). 88p. (YA). (gr. 8-12). pap. 6.95 *(978-1-78112-109-2(5))*; lib. bdg. 22.60 *(978-1-78112-110-8(9))* Lerner Publishing Group.

Hope, Laura Lee. Outdoor Girls in the Saddle. 2006. 26.95 *(978-1-4218-2983-8(5))*; pap. 11.95 *(978-1-4218-3083-4(3))* 1st World Publishing, Inc.

Kesselring, Mari & Epelbaum, Mariano. Tuned Out. Epelbaum, Mariano, illus. 2015. (ENG., Illus.). 64p. (J). pap. 8.95 *(978-1-63235-099-2(8))* RiverStream Publishing.

Koski, Mary B. Impatient Pamela Calls 9-1-1. Brown, Dan, illus. 2nd ed. 2004. (Impatient Pamela Ser.). (ENG.). 32p. (J). (gr. 1-3). 14.95 *(978-1-930650-09-1(4))* mTrellis Publishing, Inc.

Mlynowski, Sarah. Gimme a Call. 2011. (ENG.). 320p. (YA). (gr. 7). pap. 9.99 *(978-0-385-73589-6(8)*, Ember) Random Hse. Children's Bks.

Ostow, Micol. What Would My Cell Phone Do? 2011. (ENG.). 272p. (YA). (gr. 7-18). 7.99 *(978-0-14-241469-9(7)*, Speak) Penguin Young Readers Group.

Publications International Ltd. Staff. Dora PNO BK Follow Music. 2008. 10p. (J). 16.98 *(978-1-4127-8996-7(6)*, PIL Kids) Publications International, Ltd.

Reynolds, Wendy. Moby for Justice. 2006. 17.00 *(978-0-8059-8861-1(0))* Dorrance Publishing Co., Inc.

School Zone Staff, ed. Talking Telephone. 2007. (J). 7.99 *(978-1-58947-873-2(8))* School Zone Publishing Co.

Slater, Teddy. Emergency, Call 911. Lewis, Anthony, illus. 2010. 16p. (J). *(978-0-545-24601-9(6))* Scholastic, Inc.

Witherow, Wendy. Miranda's Makeover. Pulley, Kelly, illus. 2007. 93p. (J). *(978-1-934306-11-6(8))* Mission City Pr., Inc.

TELESCOPES

Bortz, Fred. Beyond Jupiter: The Story of Planetary Astronomer Heidi Hammel. 2006. (ENG., Illus.). 128p. (gr. 7-9). per. 19.95 *(978-0-309-09552-5(2)*, Joseph Henry Pr.) National Academies Pr.

Building Blocks of Science: Sky Watchers Teacher's Guide. 2007. (Illus.). ring bd. *(978-0-89278-325-0(7))* Carolina Biological Supply Co.

Bullock, Linda. Looking Through a Telescope. 2004. (Rookie Read-About Science Ser.). (ENG., Illus.). 32p. (J). (gr. 1-2). pap. 4.95 *(978-0-516-27906-0(8)*, Children's Pr.) Scholastic Library Publishing.

Castaldo, Nancy F. Leap into Space: Exploring the Universe & Your Place in It. McRae, Patrick, illus. 2008. (ENG.). 128p. (J). (gr. 3-7). 16.99 *(978-0-8249-6815-1(8))*; pap. 12.99 *(978-0-8249-6816-8(6))* Worthy Publishing. (Ideal Pubns.).

Gibson, Brylee. The World Beyond Earth. 2007. (Connectors Ser.). (gr. 2-5). pap. (978-1-877453-11-3(0)) Global Education Systems Ltd.

Jefferis, David. Star Spotters: Telescopes & Observatories. 2008. (Exploring Our Solar System Ser.). (ENG., Illus.). 32p. (J). (gr. 3-8). lib. bdg. (978-0-7787-3725-4(X)); (gr. 4-9). pap. (978-0-7787-3742-1(X)) Crabtree Publishing Co.

Kuskowski, Alex. Stargazing, 1 vol. 2015. (ENG., Illus.). 24p. (J). (978-1-62403-746-7(1)) ABDO Publishing Co.

Lin, Yoming S. Galileo & the Telescope. 2012. (Eureka! Ser.). (Illus.). 24p. (J). (gr. 3-6). lib. bdg. 22.60 (978-1-4488-5030-3(4)) Rosen Publishing Group, Inc., The.

Mattern, Joanne. The Telescope: Looking into Space. (Technology That Changed the World Ser.). 24p. 2009. (gr. 2-3). 42.50 (978-1-60853-279-7(8)) 2003. (Illus.). (J). lib. bdg. 22.60 (978-0-8239-6489-5(2)) Rosen Publishing Group, Inc., The. (PowerKids Pr.).

Orr, Tamra. The Telescope. 2004. (Inventions That Shaped the World Ser.). (ENG., Illus.). 80p. (J). 30.50 (978-0-531-12344-7(8), Watts, Franklin) Scholastic Library Publishing.

Orr, Tamra B. The Telescope. 2006. (Inventions That Shaped the World Ser.). (Illus.). 80p. (gr. 5-8). 19.95 (978-0-7569-6863-2(1)) Perfection Learning Corp.

Phoenix International Staff, illus. Thomas & the Telescope. 2014. 12p. (J). bds. 17.98 (978-1-4508-7993-4(4), 1450879934) Phoenix International Publications, Inc.

Rau, Heather. Through My Telescope. 2013. (Rosen Readers Ser.). (ENG.). 24p. (J). (gr. 3-4). pap. 8.25 (978-1-4777-2617-4(9)); pap. 49.50 (978-1-4777-2618-1(7)) Rosen Publishing Group, Inc., The. (Rosen Classroom).

Rosewald, Mary. Tara's Telescope. 2013. (InfoMax Readers Ser.). (ENG.). 24p. (J). (gr. 3-4). pap. 8.25 (978-1-4777-2655-6(1)); pap. 49.50 (978-1-4777-2656-3(X)) Rosen Publishing Group, Inc., The. (Rosen Classroom).

Roza, Greg. The Hubble Space Telescope: Understanding & Representing Numbers in the Billions. (PowerMath: Proficiency Plus Ser.). 32p. 2009. (gr. 4-5). 47.90 (978-1-60851-422-9(6)) 2005. (Illus.). (J). (gr. 3-6). lib. bdg. 25.25 (978-1-4042-2931-0(0)) Rosen Publishing Group, Inc., The. (PowerKids Pr.).

—The Hubble Space Telescope: Understanding & Representing Numbers up to 1 Billion. 2009. (Math for the REAL World Ser.). (ENG., Illus.). 32p. (gr. 5-6). pap. 10.00 (978-1-4042-5129-8(4)) Rosen Publishing Group, Inc., The.

Simon, Seymour. Destination: Space. 2004. (ENG.). 32p. (J). pap. 6.99 (978-0-06-059681-1(3), Harper Trophy) HarperCollins Pubs.

Sparrow, Giles. Observing the Universe. 2006. (Secrets of the Universe Ser.). (Illus.). 48p. (gr. 6-12). pap. 14.05 (978-0-8368-7284-2(3)); lib. bdg. 31.00 (978-0-8368-7277-4(0)) Stevens, Gareth Publishing LLLP. (Gareth Stevens Secondary Library).

Stefoff, Rebecca. Microscopes & Telescopes. 2006. (Great Inventions Ser.). (Illus.). 128p. (J). (gr. 3-7). lib. bdg. 39.93 (978-0-7614-2230-3(7), Benchmark Bks.) Marshall Cavendish Corp.

Telescopes & Space Probes. 2006. (World Book's Solar System & Space Exploration Library). (Illus.). 63p. (J). (978-0-7166-9510-3(3)) World Bk., Inc.

Villard, Ray. Supertelescopios: Por dentro y por fuera (Large Telescopes: Inside & Out) 2009. (Tecnología: Mapas para el Futuro Ser.). (SPA.). 48p. (gr. 4-4). 53.00 (978-1-60853-290-2(9), Editorial Buenas Letras) Rosen Publishing Group, Inc., The.

Villard, Raymond. Large Telescopes: Inside & Out. 2009. (Technology: Blueprints of the Future Ser.). 48p. (gr. 4-4). 53.00 (978-1-60853-283-4(6)) Rosen Publishing Group, Inc., The.

World Book, Inc Staff, contrib. by. Observatories on Earth. 2010. (J). (978-0-7166-9553-0(7)) World Bk., Inc.

—Telescopes & Space Probes. (J). 2010. (978-0-7166-9541-7(3)) 2nd ed. 2006. (Illus.). 64p. (978-0-7166-9520-2(0)) World Bk., Inc.

TELETUBBIES (FICTITIOUS CHARACTERS)—FICTION

Davenport, Andrew. Here Come the Teletubbies. 2004. (Illus.). (J). (gr. -1-2). spiral bd. (978-0-616-03029-5(0)); spiral bd. (978-0-616-04551-0(4)) Canadian National Institute for the Blind/Institut National Canadien pour les Aveugles.

—Teletubbies (Ce p'Tit Agneau) 2004. (J). (gr. -1-2). spiral bd. (978-0-616-03071-4(1)) Canadian National Institute for the Blind/Institut National Canadien pour les Aveugles.

Follow the Leader. 2003. (J). per. (978-1-57657-861-2(5)) Paradise Pr., Inc.

TELEVISION

Berger, Melvin. Telephones, Televisions, & Toilets. (Discovery Readers Ser.). (ENG.). 48p. (J). pap. 3.95 (978-0-8249-5311-9(8), Ideal Pubns.) Worthy Publishing.

Bernay, Emma, ed. Television. 2007. (Introducing Issues with Opposing Viewpoints Ser.). (ENG., Illus.). 119p. (YA). (gr. 7-12). lib. bdg. 36.95 (978-0-7377-3853-7(7)) Cengage Gale.

Bodden, Valerie. Television. 2008. (Media Sources Ser.). (Illus.). 24p. (J). lib. bdg. 24.25 (978-1-58341-559-7(9), Creative Education) Creative Co., The.

Cantor, Joanne. Teddy's TV Troubles. Lowes, Tom, illus. 2004. 36p. (J). mass mkt. 16.95 (978-0-9647663-7-2(X)) HenschelHAUS Publishing.

Chmielewski, Gary. How Did That Get to My House? Television. 2009. (Community Connections: How Did That Get to My House? Ser.). (ENG.). 24p. (gr. 2-5). lib. bdg. 25.64 (978-1-60279-476-4(6), 200247) Cherry Lake Publishing.

Clark, Katie. Animal Actors. 2013. (We Work! Animals with Jobs Ser.). (Illus.). 24p. (J). (gr. -1-3). lib. bdg. 21.32 (978-1-61772-897-6(7)) Bearport Publishing Co., Inc.

Enz, Tammy. Terrific Tale of Television Technology. Pop Art Properties Staff, illus. 2013. (STEM Adventures Ser.). (ENG.). 32p. (gr. 3-4). 30.65 (978-1-4765-0138-3(6), Graphic Library); pap. 8.95 (978-1-4765-3458-9(6)) Capstone Press of Coughlan Cos.

Gibson, Karen. What It's Like to Be George Lopez. de la Vega, Eida, tr. from ENG. 2011. (What It's Like to Be... = Que Se Sienta Al Ser... Ser.). (SPA., Illus.). 32p. (J). (gr. -1-2). lib. bdg. 25.70 (978-1-58415-991-9(X)) Mitchell Lane Pubs., Inc.

Haerens, Margaret. Television. 2011. (Opposing Viewpoints Ser.). 240p. pap. 29.45 (978-0-7377-5244-1(0)); (ENG.). 224p. (gr. 12-12). lib. bdg. 48.80 (978-0-7377-5243-4(2)) Cengage Gale. (Greenhaven Pr., Inc.).

Hirschmann, Kris. HDTV - High Definition Television. 2010. (Great Idea Ser.). 48p. (J). (gr. 4-6). lib. bdg. 26.60 (978-1-59953-379-7(0)) Norwood Hse. Pr.

La Bella, Laura. Hulu & Jason Kilar, 1 vol. 2015. (ENG.). 128p. (YA). 35.60 (978-1-4777-7921-7(3), Rosen Young Adult) Rosen Publishing Group, Inc., The.

Mattern, Joanne. The Television: Window to the World. (Technology That Changed the World Ser.). 24p. 2009. (gr. 2-3). 42.50 (978-1-60853-280-3(1)) 2003. (Illus.). (J). lib. bdg. 22.60 (978-0-8239-6493-2(0)) Rosen Publishing Group, Inc., The. (PowerKids Pr.).

Mullins, Matt. Scriptwriter. 2011. (21st Century Skills Library: Cool Arts Careers Ser.). (ENG.). 32p. (gr. 4-8). lib. bdg. 28.50 (978-1-61080-135-5(0), 201148) Cherry Lake Publishing.

Nagle, Jeanne M. Careers in Television. 2009. (Career Resource Library). 192p. (gr. 7-12). 63.90 (978-1-60853-404-3(9)) Rosen Publishing Group, Inc., The.

Picou, Lin. TV, Yes or No. 2015. (ENG.). 24p. (gr. k-3). 28.50 (978-1-63430-345-3(8)) Rourke Educational Media.

Richter, Joanne. Inventing the Television. 2006. (Breakthrough Inventions Ser.). (ENG., Illus.). 32p. (J). (gr. 4-7). pap. (978-0-7787-2835-1(8)); lib. bdg. (978-0-7787-2813-9(7)) Crabtree Publishing Co.

Somervill, Barbara. Actor. 2011. (21st Century Skills Library: Cool Arts Careers Ser.). (ENG.). 32p. (gr. 4-8). lib. bdg. 28.50 (978-1-61080-129-4(6), 201136) Cherry Lake Publishing.

Spilsbury, Richard & Spilsbury, Louise. The Television, 1 vol. 2011. (Tales of Invention Ser.). (ENG.). 32p. (gr. 3-5). pap. 8.95 (978-1-4329-4890-0(3)); 30.65 (978-1-4329-4881-8(4)) Heinemann-Raintree. (NA-h).

Teitelbaum, Michael. Television. 2008. (21st Century Skills Innovation Library: Innovation in Entertainment Ser.). (ENG., Illus.). 32p. (gr. 4-8). lib. bdg. 28.50 (978-1-60279-263-0(1), 200146) Cherry Lake Publishing.

Wheeler, Jill C. Reality TV Titans. 2015. (Reality TV Titans Ser.: Vol. 6). (ENG.). 32p. (J). (gr. -1-3). lib. bdg. 162.42 (978-1-62403-816-7(6)) ABDO Publishing Co.

Wyckoff, Edwin Brit. The Teen Who Invented Television: Philo T. Farnsworth & His Awesome Invention. 2007. (Genius at Work! Great Inventor Biographies Ser.). (Illus.). 32p. (J). (gr. 4-7). lib. bdg. 23.94 (978-0-7660-2845-6(3), Enslow Elementary) Enslow Pubs., Inc.

TELEVISION—BROADCASTING

see Television Broadcasting

TELEVISION—FICTION

Adams, Karin. No TV? No Fair!, 1 vol. 2010. (Lorimer Streetlights Ser.). (ENG.). 120p. (J). (gr. 2-4). 8.95 (978-1-55277-471-7(6), 9781552774717) Lorimer, James & Co., Ltd., Pubs. CAN. Dist: Casemate Pubs. & Bk. Distributors, LLC.

Atinsky, Steve. Tyler on Prime Time. 2004. 176p. (J). (gr. 5-9). pap. 29.00 incl. audio (978-0-8072-2279-9(8), Listening Library) Random Hse. Audio Publishing Group.

Auerbach, Annie. Spongebob Superstar, Vol. 5. 2004. 64p. (J). (gr. 2-5). pap. 17.00 incl. audio (978-1-4000-8628-3(0), Listening Library) Random Hse. Audio Publishing Group.

Bell, Christine. Oh No! the Television Won't Work! 2005. (Illus.). 52p. pap. (978-1-84401-340-1(5)) Athena Pr.

Berenstain, Stan, et al. The Berenstain Bears Discover God's Creation, 1 vol. 2010. (Berenstain Bears/Living Lights Ser.). (ENG.). 40p. (J). (gr. -1-2). 6.99 (978-0-310-71936-6(4)) Zonderkidz.

Bonin, Liane. Pretty on the Outside: Fame Unlimited. 2007. 288p. (YA). pap. 9.99 (978-0-451-22122-3(2), N A L Trade) Penguin Publishing Group.

Carlson, Melody. Premiere, 1 vol. 2014. (On the Runway Ser.). (ENG.). 224p. (YA). pap. 9.99 (978-0-310-74728-4(7)) Zondervan.

—Spotlight, 1 vol. 2014. (On the Runway Ser.). (ENG.). 224p. (YA). pap. 9.99 (978-0-310-74821-2(6)) Zondervan.

Christensen-Jowers, Rae. A Day I Spent Without Tv. 2011. 24p. pap. 12.79 (978-1-4634-2202-8(4)) AuthorHouse.

Collins, Suzanne. Catching Fire. 2009. (Hunger Games Trilogy: Bk. 2). (YA). 74.99 (978-1-61574-572-2(6)) Findaway World, LLC.

—Catching Fire. 2009. 12.04 (978-0-7848-3842-6(9), Everbind) Marco Bk. Co.

—Catching Fire. 2011. 480p. pap. (978-1-4071-3209-9(1)) Scholastic.

—Catching Fire. (Hunger Games Ser.: 2). (ENG.). (gr. 7). 2014. 448p. (YA). pap. 12.99 (978-0-545-79188-5(X), Tangerine Pr.) 2013. 400p. (YA). pap. 12.99 (978-0-545-58617-7(8), Scholastic Pr.) 2010. (Illus.). 400p. (J). lib. bdg. 22.99 (978-0-545-31059-8(8), Scholastic Pr.) 2009. 400p. (J). 18.99 (978-0-439-02349-8(1), Scholastic Pr.) Scholastic, Inc.

—Catching Fire. l.t. ed. (Hunger Games Trilogy: 2). (ENG.). (YA). 2012. 498p. (gr. 7-12). pap. 14.99 (978-1-59413-585-9(1), Large Print Pr.) 2009. 500p. 23.95 (978-1-4104-2044-2(2)) Thorndike Pr.

—Catching Fire. 2013. (Hunger Games Trilogy Ser.: 2). lib. bdg. 24.50 (978-0-606-32025-2(3), Turtleback) Turtleback Bks.

—Catching Fire. 2011. (Hunger Games Trilogy: Bk. 2). (CHI.). 344p. (YA). (gr. 7-12). pap. (978-7-5063-5566-7(3)) Writers' Publishing Hse.

—EN LLAMAS. 2012. (Hunger Games Trilogy: Bk. 2). (SPA.). 416p. (J). pap. 19.99 (978-84-272-0213-9(X)) Molino, Editorial ESP. Dist: Lectorum Pubns., Inc.

—En Llamas, Bk. 2. 2010. (Hunger Games Trilogy: Bk. 2).Tr. of Catching Fire. (SPA.). 416p. (J). (gr. 8-12). pap. 19.99 (978-84-272-0000-5(5)) Lectorum Pubns., Inc.

—The Hunger Games. 2009. (Hunger Games Trilogy: Bk. 1). 10.85 (978-0-7848-3801-3(1), Everbind) Marco Bk. Co.

—The Hunger Games. 2010. (Hunger Games Trilogy: Bk. 1). (ENG.). 374p. (gr. 7-12). 21.00 (978-1-60686-581-1(1)) Perfection Learning Corp.

—The Hunger Games. Fournier, Guillaume, tr. 2011. (Hunger Games Trilogy: Bk. 1). (FRE.). 398p. (YA). (gr. 7-12). pap. (978-2-266-18269-0(2)) Presses Pocket.

—The Hunger Games. 2011. (Hunger Games Trilogy: 1). (YA). 69.75 (978-1-4561-3196-8(6)) Recorded Bks., Inc.

—The Hunger Games. 2010. (Hunger Games Ser.: 1). (ENG.). 384p. (J). (gr. 7-18). pap. 10.99 (978-0-439-02352-8(1), Scholastic Pr.) Scholastic, Inc.

—The Hunger Games. O'Brien, Tim, illus. 2009. 448p. pap. (978-1-4071-0908-4(1), Scholastic) Scholastic, Inc.

—The Hunger Games. (Hunger Games Ser.: 1). (ENG.). (gr. 7). 2008. 384p. (J). 18.99 (978-0-439-02348-1(3), Scholastic Pr.) 2012. 384p. (J). pap. 12.99 (978-0-545-42511-7(5))Set. 2014. (YA). pap. 38.97 (978-0-545-79191-5(X), Scholastic Pr.) Scholastic, Inc.

—The Hunger Games. l.t. ed. (Hunger Games Trilogy: Bk. 1). (ENG.). (YA). 2012. 484p. (gr. 7-12). pap. 14.99 (978-1-59413-587-3(8), Large Print Pr.) 2009. 486p. 23.95 (978-1-4104-1986-6(X)) Thorndike Pr.

—The Hunger Games. 2010. (Hunger Games Trilogy Ser.: 1). lib. bdg. 22.10 (978-1-4178-3173-9(1), Turtleback) Turtleback Bks.

—The Hunger Games. 2010. (Hunger Games Trilogy: Bk. 1). (CHI.). 324p. (YA). (gr. 7-12). pap. (978-7-5063-5153-9(6)) Writers' Publishing Hse.

—The Hunger Games Trilogy Set: The Hunger Games; Catching Fire; Mockingjay. 2010. (Hunger Games Ser.: 1). (ENG.). (J). (gr. 7-18). 53.97 (978-0-545-26535-5(5), Scholastic Pr.) Scholastic, Inc.

—Los Juegos del Hambre. 2009. (Hunger Games Trilogy: Bk. 1).Tr. of Hunger Games. (SPA.). pap. 19.99 (978-84-9867-539-9(1)) RBA Libros, S.A. ESP. Dist: Lectorum Pubns., Inc.

—LOS JUEGOS DEL HAMBRE. 2012. (Hunger Games Trilogy: Bk. 1). (SPA.). 400p. (J). pap. 19.99 (978-84-272-0212-2(1)) Molino, Editorial ESP. Dist: Lectorum Pubns., Inc.

—Mockingjay. 2011. (Hunger Games Trilogy: Bk. 3). (CHI.). 435p. (YA). (gr. 7-12). pap. (978-986-213-216-6(7)) Locus Publishing Co.

—Mockingjay. (Hunger Games Trilogy: 3). (YA). 2011. 77.75 (978-1-4561-3203-3(2)) 2010. 75.75 (978-1-4561-3205-7(9)) 2010. 1.25 (978-1-4640-2636-2(X)) Recorded Bks., Inc.

—Mockingjay. 2011. (Hunger Games Ser.: Vol. 3). (ENG.). 448p. (YA). (gr. 8-12). pap. (978-1-4071-3210-5(5)) Scholastic Canada, Ltd.

—Mockingjay. 2014. (Hunger Games Ser.: 3). (ENG.). 448p. (YA). (gr. 7). pap. 12.99 (978-0-545-79190-8(1), Scholastic Pr.) 2014. (Hunger Games Ser.: 3). (ENG.). 400p. (YA). (gr. 7). pap. 12.99 (978-0-545-78829-8(3), Scholastic Paperbacks) 2014. (Hunger Games Ser.: 3). (ENG.). 400p. (J). (gr. 7). pap. 12.99 (978-0-545-66326-7(1), Scholastic Pr.) 2010. (Hunger Games Ser.: 3). (ENG.). 400p. (J). (gr. 7-7). lib. bdg. 22.99 (978-0-545-31060-4(1), Scholastic Pr.) 2010. (Hunger Games Ser.: 3). (ENG.). 400p. (J). (gr. 7-18). 18.99 (978-0-439-02351-1(3), Scholastic Pr.) 2010. pap. (978-0-439-02354-2(8), Scholastic Pr.) Scholastic, Inc.

—Mockingjay. l.t. ed. (Hunger Games Trilogy: Bk. 3). (ENG.). (YA). 2012. 502p. (gr. 7-12). pap. 14.99 (978-1-59413-586-6(X), Large Print Pr.) 2010. 503p. 23.99 (978-1-4104-2841-7(9)) Thorndike Pr.

—Mockingjay. 2014. (Hunger Games Trilogy Ser.: 3). lib. bdg. 24.50 (978-0-606-36328-0(9)); lib. bdg. 24.50 (978-0-606-35133-1(7)) Turtleback Bks.

Collins, Yvonne & Rideout, Sandy. The Black Sheep. 2007. 348p. (J). (978-1-4287-4665-7(X)) Hyperion Pr.

Conrad, Lauren. The Fame Game. 2012. (YA). (Fame Game Ser.: 1). (ENG.). 336p. (gr. 9). pap. 10.99 (978-0-06-207519-2(5)); 313p. 12.99 (978-0-06-209271-7(5)) HarperCollins Pubs.

—L. A. Candy. (L. A. Candy Ser.: 1). (ENG.). (YA). (gr. 9-18). 2010. 352p. pap. 9.99 (978-0-06-176759-3(X)) 2009. 336p. 17.99 (978-0-06-176758-6(1)) HarperCollins Pubs.

—Starstruck. (YA). 2013. (Fame Game Ser.: 2). (ENG.). 320p. (gr. 9). pap. 10.99 (978-0-06-207982-4(4)) 2012. (Fame Game Ser.: 2). (ENG.). 304p. (gr. 9). 18.99 (978-0-06-207980-0(8)) 2012. 352p. pap. (978-0-06-220964-1(7)) HarperCollins Pubs.

—Sugar & Spice. (YA). 2011. (L. A. Candy Ser.: 3). (ENG.). 288p. (gr. 9). pap. 9.99 (978-0-06-176763-0(8)) 2010. (L. A. Candy Ser.: 3). (ENG.). 288p. (gr. 9-18). 17.99 (978-0-06-176762-3(X)) 2010. 279p. 9.99 (978-0-06-201148-0(0)) HarperCollins Pubs.

—Sweet Little Lies. 2010. (L. A. Candy Ser.: 2). (YA). (ENG.). 336p. (gr. 9). pap. 9.99 (978-0-06-176761-6(1)); 309p. 9.99 (978-0-06-198572-0(4)) HarperCollins Pubs.

Cooney, Caroline B. If the Witness Lied. 2010. (ENG.). 224p. (YA). (gr. 7). pap. 8.99 (978-0-385-73449-3(2), Ember) Random Hse. Children's Bks.

Damico, Gina. Waste of Space. 2017. (ENG.). 400p. (YA). (gr. 9). 17.99 (978-0-544-63316-2(4), HMH Books For Young Readers) Houghton Mifflin Harcourt Publishing Co.

Darke, J. A. Fade to Black. Evans, Neil, illus. 2016. (Spine Shivers Ser.). (ENG.). 128p. (gr. 3-4). lib. bdg. 26.65 (978-1-4965-3070-7(5)) Stone Arch Bks.

DeVillers, Julia & Roy, Jennifer. Double Feature. 2012. (Mix Ser.). (ENG.). 288p. (J). (gr. 4-8). pap. 7.99 (978-1-4424-3403-5(1), Aladdin) Simon & Schuster Children's Publishing.

DeVillers, Julia & Roy, Jennifer Rozines. Double Feature. 2012. (ENG.). 272p. (J). (gr. 4-8). 16.99 (978-1-4424-3402-8(3), Aladdin) Simon & Schuster Children's Publishing.

Donaldson, Julia. The Quick Brown Fox Cub. 2006. (Red Bananas Ser.). (ENG., Illus.). 48p. (J). (gr. -1-3). lib. bdg. (978-0-7787-1080-6(7)) Crabtree Publishing Co.

Dussling, Jennifer. Whatcha Got? Wummer, Amy, illus. 2004. (Social Studies Connects). 32p. (J). (gr. 1-3). pap. 5.95 (978-1-57565-143-9(2)) Kane Press, Inc.

Fisher, Carolyn. The Snow Show. 2008. (ENG., Illus.). 48p. (J). (gr. k-5). 17.00 (978-0-15-206019-0(7)) Houghton Mifflin Harcourt Publishing Co.

Green, D. L. Zeke Meeks vs the Horrifying TV-Turnoff Week, 1 vol. Alves, Josh, illus. 2012. (Zeke Meeks Ser.). (ENG.). 128p. (gr. 2-2). pap. 5.95 (978-1-4048-7220-2(5)); lib. bdg. 22.65 (978-1-4048-6804-5(6)) Picture Window Bks. (Zeke Meeks).

Greene, Janice. The Plot, 1 vol. unabr. ed. 2010. (Q Reads Ser.). (ENG.). 32p. (YA). (gr. 9-12). pap. 6.95 (978-1-61651-204-0(0)) Saddleback Educational Publishing, Inc.

Greene, Kimberly. My Life on TV. 2011. (My Sister's a Pop Star Ser.). 320p. (J). pap. 5.99 (978-0-7945-2901-7(1), Usborne) EDC Publishing.

—My Sister's a Pop Star. 2011. (My Sister's a Pop Star Ser.). 277p. (J). pap. 5.99 (978-0-7945-2899-7(6), Usborne) EDC Publishing.

Gurevich, Margaret. Chloe by Design, 1 vol. Hagel, Brooke, illus. 2014. (Chloe by Design Ser.). (ENG.). 96p. (gr. 5-8). 101.28 (978-1-4342-9379-4(3)) Stone Arch Bks.

—Chloe by Design: Making the Cut, 1 vol. Hagel, Brooke, illus. 2014. (Chloe by Design Ser.). (ENG.). 384p. (gr. 4-8). 14.95 (978-1-62370-112-3(0)) Capstone Young Readers of Coughlan Cos.

—Design Destiny, 1 vol. Hagel, Brooke, illus. 2014. (Chloe by Design Ser.). (ENG.). 96p. (gr. 5-8). 25.32 (978-1-4342-9180-6(4)) Stone Arch Bks.

Harper, Charise Mericle. Lights, Camera, Cook! Blard-Quintard, Aurélie, illus. 2017. (Next Best Junior Chef Ser.: 1). (ENG.). 192p. (J). (gr. 2-5). 12.99 **(978-0-544-91260-1(8)**, HMH Books For Young Readers) Houghton Mifflin Harcourt Publishing Co.

Harrison, John. Fergal Onions. 2005. (Illus.). 32p. pap. (978-0-7022-3481-1(8)) Univ. of Queensland Pr.

Hiaasen, Carl. Chomp. (ENG.). 304p. (J). (gr. 5). 2013. pap. 8.99 (978-0-375-86827-6(5), Ember) 2012. 16.99 (978-0-375-86842-9(9), Knopf Bks. for Young Readers) Random Hse. Children's Bks.

—Chomp. l.t. ed. 2012. (ENG.). 364p. 23.99 (978-1-4104-5101-9(1)) Thorndike Pr.

—Chomp. 2013. lib. bdg. 19.65 (978-0-606-27006-9(X), Turtleback) Turtleback Bks.

Johnson, Gabriel. Heroes of Dreams: A Heroic Dream Begins. 2011. 33p. (J). pap. 18.95 (978-1-4327-7413-4(1)) Outskirts Pr., Inc.

Kain, P. G. Famous for Thirty Seconds. 2012. (Commercial Breaks Ser.: 1). (ENG.). 320p. (J). (gr. 4-8). pap. 6.99 (978-1-4169-9786-3(5), Aladdin) Simon & Schuster Children's Publishing.

Kimpton, Diana. Princess Ellie's Royal Jamboree No. 11. Finlay, Lizzie, illus. 11th ed. 2008. (ENG.). 96p. (gr. 1-4). pap. 3.99 (978-1-4231-1531-1(7)) Hyperion Pr.

—Princess Ellie's Snowy Ride. Finlay, Lizzie, illus. 2007. (Pony-Crazed Princess Ser.). 90p. (J). 11.65 (978-0-7569-8352-9(5)) Perfection Learning Corp.

Leblanc, Louise. Maddie on TV. Cummins, Sarah, tr. from FRE. Gay, Marie-Louise, illus. 2003. (Formac First Novels Ser.: 48). (ENG.). 64p. (J). (gr. 2-5). 14.95 (978-0-88780-613-1(9), 9780887806131) Formac Publishing Co., Ltd. CAN. Dist: Casemate Pubs. & Bk. Distributors, LLC.

Lee, G. I Want My Kitty Cat Tv! Scott, E., illus. 2012. 24p. pap. 24.95 (978-1-4626-6610-2(8)) America Star Bks.

Levine, Deborah A. & Riley, JillEllyn. Kitchen Chaos. Espinosa, Leo, illus. 2015. (Saturday Cooking Club Ser.: 1). (ENG.). 336p. (J). (gr. 4-9). 17.99 (978-1-4424-9939-3(7), Aladdin) Simon & Schuster Children's Publishing.

London, C. Alexander. We Are Not Eaten by Yaks. (Accidental Adventure Ser.: 1). (ENG.). (J). (gr. 3-7). 2013. 384p. pap. 7.99 (978-0-14-242056-0(5), Puffin Books) 2011. 224p. 12.99 (978-0-399-25487-1(0), Philomel Bks.) Penguin Young Readers Group.

—We Dine with Cannibals. 2013. (Accidental Adventure Ser.: 2). (ENG.). 384p. (J). (gr. 3-7). pap. 7.99 (978-0-14-242474-2(9), Puffin Books) Penguin Young Readers Group.

McCarty, Peter. Chloe. McCarty, Peter, illus. 2012. (Illus.). 40p. (J). (gr. -1-1). (ENG.). 16.99 (978-0-06-114291-8(3)); lib. bdg. 17.89 (978-0-06-114292-5(1)) HarperCollins Pubs.

McLaughlin, Emma & Kraus, Nicola. The Real Real. 2009. (ENG.). 336p. (YA). (gr. 9). pap. 9.99 (978-0-06-172042-0(9)) HarperCollins Pubs.

McOmber, Rachel B., ed. McOmber Phonics Storybooks: On TV. rev. ed. (Illus.). (J). (978-0-944991-17-6(3)) Swift Learning Resources.

—McOmber Phonics Storybooks: The TV Box. rev. ed. (Illus.). (J). (978-0-944991-18-3(1)) Swift Learning Resources.

—McOmber Phonics Storybooks: The Video Show. rev. ed. (Illus.). (J). (978-0-944991-63-3(7)) Swift Learning Resources.

Moreta, Gladys & Picou, Lin. Puppy Trouble. Reese, Bob, illus. 2011. (ENG.). 24p. (gr. 1-2). pap. 8.95 (978-1-61236-018-8(1)) Rourke Educational Media.

O'Toole, Detra. Ty-Ty Quackers & the Hidden Treasure: Biblical Lessons with Barnyard Fun. 2009. 32p. pap. 13.99 (978-1-4343-6799-0(1)) AuthorHouse.

Otte, John W. Failstate, 1 vol. 2012. (Failstate Ser.: 1). (ENG.). 416p. (YA). pap. 15.99 (978-1-935929-48-2(8), Enclave) Gilead Publishing, LLC.

Papademetriou, Lisa & Minsky, Terri. A Very Lizzie Summer. 2005. (Lizzie Mcguire Super Special Ser.). (Illus.). 265p. (J). (978-1-4155-9625-8(5)) Disney Pr.

Patterson, James & Grabenstein, Chris. Pottymouth & Stoopid. Gilpin, Stephen, illus. 2017. (ENG.). 336p. (J). (gr. 3-7). 13.99 (978-0-316-34963-5(1)) Little Brown & Co.

Petroff, Shani. Careful What You Wish For. McKenney, J. David, illus. 2010. (Bedeviled Ser.: 3). (ENG.). 240p. (J). (gr. 3-7). pap. 6.99 (978-0-448-45113-8(1), Grosset & Dunlap) Penguin Young Readers Group.

Proimos, James. Todd's TV. Proimos, James, illus. 2010. (ENG., Illus.). 40p. (J). (gr. -1-3). 15.99 (978-0-06-170985-2(9), Tegen, Katherine Bks) HarperCollins Pubs.

Russell, Rachel Renée. Tales from a Not-So-Glam TV Star. 2014. (Dork Diaries: 7). lib. bdg. 25.75 (978-0-606-36240-5(1)) Turtleback Bks.

Stine, R. L. Rotten School #16: Dumb Clucks. Park, Trip, illus. 4.99 (978-0-06-123280-0(7)) HarperCollins Pubs.

Tait, Anne. Li Jun & the Iron Road. 2015. (ENG., Illus.). 216p. (YA). pap. 10.99 (978-1-4597-3142-4(5)) Dundurn CAN. Dist: Ingram Publisher Services.

Tayleur, Karen. Famous (Scholastic) The Awesome Life of David Mortimore Baxter. Garvey, Brann, illus. 2009. (David Mortimore Baxter Ser.). 88p. pap. 0.80 (978-1-4342-2503-0(8), David Mortimore Baxter) Stone Arch Bks.

Thaler, Mike. Groundhog Day from Black Lagoon. Lee, Jared, illus. 2015. 64p. (J). (978-0-545-78520-4(0)) Scholastic, Inc.

Waters, Summer. High Tide. 2010. (Silver Dolphins Ser.: 9). (ENG.). 176p. (J). (gr. 2-4). pap. 7.99

(978-0-00-736749-8(X), HarperCollins Children's Bks.) HarperCollins Pubs. Ltd. GBR. Dist: HarperCollins Pubs.

White, Andrea. Surviving Antarctica: Reality TV 2083. 2005. 336p. (J). (gr. 7-18). 16.99 (978-0-06-055454-5(1), HarperCollins) HarperCollins Pubs.

Williams, Kathryn. Pizza, Love, & Other Stuff That Made Me Famous. 2013. (ENG.). 256p. (YA). (gr. 7-12). pap. 11.99 (978-1-250-02745-0(4), 9781250027450) Square Fish.

Young, Judy. The Missing Grizzly Cubs. 2016. (Wild World of Buck Bray Ser.). (ENG.). 240p. (J). (gr. 3-6). 16.99 (978-1-58536-970-6(5), 204107) Sleeping Bear Pr.

Zink, Rui. The Boy Who Did Not Like Television. Dreher, Patrick, tr. from POR. Ramos, Manuel Joao, illus. 2004. (ENG.). 24p. (J). (978-1-931561-96-9(6)) MacAdam/Cage Publishing, Inc.

TELEVISION—HISTORY

Carson, Mary Kay. Who Invented Television? — Philo Farnsworth. 2012. (I Like Inventors! Ser.). 24p. (J). (gr. k-3). 22.60 (978-0-7660-3974-2(9), Enslow Elementary) Enslow Pubs., Inc.

—Who Invented Television? Philo Farnsworth. 2012. (I Like Inventors! Ser.). (Illus.). 24p. (J). (gr. k-3). pap. 7.95 (978-1-4644-0134-3(9), Enslow Elementary) Enslow Pubs., Inc.

Eboch, M. M. History of Television, 1 vol. 2014. (Essential Library of Cultural History Ser.). (ENG., Illus.). 112p. (YA). (gr. 6-12). lib. bdg. 35.64 (978-1-62403-556-2(6), 1383008, Essential Library) ABDO Publishing Co.

Krull, Kathleen. The Boy Who Invented TV: The Story of Philo Farnsworth. Couch, Greg, illus. (ENG.). 40p. (J). (gr. 1-4). 2014. 7.99 (978-0-385-75557-3(0), Dragonfly Bks.) 2009. 16.99 (978-0-375-84561-1(5), Knopf Bks. for Young Readers) Random Hse. Children's Bks.

Meucci, Sandra. Antonio & the Electric Scream: The Man Who Invented the Telephone. 2010. 138p. (J). pap. (978-0-8283-2197-6(3)) Branden Bks.

Nardo, Don. The History of Television. 2009. (World History Ser.). (ENG., Illus.). 128p. (J). 34.95 (978-1-4205-0162-9(3), 1304738, Lucent Bks.) Cengage Gale.

O'Shei, Tim. Philo T. Farnsworth: Visionary Inventor of Television. 2008. (Inventors Who Changed the World Ser.). (Illus.). 128p. (J). (gr. 6-18). lib. bdg. 34.60 (978-1-59845-075-0(1), MyReportLinks.com Bks.) Enslow Pubs., Inc.

Otfinoski, Steven. Television. 2006. (Great Inventions Ser.). (Illus.). 128p. (gr. 8-7). lib. bdg. 29.95 (978-0-7614-2228-0(5), Benchmark Bks.) Marshall Cavendish Corp.

Wyckoff, Edwin Brit. The Man Who Invented Television: The Genius of Philo T. Farnsworth. 2013. (Genius Inventors & Their Great Ideas Ser.). 48p. (J). (gr. 3-4). pap. 8.95 (978-1-4644-0209-8(4)); (Illus.). 25.27 (978-0-7660-4139-4(5)) Enslow Pubs., Inc. (Enslow Elementary).

TELEVISION—PRODUCTION AND DIRECTION

Blount, Diana. TV Production Student Activity Book. Matthews, Douglas L., ed. 2003. (Illus.). stu. ed., per., wbk. ed. (978-1-931680-51-6(5), Expert Systems for Teachers) Teaching Point, Inc.

Dunkleberger, Amy. So You Want to Be a Film or TV Director? 2007. (Careers in Film & Television Ser.). (Illus.). 128p. (J). (gr. 6-9). lib. bdg. 33.27 (978-0-7660-2738-1(4)) Enslow Pubs., Inc.

Holub, Joan. Who Was Jim Henson? Harrison, Nancy, illus. 2010. (Who Was? Ser.). (ENG.). 112p. (J). (gr. 3-7). pap. 5.99 (978-0-448-45406-1(8), Grosset & Dunlap) Penguin Young Readers Group.

Mattern, Joanne. Tyler Perry. 2012. (J). lib. bdg. 25.70 (978-1-61228-334-0(9)) Mitchell Lane Pubs., Inc.

Sheen, Barbara. J. J. Abrams. 2015. (People in the News Ser.). (ENG., Illus.). 128p. (J). (gr. 7-10). 39.40 (978-1-4205-1249-6(8), Lucent Bks.) Cengage Gale.

Uschan, Michael V., ed. Tyler Perry. 2010. (People in the News Ser.). (ENG.). 96p. (YA). (gr. 7-12). 33.95 (978-1-4205-0309-8(X)) Cengage Gale.

TELEVISION—VOCATIONAL GUIDANCE

Colby, Jennifer. TV Station. 2016. (21st Century Junior Library: Explore a Workplace Ser.). (ENG., Illus.). 24p. (J). (gr. 2-5). 27.07 (978-1-63471-079-4(7), 208395) Cherry Lake Publishing.

Dunkleberger, Amy. So You Want to Be a Film or TV Director? 2007. (Careers in Film & Television Ser.). (Illus.). 128p. (J). (gr. 6-9). lib. bdg. 33.27 (978-0-7660-2738-1(4)) Enslow Pubs., Inc.

—So You Want to Be a Film or TV Screenwriter? 2007. (Careers in Film & Television Ser.). (Illus.). 128p. (J). (gr. 6-9). lib. bdg. 33.27 (978-0-7660-2645-2(0)) Enslow Pubs., Inc.

Horn, Geoffrey M. Camera Operator. 2009. (Cool Careers: on the Go Ser.). 32p. (gr. 5-8). pap. 10.50 (978-1-4339-0165-2(X)); (YA). lib. bdg. 26.00 (978-1-4339-0001-3(7)) Stevens, Gareth Publishing LLLP.

McAlpine, Margaret. Working in Film & Television. 2004. (My Future Career Ser.). (Illus.). 64p. (gr. 3-7). lib. bdg. 27.00 (978-0-8368-4237-1(5), Gareth Stevens Learning Library) Stevens, Gareth Publishing LLLP.

Nagle, Jeanne M. Careers in Television. 2005. (Career Resource Library). (Illus.). 192p. (YA). (gr. 7-12). lib. bdg. 34.60 (978-0-8239-3187-3(0)) Rosen Publishing Group, Inc., The.

Otfinoski, Steve. Television: From Concept to Consumer. 2014. (Calling All Innovators: a Career for You Ser.). (ENG.). 64p. (J). pap. 8.95 (978-0-531-21071-0(5)) Scholastic Library Publishing.

Otfinoski, Steven. Television. 2014. (Calling All Innovators: a Career for You Ser.). (ENG.). 64p. (J). lib. bdg. 32.00 (978-0-531-20612-6(2)) Scholastic Library Publishing.

Raatma, Lucia. Working at a TV Station. 2011. (21st Century Junior Library: Careers Ser.). (ENG.). 24p. (gr. 2-5). lib. bdg. 25.64 (978-1-60279-980-6(6), 200950) Cherry Lake Publishing.

Rauf, Don & Vescia, Monique. Hollywood. 2016. (Bright Futures Press: Choose Your Own Career Adventure Ser.). (ENG., Illus.). 32p. (J). (gr. 4-6). 29.93 (978-1-63471-911-7(5), 208965) Cherry Lake Publishing.

TELEVISION BROADCASTING

see also Television in Politics

Apel, Melanie. Cool Careers Without College for Film & Television Buffs. 2008. (Cool Careers Without College Ser.). (Illus.). 144p. (YA). (gr. 7-12). lib. bdg. 35.95 (978-1-4042-1429-3(1)) Rosen Publishing Group, Inc., The.

Centore, Michael. Entertainment Industry, Vol. 10. 2016. (Stem in Current Events Ser.). (Illus.). 64p. (J). (gr. 7). 23.95 (978-1-4222-3590-4(4)) Mason Crest.

Connolly, Sean. Getting the Message: Television & Radio. 2010. 34.25 (978-1-59920-350-8(2)) Black Rabbit Bks.

Crabtree, Marc. Meet My Neighbor, the News Camera Operator. 2012. (ENG., Illus.). 24p. (J). (978-0-7787-4560-0(0)); pap. (978-0-7787-4565-5(1)) Crabtree Publishing Co.

Gilbert, Sara. Built for Success: the Story of CNN. 2013. (Built for Success Ser.). (ENG.). 48p. (J). (gr. 4-7). pap. 12.00 (978-0-89812-760-7(2), Creative Paperbacks) Creative Co., The.

—Built for Success: the Story of MTV. 2015. (Built for Success Ser.). (ENG.). 48p. (J). (gr. 5-8). pap. 12.00 (978-0-89812-982-3(6), Creative Paperbacks) Creative Co., The.

—The Story of CNN. 2012. (Built for Success Ser.). 48p. (gr. 5-12). 23.95 (978-1-60818-175-9(8), Creative Education) Creative Co., The.

—The Story of MTV. 2014. 48p. (978-1-60818-395-1(5), Creative Education) Creative Co., The.

Green, Sara. Espn. 2017. (Brands We Know Ser.). (ENG.). 24p. (J). (gr. 3-8). lib. bdg. 25.95 **(978-1-62617-651-5(5)**, Pilot Bks.) Bellwether Media.

Green, Sara. Nickelodeon. 2016. (ENG., Illus.). 24p. (J). (gr. 3-8). 25.95 (978-1-62617-411-5(3), Pilot Bks.) Bellwether Media.

Hutchings, Amy & Nations, Susan. What Happens at a TV Station? 2009. (Where People Work Ser.). 24p. (J). (gr. -1-3). lib. bdg. 22.00 (978-1-4339-0070-9(X), Weekly Reader Leveled Readers) Stevens, Gareth Publishing LLLP.

—What Happens at a TV Station? (¿Qué pasa en una emisora de Televisión?) 2009. (Where People Work Ser.). 24p. (gr. -1-3). pap. 8.15 (978-1-4339-0134-8(X)); (SPA & ENG.). pap. 8.15 (978-1-4339-0142-3(0)) Stevens, Gareth Publishing LLLP. (Weekly Reader Leveled Readers).

—What Happens at a TV Station?/¿Qué Pasa en Una Emisora de Televisión? 2009. (Where People Work/Dónde Trabaja la Gente? Ser.). (SPA & ENG.). 24p. (J). (gr. -1-3). lib. bdg. 22.00 (978-1-4339-0078-5(5), Weekly Reader Leveled Readers) Stevens, Gareth Publishing LLLP.

McAlpine, Margaret. Working in Film & Television. 2004. (My Future Career Ser.). (Illus.). 64p. (gr. 3-7). lib. bdg. 27.00 (978-0-8368-4237-1(5), Gareth Stevens Learning Library) Stevens, Gareth Publishing LLLP.

Minden, Cecilia & Cupp, Dave. TV-Station Secrets. 2008. (Reading Rocks! Ser.). (ENG., Illus.). 32p. (J). (gr. 2-5). 28.50 (978-1-60253-104-8(8), 200766) Child's World, Inc., The.

Mooney, Carla. Asking Questions about How the News Is Created. 2015. (21st Century Skills Library: Asking Questions about Media Ser.). (ENG., Illus.). 32p. (J). (gr. 4-8). 29.93 (978-1-63362-489-4(7), 206864) Cherry Lake Publishing.

Otfinoski, Steve. Television: From Concept to Consumer. 2014. (Calling All Innovators: a Career for You Ser.). (ENG.). 64p. (J). pap. 8.95 (978-0-531-21071-0(5)) Scholastic Library Publishing.

Otfinoski, Steven. Television. 2014. (Calling All Innovators: a Career for You Ser.). (ENG.). 64p. (J). lib. bdg. 32.00 (978-0-531-20612-6(2)) Scholastic Library Publishing.

Paddington, Whit. Behind the Scenes at a Newscast. 2014. (VIP Tours Ser.). 48p. (J). (gr. 4-6). 31.36 (978-1-62713-031-8(4)) Cavendish Square Publishing.

Pelusey, Michael & Pelusey, Jane. Film & Television. 2005. (Media Ser.). (Illus.). 32p. (gr. 5-8). lib. bdg. 21.95 (978-0-7910-8802-9(2), Chelsea Hse.) Facts On File, Inc.

Peppas, Lynn. Miley Cyrus. 2010. (Superstars! Ser.). (ENG.). 32p. (J). (gr. 3-6). lib. bdg. (978-0-7787-7250-7(0)) Crabtree Publishing Co.

Raatma, Lucia. Working at a TV Station. 2011. (21st Century Junior Library: Careers Ser.). (ENG.). 24p. (gr. 2-5). lib. bdg. 25.64 (978-1-60279-980-6(6), 200950) Cherry Lake Publishing.

Reeves, Diane Lindsey. TV Journalist. 2008. (Virtual Apprentice Ser.). (Illus.). 64p. (gr. 4-9). per. 9.95 (978-0-8160-7553-9(0), Checkmark Bks.) Facts On File, Inc.

Riggs, Thomas. Reality TV. Greenhaven Press Editors, ed. 2013. (At Issue Ser.). (ENG.). 128p. (gr. 10-12). pap. 27.80 (978-0-7377-6196-2(2)); lib. bdg. 39.40 (978-0-7377-6195-5(4)) Cengage Gale. (Greenhaven Pr., Inc.).

Robinson, Tom. The Evolution of News Reporting, 1 vol. 2010. (Essential Viewpoints Set 5 Ser.). (ENG.). 112p. (J). (gr. 6-12). lib. bdg. 35.64 (978-1-61613-521-8(2), Essential Library) ABDO Publishing Co.

Shapiro, Marc & Ooten, Tara Broeckel. Selena Gomez - Fame. 2012. (ENG., Illus.). 40p. (YA). pap. 7.99 (978-1-4507-6679-1(X)) Bluewater Productions, Inc.

Shofner, Shawndra. How it Happens: At the T. V. Station. 2008. (How It Happens Ser.). (YA). (gr. 2-5). lib. bdg. 21.95 (978-1-934545-07-2(4)) Oliver Pr., Inc.

Spangenburg, Ray & Moser, Kit. TV News: Can It Be Trusted? 2003. (Issues in Focus Ser.). (Illus.). 128p. (J). (gr. 6-12). lib. bdg. 26.60 (978-0-7660-1942-3(X)) Enslow Pubs., Inc.

Teitelbaum, Michael. Sports Broadcasting. 2008. (21st Century Skills Innovation Library: Innovation in Entertainment Ser.). (ENG., Illus.). 32p. (gr. 4-8). lib. bdg. 28.50 (978-1-60279-216-6(X), 200147) Cherry Lake Publishing.

—Television. 2008. (21st Century Skills Innovation Library: Innovation in Entertainment Ser.). (ENG., Illus.). 32p. (gr. 4-8). lib. bdg. 28.50 (978-1-60279-263-0(1), 200146) Cherry Lake Publishing.

TV Journalist. 2008. (Virtual Apprentice Ser.). (Illus.). 64p. (gr. 4-9). 29.95 (978-0-8160-6753-4(8), Ferguson Publishing Co.) Facts On File, Inc.

Walters, John. Sports Broadcasting, Vol. 10. Ferrer, Al, ed. 2015. (Careers off the Field Ser.). (Illus.). 64p. (J). (gr. 7). 23.95 (978-1-4222-3271-2(9)) Mason Crest.

Weil, Jamie. Asking Questions about What's on Television. 2015. (21st Century Skills Library: Asking Questions about Media Ser.). (ENG., Illus.). 32p. (J). (gr. 4-8). pap. 14.21 (978-1-63362-509-9(5), 206881) Cherry Lake Publishing.

TELEVISION BROADCASTING—BIOGRAPHY

Banting, Erinn. Katie Couric. 2007. (Remarkable People Ser.). (Illus.). 24p. (J). (gr. 4-6). pap. 8.95 (978-1-59036-644-8(1)); lib. bdg. 24.45 (978-1-59036-643-1(3)) Weigl Pubs., Inc.

Barbara Walters. 2010. (Women of Achievement Ser.). (Illus.). 128p. (J). (gr. 6-12). 35.00 (978-1-60413-686-9(3), Chelsea Hse.) Facts On File, Inc.

Blashfield, Jean F. Oprah Winfrey. 2003. (Trailblazers of the Modern World Ser.). (ENG & SPA., Illus.). 48p. (gr. 5-12). pap. 14.05 (978-0-8368-5247-9(8), Gareth Stevens Secondary Library) Stevens, Gareth Publishing LLLP.

Boone, Mary. Jennette McCurdy. 2010. (Robbie Reader Ser.). (Illus.). 32p. (YA). (gr. 2-5). lib. bdg. 25.70 (978-1-58415-900-1(6)) Mitchell Lane Pubs., Inc.

Brown, Jonatha A. Oprah Winfrey. 2004. (People We Should Know Ser.). (Illus.). 24p. (gr. 1-4). pap. 8.15 (978-0-8368-4319-4(3)); (ENG & SPA., pap. 8.15 (978-0-8368-4361-3(4)); lib. bdg. 22.00 (978-0-8368-4312-5(6)) Stevens, Gareth Publishing LLLP. (Weekly Reader Leveled Readers).

—Oprah Winfrey. Acosta, Tatiana & Gutierrez, Guillermo, trs. 2004. (Gente Que Hay Que Conocer Ser.). (SPA., Illus.). 24p. (gr. 1-4). lib. bdg. 22.00 (978-0-8368-4354-5(1), Weekly Reader Leveled Readers) Stevens, Gareth Publishing LLLP.

Davidson, Amy. Elle Fanning. 2012. (Rising Stars Ser.). (Illus.). 32p. (J). (gr. 3-6). 25.25 (978-1-4339-7280-5(8)); pap. 10.50 (978-1-4339-7281-2(6)) Stevens, Gareth Publishing LLLP.

—Kendall Jenner. 2012. (Rising Stars Ser.). (Illus.). 32p. (J). (gr. 3-6). 25.25 (978-1-4339-7288-1(3)); pap. 10.50 (978-1-4339-7289-8(1)) Stevens, Gareth Publishing LLLP.

Dougherty, Terri. Tyra Banks. 2009. (People in the News Ser.). (Illus.). 128p. (YA). (gr. 7-12). 33.95 (978-1-4205-0161-2(5)) Cengage Gale.

Edgers, Geoff, et al. Who Was Julia Child? Harrison, Nancy & Putra, Dede, illus. 2015. (Who Was? Ser.). (ENG.). 112p. (J). (gr. 3-7). 5.99 (978-0-448-48297-2(5), Grosset & Dunlap) Penguin Young Readers Group.

Gagne, Tammy. Day by Day with Bindi Sue Irwin. 2012. 32p. (J). (gr. -1-2). lib. bdg. 25.70 (978-1-61228-326-5(8)) Mitchell Lane Pubs., Inc.

Klein, Rebecca. Jimmy Fallon, 01 vols., 1. 2016. (Giants of Comedy Ser.). (ENG., Illus.). 112p. (J). 35.60 (978-1-4994-6254-8(9), Rosen Young Adult) Rosen Publishing Group, Inc., The.

Krohn, Katherine E. Oprah Winfrey. (Just the Facts Biographies Ser.). (Illus.). 112p. 2004. (ENG.). (gr. 5-12). lib. bdg. 27.93 (978-0-8225-2472-4(4)) 2003. (J). (gr. 6-18). pap. 7.95 (978-0-8225-5000-6(8)) Lerner Publishing Group.

Lee, T. S. The Oprah Winfrey Story: The First Oprah Winfrey Comic Biography. 2010. 190p. (J). pap. 14.95 (978-0-9819542-6-4(X)) DASANBOOKS.

Meltzer, Brad. I Am Jim Henson. Eliopoulos, Christopher, illus. 2017. (Ordinary People Change the World Ser.). (ENG.). 40p. (J). (gr. k-3). 14.99 (978-0-525-42850-3(X), Dial Bks) Penguin Young Readers Group.

Paprocki, Sherry Beck. Ellen Degeneres: Entertainer. 2009. (Women of Achievement Ser.). (Illus.). 136p. (gr. 6-12). 35.00 (978-1-60413-082-9(2), Chelsea Hse.) Facts On File, Inc.

Payment, Simone. Michael J. Fox: Parkinson's Disease Research Advocate. 2009. (Celebrity Activists Ser.). 112p. (gr. 8-8). 66.50 (978-1-61511-831-1(4)) Rosen Publishing Group, Inc., The.

Schuman, Michael A. Tina Fey: TV Comedy Superstar. 2011. (People to Know Today Ser.). (Illus.). 112p. (J). (gr. 7-12). lib. bdg. 33.27 (978-0-7660-3557-7(3)) Enslow Pubs., Inc.

Seba, Jaime. Ellen DeGeneres: From Comedy Club to Talk Show. 2012. (Illus.). 64p. (J). pap. (978-1-4222-2308-6(6)); (gr. 7-8). 22.95 (978-1-4222-2297-3(7)) Mason Crest.

Snyder, Gail. Brooke Knows Best. 2010. (Major Reality Shows Ser.). 48p. (YA). (gr. 7-18). lib. bdg. 19.95 (978-1-4222-1680-4(2)) Mason Crest.

Spilsbury, Richard. Simon Cowell, 1 vol. 2012. (Titans of Business Ser.). (ENG.). 48p. (gr. 4-6). pap. 9.95 (978-1-4329-6434-4(8)); lib. bdg. 32.65 (978-1-4329-6427-6(5)) Heinemann-Raintree. (NA-h).

Tieck, Sarah. Miley Cyrus CD & Book. 2010. (Big Buddy Biographies CD+Book Ser.). 32p. (gr. 2-5). audio compact disk 57.00 (978-1-61613-306-1(6), Big Buddy Bks.) ABDO Publishing Co.

—Miley Cyrus Site CD & Book. 2010. (Big Buddy Biographies Site CD+Book Ser.). 32p. (gr. 2-5). cd-rom 85.57 (978-1-61613-278-1(7), Big Buddy Bks.) ABDO Publishing Co.

Tina Fey. 2010. (Women of Achievement Ser.). (Illus.). 136p. (J). (gr. 6-12). 35.00 (978-1-60413-709-5(6), Chelsea Hse.) Facts On File, Inc.

Todd, Anne M. Tyra Banks. 2009. (Women of Achievement Ser.). (Illus.). 120p. (gr. 6-12). 35.00 (978-1-60413-462-9(3), Chelsea Hse.) Facts On File, Inc.

Tometich, Annabelle. Today's 12 Hottest TV Superstars. 2015. (ENG., Illus.). 32p. (J). (978-1-63235-023-7(8)) Pr. Room Editions LLC.

TELEVISION IN POLITICS

Ruschmann, Paul. The FCC/Broadcast Regulations. Marzilli, Alan, ed. 2004. (Point/Counterpoint Ser.). (Illus.). 112p. (C). (gr. 9-13). 35.00 (978-0-7910-8363-5(2), Chelsea Hse.) Facts On File, Inc.

TELEVISION PLAYS

Crompton, Richmal. Just William As Seen on TV. 2003. (ENG., Illus.). 176p. (J). pap. 6.95 (978-0-333-62802-7(0)) Macmillan Pubs., Ltd. GBR. Dist: Trafalgar Square Publishing.

Jozsa, Orsolya. Meaning & Perspective in Tom Stoppard's Three Plays - Rosencrantz & Guildenstern Are Dead, Jumpers, Dogg's Hamlet Cahoot's MacBeth. 2008. 52p. pap. (978-3-639-02075-5(8)) AV Akademikerverlag GmbH & Co. KG.

TELEVISION PROGRAMS

Anniss, Matthew. Create Your Own Movie or TV Show. 2016. (Media Genius Ser.). (ENG.). 48p. (gr. 5-8). lib. bdg. 33.32 (978-1-4109-8110-3(X)) Heinemann-Raintree.

Baby Boomers, 5 cass.; set. 2004. (People's Century Ser.). (gr. 7-18). 59.95 incl. VHS (978-1-57807-186-9(0), WG590) WGBH Boston Video.

Bailey, Diane. America's Best Dance Crew. 2010. (Major Competitive Reality Shows Ser.). 48p. (YA). (gr. 7-18). pap. 7.95 (978-1-4222-1932-4(1)); lib. bdg. 19.95 (978-1-4222-1669-9(1)) Mason Crest.

BBC Staff, et al. The Companion's Companion. 2017. (ENG., Illus.). 176p. (J). 14.99 **(978-1-4059-2969-1(3)**, 9781405929691) Penguin Bks., Ltd. GBR. Dist: Diamond Comic Distributors, Inc.

Bednar, Chuck. American Idol Profiles Index: Top Finalists from Each Season (82 Contestants) 2009. (Dream Big: American Idol Superstars Ser.). 64p. (YA). (gr. 5-18). pap. 9.95 (978-1-4222-1593-7(8)) Mason Crest.

—Insights into American Idol. 2009. (Dream Big: American Idol Superstars Ser.). 64p. (YA). (gr. 5-18). pap. 9.95 (978-1-4222-1600-2(4)); lib. bdg. 22.95 (978-1-4222-1514-2(8)) Mason Crest.

Bennett, Adelaide. Global Legends & Lore: Vampires & Werewolves Around the World. 2010. (Making of a Monster Ser.). 64p. (YA). (gr. 7-18). lib. bdg. 22.95 (978-1-4222-1810-5(4)) Mason Crest.

Brennan, Kristine. The City. 2010. (Major Reality Shows Ser.). 48p. (YA). (gr. 7-18). pap. 7.95 (978-1-4222-1944-7(5)); lib. bdg. 19.95 (978-1-4222-1681-1(0)) Mason Crest.

British Broadcasting Corporation Staff. Companion Compendium. 2013. (ENG., Illus.). 160p. (J). 10.99 (978-1-4059-0748-4(7)) Penguin Bks., Ltd. GBR. Dist: Diamond Bk. Distributors.

Britton, Felicity. The Glee Cast: Inspiring Gleek Mania. 2012. (USA TODAY Lifeline Biographies Ser.). (ENG., Illus.). 112p. (gr. 6-12). lib. bdg. 34.60 (978-0-7613-8639-1(4)) Lerner Publishing Group.

Cane, David A. Nitro Circus. 2010. (Major Reality Shows Ser.). 48p. (YA). (gr. 7-18). lib. bdg. 19.95 (978-1-4222-1687-3(X)) Mason Crest.

Capek, Michael. Zorro. 2017. 25.70 (978-1-61228-972-4(X)) Mitchell Lane Pubs., Inc.

Cashin, John. Keeping up with the Kardashians. 2010. (Major Reality Shows Ser.). (Illus.). 48p. (J). (gr. 7-18). pap. 7.95 (978-1-4222-1948-5(8), 1318043); lib. bdg. 19.95 (978-1-4222-1685-9(3), 1318043) Mason Crest.

Clark, Travis. Punk'd. 2010. (Major Reality Shows Ser.). 48p. (YA). (gr. 7-18). pap. 7.95 (978-1-4222-1951-5(8)); lib. bdg. 19.95 (978-1-4222-1688-0(8)) Mason Crest.

—Survivor. 2010. (Major Competitive Reality Shows Ser.). 48p. (YA). (gr. 7-18). lib. bdg. 19.95 (978-1-4222-1678-1(0)) Mason Crest.

Cooke, C. W. Fame: The Cast of Glee. 2011. (ENG., Illus.). 40p. (YA). pap. 7.99 (978-1-4507-4429-4(X)) Bluewater Productions, Inc.

The Dangerous Book of Monsters. 2015. (ENG., Illus.). 176p. (J). 16.99 (978-1-4059-2003-2(3), 9781405920032) Penguin Bks., Ltd. GBR. Dist: Diamond Comic Distributors, Inc.

Dimartino, Konietzko & DiMartino, Michael Dante. The Legend of Korra, Bk. 3. 2015. (ENG., Illus.). 186p. (gr. 3-7). 34.99 (978-1-61655-565-8(3)) Dark Horse Comics.

DiMartino, Michael Dante. Legend of Korra, Bk. 2. 2014. (ENG., Illus.). 186p. (gr. 3-7). 34.99 (978-1-61655-462-0(2)) Dark Horse Comics.

Donovan, Sandy. Movies & TV Top Tens. 2014. (Entertainment's Top 10 Ser.). (ENG., Illus.). 32p. (gr. 5-8). lib. bdg. 26.60 (978-1-4677-3840-8(9), Lerner Pubns.) Lerner Publishing Group.

Dorling Kindersley Publishing Staff. Blast Off! 2010. (DK Readers Ser.). (ENG.). 32p. (J). (gr. -1-1). 14.99 (978-0-7566-6879-2(4), DK Children) Dorling Kindersley Publishing, Inc.

—Blast Off!, Pre-Level 1. 2010. (DK Readers Ser.). (ENG.). 32p. (J). (gr. -1-1). pap. 3.99 (978-0-7566-6692-7(9), DK Children) Dorling Kindersley Publishing, Inc.

—Character Encyclopedia. 2017. (ENG.). 176p. (J). (gr. 1-4). 19.99 **(978-1-4654-6325-8(9)**, DK Children) Dorling Kindersley Publishing, Inc.

—Don't Wake the Zillo Beast! 2011. (DK Readers Ser.). (ENG.). 32p. (J). (gr. -1-1). 3.99 (978-0-7566-8279-8(7), DK Children) Dorling Kindersley Publishing, Inc.

—Rebel Power! 2015. (DK Readers Ser.). (ENG., Illus.). 48p. (J). (gr. 1-3). 14.99 (978-1-4654-3595-8(6)); pap. 3.99 (978-1-4654-3596-5(4)) Dorling Kindersley Publishing, Inc. (DK Children).

—Rebels - Epic Battles. 2015. (ENG.). 144p. (J). (gr. 3-7). 16.99 (978-1-4654-3591-0(3), DK Children) Dorling Kindersley Publishing, Inc.

—Star Wars Vile Villains Ultimate Sticker Collection. 2015. (ENG.). 96p. (J). (gr. 1-4). pap. 12.99 (978-1-4654-4204-8(9)) Dorling Kindersley Publishing, Inc.

Dorling Kindersley Publishing Staff & Dubowski, Cathy East. Ahsoka in Action!, Level 1. 2012. (DK Readers Ser.). (ENG., Illus.). 32p. (J). (gr. k-4). pap. 3.99 (978-1-4654-0583-8(6), DK Children) Dorling Kindersley Publishing, Inc.

Dorling Kindersley Publishing Staff & East Dubowski, Cathy. Ahsoka in Action! 2012. (DK Readers Ser.). (ENG., Illus.). 32p. (J). (gr. k-4). 14.99 (978-1-4654-0584-5(4), DK Children) Dorling Kindersley Publishing, Inc.

—Masters of the Force. 2012. (DK Readers Ser.). (ENG.). 32p. (J). (gr. -1-1). pap. 3.99 (978-1-4654-0585-2(2), DK Children) Dorling Kindersley Publishing, Inc.

Dorling Kindersley Publishing Staff & Hibbert, Clare. The Clone Wars - Jedi Heroes. 2010. (DK Readers Ser.). (ENG.). 48p. (J). (gr. 2-4). pap. 3.99 (978-0-7566-6689-7(9), DK Children) Dorling Kindersley Publishing, Inc.

Dorling Kindersley Publishing Staff, et al. Absolutely Everything You Need to Know. 2015. (ENG., Illus.). 200p. (J). (gr. 3-7). 19.99 (978-1-4654-3785-3(1), DK Children) Dorling Kindersley Publishing, Inc.

—Character Encyclopedia. 2013. (ENG.). 208p. (gr. 2-7). 16.99 (978-1-4654-0267-7(5), DK) Dorling Kindersley Publishing, Inc.

—Planets in Peril. 2010. (DK Readers Ser.). (ENG.). 48p. (J). (gr. 3-7). pap. 3.99 (978-0-7566-6690-3(2), DK Children) Dorling Kindersley Publishing, Inc.

Dougherty, Terry. Rob Dyrdek's Fantasy Factory. 2010. (Major Reality Shows Ser.). 48p. (YA). (gr. 7-18). pap. 7.95 (978-1-4222-1952-2(6)); lib. bdg. 19.95 (978-1-4222-1689-7(6)) Mason Crest.

Downey, Glen R. The 10 Most Memorable TV Moments. 2008. 14.99 (978-1-55448-544-4(4)) Scholastic Library Publishing.

Englart, Mindi. Televison Show. 2003. (Made in the USA Ser.). 32p. (YA). 24.94 *(978-1-56711-413-3(X),* Blackbirch Pr., Inc.) Cengage Gale.

ESCAPE! Because Accidents Happen: Abandon Ship. 2004. (NOVA Ser.). (gr. 7-18). 19.95 incl. VHS *(978-1-57807-158-6(5),* WG2607) WGBH Boston Video.

Ferris, Julie. Ultimate Sticker Collection: Star Wars: the Force Awakens Stickerscapes. 2015. (Ultimate Sticker Collections). (ENG.). 96p. (J). (gr. 1-4). pap. 12.99 *(978-1-4654-3786-0(X),* DK Children) Dorling Kindersley Publishing, Inc.

Fisher, Diana, illus. Watch Me Draw Disney's Little Einsteins Amazing Missions. 2012. (J). *(978-1-936309-43-6(2))* Quarto Publishing Group USA.

Gilbert, Elizabeth T., illus. Watch Me Draw Tiggerific Tales. 2013. (Watch Me Draw Ser.). 24p. (gr. -1-2). 25.65 *(978-1-936309-87-0(4))* Quarto Publishing Group USA.

Gitlin, Martin. The Hills. 2010. (Major Reality Shows Ser.). 48p. (YA). (gr. 7-18). pap. 7.95 *(978-1-4222-1946-1(1));* lib. bdg. 19.95 *(978-1-4222-1683-5(7))* Mason Crest.

—My Super Sweet 16. 2010. (Major Reality Shows Ser.). 48p. (YA). (gr. 7-18). lib. bdg. 19.95 *(978-1-4222-1686-6(1))* Mason Crest.

Grayson, Robert. The Biggest Loser. 2010. (Major Competitive Reality Shows Ser.). 48p. (YA). (gr. 7-18). pap. 7.95 *(978-1-4222-1935-5(6));* lib. bdg. 19.95 *(978-1-4222-1672-9(1))* Mason Crest.

—Dancing with the Stars. 2010. (Major Competitive Reality Shows Ser.). 48p. (YA). (gr. 7-18). pap. 7.95 *(978-1-4222-1936-2(4));* lib. bdg. 19.95 *(978-1-4222-1673-6(X))* Mason Crest.

Green, Sara. Nickelodeon. 2016. (ENG., Illus.). 24p. (J). (gr. 3-8). 25.95 *(978-1-62617-411-5(3),* Pilot Bks.) Bellwether Media.

Hall, Susan T., illus. Watch Me Draw Diego's Animal Adventures. 2013. (Watch Me Draw Ser.). 24p. (J). (gr. -1-2). 25.65 *(978-1-936309-88-7(2))* Quarto Publishing Group USA.

Hasbro Staff. The Elements of Harmony: Friendship Is Magic. 2013. (ENG.). 256p. (J). (gr. 7-17). 18.00 *(978-0-316-24754-2(5))* Little, Brown Bks. for Young Readers.

Hasday, Judy. So You Think You Can Dance. 2010. (Major Competitive Reality Shows Ser.). 48p. (YA). (gr. 7-18). lib. bdg. 19.95 *(978-1-4222-1677-4(2))* Mason Crest.

Hermansson, Casie. Parental Guidance Ratings. 2013. (Hot Topics in Media EBook Ser.). (ENG.). 48p. (J). pap. 15.64 *(978-1-61783-784-5(9));* (gr. 3-6). lib. bdg. 32.79 *(978-1-61783-734-0(2))* ABDO Publishing Co.

Holub, Joan. Who Was Jim Henson? Harrison, Nancy, illus. 2010. (Who Was? Ser.). (ENG.). 112p. (J). (gr. 3-7). pap. 5.99 *(978-0-448-45406-1(8),* Grosset & Dunlap) Penguin Young Readers Group.

Indovino, Shaina C. Simon Cowell: From the Mailroom to Idol Fame. 2012. (Extraordinary Success with a High School Diploma or Less Ser.). 64p. (J). (gr. 7-8). 22.95 *(978-1-4222-2296-6(9))* Mason Crest.

Indovino, Shaina Carmel. Simon Cowell: From the Mailroom to Idol Fame. 2012. pap. *(978-1-4222-2307-9(8))* Mason Crest.

Kidder, Lisa & Kidder, Lisa Damian. Glee Totally Unofficial: The Ultimate Guide to the Smash-Hit High School Musical. Triumph Books Staff, ed. 2010. (ENG., Illus.). 128p. (J). (gr. 7). pap. 14.95 *(978-1-60078-498-9(4))* Triumph Bks.

Konietzko, Bryan & DiMartino, Michael Dante. Avatar: The Last Airbender. 2010. (Avatar: the Last Airbender Ser.). (ENG., Illus.). 184p. 34.99 *(978-1-59582-504-9(5))* Dark Horse Comics.

Kopp, Megan. Reality Television. 2013. (Hot Topics in Media EBook Ser.). (ENG.). 48p. (J). pap. 15.64 *(978-1-61783-785-2(7));* (gr. 3-6). lib. bdg. 32.79 *(978-1-61783-735-7(0))* ABDO Publishing Co.

Kowalski, Emma. American Idol. 2010. (Major Competitive Reality Shows Ser.). 48p. (YA). (gr. 7-18). pap. 7.95 *(978-1-4222-1931-7(3));* lib. bdg. 19.95 *(978-1-4222-1668-2(3))* Mason Crest.

—America's Next Top Model. 2010. (Major Competitive Reality Shows Ser.). 48p. (YA). (gr. 7-18). pap. 7.95 *(978-1-4222-1934-8(8));* lib. bdg. 19.95 *(978-1-4222-1671-2(3))* Mason Crest.

—Project Runway. 2010. (Major Competitive Reality Shows Ser.). 48p. (YA). (gr. 7-18). pap. 7.95 *(978-1-4222-1938-6(0));* lib. bdg. 19.95 *(978-1-4222-1675-0(6))* Mason Crest.

—Run's House. 2010. (Major Reality Shows Ser.). 48p. (YA). (gr. 7-18). pap. 7.95 *(978-1-4222-1953-9(4));* lib. bdg. 19.95 *(978-1-4222-1690-3(X))* Mason Crest.

MacKinnon, J. Beyblade: Official Handbook. 2003. (Illus.). 69p. (J). *(978-0-439-62860-0(1))* Scholastic, Inc.

Magid, Jennifer. Miley Cyrus/Hannah Montana. 2008. (Today's Superstars). 32p. (YA). (gr. 4-7). lib. bdg. 31.95 *(978-0-8368-9236-9(4))* Stevens, Gareth Publishing LLLP.

Major Competitive Reality Shows, 11 vols., Set. Incl. American Idol. Kowalski, Emma. pap. 7.95 *(978-1-4222-1931-7(3));* America's Best Dance Crew. Bailey, Diane. pap. 7.95 *(978-1-4222-1932-4(1));* America's Got Talent. Whiting, Jim. pap. 7.95 *(978-1-4222-1933-1(X));* America's Next Top Model. Kowalski, Emma. pap. 7.95 *(978-1-4222-1934-8(8));* Biggest Loser. Grayson, Robert. pap. 7.95 *(978-1-4222-1935-5(6));* Dancing with the Stars. Grayson, Robert. pap. 7.95 *(978-1-4222-1936-2(4));* Making the Band. Schweitzer, Karen. pap. 7.95 *(978-1-4222-1937-9(2));* Project Runway. Kowalski, Emma. pap. 7.95 *(978-1-4222-1938-6(0));* Real World. Schweitzer, Karen. pap. 7.95 *(978-1-4222-1939-3(9));* So You Think You Can Dance. Hasday, Judy. pap. 7.95 *(978-1-4222-1940-9(2));* Survivor. Clark, Travis. pap. 7.95 *(978-1-4222-1941-6(0));* 48p. (YA). (gr. 7-18). 2010. 2011. Set pap. 87.45 *(978-1-4222-1930-0(5));* Set lib. bdg. 219.45 *(978-1-4222-1667-5(5))* Mason Crest.

Major Reality Shows, 11 vols., Set. Incl. Brooke Knows Best. Snyder, Gail. (YA). pap. 7.95 *(978-1-4222-1943-0(7));* City. Brennan, Kristine. (YA). pap. 7.95 *(978-1-4222-1944-7(5));* Guys from Jackass Go Out on Their Own. Marcovitz, Hal. (YA). pap. 7.95 *(978-1-4222-1945-4(3));* Hills. Gitlin, Martin. (YA). pap. 7.95 *(978-1-4222-1946-1(1));* Jackass. Marcovitz, Hal. (Illus.). (YA). pap. 7.95 *(978-1-4222-1947-8(X));* Keeping up with the Kardashians. Cashin, John. (Illus.). (J). pap. 7.95 *(978-1-4222-1948-5(8),* 1318043); My Super Sweet 16. Gitlin, Martin. (YA). pap. 7.95 *(978-1-4222-1949-2(6));* Nitro Circus. Cane, David A. (YA). pap. 7.95 *(978-1-4222-1950-8(X));* Punk'd. Clark, Travis. (YA). pap. 7.95 *(978-1-4222-1951-5(8));* Rob Dyrdek's Fantasy Factory. Dougherty, Terry. (YA). pap. 7.95 *(978-1-4222-1952-2(6));* Run's House. Kowalski, Emma. (YA). pap. 7.95 *(978-1-4222-1953-9(4));* 48p. (gr. 7-18). 2010. 2011. Set pap. 87.45 *(978-1-4222-1942-3(9));* Set lib. bdg. 219.45 *(978-1-4222-1679-8(9))* Mason Crest.

Mara, Wil. Oprah Winfrey. 2005. (Rookie Biographies Ser.). (ENG., Illus.). 32p. (J). (gr. 1-2). per. 4.95 *(978-0-516-25819-5(2),* Children's Pr.) Scholastic Library Publishing.

Marcovitz, Hal. The Guys from Jackass Go Out on Their Own. 2010. (Major Reality Shows Ser.). 48p. (YA). (gr. 7-18). pap. 7.95 *(978-1-4222-1945-4(3));* lib. bdg. 19.95 *(978-1-4222-1682-8(9))* Mason Crest.

—Jackass. 2010. (Major Reality Shows Ser.). 48p. (YA). (gr. 7-18). lib. bdg. 19.95 *(978-1-4222-1684-2(5));* (Illus.). pap. 7.95 *(978-1-4222-1947-8(X))* Mason Crest.

McCarthy, Rebecca & Sugar, Rebecca. Guide to the Crystal Gems. 2015. (Steven Universe Ser.). (ENG.). 96p. (J). (gr. 3-7). 9.99 *(978-0-8431-8316-0(0),* Cartoon Network Books) Penguin Young Readers Group.

Meltzer, Brad. I Am Jim Henson. Eliopoulos, Christopher, illus. 2017. (Ordinary People Change the World Ser.). (ENG.). 40p. (J). (gr. k-3). 14.99 *(978-0-525-42850-3(X),* Dial Bks) Penguin Young Readers Group.

Milvy, Erika & Chagollan, Samantha. 101 TV Shows to See Before You Grow Up: Be Your Own TV Critic— The Must-see TV List for Kids. 2017. (101 Things Ser.). (ENG., Illus.). 144p. (J). (gr. 3-7). pap. 12.95 *(978-1-63322-277-9(2),* Walter Foster Jr) Quarto Publishing Group USA.

Mooney, Carla. The Creators & Cast of Glee. 2012. (People in the News Ser.). (ENG., Illus.). 128p. (gr. 7-10). lib. bdg. 39.40 *(978-1-4205-0789-8(3),* Lucent Bks.) Cengage Gale.

Morreale, Marie. The Cast of Girl Meets World. 2015. (ENG.). 48p. lib. bdg. *(978-0-531-21572-2(5))* Children's Pr., Ltd.

Mystery of the Senses, 5 cass.; set. 2004. (NOVA Ser.). (gr. 7-18). 69.95 incl. VHS *(978-1-884738-57-9(5),* WG2214) WGBH Boston Video.

Ninety in The 90's. 2004. (Wgbh Specials Ser.). (gr. 7-18). 19.95 *(978-1-57807-458-7(4),* WG080) WGBH Boston Video.

The Official Doctionary. 2012. (ENG., Illus.). 176p. (J). 15.99 *(978-1-4059-0896-2(3),* 9781405908962) Penguin Bks., Ltd. GBR. Dist: Diamond Comic Distributors, Inc.

Olson, Martin. The Adventure Time Encyclopaedia: Inhabitants, Lore, Spells, & Ancient Crypt Warnings of the Land of Ooo Circa 19. 56 B. G. E. - 501 A. G. E. French, Renee et al, illus. 2013. (ENG.). 160p. 19.95 *(978-1-4197-0564-9(4),* Abrams Image) Abrams, Inc.

Olson, Martin, et al. Adventure Time: The Enchiridion & Marcy's Super Secret. Millionaire, Tony et al, illus. 2015. (ENG.). 224p. 24.95 *(978-1-4197-0449-9(4))* Abrams, Inc.

Ooten, Tara Broeckel & Cooke, C. W. Fame: Justin Bieber. 2010. (Illus.). 32p. pap. 3.99 *(978-1-4507-0888-3(9))* Bluewater Productions, Inc.

Paddington, Whit. Behind the Scenes at an Animated TV Show. 2014. (VIP Tours Ser.). 48p. (J). (gr. 4-6). lib. bdg. 31.36 *(978-1-62713-022-6(5))* Cavendish Square Publishing.

Penguin UK. Doctor Who. 12th rev. ed. 2016. (ENG., Illus.). 224p. (YA). 20.00 *(978-1-4059-2677-5(5),* 9781405926775) Penguin Bks., Ltd. GBR. Dist: Diamond Comic Distributors, Inc.

Publications International Ltd. Staff, ed. Busy Day - Baby's First Look & Find Sesame. 2011. 14p. (J). bds. 3.75 net. *(978-1-4508-1674-8(6))* Publications International, Ltd.

Pudsey. Pudsey: A Pup Star's Story. 2013. (ENG., Illus.). 272p. (YA). (gr. 3-5). pap. 10.99 *(978-0-349-00165-4(0))* Little, Brown Book Group Ltd. GBR. Dist: Hachette Bk. Group.

Quan-D'Eramo, Sandra. The 10 Best TV Game Shows. 2008. 14.99 *(978-1-55448-494-2(4))* Scholastic Library Publishing.

Rowe, Brooke. What TV Show Should You Be On? 2016. (Illus.). 32p. (J). *(978-1-63470-509-7(2))* Cherry Lake Publishing.

Rowlands, Caroline. Where Equestria Comes to Life! 2017. (IExplore Ser.). (ENG.). 32p. (J). (gr. -1). 14.95 ***(978-1-78312-245-5(5))*** Carlton Kids GBR. Dist: Sterling Publishing Co., Inc.

Salamoff, Paul. The Cast of Doctor Who. 2012. (ENG., Illus.). 40p. pap. 7.99 *(978-1-4507-8451-1(8))* Bluewater Productions, Inc.

Sanna, Emily. Pop Monsters: The Modern-Day Craze for Vampires & Werewolves. 2010. (Making of a Monster Ser.). 64p. (YA). (gr. 7-18). lib. bdg. 22.95 *(978-1-4222-1806-8(6))* Mason Crest.

Santillan, Jorge. When's the Doctor? 2012. (ENG., Illus.). 40p. (YA). 14.99 *(978-1-4059-0849-8(1),* 9781405908498) Penguin Bks., Ltd. GBR. Dist: Diamond Comic Distributors, Inc.

Sarandon, Susan, narrated by. Dying to Be Thin. 2004. (NOVA Ser.). (gr. 4-18). 19.95 *(978-1-57807-232-3(8),* WG2707) WGBH Boston Video.

Schweitzer, Karen. Making the Band. 2010. (Major Competitive Reality Shows Ser.). 48p. (YA). (gr. 7-18). pap. 7.95 *(978-1-4222-1937-9(2));* lib. bdg. 19.95 *(978-1-4222-1674-3(8))* Mason Crest.

—The Real World. 2010. (Major Competitive Reality Shows Ser.). 48p. (YA). (gr. 7-18). pap. 7.95 *(978-1-4222-1939-3(9));* lib. bdg. 19.95 *(978-1-4222-1676-7(4))* Mason Crest.

Sesame Street Workshop Staff. Shalom Sesame DVD Set, 5 DVDs. 2011. (J). 59.95 *(978-1-56086-706-7(X))* Sisu Home Entertainment, Inc.

Sesame Workshop Staff. Shalom Sesame Set. 2011. 59.95 *(978-1-56086-707-4(8))* Sisu Home Entertainment, Inc.

Snyder, Gail. Brooke Knows Best. 2010. (Major Reality Shows Ser.). 48p. (YA). (gr. 7-18). pap. 7.95 *(978-1-4222-1943-0(7))* Mason Crest.

Spencer, Liv. The Miranda Cosgrove & iCarly Spectacular! Unofficial & Unstoppable. 2010. (ENG., Illus.). 142p. (J). (gr. 4-7). pap. *(978-1-55022-929-5(X))* Filmer Ltd.

Stewart, Mark. Television Moments. 2009. (Ultimate 10: Entertainment Ser.). (ENG.). 48p. (J). (gr. 4-8). pap. 10.50 *(978-1-4339-2214-5(2));* (YA). (gr. 5-9). lib. bdg. 31.00 *(978-0-8368-9166-9(X))* Stevens, Gareth Publishing LLLP.

Sublette, Guen. Here's Lookin' at Lizzie. *(978-0-312-32669-2(6))* St. Martin's Pr.

Tieck, Sarah. American Idol Host & Judges, 1 vol. 2010. (Big Buddy Biographies Set 4 Ser.). (ENG.). 32p. (J). (gr. 2-5). 28.50 *(978-1-60453-969-1(0))* ABDO Publishing Co.

Twin Talk: Advice from a TV Talk Show. 2005. (Illus.). 37p. *(978-0-439-12406-5(9))* Scholastic, Inc.

Various. The Official Annual 2017. 2016. (ENG., Illus.). 64p. (YA). 12.99 *(978-1-4059-2649-2(X),* 9781405926492) Penguin Bks., Ltd. GBR. Dist: Diamond Comic Distributors, Inc.

West, Tracey. Battle Match Up. 2010. (Bakugan Ser.). (ENG.). 16p. (J). (gr. 2-5). pap. 7.99 *(978-0-545-25182-2(6))* Scholastic, Inc.

—Yu-Gi-Oh! 2016. (Yu-Gi-Oh! Ser.). (ENG., Illus.). 144p. (J). (gr. 3-7). pap. 8.99 *(978-0-545-94075-7(3))* Scholastic, Inc.

Whiting, Jim. American Idol Judges. (Modern Role Models Ser.). (YA). 2010. (Illus.). 64p. (gr. 7-12). lib. bdg. 22.95 *(978-1-4222-0496-2(0))* 2007. pap. 9.95 *(978-1-4222-0783-3(8))* Mason Crest.

—America's Got Talent. 2010. (Major Competitive Reality Shows Ser.). 48p. (YA). (gr. 7-18). pap. 7.95 *(978-1-4222-1933-1(X));* lib. bdg. 19.95 *(978-1-4222-1670-5(5))* Mason Crest.

Winick, Judd. Pedro & Me: Friendship, Loss, & What I Learned. 2009. (ENG., Illus.). 192p. (YA). (gr. 9-13). pap. 19.99 *(978-0-8050-8964-6(0),* 9780805089646) Square Fish.

Winnick, Judd. Pedro & Me. 2011. 14.10 *(978-0-7848-3537-1(3),* Everbind) Marco Bk. Co.

Woog, Adam. Reality TV. 2007. (Ripped from the Headlines Ser.). 64p. (YA). (gr. 7-12). 23.95 *(978-1-60217-005-6(3))* Erickson Pr.

Zerkin, Becca, et al. The Walking Dead: the Pop-Up Book. Jackson, Sally Elizabeth, illus. 2015. (ENG.). 5p. 65.00 *(978-1-60887-444-6(3))* Insight Editions.

TEMPERANCE

Berry, Joy Wilt. A Book about Overdoing It. 2005. (Illus.). (J). *(978-0-7172-8575-4(8))* Scholastic, Inc.

Beyer, Mark. Temperance & Prohibition: The Movement to Pass Anti-Liquor Laws in America. 2006. (Progressive Movement, 1900-1920 — Efforts to Reform America's New Industrial Society Ser.). (Illus.). 32p. (ENG.). (gr. 4-8). pap. 10.00 *(978-1-4042-0861-2(5));* (YA). (gr. 5-9). lib. bdg. 22.50 *(978-1-4042-0195-8(5))* Rosen Publishing Group, Inc., The.

—Temperance & Prohibition: The Movement to Pass Anti-liquor Laws in America. 2009. (Progressive Movement 1900-1920: Efforts to Reform America's New Industrial Society Ser.). 32p. (gr. 3-4). 47.90 *(978-1-60854-171-3(1))* Rosen Publishing Group, Inc., The.

Blumenthal, Karen. Bootleg: Murder, Moonshine, & the Lawless Years of Prohibition. 2013. (ENG., Illus.). 176p. (YA). (gr. 7-12). pap. 13.99 *(978-1-250-03427-4(2),* 9781250034274) Square Fish.

Dunn, John M. Prohibition. 2010. (American History Ser.). (Illus.). 128p. (J). 34.80 *(978-1-4205-0134-6(8),* Lucent Bks.) Cengage Gale.

Worth, Richard. Teetotalers & Saloon Smashers: The Temperance Movement & Prohibition. 2009. (America's Living History Ser.). (Illus.). 128p. (J). (gr. 5-9). lib. bdg. 33.27 *(978-0-7660-2908-8(5))* Enslow Pubs., Inc.

TEMPERATURE

see also Heat; Low Temperatures; Thermometers

Auch, Alison. All about Temperature, 1 vol. 2010. (Physical Science Ser.). (ENG.). 24p. (gr. k-1). lib. bdg. 26.65 *(978-1-4296-6608-4(0),* Pebble Plus) Capstone Press of Coughlan Cos.

—Todo Sobre la Temperatura. 2011. (Ciencia Física/Physical Science Ser.).Tr. of All about Temperature. (SPA, ENG & MUL.). 24p. (gr. k-1). 26.65 *(978-1-4296-6904-7(7))* Capstone Press of Coughlan Cos.

Bailer, Darice. Measuring Temperature. Petelinsek, Kathleen, illus. 2014. (Explorer Junior Library: Math Explorer Junior Ser.). (ENG.). 24p. (J). (gr. 1-4). 28.50 *(978-1-62431-648-7(4),* 203104) Cherry Lake Publishing.

Boothroyd, Jennifer. What Is Today's Weather? 2014. (First Step Nonfiction - Let's Watch the Weather Ser.). (Illus.). 24p. (gr. k-2). pap. 6.95 *(978-1-4677-4500-0(6));* (ENG., lib. bdg. 23.93 *(978-1-4677-3916-0(2),* Lerner Pubns.) Lerner Publishing Group.

Burslem, Tobe. Bermendani. 2011. 28p. pap. 21.99 *(978-1-4628-5490-5(7))* Xlibris Corp.

Doudna, Kelly. If You Prefer, I'll Use a Thermometer!, 1 vol. 2007. (Science Made Simple Ser.). (ENG., Illus.). 24p. (J). (gr. k-3). lib. bdg. 24.21 *(978-1-59928-594-8(0),* SandCastle) ABDO Publishing Co.

—Super Simple Things to Do with Temperature: Fun & Easy Science for Kids, 1 vol. 2011. (Super Simple Science Ser.). (ENG., Illus.). 24p. (J). (gr. k-3). lib. bdg. 25.65 *(978-1-61714-676-3(5))* ABDO Publishing Co.

Fiedler, Julie. Learning about Heat & Temperature with Graphic Organizers. (Graphic Organizers in Science Ser.). 24p. (gr. 3-4). 2009. 42.50 *(978-1-61513-039-9(X),* PowerKids Pr.) 2006. (Illus.). (YA). lib. bdg. 22.60 *(978-1-4042-3408-6(X))* Rosen Publishing Group, Inc., The.

Frisch-Schmoll, Joy. Temperature. 2008. (Simple Science Ser.). (Illus.). 24p. (J). (gr. -1). lib. bdg. 16.95 *(978-1-58341-579-5(3),* Creative Education) Creative Co., The.

Gardner, Robert. How Hot Is Hot? Science Projects with Temperature. 2015. (Hot Science Experiments Ser.). 48p. (J). (gr. 3-4). 25.27 *(978-0-7660-6605-2(3));* pap. 8.95 *(978-0-7660-6606-9(1),* Enslow Elementary) Enslow Pubs., Inc.

—Melting, Freezing, & Boiling Science Projects with Matter. 2006. (Fantastic Physical Science Experiments Ser.). (Illus.). 48p. (J). (gr. 4-7). lib. bdg. 25.27 *(978-0-7660-2589-9(6),* Enslow Elementary) Enslow Pubs., Inc.

—Really Hot Science Projects with Temperature: How Hot Is It? How Cold Is It? 2003. (Sensational Science Experiments Ser.). (Illus.). 48p. (J). lib. bdg. 25.27 *(978-0-7660-2015-3(0))* Enslow Pubs., Inc.

Gardner, Robert & Kemer, Eric. Easy Genius Science Projects with Temperature & Heat: Great Experiments & Ideas. 2009. (Easy Genius Science Projects Ser.). (Illus.). 128p. (J). (gr. 5-9). lib. bdg. 33.27 *(978-0-7660-2939-2(5))* Enslow Pubs., Inc.

Gardner, Robert & Kemer, Eric. Experiments with Temperature & Heat. 2017. (Science Whiz Experiments Ser.). 128p. (gr. 5-5). lib. bdg. 37.27 ***(978-0-7660-8682-1(8))*** Enslow Pubs., Inc.

Gish, Melissa. Temperature. 2005. (My First Look at Science Ser.). (Illus.). 24p. (J). (gr. k-3). lib. bdg. 15.95 *(978-1-58341-375-3(8),* Creative Education) Creative Co., The.

Gosman, Gillian. What Do You Know about Earth's Atmosphere? 2013. (20 Questions: Earth Science Ser.). 24p. (J). (gr. 3-6). pap. 8.25 *(978-1-4488-9856-5(0));* pap. 49.50 *(978-1-4488-9857-2(9));* lib. bdg. 22.60 *(978-1-4488-9699-8(1))* Rosen Publishing Group, Inc., The. (PowerKids Pr.).

Hidalgo, Maria. Heat. 2006. (My First Look at Weather Ser.). (Illus.). 24p. (J). (gr. -1-3). lib. bdg. 15.95 *(978-1-58341-449-1(5),* Creative Education) Creative Co., The.

Hughes, Susan. Is It Hot or Cold? 2012. (ENG., Illus.). 24p. (J). *(978-0-7787-2049-2(7));* pap. *(978-0-7787-2056-0(X))* Crabtree Publishing Co.

Jennings, Terry. Hot & Cold. 2009. (Science Alive Ser.). (Illus.). 32p. (J). (gr. -1-2). pap. *(978-1-897563-55-7(8))* Saunders Bk. Co.

Jennings, Terry J. Hot & Cold. 2009. (J). 28.50 *(978-1-59920-274-7(3))* Black Rabbit Bks.

Johnson, Robin. What Is Temperature? 2012. (ENG.). 24p. (J). *(978-0-7787-0755-4(5));* (Illus.). pap. *(978-0-7787-0762-2(8))* Crabtree Publishing Co.

Kukla, Lauren. Temperature at Work, 1 vol. 2016. (ENG., Illus.). 24p. (J). *(978-1-68078-144-1(8))* ABDO Publishing Co.

Lilly, Melinda. Hot & Cold. 2005. (ENG.). 24p. (gr. 1-4). pap. 8.95 *(978-1-62717-259-2(9))* Rourke Educational Media.

Manolis, Kay. Temperature. (Illus.). 24p. (J). 2009. pap. *(978-1-60014-432-5(2),* Blastoff! Readers) 2007. (ENG., lib. bdg. 25.95 *(978-1-60014-100-3(5))* Bellwether Media.

—Temperature. 2007. (Blastoff! Readers Ser.). (ENG.). 24p. (J). (gr. k-2). 20.00 *(978-0-531-14729-0(0),* Children's Pr.) Scholastic Library Publishing.

Marshall Cavendish Benchmark, prod. Hot/Cold. 2nd rev. ed. 2011. (Bookworms 2nd Edition: Opposites Ser.). 16p. (gr. k-1). 21.36 *(978-0-60870-409-5(2))* Marshall Cavendish Corp.

Minden, Cecilia. Hot & Cold. 2016. (21st Century Basic Skills Library: Animal Opposites Ser.). (ENG.). 24p. (J). (gr. k-3). 24.21 *(978-1-63470-473-1(8),* 207623) Cherry Lake Publishing.

Moore, Rob. Why Does Water Evaporate? 2010. (Solving Science Mysteries Ser.). (Illus.). 24p. (J). pap. 8.25 *(978-1-61531-915-2(8),* PowerKids Pr.); (YA). (gr. 3-6). lib. bdg. 22.60 *(978-1-61531-892-6(5))* Rosen Publishing Group, Inc., The.

Rustad, Martha E. H. Today Is a Hot Day. 2017. (What Is the Weather Today? Ser.). (ENG., Illus.). 24p. (gr. k-1). lib. bdg. 21.99 *(978-1-5157-4923-3(1),* Pebble Bks.) Capstone Press of Coughlan Cos.

Schmauss, Judy Kentor. Too, Too Hot! Kaminski, Karol, illus. 2006. (Reader's Clubhouse Level 1 Reader Ser.). (ENG.). 24p. (J). (gr. 1-4). pap. 3.99 *(978-0-7641-3285-8(7))* Barron's Educational Series, Inc.

—Too, Too Hot! 2006. (Illus.). 24p. (J). lib. bdg. 11.00 *(978-1-4242-1587-4(0))* Dingles & Co.

Schuetz, Kristin. Temperature. 2015. (Understanding Weather Ser.). (ENG., Illus.). 24p. (J). (gr. k-3). lib. bdg. 25.95 *(978-1-62617-255-5(2),* Blastoff! Readers) Bellwether Media.

Sheehan, Thomas F. Para Calentarse, para Refrescarse (Keeping Warm, Keeping Cool) Sarfatti, Esther, tr. 2005. (Ciencia Citadina Ser.). (ENG & SPA., Illus.). 24p. (J). (gr. 3-7). lib. bdg. 21.36 *(978-1-59515-666-2(6))* Rourke Educational Media.

Smith, Sian. Hot & Cold, 1 vol. 2014. (Opposites Ser.). (ENG.). 24p. (gr. -1-1). pap. 5.99 *(978-1-4846-0334-5(6),* Acorn) Heinemann-Raintree.

Solway, Andrew. Secrets of Heat & Cold. 2010. (Science Secrets Ser.). 32p. (gr. 4). 28.50 *(978-1-60870-136-4(7))* Marshall Cavendish GBR. Dist: Marshall Cavendish Corp.

Stille, Darlene R. Temperature: Heating up & Cooling Down, 1 vol. Boyd, Sheree, illus. 2004. (Amazing Science Ser.). (ENG.). 24p. (gr. k-4). per. 8.95 *(978-1-4048-0345-9(9))* Picture Window Bks.

Sullivan, Navin. Temperature. 2006. (Measure Up! Ser.). (Illus.). 48p. (gr. 4-7). lib. bdg. 31.36 *(978-0-7614-2322-5(2),* Benchmark Bks.) Marshall Cavendish Corp.

Sundance/Newbridge LLC Staff. Time & Temperature. 2004. (Reading PowerWorks Ser.). (gr. 1-3). 37.50 *(978-0-7608-8976-3(7));* pap. 6.10 *(978-0-7608-8977-0(5))* Sundance/Newbridge Educational Publishing.

Woodford, Chris. Temperature. 2012. (Measure up Math Ser.). (Illus.). 32p. (J). (gr. 4-6). 26.60 *(978-1-4339-7449-6(5));* pap. 10.50 *(978-1-4339-7450-2(9))* Stevens, Gareth Publishing LLLP. (Gareth Stevens Learning Library).

TEMPERATURE MEASUREMENTS

Bailer, Darice. Measuring Temperature. Petelinsek, Kathleen, illus. 2014. (Explorer Junior Library: Math Explorer Junior Ser.). (ENG.). 24p. (J). (gr. 1-4). 28.50 *(978-1-62431-648-7(4),* 203104) Cherry Lake Publishing.

Gordon, Fernando. Anders Celsius, 1 vol. 2016. (ENG., Illus.). 24p. (J). *(978-1-68078-153-3(7))* ABDO Publishing Co.

Hinton, John. Hot or Cold? Describe & Compare Measurable Attributes. 2013. (Rosen Math Readers Ser.). (ENG.). 16p. (J). (gr. k-1). pap. 42.00 *(978-1-4777-1627-4(0));* (Illus.). pap. 7.00 *(978-1-4777-1626-7(2))* Rosen Publishing Group, Inc., The. (Rosen Classroom).

Lin, Yoming S. Fahrenheit, Celsius, & Their Temperature Scales. 2012. (Eureka! Ser.). (Illus.). 24p. (YA). (gr. 3-6). lib. bdg. 22.60 *(978-1-4488-5035-8(5))* Rosen Publishing Group, Inc., The.

Lipschultz, Wes. Is It Hot or Cold? Learning to Use a Thermometer. 2009. (Math for the REAL World Ser.). 12p. (gr. 1-2). pap. 5.90 *(978-0-8239-8848-8(1),* Rosen Classroom) Rosen Publishing Group, Inc., The.

Manolis, Kay. Temperature. (Illus.). 24p. (J). 2009. pap. *(978-1-60014-432-5(2),* Blastoff! Readers) 2007. (ENG., lib. bdg. 25.95 *(978-1-60014-100-3(5))* Bellwether Media.

—Temperature. 2007. (Blastoff! Readers Ser.). (ENG.). 24p. (J). (gr. k-2). 20.00 *(978-0-531-14729-0(0),* Children's Pr.) Scholastic Library Publishing.

Moore, Rob. Why Does Water Evaporate? 2010. (Solving Science Mysteries Ser.). (Illus.). 24p. (J). pap. 8.25 *(978-1-61531-915-2(8),* PowerKids Pr.); (YA). (gr. 3-6). lib. bdg. 22.60 *(978-1-61531-892-6(5))* Rosen Publishing Group, Inc., The.

—Why Does Water Evaporate? All about Heat & Temperature. 2010. (Illus.). 24p. (J). 49.50 *(978-1-61531-916-9(6),* 1307166, PowerKids Pr.) Rosen Publishing Group, Inc., The.

Polinsky, Paige V. Super Simple Experiments with Heat & Cold: Fun & Innovative Science Projects. 2016. (ENG., Illus.). 32p. (J). *(978-1-68078-170-0(7))* ABDO Publishing Co.

Rand, Casey. Temperature, 1 vol. 2010. (Measure It! Ser.). (ENG., Illus.). 32p. (gr. 3-6). 33.32 *(978-1-4329-3767-6(7));* pap. 8.29 *(978-1-4329-3773-7(1))* Heinemann-Raintree. (Heinemann InfoSearch).

Roberts, Abigail B. Using a Thermometer. 2017. (Super Science Tools Ser.). 24p. (gr. 1-2). pap. 48.90 ***(978-1-4824-6410-8(1))*** Stevens, Gareth Publishing LLLP.

Stille, Darlene R. & Picture Window Books Staff. La Temperatura: Caliente y Frío. Robledo, Sol, tr. from ENG. Boyd, Sheree, illus. 2007. (Ciencia Asombrosa Ser.). (SPA.). 24p. (gr. k-4). 26.65 *(978-1-4048-3234-3(3))* Picture Window Bks.

Vogel, Julia. Measuring Temperature. Marten, Luanne, illus. 2012. (Simple Measurement Ser.). (ENG.). 24p. (J). (gr. -1-2). 27.07 *(978-1-61473-280-8(9),* 204985) Child's World, Inc., The.

Webb, Barbara L. Hot or Cold? 2012. (ENG.). 24p. (gr. -1-1). pap. 8.95 *(978-1-61810-202-7(8))* Rourke Educational Media.

Woodford, Chris. Temperature. 2012. (Measure up Math Ser.). (Illus.). 32p. (J). (gr. 4-6). 26.60 *(978-1-4339-7449-6(5));* pap. 10.50 *(978-1-4339-7450-2(9))* Stevens, Gareth Publishing LLLP. (Gareth Stevens Learning Library).

TEMPERATURES, LOW

see Low Temperatures

TEMPLES

Barnes, Kathleen. I Love to See the Temple Reprint. 2009. 32p. pap. 8.95 *(978-1-60641-112-4(8))* Deseret Bk. Co.

Bodden, Valerie. Temples. 2007. (Built to Last Ser.). (Illus.). 24p. (J). (gr. 3-7). lib. bdg. 24.25 *(978-1-58341-560-3(2),* Creative Education) Creative Co., The.

D'Escery, Claire. Temples Dot the Earth. 2016. (ENG.). (J). bds. 9.99 *(978-1-4621-1842-7(9))* Cedar Fort, Inc./CFI Distribution.

Jani, Mahendra & Jani, Vandana. What You Will See Inside a Hindu Temple. Bhargava, Neirah & Dave, Vijay, photos by. 2005. (What You Will See Inside ... Ser.). (ENG., Illus.). 32p. (J). (gr. 3-7). 17.99 *(978-1-59473-116-7(0),* 9781594731167, Skylight Paths Publishing) LongHill Partners, Inc.

Levy, Leah. The Waiting Wall. Rosenfeld, D. L. & Leverton, Yossi, eds. 2009. (Illus.). 26p. (J). (gr. -1-1). 12.95 *(978-1-929628-49-0(8))* Hachai Publishing.

Rose, Simon. Sri Harmandir Sahib. 2014. (J). *(978-1-4896-2609-7(3))* Weigl Pubs., Inc.

TEN COMMANDMENTS

Allen, Jan. Now I Know the 10 Commandments. Allen, Russ, illus. 2005. 32p. (J). (gr. k-5). *(978-0-9765514-0-9(3))* Light Bugs Publishing.

Alsbrooks, Stephanie. The Ten Commandments: The Second Commandment. 2004. (J). bds. 9.99 *(978-1-4183-0000-5(4))* Christ Inspired, Inc.

Bianchi, Andrew. 10 Rulz. 2005. (Illus.). 128p. pap. *(978-1-84427-053-8(X))* Scripture Union.

Cameron, William J. You & the Ten Commandments. Bacon, Irving R., illus. 2011. 210p. 44.95 *(978-1-258-08112-6(1))* Literary Licensing, LLC.

CrossStaff Publishing, creator. The Ten Commandments Movie Coloring Book: Part 1. 2007. (Epic Stories of the Bible Ser.). (Illus.). 32p. (J). (gr. -1-3). 5.99 *(978-0-9743876-1-1(4))* CrossStaff Publishing.

David C. Cook Publishing Company Staff. The Ten Commandments. 2003. (My Jesus Pocket Bks.). (Illus.). 32p. (J). (gr. -1-3). pap., pap. 8.90 *(978-1-55513-859-2(4),* 1555138594) Cook, David C.

Dobson, Shirley, contrib. by. God's Ten Best: The Ten Commandments Comic & Activity Book. 2004. 16p. act. bk. ed. 1.49 *(978-0-8307-3060-5(5),* Gospel Light) Gospel Light Pubns.

Escalera, Manuel Silva. Cassandrita y Los Sabios: De Los 10 Mandamientos y Filosofía. 2012. (SPA.). 108p. (gr. -1). pap. 14.95 *(978-1-4772-0516-7(0))* AuthorHouse.

Forster, Pamela R. Honor Your Father & Mother: The Fifth Commandment for Little Ones. 2006. (J). spiral bd. 10.00 *(978-1-891206-23-8(0))* Doorposts.

Jenkins, Sharon I. Remember the Ten Commandments with Jam & Jean Jellybean. Jenkins, Sharon I., illus. l.t. ed. 2006. (Illus.). 32p. (J). (gr. -1-3). per. 10.99 *(978-1-59879-240-9(7))* Lifevest Publishing, Inc.

Killian, Rick & Yaxley, Trevor. The Making of the Ten Commandments. 2008. (Illus.). 120p. 16.99 *(978-0-9743876-8-0(1))* CrossStaff Publishing.

Lovasik, Lawrence G. Los Diez Mandamientos. (Illus.). (J). 1.50 *(978-0-89942-469-9(4))* Catholic Bk. Publishing Corp.

MacKenzie, Carine. God, the Ten Commandments & Jesus. 2003. (ENG.). 48p. (J). 12.99 *(978-1-85792-850-1(4),* 2c94907f-0368-4d78-82a2-be1bc134e3fd) Christian Focus Pubns. GBR. Dist: Bookmasters Distribution.

Manhardt, Laurie Watson. Friends of God: Catholic Bible Study for Children. Co, Aileen & Dayton, Melissa, illus. 2006. (Come & See Kids Ser.). 124p. (J). (gr. -1-2). per. 9.95 *(978-1-931018-41-8(3))* Emmaus Road Publishing.

Mathews, Janice. Jack & the 10 Rules. 2012. 32p. (J). 7.99 *(978-0-8280-2690-1(4))* Review & Herald Publishing Assn.

McGinnis, Mary Lane. The Ten Commandments for Children. 2012. 24p. pap. 10.99 *(978-1-4624-0084-3(1),* Inspiring Voices) Author Solutions, Inc.

McNeil, Niki, et al. HOCPP 1134 10 Commandments. 2006. spiral bd. 16.00 *(978-1-60308-134-4(8))* In the Hands of a Child.

Murphy, W. Ten Commandments for Children. Date not set. (J). (gr. -1-3). pap. 1.95 *(978-0-88271-159-1(8))* Regina Pr., Malhame & Co.

Naha, Ed. The Ten Commandments Movie Storybook. 2007. (Epic Stories of the Bible Ser.). (Illus.). 77p. (J). (gr. -1-3). 14.99 *(978-0-9743876-4-2(9))* CrossStaff Publishing.

Nolan, Allia Zobel. The Ten Commandments for Little Ones. Samuel, Janet, illus. 2009. (ENG.). 32p. (J). 14.99 *(978-0-7369-2545-7(7))* Harvest Hse. Pubs.

Notto, E. T. Light of God Bible Books: Book 1 (Creation, God's Commandments, Faith) 2008. 52p. pap. 22.49 *(978-1-4389-1702-3(3))* AuthorHouse.

Ostrowski, Thaddeus & Smith, Robert J. Primary Source Readings in Christian Morality. 2008. (J). pap. 12.50 *(978-0-88489-989-1(6))* St. Mary's Pr. of MN.

Pingry, Patricia A. The Story of the Ten Commandments. 2011. (Little Bible Bks.). 22p. (J). (gr. -1-k). bds. 6.99 *(978-0-8249-1855-2(X),* Ideal Pubns.) Worthy Publishing.

—The Story of the Ten Commandments. Venturi-Pickett, Stacy, illus. (ENG.). (J). 2008. 32p. (gr. k-3). pap. 3.99 *(978-0-8249-5554-0(4))* 2006. 26p. (gr. -1-3). bds. 10.95 *(978-0-8249-6656-0(2))* Worthy Publishing. (Ideal Pubns.).

Piscitelli, Donna & Gortler, Rosemarie. Living the 10 Commandments for Children. Sternhagen, Mimi, illus. 2006. 48p. (J). pap. 6.95 *(978-1-59276-231-6(X))* Our Sunday Visitor, Publishing Div.

Richards, Virginia Helen. The Ten Commandments. Richards, Virginia Helen & Halpin, D. Thomas, illus. 2007. (J). 1.95 *(978-0-8198-7420-7(5))* Pauline Bks. & Media.

Rock, Lois & Lush, Debbie. The Lord's Prayer & Ten Commandments: Bible Words to Know & Treasure. 2008. (ENG., Illus.). 64p. (J). (gr. -1-2). 5.99 *(978-0-7459-4941-3(X))* Lion Hudson PLC GBR. Dist: Independent Pubs. Group.

Rosenfeld, Dina. It's Called Kibud Av Va'Eim: A Story about Honoring Parents. Ebert, Len, illus. 2014. 20p. (J). 10.95 *(978-1-929628-78-0(1))* Hachai Publishing.

Scrimshire, Hazel. God's Little Guidebooks, 10 vols., Set. 2009. (Colour Bks.). (ENG., Illus.). 16p. (J). 10.99 *(978-1-84550-445-8(3),* a17a7504-3098-43b2-8ca7-6e0bf53300ab) Christian Focus Pubns. GBR. Dist: Bookmasters Distribution.

Topek, Susan R. Ten Good Rules. Schanzer, Rosalyn, illus. 2004. (General Jewish Interest Ser.). 24p. (J). (gr. -1-1). pap. 6.95 *(978-0-929371-30-6(5),* Kar-Ben Publishing) Lerner Publishing Group.

Topek, Susan Remick. Ten Good Rules: A Counting Book. Cohen, Tod, photos by. 2007. (ENG., Illus.). 24p. (J). (gr. -1-1). lib. bdg. 15.95 *(978-0-8225-7293-0(1),* Kar-Ben Publishing) Lerner Publishing Group.

—Ten Good Rules: A Ten Commandments Counting Book. Cohen, Tod, photos by. 2007. (ENG., Illus.). 24p. (J). (gr. -1-1). per. 7.95 *(978-1-58013-209-1(X),* Kar-Ben Publishing) Lerner Publishing Group.

Trahan, Kendra Swain. Following Jesus: Obeying His Commandments (Children's Version) 2006. (Illus.). 35p. (J). (gr. -1-3). per. 14.99 *(978-1-59879-201-0(6))* Lifevest Publishing, Inc.

Van Leeuwen, Wendy. The Ten Commandments Activity Book. 2007. (Illus.). 16p. (J). pap. 1.89 *(978-1-59317-210-7(9))* Warner Pr., Inc.

Vecchini, Silvia. The 10 Commandments Explained. Vincenti, Antonio, illus. 2015. (J). 6.95 *(978-0-8198-7523-5(6))* Pauline Bks. & Media.

VonSeggen, Liz. The Ten Commandments: Teaching Unit. rev. ed. 2003. (Illus.). 228p. (J). spiral bd. 45.00 *(978-1-58302-247-4(3))* One Way St., Inc.

Walker, Joni. Gods Ten Commandments. 2004. (Follow & Do Ser.). (Illus.). 32p. (J). 7.49 *(978-0-7586-0227-5(8))* Concordia Publishing Hse.

Warner Press, creator. The Ten Commandments Coloring Book. 2009. (Illus.). 16p. (J). (gr. -1-2). pap. 11.34 *(978-1-59317-340-1(7))* Warner Pr., Inc.

The 10 Commandments. (Illus.). 16p. (J). pap. 1.50 *(978-0-87162-872-5(4),* E6037) Warner Pr., Inc.

TENNESSEE

Barrett, Tracy. Tennessee. 2nd rev. ed. 2006. (Celebrate the States Ser.). (Illus.). 144p. (gr. 6-7). lib. bdg. 42.79 *(978-0-7614-2151-1(3),* Benchmark Bks.) Marshall Cavendish Corp.

Bausum, Ann. Marching to the Mountaintop: How Poverty, Labor Fights, & Civil Rights Set the Stage for Martin Luther King Jr.'s Final Hours. 2012. (ENG., Illus.). 112p. (J). (gr. 5-9). lib. bdg. 28.90 *(978-1-4263-0940-3(6),* National Geographic Children's Bks.) National Geographic Society.

Brown, Vanessa. Tennessee. Brusca, María Cristina, tr. from ENG. 2006. (Bilingual Library of the United States of America Ser.: Set 2). (ENG & SPA., Illus.). 32p. (J). (gr. 3-6). lib. bdg. 25.25 *(978-1-4042-3108-5(0))* Rosen Publishing Group, Inc., The.

Davidson, Tish. East South-Central States: Kentucky & Tennessee, Vol. 19. 2015. (Let's Explore the States Ser.). (Illus.). 64p. (J). (gr. 5). 23.95 *(978-1-4222-3322-1(7))* Mason Crest.

Downey, Tika. Tennessee: The Volunteer State. 2010. (Our Amazing States Ser.). (ENG.). 24p. (J). lib. bdg. 22.60 *(978-1-4358-9352-8(2),* PowerKids Pr.) Rosen Publishing Group, Inc., The.

Herman, Gail. Who Was Davy Crockett? Squier, Robert & Harrison, Nancy, illus. 2013. (Who Was? Ser.). (ENG.). 112p. (J). (gr. 3-7). 5.99 *(978-0-448-46704-7(6),* Grosset & Dunlap) Penguin Young Readers Group.

Jarnow, Jesse. Davy Crockett: Defensor de la frontera (Davy Crockett: Frontier Hero) 2009. (Grandes personajes en la historia de los Estados Unidos (Famous People in American History) Ser.). (SPA.). 32p. (gr. 2-3). 47.90 *(978-1-61512-797-9(6),* Editorial Buenas Letras) Rosen Publishing Group, Inc., The.

—Davy Crockett: Frontier Hero / Defensor de la Frontera. 2009. (Famous People in American History/Grandes personajes en la historia de los Estados Unidos Ser.). (ENG & SPA.). 32p. (gr. 2-3). 47.90 *(978-1-61512-543-2(4),* Editorial Buenas Letras) Rosen Publishing Group, Inc., The.

Johnston, Marianne. Davy Crockett. 2009. (American Legends Ser.). 24p. (gr. 3-3). 42.50 *(978-1-61511-381-1(9),* PowerKids Pr.) Rosen Publishing Group, Inc., The.

Knapp, Ron. Tennessee: A MyReportLinks. Com Book. 2003. (States Ser.). (Illus.). 48p. (J). lib. bdg. 25.26 *(978-0-7660-5120-1(X),* MyReportLinks.com Bks.) Enslow Pubs., Inc.

Kunstler, James Howard. Davy Crockett, 1 vol. Brodner, Steve, illus. 2004. (Rabbit Ears-A Classic Tale Ser.). (ENG.). 36p. (gr. k-5). 25.65 *(978-1-59197-762-9(2))* Spotlight.

Marsh, Carole. The Big Tennessee Reproducible Activity Book! 2004. (Carole Marsh Tennessee Bks.). (Illus.). 96p. (gr. 2-6). per. 9.95 *(978-0-7933-9957-4(2))* Gallopade International.

—My First Book about Tennessee. 2004. (Carole Marsh Tennessee Bks.). 32p. (J). (gr. k-4). pap. 7.95 *(978-0-7933-9899-7(1))* Gallopade International.

—Tennessee Current Events Projects: 30 Cool, Activities, Crafts, Experiments & More for Kids to Do to Learn about Your State! 2003. (Tennessee Experience Ser.). 32p. (gr. k-5). pap. 5.95 *(978-0-635-02061-1(0),* Marsh, Carole Bks.) Gallopade International.

—The Tennessee Experience Pocket Guide. 2004. (Carole Marsh Tennessee Bks.). (Illus.). 96p. (J). (gr. 3-8). pap. 6.95 *(978-0-7933-9928-4(9))* Gallopade International.

—Tennessee Geography Projects: 30 Cool, Activities, Crafts, Experiments & More for Kids to Do to Learn about Your State! 2003. (Tennessee Experience Ser.). 32p. (gr. k-5). pap. 5.95 *(978-0-635-01860-1(8),* Marsh, Carole Bks.) Gallopade International.

—Tennessee Government Projects: 30 Cool, Activities, Crafts, Experiments & More for Kids to Do to Learn about Your State! 2003. (Tennessee Experience Ser.). 32p. (gr. k-5). pap. 5.95 *(978-0-635-01961-5(2),* Marsh, Carole Bks.) Gallopade International.

—Tennessee Jeopardy! Answers & Questions about Our State! Line Art Staff, illus. 2004. 32p. (J). (gr. 3-8). pap. 7.95 *(978-0-7933-9812-6(6))* Gallopade International.

—Tennessee People Projects: 30 Cool, Activities, Crafts, Experiments & More for Kids to Do to Learn about Your State! 2003. (Tennessee Experience Ser.). 32p. (gr. k-5). pap. 5.95 *(978-0-635-02011-6(4),* Marsh, Carole Bks.) Gallopade International.

—Tennessee Symbols & Facts Projects: 30 Cool, Activities, Crafts, Experiments & More for Kids to Do to Learn about Your State! 2003. (Tennessee Experience Ser.). 32p. (gr. k-5). pap. 5.95 *(978-0-635-01911-0(6),* Marsh, Carole Bks.) Gallopade International.

—The Terrific Tennessee Coloring Book! 2004. (Carole Marsh Tennessee Bks.). (Illus.). 32p. (J). (gr. k-2). 3.95 *(978-0-7933-9870-6(3))* Gallopade International.

McNamara, Connie. My First University of Tennessee Words. 2004. (J). bds. 11.95 *(978-0-9759703-3-1(X))* Shamrock Publishing, Inc.

Mis, M. S. How to Draw Tennessee's Sights & Symbols. 2009. (Kid's Guide to Drawing America Ser.). 32p. (gr. k-k). 50.50 *(978-1-61511-096-4(8),* PowerKids Pr.) Rosen Publishing Group, Inc., The.

Moriarty, J. T. Davy Crockett: Frontier Hero. 2009. (Primary Sources of Famous People in American History Ser.). 32p. (gr. 2-3). 47.90 *(978-1-60851-670-4(9))* Rosen Publishing Group, Inc., The.

Murray, Julie. Tennessee, 1 vol. 2006. (United States Ser.). (ENG., Illus.). 32p. (gr. 2-4). 27.07 *(978-1-59197-701-8(0),* Buddy Bks.) ABDO Publishing Co.

Parker, Bridget. Tennessee. 2016. (States Ser.). (ENG., Illus.). 32p. (gr. 3-4). lib. bdg. 27.32 *(978-1-5157-0430-0(0))* Next Page Pr., The.

Petreycik, Rick. Tennessee. 2006. (It's My State! Ser.). (Illus.). 80p. (J). (gr. 4-7). lib. bdg. 21.95 *(978-0-7614-1909-9(8),* Benchmark Bks.) Marshall Cavendish Corp.

Petreyick, Rick. Tennessee. 2013. (It's My State 2nd Ed 5 Ser.). 80p. (J). (gr. 4-8). pap. 17.64 *(978-1-62712-104-0(8))* Cavendish Square Publishing.

Shoulders, Michael. Count on Us: A Tennessee Number Book. Langton, Bruce, illus. 2003. (Count Your Way Across the U. S. A. Ser.). (ENG.). 40p. (J). 16.95 *(978-1-58536-131-1(3))* Sleeping Bear Pr.

Sirvaitis, Karen. Tennessee. 2012. (J). lib. bdg. 25.26 *(978-0-7613-4558-9(2),* Lerner Pubns.) Lerner Publishing Group.

Skogen, J. M. Memphis Grizzlies. 2014. (On the Hardwood Ser.). 48p. (gr. 3-8). pap. 8.95 *(978-1-61570-917-5(7))* Scobre Pr. Corp.

Skogen, J. m. & Skogen, J. M. Memphis Grizzlies. 2014. (On the Hardwood Ser.). (gr. 3-8). 27.93 *(978-1-61570-918-2(5))* Scobre Pr. Corp.

Sparkman, Winette. Tennessee Trailblazers. Laughbaum, Steve & Crutchfield, Jim, illus. 56p. (J). pap., wbk. ed., act. bk. ed. 6.95 *(978-0-9634824-1-9(6))* March Media, Inc.

Sullivan, E. J. T Is for Tennessee. Cross, Neal, illus. 2007. (State Alphabet Bks.). 24p. (J). (gr. -1-3). *(978-1-58173-527-7(8))* Sweetwater Pr.

Valzania, Kimberly. Tennessee. 2003. (Rookie Read-About Geography Ser.). (ENG., Illus.). 32p. (J). (gr. 1-2). 20.50 *(978-0-516-22699-6(1),* Children's Pr.) Scholastic Library Publishing.

VanVoorst, Jenny Fretland. What's Great about Tennessee? 2014. (Our Great States Ser.). (ENG.). 32p. (gr. 2-5). lib. bdg. 26.60 *(978-1-4677-3392-2(X),* Lerner Pubns.) Lerner Publishing Group.

Weatherly, Myra S. Tennessee. 2008. (ENG.). 80p. (J). pap. 7.95 *(978-0-531-20814-4(1),* Children's Pr.) Scholastic Library Publishing.

Winders, Richard Bruce. Davy Crockett: The Legend of the Wild Frontier. 2009. (Library of American Lives & Times Ser.). 112p. (gr. 5-5). 69.20 *(978-1-60853-476-0(6))* Rosen Publishing Group, Inc., The.

TENNESSEE—FICTION

Altsheler, Joseph A. The Guns of Shiloh. 2006. (Civil War Ser.: Vol. 2). 292p. (J). reprint ed. 28.95 *(978-1-4218-1774-3(8));* pap. 13.95 *(978-1-4218-1874-0(4))* 1st World Publishing, Inc. (1st World Library - Literary Society).

—The Guns of Shiloh. l.t. ed. (Civil War Ser.: Vol. 2). (J). 2007. (ENG.). 260p. per. 23.99 *(978-1-4346-7681-8(1))* 2010. (ENG.). 356p. (gr. 4-7). reprint ed. pap. 32.75 *(978-1-177-56053-5(4))* 2008. 264p. reprint ed. 28.99 *(978-0-554-29459-9(1))* 2008. 264p. reprint ed. 25.99 *(978-0-554-38762-8(X))* 2007. 240p. reprint ed. per. 20.99 *(978-1-4346-7680-1(3))* Creative Media Partners, LLC.

—The Guns of Shiloh. 2006. (Civil War Ser.: Vol. 2). (J). reprint ed. pap. *(978-1-4065-0813-0(6))* Dodo Pr.

—The Guns of Shiloh. 2006. (Civil War Ser.: Vol. 2). (J). reprint ed. pap. *(978-1-4068-0745-5(1))* Echo Library.

—The Guns of Shiloh. 2010. 156p. pap. 24.39 *(978-1-152-46676-0(3));* (Civil War Ser.: Vol. 2). (Illus.). (J). (gr. 4-7). reprint ed. pap. 19.99 *(978-1-153-70505-9(2))* General Bks. LLC.

—The Guns of Shiloh. (Civil War Ser.: Vol. 2). (J). 2010. 216p. pap. *(978-1-4076-3068-7(7))* 2012. 362p. reprint ed. pap. *(978-1-290-02433-4(2))* HardPr.

—The Guns of Shiloh. 2003. (Civil War Ser.: Vol. 2). 232p. (J). reprint ed. pap. 36.99 *(978-1-4043-5087-8(X))* IndyPublish.com.

—The Guns of Shiloh. (Civil War Ser.: Vol. 2). (J). reprint ed. 2010. 226p. (gr. 4-7). 31.96 *(978-1-169-29437-0(5))* 2010. 226p. (gr. 4-7). pap. 19.96 *(978-1-162-69671-3(0))* 2010. 39.95 *(978-1-161-46536-5(7))* 2004. pap. 1.99 *(978-1-4192-6520-4(2))* 2004. pap. 24.95 *(978-1-4191-6520-7(8))* Kessinger Publishing, LLC.

—The Guns of Shiloh. (Civil War Ser.: Vol. 2). reprint ed. 2008. 228p. (J). pap. 14.45 *(978-1-60597-269-5(X))* 2007. 232p. per. 12.45 *(978-1-60424-259-1(0))* Standard Pubns., Inc. (Book Jungle).

—The Guns of Shiloh. 2011. (Civil War Ser.: Vol. 2). 260p. (J). (gr. 4-7). reprint ed. pap. *(978-3-8424-2812-6(X))* Tredition GmbH.

—The Guns of Shiloh. 2009. (Civil War Ser.: Vol. 2). 278p. (J). (gr. 4-7). reprint ed. pap. 16.95 *(978-1-933573-83-0(X))* Zeezok Publishing, LLC.

—The Sword of Antietam: A Story of the Nation's Crisis. 2006. (Civil War Ser.: Vol. 4). 296p. (J). reprint ed. 28.95 *(978-1-4218-1776-7(4));* pap. 13.95 *(978-1-4218-1876-4(0))* 1st World Publishing, Inc. (1st World Library - Literary Society).

—The Sword of Antietam: A Story of the Nation's Crisis. l.t. ed. (Civil War Ser.: Vol. 4). (J). reprint ed. 2006. 262p. pap. 23.99 *(978-1-4264-2714-5(X))* 2011. 358p. (gr. 4-7). pap. 32.75 *(978-1-245-13385-2(3))* 2008. 264p. 28.99 *(978-0-554-22582-1(4))* 2008. 264p. 25.99 *(978-0-554-31885-1(7))* 2007. (ENG.). 242p. pap. 20.99 *(978-1-4264-2657-5(7))* Creative Media Partners, LLC.

—The Sword of Antietam: A Story of the Nation's Crisis. 2006. (Civil War Ser.: Vol. 4). (J). reprint ed. pap. *(978-1-4065-0825-3(X))* Dodo Pr.

—The Sword of Antietam: A Story of the Nation's Crisis. 2007. (Civil War Ser.: Vol. 4). 176p. (J). reprint ed. per. *(978-1-4068-1690-7(6))* Echo Library.

—The Sword of Antietam: A Story of the Nation's Crisis. 2010. (Civil War Ser.: Vol. 4). (Illus.). 160p. (J). (gr. 4-7). reprint ed. pap. 19.99 *(978-1-153-72276-6(3))* General Bks. LLC.

—The Sword of Antietam: A Story of the Nation's Crisis. 2010. (Civil War Ser.: Vol. 4). 224p. (J). reprint ed. pap. *(978-1-4076-4642-8(7))* HardPr.

—The Sword of Antietam: A Story of the Nation's Crisis. (Civil War Ser.: Vol. 4). (J). reprint ed. 2010. 352p. (gr. 4-7). 37.56 *(978-1-163-20537-2(0))* 2010. 352p. (gr. 4-7). pap. 25.56 *(978-1-162-77564-7(5))* 2005. 352p. 46.95 *(978-1-4326-1485-0(1))* 2004. pap. 1.99 *(978-1-4192-8469-4(X))* Kessinger Publishing, LLC.

—The Sword of Antietam: A Story of the Nation's Crisis. 2009. (Civil War Ser.: Vol. 4). (J). reprint ed. pap. 16.95 *(978-1-933573-85-4(6))* Zeezok Publishing, LLC.

Bare, Bart. Girl. 2010. 188p. (YA). pap. 11.95 *(978-0-9825396-4-4(9))* Canterbury Hse. Publishing, Ltd.

Bougie, Matt. The Bell Witch: Ghost of Tennessee. Greenan, Amy, illus. 2016. (American Legends & Folktales Ser.). 32p. (J). pap. 10.58 *(978-1-5026-2220-4(3))* Cavendish Square Publishing.

Brouwer, Sigmund. Rock the Boat, 1 vol. 2015. (Orca Limelights Ser.). (ENG.). 128p. (J). (gr. 6-9). pap. 9.95 *(978-1-4598-0455-5(4))* Orca Bk. Pubs. USA.

Bryant, Jen. Ringside 1925: Views from the Scopes Trial. 2009. (ENG.). 240p. (J). (gr. 5). 7.99 *(978-0-440-42189-4(6),* Yearling) Random Hse. Children's Bks.

Carr, Patrick W. The Legend's Granddaughter: Not Quite Super, Book 1. Dabbs, Douglas, illus. 2007. 281p. (J). pap. *(978-0-9793168-0-7(4))* NQSBks.

Coleman, Evelyn. Circle of Fire. 2009. (Mysteries Through Time Ser.). 160p. (YA). (gr. 4-8). 31.95 *(978-1-60754-191-2(2));* pap. 15.25 *(978-1-60754-192-9(0))* Windmill Bks.

Crist-Evans, Craig. Moon over Tennessee: A Boy's Civil War Journal. Christensen, Bonnie, illus. 2003. (ENG.). 64p. (J). (gr. 5-7). pap. 8.95 *(978-0-618-31107-1(6))* Houghton Mifflin Harcourt Publishing Co.

Donaldson, Joan. On Viney's Mountain. 2009. (ENG.). 192p. (YA). (gr. 5-18). 16.95 *(978-0-8234-2129-9(5))* Holiday Hse., Inc.

Dorr, Shay. Khloe Dutch! 2011. 48p. pap. 8.95 *(978-1-4502-8332-8(2))* iUniverse, Inc.

Dowell, Frances O'Roark. Where I'd Like to Be. 2004. (Aladdin Fiction Ser.). 232p. (gr. 5-9). 17.00 *(978-0-7569-4357-8(4))* Perfection Learning Corp.

—Where I'd Like to Be. (ENG., (J). (gr. 5-9). 2003. Illus.). 240p. 17.99 *(978-0-689-84420-1(4))* 2004. 256p. reprint ed. pap. 7.99 *(978-0-689-87067-5(1))* Simon & Schuster Children's Publishing. (Atheneum Bks. for Young Readers).

—Where I'd Like to Be. l.t. ed. 2003. 162p. (J). 22.95 *(978-0-7862-5741-6(5))* Thorndike Pr.

Dudley, Marie Luther. Tennessee Ocean Frogs. Primm, Patricia, illus. 2008. 24p. pap. 24.95 *(978-1-60474-261-9(5))* America Star Bks.

Duncan Gurley, Ann. Esbe's Halo. 2009. 108p. (J). pap. 15.95 *(978-1-4327-3453-4(9))* Outskirts Pr., Inc.

Elmendorf, Dana. South of Sunshine. 2016. (ENG.). 256p. (YA). (gr. 8-12). 16.99 *(978-0-8075-7568-0(2))* Whitman, Albert & Co.

Faulkerson, Jeffery A. It's Good to Be Golden: The Stranger in the Shadows. 2008. 26p. pap. 24.95 *(978-1-60441-863-7(X))* America Star Bks.

Frillman, K. Country Stars: The Road Less Traveled. 2007. 348p. per. 21.95 *(978-1-4303-1234-5(3))* Lulu Pr., Inc.

Gamble, Adam. Good Night Tennessee. Veno, Joe, illus. 2007. (Good Night Our World Ser.). (ENG.). 20p. (J). (gr. k — 1). bds. 9.95 *(978-1-60219-019-1(4))* Good Night Bks.

T
U
V

Godfrey, John. The Green Enamel Kid. 2008. 64p. per. 9.95 (978-1-4357-0508-1(4)) Lulu Pr., Inc.

Grant, Natalie. The Miracle in Music City, 1 vol. 2016. (Faithgirlz / Glimmer Girls Ser.). (ENG.). 208p. (J). pap. 8.99 (978-0-310-75250-9(7)) Zonderkidz.

Gratz, Alan. Something Rotten. 2009. (ENG.). 224p. (YA). (gr. 7-18). 7.99 (978-0-14-241297-8(X), Puffin Books) Penguin Young Readers Group.

—Something Wicked. 2009. (ENG.). 288p. (YA). (gr. 7-18). 7.99 (978-0-14-241496-5(4), Puffin Books) Penguin Young Readers Group.

Green, Connie Jordan. The War at Home. 2nd ed. 2003. 144p. (J). pap. 15.00 (978-0-916078-75-1(2)) Iris Publishing Group, Inc., The.

Guiffre, William A. Eddie, the Elf Who Would Be Elvis. Fannon, Chris, illus. 2011. (ENG.). 40p. (J). 17.95 (978-0-9830172-0-2(4)); pap. 9.95 (978-0-9830172-1-9(2)) Bks. for Children Publishing.

Gunderson, Jessica. The Songs of Stones River: A Civil War Novel. 2015. (Civil War Ser.). (ENG., Illus.). 96p. (gr. 4-4). lib. bdg. 26.65 (978-1-4342-9703-7(9)) Stone Arch Bks.

Harrison, Emma. Escaping Perfect. 2016. (ENG., Illus.). 336p. (YA). (gr. 9). 17.99 (978-1-4814-4212-1(0), Simon Pulse) Simon Pulse.

Hembree, G. Wil. The Willisby Orphans: In the Keys to the Bottomless Pit. 2011. 552p. (gr. -1 — 1). 44.95 (978-1-4497-2366-8(7)); pap. 34.95 (978-1-4497-2365-1(9)) Author Solutions, Inc. (WestBow Pr.).

Higginbotham, Mary. Only Feature. 2012. 56p. pap. 16.95 (978-1-4626-7953-9(6)) America Star Bks.

Hodgin, Molly. Tenney's Journal. 2017. (American Girl: Tenney Grant Ser.). (ENG.). 160p. (J). (gr. 3-7). 11.99 (978-1-338-13704-0(2)) Scholastic, Inc.

Holley, Marietta. Samantha at the World's Fair. 2007. (ENG.). 428p. pap. 26.99 (978-1-4264-5101-0(6)) Creative Media Partners, LLC.

Huggins, Peter. In the Company of Owls. Goodman Koz, Paula, illus. 2008. (ENG.). 96p. (J). 15.95 (978-1-58838-036-4(X), NewSouth Bks.) NewSouth, Inc.

Isbell, Rebecca & Buchanan, Marilyn. Everyone Has a Story to Tell. Bledsoe, Wiliam B., illus. 2004. (J). 14.95 (978-0-9755906-0-7(X)) Olde Town Publishing.

Jacobs, Lily. The Littlest Bunny in Nashville. Dunn, Robert, illus. 2016. (ENG.). 32p. (J). (-7). 9.99 (978-1-4926-3351-8(8), 9781492633518, Sourcebooks Jabberwocky) Sourcebooks, Inc.

—The Littlest Bunny in Tennessee: An Easter Adventure. Dunn, Robert, illus. 2015. (ENG.). 32p. (J). (-3). 9.99 (978-1-4926-1207-0(3), Sourcebooks Jabberwocky) Sourcebooks, Inc.

James, Eric. A Halloween Scare in Tennessee. Le Ray, Marina, illus. 2014. (ENG.). 32p. (J). (-5). 9.99 (978-1-4926-0630-7(8), 9781492606307, Sourcebooks Jabberwocky) Sourcebooks, Inc.

—Santa's Sleigh Is on Its Way to Tennessee. Dunn, Robert, illus. 2015. (ENG.). 32p. (J). (-2). 12.99 (978-1-4926-2752-4(6), Sourcebooks Jabberwocky) Sourcebooks, Inc.

Jamison, Jo Lynn & Elliott, Lela Mae. Siren's Call of the Caves, 1 vol. 2009. 55p. pap. 16.95 (978-1-4489-8627-9(3)) PublishAmerica, Inc.

John Philip Duck. 2004. (J). 29.95 incl. audio compact disk (978-0-8045-4127-5(2)); 27.95 incl. audio (978-0-8045-6932-3(0)) Spoken Arts, Inc.

Johnson, Allen, Jr. My Brother's Story. McMorris, Kelley, illus. 2014. (Blackwater Novels Ser.: Vol. 1). (ENG.). 191p. (J). (gr. 4-7). 14.99 (978-1-933725-37-6(0)) Premium Pr. America.

Johnston, Tony. Bone by Bone by Bone. 2007. (ENG.). 192p. (YA). (gr. 7-12). 29.99 (978-1-59643-113-3(X), 9781596431133) Roaring Brook Pr.

Keith, Patty J. Will You Be My Friend? Even If I Am Different from You. Keith, Patty J., photos by. 2013. (Illus.). 36p. pap. 12.95 (978-0-615-78050-4(4)) Patty's Blooming Words.

Kenneally, Miranda. Racing Savannah, 1 vol. unabr. ed. 2015. (Hundred Oaks Ser.: Bk. 4). (ENG.). (YA). (gr. 7-9). 14.99 (978-1-5012-1560-5(4), 9781501215605, Audible Studios on Brilliance Audio) Brilliance Publishing, Inc.

—Racing Savannah. 2013. (Hundred Oaks Ser.: Bk. 4). (ENG.). 304p. (YA). (gr. 7-12). pap. 9.99 (978-1-4022-8476-2(4), 9781402284762) Sourcebooks, Inc.

—Things I Can't Forget. 2013. (Hundred Oaks Ser.: Bk. 3). (ENG.). 320p. (YA). (gr. 7-12). pap. 9.99 (978-1-4022-7190-8(5), 9781402271908) Sourcebooks, Inc.

Kidd, Ronald. Monkey Town: The Summer of the Scopes Trial. 2011. (ENG.). 288p. (YA). (gr. 7). pap. 13.99 (978-1-4424-4211-5(5), Simon Pulse) Simon Pulse.

Lee, Dakota. Flash of Freedom. 2009. 128p. pap. 11.95 (978-0-595-52557-7(1)) iUniverse, Inc.

Lloyd, Natalie. The Key to Extraordinary. (ENG.). 240p. (J). (gr. 3-7). 2017. pap. 6.99 **(978-0-545-55276-9(1))** 2016. 16.99 (978-0-545-55274-5(5)) Scholastic, Inc. (Scholastic Pr.).

Lloyd, Natalie. A Snicker of Magic. (ENG.). 320p. (J). (gr. 3-7). 2015. pap. 6.99 (978-0-545-55273-8(7)) 2014. 16.99 (978-0-545-55270-7(2)) Scholastic, Inc. (Scholastic Pr.).

—A Snicker of Magic. 2015. lib. bdg. 17.20 (978-0-606-37089-9(7)) Turtleback Bks.

Lloyd, Natalie, et al. A Snicker of Magic. 2014. (ENG.). mass mkt. (978-0-545-68447-7(1)) Scholastic, Inc.

Loyd, Todd. Dark Ride. 2012. (ENG.). 320p. (YA). (gr. 7-9). pap. 15.00 (978-1-936487-22-6(5), 1936487225) Franklin Green Publishing.

MacKay, Lisa. Nick Finds a Home. 2009. 32p. pap. 12.99 (978-1-4490-3245-6(1)) AuthorHouse.

Madden, Kerry. Jessie's Mountain. 2008. (ENG.). 320p. (J). (gr. 3-7). 16.99 (978-0-670-06154-9(9), Viking Books for Young Readers) Penguin Young Readers Group.

Martone, Ginny. Trouble at Big Bear Falls. 2011. 90p. pap. 19.95 (978-1-4626-2558-1(4)) America Star Bks.

Mary E. Gale. Mountain Boy in the City. 2009. 136p. 21.95 (978-1-4401-6771-3(0)); pap. 11.95 (978-1-4401-6773-7(7)) iUniverse, Inc.

McDaniel, Lurlene. The Year of Chasing Dreams. (ENG.). 336p. (YA). (gr. 7). 2015. pap. 9.99 (978-0-385-74174-3(X), Ember) 2014. 16.99 (978-0-385-74173-6(1), Delacorte Pr.) Random Hse. Children's Bks.

—The Year of Luminous Love. (ENG.). 384p. (YA). (gr. 7). 2014. pap. 9.99 (978-0-385-74172-9(3), Ember) 2013. 16.99 (978-0-385-74171-2(5), Delacorte Bks. for Young Readers) Random Hse. Children's Bks.

McKissack, Patricia C. Abby Takes a Stand. James, Gordon C., illus. 2007. 104p. (J). (978-0-439-02797-7(7)) Scholastic, Inc.

—Abby Takes a Stand. James, Gordon C. et al, illus. 2006. (Scraps of Time Ser.). (ENG.). 128p. (J). (gr. 3-7). 6.99 (978-0-14-240687-8(2), Puffin Books) Penguin Young Readers Group.

—Goin' Someplace Special. Pinkney, Jerry, illus. 2008. (ENG.). 40p. (J). (gr. -1-3). 7.99 (978-1-4169-2735-8(2), Aladdin) Simon & Schuster Children's Publishing.

—The Home-Run King. 2009. (Scraps of Time Ser.). (ENG.). 112p. (J). (gr. 3-7). 6.99 (978-0-14-241459-0(X), Puffin Books) Penguin Young Readers Group.

—Tippy Lemmey. Keeter, Susan, illus. 2003. (Ready-for-Chapters Ser.). 59p. (gr. 2-5). lib. bdg. 15.00 (978-0-7569-1432-5(9)) Perfection Learning Corp.

Miller, Kirsten. The Eternal Ones: What If Love Refused to Die? 2011. (ENG.). 432p. (YA). (gr. 7-18). 9.99 (978-1-59514-375-4(0), Razorbill) Penguin Young Readers Group.

Miller, Pat Zietlow. The Quickest Kid in Clarksville. Morrison, Frank, illus. 2016. (ENG.). 40p. (J). (gr. k-3). 16.99 (978-1-4521-2936-5(3)) Chronicle Bks. LLC.

Moonshower, Candie. The Legend of Zoey. 2007. (ENG.). 224p. (J). (gr. 3-7). 6.99 (978-0-440-23924-6(9), Yearling) Random Hse. Children's Bks.

Murdoch, Emily. If You Find Me. (ENG.). (YA). (gr. 7). 2014. 288p. pap. 10.99 (978-1-250-03327-7(6), 9781250033277) 2013. 256p. 17.99 (978-1-250-02152-6(9), 9781250021526) St. Martin's Pr. (St. Martin's Griffin).

Nilsson, Al. The Tennessee Tater. Nilsson, Al, illus. 2003. (Illus.). (YA). per. (978-0-9741294-9-5(6), MSP) Main St Publishing, Inc.

O'Neill, Elizabeth. Alfred Visits Tennessee. 2006. (Illus.). 24p. 12.00 (978-0-9771836-5-4(3)) Global Business Information Strategies, Inc.

Payne, C. C. Lula Bell on Geekdom, Freakdom, & the Challenges of Bad Hair, 0 vols. 2012. (ENG.). 276p. (J). (gr. 3-7). 16.99 (978-0-7614-6225-5(2), 9780761462255, Amazon Children's Publishing) Amazon Publishing.

Pfeffer, Susan Beth. The Shade of the Moon. (Life As We Knew It Ser.: 4). (ENG.). 304p. (YA). (gr. 7). 2014. pap. 8.99 (978-0-544-33615-5(1), HMH Books For Young Readers) 2013. 17.99 (978-0-547-81337-0(6)) Houghton Mifflin Harcourt Publishing Co.

Polacco, Patricia. John Philip Duck. Polacco, Patricia, illus. 2004. (ENG., Illus.). 48p. (J). (gr. k-4). 17.99 (978-0-399-24262-5(7), Philomel Bks.) Penguin Young Readers Group.

Ray, Christie Jones & Ray, Christie Jones. Fox Family of Franklin. 2012. (Illus.). 16p. pap. 10.00 (978-0-9853223-3-5(0)) Rose Water Cottage Pr.

Reed, Vernon. Children of the Hollow. 2006. (ENG.). 188p. per. 24.95 (978-1-4241-3668-1(7)) PublishAmerica, Inc.

Reinhardt, Dana. How to Build a House. 2009. (ENG.). 240p. (YA). (gr. 9-11). pap. 8.99 (978-0-375-84454-6(6), Ember) Random Hse. Children's Bks.

Rennison, Louise. Then He Ate My Boy Entrancers: More Mad, Marvy Confessions of Georgia Nicolson. (Confessions of Georgia Nicolson Ser.: 6). 2006. (ENG.). 336p. (YA). (gr. 8-12). pap. 9.99 (978-0-06-058939-4(6)) 2005. 320p. (J). lib. bdg. 16.89 (978-0-06-058938-7(8)) HarperCollins Pubs. (HarperTeen).

Rhodes, O. K. & Spencer, Octavia. The Case of the Time-Capsule Bandit. To, Vivienne, illus. 2013. (Randi Rhodes, Ninja Detective Ser.: 1). (ENG.). 224p. (J). (gr. 3-7). 16.99 (978-1-4424-7681-3(8), Simon & Schuster Bks. For Young Readers) Simon & Schuster Bks. For Young Readers.

Saveley, Barb. Dusky II: Journey of Tears. 2010. 40p. 18.95 (978-1-4389-8243-4(7)) AuthorHouse.

Schwabach, Karen. The Hope Chest. 2010. (ENG.). 288p. (J). (gr. 3-7). 7.99 (978-0-375-84096-8(6), Yearling) Random Hse. Children's Bks.

Silvano, Wendi. Love Is All Around Tennessee. Czernichowska, Joanna, illus. 2016. (ENG.). 32p. (J). (-6). 12.99 (978-1-4926-2964-1(2), Sourcebooks Jabberwocky) Sourcebooks, Inc.

Singer, Sarah Jane. Two Bullets for Sergeant Franks. 2003. (Illus.). 112p. (YA). pap. 7.99 (978-0-9721216-9-9(2), 0972121692) Computer Classics (R).

Smallman, Steve. Santa Is Coming to Chattanooga. Dunn, Robert, illus. 2015. (ENG.). 32p. (J). (-3). 9.99 (978-1-4926-2651-0(1), Sourcebooks Jabberwocky) Sourcebooks, Inc.

—Santa Is Coming to Memphis. Dunn, Robert, illus. 2015. (ENG.). 32p. (J). (-3). 9.99 (978-1-4926-2643-5(0), Sourcebooks Jabberwocky) Sourcebooks, Inc.

—Santa Is Coming to Nashville. Dunn, Robert, illus. 2014. (ENG.). 32p. (J). (-3). 9.99 (978-1-4926-0718-2(5), Sourcebooks Jabberwocky) Sourcebooks, Inc.

—Santa Is Coming to Tennessee. Dunn, Robert, illus. 2013. (ENG.). 32p. (J). (-3). 9.99 (978-1-4022-8806-7(9), Sourcebooks Jabberwocky) Sourcebooks, Inc.

—Santa Is Coming to the Great Smoky Mountains. Dunn, Robert, illus. 2013. (ENG.). 32p. (J). (-3). 9.99 (978-1-4022-9033-6(0), Sourcebooks Jabberwocky) Sourcebooks, Inc.

Smith, Robert F. Bitten: A Romantic Comedy. 2008. (YA). pap. (978-1-59038-904-1(2)) Deseret Bk. Co.

Snyder, Laurel. Penny Dreadful. Halpin, Abigail, illus. 2011. (ENG.). 320p. (J). (gr. 3-7). 8.99 (978-0-375-86169-7(6), Yearling) Random Hse. Children's Bks.

Spruill, Beverle. The Dream Box. 2009. 24p. pap. 13.50 (978-1-4490-3783-3(6)) AuthorHouse.

Steele, William O. Flaming Arrows. 2004. (ENG., Illus.). 160p. (J). (gr. 2-5). pap. 11.95 (978-0-15-205213-3(5)) Houghton Mifflin Harcourt Publishing Co.

Supplee, Suzanne. Artichoke's Heart. 2009. (ENG.). 288p. (YA). (gr. 7-18). 8.99 (978-0-14-241427-9(1), Speak) Penguin Young Readers Group.

—Somebody Everybody Listens To. 2011. (ENG.). 288p. (YA). (gr. 7-18). 8.99 (978-0-14-241886-4(2), Speak) Penguin Young Readers Group.

Taylor, Pearl Fleming. Snowbird Weenie, 1 vol. 2009. 59p. pap. 16.95 (978-1-60836-745-0(2)) America Star Bks.

Tugman, Etta. Smokey Mountain Bears. 2006. 9.00 (978-0-8059-8189-6(6)) Dorrance Publishing Co., Inc.

Turner, Thomas N. Country Music Night Before Christmas, 1 vol. Rice, James, illus. 2003. (Night Before Christmas Ser.). (ENG.). 32p. (J). (gr. k-3). 16.99 (978-1-58980-148-6(2)) Pelican Publishing Co., Inc.

Tyler-Vaughn, Savanna. Flour Sack Wear. 2006. (ENG.). 48p. per. 16.95 (978-1-4241-2501-2(4)) America Star Bks.

Tyre, Lisa Lewis & Airgood, Ellen. Last in a Long Line of Rebels. 2015. (ENG.). 288p. (J). (gr. 5). 16.99 (978-0-399-16838-3(9), Nancy Paulsen Books) Penguin Young Readers Group.

Vawter, Vince. Paperboy. 2014. (ENG.). 240p. (J). (gr. 5). pap. 7.99 (978-0-307-93151-1(X), Yearling) Random Hse. Children's Bks.

Watts, Julia. Secret City. 2013. (ENG.). 264p. (gr. 7). pap. 11.95 (978-1-59493-390-5(1)) Bella Bks., Inc.

White-Adams, Beverly. The Adventures of Rusty: Rusty Goes to Tennessee the Adventures Continue Vol. 4. 2013. 32p. pap. 17.25 (978-1-4669-8583-4(6)) Trafford Publishing.

Yancey, Rick. Alfred Kropp: the Seal of Solomon. 2015. (Alfred Kropp Ser.). (ENG.). 352p. (YA). (gr. 7). pap. 9.99 (978-1-61963-917-1(3), 9781619639171, Bloomsbury USA Childrens) Bloomsbury Publishing USA.

TENNESSEE—HISTORY

Bailey, Diane. Tennessee: Past & Present. 2010. (United States: Past & Present Ser.). (ENG., Illus.). 48p. (J). pap. 11.75 (978-1-4358-8494-6(9)); lib. bdg. 29.25 (978-1-4358-3522-1(0)) Rosen Publishing Group, Inc., The. (Rosen Reference).

Bobrick, Benson. The Battle of Nashville. 2010. (ENG., Illus.). 144p. (J). (gr. 3-7). 19.99 (978-0-375-84887-2(8), Knopf Bks. for Young Readers) Random Hse. Children's Bks.

Brown, Vanessa. Tennessee. 2009. (Bilingual Library of the United States of America Ser.). (ENG & SPA.). 32p. (gr. 2-2). 47.90 (978-1-60853-386-2(7), Editorial Buenas Letras) Rosen Publishing Group, Inc., The.

Chemerka, William R. Davy Crockett from a to Z, 1 vol. Dillon, Wade, illus. 2013. (ENG.). 32p. (J). (gr. k-3). 16.99 (978-1-4556-1835-4(7)) Pelican Publishing Co., Inc.

Dean, Arlan. The Wilderness Trail: From the Shenandoah Valley to the Ohio River. 2009. (Famous American Trails Ser.). 24p. (gr. 3-3). 42.50 (978-1-61512-493-0(4), PowerKids Pr.) Rosen Publishing Group, Inc., The.

Downey, Tika. Tennessee: The Volunteer State. 2010. (Our Amazing States Ser.). (ENG.). 24p. (J). pap. 8.25 (978-1-4358-9800-4(1), PowerKids Pr.) Rosen Publishing Group, Inc., The.

English, D. N. Downtown Wanderings & Memories. 2nd ed. 2003. (Illus.). 190p. (YA). pap. (978-0-9741294-8-8(8), MSP) Main St Publishing, Inc.

Furstinger, Nancy. Davy Crockett. 2003. (Folk Heroes Ser.). (Illus.). 24p. (J). lib. bdg. 24.45 (978-1-59036-073-6(7)) Weigl Pubs., Inc.

Gish, Melissa. Tennessee. 2009. (This Land Called America Ser.). (Illus.). 32p. (YA). (gr. 3-6). 19.95 (978-1-58341-795-9(8)) Creative Co., The.

Hama, Larry. The Battle of Shiloh: Surprise Attack! Moore, Scott, illus. 2007. (Graphic Battles of the Civil War Ser.). (ENG.). 48p. (YA). (gr. 4-7). lib. bdg. 31.95 (978-1-4042-0779-0(1)) Rosen Publishing Group, Inc., The.

Harmon, Leesa, et al. Bullets & Bayonets: A Battle of Frankin Primer. 2014. (ENG.). 117p. 25.00 (978-0-9911915-2-9(8), Academy Park Pr.) Williamson County Public Library.

Herman, Gail. Who Was Davy Crockett? 2013. (Who Was... ? Ser.). lib. bdg. 16.00 (978-0-606-32133-4(0), Turtleback) Turtleback Bks.

Hicks, Kyra E. Martha Ann's Quilt for Queen Victoria. Födi, Lee Edward, illus. 2012. 32p. (J). pap. 12.95 (978-0-9824796-8-1(9)) Black Threads Pr.

Jerome, Kate B. Lucky to Live in Tennessee. 2017. (Arcadia Kids Ser.). (ENG., Illus.). 32p. (J). 16.99 **(978-0-7385-2790-1(4))** Arcadia Publishing.

—The Wise Animal Handbook Tennessee. 2017. (Arcadia Kids Ser.). (ENG., Illus.). 32p. (J). 16.99 **(978-0-7385-2844-1(7))** Arcadia Publishing.

Lantier-Sampon, Patricia. Tennessee. 2005. (Portraits of the States Ser.). (Illus.). 32p. (gr. 2-6). pap. 10.50 (978-0-8368-4653-9(2)); lib. bdg. 26.00 (978-0-8368-4634-8(6)) Stevens, Gareth Publishing LLLP. (Gareth Stevens Learning Library).

Marsh, Carole. Exploring Tennessee Through Project-Based Learning: Geography, History, Government, Economics & More. 2016. (Tennessee Experience Ser.). (ENG.). (J). pap. 9.99 (978-0-635-12366-4(5)) Gallopade International.

—Tennessee History Projects: 30 Cool, Activities, Crafts, Experiments & More for Kids to Do to Learn about Your State! 2003. (Tennessee Experience Ser.). 32p. (gr. k-5). pap. 5.95 (978-0-635-01811-3(X), Marsh, Carole Bks.) Gallopade International.

Marthal, Barbara G. Fighting for Freedom: A Documented Story. 2012. 28p. pap. 19.99 (978-1-4772-2922-4(1)) AuthorHouse.

McDowell, Pamela. Tennessee: The Volunteer State. 2012. (J). (978-1-61913-405-8(5)); pap. (978-1-61913-406-5(3)) Weigl Pubs., Inc.

McMillan, Jenna. East Tennessee from a to Z. Patients from East Tennessee Children's Hospital, illus. 2013. (ENG.). 26p. 20.00 (978-0-9830954-2-2(6)) Books by Kids LLC.

Ollhoff, Jim. Tennessee, 1 vol. 2009. (United States Ser.). (ENG., Illus.). 48p. (YA). (gr. 2-5). 27.07 (978-1-60453-678-2(0)) ABDO Publishing Co.

Petreycik, Rick & McGeveran, William. Tennessee. 2nd ed. 2013. (Illus.). 80p. (J). (gr. 4-8). 31.36 (978-0-7614-8003-7(X)) Cavendish Square Publishing.

Publications International Ltd. Staff, et al. Yesterday & Today Nashville. 2010. 192p. 24.95 (978-1-4127-6199-4(9)) Publications International, Ltd.

Robinson, Tom. Tennessee Titans, 1 vol. 2010. (Inside the NFL Ser.). (ENG.). 48p. (YA). (gr. 3-6). lib. bdg. 32.79 (978-1-61714-031-0(7)) ABDO Publishing Co.

Semchuk, Rosann. Tennessee. 2011. (Guide to American States Ser.). (Illus.). 48p. (YA). (gr. 3-6). 29.99 (978-1-61690-815-7(7)); (J). (978-1-61690-491-3(7)) Weigl Pubs., Inc.

—Tennessee: The Volunteer State. 2016. (J). (978-1-4896-4944-7(1)) Weigl Pubs., Inc.

Shoulders, Michael. Little Tennessee. 2012. (My Little State Ser.). (ENG., Illus.). 22p. (J). 9.95 (978-1-58536-201-1(8)) Sleeping Bear Pr.

Somervill, Barbara A. Tennessee. rev. ed. 2014. (ENG.). 144p. (J). lib. bdg. 40.00 (978-0-531-28294-6(5)) Scholastic Library Publishing.

Sullivan, Laura L., et al. Tennessee. 2015. (It's My State! (r) Ser.). (ENG., Illus.). 80p. (J). (gr. 4-4). 34.21 (978-1-62713-225-1(2)) Cavendish Square Publishing.

Tieck, Sarah. Tennessee, 1 vol. 2012. (Explore the United States Ser.). (ENG., Illus.). 32p. (J). (gr. 2-5). lib. bdg. 28.50 (978-1-61783-381-6(9), Big Buddy Bks.) ABDO Publishing Co.

VanVoorst, Jenny. What's Great about Tennessee? 2014. (Our Great States Ser.). (ENG., Illus.). 32p. (gr. 2-5). pap. 7.95 (978-1-4677-4542-0(1)) Lerner Publishing Group.

Winders, Richard Bruce. Davy Crockett: The Legend of the Wild Frontier. 2005. (Library of American Lives & Times). (Illus.). 112p. (YA). (gr. 4-8). lib. bdg. 34.60 (978-0-8239-5747-7(0)) Rosen Publishing Group, Inc., The.

TENNIS

Armentrout, David & Armentrout, Patricia. Annika Sorenstam.. 2004. (Discover the Life of a Sports Star Ser.). (Illus.). 24p. (gr. 1-4). lib. bdg. (978-1-59515-130-8(3)) Rourke Educational Media.

Bow, Patricia. Tennis Science. 2008. (Sports Science Ser.). (ENG., Illus.). 32p. (J). (gr. 4-6). pap. (978-0-7787-4556-3(2)); lib. bdg. (978-0-7787-4539-6(2)) Crabtree Publishing Co.

Bratton, Deboral B. & Bratton, Ashley D. Record-a-Sport Tennis Organizer. Bratton, Deboral B. & Bratton, Ashley D., eds. 2003. (Illus.). (gr. 1-18). 18.95 (978-1-931746-06-9(0)) Sport Your Stuff Corp.

Brown, Jonatha A. Tennis. 2004. (My Favorite Sport Ser.). (Illus.). 24p. (gr. 1-4). pap. 8.15 (978-0-8368-4349-1(5)); lib. bdg. 22.00 (978-0-8368-4342-2(8)) Stevens, Gareth Publishing LLLP. (Weekly Reader Leveled Readers).

Bussiere, Desireé. Tennis by the Numbers, 1 vol. 2013. (Sports by the Numbers Ser.). (ENG.). 24p. (J). (gr. k-3). lib. bdg. 24.21 (978-1-61783-847-7(0), SandCastle) ABDO Publishing Co.

Challen, Paul. Smash It Tennis. 2010. (ENG., Illus.). 32p. (J). pap. (978-0-7787-3177-1(4)); lib. bdg. (978-0-7787-3145-0(6)) Crabtree Publishing Co.

Consistent Tennis Wins. 2004. per. 14.95 (978-0-9727444-1-6(X)) Avery's, Tom Totally Tennis.

Crossingham, John & Kalman, Bobbie. Le Tennis. 2008. (FRE.). 32p. (J). pap. 9.95 (978-2-89579-184-3(8)) Bayard Canada Livres CAN. Dist: Crabtree Publishing Co.

Derr, Aaron. Tennis: An Introduction to Being a Good Sport. Angle, Scott, illus. 2017. (Start Smart (tm) — Sports Ser.). (ENG.). 32p. (J). (gr. k-3). lib. bdg. 26.65 (978-1-63440-133-3(6)); 39.99 **(978-1-63440-145-6(X))** Red Chair Pr.

Donohue, Moira Rose & Scott, Clarke C. Arthur R. Ashe, Jr. 2012. (Illus.). 32p. (J). (978-1-935884-58-3(1)); pap. (978-1-935884-64-4(6)) State Standards Publishing, LLC.

Douglas, Paul & Spieler, Marlena. Tennis: Breaks down the Subject into 101 Easy-to-Grasp Tips. 2004. (101 Essential Tips Ser.). (ENG., Illus.). 72p. pap. 5.00 (978-0-7566-0225-3(4), DK) Dorling Kindersley Publishing, Inc.

Drewett, Jim. How to Improve at Tennis. 2007. (How to Improve At- Ser.). (ENG., Illus.). 48p. (J). (gr. 3-7). pap. (978-0-7787-3593-9(1)); lib. bdg. (978-0-7787-3571-7(0)) Crabtree Publishing Co.

Ganeri, Anita. Super Active Tennis. (Illus.). 126p. pap. (978-0-340-76446-6(5)) Hodder & Stoughton.

Gifford, Clive. Tennis. 2016. (Great Sporting Events Ser.). (ENG., Illus.). 32p. (J). (gr. 4-6). pap. 11.99 (978-1-4451-4961-5(3), Franklin Watts) Hachette Children's Group GBR. Dist: Hachette Bk. Group.

—Tennis. 2009. (Tell Me about Sports Ser.). 32p. (gr. 3-5). 28.50 (978-0-7614-4463-3(7)) Marshall Cavendish Corp.

Gitlin, Martin. Billie Jean King: Tennis Star & Social Activist, 1 vol. 2011. (Legendary Athletes Ser.). (ENG., Illus.). 112p. (YA). (gr. 7-12). 34.22 (978-1-61714-757-9(5)) ABDO Publishing Co.

—Tennis, 1 vol. 2012. (ENG.). 64p. 32.79 (978-1-61783-147-8(6), SportsZone) ABDO Publishing Co.

—Wimbledon, 1 vol. 2013. (Sports' Great Championships Ser.). (ENG.). 64p. (J). (gr. 4-6). lib. bdg. 32.79 (978-1-61783-674-9(5), SportsZone) ABDO Publishing Co.

Goldsworthy, Steve. Tennis. 2013. (J). (978-1-62127-504-6(3)); pap. (978-1-62127-507-7(8)) Weigl Pubs., Inc.

Guillermo-Newton, Judith. Competitive Tennis for Girls. 2005. (SportsGirl Ser.). (Illus.). 64p. (YA). (gr. 5-9). lib. bdg. 31.95 (978-0-8239-3407-2(1)) Rosen Publishing Group, Inc., The.

Guillermo-Newton, Judy. Competitive Tennis for Girls. 2009. (SportsGirl Ser.). 64p. (gr. 5-8). 58.50 (978-1-60853-194-3(5), Rosen Reference) Rosen Publishing Group, Inc., The.

Hoena, Blake. Tennis. 2015. (J). lib. bdg. 25.65 (978-1-62031-183-7(6), Bullfrog Bks.) Jump! Inc.

Kubik, Jeff. Wimbledon. (J). 2013. 28.55 (978-1-62127-370-7(9)) 2013. pap. 13.95 (978-1-62127-375-2(X)) 2007. (Illus.). 32p. (gr. 4-7). lib. bdg. 26.00 (978-1-59036-697-4(2)) 2007. (Illus.). 32p. (gr. 4-7). per. 9.95 (978-1-59036-698-1(0)) Weigl Pubs., Inc.

Lagunilla, Cheryl, told to. The ABC's of Tennis. 2003. (Illus.). (J). lib. bdg. 24.95 (978-0-9726419-0-6(4)) GHL Publishing LLC.

Laughlin, Kara L. Tennis. 2016. (Beginning Sports Ser.). (ENG.). 24p. (J). (gr. k-3). 27.07 (978-1-5038-0782-2(7), 210610) Child's World, Inc., The.

Luke, Andrew. Tennis, Vol. 13. 2016. (Inside the World of Sports Ser.). (ENG.). 80p. (J). (gr. 7-12). 24.95 (978-1-4222-3466-2(5)) Mason Crest.

Mallick, Nita & Guillermo-Newton, Judith. Tennis: Girls Rocking It, 01 vols., 1. 2016. (Title IX Rocks! Ser.). (ENG., Illus.). 64p. (J). 32.95 (978-1-5081-7041-9(X), Rosen Young Adult) Rosen Publishing Group, Inc., The.

Marsico, Katie. Tennis. 2008. (21st Century Skills Library: Real World Math Ser.). (ENG., Illus.). 32p. (gr. 4-8). lib. bdg. 28.50 (978-1-60279-248-7(8), 200127) Cherry Lake Publishing.

McDougall, Chros. Arthur Ashe: Tennis Great & Civil Rights Leader, 1 vol. 2011. (Legendary Athletes Ser.). (ENG., Illus.). 112p. (YA). (gr. 7-12). 34.22 (978-1-61714-753-1(2)) ABDO Publishing Co.
Mooney, Carla. Tennis. 2013. (Science Behind Sports Ser.). (ENG., Illus.). 128p. (gr. 7-10). lib. bdg. 39.40 (978-1-4205-0928-1(4), Lucent Bks.) Cengage Gale.
Otten, Jack. Tenis. 2004. (Entrenamiento Deportivo (Sports Training) Ser.). (SPA & ENG., Illus.). 24p. (J). lib. bdg. 22.60 (978-0-8239-6848-0(0), Editorial Buenas Letras) Rosen Publishing Group, Inc., The.
—Tenis (Tennis) 2009. (Entrenamiento deportivo (Sports Training) Ser.). (SPA.). 24p. (gr. 1-2). 42.50 (978-1-61512-271-4(0), Editorial Buenas Letras) Rosen Publishing Group, Inc., The.
—Tennis. 2009. (Sports Training Ser.). 24p. (gr. 1-2). 42.50 (978-1-60853-189-9(9), PowerKids Pr.) Rosen Publishing Group, Inc., The.
Rausch, David. United States Tennis Association. 2014. (Major League Sports Ser.). (ENG.). 24p. (J). (gr. 3-7). 25.95 (978-1-62617-138-1(6), Epic Bks.) Bellwether Media.
Sanchez Vicario, Arantxa. Jovenes Tenistas. (SPA.). 46p. (YA). (gr. 2-18). 16.76 (978-84-272-4967-7(5)) Molino, Editorial ESP. Dist: Lectorum Pubns., Inc.
Stauffacher, Sue. Nothing but Trouble: The Story of Althea Gibson. Couch, Greg, illus. 2011. (ENG.). 40p. (J). (gr. -1-2). pap. 7.99 (978-0-375-86544-2(6), Dragonfly Bks.) Random Hse. Children's Bks.
Sterling Publishing Co., Inc. My First Tennis Book. 2016. (First Sports Ser.). (ENG., Illus.). 22p. (J). (— 1). bds. 6.95 (978-1-4549-1975-9(2)) Sterling Publishing Co., Inc.
Stewart, Mark. Rafael Nadal. 2009. (Today's Superstars Ser.). (ENG.). 48p. (J). (gr. 5-8). pap. 14.05 (978-1-4339-2158-2(8)); lib. bdg. 31.95 (978-1-4339-1965-7(6)) Stevens, Gareth Publishing LLLP.
Venus & Serena Williams. 2015. (Quotes from the Greatest Athletes Ser.). (ENG.). (J). lib. bdg. 12.95 (978-1-4896-3385-9(5), AV2 by Weigl) Weigl Pubs., Inc.
Wells, Don. For the Love of Tennis. 2005. (For the Love of Sports Ser.). (Illus.). 24p. (J). (gr. 4-6). lib. bdg. 24.45 (978-1-59036-298-3(5)) Weigl Pubs., Inc.
—Tennis. 2005. (For the Love of Sports Ser.). (Illus.). 24p. (J). (gr. 3-7). per. 8.95 (978-1-59036-302-7(7)) Weigl Pubs., Inc.
Wells, Donald. Tennis. 2010. (In the Zone Ser.). (Illus.). 32p. (J). (gr. 3-5). pap. 11.95 (978-1-60596-905-3(2)); lib. bdg. 25.70 (978-1-60596-904-6(4)) Weigl Pubs., Inc.
Wendorff, Anne. Tennis. 2009. (My First Sports Ser.). (ENG., Illus.). 24p. (J). (gr. 2-5). lib. bdg. 25.95 (978-1-60014-328-1(8), Blastoff! Readers) Bellwether Media.
Woods, Mark & Owen, Ruth. Ace! 2010. (Top Score Maths Ser.). (Illus.). 32p. pap. (978-0-237-54280-1(3)) Evans Brothers, Ltd.
—Ace! Tennis Facts & Stats. 2011. (Top Score Math Ser.). (Illus.). 32p. (J). (gr. 3-6). lib. bdg. 26.60 (978-1-4339-4986-9(5)) Stevens, Gareth Publishing LLLP.

TENNIS—BIOGRAPHY

Anniss, Matt. Venus & Serena Williams in the Community, 1 vol., 1. 2014. (Making a Difference: Athletes Who Are Changing the World Ser.). (ENG.). 48p. (J). (gr. 5-8). 25.85 (978-1-62275-170-9(1)) Rosen Publishing Group, Inc., The.
Bailey, Diane. Venus & Serena Williams: Tennis Champions. 2010. (Sports Families Ser.). 48p. (ENG.). (J). pap. 11.75 (978-1-4358-8520-2(1), Rosen Reference); (YA). (gr. 5-8). lib. bdg., E-Book 53.00 (978-1-4488-0124-4(9)); (Illus.). (YA). (gr. 4-7). lib. bdg. 29.25 (978-1-4358-3552-8(2)) Rosen Publishing Group, Inc., The.
Boehme, Gerry. Serena Williams: Setting New Standards. 2017. (J). **(978-1-5026-2762-9(0))** Cavendish Square Publishing.
Brown, Jonatha A. Venus & Serena Williams. 2005. (People to Know Ser.). (Illus.). 24p. (gr. 1-4). pap. 8.15 (978-0-8368-4477-1(7)); lib. bdg. 22.00 (978-0-8368-4470-2(X)) Stevens, Gareth Publishing LLLP. (Weekly Reader Leveled Readers).
Christopher, Matt. Serena Williams: Legends in Sports. 2017. (ENG., Illus.). 144p. (J). (gr. 3-7). pap. 6.99 **(978-0-316-47180-0(1))** Little, Brown Bks. for Young Readers.
Deans, Karen. Playing to Win: The Story of Althea Gibson. Brown, Elbrite, illus. 2007. (ENG.). 32p. (J). (gr. -1-3). 16.95 (978-0-8234-1926-5(6)) Holiday Hse., Inc.
Donaldson, Madeline. Venus & Serena Williams. (Amazing Athletes Ser.). 32p. 2005. (Illus.). (gr. 3-4). lib. bdg. 22.60 (978-0-8225-3316-0(2)) 2nd rev. ed. 2011. (J). pap. 45.32 (978-0-7613-7654-5(2)) 2nd rev. ed. 2011. (ENG., Illus.). (J). (gr. 2-5). pap. 7.95 (978-0-7613-7463-3(9)) Lerner Publishing Group.
—Venus & Serena Williams. rev. ed. 2007. (Amazing Athletes Ser.). (ENG., Illus.). 32p. (gr. 2-5). lib. bdg. 25.26 (978-0-8225-7595-5(7)) Lerner Publishing Group.
Dorrie, Roxanne. Venus & Serena Williams: The Smashing Sisters. 2003. (High Five Reading - Red Ser.). (ENG., Illus.). 48p. (gr. 3-4). per. 9.00 (978-0-7368-2827-7(3), High Five Reading (RBL)) Capstone Press of Coughlan Cos.
Feldman, Heather. Venus Williams, Tennis Champion/Campeona del Tenis. De Leon, Mauricio Velzaquez, tr. 2008. (Reading Power Ser.). (ENG., Illus.). 24p. (gr. 1-6). per. 8.85 (978-0-8239-6212-9(1)) Rosen Publishing Group, Inc., The.
Fishman, Jon M. Serena Williams. 2016. (Amazing Athletes Ser.). (ENG., Illus.). 32p. (J). (gr. 2-5). 26.65 (978-1-5124-1334-2(8)) Lerner Publishing Group.
Franzen, Lenore. Venus Williams. 2003. (Ovations Ser.). (Illus.). 32p. (J). (978-1-58341-249-7(2), Creative Education) Creative Co., The.
Gale Editor & Greenhaven Press Editors, eds. Roger Federer. 2011. (People in the News Ser.). (Illus.). 128p. (YA). (gr. 9-12). lib. bdg. 33.95 (978-1-4205-0611-2(0)) Cengage Gale.
Gifford, Clive. Andy Murray. 2017. (Inspirational Lives Ser.). (ENG., Illus.). 32p. (J). (gr. 4-6). pap. 11.99 (978-0-7502-9495-9(7), Wayland) Hachette Children's Group GBR. Dist: Hachette Bk. Group.
Gitlin, Marty. Best Tennis Players of All Time, 1 vol. 2014. (Sports' Best Ever Ser.). (ENG., Illus.). 64p. (J). (gr. 3-6). lib. bdg. 32.79 (978-1-62403-622-4(8), SportsZone) ABDO Publishing Co.
Glaser, Jason. Maria Sharapova. (Sports Idols Ser.). 24p. (gr. 2-3). 2009. 42.50 (978-1-60853-142-4(2), PowerKids Pr.) 2008. (Illus.). (J). lib. bdg. 22.60 (978-1-4042-4181-7(7)) Rosen Publishing Group, Inc., The.
—Roger Federer. 2011. (Today's Sports Greats Ser.). (Illus.). 32p. (gr. 4-6). (J). pap. 10.50 (978-1-4339-5872-4(4), Gareth Stevens Learning Library); (YA). lib. bdg. 26.60 (978-1-4339-5870-0(8)) Stevens, Gareth Publishing LLLP.
Hubbard, Crystal & Belford, Kevin. Game, Set, Match, Champion Arthur Ashe. (ENG., Illus.). 48p. (J). (gr. 2-5). 2016. pap. 11.95 **(978-1-62014-316-2(X))** 2010. 19.95 (978-1-60060-366-2(1)) Lee & Low Bks., Inc.
Kortemeier, Todd. Superstars of Pro Tennis. 2016. (Pro Sports Superstars Ser.). (ENG., Illus.). 24p. (J). (gr. 1-4). 20.95 (978-1-60753-941-4(1)) Amicus Publishing.
Mantell, Paul. Arthur Ashe: Young Tennis Champion. Henderson, Meryl, illus. 2006. (Childhood of Famous Americans Ser.). 213p. (J). 13.65 (978-0-7569-6387-3(7)) Perfection Learning Corp.
Marcovitz, Hal. Venus & Serena Williams. 2012. (Role Model Athletes Ser.). 64p. (J). (gr. 7). 22.95 (978-1-4222-2714-5(6)) Mason Crest.
Morgan, Terri. Venus & Serena Williams: Grand Slam Sisters. (Sports Achievers Biographies Ser.). (Illus.). 2005. 80p. (gr. 7-12). lib. bdg. 22.60 (978-0-8225-3684-0(6)) 2003. 64p. (J). (gr. 4-9). pap. 5.95 (978-0-8225-9866-4(3), Carolrhoda Bks.) Lerner Publishing Group.
Nagelhout, Ryan. Serena Williams. 2016. (Sports MVPs Ser.). (Illus.). 24p. (J). (gr. 2-1). 22.60 (978-1-4824-4642-5(1)) Stevens, Gareth Publishing LLLP.
Peters, Gregory N. Serena & Venus Williams Tennis Stars, 1 vol. 2014. (Sports & Recreation Ser.). (ENG.). 48p. (gr. 4-12). 31.99 (978-1-4765-8075-3(8)) Capstone Press of Coughlan Cos.
Pina, Andrew & Uschan, Michael. Serena Williams: Tennis Ace. 2017. (People in the News Ser.). 104p. (YA). (gr. 7-7). lib. bdg. 39.40 **(978-1-5345-6027-7(0)**, Lucent Pr.) Greenhaven Publishing LLC.
Porter, Esther. Serena Williams. 2016. (Women in Sports Ser.). (ENG., Illus.). 24p. (gr. k-1). pap. 6.95 (978-1-4914-8569-9(8), Pebble Plus) Capstone Press of Coughlan Cos.
Rajczak Nelson, Kristen. Serena Williams: Tennis Star. 2016. (Junior Biographies Ser.). (Illus.). 24p. (J). pap. 9.35 (978-0-7660-8181-9(8)) Enslow Pubs., Inc.
Raum, Elizabeth. Pro Sports Biographies: Serena Williams. 2017. (Pro Sports Biographies Ser.). (ENG.). 24p. (J). (gr. 1-3). pap. 8.99 **(978-1-68152-170-1(9))** Amicus.
Sapet, Kerrily. Maria Sharapova. 2007. (Role Model Athletes Ser.). (Illus.). 64p. (YA). pap. 9.95 (978-1-4222-0777-2(3)) Mason Crest.
Savage, Jeff. Annika Sorenstam. 2005. (Amazing Athletes Ser.). (Illus.). 32p. (J). (gr. 2-5). lib. bdg. 23.93 (978-0-8225-2428-1(7)); pap. 7.95 (978-0-8225-3107-4(0)) Lerner Publishing Group.
—Maria Sharapova. (Amazing Athletes Ser.). 2008. (Illus.). 32p. (J). (gr. -1). per. 6.95 (978-0-8225-8977-8(X), First Avenue Editions) 2008. pap. 40.95 (978-0-8225-9489-5(7)) 2008. (ENG., Illus.). 32p. (gr. 2-5). lib. bdg. 25.26 (978-0-8225-8836-8(6)) 2014. (ENG., Illus.). 32p. (gr. 2-5). pap. 7.95 (978-1-4677-2643-6(5)) Lerner Publishing Group.
—Roger Federer. 2009. pap. 40.95 (978-0-7613-4778-1(X)); (ENG.). 32p. (gr. 2-5). 25.26 (978-0-8225-9995-1(3)); (ENG.). 32p. (gr. 2-5). pap. 7.95 (978-1-58013-793-5(8), First Avenue Editions) Lerner Publishing Group.
Shepherd, Jodie. Serena Williams: A Champion on & off the Court. 2016. (Rookie Biographies(tm) Ser.). (ENG., Illus.). 32p. (J). lib. bdg. 25.00 (978-0-531-21684-2(5), Children's Pr.) Scholastic Library Publishing.
Shoup, Kate. Billie Jean King: The Battle of the Sexes & Title IX. 2016. (Game-Changing Athletes Ser.). (ENG.). 112p. (YA). (gr. 9-9). 42.79 (978-1-5026-1053-9(1)) Cavendish Square Publishing.
Shoup, Kate & Cunningham, Meghan Engsberg. Serena Williams: International Tennis Superstar. 2016. (Leading Women Ser.). 112p. (J). (gr. 7-7). 39.93 (978-1-5026-2014-9(6)) Cavendish Square Publishing.
Stanmyre, Jackie. Althea Gibson & Arthur Ashe. 2016. (Game-Changing Athletes Ser.). (ENG., Illus.). 112p. (J). (gr. 9-9). 42.79 (978-1-5026-1037-9(X)) Cavendish Square Publishing.
Stewart, Mark. Maria Sharapova. 2009. (Today's Superstars Ser.). 48p. (J). (gr. 5-8). pap. 14.05 (978-1-4339-2160-5(X)); lib. bdg. 31.95 (978-1-4339-1967-1(2)) Stevens, Gareth Publishing LLLP.
Swanson, June. Venus & Serena Williams. Burke, Susan S., illus. 2003. (You Must Be Joking! Riddle Bks.). 32p. (J). (gr. 2-5). pap. 5.95 (978-0-8225-9842-8(6)) Lerner Publishing Group.
Todd, Anne M. Venus & Serena Williams. 2009. (Women of Achievement Ser.). (Illus.). 144p. (gr. 6-12). 35.00 (978-1-60413-461-2(5), Chelsea Hse.) Facts On File, Inc.
Wilson, Mike. The Williams Sisters: Venus & Serena. 2005. (ENG., Illus.). 32p. pap. 8.50 (978-0-340-84876-0(6)) Cambridge Univ. Pr.
Wright, David K. The Life of Arthur Ashe: Smashing the Color Barrier in Tennis. 2015. (Legendary African Americans Ser.). 96p. (J). (gr. 6-12). 27.94 (978-0-7660-6260-3(0)); pap. 10.95 (978-0-7660-6261-0(9)) Enslow Pubs., Inc.

TENNIS—FICTION

Adler, David A. The Tennis Trophy Mystery. Natti, Susanna, illus. 2005. (Cam Jansen Ser.: 23). (ENG.). 64p. (J). (gr. 2-5). 4.99 (978-0-14-240290-0(7), Puffin Books) Penguin Young Readers Group.
Arena, Felice & Kettle, Phil. Tennis Ace. Boyer, Susy, illus. 2004. (J). pap. (978-1-59336-360-4(5)) Mondo Publishing.
Bates, Sonya. Topspin, 1 vol. 2013. (Orca Sports Ser.). (ENG.). 160p. (YA). (gr. 6-10). pap. 9.95 (978-1-4598-0385-5(X)) Orca Bk. Pubs. USA.
Bates, Sonya Spreen. Topspin. 2013. 147p. (J). (978-1-4598-0647-4(6)) Orca Bk. Pubs.
Berman, Ron. The Kid from Courage. 2005. (Dream Ser.). (Illus.). 150p. (gr. 3-8). pap. 9.95 (978-0-9708992-2-4(X)) Scobre Pr. Corp.
Crouch, Cheryl Lynne. Tennis Shoes Trouble. 2006. 48p. 6.50 (978-0-8341-2227-7(8)) Beacon Hill Pr. of Kansas City.
Digby, Anne. The Tennis Term at Trebizon. 2016. (Trebizon Ser.). (ENG., Illus.). 192p. (J). (gr. 3-6). pap. 10.99 **(978-1-4052-8068-6(9))** Egmont Bks., Ltd. GBR. Dist: Independent Pubs. Group.
Dzidrums, Christine. Princess Dessabelle: Tennis Star. Muths, Tohn Fayette, illus. 2013. 50p. pap. 10.99 (978-1-938438-34-9(5)) Creative Media Publishing.
Egart, Patricia. Alley Learns Something New. 2012. (ENG., Illus.). 32p. pap. 8.95 (978-0-9831839-3-8(7)) Amber Skye Publishing LLC.
Feinstein, John. Vanishing Act: Mystery at the U. S. Open. 2008. (Sports Beat Ser.). (ENG.). 304p. (J). (gr. 3-7). 7.99 (978-0-440-42125-2(X), Yearling) Random Hse. Children's Bks.
Flint, Shamini. Diary of a Tennis Prodigy. Heinrich, Sally, illus. 2016. (Diary of A... Ser.). (ENG.). 112p. (J). (gr. 2-6). 8.99 (978-1-76029-088-7(2)) Allen & Unwin AUS. Dist: Independent Pubs. Group.
Harrison, Lisi, creator. Dylan. 2008. (Clique Ser.). (ENG.). 144p. (YA). (gr. 10-17). pap. 6.99 (978-0-316-03565-1(3), Poppy) Little, Brown Bks. for Young Readers.
Hellman, Charles. Adventures in SportsLand - the Tennis Bully (with accompanying CD) Tintilli, Robert, illus. 2008. (Adventures in SportsLand: the Bully Ser.). 32p. (J). (gr. -1-3). 19.95 (978-0-935938-32-6(X)) Stogo, Malcolm Assocs.
Hellman, Charles S. & Tintilli, Robert A. The Tennis Bully. 2013. 34p. pap. 9.25 (978-0-935938-24-1(9)) LuckySports.
Horowitz, Anthony. Skeleton Key. Kanako & Yuzuru, illus. 2009. (Alex Rider Ser.: Bk. 3). (ENG.). 176p. (J). (gr. 5-18). pap. 14.99 (978-0-399-25418-5(8), Philomel Bks.) Penguin Young Readers Group.
—Skeleton Key. (Alex Rider Ser.: Bk. 3). (ENG.). (J). (gr. 5-18). 2006. 368p. 8.99 (978-0-14-240614-4(7), Puffin Books) 2003. 240p. 17.99 (978-0-399-23777-5(1), Philomel Bks.) Penguin Young Readers Group.
Hutton, Sam. Final Shot. 2010. (Special Agents Ser.: 2). (ENG.). 224p. (J). (gr. 5-7). pap. 9.99 (978-0-00-714844-8(5)) HarperCollins Pubs. Ltd. GBR. Dist: HarperCollins Pubs.
Jaimet, Kate. Break Point, 1 vol. 2013. (Orca Sports Ser.). (ENG.). 176p. (YA). (gr. 6-10). pap. 9.95 (978-1-4598-0352-7(3)) Orca Bk. Pubs. USA.
Jenkins, Jerry B. & Fabry, Chris. Double Fault. 2005. (Red Rock Mysteries Ser.: 7). (ENG.). 272p. (YA). pap. 6.99 (978-1-4143-0146-4(4), Tyndale Kids) Tyndale Hse. Pubs.
Maddox, Jake. Tennis Trouble. Mourning, Tuesday, illus. 2008. (Jake Maddox Girl Sports Stories Ser.). (ENG.). 72p. (gr. 2-3). 25.32 (978-1-4342-0781-4(1)) Stone Arch Bks.
McG, Shane. Tennis, Anyone? McG, Shane, illus. 2007. (ENG., Illus.). 40p. (J). (gr. k-3). 16.95 (978-0-8225-6901-5(9), Carolrhoda Bks.) Lerner Publishing Group.
McKnight, Marty. Jim Nasium Is a Tennis Mismatch. Jones, Chris, illus. 2016. (Jim Nasium Ser.). (ENG.). 88p. (gr. 2-3). lib. bdg. 25.32 (978-1-4965-3026-4(8)) Stone Arch Bks.
Meadows, Daisy. Alice the Tennis Fairy. 2010. (Sports Fairies Ser.: 6). (ENG.). 80p. (J). (gr. 2-5). 4.99 (978-0-545-20257-2(4), Scholastic Paperbacks) Scholastic, Inc.
Priebe, Val. I Don't Want to Live on the Tennis Court, 1 vol. Santillan, Jorge H., illus. 2012. (Sports Illustrated Kids Victory School Superstars Ser.). (ENG.). 56p. (gr. 1-3). pap. 5.95 (978-1-4342-3868-9(7)); lib. bdg. 26.65 (978-1-4342-3761-3(3)) Stone Arch Bks.
Rizzuto, Katherine. Poodles Don't Play Tennis. Murphy, Liz, illus. 2013. (ENG.). 32p. (J). 19.99 (978-1-938501-06-7(3)) Turn the Page Publishing.
Seles, Monica. Love Match. 2014. (Academy Ser.). (ENG.). 224p. (YA). (gr. 7). pap. 9.99 (978-1-59990-902-8(2), 9781599909028, Bloomsbury USA Childrens) Bloomsbury Publishing USA.
Seles, Monica & LaRosa, James. Game On. 2013. (Academy Ser.). (ENG.). 256p. (YA). (gr. 7). 17.99 (978-1-59990-976-9(6), 9781599909769); pap. 9.99 (978-1-59990-901-1(4), 9781599909011) Bloomsbury Publishing USA. (Bloomsbury USA Childrens).
Shull, Megan. Amazing Grace. 2006. (ENG.). 256p. (gr. 6-9). pap. 6.99 (978-0-7868-5691-6(2)) Hyperion Pr.

TENPINS

see Bowling

TENTS

Smith, Sian. Homes That Move, 1 vol. 2013. (Where We Live Ser.). (ENG.). 24p. (gr. -1-1). pap. 6.95 (978-1-4329-8072-6(6), Acorn) Heinemann-Raintree.
Zayauskas, Victoria. The Tent. 2011. 20p. pap. 10.50 (978-1-4634-2480-0(9)) AuthorHouse.

TERESA, MOTHER, 1910-1997

Fitzpatrick, Anne. Mother Teresa. 2005. (Genius Ser.). (Illus.). 48p. (J). (gr. 5-9). lib. bdg. 21.95 (978-1-58341-330-2(8), Creative Education) Creative Co., The.
Ganeri, Anita. Mother Teresa's Alms Bowl. Radford, Karen & Noyes, Leighton, illus. 2008. (Stories of Great People Ser.). (ENG.). 40p. (J). (gr. 3-8). pap. (978-0-7787-3712-4(8)) Crabtree Publishing Co.
Ganeri, Anita & Bailey, Gerry. Mother Teresa's Alms Bowl. 2008. (Stories of Great People Ser.). (ENG., Illus.). 40p. (J). (gr. 3-8). lib. bdg. (978-0-7787-3690-5(3)) Crabtree Publishing Co.
Gigliotti, Jim & dePaola, Tomie. Who Was Mother Teresa? Harrison, Nancy, illus. 2015. (Who Was? Ser.). (ENG.). 112p. (J). (gr. 3-7). 5.99 (978-0-448-48299-6(1), Grosset & Dunlap) Penguin Young Readers Group.
Glavich, Mary Kathleen. Blessed Teresa of Calcutta: Missionary of Charity. Kiwak, Barbara, tr. Kiwak, Barbara, illus. 2003. (Encounter the Saints Ser.: Vol. 17). 136p. (J). pap. 7.95 (978-0-8198-1160-8(2), 332-024) Pauline Bks. & Media.
Gold, Maya & Dorling Kindersley Publishing Staff. Mother Teresa. 2008. (DK Biography Ser.). (ENG., Illus.). 128p. (J). (gr. 5-12). pap. 6.99 (978-0-7566-3860-1(1), DK Children) Dorling Kindersley Publishing, Inc.
Haldy, Emma E. Mother Teresa. Bane, Jeff, illus. 2017. (My Early Library: My Itty-Bitty Bio Ser.). (ENG.). 24p. (J). (gr. k-1). lib. bdg. 28.50 (978-1-63472-154-7(3), 209188) Cherry Lake Publishing.
Harrison, Paul. Mother Teresa. 2017. (ENG., Illus.). 32p. (J). (gr. 4-6). pap. 6.99 (978-0-7502-9877-3(4), Wayland) Hachette Children's Group GBR. Dist: Hachette Bk. Group.
Helfand, Lewis. Mother Teresa: Saint of the Slums. Banerjee, Sankha & Nagar, Sachin, illus. 2013. (Campfire Graphic Novels Ser.). (ENG.). 88p. (YA). (gr. 5). pap. 11.99 (978-93-80028-70-5(9), Campfire) Steerforth Pr.
Jones, Brenn. Learning about Love from the Life of Mother Teresa. 2009. (Character Building Book Ser.). 24p. (gr. 2-3). 42.50 (978-1-61511-001-8(1), PowerKids Pr.) Rosen Publishing Group, Inc., The.
Kudlinski, Kathleen. Mother Teresa: Friend to the Poor. 2006. 171p. (J). lib. bdg. 18.46 (978-1-4242-1731-1(8)) Fitzgerald Bks.
Miller, Jennifer A. Mother Teresa. 2009. (History Maker Biographies Ser.). (Illus.). 48p. (J). (gr. 3-6). 26.60 (978-1-58013-702-7(4), Lerner Pubns.) Lerner Publishing Group.
Nelson, Robin. Mother Teresa: A Life of Caring. (Pull Ahead Books-Biographies Ser.). (Illus.). 32p. 2007. (ENG.). (gr. k-3). pap. 7.95 (978-0-8225-6433-1(5)) 2006. (J). (gr. 3-7). lib. bdg. 22.60 (978-0-8225-6384-6(3), Lerner Pubns.) Lerner Publishing Group.
Rustad, Martha E. H. & Weiss, Ellen. Mother Teresa: A Life of Kindness. 2007. (People of Character Ser.). (ENG., Illus.). 24p. (J). (gr. 2-5). lib. bdg. 25.95 (978-1-60014-092-1(0)) Bellwether Media.
Slavicek, Louise Chipley. Mother Teresa: Caring for the World's Poor. 2007. (Modern Peacemakers Ser.). (Illus.). 113p. (YA). (gr. 9-12). lib. bdg. 30.00 (978-0-7910-9433-4(2)) Facts On File, Inc.
Sullivan, Anne Marie. Mother Teresa: Religious Humanitarian. 2013. (People of Importance Ser.: 21). (Illus.). 32p. (J). (gr. 4-18). 19.95 (978-1-4222-2853-1(3)) Mason Crest.
—Mother Theresa: Religious Humanitarian. 2004. (Great Names Ser.). (Illus.). 32p. (J). (gr. 3-18). lib. bdg. 19.95 (978-1-59084-142-6(5)) Mason Crest.
Trussell-Cullen, Alan. Mother Teresa. 2009. pap. 13.25 (978-1-60559-066-0(5)) Hameray Publishing Group, Inc.
Valentine, Emily. Mother Teresa: With a Discussion of Compassion. 2004. (Values in Action Ser.). (J). (978-1-59203-070-5(X)) Learning Challenge, Inc.

TERESA, OF AVILA, SAINT, 1515-1582

Wallace, Susan Helen. Saint Teresa of Avila: Joyful in the Lord. Kiwak, Barbara, illus. 2008. (Encounter the Saints Ser.: No. 24). 106p. (J). (gr. 4-7). pap. 7.95 (978-0-8198-7116-9(8)) Pauline Bks. & Media.

TERMITES

Bodden, Valerie. Creepy Creatures: Termites. 2013. (Creepy Creatures Ser.). (ENG., Illus.). 24p. (J). (gr. 1-3). pap. 7.99 (978-0-89812-798-0(X), Creative Paperbacks) Creative Co., The.
—Termites. 2013. (Illus.). 24p. (J). 25.65 (978-1-60818-235-0(5), Creative Education) Creative Co., The.
Chung, Liz. Termites. 2016. (Dig Deep! Bugs That Live Underground Ser.). 24p. (J). (gr. 3-3). pap. 8.25 (978-1-4994-2062-3(5), PowerKids Pr.) Rosen Publishing Group, Inc., The.
George, Lynn. Termites: Mound Builders. 2010. (Animal Architects Ser.). (ENG.). 24p. (J). pap. 8.25 (978-1-4488-1353-7(0)); lib. bdg. 22.60 (978-1-4488-0696-6(8)) Rosen Publishing Group, Inc., The. (PowerKids Pr.).
Gray, Susan H. & Somervill, Barbara A. Termite. 2009. (21st Century Skills Library: Animal Invaders Ser.). (ENG.). 32p. (gr. 4-8). lib. bdg. 28.50 (978-1-60279-330-9(1), 200226) Cherry Lake Publishing.
Harasymiw, Mark J. Termites. 2014. (Animals of Mass Destruction Ser.). 32p. (J). (gr. 2-5). pap. 63.00 (978-1-4824-1041-9(9)); pap. 10.50 (978-1-4824-1042-6(7)) Stevens, Gareth Publishing LLLP.
Markle, Sandra. Termites. 2008. pap. 52.95 (978-1-58013-287-9(1)) Lerner Publishing Group.
—Termites: Hardworking Insect Families. 2008. (Insect World Ser.). (ENG., Illus.). 48p. (gr. 4-8). lib. bdg. 27.93 (978-0-8225-7301-2(6), Lerner Pubns.) Lerner Publishing Group.
Murray, Julie. Termites, 1 vol. 2010. (Big Buddy Bks.). (ENG.). 32p. (J). (gr. 2-5). 28.50 (978-1-61613-488-4(7)) ABDO Publishing Co.
Petrie, Kristin. Termites, 1 vol. 2009. (Bugs! Ser.). (ENG.). 32p. (gr. 3-6). 27.07 (978-1-60453-071-1(5), Checkerboard Library) ABDO Publishing Co.
Porter, Esther. Termites, 1 vol. 2013. (Creepy Crawlers Ser.). (ENG., Illus.). 24p. (gr. k-1). lib. bdg. 26.65 (978-1-4765-2065-0(8), Pebble Plus) Capstone Press of Coughlan Cos.
Rodger, Marguerite. Termites & Other Home Wreckers. 2010. (Creepy Crawlies Ser.). (ENG.). 32p. (J). (gr. 3-6). (978-0-7787-2503-9(0)); pap. (978-0-7787-2510-7(3)) Crabtree Publishing Co.
Schuetz, Kari. Termites. 2015. (Creepy Crawlies Ser.). (ENG., Illus.). 24p. (J). (gr. k-3). lib. bdg. 25.95 (978-1-62617-228-9(5), Blastoff! Readers) Bellwether Media.
Schuh, Mari. Termites. 2014. (Illus.). 24p. (J). lib. bdg. 25.65 (978-1-62031-087-8(2), Bullfrog Bks.) Jump! Inc.
Squire, Ann O. Termites. 2003. (True Bks.). (ENG., Illus.). 48p. (J). 25.00 (978-0-516-22660-6(6), Children's Pr.) Scholastic Library Publishing.
Yomtov, Nel. From Termite Den to Office Building. 2014. (21st Century Skills Innovation Library: Innovations from Nature Ser.). (ENG., Illus.). 32p. (J). (gr. 4-8). 28.50 (978-1-62431-755-2(3), 203288) Cherry Lake Publishing.

TERMITES—FICTION

Caple, Kathy. Termite Tales. Caple, Kathy, illus. 2009. (Brand New Readers Ser.). (ENG., Illus.). 48p. (J). (gr. -1-3). pap. 5.99 (978-0-7636-3901-3(X)) Candlewick Pr.
Laden, Nina. Roberto: the Insect Architect. 2016. (ENG., Illus.). 40p. (J). (gr. k-3). 7.99 (978-1-4521-5646-0(8)) Chronicle Bks. LLC.
Provenzale, Joseph C. The Teeny, Tiny Termite. 2012. 32p. pap. 21.99 (978-1-4691-9075-4(3)) Xlibris Corp.
Rouss, Sylvia. The Littlest Pair. Hannon, Holly, illus. 2005. 32p. (J). pap. 9.95 (978-1-930143-18-0(4), Devora Publishing) Simcha Media Group.

T U V

Weston Woods Staff, creator. Roberto the Insect Architect. 2005. (J). 29.95 (978-0-439-80455-4(8)) Weston Woods Studios, Inc.

TERRARIUMS

see also Gardens, Miniature

Bearce, Stephanie. A Kid's Guide to Making a Terrarium. 2009. (Gardening for Kids Ser.). (Illus.). 48p. (J). (gr. 3-6). lib. bdg. 29.95 (978-1-58415-813-4(1)) Mitchell Lane Pubs., Inc.

Janning, Scarlett. Therese's Terrarium. 2013. (Rosen Readers Ser.). (ENG.). 24p. (J). (gr. 3-4). pap. 49.50 (978-1-4777-2537-5(7)); pap. 8.25 (978-1-4777-2536-8(9)) Rosen Publishing Group, Inc., The. (Rosen Classroom).

Lunis, Natalie. Making a Terrarium. 2011. (Early Connections Ser.). (J). (978-1-61672-612-6(1)) Benchmark Education Co.

TERRESTRIAL PHYSICS

see Geophysics

TERROR, REIGN OF

see France—History—Revolution, 1789-1799

TERRORISM

see also Bombings; Sabotage

Amer, Joseph. The War on Terror. 2005. (Behind the News Ser.). (Illus.). 112p. (J). (gr. 5-18). lib. bdg. 24.95 (978-1-881508-68-7(4)) Oliver Pr., Inc.

Anderson, Dale. The Terrorist Attacks of September, 11, 2001. 2003. (Landmark Events in American History Ser.). (Illus.). 48p. (gr. 5-12). pap. 14.05 (978-0-8368-5408-4(X), Gareth Stevens Secondary Library) Stevens, Gareth Publishing LLLP.

Anderson, Wayne. The ETA: Spain's Basque Terrorists. (Inside the World's Most Infamous Terrorist Organizations Ser.). 64p. 2009. (gr. 5-5). 58.50 (978-1-61513-578-3(2)) 2005. (Illus.). (YA). (gr. 7-12). lib. bdg. 31.95 (978-0-8239-3818-6(2)) Rosen Publishing Group, Inc., The.

Andryszewski, Tricia. Terrorism in America. 2003. (Headliners Ser.). (Illus.). 64p. (J). (gr. 5-8). lib. bdg. 25.90 (978-0-7613-2803-2(3), Millbrook Pr.) Lerner Publishing Group.

Anniss, Matt. Terrorism. 2013. (Illus.). 48p. (J). (gr. 4-8). pap. 14.05 (978-1-4339-9497-5(6)); pap. 84.30 (978-1-4339-9498-2(4)); (ENG., lib. bdg. 31.95 (978-1-4339-9496-8(8)) Stevens, Gareth Publishing LLLP.

Baer, Suzie. Peru's MRTA: Tupac Amaru Revolutionary Movement. 2005. (Inside the World's Most Infamous Terrorist Organizations Ser.). (Illus.). 64p. (YA). (gr. 7-12). lib. bdg. 31.95 (978-0-8239-3824-7(7)) Rosen Publishing Group, Inc., The.

Baldino, Greg. Investigating the Boston Marathon Bombings. 2017. (Terrorism in the 21st Century: Causes & Effects Ser.). 64p. (gr. 12-11). 34.45 **(978-1-5081-7457-8(1)**, Rosen Young Adult) Rosen Publishing Group, Inc., The.

Benoit, Peter. September 11, 2001: The 10th Anniversary. 2011. (Cornerstones of Freedom, Third Ser.). (Illus.). 64p. (J). (gr. 4-6). lib. bdg. 30.00 (978-0-531-25040-2(7), Children's Pr.) Scholastic Library Publishing.

—September 11 Then & Now. 2011. (True Bk Ser.). (ENG., Illus.). 48p. (J). pap. 6.95 (978-0-531-26629-8(X)); (gr. 3-5). lib. bdg. 29.00 (978-0-531-25424-0(0)) Scholastic Library Publishing. (Children's Pr.).

—September 11 We Will Never Forget No. 11. 2011. (Cornerstones of Freedom, Third Ser.). (ENG., Illus.). 64p. (J). pap. 8.95 (978-0-531-26565-9(X), Children's Pr.) Scholastic Library Publishing.

Berlatsky, Noah. The War on Terror. 2012. (Global Viewpoints Ser.). (ENG., Illus.). 224p. (gr. 10-12). pap. 31.70 (978-0-7377-6447-5(3), Greenhaven Pr., Inc.) Cengage Gale.

Berlatsky, Noah, ed. The War on Terror. 2012. (Global Viewpoints Ser.). (ENG., Illus.). 224p. (J). (gr. 10-12). lib. bdg. 40.45 (978-0-7377-6271-6(3), Greenhaven Pr., Inc.) Cengage Gale.

Beyer, Mark. Homeland Security & Weapons of Mass Destruction: How Prepared Are We? (Library of Weapons of Mass Destruction Ser.). 64p. 2009. (gr. 5-5). 58.50 (978-1-60853-952-9(0)) 2004. (Illus.). (J). lib. bdg. 31.95 (978-1-4042-0289-4(7)) Rosen Publishing Group, Inc., The.

Blohm, Craig E. Catastrophic Events of The 2000s. 2013. (YA). lib. bdg. (978-1-60152-522-2(2)) ReferencePoint Pr., Inc.

Bodden, Valerie. The 9/11 Terror Attacks: Days of Change. 2015. (Illus.). 80p. (J). (978-1-60818-529-0(X), Creative Education) Creative Co., The.

Brewer, Paul. The Lima Embassy Siege & Latin American Terrorism. 2006. (Terrorism in Today's World Ser.). (Illus.). 48p. (gr. 5-12). pap. 14.05 (978-0-8368-6564-6(2)); lib. bdg. 31.00 (978-0-8368-6557-8(X)) Stevens, Gareth Publishing LLLP. (Gareth Stevens Secondary Library).

Brown, Don. America Is under Attack: September 11, 2001: the Day the Towers Fell. 2014. (Actual Times Ser.: 4). (ENG., Illus.). 64p. (J). (gr. 1-5). pap. 9.99 (978-1-250-04415-0(4), 9781250044150) Square Fish.

—America Is under Attack Vol. 4: The Day the Towers Fell - September 11, 2001. 2011. (Actual Times Ser.: 4). (ENG., Illus.). 64p. (J). (gr. 1-5). 16.99 (978-1-59643-694-7(8), 9781596436947) Roaring Brook Pr.

Brownell, Richard. The Oklahoma City Bombing. 2007. (Crime Scene Investigations Ser.). (ENG., Illus.). 104p. (YA). (gr. 7-12). lib. bdg. 35.45 (978-1-59018-843-9(8)) Cengage Gale.

Broyles, Janell. Chemical & Biological Weapons in a Post-9/11 World. (Library of Weapons of Mass Destruction Ser.). 64p. 2009. (gr. 5-5). 58.50 (978-1-60853-951-2(2)) 2004. (Illus.). (J). lib. bdg. 31.95 (978-1-4042-0288-7(9)) Rosen Publishing Group, Inc., The.

Buell, Tonya. The Crash of United Flight 93 on September 11, 2001. 2005. (Terrorist Attacks Ser.). (Illus.). 64p. (YA). (gr. 7-12). lib. bdg. 31.95 (978-0-8239-3857-5(3)) Rosen Publishing Group, Inc., The.

—The Crash of United Flight 93 on September 11 2001. 2009. (Terrorist Attacks Ser.). 64p. (gr. 5-5). 58.50 (978-1-60853-316-9(6)) Rosen Publishing Group, Inc., The.

Burnett, Betty. The Attack on the U. S. S. Cole in Yemen on October 12, 2000. 2005. (Terrorist Attacks Ser.). (Illus.). 64p. (YA). (gr. 7-12). lib. bdg. 31.95 (978-0-8239-3860-5(3)) Rosen Publishing Group, Inc., The.

—The Attack on the USS Cole in Yemen on October 12 2000. 2009. (Terrorist Attacks Ser.). 64p. (gr. 5-5). 58.50 (978-1-60853-311-4(5)) Rosen Publishing Group, Inc., The.

Bursztyn, Alberto M., ed. Childhood Psychological Disorders: Current Controversies, 1 vol. 2011. (Making Sense of Psychology Ser.). 206p. (C). 49.00 (978-0-313-33696-6(2), GR3696, Greenwood) ABC-CLIO, LLC.

Byers, Ann. Lebanon's Hezbollah. 2009. (Inside the World's Most Infamous Terrorist Organizations Ser.). 64p. (gr. 5-5). 58.50 (978-1-61513-576-9(6)) Rosen Publishing Group, Inc., The.

Campbell, Geoffrey A. A Vulnerable America: An Overview of National Security. 2007. (Lucent Library of Homeland Security). (ENG., Illus.). 112p. (J). 30.85 (978-1-59018-383-0(5), Lucent Bks.) Cengage Gale.

Challen, Paul C. Surviving 9/11. 2015. (Surviving Disaster Ser.). (ENG., Illus.). 48p. (J). (gr. 5-6). 30.25 (978-1-4994-3657-0(2), Rosen Central) Rosen Publishing Group, Inc., The.

Ching, Jacqueline. Cyberterrorism. 2010. (Doomsday Scenarios: Separating Fact from Fiction Ser.). 64p. (YA). (gr. 5-8). E-Book 58.50 (978-1-4488-1205-9(4)) Rosen Publishing Group, Inc., The.

Corrigan, Jim. Causes of the War on Terrorism. 2009. (J). lib. bdg. (978-1-59556-035-3(1)) OTTN Publishing.

Crawford, Steve. War on Terror. 2010. (FAYFT: Modern Military History Ser.). 64p. (gr. 4-10). 39.95 (978-1-933834-53-5(6)) Brown Bear Bks.

Croce, Nicholas, ed. Anarchism, Revolution, & Terrorism. 2014. (Political & Economic Systems Ser.). 312p. (J). (gr. 9-12). 45.00 (978-1-62275-353-6(4)) Rosen Publishing Group, Inc., The.

Decker, Janet M., et al. Anthrax. 2nd rev. ed. 2008. (Deadly Diseases & Epidemics Ser.). (Illus.). 144p. (C). (gr. 9-18). 34.95 (978-1-60413-233-5(7), Chelsea Hse.) Facts On File, Inc.

Derkins, Susie. The Irish Republican Army. (Inside the World's Most Infamous Terrorist Organizations Ser.). 64p. 2009. (gr. 5-5). 58.50 (978-1-61513-579-0(0)) 2005. (Illus.). (YA). (gr. 7-12). lib. bdg. 31.95 (978-0-8239-3822-3(0)) Rosen Publishing Group, Inc., The.

Doak, Robin S. Homeland Security. 2011. (Cornerstones of Freedom, Third Ser.). (Illus.). 64p. (J). (ENG.). pap. 8.95 (978-0-531-26561-1(7)); lib. bdg. 30.00 (978-0-531-25036-5(9)) Scholastic Library Publishing. (Children's Pr.).

Docalavich, Heather. Antiterrorism Policy & Fighting Fear, Vol. 10. Russett, Bruce, ed. 2015. (United Nations: Leadership & Challenges in a Global World Ser.). (Illus.). 88p. (J). (gr. 7). lib. bdg. 24.95 (978-1-4222-3428-0(2)) Mason Crest.

Doeden, Matt. Impact: The Story of the September 11 Terrorist Attacks. 2015. (Tangled History Ser.). (ENG.). 112p. (gr. 3-4). lib. bdg. 31.99 (978-1-4914-7079-4(8)) Capstone Press of Coughlan Cos.

Donovan, Sandy. Protecting America: A Look at the People Who Keep Our Country Safe. 2003. (How Government Works). (ENG., Illus.). 56p. (gr. 4-8). lib. bdg. 25.26 (978-0-8225-1345-2(5)) Lerner Publishing Group.

Downing, David. The Debate about Terrorist Tactics. 2007. (Ethical Debates Ser.). (Illus.). 48p. (YA). (gr. 5-9). lib. bdg. 29.25 (978-1-4042-3757-5(7)) Rosen Publishing Group, Inc., The.

Emergency Response to Terrorism. 2nd ed. 2003. cd-rom 89.95 (978-0-9746186-0-9(8)) RESPONDER911, Inc.

Espejo, Roman. Bioterrorism. 2012. (Opposing Viewpoints Ser.). (ENG., Illus.). 224p. (gr. 10-12). lib. bdg. 48.80 (978-0-7377-6474-1(0), Greenhaven Pr., Inc.) Cengage Gale.

—Civil Liberties. 2009. (Opposing Viewpoints Ser.). (ENG., Illus.). 240p. (YA). (gr. 10-12). pap. 29.45 (978-0-7377-4355-5(7), LML02109-245310);No. 9. pap. 42.95 (978-0-7377-4356-2(5), LML02109-245369) Cengage Gale. (Greenhaven Pr., Inc.).

Espejo, Roman, ed. Bioterrorism. 2012. (Opposing Viewpoints Ser.). (ENG., Illus.). 240p. (gr. 10-12). pap. 29.45 (978-0-7377-6475-8(9), Greenhaven Pr., Inc.) Cengage Gale.

Farrell, Courtney. Terror at the Munich Olympics, 1 vol. 2010. (Essential Events Set 4 Ser.). (ENG.). 112p. (J). (gr. 6-12). lib. bdg. 35.64 (978-1-60453-945-5(3)) ABDO Publishing Co.

Feinstein, Stephen. Critical Perspectives on Terrorism. 2016. (Analyzing the Issues Ser.). 208p. (YA). lib. bdg. 47.93 (978-0-7660-8127-7(3)) Enslow Pubs., Inc.

Ferguson, Amanda. The Attack Against the U. S. Embassies in Kenya & Tanzania. (Terrorist Attacks Ser.). 64p. 2009. (gr. 5-5). 58.50 (978-1-60853-309-1(3)) 2005. (Illus.). (J). (gr. 7-12). lib. bdg. 31.95 (978-0-8239-3652-6(X)) Rosen Publishing Group, Inc., The.

Freedman, Jeri. America Debates Civil Liberties & Terrorism. 2009. (America Debates Ser.). 64p. (gr. 5-6). 58.50 (978-1-61511-331-6(2), Rosen Reference) Rosen Publishing Group, Inc., The.

Friedman, Lauri S. Terrorism. 2010. (Introducing Issues with Opposing Viewpoints Ser.). (ENG.). 144p. (gr. 7-10). 42.00 (978-0-7377-4944-1(X), Greenhaven Pr., Inc.) Cengage Gale.

Friedman, Mark. America's Struggle with Terrorism. 2011. (Cornerstones of Freedom, Third Ser.). 64p. (J). (ENG.). pap. 8.95 (978-0-531-26551-2(X)); lib. bdg. 30.00 (978-0-531-25026-6(1)) Scholastic Library Publishing. (Children's Pr.).

Gard, Carolyn. The Attack on the Pentagon on September 11, 2001. 2005. (Terrorist Attacks Ser.). (Illus.). 64p. (YA). (gr. 7-12). lib. bdg. 31.95 (978-0-8239-3858-2(1)) Rosen Publishing Group, Inc., The.

—The Attack on the Pentagon on September 11 2001. 2009. (Terrorist Attacks Ser.). 64p. (gr. 5-5). 58.50 (978-1-60853-310-7(7)) Rosen Publishing Group, Inc., The.

—The Attacks on the World Trade Center: February 26, 1993, & September 11, 2001. 2005. (Terrorist Attacks Ser.). (Illus.). 64p. (YA). (gr. 5-9). lib. bdg. 31.95 (978-0-8239-3657-1(0)) Rosen Publishing Group, Inc., The.

Giordano, Geraldine. The Oklahoma City Bombing. (Terrorist Attacks Ser.). 64p. 2009. (gr. 5-5). 58.50 (978-1-60853-318-3(2)) 2005. (Illus.). (YA). (gr. 7-12). lib. bdg. 31.95 (978-0-8239-3655-7(4)) Rosen Publishing Group, Inc., The.

Goodman, Michael E. Modern Spies. 2015. (Illus.). 48p. (J). (978-1-60818-600-6(8), Creative Education) Creative Co., The.

—Modern Spies: Wartime Spies. 2016. (Wartime Spies Ser.). (ENG., Illus.). 48p. (J). (gr. 5-9). pap. 12.00 (978-1-62832-205-7(5), Creative Paperbacks) Creative Co., The.

Green, Robert. Terrorism. 2008. (21st Century Skills Library: Global Perspectives Ser.). (ENG.). 32p. (gr. 4-8). lib. bdg. 28.50 (978-1-60279-125-1(2), 200110) Cherry Lake Publishing.

Greenberger, Robert. Suicide Bombers. (In the News Ser.). 64p. 2009. (gr. 6-6). 58.50 (978-1-61513-490-8(5)) 2006. (Illus.). (YA). (gr. 7-12). lib. bdg. 31.95 (978-1-4042-0977-0(8)) Rosen Publishing Group, Inc., The.

Gregory, Josh. The Hunt for Bin Laden: Operation Neptune Spear. 2013. (ENG.). 64p. (J). 30.00 (978-0-531-28209-0(0)); pap. 8.95 (978-0-531-27674-7(0)) Scholastic Library Publishing.

Gunderson, Cory Gideon. Islamic Fundamentalism. 2003. (World in Conflict-the Middle East Ser.). 32p. (gr. 4-8). 27.07 (978-1-59197-411-6(9), Abdo & Daughters) ABDO Publishing Co.

—Terrorist Groups. 2003. (World in Conflict-the Middle East Ser.). 32p. (gr. 4-8). 27.07 (978-1-59197-413-0(5), Abdo & Daughters) ABDO Publishing Co.

Gunderson, Jessica. Methods of Warfare. 2011. (War on Terror Ser.). (J). (gr. 5-9). 34.25 (978-1-60818-101-8(4)) Creative Co., The.

—Pivotal Moments. 2011. (War on Terror Ser.). (J). (gr. 5-9). 34.25 (978-1-60818-102-5(2)) Creative Co., The.

Halberstam, David. Firehouse. 2003. (ENG., Illus.). 208p. (gr. 8-17). pap. 16.00 (978-0-7868-8851-1(2)) Hyperion Pr.

Hampton, Wilborn. September 11, 2001: Attack on New York City. 2011. (ENG., Illus.). 160p. (J). (gr. 5). pap. 12.99 (978-0-7636-5767-3(0)) Candlewick Pr.

Harris, Nathaniel. Terrorism. 2004. (21st Century Issues Ser.). (Illus.). 48p. (gr. 5-12). lib. bdg. 31.00 (978-0-8368-5645-3(7), Gareth Stevens Secondary Library) Stevens, Gareth Publishing LLLP.

Hasan, Tahara. Anthrax Attacks Around the World. 2005. (Terrorist Attacks Ser.). (Illus.). 64p. (YA). (gr. 7-12). lib. bdg. 31.95 (978-0-8239-3859-9(X)) Rosen Publishing Group, Inc., The.

Haugen, David M. Can the War on Terrorism Be Won? 2007. (At Issue Ser.). (ENG., Illus.). 128p. (gr. 10-12). 39.40 (978-0-7377-1973-4(7), Greenhaven Pr., Inc.) Cengage Gale.

—Terrorism. 2008. (Issues on Trial Ser.). (ENG., Illus.). 240p. (gr. 10-12). 48.30 (978-0-7377-3982-4(7), Greenhaven Pr., Inc.) Cengage Gale.

Haugen, David M. & Musser, Susan. Can the War on Terrorism Be Won? 2007. (At Issue Ser.). (ENG., Illus.). 128p. (gr. 10-12). pap. 27.80 (978-0-7377-1974-1(5), Greenhaven Pr., Inc.) Cengage Gale.

Haugen, David M., et al. Iraq. 2009. (Opposing Viewpoints Ser.). (ENG., Illus.). 240p. (YA). (gr. 10-12). 29.45 (978-0-7377-4525-2(8), LML02109-246006);No. 9. pap. 42.95 (978-0-7377-4524-5(X), LML02109-245978) Cengage Gale. (Greenhaven Pr., Inc.).

Haulley, Fletcher. Critical Perspectives on 9/11. 2005. (Critical Anthologies of Nonfiction Writing Ser.). 176p. (J). (gr. 7-12). lib. bdg. 37.95 (978-1-4042-0060-9(6)) Rosen Publishing Group, Inc., The.

—The Deparment of Homeland Security. 2005. (This Is Your Government Ser.). (Illus.). 64p. (J). (gr. k-3). lib. bdg. 31.95 (978-1-4042-0209-2(9)) Rosen Publishing Group, Inc., The.

—The Department of Homeland Security. (This Is Your Government Ser.). 64p. 2009. (gr. 5-6). 58.50 (978-1-60854-371-7(4), Rosen Reference) 2006. (ENG., Illus.). (gr. 4-8). per. 12.95 (978-1-4042-0662-5(0)) Rosen Publishing Group, Inc., The.

Heing, Bridey. The Children Soldiers of ISIS. 2017. (J). **(978-0-7660-9211-2(9))** Enslow Pubs., Inc.

Hibbert, Adam. Terrorism. 2003. (In the News Ser.). (J). lib. bdg. 24.25 (978-1-58340-395-2(7)) Black Rabbit Bks.

Hiber, Amanda. Islamic Militancy. 2009. (Opposing Viewpoints Ser.). (ENG., Illus.). 224p. (gr. 10-12). pap. 33.80 (978-0-7377-4217-6(8), LML02109-243140); lib. bdg. 48.80 (978-0-7377-4216-9(X), LML02109-243107) Cengage Gale. (Greenhaven Pr., Inc.).

—Should Governments Negotiate with Terrorists? 2008. (At Issue Ser.). (ENG., Illus.). 128p. (gr. 10-12). pap. 27.80 (978-0-7377-3933-6(9), Greenhaven Pr., Inc.); 80-128p. (YA). (gr. 9-12). pap. 34.45 (978-0-7377-3932-9(0)) Cengage Gale.

Hinton, Kerry. Terrorist Attack: A Practical Survival Guide. 2009. (Library of Emergency Preparedness Ser.). 64p. (gr. 6-6). 58.50 (978-1-60853-597-2(5), Rosen Reference) Rosen Publishing Group, Inc., The.

Hunt, Jilly. Fight Against War & Terrorism. 2017. (Beyond the Headlines! Ser.). (ENG.). 48p. (gr. 4-6). lib. bdg. 33.32 **(978-1-4846-4142-2(6)**, Heinemann InfoSearch) Heinemann-Raintree.

Hunter, Nick. Terrorism & Security, 1 vol. 2011. (Hot Topics Ser.). (ENG.). 56p. (gr. 7-8). 34.65 (978-1-4329-4873-3(3)); pap. 10.95 (978-1-4329-6207-4(8)) Heinemann-Raintree. (NA-h).

Immell, Myra. Homeland Security. 2009. (At Issue Ser.). (ENG., Illus.). 128p. (gr. 10-12). pap. 27.80 (978-0-7377-4421-7(9)) Cengage Gale.

Immell, Myra, ed. Homeland Security. 2009. (At Issue Ser.). (ENG., Illus.). 128p. (gr. 10-12). 39.40 (978-0-7377-4420-0(0)) Cengage Gale.

Innes, Brian. Global Terrorism, Vol. 20. Gomez, Manny, ed. 2016. (Crime & Detection Ser.). 96p. (J). (gr. 7). 24.95 (978-1-4222-3481-5(9)) Mason Crest.

—International Terrorism. 2004. (Crime & Detection Ser.). (Illus.). 96p. (YA). (gr. 7-18). lib. bdg. 22.95 (978-1-59084-371-0(1)) Mason Crest.

Inside the World's Most Infamous Terrorist Organizations. 2005. (Illus.). 64p. (gr. 7-12). lib. bdg. 212.00 (978-0-8239-4062-2(4)) Rosen Publishing Group, Inc., The.

Isaacs, April, ed. Critical Perspectives on Al Qaeda. 2009. (Critical Anthologies of Nonfiction Writing Ser.). 184p. (gr. 8-8). 63.90 (978-1-61512-073-4(4)) Rosen Publishing Group, Inc., The.

January, Brendan. Isis: The Global Face of Terrorism. 2017. (ENG.). (J). (gr. 8-12). 37.32 **(978-1-5124-2998-5(8)**, Twenty-First Century Bks.) Lerner Publishing Group.

Kaspar, Anna. A Look at Pluto & Other Dwarf Planets. 2007. (Astronomy Now! Ser.). (Illus.). 24p. (YA). (gr. 2-5). lib. bdg. 22.60 (978-1-4042-3824-4(7)) Rosen Publishing Group, Inc., The.

Katz, Samuel M. At Any Cost: National Liberation Terrorism. 2003. (Terrorists Ser.). (Illus.). 72p. (J). (gr. 6-12). 26.60 (978-0-8225-0949-3(0)) Lerner Publishing Group.

—Global Counterstrike: International Counterterrorism. 2005. (Terrorist Dossiers Ser.). (Illus.). 72p. (J). (gr. 6-12). 26.60 (978-0-8225-1566-1(0)) Lerner Publishing Group.

—Jerusalem or Death: Palestinian Terrorism. 72p. (YA). (gr. 9-18). 19.95 (978-1-58013-208-4(1), Kar-Ben Publishing); 2003. (Illus.). (J). (gr. 6-12). 26.60 (978-0-8225-4033-5(9)) Lerner Publishing Group.

—Raging Within: Ideological Terrorism. 2003. (Terrorist Dossiers Ser.). (Illus.). 72p. (J). (gr. 6-12). 26.60 (978-0-8225-4032-8(0)) Lerner Publishing Group.

—U. S. Counterstrike: American Counterterrorism. 2005. (Terrorist Dossiers Ser.). (Illus.). 72p. (J). (gr. 6-12). 26.60 (978-0-8225-1569-2(5)) Lerner Publishing Group.

Keeter, Hunter. The U. S. Homeland Security Forces. 2004. (America's Armed Forces Ser.). (Illus.). 48p. (gr. 5-12). lib. bdg. 31.00 (978-0-8368-5682-8(1), Gareth Stevens Secondary Library) Stevens, Gareth Publishing LLLP.

Kennan, Caroline. The Rise of ISIS: The Modern Age of Terrorism. 2017. (World History Ser.). 104p. (YA). (gr. 7-7). lib. bdg. 39.90 **(978-1-5345-6056-7(4)**, Lucent Pr.) Greenhaven Publishing LLC.

Kerrigan, Michael. The Department of Homeland Security. 2004. (Rescue & Prevention Ser.). (Illus.). 96p. (J). (gr. 7-18). lib. bdg. 22.95 (978-1-59084-409-0(2)) Mason Crest.

Kerrigan, Michael. Homeland Security. 2017. (J). **(978-1-4222-3767-0(2))** Mason Crest.

Kiland, Taylor Baldwin, et al. Fighter Planes: Masters of the Sky. 2015. (Military Engineering in Action Ser.). (ENG.). 48p. (J). (gr. 6-6). 27.93 (978-0-7660-6910-7(9)) Enslow Pubs., Inc.

Koestler-Grack, Rachel A. The Department of Homeland Security. 2007. (U. S. Government Ser.). (Illus.). 104p. (J). (gr. 5-9). lib. bdg. 30.00 (978-0-7910-9286-6(0)) Facts On File, Inc.

Kowalski, Kathiann M. A Pro/con Look at Homeland Security: Safety vs. Liberty After 9/11. 2008. (Issues in Focus Today Ser.). (Illus.). 112p. (J). (gr. 3-7). lib. bdg. 33.27 (978-0-7660-2914-9(X)) Enslow Pubs., Inc.

Koya, Lena & Buell, Tonya. Investigating the Crash of Flight 93. 2017. (Terrorism in the 21st Century: Causes & Effects Ser.). 64p. (gr. 12-11). 34.45 **(978-1-5081-7459-2(8)**, Rosen Young Adult) Rosen Publishing Group, Inc., The.

Koya, Lena & Gard, Carolyn. Investigating the Attack on the Pentagon. 2017. (Terrorism in the 21st Century: Causes & Effects Ser.). 64p. (J). (gr. 12-11). 34.45 **(978-1-5081-7453-0(9)**, Rosen Young Adult) Rosen Publishing Group, Inc., The.

—Investigating the Attacks on the World Trade Center. 2017. (Terrorism in the 21st Century: Causes & Effects Ser.). 64p. (J). (gr. 12-11). 34.45 **(978-1-5081-7455-4(5)**, Rosen Young Adult) Rosen Publishing Group, Inc., The.

La Bella, Laura. The People Behind Deadly Terrorist Attacks. 2016. (Psychology of Mass Murderers Ser.). (Illus.). 144p. (J). (gr. 8-8). 37.27 (978-0-7660-7775-1(6)) Enslow Pubs., Inc.

Langwith, Jacqueline, ed. Bioterrorism. 2008. (Opposing Viewpoints Ser.). (ENG., Illus.). 258p. (YA). (gr. 7-12). 29.45 (978-0-7377-3991-6(6)); lib. bdg. 42.95 (978-0-7377-3990-9(8)) Cengage Gale. (Greenhaven Pr., Inc.).

Levin, Jack. Domestic Terrorism. 2006. (Roots of Terrorism Ser.). (Illus.). 93p. (gr. 6-12). lib. bdg. 35.00 (978-0-7910-8683-4(6), Chelsea Hse.) Facts On File, Inc.

Lunis, Natalie & Pushies, Fred J. The Takedown of Osama Bin Laden. 2012. (Special Ops Ser.). 32p. (J). (gr. 2-7). lib. bdg. 25.27 (978-1-61772-459-6(9)) Bearport Publishing Co., Inc.

Lusted, Marcia Amidon. Capture & Killing of Osama Bin Laden, 1 vol. 2011. (Essential Events Set 7 Ser.). (ENG.). 112p. (J). (gr. 6-12). lib. bdg. 35.64 (978-1-61783-180-5(8)) ABDO Publishing Co.

Luxenberg, Alan H. Radical Islam. 2010. (World of Islam Ser.). (Illus.). 64p. (YA). (gr. 4-7). lib. bdg. 22.95 (978-1-4222-0536-5(3)) Mason Crest.

Malisow, Ben. Terrorism. 2008. (Criminal Investigations Ser.). (Illus.). 144p. (J). (gr. 9-12). 35.00 (978-0-7910-9412-9(X), Chelsea Hse.) Facts On File, Inc.

Marcovitz, Harold. Privacy Rights & the Patriot Act, 1 vol. 2008. (Essential Viewpoints Set 2 Ser.). (ENG., Illus.). 112p. (J). (gr. 6-12). lib. bdg. 35.64 (978-1-60453-059-9(6)) ABDO Publishing Co.

Margulies, Philip. Al-Qaeda: Osama Bin Laden's Army of Terrorists. 2005. (Inside the World's Most Infamous Terrorist Organizations Ser.). (Illus.). 64p. (YA). (gr. 7-12). lib. bdg. 31.95 (978-0-8239-3817-9(4)) Rosen Publishing Group, Inc., The.

Margulies, Phillip. Al Qaeda: Osama bin Laden's Army of Terrorists. 2009. (Inside the World's Most Infamous Terrorist Organizations Ser.). 64p. (gr. 5-5). 58.50 (978-1-61513-573-8(1)) Rosen Publishing Group, Inc., The.

Maybury, Richard J. World War II: The Rest of the Story & How It Affects You Today, 1930 to September 11 2001. Williams, Jane A., ed. rev. ed. 2003. ("Uncle Eric" Bk.: 11). (ENG., Illus.). 349p. pap. 19.95 (978-0-942617-43-6(6)) Bluestocking Pr.

McCabe, Matthew. 12 Things to Know about Terrorism. 2015. (ENG., Illus.). 32p. (J). (978-1-63235-033-6(5)) Pr. Room Editions LLC.

Merino, Noel. Civil Liberties. 2013. (Opposing Viewpoints Ser.). (ENG., Illus.). 224p. (gr. 10-12). pap. 33.80 (978-0-7377-6305-8(1), Greenhaven Pr., Inc.) Cengage Gale.

Merino, Noël. Civil Liberties. 2013. (Opposing Viewpoints Ser.). (ENG., Illus.). 224p. (gr. 10-12). lib. bdg. 48.80 (978-0-7377-6304-1(3), Greenhaven Pr., Inc.) Cengage Gale.

Miller, Debra A. The Middle East. 2007. (Current Controversies Ser.). (ENG., Illus.). 224p. (gr. 10-12). 46.40 (978-0-7377-3960-2(6)); pap. 32.00 (978-0-7377-3961-9(4), Greenhaven Pr., Inc.) Cengage Gale.

—The Patriot Act. 2007. (Hot Topics Ser.). (ENG., Illus.). 112p. (YA). (gr. 7-12). lib. bdg. 33.95 *(978-1-59018-981-8(7),* LML02109-229790) Cengage Gale.

—Terrorism. 2008. (Hot Topics Ser.). (ENG., Illus.). 112p. (J). (gr. 3-7). lib. bdg. 33.95 *(978-1-4205-0051-6(1),* Lucent Bks.) Cengage Gale.

Miller, Mara. Remembering September 11, 2001: What We Know Now. 2010. (Issues in Focus Today Ser.). 112p. (J). (gr. 7-12). 33.27 *(978-0-7660-2931-6(X))* Enslow Pubs., Inc.

—Terrorist Attacks: Disaster & Survival. 2005. (Deadly Disasters Ser.). (Illus.). 48p. (J). (gr. 4-10). lib. bdg. 25.27 *(978-0-7660-2385-7(0))* Enslow Pubs., Inc.

Miller, Raymond H. The War in Afghanistan. 2003. (American War Library). (ENG., Illus.). 112p. (J). 30.85 *(978-1-59018-331-1(2),* Lucent Bks.) Cengage Gale.

Mullins, Matt. Homeland Security. 2010. (21st Century Skills Library: Citizens & Their Governments Ser.). (ENG.). 32p. (gr. 4-8). lib. bdg. 28.50 *(978-1-60279-633-1(5),* 200338) Cherry Lake Publishing.

Murdico, Suzanne J. Osama Bin Laden. 2007. (Middle East Leaders Ser.). (Illus.). 112p. (J). (gr. 3-7). lib. bdg. 34.60 *(978-1-4042-0875-9(5),* Rosen Reference) Rosen Publishing Group, Inc., The.

—Osama bin Laden. 2009. (Middle East Leaders Ser.). 112p. (gr. 5-8). 66.50 *(978-1-61514-647-5(4),* Rosen Reference) Rosen Publishing Group, Inc., The.

Nardo, Don. Cause & Effect: The War on Terror. 2017. (ENG.). 80p. (YA). (gr. 5-12). ***(978-1-68282-170-1(6))*** ReferencePoint Pr., Inc.

Nardo, Don. Massacre in Munich: How Terrorists Changed the Oylmpics & the World. 2016. (Captured History Sports Ser.). (ENG., Illus.). 64p. (gr. 5-7). lib. bdg. 34.65 *(978-0-7565-5292-3(3),* CPB Grades 4-8) Compass Point Bks.

Natural Disasters. 2014. 48p. (J). *(978-1-4222-3044-2(9))* Mason Crest.

Orr, Tamra. Egyptian Islamic Jihad. 2009. (Inside the World's Most Infamous Terrorist Organizations Ser.). 64p. (gr. 5-5). 58.50 *(978-1-61513-574-5(X))* Rosen Publishing Group, Inc., The.

parks, peggy j. Cyberterrorism. 2012. (Illus.). 96p. (J). lib. bdg. *(978-1-60152-264-1(9))* ReferencePoint Pr., Inc.

Paul, Michael. Oklahoma City & Anti-Government Terrorism. 2006. (Terrorism in Today's World Ser.). (Illus.). 48p. (gr. 5-12). pap. 14.05 *(978-0-8368-6565-3(0));* lib. bdg. 31.00 *(978-0-8368-6558-5(8))* Stevens, Gareth Publishing LLLP. (Gareth Stevens Secondary Library).

—Pan Am 103 & State-Sponsored Terrorism. 2006. (Terrorism in Today's World Ser.). (Illus.). 48p. (gr. 5-12). pap. 14.05 *(978-0-8368-6566-0(9));* lib. bdg. 31.00 *(978-0-8368-6559-2(6))* Stevens, Gareth Publishing LLLP. (Gareth Stevens Secondary Library).

Pavlovic, Zoran. Terrorism & Security. 2009. (Global Connections Ser.). (Illus.). 120p. (gr. 5-8). 35.00 *(978-1-60413-282-3(5),* Chelsea Hse.) Facts On File, Inc.

Peppas, Lynn & Newton, Sydney. Terrorism Alert! 2005. (Disaster Alert! Ser.). (ENG., Illus.). 32p. (J). (gr. 4-7). pap. *(978-0-7787-1617-4(1));* lib. bdg. *(978-0-7787-1585-6(X))* Crabtree Publishing Co.

Perl, Lila. Terrorism. 2003. (Open for Debate Ser.). (Illus.). 128p. (gr. 7-18). lib. bdg. 42.79 *(978-0-7614-1583-1(1),* Benchmark Bks.) Marshall Cavendish Corp.

Perliger, Arie. Middle Eastern Terrorism. Eubank, Bill, ed. 2006. (Roots of Terrorism Ser.). (Illus.). 111p. (gr. 6-12). 35.00 *(978-0-7910-8309-3(8),* Chelsea Hse.) Facts On File, Inc.

Pierce, Alan. September 11 2001, 1 vol. 2005. (American Moments Set Ii Ser.). (ENG.). 48p. (gr. 4-8). 27.07 *(978-1-59197-735-3(5),* Abdo & Daughters) ABDO Publishing Co.

Porterfield, Jason. Terrorism, Dirty Bombs, & Weapons of Mass Destruction. (Library of Weapons of Mass Destruction Ser.). 64p. 2009. (gr. 5-5). 58.50 *(978-1-60853-954-3(7))* 2004. (Illus.). (J). lib. bdg. 31.95 *(978-1-4042-0291-7(9))* Rosen Publishing Group, Inc., The.

Publishers, Chelsea House, creator. The Roots of Terrorism, 6 vols., Set. 2006. (Roots of Terrorism Ser.). (gr. 6-12). 210.00 *(978-0-7910-9322-1(0),* Chelsea Hse.) Facts On File, Inc.

Rice Jr., Earle. Al Qaeda. 2017. lib. bdg. 29.95 ***(978-1-68020-047-8(X))*** Mitchell Lane Pubs., Inc.

—Islamic State. 2017. lib. bdg. 29.95 ***(978-1-68020-055-3(0))*** Mitchell Lane Pubs., Inc.

Roleff, Tamara L., ed. The World Trade Center Attack. 2003. (History Firsthand Ser.). (Illus.). 202p. (YA). (gr. 7-10). pap. 21.20 *(978-0-7377-1469-2(7),* Greenhaven Pr., Inc.) Cengage Gale.

Romano, Amy. Germ Warfare. (Germs: the Library of Disease-Causing Organisms Ser.). 48p. 2009. (gr. 5-5). 53.00 *(978-1-61512-716-0(X))* 2004. (Illus.). (gr. 7-12). lib. bdg. 29.25 *(978-0-8239-4493-4(X))* Rosen Publishing Group, Inc., The.

Rosaler, Maxine. Hamas: (Rev) Palestinian Terrorists. 2005. (Inside the World's Most Infamous Terrorist Organizations Ser.). (Illus.). 64p. (J). (gr. -1-7). lib. bdg. 31.95 *(978-1-4042-0634-2(5))* Rosen Publishing Group, Inc., The.

Rudolph, Jessica. CIA Paramilitary Operatives in Action. 2013. (Special Ops II Ser.). 32p. (J). (gr. 2-7). lib. bdg. 26.60 *(978-1-61772-892-1(6))* Bearport Publishing Co., Inc.

Rudy, Lisa Jo. Bioterror: Deadly Invisible Weapons. 2007. (24/7: Science Behind the Scenes Ser.). (ENG., Illus.). 64p. (J). (gr. 9-12). 29.00 *(978-0-531-12080-4(5),* Watts, Franklin) Scholastic Library Publishing.

Ruffin, David C. The Duties & Responsibilities of the Secretary of Homeland Security. (Your Government in Action Ser.). 32p. (gr. 3-3). 2009. 43.90 *(978-1-60854-918-4(6))* 2005. (Illus.). (J). lib. bdg. 23.95 *(978-1-4042-2693-7(1))* Rosen Publishing Group, Inc., The. (PowerKids Pr.).

Samuels, Charlie. Timeline of the War on Terror. 2011. (Americans at War: a Gareth Stevens Timeline Ser.). (Illus.). 48p. (J). (gr. 6-8). pap. 14.05 *(978-1-4339-5924-0(0));* lib. bdg. 31.95 *(978-1-4339-5922-6(4))* Stevens, Gareth Publishing LLLP. (Gareth Stevens Secondary Library).

Santora, Maureen Crethan. The Day the Towers Fell: The Story of September 11, 2001. Santora, Maureen Crethan, illus. 2008. (Illus.). 32p. (J). 31.99 *(978-1-4257-7872-9(0))* Xlibris Corp.

—My Son Christopher: A 9/11 Mother's Tale of Remembrance. 2008. 36p. 31.99 *(978-1-4363-3044-2(0))* Xlibris Corp.

Scheppler, Bill. Guantánamo Bay & Military Tribunals: The Detention & Trial of Suspected Terrorists. 2009. (Frontline Coverage of Current Events Ser.). 48p. (gr. 5-5). 53.00 *(978-1-61512-655-2(4))* Rosen Publishing Group, Inc., The.

—The USA Patriot Act: Antiterror Legislation in Response To 9/11. (Library of American Laws & Legal Principles Ser.). 48p. 2009. (gr. 5-8). 53.00 *(978-1-60853-466-1(9),* Rosen Reference) 2005. (Illus.). (YA). (gr. 7-12). lib. bdg. 29.25 *(978-1-4042-0457-7(1))* Rosen Publishing Group, Inc., The.

Schmermund, Elizabeth, ed. Domestic Terrorism. 2017. (At Issue Ser.). 128p. (J). (gr. 10-12). pap. 27.80 ***(978-1-5345-0039-6(1));*** lib. bdg. 39.40 ***(978-1-5345-0015-0(4))*** Greenhaven Publishing LLC. (Greenhaven Publishing).

Schorr, Loretta. Attacked, 1 vol. unabr. ed. 2012. (Astonishing Headlines Ser.). (ENG.). 92p. (YA). (gr. 9-12). 8.95 *(978-1-61651-918-6(5))* Saddleback Educational Publishing, Inc.

Shahak, Bat-Chen. The Bat-Chen Diaries. Rubanenko, Diana, tr. from HEB. 2008. (Israel Ser.). (ENG., Illus.). 112p. (J). (gr. 5-7). lib. bdg. 16.95 *(978-0-8225-8807-8(2));* per. 7.95 *(978-0-8225-7223-7(0))* Lerner Publishing Group. (Kar-Ben Publishing).

Sheen, Barbara. Nuclear Weapons. 2007. (Ripped from the Headlines Ser.). 64p. (YA). (gr. 7-12). 23.95 *(978-1-60217-004-9(5))* Erickson Pr.

Sherrow, Victoria. Homegrown Terror: The Oklahoma City Bombing. 2012. (Disasters — People in Peril Ser.). (Illus.). 48p. (J). (gr. 5-18). lib. bdg. 25.27 *(978-0-7660-4016-8(X))* Enslow Pubs., Inc.

Shostak, Arthur B., ed. Defeating Terrorism/Developing Dreams: Beyond 9/11 & the Iraq War. 2005. (Defeating Terrorism/Developing Dreams: Beyond 9/11 & the Iraq War Ser.). (Illus.). 185p. (gr. 6-12). 159.75 *(978-0-7910-8421-2(3),* Chelsea Hse.) Facts On File, Inc.

Shuchart, John & Scearcy, Steve. Kids' Letters to Terrorists. 2003. (ENG., Illus.). 148p. pap. 9.95 *(978-1-932181-00-5(8),* PP8100) Personhood Pr.

Silate, Jennifer. Terrorist Attack: True Stories of Survival. (Survivor Stories Ser.). 48p. (gr. 5-5). 2009. 53.00 *(978-1-60853-257-5(7),* Rosen Reference) 2007. (Illus.). (YA). lib. bdg. 29.25 *(978-1-4042-1001-1(6))* Rosen Publishing Group, Inc., The.

Silverstein Gray, Judy & Baldwin Kiland, Taylor. Cyber Technology: Using Computers to Fight Terrorism. 2016. (Military Engineering in Action Ser.). 48p. (J). (gr. 6-5). pap. 11.70 *(978-0-7660-7535-1(4))* Enslow Pubs., Inc.

Sonneborn, Liz. Murder at the 1972 Olympics in Munich. 2009. (Terrorist Attacks Ser.). 64p. (gr. 5-5). 58.50 *(978-1-60853-308-4(5))* Rosen Publishing Group, Inc., The.

Souter, Gerry & Souter, Janet. War in Afghanistan & Iraq: The Daily Life of the Men & Women Serving in Afghanistan & Iraq. Carlton Books Staff, ed. 2011. (ENG., Illus.). 48p. (J). (gr. 3). 16.95 *(978-1-84732-895-3(4))* Carlton Bks., Ltd. GBR. Dist: Sterling Publishing Co., Inc.

Spies, Karen Bornemann. Pan Am Flight 103: Terrorism over Lockerbie. 2003. (American Disasters Ser.). (Illus.). 48p. (J). (gr. 4-10). lib. bdg. 23.93 *(978-0-7660-1788-7(5))* Enslow Pubs., Inc.

Steele, Philip. Hostage Takers. 2016. (Illus.). 48p. (J). *(978-0-7787-2587-9(1))* Crabtree Publishing Co.

Stefoff, Rebecca. The Patriot ACT. 2010. (Landmark Legislation Ser.). 128p. (YA). (gr. 7-12). 39.93 *(978-1-60870-042-4(9))* Marshall Cavendish Corp.

—Security V. Privacy. 2007. (Open for Debate Ser.). (Illus.). 128p. (gr. 7-7). lib. bdg. 42.79 *(978-0-7614-2578-6(0),* Benchmark Bks.) Marshall Cavendish Corp.

Stein, R. Conrad. The Oklahoma City National Memorial. 2003. (Cornerstones of Freedom Ser.). (ENG., Illus.). 48p. (YA). (gr. 4-7). 26.00 *(978-0-516-24205-7(9))* Scholastic Library Publishing.

Stephens, Ronald, ed. Terrorism & Perceived Terrorism Threats. 2014. (Safety First Ser.: 11). 48p. (J). (gr. 5-18). 20.95 *(978-1-4222-3055-8(4))* Mason Crest.

Sterngass, Jon. Terrorism. 2011. (Debating the Issues Ser.). 64p. (gr. 6). 32.79 *(978-0-7614-4977-5(9))* Marshall Cavendish GBR. Dist: Marshall Cavendish Corp.

Stewart, Gail B. Defending the Borders: The Role of Border & Immigration Control. 2003. (Lucent Library of Homeland Security). (Illus.). 112p. (J). 29.95 *(978-1-59018-376-2(2),* Lucent Bks.) Cengage Gale.

Stinson, Doug. Protecting the Nation's Borders. 2005. (At Issue Ser.). (ENG.). 80-128p. (gr. 10-12). pap. 24.45 *(978-0-7377-2740-1(3),* Greenhaven Pr., Inc.) Cengage Gale.

Stinson, Douglass, ed. Protecting America's Borders. 2005. (At Issue Ser.). 94p. (YA). (gr. 10-13). lib. bdg. 29.95 *(978-0-7377-2739-5(X),* Greenhaven Pr., Inc.) Cengage Gale.

Terrorism. 2010. (Key Concepts in American History Ser.). (Illus.). 128p. (gr. 6-12). 45.00 *(978-1-60413-226-7(4),* Chelsea Hse.) Facts On File, Inc.

Terrorism. 2006. (Understanding Global Issues Ser.). (Illus.). 56p. per. 11.95 *(978-1-59036-508-3(9))* Weigl Pubs., Inc.

Terrorism in the 21st Century: Causes & Effects. 2017. (Terrorism in the 21st Century: Causes & Effects Ser.). 64p. (gr. 12-11). 206.70 ***(978-1-4994-6638-6(2),*** Rosen Young Adult) Rosen Publishing Group, Inc., The.

Terrorist Attacks. 2005. (Illus.). 64p. (gr. 7-12). lib. bdg. 239.40 *(978-0-8239-4077-6(2))* Rosen Publishing Group, Inc., The.

Terrorist Attacks Set 1. 2005. (Illus.). (gr. 7-12). lib. bdg. 159.00 *(978-0-8239-3900-8(6))* Rosen Publishing Group, Inc., The.

Terrorist Attacks Set 2. 2005. (Illus.). 64p. (gr. 7-12). lib. bdg. 159.00 *(978-0-8239-4063-9(2))* Rosen Publishing Group, Inc., The.

Tomkies, Kelly Kagamas. The National Counterterrorism Center. 2017. (J). ***(978-1-4222-3766-3(4))*** Mason Crest.

Torr, James D. Responding to Attack: Firefighters & Police. 2003. (Lucent Library of Homeland Security). (Illus.). 112p. (J). 30.85 *(978-1-59018-375-5(4),* Lucent Bks.) Cengage Gale.

Torres, John. How Barack Obama Fought the War on Terrorism. 2017. (Presidents at War Ser.). 128p. (J). (gr. 8-8). lib. bdg. 37.27 ***(978-0-7660-8535-0(X))*** Enslow Pubs., Inc.

Townsend, Chris. Global Recruitment by ISIS. 2017. (J). ***(978-0-7660-9212-9(7))*** Enslow Pubs., Inc.

—ISIS Hostages. 2017. (J). ***(978-0-7660-9217-4(8))*** Enslow Pubs., Inc.

—Life under the Caliphate. 2017. (J). ***(978-0-7660-9218-1(6))*** Enslow Pubs., Inc.

—The Violent Rise of ISIS. 2017. (J). ***(978-0-7660-9210-5(0))*** Enslow Pubs., Inc.

Uschan, Michael V. The Beslan School Siege & Separatist Terrorism. 2006. (Terrorism in Today's World Ser.). (Illus.). 48p. (gr. 5-12). pap. 14.05 *(978-0-8368-6563-9(4));* lib. bdg. 31.00 *(978-0-8368-6556-1(1))* Stevens, Gareth Publishing LLLP. (Gareth Stevens Secondary Library).

—Suicide Bombings in Israel & Palestinian Terrorism. 2006. (Terrorism in Today's World Ser.). (Illus.). 48p. (gr. 5-12). pap. 14.05 *(978-0-8368-6568-4(5));* lib. bdg. 31.00 *(978-0-8368-6561-5(8))* Stevens, Gareth Publishing LLLP. (Gareth Stevens Secondary Library).

Webb, Glenn. Critical World Issues: Terrorism, Vol. 16. 2016. (Critical World Issues Ser.: Vol. 16). (ENG., Illus.). 112p. (J). (gr. 7-12). 25.95 *(978-1-4222-3661-1(7))* Mason Crest.

Weil, Ann. Terrorism, 1 vol. unabr. ed. 2012. (Disasters Ser.). (ENG.). 92p. (YA). (gr. 9-12). 8.95 *(978-1-61651-936-0(3))* Saddleback Educational Publishing, Inc.

Weinberg, Leonard & Eubank, William L. What Is Terrorism? 2006. (Roots of Terrorism Ser.). (Illus.). 120p. (gr. 6-12). lib. bdg. 35.00 *(978-0-7910-8305-5(5),* Chelsea Hse.) Facts On File, Inc.

Wells, Donald, ed. Terrorism. 2006. (Understanding Global Issues Ser.). (Illus.). 56p. (J). (gr. 3-7). lib. bdg. 28.50 *(978-1-59036-234-1(9))* Weigl Pubs., Inc.

Wicker, R. Doug. The Bombing of Pan Am Flight 103. (Terrorist Attacks Ser.). 64p. 2009. (gr. 5-5). 58.50 *(978-1-60853-315-2(8))* 2005. (Illus.). (YA). (gr. 7-12). lib. bdg. 31.95 *(978-0-8239-3656-4(2))* Rosen Publishing Group, Inc., The.

Williams, Brian. America under Attack. 2003. (Dates with History Ser.). 45p. (J). lib. bdg. 28.50 *(978-1-58340-406-5(6))* Black Rabbit Bks.

Wilson, Mike. Terrorism. 2008. (Opposing Viewpoints Ser.). (ENG., Illus.). 224p. (gr. 10-12). 48.80 *(978-0-7377-4234-3(8),* LML01709-243116); pap. 33.80 *(978-0-7377-4235-0(6),* LML01709-243151) Cengage Gale. (Greenhaven Pr., Inc.).

Wimmer, Teresa. Causes. 2011. (War on Terror Ser.). (Illus.). 48p. (J). (gr. 5-9). 34.25 *(978-1-60818-097-4(2))* Creative Co., The.

—Controversies. 2011. (War on Terror Ser.). (Illus.). 48p. (J). (gr. 5-9). 34.25 *(978-1-60818-098-1(0))* Creative Co., The.

—Ideology & Information. 2011. (War on Terror Ser.). (Illus.). 48p. (J). (gr. 5-9). 34.25 *(978-1-60818-099-8(9))* Creative Co., The.

—Important Figures. 2011. (War on Terror Ser.). (Illus.). 48p. (J). (gr. 5-9). 34.25 *(978-1-60818-100-1(6))* Creative Co., The.

Woolf, Alex. Osama Bin Laden. 2004. (A&E Biography Ser.). (Illus.). 112p. (J). 29.27 *(978-0-8225-5003-7(2),* Lerner Pubns.) Lerner Publishing Group.

—Terrorism. 2011. (Global Issues Ser.). (Illus.). 48p. (YA). (gr. 5-8). lib. bdg. 29.25 *(978-1-4488-1881-5(8),* Rosen Reference) Rosen Publishing Group, Inc., The.

Wright, John D. Counterterrorist Forces with the CIA. 2004. (Rescue & Prevention Ser.). (Illus.). 96p. (YA). (gr. 7-18). lib. bdg. 22.95 *(978-1-59084-407-6(6))* Mason Crest.

Yomtov, Nel. Counterterrorism. 2016. (Military Missions Ser.). (ENG., Illus.). 24p. (J). (gr. 3-7). 25.95 *(978-1-62617-434-4(2),* Epic Bks.) Bellwether Media.

Zelinger, Laurie E. Please Explain Terrorism to Me: A Story for Children, PEARLS of Wisdom for Their Parents. Israeli, Ann, illus. 2016. (J). pap. *(978-1-61599-291-1(X))* Loving Healing Pr., Inc.

Zullo, Allan. Heroes of 9/11. 2011. (Illus.). 181p. (J). pap. *(978-0-545-25506-6(6))* Scholastic, Inc.

TERRORISM—FICTION

Appleton, Victor. The Robot Olympics. 2007. (Tom Swift, Young Inventor Ser.). (ENG.). 160p. (gr. 4-7). 27.07 *(978-1-59961-351-2(4))* Spotlight.

Aronson, Sarah. Believe. 2013. (ENG.). 296p. (YA). (gr. 7-12). 17.95 *(978-1-4677-0697-1(3),* Carolrhoda Lab™) Lerner Publishing Group.

Barry, Dave. The Worst Class Trip Ever. 2015. (Class Trip Ser.). (ENG.). 224p. (J). (gr. 3-7). 13.99 *(978-1-4847-0849-1(0))* Disney Pr.

Baskin, Nora Raleigh. Nine, Ten: A September 11 Story. 2016. (ENG., Illus.). 208p. (J). (gr. 3-7). 16.99 *(978-1-4424-8506-8(X))* Simon & Schuster Children's Publishing.

Blackman, Malorie. Black & White. 2007. (ENG.). 512p. (YA). (gr. 9-12). pap. 12.99 *(978-1-4169-0017-7(9),* Simon & Schuster Bks. For Young Readers) Simon & Schuster Bks. For Young Readers.

Bowen, Carl & Fuentes, Benny. Dragon Teeth. Tortosa, Wilson, illus. 2015. (Shadow Squadron Ser.). (ENG.). 112p. (gr. 4-8). lib. bdg. 26.65 *(978-1-4965-0383-1(X))* Stone Arch Bks.

—Long Shadow. Tortosa, Wilson, illus. 2015. (Shadow Squadron Ser.). (ENG.). 112p. (gr. 4-8). pap. 5.95 *(978-1-4965-0388-6(0))* Stone Arch Bks.

—Steel Hammer. Tortosa, Wilson, illus. 2015. (Shadow Squadron Ser.). (ENG.). 112p. (gr. 4-8). lib. bdg. 26.65 *(978-1-4965-0385-5(6))* Stone Arch Bks.

—White Needle, 1 vol. Tortosa, Wilson, illus. 2014. (Shadow Squadron Ser.). (ENG.). 112p. (gr. 4-8). 26.65 *(978-1-4342-6398-8(3))* Stone Arch Bks.

Bradford, Chris. Recruit, Bk. 1. 2017. (Bodyguard Ser.). (ENG.). 272p. (J). (gr. 5). pap. 8.99 *(978-1-5247-3697-2(X),* Philomel Bks.) Penguin Young Readers Group.

Bradley, F. T. The Alias Men. 2015. (Double Vision Ser.: 3). (ENG.). 256p. (J). (gr. 3-7). pap. 6.99 *(978-0-06-210444-1(6))* HarperCollins Pubs.

—Double Vision: The Alias Men. 2014. (Double Vision Ser.: 3). (ENG.). 256p. (J). (gr. 3-7). 16.99 *(978-0-06-210443-4(8))* HarperCollins Pubs.

Bunting, Eve. The Man with the Red Bag. 2007. 230p. (J). (gr. 5-9). 15.99 *(978-0-06-081828-9(X),* Cotler, Joanna Books) HarperCollins Pubs.

Burns, Joanne. What Is Heaven Like? 2005. 35p. (J). 10.99 *(978-1-4116-3360-5(1))* Lulu Pr., Inc.

Burrows, Jennifer S. Most Beautiful. 2012. (ENG.). 50p. (J). (gr. 4-7). pap. 9.99 *(978-0-89824-376-5(9))* Royal Fireworks Publishing Co.

Butcher, Andrew & Butcher, Andrew J. Factoria Frankestein. Morales, Andrea, tr. 2004. (SPA., Illus.). 240p. *(978-84-95618-57-3(5),* Umbriel) Ediciones Urano S. A.

Carter, Ally. United We Spy (10th Anniversary Edition) 2016. (Gallagher Girls Ser.). (ENG.). 320p. (YA). (gr. 5-9). pap. 9.99 *(978-1-4847-8508-9(8))* Hyperion Bks. for Children.

Chima, Cinda Williams. The Enchanter Heir. 2013. 464p. 18.99 *(978-1-4231-8789-9(X))* Disney Pr.

Clancy, Tom. Patriot Games. 2013. (gr. 7-12). 20.85 *(978-0-8335-1643-5(4),* Turtleback) Turtleback Bks.

Cooney, Caroline B. The Terrorist. 2012. (ENG.). 144p. (YA). pap. 6.99 *(978-1-4532-7467-5(7))* Open Road Integrated Media, Inc.

Cray, Jordan. Firestorm. 2009. (Danger. com Ser.: 2). (ENG.). 208p. (YA). (gr. 7). pap. 9.99 *(978-1-4169-9846-4(2),* Simon Pulse) Simon Pulse.

Dashner, James. The Eye of Minds. 2013. 310p. (YA). *(978-0-385-38370-7(3),* Delacorte Pr) Random House Publishing Group.

—The Eye of Minds. (Mortality Doctrine Ser.). (ENG.). (YA). (gr. 7). 2014. 342p. pap. 9.99 *(978-0-385-74140-8(5),* Ember) 2013. 320p. 18.99 *(978-0-385-74139-2(1),* Delacorte Pr.) Random Hse. Children's Bks.

—The Game of Lives. 2015. (Mortality Doctrine Ser.). (ENG.). 352p. (YA). (gr. 7). lib. bdg. 21.99 *(978-0-375-99003-8(8));* 18.99 *(978-0-385-74143-9(X))* Random Hse. Children's Bks. (Delacorte Pr.).

—The Game of Lives (the Mortality Doctrine, Book Three) 2017. (Mortality Doctrine Ser.: 3). (ENG.). 384p. (YA). (gr. 7). pap. 9.99 ***(978-0-385-74144-6(8),*** Ember) Random Hse. Children's Bks.

Dashner, James. The Rule of Thoughts. (Mortality Doctrine Ser.). (ENG.). (YA). (gr. 7). 2014. 336p. 18.99 *(978-0-385-74141-5(3),* Delacorte Pr.)Bk. 2. 2016. 352p. pap. 9.99 *(978-0-385-74142-2(1),* Ember) Random Hse. Children's Bks.

David, Christopher. Denholme & the Skeleton Mystery. 2006. 274p. pap. 22.52 *(978-1-4120-8014-9(2))* Trafford Publishing.

Davidson, Jenny. The Explosionist. 2008. 464p. (YA). (gr. 7-18). lib. bdg. 18.89 *(978-0-06-123976-2(3),* HarperTeen) HarperCollins Pubs.

Davies, Stephen. Blood & Ink. 2017. (ENG.). 224p. (YA). (gr. 7). lib. bdg. 17.99 ***(978-1-58089-790-7(8),*** Charlesbridge Teen) Charlesbridge Publishing, Inc.

Davies, Stephen. Outlaw. 2011. (ENG.). 304p. (YA). (gr. 7). 16.99 *(978-0-547-39017-8(3))* Houghton Mifflin Harcourt Publishing Co.

Deuker, Carl & Perry, Thomas. Runner. 2007. (ENG.). 224p. (YA). (gr. 7-12). pap. 8.99 *(978-0-618-73505-1(4))* Houghton Mifflin Harcourt Publishing Co.

Doctorow, Cory. Little Brother. (ENG.). (YA). (gr. 8-13). 2010. 432p. pap. 12.99 *(978-0-7653-2311-8(7),* 9780765323118) 2008. 384p. 19.99 *(978-0-7653-1985-2(3),* 9780765319852) Doherty, Tom Assocs., LLC. (Tor Teen).

—Little Brother. 2010. (YA). lib. bdg. 24.50 *(978-0-606-14347-9(5),* Turtleback) Turtleback Bks.

Dowd, Siobhan. Bog Child. 2010. (ENG.). 336p. (YA). (gr. 7). pap. 9.99 *(978-0-375-84135-4(0))* Fickling, David Bks. GBR. Dist: Penguin Random Hse. LLC.

Dunlop, Ed. Sherlock Jones: The Assassination Plot. 2004. 116p. (J). 8.99 *(978-1-59166-315-7(6))* BJU Pr.

Ellis, Deborah. The Breadwinner Trilogy, 1 vol. 2009. (ENG.). 520p. (J). (gr. 4-9). pap. 18.95 *(978-0-88899-959-7(3))* Groundwood Bks. CAN. Dist: Publishers Group West (PGW).

Everheart, Chris. Demolition Day, 1 vol. Arcana Studio Staff, illus. 2010. (Recon Academy Ser.). (ENG.). 64p. (gr. 3-3). 26.65 *(978-1-4342-1917-6(8),* Recon Academy) Stone Arch Bks.

—The Hidden Face of Fren-Z, 1 vol. 2009. (Recon Academy Ser.). (ENG.). 64p. (gr. 3-3). lib. bdg. 26.65 *(978-1-4342-1165-1(7),* Recon Academy) Stone Arch Bks.

—Mixed Signals, 1 vol. Arcana Studio Staff, illus. 2010. (Recon Academy Ser.). (ENG.). 64p. (gr. 3-3). 26.65 *(978-1-4342-1915-2(1),* Recon Academy) Stone Arch Bks.

—Nuclear Distraction, 1 vol. 2009. (Recon Academy Ser.). (ENG.). 64p. (gr. 3-3). lib. bdg. 26.65 *(978-1-4342-1167-5(3),* Recon Academy) Stone Arch Bks.

—Prep Squadron, 1 vol. 2009. (Recon Academy Ser.). (ENG.). 64p. (gr. 3-3). lib. bdg. 26.65 *(978-1-4342-1168-2(1),* Recon Academy) Stone Arch Bks.

—Shadow Cell Scam, 1 vol. 2009. (Recon Academy Ser.). (ENG.). 64p. (gr. 3-3). lib. bdg. 26.65 *(978-1-4342-1166-8(5),* Recon Academy) Stone Arch Bks.

—Storm Surge, 1 vol. Arcana Studio Staff, illus. 2010. (Recon Academy Ser.). (ENG.). 64p. (gr. 3-3). 26.65 *(978-1-4342-1918-3(6),* Recon Academy) Stone Arch Bks.

—Teen Agent, 1 vol. Arcana Studio Staff, illus. 2010. (Recon Academy Ser.). (ENG.). 64p. (gr. 3-3). 26.65 *(978-1-4342-1916-9(X),* Recon Academy) Stone Arch Bks.

Floreen, Tim. Willful Machines. 2016. (ENG., Illus.). 384p. (YA). (gr. 9). pap. 10.99 *(978-1-4814-3278-8(8),* Simon Pulse) Simon Pulse.

Girard, Geoffrey. Truthers. 2017. (ENG.). 360p. (YA). (gr. 7-12). 17.99 *(978-1-5124-2779-0(9))* Lerner Publishing Group.

Grainger, A. J. Captive. 2016. (ENG.). 272p. (YA). (gr. 7). pap. 11.99 *(978-1-4814-2904-7(3))* Simon & Schuster Children's Publishing.

Gratz, Alan. Code of Honor. 2015. (ENG.). 288p. (J). (gr. 7). 17.99 *(978-0-545-69519-0(8),* Scholastic Pr.) Scholastic, Inc.

Hayes, Rosemary. Mixing It. 2007. (ENG.). 192p. (J). (gr. 4-7). per. *(978-1-84507-495-1(5))* Rough Guides, Ltd.

Heneghan, James B. Torn Away, 1 vol. 2003. (ENG.). 256p. (YA). (gr. 8-12). pap. 9.95 *(978-1-55143-263-2(3))* Orca Bk. Pubs. USA.

Higgins, Jack & Richards, Justin. First Strike. 2011. (Rich & Jade Ser.: Bk. 4). (ENG.). 240p. (YA). (gr. 7-18). 8.99 *(978-0-14-241909-0(5),* Speak) Penguin Young Readers Group.

—Sharp Shot. 2010. (Rich & Jade Ser.: Bk. 3). (ENG.). 240p. (YA). (gr. 7-18). 8.99 *(978-0-14-241730-0(0),* Speak) Penguin Young Readers Group.

T
U
V

Horowitz, Anthony. Ark Angel. (Alex Rider Ser.: Bk. 6). (ENG.). (J). (gr. 5-18). 2007. 352p. 8.99 (978-0-14-240738-7(0), Puffin Books) 2006. 336p. 17.99 (978-0-399-24152-9(3), Philomel Bks.) Penguin Young Readers Group.
—Ark Angel. 2007. (Alex Rider Ser.: Bk. 6). 326p. (gr. 5-9). 19.00 (978-0-7569-8134-1(4)) Perfection Learning Corp.
—Ark Angel. 2007. (Alex Rider Ser.: 6). 326p. lib. bdg. 19.65 (978-1-4177-7664-1(1), Turtleback) Turtleback Bks.
—Scorpia. (Alex Rider Ser.). (ENG.). (J). (gr. 5-18). 2006. 416p. pap. 8.99 (978-0-14-240578-9(7), Puffin Books) 2005. 336p. 17.99 (978-0-399-24151-2(5), Philomel Bks.) Penguin Young Readers Group.
—Scorpia Rising. (Alex Rider Ser.). (ENG.). (J). (gr. 5-18). 2012. 432p. 8.99 (978-0-14-241985-4(0), Puffin Books) 2011. 416p. 17.99 (978-0-399-25057-6(3), Philomel Bks.) Penguin Young Readers Group.
—Scorpia Rising, 9 vols. (J). 2012. 90.75 (978-1-4561-3363-4(2)) 2012. 1.25 (978-1-4640-0577-0(X)) 2012. 256.75 (978-1-4561-3362-7(4)) 2011. 122.75 (978-1-4561-3365-8(9)) 2011. 120.75 (978-1-4561-3367-2(5)) Recorded Bks., Inc.
—Scorpia Rising. 2012. (Alex Rider Ser.: 9). lib. bdg. 19.65 (978-0-606-23638-6(4), Turtleback) Turtleback Bks.
—Skeleton Key. Kanako & Yuzuru, illus. 2009. (Alex Rider Ser.: Bk. 3). (ENG.). 176p. (J). (gr. 5-18). pap. 14.99 (978-0-399-25418-5(8), Philomel Bks.) Penguin Young Readers Group.
—Skeleton Key. (Alex Rider Ser.: Bk. 3). (ENG.). (J). (gr. 5-18). 2006. 368p. 8.99 (978-0-14-240614-4(7), Puffin Books) 2003. 240p. 17.99 (978-0-399-23777-5(1), Philomel Bks.) Penguin Young Readers Group.
—Stormbreaker. Damerum, Kanako et al, illus. 2006. (Alex Rider Ser.). (ENG.). 144p. (J). (gr. 5-18). pap. 14.99 (978-0-399-24633-3(9), Philomel Bks.) Penguin Young Readers Group.
—Stormbreaker. 2006. (Alex Rider Ser.: Bk. 1). (ENG.). 304p. (J). (gr. 5-18). 8.99 (978-0-14-240611-3(2), Puffin Books) Penguin Young Readers Group.
—Stormbreaker. 2004. (Alex Rider Ser.: Bk. 1). 208p. (J). (gr. 4-7). pap. 38.00 incl. audio (978-0-8072-2277-5(1), Listening Library) Random Hse. Audio Publishing Group.
Jenkins, Jerry B. & Fabry, Chris. Dead End. 2006. (Red Rock Mysteries Ser.: 15). (ENG.). 248p. (YA). (gr. 3-7). per. 6.99 (978-1-4143-0154-9(5), Tyndale Kids) Tyndale Hse. Pubs.
Jones, Don. When the Firewood Comes. 2009. 86p. pap. 19.95 (978-1-4489-9667-4(8)) America Star Bks.
Kalkowski, John. Red Cell. 2010. 164p. 21.95 (978-1-4502-1209-0(3)) iUniverse, Inc.
Kass, Pnina Moed. Real Time. 2006. (ENG.). 192p. (YA). (gr. 7-12). reprint ed. pap. 7.99 (978-0-618-69174-6(X)) Houghton Mifflin Harcourt Publishing Co.
Klavan, Andrew. Hostage Run, 1 vol. 2016. (MindWar Trilogy Ser.). (ENG.). 352p. (YA). pap. 9.99 (978-1-4016-8897-4(7)) Nelson, Thomas Inc.
—The Last Thing I Remember, 1 vol. 2010. (Homelanders Ser.: 1). (ENG.). 352p. (YA). pap. 9.99 (978-1-59554-586-2(7)) Nelson, Thomas Inc.
Klein. Operation Firestorm. (Bloomfield 3-in-1 Mini Ser.). (J). 17.99 (978-1-56871-309-0(6)) Targum Pr., Inc.
Kuipers, Alice. Lost for Words. 2010. 224p. (YA). (gr. 8-18). 16.99 (978-0-06-142922-4(8), HarperTeen) HarperCollins Pubs.
Langston, Laura. In Plain Sight. 2017. (Orca Soundings Ser.). lib. bdg. 20.80 **(978-0-606-40455-6(4))** Turtleback Bks.
Lebbon, Tim. Contagion. 2013. (Toxic City Ser.). (ENG.). 219p. (J). (gr. 7). 17.99 (978-1-61614-821-8(7)) Prometheus Bks., Pubs.
Lee, Fonda. Exo. 2017. (ENG.). 384p. (J). (gr. 7). 17.99 (978-0-545-93343-8(9), Scholastic Pr.) Scholastic, Inc.
Levithan, David. Love Is the Higher Law. 2010. (ENG.). 176p. (YA). (gr. 7). pap. 9.99 (978-0-375-83469-1(9), Knopf Bks. for Young Readers) Random Hse. Children's Bks.
Levy, Marilyn. Checkpoints. 2009. (ENG.). 256p. (gr. 7). pap. 14.95 (978-0-8276-0870-2(5)) Jewish Pubn. Society.
Logie, Mark. Storm Troopers Tz9. 2011. 108p. pap. (978-0-7552-1333-7(5)) Authors OnLine, Ltd.
McKay, Sharon E. Thunder over Kandahar. Gerszak, Rafal, photos by. 2010. (ENG., Illus.). 264p. (YA). (gr. 7-12). 19.95 (978-1-55451-267-6(0), 9781554512676); 3rd ed. pap. 12.95 (978-1-55451-266-9(2), 9781554512669) Annick Pr., Ltd. CAN. Dist: Publishers Group West (PGW).
McKenzie, Sophie. Every Second Counts. 2016. 405p. (YA). pap. (978-1-4814-3927-5(8)) Simon & Schuster Children's Publishing.
—In a Split Second. 2015. (ENG., Illus.). 368p. (YA). (gr. 7). 17.99 (978-1-4814-1394-7(5)) Simon & Schuster Children's Publishing.
Meminger, Neesha. Shine, Coconut Moon. 2010. (ENG.). 256p. (YA). (gr. 9). pap. 10.99 (978-1-4424-0305-5(5), McElderry, Margaret K. Bks.) McElderry, Margaret K. Bks.
Mohsenian, Javad. 9/11 Children. 2006. (ENG.). 128p. per. 10.95 (978-0-7414-3218-6(8)) Infinity Publishing.
Monaghan, Annabel. Double Digit. (ENG.). 192p. (YA). (gr. 7). 2015. pap. 7.99 (978-0-544-33620-9(8), HMH Books For Young Readers) 2014. 16.99 (978-0-544-10577-5(X)) Houghton Mifflin Harcourt Publishing Co.
—A Girl Named Digit: Under Cover, under Pressure, under Estimated. 2013. (ENG.). 192p. (YA). (gr. 7). pap. 8.99 (978-0-544-02248-5(3)) Houghton Mifflin Harcourt Publishing Co.
—A Girl Named Digit: Undercover, under Pressure, & Underestimated. 2012. (ENG., Illus.). 192p. (YA). (gr. 7). 16.99 (978-0-547-66852-9(X)) Houghton Mifflin Harcourt Publishing Co.
Morris, Robert. Grandma Ursu, Think Blue. 2003. (Illus.). 32p. (J). 15.95 (978-0-9741634-0-6(6)) Ursu Pubns.
Muchamore, Robert. The Recruit. Aggs, John, illus. 2012. (ENG.). 176p. (YA). (gr. 7-17). pap. 12.99 (978-1-4449-0318-8(7)) Hodder & Stoughton GBR. Dist: Hachette Bk. Group.
—The Recruit. 2010. (Cherub Ser.: 1). (ENG.). 352p. (YA). (gr. 7). pap. 11.99 (978-1-4424-1360-3(3)); 17.99 (978-1-4169-9940-9(X)) Simon Pulse. (Simon Pulse).
—The Sleepwalker. 2015. (Cherub Ser.: 9). (ENG., Illus.). 336p. (YA). (gr. 7). 17.99 (978-1-4814-5663-0(6), Simon Pulse) Simon Pulse.
Norris, Elizabeth. Unraveling. (Unraveling Ser.: 1). (ENG.). (YA). (gr. 8). 2013. 480p. pap. 9.99 (978-0-06-210374-1(1)) 2012. 464p. 17.99 (978-0-06-210373-4(3)) HarperCollins Pubs.
O'Malley Cerra, Kerry. Just a Drop of Water. 2014. (ENG.). 320p. (J). (gr. 2-7). 14.95 (978-1-62914-613-3(7), Sky Pony Pr.) Skyhorse Publishing Co., Inc.
Peretti, Frank E. Trapped at the Bottom of the Sea. 2004. (Cooper Kids Adventure Ser.: No. 4). 144p. (gr. 4-7). 5.99 (978-0-89107-594-3(1)); Vol. 4. (J). (gr. 3-6). pap. 6.99 (978-1-58134-621-3(2)) Crossway.
Plum-Ucci, Carol. Fire Will Fall. 2011. (ENG.). 492p. (YA). (gr. 9). pap. 25.99 (978-0-547-55007-7(3)) Houghton Mifflin Harcourt Publishing Co.
Prose, Francine. Bullyville. 2007. 260p. (YA). (gr. 7-12). 16.99 (978-0-06-057497-0(6)); lib. bdg. 17.89 (978-0-06-057498-7(4)) HarperCollins Pubs. (HarperTeen).
Readler, Blaine C. Under the Radar: The Spy Drone Adventure. 2006. (ENG.). 248p. (J). (gr. 7-12). per. (978-1-933255-18-7(8)) DNA Pr.
Rees, Celia. This Is Not Forgiveness. 2012. (ENG.). 288p. (YA). (gr. 9-12). 17.99 (978-1-59990-776-5(3), 9781599907765, Bloomsbury USA Childrens) Bloomsbury Publishing USA.
Rhodes, Jewell Parker. Towers Falling. 2016. (ENG., Illus.). 240p. (J). (gr. 3-7). 16.99 (978-0-316-26222-4(6)) Little, Brown Bks. for Young Readers.
Saddleback Educational Publishing Staff, ed. Neptune, 1 vol. unabr. ed. 2011. (Heights Ser.). (ENG.). 50p. (gr. 5-8). pap. 7.95 (978-1-61651-285-9(7)) Saddleback Educational Publishing, Inc.
Seabrooke, Brenda. Stonewolf. 2004. (ENG.). 240p. (J). (gr. 7-18). tchr. ed. 16.95 (978-0-8234-1848-0(0)) Holiday Hse., Inc.
Smibert, Angie. The Forgetting Curve, 0 vols. 2012. (Memento Nora Ser.: 2). (ENG.). 192p. (YA). (gr. 8-12). 16.99 (978-0-7614-6265-1(1), 9780761462651, Amazon Children's Publishing) Amazon Publishing.
—Memento Nora, 0 vols. 2013. (Memento Nora Ser.: 1). (ENG.). 192p. (J). (gr. 7-10). pap. 9.99 (978-1-4778-1624-0(0), 9781477816240, Amazon Children's Publishing) Amazon Publishing.
Smith, Dan. Boy X. 2017. (J). **(978-1-338-17150-1(X))** Scholastic, Inc.
Smith, Roland. Independence Hall. (I, Q Ser.: Bk. 1). (ENG., 312p. (gr. 5-9). 2009. Illus.). (J). 15.95 (978-1-58536-468-8(1)) 2008. (YA). pap. 8.95 (978-1-58536-325-4(1)) Sleeping Bear Pr.
—The White House. 2010. (I, Q Ser.: Bk. 2). (ENG.). 256p. (YA). (gr. 6-8). 15.95 (978-1-58536-478-7(9), 202191); pap. 8.95 (978-1-58536-456-5(8), 202378) Sleeping Bear Pr.
Smith, Roland & Spradlin, Michael P. The Windy City, Bk.5. 2014. (I, Q Ser.). (ENG.). 240p. (YA). (gr. 5-7). 9.99 (978-1-58536-823-5(7), 202902) Sleeping Bear Pr.
Spradlin, Michael P. & Smith, Roland. Alcatraz. 2014. (I, Q Ser.). (ENG.). 272p. (J). (gr. 5-7). 16.99 (978-1-58536-826-6(1), 203667); pap. 9.99 (978-1-58536-825-9(3), 203727) Sleeping Bear Pr.
Stanley, Diane. Saving Sky. (ENG.). 208p. (J). (gr. 3-7). 2012. pap. 6.99 (978-0-06-123907-6(0)) 2010. 15.99 (978-0-06-123905-2(4)) HarperCollins Pubs.
Strasser, Todd. American Terrorist. 2017. (YA). pap. (978-1-4814-6134-4(6), Simon & Schuster Bks. For Young Readers) Simon & Schuster Bks. For Young Readers.
Stratton, Allan. Borderline. (ENG.). (YA). (gr. 8). 2012. 320p. pap. 9.99 (978-0-06-145113-3(4)) 2010. (Illus.). 304p. 16.99 (978-0-06-145111-9(8)) HarperCollins Pubs. (HarperTeen).
Tarshis, Lauren. I Survived the Attacks of September 11, 2001. 2012. (I Survived Ser.: 6). (ENG.). 112p. (J). (gr. 2-5). pap. 4.99 (978-0-545-20700-3(2), Scholastic Paperbacks) Scholastic, Inc.
—I Survived the Attacks of September 11, 2001. 2012. (I Survived . Ser.: No. 6). lib. bdg. 14.75 (978-0-606-26205-7(9), Turtleback) Turtleback Bks.
Taylor, Ed. The Dirty Bombers: Terrorism with a Twist. 2013. (ENG.). 192p. pap. (978-1-78306-044-3(1)) Troubador Publishing Ltd.
Terry, Teri. Fractured. 2014. (Slated Ser.: 2). (ENG.). 352p. (YA). (gr. 7). pap. 9.99 (978-0-14-242504-6(4), Speak) Penguin Young Readers Group.
Trout, Richard. Czar of Alaska: The Cross of Charlemagne, 1 vol. 2005. (MacGregor Family Adventure Ser.: 4). (ENG.). 256p. (YA). (gr. k-3). 16.99 (978-1-58980-328-2(0)) Pelican Publishing Co., Inc.
Tzvieli, Neta. The Private Eyes & the Mysterious Submarine. 2009. 149p. 17.99 (978-1-59826-286-5(6)) Feldheim Pubs.
Walsh, Alice. A Long Way from Home, 1 vol. 2012. (ENG.). 232p. (J). (gr. 6-8). 11.95 (978-1-926920-79-5(1)) Second Story Pr. CAN. Dist: Orca Bk. Pubs. USA.
Walters, Eric. We All Fall Down. 2006. (ENG.). 192p. (J). (gr. 5). pap. 9.99 (978-0-385-66192-8(4), Doubleday Canada) Penguin Random House Canada Young Readers CAN. Dist: Penguin Random Hse. LLC.
Waudby, Jeannie. One of Us. 2015. (ENG.). 320p. (YA). (gr. 7). 16.95 (978-0-7624-5799-1(6), Running Pr. Kids) Running Pr. Bk. Pubs.
Wells, Robison. Blackout. (Blackout Ser.: 1). (ENG.). (YA). (gr. 8). 2014. 448p. pap. 9.99 (978-0-06-202613-2(5)) 2013. 432p. 17.99 (978-0-06-202612-5(7)) HarperCollins Pubs. (HarperTeen).
—Dead Zone. 2014. (Blackout Ser.: 2). (ENG.). 384p. (YA). (gr. 8). 17.99 (978-0-06-227502-8(X), HarperTeen) HarperCollins Pubs.
Williams, David Morgan. Ebony & Ivory. 2007. (ENG.). 136p. (J). pap. 11.95 (978-0-86243-972-9(8)) Y Lolfa GBR. Dist: Dufour Editions, Inc.
Willis, Meredith Sue. Meli's Way. 2015. 178p. (YA). (978-1-932727-15-9(9)) Montemayor Pr.
Woolston, Blythe. Black Helicopters. 2015. (ENG.). 176p. (YA). (gr. 9). pap. 7.99 (978-0-7636-7171-6(1)) Candlewick Pr.
Zucker, Jonny. Stunt Girl. 2009. pap. 1.00 (978-1-4074-4531-1(6)) Recorded Bks., Inc.

TESLA, NIKOLA, 1856-1943

Aldrich, Lisa J. Nikola Tesla & the Taming of Electricity. 2005. (Profiles in Science Ser.). (Illus.). 160p. (J). (gr. 3-7). lib. bdg. 26.95 (978-1-931798-46-4(X)) Reynolds, Morgan Inc.
Diggory, Nikki. Inventor Nikola Tesla. 2013. (Rosen Readers Ser.). (ENG.). 24p. (J). (gr. 3-4). pap. 49.50 (978-1-4777-2507-8(5)); pap. 8.25 (978-1-4777-2506-1(7)) Rosen Publishing Group, Inc., The. (Rosen Classroom).
Hardyman, Robyn. Nikola Tesla & Thomas Edison. 2014. (Dynamic Duos of Science Ser.). 48p. (YA). (gr. 5-8). pap. 84.30 (978-1-4824-1285-7(3)) Stevens, Gareth Publishing LLLP.
Jacobson, Fiona. Nikola Tesla Lights the World. 2013. (InfoMax Readers Ser.). (ENG.). 24p. (J). (gr. 3-4). pap. 8.25 (978-1-4777-2510-8(5)); pap. 49.50 (978-1-4777-2511-5(3)) Rosen Publishing Group, Inc., The. (Rosen Classroom).
Kulling, Monica & Slavin, Bill. Zap! Nikola Tesla Takes Charge. 2016. (Great Idea Ser.). (ENG., Illus.). 32p. (J). (gr. k-3). 17.99 (978-1-77049-522-7(3), Tundra Bks.) Tundra Bks. CAN. Dist: Penguin Random Hse. LLC.
Marsico, Katie. Inventor, Engineer, & Physicist Nikola Tesla. 2017. (STEM Trailblazer Bios Ser.). (ENG.). 32p. (J). (gr. 2-5). 26.65 **(978-1-5124-3448-4(5))** Lerner Publishing Group.
McPherson, Stephanie Sammartino. War of the Currents: Thomas Edison vs. Nikola Tesla. 2012. (Scientific Rivalries & Scandals Ser.). (ENG., Illus.). 64p. (J). (gr. 6-12). lib. bdg. 33.27 (978-0-7613-5487-1(5)) Lerner Publishing Group.
O'Shei, Tim. Marconi & Tesla: Pioneers of Radio Communication. 2008. (Inventors Who Changed the World Ser.). (Illus.). 128p. (J). (gr. 3-7). lib. bdg. 34.60 (978-1-59845-076-7(X), MyReportLinks.com Bks.) Enslow Pubs., Inc.
Rusch, Elizabeth. Electrical Wizard. 2015. (Candlewick Biographies Ser.). lib. bdg. 14.75 (978-0-606-36873-5(6)) Turtleback Bks.
—Electrical Wizard: How Nikola Tesla Lit up the World. Dominguez, Oliver, illus. (Candlewick Biographies Ser.). (ENG.). (J). 2015. 56p. (gr. 3-7). 14.99 (978-0-7636-7978-1(X)) 2013. 40p. (gr. 2-5). 16.99 (978-0-7636-5855-7(3)) Candlewick Pr.
Yount, Lisa. Nikola Tesla. 2011. (Trailblazers in Science & Technology Ser.). 146p. (gr. 6-12). 35.00 (978-1-60413-670-8(7), Chelsea Hse.) Facts On File, Inc.

TEST PILOTS

see Air Pilots; Airplanes—Testing

TESTS

see Educational Tests and Measurements

TEXAS

Barenblat, Rachel. Texas. Porras, Carlos & D'Andrea, Patricia, trs. from ENG. 2003. (World Almanac Biblioteca de los Estados). (SPA., Illus.). 48p. (gr. 4-9). lib. bdg. 31.00 (978-0-8368-5547-0(7), Gareth Stevens Learning Library) Stevens, Gareth Publishing LLLP.
Bodden, Valerie. Texas. 2010. (Let's Explore America Ser.). 24p. (J). (gr. k-2). 19.95 (978-1-58341-837-6(7)) Creative Co., The.
Boehm Jerome, Kate. Austin & the State of Texas: Cool Stuff Every Kid Should Know. 2011. (Arcadia Kids Ser.). (ENG., Illus.). 48p. (J). (gr. 3-6). pap. 9.99 (978-1-4396-0088-7(0)) Arcadia Publishing.
Bredeson, Carmen. Texas. (Rookie Espanol: Geografia Ser.). (J). (gr. k-2). 2005. (SPA., Illus.). 32p. pap. 5.95 (978-0-516-25516-3(9), Children's Pr.) 2004. 19.50 (978-0-516-25110-3(4), Watts, Franklin) Scholastic Library Publishing.
Caravantes, Peggy. O. Henry: William Sidney Porter: Texas Cowboy Writer. 2003. (J). (978-1-57168-768-5(8), Eakin Pr.) Eakin Pr.
Davis, Lucile. The Caddo of Texas. 2009. (Library of Native Americans Ser.). 64p. (gr. 4-4). 58.50 (978-1-60853-743-3(9), PowerKids Pr.) Rosen Publishing Group, Inc., The.
Doeden, Matt. Yao Ming. 2009. (Sports Heroes & Legends Ser.). (ENG.). 120p. (gr. 5-12). 30.60 (978-0-7613-4227-4(3)) Lerner Publishing Group.
Downey, Tika. Texas: The Lone Star State. (Illus.). 24p. (J). 2010. pap. 8.25 (978-1-4358-3344-9(9), 1300531) 2009. lib. bdg. 22.60 (978-1-4042-8112-7(6), 1300531) Rosen Publishing Group, Inc., The. (PowerKids Pr.).
Flatt, Lizann. Life in an Industrial City. 2010. (Learn about Urban Life Ser.). (ENG., Illus.). 32p. (J). (gr. 4-9). pap. (978-0-7787-7402-0(3)); lib. bdg. (978-0-7787-7392-4(2)) Crabtree Publishing Co.
Flynn, Jean. Texas Women Who Dared to Be First. 2004. (Illus.). 144p. (gr. 4-7). 18.95 (978-1-57168-232-1(5)) Eakin Pr.
Gamble, Adam & Jasper, Mark. Good Night Austin. Palmer, Ruth & Veno, Joe, illus. 2015. (Good Night Our World Ser.). (ENG.). 20p. (J). (— 1). bds. 9.95 (978-1-60219-233-1(2)) Good Night Bks.
Garza, Carmen Lomas, illus. In My Family. 2011.Tr. of En Mi Familia. (ENG & SPA.). 32p. (C). (gr. 1-4). pap. 24.95 (978-0-89239-163-9(4)) National Geographic School Publishing, Inc.
Golden, Nancy. Life with the Comanches: The Kidnapping of Cynthia Ann Parker. 2009. (Great Moments in American History Ser.). 32p. (gr. 3-3). 47.90 (978-1-61513-146-4(9)) Rosen Publishing Group, Inc., The.
Gregory, Josh. Texas. 2017. (True Book — My United States Ser.). (ENG.). 48p. (J). pap. 7.95 **(978-0-531-23293-4(X)**, Children's Pr.) Scholastic Library Publishing.
Hanson-Harding, Alexandra. Texas. 2008. (From Sea to Shining Sea, Second Ser.). (ENG., Illus.). 80p. (J). (gr. 3-5). pap. 7.95 (978-0-531-18809-5(4), Children's Pr.) Scholastic Library Publishing.
Herold, Vickey. A Cattle Town: Forth Worth. 2006. (J). pap. (978-1-4108-6427-7(8)) Benchmark Education Co.
Kadair, Deborah Ousley. I Spy in the Texas Sky, 1 vol. Kadair, Deborah Ousley, illus. 2009. (ENG., Illus.). 32p. (J). (gr. k-3). 16.99 (978-1-58980-654-2(9)) Pelican Publishing Co., Inc.
Levy, Janey. Juneteenth: Celebrating the End of Slavery. (Reading Room Collection 2 Ser.). 24p. 2009. (gr. 3-4). 42.50 (978-1-60851-976-7(7), PowerKids Pr.) 2003. (Illus.). (J). lib. bdg. 22.60 (978-0-8239-3711-0(9)) Rosen Publishing Group, Inc., The.
Marsh, Carole. Texas Current Events Projects: 30 Cool, Activities, Crafts, Experiments & More for Kids to Do to Learn about Your State! 2003. (Texas Experience Ser.). 32p. (gr. k-5). pap. 5.95 (978-0-635-02062-8(9), Marsh, Carole Bks.) Gallopade International.
—Texas Geography Projects: 30 Cool, Activities, Crafts, Experiments & More for Kids to Do to Learn about Your State! 2003. (Texas Experience Ser.). 32p. (gr. k-5). pap. 5.95 (978-0-635-01861-8(6), Marsh, Carole Bks.) Gallopade International.
—Texas Government Projects: 30 Cool, Activities, Crafts, Experiments & More for Kids to Do to Learn about Your State! 2003. (Texas Experience Ser.). 32p. (gr. k-5). pap. 5.95 (978-0-635-01962-2(0), Marsh, Carole Bks.) Gallopade International.
—Texas People Projects: 30 Cool, Activities, Crafts, Experiments & More for Kids to Do to Learn about Your State! 2003. (Texas Experience Ser.). 32p. (gr. k-5). pap. 5.95 (978-0-635-02012-3(2), Marsh, Carole Bks.) Gallopade International.
—Texas Symbols & Facts Projects: 30 Cool, Activities, Crafts, Experiments & More for Kids to Do to Learn about Your State! 2003. (Texas Experience Ser.). 32p. (gr. k-5). pap. 5.95 (978-0-635-01912-7(4), Marsh, Carole Bks.) Gallopade International.
McAdam, Claudia Cangilla. Do You See What I See? Texas. 2007. (Illus.). (J). (gr. 3-7). 14.95 (978-1-56579-589-1(X), Westcliffe Pubs.) Bower Hse.
McNeil, Niki, et al. HOCPP 1120 Texas. 2006. spiral bd. 24.00 (978-1-60308-120-7(8)) In the Hands of a Child.
Murray, Julie. Texas, 1 vol. 2006. (United States Ser.). (ENG., Illus.). 32p. (gr. 2-4). 27.07 (978-1-59197-702-5(9), Buddy Bks.) ABDO Publishing Co.
Obregon, Jose Maria. Texas. De Leon, Mauricio Velzaquez, tr. 2005. (Bilingual Library of the United States of America Ser.: Set 1). (ENG & SPA., Illus.). 32p. (J). (gr. 3-6). lib. bdg. 25.25 (978-1-4042-3109-2(9)) Rosen Publishing Group, Inc., The.
Obregón, José María. Texas. 2009. (Bilingual Library of the United States of America Ser.). 32p. (gr. 2-2). 47.90 (978-1-60853-387-9(5), Editorial Buenas Letras) Rosen Publishing Group, Inc., The.
Parker, Bridget. Texas. 2016. (States Ser.). (ENG., Illus.). 32p. (gr. 3-4). lib. bdg. 27.32 (978-1-5157-0431-7(9)) Next Page Pr., The.
Parker, Janice. Texas: The Lone Star State. 2016. (J). **(978-1-5105-2095-0(3))** SmartBook Media, Inc.
Pelta, Kathy. Texas. (J). 2012. lib. bdg. 25.26 (978-0-7613-4559-6(0), Lerner Pubns.) 2nd rev. exp. ed. 2003. (Illus.). 84p. (gr. 3-6). pap. 6.95 (978-0-8225-4142-4(4)) Lerner Publishing Group.
Peppas, Lynn. Why Charles Goodnight Matters to Texas. 2014. (Illus.). 32p. (J). lib. bdg. 26.25 (978-1-4777-0907-8(X)) Rosen Publishing Group, Inc., The.
—Why Martín de Léon Matters to Texas. 2014. (Illus.). 32p. (J). lib. bdg. 26.25 (978-1-4777-0916-0(9)) Rosen Publishing Group, Inc., The.
Perry, Lucinda. The Ninth Child: Third Edition. 2008. 256p. pap. 19.95 (978-0-595-52455-6(9)) iUniverse, Inc.
Puck. 123 Texas. Somers, Kevin, illus. 2009. (Cool Counting Bks.). (ENG.). 22p. (J). (gr. k — 1). bds. 8.95 (978-0-9796213-6-9(4)) Duo Pr. LLC.
Rappoport, Ken. Texas a & M Aggies, 1 vol. 2013. (Inside College Football Set 2 Ser.). (ENG.). 48p. (J). (gr. 3-6). lib. bdg. 32.79 (978-1-61783-657-2(5), SportsZone) ABDO Publishing Co.
Salch, Megan. 100+ Activities for Houston Kids 2006. 2005. (Illus.). 40p. pap. 19.95 (978-0-9776154-0-7(5)) Salch, Megan F.
Sanford, William R. & Green, Carl R. Richard King: Courageous Texas Cattleman. 2012. (Courageous Heroes of the American West Ser.). (Illus.). 48p. (J). pap. 8.95 (978-1-4644-0088-9(1)) Enslow Pubs., Inc.
Sasek, Miroslav. This Is Texas. 2006. (This Is ... Ser.). (ENG., Illus.). 64p. (J). (gr. 2-12). 17.95 (978-0-7893-1389-8(8)) Universe Publishing.
Smith, Karla. All Around Texas: Regions & Resources. 2003. (Heinemann State Studies). (Illus.). 48p. (J). lib. bdg. 27.07 (978-1-4034-0686-6(3)) Heinemann-Raintree.
Somervill, Barbara A. Texas. 2011. (America the Beautiful, Third Ser.). (Illus.). 144p. (J). pap. 12.95 (978-0-531-22918-7(1), Children's Pr.) Scholastic Library Publishing.
—Texas (Revised Edition) 2014. (America the Beautiful Ser.: 3). (ENG., Illus.). 144p. (J). lib. bdg. 40.00 (978-0-531-24898-0(4)) Scholastic Library Publishing.
Stumpff, April D. & Messersmith, Patrick. Ann Richards: A Woman's Place Is in the Dome. 2006. (Stars of Texas Ser.: 6). (ENG., Illus.). 80p. (gr. 4-7). 14.95 (978-1-933337-12-8(5)) State Hse. Pr.
Tingle, Tim. Saltypie: A Choctaw Journey from Darkness into Light. Clarkson, Karen, illus. 2010. (ENG.). 40p. (J). (gr. 2-6). 17.95 (978-1-933693-67-5(3)) Cinco Puntos Pr.
Wade, Mary Dodson. Uniquely Texas. 2003. (Heinemann State Studies). (Illus.). 48p. (J). lib. bdg. 27.07 (978-1-4034-0691-0(X)) Heinemann-Raintree.
Walker, Paul Robert. Remember the Alamo: Texians, Tejanos, & Mexicans Tell Their Stories. 2007. (Remember Ser.). (ENG., Illus.). 64p. (gr. 5-8). lib. bdg. 27.90 (978-1-4263-0011-0(5), National Geographic Children's Bks.) National Geographic Society.
Weintraub, A. How to Draw Texas's Sights & Symbols. 2009. (Kid's Guide to Drawing America Ser.). 32p. (gr. k-k). 50.50 (978-1-61511-097-1(6), PowerKids Pr.) Rosen Publishing Group, Inc., The.
White, Andrea & Mimi, Vance. Tummies on the Run. Shepperson, Rob, illus. 2012. 32p. pap. 11.95 (978-1-60898-134-2(7)) namelos llc.

TEXAS—FICTION

Alegria, Malin. Border Town #2: Quince Clash. 2012. (Border Town Ser.). (ENG.). 192p. (J). (gr. 7). pap. 5.99 (978-0-545-40241-5(7), Scholastic Paperbacks) Scholastic, Inc.
—Pueblo Fronterizo No. 2: Guerra de Quinceañeras. 2013. (Pueblo Fronterizo Ser.: 2). (SPA.). 208p. (J). (gr. 7). pap. 5.99 (978-0-545-56565-3(0), Scholastic en Espanol) Scholastic, Inc.
Alikhan, Salima. The Pied Piper of Austin, 1 vol. Alikhan, Salima, illus. 2009. (ENG., Illus.). 32p. (J). (gr. k-3). 16.99 (978-1-58980-629-0(8)) Pelican Publishing Co., Inc.

Alter, Judy. Sam Houston Is My Hero. 2003. (Chaparral Bks.). (ENG.). 130p. (J). pap. 11.95 (978-0-87565-277-1(8)) Texas Christian Univ. Pr.

Altsheler, Joseph A. The Texan Scouts. 2007. (Texan Ser.: Vol. 2). 272p. reprint ed. per. 10.45 (978-1-60424-305-5(8), Book Jungle) Standard Pubns., Inc.

—The Texan Scouts: A Story of the Alamo & Goliad. 2006. (Texan Ser.). 352p. (J). reprint ed. pap. 15.95 (978-1-4218-1881-8(7), 1st World Library - Literary Society) 1st World Publishing, Inc.

—The Texan Scouts: A Story of the Alamo & Goliad. l.t. ed. (Texan Ser.: Vol. 2). (J). reprint ed. 2007. (ENG.). 316p. pap. 24.99 (978-1-4264-3365-8(4)) 2010. 376p. (gr. 4-7). pap. 33.75 (978-1-177-24805-1(0)) 2008. 320p. 29.99 (978-0-554-22920-1(X)) 2008. 320p. 28.99 (978-0-554-32223-0(4)) 2007. (ENG.). 282p. pap. 21.99 (978-1-4264-3310-8(7)) Creative Media Partners, LLC.

—The Texan Scouts: A Story of the Alamo & Goliad. 2006. (Texan Ser.: Vol. 2). (J). reprint ed. pap. (978-1-4065-0826-0(8)) Dodo Pr.

—The Texan Scouts: A Story of the Alamo & Goliad. 2007. (Texan Ser.: Vol. 2). 208p. (J). reprint ed. per. (978-1-4068-1691-4(4)) Echo Library.

—The Texan Scouts: A Story of the Alamo & Goliad. 2010. (Texan Ser.: Vol. 2). (Illus.). 184p. (J). (gr. 4-7). reprint ed. pap. 19.99 (978-1-4432-3075-9(8)) General Bks. LLC.

—The Texan Scouts: A Story of the Alamo & Goliad. (Texan Ser.: Vol. 2). (J). reprint ed. 2012. 380p. (gr. 4-7). pap. (978-1-290-32714-5(9)) 2010. 258p. pap. (978-1-4076-1525-7(4)) HardPr.

—The Texan Scouts: A Story of the Alamo & Goliad. (Texan Ser.: Vol. 2). (J). reprint ed. 2011. 362p. (gr. 4-7). 46.95 (978-1-169-83723-2(9)) 2010. 362p. (gr. 4-7). 37.56 (978-1-163-21368-1(3)) 2010. 362p. (gr. 4-7). pap. 25.56 (978-1-162-64067-9(7)) 2004. 360p. 46.95 (978-1-4326-1538-3(6)) 2004. pap. 31.95 (978-1-4179-1479-1(3)) Kessinger Publishing, LLC.

—The Texan Scouts: A Story of the Alamo & Goliad. 2008. (Texan Ser.: Vol. 2). 364p. (J). reprint ed. per. (978-1-4086-5013-4(4)) Read Bks.

—The Texan Scouts: A Story of the Alamo & Goliad. 2011. (Texan Ser.: Vol. 1). 290p. (J). (gr. 4-7). reprint ed. pap. (978-3-8424-7933-3(6)) Tredition GmbH.

—The Texan Star: The Story of a Great Fight for Liberty. 2006. (Texan Ser.: Vol. 1). 364p. (J). reprint ed. 31.95 (978-1-4218-1782-8(9)); pap. 15.95 (978-1-4218-1882-5(5)) 1st World Publishing, Inc. (1st World Library - Literary Society).

—The Texan Star: The Story of a Great Fight for Liberty. (Texan Ser.: Vol. 1). (J). reprint ed. 26.95 (978-0-8488-0729-0(4)) Amereon Ltd.

—The Texan Star: The Story of a Great Fight for Liberty. (Texan Ser.: Vol. 1). (J). 2010. 398p. pap. 33.75 (978-1-145-48797-0(1)) 2007. (ENG.). 328p. pap. 24.99 (978-1-4264-9137-5(9)) 2010. 398p. (gr. 4-7). reprint ed. pap. 33.75 (978-1-177-71810-3(3)) 2008. 332p. reprint ed. 28.99 (978-0-554-34751-6(2)) 2008. 332p. reprint ed. 29.99 (978-0-554-25448-7(4)) 2007. (ENG.). 296p. reprint ed. pap. 21.99 (978-1-4264-9083-5(6)) Creative Media Partners, LLC.

—The Texan Star: The Story of a Great Fight for Liberty. 2006. (Texan Ser.: Vol. 1). (J). reprint ed. pap. (978-1-4065-0827-7(6)) Dodo Pr.

—The Texan Star: The Story of a Great Fight for Liberty. 2007. (Texan Ser.: Vol. 1). 216p. (J). reprint ed. per. (978-1-4068-1692-1(2)) Echo Library.

—The Texan Star: The Story of a Great Fight for Liberty. (Texan Ser.: Vol. 1). (J). reprint ed. 2010. 192p. (gr. 4-7). pap. 19.99 (978-1-4432-0955-7(4)) 2009. 228p. pap. 12.02 (978-1-150-78580-1(2)) General Bks. LLC.

—The Texan Star: The Story of a Great Fight for Liberty. 2010. (Texan Ser.: Vol. 1). 268p. (J). reprint ed. pap. (978-1-4076-1570-7(X)) HardPr.

—The Texan Star: The Story of a Great Fight for Liberty. 2011. (Texan Ser.: Vol. 1). 304p. (J). (gr. 4-7). reprint ed. pap. (978-3-8424-7958-6(1)) Tredition GmbH.

—The Texan Triumph: A Romance of the San Jacinto Campaign. (Texan Ser.: Vol. 3). (J). reprint ed. 24.95 (978-0-8488-0731-3(6)) Amereon Ltd.

Ames, Joseph B. Pete Cow Puncher a Story of the Texas Plains. Perard, Victor, illus. 2005. reprint ed. pap. 31.95 (978-0-7661-9421-2(3)) Kessinger Publishing, LLC.

Anderson, T. Neill. City of the Dead: Galveston Hurricane 1900. 2013. (J). pap. 16.95 (978-1-58089-515-6(8)); (ENG., Illus.). 144p. (YA). (gr. 7). 16.95 (978-1-58089-514-9(X)) Charlesbridge Publishing, Inc.

Archer, Jennifer. Through Her Eyes. 2012. (ENG.). 400p. (YA). (gr. 8). pap. 9.99 (978-0-06-183459-2(9), HarperTeen) HarperCollins Pubs.

Aryal, Aimee. How 'Bout Them Cowboys! De Angel, Miguel, illus. 2007. 24p. (J). 17.95 (978-1-932888-90-4(X)) Mascot Bks., Inc.

—How 'Bout Them Cowboys! Coloring Book. 2007. (YA). pap. 4.95 (978-1-932888-77-5(2)) Mascot Bks., Inc.

Aunt Julie. Paddleduck! #2: Julie, Living in Texas. 2011. 56p. pap. (978-1-4269-6656-9(3)) Trafford Publishing (UK) Ltd.

Badeaux, Dewey. Sam & Skully. Ball, Lauren, illus. 2013. 126p. pap. 12.99 (978-0-9884057-4-5(1)) Alligator Pr.

Bass, William E. Santa Revisits His Secret Little Helper. Salazar, Vivian, illus. 2012. 26p. 24.95 (978-1-4626-5396-6(0)) America Star Bks.

Bauer, Joan. Rules of the Road. 2005. (ENG.). 208p. (YA). (gr. 7-7). pap. 8.99 (978-0-14-240425-6(X), Speak) Penguin Young Readers Group.

Bauld, Jane Scoggins. Hector Visits His Country Cousin, Vol. 3. Laronde, Gary, illus. 2003. (Hector's Escapades Ser.). 25p. (gr. -1). per. 7.95 (978-1-57168-676-3(2)) Eakin Pr.

Bedford, David A. Angela. 2009. 190p. 25.50 (978-1-60860-755-6(0), Eloquent Bks.) Strategic Book Publishing & Rights Agency (SBPRA).

Bertrand, Diane Gonzales. The F Factor. 2010. 256p. (YA). (gr. 6-18). pap. 12.95 (978-1-55885-598-4(X), Piñata Books) Arte Publico Pr.

Bhakta, Sanjini. My Life as a Dollar Bill. 2010. 28p. pap. 12.95 (978-1-4520-6152-8(1)) AuthorHouse.

Blair, Eric. Pecos Bill, 1 vol. Chambers-Goldberg, Micah, illus. 2013. (My First Classic Story Ser.).Tr. of Pecos Bill. (ENG.). 32p. (gr. k-3). pap. 7.10 (978-1-4795-1860-9(3), My First Classic Story) Picture Window Bks.

Blue, Parker. Catch Me. 2015. (ENG., Illus.). 222p. (J). pap. 14.95 (978-1-61194-623-9(9)) BelleBks., Inc.

Borgia, Mary. Tales of the Texas Mermaid: The Boot. 2006. (Illus.). 47p. (J). 17.95 (978-0-9778451-0-1(9)) Goretti Publishing.

—Tales of the Texas Mermaid: The Charro. 2007. (J). 17.95 (978-0-9778451-1-8(7)) Goretti Publishing.

Borntrager, Mary Christner. Polly. 2015. (ENG.). 176p. (YA). (gr. 4-7). pap. 9.99 (978-0-8361-3670-8(5)) Herald Pr.

Bradley, Sharon. Walking Away from Texas. 2004. 112p. (YA). pap. 10.95 (978-0-595-32672-3(2)) iUniverse, Inc.

Brehm, David L. Willy Nilly Volume 1. Claerhout, Paul, illus. 2013. 94p. (J). pap. 19.95 (978-0-9860669-0-0(7)) Blue Logic Publishing.

Brett, Jan. Armadillo Rodeo. Brett, Jan, illus. 2004. (ENG., Illus.). 32p. (J). (gr. -1-3). pap. 6.99 (978-0-14-240125-5(0), Puffin Books) Penguin Young Readers Group.

A Brother's Sin. 2008. 84p. pap. 9.95 (978-1-934335-21-5(5)) WordWright.biz, Inc.

Bryant, Annie. Isabel's Texas Two-Step. 2008. (Beacon Street Girls Ser.: No. 5). (ENG.). 256p. (J). (gr. 4-8). pap. 7.99 (978-1-4169-6423-0(1), Aladdin) Simon & Schuster Children's Publishing.

Burns, A. M. & Ricci, Caitlin. Running with the Pack. 2016. (ENG., Illus.). (YA). pap. 14.99 (**978-1-63477-063-7(3)**, Harmony Ink Pr.) Dreamspinner Pr.

Bynum, Janie. The Twelve Days of Christmas in Texas. 2016. (Twelve Days of Christmas in America Ser.). (ENG., Illus.). 22p. (J). (— 1). bds. 7.95 (978-1-4549-2059-5(9)) Sterling Publishing Co., Inc.

—The Twelve Days of Christmas in Texas. Bynum, Janie, illus. 2009. (Twelve Days of Christmas in America Ser.). (ENG., Illus.). 40p. (J). (gr. k). 12.95 (978-1-4027-6350-2(6)) Sterling Publishing Co., Inc.

Cagan, Kayla. Piper Perish. 2017. (ENG., Illus.). 416p. (YA). 17.99 (978-1-4521-5583-8(6)) Chronicle Bks. LLC.

Caine, Rachel, pseud. Bite Club, 10 vols. 2011. (Morganville Vampires Ser.: 10). (ENG.). 368p. (YA). (gr. 9). pap. 9.99 (978-0-451-23468-1(5), Berkley) Penguin Publishing Group.

—Bitter Blood. 2013. (Morganville Vampires Ser.: 13). (ENG.). 432p. (YA). (gr. 9). pap. 9.99 (978-0-451-41424-3(1), Berkley) Penguin Publishing Group.

—Black Dawn. 2012. (Morganville Vampires Ser.: 12). (ENG.). 400p. (YA). (gr. 9). pap. 9.99 (978-0-451-23793-4(5), Berkley) Penguin Publishing Group.

—Carpe Corpus. 2009. (Morganville Vampires Ser.: 6). (ENG.). 256p. (YA). (gr. 9-18). mass mkt. 7.99 (978-0-451-22719-5(0), Berkley) Penguin Publishing Group.

—Feast of Fools. 2008. (Morganville Vampires Ser.: Bk. 4). 256p. (YA). lib. bdg. 20.00 (978-1-4242-4702-8(0)) Fitzgerald Bks.

—Feast of Fools. 2008. (Morganville Vampires Ser.: 4). (ENG.). 256p. (YA). (gr. 9-18). mass mkt. 7.99 (978-0-451-22463-7(9), Berkley) Penguin Publishing Group.

—Ghost Town, 9 vols. 2011. (Morganville Vampires Ser.: 9). (ENG.). 368p. (YA). (gr. 9-18). 9.99 (978-0-451-23291-5(7), Berkley) Penguin Publishing Group.

—Kiss of Death, 8 vols. 2010. (Morganville Vampires Ser.: 8). (ENG.). 256p. (YA). (gr. 9-18). 6.99 (978-0-451-22973-1(8), Berkley) Penguin Publishing Group.

—Last Breath, 11 vols. 2012. (Morganville Vampires Ser.: 11). (ENG.). 368p. (YA). (gr. 9). 9.99 (978-0-451-23580-0(0), Berkley) Penguin Publishing Group.

—Lord of Misrule. 2009. (Morganville Vampires Ser.: Bk. 5). 352p. (YA). lib. bdg. 20.00 (978-1-4242-4704-2(7)) Fitzgerald Bks.

—Lord of Misrule. 2009. (Morganville Vampires Ser.: 5). (ENG.). 256p. (YA). (gr. 9-18). mass mkt. 7.99 (978-0-451-22572-6(4), Berkley) Penguin Publishing Group.

—Midnight Alley. 2007. (Morganville Vampires Ser.: Bk. 3). 256p. (YA). lib. bdg. 20.00 (978-1-4242-4705-9(5)) Fitzgerald Bks.

—Midnight Alley. 2007. (Morganville Vampires Ser.: 3). (ENG.). 256p. (YA). (gr. 9-18). mass mkt. 7.99 (978-0-451-22238-1(5), Berkley) Penguin Publishing Group.

—The Morganville Vampires. (Morganville Vampires Ser.: Bks. 3-4). (ENG.). 464p. (YA). (gr. 9-18). Vol. 2. 2010. 9.99 (978-0-451-23289-2(5)) Vol. 3. 2011. 9.99 (978-0-451-23355-4(7)) Vol. 4. 2011. 9.99 (978-0-451-23426-1(X)) Penguin Publishing Group. (Berkley).

Campbell, Isaiah. AbrakaPOW. 2016. (ENG., Illus.). 400p. (J). (gr. 3-7). 16.99 (978-1-4814-2634-3(6), Simon & Schuster Bks. For Young Readers) Simon & Schuster Bks. For Young Readers.

Canales, Viola. The Tequila Worm. 2007. (ENG., Illus.). 208p. (YA). (gr. 7-11). pap. 7.99 (978-0-375-84089-0(3), Lamb, Wendy Bks.) Random Hse. Children's Bks.

Casad, Mary Brooke. Bluebonnet at the State Fair of Texas, 1 vol. Binder, Pat, illus. 2010. (ENG.). 40p. (J). (gr. k-3). pap. 8.95 (978-1-58980-830-0(4)) Pelican Publishing Co., Inc.

Casad, Mary Brooke. Bluebonnet at the Texas State Capitol, 1 vol. Vincent, Benjamin, illus. 2017. (Bluebonnet Ser.). (ENG.). 32p. (gr. -1-3). 9.95 (**978-1-4556-2363-1(6)**) Pelican Publishing Co., Inc.

Casad, Mary Brooke & Brooke Casad, Mary. Bluebonnet at the East Texas Oil Museum, 1 vol. Vincent, Benjamin, illus. 2005. (Bluebonnet Ser.). (ENG.). 32p. (J). (gr. k-3). 16.99 (978-1-58980-358-9(2)) Pelican Publishing Co., Inc.

Castilla, Julia Mercedes. Strange Parents. 2009. 144p. (J). (gr. 6-18). pap. 9.95 (978-1-55885-590-8(4), Piñata Books) Arte Publico Pr.

Chrismer, Melanie. Phoebe Clappsaddle for Sheriff, 1 vol. Roeder, Virginia M., illus. 2003. (ENG.). 32p. (J). (gr. k-3). 16.99 (978-1-58980-127-1(X)) Pelican Publishing Co., Inc.

—Phoebe Clappsaddle Has a Tumbleweed Christmas, 1 vol. Roeder, Virginia M., illus. 2004. (ENG.). 32p. (J). (gr. k-3). 16.99 (978-1-58980-241-4(1)) Pelican Publishing Co., Inc.

Christian, Diana. The Lucky Seven. 2005. 71p. pap. 19.95 (978-1-4137-5471-1(6)) America Star Bks.

Clement-Moore, Rosemary. Texas Gothic. 2012. (ENG.). 416p. (YA). (gr. 9). pap. 10.99 (978-0-385-73694-7(0), Ember) Random Hse. Children's Bks.

Clifton, Lutricia. Seeking Cassandra. 2016. (ENG.). 192p. (J). 16.95 (978-0-8234-3560-9(1)) Holiday Hse., Inc.

Clifton Wisler, G. All for Texas. 2004. 140p. (J). lib. bdg. 16.92 (978-1-4242-0767-1(3)) Fitzgerald Bks.

Colburn, Cherie Foster. Bloomin' Tales: Legends of Seven Favorite Texas Wildflowers. Hein, Joy Fisher, illus. 2012. (ENG.). 64p. (J). (gr. 4-4). 24.95 (978-1-936474-18-9(2), 91c14e7a-1c5d-4381-b022-da21965048db) Bright Sky Pr.

Cooner, Donna. Worthy. 2017. (ENG.). 288p. (J). (gr. 7). 17.99 (978-0-545-90393-6(9)) Scholastic, Inc.

Cooper, Floyd. Juneteenth for Mazie. Cooper, Floyd, illus. 2015. (Fiction Picture Bks.). (ENG., Illus.). 40p. (gr. 1-2). lib. bdg. 25.32 (978-1-4795-5819-3(2), Fiction Picture Bks.) Picture Window Bks.

Corgliano, K. L. Millie & Me, 1 vol. 2009. 29p. pap. 24.95 (978-1-60813-935-4(2)) America Star Bks.

Cousins Camp. 2010. 32p. pap. 12.99 (978-1-4490-8387-8(0)) AuthorHouse.

Crawford, Ann Fears. Keechee: The Witch of the Woods. 2005. (J). (978-1-931823-21-0(9)) Halcyon Pr.

Crowley, Suzanne. The Very Ordered Existence of Merilee Marvelous. 2007. 380p. (J). (gr. 5-9). 16.99 (978-0-06-123197-1(5), Greenwillow Bks.) HarperCollins Pubs.

Crownover, Rebecca. Texas Farm Girl. Daigle, Brian, illus. 2013. (ENG.). (J). (gr. -1-3). 14.95 (978-1-62086-265-0(4)) Mascot Bks., Inc.

Cuate, Melodie A. Journey to la Salle's Settlement. 2010. (Mr. Barrington's Mysterious Trunk Ser.). (ENG., Illus.). 184p. (J). lib. bdg. 18.95 (978-0-89672-704-5(1)) Texas Tech Univ. Pr.

Cummings, W. L. A Far West Texas Christmas, 1 vol. 2009. 25p. pap. 19.95 (978-1-4489-9402-1(0)) PublishAmerica, Inc.

Czerw, Nancy Carpenter. Itty & Bitty - On the Road. Berlin, Rose Mary, illus. 2008. (Itty & Bitty Ser.: 3). (ENG.). 32p. (J). (gr. -1-3). 16.95 (978-0-9755618-4-3(7)) McWitty Pr., Inc.

Dahlstrom, S. J. Texas Grit: the Adventures of Wilder Good #2. 2014. (Adventures of Wilder Good Ser.). (ENG.). 141p. (J). (gr. 3). pap. 7.95 (978-1-58988-094-8(3)) Dry, Paul Bks., Inc.

Davis, David. Ten Texas Babies, 1 vol. Jackson, Shelley & Crosby, Jeff, illus. 2014. (ENG.). 32p. (J). (gr. k-3). 16.99 (978-1-4556-1874-3(8)) Pelican Publishing Co., Inc.

—Texas Aesop's Fables, 1 vol. Ward, Sue Marshall, illus. 2008. (ENG.). 32p. (J). (gr. k-3). 16.99 (978-1-58980-569-9(0)) Pelican Publishing Co., Inc.

—Texas Zeke & the Longhorn, 1 vol. Stacy, Alan, illus. 2006. (ENG.). 32p. (J). (gr. k-3). 16.99 (978-1-58980-348-0(5)) Pelican Publishing Co., Inc.

Davis, Peg. After the Storm: A Napoleon & Marigold Adventure. 2009. 40p. pap. 16.50 (978-1-60860-222-3(2), Eloquent Bks.) Strategic Book Publishing & Rights Agency (SBPRA).

—Napoleon & Marigold. 2008. 24p. pap. 13.50 (978-1-60693-114-1(8), Eloquent Bks.) Strategic Book Publishing & Rights Agency (SBPRA).

Dean, Carolee. Comfort. 2004. (ENG.). 256p. (YA). (gr. 7-18). pap. 14.95 (978-0-618-43912-6(9)) Houghton Mifflin Harcourt Publishing Co.

—Take Me There. 2010. (ENG.). 336p. (YA). (gr. 9-18). pap. 8.99 (978-1-4169-8950-9(1), Simon Pulse) Simon Pulse.

Decter, Ed. VIP Lounge. 2009. (Chloe Gamble Ser.). (ENG.). 352p. (YA). (gr. 9-18). pap. 9.99 (978-1-4169-5436-1(8), Simon Pulse) Simon Pulse.

Dell, Pamela. Blood in the Water: A Story of Friendship During the Mexican War. 2003. (Scrapbooks of America Ser.). (ENG., Illus.). 48p. (J). (gr. 3-6). 32.79 (978-1-59187-042-5(9), 200805) Child's World, Inc., The.

Delp, Randy. The Ugly Bug & the Beautiful Butterfly. 2011. 76p. pap. (978-1-4269-5354-5(2)) Trafford Publishing (UK) Ltd.

Dillon, Kimberly M. The Ghosts of Wolf Creek. 2008. 73p. pap. 19.95 (978-1-60563-996-3(6)) America Star Bks.

Dromgoole, Glenn. Good Night Little Texan. Clack, Barbra, illus. 2012. (ENG.). 24p. (J). (gr. k-2). 15.95 (978-1-936474-10-3(7), 9781936474103) Bright Sky Pr.

Dyer, Jonah Lisa & Dyer, Stephen. The Season. 2016. (ENG.). 352p. (YA). (gr. 9). 17.99 (978-0-451-47634-0(4), Viking Books for Young Readers) Penguin Young Readers Group.

Edgell, Ernest. The Cowbears of Texas: The Hero. Haycraft, Marilynn J., illus. 2004. 25p. pap. 24.95 (978-1-4137-3507-9(X)) PublishAmerica, Inc.

Elliott, Alan. Willy the Texas Longhorn, 1 vol. Ford, Stephanie, illus. 2013. (ENG.). 32p. (J). (gr. k-3). 16.99 (978-1-4556-1870-5(5)) Pelican Publishing Co., Inc.

Ellsberry, Sharon. The Spaniel Family Goes to the State Fair. Espinosa, Chris, illus. 2004. 24p. (J). 9.00 (978-0-9724637-2-0(0)) Sky Rocket Pr.

Enderle, Dotti. Crosswire. 2010. (ENG.). 144p. (J). (gr. 4-6). 17.95 (978-1-59078-751-9(X), Calkins Creek) Boyds Mills Pr.

—The Fat Stock Stampede at the Houston Livestock Show & Rodeo, 1 vol. Galey, Chuck, illus. 2008. (ENG.). 32p. (J). (gr. 1-3). 16.99 (978-1-58980-443-2(0)) Pelican Publishing Co., Inc.

—Granny Gert & the Bunion Brothers, 1 vol. Kulka, Joe, illus. 2006. (ENG.). 32p. (J). (gr. k-3). 16.99 (978-1-58980-373-2(6)) Pelican Publishing Co., Inc.

Enderle, Dotti & Galey, Chuck. The Cotton Candy Catastrophe at the Texas State Fair, 1 vol. 2004. (ENG., Illus.). 32p. (J). (gr. k-3). 16.99 (978-1-58980-189-9(X)) Pelican Publishing Co., Inc.

Epner, Paul. Herbert Hilligan's Lone Star Adventure. Kuon, Vuthy & Nguyen, Duke, illus. 2003. 32p. (J). 15.95 (978-0-9743335-3-3(0)) Imaginative Publishing, Ltd.

Erdman, Loula G. The Wind Blows Free. 2006. (Living History Library). 271p. (YA). (gr. 6). pap. 12.95 (978-1-932350-09-8(8)) Bethlehem Bks.

Erdman, Loula Grace. The Good Land. 2008. (Living History Library). 185p. (YA). (gr. 6). pap. 12.95 (978-1-932350-13-5(6)) Bethlehem Bks.

Erickson, John R. The Big Question. Holmes, Gerald L., illus. 2012. 128p. (J). pap. (978-1-59188-160-5(9)) Maverick Bks.

—The Big Question. Holmes, Gerald L., illus. 2012. (Hank the Cowdog Ser.: Vol. 60). (ENG.). 128p. (J). (gr. 3-6). 15.99 (978-1-59188-260-2(5)) Maverick Bks., Inc.

—The Case of the Blazing Sky. Holmes, Gerald L., illus. 2011. (Hank the Cowdog Ser.). (ENG.). 129p. (J). (gr. 3-6). pap. 5.99 (978-1-59188-151-3(X)) Maverick Bks., Inc.

—The Case of the Booby-Trapped Pickup. Holmes, Gerald L., illus. 2011. (Hank the Cowdog Ser.). (ENG.). 129p. (J). (gr. 3-6). pap. 5.99 (978-1-59188-149-0(8)) Maverick Bks., Inc.

—The Case of the Coyote Invasion. Holmes, Gerald L., illus. 2011. (Hank the Cowdog Ser.: No. 56). (ENG.). 132p. (J). (gr. 3-6). pap. 5.99 (978-1-59188-156-8(0)) Maverick Bks., Inc.

—The Case of the Dinosaur Birds. Holmes, Gerald L., illus. 2011. (Hank the Cowdog Ser.). (ENG.). 125p. (J). (gr. 3-6). pap. 5.99 (978-1-59188-154-4(4)) Maverick Bks., Inc.

—The Case of the Mysterious Voice. Holmes, Gerald L., illus. 2012. (Hank the Cowdog (Quality) Ser.: Vol. 58). (ENG.). 123p. (J). (gr. 3-6). pap. 5.99 (978-1-59188-158-2(7)) Maverick Bks., Inc.

—The Case of the Perfect Dog. Holmes, Gerald L., illus. 2012. 127p. (J). (978-1-59188-259-6(1)) Maverick Bks.

—The Case of the Perfect Dog. Holmes, Gerald L., illus. 2012. (Hank the Cowdog (Quality) Ser.). (ENG.). 127p. (J). (gr. 3-6). pap. 5.99 (978-1-59188-159-9(5)) Maverick Bks., Inc.

—The Case of the Secret Weapon. Holmes, Gerald L., illus. 2011. (Hank the Cowdog Ser.). (ENG.). 125p. (J). (gr. 3-6). pap. 5.99 (978-1-59188-155-1(2)) Maverick Bks., Inc.

—The Disappearance of Drover. Holmes, Gerald L., illus. 2011. (Hank the Cowdog Ser.). (ENG.). 122p. (J). (gr. 3-6). pap. 5.99 (978-1-59188-157-5(9)) Maverick Bks., Inc.

—Drover's Secret Life. Holmes, Gerald L., illus. 2011. (Hank the Cowdog Ser.). (ENG.). 118p. (J). (gr. 3-6). pap. 5.99 (978-1-59188-153-7(6)) Maverick Bks., Inc.

Erickson, John R. & Holmes, Gerald L., illus. The Case of the Prowling Bear. 2013. 126p. (J). (978-1-59188-261-9(3)) Maverick Bks.

Estevis, Anne. Chicken Foot Farm. 2008. 154p. (J). (gr. 6-18). pap. 10.95 (978-1-55885-505-2(X), Piñata Books) Arte Publico Pr.

—Down Garrapata Road. 2003. 128p. (J). pap. 12.95 (978-1-55885-397-3(9)) Arte Publico Pr.

Fehlbaum, Beth. Big Fat Disaster. (ENG.). (YA). 2015. 286p. pap. 9.99 (978-1-4405-9267-6(5)) 2014. 288p. 17.99 (978-1-4405-7048-3(5)) Simon Pulse. (Simon Pulse).

—Hope in Patience. 2010. 312p. (YA). (gr. 8-18). 16.95 (978-1-934813-41-6(9)) Westside Bks.

Fern, Tracey E. Buffalo Music. Castillo, Lauren, illus. 2008. (ENG.). 32p. (J). (gr. -1-3). 17.99 (978-0-618-72341-6(2)) Houghton Mifflin Harcourt Publishing Co.

Fields, Jan. Chase the Chupacabra, 1 vol. Brundage, Scott, illus. 2014. (Monster Hunters Ser.). (ENG.). 80p. (J). (gr. 8-12). 27.07 (978-1-62402-044-5(5)) Magic Wagon.

Fisher, Karianne M. A Pup Named Moose. 2011. 20p. pap. 24.95 (978-1-4512-3373-5(6)) America Star Bks.

Fisher, Karianne Marie. In a Land Called Hogeye, 1 vol. 2010. 24p. pap. 24.95 (978-1-4489-8798-6(9)) PublishAmerica, Inc.

Fitzgibbon, Diana. Somewhere in Texas. Gonzales, Diana, ed. Del Toro, Mark, illus. 2004. 32p. (J). (978-0-9747587-0-1(1)) Mike-Auri Bks.

Flemmer, Chip. Out of Texas, 1 vol. 2010. 183p. pap. 24.95 (978-1-4489-2918-4(0)) America Star Bks.

Freeman, Shannon. Traumatized. 2014. (Port City High Ser.: 7). (YA). lib. bdg. 20.80 (978-0-606-36619-9(9)) Turtleback Bks.

G & G Wilcox. Tex, the Little Caterpillar from Texas. 2009. 68p. pap. 41.99 (978-1-4363-6494-2(9)) Xlibris Corp.

Gaard, Betty. Jericho Ride. 2003. (Illus.). 165p. (J). pap. 8.99 (978-1-57924-968-7(X)) BJU Pr.

Galbraith, Julie. Stable Ground: The Riding Series #1. 2013. 136p. pap. (978-1-927794-05-0(6)) Lechner Syndications.

Gamble, Adam. Good Night Texas. Veno, Joe & Kelly, Cooper, illus. 2nd ed. 2011. (Good Night Our World Ser.). (ENG.). 20p. (J). (gr. k — 1). bds. 9.95 (978-1-60219-053-5(4)) Good Night Bks.

Gamble, Adam & Jasper, Mark. Buenas Noches, Texas. 2013. (Buenas Noches Ser.). (SPA & ENG., Illus.). 20p. (J). (— 1). bds. 9.95 (978-1-60219-093-1(3)) Good Night Bks.

Garza, Xavier. Creepy Creatures & Other Cucuys. 2004. (Illus.). 144p. pap. 9.95 (978-1-55885-410-9(X), Piñata Books) Arte Publico Pr.

Garza, Xavier, illus. Maximilian & the Mystery of the Guardian Angel. 2011. (Max's Lucha Libre Adventures Ser.). (SPA & ENG.). 160p. (J). (gr. 5-8). pap. 12.95 (978-1-933693-98-9(3)) Cinco Puntos Pr.

Gentry, Jennifer Mills. Maria's 4th of July. 2011. 32p. pap. 24.95 (978-1-4560-7300-8(1)) America Star Bks.

Gibbs, Stuart. Poached. 2014. (FunJungle Ser.). (ENG., Illus.). 352p. (J). (gr. 3-7). 17.99 (978-1-4424-6777-4(0), Simon & Schuster Bks. For Young Readers) Simon & Schuster Bks. For Young Readers.

Gipson, Fred. Old Yeller. Date not set. 192p. (J). 20.95 (978-0-8488-2273-6(0)) Amereon Ltd.

—Old Yeller. 2009. (Perennial Classics Ser.). 132p. (gr. 4-7). 20.85 (978-0-613-85744-4(5), Turtleback) Turtleback Bks.

Gipson, Fred & Polson, Steven. Old Yeller. 2009. (Perennial Classics Ser.). (ENG., Illus.). 144p. (gr. 4-7). pap. 12.99 (978-0-06-093547-4(2), Harper Perennial) HarperCollins Pubs.

Goode, John. 151 Days. 2016. (ENG., Illus.). (J). 32.99 (**978-1-63477-925-8(8)**) 2014. 350p. pap. 17.99 (978-1-62798-747-9(9)) Dreamspinner Pr. (Harmony Ink Pr.).

Gribnau, Joe. Kick the Cowboy, 1 vol. Tans, Adrian, illus. 2009. (ENG.). 32p. (J). (gr. k-3). 16.99 (978-1-58980-605-4(0)) Pelican Publishing Co., Inc.

Griffin, Kitty & Combs, Kathy. Stinker & the Onion Princess. Manders, John, illus. 2005. (J). (978-0-8037-2976-6(6), Dial) Penguin Publishing Group.

Gurevich, Margaret. Gina's Balance. 2016. (What's Your Dream? Ser.). (ENG., Illus.). 96p. (gr. 3-4). lib. bdg. 25.32 (978-1-4965-3443-9(3)) Capstone Press of Coughlan Cos.

Haden, Robbie. Run Girl Run. 2013. 116p. 28.95 (978-1-4525-6779-2(4)); pap. 11.99 (978-1-4525-6777-8(8)) Author Solutions, Inc. (Balboa Pr.).

Hale, Marian. Dark Water Rising. 2010. (ENG.). 256p. (J). (gr. 5-9). pap. 7.99 (978-0-312-62908-3(7), 9780312629083) Square Fish.

—The Goodbye Season. 2009. (ENG.). 288p. (YA). (gr. 7-12). 16.99 (978-0-8050-8855-7(5), 9780805088557, Holt, Henry & Co. Bks. For Young Readers) Holt, Henry & Co.

—The Truth about Sparrows. 2007. (ENG.). 288p. (YA). (gr. 7-12). per. 9.99 (978-0-312-37133-3(0), 9780312371333) Square Fish.

Harper, Jo. Mayor Jalapeno Hal from Presidio, Texas. 2003. (Illus.). (J). (978-1-57168-767-8(X), Eakin Pr.) Eakin Pr.

T
U
V

Harper, Suzanne. A Gaggle of Goblins. 2012. (Unseen World of Poppy Malone Ser.: 1). (ENG.). 320p. (J). (gr. 3-7). pap. 6.99 (978-0-06-199609-2(2), Greenwillow Bks.) HarperCollins Pubs.
—A Gust of Ghosts. (ENG.). 320p. (J). (gr. 3-7). 2075. 6.99 (978-0-06-199612-2(2)) 2012. (Unseen World of Poppy Malone Ser.: 2). 16.99 (978-0-06-199610-8(6)) HarperCollins Pubs. (Greenwillow Bks.).
—A Mischief of Mermaids. 2013. (Unseen World of Poppy Malone Ser.: 3). (ENG.). 288p. (J). (gr. 3-7). 16.99 (978-0-06-199613-9(0), Greenwillow Bks.) HarperCollins Pubs.
—The Unseen World of Poppy Malone No. 1: A Gaggle of Goblins. 2011. (Unseen World of Poppy Malone Ser.: 1). (ENG., Illus.). 304p. (J). (gr. 3-7). 16.99 (978-0-06-199607-8(6), Greenwillow Bks.) HarperCollins Pubs.
Harrington, Karen. Sure Signs of Crazy. (ENG.). (J). 2014. 304p. (gr. 5-17). pap. 7.99 (978-0-316-21049-2(8)) 2013. 288p. (gr. 4-17). 17.00 (978-0-316-21058-4(7)) Little, Brown Bks. for Young Readers.
Heasley, Gwendolyn. Where I Belong. 2011. (Where I Belong Ser.: 1). (ENG.). 304p. (YA). (gr. 8-18). pap. 9.99 (978-0-06-197884-5(1), HarperTeen) HarperCollins Pubs.
Hees, Miriam. The Adventures of Jilly & Brad: Noises in the Attic. Kinneman, D. Michael, illus. 2003. 128p. (J). pap. 5.95 (978-0-9718348-4-2(9)) Blooming Tree Pr.
Heflin, Ronald. Caddo Lake. 2011. 156p. pap. 24.95 (978-1-4626-0093-9(X)) America Star Bks.
Herbert Hilligan & His Magical Adventure Curriculum Guide. 2004. ring bd. 24.95 (978-0-9743335-4-0(9)) Imaginative Publishing, Ltd.
Herbert Hilligan's Lone Star Adventure Curriculum Guide. 2004. ring bd. 24.95 (978-0-9743335-7-1(3)) Imaginative Publishing, Ltd.
Higman, Anita. The Living Darkness: Texas Caves. 2nd ed. 2003. (Illus.). xiii, 93p. (J). (978-1-57168-783-8(1), Eakin Pr.) Eakin Pr.
Hobbs, Will. Take Me to the River. (ENG.). (J). (gr. 5). 2012. 208p. pap. 6.99 (978-0-06-074146-4(5)) 2011. 192p. 15.99 (978-0-06-074144-0(9)) HarperCollins Pubs.
Holt, Kimberly Willis. Dancing in Cadillac Light. 2003. (ENG.). 176p. (J). (gr. 5-9). 5.99 (978-0-698-11970-3(3), Puffin Books) Penguin Young Readers Group.
—Dancing in Cadillac Light. 2004. 176p. (J). (gr. 4-7). pap. 36.00 incl. audio (978-0-8072-2095-5(7), Listening Library) Random Hse. Audio Publishing Group.
—When Zachary Beaver Came to Town. unabr. ed. 2004. 227p. (J). (gr. 5-9). pap. 36.00 incl. audio (978-0-8072-8394-3(0), Listening Library) Random Hse. Audio Publishing Group.
—When Zachary Beaver Came to Town. 2011. (ENG.). 256p. (J). (gr. 5-9). pap. 7.99 (978-0-312-63212-0(6), 9780312632120) Square Fish.
Honeyman, Kay. Interference. 2016. (ENG.). 352p. (YA). (gr. 7). 17.99 (978-0-545-81232-0(1), Levine, Arthur A. Bks.) Scholastic, Inc.
Huling, Jan. Puss in Cowboy Boots. Huling, Phil, illus. 2007. (ENG.). 40p. (J). (gr. 1-4). 11.99 (978-1-4169-6749-1(4), Simon & Schuster/Paula Wiseman Bks.) Simon & Schuster/Paula Wiseman Bks.
Inagaki, Riichiro. Eyeshield 21, Vol. 12. Murata, Yusuke, illus. 2007. (ENG.). 208p. pap. 9.99 (978-1-4215-1061-3(8)) Viz Media.
—Eyeshield 21, Vol. 13. Murata, Yusuke, illus. 2007. (ENG.). 216p. pap. 7.99 (978-1-4215-1062-0(6)) Viz Media.
Ing, Dean. It's up to Charlie Hardin. 2015. (Baen Ser.: 1). (ENG.). 256p. (YA). (gr. 5). 16.99 (978-1-4767-8030-6(7)) Baen Bks.
Isaacs, Anne. Meanwhile, Back at the Ranch. Hawkes, Kevin, illus. 2014. (ENG.). 56p. (J). (gr. k-4). 17.99 (978-0-375-86745-3(7), Schwartz & Wade Bks.) Random Hse. Children's Bks.
Jackson, Laura Gower. The Snowman & the Magic Eyeglasses. 2010. 24p. 11.99 (978-1-4520-3544-4(X)) AuthorHouse.
Jackson, Sarah. Preep of Old Washington Square: A Collection of East Texas Tales. Jenkins, Delores, illus. l.t. ed. 2005. 48p. (J). 16.95 (978-1-931823-25-8(1)) Halcyon Pr., Ltd.
Jacobs, Lily. The Littlest Bunny in Austin. Dunn, Robert, illus. 2016. (ENG.). 32p. (J). (-7). 9.99 (978-1-4926-3347-1(X), 9781492633471, Sourcebooks Jabberwocky) Sourcebooks, Inc.
—The Littlest Bunny in Dallas. Dunn, Robert, illus. 2016. (ENG.). 32p. (J). (-7). 9.99 (978-1-4926-3349-5(6), 9781492633495, Sourcebooks Jabberwocky) Sourcebooks, Inc.
—The Littlest Bunny in Texas: An Easter Adventure. Dunn, Robert, illus. 2015. (ENG.). 32p. (J). (-3). 9.99 (978-1-4926-1210-0(3), Sourcebooks Jabberwocky) Sourcebooks, Inc.
James, Eric. A Halloween Scare in Texas. Le Ray, Marina, illus. 2014. (ENG.). 32p. (J). (-5). 9.99 (978-1-4926-0633-8(2), 9781492606338, Sourcebooks Jabberwocky) Sourcebooks, Inc.
—Santa's Sleigh Is on Its Way to Texas. Dunn, Robert, illus. 2015. (ENG.). 32p. (J). (-2). 12.99 (978-1-4926-2739-5(9), Sourcebooks Jabberwocky) Sourcebooks, Inc.
(Jerry) Deal, Gerald R. Famous Dog Chowski. 2013. 44p. pap. 20.72 (978-1-4669-9707-3(9)) Trafford Publishing.
Johansson, J. R. The Row. O'Malley, Janine, ed. 2016. (ENG.). 352p. (YA). 17.99 (978-0-374-30025-8(9), 9780374300258, Farrar, Straus & Giroux (BYR)) Farrar, Straus & Giroux.
Jones, Patrick. Raising Heaven. 2015. (J). 9.99 (978-1-4677-7697-4(1)); (ENG.). 96p. (gr. 6-12). lib. bdg. 27.99 (978-1-4677-5802-4(7)) Lerner Publishing Group.
Jones, Ralph E. The Adventures of Kele: Boy of the Rock Shelter. 2012. 156p. pap. 41.99 (978-1-4772-9405-5(8)); 56p. pap. 24.99 (978-1-4685-7696-2(8)) AuthorHouse.
Julie, Aunt. State Symbols of Texas - Paddleduck #8. 2012. 50p. pap. 5.95 (978-1-105-91163-7(2)) Lulu Pr., Inc.
Karr, Kathleen. Exiled: Memoirs of a Camel, 0 vols. 2006. (ENG.). 242p. (gr. 5-8). pap. 9.99 (978-0-7614-5291-1(5), 9780761452911, Amazon Children's Publishing) Amazon Publishing.
Kearby, Mike. The Trail Drives, No. 2. White, Mack, illus. 2015. (Texas Tales Illustrated Ser.). (ENG.). 24p. pap. 5.95 (978-0-87565-608-3(0)) Texas Christian Univ. Pr.
Kelly, David A. The Astro Outlaw. 2012. (Ballpark Mysteries Ser.: Bk. 4). lib. bdg. 14.75 (978-0-606-23861-8(1), Turtleback) Turtleback Bks.
—The Rangers Rustlers. Meyers, Mark, illus. 2016. (Ballpark Mysteries Ser.: Bk. 12). (ENG.). 112p. (J). (gr. 1-4). pap. 4.99 (978-0-385-37881-9(5), Random Hse. Bks. for Young Readers) Random Hse. Children's Bks.
Kelly, Jacqueline. Counting Sheep: Calpurnia Tate, Girl Vet. White, Teagan & Meyer, Jennifer L., illus. 2017. (Calpurnia Tate, Girl Vet Ser.). (ENG.). 112p. (J). 15.99 (978-1-62779-870-9(6), 9781627798709, Holt, Henry & Co. Bks. For Young Readers) Holt, Henry & Co.
—The Curious World of Calpurnia Tate. 2015. (Calpurnia Tate Ser.: 2). (ENG.). 320p. (J). (gr. 4-7). 16.99 (978-0-8050-9744-3(9), 9780805097443, Holt, Henry & Co. Bks. For Young Readers) Holt, Henry & Co.
—The Curious World of Calpurnia Tate. 2017. (Calpurnia Tate Ser.: 2). (J). lib. bdg. 18.40 **(978-0-606-39939-5(9))** Turtleback Bks.
—La Evolución de Calpurnia Tate. 2010.Tr. of Evolution of Calpurnia Tate. (SPA.). 272p. (YA). pap. 20.95 (978-84-9918-103-5(1)) Roca Editorial ESP. Dist: Spanish Pubs., LLC.
—La Evolucion de Calpurnia Tate, Vol. 2. 2011.Tr. of Evolution of Calpurnia Tate. (SPA.). 272p. pap. 12.95 (978-84-92833-15-3(7)) Roca Editorial ESP. Dist: Spanish Pubs., LLC.
—The Evolution of Calpurnia Tate. 2009. (Calpurnia Tate Ser.: 1). (ENG.). 352p. (J). (gr. 4-7). 17.99 (978-0-8050-8841-0(5), 9780805088410, Holt, Henry & Co. Bks. For Young Readers) Holt, Henry & Co.
—The Evolution of Calpurnia Tate. 2010. 340p. 18.00 (978-1-60686-849-2(7)) Perfection Learning Corp.
—The Evolution of Calpurnia Tate. 2011. (Calpurnia Tate Ser.: 1). (ENG.). 368p. (J). (gr. 4-7). pap. 7.99 (978-0-312-65930-1(X), 9780312659301) Square Fish.
—The Evolution of Calpurnia Tate. 2011. (Calpurnia Tate Ser.: 1). (J). lib. bdg. 18.40 (978-0-606-20974-8(3), Turtleback) Turtleback Bks.
—Skunked! White, Teagan & Meyer, Jennifer L., illus. 2016. (Calpurnia Tate, Girl Vet Ser.). (ENG.). 112p. (J). 15.99 (978-1-62779-868-6(4), 9781627798686, Holt, Henry & Co. Bks. For Young Readers) Holt, Henry & Co.
Kelly, Jacqueline. Who Gives a Hoot?: Calpurnia Tate, Girl Vet. Meyer, Jennifer L., illus. 2017. (Calpurnia Tate, Girl Vet Ser.). (ENG.). 112p. (J). 15.99 **(978-1-62779-873-0(0)**, 9781627798730, Holt, Henry & Co. Bks. For Young Readers) Holt, Henry & Co.
Kerr, P. B., pseud. One Small Step. 2009. (ENG.). 320p. (J). (gr. 3-9). pap. 8.99 (978-1-4169-4214-6(9), McElderry, Margaret K. Bks.) McElderry, Margaret K. Bks.
Ketteman, Helen. The Three Little Gators. Terry, Will, illus. 2009. (ENG.). 32p. (J). (gr. -1-3). 16.99 (978-0-8075-7824-7(X)) Whitman, Albert & Co.
—Waynetta & the Cornstalk: A Texas Fairy Tale. Greenseid, Diane, illus. 2012. (ENG.). 32p. (J). (gr. -1-3). pap. 7.99 (978-0-8075-8688-4(9)) Whitman, Albert & Co.
Kimmel, Eric A. Jack & the Giant Barbecue, 0 vols. Manders, John, illus. 2012. (ENG.). 32p. (J). (gr. 1-3). 17.99 (978-0-7614-6128-9(0), 9780761461289, Amazon Children's Publishing) Amazon Publishing.
—The Lady in the Blue Cloak: Legends from the Texas Missions. Guevara, Susan, illus. 2006. (ENG.). 40p. (J). (gr. 6-10). 16.95 (978-0-8234-1738-4(7)) Holiday Hse., Inc.
Kornechak, Marilyn Gilbert. Paisano Pete: Snake-Killer Bird. Eckhardt, Jason C., illus. 2003. 100p. (J). (gr. 3-7). per. 11.95 (978-1-57168-770-8(X), Eakin Pr.) Eakin Pr.
Kountz, Charity. Jason, Lizzy & the Snowman Village. Klock, Kimberly, illus. 2013. 132p. 24.99 (978-0-9859601-1-7(6)) Texas Pride Publishing.
Kralovansky, Susan. Twelve Cowboys Ropin', 1 vol. Kralovansky, Susan, illus. 2015. (ENG., Illus.). 32p. (J). (gr. k-3). 16.99 (978-1-4556-2081-4(5)) Pelican Publishing Co., Inc.
Krueger, Kathryn L. Road to Grandma's House. 2005. 128p. pap. 13.95 (978-1-59800-366-6(6)) Outskirts Pr., Inc.
Krulik, Nancy. She's Got the Beat. 2010. (Romantic Comedies Ser.). (ENG.). 320p. (YA). (gr. 9). pap. 14.99 (978-1-4424-1419-8(7), Simon Pulse) Simon Pulse.
Krulik, Nancy & dePaola, Tomie. Rootin' Tootin' Cow Dog #8. Braun, Sebastien, illus. 2015. (Magic Bone Ser.: 8). (ENG.). 128p. (J). (gr. 1-3). bds. 4.99 (978-0-448-48097-8(2), Grosset & Dunlap) Penguin Young Readers Group.
Lackey, Mercedes & Edghill, Rosemary. Dead Reckoning. 2012. (ENG.). 336p. (YA). (gr. 7-12). 16.99 (978-1-59990-684-3(8), 9781599906843, Bloomsbury USA Childrens) Bloomsbury Publishing USA.
Lake, Julie. Galveston's Summer of the Storm. 2003. (Chaparral Bks.). (ENG.). 158p. pap. 17.95 (978-0-87565-272-6(7)) Texas Christian Univ. Pr.
Lansdale, Joe R. All the Earth, Thrown to the Sky. 2012. (ENG.). 252p. (YA). (gr. 7). pap. 8.99 (978-0-385-73932-0(X), Ember) Random Hse. Children's Bks.
Lasher, Olga Rivera. La Historieta (the Storyteller) 2008. 88p. per. 7.95 (978-1-4327-0914-3(3)) Outskirts Pr., Inc.
Ledford, Mary"Aunt Sissy"Ledlowtranette. Cowboy Will & the Magic Rope. 2012. 32p. pap. 19.99 (978-1-4772-5167-6(7)) AuthorHouse.
Lindsey, Julie Anne. Reinventing Chloe. 2013. 278p. pap. 13.99 (978-1-62237-152-5(6)) Turquoise Morning Pr.
Literature Connections English: ... & the Earth Did Not Devour Him. 2004. (gr. 6-12). (978-0-395-77139-6(0), 2-70217) Holt McDougal.
Loftin, Nikki. Wish Girl. 2015. (ENG.). 256p. (J). (gr. 3-7). 16.99 (978-1-59514-686-1(5), Razorbill) Penguin Young Readers Group.
Love, D. Anne. Picture Perfect. 2010. (ENG.). 304p. (YA). (gr. 7). pap. 8.99 (978-0-689-87391-1(3), McElderry, Margaret K. Bks.) McElderry, Margaret K. Bks.
Lupica, Mike. Qb 1. 2013. (ENG.). 272p. (J). (gr. 5). 17.99 (978-0-399-25228-0(2), Philomel Bks.) Penguin Publishing Group.
—Qb 1. 2014. (ENG.). 288p. (J). (gr. 5). pap. 7.99 (978-0-14-751152-2(6), Puffin Books) Penguin Young Readers Group.
MacHalek, Bj. The Adventures of a Noble Duchess: Duchess on Yard Patrol. 2012. 32p. pap. 17.37 (978-1-4389-6886-5(8)) AuthorHouse.
Mackey, Weezie Kerr. Throwing Like a Girl, 0 vols. 2010. (ENG.). 272p. (YA). (gr. 7-9). pap. 9.99 (978-0-7614-5606-3(6), 9780761456063, Amazon Children's Publishing) Amazon Publishing.
Magsamen, Sandra. I Love Texas (an ABC Adventure) 2015. (ENG.). 40p. (J). (-5). 12.99 (978-1-4926-2835-4(2), Sourcebooks Jabberwocky) Sourcebooks, Inc.
Maliszewski, Julia. Grandmas Got the Goodies. 2013. 28p. pap. 14.93 (978-1-4669-8718-0(9)) Trafford Publishing.
Mangum, James A. & Spires, Sidney. The Fairy the Chupacabra & Those Marfa Lights: A West Texas Fable. Mangum, James A., illus. 2008. (Illus.). 32p. (J). 17.95 (978-0-9798391-5-3(7)) Hardy, John M. Publishing Co.
Manley, Candace. Skeeter's Dream. 2010. (ENG.). 192p. (J). (gr. 7-18). pap. 14.95 (978-0-9785634-8-6(4)) La Frontera Publishing.
Mantell, Paul & Christopher, Matt. Snowboard Champ. 2005. (Matt Christopher Sports Ser.). 146p. (gr. 3-7). 16.00 (978-0-7569-5198-6(4)) Perfection Learning Corp.
Marquith, M. Delmore. Flying Buddies of Texas. 2012. 250p. 46.95 (978-1-258-22955-9(2)); pap. 31.95 (978-1-258-24387-6(3)) Literary Licensing, LLC.
Marsh, Carole. The Mystery at Rattlesnake Ridge. 2014. (Wildlife Mysteries Ser.). (ENG., Illus.). 158p. (J). (gr. 2-9). pap. 7.99 (978-0-635-11188-3(8), Marsh, Carole Bks.) Gallopade International.
Martin, Bridgitt. Bunny & the Amazing Gift: God Cares for All His Creation. 2013. 28p. pap. 13.99 (978-1-4908-0952-6(X), WestBow Pr.) Author Solutions, Inc.
Martin, Joan Watson. Inventing Chloe. 2008. 140p. 19.95 (978-1-934335-25-3(8)); pap. 9.95 (978-1-934335-24-6(X)) WordWright.biz, Inc. (One Night Bks.).
Martin, LaJoyce. The Silver Ghost. 2004. (Illus.). 161p. (J). pap. 9.99 (978-1-56722-643-0(4)) Word Aflame Pr.
Marusak, Elaine. Truly Tales & Girl Fish Stories. 2006. 93p. pap. 16.95 (978-1-4241-3244-7(4)) PublishAmerica, Inc.
Marusak, Elaine Truly. Truly Tales: Aunt Gertie & Uncle George's Haunted House. 2007. (ENG.). 84p. per. 19.95 (978-1-4241-5959-8(8)) America Star Bks.
Mastrud, Karen. Fucious. 2012. 34p. 24.95 (978-1-61863-419-1(4)) Bookstand Publishing.
—Fucious: The True Story of the Ugly Duckling. Margolis, Al, illus. 2012. 32p. (J). 24.95 (978-1-61863-414-6(3)) Bookstand Publishing.
Mathieu, Jennifer. Devoted. 2015. (ENG.). 336p. (YA). (gr. 7). 16.99 (978-1-59643-911-5(4), 9781596439115) Roaring Brook Pr.
Mathieu, Jennifer. Moxie. 2017. (YA). pap. **(978-1-250-10426-7(2))** Roaring Brook Pr.
Mayhall, Robin. He Loves Me, He Loves Me Not. Cella, Kristen & Tiede, Dirk, illus. 2013. (My Boyfriend Is a Monster Ser.: 7). (ENG.). 128p. (YA). (gr. 7-12). lib. bdg. 29.27 (978-0-7613-6005-6(0), Graphic Universe™) Lerner Publishing Group.
—He Loves Me, He Loves Me Not. Cella, Kristen et al, illus. 2013. (My Boyfriend Is a Monster Ser.: 7). (ENG.). 128p. (YA). (gr. 7-12). pap. 9.95 (978-0-7613-8548-6(7), Graphic Universe™) Lerner Publishing Group.
McBride-Smith, Barbara. Greek Myths, Western Style: Toga Tales with an Attitude. 2005. (ENG.). 128p. (J). (gr. 5-17). pap. 8.95 (978-0-87483-617-2(4)) August Hse. Pubs., Inc.
McBride, Susan. The Debs: Gloves Off. 2010. (YA). (978-0-385-73796-8(3)); (978-0-385-90703-3(6)) Random House Publishing Group. (Delacorte Pr).
McCall, Guadalupe Garcia. Shame the Stars, 1 vol. 2016. (ENG.). 320p. (YA). 19.95 (978-1-62014-278-3(3)) Lee & Low Bks., Inc.
—Summer of the Mariposas. 2012. (ENG.). 352p. (YA). 19.95 (978-1-60060-900-8(7), Tu Bks.) Lee & Low Bks., Inc.
—Under the Mesquite. 2013. (ENG., Illus.). 224p. (J). (gr. 7-18). 17.95 (978-1-60060-429-4(3)) Lee & Low Bks., Inc.
McLellan, Sean. The Red Booted Chicken. 2009. 48p. (J). pap. 17.49 (978-1-4389-5610-7(X)) AuthorHouse.
McMahon, P. J. Case of the Psychic Hamster. Manders, John, illus. 2005. 153p. (J). lib. bdg. 15.38 (978-1-4242-0404-5(6)) Fitzgerald Bks.
—Case of the Singing Sea Dragons. Manders, John, illus. 2005. 153p. (J). lib. bdg. 15.38 (978-1-4242-0406-9(2)) Fitzgerald Bks.
McManis, Margaret. The Wild Texas Stampede!, 1 vol. Dupree, Bruce, illus. 2008. (ENG.). 32p. (J). (gr. 1-3). 16.99 (978-1-58980-568-2(2)) Pelican Publishing Co., Inc.
Meyer, Carolyn. Jubilee Journey. 2007. (ENG., Illus.). 288p. (J). (gr. 5-7). pap. 17.95 (978-0-15-205845-6(1)) Houghton Mifflin Harcourt Publishing Co.
—Jubilee Journey. 2007. 271p. (J). (gr. 5-9). 14.60 (978-0-7569-6682-9(5)) Perfection Learning Corp.
—White Lilacs. 2007. (ENG., Illus.). 256p. (J). (gr. 2-5). pap. 8.99 (978-0-15-205851-7(6)) Houghton Mifflin Harcourt Publishing Co.
—White Lilacs. 2006. (Illus.). 242p. (gr. 4-7). 16.95 (978-0-7569-6683-6(3)) Perfection Learning Corp.
Michael, Todd. Texas State Bird Pageant. Randall, Lee Brandt, illus. 2005. 32p. (J). (gr. -1-3). 16.95 (978-1-893062-75-7(9)) Quail Ridge Pr., Inc.
Minton, Ross. Baseball, from the Street to the Diamond, 1 vol. 2010. 94p. pap. 19.95 (978-1-4489-4918-2(1)) America Star Bks.
Mitchell, Carolann. The Song of the Snow. 2011. 68p. (gr. 4-6). pap. 8.95 (978-0-595-46609-2(5)) iUniverse, Inc.
Moberg, Julia. Skies over Sweetwater. 2007. (ENG.). 152p. (gr. 7-18). per. 15.00 (978-0-9792371-2-6(2)) Keene Publishing.
Moceanu, Dominique & Thompson, Alicia. Reaching High. 2012. (Go-For-Gold Gymnasts Ser.). (ENG.). 224p. (J). (gr. 5-9). pap. 5.99 (978-1-4231-3657-6(8)) Hyperion Pr.
Moss, Patricia Crocker. Dillie's Encounter with the Bucket Man. 2010. 36p. pap. 21.99 (978-1-4535-4460-0(7)) Xlibris Corp.
Moulder, Holly. Crystal City Lights. 2013. (ENG.). 190p. (J). pap. 8.99 (978-0-9885295-0-2(5)) Blue Marlin Pubns.
Mowry, Tia & Mowry, Tamera. Double Vision. 2015. (Twintuition Ser.: 1). (ENG.). 208p. (J). (gr. 3-7). 16.99 (978-0-06-237286-4(6)) HarperCollins Pubs.
Murphy, Julie. Dumplin. (YA). (gr. 8). 2017. 400p. pap. 9.99 (978-0-06-232719-2(4)) 2015. (ENG.). 384p. 17.99 (978-0-06-232718-5(6)) HarperCollins Pubs.
—Dumplin. 2017. (YA). lib. bdg. 20.85 **(978-0-606-39647-9(0))** Turtleback Bks.
Murray, Pamela. Pirates of Texas. 2012. 28p. (-18). pap. 24.95 (978-1-4626-9996-4(0)) America Star Bks.
Myers, Anna. Tumbleweed Baby. Vess, Charles, illus. 2014. (ENG.). 32p. (J). (gr. k-2). 16.95 (978-1-4197-1232-6(2), Abrams Bks. for Young Readers) Abrams, Inc.
Neighbors, Jared. Rivals, 1 vol. 2009. 73p. pap. 19.95 (978-1-61582-021-4(3)) America Star Bks.
Nichols, Travis. Matthew Meets the Man. 2012. (ENG., Illus.). 176p. (YA). (gr. 6-9). 24.99 (978-1-59643-545-2(3), 9781596435452) Roaring Brook Pr.
Nielson, Ane O. The Lone Star G Brand on My Behind. 2004. (Illus.). 96p. (J). per. 9.95 (978-1-930580-56-5(8), Luminary Media Group) Pine Orchard, Inc.
Norton, Tamra. Comfortable in My Own Genes: A Novel. 2004. 175p. pap. 15.95 (978-1-55517-772-0(7)) Cedar Fort, Inc./CFI Distribution.
O Flatharta, Antoine. Hurry & the Monarch. So, Meilo, illus. 2009. (ENG.). 40p. (J). (gr. k-3). pap. 7.99 (978-0-385-73719-7(X), Dragonfly Bks.) Random Hse. Children's Bks.
O'Kane, George & McEntee, Bill, illus. Hook Em's Colorful Campus Tour - University of Texas A-Z: Forty Acres (A-Z) 2004. (J). 9.99 (978-1-933069-01-2(5)) Odd Duck Ink, Inc.
O'Neill, Elizabeth. Alfred Visits Texas. 2007. 24p. (J). pap. 12.00 (978-0-9790240-9-2(9)) Global Business Information Strategies, Inc.
Pascal, Francine. The Ruling Class. 2010. (ENG.). 208p. (YA). (gr. 9). pap. 10.99 (978-1-4424-1423-5(5), Simon Pulse) Simon Pulse.
Patchin, Frank Gee. The Pony Rider Boys in Texas: Or- the Veiled Riddle of the Plains. 2007. (ENG.). 166p. pap. 19.99 (978-1-4346-3536-5(8)); 182p. pap. 21.99 (978-1-4346-3537-2(6)) Creative Media Partners, LLC.
Paulsen, Gary. Canyons. 2011. (ENG.). 192p. (YA). (gr. 7). pap. 7.99 (978-0-385-74234-4(7), Ember) Random Hse. Children's Bks.
—Canyons. 2011. 184p. (gr. 4-7). lib. bdg. 18.40 (978-0-8335-6467-2(6), Turtleback) Turtleback Bks.
—The Legend of Bass Reeves: Being the True & Fictional Account of the Most Valiant Marshal in the West. 2008. (ENG., Illus.). 160p. (YA). (gr. 7-9). mass mkt. 6.99 (978-0-553-49429-7(5), Laurel Leaf) Random Hse. Children's Bks.
Payton, Belle. Two Cool for School. 2014. (It Takes Two Ser.: 2). (ENG., Illus.). 160p. (J). (gr. 3-7). 16.99 (978-1-4814-0645-1(0), Simon Spotlight) Simon Spotlight.
—A Whole New Ball Game. 2014. (It Takes Two Ser.: 1). (ENG., Illus.). 160p. (J). (gr. 3-7). 16.99 (978-1-4814-0642-0(6)); pap. 6.99 (978-1-4814-0641-3(8)) Simon Spotlight. (Simon Spotlight).
Pearl, Paige. ARTLANTICA: the Secret Kingdom Beneath Galveston Island. 2008. 38p. 18.95 (978-1-4357-0389-6(8)) Lulu Pr., Inc.
Pearson, Mary E. A Room on Lorelei Street. 2008. (ENG.). 288p. (YA). (gr. 9-13). pap. 19.99 (978-0-312-38019-9(4), 9780312380199) Square Fish.
Penson, Mary. Billy Bardin & the Witness Tree. 2004. (Chaparral Bks.). (ENG.). 146p. (J). pap. 11.95 (978-0-87565-283-2(2)) Texas Christian Univ. Pr.
Penson, Mary E. Martha Mary Overstreet, M. D. 2007. (Chaparral Bks.). (ENG.). 142p. (J). per. 11.95 (978-0-87565-345-7(6)) Texas Christian Univ. Pr.
Pérez, Ashley Hope. Out of Darkness. 2015. (ENG., Illus.). 408p. (YA). (gr. 8-12). 18.99 (978-1-4677-4202-3(3), Carolrhoda Lab™) Lerner Publishing Group.
Peschke, M. Vacation Queen. Mourning, Tuesday, illus. 2016. (Kylie Jean Ser.). (ENG.). 112p. (gr. 2-3). 8.95 (978-1-5158-0059-0(8)) Picture Window Bks.
Peschke, Marci. Blueberry Queen, 1 vol. Mourning, Tuesday, illus. 2011. (Kylie Jean Ser.). (ENG.). 112p. (gr. 2-3). pap. 5.95 (978-1-4048-6615-7(9)); lib. bdg. 22.65 (978-1-4048-6756-7(2)) Picture Window Bks. (Kylie Jean).
—Cooking Queen. Mourning, Tuesday, illus. 2017. (Kylie Jean Ser.). (ENG.). 112p. (gr. 2-3). lib. bdg. 22.65 **(978-1-4795-9899-1(2)**, Kylie Jean) Picture Window Bks.
—Dancing Queen, 1 vol. Mourning, Tuesday, illus. 2012. (Kylie Jean Ser.). (ENG.). 112p. (gr. 2-3). pap. 5.95 (978-1-4048-7209-7(4)); lib. bdg. 22.65 (978-1-4048-6798-7(8)) Picture Window Bks. (Kylie Jean).
—Drama Queen, 1 vol. Mourning, Tuesday, illus. 2011. (Kylie Jean Ser.). (ENG.). 112p. (gr. 2-3). lib. bdg. 22.65 (978-1-4048-6757-4(0), Kylie Jean) Picture Window Bks.
—Drama Queen, 1 vol. Mourning, Tuesday, illus. 2011. (Kylie Jean Ser.). (ENG.). 112p. (gr. 2-3). pap. 5.95 (978-1-4048-6616-4(7), Kylie Jean) Picture Window Bks.
—Fashion Queen. Mourning, Tuesday, illus. 2015. (Kylie Jean Ser.). (ENG.). 112p. (gr. 2-3). 8.95 (978-1-4795-5881-0(8), Kylie Jean) Picture Window Bks.
—Fishing Queen. Mourning, Tuesday, illus. 2017. (Kylie Jean Ser.). (ENG.). 112p. (gr. 2-3). lib. bdg. 22.65 **(978-1-4795-9900-4(X)**, Kylie Jean) Picture Window Bks.
—Football Queen, 1 vol. Mourning, Tuesday, illus. 2012. (Kylie Jean Ser.). (ENG.). 112p. (gr. 2-3). pap. 5.95 (978-1-4048-7210-3(8)); lib. bdg. 22.65 (978-1-4048-6799-4(6)) Picture Window Bks. (Kylie Jean).
—Green Queen, 1 vol. Mourning, Tuesday, illus. 2014. (Kylie Jean Ser.). (ENG.). 112p. (gr. 2-3). 22.65 (978-1-4795-2351-1(8), Kylie Jean) Picture Window Bks.
—Gymnastics Queen. Mourning, Tuesday, illus. 2016. (Kylie Jean Ser.). (ENG.). 112p. (gr. 2-3). lib. bdg. 22.65 (978-1-5158-0052-1(0)) Picture Window Bks.
—Hoop Queen, 1 vol. Mourning, Tuesday, illus. 2011. (Kylie Jean Ser.). (ENG.). 112p. (gr. 2-3). lib. bdg. 22.65 (978-1-4048-5962-3(4), Kylie Jean) Picture Window Bks.
—Hoop Queen, 1 vol. Mourning, Tuesday, illus. 2011. (Kylie Jean Ser.). (ENG.). 112p. (gr. 2-3). pap. 5.95 (978-1-4048-6617-1(5), Kylie Jean) Picture Window Bks.

—Rodeo Queen, 1 vol. Mourning, Tuesday, illus. 2011. (Kylie Jean Ser.). (ENG.). 112p. (gr. 2-3). pap. 5.95 *(978-1-4048-6618-8(3))*; lib. bdg. 22.65 *(978-1-4048-5961-6(6))* Picture Window Bks. (Kylie Jean).
—Singing Queen, 1 vol. Mourning, Tuesday, illus. 2012. (Kylie Jean Ser.). (ENG.). 112p. (gr. 2-3). pap. 5.95 *(978-1-4048-7211-0(6))*; lib. bdg. 22.65 *(978-1-4048-6800-7(3))* Picture Window Bks. (Kylie Jean).
—Soccer Queen. Mourning, Tuesday, illus. 2015. (Kylie Jean Ser.). (ENG.). 112p. (gr. 2-3). 22.65 *(978-1-4795-5882-7(6)*, Kylie Jean) Picture Window Bks.
—Spelling Queen, 1 vol. Mourning, Tuesday, illus. 2012. (Kylie Jean Ser.). (ENG.). 112p. (gr. 2-3). pap. 5.95 *(978-1-4048-7212-7(4))*; lib. bdg. 22.65 *(978-1-4048-6801-4(1))* Picture Window Bks. (Kylie Jean).
—Vacation Queen. Mourning, Tuesday, illus. 2016. (Kylie Jean Ser.). (ENG.). 112p. (gr. 2-3). lib. bdg. 22.65 *(978-1-5158-0058-3(X))* Picture Window Bks.
—Valentine Queen, 1 vol. Mourning, Tuesday, illus. 2014. (Kylie Jean Ser.). (ENG.). 112p. (gr. 2-3). 22.65 *(978-1-4795-2352-8(6)*, Kylie Jean) Picture Window Bks.
Petit, Denice. Twenty-Two Turtles. 2013. (ENG.). 34p. (J). pap. 15.95 *(978-1-4327-9875-8(8))* Outskirts Pr., Inc.
Pierotti, Jr. Toward the Setting Sun. 2007. 268p. per. 17.95 *(978-0-595-45469-3(0))* iUniverse, Inc.
Pittman, Seth. Raggy's Island. 2010. 124p. pap. 9.95 *(978-0-557-59557-0(6))* Lulu Pr., Inc.
Platt, Randall Beth. Liberty's Christmas. 2012. (ENG.). 224p. (YA). (gr. 7-12). 19.95 *(978-0-89672-766-3(1))* Texas Tech Univ. Pr.
Powell, Lenora Y. Ardo: The Mysterious New House. 2008. 105p. pap. 19.95 *(978-1-60672-133-9(X))* America Star Bks.
Rand, Johnathan. Freddie Fernortner #11: Tadpole Trouble. 2010. 95p. (J). pap. 4.99 *(978-1-893699-29-8(3))* AudioCraft Publishing, Inc.
Ransom, Candice. The Night of the Hurricane's Fury. Tong, Paul, illus. (On My Own History Ser.). 48p. 2011. (J). pap. 39.62 *(978-0-7613-7621-7(6)*, First Avenue Editions) 2011. (ENG.). (gr. 2-4). pap. 6.95 *(978-0-7613-3940-3(X)*, First Avenue Editions) 2009. (ENG.). (gr. 2-4). 25.26 *(978-0-8225-7893-2(X))* Lerner Publishing Group.
Reeves, Dia. Bleeding Violet. 2010. (ENG.). 480p. (YA). (gr. 9). pap. 20.99 *(978-1-4169-8619-5(7)*, Simon Pulse) Simon Pulse.
—Slice of Cherry. 2011. (ENG.). (YA). (gr. 9). 528p. pap. 9.99 *(978-1-4169-8621-8(9))*; 512p. 16.99 *(978-1-4169-8620-1(0))* Simon Pulse. (Simon Pulse).
Restrepo, Bettina. Illegal. 2011. (ENG.). 272p. (YA). (gr. 8-18). 17.99 *(978-0-06-195342-2(3)*, Tegen, Katherine Bks) HarperCollins Pubs.
Rice, David. Crazy Loco. 2008. 135p. 16.00 *(978-0-7569-8951-4(5))* Perfection Learning Corp.
Rice, David & Garcia, Mike D. Heart-Shaped Cookies. 2011. (YA). pap. *(978-1-931010-79-5(X))* Bilingual Pr./Editorial Bilingue.
Rinaldi, Ann. Come Juneteenth. 2009. (ENG., Illus.). 256p. (YA). (gr. 7). pap. 7.99 *(978-0-15-206392-4(7))* Houghton Mifflin Harcourt Publishing Co.
Rizzo, Cynthia Marie. Julie & the Unicorn. 2003. 49p. pap. 16.95 *(978-1-4137-0785-4(8))* PublishAmerica, Inc.
Roach, Joyce Gibson, tr. Cowgirl of the Rocking R. 2003. (J). *(978-0-9726573-0-3(4))* Crosswinds Bks.
Roberts, Tina. Dream Watchman: Quest for the Missing Talisman Book I. 2011. 244p. pap. 15.95 *(978-1-60976-636-8(9)*, Eloquent Bks.) Strategic Book Publishing & Rights Agency (SBPRA).
Robinson, Gary. Danny Blackgoat, Rugged Road to Freedom. 2014. (ENG.). (YA). pap. 9.95 *(978-1-939053-05-3(6)*, 7th Generation) Book Publishing Co.
Sachar, Louis. Hoyos. 2003. (SPA.). (gr. 5-8). lib. bdg. 25.75 *(978-0-613-64523-2(5)*, Turtleback) Turtleback Bks.
Saldaña, Jr. A Good Long Way. 2010. 128p. (J). (gr. 6-18). pap. 10.95 *(978-1-55885-607-3(2)*, Piñata Books) Arte Publico Pr.
Saldana, Rene, Jr. The Jumping Tree. 2008. 181p. (gr. 5-7). 16.50 *(978-0-7569-8950-7(7))* Perfection Learning Corp.
Saldana, Rene. The Whole Sky Full of Stars. 2008. (ENG.). 144p. (YA). (gr. 7-11). mass mkt. 5.99 *(978-0-440-23791-4(2)*, Laurel Leaf) Random Hse. Children's Bks.
Sally Spencer. Juanita's Flowers. Phil Brannan & Sunni Brannan, illus. 2009. 32p. pap. 14.49 *(978-1-4389-4841-6(7))* AuthorHouse.
Sanders, Russell. All You Need Is Love. 2017. 220p. pap. 14.99 ***(978-1-63533-321-3(0)***, Harmony Ink Pr.) Dreamspinner Pr.
Sargent, Dave & Sargent, Pat. Grady: (Dappled Grey) Proud to Be an American, 30 vols., Vol. 30. Lenoir, Jane, illus. 2003. (Saddle up Ser.: Vol. 30). 42p. (J). lib. bdg. 23.60 *(978-1-56763-813-4(9))* Ozark Publishing.
—Grady: Proud to Be an American, 30 vols. Lenoir, Jane, illus. 2003. (Saddle up Ser.: Vol. 30). 42p. (J). pap. 10.95 *(978-1-56763-814-1(7))* Ozark Publishing.
Schlosser, S. E. Spooky Texas: Tales of Hauntings, Strange Happenings, & Other Local Lore. Hoffman, Paul G., illus. 2008. (Spooky Ser.). (ENG.). 200p. pap. 14.95 *(978-0-7627-4853-2(2))* Globe Pequot Pr., The.
Schult, Sherry. There's a Horse in My Closet..., 1 vol. 2010. 48p. pap. 16.95 *(978-1-4489-5412-4(6))* PublishAmerica, Inc.
Seals, Hollie. When You Can't Find the Words. 2007. 144p. per. 11.95 *(978-0-595-45023-7(7))* iUniverse, Inc.
Shafer, Patty. Annie the Texas Ranch Dog - Danger at Lost Maples. Retzlaff, Shay, illus. 2012. (ENG.). 96p. (J). pap. 9.95 *(978-1-61899-009-9(8)*, Tadpole Pr. 4 Kids) Smooth Sailing Pr., LLC.
—Annie the Texas Ranch Dog - Injured Hero. Retzlaff, Shay, illus. 2012. 96p. (J). pap. 9.95 *(978-1-61899-008-2(X)*, Tadpole Pr. 4 Kids) Smooth Sailing Pr., LLC.
—Annie the Texas Ranch Dog - New Life in Utopia. Retzlaff, Shay, illus. 2012. 96p. (J). pap. 9.95 *(978-1-61899-007-5(1)*, Tadpole Pr. 4 Kids) Smooth Sailing Pr., LLC.
Silvano, Wendi. Love Is All Around Texas. Czernichowska, Joanna, illus. 2016. (ENG.). 32p. (J). (-6). 12.99 *(978-1-4926-2965-8(0)*, Sourcebooks Jabberwocky) Sourcebooks, Inc.
Simmons, Lynn. Bo & the Christmas Bandit, 1 vol. Lyne, Alison, illus. 2009. (Bo Ser.). (ENG.). 128p. (J). (gr. 3-6). pap. 8.95 *(978-1-58980-723-5(5))* Pelican Publishing Co., Inc.
Simmons, Ted. Diablo Creek. 2007. (ENG.). 168p. (YA). pap. *(978-0-9776958-7-4(5))* CyPress Pubns.
Smallman, Steve. Santa Is Coming to Austin. Dunn, Robert, illus. 2013. (ENG.). 32p. (J). (-3). 9.99 *(978-1-4022-8973-6(1)*, Sourcebooks Jabberwocky) Sourcebooks, Inc.
—Santa Is Coming to Dallas. Dunn, Robert, illus. 2014. (ENG.). 32p. (J). (-3). 9.99 *(978-1-4926-0700-7(2)*, Sourcebooks Jabberwocky) Sourcebooks, Inc.
—Santa Is Coming to el Paso. Dunn, Robert, illus. 2015. (ENG.). 32p. (J). (-3). 9.99 *(978-1-4926-2634-3(1)*, Sourcebooks Jabberwocky) Sourcebooks, Inc.
—Santa Is Coming to Houston. Dunn, Robert, illus. 2015. (ENG.). 32p. (J). (-3). 9.99 *(978-1-4926-2631-2(7)*, Sourcebooks Jabberwocky) Sourcebooks, Inc.
—Santa Is Coming to Lubbock. Dunn, Robert, illus. 2013. (ENG.). 32p. (J). (-3). 9.99 *(978-1-4022-9136-4(1)*, Sourcebooks Jabberwocky) Sourcebooks, Inc.
—Santa Is Coming to Texas. Dunn, Robert, illus. 2012. (ENG.). 32p. (J). (-3). 9.99 *(978-1-4022-7512-8(9)*, Sourcebooks Jabberwocky) Sourcebooks, Inc.
Smallman, Steve, et al. My First Santa's Coming to Texas. Dunn, Robert, illus. 2015. (ENG.). 18p. (J). bds. 9.99 *(978-1-4926-2870-5(0)*, Sourcebooks Jabberwocky) Sourcebooks, Inc.
Smart, Kimberly. A New Home for Gabril. 2008. 32p. 15.95 *(978-1-4357-0762-7(1))* Lulu Pr., Inc.
Smith, Cynthia Leitich. Blessed. (Tantalize Ser.). (ENG., Illus.). (YA). (gr. 9). 2012. 464p. pap. 8.99 *(978-0-7636-5479-5(5))* 2011. 480p. 17.99 *(978-0-7636-4326-3(2))* Candlewick Pr.
—Tantalize. 2007. (Tantalize Ser.). (ENG., Illus.). 336p. (YA). (gr. 9-12). 16.99 *(978-0-7636-2791-1(7))* Candlewick Pr.
Smith, Debra. Hattie Marshall & the Dangerous Fire, 1 vol. 2007. (Hattie Marshall Ser.). (ENG.). 128p. (J). (gr. 3-6). per. 7.95 *(978-1-58980-492-0(9))* Pelican Publishing Co., Inc.
Smith, Debra West. Hattie Marshall & the Prowling Panther, 1 vol. 2005. (Hattie Marshall Ser.). (ENG.). 144p. (J). (gr. 4-6). pap. 7.95 *(978-1-56554-940-1(6))* Pelican Publishing Co., Inc.
Smith, Greg Leitich. Chronal Engine. Henry, Blake, illus. 2013. (ENG.). 192p. (J). (gr. 5-7). pap. 6.99 *(978-0-544-02277-5(7))* Houghton Mifflin Harcourt Publishing Co.
Spradlin, Joe. Sugar. 2007. 48p. per. 14.95 *(978-1-4327-0200-7(9))* Outskirts Pr., Inc.
Stauffer, Sharon. Cornfield Baby: And Other Nature Surprises. 2003. (Illus.). 179p. 8.40 *(978-0-7399-2314-6(5)*, 2344) Rod & Staff Pubs., Inc.
Stern, Jacqueline. The Ghosts of Goliad. 2003. iii, 165p. (J). 17.95 *(978-1-57168-785-2(8)*, Eakin Pr.) Eakin Pr.
—The Haunted Tunnel. 96p. 8.95 *(978-1-57168-310-6(0))* Eakin Pr.
Stephenson, Lynda. Dancing with Elvis. (YA). (gr. 7). 2006. (ENG.). 331p. per. 8.00 *(978-0-8028-5300-4(5))* 2005. 323p. 17.00 *(978-0-8028-5293-9(9))* Eerdmans, William B. Publishing Co. (Eerdmans Bks For Young Readers).
Stone, B. J. Girl on the Bluff. (Illus.). 160p. 8.95 *(978-1-57168-297-0(X))* Eakin Pr.
Stone, Jeff. Five Ancestors Out of the Ashes: Phoenix. 2013. (Five Ancestors Out of the Ashes Ser.: 1). (ENG.). 304p. (J). (gr. 4-7). 6.99 *(978-0-375-87097-2(0)*, Yearling) Random Hse. Children's Bks.
—Five Ancestors Out of the Ashes #1: Phoenix. 2012. (Five Ancestors Out of the Ashes Ser.). (ENG.). 288p. (J). (gr. 4-7). 16.99 *(978-0-375-87018-7(0)*, Random Hse. Bks. for Young Readers) Random Hse. Children's Bks.
Stork, Francisco X. The Memory of Light. 2016. (Arthur a Levine Novel Bks.). (ENG.). 336p. (YA). (gr. 7). 17.99 *(978-0-545-47432-0(9))* Scholastic, Inc.
Strauss, Kevin. Pecos Bill Invents the Ten-Gallon Hat, 1 vol. Harrington, David, illus. 2012. (ENG.). 32p. (J). (gr. k-3). 16.99 *(978-1-4556-1502-5(1))* Pelican Publishing Co., Inc.
Stripland, Rubye Weldon. Lucy Bell, Queen of the Pasture. 2008. 92p. pap. 10.95 *(978-1-4357-1472-4(5))* Lulu Pr., Inc.
—Lucy Bell, Queen of the Pasture Book Four. 2009. 94p. pap. 10.96 *(978-1-4357-4742-5(9))* Lulu Pr., Inc.
—Lucy Bell, Queen of the Pasture, Book Three. 2008. 90p. pap. 10.95 *(978-1-4357-3418-0(1))* Lulu Pr., Inc.
—Lucy Bell, Queen of the Pasture Book Two. 2008. 100p. pap. 10.95 *(978-1-4357-1895-1(X))* Lulu Pr., Inc.
Sully, Katherine. Night-Night Texas. Kolanovic, Dubravka & Poole, Helen, illus. 2016. (ENG.). 20p. (J). (-1). bds. 9.99 *(978-1-4926-3936-7(2)*, 9781492639367, Sourcebooks Jabberwocky) Sourcebooks, Inc.
Tata, Cb. Ernie the Eagle Goes to Texas. Hanley, Zachary, illus. 2012. 44p. 24.95 *(978-1-4626-5374-4(X))* America Star Bks.
Tingle, Tim. Danny Blackgoat, Navajo Prisoner. 2013. (PathFinders Ser.). (ENG.). 151p. (YA). pap. 9.95 *(978-1-939053-03-9(X)*, 7th Generation) Book Publishing Co.
Tingle, Tim & Moore, Doc. More Spooky Texas Tales. Benas, Jeanne A., illus. 2010. (ENG.). 104p. (J). (gr. 4-7). lib. bdg. 18.95 *(978-0-89672-700-7(9))* Texas Tech Univ. Pr.
Tingle, Tim & Moore, James W. Spooky Texas Tales. Miller, Gina, illus. 2005. x, 85p. (J). pap. *(978-0-89672-566-9(9))* Texas Tech Univ. Pr.
Townsend, Tom. Powderhorn Passage. 112p. 9.95 *(978-1-57168-433-2(6))* Eakin Pr.
Trenchard, Robert. The Francine Frog Fiasco. 2008. 265p. (J). pap. 13.99 *(978-0-615-20974-6(2))* Soxwings Publishing.
Treviño, Hilda L. Ladybugs on a Mission. 2013. 70p. (gr. 4-6). pap. 8.95 *(978-1-4759-7762-2(X))* iUniverse, Inc.
Tribolet, Leslie L. Danny's Tale: Adventures of an Arabian Horse in his Own Words. 2010. (Illus.). 112p. 24.95 *(978-1-4490-6065-7(X))*; pap. 14.95 *(978-1-4490-6064-0(1))* AuthorHouse.
Turner, Juliette. That's Not Hay in My Hair, 1 vol. 2016. (ENG.). 240p. (J). pap. 8.99 *(978-0-310-73244-0(1))* Zonderkidz.
Vermillion, Patricia. ¿Chili Texano? ¡Ay Dios! Guadalupe, Jezabel, tr. from ENG. Smith, Kuleigh, illus. 2013. (SPA & ENG.). 40p. 21.95 *(978-0-87565-584-0(X))* Texas Christian Univ. Pr.
—Texas Chili? Oh My! Smith, Kuleigh, illus. 2013. (ENG.). 40p. 21.95 *(978-0-87565-568-0(8))* Texas Christian Univ. Pr.
Villareal, Ray. Alamo Wars. 2008. 187p. (J). (gr. 6-18). pap. 10.95 *(978-1-55885-513-7(0)*, Piñata Books) Arte Publico Pr.
—Who's Buried in the Garden? 2009. 160p. (YA). (gr. 6-18). pap. 10.95 *(978-1-55885-546-5(7)*, Piñata Books) Arte Publico Pr.
Walker, Melissa. Small Town Sinners. 2011. (ENG.). 288p. (YA). (gr. 9-12). 16.99 *(978-1-59990-527-3(2)*, 9781599905273, Bloomsbury USA Childrens) Bloomsbury Publishing USA.
Walthers, Joanie. The Fish Smuggler. Walthers, Don, illus. 2013. (ENG.). 24p. (J). 19.95 *(978-1-4787-1167-4(1))* Outskirts Pr., Inc.
Webb, Susan. A Tale of Two Brothers. 2012. 24p. pap. 12.95 *(978-1-4497-6053-3(8)*, WestBow Pr.) Author Solutions, Inc.
Webster-Tyson, Paulette L. I Gotta Get a Nickname! 2011. 32p. (gr. -1-2). pap. 17.25 *(978-1-4269-5625-6(8))* Trafford Publishing.
Weihrich, Carroll. On Jim Street. 2003. 144p. 24.50 *(978-1-932621-19-8(9))*; per. 15.00 *(978-1-932621-18-1(0))* Open Bk. Publishing.
Weldon, Stayton. Whitey on the Ranch. Anderson-Shorter, Susan, illus. 2010. 52p. pap. 12.95 *(978-1-4490-5474-8(9))* AuthorHouse.
Wells, Tom. Strange Seasons: Summer. 2008. 212p. 24.95 *(978-0-595-50888-4(X))*; pap. 14.95 *(978-0-595-52016-9(2))* iUniverse, Inc.
White, Tom. Lost in the Texas Desert. 2004. (Illus.). 132p. per. 7.95 *(978-0-9753611-0-8(4))* Arlington Pubns.
Williams, Lori Aurelia. When Kambia Elaine Flew in from Neptune. unabr. ed. 2004. 246p. (J). (gr. 7-18). pap. 50.00 incl. audio *(978-0-8072-8851-1(9)*, Listening Library) Random Hse. Audio Publishing Group.
Wilsdon, Christina. A Wild Ride in Texas. Jaekel, Susan, illus. 2006. 26p. (J). 7.99 *(978-1-59939-011-6(6))* Cornerstone Pr.
Woolley, Bryan. Mr. Green's Magnificent Machine. Arbuckle, Scott, illus. 2003. 32p. 15.95 *(978-1-57168-606-0(1))* Eakin Pr.
Worcester, Daryl D. Traves Travislot's Going South for the Winter. 2011. 46p. pap. 16.95 *(978-1-4626-1091-4(9))* America Star Bks.
Wright, Lynda. Flowers for Addison. 2012. 24p. pap. 24.95 *(978-1-4626-5787-2(7))* America Star Bks.
Ziegler, Jennifer. How Not to Be Popular. 2010. (ENG.). 348p. (YA). (gr. 7). mass mkt. 8.99 *(978-0-440-24024-2(7)*, Delacorte Bks. for Young Readers) Random Hse. Children's Bks.
—Revenge of the Angels. 2015. (ENG.). 256p. (J). (gr. 3-7). 16.99 *(978-0-545-83899-3(1)*, Scholastic Pr.) Scholastic, Inc.

TEXAS—HISTORY

Alter, Judy. Martín de León: Tejano Empresario. Messersmith, Patrick, illus. 2007. (Stars of Texas Ser.: 4). (ENG.). 72p. (gr. 4-7). 14.95 *(978-1-933337-08-1(7))* State Hse. Pr.
—Mirabeau B. Lamar: Second President of Texas. Messersmith, Patrick, illus. 2005. (Stars of Texas Ser.: 2). (ENG.). 72p. (gr. 4-7). 17.95 *(978-1-880510-97-1(9))* State Hse. Pr.
—Miriam Ma Ferguson: First Woman Governor of Texas. Messersmith, Patrick, illus. 2006. (Stars of Texas Ser.: 3). (ENG.). 72p. (gr. 4-7). 17.95 *(978-1-933337-01-2(X))* State Hse. Pr.
Altman, Linda Jacobs & Benduhn, Tea. Texas. 2nd rev. ed. 2010. (It's My State! Ser.). 80p. (gr. 3-18). lib. bdg. 31.36 *(978-1-60870-059-2(3))* Marshall Cavendish Corp.
Amberson, Mary. A Brave Boy & a Good Soldier: John C. C. Hill & the Texas Expedition to Mier. 2006. (ENG., Illus.). 100p. (J). (gr. 3-7). 24.95 *(978-0-87611-214-4(9))* Texas State Historical Assn.
Antonio Lopez de Santa Anna. 2010. (Great Hispanic Heritage Ser.). (Illus.). 104p. (gr. 6-12). 35.00 *(978-1-60413-734-7(7)*, Chelsea Hse.) Facts On File, Inc.
Baker, Karle Wilson. Texas Flag Primer. 2005. reprint ed. pap. 20.95 *(978-0-7661-9572-1(4))* Kessinger Publishing, LLC.
Bauer, Marion Dane. Celebrating Texas: 50 States to Celebrate. Canga, C. B., illus. 2013. (Green Light Readers Level 3 Ser.). (ENG.). 40p. (J). (gr. 1-4). 12.99 *(978-0-547-98395-0(6))*; pap. 3.99 *(978-0-547-89786-8(3))* Houghton Mifflin Harcourt Publishing Co.
Belviso, Meg & Pollack, Pamela. What Was the Alamo? 2013. (What Was... ? Ser.). lib. bdg. 16.00 *(978-0-606-32129-7(2)*, Turtleback) Turtleback Bks.
Berman, Ron. Houston Rockets. 2013. (On the Hardwood Ser.). (ENG., Illus.). 48p. (gr. 3-8). pap. 8.95 *(978-1-61570-837-6(5))* Scobre Pr. Corp.
Bodden, Valerie. Samuel Houston: Army Leader & Historic Politician, 1 vol. 2010. (Military Heroes Ser.). (ENG.). 112p. (J). (gr. 6-12). lib. bdg. 35.64 *(978-1-60453-962-2(3))* ABDO Publishing Co.
Boehm Jerome, Kate. Houston, Tx: Cool Stuff Every Kid Should Know. 2010. (Arcadia Kids Ser.). (ENG., Illus.). 48p. (J). (gr. 3-6). pap. 9.99 *(978-1-4396-0066-5(X))* Arcadia Publishing.
Boys and Girls Club of Greater Fort Worth. T Is for Texas: Written by Kids for Kids. McCann, Michelle, ed. 2014. (See My State Ser.). (ENG., Illus.). 32p. (J). (gr. -1-3). 13.99 *(978-0-88240-989-4(1)*, 9780882409894, West Winds Pr.) Graphic Arts Ctr. Publishing Co.
Branson, Michelle. Texas Doodles, 1 vol. 2014. (ENG., Illus.). 240p. (J). pap. 9.99 *(978-1-4236-3634-2(1))* Gibbs Smith, Publisher.
Bredeson, Carmen & Dodson Wade, Mary. Texas. 2nd rev. ed. 2005. (Celebrate the States Ser.). (Illus.). 144p. (gr. 6-2). lib. bdg. 42.79 *(978-0-7614-1736-1(2)*, Benchmark Bks.) Marshall Cavendish Corp.
Brown, Jonatha A. Texas. 2005. (Portraits of the States Ser.). (Illus.). 32p. (gr. 2-6). pap. 10.50 *(978-0-8368-4654-6(0))*; lib. bdg. 26.00 *(978-0-8368-4635-5(4))* Stevens, Gareth Publishing LLLP. (Gareth Stevens Learning Library).
Burke, Johanna. The American Civil War in Texas. 2010. (Spotlight on Texas Ser.). (Illus.). 32p. (J). (gr. 3-4). (ENG.). pap. 11.75 *(978-1-61532-472-9(0))*; lib. bdg. 25.25 *(978-1-61532-474-3(7))* Rosen Publishing Group, Inc., The.
Cameron, Charles. Why Lizzie Johnson Matters to Texas. 2014. (Illus.). 32p. (J). lib. bdg. 26.25 *(978-1-4777-0908-5(8))* Rosen Publishing Group, Inc., The.
—Why Richard King Matters to Texas. 2014. (Illus.). 32p. (J). lib. bdg. 26.25 *(978-1-4777-0910-8(X))* Rosen Publishing Group, Inc., The.
Cane, Sutter. Governing Texas: Local, State, & National Governments. 2010. (Spotlight on Texas Ser.). (ENG., Illus.). 32p. (J). (gr. 3-4). pap. 11.75 *(978-1-61532-481-1(X))*; lib. bdg. 26.25 *(978-1-61532-483-5(6))* Rosen Publishing Group, Inc., The.
Caravantes, Peggy. American in Texas: The Story of Sam Houston. 2004. (Notable Americans Ser.). (Illus.). 144p. (YA). (gr. 6-12). 23.95 *(978-1-931798-19-8(2))* Reynolds, Morgan Inc.
Chemerka, William R. The Alamo from A to Z, 1 vol. Dillon, Wade, illus. 2011. (ENG.). 32p. (J). (gr. k-3). 16.99 *(978-1-4556-1461-5(0))* Pelican Publishing Co., Inc.
—Juan Seguin. Collins, Don, illus. 2012. (ENG.). 64p. (J). 16.95 *(978-1-933979-79-3(8)*, 9781933979793) Bright Sky Pr.
Chrismer, Melanie. Lone Star Legacy: The Texas Rangers Then & Now, 1 vol. 2016. (ENG., Illus.). 144p. (J). (gr. 4-7). pap. 16.95 *(978-1-4556-2104-0(8))* Pelican Publishing Co., Inc.
Christian, Betsy & Christian, George. For the Love of Texas: Tell Me about the Colonists! Gruszka, Chris A., illus. 2013. Orig. Title: For the Love of Texas: Tell Me about the Colonists! (ENG.). 112p. (J). (gr. 4-7). 14.99 *(978-1-62619-159-4(X)*, History Pr., The) Arcadia Publishing.
—For the Love of Texas: Tell Me about the Revolution! Gruszka, Chris A., illus. 2013. Orig. Title: For the Love of Texas: Tell Me about the Revolution! (ENG.). 128p. (gr. 4-7). 14.99 *(978-1-62619-160-0(3)*, History Pr., The) Arcadia Publishing.
Clinton, Greg. Life in Contemporary Texas. 2014. (Spotlight on Texas Ser.). (ENG.). 32p. (J). (gr. 3-4). 26.25 *(978-1-4777-4506-9(8)*, Rosen Classroom) Rosen Publishing Group, Inc., The.
—Texas During Reconstruction. 2014. (Spotlight on Texas Ser.). (ENG.). 32p. (J). (gr. 3-4). 26.25 *(978-1-4777-4517-5(3)*, Rosen Classroom) Rosen Publishing Group, Inc., The.
Connery-Boyd, Peg. Texas. 2016. (Hawk's Nest Activity Bks.: 0). (ENG.). 64p. (J). (-3). pap. 8.99 *(978-1-4926-3967-1(2)*, 9781492639671, Sourcebooks Jabberwocky) Sourcebooks, Inc.
Connors, Kathleen. Let's Explore the Southwest. 2013. (Road Trip: Exploring America's Regions Ser.). 24p. (J). (gr. 2-5). pap. 8.15 *(978-1-4339-9150-9(0))*; (ENG., Illus.). lib. bdg. 22.60 *(978-1-4339-9149-3(7))* Stevens, Gareth Publishing LLLP.
Corporate Contributor. Drew Brees. 2012. (ENG.). 32p. (J). *(978-0-7787-7616-1(6))*; pap. *(978-0-7787-7629-1(8))* Crabtree Publishing Co.
Crane, Carol. Little Texas. Monroe, Michael Glenn, illus. 2010. (My Little State Ser.). (ENG.). 22p. (J). 9.95 *(978-1-58536-488-6(6))* Sleeping Bear Pr.
Curry, Jane Louise. Hold up the Sky: And Other Native American Tales from Texas & The. Watts, James, illus. 2010. (ENG.). 176p. (J). (gr. 3-7). pap. 9.99 *(978-1-4424-2155-4(X)*, McElderry, Margaret K. Bks.) McElderry, Margaret K. Bks.
Drez, Jennifer & Bumstead, Robin. Goodnight Cowtown. Voight, Lisa, illus. 2012. 40p. (J). 17.95 *(978-0-615-54492-2(4))* Petit Chou Chou, LLC.
Durden-Nelson, Mae. I Just Called Her Momma. 2003. (Illus.). xii, 162p. (J). 18.95 *(978-1-57168-714-2(9))* Eakin Pr.
Early American Wars, 4 vols., Set. Incl. American Revolutionary War. Marston, Daniel & O'Neill, Robert John. lib. bdg. 33.25 *(978-1-4488-1331-5(X))*; Texas War of Independence. Huffines, Alan C. lib. bdg. 33.25 *(978-1-4488-1332-2(8))*; War of 1812: The Fight for American Trade Rights. Benn, Carl. lib. bdg. 33.25 *(978-1-4488-1333-9(6))*; (YA). (gr. 9-18). 2011. (Early American Wars Ser.). (Illus.). 96p. 2011. Set lib. bdg. 127.80 *(978-1-4488-1387-2(5))* Rosen Publishing Group, Inc., The.
Edmondson, J. R. Jim Bowie: Frontier Legend, Alamo Hero. 2009. (Library of American Lives & Times Ser.). 112p. (gr. 5-5). 69.20 *(978-1-60853-488-3(X))* Rosen Publishing Group, Inc., The.
Egan, Tracie. Francisca Alavez, the Angel of Goliad. 2004. (Famous People in American History Ser.). (ENG., Illus.). 32p. (gr. 4-8). pap. 10.00 *(978-0-8239-4181-0(7))* Rosen Publishing Group, Inc., The.
—Francisca Alvarez: El angel de Goliad. 2004. (Grandes personajes en la historia de los Estados Unidos Ser.). (SPA.). 32p. (gr. 3-6). pap. 10.00 *(978-0-8239-4227-5(9)*, Rosen Classroom) Rosen Publishing Group, Inc., The.
—Francisca Alvarez: El ángel de Goliad (Francisca Alvarez: the Angel of Goliad) 2009. (Grandes personajes en la historia de los Estados Unidos (Famous People in American History) Ser.). (SPA.). 32p. (gr. 2-3). 47.90 *(978-1-61512-798-6(4)*, Editorial Buenas Letras) Rosen Publishing Group, Inc., The.
—Francisca Alvarez: The Angel of Goliad. 2009. (Primary Sources of Famous People in American History Ser.). 32p. (gr. 2-3). 47.90 *(978-1-60851-675-9(X))* Rosen Publishing Group, Inc., The.
—Francisca Alvarez: The Angel of Goliad / el ángel de Goliad. 2009. (Famous People in American History/Grandes personajes en la historia de los Estados Unidos Ser.). (ENG & SPA.). 32p. (gr. 2-3). 47.90 *(978-1-61512-544-9(2)*, Editorial Buenas Letras) Rosen Publishing Group, Inc., The.
Ellis, Paula. Texas Activity Book, 1 vol. Nitzsche, Shane, illus. 2012. (Color & Learn Ser.). (ENG.). 64p. (J). (gr. 2-3). pap. 5.95 *(978-1-59193-376-2(5))* Adventure Pubns.
Espinosa, Chris & Rawlett, Robert. Rocket Megabyte's Texas Adventure. Espinosa, Chris, illus. 2004. (Illus.). 68p. (J). 14.00 *(978-0-9724637-1-3(2))* Sky Rocket Pr.
Fehrenbach, T. R. Lone Star: The Story of Texas. 2003. (Illus.). xxxii, 600p. (J). 60.00 *(978-0-13-058625-4(0))* Prentice Hall PTR.
Fein, Eric. Outnumbered: Davy Crockett's Final Battle at the Alamo. 2009. (Great Moments in American History Ser.). 32p. (gr. 3-3). 47.90 *(978-1-61513-148-8(5))* Rosen Publishing Group, Inc., The.
Fisher, Doris. Army Camels: Texas Ships of the Desert, 1 vol. Buckner, Julie, illus. 2013. (ENG.). 32p. (J). (gr. k-3). 16.99 *(978-1-4556-1823-1(3))* Pelican Publishing Co., Inc.

Flynn, Jean. Henry B. Gonzalez: Rebel with a Cause. 2003. (Illus.). v, 140p. (J). 16.95 (978-1-57168-780-7(7), Eakin Pr.) Eakin Pr.

Fradin, Dennis Brindell. The Alamo. 2006. (Turning Points in U. S. History Ser.). (Illus.). 46p. (J). (gr. 3-7). lib. bdg. 29.93 (978-0-7614-2127-6(0), Benchmark Bks.) Marshall Cavendish Corp.

Francis, Peter, illus. God Bless Texas, 1 vol. 2016. (Land That I Love Book Ser.). (ENG.). 18p. (J). bds. 9.99 (978-0-310-75343-8(0)) Zonderkidz.

Gamble, Adam & Jasper, Mark. Good Night Houston. Veno, Joe, illus. 2016. (Good Night Our World Ser.). (ENG.). 20p. (J). (— 1). bds. 9.95 (978-1-60219-504-2(8)) Good Night Bks.

Garland, Sherry. Voices of the Alamo, 1 vol. Himler, Ronald, illus. 2017. (Voices of History Ser.). (ENG.). 40p. (J). (gr. 3-3). 17.99 (978-1-58980-222-3(5)) Pelican Publishing Co., Inc.

Gendell, Megan. The Spanish Missions of Texas. 2010. (True Book(tm), a — Spanish Missions Ser.). (ENG.). 48p. (J). (gr. 2-5). 31.00 (978-0-531-20580-8(0)); (Illus.). pap. 6.95 (978-0-531-21243-1(2)) Scholastic Library Publishing.

Gibson, Karen Bush. Texas History for Kids: Lone Star Lives & Legends, with 21 Activites. 2015. (For Kids Ser.). (ENG., Illus.). 144p. (J). (gr. 4). pap. 16.95 (978-1-61374-989-0(9)) Chicago Review Pr., Inc.

Goldsworthy, Steve. El Alamo. 2013. (Iconos Americanos Ser.). (SPA., Illus.). 24p. (J). (gr. k-2). lib. bdg. 27.13 (978-1-62127-615-9(5), AV2 by Weigl) Weigl Pubs., Inc.

Haley, James. Stephen Austin & the Founding of Texas. 2009. (Library of American Lives & Times Ser.). 112p. (gr. 5-5). 69.20 (978-1-60853-506-4(1)) Rosen Publishing Group, Inc., The.

Haley, James L. Stephen F. Austin & the Founding of Texas. 2005. (Library of American Lives & Times). (Illus.). 112p. (YA). (gr. 4-8). lib. bdg. 34.60 (978-0-8239-5738-5(1)) Rosen Publishing Group, Inc., The.

Harasymiw, Therese. Causes & Effects of the Texas Revolution. 2010. (Spotlight on Texas Ser.). (Illus.). 32p. (J). (gr. 3-4). (ENG.). pap. 11.75 (978-1-61532-466-8(6)); lib. bdg. 25.25 (978-1-61532-468-2(2)) Rosen Publishing Group, Inc., The.

Herold, Vickey. Discover a Cattle Town: Forth Worth. 2006. (J). pap. (978-1-4108-6430-7(8)) Benchmark Education Co.

Hoffman, Mary Ann. The Alamo. 2010. (Spotlight on Texas Ser.). (ENG., Illus.). 32p. (J). (gr. 3-4). lib. bdg. 26.25 (978-1-61532-461-3(5)) Rosen Publishing Group, Inc., The.

Hollmann, Robert E. William Barret Travis. 2012. (ENG.). 130p. pap. 9.95 (978-0-9779863-9-2(X)) Fireside Pr., Inc.

Holt, Rinehart and Winston Staff. Holt Texas! 3rd ed. 2003. (SPA., Illus.). 83.00 (978-0-03-073767-1(2)) Holt McDougal.

Hopkins, Jackie Mims. Our Texas. Spearing, Craig J., illus. 2010. (ENG.). 44p. (J). (gr. 1-4). pap. 8.95 (978-1-57091-726-4(4)) Charlesbridge Publishing, Inc.

Hughes, Bill. Texas History Coloring Book & Punch Out Playset. 2004. (Illus.). 16p. (J). 4.95 (978-0-9746784-0-5(6)) Great Big Comics, Big Tex Films.

Isecke, Harriet. Finding Texas: Exploration in New Lands, 1 vol. 2012. (Primary Source Readers Ser.). (ENG.). 32p. (J). (gr. 4-4). pap. 8.99 (978-1-4333-5042-9(4)) Teacher Created Materials, Inc.

—Stephen F. Austin: The Father of Texas, 1 vol. 2012. (Primary Source Readers Ser.). (ENG.). 32p. (J). (gr. 3-3). pap. 8.99 (978-1-4333-5045-0(9)) Teacher Created Materials, Inc.

—Texas en el Siglo XX (Texas in the 20th Century) 2013. (Primary Source Readers Ser.). (SPA.). lib. bdg. 19.65 (978-0-606-31872-3(0), Turtleback) Turtleback Bks.

—Texas Hoy: Guiando a los Estados Unidos Hacia el Futuro. 2013. (Primary Source Readers (Spanish) Ser.). (SPA.). lib. bdg. 19.65 (978-0-606-31874-7(7), Turtleback) Turtleback Bks.

—Texas in the 20th Century: Building Industry & Community, 1 vol. 2012. (Primary Source Readers Ser.). (ENG.). 32p. (J). (gr. 4-4). pap. 8.99 (978-1-4333-5209-6(5)) Teacher Created Materials, Inc.

—Texas Today: Leading America into the Future, 1 vol. 2012. (Primary Source Readers Ser.). (ENG.). 32p. (J). (gr. 4-4). pap. 8.99 (978-1-4333-5053-5(X)) Teacher Created Materials, Inc.

Isecke, Harriet & Kuligowski, Stephanie. Descubriendo Texas. 2013. (Primary Source Readers Ser.). (SPA.). lib. bdg. 19.65 (978-0-606-31862-4(3), Turtleback) Turtleback Bks.

—Stephen F. Austin: El Padre de Texas / Stephen F. Austin - The Father of Texas. 2013. (Primary Source Readers Ser.). (SPA.). lib. bdg. 19.65 (978-0-606-31865-5(8), Turtleback) Turtleback Bks.

Jackson, Jack. New Texas History Movies. 2007. (ENG., Illus.). 50p. pap. 9.95 (978-0-87611-223-6(8)) Texas State Historical Assn.

Jackson, Jack & Magruder, Jana. New Texas History Movies. Jackson, Jack, illus. 2007. (ENG., Illus.). 66p. pap. 19.95 (978-0-87611-231-1(9)) Texas State Historical Assn.

Jackson, Sarah. Preep II: More Tales of Early Texas. Jenkins, Delores, illus. 2007. 48p. (J). 19.95 (978-1-931823-52-4(9)) Halcyon Pr., Ltd.

James, Trisha. Cattle & Oil: The Growth of Texas Industries. 2010. (Spotlight on Texas Ser.). (ENG., Illus.). 32p. (J). (gr. 3-4). pap. 11.75 (978-1-61532-475-0(5)); lib. bdg. 26.25 (978-1-61532-477-4(1)) Rosen Publishing Group, Inc., The.

—Celebrating Texas: Patriotic Symbols & Landmarks. 2010. (Spotlight on Texas Ser.). (Illus.). 32p. (J). (gr. 3-4). (ENG.). pap. 11.75 (978-1-61532-484-2(4)); lib. bdg. 25.25 (978-1-61532-486-6(0)) Rosen Publishing Group, Inc., The.

Jerome, Kate B. Lucky to Live in Texas. 2017. (Arcadia Kids Ser.). (ENG., Illus.). 32p. (J). 16.99 (978-0-7385-2769-7(6)) Arcadia Publishing.

—The Wise Animal Handbook Texas. 2017. (Arcadia Kids Ser.). (ENG., Illus.). 32p. (J). 16.99 (978-0-7385-2845-8(5)) Arcadia Publishing.

Johnson, Robin. Why Mirabeau Lamar Matters to Texas. 2014. (Illus.). 32p. (J). lib. bdg. 26.25 (978-1-4777-0915-3(0)) Rosen Publishing Group, Inc., The.

Kearby, Mike. Texas Tales Illustrated: The Revolution. White, Mack, illus. 2011. (Texas Tales Illustrated Ser.: 1). (ENG.). 32p. (J). (gr. k-7). pap. 6.95 (978-0-87565-429-4(0)); pap. 6.95 (978-0-87565-439-3(8)) Texas Christian Univ. Pr.

Kenney, Karen Latchana. The Lonesome Star: A Story about Texas, 1 vol. 2008. (Fact & Fable: State Stories Ser.). (ENG., Illus.). 24p. (J). (gr. -1-2). 25.65 (978-1-60453-184-8(3)) ABDO Publishing Co.

King, M. G. Librarian on the Roof! A True Story. Gilpin, Stephen, illus. 2010. (ENG.). 32p. (J). (gr. 1-3). 16.99 (978-0-8075-4512-6(0)) Whitman, Albert & Co.

Kleinmartin, Hex, et al. Texas. 2015. (J). lib. bdg. (978-1-62712-769-1(0)); (ENG., Illus.). 80p. (gr. 4-4). 34.21 (978-1-5026-0017-2(X)) Cavendish Square Publishing.

Koceich, Matt. My Texas. 2015. (ENG.). 50p. (J). (gr. 4-8). pap. 8.95 (978-1-61821-435-5(7)) Prufrock Pr.

Kuligowski, Stephanie. La Colonizacion de Texas / the Colonization of Texas. 2013. (Primary Source Readers Ser.). (SPA.). lib. bdg. 19.65 (978-0-606-31864-8(X), Turtleback) Turtleback Bks.

—The Colonization of Texas: Missions & Settlers, 1 vol. 2012. (Primary Source Readers Ser.). (ENG.). 32p. (J). (gr. 4-4). pap. 8.99 (978-1-4333-5044-3(0)) Teacher Created Materials, Inc.

—La Salle: Early Texas Explorer, 1 vol. 2012. (Primary Source Readers Ser.). (ENG.). 32p. (J). (gr. 3-3). pap. 8.99 (978-1-4333-5043-6(2)) Teacher Created Materials, Inc.

—La Salle: Uno de los Primeros Exploradores de Texas. 2013. (Primary Source Readers Ser.). (SPA.). lib. bdg. 19.65 (978-0-606-31863-1(1), Turtleback) Turtleback Bks.

Laird, Johnna M. Southwest: New Mexico, Oklahoma, Texas, Vol. 19. 2015. (Let's Explore the States Ser.). (Illus.). 64p. (J). (gr. 5). 23.95 (978-1-4222-3334-4(0)) Mason Crest.

Lanser, Amanda. What's Great about Texas? 2014. (Our Great States Ser.). (ENG., Illus.). 32p. (gr. 2-5). pap. 7.95 (978-1-4677-4534-5(0)); lib. bdg. 26.60 (978-1-4677-3348-9(2), Lerner Pubns.) Lerner Publishing Group.

Let's Explore the Southwest. 2013. (Road Trip: Exploring America's Regions Ser.). 24p. (J). (gr. 2-5). pap. 48.90 (978-1-4339-9151-6(9)) Stevens, Gareth Publishing LLLP.

Levy, Janey. The Battle of the Alamo. 2009. (Real Life Readers Ser.). 32p. (gr. 4-5). pap. 10.00 (978-1-4358-0167-7(9), Rosen Classroom); (gr. 4-4). 47.90 (978-1-61511-369-9(X), PowerKids Pr.); (J). (gr. 3-4). lib. bdg. 25.25 (978-1-4358-2991-6(3), PowerKids Pr.) Rosen Publishing Group, Inc., The.

Levy, Janey & Donnell, Kerri. The Missions of Texas. 2010. (Spotlight on Texas Ser.). (Illus.). 32p. (J). (gr. 3-4). (ENG.). pap. 11.75 (978-1-61532-456-9(9)); 25.25 (978-1-61532-465-1(8)) Rosen Publishing Group, Inc., The.

Magruder, Jana & Amberson, Mary. A Brave Boy & a Good Soldier Educator Guide: John C. C. Hill & the Texas Expedition to Mier. 2006. (ENG., Illus.). 100p. pap., tchr.'s training gde. ed. 19.95 (978-0-87611-229-8(7)) Texas State Historical Assn.

Marfa, Isabelle. The Land & Resources of Texas: Shaping the Growth of the State. 2010. (Spotlight on Texas Ser.). (ENG., Illus.). 32p. (J). (gr. 3-4). pap. 11.75 (978-1-61532-478-1(X)); lib. bdg. 26.25 (978-1-61532-480-4(1)) Rosen Publishing Group, Inc., The.

Marsh, Carole. Exploring Texas Through Project-Based Learning: Geography, History, Government, Economics & More. 2016. (Texas Experience Ser.). (ENG.). (J). pap. 9.99 (978-0-635-12367-1(3)) Gallopade International.

—Texas History Projects: 30 Cool, Activities, Crafts, Experiments & More for Kids to Do to Learn about Your State! 2003. (Texas Experience Ser.). 32p. (gr. k-5). pap. 5.95 (978-0-635-01812-0(8), Marsh, Carole Bks.) Gallopade International.

Marsico, Katie. The Rio Grande. 2013. (Explorer Library: Social Studies Explorer Ser.). (ENG.). 32p. (J). (gr. 4-8). 28.50 (978-1-62431-012-6(5), 202499); pap. 14.21 (978-1-62431-036-2(2), 202501) Cherry Lake Publishing.

Mattern, Joanne. The Alamo. 2014. (ENG.). 32p. (gr. 3-6). 32.79 (978-1-62717-740-5(X)) Rourke Educational Media.

—La Anexion de Texas /The Annexation of Texas. 2013. (Primary Source Readers Ser.). (SPA.). lib. bdg. 19.65 (978-0-606-31868-6(2), Turtleback) Turtleback Bks.

—The Annexation of Texas: From Republic to Statehood, 1 vol. 2012. (Primary Source Readers Ser.). (ENG.). 32p. (J). (gr. 4-4). pap. 8.99 (978-1-4333-5048-1(3)) Teacher Created Materials, Inc.

—Sam Houston: A Fearless Statesman, 1 vol. 2012. (Primary Source Readers Ser.). (ENG.). 32p. (J). (gr. 3-3). pap. 8.99 (978-1-4333-5049-8(1)) Teacher Created Materials, Inc.

McAneney, Caitlin. Becoming Texas: Early Statehood. 2014. (Spotlight on Texas Ser.). (ENG.). 32p. (J). (gr. 3-4). 26.25 (978-1-4777-4527-4(0), Rosen Classroom) Rosen Publishing Group, Inc., The.

McCartney, Tania. A Texas Year: Twelve Months in the Life of Texan Kids. Snerling, Tina, illus. 2016. (Kids' Year Ser.). (ENG.). 32p. (J). (gr. -1-3). 17.99 (978-1-925335-06-4(2), EK Bks.) Exisle Publishing Pty Ltd. AUS. Dist: Hachette Bk. Group.

McGowen, Tom. The Alamo. 2017. (J). **(978-0-531-22617-9(4)**, Orchard Bks.) Scholastic, Inc.

McKinley, Fred B. Chinqua Where? The Spirit of Rural America, 1947-1955. Blassingame, Calvin, illus. 2003. 319p. 24.95 (978-0-9729655-0-7(5)) Willow Creel Publishing Co.

Miller, Barbara Kiely. Sam Houston. 2007. (Grandes Personajes (Great Americans) Ser.). 24p. (gr. 1-4). (SPA.). pap. 8.15 (978-0-8368-8336-7(5)); pap. 8.15 (978-0-8368-8323-7(3)); lib. bdg. 22.00 (978-0-8368-8316-9(0)); (SPA., Illus.). lib. bdg. 22.00 (978-0-8368-8329-9(2)) Stevens, Gareth Publishing LLLP. (Weekly Reader Leveled Readers).

Mitchell, Mark. Raising la Belle. Mitchell, Mark, illus. (Professor Wigglestix & the Weather Ser.). (Illus.). 112p. 10.95 (978-1-57168-703-6(3)) Eakin Pr.

Moore, Jess. The Economy of Texas. 2014. (Spotlight on Texas Ser.). (ENG.). 32p. (J). (gr. 3-4). pap. 11.75 (978-1-4777-4512-0(2), Rosen Classroom) Rosen Publishing Group, Inc., The.

—Texas During the Great Depression. 2014. (Spotlight on Texas Ser.). (ENG.). 32p. (J). (gr. 3-4). 26.25 (978-1-4777-4511-3(4), Rosen Classroom) Rosen Publishing Group, Inc., The.

Mountjoy, Shane. The Alamo: The Battle for Texas. 2009. (Milestones in American History Ser.). (Illus.). 144p. (gr. 6-12). 35.00 (978-1-60413-056-0(3), Chelsea Hse.) Facts On File, Inc.

Nagle, Jeanne M. Texas: Past & Present. 2009. (Illus.). 48p. (J). 70.50 (978-1-4358-5573-1(6)); pap. 11.75 (978-1-4358-5572-4(8)); (ENG., lib. bdg. 29.25 (978-1-4358-5287-7(7)) Rosen Publishing Group, Inc., The. (Rosen Reference).

National Geographic Learning. Jari's Year. 2009. (Inside the USA Ser.). (ENG., Illus.). 16p. (C). pap. 13.95 (978-0-7362-7065-6(5)) CENGAGE Learning.

Nelson, Kristin L. The Alamo. (Lightning Bolt Books (tm) — Famous Places Ser.). (ENG.). 32p. (gr. k-2). 2010. lib. bdg. 26.60 (978-0-7613-6017-9(4), Lerner Pubns.) 2003. (Illus.). pap. 7.95 (978-0-8225-3760-1(5)) 2003. (Illus.). lib. bdg. 22.60 (978-0-8225-3599-7(8)) Lerner Publishing Group.

Nelson, Robin. Juneteenth. 2009. (First Step Nonfiction - American Holidays Ser.). (ENG.). 24p. (gr. k-2). 23.93 (978-0-7613-4934-1(0)) Lerner Publishing Group.

O'Hern, Kerri & Riehecky, Janet. The Battle of the Alamo. 2006. (Graphic Histories Ser.). (Illus.). 32p. (gr. 5-8). pap. 10.50 (978-0-8368-6253-9(8)) Stevens, Gareth Publishing LLLP.

O'Hern, Kerri, et al. La Batalla de el Álamo. 2007. (Historias Graficas (Graphic Histories) Ser.). (SPA., Illus.). 32p. (gr. 5-8). pap. 10.50 (978-0-8368-7900-1(7)); lib. bdg. 27.00 (978-0-8368-7893-6(0)) Stevens, Gareth Publishing LLLP.

Ollhoff, Jim. Texas, 1 vol. 2009. (United States Ser.). (ENG., Illus.). 48p. (YA). (gr. 2-5). 27.07 (978-1-60453-679-9(9)) ABDO Publishing Co.

Otfinoski, Steven. The Story of Juneteenth: An Interactive History Adventure. 2015. (You Choose: History Ser.). (ENG., Illus.). 112p. (gr. 3-4). lib. bdg. 31.99 (978-1-4914-1802-4(8), You Choose Bks.) Capstone Press of Coughlan Cos.

Owens, Sharon. Immigration & Migration in Texas. 2014. (Spotlight on Texas Ser.). (ENG.). 32p. (J). (gr. 3-4). 26.25 (978-1-4777-4522-9(X), Rosen Classroom) Rosen Publishing Group, Inc., The.

Paradis. Texas Monsters. Paradis, illus. 2017. (ENG., Illus.). 22p. (gr. -1). bds. 9.99 **(978-2-924734-07-0(X))** City Monsters Bks. CAN. Dist: Publishers Group West (PGW).

Parker, Janice. Texas. 2011. (Guide to American States Ser.). (Illus.). 48p. (YA). (gr. 3-6). 29.99 (978-1-61690-816-4(5)); (J). (978-1-61690-492-0(5)) Weigl Pubs., Inc.

—Texas: The Lone Star State. 2016. (J). (978-1-4896-4947-8(6)) Weigl Pubs., Inc.

Peppas, Lynn. The Battle of the Alamo. 2017. 48p. (J). **(978-0-7787-3940-1(6))** Crabtree Publishing Co.

—Why Anson Jones Matters to Texas. 2014. (Illus.). 32p. (J). lib. bdg. 26.25 (978-1-4777-0911-5(8)) Rosen Publishing Group, Inc., The.

—Why Cabeza de Vaca Matters to Texas. 2014. (Illus.). 32p. (J). lib. bdg. 26.25 (978-1-4777-0913-9(4)) Rosen Publishing Group, Inc., The.

—Why Francisco Coronado Matters to Texas. 2014. (Illus.). 32p. (J). lib. bdg. 26.25 (978-1-4777-0909-2(6)) Rosen Publishing Group, Inc., The.

—Why José Antonio Navarro Matters to Texas. 2014. (Illus.). 32p. (J). lib. bdg. 26.25 (978-1-4777-0936-8(3)) Rosen Publishing Group, Inc., The.

—Why Sam Houston Matters to Texas. 2014. (Illus.). 32p. (J). lib. bdg. 26.25 (978-1-4777-0912-2(6)) Rosen Publishing Group, Inc., The.

—Why Sieur de La Salle Matters to Texas. 2014. (Illus.). 32p. (J). lib. bdg. 26.25 (978-1-4777-0917-7(7)) Rosen Publishing Group, Inc., The.

—Why Stephen F. Austin Matters to Texas. 2014. (Illus.). 32p. (J). lib. bdg. 26.25 (978-1-4777-0914-6(2)) Rosen Publishing Group, Inc., The.

Peterson, Sheryl. Texas. Kania, Matt, illus. 2009. (This Land Called America Ser.). 32p. (YA). (gr. 3-6). 19.95 (978-1-58341-796-6(6)) Creative Co., The.

Petrick, Neila Skinner. Jane Wilkinson Long: Texas Pioneer, 1 vol. Haynes, Joyce, illus. 2004. (ENG.). 32p. (J). (gr. k-3). 16.99 (978-1-58980-147-9(4)) Pelican Publishing Co., Inc.

Phan, Sandy. American Indians in Texas: Conflict & Survival, 1 vol. 2012. (Primary Source Readers Ser.). (ENG.). 32p. (J). (gr. 4-4). pap. 8.99 (978-1-4333-5040-5(8)) Teacher Created Materials, Inc.

—The Caddo & Comanche: American Indians Tribes in Texas, 1 vol. 2012. (Primary Source Readers Ser.). (ENG.). 32p. (J). (gr. 3-3). pap. 8.99 (978-1-4333-5041-2(6)) Teacher Created Materials, Inc.

—Los Caddo y los Comanche. 2013. (Primary Source Readers Ser.). (SPA.). lib. bdg. 19.65 (978-0-606-31861-7(5), Turtleback) Turtleback Bks.

—Los Indigenas Americanos de Texas (American Indians in Texas) 2013. (Primary Source Readers Ser.). (SPA.). lib. bdg. 19.65 (978-0-606-31860-0(7), Turtleback) Turtleback Bks.

Pickman, Richard. Anglo-American Colonization of Texas. 2010. (Spotlight on Texas Ser.). (ENG.). 32p. (J). (gr. 3-4). pap. 11.75 (978-1-61532-462-0(3)); (Illus.). lib. bdg. 26.25 (978-1-61532-464-4(X)) Rosen Publishing Group, Inc., The.

Pratt, Laura. Texas: The Lone Star State. 2012. (J). (978-1-61913-407-2(1)); pap. (978-1-61913-408-9(X)) Weigl Pubs., Inc.

Raatma, Lucia. Barbara Jordan. 2013. (Leading Women 2 Ser.). 96p. (YA). (gr. 7-12). pap. 19.99 (978-1-62712-114-9(5)) Cavendish Square Publishing.

Rajczak, Kristin. The Civil Rights Movement in Texas. 2014. (Spotlight on Texas Ser.). (ENG., Illus.). 32p. (J). (gr. 3-4). 26.25 (978-1-4777-4562-5(9), Rosen Classroom) Rosen Publishing Group, Inc., The.

Rajczak, Michael. Texas Geography. 2014. (Spotlight on Texas Ser.). (ENG.). 32p. (J). (gr. 3-4). 26.25 (978-1-4777-4532-8(7), Rosen Classroom) Rosen Publishing Group, Inc., The.

Randolph, Joanne. The Angel of Goliad: Francisca Alvarez & the Texas War for Independence. 2009. (Great Moments in American History Ser.). 32p. (gr. 3-3). 47.90 (978-1-61513-151-8(5)) Rosen Publishing Group, Inc., The.

Rasinski, Timothy. Reader's Theater Scripts: Texas History, 1 vol. rev. ed. 2014. (Reader's Theater Scripts Ser.). (ENG., Illus.). 176p. (gr. 4-7). pap. 19.99 (978-1-4258-1009-2(8)) Shell Educational Publishing.

Riehecky, Janet & O'Hern, Kerri. The Battle of the Alamo. McHargue, D., illus. 2006. (Graphic Histories Ser.). 32p. (gr. 5-8). lib. bdg. 27.00 (978-0-8368-6201-0(5)) Stevens, Gareth Publishing LLLP.

RJF Publishing Staff & Burgan, Michael. The Alamo. 2009. (Symbols of American Freedom Ser.). 48p. (gr. 4-6). 30.00 (978-1-60413-512-1(3), Chelsea Clubhouse) Facts On File, Inc.

Roberts, Russell. The Life & Times of Stephen F. Austin. 2007. (Profiles in American History Ser.). (Illus.). 48p. (J). (gr. 4-7). lib. bdg. 29.95 (978-1-58415-531-7(0)) Mitchell Lane Pubs., Inc.

—Texas Joins the United States. 2007. (Building America Ser.). (Illus.). 48p. (J). (gr. 4-8). lib. bdg. 29.95 (978-1-58415-550-8(7)) Mitchell Lane Pubs., Inc.

Rodgers, Kelly. Leaders in the Texas Revolution: United for a Cause, 1 vol. 2012. (Primary Source Readers Ser.). (ENG.). 32p. (J). (gr. 3-3). pap. 8.99 (978-1-4333-5047-4(5)) Teacher Created Materials, Inc.

—Lideres de la Revolucion de Texas (Leaders in the Texas Revolution) 2013. (Primary Source Readers Ser.). (SPA.). lib. bdg. 19.65 (978-0-606-31867-9(4), Turtleback) Turtleback Bks.

—La Revolucion de Texas. 2013. (Primary Source Readers Ser.). (SPA.). lib. bdg. 19.65 (978-0-606-31866-2(6), Turtleback) Turtleback Bks.

—The Texas Revolution: Fighting for Independence, 1 vol. 2012. (Primary Source Readers Ser.). (ENG.). 32p. (J). (gr. 4-4). pap. 8.99 (978-1-4333-5046-7(7)) Teacher Created Materials, Inc.

Roza, Greg. Early Explorers of Texas. 2010. (Spotlight on Texas Ser.). (Illus.). 32p. (J). (gr. 3-4). (ENG.). pap. 11.75 (978-1-61532-454-5(2)); lib. bdg. 25.25 (978-1-61532-489-7(5)) Rosen Publishing Group, Inc., The.

—The Karankawa of Texas. 2009. (Library of Native Americans Ser.). 64p. (gr. 4-4). 58.50 (978-1-60853-748-8(X), PowerKids Pr.) Rosen Publishing Group, Inc., The.

—Texas Cities: Then & Now. 2014. (Spotlight on Texas Ser.). (ENG.). 32p. (J). (gr. 3-4). 26.25 (978-1-4777-4551-9(3), Rosen Classroom) Rosen Publishing Group, Inc., The.

Rubin, Donna. Log Cabin Kitty. Halbower, Susan J., illus. 2012. 56p. pap. 20.00 (978-0-87565-503-1(3)) Texas Christian Univ. Pr.

Ruffin, Frances E. The Alamo. 2006. (Places in American History Ser.). (Illus.). 24p. (gr. 1-4). pap. 8.15 (978-0-8368-6414-4(X)); lib. bdg. 22.00 (978-0-8368-6407-6(7)) Stevens, Gareth Publishing LLLP. (Weekly Reader Leveled Readers).

Sanford, William R. & Green, Carl R. Richard King: Courageous Texas Cattleman. 2012. (Courageous Heroes of the American West Ser.). (Illus.). 48p. (J). (gr. 5-18). 22.60 (978-0-7660-4003-8(8)) Enslow Pubs., Inc.

Scher, Linda. The Texas City Disaster. 2007. (Code Red Ser.). (Illus.). 32p. (YA). (gr. 2-5). lib. bdg. 25.27 (978-1-59716-363-7(5)) Bearport Publishing Co., Inc.

Schwartz, Heather. Lizzie Johnson: Texan Cowgirl, 1 vol. 2012. (Primary Source Readers Ser.). (ENG.). 32p. (J). (gr. 3-3). pap. 8.99 (978-1-4333-5051-1(3)) Teacher Created Materials, Inc.

—War, Cattle, & Cowboys: Texas as a Young State, 1 vol. 2012. (Primary Source Readers Ser.). (ENG.). 32p. (J). (gr. 4-4). pap. 8.99 (978-1-4333-5050-4(5)) Teacher Created Materials, Inc.

Shoup, Kate. Texas & the Mexican War. 2016. (Expanding America Ser.). (ENG., Illus.). 96p. (J). (gr. 8-8). 42.79 (978-1-5026-0964-9(9)) Cavendish Square Publishing.

Siegfried Holtz, Eric & Barenblat, Rachel. Texas. 2003. (World Almanac Biblioteca de los Estados). (SPA., Illus.). 48p. (gr. 4-9). pap. 14.05 (978-0-8368-5554-8(X), Gareth Stevens Learning Library) Stevens, Gareth Publishing LLLP.

Skewes, John & Mullin, Michael. Larry Gets Lost in Texas. Skewes, John, illus. 2010. (Larry Gets Lost Ser.). (ENG., Illus.). 32p. (J). (gr. -1-2). 17.99 (978-1-57061-680-8(9), Little Bigfoot) Sasquatch Bks.

Smith, Andrea P. Jim Bowie. 2012. (Illus.). 24p. (J). 63.60 (978-1-4488-5231-4(5)); pap. 10.60 (978-1-4488-5230-7(7)); lib. bdg. 25.25 (978-1-4488-5196-6(3)) Rosen Publishing Group, Inc., The. (PowerKids Pr.).

Sorrels, Roy. The Legend of the Alamo. 2012. (Stories in American History Ser.). (Illus.). 128p. (J). (gr. 5-18). 33.27 (978-0-7660-3952-0(8)) Enslow Pubs., Inc.

South, Victor. Remember the Alamo: Americans Fight for Texas, 1820-1845. 2012. (J). pap. (978-1-4222-2416-8(3)) Mason Crest.

—Remember the Alamo: Americans Fight for Texas, 1820-1845. Rakove, Jack N., ed. 2012. (How America Became America Ser.). 48p. (J). (gr. 3-4). 19.95 (978-1-4222-2402-1(3)) Mason Crest.

Spotlight on Texas: Set 2. 2014. (Spotlight on Texas Ser.). (ENG.). 32p. (J). (gr. 3-4). 315.00 (978-1-4777-4561-8(0), Rosen Classroom) Rosen Publishing Group, Inc., The.

Spotlight on Texas: The Growth & Development of the Lone Star State, 12 vols., Set. Incl. Alamo. Hoffman, Mary Ann. lib. bdg. 26.25 (978-1-61532-461-3(5)); American Civil War in Texas. Burke, Johanna. lib. bdg. 25.25 (978-1-61532-474-3(7)); Anglo-American Colonization of Texas. Pickman, Richard. lib. bdg. 26.25 (978-1-61532-464-4(X)); Cattle & Oil: The Growth of Texas Industries. James, Trisha. lib. bdg. 26.25 (978-1-61532-477-4(1)); Causes & Effects of the Texas Revolution. Harasymiw, Therese. lib. bdg. 25.25 (978-1-61532-468-2(2)); Celebrating Texas: Patriotic Symbols & Landmarks. James, Trisha. lib. bdg. 25.25 (978-1-61532-486-6(0)); Early Explorers of Texas. Roza, Greg. lib. bdg. 25.25 (978-1-61532-489-7(5)); Governing Texas: Local, State, & National Governments. Cane, Sutter. lib. bdg. 26.25 (978-1-61532-483-5(6)); Land & Resources of Texas: Shaping the Growth of the State. Marfa, Isabelle. lib. bdg. 26.25 (978-1-61532-480-4(1)); (J). (gr. 3-4). (Spotlight on Texas Ser.). (ENG., Illus.). 32p. 2010. Set lib. bdg. 183.75 (978-1-61532-856-7(4), PowerKids Pr.) Rosen Publishing Group, Inc., The.

The State of Texas 8-Book Set. 2014. (Primary Source Readers Ser.). (ENG., Illus.). 32p. (gr. 4-5). spiral bd. 71.92 (978-1-4938-0876-2(1)) Teacher Created Materials, Inc.

Steele, Christy. Texas Joins the United States. 2005. (America's Westward Expansion Ser.). (Illus.). 48p. (gr. 5-12). lib. bdg. 31.00 (978-0-8368-5791-7(7), Gareth

Stevens Secondary Library) Stevens, Gareth Publishing LLLP.

Steinagle, Jason. Citizenship: What It Means to Be from Texas. 2014. (Spotlight on Texas Ser.). (ENG., Illus.). 32p. (J). (gr. 3-4). 26.25 *(978-1-4777-4546-5(7),* Rosen Classroom) Rosen Publishing Group, Inc., The.

Teitelbaum, Michael. Texas, 1527-1836. 2006. (National Geographic Voices from ColonialAmerica Ser.). (ENG., Illus.). 112p. (J). (gr. 5-9). lib. bdg. 32.90 *(978-0-7922-6682-2(X),* National Geographic Children's Bks.) National Geographic Society.

Temple, Teri & Temple, Bob. Remember the Alamo. 2006. (Events in American History Ser.). (Illus.). 48p. (YA). (gr. 3-6). lib. bdg. 31.36 *(978-1-60044-125-7(4))* Rourke Educational Media.

Tieck, Sarah. Texas, 1 vol. 2012. (Explore the United States Ser.). (ENG.). 32p. (J). (gr. 2-5). lib. bdg. 28.50 *(978-1-61783-382-3(7),* Big Buddy Bks.) ABDO Publishing Co.

Torres, John Albert. The Texas Fight for Independence: From the Alamo to San Jacinto. 2006. (Wild History of the American West Ser.). (Illus.). 128p. (J). (gr. 5-9). lib. bdg. 34.60 *(978-1-59845-011-8(5),* MyReportLinks.com Bks.) Enslow Pubs., Inc.

Turner, Carolyn. Sam Houston. 2010. pap. 9.95 *(978-1-61690-066-3(0));* 24p. (J). (gr. 2-4). lib. bdg. 25.70 *(978-1-61690-065-6(2))* Weigl Pubs., Inc.

Wade, Mary Dodson. Henrietta King: La Patrona. Farnsworth, Bill, illus. 2012. (ENG.). 64p. 16.95 *(978-1-933979-63-2(1),* 7e8171df-3905-4241-a084-108e6384ddaf) Bright Sky Pr.

—Henrietta King: Loving the Land. Farnsworth, Bill, illus. 2011. (ENG.). 24p. 16.95 *(978-1-933979-64-9(X),* dcf39346-020e-471d-9505-349b26473e11) Bright Sky Pr.

—Sam Houston: Standing Firm. Fisher Hein, Joy, illus. 2009. (ENG.). 24p. (J). (gr. k-2). 16.95 *(978-1-933979-13-7(5),* b21386f0-913f-4469-aac4-6dc1e0ccf68c) Bright Sky Pr.

—Stephen F. Austin: Keeping Promises. 2012. (Texas Heroes for Young Readers Ser.). (ENG.). 24p. (J). (gr. k-2). 16.95 *(978-1-933979-11-3(9))* Bright Sky Pr.

—Texas History. 2003. (Heinemann State Studies). (Illus.). 48p. (J). lib. bdg. 27.07 *(978-1-4034-0687-3(1))* Heinemann-Raintree.

—Texas Plants & Animals. 2003. (Heinemann State Studies). (Illus.). 48p. (J). lib. bdg. 27.07 *(978-1-4034-0690-3(1))* Heinemann-Raintree.

Walker, Paul Robert. Remember the Alamo: Texians, Tejanos, & Mexicans Tell Their Stories. 2015. (ENG., Illus.). 64p. (J). (gr. 5). pap. 7.99 *(978-1-4263-2249-5(6),* National Geographic Children's Bks.) National Geographic Society.

Warrick, Karen Clemens. Alamo: Victory or Death on the Texas Frontier. 2008. (America's Living History Ser.). (Illus.). 128p. (J). (gr. 5-9). lib. bdg. 33.27 *(978-0-7660-2937-8(9))* Enslow Pubs., Inc.

Wimberley, John. Life in the Republic of Texas. 2010. (Spotlight on Texas Ser.). (ENG., Illus.). 32p. (J). (gr. 3-4). 26.25 *(978-1-61532-471-2(2));* pap. 11.75 *(978-1-61532-469-9(0))* Rosen Publishing Group, Inc., The.

Winter, Jonah. Born & Bred in the Great Depression. Root, Kimberly Bulcken, illus. 2011. (ENG.). 40p. (J). (gr. k-4). 17.99 *(978-0-375-86197-0(1),* Schwartz & Wade Bks.) Random Hse. Children's Bks.

Woodward, Mac. Sam Houston: For Texas & the Union. 2009. (Library of American Lives & Times Ser.). 112p. (gr. 5-5). 69.20 *(978-1-60853-504-0(5))* Rosen Publishing Group, Inc., The.

Woodward, Walter M. Sam Houston: For Texas & the Union. 2005. (Library of American Lives & Times). (Illus.). 112p. (YA). (gr. 4-8). lib. bdg. 34.60 *(978-0-8239-5739-2(X))* Rosen Publishing Group, Inc., The.

Worth, Richard. The Texas War of Independence. 2008. (Hispanic America Ser.). 80p. (gr. 5-18). lib. bdg. 34.21 *(978-0-7614-2934-0(4),* Benchmark Bks.) Marshall Cavendish Corp.

TEXAS RANGERS

Newton, Michael. The Texas Rangers. 2010. (Law Enforcement Agencies Ser.). (Illus.). 128p. (gr. 6-12). 35.00 *(978-1-60413-626-5(X),* Chelsea Hse.) Facts On File, Inc.

TEXAS RANGERS (BASEBALL TEAM)

Basen, Ryan. Texas Rangers, 1 vol. 2011. (Inside MLB Ser.). (ENG., Illus.). 48p. (YA). (gr. 3-6). lib. bdg. 32.79 *(978-1-61714-061-7(9))* ABDO Publishing Co.

Connery-Boyd, Peg. Texas Rangers. 2016. (Hawk's Nest Activity Bks.: 0). (ENG.). 64p. (J). (gr. k-3). pap., act. bk. ed. 8.99 *(978-1-4926-3565-9(0))* Sourcebooks, Inc.

Gilbert, Sara. The Story of the Texas Rangers. 2011. (Baseball: the Great American Game Ser.). (Illus.). 48p. (J). (gr. 5-8). lib. bdg. 34.25 *(978-1-60818-058-5(1),* Creative Education) Creative Co., The.

Lace, William W. Nolan Ryan: Hall of Fame Baseball Superstar. 2014. (Hall of Fame Sports Greats Ser.). 64p. (J). (gr. 4-9). pap. 9.95 *(978-1-62285-026-6(2))* Enslow Pubs., Inc.

Monnig, Alex. Texas Rangers. 2014. (Favorite Baseball Teams Ser.). (ENG.). 32p. (J). (gr. 1-4). 28.50 *(978-1-62323-980-0(X),* 206757) Child's World, Inc., The.

Richardson, Adele. The Story of the Texas Rangers. 2007. (Baseball, the Great American Game Ser.). (Illus.). 48p. (YA). (gr. 4-7). lib. bdg. 32.80 *(978-1-58341-502-3(5))* Creative Co., The.

Stewart, Mark. The Texas Rangers. 2012. (Team Spirit Ser.). 48p. (J). (gr. 3-6). lib. bdg. 29.27 *(978-1-59953-499-2(1))* Norwood Hse. Pr.

TEXTILE FABRICS

see Textile Industry

TEXTILE INDUSTRY

see also Cotton Manufacture; Dyes and Dyeing; Tapestry; Weaving

also names of special textile fabrics, (e.g. Silk); and names of articles manufactured, e.g. Carpets

Carlson, Laurie. Knit, Hook, & Spin: A Kid's Activity Guide to Fiber Arts & Crafts. 2016. (ENG., Illus.). 144p. (J). (gr. 4-7). pap. 14.99 *(978-1-61373-400-1(X))* Chicago Review Pr., Inc.

Dickerson, Jennifer. Mini Flower Loom Crafts: 18 Super Simple Projects. 2015. (ENG., Illus.). 32p. 9.95 *(978-1-63186-483-4(1),* 9781631864834) Taunton Pr., Inc.

Hoffmann, Sara. Made of Cloth. 2012. (First Step Nonfiction - Exploring Materials Ser.). (ENG., Illus.). 8p. (gr. -1-1). pap. 4.95 *(978-1-4677-0503-5(9),* Lerner Pubns.) Lerner Publishing Group.

Kinsner, Kathy. Fabric Around the World. 2004. (Shared Connections Ser.). (J). instr.'s gde. ed. 27.00 *(978-1-4108-1622-1(2))* Benchmark Education Co.

—Fabric Around the World: Small Book. 2004. (Shared Connections Ser.). (J). pap. *(978-1-4108-1646-7(X))* Benchmark Education Co.

Limós, Anna. Easy Cloth Crafts in 5 Steps. 2008. (Easy Crafts in 5 Steps Ser.). (Illus.). 32p. (J). (gr. 3-7). lib. bdg. 23.94 *(978-0-7660-3084-8(9),* Enslow Elementary) Enslow Pubs., Inc.

Mara, Wil. From Sharks to... Swimsuits. 2012. (21st Century Skills Innovation Library: Innovations from Nature Ser.). (ENG.). 32p. (gr. 4-8). 28.50 *(978-1-61080-499-8(6),* 202109); pap. 14.21 *(978-1-61080-673-2(5),* 202283) Cherry Lake Publishing.

Mitchell, Melanie S. Cloth. 2003. (First Step Nonfiction - Materials Ser.). (ENG., Illus.). 24p. (gr. k-2). lib. bdg. 23.93 *(978-0-8225-4616-0(7))* Lerner Publishing Group.

Morris, Neil. Textiles. 2010. (Materials That Matter Ser.). 32p. (YA). (gr. 4-7). 28.50 *(978-1-60753-069-5(4))* Amicus Publishing.

Nelson, Robin. From Cotton to T-Shirt. 2013. (Start to Finish, Second Series: Everyday Products Ser.). (ENG., Illus.). 24p. (gr. k-3). pap. 6.95 *(978-0-7613-8572-1(X))* Lerner Publishing Group.

—From Sheep to Sweater. 2013. (Start to Finish, Second Series: Everyday Products Ser.). (ENG., Illus.). 24p. (gr. k-3). pap. 6.95 *(978-0-7613-8575-2(4));* lib. bdg. 23.93 *(978-0-7613-6564-8(8),* Lerner Pubns.) Lerner Publishing Group.

Poratto, Maria Laura. Costura para Ninos. 2004. (SPA., Illus.). 48p. (J). pap. 7.95 *(978-987-550-297-0(9))* Longseller S.A. ARG. Dist: Libros Sin Fronteras.

Rosen Publishing Staff. American History Arts & Crafts, 1 vol. 2015. (American History Arts & Crafts Ser.). (ENG.). 32p. (J). 165.00 *(978-1-4777-5727-7(9),* PowerKids Pr.) Rosen Publishing Group, Inc., The.

Senker, Cath. Immigrants & Refugees. 2012. (Mapping Global Issues Ser.). 48p. (J). (gr. 7-9). lib. bdg. 34.25 *(978-1-59920-509-0(2))* Black Rabbit Bks.

Sohn, Emily & Klobuchar, Lisa. Fabric: It's Got You Covered! 2011. (IScience Readers Ser.). 24p. (J). (gr. k-2). lib. bdg. 21.27 *(978-1-59953-406-0(1))* Norwood Hse. Pr.

Spilsbury, Louise. Tapestries & Textiles. 2009. (Stories in Art Ser.). (Illus.). 30p. (J). lib. bdg. 26.50 *(978-1-4042-4436-8(0))* Rosen Publishing Group, Inc., The.

Storey, Rita. Wool & Cotton. 2007. (How We Use Materials/Watts Ser.). (Illus.). 30p. (J). (gr. 4-7). lib. bdg. 28.50 *(978-1-59920-001-9(5))* Black Rabbit Bks.

Thomson, Ruth. What Are Textiles? 2005. (Art's Alive! Ser.). (Illus.). 30p. (J). (gr. 3-7). lib. bdg. 27.10 *(978-1-932889-90-1(6))* Sea-To-Sea Pubns.

Tiner, John Hudson. Cloth. 2003. (Matter & Materials Ser.). (J). *(978-1-58417-162-1(6)); (978-1-58417-168-3(5))* Lake Street Pubs.

Top That Publishing Staff, ed. Funky Fabrics. 2004. (Creative Studios Ser.). (Illus.). 48p. (J). *(978-1-84510-249-4(5))* Top That! Publishing PLC.

Toth-Chernin, Jan. E-Textiles. 2013. (21st Century Skills Innovation Library: Makers As Innovators Ser.). (ENG., Illus.). 32p. (J). (gr. 4-8). pap. 14.21 *(978-1-62431-272-4(1),* 202882); lib. bdg. 28.50 *(978-1-62431-140-6(7),* 202880) Cherry Lake Publishing.

Warwick, Ellen. Injeanuity. Lum, Bernice, illus. 2006. (Planet Girl Ser.). (ENG.). 80p. (J). (gr. 7-12). 12.95 *(978-1-55337-681-1(1))* Kids Can Pr., Ltd. CAN. Dist: Hachette Bk. Group.

Wyckoff, Edwin Brit. The Woman Who Invented the Thread That Stops Bullets: The Genius of Stephanie Kwolek. 2013. (Genius Inventors & Their Great Ideas Ser.). 48p. (J). (gr. 3-4). pap. 8.95 *(978-1-4644-0211-1(6),* Enslow Elementary); (Illus.). 25.27 *(978-0-7660-4141-7(7))* Enslow Pubs., Inc.

TEXTILE PAINTING

DaSilva, Barbara, ed. Textiles: Vintage Images of America's Living Past. 2009. (Applewood's Pictorial America Ser.). (ENG.). 56p. pap. 9.95 *(978-1-60889-013-2(9))* Applewood Bks.

THACKERAY, WILLIAM MAKEPEACE, 1811-1863

Salmon, Richard. William Makepeace Thackeray. 2005. (ENG.). 128p. (C). pap. 19.95 *(978-0-7463-0996-4(1))* Northcote Hse. Publishers, Ltd. GBR. Dist: Casemate Academic.

THAILAND

Aloian, Molly. Cultural Traditions in Thailand. 2012. (ENG.). 32p. (J). *(978-0-7787-7519-5(4));* (Illus.). pap. *(978-0-7787-7524-9(0))* Crabtree Publishing Co.

Brown, Janet. B Is for Bangkok. Q, Likit, illus. 2011. (Alphabetical World Ser.). (ENG.). 47p. (J). (gr. k-4). 12.95 *(978-1-934159-26-2(3))* ThingsAsian Pr.

Donaldson, Madeline. Thailand. 2011. (Country Explorers Ser.). (ENG., Illus.). 48p. (J). (gr. 2-4). lib. bdg. 29.27 *(978-0-7613-6414-6(5))* Lerner Publishing Group.

Furstinger, Nancy. Bangkok, 1 vol. 2005. (Cities Set 1 Ser.). (ENG., Illus.). 32p. (gr. k-6). 27.07 *(978-1-59197-852-7(1),* Checkerboard Library) ABDO Publishing Co.

Hill, Valerie. Thailand. 2004. (Ask about Asia Ser.). (Illus.). 48p. (J). (gr. 4-18). lib. bdg. 19.95 *(978-1-59084-205-8(7))* Mason Crest.

Meachen Rau, Dana. Thailand. 2006. (Discovering Cultures Ser.). (Illus.). 48p. (J). (gr. 3-7). lib. bdg. 28.50 *(978-0-7614-1989-1(6),* Benchmark Bks.) Marshall Cavendish Corp.

Phillips, Douglas A. Thailand. 2007. (Modern World Nations Ser.). (Illus.). 108p. (YA). (gr. 7-12). lib. bdg. 35.00 *(978-0-7910-9250-7(X))* Facts On File, Inc.

Raatma, Lucia. It's Cool to Learn about Countries: Thailand. 2012. (Explorer Library: Social Studies Explorer Ser.). (ENG.). 48p. (gr. 4-8). 31.36 *(978-1-61080-441-7(4),* 202051); pap. 15.64 *(978-1-61080-615-2(8),* 202225) Cherry Lake Publishing.

Russell, Elaine & Meesukhon, Patcharee. All about Thailand: Stories, Songs & Crafts for Kids. Yeesman, Vinit, illus. 2016. (ENG.). 64p. (J). (gr. 3-6). 14.95 *(978-0-8048-4427-7(5))* Tuttle Publishing.

Sheen, Barbara. Foods of Thailand. 2006. (Taste of Culture Ser.). (ENG., Illus.). 64p. (J). (gr. 3-7). lib. bdg. 28.75 *(978-0-7377-3037-1(4),* Greenhaven Pr., Inc.) Cengage Gale.

Sobol, Richard, photos by. An Elephant in the Backyard. 2004. (Illus.). (J). *(978-0-525-46970-4(2),* Dutton Juvenile) Penguin Publishing Group.

Taus-Bolstad, Stacy. Thailand in Pictures. 2nd ed. 2003. (Visual Geography Series, Second Ser.). (ENG., Illus.). 80p. (gr. 5-12). 31.93 *(978-0-8225-0939-4(3))* Lerner Publishing Group.

Tecco, Betsy Dru. How to Draw Thailand's Sights & Symbols. 2009. (Kid's Guide to Drawing the Countries of the World Ser.). 48p. (gr. 4-4). 53.00 *(978-1-61511-127-5(1),* PowerKids Pr.) Rosen Publishing Group, Inc., The.

Thailand. 2014. (ENG.). 144p. (J). lib. bdg. 40.00 *(978-0-531-20791-8(9))* Scholastic Library Publishing.

THAILAND—FICTION

Ayer, Jacqueline, creator. Nu Dang & His Kite. 2017. (ENG.). 40p. (J). (gr. -1-3). 16.95 *(978-1-59270-231-2(7))* Enchanted Lion Bks., LLC.

—The Paper-Flower Tree. 2017. (ENG.). 40p. (J). (gr. -1-3). 16.95 *(978-1-59270-224-4(4))* Enchanted Lion Bks., LLC.

Bridges, Shirin Yim. The Umbrella Queen. Yoo, Taeeun, illus. 2008. (ENG.). 40p. (J). (gr. k-3). 16.99 *(978-0-06-075040-4(5),* Greenwillow Bks.) HarperCollins Pubs.

Fleischman, Sid. The White Elephant. McGuire, Robert, illus. 2006. 112p. (J). (gr. 3-6). lib. bdg. 16.89 *(978-0-06-113137-0(7));* 15.99 *(978-0-06-113136-3(9))* HarperCollins Pubs. (Greenwillow Bks.).

Gilligan, Shannon. The Case of the Silk King. Pornkerd, Vorrarit et al, illus. 2006. (Choose Your Own Adventure Ser.). 144p. (J). (gr. 4-8). per. 6.99 *(978-1-933390-14-7(X),* CHCL14) Chooseco LLC.

—The Case of the Silk King. 2005. 116p. (J). pap. *(978-0-7608-9702-7(6))* Sundance/Newbridge Educational Publishing.

Harris, R. P. Tua & the Elephant. Yoo, Taeeun, illus. 2012. (ENG.). 204p. (J). (gr. 3-7). 16.99 *(978-0-8118-7781-7(7))* Chronicle Bks. LLC.

Joo, Mi-hwa. I Am a Little Monk: Thailand. Cowley, Joy, ed. Gahng, Hwa-kyeong, illus. 2015. (Global Kids Storybooks Ser.). (ENG.). 32p. (gr. 1-4). 7.99 *(978-1-925246-58-2(2));* 26.65 *(978-1-925246-06-3(X));* 26.65 *(978-1-925246-32-2(9))* ChoiceMaker Pty. Ltd., The AUS. (Big and SMALL). Dist: Lerner Publishing Group.

—I Am a Little Monk: Thailand. Cowley, Joy, ed. Gahng, Hwa-kyeong, illus. 2015. (Global Kids Storybooks Ser.). (ENG.). 32p. (J). (gr. 1-4). pap. 7.99 *(978-1-925233-47-6(2))* Lerner Publishing Group.

Jordan, Lana. The Sleepytime Ponies Trick a Trickster. Allen, Kd & Giraud, Teresa, illus. 2004. 32p. (J). 12.95 *(978-0-9710696-1-9(1))* Jorlan Publishing, Inc.

Martin, Tamra. My Wish, Our Little Oat. Tinker, Jason, illus. 2007. 36p. (J). 21.99 *(978-1-59879-522-6(8),* Lifevest) Lifevest Publishing, Inc.

Oliviero, Jamie. Som See & the Magic Elephant. Kelly, Jo'Anne, illus. 2005. 27p. (J). (gr. -1-2). reprint ed. 17.00 *(978-0-7567-8929-9(X))* DIANE Publishing Co.

Pedigo, Kim Tran. Having Fun with Kandai the Elephant. 2nd ed. 2013. (Illus.). 34p. pap. 11.95 *(978-0-9885603-1-4(3))* Outrival Publishing.

—Kandai the Elephant Goes Bananas. 2013. 32p. pap. 11.95 *(978-0-9885603-0-7(5));* 2nd ed. 17.95 *(978-0-9885603-2-1(1))* Outrival Publishing.

Petit, Denice. Twenty-Two Turtles. 2013. (ENG.). 34p. (J). pap. 15.95 *(978-1-4327-9875-8(8))* Outskirts Pr., Inc.

Shadowboxer. 2014. (ENG.). 288p. (J). (gr. 8). pap. 9.99 *(978-1-78108-282-9(0),* Ravenstone) Rebellion GBR. Dist: Simon & Schuster, Inc.

Towe, H.P. Mr. Monkey Sees & Mr. Monkey Do. 2013. 24p. pap. 14.93 *(978-1-4669-8760-9(X))* Trafford Publishing.

VanArsdale, Anthony, illus. The Detour of the Elephants. 2017. (Boxcar Children Great Adventure Ser.: 3). (ENG.). 144p. (J). (gr. 1-5). 6.99 ***(978-0-8075-0685-1(0))*** Whitman, Albert & Co.

THAMES RIVER AND VALLEY

Manning, Paul. The Thames. (River Adventures Ser.). 2014. (J). lib. bdg. 31.35 *(978-1-59920-918-0(7))* 2013. 48p. (gr. 5-11). lib. bdg. 37.10 *(978-1-59920-924-1(1))* Black Rabbit Bks.

THANKSGIVING DAY

Adams, Colleen. The True Story of the First Thanksgiving. 2009. (What Really Happened? Ser.). 24p. (gr. 2-3). 42.50 *(978-1-60854-769-2(8),* PowerKids Pr.); (Illus.). (YA). (gr. 3-6). lib. bdg. 22.60 *(978-1-4042-4476-4(X))* Rosen Publishing Group, Inc., The.

Adams, Michelle Medlock. What Is Thanksgiving? Wummer, Amy, illus. (What Is... Ser.). (J). 2014. 22p. bds. 6.99 *(978-0-8249-1938-2(6))* 2009. (ENG.). 20p. (gr. -1-k). bds. 6.99 *(978-0-8249-1826-2(6))* Worthy Publishing. (Ideal Pubns.).

Allegra, Mike. Sarah Gives Thanks: How Thanksgiving Became a National Holiday. Gardner, David, illus. 2012. (ENG.). 32p. (J). (gr. 1-3). 16.99 *(978-0-8075-7239-9(X))* Whitman, Albert & Co.

Anderson, Laurie Halse. Thank You, Sarah: The Woman Who Saved Thanksgiving. Faulkner, Matt, illus. 2005. (ENG.). 40p. (J). (gr. k-3). 7.99 *(978-0-689-85143-8(X),* Simon & Schuster Bks. For Young Readers) Simon & Schuster Bks. For Young Readers.

Appleby, Alex. Feliz Da de Accin de Gracias! / Happy Thanksgiving!, Vol. 1. 2014. (¡Felices Fiestas! / Happy Holidays! Ser.). (SPA & BYN.). 24p. (J). (gr. k-k). 22.60 *(978-1-4339-9968-0(4))* Stevens, Gareth Publishing LLLP.

—Happy Thanksgiving!, Vol. 1. 2014. (Happy Holidays! Ser.). (ENG., Illus.). 24p. (J). (gr. k-k). 22.60 *(978-1-4339-9947-5(1))* Stevens, Gareth Publishing LLLP.

Balfour, Barbara. Thanksgiving Day. 2006. (American Holidays Ser.). (Illus.). 24p. (J). (gr. 3-7). lib. bdg. 24.45 *(978-1-59036-405-5(8));* per. 8.95 *(978-1-59036-408-6(2))* Weigl Pubs., Inc.

Bartlett, Robert Merrill. The Story of Thanksgiving. Comport, Sally Wern, illus. rev. ed. 2004. 30p. (J). (gr. k-4). reprint ed. *(978-0-7567-7757-9(7))* DIANE Publishing Co.

—The Story of Thanksgiving. Comport, Sally Wern, illus. Date not set. 40p. (J). (gr. 2-5). 5.99 *(978-0-06-446238-9(2))* HarperCollins Pubs.

Bodden, Valerie. Thanksgiving. 2005. (My First Look at Holidays Ser.). (Illus.). 24p. (J). (gr. k-3). lib. bdg. 15.95 *(978-1-58341-370-8(7),* Creative Education) Creative Co., The.

Brignaud, Pierre & Sévigny, Eric, illus. Happy Thanksgiving! 2nd ed. 2012. (Confetti Ser.). (ENG.). 24p. (J). (gr. -1-1). pap. 4.99 *(978-2-89718-021-8(8))* Caillouet, Gerry.

Bruchac, Margaret M. & Grace, Catherine O'Neill. 1621: A New Look at Thanksgiving. Coulson, Cotton & Brimberg, Sisse, photos by. 2004. (I Am American Ser.). (ENG., Illus.). 48p. (J). (gr. 3-7). pap. 7.95 *(978-0-7922-6139-1(9),* National Geographic Children's Bks.) National Geographic Society.

Bullard, Lisa. Grace's Thanksgiving. Saunders, Katie, illus. 2012. (Cloverleaf Books (tm) — Fall & Winter Holidays Ser.). (ENG.). 24p. (gr. k-2). 6.95 *(978-0-7613-8589-9(4));* lib. bdg. 23.93 *(978-0-7613-5076-7(4))* Lerner Publishing Group. (Millbrook Pr.).

Coffelt, Soraya Diase. It's Not about You Mrs. Turkey: A Love Letter about the True Meaning of Thanksgiving. 2015. (Love Letters Book Ser.). (ENG., Illus.). 32p. (J). pap. 8.99 *(978-1-63047-636-6(6))* Morgan James Publishing.

Colman, Penny. Thanksgiving: The True Story. 2008. (ENG., Illus.). 160p. (YA). (gr. 5-11). 29.99 *(978-0-8050-8229-6(8),* Holt, Henry & Co. Bks. For Young Readers) Holt, Henry & Co.

Connors, Kathleen. The First Thanksgiving, Vol. 1. 2014. (What You Didn't Know about History Ser.). (Illus.). 24p. (J). (gr. 2-3). (ENG.). 22.60 *(978-1-4824-0581-1(4));* pap. 8.15 *(978-1-4824-0582-8(2))* Stevens, Gareth Publishing LLLP.

Crane, Carol. P Is for Pilgrim: A Thanksgiving Alphabet. Urban, Helle, illus. rev. ed. 2007. (ENG.). 40p. (J). (gr. k-6). 7.95 *(978-1-58536-353-7(7))* Sleeping Bear Pr.

Crawford, Laura. The Pilgrims' Thanksgiving from A to Z, 1 vol. Hierstein, Judith, illus. 2005. (ENG.). 32p. (J). (gr. k-3). per. 8.99 *(978-1-58980-238-4(1))* Pelican Publishing Co., Inc.

Dash, Meredith. Dia de Accion de Gracias. 2015. (Días Festivos Ser.). (SPA & ENG., Illus.). 24p. (gr. k-1). pap. 7.95 *(978-1-4966-0415-6(6))* Capstone Classroom.

—Thanksgiving, 1 vol. 2014. (National Holidays Ser.). (ENG., Illus.). 24p. (J). (gr. 4-8). lib. bdg. 28.50 *(978-1-62970-047-2(9))* ABDO Publishing Co.

Dayton, Connor. Thanksgiving. 2012. (American Holidays Ser.). (ENG., Illus.). 24p. (J). (gr. k-3). pap. 8.25 *(978-1-4488-6240-5(X));* lib. bdg. 22.60 *(978-1-4488-6141-5(1))* Rosen Publishing Group, Inc., The. (PowerKids Pr.).

—Thanksgiving: Día de Accion de Gracias. Alamán, Eduardo, tr. from ENG. 2012. (American Holidays / Celebraciones en los Estados Unidos Ser.). (ENG & SPA.). 24p. (gr. k-3). lib. bdg. 22.60 *(978-1-4488-6707-3(X),* PowerKids Pr.) Rosen Publishing Group, Inc., The.

Dean, Sheri. Thanksgiving. 2010. (Our Country's Holidays Ser.). (ENG.). 24p. (J). (gr. k-3). pap. 8.15 *(978-1-4339-3927-3(4));* lib. bdg. 22.60 *(978-1-4339-3926-6(6))* Stevens, Gareth Publishing LLLP.

—Thanksgiving/Día de Acción de Gracias. 2006. (Our Country's Holidays/ Las fiestas de nuestra nacion Ser.). (SPA., Illus.). 24p. (gr. k-3). pap. 8.15 *(978-0-8368-6530-1(8),* Weekly Reader Leveled Readers) Stevens, Gareth Publishing LLLP.

Dear Santa: Individual Title Six-Packs. (Literatura 2000 Ser.). (gr. k-1). 28.00 *(978-0-7635-0048-1(8))* Rigby Education.

DeRubertis, Barbara. Let's Celebrate Thanksgiving Day. Sperling, Thomas, illus. 2013. (Holidays & Heroes Ser.). 32p. (gr. 1-3). pap. 7.95 *(978-1-57565-636-6(1))* Kane Press, Inc.

deRubertis, Barbara. Let's Celebrate Thanksgiving Day. Sperling, Thomas, illus. 2014. (Holidays & Heroes Ser.). 32p. (gr. 1-3). lib. bdg. 25.26 *(978-1-57565-723-3(6))* Kane Press, Inc.

Douglas, Punchye. Safari Oklahoma Presents: Thanksgiving History Coloring Book. (Illus.). 16p. (J). (gr. k-6). 5.00 *(978-0-9703183-3-6(2))* Douglas, Bettye Forum, Inc., The.

Englar, Mary. The Pilgrims & the First Thanksgiving, 1 vol. McDonnell, Peter, illus. 2006. (Graphic History Ser.). (ENG.). 32p. (gr. 3-4). 8.10 *(978-0-7368-9656-6(2));* 30.65 *(978-0-7368-5492-4(4))* Capstone Press of Coughlan Cos. (Graphic Library).

Erlbach, Arlene & Erlbach, Herbert. Fun Thanksgiving Day Crafts. 2015. (Kid Fun Holiday Crafts! Ser.). 32p. (J). (gr. 3-4). pap. 7.95 *(978-0-7660-6251-1(1),* Enslow Elementary) Enslow Pubs., Inc.

—Thanksgiving Day Crafts. Ponte, June, illus. 2005. (Fun Holiday Crafts Kids Can Do! Ser.). 32p. (J). lib. bdg. 23.94 *(978-0-7660-2345-1(1),* Enslow Elementary) Enslow Pubs., Inc.

Felix, Rebecca. We Celebrate Thanksgiving in Fall. 2013. (J). *(978-1-61080-979-5(3));* (ENG.). 24p. 22.79 *(978-1-61080-904-7(1),* 202595); (ENG.). 24p. pap. 12.79 *(978-1-61080-929-0(7),* 202597) Cherry Lake Publishing.

Gibbons, Gail. Thanksgiving Is... (ENG., Illus.). 32p. (J). 2005. pap. 7.99 *(978-0-8234-1979-1(7))* 2004. tchr. ed. 17.95 *(978-0-8234-1849-7(9))* Holiday Hse., Inc.

Gleisner, Jenna Lee. Celebrating Thanksgiving. 2017. (Welcome, Fall! Ser.). (ENG.). 24p. (J). (gr. -1-2). lib. bdg. 27.07 *(978-1-5038-1662-6(1),* 211498) Child's World, Inc., The.

Goeller, Dorothy. Thanksgiving Day. 2010. (All about Holidays Ser.). (Illus.). 24p. (J). 22.60 *(978-0-7660-3809-7(2));* pap. 7.95 *(978-1-59845-178-8(2))* Enslow Pubs., Inc. (Enslow Elementary).

Grack, Rachel. Thanksgiving. 2017. (Thanksgiving Ser.). 24p. (J). (gr. k-3). pap. 6.99 ***(978-1-61891-277-0(1));*** (ENG., Illus.). lib. bdg. 25.95 *(978-1-62617-598-3(5))* Bellwether Media. (Blastoff! Readers).

Gunderson, Jessica. The Pilgrims' First Thanksgiving, 1 vol. Lucke, Deb, illus. (Thanksgiving Ser.). (ENG.). 24p. (gr. 1-2). 2011. pap. 8.95 *(978-1-4048-6720-8(1))* 2010. lib. bdg. 27.32 *(978-1-4048-6285-2(4))* Picture Window Bks.

—Thanksgiving Then & Now, 1 vol. Shin, Hayoung, illus. (Thanksgiving Ser.). (ENG.). 24p. (gr. 1-2). 2011. pap. 8.95

T U V

(978-1-4048-6723-9(6)) 2010. lib. bdg. 27.32 (978-1-4048-6286-9(2)) Picture Window Bks.

Happy Thanksgiving. 32p. (J). 2.69 (978-0-7847-1128-6(3)) Standard Publishing.

Happy Thanksgiving Coloring Book. 2006. 16p. (J). pap. 1.99 (978-0-7847-1744-8(3), 04370) Standard Publishing.

Harte, May. Thanksgiving. 2009. (My Library of Holidays Ser.). 24p. (gr. 1-1). 37.50 (978-1-61514-697-0(0), PowerKids Pr.) Rosen Publishing Group, Inc., The.

Haugen, Brenda. Thanksgiving. Ouren, Todd, illus. 2003. (Holidays & Celebrations Ser.). (ENG.). 24p. (gr. k-3). 26.65 (978-1-4048-0191-2(X)) Picture Window Bks.

Hayes, Dan, illus. The Thanksgiving. 24p. (J). pap., act. bk. ed. 7.95 (978-0-8249-5324-9(X), Ideal Pubns.) Worthy Publishing.

Heiligman, Deborah. Celebrate Thanksgiving: With Turkey, Family, & Counting Blessings. 2006. (Holidays Around the World Ser.). (ENG., Illus.). 32p. (J). (gr. 1-4). 15.95 (978-0-7922-5928-2(9)); 23.90 (978-0-7922-5929-9(7)) National Geographic Society. (National Geographic Children's Bks.).

—Celebrate Thanksgiving: With Turkey Family & Counting Blessings. 2017. (Holidays Around the World Ser.). (ENG., Illus.). 32p. (J). (gr. 1-4). pap. 7.99 (978-1-4263-2847-3(8), National Geographic Children's Bks.) National Geographic Society.

—Holidays Around the World: Celebrate Thanksgiving. 2017. (Holidays Around the World Ser.). (ENG.). 32p. (J). (gr. 1-4). lib. bdg. 17.90 (978-1-4263-2848-0(6), National Geographic Children's Bks.) National Geographic Society.

Heiligman, Deborah & National Geographic Kids Staff. Celebrate Thanksgiving: With Turkey, Family, & Counting Blessings. 2008. (Holidays Around the World Ser.). (ENG., Illus.). 32p. (J). (gr. 1-4). 6.95 (978-1-4263-0292-3(4), National Geographic Children's Bks.) National Geographic Society.

Heinrichs, Ann. Thanksgiving. Jordan, Charles, illus. 2013. (Holidays & Celebrations Ser.). (ENG.). 32p. (J). (gr. k-3). 27.07 (978-1-62323-513-0(8), 206286) Child's World, Inc., The.

Herrington, Lisa M. Thanksgiving. 2013. (ENG.). 32p. (J). 23.00 (978-0-531-27206-0(0)); pap. 5.95 (978-0-531-27356-2(3)) Scholastic Library Publishing.

Hinkler Books, ed. Baby's First Thanksgiving. 2012. (Baby's First Ser.). 24p. (J). bds. 5.99 (978-1-74308-537-0(0)) Hinkler Bks. Pty. Ltd. AUS. Dist: Ideals Pubns.

Holub, Joan. What Was the First Thanksgiving? 2013. (What Was? Ser.). (ENG., Illus.). 112p. (J). (gr. 3-7). pap. 5.99 (978-0-448-46463-3(2), Penguin Workshop) Penguin Young Readers Group.

—What Was the First Thanksgiving? 2013. (What Was... ? Ser.). lib. bdg. 16.00 (978-0-606-31687-3(6), Turtleback) Turtleback Bks.

Jones, Karl & Price, Stern. Thanksgiving Activity Book. Chou, Joey, illus. 2015. (ENG.). 16p. (J). (gr. 3-7). bds. 9.99 (978-0-8431-8296-5(2), Price Stern Sloan) Penguin Young Readers Group.

Kenan, Tessa. It's Thanksgiving! 2016. (Bumba Books (tm) — It's a Holiday! Ser.). (ENG., Illus.). 24p. (J). (gr. -1-1). 25.32 (978-1-5124-1429-5(8)) Lerner Publishing Group.

Keogh, Josie. Thanksgiving. 2013. (PowerKids Readers: Happy Holidays! Ser.). (ENG., Illus.). 24p. (J). (gr. k-2). pap. 8.25 (978-1-4488-9704-9(1)); lib. bdg. 22.60 (978-1-4488-9624-0(X)) Rosen Publishing Group, Inc., The. (PowerKids Pr.).

—Thanksgiving: Día de Acción de Gracias. Alamán, Eduardo, tr. from ENG. 2013. (PowerKids Readers: Happy Holidays! / !Felices Fiestas! Ser.). (ENG & SPA., Illus.). 24p. (gr. k-2). lib. bdg. 22.60 (978-1-4488-9967-8(2), PowerKids Pr.) Rosen Publishing Group, Inc., The.

Kessel, Joyce K. Squanto & the First Thanksgiving. Donze, Lisa, illus. rev. ed. 2003. (On My Own Holidays Ser.). (ENG.). 48p. (gr. 2-4). pap. 6.95 (978-1-57505-585-5(6)); lib. bdg. 25.26 (978-0-87614-941-6(7)) Lerner Publishing Group.

—Squanto y el Primer Dia de Accion de Gracias. Donze, Lisa, illus. 2007. (Yo Solo - Festividades (on My Own - Holidays) Ser.). 48p. (J). (gr. 4-7). per. 6.95 (978-0-8225-7795-9(X)) Lerner Publishing Group.

—Squanto y el Primer Día de Acción de Gracias. Translations.com Staff, tr. from ENG. Donze, Lisa, illus. 2007. (Yo Solo - Festividades (on My Own - Holidays) Ser.). (SPA.). 48p. (gr. 2-4). lib. bdg. 25.26 (978-0-8225-7792-8(5)) Lerner Publishing Group.

—Squanto Y el Primer Dia de Accion de Gracias; Squanto & the First Thanksgiving. 2008. pap. 40.95 (978-0-8225-9678-3(4)) Lerner Publishing Group.

Kule, Elaine A. Celebrate Thanksgiving Day. 2006. (Celebrate Holidays Ser.). (Illus.). 112p. (J). (gr. 3-7). lib. bdg. 33.27 (978-0-7660-2578-3(0)) Enslow Pubs., Inc.

Landau, Elaine. Celebrate the First Thanksgiving with Elaine Landau. 2006. (Explore Colonial America with Elaine Landau Ser.). (Illus.). 48p. (J). (gr. 3-7). lib. bdg. 25.27 (978-0-7660-2556-1(X), Enslow Elementary) Enslow Pubs., Inc.

—What Is Thanksgiving? 2011. (I Like Holidays! Ser.). (Illus.). 24p. (J). (gr. k-18). pap. 7.95 (978-1-59845-294-5(0), Enslow Elementary); (gr. 1-4). lib. bdg. 22.60 (978-0-7660-3701-4(0)) Enslow Pubs., Inc.

Lawrence, Elizabeth K. Celebrate Thanksgiving. 2015. (Our Holidays Ser.). (ENG., Illus.). 24p. (J). (gr. 1-1). pap. 8.22 (978-1-5026-0412-5(4)) Cavendish Square Publishing.

Lee, Sally. A Short History of Thanksgiving. 2015. (Holiday Histories Ser.). (ENG., Illus.). 24p. (gr. k-1). lib. bdg. 26.65 (978-1-4914-6097-9(0)) Capstone Press of Coughlan Cos.

Ludgate, Kevin. Pilgrim Village: A Thanksgiving Diorama, 1 vol. 2010. (ENG., Illus.). 32p. (J). pap. 9.99 (978-0-7643-3563-1(4), 9780764335631) Schiffer Publishing, Ltd.

Lynette, Rachel. Let's Throw a Thanksgiving Party! 2011. (J). 49.50 (978-1-4488-2736-7(1)); pap. 8.25 (978-1-4488-2735-0(3)); lib. bdg. 22.60 (978-1-4488-2573-8(3)) Rosen Publishing Group, Inc., The. (PowerKids Pr.).

Mackall, Dandi. The Fantastic Gifts of Fall. 2017. (Seasons Ser.). (ENG., Illus.). 32p. (J). (gr. -1-3). pap. 3.99 (978-1-4627-4517-3(2), B&H Kids) B&H Publishing Group.

Marzollo, Jean. I Spy Thanksgiving. Wick, Walter, illus. 2011. (Scholastic Reader Level 1 Ser.). (ENG.). 32p. (J). (gr. -1-2). pap. 3.99 (978-0-545-22094-1(7), Cartwheel Bks.) Scholastic, Inc.

Matters, Print & Morrill, Ann. Thanksgiving & Other Harvest Festivals. 2009. (Holidays & Celebration Ser.). (Illus.). 104p. (gr. 5-8). 40.00 (978-1-60413-096-6(2), Chelsea Hse.) Facts On File, Inc.

McGee, Randel. Paper Crafts for Thanksgiving. 2011. (Paper Craft Fun for Holidays Ser.). (Illus.). 48p. (J). (gr. 2-5). lib. bdg. 25.27 (978-0-7660-3722-9(3)); (gr. 3-18). pap. 8.95 (978-1-59845-336-2(X), Enslow Elementary) Enslow Pubs., Inc.

McGill, Jordan, ed. Thanksgiving. 2011. (J). (gr. 3-5). pap. 12.95 (978-1-61690-686-3(3), AV2 by Weigl); (Illus.). 24p. (gr. 2-5). 27.13 (978-1-61690-680-1(4)) Weigl Pubs., Inc.

Mercer, Abbie. Happy Thanksgiving. (Holiday Fun Ser.). 24p. 2009. (gr. 2-3). 42.50 (978-1-61513-378-9(X), PowerKids Pr.) 2007. (Illus.). (J). (gr. -1-3). lib. bdg. 22.60 (978-1-4042-3807-7(7)) Rosen Publishing Group, Inc., The.

Merrick, Patrick. Thanksgiving Turkeys. 2015. (Our Holiday Symbols Ser.). (ENG.). 24p. (J). (gr. 1-4). 25.64 (978-1-63143-747-2(X), 208556) Child's World, Inc., The.

Metaxas, Eric. Squanto & the First Thanksgiving: The Legendary American Tale. Donato, Michael A., illus. 2004. 36p. (J). (gr. 3-8). reprint ed. 19.00 (978-0-7567-7123-2(4)) DIANE Publishing Co.

Morey, Allan. Thanksgiving Day. Hartley, Brian, illus. 2017. (Holidays in Rhythm & Rhyme Ser.). (ENG.). 24p. (gr. 1-3). 33.99 (978-1-68410-055-2(0)) Cantata Learning.

Morrison, Jessica. Thanksgiving. 2010. (Illus.). 24p. (978-1-55388-613-6(5)); pap. (978-1-55388-614-3(3)) Weigl Educational Pubs. Ltd.

Muehlenhardt, Amy Bailey. Thanksgiving Crafts, 1 vol. Takvorian, Nadine, illus. 2010. (Thanksgiving Ser.). (ENG.). 24p. (gr. 1-2). lib. bdg. 27.32 (978-1-4048-6282-1(X)) Picture Window Bks.

Murray, Julie. Thanksgiving, 1 vol. 2003. (Holidays Ser.). (ENG.). 24p. (gr. k-4). 25.65 (978-1-57765-956-3(2), Buddy Bks.) ABDO Publishing Co.

Nelson, Robin. Thanksgiving. 2009. (First Step Nonfiction - American Holidays Ser.). (ENG.). 24p. (gr. k-2). 23.93 (978-0-7613-4901-3(4)); (Illus.). pap. 6.95 (978-0-7613-5029-3(2), 1299384, Lerner Pubns.) Lerner Publishing Group.

Owen, Ruth. Thanksgiving Origami. 2012. (Holiday Origami Ser.). (ENG., Illus.). 32p. (J). (gr. 3-6). pap. 11.75 (978-1-4488-7923-6(X), PowerKids Pr.) Rosen Publishing Group, Inc., The.

Peppas, Lynn. Thanksgiving. 2009. (Celebrations in My World Ser.). (ENG., Illus.). 32p. (J). (gr. -1-3). pap. (978-0-7787-4309-5(8)) Crabtree Publishing Co.

Perry, Rex, illus. Over the River & Through the Woods. 2004. 24p. (J). lib. bdg. 8.00 (978-1-4242-0640-7(5)) Fitzgerald Bks.

Pettiford, Rebecca. Día de Acción de Gracias. 2015.Tr. of Thanksgiving Day. (SPA., Illus.). 24p. (J). lib. bdg. (978-1-62031-240-7(9), Bullfrog Bks.) Jump! Inc.

—Thanksgiving. 2015. (Illus.). 24p. (J). lib. bdg. (978-1-62031-186-8(0), Bullfrog Bks.) Jump! Inc.

Ponto, Joanna. Thanksgiving. 2016. (Story of Our Holidays Ser.). (Illus.). 32p. (J). (gr. 3-3). pap. 10.52 (978-0-7660-7631-0(8)) Enslow Pubs., Inc.

Rader, Laura & Utt, Mary Ann, illus. A Child's Story of Thanksgiving. 24p. (J). 7.95 (978-0-8249-5327-0(4), Ideal Pubns.) Worthy Publishing.

Randall, Ronne. Thanksgiving Sweets & Treats. 2012. (Holiday Cooking for Kids! Ser.). (ENG., Illus.). 32p. (J). (gr. 3-6). 26.50 (978-1-4488-8082-9(3)); pap. 11.75 (978-1-4488-8129-1(3)) Windmill Bks.

Robertson, Brynn, compiled by. Standard Christmas Program Book: Poems & Programs for Christmas & Thanksgiving. 2006. (Illus.). 48p. pap. 6.99 (978-0-7847-1647-2(1)) Standard Publishing.

Rooney, Ronnie. Thanksgiving Recipes, 1 vol. Rooney, Ronnie, illus. 2010. (Thanksgiving Ser.). (ENG., Illus.). 24p. (gr. 1-2). lib. bdg. 27.32 (978-1-4048-6283-8(8)) Picture Window Bks.

Ross, Kathy. All New Crafts for Thanksgiving. Holm, Sharon Lane, illus. 2005. 48p. (gr. k-2). (J). per. 7.95 (978-0-7613-2394-5(5), First Avenue Editions); (ENG.). lib. bdg. 25.26 (978-0-7613-2922-0(6), Millbrook Pr.) Lerner Publishing Group.

Samo, Melissa. If You Were a Kid at the First Thanksgiving Dinner. Farré, Lluís, illus. 2017. (If You Were a Kid Ser.). (ENG.). 32p. (J). pap. 7.95 (978-0-531-23097-8(X), Children's Pr.) Scholastic Library Publishing.

Santella, Andrew. The First Thanksgiving. 2003. (Cornerstones of Freedom Ser.). (ENG., Illus.). 48p. (YA). (gr. 4-7). 26.00 (978-0-516-24204-0(0)) Scholastic Library Publishing.

Samo, Melisa. If You Were a Kid at the First Thanksgiving Dinner. 2017. (If You Were a Kid Ser.). (ENG., Illus.). 32p. (J). lib. bdg. 26.00 (978-0-531-22383-3(3), Children's Pr.) Scholastic Library Publishing.

Skarmeas, Nancy J. The Story of Thanksgiving. Venturi-Pickett, Stacy, illus. 2012. 22p. (J). bds. 6.99 (978-0-8249-1883-5(5), Ideal Pubns.) Worthy Publishing.

Smith, Andrea P. The First Thanksgiving. 2012. (Illus.). 24p. (J). 63.60 (978-1-4488-5213-0(7)); pap. 10.60 (978-1-4488-5212-3(9)); lib. bdg. 25.25 (978-1-4488-5187-4(4)) Rosen Publishing Group, Inc., The. (PowerKids Pr.).

Stiegemeyer, Julie. Thanksgiving: A Harvest Celebration. Benoit, Renne, illus. 2003. 32p. (J). 13.49 (978-0-7586-0530-6(7)) Concordia Publishing Hse.

Stilwell, Norma Mintum. A Thought for Thanksgiving. Bingham, Pamela E., illus. 2011. 24p. pap. 14.95 (978-1-936343-93-5(2)) Peppertree Pr., The.

Sweet, Melissa. Balloons over Broadway: The True Story of the Puppeteer of Macy's Parade. 2011. (ENG., Illus.). 40p. (J). (gr. -1-3). 17.99 (978-0-547-19945-0(7)) Houghton Mifflin Harcourt Publishing Co.

Tani, Branca. Art for Thanksgiving. 2015. (Rosen REAL Readers: STEM & STEAM Collection). (ENG.). 8p. pap. 5.46 (978-1-4994-9698-7(2), Rosen Classroom) Rosen Publishing Group, Inc., The.

Trueit, Trudi Strain. Thanksgiving. 2010. (Benchmark Rebus: Holiday Fun Ser.). 24p. (gr. k-1). 15.95 (978-0-7614-4888-4(8)) Marshall Cavendish Corp.

Vidrine, Beverly Barras. Thanksgiving Day Alphabet, 1 vol. Lyne, Alison D., illus. 2006. (ENG.). 32p. (J). (gr. k-3). 8.95 (978-1-58980-338-1(8)) Pelican Publishing Co., Inc.

Walker, Nan. Thanksgiving Then & Now. 2011. (Early Connections Ser.). (J). (978-1-61672-378-1(5)) Benchmark Education Co.

Webster, Christine. How to Draw Thanksgiving Symbols. 2009. (Kid's Guide to Drawing Ser.). 24p. (gr. 3-3). 47.90 (978-1-61511-041-4(0), PowerKids Pr.) Rosen Publishing Group, Inc., The.

Wesemann, Tim. Tassel-Free Living for Grads: God's Grace for Grads. 2003. (Illus.). 64p. (YA). 9.99 (978-0-9718985-8-5(8)) C T A, Inc.

Williams, Colleen Madonna Flood. My Adventure on Thanksgiving Day. 2006. 44p. (J). 8.99 (978-1-59092-557-7(2)) Blue Forge Pr.

Yero, Judith Lloyd. The Mayflower Compact. 2006. (American Documents Ser.). (ENG., Illus.). 40p. (J). (gr. 5-9). 15.95 (978-0-7922-5891-9(6)); lib. bdg. 23.90 (978-0-7922-5892-6(4)) National Geographic Society. (National Geographic Children's Bks.).

Zocchi, Judy. On Thanksgiving Day. Wallis, Rebbeca, illus. 2005. (Holiday Happenings Ser.). 32p. (J). pap. 10.95 (978-1-59646-212-0(4)) Dingles & Co.

—On Thanksgiving Day. Wallis, Rebecca, illus. 2005. (Holiday Happenings Ser.). 32p. (J). per. 10.95 (978-1-59646-213-7(2)) Dingles & Co.

—On Thanksgiving Day/el Día de Acción de Gracias. Wallis, Rebecca, illus. 2005. (Holiday Happenings Ser.).Tr. of Día de Acción de Gracias. (ENG & SPA.). 32p. (J). pap. 10.95 (978-1-59646-214-4(0)); lib. bdg. 21.65 (978-1-891997-75-4(0)); per. 10.95 (978-1-59646-215-1(9)) Dingles & Co.

THANKSGIVING DAY—FICTION

Alcott, Louisa May. An Old-Fashioned Thanksgiving. Wheeler, Jody, illus. 2010. 40p. (J). (gr. -1-3). 14.99 (978-0-8249-5620-2(6), Ideal Pubns.) Worthy Publishing.

Anastos, Ernie. Ernie & the Big Newz. 2007. 32p. pap. 15.95 (978-0-9705100-5-1(5)) NK Pubns.

Anderson, Derek, et al. Over the River: A Turkey's Tale. 2005. (ENG., Illus.). 40p. (J). (gr. -1-3). 15.99 (978-0-689-87635-6(1), Simon & Schuster Bks. For Young Readers) Simon & Schuster Bks. For Young Readers.

Auch, Mary Jane. Beauty & the Beaks: A Turkey's Cautionary Tale. Auch, Herm & Auch, Mary Jane, illus. 2007. (ENG.). 32p. (J). (gr. -1-3). 17.95 (978-0-8234-1990-6(8)) Holiday Hse., Inc.

Balaban, Mariah. Scooby-Doo & the Thanksgiving Terror, 1 vol. Duendes Del Sur Staff, illus. 2012. (Scooby-Doo! Set 2 Ser.: No. 2). (ENG.). 24p. (J). (gr. k-3). lib. bdg. 24.21 (978-1-59961-870-8(2)) Spotlight.

Balian, Lorna. Sometimes It's Turkey, Sometimes It's Feathers, 1 vol. 2003. (ENG., Illus.). 32p. (J). 14.95 (978-1-932065-33-6(4)); pap. 5.95 (978-1-932065-41-1(5)) Star Bright Bks., Inc.

Banks, Steven. Thanks a Lot, Robo-Turkey! LaPadula, Tom, illus. 2005. (Adventures of Jimmy Neutron Ser.: 10). 24p. (J). lib. bdg. 15.00 (978-1-59054-787-8(X)) Fitzgerald Bks.

Barbara, Cohen. Molly's Pilgrim. 97th rev. ed. 2014. (ENG.). 32p. (J). (gr. 1-5). 8.24 (978-1-63245-244-3(8)) Lectorum Pubns., Inc.

Barbo, Maria S. & Bridwell, Norman. Thanksgiving Parade. Artful Doodlers, illus. 2010. (J). (978-0-545-25332-1(2)) Scholastic, Inc.

Berenstain, Mike, et al. The Berenstain Bears Give Thanks, 1 vol. Berenstain, Stan, illus. 2009. (Berenstain Bears/Living Lights Ser.). (ENG.). 32p. (J). (gr. -1-2). pap. 3.99 (978-0-310-71251-0(3)) Zonderkidz.

Bildner, Phil. Turkey Bowl. Payne, C. F., illus. 2008. (ENG.). 32p. (J). (gr. k-3). 15.99 (978-0-689-87896-1(6), Simon & Schuster Bks. For Young Readers) Simon & Schuster Bks. For Young Readers.

Bourgeois, Paulette. Franklin y el Dia de Accion de Gracias. Varela, Alejandra López, tr. Clark, Brenda, illus.Tr. of Franklin's Thanksgiving. (SPA.). (J). (gr. k-2). 10.95 (978-1-930332-07-2(6), LC30184) Lectorum Pubns., Inc.

Brown, L. McDougal's Feast. 2013. (ENG.). 24p. (J). pap. 11.95 (978-1-4787-0596-3(5)) Outskirts Pr., Inc.

Bunting, Eve. Frog & Friends Celebrate Thanksgiving, Christmas, & New Year's Eve. Masse, Josée, illus. 2015. (I AM a READER!: Frog & Friends Ser.). (ENG.). 40p. (J). (gr. 1-2). 9.99 (978-1-58536-897-6(0), 203949) Sleeping Bear Pr.

Burton, Jeffrey. The Itsy Bitsy Pilgrim. Rescek, Sanja, illus. 2016. (Itsy Bitsy Ser.). (ENG.). 16p. (J). (gr. -1 — 1). bds. 5.99 (978-1-4814-6852-7(9), Little Simon) Little Simon.

Bush, Leanne. Sarah's Happy Harvest Time, 1 vol. Briggs, Charlotte, illus. 2009. 32p. pap. 24.95 (978-1-60813-818-0(6)) America Star Bks.

Cazet, Denys. Minnie & Moo & the Thanksgiving Tree. 2003. (Minnie & Moo Ser.). (Illus.). 48p. (J). (gr. -1-2). pap. 31.95 incl. audio compact disk (978-1-59112-586-0(3)) Live Oak Media.

Cohen, Barbara. Molly's Pilgrim. Duffy, Daniel Mark & Deraney, Michael J., illus. 97th rev. ed. 2005. (ENG.). 32p. (J). (gr. 2-5). pap. 3.99 (978-0-688-16280-1(0)) HarperCollins Pubs.

—Molly's Pilgrim. (Literature to Go Ser.). pap., tchr. ed. incl. VHS (978-0-7919-2685-7(0)) Phoenix Films & Video.

Cole, Joanna. The Magic School Bus at the First Thanksgiving. Bracken, Carolyn, illus. 2006. (J). pap. (978-0-439-89935-2(4)) Scholastic, Inc.

Cox, Judy. One Is a Feast for Mouse: A Thanksgiving Tale. Ebbeler, Jeffrey, illus. 2009. (ENG.). 32p. (J). (gr. -1-3). pap. 7.99 (978-0-8234-2231-9(3)) Holiday Hse., Inc.

Davis, Nancy & Davis, Kathryn Lynn. The First Thanksgiving. Davis, Nancy & Davis, Kathryn Lynn, illus. 2010. (ENG., Illus.). 14p. (J). (gr. -1 — 1). bds. 5.99 (978-1-4424-0807-4(3), Little Simon) Little Simon.

Dean, James & Dean, Kimberly. The First Thanksgiving. Dean, James, illus. 2013. (Pete the Cat Ser.). (ENG.). 16p. (J). (gr. -1-3). 6.99 (978-0-06-219869-3(6), HarperFestival) HarperCollins Pubs.

Dellinger, Hampton. Thanks for Nothing: How Willie & Abe Saved Thanksgiving. 2008. 24p. 12.99 (978-0-615-24971-1(X)) Dellinger, Hampton.

dePaola, Tomie. My First Thanksgiving. 2008. (ENG.). 14p. (J). (gr. -1-k). bds. 5.99 (978-0-448-44857-2(2), Grosset & Dunlap) Penguin Young Readers Group.

Devlin, Wende. Cranberry Thanksgiving. Devlin, Harry, illus. 2012. (ENG.). 32p. (J). (gr. -1-3). 18.95 (978-1-930900-63-9(5)) Purple Hse. Pr.

Dickinson, Asa Don. Good Cheer Stories Every Child Should Know. 2007. 242p. pap. 20.99 (978-1-4346-3438-2(8)); (ENG.). 268p. pap. 23.99 (978-1-4346-3439-9(6)) Creative Media Partners, LLC.

Donovan, Dan. Holiday Tails! 2011. 48p. pap. 19.26 (978-1-4520-9628-5(7)) AuthorHouse.

Elliott, Laura Malone. Thanksgiving Day Thanks. Munsinger, Lynn, illus. 2013. (ENG.). 32p. (J). (gr. -1-3). 17.99 (978-0-06-000236-7(0)) HarperCollins Pubs.

Evans, Karen & Urmston, Kathleen. Thanksgiving. Kaeden Corp. Staff, ed. Graves, Dennis, illus. 2006. (ENG.). 12p. (gr. k-2). pap. 7.95 (978-1-879835-57-3(6), Kaeden Bks.) Kaeden Corp.

Evans, Rhonda Boone. Thanksgiving with the Lumpkins. 2009. 40p. pap. 16.50 (978-1-60860-783-9(6), Eloquent Bks.) Strategic Book Publishing & Rights Agency (SBPRA).

Fearing, Mark. The Great Thanksgiving Escape. Fearing, Mark, illus. (ENG., Illus.). 32p. (J). (gr. k-3). 2017. 6.99 (978-0-7636-9511-8(4)) 2014. 15.99 (978-0-7636-6306-3(9)) Candlewick Pr.

Flor Ada, Alma. Celebrate Thanksgiving Day with Beto & Gaby. Hayes, Joe & Franco, Sharon, trs. Rueda, Claudia, illus. 2006. (Cuentos para Celebrar / Stories to Celebrate Ser.). 30p. (gr. k-6). per. 11.95 (978-1-59820-133-8(6)) Santillana USA Publishing Co., Inc.

Freeman, Martha. Who Stole Grandma's Million-Dollar Pumpkin Pie? 2009. (Chickadee Court Mystery Ser.). (ENG.). 256p. (J). (gr. 3-7). 16.95 (978-0-8234-2215-9(1)) Holiday Hse., Inc.

Friedman, Laurie. Mallory Makes a Difference. Kalis, Jennifer, illus. 2017. (Mallory Ser.: 28). (ENG.). 152p. (gr. 2-5). 15.95 (978-1-4677-5032-5(8)) Lerner Publishing Group.

Friedman, Laurie. Thanksgiving Rules. Murfin, Teresa, illus. 2009. (Carolrhoda Picture Bks.). (ENG.). 32p. (J). (gr. k-3). 16.95 (978-0-8225-7983-0(9)) Lerner Publishing Group.

Gibson, Sherri L. In the Mind of a Child: Children's Stories. 2013. 36p. pap. 24.95 (978-1-62709-750-5(3)) America Star Bks.

Goodspeed, Judy. Perky Turkey's Perfect Plan. (Illus.). 22p. (J). 2007. per. 11.99 (978-0-9797574-3-3(6)) 2006. lib. bdg. 24.95 (978-0-9778651-1-6(8)) Dragonfly Publishing, Inc.

—Perky Turkey's Perfect Plan. Taylor, Chet, illus. 2005. 22p. (J). 18.99 (978-0-9765786-0-4(3)) Dragonfly Publishing, Inc.

Greene, Rhonda Gowler. The Very First Thanksgiving Day. Gaber, Susan, illus. 2006. (ENG.). 32p. (J). (gr. -1-1). 6.99 (978-1-4169-1916-2(3), Atheneum Bks. for Young Readers) Simon & Schuster Children's Publishing.

Gutman, Dan. Dr. Carbles Is Losing His Marbles! Paillot, Jim, illus. 2007. (My Weird School Ser.: 19). 112p. (J). (ENG.). (gr. 1-5). pap. 4.99 (978-0-06-123477-4(X)); (gr. 2-5). lib. bdg. 15.89 (978-0-06-123478-1(8)) HarperCollins Pubs.

—Dr. Carbles Is Losing His Marbles! Paillot, Jim, illus. 2007. (My Weird School Ser.: No. 19). 99p. (J). (gr. 2-5). 11.65 (978-0-7569-8810-4(1)) Perfection Learning Corp.

Hallinan, P. K. Thanksgiving at Our House. 2006. (ENG., Illus.). 32p. (J). (gr. -1-3). 9.85 (978-0-8249-5534-2(X), 1262730, Ideal Pubns.) Worthy Publishing.

—Today Is Thanksgiving! Hallinan, P. K., illus. 2008. (ENG., Illus.). 26p. (J). (gr. -1-k). bds. 6.99 (978-0-8249-6727-7(5), Ideal Pubns.) Worthy Publishing.

Hapka, Cathy, pseud. Giving Thanks. Byrne, Mike, illus. 2014. 32p. (J). pap. (978-0-545-75841-3(6)) Scholastic, Inc.

Harley, Bill. Charlie Bumpers vs. the Perfect Little Turkey, 1 vol. Gustavson, Adam, illus. (Charlie Bumpers Ser.: 4). (ENG.). (J). (gr. 2-4). 2016. 176p. pap. 6.95 (978-1-56145-963-6(1)) 2015. 164p. 13.95 (978-1-56145-835-6(X)) Peachtree Pubs.

—Charlie Bumpers vs. the Puny Pirates, 1 vol. Gustavson, Adam, illus. (Charlie Bumpers Ser.). (ENG.). (J). (gr. 2-4). 2017. 186p. pap. 6.95 (978-1-68263-001-3(3)) 2016. 160p. 14.95 (978-1-56145-939-1(9)) Peachtree Pubs.

Hawley, Mabel C. Four Little Blossoms Through the Holidays. 2005. pap. 22.95 (978-1-4179-9003-0(1)) Kessinger Publishing, LLC.

Higgins, M. G. Party of Nine. Taylor, Jo, illus. 2016. (Sibling Split Ser.). (ENG.). 112p. (gr. 2-3). lib. bdg. 25.32 (978-1-4965-2592-5(2)) Stone Arch Bks.

Hill, Eric. Spot's Thanksgiving. Hill, Eric, illus. 2016. (Spot Ser.). (ENG., Illus.). 10p. (J). (gr. -1-k). bds. 6.99 (978-0-399-24186-4(8), Warne) Penguin Young Readers Group.

Hillert, Margaret. Why We Have Thanksgiving. Marchesi, Stephen, illus. 2016. (BeginningtoRead Ser.). (ENG.). 32p. (J). (gr. 1-2). 22.60 (978-1-59953-809-9(1)) Norwood Hse. Pr.

Holub, Joan. More Snacks! A Thanksgiving Play. Terry, Will, illus. 2006. (Ant Hill Ser.: 1). (ENG.). 24p. (J). (gr. -1-k). pap. 3.99 (978-1-4169-0954-5(0)); lib. bdg. 11.89 (978-1-4169-2559-0(7)) Simon Spotlight. (Simon Spotlight).

Honeycutt, Scarlet. Turkeys in Disguise. Aarvig, Cindy, illus. 2007. 48p. per. 24.95 (978-1-4137-4035-6(9)) America Star Bks.

Horowitz, Dave. The Ugly Pumpkin. Horowitz, Dave, illus. 2008. (ENG., Illus.). 40p. (J). (gr. -1-k). pap. 6.99 (978-0-14-241145-2(0), Puffin Books) Penguin Young Readers Group.

Hurley, Wes. How the Winter Frog Came to Was: Or, How to Get a Nice Surprise on Thanksgiving! Lee, Susan, illus. 2007. 36p. per. 24.95 (978-1-4241-8395-1(2)) America Star Bks.

James, Cheryl D. Leah's Treasure Book. 2012. 36p. pap. 16.99 (978-1-4624-0422-3(7), Inspiring Voices) Author Solutions, Inc.

Johnston, Teresa. Thanksgiving for Emily Ann. Newton, Vanessa Brantley, illus. 2014. (ENG.). 32p. (J). (gr. -1-k). 6.99 (978-0-545-43413-3(0), Cartwheel Bks.) Scholastic, Inc.

Jones, Kia. The Adventures of Shamya & Friends: The Thanksgiving Day Wish. 2009. 28p. pap. 12.49 (978-1-4389-5127-0(2)) AuthorHouse.

Jones, Marcia Thornton & Dadey, Debbie. Wizards Do Roast Turkeys. Dreidemy, Joëlle, illus. 2007. 64p. (J). pap. *(978-0-545-00235-6(4))* Scholastic, Inc.
Jules, Jacqueline. Duck for Turkey Day. Mitter, Kathryn, illus. (ENG.). 32p. (J). 2017. (gr. k-2). pap. 7.99 ***(978-0-8075-1735-2(6))*** 2009. (gr. 1-3). 16.99 *(978-0-8075-1734-5(8))* Whitman, Albert & Co.
Kann, Victoria. Pinkalicious - Thanksgiving Helper. Kann, Victoria, illus. 2014. (Pinkalicious Ser.). (ENG., Illus.). 24p. (J). (gr. -1-3). pap. 6.99 *(978-0-06-218774-1(0),* HarperFestival) HarperCollins Pubs.
Katschke, Judy. First Grade Feast!/By Judy Katschke; Illustrated by Clare Elsom. Elsom, Clare, illus. 2014. 32p. (J). pap. *(978-0-545-75844-4(0))* Scholastic, Inc.
Kennedy, Anne Vittur. One Big Turkey, 1 vol. 2016. (ENG., Illus.). 20p. (J). bds. 8.99 *(978-0-7180-8711-1(9))* Nelson, Thomas Inc.
Kimmelman, Leslie. Round the Turkey: A Grateful Thanksgiving. Cote, Nancy, illus. 2012. (J). 34.28 *(978-1-61913-130-9(7))* Weigl Pubs., Inc.
Klein, Abby. Thanks for Giving. McKinley, John, illus. 2009. (Ready, Freddy! Reader List: No. 4). 32p. (J). pap. *(978-0-545-14176-5(1))* Scholastic, Inc.
—Thanksgiving Turkey Trouble. McKinley, John, illus. 2008. (Ready, Freddy! Ser.: Bk. 15). 95p. (gr. -1-3). 16.00 *(978-0-7569-8838-8(1))* Perfection Learning Corp.
Klimo, Kate. Dash. 2014. (Dog Diaries: 5). lib. bdg. 18.40 *(978-0-606-36021-0(2))* Turtleback Bks.
—Dog Diaries #5: Dash. Jessell, Tim, illus. 2014. (Dog Diaries). (ENG.). 160p. (J). (gr. 2-5). pap. 7.99 *(978-0-385-37338-8(4),* Random Hse. Bks. for Young Readers) Random Hse. Children's Bks.
Kroll, Virginia. The Thanksgiving Bowl, 1 vol. O'Neill, Philomena, illus. 2007. (ENG.). 32p. (J). (gr. k-3). 16.99 *(978-1-58980-365-7(5))* Pelican Publishing Co., Inc.
Krulik, Nancy. Don't Be Such a Turkey! John and Wendy Staff, illus. 2010. (Katie Kazoo, Switcheroo Ser.). (ENG.). 160p. (J). (gr. 2-4). pap. 4.99 *(978-0-448-45448-1(3),* Grosset & Dunlap) Penguin Young Readers Group.
Lois, Lowry. Gooney Bird & the Room Mother. Thomas, Middy, illus. 2006. (Gooney Bird Ser.: No. 2). (ENG.). 80p. (J). (gr. 3-7). 5.99 *(978-0-440-42133-7(0),* Yearling) Random Hse. Children's Bks.
Longstreet, Barbara, et al. Woodsey School Kids Thanksgiving Feast. 2004. 28p. pap. 24.95 *(978-1-4137-1992-5(9))* PublishAmerica, Inc.
Mackall, Dandi Daley. Thank You for Thanksgiving. Walker, John, illus. 2008. 32p. (J). (gr. -1). 13.49 *(978-0-7586-1500-8(0))* Concordia Publishing Hse.
Maloney, Peter & Zekauskas, Felicia. Thanks for Nothing! 2003. (Illus.). 31p. (J). *(978-0-439-55360-5(1))* Scholastic, Inc.
Manushkin, Fran. Katie Saves Thanksgiving, 1 vol. Lyon, Tammie, illus. 2010. (Katie Woo Ser.). (ENG.). 32p. (gr. k-2). lib. bdg. 21.32 *(978-1-4048-5988-3(8));* pap. 5.95 *(978-1-4048-6367-5(2))* Picture Window Bks.
Markes, Julie. Thanks for Thanksgiving. Barrette, Doris, illus. (ENG.). 32p. (J). (gr. -1-3). 2008. pap. 6.99 *(978-0-06-051098-5(6))* 2004. 12.99 *(978-0-06-051096-1(X))* HarperCollins Pubs.
Markes, Julie. Thanks for Thanksgiving Board Book. Barrette, Doris, illus. 2017. 32p. (J). (gr. -1 — 1). bds. 7.99 ***(978-0-06-264331-5(2),*** HarperFestival) HarperCollins Pubs.
Martin, Ann M. Needle & Thread. 2007. (Main Street Ser.). (Illus.). 205p. (J). (gr. 4-7). 14.65 *(978-0-7569-8328-4(2))* Perfection Learning Corp.
—Needle & Thread. Andreasen, Dan, illus. 2007. 205p. (J). pap. *(978-0-545-03660-3(7))* Scholastic, Inc.
Mayer, Mercer. Just a Special Thanksgiving. Mayer, Mercer, illus. 2015. (Little Critter Ser.). (ENG., Illus.). 24p. (J). (gr. -1-2). pap. 4.99 *(978-0-06-147811-6(3),* HarperFestival) HarperCollins Pubs.
—Just a Special Thanksgiving. 2015. (Little Critter Ser.). (J). lib. bdg. 14.75 *(978-0-606-37605-1(4))* Turtleback Bks.
Mayr, Diane. Run, Turkey, Run! Rader, Laura, illus. 2009. (ENG.). 32p. (J). (gr. -1-2). pap. 7.99 *(978-0-8027-8481-0(X),* 9780802784810, Bloomsbury USA Childrens) Bloomsbury Publishing USA.
McCue, Lisa, illus. Corduroy's Thanksgiving. 2006. (Corduroy Ser.). (ENG.). 16p. (J). (gr. -1 — 1). bds. 5.99 *(978-0-670-06108-2(5),* Viking Books for Young Readers) Penguin Young Readers Group.
McDonald, Megan. Judy Moody & Stink: the Wishbone Wish. Reynolds, Peter H., illus. 2015. (Judy Moody Ser.). (ENG.). 128p. (J). (gr. 1-4). 14.99 *(978-0-7636-7206-5(8))* Candlewick Pr.
—The Wishbone Wish. Reynolds, Peter H., illus. 2016. (Judy Moody & Stink Ser.: 4). (ENG.). 116p. (J). (gr. 1-4). lib. bdg. 18.40 *(978-0-606-39093-4(6))* Turtleback Bks.
McGrath, Barbara Barbieri & Tagel, Peggy. Thanksgiving Counting. 2016. (First Celebrations Ser.). (ENG., Illus.). 12p. (J). (— 1). bds. 6.95 *(978-1-58089-534-7(4))* Charlesbridge Publishing, Inc.
McGuirk, Leslie. Gobble, Gobble, Tucker! McGuirk, Leslie, illus. 2014. (ENG., Illus.). 32p. (J). (-k). bds. 7.99 *(978-0-7636-6887-7(7))* Candlewick Pr.
McNamara, Margaret. Happy Thanksgiving. Gordon, Mike, illus. 2005. (Robin Hill School Ser.). (ENG.). 32p. (J). (gr. -1-1). pap. 3.99 *(978-1-4169-0505-9(7),* Simon Spotlight) Simon Spotlight.
Meddaugh, Susan. Martha Speaks: Thanksgiving Reunion (Chapter Book) 2013. (Martha Speaks Ser.). (ENG., Illus.). 96p. (J). (gr. 1-4). 14.99 *(978-0-547-86580-5(5))* Houghton Mifflin Harcourt Publishing Co.
—Thanksgiving Reunion. 2013. (Martha Speaks Ser.). (ENG., Illus.). 96p. (J). (gr. 1-4). pap. 5.99 *(978-0-547-86581-2(3))* Houghton Mifflin Harcourt Publishing Co.
Melmed, Laura Krauss. This First Thanksgiving Day: A Counting Story. Buehner, Mark, illus. 2003. (ENG.). 32p. (J). (gr. -1-3). pap. 6.99 *(978-0-06-054184-2(9))* HarperCollins Pubs.
Menard, Michele R. The Thanksgiving Ring. 2013. 56p. 24.95 *(978-0-9891734-8-3(8))* Four Menards, The.
Metzger, Steve. The Amazing Turkey Rescue. Paillot, Jim, illus. 2007. (J). ***(978-0-545-01420-5(4))*** Scholastic, Inc.
Metzger, Steve. The Great Turkey Race. Paillot, Jim, illus. 2006. (J). *(978-0-439-85930-1(1))* Scholastic, Inc.
Miller, Pat Zietlow. Sharing the Bread: An Old-Fashioned Thanksgiving Story. McElmurry, Jill, illus. 2015. (ENG.). 32p. (J). (gr. -1-3). 17.99 *(978-0-307-98182-0(7),* Schwartz & Wade Bks.) Random Hse. Children's Bks.
Moon, Alice. Lucky's Special Thanksgiving. 2007. (Illus.). (J). pap. 9.95 *(978-0-9795831-2-4(8))* PeachMoon Publishing.
Morrison, Jessica. Le Jour de L'Action de Grâce: Les Célébrations Canadiennes. Karvonen, Tanjah, tr. from ENG. 2011. (FRE.). 24p. (gr. k-3). *(978-1-77071-400-7(6))* Weigl Educational Pubs. Ltd.
Morse, William A. and & Morse, William A. And Dana Jo. Kurkle Kids: Spirit of America. 2009. 44p. pap. 16.99 *(978-1-4490-1009-6(1))* AuthorHouse.
Neely, Kirk H. Santa Almost Got Caught: Stories for Thanksgiving, Christmas, & the New Year. Cash, Emory, illus. 2011. 152p. pap. 14.99 *(978-1-4575-0477-8(4))* Dog Ear Publishing, LLC.
Oceanak, Karla. Finicky. Spanjer, Kendra, illus. 2012. (Aldo Zelnick Comic Novel Ser.: 6). (ENG.). 160p. (J). (gr. 3-7). 12.95 *(978-1-934649-24-4(4))* Bailiwick Pr.
O'Connor, Jane. Fancy Nancy: Our Thanksgiving Banquet. Glasser, Robin Preiss, illus. 2011. (Fancy Nancy Ser.). (ENG.). 24p. (J). (gr. -1-3). pap. 4.99 *(978-0-06-123598-6(9),* HarperFestival) HarperCollins Pubs.
Olson, Nancy. Thanksgiving at Grandma's. Marino, Michael F., illus. 2009. 24p. pap. 10.95 *(978-1-4251-8909-9(1))* Trafford Publishing.
Osborne, Mary Pope, et al. Jueves de Acción de Gracias. Murdocca, Sal, illus. 2014. 27. (SPA.). 88p. (J). (gr. 2-4). pap. 5.99 *(978-1-933032-94-8(4))* Lectorum Pubns., Inc.
Parish, Herman. Amelia Bedelia Talks Turkey. Sweat, Lynn, illus. (I Can Read Level 2 Ser.). (ENG.). 64p. (J). (gr. k-3). 2009. pap. 3.99 *(978-0-06-084354-0(3))* 2008. 16.99 *(978-0-06-084352-6(7))* HarperCollins Pubs. (Greenwillow Bks.).
—Amelia Bedelia Talks Turkey. Parish, Herman & Sweat, Lynn, illus. 2008. (Amelia Bedelia Ser.). 64p. (J). (gr. k-4). lib. bdg. 17.89 *(978-0-06-084353-3(5),* Greenwillow Bks.) HarperCollins Pubs.
Park, Barbara. Turkeys We Have Loved & Eaten, No. 28. Brunkus, Denise, illus. 2012. (Junie B. Jones Ser.: 28). (ENG.). 144p. (J). (gr. 1-4). lib. bdg. 14.99 *(978-0-375-97063-4(0),* Random Hse. Bks. for Young Readers) Random Hse. Children's Bks.
—Turkeys We Have Loved & Eaten (and Other Thankful Stuff), No. 28. Brunkus, Denise, illus. 2012. (Junie B. Jones Ser.). (ENG.). 144p. (J). (gr. 1-4). 11.99 *(978-0-375-87063-7(6),* Random Hse. Bks. for Young Readers) Random Hse. Children's Bks.
—Turkeys We Have Loved & Eaten (and Other Thankful Stuff) 2014. (Junie B. Jones Ser.: 28). lib. bdg. 14.75 *(978-0-606-36015-9(8))* Turtleback Bks.
Peacock, L. A. The Truth (and Myths) about Thanksgiving. Wigsby, Nick, illus. 2013. 89p. (J). pap. *(978-0-545-56846-3(3))* Scholastic, Inc.
Peterson, Joel & Rogers, Jacqueline, illus. The Littles & the Surprise Thanksgiving Guests. 2004. (Littles First Readers Ser.). 105p. (J). *(978-0-439-68704-1(7))* Scholastic, Inc.
Priddy, Roger. Alphaprints: Gobble Gobble. 2016. (Alphaprints Ser.). (ENG.). 10p. (J). bds. 7.99 *(978-0-312-52057-1(3),* 9780312520571, Priddy Bks.) St. Martin's Pr.
—Bright Baby: Happy Thanksgiving. 2015. (Bright Baby Ser.). (ENG.). 16p. (J). (gr. -1 — 1). bds. 4.99 *(978-0-312-51871-4(4),* 9780312518714, Priddy Bks.) St. Martin's Pr.
Rains, Deborah Jane. Cuddles & Snuggles. 2011. 24p. pap. 24.95 *(978-1-4489-3917-6(8))* America Star Bks.
—St Patrick's Day with Cuddles & Snuggles. 2011. 16p. pap. 24.95 *(978-1-4489-4926-7(2))* America Star Bks.
—Thanksgiving with Cuddles & Snuggles, 1 vol. 2010. 20p. 24.95 *(978-1-4489-4924-3(6))* PublishAmerica, Inc.
Rey, H. A. Happy Thanksgiving. 2010. (Curious George Ser.). (ENG., Illus.). 14p. (J). (gr. -1 — 1). bds. 7.99 *(978-0-547-13106-1(2))* Houghton Mifflin Harcourt Publishing Co.
Roberts, Bethany. Thanksgiving Mice! Cushman, Doug, illus. 2005. (ENG.). 32p. (J). (gr. -1 — 1). 5.95 *(978-0-618-60486-9(3))* Houghton Mifflin Harcourt Publishing Co.
Roe, E. P. Three Thanksgiving Kisses. 2004. reprint ed. pap. 15.95 *(978-1-4191-8991-3(3))* Kessinger Publishing, LLC.
Roy, Ronald. November Night. Gurney, John Steven, illus. 2014. (Calendar Mysteries Ser.: 11). (ENG.). 80p. (J). (gr. 1-4). 4.99 *(978-0-385-37165-0(9),* Random Hse. Bks. for Young Readers) Random Hse. Children's Bks.
—Turkey Trouble on the National Mall. Bush, Timothy, illus. 2012. (Capital Mysteries Ser.: 14). (ENG.). 96p. (J). (gr. 1-4). 4.99 *(978-0-307-93220-4(6),* Random Hse. Bks. for Young Readers) Random Hse. Children's Bks.
Ruelle, Karen Gray. The Thanksgiving Beast Feast. (Holiday House Readers Ser.). (ENG., Illus.). 32p. (J). (gr. k-3). pap. 4.95 *(978-0-8234-1802-2(2))* Holiday Hse., Inc.
—The Thanksgiving Beast Feast Level 2: A Holiday House Reader. Ruelle, Karen Gray, illus. (ENG., Illus.). 32p. (J). (gr. k-3). tchr. ed. 15.95 *(978-0-8234-1511-3(2))* Holiday Hse., Inc.
Rylant, Cynthia. Annie & Snowball & the Thankful Friends. Stevenson, Suçie, illus. (Annie & Snowball Ser.: 10). (ENG.). 40p. (J). (gr. k-2). 2012. pap. 3.99 *(978-1-4169-7202-0(1))* 2011. 15.99 *(978-1-4169-7200-6(5))* Simon Spotlight. (Simon Spotlight).
—Annie & Snowball & the Thankful Friends. 2012. (Annie & Snowball Ready-To-Read Ser.). lib. bdg. 13.55 *(978-0-606-26917-9(7),* Turtleback) Turtleback Bks.
Santa's Thanksgiving. 2005. (J). 5.95 *(978-0-9769321-0-9(5))* Steingart, Nathan Publishing.
Schulz, Charles. Charlie Brown Thanksgiving, 1 vol. 2013. (Peanuts Picture Bks.). (ENG.). 24p. (J). (gr. -1-4). lib. bdg. 24.21 *(978-1-61479-030-3(2))* ABDO Publishing Co.
—Snoopy's Thanksgiving. 2014. (Peanuts Seasonal Ser.: 0). (ENG., Illus.). 64p. 9.99 *(978-1-60699-778-9(5),* 699778) Fantagraphics Bks.
Scieszka, Jon. Trucksgiving. Shannon, David et al, illus. 2010. (Jon Scieszka's Trucktown Ser.). (ENG.). 24p. (J). (gr. -1-1). 16.99 *(978-1-4169-4157-6(6));* pap. 3.99 *(978-1-4169-4146-0(0))* Simon Spotlight. (Simon Spotlight).
Shore, Diane Z. This Is the Feast. Lloyd, Megan, illus. 2011. (ENG.). 32p. (J). (gr. -1-3). pap. 6.99 *(978-0-06-443850-6(3))* HarperCollins Pubs.
Silvano, Wendi. Turkey Trouble, 0 vols. 2009. (ENG., Illus.). 32p. (J). (gr. -1-2). 15.99 *(978-0-7614-5529-5(9),* 9780761455295, Two Lions) Amazon Publishing.
Slater, Teddy. The Best Thanksgiving Ever! Long, Ethan, illus. 2007. (ENG.). 24p. (J). (gr. -1-3). pap. 5.99 *(978-0-439-87390-1(8),* Cartwheel Bks.) Scholastic, Inc.
Spinelli, Eileen. The Perfect Thanksgiving. Adinolfi, JoAnn, illus. 2007. (ENG.). 32p. (J). (gr. -1-2). 7.99 *(978-0-312-37505-8(0),* 9780312375058) Square Fish.
—Thanksgiving at the Tappletons' Cocca-Leffler, Maryann, illus. 2015. (ENG.). 32p. (J). (gr. -1-3). pap. 6.99 *(978-0-06-236397-8(2))* HarperCollins Pubs.
—Thanksgiving at the Tappletons' Lloyd, Megan, illus. 2005. (gr. -1-3). 17.00 *(978-0-7569-5762-9(1))* Perfection Learning Corp.
Stanley, Diane. Thanksgiving on Plymouth Plantation. Berry, Holly, illus. 2004. (Time-Traveling Twins Ser.). (ENG.). 48p. (J). (gr. k-5). 16.99 *(978-0-06-027069-8(1))* HarperCollins Pubs.
Star, Nancy. The Case of the Thanksgiving Thief. Bernardin, James, illus. 2004. 79p. (J). *(978-0-439-67261-0(9))* Scholastic, Inc.
Steinberg, Jessica. Not This Turkey! Pike, Amanda, illus. 2016. (ENG.). 32p. (J). (gr. -1-3). 16.99 *(978-0-8075-7908-4(4))* Whitman, Albert & Co.
Stern, Ricki. Mission Impossible. Date not set. (Beryl E. Bean Ser.: Vol. 3). (Illus.). (J). lib. bdg. 15.89 *(978-0-06-028773-3(X),* Harper Trophy) HarperCollins Pubs.
Stone Arch Books. Halloween & Thanksgiving, 1 vol. Nguyen, Dustin, illus. 2014. (Batman: Li'l Gotham Ser.). (ENG.). 32p. (gr. 2-3). 22.60 *(978-1-4342-9208-7(8))* Stone Arch Bks.
Stone, Tanya Lee. T Is for Turkey: A True Thanksgiving Story. Kelley, Gerald, illus. 2009. (ENG.). 24p. (J). (gr. -1-k). mass mkt. 4.99 *(978-0-8431-2570-2(5),* Price Stern Sloan) Penguin Young Readers Group.
Suhay, Lisa. Pardon Me, It's Ham, Not Turkey. Barcita, Pamela, illus. 2007. (J). (gr. -1-3). 17.95 *(978-1-933982-01-4(2))* Bumble Bee Publishing.
Sullivan, Maureen & Josephs, Alison. Ankle Soup: A Thanksgiving Story. Josephs, Alison, illus. 2008. (Illus.). 32p. 17.95 *(978-0-9820381-0-9(0))* McJo InkWorks.
Tamaja Press & Tillman, Gloria J. Teeth for Thanksgiving. 2017. (ENG., Illus.). 36p. (J). lib. bdg. 12.99 *(978-0-9841260-7-1(4))* Tamaja Pr.
Taylor, Helen L. Little Pilgrim's Progress: From John Bunyan's Classic. 2006. (ENG., Illus.). 336p. (gr. -1-3). per. 8.99 *(978-0-8024-4924-5(7))* Moody Pubs.
Thaler, Mike. The Thanksgiving Day from the Black Lagoon. Lee, Jared, illus. 2009. 64p. (J). *(978-0-545-16812-0(0))* Scholastic, Inc.
Wheeler, Lisa. Turk & Runt: A Thanksgiving Comedy. Ansley, Frank, illus. 2005. (ENG.). 32p. (J). (gr. -1-2). 7.99 *(978-1-4169-0714-5(9),* Atheneum Bks. for Young Readers) Simon & Schuster Children's Publishing.
Wilce, Colin. The Youngsters' Adventure & Thanksgiving (Rabbit Brook Tales Volume 4) 2007. 80p. pap. 17.95 *(978-1-84753-202-2(0))* Lulu Pr., Inc.
Williams, Jacklyn. Feliz Dia de Gracias, Gus!, 1 vol. Abello, Patricia, tr. from ENG. Cushman, Doug, illus. 2006. (Read-It! Readers en Español: Gus el Erizo Ser.). (SPA.). 32p. (gr. k-3). lib. bdg. 19.99 *(978-1-4048-2690-8(4),* Easy Readers) Picture Window Bks.
Wood, Francis Eugene. Autumn's Reunion: A Story of Thanksgiving. Dean, Tina & Marken, Jon, eds. McDermott, Robert W., illus. 2006. 47p. pap. 8.00 *(978-0-9746372-2-8(X))* Tip-Of-The-Moon Publishing Co.

THEATER

see also Acting; Actors and Actresses; Ballet; Bible Plays; Opera; Puppets; Theaters

Alexander, Martha, et al. Teatro para Niños. Tenorio, Miguel A., ed. 2005. (SPA & ENG.). 246p. (J). (gr. 4-7). pap. 14.95 *(978-968-860-739-8(8))* Editorial Pax MEX. Dist: Independent Pubs. Group.
Berne, Emma Carlson. William Shakespeare: Playwright & Poet, 1 vol. 2008. (Essential Lives Set 2 Ser.). (ENG., Illus.). 112p. (J). (gr. 6-12). lib. bdg. 35.64 *(978-1-60453-042-1(1))* ABDO Publishing Co.
Blackwell, Su & Fletcher, Corina. The Sleeping Beauty Theatre. 2015. (ENG., Illus.). 32p. (J). (gr. 1-5). 29.95 *(978-0-500-65054-7(3),* 565054) Thames & Hudson.
Clements, Gillian. Tudor Theatre. 2009. (Building History Ser.). (Illus.). 32p. (J). (gr. 3-5). 27.10 *(978-1-59771-147-0(0))* Sea-To-Sea Pubns.
Cobb, Lisa Kaniut. Literary Ideas & Scripts for Young Playwrights, 1 vol. 2004. (Illus.). 192p. (J). pap. 32.00 *(978-1-59158-071-3(4),* LU0714, Libraries Unlimited) ABC-CLIO, LLC.
Cohan, George M. & Schwaeber, Barbie. Give My Regards to Broadway. Newsom, Carol, illus. 2008. (American Favorites Ser.). (ENG.). 32p. (J). (gr. -1-3). 14.95 *(978-1-59249-726-3(8));* 8.95 *(978-1-59249-727-0(6))* Soundprints.
Culp, Jennifer. What Is a Play?, 1 vol. 2015. (ENG., Illus.). 32p. (J). 23.45 *(978-1-62275-668-1(1),* Britannica Educational Publishing) Rosen Publishing Group, Inc., The.
Donovan, Sandy. Music & Theater Top Tens. 2014. (Entertainment's Top 10 Ser.). (Illus.). 32p. (J). (gr. 5-8). lib. bdg. 26.60 *(978-1-4677-3843-9(3),* Lerner Pubns.) Lerner Publishing Group.
Dorling Kindersley Publishing Staff. Shakespeare. 2015. (DK Eyewitness Bks.). (ENG., Illus.). 72p. (J). (gr. 3-7). pap. 9.99 *(978-1-4654-3185-1(3),* DK Children) Dorling Kindersley Publishing, Inc.
Draper, Penny. Breaking Big, 1 vol. 2016. (Orca Limelights Ser.). (ENG.). 144p. (J). (gr. 6-9). pap. 9.95 *(978-1-4598-0923-9(8))* Orca Bk. Pubs. USA.
Dunleavy, Deborah. The Jumbo Book of Drama. Kurisu, Jane, tr. Kurisu, Jane, illus. 2004. (Jumbo Bks.). (ENG.). 208p. (J). (gr. 4-6). 14.95 *(978-1-55337-008-6(2))* Kids Can Pr., Ltd. CAN. Dist: Hachette Bk. Group.
Emmer, Rae. Drama Club. 2009. (School Activities Ser.). 24p. (gr. 1-1). 42.50 *(978-1-60852-998-8(3),* PowerKids Pr.) Rosen Publishing Group, Inc., The.
—Drama Club / Club de Teatro. 2009. (School Activities / Actividades escolares Ser.). (ENG & SPA.). 24p. (gr. 1-2). 42.50 *(978-1-60853-004-5(3),* Editorial Buenas Letras) Rosen Publishing Group, Inc., The.
Evans, Cheryl & Smith, Lucy. Acting & Theatre. Evans, Cheryl, ed. Jude, Conny, illus. Putsman, Helen, photos by. 2008. (Acting & Theatre Ser.). 64p. (J). pap. 8.99 *(978-0-7945-2216-2(5),* Usborne) EDC Publishing.
Firth, Melissa. Behind the Scenes at a Play. 2014. (VIP Tours Ser.). 48p. (J). (gr. 4-6). 31.36 *(978-1-62713-019-6(5))* Cavendish Square Publishing.
Gallegos, Manuel. Mi Primer Teatro. 2003. (J). *(978-956-240-371-9(8))* Arrayán Editores S.A.
Hilliam, David. William Shakespeare: England's Greatest Playwright & Poet. 2009. (Rulers, Scholars, & Artists of the Renaissance Ser.). 112p. (gr. 5-8). 66.50 *(978-1-60852-945-2(2),* Rosen Reference) Rosen Publishing Group, Inc., The.
In the Movies, 6 vols. (Book2WebTM Ser.). (gr. 4-8). 36.50 *(978-0-322-02982-8(1))* Wright Group/McGraw-Hill.
Kenney, Karen Latchana. Cool Costumes: How to Stage Your Very Own Show, 1 vol. 2010. (Cool Performances Ser.). (ENG., Illus.). 32p. (gr. 3-6). 28.50 *(978-1-60453-714-7(0),* Checkerboard Library) ABDO Publishing Co.
—Cool Special Effects: How to Stage Your Very Own Show, 1 vol. 2010. (Cool Performances Ser.). (ENG., Illus.). 32p. (gr. 3-6). 28.50 *(978-1-60453-719-2(1),* Checkerboard Library) ABDO Publishing Co.
Lewis, Jan, illus. Performance. 2012. (First Time Ser.). (ENG.). 24p. (J). *(978-1-84643-487-7(4))* Child's Play International Ltd.
Madl-Palfi, L. & Tujner-Marko, B. Kaspertheater Rund ums Jahr. (Illus.). 144p. pap. *(978-3-12-675640-2(9))* Klett, Ernst, Verlag GmbH DEU. Dist: International Bk. Import Service, Inc.
Malam, John. Theater: From First Rehearsal to Opening Night! a Building Works Book. Malam, John, illus. 2006. (Illus.). 32p. (J). (gr. k-4). 17.00 *(978-1-4223-5179-6(3))* DIANE Publishing Co.
Manning, Mick & Granström, Brita, illus. Drama School. 2009. (ENG.). 48p. (J). (gr. 2-5). 17.95 *(978-1-84507-845-4(4),* Frances Lincoln); pap. 9.95 *(978-1-84507-846-1(2),* Frances Lincoln Children's Bks.) Quarto Publishing Group UK GBR. Dist: Hachette Bk. Group.
Manning, Mick, et al. Teatro. 2006. (Mi Primer Libro Ser.). (SPA., Illus.). 48p. (J). (gr. 2-3). 17.99 *(978-84-241-1311-7(X))* Everest Editora ESP. Dist: Lectorum Pubns., Inc.
Matthews, Sheelagh. The Sydney Opera House. 2008. (Structural Wonders Ser.). (Illus.). 32p. (J). (gr. 4-6). pap. 9.95 *(978-1-59036-937-1(8))* Weigl Pubs., Inc.
Meister, Cari. El Teatro. 2016. (Los Primeros Viajes Escolares (First Field Trips)).Tr. of Theater. 24p. (J). (gr. k-2). lib. bdg. 25.65 *(978-1-62031-332-9(4),* Bullfrog Bks.) Jump! Inc.
—Theater. Fretland VanVoorst, Jenny, ed. 2016. (First Field Trips). 24p. (J). (gr. k-2). lib. bdg. 25.65 *(978-1-62031-298-8(0),* Bullfrog Bks.) Jump! Inc.
Owings, Lisa. What Are Plays? 2014. (Name That Text Type! Ser.). (Illus.). 32p. (gr. 2-4). pap. 7.95 *(978-1-4677-4520-8(0));* (ENG.). lib. bdg. 26.60 *(978-1-4677-4060-9(8),* Lerner Pubns.) Lerner Publishing Group.
Rauf, Don. Music in Theater. 2016. (Exploring Theater Ser.). 96p. (J). lib. bdg. 42.79 *(978-1-5026-2271-6(8))* Cavendish Square Publishing.
Rauf, Don & Vescia, Monique. Choose Your Own Career Adventure on Broadway. 2016. (Bright Futures Press: Choose Your Own Career Adventure Ser.). (ENG.). 32p. (J). (gr. 4-6). 29.93 *(978-1-63471-909-4(3),* 208957) Cherry Lake Publishing.
Regan, Lisa. Broadway Star. 2012. (Stage School Ser.). (ENG., Illus.). 32p. (J). (gr. 3-6). 25.25 *(978-1-4488-8092-8(0));* pap. 10.00 *(978-1-4488-8151-2(X))* Windmill Bks.
Schanker, Harry H., et al. The Stage & the School. 9th ed. 2004. (STAGE & SCHOOL Ser.). (ENG., Illus.). 672p. (gr. 9-12). stu. ed. 102.00 *(978-0-07-861627-3(1),* 0078616271) McGraw-Hill Higher Education.
Zimmerman, Suzi. Introduction to Theatre Arts: An Action Handbook for Middle Grade & High School Students & Teachers. 2007. (ENG., Illus.). 255p. stu. ed., per. 24.95 *(978-1-56608-148-1(3))* Meriwether Publishing, Ltd.

THEATER—FICTION

Adrian, Emily. Like It Never Happened. 2015. (ENG.). 368p. (J). (gr. 9). 17.99 *(978-0-525-42823-7(2),* Dial Bks) Penguin Young Readers Group.
Aliki. Play's the Thing. Aliki, illus. 2005. (ENG., Illus.). 32p. (J). 16.99 *(978-0-06-074355-0(7))* HarperCollins Pubs.
Alsenas, Linas. Beyond Clueless. 2015. (ENG.). 256p. (YA). (gr. 7-11). 16.95 *(978-1-4197-1496-2(1),* Amulet Bks.) Abrams, Inc.
Andrews, Julie & Hamilton, Emma Walton. The Great American Mousical. Walton, Tony, illus. 2006. (Julie Andrews Collection). (J). (gr. k-4). 160p. 15.99 *(978-0-06-057918-0(8),* Julie Andrews Collection); 147p. lib. bdg. 16.89 *(978-0-06-057919-7(6))* HarperCollins Pubs.
Appelt, Kathi. Bat Jamboree. Sweet, Melissa, illus. 2004. 17.00 *(978-0-7569-4074-4(5))* Perfection Learning Corp.
Archer, Nick & McDonald, Megan. Rule of Three. 2010. (Sisters Club Ser.: 2). (ENG., Illus.). 240p. (J). (gr. 3-7). pap. 5.99 *(978-0-7636-4830-5(2))* Candlewick Pr.
—Rule of Three. Consolazio, Pamela A., illus. 2009. (Sisters Club Ser.: 2). (ENG.). 240p. (J). (gr. 3-7). 15.99 *(978-0-7636-4153-5(7))* Candlewick Pr.
Avi. Romeo & Juliet Together (and Alive!) at Last. 2012. (ENG.). 128p. (J). (gr. 5-9). pap. 6.99 *(978-0-545-43097-5(6),* Scholastic Paperbacks) Scholastic, Inc.
Barkley, Callie. All about Ellie. Riti, Marsha, illus. 2013. (Critter Club Ser.: 2). (ENG.). 128p. (J). (gr. k-2). 15.99 *(978-1-4424-5789-8(9));* pap. 5.99 *(978-1-4424-5788-1(0))* Little Simon. (Little Simon).
—All about Ellie. 2013. (Critter Club Ser.: 2). lib. bdg. 16.00 *(978-0-606-27024-3(8),* Turtleback) Turtleback Bks.
Barshaw, Ruth McNally. The Show Must Go On. Barshaw, Ruth McNally, illus. 2013. (Ellie Mcdoodle Diaries). (ENG., Illus.). 176p. (YA). (gr. 3-6). 12.99 *(978-1-61963-059-8(1),*

TUV

9781619630598, Bloomsbury USA Childrens) Bloomsbury Publishing USA.

Berenstain, Mike. The Berenstain Bears Blessed Are the Peacemakers, 1 vol. 2014. (Berenstain Bears/Living Lights Ser.). (ENG.). 24p. (J). pap. 3.99 *(978-0-310-73481-9(9))* Zonderkidz.

Berenstain, Mike, et al. The Berenstain Bears Give Thanks, 1 vol. Berenstain, Stan, illus. 2009. (Berenstain Bears/Living Lights Ser.). (ENG.). 32p. (J). (gr. -1-2). pap. 3.99 *(978-0-310-71251-0(3))* Zonderkidz.

Bergen, Lara. Drama Queen. 2007. 164p. (J). pap. *(978-0-545-03702-0(6))* Scholastic, Inc.

Bjorkman, Lauren. My Invented Life. 2009. (ENG.). 240p. (YA). (gr. 9-13). 27.99 *(978-0-8050-8950-9(0),* Holt, Henry & Co. Bks. For Young Readers) Holt, Henry & Co.

Blubaugh, Penny. Blood & Flowers. 2011. (ENG.). 352p. (YA). (gr. 8-18). 16.99 *(978-0-06-172862-4(4),* HarperTeen) HarperCollins Pubs.

Blume, Judy. The One in the Middle Is the Green Kangaroo. Ohi, Debbie Ridpath, illus. 2014. (ENG.). 48p. (J). (gr. 1-5). pap. 5.99 *(978-1-4814-1131-8(4),* Atheneum Bks. for Young Readers) Simon & Schuster Children's Publishing.

Bond, Felicia. The Halloween Play. Bond, Felicia, illus. 2008. Orig. Title: The Halloween Performance. (ENG., Illus.). 32p. (J). (gr. -1-1). pap. 7.99 *(978-0-06-135796-1(0))* HarperCollins Pubs.

Booth, Molly. Saving Hamlet. 2016. (ENG.). 352p. (YA). (gr. 7-12). 17.99 *(978-1-4847-5274-6(0))* Hyperion Bks. for Children.

Bowe, Julie. So Much Drama. 2016. (Victoria Torres, Unfortunately Average Ser.). (ENG., Illus.). 160p. (gr. 4-4). pap. 5.95 *(978-1-4965-3807-9(2));* lib. bdg. 26.65 *(978-1-4965-3799-7(8))* Stone Arch Bks.

Brown, Monica. Drama Queen. 2016. (Lola Levine Ser.: 2). (J). lib. bdg. 16.00 *(978-0-606-38329-5(8))* Turtleback Bks.

—Lola Levine, Drama Queen. 2016. (Lola Levine Ser.: 2). (ENG., Illus.). (J). (gr. 1-5). 112p. pap. 5.99 *(978-0-316-25842-5(3));* 96p. 15.99 *(978-0-316-25843-2(1))* Little, Brown Bks. for Young Readers.

Cabot, Meg. Stage Fright. 2010. (Allie Finkle's Rules for Girls Ser.: 4). (ENG.). 240p. (J). (gr. 3-7). 6.99 *(978-0-545-04046-4(9))* Scholastic, Inc.

Calin, Marisa. Between You & Me. 2012. (ENG.). 256p. (YA). (gr. 7-12). 16.99 *(978-1-59990-758-1(5),* 9781599907581, Bloomsbury USA Childrens) Bloomsbury Publishing USA.

Carretero, Mónica. ROLY-POLIES. 2011. (Mini-Animalist Ser.). (ENG., Illus.). 32p. (J). (gr. k-2). *(978-84-938240-1-3(1))* D P & G Military Pubs.

The Case of the Vanishing Emerald. 2015. (Mysteries of Maisie Hitchins Ser.: 2). (ENG., Illus.). 176p. (J). (gr. 2-5). 14.99 *(978-0-544-33927-9(4),* HMH Books For Young Readers) Houghton Mifflin Harcourt Publishing Co.

Caveney, Philip. Night on Terror Island. 2013. (ENG.). 240p. (J). (gr. 4-6). pap. 12.99 *(978-1-84939-270-9(6))* Andersen Pr. GBR. Dist: Independent Pubs. Group.

Chen, Bill. The Musical. Sun, Jun, illus. 2013. (J). *(978-0-9845523-1-3(6))* Heryin Publishing Corp.

Cherry, Alison. Look Both Ways. 2016. (ENG.). 304p. (YA). (gr. 7). 17.99 *(978-0-553-51186-4(6),* Delacorte Pr.) Random Hse. Children's Bks.

Cocca-Leffler, Maryann, illus. Spotlight on Stacey. 2007. (Social Studies Connects). 32p. (J). (gr. -1-3). pap. 5.95 *(978-1-57565-236-8(6))* Kane Press, Inc.

Cocks, Heather & Morgan, Jessica. Spoiled. 2012. (ENG.). 384p. (YA). (gr. 10-17). pap. 10.00 *(978-0-316-09827-4(2),* Poppy) Little, Brown Bks. for Young Readers.

Condie, Ally. Summerlost. (ENG.). 272p. (J). (gr. 5). 2017. 8.99 *(978-0-399-18721-6(9),* Puffin Books) 2016. 17.99 *(978-0-399-18719-3(7),* Dutton Books for Young Readers) Penguin Young Readers Group.

—Summerlost. 2017. lib. bdg. 19.65 ***(978-0-606-40105-0(9))*** Turtleback Bks.

Conford, Ellen. Annabel the Actress Starring in the Hound of the Barkervilles. Andriani, Renee W., illus. 2004. (Annabel the Actress Ser.). 83p. (gr. 2-5). 14.00 *(978-0-7569-2180-4(5))* Perfection Learning Corp.

Creech, Sharon. Replay. (J). (gr. 3-7). 2013. (ENG.). 224p. pap. 6.99 *(978-0-06-054021-0(4))* 2005. 240p. lib. bdg. 16.89 *(978-0-06-054020-3(6),* Cotler, Joanna Books) HarperCollins Pubs.

Culbertson, Kim. Instructions for a Broken Heart. 2011. (ENG.). 304p. (YA). (gr. 7-12). pap. 9.99 *(978-1-4022-4302-8(2))* Sourcebooks, Inc.

Dahl, Michael. Curtains! A High School Musical Mystery. Prothero, Tiffany, illus. 2008. (Vortex Bks.). (ENG.). 112p. (gr. 2-3). 26.65 *(978-1-4342-0801-9(X),* Vortex Bks.) Stone Arch Bks.

Day, Susie. My Invisible Boyfriend. 2010. (ENG.). 288p. (J). (gr. 7-18). 16.99 *(978-0-545-07354-7(5),* Scholastic Pr.) Scholastic, Inc.

De Baun, Hillary Hall. The Last Stop Before Heaven. Cooper, Floyd, illus. 2012. (ENG.). 236p. (J). pap. 9.00 *(978-0-8028-5398-1(6),* Eerdmans Bks For Young Readers) Eerdmans, William B. Publishing Co.

Dee, Barbara. Star-Crossed. 2017. (ENG., Illus.). 288p. (J). (gr. 4-8). 16.99 *(978-1-4814-7848-9(6),* Simon & Schuster/Paula Wiseman Bks.) Simon & Schuster/Paula Wiseman Bks.

—Trauma Queen. 2011. (Mix Ser.). (ENG.). 272p. (J). (gr. 4-8). pap. 6.99 *(978-1-4424-0923-1(1),* Aladdin) Simon & Schuster Children's Publishing.

dePaola, Tomie. Stagestruck. dePaola, Tomie, illus. 2007. (ENG., Illus.). 32p. (J). (gr. -1-3). pap. 6.99 *(978-0-14-240899-5(9),* Puffin Books) Penguin Young Readers Group.

—Stagestruck. dePaola, Tomie, illus. 2007. (Illus.). (gr. -1-3). 17.00 *(978-0-7569-8159-4(X))* Perfection Learning Corp.

Destiny, A. & Helms, Rhonda. Never Too Late. 2015. (Flirt Ser.). (ENG., Illus.). 224p. (YA). (gr. 7). pap. 9.99 *(978-1-4814-5188-8(X),* Simon Pulse) Simon Pulse.

DiTerlizzi, Tony. Kenny & the Dragon. 2008. (Playaway Children Ser.). (J). (gr. 3-7). 39.99 *(978-1-60640-958-9(1))* Findaway World, LLC.

—Kenny & the Dragon. DiTerlizzi, Tony, illus. (ENG., Illus.). (J). (gr. 3-7). 2012. 176p. pap. 8.99 *(978-1-4424-3651-0(4))* 2008. 160p. 17.99 *(978-1-4169-3977-1(6))* Simon & Schuster Bks. For Young Readers. (Simon & Schuster Bks. For Young Readers).

—Kenny & the Dragon. DiTerlizzi, Tony, illus. 2008. (Illus.). 160p. (J). (gr. 3-7). 15.99 Simon & Schuster Children's Publishing.

Dixon, Franklin W. Talent Show Tricks. David, Matt, illus. 2016. (Hardy Boys Clue Book Ser.: 4). (ENG.). 96p. (J). (gr. 1-4). pap. 5.99 *(978-1-4814-5180-2(4),* Aladdin) Simon & Schuster Children's Publishing.

Donnelly, Rebecca. How to Stage a Catastrophe. 2017. (ENG.). 256p. (gr. 4-7). 12.95 *(978-1-62370-807-8(9))* Capstone Young Readers of Coughlan Cos.

Doudna, Kelly. Jellyfish Role, 1 vol. Chawla, Neena, illus. 2007. (Critter Chronicles Ser.). (ENG.). 24p. (J). (gr. k-3). lib. bdg. 24.21 *(978-1-59928-446-0(4),* SandCastle) ABDO Publishing Co.

Federle, Tim. Better Nate Than Ever. 2013. (ENG., Illus.). 288p. (J). (gr. 4-8). 17.99 *(978-1-4424-4689-2(7),* Simon & Schuster Bks. For Young Readers) Simon & Schuster Bks. For Young Readers.

—Five, Six, Seven, Nate! (ENG., Illus.). (J). (gr. 5-9). 2015. 320p. pap. 7.99 *(978-1-4424-4695-3(1))* 2014. 304p. 16.99 *(978-1-4424-4693-9(5))* Simon & Schuster Bks. For Young Readers. (Simon & Schuster Bks. For Young Readers).

Fiedler, Lisa & Wallach, Anya. Showstopper! 2015. (Stagestruck Ser.). (ENG.). 280p. (J). (gr. 4-6). 11.99 *(978-1-58536-925-6(X),* 203948) Sleeping Bear Pr.

Fields, Jan. Ghost Light Burning: An Up2U Mystery Adventure, 1 vol. Fabbretti, Valerio, illus. 2015. (ENG.). 80p. (J). *(978-1-62402-092-6(5))* Magic Wagon.

Friedman, Laurie. Mallory in the Spotlight. Kalis, Jennifer, illus. (Mallory Ser.). 2011. pap. 33.92 *(978-0-7613-8359-8(X),* Darby Creek) 2011. (ENG.). 160p. (J). (gr. 2-5). pap. 5.95 *(978-0-7613-3948-9(5),* Darby Creek) 2010. (ENG.). 160p. (J). (gr. 2-5). 15.95 *(978-0-8225-8884-9(6),* Carolrhoda Bks.) Lerner Publishing Group.

Gallagher, Toni. Twist My Charm - The Popularity Spell. 2015. (Twist My Charm Ser.). (ENG.). 272p. (J). (gr. 3-7). 16.99 *(978-0-553-51115-4(7),* Random Hse. Bks. for Young Readers) Random Hse. Children's Bks.

Giff, Patricia Reilly. Star Time. Bright, Alasdair, illus. 2011. (Zigzag Kids Ser.). (ENG.). 80p. (J). (gr. 1-4). 4.99 *(978-0-375-85912-0(8),* Yearling) Random Hse. Children's Bks.

Gilman, Grace. Dixie. McConnell, Sarah, illus. 2011. (I Can Read Level 1 Ser.). (ENG.). 32p. (J). (gr. -1-3). 16.99 *(978-0-06-171914-1(5));* pap. 3.99 *(978-0-06-171913-4(7))* HarperCollins Pubs.

Giulieri, Anne. In the Playhouse, 1 vol. Aranda, Omar, illus. 2012. (Engage Literacy Magenta Ser.). (ENG.). 32p. (gr. k-2). pap. 5.99 *(978-1-4296-8852-9(1),* Engage Literacy) Capstone Press of Coughlan Cos.

Grabenstein, Chris. The Hanging Hill. 2010. (Haunted Mystery Ser.: 2). (ENG.). 336p. (J). (gr. 3-7). pap. 6.99 *(978-0-375-84700-4(6),* Yearling) Random Hse. Children's Bks.

Green, D. L. Zeke Meeks vs the Crummy Class Play, 1 vol. Alves, Josh, illus. 2014. (Zeke Meeks Ser.). (ENG.). 128p. (gr. 2-2). 22.65 *(978-1-4795-4827-9(8),* Zeke Meeks) Picture Window Bks.

Green, John. Will Grayson, Will Grayson. 2011. lib. bdg. 22.10 *(978-0-606-15358-4(6),* Turtleback) Turtleback Bks.

Green, John & Levithan, David. Will Grayson, Will Grayson. 2015. (SPA.). 336p. (YA). (gr. 7). pap. 12.95 *(978-1-101-91070-2(4),* Vintage Espanol) Knopf Doubleday Publishing Group.

—Will Grayson, Will Grayson. (ENG., (YA). (gr. 9-18). 2011. Illus.). 352p. 10.99 *(978-0-14-241847-5(1),* Speak) 2010. 320p. 17.99 *(978-0-525-42158-0(0),* Dutton Books for Young Readers) Penguin Young Readers Group.

Greenwald, Tommy. Charlie Joe Jackson's Guide to Extra Credit. Coovert, J. P., illus. 2012. (Charlie Joe Jackson Ser.: 2). (ENG.). 272p. (J). (gr. 4-7). 15.99 *(978-1-59643-692-3(1),* 9781596436923) Roaring Brook Pr.

—Charlie Joe Jackson's Guide to Extra Credit. Coovert, J. P., illus. 2013. (Charlie Joe Jackson Ser.: 2). (ENG.). 288p. (J). (gr. 4-7). pap. 7.99 *(978-1-250-01670-6(3),* 9781250016706) Square Fish.

—Charlie Joe Jackson's Guide to Extra Credit. 2013. (Charlie Joe Jackson's Guide Ser.: 2). (J). lib. bdg. 18.40 *(978-0-606-28461-5(3),* Turtleback) Turtleback Bks.

Guest, Elissa Haden. Iris & Walter - The School Play. Davenier, Christine, illus. 2006. (Iris & Walter Ser.). 44p. (gr. 1-4). 15.95 *(978-0-7569-6679-9(5))* Perfection Learning Corp.

Gutman, Dan. Miss Laney Is Zany! 2010. (My Weird School Daze Ser.: 8). (J). lib. bdg. 14.75 *(978-0-606-10112-7(8),* Turtleback) Turtleback Bks.

Hale, Bruce. Give My Regrets to Broadway. 2005. (Chet Gecko Mystery Ser.). (Illus.). 115p. (gr. 3-7). 16.00 *(978-0-7569-5247-1(6))* Perfection Learning Corp.

Hamilton, Rachel. Louie Takes the Stage! (Unicorn in New York #2) 2017. (Unicorn in New York Ser.: 2). (ENG.). 128p. (J). (gr. 2-5). pap. 4.99 ***(978-1-338-05512-2(7),*** Scholastic Paperbacks) Scholastic, Inc.

Harley, Bill. Charlie Bumpers vs. the Really Nice Gnome, 1 vol. Gustavson, Adam, illus. (Charlie Bumpers Ser.). (ENG.). 160p. (J). (gr. 2-4). 2015. pap. 6.95 *(978-1-56145-831-8(7))* 2014. 13.95 *(978-1-56145-740-3(X))* Peachtree Pubs.

Hayes, John C. Splurge & the Theatre of Magic. 2008. 348p. pap. 22.00 *(978-1-84426-500-8(5))* Upfront Publishing Ltd. GBR. Dist: Printondemand-worldwide.com.

Henson, Heather. Here's How I See It — Here's How It Is. 2010. (ENG., Illus.). 304p. (J). (gr. 5-9). pap. 6.99 *(978-1-4169-9773-3(3),* Atheneum Bks. for Young Readers) Simon & Schuster Children's Publishing.

Higginson, Hadley. Keeker & the Springtime Surprise. Perrett, Lisa, illus. 2007. (Keeker & the Sneaky Pony Ser.: KEEK). (ENG.). 58p. (J). (gr. k-3). per. 4.99 *(978-0-8118-5599-0(6))* Chronicle Bks. LLC.

Hill, Grace Brooks. The Corner House Girls in a Play. 2011. (Illus.). 154p. pap. 9.99 *(978-1-61203-171-2(4))* Bottom of the Hill Publishing.

Hoffman, Mary. Amazing Grace. (Illus.). 32p. (J). (ARA & ENG.). *(978-1-85430-334-9(1),* 93433); (ENG & VIE., *(978-1-85430-340-0(6),* 93435) Little Tiger Pr. Group.

—Encore, Grace! 2011. (ENG.). 112p. (J). (gr. 3-7). 5.99 *(978-0-14-241854-3(4),* Puffin Books) Penguin Young Readers Group.

Holden, Pam. Our Puppet Show. 2015. (ENG., Illus.). 16p. (-1). pap. *(978-1-77654-072-3(7),* Red Rocket Readers) Flying Start Bks.

Holm, Jennifer L. & Holm, Matthew. The Musical. Holm, Jennifer L. & Holm, Matthew, illus. 2009. (Babymouse Ser.: 10). (ENG., Illus.). 96p. (J). (gr. 2-5). pap. 6.99 *(978-0-375-84388-4(4));* lib. bdg. 12.99 *(978-0-375-93791-0(9))* Random Hse. Children's Bks. (Random Hse. Bks. for Young Readers).

Hopkins, Cathy. The Princess of Pop. 2012. (Truth or Dare Ser.). (ENG.). 224p. (YA). (gr. 7). pap. 10.99 *(978-1-4424-6057-7(1),* Simon Pulse) Simon Pulse.

Hopkins, Lee Bennett. Full Moon & Star. Hall, Marcellus, illus. 2011. (ENG.). 32p. (J). (gr. -1-k). 16.95 *(978-1-4197-0013-2(8),* Abrams Bks. for Young Readers) Abrams, Inc.

Horowitz, Anthony. The Devil & His Boy. 2007. (ENG.). 192p. (J). (gr. 3-7). 6.99 *(978-0-14-240797-4(6),* Puffin Books) Penguin Young Readers Group.

Hughes, Virginia. Peggy Finds the Theater. Leone, Sergio, illus. 2011. 186p. 42.95 *(978-1-258-10513-6(6))* Literary Licensing, LLC.

Jakubowski, Michele. Dodgeball, Drama, & Other Dilemmas. Montalto, Luisa, illus. 2013. (Sidney & Sydney Ser.). (ENG.). 128p. (gr. 1-3). 8.95 *(978-1-4795-2116-6(7));* lib. bdg. 25.32 *(978-1-4048-8061-0(5))* Picture Window Bks.

—Sidney & Sydney, 1 vol. 2014. (Sidney & Sydney Ser.). (ENG.). 128p. (gr. 1-3). 75.96 *(978-1-4795-5749-3(8))* Picture Window Bks.

Jellen, Michelle. Spain or Shine. 2005. (S. A. S. S. Ser.). (ENG., Illus.). 224p. (YA). (gr. 7-7). 7.99 *(978-0-14-240368-6(7),* Speak) Penguin Young Readers Group.

Jones, Traci L. Silhouetted by the Blue. 2011. (ENG.). 208p. (J). (gr. 5-9). 16.99 *(978-0-374-36914-9(3),* 9780374369149, Farrar, Straus & Giroux (BYR)) Farrar, Straus & Giroux.

Kear, Nicole C. The Fix-It Friends: the Show Must Go On. Dockray, Tracy, illus. 2017. (Fix-It Friends Ser.: 3). (ENG.). 160p. (J). pap. 5.99 ***(978-1-250-08668-6(X),*** 9781250086686) Imprint IND. Dist: Macmillan.

Keenan-Bolger, Andrew, et al. Jack & Louisa - Act 1. Webster, Kyle T., illus. 2015. (Jack & Louisa Ser.: 1). (ENG.). 240p. (J). (gr. 3-7). bds. 16.99 *(978-0-448-47839-5(0),* Grosset & Dunlap) Penguin Young Readers Group.

Kehret, Peg. Backstage Fright. 2008. (ENG.). 128p. (J). (gr. 3-7). pap. 7.99 *(978-1-4169-9107-6(7),* Simon & Schuster/Paula Wiseman Bks.) Simon & Schuster/Paula Wiseman Bks.

Kirby, Stan. Captain Awesome Saves the Winter Wonderland. O'Connor, George, illus. 2012. (Captain Awesome Ser.: 6). (ENG.). 128p. (J). (gr. k-4). 16.99 *(978-1-4424-4335-8(9));* pap. 5.99 *(978-1-4424-4334-1(0))* Little Simon. (Little Simon).

—Captain Awesome Saves the Winter Wonderland. 2012. (Captain Awesome Ser.: 6). lib. bdg. 16.00 *(978-0-606-26894-3(4),* Turtleback) Turtleback Bks.

Klein, Abby. Thanksgiving Turkey Trouble. McKinley, John, illus. 2008. (Ready, Freddy! Ser.: Bk. 15). 95p. (gr. -1-3). 16.00 *(978-0-7569-8838-8(1))* Perfection Learning Corp.

Klein, Jen. Summer Unscripted. 2017. (ENG.). 320p. (YA). (gr. 7). 17.99 ***(978-1-5247-0004-1(5),*** Random Hse. Bks. for Young Readers) Random Hse. Children's Bks.

Klein, Lisa. Love Disguised. 2013. (ENG., Illus.). 320p. (YA). (gr. 7). 17.99 *(978-1-59990-968-4(5),* 9781599909684, Bloomsbury USA Childrens) Bloomsbury Publishing USA.

Kline, Suzy & Remkiewicz, Frank. Horrible Harry Bugs the Three Bears. Remkiewicz, Frank & Remkiewicz, illus. 2009. (Horrible Harry Ser.). (ENG.). 80p. (J). (gr. 2-4). 4.99 *(978-0-14-241295-4(3),* Puffin Books) Penguin Young Readers Group.

Knudson, Mike & Wilkinson, Steve. Raymond & Graham Rule the School. Curtis, Stacy, illus. 2009. (Raymond & Graham Ser.). (ENG.). 144p. (J). (gr. 3-7). 6.99 *(978-0-14-241426-2(3),* Puffin Books) Penguin Young Readers Group.

Koja, Kathe. Talk. 2008. (ENG.). 144p. (YA). (gr. 7-12). per. 16.99 *(978-0-312-37605-5(7),* 9780312376055) Square Fish.

Korman, Gordon. No More Dead Dogs. 2017. Orig. Title: Touchdown Stage Left. (J). lib. bdg. 17.20 ***(978-0-606-40570-6(4))*** Turtleback Bks.

Krishnaswami, Uma. El árbol Más Feliz: Un Cuento Sobre Yoga. Jeyaveeran, Ruth, illus. 2008.Tr. of Happiest Tree: a Yoga Story. (SPA.). 32p. (J). pap. 10.95 *(978-1-62014-149-6(3))* Lee & Low Bks., Inc.

Krossing, Karen. Cut the Lights, 1 vol. 2013. (Orca Limelights Ser.). (ENG.). 136p. (J). (gr. 6-9). pap. 9.95 *(978-1-4598-0413-5(9))* Orca Bk. Pubs. USA.

Krulik, Nancy. Holly's Jolly Christmas. John and Wendy Staff, illus. 2009. (Katie Kazoo, Switcheroo Ser.: No. 8). (ENG.). 160p. (J). (gr. 2-4). pap. 4.99 *(978-0-448-45218-0(9),* Grosset & Dunlap) Penguin Young Readers Group.

—No Biz Like Show Biz. John and Wendy Staff, illus. 2007. (Katie Kazoo, Switcheroo Ser.: 24). (ENG.). 80p. (J). (gr. 2-4). pap. 4.99 *(978-0-448-44440-6(2),* Grosset & Dunlap) Penguin Young Readers Group.

—The Twelve Burps of Christmas. Blecha, Aaron, illus. 2012. (George Brown, Class Clown Ser.: No. 1). (ENG.). 192p. (J). (gr. 2-4). pap. 5.99 *(978-0-448-45680-5(X),* Grosset & Dunlap) Penguin Young Readers Group.

—The Twelve Burps of Christmas. 2012. (George Brown, Class Clown Ser.: No. 1). lib. bdg. 16.00 *(978-0-606-26652-9(6),* Turtleback) Turtleback Bks.

Landon, Kristen. Life in the Pit. 2008. (ENG., Illus.). 248p. (YA). (gr. 5-13). pap. 8.95 *(978-1-933831-08-4(1))* Blooming Tree Pr.

Lazebnik, Claire. The Trouble with Flirting. 2013. (ENG.). 336p. (YA). (gr. 8). pap. 9.99 *(978-0-06-192127-8(0),* HarperTeen) HarperCollins Pubs.

Levy, Janice. Showtime for Flip-Flop, 1 vol. Madden, Colleen M., illus. 2011. (Flip-Flop Adventure Ser.). (ENG.). 32p. (J). (gr. k-3). 28.50 *(978-1-61641-654-6(8))* Magic Wagon.

Lewman, David. The Case of the Plagued Play. 2013. (Club CSI Ser.: 6). (ENG., Illus.). 160p. (J). (gr. 3-7). 15.99 *(978-1-4424-7261-7(8));* pap. 6.99 *(978-1-4424-7260-0(X))* Simon Spotlight. (Simon Spotlight).

Lin, Grace. The Year of the Dog. 2007. (Pacy Lin Novel Ser.). (ENG., Illus.). 160p. (J). (gr. 3-7). per. 6.99 *(978-0-316-06002-8(X))* Little, Brown Bks. for Young Readers.

—The Year of the Dog. 2007. (Illus.). 134p. (gr. 3-7). 16.00 *(978-0-7569-8143-3(3))* Perfection Learning Corp.

Lithgow, John. Marsupial Sue Presents the Runaway Pancake. Davis, Jack E., illus. 2008. (ENG.). 40p. (J). (gr. -1-3). 7.99 *(978-0-689-87848-0(6),* Simon & Schuster Bks. For Young Readers) Simon & Schuster Bks. For Young Readers.

Lithgow, John & Davis, Jack E. Marsupial Sue Presents the Runaway Pancake. 2005. (ENG., Illus.). 40p. (J). (gr. -1-3). 19.99 *(978-0-689-87847-3(8),* Simon & Schuster Bks. For Young Readers) Simon & Schuster Bks. For Young Readers.

Lorimer, Janet. The Bad Luck Play, 1 vol. unabr. ed. 2010. (Q Reads Ser.). (ENG.). 32p. (YA). (gr. 9-12). pap. 6.95 *(978-1-61651-198-2(2))* Saddleback Educational Publishing, Inc.

MacDonald, Bailey. Wicked Will: A Mystery of Young William Shakespeare. 2010. (ENG.). 224p. (J). (gr. 4-7). pap. 5.99 *(978-1-4169-8661-4(8),* Aladdin) Simon & Schuster Children's Publishing.

—Wicked Will: A Mystery of Young William Shakespeare. 2009. (ENG.). 208p. (J). (gr. 4-7). 16.99 *(978-1-4169-8660-7(X),* Simon & Schuster/Paula Wiseman Bks.) Simon & Schuster/Paula Wiseman Bks.

MacDonald, Maryann. Starring Francie O'Leary. Richards, Virginia Helen, illus. 2010. 64p. (J). (gr. 1-3). pap. 6.95 *(978-0-8198-7132-9(X))* Pauline Bks. & Media.

Mackall, Dandi Daley. Natalie Really Very Much Wants to Be a Star, 1 vol. Blakeslee, Lys, illus. 2009. (That's Nat! Ser.). (ENG.). 96p. (J). (gr. 1-4). pap. 4.99 *(978-0-310-71567-2(9))* Zonderkidz.

Mantchev, Lisa. Eyes Like Stars. 2010. (Theatre Illuminata Ser.: 1). (ENG.). 384p. (YA). (gr. 7-12). pap. 11.99 *(978-0-312-60866-8(7),* 9780312608668) Square Fish.

—Perchance to Dream. 2011. (Theatre Illuminata Ser.: 2). (ENG.). 368p. (YA). (gr. 7-12). pap. 9.99 *(978-0-312-67510-3(0),* 9780312675103) Square Fish.

Manushkin, Fran. Star of the Show, 1 vol. Lyon, Tammie, illus. 2011. (Katie Woo Ser.). (ENG.). 32p. (gr. k-2). pap. 5.95 *(978-1-4048-6613-3(2));* lib. bdg. 21.32 *(978-1-4048-6515-0(2))* Picture Window Bks.

Marsh, Robert. Monster & Me, 1 vol. Percival, Tom, illus. 2009. (Monster & Me Ser.). (ENG.). 40p. (gr. 1-3). lib. bdg. 23.99 *(978-1-4342-1589-5(X),* Graphic Sparks) Stone Arch Bks.

Martin, Ann M. Needle & Thread. 2007. (Main Street Ser.). (Illus.). 205p. (J). (gr. 4-7). 14.65 *(978-0-7569-8328-4(2))* Perfection Learning Corp.

—Needle & Thread. Andreasen, Dan, illus. 2007. 205p. (J). pap. *(978-0-545-03660-3(7))* Scholastic, Inc.

Martin, C. K. Kelly. The Lighter Side of Life & Death. 2010. (YA). pap. *(978-0-375-84590-1(9))* Random Hse. Children's Bks.

McCaughrean, Geraldine. The Glorious Adventures of the Sunshine Queen. 2011. 336p. (J). (gr. 5). 16.99 *(978-0-06-200806-0(4))* HarperCollins Pubs.

McCowan, Patricia. Upstaged, 1 vol. 2016. (Orca Limelights Ser.). (ENG.). 160p. (J). (gr. 6-9). pap. 9.95 *(978-1-4598-1004-4(X))* Orca Bk. Pubs. USA.

McDaniel, Lurlene. The End of Forever. 2013. (ENG.). 320p. (YA). (gr. 7). pap. 8.99 *(978-0-385-74380-8(7),* Ember) Random Hse. Children's Bks.

Mcgaffey, Kenneth. The Sorrows of a Show Girl. 2005. 144p. pap. 10.95 *(978-1-4218-1579-4(6),* 1st World Library - Literary Society) 1st World Publishing, Inc.

—The Sorrows of a Show Girl. 2004. reprint ed. pap. 15.95 *(978-1-4191-8297-6(8))* Kessinger Publishing, LLC.

McGaffey, Kenneth. The Sorrows of A Show Girl. 2004. reprint ed. pap. 1.99 *(978-1-4192-8297-3(2))* Kessinger Publishing, LLC.

McMullan, Kate. Help! It's Parent's Day at DSA, 1 vol. Basso, Bill, illus. 2006. (Dragon Slayers' Academy Ser.: No. 10). (ENG.). 112p. (gr. 1-7). 24.21 *(978-1-59961-125-9(2))* Spotlight.

Messner, Kate. Marty McGuire. Floca, Brian, illus. 2011. (ENG.). 144p. (J). (gr. 2-5). pap. 5.99 *(978-0-545-14246-5(6),* Scholastic Pr.) Scholastic, Inc.

Mörchen, Roland. Wir Gehen Ins Fernsehstudio. Kiefer, Katja, illus. 2010. (ENG.). 40p. (J). (gr. 3-7). 19.99 *(978-3-487-08836-5(3))* Olms, Georg Verlag AG DEU. Dist: Independent Pubs. Group.

Morgan, Melissa J. Freaky Tuesday, 17 vols. 2007. (Camp Confidential Ser.: 17). (ENG.). 160p. (J). (gr. 3-7). pap. 4.99 *(978-0-448-44651-6(0),* Grosset & Dunlap) Penguin Young Readers Group.

Moulton, Erin E. Tracing Stars. 2013. (ENG.). 256p. (J). (gr. 3-7). pap. 6.99 *(978-0-14-242653-1(9),* Puffin Books) Penguin Young Readers Group.

Mullarkey, Lisa. The Biggest Star by Far, 1 vol. Harris, Phyllis, illus. 2009. (Katharine the Almost Great Ser.: No. 1). (ENG.). 80p. (J). (gr. 1-4). 27.07 *(978-1-60270-581-4(X))* Magic Wagon.

Mullarkey, Lisa & Mullarkey, John. Get Ella to the Apollo, 1 vol. Bernard, Courtney, illus. 2015. (ENG.). 128p. (J). *(978-1-62402-087-2(9))* Magic Wagon.

—Shakespeare Saves the Globe, 1 vol. Bernard, Courtney, illus. 2015. (ENG.). 128p. (J). *(978-1-62402-090-2(9))* Magic Wagon.

Mullins, Julie. School Play Stars. Maddock, Monika, illus. 2005. (Girlz Rock! Ser.). (J). pap. *(978-1-59336-706-0(6))* Mondo Publishing.

Naylor, Phyllis Reynolds. I Like Him, He Likes Her: Alice Alone; Simply Alice; Patiently Alice. 2010. (Alice Ser.). (ENG.). 640p. (YA). (gr. 7). pap. 12.99 *(978-1-4424-0978-1(9),* Atheneum Bks. for Young Readers) Simon & Schuster Children's Publishing.

—Incredibly Alice. (Alice Ser.: 23). (ENG., (YA). (gr. 9). 2012. Illus.). 304p. pap. 8.99 *(978-1-4169-7556-4(X))* 2011. 288p. 16.99 *(978-1-4169-7553-3(5))* Simon & Schuster Children's Publishing. (Atheneum Bks. for Young Readers).

—Simply Alice. 2003. (Alice Ser.: 14). (ENG., Illus.). 240p. (YA). (gr. 7). mass mkt. 5.99 *(978-0-689-85965-6(1),* Simon Pulse) Simon Pulse.

Nees, Susan. School Play. 2013. (Missy's Super Duper Royal Deluxe Ser.: 3). (ENG., Illus.). 80p. (J). (gr. k-2). pap. 4.99 *(978-0-545-43853-7(5))* Scholastic, Inc.

Night, P. J. The Show Must Go On! 2011. (You're Invited to a Creepover Ser.: 4). (ENG.). 160p. (J). (gr. 3-7). pap. 6.99 *(978-1-4424-2905-5(4),* Simon Spotlight) Simon Spotlight.

—Show Must Go On!, 1 vol. 2013. (You're Invited to a Creepover Ser.). (ENG.). 160p. (J). (gr. 3-6). lib. bdg. 24.21 *(978-1-61479-063-1(9),* Essential Library) ABDO Publishing Co.

—The Show Must Go On! 2011. (Creepover Ser.: 4). lib. bdg. 16.00 *(978-0-606-23748-2(8),* Turtleback) Turtleback Bks.

Osborne, Mary Pope, et al. Miedo Escénico en una Noche de Verano. Murdocca, Sal, illus. 2014. 25. (SPA.). 86p. (J). (gr. 2-4). pap. 5.99 *(978-1-933032-92-4(8))* Lectorum Pubns., Inc.

—A Time to Dance: Virginia's Civil War Diary. 2003. (My America Ser.). (ENG.). 112p. (J). 12.95 *(978-0-439-44341-8(5))* Scholastic, Inc.

O'Shaughnessy McKenna, Colleen. Third Grade Wedding Bells? Roth, Stephanie, illus. 2006. (Third Grade Ser.). (ENG.). 160p. (J). (gr. 2-5). 15.95 *(978-0-8234-1943-2(6))* Holiday Hse., Inc.

Paratore, Coleen Murtagh. Willa by Heart. 2008. (Wedding Planner's Daughter Ser.). (ENG.). 240p. (J). (gr. 3-7). 15.99 *(978-1-4169-4076-0(6),* Simon & Schuster Bks. For Young Readers) Simon & Schuster Bks. For Young Readers.

—Willa by Heart. 2009. (Wedding Planner's Daughter Ser.). (ENG.). 240p. (J). (gr. 4-8). pap. 6.99 *(978-1-4169-7470-3(9),* Aladdin) Simon & Schuster Children's Publishing.

Parish, Herman. Amelia Bedelia Talks Turkey. Sweat, Lynn, illus. 2008. (Amelia Bedelia Ser.). (ENG.). 64p. (J). (gr. k-4). 16.99 *(978-0-06-084352-6(7),* Greenwillow Bks.) HarperCollins Pubs.

—Amelia Bedelia Talks Turkey. Parish, Herman & Sweat, Lynn, illus. 2008. (Amelia Bedelia Ser.). 64p. (J). (gr. k-4). lib. bdg. 17.89 *(978-0-06-084353-3(5),* Greenwillow Bks.) HarperCollins Pubs.

Park, Barbara. Shipwrecked, No. 23. Brunkus, Denise, illus. 2005. (Junie B. Jones Ser.: No. 6). (ENG.). 96p. (J). (gr. 1-4). mass mkt. 4.99 *(978-0-375-82805-8(2),* Random Hse. Bks. for Young Readers) Random Hse. Children's Bks.

Patterson, James & Grabenstein, Chris. Jacky Ha-Ha. Kerascoët, illus. 2016. (ENG.). 384p. (J). (gr. 3-7). 13.99 *(978-0-316-26249-1(8),* Jimmy Patterson) Little Brown & Co.

—Jacky Ha-Ha. 2017. (Jacky Ha-Ha Ser.). (J). lib. bdg. 18.40 ***(978-0-606-40732-8(4))*** Turtleback Bks.

Patterson, Nancy Ruth. A Simple Gift. 2009. 128p. (gr. 3-7). pap. 10.95 *(978-1-4401-1206-5(1))* iUniverse, Inc.

Perez, Marlene. The Comeback. 2009. (ENG.). 208p. (J). (gr. 7). pap. 8.99 *(978-0-545-08807-7(0))* Scholastic, Inc.

Perl, Erica S. The Capybara Conspiracy: A Novel in Three Acts. 2016. (ENG.). 192p. (J). (gr. 5). 16.99 *(978-0-399-55171-0(9),* Knopf Bks. for Young Readers) Random Hse. Children's Bks.

Perlov, Betty Rosenberg. Rifka Takes a Bow. Kawa, Cosei, illus. 2013. (ENG.). 32p. (J). (gr. k-3). 17.95 *(978-0-7613-8127-3(9));* 7.95 *(978-0-7613-8128-0(7))* Lerner Publishing Group. (Kar-Ben Publishing).

Peschke, Marci. Drama Queen, 1 vol. Mourning, Tuesday, illus. 2011. (Kylie Jean Ser.). (ENG.). 112p. (gr. 2-3). lib. bdg. 22.65 *(978-1-4048-6757-4(0),* Kylie Jean) Picture Window Bks.

—Drama Queen, 1 vol. Mourning, Tuesday, illus. 2011. (Kylie Jean Ser.). (ENG.). 112p. (gr. 2-3). pap. 5.95 *(978-1-4048-6616-4(7),* Kylie Jean) Picture Window Bks.

Petroff, Shani. Daddy's Little Angel, No. 1. McKenney, J. David, illus. 2009. (Bedeviled Ser.: 1). (ENG.). 240p. (J). (gr. 5-7). pap. 7.99 *(978-0-448-45111-4(5),* Grosset & Dunlap) Penguin Young Readers Group.

—Romeo & What's Her Name. 2017. (ENG.). 224p. (YA). pap. 9.99 *(978-1-250-11114-2(5),* 9781250111142) Feiwel & Friends.

Phillips, Ruby Ann. The Great & Powerful, 1 vol. Isik, Semur, illus. 2014. (Krystal Ball Ser.). (ENG.). 112p. (gr. 2-3). 25.32 *(978-1-4795-2179-1(5))* Picture Window Bks.

Polacco, Patricia. Mr. Wayne's Masterpiece. Polacco, Patricia, illus. 2014. (ENG., Illus.). 40p. (J). (gr. k-3). 17.99 *(978-0-399-16095-0(7),* G.P. Putnam's Sons Books for Young Readers) Penguin Young Readers Group.

Polonsky, Ami. Gracefully Grayson. 2016. (ENG., Illus.). 250p. (J). (gr. 5-9). pap. 8.99 *(978-1-4847-2365-4(1))* Hyperion Bks. for Children.

—Gracefully Grayson. 2014. (ENG.). 256p. (J). (gr. 5-9). 16.99 *(978-1-4231-8527-7(7))* Hyperion Pr.

Poydar, Nancy. Bunny Business. 2003. (ENG., Illus.). 32p. (J). (gr. k-3). tchr. ed. 16.95 *(978-0-8234-1771-1(9))* Holiday Hse., Inc.

Primavera, Elise. Louise the Big Cheese. Goode, Diane, illus. 2011. (ENG.). 40p. (J). (gr. k-3). 6.99 *(978-1-4424-2066-3(9),* Simon & Schuster/Paula Wiseman Bks.) Simon & Schuster/Paula Wiseman Bks.

—Louise the Big Cheese: Divine Diva. Goode, Diane, illus. 2009. (ENG.). 40p. (J). (gr. k-3). 16.99 *(978-1-4169-7180-1(7),* Simon & Schuster/Paula Wiseman Bks.) Simon & Schuster/Paula Wiseman Bks.

Rae, Kristin. What You Always Wanted: An If Only Novel. 2016. (If Only... Ser.). (ENG.). 320p. (YA). pap. 9.99 *(978-1-61963-345-2(0),* 9781619633452, Bloomsbury USA Childrens) Bloomsbury Publishing USA.

Rasheed, Leila. Doughnuts, Dreams & Drama Queens. 2013. (Fantastic Diary of Bathsheba Claric de Trop Ser.). 299p. (J). pap. 5.99 *(978-0-7945-3030-3(3),* Usborne) EDC Publishing.

Reich, Susanna. Penelope Bailey Takes the Stage, 1 vol. 2006. (ENG.). 32p. (J). (gr. 3-7). 16.95 *(978-0-7614-5287-4(7))* Marshall Cavendish Corp.

Rennison, Louise. Are These My Basoomas I See Before Me? Final Confessions of Georgia Nicolson. 2010. (Confessions of Georgia Nicolson Ser.: 10). (ENG.). 336p. (YA). (gr. 8-9). pap. 8.99 *(978-0-06-145937-5(2),* HarperTeen) HarperCollins Pubs.

Ribar, Lindsay. The Art of Wishing. (ENG.). (YA). (gr. 7). 2014. 336p. pap. 9.99 *(978-0-14-242529-9(X),* Speak) 2013. 320p. 17.99 *(978-0-8037-3827-0(7),* Dial Bks) Penguin Young Readers Group.

—The Fourth Wish. 2014. (Art of Wishing Ser.). (ENG.). 368p. (YA). (gr. 7). 17.99 *(978-0-8037-3828-7(5),* Kathy Dawson Books) Penguin Young Readers Group.

Roberts, Bethany. Thanksgiving Mice! Cushman, Doug, illus. 2005. (ENG.). 32p. (J). (gr. -1 — 1). 5.95 *(978-0-618-60486-9(3))* Houghton Mifflin Harcourt Publishing Co.

Ruditis, Paul. Entrances & Exits. 2008. (Drama! Ser.). (ENG.). 256p. (YA). (gr. 9). pap. 12.99 *(978-1-4169-5906-9(8),* Simon Pulse) Simon Pulse.

Rylant, Cynthia. Annie & Snowball & the Shining Star. Stevenson, Suçie, illus. (Annie & Snowball Ser.: 6). (ENG.). 40p. (J). (gr. k-2). 2010. pap. 3.99 *(978-1-4169-3950-4(4))* 2009. 16.99 *(978-1-4169-3946-7(6))* Simon Spotlight. (Simon Spotlight).

Schindler, Holly. Spark. 2016. 304p. (YA). (gr. 8). 17.99 *(978-0-06-222023-3(3),* HarperTeen) HarperCollins Pubs.

Schotter, Roni. Purim Play, 0 vols. Hafner, Marylin, illus. 2010. (ENG.). 34p. (J). (gr. -1-2). pap. 6.99 *(978-0-7614-5800-5(X),* 9780761458005, Amazon Children's Publishing) Amazon Publishing.

Schreiber, Elisheva. The Miniature Puppet Theater Book. Pollack, Gadi & Markovitch, Evegeny, illus. (J). 14.95 *(978-1-58330-617-8(X))* Feldheim Pubs.

Schreiber, Joe. Lenny Cyrus, School Virus. Smith, Matt, illus. 2014. (ENG.). 288p. (J). (gr. 5-7). pap. 6.99 *(978-0-544-33628-5(3),* HMH Books For Young Readers) Houghton Mifflin Harcourt Publishing Co.

Schusterman, Michelle. Theater of Forever & Ever. 2017. (ENG.). 224p. (J). (gr. 3-7). 16.99 *(978-0-399-55066-9(6),* Random Hse. Bks. for Young Readers) Random Hse. Children's Bks.

Scieszka, Jon. SPHDZ Book #2! Prigmore, Shane, illus. 2011. (Spaceheadz Ser.: 2). (ENG.). 256p. (J). (gr. 2-5). pap. 7.99 *(978-1-4169-7954-8(9),* Simon & Schuster Bks. For Young Readers) Simon & Schuster Bks. For Young Readers.

Scott, Kieran. Geek Magnet. 2009. (ENG.). 320p. (YA). (gr. 7-18). 8.99 *(978-0-14-241417-0(4),* Speak) Penguin Young Readers Group.

Selznick, Brian. The Marvels. 2016. (CHI.). (J). ***(978-986-479-039-5(0))*** Commonwealth Publishing Co., Ltd.

—The Marvels. Selznick, Brian, illus. 2015. (ENG., Illus.). 672p. (J). (gr. 5-7). 32.99 *(978-0-545-44868-0(9),* Scholastic Pr.) Scholastic, Inc.

Shulman, Dee. On Stage in America. 2012. (My Totally Secret Diary Ser.). (ENG., Illus.). 144p. (J). (gr. 2-4). pap. 12.99 *(978-1-86230-423-9(8),* Red Fox) Random House Children's Books GBR. Dist: Independent Pubs. Group.

Sinclair, Gardine. Mystery at Stageschool. 2013. 190p. (J). pap. *(978-1-78299-388-9(6))* FeedARead.com.

Sloan, Brian. Tale of Two Summers. 2014. (ENG., Illus.). 256p. (YA). (gr. 7). pap. 12.99 *(978-1-4169-5794-2(4),* Simon & Schuster Bks. For Young Readers) Simon & Schuster Bks. For Young Readers.

Sloan, Holly Goldberg. Short. 2017. (ENG.). 304p. (J). (gr. 3-7). 16.99 *(978-0-399-18621-9(2),* Dial Bks) Penguin Young Readers Group.

Snyder, Zilpha Keatley. William's Midsummer Dreams. (ENG., (J). (gr. 3-7). 2012. Illus.). 240p. pap. 6.99 *(978-1-4424-1998-8(9))* 2011. 224p. 16.99 *(978-1-4424-1997-1(0))* Simon & Schuster Children's Publishing. (Atheneum Bks. for Young Readers).

Spirn, Michele Sobel. I Am the Turkey. Allen, Joy, illus. 2007. (I Can Read Bks.). 48p. (gr. -1-3). 14.00 *(978-0-7569-8055-9(0))* Perfection Learning Corp.

Spirn, Michele Sobel & Spirn, Michele S. I Am the Turkey. Allen, Joy, illus. (I Can Read Level 2 Ser.). 48p. (J). (gr. k-3). 2006. (ENG.). pap. 3.99 *(978-0-06-053232-1(7))* 2004. 15.99 *(978-0-06-053230-7(0))* HarperCollins Pubs.

Stahler, David, Jr. Spinning Out. 2011. (ENG.). 288p. (YA). (gr. 7-17). 16.99 *(978-0-8118-7780-0(9))* Chronicle Bks. LLC.

Stewart, Shawn. Donny & the Doorman's Nightmare. 2004. 54p. pap. 8.11 *(978-1-4116-2188-6(3))* Lulu Pr., Inc.

Stine, R. L. The 12 Screams of Christmas. 2014. (Goosebumps Most Wanted Ser.). lib. bdg. 18.40 *(978-0-606-36066-1(2))* Turtleback Bks.

Strohm, Stephanie Kate. The Taming of the Drew. 2016. (ENG.). 304p. (J). (gr. 6). 17.99 *(978-1-5107-0215-8(6),* Sky Pony Pr.) Skyhorse Publishing Co., Inc.

Surviving the Applewhites. (J). tchr. ed. *(978-0-06-058369-9(X))* HarperCollins Pubs.

Sutherland, Tui T. This Must Be Love. 256p. (J). 2005. pap. 7.99 *(978-0-06-056477-3(6),* Harper Trophy) 2004. (gr. 7-18). lib. bdg. 16.89 *(978-0-06-056476-6(8))* HarperCollins Pubs.

Telgemeier, Raina. Drama. 2012. (ENG., Illus.). 240p. (J). (gr. 5-9). 24.99 *(978-0-545-32698-8(2));* pap. 10.99 *(978-0-545-32699-5(0))* Scholastic, Inc. (Graphix).

—Drama. 2012. lib. bdg. 22.10 *(978-0-606-26738-0(7),* Turtleback) Turtleback Bks.

Terrell, Brandon. High Drama. 2015. (ENG.). 112p. (YA). (gr. 6-12). 27.99 *(978-1-4677-5710-2(1))* Lerner Publishing Group.

Thompson, Jan & Sharpe, Jaime. Amara's Magical Playhouse: The Adventure Begins. 2010. 108p. pap. 37.99 *(978-1-4520-8284-4(7))* AuthorHouse.

Thompson, Ricki. City of Cannibals. 2010. (ENG.). 269p. (YA). (gr. 9-12). 18.95 *(978-1-59078-623-9(8),* Front Street) Boyds Mills Pr.

Tillworth, Mary. King for a Day! (PAW Patrol) Jackson, Mike, illus. 2016. (Step into Reading Ser.). (ENG.). 24p. (J). (gr. -1-1). 4.99 *(978-1-101-93684-9(3),* Random Hse. Bks. for Young Readers) Random Hse. Children's Bks.

Tirabassi, Maren C. Footlights & Fairy Dust: Matt & Maria Go to the Theatre. Kramer, Brandie, illus. 2007. (ENG.). 48p. (J). (gr. 2-7). pap. 14.95 *(978-1-933002-26-2(3))* PublishingWorks.

Trigiani, Adriana. Viola in the Spotlight. 2012. (Viola Ser.: 2). (ENG.). 288p. (YA). (gr. 8). pap. 8.99 *(978-0-06-145107-2(X),* HarperTeen) HarperCollins Pubs.

Understudies: Individual Title Six-Packs. (Bookweb Ser.). 32p. (gr. 4-18). 34.00 *(978-0-7635-3724-1(1))* Rigby Education.

Verdi, Jessica. My Life after Now. 2013. (ENG.). 304p. (YA). (gr. 7-12). pap. 9.99 *(978-1-4022-7785-6(7),* 9781402277856) Sourcebooks, Inc.

Villareal, Ray. Alamo Wars. 2008. 187p. (J). (gr. 6-18). pap. 10.95 *(978-1-55885-513-7(0),* Piñata Books) Arte Publico Pr.

Vinopol, Corinne & Bednarczyk, Angela. ASL Tales & Games for Kids - Biscuit Blvd: Computer Software in American Sign Language. 2004. (J). cd-rom 34.95 *(978-0-9667589-9-3(4))* Institute for Disabilities Research & Training, Inc.

Warner, Gertrude Chandler, creator. The Ghost at the Drive-In Movie. 2008. (Boxcar Children Mysteries Ser.: 116). (ENG.). 128p. (J). (gr. 1-5). pap. 5.99 *(978-0-8075-5578-1(9))* Whitman, Albert & Co.

Watson, Cristy. On Cue, 1 vol. 2016. (Orca Currents Ser.). (ENG.). 144p. (J). (gr. 5-9). pap. 9.95 *(978-1-4598-1105-8(4))* Orca Bk. Pubs. USA.

Weatherly, Lee. Child X. 2004. 211p. 16.00 *(978-0-7569-3211-4(4))* Perfection Learning Corp.

Webb, Holly. The Case of the Vanishing Emerald. Lindsay, Marion, illus. 2016. (Mysteries of Maisie Hitchins Ser.: 2). (ENG.). 176p. (J). (gr. 2-5). pap. 5.99 *(978-0-544-66851-5(0),* HMH Books For Young Readers) Houghton Mifflin Harcourt Publishing Co.

Wesley, Valerie Wilson. How to Almost Ruin Your School Play. 2005. (Illus.). 105p. (J). lib. bdg. 15.00 *(978-1-4242-0645-2(6))* Fitzgerald Bks.

West, Jacqueline. Dreamers Often Lie. 2016. (ENG.). 368p. (YA). (gr. 7). 17.99 *(978-0-8037-3863-8(3),* Dial Bks) Penguin Young Readers Group.

Whitten, A. J. The Cellar. 2011. (ENG.). 288p. (YA). (gr. 7-18). pap. 16.99 *(978-0-547-23253-9(5))* Houghton Mifflin Harcourt Publishing Co.

Wilkinson, Lili. Pink. (ENG.). 320p. (YA). (gr. 8). 2012. pap. 9.99 *(978-0-06-192654-9(X))* 2011. 16.99 *(978-0-06-192653-2(1))* HarperCollins Pubs. (HarperTeen).

Williams, Julie. Drama Queens in the House. 2014. (ENG.). 432p. (YA). (gr. 7). 17.99 *(978-1-59643-735-7(9),* 9781596437357) Roaring Brook Pr.

Winkler, Henry & Oliver, Lin. The Curtain Went Up, My Pants Fell Down. Watson, Jesse Joshua, illus. 2007. (Hank Zipzer Ser.: 11). (ENG.). 160p. (J). (gr. 3-7). pap. 5.99 *(978-0-448-44267-9(1),* Grosset & Dunlap) Penguin Young Readers Group.

Yee, Lisa. Bobby the Brave (Sometimes) Santat, Dan, illus. 2012. (ENG.). 160p. (J). (gr. 2-5). pap. 5.99 *(978-0-545-05595-6(4),* Levine, Arthur A. Bks.) Scholastic, Inc.

—Warp Speed. (ENG.). 320p. (J). 2013. (gr. 3-7). pap. 6.99 *(978-0-545-15400-0(6))* 2011. (gr. 4-7). 16.99 *(978-0-545-12276-4(7))* Scholastic, Inc. (Levine, Arthur A. Bks.).

Young, Judy. Star in a Play. Sullivan, Dana, illus. 2015. (I AM a READER: Digger & Daisy Ser.). (ENG.). 32p. (J). (gr. k-2). 9.99 *(978-1-58536-929-4(2),* 203950) Sleeping Bear Pr.

Zann, Tara. Wild Child: Forest's First Day of School. Ermos, George & Widdowson, Dan, illus. 2017. (Wild Child Ser.: 2). (ENG.). 144p. (J). pap. 5.99 *(978-1-250-10387-1(8),* 9781250103871) Imprint IND. Dist: Macmillan.

THEATER—HISTORY

Carew-Miller, Anna. William Shakespeare: Great English Playwright & Poet. 2013. (People of Importance Ser.: 21). (Illus.). 32p. (J). (gr. 4-18). 19.95 *(978-1-4222-2859-3(2))* Mason Crest.

Hilliam, David. William Shakespeare: England's Greatest Playwright & Poet. 2004. (Rulers, Scholars, & Artists of the Renaissance Ser.). (Illus.). 112p. lib. bdg. 34.60 *(978-1-4042-0318-1(4))* Rosen Publishing Group, Inc., The.

Hosein, Ann. The History of Theatre. 2015. (Britannica Guide to the Visual & Performing Arts Ser.). (ENG., Illus.). 128p. (J). (gr. 9-10). 45.00 *(978-1-68048-082-5(0),* Britannica Educational Publishing) Rosen Publishing Group, Inc., The.

McDonnell, Kathleen. Putting on a Show: Theater for Young People, 1 vol. 2005. (ENG., Illus.). 226p. (J). (gr. 4-9). pap. 14.95 *(978-1-896764-89-4(4))* Second Story Pr. CAN. Dist: Orca Bk. Pubs. USA.

Morley, Jacqueline. You Wouldn't Want to Be a Shakespearean Actor! Some Roles You Might Not Want to Play. Antram, David, illus. 2010. (You Wouldn't Want to Ser.). (ENG.). 32p. (J). (gr. 3-18). pap. 9.95 *(978-0-531-22826-5(6))* Scholastic Library Publishing.

Morley, Jacqueline & Salariya, David. You Wouldn't Want to Be a Shakespearean Actor! Some Roles You Might Not Want to Play. Antram, David, illus. 2010. (You Wouldn't Want to Ser.). (ENG.). 32p. (J). 29.00 *(978-0-531-20471-9(5))* Scholastic Library Publishing.

Rosen, Michael. Shakespeare: His Work & His World. Ingpen, Robert R., illus. 2006. (ENG.). 96p. (J). (gr. 7-11). pap. 10.99 *(978-0-7636-3201-4(5))* Candlewick Pr.

Shuter, Jane. Shakespeare & the Theater, 1 vol. 2014. (Shakespeare Alive Ser.). (ENG.). 64p. (gr. 7-8). lib. bdg. 37.32 *(978-1-4329-9630-7(4))* Heinemann-Raintree.

—Shakespeare & the Theatre, 1 vol. 2014. (Shakespeare Alive Ser.). (ENG.). 64p. (gr. 7-8). pap. 10.95 *(978-1-4329-9634-5(7))* Heinemann-Raintree.

Shuter, Jane & Shuter, Paul. Shakespeare Alive, 1 vol. 2014. (Shakespeare Alive Ser.). (ENG.). 32p. (gr. 7-8). lib. bdg. 111.96 *(978-1-4329-9632-1(0))* Heinemann-Raintree.

Sitarz, Paula Gaj. The Curtain Rises Vol. 1: A History of Theatre from Its Origins in Greek & Roman Times Through the English Restoration. Landes, William-Alan, ed. 2003. (Illus.). 144p. (YA). (gr. 5-12). pap. 28.00 *(978-0-88734-685-9(5))* Players Pr., Inc.

Woollard, Mary. An Illustrated Guide to Staging History. unabr. ed. 2003. (Illus.). 302p. (YA). (gr. 4-12). pap. 30.00 *(978-0-85343-624-9(X))* Miller, J. Garnet Ltd. GBR. Dist: Empire Publishing Service.

THEATER—PRODUCTION AND DIRECTION

Freedman, Jeri. Directing in Theater. 2016. (Exploring Theater Ser.). 96p. (J). lib. bdg. 42.79 *(978-1-5026-2283-9(1))* Cavendish Square Publishing.

Garrett, Dan, ed. Masks & Faces. 11th ed. 2003. (Drama Workshop Plays Ser.). (Illus.). 96p. (Orig.). (YA). (gr. 6-12). pap. 15.00 *(978-0-333-36056-9(7))* Macmillan Education, Ltd. GBR. Dist: Players Pr., Inc.

—Scapegoats. 11th ed. 2003. (Drama Workshop Plays Ser.). (Illus.). 96p. (Orig.). (YA). (gr. 6-12). pap. 15.00 *(978-0-333-36055-2(9))* Macmillan Education, Ltd. GBR. Dist: Players Pr., Inc.

Guillain, Charlotte. Writing & Staging Adventure Plays. 2016. (Writing & Staging Plays Ser.). (ENG., Illus.). 48p. (gr. 4-6). lib. bdg. 33.32 *(978-1-4846-2770-9(9),* Heinemann InfoSearch) Heinemann-Raintree.

—Writing & Staging Funny Plays. 2016. (Writing & Staging Plays Ser.). (ENG., Illus.). 48p. (gr. 4-6). lib. bdg. 33.32 *(978-1-4846-2769-3(5),* Heinemann InfoSearch) Heinemann-Raintree.

—Writing & Staging Myths & Legends. 2016. (Writing & Staging Plays Ser.). (ENG., Illus.). 48p. (gr. 4-6). lib. bdg. 33.32 *(978-1-4846-2772-3(5),* Heinemann InfoSearch) Heinemann-Raintree.

—Writing & Staging Real-Life Plays. 2016. (Writing & Staging Plays Ser.). (ENG., Illus.). 48p. (gr. 4-6). lib. bdg. 33.32 *(978-1-4846-2771-6(7),* Heinemann InfoSearch) Heinemann-Raintree.

Harmon, Don. Producing in Theater. 2016. (Exploring Theater Ser.). 96p. (J). lib. bdg. 42.79 *(978-1-5026-2281-5(5))* Cavendish Square Publishing.

Kenney, Karen Latchana. Cool Productions: How to Stage Your Very Own Show, 1 vol. 2010. (Cool Performances Ser.). (ENG., Illus.). 32p. (gr. 3-6). 28.50 *(978-1-60453-716-1(7),* Checkerboard Library) ABDO Publishing Co.

Poulsson, Emilie. Finger Plays for Nursery & Kindergarten. Bridgman, L. T., illus. 70th ed. 2011. (Dover Children's Activity Bks.). (ENG.). 80p. (J). (gr. 4-7). reprint ed. pap. 8.95 *(978-0-486-22588-3(7))* Dover Pubns., Inc.

Wallace, Nancy K. Farmyard Security: A Readers' Theater Script & Guide. 2013. (Readers' Theater: How to Put on a Production Ser.). 32p. (J). (gr. 2-6). lib. bdg. 28.50 *(978-1-61641-985-1(7),* Looking Glass Library- Nonfiction) Magic Wagon.

—Fettuccine & Four-Leaf Clovers: A Readers' Theater Script & Guide, 1 vol. Mata, Nina, illus. 2016. (ENG.). 32p. (J). *(978-1-62402-112-1(3))* Magic Wagon.

—Hair Today, Gone Tomorrow: A Readers' Theater Script & Guide. 2013. (Readers' Theater: How to Put on a Production Ser.). 32p. (J). (gr. 2-6). lib. bdg. 28.50 *(978-1-61641-986-8(5),* Looking Glass Library- Nonfiction) Magic Wagon.

—Pricked Pinkies: A Readers' Theater Script & Guide. 2013. (Readers' Theater: How to Put on a Production Ser.). 32p. (J). (gr. 2-6). lib. bdg. 28.50 *(978-1-61641-987-5(3),* Looking Glass Library- Nonfiction) Magic Wagon.

THEATERS

Capaccio, George. Lighting & Sound in Theater. 2016. (Exploring Theater Ser.). 96p. (J). lib. bdg. 42.79 *(978-1-5026-2275-4(0))* Cavendish Square Publishing.

Clements, Gillian. Tudor Theatre. 2009. (Building History Ser.). (Illus.). 32p. (J). (gr. 3-5). 27.10 *(978-1-59771-147-0(0))* Sea-To-Sea Pubns.

Cohn, Jessica. On the Job in the Theater. Scheuer, Lauren, illus. 2016. (Core Content Social Studies — on the Job Ser.). (ENG.). 32p. (J). (gr. 2-5). lib. bdg. 26.65 *(978-1-63440-113-5(1))* Red Chair Pr.

Harman, Paul. A Guide to UK Theatre for Young Audiences. Harman, Paul, ed. 2010. (ENG.). 104p. (J). pap. 18.95 *(978-1-906582-09-8(2))* Aurora Metro Pubns. Ltd. GBR. Dist: Consortium Bk. Sales & Distribution.

Kreisman, Rachelle. Things We Do: A Kids' Guide to Community Activity. Haggerty, Tim, illus. 2015. (Start Smart: Community Ser.). (ENG.). 32p. (gr. 1-3). 26.65 *(978-1-937529-51-2(7))* Red Chair Pr.

Matthews, Sheelagh. The Sydney Opera House. 2008. (Structural Wonders Ser.). (Illus.). 32p. (J). (gr. 4-6). lib. bdg. 26.00 *(978-1-59036-936-4(X))* Weigl Pubs., Inc.

Rose, Simon. Colosseum. 2012. (J). 27.13 *(978-1-61913-249-8(4));* pap. 12.95 *(978-1-61913-255-9(9))* Weigl Pubs., Inc.

Shofner, Shawndra. Sydney Opera House. 2006. (Modern Wonders of the World Ser.). (Illus.). 32p. (J). (gr. 4-7). lib. bdg. 18.95 *(978-1-58341-442-2(8),* Creative Education) Creative Co., The.

THEATERS—STAGE SETTING AND SCENERY

Beaton, Clare. Make Your Own Theatre Cinderella. 2014. (Make Your Own Ser.). (ENG.). 20p. (J). (gr. k-2). pap. 7.99 *(978-1-905710-18-8(6))* B Small Publishing GBR. Dist: Independent Pubs. Group.

—Snow White. 2014. (Make Your Own Ser.). (ENG.). 20p. (J). (gr. k-2). pap. 7.99 *(978-1-905710-32-4(1))* B Small Publishing GBR. Dist: Independent Pubs. Group.

Bryan, Bethany. Set Design & Prop Making in Theater. 2016. (Exploring Theater Ser.). 96p. (J). lib. bdg. 42.79 *(978-1-5026-2279-2(3))* Cavendish Square Publishing.

Cobb, Vicki. On Stage. 2008. pap. 52.95 *(978-0-8225-9450-5(1))* Lerner Publishing Group.

—On Stage. Gold, Michael, photos by. 2005. (Where's the Science Here? Ser.). (ENG., Illus.). 48p. (gr. 3-5). lib. bdg. 23.93 *(978-0-7613-2774-5(6),* Millbrook Pr.) Lerner Publishing Group.

Kenney, Karen Latchana. Cool Sets & Props: How to Stage Your Very Own Show, 1 vol. 2010. (Cool Performances Ser.). (ENG., Illus.). 32p. (gr. 3-6). 28.50 *(978-1-60453-718-5(3),* Checkerboard Library) ABDO Publishing Co.

Larson, Jeff. FX! Lighting & Sound (Grade 7) 2017. (TIME for KIDS(r) Nonfiction Readers Ser.). (Illus.). 64p. (gr. 7-7). pap. 10.99 ***(978-1-4938-3612-3(9))*** Teacher Created Materials, Inc.

Woollard, Mary. An Illustrated Guide to Staging History. unabr. ed. 2003. (Illus.). 302p. (YA). (gr. 4-12). pap. 30.00 *(978-0-85343-624-9(X))* Miller, J. Garnet Ltd. GBR. Dist: Empire Publishing Service.

THEATRICAL COSTUME

see Costume

THEATRICAL MAKEUP

Craig, Jonathan & Light, Bridget. Special Effects Make-Up Artist: The Coolest Jobs on the Planet, 1 vol. 2013. (Coolest Jobs on the Planet Ser.). (ENG.). 48p. (gr. 5-8). 32.65 *(978-1-4109-5486-2(2));* pap. 8.99 *(978-1-4109-5491-6(9))* Heinemann-Raintree.

Hammelef, Danielle S. Mind-Blowing Makeup in Special Effects. 2015. (Awesome Special Effects Ser.). (ENG., Illus.). 32p. (gr. 1-2). lib. bdg. 26.65 *(978-1-4914-2002-7(2))* Capstone Press of Coughlan Cos.

Kenney, Karen Latchana. Cool Makeup: How to Stage Your Very Own Show, 1 vol. 2010. (Cool Performances Ser.). (ENG., Illus.). 32p. (gr. 3-6). 28.50 *(978-1-60453-715-4(9),* Checkerboard Library) ABDO Publishing Co.

TUV

Larson, Jessica. FX! Makeup & Costumes (Grade 7) 2017. (TIME for KIDS(r) Nonfiction Readers Ser.). (Illus.). 64p. (gr. 7-7). pap. 10.99 ***(978-1-4938-3613-0(7))*** Teacher Created Materials, Inc.

Mason, Helen. Makeup Artist. 2014. (Creative Careers Ser.). 48p. (J). (gr. 4-8). pap. 84.30 *(978-1-4824-1303-8(5))* Stevens, Gareth Publishing LLLP.

THEATRICAL SCENERY

see Theaters—Stage Setting and Scenery

THEFT

Berry, Joy. Help Me Be Good about Stealing. 2009. (Help Me Be Good Ser.). 32p. pap. 7.95 *(978-1-60577-124-3(4))* Berry, Joy Enterprises.

Berry, Joy Wilt. A Book about Stealing. 2005. (Illus.). (J). *(978-0-7172-8585-3(5))* Scholastic, Inc.

Booth, Jack. The 10 Most Daring Heists. 2007. (J). 14.99 *(978-1-55448-486-7(3))* Scholastic Library Publishing.

Guillain, Charlotte. Great Art Thefts, 1 vol. 2013. (Treasure Hunters Ser.). (ENG.). 48p. (gr. 5-8). pap. 9.25 *(978-1-4109-4958-5(3))*; lib. bdg. 29.99 *(978-1-4109-4951-6(6))* Heinemann-Raintree.

Hanel, Rachael. Identity Theft. 2010. (Controversy! 2 Ser.). 112p. (gr. 7-18). 37.07 *(978-0-7614-4901-0(9))* Marshall Cavendish GBR. Dist: Marshall Cavendish Corp.

Kiesbye, Stefan. Identity Theft. 2011. (At Issue Ser.). (ENG.). 128p. (gr. 10-12). 39.40 *(978-0-7377-5582-4(2))*; pap. 27.80 *(978-0-7377-5583-1(0)*, Greenhaven Pr., Inc.) Cengage Gale.

Larsen, Carolyn. My Stuff, Your Stuff: A Book about Stealing. O'Connor, Tim, illus. 2017. (Growing God's Kids Ser.). (ENG.). 32p. (J). pap. 4.99 *(978-0-8010-0991-4(X))* Baker Bks.

Maule, David. Stealing High Beginning Book with Online Access. 2014. (ENG.). 24p. (J). pap. 9.50 *(978-1-107-67774-6(2))* Cambridge Univ. Pr.

Sheinkin, Steve. Lincoln's Grave Robbers. 2013. (ENG.). 224p. (J). (gr. 5-9). 16.99 *(978-0-545-40572-0(6)*, Scholastic Pr.) Scholastic, Inc.

Vacca, John, et al. Identity Theft. 2012. (Cybersafety Ser.). (Illus.). 135p. (gr. 6-12). 39.95 *(978-1-60413-700-2(2))* Facts On File, Inc.

whiting, jim. Identity Theft. 2012. (Illus.). 96p. (J). lib. bdg. *(978-1-60152-454-6(4))* ReferencePoint Pr., Inc.

Wood, Alix. Body Snatching. Wood, Alix, illus. 2013. (Why'd They Do That? Strange Customs of the Past Ser.). (Illus.). 32p. (J). (gr. 4-6). pap. 10.50 *(978-1-4339-9573-6(5))* Stevens, Gareth Publishing LLLP.

—Body Snatching. 2013. (Why'd They Do That? Strange Customs of the Past Ser.). (ENG., Illus.). 32p. (J). (gr. 4-6). lib. bdg. 26.60 *(978-1-4339-9572-9(7))* Stevens, Gareth Publishing LLLP.

Wood, Alix, illus. Body Snatching. 2013. (Why'd They Do That? Strange Customs of the Past Ser.). 32p. (J). (gr. 4-6). pap. 63.00 *(978-1-4339-9574-3(3))* Stevens, Gareth Publishing LLLP.

THEFT—FICTION

Abdo, Kenny. All for a Game, 1 vol. Doucet, Bob, illus. 2013. (Haven't Got a Clue! Ser.). (ENG.). 80p. (J). (gr. 3-6). lib. bdg. 27.07 *(978-1-61641-950-9(4)*, Calico Chapter Bks) Magic Wagon.

Adler, David A. Bones & the Big Yellow Mystery, No. 1. Newman, Barbara Johansen, illus. 2008. (Bones Ser.: 1). (ENG.). 32p. (J). (gr. 1-3). mass mkt. 3.99 *(978-0-14-241042-4(X)*, Penguin Young Readers) Penguin Young Readers Group.

—Cam Jansen & the Joke House Mystery. Allen, Joy, illus. 2014. (Cam Jansen Ser.: 34). (ENG.). 64p. (J). (gr. 2-5). 14.99 *(978-0-670-01262-6(9)*, Viking Books for Young Readers) Penguin Young Readers Group.

—Cam Jansen & the Millionaire Mystery. Allen, Joy, illus. 2013. (Cam Jansen Ser.: 32). (ENG.). 64p. (J). (gr. 2-5). pap. 4.99 *(978-0-14-242747-7(0)*, Puffin Books) Penguin Young Readers Group.

—The Valentine Baby Mystery. Natti, Susanna, illus. 25th ed. 2006. (Cam Jansen Ser.: 25). (ENG.). 80p. (J). (gr. 2-5). 4.99 *(978-0-14-240694-6(5)*, Puffin Books) Penguin Young Readers Group.

Aldridge, Janet. The Meadow-Brook Girls by the Sea, or Th. 2006. pap. *(978-1-4065-0693-8(1))* Dodo Pr.

Alexander, Carol. The Book Thief. Friedland, Joyce & Kessler, Rikki, eds. 2009. (Novel-Ties Ser.). (Illus.). 40p. pap. 16.95 *(978-0-7675-4277-7(0))* Learning Links Inc.

Allen, Elise & Stanford, Halle. Spring's Sparkle Sleepover. Pooler, Paige, illus. 2015. (Enchanted Sisters Ser.). (ENG.). 128p. (J). (gr. 2-4). 15.99 *(978-1-61963-296-7(9)*, 9781619632967); pap. 5.99 *(978-1-61963-269-1(1)*, 9781619632691) Bloomsbury Publishing USA. (Bloomsbury USA Childrens).

Aretha, David. A Hall Lot of Trouble at Cooperstown: The Baseball Geeks Adventures Book 1. 2014. (Baseball Geeks Adventures Ser.). (Illus.). 96p. (J). (gr. 4-7). 17.95 *(978-1-62285-118-8(8))* Enslow Pubs., Inc.

Ashby, Freya Katrina. Summer at the Dunes: A Deirdre Carlisle Mystery. 2007. 108p. per. 9.95 *(978-0-595-43663-7(3))* iUniverse, Inc.

Atkins, Ron. Abby & the Bicycle Caper. 2004. 48p. pap. 8.95 *(978-0-595-30565-0(2))* iUniverse, Inc.

Balliett, Blue. Pieces & Players. 2015. (ENG., Illus.). 320p. (J). (gr. 3-7). 17.99 *(978-0-545-29990-9(X)*, Scholastic Pr.) Scholastic, Inc.

Bancks, Tristan. Noob, Crimebuster. Gorissen, Dean, illus. 2015. (Legends in Their Own Lunchbox Ser.). (ENG.). 48p. (gr. 1-2). pap. 7.99 *(978-1-4966-0241-1(2)*, Legends in Their Own Lunchbox) Capstone Classroom.

Barnett, Mac. Danger Goes Berserk. Myers, Matthew, illus. 2013. (Brixton Brothers Ser.: 4). (ENG.). 256p. (J). (gr. 3-7). pap. 7.99 *(978-1-4424-3978-8(5)*, Simon & Schuster Bks. For Young Readers) Simon & Schuster Bks. For Young Readers.

Barnett, Mac, et al. The Clock Without a Face. Teplin, Scott & Rex, Adam, illus. 2010. (ENG.). 30p. (gr. 2-18). bds. 19.95 *(978-1-934781-71-5(1))* McSweeney's Publishing.

Beauvais, Clémentine. Gargoyles Gone AWOL. Horne, Sarah, illus. 2015. (Sesame Seade Mystery Ser.: 2). (ENG.). 208p. (J). (gr. 2-6). 16.95 *(978-0-8234-3205-9(X))* Holiday Hse., Inc.

Bellingham, Brenda. Lilly's Special Gift. 2005. (Illus.). 59p. (J). lib. bdg. 12.00 *(978-1-4242-1204-0(9))* Fitzgerald Bks.

Braffet, Holly, illus. Kekoa & the Egg Mystery. 2010. (ENG.). 32p. (J). (gr. -1-2). 14.95 *(978-1-933067-35-3(7))* Beachhouse Publishing, LLC.

Brezenoff, Steve. Ballgame with No One at Bat. 2013. (Field Trip Mysteries Ser.). (ENG.). 88p. (gr. 2-3). pap. 35.70 *(978-1-4342-6230-1(8))* Stone Arch Bks.

—The Ballgame with No One at Bat. Calo, Marcos, illus. 2013. (Field Trip Mysteries Ser.). (ENG.). 88p. (gr. 2-3). pap. 6.10 *(978-1-4342-6211-0(1))*; lib. bdg. 25.32 *(978-1-4342-5978-3(1))* Stone Arch Bks.

—The Carnival Caper: An Interactive Mystery Adventure. Calo, Marcos, illus. 2017. (You Choose Stories: Field Trip Mysteries Ser.). (ENG.). 112p. (gr. 3-7). lib. bdg. 32.65 *(978-1-4965-2645-8(7))* Stone Arch Bks.

—The Case of the Counterfeit Painting. Weber, Lisa K., illus. 2016. (Museum Mysteries Ser.). (ENG.). 128p. (gr. 2-3). pap. 6.95 *(978-1-4965-2522-2(1))*; lib. bdg. 26.65 *(978-1-4965-2518-5(3))* Stone Arch Bks. (Museum Mysteries).

—Dinosaur That Disappeared. 2013. (Field Trip Mysteries Ser.). (ENG.). 88p. (gr. 2-3). pap. 35.70 *(978-1-4342-6233-2(2))* Stone Arch Bks.

—The Dinosaur That Disappeared, 1 vol. Calo, Marcos, illus. 2013. (Field Trip Mysteries Ser.). (ENG.). 88p. (gr. 2-3). pap. 6.10 *(978-1-4342-6213-4(8))*; lib. bdg. 25.32 *(978-1-4342-5960-6(3))* Stone Arch Bks.

—The Disappearing Fruit: An Interactive Mystery Adventure. Calo, Marcos, illus. 2017. (You Choose Stories: Field Trip Mysteries Ser.). (ENG.). 112p. (gr. 3-7). lib. bdg. 32.65 *(978-1-4965-2643-4(0))* Stone Arch Bks.

Brezenoff, Steven. Case of the Counterfeit Painting. Weber, Lisa K., illus. 2017. 118p. (J). pap. *(978-1-4965-2530-7(2))* Stone Arch Bks.

—The Case of the Stolen Sculpture. Weber, Lisa K., illus. 2015. (Museum Mysteries Ser.). (ENG.). 128p. (gr. 2-3). lib. bdg. 26.65 *(978-1-4342-9686-3(5))* Stone Arch Bks.

Bright, J. E. Batman vs. Catwoman, 1 vol. Levins, Tim, illus. 2013. (DC Super Heroes Ser.). (ENG.). 56p. (gr. 2-3). lib. bdg. 26.65 *(978-1-4342-6013-0(5))* Stone Arch Bks.

Bright, Philip & Ramos, Sarah. Jimmy Rat. 2008. (Illus.). 32p. pap. 17.95 *(978-0-9556105-9-2(1))* Picnic Publishing Ltd. GBR. Dist: Trans-Atlantic Pubns., Inc.

Broad, Michael. Ghost Diamond!, No. 1. Broad, Michael, illus. 2011. (Agent Amelia Ser.: 1). (ENG., Illus.). 144p. (J). (gr. 2-5). pap. 5.95 *(978-0-7613-8060-3(4)*, Darby Creek); lib. bdg. 22.60 *(978-0-7613-8056-6(6))* Lerner Publishing Group.

—#1 Ghost Diamond! 2011. (Agent Amelia Ser.). pap. 33.92 *(978-0-7613-8341-3(7)*, Darby Creek) Lerner Publishing Group.

Brown, Jeff. Framed in France. Pamintuan, Macky, illus. 2014. (Flat Stanley's Worldwide Adventures Ser.: 11). (ENG.). 128p. (J). (gr. 1-5). 15.99 *(978-0-06-218985-1(9))*; pap. 4.99 *(978-0-06-218984-4(0))* HarperCollins Pubs.

Brown, Marc. Arthur & the Mystery of the Stolen Bike. 2012. (ENG., Illus.). 64p. (J). (gr. 1-4). pap. 4.99 *(978-0-316-13363-0(9))* Little, Brown Bks. for Young Readers.

Carter, Ally. Heist Society. 2011. (Heist Society Novel Ser.). (ENG.). 304p. (J). (gr. 5-9). pap. 9.99 *(978-1-4231-1661-5(5))* Hyperion Pr.

Cazet, Denys. Minnie & Moo: The Case of the Missing Jelly Donut. Cazet, Denys, illus. 2007. (Minnie & Moo Ser.). (Illus.). 45p. (J). (gr. -1-3). pap. 29.95 incl. audio *(978-1-4301-0088-1(5))* Live Oak Media.

Chandra, Rohini S. The Dragon in the Candle Jar. 2013. 52p. pap. 16.95 *(978-1-4626-9842-4(5))* America Star Bks.

Cheshire, Simon. The Treasure of Dead Man's Lane & Other Case Files: Saxby Smart, Private Detective: Book 2. Alley, R. W., illus. 2011. (Saxby Smart, Private Detective Ser.: 2). (ENG.). 224p. (J). (gr. 3-7). pap. 8.99 *(978-0-312-67434-2(1)*, 9780312674342) Square Fish.

Choksi, Sean. The Theft of Time. 2010. 67p. pap. 14.95 *(978-1-4327-6598-9(1))* Outskirts Pr., Inc.

Clark, Sherryl. Kim's Pet Scoop. McKenzie, Heath, illus. 2015. (J). pap. *(978-1-4966-0238-1(2))* Capstone Classroom.

Clements, Andrew. The Map Trap. Andreasen, Dan, illus. 2016. (ENG.). 160p. (J). (gr. 3-7). pap. 7.99 *(978-1-4169-9728-3(8))* Simon & Schuster Children's Publishing.

—The Map Trap. LaMarche, Jim & Andreasen, Dan, illus. 2014. (ENG.). 144p. (J). (gr. 3-7). 17.99 *(978-1-4169-9727-6(X)*, Atheneum Bks. for Young Readers) Simon & Schuster Children's Publishing.

—The Map Trap. 2016. lib. bdg. 18.40 *(978-0-606-38977-8(6))* Turtleback Bks.

Cobb, Amy. Dude, Where's My Saxophone?, 1 vol. Cattish, Anna, illus. 2015. (ENG.). 112p. (J). *(978-1-62402-073-5(9))* Magic Wagon.

Couloumbis, Audrey. Say Yes. 2003. (ENG.). 208p. (J). (gr. 3-7). pap. 7.99 *(978-0-14-250186-3(7)*, Speak) Penguin Young Readers Group.

Cushman, Doug, illus. Dirk Bones & the Mystery of the Missing Books. 2009. (I Can Read Level 1 Ser.). (ENG.). 32p. (J). (gr. -1-3). 16.99 *(978-0-06-073768-9(9))* HarperCollins Pubs.

Dahl, Michael. Blood Shark! Sinkovec, Igor, illus. 2015. (Igor's Lab of Fear Ser.). (ENG.). 40p. (gr. 1-3). lib. bdg. 23.99 *(978-1-4965-0456-2(9))* Stone Arch Bks.

—The Clown Prince of Cards. Vecchio, Luciano, illus. 2016. (Batman Tales of the Batcave Ser.). (ENG.). 40p. (gr. 1-3). lib. bdg. 24.65 *(978-1-4965-4013-3(1)*, DC Super Heroes) Stone Arch Bks.

—Dragon Theft Auto, 1 vol. Rong, Yap Kun, illus. 2010. (Dragonblood Ser.). (ENG.). 40p. (gr. 1-3). pap. 6.25 *(978-1-4342-2310-4(8)*, Zone Bks.) Stone Arch Bks.

—Dragon Theft Auto, 1 vol. Evans, Mark & Kun Rong, Yap, illus. 2009. (Dragonblood Ser.). (ENG.). 40p. (gr. 1-3). 23.99 *(978-1-4342-1264-1(5)*, Zone Bks.) Stone Arch Bks.

—The Thirteenth Mystery. Weber, Lisa K., illus. (Hocus Pocus Hotel Ser.). (ENG.). 224p. (gr. 2-3). 2016. pap. 7.95 *(978-1-4965-0755-6(X))* 2014. 10.95 *(978-1-4342-6509-8(9))* Stone Arch Bks.

Dakers, Diane. Bad Business, 1 vol. 2015. (Orca Currents Ser.). (ENG.). 128p. (J). (gr. 5-9). pap. 9.95 *(978-1-4598-0969-7(6))* Orca Bk. Pubs. USA.

Davies, Matt. Ben Rides On. 2013. (ENG., Illus.). 32p. (J). (gr. -1-2). 17.99 *(978-1-59643-794-4(4)*, 9781596437944) Roaring Brook Pr.

Davies, Nicola. The Promise. Carlin, Laura, illus. 2014. (ENG.). 40p. (J). (gr. k-4). 16.99 *(978-0-7636-6633-0(5))* Candlewick Pr.

Devargas, Casey Anthony. The Kindergarten Treasure. 2012. 44p. pap. 7.00 *(978-0-9859042-0-3(8))* CD Publishing.

Dhami, Narinder. Samosa Thief. Blundell, Tony, illus. 2005. (ENG.). 24p. (J). lib. bdg. 23.65 *(978-1-59646-708-8(8))* Dingles & Co.

DiCamillo, Kate. Mercy Watson Fights Crime. Van Dusen, Chris, illus. 2010. (Mercy Watson Ser.: 3). (ENG.). 80p. (J). (gr. 1-4). pap. 5.99 *(978-0-7636-4952-4(X))* Candlewick Pr.

—Mercy Watson Fights Crime. DiCamillo, Kate & Van Dusen, Chris, illus. 2006. (Mercy Watson Ser.: 3). (ENG.). 80p. (J). (gr. k-3). 14.99 *(978-0-7636-2590-0(6))* Candlewick Pr.

—Mercy Watson Fights Crime. 2010. (Mercy Watson Ser.: Bk. 3). lib. bdg. 16.00 *(978-0-606-14927-3(9)*, Turtleback) Turtleback Bks.

Dickson, Louise. The Disappearing Magician. Cupples, Pat, illus. 2007. (Kids Can Read Ser.). (ENG.). 32p. (J). (gr. 1-2). 3.95 *(978-1-55453-034-2(2))* Kids Can Pr., Ltd. CAN. Dist: Hachette Bk. Group.

Dionne, Erin. Moxie & the Art of Rule Breaking: A 14-Day Mystery. 2013. (ENG.). 256p. (J). (gr. 5). 16.99 *(978-0-8037-3871-3(4)*, Dial Bks) Penguin Young Readers Group.

Disney Book Group Staff. Sheriff Callie's Wild West Peck's Trail Mix Mix-Up. Disney Storybook Art Team, illus. 2015. (World of Reading Ser.). (ENG.). 32p. (J). (gr. -1-k). pap. 3.99 *(978-1-4847-1566-6(7))* Disney Pr.

Dixon, Franklin W. The Bicycle Thief. Burroughs, Scott, illus. 2011. (Hardy Boys: the Secret Files Ser.: 6). (ENG.). 96p. (J). (gr. 1-4). pap. 5.99 *(978-1-4169-9396-4(7)*, Aladdin) Simon & Schuster Children's Publishing.

—The Curse of the Ancient Emerald. 2015. (Hardy Boys Adventures Ser.: 9). (ENG., Illus.). 128p. (J). (gr. 3-7). pap. 6.99 *(978-1-4814-2475-2(0)*, Aladdin) Simon & Schuster Children's Publishing.

—Ship of Secrets. 2014. (Hardy Boys: Secret Files Ser.: 15). lib. bdg. 14.75 *(978-0-606-35781-4(5))* Turtleback Bks.

—Showdown at Widow Creek. 2016. (Hardy Boys Adventures Ser.: 11). (ENG., Illus.). 128p. (J). (gr. 3-7). 17.99 *(978-1-4814-3878-0(6)*, Aladdin) Simon & Schuster Children's Publishing.

Douglas, Erin. Get That Pest! Yee, Wong Herbert, illus. 2003. (Green Light Readers Level 2 Ser.). (ENG.). 24p. (J). (gr. -1-3). pap. 3.95 *(978-0-15-204833-4(2))* Houghton Mifflin Harcourt Publishing Co.

Duddle, Jonny. The Jolley-Rogers & the Ghostly Galleon. Duddle, Jonny, illus. 2016. (ENG., Illus.). 160p. (J). (gr. 1-4). pap. 6.99 *(978-0-7636-8910-0(6)*, Templar) Candlewick Pr.

Duk, Lor. The Firestorm Heart: A Dragon Friend Story. 2010. 236p. pap. 15.95 *(978-1-4401-9474-0(2))* iUniverse, Inc.

Eason, Sarah. Hand It over, Harry: Don't Steal. 2013. (You Choose Ser.). 32p. (J). (gr. k-3). pap. 7.95 *(978-1-4644-0561-7(1)*, Enslow Elementary) Enslow Pubs., Inc.

Eggleton, Jill. Mickey Maloney's Missing Bag. Pye, Trevor, illus. 2004. (Rigby Sails Early Ser.). (ENG.). 16p. (gr. 1-2). pap. 6.95 *(978-0-7578-9299-8(X))* Houghton Mifflin Harcourt Publishing Co.

Elliott, Rebecca. A Woodland Wedding. Elliott, Rebecca, illus. 2016. (Owl Diaries: 3). (ENG., Illus.). 80p. (J). (gr. k-2). 15.99 *(978-0-545-82558-0(X))* Scholastic, Inc.

Escoffier, Michaël. Brief Thief. Di Giacomo, Kris, illus. 2013. (ENG.). 32p. (J). (gr. -1-3). 16.95 *(978-1-59270-131-5(0))* Enchanted Lion Bks., LLC.

Everett, George W. G. W. Frog & the Pumpkin Patch Bandit. 2010. 40p. 16.95 *(978-1-4497-0759-0(9)*, WestBow Pr.) Author Solutions, Inc.

Fanning, Kieran. Code Crackers: Trapdoor to Treachery. 2010. (Dover Children's Classics Ser.). (ENG.). 128p. (J). (gr. 3-5). pap. 5.99 *(978-0-486-47880-7(7))* Dover Pubns., Inc.

Fenn, Jennifer. Flight Risk. 2017. (ENG.). 384p. (YA). 17.99 *(978-1-62672-760-1(0)*, 9781626727601) Roaring Brook Pr.

Fertig, Dennis. Something Rotten at Village Market. McMahon, Bob, tr. McMahon, Bob, illus. 2003. 60p. 11.60 net. *(978-0-7398-5170-8(5))* Steck-Vaughn.

Fisch, Sholly, et al. Bottle of the Planets. 2015. (All-New Batman: the Brave & the Bold Ser.). (ENG., Illus.). 32p. (gr. 2-3). lib. bdg. 22.60 *(978-1-4342-9658-0(X))* Stone Arch Bks.

Flegg, Aubrey. In the Claws of the Eagle Vol. 3. 2006. (Louise Trilogy Ser.: 03). (ENG.). 288p. (J). pap. 12.95 *(978-0-86278-827-8(7))* O'Brien Pr., Ltd., The IRL. Dist: Dufour Editions, Inc.

Foster, Martha S. Ginger Box. Geer, Charles, illus. 2011. 126p. 40.95 *(978-1-258-06588-1(6))* Literary Licensing, LLC.

Gosling, Sharon. The Diamond Thief. 2014. (Diamond Thief Ser.). (ENG.). 336p. (gr. 9-12). 16.95 *(978-1-63079-002-8(8))* Switch Pr.

Gottesfeld, Jeff. The Bank of Badness, 1 vol. 2013. (Robinson's Hood Ser.). (ENG.). (gr. 5-8). pap. 8.95 *(978-1-62250-001-7(6))* Saddleback Educational Publishing, Inc.

—The Bank of Badness. 2013. (Robinson's Hood Ser.: 2). lib. bdg. 19.60 *(978-0-606-27019-9(1)*, Turtleback) Turtleback Bks.

—Chopped!, 1 vol. 2013. (Robinson's Hood Ser.). (ENG.). (gr. 5-8). pap. 8.95 *(978-1-62250-002-4(4))* Saddleback Educational Publishing, Inc.

—Chopped! 2013. (Robinson's Hood Ser.: 3). lib. bdg. 19.60 *(978-0-606-27020-5(5)*, Turtleback) Turtleback Bks.

Grant, Vicki. Identificación, 1 vol. 2009. (Spanish Soundings Ser.). (SPA.). 112p. (YA). (gr. 8-12). pap. 9.95 *(978-1-55469-134-0(6))* Orca Bk. Pubs. USA.

Graves, Judith. Exposed, 1 vol. 2015. (Retribution Ser.). (ENG.). 144p. (YA). (gr. 8-12). pap. 9.95 *(978-1-4598-0722-8(7))* Orca Bk. Pubs. USA.

Griffin, N. Smashie Mcperter & the Mystery of Room 11. Hindley, Kate, illus. 2015. (ENG.). 256p. (J). (gr. 2-5). 15.99 *(978-0-7636-6145-8(7))* Candlewick Pr.

Grisham, John. The Accused. (Theodore Boone Ser.: 3). (ENG.). (J). (gr. 3-7). 2013. 304p. pap. 8.99 *(978-0-14-242613-5(X)*, Puffin Books) 2012. 288p. 16.99 *(978-0-525-42576-2(4)*, Dutton Books for Young Readers) Penguin Young Readers Group.

—The Accused. 2013. (Theodore Boone Ser.: 3). lib. bdg. 18.40 *(978-0-606-31696-5(5)*, Turtleback) Turtleback Bks.

Gutman, Dan. Babe Ruth & the Ice Cream Mess. Garvin, Elaine, illus. 2004. (Ready-To-read COFA Ser.). (ENG.). 32p. (J). (gr. k-2). pap. 3.99 *(978-0-689-85529-0(X)*, Simon Spotlight) Simon Spotlight.

Hale, Bruce. Hiss Me Deadly. Hale, Bruce, illus. 2009. (Chet Gecko Ser.: 13). (ENG., Illus.). 128p. (J). (gr. 2-5). pap. 5.99 *(978-0-15-206424-2(9))* Houghton Mifflin Harcourt Publishing Co.

—School for SPIES Thicker Than Water. Dorman, Brandon, illus. 2015. (ENG.). 368p. (J). (gr. 3-7). pap. 6.99 *(978-1-4231-7106-5(3))* Hyperion Bks. for Children.

Harvey, Jacqueline. Alice-Miranda in Paris. 2015. (Alice-Miranda Ser.: 7). (ENG.). 336p. (J). (gr. 3-7). 9.99 *(978-1-74275-288-4(8))* Random Hse. Australia AUS. Dist: Independent Pubs. Group.

Hautman, Pete. How to Steal a Car. 2009. (ENG.). 176p. (J). (gr. 7-18). 16.99 *(978-0-545-11318-2(0)*, Scholastic Pr.) Scholastic, Inc.

Heath, Jack. Money Run. 2013. (ENG.). 256p. (J). (gr. 7). 17.99 *(978-0-545-51266-4(2))* Scholastic, Inc.

Henry, April. Girl, Stolen. 2010. (Girl, Stolen Ser.). (ENG.). 224p. (YA). (gr. 7-12). 18.99 *(978-0-8050-9005-5(3)*, 9780805090055, Holt, Henry & Co. Bks. For Young Readers) Holt, Henry & Co.

Hood, Susan. Pup & Hound Catch a Thief. Hendry, Linda, illus. 2007. (Kids Can Read Ser.). (ENG.). 32p. (J). (gr. k-1). 3.95 *(978-1-55337-973-7(X))* Kids Can Pr., Ltd. CAN. Dist: Hachette Bk. Group.

Hope, Lee Laura. Six Little Bunkers at Aunt Jo's. 2007. (ENG.). 144p. pap. 18.99 *(978-1-4346-3234-0(2))*; 156p. pap. 21.99 *(978-1-4346-3235-7(0))* Creative Media Partners, LLC.

Hughes, Shirley. Digby o'Day & the Great Diamond Robbery. Vulliamy, Clara, illus. 2015. (ENG.). 136p. (J). (gr. k-3). 12.99 *(978-0-7636-7445-8(1))* Candlewick Pr.

Hunt, Elizabeth Singer. The Caper of the Crown Jewels, Bk. 4. 2008. (Secret Agent Jack Stalwart Ser.: 4). (ENG., Illus.). 144p. (J). (gr. 1-4). per. 5.99 *(978-1-60286-013-1(0)*, Weinstein Bks.) Perseus Bks. Group.

—The Mystery of the Mona Lisa, Bk. 3. Williamson, Brian, illus. 2007. (Secret Agent Jack Stalwart Ser.: 3). (ENG.). 128p. (J). (gr. 1-4). per. 5.99 *(978-1-60286-001-8(7)*, Weinstein Bks.) Perseus Bks. Group.

—Theft of the Samurai Sword: Japan #11. 2009. (ENG., Illus.). 128p. (J). lib. bdg. 15.38 *(978-1-4242-4452-2(8))* Fitzgerald Bks.

Hunt, Elizabeth Singer & Weinstein Books Staff. The Theft of the Samurai Sword: Japan. Williamson, Brian, illus. 2009. (Secret Agent Jack Stalwart Ser.: 11). (ENG.). 128p. (J). (gr. 1-4). pap. 5.99 *(978-1-60286-098-8(X)*, Weinstein Bks.) Perseus Bks. Group.

Hutchins, Hazel. The Great Bike Rescue, 1 vol. 2013. (Orca Young Readers Ser.). (ENG.). 112p. (J). (gr. 3-6). pap. 7.95 *(978-1-4598-0478-4(3))* Orca Bk. Pubs. USA.

Hyder, M. A. Donia: Stolen Raindrops or Honour among Thieves. 2011. (Illus.). 364p. pap. 20.53 *(978-1-4567-7428-8(X))* AuthorHouse.

Hymas, Allison K. Under Locker & Key. 2017. (Max Ser.). (ENG., Illus.). 256p. (J). (gr. 4-8). pap. 7.99 *(978-1-4814-6342-3(X)*, Simon & Schuster/Paula Wiseman Bks.) Simon & Schuster/Paula Wiseman Bks.

Inches, Alison. Súper Bebés! Miller, Victoria, illus. 2006. (Dora la Exploradora Ser.). (SPA.). 24p. (J). (gr. -1-3). pap. 3.99 *(978-1-4169-2461-6(2)*, Libros Para Ninos) Libros Para Ninos.

Ish-Kishor, Sulamith. A Boy of Old Prague. Shahn, Ben, illus. 2008. (Dover Children's Classics Ser.). (ENG.). 96p. (J). (gr. 4-6). pap. 3.99 *(978-0-486-46766-5(X))* Dover Pubns., Inc.

Ius, Dawn. Overdrive. 2016. (ENG., Illus.). 352p. (YA). (gr. 9). 17.99 *(978-1-4814-3944-2(8)*, Simon Pulse) Simon Pulse.

Jackson, Ellen. The Cupcake Thief. 2008. pap. 34.95 *(978-1-58013-765-2(2))* Kane Press, Inc.

—The Cupcake Thief. Sims, Blanche, illus. 2007. (Social Studies Connects). 32p. (J). (gr. -1-3). pap. 5.95 *(978-1-57565-247-4(1))* Kane Press, Inc.

Jacobson, Rick. The Mona Lisa Caper. Jacobson, Rick & Fernandez, Laura, illus. 2005. (ENG.). 24p. (J). (gr. k-3). 16.99 *(978-0-88776-726-5(5)*, Tundra Bks.) Tundra Bks. CAN. Dist: Penguin Random Hse. LLC.

Jakubowski, Michele. The Professor's Discovery. Pinelli, Amerigo, illus. 2016. (Sleuths of Somerville Ser.). (ENG.). 144p. (gr. 4-6). lib. bdg. 25.99 *(978-1-4965-3177-3(9))* Stone Arch Bks.

—The Professor's Discovery. Pinelli, Amerigo, illus. 2017. (Sleuths of Somerville Ser.). (ENG.). 144p. (gr. 4-6). pap. 6.95 *(978-1-4965-3181-0(7))* Stone Arch Bks.

James, Dalton. The Sneakiest Pirates. 2008. 20p. pap. 10.95 *(978-1-4327-2477-1(0))* Outskirts Pr., Inc.

Jennings, Sharon. Jingle Bats. Mulloy, Kalle, illus. 72p. pap. *(978-1-897039-22-9(0))* High Interest Publishing (HIP).

Jewel Robbery. 2008. (Looney Tunes 8*8 Ser.). 24p. pap. *(978-1-4075-2632-4(4))*; pap. *(978-1-4075-2642-3(1))* Parragon, Inc.

Jonell, Lynne. Emmy & the Home for Troubled Girls. Bean, Jonathan, illus. 2010. (Emmy & the Rat Ser.: 2). (ENG.). 384p. (J). (gr. 4-7). pap. 12.99 *(978-0-312-60873-6(X)*, 9780312608736) Square Fish.

Jones, Allan Frewin. Blood Stone, Vol. 6. 6th ed. 2003. (ENG.). 176p. (J). mass mkt. *(978-0-330-37476-7(1)*, Pan) Pan Macmillan.

Judge, Chris. The Snow Beast. Judge, Chris, illus. 2015. (ENG., Illus.). 32p. (J). (gr. -1-3). 17.99 *(978-1-4677-9313-1(2))* Andersen Pr. GBR. Dist: Lerner Publishing Group.

Juslin, Lee. Nurse Frosty Saves the Day. 2009. 35p. pap. 22.00 *(978-0-557-09486-8(0))* Lulu Pr., Inc.

Keene, Carolyn. The Apple Bandit. Jones, Jan Naimo, illus. 2005. (Nancy Drew Notebooks). 74p. (J). (gr. 1-4). 11.65 *(978-0-7569-6505-1(5))* Perfection Learning Corp.

—The Cinderella Ballet Mystery, 1 vol. Pamintuan, Macky, illus. 2007. (Nancy Drew & the Clue Crew Ser.). (ENG.). 83p. (gr. 1-4). 24.21 *(978-1-59961-345-1(X))* Spotlight.

—The Nancy Drew & the Clue Crew Collection: Sleepover Sleuths; Scream for Ice Cream; Pony Problems; the

Cinderella Ballet Mystery; Case of the Sneaky Snowman. Pamintuan, Macky, illus. 2014. (Nancy Drew & the Clue Crew Ser.). (ENG.). 480p. (J). (gr. 1-4). pap. 29.99 *(978-1-4814-1472-2(0)*, Aladdin) Simon & Schuster Children's Publishing.

—The Orchid Thief. 19th ed. 2006. (Nancy Drew (All New) Girl Detective Ser.: 19). (ENG.). 144p. (J). (gr. 3-7). pap. 5.99 *(978-1-4169-0980-4(X)*, Aladdin) Simon & Schuster Children's Publishing.

—Scream for Ice Cream, 1 vol. Pamintuan, Macky, illus. 2007. (Nancy Drew & the Clue Crew Ser.). (ENG.). 89p. (gr. 1-4). 24.21 *(978-1-59961-347-5(6))* Spotlight.

—Sleepover Sleuths, 1 vol. Pamintuan, Macky, illus. 2007. (Nancy Drew & the Clue Crew Ser.). (ENG.). 81p. (gr. 1-4). 24.21 *(978-1-59961-348-2(4))* Spotlight.

—Time Thief. Pamintuan, Macky, illus. 2011. (Nancy Drew & the Clue Crew Ser.: 28). (ENG.). 96p. (J). (gr. 1-4). pap. 5.99 *(978-1-4169-9458-9(0)*, Aladdin) Simon & Schuster Children's Publishing.

Kehret, Peg & the Cat, Pete. Spy Cat. 2008. (Pete the Cat Ser.). (ENG.). 192p. (J). (gr. 3-7). 5.99 *(978-0-14-241219-0(8)*, Puffin Books) Penguin Young Readers Group.

Kelly, David A. The Fenway Foul-Up. Meyers, Mark, illus. 2011. (Ballpark Mysteries Ser.: Bk. 1). (ENG.). 112p. (J). (gr. 1-4). pap. 4.99 *(978-0-375-86703-3(1)*, Random Hse. Bks. for Young Readers) Random Hse. Children's Bks.

Kline, Suzy. Horrible Harry Takes the Cake. Remkiewicz, Frank, illus. 2007. (Horrible Harry Ser.). (ENG.). 64p. (J). (gr. 2-4). 4.99 *(978-0-14-240939-8(1)*, Puffin Books) Penguin Young Readers Group.

Korman, Gordon. Framed. (J). 2011. (ENG.). 240p. (gr. 3-7). pap. 6.99 *(978-0-545-19763-2(5)*, Scholastic Paperbacks) 2010. *(978-0-545-27081-6(2)*, Scholastic Pr.) 2010. (Swindle Ser.: 3). (ENG.). 240p. (gr. 4-7). 16.99 *(978-0-545-17849-5(5)*, Scholastic Pr.) Scholastic, Inc.

—Jingle (Swindle #8) 2016. (Swindle Ser.: 8). (ENG.). 208p. (J). (gr. 3-7). 16.99 *(978-0-545-86142-7(X)*, Scholastic Pr.) Scholastic, Inc.

—Zoobreak. 2009. 230p. (J). *(978-0-545-20027-1(X)*, Scholastic Pr.) Scholastic, Inc.

Kowitt, H. N. The Loser List. 2011. (ENG.). 224p. (J). (gr. 3-7). 9.99 *(978-0-545-24004-8(2)*, Scholastic Paperbacks) Scholastic, Inc.

Kropp, Alex. Hacker! (Illus.). 93p. *(978-1-897039-09-0(3))* High Interest Publishing (HIP).

Kulper, Kendall. Drift & Dagger. 2015. (ENG.). 368p. (YA). (gr. 7-17). 18.00 *(978-0-316-40453-2(5))* Little, Brown Bks. for Young Readers.

Kysiak, Penelope Ann. You Can't Steal One's Wishes, 1 vol. 2009. 35p. pap. 24.95 *(978-1-60749-149-1(4))* America Star Bks.

Lagonegro, Melissa. Super Agents. 2016. (Step into Reading Ser.). (ENG., Illus.). 24p. (J). (gr. -1-1). pap. 4.99 *(978-1-101-93140-0(X)*, Random Hse. Bks. for Young Readers) Random Hse. Children's Bks.

Lee, HaeDa. Ida's Present. Kim, InHyeon, illus. 2014. (MySELF Bookshelf Ser.). (ENG.). 32p. (J). (gr. k-2). pap. 11.94 *(978-1-60357-694-9(0))*; lib. bdg. 25.27 *(978-1-59953-659-0(5))* Norwood Hse. Pr.

Levins, Sandra. Bumblebee Bike. Keay, Claire, illus. 2014. (J). *(978-1-4338-1645-1(8))*; 32p. pap. *(978-1-4338-1646-8(6))* American Psychological Assn. (Magination Pr.).

Lewis, J. Patrick. The Stolen Smile. Kelley, Gary, illus. 2nd ed. 2015. (ENG.). 40p. (J). (gr. 2-4). 16.99 *(978-1-56846-281-3(6)*, Creative Editions) Creative Co., The.

Lockwood, Vicki. The Magnificent Lizzie Brown & the Ghost Ship. Hans, Stephanie, illus. 2015. (Magnificent Lizzie Brown Ser.). (ENG.). 200p. (gr. 5-9). lib. bdg. 26.65 *(978-1-4342-9806-5(X))* Stone Arch Bks.

London, Jack. The Call of the Wild. Moser, Barry, illus. 2011. (ENG.). 144p. (J). (gr. 4-9). pap. 8.99 *(978-1-4424-3411-0(2)*, Simon & Schuster Bks. For Young Readers) Simon & Schuster Bks. For Young Readers.

—La Llamada de la Naturaleza. 2003. (Historias de Siempre Ser.).Tr. of Call of the Wild. (SPA., Illus.). 92p. (J). (gr. 5-8). pap. 10.95 *(978-84-204-5731-4(0))* Santillana USA Publishing Co., Inc.

Lorimer, Janet. The Tiger Lily Code, 1 vol. unabr. ed. 2010. (Q Reads Ser.). (ENG.). 32p. (YA). (gr. 9-12). pap. 6.95 *(978-1-61651-195-1(8))* Saddleback Educational Publishing, Inc.

Lowery, Rae. The Case of the Pack-Rat Park. 2008. 57p. pap. 19.95 *(978-1-60610-426-2(8))* America Star Bks.

Lucky, A. E. Kyle the Detective, 1 vol. 2010. 70p. pap. 19.95 *(978-1-4512-2042-1(1))* America Star Bks.

Ludwig, Elisa. Pretty Crooked. 2012. (Pretty Crooked Trilogy Ser.: 1). (ENG.). 368p. (YA). (gr. 8). 17.99 *(978-0-06-206606-0(4)*, Tegen, Katherine Bks) HarperCollins Pubs.

Lysiak, Hilde & Lysiak, Matthew. Hero Dog! Lew-Vriethoff, Joanne, illus. 2017. (Hilde Cracks the Case Ser.: 1). (ENG.). 96p. (J). (gr. 1-3). pap. 4.99 ***(978-1-338-14155-9(4))*** Scholastic, Inc.

Maddox, Jake. Caught Stealing. Aburtov, Jesus Aburto, illus. 2015. (Jake Maddox Sports Stories Ser.). (ENG.). 72p. (gr. 2-3). lib. bdg. 25.32 *(978-1-4965-0493-7(3))* Stone Arch Bks.

Malaspina, Ann. Guinea Fowl & Rabbit Get Justice: An African Folktale. Wendland, Paula, illus. 2013. (Folktales from Around the World Ser.). (ENG.). 24p. (J). (gr. k-3). 28.50 *(978-1-62323-614-4(2)*, 206381) Child's World, Inc., The.

Marciano, John Bemelmans. Madeline & the Old House in Paris. 2013. (Madeline Ser.). (ENG.). 48p. (J). (gr. -1-2). 17.99 *(978-0-670-78485-1(0)*, Viking Books for Young Readers) Penguin Young Readers Group.

Marois, Andre. The Sandwich Thief. Doyon, Patrick, illus. 2016. (ENG.). 160p. (J). (gr. 1-4). 14.99 *(978-1-4521-4659-1(4))* Chronicle Bks. LLC.

Maynard, Adam G. The Adventures of Dynamo Dog & the Case of the Missing Jewelery. 2010. 24p. 15.49 *(978-1-4490-9186-6(5))* AuthorHouse.

Mazer, Anne. Now You See It, Now You Don't. 2005. (Amazing Days of Abby Hayes Ser.: Bk. 15). (Illus.). 126p. (J). (gr. 4-7). 12.65 *(978-0-7569-5932-6(2))* Perfection Learning Corp.

McClintock, Norah. Marked, 1 vol. 2008. (Orca Currents Ser.). (ENG.). (J). (gr. 5-9). 128p. pap. 9.95 *(978-1-55143-992-1(1))*; 112p. lib. bdg. 16.95 *(978-1-55143-994-5(8))* Orca Bk. Pubs. USA.

—Marqué, 1 vol. 2011.Tr. of Marked. (FRE.). 128p. (J). (gr. 5-9). pap. 9.95 *(978-1-55469-855-4(3))* Orca Bk. Pubs. USA.

—Nowhere to Turn. 2012. (Robyn Hunter Mysteries Ser.: 6). (ENG.). 240p. (YA). (gr. 6-12). pap. 8.95 *(978-0-7613-9398-6(6)*, Darby Creek) Lerner Publishing Group.

—Watch Me, 1 vol. 2008. (Orca Currents Ser.). (ENG.). (J). (gr. 5-9). 112p. 16.95 *(978-1-55469-040-4(4))*; 128p. pap. 9.95 *(978-1-55469-039-8(0))* Orca Bk. Pubs. USA.

Meadows, Daisy. Emily, the Emerald Fairy. Ripper, Georgie, illus. 2005. 65p. (J). pap. *(978-0-545-01190-7(6))* Scholastic, Inc.

Meadows, Thomas. The Tales of Tommy Tucker: Pizza Pie Patty! 2013. 36p. pap. 17.25 *(978-1-4669-8894-1(0))* Trafford Publishing.

Meddaugh, Susan. Martha Speaks: Secret Agent Dog (Chapter Book) 2012. (Martha Speaks Ser.). (ENG., Illus.). 96p. (J). (gr. 1-4). pap. 5.99 *(978-0-547-57660-2(9))* Houghton Mifflin Harcourt Publishing Co.

Metz, Melinda. S. M. A. R. T. S. & the Invisible Robot. McKenzie, Heath, illus. 2015. (S. M. A. R. T. S. Ser.). (ENG.). 128p. (gr. 3-6). 22.65 *(978-1-4965-0463-0(1))* S.M.A.R.T.S. Learning System.

Meyerhoff, Jenny. Pumpkin Spice. Chatelain, Éva, illus. 2015. (Friendship Garden Ser.: 2). (ENG.). 144p. (J). (gr. 2-5). pap. 5.99 *(978-1-4814-3909-1(X)*, Aladdin) Simon & Schuster Children's Publishing.

—Pumpkin Spice. 2015. (Friendship Garden Ser.: 2). lib. bdg. 16.00 *(978-0-606-37833-8(2))* Turtleback Bks.

Montgomery-Higham, Amanda. Max & the Doglins. 2007. (Child's Play Library). (ENG., Illus.). 32p. (J). (gr. 2-3). pap. *(978-1-84643-043-5(7))* Child's Play International Ltd.

Montgomery, Lewis B. The Case of the Locked Box. Wummer, Amy, illus. 2013. (ENG.). (J). (gr. 2-4). (Milo & Jazz Mysteries (r) Ser.: Vol. 11). 112p. pap. 6.95 *(978-1-57565-626-7(4))*; (Milo & Jazz Mysteries Ser.: Vol. 11). 106p. lib. bdg. 22.60 *(978-1-57565-625-0(6))* Kane Press, Inc.

Murphy, Bonnie S. The Puzzle Piece Thief. 2010. 28p. pap. 15.99 *(978-1-4500-2649-9(4))* Xlibris Corp.

Ofelia, Dumas Lachtman. Big Enough Bastante Grande. Enrique, Sanchez, illus. 2008. 32p. (J). pap. 7.95 *(978-1-55885-239-6(5))* Arte Publico Pr.

Oldfield, Jenny. Crazy Horse. 2009. (Horses of Half Moon Ranch Ser.: 3). (ENG.). 160p. (J). (gr. 4-7). pap. 9.99 *(978-1-4022-1702-9(1)*, Sourcebooks Jabberwocky) Sourcebooks, Inc.

Olin, Sean. Reckless Hearts. 2015. (Wicked Games Ser.: 2). (ENG.). 336p. (YA). (gr. 9). 17.99 *(978-0-06-219241-7(8)*, Tegen, Katherine Bks) HarperCollins Pubs.

Oliver, Andrew. Scrambled. 2007. 288p. (J). per. 12.95 *(978-0-9661009-8-3(0))* Adams-Pomeroy Pr.

Oliver Optic. Poor & Proud: Or the Fortunes of Katy Redburn: a Story for Young. l.t. ed. 2007. 444p. pap. 21.99 *(978-1-4264-9954-8(X))* Creative Media Partners, LLC.

O'Reilly, Sean. The Monster Crooks, 1 vol. 2011. (Mighty Mighty Monsters Ser.). (ENG.). 48p. (gr. 2-3). lib. bdg. 23.99 *(978-1-4342-3216-8(6))* Stone Arch Bks.

—The Monster Crooks, 1 vol. Arcana Studio Staff, illus. 2012. (Mighty Mighty Monsters Ser.). (ENG.). 48p. (gr. 2-3). pap. 6.10 *(978-1-4342-4610-3(8))* Stone Arch Bks.

—The Toy Snatcher, 1 vol. Arcana Studio Staff, illus. 2012. (Mighty Mighty Monsters Ser.). (ENG.). 48p. (gr. 2-3). pap. 6.10 *(978-1-4342-4612-7(4))* Stone Arch Bks.

Ott, Alexandra. Rules for Thieves. 2017. (Rules for Thieves Ser.: 1). (ENG., Illus.). 320p. (J). (gr. 3-7). 17.99 ***(978-1-4814-7274-6(7)***, Aladdin) Simon & Schuster Children's Publishing.

—Rules for Thieves. 2017. (J). pap. ***(978-1-4814-7275-3(5)***, Simon & Schuster/Paula Wiseman Bks.) Simon & Schuster/Paula Wiseman Bks.

Padma, T. V. The Cleverest Thief. 2008. (Story Cove Ser.). (ENG., Illus.). 32p. (J). (gr. -1-3). pap. 4.95 *(978-0-87483-882-4(7))* August Hse. Pubs., Inc.

Papp, Robert, illus. Monkey Trouble. 2011. (Boxcar Children Mysteries Ser.: 127). (ENG.). 128p. (J). (gr. 1-5). pap. 5.99 *(978-0-8075-5240-7(2))* Whitman, Albert & Co.

Park, Barbara. Junie B. Jones Is Not a Crook. unabr. ed. 2004. (Junie B. Jones Ser.: No. 9). 67p. (J). (gr. k-3). pap. 17.00 incl. audio *(978-0-8072-0530-3(3)*, Listening Library) Random Hse. Audio Publishing Group.

Pearce, Margaret. Jumping into Trouble Book 3: Missing! a Horse. 2013. 66p. pap. *(978-1-922066-61-9(3))* Writers Exchange E-Publishing.

Pearson, Carol Lynn. A Christmas Thief. 2008. 80p. 12.99 *(978-1-59955-184-5(5))* Cedar Fort, Inc./CFI Distribution.

Peck, Robert Newton. Horse Thief. 2003. 277p. (YA). (gr. 7). 13.65 *(978-0-7569-1461-5(2))* Perfection Learning Corp.

Pennypacker, Sara & Brown, Jeff. The Great Egyptian Grave Robbery. Pamintuan, Macky, illus. 2009. (Flat Stanley's Worldwide Adventures Ser.: 2). (ENG.). 96p. (J). (gr. 2-5). pap. 4.99 *(978-0-06-142992-7(9))* HarperCollins Pubs.

—The Great Egyptian Grave Robbery No. 2. Pamintuan, Macky, illus. 2009. (Flat Stanley's Worldwide Adventures Ser.: 2). (ENG.). 96p. (J). (gr. 2-5). 15.99 *(978-0-06-142993-4(7))* HarperCollins Pubs.

Perelman, Helen. Taffy Trouble. Waters, Erica-Jane, illus. 2015. (Candy Fairies Ser.: 16). (ENG.). 128p. (J). (gr. -1-5). pap. 5.99 *(978-1-4814-0613-0(2)*, Aladdin) Simon & Schuster Children's Publishing.

Phillips, Dee. Joyride, 1 vol. unabr. ed. 2011. (Right Now! Ser.). (ENG., Illus.). 45p. (YA). (gr. 9-12). pap. 8.95 *(978-1-61651-251-4(2))* Saddleback Educational Publishing, Inc.

Pick, Alice. Jamey's Promise, 1 vol. 2009. 61p. pap. 19.95 *(978-1-61582-547-9(9))* America Star Bks.

Polak, Monique. Home Invasion. 2006. (Orca Soundings Ser.). 105p. (gr. 7-11). 19.95 *(978-0-7569-6871-7(2))* Perfection Learning Corp.

Ponti, James. Framed! 2016. (Framed! Ser.: 1). (ENG., Illus.). 304p. (J). (gr. 3-7). 17.99 *(978-1-4814-3630-4(9)*, Aladdin) Simon & Schuster Children's Publishing.

Pratcher, Roger & Pratcher, Birgit. June Bear Adventures: The Missing Pies. 2007. 236p. per. 11.95 *(978-1-4327-0352-3(8))* Outskirts Pr., Inc.

Preller, James. Jigsaw Jones: The Case of the Smelly Sneaker. 2017. (Jigsaw Jones Mysteries Ser.). (ENG.). 96p. (J). pap. 4.99 *(978-1-250-11080-0(7)*, 9781250110800) Feiwel & Friends.

Prineas, Sarah. The Magic Thief. Caparo, Antonio Javier, illus. 2008. (Magic Thief Ser.: 1). (ENG.). 432p. (J). (gr. 5-9). 16.99 *(978-0-06-137587-3(X))* HarperCollins Pubs.

Quinn, Spencer, pseud. ARF - A Bowser & Birdie Novel. 2016. (ENG.). 304p. (J). (gr. 3-7). 16.99 *(978-0-545-64334-4(1)*, Scholastic Pr.) Scholastic, Inc.

—Woof. (Bowser & Birdie Mystery Ser.). (ENG.). 304p. (J). (gr. 3-7). 2016. pap. 7.99 *(978-0-545-64332-0(5))* 2015. 16.99 *(978-0-545-64331-3(7)*, Scholastic Pr.) Scholastic, Inc.

—Woof. 2016. lib. bdg. 18.40 *(978-0-606-39011-8(1))* Turtleback Bks.

Rabley, Stephen. Marcel & Mona Lisa Book, Pack. 2nd ed. 2016. (ENG., Illus.). 16p. pap. 14.65 incl. audio compact disk ***(978-1-4058-8064-0(3))*** Pearson Education.

Random House. The Great Train Mystery. 2013. (Spongebob Squarepants Step into Reading Ser.). lib. bdg. 13.55 *(978-0-606-35116-4(7))* Turtleback Bks.

Random House Staff. The Great Train Mystery (SpongeBob SquarePants) Random House Staff, illus. 2013. (Step into Reading Ser.). (ENG., Illus.). 32p. (J). (gr. -1-1). pap. 3.99 *(978-0-449-81441-3(6)*, Random Hse. Bks. for Young Readers) Random Hse. Children's Bks.

Rankine-Van Wassenhoven, Jacqueline. Who Stole Grandpa's Teeth? 2008. 20p. 10.94 *(978-1-4357-0522-7(X))* Lulu Pr., Inc.

Redbank, Tennant. The Beach Bandit. 2016. (Barbie Chapters Ser.). (ENG., Illus.). 64p. (J). (gr. 1-4). lib. bdg. 12.99 *(978-0-375-97413-7(X)*, Random Hse. Bks. for Young Readers) Random Hse. Children's Bks.

Richardson, E. E. The Curse Box. 2013. (ENG.). 64p. (YA). (gr. 6-12). pap. 6.95 *(978-1-78112-176-4(1))*; lib. bdg. 22.60 *(978-1-78112-175-7(3))* Lerner Publishing Group.

Rinaldi, Ann. An Acquaintance with Darkness. 2005. (Great Episodes Ser.). 374p. (gr. 7-12). 18.00 *(978-0-7569-5040-8(6))* Perfection Learning Corp.

Robins, Eleanor. Aztec Ring Mystery, 1 vol. unabr. ed. 2011. (Carter High Mysteries Ser.). (ENG.). 46p. (YA). (gr. 9-12). 7.95 *(978-1-61651-561-4(9))* Saddleback Educational Publishing, Inc.

—Drama Club Mystery, 1 vol. unabr. ed. 2011. (Carter High Mysteries Ser.). (ENG.). 47p. (YA). (gr. 9-12). 7.95 *(978-1-61651-562-1(7))* Saddleback Educational Publishing, Inc.

Rogers, Bud & Martin, Gary. The Witch of Endor, 1 vol. Cariello, Sergio, illus. 2008. (Z Graphic Novels / Son of Samson Ser.). (ENG.). 160p. (J). pap. 6.99 *(978-0-310-71283-1(1))* Zonderkidz.

Rowley, M'lin. Knights of Right, BK 4: The Fiery Gloves. 2010. 80p. (J). pap. 6.99 *(978-1-60641-241-1(8)*, Shadow Mountain) Shadow Mountain Publishing.

Roy, Ron. The Missing Mummy. (A to Z Mystery Ser.: Vol. 13). (J). 11.32 *(978-0-7383-3465-3(0))* Booksource, The.

—Mystery at the Washington Monument. Bush, Timothy, illus. 2007. (Capital Mysteries Ser.: No. 8). 87p. (gr. 1-4). 15.00 *(978-0-7569-7845-7(9))* Perfection Learning Corp.

—September Sneakers. 2013. (Calendar Mysteries Ser.: 9). lib. bdg. 14.75 *(978-0-606-32231-7(0)*, Turtleback) Turtleback Bks.

—A Thief at the National Zoo. Bush, Timothy, illus. 2008. (Capital Mysteries Ser.: No. 9). 87p. (gr. k-3). 15.00 *(978-0-7569-8329-1(0))* Perfection Learning Corp.

—A Thief at the National Zoo. Bush, Timothy, illus. 2007. (Capital Mysteries Ser.: No. 9). (ENG.). 96p. (J). (gr. 1-4). per. 4.99 *(978-0-375-84804-9(5)*, Random Hse. Bks. for Young Readers) Random Hse. Children's Bks.

—Trouble at the Treasury. Bush, Timothy, illus. 2006. (Capital Mysteries Ser.: No. 7). (ENG.). 96p. (J). (gr. 1-4). per. 4.99 *(978-0-375-83969-6(0)*, Random Hse. Bks. for Young Readers) Random Hse. Children's Bks.

Ryan, Carrie & Davis, John Parke. The Map to Everywhere. 2014. (Map to Everywhere Ser.: Bk. 1). (ENG., Illus.). 448p. (J). (gr. 3-7). 17.00 *(978-0-316-24077-2(X))* Little Brown & Co.

Santopolo, Jill. The Nina, the Pinta, & the Vanishing Treasure. 2009. (Alec Flint Mystery Ser.: 1). (ENG.). 192p. (J). (gr. 2-5). pap. 6.99 *(978-0-439-90353-0(X)*, Scholastic Paperbacks) Scholastic, Inc.

Schraff, Anne. Like a Broken Doll. 2011. (Urban Underground — Harriet Tubman High School Ser.). (YA). lib. bdg. 20.80 *(978-0-606-14799-6(3)*, Turtleback) Turtleback Bks.

—Stolen Treasure. 2014. (Red Rhino Ser.). (J). lib. bdg. 18.40 *(978-0-606-36203-0(7))* Turtleback Bks.

Scott, Elizabeth. Stealing Heaven. 2009. (ENG.). 336p. (YA). (gr. 8). pap. 8.99 *(978-0-06-112282-8(3)*, HarperTeen) HarperCollins Pubs.

Shepard, Sara. Crushed. 2014. (Pretty Little Liars Ser.: 13). (ENG.). 368p. (YA). (gr. 9). pap. 10.99 *(978-0-06-219972-0(2)*, HarperTeen) HarperCollins Pubs.

Skead, Robert. Elves Can't Kick. 2005. 84p. per. 7.99 *(978-1-929478-66-8(6))* Cross Training Publishing.

Snicket, Lemony, pseud. Who Could That Be at This Hour? Seth, illus. (All the Wrong Questions Ser.: 1). (ENG.). (J). (gr. 3-17). 2014. 288p. pap. 7.99 *(978-0-316-33547-8(9))* 2012. 272p. 15.99 *(978-0-316-12308-2(0))* Little, Brown Bks. for Young Readers.

Snicket, Lemony, pseud & Seth. Who Could That Be at This Hour? 2012. *(978-0-316-24771-9(5))* Little Brown & Co.

Song, Amira. Horse Lovers Forever. 2012. 64p. pap. *(978-1-4602-0144-2(2))* FriesenPress.

Sonneborn, Scott. The Computer Meltdown. Lozano, Omar, illus. 2015. (North Police Ser.). (ENG.). 32p. (gr. k-2). lib. bdg. 21.32 *(978-1-4795-6485-9(0))* Picture Window Bks.

Spector, Baron. Tracking Your Nightmare, 1 vol. Kneupper, Setch, illus. 2012. (Graveyard Diaries Ser.). (ENG.). 128p. (J). (gr. 3-8). lib. bdg. 27.07 *(978-1-61641-898-4(2)*, Calico Chapter Bks) Magic Wagon.

Spencer, Katherine. More Than Friends: A Saving Grace Novel. 2008. (Saving Grace Ser.). (ENG., Illus.). 224p. (YA). (gr. 7-12). pap. 14.95 *(978-0-15-205746-6(3))* Houghton Mifflin Harcourt Publishing Co.

Stephens, Sarah Hines. Catwoman's Purrfect Plot. Vecchio, Luciano, illus. 2017. (Batman & Robin Adventures Ser.). (ENG.). 88p. (gr. 2-3). lib. bdg. 26.65 ***(978-1-4965-5349-2(7)***, DC Super Heroes) Stone Arch Bks.

Stevenson, Steve. The Crown of Venice, No. 7. Turconi, Stefano, illus. 2014. (Agatha: Girl of Mystery Ser.: 7). (ENG.). 144p. (J). (gr. 2-5). 5.99 *(978-0-448-46225-7(7)*, Grosset & Dunlap) Penguin Young Readers Group.

—The Crown of Venice. 2014. (Agatha Girl of Mystery Ser.: 7). lib. bdg. 16.00 *(978-0-606-36164-4(2))* Turtleback Bks.

Stilton, Geronimo. Don't Wake the Dinosaur! 2014. (Geronimo Stilton Cavemice Ser.: 6). (ENG.). 128p. (J). (gr. 2-5). pap. 7.99 *(978-0-545-65603-0(6)*, Scholastic Paperbacks) Scholastic, Inc.

—Don't Wake the Dinosaur! 2014. (Geronimo Stilton Cavemice Ser.: 6). lib. bdg. 18.40 *(978-0-606-36057-9(3))* Turtleback Bks.

Stilton, Geronimo & Stilton, Thea. Thea Stilton & the Mystery in Paris. 2010. (Thea Stilton Ser.: 5). (ENG.). 176p. (J). (gr. 2-5). pap. 8.99 *(978-0-545-22773-5(9)*, Scholastic Paperbacks) Scholastic, Inc.

Stilton, Thea. Thea Stilton & the Blue Scarab Hunt. 2012. (Thea Stilton Ser.: 11). lib. bdg. 19.65 *(978-0-606-26183-8(4)*, Turtleback) Turtleback Bks.

—Thea Stilton & the Hollywood Hoax. 2016. (Thea Stilton Ser.: 23). lib. bdg. 18.40 *(978-0-606-38799-6(4))* Turtleback Bks.

—Thea Stilton & the Prince's Emerald. 2012. (Thea Stilton Ser.: 12). lib. bdg. 19.65 *(978-0-606-26534-8(1)*, Turtleback) Turtleback Bks.

Summy, Barrie. I So Don't Do Famous. 2012. (ENG.). 304p. (J). (gr. 5). 7.99 *(978-0-385-73791-3(2)*, Yearling) Random Hse. Children's Bks.

Taylor, Joseph. Allison Investigates. 2009. 202p. pap. 12.95 *(978-0-9815894-1-1(3))* Four Star Publishing.

Terrell, Brandon. The Vanishing Treasure. Epelbaum, Mariano, illus. 2017. (Snoops, Inc Ser.). (ENG.). 112p. (gr. 4-6). lib. bdg. 26.65 *(978-1-4965-4345-5(9))* Stone Arch Bks.

Titus, Eve. Basil in Mexico. Galdone, Paul, illus. 2016. (Great Mouse Detective Ser.: 3). (ENG.). 112p. (J). (gr. 1-4). pap. 5.99 *(978-1-4814-6407-9(8)*, Aladdin) Simon & Schuster Children's Publishing.

Toliver, Wendy. Lifted. 2010. (ENG.). 352p. (YA). (gr. 9-18). pap. 9.99 *(978-1-4169-9048-2(8)*, Simon Pulse) Simon Pulse.

Top Ten Clues You're Clueless. 2014. (ENG.). 304p. (YA). (gr. 8). pap. 9.99 *(978-0-06-227242-3(X))* HarperCollins Pubs.

Tosten, S. Kennedy. Troy's Amazing Universe Bk. 2: T for Toy. 2004. (Illus.). 149p. (YA). (gr. 2-18). pap. 13.95 *(978-0-9743185-1-6(5))* Brite Pr.

Umansky, Kaye. Solomon Snow & the Stolen Jewel. Nash, Scott, illus. 2007. (ENG.). 256p. (J). (gr. 2-5). 12.99 *(978-0-7636-2793-5(3))* Candlewick Pr.

Vernon, Ursula. The Case of the Toxic Mutants. 2013. (Dragonbreath Ser.: 9). (ENG., Illus.). 208p. (J). (gr. 3-7). 12.99 *(978-0-8037-3847-8(1)*, Dial Bks) Penguin Young Readers Group.

Vicente, Alidis. The Missing Chancleta & Other Top-Secret Cases / la Chancleta Perdida y Otros Casos Secretos. 2013. (SPA & ENG., Illus.). 64p. (J). pap. 9.95 *(978-1-55885-779-7(6)*, Piñata Books) Arte Publico Pr.

Wallace, Karen. Diamond Takers. 2007. (Lady Violet Mysteries Ser.: 3). (ENG.). 240p. (J). (gr. 4-7). pap. 9.95 *(978-1-4169-0100-6(0)*, Simon & Schuster Children's) Simon & Schuster, Ltd. GBR. Dist: Simon & Schuster, Inc.

Wallace, Nancy K. Presumed Missing, 1 vol. Chronister, Amanda, illus. 2013. (Abby & the Book Bunch Ser.). (ENG.). 80p. (J). (gr. 2-5). 27.07 *(978-1-61641-917-2(2))* Magic Wagon.

Watson, Jude. Sting. 2016. (ENG.). 272p. (J). (gr. 3-7). 16.99 *(978-0-545-86346-9(5)*, Scholastic Pr.) Scholastic, Inc.

Wells, Marcia. Doom at Grant's Tomb. Calo, Marcos, illus. 2017. (Eddie Red Undercover Ser.: 3). (ENG.). (J). (gr. 5-7). lib. bdg. 17.20 ***(978-0-606-39813-8(9))*** Turtleback Bks.

—Mystery in Mayan Mexico. Calo, Marcos, illus. 2016. (Eddie Red Undercover Ser.: 2). (ENG.). 224p. (J). (gr. 5-7). pap. 7.99 *(978-0-544-66850-8(2)*, HMH Books For Young Readers) Houghton Mifflin Harcourt Publishing Co.

—Mystery on Museum Mile. Calo, Marcos, illus. 2014. (Eddie Red Undercover Ser.: 1). (ENG.). 256p. (J). (gr. 5-7). 16.99 *(978-0-544-23833-6(8)*, HMH Books For Young Readers) Houghton Mifflin Harcourt Publishing Co.

West, Tracey. Secret of the Water Dragon. Howells, Graham & Jones, Damien, illus. 2015. (Dragon Masters Ser.: 3). (ENG.). 96p. (J). (gr. 1-3). pap. 4.99 *(978-0-545-64628-4(6))* Scholastic, Inc.

White, Paul. Jungle Doctor in Slippery Places. 2011. (Flamingo Fiction 9-13s Ser.). (ENG., Illus.). 160p. (J). (gr. 4-7). pap. 8.99 *(978-1-84550-298-0(1)*, ad8bbad9-6595-4aeb-8c4f-f089b189b088) Christian Focus Pubns. GBR. Dist: Bookmasters Distribution.

Widmark, Martin. The Diamond Mystery, No. 1. Willis, Helena, illus. 2014. (Whodunit Detective Agency Ser.: 1). (ENG.). 80p. (J). (gr. 2-4). 5.99 *(978-0-448-48066-4(2)*, Grosset & Dunlap) Penguin Young Readers Group.

Woodson, Marion. Dinosaur Fever. 2008. (ENG.). 160p. (J). (gr. 4). pap. 11.99 *(978-1-55002-690-0(9)*, Sandcastle Bks.) Dundurn CAN. Dist: Ingram Publisher Services.

Yee, Paul. Shu-Li & Tamara, 1 vol. Wang, Shaoli, illus. 2008. (ENG.). 72p. (J). (gr. 1-4). per. 7.95 *(978-1-896580-93-7(9))* Tradewind Bks. CAN. Dist: Orca Bk. Pubs. USA.

THEOLOGY

see also Baptism; Christianity; Church; Ethics; Faith; God; Jesus Christ; Religion; Religion and Science; Spiritual Life; Worship

Arbo, Barbara. Scriptures for Kids. Ross, Melissa, illus. 2013. 24p. 19.95 *(978-1-61633-402-4(9))*; pap. 10.95 *(978-1-61633-403-1(7))* Guardian Angel Publishing, Inc.

Berlatsky, Noah. The Catholic Church. 2010. (Opposing Viewpoints Ser.). (ENG.). 240p. 42.95 *(978-0-7377-5104-8(5))*; 224p. (gr. 10-12). pap. 33.80 *(978-0-7377-5105-5(3))* Cengage Gale. (Greenhaven Pr., Inc.).

Colkmire, Lance. Know It, Live It: Helping Kids Embrace Pentecostal Teachings. 2004. (Illus.). (J). per. 9.99 *(978-0-87148-468-0(4))* Pathway Pr.

Crompton, Samuel Willard. Emanuel Swedenborg. 2004. (Spiritual Leaders & Thinkers Ser.). (Illus.). 120p. (J). (gr. 9-13). 30.00 *(978-0-7910-8102-0(8)*, Chelsea Hse.) Facts On File, Inc.

TUV

Dant, Jennifer. Everybody Is Important: A Kids' Guide to Our Seven Principles. 2010. (J). pap. 6.00 (978-1-55896-564-5(5), Skinner Hse. Bks.) Unitarian Universalist Assn.
Davenport, Jeff. God Is Really, Really Real: 30 Easily Taught Bible Doctrines. Looney, Bill, illus. 2015. (ENG.). 96p. (J). 15.99 (978-0-89221-738-0(3)) New Leaf Pub. Group.
Discover 1 John. (Discover Your Bible Ser.). (KOR.). (J). pap., stu. ed. 2.75 (978-1-55883-240-4(8), 600220) C R C World Literature Ministries/Libros Desafio.
Una Historia Que no Cesa, 2 vols. 2003. (SPA., Illus.). 240p. (YA). 24.95 (978-0-915741-18-2(0)) Stampley, C. D. Enterprises, Inc.
Is There Really a God? 2003. (BUL.). (YA). 0.75 (978-1-893345-14-0(9)) Answers in Genesis Ministries.
Meade, Starr. Mighty Acts of God: A Family Bible Story Book. O'Connor, Tim, illus. 2010. 288p. (J). 24.99 (978-1-4335-0604-8(1)) Crossway.
Mudge, Michael. Spiritual Warfare Basic Training. 2012. 44p. pap. 21.99 (978-1-4772-8539-8(3)) AuthorHouse.
Peckham, Lori, ed. Guide's Greatest Grace Stories. 2008. 160p. pap. 11.99 (978-0-8280-2390-0(5)) Review & Herald Publishing Assn.
Pierce, Seth J. What We Believe for Teens. 2007. (J). pap. 11.99 (978-0-8163-2213-8(9)) Pacific Pr. Publishing Assn.
Reynolds, Ralph V. Dividing the Word of Truth. 193p. (YA). (gr. 9). pap. 14.95 (978-1-877917-08-0(7)) Alpha Bible Pubns.
—Usando Bien la Palabra de Verdad. Geissler, Darry & Geissler, Kimberly, eds. Crossley, Darry, tr. (SPA.). 220p. (Orig.). (YA). pap. 14.95 (978-1-877917-12-7(5)) Alpha Bible Pubns.
Shewan, Edward. Manual of Christian Doctrine, Answer Key. 2004. pap. 3.95 (978-1-930367-99-9(6), CLP10091) Christian Liberty Pr.
Strobel, Lee. Case for Grace for Kids, 1 vol. 2015. (ENG., Illus.). 176p. (J). pap. 7.99 (978-0-310-73656-1(0)) Zonderkidz.
Thomas, Jerry D. & Thomas, Kitty. Step by Step: Helping Children Understand the Principles of Steps to Christ. 2008. (J). pap. 11.99 (978-0-8163-2277-0(5)) Pacific Pr. Publishing Assn.
Through Christ Our Lord. (YA). (gr. 9-12). 19.00 (978-1-931555-42-5(7)) Our Lady of Victory Schl.
Tyner, Stuart. The Meanest Man in the Army: And Other Stories of Grace. 2014. (ENG.). (J). pap. 12.99 (978-0-8280-2729-8(3)) Review & Herald Publishing Assn.

THEOLOGY, DEVOTIONAL
see Prayers

THEORETICAL CHEMISTRY
see Chemistry, Physical and Theoretical

THEORY OF NUMBERS
see Number Theory

THEORY OF SETS
see Set Theory

THEOTOCOPULI, DOMINICO, CALLED EL GRECO, 1541?-1614
see Greco, 1541?-1614

THERESE, DE LISIEUX, SAINT, 1873-1897
Glavich, Mary Kathleen. Saint Therese of Lisieux: The Way of Love. Esquinaldo, Virginia, tr. Esquinaldo, Virginia, illus. 2003. (Encounter the Saints Ser.). 132p. (J). pap. 5.95 (978-0-8198-7074-2(9), 332-370) Pauline Bks. & Media.
Monahan, Joan. St. Therese of Lisieux: Missionary of Love. 2003. (Illus.). 144p. 9.95 (978-0-8091-6710-4(7), 6710-7) Paulist Pr.

THERMODYNAMICS
see also Heat; Quantum Theory
Berne, Emma Carlson. Hot! Heat Energy. 2013. (Energy Everywhere Ser.). (ENG., Illus.). 24p. (J). (gr. 3-6). pap. 8.25 (978-1-4488-9752-0(1)); lib. bdg. 22.60 (978-1-4488-9647-9(9)) Rosen Publishing Group, Inc., The. (PowerKids Pr.).
Jennings, Terry J. Hot & Cold. 2009. (J). 28.50 (978-1-59920-274-7(3)) Black Rabbit Bks.
Lawrence, Ellen. Heat. 2016. (FUN-Damental Experiments Ser.). (ENG., Illus.). 24p. (J). (gr. -1-3). 17.95 (978-1-943553-19-8(X)) Bearport Publishing Co., Inc.
Lindeen, Mary. Hot & Cold. 2017. (BeginningtoRead Ser.). (ENG.). 32p. (J). (-2). 22.60 **(978-1-59953-883-9(0))**; pap. 11.94 **(978-1-68404-102-2(3))** Norwood Hse. Pr.
Magloff, Lisa. Experiments with Heat & Energy. 2010. (Cool Science Ser.). 32p. (J). (gr. 5-6). lib. bdg. 28.00 (978-1-4339-3450-6(7)); (Illus.). pap. 10.50 (978-1-4339-3451-3(5)) Stevens, Gareth Publishing LLLP. (Gareth Stevens Learning Library).
McPartland, Randall. Understanding the Laws of Thermodynamics. 2015. (J). lib. bdg. (978-1-62713-429-3(8)) Cavendish Square Publishing.
Rivera, Sheila. Heating. 2007. (First Step Nonfiction - Changing Matter Ser.). (ENG., Illus.). 8p. (gr. -1-1). pap. 4.95 (978-0-8225-6415-7(7)) Lerner Publishing Group.
Steinberg, Lynnae D. What Is Heat Energy? 2017. (Let's Find Out! Forms of Energy Ser.). 32p. (J). (gr. 6-8). pap. 12.90 **(978-1-68048-701-5(9)**, Britannica Educational Publishing) Rosen Publishing Group, Inc., The.
Thomas, Isabel. Experiments with Heating & Cooling. 2015. (Read & Experiment Ser.). (ENG., Illus.). 32p. (gr. 2-4). 30.65 (978-1-4109-6839-5(1), Raintree Perspectives) Heinemann-Raintree.

THERMOMETERS
see also Temperature
Doudna, Kelly. If You Prefer, I'll Use a Thermometer!, 1 vol. 2007. (Science Made Simple Ser.). (ENG., Illus.). 24p. (J). (gr. k-3). lib. bdg. 24.21 (978-1-59928-594-8(0), SandCastle) ABDO Publishing Co.
Hanson, Anders. Meteorologist's Tools, 1 vol. 2011. (Professional Tools Ser.). (ENG., Illus.). 24p. (J). (gr. 3-5). lib. bdg. 25.65 (978-1-61613-580-5(8), Super SandCastle) ABDO Publishing Co.
Johnson, Robin. What Is Temperature? 2012. (ENG.). 24p. (J). (978-0-7787-0755-4(5)); (Illus.). pap. (978-0-7787-0762-2(8)) Crabtree Publishing Co.
Lin, Yoming S. Fahrenheit, Celsius, & Their Temperature Scales. 2012. (Eureka! Ser.). (Illus.). 24p. (YA). (gr. 3-6). lib. bdg. 22.60 (978-1-4488-5035-8(5)) Rosen Publishing Group, Inc., The.
Lipschultz, Wes. Is It Hot or Cold? Learning to Use a Thermometer. 2009. (Math for the REAL World Ser.). 12p. (gr. 1-2). pap. 5.90 (978-0-8239-8848-8(1), Rosen Classroom) Rosen Publishing Group, Inc., The.
Metz, Lorijo. Using Thermometers. 2013. (Science Tools Ser.). (ENG., Illus.). 24p. (J). (gr. 3-6). 22.60 (978-1-4488-9684-4(3)); pap. 8.25 (978-1-4488-9826-8(9)) Rosen Publishing Group, Inc., The. (PowerKids Pr.).
Rivera, Sheila. Thermometer. 2006. (First Step Nonfiction - Simple Tools Ser.). (ENG., Illus.). 8p. (gr. -1-1). pap. 4.95 (978-0-8225-5711-1(8), Lerner Pubns.) Lerner Publishing Group.
Roberts, Abigail B. Using a Thermometer. 2017. (Super Science Tools Ser.). 24p. (gr. 1-2). pap. 48.90 **(978-1-4824-6410-8(1))** Stevens, Gareth Publishing LLLP.
Sullivan, Navin. Temperature. 2006. (Measure Up! Ser.). (Illus.). 48p. (gr. 4-7). lib. bdg. 31.36 (978-0-7614-2322-5(2), Benchmark Bks.) Marshall Cavendish Corp.
Webb, Barbara L. Hot or Cold? 2012. (ENG.). 24p. (gr. -1-1). pap. 8.95 (978-1-61810-202-7(8)) Rourke Educational Media.

THERMOMETERS AND THERMOMETRY
see Temperature Measurements; Thermometers

THERMOPOLIS, MIA (FICTITIOUS CHARACTER)—FICTION
Cabot, Meg. In Waiting. 2008. (Princess Diaries: 4). (ENG.). 256p. (YA). (gr. 8). pap. 9.99 (978-0-06-154364-7(0), HarperTeen) HarperCollins Pubs.
—The Princess Diaries. 2008. (Princess Diaries: 1). (ENG.). 256p. (YA). (gr. 8). pap. 9.99 (978-0-06-147993-9(4))Vols. 1-3. Set. 2006. (Princess Diaries: Vol. I). (J). pap., pap. 19.99 (978-0-06-115389-1(3)) HarperCollins Pubs. (HarperTeen).
—The Princess Diaries. 2008. 20.00 (978-0-7569-8793-0(8)) Perfection Learning Corp.
—The Princess Diaries. unabr. ed. 2004. (Princess Diaries: Vol. I). 240p. (J). (gr. 7-18). pap. 38.00 incl. audio (978-0-8072-0669-0(5), Listening Library) Random Hse. Audio Publishing Group.
—The Princess Diaries. 2008. (Princess Diaries: 1). (YA). lib. bdg. 20.85 (978-1-4178-2328-4(3), Turtleback) Turtleback Bks.
—The Princess Diaries Box Set: The Princess Diaries; Princess in the Spotlight; Princess in Love. 2003. (Princess Diaries). 304p. (gr. 7-18). pap. 19.99 (978-0-06-058745-1(8)) HarperCollins Pubs.

THESEUS (GREEK MYTHOLOGY)
Davis, Graeme. Theseus & the Maze of the Minotaur. 2015. (Heroes & Legends Ser.). (ENG., Illus.). 80p. (J). (gr. 7-8). 35.60 (978-1-4994-6178-7(X), Rosen Young Adult) Rosen Publishing Group, Inc., The.
Ehrmann, Johanna. Theseus & the Minotaur, 1 vol., 1. 2014. (Jr. Graphic Myths: Greek Heroes Ser.). (ENG.). 24p. (J). (gr. 3-6). 26.25 (978-1-4777-6236-3(1), PowerKids Pr.) Rosen Publishing Group, Inc., The.
Hoena, B. A. Theseus & the Minotaur: A Graphic Retelling. 2015. (Ancient Myths Ser.). (ENG., Illus.). 32p. (gr. 3-4). lib. bdg. 30.65 (978-1-4914-2075-1(8), Graphic Library) Capstone Press of Coughlan Cos.
Hoena, Blake. The Quest of Theseus: An Interactive Mythological Adventure. Arcabascio, Carolyn, illus. 2017. (You Choose: Ancient Greek Myths Ser.). (ENG.). 112p. (gr. 3-4). pap. 6.95 (978-1-5157-4826-7(X), You Choose Bks.) Capstone Press of Coughlan Cos.
—The Quest of Theseus: An Interactive Mytholoical Adventure. Arcabascio, Carolyn, illus. 2017. (You Choose: Ancient Greek Myths Ser.). (ENG.). 112p. (gr. 3-4). lib. bdg. 31.99 (978-1-5157-4821-2(9)) Capstone Press of Coughlan Cos.
Jeffrey, Gary. Theseus Battles the Minotaur. 2012. (Graphic Mythical Heroes Ser.). (Illus.). 24p. (J). (gr. 3-5). pap. 8.15 (978-1-4339-7528-8(9)); lib. bdg. 23.95 (978-1-4339-7527-1(0)) Stevens, Gareth Publishing LLLP.
Limke, Jeff. Theseus: Battling the Minotaur. 2009. pap. 52.95 (978-0-7613-4761-3(5)) Lerner Publishing Group.
—Theseus: Battling the Minotaur. McCrea, John, illus. (Graphic Myths & Legends Ser.). (ENG.). 48p. (gr. 4-8). 2008. pap. 8.95 (978-0-8225-8517-6(0)) 2007. (J). lib. bdg. 27.93 (978-0-8225-6756-1(3), Graphic Universe™) Lerner Publishing Group.
McCaughrean, Geraldine, retold by. Theseus. 2005. (Heroes Ser.). (ENG., Illus.). 120p. (J). (gr. 4-10). 17.95 (978-0-8126-2739-8(3)) Cricket Bks.
Nagle, Frances. The Minotaur. 2016. (Monsters! Ser.). (Illus.). 32p. (J). (gr. 2-1). pap. 10.50 (978-1-4824-4871-9(8)) Stevens, Gareth Publishing LLLP.
Tracy, Kathleen. Theseus. 2007. (Profiles in Greek & Roman Mythology Ser.). (Illus.). 48p. (YA). (gr. 4-7). lib. bdg. 29.95 (978-1-58415-554-6(X)) Mitchell Lane Pubs., Inc.

THIEVES
see Robbers and Outlaws

THINKING
see Thought and Thinking

THIRTY YEARS' WAR, 1618-1648
Roscoe, Kelly, ed. The Emergence of Modern Europe. 2017. (Power & Religion in Medieval & Renaissance Times Ser.). 112p. (gr. 14-15). 36.25 **(978-1-68048-621-6(7)**, Britannica Educational Publishing) Rosen Publishing Group, Inc., The.

THOMAS, A BECKET, SAINT, 1118?-1170
Hilliam, David. Thomas Becket: English Saint & Martyr. 2009. (Leaders of the Middle Ages Ser.). 112p. (gr. 5-8). 66.50 (978-1-61513-902-6(8), Rosen Reference) Rosen Publishing Group, Inc., The.

THOMAS, AQUINAS, SAINT, 1225?-1274
Trouvé, Marianne Lorraine. Saint Thomas Aquinas: Missionary of Truth. Morrison, Cathy, illus. 2015. 137p. (J). pap. 8.95 (978-0-8198-9026-9(X)) Pauline Bks. & Media.

THOMAS MORE, SAINT, 1478-1535
see More, Thomas, Sir, Saint, 1478-1535

THOMAS THE TANK ENGINE (FICTITIOUS CHARACTER)—FICTION
Awdry, W. Brave Little Engines (Thomas & Friends) Durk, Jim, illus. 2014. (Deluxe Paint Box Book Ser.). (ENG.). 128p. (J). (gr. -1-2). pap. 7.99 (978-0-385-38510-7(2), Golden Bks.) Random Hse. Children's Bks.
—Bust My Buffers! (Thomas & Friends) 2014. (Color Plus 1,000 Stickers Ser.). (ENG.). 64p. (J). (gr. -1-2). pap. 9.99 (978-0-385-38537-4(4), Golden Bks.) Random Hse. Children's Bks.
—A Ghost on the Track (Thomas & Friends) 2015. (Step into Reading Ser.). (ENG., Illus.). 24p. (J). (gr. -1-1). 4.99 (978-0-553-52168-9(3), Random Hse. Bks. for Young Readers) Random Hse. Children's Bks.
—Go, Go, Thomas! 2013. (Thomas & Friends 8X8 Ser.). lib. bdg. 14.75 (978-0-606-26992-6(4), Turtleback) Turtleback Bks.
—The Good Sport. Courtney, Richard, illus. 2016. 24p. (J). **(978-1-5182-1481-3(9))** Random Hse., Inc.
—Hero of the Rails. Golden Books Staff, illus. 2010. (Little Golden Book Ser.). (ENG.). 24p. (J). (gr. -1-k). 4.99 (978-0-375-85950-2(0), Golden Bks.) Random Hse. Children's Bks.
—Legend of the Lost Treasure. 2015. (Little Golden Book Ser.). (ENG., Illus.). 24p. (J). (-k). 4.99 (978-0-553-52074-3(1), Golden Bks.) Random Hse. Children's Bks.
—The Lost Crown of Sodor. 2013. (Thomas & Friends 8X8 Ser.). lib. bdg. 13.55 (978-0-606-32227-0(2), Turtleback) Turtleback Bks.
—The Lost Ship. Courtney, Richard, illus. 2015. (Step into Reading Ser.). (ENG.). 32p. (J). (gr. -1-1). 3.99 (978-0-553-52171-9(3), Random Hse. Bks. for Young Readers) Random Hse. Children's Bks.
—Not So Fast, Bash & Dash! 2013. (Thomas & Friends Step into Reading Ser.). lib. bdg. 13.55 (978-0-606-32228-7(0), Turtleback) Turtleback Bks.
—Ride the Rails with Thomas (Thomas & Friends) Stubbs, Tommy, illus. 2015. (Pictureback(R) Ser.). (ENG.). 24p. (J). (gr. -1-2). 5.99 (978-0-385-38538-1(2), Random Hse. Bks. for Young Readers) Random Hse. Children's Bks.
—The Rocket Returns. 2014. (Thomas & Friends Step into Reading Ser.). lib. bdg. 13.55 (978-0-606-35207-9(4)) Turtleback Bks.
—Runaway Engine! Stubbs, Tommy, illus. 2011. (Pictureback(R) Ser.). (ENG.). 16p. (J). (gr. -1-2). pap. 4.99 (978-0-375-87253-2(1), Random Hse. Bks. for Young Readers) Random Hse. Children's Bks.
—Santa's Little Engine. 2014. (Thomas & Friends Step into Reading Ser.). lib. bdg. 13.55 (978-0-606-36014-2(X)) Turtleback Bks.
—Secret of the Green Engine. 2012. (Thomas & Friends Step into Reading Ser.). lib. bdg. 13.55 (978-0-606-26804-2(9), Turtleback) Turtleback Bks.
—Sodor's Legend of the Lost Treasure. 2015. (Big Golden Book Ser.). (ENG., Illus.). 32p. (J). (gr. -1-2). 9.99 (978-0-553-52076-7(8), Golden Bks.) Random Hse. Children's Bks.
—Story Time Collection. Courtney, Richard & Stubbs, Tommy, illus. 2014. (ENG.). 320p. (J). (gr. -1-2). 15.99 (978-0-553-49678-9(6), Random Hse. Bks. for Young Readers) Random Hse. Children's Bks.
—Tale of the Brave. 2014. (Little Golden Book Ser.). (ENG., Illus.). 24p. (J). (-k). 4.99 (978-0-385-37916-8(1), Golden Bks.) Random Hse. Children's Bks.
—Tale of the Brave (Thomas & Friends) Stubbs, Tommy, illus. 2014. (Big Golden Book Ser.). (ENG.). 48p. (J). (gr. -1-2). 9.99 (978-0-385-37915-1(3), Golden Bks.) Random Hse. Children's Bks.
—Thomas' 123 Book. Courtney, Richard, illus. 2013. (Pictureback(R) Ser.). (ENG.). 24p. (J). (gr. -1-2). pap. 3.99 (978-0-307-98203-2(3), Random Hse. Bks. for Young Readers) Random Hse. Children's Bks.
—Thomas' 123 Book. 2013. (Thomas & Friends 8X8 Ser.). lib. bdg. 13.55 (978-0-606-26991-9(6), Turtleback) Turtleback Bks.
—Thomas & Fire Engine Flynn Book & CD (Thomas & Friends) 2016. (Pictureback(R) Ser.). (ENG., Illus.). 24p. (J). (gr. -1-2). pap. 6.99 (978-1-101-93829-4(3), Random Hse. Bks. for Young Readers) Random Hse. Children's Bks.
—Thomas & Friends: Fast Work! Storybook & Seek-And-Find Activities. Chilvers, Nigel, illus. 2016. (ENG.). 10p. (J). (gr. -1-k). bds. 10.99 (978-0-7944-3592-9(0)) Studio Fun International.
—Thomas & Friends: Movie Theater Storybook & Movie Projector. 2016. (Movie Theater Ser.: 1). (ENG.). 32p. (J). (gr. -1-1). 19.99 (978-0-7944-3705-3(2), Reader's Digest Children's Bks.) Studio Fun International.
—Thomas Comes to Breakfast. Courtney, Richard, illus. 2004. (Step into Reading Ser.). (ENG.). 32p. (J). (gr. -1-1). pap. 3.99 (978-0-375-82892-8(3), Random Hse. Bks. for Young Readers) Random Hse. Children's Bks.
—Thomas Saves Easter! Stubbs, Tommy, illus. 2013. (Glitter Board Book Ser.). (ENG.). 12p. (J). (-k). bds. 6.99 (978-0-307-98158-5(4), Golden Bks.) Random Hse. Children's Bks.
—Thomas the Tank Engine: the Very First Stories (Thomas & Friends) 2015. (ENG., Illus.). 40p. (J). (gr. -1-3). 16.99 (978-0-553-52335-5(X), Random Hse. Bks. for Young Readers) Random Hse. Children's Bks.
—Treasure on the Tracks. 2013. (Thomas & Friends Step into Reading Ser.). lib. bdg. 13.55 (978-0-606-32229-4(9), Turtleback) Turtleback Bks.
Awdry, Wilbert V. Fast Train, Slow Train (Thomas & Friends) 2014. (Big Bright & Early Board Book Ser.). (ENG., Illus.). 24p. (J). (— 1). bds. 6.99 (978-0-385-37408-8(9), Random Hse. Bks. for Young Readers) Random Hse. Children's Bks.
—Go, Go, Thomas! - Express Coming Through. Random House Staff, illus. 2013. (Pictureback(R) Ser.). (ENG.). 32p. (J). (gr. -1-2). pap. 4.99 (978-0-307-98216-2(5), Random Hse. Bks. for Young Readers) Random Hse. Children's Bks.
—King of the Railway. Golden Books Staff, illus. 2013. (Little Golden Book Ser.). (ENG.). 24p. (J). (gr. -1-1). 4.99 (978-0-449-81537-3(4), Golden Bks.) Random Hse. Children's Bks.
—My Red Railway Book Box. Stubbs, Tommy, illus. 2008. (Bright & Early Board Books(TM) Ser.). (ENG.). 96p. (J). (— 1). bds. 14.99 (978-0-375-84322-8(1), Random Hse. Bks. for Young Readers) Random Hse. Children's Bks.
—Risky Rails! 2012. (Thomas & Friends 8X8 Ser.). lib. bdg. 13.55 (978-0-606-26803-5(0), Turtleback) Turtleback Bks.
—Rolling on the Rails. Golden Books Staff, illus. 2011. (Thomas & Friends Ser.). (ENG.). 12p. (J). (gr. k — 1). bds. 8.99 (978-0-375-87304-1(X), Golden Bks.) Random Hse. Children's Bks.
—Search & Rescue! (Thomas & Friends) Random House Staff, illus. 2012. (Pictureback(R) Ser.). (ENG.). 16p. (J). (gr. -1-2). pap. 4.99 (978-0-307-93029-3(7), Random Hse. Bks. for Young Readers) Random Hse. Children's Bks.
—Tales of Discovery. Golden Books Staff, illus. 2011. (Padded Board Book Ser.). (ENG.). 30p. (J). (gr. k — 1). bds. 11.99 (978-0-375-87192-4(6), Golden Bks.) Random Hse. Children's Bks.
—Thomas & the Shark. Courtney, Richard, illus. 2013. (Step into Reading Ser.). (ENG.). 32p. (J). (gr. -1-1). pap. 3.99 (978-0-307-98200-1(9), Random Hse. Bks. for Young Readers) Random Hse. Children's Bks.
—Thomas & the Shark. 2013. (Thomas & Friends Step into Reading Ser.). lib. bdg. 13.55 (978-0-606-26996-4(7), Turtleback) Turtleback Bks.
—Thomas' Christmas Star. Durk, Jim, illus. 2013. (Color Plus Card Stock Ser.). (ENG.). 48p. (J). (gr. -1-2). pap. 3.99 (978-0-449-81880-0(2), Golden Bks.) Random Hse. Children's Bks.
—Thomas' Giant Puzzle Book (Thomas & Friends) Durk, Jim, illus. 2012. (Giant Coloring Book Ser.). (ENG.). 40p. (J). (gr. -1-2). pap. 9.99 (978-0-307-97690-1(4), Golden Bks.) Random Hse. Children's Bks.
—Thomas in Charge/Sodor's Steamworks. Random House Staff, illus. 2012. (Pictureback(R) Ser.). (ENG.). 32p. (J). (gr. -1-2). pap. 4.99 (978-0-307-93119-1(6), Random Hse. Bks. for Young Readers) Random Hse. Children's Bks.
—Up, up & Away! Golden Books Staff & Durk, Jim, illus. 2013. (Color Plus Chunky Crayons Ser.). (ENG.). 48p. (J). (gr. -1-1). pap. 3.99 (978-0-307-98199-8(1), Golden Bks.) Random Hse. Children's Bks.
Awdry, Wilbert V. & Awdry, W. Blue Train, Green Train. Stubbs, Tommy, illus. 2007. (Bright & Early Board Books(TM) Ser.). (ENG.). 24p. (J). (— 1). bds. 4.99 (978-0-375-83984-9(4), Random Hse. Bks. for Young Readers) Random Hse. Children's Bks.
—Thomas & the Hide & Seek Animals. Bell, Owain, illus. 2007. (Thomas & Friends Ser.). (ENG.). 24p. (J). (gr. -1-k). 5.99 (978-0-375-84173-6(3), Random Hse. Bks. for Young Readers) Random Hse. Children's Bks.
Awdry, Wilbert V. & Wrecks, Billy. Thomas Looks up (Thomas & Friends) Random House Staff, illus. 2012. (ENG.). 16p. (J). (gr. k-k). 7.99 (978-0-307-93092-7(0), Random Hse. Bks. for Young Readers) Random Hse. Children's Bks.
Boutavant, Marc, illus. All Aboard Train Matching Game. 2016. (ENG.). 36p. (J). (gr. -1-17). bds. 14.99 (978-1-4521-4861-8(9)) Chronicle Bks. LLC.
Feldman, Thea. Thomas & Friends: Best Day Ever! 2015. (ENG.). 12p. (J). (gr. -1-k). 15.99 (978-0-7944-3512-7(2), Reader's Digest Children's Bks.) Studio Fun International.
From Self to God. 2010. (ENG.). 140p. 21.95 (978-1-4502-2116-0(5)) iUniverse, Inc.
Golden Books. Thomas & Friends 6-Movie Coloring Collection. Durk, Jim, illus. 2016. (Jumbo Coloring Book Ser.). (ENG.). 224p. (J). (gr. -1-2). pap. 5.99 (978-1-101-94019-8(0), Golden Bks.) Random Hse. Children's Bks.
—Thomas & Friends Summer 2016. 2016. (Little Golden Book Ser.). (ENG., Illus.). 24p. (J). (-k). 4.99 (978-1-101-93756-3(4), Golden Bks.) Random Hse. Children's Bks.
—Thomas & Friends Summer 2017 Movie Big Golden Book (Thomas & Friends) Stubbs, Tommy, illus. 2017. (Big Golden Book Ser.). (ENG.). 32p. (J). (gr. -1-2). 9.99 **(978-1-5247-1662-2(6)**, Golden Bks.) Random Hse. Children's Bks.
—Thomas & the Blue Streak. 2016. (Coloring Book Ser.). (ENG., Illus.). 128p. (J). (gr. -1-2). pap. 5.99 (978-1-101-93199-8(X), Golden Bks.) Random Hse. Children's Bks.
—Thomas & the Dinosaur (Thomas & Friends) Lapadula, Thomas, illus. 2015. (Little Golden Book Ser.). (ENG.). 24p. (J). (-k). 4.99 (978-0-553-49681-9(6), Golden Bks.) Random Hse. Children's Bks.
—Thomas & the Easter Eggs (Thomas & Friends) 2016. (Little Golden Book Ser.). (ENG., Illus.). 24p. (J). (gr. -1-k). 4.99 (978-1-101-93252-0(X), Golden Bks.) Random Hse. Children's Bks.
—Thomas' No. 1 Book of Fun (Thomas & Friends) 2017. (ENG.). 80p. (J). (gr. -1-2). pap. 6.99 (978-1-5247-1437-6(2), Golden Bks.) Random Hse. Children's Bks.
—Thomas on the Moon (Thomas & Friends) 2017. (Little Golden Book Ser.). (ENG., Illus.). 24p. (J). (-k). 4.99 (978-0-399-55853-5(5), Golden Bks.) Random Hse. Children's Bks.
Golden Books Staff. Travel with Thomas. Santanach, Tino, illus. 2007. (Deluxe Coloring Book Ser.). (ENG.). 96p. (J). (gr. -1-2). pap. 3.99 (978-0-375-83953-5(4), Golden Bks.) Random Hse. Children's Bks.
Golden Books Staff, illus. Favorites: Thomas Breaks a Promise - Thomas & the Big, Big Bridge/May the Best Engine Win! 2009. (Little Golden Book Favorites Ser.). (ENG.). 80p. (J). (gr. -1-2). 7.99 (978-0-375-85554-2(8), Golden Bks.) Random Hse. Children's Bks.
Here Comes Thomas! 2015. (ENG.). 24p. (J). (gr. -1-k). 18.99 (978-0-7944-3226-3(3), Reader's Digest Children's Bks.) Studio Fun International.
Hooke, R. Schuyler & Awdry, W. Thomas & the Great Discovery. Stubbs, Tommy, illus. 2009. (Little Golden Book Ser.). (ENG.). 24p. (J). (gr. -1-2). 4.99 (978-0-375-85153-7(4), Golden Bks.) Random Hse. Children's Bks.
Phoenix International Staff, illus. Thomas & Friends(tm)I Can Drive! 2015. 12p. (J). bds. (978-1-4508-8632-1(9), 1450886329) Publications International, Ltd.
Publications International Ltd. Staff, creator. Thomas & Friends Musical Pop-up Treasury. 2007. (Thomas & Friends Ser.). (Illus.). 24p. (gr. -1). 15.98 (978-1-4127-9293-6(2)) Publications International, Ltd.
Publications International Ltd. Staff, ed. Book Block(tm) Thomas & Friends (tm) 12 Board Books. 2015. 10p. (J). 12.98 (978-1-4508-9373-2(2), 1450893732) Publications International, Ltd.

—Right on Time Rescues. 2010. 14p. (J). bds. 16.98 *(978-1-4127-1872-1(4))* Phoenix International Publications, Inc.
—Thomas & Friends: A Busy Day on Sodor. 2009. (Illus.). 18p. (J). bds. 10.98 *(978-1-4127-1735-9(3)*, PIL Kids) Publications International, Ltd.
—Thomas & Friends: Engine Roll Call. 2011. 8p. (J). bds. 7.98 *(978-1-4508-1435-5(2))* Publications International, Ltd.
—Thomas & Friends: Let's Go, Thomas! 2010. 14p. (J). 17.98 *(978-1-4508-0212-3(5))* Phoenix International Publications, Inc.
—Thomas & Friends: Lights, Music & Me! 2011. 14p. (J). bds. 10.98 *(978-1-4508-1562-8(6))* Publications International, Ltd.
—Thomas & Friends: Play-a-Tune Puzzle Book. 2010. 10p. (J). bds. 13.98 *(978-1-60553-756-6(X))* Publications International, Ltd.
—Thomas & Friends: Super Look & Find Activity Pad with Stickers. 2011. 64p. (J). 10.98 *(978-1-4508-1563-5(4))* Publications International, Ltd.
—Thomas & Friends Super Look & Find Activity Pad. 2011. 64p. (J). 10.98 *(978-1-4508-1863-6(3))*; 13.98 *(978-1-4508-1199-6(X))* Publications International, Ltd.
—Thomas Great to be Engine Little Sound. 2011. 12p. 9.98 *(978-1-4508-0872-9(7))* Phoenix International Publications, Inc.
—Thomas Songs Play & Learn. 2010. 24p. (J). 12.98 *(978-1-4508-0115-7(3))* Phoenix International Publications, Inc.
—Thomas the Tank Good Morning Engines. 12p. (J). bds. *(978-0-7853-8282-9(8)*, 0785382828) Phoenix International Publications, Inc.
—Trains. 2011. 12p. (J). bds. 13.98 *(978-1-4508-1138-5(8))* Publications International, Ltd.
Random House. The Best Engines Ever. 2016. (Pictureback(R) Ser.). (ENG., Illus.). 24p. (J). (gr. -1-2). 4.99 *(978-1-101-93197-4(3)*, Random Hse. Bks. for Young Readers) Random Hse. Children's Bks.
—Dinos & Discoveries/Emily Saves the World, 2 bks. in 1. 2015. (Pictureback(R) Ser.). (ENG., Illus.). 24p. (J). (gr. -1-2). 4.99 *(978-0-553-50870-3(9)*, Random Hse. Bks. for Young Readers) Random Hse. Children's Bks.
—Five Tank Engine Tales (Thomas & Friends) Courtney, Richard, illus. 2015. (Step into Reading Ser.). (ENG.). 160p. (J). (gr. -1-1). pap. 7.99 *(978-0-385-38496-4(3)*, Random Hse. Bks. for Young Readers) Random Hse. Children's Bks.
—My Thomas Potty Book (Thomas & Friends) 2016. (ENG., Illus.). 14p. (J). (gr. -1 — 1). bds. 9.99 *(978-1-101-93427-2(1)*, Random Hse. Bks. for Young Readers) Random Hse. Children's Bks.
—Reds Against Blues! (Thomas & Friends) Courtney, Richard, illus. 2016. (Step into Reading Ser.). (ENG.). 24p. (J). (gr. -1-1). 4.99 *(978-1-101-93284-1(8)*, Random Hse. Bks. for Young Readers) Random Hse. Children's Bks.
—Thomas & Gordon (Thomas & Friends) Dalby, C. Reginald, illus. 2016. (ENG.). 24p. (J). (— 1). bds. 6.99 *(978-1-101-93139-4(6)*, Random Hse. Bks. for Young Readers) Random Hse. Children's Bks.
—Thomas at the Steelworks/Friends to the Rescue. 2017. (Pictureback(R) Ser.). (ENG., Illus.). 24p. (J). (gr. -1-2). pap. 4.99 ***(978-1-5247-1655-4(3)***, Random Hse. Bks. for Young Readers) Random Hse. Children's Bks.
—Thomas' Color Book (Thomas & Friends) Courtney, Richard, illus. 2017. (Pictureback(R) Ser.). (ENG.). 24p. (J). (gr. -1-2). 4.99 *(978-1-101-93723-5(8)*, Random Hse. Bks. for Young Readers) Random Hse. Children's Bks.
—Thomas Counts on Christmas (Thomas & Friends) 2016. (ENG., Illus.). 12p. (J). (— 1). bds. 6.99 *(978-0-385-37390-6(2)*, Random Hse. Bks. for Young Readers) Random Hse. Children's Bks.
—Thomas' Railway Friends (Thomas & Friends) 2016. (ENG., Illus.). 16p. (J). (— 1). bds. 7.99 *(978-0-399-55214-4(6)*, Random Hse. Bks. for Young Readers) Random Hse. Children's Bks.
—5-Minute Stories - The Sleepytime Collection. 2016. (ENG., Illus.). 160p. (J). (gr. -1-2). 12.99 *(978-0-399-55207-6(3)*, Random Hse. Bks. for Young Readers) Random Hse. Children's Bks.
Random House Disney Staff. Thomas & Friends the Great Railway Show/off to the Races. Stubbs, Tommy, illus. 2016. (Pictureback(R) Ser.). (ENG.). 24p. (J). (gr. -1-2). 4.99 *(978-1-101-93202-5(3)*, Random Hse. Bks. for Young Readers) Random Hse. Children's Bks.
—A Valentine for Percy (Thomas & Friends) Courtney, Richard, illus. 2015. (Step into Reading Ser.). (ENG.). 24p. (J). (gr. -1-1). 4.99 *(978-1-101-93287-2(2)*, Random Hse. Bks. for Young Readers) Random Hse. Children's Bks.
Random House Staff. Railway Adventures. Random House Staff, illus. 2010. (Step into Reading Ser.). (ENG., Illus.). 160p. (J). (gr. -1-1). pap. 7.99 *(978-0-375-86653-1(1)*, Random Hse. Bks. for Young Readers) Random Hse. Children's Bks.
Smith, Geof. Thomas & Friends the Great Race. 2016. (Big Golden Book Ser.). (ENG., Illus.). 32p. (J). (gr. -1-2). 9.99 *(978-1-101-93798-3(X)*, Golden Bks.) Random Hse. Children's Bks.
Stubbs, Tommy, illus. A Crack in the Track. 2004. (Bright & Early Board Books(TM) Ser.). (ENG.). 24p. (J). (— 1). bds. 4.99 *(978-0-375-82755-6(2)*, Random Hse. Bks. for Young Readers) Random Hse. Children's Bks.
—Thomas & Friends Little Golden Book Library (Thomas & Friends), 5 vols. 2013. (ENG.). 120p. (J). (-k). 24.95 *(978-0-449-81482-6(3)*, Golden Bks.) Random Hse. Children's Bks.
Thomas & Friends, Thomas &. Thomas & Friends: Thomas Speeds Along. 2015. (Lift-The-Flap Ser.: 1). (ENG.). 10p. (J). (gr. -1-k). 11.99 *(978-0-7944-3480-9(0)*, Reader's Digest Children's Bks.) Studio Fun International.
Thomas The Tank Engine & Egmont Staff. Thomas & Friends. 2008. (Illus.). 140p. *(978-0-603-56338-6(4))* Egmont Bks., Ltd.
Thomas the Tank Engine. 2012. *(978-0-7948-3764-8(6))* Egmont Bks., Ltd.
Webster, Christy. Get Rolling with Phonics (Thomas & Friends) 2016. (Step into Reading Ser.). (ENG., Illus.). 144p. (J). (gr. -1-2). pap. 12.99 *(978-1-101-93726-6(2)*, Random Hse. Bks. for Young Readers) Random Hse. Children's Bks.
Webster, Christy. Thomas' Opposites Book (Thomas & Friends) Courtney, Richard, illus. 2017. (Pictureback(R) Ser.). (ENG.). 24p. (J). (gr. -1-2). pap. 4.99 ***(978-1-5247-1604-2(9)***, Random Hse. Bks. for Young Readers) Random Hse. Children's Bks.
Webster, Christy & Awdry, W. Thomas & Friends Summer 2016 Movie Step into Reading (Thomas & Friends) Courtney, Richard, illus. 2016. (Step into Reading Ser.). (ENG.). 24p. (J). (gr. -1-1). 4.99 *(978-1-101-94031-0(X)*, Random Hse. Bks. for Young Readers) Random Hse. Children's Bks.

THOMSON, J. J. (JOSEPH JOHN), SIR, 1856-1940

Sherman, Josepha. J. J. Thomson & the Discovery of Electrons. 2005. (Uncharted, Unexplored, & Unexplained Ser.). (Illus.). 48p. (J). (gr. 4-8). lib. bdg. 29.95 *(978-1-58415-370-2(9))* Mitchell Lane Pubs., Inc.

THOREAU, HENRY DAVID, 1817-1862

Burleigh, Robert. If You Spent a Day with Thoreau at Walden Pond. Minor, Wendell, illus. 2012. (ENG.). 36p. (J). (gr. k-4). 17.99 *(978-0-8050-9137-3(8)*, 9780805091373, Holt, Henry & Co. Bks. For Young Readers) Holt, Henry & Co.
Coddington, Andrew. Henry David Thoreau: Writer of the Transcendentalist Movement. 2016. (Great American Thinkers Ser.). 128p. (J). (gr. 9-9). 45.64 *(978-1-5026-1928-0(8))* Cavendish Square Publishing.
Locker, Thomas. Walking with Henry: The Life & Works of Henry David Thoreau. 2011. (ENG., Illus.). 32p. (J). (gr. -1-5). pap. 9.95 *(978-1-55591-016-7(5))* Fulcrum Publishing.
McCarthy, Pat. Henry David Thoreau: Writer, Thinker, Naturalist. 2003. (Historical American Biographies Ser.). (Illus.). 128p. (J). (gr. 6-12). lib. bdg. 26.60 *(978-0-7660-1978-2(0))* Enslow Pubs., Inc.
McCurdy, Michael. Walden Then & Now: An Alphabetical Tour of Henry Thoreau's Pond. McCurdy, Michael, illus. 2010. (ENG., Illus.). 32p. (J). (gr. k-12). 16.95 *(978-1-58089-253-7(1))* Charlesbridge Publishing, Inc.
Meltzer, Milton. Henry David Thoreau: A Biography. 2007. (Literary Greats Ser.). (ENG., Illus.). 160p. (gr. 7-12). lib. bdg. 33.26 *(978-0-8225-5893-4(9)*, Twenty-First Century Bks.) Lerner Publishing Group.
Niver, Heather Moore. Henry David Thoreau: Author of Civil Disobedience. 2017. (J). ***(978-1-5383-8113-7(3))***; pap. ***(978-1-5383-8112-0(5))*** Rosen Publishing Group, Inc., The. (Rosen Young Adult).
Olson, Steven P. Henry David Thoreau: American Naturalist, Writer, & Transcendentalist. 2009. (Library of American Thinkers Ser.). 112p. (gr. 6-6). 66.50 *(978-1-60853-513-2(4)*, Rosen Reference) Rosen Publishing Group, Inc., The.
Porcellino, John. Thoreau at Walden. Porcellino, John, illus. 2009. (ENG., Illus.). 112p. (J). (gr. 5-18). pap. 9.99 *(978-1-4231-0039-3(5))* Hyperion Pr.
Schnur, Steven. Henry David's House. Fiore, Peter M., illus. 2007. (ENG.). 32p. (J). (gr. k-3). pap. 7.95 *(978-0-88106-117-8(4))* Charlesbridge Publishing, Inc.
Smith, Corinne Hosfeld. Henry David Thoreau for Kids: His Life & Ideas, with 21 Activities. 2016. (For Kids Ser.). (ENG., Illus.). 128p. (J). (gr. 4). pap. 16.95 *(978-1-61373-146-8(9))* Chicago Review Pr., Inc.
Thoreau, Henry. Walking. Clifton Johnson, illus. 2010. 100p. pap. 3.49 *(978-1-60386-305-6(2)*, Watchmaker Publishing) Wexford College Pr.

THOROUGHFARES

see Roads; Streets

THORPE, JIM, 1888-1953

Bruchac, Joseph. Jim Thorpe, Original All-American. 2008. (ENG.). 288p. (YA). (gr. 7-18). 9.99 *(978-0-14-241233-6(3)*, Speak) Penguin Young Readers Group.
Cain, Marie Mowery. Who Was Jim Thorpe? 2013. (Big Books, Red Ser.). (ENG & SPA., Illus.). 16p. pap. 33.00 *(978-1-59246-226-1(X))* Big Books, by George!
Fandel, Jennifer. Jim Thorpe: Greatest Athlete in the World, 1 vol. Whigham, Rod, illus. 2008. (Graphic Biographies Ser.). (ENG.). 32p. (gr. 3-4). per. 8.10 *(978-1-4296-1773-4(X)*, Graphic Library) Capstone Press of Coughlan Cos.
Golus, Carrie. Jim Thorpe. 2008. pap. 58.95 *(978-0-8225-9399-7(8))* Lerner Publishing Group.
Jim Thorpe, Mejor Atleta del Mundo. 2003. (Notas Biograficas Ser.). (SPA., Illus.). pap. 48.95 *(978-0-8136-5916-9(7))* Modern Curriculum Pr.
Schuman, Michael A. Jim Thorpe: "There's No Such Thing as 'Can't' 2009. (Americans—the Spirit of a Nation Ser.). (Illus.). 128p. (J). (gr. 5-12). lib. bdg. 33.27 *(978-0-7660-3021-3(0))* Enslow Pubs., Inc.
Sheinkin, Steve. Undefeated: Jim Thorpe & the Carlisle Indian School Football Team. Hsu, Connie, ed. 2017. (ENG., Illus.). 288p. (J). 19.99 *(978-1-59643-954-2(8)*, 9781596439542) Roaring Brook Pr.

THOUGHT AND THINKING

see also Intellect; Logic; Perception; Reasoning

Athans, Sandra K. & Parente, Robin W. Tips & Tricks for Determining Point of View & Purpose. 2014. (Common Core Readiness Guide to Reading Ser.). 80p. (J). (gr. 5-8). 32.95 *(978-1-4777-7555-4(2)*, Rosen Reference) Rosen Publishing Group, Inc., The.
—Tips & Tricks for Evaluating an Argument & Its Claims. 2014. (Common Core Readiness Guide to Reading Ser.). 80p. (YA). (gr. 5-8). 32.95 *(978-1-4777-7559-2(5))* Rosen Publishing Group, Inc., The.
Baker, Michael. Mind Benders Level 1: Deductive Thinking Skills. 2013. (Mind Benders Ser.). 56p. (gr. -1-k). pap. 9.99 *(978-0-89455-872-6(2))* Critical Thinking Co., The.
—Mind Benders Level 2: Deductive Thinking Skills. 2013. (Mind Benders Ser.). 64p. (gr. 1-2). pap. 9.99 *(978-0-89455-873-3(0))* Critical Thinking Co., The.
Black, Howard & Parks, Sandra. Building Thinking Skills Level 1. 2013. (Building Thinking Skills Ser.). (ENG.). 376p. (gr. 2-3). pap. 29.99 *(978-1-60144-149-2(5))* Critical Thinking Co., The.
—Building Thinking Skills Level 2. 2013. (Building Thinking Skills Ser.). (ENG.). 408p. (gr. 4-6). pap. 29.99 *(978-1-60144-150-8(9))* Critical Thinking Co., The.
Bluedorn, Nathaniel & Bluedorn, Hans. The Thinking Toolbox. 2005. (Illus.). 234p. (J). per. 22.00 *(978-0-9745315-1-9(0)*, 4000) Christian Logic.
Bright & Beyond - Thinking. 2004. (J). *(978-0-9763648-1-8(6))* Pal Toys, LLC.
Buzan, Tony. Mind Maps for Kids: The Shortcut to Success at School. 2005. (ENG., Illus.). 128p. pap. 19.95 *(978-0-00-715133-2(0)*, HarperThorsons) HarperCollins Pubs. Ltd. GBR. Dist: HarperCollins Pubs.
Carr, Mary. Great Chocolate Caper: Mystery That Teaches Logic Skills. 2005. 64p. pap. 11.95 *(978-1-59363-035-5(2))* Prufrock Pr.
Critical Thinking Publishing Staff, et al. Can You Find Me? K-1: Reading, Math, Science, Social Studies. 2010. (Can You Find Me? Ser.). (ENG., Illus.). 112p. (gr. k-1). pap. 14.99 *(978-0-89455-794-1(7))* Critical Thinking Co., The.
—Can You Find Me? PreK: Reading, Math, Science, Social Studies. 2011. (Can You Find Me? Ser.). (ENG.). 112p. (gr. -1 — 1). pap. 14.99 *(978-0-89455-793-4(9))* Critical Thinking Co., The.
Critical Thinking-What's Wrong with This Picture? (Gr. 1-3) 2003. (J). *(978-1-58232-066-3(7))* ECS Learning Systems, Inc.
Donahue, Jill Lynn. Being Considerate. Previn, Stacey, illus. 2007. (Way to Be! Ser.). (ENG.). 24p. (gr. -1-2). lib. bdg. 26.65 *(978-1-4048-3777-5(9))* Picture Window Bks.
Draze, Dianne. First Time Analogies. 2005. (ENG.). 48p. (-2). pap. 14.95 *(978-1-59363-073-7(5))* Prufrock Pr.
Free Spirit Publishing. Stay Positive in a Jar: Tips, Quotes, & Questions to Spark Upbeat Thoughts & Attitudes. 2017. (In a Jar(r) Ser.). (ENG.). (J). 9.99 ***(978-1-63198-201-9(X))*** Free Spirit Publishing, Inc.
Friedman, Lauri S. Nuclear Power. 2009. (Introducing Issues with Opposing Viewpoints Ser.). (ENG., Illus.). 144p. (gr. 10-12). 42.00 *(978-0-7377-4482-8(0))* Cengage Gale.
Gordon, Carol. Super Smart Information Strategies: Make the Grade. 2010. (Explorer Library: Information Explorer Ser.). (ENG.). 32p. (gr. 4-8). pap. 14.21 *(978-1-61080-259-8(4)*, 200907); lib. bdg. 28.50 *(978-1-60279-642-3(4)*, 200345) Cherry Lake Publishing.
Hay, Louise L. I Think, I Am! Teaching Kids the Power of Affirmations. Schwarz, Manuela, illus. 2008. (ENG.). 32p. (gr. -1-2). 15.99 *(978-1-4019-2208-5(2))* Hay Hse., Inc.
Heinrich, Erik. Survival Debate: A Rip-Roaring Game of Either-Or Questions. 2012. (This or That? Ser.). (ENG., Illus.). 32p. (gr. 3-4). lib. bdg. 27.99 *(978-1-4296-8594-8(8))* Capstone Press of Coughlan Cos.
—This or That Survival Debate: A Rip-Roaring Game of Either - Or Questions. 2012. (This or That? Ser.). (ENG., Illus.). 32p. (gr. 3-4). pap. 8.29 *(978-1-4296-9278-6(2))* Capstone Press of Coughlan Cos.
—This or That Survival Debate: A Rip-Roaring Game of Either/or Questions. 2012. (This or That? Ser.). (ENG.). 32p. (gr. 3-4). pap. 47.70 *(978-1-4296-9279-3(0)*, Edge Bks.) Capstone Press of Coughlan Cos.
Heinrich, Erik, et al. This or That? 2012. (This or That? Ser.). (ENG.). 32p. (gr. 3-4). 111.96 *(978-1-4296-9147-5(6)*, Edge Bks.) Capstone Press of Coughlan Cos.
Imagine That! Celebrating God's Gift of Creative Thinking. (Imagine That! Activity Bks.). (Illus.). 48p. (J). (gr. k-3). pap. 5.95 *(978-0-87162-832-9(5)*, E2300); (gr. 3-7). pap. 5.95 *(978-0-87162-834-3(1)*, E2301) Warner Pr., Inc.
Jerome, Kate Boehm & National Geographic Learning Staff. Thinking It Through. 2007. (Reading Expeditions Ser.). (ENG., Illus.). 24p. (J). pap. 14.95 *(978-0-7922-4593-3(8))* CENGAGE Learning.
Johnson, Robin. Above & Beyond with Creativity & Innovation. 2016. (Fueling Your Future! Going above & Beyond in the 21st Cent Ser.). (ENG., Illus.). 48p. (J). (gr. 5-8). *(978-0-7787-2831-3(5))* Crabtree Publishing Co.
Kopp, Megan. Above & Beyond with Critical Thinking & Problem Solving. 2016. (Fueling Your Future! Going above & Beyond in the 21st Cent Ser.). (ENG.). 48p. (J). (gr. 5-8). *(978-0-7787-2842-9(0))* Crabtree Publishing Co.
Kuskowski, Alex. Cool Thinking: Healthy & Fun Ways to Train Your Brain, 1 vol. 2012. (Cool Health & Fitness Ser.). (ENG.). 32p. (J). (gr. 3-6). lib. bdg. 27.07 *(978-1-61783-430-1(0)*, Checkerboard Library) ABDO Publishing Co.
Lanza, Janet & Flahive, Lynn. Blooming Category Activities. 2006. (ACE., Illus.). 190p. (J). per. 37.95 *(978-0-7606-0654-4(4))* LinguiSystems, Inc.
Levin, Daniel T. & Hammer, David. Becoming a Responsive Science Teacher: Focusing on Student Thinking in Secondary Science. 2012. (ENG.). 270p. (J). pap. *(978-1-936959-05-1(4))* National Science Teachers Assn.
Levine, Melvin D., contrib. by. Developing Minds Library, 22 cass.; set. 2004. (gr. -1-18). stu. ed. 499.95 incl. VHS *(978-1-57807-643-7(9)*, WG1166) WGBH Boston Video.
The Library of Higher Order of Thinking Skills. (YA). (gr. 5-8). 143.70 *(978-1-4042-0624-3(8)*, Rosen Reference) Rosen Publishing Group, Inc., The.
Meister, Cari. Totally Wacky Facts about the Human Mind. 2016. (Mind Benders Ser.). (ENG., Illus.). 112p. (gr. 1-3). lib. bdg. 23.32 *(978-1-4914-8361-9(X))* Capstone Press of Coughlan Cos.
Metzroth, Rupert A. Think for Yourself. 2004. (Illus.). 170p. per. 18.95 *(978-1-931934-30-5(4))* Back Yard Pub.
Meyer, Joyce & Hafer, Todd. Battlefield of the Mind - For Teens: Winning the Battle in Your Mind. annot. ed. 2006. (ENG.). 176p. (YA). (gr. 8-17). per. 14.00 *(978-0-446-69764-4(8)*, Faithwords) Hachette Nashville.
Meyer, Joyce & Moore, Karen. Battlefield of the Mind for Kids. 2006. (ENG., Illus.). 192p. (J). (gr. 3-7). per. 12.00 *(978-0-446-69125-3(9)*, Faithwords) Hachette Nashville.
Morrison, Matthew. Big Questions: Incredible Adventures in Thinking. Chalk, Gary, illus. 2007. (ENG.). 204p. (J). (gr. 4-8). pap. 7.95 *(978-1-84046-670-6(7))* Icon Bks., Ltd. GBR. Dist: Publishers Group Canada.
Murrie, Matthew & McHugh, Andrew R. The Book of What If... ? Questions & Activities for Curious Minds. (ENG., Illus.). 240p. (J). (gr. 3-7). 2017. pap. 12.99 *(978-1-58270-528-6(3))* 2016. 17.99 *(978-1-58270-529-3(1))* Aladdin/Beyond Words.
O'Hearn, Michael, et al. This or That? 2012. (This or That? Ser.). (ENG.). 32p. (gr. 3-4). pap. 190.80 *(978-1-4296-9281-6(2))*; pap. 31.80 *(978-1-4296-9280-9(4))* Capstone Press of Coughlan Cos. (Edge Bks.).
Price, Joan A. Ancient & Hellenistic Thought. 2008. (Understanding Philosophy Ser.). (Illus.). 118p. (C). (gr. 9). lib. bdg. 35.00 *(978-0-7910-8739-8(5)*, Chelsea Hse.) Facts On File, Inc.
—Contemporary Thought. 2008. (Understanding Philosophy Ser.). (Illus.). 160p. (YA). (gr. 9-12). lib. bdg. 35.00 *(978-0-7910-8792-3(1))* Facts On File, Inc.
Rando, Caterina. You Can Think Differently. 2017. (Be Your Best Self Ser.). 158p. (J). (gr. 12-14). 44.60 ***(978-1-4994-6666-9(8)***, Rosen Young Adult) Rosen Publishing Group, Inc., The.
Raum, Elizabeth, et al. Let's Think About, 1 vol. 2014. (Let's Think About Ser.). (ENG.). 48p. (gr. 3-6). 133.28 *(978-1-4846-0294-2(3)*, Heinemann InfoSearch) Heinemann-Raintree.
Risby, Bonnie. Logic Countdown. 2005. (Blast off with Logic Ser.: 1). (ENG.). 64p. (Orig.). (gr. 3-4). pap. 14.95 *(978-1-59363-087-4(5)*, 9781593630874) Prufrock Pr.
—Logic Liftoff. 2005. (Blast off with Logic Ser.: 2). (ENG.). 64p. (Orig.). (gr. 4-6). pap. 14.95 *(978-1-59363-088-1(3))* Prufrock Pr.
—Logic Safari. 2005. (Logic Safari Ser.: 1). (ENG.). Bk. 1. 32p. (gr. 2-3). pap. 12.95 *(978-1-59363-089-8(1))*Bk. 2. 32p. (gr. 3-4). pap. 12.95 *(978-1-59363-090-4(5))* Vol. 3. 36p. (gr. 5-6). pap. 12.95 *(978-1-59363-091-1(3))* Prufrock Pr.
Risby, Bonnie & Risby, Robby. Lollipop Logic: Critical Thinking Activities. 2005. (Lollipop Logic Ser.). (ENG.). 64p. (-2). pap. 12.95 *(978-1-59363-092-8(1))* Prufrock Pr.
Rodriguez, Ana Maria. A Day in the Life of the Brain. 2006. (Brain Works). (Illus.). 112p. (YA). (gr. 5-9). 32.95 *(978-0-7910-8947-7(9))* Facts On File, Inc.
Rosen Publishing Staff. The Guide for Curious Minds: Set 2, 1 vol. 2015. (Guide for Curious Minds Ser.). (ENG.). 136p. (YA). 191.25 *(978-1-4777-8131-9(5)*, Rosen Young Adult) Rosen Publishing Group, Inc., The.
Roy, Gregory & Roy, Jennifer Rozines. Graphing in the Desert. 2006. (Math All Around Ser.). (Illus.). 32p. (gr. 2-7). lib. bdg. 29.93 *(978-0-7614-2262-4(5)*, Benchmark Bks.) Marshall Cavendish Corp.
Roy, Jennifer Rozines & Roy, Gregory. Graphing in the Desert. 2007. (Math All Around Ser.). (Illus.). 31p. (J). (gr. 3-7). pap. 6.99 *(978-0-7614-3382-8(1)*, Benchmark Bks.) Marshall Cavendish Corp.
—Multiplication on the Farm. (Math All Around Ser.). (Illus.). 2007. 31p. (J). (gr. -1-3). pap. 6.99 *(978-0-7614-3386-6(4))* 2006. 32p. (gr. 2-7). lib. bdg. 29.93 *(978-0-7614-2268-6(4))* Marshall Cavendish Corp. (Benchmark Bks.).
—Subtraction at School. 2007. (J). pap. 6.99 *(978-0-7614-3409-2(7))* Marshall Cavendish Corp.
School Zone Publishing Company Staff. Thinking Skills Bilingual. 2007. (ENG.). 64p. (J). pap. 2.69 *(978-1-58947-975-3(0))* School Zone Publishing Co.
Sleeping Bear Editor, ed. Diary of an American Kid. 2011. (Country Journal Ser.). (ENG.). 128p. (J). (gr. 4-8). pap. 9.95 *(978-1-58536-171-7(2)*, 202262) Sleeping Bear Pr.
Spalding, Maddie. 12 Tips to Maintain Brain Health. 2017. (Healthy Living Ser.). (ENG., Illus.). 32p. (J). (gr. 3-6). 21.95 *(978-1-63235-368-9(7))* Pr. Room Editions LLC.
Spalding, Maddie & Ventura, Marne. 12 Tips to Maintain Brain Health. 2016. (Healthy Living Ser.). (ENG., Illus.). 32p. (J). pap. 9.95 *(978-1-63235-386-3(5))* Pr. Room Editions LLC.
Spiegel, Al. Ideas. Mortimer, Mitch, illus. 2003. 32p. (J). lib. bdg. 13.99 *(978-0-9743553-0-6(5))* Crazy Man Press, LLC.
Thornton, Geoffrey. What's Wrong? Visual Adventures in Critical Thinking. 2007. 32p. per. 19.95 *(978-1-59858-296-3(8))* Dog Ear Publishing, LLC.
Zimmer, Gretchen. Stinkin' Thinkin' 2012. (ENG.). (J). pap. 10.95 *(978-1-4675-2929-7(X))* Independent Pub.

THOUGHT TRANSFERENCE

see also Clairvoyance; Extrasensory Perception; Hypnotism

Bristol, Claude M. The Magic of Believing for Young People. 2008. 148p. pap. *(978-1-60796-063-8(X))* Editorial Benei Noaj.
Brunke, Dawn Baumann. Animal Voices, Animal Guides: Discover Your Deeper Self Through Communication with Animals. 2nd ed. 2009. (ENG.). 256p. pap. 16.00 *(978-1-59143-098-8(4))* Bear & Co.
—Awakening to Animal Voices: A Teen Guide to Telepathic Communication with All Life. 2004. (ENG., Illus.). 272p. (YA). (gr. 7-12). pap. 14.95 *(978-0-89281-136-6(6)*, Healing Arts Pr.) Inner Traditions International, Ltd.
Fullman, Joe. Mind Tricks. 2009. (Magic Handbook Ser.). (ENG., Illus.). 32p. (J). (gr. 3-12). pap. 6.95 *(978-1-55407-571-3(8)*, 9781554075713) Firefly Bks., Ltd.
Heos, Bridget. Do You Really Want to Visit Uranus? Fabbri, Daniele, illus. 2013. (Do You Really Want to Visit... ? Ser.). (ENG.). 24p. (gr. 1-4). 27.10 *(978-1-60753-202-6(6))* Amicus Publishing.
Lane, Mike. Mind Magic. Mostyn, David, illus. 2012. (Miraculous Magic Tricks Ser.). 32p. (J). (gr. 3-6). pap. 11.75 *(978-1-4488-6735-6(5))*; lib. bdg. 26.50 *(978-1-61533-514-5(5))* Windmill Bks.
Tilden, Thomasine E. Lewis. Mind Games! Can a Psychic Tell What You're Thinking? 2011. (J). pap. *(978-0-545-32943-9(4))* Scholastic, Inc.
Turnbull, Stephanie. Do You Really Want to Visit Uranus? 2011. (Secrets of Magic Ser.). 32p. (gr. 4-7). lib. bdg. 31.35 *(978-1-59920-498-7(3))* Black Rabbit Bks.
—Mind-Reading Tricks. 2011. (ENG., Illus.). 32p. (J). pap. 10.95 *(978-1-77092-044-6(7))* Saunders Bk. Co. CAN. Dist: RiverStream Publishing.

THREATENED PLANTS

see Endangered Plants

THREATENED SPECIES

see Endangered Species

THREE MUSKETEERS (FICTITIOUS CHARACTERS)—FICTION

Dumas, Alexandre. Los Tres Mosqueteros.Tr. of Trois Mousquetaires. (SPA.). (J). 2.49 *(978-968-890-125-0(3))* Edivision Compania Editorial, S.A. de C.V. MEX. Dist: Continental Bk. Co., Inc.
Golden Books Staff. Barbie & the Three Musketeers. 2009. (Little Golden Book Ser.). (ENG., Illus.). 24p. (J). (gr. -1-2). 3.99 *(978-0-375-85448-4(7)*, Golden Bks.) Random Hse. Children's Bks.
—Barbie & the Three Musketeers. Golden Books Staff, illus. 2009. (Pictureback(R) Ser.). (ENG., Illus.). 16p. (J). (gr. -1-2). pap. 3.99 *(978-0-375-85446-0(0)*, Golden Bks.) Random Hse. Children's Bks.

T U V

THUNDERSTORMS

see also Lightning

Adams, Renee. Can Thunder Hurt Me? Adams, Renee, illus. 2012. (Illus.). 24p. pap. 17.99 *(978-1-4685-5852-4(8))* AuthorHouse.

Bailer, Darice. Why Does It Thunder & Lightning? 2010. (Tell Me Why, Tell Me How 4 Ser.). 32p. (gr. 3-5). 29.93 *(978-0-7614-4825-9(X))* Marshall Cavendish Corp.

Bodden, Valerie. Our Wonderful Weather: Thunderstorms. 2014. (Our Wonderful Weather Ser.). (ENG., Illus.). 24p. (J). (gr. 1-3). pap. 9.99 *(978-0-89812-724-9(6)*, Creative Paperbacks) Creative Co., The.

—Thunderstorms. 2012. (Illus.). 24p. (J). 25.65 *(978-1-60818-149-0(9)*, Creative Education) Creative Co., The.

Boothroyd, Jennifer. What Is Severe Weather? 2014. (First Step Nonfiction - Let's Watch the Weather Ser.). (Illus.). 24p. (gr. k-2). pap. 6.95 *(978-1-4677-4499-7(9))* Lerner Publishing Group.

Broeders, Rebecca. How to Survive a Thunderstorm. 2012. 20p. pap. 17.99 *(978-1-4685-7672-6(0))* AuthorHouse.

Cox-Cannons, Helen. Thunder & Lightning, 1 vol. 2014. (Weather Wise Ser.). (ENG., Illus.). 24p. (gr. -1-1). 22.65 *(978-1-4846-0548-6(9)*, Acorn) Heinemann-Raintree.

Doeden, Matt. Thunderstorms. 2008. pap. 40.95 *(978-0-8225-9444-4(7))*; (ENG., Illus.). 32p. lib. bdg. 22.60 *(978-0-8225-7908-3(1)*, Lerner Pubns.) Lerner Publishing Group.

Galiano, Dean. Thunderstorms & Lightning. (Weather Watcher's Library). 48p. (gr. 5-8). 2009. 53.00 *(978-1-60854-275-8(0))* 2003. (Illus.). (YA). lib. bdg. 23.95 *(978-0-8239-3093-7(9)*, WETHLI) Rosen Publishing Group, Inc., The. (Rosen Reference).

Gonzales, Doreen. Thunderstorms. 2012. (Killer Disasters Ser.). (ENG., Illus.). 24p. (J). (gr. 3-6). 22.60 *(978-1-4488-7443-9(2))*; pap. 8.25 *(978-1-4488-7516-0(1))* Rosen Publishing Group, Inc., The. (PowerKids Pr.).

Gustaitis, Joseph Alan. Storm Chasers. 2010. (Benchmark Rockets: Dirty & Dangerous Jobs Ser.). 32p. (J). (gr. 3-6). 28.50 *(978-1-60870-179-7(4))* Marshall Cavendish Corp.

Hansen, Grace. Truenos y Relampagos. 2016. (Clima Ser.). (SPA.). 24p. (J). (gr. 1-6). pap. 7.95 *(978-1-4966-0695-2(7))* Capstone Classroom.

Higgins, Nadia. It's a Thunderstorm!, 1 vol. Ward, Damian, illus. 2010. (Weather Watchers Ser.). (ENG.). 32p. (J). (gr. k-3). 28.50 *(978-1-60270-729-0(4))* Magic Wagon.

Jensen, Belinda. A Party for Clouds: Thunderstorms. Kurilla, Renee, illus. 2016. (Bel the Weather Girl Ser.). (ENG.). 24p. (J). (gr. -1-3). 25.32 *(978-1-4677-7959-3(8)*, Millbrook Pr.) Lerner Publishing Group.

Johnson, Robin. What Is a Thunderstorm? 2016. (ENG., Illus.). 24p. (J). *(978-0-7787-2400-1(X))* Crabtree Publishing Co.

Lawrence, Ellen. What Is Lightning? 2015. (Weather Wise Ser.). (ENG., Illus.). 24p. (J). (gr. -1-3). lib. bdg. 23.93 *(978-1-62724-863-1(3))* Bearport Publishing Co., Inc.

McAuliffe, Bill. Thunderstorms. 2017. (J). ***(978-1-60818-827-7(2)***, Creative Education) 2010. 40p. (YA). (gr. 4-7). lib. bdg. 23.95 *(978-1-58341-930-4(6))* Creative Co., The.

Mezzanotte, Jim. Thunderstorms. (Wild Weather Ser.). 24p. 2009. (ENG.). (J). (gr. k-3). pap. 8.15 *(978-1-4339-2364-7(5))* 2009. (J). (gr. k-3). lib. bdg. 22.00 *(978-1-4339-2350-0(5))* 2007. (Illus.). (gr. 1-4). pap. 8.15 *(978-0-8368-7922-3(8))* 2007. (Illus.). (gr. 1-4). lib. bdg. 22.00 *(978-0-8368-7915-5(5))* Stevens, Gareth Publishing LLLP. (Weekly Reader Leveled Readers).

—Tormentas Eléctricas. 2007. (Tormentas (Storms) Ser.). (SPA., Illus.). 24p. (gr. 1-4). pap. 8.15 *(978-0-8368-8081-6(1))*; lib. bdg. 22.00 *(978-0-8368-8074-8(9))* Stevens, Gareth Publishing LLLP. (Weekly Reader Leveled Readers).

—Tormentas Eléctricas (Thunderstorms) 2009. (Tiempo extremo Ser.). (SPA.). 24p. (J). (gr. k-3). pap. 8.15 *(978-1-4339-2371-5(8))*; lib. bdg. 22.00 *(978-1-4339-2357-9(2))* Stevens, Gareth Publishing LLLP. (Weekly Reader Leveled Readers).

Rehberg, Emily. Thunder Is Not Scary. Craig, Branden Chapin & Chapin, Jimmy, illus. 2013. 26p. pap. 12.00 *(978-0-9800108-3-1(7))* Bilbo Bks.

Stiefel, Chana. Thunderstorms. 2009. (True Book(tm), a — Earth Science Ser.). (ENG., 48p. (J). Illus.). (gr. 2-5). 31.00 *(978-0-531-16884-4(0))*; pap. 6.95 *(978-0-531-21352-0(8)*, Children's Pr.) Scholastic Library Publishing.

Thomas, Rick & Picture Window Books Staff. ¡Rambum! ¡Pum! Un Libro Sobre Tormentas. Robledo, Sol, tr. from ENG. Shea, Denise, illus. 2007. (Ciencia Asombrosa: el Tiempo Ser.). (SPA.). 24p. (gr. -1-3). 26.65 *(978-1-4048-3227-5(0))* Picture Window Bks.

World Book, Inc Staff, contrib. by. Thunderstorms. (J). 2007. *(978-0-7166-9812-8(9))* 2nd ed. 2009. (Illus.). 47p. *(978-0-7166-9828-9(5))* World Bk., Inc.

THUNDERSTORMS—FICTION

Adams, William J. Hate that Thunder. Stiglich, Tom, illus. 2005. 24p. (J). pap. 8.95 *(978-0-9772757-0-0(1))* Mandy & Andy Bks., Inc.

—Hate That Thunder/Odio Ese Trueno, 1 vol. Stiglich, Tom, illus. 2007. (Mandy & Andy Bks.). (ENG & SPA.). 49p. (J). (gr. k-2). per. 10.95 *(978-0-9772757-1-7(X))* Mandy & Andy Bks., Inc.

Batson, Susann. Scaredy: A Cloud Afraid of Thunder. 2010. 16p. pap. 9.95 *(978-1-61633-053-8(8))* Guardian Angel Publishing, Inc.

Beeke, Joel R. & Kleyn, Diana. How God Used a Thunderstorm. Anderson, Jeff, illus. 2007. (Building on the Rock Ser.). (ENG.). 176p. (J). pap. 8.99 *(978-1-85792-815-0(6)*, 9781857928150, CF4Kids) Christian Focus Pubns. GBR. Dist: Bookmasters Distribution.

Berenstain, Jan & Berenstain, Mike. Bear Country Blessings, 1 vol. 2013. (Berenstain Bears/Living Lights Ser.). (ENG.). 96p. (J). 7.99 *(978-0-310-73503-8(3))* Zonderkidz.

Blackman, Christy. Mr. Thunder Is Here, but There's No Reason to Fear. 2008. 36p. pap. 24.95 *(978-1-60441-695-4(5))* America Star Bks.

Bluemle, Elizabeth. Tap Tap Boom Boom. Karas, G. Brian, illus. 2014. (ENG.). 32p. (J). (gr. -1-2). 16.99 *(978-0-7636-5696-6(8))* Candlewick Pr.

Brewer, Janey. Mist & Moonlight. 2007. 76p. per. 19.95 *(978-1-4241-9525-1(X))* America Star Bks.

Bright, Belle. Crash, Bang, Boom, Zing. Bright, Michael, illus. 2009. 12p. pap. 24.95 *(978-1-60749-383-9(7))* America Star Bks.

Brown, Peter. Flight of the Dodo. 2010. (ENG., Illus.). 32p. (J). (gr. -1-3). pap. 7.99 *(978-0-316-08339-3(9))* Little, Brown Bks. for Young Readers.

Carol Henson Keesee. The Angry Thunderstorm. Rachel Henson, illus. 2009. 40p. pap. 20.00 *(978-1-4389-4334-3(2))* AuthorHouse.

Cazet, Denys. Minnie & Moo Meet Frankenswine. Cazet, Denys, illus. 2004. (Readalongs for Beginning Readers Ser.). (Illus.). 28.95 incl. audio compact disk *(978-1-59112-876-2(5))*; (J). 25.95 incl. audio *(978-1-59112-262-3(7))*; (J). pap. 29.95 incl. audio *(978-1-59112-263-0(5))* Live Oak Media.

—Minnie & Moo Meet Frankenswine, 4 bks. 2004. (Readalongs for Beginning Readers Ser.). (Illus.). 48p. (J). (gr. -1-2). pap. 31.95 incl. audio compact disk *(978-1-59112-877-9(3))* Live Oak Media.

Crum, Shutta. Thunder-Boomer! Thompson, Carol, illus. 2009. (ENG.). 40p. (J). (gr. -1-3). 17.99 *(978-0-618-61865-1(1))* Houghton Mifflin Harcourt Publishing Co.

D'Agata, Tabatha Jean. Storm Tunes: Yes, I Can Read! Nature Series, Book 2. Lineberger, Judy, illus. 2006. (Yes, I Can Read! Ser.: Bk. 2). 30p. (J). pap. 6.95 *(978-1-934138-02-1(9))* Bouncing Ball Bks., Inc.

Gorbachev, Valeri. Catty Jane Who Hated the Rain. Gorbachev, Valeri, illus. 2012. (ENG., Illus.). 32p. (J). (gr. -1-3). 16.95 *(978-1-59078-700-7(5))* Boyds Mills Pr.

Graber, Lois, illus. A Song in the Storm. 2012. 32p. (J). *(978-0-7399-2445-7(1))* Rod & Staff Pubs., Inc.

High, Gracia. I am not going to sleep Now. 2004. 21p. pap. 24.95 *(978-1-4137-3000-5(0))* PublishAmerica, Inc.

Hileman, Jane & Pitt, Marilyn. The Storm. Bianchi, John, illus. 2011. (Power 50 - Potato Chip Bks). 12p. pap. 33.92 *(978-1-61541-233-4(6))* American Reading Co.

Hill, Susan & Sewell, Anna. Black Beauty & the Thunderstorm. Farnsworth, Bill, illus. 2011. (My Readers Ser.). (ENG.). 48p. (J). (gr. 1-3). pap. 3.99 *(978-0-312-64721-6(2)*, 9780312647216) Square Fish.

Hobbie, Holly. You Are My Sunshine. 2010. (Toot & Puddle Ser.: 3). (ENG., Illus.). 32p. (J). (gr. -1-3). pap. 7.99 *(978-0-316-16703-1(7))* Little, Brown Bks. for Young Readers.

Hulst, W. G. van de & Hulst, Willem G. van de, illus. Through the Thunderstorm. 2014. (J). *(978-1-928136-02-6(8))* Inheritance Pubns.

Leslie, Lashawn. Thundermonsters. 2012. 16p. pap. 15.99 *(978-1-4772-5422-6(6))* AuthorHouse.

Lignell, Kirk. Listen to the Raindrops: Featuring the Storm Song. Lignell, Brent, illus. 2007. 32p. (J). (gr. -1-3). 17.95 *(978-1-932399-15-8(1))* Huron River Pr.

McNaughton, Karen. What Makes the Thunder? 2011. 24p. pap. 11.50 *(978-1-60976-224-7(X)*, Eloquent Bks.) Strategic Book Publishing & Rights Agency (SBPRA).

Merkel, Tara & Monahan, Ryan. The Thunderstorm. 2007. 20p. per. 11.00 *(978-1-4343-0585-5(6))* AuthorHouse.

Moss, Miriam. Wiley & Jasper. Bucker, Jutta, tr. Bucker, Jutta, illus. 2003. (J). 25p. pap. *(978-1-59336-061-0(4))*; 32p. 15.95 *(978-1-59336-060-3(6))* Mondo Publishing.

Norton, Jack, Jr., as told by. Brave from Thunders. 2003. pap. 15.00 *(978-0-9740071-3-7(7))* Ctr. for the Affirmation of Responsible Education.

Pitt, Marilyn & Sanchez, Lucia M. La Tormenta: The Storm. Bianchi, John, illus. 2011. (poder de 50 - Libros papas fritas Ser.). (SPA.). 12p. pap. 33.92 *(978-1-61541-441-3(X))* American Reading Co.

Polacco, Patricia. Thunder Cake. 2015. 32p. pap. 8.00 *(978-1-61003-536-1(4))* Center for the Collaborative Classroom.

Rivera-Ashford, Roni Capin & Johnson, Richard. Hip Hip Hooray, It's Monsoon Day! 2007. (ENG & SPA.). (YA). pap. 15.95 *(978-1-886679-36-8(3))* Arizona Sonora Desert Museum Pr.

Seeger, Laura Vaccaro. Walter Was Worried. Seeger, Laura Vaccaro, illus. 2016. (ENG., Illus.). 40p. (J). 14.99 *(978-1-62672-251-4(X)*, 9781626722514) Roaring Brook Pr.

Spear, Lisa D. Thunderburps. Baker, David, illus. 2012. 26p. 24.95 *(978-1-4626-0793-8(4))* America Star Bks.

Testa, Maggie. Daniel Gets Scared. 2015. (Daniel Tiger's Neighborhood Ready-To-Read Ser.). lib. bdg. 13.55 *(978-0-606-36243-4(7))* Turtleback Bks.

Torres, J. The Sound of Thunder. Hicks, Faith Erin, illus. 2014. (Bigfoot Boy Ser.). (ENG.). 100p. (J). (gr. 2-5). 17.95 *(978-1-894786-58-4(0))*; pap. 9.95 *(978-1-894786-59-1(9))* Kids Can Pr., Ltd. CAN. Dist: Hachette Bk. Group.

TIBET AUTONOMOUS REGION (CHINA)

Deasy, H. H. P. In Tibet & Chinese Turkestan: Being the Record of Three Years' Exploration. 2008. 95.00 *(978-1-57898-702-3(4))*; pap. *(978-1-57898-703-0(2))* Martino Fine Bks.

Dolphin, Laurie. Our Journey from Tibet. Johnson, Nancy Jo, photos by. 2006. (Illus.). 40p. (J). (gr. k-4). 16.00 *(978-0-7567-9812-3(4))* DIANE Publishing Co.

Gray, Nick & Scandiffio, Laura. Escape from Tibet: A True Story. 2014. (ENG., Illus.). 164p. (YA). (gr. 6-12). pap. 12.95 *(978-1-55451-662-9(5)*, 9781554516629) Annick Pr., Ltd. CAN. Dist: Publishers Group West (PGW).

Haerens, Margaret. Tibet. 2014. (Opposing Viewpoints Ser.). (ENG.). 224p. pap. 33.80 *(978-0-7377-7363-7(4)*, Greenhaven Pr., Inc.) Cengage Gale.

Harris, Joseph. Tibet. 2009. (Global Hotspots Ser.). 32p. (gr. 5-18). lib. bdg. 18.56 *(978-0-7614-4762-7(8))* Marshall Cavendish Corp.

Hay, Jeff. Tibet. Greenhaven Press Editors & Gale Editors, eds. 2014. (Genocide & Persecution Ser.). (ENG., Illus.). 240p. (gr. 10-12). lib. bdg. 42.00 *(978-0-7377-6901-2(7)*, Greenhaven Pr., Inc.) Cengage Gale.

Hellstrom, Travis. My Day with the Dalai Lama: A Coloring Book for All Ages. Hoyle, Leighanna, illus. 2017. (ENG.). 48p. (J). (gr. -1-2). pap. 5.99 *(978-1-57826-639-5(4)*, Hatherleigh Pr.) Hatherleigh Co., Ltd., The.

Kummer, Patricia K. Enchantment of the World: Tibet. 2003. (Enchantment of the World Ser.). (ENG., Illus.). 144p. (YA). (gr. 5-9). 39.00 *(978-0-516-22693-4(2))* Scholastic Library Publishing.

Levy, Patricia & Bosco, Don. Tibet. 2nd rev. ed. 2006. (Cultures of the World Ser.). (Illus.). 144p. (gr. 6). lib. bdg. 42.79 *(978-0-7614-2076-7(2)*, Benchmark Bks.) Marshall Cavendish Corp.

Levy, Patricia, et al. Tibet. 3rd enl. ed. 2016. (Cultures of the World (Third Edition) (r) Ser.). 144p. (J). 47.07 *(978-1-5026-2213-6(0))* Cavendish Square Publishing.

Nagle, Jeanne. The 14th Dalai Lama: Spiritual Leader of Tibetan Buddhists. 2017. (J). ***(978-1-5081-7745-6(7))***; pap. ***(978-1-5383-8079-6(X))*** Rosen Publishing Group, Inc., The.

Senker, Cath. The Dalai Lama: His Life & Work. 2016. (ENG., Illus.). 32p. (J). (gr. 4-6). 16.99 *(978-0-7502-9768-4(9)*, Wayland) Hachette Children's Group GBR. Dist: Hachette Bk. Group.

Sonneborn, Liz. Tibet. 2016. (Enchantment of the World(tm) Ser.). (ENG., Illus.). 144p. (J). lib. bdg. 40.00 *(978-0-531-21888-4(0)*, Children's Pr.) Scholastic Library Publishing.

TIBET AUTONOMOUS REGION (CHINA)—FICTION

Caravan. 2007. (Choose Your Own Adventure - Dragonlarks Ser.). (Illus.). 64p. (J). (gr. 4-7). pap. 7.99 *(978-1-933390-54-3(9))* Chooseco LLC.

Carlson, Dale Bick. The Mountain of Truth. Nicklaus, Carol, illus. 2nd ed. 2005. (ENG.). 169p. (gr. 8-12). reprint ed. pap. 14.95 *(978-1-884158-30-8(7))* Team Kreskin Productions, LLC.

Giancamilli, Vanessa. Gecko Gathering. Kest, Kristin, illus. 2005. (Soundprints' Amazing Animal Adventures! Ser.). (ENG.). (J). (gr. -1-2). 32p. 9.95 *(978-1-59249-323-4(8)*, PS7157); 36p. 2.95 *(978-1-59249-289-3(4)*, S7157); 36p. 15.95 *(978-1-59249-288-6(6)*, B7107); 36p. pap. 6.95 *(978-1-59249-290-9(8)*, S7107); 32p. 19.95 *(978-1-59249-321-0(1)*, BC7107) Soundprints.

Halpern, Gina. Where Is Tibet? Halpern, Gina, illus. 2nd ed. 2011. (ENG., Illus.). 48p. (J). (gr. -1-2). pap. 14.95 *(978-1-55939-383-6(1)*, Snow Lion Publications, Inc.) Shambhala Pubns., Inc.

Hergé. Tintin au Tibet.Tr. of Tintin in Tibet. (J). (gr. 7-9). ring bd. 24.95 *(978-0-8288-5092-6(5))* French & European Pubns., Inc.

—Tintin en Tibet. (SPA., Illus.). 62p. (J). 24.95 *(978-0-8288-4996-8(X))* French & European Pubns., Inc.

—Tintin in Tibet. Orig. Title: Tintin au Tibet. (Illus.). 62p. (J). 24.95 *(978-0-8288-5001-8(1))* French & European Pubns., Inc.

Hergé & Egmont Books Staff. Tintin in Tibet. 2003. Orig. Title: Tintin au Tibet. (ENG., Illus.). 64p. *(978-1-4052-0819-2(8))* Egmont Bks., Ltd.

Moffett, Rodney. The Eighth Crest. 2006. (ENG.). 228p. per. 24.95 *(978-1-4241-3907-1(4))* PublishAmerica, Inc.

Rose, Naomi. Tibetan Tales for Little Buddhas. 2003. (TIB & ENG., Illus.). 64p. (J). pap. 16.95 *(978-1-57416-081-9(8))* Clear Light Pubs.

Soros, Barbara. Tenzin's Deer. Mayer, Danuta, illus. (ENG.). 32p. (J). (gr. 2-4). 2007. pap. 7.99 *(978-1-84686-130-7(6))* 2005. 16.99 *(978-1-905236-57-2(3))* Barefoot Bks., Inc.

Thorney, Zedar. Red Star Red Tar. 2010. 66p. pap. 20.00 *(978-1-60860-360-2(1)*, Eloquent Bks.) Strategic Book Publishing & Rights Agency (SBPRA).

TIDAL WAVES

see Ocean Waves

TIDES

Brasch, Nicolas. Times, Tides, & Revolutions. 2010. (Science Behind Ser.). 32p. lib. bdg. 28.50 *(978-1-59920-563-2(7))* Black Rabbit Bks.

Declus, Jennifer. What Might I Find in a Tidepool. Kalasea, illus. 2004. (J). *(978-0-9743690-4-4(7))* Britt Allcroft Productions.

Dickmann, Nancy. Harnessing Wave & Tidal Energy. 2016. (Future of Power Ser.). 00032p. (J). (gr. 4-5). pap. 10.00 *(978-1-4994-3213-8(5)*, PowerKids Pr.) Rosen Publishing Group, Inc., The.

Richter, Al. Ocean Tides. (Reading Room Collection 1 Ser.). 16p. 2009. (gr. 2-3). 37.50 *(978-1-60851-947-7(3))* 2006. (Illus.). (J). (gr. 3-7). lib. bdg. 17.25 *(978-1-4042-3343-0(1))* Rosen Publishing Group, Inc., The. (PowerKids Pr.).

TIDES—FICTION

Herman, Gail. The Creeping Tide. Nez, John, illus. 2003. (Science Solves It! Ser.). 32p. (J). pap. 5.95 *(978-1-57565-128-6(9))* Kane Press, Inc.

McClure, Nikki. Waiting for High Tide. 2016. (ENG., Illus.). 48p. (J). (gr. k-2). 19.95 *(978-1-4197-1656-0(5)*, Abrams Bks. for Young Readers) Abrams, Inc.

Rey, H. A. & Rey, Margret. Chasing Waves. 2014. (Curious George Ser.). (ENG., Illus.). 24p. (J). (gr. -1-3). pap. 4.99 *(978-0-544-24004-9(9)*, HMH Books For Young Readers) Houghton Mifflin Harcourt Publishing Co.

TIGER

Amstutz, Lisa. Tigers on the Hunt. 2017. (Searchlight Books (tm) — Predators Ser.). (ENG.). (J). (gr. 3-5). pap. 9.99 ***(978-1-5124-5613-4(6))***; (Illus.). lib. bdg. 30.65 ***(978-1-5124-3400-2(0))*** Lerner Publishing Group.

Antle, Bhagavan. The Tiger Cubs & the Chimp: The True Story of How Anjana the Chimp Helped Raise Two Baby Tigers. Antle, Bhagavan, illus. Bland, Barry, photos by. 2013. (ENG., Illus.). 32p. (J). (gr. -1-3). 16.99 *(978-0-8050-9319-3(2)*, 9780805093193, Holt, Henry & Co. Bks. For Young Readers) Holt, Henry & Co.

Archer, Claire. Tigers, 1 vol. 2014. (Big Cats Ser.). (ENG.). 24p. (J). (gr. 4-8). lib. bdg. 28.50 *(978-1-62970-006-9(1))* ABDO Publishing Co.

Archer, Claire, et al. Tigres. 2015. (Grandes Felinos Ser.). (SPA., Illus.). 24p. (gr. k-1). pap. 7.95 *(978-1-4966-0467-5(9))* Capstone Classroom.

AZ Books, creator. Hello, I'm Tiger! 2012. (Who Lives in the Book? Ser.). (ENG., Illus.). 10p. (J). (gr. -1-k). bds. 11.95 *(978-1-61889-211-9(8))* AZ Bks. LLC.

Baker, David G. & Stewart, Margaret Taylor. Tales of Mike the Tiger: Facts & Fun for Everyone. Lockwood, C. C., photos by. 2006. (ENG., Illus.). 144p. (gr. 4-7). 19.95 *(978-0-8071-3118-3(0)*, 9780807131183) Louisiana State Univ. Pr.

Barnes, Julia. The Secret Lives of Tigers. 2007. (Secret Lives of Animals Ser.). (Illus.). 32p. (gr. 2-6). lib. bdg. 26.00 *(978-0-8368-7659-8(8)*, Gareth Stevens Learning Library) Stevens, Gareth Publishing LLLP.

—101 Facts about Tigers. 2004. (One Hundred One Facts about Predators Ser.). (Illus.). 32p. (gr. 1-4). lib. bdg. 26.00 *(978-0-8368-4041-4(0)*, Gareth Stevens Learning Library) Stevens, Gareth Publishing LLLP.

Bergeron, Alain M., et al. Les Tigres. 2010. (FRE., Illus.). 64p. (J). pap. 8.95 *(978-2-89435-465-0(7))* Quintin Pubs./Editions Michel Quintin CAN. Dist: Crabtree Publishing Co.

Big Cats. 2014. (Animal Q & A Ser.). (Illus.). 24p. (J). (gr. k-3). lib. bdg. 23.60 *(978-1-4777-9182-0(5))* Windmill Bks.

Bodden, Valerie. Amazing Animals - Tigers. 2009. (Amazing Animals Ser.). 24p. (J). (gr. 1-5). 24.25 *(978-1-58341-720-1(6)*, Creative Education) Creative Co., The.

—Amazing Animals: Tigers. 2011. (Amazing Animals Ser.). (ENG.). 24p. (J). (gr. 1-3). pap. 8.99 *(978-0-89812-745-4(9)*, Creative Paperbacks) Creative Co., The.

Books Are Fun 8 Title Animal Lives Set: Tigers. 2006. (J). *(978-1-59566-312-2(6))* QEB Publishing Inc.

Boothroyd, Jennifer. From Cub to Tiger. 2016. (Start to Finish, Second Ser.). (ENG., Illus.). 24p. (J). (gr. k-3). lib. bdg. 23.99 *(978-1-5124-1832-3(3)*, Lerner Pubns.) Lerner Publishing Group.

Bortolotti, Dan. Tiger Rescue: Changing the Future for Endangered Wildlife. 2003. (Firefly Animal Rescue Ser.). (ENG., Illus.). 64p. (J). (gr. 5-18). 19.95 *(978-1-55297-599-2(1)*, 9781552975992); pap. 9.95 *(978-1-55297-558-9(4)*, 9781552975589) Firefly Bks., Ltd.

Bowman, Donna H. Big Cats. Wald, Christina, illus. 2008. (ENG.). 24p. (J). (gr. 3-18). 19.95 *(978-1-58117-781-7(X)*, Intervisual/Piggy Toes) Bendon, Inc.

Brayley, Genevieve. Noah Saves the Tigers. 2010. 28p. pap. 28.03 *(978-1-4500-3077-9(7))* Xlibris Corp.

Brown, Penny & Washington, Joi. How the Tiger Takes Care of Her Babies. Washington, Joi, illus. 2012. (1B Animal Behaviors Ser.). (ENG., Illus.). 24p. (J). pap. 5.99 *(978-1-61406-172-4(6))* American Reading Co.

Butterworth, Nick. Tiger in the Snow! 2008. (ENG., Illus.). 32p. 9.95 *(978-0-00-725774-4(0))* HarperCollins Pubs. Ltd. GBR. Dist: Independent Pubs. Group.

Clark, Willow. Bengal Tigers. 2012. (Animals of Asia Ser.). (ENG., Illus.). 24p. (J). (gr. 1-5). 22.60 *(978-1-4488-7417-0(3))*; pap. 8.25 *(978-1-4488-7490-3(4))* Rosen Publishing Group, Inc., The. (PowerKids Pr.).

Claybourne, Anna. Tiger. 2012. (Animals on the Edge Ser.). (ENG., Illus.). 48p. (gr. 3-8). pap. 12.00 *(978-1-4081-4957-7(5)*, 9781408149577, Bloomsbury USA Childrens) Bloomsbury Publishing USA.

—Tigers, 1 vol. 2014. (Living in the Wild: Big Cats Ser.). (ENG.). 48p. (gr. 3-6). lib. bdg. 33.32 *(978-1-4329-8110-5(2)*, Heinemann InfoSearch) Heinemann-Raintree.

Crossley, Laura C. Three Little Tiger Cubs: A Journey Through the Seasons with a Mom & Her Cubs. 2005. (ENG., Illus.). 29p. (J). (gr. -1-3). per. 19.99 *(978-1-59926-853-8(1))* Xlibris Corp.

Davies, Ann & Davies, Gill. The One Tiger. 2008. (Illus.). 32p. (J). pap. 7.99 *(978-1-905470-23-5(1))* SeaSquirt Pubns. GBR. Dist: Basic Distribution, Inc.

Eason, Sarah. Save the Tiger. Geeson, Andrew & Veldhoven, Marijke, illus. 2009. (Save the... Ser.). 32p. (J). (gr. 2-5). lib. bdg. 25.25 *(978-1-4358-2813-1(5))* Rosen Publishing Group, Inc., The.

Esbaum, Jill. Explore My World Tigers. 2016. (Explore My World Ser.). (ENG., Illus.). 32p. (J). (gr. -1-2). pap. 4.99 *(978-1-4263-2426-0(X)*, National Geographic Children's Bks.) National Geographic Society.

Eszterhas, Suzi. Tiger. 2016. (ENG., Illus.). 32p. (J). (gr. -1-2). pap. 9.99 *(978-1-84780-656-7(2)*, Frances Lincoln) Quarto Publishing Group UK GBR. Dist: Littlehampton Bk Services, Ltd.

Eszterhas, Suzi, photos by. Tiger. 2014. (Eye on the Wild Ser.). (ENG., Illus.). 32p. (J). (gr. -1-2). 15.99 *(978-1-84780-517-1(5)*, Frances Lincoln) Quarto Publishing Group UK GBR. Dist: Hachette Bk. Group.

Feldman, Thea. Katya's Busy Morning. 2006. (Illus.). (J). *(978-0-696-23292-3(8))* Meredith Bks.

Firestone, Mary. Top 50 Reasons to Care about Tigers: Animals in Peril. 2010. (Top 50 Reasons to Care about Endangered Animals Ser.). (Illus.). 104p. (J). (gr. 5-9). 33.27 *(978-0-7660-3452-5(6))* Enslow Pubs., Inc.

Franchino, Vicky. Tigers. 2012. (Nature's Children Ser.). (ENG.). 48p. (J). pap. 6.95 *(978-0-531-25484-4(4))* Scholastic Library Publishing.

—Tigers - Nature's Children. 2012. (ENG.). 48p. (J). lib. bdg. 28.00 *(978-0-531-26839-1(X))* Scholastic Library Publishing.

Frost, Helen. Sabertooth Cat [Scholastic]. Hughes, Jon, illus. 2009. (Dinosaurs & Prehistoric Animals Ser.). 24p. (gr. k-1). pap. 1.00 *(978-1-4296-4249-1(1)*, Pebble Plus) Capstone Press of Coughlan Cos.

—Tigers [Scholastic]. 2011. (Rain Forest Animals Ser.). 24p. pap. 0.50 *(978-1-4296-6311-3(1)*, Pebble Bks.) Capstone Press of Coughlan Cos.

Gaines, Richard Marshall. When Tigers Attack! 2006. (When Wild Animals Attack! Ser.). (Illus.). 48p. (J). (gr. 4-10). lib. bdg. 25.27 *(978-0-7660-2665-0(5))* Enslow Pubs., Inc.

Galvin, Laura Gates. Tiger Cub See-and-Do. Cohen, Jessie, illus. 2005. (Let's Go to the Zoo! Ser.). (ENG.). 16p. (J). (gr. -1-k). 5.95 *(978-1-56899-856-5(2)*, B9006) Soundprints.

Gareth Stevens Publishing Staff, contrib. by. Tigers. 2004. (All about Wild Animals Ser.). (Illus.). 32p. (gr. k-4). lib. bdg. 26.00 *(978-0-8368-4189-3(1)*, Gareth Stevens Learning Library) Stevens, Gareth Publishing LLLP.

Gilbert, Sara. Ice Age Mega Beasts: Saber-Toothed Cats. 2017. (Ice Age Mega Beasts Ser.). (ENG., Illus.). 24p. (J). (gr. 1-3). pap. 8.99 ***(978-1-62832-377-1(9)***, Creative Paperbacks) Creative Co., The.

Gilbert, Sara. Saber-Toothed Cats. 2017. (Illus.). 23p. (J). *(978-1-60818-769-0(1)*, Creative Education) Creative Co., The.

Goecke, Michael P. Saber-Toothed Cat, 1 vol. 2003. (Prehistoric Animals Ser.). (ENG.). 24p. (gr. k-4). 25.65 *(978-1-57765-970-9(8)*, Buddy Bks.) ABDO Publishing Co.

Goldish, Meish. Siberian Tiger: The World's Biggest Cat. 2010. (More SuperSized! Ser.). (Illus.). 24p. (J). (gr. k-3). lib. bdg. 22.61 *(978-1-936087-28-0(6))* Bearport Publishing Co., Inc.

Goodman, Susan E. Saber-Toothed Cats. Maguire, Kerry, illus. (On My Own Science Ser.). 48p. 2006. (ENG.). (gr. 2-4). per. 6.95 (978-1-57505-851-1(0), First Avenue Editions) 2005. (J). (gr. 3-7). lib. bdg. 25.26 (978-1-57505-759-0(X)) Lerner Publishing Group.

Green, Carl R. The Tiger: A MyReportLinks.com Book. 2003. (Endangered & Threatened Animals Ser.). (Illus.). 48p. (J). (gr. 4-10). lib. bdg. 26.60 (978-0-7660-5059-4(9), MyReportLinks.com Bks.) Enslow Pubs., Inc.

Gregoire, Maryellen. Un Cachorro de Tigre (a Tiger Cub) 2012. (Wonder Readers Spanish Emergent Ser.). (SPA.). 8p. (gr. -1-1). pap. 35.94 (978-1-62065-573-3(X)) Capstone Press of Coughlan Cos.

—A Tiger Cub, 1 vol. 2012. (Wonder Readers Emergent Level Ser.). (ENG.). 32p. (gr. -1-1). pap. 5.99 (978-1-4296-7788-2(0), Wonder Readers) Capstone Press of Coughlan Cos.

Guarnotta, Lucia, illus. We Are Tigers. 2006. (We Are... Ser.). 40p. (gr. -1-k). bds. (978-2-7641-1456-8(7)) Tormont Pubns.

Guillain, Charlotte, et al. Living in the Wild: Big Cats, 1 vol. 2014. (Living in the Wild: Big Cats Ser.). (ENG.). 48p. (gr. 3-6). lib. bdg. 199.92 (978-1-4329-8111-2(0), Heinemann InfoSearch) Heinemann-Raintree.

Hall, Margaret. Tigers & Their Cubs. 2007. (Animal Offspring Ser.). (ENG.). 24p. (gr. k-1). pap. 41.70 (978-1-4296-0565-6(0), Pebble Plus) Capstone Press of Coughlan Cos.

Hanel, Rachael. Tigers. 2008. (Living Wild Ser.). (Illus.). 46p. (J). (gr. 4-6). lib. bdg. 22.95 (978-1-58341-660-0(9), Creative Education) Creative Co., The.

Hegel, Claudette. Tigers, 1 vol. 2012. (Big Cats Ser.). (ENG.). 32p. (gr. 3-4). lib. bdg. 27.99 (978-1-4296-7646-5(9), Edge Bks.) Capstone Press of Coughlan Cos.

Hendrix, Emilia. Tigers & Cubs. 2016. (Animal Family Ser.). (ENG.). 24p. (J). (gr. k-k). pap. 8.15 (978-1-4824-3791-1(0)) Stevens, Gareth Publishing LLLP.

Hirsch, Rebecca E. Siberian Tigers: Camouflaged Hunting Mammals. 2015. (Comparing Animal Traits Ser.). (ENG., Illus.). 32p. (J). (gr. 2-4). pap. 8.99 (978-1-4677-6065-2(X), Lerner Pubns.) Lerner Publishing Group.

Hoff, Mary King. Tigers. 2005. (Wild World of Animals (Creative Education) Ser.). (Illus.). 32p. (J). (gr. 2-5). lib. bdg. 18.95 (978-1-58341-355-5(3), Creative Education) Creative Co., The.

Jazynka, Kitson. National Geographic Kids Mission: Tiger Rescue: All about Tigers & How to Save Them. 2015. (NG Kids Mission: Animal Rescue Ser.). (ENG., Illus.). 112p. (J). (gr. 5). pap. 12.99 (978-1-4263-1895-5(2), National Geographic Children's Bks.) National Geographic Society.

Jenkins, Martin. Can We Save the Tiger? White, Vicky, illus. 2014. (ENG.). 56p. (J). (gr. k-3). 9.99 (978-0-7636-7378-9(1)) Candlewick Pr.

Kalman, Bobbie. Endangered Tigers. 2008. (FRE.). 32p. (J). pap. 9.95 (978-2-89579-204-8(6)) Bayard Canada Livres CAN. Dist: Crabtree Publishing Co.

—Endangered Tigers. 2004. (Earth's Endangered Animals Ser.). (ENG., Illus.). 32p. (J). pap. (978-0-7787-1896-3(4)) Crabtree Publishing Co.

Katirgis, Jane & Green, Carl R. Endangered Tigers. 2015. (Wildlife at Risk Ser.). (ENG.). 48p. (J). (gr. 6-6). pap. 11.70 (978-0-7660-6904-6(4)); (Illus.). 27.93 (978-0-7660-6906-0(0)) Enslow Pubs., Inc.

Kuskowski, Alex. Tigers, 1 vol. 2014. (Zoo Animals Ser.). (ENG.). 24p. (J). (gr. k-3). lib. bdg. 24.21 (978-1-62403-275-2(3), SandCastle) ABDO Publishing Co.

Landau, Elaine. Fierce Cats. 2003. (Fearsome, Scary, & Creepy Animals Ser.). (Illus.). 48p. (J). (gr. 1-4). lib. bdg. 23.93 (978-0-7660-2062-7(2)) Enslow Pubs., Inc.

Latta, Jan. Timba el Tigre. 2007. (Familias de animales salvajes (Wild Animal Families) Ser.). (SPA., Illus.). 24p. (gr. 1-4). lib. bdg. 24.00 (978-0-8368-7971-1(6), Gareth Stevens Learning Library) Stevens, Gareth Publishing LLLP.

—Timba the Tiger. 2007. (Wild Animal Families Ser.). (Illus.). 24p. (gr. 1-4). pap. 8.15 (978-0-8368-7779-3(9)); lib. bdg. 24.00 (978-0-8368-7772-4(1)) Stevens, Gareth Publishing LLLP. (Gareth Stevens Learning Library).

Leaf, Christina. Baby Tigers. 2015. (Super Cute! Ser.). (ENG., Illus.). 24p. (J). (gr. k-3). lib. bdg. 25.95 (978-1-62617-173-2(4), Blastoff! Readers) Bellwether Media.

Ledu-Frattini, Stephanie. The Tiger. Uhlig, Elizabeth, tr. from FRE. Sah, Anup, photos by. 2004. (Animal Close-Ups Ser.). (Illus.). 28p. (J). pap. 6.95 (978-1-57091-373-0(0)) Charlesbridge Publishing, Inc.

Macheske, Felicia. Striped Stalkers: Tiger. 2017. (Guess What Ser.). (ENG., Illus.). 24p. (J). (gr. k-2). lib. bdg. 28.50 (978-1-63472-172-1(1), 209260) Cherry Lake Publishing.

Macken, JoAnn Early. Tigers: Los Tigres. 2004. (Animals I See at the Zoo/ Animales que veo en el zoologico (bilingual) Ser.). (SPA., Illus.). 24p. (gr. k-3). pap. 8.15 (978-0-8368-4391-0(6), Weekly Reader Leveled Readers) Stevens, Gareth Publishing LLLP.

—Tigers (Los Tigres) 2004. (Animals I See at the Zoo/ Animales que veo en el zoologico Ser.). (SPA., Illus.). 24p. (gr. k-3). lib. bdg. 22.00 (978-0-8368-4386-6(X), Weekly Reader Leveled Readers) Stevens, Gareth Publishing LLLP.

Maclaine, James. Tigers IR. 2012. (Beginner's Nature Ser.). 32p. (J). bds. 4.99 (978-0-7945-3286-4(1), Usborne) EDC Publishing.

Macleod, Steve. Soy el Tigre. 2012. (SPA.). (J). (978-1-61913-179-8(X)) Weigl Pubs., Inc.

—Tiger. 2011. (J). 27.13 (978-1-61690-853-9(X)); pap. 12.95 (978-1-61690-854-6(8)) Weigl Pubs., Inc.

Markert, Jenny. Tigers. 2015. (Animals of the Rain Forest Ser.). (ENG.). 24p. (J). (gr. 2-5). 27.07 (978-1-63143-752-6(6), 208581) Child's World, Inc., The.

Marsh, Laura. National Geographic Readers: Tigers. 2012. (Readers Ser.). (ENG., Illus.). 32p. (J). (gr. k-3). lib. bdg. 13.90 (978-1-4263-0912-0(0), National Geographic Children's Bks.) National Geographic Society.

—Tigers. 2012. (Readers Ser.). (ENG., Illus.). 32p. (J). (gr. k-3). pap. 3.99 (978-1-4263-0911-3(2), National Geographic Children's Bks.) National Geographic Society.

McRae, Anne & Morris, Neil. Celia the Tiger. De Luca, Daniela, illus. 2017. (J). **(978-0-7166-3524-6(0))** World Bk., Inc.

Meister, Cari. Do You Really Want to Meet a Tiger? Fabbri, Daniele, illus. 2015. (Do You Really Want to Meet...? Ser.). 24p. (J). 27.10 (978-1-60753-459-4(2)) Amicus Publishing.

—Tigers. 2015. (J). lib. bdg. 25.65 (978-1-62031-169-1(0), Bullfrog Bks.) Jump! Inc.

Montgomery, Sy. The Man-Eating Tigers of Sundarbans. Briggs, Eleanor, photos by. 2004. (ENG., Illus.). 64p. (J). (gr. 5-7). pap. 7.99 (978-0-618-49490-3(1)) Houghton Mifflin Harcourt Publishing Co.

—The Man-Eating Tigers of Sundarbans. Briggs, Eleanor, photos by. 2004. (Illus.). 57p. (J). 14.60 (978-0-7569-5180-1(1)) Perfection Learning Corp.

Moore, S. Tiger Talk: Learning the T Sound. 2009. (PowerPhonics Ser.). 24p. (gr. 1-1). 39.90 (978-1-60851-475-5(7), PowerKids Pr.) Rosen Publishing Group, Inc., The.

Morgan, Sally. Amazing Animals - Tigers. 2010. (Amazing Animal Hunters Ser.). 32p. (J). 28.50 (978-1-60753-049-7(X)) Amicus Publishing.

—Amazing Animals - Tigers. 2004. (QEB Animal Lives Ser.). (Illus.). 32p. (J). lib. bdg. 18.95 (978-1-59566-035-0(6)) QEB Publishing Inc.

—Amazing Animals - Tigers. 2012. (Illus.). 32p. (gr. 3-5). pap. 8.95 (978-1-926722-53-5(1)) Saunders Bk. Co. CAN. Dist: RiverStream Publishing.

Morgan, Sally & Martineau, Susan. Amazing Animals - Tigers. 2011. (Positive Steps Ser.). 32p. (gr. 2-5). lib. bdg. 31.35 (978-1-59920-489-5(4)) Black Rabbit Bks.

Murray, Julie. Tigers, 1 vol. (Asian Animals Ser.). (ENG.). 2013. 32p. (J). (gr. 2-5). lib. bdg. 28.50 (978-1-61783-558-2(7), Big Buddy Bks.) 2003. 24p. (gr. k-4). 25.65 (978-1-57765-646-3(6), Buddy Bks.) ABDO Publishing Co.

Nobleman, Marc Tyler. Tigers. 2008. (Endangered! Ser.). 48p. (gr. 3-18). lib. bdg. 29.93 (978-0-7614-2986-9(7), Benchmark Bks.) Marshall Cavendish Corp.

O'Neal, Claire. Threat to the Bengal Tiger. 2008. (On the Verge of Extinction Ser.). (Illus.). 32p. (J). (gr. 1-5). lib. bdg. 25.70 (978-1-58415-688-8(0)) Mitchell Lane Pubs., Inc.

Owen, Ruth. Tiger Cubs. (Wild Baby Animals Ser.). 24p. (J). (gr. k-3). 2016. (ENG.). pap. 7.95 **(978-1-944998-39-4(X))** 2011. lib. bdg. 19.96 (978-1-61772-158-8(1)) 2011. lib. bdg., E-Book 39.93 (978-1-61772-245-5(6)) Bearport Publishing Co., Inc.

Owings, Lisa. Tiger Attack. 2012. (Animal Attacks Ser.). (ENG., Illus.). 24p. (J). (gr. 3-7). lib. bdg. 25.95 (978-1-60014-792-0(5), Torque Bks.) Bellwether Media.

Pallotta, Jerry. Lion vs. Tiger. Bolster, Rob, illus. 2016. (Who Would Win? Ser.). (ENG.). 32p. (J). (gr. 2-5). pap. 3.99 (978-0-545-17571-5(2)) Scholastic, Inc.

Pearl, Norman. Tigers: Hunters of Asia. 2009. (Powerful Predators Ser.). 24p. (gr. 2-3). 42.50 (978-1-60851-350-5(5)); (Illus.). (J). (gr. 3-4). lib. bdg. 22.60 (978-1-4042-4507-5(3)) Rosen Publishing Group, Inc., The. (PowerKids Pr.).

Pelusey, Michael & Pelusey, Jane. Tigers & Lions. 2008. (Zoo Animals Ser.). 32p. (gr. 2-3). lib. bdg. 18.56 (978-0-7614-3151-0(9), Benchmark Bks.) Marshall Cavendish Corp.

Peterson, Megan Cooley & Rustad, Martha E. H. Bengal Tigers Are Awesome! 2015. (Awesome Asian Animals Ser.). (ENG., Illus.). 32p. (gr. 1-2). lib. bdg. 27.32 (978-1-4914-3903-6(3)) Capstone Press of Coughlan Cos.

Pingry, Patricia A. & Sharp, Chris. Baby Tiger. 2003. (San Diego Zoo Animal Library). (ENG., Illus.). 24p. (J). bds. 6.95 (978-0-8249-6527-3(2), Ideal Pubns.) Worthy Publishing.

Poitier, Anton. Once I Was a Comic... But Now I'm a Book about Tigers. Evans, Melvyn, illus. 2010. 24p. (J). (gr. k-3). 7.99 (978-0-8416-7201-7(6)) Hammond World Atlas Corp.

Portman, Michael. Tigers in Danger. 2011. (Animals at Risk Ser.). (Illus.). 24p. (J). (gr. 2-5). pap. 8.15 (978-1-4339-5812-0(0)); lib. bdg. 22.60 (978-1-4339-5810-6(4)) Stevens, Gareth Publishing LLLP. (Gareth Stevens Learning Library).

Quality Productions Staff. Tigres. Rountree, Monica, tr. 2003. (Zoobooks Ser.). Orig. Title: Tigers. (SPA., Illus.). 24p. (J). (gr. k-6). lib. bdg. 15.95 (978-1-888153-75-0(X)) Wildlife Education, Ltd.

Reher, Matt. Could a Tiger Be My Pet? 2016. (1B Animal Behaviors Ser.). (ENG., Illus.). 24p. (J). pap. 5.99 (978-1-63437-448-4(7)) American Reading Co.

Riddolls, Tom. Tigers. 2014. (J). pap. (978-1-4896-0931-1(8)) Weigl Pubs., Inc.

Riggs, Kate. Seedlings: Tigers. 2014. (Seedlings Ser.). (ENG.). 24p. (J). (gr. -1-k). pap. 6.99 (978-0-89812-889-5(7), Creative Paperbacks) Creative Co., The.

—Tigers. 2013. (J). 25.65 (978-1-60818-344-9(0), Creative Education) Creative Co., The.

Ring, Susan. Project Tiger. Marshall, Diana & Nault, Jennifer, eds. 2003. (Zoo Life Ser.). (Illus.). 24p. (J). pap. 8.95 (978-1-59036-061-3(3)) Weigl Pubs., Inc.

Ringstad, Arnold. Tigers. 2015. (Wild Cats Ser.). (Illus.). 24p. (J). 27.10 (978-1-60753-605-5(6)) Amicus Publishing.

Ritchey, Kate & Bader, Bonnie. Lion, Tiger, & Bear, Level 4. 2015. (Penguin Young Readers, Level 4 Ser.). (ENG., Illus.). 48p. (J). (gr. 3-4). pap. 3.99 (978-0-448-48336-8(X), Penguin Young Readers) Penguin Young Readers Group.

Rober, Harold. Saber-Toothed Cat. 2017. (Bumba Books (tm) — Dinosaurs & Prehistoric Beasts Ser.). (ENG.). 24p. (J). (gr. -1-1). 12.99 **(978-1-5124-3717-1(4))**; 38.65 **(978-1-5124-3716-4(6))**; 38.65 **(978-1-5124-2739-4(X))** Lerner Publishing Group. (Lerner Pubns.).

Rober, Harold T. Saber-Toothed Cat. 2017. (Bumba Books (tm) — Dinosaurs & Prehistoric Beasts Ser.). (ENG., Illus.). 24p. (J). (gr. -1-1). 25.32 (978-1-5124-2645-8(8)) Lerner Publishing Group.

Rober, Harold T. El Tigre Dientes de Sable. 2017. (Bumba Books (tm) en Español — Dinosaurios y Bestias Prehistóricas (Dinosaurs & Prehistoric Beasts) Ser.). (SPA.). 24p. (J). (gr. -1-1). 25.32 **(978-1-5124-4119-2(8))** Lerner Publishing Group.

Royston, Angela. Save the Tiger, 1. 2014. (Animal SOS! Ser.). (ENG.). 32p. (J). (gr. k-5). 26.25 (978-1-4777-6029-1(6), Windmill Bks.) Rosen Publishing Group, Inc., The.

Salzmann, Mary Elizabeth. Baby Tigers, 1 vol. 2014. (Baby Animals Set 2 Ser.). (ENG.). 24p. (J). (gr. -1-3). 24.21 (978-1-62403-512-8(4)) ABDO Publishing Co.

Schafer, Susan & Robinson, Fay. Tigers. 2009. (Benchmark Rockets Ser.). 24p. (gr. 1-18). 24.21 (978-0-7614-4345-2(2), Benchmark Bks.) Marshall Cavendish Corp.

Scheunemann, Pam. Tigers Roar!, 1 vol. 2009. (Animal Sounds Set 1 Ser.). (ENG., Illus.). 24p. (J). (gr. k-3). lib. bdg. 24.21 (978-1-60453-572-3(5), SandCastle) ABDO Publishing Co.

Server, Lee. Tigers - Pb: A Portrait of the Animal World. 2013. (Portrait of the Animal World Ser.). (Illus.). 72p. pap. 9.95 (978-1-59764-319-1(X)) New Line Bks.

Sexton, Colleen. The Bengal Tiger. 2011. (Nature's Deadliest Ser.). (ENG., Illus.). 24p. (YA). (gr. 3-8). lib. bdg. 25.95 (978-1-60014-663-3(5), Pilot Bks.) Bellwether Media.

Simpson, Phillip. All about Tigers: A Description Text, 1 vol. 2014. (Text Structures Ser.). (ENG.). 32p. (gr. 1-3). pap. 7.99 (978-1-4846-0413-7(X), Heinemann First Library) Heinemann-Raintree.

Sirota, Lyn A. Bengal Tigers, 1 vol. 2010. (Asian Animals Ser.). (ENG.). 24p. (gr. k-1). pap. 7.29 (978-1-4296-4843-1(0)); 26.65 (978-1-4296-4032-9(4)); pap. 41.70 (978-1-4296-5093-9(1)) Capstone Press of Coughlan Cos. (Pebble Plus).

Smith, Lucy Sackett. Tigers: Prowling Predators. 2009. (Mighty Mammals Ser.). 24p. (J). (ENG.). pap. 8.25 (978-1-4358-3285-5(X), PowerKids Pr.); (Illus.). lib. bdg. 22.60 (978-1-4042-8107-3(X)) Rosen Publishing Group, Inc., The.

Soundprints, creator. Tiger Cub See-and-Do. 2011. (Let's Go to the Zoo! Ser.). (ENG., Illus.). 16p. (gr. -1). 5.95 (978-1-60727-460-5(4)) Soundprints.

Stanley, Elizabeth. Tyger! Tyger! 2007. (ENG., Illus.). 32p. (J). (gr. -1-3). 16.95 (978-1-59270-068-4(3)) Enchanted Lion Bks., LLC.

Steffora, Tracey. Animal Math: Adding, Taking Away, & Skip Counting, 1 vol. 2014. (Animal Math Ser.). (ENG.). 32p. (gr. -1-1). 29.99 (978-1-4846-0061-0(4), NA-h) Heinemann-Raintree.

—Taking Away with Tigers, 1 vol. 2013. (Animal Math Ser.). (ENG.). 24p. (gr. -1-1). 22.65 (978-1-4329-7563-0(3)); pap. 6.95 (978-1-4329-7570-8(6)) Heinemann-Raintree. (NA-h).

Stone, Lynn M. Tigers. 2004. (Nature Watch Ser.). (ENG.). 48p. (gr. 4-8). 27.93 (978-1-57505-578-7(3), Carolrhoda Bks.) Lerner Publishing Group.

Stone, Tanya Lee. Tigers. 2003. (Wild Wild World Ser.). 24p. (YA). 24.94 (978-1-56711-826-1(7), Blackbirch Pr., Inc.) Cengage Gale.

Thomas, Isabel. Lion vs. Tiger. 2017. (Animal Rivals Ser.). (ENG.). 24p. (gr. k-2). lib. bdg. 23.32 **(978-1-4846-4073-9(X)**, Heinemann Read & Learn) Heinemann-Raintree.

Thomson, Sarah L. Amazing Tigers! 2005. (I Can Read Level 2 Ser.). (ENG., Illus.). 32p. (J). (gr. k-3). pap. 3.99 (978-0-06-054452-2(X)) HarperCollins Pubs.

Ticktock Media, Ltd. Staff. What Do Tigers Do? 2008. (What Do Animals Do? Ser.). (ENG.). 10p. (J). (gr. k — 1). bds. 4.95 (978-1-84696-794-8(5), TickTock Books) Octopus Publishing Group GBR. Dist: Independent Pubs. Group.

Tigers. 2003. (J). per. (978-1-57657-946-6(8)) Paradise Pr., Inc.

Tigers: Level R, 6 vols. (Wonder Worldtm Ser.). 48p. 44.95 (978-0-7802-7068-8(1)) Wright Group/McGraw-Hill.

Tiger's Tail. Date not set. (Touch & Feel Ser.). (J). 4.98 (978-0-7525-9570-2(9)) Parragon, Inc.

Toufexis, George. Extreme Lions & Tigers Tattoos. 2011. (Dover Tattoos Ser.). (ENG.). 4p. (J). (gr. 1-4). pap. 1.50 (978-0-486-48184-5(0)) Dover Pubns., Inc.

Turnbull, Stephanie. Tiger. 2013. (Big Beasts Ser.). (Illus.). 24p. (gr. k-3). 28.50 (978-1-59920-837-4(7)) Black Rabbit Bks.

Unwin, Mike. Why Do Tigers Have Stripes? Morton, Robert et al, illus. 2006. (Usborne Starting Point Science Ser.). 22p. (J). (gr. 1-4). pap. 4.99 (978-0-7945-1408-2(1), Usborne) EDC Publishing.

Vogel, Elizabeth. Tigers. 2009. (Big Cats (Powerkids Readers) Ser.). 24p. (gr. 1-1). 37.50 (978-1-61511-572-3(2), PowerKids Pr.) Rosen Publishing Group, Inc., The.

Vogel, Julia. Tigers: Built for the Hunt. 2015. (Predator Profiles Ser.). (ENG., Illus.). 24p. (gr. 1-2). lib. bdg. 25.32 (978-1-4914-5036-9(3)) Capstone Press of Coughlan Cos.

Von Zumbusch, Amelie. Tigers: World's Largest Cats. 2007. (Dangerous Cats Ser.). (Illus.). 24p. (J). (gr. 3-7). lib. bdg. 22.60 (978-1-4042-3632-5(5)) Rosen Publishing Group, Inc., The.

von Zumbusch, Amelie. Tigers: World's Largest Cats. 2009. (Dangerous Cats Ser.). 24p. (gr. 2-3). 42.50 (978-1-61512-131-1(5), PowerKids Pr.) Rosen Publishing Group, Inc., The.

Watson, Galadriel Findlay. Tigers. 2008. (Amazing Animals Ser.). (Illus.). 24p. (J). (gr. 2-4). pap. 8.95 (978-1-59036-963-0(7)); lib. bdg. 24.45 (978-1-59036-962-3(9)) Weigl Pubs., Inc.

Watt, E. Melanie. Tigers. 2012. (Animals on the Brink Ser.). (ENG., Illus.). 48p. (J). (gr. 4-7). pap. 14.95 (978-1-61913-432-4(2)); lib. bdg. 29.99 (978-1-61913-431-7(4)) Weigl Pubs., Inc. (AV2 by Weigl).

Wells, Robert E. Can We Share the World with Tigers? Wells, Robert E., illus. 2012. (Wells of Knowledge Science Ser.). (ENG., Illus.). 32p. (J). (gr. 1-3). 16.99 (978-0-8075-1055-1(6)) Whitman, Albert & Co.

West, David. Sabertooth Tiger. Poluzzi, Alessandro, illus. 2017. (Graphic Prehistoric Animals Ser.). 32p. (gr. 3-7). lib. bdg. 31.35 (978-1-62588-411-4(7)) Black Rabbit Bks.

Whyte, Elizabeth. Tigers. 2012. (Killer Cats Ser.). (Illus.). 24p. (J). (gr. 2-5). pap. 8.15 (978-1-4339-7016-0(3)); lib. bdg. 22.60 (978-1-4339-7015-3(5)) Stevens, Gareth Publishing LLLP.

Wildlife Education. Tigers. 2007. (Illus.). (J). 5.99 (978-1-932396-35-5(7), Critters Up Close) Wildlife Education, Ltd.

Wildlife Education, contrib. by. Tigers. 2005. (Zootles Ser.). (Illus.). 23p. (J). (gr. -1-k). lib. bdg. 10.95 (978-1-932396-10-2(1)) Wildlife Education, Ltd.

Wilsdon, Christina. Tigers. (Amazing Animals Ser.). 48p. 2009. (gr. 2-6). pap. 10.50 (978-1-4339-2020-2(4), Gareth Stevens Learning Library) 2008. (J). (gr. 3-6). lib. bdg. 28.00 (978-0-8368-9103-4(1)) Stevens, Gareth Publishing LLLP.

—Tigers. 2007. (J). (978-1-59939-117-5(1), Reader's Digest Young Families, Inc.) Studio Fun International.

Yoyo Books Staff. We are Tigers. 2005. 40p. bds. (978-90-5843-818-8(X)) YoYo Bks.

Zeiger, Jennifer. Saber-Toothed Cat. 2015. (21st Century Junior Library: Dinosaurs & Prehistoric Creatures Ser.). (ENG., Illus.). 24p. (J). (gr. 2-5). lib. bdg. 27.07 (978-1-63362-386-6(6), 206964) Cherry Lake Publishing.

Zobel, Derek. Tigers. 2011. (Animal Safari Ser.). (ENG., Illus.). 24p. (J). (gr. k-3). lib. bdg. 25.95 (978-1-60014-610-7(4), Blastoff! Readers) Bellwether Media.

TIGER—FICTION

Abraham, Rayna M. Just Imagine: Rayna Abraham's Creative Collection for Kids. 2011. 44p. pap. 16.59 (978-1-4634-1529-7(X)) AuthorHouse.

Adams, Pam. Tiger. 2005. (ENG., Illus.). 12p. (J). (gr. -1-k). bds. (978-1-904550-28-0(2)) Child's Play International Ltd.

Adams, Richard. The Tyger Voyage. Bayley, Nicola, illus. 2013. 32p. (J). 15.95 net. (978-1-56792-491-6(3)) Godine, David R. Pub.

Amazing Mallika - Evaluation Guide: Evaluation Guide. 2006. (J). (978-1-55942-398-4(6)) Witcher Productions.

Angel, Ido. Vipo in Moscow: The Siberian Tiger Is Hungry! 2015. (AV2 Animated Storytime Ser.). (ENG.). (J). lib. bdg. 29.99 (978-1-4896-3914-1(4), AV2 by Weigl) Weigl Pubs., Inc.

Annaud, Jean-Jacques, et al. Two Brothers: The Tale of Kumal & Sangha. novel ed. 2005. (Novelization for Young Readers Ser.). (ENG., Illus.). 192p. pap. 7.95 (978-1-55704-632-1(8), William Morrow Paperbacks) HarperCollins Pubs.

Aryal, Aimee. Hello Tiger! Graybill, Joni, illus. 2004. 24p. (J). 19.95 (978-1-932888-25-6(X)) Mascot Bks., Inc.

Aubuchon, Hope L. Tiger, Ruler of the Universe. 2009. 48p. pap. 24.95 (978-1-60749-896-4(0)) America Star Bks.

Ayers, Linda. Tiger Does the Write Thing. Hunt, Jane, illus. l.t. ed. 2005. 35p. (J). per. 7.95 (978-0-9760505-4-4(4)) Blue Thistle Pr.

—Tiger Goes Collecting. Hunt, Jane, illus. l.t. ed. 2004. 55p. (J). per. 7.95 (978-0-9760505-2-0(8)) Blue Thistle Pr.

AZ Books. Tiger & His Stripes. 2013. (Amusing Stories Ser.). (ENG.). 10p. (J). (-k). bds. 7.95 (978-1-61889-307-9(6)) AZ Bks. LLC.

AZ Books Staff. Who Is the Tiger Looking For? Gridina, Anna, ed. 2012. (Who Is There Ser.). (ENG.). 10p. (J). (-k). bds. 11.95 (978-1-61889-037-5(9)) AZ Bks. LLC.

Baby Tiger's Blanket. 2005. (Georgie Giraffe Chapter Ser.). (J). 7.67 (978-1-932570-44-1(6)) Pioneer Valley Bks.

Banks, Kate. Close Your Eyes. Hallensleben, Georg, illus. 2015. (ENG.). 36p. (J). (gr. -1-1). bds. 7.99 (978-0-374-30101-9(8), 9780374301019, Farrar, Straus & Giroux (BYR)) Farrar, Straus & Giroux.

Banks, Lynne Reid. Tiger, Tiger. 2007. (ENG.). 208p. (YA). (gr. 7-11). mass mkt. 6.99 (978-0-440-42044-6(X), Laurel Leaf) Random Hse. Children's Bks.

Bannerman, Helen. The Boy & the Tigers. Petrone, Valeria, illus. 2004. (Little Golden Book Ser.). (ENG.). 24p. (J). (gr. -1-2). 4.99 (978-0-375-82719-8(6), Golden Bks.) Random Hse. Children's Bks.

—Little Black Sambo. 2007. (Illus.). 72p. per. 11.45 (978-1-59462-581-7(6), Book Jungle) Standard Pubns., Inc.

—Short Works of Helen Bannerman. l.t. ed. 2007. (ENG.). 54p. pap. 18.99 (978-1-4346-4066-6(3)) Creative Media Partners, LLC.

—The Story of Little Babaji. 2004. (Illus.). (J). (gr. -1-18). spiral bd. (978-0-616-14615-6(9)) Canadian National Institute for the Blind/Institut National Canadien pour les Aveugles.

—The Story of Little Black Sambo. 2007. pap. 7.99 (978-1-59986-912-4(8), FQ Classics) Filiquarian Publishing, LLC.

Barkow, Henriette. Buri & the Marrow. Finlay, Lizzie, illus. 2004. (ENG & FRE.). 24p. (J). pap. (978-1-85269-583-5(8)) Mantra Lingua.

Beck, Lynn G. & Sesa. Powercat, the Pacific Tiger. 2012. (J). 14.95 (978-1-937406-00-4(8)) Mascot Bks., Inc.

Berkeley, Jon. The Palace of Laughter. Dorman, Brandon, illus. (Wednesday Tales Ser.: No. 1). (J). (gr. 3-7). 2007. (ENG.). 464p. pap. 8.99 (978-0-06-075509-6(1)) 2006. 427p. 16.99 (978-0-06-075507-2(5), Julie Andrews Collection) HarperCollins Pubs.

—The Tiger's Egg. Dorman, Brandon, illus. (Wednesday Tales Ser.: No. 2). (J). 2009. (ENG.). 432p. pap. 7.99 (978-0-06-075512-6(1), Harper Trophy) 2007. 416p. (gr. 3-7). 16.99 (978-0-06-075510-2(5), Julie Andrews Collection) HarperCollins Pubs.

Bonnell, Kris. What Tigers Do. 2006. (J). pap. 5.95 (978-1-933727-41-7(1)) Reading Reading Bks., LLC.

Brennan, Sarah. The Tale of Temujin. Harrison, Harry, illus. 2012. (ENG.). 32p. (J). (978-1-937160-23-4(8)) Auspicious Times.

Bright, J. E. The Fastest Pet on Earth, 1 vol. Baltazar, Art, illus. 2011. (DC Super-Pets Ser.). (ENG.). 56p. (gr. 2-2). pap. 4.95 (978-1-4048-6623-2(X)); lib. bdg. 23.99 (978-1-4048-6264-7(1)) Picture Window Bks. (DC Super-Pets).

Brooks, John. The Sundarbans Tiger. 2006. 115p. (J). pap. 13.58 (978-0-9661789-4-4(7)) Canis Lupus Productions.

Brown, Peter. Mr. Tiger Goes Wild. 2013. (ENG.). 48p. (J). 126.00 (978-0-316-25551-6(3)); (Illus.). (gr. -1-1). 18.00 (978-0-316-20063-9(8)) Little, Brown Bks. for Young Readers.

Burchett, Jan & Vogler, Sara. Poacher Panic, 1 vol. Le Feyer, Diane, illus. 2012. (Wild Rescue Ser.). (ENG.). 152p. (gr. 3-6). 9.95 (978-1-4342-4593-9(4)); lib. bdg. 25.32 (978-1-4342-3286-1(7)) Stone Arch Bks.

Cadet, John. The Kangaroo's Adventure. 2012. 24p. pap. 24.95 (978-1-4560-2861-9(8)) America Star Bks.

Chan, Janette Shipston. The Tiny Tiger. 2010. 24p. (J). 13.50 (978-1-4520-4106-3(7)) AuthorHouse.

Child, Lauren. Maude: The Not-So-Noticeable Shrimpton. Krauss, Trisha, illus. 2013. (ENG.). 32p. (J). (gr. k-3). 16.99 (978-0-7636-6515-9(0)) Candlewick Pr.

Chin, Oliver. The Year of the Tiger: Tales from the Chinese Zodiac. Roth, Justin, illus. 2010. (Tales from the Chinese Zodiac Ser.). (ENG.). 36p. (J). (gr. -1-3). 15.95 (978-1-59702-020-6(6)) Immedium.

Christie, Jacky. Roger's Big Adventure. 2005. (J). pap. 8.00 (978-0-8059-6889-7(X)) Dorrance Publishing Co., Inc.

Cline, Renee. Kawndra the Tiger. 2009. 28p. pap. 15.49 (978-1-4389-6484-3(6)) AuthorHouse.

Cook, Sherry & Johnson, Terri. Timothy Tornado, 26. Kuhn, Jesse, illus. l.t. ed. 2006. (Quirkles — Exploring Phonics through Science Ser.: 20). 32p. 7.99 (978-1-933815-19-0(1), Quirkles, The) Creative 3, LLC.

T U V

Corris, Charles R. Donald Ditz & the Red Tiger, 1 vol. 2010. 64p. pap. 19.95 (978-1-4512-2193-0(2)) America Star Bks.

Counts, Monika, illus. LSU Countdown to Touchdown. 2010. (Countdown to Touchdown Ser.). 20p. 14.95 (978-1-61524-081-4(0), Intervisual/Piggy Toes) Bendon, Inc.

Daniel Visits the Doctor. 2014. (Daniel Tiger's Neighborhood Ser.). (ENG., Illus.). 24p. (J). (gr. -1-1). pap. 3.99 (978-1-4814-1734-1(7), Simon Spotlight) Simon Spotlight.

De Luca, Daniela. Celia the Tiger. 2008. (It's a Wildlife, Buddy! Ser.). (ENG., Illus.). 30p. (J). (gr. -1-1). 12.95 (978-88-6098-089-2(5)) McRae Bks. Srl ITA. Dist: Independent Pubs. Group.

Derrick, David G., Jr., illus. I'm the Scariest Thing in the Jungle! 2013. (ENG.). 36p. (J). (gr. -1-3). 15.95 (978-1-59702-087-9(7)) Immedium.

Derubertis, Barbara. Tessa Tiger's Temper Tantrums. Alley, R. W., illus. 2011. (Animal Antics A to Z Set III Ser.). pap. 45.32 (978-0-7613-8429-8(4)) Kane Press, Inc.

deRubertis, Barbara. Tessa Tiger's Temper Tantrums. Alley, R. W., illus. 2011. (Animal Antics A to Z Ser.). 32p. (J). pap. 7.95 (978-1-57565-345-7(1)); lib. bdg. 22.60 (978-1-57565-353-2(2)) Kane Press, Inc.

deRubertis, Barbara & DeRubertis, Barbara. Tessa Tiger's Temper Tantrums. Alley, R. W., illus. 2012. (Animal Antics A to Z Ser.). 32p. (J). (gr. 2 — 1). cd-rom 7.95 (978-1-57565-413-3(X)) Kane Press, Inc.

DiCamillo, Kate. The Tiger Rising. (ENG.). (J). (gr. 5). 2015. 144p. pap. 6.99 (978-0-7636-8087-9(7)) 2011. (Illus.). 128p. 15.99 (978-0-7636-5270-8(9)) Candlewick Pr.

—The Tiger Rising. Sheban, Chris, illus. 2006. 144p. (J). (gr. 5). pap. 5.99 (978-0-7636-2916-8(2)) Candlewick Pr.

—The Tiger Rising. aut. ed. 2011. (ENG., Illus.). 128p. (J). (gr. 5). 50.00 (978-0-7636-5383-5(7)) Candlewick Pr.

—The Tiger Rising. unabr. ed. 2004. (Middle Grade Cassette Librariestm Ser.). 128p. (J). (gr. 5-9). pap. 29.00 incl. audio (978-0-8072-0998-1(8), S YA 285 SP, Listening Library) Random Hse. Audio Publishing Group.

Dietl, Erhard. A Veces Quisiera Ser un Tigre. (Torre de Papel Ser.). (SPA., Illus.). (J). 7.95 (978-958-04-5040-5(4)) Norma S.A. COL. Dist: Distribuidora Norma, Inc.

Dowson, Nick. Tigress. Chapman, Jane, illus. 2008. (Read, Listen, & Wonder Ser.). (ENG.). 32p. (J). (gr. -1-3). pap. 8.99 (978-0-7636-3872-6(2)) Candlewick Pr.

—Tigress, Pack. Chapman, Jane, illus. 2008. (Read, Listen, & Wonder Ser.). (ENG.). 32p. (J). (gr. -1-3). pap. 9.99 (978-0-7636-4189-4(8)) Candlewick Pr.

—Tigress: Read & Wonder. Chapman, Jane, illus. 2007. (Read & Wonder Ser.). (ENG.). 32p. (J). (gr. -1-3). pap. 6.99 (978-0-7636-3314-1(3)) Candlewick Pr.

Durant, Alan. If You Go Walking in Tiger Wood. Boon, Debbie, illus. 2005. (ENG.). 100p. (J). (gr. -1-k). pap. 9.99 (978-0-00-710390-4(5), HarperSport) HarperCollins Pubs. Ltd. GBR. Dist: Independent Pubs. Group.

Eliot, Margaret. Cat & Tiger Go to the Seaside. 2012. 24p. pap. 28.03 (978-1-4691-7674-1(2)) Xlibris Corp.

Ellie. Bengal & Sengal. 2006. (J). pap. 8.00 (978-0-8059-7273-3(0)) Dorrance Publishing Co., Inc.

Elliott, Rebecca. The Last Tiger. Elliott, Rebecca, illus. 2013. (ENG., Illus.). 32p. (J). (gr. k-2). pap. 8.99 (978-0-7459-6349-5(8)) Lion Hudson PLC GBR. Dist: Independent Pubs. Group.

Flood, Pansie Hart. Tiger Turcotte Takes on the Know-It-All. Wummer, Amy, illus. 2005. 72p. (J). (gr. 1-4). pap. 6.95 (978-1-57505-900-6(2)) Lerner Publishing Group.

Forsythe, Amanda J. The Contabulous Adventures of M E. 2012. 28p. 24.95 (978-1-4626-6531-0(4)) America Star Bks.

Friedman, Becky. Daniel Goes to School. 2014. (Daniel Tiger's Neighborhood 8X8 Ser.). lib. bdg. 13.55 (978-0-606-35756-2(4)) Turtleback Bks.

—Daniel Learns to Share. 2016. (Simon & Schuster Ready-To-Read Level 1 Ser.). lib. bdg. 13.55 **(978-0-606-39754-4(X))** Turtleback Bks.

—Daniel Tries a New Food. 2015. (Daniel Tiger's Neighborhood 8X8 Ser.). lib. bdg. 13.55 (978-0-606-37874-1(X)) Turtleback Bks.

—Daniel Visits the Doctor. 2014. (Daniel Tiger's Neighborhood 8X8 Ser.). lib. bdg. 13.55 (978-0-606-36112-5(X)) Turtleback Bks.

—Daniel's First Fireworks. 2016. (Daniel Tiger's Neighborhood 8X8 Ser.). lib. bdg. 13.55 (978-0-606-38990-7(3)) Turtleback Bks.

—Daniel's Winter Adventure. Fruchter, Jason, illus. 2016. (Daniel Tiger's Neighborhood 8X8 Ser.). (ENG.). 24p. (gr. -1-2). 13.55 (978-0-606-39247-1(5)) Turtleback Bks.

—What Is Daniel Wearing? Fruchter, Jason, illus. 2015. (Daniel Tiger's Neighborhood Ser.). (ENG.). 14p. (J). (gr. -1 — 1). 8.99 (978-1-4814-2899-6(3), Simon Spotlight) Simon Spotlight.

Fruchter, Jason, illus. The Baby Is Here! 2015. (Daniel Tiger's Neighborhood Ser.). (ENG.). 24p. (J). (gr. -1-2). pap. 3.99 (978-1-4814-3013-5(0), Simon Spotlight) Simon Spotlight.

—Big Enough to Help. 2015. (Daniel Tiger's Neighborhood Ser.). (ENG.). 24p. (J). (gr. -1-1). pap. 5.99 (978-1-4814-2942-9(6), Simon Spotlight) Simon Spotlight.

—Daniel Feels Left Out. 2015. (Daniel Tiger's Neighborhood Ser.). (ENG.). 32p. (J). (gr. -1-k). 16.99 (978-1-4814-3836-0(0), Simon Spotlight) Simon Spotlight.

—Daniel Plays at School. 2016. (Daniel Tiger's Neighborhood Ser.). (ENG.). 32p. (J). (gr. -1-k). pap. 3.99 (978-1-4814-6102-3(8), Simon Spotlight) Simon Spotlight.

—Daniel's First Fireworks. 2016. (Daniel Tiger's Neighborhood Ser.). (ENG.). 24p. (J). (gr. -1-2). pap. 3.99 (978-1-4814-6053-8(6), Simon Spotlight) Simon Spotlight.

—Daniel's First Sleepover. 2015. (Daniel Tiger's Neighborhood Ser.). (ENG.). 24p. (J). (gr. -1-2). pap. 3.99 (978-1-4814-2893-4(4), Simon Spotlight) Simon Spotlight.

—Daniel's New Friend. 2015. (Daniel Tiger's Neighborhood Ser.). (ENG.). 24p. (J). (gr. -1-2). pap. 3.99 (978-1-4814-3543-7(4), Simon Spotlight) Simon Spotlight.

—Friends Help Each Other. 2014. (Daniel Tiger's Neighborhood Ser.). (ENG.). 32p. (J). (gr. -1-k). pap. 3.99 (978-1-4814-0366-5(4), Simon Spotlight) Simon Spotlight.

—Happy Love Day, Daniel Tiger! 2015. (Daniel Tiger's Neighborhood Ser.). (ENG.). 14p. (J). (gr. -1-2). bds. 6.99 (978-1-4814-4855-0(2), Simon Spotlight) Simon Spotlight.

—How Is Daniel Feeling? 2015. (Daniel Tiger's Neighborhood Ser.). (ENG.). 14p. (J). (gr. -1-k). bds. 10.99 (978-1-4814-3856-8(5), Simon Spotlight) Simon Spotlight.

—I Love You, Dad. 2015. (Daniel Tiger's Neighborhood Ser.). (ENG.). 26p. (J). (gr. -1-k). bds. 8.99 (978-1-4814-5736-1(5), Simon Spotlight) Simon Spotlight.

—What Time Is It, Daniel Tiger? 2016. (Daniel Tiger's Neighborhood Ser.). (ENG.). 14p. (J). (gr. -1-k). bds. 10.99 (978-1-4814-6934-0(7), Simon Spotlight) Simon Spotlight.

—You're Still You! 2016. (Daniel Tiger's Neighborhood Ser.). (ENG.). 12p. (J). (gr. -1-k). bds. 5.99 (978-1-4814-6743-8(3), Simon Spotlight) Simon Spotlight.

Gleeson, Brian. The Tiger & the Brahmin, 1 vol. Vargo, Kurt, illus. 2005. (Rabbit Ears: A Classic Tale Ser.). (ENG.). 36p. (gr. 2-7). 25.65 (978-1-59679-347-7(3)) Spotlight.

Gorbachev, Valeri. Cats Are Cats. Gorbachev, Valeri, illus. 2014. (ENG., Illus.). 32p. (J). (gr. -1-3). 16.95 (978-0-8234-3052-9(9)) Holiday Hse., Inc.

Grambling, Lois G. Can I Bring Saber to New York, Ms. Mayor? Love, Judy, illus. 2014. (Prehistoric Pets Ser.). (ENG.). 32p. (J). (gr. k-3). 17.95 (978-1-58089-570-5(0)) Charlesbridge Publishing, Inc.

Hale, Bruce. Danny & the Dinosaur & the New Puppy. 2015. (I Can Read! Level 1 Ser.). (J). lib. bdg. 13.55 (978-0-606-37608-2(9)) Turtleback Bks.

Hamburg, Jennifer. Daniel Goes to the Playground. 2015. (Daniel Tiger's Neighborhood 8X8 Ser.). lib. bdg. 13.55 (978-0-606-38256-4(9)) Turtleback Bks.

Hamilton, Linda. Smile & Say Cheetah! Brown, Kevin, illus. 2005. (978-1-933248-00-4(9)) World Quest Learning.

Harris, Wendy. Daniel Visits the Library. 2015. (Daniel Tiger's Neighborhood Ready-To-Read Ser.). lib. bdg. 13.55 (978-0-606-37875-8(8)) Turtleback Bks.

Harvey, Charlene A. The Adventures of the Tiger Club. 2011. 14p. pap. 10.99 (978-1-61215-027-7(6)) Salem Author Services.

Hoffmire, Baird, illus. How Tiger Got His Stripes: A Folktale from Vietnam. 2006. (Story Cove Ser.). (ENG.). 32p. (J). (gr. -1-3). pap. 4.95 (978-0-87483-799-5(5)) August Hse. Pubs., Inc.

Houck, Colleen. Tiger's Curse, Bk. 1. 2012. (Tiger's Curse Ser.: Bk. 1). (ENG.). 456p. (J). (gr. 7). pap. 9.95 (978-1-4549-0249-2(3)) Sterling Publishing Co., Inc.

—Tiger's Curse. 2012. (Tiger's Curse Ser.: Bk. 1). lib. bdg. 20.80 (978-0-606-23822-9(0), Turtleback) Turtleback Bks.

—Tiger's Destiny. (Tiger's Curse Ser.: Bk. 4). (ENG.). 464p. (J). (gr. 7). 2015. pap. 9.95 (978-1-4549-0356-7(2)) 2012. 17.95 (978-1-4027-9843-6(1)) Sterling Publishing Co., Inc.

—Tiger's Quest. (Tiger's Curse Ser.: Bk. 2). (ENG.). (J). (gr. 7). 2013. 512p. pap. 9.95 (978-1-4549-0358-1(9)) 2011. 496p. 17.95 (978-1-4027-8404-0(X)) Sterling Publishing Co., Inc.

—Tiger's Voyage. (Tiger's Curse Ser.: Bk. 3). (ENG.). (J). (gr. 7). 2014. 568p. pap. 9.95 (978-1-4549-0357-4(0))Bk. 3. 2011. 560p. 17.95 (978-1-4027-8405-7(8)) Sterling Publishing Co., Inc.

Huang, Yu-Hsuan, illus. Baby Tiger: Finger Puppet Book. 2016. (ENG.). 12p. (J). (gr. -1 — 1). bds. 6.99 (978-1-4521-4236-4(X)) Chronicle Bks. LLC.

Ipcar, Dahlov. Stripes & Spots, 1 vol. 2012. (ENG.). 42p. (J). 17.95 (978-1-934031-70-4(4), 2e66d329-f317-4896-abd2-ae101e429c86) Islandport Pr., Inc.

Irwin, Bindi & Black, Jess. Roar! 2011. (Bindi's Wildlife Adventures Ser.: 6). (ENG.). 112p. (J). (gr. 3-6). pap. 4.99 (978-1-4022-5931-9(X), Sourcebooks Jabberwocky) Sourcebooks, Inc.

Izquierdo, Ana, tr. Caritas Felices: Winnie-the-Pooh. 2007. (Disney Winnie the Pooh (SilverDolphin) Ser.). (SPA., Illus.). 10p. (J). (gr. -1). bds. (978-970-718-393-3(4), Silver Dolphin en Español) Advanced Marketing, S. de R. L. de C. V.

Johnson, Julia. Cheetah's Tale. Stacey International Staff, ed. Keeble, Susan, illus. 2004. (ENG.). 56p. 16.95 (978-1-900988-87-2(9), Stacey International) Stacey Publishing GBR. Dist: Casemate Pubs. & Bk. Distributors, LLC.

Jones, Thomas Rumsey. Boris: The Bengal Tiger. Eguiguren, India J. & Eguiguren, A. R., illus. 2013. 46p. pap. 5.99 (978-1-883378-81-3(8)) Sun on Earth Bks.

Kasza, Keiko. The Rat & the Tiger. 2007. (ENG., Illus.). 32p. (J). (gr. -1-2). pap. 6.99 (978-0-14-240900-8(6), Puffin Books) Penguin Young Readers Group.

Katie, Byron & Wilhelm, Hans. Tiger-Tiger, Is It True? Four Questions to Make You Smile Again. 2009. (ENG., Illus.). 32p. 14.95 (978-1-4019-2560-4(X), 1076) Hay Hse., Inc.

Katz, Karen. Roar, Roar, Baby! Katz, Karen, illus. 2015. (ENG., Illus.). 14p. (J). (gr. -1 — 1). bds. 6.99 (978-1-4814-1788-4(6), Little Simon) Little Simon.

Kerr, Judith. The Judith Kerr Treasury. 2014. (ENG., Illus.). 176p. (J). 29.99 (978-0-00-758653-0(1), HarperCollins Children's Bks.) HarperCollins Pubs. Ltd. GBR. Dist: HarperCollins Pubs.

—The Tiger Who Came to Tea. Kerr, Judith, illus. 2009. (ENG., Illus.). 32p. (J). (gr. -1-2). 17.99 (978-0-7636-4563-2(X)) Candlewick Pr.

—The Tiger Who Came to Tea. 2006. pap. (978-0-06-052468-5(5)) HarperCollins Canada, Ltd.

Khan, Nicholai. Nicho the Tiger - Create Your World. 2011. (Illus.). 28p. (J). 14.95 (978-0-9820801-2-2(3)) Nicho The Tiger LLC.

Khanna, Balraj. Rajah: King of the Jungle. 2011. (ENG.). 112p. 16.95 (978-1-935677-03-1(9)) Mapin Publishing Pvt. Ltd IND. Dist: National Bk. Network.

King-Chai, Sharon. Snail Mail. 2017. (ENG., Illus.). 32p. (J). (gr. -1-k). 17.99 (978-1-4449-2254-7(8)) Hachette Children's Group GBR. Dist: Hachette Bk. Group.

Kinney, Kendall. Tiger Tails. 2004. 68p. (J). per. 10.95 (978-1-932196-21-4(8)) WordWright.biz, Inc.

Kite, Justin. Even Tigers Need to Sleep. 2012. 24p. pap. 28.03 (978-1-4691-8880-5(5)) Xlibris Corp.

Kleinman, Estelle. Tears of a Tiger. Friedland, Joyce & Kessler, Rikki, eds. 2008. (Novel-Ties Ser.). (Illus.). 31p. pap. 16.95 (978-0-7675-4259-3(2)) Learning Links Inc.

Kraus, Robert. Leo, el Retaño Tardio. Mlawer, Teresa, tr. Aruego, Jose, illus.Tr. of Leo the Late Bloomer. (SPA.). (J). (gr. k-1). pap. 7.95 (978-1-930332-02-7(5), LC30358) Lectorum Pubns., Inc.

Kung, Annie, tr. Auntie Tigress & Other Favorite Chinese Folk Tales. Wang, Eva, illus. 2006. (ENG.). 48p. (J). (gr. -1). lib. bdg. 16.50 (978-1-933327-29-7(4)) Purple Bear Bks., Inc.

Lambert, Jonny. Tiger Tiger. Lambert, Jonny, illus. 2017. (ENG., Illus.). 32p. (J). (gr. -1-2). 16.99 **(978-1-68010-044-0(0))** Tiger Tales.

LaRochelle, David. It's a Tiger! Tankard, Jeremy, illus. 2012. (ENG.). 36p. (J). (gr. -1-k). 16.99 (978-0-8118-6925-6(3)) Chronicle Bks. LLC.

Lee, Lucas Taekwon. The Legend of Baeoh: How Baeoh Got His Stripes. Forward, Max, illus. 2007. (ENG.). 36p. (J). (gr. 1-2). 17.95 (978-1-931741-88-0(3)) Reed, Robert D. Pubs.

Lindgren, Barbro. Soda Pop. Adbage, Lisen, illus. 2017. (ENG.). 112p. (J). (gr. 3-5). 16.99 **(978-1-77657-010-2(3))** Gecko Pr. NZL. Dist: Lerner Publishing Group.

Litton, Jonathan. Planet Pop-Up: Tiger Takes Off. Anderson, Nicola, illus. 2015. (Planet Pop-Up Ser.). (ENG.). 12p. (J). (gr. -1). 12.95 (978-1-62686-373-6(3), Silver Dolphin Bks.) Readerlink Distribution Services, LLC.

London, Jonathan. Little Lost Tiger, 0 vols. Spirin, Ilya, illus. 2012. (ENG.). 32p. (J). (gr. k-3). 17.99 (978-0-7614-6130-2(2), 9780761461302, Amazon Children's Publishing) Amazon Publishing.

Long, Ethan. Lion & Tiger & Bear: Tag! You're It! 2016. (Lion & Tiger & Bear Ser.). (ENG., Illus.). 40p. (J). (gr. k-2). 14.95 (978-1-4197-1896-0(7)) Abrams, Inc.

Lorenz, Jinye. Ryong's Story: Extended Version of Grandfather, the Tiger & Ryong. Lorenz, Virginia O., ed. 2006. (Illus.). 135p. (YA). per. 14.95 (978-1-888350-11-1(3)) Lighted Lamp Pr.

Lumry, Amanda & Hurwitz, Laura. Tigers in Terai. McIntyre, Sarah, illus. 2nd rev. ed. 2007. (Adventures of Riley (Unnumberd) Ser.). 36p. (J). (gr. -1-3). 15.95 (978-1-60040-003-2(5)) Centro Bks., LLC.

—Tigers in Terai. McIntyre, Sarah, illus. (Adventures of Riley Ser.). 36p. 2003. 15.95 (978-0-9662257-7-8(5)) 2nd ed. 2007. (978-0-9748411-6-8(1)) Eaglemont Pr.

Malone, Geoffrey. Tiger! 2006. (ENG.). 304p. (J). (gr. 4-6). pap. 10.95 (978-0-340-89358-6(3)) Hachette Children's Group GBR. Dist: Hachette Bk. Group.

Marinaro, Stacy. Carter Finds a Tiger. 2009. 19p. 12.50 (978-0-578-02365-6(2)) Marinaro, Stacy.

Marlow, Herb. The Tiger's Den. Head, Pat, illus. 2003. 22p. (J). 19.95 (978-1-893595-37-8(4)) Four Seasons Bks., Inc.

Marsh, Carole. The Mystery in Las Vegas. 2009. (Real Kids, Real Places Ser.). (Illus.). 145p. (J). lib. bdg. 18.99 (978-0-635-07045-6(6), Marsh, Carole Mysteries) Gallopade International.

Mathis, Tabitha. The Princess & the Tyger. 2012. 28p. pap. 24.95 (978-1-4626-8265-2(0)) America Star Bks.

Mcdoogle, Farrah. Thank You Day. 2014. (Daniel Tiger's Neighborhood Ready-To-Read Ser.). lib. bdg. 13.55 (978-0-606-35449-3(2)) Turtleback Bks.

McGonagle, Joanne L. The Tiniest Tiger. 2008. (ENG.). 52p. pap. 15.00 (978-1-4196-8467-8(1)) CreateSpace Independent Publishing Platform.

Michaelis, Antonia. Tiger Moon. 2009. (ENG.). 480p. (YA). (gr. 7-11). pap. 9.95 (978-0-8109-4499-2(5), Amulet Bks.) Abrams, Inc.

Millhouse, Jackie. The Tiger & the General. Girouard, Patrick, illus. 2007. (J). (978-1-932911-32-9(4)) World Tribune Pr.

Milne, A. A. In Which It Is Shown That Tiggers Don't Climb Trees. Shepard, Ernest H., illus. unabr. ed. (Classic Pooh Treasury Ser.). (J). incl. audio (978-1-57375-529-0(X), 71414) Audioscope.

—Pu Baut ein Haus.Tr. of Pooh Builds a House. (GER.). (J). pap. 12.95 (978-3-423-07395-0(0)) Deutscher Taschenbuch Verlag GmbH & Co KG DEU. Dist: Distribooks, Inc.

—Tigger Tales. Shepard, Ernest H., illus. 2006. 36p. (J). (gr. k-4). reprint ed. 15.00 (978-1-4223-5453-7(9)) DIANE Publishing Co.

Minz-Kammer, Koda. Pinpot Tiger & the Lost Monkey. 2008. 54p. pap. 20.00 (978-0-557-01646-4(0)) Lulu Pr., Inc.

Moynahan, Jamie. Tiger Bunnies. 2009. (Illus.). 16p. pap. 9.49 (978-1-4389-7000-4(5)) AuthorHouse.

Murakami, Jon & Yeh, Phil. The Winged Tiger & the Dragons of Hawaii. 2005. 48p. pap. 11.95 (978-0-9755635-0-2(5)) Eastwind Studios.

Nagda, Ann Whitehead. A Tiger Tale. Kratter, Paul, illus. (Soundprints' Amazing Animal Adventures! Ser.). (ENG.). 36p. (J). 2005. (gr. -1-2). 2.95 (978-1-59249-044-8(1), S7151) 2005. (gr. -1-2). 15.95 (978-1-59249-042-4(5), B7101) 2005. (gr. -1-2). pap. 6.95 (978-1-59249-043-1(3), S7101) 2005. (gr. -1-2). 19.95 (978-1-59249-388-3(2), BC7101) 2005. (gr. 2-2). 8.95 (978-1-59249-389-0(0), SC7101) 2003. (gr. -1-3). 9.95 (978-1-59249-057-8(3), PS7151) Soundprints.

Naughton, Patrick. Colonel Tiger on the Raft. 2010. 76p. pap. 12.95 (978-1-4452-6095-2(6)) Lulu Pr., Inc.

Newton-Kowalsky, Jacqueline. Itsy Bitsy Stories for Itsy Bitsy Tigers. 2012. 32p. pap. (978-1-77097-138-7(6)) FriesenPress.

Nowra, Louis. Into That Forest, 0 vols. 2013. (ENG.). 160p. (YA). (gr. 7-9). 16.99 (978-1-4778-1725-4(5), 9781477817254, Amazon Children's Publishing); 162p. 16.99 (978-1-4778-6725-9(2)) Amazon Publishing.

O'Campo, Allicia. Tinky Goes to North Americ. 2009. 28p. pap. 15.50 (978-1-60860-412-8(8), Eloquent Bks.) Strategic Book Publishing & Rights Agency (SBPRA).

Osborne, Mary Pope. Tigers at Twilight. unabr. ed. 2004. (Magic Tree House Ser.: No. 19). 72p. (J). (gr. k-3). pap. 17.00 incl. audio (978-0-8072-0928-8(7), S FTR 251 SP, Listening Library) Random Hse. Audio Publishing Group.

Osborne, Mary Pope, et al. Tigres Al Anochecer. Murdocca, Sal, illus. 2008. (Casa del Arbol Ser.: 19).Tr. of Tigers at Twilight. (SPA.). (J). (gr. 2-4). pap. 5.99 (978-1-933032-49-8(9)) Lectorum Pubns., Inc.

Ostermeyer, Tim, photos by. Titus & Tiana: Lesson for Baby Tigers. 2011. (Illus.). 18.95 (978-0-9794228-6-7(8)) Ostermeyer Photography.

Owens, Jeanette. The Adventures of Raj: The Snow Tiger. 2012. (Illus.). 28p. pap. 19.99 (978-1-4678-8937-7(7)) AuthorHouse.

PaleoJoe & Caszatt-Allen, Wendy. Secret Sabertooth. 2007. (PaleoJoe's Dinosaur Detective Club Ser.: 3). (ENG., Illus.). 168p. (J). (gr. 2-5). pap. 8.95 (978-1-934133-10-1(8), Mackinac Island Press, Inc.) Charlesbridge Publishing, Inc.

Parish, Scott. Tigre a la Mesa. 2005. 14p. (J). 10.00 (978-1-4116-6003-8(X)) Lulu Pr., Inc.

Parragon Staff. Tigger's Adventure. 2010. (Disney Diecut Classics). 72p. (J). (gr. -1-1). (978-1-4075-8903-9(2)) Parragon, Inc.

Partis, Joanne. Stripe. Partis, Joanne, illus. (Carolrhoda Picture Books Ser.). (Illus.). 32p. (J). 2004. pap. 6.95 (978-1-57505-667-8(4)) 2003. (gr. -1-3). 14.95 (978-1-57505-450-6(7)) Lerner Publishing Group.

—Stripe's Naughty Sister. 2003. (Picture Bks.). (Illus.). 32p. (J). (gr. -1-3). 15.95 (978-0-87614-466-4(0), Carolrhoda Bks.) Lerner Publishing Group.

Pelley, Kathleen T. Raj the Bookstore Tiger. Keiser, Paige, illus. 2011. (ENG.). 32p. (J). (gr. -1-3). 15.95 (978-1-58089-230-8(2)) Charlesbridge Publishing, Inc.

Pendergrass, Daphne. Daniel Plays at School. 2016. (Daniel Tiger's Neighborhood Ready-To-Read Ser.). lib. bdg. 13.55 (978-0-606-38991-4(1)) Turtleback Bks.

Perkins, Mitali. Tiger Boy. 2017. (ENG.). 144p. (J). (gr. 2-5). pap. 6.99 (978-1-58089-661-0(8)) Charlesbridge Publishing, Inc.

—Tiger Boy. Hogan, Jamie, illus. 2015. (ENG.). 144p. (J). (gr. 2-5). lib. bdg. 14.95 (978-1-58089-660-3(X)) Charlesbridge Publishing, Inc.

Peters, Andrew. The Tiger & the Wise Man. Mayo, Diana, illus. 2010. (Traditional Tales with a Twist Ser.). (ENG.). 32p. (J). (gr. -1-2). audio compact disk (978-1-84643-346-7(0)) Child's Play International Ltd.

Peters, Andrew Fusek. The Tiger & the Wise Man. Mayo, Diana, illus. 2004. (Traditional Tales with a Twist Ser.). (ENG.). 32p. (J). (gr. 2-3). (978-1-904550-07-5(X)) Child's Play International Ltd.

Pogo the Clown. The Littlest Tiger: Harley's Great Adventures. Miller, Richard, illus. 2004. (J). 12.95 (978-0-9755253-2-6(8)) Chiliric Pubns.

Powell, Richard. Timmy Tiger. Rhodes, Katie, illus. 2004. (Fuzzy Friends Ser.). 10p. (J). 7.95 (978-1-58925-722-1(7)) Tiger Tales.

Prebeg, Rick. You've Got Cheetah Mail. Prebeg, Rick, photos by. 2005. (Illus.). (J). (978-1-933248-11-0(4)) World Quest Learning.

Priddy, Roger. Tiger - Animal Buddies. 2015. (Animal Buddies Ser.). (ENG., Illus.). 8p. (J). (gr. -1 — 1). bds. 5.99 (978-0-312-51865-3(X), 9780312518653, Priddy Bks.) St. Martin's Pr.

Proimos, James, Jr. Knuckle & Potty Destroy Happy World. Proimos, James, Jr., illus. 2012. (ENG., Illus.). 80p. (J). (gr. 2-5). 12.99 (978-0-8050-9155-7(6), 9780805091557, Holt, Henry & Co. Bks. For Young Readers) Holt, Henry & Co.

Publications International Ltd. Staff, ed. Potty Time with Tiger: Boy. 2010. (J). bds. 5.98 (978-1-4127-6915-0(9)) Publications International, Ltd.

—Potty Time with Tiger: Girl. 2010. (SPA.). (J). bds. 5.98 (978-1-4127-6916-7(7)) Publications International, Ltd.

—A Ring-A-Ling Day! 2009. 12p. (J). bds. 11.98 (978-1-4127-9614-9(8), PIL Kids) Publications International, Ltd.

Rayner, Catherine. Augustus & His Smile. Rayner, Catherine, illus. 2016. (ENG., Illus.). 32p. (J). (gr. -1-2). 16.99 (978-1-68010-005-1(X)) Tiger Tales.

Rayner, Catherine. One Happy Tiger. Rayner, Catherine, illus. 2017. (ENG., Illus.). 24p. (J). (gr. -1-1). bds. 9.99 **(978-1-58925-234-9(9))** Tiger Tales.

Redbank, Tennant. The Great Mountain Adventure. RH Disney et al, illus. 2016. (Disney Chapters Ser.). (ENG.). 64p. (J). (gr. 1-4). 5.99 (978-0-7364-3636-6(7), RH/Disney) Random Hse. Children's Bks.

—The Kitchen Catastrophe. The Disney Storybook Art Team & Batson, Alan, illus. 2016. (Disney Chapters Ser.). (ENG.). 64p. (J). (gr. 1-4). 5.99 (978-0-7364-3643-4(X), RH/Disney) Random Hse. Children's Bks.

Rigo, L. & Caviezel, Giovanni, illus. Little Tiger. 2010. (Look at Me Bks.). (ENG.). 10p. (J). (gr. -1-k). bds. 8.99 (978-0-7641-6326-5(4)) Barron's Educational Series, Inc.

Rigo, Laura, illus. Little Tiger. 2017. (Mini Look at Me Bks.). (ENG.). 10p. (J). (gr. -1 — 1). bds. 4.99 (978-0-7641-6881-9(9)) Barron's Educational Series, Inc.

Robert, Kraus. Leo the Late Bloomer. 2014. (Trophy Picture Bks). (ENG.). 32p. (J). (gr. k-3). 11.24 (978-1-63245-278-8(2)) Lectorum Pubns., Inc.

Ross, Dev. We Both Read Bilingual Edition-Frank & the Tiger/Sapi y el Tigre. Canetti, Yanitzia, tr. from ENG. Reinhart, Larry, illus. 2014. (We Both Read - Level K-1 (Quality) Ser.). (ENG & SPA.). 44p. (J). (gr. k-1). pap. 4.99 (978-1-60115-058-5(X)) Treasure Bay, Inc.

—We Both Read-Frank & the Tiger. Reinhart, Larry, illus. 2011. 44p. (J). 9.95 (978-1-60115-259-6(0)) Treasure Bay, Inc.

Ross, Patrick. Oliver: The Great Escape. Burcham, David, illus. 2009. 34p. pap. 24.95 (978-1-60749-151-4(6)) America Star Bks.

Roth, Carol. Hold Your Temper, Tiger. Rashin, illus. 2017. (ENG.). 32p. (J). (gr. -1-3). 17.95 (978-0-7358-4274-8(4)) North-South Bks., Inc.

Rouncville, Bibi. Bog Nymphs & Tiger Stones. 2008. 52p. pap. 15.50 (978-1-4357-3966-6(3)) Lulu Pr., Inc.

Roy, Ron. A Thief at the National Zoo. Bush, Timothy, illus. 2008. (Capital Mysteries Ser.: No. 9). 87p. (gr. k-3). 15.00 (978-0-7569-8329-1(0)) Perfection Learning Corp.

—A Thief at the National Zoo. Bush, Timothy, illus. 2007. (Capital Mysteries Ser.: No. 9). (ENG.). 96p. (J). (gr. 1-4). per. 4.99 (978-0-375-84804-9(5), Random Hse. Bks. for Young Readers) Random Hse. Children's Bks.

Rubio, Gabriela. Terrible/Terrible. 2006. (Jardin de los Ninos (Ediciones Ekare) Ser.). (SPA., Illus.). 22p. (J). (gr. 3-5). (978-84-933060-7-6(X)) Ekare, Ediciones.

Rubio, Gabriela & Rubio Márquez, Gabriela. Se Acabo! 2004. (SPA., Illus.). 30p. (J). 6.50 (978-84-348-7875-4(5)) SM Ediciones ESP. Dist: Lectorum Pubns., Inc.

Ruddra, Anshumani. Dorje's Stripes. A-Park, Gwangjo & A-Park, Jung, illus. 2011. (ENG.). 40p. (J). (gr. k-4). 9.99 (978-1-935279-98-3(X)) Kane Miller.

Safari Press Staff, ed. Book Buddy - Tiger with Story Book. (Illus.). 10p. (J). (gr. -1-3). reprint ed. pap. (978-1-881469-85-8(9)) Safari, Ltd.

Samoun, Abigail. How Tiger Says Thank You! Watts, Sarah, illus. 2015. (Little Traveler Ser.). (ENG & MUL.). 22p. (J). (gr.

-1-k). bds. 6.95 *(978-1-4549-1497-6(1))* Sterling Publishing Co., Inc.

Samson, Lucretia. Hungry Tiger & Clever Rabbit: A Tale from Korea. Bijoo, Adrian, illus. 2016. 24p. (J). pap. *(978-1-927244-58-6(7))* Clean Slate Pr. Ltd.

—Hungry Tiger & Clever Rabbit (Big Book Edition) A Tale from Korea. Bijoo, Adrian, illus. 2016. 24p. (J). pap. *(978-1-927244-68-5(4))* Flying Start Bks.

Sanner, Jennifer Jackson, ed. The Three Little Jayhawks. Pearson, Larry Leroy, illus. 2006. 40p. (J). per. 20.00 *(978-0-9742918-1-9(1))* Kansas Alumni Assoc.

Santomero, Angela C. Big Brother Daniel. Fruchter, Jason, illus. 2015. (Daniel Tiger's Neighborhood Ser.). (ENG.). 14p. (J). (gr. -1-k). bds. 5.99 *(978-1-4814-3172-9(2)*, Simon Spotlight) Simon Spotlight.

—Daniel's First Sleepover. 2015. (Daniel Tiger's Neighborhood 8X8 Ser.). lib. bdg. 13.55 *(978-0-606-36315-0(7))* Turtleback Bks.

—Goodnight, Daniel Tiger. Style Guide Staff, illus. 2014. (Daniel Tiger's Neighborhood Ser.). (ENG.). 26p. (J). (gr. -1-2). 12.99 *(978-1-4814-0048-0(7)*, Simon Spotlight) Simon Spotlight.

—Goodnight, Daniel Tiger. 2014. (Daniel Tiger's Neighborhood 8X8 Ser.). lib. bdg. 13.55 *(978-0-606-36113-2(8))* Turtleback Bks.

—Merry Christmas, Daniel Tiger! Fruchter, Jason, illus. 2015. (Daniel Tiger's Neighborhood Ser.). (ENG.). 14p. (J). (gr. -1-2). bds. 6.99 *(978-1-4814-4660-0(6)*, Simon Spotlight) Simon Spotlight.

Scelsa, Greg. Rhyme Time. Faulkner, Stacey, ed. Hanke, Karen, illus. 2006. (J). pap. 2.99 *(978-1-59198-323-1(1))* Creative Teaching Pr., Inc.

Schulz, Charles. Alle Achtung. Herbst, Gabriele & Rolle, Ekkehard, trs. from ENG. (Snoopy & die Peanuts Ser.: Vol. 5). (GER., Illus.). 128p. (J). pap. *(978-3-8105-1818-7(2))* Kruger, Wolfgang Verlag, GmbH DEU. Dist: International Bk. Import Service, Inc.

Schwartz, Betty & Seresin, Lynn. Ten Playful Tigers: A Touch-And-Feel Counting Book. Powell, Luciana Navarro, illus. 2015. (Back-And-Forth Bks.). (ENG.). 22p. (gr. -1 — 1). bds. 9.99 *(978-1-62370-233-5(X))* Capstone Young Readers of Coughlan Cos.

Seidon, Bonnie Bale. The Adventures of Trevor & the Tiger. 2012. 104p. 21.79 *(978-1-4669-4389-6(0))*; pap. 11.79 *(978-1-4669-4391-9(2))* Trafford Publishing.

Shaw, Natalie. I'm Feeling Happy. Fruchter, Jason, illus. 2016. (Daniel Tiger's Neighborhood Ser.). (ENG.). 14p. (J). (gr. -1 — 1). bds. 5.99 *(978-1-4814-6178-8(8)*, Simon Spotlight) Simon Spotlight.

—I'M Feeling Silly. Fruchter, Jason, illus. 2016. (Daniel Tiger's Neighborhood Ser.). (ENG.). 14p. (J). (gr. -1 — 1). bds. 5.99 *(978-1-4814-6815-2(4)*, Simon Spotlight) Simon Spotlight.

—Meet the Neighbors! Style Guide Staff, illus. 2014. (Daniel Tiger's Neighborhood Ser.). (ENG.). 16p. (J). (gr. -1-k). bds. 7.99 *(978-1-4424-9837-2(4)*, Simon Spotlight) Simon Spotlight.

Simon, Mary Manz. Tiger Forgives. Clearwater, Linda & Couri, Kathy, illus. 2006. (First Virtues for Toddlers Ser.). 20p. (J). 5.99 *(978-0-7847-1413-3(4)*, 04065) Standard Publishing.

Sky Koster, Amy. Cute, Sweet, & Petite! (Disney Princess: Palace Pets) Random House Disney Staff, illus. 2015. (Big Golden Book Ser.). (ENG.). 64p. (J). (gr. -1-2). 9.99 *(978-0-7364-3412-6(7)*, Golden/Disney) Random Hse. Children's Bks.

Smith, Sherri. Counting with Mike the Tiger. Walsh, D. T., illus. 2013. (ENG.). (J). (gr. -1-k). 14.95 *(978-1-62086-349-7(9))* Mascot Bks., Inc.

—Mike the Tiger Teaches the Alphabet. Walsh, D. T., illus. 2013. (ENG.). (J). (gr. -1-k). 14.95 *(978-1-62086-348-0(0))* Mascot Bks., Inc.

Snowflake Day! 2014. (Daniel Tiger's Neighborhood Ser.). (ENG., Illus.). 14p. (J). (gr. -1-k). bds. 5.99 *(978-1-4814-1771-6(1)*, Simon Spotlight) Simon Spotlight.

Snyder, Betsy E. Have You Ever Tickled a Tiger? 2009. (ENG., Illus.). 14p. (J). (gr. k — 1). 9.99 *(978-0-375-84396-9(5)*, Random Hse. Bks. for Young Readers) Random Hse. Children's Bks.

So-Un, Kim. The Tigers of the Kumgang Mountains: A Korean Folktale. Kyoung-Sim, Jeong, illus. 2005. (ENG.). 1p. (J). (gr. 4-11). 16.95 *(978-0-8048-3653-1(1))* Tuttle Publishing.

Soli, Doris. Jango the Little Dragon: The Wondrous Adventures of Little Dragon. 2011. (Illus.). 36p. pap. 17.07 *(978-1-4567-8487-4(0))* AuthorHouse.

Spagnoli, Cathy. Nine-In-One:Grr! Grr! Hom, Nancy, illus. 2013. (ENG.). 32p. (J). (gr. -1-5). pap. 9.95 *(978-0-89239-048-9(4))* Lee & Low Bks., Inc.

Sparrow, Steve. The Wooden Tiger. 2009. 52p. pap. *(978-1-84923-773-4(5))* YouWriteOn.

Spinner, Cala. A Busy Day in the Neighborhood. Fruchter, Jason, illus. 2017. (Daniel Tiger's Neighborhood Ser.). (ENG.). 12p. (J). (gr. -1-k). bds. 14.99 *(978-1-4814-8583-8(0)*, Simon Spotlight) Simon Spotlight.

Spreng, Robert C. The Tahoe Tiger & the Lahontan Lion. 2008. 38p. pap. 14.50 *(978-0-557-02370-7(X))* Lulu Pr., Inc.

Stewart, Lizzy. There's a Tiger in the Garden. 2016. (ENG., Illus.). 40p. (J). pap. 9.99 *(978-1-84780-807-3(7))*; 18.99 *(978-1-84780-806-6(9))* Quarto Publishing Group UK GBR. (Frances Lincoln Children's Bks.). Dist: Littlehampton Bk Services, Ltd.

Stockland, Patricia M. Tiger Toothache, 1 vol. Haugen, Ryan, illus. 2008. (Safari Friends Ser.). (ENG.). 32p. (gr. -1-3). 28.50 *(978-1-60270-087-1(7)*, Looking Glass Library) ABDO Publishing Co.

Studio Mouse Staff. Pooh & Eeyore, Pooh & Tigger. rev. ed. 2004. (Friends Collection). (ENG., Illus.). 36p. (J). (gr. -1-3). 15.99 *(978-1-59069-390-2(6)*, 1A302) Studio Mouse LLC.

—Pooh & Tigger. 2008. (ENG., Illus.). 36p. (J). (gr. -1). 7.99 *(978-1-59069-417-6(1))* Studio Mouse LLC.

Style Guide Staff & Fruchter, Jason, illus. Daniel Goes to School. 2014. (Daniel Tiger's Neighborhood Ser.). (ENG.). 24p. (J). (gr. -1-7). pap. 3.99 *(978-1-4814-0318-4(4)*, Simon Spotlight) Simon Spotlight.

Style Guide Staff & Garwood, Gord, illus. Thank You Day. 2014. (Daniel Tiger's Neighborhood Ser.). (ENG.). 24p. (J). (gr. -1-k). pap. 3.99 *(978-1-4424-9833-4(1)*, Simon Spotlight) Simon Spotlight.

Sykes, Julie. I Don't Want to Go to Bed! Warnes, Tim, illus. 2013. (ENG.). 32p. (J). *(978-1-58925-148-9(2))* Tiger Tales.

Taylor, Thomas. The Loudest Roar. 2003. (Illus.). (J). pap. *(978-0-439-50131-6(8)*, Levine, Arthur A. Bks.) Scholastic, Inc.

Teckentrup, Britta. Don't Wake up the Tiger. Teckentrup, Britta, illus. 2016. (ENG., Illus.). 30p. (J). (-k). 15.99 *(978-0-7636-8996-4(3)*, Nosy Crow) Candlewick Pr.

Tenbeth, Kate. Burly & Grum & the Tiger's Tale. Jones, Rob, illus. 2013. 36p. pap. *(978-0-9572119-7-1(X))* Magic Toy Bks.

Testa, Maggie. Daniel Plays Ball. 2014. (Daniel Tiger's Neighborhood Ready-To-Read Ser.). lib. bdg. 13.55 *(978-0-606-36114-9(6))* Turtleback Bks.

—Friends Are the Best! Style Guide, Style & Fruchter, Jason, illus. 2014. (Daniel Tiger's Neighborhood Ser.). (ENG.). 12p. (J). (gr. -1-k). bds. 5.99 *(978-1-4424-9547-0(2)*, Simon Spotlight) Simon Spotlight.

—A Ride Through the Neighborhood. Style Guide Staff, illus. 2014. (Daniel Tiger's Neighborhood Ser.). (ENG.). 12p. (J). (gr. -1-1). bds. 6.99 *(978-1-4424-9839-6(0)*, Simon Spotlight) Simon Spotlight.

Thurber, James. The Tiger Who Would Be King. Yoon, JooHee, illus. 2015. (ENG.). 40p. (J). (gr. k-4). 18.95 *(978-1-59270-182-7(5))* Enchanted Lion Bks., LLC.

The Tiger's Stripes & the Water Buffalo's Teeth. 2010. 40p. 19.57 *(978-1-4269-3110-9(7))* Trafford Publishing.

Tommy's Tummy Ache: Individual Title Six-Packs. (Literatura 2000 Ser.). (gr. -1-1). 28.00 *(978-0-7635-0015-3(1))* Rigby Education.

Turnbull, Victoria. The Sea Tiger. Turnbull, Victoria, illus. 2015. (ENG., Illus.). 40p. (J). (gr. -1-2). 16.99 *(978-0-7636-7986-6(0)*, Templar) Candlewick Pr.

Wallace Hunchak, Lisa. It Could Happen. 2013. 32p. pap. 17.25 *(978-1-4669-7130-1(4))* Trafford Publishing.

Walsh, Joanna. I Love Mom. Abbot, Judi, illus. 2014. (ENG.). 32p. (J). (gr. -1-3). 16.99 *(978-1-4814-2808-8(X)*, Simon & Schuster/Paula Wiseman Bks.) Simon & Schuster/Paula Wiseman Bks.

Walters, Eric. Tiger by the Tail. 2009. (ENG.). 176p. (J). (gr. 6). pap. *(978-1-55488-175-8(7))* Beach Holme Pubs., Ltd.

Wang, Eva, illus. Auntie Tigress & Other Favorite Chinese Folk Tales. 2006. (ENG.). 48p. (J). 15.95 *(978-1-933327-28-0(6))* Purple Bear Bks., Inc.

Warnes, Tim & Sykes, Julie. Bathtime, Little Tiger! Warnes, Tim, illus. 2003. (Little Tiger Lift-the-Flap Ser.). (Illus.). 12p. (J). 5.95 *(978-1-58925-693-4(X))* Tiger Tales.

—Hide & Seek, Little Tiger. Warnes, Tim, illus. 2003. (Little Tiger Lift-the-Flap Ser.). (Illus.). 14p. (J). 5.95 *(978-1-58925-694-1(8))* Tiger Tales.

Warren, Vince H. The Adventures of Meka & Her Two Cubs. 2013. (ENG.). 28p. (J). pap. 7.95 *(978-1-4787-0308-2(3))* Outskirts Pr., Inc.

Watt, Fiona. That's Not My Tiger. Wells, Rachel, illus. 2010. (Touchy-Feely Board Bks.). 10p. (J). bds. 8.99 *(978-0-7945-2820-1(1))* EDC Publishing.

Watterson, William. Achtung, Fertig, Los! Goetting, Waltraud, tr. from ENG. (Calvin & Hobbes Ser.: Vol. 8). (GER., Illus.). 64p. (J). pap. *(978-3-8105-0336-7(3))* Kruger, Wolfgang Verlag, GmbH DEU. Dist: International Bk. Import Service, Inc.

—Alles unter Kontrolle. Goetting, Waltraud, tr. from ENG. (Calvin & Hobbes Ser.: Vol. 3). (GER., Illus.). 64p. (J). pap. *(978-3-8105-0330-5(4))* Kruger, Wolfgang Verlag, GmbH DEU. Dist: International Bk. Import Service, Inc.

—Auf dem Sprung. Goetting, Waltraud, tr. from ENG. (Calvin & Hobbes Ser.: Bk. 1). (GER., Illus.). 96p. (J). pap. *(978-3-8105-0320-6(7))* Kruger, Wolfgang Verlag, GmbH DEU. Dist: International Bk. Import Service, Inc.

—Bloss nicht Aergern. Goetting, Waltraud, tr. from ENG. (Calvin & Hobbes Ser.: Bk. 3). (GER., Illus.). 96p. (J). pap. *(978-3-8105-0322-0(3))* Kruger, Wolfgang Verlag, GmbH DEU. Dist: International Bk. Import Service, Inc.

—Calvin & Hobbes: Das Jubilaumsalbum, 10 vols. Bartoszko, Alexandra, tr. from ENG. (Calvin & Hobbes Ser.). (GER., Illus.). 208p. (J). *(978-3-8105-0370-1(3))* Kruger, Wolfgang Verlag, GmbH DEU. Dist: International Bk. Import Service, Inc.

—Einfach Umwerfend. Goetting, Waltraud, tr. from ENG. (Calvin & Hobbes Ser.: Vol. 13). (GER., Illus.). 48p. (J). pap. *(978-3-8105-0350-3(9))* Kruger, Wolfgang Verlag, GmbH DEU. Dist: International Bk. Import Service, Inc.

—Enorm in Form. Goetting, Waltraud, tr. from ENG. (Calvin & Hobbes Ser.: Vol. 9). (GER., Illus.). 64p. (J). pap. *(978-3-8105-0340-4(1))* Kruger, Wolfgang Verlag, GmbH DEU. Dist: International Bk. Import Service, Inc.

—Feine Freunde. Goetting, Waltraud, tr. from ENG. (Calvin & Hobbes Ser.: Vol. 15). (GER., Illus.). 80p. (J). pap. *(978-3-8105-0353-4(3))* Kruger, Wolfgang Verlag, GmbH DEU. Dist: International Bk. Import Service, Inc.

—Fix & Fertig. Goetting, Waltraud, tr. from ENG. (Calvin & Hobbes Ser.: Bk. 2). (GER., Illus.). 96p. (J). pap. *(978-3-8105-0321-3(5))* Kruger, Wolfgang Verlag, GmbH DEU. Dist: International Bk. Import Service, Inc.

—Ganz schoen Daneben. Goetting, Waltraud, tr. from ENG. (Calvin & Hobbes Ser.: Vol. 7). (GER., Illus.). 64p. (J). pap. *(978-3-8105-0335-0(5))* Kruger, Wolfgang Verlag, GmbH DEU. Dist: International Bk. Import Service, Inc.

—Immer mit der Ruhe. Goetting, Waltraud, tr. from ENG. (Calvin & Hobbes Ser.: Vol. 4). (GER., Illus.). 64p. (J). pap. *(978-3-8105-0331-2(2))* Kruger, Wolfgang Verlag, GmbH DEU. Dist: International Bk. Import Service, Inc.

—Immer Voll Drauf. Goetting, Waltraud, tr. from ENG. (Calvin & Hobbes Ser.: Vol. 5). (GER., Illus.). 64p. (J). pap. *(978-3-8105-0332-9(0))* Kruger, Wolfgang Verlag, GmbH DEU. Dist: International Bk. Import Service, Inc.

—Jetzt Erst Recht. Goetting, Waltraud, tr. from ENG. (Calvin & Hobbes Ser.: Vol. 10). (GER., Illus.). 64p. (J). pap. *(978-3-8105-0339-8(8))* Kruger, Wolfgang Verlag, GmbH DEU. Dist: International Bk. Import Service, Inc.

—Jetzt geht's Rund. Goetting, Waltraud, tr. from ENG. (Calvin & Hobbes Ser.: Vol. 1). (GER., Illus.). 64p. (J). pap. *(978-3-8105-0328-2(2))* Kruger, Wolfgang Verlag, GmbH DEU. Dist: International Bk. Import Service, Inc.

—Mach mir den Tiger. Goetting, Waltraud, tr. from ENG. (Calvin & Hobbes Ser.: Vol. 11). (GER., Illus.). 64p. (J). pap. *(978-3-8105-0341-1(X))* Kruger, Wolfgang Verlag, GmbH DEU. Dist: International Bk. Import Service, Inc.

—Die Phantastischen Zwei. Goetting, Waltraud, tr. from ENG. (Calvin & Hobbes Ser.: Vol. 14). (GER., Illus.). 80p. (J). pap. *(978-3-8105-0351-0(7))* Kruger, Wolfgang Verlag, GmbH DEU. Dist: International Bk. Import Service, Inc.

—Steil nach Oben. Goetting, Waltraud, tr. from ENG. (Calvin & Hobbes Ser.: Vol. 6). (GER., Illus.). 64p. (J). pap. *(978-3-8105-0333-6(9))* Kruger, Wolfgang Verlag, GmbH DEU. Dist: International Bk. Import Service, Inc.

—Tierisch Lyrisch. Goetting, Waltraud, tr. from ENG. (Calvin & Hobbes Ser.: Vol. 12). (GER., Illus.). 64p. (J). pap. *(978-3-8105-0349-7(5))* Kruger, Wolfgang Verlag, GmbH DEU. Dist: International Bk. Import Service, Inc.

Watts, Katherine. Tiger Tails. 2008. 76p. pap. 35.95 *(978-0-9556878-0-8(2))* Watts, Katherine GBR. Dist: Lulu Pr., Inc.

Weintroub, Alex. Tilly the Tiger. 2016. (ENG.). 29p. (J). 13.95 *(978-1-78612-173-8(5)*, 63cc1d78-3724-4839-8c26-0d9982b47cd0) Austin, Stan AUS. Dist: Bookmasters Distribution.

Willis, Jeanne. Supercat vs the Pesky Pirate (Supercat, Book 3) 2015. (Supercat Ser.: 3). (ENG., Illus.). 224p. (J). pap. 5.99 *(978-0-00-812470-0(1)*, HarperCollins Children's Bks.) HarperCollins Pubs. Ltd. GBR. Dist: HarperCollins Pubs.

Wilson, Essdale. Horses, Tigers & Neighbors. 2007. 160p. per. 24.95 *(978-1-4241-5811-9(7))* America Star Bks.

Yeoman, John. Quentin Blake's Amazing Animal Stories. Blake, Quentin, illus. 2012. (ENG.). 124p. (J). (gr. 2-4). 19.99 *(978-1-84365-195-6(5)*, Pavilion Children's Books) Pavilion Bks. GBR. Dist: Independent Pubs. Group.

Zahradka, Miroslav. The Un-Terrible Tiger. Zahradka, Miroslav, illus. (Illus.). 32p. (J). (gr. -1-3). 12.95 *(978-0-87592-056-6(X))* Scroll Pr., Inc.

TIGERS

see Tiger

TIGRIS RIVER VALLEY

Miller, Gary G. & Miller, Gary. The Tigris & Euphrates: Rivers of the Fertile Crescent. 2010. (Rivers Around the World Ser.). (ENG., Illus.). 32p. (J). (gr. 5-8). pap. *(978-0-7787-7471-6(6))*; lib. bdg. *(978-0-7787-7448-8(1))* Crabtree Publishing Co.

Mountjoy, Shane. The Tigris & Euphrates Rivers. 2004. (Rivers in World History Ser.). (Illus.). 120p. (C). (gr. 9-13). 32.50 *(978-0-7910-8246-1(6)*, Chelsea Hse.) Facts On File, Inc.

Rice Jr., Earle. The Tigris/Euphrates River. 2012. (Illus.). 47p. (J). lib. bdg. 29.95 *(978-1-61228-298-5(9))* Mitchell Lane Pubs., Inc.

TIMBER

see Forests and Forestry; Lumber and Lumbering; Trees; Wood

TIME

see also Calendars; Clocks and Watches

Adams, Colleen. A Weekend in the City: Adding & Subtracting Times to the Nearest Minute. 2009. (PowerMath Ser.). (ENG., Illus.). 24p. (gr. 3-4). pap. 8.25 *(978-0-8239-8897-6(X)*, PowerKids Pr.) Rosen Publishing Group, Inc., The.

Adamson, Thomas K. & Adamson, Heather. How Do You Measure Time?, 1 vol. 2011. (Measure It! Ser.). (ENG.). 32p. (gr. 1-2). pap. 8.10 *(978-1-4296-6332-8(4)*, Aplus Bks.) Capstone Press of Coughlan Cos.

Adamson, Thomas K. and Heather. How Do You Measure Time? 2011. (Measure It! Ser.). (ENG.). 32p. (gr. 1-2). pap. 47.70 *(978-1-4296-6459-2(2)*, Aplus Bks.) Capstone Press of Coughlan Cos.

Adamson, Tom & Adamson, Heather. How Do You Measure Time?, 1 vol. 2010. (Measure It! Ser.). (ENG.). 32p. (gr. 1-2). lib. bdg. 27.32 *(978-1-4296-4459-4(1)*, Aplus Bks.) Capstone Press of Coughlan Cos.

Adler, David. Time Zones. Miller, Edward, illus. 2011. (ENG.). 32p. (J). pap. 7.95 *(978-0-8234-2385-9(9))* Holiday Hse., Inc.

Adler, David A. Time Zones. Miller, Edward, III, illus. 2010. (ENG.). 32p. (J). (gr. 1-5). 17.95 *(978-0-8234-2201-2(1))* Holiday Hse., Inc.

Amery, H. Telling the Time. 2004. (Treasury of Farmyard Tales Ser.). (SPA.). 24p. (J). (gr. -1-18). 8.95 *(978-0-7945-0146-4(X)*, Usborne) EDC Publishing.

Amery, Heather. Telling the Time. Tyler, Jenny & Lacey, Minna, eds. Cartwright, Stephen, illus. 2007. (Usborne Farmyard Tales Ser.). 24p. (J). (gr. -1-2). bds. 12.99 *(978-0-7945-1519-5(3)*, Usborne) EDC Publishing.

Andrus, Aubre & Bluth, Karen. Me Time: How to Manage a Busy Life. Collignon, Veronica, illus. 2017. (Stress-Busting Survival Guides). (ENG.). 48p. (gr. 4-5). lib. bdg. 31.32 ***(978-1-5157-6821-0(X))*** Capstone Press of Coughlan Cos.

Arias, Lisa. Time Travel: Intervals & Elapsed Time. 2014. (ENG.). 32p. (gr. 3-6). 32.79 *(978-1-62717-706-1(X))* Rourke Educational Media.

Bailer, Darice. Measuring Time with a Calendar. Petelinsek, Kathleen, illus. 2014. (Explorer Junior Library: Math Explorer Junior Ser.). (ENG.). 24p. (J). (gr. 1-4). 28.50 *(978-1-62431-649-4(2)*, 203108) Cherry Lake Publishing.

Baxter, Nicola. Learn to Tell Time: With Magnets to Use Again & Again! Elliott, Rebecca, illus. 2013. (ENG.). 16p. (J). (gr. -1-12). bds. 17.99 *(978-1-84322-638-3(3)*, Armadillo) Anness Publishing GBR. Dist: National Bk. Network.

Benchmark Education Company, LLC Staff, compiled by. Measuring Time: Theme Set. 2006. (J). 274.00 *(978-1-4108-7074-2(X))* Benchmark Education Co.

—Telling Time. 2006. (J). 235.00 *(978-1-4108-7050-6(2))* Benchmark Education Co.

Berendes, Mary. Days & Times (Los Dias y Las Horas) Petelinsek, Kathleen, illus. 2008. (WordBooks/Libros de Palabras Ser.). (ENG.). 24p. (J). (gr. k-3). 25.64 *(978-1-59296-990-6(9)*, 201090) Child's World, Inc., The.

Bernardi, Philip & Havens, Diane. Twice upon a Time. 2003. (Theater for Young Audiences Ser.). (Illus.). 24p. (J). (gr. k-6). pap. 6.00 *(978-0-88734-425-1(9))* Players Pr., Inc.

Bernhard, Durga. While You Are Sleeping. 2011. (J). pap. 14.95 *(978-1-57091-474-4(5))* Charlesbridge Publishing, Inc.

—While You Are Sleeping. Bernhard, Durga, illus. 2011. (ENG., Illus.). 24p. (J). (gr. k-3). 14.95 *(978-1-57091-473-7(7))* Charlesbridge Publishing, Inc.

Boswell, Kelly. Timelines, Timelines, Timelines!, 1 vol. 2013. (Displaying Information Ser.). (ENG.). 32p. (gr. 1-2). 27.32 *(978-1-4765-0261-8(7))*; pap. 8.95 *(978-1-4765-3338-4(5))* Capstone Press of Coughlan Cos. (Aplus Bks.).

Branley, Franklyn M. What Makes Day & Night. Dorros, Arthur, illus. 2015. (Let's-Read-And-Find-Out Science 2 Ser.). (ENG.). 32p. (J). (gr. -1-3). pap. 6.99 *(978-0-06-238197-2(0))* HarperCollins Pubs.

Brasch, Nicolas. Times, Tides, & Revolutions. 2010. (Science Behind Ser.). 32p. lib. bdg. 28.50 *(978-1-59920-563-2(7))* Black Rabbit Bks.

Brooks, Marigold. It's Time for Summer Camp. 2017. (Let's Tell Time Ser.). 24p. (gr. 4-6). 23.60 ***(978-1-5081-5726-7(X)***, PowerKids Pr.) Rosen Publishing Group, Inc., The.

Burstein, John. Keeping Track of Time: Go Fly a Kite! Destiny Images Staff, illus. 2003. (Math Monsters Ser.). 24p. (J). (gr. k-4). lib. bdg. 21.00 *(978-0-8368-3810-7(6)*, Weekly Reader Leveled Readers) Stevens, Gareth Publishing LLLP.

Burton, Margie, et al. Keeping Time. 2011. (Early Connections Ser.). (J). *(978-1-61672-524-2(9))* Benchmark Education Co.

Bussiere, Desirée. What in the World Is a Leap Year? & Other Time Measurements, 1 vol. 2013. (Let's Measure More Ser.). (ENG.). 24p. (J). (gr. -1-3). lib. bdg. 24.21 *(978-1-61783-597-1(8)*, SandCastle) ABDO Publishing Co.

Carson-Dellosa Publishing Staff. Time & Money. 2006. (ENG., Illus.). 54p. (gr. k-3). 2.99 *(978-0-7696-6480-4(6)*, Brighter Child) Carson-Dellosa Publishing, LLC.

Cernek, Kim. Build-a-Skill Instant Books Time & Money. Faulkner, Stacey, ed. Campbell, Jenny & Tom, Darcy, illus. 2007. (J). 4.99 *(978-1-59198-417-7(3))* Creative Teaching Pr., Inc.

Chanko, Pamela. Shoe Box Learning Centers: Time & Measurement: 30 Instant Centers with Reproducible Templates & Activities That Help Kids Practice Important Math Skills-Independently! 2012. (ENG.). 80p. (gr. k-2). pap. 12.99 *(978-0-545-46873-2(6)*, Teaching Resources) Scholastic, Inc.

Cifuentes, Carolina. What Time Is It? Calitri, Susan Chapman, illus. 2010. (My World Ser.).Tr. of Que Hora Es? (ENG.). 24p. (J). (gr. -1-1). lib. bdg. 22.60 *(978-1-60754-954-3(9))* Windmill Bks.

Cifuentes, Carolina, ed. What Time Is It? Calitri, Susan Chapman, illus. 2010. (My World Ser.).Tr. of Que Hora Es? (ENG.). 24p. (J). (gr. -1-1). pap. 8.15 *(978-1-61533-041-6(0))* Windmill Bks.

Clark, Claire. The Calendar. 2012. (Calendar Ser.). (ENG.). 24p. (gr. k-1). pap. 166.80 *(978-1-4296-8339-5(2))*; lib. bdg. 79.95 *(978-1-4296-8115-5(2))* Capstone Press of Coughlan Cos. (Pebble Plus).

—How Long Is a Day? 2012. (Calendar Ser.). (ENG.). 24p. (gr. k-1). pap. 41.70 *(978-1-4296-8334-0(1)*, Pebble Plus) Capstone Press of Coughlan Cos.

—How Long Is a Month? 2012. (Calendar Ser.). (ENG.). 24p. (gr. k-1). pap. 41.70 *(978-1-4296-8335-7(X)*, Pebble Plus) Capstone Press of Coughlan Cos.

—How Long Is a Week? 2012. (Calendar Ser.). (ENG.). 24p. (gr. k-1). pap. 41.70 *(978-1-4296-8336-4(8)*, Pebble Plus) Capstone Press of Coughlan Cos.

—How Long Is a Year? 2012. (Calendar Ser.). (ENG.). 24p. (gr. k-1). pap. 41.70 *(978-1-4296-8337-1(6)*, Pebble Plus) Capstone Press of Coughlan Cos.

Cleary, Brian P. A Second, a Minute, a Week with Days in It: A Book about Time. Gable, Brian, illus. (ENG.). 32p. (gr. k-3). 2015. pap. 6.95 *(978-1-4677-2050-2(X))* 2013. lib. bdg. 16.95 *(978-0-8225-7883-3(2))* Lerner Publishing Group. (Millbrook Pr.).

Collins Easy Learning & HarperCollins UK Staff. Telling the Time Practice. 2011. (Collins Easy Learning Age 7-11 Ser.). (ENG.). 64p. (J). pap. 6.99 *(978-0-00-746163-9(1))* HarperCollins Pubs. Ltd. GBR. Dist: Independent Pubs. Group.

Collins Easy Learning Staff, et al. Telling the Time Ages 5-7. 2015. (Collins Easy Learning Ser.). (ENG.). 32p. (J). (gr. k-2). pap. 6.95 *(978-0-00-813437-2(5))* HarperCollins Pubs. Ltd. GBR. Dist: Independent Pubs. Group.

—Telling the Time, Ages 7-9. 2015. (Collins Easy Learning Ser.). (ENG.). 32p. (J). (gr. 2-4). pap. 6.95 *(978-0-00-813425-9(1))* HarperCollins Pubs. Ltd. GBR. Dist: Independent Pubs. Group.

Conklin, Wendy. Fun & Games: Clockwork Carnival: Measuring Time (Grade 3) 2017. (Mathematics Readers Ser.). (Illus.). 32p. (gr. 3-3). 8.99 ***(978-1-4807-5805-6(1))*** Teacher Created Materials, Inc.

Dapice, Carmine. Lets Rhyme with Time. 2013. 38p. pap. 13.95 *(978-1-4497-8822-3(X)*, WestBow Pr.) Author Solutions, Inc.

Davies, Ann & Ne, Harriet. What Time Is It? Asks Elephant. (Illus.). 10p. (J). pap. 15.95 *(978-1-85479-262-4(8))* O'Mara, Michael Bks., Ltd. GBR. Dist: Trans-Atlantic Pubns., Inc.

Davies, Kate, illus. Tick Tock! Tell the Time: Follow Liam Through His Busy Day. 2017. (ENG.). 10p. (J). (gr. -1-2). bds. 8.99 *(978-0-7641-6874-1(6))* Barron's Educational Series, Inc.

de Klerk, Roger, illus. Foxy Learns to Tell Time. 2009. (Foxy Learns Ser.). 16p. (J). pap. 4.95 *(978-1-59496-180-9(8))* Teora USA LLC.

Dick, Judy. Sacred Time: The Jewish Calendar & Life Cycle. 2012. (J). *(978-0-87441-863-7(1))* Behrman Hse., Inc.

Donovan, Sandra. Teen Wise Guide to Time Management. 2012. (USA TODAY Teen Wise Guides: Time, Money, & Relationships Ser.). (ENG.). 64p. (gr. 8-12). lib. bdg. 31.93 *(978-0-7613-7019-2(6))* Lerner Publishing Group.

Dorling Kindersley Publishing Staff. My First Day & Night. 2017. (My First Bks.). (ENG.). 36p. (J). (— 1). bds. 5.99 ***(978-1-4654-6142-1(6)***, DK Children) Dorling Kindersley Publishing, Inc.

Dowdy, Penny. Time. 2008. (My Path to Math Ser.). (ENG., Illus.). 24p. (J). (gr. k-3). pap. *(978-0-7787-4362-0(4))*; lib. bdg. *(978-0-7787-4344-6(6))* Crabtree Publishing Co.

Estellon, Pascale. It's about Time: Untangling Everything You Need to Know about Time, 0 vols. 2014. (ENG., Illus.). 48p. (J). (gr. k-4). 18.95 *(978-1-77147-006-3(2)*, Owlkids) Owlkids Bks. Inc. CAN. Dist: Publishers Group West (PGW).

Faulkner, Keith & Tyger, Rory. Time's Up! Faulkner, Keith & Tyger, Rory, illus. Lambert, Jonathan, illus. 2003. (J). *(978-0-439-56155-6(8))* Scholastic, Inc.

Feldman, Thea. Kingfisher Readers L1: Time. 2014. (Kingfisher Readers Ser.). (ENG., Illus.). 32p. (J). (gr. k-3).

TUV

12.99 *(978-0-7534-7142-5(6)*, 9780753471425, Kingfisher) Roaring Brook Pr.

Fischer, James. Keeping Your Business Organized: Time Management & Workflow. Madrian, Brigitte, ed. 2013. (Young Adult Library of Small Business & Finance Ser.). (Illus.). 64p. (J). (gr. 7-18). pap. 12.95 *(978-1-4222-2982-8(3))* Mason Crest.

—Time Math. 2013. (Math 24/7 Ser.: 10). 48p. (J). (gr. 5-18). 19.95 *(978-1-4222-2910-1(6))* Mason Crest.

Flash Kids Editors, ed. Time & Money: Grade 1 (Flash Skills) 2010. (Flash Skills Ser.). (ENG.). 64p. (J). pap. 3.95 *(978-1-4114-3450-9(1)*, Spark Publishing Group) Sterling Publishing Co., Inc.

Formichelli, Linda & Martin, W. Eric. Timekeeping: Explore the History & Science of Telling Time with 15 Projects. Carbaugh, Sam, illus. 2012. (Build It Yourself Ser.). (ENG.). 128p. (J). (gr. 3-7). 21.95 *(978-1-61930-136-8(9))* Open City Bks.

Formichelli, Linda, et al. Timekeeping: Explore the History & Science of Telling Time with 15 Projects. Carbaugh, Samuel, illus. 2012. (Build It Yourself Ser.). (ENG.). 128p. (J). (gr. 3-7). pap. 15.95 *(978-1-61930-033-0(8))* Open City Bks.

Fortuna, Lois. Getting Ready for School. 2016. (We Can Do It! Ser.). (ENG.). 24p. (J). (gr. k-k). pap. 8.15 *(978-1-4824-3799-7(6))* Stevens, Gareth Publishing LLLP.

Gaddi, Rosalie. Austin's Airplane Adventure: Solve Problems Involving Measurement. 2014. (Rosen Common Core Math Readers Ser.). (ENG., Illus.). 24p. (J). (gr. 3-4). pap. 8.25 *(978-1-4777-4915-9(2)*, PowerKids Pr.) Rosen Publishing Group, Inc., The.

Gardner, Robert & Conklin, Joshua. A Kid's Book of Experiments with Time. 2016. (Surprising Science Experiments Ser.). (ENG., Illus.). 48p. (J). (gr. 4-4). pap. 11.70 *(978-0-7660-7272-5(X))* Enslow Pubs., Inc.

Gerard, Franck J. Time Waits for No One! Prioritize to Change Your Life! 2005. (Illus.). 90p. per., training bk. ed. 14.99 net. *(978-0-9772685-0-4(0))* ABC Pubs.

Gleick, Beth. Time Is When. Jocelyn, Marthe, illus. 2008. (ENG.). 32p. (J). (gr. -1-2). 15.95 *(978-0-88776-870-5(9)*, Tundra Bks.) Tundra Bks. CAN. Dist: Penguin Random Hse. LLC.

Green, Jen. Day & Night. 2008. (Our Earth Ser.). (Illus.). 24p. (J). (gr. 1-4). lib. bdg. 22.60 *(978-1-4042-4275-3(9))* Rosen Publishing Group, Inc., The.

Greenes, Carol, et al. Time & Money. 2003. (Illus.). 60p. (J). (gr. -1-3). 16.95 *(978-0-7690-0004-6(5))* Seymour, Dale Pubns.

Greenwell, Jessica. Wipe-Clean Telling the Time. Scott, Kimberley, illus. 2013. (Usborne Wipe-Clean Ser.). (ENG.). 20p. (J). (gr. -1-3). pap. 7.99 *(978-0-7945-3403-5(1)*, Usborne) EDC Publishing.

Guillain, Charlotte. Music: From the Voice to Electronica. 2010. (Timeline History Ser.). (ENG., Illus.). 32p. (gr. 3-5). 29.99 *(978-1-4329-3808-6(8)*, NA-h) Heinemann-Raintree.

Haslam, Andrew, et al. Time. (Make It Work! Ser.). (Illus.). 48p. (J). pap. 7.99 *(978-0-590-24915-7(0))*; pap. 16.99 *(978-0-590-24914-0(2))* Scholastic, Inc.

Havener, Katherine. Nursies When the Sun Shines: A Little Book on Night Weaning. Burrier, Sara, illus. 2nd ed. 2013. 20p. (J). pap. 9.99 *(978-0-615-75642-4(5))* Elea Pr.

Heddle, Becca. What's up with Time? Rowe, Alan, illus. 2017. (ENG.). 48p. (J). pap. 8.99 ***(978-0-00-820884-4(0))*** HarperCollins Pubs. Ltd. GBR. Dist: Independent Pubs. Group.

Heos, Bridget. Telling Time. Longhi, Katya, illus. 2015. (Math World Ser.). 24p. (J). lib. bdg. 27.10 *(978-1-60753-461-7(4))* Amicus Publishing.

Hoffman, Juliet. 24 Hours: From Day to Night. 2009. (Real Life Readers Ser.). 12p. (gr. 1-2). pap. 5.90 *(978-1-4042-7925-4(3)*, Rosen Classroom) Rosen Publishing Group, Inc., The.

Holt, Rinehart and Winston Staff. Horizons: Time for Kids Collection, 18 vols. 2003. (Harcourt Horizons Ser.). (Illus.). (gr. k-18). 63.70 *(978-0-15-333097-1(X))* Harcourt Schl. Pubs.

Hubbard, Ben. Top 10 Longest. 2010. (ENG., Illus.). 32p. (J). pap. *(978-0-7787-7510-2(0))*; lib. bdg. *(978-0-7787-7489-1(9))* Crabtree Publishing Co.

Hutchins, Hazel. A Second Is a Hiccup: A Child's Book of Time. Denton, Kady MacDonald, illus. 2008. (J). 16.99 *(978-0-439-83110-9(5)*, Levine, Arthur A. Bks.) Scholastic, Inc.

Hutmacher, Kimberly M. Hours. 2012. (It's about Time Ser.). (ENG.). 24p. (gr. k-1). pap. 35.70 *(978-1-4296-9351-6(7))*; (Illus.). pap. 6.29 *(978-1-4296-9350-9(9))* Capstone Press of Coughlan Cos. (Pebble Bks.).

—Hours, 1 vol. 2012. (It's about Time Ser.). (ENG., Illus.). 24p. (gr. k-1). lib. bdg. 21.99 *(978-1-4296-8577-1(8)*, Pebble Bks.) Capstone Press of Coughlan Cos.

—It's about Time. 2012. (It's about Time Ser.). (ENG.). 24p. (gr. k-1). pap. 17.85 *(978-1-4296-9356-1(8))*; pap. 107.10 *(978-1-4296-9357-8(6))*; lib. bdg. 65.97 *(978-1-4296-9165-9(4))* Capstone Press of Coughlan Cos. (Pebble Bks.).

—Minutes. 2012. (It's about Time Ser.). (ENG.). 24p. (gr. k-1). pap. 35.70 *(978-1-4296-9353-0(3))*; (Illus.). pap. 6.29 *(978-1-4296-9352-3(5))*; (Illus.). lib. bdg. 21.99 *(978-1-4296-8576-4(X))* Capstone Press of Coughlan Cos. (Pebble Bks.).

—Seconds. 2012. (It's about Time Ser.). (ENG.). 24p. (gr. k-1). pap. 35.70 *(978-1-4296-9355-4(X))*; pap. 6.29 *(978-1-4296-9354-7(1))* Capstone Press of Coughlan Cos. (Pebble Bks.).

—Seconds, 1 vol. 2012. (It's about Time Ser.). (ENG.). 24p. (gr. k-1). lib. bdg. 21.99 *(978-1-4296-8575-7(1)*, Pebble Bks.) Capstone Press of Coughlan Cos.

Jackson, Dona. Let's Get Moving! Tell & Write Time. 2013. (InfoMax Math Readers Ser.). (ENG.). 24p. (J). (gr. 1-2). pap. 49.50 *(978-1-4777-2176-6(2))*; (Illus.). pap. 8.25 *(978-1-4777-2175-9(4))* Rosen Publishing Group, Inc., The. (Rosen Classroom).

Jackson, Lora Z. Around the Clock: A Story about Telling Time. Martin, Miles J., illus. 2011. 58p. 36.95 *(978-1-258-06483-9(9))* Literary Licensing, LLC.

Jenkins, Steve. Just a Second: A Different Way to Look at Time. 2011. (ENG., Illus.). 40p. (J). (gr. -1-3). 17.99 *(978-0-618-70896-3(0))* Houghton Mifflin Harcourt Publishing Co.

Jones, Tammy. What Is the Time? 2009. (Sight Word Readers Set A Ser.). (J). 3.49 net. *(978-1-60719-150-6(4))* Newmark Learning LLC.

Kalman, Bobbie. ¿Qué Es el Tiempo? 2009. (SPA.). 24p. (J). *(978-0-7787-8703-7(6))*; pap. *(978-0-7787-8742-6(7))* Crabtree Publishing Co.

—What Time Is It? 2008. (Looking at Nature Ser.). (ENG., Illus.). 24p. (J). (gr. -1-2). pap. *(978-0-7787-3345-4(9))*; lib. bdg. *(978-0-7787-3325-6(4))* Crabtree Publishing Co.

Karapetkova, Holly. Seconds, Minutes, & Hours. 2009. (Illus.). 24p. (J). lib. bdg. 22.79 *(978-1-60694-379-3(0))* Rourke Educational Media.

Katirgis, Jane. Day & Night. 2011. (All about Opposites Ser.). (Illus.). 24p. (J). (gr. -1-18). pap. 7.95 *(978-1-59845-262-4(2)*, Enslow Elementary); (gr. k-3). lib. bdg. 22.60 *(978-0-7660-3915-5(3))* Enslow Pubs., Inc.

Kay, Jill. Fernando Exercises! 2013. (Core Math Skills: Measurement & Geometry Ser.). 24p. (J). (gr. 1-2). 22.60 *(978-1-4777-2228-2(9))*; (ENG.). pap. 8.25 *(978-1-4777-2106-3(1))* Rosen Publishing Group, Inc., The. (Rosen Classroom).

—Fernando Exercises! Tell & Write Time. 2013. (Rosen Math Readers Ser.). (ENG.). 24p. (J). (gr. 1-2). pap. 49.50 *(978-1-4777-2107-0(X)*, Rosen Classroom) Rosen Publishing Group, Inc., The.

Kompelien, Tracy. I Can Tell Time with a Rhyme!, 1 vol. 2007. (Math Made Fun Ser.). (ENG., Illus.). 24p. (J). (gr. k-3). lib. bdg. 24.21 *(978-1-59928-525-2(8)*, SandCastle) ABDO Publishing Co.

Koscielniak, Bruce. About Time: A First Look at Time & Clocks. (ENG., Illus.). 32p. (J). (gr. 2-5). 2013. pap. 7.99 *(978-0-544-10512-6(5))* 2004. tchr. ed. 17.99 *(978-0-618-39668-9(3))* Houghton Mifflin Harcourt Publishing Co.

—About Time: A First Look at Time & Clocks. 2013. lib. bdg. 18.40 *(978-0-606-33538-6(2)*, Turtleback) Turtleback Bks.

Krech, Bob & Novelli, Joan. 50 Fill-In Math Word Problems - Time & Measurement: Engaging Story Problems for Students to Read, Fill-In, Solve, & Sharpen Their Math Skills. 2009. (50 Fill-in Math Word Problems Ser.). (ENG.). 64p. (gr. 2-3). pap. 11.99 *(978-0-545-07483-4(5)*, Teaching Resources) Scholastic, Inc.

Krieg, Katherine. How Many Days? 2015. (Measuring Time Ser.). (ENG., Illus.). 16p. (J). (gr. k-2). 17.95 *(978-1-60753-723-6(0))* Amicus Publishing.

—How Many Hours? 2015. (Measuring Time Ser.). (ENG., Illus.). 16p. (J). (gr. k-2). 17.95 *(978-1-60753-722-9(2))* Amicus Publishing.

—How Many Minutes? 2015. (Measuring Time Ser.). (ENG., Illus.). 16p. (J). (gr. k-2). 17.95 *(978-1-60753-721-2(4))* Amicus Publishing.

—How Many Months? 2015. (Measuring Time Ser.). (ENG., Illus.). 16p. (J). (gr. k-2). 17.95 *(978-1-60753-725-0(7))* Amicus Publishing.

—How Many Seconds? 2015. (Measuring Time Ser.). (ENG., Illus.). 16p. (J). (gr. k-2). 17.95 *(978-1-60753-720-5(6))* Amicus Publishing.

—How Many Weeks? 2015. (Measuring Time Ser.). (ENG., Illus.). 16p. (J). (gr. k-2). 17.95 *(978-1-60753-724-3(9))* Amicus Publishing.

—How Many Years? 2015. (Measuring Time Ser.). (Illus.). 16p. (J). (gr. k-2). 17.95 *(978-1-60753-726-7(5))* Amicus Publishing.

Kumon Publishing, creator. Easy Telling Time Write & Wipe! 2007. (Kumon Flash Cards Ser.). (ENG., Illus.). (J). 9.95 *(978-1-933241-45-6(4))* Kumon Publishing North America, Inc.

Kumon Publishing North America, creator. My Book of Easy Telling Time: Learning about Hours & Half-Hours. 2006. (Kumon Workbooks Ser.). (Illus.). 80p. (J). (gr. -1-1). per. 7.95 *(978-1-933241-26-5(8))* Kumon Publishing North America, Inc.

—My Book of Telling Time: Learning about Minutes. 2006. (Kumon Workbooks Ser.). (Illus.). 80p. (J). (gr. k-2). per. 7.95 *(978-1-933241-27-2(6))* Kumon Publishing North America, Inc.

Learn to Tell the Time. 2003. (Illus.). (J). bds. 4.98 *(978-1-4054-1145-5(7))* Parragon, Inc.

Let's Tell Time. 2017. (Let's Tell Time Ser.). 24p. (gr. 4-6). 94.40 ***(978-1-5081-5782-3(0))***; pap. 33.00 ***(978-1-5081-5801-1(0))*** Rosen Publishing Group, Inc., The. (PowerKids Pr.).

Let's Tell Time. 2003. 16p. (J). 3.79 *(978-1-58792-052-3(2))* Trend Enterprises, Inc.

Levy, Janey. Keeping Time Through the Ages: The History of Tools Used to Measure Time. (PowerMath Ser.). (Illus.). 32p. 2009. (ENG.). (J). (gr. 4-5). pap. 10.00 *(978-0-8239-8917-1(8))* 2004. (J). lib. bdg. 25.25 *(978-0-8239-8993-5(3))* Rosen Publishing Group, Inc., The. (PowerKids Pr.).

Lift-The-Flap Telling the Time. 2017. (Advanced Lift-The-Flap BDs* Ser.). (ENG.). (J). bds. 14.99 ***(978-0-7945-3865-1(7)***, Usborne) EDC Publishing.

Lindeen, Mary. Friday, 1 vol. Gonzalez, Javier A., illus. 2008. (Days of the Week Ser.). (ENG.). 24p. (J). (gr. -1-k). 27.07 *(978-1-60270-101-4(6))* Magic Wagon.

—Monday, 1 vol. Gonzalez, Javier A., illus. 2008. (Days of the Week Ser.). (ENG.). 24p. (J). (gr. -1-k). 27.07 *(978-1-60270-097-0(4))* Magic Wagon.

—Saturday, 1 vol. Gonzalez, Javier A., illus. 2008. (Days of the Week Ser.). (ENG.). 24p. (J). (gr. -1-k). 27.07 *(978-1-60270-102-1(4))* Magic Wagon.

—Sunday, 1 vol. Gonzalez, Javier A., illus. 2008. (Days of the Week Ser.). (ENG.). 24p. (J). (gr. -1-k). 27.07 *(978-1-60270-096-3(6))* Magic Wagon.

—Thursday, 1 vol. Gonzalez, Javier A., illus. 2008. (Days of the Week Ser.). (ENG.). 24p. (J). (gr. -1-k). 27.07 *(978-1-60270-100-7(8))* Magic Wagon.

—Tuesday, 1 vol. Gonzalez, Javier A., illus. 2008. (Days of the Week Ser.). (ENG.). 24p. (J). (gr. -1-k). 27.07 *(978-1-60270-098-7(2))* Magic Wagon.

—Wednesday, 1 vol. Gonzalez, Javier A., illus. 2008. (Days of the Week Ser.). (ENG.). 24p. (J). (gr. -1-k). 27.07 *(978-1-60270-099-4(0))* Magic Wagon.

—The Week, 1 vol. Gonzalez, Javier A., illus. 2008. (Days of the Week Ser.). (ENG.). 24p. (gr. -1-1). 27.07 *(978-1-60270-103-8(2)*, Looking Glass Library- Nonfiction) Magic Wagon.

Lionni, Leo. When? 2014. (ENG., Illus.). 16p. (J). (— 1). bds. 5.99 *(978-0-385-75408-8(6)*, Knopf Bks. for Young Readers) Random Hse. Children's Bks.

Llewellyn, Claire. Day & Night. 2006. (I Know That, Cycles of Nature Set Ser.). (Illus.). 24p. (J). (gr. -1-3). lib. bdg. 22.80 *(978-1-59771-018-3(0))* Sea-To-Sea Pubns.

Loughran, Donna. Time Ticks By: How Do You Read a Clock? 2013. (IMath Ser.). (Illus.). 24p. (J). (gr. k-2). pap. 11.94 *(978-1-60357-490-7(5))* Norwood Hse. Pr.

Loughran, Donna & Brunner-Jass, Renata. Field of Play: Measuring Distance, Rate, & Time. 2013. (IMath Ser.). (Illus.). 48p. (J). (gr. 5-6). pap. 11.94 *(978-1-60357-510-2(3))*; lib. bdg. 23.94 *(978-1-59953-571-6(8))* Norwood Hse. Pr.

Macdonald, Fiona. You Wouldn't Want to Live Without Clocks & Calendars! Antram, David, illus. 2015. (You Wouldn't Want to Live Without... Ser.). (ENG.). 32p. (J). lib. bdg. 29.00 *(978-0-531-21928-7(3)*, Watts, Franklin) Scholastic Library Publishing.

—You Wouldn't Want to Live Without Clocks & Calendars! 2015. (You Wouldn't Want to Live Without Ser.). lib. bdg. 20.80 *(978-0-606-37469-9(8))* Turtleback Bks.

MacDonald, Lucy. You Can Manage Your Time. 2017. (Be Your Best Self Ser.). 158p. (gr. 12-14). lib. bdg. 44.60 ***(978-1-5383-8002-4(1)***, Rosen Young Adult) Rosen Publishing Group, Inc., The.

Meachen Rau, Dana. Space & Time. 2008. (Earth Matters Ser.). 32p. (gr. 1-2). lib. bdg. 15.95 *(978-0-7614-3049-0(0)*, Benchmark Bks.) Marshall Cavendish Corp.

—Space & Time/El Tiempo y Espacio. 2008. (Earth Matters/El Planeta Es Importante Ser.). (SPA & ENG.). 32p. (gr. k-1). lib. bdg. 15.95 *(978-0-7614-3496-2(8)*, Benchmark Bks.) Marshall Cavendish Corp.

—El Tiempo y el Espacio. 2008. (Planeta Es Importante Ser.). (SPA.). 32p. (gr. 1-2). lib. bdg. 15.95 *(978-0-7614-3470-2(4)*, Benchmark Bks.) Marshall Cavendish Corp.

Meyers, Nancy. Doodles Time. Meyers, Nancy, illus. 2012. (Doodles Ser.). (ENG., Illus.). 64p. (J). (gr. k-5). pap. 7.95 *(978-1-61608-670-1(X)*, 608670, Sky Pony Pr.) Skyhorse Publishing Co., Inc.

Miglis, Jenny. My Talking Clock: Hannah's Busy Day. 2005. 12p. bds. 9.95 *(978-1-932915-06-8(0))* Sandvik Publishing.

Minden, Cecilia. It Is about Time! 2010. (21st Century Basic Skills Library: Measurements Ser.). (ENG.). 24p. (gr. k-3). lib. bdg. 22.79 *(978-1-60279-847-2(8)*, 200560) Cherry Lake Publishing.

Minhós Martins, Isabel. The World in a Second. Carvalho, Bernardo, illus. 2015. (ENG.). 56p. (J). (gr. -1-3). 18.95 *(978-1-59270-157-5(4))* Enchanted Lion Bks., LLC.

Moffatt, Judith, illus. Slide & Discover: It's Time! 2005. (Slide & Discover Ser.). 8p. (J). bds. 7.95 *(978-1-58117-247-8(8)*, Intervisual/Piggy Toes) Bendon, Inc.

Moldovo, Eustacia & Murphy, Patricia J. Learning to Tell Time with Puppies & Kittens. 2017. (J). pap. ***(978-0-7660-9075-0(2))*** Enslow Pubs., Inc.

Moran, Lisa. Making a Difference SB1 the Gift of Time. 2010. (Connect to Literacy Ser.). 8p. pap. *(978-1-4334-0503-7(2))* Millmark Education.

Murphy, Patricia J. Telling Time with Puppies & Kittens. 2007. (Puppy & Kitten Math Ser.). (Illus.). 32p. (J). (gr. 1-2). lib. bdg. 23.94 *(978-0-7660-2728-2(7)*, Enslow Elementary) Enslow Pubs., Inc.

Murphy, Stuart J. It's about Time! Speirs, John, illus. 2005. (MathStart Ser.). 40p. (J). 16.99 *(978-0-06-055768-3(0))*; (ENG.). (gr. -1). pap. 5.99 *(978-0-06-055769-0(9))* HarperCollins Pubs.

—It's about Time! Speirs, John, illus. 2005. (Mathstart Ser.). 33p. (gr. -1-3). 16.00 *(978-0-7569-5224-2(7))* Perfection Learning Corp.

—Rodeo Time. Wenzel, David T., illus. 2006. (MathStart 3 Ser.). (ENG.). 40p. (J). (gr. 2-5). pap. 5.99 *(978-0-06-055779-9(6))* HarperCollins Pubs.

Nadeau, Isaac. Learning about Earth's Cycles with Graphic Organizers. (Graphic Organizers in Science Ser.). 24p. 2009. (gr. 3-4). 42.50 *(978-1-61513-029-0(2))* 2006. (ENG., Illus.). (gr. 4-6). pap. 8.25 *(978-1-4042-5044-4(1))* 2005. (Illus.). (J). (gr. 3-7). lib. bdg. 22.60 *(978-1-4042-2807-8(1))* Rosen Publishing Group, Inc., The. (PowerKids Pr.).

Nagelhout, Ryan. Time Zones. 2014. (Map Basics Ser.). 24p. (J). (gr. 2-5). 22.60 *(978-1-4824-1068-6(0))* Stevens, Gareth Publishing LLLP.

Nelson, Robin. Day & Night. 2010. (First Step Nonfiction - Discovering Nature's Cycles Ser.). (ENG., Illus.). 24p. (gr. k-2). lib. bdg. 23.93 *(978-0-7613-4576-3(0))* Lerner Publishing Group.

Pezzimenti, Grace. Busy Families: Learning to Tell Time by the Hour. (Math for the Real World: Early Emergent Ser.). (ENG., Illus.). 8p. (gr. k-1). 2009. pap. 5.15 *(978-0-8239-8912-6(7))* 2004. 29.95 *(978-0-8239-7627-0(0))* Rosen Publishing Group, Inc., The.

Pistoia, Sara. Time. 2016. (J). *(978-1-4896-5122-8(5))* Weigl Pubs., Inc.

Prior, Jennifer Overend & Prior, Jennifer. Time & Money: 14 Reproducible Games That Help Struggling Learners Practice & Really Master Basic Time & Money Skills. 2007. (Math Games to Master Basic Skills Ser.). (ENG., Illus.). 48p. pap. 10.99 *(978-0-439-55414-5(4)*, Teaching Resources) Scholastic, Inc.

Race Against Time: Individual Title Six-Packs. (Bookweb Ser.). 32p. (gr. 4-18). 34.00 *(978-0-7635-3745-6(4))* Rigby Education.

Rajczak Nelson, Kristen. How Do You Gain Time When You Fly West? And Other FAQS about Time & Travel. 2016. (Q & a: Life's Mysteries Solved! Ser.). 32p. (J). (gr. 4-3). pap. 10.50 *(978-1-4824-4752-1(5))* Stevens, Gareth Publishing LLLP.

Randolph, Joanne. All about a Day. 2009. (It's about Time Ser.). 24p. (gr. 1-1). 42.50 *(978-1-61513-630-8(4)*, PowerKids Pr.) Rosen Publishing Group, Inc., The.

—All about a Day/Los Días. 2009. (It's about Time/Los libros del tiempo Ser.). (SPA.). 24p. (gr. 1-1). 42.50 *(978-1-61513-626-1(6)*, Editorial Buenas Letras) Rosen Publishing Group, Inc., The.

—All about A Day/Los Días. Brusca, Maria Cristina, tr. from ENG. 2007. (It's about Time / Los Libros Del Tiempo Ser.). (ENG & SPA., Illus.). 24p. (J). (gr. k-2). lib. bdg. 22.60 *(978-1-4042-7627-7(0))* Rosen Publishing Group, Inc., The.

—All about an Hour. (It's about Time Ser.). 24p. 2009. (gr. 1-1). 42.50 *(978-1-61513-631-5(2)*, PowerKids Pr.) 2007. (Illus.). (J). (gr. k-2). lib. bdg. 22.60 *(978-1-4042-3766-7(6))* Rosen Publishing Group, Inc., The.

—All about an Hour/Las Horas. 2009. (It's about Time/Los libros del tiempo Ser.). (SPA.). 24p. (gr. 1-1). 42.50 *(978-1-61513-627-8(4)*, Editorial Buenas Letras) Rosen Publishing Group, Inc., The.

—All about an Hour/Las Horas. Brusca, Maria Cristina, tr. from ENG. 2007. (It's about Time / Los Libros Del Tiempo Ser.). (ENG & SPA., Illus.). 24p. (J). (gr. k-2). lib. bdg. 22.60 *(978-1-4042-7626-0(2))* Rosen Publishing Group, Inc., The.

Rau, Dana Meachen. Day & Night/El Día y la Noche. 2009. (Bookworms Ser.). (SPA & ENG.). 32p. (gr. 1-2). lib. bdg. 15.95 *(978-0-7614-4788-7(1))* Marshall Cavendish Corp.

Raum, Elizabeth, et al. You Choose: Historical Eras. 2016. (You Choose: Historical Eras Ser.). (ENG.). 112p. lib. bdg. 127.96 *(978-1-5157-4025-4(0)*, You Choose Bks.) Capstone Press of Coughlan Cos.

Reid, Stephanie. Time, 1 vol. 2012. (Early Childhood Themes Ser.). (ENG.). 16p. (J). (gr. -1-2). pap. 6.99 *(978-1-4333-3489-4(5))*; pap. 19.99 *(978-1-4333-3490-0(9))* Teacher Created Materials, Inc.

Rice, Dona Herweck. Day & Night, 1 vol. 2012. (Early Childhood Themes Ser.). (ENG.). 16p. (J). (gr. -1-2). pap. 19.99 *(978-1-4333-3492-4(5))* Teacher Created Materials, Inc.

—Day & Night: Time, 1 vol. 2012. (Early Childhood Themes Ser.). (ENG.). 16p. (J). (gr. -1-2). pap. 6.99 *(978-1-4333-3491-7(7))* Teacher Created Materials, Inc.

Robinson, Fay. It's 6 P. M. 2016. (Spring Forward Ser.). (J). (gr. 1). *(978-1-4900-9370-3(2))* Benchmark Education Co.

Roegiers, Maud. Take the Time: Mindfulness for Kids. 2010. (Illus.). 32p. (J). (gr. -1-3). 14.95 *(978-1-4338-0794-7(7))*; pap. 9.95 *(978-1-4338-0796-1(3))* American Psychological Assn. (Magination Pr.).

Roper, Dawn. 30 Fun Ways to Learn about Time & Money. 2011. (30 Fun Ways to Learn Ser.). (ENG.). 80p. (gr. -1-k). pap. 12.95 *(978-0-87659-370-7(8)*, Gryphon House Inc) Gryphon Hse., Inc.

Rosa-Mendoza, Gladys. My Week/Mi Semana. Wesley, Milliana, ed. Grosshauser, Peter, illus. 2007. (English Spanish Foundations Ser.). (gr. -1-k). bds. 6.95 *(978-1-931398-25-1(9))* Me+Mi Publishing.

—What Time Is It? Cifuentes, Carolina, ed. 2004. (English-Spanish Foundations Ser.: Vol. 7).Tr. of Que Hora Es? (ENG & SPA., Illus.). 20p. (J). (gr. -1-4). bds. 6.95 *(978-0-9679748-9-7(5))* Me+Mi Publishing.

Scheunemann, Pam. Time - 6 Titles. 2008. (Time Ser.: 6). (ENG., Illus.). 24p. (J). (gr. k-3). lib. bdg. 145.26 *(978-1-60453-014-8(6)*, SandCastle) ABDO Publishing Co.

—Time to Learn about Past, Present & Future, 1 vol. 2008. (Time Ser.). (ENG., Illus.). 24p. (J). (gr. k-3). lib. bdg. 24.21 *(978-1-60453-017-9(0))* ABDO Publishing Co.

—Time to Learn about Seconds, Minutes & Hours, 1 vol. 2008. (Time Ser.). (ENG., Illus.). 24p. (J). (gr. k-3). lib. bdg. 24.21 *(978-1-60453-019-3(7))* ABDO Publishing Co.

—Time to Learn about Weeks & Months, 1 vol. 2008. (Time Ser.). (ENG., Illus.). 24p. (J). (gr. k-3). lib. bdg. 24.21 *(978-1-60453-020-9(0))* ABDO Publishing Co.

School Zone Interactive Staff. Time, Money & Fractions. rev. ed. 2004. (ENG.). 64p. (J). (gr. k-2). 15.99 *(978-1-58947-832-9(0))* School Zone Publishing Co.

School Zone Staff. Time & Money. 2004. (ENG.). 56p. (J). 2.79 *(978-1-58947-990-6(4))* School Zone Publishing Co.

School Zone Staff, ed. Time & Money. 2005. (ENG.). 26p. (J). (gr. 1-2). pap. 3.79 *(978-1-58947-788-9(X))* School Zone Publishing Co.

—Time, Money & Fractions. 2003. (ENG.). (J). (gr. 1-2). cd-rom 19.99 *(978-1-58947-930-2(0))* School Zone Publishing Co.

The Science of Time. 2016. (Illus.). 48p. (J). *(978-1-4222-3516-4(5))* Mason Crest.

Sharp, Jean. Telling Time All the Time. 2008. (Math in Our World - Level 2 Ser.). 24p. (gr. 1-4). pap. 8.15 *(978-0-8368-9010-5(8))*; (Illus.). lib. bdg. 22.00 *(978-0-8368-9001-3(9))* Stevens, Gareth Publishing LLLP. (Weekly Reader Leveled Readers).

—Vamos a Decir la Hora Todo el Tiempo. 2008. (Matemáticas en Nuestro Mundo - Nivel 2 (Math in Our World - Level 2) Ser.). (SPA., Illus.). 24p. (gr. 1-4). lib. bdg. 22.00 *(978-0-8368-9019-8(1)*, Weekly Reader Leveled Readers) Stevens, Gareth Publishing LLLP.

—Vamos a Decir La Hora Todo El Tiempo. 2008. (Las Matemáticas en Nuestro Mundo Ser.). (SPA.). 24p. (gr. 1-4). pap. 8.15 *(978-0-8368-9028-0(0)*, Weekly Reader Leveled Readers) Stevens, Gareth Publishing LLLP.

Shaskan, Trisha Speed. If You Were a Minute, 1 vol. Carabelli, Francesca, illus. 2009. (Math Fun Ser.). (ENG.). 24p. (gr. 2-4). pap. 7.95 *(978-1-4048-5202-0(6))*; lib. bdg. 27.99 *(978-1-4048-5201-3(8))* Picture Window Bks.

Sherman, Josepha. How Do We Know the Nature of Time. (Great Scientific Questions & the Scientists Who Answered Them Ser.). 112p. (gr. 7-12). 2009. 63.90 *(978-1-61513-205-8(8))* 2005. (Illus.). (J). lib. bdg. 34.60 *(978-1-4042-0073-9(8))* Rosen Publishing Group, Inc., The.

Steck-Vaughn Staff. At-Home Workbooks: Time. 2004. (Illus.). pap., wbk. ed. *(978-0-7398-8538-3(3))* Steck-Vaughn.

—Early Math: Time I. 2005. pap. 2.99 *(978-1-4190-0327-1(5))* Steck-Vaughn.

—Early Math: Time II. 2005. pap. 2.99 *(978-1-4190-0337-0(2))* Steck-Vaughn.

Steffora, Tracey. Days of the Week, 1 vol. 2011. (Measuring Time Ser.). (ENG.). 24p. (gr. -1-1). 22.65 *(978-1-4329-4901-3(2))*; pap. 6.29 *(978-1-4329-4908-2(X))* Heinemann-Raintree. (Acorn).

—Días de la Semana. 2011. (Medir el Tiempo Ser.). (SPA.). 24p. (gr. -1-1). 22.65 *(978-1-4329-5629-5(9))*; pap. 6.29 *(978-1-4329-5636-3(1))* Heinemann-Raintree. (Bellota).

—Estaciones del Año. 2011. (Medir el Tiempo Ser.). (SPA.). 24p. (gr. -1-1). 22.65 *(978-1-4329-5632-5(9))*; pap. 6.29 *(978-1-4329-5639-4(6))* Heinemann-Raintree. (Bellota).

—Horas del Día. 2011. (Medir el Tiempo Ser.). (SPA.). 24p. (gr. -1-1). 22.65 *(978-1-4329-5633-2(7))*; pap. 6.29 *(978-1-4329-5640-0(X))* Heinemann-Raintree. (Bellota).

—Horas, Minutos y Segundos. 2011. (Medir el Tiempo Ser.). (SPA.). 24p. (gr. -1-1). 22.65 *(978-1-4329-5630-1(2))*; pap. 6.29 *(978-1-4329-5637-0(X))* Heinemann-Raintree. (Bellota).

—Hours, Minutes, & Seconds, 1 vol. 2011. (Measuring Time Ser.). (ENG.). 24p. (gr. -1-1). 22.65 *(978-1-4329-4900-6(4)*, Acorn) Heinemann-Raintree.

—Measuring Time, 6 vols., Set. Incl. Days of the Week. pap. 6.29 *(978-1-4329-4908-2(X))*; Seasons of the Year. pap. 6.29 *(978-1-4329-4909-9(8))*; Times of the Day. pap. 6.29 *(978-1-4329-4910-5(1))*; (gr. -1-1). (Measuring Time Ser.). (ENG.). 24p. 2011. Set pap. 18.87 *(978-1-4329-4913-6(6))*; Set lib. bdg. 90.60 *(978-1-4329-4906-8(3))* Heinemann-Raintree. (Acorn).

—Medir el Tiempo. 2011. (Medir el Tiempo Ser.). (SPA.). 24p. (gr. -1-1). lib. bdg. 135.90 *(978-1-4329-5634-9(5)*, Bellota) Heinemann-Raintree.

—Meses del Año. 2011. (Medir el Tiempo Ser.). (SPA.). 24p. (gr. -1-1). 22.65 *(978-1-4329-5631-8(0))*; pap. 6.29 *(978-1-4329-5638-7(8))* Heinemann-Raintree. (Bellota).

—Months of the Year, 1 vol. 2011. (Measuring Time Ser.). (ENG.). 24p. (gr. -1-1). 22.65 *(978-1-4329-4905-1(5)*, Acorn) Heinemann-Raintree.

—Relojes y Calendarios. 2011. (Medir el Tiempo Ser.). (SPA.). 24p. (gr. -1-1). pap. 6.29 *(978-1-4329-5635-6(3)*, Bellota) Heinemann-Raintree.

—Seasons of the Year, 1 vol. 2011. (Measuring Time Ser.). (ENG.). 24p. (gr. -1-1). pap. 6.29 *(978-1-4329-4909-9(8)*, Acorn) Heinemann-Raintree.

—Times of the Day, 1 vol. 2011. (Measuring Time Ser.). (ENG.). 24p. (gr. -1-1). 22.65 *(978-1-4329-4903-7(9))*; pap. 6.29 *(978-1-4329-4910-5(1))* Heinemann-Raintree. (Acorn).

—What Is Time?, 1 vol. 2011. (ENG.). 24p. (gr. -1-1). pap. 8.95 *(978-1-4329-5502-1(0))*; 25.99 *(978-1-4329-5357-7(5))* Heinemann-Raintree. (Acorn Read-Aloud).

Studio Mouse Staff. Time to Learn!, 4 vols. rev. ed. 2007. (ENG., Illus.). 4x20p. (J). (gr. -1-k). 14.99 *(978-1-59069-564-7(X))* Studio Mouse LLC.

Sullivan, Navin. Time. 2006. (Measure Up! Ser.). (Illus.). 48p. (gr. 4-3). lib. bdg. 31.36 *(978-0-7614-2321-8(4)*, Benchmark Bks.) Marshall Cavendish Corp.

Sundance/Newbridge LLC Staff. Time & Temperature. 2004. (Reading PowerWorks Ser.). (gr. 1-3). 37.50 *(978-0-7608-8976-3(7))*; pap. 6.10 *(978-0-7608-8977-0(5))* Sundance/Newbridge Educational Publishing.

Tell Me the Time. (First Bks.: No. S808-3). (Illus.). (J). (gr. -1). pap. 3.95 *(978-0-7214-5054-4(7)*, Dutton Juvenile) Penguin Publishing Group.

Tell the Time. 2004. (Wall Charts Ser.). (J). 4.99 *(978-1-904586-22-7(8))*; 32p. wbk. ed. 3.99 *(978-1-904586-16-6(3))* Byeway Bks.

Thomas, Mary Ann. Our Train Trip: Learning to Add Times by the Half Hour. 2009. (Math for the REAL World Ser.). 12p. (gr. 1-2). pap. 5.90 *(978-0-8239-8849-5(X)*, Rosen Classroom) Rosen Publishing Group, Inc., The.

Thornborough, Kathy. Days & Times. Petelinsek, Kathleen, illus. 2014. (Talking Hands Ser.). (ENG.). 24p. (J). (gr. k-3). 25.64 *(978-1-62687-316-2(X)*, 207156) Child's World, Inc., The.

Time. (Make it Work Ser.). 42p. (J). (gr. 4-8). pap. *(978-1-882210-40-4(9))* Action Publishing, Inc.

Time - Set 1: What Time Is It. 2005. (J). spiral bd. 23.40 *(978-0-9770248-6-5(5))* Sidedoor Publishing LLC.

Time for a Party, 6, Pack. (Discovery World Ser.). 16p. (gr. 1-2). 28.00 *(978-0-7635-8457-3(6))* Rigby Education.

Time, Inc. Library Bound Titles [Capstone Sole Source]. 2010. (Time, Inc. Library-Bound Titles Ser.). 139.96 *(978-1-4296-5885-0(1))* Capstone Press of Coughlan Cos.

Top That Publishing Staff, ed. Lets Explore Time. 2004. (Fun Kits Ser.). (Illus.). 48p. (J). *(978-1-84510-246-3(0))* Top That! Publishing PLC.

Tyler, Jenny & Gee, R. Time. Bryant-Mole, K., ed. rev. ed. 2004. (First Learning Ser.). (ENG., Illus.). 1p. (J). (gr. -1-3). pap., act. bk. ed. 4.95 *(978-0-7460-3806-2(2))* EDC Publishing.

Wadsworth, Pamela. Golwg Gyntaf Ar Amser a Gofod. 2005. (WEL., Illus.). 24p. pap. *(978-1-85596-248-4(9))* Dref Wen.

Walker, Nan. Day Camp. 2011. (Early Connections Ser.). (J). *(978-1-61672-347-7(5))* Benchmark Education Co.

Walpole, Brenda. I Wonder Why the Sun Rises: And Other Questions about Time & Seasons. 2011. (I Wonder Why Ser.). (ENG., Illus.). 32p. (J). (gr. k-3). pap. 6.99 *(978-0-7534-6529-5(9)*, 9780753465295, Kingfisher) Roaring Brook Pr.

—I Wonder Why the Sun Rises & Other Questions about Time & Seasons. 2008. (I Wonder Why Ser.). (Illus.). 32p. (gr. k-3). 17.00 *(978-0-7569-9054-1(8))* Perfection Learning Corp.

Wilkin, Jennifer. Time Zones, Vol. 4. 2nd ed. 2015. (Time Zones Second Edition Ser.). (ENG.). 144p. (C). pap., stu. ed. 54.95 *(978-1-305-51074-6(7))* Cengage Heinle.

Wilmes, Liz, et al. Circle Time Book: For Holiday & Seasons. Dane, Donna, illus. 2004. 128p. (J). pap. 12.95 *(978-0-943452-00-5(7)*, 20002) Building Blocks, LLC.

Woodford, Chris. Time. 2012. (Measure up Math Ser.). (Illus.). 32p. (J). (gr. 4-6). 26.60 *(978-1-4339-7453-3(3))*; pap. 10.50 *(978-1-4339-7454-0(1))* Stevens, Gareth Publishing LLLP. (Gareth Stevens Learning Library).

Woods, Sadie. It's Time for the Soccer Game. 2017. (Let's Tell Time Ser.). 24p. (gr. 4-6). 23.60 ***(978-1-5081-5727-4(8)***, PowerKids Pr.) Rosen Publishing Group, Inc., The.

TIME—FICTION

Adams, Colleen. The Big Day! 2006. (Neighborhood Readers Ser.). (ENG.). 8p. (gr. -1-3). pap. 5.15 *(978-1-4042-5708-5(X)*, Rosen Classroom) Rosen Publishing Group, Inc., The.

Ahn, Somin. One Minute. 2016. (ENG., Illus.). 36p. (J). (gr. -1-k). 15.99 *(978-1-4521-5564-7(X))* Chronicle Bks. LLC.

Baldwin, J. R. Ashley & Mr. Sunshine. 2009. 24p. pap. 24.95 *(978-1-60836-180-9(2))* America Star Bks.

Barchers, Suzanne I. Late Kate, 1 vol. 2011. (Targeted Phonics Ser.). (ENG.). 16p. (J). (gr. k-2). pap. 5.99 *(978-1-4333-2906-7(9))* Teacher Created Materials, Inc.

Bostrom, Kathleen Long. Good Morning, God! Lyon, Tammie, illus. 2014. 20p. (J). bds. 6.99 *(978-0-8249-1939-9(4)*, Ideal Pubns.) Worthy Publishing.

Britt, Paige. The Lost Track of Time. 2016. (ENG.). 320p. (J). (gr. 3-7). pap. 9.99 *(978-0-545-53813-8(0)*, Scholastic Pr.) Scholastic, Inc.

—The Lost Track of Time. White, Lee, illus. 2015. (ENG.). 320p. (J). (gr. 3-7). 17.99 *(978-0-545-53812-1(2)*, Scholastic Pr.) Scholastic, Inc.

Bryson, Theresa. Farm Alarm. 2011. (Early Connections Ser.). (J). *(978-1-61672-350-7(5))* Benchmark Education Co.

Buckley, Michael. Magic & Other Misdemeanors. Ferguson, Peter, illus. 2008. (Sisters Grimm Ser.). (ENG.). 304p. (J). (gr. 3-7). pap. 7.95 *(978-0-8109-7263-6(8)*, Amulet Bks.) Abrams, Inc.

Butler, Dori. Late Again! 2005. (J). pap. *(978-1-4108-4209-1(6))* Benchmark Education Co.

Charlesworth, Kate & Gribbin, John. The Cartoon History of Time. 2013. (ENG., Illus.). 64p. pap. 19.95 *(978-0-486-49097-7(1))* Dover Pubns., Inc.

Cirrone, Dorian. The First Last Day. (ENG., Illus.). 240p. (J). (gr. 3-7). 2017. pap. 7.99 ***(978-1-4814-5814-6(0))*** 2016. 17.99 *(978-1-4814-5813-9(2))* Simon & Schuster Children's Publishing. (Aladdin).

Coates, Kimberly & Coates, Ashley. If I Only Knew How to Tell Time. 2013. 32p. pap. 19.99 *(978-1-4772-9963-0(7))* AuthorHouse.

Cole, Bob. Power Reading: Chapter/Sci-Fi/Time Warp. Ford, David, illus. 2004. 25p. (J). (gr. 4-18). vinyl bd. 39.95 *(978-1-883186-60-9(9)*, PPSF3) National Reading Styles Institute, Inc.

Cousins, Lucy. Maisy's First Clock. Cousins, Lucy, illus. 2011. (Maisy Ser.). (ENG., Illus.). 16p. (J). (gr. k-k). bds. 14.99 *(978-0-7636-5095-7(1))* Candlewick Pr.

Cuyler, Margery. Tick Tock Clock. Neubecker, Robert, illus. 2012. (My First I Can Read Ser.). (ENG.). 32p. (J). (gr. -1 — 1). 16.99 *(978-0-06-136309-2(X))*; pap. 3.99 *(978-0-06-136311-5(1))* HarperCollins Pubs.

Dahl, Michael. The Lost Page. Evergreen, Nelson, illus. 2015. (Library of Doom: the Final Chapters Ser.). (ENG.). 40p. (gr. 1-3). 23.99 *(978-1-4342-9679-5(2))* Stone Arch Bks.

Danziger, Paula. It's Justin Time, Amber Brown. Ross, Tony, illus. (Amber Brown Ser.). 9.95 *(978-1-59112-294-4(5))* Live Oak Media.

—Justo a Tiempo, Ambar Dorado. Ross, Tony, illus. 2007. (Amber Brown Ser.). (SPA.). 48p. (gr. k-3). per. 8.95 *(978-1-59820-595-4(1)*, Alfaguara) Santillana USA Publishing Co., Inc.

Darlison, A. Keeping It Real. 2016. (Netball Gems Ser.: 6). (ENG., Illus.). 160p. (J). (gr. 3-6). pap. 8.99 *(978-0-14-378115-8(4))* Random Hse. Australia AUS. Dist: Independent Pubs. Group.

Derrick, Patricia. Mr. Walrus & the Old School Bus. Martinez, J-P Loppo, illus. 2007. 32p. 18.95 incl. audio compact disk *(978-1-933818-13-9(1))* Animalations.

Dodd, Emma, illus. Tick Tock Dog: A Tell the Time Book - with a Special Movable Clock! 2016. (ENG.). 12p. (J). (gr. -1-12). bds. 14.99 *(978-1-86147-718-7(X)*, Armadillo) Anness Publishing GBR. Dist: National Bk. Network.

Fearing, Mark. Dilly Dally Daisy. 2015. (ENG., Illus.). 32p. (J). (gr. -1-k). 16.99 *(978-0-8037-4065-5(4)*, Dial Bks) Penguin Young Readers Group.

Ficocelli, Elizabeth. Kid Tea. Dibley, Glin, illus. 2009. 32p. (J). (gr. -1). bds. 7.99 *(978-0-7614-5533-2(7))* Marshall Cavendish Corp.

Freeman, Tor. Benji Bear's Busy Day. Freeman, Tor, illus. 2015. (ENG., Illus.). 18p. (J). (-k). bds. 17.99 *(978-1-5098-0111-4(1))* Pan Macmillan GBR. Dist: Independent Pubs. Group.

Fruchter, Jason, illus. What Time Is It, Daniel Tiger? 2016. (Daniel Tiger's Neighborhood Ser.). (ENG.). 14p. (J). (gr. -1-k). bds. 10.99 *(978-1-4814-6934-0(7)*, Simon Spotlight) Simon Spotlight.

Garrity, Jennifer Johnson. Calendar Quest: A 5,000 Year Trek Through Western History with Father Time. 2004. (ENG., Illus.). 160p. (J). per. 14.00 *(978-0-9770704-0-4(9)*, CQ-001, Tools For Young Historians) BrimWood Pr.

Harris, Trudy. The Clock Struck One: A Time-Telling Tale. Hartman, Carrie, illus. 2009. (Math Is Fun! Ser.). (ENG.). 32p. (gr. k-2). 19.99 *(978-0-8225-9067-5(0)*, Millbrook Pr.) Lerner Publishing Group.

Havercroft, Elizabeth. A Year in the World of Dinosaurs. 2009. (Time Goes By Ser.). (ENG.). 24p. (gr. k-3). pap. 6.95 *(978-1-58013-802-4(0)*, First Avenue Editions) Lerner Publishing Group.

Hennessy, B. G. Mr. Ouchy's First Day. Meisel, Paul, illus. 2007. (J). (gr. k-3). 29.95 incl. audio compact disk *(978-0-8045-4160-2(4))*; 27.95 incl. audio *(978-0-8045-6946-0(0))* Spoken Arts, Inc.

Herbauts, Anne. Monday. 2006. (ENG., Illus.). 36p. (J). (gr. -1-3). 16.95 *(978-1-59270-057-8(8))* Enchanted Lion Bks., LLC.

Howard, Cheryl L. Duster Dustbunny's Seven Days of the Week & Twelve Months in a Year. 2009. (Illus.). 48p. pap. 17.50 *(978-1-60860-787-7(9)*, Eloquent Bks.) Strategic Book Publishing & Rights Agency (SBPRA).

It's Time. 2016. (It's Time Ser.). 24p. (gr. 1-1). 94.40 *(978-1-4994-2431-7(0))*; pap. 33.00 *(978-1-4994-2488-1(4))* Rosen Publishing Group, Inc., The. (PowerKids Pr.).

Jakubowski, Kristan E. Paint the Town. 2008. 24p. pap. 11.85 *(978-1-4343-6912-3(9))* AuthorHouse.

James, Lincoln. Sal Sleeps In. 2006. (Neighborhood Readers Ser.). (ENG.). 8p. (gr. -1-3). pap. 5.15 *(978-1-4042-5780-1(2)*, Rosen Classroom) Rosen Publishing Group, Inc., The.

Jocelyn, Marthe, ed. First Times: Stories Selected by Marthe Jocelyn. 2007. (ENG.). 200p. (YA). (gr. 5-8). pap. 9.95 *(978-0-88776-777-7(X)*, Tundra Bks.) Tundra Bks. CAN. Dist: Penguin Random Hse. LLC.

Jones, Christianne C. Morning Mystery, 1 vol. Simard, Remy, illus. 2010. (My First Graphic Novel Ser.). (ENG.). 32p. (gr. k-2). lib. bdg. 24.65 *(978-1-4342-1890-2(2)*, My First Graphic Novel) Stone Arch Bks.

Kondrchek, Jamie. My Favorite Time of Day (Mi Hora Preferida del Dia) Vega, Eida de la, tr. from ENG. Rasemas, Joe, illus. 2009. (Day in the Life Ser.). (SPA & ENG.). 32p. (J). (gr. -1-1). lib. bdg. 25.70 *(978-1-58415-837-0(9))* Mitchell Lane Pubs., Inc.

Kovanchak, Danielle. It's about Time. 2009. 44p. pap. 16.99 *(978-1-4389-7023-3(4))* AuthorHouse.

Krivitzky, Nathan & Nathan, Krivitzky. Always Late Nate. O'Connell, Dave, illus. 2009. (ENG.). 32p. (J). pap. 10.95 *(978-1-933916-41-5(9))* Nelson Publishing & Marketing.

Kubler, Annie, illus. What's the Time, Mr. Wolf? 2003. (Finger Puppet Bks.). (ENG.). 24p. (J). (gr. 1-1). *(978-0-85953-944-9(X))* Child's Play International Ltd.

little bee books, little bee. A Day with Cinderella. 2015. (ENG., Illus.). 16p. (J). (gr. -1-1). 8.99 *(978-1-4998-0061-6(4))* Little Bee Books Inc.

Lowery, Mark A. Magic Time, Time Is Magical. 2012. 154p. pap. 19.95 *(978-1-62709-345-3(1))* America Star Bks.

Marshall, Wendy. The O'Clocks: Mr. O'Clock Goes to A Party. 2008. 40p. pap. 18.49 *(978-1-4389-2403-8(8))* AuthorHouse.

Mass, Wendy. 11 Birthdays. (ENG.). 272p. (J). (gr. 3-7). 2010. pap. 6.99 *(978-0-545-05240-5(8)*, Scholastic Paperbacks) 2009. 17.99 *(978-0-545-05239-9(4)*, Scholastic Pr.) Scholastic, Inc.

—11 Birthdays. 2010. (Willow Falls Ser.: 1). lib. bdg. 17.20 *(978-0-606-13990-8(7)*, Turtleback) Turtleback Bks.

Millman, M. C. Time Will Tell. 2004. 272p. (YA). 19.95 *(978-1-932443-25-7(8)*, TWTH) Judaica Pr., Inc., The.

Molesworth & Molesworth, Mary Louisa S. The Cuckoo Clock. 2008. 112p. 23.95 *(978-1-60664-856-8(X))*; pap. 9.95 *(978-1-60664-103-3(4))* Aegypan.

MUSS, Anon E. Time Portal. 2010. 221p. pap. 11.84 *(978-0-557-46606-1(7))* Lulu Pr., Inc.

My Time on Nantucket. 2005. (J). cd-rom 11.95 *(978-0-9755078-2-7(6))* Sweet Punkin Pr.

Myers, Bill. Baseball for Breakfast: The Story of a Boy Who Hated to Wait. Riccio, Frank, illus. 2005. 29p. (J). (gr. 4-8). reprint ed. 15.00 *(978-0-7567-9248-0(7))* DIANE Publishing Co.

O'Mara, Blanche. A Year with Carmen. 2006. (Neighborhood Readers Ser.). (ENG.). 12p. (gr. 1-3). pap. 5.90 *(978-1-4042-6835-7(9)*, Rosen Classroom) Rosen Publishing Group, Inc., The.

Omololu, C. J. When It's Six O'Clock in San Francisco: A Trip Through Time Zones. DuBurke, Randy, illus. 2009. (ENG.). 32p. (J). (gr. -1-3). 16.99 *(978-0-618-76827-1(0))* Houghton Mifflin Harcourt Publishing Co.

Peck, Dale. Drift House: The First Voyage. 2006. (ENG.). 464p. (YA). (gr. 5). per. 7.95 *(978-1-59990-005-6(X)*, 9781599900056, Bloomsbury USA Childrens) Bloomsbury Publishing USA.

Pilegard, Virginia Walton. The Warlord's Alarm, 1 vol. Debon, Nicolas, illus. 2006. (Warlord's Ser.). (ENG.). 32p. (J). (gr. k-3). 16.99 *(978-1-58980-378-7(7))* Pelican Publishing Co., Inc.

Poulin, Andree. The Best Time. Beha, Philippe, illus. 2009. (My First Stories Ser.). 24p. (J). (gr. -1-3). 22.60 *(978-1-60754-350-3(8))*; pap. 8.15 *(978-1-60754-351-0(6))* Windmill Bks.

Poulin, Andrée. The Worst Time. Beha, Philippe, illus. 2009. (My First Stories Ser.). 24p. (J). (gr. -1-3). 22.60 *(978-1-60754-367-1(2))*; pap. 8.15 *(978-1-60754-368-8(0))* Windmill Bks.

Publications International Ltd. Staff, ed. Exploring Time with Dora Clock. 2004. 10p. (J). bds. 16.98 *(978-1-4127-3050-1(3)*, 7228800) Publications International, Ltd.

—Spongebob Clock It's Time Sound Book. 2004. 10p. (J). bds. 16.98 *(978-1-4127-3030-3(9)*, 7226500) Publications International, Ltd.

Ruebush, McKenna. Enter a Glossy Web. Zollars, Jaime, illus. 2016. (ENG.). 400p. (YA). 16.99 *(978-1-62779-370-4(4)*, 9781627793704, Holt, Henry & Co. Bks. For Young Readers) Holt, Henry & Co.

Ruffenach, Jessie, ed. Baby Learns about Time. Thomas, Peter, tr. from ENG. Blacksheep, Beverly, illus. 2005. (NAV & ENG.). 16p. (J). (gr. 4-7). 7.95 *(978-1-893354-64-7(4))* Salina Bookshelf Inc.

Rupp, Rebecca. Journey to the Blue Moon: In Which Time Is Lost & Then Found Again. 2006. (ENG., Illus.). 272p. (J). (gr. 5-7). 15.99 *(978-0-7636-2544-3(2))* Candlewick Pr.

Salerni, Dianne K. The Eighth Day. McClellan, David, illus. (Eighth Day Ser.: 1). (ENG.). (J). (gr. 3-7). 2015. 336p. pap. 6.99 *(978-0-06-227216-4(0))* 2014. 320p. 16.99 *(978-0-06-227215-7(2))* HarperCollins Pubs.

—The Inquisitor's Mark. 2015. (Eighth Day Ser.: 2). (ENG.). 368p. (J). (gr. 3-7). pap. 6.99 *(978-0-06-227219-5(5))* HarperCollins Pubs.

Scholastic, Inc. Staff, contrib. by. It Is Time For... 2014. (Rookie Toddler(r) Ser.). (ENG.). 12p. (J). bds. 6.95 *(978-0-531-20916-5(4))* Scholastic Library Publishing.

Schuepbach, Lynnette. Cat Time. 2006. 28p. pap. 12.95 *(978-0-9759613-2-2(2))* Creative Sources.

Simon, Jenne. Tell the Time! Hino, Sachiho, illus. 2015. (J). *(978-0-545-74720-2(1))* Scholastic, Inc.

Smith, C. Michelle. Skeeter Sneeter Doodlebop. Foreman, A., illus. 2009. 24p. pap. 15.63 *(978-1-934840-54-2(8))* Nimble Bks. LLC.

Specter, Baron. The Spooky Short Sands Shipwreck: #4, 1 vol. Evans, Dustin, illus. 2010. (Ghostly Graphic Adventures Ser.). (ENG.). 32p. (J). (gr. 3-6). 28.50 *(978-1-60270-773-3(1))* ABDO Publishing Co.

Stilton, Geronimo. The Hour of Magic. 2016. (ENG.). 320p. (J). (gr. 2-5). 14.99 *(978-0-545-82336-4(6))* Scholastic, Inc.

Thompson, Kate. I Can Tell the Time. Green, Barry, illus. 2014. (I Can Bks.). (ENG.). 12p. (J). (gr. -1). 7.99 *(978-1-78244-825-9(X))* Top That! Publishing PLC GBR. Dist: Independent Pubs. Group.

Time Goes By, 8 vols., Set. Incl. Day at a Zoo. Harrison, Sarah. (J). lib. bdg. 22.60 *(978-1-58013-554-2(4))*; Day at an Airport. Harrison, Sarah. (J). lib. bdg. 22.60 *(978-1-58013-551-1(X))*; Day in a City. Harris, Nicholas. (J). lib. bdg. 22.60 *(978-1-58013-552-8(8))*; Year at a Construction Site. Harris, Nicholas. (J). lib. bdg. 22.60 *(978-1-58013-549-8(8))*; Year at a Farm. Harris, Nicholas. lib. bdg. 22.60 *(978-1-58013-553-5(6))*; Year in a Castle. Coombs, Rachel. (J). lib. bdg. 22.60 *(978-1-58013-550-4(1))*; Year in the World of Dinosaurs. Havercroft, Elizabeth. lib. bdg. 22.60 *(978-1-58013-548-1(X))*; Year on a Pirate Ship. Havercroft, Elizabeth. lib. bdg. 22.60 *(978-1-58013-547-4(1))*; (Illus.). 24p. (gr. k-3). 2008. (Time Goes By Ser.). (ENG.). 2008. Set lib. bdg. 113.00 *(978-1-58013-546-7(3))* Lerner Publishing Group.

Time Slime. 2003. 156p. (YA). (gr. 5-12). pap. 7.95 *(978-0-9702176-3-9(3)*, 0004) Night Howl Productions.

Tulien, Sean, et al. Clock King's Time Bomb, 1 vol. Schoening, Dan, illus. 2011. (Flash Ser.). (ENG.). 56p. (gr. 2-3). pap. 4.95 *(978-1-4342-3412-4(6))*; lib. bdg. 26.65 *(978-1-4342-2626-6(3))* Stone Arch Bks. (DC Super Heroes).

Turley, Sandy. The Clock & the Mouse: A Teaching Rhyme about Time. Peterson, Sara & Lindstrom, Brita, illus. 2006. 32p. (J). lib. bdg. 26.95 *(978-0-9778548-0-6(9))* Helps4Teachers.

Vitale, Samantha. Wasted Time. 2007. 56p. per. 16.95 *(978-1-4241-7436-2(8))* America Star Bks.

What Time Is It Jeanne-Marie. 2005. (Illus.). 34p. (J). mass mkt. 9.99 *(978-0-9740599-7-6(8))* Omnibus Publishing.

Whybrow, Ian, et al. Owain A'r Cloc. 2005. (WEL., Illus.). 20p. 6.99 *(978-1-84323-366-4(5))* Gomer Pr. GBR. Dist: Gomer Pr.

Williams, David K. & Williams, David. Tick Tock. Ovresat, Laura, illus. 2006. (Green Light Readers Level 1 Ser.). (ENG.). 24p. (J). (gr. -1-3). pap. 3.95 *(978-0-15-205605-6(X))* Houghton Mifflin Harcourt Publishing Co.

Winfrey, Michelle/w. It's My Birthday... Finally! A Leap Year Story. 2007. (Illus.). 96p. (J). per. 11.95 *(978-0-9727179-5-3(1))* Hobby Hse. Publishing Group.

Woodruff, Liza, illus. What Time Is It? 2005. (My First Reader Ser.). (ENG.). 32p. (J). (gr. k-4). per. 3.95 *(978-0-516-25279-7(8)*, Children's Pr.) Scholastic Library Publishing.

Woodruff, Liza & Demar, Regier. What Time Is It? Woodruff, Liza, illus. 2005. (My First Reader Ser.). (ENG., Illus.). 32p. (J). (gr. k-1). 18.50 *(978-0-516-25180-6(5)*, Children's Pr.) Scholastic Library Publishing.

TIME—POETRY

Low, Elizabeth Cothen. Big Book of Seasons, Holidays, & Weather: Rhymes, Fingerplays, & Songs for Children. 2011. (ENG., Illus.). 156p. E-Book *(978-1-59884-624-9(8)*, Libraries Unlimited) ABC-CLIO, LLC.

Smith, Marie & Smith, Roland. T Is for a Time. Graef, Renee, illus. 2015. (ENG.). 40p. (J). (gr. 2-5). 16.99 *(978-1-58536-512-8(2)*, 203809) Sleeping Bear Pr.

Wright, Blanche Fisher, illus. Real Mother Goose Clock Book. 22p. (J). (gr. -1-2). 6.95 *(978-1-56288-095-8(0))* Checkerboard Pr., Inc.

TIME TRAVEL

Arias, Lisa. Time Travel: Intervals & Elapsed Time. 2014. (ENG.). 32p. (gr. 3-6). 32.79 *(978-1-62717-706-1(X))* Rourke Educational Media.

Fast Forward, 6 vols., Set. Incl. Castles Through Time. Harris, Nicolas. lib. bdg. 25.25 *(978-1-4358-2798-1(8))*; Dinosaurs Through Time. Harris, Nicolas. Dennis, Peter, illus. lib. bdg. 25.25 *(978-1-4358-2802-5(X))*; Earthquakes Through Time. Harris, Nicolas. lib. bdg. 25.25 *(978-1-4358-2803-2(8))*; Pyramids Through Time. Harris, Nicolas. lib. bdg. 25.25 *(978-1-4358-2801-8(1))*; Volcanoes Through Time. Harris, Nicolas. lib. bdg. 25.25 *(978-1-4358-2800-1(3))*; Wild West Through Time. Aston, Claire. lib. bdg. 25.25 *(978-1-4358-2799-8(6))*; 32p. (YA). (gr. 2-5). 2009. Set lib. bdg. 143.70 *(978-1-4358-2819-3(4)*, PowerKids Pr.) Rosen Publishing Group, Inc., The.

T
U
V

Hamilton, John. Time Travel, 1 vol. 2006. (World of Science Fiction Ser.). (ENG., Illus.). 32p. (gr. 4-7). 27.07 *(978-1-59679-996-7(X)*, Abdo & Daughters) ABDO Publishing Co.

Hunter, Nick. Is Time Travel Possible? 2016. (Top Secret! Ser.). (ENG., Illus.). 48p. (gr. 4-6). lib. bdg. 33.32 *(978-1-4109-8162-2(2))* Heinemann-Raintree.

Kallen, Stuart A. Time Travel. 2009. (Mysterious Encounters Ser.). 48p. (J). 29.00 *(978-0-7377-4573-3(8)*, Kidhaven) Cengage Gale.

TIME TRAVEL—FICTION

Abbott, Tony. The Moon Scroll. Jessell, Tim, illus. 2004. (Secrets of Droon Ser.: No. 15). 129p. (gr. 2-5). 15.00 *(978-0-7569-3946-5(1))* Perfection Learning Corp.

Aguirre, Ann. Infinite Risk. 2016. (Immortal Game Ser.: 3). (ENG.). 384p. (YA). 17.99 *(978-1-250-02465-7(X)*, 9781250024657) Feiwel & Friends.

Akins, Karen. Loop. 2014. (ENG.). 336p. (YA). (gr. 7-12). 18.99 *(978-1-250-03098-6(6)*, 9781250030986, St. Martin's Griffin) St. Martin's Pr.

—Twist. 2015. (ENG.). 336p. (YA). (gr. 7-12). 18.99 *(978-1-250-03100-6(1)*, 9781250031006, St. Martin's Griffin) St. Martin's Pr.

Alexander, Lloyd. Time Cat: The Remarkable Journeys of Jason & Gareth. 2012. (ENG., Illus.). 240p. (J). (gr. 3-7). pap. 7.99 *(978-0-312-63213-7(4)*, 9780312632137) Square Fish.

Alfred Oscar Valentine: Tales from Spoon Creek. 2005. (J). *(978-0-9766894-4-7(8))* Stanley, Donna Lacy.

Anderson, Jessica. Brownies with Benjamin Franklin. 2016. (Time Hop Sweets Shop Ser.). (ENG.). 32p. (gr. k-3). 25.65 *(978-1-68191-375-9(5))* Rourke Educational Media.

Andrews, Jane. Ten Boys Who Lived on the Road from Long Ago to Now (Yesterday's Classics) 2006. (J). 9.95 *(978-1-59915-064-2(6))* Yesterday's Classics.

Anzalone, Karen. Time in a Bottle. 2003. 100p. (YA). pap. 9.00 *(978-0-7599-3840-3(7))* Hard Shell Word Factory.

Asch, Frank. Time Twister: Journal 3 of a Cardboard Genius. Asch, Frank, illus. 2008. (Journals of a Cardboard Genius Ser.). (ENG., Illus.). 144p. (J). (gr. 2-5). pap. 5.95 *(978-1-55453-231-5(0))* Kids Can Pr., Ltd. CAN. Dist: Hachette Bk. Group.

Aureliani, Franco. Dino-Mike! Aureliani, Franco, illus. 2015. (Dino-Mike! Ser.). (ENG., Illus.). 128p. (gr. 1-3). lib. bdg. 101.28 *(978-1-4965-0311-4(2)*, Dino-Mike!) Stone Arch Bks.

—Dino-Mike & the Jurassic Portal. Aureliani, Franco, illus. 2015. (Dino-Mike! Ser.). (ENG., Illus.). 128p. (gr. 1-3). lib. bdg. 25.32 *(978-1-4342-9630-6(X))* Stone Arch Bks.

—Dino-Mike & the Museum Mayhem. Aureliani, Franco, illus. 2015. (Dino-Mike! Ser.). (ENG., Illus.). 128p. (gr. 1-3). lib. bdg. 25.32 *(978-1-4342-9628-3(8)*, Dino-Mike!) Stone Arch Bks.

—Dino-Mike & the T. Rex Attack. Aureliani, Franco, illus. 2015. (Dino-Mike! Ser.). (ENG., Illus.). 128p. (gr. 1-3). lib. bdg. 25.32 *(978-1-4342-9627-6(X))* Stone Arch Bks.

—Dino-Mike & the Underwater Dinosaurs. Aureliani, Franco, illus. 2015. (Dino-Mike! Ser.). (ENG., Illus.). 128p. (gr. 1-3). lib. bdg. 25.32 *(978-1-4342-9629-0(6))* Stone Arch Bks.

Aureliani, Franco, illus. Dino-Mike & the Museum Mayhem. 2015. (J). lib. bdg. *(978-1-4062-9391-3(1))* Stone Arch Bks.

Avery, Ben. Tunnel Twist-Up, 1 vol., Vol. 4. Gaudiamo, Adi Darda, illus. 2008. (Z Graphic Novels / TimeFlyz Ser.). (ENG.). 160p. (J). (gr. 4-7). pap. 6.99 *(978-0-310-71364-7(1))* Zondervan.

Avery, Ben & Zondervan Staff. Time Trap, 1 vol. Wong, Scott, illus. 2009. (Z Graphic Novels / TimeFlyz Ser.). (ENG.). 160p. (J). pap. 6.99 *(978-0-310-71366-1(8))* Zondervan.

Avi. Something Upstairs. 2010. (ENG.). 144p. (J). (gr. 3-7). 5.99 *(978-0-545-21491-9(2)*, Scholastic Pr.) Scholastic, Inc.

—Something Upstairs. 2010. lib. bdg. 16.00 *(978-0-606-14682-1(2)*, Turtleback) Turtleback Bks.

Ayasta, Ayasta. Star. 2007. 117p. 34.95 *(978-1-4303-1520-9(2))* Lulu Pr., Inc.

Ayers, Linda. The Time Bridge Travelers, 3 bks., Bk. 1. Ayers, Ryan, illus. 56p. (J). 2006. 13.95 *(978-0-9760505-8-2(7))* 2004. per. 7.95 *(978-0-9760505-0-6(1))* Blue Thistle Pr.

—The Time Bridge Travelers & the Mysterious Map, 3 bks., Bk. 2. Ayers, Ryan, illus. l.t. ed. (Time Bridge Travelers Ser.: 2). 80p. (J). 2006. 13.95 *(978-0-9760505-6-8(0))* 2005. per. 7.95 *(978-0-9760505-3-7(6))* Blue Thistle Pr.

—The Time Bridge Travelers & the Time Travel Station, 3 bks., Bk. 3. Ayers, Ryan, illus. l.t. ed. 2007. (Time Bridge Travelers Ser.: 3). 140p. (J). lib. bdg. 16.95 *(978-0-9786302-8-7(9))*; per. 7.95 *(978-0-9786302-7-0(0))* Blue Thistle Pr.

Bagdanov, Patricia. The Adventures of Charlie & a Dragon Named Trevor. 2013. 26p. pap. 16.95 *(978-1-63004-985-0(9))* PublishAmerica, Inc.

Baggott, Julianna. The Prince of Fenway Park. 2011. (ENG.). 352p. (J). (gr. 3-7). pap. 6.99 *(978-0-06-087244-1(6))* HarperCollins Pubs.

Bailer, Darice. The Last Rail. 2011. (ENG.). 32p. (J). 9.95 *(978-1-60727-173-4(7))* Soundprints.

—The Pony Express. Antonishak, Tom, illus. 3rd ed. 2003. (Soundprints' Read-and-Discover Ser.). (ENG.). 48p. (J). (gr. -1-3). pap. 3.95 *(978-1-59249-019-6(0)*, S2008) Soundprints.

Baldwin, Quinn. Crossover. 2011. 168p. pap. 15.00 *(978-0-557-74844-0(5))* Lulu Pr., Inc.

Banks, Steven. Lost in Time. The Artifact Group, illus. 2006. 22p. (J). lib. bdg. 15.00 *(978-1-4242-0977-4(3))* Fitzgerald Bks.

Baraitser, Marion. Home Number One. 2006. (Illus.). 63p. (YA). pap. *(978-0-9529426-7-2(4))* Loki Books Ltd.

Barnett, Mac. Oh No! Not Again! Or How I Built a Time Machine to Save History - Or at Least My History Grade. Santat, Dan, illus. 2012. (Oh No! Picture Book Ser.). (ENG.). 40p. (J). (gr. -1-k). 17.99 *(978-1-4231-4912-5(2))* Hyperion Pr.

Barron, T. A. The Ancient One. 2003. (Illus.). 304p. 14.65 *(978-0-7569-6642-3(6))* Perfection Learning Corp.

Barron, Tom. The Ancient One. 2016. (ENG.). 320p. (J). (gr. 5). 8.99 *(978-1-101-99702-4(8)*, Puffin Books) Penguin Young Readers Group.

Barrowman, John & Barrowman, Carole E. Book of Beasts. 2016. (Hollow Earth Ser.). (ENG.). 336p. (J). (gr. 3-7). pap. 7.99 *(978-1-4814-4231-2(7)*, Simon & Schuster/Paula Wiseman Bks.) Simon & Schuster/Paula Wiseman Bks.

—Conjuror. 2016. (Orion Chronicles Ser.). (ENG.). 320p. (YA). (gr. 7). 16.99 *(978-1-78185-637-6(0))* Head of Zeus GBR. Dist: Independent Pubs. Group.

Barrows, Annie. The Magic Half. 2008. (ENG.). 224p. (YA). (gr. 3-7). 16.99 *(978-1-59990-132-9(3)*, 9781599901329, Bloomsbury USA Childrens) Bloomsbury Publishing USA.

—Magic in the Mix. (ENG.). 288p. (YA). (gr. 3-6). 2015. pap. 7.99 *(978-1-61963-798-6(7)*, 9781619637986) 2014. 16.99 *(978-1-61963-482-4(1)*, 9781619634824) Bloomsbury Publishing USA. (Bloomsbury USA Childrens).

Basic, Zdenko & Sumberac, Manuel, illus. Steampunk: H. G. Wells. 2013. (ENG.). 408p. (YA). (gr. 7-17). 18.95 *(978-0-7624-4444-1(4)*, Running Pr. Kids) Running Pr. Bk. Pubs.

Baskin, Nora Raleigh. Subway Love. 2014. (ENG.). 224p. (YA). (gr. 9). 16.99 *(978-0-7636-6845-7(1))* Candlewick Pr.

Bateman, Jordan. Dunamis Heroes: Issue #1: the Lost Kingdom. Save, Ken, illus. 2007. 120p. (J). per. *(978-0-9781953-0-4(2))* Dunamis Media.

Bauer, Christina. The Pirate Queen: A Timewalker Journey. 2005. 280p. (YA). 14.99 *(978-1-59092-224-8(7))* Blue Forge Pr.

Bauer, Marion Dane. The Blue Ghost. Wang, Suling, illus. 2006. (Stepping Stone Book Ser.). (ENG.). 96p. (J). (gr. 1-4). 3.99 *(978-0-375-83339-7(0)*, Random Hse. Bks. for Young Readers) Random Hse. Children's Bks.

Beckman, Thea. Crusade in Jeans. 2011. (ENG.). 307p. (J). (gr. 6). pap. 9.95 *(978-1-935954-07-1(5)*, 9781935954071) Lemniscaat USA.

Bell, Ted. Nick of Time. 2009. (Nick Mciver Adventures Through Time Ser.: 1). (ENG., Illus.). 464p. (J). (gr. 5-9). pap. 8.99 *(978-0-312-58143-5(2)*, 9780312581435) Square Fish.

—The Time Pirate. 2011. (Nick Mciver Adventures Through Time Ser.: 2). (ENG., Illus.). 480p. (J). (gr. 5-9). pap. 10.99 *(978-0-312-66549-4(0)*, 9780312665494) Square Fish.

Bellairs, John. The House with a Clock in Its Walls. Gorey, Edward, illus. 2004. (Lewis Barnavelt Ser.: Bk. 1). (ENG.). 192p. (J). (gr. 3-7). pap. 6.99 *(978-0-14-240257-3(5)*, Puffin Books) Penguin Young Readers Group.

—The House with a Clock in Its Walls. (Lewis Barnavelt Ser.: Bk. 1). 179p. (J). (gr. 4-6). pap. 4.50 *(978-0-8072-1423-7(X)*, Listening Library) Random Hse. Audio Publishing Group.

Benderly, Beryl Lieff. Jason's Miracle: A Hanukkah Story. 2004. 114p. (J). (gr. 4-8). reprint ed. *(978-0-7567-7792-0(5))* DIANE Publishing Co.

Benton, Jim. The Fran That Time Forgot. Benton, Jim, illus. 4th ed. 2005. (Franny K. Stein, Mad Scientist Ser.: 4). (ENG., Illus.). 112p. (J). (gr. 2-5). mass mkt. 5.99 *(978-0-689-86298-4(9))*; 16.99 *(978-0-689-86294-6(6))* Simon & Schuster Bks. For Young Readers. (Simon & Schuster Bks. For Young Readers).

—The Fran That Time Forgot, 1 vol. Benton, Jim, illus. 2011. (Franny K. Stein, Mad Scientist Ser.). (ENG., Illus.). 112p. (gr. 3-6). 24.21 *(978-1-59961-820-3(6))* Spotlight.

—The Fran with Four Brains, 1 vol. Benton, Jim, illus. 2011. (Franny K. Stein, Mad Scientist Ser.). (ENG., Illus.). 112p. (gr. 3-6). 24.21 *(978-1-59961-822-7(2))* Spotlight.

Berard, Robin M. King Tut & the Girl Who Loved Him: The Strange Adventures of Johanna Wilson. 2007. 212p. per. 12.95 *(978-1-58348-477-7(9)*, iUniverse Star) iUniverse, Inc.

Berrios, Frank. Time Travel Mater (Disney/Pixar Cars) RH Disney Staff, illus. 2013. (Pictureback(R) Ser.). (ENG.). 16p. (J). (gr. -1-2). 3.99 *(978-0-7364-3107-1(1)*, RH/Disney) Random Hse. Children's Bks.

Bessey, Siân Ann. Escape from Germany. 2004. 183p. (J). *(978-1-59156-436-2(0))* Covenant Communications.

—Uprising in Samoa: A Novel. 2004. 178p. (J). *(978-1-59156-890-2(0))* Covenant Communications.

Bethany: Adventures of the Mighty Mustard Seed. 2004. Orig. Title: Bethany in Beulah Land. (J). mass mkt. 12.95 *(978-0-9745440-0-7(0))* McKatlib Pr.

Beveridge, Cathy. Stormstruck. 2006. (ENG., Illus.). 214p. (J). pap. *(978-1-55380-041-5(9))* Ronsdale Pr.

Biggs, Stephen. The Time Barrel. 2009. 152p. pap. *(978-1-84923-434-4(5))* YouWriteOn.

Bilgrey, Marc. And Don't Forget to Rescue the Other Princess. 2009. 252p. 25.95 *(978-1-59414-744-9(2)*, Five Star) Cengage Gale.

Bishop, Mary Harelkin & Coteau Books Staff. Tunnels of Tyranny: A Fourth Moose Jaw Adventure, 1 vol. 2005. (Moose Jaw Adventure Ser.). (ENG.). 248p. (J). (gr. 4-7). pap. 7.95 *(978-1-55050-316-6(2))* Coteau Bks. CAN. Dist: Orca Bk. Pubs. USA.

Blair, Margaret Whitman. The Sand Castle: Blockade Running & the Battle of Fort Fisher. 2005. (White Mane Kids Ser.: 17). (Illus.). 187p. (J). (gr. 4-7). per. 8.95 *(978-1-57249-346-9(1)*, White Mane Kids) White Mane Publishing Co., Inc.

Bloor, Edward. London Calling. 2008. (ENG., Illus.). 304p. (YA). (gr. 7-9). per. 8.99 *(978-0-375-84363-1(9)*, Ember) Random Hse. Children's Bks.

Bobulski, Chelsea. The Wood. 2017. (ENG.). 320p. (YA). 17.99 *(978-1-250-09426-1(7)*, 9781250094261) Feiwel & Friends.

Bodeen, S. A. Trapped. 2016. (Shipwreck Island Ser.: 3). (ENG.). 160p. (J). 16.99 *(978-1-250-02781-8(0)*, 9781250027818) Feiwel & Friends.

Boeve, Eunice. Echoes of Kansas Past. Peterson-Shea, Julie, illus. 2012. 176p. pap. 10.99 *(978-0-9851196-9-0(1))* Rowe Publishing and Design.

Bold, Emily. Breath of Yesterday, 0 vols. Bell, Katja, tr. from GER. 2014. (Curse Ser.: 2). (ENG.). 376p. (YA). (gr. 9-12). pap. 9.99 *(978-1-4778-4714-5(6)*, 9781477847145) Amazon Publishing.

Bolte, Marissa. Arrested for Witchcraft! Nickolas Flux & the Salem Witch Trials, 1 vol. Ginevra, Dante, illus. 2014. (Nickolas Flux History Chronicles Ser.). (ENG.). (gr. 3-4). 40p. pap. 7.95 *(978-1-4765-5151-7(0))*; 32p. lib. bdg. 30.65 *(978-1-4765-3947-8(2))* Capstone Press of Coughlan Cos. (Graphic Library).

Bond, Nancy. A String in the Harp. 2006. (ENG.). 384p. (J). (gr. 5-9). pap. 8.99 *(978-1-4169-2771-6(9)*, Aladdin) Simon & Schuster Children's Publishing.

Boniface, William. The Extraordinary Adventures of Ordinary Boy. Gilpin, Stephen, illus. 2008. (Extraordinary Adventures of Ordinary Boy Ser.: 2). (ENG.). 368p. (J). (gr. 3-7). pap. 6.99 *(978-0-06-077469-1(X))* HarperCollins Pubs.

Booth, Molly. Saving Hamlet. 2016. (ENG.). 352p. (YA). (gr. 7-12). 17.99 *(978-1-4847-5274-6(0))* Hyperion Bks. for Children.

Bosch, Pseudonymous. This Isn't What It Looks Like. (Secret Ser.: 4). (ENG.). (J). (gr. 3-7). 2011. 448p. pap. 8.99 *(978-0-316-07624-1(4))* 2010. 432p. 17.00 *(978-0-316-07625-8(2))* Little, Brown Bks. for Young Readers.

Boston, L. M. The Stones of Green Knowe. Boston, Peter, illus. 2006. (Green Knowe Ser.: 6). (ENG.). 144p. (J). (gr. 2-5). pap. 10.95 *(978-0-15-205566-0(5))* Houghton Mifflin Harcourt Publishing Co.

Bow, James. The Young City: The Unwritten Books. 2008. (Unwritten Bks.: 3). (ENG.). 264p. (YA). (gr. 7). pap. 12.99 *(978-1-55002-846-1(4))* Dundurn CAN. Dist: Ingram Publisher Services.

Boyce, Frank Cottrell. Chitty Chitty Bang Bang & the Race Against Time. Berger, Joe, illus. (Chitty Chitty Bang Bang Ser.). (ENG.). 240p. (J). (gr. 4-7). 2014. pap. 6.99 *(978-0-7636-6931-7(8))* 2013. 15.99 *(978-0-7636-5982-0(7))* Candlewick Pr.

—Chitty Chitty Bang Bang Flies Again. Berger, Joe, illus. 2013. (Chitty Chitty Bang Bang Ser.). (ENG.). 224p. (J). (gr. 4-7). pap. 6.99 *(978-0-7636-6353-7(0))* Candlewick Pr.

Bracken, Alexandra. Passenger. 2016. (Passenger Ser.). (ENG.). 512p. (YA). (gr. 9-17). pap. 9.99 *(978-1-4847-3279-3(0))* Disney Pr.

—Passenger. 2016. (Passenger Ser.). (ENG.). 496p. (YA). (gr. 9-12). 17.99 *(978-1-4847-1577-2(2))* Hyperion Bks. for Children.

—Wayfarer. 2017. (Passenger Ser.). (ENG.). 544p. (YA). (gr. 9-17). 17.99 *(978-1-4847-1576-5(4))* Hyperion Bks. for Children.

Bradbury, Ray. The Halloween Tree. (J). 20.95 *(978-0-8488-0432-9(5))* Amereon Ltd.

—The Halloween Tree. Eller, Jon, ed. Bradbury, Ray & Mugnaini, Joe, illus. 2005. 494p. (J). (gr. 4-12). per. 75.00 *(978-1-887368-80-3(9))* Gauntlet, Inc.

—The Halloween Tree. Mugnaini, Joseph, illus. 2007. (ENG.). 160p. (J). (gr. 3-7). reprint ed. 15.99 *(978-0-394-82409-3(1)*, Knopf Bks. for Young Readers) Random Hse. Children's Bks.

Bradley, Timothy J. Time Jump, Bk. 3. 2014. (Sci Hi Ser.). (ENG.). 232p. (J). (gr. 3-6). lib. bdg. 26.96 *(978-1-4807-4217-8(1))* Teacher Created Materials, Inc.

Brashares, Ann. The Here & Now. 2014. 242p. (YA). *(978-0-385-39008-8(4)*, Delacorte Pr) Random House Publishing Group.

—The Here & Now. (ENG.). 256p. (YA). (gr. 7). 2015. pap. 10.99 *(978-0-385-73683-1(5)*, Ember) 2014. 18.99 *(978-0-385-73680-0(0)*, Delacorte Pr.) Random Hse. Children's Bks.

Brennan, Herbie. The Doomsday Box: A Shadow Project Adventure. 2011. (Shadow Project Ser.: 2). (ENG.). 352p. (J). (gr. 5). pap. 6.99 *(978-0-06-175650-4(4))* HarperCollins Pubs.

Brezenoff, Steve. Overboard, 1 vol. Murphy, Scott, illus. 2012. (Return to Titanic Ser.). (ENG.). 112p. (gr. 2-3). pap. 6.95 *(978-1-4342-3912-9(8))*; lib. bdg. 25.32 *(978-1-4342-3302-8(2))* Stone Arch Bks. (Return to Titanic).

—Stowaways, 1 vol. Murphy, Scott, illus. 2012. (Return to Titanic Ser.). (ENG.). 112p. (gr. 2-3). pap. 6.95 *(978-1-4342-3910-5(1))*; lib. bdg. 25.32 *(978-1-4342-3300-4(6))* Stone Arch Bks. (Return to Titanic).

—Time Voyage, 1 vol. Murphy, Scott, illus. 2012. (Return to Titanic Ser.). (ENG.). 112p. (gr. 2-3). pap. 6.95 *(978-1-4342-3909-9(8))*; lib. bdg. 25.32 *(978-1-4342-3299-1(9))* Stone Arch Bks. (Return to Titanic).

—An Unsinkable Ship, 1 vol. Murphy, Scott, illus. 2012. (Return to Titanic Ser.). (ENG.). 112p. (gr. 2-3). pap. 6.95 *(978-1-4342-3911-2(X))*; lib. bdg. 25.32 *(978-1-4342-3301-1(4))* Stone Arch Bks. (Return to Titanic).

Briggs, Elizabeth. Future Shock. 2016. (YA). (Future Shock Ser.: 1). (ENG.). 288p. (gr. 8-12). pap. 9.99 *(978-0-8075-2680-4(0))*; *(978-0-8075-2683-5(5))*; (Future Shock Ser.: 1). (ENG.). 272p. (gr. 8-12). 16.99 *(978-0-8075-2682-8(7))* Whitman, Albert & Co.

Briggs, Elizabeth. Future Threat. 2017. (Future Shock Ser.: 2). (ENG.). 272p. (YA). (gr. 8-12). 16.99 *(978-0-8075-2684-2(3))*; pap. 9.99 ***(978-0-8075-2686-6(X))*** Whitman, Albert & Co.

Brodien-Jones, Chris. The Glass Puzzle. 2013. (Illus.). 319p. (J). *(978-0-385-74298-6(3)*, Delacorte Pr) Random House Publishing Group.

Brodien-Jones, Christine. The Glass Puzzle. 2013. (ENG., Illus.). 336p. (J). (gr. 4-7). 16.99 *(978-0-385-74297-9(5)*, Delacorte Bks. for Young Readers) Random Hse. Children's Bks.

Buckley-Archer, Linda. The Time Quake. (Gideon Trilogy Ser.: 3). (ENG.). 464p. (J). (gr. 5-9). 2010. pap. 9.99 *(978-1-4169-1530-0(3))* 2009. 17.99 *(978-1-4169-1529-4(X))* Simon & Schuster Bks. For Young Readers. (Simon & Schuster Bks. For Young Readers).

—The Time Travelers. (Gideon Trilogy Ser.: 1). (ENG.). 416p. (J). (gr. 5-9). 2012. 17.99 *(978-1-4424-6551-0(4))* 2007. pap. 8.99 *(978-1-4169-1526-3(5))* Simon & Schuster Bks. For Young Readers. (Simon & Schuster Bks. For Young Readers).

Buckley, Michael. Attack of the Bullies. 2013. (Nerds Ser.). (ENG.). 336p. (YA). (gr. 3-7). 16.95 *(978-1-4197-0857-2(0)*, Amulet Bks.) Abrams, Inc.

Buehrlen, M. G. The Fifty-Seven Lives of Alex Wayfare. 2015. (ENG., Illus.). 324p. pap. 15.99 *(978-1-62681-872-9(X))* Diversion Publishing Corp.

—The Untimely Deaths of Alex Wayfare. 2016. (ENG.). 232p. pap. 15.99 *(978-1-68230-058-9(7))* Diversion Publishing Corp.

Burgess, Barbara. The Magic Manuscript: The Nine Companions. 2013. 234p. pap. 12.99 *(978-0-9918574-3-2(7))* Sulby Hall Publishing.

—The Magic Manuscript: Voyage to Eve Ilion. 2013. 202p. pap. 9.99 *(978-0-9918574-4-9(5))* Sulby Hall Publishing.

Burnell, Pamela H. The Light Keeper: An Epps Kids Mystery. 2008. 76p. pap. 19.95 *(978-1-60474-847-5(8))* America Star Bks.

Bush, Maureen. The Nexus Ring, 1 vol. 2007. (Veil of Magic Ser.: 1). (ENG.). 136p. (J). (gr. 3-6). per. 6.95 *(978-1-55050-362-3(6))* Coteau Bks. CAN. Dist: Orca Bk. Pubs. USA.

Bush, Penelope. Alice in Time. 2011. (ENG., Illus.). 208p. (YA). (gr. 7-18). 17.95 *(978-0-8234-2329-3(8))* Holiday Hse., Inc.

Butler, Dori. The Time Capsule. 2005. (J). pap. *(978-1-4108-4198-8(7))* Benchmark Education Co.

Buzbee, Lewis. Bridge of Time. 2013. (ENG.). 320p. (J). (gr. 5-9). pap. 14.99 *(978-1-250-02734-4(9)*, 9781250027344) Square Fish.

Byng, Georgia. Molly Moon, Micky Minus, & the Mind Machine. (Molly Moon Ser.: 4). (ENG.). (J). (gr. 3-7). 2008. 416p. pap. 7.99 *(978-0-06-075038-1(3))* 2007. 384p. 16.99 *(978-0-06-075036-7(7))* HarperCollins Pubs.

—Molly Moon Viaja a Traes del Tiempo. Crispin, Maria Dolores, tr. 2005. (SPA.). 350p. *(978-84-675-0570-2(2))* SM Ediciones.

—Molly Moon's Hypnotic Time Travel Adventure. (ENG.). 400p. (J). 2006. (Molly Moon Ser.: 3). (gr. 3-7). pap. 7.99 *(978-0-06-075034-3(0))* 2005. (Illus.). 16.99 *(978-0-06-075032-9(4))* HarperCollins Pubs.

—Molly Moon's Hypnotic Time Travel Adventure. 2007. (Molly Moon Ser.). (Illus.). 392p. (gr. 3-7). 18.00 *(978-0-7569-7761-0(4))* Perfection Learning Corp.

—Molly Moon's Hypnotic Time-Travel Adventure. 2005. (Illus.). 400p. (J). lib. bdg. 18.89 *(978-0-06-075033-6(2))* HarperCollins Pubs.

Cabot, Meg. Shadowland & Ninth Key. 2010. (Mediator Ser.). (ENG.). 544p. (YA). (gr. 8). pap. 9.99 *(978-0-06-204020-6(0)*, HarperTeen) HarperCollins Pubs.

—Twilight. 2005. (Mediator Ser.: No. 6). (ENG.). 256p. (J). 15.99 *(978-0-06-072467-2(6))* HarperCollins Pubs.

Cameron, Ian. Stirling Bridge. (Illus.). 32p. pap. 6.95 *(978-1-899827-07-7(2))* Scottish Children's Pr. GBR. Dist: Wilson & Assocs.

Card, Orson Scott. Pathfinder. (ENG.). 672p. (YA). (gr. 7). 2011. pap. 12.99 *(978-1-4169-9179-3(4))* 2010. 19.99 *(978-1-4169-9176-2(X))* Simon Pulse. (Simon Pulse).

—Pathfinder. l.t. ed. 2011. (Pathfinder Ser.). (ENG.). 802p. 23.99 *(978-1-4104-3681-8(0))* Thorndike Pr.

—Ruins. (ENG.). 544p. (YA). (gr. 7). 2013. pap. 12.99 *(978-1-4169-9180-9(8))* 2012. 18.99 *(978-1-4169-9177-9(8))* Simon Pulse. (Simon Pulse).

—Visitors. 2015. (ENG., Illus.). 608p. (YA). (gr. 7). pap. 12.99 *(978-1-4169-9181-6(6)*, Simon Pulse) Simon Pulse.

Carpenter, Chad. Morry Moose's Time-Traveling Outhouse Adventure. 2013. (ENG.). 48p. (J). pap. 12.95 *(978-1-62343-163-1(8))* Willow Creek Pr., Inc.

Carter, Rachel. Find Me Where the Water Ends. 2014. (ENG.). 352p. (YA). (gr. 9). 17.99 *(978-0-06-208111-7(X)*, HarperTeen) HarperCollins Pubs.

—So Close to You. 2013. (ENG.). 336p. (YA). (gr. 9). pap. 9.99 *(978-0-06-208106-3(3)*, HarperTeen) HarperCollins Pubs.

—This Strange & Familiar Place. 2013. (ENG.). 272p. (YA). (gr. 9). 17.99 *(978-0-06-208108-7(X)*, HarperTeen) HarperCollins Pubs.

Castellan, Andrea. Mickey Mouse & the Orbiting Nightmare. 2011. (ENG., Illus.). 128p. (J). pap. *(978-1-60886-630-4(0))* Boom! Studios.

Chapman, Bob. Visitors. 2006. 304p. pap. *(978-1-84401-693-8(5))* Athena Pr.

Cheasebro, Margaret. The Healing Tree. 2015. (ENG.). 304p. (YA). 15.95 *(978-1-937240-60-8(6))* Casa de Snapdragon LLC.

Childress, Jamie. Galactic Treasure Hunt #4: Lost in Time. Braun, Chris, illus. 2008. (Galactic Treasure Hunt Ser.). (ENG.). 176p. (J). pap. 5.99 *(978-1-931882-89-7(4))* Adventures Unlimited Pr.

Citra, Becky. Jeremy & the Enchanted Theater. Milne, Jessica, illus. 2004. 64p. (J). lib. bdg. 20.00 *(978-1-4242-1258-3(8))* Fitzgerald Bks.

—Jeremy & the Fantastic Flying Machine, 1 vol. Milne, Jessica, illus. 2008. (Orca Echoes Ser.). (ENG.). 64p. (J). (gr. 2-3). pap. 6.95 *(978-1-55143-950-1(6))* Orca Bk. Pubs. USA.

Clarizio, Laura. Traveling Through Time: If I Had a Magic Carpet IV. 2012. 100p. 21.95 *(978-1-4489-3229-0(7))* America Star Bks.

Clark, Hattie Mae. It Happened at a Hanging. 2003. (Single Titles Ser.: up). (ENG.). 160p. (YA). (gr. 7-12). lib. bdg. 18.95 *(978-0-7613-2521-5(2)*, Millbrook Pr.) Lerner Publishing Group.

Clark, Henry. The Book That Proves Time Travel Happens. 2015. (ENG., Illus.). 416p. (J). (gr. 3-7). 17.00 *(978-0-316-40617-8(1))* Little Brown & Co.

Cockcroft, Jason. Counter Clockwise. 2009. 208p. (J). lib. bdg. 16.89 *(978-0-06-125555-7(6))*; (ENG., Illus.). (gr. 5-18). 15.99 *(978-0-06-125554-0(8))* HarperCollins Pubs. (Tegen, Katherine Bks).

Cohagan, Carolyn. The Lost Children. 2011. (ENG.). 320p. (J). (gr. 3-7). pap. 7.99 *(978-1-4169-8617-1(0)*, Aladdin) Simon & Schuster Children's Publishing.

—The Lost Children. 2010. (ENG.). 320p. (J). (gr. 3-7). 16.99 *(978-1-4169-8616-4(2)*, Simon & Schuster/Paula Wiseman Bks.) Simon & Schuster/Paula Wiseman Bks.

Cohen, Rich. Alex & the Amazing Time Machine. Murphy, Kelly, illus. 2013. (ENG.). 176p. (J). (gr. 3-7). pap. 6.99 *(978-1-250-02729-0(2)*, 9781250027290) Square Fish.

Colfer, Eoin. The Forever Man. 2015. (Warp Ser.). (ENG.). 352p. (YA). (gr. 7-12). 17.99 *(978-1-4847-2603-7(0))* Hyperion Bks. for Children.

—The Hangman's Revolution. 2014. (W. A. R. P. Ser.: Bk. 2). (ENG.). 384p. (YA). (gr. 7-12). 17.99 *(978-1-4231-6163-9(7))* Disney Pr.

—The Hangman's Revolution. 2015. (Warp Ser.). (ENG.). 400p. (YA). (gr. 7-12). pap. 9.99 *(978-1-4231-6498-2(9))* Hyperion Bks. for Children.

—The Time Paradox. 2009. (Artemis Fowl Ser.). (ENG.). 448p. (J). (gr. 5-9). pap. 8.99 *(978-1-4231-0837-5(X))* Hyperion Pr.

—The Time Paradox. 2009. (Artemis Fowl Ser.: 6). (J). lib. bdg. 19.65 *(978-0-606-10579-8(4)*, Turtleback) Turtleback Bks.

Collard, Sneed B., III. Dog 4491. 2013. (Illus.). 256p. (J). 13.99 *(978-0-9844460-4-9(4))* Bucking Horse Bks.

Collard, Sneed B., 3rd. Dog 4491. 2013. (ENG., Illus.). 256p. (J). pap. 8.00 *(978-0-9844460-5-6(2))* Mountain Pr. Publishing Co., Inc.

Collins, Terry, et al. Nickolas Flux History Chronicles, 1 vol. Simmons, Mark, illus. 2014. (Nickolas Flux History Chronicles Ser.). (ENG.). 32p. (gr. 3-4). 122.60 *(978-1-4914-0255-9(5)*, Graphic Library) Capstone Press of Coughlan Cos.

Columbus, Chris & Vizzini, Ned. Battle of the Beasts. Call, Greg, illus. 2015. (House of Secrets Ser.: 2). (ENG.). 480p. (J). (gr. 3-7). pap. 7.99 *(978-0-06-219250-9(7))* HarperCollins Pubs.

The Complete Gideon Trilogy: The Time Travelers; the Time Thief; the Time Quake. 2014. (Gideon Trilogy Ser.). (ENG., Illus.). 1424p. (J). (gr. 5-9). pap. 26.99 *(978-1-4814-2613-8(3)*, Simon & Schuster Bks. For Young Readers) Simon & Schuster Bks. For Young Readers.

Connolly, Kara. No Good Deed. 2017. (ENG.). 352p. (YA). (gr. 9). 17.99 ***(978-0-385-74393-8(9))***; lib. bdg. 20.99 ***(978-0-375-99140-0(9))*** Random Hse. Children's Bks. (Delacorte Pr.).

Cooper, Clare. Time Ball. 2003. (ENG.). 72p. pap. 11.95 *(978-1-84323-255-1(3))* Beekman Bks., Inc.

Coughlin, Shirley. Toby & the Pirates. 2012. 58p. pap. 13.00 *(978-1-61204-745-4(9)*, Strategic Bk. Publishing) Strategic Book Publishing & Rights Agency (SBPRA).

Cowden, Matt. Emma Mcdougal & the Quest for Father Time. Black, Ilene, illus. 2008. 190p. (J). 24.95 *(978-0-9799189-0-2(1))* His Work Christian Publishing.

Crawford, Charlene E. Adventures with Granny in the Garden. 2006. (J). pap. 7.95 *(978-1-882185-69-6(2))* Cornerstone Publishing, Inc.

Crawford, Quinton Douglass. Moochie the Soochie Visits the Peace People. 2007. 27p. 12.50 *(978-0-615-14879-3(4))* Crawford, Quinton Douglass.

Cross, Julie. Tempest. 2012. (Tempest Trilogy Ser.: 1). (ENG.). (YA). (gr. 9-12). 368p. pap. 9.99 *(978-1-250-01120-6(5)*, 9781250011206); 352p. 17.99 *(978-0-312-56889-4(4)*, 9780312568894) St. Martin's Pr. (St. Martin's Griffin).

—Timestorm: A Tempest Novel. 2014. (Tempest Trilogy Ser.: 3). (ENG.). 368p. (YA). (gr. 9-12). 18.99 *(978-0-312-56891-7(6)*, 9780312568917, St. Martin's Griffin) St. Martin's Pr.

—Vortex. 2013. (Tempest Trilogy Ser.: 2). (ENG.). 368p. (YA). (gr. 9-12). 18.99 *(978-0-312-56890-0(8)*, 9780312568900, St. Martin's Griffin) St. Martin's Pr.

—Vortex: A Tempest Novel. 2013. (Tempest Trilogy Ser.: 2). (ENG.). 384p. (YA). (gr. 9-12). pap. 9.99 *(978-1-250-04478-5(2)*, 9781250044785, St. Martin's Griffin) St. Martin's Pr.

Cuate, Melodie A. Journey to la Salle's Settlement. 2010. (Mr. Barrington's Mysterious Trunk Ser.). (ENG., Illus.). 184p. (J). lib. bdg. 18.95 *(978-0-89672-704-5(1))* Texas Tech Univ. Pr.

—Journey to the Alamo. 2006. (Mr. Barrington's Mysterious Trunk Ser.). (Illus.). 144p. (J). (gr. 4-7). 18.95 *(978-0-89672-592-8(8))* Texas Tech Univ. Pr.

Cunningham, Mary. The Magic Medallion. 2006. (Cynthia's Attic Ser.). 158p. (J). (gr. 4-7). per. 9.99 *(978-1-59080-460-5(0))* Echelon Press Publishing.

Curley, Marianne. Key. 2011. (Guardians of Time Ser.). (ENG.). 416p. (YA). (gr. 7). pap. 9.99 *(978-1-59990-545-7(0)*, 9781599905457, Bloomsbury USA Childrens) Bloomsbury Publishing USA.

—Old Magic. 2009. (ENG.). 400p. (YA). (gr. 7-18). pap. 9.99 *(978-1-4169-8991-2(9),* Simon Pulse) Simon Pulse.

Curry, Jane Louise. The Black Canary. 2005. (ENG., Illus.). 288p. (J). (gr. 5-9). 18.99 *(978-0-689-86478-0(7),* McElderry, Margaret K. Bks.) McElderry, Margaret K. Bks.

Dalton, Annie. Budding Star: Mission - Rescue a Pop Princess. 2008. (Mel Beeby Agent Angel Ser.). (ENG.). 208p. (J). (gr. 4-7). pap. 6.95 *(978-0-00-720478-6(7))* HarperCollins Pubs. Ltd. GBR. Dist: Independent Pubs. Group.

—The Divine Collection: Three Amazing Missions in One Book! 2008. (Mel Beeby Agent Angel Ser.). (ENG., Illus.). 608p. (J). (gr. 4-7). pap. 19.95 *(978-0-00-719074-4(3))* HarperCollins Pubs. Ltd. GBR. Dist: Independent Pubs. Group.

—Fighting Fit: Mission - Get into the Gladiator Groove! 2009. (Mel Beeby, Agent Angel Ser.: 6). (ENG.). 192p. (J). (gr. 4-7). pap. 7.99 *(978-0-00-720476-2(0))* HarperCollins Pubs. Ltd. GBR. Dist: HarperCollins Pubs.

—Flying High, No. 3. 2003. (Angels Unlimited Ser.). (ENG., Illus.). 144p. (J). pap. 4.99 *(978-0-06-008817-0(6))* HarperCollins Pubs.

—Flying High: Mission - Prepare to Party! 2010. (Mel Beeby, Agent Angel Ser.: 3). (ENG.). 144p. (J). (gr. 4-7). pap. 7.99 *(978-0-00-720473-1(6))* HarperCollins Pubs. Ltd. GBR. Dist: HarperCollins Pubs.

—Fogging Over: Mission - Take a Trip down Under. 2010. (Mel Beeby, Agent Angel Ser.: 5). (ENG.). 160p. (J). (gr. 4-7). pap. 7.99 *(978-0-00-720475-5(2))* HarperCollins Pubs. Ltd. GBR. Dist: HarperCollins Pubs.

—Losing the Plot: Mission: Rescue a Teenage Trio! 2008. (Mel Beeby Agent Angel Ser.). (ENG.). 160p. (J). (gr. 4-7). pap. 6.95 *(978-0-00-720472-4(8))* HarperCollins Pubs. Ltd. GBR. Dist: Independent Pubs. Group.

—Making Waves: Mission - Foil the Pirates. 2010. (Mel Beeby, Agent Angel Ser.: 7). (ENG.). 208p. (J). (gr. 4-7). pap. 9.99 *(978-0-00-720477-9(9))* HarperCollins Pubs. Ltd. GBR. Dist: HarperCollins Pubs.

—Winging It: Mission: Enrol at Angel School! 2008. (Mel Beeby Agent Angel Ser.). (ENG.). 144p. (J). (gr. 4-7). pap. 6.95 *(978-0-00-720471-7(X))* HarperCollins Pubs. Ltd. GBR. Dist: Independent Pubs. Group.

Dashner, James. A Mutiny in Time. (Infinity Ring Ser.: 1). (ENG.). 192p. (J). (gr. 3-7). 2015. pap. 6.99 *(978-0-545-90016-4(6))* 2012. 12.99 *(978-0-545-38696-8(9))* 2012. 16.99 *(978-0-545-48321-6(2))* Scholastic, Inc.

Dateno, Maria Grace. Courageous Quest. Cunningham, Paul, illus. 2014. 81p. (J). pap. 5.95 *(978-0-8198-1628-3(0))* Pauline Bks. & Media.

—Danger at Sea. Cunningham, Paul, illus. 2013. 80p. (J). pap. 5.95 *(978-0-8198-1891-1(7))* Pauline Bks. & Media.

—Discovery at Dawn. Cunningham, Paul, illus. 2014. (ENG.). 79p. (J). pap. 5.95 *(978-0-8198-1895-9(X))* Pauline Bks. & Media.

—Mystery of the Missing Jars. Cunningham, Paul, illus. 2014. 77p. (J). 5.95 *(978-0-8198-4922-9(7))* Pauline Bks. & Media.

David, Erica. Mr. Peabody & Sherman Big Golden Book (Mr. Peabody & Sherman) Laguna, Fabio & Spaziante, Patrick, illus. 2014. (Big Golden Book Ser.). (ENG.). 48p. (J). (gr. k-4). 9.99 *(978-0-385-37142-1(X),* Golden Bks.) Random Hse. Children's Bks.

—Mr. Peabody & Sherman Junior Novelization (Mr. Peabody & Sherman) Random House, illus. 2014. (Junior Novel Ser.). (ENG.). 128p. (J). (gr. 2-5). 5.99 *(978-0-385-37141-4(1),* Random Hse. Bks. for Young Readers) Random Hse. Children's Bks.

Davie, Jan. Apollo Cafe. 2005. 76p. pap. *(978-1-84401-565-8(3))* Athena Pr.

Davies, Linda. Longbow Girl. 2016. (ENG.). 336p. (J). (gr. 7). 17.99 *(978-0-545-85345-3(1),* Chicken Hse., The) Scholastic, Inc.

De la Peña, Matt. Curse of the Ancients. 2015. (Infinity Ring Ser.: 4). (ENG.). 192p. (J). (gr. 3-7). pap. 6.99 *(978-0-545-90119-2(7))* Scholastic, Inc.

—Curse of the Ancients. 2015. (Infinity Ring Ser.: 4). lib. bdg. 17.20 *(978-0-606-37789-8(1))* Turtleback Bks.

de los Santos, Marisa & Teague, David. Saving Lucas Biggs. (ENG.). (J). (gr. 3-7). 2015. 320p. pap. 6.99 *(978-0-06-227463-2(5))* 2014. 288p. 16.99 *(978-0-06-227462-5(7))* HarperCollins Pubs.

Deborah Strandberg, Rebecca Reynolds and. Trammler Triplet Tales #2 - HIDDEN in TIME. 2007. 116p. pap. 8.94 *(978-1-4303-2097-5(4))* Lulu Pr., Inc.

—Trammler Triplet Tales-Adventure #3 SEEKING the SOURCE. 2007. 175p. pap. 11.38 *(978-1-4303-1197-3(5))* Lulu Pr., Inc.

Deering, Leta. Patriotic Samáand the Mendez Twins at the Alamo. 2008. 112p. pap. 19.95 *(978-1-60610-689-1(9))* America Star Bks.

Deutsch, Stacia & Cohon, Rhody. Bell's Breakthrough. Wenzel, David, illus. 2013. (Blast to the Past Ser.: 3). (ENG.). 128p. (J). (gr. 2-5). pap. 5.99 *(978-1-4424-9536-4(7),* Simon & Schuster/Paula Wiseman Bks.) Simon & Schuster/Paula Wiseman Bks.

—Disney's Dream. Wenzel, David, illus. 2013. (Blast to the Past Ser.: 2). (ENG.). 128p. (J). (gr. 2-5). pap. 6.99 *(978-1-4424-9535-7(9),* Simon & Schuster/Paula Wiseman Bks.) Simon & Schuster/Paula Wiseman Bks.

—Lincoln's Legacy. Wenzel, David, illus. 2005. (Blast to the Past Ser.: 1). (ENG.). 112p. (J). (gr. 2-5). pap. 6.99 *(978-0-689-87024-8(8),* Simon & Schuster/Paula Wiseman Bks.) Simon & Schuster/Paula Wiseman Bks.

Deutsch/Cohon. Disney's Dream. Wenzel, David, illus. 2005. 108p. (J). lib. bdg. 16.92 *(978-1-4242-1714-4(8))* Fitzgerald Bks.

Dinsdale, Christopher. Broken Circle. 2004. (ENG.). 104p. (J). pap. 7.95 *(978-1-894917-15-5(4),* Napoleon & Co.) Dundum CAN. Dist: Ingram Publisher Services.

Disney Book Group Staff. Gravity Falls Once upon a Swine. Disney Storybook Artists Staff & No New Art Needed, illus. 2014. (Gravity Falls Chapter Book Ser.: 2). (ENG.). 112p. (J). (gr. 1-3). pap. 4.99 *(978-1-4847-1140-8(8))* Disney Pr.

—Teen Beach 2. 2015. (ENG.). 128p. (J). (gr. 5-9). pap. 5.99 *(978-1-4847-1077-7(0))* Disney Pr.

Disney Book Group Staff & Miller, Bryan Q. Disney Comics Tomorrowland. Jones, Kelley, illus. 2014. (Disney Original Graphic Novel Ser.: 1). (ENG.). 176p. (J). (gr. 3-7). pap. 12.99 *(978-1-4231-6229-2(3))* Disney Pr.

Disney Press Staff. Once upon a Swine. 2014. (Gravity Falls Ser.: 2). (J). lib. bdg. 14.75 *(978-0-606-35916-0(8))* Turtleback Bks.

Divakaruni, Chitra Banerjee. The Mirror of Fire & Dreaming. 2007. (ENG.). 336p. (J). (gr. 3-7). pap. 14.99 *(978-1-4169-1768-7(3),* Aladdin) Simon & Schuster Children's Publishing.

Dorfman, Joaquin. The Long Wait for Tomorrow. 2009. (YA). *(978-0-375-84696-0(4))* Random Hse., Inc.

Doty, Jean Slaughter. Can I Get There by Candlelight? 2012. (ENG.). 128p. (YA). (gr. 7). pap. 7.99 *(978-1-4424-8608-9(2),* Simon & Schuster Bks. For Young Readers) Simon & Schuster Bks. For Young Readers.

Douglas, Helen. After Eden. 2013. (ENG.). 288p. (YA). (gr. 7). 17.99 *(978-1-61963-130-4(X),* 9781619631304, Bloomsbury USA Childrens) Bloomsbury Publishing USA.

—Chasing Stars. 2016. (ENG.). 352p. (YA). 17.99 *(978-1-61963-410-7(4),* 9781619634107, Bloomsbury USA Childrens) Bloomsbury Publishing USA.

Dowding, Philippa. Carter & the Curious Maze. 2016. (Weird Stories Gone Wrong Ser.: 3). (ENG., Illus.). 136p. (J). pap. 9.99 *(978-1-4597-3249-0(9))* Dundum CAN. Dist: Ingram Publisher Services.

Downer, Ann. Hatching Magic. Rayyan, Omar, illus. 2004. 242p. 16.00 *(978-0-7569-3481-1(8))* Perfection Learning Corp.

Downie, Mary Alice & Downie, John. Alison's Ghosts, 1 vol. 2008. (Lorimer Streetlights Ser.). (ENG.). 104p. (J). (gr. 2-4). 8.95 *(978-1-55277-013-9(3),* 9781552770139) Lorimer, James & Co., Ltd., Pubs. CAN. Dist: Casemate Pubs. & Bk. Distributors, LLC.

Drexler, Sam & Shelby, Fay. Murder in Bozeman. 2005. (Erika & Oz Adventures in American History Ser.: Vol. 2). 152p. (YA). (gr. 9-12). pap. 9.99 *(978-0-9669988-2-5(0))* Aunt Strawberry Bks.

Duey, Kathleen. Leonardo. Epstein, Eugene, illus. 2009. (Time Soldiers Ser.). (ENG.). (J). (gr. k-2). 95p. 9.95 *(978-1-929945-89-4(2))*;Bk. 8. 48p. 15.95 *(978-1-929945-88-7(4))* Big Guy Bks., Inc.

—Rex. Epstein, Eugene, illus. Gould, Robert, photos by. 2003. (Time Soldiers Ser.: Bk. 1). (ENG.). 48p. (J). (gr. k-2). pap. 7.95 *(978-1-929945-20-7(5))* Big Guy Bks., Inc.

—Rex. Epstein, Eugene, illus. 2006. (Time Soldiers Ser.: Bk. 1). 96p. (J). (gr. -1-7). lib. bdg. 24.21 *(978-1-59961-227-0(5))* Spotlight.

—Rex 2. Epstein, Eugene, illus. Gould, Robert, photos by. 2003. (Time Soldiers Ser.: Bk. 2). (ENG.). 48p. (J). (gr. k-2). pap. 8.95 *(978-1-929945-27-6(2))* Big Guy Bks., Inc.

—Rex2. Epstein, Eugene, illus. Gould, Robert, photos by. 2007. (Time Soldiers Ser.). (ENG.). 96p. (gr. -1-7). 24.21 *(978-1-59961-228-7(3))* Spotlight.

—Samurai. Epstein, Eugene, illus. Gould, Robert, photos by. 2007. (Time Soldiers Ser.). (ENG.). 96p. (gr. k-2). 24.21 *(978-1-59961-229-4(1))* Spotlight.

Duey, Kathleen & Gould, Robert. Rex 2. Epstein, Eugene, illus. Gould, Robert, photos by. 2003. (Soldados de Tiempo Libro: Vol. 2). (SPA & ENG.). 48p. (J). (gr. k-4). pap. 8.95 *(978-1-929945-36-8(1))* Big Guy Bks., Inc.

—Rex2. Epstein, Eugene, illus. Gould, Robert, photos by. 2003. (Time Soldiers Ser.). 48p. (J). (gr. 4-7). 17.10 *(978-0-7569-3472-9(9))* Perfection Learning Corp.

Dyer, K. C. Shades of Red: An Eagle Glen Trilogy Book. 2005. (Eagle Glen Trilogy Ser.: 3). (ENG.). 272p. (YA). (gr. 7). pap. 12.99 *(978-1-55002-545-3(7))* Dundum CAN. Dist: Ingram Publisher Services.

Eade, Oliver. The Terminus. 2013. 264p. pap. *(978-1-909411-26-5(4))* Mauve Square Publishing.

Earl, Cheri Pray & Williams, Carol Lynch. Secret in Pennsylvania. 2009. (J). *(978-1-56145-477-8(X),* Peachtree Junior) Peachtree Pubs.

Falcone, L. M. Walking with the Dead. 2005. (ENG., Illus.). 200p. (J). (gr. 4-7). 7.95 *(978-1-55337-709-2(5))* Kids Can Pr., Ltd. CAN. Dist: Hachette Bk. Group.

Falkner, Brian. The Project. 2012. (ENG.). 288p. (YA). (gr. 7). pap. 8.99 *(978-0-375-87188-7(8),* Ember) Random Hse. Children's Bks.

Fanning, Kieran. The Black Lotus: The Samurai Wars. 2016. (ENG.). 304p. (J). (gr. 3-7). 16.99 *(978-0-545-94028-3(1),* Chicken Hse., The) Scholastic, Inc.

—Code Crackers: Voyage to Victory. 2010. (Dover Children's Classics Ser.). (ENG., Illus.). 128p. (J). (gr. 3-5). pap. 5.99 *(978-0-486-47881-4(5))* Dover Pubns., Inc.

Farmer, Penelope. Charlotte Sometimes. 2017. (ENG., Illus.). 208p. (gr. 7-9). pap. 9.99 *(978-1-68137-104-7(9),* NYRB Kids) New York Review of Bks., Inc., The.

Feldman, Ruth Tenzer. The Ninth Day. 2013. (Blue Thread Saga Ser.). (ENG., Illus.). 288p. (YA). pap. 13.95 *(978-1-932010-65-7(3),* 9781932010657) Ooligan Pr.

Finn, Perdita. Crashing the Party. Dorman, Brandon, illus. 2007. 109p. (J). *(978-0-439-74436-2(9))* Scholastic, Inc.

—Going for the Gold. 2007. 118p. (J). *(978-0-439-89208-7(2))* Scholastic, Inc.

—Stealing the Show. Moran, Mike, illus. 2006. (Time Flyers Ser.: Vol. 1). 109p. (J). pap. *(978-0-439-74433-1(4))* Scholastic, Inc.

Fisher, Catherine. The Slanted Worlds. 2015. (Obsidian Mirror Ser.: 2). (ENG.). 384p. (YA). (gr. 7). pap. 9.99 *(978-0-14-242678-4(4),* Speak) Penguin Young Readers Group.

Fleischman, Sid. The 13th Floor: A Ghost Story. Sís, Peter, illus. 2007. (ENG.). 240p. (J). (gr. 3-7). per. 6.99 *(978-0-06-134503-6(2),* Greenwillow Bks.) HarperCollins Pubs.

Fleming, Ian. Chitty Chitty Bang Bang. Berger, Joe, illus. 2013. (Chitty Chitty Bang Bang Ser.). (ENG.). 160p. (J). (gr. 4-7). pap. 6.99 *(978-0-7636-6666-8(1))* Candlewick Pr.

Focus on the Family Staff & Hering, Marianne. Light in the Lions' Den. 2017. (AIO Imagination Station Bks.: 19). (ENG.). 144p. (J). pap. 4.99 *(978-1-58997-878-2(1))* Focus on the Family Publishing.

Fogarty, Paula. Slave of the Lamp. l.t. ed. 2013. 354p. pap. *(978-1-4596-6705-1(0))* ReadHowYouWant.com, Ltd.

Fontes, Justine & Fontes, Ron. Casebook: The Bermuda Triangle. 2009. (Top Secret Graphica Mysteries Ser.). (Illus.). 48p. (YA). (gr. 2-6). 29.25 *(978-1-60754-591-0(8))*; pap. 11.75 *(978-1-60754-592-7(6))* Windmill Bks.

Foreman, Colin. A Moment Comes. Colin Foreman. 2007. (Keepers & Seekers Ser.). (ENG., Illus.). 320p. pap. *(978-0-9548949-2-4(8))* Myroy Bks. Ltd.

Fox Mazer, Norma. Saturday, the Twelfth of October. 2015. (ENG.). 274p. (J). (gr. 3). pap. 13.95 *(978-1-939601-31-5(2))* Ig Publishing, Inc.

Franco, Franco. Dino-Mike! Franco, Franco, illus. 2015. (Dino-Mike! Ser.). (ENG., Illus.). 128p. (gr. 1-3). pap. 23.80 *(978-1-4965-2233-7(8),* Dino-Mike!) Stone Arch Bks.

Franco, Franco & Garcia, Eduardo. Dino-Mike & the Living Fossils. Franco, Franco, illus. 2016. (Dino-Mike! Ser.). (ENG., Illus.). 128p. (gr. 1-3). lib. bdg. 25.32 *(978-1-4965-2489-8(6),* Dino-Mike!) Stone Arch Bks.

Friedman, Stanley. Quantum Outlaws. 2010. 210p. pap. 11.95 *(978-1-935630-09-8(1))* Bellissima Publishing, LLC.

Funk, Rachel. Christabelle in the Museum of Time. 2007. 217p. pap. 14.95 *(978-1-4303-2572-7(0))* Lulu Pr., Inc.

Gardner, Sally. The Door That Led to Where. 2016. (ENG.). 288p. (YA). (gr. 7). 17.99 *(978-0-399-54997-7(8),* Delacorte Pr.) Random Hse. Children's Bks.

Garfinkle, D. L. Stuck in the 70's. 2007. 182p. (YA). *(978-1-4287-4661-9(7))* Penguin Publishing Group.

Gaston County Museum of Art & History, ed. The Secret Adventures of Hamster Sam: Attack of the Evil Boll Weevils! 2008. (Illus.). 32p. (J). 15.95 *(978-0-9798445-0-8(9))* DM Creative.

Gayle, Sharon Shavers. Emma's Escape: A Story of America's Underground Railroad. Velasquez, Eric, illus. 3rd ed. 2003. (Soundprints' Read-and-Discover Ser.). (ENG.). 48p. (J). (gr. -1-3). pap. 3.95 *(978-1-59249-021-9(2),* S2009) Soundprints.

Gibbons, Alan. Renegade. 2010. (ENG., Illus.). 336p. (YA). (gr. 7-17). 8.99 *(978-1-4440-0079-5(9),* Orion Children's Bks.) Hachette Children's Group GBR. Dist: Hachette Bk. Group.

—Scared to Death. 2010. (ENG., Illus.). 352p. (J). (gr. 4-6). pap. 8.99 *(978-1-4440-0143-3(4),* Orion Children's Bks.) Hachette Children's Group GBR. Dist: Hachette Bk. Group.

Gibbs, Stuart. Double Cross. 2013. (Last Musketeer Ser.: 3). (ENG.). 256p. (J). (gr. 3-7). 16.99 *(978-0-06-204844-8(9))* HarperCollins Pubs.

—The Last Musketeer. 2012. (Last Musketeer Ser.: 1). (ENG.). 272p. (J). (gr. 3-7). pap. 6.99 *(978-0-06-204839-4(2))* HarperCollins Pubs.

—Traitor's Chase. 2012. (Last Musketeer Ser.: 2). (ENG.). 256p. (J). (gr. 3-7). 16.99 *(978-0-06-204841-7(4))* HarperCollins Pubs.

Gier, Kerstin. Emerald Green. Bell, Anthea, tr. 2013. (Ruby Red Trilogy Ser.: Vol. 3). (ENG.). 464p. (YA). (gr. 7). 17.99 *(978-0-8050-9267-7(6),* 9780805092677, Holt, Henry & Co. Bks. For Young Readers) Holt, Henry & Co.

—Ruby Red. Bell, Anthea, tr. from GER. 2011. (Ruby Red Trilogy Ser.: 1). (ENG.). 336p. (YA). (gr. 7-12). 18.99 *(978-0-8050-9252-3(8),* 9780805092523, Holt, Henry & Co. Bks. For Young Readers) Holt, Henry & Co.

—Ruby Red. Bell, Anthea, tr. 2012. (Ruby Red Trilogy Ser.: 1). (ENG.). 352p. (YA). (gr. 7-12). pap. 10.99 *(978-0-312-55151-3(7),* 9780312551513) Square Fish.

—Sapphire Blue. Bell, Anthea, tr. from GER. 2012. (Ruby Red Trilogy Ser.: 2). (ENG.). 368p. (YA). (gr. 7). 18.99 *(978-0-8050-9266-0(8),* 9780805092660, Holt, Henry & Co. Bks. For Young Readers) Holt, Henry & Co.

—Sapphire Blue. Bell, Anthea, tr. 2013. (Ruby Red Trilogy Ser.: 2). (ENG.). 384p. (YA). (gr. 7). pap. 10.99 *(978-1-250-03416-8(7),* 9781250034168) Square Fish.

Giles, Katharine. The Princess of Skye, an Archer Adventure. 2013. (ENG.). 280p. (YA). pap. 12.99 *(978-1-939927-79-8(X))* Telemachus Pr., LLC.

Gingrich, Callista & Arciero, Susan. Yankee Doodle Dandy. 2013. (Ellis the Elephant Ser.). (ENG., Illus.). 40p. (J). (gr. -1-3). 14.95 *(978-1-62157-087-5(8),* Regnery Kids) Regnery Publishing, Inc., An Eagle Publishing Co.

Gleason, Colleen. The Clockwork Scarab. 2013. (Stoker & Holmes Ser.: 1). (ENG.). 356p. (YA). (gr. 7-12). 17.99 *(978-1-4521-1070-7(0))* Chronicle Bks. LLC.

Goodman, Alison. Singing the Dogstar Blues. 2008. 240p. (YA). *(978-0-7322-8863-1(0))* HarperCollins Pubs. Australia.

Gordon, Fran & Tischler, Faye. Dutch Double. 2007. (Illus.). 88p. pap. 15.95 *(978-1-59299-242-3(0))* Inkwater Pr.

Gould, Robert & Duey, Kathleen. Time Soldiers. 2005. 384p. pap. 16.95 *(978-1-929945-60-3(4))* Big Guy Bks., Inc.

—Time Soldiers - Rex. Epstein, Eugene, illus. Gould, Robert, photos by. 2005. (Time Soldiers Ser.: Bk. 1). (ENG.). 96p. (J). (gr. k-2). per. 5.95 *(978-1-929945-53-5(1))*; per. 5.95 *(978-1-929945-54-2(X))* Big Guy Bks., Inc.

Graham, J. Lee. In the Nick of Time. 2008. 108p. pap. 10.95 *(978-0-595-52621-5(7))* iUniverse, Inc.

Green, John. Sparta! Warriors of the Ancient World. 2013. (Dover History Coloring Book Ser.). (ENG.). 32p. (gr. 3-12). pap. 3.99 *(978-0-486-49813-3(1))* Dover Pubns., Inc.

Greenburg, Dan. It's Itchcraft!, 30 vols. Davis, Jack E., illus. 2003. (Zack Files Ser.: 30). (ENG.). 128p. (J). (gr. 2-5). pap. 4.99 *(978-0-448-42888-8(1),* Grosset & Dunlap) Penguin Young Readers Group.

—It's Itchcraft! Davis, Jack E., illus. 2004. (Zack Files Ser.). 118p. lib. bdg. 15.00 *(978-0-7569-2238-2(0))* Perfection Learning Corp.

Greenburg, J. C. In the Ice Age. Gerardi, Jan, illus. 2005. (Andrew Lost Ser.: 12). (ENG.). 96p. (J). (gr. 1-4). 3.99 *(978-0-375-82952-9(0),* Random Hse. Bks. for Young Readers) Random Hse. Children's Bks.

—In Time. Gerardi, Jan, illus. 2004. (Andrew Lost Ser.: 9). (ENG.). 96p. (J). (gr. 1-4). 3.99 *(978-0-375-82949-9(0),* Random Hse. Bks. for Young Readers) Random Hse. Children's Bks.

—On Earth. Gerardi, Jan, illus. 10th ed. 2005. (Andrew Lost Ser.: 10). (ENG.). 96p. (J). (gr. 1-4). 3.99 *(978-0-375-82950-5(4),* Random Hse. Bks. for Young Readers) Random Hse. Children's Bks.

—With the Dinosaurs. Gerardi, Jan, illus. 2005. (Andrew Lost Ser.: 11). (ENG.). 96p. (J). (gr. 1-4). 3.99 *(978-0-375-82951-2(2),* Random Hse. Bks. for Young Readers) Random Hse. Children's Bks.

Greenspan, Paul. Crystal of Dreams. 2007. 192p. pap. 12.96 *(978-0-615-13477-2(7))* Flying Cloud Bks.

Guibord, Maurissa. Warped. 2012. (ENG.). 348p. (YA). (gr. 7). pap. 9.99 *(978-0-385-73892-7(7),* Ember) Random Hse. Children's Bks.

Gutman, Dan. Abner & Me. 2007. (Baseball Card Adventures Ser.). (ENG., Illus.). 176p. (J). (gr. 5-9). pap. 5.99 *(978-0-06-053445-5(1))* HarperCollins Pubs.

—Abner & Me. 2007. (Baseball Card Adventures Ser.). (Illus.). 166p. (gr. 5-9). 16.00 *(978-0-7569-7920-1(X))* Perfection Learning Corp.

—Honus & Me. 2003. (Baseball Card Adventures Ser.). (ENG., Illus.). 144p. (J). (gr. 5-9). pap. 6.99 *(978-0-380-78878-1(0))* HarperCollins Pubs.

—Honus & Me. 2003. (Baseball Card Adventures Ser.). (J). (gr. 3-6). lib. bdg. 16.00 *(978-0-613-07982-2(5),* Turtleback) Turtleback Bks.

—Jackie & Me. 2005. (Baseball Card Adventures Ser.). (Illus.). 145p. (YA). (gr. 4-8). reprint ed. 20.00 *(978-0-7567-9569-6(9))* DIANE Publishing Co.

—Jim & Me. 2010. (Baseball Card Adventures Ser.). (ENG.). 224p. (J). (gr. 5-9). pap. 6.99 *(978-0-06-059496-1(9))* HarperCollins Pubs.

—Jim & Me. 2010. (Baseball Card Adventures Ser.). (J). lib. bdg. 17.20 *(978-0-606-09536-5(5),* Turtleback) Turtleback Bks.

—The Lincoln Project. 2016. (Flashback Four Ser.: 1). 240p. (J). (gr. 3-7). 16.99 *(978-0-06-237441-7(9))* HarperCollins Pubs.

—Mickey & Me. 2004. (Baseball Card Adventures Ser.). (ENG., Illus.). 160p. (J). (gr. 5-9). pap. 5.99 *(978-0-06-447258-6(2))* HarperCollins Pubs.

—Mickey & Me. 2004. (Baseball Card Adventures Ser.). (J). lib. bdg. 16.00 *(978-0-613-99233-6(4),* Turtleback) Turtleback Bks.

—Ray & Me. (Baseball Card Adventures Ser.). (ENG.). 192p. (J). (gr. 5-9). 2011. pap. 6.99 *(978-0-06-123483-5(4))* 2009. (Illus.). 16.99 *(978-0-06-123481-1(8))* HarperCollins Pubs.

—Roberto & Me. (Baseball Card Adventures Ser.). (ENG.). 192p. (J). (gr. 5-9). 2012. pap. 5.99 *(978-0-06-123486-6(9))* 2010. 16.99 *(978-0-06-123484-2(2))* HarperCollins Pubs.

—Roberto & Me. 2012. (Baseball Card Adventures Ser.). (J). lib. bdg. 16.00 *(978-0-606-23591-4(4),* Turtleback) Turtleback Bks.

—Satch & Me. (Baseball Card Adventures Ser.). (ENG.). 192p. (J). (gr. 5-9). 2009. pap. 5.99 *(978-0-06-059493-0(4))* 2006. (Illus.). 16.99 *(978-0-06-059491-6(8))* HarperCollins Pubs. (Amistad).

—Satch & Me. 2009. (Baseball Card Adventures Ser.). (J). lib. bdg. 16.00 *(978-0-606-00023-9(2),* Turtleback) Turtleback Bks.

—Shoeless Joe & Me. 2003. (Baseball Card Adventures Ser.). (ENG., Illus.). 176p. (J). (gr. 5-9). pap. 6.99 *(978-0-06-447259-3(0))* HarperCollins Pubs.

—Shoeless Joe & Me. 2003. (Baseball Card Adventures Ser.). (Illus.). 163p. (gr. 3-7). 16.00 *(978-0-7569-1438-7(8))* Perfection Learning Corp.

—Shoeless Joe & Me. 2003. (Baseball Card Adventures Ser.). (J). (gr. 3-6). lib. bdg. 16.00 *(978-0-613-61816-8(5),* Turtleback) Turtleback Bks.

—Ted & Me. 2012. (Baseball Card Adventures Ser.). (Illus.). 208p. (J). (gr. 5-9). (ENG.). 15.99 *(978-0-06-123487-3(7))*; lib. bdg. 16.89 *(978-0-06-123488-0(5))* HarperCollins Pubs.

—Willie & Me. 2015. (Baseball Card Adventures Ser.: 12). (ENG.). 176p. (J). (gr. 3-7). 16.99 *(978-0-06-170404-8(0))* HarperCollins Pubs.

Haddix, Margaret Peterson. Caught. 2013. (Missing Ser.: 5). (ENG., Illus.). 368p. (J). (gr. 3-7). pap. 7.99 *(978-1-4169-8983-7(8),* Simon & Schuster Bks. For Young Readers) Simon & Schuster Bks. For Young Readers.

—Caught. 2013. (Missing Ser.: 5). lib. bdg. 18.40 *(978-0-606-27045-8(0),* Turtleback) Turtleback Bks.

—Found. (Missing Ser.: 1). (ENG.). (J). (gr. 3-7). 2009. 336p. pap. 7.99 *(978-1-4169-5421-7(X))* 2008. 320p. 17.99 *(978-1-4169-5417-0(1))* Simon & Schuster Bks. For Young Readers. (Simon & Schuster Bks. For Young Readers).

—Redeemed. 2015. (Missing Ser.: 8). (ENG.). 416p. (J). (gr. 3-7). 17.99 *(978-1-4424-9756-6(4),* Simon & Schuster Bks. For Young Readers) Simon & Schuster Bks. For Young Readers.

—Redeemed. 2016. (Missing Ser.: 8). lib. bdg. 18.40 *(978-0-606-39234-1(3))* Turtleback Bks.

—Revealed. 2015. (Missing Ser.: 7). lib. bdg. 19.65 *(978-0-606-37847-5(2))* Turtleback Bks.

—Risked. 2013. (Missing Ser.: Bk. 6). (ENG., Illus.). 320p. (J). (gr. 3-7). 16.99 *(978-1-4169-8984-4(6),* Simon & Schuster Bks. For Young Readers) Simon & Schuster Bks. For Young Readers.

—Risked. 2014. (Missing Ser.: 6). lib. bdg. 19.65 *(978-0-606-36096-8(4))* Turtleback Bks.

—Torn. (Missing Ser.: 4). (ENG.). (J). (gr. 3-7). 2012. 368p. pap. 8.99 *(978-1-4169-8981-3(1))* 2011. 352p. 17.99 *(978-1-4169-8980-6(3))* Simon & Schuster Bks. For Young Readers. (Simon & Schuster Bks. For Young Readers).

—Torn. l.t. ed. 2011. (Missing Ser.: Bk. 4). (ENG.). 368p. 23.99 *(978-1-4104-4078-5(8))* Thorndike Pr.

—Torn. 2012. (Missing Ser.: 4). lib. bdg. 18.40 *(978-0-606-26333-7(0),* Turtleback) Turtleback Bks.

Hahn, Mary Downing. The Doll in the Garden; The Old Willis Place. 2009. pap. 11.90 *(978-0-547-37542-7(5))* Houghton Mifflin Harcourt Trade & Reference Pubs.

Handford, Martin. Where's Waldo? 2007. (Where's Waldo? Ser.). (Illus.). 24p. (gr. 4-7). lib. bdg. 18.40 *(978-1-4178-2424-3(7),* Turtleback) Turtleback Bks.

—Where's Waldo Now? Handford, Martin, illus. 25th anniv. deluxe ed. 2012. (Where's Waldo? Ser.). (ENG., Illus.). 32p. (J). (gr. k-4). 16.99 *(978-0-7636-4526-7(5))* Candlewick Pr.

Hansen, Justin LaRocca. Brothers Unite. 2016. (Secondhand Heroes Ser.). (ENG., Illus.). 160p. (J). (gr. 3-7). pap. 10.99 *(978-0-8037-4094-5(8),* Dial Bks) Penguin Young Readers Group.

Hansen, Lynne. Reckless Revolution. 2007. (YA). *(978-1-4114-9672-9(8),* Spark Publishing Group) Sterling Publishing Co., Inc.

—Shades of Blue & Gray. 2007. (YA). pap. *(978-1-4114-9674-3(4),* Spark Publishing Group) Sterling Publishing Co., Inc.

—A Time for Witches. 2007. (YA). *(978-1-4114-9671-2(X),* Spark Publishing Group) Sterling Publishing Co., Inc.

Hardie, Richard. Leap of Faith. 2013. (Illus.). 272p. pap. *(978-1-909841-26-0(9))* Crooked Cat Publishing.

Hardman, Ron & Hardman, Jessica. Shadow Fox: Sons of Liberty. Barnecut, Suzanne, ed. Harrigan, Mike, illus. 2010. (Shadow Fox Ser.). 186p. (J). (gr. 4-8). 22.99 *(978-0-9819607-1-5(5))* Fox Run Pr., LLC.

—Shadow Fox: Sons of Liberty. Barnecut, Suzanne, ed. Harrigan, Mike, illus. 2010. (Shadow Fox Ser.). 186p. (J). (gr. 4-8). pap. 11.99 *(978-0-9819607-0-8(7))* Fox Run Pr., LLC.

—Shadow Fox: Sons of Liberty Teacher's Edition. Barnecutt, Suzanne, ed. Harrigan, Mike, illus. 2010. (Shadow Fox Ser.: 1). 186p. (J). 34.99 *(978-0-9819607-2-2(3))* Fox Run Pr., LLC.

Harelkin, Mary. Tunnels of Treachery, 1 vol. 2003. (Moose Jaw Adventure Ser.: Vol. 3). (ENG., Illus.). 304p. (J). (gr. 4-7). pap. 7.95 *(978-1-55050-270-1(0))* Coteau Bks. CAN. Dist: Orca Bk. Pubs. USA.

Harness, Cheryl. Ghosts of the Civil War. Harness, Cheryl, illus. 2004. (ENG., Illus.). 48p. (J). (gr. 2-5). 8.99 *(978-0-689-86992-1(4),* Simon & Schuster Bks. For Young Readers) Simon & Schuster Bks. For Young Readers.

Harris, Rachel. A Tale of Two Centuries. 2013. (Entangled Teen Ser.). (ENG.). 320p. (YA). (gr. 7-12). pap. 9.99 *(978-1-62266-012-4(9),* 9781622660124) Entangled Publishing, LLC.

Harris, Stanley. The First Shot: A Tale of a Boy's Trip Through Time to the Battle of Lexington. 2007. per. *(978-1-59872-958-0(6))* Instant Pub.

Harrison, Mette Ivie. The Princess & the Bear. 2010. (ENG.). 352p. (YA). (gr. 8). pap. 8.99 *(978-0-06-155316-5(6),* HarperTeen) HarperCollins Pubs.

Hautman, Pete. Mr. Was. 2012. (ENG.). 240p. (YA). (gr. 7). pap. 8.99 *(978-1-4424-3337-3(X),* Simon & Schuster Bks. For Young Readers) Simon & Schuster Bks. For Young Readers.

Hehir, Tim. Julius & the Soul-Catcher. 2016. (ENG., Illus.). 368p. (J). (gr. 5-9). 9.95 *(978-1-925240-17-7(7))* Text Publishing Co. AUS. Dist: Consortium Bk. Sales & Distribution.

Heilig, Heidi. The Girl from Everywhere. 2016. 464p. (YA). (gr. 8). 17.99 *(978-0-06-238075-3(3),* Greenwillow Bks.) HarperCollins Pubs.

Heimerdinger, Chris. Drums of Desolation: A Novel. 2014. 419p. (YA). *(978-1-62108-821-9(9))* Covenant Communications.

—Escape from Zarahemla. 2011. 263p. (YA). pap. *(978-1-60861-539-1(1))* Covenant Communications.

—Kingdoms & Conquerors: A Novel. 2005. 434p. (YA). *(978-1-59156-740-0(8))* Covenant Communications.

—Tower of Thunder Vol. 9: A Novel. 2004. (Tennis Shoes Adventure Ser.). 406p. pap. 14.95 *(978-1-59156-177-4(9))* Covenant Communications, Inc.

—The Warriors of Cumorah, Vol. 8. 2004. (Tennis Shoes Adventure Ser.). xi, 394p. pap. 14.95 *(978-1-57734-922-8(9))* Covenant Communications, Inc.

Helwani, Najiyah Diana. Sophia's Journal: Time Warp 1857. 2008. (YA). per. *(978-0-9793577-2-5(1))* Muslim Writers Publishing.

Hemphill, Michael & Angleberger, Tom. Stonewall Hinkleman & the Battle of Bull Run. 2014. (ENG.). 192p. (J). (gr. 3-7). pap. 7.99 *(978-0-14-751182-9(8),* Puffin Books) Penguin Young Readers Group.

Hendey, Lisa M. The Whisper in the Ruins. Bower, Jenn, illus. 2016. (Chime Travelers Ser.: 3). (ENG.). 128p. (J). (gr. 2-5). pap. 6.99 *(978-1-63253-036-3(8),* Servant Bks.) Franciscan Media.

Henn, Pamela. Nick & Slim: The Legend of the Falcon Mine. 2006. (Illus.). 472p. (YA). 19.95 *(978-0-9760654-0-1(1))* White Wolf Studio, Inc.

Hering, Marianne. In Fear of the Spear. 2016. (AIO Imagination Station Bks.: 17). (ENG.). 144p. (J). pap. 4.99 *(978-1-58997-804-1(8))* Focus on the Family Publishing.

—Trouble on the Orphan Train. 2016. (AIO Imagination Station Bks.: 18). (ENG.). 144p. (J). pap. 4.99 *(978-1-58997-805-8(6))* Focus on the Family Publishing.

Hernandez, David. Land of the Pharaohs, 1 vol. 2003. (Adventures of Toby Digz Ser.: 1). (ENG., Illus.). 96p. pap. 5.99 *(978-1-4003-0195-9(5))* Nelson, Thomas Inc.

—The Mighty Armor, 1 vol., Vol. 2. 2003. (Adventures of Toby Digz Ser.: 2). (ENG., Illus.). 96p. pap. 5.99 *(978-1-4003-0196-6(3))* Nelson, Thomas Inc.

Higgins, Lawrence. Demons & Dragons: Time, Space & Magic. 2010. (ENG., Illus.). 93p. pap. 20.99 *(978-1-906791-68-1(6))* Arena Bks. GBR. Dist: Lightning Source UK, Ltd.

Hill, C. J. Echo in Time. 2014. 387p. (YA). *(978-0-06-212395-4(5))* HarperCollins Pubs.

—Erasing Time. 2012. (Erasing Time Ser.: 1). (ENG.). 368p. (YA). (gr. 8). 17.99 *(978-0-06-212392-3(0),* Tegen, Katherine Bks) HarperCollins Pubs.

Hillyer, Lexa. Proof of Forever. 352p. (YA). (gr. 8). 2016. pap. 9.99 *(978-0-06-233038-3(1))* 2015. (ENG.). 17.99 *(978-0-06-233037-6(3))* HarperCollins Pubs. (HarperTeen).

Hoffman, Mary. Special Powers. 200p. pap. *(978-0-340-62670-2(4))* Hodder & Stoughton.

Holliday, Susan. The Time Street Gang & the Rag & Bone Boy. Lt. ed. 2007. 132p. pap. *(978-1-905665-64-8(4))* Pollinger In Print.

Hood, Ann. Anastasia Romanov: The Last Grand Duchess. Zilber, Denis, illus. 2014. (Treasure Chest Ser.: 10). (ENG.). 240p. (J). (gr. 3-7). 15.99 *(978-0-448-46770-2(4));*No. 10. 6.99 *(978-0-448-46771-9(2))* Penguin Young Readers Group. (Grosset & Dunlap).

—Clara Barton: Angel of the Battlefield. Kwasney, Karl et al, illus. 2012. (Treasure Chest Ser.: 1). (ENG.). 208p. (J). (gr. 3-7). pap. 6.99 *(978-0-448-45467-2(X),* Grosset & Dunlap) Penguin Young Readers Group.

—Crazy Horse: Brave Warrior. Altmann, Scott & Zilber, Denis, illus. 2013. (Treasure Chest Ser.: 5). (ENG.). 192p. (J). (gr. 3-7). pap. 6.99 *(978-0-448-45728-4(8),* Grosset & Dunlap) Penguin Young Readers Group.

—Harry Houdini: Prince of Air. Altmann, Scott & Zilber, Denis, illus. 2012. (Treasure Chest Ser.: 4). (ENG.). 208p. (J). (gr. 3-7). pap. 6.99 *(978-0-448-45470-2(X),* Grosset & Dunlap) Penguin Young Readers Group.

—Prince of Air, No. 4. Altmann, Scott & Zilber, Denis, illus. 2012. (Treasure Chest Ser.: 4). (ENG.). 208p. (J). (gr. 3-7). 15.99 *(978-0-448-45474-0(2),* Grosset & Dunlap) Penguin Young Readers Group.

—Queen Liliuokalani: Royal Prisoner. Altmann, Scott & Zilber, Denis, illus. 2013. (Treasure Chest Ser.: 6). (ENG.). 176p. (J). (gr. 3-7). 15.99 *(978-0-448-45739-0(3));* pap. 6.99 *(978-0-448-45729-1(6))* Penguin Young Readers Group. (Grosset & Dunlap).

Hood, Ann & Altmann, Scott. Angel of the Battlefield. Kwasney, Karl & Zilber, Denis, illus. 2012. (Treasure Chest Ser.: 1). (ENG.). 240p. (J). (gr. 3-7). 15.99 *(978-0-448-45471-9(8),* Grosset & Dunlap) Penguin Young Readers Group.

Hopper, Ada. Don't Disturb the Dinosaurs. Ricks, Sam, illus. 2016. (DATA Set Ser.: 2). (ENG.). 128p. (J). (gr. k-4). pap. 5.99 *(978-1-4814-5731-6(4),* Little Simon) Little Simon.

Horender, Philip M. A Brave New Mouse: Ellis Island Approved Immigrant, 1 vol. Wolek, Guy, illus. 2013. (Maximilian P. Mouse, Time Traveler Ser.). (ENG.). 112p. (J). (gr. 3-6). lib. bdg. 27.07 *(978-1-61641-961-5(X),* Calico Chapter Bks) Magic Wagon.

—Head West, Young Mouse: Transcontinental Railroad Traveler, 1 vol. Wolek, Guy, illus. 2013. (Maximilian P. Mouse, Time Traveler Ser.). (ENG.). 112p. (J). (gr. 3-6). lib. bdg. 27.07 *(978-1-61641-959-2(8),* Calico Chapter Bks) Magic Wagon.

—Homeward Bound: Civil Rights Mouse Leader, 1 vol. Wolek, Guy, illus. 2013. (Maximilian P. Mouse, Time Traveler Ser.). (ENG.). 112p. (J). (gr. 3-6). lib. bdg. 27.07 *(978-1-61641-962-2(8),* Calico Chapter Bks) Magic Wagon.

—The Mighty Maximilian: Samuel Clemens's Traveling Companion, 1 vol. Wolek, Guy, illus. 2013. (Maximilian P. Mouse, Time Traveler Ser.). (ENG.). 112p. (J). (gr. 3-6). lib. bdg. 27.07 *(978-1-61641-960-8(1),* Calico Chapter Bks) Magic Wagon.

—Patriotic Mouse: Boston Tea Party Participant, 1 vol. Wolek, Guy, illus. 2013. (Maximilian P. Mouse, Time Traveler Ser.). (ENG.). 112p. (J). (gr. 3-6). lib. bdg. 27.07 *(978-1-61641-957-8(1),* Calico Chapter Bks) Magic Wagon.

—Yankee Mouse: Gettysburg Address Observer, 1 vol. Wolek, Guy, illus. 2013. (Maximilian P. Mouse, Time Traveler Ser.). (ENG.). 112p. (J). (gr. 3-6). lib. bdg. 27.07 *(978-1-61641-958-5(X),* Calico Chapter Bks) Magic Wagon.

Hosie, Donna. The Devil's Dreamcatcher. (ENG.). (YA). (gr. 10). 2016. 272p. pap. 7.99 *(978-0-8234-3693-4(4))* 2015. 288p. 16.95 *(978-0-8234-3390-2(0))* Holiday Hse., Inc.

—The Devil's Intern. 2014. (ENG.). 288p. (YA). (gr. 10-12). 16.95 *(978-0-8234-3195-3(9))* Holiday Hse., Inc.

Howard, Martin. Shaun the Sheep: Blast to the Past. Janes, Andy, illus. 2017. (Tales from Mossy Bottom Farm Ser.: 6). (ENG.). 112p. (J). (gr. k-3). pap. 4.99 *(978-0-7636-9093-9(7),* Candlewick Entertainment) Candlewick Pr.

Hubbell, Mary A. The Miracle of Annie's Ring. 2010. 138p. pap. 11.50 *(978-1-60911-530-2(9),* Eloquent Bks.) Strategic Book Publishing & Rights Agency (SBPRA).

Hulme-Cross, Benjamin. The Egyptian Warrior. 2016. (Warrior Heroes Ser.). (ENG., Illus.). 176p. (J). (gr. 6-9). *(978-0-7787-2864-1(1))* Crabtree Publishing Co.

—The Gladiator's Victory. Rinaldi, Angelo, illus. 2015. (ENG.). 160p. (J). *(978-0-7787-1764-5(X))* Crabtree Publishing Co.

—The Knight's Enemies. Rinaldi, Angelo, illus. 2015. (ENG.). 160p. (J). *(978-0-7787-1765-2(8))* Crabtree Publishing Co.

—The Samurai's Assassin. Rinaldi, Angelo, illus. 2015. (ENG.). 160p. (J). *(978-0-7787-1766-9(6))* Crabtree Publishing Co.

—The Spartan's March. 2016. (Warrior Heroes Ser.). (ENG., Illus.). 176p. (J). (gr. 6-9). *(978-0-7787-2865-8(X))* Crabtree Publishing Co.

—The Viking's Revenge. Rinaldi, Angelo, illus. 2015. (ENG.). 160p. (J). *(978-0-7787-1767-6(4))* Crabtree Publishing Co.

Hurmence, Belinda. A Girl Called Boy. 2006. (ENG.). 176p. (J). (gr. 5-7). pap. 12.95 *(978-0-618-68925-5(7))* Houghton Mifflin Harcourt Publishing Co.

Hurst, Melissa E. The Edge of Forever. 2015. (ENG.). 272p. (J). (gr. 6). pap. 14.99 *(978-1-63220-424-0(X),* Sky Pony Pr.) Skyhorse Publishing Co., Inc.

Jakobsen, Lars. The Mysterious Manuscript. Jakobsen, Lars, illus. 2012. (Mortensen's Escapades Ser.: 1). (ENG., Illus.). 48p. (gr. 6-12). pap. 6.95 *(978-0-8225-9409-3(9));* lib. bdg. 27.93 *(978-0-7613-7883-9(9))* Lerner Publishing Group. (Graphic Universe™).

—The Red Ruby. Jakobsen, Lars, illus. 2013. (Mortensen's Escapades Ser.: 3). (ENG., Illus.). 48p. (gr. 6-12). pap. 6.95 *(978-1-4677-0729-9(5),* Graphic Universe™) Lerner Publishing Group.

—The Santa Fe Jail. Jakobsen, Lars, illus. 2012. (Mortensen's Escapades Ser.: 2). (ENG., Illus.). 48p. (gr. 6-12). pap. 6.95 *(978-0-8225-9421-5(8));* lib. bdg. 27.93 *(978-0-7613-7886-0(3))* Lerner Publishing Group. (Graphic Universe™).

—The Secret Mummy. Jakobsen, Lars, illus. 2013. (Mortensen's Escapades Ser.: 4). (ENG., Illus.). 48p. (gr. 6-12). pap. 6.95 *(978-1-4677-0730-5(9));* lib. bdg. 27.93 *(978-0-7613-7915-7(0))* Lerner Publishing Group. (Graphic Universe™).

Jakobsen, Lars & Chapman, Robyn. The Red Ruby. Jakobsen, Lars, illus. 2013. (Mortensen's Escapades Ser.: 3). (ENG., Illus.). 48p. (gr. 6-12). lib. bdg. 27.93 *(978-0-7613-7914-0(2),* Graphic Universe™) Lerner Publishing Group.

Jane, Yolen. The Devil's Arithmetic. 2014. (ENG.). 176p. (J). 11.24 *(978-1-63245-218-4(9))* Lectorum Pubns., Inc.

Jarman, Julia. The Magic Scooter. 2015. (Race Further with Reading Ser.). (ENG., Illus.). 48p. (J). *(978-0-7787-2086-7(1))* Crabtree Publishing Co.

—The Time-Travelling Cat & the Aztec Sacrifice. 2006. (Time-Travelling Cat Ser.). (ENG., Illus.). 160p. (J). (gr. 3-6). pap. 12.99 *(978-1-84270-516-2(4))* Andersen Pr. GBR. Dist: Independent Pubs. Group.

—The Time-Travelling Cat & the Egyptian Goddess. 2007. (Time-Travelling Cat Ser.: 1). (ENG.). 128p. (J). (gr. 4-7). per. 12.99 *(978-1-84270-521-6(0))* Andersen Pr. GBR. Dist: Independent Pubs. Group.

—Time-Travelling Cat & the Great Victorian Stink. 2011. (Time-Travelling Cat Ser.: 6). (ENG.). 160p. (J). (gr. 4-7). pap. 12.99 *(978-1-84939-019-4(3))* Andersen Pr. GBR. Dist: Independent Pubs. Group.

—The Time-Travelling Cat & the Roman Eagle. (Illus.). (J). 128p. 16.95 *(978-0-86264-861-9(0));* 2008. (Time-Travelling Cat Ser.: 3). (ENG., 156p. (gr. 4-7). pap. 13.99 *(978-1-84270-617-6(9))* Andersen Pr. GBR. Dist: Trafalgar Square Publishing, Independent Pubs. Group.

—The Time-Travelling Cat & the Viking Terror. 2008. (Time-Travelling Cat Ser.: 4). (ENG., Illus.). 176p. (J). (gr. 4-7). pap. 11.99 *(978-1-84270-686-2(1))* Andersen Pr. GBR. Dist: Independent Pubs. Group.

Jeb. Destinations in Time. 2008. 101p. pap. 19.95 *(978-1-60672-653-2(6))* America Star Bks.

Johnson, Cara. Looking Forward Back: The Dream Travelers Book Three. 2008. 162p. (J). per. 9.99 *(978-0-9768870-3-4(7))* Whirling Dirvish Publishing.

Johnson, Charles & Johnson, Elisheba. The Adventures of Emery Jones, Boy Science Wonder: Bending Time. Johnson, Charles, illus. 2013. (Illus.). 110p. pap. 9.99 *(978-1-62015-181-5(2),* Booktrope Editions) Booktrope.

Jones, Chris. Cameron Jack & the Ghosts of World War 2. 2010. 120p. pap. 12.49 *(978-1-4520-2839-2(7))* AuthorHouse.

Jones, Diana Wynne. A Tale of Time City. 2012. (ENG.). 384p. (YA). (gr. 7-18). 9.99 *(978-0-14-242015-7(8),* Firebird) Penguin Young Readers Group.

The Journal: Dear Future II: Individual Title Six-Packs. (Action Packs Ser.). 104p. (gr. 3-5). 44.00 *(978-0-7635-8417-7(7))* Rigby Education.

Karre, Elizabeth. No Regrets. 2014. (Gift Ser.). (ENG.). 120p. (YA). (gr. 6-12). pap. 7.95 *(978-1-4677-4480-5(8),* Darby Creek); lib. bdg. 27.93 *(978-1-4677-3512-4(4))* Lerner Publishing Group.

Kassirer, Sue. Thar She Blows! Whaling in The 1860s. Fridell, Pat, illus. 2007. 32p. (J). 15.00 *(978-1-4223-6721-6(5))* DIANE Publishing Co.

Kehret, Peg. Flood Disaster. 2008. (ENG.). 160p. (J). (gr. 3-7). pap. 8.99 *(978-1-4169-9109-0(3),* Simon & Schuster/Paula Wiseman Bks.) Simon & Schuster/Paula Wiseman Bks.

Kennedy Center Staff. Unleashed: The Lives of White House Pets. Hoyt, Ard, illus. 2011. (ENG.). 112p. (J). (gr. 2-5). pap. 5.99 *(978-1-4169-4862-9(7),* Simon & Schuster Bks. For Young Readers) Simon & Schuster Bks. For Young Readers.

Kessler, Jackie Morse. Loss. 2012. (Riders of the Apocalypse Ser.: 3). (ENG.). 272p. (YA). (gr. 7). pap. 8.99 *(978-0-547-71215-4(4))* Houghton Mifflin Harcourt Publishing Co.

—Loss. 2012. (Riders of the Apocalypse Ser.: 3). lib. bdg. 19.65 *(978-0-606-24742-9(4),* Turtleback) Turtleback Bks.

Kessler, Liz. A Year Without Autumn. (ENG.). 304p. (J). (gr. 4-7). 2012. pap. 7.99 *(978-0-7636-6060-4(4))* 2011. (Illus.). 15.99 *(978-0-7636-5595-2(3))* Candlewick Pr.

Kimmel, Eric A. Scarlett & Sam: Escape from Egypt. Stevanovic, Ivica, illus. 2015. (J). 6.99 *(978-1-4677-6207-6(5));* (ENG.). 168p. (gr. 1-3). lib. bdg. 15.95 *(978-1-4677-3850-7(6))* Lerner Publishing Group. (Kar-Ben Publishing).

Kirby, Matthew J. Cave of Wonders. 2013. (Infinity Ring Ser.: 5). (ENG.). 192p. (J). (gr. 3-7). 12.99 *(978-0-545-38700-2(0));* 16.99 *(978-0-545-48460-2(X))* Scholastic, Inc.

Klass, David. Timelock. 2009. (Caretaker Trilogy Ser.: 3). (ENG.). 256p. (YA). (gr. 9-12). 17.99 *(978-0-374-32309-7(7),* 9780374323097, Farrar, Straus & Giroux (BYR)) Farrar, Straus & Giroux.

—Timelock. 2010. (Caretaker Trilogy Ser.: 3). (ENG.). 272p. (YA). (gr. 9-12). pap. 8.99 *(978-0-312-60863-7(2),* 9780312608637) Square Fish.

Kramer, Alan & Kramer, Candice. The Star-Spangled Banner Story. 2005. (J). pap. *(978-1-4108-4203-9(7))* Benchmark Education Co.

Kriyananda, Swami. The Time Tunnel: A Tale for All Ages & for the Child in You. 2013. (ENG., Illus.). 180p. (J). (gr. 3-7). 14.95 *(978-1-56589-270-5(4))* Crystal Clarity Pubs.

Larsen, Angela Sage. Keeping Secrets, Bk. 2. 2012. (Fifties Chix Ser.: 2). (ENG.). 220p. (YA). pap. 9.95 *(978-1-60746-367-2(9),* Premiere) FastPrncil, Inc.

—Third Time's a Charm, Bk. 3. 2013. (Fifties Chix Ser.: 3). (ENG.). 200p. (YA). pap. 9.95 *(978-1-60746-155-5(2),* Premiere) FastPrncil, Inc.

—Till the End of Time. 2013. (Fifties Chix Ser.: 5). (ENG.). 200p. (YA). pap. 9.95 *(978-1-60746-468-6(3),* Premiere) FastPrncil, Inc.

Laurence, Margaret. The Olden Days Coat. Wood, Muriel, illus. 2004. (ENG.). 32p. (J). (gr. 2-5). pap. 8.99 *(978-0-88776-704-3(4),* Tundra Bks.) Tundra Bks. CAN. Dist: Penguin Random Hse. LLC.

Leighton-Porter, Wendy. The Shadow of Camelot. 2013. 262p. pap. *(978-1-909411-06-7(X))* Mauve Square Publishing.

L'Engle, Madeleine. An Acceptable Time. 2007. (Wrinkle in Time Quintet Ser.: 5). (ENG.). 384p. (J). (gr. 5-9). per. 6.99 *(978-0-312-36858-6(5),* 9780312368586) Square Fish.

—Many Waters. 2007. (Wrinkle in Time Quintet Ser.: 3). (ENG.). 368p. (J). (gr. 5-9). per. 6.99 *(978-0-312-36857-9(7),* 9780312368579) Square Fish.

Lewis, Anne. Dragonchild. 2003. (Bwgan-Wood Ser.: 3). (ENG., Illus.). 208p. (J). (gr. 3-6). pap. 7.95 *(978-1-870206-55-6(X))* Honno Welsh Women's Pr. GBR. Dist: Independent Pubs. Group.

Limbaugh, Rush H., III. Rush Revere & the Brave Pilgrims: Time-Travel Adventures with Exceptional Americans. 2013. (ENG., Illus.). 224p. 19.99 *(978-1-4767-5586-1(8),* Threshold Editions) Threshold Editions.

—Rush Revere & the First Patriots: Time-Travel Adventures with Exceptional Americans. 2014. (Rush Revere Ser.: 2). (ENG., Illus.). 256p. 19.99 *(978-1-4767-5588-5(4),* Threshold Editions) Threshold Editions.

Limbaugh, Rush H., III & Limbaugh, Kathryn Adams. Rush Revere & the American Revolution. 2014. (ENG.). 256p. 19.99 *(978-1-4767-8987-3(8),* Threshold Editions) Threshold Editions.

—Rush Revere & the Presidency. 2016. (Rush Revere Ser.: 5). (ENG., Illus.). 272p. (gr. 4-7). 19.99 *(978-1-5011-5689-2(6),* Threshold Editions) Threshold Editions.

Liparulo, Robert. Gatekeepers, 1 vol. 2009. (Dreamhouse Kings Ser.: 3). (ENG.). 320p. pap. 9.99 *(978-1-59554-729-3(0))* Nelson, Thomas Inc.

—Watcher in the Woods, 1 vol. 2009. (Dreamhouse Kings Ser.: 2). (ENG.). 304p. pap. 9.99 *(978-1-59554-728-6(2))* Nelson, Thomas Inc.

—Whirlwind, 1 vol. 2010. (Dreamhouse Kings Ser.: 5). (ENG.). 320p. pap. 9.99 *(978-1-59554-892-4(0))* Nelson, Thomas Inc.

Litrel, Suzanne M. Jackie Tempo & the Emperor's Seal. 2007. 172p. (YA). per. 13.95 *(978-0-595-46822-5(5))* iUniverse, Inc.

Little, Kimberley Griffiths. The Last Snake Runner. 2006. 201p. (YA). (gr. 7-10). reprint ed. 16.00 *(978-1-4223-5838-2(0))* DIANE Publishing Co.

Long, David. Diary of a Time Traveler: Travel the Globe & Meet History's Most Interesting Characters. Stevenson, Nicholas, illus. 2015. (ENG.). 64p. (J). (gr. 2-5). 22.99 *(978-1-84780-704-5(6),* Wide Eyed Editions) Quarto Publishing Group UK GBR. Dist: Hachette Bk. Group.

Lopez, David Mark. Maddie's Magic Markers: Ride Like an Indian. 2006. (J). (gr. 3-7). *(978-0-9744097-1-9(5))* Lopez, David.

—Run Like a Fugitive. 2006. (J). (gr. 4-8). *(978-0-9744097-2-6(3))* Lopez, David.

—Walk Like an Egyptian. 2006. (J). (gr. 3-7). *(978-0-9744097-0-2(7))* Lopez, David.

Lovett, Vienna. Mission from God. 2013. 256p. *(978-1-77069-833-8(7))* Word Alive Pr.

Lowell, Susan. The Great Grand Canyon Time Train. Shroades, John / W., illus. 2011. 32p. (J). 15.95 *(978-1-933855-63-9(0))* Rio Nuevo Pubs.

MacCullough, Carolyn. Once a Witch. 2010. (ENG.). 320p. (YA). (gr. 7). pap. 8.99 *(978-0-547-41730-1(6))* Houghton Mifflin Harcourt Publishing Co.

MacHale, D. J. The Never War. 2003. (Pendragon Ser.: 3). (ENG., Illus.). 352p. (J). (gr. 5-9). pap. 9.99 *(978-0-7434-3733-2(0),* Aladdin) Simon & Schuster Children's Publishing.

—Pendragon: The Merchant of Death; The Lost City of Fear; The Never War; The Reality Bug; Black Water. 2013. (Pendragon Ser.). (ENG., Illus.). 1968p. (J). (gr. 5-9). pap. 49.99 *(978-1-4424-9926-3(5),* Simon & Schuster/Paula Wiseman Bks.) Simon & Schuster/Paula Wiseman Bks.

Madonia, Kristen-Paige. Invisible Fault Lines. 2016. (ENG.). 320p. (YA). (gr. 7). 17.99 *(978-1-4814-3071-5(8),* Simon & Schuster Bks. For Young Readers) Simon & Schuster Bks. For Young Readers.

Maes, Nicholas. Laughing Wolf. 2009. (Felix Taylor Adventure Ser.: 1). (ENG.). 248p. (J). (gr. 7-18). pap. 10.99 *(978-1-55488-385-1(7),* Dundurn Pr.) Dundurn CAN. Dist: Ingram Publisher Services.

Mahy, Margaret. Maddigan's Fantasia. 2012. (ENG.). 512p. (J). (gr. 5-9). pap. 22.99 *(978-1-4424-6053-9(9),* McElderry, Margaret K. Bks.) McElderry, Margaret K. Bks.

Maihack, Mike. Secret of the Time Tablets (Cleopatra in Space #3) 2016. (Cleopatra in Space Ser.: 3). (ENG.). 192p. (J). (gr. 3-7). pap. 12.99 *(978-0-545-83867-2(3),* Graphix) Scholastic, Inc.

—The Thief & the Sword. 2015. (Cleopatra in Space Ser.: 2). (ENG., Illus.). 192p. (J). (gr. 3-7). 22.99 *(978-0-545-52844-3(5),* Graphix) Scholastic, Inc.

Malcolm, Jahnna N. Pirate's Revenge. Comport, Sally Wern, illus. 2003. 77p. (J). *(978-1-931020-09-1(4))* HOP, LLC.

Malone, Marianne. The Pirate's Coin.. Call, Greg, illus. 2014. (Sixty-Eight Rooms Adventures Ser.). (ENG.). 240p. (J). (gr. 3-7). 7.99 *(978-0-307-97720-5(X),* Yearling) Random Hse. Children's Bks.

—The Secret of the Key: a Sixty-Eight Rooms Adventure. 2015. (Sixty-Eight Rooms Adventures Ser.). (ENG., Illus.). 256p. (J). (gr. 3-7). 6.99 *(978-0-307-97724-3(2),* Yearling) Random Hse. Children's Bks.

—Stealing Magic. Call, Greg, illus. (Sixty-Eight Rooms Adventures Ser.). (ENG.). (J). (gr. 3-7). 2013. 272p. pap. 6.99 *(978-0-375-86790-3(2),* Yearling) 2012. 256p. 16.99 *(978-0-375-86819-1(4),* Random Hse. Bks. for Young Readers) Random Hse. Children's Bks.

Mancusi, Mari. Shattered. (Scorched Ser.: 2). (ENG.). (YA). 2015. 416p. (gr. 8-12). pap. 9.99 *(978-1-4926-0869-1(6))* 2014. 400p. (gr. 7-12). 16.99 *(978-1-4022-8461-8(6),* 9781402284618) Sourcebooks, Inc.

Mangum, Lisa. The Forgotten Locket. (YA). 2012. pap. 8.99 *(978-1-60907-017-5(8))* 2011. (Hourglass Door Trilogy: Bk. 3). 416p. (gr. 3-18). 18.99 *(978-1-60908-049-5(1))* Deseret Bk. Co.

—The Hourglass Door. (Hourglass Door Trilogy: Bk. 1). (YA). 2010. 408p. mass mkt. 7.99 *(978-1-60641-679-2(0))* 2009. 432p. (gr. 9-18). 18.95 *(978-1-60641-093-6(8))* Shadow Mountain Publishing. (Shadow Mountain).

Mansbach, Adam & Zweibel, Alan. Benjamin Franklin: Huge Pain in My... 2017. (Benjamin Franklin Ser.). (ENG.). 224p. (J). (gr. 5-9). pap. 7.99 *(978-1-4847-2537-5(9))* Hyperion Bks. for Children.

Mansbach, Adam & Zwiebel, Alan. Benjamin Franklin: You've Got Mail. 2017. (Benjamin Franklin Ser.). (ENG.). 224p. (J). (gr. 5-9). 12.99 *(978-1-4847-1305-1(2))* Hyperion Bks. for Children.

Mansfield, Keith. Johnny Mackintosh & the Spirit of London. 2010. (Johnny Mackintosh,Johnny Mackintosh Trilogy Ser.: 1). (ENG.). 352p. (J). (gr. 4-6). pap. 8.99 *(978-1-84724-774-2(1))* Quercus GBR. Dist: Hachette Bk. Group.

Masciola, Carol. The Yearbook. 2015. (ENG.). 224p. (YA). 17.99 *(978-1-4405-8897-6(X),* Simon Pulse) Simon Pulse.

Mass, Wendy. The Last Present. (ENG.). 256p. (J). (gr. 3-7). 2015. pap. 6.99 *(978-0-545-31017-8(2))* 2013. 16.99 *(978-0-545-31016-1(4),* Scholastic Pr.) Scholastic, Inc.

Mawhinney, Art, illus. Dora & Diego Help the Dinosaur. 2011. (Dora & Diego Ser.). (ENG.). 24p. (J). pap. 3.99 *(978-1-4424-1400-6(6),* Simon Spotlight/Nickelodeon) Simon Spotlight/Nickelodeon.

Maxwell, Lisa. The Last Magician. 2017. (ENG., Illus.). 512p. (YA). (gr. 9). 18.99 *(978-1-4814-3207-8(9),* Simon Pulse) Simon Pulse.

McBrier, Page. Abracadabra Tut. 2014. (ENG.). (J). pap. 9.99 *(978-0-9960794-0-2(8))* Palm Canyon Pr.

McCLOUD, Scott. Seonimod, 1 vol. Austin, Terry & Burchett, Rick, illus. 2013. (Superman Adventures Ser.). (ENG.). 32p. (gr. 2-3). lib. bdg. 22.60 *(978-1-4342-4711-7(2))* Stone Arch Bks.

McCranie, Stephen. Mal & Chad - The Biggest, Bestest Time Ever! McCranie, Stephen, illus. 2011. (Mal & Chad Ser.: 1). (ENG., Illus.). 224p. (J). (gr. 3-7). 9.99

(978-0-399-25221-1(5), Philomel Bks.) Penguin Young Readers Group.

McCusker, Paul. Out of Time, 1 vol. 2009. (Time Thriller Trilogy Ser.: Bk. 2). (ENG., Illus.). 240p. (YA). (gr. 8-11). pap. 9.99 *(978-0-310-71437-8(0))* Zondervan.

—Strange Journey Back. 2006. (Adventures in Odyssey Bks.: No. 1). (ENG., Illus.). 304p. (J). (gr. 3-7). per. 15.99 *(978-1-58997-325-1(9))* Tyndale Hse. Pubs.

McCusker, Paul & Elmer, Robert. Ripple Effect, 1 vol., Bk. 1. 2008. (Time Thriller Trilogy Ser.: Bk. 1). (ENG., Illus.). 224p. (YA). (gr. 8-11). pap. 9.99 *(978-0-310-71436-1(2))* Zondervan.

McDonnell, Kathleen. The Shining World, 1 vol. 2003. (Notherland Journeys Ser.: 2). (ENG.). 240p. (YA). (gr. 7-9). pap. 6.95 *(978-1-896764-79-5(7))* Second Story Pr. CAN. Dist: Orca Bk. Pubs. USA.

McGowan, Michael. Newton Time Machine. 2008. (ENG., Illus.). 216p. (J). pap. 11.99 *(978-0-00-639550-8(3)*, Harper Trophy) HarperCollins Pubs.

McGrath, Robin. Livyers World. 2007. (ENG.). 150p. (J). (gr. 4-7). per. *(978-1-897174-15-9(2))* Creative Bk. Publishing.

McMann, Lisa. The Trap Door. (Infinity Ring Ser.: 3). (ENG.). 192p. (J). (gr. 3-7). 2015. pap. 6.99 *(978-0-545-90109-3(X))* 2013. 16.99 *(978-0-545-48456-5(1))* 2013. (Illus.). 12.99 *(978-0-545-38698-2(5))* Scholastic, Inc.

—The Trap Door. 2015. (Infinity Ring Ser.: 3). lib. bdg. 17.20 *(978-0-606-37788-1(3))* Turtleback Bks.

McMasters, Gretchen. Aesock's Travels & Los Viajes de Aesock: Lights, Camera, Edison! & Luz, Cámara, Edison. 2004. (Aesock's Travels & Los Viajes de Aesock Ser.: 1). (ENG & SPA., Illus.). 160p. (J). pap. 5.99 *(978-0-9713756-9-7(0))* Stargazer Publishing Co.

McMullan, Kate. Countdown to the Year 1000, 1 vol. Basso, Bill, illus. 2007. (Dragon Slayers' Academy Ser.: No. 8). (ENG.). 107p. (gr. 2-5). 24.21 *(978-1-59961-376-5(X))* Spotlight.

McMullen, Sean. Before the Storm. 2009. 262p. (Orig.). pap. 13.95 *(978-1-879462-50-2(8)*, Ford Street Publishing) Hybrid Pubs. AUS. Dist: International Publishers Marketing.

McSkimming, Geoffrey. Phyllis Wong & the Waking of the Wizard. 2016. (Phyllis Wong Ser.). (ENG.). 400p. (J). (gr. 3-7). pap. 12.99 *(978-1-76011-338-4(7))* Allen & Unwin AUS. Dist: Independent Pubs. Group.

Messner, Kate. Danger in Ancient Rome. McMorris, Kelley, illus. 2015. (Ranger in Time Ser.: 2). (ENG.). 160p. (J). (gr. 2-5). pap. 5.99 *(978-0-545-63917-0(4)*, Scholastic Pr.) Scholastic, Inc.

—Escape from the Great Earthquake. McMorris, Kelley, illus. 2017. (Ranger in Time Ser.: 6). (ENG.). 160p. (J). (gr. 2-5). pap. 5.99 ***(978-0-545-90983-9(X))*** Scholastic, Inc.

—Land of Fire & Ice. McMorris, Kelley, illus. 2017. (Ranger in Time Ser.: 5). (ENG.). 160p. (J). (gr. 2-5). pap. 5.99 *(978-0-545-90978-5(3))* Scholastic, Inc.

—Long Road to Freedom. McMorris, Kelley, illus. 2015. (Ranger in Time Ser.: 3). (ENG.). 160p. (J). (gr. 2-5). pap. 5.99 *(978-0-545-63920-0(4))* Scholastic, Inc.

—Race to the South Pole. McMorris, Kelley, illus. 2016. (Ranger in Time Ser.: 4). (ENG.). 160p. (J). (gr. 2-5). pap. 5.99 *(978-0-545-63925-5(5))* Scholastic, Inc.

—Rescue on the Oregon Trail. McMorris, Kelley, illus. 2015. (Ranger in Time Ser.: 1). (ENG.). 144p. (J). (gr. 2-5). pap. 5.99 *(978-0-545-63914-9(X)*, Scholastic Pr.) Scholastic, Inc.

Metz, Melinda. Raven's Point. 2005. pap. *(978-0-06-052373-2(5))* HarperCollins Canada, Ltd.

Meyer, William. The Secret of the Scarab Beetle. 2016. (Horace J. Edwards & the Time Keepers Ser.). (ENG., Illus.). 230p. (J). (gr. 4-6). pap. 9.99 *(978-1-58536-939-3(X)*, 204089); 16.99 *(978-1-58536-938-6(1)*, 204031) Sleeping Bear Pr.

Miguel Carbonell. King Tut's Tomb Robbers. 2010. 180p. 23.95 *(978-1-4502-1638-8(2))*; pap. 13.95 *(978-1-4502-1637-1(4))* iUniverse, Inc.

Miller, Bryan Q. Space Mountain: A Graphic Novel. 2014. (J). lib. bdg. 24.50 *(978-0-606-35260-4(0))* Turtleback Bks.

Mlynowski, Sarah. Gimme a Call. 2011. (ENG.). 320p. (YA). (gr. 7). pap. 9.99 *(978-0-385-73589-6(8)*, Ember) Random Hse. Children's Bks.

Monir, Alexandra. Timekeeper. (ENG.). (YA). (gr. 7). 2014. 304p. pap. 8.99 *(978-0-385-73841-5(2)*, Ember) 2013. 288p. 16.99 *(978-0-385-73840-8(4)*, Delacorte Bks. for Young Readers) Random Hse. Children's Bks.

—Timeless. 2012. (ENG.). 300p. (YA). (gr. 7). pap. 8.99 *(978-0-385-73839-2(0)*, Ember) Random Hse. Children's Bks.

Monson, Marianne. Escape from Egypt. 2010. (J). *(978-1-60641-670-9(7))* Deseret Bk. Co.

—Pioneer Puzzle. 2010. (J). *(978-1-60641-669-3(3))* Deseret Bk. Co.

Montgomery, R. A. House of Danger. 2005. (Choose Your Own Adventure Ser.). (Illus.). 108p. (gr. 4-8). pap. 5.50 *(978-0-7608-9694-5(1))* Sundance/Newbridge Educational Publishing.

—House of Danger. Sundaravej, Sittisan, illus. 2006. (Choose Your Own Adventure Ser.: No. 6). 144p. (J). (gr. 4-8). per. 6.99 *(978-1-933390-06-2(9)*, CHCL06) Chooseco LLC.

—Island of Time. Louie, Wes & Cannella, Marco, illus. 2008. 144p. (J). (gr. 2-7). pap. 6.99 *(978-1-933390-28-4(X))* Chooseco LLC.

—The Trail of Lost Time. 2011. (Illus.). 144p. (J). mass mkt. 6.99 *(978-1-937133-03-0(6))* Chooseco LLC.

Moonshower, Candie. The Legend of Zoey. 2007. (ENG.). 224p. (J). (gr. 3-7). 6.99 *(978-0-440-23924-6(9)*, Yearling) Random Hse. Children's Bks.

Morrison, Michele. The Comet's Tale. 2007. 136p. pap. 16.95 *(978-1-84753-634-1(4))* Lulu Pr., Inc.

Moss, Marissa. Mira's Diary: California Dreaming. Moss, Marissa, illus. 2016. (ENG., Illus.). 190p. (J). (gr. 2-8). 12.99 *(978-1-939547-22-4(9))* Creston Bks.

—The Pharaoh's Secret. 2009. (ENG., Illus.). 320p. (J). (gr. 3-7). 16.95 *(978-0-8109-8378-6(8)*, Amulet Bks.) Abrams, Inc.

Moss, Marissa, illus. Mira's Diary: Bombs over London. 2014. (ENG.). 190p. (J). (gr. 2-8). 12.99 *(978-1-939547-12-5(1))* Creston Bks.

Mould, Paul, ed. The Magnificent Six. 2007. (Illus.). 52p. pap. *(978-1-58690-048-9(X))* Mould, Paul Publishing.

Muir, Sabine. Meeting Wolfie: A Story about Mozart. 2006. 129p. pap. 19.95 *(978-1-4241-3968-2(6))* PublishAmerica, Inc.

Mullarkey, Lisa & Mullarkey, John. Get Ella to the Apollo, 1 vol. Bernard, Courtney, illus. 2015. (ENG.). 128p. (J). *(978-1-62402-087-2(9))* Magic Wagon.

—Mary Molds a Monster, 1 vol. Bernard, Courtney, illus. 2015. (ENG.). 128p. (J). *(978-1-62402-088-9(7))* Magic Wagon.

—Monet Changes Mediums, 1 vol. Bernard, Courtney, illus. 2015. (ENG.). 128p. (J). *(978-1-62402-089-6(5))* Magic Wagon.

—Shakespeare Saves the Globe, 1 vol. Bernard, Courtney, illus. 2015. (ENG.). 128p. (J). *(978-1-62402-090-2(9))* Magic Wagon.

Murrell, Belinda. The Locket of Dreams. (ENG.). 288p. (J). (gr. 4-7). 2015. pap. 12.99 *(978-0-85798-695-5(3))* 2nd ed. 2013. 17.99 *(978-0-85798-021-2(1))* Random Hse. Australia AUS. Dist: Independent Pubs. Group.

—The Lost Sapphire. 2016. (ENG.). 288p. (YA). (gr. 4-7). pap. 12.99 *(978-1-925324-11-2(7))* Random Hse. Australia AUS. Dist: Independent Pubs. Group.

Myers, Bill. Choices: A Truth Seekers Novel. 2014. (Truth Seekers Ser.). (ENG.). 224p. (J). (gr. 4-8). 10.99 *(978-1-4336-9081-5(0)*, B&H Kids) B&H Publishing Group.

Mystery of the Maya: Choose Your Own Adventure. 2004. per. 5.95 *(978-0-9745356-3-0(X))* Chooseco LLC.

Narine, Vidya D. Kari. 2011. 66p. 24.99 *(978-1-4568-5348-8(1))*; pap. 15.99 *(978-1-4568-5347-1(3))* Xlibris Corp.

Nelson, Peter. Herbert's Wormhole. Rao, Rohitash, illus. 2010. (Herbert's Wormhole Ser.: 1). (ENG.). 304p. (J). (gr. 3-7). pap. 6.99 *(978-0-06-168870-6(3))* HarperCollins Pubs.

—Herbert's Wormhole: AeroStar & the 3 1/2-Point Plan of Vengeance. Rao, Rohitash, illus. 2013. (Herbert's Wormhole Ser.: 3). (ENG.). 352p. (J). (gr. 3-7). 12.99 *(978-0-06-201220-3(7))* HarperCollins Pubs.

—Herbert's Wormhole: The Rise & Fall of el Solo Libre. Rao, Rohitash, illus. 2014. (Herbert's Wormhole Ser.: 2). (ENG.). 336p. (J). (gr. 3-7). pap. 6.99 *(978-0-06-201219-7(3))* HarperCollins Pubs.

—The Rise & Fall of el Solo Libre. Rao, Rohitash, illus. 2012. (Herbert's Wormhole Ser.: 2). (ENG.). 320p. (J). (gr. 3-7). 12.99 *(978-0-06-201218-0(5))* HarperCollins Pubs.

Nesbit, E. The House of Arden. 2006. 184p. (gr. 3-7). per. 14.95 *(978-1-59818-967-4(0))*; 26.95 *(978-1-59818-181-4(5))* Aegypan.

—The House of Arden. 2006. (New York Review Children's Collection). (ENG.). 260p. (J). (gr. 4-7). 17.95 *(978-1-59017-202-5(7)*, NYR Children's Collection) New York Review of Bks., Inc., The.

—The Story of the Amulet. 2010. (CHI.). 270p. (YA). pap. *(978-986-146-634-7(7))* Storm & Stress Publishing Co, Ltd.

—The Story of the Amulet. 2009. 176p. (gr. -1-7). pap. 4.95 *(978-1-60459-694-6(5))* Wilder Pubns., Corp.

Nesbø, Jo. Bubble in the Bathtub. Chace, Tara F., tr. Lowery, Mike, illus. 2011. (Doctor Proctor's Fart Powder Ser.). (ENG.). 448p. (J). (gr. 3-7). pap. 7.99 *(978-1-4169-7975-3(1)*, Aladdin) Simon & Schuster Children's Publishing.

—Bubble in the Bathtub. Chace, Tara, tr. from NOR. Lowery, Mike, illus. 2011. (Doctor Proctor's Fart Powder Ser.). (ENG.). 432p. (J). (gr. 3-7). 17.99 *(978-1-4169-7974-6(3)*, Aladdin) Simon & Schuster Children's Publishing.

Neubecker, Robert. Racing the Waves. 2014. (Tales of the Time Dragon Ser.: 2). (ENG.). 32p. (J). (gr. 1-3). 15.99 *(978-0-545-54903-5(5))* Scholastic, Inc.

Nickel, Scott. Back to the Ice Age. Corts, Enrique, illus. 2008. (Graphic Sparks Ser.). (ENG.). 40p. (gr. 1-3). pap. 5.95 *(978-1-4342-0500-1(2)*, Graphic Sparks) Stone Arch Bks.

—Blast to the Past. Harpster, Steve, illus. 2006. (Graphic Sparks Ser.). (ENG.). 40p. (gr. 1-3). 5.95 *(978-1-59889-167-6(7)*, Graphic Sparks) Stone Arch Bks.

—T. Rex vs Robo-Dog 3000. Corts, Enrique, illus. 2008. (Graphic Sparks Ser.). (ENG.). 40p. (gr. 1-3). pap. 5.95 *(978-1-4342-0857-6(5)*, Graphic Sparks) Stone Arch Bks.

Nielsen, Jennifer A. Behind Enemy Lines. 2016. (Infinity Ring Ser.: 6). (ENG.). 192p. (J). (gr. 3-7). pap. 6.99 *(978-0-545-90121-5(9)*, Scholastic Pr.) Scholastic, Inc.

—Behind Enemy Lines. 2016. (Infinity Ring Ser.: 6). lib. bdg. 17.20 *(978-0-606-38623-4(8))* Turtleback Bks.

North, Ryan. Adventure Time, Vol. 3. 2013. (Adventure Time Graphic Novels Ser.: 3). lib. bdg. 26.95 *(978-0-606-35462-2(X))* Turtleback Bks.

—Adventure Time Volume 2. 2013. (Adventure Time Graphic Novels Ser.: 2). lib. bdg. 26.95 *(978-0-606-35461-5(1))* Turtleback Bks.

Norton, Andre. Key Out of Time. 2007. 140p. per. 11.95 *(978-1-60312-081-4(5))* Aegypan.

—The Time Traders. 2007. 236p. per. 12.95 *(978-1-4218-2734-6(4))*; 27.95 *(978-1-4218-2634-9(8))* 1st World Publishing, Inc. (1st World Library - Literary Society).

—The Time Traders. 2007. 172p. pap. 19.99 *(978-1-4264-9591-5(9))*; (ENG.). 194p. pap. 21.99 *(978-1-4264-9972-2(8))* Creative Media Partners, LLC.

—The Time Traders. 2006. pap. *(978-1-4068-3561-8(7))* Echo Library.

Noyes, Deborah. Plague in the Mirror. 2013. (ENG.). 272p. (YA). (gr. 9). 16.99 *(978-0-7636-5980-6(0))* Candlewick Pr.

O'Brien, Johnny. Day of Deliverance. Hardcastle, Nick, illus. 2010. (Jack Christie Adventure Ser.: 2). (ENG.). 192p. (J). (gr. 4-7). 15.99 *(978-0-7636-5075-9(7)*, Templar) Candlewick Pr.

—Day of the Assassins. Hardcastle, Nick, illus. 2010. (Jack Christie Adventure Ser.: 1). (ENG.). 224p. (J). (gr. 4-7). pap. 6.99 *(978-0-7636-4995-1(3)*, Templar) Candlewick Pr.

—Day of the Assassins: A Jack Christie Novel. Hardcastle, Nick, illus. 2009. (Jack Christie Adventure Ser.: 1). (ENG.). 224p. (J). (gr. 4-7). 15.99 *(978-0-7636-4595-3(8)*, Templar) Candlewick Pr.

Oda, Matthew K. The Time MacHine: Mario's Box A Journey into Creativity. 2011. 36p. pap. 24.95 *(978-1-4626-3892-5(9))* America Star Bks.

Oppenlander, Annette. Escape from the Past: The Duke's Wrath. 2015. (ENG.). 299p. (YA). (gr. 8-17). pap. 12.95 *(978-1-84694-973-9(4)*, Lodestone Bks.) Hunt, John Publishing Ltd. GBR. Dist: National Bk. Network.

—Escape from the Past: The Kid (book 2) 2016. (ENG.). 304p. (YA). (gr. 8-17). pap. 12.95 *(978-1-78535-213-3(X)*, Lodestone Bks.) Hunt, John Publishing Ltd. GBR. Dist: National Bk. Network.

Osborne, Mary Pope. Abe Lincoln at Last! Murdocca, Sal, illus. 2013. (Magic Tree House Merlin Mission Ser.: 19). (ENG.). 144p. (J). (gr. 2-5). 5.99 *(978-0-375-86797-2(X)*, Random Hse. Bks. for Young Readers) Random Hse. Children's Bks.

—Abe Lincoln at Last! 2013. (Magic Tree House Merlin Missions Ser.: 19). lib. bdg. 16.00 *(978-0-606-35563-6(4))* Turtleback Bks.

—Barcos Vikingos Al Amanecer. Brovelli, Marcela, tr. from ENG. Murdocca, Sal, illus. 2007. (Casa del Arbol Ser.: 15). (SPA.). 73p. (J). per. 5.99 *(978-1-933032-21-4(9))* Lectorum Pubns., Inc.

—A Big Day for Baseball. Murdocca, Sal, illus. 2017. (Magic Tree House Ser.: 29). (ENG.). (J). (gr. 1-4). 80p. 13.99 ***(978-1-5247-1308-9(2))***; 96p. lib. bdg. 16.99 ***(978-1-5247-1309-6(0))*** Random Hse. Children's Bks. (Random Hse. Bks. for Young Readers).

—Blizzard of the Blue Moon. Murdocca, Sal, illus. 2007. (Magic Tree House Merlin Mission Ser.: 8). (ENG.). 144p. (J). (gr. 2-5). 5.99 *(978-0-375-83038-9(3)*, Random Hse. Bks. for Young Readers) Random Hse. Children's Bks.

—Buffalo Before Breakfast. 2004. (Magic Tree House Ser.: No. 18). 72p. (J). (gr. k-3). pap. 17.00 incl. audio *(978-0-8072-0927-1(9)*, Listening Library) Random Hse. Audio Publishing Group.

—El Caballero Del Alba. 2004. (Casa del Arbol Ser.: 2). (SPA.). (J). pap. 5.99 *(978-1-930332-50-8(5))* Lectorum Pubns., Inc.

—Carnival at Candlelight. Murdocca, Sal, illus. 2006. (Magic Tree House Merlin Mission Ser.: 5). (ENG.). 144p. (J). (gr. 2-5). 5.99 *(978-0-375-83034-1(0)*, Random Hse. Bks. for Young Readers) Random Hse. Children's Bks.

—Un Castillo Embrujado en la Noche de Halloween. 2015. (Casa De árbol Ser.: 30). (SPA., Illus.). 144p. (J). (gr. 2-4). pap. 5.99 *(978-1-63245-533-8(1))* Lectorum Pubns., Inc.

—Christmas in Camelot. Murdocca, Sal, illus. 2009. (Magic Tree House Merlin Mission Ser.: 1). (ENG.). 144p. (J). (gr. 2-5). 5.99 *(978-0-375-85812-3(1)*, Random Hse. Bks. for Young Readers) Random Hse. Children's Bks.

—Christmas in Camelot. 2009. (Magic Tree House Merlin Missions Ser.: 1). lib. bdg. 16.00 *(978-0-606-06386-9(2)*, Turtleback) Turtleback Bks.

—Civil War on Sunday. unabr. ed. 2004. (Magic Tree House Ser.: No. 21). 76p. (J). (gr. k-3). pap. 17.00 incl. audio *(978-0-8072-0930-1(9)*, S FTR 253 SP, Listening Library) Random Hse. Audio Publishing Group.

—A Crazy Day with Cobras. Murdocca, Sal, illus. (ENG.). (J). 2012. (Magic Tree House Merlin Missions Ser.: No. 17). 144p. (gr. 1-4). 5.99 *(978-0-375-86795-8(3))* 2011. (Magic Tree House Merlin Mission Ser.: 45). 128p. (gr. 2-5). 12.99 *(978-0-375-86823-8(2))* Random Hse. Children's Bks. (Random Hse. Bks. for Young Readers).

—A Crazy Day with Cobras. 2012. (Magic Tree House Merlin Missions Ser.: 17). lib. bdg. 16.00 *(978-0-606-26997-1(5)*, Turtleback) Turtleback Bks.

—Danger in the Darkest Hour. Murdocca, Sal, illus. 2015. (Stepping Stone Book Ser.: No. 1). (ENG.). 192p. (J). (gr. 2-5). 14.99 *(978-0-553-49772-4(3)*, Random Hse. Bks. for Young Readers) Random Hse. Children's Bks.

—Dark Day in the Deep Sea. 2009. (Magic Tree House Merlin Missions Ser.: 11). lib. bdg. 16.00 *(978-0-606-01778-7(X)*, Turtleback) Turtleback Bks.

—Day of the Dragon King. unabr. ed. 2004. (Magic Tree House Ser.: No. 14). 68p. (J). (gr. k-3). pap. 17.00 incl. audio *(978-0-8072-0783-3(7)*, S FTR 242 SP, Listening Library) Random Hse. Audio Publishing Group.

—Dinosaurios Al Atardecer. 2004. (Casa del Arbol Ser.: 1). (SPA.). (J). pap. 5.99 *(978-1-930332-49-2(1))* Lectorum Pubns., Inc.

—Dinosaurios al Atardecer. 2003. (Magic Tree House Ser.: 1). (SPA.). (gr. 3-6). lib. bdg. 16.00 *(978-0-613-64486-0(7)*, Turtleback) Turtleback Bks.

—Dinosaurs Before Dark. unabr. ed. 2004. (Magic Tree House Ser.: No. 1). 68p. (J). (gr. k-5). pap. 17.00 incl. audio *(978-0-8072-0330-9(0)*, FTR208SP, Listening Library) Random Hse. Audio Publishing Group.

—Dinosaurs Before Dark. Murdocca, Sal, illus. 20th anniv. ed. 2012. (Magic Tree House Ser.: 1). (ENG.). 96p. (J). (gr. k-3). 14.99 *(978-0-375-86988-4(3)*, Random Hse. Bks. for Young Readers) Random Hse. Children's Bks.

—Dogs in the Dead of Night. Murdocca, Sal, illus. 2013. (Magic Tree House (R) Merlin Mission Ser.: 18). (ENG.). 144p. (J). (gr. 2-5). 5.99 *(978-0-375-86796-5(1)*, Random Hse. Bks. for Young Readers) Random Hse. Children's Bks.

—Dogs in the Dead of Night. 2013. (Magic Tree House Merlin Missions Ser.: 18). lib. bdg. 16.00 *(978-0-606-31939-3(5)*, Turtleback) Turtleback Bks.

—Dragon of the Red Dawn. Murdocca, Sal, illus. 2008. (Magic Tree House Merlin Mission Ser.: 9). (ENG.). 144p. (J). (gr. 2-5). 5.99 *(978-0-375-83728-9(0)*, Random Hse. Bks. for Young Readers) Random Hse. Children's Bks.

—Earthquake in the Early Morning. unabr. ed. 2004. (Magic Tree House Ser.: No. 24). 71p. (J). (gr. k-3). pap. 17.00 incl. audio *(978-0-8072-0933-2(3)*, S FTR 256 SP, Listening Library) Random Hse. Audio Publishing Group.

—A Ghost Tale for Christmas Time. Murdocca, Sal, illus. (Magic Tree House Merlin Mission Ser.: No. 16). (ENG.). (J). (gr. 2-5). 2012. 144p. pap. 5.99 *(978-0-375-85653-2(6))* 2010. 128p. 12.99 *(978-0-375-85652-5(8))* Random Hse. Children's Bks. (Random Hse. Bks. for Young Readers).

—A Ghost Tale for Christmas Time. 2012. (Magic Tree House Merlin Missions Ser.: 16). lib. bdg. 16.00 *(978-0-606-26808-0(1)*, Turtleback) Turtleback Bks.

—Ghost Town at Sundown. unabr. ed. 2004. (Magic Tree House Ser.: No. 10). 73p. (J). (gr. k-3). pap. 17.00 incl. audio *(978-0-8072-0535-8(4)*, Listening Library) Random Hse. Audio Publishing Group.

—A Good Night for Ghosts. 2010. (Magic Tree House Merlin Missions Ser.: No. 14). (Illus.). 157p. (J). pap. *(978-4-8401-3411-8(1))* Fukuinkan Shoten.

—A Good Night for Ghosts. Murdocca, Sal, illus. (Magic Tree House Merlin Mission Ser.: 14). (ENG.). (J). (gr. 2-5). 2011. 144p. 5.99 *(978-0-375-85649-5(8))* 2009. 128p. 12.99 *(978-0-375-85648-8(X))* Random Hse. Children's Bks. (Random Hse. Bks. for Young Readers).

—Haunted Castle on Hallows Eve. Murdocca, Sal, illus. 2010. (Magic Tree House Merlin Mission Ser.: 2). (ENG.). 144p. (J). (gr. 2-5). pap. 5.99 *(978-0-375-86090-4(8)*, Random Hse. Bks. for Young Readers) Random Hse. Children's Bks.

—Haunted Castle on Hallows Eve. 2010. (Magic Tree House Merlin Missions Ser.: 2). lib. bdg. 16.00 *(978-0-606-13992-2(3)*, Turtleback) Turtleback Bks.

—High Tide in Hawaii. Murdocca, Sal, illus. 2003. (Magic Tree House (R) Ser.: 28). (ENG.). 96p. (J). (gr. 1-4). pap. 5.99 *(978-0-375-80616-2(4)*, Random Hse. Bks. for Young Readers) Random Hse. Children's Bks.

—High Tide in Hawaii. 2003. (Magic Tree House Ser.: 28). (gr. k-3). lib. bdg. 16.00 *(978-0-613-62386-5(X)*, Turtleback) Turtleback Bks.

—High Time for Heroes. Murdocca, Sal, illus. 2016. (Magic Tree House Merlin Mission Ser.: 23). (ENG.). 144p. (J). (gr. 2-5). 5.99 *(978-0-307-98052-6(9)*, Random Hse. Bks. for Young Readers) Random Hse. Children's Bks.

—La Hora de Los Juegos Olimpicos. Brovelli, Marcela, tr. Murdocca, Sal, illus. 2007. (Casa del Arbol Ser.: 16).Tr. of Hour of the Olympics Games. (ENG & SPA.). 68p. (J). per. 5.99 *(978-1-933032-22-1(7))* Lectorum Pubns., Inc.

—Hour of the Olympics. unabr. ed. 2004. (Magic Tree House Ser.: No. 16). 70p. (J). (gr. k-3). pap. 17.00 incl. audio *(978-0-8072-0785-7(3)*, LFTR 244 SP, Listening Library) Random Hse. Audio Publishing Group.

—Hurry up, Houdini! Murdocca, Sal, illus. 2013. (Magic Tree House Merlin Missions Ser.: No. 22). (ENG.). 128p. (J). (gr. 2-5). 12.99 *(978-0-307-98045-8(6)*, Random Hse. Bks. for Young Readers) Random Hse. Children's Bks.

—Hurry up, Houdini! 2015. (Magic Tree House Merlin Missions Ser.: 22). lib. bdg. 16.00 *(978-0-606-37718-8(2))* Turtleback Bks.

—The Knight at Dawn. unabr. ed. 2004. (Magic Tree House Ser.: No. 2). 66p. (J). (gr. k-3). pap. 17.00 incl. audio *(978-0-8072-0331-6(9)*, Listening Library) Random Hse. Audio Publishing Group.

—The Knight at Dawn. Murdocca, Sal, illus. 20th anniv. ed. 2013. (Magic Tree House Ser.). (ENG.). 96p. (J). (gr. 1-4). 14.99 *(978-0-449-81822-0(5)*, Random Hse. Bks. for Young Readers) Random Hse. Children's Bks.

—Leprechaun in Late Winter. Murdocca, Sal, illus. (Magic Tree House Merlin Mission Ser.: No. 15). (ENG.). 128p. (J). (gr. 2-5). 2012. 5.99 *(978-0-375-85651-8(X))* 2010. 12.99 *(978-0-375-85650-1(1))* Random Hse. Children's Bks. (Random Hse. Bks. for Young Readers).

—Leprechaun in Late Winter. 2012. (Magic Tree House Merlin Missions Ser.: 15). lib. bdg. 16.00 *(978-0-606-23860-1(3)*, Turtleback) Turtleback Bks.

—Una Momia Al Amanecer. 2004. (Casa del Arbol Ser.: 3). (SPA.). (J). pap. 5.99 *(978-1-930332-51-5(3))* Lectorum Pubns., Inc.

—Una Momia en la Manana. 2003. (Magic Tree House Ser.: 3). (SPA.). (gr. 3-6). lib. bdg. 16.00 *(978-0-613-64609-3(6)*, Turtleback) Turtleback Bks.

—Monday with a Mad Genius. Murdocca, Sal, illus. (Magic Tree House Merlin Mission Ser.: 10). (ENG.). (J). (gr. 2-5). 2009. 144p. 5.99 *(978-0-375-83730-2(2))* 2007. 128p. 11.99 *(978-0-375-83729-6(9))* Random Hse. Children's Bks. (Random Hse. Bks. for Young Readers).

—Monday with a Mad Genius. 2009. (Magic Tree House Merlin Missions Ser.: 10). lib. bdg. 16.00 *(978-0-606-01777-0(1)*, Turtleback) Turtleback Bks.

—Moonlight on the Magic Flute. Murdocca, Sal, illus. 2010. (Magic Tree House Merlin Mission Ser.: No. 13). (ENG.). 144p. (J). (gr. 2-5). pap. 5.99 *(978-0-375-85647-1(1)*, Random Hse. Bks. for Young Readers) Random Hse. Children's Bks.

—Navidad en Camelot. 2015. (Casa De árbol Ser.: 29). (SPA., Illus.). 144p. (J). (gr. 2-4). pap. 5.99 *(978-1-63245-532-1(3))* Lectorum Pubns., Inc.

—Night of the New Magicians. Murdocca, Sal, illus. 2007. (Magic Tree House Merlin Mission Ser.: 7). (ENG.). 144p. (J). (gr. 2-5). 5.99 *(978-0-375-83036-5(7)*, Random Hse. Bks. for Young Readers) Random Hse. Children's Bks.

—Night of the New Magicians. 2007. (Magic Tree House Merlin Missions Ser.: 7). lib. bdg. 16.00 *(978-1-4177-9108-8(X)*, Turtleback) Turtleback Bks.

—Night of the Ninth Dragon. Murdocca, Sal, illus. 2016. (Magic Tree House Merlin Missions Ser.: No. 27). (ENG.). 144p. (J). (gr. 2-5). 13.99 *(978-0-553-51089-8(4)*, Random Hse. Bks. for Young Readers) Random Hse. Children's Bks.

—La Noche de los Ninjas. 2004. (Casa del Arbol Ser.: 5).Tr. of Night of the Ninjas. (SPA., Illus.). (J). pap. 5.99 *(978-1-930332-66-9(1))* Lectorum Pubns., Inc.

—Piratas Despues Del Mediodia. 2004. (Casa del Arbol Ser.: 4). (SPA.). (J). pap. 5.99 *(978-1-930332-52-2(1))* Lectorum Pubns., Inc.

—Piratas Despues del Mediodia. 2003. (Magic Tree House Ser.: 4). (SPA.). (gr. 3-6). lib. bdg. 16.00 *(978-0-613-64578-2(2)*, Turtleback) Turtleback Bks.

—Revolutionary War on Wednesday. unabr. ed. 2004. (Magic Tree House Ser.: No. 22). 69p. (J). (gr. k-3). pap. 17.00 incl. audio *(978-0-8072-0931-8(7)*, S FTR 254 SP, Listening Library) Random Hse. Audio Publishing Group.

—Season of the Sandstorms. 2014. (Magic Tree House Merlin Missions Ser.: No. 6). 15.00 *(978-1-63419-681-9(3))* Perfection Learning Corp.

—Season of the Sandstorms. Murdocca, Sal, illus. 2006. (Magic Tree House Merlin Mission Ser.: No. 6). (ENG.). 144p. (J). (gr. 2-5). 5.99 *(978-0-375-83032-7(4)*, Random Hse. Bks. for Young Readers) Random Hse. Children's Bks.

—Shadow of the Shark. 2017. (Magic Tree House Merlin Mission Ser.: 25). (ENG., Illus.). 144p. (J). (gr. 2-5). 5.99 ***(978-0-553-51084-3(3)***, Random Hse. Bks. for Young Readers) Random Hse. Children's Bks.

—Shadow of the Shark. Murdocca, Sal, illus. 2015. (Magic Tree House Merlin Mission Ser.: No. 25). (ENG.). 144p. (J). (gr. 2-5). lib. bdg. 15.99 *(978-0-553-51082-9(7)*, Random Hse. Bks. for Young Readers) Random Hse. Children's Bks.

—Soccer on Sunday. Murdocca, Sal, illus. (Magic Tree House Merlin Missions Ser.: No. 24). (ENG.). (J). (gr. 2-5). 2016. 144p. 5.99 *(978-0-307-98056-4(1))* 2014. 128p. 12.99 *(978-0-307-98053-3(7))* Random Hse. Children's Bks. (Random Hse. Bks. for Young Readers).

—Stallion by Starlight. Murdocca, Sal, illus. (Magic Tree House Merlin Mission Ser.: No. 21). (ENG.). (J). (gr. 2-5). 2014.

T
U
V

144p. pap. 5.99 (978-0-307-98044-1(8)) 2013. 128p. lib. bdg. 15.99 (978-0-307-98042-7(1)) Random Hse. Children's Bks. (Random Hse. Bks. for Young Readers).

—Stallion by Starlight. 2014. (Magic Tree House Merlin Missions Ser.: 21). lib. bdg. 16.00 (978-0-606-36411-9(0)) Turtleback Bks.

—Summer of the Sea Serpent. Murdocca, Sal, illus. 2011. (Magic Tree House Merlin Mission Ser.: No. 3). (ENG.). 144p. (J). (gr. 2-5). 5.99 (978-0-375-86491-9(1), Random Hse. Bks. for Young Readers) Random Hse. Children's Bks.

—Una Tarde en el Amazonas. 2004. (Casa del Arbol Ser.: 6).Tr. of Afternoon on the Amazon. (SPA., Illus.). 66p. (J). pap. 5.99 (978-1-930332-67-6(X)) Lectorum Pubns., Inc.

—Un Tigre Dientes de Sable en el Ocaso. 2004. (Casa del Arbol Ser.: 7).Tr. of Sunset of the Sabretooth. (SPA., Illus.). (J). pap. 5.99 (978-1-930332-68-3(8)) Lectorum Pubns., Inc.

—Tonight on the Titanic. unabr. ed. 2004. (Magic Tree House Ser.: No. 17). 71p. (J). (gr. k-3). pap. 17.00 incl. audio (978-0-8072-0926-4(0), S FTR 249 SP, Listening Library) Random Hse. Audio Publishing Group.

—Twister on Tuesday. 2004. (Magic Tree House Ser.: No. 23). 70p. (J). (gr. k-3). pap. 17.00 incl. audio (978-0-8072-9932-6(4), Listening Library) Random Hse. Audio Publishing Group.

—Vacaciones Al Pie de un Volcan. Brovelli, Marcela, tr. from ENG. Murdocca, Sal, illus. 2007. (Casa del Arbol Ser.: 13).Tr. of Vacation under the Colcano. (SPA.). 74p. (J). per. 5.99 (978-1-933032-19-1(7)) Lectorum Pubns., Inc.

—Vacation under the Volcano. unabr. ed. 2004. (Magic Tree House Ser.: No. 13). 74p. (J). (gr. k-3). pap. 17.00 incl. audio (978-0-8072-0782-6(9), LFTR 241 SP, Listening Library) Random Hse. Audio Publishing Group.

—El Verano de la Serpiente Marina. 2015. (Casa De árbol Ser.: 31). (SPA., Illus.). 144p. (J). (gr. 2-4). pap. 5.99 (978-1-63245-534-5(X)) Lectorum Pubns., Inc.

—Viking Ships at Sunrise. unabr. ed. 2004. (Magic Tree House Ser.: No. 15). 71p. (J). (gr. k-3). pap. 17.00 incl. audio (978-0-8072-0784-0(5), LFTR 243 SP, Listening Library) Random Hse. Audio Publishing Group.

Osborne, Mary Pope & Murdocca, Sal. Esta Noche en el Titanic. Murdocca, Sal, illus. 2008. (Casa del Arbol Ser.: 17).Tr. of Tonight on the Titanic. (SPA., Illus.). (J). (gr. 2-4). pap. 5.99 (978-1-933032-47-4(2)) Lectorum Pubns., Inc.

Osborne, Mary Pope & Osborne, Magic Tree. Dark Day in the Deep Sea. Murdocca, Sal, illus. 2009. (Magic Tree House Merlin Mission Ser.: 11). (ENG.). 144p. (J). (gr. 2-5). 5.99 (978-0-375-83732-6(9), Random Hse. Bks. for Young Readers) Random Hse. Children's Bks.

Osborne, Mary Pope & PLC Editors Staff. Carnival at Candlelight. Murdocca, Sal, illus. 2006. (Magic Tree House Merlin Missions Ser.: No. 5). 105p. (gr. 2-6). 15.00 (978-0-7569-6690-4(6)) Perfection Learning Corp.

Osborne, Mary Pope, et al. Buenos Días, Gorilas. Murdocca, Sal, illus. 2014. 26. (SPA.). 88p. (J). (gr. 2-4). pap. 5.99 (978-1-933032-93-1(6)) Lectorum Pubns., Inc.

—Búfalos Antes Del Desayuno. Murdocca, Sal, illus. 2008. (Casa del Arbol Ser.: 18).Tr. of Buffalo Before Breakfast. (SPA.). (J). (gr. 2-4). pap. 5.99 (978-1-933032-48-1(0)) Lectorum Pubns., Inc.

—Carnaval a Media Luz. Murdocca, Sal, illus. 2016. (SPA.). (J). (gr. 2-4). pap. 5.99 **(978-1-63245-643-4(5))** Lectorum Pubns., Inc.

—La Estación de Las Tormentas de Arena. Murdocca, Sal, illus. 2016. (SPA.). (J). (gr. 2-4). pap. 5.99 **(978-1-63245-644-1(3))** Lectorum Pubns., Inc.

—Jueves de Acción de Gracias. Murdocca, Sal, illus. 2014. 27. (SPA.). 88p. (J). (gr. 2-4). pap. 5.99 (978-1-933032-94-8(4)) Lectorum Pubns., Inc.

—Maremoto en Hawái. Murdocca, Sal, illus. 2014. 28. (SPA.). 88p. (J). (gr. 2-4). pap. 5.99 (978-1-933032-95-5(2)) Lectorum Pubns., Inc.

—Miedo Escénico en una Noche de Verano. Murdocca, Sal, illus. 2014. 25. (SPA.). 86p. (J). (gr. 2-4). pap. 5.99 (978-1-933032-92-4(8)) Lectorum Pubns., Inc.

—La Noche de los Nuevos Magos. Murdocca, Sal, illus. 2016. (SPA.). (J). (gr. 2-4). pap. 5.99 **(978-1-63245-645-8(1))** Lectorum Pubns., Inc.

—Tormenta de Nieve en Luna Azul. Murdocca, Sal, illus. 2016. (SPA.). (J). (gr. 2-4). pap. 5.99 **(978-1-63245-646-5(X))** Lectorum Pubns., Inc.

Osterweil, Adam & Smith, Craig. The Baseball Card Kid. Smith, Craig, illus. 2009. (ENG., Illus.). 199p. (J). (gr. 3-7). 17.95 (978-1-59078-526-3(6), Front Street) Boyds Mills Pr.

Owen, James A. The Dragon's Apprentice. Owen, James A., illus. (Chronicles of the Imaginarium Geographica Ser.: 5). (ENG., Illus.). (YA). (gr. 7). 2012. 400p. pap. 9.99 (978-1-4169-5898-7(3)) 2010. 384p. 17.99 (978-1-4169-5897-0(5)) Simon & Schuster Bks. For Young Readers. (Simon & Schuster Bks. For Young Readers).

—The Dragons of Winter. Owen, James A., illus. (Chronicles of the Imaginarium Geographica Ser.: 6). (ENG., Illus.). (YA). (gr. 7). 2013. 416p. pap. 9.99 (978-1-4424-1224-8(0)) 2012. 400p. 17.99 (978-1-4424-1223-1(2)) Simon & Schuster Bks. For Young Readers. (Simon & Schuster Bks. For Young Readers).

—Fall of the Dragons: The Dragon's Apprentice; the Dragons of Winter; the First Dragon. 2016. (Age of Dragons Ser.: 3). (ENG., Illus.). 1056p. pap. 21.99 (978-1-4814-2998-6(1), SAGA Press) Simon & Schuster Bks. For Young Readers.

—The First Dragon. Owen, James A., illus. (Chronicles of the Imaginarium Geographica Ser.: 7). (ENG., Illus.). 304p. (YA). (gr. 7). 2014. pap. 12.99 (978-1-4424-1227-9(5)) 2013. 17.99 (978-1-4424-1226-2(7)) Simon & Schuster Bks. For Young Readers. (Simon & Schuster Bks. For Young Readers).

—Here, There Be Dragons. 2008. (Playaway Children Ser.). (YA). (gr. 7-12). 59.99 (978-1-60640-959-6(X)) Findaway World, LLC.

—Here, There Be Dragons. Owen, James A., illus. (Chronicles of the Imaginarium Geographica Ser.: 1). (ENG., Illus.). (YA). (gr. 7-12). 2007. 352p. pap. 11.99 (978-1-4169-1228-6(2)) 2006. 336p. 21.99 (978-1-4169-1227-9(4)) Simon & Schuster Bks. For Young Readers. (Simon & Schuster Bks. For Young Readers).

—The Indigo King. Owen, James A., illus. (Chronicles of the Imaginarium Geographica Ser.: 3). (ENG., Illus.). (YA). (gr. 7). 2010. 400p. pap. 12.99 (978-1-4169-5108-7(3)) 2008. 384p. 17.99 (978-1-4169-5107-0(5)) Simon & Schuster Bks. For Young Readers. (Simon & Schuster Bks. For Young Readers).

—The Search for the Red Dragon. Owen, James A., illus. 2008. (Chronicles of the Imaginarium Geographica Ser.: 2). (ENG., Illus.). (YA). (gr. 7). 400p. pap. 9.99 (978-1-4169-4851-3(1)); 384p. 17.99 (978-1-4169-4850-6(3)) Simon & Schuster Bks. For Young Readers. (Simon & Schuster Bks. For Young Readers).

—The Shadow Dragons. Owen, James A., illus. 2009. (Chronicles of the Imaginarium Geographica Ser.: 4). (ENG., Illus.). 432p. (YA). (gr. 7-18). 21.99 (978-1-4169-5879-6(7), Simon & Schuster Bks. For Young Readers) Simon & Schuster Bks. For Young Readers.

Oxridge, Panama. Justin Thyme. 2012. (Tartan of Thyme Ser.). (Illus.). 368p. (YA). (gr. 5-12). pap. 9.99 (978-0-9567122-8-8(2)) Lerner Publishing Group.

—Justin Thyme. Poxmage, Adrian, illus. 2011. (Tartan of Thyme Ser.). 368p. (YA). 18.99 (978-0-9562315-9-8(4)) Lerner Publishing Group.

Packard, Edward. Return to the Cave of Time. Willis, Drew, illus. 2012. (U-Ventures Ser.). (ENG.). 160p. (Orig.). (J). (gr. 3-7). pap. 5.99 (978-1-4424-3427-1(9), Simon & Schuster Bks. For Young Readers) Simon & Schuster Bks. For Young Readers.

Palmer, Robin. Once upon a Kiss. 2016. (ENG.). 304p. (YA). (gr. 7). pap. 9.99 (978-0-14-750988-8(2), Speak) Penguin Young Readers Group.

Panckridge, Michael & Lee, Brett. Toby Jones & the Clash with Father Time. 5th ed. 2007. 208p. (978-0-207-20047-2(5)) HarperCollins Pubs. Australia.

Park, Linda Sue. Archer's Quest. 2008. (ENG., Illus.). 176p. (J). (gr. 3-7). 6.99 (978-0-440-42204-4(3), Yearling) Random Hse. Children's Bks.

Parton, Paula. Room 17 'Where History Comes Alive!' Book Ii, Explorers. 2008. 120p. pap. 8.95 (978-0-9794815-3-6(8)) Bellissima Publishing, LLC.

Pathfinder Trilogy: Pathfinder; Ruins; Visitors. 2014. (ENG., Illus.). 1824p. (YA). (gr. 7). 59.99 (978-1-4814-2698-5(2), Simon Pulse) Simon Pulse.

Pati, Geeta. Finny's Voyage Through the Universe: Nebula, Supernova, Open Star Cluster. 2007. 100p. per. 11.95 (978-1-59526-422-0(1), Llumina Pr.) Aeon Publishing Inc.

Patterson, James. Demons & Druids. 2011. (Daniel X Ser.: 3). (ENG.). 304p. (J). (gr. 3-7). pap., pap. 8.00 (978-0-316-03830-0(X), Jimmy Patterson) Little Brown & Co.

Patterson, James & Sadler, Adam. Demons & Druids. l.t. ed. 2010. (Daniel X Ser.: 3). (ENG.). 320p. 29.99 (978-0-316-08731-5(9), Jimmy Patterson) Little Brown & Co.

Paulsen, Gary & Roberts, Esyllt Nest. Plygu Amser. 2005. (WEL.). 80p. pap. (978-0-86381-683-3(5)) Gwasg Carreg Gwalch.

Paz, Diana. Timespell. 2013. 312p. pap. 14.99 (978-1-936850-21-1(4)) Rhemalda Publishing.

Peacock, L. A. Panic in Pompeii. Hale, Nathan, illus. 2011. 92p. (J). pap. (978-0-545-34062-5(4)) Scholastic, Inc.

—Terror at Troy. Hale, Nathan, illus. 2012. 90p. (J). (978-0-545-34063-2(2)) Scholastic, Inc.

Pearson, Ridley. Disney Lands. 2015. (Kingdom Keepers: Bk. 1). (ENG., Illus.). 352p. (J). (gr. 4-7). 17.99 (978-1-4231-8431-7(9)) Hyperion Bks. for Children.

—Kingdom Keepers the Return. 2017. (Kingdom Keepers Ser.). (ENG.). 480p. (J). (gr. 5-9). 17.99 (978-1-4231-8433-1(5)) Hyperion Bks. for Children.

—Kingdom Keepers: the Return Book Two Legacy of Secrets. 2017. (Kingdom Keepers: the Return Ser.). (ENG.). 416p. (J). (gr. 3-7). pap. 8.99 (978-1-4847-3414-8(9)) Hyperion Bks. for Children.

—The Return: Legacy of Secrets. 2016. (Kingdom Keepers Ser.: Bk. 2). (ENG., Illus.). 394p. (J). (gr. 5-9). 17.99 (978-1-4231-8432-4(7)) Hyperion Bks. for Children.

Pease, D. Robert. Noah Zarc: Cataclysm. 2nd l.t. ed. 2013. 2. (ENG.). 234p. (gr. 3-8). pap. 11.95 (978-1-62253-406-7(9)) Evolved Publishing.

—Noah Zarc: Omnibus. l.t. ed. 2013. 4. (ENG.). 630p. (gr. 3-8). 36.95 (978-1-62253-410-4(7)) Evolved Publishing.

Penner, Stephen. Professor Barrister's Dinosaur Mysteries #2: The Case of the Armored Allosaurus. 2010. 54p. pap. 19.60 (978-1-60888-018-8(4)) Nimble Bks. LLC.

Perrin, Randy, et al. Time Like a River. 2004. 144p. (gr. 5-18). 14.95 (978-1-57143-061-8(X)) RDR Bks.

Phelps, Donna & Phelps, Cameron. Cameron & the Dinosaur Heroes. 2011. 128p. 21.23 (978-1-4567-2476-4(2)); pap. 10.68 (978-1-4389-6353-2(X)) AuthorHouse.

Pilkey, Dav. The Adventures of Ook & Gluk, Kung-Fu Cavemen from the Future. Pilkey, Dav, illus. (Captain Underpants Ser.). (ENG., Illus.). 176p. (J). (gr. 2-5). 2011. 5.99 (978-0-545-38577-0(6)) 2010. 9.99 (978-0-545-17530-2(5)) Scholastic, Inc.

—The Adventures of Ook & Gluk, Kung-Fu Cavemen from the Future. 2011. lib. bdg. 16.00 (978-0-606-16381-1(6), Turtleback) Turtleback Bks.

—Las Aventuras de Uuk y Gluk, Cavernicolas del Futuro y Maestros de Kung Fu. Pilkey, Dav, illus. 2011. (Captain Underpants Ser.). (SPA., Illus.). 176p. (J). (gr. 2-5). pap. 5.99 (978-0-545-27916-1(X), Scholastic en Espanol) Scholastic, Inc.

—Captain Underpants & the Revolting Revenge of the Radioactive Robo-Boxers. Pilkey, Dav, illus. 2013. (Captain Underpants Ser.: 10). (ENG., Illus.). 192p. (J). (gr. 2-5). 9.99 (978-0-545-17536-4(4)) Scholastic, Inc.

—Captain Underpants & the Revolting Revenge of the Radioactive Robo-Boxers. 2013. (Captain Underpants Ser.: 10). lib. bdg. 20.85 (978-0-606-31563-0(2), Turtleback) Turtleback Bks.

Pilkey, Dav & Beard, George. The Adventures of Ook & Gluk, Kung-Fu Cavemen from the Future. 2010. lib. bdg. 20.85 (978-0-606-15003-3(X), Turtleback) Turtleback Bks.

Plante, Raymond. Le Monde de Xéros. Delezenne, Christine, illus. 2004. (Roman Jeunesse Ser.). (FRE.). 96p. (J). (gr. 4-7). pap. (978-2-89021-615-0(2)) Diffusion du livre Mirabel (DLM).

Post, Bobby. The Adventures of Jimmy. 2007. 48p. per. 16.95 (978-1-4137-8704-7(5)) America Star Bks.

Poteat, Bruce S. Evil Deception. 2013. 192p. (gr. 10-12). 30.95 (978-1-4497-9565-8(X)); pap. 13.95 (978-1-4497-9570-2(6)) Author Solutions, Inc. (WestBow Pr.).

Potter, David. The Left Behinds: Abe Lincoln & the Selfie That Saved the Union. 2016. (Left Behinds Ser.). (ENG.). 304p. (J). (gr. 3-7). 16.99 (978-0-385-39060-6(2), Crown Books For Young Readers) Random Hse. Children's Bks.

—The Left Behinds: the IPhone That Saved George Washington. 2016. (Left Behinds Ser.). (ENG.). 368p. (J). (gr. 3-7). 7.99 (978-0-385-39059-0(9), Yearling) Random Hse. Children's Bks.

Prévost, Guillaume & Rodarmor, William. The Circle of Gold: The Book of Time III. 2009. (J). pap. (978-0-439-88382-5(2), Levine, Arthur A. Bks.) Scholastic, Inc.

Price, Susan. A Sterkarm Kiss. 2004. (ENG.). 288p. (J). (gr. 7-18). 16.99 (978-0-06-072197-8(9)) HarperCollins Pubs.

Prior, Natalie Jane & Prior, Natalie. Lily Quench & the Treasure of Mote Ely, Vol. 3. 2004. (ENG., Illus.). 160p. (J). (gr. 3-7). 6.99 (978-0-14-240022-7(X), Puffin Books) Penguin Young Readers Group.

Pullman, Philip. The Adventures of John Blake: Mystery of the Ghost Ship. Fordham, Fred, illus. 2017. (ENG.). 160p. (J). (gr. 3-7). 19.99 **(978-1-338-14912-8(1)**, Graphix) Scholastic, Inc.

—The Adventures of John Blake: Mystery of the Ghost Ship. Fordham, Fred, illus. 2017. lib. bdg. 33.05 **(978-0-606-40195-1(4))** Turtleback Bks.

Quinn, K. A. S. The Queen Alone. 2015. (Chronicles of the Tempus Ser.). (ENG.). 328p. (J). (gr. 4-7). pap. 10.99 (978-1-84887-056-7(6)) Atlantic Bks., Ltd. GBR. Dist: Independent Pubs. Group.

Quintana, Adrienne. Eruption. 2015. 282p. (YA). pap. 16.99 (978-1-4621-1536-5(5)) Cedar Fort, Inc./CFI Distribution.

Rabin, Staton. Black Powder. 2005. (ENG.). 256p. (YA). (gr. 7-9). 16.95 (978-0-689-86876-4(6), McElderry, Margaret K. Bks.) McElderry, Margaret K. Bks.

Ramsay, Elizabeth. The Burning Light. Katz, Avi, illus. 2005. 144p. (J). (gr. 4-9). 14.95 (978-1-930143-43-2(5)); pap. 9.95 (978-1-930143-44-9(3)) Simcha Media Group. (Devora Publishing).

Rau, Dana Meachen. Moon Walk. Buchs, Thomas, illus. 2004. (Soundprints' Read-and-Discover Ser.). 48p. (gr. -1-3). 13.95 (978-0-7569-3370-8(6)) Perfection Learning Corp.

Rechlin, Ted. ComicQuest TIME TRAVEL TROUBLE. 2013. (Dover Children's Activity Bks.). (ENG.). 48p. (J). (gr. 3-8). pap. 4.99 (978-0-486-49949-9(9)) Dover Pubns., Inc.

Reed, Wilfred. Andy & Mark & the Time Machine: Custer's Last Stand. 2003. 240p. (YA). pap. 15.95 (978-0-595-26496-4(4), Writers Club Pr.) iUniverse, Inc.

Reeve, Philip. Starcross: A Stirring Adventure of Spies, Time Travel & Curious Hats. Wyatt, David, illus. 2007. (ENG.). 384p. (YA). (gr. 5-18). 16.95 (978-1-59990-121-3(8), 9781599901213, Bloomsbury USA Childrens) Bloomsbury Publishing USA.

Reger, Rob & Gruner, Jessica. Dark Times. Reger, Rob & Parker, Buzz, illus. 2011. (Emily the Strange Ser.: 3). (ENG.). 248p. (YA). (gr. 8). pap. 8.99 (978-0-06-145237-6(8)) HarperCollins Pubs.

Reid, Kate. Operation Timewarp. 2003. 195p. pap. (978-1-84255-203-2(1), Orion Children's Bks.) Hachette Children's Group.

Reinhardt, Dana. Odessa Again. 2013. (ENG., Illus.). 208p. (J). (gr. 3-7). 15.99 (978-0-385-73956-6(7), Lamb, Wendy Bks.) Random Hse. Children's Bks.

Reiss, Kathryn. Paint by Magic. 2003. (ENG.). 288p. (J). (gr. 5-7). pap. 17.95 (978-0-15-204925-6(8)) Houghton Mifflin Harcourt Publishing Co.

—Paint by Magic. 2003. (Time Travel Mysteries Ser.). 271p. (J). (gr. 5). 14.60 (978-0-7569-4210-6(1)) Perfection Learning Corp.

—Pale Phoenix. 2003. (ENG., Illus.). 336p. (J). (gr. 5-7). pap. 15.95 (978-0-15-204927-0(4)) Houghton Mifflin Harcourt Publishing Co.

Revealed. 2014. (Missing Ser.: 7). (ENG., Illus.). 448p. (J). (gr. 3-7). 18.99 (978-1-4169-8986-8(2), Simon & Schuster Bks. For Young Readers) Simon & Schuster Bks. For Young Readers.

Richards, Justin. Rewind Assassin. 2007. (Time Runners Ser.: 2). (ENG.). 208p. (J). (gr. 4-7). pap. 8.99 (978-1-4169-2643-6(7)) Simon & Schuster, Ltd. GBR. Dist: Simon & Schuster, Inc.

Richardson, J. J. It's about Time. 2008. (ENG.). 92p. pap. 12.99 (978-1-4196-5707-8(0)) CreateSpace Independent Publishing Platform.

Riddleburger, Sam & Michael Hemphill. Stonewall Hinkleman & the Battle of Bull Run. 2014. lib. bdg. 18.40 (978-0-606-35709-8(2)) Turtleback Bks.

Riggs, Ransom. Library of Souls. 2015. (Miss Peregrine's Peculiar Children Ser.: Bk. 3). (ENG., Illus.). 464p. (YA). (gr. 9). 18.99 (978-1-59474-758-8(X)) Quirk Bks.

—Library of Souls. 2017. (Miss Peregrine's Peculiar Children Ser.: 3). (ENG.). (YA). (gr. 9). lib. bdg. 23.30 **(978-0-606-39808-4(2))** Turtleback Bks.

Riley, Lehman & Austin, Megan. The Life of Babe Didrikson: "Greatness Is Never Forgotten" Wallace, Joshua, illus. 2005. 47p. (J). pap. (978-0-9760523-2-6(6)) Matter of Africa America Time.

Riley, Lehman C. Meeting Dr. Martin Luther King. 2004. (Adventures of Papa Lemon's Little Wanderers Ser.: Bk. 1). 35p. (978-0-9760523-0-2(X)) Matter of Africa America Time.

Rits, Susan Katherine. The Pirates of Bair Island. 2013. 234p. pap. 12.99 (978-0-9894891-1-9(6)) Imprint.li.

Rocan, Susan. Withershins. 2008. (Spirit Quest Ser.: 1). (ENG.). 225p. (YA). (gr. 12-14). pap. 14.95 (978-1-894283-75-5(9)) Great Plains Pubns. CAN. Dist: Publishers Group Canada.

Rogers, Gregory. The Hero of Little Street. Rogers, Gregory, illus. 2012. (ENG., Illus.). 32p. (J). (gr. k-3). 17.99 (978-1-59643-729-6(4), 9781596437296) Roaring Brook Pr.

Rose, John. Wikker. 2007. 248p. pap. 17.95 (978-1-4303-1523-0(7)) Lulu Pr., Inc.

Rose, Simon. The Sorcerer's Letterbox, 1 vol. 2004. (ENG., Illus.). 114p. (J). (gr. 4-6). per. 7.95 (978-1-896580-52-4(1)) Tradewind Bks. CAN. Dist: Orca Bk. Pubs. USA.

—The Time Camera, 1 vol. 2012. (ENG., Illus.). 96p. (J). (gr. 3-6). pap. 9.95 (978-1-896580-09-8(2)) Tradewind Bks. CAN. Dist: Orca Bk. Pubs. USA.

Rosenow, Ty. The Historical Adventures of Thomas Balfour. 2012. 186p. pap. 17.95 (978-1-105-94011-8(X)) Lulu Pr., Inc.

Rowley, M'lin. The Silver Coat. 2009. (Knights of Right Ser.: Bk. 2). 71p. (J). (gr. 1-5). pap. 6.99 (978-1-60641-104-9(7), Shadow Mountain) Shadow Mountain Publishing.

Rowleym'Lin. Knights of Right, BK 3: The Warrior's Guard. 2010. 80p. (J). pap. 6.99 (978-1-60641-240-4(X), Shadow Mountain) Shadow Mountain Publishing.

Ruby, Anne. Children of the Sea. Meier, Ty, illus. 2007. (YA). per. (978-0-9787881-0-0(9)) Seachild.

Ryan, Carrie. Divide & Conquer. (Infinity Ring Ser.: 2). (ENG.). 192p. (J). (gr. 3-7). 2015. pap. 6.99 (978-0-545-90017-1(4)) 2012. 16.99 (978-0-545-48455-8(3)) 2012. 12.99 (978-0-545-38697-5(7)) Scholastic, Inc.

Sabuda, Robert. Uh-Oh, Leonardo! The Adventures of Providence Traveler. Sabuda, Robert, illus. 2007. (ENG., Illus.). 48p. (J). (gr. k-3). 12.99 (978-1-4169-6164-2(X), Aladdin) Simon & Schuster Children's Publishing.

Sage, Angie. Physik. Zug, Mark, illus. (Septimus Heap Ser.: 3). (ENG.). (J). (gr. 4-7). 2007. 560p. 17.99 (978-0-06-057737-7(1))Bk. 3. 2008. 576p. pap. 7.99 (978-0-06-057739-1(8)) HarperCollins Pubs. (Tegen, Katherine Bks).

—Physik, 11 vols. 2007. (Septimus Heap Ser.: 3). (J). (SPA.). 131.75 (978-1-4281-4582-5(6)); 133.75 (978-1-4281-4580-1(X)); 113.75 (978-1-4281-4576-4(1)); 1.25 (978-1-4281-4573-3(7)); 277.75 (978-1-4281-4577-1(X)); 111.75 (978-1-4281-4578-8(8)) Recorded Bks., Inc.

—Physik. 2008. (Septimus Heap Ser.: 3). (J). lib. bdg. 18.40 (978-1-4178-1565-4(5), Turtleback) Turtleback Bks.

—Queste. Zug, Mark, illus. (Septimus Heap Ser.: 4). (ENG.). (J). (gr. 4). 2009. 624p. pap. 7.99 (978-0-06-088209-9(3)) 2008. 608p. 17.99 (978-0-06-088207-5(7)) HarperCollins Pubs. (Tegen, Katherine Bks).

—Queste. Zug, Mark, illus. 2009. (Septimus Heap Ser.: 4). 596p. (J). lib. bdg. 18.40 (978-0-606-02607-9(X), Turtleback) Turtleback Bks.

Sales, Leila. Once Was a Time: An Alliteration Adventure. 2016. (ENG., Illus.). 272p. (J). (gr. 5-17). 16.99 (978-1-4521-4009-4(X)) Chronicle Bks. LLC.

Sargent, Alan E. Fortitude: The Adventures of the Esteem Team. Wade, Jerry, illus. 2013. 84p. pap. 10.95 (978-1-62516-984-6(1), Strategic Bk. Publishing) Strategic Book Publishing & Rights Agency (SBPRA).

Saunders, Kate. Beswitched. 2012. (ENG.). 272p. (J). (gr. 4-7). 7.99 (978-0-375-87329-4(5), Yearling) Random Hse. Children's Bks.

—The Curse of the Chocolate Phoenix: A Companion to the Whizz Pop Chocolate Shop. 2015. (ENG.). 272p. (J). (gr. 5). 19.99 (978-0-375-99183-7(2), Delacorte Bks. for Young Readers) Random Hse. Children's Bks.

Savage, Jeffrey S. The Fourth Nephite: Return to Palmyra, Bk. 2. 2011. audio compact disk 29.99 (978-1-60908-073-0(4)) Deseret Bk. Co.

Scieszka, Jon. Da Wild, Da Crazy, Da Vinci. McCauley, Adam, illus. 2006. (Time Warp Trio Ser.: No. 14). 72p. (gr. 4-7). 15.00 (978-0-7569-6677-5(9)) Perfection Learning Corp.

—The Good, the Bad, & the Goofy. Smith, Lane, illus. 2005. (Time Warp Trio Ser.: No. 3). 70p. (gr. 4-7). 15.00 (978-0-7569-5876-3(8)) Perfection Learning Corp.

—Hey Kid, Want to Buy a Bridge? McCauley, Adam, illus. 2005. (Time Warp Trio Ser.: No. 11). 74p. (gr. 4-7). 15.00 (978-0-7569-5988-3(8)) Perfection Learning Corp.

—It's All Greek to Me. Smith, Lane, illus. 2006. (Time Warp Trio Ser.: No. 8). 71p. (gr. 4-7). 15.00 (978-0-7569-6780-2(5)) Perfection Learning Corp.

—Marco? Polo!, No. 16. McCauley, Adam, illus. 2008. (Time Warp Trio Ser.: 16). (ENG.). 96p. (J). (gr. 2-4). 5.99 (978-0-14-241177-3(9), Puffin Books) Penguin Young Readers Group.

—Marco? Polo! McCauley, Adam, illus. 2008. (Time Warp Trio Ser.: No. 16). 90p. (J). (gr. 4-6). 12.65 (978-0-7569-8923-1(X)) Perfection Learning Corp.

—Me Oh Maya. McCauley, Adam, illus. 2005. (Time Warp Trio Ser.: 13). (ENG.). 96p. (J). (gr. 2-4). 5.99 (978-0-14-240300-6(8), Puffin Books) Penguin Young Readers Group.

—Me Oh Maya. McCauley, Adam, illus. 2005. (Time Warp Trio Ser.: No. 13). 69p. (gr. 2-6). 15.00 (978-0-7569-5060-6(0)) Perfection Learning Corp.

—Oh Say, I Can't See, No. 15. McCauley, Adam, illus. 2007. (Time Warp Trio Ser.: 15). (ENG.). 80p. (J). (gr. 2-4). 5.99 (978-0-14-240808-7(5), Puffin Books) Penguin Young Readers Group.

—El Pirata Barbanegra. Smith, Lane, illus. (SPA.). (J). (gr. 5-8). 7.95 (978-958-04-3401-6(8), NR8584) Norma S.A. COL. Dist: Distribuidora Norma, Inc., Lectorum Pubns., Inc.

—Sam Samurai. McCauley, Adam, illus. 2004. (Time Warp Trio Ser.: 10). (ENG.). 96p. (J). (gr. 2-4). pap. 5.99 (978-0-14-240088-3(2), Puffin Books) Penguin Young Readers Group.

—Sam Samurai. McCauley, Adam, illus. 2006. (Time Warp Trio Ser.: No. 10). 85p. (gr. 4-7). 15.00 (978-0-7569-6779-6(1)) Perfection Learning Corp.

—See You Later, Gladiator. McCauley, Adam, illus. 2004. (Time Warp Trio Ser.: 9). (ENG.). 96p. (J). (gr. 2-4). pap. 5.99 (978-0-14-240117-0(X), Puffin Books) Penguin Young Readers Group.

—See You Later, Gladiator. McCauley, Adam, illus. 2004. (Time Warp Trio Ser.: No. 9). 87p. (J). (gr. 4-7). 12.65 (978-0-7569-5986-9(1)) Perfection Learning Corp.

—Tut, Tut. Smith, Lane, illus. 2004. (Time Warp Trio Ser.: No. 6). 74p. (gr. 4-7). 15.00 (978-0-7569-4050-8(8)) Perfection Learning Corp.

—Viking It & Liking It. McCauley, Adam, illus. 2004. (Time Warp Trio Ser.: 12). (ENG.). 96p. (J). (gr. 2-4). pap. 5.99 (978-0-14-240002-9(5), Puffin Books) Penguin Young Readers Group.

—Viking It & Liking It. McCauley, Adam, illus. 2004. (Time Warp Trio Ser.: No. 12). 73p. (gr. 2-6). 15.00 (978-0-7569-2589-5(4)) Perfection Learning Corp.

—Viking It & Liking It. 2004. (Time Warp Trio Ser.: 12). 16.00 (978-1-4176-3613-6(0), Turtleback) Turtleback Bks.

—Your Mother Was a Neanderthal. Smith, Lane, illus. 2004. (Time Warp Trio Ser.: 4). (ENG.). 80p. (J). (gr. 2-4). pap. 5.99 (978-0-14-240048-7(3), Puffin Books) Penguin Young Readers Group.

—Your Mother Was a Neanderthal. Smith, Lane, illus. 2006. (Time Warp Trio Ser.: No. 4). 78p. (gr. 4-7). 15.00 *(978-0-7569-6782-6(1))* Perfection Learning Corp.

—Your Mother Was a Neanderthal. Smith, Lane, illus. 2004. (Time Warp Trio Ser.: 4). 78p. (J). 16.00 *(978-1-4176-3603-7(3))* Turtleback Bks.

—2095. Smith, Lane, illus. 2004. (Time Warp Trio Ser.: 5). (ENG.). 80p. (J). (gr. 2-4). pap. 5.99 *(978-0-14-240044-9(0),* Puffin Books) Penguin Young Readers Group.

—2095. Smith, Lane, illus. 2005. (Time Warp Trio Ser.: No. 5). 72p. (gr. 4-7). 15.00 *(978-0-7569-5989-0(6))* Perfection Learning Corp.

Seegert, Scott. Vordak the Incomprehensible: Time Travel Trouble. Martin, John, illus. 2013. (Vordak the Incomprehensible Ser.). (ENG.). 192p. (J). (gr. 5). 13.99 *(978-0-60684-461-8(X),* Darby Creek) Lerner Publishing Group.

Seven, John. The Alchemist War, 1 vol. Phillips, Craig, illus. 2013. (Time-Tripping Faradays Ser.). (ENG.). 160p. (gr. 4-5). 9.95 *(978-1-62370-011-9(6));* (YA). pap. 5.95 *(978-1-4342-6438-1(6));* (gr. 4-5). lib. bdg. 26.65 *(978-1-4342-6028-4(3))* Stone Arch Bks.

—The Dragon of Rome, 1 vol. Phillips, Craig, illus. 2013. (Time-Tripping Faradays Ser.). (ENG.). 160p. (gr. 4-5). 9.95 *(978-1-62370-012-6(4));* lib. bdg. 26.65 *(978-1-4342-6029-1(1))* Stone Arch Bks.

—The Outlaw of Sherwood Forest, 1 vol. Hans, Stephanie, illus. 2014. (Time-Tripping Faradays Ser.). (ENG.). 192p. (gr. 4-5). lib. bdg. 26.65 *(978-1-4342-9174-5(X))* Stone Arch Bks.

—The Terror of the Tengu, 1 vol. Hans, Stephanie, illus. 2014. (Time-Tripping Faradays Ser.). (ENG.). 192p. (gr. 4-5). 26.65 *(978-1-4342-9173-8(1))* Stone Arch Bks.

—The Time-Tripping Faradays. Phillips, Craig, illus. 2013. (Time-Tripping Faradays Ser.). (ENG.). 160p. (gr. 4-5). 53.30 *(978-1-4342-8994-0(X))* Stone Arch Bks.

Seven, John & Phillips, Craig. The Dragon of Rome, 1 vol. 2013. (ENG.). 160p. (YA). pap. *(978-1-4342-6439-8(4))* Stone Arch Bks.

Shapiro, David R. Blunderbuss Wanderlust: Being an Account of the Temporal Travels of Colonel Victor Von Vector & the Eras of His Ways. Herndon, Christopher, illus. 2nd ed. 2016. (ENG.). 44p. (J). (gr. 4-7). 14.99 *(978-1-940052-13-7(0))* Craigmore Creations.

—Terra Tempo: The Four Corners of Time. Herndon, Christopher, illus. 2013. (Terra Tempo Ser.). (ENG.). 264p. (J). pap. 17.99 *(978-0-9844422-6-3(X))* Craigmore Creations.

—Terra Tempo Vol. 3: The Academy of Planetary Evolution. Herndon, Christopher, illus. 2014. (Terra Tempo Ser.). (ENG.). 182p. (J). (gr. 2-4). pap. 17.99 *(978-1-940052-09-0(2))* Craigmore Creations.

Shaw, Alexander William. The Adventures of A Teenage Time Traveller. 2009. 84p. pap., pap. 12.95 *(978-0-9561592-2-9(2))* Hetman Publishing GBR. Dist: Lulu Pr., Inc.

Shay, Michael K. A Flash in Time: A Novel. 2016. (J). pap. *(978-1-63293-141-2(9))* Sunstone Pr.

Sheley, Kristen. Partners in Time #4: Family Matters. 2008. 216p. pap. 15.95 *(978-0-595-51850-0(8))* iUniverse, Inc.

—Partners in Time #5: A Change of Course. 2010. 236p. 25.95 *(978-1-4502-6658-1(4));* pap. 15.95 *(978-1-4502-6657-4(6))* iUniverse, Inc.

Sherry, Kevin. Monsters on the Run. 2015. (Yeti Files Ser.: 2). (ENG., Illus.). 128p. (J). (gr. 2-5). 8.99 *(978-0-545-55619-4(8),* Scholastic Pr.) Scholastic, Inc.

Silverthorne, Judith. Dinosaur Breakout, 1 vol. 2004. (Dinosaur Adventure Ser.). (ENG.). 208p. (J). (gr. 4-7). pap. 6.95 *(978-1-55050-294-7(8))* Coteau Bks. CAN. Dist: Orca Bk. Pubs. USA.

—The Secret of Sentinel Rock. 2007. (From Many Peoples Ser.). (Illus.). 159p. (J). (gr. 3-5). per. *(978-1-55050-386-9(3))* Coteau Bks.

—The Secret of the Stone House, 1 vol. 2005. (From Many Peoples Ser.). (ENG., Illus.). 224p. (J). (gr. 4-7). pap. 7.95 *(978-1-55050-325-8(1))* Coteau Bks. CAN. Dist: Orca Bk. Pubs. USA.

Simonds, Kevin. The Tomb of Father Time. 2011. 178p. pap. 24.95 *(978-1-4626-2739-4(0))* America Star Bks.

Smith, Greg Leitich. Borrowed Time. 2015. (ENG., Illus.). 192p. (J). (gr. 5-7). 16.99 *(978-0-544-23711-7(0))* Houghton Mifflin Harcourt Publishing Co.

—Chronal Engine. Henry, Blake, illus. 2013. (ENG.). 192p. (J). (gr. 5-7). pap. 6.99 *(978-0-544-02277-5(7))* Houghton Mifflin Harcourt Publishing Co.

Smith, Lindsay. A Darkly Beating Heart. 2016. (ENG.). 272p. (YA). 17.99 *(978-1-62672-044-2(4),* 9781626720442) Roaring Brook Pr.

Smith, Molly. Border Breakdown: The Fall of the Berlin Wall. 2011. (ENG.). (J). 9.95 *(978-1-60727-113-0(3))* Soundprints.

Snider, Cindy Gay. Finding Anna Bee. Chambers, Mary, illus. 2007. 163p. (J). (gr. 3-7). per. 9.99 *(978-0-8361-9392-3(X))* Herald Pr.

Solice, Deborah. The Eye of the Undead: The Hidden Channel: an Adventure Series in Time. l.t. ed. 2005. (ENG., Illus.). 100p. (J). per. 7.59 *(978-1-933300-01-6(9))* Wandering Sage Pubns., LLC.

Sommer, Carl. Fast Forward. Budwine, Greg, illus. 2009. (Quest for Success Ser.). (ENG.). 56p. (YA). pap. 4.95 *(978-1-57537-277-8(0));* lib. bdg. 12.95 *(978-1-57537-252-5(5))* Advance Publishing, Inc.

—Fast Forward(Avance Acelarado) Budwine, Greg, illus. 2009. (Quest for Success Bilingual Ser.). (SPA & ENG.). 104p. (YA). lib. bdg. 14.95 *(978-1-57537-227-3(4))* Advance Publishing, Inc.

—Time Remote! Budwine, Greg, illus. 2014. (J). pap. *(978-1-57537-970-8(8))* Advance Publishing, Inc.

—Time Remote! 2003. (Another Sommer-Time Story Ser.). (Illus.). 48p. (J). (gr. 1-4). 16.95 incl. audio *(978-1-57537-561-8(3))* Advance Publishing, Inc.

—Time Remote! Budwine, Greg, illus. 2003. (Another Sommer-Time Story Ser.). (ENG.). 48p. (J). (gr. 1-4). 16.95 incl. audio compact disk *(978-1-57537-512-0(5))* Advance Publishing, Inc.

—Time Remote!(El Control Del Tiempo!) Budwine, Greg, illus. 2009. (Another Sommer-Time Story Bilingual Ser.). (SPA & ENG.). 48p. (J). lib. bdg. 16.95 *(978-1-57537-170-2(7))* Advance Publishing, Inc.

Soup, Cuthbert. Another Whole Nother Story. Timmins, Jeffrey Stewart, illus. (Whole Nother Story Ser.). (ENG.). (YA). (gr. 3-6). 2012. 320p. pap. 7.99 *(978-1-59990-737-6(2),* 9781599907376) 2010. 304p. 16.99 *(978-1-59990-436-8(5),* 9781599904368) Bloomsbury Publishing USA. (Bloomsbury USA Childrens).

—No Other Story. (Whole Nother Story Ser.). (ENG., Illus.). 256p. (YA). (gr. 3-6). 2013. pap. 7.99 *(978-1-61963-120-5(2),* 9781619631205) 2012. 16.99 *(978-1-59990-824-3(7),* 9781599908243) Bloomsbury Publishing USA. (Bloomsbury USA Childrens).

Specter, Baron. Chasing Whales Aboard the Charles W. Morgan, 1 vol., Bk. 2. Evans, Dustin, illus. 2010. (Ghostly Graphic Adventures Ser.). (ENG.). 32p. (gr. 4-6). 28.50 *(978-1-60270-771-9(5),* Graphic Planet- Fiction) ABDO Publishing Co.

—Dodging Danger on the Dartmouth, 1 vol., Bk. 1. Evans, Dustin, illus. 2010. (Ghostly Graphic Adventures Ser.). (ENG.). 32p. (J). (gr. 3-6). 28.50 *(978-1-60270-770-2(7))* ABDO Publishing Co.

—The Lighthouse of Terror, 1 vol., Bk. 3. Evans, Dustin, illus. 2010. (Ghostly Graphic Adventures Ser.). (ENG.). 32p. (J). (gr. 3-6). 28.50 *(978-1-60270-772-6(3))* ABDO Publishing Co.

Stanchfield, Justin. Timewalker. 2011. (Fiction Ser.). 330p. (J). pap. 5.99 *(978-0-7945-3032-7(X),* Usborne) EDC Publishing.

Stanley, Diane. Thanksgiving on Plymouth Plantation. Berry, Holly, illus. 2004. (Time-Traveling Twins Ser.). (ENG.). 48p. (J). (gr. k-5). 16.99 *(978-0-06-027069-8(1))* HarperCollins Pubs.

Stanton, Angie. Waking in Time. 2017. (ENG.). 360p. (gr. 9-12). 17.95 *(978-1-63079-070-7(2))* Switch Pr.

Starobinets, Anna. Catlantis. Bugaeva, Jane, tr. from RUS. Klimowski, Andrzej, illus. 2016. (ENG.). 136p. (J). (gr. 3-7). 16.95 *(978-1-68137-000-2(X),* NYR Children's Collection) New York Review of Bks., Inc., The.

Steinkraus, Kyla. Dessert with Daniel Boone. 2016. (Time Hop Sweets Shop Ser.). (ENG.). 32p. (gr. k-3). 25.65 *(978-1-68191-373-5(9))* Rourke Educational Media.

Stewart, Dianne C. Quimbaya. 2008. (ENG.). 200p. (gr. 1-18). pap. 8.95 *(978-0-9667359-8-7(6),* BeanPole Bks.) Harren Communications, LLC.

Stewart, Yale. Escape from Future World!, 1 vol. Stewart, Yale, illus. 2014. (Amazing Adventures of Superman! Ser.). (ENG., Illus.). 32p. (gr. k-2). lib. bdg. 25.32 *(978-1-4795-5732-5(3),* DC Super Heroes) Stone Arch Bks.

Stilton, Geronimo. Back in Time. 2015. (Geronimo Stilton Special Edition: the Journey Through Time Ser.: 2). (ENG.). 320p. (J). (gr. 2-5). 14.99 *(978-0-545-74618-2(3),* Scholastic Paperbacks) Scholastic, Inc.

—Journey Through Time. 2014. (Geronimo Stilton Special Edition Ser.). (ENG.). 320p. (J). (gr. 2-5). 14.99 *(978-0-545-55623-1(6),* Scholastic Paperbacks) Scholastic, Inc.

—The Race Against Time: The Third Journey Through Time. 2016. (Geronimo Stilton Journey Through Time Ser.: 3). (ENG.). 320p. (J). (gr. 2-5). 14.99 *(978-0-545-87241-6(3),* Scholastic Paperbacks) Scholastic, Inc.

Stilton, Geronimo, et al. The Journey Through Time. 2014. (Illus.). 94p. (J). *(978-0-545-61129-9(6))* Scholastic, Inc.

Stokes, Jordan & Belinkie, Matt. Gilded Delirium. 2007. (YA). pap. *(978-1-4114-9670-5(1),* Spark Publishing Group) Sterling Publishing Co., Inc.

Strasser, Todd. Abe Lincoln for Class President. 2010. 144p. pap. 10.95 *(978-1-4502-1244-1(1))* iUniverse, Inc.

Stuart, Raff. A Roman Odyssey: Book One of the chronicles of Adam Black the Teenage Time Traveller. 2009. 228p. pap. 14.49 *(978-1-4389-7407-1(8))* AuthorHouse.

Sullivan, Michael John & Petrone, Susan. The Sockkids Meet Lincoln. 2013. 42p. pap. 10.99 *(978-0-9727077-7-0(8))* Scribe Publishing.

Suphandagi, Lale. The Dream Bird. 2013. (ENG., Illus.). 54p. (J). (gr. k-1). pap. 9.95 *(978-1-59784-282-2(6))* Tughra Bks.

Sutherland, Tui T. So This Is How It Ends. 2006. (Avatars Ser.: Bk. 1). 353p. (YA). (gr. 7-12). 16.99 *(978-0-06-075024-4(3),* Eos) HarperCollins Pubs.

Swindells, Robert. In the Nick of Time. 2008. (ENG.). 224p. (YA). (gr. 7-18). 12.99 *(978-0-552-55585-2(1))* Transworld Publishers Ltd. GBR. Dist: Independent Pubs. Group.

—Timesnatch. Riley, Jon, illus. 2008. (ENG.). 176p. (YA). (gr. 7). pap. 12.99 *(978-0-552-55592-0(4),* Corgi) Transworld Publishers Ltd. GBR. Dist: Independent Pubs. Group.

Tanigawa, Nagaru. The Intrigues of Haruhi Suzumiya. 2012. (Haruhi Suzumiya Ser.: 7). (ENG.). 288p. (YA). (gr. 10-17). 15.99 *(978-0-316-03895-9(4));* pap. 18.00 *(978-0-316-03896-6(2))* Little, Brown Bks. for Young Readers.

Taylor, Janet B. Into the Dim. 2016. (ENG.). 432p. (YA). (gr. 9). 17.99 *(978-0-544-60200-7(5),* HMH Books For Young Readers) Houghton Mifflin Harcourt Publishing Co.

—Sparks of Light. 2017. (ENG.). 448p. (YA). (gr. 9). 16.99 *(978-0-544-60957-0(3),* HMH Books For Young Readers) Houghton Mifflin Harcourt Publishing Co.

Taylor, Thomas. Haunters. 2013. 327p. (J). *(978-0-545-50253-5(3))* Scholastic, Inc.

Terrell, Brandon. Grit & Gold. Max, Iman & Garcia, Eduardo, illus. 2016. (Time Machine Magazine Ser.). (ENG.). 128p. (gr. 3-4). lib. bdg. 22.65 *(978-1-4965-2597-0(3))* Capstone Press of Coughlan Cos.

—Pluck & Perfection. Max, Iman, illus. 2016. (Time Machine Magazine Ser.). (ENG.). 128p. (gr. 3-4). lib. bdg. 22.65 *(978-1-4965-2595-6(7))* Capstone Press of Coughlan Cos.

—Time Machine Magazine. 2016. (Time Machine Magazine Ser.). (ENG.). 128p. (gr. 3-4). 90.60 *(978-1-4965-2742-4(9))* Capstone Press of Coughlan Cos.

—Valor & Victory. Max, Iman, illus. 2016. (Time Machine Magazine Ser.). (ENG.). 128p. (gr. 3-4). lib. bdg. 22.65 *(978-1-4965-2594-9(9))* Capstone Press of Coughlan Cos.

Terrill, Cristin. All Our Yesterdays. 2014. (All Our Yesterdays Ser.). (ENG.). 368p. (YA). (gr. 7-12). pap. 9.99 *(978-1-4231-8524-6(2))* Hyperion Bks. for Children.

—All Our Yesterdays. 2013. (All Our Yesterdays Ser.). (ENG.). 368p. (YA). (gr. 7-12). 17.99 *(978-1-4231-7637-4(5))* Hyperion Pr.

A Theft in Time: Timedetectors II, 6 Pack. (Action Packs Ser.). 120p. (gr. 3-5). 44.00 *(978-0-7635-8425-2(8))* Rigby Education.

There's No Room for You, Maddie Morrison. 2006. (J). per. 6.99 *(978-0-9786117-0-5(5))* Neal Morgan Publishing.

Thompson, Lisa. In Search of the Egyptian Queen. Cantell, Brenda, illus. 2006. (Treasure Trackers Ser.). 80p. (J). (gr. 3-4). lib. bdg. 19.00 *(978-0-7910-8874-6(X))* Facts On File, Inc.

Thorne, Bella. Autumn's Wish. (ENG.). 320p. (YA). (gr. 7). 2017. pap. 9.99 ***(978-0-385-74438-6(2),*** Ember) 2016. 18.99 *(978-0-385-74437-9(4),* Delacorte Pr.) Random Hse. Children's Bks.

Thorne MBE, Tony. The junior philosophical Society. 2007. 114p. pap. 12.95 *(978-1-4116-9623-5(9))* Lulu Pr., Inc.

Time, Nicholas O. Going, Going, Gone. 2016. (In Due Time Ser.: 1). (ENG., Illus.). 160p. (J). (gr. 3-7). pap. 6.99 *(978-1-4814-6729-2(8),* Simon Spotlight) Simon Spotlight.

—Going, Going, Gone. 2016. (In Due Time Ser.: 1). lib. bdg. 17.20 *(978-0-606-38985-3(7))* Turtleback Bks.

Time Slime. 2003. 156p. (YA). (gr. 5-12). pap. 7.95 *(978-0-9702176-3-9(3),* 0004) Night Howl Productions.

Tomasi-Dubois, Mary. Danger in the Jeweled City: A Matt & Heather Thriller. 2007. 188p. (YA). per. 15.95 *(978-0-9798633-5-6(X))* Robertson Publishing.

Torres, J. Charge of the Army Eternal, 1 vol. Davis, Dan & Suriano, Andy, illus. 2013. (Batman: the Brave & the Bold Ser.). (ENG.). 32p. (gr. 2-3). 22.60 *(978-1-4342-4706-3(6))* Stone Arch Bks.

Triana, Gaby. Summer of Yesterday. 2014. (ENG., Illus.). 272p. (YA). (gr. 9). pap. 9.99 *(978-1-4814-0130-2(0),* Simon Pulse) Simon Pulse.

Trine, Greg. The Brotherhood of the Traveling Underpants. 2009. (Melvin Beederman Superhero Ser.: 7). (J). lib. bdg. 19.65 *(978-0-606-01751-0(8),* Turtleback) Turtleback Bks.

—Pinkbeard's Revenge. Dormer, Frank W., illus. (Adventures of Jo Schmo Ser.: 4). (ENG.). 128p. (J). (gr. 1-4). 2015. pap. 5.99 *(978-0-544-45601-3(7),* HMH Books For Young Readers) 2013. 12.99 *(978-0-547-80797-3(X))* Houghton Mifflin Harcourt Publishing Co.

—Wyatt Burp Rides Again. Dormer, Frank W., illus. 2014. (Adventures of Jo Schmo Ser.: 2). (ENG.). 112p. (J). (gr. 1-4). pap. 5.99 *(978-0-544-01899-0(0),* HMH Books For Young Readers) Houghton Mifflin Harcourt Publishing Co.

Turetsky, Bianca. The Time-Traveling Fashionista on Board the Titanic. 2012. (Time-Traveling Fashionista Ser.: 1). (ENG.). 272p. (J). (gr. 3-7). pap. 12.99 *(978-0-316-10544-6(9),* Poppy) Little, Brown Bks. for Young Readers.

Valentine, James. The Future Is Unknown. 2007. (TimeJumpers Ser.: 3). (ENG.). 288p. (J). (gr. 3-7). pap. 13.99 *(978-0-689-87354-6(9),* Aladdin) Simon & Schuster Children's Publishing.

—The Present Never Happens. 2007. (TimeJumpers Ser.: 2). (ENG.). 304p. (J). (gr. 3-7). pap. 13.99 *(978-1-4169-3956-6(3),* Simon & Schuster/Paula Wiseman Bks.) Simon & Schuster/Paula Wiseman Bks.

Vande Velde, Vivian. A Well-Timed Enchantment. 2006. (ENG., Illus.). 240p. (J). (gr. 5-7). pap. 13.95 *(978-0-15-204919-5(3))* Houghton Mifflin Harcourt Publishing Co.

—23 Minutes. 2016. (ENG.). 176p. (J). (gr. 6-10). 16.95 *(978-1-62979-441-9(4))* Boyds Mills Pr.

Vaupel, Robin. Rules of the Universe. 2007. (ENG.). 192p. (J). (gr. 3-7). 16.95 *(978-0-8234-1811-4(1))* Holiday Hse., Inc.

VIZ Media Staff & Straffi, Iginio. WINX Club, Vol. 6. 2013. (ENG.). 96p. (J). pap. 6.99 *(978-1-4215-4203-4(X))* Viz Media.

Walker, Rysa. Timebound, 0 vols. 2014. (Chronos Files Ser.: 1). (ENG.). 374p. (YA). (gr. 7-12). pap. 14.95 *(978-1-4778-4815-9(0),* 9781477848159) Amazon Publishing.

—Time's Divide, 0 vols. 2015. (Chronos Files Ser.: 3). (ENG.). 543p. (YA). (gr. 7-12). pap. 12.95 *(978-1-5039-4658-3(4),* 9781503946583, Skyscape) Amazon Publishing.

—Time's Edge, 0 vols. 2014. (Chronos Files Ser.: 2). (ENG.). 450p. (J). (gr. 7-12). pap. 9.99 *(978-1-4778-2582-2(7),* 9781477825822, Skyscape) Amazon Publishing.

Waring, Scott C. West's Time MacHine. 2007. 200p. 24.95 *(978-0-595-88775-0(9));* per. 14.95 *(978-0-595-41887-9(2))* iUniverse, Inc.

Wartik, David J. The VonNesta Project: Camp Fingerlake. 2007. 148p. per. 13.95 *(978-1-60145-394-5(9))* Booklocker.com, Inc.

Wayne, Matt. Menace of the Time Thief, 1 vol. Suriano, Andy & Davis, Dan W., illus. 2012. (Batman: the Brave & the Bold Ser.). (ENG.). 32p. (gr. 2-3). lib. bdg. 22.60 *(978-1-4342-4548-9(9))* Stone Arch Bks.

Welford, Ross. Time Traveling with a Hamster. 2016. (ENG.). 432p. (J). (gr. 3-7). 16.99 *(978-0-399-55149-9(2),* Schwartz & Wade Bks.) Random Hse. Children's Bks.

Wells, H. G. The Time Machine. 2008. (Bring the Classics to Life Ser.). (Illus.). 72p. (gr. 4-12). pap., act. bk. ed. 10.95 *(978-0-931334-43-6(8),* EDCTR-403B) EDCON Publishing Group.

—The Time Machine. 2004. (Fast Track Classics Ser.). (Illus.). 48p. (J). pap. *(978-0-237-52406-7(6))* Evans Brothers, Ltd.

—The Time Machine. Howell, Troy, illus. 2008. (Classic Starts(tm) Ser.). (ENG.). 160p. (J). (gr. 2-4). 6.95 *(978-1-4027-4582-9(6))* Sterling Publishing Co., Inc.

—The Time Machine. Edens, John, illus. 2005. (Reader's Workshop Ser.). (ENG.). 80p. (C). pap. 17.95 *(978-0-7362-2790-2(3))* CENGAGE Learning.

—The Time Machine, 1 vol. 2010. (Illustrated Classics Ser.). (ENG., Illus.). 64p. (YA). (gr. 9-12). per. 9.95 *(978-1-56254-944-2(8))* Saddleback Educational Publishing, Inc.

Wesley, Mary. Haphazard House. Date not set. (Sky Bks.). 200p. pap. 54.75 *(978-0-582-08108-6(4))* Addison-Wesley Longman, Ltd. GBR. Dist: Trans-Atlantic Pubns., Inc.

Weston, Greg. Charlie Cornwall & the Historymakers. 2011. 460p. pap. 25.50 *(978-1-4467-8713-7(3))* Lulu Pr., Inc.

Weston, Martha. Dr. Clock-Sicle: A Holiday House Reader, Level 1. (ENG., Illus.). 32p. (J). (gr. k-3). tchr. ed. 14.95 *(978-0-8234-1825-1(1))* Holiday Hse., Inc.

White, Andrea. Windows on the World. 2011. 238p. (J). 18.95 *(978-1-60898-105-2(3));* pap. 9.95 *(978-1-60898-106-9(1))* namelos llc.

Whitler, Larry. Oreo & Braun XOB the Full Circle Quest. 2007. 207p. pap. 14.95 *(978-1-4116-6080-9(3))* Lulu Pr., Inc.

Whitman, Emily. Wildwing. 2010. (ENG.). 368p. (YA). (gr. 8-18). 16.99 *(978-0-06-172452-7(1),* Greenwillow Bks.) HarperCollins Pubs.

Wickham, Martha. Mysterious Journey. 2011. (ENG.). 32p. (J). 9.95 *(978-1-60727-179-6(6))* Soundprints.

Williams, Carol Lynch & Earl, Cheri Pray. Wizard of Menlo Park, New Jersey. Oliphant, Manelle, illus. 2014. (Just in Time Ser.). (ENG.). 140p. (J). pap. 9.95 *(978-1-938301-77-3(3))* Familius LLC.

Williams, David Morgan. Xcalibur, Merlin & the Teeth of the Dragon. 2015. (ENG.). 160p. (J). pap. 13.00 *(978-1-84771-823-5(X))* Y Lolfa GBR. Dist: Dufour Editions, Inc.

Williams, Maiya. The Golden Hour. 2006. (ENG.). 288p. (J). (gr. 5-10). per. 5.95 *(978-0-8109-9216-0(7))* Abrams, Inc.

Wilson, N. D. Outlaws of Time: the Legend of Sam Miracle. 2017. (Outlaws of Time Ser.: 1). 352p. (J). (gr. 3-7). pap. 6.99 *(978-0-06-232727-7(5),* Tegen, Katherine Bks) HarperCollins Pubs.

Wincik, Stephanie. The Journey: A Northern Lights Adventure. 2007. 111p. (J). per. 9.99 *(978-0-9725650-4-2(3))* One Horse Pr.

Wingard, Lucinda. The Turn-Around Bird. 2012. 296p. pap. 16.00 *(978-0-9848400-1-4(X))* Plicata Pr. LLC.

Wiseman, David. Jeremy Visick. 2005. 176p. (YA). (gr. 5-18). 21.25 *(978-0-8446-7271-7(8),* 3594) Smith, Peter Pub., Inc.

Wishinsky, Frieda. Yikes, Vikings! Griffiths, Dean & Owlkids Books Inc. Staff, illus. 2007. (Canadian Flyer Adventures Ser.: 4). (ENG.). 96p. (J). (gr. 1-4). per. 7.95 *(978-1-897066-97-3(X),* Maple Tree Pr.) Owlkids Bks. Inc. CAN. Dist: Publishers Group West (PGW).

Woodfield, Gary. The Time Thief. 2004. (J). per. 19.95 *(978-0-9761289-2-2(6))* Nightengale Pr.

Woodruff, Elvira. George Washington's Spy. 2012. lib. bdg. 17.20 *(978-0-606-26216-3(4),* Turtleback) Turtleback Bks.

Wrecks, Billy. Time-Travel Trouble! 2014. (Step into Reading Level 2 Ser.). lib. bdg. 13.55 *(978-0-606-36281-8(9))* Turtleback Bks.

Yamada, Debbie Leung. Striking It Rich: Treasures from Gold Mountain. Tang, You-shan, illus. l.t. ed. 2004. 128p. (J). (gr. 4-8). pap. 13.95 *(978-1-879965-21-8(6))* Polychrome Publishing Corp.

Yep, Laurence & Ryder, Joanne. A Dragon's Guide to Making Perfect Wishes. 2017. (Dragon's Guide Ser.: 3). (ENG.). 240p. (J). (gr. 3-7). 16.99 *(978-0-385-39236-5(2),* Crown Books For Young Readers) Random Hse. Children's Bks.

Yolen, Jane. The Devil's Arithmetic. 2004. (Puffin Modern Classics Ser.). (ENG.). 176p. (J). (gr. 5-3). pap. 7.99 *(978-0-14-240109-5(9),* Puffin Books) Penguin Young Readers Group.

Yomtov, Nel, et al. Nickolas Flux History Chronicles, 1 vol. Ginevra, Dante, illus. 2014. (Nickolas Flux History Chronicles Ser.). (ENG.). 32p. (gr. 3-4). lib. bdg. 122.60 *(978-1-4765-7310-6(7),* Graphic Library) Capstone Press of Coughlan Cos.

Yomtov, Nelson. Titanic Disaster! Nickolas Flux & the Sinking of the Great Ship. Simmons, Mark, illus. 2015. (Nickolas Flux History Chronicles Ser.). (ENG.). 32p. (gr. 3-4). lib. bdg. 30.65 *(978-1-4914-2070-6(7),* Graphic Library) Capstone Press of Coughlan Cos.

—Trapped in Antarctica! Nickolas Flux & the Shackleton Expedition. Simmons, Mark, illus. 2015. (Nickolas Flux History Chronicles Ser.). (ENG.). 32p. (gr. 3-4). lib. bdg. 30.65 *(978-1-4914-2069-0(3),* Graphic Library) Capstone Press of Coughlan Cos.

TIMOTHY (BIBLICAL FIGURE)

Rottmann, Erik. Timothy Joins Paul. Snyder, Joel, illus. 2005. (ENG.). 16p. (J). 1.99 *(978-0-7586-0506-1(4))* Concordia Publishing Hse.

TINTIN (FICTITIOUS CHARACTER)—FICTION

Gilchrist, Ellen. Adventures of TinTin. 2009. Vol. 6. pap. 18.99 *(978-0-316-18990-3(1))* Vol. 7. pap. 18.99 *(978-0-316-18992-7(8))* Little, Brown Bks. for Young Readers.

Hergé. The Adventures of Tintin, 8. collector's gif. ed. Set. 2008. (ENG.). (gr. 3-17). 165.00 *(978-0-316-00668-2(8))* Vol. 1. 2009. 192p. 18.99 *(978-0-316-18979-8(0))* Vol. 2. 2009. 192p. 18.99 *(978-0-316-18983-5(9))* Vol. 3. 2009. 192p. 18.99 *(978-0-316-18986-6(3))* Vol. 4. 2009. 192p. 18.99 *(978-0-316-18987-3(1))* Little, Brown Bks. for Young Readers.

—America. Orig. Title: Tintin en Amerique. (Illus.). 62p. (J). 24.95 *(978-0-8288-5000-1(3))* French & European Pubns., Inc.

—America. 2004. (Adventures of Tintin Ser.). Orig. Title: Tintin en Amerique. (Illus.). 124p. 24.95 *(978-0-86719-904-8(0))* Last Gasp of San Francisco.

—The Black Island. (Illus.). 62p. (J). 19.95 *(978-0-8288-5012-4(7))* French & European Pubns., Inc.

—The Black Island. 2012. (Adventures of Tintin: Young Readers Edition Ser.). (ENG., Illus.). 96p. (J). (gr. 3-17). pap. 11.00 *(978-0-316-13387-6(6))* Little, Brown Bks. for Young Readers.

—The Blue Lotus. (Illus.). (J). 19.95 *(978-0-8288-5480-1(7))* French & European Pubns., Inc.

—The Blue Lotus. 2011. (Adventures of Tintin: Young Readers Edition Ser.). (ENG., Illus.). 96p. (J). (gr. 3-17). pap. 9.99 *(978-0-316-13382-1(5))* Little, Brown Bks. for Young Readers.

—The Broken Ear. (Illus.). 62p. (J). 24.95 *(978-0-8288-5086-5(0))* French & European Pubns., Inc.

—The Broken Ear. 2011. (Adventures of Tintin: Young Readers Edition Ser.). (ENG., Illus.). 96p. (J). (gr. 3-17). pap. 11.00 *(978-0-316-13385-2(X))* Little, Brown Bks. for Young Readers.

—The Calculus Affair. (Illus.). 62p. (J). 19.95 *(978-0-8288-5014-8(3))* French & European Pubns., Inc.

—The Castafiore Emerald. (Illus.). 62p. (J). 19.95 *(978-0-8288-5016-2(X))* French & European Pubns., Inc.

—El Cetro de Ottokar. 2007. (Aventuras de Tintin Ser.). (SPA., Illus.). 62p. reprint ed. 22.95 *(978-1-59497-345-1(8))* Public Square Bks.

—Cigars of the Pharaoh.Tr. of Cigares du Pharoan. (Illus.). 62p. (J). 19.95 *(978-0-8288-5021-6(6))* French & European Pubns., Inc.

T
U
V

—Cigars of the Pharaoh. 2011. (Adventures of Tintin: Young Readers Edition Ser.).Tr. of Cigares du Pharaon. (ENG., Illus.). 96p. (J). (gr. 3-17). pap. 11.00 *(978-0-316-13388-3(4))* Little, Brown Bks. for Young Readers.
—The Crab with the Golden Claws. (Illus.). 62p. (J). (gr. 3-8). 19.95 *(978-0-8288-5023-0(2))* French & European Pubns., Inc.
—The Crab with the Golden Claws. 2012. (Adventures of Tintin: Young Readers Edition Ser.). (ENG., Illus.). 96p. (J). (gr. 3-17). pap. 8.99 *(978-0-316-19876-9(5))* Little, Brown Bks. for Young Readers.
—Le Crabe aux Pinces d'Or.Tr. of Crab with the Golden Claws. (FRE., Illus.). (J). (gr. 7-9). ring bd. 19.95 *(978-0-8288-5025-4(9))* French & European Pubns., Inc.
—Destination Moon.Tr. of Objectif Lune. (J). (gr. 3-8). ring bd. 19.95 *(978-0-8288-5026-1(7))*; (Illus.). 62p. 19.95 *(978-0-8288-5027-8(5))* French & European Pubns., Inc.
—Flight 714. (Illus.). 62p. (J). 19.95 *(978-0-8288-5034-6(8))* French & European Pubns., Inc.
—L' Ile Noire.Tr. of Black Island. (FRE., Illus.). (J). (gr. 7-9). ring bd. 19.95 *(978-0-8288-5039-1(9))* French & European Pubns., Inc.
—La Isla Negra. 2007. (Aventuras de Tintin Ser.). (SPA., Illus.). 62p. reprint ed. 22.95 *(978-1-59497-344-4(X))* Public Square Bks.
—King Ottokar's Sceptre. (Illus.). 62p. (J). 19.95 *(978-0-8288-5044-5(5))* French & European Pubns., Inc.
—King Ottokar's Sceptre. 2012. (Adventures of Tintin: Young Readers Edition Ser.). (ENG., Illus.). 96p. (J). (gr. 3-17). pap. 8.99 *(978-0-316-13383-8(3))* Little, Brown Bks. for Young Readers.
—Land of Black Gold. Orig. Title: Tintin au Pays de l'Or Noir. (Illus.). 62p. (J). 19.95 *(978-0-8288-5048-3(8))* French & European Pubns., Inc.
—El Loto Azul.Tr. of Blue Lotus. (SPA., Illus.). 62p. (J). 19.95 *(978-0-8288-5049-0(6))* French & European Pubns., Inc.
—El Loto Azul. (Tintin Ser.).Tr. of Blue Lotus. (SPA.). 64p. (J). 14.95 *(978-84-261-1418-1(0))* Juventud, Editorial ESP. Dist: Distribooks, Inc.
—Le Lotus Bleu.Tr. of Blue Lotus. (FRE.). (J). (gr. 2-9). 19.95 *(978-0-8288-5050-6(X))* French & European Pubns., Inc.
—Objectif Lune.Tr. of Destination Moon. (FRE., Illus.). (J). (gr. 7-9). ring bd. 19.95 *(978-0-8288-5051-3(8))* French & European Pubns., Inc.
—On a Marche sur la Lune. (Tintin Ser.).Tr. of Explorers on the Moon. (FRE.). (J). pap. 21.95 *(978-2-203-00116-9(X))* Casterman, Editions FRA. Dist: Distribooks, Inc.
—On a Marche sur la Lune.Tr. of Explorers on the Moon. (FRE., Illus.). (J). (gr. 7-9). ring bd. 19.95 *(978-0-8288-5053-7(4))* French & European Pubns., Inc.
—L' Oreille Cassee.Tr. of Broken Ear. (FRE., Illus.). 62p. (J). 19.95 *(978-0-8288-5054-4(2))* French & European Pubns., Inc.
—Prisoners of the Sun. (Illus.). 62p. (J). 24.95 *(978-0-8288-5056-8(9))* French & European Pubns., Inc.
—Prisoners of the Sun. 2014. (Adventures of Tintin: Young Readers Edition Ser.). (ENG., Illus.). 96p. (J). (gr. 3-17). pap. 9.00 *(978-0-316-40917-9(0))* Little, Brown Bks. for Young Readers.
—Red Rackham's Treasure. Orig. Title: Tresor de Rackham le Rouge. (Illus.). 62p. (J). 24.95 *(978-0-8288-5057-5(7))* French & European Pubns., Inc.
—Red Rackham's Treasure. 2011. (Adventures of Tintin: Young Readers Edition Ser.). Orig. Title: Tresor de Rackham le Rouge. (ENG., Illus.). 96p. (J). (gr. 3-17). pap. 9.99 *(978-0-316-13384-5(1))* Little, Brown Bks. for Young Readers.
—The Red Sea Sharks. (Illus.). (J). (gr. 3-8). 24.95 *(978-0-8288-5058-2(5))* French & European Pubns., Inc.
—Secret de la Licorne.Tr. of Secret of the Unicorn. (FRE., Illus.). (J). (gr. 7-9). 24.95 *(978-0-8288-5065-0(8))* French & European Pubns., Inc.
—The Secret of the Unicorn. Orig. Title: Secret de la Licorne. (Illus.). 62p. (J). 24.95 *(978-0-8288-5066-7(6))* French & European Pubns., Inc.
—The Secret of the Unicorn. Orig. Title: Secret de la Licorne. (ENG., Illus.). (J). (gr. 3-17). 2012. 64p. 60.00 *(978-0-316-23055-1(3))* 2011. 96p. pap. 9.99 *(978-0-316-13386-9(8))* Little, Brown Bks. for Young Readers.
—Sept Boules de Cristal. (FRE., Illus.). (J). (gr. 7-9). 24.95 *(978-0-8288-5069-8(0))* French & European Pubns., Inc.
—The Seven Crystal Balls. (Illus.). 62p. (J). (gr. 3-8). 24.95 *(978-0-8288-5071-1(2))* French & European Pubns., Inc.
—The Seven Crystal Balls. 2014. (Adventures of Tintin: Young Readers Edition Ser.). (ENG., Illus.). 96p. (J). (gr. 3-17). pap. 9.00 *(978-0-316-40918-6(9))* Little, Brown Bks. for Young Readers.
—The Shooting Star. (Illus.). (J). (gr. 3-8). ring bd. 24.95 *(978-0-8288-5073-5(9))* French & European Pubns., Inc.
—The Shooting Star. 2012. (Adventures of Tintin: Young Readers Edition Ser.). (ENG., Illus.). 96p. (J). (gr. 3-7). pap. 8.99 *(978-0-316-19875-2(7))* Little, Brown Bks. for Young Readers.
—Tintin: Descubro Las Letras. 2004. (SPA.). 24p. 19.95 *(978-1-59497-066-5(1))* Public Square Bks.
—Tintin: El cangrejo de las pinzas de Oro. 2007. (SPA., Illus.). 64p. reprint ed. 22.95 *(978-1-59497-346-8(6))* Public Square Bks.
—Tintin & Alph-Art. 2007. (Adventures of Tintin: Original Classic Ser.). (ENG., Illus.). 64p. (gr. 3-17). pap. 11.99 *(978-0-316-00375-9(1))* Little, Brown Bks. for Young Readers.
—Tintin & the Golden Fleece. (J). (gr. 3-8). 24.95 *(978-0-8288-5087-2(9))* French & European Pubns., Inc.
—Tintin & the Lake of Sharks. (Illus.). 62p. (J). 24.95 *(978-0-416-78950-8(1))* French & European Pubns., Inc.
—Tintin & the Picaros. Orig. Title: Tintin et les Picaros. (Illus.). 62p. (J). 24.95 *(978-0-8288-5089-6(5))* French & European Pubns., Inc.
—Tintin au Congo. (FRE., Illus.). (J). (gr. 7-9). 24.95 *(978-0-8288-5090-2(9))* French & European Pubns., Inc.
—Tintin au Pays de l'Or Noir.Tr. of Land of Black Gold. (FRE.). (J). (gr. 7-9). 24.95 *(978-0-8288-5091-9(7))* French & European Pubns., Inc.
—Tintin au Tibet.Tr. of Tintin in Tibet. (J). (gr. 7-9). ring bd. 24.95 *(978-0-8288-5092-6(5))* French & European Pubns., Inc.
—Tintin en Amerique. Orig. Title: Tintin in America. (Illus.). 62p. (J). (SPA.). 24.95 *(978-0-8288-5094-0(1))*; (FRE., 24.95 *(978-0-8288-5093-3(3))* French & European Pubns., Inc.
—Tintin en el Congo. (SPA., Illus.). 62p. (J). 24.95 *(978-0-8288-5095-7(X))* French & European Pubns., Inc.
—Tintin en el Pais del Oro Negro.Tr. of Land of Black Gold. (SPA., Illus.). 62p. (J). 24.95 *(978-0-8288-4995-1(1))* French & European Pubns., Inc.
—Tintin en Tibet. (SPA., Illus.). 62p. (J). 24.95 *(978-0-8288-4996-8(X))* French & European Pubns., Inc.
—Tintin et les Picaros.Tr. of Tintin & the Picaros. (FRE., Illus.). 62p. (J). 24.95 *(978-0-8288-4997-5(8))* French & European Pubns., Inc.
—Tintin im Amerika.Tr. of Tintin in America. (GER., Illus.). 62p. (J). pap. 24.95 *(978-0-8288-4999-9(4))* French & European Pubns., Inc.
—Tintin im Kongo. (GER., Illus.). 62p. (J). pap. 24.95 *(978-0-8288-4998-2(6))* French & European Pubns., Inc.
—Tintin in America. 2011. (Adventures of Tintin: Young Readers Edition Ser.). Orig. Title: Tintin en Amerique. (ENG., Illus.). 96p. (J). (gr. 3-17). pap. 9.99 *(978-0-316-13380-7(9))* Little, Brown Bks. for Young Readers.
—Tintin in the Land of the Soviets. 2007. (Adventures of Tintin: Original Classic Ser.). (ENG., Illus.). 144p. (gr. 3-17). pap. 13.99 *(978-0-316-00374-2(3))* Little, Brown Bks. for Young Readers.
—Tintin in Tibet. Orig. Title: Tintin au Tibet. (Illus.). 62p. (J). 24.95 *(978-0-8288-5001-8(1))* French & European Pubns., Inc.
—Tintin y los Picaros. (SPA., Illus.). 62p. (J). 24.95 *(978-0-8288-5002-5(X))* French & European Pubns., Inc.
—Tresor de Rackham le Rouge.Tr. of Red Rackham's Treasure. (FRE., Illus.). 62p. (J). (gr. 7-9). 24.95 *(978-0-8288-5003-2(8))* French & European Pubns., Inc.
—Le Tresor de Rackham le Rouge. (Tintin Ser.). (FRE., Illus.). 62p. (J). pap. 21.95 *(978-2-203-00111-4(9))* Casterman, Editions FRA. Dist: Distribooks, Inc.
—Vol 714 Pour Sydney Vol. 714: Flight 714 for Sydney. (FRE., Illus.). 62p. 21.95 *(978-2-203-00121-3(6))* Casterman, Editions FRA. Dist: Distribooks, Inc.
Hergé & Egmont Books Staff. Tintin & the Picaros. 2003. Orig. Title: Tintin et les Picaros. (ENG.). 64p. *(978-1-4052-0823-9(6))* Egmont Bks., Ltd.
—Tintin in Tibet. 2003. Orig. Title: Tintin au Tibet. (ENG., Illus.). 64p. *(978-1-4052-0819-2(8))* Egmont Bks., Ltd.
Hergé & I, Herge-tintin Rustica. Tintin en Amerique. (Tintin Ser.). Orig. Title: Tintin in America. (SPA.). 64p. (J). 14.95 *(978-84-261-1400-6(8))* Juventud, Editorial ESP. Dist: Distribooks, Inc.
—Tintin en el Congo. (Tintin Ser.). (SPA.). 64p. (J). 14.95 *(978-84-261-1401-3(6))* Juventud, Editorial ESP. Dist: Distribooks, Inc.
Hergé & Iii, Herge-tintin Rustica. Tintin el Pais del Oro Negro. (Tintin Ser.). (SPA., Illus.). 64p. (J). 14.95 *(978-84-261-1402-0(4))* Juventud, Editorial ESP. Dist: Distribooks, Inc.
Hergé & Iv, Herge-tintin Rustica. Tintin y los Picaros. (Tintin Ser.). (SPA.). 64p. (J). 14.95 *(978-84-261-1389-4(3))* Juventud, Editorial ESP. Dist: Distribooks, Inc.
Hergé, et al. Aterrizaje en la Luna. (Tintin Ser.). (SPA.). 64p. (J). 14.95 *(978-84-261-1412-9(1))* Juventud, Editorial ESP. Dist: Distribooks, Inc.
Peters, Stephanie. The Adventures of Tintin: The Chapter Book. 2011. (J). lib. bdg. 14.75 *(978-0-606-23444-3(6))*, Turtleback) Turtleback Bks.
Surhone, Lambert M., et al, eds. The Adventures of Tintin: Secret of the Unicorn. 2010. 124p. pap. *(978-613-0-99918-6(6))* AV Akademikerverlag GmbH & Co. KG.

TIRES, RUBBER

Allman, Toney. Recycled Tires. 2009. (Great Idea Ser.). (ENG., Illus.). 48p. (J). (gr. 4-6). lib. bdg. 26.60 *(978-1-59953-197-7(6))* Norwood Hse. Pr.
Ridley, Sarah. A Rubber Tire. 2006. (How It's Made Ser.). (Illus.). 32p. (gr. 1-4). lib. bdg. 26.00 *(978-0-8368-6295-9(3))*, Gareth Stevens Learning Library) Stevens, Gareth Publishing LLLP.

TITANIC (STEAMSHIP)

Adams, Simon. Titanic. 2014. (DK Eyewitness Bks.). (ENG.). 72p. (J). (gr. 3-7). pap. 9.99 *(978-1-4654-2057-2(6))*, DK Children) Dorling Kindersley Publishing, Inc.
Aldridge, Rebecca. The Sinking of the Titanic. 2008. (Great Historic Disasters Ser.). (Illus.). 112p. (gr. 5-8). lib. bdg. 35.00 *(978-0-7910-9643-7(2))*, Chelsea Hse.) Facts On File, Inc.
Amstutz, Lisa J. Titanic, 1 vol. 2014. (Digging up the Past Ser.). (ENG.). 112p. (J). (gr. 6-12). lib. bdg. 35.64 *(978-1-62403-238-7(9))*, Essential Library) ABDO Publishing Co.
Benoit, Peter. The Titanic. 2013. (Cornerstones of Freedom™, Third Ser.). (ENG., Illus.). 64p. (J). pap. 8.95 *(978-0-531-21965-2(8))*; lib. bdg. 30.00 *(978-0-531-23607-9(2))* Scholastic Library Publishing.
—The Titanic Disaster. 2011. (J). pap. *(978-0-531-29026-2(3))* Children's Pr., Ltd.
—The Titanic Disaster. 2011. (True Bks.). 48p. (J). (gr. 3-5). 29.00 *(978-0-531-20627-0(0))*; (ENG.). pap. 6.95 *(978-0-531-28996-9(6))* Scholastic Library Publishing. (Children's Pr.).
Brown, Don. All Stations! Distress! April 15, 1912: the Day the Titanic Sank. Brown, Don, illus. 2010. (Actual Times Ser.: 2). (ENG., Illus.). 64p. (J). (gr. 1-5). pap. 8.99 *(978-1-59643-644-2(1)*, 9781596436442) Square Fish.
Burgan, Michael. Finding the Titanic: How Images from the Ocean Depths Fueled Interest in the Doomed Ship. 2017. (Captured Science History Ser.). (ENG.). 64p. (gr. 5-7). lib. bdg. 34.65 **(978-0-7565-5640-2(6)**, CPB Grades 4-8) Compass Point Bks.
Burgan, Michael. Titanic: Truth & Rumors. Doty, Eldon, illus. 2010. (Truth & Rumors Ser.). (ENG.). 32p. (gr. 3-4). lib. bdg. 27.99 *(978-1-4296-3951-4(2))*, Edge Bks.) Capstone Press of Coughlan Cos.
Burlingame, Jeff. The Titanic Tragedy. 2011. (Perspectives on 3 Ser.). 112p. (gr. 7). 39.93 *(978-1-60870-450-7(5))* Marshall Cavendish Corp.
Callery, Sean. Titanic. 2014. (Scholastic Discover More Ser.). (ENG.). 112p. (J). (gr. 5-9). 15.99 *(978-0-545-50512-3(7))*, Scholastic Reference) Scholastic, Inc.
Caper, William. Nightmare on the Titanic. 2007. (Code Red Ser.). (Illus.). 32p. (YA). (gr. 2-5). lib. bdg. 25.27 *(978-1-59716-362-0(7))* Bearport Publishing Co., Inc.
Carson, Mary Kay. What Sank the World's Biggest Ship? And Other Questions About... The Titanic. Elliott, Mark, illus. 2012. (Good Question! Ser.). (ENG.). 32p. (J). pap. 5.95 *(978-1-4027-8733-1(2))* Sterling Publishing Co., Inc.
Chrisp, Peter. Explore Titanic: Breathtaking New Pictures, Recreated with Digital Technology, 2 vols. Vongprapachanh, Somchith, illus. 2011. (ENG.). 40p. (J). (gr. 4-9). 18.99 *(978-1-4380-7159-6(0))* Barron's Educational Series, Inc.
Claybourne, Anna & Daynes, Katie. Titanic. McNee, Ian, illus. 2006. (Usborne Young Reading Ser.). 64p. (J). (gr. 3-7). 8.99 *(978-0-7945-1269-9(0)*, Usborne) EDC Publishing.
Denenberg, Barry. Titanic Sinks! Experience the Titanic's Doomed Voyage in This Unique Presentation of Fact & Fiction. 2011. (ENG., Illus.). 72p. (J). (gr. 4-7). 19.99 *(978-0-670-01243-5(2))*, Viking Books for Young Readers) Penguin Young Readers Group.
Doeden, Matt. The Sinking of the Titanic, 1 vol. Barnett, Charles, III & Miller, Phil, illus. 2005. (Graphic History Ser.). (ENG.). 32p. (gr. 3-4). per. 8.10 *(978-0-7368-5247-0(6))*, Graphic Library) Capstone Press of Coughlan Cos.
—The Sinking of the Titanic, 1 vol. Barnett, Charles, III et al, illus. 2005. (Graphic History Ser.). (ENG.). 32p. (gr. 3-4). 30.65 *(978-0-7368-3834-4(1))*, Graphic Library) Capstone Press of Coughlan Cos.
Dorling Kindersley Publishing Staff. The Story of the Titanic. Noon, Steve, illus. 2012. (ENG.). 48p. (J). (gr. 3-7). 17.99 *(978-0-7566-9171-4(0))*, DK Children) Dorling Kindersley Publishing, Inc.
Dougherty, Terri. The Search for the Titanic: Finding the Ship's Watery Grave, 1 vol. 2014. (Titanic Perspectives Ser.). (ENG.). 48p. (gr. 3-4). 31.99 *(978-1-4914-0418-8(3))* Capstone Press of Coughlan Cos.
—The Titanic's Crew: Working Aboard the Great Ship, 1 vol. 2014. (Titanic Perspectives Ser.). (ENG., Illus.). 48p. (gr. 3-4). 31.99 *(978-1-4914-0420-1(5))* Capstone Press of Coughlan Cos.
Dougherty, Terri, et al. Titanic Perspectives, 1 vol. 2014. (Titanic Perspectives Ser.). (ENG.). 48p. (gr. 3-4). 127.96 *(978-1-4914-0899-5(5))* Capstone Press of Coughlan Cos.
Driscoll, Laura. Titanic: The Story Lives On! Kayganich, Bob, illus. 2012. (Penguin Young Readers, Level 4 Ser.). (ENG.). 48p. (J). (gr. 3-4). mass mkt. 3.99 *(978-0-448-45757-4(1))*, Penguin Young Readers) Penguin Young Readers Group.
Dubowski, Mark. DK Readers L3: Titanic: The Disaster That Shocked the World! 2015. (DK Readers Ser.). (ENG., Illus.). 64p. (J). (gr. 2-4). pap. 3.99 *(978-1-4654-2840-0(2))*, DK Children) Dorling Kindersley Publishing, Inc.
Dunn, Joe. The Titanic, 1 vol. 2007. (Graphic History Ser.). (ENG., Illus.). 32p. (gr. 3-6). 28.50 *(978-1-60270-079-6(6))*, Graphic Planet- Nonfiction) ABDO Publishing Co.
Fedyszyn, Kirra. Molly Brown. 2014. (Jr. Graphic American Legends Ser.). (Illus.). 24p. (J). (gr. 3-6). pap. 10.60 *(978-1-4777-7201-0(4))*, PowerKids Pr.) Rosen Publishing Group, Inc., The.
Fitzgerald, Dawn. Robert Ballard: Discovering the Titanic & Beyond. 2004. (Gateway Biography Ser.). 48p. (J). lib. bdg. 26.65 *(978-0-7613-2836-0(X))*, Millbrook Pr.) Lerner Publishing Group.
Fullman, Joe. The Story of Titanic for Children. 2016. (ENG., Illus.). 48p. (J). (gr. 3). 17.95 *(978-1-78312-149-6(1))* Carlton Kids GBR. Dist: Sterling Publishing Co., Inc.
Gaetan-Beltran, Daniel. The Titanic. 2015. (Perspectives on Modern World History Ser.). (ENG., Illus.). 224p. (J). (gr. 10-12). 47.80 *(978-0-7377-7310-1(3))*, Greenhaven Pr., Inc.) Cengage Gale.
Ganeri, Anita & West, David. The Sinking of the Titanic & Other Shipwrecks. 2011. (Incredible True Adventures Ser.). (ENG.). 48p. (YA). (gr. 5-8). pap. 11.75 *(978-1-4488-6663-2(4))*; lib. bdg. 29.25 *(978-1-4488-6659-5(6))* Rosen Publishing Group, Inc., The. (Rosen Reference).
Gunderson, Jessica. Your Life as a Cabin Attendant on the Titanic. Dougherty, Rachel, illus. 2012. (Way It Was Ser.). (ENG.). 32p. (gr. 2-3). pap. 8.95 *(978-1-4048-7248-6(5))*; lib. bdg. 26.65 *(978-1-4048-7158-8(6))* Picture Window Bks.
Hopkinson, Deborah. Titanic: Voices from the Disaster. (J). 2014. (ENG.). 304p. (gr. 3-7). pap. 7.99 *(978-0-545-11675-6(9)*, Scholastic Paperbacks) 2012. (ENG., Illus.). 304p. (gr. 3-7). 17.99 *(978-0-545-11674-9(0))*, Scholastic Pr.) 2012. (Illus.). 289p. pap. 8.95 *(978-0-545-43677-9(X)*, Scholastic Pr.) Scholastic, Inc.
Jenkins, Martin. Titanic. Sanders, Brian, illus. 2012. (ENG.). 32p. (J). (gr. 3-7). pap. 6.99 *(978-0-7636-6034-5(5))* Candlewick Pr.
—Titanic: Disaster at Sea. 2012. lib. bdg. 17.20 *(978-0-606-23811-3(5))*, Turtleback) Turtleback Bks.
Johnson, Robin. Titanic. 2012. (ENG.). 48p. (J). *(978-0-7787-7929-2(7))*; (gr. 2-6). pap. *(978-0-7787-7938-4(6))* Crabtree Publishing Co.
Kupperberg, Paul. The Tragedy of the Titanic. 2009. (When Disaster Strikes! Ser.). 48p. (gr. 5-8). 53.00 *(978-1-60854-782-1(5))*, Rosen Reference) Rosen Publishing Group, Inc., The.
—The Tragedy of the Titanic: When Disaster Strikes! 2005. (When Disaster Strikes! Ser.). (Illus.). 48p. (YA). (gr. 5-8). lib. bdg. 29.25 *(978-0-8239-3679-3(1))* Rosen Publishing Group, Inc., The.
Lassieur, Allison. Can You Survive the Titanic? An Interactive Survival Adventure, 1 vol. 2011. (You Choose: Survival Ser.). (ENG.). 112p. (gr. 3-4). pap. 6.95 *(978-1-4296-7351-8(6))*; pap. 41.70 *(978-1-4296-7352-5(4))*; lib. bdg. 31.99 *(978-1-4296-6586-5(6))* Capstone Press of Coughlan Cos. (You Choose Bks.).
Lohse, Joyce B. Unsinkable: The Molly Brown Story. 2006. (Now You Know Bio Ser.). (Illus.). 76p. (J). pap. 8.95 *(978-0-86541-081-7(X))* Filter Pr., LLC.
Lorbiecki, Marybeth. Escaping Titanic: A Young Girl's True Story of Survival, 1 vol. Lorbiecki, Marybeth & Heinzen, Kory S., illus. 2012. (ENG.). 32p. (gr. 3-5). pap. 8.95 *(978-1-4048-7235-6(3))*; lib. bdg. 28.65 *(978-1-4048-7143-4(8))* Picture Window Bks.
Lusted, Marcia Amidon. The Sinking of the Titanic: A History Perspectives Book. 2013. (Perspectives Library). (ENG., Illus.). 32p. (J). (gr. 4-8). 28.50 *(978-1-62431-421-6(X)*, 202804); pap. 14.21 *(978-1-62431-497-1(X)*, 202806) Cherry Lake Publishing.
Matsen, Bradford. The Incredible Quest to Find the Titanic. 2003. (Incredible Deep-Sea Adventures Ser.). (Illus.). 48p. (J). lib. bdg. 25.27 *(978-0-7660-2191-4(2))* Enslow Pubs., Inc.
McCollum, Sean, et al. Eyewitness to Titanic. 2015. (ENG., Illus.). 160p. (gr. 3-4). pap. 9.95 *(978-1-62370-131-4(7))* Capstone Young Readers of Coughlan Cos.
McDonnell, Vincent. Titanic Tragedy. 2007. (ENG.). 160p. (J). (gr. -1-3). per. 12.95 *(978-1-905172-41-2(9))* Collins Pr., The IRL. Dist: Dufour Editions, Inc.
McPherson, Stephanie Sammartino. Iceberg, Right Ahead! The Tragedy of the Titanic. (ENG., Illus.). 112p. (gr. 6-12). 2015. 34.65 *(978-1-4677-5932-8(5)*, Lerner Digital) 2011. lib. bdg. 33.26 *(978-0-7613-6756-7(X))* Lerner Publishing Group.
Ohlin, Nancy. The Titanic. Larkum, Adam, illus. 2016. (Blast Back! Ser.). (ENG.). 112p. (J). (gr. 2-5). pap. 5.99 *(978-1-4998-0273-3(0))* Little Bee Books Inc.
Otfinoski, Steven. Smooth Sea & a Fighting Chance: The Story of the Sinking of Titanic. 2016. (Tangled History Ser.). (ENG., Illus.). 112p. (gr. 3-4). lib. bdg. 31.99 *(978-1-4914-8453-1(5))* Capstone Press of Coughlan Cos.
Park, Louise. The Sinking of the Titanic. 2013. (Discovery Education: Sensational True Stories Ser.). (ENG., Illus.). 32p. (J). (gr. 3-6). pap. 10.00 *(978-1-4777-0099-0(4))*; lib. bdg. 25.25 *(978-1-4777-0057-0(9))* Rosen Publishing Group, Inc., The. (PowerKids Pr.).
Price, Sean, et al, contrib. by. Passengers of the Titanic: Traveling on an Ill-Fated Ship, 1 vol. 2014. (Titanic Perspectives Ser.). (ENG., Illus.). 48p. (gr. 3-4). 31.99 *(978-1-4914-0421-8(3))* Capstone Press of Coughlan Cos.
Ruffin, Frances E. Unsinkable Molly Brown. 2009. (American Legends Ser.). 24p. (gr. 3-3). 42.50 *(978-1-61511-377-4(0)*, PowerKids Pr.) Rosen Publishing Group, Inc., The.
Shea, Therese. The Sinking of the Titanic. 2015. (Doomed! Ser.). (ENG.). 32p. (J). (gr. 4-5). pap. 10.50 *(978-1-4824-2944-2(6))* Stevens, Gareth Publishing LLLP.
Shoulders, Debbie & Shoulders, Michael. T Is for Titanic: A Titanic Alphabet. van Frankenhuyzen, Gijsbert, illus. 2011. (ENG.). 32p. (gr. k-5). 17.95 *(978-1-58536-176-2(3))* Sleeping Bear Pr.
Spangenburg, Ray, et al. Robert Ballard. 2009. (Makers of Modern Science Ser.). (Illus.). 176p. (gr. 6-12). 35.00 *(978-0-8160-6173-0(4))*, Chelsea Hse.) Facts On File, Inc.
Stewart, David. You Wouldn't Want to Sail on the Titanic! 2013. (You Wouldn't Want To Ser.). lib. bdg. 20.80 *(978-0-606-31630-9(2))*, Turtleback) Turtleback Bks.
—You Wouldn't Want to Sail on the Titanic! One Voyage You'D Rather Not Make. Antram, David, illus. rev. ed. 2013. (You Wouldn't Want to... Ser.). (ENG.). 40p. (J). pap. 9.95 *(978-0-531-24505-7(5))*, Watts, Franklin) Scholastic Library Publishing.
Stewart, Melissa. National Geographic Readers: Titanic. 2012. (Readers Ser.). (ENG.). 48p. (J). (gr. 1-4). lib. bdg. 13.90 *(978-1-4263-1060-7(9))*, National Geographic Children's Bks.) National Geographic Society.
Stewart, Melissa & National Geographic Kids Staff. Titanic. 2012. (Readers Ser.). (ENG., Illus.). 48p. (J). (gr. 1-4). pap. 3.99 *(978-1-4263-1059-1(5))*, National Geographic Children's Bks.) National Geographic Society.
Stone, Adam. The Titanic Disaster. 2014. (Disaster Stories Ser.). (ENG.). 24p. (J). (gr. 3-8). 29.95 *(978-1-62617-154-1(8))*, Black Sheep) Bellwether Media.
Temple, Bob. The Titanic: An Interactive History Adventure. 2016. (You Choose: History Ser.). (ENG.). 112p. (gr. 3-4). pap. 6.95 *(978-1-5157-3388-1(2))*; lib. bdg. 31.99 *(978-1-5157-3385-0(8))* Capstone Press of Coughlan Cos. (You Choose Bks.).
—The Titanic [Scholastic]: An Interactive History Adventure. 2010. (You Choose: History Ser.). 112p. pap. 0.86 *(978-1-4296-5119-6(9))*, You Choose Bks.) Capstone Press of Coughlan Cos.
Vander Hook, Sue. The Titanic, 1 vol. 2008. (Essential Events Set 2 Ser.). (ENG., Illus.). 112p. (J). (gr. 6-12). lib. bdg. 35.64 *(978-1-60453-051-3(0))* ABDO Publishing Co.
Weldon, Christine. Children of the Titanic, 1 vol. 2012. (ENG., Illus.). 92p. (J). (gr. 2-4). pap. 14.95 *(978-1-55109-892-0(X))* Nimbus Publishing, Ltd. CAN. Dist: Orca Bk. Pubs. USA.
Whiting, Jim. The Sinking of the Titanic. 2006. (Monumental Milestones Ser.). (Illus.). 48p. (J). (gr. 3-7). lib. bdg. 29.95 *(978-1-58415-472-3(1))* Mitchell Lane Pubs., Inc.
Wishinsky, Frieda. Remembering the Titanic. 2012. (Scholastic Reader Level 3 Ser.). (ENG.). 32p. (J). (gr. 1-3). pap. 3.99 *(978-0-545-35844-6(2))*, Scholastic Paperbacks) Scholastic, Inc.
Yasuda, Anita. Sinking of the Titanic, 1 vol. 2013. (History's Greatest Disasters Ser.). (ENG.). 48p. (J). (gr. 3-6). lib. bdg. 32.79 *(978-1-61783-960-3(4))* ABDO Publishing Co.
—Sinking of the Titanic Paperback. 2013. (J). 15.64 *(978-1-62403-025-3(4))*, Core Library) ABDO Publishing Co.
Zullo, Allan. Titanic: Young Survivors. 2015. (Ten True Tales Ser.). (ENG.). 192p. (J). (gr. 3-7). pap. 5.99 *(978-0-545-81839-1(7))*, Scholastic Nonfiction) Scholastic, Inc.

TITANIC (STEAMSHIP)—FICTION

Brezenoff, Steve. Overboard, 1 vol. Murphy, Scott, illus. 2012. (Return to Titanic Ser.). (ENG.). 112p. (gr. 2-3). pap. 6.95 *(978-1-4342-3912-9(8))*; lib. bdg. 25.32 *(978-1-4342-3302-8(2))* Stone Arch Bks. (Return to Titanic).
—Stowaways, 1 vol. Murphy, Scott, illus. 2012. (Return to Titanic Ser.). (ENG.). 112p. (gr. 2-3). pap. 6.95 *(978-1-4342-3910-5(1))*; lib. bdg. 25.32 *(978-1-4342-3300-4(6))* Stone Arch Bks. (Return to Titanic).
—Time Voyage, 1 vol. Murphy, Scott, illus. 2012. (Return to Titanic Ser.). (ENG.). 112p. (gr. 2-3). pap. 6.95 *(978-1-4342-3909-9(8))*; lib. bdg. 25.32 *(978-1-4342-3299-1(9))* Stone Arch Bks. (Return to Titanic).
—An Unsinkable Ship, 1 vol. Murphy, Scott, illus. 2012. (Return to Titanic Ser.). (ENG.). 112p. (gr. 2-3). pap. 6.95 *(978-1-4342-3911-2(X))*; lib. bdg. 25.32 *(978-1-4342-3301-1(4))* Stone Arch Bks. (Return to Titanic).

Bunting, Eve. S. O. S. Titanic. 2012. (ENG.). 256p. (YA). (gr. 7-12). pap. 7.99 *(978-0-15-201305-9(9))* Houghton Mifflin Harcourt Publishing Co.

Crew, Gary. Pig on the Titanic: A True Story. Whatley, Bruce, illus. 2005. 32p. (J). 15.99 *(978-0-06-052305-3(0))* HarperCollins Pubs.

Crisp, Marty. Titanicat. Papp, Robert, illus. 2008. (ENG.). 40p. (J). (gr. k-6). 17.95 *(978-1-58536-355-1(3))* Sleeping Bear Pr.

Croy, Anita. Titanic: The Search for the Lost Fugitives. Posen, Mick, illus. 2012. (ENG.). 48p. (J). (gr. 3-7). 16.99 *(978-0-7534-6672-8(4)*, 9780753466728, Kingfisher) Roaring Brook Pr.

Duey, K. & Bale, K. A. Salvados! Titanic. 2003. (Survival Ser.).Tr. of Survival! Titanic. (SPA.). (J). pap. 9.95 *(978-0-9715256-4-1(1))* Planeta Publishing Corp.

Duey, Kathleen & Bale, Karen A. Titanic: April 1912. 2014. (Survivors Ser.). (ENG., Illus.). 192p. (J). (gr. 3-7). pap. 7.99 *(978-1-4424-9051-2(9)*, Aladdin) Simon & Schuster Children's Publishing.

—Titanic: April 1912. 2014. (Survivors Ser.). (ENG., Illus.). 192p. (J). (gr. 3-7). 15.99 *(978-1-4424-9052-9(7)*, Simon & Schuster/Paula Wiseman Bks.) Simon & Schuster/Paula Wiseman Bks.

Gray, Claudia. Fateful. (ENG.). (YA). (gr. 9). 2012. 352p. pap. 9.99 *(978-0-06-200621-9(5))* 2011. 336p. 17.99 *(978-0-06-200620-2(7))* HarperCollins Pubs. (HarperTeen).

Harrison, Cora. Titanic Voyage from Drumshee. 2nd ed. 2003. (Drumshee Timeline Ser.). 134p. (J). (gr. 4-7). per. *(978-0-86327-905-8(8))* Wolfhound Pr.

Korman, Gordon. Collision Course, Bk. 2. 2011. (Titanic Ser.: 2). (ENG.). 160p. (J). (gr. 3-7). pap. 6.99 *(978-0-545-12332-7(1)*, Scholastic Paperbacks) Scholastic, Inc.

—Titanic. 2011. (Titanic Ser.: 3). (ENG.). 176p. (J). (gr. 3-7). pap. 6.99 *(978-0-545-12333-4(X)*, Scholastic Paperbacks) Scholastic, Inc.

—Unsinkable, Bk. 1. 2011. (Titanic Ser.: 1). (ENG.). 160p. (J). (gr. 3-7). pap. 6.99 *(978-0-545-12331-0(3)*, Scholastic Paperbacks) Scholastic, Inc.

Luper, Eric. The Titanic Treasure. 2017. (Key Hunters Ser.: 5). (ENG.). 128p. (J). (gr. 2-5). pap. 4.99 ***(978-1-338-14926-5(1)***, Scholastic Paperbacks) Scholastic, Inc.

—The Titanic Treasure (Key Hunters #5) 2017. (Key Hunters Ser.: 5). (ENG.). 128p. (J). (gr. 2-5). lib. bdg. 16.99 ***(978-1-338-14927-2(X)***, Scholastic Paperbacks) Scholastic, Inc.

Mone, Gregory. Dangerous Waters: An Adventure on Titanic. 2012. (ENG.). 240p. (J). (gr. 4-7). 16.99 *(978-1-59643-673-2(5)*, 9781596436732) Roaring Brook Pr.

—Dangerous Waters: An Adventure on Titanic. 2013. (ENG.). 256p. (J). (gr. 4-7). pap. 7.99 *(978-1-250-01671-3(1)*, 9781250016713) Square Fish.

Morpurgo, Michael. Kaspar the Titanic Cat. Foreman, Michael, illus. 2012. 208p. (J). (gr. 3-7). 16.99 *(978-0-06-200618-9(5))* HarperCollins Pubs.

Osborne, Mary Pope. Tonight on the Titanic. unabr. ed. 2004. (Magic Tree House Ser.: No. 17). 71p. (J). (gr. k-3). pap. 17.00 incl. audio *(978-0-8072-0926-4(0)*, S FTR 249 SP, Listening Library) Random Hse. Audio Publishing Group.

Osborne, Mary Pope & Murdocca, Sal. Esta Noche en el Titanic. Murdocca, Sal, illus. 2008. (Casa del Arbol Ser.: 17).Tr. of Tonight on the Titanic. (SPA., Illus.). (J). (gr. 2-4). pap. 5.99 *(978-1-933032-47-4(2))* Lectorum Pubns., Inc.

Osterweil, Adam & Smith, Craig. The Baseball Card Kid. Smith, Craig, illus. 2009. (ENG., Illus.). 199p. (J). (gr. 3-7). 17.95 *(978-1-59078-526-3(6)*, Front Street) Boyds Mills Pr.

Peters, Stephanie True. The First & Final Voyage: The Sinking of the Titanic, 1 vol. Proctor, Jon, illus. 2008. (Historical Fiction Ser.). (ENG.). 56p. (gr. 2-3). pap. 6.25 *(978-1-4342-0494-3(4)*, Graphic Flash) Stone Arch Bks.

Phillips, Dee. Titanic. 2014. (Yesterday's Voices Ser.). (YA). lib. bdg. 19.60 *(978-0-606-35583-4(9))* Turtleback Bks.

Schillow, Ned W. and Schillow. Titanic Hearts. 2007. 100p. per. 10.00 *(978-1-4257-3842-6(7))* Xlibris Corp.

Scholastic, Inc. Staff & Watson, Jude. Doublecross - Mission Titanic, Bk. 1. 2015. (39 Clues: Doublecross Ser.: 1). (ENG.). 224p. (J). (gr. 3-7). 12.99 *(978-0-545-76719-4(9))* Scholastic, Inc.

Smyth, Jimmy. Titanic the Untold Story. 2013. 34p. pap. *(978-0-9569314-4-3(8))* Smith, Jimmy.

Tarshis, Lauren. I Survived the Sinking of the Titanic 1912. 2010. (I Survived Ser.: 1). (ENG., Illus.). 112p. (J). (gr. 2-5). 4.99 *(978-0-545-20694-5(4)*, Scholastic Paperbacks) Scholastic, Inc.

—I Survived the Sinking of the Titanic 1912. 2010. (I Survived . Ser.: No. 1). lib. bdg. 14.75 *(978-0-606-23741-3(0)*, Turtleback) Turtleback Bks.

Tharp, Jason. Monsta Doodle, Bk. 1. 2016. (Super Monsta Friends Ser.: 2). (ENG.). 128p. (J). (gr. 2-5). pap. 12.99 *(978-0-545-83964-8(5))* Scholastic, Inc.

Wallace, Jim. Terror on the Titanic. Sundaravej, Sittisan & Barchus, Nathan, illus. 2007. (Choose Your Own Adventure Ser.: No. 24). (ENG.). 122p. (J). (gr. 4-7). pap. 6.99 *(978-1-933390-24-6(7))* Chooseco LLC.

Warner, Michael N. The Titanic Game. Ordaz, Frank, illus. 2007. (ENG.). 208p. (J). pap. 11.95 *(978-0-9744446-2-8(6))* All About Kids Publishing.

Watson, Jude. Mission Titanic. 2015. (39 Clues: Doublecross Ser.: 1). (ENG.). 224p. (J). (gr. 3-7). 12.99 *(978-0-545-74781-3(3))* Scholastic, Inc.

Watts, Irene N. No Moon. 2010. (ENG.). 240p. (YA). (gr. 5). pap. 12.95 *(978-0-88776-971-9(3)*, Tundra Bks.) Tundra Bks. CAN. Dist: Penguin Random Hse. LLC.

White, Ellen Emerson. Voyage on the Great Titanic. 2010. (Dear America Ser.). (ENG., Illus.). 208p. (J). (gr. 3-7). 12.99 *(978-0-545-23834-2(X)*, Scholastic Pr.) Scholastic, Inc.

Wishinsky, Frieda. SOS! Titanic! Eid, Jean-Paul & Owlkids Books Inc. Staff, illus. 2010. (Canadian Flyer Adventures Ser.: 14). (ENG.). 96p. (J). (gr. 1-4). pap. 7.95 *(978-1-897349-78-6(5)*, Maple Tree Pr.) Owlkids Bks. Inc. CAN. Dist: Publishers Group West (PGW).

Yomtov, Nelson. Titanic Disaster! Nickolas Flux & the Sinking of the Great Ship. Simmons, Mark, illus. 2015. (Nickolas Flux History Chronicles Ser.). (ENG.). 32p. (gr. 3-4). lib. bdg. 30.65 *(978-1-4914-2070-6(7)*, Graphic Library) Capstone Press of Coughlan Cos.

Zullo, Allan. Titanic Young Survivors. 2012. 181p. (J). *(978-0-545-33315-3(6))* Scholastic, Inc.

TITHES

MacKenzie, Catherine. George Müller: Does Money Grow on Trees? 2012. (Little Lights Ser.). (ENG., Illus.). 24p. (J). (gr. -1-3). 7.99 *(978-1-84550-110-5(1)*, af11d222-af25-41e4-93d0-1d014d537a0d) Christian Focus Pubns. GBR. Dist: Bookmasters Distribution.

Mathews, Janice. Jack Gives Back. 2012. (J). 7.99 *(978-0-8280-2667-3(X))* Review & Herald Publishing Assn.

TITIAN, APPROXIMATELY 1488-1576

Venezia, Mike. Getting to Know the World's Greatest Artists - Titian. Venezia, Mike, illus. 2003. (Getting to Know the World's Greatest Artists Ser.). (ENG., Illus.). 32p. (J). (gr. 3-4). pap. 6.95 *(978-0-516-26975-7(5)*, Children's Pr.) Scholastic Library Publishing.

—Titian. Venezia, Mike, illus. 2003. (Getting to Know World Artists Ser.). (ENG., Illus.). 32p. (J). 28.00 *(978-0-516-22575-3(8)*, Children's Pr.) Scholastic Library Publishing.

TIZIANO, APPROXIMATELY 1488-1576

see Titian, approximately 1488-1576

TOADS

see Frogs

TOADSTOOLS

see Mushrooms

TOBACCO HABIT

Connolly, Sean. Tobacco. 2006. (Straight Talking Ser.). (Illus.). 46p. (YA). (gr. 4-7). lib. bdg. 32.80 *(978-1-58340-649-6(2))* Black Rabbit Bks.

—Tobacco. 2009. (Straight Talking Ser.). (Illus.). 48p. (YA). (gr. 8-12). pap. *(978-1-895058-55-0(4))* Saunders Bk. Co.

Davani, Keyvan. SmokeReality. 2007. 160p. pap. 13.95 *(978-1-84753-552-8(6))* Lulu Pr., Inc.

Green, Carl R. Nicotine & Tobacco: A Myreportlinks. com Book. 2005. (Drugs Ser.). (Illus.). 48p. (J). (gr. 4-10). lib. bdg. 26.60 *(978-0-7660-5283-3(4)*, MyReportLinks.com Bks.) Enslow Pubs., Inc.

Hasan, Heather. Caffeine & Nicotine. 2009. (Drug Abuse & Society Ser.). (YA). (gr. 7-12). lib. bdg. 31.95 *(978-1-4358-5015-6(7))* Rosen Publishing Group, Inc., The.

Holt, Rinehart and Winston Staff. A Lifetime of Health Chptr. 11: Tobacco. 4th ed. Date not set. pap. 11.20 *(978-0-03-068103-5(0))* Holt McDougal.

Horsfield, Alan & Horsfield, Elaine. Talking about the Dangers of Alcohol, Tobacco, & Caffeine. 2010. (Healthy Living Ser.). (Illus.). 32p. (YA). (gr. 3-6). lib. bdg. 26.00 *(978-1-4339-3661-6(5))* Stevens, Gareth Publishing LLLP.

Hunnicutt, Susan C. Tobacco & Smoking. 2008. (Opposing Viewpoints Ser.). (ENG., Illus.). 222p. (YA). (gr. 10-12). 27.50 *(978-0-7377-4243-5(7)*, LML01709-243155); pap. 39.70 *(978-0-7377-4242-8(9)*, LML01709-243120) Cengage Gale. (Greenhaven Pr., Inc.).

Hunter, David. Born to Smoke: Nicotine & Genetics. 2009. (Illus.). 112p. (J). 26.95 *(978-1-4222-0230-2(5)*, 1291227) Mason Crest.

—But Smoking Makes Me Happy: The Link Between Nicotine & Depression. 2009. (Illus.). 112p. (J). pap. 26.95 *(978-1-4222-1335-3(8))* Mason Crest.

—Thousands of Deadly Chemicals: Smoking & Health. 2007. (Tobacco: the Deadly Drug Ser.). (Illus.). 112p. (YA). pap. 12.95 *(978-1-4222-0817-5(6))* Mason Crest.

Jones, David C. One Person to Another: Smoking, Chewing Tobacco & Young Peopole. l.t. ed. 2003. 20p. (YA). 4.00 *(978-1-878400-17-8(7))* Dolphin Publishing.

Keyishian, Elizabeth. Smoking. rev. ed. 2005. (Need to Know Library). (Illus.). 64p. (J). (gr. 7-12). lib. bdg. 31.95 *(978-0-8239-4092-9(6))* Rosen Publishing Group, Inc., The.

Malaspina, Ann. False Images, Deadly Promises: Smoking & the Media. 2007. (Tobacco: the Deadly Drug Ser.). (Illus.). 112p. (YA). pap. 12.95 *(978-1-4222-0812-0(5))* Mason Crest.

Mason, Paul. Know the Facts about Drinking & Smoking. 2009. (J). 70.50 *(978-1-4358-5463-5(2))*; (ENG.). 48p. (YA). pap. 11.75 *(978-1-4358-5462-8(4))* Rosen Publishing Group, Inc., The. (Rosen Reference).

Miller, Heather. Smoking. 2008. (21st Century Skills Library: Health at Risk Ser.). (ENG., Illus.). 32p. (J). (gr. 4-8). lib. bdg. 28.50 *(978-1-60279-286-9(0)*, 200135) Cherry Lake Publishing.

Price, Sean. Nicotine. 2008. (Junior Drug Awareness Ser.). (Illus.). 120p. (gr. 5-8). 30.00 *(978-0-7910-9696-3(3)*, Chelsea Hse.) Facts On File, Inc.

Sharp, Katie John. Smokeless Tobacco: Not a Safe Alternative. 2009. (Illus.). 112p. (J). pap. 26.95 *(978-1-4222-1332-2(3)*, 1291227) Mason Crest.

—Teenagers & Tobacco: Nicotine & the Adolescent Brain. 2007. (Tobacco: the Deadly Drug Ser.). (Illus.). 112p. (YA). (gr. 3-7). pap. 12.95 *(978-1-4222-0816-8(8))* Mason Crest.

Smoking. 2008. (Current Controversies Ser.). (Illus.). 176-240p. (gr. 10-12). 36.20 *(978-0-7377-3293-1(8))*; pap. 24.95 *(978-0-7377-3294-8(6))* Cengage Gale. (Greenhaven Pr., Inc.).

Walker, Ida. Addiction in America: Society, Psychology & Heredity. 2012. (Illus.). 128p. (J). *(978-1-4222-2424-3(4))*; *(978-1-4222-2443-4(0))* Mason Crest.

Wilcox, Christine. Thinking Critically: E-Cigarettes & Vaping. 2016. (Thinking Critically Ser.). (ENG., Illus.). 80p. (J). (gr. 5-12). 38.60 *(978-1-60152-956-5(2))* ReferencePoint Pr., Inc.

TOES

see Foot

TOILET

see Beauty, Personal

TOILET PREPARATIONS

see Cosmetics

TOILET TRAINING

Aaron-Barrada, prod. PottieStickers 3-pack Sports Equipment, Seashells & Butterflies: How to Toilet Train in 7 Days with Success with the #1 Portable Toilet Training Reward System for today's family-on-the-go-lifestyle... because consistency Counts!, 3 vols. 2004. (Illus.). 6p. (J). 9.99 *(978-0-9768671-1-1(7))* Aaron-Barrada, Inc.

Aaron-Barrada, Tammie, creator. PottieStickers 3-Pack Fireflies, Kites & Fish Tank: How to Toilet Train in 7 Days with Success with the #1 Portable Toilet Training Reward System for Today's Family-on-the-Go-Lifestyle... Because Consistency Counts!, 3 vols. 2004. (Illus.). 6p. (J). 9.99 *(978-0-9768671-2-8(5))* Aaron-Barrada, Inc.

—PottieStickers 3-Pack Tools, Sea Horses & Flowers: How to Toilet Train in 7 Days with Success! #1 Portable Toilet Training Reward System for today's family-on-the-go-lifestyle... because consistency Counts! 2004. Orig. Title: #1 Portable Toilet Training Reward System for today's family-on-the-go-lifestyle... because consistency Counts! (Illus.). 6p. (J). 9.99 *(978-0-615-12767-5(3))* Aaron-Barrada, Inc.

Berry, Joy. Teach Me about Potty Training. 2009. (ENG.). 40p. (J). (gr. k — 1). bds. 7.95 *(978-1-60577-011-6(6))* Berry, Joy Enterprises.

—Teach Me about Potty Training (Boys) 2009. (Teach Me About Ser.). 40p. 7.95 incl. lp *(978-1-60577-033-8(7))* Berry, Joy Enterprises.

Brooks, Felicity & Allen, Francesca. Baby's Potty. Wells, Rachel, illus. 2006. (Baby's Day Board Book Ser.). 10p. (J). (gr. -1). bds. 8.99 *(978-0-7945-1362-7(X)*, Usborne) EDC Publishing.

Chapman, Jared. Vegetables in Underwear. 2017. (ENG., Illus.). 22p. (J). (gr. -1-k). bds. 7.95 *(978-1-4197-2377-3(4)*, Abrams Appleseed) Abrams, Inc.

Dorling Kindersley Publishing Staff. Boys' Noisy Potty Book. 2014. (ENG.). 10p. (J). (gr. -1-k). bds. 12.99 *(978-1-4654-1664-3(1)*, DK Children) Dorling Kindersley Publishing, Inc.

—Boys' Potty Time. 2010. (ENG., Illus.). 14p. (J). (gr. -1-k). bds. 7.99 *(978-0-7566-5884-7(5)*, DK Children) Dorling Kindersley Publishing, Inc.

—Girls' Noisy Potty Book. 2014. (ENG.). 10p. (J). (gr. -1-k). bds. 12.99 *(978-1-4654-1663-6(3)*, DK Children) Dorling Kindersley Publishing, Inc.

—Girl's Potty Time. 2010. (ENG., Illus.). 14p. (J). (gr. -1-k). bds. 7.99 *(978-0-7566-5885-4(3)*, DK Children) Dorling Kindersley Publishing, Inc.

Foote, Tracy. My Potty Reward Stickers for Boys: 126 Boy Potty Training Stickers & Chart to Motivate Toilet Training. 4th ed. 2006. (J). per. 7.95 *(978-0-9708226-8-0(5))* TracyTrends.

—My Potty Reward Stickers for Boys: 126 Boy Stickers & Chart to Motivate Toilet Training. 2003. (J). 7.95 *(978-0-9708226-6-6(9))* TracyTrends.

—My Potty Reward Stickers for Girls: 126 Girl Potty Training Stickers & Chart to Motivate Toilet Training. 4th ed. 2006. (Illus.). (J). 7.95 *(978-0-9708226-7-3(7))* TracyTrends.

—My Potty Reward Stickers for Girls: 126 Girl Stickers & Chart to Motivate Toilet Training. 3rd rev. ed. 2003. (J). 7.95 *(978-0-9708226-5-9(0))* TracyTrends.

Frankel, Alona. Mi Bacinica y Yo (para El) 2013. (SPA., Illus.). 44p. (J). (gr. -1 — 1). 7.95 *(978-1-77085-402-4(9)*, 9781770854024) Firefly Bks., Ltd.

—Mi Bacinica y Yo (para Ella) 2013. (SPA., Illus.). 44p. (J). (gr. -1 — 1). 7.95 *(978-1-77085-403-1(7)*, 9781770854031) Firefly Bks., Ltd.

—Once upon a Potty - - Girl. Frankel, Alona, illus. 2007. (Once upon a Potty Ser.). (ENG., Illus.). 40p. (J). (gr. -1 — 1). 7.95 *(978-1-55407-284-2(0)*, 9781554072842) Firefly Bks., Ltd.

—Once upon a Potty — Boy. 2014. (Once upon a Potty Ser.). (ENG., Illus.). 24p. (J). (gr. -1 — 1). bds. 6.95 *(978-1-77085-404-8(5)*, 9781770854048) Firefly Bks., Ltd.

—Once upon a Potty — Girl. 2014. (Once upon a Potty Ser.). (ENG., Illus.). 24p. (J). (gr. -1 — 1). bds. 6.95 *(978-1-77085-405-5(3)*, 9781770854055) Firefly Bks., Ltd.

—Once upon a Potty - Boy. Frankel, Alona, illus. 2007. (Once upon a Potty Ser.). (ENG., Illus.). 40p. (J). (gr. -1 — 1). 7.95 *(978-1-55407-283-5(2)*, 9781554072835) Firefly Bks., Ltd.

Gordon, Rachel & Gold, Claudia. Potty Palooza: A Step-by-Step Guide to Using a Potty. Bergmann, Sarah, illus. 2013. (ENG.). 32p. (J). (gr. k — 1). bds. 8.95 *(978-0-7611-7485-1(0)*, 17485) Workman Publishing Co., Inc.

Hochman, David & Kennison, Ruth. The Potty Train. Anderson, Derek, illus. 2008. (ENG.). 32p. (J). (gr. -1-k). 9.99 *(978-1-4169-2833-1(2)*, Simon & Schuster Bks. For Young Readers) Simon & Schuster Bks. For Young Readers.

Inserra, Rosa. Captain of the Toilet. 2013. (Toilet Tales! Ser.). (ENG., Illus.). 10p. (J). (gr. -1-k). bds. 8.99 *(978-0-7641-6658-7(1))* Barron's Educational Series, Inc.

Knickerbocker-Silva, Heather. Tinkle, Tinkle When I Go to the Potty. 2009. 40p. pap. 13.95 *(978-1-59858-826-2(5))* Dog Ear Publishing, LLC.

Kroha, Kristin V. Sophie's Magic Underwear. 2012. (ENG., Illus.). 32p. (J). (gr. -1-2). 7.95 *(978-0-9848657-0-3(5))* Lesson Ladder.

Lansky, Bruce & Pottle, Robert. Tinkle, Tinkle, Little Tot: Songs & Rhymes for Toilet Training. Blake, Anne Catharine, illus. 2005. 32p. (J). 8.95 *(978-0-88166-492-8(8)*, 1182) Meadowbrook Pr.

Lewis, Bisa. Let's Potty! Floyd, John, Jr., illus. 2006. (J). bds. 6.99 *(978-1-934214-12-1(4))* OurRainbow Pr., LLC.

L'Heureux, Christine. Caillou: No More Diapers. Brignaud, Pierre, illus. 2011. (Hand in Hand Ser.). (ENG.). 24p. (J). (gr. -1-k). 5.95 *(978-2-89450-840-4(9))* Caillouet, Gerry.

—Caillou, No More Diapers. Brignaud, Pierre, illus. 2016. (Potty Training Ser.: 2). (ENG.). 24p. (J). (gr. -1-k). bds. 7.99 *(978-2-89718-296-0(2))* Caillouet, Gerry.

Macaulay, David & Keenan, Sheila. Toilet: How It Works. 2015. (ENG., Illus.). 32p. (J). (gr. 1-4). 17.99 *(978-1-62672-214-9(5)*, 9781626722149, Macaulay, David Studio) Roaring Brook Pr.

Mandell, Sabain. Www.AdorableDiapers.Com Presents How to Create Personalized Diapers for Kids! 2011. 32p. (gr. -1). pap. 19.99 *(978-1-4520-9987-3(1))* AuthorHouse.

Mastel, Julie. Jesus Was with Me All Along: A Book about Bedwetting. 2013. 36p. pap. 15.95 *(978-1-4497-8321-1(X)*, WestBow Pr.) Author Solutions, Inc.

Mcaleer, Sarah & McAleer, Kathleen. Don't Tee Tee in Your Tutu: A Potty Training Book for Young Ballerinas. 2009. 28p. pap. 13.99 *(978-1-4389-4029-8(7))* AuthorHouse.

Morgan, Richard. Zoo Poo: A First Toilet Training Book. 2004. (ENG., Illus.). 24p. (J). pap. 5.95 *(978-0-7641-2767-0(5))* Barron's Educational Series, Inc.

—Zoo Poo: A First Toilet Training Book. 2004. (gr. -1-2). lib. bdg. 15.95 *(978-0-613-81357-0(X)*, Turtleback) Turtleback Bks.

Piggy Toes Press, creator. Let's Go Potty! 2008. (ENG., Illus.). 14p. (gr. -1-k). 8.95 *(978-1-58117-688-9(0)*, Intervisual/Piggy Toes) Bendon, Inc.

—Let's Go Potty for Boys. 2008. (ENG., Illus.). 14p. (gr. -1-k). bds. 8.95 *(978-1-58117-689-6(9)*, Intervisual/Piggy Toes) Bendon, Inc.

Pinnington, Andrea & Dorling Kindersley Publishing Staff. Big Boys Use the Potty! 2005. (ENG., Illus.). 12p. (J). (gr. -1-k). bds. 6.99 *(978-0-7566-1451-5(1)*, DK Children) Dorling Kindersley Publishing, Inc.

Priddy, Roger. Potty Time Training Pack: A Friendly Reassuring Way to Help Your Child Learn to Use a Potty. 2007. (Potty Time Training Pack Ser.). (ENG., Illus.). 18p. (J). (— 1). 12.95 *(978-0-312-49977-8(9)*, 9780312499778, Priddy Bks.) St. Martin's Pr.

Publications International Ltd. Staff. Once upon a Potty. 2010. 8p. (J). bds. 7.98 *(978-1-60553-416-9(1))* Phoenix International Publications, Inc.

Publications International Ltd. Staff & Frankel, Alana. Once upon a Potty Girl. 2010. 8p. (J). bds. 7.98 *(978-1-60553-417-6(X))* Phoenix International Publications, Inc.

Sanschagrin, Joceline. Caillou. Brignaud, Pierre, illus. 2016. (Hand in Hand Ser.). (ENG.). 24p. (J). (gr. -1-k). bds. 12.99 *(978-2-89718-344-8(6))* Caillouet, Gerry.

—Caillou: Potty Time. Brignaud, Pierre, illus. 4th ed. 2010. (Hand in Hand Ser.). (ENG.). 24p. (J). (gr. -1-k). 5.95 *(978-2-89450-749-0(6))* Figment.

—Caillou, Potty Time. Brignaud, Pierre, illus. 2016. (Hand in Hand Ser.: 1). (ENG.). 24p. (J). (gr. -1-k). bds. 7.99 *(978-2-89718-295-3(4))* Caillouet, Gerry.

Sawyer, Parker K. Potty Time! Moroney, Christopher, illus. 2006. (Sesame Beginnings Ser.). (ENG.). 12p. (J). (gr. k — 1). bds. 5.99 *(978-0-375-83695-4(0)*, Random Hse. Bks. for Young Readers) Random Hse. Children's Bks.

Spector, Todd. How to Pee: Potty Training for Boys. Chung, Arree, illus. 2015. (ENG.). 40p. (J). (— 1). 12.99 *(978-0-8050-9773-3(2)*, 9780805097733, Holt, Henry & Co. Bks. For Young Readers) Holt, Henry & Co.

—How to Pee: Potty Training for Girls. Chung, Arree, illus. 2016. (ENG.). 40p. (J). 12.99 *(978-1-62779-297-4(X)*, 9781627792974, Holt, Henry & Co. Bks. For Young Readers) Holt, Henry & Co.

Tucker, Jason. Ferdinand Uses the Potty. West, D. E., illus. 2009. (J). pap. 13.95 *(978-1-932690-82-8(4))* Loving Healing Pr., Inc.

Verdick, Elizabeth. Diapers Are Not Forever. Heinlen, Marieka, illus. (Best Behavior Ser.). (ENG & SPA.). 24p. (J). 2014. bds. 7.95 *(978-1-57542-429-3(0))* 2008. bds. 7.95 *(978-1-57542-296-1(4))* Free Spirit Publishing, Inc.

Vestergaard, Hope. Potty Animals: What to Know When You've Gotta Go! Petrone, Valeria, illus. 2010. (ENG.). 32p. (J). (gr. -1-1). 14.95 *(978-1-4027-5996-3(7))* Sterling Publishing Co., Inc.

Willems, Mo. Time to Pee! Willems, Mo, illus. 2003. (ENG., Illus.). 40p. (J). (gr. -1-k). 16.99 *(978-0-7868-1868-6(9))* Hyperion Pr.

Young, Caroline. Guide to Potty Training Internet-Referenced. 2010. (Parent's Guides). 64p. (J). pap. 9.99 *(978-0-7945-2107-3(X)*, Usborne) EDC Publishing.

TOILET TRAINING—FICTION

Ann. We Call Him Puddles. 2007. 24p. per. 24.95 *(978-1-4241-8738-6(9))* America Star Bks.

Apple, Sam. The Saddest Toilet in the World. Ricks, Sam, illus. 2016. (ENG.). 32p. (J). (gr. -1-2). 17.99 *(978-1-4814-5122-2(7)*, Aladdin) Simon & Schuster Children's Publishing.

Barksdale, Miechel & Dunn, Richard. Mommy, Its Time to Go Pee. 2010. 32p. pap. 12.99 *(978-1-4490-6860-8(X))* AuthorHouse.

Berenstain, Jan & Berenstain, Mike. The Berenstain Bears' Valentine Party. 2008. (Berenstain Bears Ser.). (ENG., Illus.). 16p. (J). (gr. -1-3). pap. 6.99 *(978-0-06-057425-3(9)*, HarperFestival) HarperCollins Pubs.

Berger, Samantha. Pirate Potty. Cartwright, Amy, illus. 2010. (ENG.). 24p. (J). (gr. -1 — 1). pap. 5.99 *(978-0-545-17295-0(0)*, Cartwheel Bks.) Scholastic, Inc.

—Princess Potty. Cartwright, Amy, illus. 2010. (ENG.). 24p. (J). (gr. -1 — 1). pap. 5.99 *(978-0-545-17296-7(9)*, Cartwheel Bks.) Scholastic, Inc.

Chou, Yih-fen. Mimi Goes Potty. Chen, Zhiyuan, illus. 2011. (J). *(978-0-9845523-9-9(1))* Heryin Publishing Corp.

—The Potty Story. Chen, Zhiyuan, illus. 2011. (J). *(978-0-9845523-8-2(3))* Heryin Publishing Corp.

Church, Caroline Jayne. Potty Time! Church, Caroline Jayne, illus. 2012. (ENG., Illus.). 10p. (J). (gr. -1-k). bds. 7.99 *(978-0-545-35080-8(8)*, Cartwheel Bks.) Scholastic, Inc.

Cole, Joanna. My Big Boy Potty. Chambliss, Maxie, illus. 2004. (ENG.). 32p. (J). (gr. -1-3). 6.99 *(978-0-688-17042-4(0))* HarperCollins Pubs.

—My Big Girl Potty. Chambliss, Maxie, illus. 2004. (ENG.). 32p. (J). (gr. -1 — 1). 6.99 *(978-0-688-17041-7(2))* HarperCollins Pubs.

Comtesse, Gavin. Hamish & the Terrible Poo. 2013. 50p. 19.89 *(978-1-4669-9760-8(5))*; pap. 9.89 *(978-1-4669-9761-5(3))* Trafford Publishing.

Cook, Julia & Jana, Laura. It's You & Me Against the Pee... & the Poop, Too! DuFalla, Anita, illus. 2011. 32p. (gr. -1). pap. 9.95 *(978-1-931636-75-9(3))* National Ctr. For Youth Issues.

Corderoy, Tracey. It's Potty Time! Pedler, Caroline, illus. 2014. (ENG.). 22p. (J). (gr. -1-k). bds. 8.99 *(978-1-58925-574-6(7))* Tiger Tales.

Crikelair, Wendy. Poopie Party. 2011. 28p. pap. 15.99 *(978-1-4628-8093-5(2))* Xlibris Corp.

Dahl, Michael. Duck Goes Potty, 1 vol. Vidal, Oriol, illus. 2010. (Hello Genius Ser.). (ENG.). 20p. (gr. 1-2). bds. 7.99 *(978-1-4048-5726-1(5))* Picture Window Bks.

Daniel Goes to the Potty. 2014. (Daniel Tiger's Neighborhood Ser.). (ENG., Illus.). 14p. (J). (gr. -1 — 1). 8.99 *(978-1-4814-2048-8(8)*, Simon Spotlight) Simon Spotlight.

De Smet, Marian & Meijer, Marja. Encerrada: Anna's Tight Squeeze. Pacheco, Laura Emilia, tr. Uitgeverij, Clavis, illus. 2004. 28p. (J). 14.95 *(978-970-29-0665-0(2))* Santillana USA Publishing Co., Inc.

DePrisco, Dorothea & McKendry, Sam. I'm a Big Kid Now. 2006. (ENG.). 36p. bds. 12.95 *(978-1-58117-523-3(X)*, Intervisual/Piggy Toes) Bendon, Inc.

Dorling Kindersley Publishing Staff. Big Girls Use the Potty! 2008. (ENG.). 20p. (J). (gr. -1-k). 3.99 *(978-0-7566-3928-0(X))*, DK Children) Dorling Kindersley Publishing, Inc.

—Big Girls Use the Potty! 2005. (ENG., Illus.). 12p. (J). (gr. -1-k). bds. 6.99 *(978-0-7566-1452-2(X))*, DK Children) Dorling Kindersley Publishing, Inc.

Edwards, W M, illus. Island Potty Party. 2007. (Playdate Kids Musical Ser.). 27p. (J). (gr. -1-3). 14.95 incl. audio compact disk *(978-1-933721-15-6(4))* Playdate Kids Publishing.

Ford, Bernette. No More Diapers for Ducky! Williams, Sam, illus. 2007. (Ducky & Piggy Ser.). (ENG.). 26p. (J). (gr. -1 — 1). bds. 7.95 *(978-1-905417-38-4(1))* Boxer Bks., Ltd. GBR. Dist: Sterling Publishing Co., Inc.

Frankel, Alona. Once upon a Potty Sound Book for Girls. Publications International Ltd. Staff, ed. 2010. 8p. (J). bds. 7.98 *(978-1-4508-0828-6(X))* Publications International, Ltd.

Froeb, Lori C. Let's Go Potty, Elmo! Pull the Tabs, Turn the Wheel, & Lift the Flap! 2015. (ENG.). 12p. (J). (gr. -1-k). bds. 10.99 *(978-0-7944-3517-2(3))*, Reader's Digest Children's Bks.) Studio Fun International.

Gaydos, Nora. Now I'm Growing! Prince of the Potty - Little Steps for Big Kids! Gutierrez, Akemi, illus. 2011. (ENG.). 30p. (J). (gr. -1-17). 8.99 *(978-1-60169-077-7(0))* Innovative Kids.

—Princess of the Potty - Little Steps for Big Kids! Gutierrez, Akemi, illus. 2011. (ENG.). 30p. (J). (gr. -1-17). 8.99 *(978-1-60169-076-0(2))* Innovative Kids.

Geis, Patricia. Good-bye Diaper! Folch, Sergio, illus. 2009. (Good Habits with Coco & Tula Ser.). 16p. (J). (gr. -1-k). bds. 11.40 *(978-1-60754-404-3(0))* Windmill Bks.

Gramma Debbie. The Poop Book. 2012. 32p. pap. 19.99 *(978-1-4772-5287-1(8))* AuthorHouse.

Hager, Kendra M. Alexander. Potty Praise for Boys & Girls. 2013. 56p. pap. 17.95 *(978-1-60911-459-6(0))*, Strategic Bk. Publishing) Strategic Book Publishing & Rights Agency (SBPRA).

Hayes, Kate. All about Poop. Garnsworthy, Marlo, ed. Vaughan, Brenna, illus. 2012. (ENG.). 38p. (J). pap. 14.95 *(978-0-9854248-0-0(X))* Pinwheel Bks.

Hodson, Sarah E. Early Social Skills Stories: Going Potty. Platt, Jason, illus. 2013. (J). *(978-0-7606-1408-2(3))* LinguiSystems, Inc.

Inserra, Rosa. Queen of the Toilet. 2013. (Toilet Tales! Ser.). (ENG.). 10p. (J). (gr. -1-k). bds. 8.99 *(978-0-7641-6659-4(X))* Barron's Educational Series, Inc.

Jackson, Nikki. Georgia & Reed's: My Potty & Me. 2012. 16p. pap. 15.99 *(978-1-4772-4516-3(2))* AuthorHouse.

Jadoul, Émile. All by Myself! 2012. (ENG.). 26p. (J). 14.00 *(978-0-8028-5411-7(7))*, Eerdmans Bks For Young Readers) Eerdmans, William B. Publishing Co.

Kramer, Paul. Do Not Dread Wetting the Bed. 2012. (ENG & ACE.). 32p. (J). (gr. -1-3). 15.95 *(978-0-9819745-0-7(3))* Aloha Wellness Pubs.

Lewison, Wendy Cheyette. The Prince & the Potty. Motoyama, Keiko, illus. 2006. (ENG.). 40p. (J). (gr. -1-3). 16.99 *(978-0-689-87808-4(7))*, Simon & Schuster Bks. For Young Readers) Simon & Schuster Bks. For Young Readers.

Lloyd-Jones, Sally. Skip to the Loo, My Darling! a Potty Book. Jeram, Anita, illus. 2016. (ENG.). 32p. (J). (-k). 11.99 *(978-0-7636-7234-8(3))* Candlewick Pr.

Make Believe Ideas. Even Pirates Poop. 2014. (ENG.). 12p. (J). bds. 9.99 *(978-1-78393-113-2(2))* Make Believe Ideas GBR. Dist: Nelson, Thomas Inc.

—Even Princesses Poop. 2014. (ENG.). 12p. (J). bds. 9.99 *(978-1-78393-112-5(4))* Make Believe Ideas GBR. Dist: Nelson, Thomas Inc.

Manushkin, Fran. Big Boy Underpants. Petrone, Valeria, illus. 2016. (ENG.). 24p. (J). (— 1). bds. 7.99 *(978-0-553-53861-8(6))*, Random Hse. Bks. for Young Readers) Random Hse. Children's Bks.

—Big Girl Panties. Petrone, Valeria, illus. 2012. (ENG.). 24p. (J). (gr. k — 1). bds. 7.99 *(978-0-307-93152-8(8))*, Robin Corey Bks.) Random Hse. Children's Bks.

Mayer, Mercer & Mayer, Gina. The New Potty. 2003. (Look-Look Ser.). (ENG., Illus.). 24p. (J). (-k). pap. 3.99 *(978-0-375-82631-3(9))*, Random Hse. Bks. for Young Readers) Random Hse. Children's Bks.

McMahon, Kara & Jordan, Apple. My Growing-Up Library. 2010. (ENG., Illus.). 12p. (J). (gr. k — 1). bds. 10.99 *(978-0-375-85984-7(5))*, Random Hse. Bks. for Young Readers) Random Hse. Children's Bks.

Munsch, Robert. I Have to Go! Martchenko, Michael, illus. 8th ed. 2010. (ENG.). 24p. (J). (gr. -1-k). bds. 7.99 *(978-1-55451-253-9(0))*, 9781554512539) Annick Pr., Ltd. CAN. Dist: Publishers Group West (PGW).

—I Have to Go! 2007. (J). 15.10 *(978-0-7569-7622-4(7))* Perfection Learning Corp.

Neis, Izzy. I Want to Potty. Shakir, Susie, illus. 2005. 10p. (J). 9.95 *(978-1-58117-422-9(5))*, Intervisual/Piggy Toes) Bendon, Inc.

Nussbaum, Dori. The Hungry Potty. 2004. 28p. per. 8.95 *(978-1-932344-67-7(5))* Thornton Publishing, Inc.

O'Brien, Melanie. No More Diapers. 2009. 18p. 10.95 *(978-1-58117-920-0(0))*, Intervisual/Piggy Toes) Bendon, Inc.

Oud, Pauline. Ian's New Potty. 2011. (ENG.). 32p. (J). (gr. k — 1). 16.95 *(978-1-60537-103-0(3))* Cobblestone Publishing Co.

Patricelli, Leslie. Potty. Patricelli, Leslie, illus. 2010. (Leslie Patricelli Board Bks.). (ENG., Illus.). 28p. (J). (gr. k — 1). bds. 6.99 *(978-0-7636-4476-5(5))* Candlewick Pr.

—Potty/Bacinica. Patricelli, Leslie, illus. 2016. (Leslie Patricelli Board Bks.). (ENG & SPA., Illus.). (J). (— 1). bds. 6.99 *(978-0-7636-8777-9(4))* Candlewick Pr.

Publications International Ltd. Staff, ed. Once upon a Potty Sound Book for Boys. 2010. 8p. (J). bds. 7.98 *(978-1-4508-0829-3(8))* Phoenix International Publications, Inc.

—Potty Time with Tiger: Boy. 2010. (J). bds. 5.98 *(978-1-4127-6915-0(9))* Publications International, Ltd.

—Potty Time with Tiger: Girl. 2010. (SPA.). (J). bds. 5.98 *(978-1-4127-6916-7(7))* Publications International, Ltd.

—Sesame Street: Elmo's Potty Book (First Look & Find) 2011. 18p. (J). bds. 7.98 *(978-1-60553-840-2(X))* Phoenix International Publications, Inc.

—Sesame Street: Potty Time Songs. 2010. 12p. (J). bds. 9.98 *(978-1-4508-0365-6(2))* Phoenix International Publications, Inc.

—Sesame Street: Potty Time with Elmo (Look & Find) 2010. 20p. (J). pap. 5.98 *(978-1-4508-1471-3(9))* Publications International, Ltd.

Random House. My Thomas Potty Book (Thomas & Friends) 2016. (ENG., Illus.). 14p. (J). (gr. -1 — 1). bds. 9.99 *(978-1-101-93427-2(1))*, Random Hse. Bks. for Young Readers) Random Hse. Children's Bks.

—P Is for Potty! (Sesame Street) Moroney, Christopher, illus. 2014. (Lift-The-Flap Ser.). (ENG.). 12p. (J). (— 1). bds. 5.99 *(978-0-385-38369-1(X))*, Random Hse. Bks. for Young Readers) Random Hse. Children's Bks.

Richmond, Marianne. Big Boys Go Potty. Richmond, Marianne, illus. 2012. (ENG., Illus.). 32p. (J). 9.99 *(978-1-4022-6659-1(6))*, Sourcebooks Jabberwocky) Sourcebooks, Inc.

—Big Girls Go Potty. Richmond, Marianne, illus. 2012. (ENG., Illus.). 32p. (J). 9.99 *(978-1-4022-6662-1(6))*, Sourcebooks Jabberwocky) Sourcebooks, Inc.

Shea, Bob. Dinosaur vs. the Potty. Shea, Bob, illus. 2012. (ENG., Illus.). 30p. (J). (gr. -1-1). bds. 6.99 *(978-1-4231-5179-1(8))* Hyperion Pr.

Slattery, Karen. Piper's Diapers. 2003. (J). pap. 9.00 *(978-0-8059-5765-5(0))* Dorrance Publishing Co., Inc.

Smart Kidz, creator. It's Potty Time for Boys. 2013. (ENG., Illus.). 12p. (J). bds. 12.99 *(978-1-891100-05-5(X))*, Smart Kids) Penton Overseas, Inc.

Snedegar, Eugenia. Ellie Goes Potty, 1 vol. 2009. 24p. pap. 24.95 *(978-1-61546-658-0(4))* America Star Bks.

Snyder, Betsy E., illus. Lily's Potty. 2010. 16p. (J). bds. *(978-1-60906-001-5(6))* Begin Smart LLC.

Trasler, Janee. Pottytime for Chickies. Trasler, Janee, illus. 2014. (Chickies Ser.). (ENG., Illus.). 24p. (J). (gr. -1 — 1). bds. 8.99 *(978-0-06-227469-4(4))*, HarperFestival) HarperCollins Pubs.

van Genechten, Guido. The Big Potty Book. 2009. (ENG.). 20p. (J). (gr. k — 1). bds. 12.95 *(978-1-60537-031-6(2))* Cobblestone Publishing Co.

Van Lieshout, Maria. I Use the Potty. 2016. (Big Kid Power Ser.). (ENG., Illus.). 28p. (J). (gr. -1 — 1). 9.99 *(978-1-4521-3535-9(5))* Chronicle Bks. LLC.

Watt, Fiona & Wells, Rachel, eds. Potty Time. 2004. (Baby's World Ser.). (ENG., Illus.). 1p. (J). (gr. -1-18). pap. 4.95 *(978-0-7460-3839-0(9))* EDC Publishing.

Wax, Wendy & Wax, Naomi. Even Firefighters Go to the Potty: A Potty Training Lift-the-Flap Story. Sisk, Clay & Gilpin, Stephen, illus. 2008. (ENG.). 22p. (J). (gr. -1-k). 7.99 *(978-1-4169-2720-4(4))*, Little Simon) Little Simon.

Wax, Wendy A. & Wax, Naomi. Even Princesses Go to the Potty. Carabelli, Francesca, illus. 2014. (ENG.). 22p. (J). (gr. -1 — 1). 7.99 *(978-1-4424-8886-1(7))*, Little Simon) Little Simon.

Whelen-Banks, Jane. Liam Goes Poo in the Toilet: A Story about Trouble with Toilet Training. 2008. (ENG., Illus.). 32p. 12.95 *(978-1-84310-900-6(X))*, 5371) Kingsley, Jessica Pubs. GBR. Dist: Macmillan Distribution Ltd.

TOKYO (JAPAN)

Akio, Irene. T Is for Tokyo. Akio, Irene, illus. 2010. (ENG., Illus.). 36p. (J). (gr. k-5). 12.95 *(978-1-934159-23-1(9))* ThingsAsian Pr.

Barber, Nicola. Tokyo. Bowden, Rob, photos by. 2006. (Global Cities Ser.). (Illus.). 61p. (gr. 5-8). 30.00 *(978-0-7910-8855-5(3))*, Chelsea Hse.) Facts On File, Inc.

—Tokyo. 2004. (Great Cities of the World Ser.). (Illus.). 48p. (gr. 5-12). lib. bdg. 31.00 *(978-0-8368-5033-8(5))*, Gareth Stevens Secondary Library) Stevens, Gareth Publishing LLLP.

Smith, Jacquelyn. Pitty the City Kitty; Tokyo. Smith, Jacquelyn & Kalafatis, John, illus. 2009. 32p. (J). 15.99 *(978-1-935479-01-7(6))* A.M. Green Publishing.

Takabayashi, Mari. I Live in Tokyo. 2004. (ENG., Illus.). 32p. (J). (gr. -1-3). reprint ed. pap. 6.95 *(978-0-618-49484-2(7))* Houghton Mifflin Harcourt Publishing Co.

Verzov, Ella & Oirechman, Chana. Moshe of Japan. 2013. (Illus.). 50p. (J). *(978-1-61465-171-0(X))* Menucha Pubs. Inc.

TOLERATION

see also Discrimination; Freedom of Religion

All about Us Interactive Packages: Here I Am. (Pebble Soup Explorations Ser.). (gr. -1-18). 52.00 *(978-0-7578-5227-5(0))* Rigby Education.

Amoroso, Cynthia. Tolerance. 2013. (Values to Live By Ser.). (ENG.). 24p. (J). (gr. -1-2). 25.64 *(978-1-62323-527-7(6))*, 206298) Child's World, Inc., The.

Baptiste, Tracey & Banas, Sharon L. Overcoming Prejudice. 2009. (Character Education Ser.). (Illus.). 128p. (gr. 6-12). 35.00 *(978-1-60413-119-2(5))*, Chelsea Hse.) Facts On File, Inc.

Burstein, John. Can We Get Along? Dealing with Differences. 2009. (Slim Goodbody's Life Skills 101 Ser.). (ENG., Illus.). 32p. (J). (gr. 3-6). pap. *(978-0-7787-4804-5(9))*; lib. bdg. *(978-0-7787-4788-8(3))* Crabtree Publishing Co.

Cassius, Sonya. My Beautiful World. 2009. (Illus.). 32p. pap. 12.99 *(978-1-4343-0061-4(7))* AuthorHouse.

Currie, Stephen. Religious Oppression. 2003. (Great Escapes Ser.). (ENG., Illus.). 112p. (J). 30.85 *(978-1-59018-280-2(4))*, Lucent Bks.) Cengage Gale.

Gay, Kathlyn. Bigotry & Intolerance: The Ultimate Teen Guide. 2015. (It Happened to Me Ser.: 35). (ENG., Illus.). 182p. pap. 30.00 *(978-1-4422-5659-0(1))* Rowman & Littlefield Publishers, Inc.

—Bigotry & Intolerance: The Ultimate Teen Guide. 2013. (It Happened to Me Ser.: 35). (ENG., Illus.). 182p. 55.00 *(978-0-8108-8360-4(0))* Scarecrow Pr., Inc.

—Cultural Diversity: Conflicts & Challenges. 2003. (It Happened to Me Ser.: 6). (ENG., Illus.). 144p. pap. 45.00 *(978-0-8108-4805-4(8))* Scarecrow Pr., Inc.

Hanes, Richard Clay, et al. Prejudice in the Modern World. 2007. (J). *(978-1-4144-0206-2(6))*; *(978-1-4144-0205-5(8))* Cengage Gale.

Hanson, Anders. Everyone Is Equal: The Kids' Book of Tolerance, 1 vol. 2014. (What We Stand For Ser.). (ENG.). 24p. (gr. 5-10). lib. bdg. 25.65 *(978-1-62403-293-6(1))*, Super SandCastle) ABDO Publishing Co.

James, Emily. How to Be Tolerant: A Question & Answer Book about Tolerance. 2017. (Character Matters Ser.). (ENG.). 32p. (gr. 1-2). lib. bdg. 27.32 ***(978-1-5157-7202-6(0))***, Aplus Bks.) Capstone Press of Coughlan Cos.

LaMachia, John. So What Is Tolerance Anyway? 2009. (Student's Guide to American Civics Ser.). 48p. (gr. 5-8). 53.00 *(978-1-61511-241-8(3))*, Rosen Reference) Rosen Publishing Group, Inc., The.

Mason, Paul. Religious Extremism. 2010. (Voices Ser.). (Illus.). 48p. pap. *(978-0-237-54219-1(6))* Evans Brothers, Ltd.

Meiners, Cheri J. Accept & Value Each Person. Johnson, Meredith, illus. 2006. (Learning to Get Along(r) Ser.). (ENG.). 40p. (J). (gr. 3-7). pap. 10.95 *(978-1-57542-203-9(4))* Free Spirit Publishing, Inc.

Munson, Derek. Pastel para Enemigos. King, Tara Calahan, illus. 2004.Tr. of Enemy Pie. (SPA.). 40p. (J). (gr. k-2). pap. 9.99 *(978-84-261-3378-6(9))* Juventud, Editorial ESP. Dist: Lectorum Pubns., Inc.

Palmer, Bill. Gallup Guides for Youth Facing Persistent Prejudice. 2012. (Gallup Guides for Youth Facing Persistent Prejudice Ser.). 64p. (J). (gr. 7-8). 22.95 *(978-1-4222-2466-3(X))* Mason Crest.

Pederson, Charles E. Racism & Intolerance. 2008. (Man's Inhumanities Ser.). (YA). (gr. 7-12). 23.95 *(978-1-60217-976-9(X))* Erickson Pr.

Pryor, Kimberley Jane. Tolerance. 2008. (Values Ser.). 32p. (J). (gr. 1-3). lib. bdg. 18.56 *(978-0-7614-3129-9(2))* Marshall Cavendish Corp.

Roberts, Jillian. What Makes Us Unique? Our First Talk about Diversity, 1 vol. Revell, Cindy, illus. 2016. (Just Enough Ser.). (ENG.). 32p. (J). (gr. k-1). 19.95 *(978-1-4598-0948-2(3))* Orca Bk. Pubs. USA.

Sanna, Ellyn. Gallup Guides for Youth Facing Persistent Prejudice Muslims. 2012. (Gallup Guides for Youth Facing Persistent Prejudice Ser.). 64p. (J). (gr. 7-8). 22.95 *(978-1-4222-2468-7(6))* Mason Crest.

—People with Mental & Physical Challenges. 2012. (Gallup Guides for Youth Facing Persistent Prejudice Ser.). 64p. (J). (gr. 7-8). 22.95 *(978-1-4222-2470-0(8))* Mason Crest.

Scheunemann, Pam. Learning about Differences, 1 vol. 2004. (Keeping the Peace Ser.). (ENG., Illus.). 24p. (J). (gr. k-3). lib. bdg. 24.21 *(978-1-59197-561-8(1))*, SandCastle) ABDO Publishing Co.

—Tolerance. 2003. (United We Stand Ser.). (ENG., Illus.). 24p. (J). (gr. k-3). lib. bdg. 24.21 *(978-1-57765-881-8(7))*, SandCastle) ABDO Publishing Co.

Thomson Gale Staff. Prejudice in the Modern World. Hanes, Sharon M., ed. rev. ed. 2007. (Prejudice in the Modern World Reference Library). (ENG.). 256p. (YA). 106.00 *(978-1-4144-0208-6(2))*, UXL) Cengage Gale.

—Prejudice in the Modern World - Almanac, 2.0. Hanes, Richard C. et al, eds. rev. ed. 2007. (Prejudice in the Modern World Reference Library). (ENG.). 462p. (YA). 191.00 *(978-1-4144-0204-8(X))*, UXL) Cengage Gale.

Thomson Gale Staff & Hermsen, Sarah. Prejudice in the Modern World: Biographies. Hanes, Richard C. & Rudd, Kelly, eds. rev. ed. 2007. (Prejudice in the Modern World Reference Library). (ENG.). 288p. (YA). 106.00 *(978-1-4144-0207-9(4))*, UXL) Cengage Gale.

—Prejudice in the Modern World: Cumulative Index. rev. ed. 2007. (Prejudice in the Modern World Reference Library). (ENG.). 34p. (YA). 5.00 *(978-1-4144-0209-3(0))*, UXL) Cengage Gale.

Webber, Diane & Mandel, Laurie. Totally Tolerant: Spotting & Stopping Prejudice. 2008. (ENG.). 112p. (J). (gr. 7-18). pap. 8.95 *(978-0-531-20525-9(8))* Scholastic Library Publishing.

TOLERATION—FICTION

Akerson, Julie Chicos. The Life of Riley the Cat. Taylor, Jennifer, illus. 2005. 28p. (J). 15.50 *(978-1-4120-5858-2(9))* Trafford Publishing.

Alary, Laura. Mira & the Big Story. Todd, Sue, illus. 2012. (ENG.). 36p. (J). 12.00 *(978-1-55896-693-2(5))*, Skinner Hse. Bks.) Unitarian Universalist Assn.

Aldrich, Jodi. Bee Mumble & Wug. 2011. 36p. (J). pap. 20.95 *(978-1-4327-6808-9(5))* Outskirts Pr., Inc.

Alimonti, Frederick & Tedesco, Ann. Tommy & the T-Tops: Helping Children Overcome Prejudice. Hazard, John, illus. 2009. (Let's Talk Ser.). (ENG.). 48p. (J). (gr. -1-4). pap. 8.95 *(978-0-88282-305-8(1))* New Horizon Pr. Pubs., Inc.

Applegate, Katherine. Wishtree. 2017. (ENG., Illus.). 224p. (J). 16.99 ***(978-1-250-04322-1(0))***, 9781250043221) Feiwel & Friends.

Baker, Ed. The Story of Kitten Cuckoo. Baker, Ed, illus. 2007. (ENG., Illus.). 32p. (J). (gr. -1-17). 15.95 *(978-1-933572-04-8(3))* Centro Bks., LLC.

Barry, Debra R. Brady Pickles. 2011. 32p. pap. 24.95 *(978-1-4626-3716-4(7))* America Star Bks.

Baynes, Jenean Atwood & Atwood, John H. Blue Spots! Yellow Spots! 2012. 28p. (-18). pap. 13.54 *(978-1-4669-4969-0(4))* Trafford Publishing.

Beck, Rachel. Bella & the Little Gray Kitten. 2011. 40p. (gr. -1). pap. 18.50 *(978-1-4567-3365-0(6))* AuthorHouse.

Bradbury, Jennifer. A Moment Comes. 2013. (ENG., Illus.). 288p. (YA). (gr. 7). 17.99 *(978-1-4169-7876-3(3))* Simon & Schuster Children's Publishing.

Carr, Elias. Jo y la Sopa Lenta. Garton, Michael, illus. 2016. (SPA.). (J). ***(978-1-5064-2097-4(4))***, Sparkhouse Pr.) Spark Hse.

Castonguay, Leo. Piper Peter. 2012. 44p. pap. 24.95 *(978-1-4626-8078-8(X))* America Star Bks.

Cook, Julia. I Want to Be the Only Dog! DuFalla, Anita, illus. 2015. (ENG.). 32p. (J). pap. 10.95 *(978-1-934490-86-0(5))* Boys Town Pr.

Defosse, Rosana Curiel. Santiago en el Pantano. Barradas, Leticia, illus. (Santiago Y Los Valores Ser.). (SPA.). 32p. (J). (gr. 3-5). pap. 7.95 *(978-970-29-0133-4(2))* Santillana USA Publishing Co., Inc.

Elliott, David. Nobody's Perfect. Zuppardi, Sam, illus. 2015. (ENG.). 32p. (J). (gr. -1-3). 16.99 *(978-0-7636-6909-6(8))* Candlewick Pr.

Ellison, Laura. Hard Rock, Hard Times: Coming of Age in Butte Montana, 1911-1917. 2005. 195p. (YA). per. *(978-0-9722217-7-1(8))* Horse Creek Pubns.

Erskine, Kathryn. Quaking. 2010. (ENG.). 256p. (YA). (gr. 7-18). 7.99 *(978-0-14-241476-7(X))*, Speak) Penguin Young Readers Group.

Flinn, Alex. Fade to Black. 2006. (ENG.). 208p. (YA). (gr. 9-12). pap. 9.99 *(978-0-06-056842-9(9))*, HarperTeen) HarperCollins Pubs.

Frost, Daniel, tr. from SPA. You, Them, & the Others. 2006. Orig. Title: Tú, ellos y los Otros. (Illus.). 111p. (J). per. 12.95 net. *(978-0-9785270-8-2(9))* Pasiteles Publishing Co.

Frye, Timea Csonka. Wishing Star: Lost in the Woods. 2013. 32p. pap. 24.95 *(978-1-63000-931-1(8))* America Star Bks.

Gilks, Tina M. My Dog Mo. 2011. 32p. pap. 17.25 *(978-1-4269-4931-9(6))* Trafford Publishing.

Harris, Robie H. Who We Are! All about Being the Same & Being Different. Westcott, Nadine Bernard, illus. 2016. (Let's Talk about You & Me Ser.). (ENG.). 40p. (J). (-k). 15.99 *(978-0-7636-6903-4(2))* Candlewick Pr.

Henderson, Barbara. Down in Mr Brown's Garden. 2009. 40p. pap. 14.75 *(978-1-60860-703-7(8))*, Strategic Bk. Publishing) Strategic Book Publishing & Rights Agency (SBPRA).

Hoblin, Paul & Hueller, Patrick. Archenemy. 2013. (Counterattack Ser.). (ENG.). 112p. (YA). (gr. 6-12). pap. 7.95 *(978-1-4677-0721-3(X))*; lib. bdg. 27.93 *(978-1-4677-0306-2(0))* Lerner Publishing Group.

Hockerman, Dennis, illus. The Country Mouse & the City Mouse: A Tale of Tolerance. 2006. (J). 6.99 *(978-1-59939-003-1(5))* Cornerstone Pr.

Hooray for Boys & Girls! 2006. (J). 15.95 *(978-0-9776837-0-3(2))* West Woods Pr.

Humphrey, Eleanor Cairns. Building Santa's Work Shop from Tales of the Crystal Cave. 2012. 268p. pap. 27.95 *(978-1-4626-7820-4(3))* America Star Bks.

Ish-Kishor, Sulamith. A Boy of Old Prague. Shahn, Ben, illus. 2008. (Dover Children's Classics Ser.). (ENG.). 96p. (J). (gr. 4-6). pap. 3.99 *(978-0-486-46766-5(X))* Dover Pubns., Inc.

Jay, Stacey. Of Beast & Beauty. 2014. (ENG.). 400p. (YA). (gr. 9). pap. 9.99 *(978-0-385-74321-1(1))*, Ember) Random Hse. Children's Bks.

Job, et al. Yakari & the Beavers. 2007. (Yakari Ser.: 3). (ENG., Illus.). 48p. (J). (gr. 4-7). per. 11.95 *(978-1-905460-09-0(0))* CineBook GBR. Dist: National Bk. Network.

Karre, Elizabeth. The Fight. 2013. (Surviving Southside Ser.). (ENG.). 128p. (YA). (gr. 6-12). pap. 7.95 *(978-1-4677-0709-1(0))* Lerner Publishing Group.

Katz, Karin Jill. There's a Fly in My Soup. 2012. 16p. pap. 15.99 *(978-1-4772-6331-0(4))* AuthorHouse.

Kelly, Keith. Peace Comes to Ajani. Kelly, Keith, illus. 2009. (Illus.). 56p. (J). pap. 9.95 *(978-0-932112-59-0(5))* Carolina Wren Pr.

Kempter, Christa & Weldin, Frauke. Wally & Mae. 2010. (ENG., Illus.). 32p. (J). (gr. -1-k). pap. 7.95 *(978-0-7358-2290-0(5))* North-South Bks., Inc.

Kerrin, Jessica Scott. Martin Bridge: Onwards & Upwards! Kelly, Joseph, illus. 2009. (Martin Bridge Ser.). (ENG.). 112p. (J). (gr. 2-5). 6.95 *(978-1-55453-161-5(6))* Kids Can Pr., Ltd. CAN. Dist: Hachette Bk. Group.

Kim, YoeongAh. The Shooting Stars Soccer Team. Lee, Hyeongjin, illus. rev. ed. 2014. (MySELF Bookshelf Ser.). (ENG.). 32p. (J). (gr. k-2). lib. bdg. 25.27 *(978-1-59953-648-4(X))* Norwood Hse. Pr.

Lash, Batton, et al. The Scrapyard Detectives: Collected Cases. 2007. (Illus.). 102p. (J). (gr. 3-5). per. *(978-0-9797193-0-1(5))* Diversity Foundation, The.

Lennon, John. Imagine. Jullien, Jean, illus. 2017. (ENG.). 32p. (J). (gr. -1-3). 18.99 ***(978-1-328-80865-3(3))***, Clarion Bks.) Houghton Mifflin Harcourt Trade & Reference Pubs.

Luchsinger, Dena. Sometimes Smart Is Good/A Veces Es Bueno Ser Listo. Jerome, Karen A., illus. 2007. (SPA & ENG.). 32p. (J). (gr. -1). 16.00 *(978-0-8028-5215-1(7))*, Eerdmans Bks For Young Readers) Eerdmans, William B. Publishing Co.

Luciani, Brigitte. A Hubbub. Gauvin, Edward, tr. from FRE. Tharlet, Eve, illus. 2010. (Mr. Badger & Mrs. Fox Ser.: 2). (ENG.). 32p. (J). (gr. k-3). pap. 6.95 *(978-0-7613-5632-5(0))*, Graphic Universe™)Bk. 2. 25.26 *(978-0-7613-5626-4(6))* Lerner Publishing Group.

—The Meeting. Burrell, Carol, tr. from FRE. Tharlet, Eve, illus. 2010. (Mr. Badger & Mrs. Fox Ser.: 1). (ENG.). 32p. (J). (gr. k-3). lib. bdg. 25.26 *(978-0-7613-5625-7(8))* Lerner Publishing Group.

—The Meeting. Burrell, Carol, tr. from FRE. Tharlet, Eve, illus. 2010. 1. (ENG.). 32p. (C). (gr. k-3). pap. 10.95 *(978-0-7613-5631-8(2))* National Geographic School Publishing, Inc.

M. Alvarado. We Are Different, but the Same. 2012. 16p. pap. 15.99 *(978-1-4685-4425-1(X))* AuthorHouse.

Mantchev, Lisa. Strictly No Elephants. Yoo, Taeeun, illus. 2015. (ENG.). 32p. (J). (gr. -1-3). 17.99 *(978-1-4814-1647-4(2))*, Simon & Schuster Bks. For Young Readers) Simon & Schuster Bks. For Young Readers.

Marin, Cheech. Cheech y el Autobus Fantasma. Fabiancic, Miriam, tr. Ramirez, Orlando L., illus. 2009. (SPA.). 32p. (J). (gr. -1-3). 17.99 *(978-0-06-113214-8(4))*, Rayo) HarperCollins Pubs.

Menchin, Scott. What Are You Waiting For? Phelan, Matt, illus. 2017. (ENG.). 32p. (J). 16.99 *(978-1-62672-152-4(1))*, 9781626721524) Roaring Brook Pr.

Moulton, Mark K. A Royal Wedding. Good, Karen H., illus. 2007. (ENG.). 32p. (J). (gr. k-3). 14.99 *(978-0-8249-8677-3(6))*, Ideal Pubns.) Worthy Publishing.

Moulton, Mark Kimball. One Enchanted Evening. Crouch, Karen Hillard, illus. 2003. 32p. (J). 14.95 *(978-0-8249-5480-2(7))*, Ideal Pubns.) Worthy Publishing.

Mullinax, Jerry. Enoree. 2009. (YA). pap. *(978-0-88092-646-1(5))* Royal Fireworks Publishing Co.

Muschla, Gary Robert. The Sword & the Cross. 2009. (YA). pap. *(978-0-88092-472-6(1))* Royal Fireworks Publishing Co.

Naylor, Phyllis Reynolds. Faith, Hope, & Ivy June. 2011. (ENG.). 288p. (J). (gr. 3-7). 6.99 *(978-0-375-84491-1(0))*, Yearling) Random Hse. Children's Bks.

Owens, Robert. Butterfly Love. 2008. 34p. pap. 16.70 *(978-0-557-01168-1(X))* Lulu Pr., Inc.

Pelley, Kathleen. The Giant King. Manning, Maurie J., tr. Manning, Maurie J., illus. 2003. (New Child & Family Press Titles Ser.). 32p. (gr. -1-4). 14.95 *(978-0-87868-880-7(3))*, 8803, Child & Family Pr.) Child Welfare League of America, Inc.

Peterson, Lois. Meeting Miss 405, 1 vol. 2008. (Orca Young Readers Ser.). (ENG.). 112p. (J). (gr. 3-6). pap. 7.95 *(978-1-55469-015-2(3))* Orca Bk. Pubs. USA.

Queen Rania of Jordan Al Abdullah Staff, et al. The Sandwich Swap. Tusa, Tricia, illus. 2010. (ENG.). 32p. (J). (gr. -1-2). 16.99 *(978-1-4231-2484-9(7))* Hyperion Pr.

Regan, Lisa. Wait Your Turn, Tilly: Be Patient. 2017. (You Choose Ser.). 32p. (J). (gr. 2-2). lib. bdg. 25.27 **(978-0-7660-8704-0(2))** Enslow Pubs., Inc.
Sagar, Marie. Jimmy's Adventures: I'm Bored & Mr. Gray Bat. 2007. 20p. (J). 7.00 *(978-0-8059-7494-2(6))* Dorrance Publishing Co., Inc.
Schmidt, René. Leaving Fletchville, 1 vol. 2008. (ENG.). 168p. (J). (gr. 3-7). pap. 9.95 *(978-1-55143-945-7(X))* Orca Bk. Pubs. USA.
Shelley, Mary. Frankenstein: With a Discussion of Tolerance. Clift, Eva, tr. Clift, Eva, illus. 2003. (Values in Action Illustrated Classics Ser.). (J). *(978-1-59203-048-4(3))* Learning Challenge, Inc.
Smithern, Beth. Cocoa Bean & Squirt. 2010. 68p. pap. 10.49 *(978-1-4520-1929-1(0))* AuthorHouse.
Storm, Hannah, frwd. Buddy Booby's Birthmark. 2006. (Illus.). 36p. (J). 21.99 *(978-0-9794413-0-1(7))*; pap. 15.99 *(978-0-9794413-1-8(5))* E & D Bks., Ltd.
Swift, Jonathan. Gulliver's Travels: And A Discussion of Tolerance. Clift, Eva, illus. 2003. (Values in Action Illustrated Classics Ser.). 191p. (J). *(978-1-59203-029-3(7))* Learning Challenge, Inc.
Taylor, Chloë. Clothes Minded. Zhang, Nancy, illus. 2015. (Sew Zoey Ser.: 11). (ENG.). 160p. (J). (gr. 3-7). pap. 6.99 *(978-1-4814-2927-6(2)*, Simon Spotlight) Simon Spotlight.
Thompson, Michael. Los Otros Osos / the Other Bears. Thompson, Michael, illus. 2013. (ENG & SPA., Illus.). (J). 16.99 *(978-1-59572-644-5(6))* Star Bright Bks., Inc.
—The Other Bears, 1 vol. Thompson, Michael, illus. 2013.Tr. of Os Outros Ursos. (ENG., Illus.). 32p. (J). 16.99 *(978-1-59572-638-4(1))*; pap. 6.99 *(978-1-59572-639-1(X))* Star Bright Bks., Inc.
Uhlberg, Myron. Dad, Jackie, & Me, 1 vol. Bootman, Colin, illus. (ENG.). 32p. (J). 2010. pap. 8.95 *(978-1-56145-531-7(8))* 2005. 16.95 *(978-1-56145-329-0(3))* Peachtree Pubs.
Vanoosting, James. Walking Mary. 2005. 144p. (J). (gr. 7-18). lib. bdg. 16.89 *(978-0-06-028472-5(2))* HarperCollins Pubs.
Vaughn, Royce, illus. Seymour Bluffs & Robert Wadlow, the Tallest Man in the World: A Story about Diversity & Tolerance. 2007. 28p. (J). 12.95 *(978-0-9728538-4-2(7))* Arnica Publishing.
Wahl, Jan. Candy Shop. Wong, Nicole, illus. 2005. (ENG.). 32p. (J). (gr. -1-3). pap. 7.95 *(978-1-57091-668-7(3))* Charlesbridge Publishing, Inc.
—Candy Shop. Wong, Nicole E., illus. 2004. (ENG.). 32p. (J). (gr. -1-3). 15.95 *(978-1-57091-508-6(3))* Charlesbridge Publishing, Inc.
Williams, Sam. Talk Peace. Moriuchi, Mique, illus. 2005. 32p. (J). 16.95 *(978-0-8234-1936-4(3))* Holiday Hse., Inc.
Wood, Douglas. Old Turtle & the Broken Truth. Muth, Jon J., illus. 2003. (ENG.). 64p. (J). (gr. -1-3). 17.99 *(978-0-439-32109-9(3))* Scholastic, Inc.
Zia, Farhana. The Garden of My Imaan, 1 vol. 2013. (ENG.). 192p. (J). (gr. 3-5). 15.95 *(978-1-56145-698-7(5))* Peachtree Pubs.

TOLKIEN, J. R. R. (JOHN RONALD RUEL), 1892-1973

Clinton, Greg. Reading & Interpreting the Works of J.R.R. Tolkien. 2016. (Lit Crit Guides). (Illus.). 176p. (J). 39.93 *(978-0-7660-8362-2(4))* Enslow Pubs., Inc.
Collins, David R. J. R. R. Tolkien. 2004. (Just the Facts Biographies Ser.). (ENG., Illus.). 112p. (gr. 5-12). lib. bdg. 27.93 *(978-0-8225-2470-0(8))* Lerner Publishing Group.
Heims, Neil. J. R. R. Tolkien. 2004. (Great Writers Ser.). (Illus.). 128p. (YA). (gr. 9-13). 31.95 *(978-0-7910-7847-1(7)*, Chelsea Hse.) Facts On File, Inc.
McAlister, Caroline. John Ronald's Dragons: the Story of J. R. R. Tolkien. Wheeler, Eliza, illus. 2017. (ENG.). 48p. (J). 18.99 *(978-1-62672-092-3(4)*, 9781626720923) Roaring Brook Pr.
Neimark, Anne E. Mythmaker: The Life of J. R. R. Tolkien, Creator of the Hobbit & the Lord of the Rings. Weinman, Brad, illus. (ENG.). 144p. (J). (gr. 5-7). 2014. pap. 7.99 *(978-0-544-02324-6(2)*, HMH Books For Young Readers) 2012. 12.99 *(978-0-547-99734-6(5))* Houghton Mifflin Harcourt Publishing Co.
Pollack, Pam & Belviso, Meg. Who Was J. R. R. Tolkien? Moore, Jonathan & Harrison, Nancy, illus. 2015. 105p. (J). *(978-1-4806-8935-0(1))* Baker & Taylor, CATS.
Pollack, Pamela D. & Belviso, Meg. Who Was J. R. R. Tolkien? Moore, Jonathan & Harrison, Nancy, illus. 2015. (Who Was? Ser.). (ENG.). 112p. (J). (gr. 3-7). 5.99 *(978-0-448-48302-3(5)*, Grosset & Dunlap) Penguin Young Readers Group.
Repun, Graciela. Master of the Rings: Inside the World of J. R. R. Tolkein. 2003. (ENG., Illus.). 176p. pap. *(978-1-84046-400-9(3)*, Wizard Books) Icon Bks., Ltd.
Wallner, Alexandra & Wallner, John C. J. R. R. Tolkien. 2011. (ENG., Illus.). 32p. (J). 17.95 *(978-0-8234-1951-7(7))* Holiday Hse., Inc.
Wheeler, Jill C. J. R. R. Tolkien, 1 vol. 2009. (Children's Authors Set 5 Ser.). (ENG.). 24p. (J). (gr. 2-5). 25.65 *(978-1-60453-080-3(4))* ABDO Publishing Co.

TONGUE

Bozzo, Linda. Amazing Animal Tongues. (Creature Features Ser.). 24p. 2009. (gr. 2-3). 42.50 *(978-1-61512-070-3(X)*, PowerKids Pr.) 2008. (Illus.). (J). (gr. 3-7). lib. bdg. 22.60 *(978-1-4042-4172-5(8))* Rosen Publishing Group, Inc., The.
Canetti, Yanitzia. La adaptación, ¡qué Sensación! Lenguas. 2010. (SPA.). 24p. (J). pap. *(978-1-59835-188-0(5)*, BrickHouse Education) Cambridge BrickHouse, Inc.
—Amazing Adaptations! Tongues. 2010. 24p. (J). pap. *(978-1-59835-213-9(X)*, BrickHouse Education) Cambridge BrickHouse, Inc.
Cusick, Dawn. Animal Tongues. 2017. (ENG., Illus.). 36p. (J). (gr. -1-3). pap. 7.99 **(978-1-58089-687-0(1))** Charlesbridge Publishing, Inc.
Fernandez, A. & Fernandez, Q. Hooray for My Taste. (Hooray for My Senses Ser.). (Illus.). (J). 19.27 *(978-1-58952-376-0(8))* Rourke Educational Media.
Hopper, Karina. Mouth & Tongue Let's Have Some Fun! Macdonald, Lisa, illus. 2010. (ENG.). 48p. pap. 9.95 *(978-1-84905-161-3(5)*, 3101) Kingsley, Jessica Pubs. GBR. Dist: Macmillan Distribution Ltd.
Kubler, Annie, illus. What Can I Taste? 2011. (Small Senses Ser.). (ENG.). 12p. (J). bds. *(978-1-84643-375-7(4))* Child's Play International Ltd.
Libra, Anna. Why Does That Taste Bad? An Inside Look at the Tongue. 2003. (J). pap. *(978-1-58417-069-3(7))*; lib. bdg. *(978-1-58417-006-8(9))* Lake Street Pubs.
Meachen Rau, Dana. Yum! A Book about Taste. Peterson, Rick, illus. 2005. (Amazing Body: the Five Senses Ser.). (ENG.). 24p. (gr. k-3). 26.65 *(978-1-4048-1021-1(8))* Picture Window Bks.
—Yum! [Scholastic]: A Book about Taste. Peterson, Rick, illus. 2010. (Amazing Body: the Five Senses Ser.). 24p. pap. 0.56 *(978-1-4048-6543-3(8)*, Nonfiction Picture Bks.) Picture Window Bks.
Pryor, Kimberley Jane. Tasting. 2003. (Senses Ser.). (Illus.). 32p. (gr. 2-4). 23.00 *(978-0-7910-7557-9(5)*, Chelsea Hse.) Facts On File, Inc.
Randolph, Joanne. Whose Tongue Is This? 2009. (Animal Clues Ser.). 24p. (gr. 1-1). 42.50 *(978-1-61511-436-8(X))*; (Illus.). (J). lib. bdg. 22.60 *(978-1-4042-4455-9(7))* Rosen Publishing Group, Inc., The. (PowerKids Pr.).
—Whose Tongue Is This? De Quién Es Esta Lengua? 2009. (Animal Clues / ¿Adivina de Quién Es? Ser.). (SPA & ENG., Illus.). 24p. (J). lib. bdg. 22.60 *(978-1-4358-2532-1(2)*, PowerKids Pr.) Rosen Publishing Group, Inc., The.
—Whose Tongue Is This? / ¿de quién es esta Lengua? 2009. (Animal Clues / ¿Adivina de Quién Es? Ser.). (ENG & SPA.). 24p. (gr. 1-1). 42.50 *(978-1-61511-442-9(4)*, Editorial Buenas Letras) Rosen Publishing Group, Inc., The.
Rustad, Martha E. H. Tasting. 2014. (Illus.). 24p. (J). lib. bdg. 25.65 *(978-1-62031-118-9(6)*, Bullfrog Bks.) Jump! Inc.
Stewart, Melissa. Terrific Tongues up Close. 2012. (Animal Bodies up Close Ser.). 24p. (J). (gr. k-3). (Illus.). pap. 7.95 *(978-1-4644-0083-4(0))*; 22.60 *(978-0-7660-3894-3(7))* Enslow Pubs., Inc. (Enslow Elementary).
Wearing, Judy. Taste. 2009. (World of Wonder Ser.). (Illus.). 24p. (J). (gr. 2-4). pap. 8.95 *(978-1-60596-057-9(8))*; lib. bdg. 24.45 *(978-1-60596-056-2(X))* Weigl Pubs., Inc.

TOOLS

see also Agricultural Machinery; Machinery

ABDO Publishing Company Staff. More Professional Tools. 2014. (More Professional Tools Ser.: 6). (ENG.). 24p. (gr. k-4). lib. bdg. 153.90 *(978-1-62403-070-3(X)*, Super SandCastle) ABDO Publishing Co.
Adams, Barbara. A World of Tools. Date not set. (Early Science Big Bks.). (Illus.). 16p. (J). (gr. -1-2). pap. 16.95 *(978-1-58273-115-5(2))* Sundance/Newbridge Educational Publishing.
Benchmark Education Company, LLC Staff, compiled by. Tools & Technology. 2006. (J). 148.00 *(978-1-4108-7034-6(0))* Benchmark Education Co.
Biskup, Agnieszka. Batarangs & Grapnels: The Science Behind Batman's Utility Belt, 1 vol. 2014. (Batman Science Ser.). (ENG.). 32p. (gr. 3-4). 27.32 *(978-1-4765-3943-0(X)*, DC Super Heroes) Stone Arch Bks.
Blevins, Wiley. Tools Scientists Use, 6 vols., Set. 2004. (Phonics Readers Books 37-72 Ser.). (ENG.). 8p. (gr. k-1). pap. 35.70 *(978-0-7368-4080-4(X)*, Phonics Readers) Capstone Press of Coughlan Cos.
Buzzeo, Toni. Whose Tools? Datz, Jim, illus. 2015. (Whose Tools? Ser.). (ENG.). 16p. (J). (gr. -1 — 1). bds. 9.95 *(978-1-4197-1431-3(7))* Abrams, Inc.
Cain, Marie Mowery. Tools Rule. 2013. (Big Books, Red Ser.). (ENG & SPA., Illus.). 16p. pap. 33.00 *(978-1-59246-212-4(X))* Big Books, by George!
Cooper, Sharon Katz. Whose Tools Are These? A Look at Tools Workers Use - Big, Sharp, & Smooth, 1 vol. Muehlenhardt, Amy Bailey, illus. 2006. (Whose Is It?: Community Workers Ser.). (ENG.). 24p. (gr. -1-2). lib. bdg. 26.65 *(978-1-4048-1602-2(X))* Picture Window Bks.
Gibbons, Gail. Tool Book. 2017. (ENG.). 18p. (J). (gr. -1 — 1). bds. 7.99 **(978-0-8234-3872-3(4))** Holiday Hse., Inc.
Gosman, Gillian. Simple Machines at School. 2014. (Simple Machines Everywhere Ser.). (Illus.). 24p. (J). (gr. k-3). pap. 49.50 *(978-1-4777-6645-3(6)*, PowerKids Pr.) Rosen Publishing Group, Inc., The.
Gregory, Josh. Drills. 2013. (21st Century Junior Library: Basic Tools Ser.). (ENG.). 24p. (J). (gr. 2-5). 25.64 *(978-1-62431-170-3(9)*, 203000); pap. 12.79 *(978-1-62431-302-8(7)*, 203002) Cherry Lake Publishing.
—Hammers. 2013. (21st Century Junior Library: Basic Tools Ser.). (ENG.). 24p. (J). (gr. 2-5). 25.64 *(978-1-62431-168-0(7)*, 202992); pap. 12.79 *(978-1-62431-300-4(0)*, 202994) Cherry Lake Publishing.
—Screwdrivers. 2013. (21st Century Junior Library: Basic Tools Ser.). (ENG.). 24p. (J). (gr. 2-5). 25.64 *(978-1-62431-169-7(5)*, 202996); pap. 12.79 *(978-1-62431-301-1(9)*, 202998) Cherry Lake Publishing.
—Wrenches. 2013. (21st Century Junior Library: Basic Tools Ser.). (ENG.). 24p. (J). (gr. 2-5). 25.64 *(978-1-62431-175-8(X)*, 203020); pap. 12.79 *(978-1-62431-307-3(8)*, 203022) Cherry Lake Publishing.
Hanson, Anders. Hammers, 1 vol. 2010. (Tools of the Trade Ser.). (ENG., Illus.). 24p. (J). (gr. k-3). lib. bdg. 24.21 *(978-1-60453-582-2(2)*, SandCastle) ABDO Publishing Co.
—Pliers, 1 vol. 2010. (Tools of the Trade Ser.). (ENG., Illus.). 24p. (J). (gr. k-3). lib. bdg. 24.21 *(978-1-60453-583-9(0)*, SandCastle) ABDO Publishing Co.
—Saws, 1 vol. 2010. (Tools of the Trade Ser.). (ENG., Illus.). 24p. (J). (gr. k-3). lib. bdg. 24.21 *(978-1-60453-584-6(9)*, SandCastle) ABDO Publishing Co.
—Tools of the Trade, 6 vols., Set. Incl. Drills. lib. bdg. 24.21 *(978-1-60453-581-5(4))*; Hammers. lib. bdg. 24.21 *(978-1-60453-582-2(2))*; Pliers. lib. bdg. 24.21 *(978-1-60453-583-9(0))*; Saws. lib. bdg. 24.21 *(978-1-60453-584-6(9))*; Screwdrivers. 24.21 *(978-1-60453-585-3(7))*; Wrenches. lib. bdg. 24.21 *(978-1-60453-586-0(5))*; (J). (gr. k-3). (Tools of the Trade Ser.: 6). (ENG., Illus.). 24p. 2010. Set lib. bdg. 145.26 *(978-1-60453-580-8(6)*, SandCastle) ABDO Publishing Co.
—Wrenches, 1 vol. 2010. (Tools of the Trade Ser.). (ENG., Illus.). 24p. (J). (gr. k-3). lib. bdg. 24.21 *(978-1-60453-586-0(5)*, SandCastle) ABDO Publishing Co.
King, Aven. A Doctor's Tools. 2015. (Community Helpers & Their Tools Ser.). (ENG., Illus.). 24p. (J). (gr. 2-3). pap. 8.25 *(978-1-4994-0838-6(2)*, PowerKids Pr.) Rosen Publishing Group, Inc., The.
Mangieri, Catherine. Using Measuring Tools. 2009. (Real Life Readers Ser.). 12p. (gr. 1-2). pap. 5.90 *(978-1-4042-7921-6(0)*, Rosen Classroom) Rosen Publishing Group, Inc., The.
Manolis, Kay. Ramps. 2009. (Simple Machines Ser.). (ENG., Illus.). 24p. (J). (gr. 2-5). lib. bdg. 25.95 *(978-1-60014-346-5(6)*, Blastoff! Readers) Bellwether Media.
—Screws. 2009. (Simple Machines Ser.). (ENG., Illus.). 24p. (J). (gr. 2-5). lib. bdg. 25.95 *(978-1-60014-322-9(9)*, Blastoff! Readers) Bellwether Media.
—Wedges. 2009. (Simple Machines Ser.). (ENG., Illus.). 24p. (J). (gr. 2-5). lib. bdg. 25.95 *(978-1-60014-323-6(7)*, Blastoff! Readers) Bellwether Media.
Marsico, Katie. Pliers. 2013. (21st Century Junior Library: Basic Tools Ser.). (ENG., Illus.). 24p. (J). (gr. 2-5). 25.64 *(978-1-62431-174-1(1)*, 203016); pap. 12.79 *(978-1-62431-306-6(X)*, 203018) Cherry Lake Publishing.
—Saws. 2013. (21st Century Junior Library: Basic Tools Ser.). (ENG.). 24p. (J). (gr. 2-5). 25.64 *(978-1-62431-171-0(7)*, 203004); pap. 12.79 *(978-1-62431-303-5(5)*, 203006) Cherry Lake Publishing.
Masterson, Josephine. My Grandfather's Workshop. 2015. (Rosen REAL Readers: STEM & STEAM Collection). (ENG.). 8p. pap. 5.46 *(978-1-4994-9708-3(3)*, Rosen Classroom) Rosen Publishing Group, Inc., The.
McFadden, Jesse. A Construction Worker's Tools. 2015. (Community Helpers & Their Tools Ser.). (ENG., Illus.). 24p. (J). (gr. 2-3). pap. 8.25 *(978-1-4994-0836-2(6)*, PowerKids Pr.) Rosen Publishing Group, Inc., The.
McKinney, Devon. A Firefighter's Tools. 2015. (Community Helpers & Their Tools Ser.). (ENG.). 24p. (J). (gr. 2-3). 23.60 *(978-1-4994-0897-3(8)*, PowerKids Pr.) Rosen Publishing Group, Inc., The.
Meachen Rau, Dana. Builders/Los Contructores. 2007. (Tools We Use/Instrumentos de Trabajo Ser.). (SPA & ENG., Illus.). 32p. (gr. k-2). lib. bdg. 15.95 *(978-0-7614-2821-3(6)*, Benchmark Bks.) Marshall Cavendish Corp.
—Los Constructores. 2007. (Instrumentos de Trabajo Ser.). (SPA., Illus.). 32p. (gr. k-2). lib. bdg. 15.95 *(978-0-7614-2797-1(X)*, Benchmark Bks.) Marshall Cavendish Corp.
Milet Publishing Staff. My First Bilingual Book - Tools. 2014. (My First Bilingual Book Ser.). (Illus.). 20p. (J). (— 1). (ENG & ARA.). bds. 7.99 *(978-1-84059-906-0(5))*; (ENG & GER., bds. 7.99 *(978-1-84059-911-4(1))*; (ENG, POL & POR., bds. 7.99 *(978-1-84059-914-5(6))*; (ENG & URD., bds. 7.99 *(978-1-84059-920-6(0))*; (SPA & ENG., bds. 7.99 *(978-1-84059-918-3(9))*; (ENG & RUS., bds. 7.99 *(978-1-84059-916-9(2))*; (ENG & TUR., bds. 7.99 *(978-1-84059-919-0(7))*; (ENG & BEN., bds. 7.99 *(978-1-84059-907-7(3))* Milet Publishing.
—My First Bilingual Book - Tools - English. 2014. (My First Bilingual Book Ser.). (ENG & VIE., Illus.). 20p. (J). (— 1). bds. 7.99 *(978-1-84059-921-3(9))* Milet Publishing.
—My First Bilingual Book - Tools - Ferramentas. 2014. (My First Bilingual Book Ser.). (POR & ENG., Illus.). 20p. (J). (— 1). bds. 7.99 *(978-1-84059-915-2(4))* Milet Publishing.
—My First Bilingual Book - Tools (English-Somali) 2014. (My First Bilingual Book Ser.). (ENG & SOM., Illus.). 20p. (J). (— 1). bds. 7.99 *(978-1-84059-917-6(0))* Milet Publishing.
—Tools. 2014. (My First Bilingual Book Ser.). (ENG & ITA., Illus.). 20p. (J). (— 1). bds. 7.99 *(978-1-84059-912-1(X))* Milet Publishing.
—Tools - My First Bilingual Book. 2014. (My First Bilingual Book Ser.). (ENG & PER., Illus.). 20p. (J). (— 1). bds. 7.99 *(978-1-84059-909-1(X))*; bds. 7.99 *(978-1-84059-908-4(1))*; bds. 7.99 *(978-1-84059-913-8(8))* Milet Publishing.
—Tools (English-French) 2014. (My First Bilingual Book Ser.). (FRE & ENG., Illus.). 20p. (J). (— 1). bds. 7.99 *(978-1-84059-910-7(3))* Milet Publishing.
Monroe, Andrea. The Science of Tools. 2003. (Living Science Ser.). (Illus.). 32p. (J). (gr. 1-3). pap. 9.95 *(978-1-930954-31-1(X))* Weigl Pubs., Inc.
Morris, Ann. Tools. Heyman, Ken, photos by. 2015. (Illus.). 32p. pap. 7.00 *(978-1-61003-622-1(0))* Center for the Collaborative Classroom.
Nelson, Robin. What Do Pliers Do? 2012. (First Step Nonfiction - Tools at Work Ser.). (ENG., Illus.). 24p. (gr. k-2). lib. bdg. 23.93 *(978-0-7613-8980-4(6)*, Lerner Pubns.) Lerner Publishing Group.
—What Does a Hammer Do? 2012. (First Step Nonfiction - Tools at Work Ser.). (ENG., Illus.). 24p. (gr. k-2). pap. 6.95 *(978-1-58013-947-2(7))*; lib. bdg. 23.93 *(978-0-7613-8976-7(8)*, Lerner Pubns.) Lerner Publishing Group.
—What Does a Level Do? 2012. (First Step Nonfiction - Tools at Work Ser.). (ENG., Illus.). 24p. (gr. k-2). pap. 6.95 *(978-1-58013-948-9(5))*; lib. bdg. 23.93 *(978-0-7613-8981-1(4)*, Lerner Pubns.) Lerner Publishing Group.
—What Does a Saw Do? 2012. (First Step Nonfiction - Tools at Work Ser.). (ENG., Illus.). 24p. (gr. k-2). pap. 6.95 *(978-1-58013-950-2(7))*; lib. bdg. 23.93 *(978-0-7613-8979-8(2)*, Lerner Pubns.) Lerner Publishing Group.
—What Does a Screwdriver Do? 2012. (First Step Nonfiction - Tools at Work Ser.). (ENG., Illus.). 24p. (gr. k-2). pap. 6.95 *(978-1-58013-951-9(5))*; lib. bdg. 23.93 *(978-0-7613-8978-1(4)*, Lerner Pubns.) Lerner Publishing Group.
—What Does a Wrench Do? 2012. (First Step Nonfiction - Tools at Work Ser.). (ENG., Illus.). 24p. (gr. k-2). pap. 6.95 *(978-1-58013-952-6(3))*; lib. bdg. 23.93 *(978-0-7613-8977-4(6)*, Lerner Pubns.) Lerner Publishing Group.
Orme, David. Amazing Gadgets. 2010. (Fact to Fiction Grafx Ser.). (Illus.). 36p. (J). lib. bdg. 16.95 *(978-1-60686-471-5(8))* Perfection Learning Corp.
Oxlade, Chris. Levers. 2009. (Simple Machines (Smart Apple Media Paperback) Ser.). (Illus.). 32p. (J). (gr. k-2). pap. 7.95 *(978-1-59920-200-6(X))* Black Rabbit Bks.
—Screws. 2009. (Simple Machines (Smart Apple Media Paperback) Ser.). (Illus.). 32p. (J). (gr. k-2). pap. 7.95 *(978-1-59920-202-0(6))* Black Rabbit Bks.
—Wedges & Ramps. 2009. (Simple Machines (Smart Apple Media Paperback) Ser.). (Illus.). 32p. (J). (gr. 4-7). pap. 7.95 *(978-1-59920-203-7(4))* Black Rabbit Bks.
Puri, Devi. Making Tools in the Wild, 01 vols., 1. 2016. (Wilderness Survival Skills Ser.). (ENG., Illus.). 24p. (J). pap. 8.25 *(978-1-5081-4327-7(7)*, PowerKids Pr.) Rosen Publishing Group, Inc., The.
Rau, Dana Meachen. Builders. 2007. (J). pap. 6.99 *(978-0-7614-3289-0(2))* Marshall Cavendish Corp.
Research Tools You Can Use. 2014. (Research Tools You Can Use Ser.). 32p. (J). (gr. 3-6). 140.70 *(978-1-62275-389-5(5))* Rosen Publishing Group, Inc., The.
Rice, Dona. Good Work. 2015. (TIME for KIDS(r) Nonfiction Readers Ser.). (ENG., Illus.). 12p. (gr. k-k). 4.99 *(978-1-4938-2141-9(5))* Teacher Created Materials, Inc.
Rice, Dona Herweck. Hit It! - History of Tools, 1 vol. 2nd rev. ed. 2012. (Nonfiction Readers Ser.). (ENG.). 32p. (J). (gr. 3-3). pap. 8.99 *(978-1-4333-3680-5(4))* Teacher Created Materials, Inc.
—Hit It! History of Tools, 1 vol. 2nd rev. ed. 2014. (TIME for KIDS(r) Nonfiction Readers Ser.). (ENG., Illus.). 32p. (J). (gr. 3-3). pap. 25.96 *(978-1-4807-1089-4(X))* Shell Educational Publishing.
Schuh, Mari. Tools for the Garden, 1 vol. 2010. (Gardens Ser.). (ENG.). 24p. (gr. k-1). lib. bdg. 21.99 *(978-1-4296-3983-5(0)*, Pebble Bks.) Capstone Press of Coughlan Cos.
Sundance/Newbridge LLC Staff. A World of Tools. 2007. (Early Science Ser.). (gr. k-3). 18.95 *(978-1-4007-6504-1(8))*; pap. 6.10 *(978-1-4007-6500-3(5))* Sundance/Newbridge Educational Publishing.
Tieck, Sarah. Screws, 1 vol. 2006. (Simple Machines Ser.). (ENG., Illus.). 24p. (gr. -1-3). 25.65 *(978-1-59679-817-5(3)*, Buddy Bks.) ABDO Publishing Co.
Tools & Machines. 2010. (Experimenting with Everyday Science Ser.). (Illus.). 184p. (gr. 6-12). 35.00 *(978-1-60413-171-0(3)*, Chelsea Hse.) Facts On File, Inc.
Truran, Stacy. Troy's Tree Fort: Measure Lengths in Standard Units. 2014. (Rosen Common Core Math Readers Ser.). (ENG.). 24p. (J). (gr. 2-3). pap. 8.25 *(978-1-4777-4784-1(2)*, Rosen Classroom) Rosen Publishing Group, Inc., The.
A Worker's Tools: Individual Title Six-Packs. (Discovery World Ser.). 16p. (gr. 1-2). 28.00 *(978-0-7635-8459-7(2))* Rigby Education.

TOOLS—FICTION

Barchers, Suzanne I. Fix It!, 1 vol. 2011. (Targeted Phonics Ser.). (ENG., Illus.). 16p. (J). (gr. k-2). pap. 5.99 *(978-1-4333-2423-9(7))* Teacher Created Materials, Inc.
Cerato, Mattia. Drew the Screw. Cerato, Mattia, illus. 2016. (I Like to Read(r) Ser.). (ENG., Illus.). 24p. (J). (gr. -1-3). 14.95 *(978-0-8234-3540-1(7))*; pap. 6.99 *(978-0-8234-3541-8(5))* Holiday Hse., Inc.
Connor, Leslie. Miss Bridie Chose a Shovel. Azarian, Mary, illus. unabr. ed. 2005. (J). (gr. k-3). 29.95 incl. audio compact disk *(978-0-8045-4135-0(3)*, SACD4135); 27.95 incl. audio *(978-0-8045-6936-1(3)*, SAC6936) Spoken Arts, Inc.
Fliess, Sue. Let's Build!, 0 vols. 2014. (ENG.). 24p. (J). (gr. -1-3). 14.99 *(978-1-4778-4724-4(3)*, 9781477847244, Amazon Children's Publishing) Amazon Publishing.
Fox, Will. Bertie Bolt. Fox, Will, illus. 2013. (ENG., Illus.). 20p. (J). pap. 6.04 *(978-1-908865-20-5(2))* Beecroft Publishing GBR. Dist: Lightning Source, Inc.
—Billy Brush. Fox, Will, illus. 2013. (ENG., Illus.). 20p. (J). pap. 6.04 *(978-1-908865-25-0(3))* Beecroft Publishing GBR. Dist: Lightning Source, Inc.
—Hector Hacksaw. Fox, Will, illus. 2013. (ENG., Illus.). 20p. (J). pap. 6.04 *(978-1-908865-28-1(8))* Beecroft Publishing GBR. Dist: Lightning Source, Inc.
—Molly Mallet. Fox, Will, illus. 2013. (ENG., Illus.). 20p. (J). pap. 6.04 *(978-1-908865-27-4(X))* Beecroft Publishing GBR. Dist: Lightning Source, Inc.
—Peggy Peg. Fox, Will, illus. 2013. (ENG., Illus.). 20p. (J). pap. 6.04 *(978-1-908865-22-9(9))* Beecroft Publishing GBR. Dist: Lightning Source, Inc.
—Rusty Nail. Fox, Will, illus. 2013. (ENG., Illus.). 20p. (J). pap. 6.04 *(978-1-908865-21-2(0))* Beecroft Publishing GBR. Dist: Lightning Source, Inc.
—Sally Screw. Fox, Will, illus. 2013. (ENG., Illus.). 20p. (J). pap. 6.04 *(978-1-908865-23-6(7))* Beecroft Publishing GBR. Dist: Lightning Source, Inc.
—Spiky Saw. Fox, Will, illus. 2013. (ENG., Illus.). 16p. (J). pap. 6.04 *(978-1-908865-26-7(1))* Beecroft Publishing GBR. Dist: Lightning Source, Inc.
—Suzy Scissors. Fox, Will, illus. 2013. (ENG., Illus.). 20p. (J). pap. 6.04 *(978-1-908865-29-8(6))* Beecroft Publishing GBR. Dist: Lightning Source, Inc.
—Twisty Drill. Fox, Will, illus. 2013. (ENG., Illus.). 16p. (J). pap. 6.04 *(978-1-908865-24-3(5))* Beecroft Publishing GBR. Dist: Lightning Source, Inc.
Fritz, Betty. Bang Bang Bang, Hammers in the Morning. 2009. (J). 16.95 *(978-1-61623-624-3(8))* Independent Pub.
Garcia, Emma. Tap Tap Bang Bang. 2013. (ENG., Illus.). 26p. (J). (— 1). bds. 6.95 *(978-1-907967-67-2(2))* Boxer Bks., Ltd. GBR. Dist: Sterling Publishing Co., Inc.
Grey, Mini. The Adventures of the Dish & the Spoon. 2015. (ENG.). 32p. (J). (gr. 1-4). 7.99 *(978-0-553-50904-5(7)*, Dragonfly Bks.) Random Hse. Children's Bks.
Handy Manny Pop-up Tool Book. 2009. 6p. 12.99 *(978-1-4231-2114-5(7))* Disney Pr.
Klein, Adria F. Hank Hammer, 1 vol. Rowland, Andrew, illus. 2011. (Tool School Ser.). (ENG.). 32p. (gr. 1-2). pap. 6.25 *(978-1-4342-3385-1(5))*; lib. bdg. 22.65 *(978-1-4342-3043-0(0))* Stone Arch Bks.
—Hank Hammer & the Puppy, 1 vol. Rowland, Andrew, illus. 2012. (Tool School Ser.). (ENG.). 32p. (gr. 1-3). pap. 6.25 *(978-1-4342-4233-4(1))*; lib. bdg. 22.65 *(978-1-4342-4020-0(7))* Stone Arch Bks.
—Sammy Saw, 1 vol. Rowland, Andrew, illus. 2011. (Tool School Ser.). (ENG.). 32p. (gr. 1-2). pap. 6.25 *(978-1-4342-3387-5(1))*; lib. bdg. 22.65 *(978-1-4342-3045-4(7))* Stone Arch Bks.
—Sammy Saw & the Campout, 1 vol. Rowland, Andrew, illus. 2012. (Tool School Ser.). (ENG.). 32p. (gr. 1-3). pap. 6.25 *(978-1-4342-4234-1(X))*; lib. bdg. 22.65 *(978-1-4342-4022-4(3))* Stone Arch Bks.
—Sophie Screwdriver, 1 vol. Rowland, Andrew, illus. 2011. (Tool School Ser.). (ENG.). 32p. (gr. 1-2). pap. 6.25 *(978-1-4342-3386-8(3))*; lib. bdg. 22.65 *(978-1-4342-3044-7(9))* Stone Arch Bks.
—Sophie Screwdriver & the Classroom, 1 vol. Rowland, Andrew, illus. 2012. (Tool School Ser.). (ENG.). 32p. (gr. 1-3). pap. 6.25 *(978-1-4342-4235-8(8))*; lib. bdg. 22.65 *(978-1-4342-4021-7(5))* Stone Arch Bks.

TUV

—Tia Tape Measure, 1 vol. Rowland, Andrew, illus. 2011. (Tool School Ser.). (ENG.). 32p. (gr. 1-2). pap. 6.25 *(978-1-4342-3388-2(X))*; lib. bdg. 22.65 *(978-1-4342-3046-1(5))* Stone Arch Bks.

—Tia Tape Measure & the Move, 1 vol. Rowland, Andrew, illus. 2012. (Tool School Ser.). (ENG.). 32p. (gr. 1-3). pap. 6.25 *(978-1-4342-4236-5(6))*; lib. bdg. 22.65 *(978-1-4342-4023-1(1))* Stone Arch Bks.

McNeil, Niki, et al. HOCPP 1070 Mike & Mary Anne the Steam Shovel. 2006. spiral bd. *(978-1-60308-070-5(8))* In the Hands of a Child.

Meltzer, Lynn. The Construction Crew. Eko-Burgess, Carrie, illus. 2011. (ENG.). 40p. (J). (gr. -1-k). 15.99 *(978-0-8050-8884-7(9))*, 9780805088847, Holt, Henry & Co. Bks. For Young Readers) Holt, Henry & Co.

Meshon, Aaron. Tools Rule! Meshon, Aaron, illus. 2014. (ENG., Illus.). 40p. (J). (gr. -1-3). 17.99 *(978-1-4424-9601-9(0))*, Atheneum Bks. for Young Readers) Simon & Schuster Children's Publishing.

Monroe, Chris. Monkey with a Tool Belt. Monroe, Chris, illus. 2008. (Carolrhoda Picture Bks.). (ENG., Illus.). 32p. (J). (gr. -1-2). lib. bdg. 16.95 *(978-0-8225-7631-0(7))*, Carolrhoda Bks.) Lerner Publishing Group.

—Monkey with a Tool Belt & the Maniac Muffins. Monroe, Chris, illus. 2016. (ENG., Illus.). 32p. (gr. -1-2). (J). 17.99 *(978-1-4677-2155-4(7))*; 35.99 *(978-1-4677-9562-3(3))* Lerner Publishing Group. (Carolrhoda Bks.).

—Monkey with a Tool Belt & the Noisy Problem. Monroe, Chris, illus. 2009. (Carolrhoda Picture Bks.). (ENG., Illus.). 32p. (J). (gr. -1-2). 16.95 *(978-0-8225-9247-1(9))* Lerner Publishing Group.

Monroe, Chris. Monkey with a Tool Belt & the School Mystery. Monroe, Chris, illus. 2017. (ENG., Illus.). 32p. (gr. -1-2). 17.99 ***(978-1-5124-3010-3(2)***, Carolrhoda Bks.) Lerner Publishing Group.

Pflugfelder, Bob & Hockensmith, Steve. Nick & Tesla's Secret Agent Gadget Battle. 2014. (Nick & Tesla Ser.: 3). (ENG., Illus.). 256p. (J). (gr. 4-7). 12.95 *(978-1-59474-676-5(1))* Quirk Bks.

Publications International Ltd. Staff, ed. Handy Manny. 2008. 16p. (J). bds. 9.98 *(978-1-4127-9373-5(4))*, PIL Kids) Publications International, Ltd.

—Handy Manny: Fiesta Fun. 2008. (J). bds. 10.98 *(978-1-4127-8867-0(6))* Publications International, Ltd.

Rockwell, Anne F. & Rockwell, Harlow. The Toolbox. Rockwell, Anne F. & Rockwell, Harlow, illus. 2006. (ENG., Illus.). 20p. (J). (gr. -1-k). bds. 7.99 *(978-0-8027-9609-7(5))*, 9780802796097, Bloomsbury USA Childrens) Bloomsbury Publishing USA.

Shulman, Lisa. Old MacDonald Had a Woodshop. Wolff, Ashley, illus. 2004. (ENG.). 32p. (J). (gr. -1-k). reprint ed. pap. 6.99 *(978-0-14-240186-6(2))*, Puffin Books) Penguin Young Readers Group.

Slater, David Michael. David Michael Slater: Missy Swiss & More - 6 Titles, 6 vols., Set. Incl. Comin' Through. Rooney, Ronnie, illus. 28.50 *(978-1-60270-008-6(7))*; Flour Girl: A Recipe for Disaster. Brooks, S. G., illus. 28.50 *(978-1-60270-009-3(5))*; Missy Swiss. Reibeling, Brandon, illus. 28.50 *(978-1-60270-010-9(9))*; Ned Loses His Head. 28.50 *(978-1-60270-011-6(7))*; Seven Ate Nine. Trover, Zachary, illus. 28.50 *(978-1-60270-012-3(5))*; Sharpest Tool in the Shed. Reibeling, Brandon, illus. 28.50 *(978-1-60270-013-0(3))*; (gr. -1-4). (Missy Swiss & More Ser.). (ENG.). 32p. 2007. 171.00 *(978-1-60270-007-9(9))*, Looking Glass Library) ABDO Publishing Co.

—The Sharpest Tool in the Shed, 1 vol. Reibeling, Brandon, illus. 2007. (Missy Swiss & More Ser.). (ENG.). 32p. (gr. -1-4). 28.50 *(978-1-60270-013-0(3))*, Looking Glass Library) ABDO Publishing Co.

Smith, Kourtney. The Adventures of Stanley the Staple. 2013. 28p. pap. 24.95 *(978-1-63004-276-9(5))* America Star Bks.

Sturges, Philemon. I Love Tools! Halpern, Shari, illus. 2006. 24p. (J). (gr. -1-1). 14.89 *(978-0-06-009288-7(2))* HarperCollins Pubs.

TOPOLOGY

Piddock, Claire. Position & Direction. 2010. (ENG., Illus.). 24p. (J). *(978-0-7787-5248-6(8))*; pap. *(978-0-7787-5295-0(X))* Crabtree Publishing Co.

TORNADOES

see also Storms

Aboff, Marcie. Tornadoes!, 1 vol. Sotirovski, Aleksandar, illus. 2012. (First Graphics: Wild Earth Ser.). (ENG.). 24p. (gr. 1-2). pap. 6.29 *(978-1-4296-7952-7(2))*; pap. 35.70 *(978-1-4296-8372-2(4))* Capstone Press of Coughlan Cos.

Armentrout, David. Tornadoes. 2009. (ENG.). 32p. pap. 3.99 *(978-0-8249-1413-4(9))*, Ideal Pubns.) Worthy Publishing.

Armour, Cy. Tornadoes & Hurricanes!, 1 vol. 2nd rev. ed. 2014. (TIME for KIDS(r) Nonfiction Readers Ser.). (ENG., Illus.). 24p. (J). (gr. 2-2). pap. 23.96 *(978-1-4807-1041-2(5))* Shell Educational Publishing.

—Tornadoes & Hurricanes!, 1 vol. 2nd rev. ed. 2011. (Nonfiction Readers Ser.). (ENG.). 24p. (J). (gr. 2-2). pap. 6.99 *(978-1-4333-3614-0(6))* Teacher Created Materials, Inc.

Aronin, Miriam. Oklahoma's Devastating May 2013 Tornado. 2014. (Code Red Ser.). 32p. (J). (gr. 2-7). lib. bdg. 25.27 *(978-1-62724-131-1(0))* Bearport Publishing Co., Inc.

Baker, John R. The Worlds Worst Tornadoes. 2016. (World's Worst Natural Disasters Ser.). (ENG., Illus.). 32p. (gr. 1-2). pap. 7.95 *(978-1-5157-1792-8(5))* Capstone Press of Coughlan Cos.

—The World's Worst Tornadoes. 2016. (World's Worst Natural Disasters Ser.). (ENG., Illus.). 32p. (gr. 1-2). lib. bdg. 26.65 *(978-1-5157-1788-1(7))* Capstone Press of Coughlan Cos.

Ball, Jacqueline A. Tornado! The 1974 Super Outbreak. 2005. (X-Treme Disasters That Changed America Ser.). 32p. (J). lib. bdg. 25.27 *(978-1-59716-009-4(1))* Bearport Publishing Co., Inc.

Berger, Melvin & Berger, Gilda. Hurricanes Have Eyes but Can't See: And Other Amazing Facts about Wild Weather. 2003. (Illus.). 48p. (J). *(978-0-439-54980-6(9))* Scholastic, Inc.

Bodden, Valerie. Our Wonderful Weather: Tornadoes. 2014. (Our Wonderful Weather Ser.). (ENG., Illus.). 24p. (J). (gr. 1-3). pap. 9.99 *(978-0-89812-923-6(0))*, Creative Paperbacks) Creative Co., The.

—Tornadoes. 2012. (Illus.). 24p. (J). 25.65 *(978-1-60818-150-6(2))*, Creative Education) Creative Co., The.

Boothroyd, Jennifer. What Is Severe Weather? 2014. (First Step Nonfiction - Let's Watch the Weather Ser.). 24p. (gr. k-2). (Illus.). pap. 6.95 *(978-1-4677-4499-7(9))*; (ENG.). lib. bdg. 23.93 *(978-1-4677-3919-1(7))*, Lerner Pubns.) Lerner Publishing Group.

Bowman, Chris. Survive a Tornado. 2016. (Survival Zone Ser.). (ENG., Illus.). 24p. (J). (gr. 3-7). 25.95 *(978-1-62617-444-3(X))*, Torque Bks.) Bellwether Media.

Brennan, Linda Crotta. We Have Tornadoes. 2014. (Tell Me Why Library). (ENG., Illus.). 24p. (J). (gr. 2-5). 25.64 *(978-1-63188-012-4(8))*, 205455) Cherry Lake Publishing.

Carson, Mary Kay. Inside Tornadoes. 2010. (Inside Ser.). (ENG., Illus.). 48p. (J). (gr. 3-6). pap. 9.95 *(978-1-4027-7781-3(7))* Sterling Publishing Co., Inc.

Cassie, Brian. Tornadoes. (Science Readers Ser.). (Illus.). 32p. (J). pap. 3.99 *(978-0-439-42505-6(0))* Scholastic, Inc.

Ceban, Bonnie J. Tornadoes: Disaster & Survival. 2005. (Deadly Disasters Ser.). (Illus.). 48p. (J). lib. bdg. 25.27 *(978-0-7660-2383-3(4))* Enslow Pubs., Inc.

Cernak, Linda. The Science of a Tornado. 2015. (21st Century Skills Library: Disaster Science Ser.). (ENG., Illus.). 32p. (J). (gr. 4-8). 29.93 *(978-1-63362-482-5(X))*, 206836) Cherry Lake Publishing.

Chambers, Catherine. Tornadoes. 2016. (Wild Weather Ser.). (ENG.). 32p. (gr. 1-3). pap. 7.99 *(978-1-4846-3586-5(8))*, NA-h) Heinemann-Raintree.

Close, Edward. Extreme Weather, 1 vol., 1. 2014. (Discovery Education: Earth & Space Science Ser.). (ENG.). 32p. (gr. 3-6). 26.25 *(978-1-4777-6194-6(2))*, PowerKids Pr.) Rosen Publishing Group, Inc., The.

Cox Cannons, Helen. Wind, 1 vol. 2014. (Weather Wise Ser.). (ENG., Illus.). 24p. (gr. -1-1). pap. 5.99 *(978-1-4846-0559-2(4))*, Acorn) Heinemann-Raintree.

Davies, Jon. Storm Chasers! on the Trail of Twisters. Rath, Robert, illus. Davies, Jon & Reed, Jim, photos by. 2007. 48p. (J). (gr. 3-7). pap. 12.95 *(978-1-56037-407-7(1))* Farcountry Pr.

Doeden, Matt. Tornadoes. 2008. pap. 40.95 *(978-0-8225-9445-1(5))*; (ENG., Illus.). 32p. lib. bdg. 22.60 *(978-0-8225-7910-6(3))*, Lerner Pubns.) Lerner Publishing Group.

Donnelly, Karen. Storms of the Past & the Future. 2009. (Earth's Changing Weather & Climate Ser.). 24p. (gr. 4-4). 42.50 *(978-1-61512-250-9(8))*, PowerKids Pr.) Rosen Publishing Group, Inc., The.

Donnelly, Karen J. Storms of the Past & the Future. 2003. (Earth's Changing Weather & Climate Ser.). (Illus.). 24p. (J). lib. bdg. 22.60 *(978-0-8239-6216-7(4))*, PowerKids Pr.) Rosen Publishing Group, Inc., The.

Dougherty, Terri. Anatomy of a Tornado. (Disasters Ser.). (ENG.). 48p. (gr. 3-4). 2011. pap. 59.70 *(978-1-4296-6445-5(2))* 2010. lib. bdg. 31.99 *(978-1-4296-5494-4(5))* Capstone Press of Coughlan Cos.

—The Worst Tornadoes of All Time. 2012. (Epic Disasters Ser.). (ENG.). 32p. (gr. 3-4). pap. 47.70 *(978-1-4296-8509-2(3))*, Edge Bks.) Capstone Press of Coughlan Cos.

Drummond, Allan. Green City. 2016. (ENG., Illus.). 40p. (J). 17.99 *(978-0-374-37999-5(8))*, 9780374379995, Farrar, Straus & Giroux (BYR)) Farrar, Straus & Giroux.

Duke, Shirley. Tornadoes. 2015. (ENG.). 48p. (gr. 3-6). 35.64 *(978-1-63430-426-9(8))* Rourke Educational Media.

Elkins, Elizabeth. Investigating Tornadoes. 2017. (Investigating Natural Disasters Ser.). (ENG., Illus.). 32p. (gr. 3-4). lib. bdg. 27.99 *(978-1-5157-4037-7(4))*, Edge Bks.) Capstone Press of Coughlan Cos.

Fradin, Judy & Fradin, Dennis. Tornado! The Story Behind These Twisting, Turning, Spinning, & Spiraling Storms. 2011. (ENG., Illus.). 64p. (J). (gr. 5-18). 16.95 *(978-1-4263-0779-9(9))*; 26.90 *(978-1-4263-0780-5(2))* National Geographic Society. (National Geographic Children's Bks.).

Friesen, Helen Lepp. Tornadoes. 2016. (J). ***(978-1-5105-2077-6(5))*** SmartBook Media, Inc.

Gibbons, Gail. Tornadoes! Gibbons, Gail, illus. 2009. (ENG., Illus.). 32p. (J). (gr. -1-3). pap. 7.99 *(978-0-8234-2274-6(7))* Holiday Hse., Inc.

—Tornadoes! 2009. (ENG., Illus.). 32p. (J). (gr. -1-3). 17.95 *(978-0-8234-2216-6(X))* Holiday Hse., Inc.

Gifford, Clive. Chasing the World's Most Dangerous Storms. 2010. (Extreme! Ser.). (ENG.). 32p. (gr. 3-4). pap. 47.70 *(978-1-4296-5123-3(7))*, Fact Finders) Capstone Press of Coughlan Cos.

Gonzales, Doreen. Tornadoes. 2012. (Killer Disasters Ser.). (ENG., Illus.). 24p. (J). (gr. 3-6). pap. 8.25 *(978-1-4488-7512-2(9))*; lib. bdg. 22.60 *(978-1-4488-7439-2(4))* Rosen Publishing Group, Inc., The. (PowerKids Pr.).

Group/McGraw-Hill, Wright. Savage Storms: Tornadoes & Hurricanes, 6 vols. (Book2WebTM Ser.). (gr. 4-8). 36.50 *(978-0-322-04424-1(3))* Wright Group/McGraw-Hill.

Gullo, Arthur. Tornadoes. 2015. (J). lib. bdg. *(978-1-62713-517-7(0))* Cavendish Square Publishing.

Hamilton, S. L. Tornadoes. 2012. 32p. 27.07 *(978-1-61783-262-8(6))*, Abdo & Daughters) ABDO Publishing Co.

Hansen, Grace. Tornadoes, 1 vol. 2016. (ENG., Illus.). 24p. (J). *(978-1-62970-935-2(2))* ABDO Publishing Co.

—Tornados. 2016. (Clima Ser.). (SPA.). 24p. (J). (gr. 1-6). pap. 7.95 *(978-1-4966-0696-9(5))* Capstone Classroom.

Harasymiw, Mark. Chasing a Tornado. 2014. (Illus.). 32p. (J). *(978-1-4824-0138-7(X))* Stevens, Gareth Publishing LLLP.

Hayden, Kate. Twisters! 2010. (DK Reader Level 2 Ser.). (gr. k-3). lib. bdg. 13.55 *(978-0-613-33171-5(0))*, Turtleback) Turtleback Bks.

Heinrichs, Ann. Storm Chaser. 2009. (21st Century Skills Library: Cool Science Careers Ser.). (ENG.). 32p. (gr. 4-8). lib. bdg. 28.50 *(978-1-60279-308-8(5))*, 200204) Cherry Lake Publishing.

Higgins, Nadia. It's a Tornado!, 1 vol. Ward, Damian, illus. 2010. (Weather Watchers Ser.). (ENG.). 32p. (J). (gr. k-3). 28.50 *(978-1-60270-730-6(8))* Magic Wagon.

Hirschmann, Kris. Twister!, 1 vol. 2008. (What's It Like Out? Ser.). (ENG.). 32p. (gr. k-6). 27.07 *(978-1-59928-946-5(6))*, Checkerboard Library) ABDO Publishing Co.

Homer, Katie. Brainstorming Creative Guide to Help Parents & Children Through Severe Weather. 2008. 32p. 19.95 *(978-1-933466-73-6(1))* Kansas City Star Bks.

Honders, Christine. A Trip Inside a Tornado. 2015. (Fantastic Science Journeys Ser.). (ENG.). 32p. (J). (gr. 2-3). pap. 10.50 *(978-1-4824-1998-6(X))* Stevens, Gareth Publishing LLLP.

Hubbard, Ben. Tornado: Perspectives on Tornado Disasters, 1 vol. 2014. (Disaster Dossiers Ser.). (ENG., Illus.). 56p. (gr. 7-8). pap. 9.49 *(978-1-4846-0189-1(0))*, NA-h) Heinemann-Raintree.

Jeffrey, Gary. Tornadoes & Superstorms. 2007. (Graphic Natural Disasters Ser.). (ENG.). 48p. (YA). 58.50 *(978-1-4488-1667-5(X))*, Rosen Reference) Rosen Publishing Group, Inc., The.

—Tornadoes & Superstorms. Riley, Terry, illus. 2007. (Graphic Natural Disasters Ser.). (ENG.). 48p. (gr. 5-8). pap. 14.05 *(978-1-4042-1985-4(4))*; (J). lib. bdg. 31.95 *(978-1-4042-1993-9(5))* Rosen Publishing Group, Inc., The.

Jensen, Belinda. The Sky Stirs up Trouble: Tornadoes. Kurilla, Renee, illus. 2016. (Bel the Weather Girl Ser.). (ENG.). 24p. (J). (gr. -1-3). 25.32 *(978-1-4677-7960-9(1))*, Millbrook Pr.) Lerner Publishing Group.

Johnson, Robin. What Is a Tornado? 2016. (ENG., Illus.). 24p. (J). *(978-0-7787-2423-0(9))* Crabtree Publishing Co.

Kallio, Jamie. 12 Things to Know about Wild Weather. 2015. (ENG., Illus.). 32p. (J). *(978-1-63235-035-0(1))* Pr. Room Editions LLC.

Lay, Kathryn. Tornado Trouble, 1 vol., Vol. 1. Wolff, Jason, illus. 2011. (Wendy's Weather Warriors Ser.). (ENG.). 80p. (gr. 2-4). 27.07 *(978-1-60270-754-2(5))*, Calico Chapter Bks) Magic Wagon.

Leathers, Daniel. Tornado Outbreak 1985. 2007. (Natural Disasters Ser.). (Illus.). 32p. (J). (gr. 1-4). lib. bdg. 25.70 *(978-1-58415-571-3(X))* Mitchell Lane Pubs., Inc.

Leavitt, Amie Jane. A Daredevil's Guide to Storm Chasing, 1 vol. 2013. (Daredevils' Guides). (ENG.). 48p. (gr. 3-4). lib. bdg. 31.99 *(978-1-4296-9984-6(1))* Capstone Press of Coughlan Cos.

Lindop, Laurie. Chasing Tornadoes. 2003. (Science on the Edge Ser.). (Illus.). 80p. (gr. 5-18). lib. bdg. 26.90 *(978-0-7613-2703-5(7))*, Twenty-First Century Bks.) Lerner Publishing Group.

Macceca, Stephanie. Tornado Trouble. 2015. (Building Fluency Through Reader's Theater Ser.). (ENG., Illus.). 32p. (gr. 3-3). pap. 7.99 *(978-1-4938-1289-9(0))* Teacher Created Materials, Inc.

McAuliffe, Bill. Tornadoes. 2017. (J). ***(978-1-60818-828-4(0))***, Creative Education) 2010. 47p. (YA). (gr. 4-7). lib. bdg. 23.95 *(978-1-58341-931-1(4))* Creative Co., The.

Meister, Cari. Tornadoes. 2015. (Illus.). 24p. (J). lib. bdg. 25.65 *(978-1-62031-225-4(5))* Jump! Inc.

Mezzanotte, Jim. Tornadoes. (Wild Weather Ser.). 24p. 2009. (ENG.). (J). (gr. k-3). pap. 8.15 *(978-1-4339-2365-4(3))* 2009. (ENG.). (J). (gr. k-3). lib. bdg. 22.00 *(978-1-4339-2351-7(3))* 2007. (Illus.). (gr. 1-4). pap. 8.15 *(978-0-8368-7923-0(6))* 2007. (Illus.). (gr. 1-4). lib. bdg. 22.00 *(978-0-8368-7916-2(3))* Stevens, Gareth Publishing LLLP. (Weekly Reader Leveled Readers).

—Tornados. 2007. (Tormentas (Storms) Ser.). (SPA., Illus.). 24p. (gr. 1-4). pap. 8.15 *(978-0-8368-8082-3(X))*; lib. bdg. 22.00 *(978-0-8368-8075-5(7))* Stevens, Gareth Publishing LLLP. (Weekly Reader Leveled Readers).

—Tornados (Tornadoes) 2009. (Tiempo extremo Ser.). (SPA.). 24p. (J). (gr. k-3). pap. 8.15 *(978-1-4339-2372-2(6))*; lib. bdg. 22.00 *(978-1-4339-2358-6(0))* Stevens, Gareth Publishing LLLP. (Weekly Reader Leveled Readers).

Miller, Ron. Chasing the Storm: Tornadoes, Meteorology, & Weather Watching. 2014. (Illus.). 64p. (gr. 6-12). lib. bdg. 33.26 *(978-1-4677-1284-2(1))*, Twenty-First Century Bks.) Lerner Publishing Group.

Minden, Cecilia. Tornadoes! 2010. (21st Century Basic Skills Library: Natural Disasters Ser.). (ENG.). 24p. (gr. k-3). lib. bdg. 22.79 *(978-1-60279-863-2(X))*, 200592) Cherry Lake Publishing.

Morris, Neil & Steele, Philip. Inside Hurricanes & Tornadoes. 2006. (Inside Nature's Disasters Ser.). (Illus.). 36p. (gr. 3-7). lib. bdg. 26.00 *(978-0-8368-7249-1(5))*, Gareth Stevens Learning Library) Stevens, Gareth Publishing LLLP.

Murray, Peter. Tornadoes. 2015. (Forces of Nature Ser.). (ENG.). 24p. (J). (gr. 2-5). 27.07 *(978-1-63143-768-7(2))*, 208608) Child's World, Inc., The.

Orr, Tamra B. Tornadoes. 2012. (21st Century Skills Library: Real World Math Ser.). (ENG., Illus.). 32p. (J). (gr. 4-8). pap. 14.21 *(978-1-61080-413-4(9))*, 201345); lib. bdg. 28.50 *(978-1-61080-326-7(4))*, 201312) Cherry Lake Publishing.

Otfinoski, Steven. Tornadoes. 2016. (True Book(tm), a — Extreme Earth Ser.). (ENG., Illus.). 48p. (J). lib. bdg. 31.00 *(978-0-531-22297-3(7))*, Children's Pr.) Scholastic Library Publishing.

Oxlade, Chris. Why Why Why Do Tornadoes Spin. 2008. 32p. pap. *(978-1-84810-004-6(3))* Miles Kelly Publishing, Ltd.

—Why Why Why... Do Tornadoes Spin? 2010. (Why Why Why Ser.). 32p. (J). (gr. 1-3). lib. bdg. 18.95 *(978-1-4222-1586-9(5))* Mason Crest.

Penner, Lucille Recht. Twisters! Gams, Allen, illus. 2009. (Step into Reading Ser.). (ENG.). 48p. (J). (gr. k-3). pap. 3.99 *(978-0-375-86224-3(2))*, Random Hse. Bks. for Young Readers) Random Hse. Children's Bks.

Person, Stephen. Saving Animals after Tornadoes. 2012. (Rescuing Animals from Disasters Ser.). 32p. (J). (gr. 2-7). lib. bdg. 25.27 *(978-1-61772-458-9(0))* Bearport Publishing Co., Inc.

Petty, Kate. The Awesome Book of Tornadoes & Other Storms. Paiva, Johannah Gilman, ed. Roberts, Peter, illus. 2014. (ENG.). 32p. (J). (gr. 3-7). 7.99 *(978-1-4867-0261-9(9))* Flowerpot Children's Pr. Inc. CAN. Dist: Cardinal Pubs. Group.

Phelan, Glen. Extreme Weather. 2007. (Reading Expeditions Ser.). (ENG., Illus.). 32p. (J). pap. 17.95 *(978-0-7922-4575-9(X))* CENGAGE Learning.

Plattner, Josh & Craig, Diane. Tornado or Dust Devil?, 1 vol. 2016. (This or That? Weather Ser.). (ENG., Illus.). 24p. (J). (gr. k-4). 25.65 *(978-1-62403-957-7(X))* ABDO Publishing Co.

Prokos, Anna. Tornadoes. 2008. (Ultimate 10 Ser.). 48p. (YA). (gr. 5-9). lib. bdg. 31.00 *(978-0-8368-9153-9(8))* Stevens, Gareth Publishing LLLP.

Rajczak, Kristen. Terrifying Tornadoes. 2012. (Angry Earth Ser.). (ENG., Illus.). 32p. (J). (gr. 3-6). pap. 10.50 *(978-1-4339-6543-2(7))*, Gareth Stevens Learning Library); lib. bdg. 26.60 *(978-1-4339-6541-8(0))* Stevens, Gareth Publishing LLLP.

Randolph, Joanne, ed. Tornado Alert! 2017. (Weather Report). 32p. (J). (gr. 3-3). pap. 10.52 ***(978-0-7660-9025-5(6))*** Enslow Pubs., Inc.

Raum, Elizabeth. Surviving Tornadoes, 1 vol. 2011. (Children's True Stories: Natural Disasters Ser.). (ENG.). 32p. (gr. 3-3). pap. 8.29 *(978-1-4109-4099-5(3))*; 30.65 *(978-1-4109-4092-6(6))* Heinemann-Raintree. (Raintree Perspectives).

—Tornado! 2016. (Natural Disasters Ser.). (ENG., Illus.). 32p. (J). (gr. k-3). 20.95 *(978-1-60753-992-6(6))* Amicus Publishing.

Rebman, Renee C. How Do Tornadoes Form? 2010. (Tell Me Why, Tell Me How 4 Ser.). 32p. (gr. 3-5). 29.93 *(978-0-7614-4828-0(4))* Marshall Cavendish Corp.

Rice, William B. Tornadoes, 1 vol. 2009. (Science Readers: a Closer Look Ser.). (ENG.). 32p. (J). (gr. 3-3). pap. 8.99 *(978-1-4333-0311-1(6))* Teacher Created Materials, Inc.

Rudolph, Jessica. Erased by a Tornado! 2010. (Disaster Survivors Ser.). (Illus.). 32p. (YA). (gr. 4-7). lib. bdg. 25.27 *(978-1-936087-52-5(9))* Bearport Publishing Co., Inc.

—Tornado. 2014. (It's a Disaster! Ser.). 24p. (J). (gr. -1-3). lib. bdg. 23.93 *(978-1-62724-126-7(4))* Bearport Publishing Co., Inc.

Rustad, Martha E. H. & Kalz, Jill. Tornadoes: Be Aware & Prepare, 1 vol. 2014. (Weather Aware Ser.). (ENG.). 32p. (gr. 1-2). lib. bdg. 27.32 *(978-1-4765-9906-9(8))* Capstone Press of Coughlan Cos.

Scavuzzo, Wendy. Tornado Alert! 3rd rev. ed. 2011. (ENG., Illus.). 32p. (J). *(978-0-7787-1594-8(9))*; (Disaster Alert! Ser.: No. 18). (gr. 3-6). pap. *(978-0-7787-1627-3(9))* Crabtree Publishing Co.

Schreiber, Ann. Twister Trouble. Speirs, John, illus. 2010. (Magic School Bus Science Chapter Bks.). (KOR.). 82p. (J). *(978-89-491-5320-9(3))* Biryongso Publishing Co.

Schuh, Mari C. Tornadoes. 2016. (Earth in Action Ser.). (ENG.). 24p. pap. 6.95 *(978-1-5157-6215-7(7))*, Pebble Plus) Capstone Press of Coughlan Cos.

—Tornadoes [Scholastic]. 2010. (Earth in Action Ser.). (ENG.). 24p. pap. 0.49 *(978-1-4296-5801-0(0))*, Pebble Plus) Capstone Press of Coughlan Cos.

Shea, Therese. When Tornadoes Touch Down. 2015. (Eye on the Sky Ser.). (ENG., Illus.). 32p. (J). (gr. 3-4). pap. 10.50 *(978-1-4824-2896-4(2))* Stevens, Gareth Publishing LLLP.

Shores, Lori. Cómo Hacer un Tornado en una Botella. Translations.com Staff, tr. from ENG. 2010. (Divertirse con la Ciencia/Hands-On Science Fun Ser.).Tr. of How to Build a Tornado in a Bottle. (SPA, ENG & MUL.). 24p. (gr. k-1). lib. bdg. 26.65 *(978-1-4296-6107-2(0))* Capstone Press of Coughlan Cos.

—How to Build a Tornado in a Bottle. 2010. (Hands-On Science Fun Ser.). (ENG.). 24p. (gr. k-1). pap. 41.70 *(978-1-4296-5578-1(X))*, Pebble Plus) Capstone Press of Coughlan Cos.

Silverstein, Alvin, et al. Tornadoes: The Science Behind Terrible Twisters. 2009. (Science Behind Natural Disasters Ser.). (Illus.). 48p. (J). (gr. 5-9). lib. bdg. 25.27 *(978-0-7660-2976-7(X))* Enslow Pubs., Inc.

Simon, Seymour. Tornadoes: All about Their Formation, Destruction, Warning Signs, & More! rev. ed. 2017. (Illus.). 32p. (J). (gr. 1-5). pap. 6.99 *(978-0-06-247032-4(9))* HarperCollins Pubs.

Sood, Malini. Hurricanes & Tornadoes. (Wild Nature Ser.). 48p. 2009. (gr. 4-5). 53.00 *(978-1-60854-794-4(9))*, PowerKids Pr.) 2007. (Illus.). (YA). (gr. 3-6). lib. bdg. 29.25 *(978-1-4042-3900-5(6))* Rosen Publishing Group, Inc., The.

Spilsbury, Louise & Spilsbury, Richard. Hurricanes & Tornadoes in Action. 2009. (Natural Disasters in Action Ser.). (ENG., Illus.). 48p. (J). (gr. 5-8). pap. 11.75 *(978-1-4358-5133-7(1))*, 1284479, Rosen Reference) Rosen Publishing Group, Inc., The.

—Terrifying Tornadoes, 1 vol. 2nd ed. 2010. (Awesome Forces of Nature Ser.). (ENG., Illus.). 32p. (gr. 3-6). 33.32 *(978-1-4329-3786-7(3))*; pap. 8.29 *(978-1-4329-3793-5(6))* Heinemann-Raintree. (Heinemann InfoSearch).

Steele, Philip, et al. Extreme Planet. 2014. (Illus.). 128p. (J). *(978-1-4351-5523-7(8))* Barnes & Noble, Inc.

Tarshis, Lauren. Tornado Terror: True Tornado Survival Stories & Amazing Facts from History & Today. 2017. (I Survived True Stories Ser.: 3). (ENG.). 176p. (J). (gr. 2-5). 12.99 *(978-0-545-91943-2(6))*, Scholastic Pr.) Scholastic, Inc.

Thomas, Rick. Twisters: A Book about Tornadoes, 1 vol. Shea, Denise, illus. 2005. (Amazing Science: Weather Ser.). (ENG.). 24p. (gr. -1-3). 26.65 *(978-1-4048-0930-7(9))* Picture Window Bks.

Thomas, Rick & Picture Window Books Staff. ¡Juush! ¡Ruum! Un Libro Sobre Tornados. Robledo, Sol, tr. from ENG. Shea, Denise, illus. 2007. (Ciencia Asombrosa: el Tiempo Ser.). (SPA.). 24p. (gr. -1-3). 26.65 *(978-1-4048-3237-4(8))* Picture Window Bks.

Thoron, Joe. Tornadoes. 2006. (Kaleidoscope Natural Disasters Ser.). (Illus.). 48p. (gr. 3-7). lib. bdg. 20.95 *(978-0-7614-2104-7(1))*, Benchmark Bks.) Marshall Cavendish Corp.

Ventura, Marne. Detecting Tornadoes. 2017. (Detecting Disasters (hardcover) Ser.). (ENG., Illus.). 32p. (J). (gr. 4-7). lib. bdg. 28.50 ***(978-1-63517-004-7(4)***, Focus Readers) North Star Editions.

Ventura, Marne. How to Survive a Tornado. 2015. (Survival Guides). (ENG.). 24p. (J). (gr. 2-5). 27.07 *(978-1-60973-161-8(1))*, 208792) Child's World, Inc., The.

WalkerTheo. THE CITY EXPERIMENT: REBUILDING GREENSBURG, KANSAS LOW INTERMEDIATE BOOK WITH ONLINE ACCESS. 2014. (ENG., Illus.). 24p. (J). pap. 9.50 *(978-1-107-62256-2(5))* Cambridge Univ. Pr.

Wendorff, Anne. Tornadoes. 2008. (Extreme Weather Ser.). (ENG., Illus.). 24p. (J). (gr. 2-5). lib. bdg. 25.95 *(978-1-60014-187-4(0))* Bellwether Media.

Woods, Michael & Woods, Mary B. Tornadoes. 2006. (Disasters up Close Ser.). (Illus.). 64p. (J). (gr. 3-7). lib. bdg. 27.93 *(978-0-8225-4714-3(7),* Lerner Pubns.) Lerner Publishing Group.

World Book, Inc Staff, contrib. by. Library of Natural Disasters, 15 vols., Set. 2007. (J). wbk. ed. 329.00 *(978-0-7166-9801-2(3))* World Bk., Inc.

—Tornadoes. (J). 2007. *(978-0-7166-9813-5(7))* 2nd ed. 2009. (Illus.). 47p. *(978-0-7166-9829-6(3))* World Bk., Inc.

TORNADOES—FICTION

Acton, Vanessa. Vortex. 2017. (Day of Disaster Ser.). (ENG.). 104p. (YA). (gr. 6-12). 26.65 *(978-1-5124-2773-8(X));* 12.99 ***(978-1-5124-3513-9(9),*** Darby Creek); 39.99 ***(978-1-5124-2780-6(2),*** Darby Creek); 39.99 ***(978-1-5124-3512-2(0),*** Darby Creek) Lerner Publishing Group.

Beard, Darleen Bailey & Beard, Darleen B. Twister. Carpenter, Nancy, illus. 2003. (ENG.). 32p. (J). (gr. -1-3). pap. 8.99 *(978-0-374-48014-1(1),* 9780374480141) Square Fish.

Bishop, Jenn. 14 Hollow Road. 2017. (ENG.). 288p. (J). (gr. 3-7). 16.99 ***(978-1-101-93875-1(7));*** lib. bdg. 19.99 ***(978-1-101-93876-8(5))*** Random Hse. Children's Bks. (Knopf Bks. for Young Readers).

Byars, Betsy. Tornado. Ben-Ami, Doron, illus. 2004. (Trophy Chapter Bks.). (ENG.). 64p. (J). (gr. 1-5). pap. 4.99 *(978-0-06-442063-1(9))* HarperCollins Pubs.

—Tornado. 2004. (J). (gr. 3-6). lib. bdg. 14.75 *(978-0-613-01485-4(5),* Turtleback) Turtleback Bks.

Christopher, Matt. Slam Dunk. 2004. (Matt Christopher Sports Ser.). 118p. (gr. 3-7). 15.00 *(978-0-7569-3046-2(4))* Perfection Learning Corp.

Clay, Shenise Tiana. The Kids Who Were Left Alone When There Was A Tornado. 2004. (J). 6.00 *(978-0-9701482-6-1(7))* Changing Lives Publishing.

Clements, Andrew. About Average. Elliott, Mark, illus. (ENG.). (J). (gr. 3-7). 2014. 144p. pap. 7.99 *(978-1-4169-9725-2(3))* 2012. 128p. 16.99 *(978-1-4169-9724-5(5))* Simon & Schuster Children's Publishing. (Atheneum Bks. for Young Readers).

Cook, Sherry & Johnson, Terri. Timothy Tornado, 26. Kuhn, Jesse, illus. l.t. ed. 2006. (Quirkles — Exploring Phonics through Science Ser.: 20). 32p. 7.99 *(978-1-933815-19-0(1),* Quirkles, The) Creative 3, LLC.

Draper, Penny. Day of the Cyclone, 1 vol. Sapergia, Barbara, ed. 2012. (Disaster Strikes! Ser.: 7). (ENG.). 176p. (J). (gr. 4-7). pap. 8.95 *(978-1-55050-481-1(9))* Coteau Bks. CAN. Dist: Orca Bk. Pubs. USA.

Duff, Jc. Tornado Watch. 2012. 32p. pap. 21.99 *(978-1-4771-1866-5(7))* Xlibris Corp.

Ellis, Melody A. An Unexpected Hero. 2009. 48p. pap. 16.95 *(978-1-60749-834-6(0))* America Star Bks.

Fields, Terri. El Domador de Tornados, 1 vol. Jacques, Laura, illus. 2016. (SPA.). 32p. (J). (gr. k-3). pap. 9.95 *(978-1-62855-747-3(8))* Arbordale Publishing.

—Tornado Tamer, 1 vol. Jacques, Laura, illus. 2016. (ENG & SPA.). 32p. (J). (gr. k-3). 17.95 *(978-1-62855-733-6(8));* pap. 9.95 *(978-1-62855-740-4(0))* Arbordale Publishing.

Fisher, Carolyn. A Twisted Tale. 2004. (Illus.). 33p. (J). (gr. k-4). reprint ed. 16.00 *(978-0-7567-8412-6(3))* DIANE Publishing Co.

Garretson, Jerri. Kansas Tall Tales: Tenth Anniversary Anthology. Garretson, Jerri & Dollar, Diane A., illus. 2008. 106p. (J). pap. 19.95 *(978-0-9659712-7-0(9))* Ravenstone Pr.

Garrett, Lyn. Horatio & the Sea Tornado. 2012. 28p. (-18). pap. 12.50 *(978-1-62212-615-6(7),* Strategic Bk. Publishing) Strategic Book Publishing & Rights Agency (SBPRA).

Geisert, Arthur, creator. Thunderstorm. (ENG., Illus.). (J). 2015. 34p. (gr. k). 60.00 *(978-1-59270-170-4(1))* 2013. 32p. (gr. -1). 17.95 *(978-1-59270-133-9(7))* Enchanted Lion Bks., LLC.

Ghigna, Charles & Ghigna, Debra. Barn Storm. Greenseid, Diane, illus. 2010. (Step into Reading Ser.). (ENG.). 32p. (J). (gr. -1-1). pap. 3.99 *(978-0-375-86114-7(9),* Random Hse. Bks. for Young Readers) Random Hse. Children's Bks.

Gutman, Dan. The Talent Show. 2010. (ENG.). 224p. (J). (gr. 3-7). 17.99 *(978-1-4169-9003-1(8),* Simon & Schuster Bks. For Young Readers) Simon & Schuster Bks. For Young Readers.

Hansen, Susan. The Flying Quilt. 2011. pap. 9.95 *(978-0-7414-6469-9(1))* Infinity Publishing.

Hoyt, Kathleen. Kerloon & Cooley. 2012. 24p. pap. *(978-1-77097-833-1(X))* FriesenPress.

Jenkins, Amanda. Tornado! 2005. (J). pap. *(978-1-4108-4212-1(6))* Benchmark Education Co.

Kennedy, Marlane. Tornado Alley. 2014. (Disaster Strikes Ser.: 2). lib. bdg. 14.75 *(978-0-606-35828-6(5))* Turtleback Bks.

King-Cargile, Gillian. The Toy & the Twister. Krull, Kevin, illus. 2015. (Stuffed Bunny Science Adventure Ser.). (ENG.). 36p. (J). (gr. k-3). 18.99 *(978-0-87580-496-5(9))* Northern Illinois Univ. Pr.

Lester, Helen. Batter up Wombat. Munsinger, Lynn, illus. 2006. (ENG.). 32p. (J). (gr. k-3). 24.80 *(978-1-4287-0160-1(5),* Follettbound) Follett School Solutions.

Long, Loren. Otis & the Tornado. Long, Loren, illus. 2011. (Otis Ser.: 2). (ENG., Illus.). 40p. (J). (gr. -1-2). 17.99 *(978-0-399-25477-2(3),* Philomel Bks.) Penguin Young Readers Group.

Marsh, Carole. The Ferocious Forest Fire Mystery. 2008. (Masters of Disasters Ser.). (Illus.). 118p. (J). (gr. 3-5). 14.95 *(978-0-635-06468-4(5));* per. 5.99 *(978-0-635-06465-3(0))* Gallopade International.

—The Treacherous Tornado Mystery. 2007. (Masters of Disasters Ser.). (Illus.). 118p. (J). (gr. 2-9). 14.95 *(978-0-635-06394-6(8));* per. 5.99 *(978-0-635-06338-0(7))* Gallopade International.

Mckenzie, Precious. Disaster Day. Mones, Marc, illus. 2012. (ENG.). 24p. (gr. 2-3). pap. 8.95 *(978-1-61810-331-4(8))* Rourke Educational Media.

McMullan, Kate. A Fine Start Bk. 3: Meg's Prairie Diary. 2003. (My America Ser.). (ENG.). 112p. (J). 12.95 *(978-0-439-37061-5(2))* Scholastic, Inc.

Messenger, Shannon. Let the Sky Fall. 2013. (Sky Fall Ser.: 1). (ENG.). (YA). (gr. 7). Illus.). 432p. pap. 10.99 *(978-1-4424-5042-4(8));* 416p. 17.99 *(978-1-4424-5041-7(X))* Simon Pulse. (Simon Pulse).

Mikkelsen, Jon. Storm Shelter. Lueth, Nathan, illus. 2008. (We Are Heroes Ser.). (ENG.). 40p. (gr. 2-3). lib. bdg. 23.99 *(978-1-4342-0787-6(0),* Keystone Bks.) Stone Arch Bks.

Osborne, Mary Pope. Twister on Tuesday. 2004. (Magic Tree House Ser.: No. 23). 70p. (J). (gr. k-3). pap. 17.00 incl. audio *(978-0-8072-9932-6(4),* Listening Library) Random Hse. Audio Publishing Group.

Saddleback Educational Publishing Staff, ed. Twister, 1 vol. unabr. ed. 2011. (Heights Ser.). (ENG.). 49p. (gr. 5-8). 7.95 *(978-1-61651-626-0(7))* Saddleback Educational Publishing, Inc.

Scott, Leah. Tincup & the Tornado. 2012. (ENG.). 34p. (J). pap. 18.95 *(978-1-4327-8826-1(4));* pap. 12.95 *(978-1-4327-8695-3(4))* Outskirts Pr., Inc.

Scrimger, Richard. Into the Ravine. 2007. (ENG.). 264p. (YA). (gr. 5-12). per. 9.95 *(978-0-88776-822-4(9),* Tundra Bks.) Tundra Bks. CAN. Dist: Penguin Random Hse. LLC.

Tarshis, Lauren. I Survived the Joplin Tornado 2011. 2015. (I Survived Ser.: 12). (ENG.). 112p. (J). (gr. 2-5). pap. 4.99 *(978-0-545-65848-5(9),* Scholastic Paperbacks) Scholastic, Inc.

Tougas, Chris. Mechanimals, 1 vol. 2012. (ENG.). 32p. (J). (gr. -1-3). 9.95 *(978-1-4598-0273-5(X))* Orca Bk. Pubs. USA.

Troupe, Thomas Kingsley. Tornado: a Twisting Tale of Survival. Fagan, Kirbi, illus. 2016. (Survive! Ser.). (ENG.). 56p. (gr. 4-6). lib. bdg. 25.32 *(978-1-4965-2556-7(6))* Stone Arch Bks.

Ward, Pat Mays. Big Mama's Storm Cellar. 2010. 24p. 14.99 *(978-1-4490-8236-9(X))* AuthorHouse.

Watkins, Elaine. Tornado Nine. 2016. (ENG.). 56p. (J). (gr. 4-6). 10.95 *(978-1-78554-532-0(9),* 4fcf26bf-8f24-4eea-8e42-40737b3c08c2) Austin, Stan AUS. Dist: Bookmasters Distribution.

TORONTO (ONT.)

Boudreau, Hélène, et al. Life in a Residential City. 2010. (Learn about Urban Life Ser.). (ENG., Illus.). 32p. (J). (gr. 3-6). pap. *(978-0-7787-7403-7(1));* lib. bdg. *(978-0-7787-7393-1(0))* Crabtree Publishing Co.

Connery-Boyd, Peg. Totally Toronto! 2016. (Hawk's Nest Activity Bks.: 0). (ENG.). 64p. (J). (-3). pap. 8.99 *(978-1-4926-3968-8(0),* 9781492639688, Sourcebooks Jabberwocky) Sourcebooks, Inc.

Covello, Paul. Toronto ABC. 2014. (ENG., Illus.). 15p. (J). bds. 10.50 *(978-1-4434-3144-6(3),* Harper Trophy) HarperCollins Pubs.

Gürth, Per-Henrik. ABC of Toronto. Gürth, Per-Henrik, illus. 2013. (ENG., Illus.). 32p. (J). (gr. -1-k). 15.95 *(978-1-77138-037-9(3))* Kids Can Pr., Ltd. CAN. Dist: Hachette Bk. Group.

Moak, Allan. A Big City Alphabet. 2009. (ABC Our Country Ser.). (ENG., Illus.). 32p. (J). (gr. -1-3). pap. 7.95 *(978-0-88776-939-9(X),* Tundra Bks.) Tundra Bks. CAN. Dist: Penguin Random Hse. LLC.

Rowe, Percy. Toronto. 2003. (Great Cities of the World Ser.). (Illus.). 48p. (gr. 5-12). lib. bdg. 31.00 *(978-0-8368-5026-0(2),* Gareth Stevens Secondary Library) Stevens, Gareth Publishing LLLP.

Schwartz, Joanne. City Alphabet, 1 vol. Beam, Matt, illus. 2009. (ENG.). 60p. (gr. -1-4). 18.95 *(978-0-88899-928-3(3))* Groundwood Bks. CAN. Dist: Publishers Group West (PGW).

TORONTO BLUE JAYS (BASEBALL TEAM)

Connery-Boyd, Peg. Toronto Blue Jays Activity Book. 2016. (Hawk's Nest Activity Bks.: 0). (ENG.). 64p. (J). (gr. k-3). pap. 8.99 *(978-1-4926-3376-1(3))* Sourcebooks, Inc.

Frisch, Aaron. Toronto Blue Jays. 2009. (World Series Champions Ser.). 23p. (J). (gr. 2-3). 24.25 *(978-1-58341-686-0(2),* Creative Education) Creative Co., The.

Gerstner, Joanne. Toronto Blue Jays, 1 vol. (Inside MLB Ser.). (ENG., 48p. (gr. 3-6). 2011. Illus.). (YA). lib. bdg. 32.79 *(978-1-61714-062-4(7))* 2014. lib. bdg. 32.79 *(978-1-62403-488-6(8),* SportsZone) ABDO Publishing Co.

Gilbert, Sara. Toronto Blue Jays. 2013. (Illus.). 24p. (J). 25.65 *(978-1-60818-273-2(8),* Creative Education) Creative Co., The.

—World Series Champs: Toronto Blue Jays. 2013. (World Series Champions Ser.). (ENG.). 24p. (J). (gr. 1-3). pap. 7.99 *(978-0-89812-824-6(2),* Creative Paperbacks) Creative Co., The.

LeBoutillier, Nate. The Story of the Toronto Blue Jays. 2011. (Illus.). 48p. (J). 35.65 *(978-1-60818-059-2(X),* Creative Education) Creative Co., The.

Shofner, Shawndra. The Story of the Toronto Blue Jays. 2007. (Baseball, the Great American Game Ser.). (Illus.). 48p. (YA). (gr. 4-7). lib. bdg. 32.80 *(978-1-58341-503-0(3))* Creative Co., The.

Stewart, Mark. The Toronto Blue Jays. 2012. (Team Spirit Ser.). 48p. (J). (gr. 3-6). lib. bdg. 29.27 *(978-1-59953-500-5(9))* Norwood Hse. Pr.

TORTOISES

see Turtles

TOTALITARIANISM

see also Communism; Dictators; National Socialism

Bailey, Diane. Dictatorship. Colton, Timothy J., ed. 2012. (Major Forms of World Government Ser.). 64p. (J). (gr. 5). 22.95 *(978-1-4222-2138-9(5))* Mason Crest.

Connolly, Sean. Dictatorship. 2012. (Systems of Government Ser.). (Illus.). 48p. (gr. 6-12). lib. bdg. 37.10 *(978-1-59920-804-6(0))* Black Rabbit Bks.

Donovan, Sandy. Lethal Leaders & Military Madmen. 2013. (ShockZone (tm) — Villains Ser.). (ENG., Illus.). 32p. (gr. 5-8). pap. 8.95 *(978-1-4677-0896-8(8))* Lerner Publishing Group.

McCarthy, Rose. Dictatorship: A Primary Source Analysis. 2009. (Primary Sources of Political Systems Ser.). 64p. (gr. 5-8). 58.50 *(978-1-60851-837-1(X))* Rosen Publishing Group, Inc., The.

TOTALITARIANISM—FICTION

Brody, Jennifer. The 13th Continuum. 2016. (Continuum Trilogy Ser.: 1). (ENG.). 416p. (YA). pap. 14.95 *(978-1-68162-254-5(8))* Turner Publishing Co.

Fukui, Isamu. Truancy. 2010. (Truancy Ser.: 1). (ENG.). 432p. (YA). (gr. 8-12). pap. 24.99 *(978-0-7653-2258-6(7),* 9780765322586, Tor Teen) Doherty, Tom Assocs., LLC.

—Truancy Origins. 2011. (Truancy Ser.: 2). (ENG.). 384p. (YA). (gr. 8-12). pap. 19.99 *(978-0-7653-2264-7(1),* 9780765322647, Tor Teen) Doherty, Tom Assocs., LLC.

Helland, Jenna. The August 5. 2015. (ENG., Illus.). 320p. (YA). (gr. 7). 16.99 *(978-0-374-38264-3(6),* 9780374382643, Farrar, Straus & Giroux (BYR)) Farrar, Straus & Giroux.

Mafi, Tahereh. Shatter Me. (Shatter Me Ser.: 1). (ENG.). (YA). (gr. 9). 2012. 464p. pap. 9.99 *(978-0-06-208550-4(6))* 2011. 352p. 17.99 *(978-0-06-208548-1(4))* HarperCollins Pubs.

—Shatter Me. 2012. (Shatter Me Ser.: 1). (YA). lib. bdg. 20.85 *(978-0-606-26868-4(5),* Turtleback) Turtleback Bks.

—Unravel Me. 2013. (Shatter Me Ser.: 2). (ENG.). (YA). (gr. 9). 496p. pap. 9.99 *(978-0-06-208554-2(9));* 480p. 17.99 *(978-0-06-208553-5(0))* HarperCollins Pubs.

—Unravel Me. 2013. (Shatter Me Ser.: 2). (YA). lib. bdg. 20.85 *(978-0-606-35049-5(7),* Turtleback) Turtleback Bks.

Maynard, Case. The Surrendered. 2016. (ENG.). 266p. (YA). (gr. 9). pap. 9.95 *(978-0-9970104-7-3(9))* Blaze Publishing, LLC.

Mourlevat, Jean-Claude. Winter's End. Bell, Anthea, tr. from FRE. 2009. (ENG., Illus.). 432p. (YA). (gr. 9-18). 17.99 *(978-0-7636-4450-5(1))* Candlewick Pr.

Patterson, James. The Fire. 2011. (Playaway Children Ser.). (ENG.). (YA). (gr. 8-12). 59.99 *(978-1-61113-385-1(8))* Hachette Audio.

Patterson, James & Dembowski, Jill. The Fire. (Witch & Wizard Ser.: 3). (ENG.). 352p. (YA). 2013. (gr. 7-17). mass mkt. 8.00 *(978-1-4555-2152-4(3))* 2011. (gr. 5-17). 17.99 *(978-0-316-10190-5(7))* Little Brown & Co. (Jimmy Patterson).

—The Fire. 2012. (Witch & Wizard Ser.: 3). (YA). lib. bdg. 20.85 *(978-0-606-26698-7(4),* Turtleback) Turtleback Bks.

Patterson, James & Raymond, Emily. The Lost. 2014. 355p. (YA). *(978-0-316-24266-0(7))* Little Brown & Co.

TOTEMS AND TOTEMISM

Crewe, Sabrina. Totem Poles. 2015. (Canadian Symbols Ser.). (ENG.). 24p. (gr. k-1). 26.65 *(978-1-4914-7092-3(5))* Capstone Press of Coughlan Cos.

Howse, Jennifer. Totem Poles: Canadian Icons. 2010. (Illus.). 24p. *(978-1-77071-574-5(6));* pap. *(978-1-77071-581-3(9))* Weigl Educational Pubs. Ltd.

Kramer, Pat. Totem Poles for Kids: A Kids Own SuperGuide. Kramer, Pat, photos by. (Illus.). 48p. (J). pap. *(978-1-55153-626-2(9))* Altitude Publishing Canada Ltd.

TOTEMS AND TOTEMISM—FICTION

Powell, Jim S. The Mystery of the Totem Trees: A Plumroy Pack Adventure. 2009. 124p. pap. 10.95 *(978-1-4401-3921-5(0))* iUniverse, Inc.

Sargent, Dave, et al. Once upon a Totem Pole Vol. 14: (Haida) Be Creative, 20 vols. Lenoir, Jane, illus. l.t. ed. 2003. (Story Keeper Ser.: 14). 42p. (J). pap. 10.95 *(978-1-56763-930-8(5));* Vol. 14. lib. bdg. 23.60 *(978-1-56763-929-2(1))* Ozark Publishing.

TOUCANS

Borgert-Spaniol, Megan. Toucans. 2014. (Animal Safari Ser.). (ENG., Illus.). 24p. (J). (gr. k-3). lib. bdg. 25.95 *(978-1-62617-065-0(7),* Blastoff! Readers) Bellwether Media.

Dunn, Mary R. Toucans, 1 vol. 2012. (South American Animals Ser.). (ENG., Illus.). 24p. (gr. k-1). lib. bdg. 26.65 *(978-1-4296-7590-1(X),* Pebble Plus) Capstone Press of Coughlan Cos.

McDonald, Mary Ann. Toucans. 2015. (Animals of the Rain Forest Ser.). (ENG.). 24p. (J). (gr. 2-5). 27.07 *(978-1-63143-753-3(4),* 208582) Child's World, Inc., The.

Ponka, Katherine. Being a Toucan. 2014. (Illus.). 32p. (J). *(978-1-4824-0130-1(4))* Stevens, Gareth Publishing LLLP.

Ryndak, Rob. Toucans. 2015. (Jungle Animals Ser.). (ENG., Illus.). 24p. (J). (gr. k-k). 22.60 *(978-1-4824-1764-7(2))* Stevens, Gareth Publishing LLLP.

Schuh, Mari. Toucans. 2014. (Illus.). 24p. (J). lib. bdg. 25.65 *(978-1-62031-113-4(5),* Bullfrog Bks.) Jump! Inc.

Suen, Anastasia. Toco Toucans: Bright Enough to Disappear. 2010. (Disappearing Acts Ser.). (Illus.). 24p. (J). (gr. k-3). lib. bdg. 22.61 *(978-1-936087-45-7(6))* Bearport Publishing Co., Inc.

Waxman, Laura Hamilton. Toco Toucans: Big-Billed Tropical Birds. 2016. (Comparing Animal Traits Ser.). (ENG., Illus.). 32p. (J). (gr. 2-4). 26.65 *(978-1-4677-9510-4(0),* Lerner Pubns.) Lerner Publishing Group.

TOUCANS—FICTION

Achrafi, Sherihan. Over the Rainbow. 2017. (ENG., Illus.). 30p. (J). pap. 28.22 ***(978-1-5245-2215-5(5))*** Xlibris Corp.

Antony, Steve. Betty Goes Bananas. 2014. (ENG., Illus.). 32p. (J). (-k). 16.99 *(978-0-553-50761-4(3),* Schwartz & Wade Bks.) Random Hse. Children's Bks.

Lehrhaupt, Adam. Warning: Do Not Open This Book! Forsythe, Matthew, illus. 2013. (ENG.). 40p. (J). (gr. -1-3). 17.99 *(978-1-4424-3582-7(8),* Simon & Schuster Bks. For Young Readers) Simon & Schuster Bks. For Young Readers.

Mayfield, Sue. I Can, You Can, Toucan! 2006. (Green Bananas Ser.). (ENG., Illus.). 48p. (J). (gr. -1-3). lib. bdg. *(978-0-7787-1032-5(7))* Crabtree Publishing Co.

—I Can, You Can, Toucan! Padua, Rochelle, illus. 2005. (Green Bananas Ser.). (ENG.). 48p. (J). (gr. k-2). pap. 5.99 *(978-1-4052-1793-4(6))* Egmont Bks., Ltd. GBR. Dist: Independent Pubs. Group.

McBrayer, Cassidy. You Can, Toucan! You Can. 2008. 20p. pap. 15.95 *(978-1-4327-1132-0(6))* Outskirts Pr., Inc.

Murguia, Bethanie Deeney. Toucans, Too. 2017. (ENG.). 40p. (J). (gr. -1-2). 17.99 ***(978-1-4998-0421-8(0))*** Little Bee Books Inc.

TOUCH

Aloian, Molly. What Is Touch? 2013. (ENG., Illus.). 24p. (J). *(978-0-7787-0968-8(X));* pap. *(978-0-7787-0991-6(4))* Crabtree Publishing Co.

Appleby, Alex. Lo Que Toco / What I Touch. 2014. (Mis Cinco Sentidos / My Five Senses Ser.). (SPA.). 24p. (J). (gr. k-2). 22.60 *(978-1-4824-0877-5(5))* Stevens, Gareth Publishing LLLP.

—What I Touch. 2014. (My Five Senses Ser.). 24p. (J). (gr. k-2). pap. 48.90 *(978-1-4824-0824-9(4));* pap. 8.15 *(978-1-4824-0823-2(6))* Stevens, Gareth Publishing LLLP.

Baggott, Stella. Baby's Very First Touchy-Feely Book. 2010. (Baby's Very First Board Bks). 10p. (J). bds. 9.99 *(978-0-7945-2647-4(0),* Usborne) EDC Publishing.

Ballard, Carol. Your Sense of Touch. 2010. (Your Body at Work Ser.). (ENG.). 32p. (YA). (gr. 2-5). lib. bdg. 26.60 *(978-1-4339-4115-3(5))* Stevens, Gareth Publishing LLLP.

Barnham, Kay. Touch. 2005. (Our Senses Ser.). (Illus.). 24p. (gr. k-3). lib. bdg. 23.00 *(978-0-8368-4410-8(6),* Gareth Stevens Learning Library) Stevens, Gareth Publishing LLLP.

Barraclough, Sue. What Can I Feel? 2005. (J). *(978-1-4034-7077-5(4));* (ENG.). 32p. pap. *(978-1-4034-7083-6(9))* Steck-Vaughn.

Beaumont, Susanna. Baby Senses Touch. 2005. (Baby Senses Ser.). (Illus.). 12p. (gr. -1-k). per., bds. *(978-1-905051-47-2(6))* Make Believe Ideas.

Bellamy, Adam. What's That I Feel? 2017. (All about My Senses Ser.). 24p. (J). (gr. k-1). lib. bdg. 22.60 ***(978-0-7660-8720-0(4))*** Enslow Pubs., Inc.

Bokhari, Raana. Allah Gave Me Two Hands & Feet. Clarke, Asiya, illus. 2015. (ENG.). 32p. (J). 8.95 *(978-0-86037-348-3(7))* Kube Publishing Ltd. GBR. Dist: Consortium Bk. Sales & Distribution.

Boothroyd, Jennifer. What Is Touch? 2009. (Lightning Bolt Books (tm) — Your Amazing Senses Ser.). (ENG.). 32p. (gr. k-2). 26.60 *(978-0-7613-4252-6(4),* Lerner Pubns.); pap. 7.95 *(978-0-7613-5018-7(7))* Lerner Publishing Group.

Brocket, Jane. Spiky, Slimy, Smooth: What Is Texture? Brocket, Jane, photos by. 2011. (Jane Brocket's Clever Concepts Ser.). (ENG., Illus.). 32p. (gr. -1-2). 26.60 *(978-0-7613-4614-2(7))* Lerner Publishing Group.

Carr, Aaron. Tacto. 2014. (SPA., Illus.). 24p. (J). *(978-1-62127-583-1(3))* Weigl Pubs., Inc.

Cotta, Susan. I Can Show You I Care: Compassionate Touch for Children. Crawford, Gregory, illus. 2003. (ENG.). 32p. (J). (gr. k-4). 18.95 *(978-1-55643-433-4(2))* North Atlantic Bks.

Cottin, Menena. The Black Book of Colors. Amado, Elisa, tr. from SPA. Faria, Rosana & Faria, Rosana, illus. 2008. (ENG.). 24p. (J). (gr. k-5). 17.95 *(978-0-88899-873-6(2))* Groundwood Bks. CAN. Dist: Publishers Group West (PGW).

Dayton, Connor. Touch. 2014. (Your Five Senses & Your Sixth Sense Ser.). (Illus.). 24p. (J). (gr. k-2). 22.60 *(978-1-4777-2855-0(4),* PowerKids Pr.) Rosen Publishing Group, Inc., The.

DeMedeiros, James. Touch. 2009. (World of Wonder Ser.). (Illus.). 24p. (J). (gr. 2-4). lib. bdg. 24.45 *(978-1-60596-058-6(6))* Weigl Pubs., Inc.

Durrie, Karen. Touch. 2012. (J). 27.13 *(978-1-61913-313-6(X));* pap. 12.95 *(978-1-61913-318-1(0))* Weigl Pubs., Inc.

Ganeri, Anita. Touch. 2013. (Senses Ser.). (Illus.). 24p. (gr. k-3). 28.50 *(978-1-59920-855-8(5))* Black Rabbit Bks.

George, Patrick. I Touch .. George, Patrick, illus. 2013. (ENG., Illus.). 36p. (J). (gr. -1-k). 12.99 *(978-1-908473-08-0(8))* PatrickGeorge GBR. Dist: Independent Pubs. Group.

Gordon, Sharon. Duro Blando. 2006. (Bookworms Ser.). (SPA & ENG., Illus.). 24p. (gr. k-1). lib. bdg. 15.95 *(978-0-7614-2368-3(0))* Marshall Cavendish Corp.

—Hard/Soft. 2007. (J). pap. 6.99 *(978-0-7614-3282-1(5))* Marshall Cavendish Corp.

—Hard/Soft/Duro/Blando. 2006. (Bookworms Ser.). (ENG & SPA., Illus.). 24p. (gr. k-1). lib. bdg. 15.95 *(978-0-7614-2448-2(2))* Marshall Cavendish Corp.

Hall, Kirsten. Animal Touch. 2005. (Animals & Their Senses Ser.). (Illus.). 24p. (gr. k-3). pap. 8.15 *(978-0-8368-4812-0(8));* lib. bdg. 22.00 *(978-0-8368-4806-9(3))* Stevens, Gareth Publishing LLLP. (Weekly Reader Leveled Readers).

—Animal Touch (El Tacto en los Animales) 2005. (Animals & Their Senses/ Los sentidos de los animales (bilingual) Ser.). (ENG & SPA., Illus.). 24p. (gr. k-3). pap. 8.15 *(978-0-8368-4824-3(1));* lib. bdg. 22.00 *(978-0-8368-4818-2(7))* Stevens, Gareth Publishing LLLP. (Weekly Reader Leveled Readers).

Hewitt, Sally. Touch That! 2008. (Let's Start Science Ser.). (ENG., Illus.). 24p. (J). (gr. 3-7). pap. *(978-0-7787-4062-9(5))* Crabtree Publishing Co.

Hidalgo, Maria. Touch. 2003. 24p. (J). lib. bdg. 21.35 *(978-1-58340-307-5(8))* Black Rabbit Bks.

Issa, Joanna. What Can I Feel?, 1 vol. 2014. (These Are My Senses Ser.). (ENG., Illus.). 24p. (gr. -1-1). pap. 5.99 *(978-1-4846-0432-8(6),* Acorn) Heinemann-Raintree.

Jordan, Apple. Smooth Rough. 2nd rev. ed. 2011. (Bookworms 2nd Edition: Opposites Ser.). 16p. (gr. k-1). 21.36 *(978-1-60870-422-4(X))* Marshall Cavendish Corp.

Kalman, Bobbie. ¿Cómo se siente al Tocarlo? 2008. (SPA.). 24p. (J). lib. bdg. *(978-0-7787-8722-8(2))* Crabtree Publishing Co.

—¿Como Se Siente Al Tocarlo? 2008.Tr. of How Does It Feel? (SPA.). 24p. (J). pap. *(978-0-7787-8731-0(1))* Crabtree Publishing Co.

Kubler, Annie, illus. What Can I Feel? 2011. (Small Senses Ser.). (ENG.). 12p. (J). bds. *(978-1-84643-374-0(6))* Child's Play International Ltd.

Kurtz, John. The World Around Us! Touch. 2011. (Dover Coloring Bks.). (ENG., Illus.). 32p. (J). (gr. k-3). pap. 4.99 *(978-0-486-48038-1(0))* Dover Pubns., Inc.

Landau, Elaine. The Sense of Touch. 2008. (True Book(tm), a — Health & the Human Body Ser.). (ENG., Illus.). 48p. (J). (gr. 2-5). 31.00 *(978-0-531-16874-5(3))* Scholastic Library Publishing.

Lay, Kathryn. Touching Their Prey: Animals with an Amazing Sense of Touch, 1 vol. Wald, Christina, illus. 2012. (Sensing Their Prey Ser.). (ENG.). 32p. (J). (gr. -1-4). lib. bdg. 28.50 *(978-1-61641-870-0(2),* Looking Glass Library) Magic Wagon.

Llewellyn, Claire. Touching. 2005. (I Know That! Ser.). (Illus.). 24p. (J). (gr. 1-3). lib. bdg. 22.80 *(978-1-932889-50-5(7))* Sea-To-Sea Pubns.

Manasco, Hunter. An Exceptional Children's Guide to Touch: Teaching Social & Physical Boundaries to Kids. Manasco, Katharine, illus. 2012. (ENG.). 72p. (J). 17.95 *(978-1-84905-871-1(7),* 6045) Kingsley, Jessica Pubs. GBR. Dist: Macmillan Distribution Ltd.

McKendry, Sam. Bless Everyone. 2006. (ENG., Illus.). 12p. (J). (gr. -1-k). 8.95 *(978-1-58117-445-8(4),* Intervisual/Piggy Toes) Bendon, Inc.

Meachen Rau, Dana. Soft & Smooth, Rough & Bumpy: A Book about Touch. Peterson, Rick, illus. 2005. (Amazing Body: the Five Senses Ser.). (ENG.). 24p. (gr. k-3). 26.65 *(978-1-4048-1022-8(6))* Picture Window Bks.

TUV

—Soft & Smooth, Rough & Bumpy [Scholastic]: A Book about Touch. Peterson, Rick, illus. 2010. (Amazing Body: the Five Senses Ser.). 24p. pap. 0.56 *(978-1-4048-6544-0(6)*, Nonfiction Picture Bks.) Picture Window Bks.
Medeiros, J. de. Touch. 2009. (World of Wonder Ser.). (Illus.). 24p. (J). (gr. 2-4). pap. *(978-1-60596-059-3(4))* Weigl Pubs., Inc.
Milet Publishing Staff. My Bilingual Book-Touch. 2014. (My Bilingual Book Ser.). (ENG & SPA., Illus.). 28p. (J). (gr. -1-k). 9.95 *(978-1-84059-848-3(4))*; 9.95 *(978-1-84059-843-8(3))* Milet Publishing.
—My Bilingual Book-Touch (English-Arabic) 2014. (My Bilingual Book Ser.). (ENG & ARA., Illus.). 28p. (J). (gr. -1-k). 9.95 *(978-1-84059-836-0(0))* Milet Publishing.
—My Bilingual Book-Touch (English-Bengali) 2014. (My Bilingual Book Ser.). (ENG & BEN., Illus.). 28p. (J). (gr. -1-k). 9.95 *(978-1-84059-837-7(9))* Milet Publishing.
—My Bilingual Book-Touch (English-Chinese) 2014. (My Bilingual Book Ser.). (ENG & CHI., Illus.). 28p. (J). (gr. -1-k). 9.95 *(978-1-84059-838-4(7))* Milet Publishing.
—My Bilingual Book-Touch (English-Farsi) 2014. (My Bilingual Book Ser.). (ENG & PER., Illus.). 28p. (J). (gr. -1-k). 9.95 *(978-1-84059-839-1(5))* Milet Publishing.
—My Bilingual Book-Touch (English-German) 2014. (My Bilingual Book Ser.). (ENG & GER., Illus.). 28p. (J). (gr. -1-k). 9.95 *(978-1-84059-841-4(7))* Milet Publishing.
—My Bilingual Book-Touch (English-Italian) 2014. (My Bilingual Book Ser.). (ENG & ITA., Illus.). 28p. (J). (gr. -1-k). 9.95 *(978-1-84059-842-1(5))* Milet Publishing.
—My Bilingual Book-Touch (English-Portuguese) 2014. (My Bilingual Book Ser.). (ENG & POR., Illus.). 28p. (J). (gr. -1-k). 9.95 *(978-1-84059-845-2(X))* Milet Publishing.
—My Bilingual Book-Touch (English-Russian) 2014. (My Bilingual Book Ser.). (ENG & RUS., Illus.). 28p. (J). (gr. -1-k). 9.95 *(978-1-84059-846-9(8))* Milet Publishing.
—My Bilingual Book-Touch (English-Somali) 2014. (My Bilingual Book Ser.). (ENG & SOM., Illus.). 28p. (J). (gr. -1-k). 9.95 *(978-1-84059-847-6(6))* Milet Publishing.
—My Bilingual Book-Touch (English-Turkish) 2014. (My Bilingual Book Ser.). (ENG & TUR., Illus.). 28p. (J). (gr. -1-k). 9.95 *(978-1-84059-849-0(2))* Milet Publishing.
—My Bilingual Book-Touch (English-Urdu) 2014. (My Bilingual Book Ser.). (ENG & URD., Illus.). 28p. (J). (gr. -1-k). 9.95 *(978-1-84059-850-6(6))* Milet Publishing.
—My Bilingual Book-Touch (English-Vietnamese) 2014. (My Bilingual Book Ser.). (ENG & VIE., Illus.). 28p. (J). (gr. -1-k). 9.95 *(978-1-84059-851-3(4))* Milet Publishing.
—Touch - My Bilingual Book. 2014. (My Bilingual Book Ser.). (ENG & FRE., Illus.). 28p. (J). (gr. -1-k). 9.95 *(978-1-84059-840-7(9))* Milet Publishing.
Mlawer, Teresa, tr. What Do I Feel? / ¿Qué Siento? Kubler, Annie, illus. 2015. (Small Senses Bilingual Ser.: 5). (ENG & SPA.). 12p. (J). bds. *(978-1-84643-721-2(0))* Child's Play International Ltd.
Morgan, Sally. How Touch Works. 2010. (Our Senses Ser.). 24p. (J). (gr. k-2). pap. 8.25 *(978-1-61532-565-8(4)*, PowerKids Pr.); (Illus.). (gr. -1-2). lib. bdg. 22.60 *(978-1-61532-556-6(5))* Rosen Publishing Group, Inc., The.
Murphy, Patricia J. Touch. 2003. (True Bks.). (ENG.). 48p. (gr. 3-5). pap. 6.95 *(978-0-516-26972-6(0)*, Children's Pr.) Scholastic Library Publishing.
Murray, Julie. I Can Touch, 1 vol. 2016. (ENG., Illus.). 24p. *(978-1-62970-929-1(8))* ABDO Publishing Co.
Nelson, Robin. El Tacto. Translations.com Staff, tr. from ENG. 2006. (Mi Primer Paso Al Mundo Real - Los Sentidos (First Step Nonfiction - Senses) Ser.). (SPA., Illus.). 24p. (gr. k-2). lib. bdg. 23.93 *(978-0-8225-6225-2(1)*, Ediciones Lerner) Lerner Publishing Group.
—El Tacto (Touching) 2006. (Mi Primer Paso al Mundo Real Ser.). (Illus.). 23p. (J). (gr. -1-3). per. 4.25 *(978-0-8225-6544-4(7)*, Ediciones Lerner) Lerner Publishing Group.
—Touching. 2005. (First Step Nonfiction Ser.). (Illus.). 24p. (gr. k-2). lib. bdg. 17.27 *(978-0-8225-1266-0(1))* Lerner Publishing Group.
Priddy, Roger. Baby Touch & Feel: Hugs. 2013. (Baby Touch & Feel Ser.). (ENG.). 10p. (J). (gr. -1 — 1). bds. 8.99 *(978-0-312-51649-9(5)*, 9780312516499, Priddy Bks.) St. Martin's Pr.
—Bright Baby Touch & Feel Hugs & Kisses. 2009. (Bright Baby Touch & Feel Ser.). (ENG.). 12p. (J). (gr. -1 — 1). bds. 4.95 *(978-0-312-50827-2(1)*, 9780312508272, Priddy Bks.) St. Martin's Pr.
Pryor, Kimberley Jane. Touching. 2003. (Senses Ser.). (Illus.). 32p. (gr. 2-4). 23.00 *(978-0-7910-7558-6(3)*, Chelsea Hse.) Facts On File, Inc.
Rivera, Sheila. How Does It Feel? (First Step Nonfiction - Properties of Matter Ser.). 2005. (ENG.). 8p. (gr. -1-1). pap. 4.95 *(978-0-8225-5405-9(4))* 2004. (J). lib. bdg. 23.99 *(978-0-8225-2863-0(0))* Lerner Publishing Group. (Lerner Pubns.).
Rustad, Martha E. H. Touching. 2014. (Illus.). 24p. (J). lib. bdg. 25.65 *(978-1-62031-119-6(4)*, Bullfrog Bks.) Jump! Inc.
Schuh, Mari. The Sense of Touch. 2007. (Senses Ser.). (ENG., Illus.). 24p. (J). (gr. 2-5). lib. bdg. 25.95 *(978-1-60014-074-7(2))* Bellwether Media.
Verdick, Elizabeth & Lisovskis, Marjorie. Reach. 2013. (Happy Healthy Baby(r) Ser.). (ENG., Illus.). 22p. (J). bds. 6.99 *(978-1-57542-424-8(X))* Free Spirit Publishing, Inc.
Vogel, Julie & Vogel, Julia. Your Sensational Sense of Touch. Squier, Robert, illus. 2011. (Sensational Senses Ser.). (ENG.). 32p. (J). (gr. k-3). lib. bdg. 27.07 *(978-1-60954-290-0(8)*, 200819) Child's World, Inc., The.
Wheeler-Toppen, Jodi Lyn. Our Skin Can Touch. 2017. (Our Amazing Senses Ser.). (ENG.). 24p. (gr. k-1). lib. bdg. 21.99 ***(978-1-5157-6715-2(9))*** Capstone Press of Coughlan Cos.

TOUCH—FICTION

Beth, Robinson. God Made Me: The Safe Touch Coloring Book. Noel, Green, illus. 2007. 20p. (J). pap. 3.99 *(978-0-9799092-0-7(1))* Robinson, Beth.
Chapman, Jane. No More Cuddles! Chapman, Jane, illus. 2015. (ENG., Illus.). 32p. (J). (gr. -1-3). 16.99 *(978-1-58925-195-3(4))* Tiger Tales.
Cole, Kathryn. That Uh-Oh Feeling: A Story about Touch, 1 vol. Leng, Qin, illus. 2016. (I'm a Great Little Kid Ser.). (ENG.). 24p. (J). (gr. 1-3). 15.95 *(978-1-927583-91-3(8))* Second Story Pr. CAN. Dist: Orca Bk. Pubs. USA.
Isadora, Rachel. I Hear a Pickle: And Smell, See, Touch, & Taste It, Too! Isadora, Rachel, illus. 2016. (ENG., Illus.). 32p. (J). (-k). 16.99 *(978-0-399-16049-3(3)*, Nancy Paulsen Books) Penguin Young Readers Group.
Jackson, Richard. Have a Look, Says Book. Hawkes, Kevin, illus. 2016. (ENG.). 48p. (J). (gr. -1-2). 17.99 *(978-1-4814-2105-8(0))* Simon & Schuster Children's Publishing.
Katz, Karen. Mommy Hugs: Lap Edition. Katz, Karen, illus. 2010. (ENG., Illus.). 26p. (J). (gr. -1 — 1). bds. 12.99 *(978-1-4424-0791-6(3)*, Little Simon) Little Simon.
Prose, Francine. Touch. 2010. (ENG.). 272p. (YA). (gr. 9). pap. 8.99 *(978-0-06-137519-4(5)*, HarperTeen) HarperCollins Pubs.
Raum, Elizabeth. Cedric & the Dragon. Crittenden, Nina Victor, illus. 2010. (J). *(978-1-934617-05-2(9)*, Alma Little) Elva Resa Publishing, LLC.
Verdick, Elizabeth & Lisovskis, Marjorie. Cuddle. 2013. (Happy Healthy Baby Ser.). (ENG., Illus.). 22p. (J). bds. 6.99 *(978-1-57542-423-1(1))* Free Spirit Publishing, Inc.
Watt, Fiona. That's Not My Kitten. Wells, Rachel, illus. rev. ed. 2006. (Touchy-Feely Board Bks.). 10p. (J). (gr. -1-k). bds. 7.99 *(978-0-7945-1266-8(6)*, Usborne) EDC Publishing.
Weston Woods Staff, creator. A Kiss for Little Bear. 2011. 18.95 *(978-0-439-72735-8(9))*; 29.95 *(978-0-439-73481-3(9))*; 38.75 *(978-0-439-72739-6(1))* Weston Woods Studios, Inc.

TOULOUSE-LAUTREC, HENRI DE, 1864-1901

Burleigh, Robert. Toulouse-Lautrec: The Moulin Rouge & the City of Light. 2006. (Illus.). 32p. (J). (gr. 4-8). 18.00 *(978-1-4223-5493-3(8))* DIANE Publishing Co.
Cook, Diane. Henri Toulouse-Lautrec: 19th Century French Painter. 2004. (Great Names Ser.). (Illus.). 32p. (J). (gr. 3-18). lib. bdg. 19.95 *(978-1-59084-155-6(7))* Mason Crest.

TOURISM

see also Travel

Bellamy, Rufus. Tourism. 2010. (Sustaining Our Environment Ser.). 48p. (J). 35.65 *(978-1-60753-138-8(0))* Amicus Publishing.
Bianchi, Sebastian & Sebastian Bianchi, A. AS Spanish: Tourism & Leisure. 2010. (SPA & ENG., Illus.). 64p. pap., wbk. ed. 13.95 *(978-0-340-99098-8(8))* Hodder Education Group GBR. Dist: Trans-Atlantic Pubns., Inc.
Burton, Margie, et al. Travel Money, U. S. A. 2011. (Early Connections Ser.). (J). *(978-1-61672-508-2(7))* Benchmark Education Co.
Ching, Jacqueline. Jobs in Green Travel & Tourism. 2010. (Green Careers Ser.). 80p. (YA). (gr. 7-12). E-Book 61.20 *(978-1-4488-0134-3(6))* Rosen Publishing Group, Inc., The.
Espejo, Roman. What Is the Impact of Tourism? 2008. (At Issue Ser.). (ENG., Illus.). 128p. (gr. 10-12). 39.40 *(978-0-7377-4120-9(1))*; pap. 27.80 *(978-0-7377-4121-6(X))* Cengage Gale. (Greenhaven Pr., Inc.).
Feldman, Heather. Dennis Tito: The First Space Tourist. 2009. (Space Firsts Ser.). 24p. (gr. 3-4). 42.50 *(978-1-60853-112-7(0)*, PowerKids Pr.) Rosen Publishing Group, Inc., The.
Goldstein, Margaret J. Private Space Travel. 2017. (Space Discovery Guides). (ENG., Illus.). 48p. (J). (gr. 4-6). 31.99 *(978-1-5124-2589-5(3))* Lerner Publishing Group.
Goldstein, Margaret J. Private Space Travel: A Space Discovery Guide. 2017. (Space Discovery Guides). (ENG.). 48p. (J). (gr. 4-6). 16.99 ***(978-1-5124-3816-1(2))***; 47.99 ***(978-1-5124-3815-4(4))***; (Illus.). 47.99 ***(978-1-5124-2797-4(7))*** Lerner Publishing Group. (Lerner Pubns.).
Goldsworthy, Steve. Travel Green. 2010. (Being Green Ser.). (Illus.). 32p. (YA). (gr. 3-6). lib. bdg. 27.13 *(978-1-61690-085-4(7))*; (J). (gr. 4-6). pap. 12.95 *(978-1-61690-086-1(5))* Weigl Pubs., Inc.
Goldsworthy, Steve. Travelling Green. 2016. (J). ***(978-1-5105-2223-7(9))*** SmartBook Media, Inc.
Goodman, Susan E. How Do You Burp in Space? And Other Tips Every Space Tourist Needs to Know. Slack, Michael H., illus. 2013. (ENG.). 80p. (J). (gr. 3-6). 16.99 *(978-1-59990-068-1(8)*, 9781599900681, Bloomsbury USA Childrens) Bloomsbury Publishing USA.
Hauser, Mindy Moser. The Vo-Tech Track to Success in Hospitality & Tourism. 2014. (Learning a Trade, Preparing for a Career Ser.). (Illus.). 80p. (J). (gr. 7-12). 34.25 *(978-1-4777-7728-2(8))* Rosen Publishing Group, Inc., The.
Inskipp, Carol. Travel & Tourism. 2009. (J). 32.80 *(978-1-59920-100-9(3))* Black Rabbit Bks.
Mason, Paul. Extreme Storms. 2012. (Disaster Watch! Ser.). 32p. (gr. 4-6). 28.50 *(978-1-59920-424-6(X))* Black Rabbit Bks.
McAlpine, Margaret. Working in Travel & Tourism. 2004. (My Future Career Ser.). (Illus.). 64p. (gr. 3-7). lib. bdg. 27.00 *(978-0-8368-4239-5(1)*, Gareth Stevens Learning Library) Stevens, Gareth Publishing LLLP.
Pasternak, Ceel. Cool Careers for Girls in Travel & Hospitality. 2003. (ENG., Illus.). 120p. (YA). (gr. 8-17). pap. 13.95 *(978-1-57023-192-6(3))* Impact Pubns.
Payment, Simone. Cool Careers Without College for People Who Love to Travel. 2009. (Cool Careers Without College Ser.). 144p. (gr. 6-6). 66.50 *(978-1-61511-980-6(9))* Rosen Publishing Group, Inc., The.
Penta, Mark, creator. Cape Cod Invasion! 2007. (Illus.). 32p. 17.95 *(978-1-933212-49-4(7)*, Commonwealth Editions) Applewood Bks.
Randolph, Joanne. Dennis Tito: First Space Tourist. 2009. (Reading Room Collection 2 Ser.). 24p. (gr. 3-4). 42.50 *(978-1-60851-962-0(7)*, PowerKids Pr.) Rosen Publishing Group, Inc., The.
—Dennis Tito, First Space Tourist. 2003. (Reading Room Collection 2 Ser.). (Illus.). 24p. (J). lib. bdg. 22.60 *(978-0-8239-3699-1(6))* Rosen Publishing Group, Inc., The.
Riley, Rowan. Great Careers with a High School Diploma: Hospitality, Human Services, & Tourism. 2008. (Great Careers with a High School Diploma Ser.). 93p. (C). (gr. 9). 32.95 *(978-0-8160-7048-0(2)*, Ferguson Publishing Co.) Facts On File, Inc.
Roza, Greg. Reducing Your Carbon Footprint on Vacation. 2009. (Your Carbon Footprint Ser.). 48p. (gr. 5-5). 53.00 *(978-1-60854-913-9(5)*, Rosen Reference) Rosen Publishing Group, Inc., The.
Smith, John D. & Warburton, Fiona. Cambridge IGCSE Travel & Tourism. 2012. (Cambridge International IGCSE Ser.). (ENG., Illus.). 265p. pap. 33.13 *(978-0-521-14922-8(3))* Cambridge Univ. Pr.
Stearman, Kaye. Travel & Tourism Careers. 2010. (In the Workplace Ser.). 48p. (J). 35.65 *(978-1-60753-096-1(1))* Amicus Publishing.
Stearman, Kaye & Savery, Annabel. Travel & Tourism. 2011. (Been There! Ser.). 32p. (gr. 3-6). lib. bdg. 31.35 *(978-1-59920-476-5(2))* Black Rabbit Bks.
Travel & Tourism. 2nd rev. ed. 2010. (What Can I Do Now? Ser.). 224p. (gr. 6-12). 32.95 *(978-0-8160-8078-6(X)*, Ferguson Publishing Co.) Facts On File, Inc.
Turner, Cherie. Adventure Tour Guides: Life on Extreme Outdoor Adventures. 2009. (Extreme Careers Ser.). 64p. (gr. 5-5). 58.50 *(978-1-61512-383-4(0)*, Rosen Reference) Rosen Publishing Group, Inc., The.
Walker, Robin & Harding, Keith. Tourism 2. 2009. (ENG., Illus.). 144p. stu. ed. 31.19 *(978-0-19-455103-8(2))* Oxford Univ. Pr., Inc.

TOURISM—FICTION

Bean, Raymond. The Curse of Mars. 2016. (Out of This World Ser.). (ENG., Illus.). 112p. (gr. 2-5). lib. bdg. 32.65 *(978-1-4965-3615-0(0))* Out of this World GBR. Dist: Capstone Pub.
—Journey to the Moon. 2016. (Out of This World Ser.). (ENG., Illus.). 112p. (gr. 2-5). lib. bdg. 32.65 *(978-1-4965-3616-7(9))* Out of this World GBR. Dist: Capstone Pub.
Class Trip, 6 vols., Set. 2009. (J). (gr. 2-5). lib. bdg. 179.70 *(978-1-58415-812-7(3))* Mitchell Lane Pubs., Inc.
Friedman, Laurie. Red, White, & True Blue Mallory. Kalis, Jennifer, illus. (Mallory Ser.: 11). (ENG.). 184p. (J). (gr. 2-5). 2010. pap. 5.95 *(978-0-7613-3946-5(9))* 2009. 15.95 *(978-0-8225-8882-5(X))* Lerner Publishing Group. (Carolrhoda Bks.).
Keyes, Diane. Spirit of the Snowpeople. Stevens, Helen, illus. 2008. (ENG.). 32p. (J). (gr. -1-3). 15.95 *(978-0-89272-710-0(1))* Down East Bks.
Spalding, Andrea. An Island of My Own. 2008. (ENG., Illus.). 112p. (YA). (gr. 8-12). pap. 11.99 *(978-1-55002-635-1(6)*, Sandcastle Bks.) Dundurn CAN. Dist: Ingram Publisher Services.

TOURIST TRADE

see Tourism

TOUSSAINT LOUVERTURE, 1743?-1803

Worth, Richard. Toussaint L'Ouverture: Fighting for Haitian Independence. 2017. (Rebels with a Cause Ser.). 128p. (J). (gr. 8-8). lib. bdg. 37.27 ***(978-0-7660-8521-3(X))*** Enslow Pubs., Inc.

TOWER OF LONDON (LONDON, ENGLAND)

Hoena, Blake. The Tower of London: A Chilling Interactive Adventure. 2016. (You Choose: Haunted Places Ser.). (ENG., Illus.). 112p. (gr. 3-4). lib. bdg. 31.99 *(978-1-5157-2579-4(0)*, You Choose Bks.) Capstone Press of Coughlan Cos.
Nelson, Drew. Haunted! the Tower of London. 2013. 32p. (J). (gr. 3-6). 26.60 *(978-1-4339-9263-6(9))*; pap. 10.50 *(978-1-4339-9264-3(7))*; pap. 63.00 *(978-1-4339-9265-0(5))* Stevens, Gareth Publishing LLLP.
Riley, Gail Blasser. Tower of London: England's Ghostly Castle. 2006. (Castles, Palaces, & Tombs Ser.). (Illus.). 32p. (YA). (gr. 2-5). lib. bdg. 25.27 *(978-1-59716-249-4(3))* Bearport Publishing Co., Inc.

TOWN OFFICERS

see Local Government

TOWN PLANNING

see City Planning

TOWNS

see Cities and Towns

TOXIC WASTES

see Hazardous Wastes

TOXICOLOGY

see Poisons

TOY AND MOVABLE BOOKS

Abbott Orloff, Chrissy. Lady Humming Fly's Lesson on Staying Safe. 2009. 80p. pap. 28.99 *(978-1-4389-9938-8(0))* AuthorHouse.
Abbott, Simon. Pop & Play: Things That Go. 2013. (ENG., Illus.). 10p. (J). (gr. -1-k). bds. 7.99 *(978-0-7534-7162-3(0)*, 9780753471623, Kingfisher) Roaring Brook Pr.
—Pop & Play: Zoo Animals. 2013. (ENG., Illus.). 10p. (J). (gr. -1-k). bds. 7.99 *(978-0-7534-7163-0(9)*, 9780753471630, Kingfisher) Roaring Brook Pr.
Abbott, Simon, illus. Cafe. 2015. (Happy Street Ser.). (ENG.). 10p. (J). (gr. -1-k). 9.99 *(978-1-4052-7057-1(8))* Egmont Bks., Ltd. GBR. Dist: Independent Pubs. Group.
—Happy Street - Post Office. 2015. (Happy Street Ser.). (ENG.). 10p. (J). (gr. -1-k). bds. 9.99 *(978-1-4052-7520-0(0))* Egmont Bks., Ltd. GBR. Dist: Independent Pubs. Group.
—Happy Street - School. 2016. (Happy Street Ser.). (ENG.). 10p. (J). (gr. -1-k). bds. 9.99 *(978-1-4052-7522-4(7))* Egmont Bks., Ltd. GBR. Dist: Independent Pubs. Group.
—Happy Street: Vet. 2016. (Happy Street Ser.). (ENG.). 10p. (J). (gr. -1-k). 9.99 *(978-1-4052-7518-7(9))* Egmont Bks., Ltd. GBR. Dist: Independent Pubs. Group.
Abel, Simone, illus. Where Is Caterpillar Look & Play. (Lamaze Ser.). bds. 8.99 *(978-1-58663-731-6(2))* Friedman, Michael Publishing Group, Inc.
Abrams Appleseed. Making Faces: A First Book of Emotions. 2017. (ENG., Illus.). 14p. (J). bds. 7.95 *(978-1-4197-2383-4(9)*, Abrams Appleseed) Abrams, Inc.
Abrams, Pam. Can I Push the Button. 2009. 14p. 10.95 *(978-1-58117-903-3(0)*, Intervisual/Piggy Toes) Bendon, Inc.
Abramson, Andra. Snoopy's Happy Day: A Peanuts Puppet Book. Whitlock, Matt, illus. 2015. (ENG.). 16p. (J). (gr. -1). bds. 9.99 *(978-1-60433-545-3(9)*, Applesauce Pr.) Cider Mill Pr. Bk. Pubs., LLC.
Acampora, Courtney. Eyes & Ears. Kushnir, Hilli, illus. 2016. (ENG.). 22p. (J). (gr. -1). bds. 12.99 *(978-1-62686-749-9(6)*, Silver Dolphin Bks.) Readerlink Distribution Services, LLC.
—Heads & Tails. Tinarelli, Beatrice, illus. 2016. (ENG.). 22p. (J). (gr. -1). bds. 12.99 *(978-1-62686-748-2(8)*, Silver Dolphin Bks.) Readerlink Distribution Services, LLC.
Accord Publishing Staff. Dinosaurs: A Mini Animotion Book. 2011. (ENG.). 12p. (J). 9.99 *(978-1-4494-0172-6(4))* Andrews McMeel Publishing.
—Numbers: A Caterpillar-Shaped Book. 2012. (ENG.). 24p. (J). 11.99 *(978-1-4494-1736-9(1))* Andrews McMeel Publishing.
—Oliver's First Christmas. Valiant, Kristi, illus. 2012. (ENG.). 14p. (J). (-k). bds. 5.99 *(978-1-4494-2245-5(4))* Andrews McMeel Publishing.
—What Do You See? A Lift-The-Flap Book. 2014. (ENG.). 12p. (J). (-k). bds. 6.99 *(978-1-4494-4385-6(0))* Andrews McMeel Publishing.
—Where Does Love Come From? Kirkova, Milena, illus. 2012. (ENG.). 18p. (J). bds. 5.99 *(978-1-4494-2884-6(3))* Andrews McMeel Publishing.
Accord Publishing Staff & Andrews McMeel Publishing, LLC Staff. Bugs. 2014. (ENG., Illus.). 12p. (J). bds. 5.99 *(978-1-4494-6055-6(0))* Andrews McMeel Publishing.
—Numbers: A Silly Slider Book. Cole, Jeff, illus. 2011. (ENG.). 12p. (J). (gr. -1-k). bds. 10.99 *(978-1-4494-0174-0(0))* Andrews McMeel Publishing.
Ackerman, Jill. Hey, Diddle Diddle! Berg, Michelle, illus. 2011. (Little Scholastic Ser.). (ENG.). 6p. (J). (gr. k — 1). 12.99 *(978-0-545-35113-3(8)*, Cartwheel Bks.) Scholastic, Inc.
—Old MacDonald: A Hand-Puppet Board Book. Berg, Michelle, illus. 2007. (Little Scholastic Ser.). (ENG.). 6p. (J). (gr. k — 1). bds. 12.99 *(978-0-545-02603-1(2))* Scholastic, Inc.
—Please & Thank You! Berg, Michelle, illus. 2011. (Little Scholastic Ser.). (ENG.). 10p. (J). (gr. k — 1). bds. 6.99 *(978-0-545-27092-2(8)*, Cartwheel Bks.) Scholastic, Inc.
—This Little Piggy. Berg, Michelle, illus. 2007. (Little Scholastic Ser.). (ENG.). 6p. (J). (gr. k — 1). bds. 12.99 *(978-0-545-03038-0(2))* Scholastic, Inc.
—Uh-Oh! I'm Sorry. Berg, Michelle, illus. 2011. (Little Scholastic Ser.). (ENG.). 10p. (J). (gr. k — 1). bds. 6.99 *(978-0-545-30745-1(7)*, Cartwheel Bks.) Scholastic, Inc.
—Welcome Summer. Davis, Nancy, illus. 2010. (Little Scholastic Ser.). (ENG.). 10p. (J). (gr. k — 1). bds. 5.99 *(978-0-545-15164-1(3)*, Cartwheel Bks.) Scholastic, Inc.
Ackerman, Jill & Landers, Ace. I Am a Train. Scholastic, Inc. Staff, ed. 2008. (ENG.). 8p. (J). (gr. -1 — 1). bds. 4.99 *(978-0-545-07962-4(4)*, Cartwheel Bks.) Scholastic, Inc.
Ackland, Nick. Colors. 2015. (Bright Beginnings Ser.). (ENG.). 20p. (J). (gr. -1 — 1). bds. 6.99 *(978-0-7641-6742-3(1))* Barron's Educational Series, Inc.
—First Words. 2015. (Bright Beginnings Ser.). (ENG.). 20p. (J). (gr. -1 — 1). bds. 6.99 *(978-0-7641-6743-0(X))* Barron's Educational Series, Inc.
—In the Jungle. McDonald, Jake, illus. 2017. (Who's Hiding? Bks.). (ENG.). 10p. (J). (gr. -1 — 1). bds. 7.99 *(978-0-7641-6876-5(2))* Barron's Educational Series, Inc.
—Little Lion in the Garden. Walshaw, Sam, illus. 2017. (Little Explorers Ser.). (ENG.). 10p. (J). (gr. -1 — 1). bds. 6.99 *(978-0-7641-6895-6(9))* Barron's Educational Series, Inc.
—Out & About. Bradley, Jennie, illus. 2017. (Busy Baby Ser.). (ENG.). 10p. (J). (gr. -1 — 1). bds. 6.99 *(978-0-7641-6893-2(2))* Barron's Educational Series, Inc.
—What Noise Does a Lion Make? Bee, Bella, illus. 2016. (What Noise Does A... Ser.). (ENG.). 10p. (J). (gr. -1 — 1). bds. 6.99 *(978-0-7641-6844-4(4))* Barron's Educational Series, Inc.
—What Noise Does an Owl Make? Bee, Bella, illus. 2016. (What Noise Does A... Ser.). (ENG.). 10p. (J). (gr. -1 — 1). bds. 6.99 *(978-0-7641-6845-1(2))* Barron's Educational Series, Inc.
Acosta, Jamey & Reid, Stephanie. Health & Safety, 1 vol. 2010. (Early Childhood Themes Ser.). (ENG., Illus.). 16p. (J). (gr. -1-2). pap. 19.99 *(978-1-4333-1809-2(1))* Shell Educational Publishing.
Acredolo, Linda & Goodwyn, Susan. I Can Sign! Playtime. 2007. (Baby Signs (Ideals) Ser.). (ENG., Illus.). 12p. (gr. -1). 9.99 *(978-0-8249-6708-6(9)*, Ideal Pubns.) Worthy Publishing.
Active Minds, 6 bks. (Illus.). (J). (gr. -1-3). lib. bdg. 71.70 *(978-1-56674-926-8(3))* Forest Hse. Publishing Co., Inc.
Adair, Amy. Jay Jay's Special Delivery. 2003. (Illus.). (J). 15.98 *(978-0-7853-8625-4(4))* Publications International, Ltd.
Adams, Ben. The Pig with the Curliest Tail. Cameron, Craig, illus. 2013. (Googly Eyes Ser.). (ENG.). 12p. (J). (gr. -1-k). bds. 6.99 *(978-1-84322-618-5(9)*, Armadillo) Anness Publishing GBR. Dist: National Bk. Network.
—Polly the Farm Puppy. Cameron, Craig, illus. 2013. (Googly Eyes Ser.). (ENG.). 12p. (J). (gr. -1-k). bds. 6.99 *(978-1-84322-319-1(8)*, Armadillo) Anness Publishing GBR. Dist: National Bk. Network.
Adams, David J. Good Night Vancouver. Veno, Joe & Rosen, Anne, illus. 2010. (Good Night Our World Ser.). (ENG.). 20p. (J). (gr. k — 1). bds. 9.95 *(978-1-60219-039-9(9))* Good Night Bks.
Adams, Jennifer. Alice in Wonderland: A Colors Primer, 1 vol. Oliver, Alison, illus. 2012. (ENG.). 22p. (gr. k-1). bds. 9.99 *(978-1-4236-2477-6(7))* Gibbs Smith, Publisher.
—Anna Karenina: A Babylit Fashion Primer, 1 vol. Oliver, Alison, illus. 2013. (ENG.). 22p. (J). (gr. k-1). bds. 9.99 *(978-1-4236-3483-6(7))* Gibbs Smith, Publisher.
—A Christmas Carol: A Babylit Colors Primer, 1 vol. Oliver, Alison, illus. 2012. (ENG.). 22p. (J). (gr. k-1). bds. 9.99 *(978-1-4236-2575-9(7))* Gibbs Smith, Publisher.
—Dracula, 1 vol. Oliver, Alison, illus. 2012. (ENG.). 22p. (J). (gr. k-1). bds. 9.99 *(978-1-4236-2480-6(7))* Gibbs Smith, Publisher.
—Edgar & the Tattle-Tale Heart Board Book, 1 vol. Stucki, Ron, illus. 2015. (ENG.). 34p. (J). bds. 9.99 *(978-1-4236-4176-6(0))* Gibbs Smith, Publisher.
—Edgar Gets Ready for Bed, 1 vol. Stucki, Ron, illus. 2014. (ENG.). 32p. (J). 16.99 *(978-1-4236-3528-4(0))* Gibbs Smith, Publisher.
—Edgar Gets Ready for Bed Board Book, 1 vol. Stucki, Ron, illus. 2015. (ENG.). 22p. (J). bds. 9.99 *(978-1-4236-4175-9(2))* Gibbs Smith, Publisher.
—Frankenstein: An Anatomy Primer, 1 vol. Oliver, Alison, illus. 2014. (ENG.). 22p. (J). (gr. k-1). bds. 9.99 *(978-1-4236-3741-7(0))* Gibbs Smith, Publisher.
—Jabberwocky: A Nonsense Primer, 1 vol. Oliver, Alison, illus. 2013. (ENG.). 22p. (J). (gr. k-1). bds. 9.99 *(978-1-4236-3408-9(X))* Gibbs Smith, Publisher.
—Jane Eyre: A Counting Primer, 1 vol. Oliver, Alison, illus. 2012. (ENG.). 22p. (J). (gr. k-1). bds. 9.99 *(978-1-4236-2474-5(2))* Gibbs Smith, Publisher.

—A Midsummer Night's Dream: A Babylit Fairies Primer, 1 vol. Oliver, Alison, illus. 2016. (ENG.). 22p. (J). bds. 9.99 (978-1-4236-4181-0(7)) Gibbs Smith, Publisher.
—Moby-Dick, 1 vol. Oliver, Alison, illus. 2013. (ENG.). 22p. (J). (gr. k-1). bds., bds. 9.99 (978-1-4236-3204-7(4)) Gibbs Smith, Publisher.
—My Little Cities: Paris. Pizzoli, Greg, illus. 2017. (ENG.). 22p. (J). (gr. -1 — 1). bds. 9.99 **(978-1-4521-5390-2(6))** Chronicle Bks. LLC.
—My Little Cities: San Francisco. Pizzoli, Greg, illus. 2017. (ENG.). 22p. (J). (gr. -1 — 1). bds. 9.99 **(978-1-4521-5391-9(4))** Chronicle Bks. LLC.
—Romeo & Juliet: A Babylit Counting Primer, 1 vol. Oliver, Alison, illus. 2011. (ENG.). 22p. (J). (gr. k-1). bds. 9.99 (978-1-4236-2205-5(7)) Gibbs Smith, Publisher.
—Sense & Sensibility: An Opposites Primer, 1 vol. Oliver, Alison, illus. 2013. (ENG.). 22p. (J). (gr. k-1). bds., bds. 9.99 (978-1-4236-3170-5(6)) Gibbs Smith, Publisher.
—Wuthering Heights: A Weather Primer, 1 vol. Oliver, Alison, illus. 2013. (ENG.). 22p. (J). (gr. k-1). bds., bds. 9.99 (978-1-4236-3173-6(0)) Gibbs Smith, Publisher.
Adams, Michelle Medlock. Hooray for Easter! Devaney, Adam, illus. 2010. 16p. (J). (gr. -1-k). 12.99 (978-0-8249-1840-8(1), Ideal Pubns.) Worthy Publishing.
—The Story of Jesus Activity Book. Reed, Lisa, illus. 2014. 18p. (J). 4.99 (978-0-8249-5659-2(1), Ideal Pubns.) Worthy Publishing.
—The Story of Noah Activity Book. Reed, Lisa, illus. 2014. 18p. (J). 4.99 (978-0-8249-5660-8(5), Ideal Pubns.) Worthy Publishing.
—What Is Thanksgiving? Wummer, Amy, illus. 2009. (ENG.). 20p. (J). (gr. -1-k). bds. 6.99 (978-0-8249-1826-2(6), Ideal Pubns.) Worthy Publishing.
—Why I Thank You, God. Koeller, Carol, illus. 2006. 20p. (J). (gr. -1). bds. 5.49 (978-0-7586-0911-3(6)) Concordia Publishing Hse.
Adams, Pam, illus. The Farmer in the Dell. 2013. (Classic Books with Holes 8x8 with CD Ser.). (ENG.). 16p. (J). (gr. -1). pap. incl. audio compact disk (978-1-84643-624-6(9)) Child's Play International Ltd.
—The First Day. 2009. 10p. (J). bds. (978-0-85953-149-8(X)) Child's Play International Ltd.
—Old Macdonald Had a Farm. 2003. (Classic Books with Holes 8x8 Ser.). (ENG.). 16p. (J). pap. (978-0-85953-135-1(X)) Child's Play International Ltd.
—There Was an Old Lady Who Swallowed a Fly. 2003. (Classic Books with Holes 8x8 Ser.). (ENG.). 16p. (J). pap. (978-0-85953-134-4(1)) Child's Play International Ltd.
—There Was an Old Lady Who Swallowed the Sea. (Classic Books with Holes Board Book Ser.). (ENG.). (J). (gr. -1-k). 2007. 14p. bds. (978-1-84643-073-2(9)) 2006. 16p. pap. incl. audio compact disk (978-1-84643-035-0(6)) Child's Play International Ltd.
—This Old Man. 2007. (Classic Books with Holes 8x8 with CD Ser.). (ENG.). 16p. (J). (gr. -1-1). pap. incl. audio compact disk (978-1-904550-63-1(0)) Child's Play International Ltd.
Adler, Victoria. All of Baby Nose to Toes. Nakata, Hiroe, illus. 2011. (ENG.). 30p. (J). (gr. k — 1). bds. 6.99 (978-0-8037-3531-6(6), Dial Bks) Penguin Young Readers Group.
Aesop Enterprise Inc. Staff & Baruzzi, Agnese. Aesop's Fables. Baruzzi, Agnese, illus. 2012. (ENG., Illus.). 16p. (J). (gr. k-2). 18.99 (978-1-85707-895-4(0)) Tango Bks. GBR. Dist: Independent Pubs. Group.
Ageledis, Ida. First Foil Poetry Seasons, 2 vols. Berg, Michelle, illus. 2005. (First Foil Poetry Haikus Ser.). 10p. (J). 6.95 (978-1-58117-188-4(9), Intervisual/Piggy Toes) Bendon, Inc.
Ahlberg, Allan. The Goldilocks Variations: A Pop-Up Book. Ahlberg, Jessica, illus. 2012. (ENG.). 40p. (J). (gr. k-4). 17.99 (978-0-7636-6268-4(2)) Candlewick Pr.
Ahlberg, Jessica. Fairy Tales for Mr. Barker: A Peek-Through Story. Ahlberg, Jessica, illus. 2016. (ENG., Illus.). 32p. (J). (-k). 15.99 (978-0-7636-8124-1(5)) Candlewick Pr.
Aigner-Clark, Julie. Baby Einstein Poemas Preciosos: Pretty Poems & Wonderful Words. Zaidi, Nadeem, illus. 2004. (SPA.). 10p. (J). 9.95 (978-970-718-210-3(5), Silver Dolphin Bks.) Readerlink Distribution Services, LLC.
—Master Pieces. Zaidi, Nadeem, illus. 2004. (SPA.). 10p. (J). 9.95 (978-970-718-211-0(3), Silver Dolphin Bks.) Readerlink Distribution Services, LLC.
Ainsworth, Kimberly. Moustache Up! A Playful Game of Opposites. Roode, Daniel, illus. 2013. (ENG.). 18p. (J). (gr. -1-k). bds. 7.99 (978-1-4424-7526-7(9), Little Simon) Little Simon.
Ajmera, Maya. Global Baby Bedtimes. 2015. (ENG., Illus.). 16p. (J). (— 1). bds. 6.95 (978-1-58089-708-2(8)) Charlesbridge Publishing, Inc.
—Global Baby Boys. 2014. (ENG., Illus.). 16p. (J). (— 1). bds. 6.95 (978-1-58089-440-1(2)) Charlesbridge Publishing, Inc.
Albee, Sarah. Elmo Says... Leigh, Tom, illus. 2009. (Big Bird's Favorites Board Bks.). (ENG.). 24p. (J). (gr. k — 1). bds. 4.99 (978-0-375-84540-6(2), Random Hse. Bks. for Young Readers) Random Hse. Children's Bks.
—Halloween ABC. Woolf, Julia, illus. 2015. (Little Golden Board Book Ser.). (ENG.). 26p. (J). (-k). bds. 7.99 (978-0-553-52422-2(4), Random Hse. Bks. for Young Readers) Random Hse. Children's Bks.
Albee, Sarah & Hood, Susan. Snappy Heads Andy Alligator. Brown, Jo, illus. 2009. (Snappy Fun Bks.). (ENG.). 10p. (J). (gr. -1 — 1). bds. 7.99 (978-0-7944-1908-0(9), Reader's Digest Children's Bks.) Studio Fun International.
—Snappy Heads Tommy T Rex. Brown, Jo, illus. 2009. (New Snappy Fun Ser.). (ENG.). 10p. (J). (gr. -1-k). bds. 7.99 (978-0-7944-1907-3(0)) Reader's Digest Assn., Inc., The.
Albers, Josef. Squares & Other Shapes: With Josef Albers. 2016. (ENG., Illus.). 30p. (gr. -1 — 1). bds. 9.95 (978-0-7148-7256-8(3)) Phaidon Pr., Inc.
Albers, Joseph. Squares & Other Shapes: With Josef Albers. 2016. (ENG., Illus.). 30p. bds. 9.95 (978-0-7148-7255-1(5)) Phaidon Pr., Inc.
Albout, Corrine & Mabire, Grégoire. All Aboard. 2011. (One by One Ser.). (Illus.). 14p. bds. (978-1-84089-687-9(6)) Zero to Ten, Ltd.
Aliens Sticker Book. (Weird & Wacky Ser.). 16p. (J). (978-2-89393-870-7(1)) Phidal Publishing, Inc./Editions Phidal, Inc.
All the Stars. 2008. (Looney Tunes Giant Floor Pad Ser.). 80p. pap. (978-1-4075-2897-7(1)) Parragon, Inc.
All Things Bright & Beautiful. 2006. 16p. (J). pap. 1.99 (978-0-7847-1588-8(2), 22135) Standard Publishing.
Allan, Nicholas. Father Christmas Needs a Wee! Allan, Nicholas, illus. 2009. (ENG., Illus.). 32p. (J). (gr. -1-k). pap. 13.99 (978-1-86230-825-1(X), Red Fox) Random House Children's Books GBR. Dist: Independent Pubs. Group.
Allen, Constance. Peekaboo, Elmo! (Sesame Street) Prebenna, David, illus. 2014. (Big Bird's Favorites Board Bks.). (ENG.). 24p. (J). (— 1). bds. 4.99 (978-0-449-81483-3(1), Random Hse. Bks. for Young Readers) Random Hse. Children's Bks.
Allen, Elise. Barbie: A Fashion Fairytale. 2010. (Illus.). (J). (978-0-7944-2167-0(9), Reader's Digest Children's Bks.) Studio Fun International.
Allen, Francesca, illus. Vacation. 2006. (Usborne Look & Say Ser.). 10p. (J). (gr. -1-k). bds. 7.99 (978-0-7945-1315-3(8), Usborne) EDC Publishing.
Allen, J. J. Hello Kitty's Fun Friend Day! 2003. (Illus.). 32p. (J). pap. (978-0-439-44917-5(0)) Scholastic, Inc.
Allen, Judy. Flip the Flaps: Dinosaurs. Humphries, Tudor, illus. 2011. (Flip the Flaps Ser.). (ENG.). 32p. (J). (gr. -1-1). pap. 6.99 (978-0-7534-6496-0(9), 9780753464960, Kingfisher) Roaring Brook Pr.
—Flip the Flaps: Whales & Dolphins. Bostock, Mike, illus. 2011. (Flip the Flaps Ser.). (ENG.). 32p. (J). (gr. -1-1). pap. 6.99 (978-0-7534-6497-7(7), 9780753464977, Kingfisher) Roaring Brook Pr.
Allen, Judy & Mendez, Simon. Flip the Flaps: Animal Homes. 2013. (Flip the Flaps Ser.). (ENG., Illus.). 32p. (J). (gr. -1-1). 6.99 (978-0-7534-6950-7(2), 9780753469507, Kingfisher) Roaring Brook Pr.
Alligator Books Staff & Fabiny, Sarah. Katie Kitten Finds a Friend. Hughes, Cathy, illus. 2012. (Squeaky Board Bks.). (ENG.). 20p. (J). bds. 4.99 (978-0-7641-6481-1(3)) Barron's Educational Series, Inc.
—Pip Puppy Looks for Mom. Hughes, Cathy, illus. 2012. (Squeaky Board Bks.). (ENG.). 18p. (J). bds. 4.99 (978-0-7641-6482-8(1)) Barron's Educational Series, Inc.
Allum, Margaret & Watson, Judy. How Many Peas in a Pod? 2006. (Illus.). 16p. pap. (978-1-921049-43-9(X)) Little Hare Bks. AUS. Dist: HarperCollins Pubs. Australia.
Alyce, Kathie. Flip Flop Block Quilts, 1 vol. 2010. (ENG., Illus.). 64p. 22.95 (978-1-57432-675-8(9), 1574326759, American Quilter's Society) Collector Bks.
Ameet Studio Staff. Enter the Dark Knight. 2016. (LEGO DC Super Heroes Ser.). (ENG.). 32p. (J). (gr. 2-5). pap., act. bk. ed. 8.99 (978-1-338-11411-9(5)) Scholastic, Inc.
American Museum of Natural History. Camouflage. 2016. (Science for Toddlers Ser.). (ENG., Illus.). 18p. (J). (gr. -1). bds. 7.95 (978-1-4549-2079-3(3)) Sterling Publishing Co., Inc.
American Museum of Natural History Staff. ABC Oceans. 2014. (AMNH ABC Board Bks.). (ENG., Illus.). 18p. (J). (gr. -1-k). bds. 7.95 (978-1-4549-1195-1(6)) Sterling Publishing Co., Inc.
—Spot the Animals: A Lift-the-Flap Book of Colors. 2012. (ENG., Illus.). 16p. (J). (gr. -1-2). bds. 6.95 (978-1-4027-7723-3(X)) Sterling Publishing Co., Inc.
America's 50 States. 2014. (Illus.). (J). (978-1-4351-5773-6(7)) Barnes & Noble, Inc.
Amery, H. Where's Curly? Cartwright, Stephen, illus. 2004. (Treasury of Farmyard Tales Ser.). 16p. (J). (gr. 1-18). pap. 7.95 (978-0-7945-0514-1(7)) EDC Publishing.
Amery, H. & Cartwright, S. Where's Rusty? 2004. (Treasury of Farmyard Tales Ser.). 10p. (J). 7.95 (978-0-7945-0545-5(7)) EDC Publishing.
Amery, Heather. The Farm. Cartwright, Stephen, illus. 2008. (Usborne Talkabout Bks.). 12p. (J). (gr. -1-3). bds. 8.99 (978-0-7945-1795-3(1), Usborne) EDC Publishing.
—Farmyard Tales Christmas Flap Bk And. 2006. 24p. 12.99 (978-0-7945-0556-1(2), Usborne) EDC Publishing.
—Red Tractor Board Book. Cartwright, Stephen, illus. 2004. (Young Farmyard Tales Board Books Ser.). 10p. (J). bds. 3.95 (978-0-7945-0469-4(8), Usborne) EDC Publishing.
—The Seaside. Cartwright, Stephen, illus. 2008. (Usborne Talkabout Bks.). 12p. (J). bds. 8.99 (978-0-7945-1794-6(3), Usborne) EDC Publishing.
—Wind-up Plane. 2009. (Wind-up Bks). 14p. (J). bds. 29.99 (978-0-7945-2534-7(2), Usborne) EDC Publishing.
—Zoo Talkabout Board Book. Cartwright, Stephen, illus. 2008. (Talkabout Board Bks). 12p. (J). bds. 8.99 (978-0-7945-1793-9(5), Usborne) EDC Publishing.
Amery, Heather & Doherty, Gillian. Wind-Up Tractor Book. 2007. (Wind-up Tractor Book Ser.). 14p. (J). bds. 25.99 (978-0-7945-1861-5(3), Usborne) EDC Publishing.
—Wind-up Train Book. 2008. (Wind-up Bks). 14p. (J). bds. 29.99 (978-0-7945-2192-9(4), Usborne) EDC Publishing.
Anastas, Margaret. Mommy's Best Kisses. Winter, Susan, illus. 2008. (ENG.). 34p. (J). (gr. -1-k). bds. 6.99 (978-0-06-124130-7(X), HarperFestival) HarperCollins Pubs.
Ander, Martin. The Hip Hop Board Book. 2012. (ENG., Illus.). 20p. 14.95 (978-91-85639-53-3(2)) Dokument förlag, Fotograf Malcolm Jacobsson SWE. Dist: SCB Distributors.
Andersen, Hans Christian. The Little Christmas Tree: With an Advent Calendar Just for You! Downer, Maggie, illus. 2015. (ENG.). 10p. (J). (gr. k-3). bds. 7.99 (978-1-86147-291-5(9), Armadillo) Anness Publishing GBR. Dist: National Bk. Network.
—The Princess & the Pea. Kolanovic, Dubravka, illus. 2014. (J). (978-1-4723-5207-1(6)) Parragon Bk. Service Ltd.
—The Snow Queen. Sumberac, Manuel, illus. 2014. (J). (978-1-4351-5587-9(4)) Barnes & Noble, Inc.
Anderson, Airlie. A Very Furry Flap Book. 2004. (Illus.). 10p. (J). bds. 5.95 (978-1-58925-701-6(4)) Tiger Tales.
Anderson, Airlie, illus. Ten Little Ducks. 2008. (Activity Bks.). (ENG.). 24p. (J). (gr. -1-1). (978-1-84643-182-1(4)) Child's Play International Ltd.
—A Very Patchy Flap Book. 2004. 10p. (J). bds. 5.95 (978-1-58925-702-3(2)) Tiger Tales.
—A Very Spotty Flap Book. 2004. 10p. (J). bds. 5.95 (978-1-58925-703-0(0)) Tiger Tales.
—A Very Stripy Flap Book. 2004. 10p. (J). bds. 5.95 (978-1-58925-704-7(9)) Tiger Tales.
Anderson, Debby. Jesus Is Alive. 2017. (Cuddle & Sing Ser.). (ENG.). 18p. (J). bds. 5.99 (978-1-4347-1115-1(3)) Cook, David C.
Anderson, Derek. Ten Pigs - An Epic Bath Adventure. 2017. (ENG.). 32p. (J). (— 1). bds. 6.99 **(978-1-338-13581-7(3)**, Cartwheel Bks.) Scholastic, Inc.
Anderson, Sara. Noisy City Day (2015 Board Book) Anderson, Sara, illus. 2015. (ENG., Illus.). 12p. (J). (gr. -1-1). bds. 10.95 (978-1-943459-00-1(2)) Sara Anderson Children's Bks.
—Noisy City Night (2015 Board Book) Anderson, Sara, illus. 2015. (ENG., Illus.). 12p. (J). (gr. -1-1). bds. 10.95 (978-1-943459-01-8(0)) Sara Anderson Children's Bks.
Andreae, Giles. Giraffes Can't Dance. Parker-Rees, Guy, illus. 2012. (ENG.). 32p. (J). (gr. -1-3). bds. 6.99 (978-0-545-39255-6(1), Cartwheel Bks.) Scholastic, Inc.
—I Love You, Baby [board Book]. Dodd, Emma, illus. 2016. (ENG.). 26p. (J). (gr. -1-k). bds. 6.99 (978-1-4847-2261-9(2)) Hyperion Bks. for Children.
—My Little World of Happy, 9 vols. Cronin, Janet, illus. 2013. (World of Happy Ser.). (ENG.). 90p. (J). (— 1). bds. 15.99 (978-1-4052-6082-4(3)) Egmont Bks., Ltd. GBR. Dist: Independent Pubs. Group.
—Rumble in Jungle. 2011. (ENG.). 24p. (J). bds. 9.95 (978-1-58925-864-8(9)) Tiger Tales.
Andrew, Carol B. Animal Alphabet: An Interactive Book to Learn about Letters. 2005. (Illus.). (J). (978-1-933577-00-5(2)) Learning Wood, LLC.
—The Colorful Secret: An Interactive Book to Learn about Colors. 2005. (Illus.). (J). (978-1-933577-01-2(0)) Learning Wood, LLC.
—Counting Dinosaurs: An Interactive Book to Learn about Numbers. 2005. (Illus.). (J). (978-1-933577-02-9(9)) Learning Wood, LLC.
—Little Farm Puppy. 2006. (Illus.). (J). (978-1-933577-05-0(3)) Learning Wood, LLC.
—My Beautiful Ballets. 2006. (Illus.). (J). (978-1-933577-04-3(5)) Learning Wood, LLC.
—Where's My Mommy? 2006. (Illus.). (J). (978-1-933577-06-7(1)) Learning Wood, LLC.
Andrews McMeel Publishing, LLC Staff. Colors. Stone, Kate, illus. 2015. (ENG.). 12p. (J). bds. 10.99 (978-1-4494-5587-3(5)) Andrews McMeel Publishing.
—Zoo Babies. 2015. (ENG.). 12p. (J). bds. 5.99 (978-1-4494-6058-7(5)) Andrews McMeel Publishing.
Andrews McMeel Publishing Staff. Dinosaurs. 2014. (ENG., Illus.). 12p. (J). bds. 5.99 (978-1-4494-6056-3(9)) Andrews McMeel Publishing.
Angleberger, Tom. Art2-D2's Guide to Folding & Doodling. 2013. (Origami Yoda Ser.). (ENG., Illus.). 176p. (J). (gr. 3-7). 12.95 (978-1-4197-0534-2(2), Amulet Bks.) Abrams, Inc.
Anholt, Catherine & Anholt, Laurence. Can You Guess? A Lift-the-Flap Birthday Party Book. 2003. (Illus.). 16p. pap. 7.95 (978-0-7112-2214-4(2)) Fleming, Randall.
Anne Paradis, Anne. Baby Caillou, Bedtime Hide & Seek: A Lift-the-Flap Book. Chouette Publishing Staff, ed. Kary, illus. 2016. (Baby Caillou Ser.). (ENG.). 10p. (J). (— 1). bds. 6.99 (978-2-89718-351-6(9)) Caillouet, Gerry.
Anness Publishing Ltd. Let's Look & See: Canadian Animals. 2014. (ENG., Illus.). 24p. (J). (gr. -1-k). bds. 6.99 (978-1-86147-377-6(X), Armadillo) Anness Publishing GBR. Dist: National Bk. Network.
—Let's Look & See: Vehicles. 2014. (ENG., Illus.). 24p. (J). (gr. -1-k). bds. 6.99 (978-1-86147-375-2(3), Armadillo) Anness Publishing GBR. Dist: National Bk. Network.
Anness Punlishing. Busy Little People: Fun Pictures & Games for Babies & Toddlers! 2015. (ENG., Illus.). 48p. bds. 9.99 (978-1-86147-629-6(9), Armadillo) Anness Publishing GBR. Dist: National Bk. Network.
—My First Book of the 50 States of America: With Maps, Dates & Fun Facts! 2015. (ENG., Illus.). 54p. bds. 9.99 (978-1-86147-628-9(0), Armadillo) Anness Publishing GBR. Dist: National Bk. Network.
Antón, Josef. Deep in the Forest: A Seek-And-Find Adventure. Brunellière, Lucie, illus. 2017. (ENG.). 14p. (J). (gr. -1-k). bds. 17.95 (978-1-4197-2351-3(0), Abrams Appleseed) Abrams, Inc.
Antonia, Miller, illus. Baby's Very First Little Book of Bunnies. 2011. (Baby's Very First Board Bks). 10p. (J). ring bd. 6.99 (978-0-7945-2955-0(0), Usborne) EDC Publishing.
—Baby's Very First Little Book of Kittens. 2011. (Baby's Very First Board Bks). 10p. (J). ring bd. 6.99 (978-0-7945-2956-7(9), Usborne) EDC Publishing.
Appel, Julie & Guglielmo, Amy. Find King Henry's Treasure. 2010. (Touch the Art Ser.). (ENG., Illus.). 24p. (J). (gr. -1-1). bds. 12.95 (978-1-4027-6324-3(7)) Sterling Publishing Co., Inc.
Applesauce Press, Applesauce & Cider Mill Press Staff. Baa Baa Black Sheep: A Spinning Sheep Pop-Up Book. 2017. (ENG.). 8p. (J). 14.95 (978-1-60433-688-7(9), Applesauce Pr.) Cider Mill Pr. Bk. Pubs., LLC.
Arai, Hiroyuki. Everyone Says Goodnight. 2016. (ENG., Illus.). 28p. (J). (gr. -1 — 1). 14.99 (978-1-4521-5139-7(3)) Chronicle Bks. LLC.
Arcturus Publishing Staff. Santa's Sleigh. 2013. (ENG., Illus.). 10p. (J). bds. 9.95 (978-1-78212-186-2(2)) Arcturus Publishing GBR. Dist: Bookmasters Distribution.
Ariel & the Lost Whirlpool. 2013. (Illus.). (J). (978-1-4351-4946-5(7)) Disney Pr.
Arita, Vera. Animals Sing Aloha. Louie, Ron, illus. 2009. (ENG.). 20p. (J). (gr. -1-1). bds. 7.95 (978-1-933067-29-2(2)) Beachhouse Publishing, LLC.
Armadillo. Kittens. 2015. (ENG., Illus.). 24p. bds. 6.99 (978-1-86147-645-6(0), Armadillo) Anness Publishing GBR. Dist: National Bk. Network.
—Let's Count 123: A Very First Number Book. 2015. (ENG., Illus.). 48p. bds. 9.99 (978-1-86147-659-3(0), Armadillo) Anness Publishing GBR. Dist: National Bk. Network.
—Let's Learn 250 Words: A Very First Reading Book. 2016. (ENG., Illus.). 48p. bds. 9.99 (978-1-86147-706-4(6), Armadillo) Anness Publishing GBR. Dist: National Bk. Network.
—Let's Look & See: Animals. 2014. (ENG., Illus.). 24p. (J). (gr. k-2). bds. 6.99 (978-1-86147-376-9(1), Armadillo) Anness Publishing GBR. Dist: National Bk. Network.
—Let's Look & See: Pets. 2014. (ENG., Illus.). 24p. (J). (gr. k-2). bds. 6.99 (978-1-86147-378-3(8), Armadillo) Anness Publishing GBR. Dist: National Bk. Network.
—Things That Go! Tractors Trucks Trains Planes Helicopters Balloons Ships Ferries Boats Bicycles Motorcycles Cars. 2016. (ENG., Illus.). 48p. (J). (gr. -1-12). bds. 9.99 (978-1-86147-693-7(0), Armadillo) Anness Publishing GBR. Dist: National Bk. Network.
Armadillo, Jeffrey. My First Animals: Over 200 Animals to Name & Learn About. Lewis, Jan, illus. 2015. (ENG.). 48p. bds. 9.99 (978-1-86147-652-4(3), Armadillo) Anness Publishing GBR. Dist: National Bk. Network.
Armadillo Press. Dog & Friends! A Box of Exciting Picture Books, 6 vols. 2017. (ENG., Illus.). 54p. (J). (gr. -1-12). bds. 14.99 (978-1-86147-640-1(X), Armadillo) Anness Publishing GBR. Dist: National Bk. Network.
Armadillo Press Staff. My Book of Baby Animals: A Fun-Packed Picture & Puzzle Book for Little Ones. 2016. (ENG., Illus.). 48p. bds. 9.99 (978-1-86147-662-3(0), Armadillo) Anness Publishing GBR. Dist: National Bk. Network.
Armadillo Publishing Staff. Baby's Bible Stories: The Birth of Jesus. Lewis, Jan, illus. 2015. (ENG.). 24p. pap. 6.99 (978-1-86147-484-1(9), Armadillo) Anness Publishing GBR. Dist: National Bk. Network.
—This Little Pig. Lewis, Jan, illus. 2015. (ENG.). 24p. bds. 6.99 (978-1-86147-486-5(5), Armadillo) Anness Publishing GBR. Dist: National Bk. Network.
—Words - Let's Look & See. 2015. (ENG., Illus.). 24p. bds. 6.99 (978-1-86147-485-8(7), Armadillo) Anness Publishing GBR. Dist: National Bk. Network.
Arno. A Tiger in My Garden: A Do-It-Yourself Pop-Up Book. 2014. (ENG.). 32p. (J). (gr. 2-5). 19.95 (978-3-7913-7193-1(2)) Prestel Verlag GmbH & Co KG. DEU. Dist: Penguin Random Hse. LLC.
Arnold, Caroline. A Panda's World. Arnold, Caroline, illus. 2015. (Caroline Arnold's Black & White Animals Ser.). (ENG., Illus.). 20p. (gr. -1-2). bds. 7.99 (978-1-4795-6354-8(4)) Picture Window Bks.
Arnold, Damon. I Am / Mirror Mirror. 2009. 50p. pap. 12.95 (978-1-58909-587-8(1)) Bookstand Publishing.
Arnold, Marsha Diane. Baby Animals Take a Bath. Tildes, Phyllis Limbacher, illus. 2017. (ENG.). 10p. (J). (— 1). bds. 6.99 (978-1-58089-538-5(7)) Charlesbridge Publishing, Inc.
—Baby Animals Take a Nap. Tildes, Phyllis Limbacher, illus. 2017. (ENG.). 10p. (J). (— 1). bds. 6.99 (978-1-58089-539-2(5)) Charlesbridge Publishing, Inc.
Arps, Melissa. Shapes. 2006. (Illus.). (J). (978-0-7364-2383-0(4)) Random Hse., Inc.
Arrenhius, Ingela. Welcome to Curiosity! The Lift-the-Flap Tour of a Very Small Town. 2017. (ENG., Illus.). 22p. (J). (gr. -1 — 1). 16.99 **(978-1-4521-6157-0(7))** Chronicle Bks. LLC.
Arrowsmith, Vicky. Sticker Dolly Dressing Costumes & Parties. 2012. (Sticker Dolly Dressing Ser.). 24p. (J). pap. 8.99 (978-0-7945-3134-8(2), Usborne) EDC Publishing.
Ashdown, Rebecca. Bob & Flo & the Missing Bucket (Board Book) 2017. (ENG., Illus.). 26p. (J). (— 1). bds. 7.99 (978-0-544-86711-6(4), HMH Books For Young Readers) Houghton Mifflin Harcourt Publishing Co.
—Bob & Flo Play Hide-And-Seek (Board Book) 2017. (ENG., Illus.). 26p. (J). (— 1). bds. 7.99 (978-0-544-85959-3(6), HMH Books For Young Readers) Houghton Mifflin Harcourt Publishing Co.
Au, May Parker. Princess Huilua & Kamapuaa. 2007.Tr. of Ke Kamalii Wahine o Huilua a me Kamapuaa. (ENG & HAW.). (J). lib. bdg. (978-0-9773495-4-8(3)) Na Kamalei Koolauloa Early Education Program.
Auerbach, Annie. Christmas Eve. 2017. (ENG.). 10p. (J). (gr. -1 — 1). bds. 6.99 **(978-0-7641-6896-3(7))** Barron's Educational Series, Inc.
Auerbach, Annie. Cindy Big Hair: A Twisted (and Teased & Braided) Cinderella Story. Maxey, David, illus. 2005. 16p. (J). 12.95 (978-1-58117-387-1(3), Intervisual/Piggy Toes) Bendon, Inc.
Augarde, Steve. Garage: A Pop-up Book. Augarde, Steve, illus. 2005. (Illus.). 10p. (J). (gr. k-4). reprint ed. 15.00 (978-0-7567-9299-2(1)) DIANE Publishing Co.
Ault, Kelly. Let's Sign, Baby! A Fun & Easy Way to Talk with Baby. Landry, Leo, illus. abr. ed. 2010. (ENG.). 40p. (J). (gr. k — 1). bds. 7.99 (978-0-547-31596-6(1)) Houghton Mifflin Harcourt Publishing Co.
Austin, Patrick. The Brave Little Tailor. Imodraj, illus. 2014. (ENG.). 16p. (J). (gr. -1-3). 7.99 (978-1-4867-0016-5(0)) Flowerpot Children's Pr. Inc. CAN. Dist: Cardinal Pubs. Group.
Austin, Richard. Pocket Piggies Colors! The Teacup Pigs of Pennywell Farm. Austin, Richard, photos by. 2014. (ENG., Illus.). 22p. (J). bds. 5.95 (978-0-7611-7980-1(1), 17980) Workman Publishing Co., Inc.
—Pocket Piggies Numbers! Featuring the Teacup Pigs of Pennywell Farm. Austin, Richard, photos by. 2014. (ENG., Illus.). 22p. (J). bds. 5.95 (978-0-7611-7979-5(8), 17979) Workman Publishing Co., Inc.
Austin, Richard, photos by. Pocket Piggies Opposites! Featuring the Teacup Pigs of Pennywell Farm. 2016. (ENG., Illus.). 22p. (J). (gr. -1 — 1). bds. 5.95 (978-0-7611-8548-2(8)) Workman Publishing Co., Inc.
Awdry, W. Go, Go, Thomas! 2013. (Thomas & Friends 8X8 Ser.). lib. bdg. 14.75 (978-0-606-26992-6(4), Turtleback) Turtleback Bks.
—Thomas & Friends - Go, Thomas Go! 2007. (Bright & Early Playtime Bks.). (ENG., Illus.). 14p. (J). (gr. k-k). 10.99 (978-0-375-83983-2(6), Random Hse. Bks. for Young Readers) Random Hse. Children's Bks.
—Thomas & Friends: Fast Work! Storybook & Seek-And-Find Activities. Chilvers, Nigel, illus. 2016. (ENG.). 10p. (J). (gr. -1-k). bds. 10.99 (978-0-7944-3592-9(0)) Studio Fun International.
—Thomas & Friends: Movie Theater Storybook & Movie Projector. 2016. (Movie Theater Ser.: 1). (ENG.). 32p. (J). (gr. -1-1). 19.99 (978-0-7944-3705-3(2), Reader's Digest Children's Bks.) Studio Fun International.
Awdry, Wilbert V. Good Night, Thomas (Thomas & Friends) Random House Staff, illus. 2012. (Glow-In-the-Dark Board Book Ser.). (ENG.). 12p. (J). (gr. k-k). bds. 6.99 (978-0-307-97697-0(1), Random Hse. Bks. for Young Readers) Random Hse. Children's Bks.
—Making Tracks! (Thomas & Friends) Golden Books Staff, illus. 2012. (Write-On/Wipe-off Activity Book Ser.). (ENG.).

TUV

12p. (J). (gr. -1-2). bds. 9.99 *(978-0-307-93002-6(5)*, Golden Bks.) Random Hse. Children's Bks.

—My Red Railway Book Box. Stubbs, Tommy, illus. 2008. (Bright & Early Board Books(TM) Ser.). (ENG.). 96p. (J). (— 1). bds. 14.99 *(978-0-375-84322-8(1)*, Random Hse. Bks. for Young Readers) Random Hse. Children's Bks.

—Rolling on the Rails. Golden Books Staff, illus. 2011. (Thomas & Friends Ser.). (ENG.). 12p. (J). (gr. k — 1). bds. 8.99 *(978-0-375-87304-1(X)*, Golden Bks.) Random Hse. Children's Bks.

—Tales of Discovery. Golden Books Staff, illus. 2011. (Padded Board Book Ser.). (ENG.). 30p. (J). (gr. k — 1). bds. 11.99 *(978-0-375-87192-4(6)*, Golden Bks.) Random Hse. Children's Bks.

—Thomas' Favorite Places & Faces. Stubbs, Tommy, illus. 2014. (Reusable Sticker Book Ser.). (ENG.). 24p. (J). (gr. -1-2). pap. 6.99 *(978-0-449-81712-4(1)*, Golden Bks.) Random Hse. Children's Bks.

AZ Books. Babies. 2013. (Guess What? Ser.). (ENG.). 10p. (J). (gr. -1 — 1). 5.95 *(978-1-61889-316-1(5))* AZ Bks. LLC.

—Big Knowledge Book. 2013. (Smart Pad Ser.). (ENG.). 14p. (J). (gr. -1-k). bds. 19.95 *(978-1-61889-444-1(7))* AZ Bks. LLC.

—Big Zoo Book. 2013. (Smart Pad Ser.). (ENG.). 14p. (J). (gr. -1-k). bds. 19.95 *(978-1-61889-418-2(8))* AZ Bks. LLC.

—Forest Animals. 2012. (Touch & Feel Ser.). (ENG.). 10p. (J). (— 1). bds. 12.95 *(978-1-61889-222-5(3))* AZ Bks. LLC.

—Forest Life. 2013. (Matching Pictures Ser.). (ENG.). 20p. (J). (gr. -1-k). spiral bd. 5.95 *(978-1-61889-308-6(4))* AZ Bks. LLC.

—Fruits. 2013. (Guess What? Ser.). (ENG.). 10p. (J). (— 1). bds. 5.95 *(978-1-61889-318-5(1))* AZ Bks. LLC.

—Prints. 2013. (Guess What? Ser.). (ENG.). 10p. (J). (— 1). bds. 5.95 *(978-1-61889-315-4(7))* AZ Bks. LLC.

—Tiger & His Stripes. 2013. (Amusing Stories Ser.). (ENG.). 10p. (J). (-k). bds. 7.95 *(978-1-61889-307-9(6))* AZ Bks. LLC.

AZ Books, creator. Brave & Smart. 2013. (Look at Me! Ser.). (ENG., Illus.). 10p. (J). (gr. -1-k). bds. 10.95 *(978-1-61889-393-2(9))* AZ Bks. LLC.

—Farm Animals. 2012. (Touch & Feel Ser.). (ENG., Illus.). 10p. (J). (gr. -1 — 1). bds. 12.95 *(978-1-61889-223-2(1))* AZ Bks. LLC.

—Kitten Searches for a Friend. 2012. (Plush Baby Ser.). (ENG., Illus.). 10p. (J). (gr. -1 — 1). bds. 11.95 *(978-1-61889-219-5(3))* AZ Bks. LLC.

—Lake Animals Moving & Talking. 2012. (Funny Trails Ser.). (ENG., Illus.). 10p. (J). (gr. -1-k). bds. 9.95 *(978-1-61889-216-4(9))* AZ Bks. LLC.

—Lamb Searches for Her Mom. 2012. (Plush Baby Ser.). (ENG., Illus.). 10p. (J). (gr. -1 — 1). 11.95 *(978-1-61889-218-8(5))* AZ Bks. LLC.

—Magic Machines. 2012. (Baby Book Ser.). (ENG., Illus.). 10p. (J). (gr. -1 — 1). bds. 4.95 *(978-1-61889-286-7(X))* AZ Bks. LLC.

—Pond Animals. 2013. (Touch & Feel Ser.). (ENG., Illus.). 10p. (J). (gr. -1-k). bds. 12.95 *(978-1-61889-224-9(X))* AZ Bks. LLC.

—Talking Train. 2012. (Lively Machines Ser.). (ENG., Illus.). 10p. (J). (gr. -1-k). bds. 10.95 *(978-1-61889-325-3(4))* AZ Bks. LLC.

—Tyler Turtle Travels to Australia. 2013. (Pop-Up: Play & Listen Ser.). (ENG., Illus.). 10p. (J). (gr. -1-k). bds. 16.95 *(978-1-61889-036-8(0))* AZ Bks. LLC.

—Walk Around a Farm. 2012. (Put Together Ser.). (ENG., Illus.). 16p. (J). (gr. -1-k). spiral bd. 6.95 *(978-1-61889-189-1(8))* AZ Bks. LLC.

—Water Animals. 2013. (Sounds Around Us Ser.). (ENG., Illus.). 16p. (J). (gr. 1-3). bds. 17.95 *(978-1-61889-283-6(5))* AZ Bks. LLC.

—What Color? 2012. (Smarty Ser.). (ENG., Illus.). 10p. (J). (gr. -1 — 1). 9.95 *(978-1-61889-249-2(5))* AZ Bks. LLC.

—What Number? 2012. (Smarty Ser.). (ENG., Illus.). 10p. (J). (gr. -1 — 1). 9.95 *(978-1-61889-248-5(7))* AZ Bks. LLC.

AZ Books Staff. About the Human Body. Petrovskaya, Olga, ed. 2012. (Million Whys Ser.). (ENG.). 12p. (J). (gr. -1-4). bds. 18.95 *(978-1-61889-058-0(1))* AZ Bks. LLC.

—Amazing Space. Ivinskaya, Snezhana, ed. 2012. (Encyclopedia with Flaps Ser.). (ENG.). 22p. (J). (gr. 1-3). bds. 13.95 *(978-1-61889-150-1(2))* AZ Bks. LLC.

—Animals. Slusar, Julia, ed. 2012. (Pull It Out Ser.). (ENG.). 10p. (J). (gr. -1 — 1). 7.95 *(978-1-61889-195-2(2))* AZ Bks. LLC.

—Babbling Pond. Tulup, Natalia, ed. 2012. (How We Speak Ser.). (ENG.). 12p. (J). (gr. -1-k). bds. 10.95 *(978-1-61889-097-9(2))* AZ Bks. LLC.

—Bear's Forest. Potapenko, Olga, ed. 2012. (Talking Plush Animals Ser.). (ENG.). 10p. (J). (gr. -1-k). bds. 10.95 *(978-1-61889-111-2(1))* AZ Bks. LLC.

—Busy Insects Moving & Talking. Dubovik, Ludmila, ed. 2012. (Funny Trails Ser.). (ENG.). 10p. (J). (gr. -1-k). bds. 9.95 *(978-1-61889-175-4(8))* AZ Bks. LLC.

—Buzzing Meadow. Tulup, Natalia, ed. 2012. (How We Speak Ser.). (ENG.). 12p. (J). (gr. -1-k). bds. 10.95 *(978-1-61889-095-5(6))* AZ Bks. LLC.

—Cinderella. Zyl, Olga, ed. 2012. (Classic Fairy Tales Ser.). (ENG.). 10p. (J). (gr. -1-k). bds. 9.95 *(978-1-61889-007-8(7))* AZ Bks. LLC.

—Colores - Colorful Animals: Colorful Animals. Gorbachenok, Ekaterina, ed. 2012. (Spanish for Kids Ser.). (ENG & SPA.). 10p. (J). (gr. -1-k). bds. 11.95 *(978-1-61889-136-5(7))* AZ Bks. LLC.

—Colors. Slusar, Julia, ed. 2012. (Pull It Out Ser.). (ENG.). 10p. (J). (gr. -1 — 1). 7.95 *(978-1-61889-193-8(6))* AZ Bks. LLC.

—Colors & Shapes. Petrovskaya, Olga, ed. 2012. (Matching Game Ser.). (ENG.). 18p. (J). (gr. -1-k). spiral bd. 4.95 *(978-1-61889-201-0(0))* AZ Bks. LLC.

—Countries & People. Borovik, Alija et al, eds. 2013. (Little Genius Ser.). (ENG.). 150p. (J). (gr. 1-3). bds. 19.95 *(978-1-61889-139-6(1))* AZ Bks. LLC.

—Discoveries & Inventions. Kazimirova, Karina, ed. 2012. (Encyclopedia with Flaps Ser.). (ENG.). 22p. (J). (gr. 1-3). bds. 13.95 *(978-1-61889-152-5(9))* AZ Bks. LLC.

—Discovering the Savanna. Gorojan, Elena, ed. 2012. (Wild Theater Ser.). (ENG.). 8p. (J). (gr. -1-3). bds. 17.95 *(978-1-61889-017-7(4))* AZ Bks. LLC.

—Exploring the Ocean. Vasilkova, Elena, ed. 2012. (Wild Theater Ser.). (ENG.). 8p. (J). (gr. -1-3). bds. 17.95 *(978-1-61889-020-7(4))* AZ Bks. LLC.

—Farm Animals. Gorojan, Elena, ed. 2012. (My First Library). (ENG.). 12p. (J). (gr. -1-k). bds. 8.95 *(978-1-61889-123-5(5))* AZ Bks. LLC.

—Farm Animals Moving & Talking. Harko, Lubov, ed. 2012. (Funny Trails Ser.). (ENG.). 10p. (J). (gr. -1-k). bds. 9.95 *(978-1-61889-174-7(X))* AZ Bks. LLC.

—Fashion Ideas. Batan, Natalia, ed. 2012. (Fashion Ideas Ser.). (ENG.). 60p. (J). bds. 15.95 *(978-1-61889-075-7(1))* AZ Bks. LLC.

—Fast Cars. Tulup, Natasha, ed. 2012. (Workshop Ser.). (ENG.). 10p. (J). (gr. -1-k). bds. 10.95 *(978-1-61889-161-7(8))* AZ Bks. LLC.

—Fast Vehicles Moving & Talking. Harko, Lubov, ed. 2012. (Funny Trails Ser.). (ENG.). 10p. (J). (gr. -1-k). bds. 9.95 *(978-1-61889-177-8(4))* AZ Bks. LLC.

—Feathered Singers. Tulup, Natalia, ed. 2012. (How We Speak Ser.). (ENG.). 12p. (J). (gr. -1-k). bds. 10.95 *(978-1-61889-096-2(4))* AZ Bks. LLC.

—Find a Pair. Petrovskaya, Olga, ed. 2012. (Matching Game Ser.). (ENG.). 18p. (J). (gr. -1-k). spiral bd. 4.95 *(978-1-61889-009-2(3))* AZ Bks. LLC.

—Find My Food & Home. Petrovskaya, Olga, ed. 2012. (Matching Game Ser.). (ENG.). 18p. (J). (gr. -1-k). spiral bd. 4.95 *(978-1-61889-010-8(7))* AZ Bks. LLC.

—Flying Planes. Tulup, Natasha, ed. 2012. (Workshop Ser.). (ENG.). 10p. (J). (gr. -1-k). 10.95 *(978-1-61889-159-4(6))* AZ Bks. LLC.

—Forest Animals. Gorojan, Elena, ed. 2012. (My First Library). (ENG.). 12p. (J). (gr. -1-k). bds. 8.95 *(978-1-61889-120-4(0))* AZ Bks. LLC.

—Forest Animals Moving & Talking. Dubovik, Ludmila, ed. 2012. (Funny Trails Ser.). (ENG.). 10p. (J). (gr. -1-k). bds. 9.95 *(978-1-61889-176-1(6))* AZ Bks. LLC.

—Frog's Pond. Potapenko, Olga, ed. 2012. (Talking Plush Animals Ser.). (ENG.). 10p. (J). (gr. -1-k). bds. 10.95 *(978-1-61889-113-6(8))* AZ Bks. LLC.

—Fruits & Vegetables. Slusar, Julia, ed. 2012. (Pull It Out Ser.). (ENG.). 10p. (J). (— 1). 7.95 *(978-1-61889-192-1(8))* AZ Bks. LLC.

—Great Warriors. Aksinovich, Natalia & Yaroshevich, Angelica, eds. 2012. (Sounds Around Us Ser.). (ENG.). 16p. (J). (gr. 1-3). bds. 17.95 *(978-1-61889-033-7(6))* AZ Bks. LLC.

—Hello, I'm Bear! Gorbachenok, Ekaterina, ed. 2012. (Who Lives in the Book? Ser.). (ENG.). 10p. (J). (-k). bds. 11.95 *(978-1-61889-070-2(0))* AZ Bks. LLC.

—Hello, I'm Horse! Gorbachenok, Ekaterina, ed. 2012. (Who Lives in the Book? Ser.). (ENG.). 10p. (J). (-k). bds. 11.95 *(978-1-61889-069-6(7))* AZ Bks. LLC.

—History & Discoveries. Shumovich, Nadegda et al, eds. 2013. (Little Genius Ser.). (ENG.). 150p. (J). (gr. 1-3). bds. 19.95 *(978-1-61889-138-9(3))* AZ Bks. LLC.

—Horse's Farm. Potapenko, Olga, ed. 2012. (Talking Plush Animals Ser.). (ENG.). 10p. (J). (gr. -1-k). bds. 10.95 *(978-1-61889-112-9(X))* AZ Bks. LLC.

—In the Forest. Ulasevich, Olga & Goncharik, Irina, eds. 2012. (Animal Sounds Ser.). (ENG.). 14p. (J). (gr. -1-k). bds. 7.95 *(978-1-61889-126-6(X))* AZ Bks. LLC.

—In the Jungle. Efimova, Tatiana, ed. 2012. (Animal Sounds Ser.). (ENG.). 14p. (J). (gr. -1-k). bds. 7.95 *(978-1-61889-125-9(1))* AZ Bks. LLC.

—In the Prairie & Desert. Efimova, Tatiana & Goncharik, Irina, eds. 2012. (Animal Sounds Ser.). (ENG.). 14p. (J). (gr. -1-k). bds. 7.95 *(978-1-61889-128-0(6))* AZ Bks. LLC.

—In the Savanna. Ulasevich, Olga & Migits, Anna, eds. 2012. (Animal Sounds Ser.). (ENG.). 14p. (J). (-k). bds. 7.95 *(978-1-61889-124-2(3))* AZ Bks. LLC.

—In the Sea & Ocean. Efimova, Tatiana, ed. 2012. (Animal Sounds Ser.). (ENG.). 14p. (J). (-k). bds. 7.95 *(978-1-61889-127-3(8))* AZ Bks. LLC.

—Jungle Animals. Gorojan, Elena, ed. 2012. (My First Library). (ENG.). 12p. (J). (-k). bds. 8.95 *(978-1-61889-121-1(9))* AZ Bks. LLC.

—Little Thumb. Zyl, Olga, ed. 2012. (Classic Fairy Tales Ser.). (ENG.). 10p. (J). (gr. -1-k). bds. 9.95 *(978-1-61889-008-5(5))* AZ Bks. LLC.

—Living Book of Dinosaurs. Latushko, Julia, ed. 2012. (Our Amazing World Ser.). (ENG.). 12p. (J). (gr. 1-3). bds. 19.95 *(978-1-61889-025-2(5))* AZ Bks. LLC.

—Living Book of the Forest. Vasilkova, Elena, ed. 2012. (Our Amazing World Ser.). (ENG.). 12p. (J). (gr. 1-3). bds. 19.95 *(978-1-61889-022-1(0))* AZ Bks. LLC.

—Living Book of the Jungle. Gasteva, Julia, ed. 2012. (Our Amazing World Ser.). (ENG.). 12p. (J). (gr. 1-3). bds. 19.95 *(978-1-61889-024-5(7))* AZ Bks. LLC.

—Living Book of the Ocean. Aksinovich, Natalia, ed. 2012. (Our Amazing World Ser.). (ENG.). 12p. (J). (gr. 1-3). bds. 19.95 *(978-1-61889-021-4(2))* AZ Bks. LLC.

—Loud Farm. Tulup, Natalia, ed. 2012. (How We Speak Ser.). (ENG.). 12p. (J). (-k). bds. 10.95 *(978-1-61889-093-1(X))* AZ Bks. LLC.

—Making Machines. Sisoj, Natalja, ed. 2012. (Modeling Clay Bks.). (ENG.). 12p. (J). (gr. -1-2). bds. 10.95 *(978-1-61889-198-3(7))* AZ Bks. LLC.

—Making the Farm. Sisoj, Natalja, ed. 2012. (Modeling Clay Bks.). (ENG.). 12p. (J). (gr. -1-2). bds. 10.95 *(978-1-61889-197-6(9))* AZ Bks. LLC.

—Making the Forest. Sisoj, Natalja, ed. 2012. (Modeling Clay Bks.). (ENG.). 12p. (J). (gr. -1-2). bds. 10.95 *(978-1-61889-199-0(5))* AZ Bks. LLC.

—Meeting Dinosaurs. Vasilkova, Elena, ed. 2012. (Wild Theater Ser.). (ENG.). 8p. (J). (gr. -1-3). bds. 17.95 *(978-1-61889-019-1(0))* AZ Bks. LLC.

—Merry Orchestra. Tulup, Natalia, ed. 2012. (Tra-La-la Ser.). (ENG.). 14p. (J). (-k). bds. 10.95 *(978-1-61889-056-6(5))* AZ Bks. LLC.

—Movie Star. Puzik, Ulijana, ed. 2012. (Lovely Charmie Ser.). (ENG.). 16p. (J). (gr. 1-3). pap. 6.95 *(978-1-61889-184-6(7))* AZ Bks. LLC.

—Musical Animals. Tulup, Natalia, ed. 2012. (Tra-La-la Ser.). (ENG.). 14p. (J). (-k). bds. 10.95 *(978-1-61889-057-3(3))* AZ Bks. LLC.

—Musical Machines. Tulup, Natalia, ed. 2012. (Tra-La-la Ser.). (ENG.). 14p. (J). (-k). bds. 10.95 *(978-1-61889-055-9(7))* AZ Bks. LLC.

—My Farm. Yaroshevich, Angelica, ed. 2012. (Open the Book-I Am Alive Ser.). (ENG.). 8p. (J). (— 1). bds. 5.95 *(978-1-61889-043-6(3))* AZ Bks. LLC.

—My Forest. Yaroshevich, Angelica, ed. 2012. (Open the Book-I Am Alive Ser.). (ENG.). 8p. (J). (— 1). bds. 5.95 *(978-1-61889-042-9(5))* AZ Bks. LLC.

—My Pets. Yaroshevich, Angelica, ed. 2012. (Open the Book-I Am Alive Ser.). (ENG.). 8p. (J). (— 1). bds. 5.95 *(978-1-61889-045-0(X))* AZ Bks. LLC.

—My Pond. Yaroshevich, Angelica, ed. 2012. (Open the Book-I Am Alive Ser.). (ENG.). 8p. (J). (— 1). bds. 5.95 *(978-1-61889-046-7(8))* AZ Bks. LLC.

—My Zoo. Yaroshevich, Angelica, ed. 2012. (Open the Book-I Am Alive Ser.). (ENG.). 8p. (J). (— 1). bds. 5.95 *(978-1-61889-044-3(1))* AZ Bks. LLC.

—Ocean Animals. Gorojan, Elena, ed. 2012. (My First Library). (ENG.). 12p. (J). (gr. -1-k). bds. 8.95 *(978-1-61889-119-8(7))* AZ Bks. LLC.

—On the Farm. Ulasevich, Olga, ed. 2012. (Animal Sounds Ser.). (ENG.). 14p. (J). (-k). bds. 7.95 *(978-1-61889-129-7(4))* AZ Bks. LLC.

—Our Cozy Forest. Zayceva, Irina, ed. 2012. (Hook-And-Loop-Pictures Ser.). (ENG.). 8p. (J). (-k). bds. 11.95 *(978-1-61889-157-0(X))* AZ Bks. LLC.

—Our Faraway Jungle. Zayceva, Irina, ed. 2012. (Hook-And-Loop-Pictures Ser.). (ENG.). 12p. (J). (-k). bds. 11.95 *(978-1-61889-158-7(8))* AZ Bks. LLC.

—Our Friendly Farm. Zayceva, Irina, ed. 2012. (Hook-And-Loop-Pictures Ser.). (ENG.). 8p. (J). (-k). bds. 11.95 *(978-1-61889-156-3(1))* AZ Bks. LLC.

—Polar Animals. Gorojan, Elena, ed. 2012. (My First Library). (ENG.). 12p. (J). (-k). bds. 8.95 *(978-1-61889-122-8(7))* AZ Bks. LLC.

—Sailing Ships. Tulup, Natasha, ed. 2012. (Workshop Ser.). (ENG.). 10p. (J). (gr. -1-k). bds. 10.95 *(978-1-61889-162-4(6))* AZ Bks. LLC.

—Sam the Auto Mechanic. Boroda, Janna, ed. 2012. (Little Master Ser.). (ENG.). 10p. (J). (gr. -1-k). bds. 10.95 *(978-1-61889-148-8(0))* AZ Bks. LLC.

—Sam the Builder. Boroda, Janna, ed. 2012. (Little Master Ser.). (ENG.). 10p. (J). (gr. -1-k). bds. 10.95 *(978-1-61889-147-1(2))* AZ Bks. LLC.

—Sam the Constructor. Boroda, Janna, ed. 2012. (Little Master Ser.). (ENG.). 10p. (J). (gr. -1-k). bds. 10.95 *(978-1-61889-149-5(9))* AZ Bks. LLC.

—Savanna Animals. Gorojan, Elena, ed. 2012. (My First Library). (ENG.). 12p. (J). (-k). bds. 8.95 *(978-1-61889-118-1(9))* AZ Bks. LLC.

—Scouting the Forest. Vasilkova, Elena, ed. 2012. (Wild Theater Ser.). (ENG.). 8p. (J). (gr. -1-3). bds. 17.95 *(978-1-61889-018-4(2))* AZ Bks. LLC.

—Secrets of Pirates. Naumovets, Elena, ed. 2012. (Mysteries of History Ser.). (ENG.). 18p. (J). (gr. 1-3). bds. 17.95 *(978-1-61889-089-4(1))* AZ Bks. LLC.

—Shapes. Slusar, Julia, ed. 2012. (Pull It Out Ser.). (ENG.). 10p. (J). (— 1). 7.95 *(978-1-61889-194-5(4))* AZ Bks. LLC.

—Sleeping Beauty. Zyl, Olga, ed. 2012. (Classic Fairy Tales Ser.). (ENG.). 10p. (J). (gr. -1-k). bds. 9.95 *(978-1-61889-006-1(9))* AZ Bks. LLC.

—Sounds of Dinosaurs. Yaroshevich, Angelica, ed. 2012. (Sounds Around Us Ser.). (ENG.). 16p. (J). (gr. 1-3). bds. 17.95 *(978-1-61889-027-6(1))* AZ Bks. LLC.

—Sounds of the Farm. Sheljagovich, Yana, ed. 2012. (Sounds Around Us Ser.). (ENG.). 16p. (J). (gr. 1-3). bds. 17.95 *(978-1-61889-029-0(8))* AZ Bks. LLC.

—Sounds of the Forest. Sheljagovich, Yana, ed. 2012. (Sounds Around Us Ser.). (ENG.). 16p. (J). (gr. 1-3). bds. 17.95 *(978-1-61889-028-3(X))* AZ Bks. LLC.

—Sounds of the Jungle. Migiz, Anna, ed. 2012. (Sounds Around Us Ser.). (ENG.). 16p. (J). (gr. 1-3). bds. 17.95 *(978-1-61889-030-6(1))* AZ Bks. LLC.

—Sounds of the Savanna & Desert. Migiz, Anna, ed. 2012. (Sounds Around Us Ser.). (ENG.). 16p. (J). (gr. 1-3). bds. 17.95 *(978-1-61889-031-3(X))* AZ Bks. LLC.

—Sounds of Wild Nature. Naumovets, Elena, ed. 2012. (Sounds Around Us Ser.). (ENG.). 16p. (J). (gr. 1-3). bds. 17.95 *(978-1-61889-026-9(3))* AZ Bks. LLC.

—Sparrow's Yard. Potapenko, Olga, ed. 2012. (Talking Plush Animals Ser.). (ENG.). 10p. (J). (gr. -1-k). bds. 10.95 *(978-1-61889-114-3(6))* AZ Bks. LLC.

—Terribly Funny Monsters. Shumovich, Nadezhda, ed. 2012. (Terribly Funny Monsters Ser.). (ENG.). 10p. (J). (gr. -1-1). bds. 15.95 *(978-1-61889-133-4(2))* AZ Bks. LLC.

—Visiting Africa. Zuk, Valentina, ed. 2012. (Lively Pictures Ser.). (ENG.). 10p. (J). (gr. -1-k). bds. 9.95 *(978-1-61889-179-2(0))* AZ Bks. LLC.

—Visiting Dinosaurs. Vol, Vera, ed. 2012. (Lively Pictures Ser.). (ENG.). 10p. (J). (gr. -1-k). bds. 9.95 *(978-1-61889-181-5(2))* AZ Bks. LLC.

—Visiting the Farm. Zuk, Valentina, ed. 2012. (Lively Pictures Ser.). (ENG.). 10p. (J). (gr. -1-k). bds. 9.95 *(978-1-61889-182-2(0))* AZ Bks. LLC.

—Visiting the Forest. Zuk, Valentina, ed. 2012. (Lively Pictures Ser.). (ENG.). 10p. (J). (gr. -1-k). bds. 9.95 *(978-1-61889-178-5(2))* AZ Bks. LLC.

—Visiting the Ocean. Lukjanenko, Anna, ed. 2012. (Lively Pictures Ser.). (ENG.). 10p. (J). (gr. -1-1). bds. 9.95 *(978-1-61889-180-8(4))* AZ Bks. LLC.

—What Do I Eat? Sisoj, Natalja, ed. 2012. (Peek-A-Boo Ser.). (ENG.). 10p. (J). (— 1). bds. 10.95 *(978-1-61889-115-0(4))* AZ Bks. LLC.

—Where's My Baby? Sisoj, Natalja, ed. 2012. (Peek-A-Boo Ser.). (ENG.). 10p. (J). (— 1). bds. 10.95 *(978-1-61889-117-4(0))* AZ Bks. LLC.

—Where's My Toy? Sisoj, Natalja, ed. 2012. (Peek-A-Boo Ser.). (ENG.). 10p. (J). (— 1). bds. 10.95 *(978-1-61889-116-7(2))* AZ Bks. LLC.

—Who Is the Bear Looking For? Sharipovas, Alesja, ed. 2012. (Who Is There Ser.). (ENG.). 10p. (J). (-k). bds. 11.95 *(978-1-61889-039-9(5))* AZ Bks. LLC.

—Who Is the Hare Looking For? Zajceva, Ira, ed. 2012. (Who Is There Ser.). (ENG.). 10p. (J). (-k). bds. 11.95 *(978-1-61889-040-5(9))* AZ Bks. LLC.

—Who Is the Lion Looking For? Shestakova, Anna, ed. 2012. (Who Is There Ser.). (ENG.). 10p. (J). (-k). bds. 11.95 *(978-1-61889-041-2(7))* AZ Bks. LLC.

—Who Is the Puppy Looking For? Gridina, Anna, ed. 2012. (Who Is There Ser.). (ENG.). 10p. (J). (-k). bds. 11.95 *(978-1-61889-038-2(7))* AZ Bks. LLC.

—Who Is the Tiger Looking For? Gridina, Anna, ed. 2012. (Who Is There Ser.). (ENG.). 10p. (J). (-k). bds. 11.95 *(978-1-61889-037-5(9))* AZ Bks. LLC.

—Who Lives in the Jungle? Gridina, Anna, ed. 2012. (Funny Animals Ser.). (ENG.). 10p. (J). (-k). bds. 8.95 *(978-1-61889-048-1(4))* AZ Bks. LLC.

—Who Lives in the Pond? Gridina, Anna, ed. 2012. (Funny Animals Ser.). (ENG.). 10p. (J). (-k). bds. 8.95 *(978-1-61889-049-8(2))* AZ Bks. LLC.

—Who Lives in the Savanna? Gridina, Anna, ed. 2012. (Funny Animals Ser.). (ENG.). 10p. (J). (-k). bds. 8.95 *(978-1-61889-050-4(6))* AZ Bks. LLC.

—Who Lives on a Farm? Gridina, Anna, ed. 2012. (Funny Animals Ser.). (ENG.). 10p. (J). (-k). bds. 8.95 *(978-1-61889-047-4(6))* AZ Bks. LLC.

—Wild Nature. Kokash, Elena et al, eds. 2013. (Little Genius Ser.). (ENG.). 150p. (J). (gr. 1-3). bds. 19.95 *(978-1-61889-140-2(5))* AZ Bks. LLC.

AZ Books Staff & Evans, Olivia. Haunted Castle. Shumovich, Nadezhda, ed. 2012. (Terribly Funny Monsters Ser.). (ENG., Illus.). 10p. (J). bds. 15.95 *(978-1-61889-134-1(0))* AZ Bks. LLC.

—Making the Zoo. Sisoj, Natalja, ed. 2012. (Modeling Clay Bk Ser.). (ENG., Illus.). 12p. (J). (gr. -1-2). bds. 10.95 *(978-1-61889-196-9(0))* AZ Bks. LLC.

B&H Kids Editorial Staff. Ambushed by the Ambassador of Ignorance/Wiping Out the Whiner Brothers, Flip-Over Book. 2017. (Bibleman Ser.). (ENG.). 32p. (J). (gr. -1-2). pap. 3.99 *(978-1-4336-4941-7(1)*, B&H Kids) B&H Publishing Group.

—Brave Queen Esther/David & the Giant Flip-Over Book. McPherson, Heath, illus. 2016. (Big Picture Interactive / the Gospel Project Ser.). (ENG.). 32p. (J). (gr. -1-3). pap. 3.99 *(978-1-4336-4329-3(4)*, B&H Kids) B&H Publishing Group.

—Braving the Big Battle with the Baroness / Repelling the Ronin of Wrong, Flip-Over Book. 2016. (Bibleman Ser.). (ENG., Illus.). 32p. (J). (gr. -1-2). pap. 3.99 *(978-1-4336-4573-0(4)*, B&H Kids) B&H Publishing Group.

—Disabling the Disobey Ray/Lighting up the Shadow of Doubt, Flip-Over Book. 2017. (Bibleman Ser.). (ENG.). 32p. (J). (gr. -1-2). pap. 3.99 *(978-1-4336-4944-8(6)*, B&H Kids) B&H Publishing Group.

—Dr. Fear's Almost Perfectly Disastrous Day / Clobbering the Crusher, Flip-Over Book. 2016. (Bibleman Ser.). (ENG., Illus.). 32p. (J). (gr. -1-2). pap. 3.99 *(978-1-4336-4574-7(2)*, B&H Kids) B&H Publishing Group.

—Easter (board Book) Conger, Holli, illus. 2017. (Little Words Matter(tm) Ser.). (ENG.). 24p. (J). (gr. -1 — 1). bds. 8.99 *(978-1-4336-4453-5(3)*, B&H Kids) B&H Publishing Group.

—If You're Happy & You Know It, Sound Book. Conger, Holli, illus. 2016. (Little Words Matter(tm) Ser.). (ENG.). 12p. (J). (gr. -1 — 1). bds. 12.99 *(978-1-4336-8678-8(3)*, B&H Kids) B&H Publishing Group.

—In the Beginning/the Great Flood Flip-Over Book. McPherson, Heath, illus. 2016. (Big Picture Interactive / the Gospel Project Ser.). (ENG.). 32p. (J). (gr. -1-3). pap. 3.99 *(978-1-4336-4328-6(6)*, B&H Kids) B&H Publishing Group.

—Jesus Loves Me, Sound Book. Conger, Holli, illus. 2015. (Little Words Matter(tm) Ser.). (ENG.). 12p. (J). (— 1). bds. 12.99 *(978-1-4336-8675-7(9)*, B&H Kids) B&H Publishing Group.

—Melting the Master of Mean / the Mayor of Maybe Doles Out Doubt, Flip-Over Book. 2016. (Bibleman Ser.). (ENG., Illus.). 32p. (J). (gr. -1-2). pap. 3.99 *(978-1-4336-4575-4(0)*, B&H Kids) B&H Publishing Group.

—Mighty Miracles/Joseph the Dreamer Flip-Over Book. McPherson, Heath, illus. 2016. (Big Picture Interactive / the Gospel Project Ser.). (ENG.). 32p. (J). (gr. -1-3). pap. 3.99 *(978-1-4336-4330-9(8)*, B&H Kids) B&H Publishing Group.

—Putting on the Full Armor of God: A Battle Plan Based on Ephesians 6. 2016. (Bibleman Ser.). (ENG., Illus.). 24p. (J). (gr. -1-2). pap. 5.99 *(978-1-4336-4577-8(7)*, B&H Kids) B&H Publishing Group.

—Stopping the Sultan of Selfishness/Fracturing the Falsehoods of the Fibbler, Flip-Over Book. 2017. (Bibleman Ser.). (ENG.). 32p. (J). (gr. -1-2). pap. 3.99 *(978-1-4336-4947-9(0)*, B&H Kids) B&H Publishing Group.

—100+ Little Bible Words (padded Board Book) 2017. (Little Words Matter(tm) Ser.). (ENG., Illus.). 38p. (J). (gr. -1 — 1). bds. 12.99 *(978-1-4336-4923-3(3)*, B&H Kids) B&H Publishing Group.

B&H Kids Editorial Staff & McPherson, Heath. The Birth of a King/Jesus Saves His People Flip-Over Book. 2016. (Big Picture Interactive / the Gospel Project Ser.). (ENG.). 32p. (J). (gr. -1-3). pap. 3.99 *(978-1-4336-4333-0(2)*, B&H Kids) B&H Publishing Group.

Baby Einstein: Let's Learn! 12 Book Block. 2013. 10p. (J). bds. 9.98 *(978-1-4508-3093-5(5)*, 1450830935) Phoenix International Publications, Inc.

Baby's Very First Touchy-Feely Christmas. 2015. (Baby's Very First Touchy-Feely Board Bks.). (ENG.). (J). 7.99 *(978-0-7945-3629-9(8)*, Usborne) EDC Publishing.

Bach, Annie. Night-Night, Forest Friends. Bach, Annie, illus. 2013. (ENG., Illus.). 24p. (J). (gr. -1-k). bds. 8.99 *(978-0-8431-7278-2(9)*, Grosset & Dunlap) Penguin Young Readers Group.

Backpack Books (Firm) Staff, contrib. by. My Big Animal Book: Includes Touch-And-Feel, Flaps, Pull-Out Tabs, & a Puzzle! 2005. (Illus.). (J). *(978-0-7607-6966-9(4))* backpackbook.

Baeten, Lieve. Curious Little Witch Board Book. 2012. (ENG., Illus.). 14p. (J). (gr. -1 — 1). bds. 9.95 *(978-0-7358-4102-4(0))* North-South Bks., Inc.

Baggott, Stella. Baby's Very First Touchy-Feely Animals Book. 2011. (Baby's Very First Ser.). 10p. (J). ring bd. 7.99 *(978-0-7945-2895-9(3)*, Usborne) EDC Publishing.

—Baby's Very First Touchy-Feely Book. 2010. (Baby's Very First Board Bks). 10p. (J). bds. 9.99 *(978-0-7945-2647-4(0)*, Usborne) EDC Publishing.

—Baby's Very First Touchy-Feely Christmas Book. Baggott, Stella, illus. 2010. (Baby's Very First Board Bks). (Illus.). 10p. (J). bds. 6.99 *(978-0-7945-2852-2(X)*, Usborne) EDC Publishing.

—Baby's Very First Touchy-Feely Lift the Flap Play Book. 2013. (Baby's Very First Board Bks). 10p. (J). ring bd. 12.99 *(978-0-7945-3386-1(8)*, Usborne) EDC Publishing.

Baggott, Stella, illus. Baby's Very First Noisy Book Farm. 2013. (Baby's Very First Noisy Book Ser.). (ENG.). 10p. (gr. -1). 15.99 *(978-0-7945-2703-7(5)*, Usborne) EDC Publishing.

Bagley, Val. Gospel Truths from the Book of Mormon. 2004. (Seek & Ye Shall Find Flap Book Ser.). (Illus.). (J). bds. 13.95 *(978-1-59156-279-5(1))* Covenant Communications, Inc.

Bagley, Val Chadwick & Mullins, Amy. My Favorite Stories from the Bible. 2006. (Illus.). 28p. (J). *(978-1-59811-173-6(6))* Covenant Communications.

—My Favorite Stories from the Book of Mormon. 2007. (Carry-Along Lift-The-Flap Book Ser.). (Illus.). (J). *(978-1-59811-385-3(2))* Covenant Communications.

Bak, Jenny. Ten Gifts from Santa Claus: A Counting Book. Harding, Niall, illus. 2011. (ENG.). 22p. (J). (gr. -1-k). 14.99 *(978-1-4052-5127-3(1))* Egmont Bks., Ltd. GBR. Dist: Independent Pubs. Group.

Baker, Keith. Quack & Count. (ENG., Illus.). (J). 2004. 24p. (gr. -1 — 1). pap. 7.99 *(978-0-15-205025-2(6))* 2003. 22p. (gr. k — 1). bds. 6.95 *(978-0-15-204751-1(4))* Houghton Mifflin Harcourt Publishing Co.

Baker, Liza. I Love You Because You're You (a StoryPlay Book) McPhail, David, illus. 2016. (ENG.). 32p. (J). (gr. -1-k). 5.99 *(978-0-545-94527-1(5)*, Cartwheel Bks.) Scholastic, Inc.

Baker-Smith, Grahame. The Twelve Days of Christmas: Panorama Pops. Baker-Smith, Grahame, illus. 2017. (Panorama Pops Ser.). (ENG., Illus.). 30p. (J). (gr. k-4). 8.99 ***(978-0-7636-9485-2(1))*** Candlewick Pr.

Baker, Sue. Oh Baby! Stockham, Jess, illus. 2006. (Blanket Babies Ser.). (ENG.). 12p. (J). (gr. -1-k). bds. *(978-1-904550-87-7(8))* Child's Play International Ltd.

Baker, Sue & Stockham, Jessica. Sleep Tight! Stockham, Jess, illus. 2006. (Blanket Babies Ser.). (ENG.). 12p. (J). (gr. -1-k). bds. *(978-1-904550-90-7(8))* Child's Play International Ltd.

Bannister, Emily, illus. Itsy Bitsy Spider. 2016. (ENG.). 10p. (J). bds. 7.99 *(978-1-62686-764-2(X)*, Silver Dolphin Bks.) Readerlink Distribution Services, LLC.

Barad, Alexis. Puppy Love. East, Jacqueline, illus. 2013. (J). *(978-0-545-47733-8(6))* Scholastic, Inc.

Barash, Chris. One Fine Shabbat. Mai-Wyss, Tatjana, illus. 2016. (ENG.). 12p. (gr. -1 — 1). (J). 5.99 *(978-1-4677-5871-0(X))*; 23.99 *(978-1-4677-9614-9(X))* Lerner Publishing Group. (Kar-Ben Publishing).

Barbas, Keri, des. Travel Scratch & Sketch. 2005. (Activity Journal Ser.). (J). 12.99 *(978-0-88088-486-0(X))* Peter Pauper Pr. Inc.

Barbie. Barbie Dreamhouse Party/ Una Fiesta de Ensueno: An English/Spanish Flap Book. 2013. (Lift-The Flap Ser.: 1). (ENG & SPA.). 10p. (J). (gr. -1-k). bds. 9.99 *(978-0-7944-2874-7(6))* Reader's Digest Assn., Inc., The.

—Barbie Find Your Talent: Book with Microphone. 2013. (Book with Microphone Ser.: 1). (ENG.). 32p. (J). (gr. -1-1). 17.99 *(978-0-7944-2914-0(9)*, Reader's Digest Children's Bks.) Studio Fun International.

Barbie: a Special Christmas. 2014. (ENG.). 16p. (J). (gr. -1-1). bds. 8.99 *(978-0-7944-3231-7(X)*, Reader's Digest Children's Bks.) Studio Fun International.

Barbie Staff. Barbie Mariposa & the Fairy Princess. 2013. (Panorama Sticker Storybook Ser.: 1). (ENG.). 20p. (J). (gr. -1-1). pap. 7.99 *(978-0-7944-2837-2(1))* Reader's Digest Assn., Inc., The.

—Barbie Mariposa & the Fairy Princess Storybook. 2013. (Storybook with Jewelry Ser.: 1). (ENG.). 24p. (J). (gr. -1-3). 11.99 *(978-0-7944-2838-9(X))* Reader's Digest Assn., Inc., The.

Barclay, Eric. Counting Dogs. Barclay, Eric, illus. 2015. (ENG., Illus.). 16p. (J). (gr. -1-k). bds. 10.99 *(978-0-545-78392-7(5)*, Cartwheel Bks.) Scholastic, Inc.

Bardaus, Anna W. Bounce, Bounce, Baby! Grove, Christine, illus. 2013. (J). *(978-0-545-61897-7(5))* Scholastic, Inc.

—Dance, Dance, Baby! Grove, Christine, illus. 2013. (J). *(978-0-545-61899-1(1))* Scholastic, Inc.

—Reach, Reach, Baby! Grove, Christine, illus. 2013. (J). *(978-0-545-61900-4(9))* Scholastic, Inc.

—Read, Read, Baby! Grove, Christine, illus. 2013. (J). *(978-0-545-61898-4(3))* Scholastic, Inc.

Barefoot Books Staff. Clare Beaton's Animal Rhymes. Beaton, Clare, illus. 2014. 14p. (J). (gr. -1-k). bds. 6.99 *(978-1-78285-080-9(5))* Barefoot Bks., Inc.

—Clare Beaton's Garden Rhymes. Beaton, Clare, illus. 2014. 14p. (J). (gr. -1-k). bds. 6.99 *(978-1-78285-081-6(3))* Barefoot Bks., Inc.

Barella, Laura, illus. The Brave Little Tailor. 2014. (Flip-Up Fairy Tales Ser.). (ENG.). 24p. (J). *(978-1-84643-654-3(0))* Child's Play International Ltd.

—Donkey Skin. 2011. (Flip-Up Fairy Tales Ser.). (ENG.). 24p. (J). audio compact disk *(978-1-84643-410-5(6))*; (gr. 2-2). *(978-1-84643-371-9(1))* Child's Play International Ltd.

—The Little Mermaid. 2010. (Flip-Up Fairy Tales Ser.). (ENG.). 24p. (J). (gr. -1-2). audio compact disk *(978-1-84643-331-3(2))* Child's Play International Ltd.

—Sleeping Beauty. 2009. (Flip-Up Fairy Tales Ser.). (ENG.). 24p. (J). (gr. -1-2). pap. *(978-1-84643-252-1(9))*; audio compact disk *(978-1-84643-295-8(2))* Child's Play International Ltd.

—The Stonecutter. 2012. (Flip-Up Fairy Tales Ser.). (ENG.). 24p. (J). audio compact disk *(978-1-84643-517-1(X))*; *(978-1-84643-478-5(5))* Child's Play International Ltd.

Barfield, Maggie. The Little Bible Storybook, 1 vol. Carpenter, Mark et al, illus. 2009. 48p. (J). bds. 9.99 *(978-0-8254-7409-5(4)*, Candle Bks.) Lion Hudson PLC GBR. Dist: Kregel Pubns.

Barker, Stephen, illus. My First Christmas. 2016. (ENG.). 12p. (J). (-k). bds. 9.99 *(978-1-62686-813-7(1)*, Silver Dolphin Bks.) Readerlink Distribution Services, LLC.

Barner, Bob. Penguins, Penguins, Everywhere! 2010. (ENG., Illus.). 20p. (J). (gr. -1 — 1). bds. 9.99 *(978-0-8118-7724-4(8))* Chronicle Bks. LLC.

Barnes, Lesley, illus. Flyaway. 2016. (ENG.). 18p. (J). (gr. -1-2). 15.99 *(978-1-84780-645-1(7)*, Frances Lincoln Children's Bks.) Quarto Publishing Group UK GBR. Dist: Hachette Bk. Group.

Barrance, Reuben & Whatmore, Candice, illus. Birthday. 2008. (Usborne Look & Say Ser.). 12p. (J). (gr. -1-3). bds. 7.99 *(978-0-7945-1988-9(1)*, Usborne) EDC Publishing.

Barron's Editorial Staff. The Nutcracker. Pagnoni, Roberta & Rigo, Laura, illus. 2015. (Little People Shape Bks.). (ENG.). 10p. (J). (gr. -1 — 1). bds. 7.99 *(978-0-7641-6796-6(0))* Barron's Educational Series, Inc.

Barron's Educational Series Staff & Rigo, L., illus. Off to School. 2010. (ENG.). 10p. (J). (gr. -1-1). bds. 7.99 *(978-0-7641-6363-0(9))* Barron's Educational Series, Inc.

Barton, Byron. My House Board Book. Barton, Byron, illus. 2017. (Illus.). 44p. (J). (gr. -1-3). bds. 7.99 *(978-0-06-233705-4(X)*, Greenwillow Bks.) HarperCollins Pubs.

Baruzzi, Agnese. Opposites: A Cut-Paper Book. Baruzzi, Agnese, illus. 2013. (ENG., Illus.). 10p. (J). (— 1). 15.99 *(978-1-85707-803-9(9))* Tango Bks. GBR. Dist: Independent Pubs. Group.

Bataille, Marion. ABC3D. 2008. (ENG.). 36p. (J). (gr. -1 — 1). 24.99 *(978-1-59643-425-7(2)*, 9781596434257) Roaring Brook Pr.

Bateson, Maggie. Dinosaur Safari. Forshaw, Louise, illus. 2014. (ENG.). 10p. (J). 14.99 *(978-1-4711-2121-0(6)*, Simon & Schuster Children's) Simon & Schuster, Ltd. GBR. Dist: Simon & Schuster, Inc.

—Fairy Unicorn Riding Stables. Comfort, Louise, illus. 2012. (ENG.). 10p. (J). (gr. -1-k). 22.99 *(978-0-230-74331-1(5))* Macmillan Pubs., Ltd. GBR. Dist: Independent Pubs. Group.

—My Pirate Adventure: A Pop-up & Play Book. Eaves, Ed, illus. 2008. (ENG.). 20p. (J). (gr. 4-7). 23.50 *(978-0-230-53036-2(2)*, Macmillan) Pan Macmillan GBR. Dist: Trans-Atlantic Pubns., Inc.

Bauer, Marion Dane. How Do I Love You? / ¿Cómo Te Quiero? Church, Caroline Jayne, illus. 2014. (SPA & ENG.). 24p. (J). (gr. -1-k). bds. 8.99 *(978-0-545-66525-4(6)*, Scholastic en Espanol) Scholastic, Inc.

—Toes, Ears, & Nose! Katz, Karen, illus. 2003. (ENG.). 16p. (J). (gr. -1 — 1). bds. 6.99 *(978-0-689-84712-7(2)*, Little Simon) Little Simon.

Bauman, Amy. Everyone Is Special! 2010. 12p. (J). (gr. -1). 9.95 *(978-1-60747-719-8(X)*, Pickwick Pr.) Phoenix Bks., Inc.

Baur, Becky. Miss Bunny's Shapes: A Fun Lift-The-Flap Book. 2017. (ENG., Illus.). 14p. (J). (— 1). bds. 8.95 *(978-1-4549-2231-5(1))* Sterling Publishing Co., Inc.

—Mr. Monkey's Numbers: A Fun Lift-The-Flap Book. 2017. (ENG., Illus.). 14p. (J). (— 1). bds. 8.95 *(978-1-4549-2230-8(3))* Sterling Publishing Co., Inc.

Baur, Laura, illus. The Riverbank. 2012. (ENG.). 36p. (J). (gr. -1-k). spiral bd. 12.99 *(978-1-85103-393-5(9))* Moonlight Publishing, Ltd. GBR. Dist: Independent Pubs. Group.

Baxter, Nicola. Bedtime Lullabies: Fall Asleep to Your Free Cd. Finn, Rebecca, illus. 2014. (ENG.). 12p. (J). (gr. -1-12). bds. 14.99 *(978-1-86147-360-8(5)*, Armadillo) Anness Publishing GBR. Dist: National Bk. Network.

—The Great Pirate Adventure: Peek Inside the 3D Windows. Goulding, June, illus. 2012. (ENG.). 12p. (J). (gr. -1-12). 16.99 *(978-1-84322-966-7(8))* Anness Publishing GBR. Dist: National Bk. Network.

—Head, Shoulders, Knees & Toes & Other Action Rhymes. Buckingham, Gabriella, illus. 2013. (ENG.). 16p. (J). (gr. -1-6). bds. 7.99 *(978-1-84322-829-5(7)*, Armadillo) Anness Publishing GBR. Dist: National Bk. Network.

—I Can Learn Times Tables: With Magnetic Numbers to Use Again & Again! Elliott, Rebecca, illus. 2013. (ENG.). 16p. (J). (gr. -1-7). bds. 17.99 *(978-1-84322-986-5(2)*, Armadillo) Anness Publishing GBR. Dist: National Bk. Network.

—Jewels for a Princess. Chaffey, Samantha, illus. 2012. (ENG.). 12p. (J). (gr. 1-6). 16.99 *(978-1-84322-926-1(9))* Anness Publishing GBR. Dist: National Bk. Network.

—Kaleidoscope Book: My First Book of Learning. Elliott, Rebecca, illus. 2013. (ENG.). 16p. bds. 16.99 *(978-1-84322-930-8(7)*, Armadillo) Anness Publishing GBR. Dist: National Bk. Network.

—Learn about Our World. Elliott, Rebecca, illus. 2013. (ENG.). 16p. (J). (gr. k-2). bds. 17.99 *(978-1-84322-985-8(4)*, Armadillo) Anness Publishing GBR. Dist: National Bk. Network.

—Learn to Count. Elliott, Rebecca, illus. 2013. (ENG.). 16p. (J). (gr. -1-2). bds. 17.99 *(978-1-84322-984-1(6)*, Armadillo) Anness Publishing GBR. Dist: National Bk. Network.

—Learn to Tell Time: With Magnets to Use Again & Again! Elliott, Rebecca, illus. 2013. (ENG.). 16p. (J). (gr. -1-12). bds. 17.99 *(978-1-84322-638-3(3)*, Armadillo) Anness Publishing GBR. Dist: National Bk. Network.

—The Mermaid & the Star. Rigby, Deborah, illus. 2025. 14p. (J). bds. *(978-1-84322-907-0(2)*, Armadillo) Anness Publishing.

—My Ballet Theatre: Peek Inside the 3-D Windows. Chaffey, Samantha, illus. 2014. (ENG.). 24p. (J). (gr. -1-12). 16.99 *(978-1-84322-949-0(8)*, Armadillo) Anness Publishing GBR. Dist: National Bk. Network.

—The Mystery of the Haunted House: Dare You Peek Through the 3-D Windows? Goulding, June, illus. 2013. (ENG.). 12p. 16.99 *(978-1-84322-754-0(1))* Anness Publishing GBR. Dist: National Bk. Network.

—Party at the Fairy Palace: Peek Inside the 3D Windows. Chaffey, Samantha, illus. 2013. (ENG.). 12p. 16.99 *(978-1-84322-725-0(8))* Anness Publishing GBR. Dist: National Bk. Network.

—Pull the Lever: Who's at Nursery? Lawson, Peter, illus. 2014. (ENG.). 8p. (J). (gr. -1-1). bds. 6.99 *(978-1-86147-393-6(1)*, Armadillo) Anness Publishing GBR. Dist: National Bk. Network.

—A Sparkly Ballet Story. Pedler, Caroline, illus. 2014. (ENG.). 14p. (J). (gr. -1-1). bds. 7.99 *(978-1-84322-546-1(8)*, Armadillo) Anness Publishing GBR. Dist: National Bk. Network.

—The Starlight Ballerina. Jones, Deborah, illus. 2025. 14p. (J). bds. *(978-1-84322-885-1(8))* Anness Publishing.

—A Visit from the Tooth Fairy: Magical Stories & a Special Message from the Little Friend Who Collects Your Baby Teeth. Manson, Beverlie, illus. 2013. (ENG.). 40p. (J). (gr. k-4). 14.99 *(978-1-84322-987-2(0)*, Armadillo) Anness Publishing GBR. Dist: National Bk. Network.

Baxter, Nicola, ed. Christmas Lullabies for Children. Finn, Rebecca, illus. 2014. (ENG.). 12p. (J). (gr. k-5). bds. 14.99 incl. audio compact disk *(978-1-84322-931-5(5)*, Armadillo) Anness Publishing GBR. Dist: National Bk. Network.

Baxter, Nicola & Adams, Ben. Freddie the Fish, Star of the Show. Cameron, Craig, illus. 2013. (Googly Eyes Ser.). (ENG.). 12p. (J). (gr. -1-k). bds. 6.99 *(978-1-84322-621-5(9)*, Armadillo) Anness Publishing GBR. Dist: National Bk. Network.

Baxter, Nicola & Francis, Jan. Traditional Fairy Tales: Eight Exciting Picture Stories for Little Ones. Parry, Jo, illus. 2013. (ENG.). 16p. (J). (gr. -1-2). 13.99 *(978-1-84322-992-6(7)*, Armadillo) Anness Publishing GBR. Dist: National Bk. Network.

Beach, Kathleen H. & Weeber, Stephanie B. Madison's Mixed-up Flower Girl Magic & Aiden's Amazing Ring Bearer Act Aiden's Amazing Ring Bearer Act. Baisley, Maryann Leake, illus. 2009. 32p. pap. 19.95 *(978-1-4251-7059-2(5))* Trafford Publishing.

BeachHouse Publishing. Geckos Go to Bed. Murakami, Jon, illus. 2008. (ENG.). 24p. (J). (gr. -1-k). bds. 8.95 *(978-1-933067-26-1(8))* Beachhouse Publishing, LLC.

Beake, Lesley & Williams, Sam. Angel & Elf: Christmas Cookies. 2014. (ENG., Illus.). 26p. (J). (— 1). bds. 6.95 *(978-1-907152-87-0(3))* Boxer Bks., Ltd. GBR. Dist: Sterling Publishing Co., Inc.

Beaton, Clare. Clare Beaton's Bedtime Rhymes. Beaton, Clare, illus. 2012. (ENG., Illus.). 14p. (J). (gr. -1-k). 6.99 *(978-1-84686-737-8(1))* Barefoot Bks., Inc.

—Clare Beaton's Farmyard Rhymes. Beaton, Clare, illus. 2012. (ENG., Illus.). 14p. (J). (gr. -1-k). 6.99 *(978-1-84686-736-1(3))* Barefoot Bks., Inc.

Beaumont, Karen. I Like Myself! Catrow, David, illus. 2010. (ENG.). 32p. (J). (gr. -1 — 1). bds. 11.99 *(978-0-547-40163-8(9))* Houghton Mifflin Harcourt Publishing Co.

—Shoe-la-La! A Storyplay Book. Leuyen, Pham, illus. 2016. (ENG.). 40p. (J). (gr. -1-k). 5.99 *(978-1-338-11555-0(3)*, Cartwheel Bks.) Scholastic, Inc.

Beauvisage, Alice. My Blankie. Beauvisage, Alice, illus. 2013. (ENG., Illus.). 12p. (J). (gr. -1-k). bds. 6.95 *(978-1-927018-08-8(0))* Simply Read Bks. CAN. Dist: Ingram Publisher Services.

Beckett-Bowman, Lucy. Sticker Dolly Dressing Bridesmaids. 2009. (Sticker Dolly Dressing Ser.). 24p. (J). pap. 8.99 *(978-0-7945-2519-4(9)*, Usborne) EDC Publishing.

—Sticker Dolly Dressing on Vacation. 2009. (Sticker Dolly Dressing Ser.). 24p. (J). pap. 8.99 *(978-0-7945-2369-5(2)*, Usborne) EDC Publishing.

—Sticker Dolly Dressing Popstars. 2009. (Sticker Dolly Dressing Ser.). 26p. (J). pap. 8.99 *(978-0-7945-2360-2(9)*, Usborne) EDC Publishing.

Bedford, David. Tails. Worthington, Leonie, illus. 2008. (ENG.). 16p. (J). (gr. k-k). 5.95 *(978-1-921272-37-0(6))* Little Hare Bks. AUS. Dist: Independent Pubs. Group.

Bedford, David & Worthington, Leonie. Big. 2006. (Illus.). 16p. pap. *(978-1-921049-22-4(7))* Little Hare Bks. AUS. Dist: HarperCollins Pubs. Australia.

—Mums. 2007. (Illus.). 16p. *(978-1-921049-78-1(2))* Little Hare Bks. AUS. Dist: HarperCollins Pubs. Australia.

—Who's Laughing? 2007. (Illus.). 16p. pap. *(978-1-921272-11-0(2))* Little Hare Bks. AUS. Dist: HarperCollins Pubs. Australia.

Beer, Barbara Vagnozzi. Jack & the Beanstalk. Vagnozzi, Barbara, illus. 2005. (Flip-Up Fairy Tales Ser.). (ENG.). 24p. (J). pap. *(978-1-904550-20-4(7))* Child's Play International Ltd.

Beeson, Samantha & Tango Books Staff. Baaah! Abbott, Simon, illus. 2003. (Noisy Pops! Ser.). (ENG.). 10p. (J). (gr. -1-k). 11.99 *(978-1-85707-573-1(0))* Tango Bks. GBR. Dist: Independent Pubs. Group.

Bell, Lucy & Everett, Melissa. Do Your Ears Hang Low? Doss, Andrea, illus. 2014. (ENG.). 20p. (J). (gr. -1-2). bds. 8.99 *(978-1-4867-0358-6(5))* Flowerpot Children's Pr. Inc. CAN. Dist: Cardinal Pubs. Group.

Bell-Martin, Janelle. Head & Shoulders, 1 vol. 2011. (Early Childhood Themes Ser.). (ENG.). 16p. (J). (gr. -1-2). pap. 19.99 *(978-1-4333-2372-0(9))* Teacher Created Materials, Inc.

—Mary Had a Little Lamb, 1 vol. 2011. (Early Childhood Themes Ser.). (ENG.). 16p. (J). (gr. -1-2). pap. 19.99 *(978-1-4333-2358-4(3))* Teacher Created Materials, Inc.

Belle, Trixie & Caruso-Scott, Melissa. Goldilocks & the Three Bears: Les Petits Fairytales. Lake, Oliver, illus. 2014. (Petits Fairytales Ser.). (ENG.). 26p. (J). (gr. -1 — 1). bds. 7.99 *(978-0-8050-9912-6(3)*, 9780805099126, Holt, Henry & Co. Bks. For Young Readers) Holt, Henry & Co.

—Little Red Riding Hood: Les Petits Fairytales. Lake, Oliver, illus. 2014. (Petits Fairytales Ser.). (ENG.). 26p. (J). (gr. -1 — 1). bds. 7.99 *(978-0-8050-9905-8(0)*, 9780805099058, Holt, Henry & Co. Bks. For Young Readers) Holt, Henry & Co.

BELTEI, Nadia. Emily's BOOKS: Coloring & Activity book, age Level: 2-3 (B&W) 2010. 39p. pap. 7.47 *(978-0-557-32886-4(1))* Lulu Pr., Inc.

Bennett, Meagan, des. Pancakes! Pancakes!, an Interactive Recipe Book. 2016. (Cook in a Book Ser.). (ENG., Illus.). 16p. 14.95 *(978-0-7148-7282-7(2))* Phaidon Pr., Inc.

Bentley, Dawn. Goodnight Bear: A Book & Night Light. Couri, Kathryn A., illus. 2005. (Stories to Share Ser.). 12p. (J). 12.95 *(978-1-58117-034-4(3)*, Intervisual/Piggy Toes) Bendon, Inc.

—Three Hungry Spiders & One Fat Fly! Twinem, Neecy, illus. 2010. (Stretchies Book Ser.). 16p. (J). (gr. -1-k). 8.99 *(978-0-8249-1460-8(0)*, Ideal Pubns.) Worthy Publishing.

—Three Stretchy Frogs. Wallis, Becky, illus. 2010. (Stretchies Book Ser.). 16p. (J). 8.99 *(978-0-8249-1459-2(7))* Hinkler Bks. Pty. Ltd. AUS. Dist: Ideals Pubns.

Bentley, Dawn & Studio Mouse Staff. Triceratops. Carr, Karen, illus. 2008. (ENG.). 24p. (J). (gr. 3-7). 4.99 *(978-1-59069-622-4(0))* Studio Mouse LLC.

—Tyrannosaurus Rex. Carr, Karen, illus. 2008. (ENG.). 24p. (J). (gr. 3-7). 4.99 *(978-1-59069-621-7(2))* Studio Mouse LLC.

Bentley, Tadgh. Little Penguin Gets the Hiccups Board Book. Bentley, Tadgh, illus. 2016. (Illus.). 34p. (J). (gr. -1 — 1). bds. 7.99 *(978-0-06-265224-9(9))* HarperCollins Pubs.

Bently, Peter. A Lark in the Ark. Chapman, Lynne, illus. 2015. (ENG.). 24p. (J). (gr. -1-k). pap. 12.99 *(978-1-4052-7508-8(1))* Egmont Bks., Ltd. GBR. Dist: Independent Pubs. Group.

—National Geographic Kids Wild Tales: Ella's Bath: A Lift-The-flap Story about Elephants. 2013. (ENG.). 20p. (J). (gr. -1-2). bds. 9.99 *(978-1-4263-1360-8(8)*, National Geographic Children's Bks.) National Geographic Society.

—National Geographic Kids Wild Tales: Twin Trouble: A Lift-The-flap Story about Bears. 2013. (ENG.). 20p. (J). (gr. -1-2). bds. 9.99 *(978-1-4263-1361-5(6)*, National Geographic Children's Bks.) National Geographic Society.

Benton, Jim. Five Stinky Socks: A Counting Book. 2015. (ENG.). 16p. (J). (— 1). bds. 5.99 *(978-0-545-64784-7(3)*, Cartwheel Bks.) Scholastic, Inc.

—Piggy Paints. 2015. (ENG.). 16p. (J). (— 1). bds. 5.99 *(978-0-545-64785-4(1)*, Cartwheel Bks.) Scholastic, Inc.

—Robot Kitties: An up & down Book. 2015. (ENG.). 16p. (J). (— 1). bds. 5.99 *(978-0-545-64786-1(X)*, Cartwheel Bks.) Scholastic, Inc.

—Where Did All the Dinos Go? Benton, Jim, illus. 2016. (ENG., Illus.). 18p. (J). (— 1). bds. 7.99 *(978-0-545-64789-2(4)*, Cartwheel Bks.) Scholastic, Inc.

—Where's My Fnurgle? 2015. (ENG.). 16p. (J). (— 1). bds. 5.99 *(978-0-545-64787-8(8)*, Cartwheel Bks.) Scholastic, Inc.

Berenstain, Jan & Berenstain, Mike. Berenstain Bears - Storybook Bible for Little Ones, 1 vol. 2015. (Berenstain Bears/Living Lights Ser.). (ENG., Illus.). 30p. (J). bds. 9.99 *(978-0-310-74941-7(7))* Zonderkidz.

—The Berenstain Bears Get Ready for School. Berenstain, Jan & Berenstain, Mike, illus. 2015. (Berenstain Bears Ser.). (ENG., Illus.). 16p. (J). (gr. -1-1). pap. 6.99 *(978-0-06-207552-9(7)*, HarperFestival) HarperCollins Pubs.

Berenstain, Jan & Berenstain, Stan. The Berenstain Bears' New Pup. Berenstain, Jan, illus. 2017. (I Can Read Level 1 Ser.). (Illus.). 40p. (J). (gr. -1-3). 9.99 *(978-0-06-257272-1(5))* HarperCollins Pubs.

Berenstain, Mike, illus. The Berenstain Bears: Easter Blessings. 2016. (J). *(978-0-8249-1967-2(X)*, Ideal Pubns.) Worthy Publishing.

—The Berenstain Bears Love One Another. 2016. (J). *(978-0-8249-1983-2(1)*, Ideal Pubns.) Worthy Publishing.

Bergen, Lara. Don't Throw That Away! A Lift-the-Flap Book about Recycling & Reusing. Snyder, Betsy E., illus. 2009. (Little Green Bks.). (ENG.). 14p. (J). (gr. -1-1). bds. 7.99 *(978-1-4169-7517-5(9)*, Little Simon) Little Simon.

—Enchanted Library, 6 vols. 2005. (Illus.). (J). *(978-0-7868-3551-5(6))*; *(978-0-7868-3547-8(8))*; *(978-0-7868-3550-8(8))*; *(978-0-7868-3546-1(X))*; *(978-0-7868-3549-2(4))*; *(978-0-7868-3548-5(6))* Disney Pr.

—Let's Dig It! Shannon, David et al, illus. 2010. (Jon Scieszka's Trucktown Ser.). (ENG.). 12p. (J). (gr. -1-k). bds. 5.99 *(978-1-4169-4190-3(8)*, Little Simon) Little Simon.

Bergen, Lara & Disney Book Group Staff. Enchanted Fashions: A Magnetic Book & Playset. Disney Storybook Artists Staff, illus. rev. ed. 2007. (Book & Magnetic Play Set Ser.). (ENG.). 16p. (J). (gr. -1 — 1). 14.99 *(978-1-4231-0752-1(7))* Disney Pr.

Berger, Carin. All Mixed Up: A Mix-and-Match Book. 2006. (ENG., Illus.). 46p. (J). (gr. -1-7). 8.95 *(978-0-8118-4966-1(X))* Chronicle Bks. LLC.

Bernd & Richter, Susan. I See You Through My Heart. 2008. bds. 8.95 *(978-1-931353-44-1(1))* Saddle Pal Creations, Inc.

Berne, Jennifer. Nighty-Night, Sleep Tight. Walker, David, illus. 2015. (Snuggle Time Stories Ser.). (ENG.). 24p. (J). (gr. -1-k). bds. 6.95 *(978-1-4549-1390-0(8))* Sterling Publishing Co., Inc.

Berrios, Frank. Let's Cruise!, 4 vols. 2006. (Illus.). (J). *(978-0-7364-2433-2(4))*; *(978-0-7364-2435-6(0))*; *(978-0-7364-2434-9(2))*; *(978-0-7364-2436-3(9))* Random Hse. Children's Bks.

—Mater to the Rescue! (Disney/Pixar Cars) Random House Disney Staff, illus. 2012. (Pictureback(R) Ser.). (ENG.). 16p. (J). (gr. -1-2). pap. 4.99 *(978-0-7364-2863-7(1)*, RH/Disney) Random Hse. Children's Bks.

—A Very Mater Christmas (Disney/Pixar Cars) Random House Disney Staff, illus. 2011. (Glitter Board Book Ser.). (ENG.). 12p. (J). (— 1). bds. 6.99 *(978-0-7364-2793-7(7)*, RH/Disney) Random Hse. Children's Bks.

Berry, Joy. I Love Mealtime. Regan, Dana, illus. 2010. (Teach Me About Ser.). (ENG.). 20p. (J). (gr. k — 1). pap. 5.99 *(978-1-60577-006-2(X))* Berry, Joy Enterprises.

—I Love Mommies & Daddies. Regan, Dana, illus. 2010. (Teach Me About Ser.). (ENG.). 20p. (J). (gr. k — 1). pap. 5.99 *(978-1-60577-001-7(9))* Berry, Joy Enterprises.

—I Love Preschool. Regan, Dana, illus. 2010. (Teach Me About Ser.). (ENG.). 20p. (J). (gr. k — 1). bds. 5.99 *(978-1-60577-015-4(9))* Berry, Joy Enterprises.

—Let's Talk about Being Patient. Smith, Maggie, illus. 2010. (Let's Talk About Ser.). (ENG.). 32p. (J). (gr. -1-k). pap. 4.99 *(978-1-60577-209-7(7))* Berry, Joy Enterprises.

Berry, Ron. Charlie the Can-Do Choo-Choo! Sharp, Chris, illus. 2006. (ENG.). 7p. (J). (gr. -1). bds. 12.95 *(978-0-8249-6678-2(3)*, Ideal Pubns.) Worthy Publishing.

—The Easter Bunny's Colorful Day! 2008. (Slide-N-Color Bks.). (Illus.). 10p. (J). (gr. -1). bds. 6.99 *(978-0-8249-6698-0(8)*, Ideal Pubns.) Worthy Publishing.

—Let Your Light Shine. 2007. (ENG., Illus.). 16p. (J). (gr. -1-k). bds. 12.99 *(978-0-8249-6723-9(2)*, Ideal Pubns.) Worthy Publishing.

—Rise & Shine! Sharp, Chris, illus. 2008. 14p. (J). bds. 12.99 *(978-0-8249-6735-2(6)*, Ideal Pubns.) Worthy Publishing.

—The Silly Safari Bus! Sharp, Chris, illus. 2008. (ENG.). 12p. (J). bds. 12.99 *(978-0-8249-6736-9(4)*, Ideal Pubns.) Worthy Publishing.

—Where Is Daddy? Smart Kids Publishing Staff, ed. 2009. (ENG.). 20p. (J). bds. 7.99 *(978-0-8249-1405-9(8)*, Ideal Pubns.) Worthy Publishing.

—Where Is Mommy? Smart Kids Publishing Staff, ed. 2009. (ENG.). 20p. (J). bds. 7.99 *(978-0-8249-1404-2(X)*, Ideal Pubns.) Worthy Publishing.

Berry, Ron & Mead, David. All Aboard! Charlie the Can-Do Choo Choo. Sharp, Chris, illus. 2009. (ENG.). 8p. 12.99 *(978-0-8249-1420-2(1)*, Ideal Pubns.) Worthy Publishing.

—The Little Drummer Boy. Sharp, Chris, illus. 2009. (ENG.). 16p. 12.99 *(978-0-8249-1429-5(5)*, Ideal Pubns.) Worthy Publishing.

Best Friends Scrapbooking. (Best Friends Club Ser.). 32p. spiral bd. *(978-1-4054-9466-3(2))* Parragon, Inc.

Bevan, Clare. Catkin the Fairy Kitten. Johnson-Isaacs, Cally, illus. 2015. (Mimi's Magical Fairy Friends Ser.: 1). (ENG.). 32p. (J). (gr. -1-2). pap. 10.99 ***(978-1-4472-7701-9(5))*** Pan Macmillan GBR. Dist: Independent Pubs. Group.

—Comet the Fairy Unicorn. Johnson-Isaacs, Cally, illus. 2015. (Mimi's Magical Fairy Friends Ser.: 3). (ENG.). 32p. (J). (gr.

T
U
V

-1-2). pap. 10.99 ***(978-1-4472-9424-5(6))*** Pan Macmillan GBR. Dist: Independent Pubs. Group.

—Freckle the Fairy Puppy. Johnson-Isaacs, Cally, illus. 2015. (Mimi's Magical Fairy Friends Ser.: 2). (ENG.). 32p. (J). (gr. -1-2). pap. 10.99 ***(978-1-4472-7700-2(7))*** Pan Macmillan GBR. Dist: Independent Pubs. Group.

—Lucky the Fairy Rabbit. Johnson-Isaacs, Cally, illus. 2017. (Mimi's Magical Fairy Friends Ser.: 5). (ENG.). 32p. (J). (gr. -1-k). pap. 10.99 ***(978-1-5098-1908-9(8))*** Pan Macmillan GBR. Dist: Independent Pubs. Group.

Bewley, Elizabeth. Choose to Recycle. Latimer, Miriam, illus. 2009. 10p. 7.95 *(978-1-58117-904-0(9)*, Intervisual/Piggy Toes) Bendon, Inc.

Beylon, Cathy. Kits Cuts Sticker Activity Book. 2003. (Dover Little Activity Bks.). (ENG., Illus.). 4p. (J). (gr. -1-5). act. bk. ed. 1.50 *(978-0-486-43011-9(1))* Dover Pubns., Inc.

Bicknell, J. Buby Baby 123_Padded. 2010. 12p. *(978-1-84879-163-3(1))* Make Believe Ideas.

—Buby Baby Colors_Padded. 2010. 12p. pap. *(978-1-84879-164-0(X))* Make Believe Ideas.

—Buby Baby Words_Padded. 2010. 12p. pap. *(978-1-84879-161-9(5))* Make Believe Ideas.

Bicknell, Joanna. All Things Bright & Beautiful. 2008. 14p. *(978-1-84610-728-3(8))* Make Believe Ideas.

—Carry-Me Pets. 2008. (Carry-Me Ser.). (Illus.). 12p. (gr. -1-k). 6.99 *(978-1-84610-720-7(2))* Make Believe Ideas GBR. Dist: Nelson, Thomas Inc.

—Googlies: Pet Pals. 2007. (Googlies Ser.). (Illus.). 14p. (gr. -1). bds. 6.95 *(978-1-84610-478-7(5))* Make Believe Ideas GBR. Dist: Nelson, Thomas Inc.

—My First BK of Animals. 2010. 16p. (J). bds. 8.99 *(978-1-84879-361-3(8))* Make Believe Ideas GBR. Dist: Nelson, Thomas Inc.

Bicknell, Joanna & Page, Nick. Finger Friends Tickle Monsters. Saunders, Katie, illus. 2007. (Finger Puppet Books Ser.). 12p. (gr. -1). bds. *(978-1-84610-427-5(0))* Make Believe Ideas.

Big Idea Entertainment, LLC & B&H Kids Editorial Staff. VeggieTales: Can You Say Peas & Thank You?, a Digital Pop-Up Book (padded) 2017. (VeggieTales Ser.). (ENG.). 20p. (J). (gr. -1-2). bds. 12.99 *(978-1-4336-9059-4(4)*, B&H Kids) B&H Publishing Group.

—VeggieTales: Show You Care & Always Share, a Digital Pop-Up Book (padded) 2017. (VeggieTales Ser.). (ENG.). 20p. (J). (gr. -1-2). bds. 12.99 *(978-1-4336-9060-0(8)*, B&H Kids) B&H Publishing Group.

—VeggieTales: Whenever You Fear, God Is near, a Digital Pop-Up Book (padded) 2017. (VeggieTales Ser.). (ENG.). 20p. (J). (gr. -1-2). bds. 12.99 *(978-1-4336-9058-7(6)*, B&H Kids) B&H Publishing Group.

Big Idea Entertainment, LLC & Neutzling, Laura. VeggieTales: a Thankful Heart Is a Happy Heart, a Digital Pop-Up Book (padded) Jones, Cory, illus. 2016. (VeggieTales Ser.). (ENG.). 22p. (J). (gr. -1-1). bds. 12.99 *(978-1-4336-9057-0(8)*, B&H Kids) B&H Publishing Group.

—VeggieTales: God Loves Us All, Big & Small, a Digital Pop-Up Book (padded) Jones, Cory, illus. 2016. (VeggieTales Ser.). (ENG.). 22p. (J). (gr. -1-1). bds. 12.99 *(978-1-4336-9007-5(1)*, B&H Kids) B&H Publishing Group.

—VeggieTales: Little Guys Can Do Big Things Too, a Digital Pop-Up Book (padded) Jones, Cory, illus. 2016. (VeggieTales Ser.). (ENG.). 22p. (J). (gr. -1-1). bds. 12.99 *(978-1-4336-9008-2(X)*, B&H Kids) B&H Publishing Group.

Biggs, Brian. Blue Bus, Red Balloon: A Book of Colors. Biggs, Brian, illus. 2013. (ENG., Illus.). 24p. (J). (gr. -1 — 1). bds. 7.99 *(978-0-06-195814-4(X))* HarperCollins Pubs.

—Good Night, Trucks: A Bedtime Book. Biggs, Brian, illus. 2013. (ENG., Illus.). 24p. (J). (gr. -1 — 1). bds. 7.99 *(978-0-06-195815-1(8))* HarperCollins Pubs.

—I'm a Firefighter. 2016. (Tinyville Town Ser.). (ENG., Illus.). 22p. (J). (gr. -1 — 1). bds. 7.95 *(978-1-4197-2134-2(8)*, Abrams Appleseed) Abrams, Inc.

—I'm a Veterinarian. 2016. (Tinyville Town Ser.). (ENG., Illus.). 22p. (J). (gr. -1 — 1). bds. 7.95 *(978-1-4197-2135-9(6)*, Abrams Appleseed) Abrams, Inc.

—Tinyville Town: I'm a Librarian. 2017. (Tinyville Town Ser.). (ENG., Illus.). 22p. (J). (gr. -1 — 1). bds. 7.95 *(978-1-4197-2322-3(7)*, Abrams Appleseed) Abrams, Inc.

Billet, Marion. The London Noisy Tube. Billet, Marion, illus. 2017. (ENG., Illus.). 10p. (J). (— 1). bds. 12.99 *(978-1-5098-0428-3(5))* Pan Macmillan GBR. Dist: Independent Pubs. Group.

—My First Camper Van. 2016. (Whizzy Wheels Ser.). (ENG., Illus.). 10p. (J). (— 1). bds. 11.99 *(978-1-5098-0426-9(9))* Pan Macmillan GBR. Dist: Independent Pubs. Group.

—My First Fire Engine. Billet, Marion, illus. 2015. (Whizzy Wheels Ser.). (ENG., Illus.). 10p. (J). (gr. -1-k). bds. 11.99 *(978-1-4472-7698-2(1))* Pan Macmillan GBR. Dist: Independent Pubs. Group.

—My First London Bus. Billet, Marion, illus. 2015. (Whizzy Wheels Ser.). (ENG., Illus.). 10p. (J). (-k). bds. 9.99 *(978-0-230-76057-8(0))* Pan Macmillan GBR. Dist: Independent Pubs. Group.

—My First London Taxi. Billet, Marion, illus. 2015. (Whizzy Wheels Ser.). (ENG., Illus.). 10p. (J). (-k). bds. 11.99 *(978-0-230-76103-2(8))* Pan Macmillan GBR. Dist: Independent Pubs. Group.

—My First Train. Billet, Marion, illus. 2015. (Whizzy Wheels Ser.). (ENG., Illus.). 10p. (J). (gr. -1-k). bds. 11.99 *(978-1-4472-7697-5(3))* Pan Macmillan GBR. Dist: Independent Pubs. Group.

—My First Truck. 2016. (Whizzy Wheels Ser.: 12). (ENG., Illus.). 10p. (J). (— 1). bds. 11.99 *(978-1-5098-0427-6(7))* Pan Macmillan GBR. Dist: Independent Pubs. Group.

Billet, Marion. My First Whizzy Wheels: Four Vehicle-Shaped Board Books in a Carry Case, 4 vols. 2016. (Whizzy Wheels Ser.). (ENG., Illus.). 40p. (J). (gr. -1-k). bds. 19.99 ***(978-1-5098-0802-1(7))*** Pan Macmillan GBR. Dist: Independent Pubs. Group.

Billet, Marion, illus. Hello! London. 2014. (Hello! Ser.). (ENG.). 10p. (J). (-k). bds. 15.99 *(978-1-4472-4682-4(9))* Pan Macmillan GBR. Dist: Independent Pubs. Group.

—London Bus. 2014. (ENG.). 12p. (J). (— 1). bds. 7.99 *(978-1-4472-5632-8(8))* Pan Macmillan GBR. Dist: Independent Pubs. Group.

—London Taxi. 2014. (ENG.). 12p. (J). (— 1). bds. 7.99 *(978-1-4472-5633-5(6))* Pan Macmillan GBR. Dist: Independent Pubs. Group.

—My First London Whizzy Wheels: Four Vehicle-Shaped Board Books in a Carry Case, 4 vols. 2016. (ENG.). 40p. (J). (gr. -1-k). 19.99 *(978-1-5098-0459-7(5))* Pan Macmillan GBR. Dist: Independent Pubs. Group.

—Noisy Farm: My First Sound Book. 2017. (ENG.). 16p. (J). (— 1). 9.99 ***(978-1-338-13220-5(2)***, Cartwheel Bks.) Scholastic, Inc.

Billet, Marion, illus. Scooter Bug. 2014. (Whizzy Wheels Ser.). (ENG.). 10p. (J). (gr. -1-k). bds. 9.99 *(978-1-4472-5763-9(4))* Pan Macmillan GBR. Dist: Independent Pubs. Group.

Bird, Benjamin. Scooby-Doo's 1-2-3 Mystery. 2015. (Scooby-Doo! Little Mysteries Ser.). (ENG., Illus.). 20p. (gr. -1 — 1). bds. 7.99 *(978-1-62370-177-2(5))* Capstone Press of Coughlan Cos.

—Scooby-Doo's ABC Mystery. 2015. (Scooby-Doo! Little Mysteries Ser.). (ENG., Illus.). 20p. (gr. -1 — 1). bds. 7.99 *(978-1-62370-175-8(9))* Capstone Press of Coughlan Cos.

—Scooby-Doo's Color Mystery. 2015. (Scooby-Doo! Little Mysteries Ser.). (ENG., Illus.). 20p. (gr. -1 — 1). bds. 7.99 *(978-1-62370-176-5(7))* Capstone Press of Coughlan Cos.

—Scooby-Doo's Shape Mystery. 2015. (Scooby-Doo! Little Mysteries Ser.). (ENG., Illus.). 20p. (gr. -1 — 1). bds. 7.99 *(978-1-62370-178-9(3))* Capstone Press of Coughlan Cos.

—Superman Colors, 1 vol. Beavers, Ethen, illus. 2014. (DC Board Bks.). (ENG.). 20p. (gr. -1 — 1). bds. 5.99 *(978-1-4795-5890-2(7))* Picture Window Bks.

—Wonder Woman ABCs, 1 vol. Beavers, Ethen, illus. 2014. (DC Board Bks.). (ENG.). 20p. (gr. -1 — 1). bds. 5.99 *(978-1-4795-5889-6(3))* Picture Window Bks.

Bird, Nicola. Go! Go! Go! Land, Fiona, illus. 2012. (ENG.). 10p. (J). (— 1). bds. 10.99 *(978-0-545-42545-2(X))* Scholastic, Inc.

Birkett, Georgie. One, Two, Peekaboo! Birkett, Georgie, illus. 2015. (Felty Flaps Ser.). (ENG., Illus.). 10p. (J). (gr. -1). bds. 9.99 *(978-1-4472-7427-8(X))* Pan Macmillan GBR. Dist: Independent Pubs. Group.

—Peekaboo! - Who Are You? Birkett, Georgie, illus. 2014. (Felty Flaps Ser.). (ENG., Illus.). 10p. (J). (gr. -1). bds. 9.99 *(978-1-4472-6098-1(8))* Pan Macmillan GBR. Dist: Independent Pubs. Group.

—Red, Blue, Peekaboo! Birkett, Georgie, illus. 2015. (Felty Flaps Ser.). (ENG., Illus.). 10p. (J). (— 1). bds. 9.99 *(978-1-4472-6099-8(6))* Pan Macmillan GBR. Dist: Independent Pubs. Group.

The Birth of Jesus Bible Sticker Book. 2003. (Illus.). 16p. (J). 2.98 *(978-1-4054-1559-0(2))* Parragon, Inc.

The Birthday Ball. 2013. (Illus.). (J). *(978-1-4351-4947-2(5))* Disney Pr.

Black, Robyn Hood. Wolves. Howard, Colin, illus. 2008. (ENG.). 24p. (J). (gr. 3-18). 19.95 *(978-1-58117-817-3(4)*, Intervisual/Piggy Toes) Bendon, Inc.

Blackstone, Stella. Cleo on the Move. Mockford, Caroline, illus. 2013. (ENG.). 24p. (J). 6.99 *(978-1-78285-056-4(2))* Barefoot Bks., Inc.

Blackstone, Stella. Hablando con Bebé. 2017. (ENG & SPA.). 14p. (J). (gr. -1 — 1). bds. 6.99 ***(978-1-78285-350-3(2))*** Barefoot Bks., Inc.

Blackstone, Stella & Barefoot Books. Baby Talk. 2015. (Illus.). 14p. (J). (gr. -1-k). bds. 6.99 *(978-1-78285-222-3(0))* Barefoot Bks., Inc.

Blackstone, Stella & Harter, Debbie. Oso en un Cuadrado. 2013. (SPA & ENG., Illus.). 24p. (J). 7.99 *(978-1-78285-030-4(9))* Barefoot Bks., Inc.

Blackstone, Stella & Scribens, Sunny. Baby's First Words. 2017. (Illus.). 30p. (J). (gr. -1-k). 14.99 ***(978-1-78285-321-3(9))*** Barefoot Bks., Inc.

—Mis Primeras Palabras. 2017. (SPA.). 30p. (J). (gr. -1-k). bds. 14.99 ***(978-1-78285-325-1(1))*** Barefoot Bks., Inc.

Blathwayt, Benedict. Dougal the Digger. Blathwayt, Benedict, illus. 2009. (ENG., Illus.). 24p. (J). (gr. -1-k). pap. 12.99 *(978-1-86230-625-7(7))* Transworld Publishers Ltd. GBR. Dist: Independent Pubs. Group.

Bleck, Linda. What's in My Truck? Bleck, Linda, illus. 2014. (ENG., Illus.). 10p. (J). (gr. -1 — 1). bds. 6.99 *(978-0-545-53525-0(5)*, Cartwheel Bks.) Scholastic, Inc.

Bledsoe, Michele. Kitty Treats Cookbook. Rupert, Chris et al, illus. 2010. (ENG.). 15p. (gr. 6). bds. 10.95 *(978-0-9753883-8-9(X))* Come & Get It Publishing.

Bloom, Jan. You Track It Weather Lab. Free Jenna Staff, ed. 2010. 12p. mass mkt. 14.99 *(978-1-60380-087-7(5))* becker&mayer! books.

Bloomsbury. Carry & Play: Christmas. 2016. (ENG.). 10p. (J). bds. 6.99 *(978-1-68119-095-2(8)*, 9781681190952, Bloomsbury Activity Bks.) Bloomsbury Publishing USA.

—Carry & Play: Snowman. 2016. (ENG.). 10p. (J). bds. 6.99 *(978-1-68119-096-9(6)*, 9781681190969, Bloomsbury Activity Bks.) Bloomsbury Publishing USA.

—Lift-The-Flap Friends: Fairy. 2016. (ENG.). 14p. (J). bds. 9.99 *(978-1-68119-098-3(2)*, 9781681190983, Bloomsbury Activity Bks.) Bloomsbury Publishing USA.

Bloomsbury USA. Baby's First Words: Animals. 2016. (ENG., Illus.). 10p. (J). bds. 5.99 *(978-1-61963-994-2(7)*, 9781619639942, Bloomsbury Activity Bks.) Bloomsbury Publishing USA.

—Carry & Play: Pumpkin. 2016. (ENG., Illus.). 10p. (J). bds. 6.99 *(978-1-61963-982-9(3)*, 9781619639829, Bloomsbury Activity Bks.) Bloomsbury Publishing USA.

—Carry & Play: Spring Friends. 2016. (ENG., Illus.). 10p. (J). (— 1). bds. 6.99 *(978-1-61963-828-0(2)*, 9781619638280, Bloomsbury Activity Bks.) Bloomsbury Publishing USA.

—Lift & Look: at School. 2016. (ENG., Illus.). 12p. (J). bds. 8.99 *(978-1-61963-997-3(1)*, 9781619639973, Bloomsbury Activity Bks.) Bloomsbury Publishing USA.

—Lift & Look: at the Park. 2016. (ENG., Illus.). 12p. (J). (— 1). bds. 8.99 *(978-1-61963-940-9(8)*, 9781619639409, Bloomsbury Activity Bks.) Bloomsbury Publishing USA.

—Lift & Look: in Space. 2016. (ENG., Illus.). 12p. (J). (— 1). bds. 8.99 *(978-1-61963-826-6(6)*, 9781619638266, Bloomsbury Activity Bks.) Bloomsbury Publishing USA.

—Lift-The-Flap Friends: Pirates. 2017. (ENG.). 14p. (J). bds. 9.99 *(978-1-68119-241-3(1)*, 9781681192413, Bloomsbury Activity Bks.) Bloomsbury Publishing USA.

—Lift-The-Flap Friends: Princess. 2017. (ENG.). 14p. (J). bds. 9.99 *(978-1-68119-240-6(3)*, 9781681192406, Bloomsbury Activity Bks.) Bloomsbury Publishing USA.

Blossom, Maggie. Wizard of Oz. Pearse, Asha, illus. 2014. (ENG.). 16p. (J). (gr. -1-4). 7.99 *(978-1-4867-0009-7(8))* Flowerpot Children's Pr. Inc. CAN. Dist: Cardinal Pubs. Group.

Blyton, Enid, et al. My First 123 & Nursery Rhymes. 2013. (ENG., Illus.). 20p. (J). bds. 11.50 *(978-1-84135-759-1(6))* Award Pubns. Ltd. GBR. Dist: Parkwest Pubns., Inc.

—My First Abc. 2013. (ENG., Illus.). 20p. (J). bds. 11.50 *(978-1-84135-757-7(X))* Award Pubns. Ltd. GBR. Dist: Parkwest Pubns., Inc.

—My First Animals. 2013. (ENG., Illus.). 20p. (J). bds. 11.50 *(978-1-84135-758-4(8))* Award Pubns. Ltd. GBR. Dist: Parkwest Pubns., Inc.

—My First Colours & Shapes. 2013. (ENG., Illus.). 20p. (J). bds. 11.50 *(978-1-84135-760-7(X))* Award Pubns. Ltd. GBR. Dist: Parkwest Pubns., Inc.

—Things That Go. 2013. (ENG.). 10p. (J). bds. 9.95 *(978-1-84135-724-9(3))* Award Pubns. Ltd. GBR. Dist: Parkwest Pubns., Inc.

—Under the Sea. 2013. (ENG.). 10p. (J). bds. 9.95 *(978-1-84135-723-2(5))* Parkwest Pubns., Inc.

Boardworks Learning Centers: Across the U. S. A. 2006. (J). bds. *(978-0-9755252-5-8(5))* Evergreen Pr. of Brainerd, LLC.

Boardworks Learning Centers: Figure It Out. 2006. (J). bds. *(978-0-9755252-4-1(7))* Evergreen Pr. of Brainerd, LLC.

Boardworks Learning Centers: I've Got It! 2006. (J). bds. *(978-0-9755252-8-9(X))* Evergreen Pr. of Brainerd, LLC.

Boardworks Learning Centers: Sentence Fixer-Uppers. 2006. (J). bds. *(978-0-9755252-7-2(1))* Evergreen Pr. of Brainerd, LLC.

Boardworks Learning Centers: Where in the World? 2006. (J). bds. *(978-0-9755252-6-5(3))* Evergreen Pr. of Brainerd, LLC.

Bolam, Emily. Dog. 2003. (Chunky Pet Bks.). (ENG., Illus.). 14p. (J). bds. 5.99 *(978-0-7641-5610-6(1))* Barron's Educational Series, Inc.

—Farmyard Friends. Bolam, Emily, illus. 2011. (ENG., Illus.). 8p. (J). (gr. -1-k). bds. 10.99 *(978-0-230-71293-5(2))* Pan Macmillan GBR. Dist: Independent Pubs. Group.

—In the Jungle. 2013. (ENG., Illus.). 10p. (J). bds. *(978-0-230-76713-3(3))* Barron's Educational Series, Inc.

Bolam, Emily, illus. In the Jungle. 2013. (Peekabooks Ser.). (ENG.). 8p. (J). (gr. -1 — 1). bds. 5.99 *(978-0-7641-6629-7(8))* Barron's Educational Series, Inc.

—Under the Sea. 2013. (Peekabooks Ser.). (ENG.). 8p. (J). (gr. -1 — 1). bds. 5.99 *(978-0-7641-6630-3(1))* Barron's Educational Series, Inc.

Bond, Michael. Paddington Bear All Day. Alley, R. W., illus. 2014. (Paddington Ser.). (ENG.). 14p. (J). (gr. -1-3). bds. 6.99 *(978-0-06-231721-6(0)*, HarperFestival) HarperCollins Pubs.

—Paddington Bear Goes to Market. Alley, R. W., illus. 2014. (Paddington Ser.). (ENG.). 14p. (J). (gr. -1-3). bds. 6.99 *(978-0-06-231722-3(9)*, HarperFestival) HarperCollins Pubs.

—Paddington Plays On. Alley, R. W., illus. 2016. (I Can Read Level 1 Ser.). 32p. (J). (gr. -1-3). pap. 3.99 *(978-0-06-243070-0(X)*, HarperCollins Pubs.

Bone, Emily. Sticker Dolly Dressing Around the World. 2011. (Sticker Dolly Dressing Ser.). 24p. (J). pap. 8.99 *(978-0-7945-2968-0(2)*, Usborne) EDC Publishing.

—Sticker Dolly Dressing Dream Jobs. 2012. (Sticker Dolly Dressing Ser.). 24p. (J). pap. 8.99 *(978-0-7945-3253-6(5)*, Usborne) EDC Publishing.

Bone, Emily & King, Colin. See Inside Trains. 2013. (Usborne Flap Book Ser.). (ENG., Illus.). 16p. (J). 13.99 *(978-0-7945-3377-9(9)*, Usborne) EDC Publishing.

Boniface, William. The Adventures of Max the Minnow. Sullivan, Don, illus. 2015. (ENG.). 26p. (J). bds. 9.99 *(978-1-4494-6490-5(4))* Andrews McMeel Publishing.

—Lights Out, Night's Out. Kirkova, Milena, illus. 2011. (ENG.). 24p. (J). pap. 6.99 *(978-1-4494-0236-5(4))* Andrews McMeel Publishing.

—There's a Dinosaur in My Soup! Poling, Kyle, illus. 2012. (ENG.). 12p. (J). (gr. -1-1). bds. 9.99 *(978-1-4424-4610-6(2)*, Little Simon) Little Simon.

Bonnet, Rosalind. Animals. rev. ed. 2013. (First Words Board Bks). 12p. (J). ring bd. 6.99 *(978-0-7945-3389-2(2)*, Usborne) EDC Publishing.

Bonnet, Rosalinde. Very First Christmas Carols. 2011. (Very First Words Board Book Ser.). 12p. (J). ring bd. 6.99 *(978-0-7945-3117-1(2)*, Usborne) EDC Publishing.

Bonnett-Rampersaud, Louise. How Do You Sleep?, 1 vol. Kest, Kristin, illus. 2008. (ENG.). 34p. (J). (gr. -1). 6.99 *(978-0-7614-5449-6(7))* Marshall Cavendish Corp.

Bonnett, Rosalind, illus. Santa Flap Book. 2012. (Flap Bks). 10p. (J). bds. 7.99 *(978-0-7945-3316-8(7)*, Usborne) EDC Publishing.

Book Company Staff. Animal World. 2003. (Novelty Bks.). (Illus.). (J). bds. 9.95 *(978-1-74047-366-8(3))* Book Co. Publishing Pty, Ltd., The AUS. Dist: Penton Overseas, Inc.

A Book of Babies. 2015. (ENG.). 24p. (J). (— 1). bds. 6.99 *(978-0-553-50779-9(6)*, Knopf Bks. for Young Readers) Random Hse. Children's Bks.

Boon, Fiona. The Story of Jesus. Ede, Lara, illus. 2014. (ENG.). 22p. (J). bds. *(978-1-78235-883-1(8))* Make Believe Ideas.

Borando, Silvia & Clerici, Lorenzo. Open up, Please! A Minibombo Book. 2016. (Minibombo Ser.). (ENG., Illus.). 24p. (J). (-k). 14.00 *(978-0-7636-9037-3(6))* Candlewick Pr.

Border, Terry. Peanut Butter's Yummy Numbers. Border, Terry, illus. 2016. (ENG., Illus.). 20p. (J). (— 1). bds. 6.99 *(978-0-399-54665-5(0)*, Philomel Bks.) Penguin Young Readers Group.

Bostrom, Kathleen Long. Rufus & Ryan Celebrate Easter! Thornburgh, Rebecca, illus. 2014. (Rufus & Ryan Ser.). 20p. (J). bds. 7.99 *(978-0-8249-1919-1(X)*, Ideal Pubns.) Worthy Publishing.

Bourgeois, Paulette. Franklin's Christmas: A Sticker Activity Book. Clark, Brenda, illus. 2003. (ENG.). 16p. (J). 6.95 *(978-1-55337-561-6(0))*; 6.95 *(978-1-55337-506-7(8))* Kids Can Pr., Ltd. CAN. Dist: Hachette Bk. Group.

Bower, Gary. Mommy Love. Bower, Jan, illus. 2012. (Little Lovable Board Bks.). (ENG.). 16p. (J). bds. 8.50 *(978-0-9845236-0-3(X))* Storybook Meadow Publishing.

Bowman, Crystal. My Christmas Stocking: Filled with God's Love, 1 vol. Gevry, Claudine, illus. 2015. (ENG.). 14p. (J). bds. 6.99 *(978-0-310-73823-7(7))* Zonderkidz.

—My Happy Pumpkin: God's Love Shining Through Me, 1 vol. 2014. (ENG.). 14p. (J). bds. 6.99 *(978-0-310-73828-2(8))* Zonderkidz.

Bowman, Donna H. Big Cats. Wald, Christina, illus. 2008. (ENG.). 24p. (J). (gr. 3-18). 19.95 *(978-1-58117-781-7(X)*, Intervisual/Piggy Toes) Bendon, Inc.

Bowman, Lucy. Sticker Dolly Dressing Fashion Long Ago. Baggott, Stella, illus. 2010. (Sticker Dolly Dressing Ser.). 24p. (J). pap. 8.99 *(978-0-7945-2547-7(4)*, Usborne) EDC Publishing.

Bowsher, Alice, illus. Lift-The-Flap & Color Jungle. 2017. (Lift-The-flap & Color Ser.). (ENG.). 10p. (J). (gr. -1-k). pap. 8.99 ***(978-1-84780-931-5(6)***, Frances Lincoln Children's Bks.) Quarto Publishing Group UK GBR. Dist: Hachette Bk. Group.

—Lift-The-Flap & Color Ocean. 2017. (Lift-The-flap & Color Ser.). (ENG.). 10p. (J). (gr. -1-k). pap. 8.99 ***(978-1-84780-932-2(4)***, Frances Lincoln Children's Bks.) Quarto Publishing Group UK GBR. Dist: Hachette Bk. Group.

Box, Su. You Are Very Special: With a Special Surprise for You Inside! Poole, Susie, illus. 2011. (ENG.). 12p. (J). (gr. -1-k). bds. 7.99 *(978-0-7459-6300-6(5))* Lion Hudson PLC GBR. Dist: Independent Pubs. Group.

Boyd, Lizi. Inside Outside. Boyd, Lizi, illus. 2013. (ENG., Illus.). 40p. (J). (gr. -1-1). 15.99 *(978-1-4521-0644-1(4))* Chronicle Bks. LLC.

Boyer, Cecile. Run, Dog! 2014. (ENG., Illus.). 48p. (J). (gr. -1-k). 16.99 *(978-1-4521-2708-8(5))* Chronicle Bks. LLC.

Boynton, Sandra. Big Box of Boynton Set 2! Snuggle Puppy! Belly Button Book! Tickle Time!, 3 vols. 2014. (ENG., Illus.). 24p. (J). (gr. k — 1). bds. 21.00 *(978-0-7611-8095-1(8)*, 18095) Workman Publishing Co., Inc.

—Eek! Halloween! 2016. (ENG., Illus.). 24p. (J). bds. 6.95 *(978-0-7611-9300-5(6))* Workman Publishing Co., Inc.

—Fuzzy Fuzzy Fuzzy! A Touch, Skritch, & Tickle Book. Boynton, Sandra, illus. 2003. (ENG., Illus.). 12p. (J). (gr. -1-k). bds. 14.99 *(978-0-689-86363-9(2)*, Little Simon) Little Simon.

—Happy Hippo, Angry Duck: A Book of Moods. Boynton, Sandra, illus. 2011. (ENG., Illus.). 16p. (J). (gr. -1-k). bds. 5.99 *(978-1-4424-1731-1(5)*, Little Simon) Little Simon.

—Tickle Time! 2012. (ENG., Illus.). 24p. (J). (gr. k-1). bds. 6.95 *(978-0-7611-6883-6(4)*, 16883) Workman Publishing Co., Inc.

—Your Personal Penguin. 2006. (ENG., Illus.). 24p. (J). (gr. k — 1). bds. 6.95 *(978-0-7611-4372-7(6)*, 14372) Workman Publishing Co., Inc.

Brainy Baby Animals. 2004. *(978-1-59394-234-2(6))* Bendon, Inc.

Brainy Baby Quad Book. 2005. (Brainy Baby Ser.). 40p. (J). bds. 10.39 *(978-1-59394-240-3(0))* Bendon, Inc.

Brandon, Wendy. Cinderbear: Board Book & Puppet Theater. Winter, Janet, illus. 2004. (J). *(978-1-883043-47-6(6))* Straight Edge Pr., The.

—The Frog Prince: Board Book & Puppet Theater. Beckes, Shirley V., illus. 2004. (J). *(978-1-883043-46-9(8))* Straight Edge Pr., The.

Brannon, Tom, illus. I Love You Valentine Songs. 2012. (J). *(978-1-4508-3303-5(9))* Phoenix International Publications, Inc.

Bratz My File. 2007. 96p. pap. *(978-1-4054-9373-4(9))* Parragon, Inc.

Braun, Sebastian. Peekaboo Baby. Braun, Sebastian, illus. 2012. (ENG., Illus.). 16p. (J). (gr. -1 — 1). bds. 6.99 *(978-0-7636-5933-2(9))* Candlewick Pr.

Braun, Sebastian, illus. I'm a Clown! 2012. (Look at Me Ser.). (ENG.). 12p. (J). bds. *(978-1-84643-472-3(6))* Child's Play International Ltd.

—I'm a Monster! 2012. (Look at Me Ser.). (ENG.). 12p. (J). bds. *(978-1-84643-470-9(X))* Child's Play International Ltd.

—I'm a Robot! 2012. (Look at Me Ser.). (ENG.). 12p. (J). bds. *(978-1-84643-469-3(6))* Child's Play International Ltd.

—I'm an Alien! 2012. (Look at Me Ser.). (ENG.). 12p. (J). bds. *(978-1-84643-471-6(8))* Child's Play International Ltd.

Braun, Sebastien. I Love My Daddy Board Book. Braun, Sebastien, illus. 2017. (Illus.). 32p. (J). (gr. -1 — 1). bds. 7.99 *(978-0-06-256425-2(0)*, Tegen, Katherine Bks) HarperCollins Pubs.

—I Love My Mommy Board Book. Braun, Sebastien, illus. 2017. (Illus.). 26p. (J). (gr. -1 — 1). bds. 7.99 *(978-0-06-256424-5(2)*, Tegen, Katherine Bks) HarperCollins Pubs.

—I Love You More. Braun, Sebastien, illus. 2013. (ENG., Illus.). 20p. (J). (gr. -1). bds. 8.95 *(978-1-58925-620-0(4))* Tiger Tales.

—One Sleepy Night. 2013. (Padded Board Books Ser.). (ENG.). 20p. (J). bds. 8.95 *(978-1-58925-619-4(0))* Tiger Tales Pubns.

—Who Can Jump? Braun, Sebastien, illus. 2014. (ENG., Illus.). 14p. (J). (— 1). bds. 6.99 *(978-0-7636-6753-5(6))* Candlewick Pr.

—Who Can Swim? Braun, Sebastien, illus. 2014. (ENG., Illus.). 14p. (J). (— 1). bds. 6.99 *(978-0-7636-6752-8(8))* Candlewick Pr.

—Who's Hiding? 2013. (ENG., Illus.). 16p. (J). (gr. -1 — 1). bds. 6.99 *(978-0-7636-5932-5(0))* Candlewick Pr.

Braun, Sebastien, illus. Santa's Noisy House. 2013. (ENG.). 12p. (J). (gr. -1-k). 17.99 *(978-0-230-76411-8(8))* Pan Macmillan GBR. Dist: Independent Pubs. Group.

—Shapes & Colors. 2012. (J). *(978-1-58865-852-4(X))* Kidsbooks, LLC.

—The Tiger Prowls: A Pop-Up Book of Wild Animals. 2016. (ENG.). 12p. (J). 16.99 *(978-1-4711-2215-6(8)*, Simon & Schuster Children's) Simon & Schuster, Ltd. GBR. Dist: Simon & Schuster, Inc.

Brett, Anna. The Fairy Creativity Book: Games, Cut-Outs, Art Paper, Stickers, & Stencils. 2017. (Creativity Bks.). (ENG.). 80p. (J). (gr. 1-6). pap. 12.99 *(978-1-4380-0967-4(4))* Barron's Educational Series, Inc.

—Magical Forest: Color & Create Your Own Beautiful 3D Scenes. 2017. (3D Colorscapes Ser.). (ENG.). 48p. (J). (gr. 3-7). bds. 10.99 *(978-0-7641-6883-3(5))* Barron's Educational Series, Inc.

Brett, Jan. Annie & the Wild Animals Send-A-Story. 2011. (Send a Story Ser.). (ENG., Illus.). 32p. (J). (gr. -1-3). pap. 4.99 *(978-0-547-56692-4(1))* Houghton Mifflin Harcourt Publishing Co.

—Gingerbread Baby. Brett, Jan, illus. 2003. (ENG., Illus.). 32p. (J). (gr. -1 — 1). bds. 7.99 *(978-0-399-24166-6(3)*, G.P. Putnam's Sons Books for Young Readers) Penguin Young Readers Group.

—Gingerbread Friends. Brett, Jan, illus. 2008. (ENG., Illus.). 32p. (J). (gr. -1-k). 17.99 *(978-0-399-25161-0(8)*, G.P. Putnam's Sons Books for Young Readers) Penguin Young Readers Group.

—The Mitten: Oversized Board Book. Brett, Jan, illus. 2014. (ENG., Illus.). 32p. (J). (gr. -1 — 1). bds. 14.99 *(978-0-399-16981-6(4)*, G.P. Putnam's Sons Books for Young Readers) Penguin Young Readers Group.

Brett, Jeannie. Little Maine. Brett, Jeannie, illus. 2010. (My Little State Ser.). (ENG., Illus.). 22p. (J). 9.95 *(978-1-58536-497-8(5))* Sleeping Bear Pr.

Brett, Tyler & Romano, Tony. False Creek. 2010. (ENG., Illus.). 22p. bds. 9.95 *(978-1-897476-66-6(3))* Simply Read Bks. CAN. Dist: Ingram Publisher Services.

Bridwell, Norman. Clifford at the Circus. Bridwell, Norman, illus. 2010. (Clifford 8x8 Ser.). (ENG., Illus.). 32p. (J). (gr. -1-3). pap. 3.99 *(978-0-545-21584-8(6)*, Cartwheel Bks.) Scholastic, Inc.

—Clifford's Family. Bridwell, Norman, illus. 2010. (Clifford 8x8 Ser.). (ENG., Illus.). 32p. (J). (gr. -1-3). pap. 3.99 *(978-0-545-21585-5(4)*, Cartwheel Bks.) Scholastic, Inc.

—Clifford's First Christmas. Bridwell, Norman, illus. 2010. (Clifford Ser.). (ENG., Illus.). 20p. (J). (gr. k — 1). bds. 6.99 *(978-0-545-21773-6(3)*, Cartwheel Bks.) Scholastic, Inc.

—Clifford's First Easter. Bridwell, Norman, illus. 2010. (Clifford Ser.). (ENG., Illus.). 14p. (J). (gr. k — 1). bds. 6.99 *(978-0-545-20010-3(5)*, Cartwheel Bks.) Scholastic, Inc.

Bridwell, Norman & Scholastic, Inc. Staff. The Big Red Dog. 2010. (Clifford Ser.). (ENG.). (J). (gr. -1-3). pap. 12.99 incl. audio compact disk *(978-0-545-25415-1(9))* Scholastic, Inc.

Bright & Beyond - Age 1. 2004. (J). *(978-0-9726170-5-5(1))* Pal Toys, LLC.

Bright & Beyond - Age 2. 2004. (J). *(978-0-9726170-6-2(X))* Pal Toys, LLC.

Bright & Beyond - Baby. 2004. (J). *(978-0-9726170-4-8(3))* Pal Toys, LLC.

Bright & Beyond - Math. 2004. (J). *(978-0-9763648-0-1(8))* Pal Toys, LLC.

Bright & Beyond - Preschool. 2004. (J). *(978-0-9726170-7-9(8))* Pal Toys, LLC.

Bright & Beyond - Reading. 2004. (J). *(978-0-9726170-8-6(6))* Pal Toys, LLC.

Bright & Beyond - Thinking. 2004. (J). *(978-0-9763648-1-8(6))* Pal Toys, LLC.

Bright & Beyond - Writing. 2004. (J). *(978-0-9726170-9-3(4))* Pal Toys, LLC.

Brighter Minds, creator. Fact Book. 2008. (DreamWorks Kung Fu Panda Ser.). (Illus.). 10p. (J). (gr. -1-3). 9.95 *(978-1-57791-420-4(1))* Brighter Minds Children's Publishing.

—Kung Fu Panda: Create-A-Story. 2008. (Illus.). 8p. (J). (gr. k-2). 9.95 *(978-1-57791-419-8(8))* Brighter Minds Children's Publishing.

—Kung Fu Panda Magnetic Storybook. 2008. (DreamWorks Kung Fu Panda Ser.). (Illus.). 10p. (J). (gr. 1-3). bds. 12.95 *(978-1-57791-421-1(X))* Brighter Minds Children's Publishing.

Brignaud, Pierre, illus. Caillou: Where Is Teddy? 2015. (Step by Step Ser.). (ENG.). 24p. (J). (gr. k-k). bds. 5.99 *(978-2-89718-173-4(7))* Caillouet, Gerry.

Britto, Romero. Where Is Friendship Bear? Britto, Romero, illus. 2010. (ENG., Illus.). 16p. (J). (gr. -1-k). 12.99 *(978-1-4169-9623-1(0)*, Little Simon) Little Simon.

Broach, Elise. Barnyard Baby. Doerrfeld, Cori, illus. 2013. (Baby Seasons Ser.). (ENG.). 14p. (J). (gr. -1 — 1). bds. 7.99 *(978-0-316-21203-8(2))* Little, Brown Bks. for Young Readers.

—Seashore Baby. 2010. (Baby Seasons Ser.). (ENG., Illus.). 14p. (J). (gr. -1 — 1). bds. 7.99 *(978-0-316-04303-8(6))* Little, Brown Bks. for Young Readers.

Broderick, Kathy. Disney Princess: Belle (Giant First Play -a- Sound) 2010. 10p. (J). bds. 17.98 *(978-1-60553-543-2(5))* Publications International, Ltd.

Brook-Piper, Holly. Animal Friends: A Touch-and-Feel Book. 2015. (ENG.). 12p. (J). (gr. -1 — 1). bds. 6.99 *(978-1-4998-0038-8(X))* Little Bee Books Inc.

—Animal Shapes: A Touch-and-Feel Book. 2015. (ENG., Illus.). 12p. (J). (gr. -1 — 1). bds. 6.99 *(978-1-4998-0039-5(8))* Little Bee Books Inc.

Brooke, Jasmine. Goldilocks & the Three Bears: Take the Temperature Test & Solve the Porridge Puzzle! 2017. (Fairy Tale Fixers: Fixing Fairy Tale Problems with STEM Ser.). 32p. (gr. 3-4). pap. 63.00 **(978-1-5382-0665-2(X))** Stevens, Gareth Publishing LLLP.

Brooke, Susan Rich, adapted by. The Lion King. 2003. (Illus.). (J). *(978-0-7853-9380-1(3))* Publications International, Ltd.

Brooke, Susan Rich & Seuss, Dr. The Cat in the Hat Flips His Lid. Enik, Ted, illus. 2003. (J). *(978-0-7853-8446-5(4))* Publications International, Ltd.

Brookes, Archer. Vampireology: The True History of the Fallen. Holt, Nick, ed. 2010. (Ologies Ser.: 9). (ENG., Illus.). 30p. (YA). (gr. 7-9). 21.99 *(978-0-7636-4914-2(7))* Candlewick Pr.

Brooks, F. & Litchfield, J. Nativity Lift-the-Flap. 2004. (First Stories Ser.). 24p. (J). 10.95 *(978-0-7945-0529-5(5))* EDC Publishing.

Brooks, Felicity. Cars. Newell, Keith, illus. 2008. (Usborne Lift & Look Ser.). 12p. (J). (gr. -1-3). bds. 9.99 *(978-0-7945-1958-2(X)*, Usborne) EDC Publishing.

—Construction Sites. Newell, Keith, illus. 2010. (Lift & Look Board Bks.). 12p. (J). bds. 9.99 *(978-0-7945-2728-0(0)*, Usborne) EDC Publishing.

—Farms lift & Look. Litchfield, Jo, illus. 2005. 12p. (J). 9.95 *(978-0-7945-0932-3(0)*, Usborne) EDC Publishing.

—Lift-out Colors Book. 2008. (Shapes & Colors Jigsaw Bks). 12p. (J). bds. 12.99 *(978-0-7945-2136-3(3)*, Usborne) EDC Publishing.

—Lift-the-Flap Counting Book. 2011. (Lift-the-Flap Bks). 14p. (J). ring bd. 11.99 *(978-0-7945-2916-1(X)*, Usborne) EDC Publishing.

—Lift-the-Flap Word Book. 2011. (Lift-the-Flap Word Book Ser.). 14p. (J). pap. 11.99 *(978-0-7945-2562-0(8)*, Usborne) EDC Publishing.

—This Is My Duck. 2008. (NoisyTouchy-Feely Board Bks). 10p. (J). (gr. -1). bds. 16.99 *(978-0-7945-2187-5(8)*, Usborne) EDC Publishing.

—This Is My Tractor. Dimitri, Simona, illus. 2009. (Noisy Touchy-Feely Board Bks). 10p. (J). bds. 16.99 *(978-0-7945-2473-9(7)*, Usborne) EDC Publishing.

—Tractors Chunky Jigsaw Book. 2005. (Chunky Jigsaw Books Ser.). 14p. (J). 7.95 *(978-0-7945-0861-6(8)*, Usborne) EDC Publishing.

—Trains Chunky Jigsaw Book. 2005. (Chunky Jigsaw Books Ser.). 14p. (J). 7.95 *(978-0-7945-0859-3(6)*, Usborne) EDC Publishing.

—Trucks Lift-and-Look. 2005. (Illus.). 12p. (J). (gr. -1-k). per., bds. 9.95 *(978-0-7945-1068-8(X)*, Usborne) EDC Publishing.

—Under the Sea Lift & Look. 2010. (Lift & Look Board Bks). 12p. (J). bds. 9.99 *(978-0-7945-2576-7(8)*, Usborne) EDC Publishing.

—Very First Animals Board Book. 2010. (Very First Words Board Bks). 10p. (J). bds. 6.99 *(978-0-7945-2479-1(6)*, Usborne) EDC Publishing.

—Very First Colors Board Book. 2010. (Very First Words Board Bks). 10p. (J). bds. 6.99 *(978-0-7945-2763-1(9)*, Usborne) EDC Publishing.

Brooks, Felicity, des. Build a Picture Trains Sticker Book. 2012. (Build a Picture Sticker Bks). 24p. (J). pap. 6.99 *(978-0-7945-3261-1(6)*, Usborne) EDC Publishing.

—Build a Picture Trucks Sticker Book. 2012. (Build a Picture Sticker Bks). 24p. (J). pap. 6.99 *(978-0-7945-3248-2(9)*, Usborne) EDC Publishing.

Brooks, Felicity & Litchfield, Jo. First Picture Animals. Van Wyk, Hanri, illus. 2008. (First Picture Board Bks.). 12p. (J). (gr. -1). bds. 11.99 *(978-0-7945-1831-8(1)*, Usborne) EDC Publishing.

Brooks, Felicity & Mackinnon, Mairi. Spanish Words & Phrases - Internet Referenced. 2008. (First Picture Spanish Ser.). (Illus.). 50p. (J). 9.99 *(978-0-7945-2229-2(7)*, Usborne) EDC Publishing.

Brooks, Felicity, et al. The Counting Train. Cartwright, Stephen, illus. 2006. (J). *(978-0-439-89922-2(2))* Scholastic, Inc.

Brooks, Susie. Five Silly Monkeys. Tarbett, Debbie, illus. 2009. (ENG.). 14p. (J). (gr. k — 1). bds. 9.99 *(978-0-545-10222-3(7)*, Cartwheel Bks.) Scholastic, Inc.

Brown, Carron. Secrets of the Seashore. Nassner, Alyssa, illus. 2014. (ENG.). 36p. (J). 12.99 *(978-1-61067-309-9(3))* Kane Miller.

Brown, Heather. Chomp! Zoo: A Pull-Tab Book. 2012. (ENG.). 12p. (J). (gr. -1-k). bds. 7.99 *(978-1-4494-2312-4(4))* Andrews McMeel Publishing.

—The Robot Book. 2013. (ENG.). 12p. (J). bds. 7.99 *(978-1-4494-3250-8(6))* Andrews McMeel Publishing.

—The Robot Book. Brown, Heather, illus. 2010. (ENG., Illus.). 12p. (J). bds. 16.99 *(978-0-7407-9725-5(5))* Andrews McMeel Publishing.

Brown, Heather & Accord Publishing Staff. Chomp! 2012. (ENG., Illus.). 12p. (J). bds. 7.99 *(978-1-4494-1016-2(2))* Andrews McMeel Publishing.

Brown, James. Farm. Brown, James, illus. 2013. (ENG., Illus.). 16p. (J). (gr. -1 — 1). bds. 6.99 *(978-0-7636-5931-8(2))* Candlewick Pr.

Brown, Janet. Goldilocks & the Three Bears (Floor Book) My First Reading Book. Morton, Ken, illus. 2013. (ENG.). 24p. (J). (gr. -1-2). pap. 6.99 *(978-1-84322-901-8(3)*, Armadillo) Anness Publishing GBR. Dist: National Bk. Network.

Brown, Margaret Wise. A Child's Good Morning Book Board Book. Katz, Karen, illus. 2016. 32p. (J). (gr. -1 — 1). bds. 7.99 *(978-0-06-233792-4(0)*, HarperFestival) HarperCollins Pubs.

—Goodnight Moon 123: A Counting Book. Hurd, Clement, illus. 2013. (ENG.). 30p. (J). (gr. -1-k). bds. 9.99 *(978-0-06-224405-5(1)*, HarperFestival) HarperCollins Pubs.

—Goodnight Moon ABC Padded Board Book: An Alphabet Book. Hurd, Clement, illus. 2013. (ENG.). 30p. (J). (gr. -1-k). bds. 9.99 *(978-0-06-224404-8(3)*, HarperFestival) HarperCollins Pubs.

—Goodnight Moon Padded Board Book. Hurd, Clement, illus. 2017. 34p. (J). (gr. -1 — 1). bds. 10.99 *(978-0-06-257309-4(8)*, HarperFestival) HarperCollins Pubs.

—Goodnight Moon/Buenas Noches, Luna. Hurd, Clement, illus. 2014. (ENG.). 34p. (J). (gr. -1-3). bds. 8.99 *(978-0-06-236791-4(9))* HarperCollins Pubs.

—Home for a Bunny. Williams, Garth, illus. 2015. (Little Golden Board Book Ser.). (ENG.). 26p. (J). (-k). bds. 7.99 *(978-0-385-39093-4(9)*, Golden Bks.) Random Hse. Children's Bks.

—The Noisy Book Board Book. Weisgard, Leonard, illus. 2017. 36p. (J). (gr. -1 — 1). bds. 7.99 **(978-0-06-248465-9(6)**, HarperFestival) HarperCollins Pubs.

—The Quiet Noisy Book Board Book. Weisgard, Leonard, illus. 2017. 34p. (J). (gr. -1 — 1). bds. 7.99 **(978-0-06-248466-6(4)**, HarperFestival) HarperCollins Pubs.

Brown, Margaret Wise. The Runaway Bunny Padded Board Book. Hurd, Clement, illus. 2017. 36p. (J). (gr. -1 — 1). bds. 9.99 *(978-0-06-245959-6(7)*, HarperFestival) HarperCollins Pubs.

Brownjohn, Emma. All Kinds of Feelings: A Lift-The-Flap Book. 2003. (All Kinds Of Ser.). (ENG., Illus.). 16p. (J). (gr. -1-k). 12.99 *(978-1-85707-596-0(X))* Tango Bks. GBR. Dist: Independent Pubs. Group.

—Help Save Our Planet. Brownjohn, Emma, illus. 2007. (Yes I Can! Ser.). (ENG., Illus.). 18p. (J). (gr. -1-k). 12.99 *(978-1-85707-701-8(6))* Tango Bks. GBR. Dist: Independent Pubs. Group.

—Yes I Can! Be Healthy. Brownjohn, Emma, illus. 2011. (Yes I Can! Ser.). (ENG., Illus.). 18p. (J). (gr. -1-k). 12.99 *(978-1-85707-734-6(2))* Tango Bks. GBR. Dist: Independent Pubs. Group.

Brownlow, Mike, illus. Dinosaurs of Doom! 2011. (Time Pirates Ser.). (ENG.). 12p. (J). (gr. k-2). bds. 24.99 *(978-0-230-74179-9(7))* Macmillan Pubs., Ltd. GBR. Dist: Independent Pubs. Group.

Broyles, Beverly Ashley, illus. Grandmother's Alligator/Burukenge Wa Nyanya Activity Guide. 2005. (ENG & SWA.). (J). 12.95 *(978-0-9703632-7-5(3))* Wakefield Connection, The.

Bruel, Nick. Bad Kitty's Tasty Treats. 2014. (Slide & Find Ser.). (ENG., Illus.). 16p. (J). (gr. -1 — 1). bds. 12.99 *(978-0-312-51723-6(8)*, 9780312517236) Roaring Brook Pr.

Bruin, Jessica. The Cube Book. 2011. (ENG., Illus.). 48p. (J). (gr. -1-1). bds. 16.95 *(978-1-77049-325-4(5)*, Tundra Bks.) Tundra Bks. CAN. Dist: Penguin Random Hse. LLC.

Bruton, Catherine. Pop! 2013. (ENG.). 496p. (YA). (gr. 7). pap. 10.99 *(978-1-4052-6133-3(1))* Egmont Bks., Ltd. GBR. Dist: Independent Pubs. Group.

Bryant, Megan E. Alphasaurus. Powell, Luciana Navarro, illus. 2012. (ENG.). 20p. (J). (gr. -1 — 1). bds. 9.99 *(978-1-4521-0748-6(3))* Chronicle Bks. LLC.

Bubble Guppies, Bubble. Bubble Guppies Come Play with Us. 2015. (Lift-The-Flap Ser.: 5). (ENG.). 10p. (J). (gr. -1-k). bds. 11.99 *(978-0-7944-3035-1(X)*, Reader's Digest Children's Bks.) Studio Fun International.

—Bubble Guppies: Let's Play, Bubble Puppy! A PeekABoo Book. 2015. (ENG.). 10p. (J). (gr. -1-k). bds. 10.99 *(978-0-7944-3470-0(3)*, Reader's Digest Children's Bks.) Studio Fun International.

Bubble Guppies Guess Who's Fin-Tastic! 2014. (Guess Who? Ser.: 1). (ENG.). 10p. (J). (gr. -1-k). bds. 10.99 *(978-0-7944-3254-6(9)*, Reader's Digest Children's Bks.) Studio Fun International.

Buck, Deanna. My First Story of the First Easter. 2008. 32p. (J). 13.95 *(978-1-59038-871-6(2))* Deseret Bk. Co.

Budnick, Madeleine. Animal Amigos! Artsy Creatures in English y Espanol. 2013. (ArteKids Ser.). (ENG & SPA., Illus.). 16p. (J). (-k). bds. 7.95 *(978-1-59534-152-5(8))* Trinity Univ. Pr.

—Black & Blanco! Engaging Art in English y Español. 2013. (ArteKids Ser.). (ENG & SPA., Illus.). 16p. (J). (-k). bds. 7.95 *(978-1-59534-154-9(4))* Trinity Univ. Pr.

Buehner, Caralyn. Snowmen All Year Board Book. Buehner, Mark, illus. 2012. (ENG.). 28p. (J). (gr. -1-k). bds. 6.99 *(978-0-8037-3905-5(2)*, Dial Bks) Penguin Young Readers Group.

Buehner, Caralyn & Buehner, Mark. The Escape of Marvin the Ape. 2010. (Illus.). 16.10 *(978-0-7569-9295-8(8))* Penguin Publishing Group.

Bug Mania. (Flip Flap Fun Book Ser.). 10p. (J). bds. *(978-2-7643-0183-8(9))* Phidal Publishing, Inc./Editions Phidal, Inc.

Bugbird, T. My Pretty Pink School Purse. Horne, J., illus. 2010. 16p. (J). 12.99 *(978-1-84879-379-8(0))* Make Believe Ideas GBR. Dist: Nelson, Thomas Inc.

Bugbird, Tim. Farm Friends Peek a Boo! 2009. (Busy Baby Ser.). (ENG., Illus.). 12p. (gr. -1-k). 7.99 *(978-1-84610-859-4(4))* Make Believe Ideas GBR. Dist: Nelson, Thomas Inc.

—Peek a Boo Baby Animals. 2008. (Peek A Boo Ser.). (Illus.). 12p. (gr. -1-k). 7.99 *(978-1-84610-858-7(6))* Make Believe Ideas GBR. Dist: Nelson, Thomas Inc.

—Peek a Boo Wacky Wild Animals. 2008. (Peek A Boo Ser.). (Illus.). 12p. (gr. -1-k). 7.99 *(978-1-84610-860-0(8))* Make Believe Ideas GBR. Dist: Nelson, Thomas Inc.

Bugs Bunny & Friends. 2008. (Super Big Coloring Book Ser.). 224p. pap. *(978-1-4075-3407-7(6))* Parragon, Inc.

Bunting, Eve. Flower Garden. Hewitt, Kathryn, illus. 2004. 28p. (gr. -1-2). 17.00 *(978-0-7569-4113-0(X))* Perfection Learning Corp.

—Scary, Scary Halloween Gift Edition. Brett, Jan, illus. 2017. (ENG.). 40p. (J). (gr. -1-3). 8.99 *(978-0-544-88034-4(X)*, HMH Books For Young Readers) Houghton Mifflin Harcourt Publishing Co.

Burke, Zoe. Charley Harper's Count the Birds. Harper, Charley, illus. 2015. (ENG.). 24p. (J). bds. 10.95 *(978-0-7649-7246-1(4)*, POMEGRANATE KIDS) Pomegranate Communications, Inc.

Burnett, Frances Hodgson. The Secret Garden. Ingpen, Robert R., illus. 2011. (Sterling Illustrated Classics Ser.). (ENG.). 240p. (J). (gr. 5-18). 19.95 *(978-1-4027-7872-8(4))* Sterling Publishing Co., Inc.

Burns, Helen Marie. Ryleigh's Little Bug Book, 1 vol. Vareberg, Gladys, illus. 2009. 24p. pap. 24.95 *(978-1-60813-701-5(5))* America Star Bks.

Burroughs, Caleb. Cars. 2006. (Look & Find Ser.). (Illus.). 18p. (J). (gr. -1-3). pap. 24.98 *(978-1-4127-3775-3(3)*, 7269900) Phoenix International Publications, Inc.

—Dora the Explorer to the Moon. Miller, Victoria, illus. 2007. (Play a Tune Tale Ser.). 16p. (J). (gr. -1-3). 12.98 *(978-1-4127-8830-4(7))* Publications International, Ltd.

—Transformers. Mawhinney, Art, illus. 2007. (Look & Find (Publications International) Ser.). 16p. (J). (gr. -1-3). 7.98 *(978-1-4127-8673-7(8))* Publications International, Ltd.

Burton, Jeffrey. Food Trucks! A Lift-The-Flap Meal on Wheels! Cooper, Jay, illus. 2016. (ENG.). 12p. (J). (gr. -1). bds. 7.99 *(978-1-4814-6521-2(X)*, Little Simon) Little Simon.

—The Itsy Bitsy Pilgrim. Rescek, Sanja, illus. 2016. (Itsy Bitsy Ser.). (ENG.). 16p. (J). (gr. -1 — 1). bds. 5.99 *(978-1-4814-6852-7(9)*, Little Simon) Little Simon.

Burton, Virginia Lee. Katy & the Big Snow. 2010. (ENG., Illus.). 38p. (J). (gr. k — 1). bds. 7.99 *(978-0-547-37145-0(4))* Houghton Mifflin Harcourt Publishing Co.

—Katy & the Big Snow Lap Board Book. 2014. (ENG., Illus.). 38p. (J). (— 1). bds. 11.99 *(978-0-544-31717-8(3)*, HMH Books For Young Readers) Houghton Mifflin Harcourt Publishing Co.

—Mike Mulligan & His Steam Shovel. 75th anniv. ed. 2014. (ENG., Illus.). 56p. (J). (gr. -1-3). 17.99 *(978-0-544-27992-6(1)*, HMH Books For Young Readers) Houghton Mifflin Harcourt Publishing Co.

Busy Builders. (Flip Flap Fun Book Ser.). 10p. (J). bds. *(978-2-7643-0138-8(3))* Phidal Publishing, Inc./Editions Phidal, Inc.

Busy City. (Flip Flap Fun Book Ser.). 10p. (J). bds. *(978-2-89393-820-2(5))* Phidal Publishing, Inc./Editions Phidal, Inc.

Butterfield, Moira. Found You, Magic Fish! Child, Jeremy, illus. 2010. (Magic Bath Bks.). (ENG.). 8p. (J). (gr. -1-k). 5.99 *(978-0-7641-9791-8(6))* Barron's Educational Series, Inc.

—Funny Face. (Baby Goldstars Changing Faces Ser.). 10p. *(978-1-4054-9703-9(3))* Parragon, Inc.

—Wake up, Magic Duck! Child, Jeremy, illus. 2010. (Magic Bath Bks.). (ENG.). 8p. (J). (gr. -1-k). 5.99 *(978-0-7641-9792-5(4))* Barron's Educational Series, Inc.

Butterworth, Nick. The Secret Path. Butterworth, Nick, illus. 2011. (Tales from Percy's Park Ser.). (ENG., Illus.). 32p. (J). pap. 11.95 *(978-0-00-715518-7(2)*, HarperCollins Children's Bks.) HarperCollins Pubs. Ltd. GBR. Dist: HarperCollins Pubs.

A Button Story. 2014. (ENG., Illus.). 26p. (J). (gr. -1 — 1). bds. 6.95 *(978-1-55451-652-0(8)*, 9781554516520) Annick Pr., Ltd. CAN. Dist: Publishers Group West (PGW).

Buzzeo, Toni. Whose Truck? Datz, Jim, illus. 2015. (Whose Tools? Ser.). (ENG.). 16p. (J). (gr. -1 — 1). bds. 9.95 *(978-1-4197-1612-6(3))* Abrams, Inc.

Bynum, Janie. The Twelve Days of Christmas in Texas. 2016. (Twelve Days of Christmas in America Ser.). (ENG., Illus.). 22p. (J). (— 1). bds. 7.95 *(978-1-4549-2059-5(9))* Sterling Publishing Co., Inc.

Cabral, Jeane. Bad Dog Ben. 2009. (Jeane Cabral Bks.). (Illus.). (J). bds. 12.99 *(978-1-934650-05-9(6))* Just For Kids Pr., LLC.

—Good Night Little Moo. Howarth, Daniel, illus. 2007. (Night Light Book Ser.). 10p. (gr. -1-k). *(978-1-84666-128-0(5)*, Tide Mill Pr.) Top That! Publishing PLC.

Cabrera, Jane. If You're Happy & You Know It! Cabrera, Jane, illus. 2010. (Illus.). 24p. (J). (gr. -1). bds. 7.95 *(978-0-8234-2227-2(5))* Holiday Hse., Inc.

—Row, Row, Row Your Boat. Cabrera, Jane, illus. 2016. (ENG., Illus.). 24p. (J). bds. 7.99 *(978-0-8234-3632-3(2))* Holiday Hse., Inc.

—Ten in the Bed. Cabrera, Jane, illus. 2010. (ENG., Illus.). 24p. (J). (gr. -1). bds. 7.95 *(978-0-8234-2258-6(5))* Holiday Hse., Inc.

Calabazza, Della & Monckeberg, Paulina. Ludovico & Ooops 2006. 2005. (Pascualina Family of Products Ser.). (ENG., Illus.). 240p. (J). (gr. 3-7). spiral bd. 11.99 *(978-956-8222-23-9(5))* Pascualina Producciones S.A.

Calder, C. J. Busy Truck, 1 vol. Rooney, Ronnie & Peterson, Shauna, illus. 2012. (Truck Buddies Ser.). (ENG.). 16p. (gr. -1-k). bds. 7.95 *(978-1-4342-4388-1(5))* Stone Arch Bks.

—Fast Truck. Rooney, Ronnie & Peterson, Shauna, illus. 2012. (Truck Buddies Ser.). (ENG.). 16p. (gr. -1-k). bds. 7.95 *(978-1-4342-4389-8(3))* Stone Arch Bks.

—Muddy Truck, 1 vol. Rooney, Ronnie & Peterson, Shauna, illus. 2012. (Truck Buddies Ser.). (ENG.). 16p. (gr. -1-k). bds. 7.95 *(978-1-4342-4390-4(7))* Stone Arch Bks.

Calino & Abbeville Press Staff. ABC Snake. Calino, illus. 2008. (ENG., Illus.). 30p. (J). (gr. k-k). 8.95 *(978-0-7892-0303-8(0)*, Abbeville Kids) Abbeville Pr., Inc.

Callahan, Sean. A Wild Day with Dad. Howarth, Daniel, illus. 2012. (ENG.). 18p. (J). (gr. -1 — 1). bds. 7.99 *(978-0-8075-2295-0(3))* Whitman, Albert & Co.

Calmenson, Stephanie. Look! Birds! Pinillos, Puy, illus. 2016. (Look! Ser.). (ENG.). 24p. (J). (gr. -1-1). 7.99 *(978-1-4998-0114-9(9))* Little Bee Books Inc.

—Look! Flowers! Pinillos, Puy, illus. 2016. (Look! Ser.). (ENG.). 24p. (J). (gr. -1-1). 7.99 *(978-1-4998-0115-6(7))* Little Bee Books Inc.

Calver, Paul & Gunzi, Christiane. Trucks. Warren Photographic Staff, photos by. 2012. (Little Noisy Bks.). (ENG., Illus.). 12p. (J). bds. 5.99 *(978-0-7641-6504-7(6))* Barron's Educational Series, Inc.

Campbell, Rod. Dear Zoo. Campbell, Rod, illus. 2005. (Dear Zoo & Friends Ser.). (ENG., Illus.). 20p. (J). (gr. -1-k). 14.99 *(978-0-689-87751-3(X)*, Little Simon) Little Simon.

—Dear Zoo. Campbell, Rod, illus. 2004. (Illus.). 16p. (J). (VIE & ENG.). bds. *(978-1-84444-183-9(0))*; (RUS & ENG., bds. *(978-1-84444-178-5(4))*; (CHI & ENG., bds. *(978-1-84444-171-6(7))* Mantra Lingua.

—Dear Zoo. 2004. (BEN & ENG., Illus.). 16p. (J). bds. *(978-1-84444-169-3(5))* Mantra Lingua.

—Dear Zoo. Campbell, Rod, illus. 2004. (Illus.). 16p. (J). (ENG & ARA.). bds. *(978-1-84444-168-6(7))*; (CHI & ENG., bds. *(978-1-84444-170-9(9))*; (ENG & ALB., bds. *(978-1-84444-167-9(9))*; (ENG & PER., bds. *(978-1-84444-172-3(5))*; (ENG & FRE., bds. *(978-1-84444-173-0(3))*; (ENG & GUJ., bds. *(978-1-84444-174-7(1))*; (ENG & HIN., bds. *(978-1-84444-175-4(X))*; (ENG & PAN., bds. *(978-1-84444-176-1(8))*; (ENG & POR., bds. *(978-1-84444-177-8(6))*; (URD & ENG., bds. *(978-1-84444-182-2(2))*; (ENG & SPA., bds. *(978-1-84444-179-2(2))*; (ENG & SOM., bds. *(978-1-84444-180-8(6))*; (ENG & TUR., bds. *(978-1-84444-181-5(4))* Mantra Lingua.

—Dear Zoo: From the Zoo. Campbell, Rod, illus. 25th ed. 2007. (ENG., Illus.). 18p. (J). (gr. -1 — 1). bds. 6.99 *(978-1-4169-4737-0(X)*, Little Simon) Little Simon.

—Dinosaurs. Campbell, Rod, illus. 2015. (Dear Zoo & Friends Ser.). (ENG., Illus.). 14p. (J). (gr. -1 — 1). bds. 6.99 *(978-1-4814-4985-4(0)*, Little Simon) Little Simon.

—Farm Animals. Campbell, Rod, illus. 2015. (Dear Zoo & Friends Ser.). (ENG., Illus.). 14p. (J). (gr. -1 — 1). bds. 6.99 *(978-1-4814-4984-7(2)*, Little Simon) Little Simon.

Campbell, S Q. Animals. 2006. (Picture Me Ser.). (Illus.). (J). *(978-1-57151-769-2(3))* Playhouse Publishing.

—Shapes. 2006. (Picture Me Ser.). (Illus.). (J). *(978-1-57151-771-5(5))* Playhouse Publishing.

Canadian Board Books. 2014. (Maple Leaf Learners Ser.). (ENG.). 20p. bds. 15.98 *(978-1-62370-434-6(0))* Capstone Young Readers of Coughlan Cos.

Candlewick Press, Candlewick. Japan: Panorama Pops. Smith, Anne, illus. 2015. (Panorama Pops Ser.). (ENG.). 30p. (J). (gr. k-4). 8.99 *(978-0-7636-7504-2(0))* Candlewick Pr.

—Shaun the Sheep Movie - Timmy in the City. Aardman Animations Staff, illus. 2015. (Tales from Mossy Bottom Farm Ser.). (ENG.). 12p. (J). (-k). bds. 7.99 *(978-0-7636-7875-3(9)*, Candlewick Entertainment) Candlewick Pr.

—The Story of Flight: Panorama Pops. Holcroft, John, illus. 2015. (ENG.). 30p. (J). (gr. k-4). 8.99 *(978-0-7636-7700-8(0))* Candlewick Pr.

Candlewick Press Staff. Creepy-Crawlies: a 3D Pocket Guide. KJA Artists Staff, illus. 2013. (Panorama Pops Ser.). (ENG.). 30p. (J). (gr. -1-2). 8.99 *(978-0-7636-6662-0(9))* Candlewick Pr.

Candy Cane Press, creator. Safe at Home! Indoor Safety. 2005. (ENG., Illus.). 14p. (J). (gr. -1-k). bds. 12.95 *(978-0-8249-6592-1(2)*, Ideal Pubns.) Worthy Publishing.

—Safe at Play: Outdoor Safety. 2005. (ENG., Illus.). 14p. (J). (gr. -1-k). bds. 12.95 *(978-0-8249-6593-8(0),* Ideal Pubns.) Worthy Publishing.

Caniac, Nina. Baby Pets Play! Caniac, Nina, illus. 2012. (ENG., Illus.). 10p. (J). (gr. -1). 12.95 *(978-2-7338-2153-4(9))* Auzou, Philippe Editions FRA. Dist: Consortium Bk. Sales & Distribution.

Cannon, Janell. Stellaluna. 2007. (ENG., Illus.). 42p. (J). (gr. -1-3). bds. 7.99 *(978-0-15-206287-3(4))* Houghton Mifflin Harcourt Publishing Co.

Capstone Press. Jelly Bear Christmas Surprise, 1 vol. 2015. (Jelly Bear Ser.). (ENG.). 10p. (gr. -1 — 1). bds. 12.99 *(978-1-62370-247-2(X))* Capstone Young Readers of Coughlan Cos.

Capucilli, Alyssa Satin. Biscuit's 123. Schories, Pat & Berlin, Rose Mary, illus. 2012. (Biscuit Ser.). (ENG.). 16p. (J). (gr. -1-1). pap. 6.99 *(978-0-06-162523-7(X),* HarperFestival) HarperCollins Pubs.

—Biscuit's Pet & Play Bedtime: A Touch & Feel Book. Schories, Pat, illus. 2017. (Biscuit Ser.). 12p. (J). (gr. -1 — 1). bds. 7.99 *(978-0-06-249039-1(7),* HarperFestival) HarperCollins Pubs.

—Katy Duck. Cole, Henry, illus. 2007. (Katy Duck Ser.). (ENG.). 16p. (J). (gr. -1-k). bds. 7.99 *(978-1-4169-1901-8(5),* Little Simon) Little Simon.

—My First Ballet Class: A Book with Foldout Pages. Jensen, Leyah, illus. Jensen, Leyah, photos by. 2011. (My First Ser.). (ENG.). 14p. (J). (gr. -1-k). 9.99 *(978-1-4424-0895-1(2),* Little Simon) Little Simon.

—My First Karate Class: A Book with Foldout Pages. Jensen, Leyah, photos by. 2012. (My First Ser.). (ENG., Illus.). 14p. (J). (gr. -1-k). 9.99 *(978-1-4424-2748-8(5),* Little Simon) Little Simon.

—My Mom & Me. Mitchell, Susan, illus. 2009. (ENG.). 16p. (J). (gr. -1-1). 7.99 *(978-1-4169-5829-1(0),* Little Simon) Little Simon.

Cara, Anwar. 5 Pillars of Islam. Zulkifli, Azhari, illus. 2015. (ENG.). 16p. (J). bds. 9.95 *(978-0-86037-574-6(9))* Kube Publishing Ltd. GBR. Dist: Consortium Bk. Sales & Distribution.

Carbone, Courtney. The Ice Box. Random House Disney Staff, illus. 2014. (Friendship Box Ser.). (ENG.). 48p. (J). (-k). bds. 10.99 *(978-0-7364-3128-6(4),* RH/Disney) Random Hse. Children's Bks.

Carle, Eric. Animal Stories: 8 Animal Stories, over 35 Sounds. 2014. 36p. (J). bds. 24.98 *(978-1-4508-8529-4(2),* 1450885292) Publications International, Ltd.

—Dream Snow. Carle, Eric, illus. 2015. (ENG., Illus.). 22p. (J). (gr. -1 — 1). bds. 9.99 *(978-0-399-17314-1(5),* Philomel Bks.) Penguin Young Readers Group.

—Have You Seen My Cat? Carle, Eric, illus. 2009. (World of Eric Carle Ser.). (ENG., Illus.). 16p. (J). bds. 7.99 *(978-1-4169-8514-3(X),* Little Simon) Little Simon.

—My First Busy Book. Carle, Eric, illus. 2015. (World of Eric Carle Ser.). (ENG., Illus.). 12p. (J). bds. 14.99 *(978-1-4814-5791-0(8),* Little Simon) Little Simon.

—My Very First Book of Animal Homes. Carle, Eric, illus. 2007. (ENG., Illus.). 20p. (J). (gr. -1 — 1). bds. 5.99 *(978-0-399-24647-0(9),* Philomel Bks.) Penguin Young Readers Group.

—My Very First Book of Motion. Carle, Eric, illus. 2007. (ENG., Illus.). 18p. (J). (gr. -1 — 1). bds. 5.99 *(978-0-399-24748-4(3),* Philomel Bks.) Penguin Young Readers Group.

—My Very First Book of Shapes / Mi Primer Libro de Figuras: Bilingual Edition. Carle, Eric, illus. 2013. (SPA & ENG., Illus.). 20p. (J). (gr. -1 — 1). bds. 5.99 *(978-0-399-16142-1(2),* Philomel Bks.) Penguin Young Readers Group.

—The Very Busy Spider. Carle, Eric, illus. 2011. (ENG., Illus.). 24p. (J). (gr. -1 — 1). bds. 15.99 *(978-0-399-25601-1(6),* Philomel Bks.) Penguin Young Readers Group.

—The Very Busy Spider. 2006. (World of Eric Carle Ser.). (ENG., Illus.). 24p. (J). (gr. -1-k). 6.99 *(978-0-448-44421-5(6),* Grosset & Dunlap) Penguin Young Readers Group.

—The Very Busy Spider's Favorite Words. Carle, Eric, illus. 2007. (World of Eric Carle Ser.). (ENG., Illus.). 20p. (J). (gr. -1-k). bds. 4.99 *(978-0-448-44703-2(7),* Grosset & Dunlap) Penguin Young Readers Group.

—The Very Hungry Caterpillar. Carle, Eric, illus. 2011. (ENG & SPA., Illus.). 32p. (J). (gr. -1-k). 21.99 *(978-0-399-25604-2(0),* Philomel Bks.) Penguin Young Readers Group.

—The Very Hungry Caterpillar. 2004. (J). (gr. -1-2). spiral bd. *(978-0-616-01610-7(7));* spiral bd. *(978-0-616-01611-4(5))* Canadian National Institute for the Blind/Institut National Canadien pour les Aveugles.

—The Very Hungry Caterpillar. 2004. (Illus.). (J). 23p. *(978-1-85269-127-1(1));* (ENG & SOM., 19p. pap. *(978-1-85269-128-8(X))* Mantra Lingua.

—The Very Hungry Caterpillar. Carle, Eric, illus. 2004. (Illus.). 20p. (J). (ENG & URD.). pap. *(978-1-85269-129-5(8));* (ENG & BEN., pap. *(978-1-85269-125-7(5));* (ENG & CHI., (gr. -1-2). pap. *(978-1-85269-126-4(3));* (ARA & ENG., (gr. -1-5). pap. *(978-1-85269-124-0(7))* Mantra Lingua.

—The Very Hungry Caterpillar. 2008. (CHI., Illus.). 32p. *(978-7-5332-5673-9(5))* Mingtian Chubanshe.

—The Very Hungry Caterpillar. Carle, Eric, illus. 2007. (ENG., Illus.). 24p. (J). (gr. -1 — 1). bds., bds. 15.99 *(978-0-399-24745-3(9),* Philomel Bks.) Penguin Young Readers Group.

—The Very Hungry Caterpillar (La Oruga Muy Hambrienta) Carle, Eric, illus. 2011. (SPA & ENG., Illus.). 24p. (J). (gr. -1 — 1). bds. 10.99 *(978-0-399-25605-9(9),* Philomel Bks.) Penguin Young Readers Group.

—The Very Hungry Caterpillar's Favorite Words. Carle, Eric, illus. 2007. (World of Eric Carle Ser.). (ENG., Illus.). 20p. (J). (gr. -1-k). bds. 3.99 *(978-0-448-44704-9(5),* Grosset & Dunlap) Penguin Young Readers Group.

—The Very Hungry Caterpillar's Finger Puppet Book. 2011. (World of Eric Carle Ser.). (ENG.). 7p. (J). (gr. -1-k). bds. 12.99 *(978-0-448-45597-6(8),* Grosset & Dunlap) Penguin Young Readers Group.

—The Very Lonely Firefly. 2012. (Penguin Young Readers, Level 2 Ser.). (ENG.). 32p. (J). (gr. 1-2). 14.99 *(978-0-448-45851-9(9));* pap. 3.99 *(978-0-448-45850-2(0))* Penguin Young Readers Group. (Penguin Young Readers).

—The Very Lonely Firefly. 2012. (Penguin Young Readers Level 2 Ser.). lib. bdg. 13.55 *(978-0-606-26069-5(2),* Turtleback) Turtleback Bks.

—What's Your Favorite Animal? Carle, Eric, illus. 2015. (ENG., Illus.). 30p. (J). (gr. -1-1). bds. 8.99 *(978-1-62779-303-2(8),* 9781627793032, Holt, Henry & Co. Bks. For Young Readers) Holt, Henry & Co.

Carle, Eric & Chronicle Books Staff. String-Alongs. 2012. (ENG., Illus.). 10p. (J). (gr. -1-17). 18.99 *(978-1-4521-0515-4(4))* Chronicle Bks. LLC.

—The World of Eric Carle the Very Hungry Caterpillar Flash Cards. 2014. (ENG., Illus.). 22p. (J). (gr. -1 — 1). 14.99 *(978-1-4521-3190-0(2))* Chronicle Bks. LLC.

Carle, Eric & Mack, Jeff. The Very Hungry Caterpillar. Carle, Eric, illus. 2015. (ENG., Illus.). 24p. (J). (gr. -1-k). bds. 19.99 *(978-0-399-17317-2(X),* Philomel Bks.) Penguin Young Readers Group.

Carpenter, Tad. Arctic Animals. 2015. (Who's That? Ser.). (ENG., Illus.). 16p. (J). (— 1). bds. 7.95 *(978-1-4549-1227-9(8))* Sterling Publishing Co., Inc.

—Barnyard Friends. 2015. (Who's That? Ser.). (ENG., Illus.). 16p. (J). (— 1). bds. 7.95 *(978-1-4549-1226-2(X))* Sterling Publishing Co., Inc.

—On the Go. 2015. (Who's That? Ser.). (ENG., Illus.). 16p. (J). (— 1). bds. 7.95 *(978-1-4549-1225-5(1))* Sterling Publishing Co., Inc.

—When I Grow Up. 2015. (Who's That? Ser.). (ENG., Illus.). 16p. (J). (— 1). bds. 7.95 *(978-1-4549-1228-6(6))* Sterling Publishing Co., Inc.

Carroll, Claudia. Shmadiggle & the Imagination Asteroid. 2008. 68p. pap. 9.95 *(978-0-557-01566-5(9))* Lulu Pr., Inc.

Carter, David. David Carter's 100: Lift the Flaps & Learn to Count! 2013. (ENG., Illus.). 20p. (J). (gr. -1-2). bds. 17.95 *(978-1-4027-8738-6(3))* Sterling Publishing Co., Inc.

Carter, David A. Alpha Bugs: A Pop-Up Alphabet. Carter, David A., illus. 2006. (David Carter's Bugs Ser.). (ENG., Illus.). 28p. (J). (gr. -1-2). 12.99 *(978-1-4169-0973-6(7),* Little Simon) Little Simon.

—B Is for Box — the Happy Little Yellow Box: A Pop-Up Book. Carter, David A., illus. 2014. (ENG., Illus.). 18p. (J). (gr. -1). 12.99 *(978-1-4814-0295-8(1),* Little Simon) Little Simon.

—Beach Bugs. Carter, David A., illus. 2008. (David Carter's Bugs Ser.). (ENG., Illus.). 16p. (J). (gr. -1-2). 12.99 *(978-1-4169-5055-4(9),* Little Simon) Little Simon.

—Bedtime Bugs. Carter, David A., illus. 2010. (David Carter's Bugs Ser.). (ENG., Illus.). 18p. (J). (gr. -1-2). 12.99 *(978-1-4169-9960-7(4),* Little Simon) Little Simon.

—The Big Bug Book. Carter, David A., illus. 2008. (David Carter's Bugs Ser.). (ENG., Illus.). 16p. (J). (gr. -1-2). 24.99 *(978-1-4169-4095-1(2),* Little Simon) Little Simon.

—Birthday Bugs. Carter, David A., illus. 2004. (David Carter's Bugs Ser.). (ENG., Illus.). 16p. (J). (gr. -1-3). 12.99 *(978-0-689-81858-5(0),* Little Simon) Little Simon.

—Bitsy Bee Goes to School. Carter, David A., illus. 2014. (David Carter's Bugs Ser.). (ENG., Illus.). 24p. (J). (gr. -1-1). pap. 3.99 *(978-1-4424-9503-6(0),* Simon Spotlight) Simon Spotlight.

—A Box of Bugs: 4 Pop-Up Concept Books. Carter, David A., illus. 2011. (David Carter's Bugs Ser.). (ENG., Illus.). 64p. (J). (gr. -1-3). 16.99 *(978-1-4424-2989-5(5),* Little Simon) Little Simon.

—Bugs That Go! A Bustling Pop-Up Book. Carter, David A., illus. 2011. (David Carter's Bugs Ser.). (ENG., Illus.). 18p. (J). (gr. -1-1). 12.99 *(978-1-4169-4097-5(9),* Little Simon) Little Simon.

—Builder Bugs: A Busy Pop-Up Book. Carter, David A., illus. 2012. (David Carter's Bugs Ser.). (ENG., Illus.). 16p. (J). (gr. -1-2). 12.99 *(978-1-4424-2648-1(9),* Little Simon) Little Simon.

—Colors: A Bugs Pop-Up Concept Book. Carter, David A., illus. 2010. (David Carter's Bugs Ser.). (ENG., Illus.). 16p. (J). (gr. -1-1). 8.99 *(978-1-4424-0830-2(8),* Little Simon) Little Simon.

—Feely Bugs. Carter, David A., illus. 2005. (David Carter's Bugs Ser.). (ENG., Illus.). 14p. (J). (gr. -1-2). 12.99 *(978-1-4169-0326-0(7),* Little Simon) Little Simon.

—Halloween Bugs, Vol. 16. Carter, David A., illus. 2003. (David Carter's Bugs Ser.). (ENG., Illus.). 14p. (J). (gr. -1-3). 12.99 *(978-0-689-85916-8(3),* Little Simon) Little Simon.

—The Happy Little Yellow Box: A Pop-Up Book of Opposites. Carter, David A., illus. 2012. (ENG., Illus.). 18p. (J). (gr. -1). 12.99 *(978-1-4169-4096-8(0),* Little Simon) Little Simon.

—The Happy Shiny Blue Circle: A Touch-And-Feel Book of Shapes. 2014. (ENG., Illus.). 16p. (J). (gr. -1-k). 14.99 *(978-1-85707-861-9(6))* Tango Bks. GBR. Dist: Independent Pubs. Group.

—Jingle Bugs: A Merry Pop-Up Book with Lights & Music! Carter, David A., illus. 2004. (David Carter's Bugs Ser.). (ENG., Illus.). 22p. (J). (gr. -1-2). 11.99 *(978-0-689-87416-1(2),* Little Simon) Little Simon.

—Merry Christmas, Bugs! Carter, David A., illus. 2014. (David Carter's Bugs Ser.). (ENG., Illus.). 24p. (J). (gr. -1-1). pap. 3.99 *(978-1-4424-9506-7(5),* Simon Spotlight) Simon Spotlight.

—One Red Dot: A Pop-Up Book for Children of All Ages. Carter, David A., illus. 2005. (ENG., Illus.). 18p. (J). (gr. -1-3). 29.99 *(978-0-689-87769-8(2),* Little Simon) Little Simon.

—Opposites: A Bugs Pop-Up Concept Book. Carter, David A., illus. 2010. (David Carter's Bugs Ser.). (ENG., Illus.). 16p. (J). (gr. -1-1). 7.99 *(978-1-4424-0829-6(4),* Little Simon) Little Simon.

—School Bugs. Carter, David A., illus. 2009. (David Carter's Bugs Ser.). (ENG., Illus.). 20p. (J). (gr. -1-2). 12.99 *(978-1-4169-5056-1(7),* Little Simon) Little Simon.

—Spring: A Pop-up Book. 2016. (Seasons Pop-Up Ser.). (ENG., Illus.). 12p. (J). (gr. -1-k). 14.95 *(978-1-4197-1912-7(2),* Abrams Appleseed) Abrams, Inc.

—Welcome to Bugland! A Fun Foldout World from David A. Carter. Carter, David A., illus. 2011. (David Carter's Bugs Ser.). (ENG., Illus.). 24p. (J). (gr. -1-3). 12.99 *(978-1-4424-1962-9(8),* Little Simon) Little Simon.

—White Noise: A Pop-Up Book for Children of All Ages. Carter, David A., illus. 2009. (ENG., Illus.). 20p. (J). (gr. -1-3). 27.99 *(978-1-4169-4094-4(4),* Little Simon) Little Simon.

—Winter. 2015. (Seasons Pop-Up Ser.). (ENG., Illus.). 12p. (J). (gr. -1-k). 14.95 *(978-1-4197-1823-6(1),* Abrams Appleseed) Abrams, Inc.

—Yellow Square: A Pop-Up Book for Children of All Ages. Carter, David A., illus. 2008. (ENG., Illus.). 20p. (J). (gr. -1-3). 19.99 *(978-1-4169-4093-7(6),* Little Simon) Little Simon.

—The 12 Bugs of Christmas: A Pop-Up Christmas Counting Book. Carter, David A., illus. 2011. (David Carter's Bugs Ser.). (ENG., Illus.). 24p. (J). (gr. -1-1). 12.99 *(978-1-4424-2649-8(7),* Little Simon) Little Simon.

—600 Black Spots: A Pop-Up Book for Children of All Ages. Carter, David A., illus. 2007. (ENG., Illus.). 20p. (J). (gr. -1-2). 25.99 *(978-1-4169-4092-0(8),* Little Simon) Little Simon.

Carter, David A. & Diaz, James. You Call That Art?! Learn about Modern Sculpture & Make Your Own. 2014. (ENG., Illus.). 48p. (J). (gr. 3-7). 24.95 *(978-1-4197-1307-1(8),* Abrams Bks. for Young Readers) Abrams, Inc.

Cartlidge, Michelle. The Mouse Christmas House: A Press-Out Model Book. (Illus.). 32p. (J). *(978-1-904613-67-1(5),* Buster Bks.) O'Mara, Michael Bks., Ltd.

Cartogna, Eileen. Jobs Around Town: Learning to Sort & Classify. (Math for the Real World: Early Emergent Ser.). (ENG., Illus.). 8p. (gr. k-1). 2009. pap. 5.15 *(978-0-8239-8910-2(0))* 2004. 29.95 *(978-0-8239-7629-4(7))* Rosen Publishing Group, Inc., The.

Cartwright, Amy, illus. Jack & the Beanstalk. 2011. (J). pap. *(978-0-545-27434-0(6),* Cartwheel Bks.) Scholastic, Inc.

Cartwright, Mary, told to. Little Book of Little Puppies. 2011. (Baby's Very First Ser.). 10p. (J). ring bd. 6.99 *(978-0-7945-2957-4(7),* Usborne) EDC Publishing.

Cartwright, Shannon. Alaska 1 2 3: Colors & Numbers. 2005. (Illus.). (J). *(978-0-9772297-0-3(X))* Taku Graphics.

Casebolt, Christan. Zoey & Bel, 1 vol. Bentley, Anita, illus. 2009. 14p. pap. 24.95 *(978-1-60813-220-1(X))* America Star Bks.

Cassidy, John. The World According to Klutz. Klutz Editors, ed. 2013. (ENG.). 300p. (J). (gr. 3). pap. 14.99 *(978-0-545-61213-5(6))* Klutz.

Casteel, Seth. Underwater Doggies Colors. 2014. (ENG., Illus.). 18p. (J). (gr. -1 — 1). bds. 6.99 *(978-0-316-37365-4(6))* Little, Brown Bks. for Young Readers.

A Castle Mystery. 2013. (Illus.). (J). *(978-1-4351-4945-8(9))* Disney Pr.

Castles & Kingdoms. 2014. (Dream Doodle Draw! Ser.). (ENG., Illus.). 96p. (J). (gr. -1-2). pap. 7.99 *(978-1-4814-1712-9(6),* Little Simon) Little Simon.

Catholic Book Publishing Staff, creator. Saints Teach Us. 2008. (St. Joseph Rattle Board Bks.). (Illus.). 14p. (gr. -1-k). bds. 4.95 *(978-0-89942-723-2(5))* Catholic Bk. Publishing Corp.

—Thank You Prayers. 2008. (St. Joseph Rattle Board Bks.). (Illus.). 14p. (gr. -1-k). bds. 4.95 *(978-0-89942-722-5(7))* Catholic Bk. Publishing Corp.

Cats & Kittens Sticker Activity Book. (My Sticker Activity Ser.). (Illus.). 12p. (J). *(978-1-4054-1178-3(3))* Parragon, Inc.

Cat's Pyjamas. Haunted House: A Touch & Feel Spooky Tour. 2013. (ENG.). 22p. (J). (gr. -1-1). 12.99 *(978-0-7641-6641-9(7))* Barron's Educational Series, Inc.

Caviezel, Giovanni. The Christmas Star. Pagnoni, Roberta, illus. 2013. (ENG.). 10p. (J). (gr. -1 — 1). bds. 6.99 *(978-0-7641-6624-2(7))* Barron's Educational Series, Inc.

—Little Elf. Mesturini, Cristina, illus. 2012. (Mini People Shape Bks.). (ENG.). 10p. (J). bds. 4.99 *(978-0-7641-6577-1(1))* Barron's Educational Series, Inc.

—Little Gingerbread Man. Donati, Giuliana, illus. (Mini People Shape Bks.). (ENG.). 10p. (J). (gr. -1-2). 2014. bds. 4.99 *(978-0-7641-6735-5(9))* 2012. bds. 7.99 *(978-0-7641-6541-2(0))* Barron's Educational Series, Inc.

—Little Snowman. Mesturini, C., illus. 2014. (Mini People Shape Bks.). (ENG.). 10p. (J). (gr. -1-2). bds. 4.99 *(978-0-7641-6737-9(5))* Barron's Educational Series, Inc.

—My Own Human Body. Mesturini, Cristina, illus. 2012. (Little People Shape Bks.). (ENG.). 10p. (J). (gr. k-2). bds. 8.99 *(978-0-7641-6570-2(4))* Barron's Educational Series, Inc.

—Nurse. Mesturini, C., illus. 2011. (Mini People Shape Bks.). (ENG.). 10p. (J). bds. 5.99 *(978-0-7641-6440-8(6))* Barron's Educational Series, Inc.

—Pirates! Mesturini, C., illus. 2011. (Mini People Shape Bks.). (ENG.). 10p. (J). bds. 5.99 *(978-0-7641-6441-5(4))* Barron's Educational Series, Inc.

—Policeman's Safety Hints. 2013. (ENG.). 12p. (J). (gr. -1-2). bds. 8.99 *(978-0-7641-6721-8(9))* Barron's Educational Series, Inc.

—Princess. Mesturini, C., illus. 2008. (Little People Shape Bks.). (ENG.). 10p. (J). (gr. k-2). bds. 10.99 *(978-0-7641-6103-2(2))* Barron's Educational Series, Inc.

—Santa. Mesturini, Cristina, illus. 2012. (Mini People Shape Bks.). (ENG.). 10p. (J). bds. 4.99 *(978-0-7641-6578-8(X))* Barron's Educational Series, Inc.

—Santa's Toyshop. Rigo, Laura, illus. 2012. (ENG.). 10p. (J). (gr. -1-k). bds. 6.99 *(978-0-7641-6546-7(1))* Barron's Educational Series, Inc.

Caviezel, Giovanni. Little Bee. 2014. (Mini-Creatures Ser.). (ENG.). 8p. (J). (gr. -1 — 1). bds. 4.99 *(978-0-7641-6713-3(8))* Barron's Educational Series, Inc.

—Little Crab. 2014. (Mini-Creatures Ser.). (ENG.). 8p. (J). (gr. -1 — 1). bds. 4.99 *(978-0-7641-6714-0(6))* Barron's Educational Series, Inc.

—Little Snail. 2014. (Mini-Creatures Ser.). (ENG.). 8p. (J). (gr. -1 — 1). bds. 4.99 *(978-0-7641-6715-7(4))* Barron's Educational Series, Inc.

Cecil, Lauren & Scholastic, Inc. Staff. Party Time! Hill, Prescott, illus. 2011. (Lalaloopsy Ser.: 2). (ENG.). 24p. (J). (gr. -1-3). pap. 3.99 *(978-0-545-37998-4(9))* Scholastic, Inc.

Cerasini, Marc. Godzilla Saves America: A Monster Showdown In 3-D! Morgan, Tom & Mounts, Paul, illus. 2006. 20p. (J). (gr. k-4). reprint ed. 12.00 *(978-1-4223-5409-4(1))* DIANE Publishing Co.

Chandler, Shannon & Accord Publishing Staff. Colors. 2011. (ENG., Illus.). 10p. (J). bds. 10.99 *(978-1-4494-0831-2(1))* Andrews McMeel Publishing.

Chanukah Treats: For Kids, by Kids. 2009. (Illus.). 16p. (J). spiral bd. *(978-0-9772560-2-0(2))* Rite Life Limited.

Chapman, Jane. Is It Christmas Yet? Chapman, Jane, illus. 2015. (ENG., Illus.). 22p. (J). (gr. -1-2). bds. 8.99 *(978-1-58925-553-1(4))* Tiger Tales.

Chapman, Jason. Who's That Singing? A Pull-the-Tab Book. Chapman, Jason, illus. 2010. (ENG., Illus.). 12p. (J). (gr. -1-1). bds. 9.99 *(978-1-4169-8736-9(3),* Little Simon) Little Simon.

—Who's That Snoring? A Pull-the-Tab Bedtime Book. Chapman, Jason, illus. 2010. (ENG., Illus.). 12p. (J). (gr. -1-1). bds. 9.99 *(978-1-4169-8937-0(4),* Little Simon) Little Simon.

Charbonnel-Bojman, Severine. My Picture Book of Animals. 2012. (ENG., Illus.). 256p. (J). (gr. -1-k). 9.95 *(978-1-77085-112-2(7),* 9781770851122) Firefly Bks., Ltd.

Charles, Faustin. The Selfish Crocodile Counting Book. Terry, Michael, illus. l.t. ed. 2008. (ENG.). 12p. (J). (gr. k-k). bds. 8.95 *(978-0-7475-9238-9(1))* Bloomsbury Publishing Plc GBR. Dist: Independent Pubs. Group.

Charles, Faustin & Beynon-Davies, Paul. The Selfish Crocodile Book of Numbers. Terry, Michael, illus. 2012. (Selfish Crocodile Ser.). (ENG.). 12p. (J). (gr. -1-k). bds. 10.99 *(978-1-4088-1451-2(X),* 9781408814512, Bloomsbury USA Childrens) Bloomsbury Publishing USA.

Charles Santore & Williams, Margery. The Velveteen Rabbit Set: Or How Toys Become Real. gif. ed. 2014. (ENG.). 48p. (J). 24.95 *(978-1-60433-335-0(9),* Applesauce Pr.) Cider Mill Pr. Bk. Pubs., LLC.

Chatterton, Martin. Can Dogs Fly? Fido's Book of Pop-up Transportation Surprises. 2005. (Illus.). 12p. (J). (gr. k-4). reprint ed. 10.00 *(978-0-7567-8838-4(2))* DIANE Publishing Co.

Chedru, Delphine. What Happens When... 2013. (ENG., Illus.). 32p. (J). (gr. k-2). 15.95 *(978-1-84976-103-1(5))* Tate Publishing, Ltd. GBR. Dist: Abrams, Inc.

Chedru, Delphine & Duisit, Bernard. This or That? 2017. (Flip Flap Pop-Up Ser.: 0). (ENG., Illus.). 16p. (gr. -1-1). 14.95 *(978-0-500-65093-6(4),* 565093) Thames & Hudson.

Cheerios Counting Songs. 2004. (Illus.). (J). *(978-0-7853-9953-7(4))* Publications International, Ltd.

Cheetham, Stephen, illus. Off to the Park! 2014. (Tactile Bks.). (ENG.). 12p. (J). *(978-1-84643-502-7(1))* Child's Play International Ltd.

Child, Jeremy. Bunny. Davies, Caroline, illus. 2013. (Rock & Rattle Bks.). (ENG.). 8p. (J). (gr. -1 — 1). bds. 3.99 *(978-0-7641-6589-4(5))* Barron's Educational Series, Inc.

—Kitty. Davies, Caroline, illus. 2013. (Rock & Rattle Bks.). (ENG.). 8p. (J). (gr. -1 — 1). bds. 3.99 *(978-0-7641-6590-0(9))* Barron's Educational Series, Inc.

—Mouse. Davies, Caroline, illus. 2013. (Rock & Rattle Bks.). (ENG.). 8p. (J). (gr. -1 — 1). bds. 3.99 *(978-0-7641-6591-7(7))* Barron's Educational Series, Inc.

—Puppy. Davies, Caroline, illus. 2013. (Rock & Rattle Bks.). (ENG.). 8p. (J). (gr. -1 — 1). bds. 3.99 *(978-0-7641-6592-4(5))* Barron's Educational Series, Inc.

—Santa. Leach, Emma, illus. 2010. (Snow Shakers Ser.). (ENG.). 8p. (J). (gr. -1-k). bds. 4.99 *(978-0-7641-6384-5(1))* Barron's Educational Series, Inc.

Child, Lydia Maria. Bitty Bear's Sleigh Ride. Ackley, Peggy Jo, illus. 2006. (J). *(978-1-59369-157-8(2))* American Girl Publishing, Inc.

Child's Play Staff. Spring. Busby, Ailie, illus. 2015. (Seasons Ser.: 4). (ENG.). 12p. (J). (gr. 1-1). bds. *(978-1-84643-741-0(5))* Child's Play International Ltd.

—Summer. Busby, Ailie, illus. 2015. (Seasons Ser.: 4). (ENG.). 12p. (J). (gr. 1-1). bds. *(978-1-84643-742-7(3))* Child's Play International Ltd.

—What's That Noise? CHOO! CHOO! Guess the Vehicle! Cocoretto, illus. 2015. (What's That Noise? Ser.: 4). (ENG.). 12p. (J). bds. *(978-1-84643-746-5(6))* Child's Play International Ltd.

—What's That Noise? SNAP! SNAP! Guess the Animal! Cocoretto, illus. 2015. (What's That Noise? Ser.: 4). (ENG.). 12p. (J). bds. *(978-1-84643-748-9(2))* Child's Play International Ltd.

—What's That Noise? TAP! TAP! Guess the Toy! Cocoretto, illus. 2015. (What's That Noise? Ser.: 4). (ENG.). 12p. (J). bds. *(978-1-84643-747-2(4))* Child's Play International Ltd.

—What's That Noise? TOOT! TOOT! Guess the Instrument! Cocoretto, illus. 2015. (What's That Noise? Ser.: 4). (ENG.). 12p. (J). bds. *(978-1-84643-749-6(0))* Child's Play International Ltd.

—Winter. Busby, Ailie, illus. 2015. (Seasons Ser.: 4). (ENG.). 12p. (J). (gr. 1-1). bds. *(978-1-84643-745-8(8))* Child's Play International Ltd.

Chilek, Laurie. Counting at the Zoo: Learning to Add 1 to One-Digit Numbers. (Math for the Real World Ser.). (ENG., Illus.). 8p. (gr. k-1). 2009. pap. 5.15 *(978-0-8239-8909-6(7))* 2004. 29.95 *(978-0-8239-7628-7(9))* Rosen Publishing Group, Inc., The.

Chorkung, illus. Sea Creatures. 2017. (First Explorers Ser.). (ENG.). 10p. (J). (— 1). bds. 8.95 ***(978-1-4549-2658-0(9))*** Sterling Publishing Co., Inc.

Chouette Publishing Staff & Paradis, Anne. Caillou: My Little Bed. Sévigny, Eric, illus. 2012. (ENG.). 10p. (J). (gr. -1-k). 9.99 *(978-2-89450-951-7(0))* Caillouet, Gerry.

Christelow, Eileen. Cinco Monitos Hacen un Pastel de Cumpleanos. 2014. (Five Little Monkeys Story Ser.).Tr. of Five Little Monkeys Bake a Birthday Cake. (ENG & SPA., Illus.). 30p. (J). (— 1). bds. 7.99 *(978-0-544-08899-3(9),* HMH Books For Young Readers) Houghton Mifflin Harcourt Publishing Co.

—Five Little Monkeys Jumping on the Bed (board Book) 2017. (Five Little Monkeys Story Ser.). (ENG., Illus.). 30p. (J). (— 1). bds. 7.99 ***(978-1-328-88456-5(2),*** HMH Books For Young Readers) Houghton Mifflin Harcourt Publishing Co.

—Five Little Monkeys Jumping on the Bed Lap Board Book. 2008. (Five Little Monkeys Story Ser.). (ENG., Illus.). 30p. (J). (gr. -1 — 1). bds. 12.99 *(978-0-547-13176-4(3))* Houghton Mifflin Harcourt Publishing Co.

—Five Little Monkeys Reading in Bed. 2014. (Five Little Monkeys Story Ser.). (ENG., Illus.). 34p. (J). (— 1). bds. 7.99 *(978-0-544-17330-9(9),* HMH Books For Young Readers) Houghton Mifflin Harcourt Publishing Co.

—Five Little Monkeys Trick-Or-Treat. 2015. (Five Little Monkeys Story Ser.). (ENG., Illus.). 36p. (J). (— 1). bds. 7.99 *(978-0-544-43062-4(X),* HMH Books For Young Readers) Houghton Mifflin Harcourt Publishing Co.

—Jumping on the Bed. 2017. (Five Little Monkeys Story Ser.). (ENG., Illus.). 30p. (J). (gr. -1 — 1). bds. 8.99 *(978-0-547-51075-0(6),* HMH Books For Young Readers) Houghton Mifflin Harcourt Publishing Co.

Christensen, Catherine, told to. Blessing the Nephite Children. 2016. (ENG.). (J). bds. 10.99 *(978-1-4621-1875-5(5))* Cedar Fort, Inc./CFI Distribution.

Christian, Cheryl. How Many? (Portuguese/English), 1 vol. Dwight, Laura, photos by. 2009. (ENG & POR., Illus.). 12p. (J). 5.95 (978-1-59572-190-7(8)) Star Bright Bks., Inc.
—What Happens Next? (Haitian Creole/English), 1 vol. Dwight, Laura, photos by. 2005. (ENG & HAT., Illus.). 12p. (J). (gr. -1). 5.95 (978-1-59572-025-2(1)) Star Bright Bks., Inc.
—What Happens Next? (Traditional Cantonese) Dwight, Laura, photos by. 2004. (CHI., Illus.). 12p. (J). bds. 5.95 (978-1-932065-63-3(6)) Star Bright Bks., Inc.
—Where Does It Go? (Haitian Creole/English), 1 vol. Dwight, Laura, photos by. 2005. (CRP & ENG., Illus.). 12p. (J). 5.95 (978-1-59572-026-9(X)) Star Bright Bks., Inc.
—Where Does It Go? (Spanish/English), 1 vol. Fiol, Maria A., tr. 2004. (Photoflaps Ser.). (ENG & SPA., Illus.). 32p. (J). bds. 5.50 (978-1-932065-59-6(8), 7187849112) Star Bright Bks., Inc.
—Where's the Baby? (Haitian Creole/English), 1 vol. Dwight, Laura, photos by. 2005. (Photoflaps Ser.). (HAT & ENG., Illus.). 12p. (J). (gr. -1). 5.95 (978-1-59572-027-6(8)) Star Bright Bks., Inc.
—Where's the Baby? (Traditional Cantonese) Dwight, Laura, photos by. 2004. (CHI., Illus.). 12p. (J). bds. 5.95 (978-1-932065-62-6(8)) Star Bright Bks., Inc.
—Where's the Kitten? (Haitian Creole/English), 1 vol. Dwight, Laura, photos by. 2005. (Photoflaps Ser.). (HAT & ENG., Illus.). 12p. (J). (gr. -1). 5.95 (978-1-59572-028-3(6)) Star Bright Bks., Inc.
—Where's the Kitten? (Russian/English), 1 vol. Dwight, Laura, photos by. 2004. (RUS & ENG., Illus.). 12p. (J). 5.95 (978-1-932065-84-8(9)) Star Bright Bks., Inc.
—Where's the Kitten? (Traditional Cantonese), 1 vol. Dwight, Laura, photos by. 2004. (CHI & ENG., Illus.). 12p. (J). 5.95 (978-1-932065-60-2(1)) Star Bright Bks., Inc.
—Where's the Puppy? (Haitian Creole/English), 1 vol. Dwight, Laura, photos by. 2005. (Photoflaps Ser.). (HAT & ENG., Illus.). 12p. (J). (gr. -1). 5.95 (978-1-59572-029-0(4)) Star Bright Bks., Inc.
—Where's the Puppy? (Russian/English), 1 vol. Dwight, Laura, photos by. 2005. (Photo Flap Bks.). (RUS & ENG., Illus.). 12p. (J). 5.95 (978-1-932065-85-5(7)) Star Bright Bks., Inc.
—Where's the Puppy? (Traditional Cantonese) Dwight, Laura, photos by. 2004. (CHI., Illus.). 12p. (J). bds. 5.95 (978-1-932065-61-9(X)) Star Bright Bks., Inc.
Christine Battuz, Christine, illus. Goodnight, Sleepy Animals: A Nightlight Book. 2016. (Nightlight Ser.). (ENG.). 14p. (J). (gr. -1-k). 12.99 (978-2-89718-338-7(1)) CrackBoom! Bks. CAN. Dist: Publishers Group West (PGW).
Christmas. (Illus.). (gr. 1-4). 3.00 (978-0-570-05521-1(0), 54-1031) Concordia Publishing Hse.
The Christmas Carol Book. (Illus.). 10p. (J). bds. (978-2-89393-929-2(5)) Phidal Publishing, Inc./Editions Phidal, Inc.
The Christmas Journey Storybook, 1 vol. 2014. (ENG., Illus.). 6p. (J). bds. 19.99 (978-1-78128-139-0(4), Candle Bks.) Lion Hudson PLC GBR. Dist: Kregel Pubns.
Christmas Stable, 1 vol. 2014. (Candle Tiny Tots Ser.). (ENG., Illus.). 16p. (J). 11.99 (978-1-78128-122-2(X), Candle Bks.) Lion Hudson PLC GBR. Dist: Kregel Pubns.
Chronicle Books Staff. New York, Baby! Jenkins, Ward, illus. 2012. (ENG.). 24p. (J). (gr. -1 — 1). 12.99 (978-1-4521-0619-9(3)) Chronicle Bks. LLC.
—Nick Jr. Nursery Rhyme Time: A Touch-and-See Activity Book. (J). 15.95 (978-0-8118-4726-1(8)) Chronicle Bks. LLC.
—San Francisco, Baby! Jenkins, Ward, illus. 2012. (ENG.). 24p. (J). (gr. -1 — 1). 12.99 (978-1-4521-0620-5(7)) Chronicle Bks. LLC.
Chronicle Books Staff & Frank, Paul. Julius!, Kit. 2009. (ENG.). 48p. (J). (gr. -1-2). act. bk. ed. 14.95 (978-0-8118-6095-6(7)) Chronicle Bks. LLC.
Chronicle Books Staff & Image Books Staff. Little Cat: Finger Puppet Book. Put, Klaartje van der, illus. 2014. (Little Finger Puppet Board Bks.). (ENG.). 12p. (J). (gr. -1 — 1). bds. 6.99 (978-1-4521-2916-7(9)) Chronicle Bks. LLC.
Chronicle Books Staff & ImageBooks Staff. Little Bee. van der Put, Klaartje, illus. 2006. (Little Finger Puppet Board Bks.: FING). (ENG.). 12p. (J). (gr. -1-7). bds. 6.99 (978-0-8118-5236-4(9)) Chronicle Bks. LLC.
—Little Moose: Finger Puppet Book. Put, Klaartje van der, illus. 2015. (ENG.). 12p. (J). (gr. -1 — 1). bds. 6.99 (978-1-4521-4231-9(9)) Chronicle Bks. LLC.
Chronicle Books Staff, et al. Little Reindeer. 2006. (Little Finger Puppet Board Bks.: FING). (ENG., Illus.). 12p. (J). (gr. -1 — 1). bds. 6.99 (978-0-8118-5457-3(4)) Chronicle Bks. LLC.
Church, Caroline Jayne. Giggle! Church, Caroline Jayne, illus. 2013. (ENG., Illus.). 10p. (J). (— 1). bds. 7.99 (978-0-545-35082-2(4), Cartwheel Bks.) Scholastic, Inc.
—I Am a Big Brother! 2015. (SPA & ENG.). 24p. (J). (gr. -1 — 1). 6.99 (978-0-545-84717-9(6), Scholastic en Espanol) Scholastic, Inc.
—I Am a Big Brother! Church, Caroline Jayne, illus. 2015. (ENG., Illus.). 24p. (J). (gr. -1 — 1). 6.99 (978-0-545-68886-4(8), Cartwheel Bks.) Scholastic, Inc.
—I Am a Big Sister! 2015. (SPA & ENG.). 24p. (J). (gr. -1 — 1). 6.99 (978-0-545-84718-6(4), Scholastic en Espanol) Scholastic, Inc.
—I Am a Big Sister! Church, Caroline Jayne, illus. 2015. (ENG., Illus.). 24p. (J). (gr. -1 — 1). 6.99 (978-0-545-68898-7(1), Cartwheel Bks.) Scholastic, Inc.
—I Love My Dinosaur. 2015. (Love Meez Ser.: 2). (ENG., Illus.). 10p. (J). (gr. -1 — 1). bds. 7.99 (978-0-545-83592-3(5), Cartwheel Bks.) Scholastic, Inc.
—I Love My Puppy. Church, Caroline Jayne, illus. 2015. (Love Meez Ser.). (ENG., Illus.). 10p. (J). (gr. -1 — 1). bds. 7.99 (978-0-545-83594-7(1), Cartwheel Bks.) Scholastic, Inc.
—I Will Love You Forever. 2016. (ENG.). 22p. (J). (gr. -1-k). bds. 8.99 (978-0-545-94200-3(4), Cartwheel Bks.) Scholastic, Inc.
—Ten Tiny Toes. Church, Caroline Jayne, illus. 2014. (ENG., Illus.). 22p. (J). (— 1). bds. 8.99 (978-0-545-53601-1(4), Cartwheel Bks.) Scholastic, Inc.
Chwast, Seymour. Tall City, Wide Country. Chwast, Seymour, illus. 2013. (ENG., Illus.). 32p. (J). (gr. -1-k). 15.99 (978-1-56846-228-8(X), Creative Editions) Creative Co., The.
Ciminera, Siobhan & Rao, Lisa. Hello, Friends! Yoe! Studio Staff, illus. 2009. (Yo Gabba Gabba! Ser.). (ENG.). 64p. (J). 4.99 (978-1-4169-7460-4(1), Simon Scribbles) Simon Scribbles.
Cinderella. 2009. (Disney Glitter Board Book Ser.). 5p. (978-1-4054-9824-1(2)) Parragon, Inc.
City. (Busy Books Large Ser.). 5p. (978-1-4054-9500-4(6)) Parragon, Inc.
Civardi, Anna. New Puppy Sticker Book. 2009. (First Experiences Sticker Book Ser.). 16p. (J). pap. 6.99 (978-0-7945-2573-6(3), Usborne) EDC Publishing.
Civardi, Anne. Going to the Dentist. 2010. (First Experiences Ser.). 16p. (J). pap. 4.99 (978-0-7945-2592-7(X), Usborne) EDC Publishing.
Clairmont, Patsy. Sleep Sweet, My Little One, 1 vol. Johannes, Shelley, illus. 2014. (ENG.). 24p. (J). bds. 12.99 (978-1-4003-2401-9(7)) Nelson, Thomas Inc.
Clark, M. H. I Am... 2011. (Growth Chart Bks.). (Illus.). (gr. -1-5). bds. 8.95 (978-1-935414-06-3(2)) Compendium, Inc., Publishing & Communications.
—I Can... 2011. (Growth Chart Bks.). (Illus.). (gr. -1-5). bds. 8.95 (978-1-932319-81-1(6)) Compendium, Inc., Publishing & Communications.
Clarke, Jane. Creaky Castle. Fox, Christyan, illus. 2013. (978-1-4351-4951-9(3)) Barnes & Noble, Inc.
—How to Bathe Your Little Dino. Birkett, Georgie, illus. 2017. 16p. (J). bds. 8.99 (978-1-61067-495-9(2)) Kane Miller.
—How to Feed Your Cheeky Monkey. Birkett, Georgie, illus. 2017. 16p. (J). bds. 8.99 (978-1-61067-497-3(9)) Kane Miller.
Clarke, Phil. Sharks. 2005. (Usborne Lift the Flap Bks.). (Illus.). 16p. (J). (gr. -1-3). 11.99 (978-0-7945-1109-8(0), Usborne) EDC Publishing.
Clarke, Phillip & Furnival, Keith. Sharks. Scott, Peter David, illus. 2005. (J). (978-0-439-86358-2(9)) Scholastic, Inc.
Clifford the Best Helper. (Illus.). 10p. (J). bds. 9.98 (978-0-7853-9948-3(8), 7208900) Publications International, Ltd.
Coat, Janik. Hippopposites. 2012. (ENG., Illus.). 38p. (J). (gr. -1 — 1). bds. 15.95 (978-1-4197-0151-1(7), Abrams Appleseed) Abrams, Inc.
Cocoretto, illus. In the Jungle. 2016. (Peekaboo! Ser.: 4). (ENG.). 12p. (J). bds. (978-1-84643-866-0(7)) Child's Play International Ltd.
—On the Farm. 2016. (Peekaboo! Ser.: 4). (ENG.). 12p. (J). bds. (978-1-84643-864-6(0)) Child's Play International Ltd.
Coffey, Michele. Let's Look at Leopards. 2003. (Real Readers - Upper Emergent Ser.). (ENG., Illus.). 12p. (gr. 1-2). pap. 5.90 (978-0-8239-6362-1(4)) Rosen Publishing Group, Inc., The.
Cohen, Alana. Heroes! White, David A., illus. 2011. (Lego City Ser.). (ENG.). 10p. (J). (gr. -1-k). bds. 9.99 (978-0-545-27439-5(7)) Scholastic, Inc.
Cohen, Miriam. Daddy's Busy Day, 1 vol. 2014. (ENG.). 32p. (J). bds. (978-1-59572-668-1(3)) Star Bright Bks., Inc.
Cohn, Arlen. Firsts. Vasconcellos, Daniel, illus. gif. ed. 2004. (ENG.). 28p. (J). bds. 9.99 (978-1-57939-168-3(0)) Andrews McMeel Publishing.
Coirault, Christine, illus. My First Book of Learning. 2009. (J). (978-1-74089-930-7(X)) Fog City Pr.
Coleman, Michelle, compiled by. My Pets. 2012. (Touch & Feel Ser.). (ENG., Illus.). 10p. (J). (— 1). bds. 12.95 (978-1-61889-221-8(5)) AZ Bks. LLC.
—Wild Animals. 2013. (Touch & Feel Ser.). (ENG., Illus.). 10p. (J). (— 1). bds. 12.95 (978-1-61889-209-6(6)) AZ Bks. LLC.
Collins, Elaine Banks. I Like Dressing Up. Floyd, John, Jr., illus. 2005. (J). bds. 5.95 (978-0-9752860-5-0(6)) OurRainbow Pr., LLC.
—See What I Can Do. Floyd, John, Jr., illus. 2006. 10p. (J). (gr. -1). bds. 5.95 (978-0-9752860-4-3(8)) OurRainbow Pr., LLC.
Collins Thoms, Susan. Noah's Ark. Stoop, Naoko, illus. 2013. (ENG.). 22p. (J). (— 1). bds. 6.95 (978-1-4027-8549-8(6)) Sterling Publishing Co., Inc.
Collison, Shauna. Heavenites Angels to Zebras Board Book with Audio CD. Nelson, Christine, illus. 2007. 26p. (J). 15.95 (978-0-9792510-0-9(1)) Revelation Products LLC.
Colman, Michelle Sinclair. Not That Tutu! Nakata, Hiroe, illus. 2013. (ENG.). 20p. (J). (— 1). bds. 7.99 (978-0-307-97698-7(X), Robin Corey Bks.) Random Hse. Children's Bks.
Combes, Mélanie, illus. Hello! Farm. 2016. (Hello! Ser.). (ENG.). 10p. (J). (gr. -1-k). bds. 16.99 (978-1-4472-7719-4(8)) Pan Macmillan GBR. Dist: Independent Pubs. Group.
Cooke, Brandy. Cupcakes! A Sweet Treat with More Than 200 Stickers. Kramer, Connie, photos by. 2011. (ENG., Illus.). 18p. (J). (gr. -1-k). bds. 6.99 (978-1-4424-2825-6(2), Little Simon) Little Simon.
—What's Following Us? Reasoner, Charles & Reasoner, John, illus. 2011. (ENG.). 20p. (J). (gr. -1 — 1). bds. 6.99 (978-1-4169-9673-6(7), Little Simon) Little Simon.
Coombs, Kate. Goodnight Mr. Darcy Board Book, 1 vol. Arnold, Alli, illus. 2015. (ENG.). 22p. (J). bds. 9.99 (978-1-4236-4177-3(9)) Gibbs Smith, Publisher.
Coombs, Kate & Austen, Jane. Goodnight Mr. Darcy: A Babylit Parody, 1 vol. 2014. (ENG., Illus.). 32p. (J). 16.99 (978-1-4236-3670-0(8)) Gibbs Smith, Publisher.
Cooney, Caroline B. I'm Going to Give You a Bear Hug!, 1 vol. Warnes, Tim, illus. 2016. (ENG.). 32p. (J). 16.99 (978-0-310-75473-2(9)) Zonderkidz.
Copenhagen Publishing Company, prod. Noah's Big Boat. 2015. (ENG.). 10p. (J). 4.99 (978-1-4964-0463-3(7), Tyndale Kids) Tyndale Hse. Pubs.
Corderoy, Tracey. It's Potty Time! Pedler, Caroline, illus. 2014. (ENG.). 22p. (J). (gr. -1-k). bds. 8.99 (978-1-58925-574-6(7)) Tiger Tales.
—Now! Warnes, Tim, illus. 2016. (ENG.). 32p. (J). (gr. -1-2). 16.99 (978-1-68010-033-4(5)) Tiger Tales.
Corke, Estelle, illus. The Gingerbread Man. 2007. (Flip-Up Fairy Tales Ser.). (ENG.). 24p. (J). audio compact disk (978-1-84643-144-9(1)); (gr. -1-2). (978-1-84643-078-7(X)) Child's Play International Ltd.
—Goldilocks & the Three Bears. (Flip-Up Fairy Tales Ser.). (ENG.). 24p. (J). 2007. (gr. -1-2). audio compact disk (978-1-84643-085-5(2)) 2005. (gr. 1-2). pap. (978-1-904550-19-8(3)) Child's Play International Ltd.
Corrigan, Kathleen. ABC, 1 vol. 2014. (Canadian Board Bks.). (ENG & FRE.). 20p. bds. 7.99 (978-1-62370-223-6(2)) Capstone Young Readers of Coughlan Cos.
—My First Colours, 1 vol. 2015. (Maple Leaf Learners Ser.). (ENG.). 20p. bds. 7.99 (978-1-62370-222-9(4)) Capstone Young Readers of Coughlan Cos.
—My First Shapes, 1 vol. 2015. (Maple Leaf Learners Ser.). (ENG.). 20p. bds. 7.99 (978-1-62370-221-2(6)) Capstone Young Readers of Coughlan Cos.
Cosgrove, Stephen. Good Night, Wheedle. James, Robin, illus. 2016. (ENG.). 20p. (J). (— 1). bds. 9.99 (978-1-63217-075-0(2), Little Bigfoot) Sasquatch Bks.
Cosmic Debris Etc., Inc. Staff, et al. Little Giraffe: Finger Puppet Book. 2009. (Little Finger Puppet Board Bks.). (ENG., Illus.). 12p. (J). (gr. -1 — 1). bds. 6.99 (978-0-8118-6787-0(0)) Chronicle Bks. LLC.
—Little Lion. 2009. (Little Finger Puppet Board Bks.). (ENG., Illus.). 12p. (J). (gr. -1 — 1). bds. 6.99 (978-0-8118-6788-7(9)) Chronicle Bks. LLC.
Cosneau, Olivia. Birds of the World: My Nature Sticker Activity Book. 2017. (ENG.). 24p. (J). (gr. k-3). pap. 7.99 (978-1-61689-566-2(7)) Princeton Architectural Pr.
—In the Age of Dinosaurs: My Nature Sticker Activity Book. 2016. (ENG., Illus.). 24p. (J). (gr. k-3). pap. 7.99 (978-1-61689-469-6(5)) Princeton Architectural Pr.
—In the Vegetable Garden: My Nature Sticker Activity Book. 2017. (ENG.). 24p. (J). (gr. k-3). pap. 7.99 (978-1-61689-571-6(3)) Princeton Architectural Pr.
Cosneau, Olivia & Duisit, Bernard. What's Up? 2017. (Flip Flap Pop-Up Ser.: 0). (ENG., Illus.). 16p. (gr. -1-1). 14.95 (978-0-500-65092-9(6), 565092) Thames & Hudson.
Costain, Meredith. Daddies Are Awesome. Lovsin, Polona, illus. 2017. (ENG.). 28p. (J). bds. 7.99 (978-1-250-10720-6(2), 9781250107206, Holt, Henry & Co. Bks. For Young Readers) Holt, Henry & Co.
Costamagna, Beatrice, illus. Crocodile Snap! 2016. (Crunchy Board Bks.). (ENG.). 12p. (J). (gr. -1-1). bds. 6.99 (978-1-4998-0201-6(3)) Little Bee Books Inc.
—Polar Bear Munch! 2016. (Crunchy Board Bks.). (ENG.). 12p. (J). (gr. -1 — 1). bds. 6.99 (978-1-4998-0345-7(1)) Little Bee Books Inc.
Cotter, Bill. Don't Push the Button! 2015. (ENG., Illus.). 24p. (J). (-3). bds. 8.99 (978-1-4926-0763-2(0)) Sourcebooks, Inc.
Cotton, Katie. Counting Lions: Portraits from the Wild. Walton, Stephen, illus. 2015. (ENG.). 40p. (J). (gr. k-12). 22.00 (978-0-7636-8207-1(1)) Candlewick Pr.
Count to Ten. (J). 26.20 (978-0-8136-8411-6(0)); 26.20 (978-0-8136-8410-9(2)); (gr. -1-3). 59.50 (978-0-8136-7942-6(7)) Modern Curriculum Pr.
Counting Cards Staff. LP-Counting: Level 1 Math. 2004. (ENG.). (J). 9.99 (978-1-59204-013-1(6)) Learning Wrap-Ups, Inc.
Coupe, Robert. Antiguo Egipto/Acient Egypt. 2011. 16p. pap. (978-607-404-320-4(5), Silver Dolphin en Español) Advanced Marketing, S. de R. L. de C. V.
Cousins, Lucy. Beep, Beep, Maisy! Cousins, Lucy, illus. 2017. (Maisy Ser.). (ENG., Illus.). 16p. (J). (-k). bds. 12.99 **(978-0-7636-9407-4(X))** Candlewick Pr.
—Count with Maisy, Cheep, Cheep, Cheep! Cousins, Lucy, illus. 2015. (Maisy Ser.). (ENG., Illus.). 32p. (J). (-k). 15.99 (978-0-7636-7643-8(8)) Candlewick Pr.
—Maisy Goes to Bed. Cousins, Lucy, illus. 2016. (Maisy Ser.). (ENG., Illus.). 16p. (J). (gr. -1-2). 14.99 (978-0-7636-9249-0(2)) Candlewick Pr.
—Maisy Goes to Preschool: A Maisy First Experiences Book. Cousins, Lucy, illus. 2010. (Maisy Ser.). (ENG., Illus.). 32p. (J). (gr. k-k). pap. 6.99 (978-0-7636-5086-5(2)) Candlewick Pr.
—Maisy's Bus. Cousins, Lucy, illus. 2017. (Maisy Ser.). (ENG., Illus.). 18p. (J). (— 1). bds. 5.99 (978-0-7636-9406-7(1)) Candlewick Pr.
—Maisy's Digger: A Go with Maisy Board Book. Cousins, Lucy, illus. 2015. (Maisy Ser.). (ENG., Illus.). 18p. (J). (— 1). bds. 5.99 (978-0-7636-8010-7(9)) Candlewick Pr.
—Maisy's First Clock. Cousins, Lucy, illus. 2011. (Maisy Ser.). (ENG., Illus.). 16p. (J). (gr. k-k). bds. 14.99 (978-0-7636-5095-7(1)) Candlewick Pr.
—Maisy's First Colors: A Maisy Concept Book. Cousins, Lucy, illus. 2013. (Maisy Ser.). (ENG., Illus.). 14p. (J). (-k). bds. 6.99 (978-0-7636-6804-4(4)) Candlewick Pr.
—Maisy's First Numbers: A Maisy Concept Book. Lucy Cousins, illus. 2013. (Maisy Ser.). (ENG.). 14p. (J). (-k). bds. 6.99 (978-0-7636-6805-1(2)) Candlewick Pr.
—Maisy's Pirate Ship: A Pop-Up-and-Play Book. Cousins, Lucy, illus. 2015. (Maisy Ser.). (ENG., Illus.). 10p. (J). (-k). 16.99 (978-0-7636-7941-5(0)) Candlewick Pr.
—Maisy's Race Car: A Go with Maisy Board Book. Cousins, Lucy, illus. 2015. (Maisy Ser.). (ENG., Illus.). 18p. (J). (— 1). bds. 5.99 (978-0-7636-8011-4(7)) Candlewick Pr.
—Maisy's Tractor. Cousins, Lucy, illus. 2015. (Maisy Ser.). (ENG., Illus.). 18p. (J). (— 1). bds. 5.99 (978-0-7636-7305-5(6)) Candlewick Pr.
—Maisy's Valentine Sticker Book. Cousins, Lucy, illus. 2005. (Maisy Ser.). (ENG., Illus.). 16p. (J). (gr. k-k). pap. 4.99 (978-0-7636-2713-3(5)) Candlewick Pr.
—Maisy's Wonderful Weather Book. 2011. (Maisy Ser.). (ENG., Illus.). 16p. (J). (gr. -1-2). 14.99 (978-0-7636-5096-4(X)) Candlewick Pr.
—Sweet Dreams, Maisy. Cousins, Lucy, illus. 2009. (Maisy Ser.). (ENG., Illus.). 32p. (J). (gr. -1-2). bds. 6.99 (978-0-7636-4532-8(X)) Candlewick Pr.
—Where Are Maisy's Friends? Cousins, Lucy, illus. 2010. (Maisy Ser.). (ENG., Illus.). 12p. (J). (-k). bds. 5.99 (978-0-7636-4669-1(5)) Candlewick Pr.
—Where Does Maisy Live? 2010. 12p. bds. 4.99 (978-976-3-64668-7(5)) Candlewick Pr.
—Where Does Maisy Live? Cousins, Lucy, illus. 2010. (Maisy Ser.). (ENG., Illus.). 12p. (J). (-k). bds. 5.99 (978-0-7636-4668-4(7)) Candlewick Pr.
—Where Is Maisy? Cousins, Lucy, illus. 2010. (Maisy Ser.). (ENG., Illus.). 14p. (J). (gr. k-k). bds. 5.99 (978-0-7636-4673-8(3)) Candlewick Pr.
Cousins, Lucy, illus. Bedtime Rhymes. 2015. (First Nursery Rhymes Ser.). (ENG.). 16p. (J). (-k). bds. 9.99 (978-1-4472-6106-3(2)) Pan Macmillan GBR. Dist: Independent Pubs. Group.
—Nursery Rhymes. 2015. (First Nursery Rhymes Ser.). (ENG.). 16p. (J). (-k). bds. 9.99 (978-1-4472-6105-6(4)) Pan Macmillan GBR. Dist: Independent Pubs. Group.
Covello, Paul. Canada 123. 2017. 30p. (J). (gr. -1-k). bds. 10.50 **(978-1-4434-5381-3(1),** Harper Trophy) HarperCollins Pubs.
Cowley, Joy. Freddy Bear & the Beach. Webb, Philip, illus. 2016. (Freddy Bear Ser.). (ENG.). 20p. (J). (gr. -1-k). bds. 12.99 (978-1-927262-56-6(9)) Upstart Pr. NZL. Dist: Independent Pubs. Group.
—Freddy Bear & the Green Peas. Webb, Philip, illus. 2016. (Freddy Bear Ser.). (ENG.). 20p. (J). (gr. -1-k). bds. 12.99 (978-1-927262-57-3(7)) Upstart Pr. NZL. Dist: Independent Pubs. Group.
—Mrs. WishyWashy & the Big Tub. 2009. pap. 8.25 (978-1-60559-233-6(1)) Hameray Publishing Group, Inc.
Cox, Katie, des. Little Hands Colors. 2009. (Little Hands (Make Believe Ideas) Ser.). (ENG., Illus.). 24p. (gr. -1-k). 6.99 (978-1-84610-959-1(0)) Make Believe Ideas GBR. Dist: Nelson, Thomas Inc.
—Little Hands First Words. 2009. (Little Hands (Make Believe Ideas) Ser.). (ENG., Illus.). 24p. (gr. -1-k). 6.99 (978-1-84610-957-7(4)) Make Believe Ideas GBR. Dist: Nelson, Thomas Inc.
—Little Hands Trucks. 2009. (Little Hands (Make Believe Ideas) Ser.). (Illus.). 24p. (gr. -1-k). 6.99 (978-1-84610-963-6(3)) Make Believe Ideas GBR. Dist: Nelson, Thomas Inc.
Cox, Katie & Make Believe Ideas Staff. Little Hands Animals. 2009. (Little Hands Ser.). (Illus.). 24p. (gr. -1-k). 6.99 (978-1-84610-958-4(2)) Make Believe Ideas GBR. Dist: Nelson, Thomas Inc.
Cox, Phil Roxbee. Big Pig on a Dig. Tyler, Jenny, ed. Cartwright, Stephen, illus. rev. ed. 2006. (Phonics Readers Ser.). 16p. (J). (gr. -1-3). pap. 6.99 (978-0-7945-1501-0(0), Usborne) EDC Publishing.
—Curly's Friends. Cartwright, Stephen, illus. rev. ed. 2005. (Usborne Farmyard Tales Touchy-Feely Ser.). 10p. (J). (gr. -1-k). bds. 7.95 (978-0-7945-1180-7(5), Usborne) EDC Publishing.
—Frog on a Log. Tyler, Jenny, ed. Cartwright, Stephen, illus. rev. ed. 2006. (Phonics Readers Ser.). 16p. (J). (gr. -1). pap. 6.99 (978-0-7945-1504-1(5), Usborne) EDC Publishing.
—Hen's Pens. Tyler, Jenny, ed. Cartwright, Stephen, illus. rev. ed. 2006. (Phonics Readers Ser.). 16p. (J). (gr. -1-3). pap. 6.99 (978-0-7945-1506-5(1), Usborne) EDC Publishing.
Cox, Phil Roxbee & Cartwright, S. Rusty's Bone. 2004. (Farmyard Tales Touchy Feely Board Bks.). (ENG., Illus.). 1p. (J). bds. 7.95 (978-0-7945-0012-2(9), Usborne) EDC Publishing.
—Wolly's Walk. 2004. (Farmyard Tales Touchy Feely Board Bks.). (ENG., Illus.). 1p. (J). bds. 7.95 (978-0-7945-0039-9(0), Usborne) EDC Publishing.
Cox, Phil Roxbee & Cartwright, Stephen. Frog on a Log. 2004. (Easy Words to Read Ser.). (Illus.). 16p. (J). (gr. 1-18). pap. 6.95 (978-0-7945-0114-3(1), Usborne) EDC Publishing.
—Hen's Pens. 2004. (Easy Words to Read Ser.). (Illus.). 16p. (J). (gr. 1-18). pap. 6.95 (978-0-7945-0113-6(3), Usborne) EDC Publishing.
—Shark in the Park. 2004. (Easy Words to Read Ser.). (Illus.). 16p. (J). (gr. 1-18). pap. 6.95 (978-0-7945-0171-6(0), Usborne) EDC Publishing.
Coxon, Michele. Where's My Kitten? (Illus.). 16p. (J). pap. 5.95 (978-1-903285-02-2(X)) Happy Cat Bks. GBR. Dist: Star Bright Bks., Inc.
Craig, Lindsey. Dancing Feet! Brown, Marc, illus. 2012. (ENG.). 32p. (J). (gr. k-k). bds. 6.99 (978-0-307-93081-1(5), Knopf Bks. for Young Readers) Random Hse. Children's Bks.
Crane, Carol. Little Georgia. Knorr, Laura, illus. 2013. (Little State Ser.). (ENG.). 20p. (J). (gr. -1-k). 9.95 (978-1-58536-203-5(4), 202355) Sleeping Bear Pr.
Crazy Animals Sticker Book. (Weird & Wacky Ser.). 16p. (J). (978-2-89393-869-1(8)) Phidal Publishing, Inc./Editions Phidal, Inc.
Creepy Crawlers Sticker Book. (Weird & Wacky Ser.). 16p. (J). (978-2-89393-872-1(8)) Phidal Publishing, Inc./Editions Phidal, Inc.
Crisp, Dan. Little Drivers Going Places! 2006. (Little Drivers Ser.). (ENG., Illus.). 14p. (J). (gr. 1-1). bds. (978-1-904550-96-9(7)) Child's Play International Ltd.
—Santa's Missing Reindeer. Crisp, Dan, illus. 2011. (ENG., Illus.). 12p. (J). (gr. -1-k). 12.99 (978-0-230-71291-1(6)) Macmillan Pubs., Ltd. GBR. Dist: Independent Pubs. Group.
—Trabajo/ Work. 2007. 14p. 10.95 (978-84-263-6452-4(7)) Vives, Luis Editorial (Edelvives) ESP. Dist: Baker & Taylor Bks.
Crisp, Dan, illus. Five Little Men in a Flying Saucer. 2005. (Classic Books with Holes Board Book Ser.). (ENG.). 14p. (J). bds. (978-1-904550-58-7(4)) Child's Play International Ltd.
—London: A Colourful City. 2012. (ENG.). 20p. (J). (gr. -1 — 1). bds. 9.99 (978-1-4052-6468-6(3)) Egmont Bks., Ltd. GBR. Dist: Independent Pubs. Group.
Croll, Carolyn, illus. The Story of Christmas. 2008. (ENG.). 96p. (gr. k-12). 16.95 (978-0-7611-5250-7(4), 15250) Workman Publishing Co., Inc.
Cronin, Doreen. Click, Clack, Moo: Cows That Type. Set. Lewin, Betsy, illus. 2009. (Click, Clack Book Ser.). (ENG.). 16p. (J). (gr. -1-k). bds. 14.99 (978-1-4169-5516-0(X), Little Simon) Little Simon.
—Farmer Brown's Barnyard. Set. Lewin, Betsy, illus. gif. ed. 2008. (Click, Clack Book Ser.). (ENG.). 106p. (J). (gr. -1-k). 18.99 (978-1-4169-5521-4(6), Little Simon) Little Simon.
Crow, Nosy. Bunny Boo Has Lost Her Teddy: A Tiny Tab Book. 2014. (Tiny Tab Ser.). (ENG.). 8p. (J). (— 1). bds. 7.99 (978-0-7636-7274-4(2), Nosy Crow) Candlewick Pr.
—Can You Say It, Too? Moo! Moo! Braun, Sebastien, illus. 2014. (Can You Say It, Too? Ser.). (ENG.). 10p. (J). (— 1). bds. 8.99 (978-0-7636-7066-5(9), Nosy Crow) Candlewick Pr.
—Can You Say It, Too? Woof! Woof! Braun, Sebastien, illus. 2014. (Can You Say It, Too? Ser.). (ENG.). 10p. (J). (— 1). bds. 8.99 (978-0-7636-6605-7(X), Nosy Crow) Candlewick Pr.
—The Coloring Book of Cards & Envelopes: Christmas. Jones, Rebecca, illus. 2016. (ENG.). 74p. (J). (gr. k-12). pap. 10.99 (978-0-7636-9242-1(5), Nosy Crow) Candlewick Pr.

T U V

—Flip Flap Farm. Scheffler, Axel, illus. 2014. (ENG.). 26p. (J). (gr. -1-2). 11.99 *(978-0-7636-7067-2(7),* Nosy Crow) Candlewick Pr.

Crowe, Caroline. Pirates in Pajamas. Knight, Tom, illus. 2017. (ENG.). 28p. (J). (gr. -1-k). bds. 7.99 ***(978-1-68010-516-2(7))*** Tiger Tales.

Crowe, Ellie. Go to Sleep, Hide & Seek. Wu, Julie, illus. 2009. 10p. (J). bds. 11.95 *(978-1-59700-759-7(5))* Island Heritage Publishing.

Crowson, Andrew. Flip Flap Christmas. Crowson, Andrew, illus. 2003. (Illus.). 12p. (J). bds. *(978-1-85602-476-1(8),* Pavilion Children's Books) Pavilion Bks.

—Flip Flap Fairytale. 2003. (Illus.). 12p. bds. *(978-1-85602-444-0(X),* Pavilion Children's Books) Pavilion Bks.

—Flip Flap People. 2003. (Illus.). 12p. bds. *(978-1-85602-443-3(1),* Pavilion Children's Books) Pavilion Bks.

—Flip Flap Prehistoric. Crowson, Andrew, illus. 2003. (Illus.). 12p. (J). pap. *(978-1-85602-474-7(1),* Pavilion Children's Books) Pavilion Bks.

—Flip Flap Safari. Crowson, Andrew, illus. 2003. (Illus.). 12p. (J). bds. *(978-1-85602-473-0(3),* Pavilion Children's Books) Pavilion Bks.

—Flip Flap Spooky. Crowson, Andrew, illus. 2003. (Illus.). 12p. (J). bds. *(978-1-85602-475-4(X),* Pavilion Children's Books) Pavilion Bks.

Crowther, Robert. Deep down under Ground: A Pop-up Book of Amazing Facts & Feats. Crowther, Robert, illus. 2004. (Illus.). 18p. (J). (gr. 3-8). reprint ed. pap. 22.00 *(978-0-7567-7179-9(X))* DIANE Publishing Co.

—Robert Crowther's Pop-Up Dinosaur ABC. Crowther, Robert, illus. 2015. (ENG., Illus.). 10p. (J). (gr. -1-3). 19.99 *(978-0-7636-7296-6(3))* Candlewick Pr.

—Ships: A Pop-Up Book. Crowther, Robert, illus. 2008. (ENG., Illus.). 10p. (J). (gr. 1-4). 17.99 *(978-0-7636-3852-8(8))* Candlewick Pr.

—Trains: A Pop-Up Railroad Book. Crowther, Robert, illus. 2016. (ENG., Illus.). 10p. (J). (gr. 1-4). 19.99 *(978-0-7636-8129-6(6))* Candlewick Pr.

Croyle, Paula. Today I'll Be a Princess. Brown, Heather, illus. 2015. (ENG.). 12p. (J). bds. 5.99 *(978-1-4494-6057-0(7))* Andrews McMeel Publishing.

Crozon, Alain. All Shook Up! 2015. (ENG., Illus.). 12p. (J). (gr. -1 — 1). bds. 10.99 *(978-1-4521-4013-1(8))* Chronicle Bks. LLC.

—Who's There? 2015. (ENG., Illus.). 10p. (J). (gr. -1 — 1). bds. 10.99 *(978-1-4521-4014-8(6))* Chronicle Bks. LLC.

Crystal, Billy. I Already Know I Love You. Sayles, Elizabeth, illus. 2008. (ENG.). 32p. (J). (gr. -1-3). bds. 7.99 *(978-0-06-145057-0(X),* HarperFestival) HarperCollins Pubs.

Cullis, Megan. Big Book of Big Trains. 2013. (Big Bks). 16p. (J). ring bd. 14.99 *(978-0-7945-3378-6(7),* Usborne) EDC Publishing.

—Sticker Dressing Heroes. 2012. (Sticker Dressing Ser.). 24p. (J). pap. 8.99 *(978-0-7945-3267-3(5),* Usborne) EDC Publishing.

Curato, Mike. Little Elliot, Big City. Curato, Mike, illus. 2016. (Little Elliot Ser.). (ENG., Illus.). 34p. (J). bds. 7.99 *(978-1-62779-698-9(3),* 9781627796989, Holt, Henry & Co. Bks. For Young Readers) Holt, Henry & Co.

Curry, Don, ed. Esape Africa. 2008. 22p. (J). 15.95 *(978-0-696-23488-0(2))* Meredith Bks.

Curry, Peter, illus. Cars & Trucks. 2016. (ENG.). 12p. (J). (gr. -1 — 1). bds. 4.99 *(978-1-4998-0199-6(8))* Little Bee Books Inc.

—Trains, Boats, & Planes. 2016. (ENG.). 12p. (J). (gr. -1 — 1). bds. 4.99 *(978-1-4998-0262-7(5))* Little Bee Books Inc.

—Zoo Animals. 2016. (ENG.). 12p. (J). (gr. -1 — 1). bds. 4.99 *(978-1-4998-0261-0(7))* Little Bee Books Inc.

da Pavlova, Chrisi È. Animal Stories from Green Lane Estate Series 5. 2012. (Illus.). 290p. pap. 22.00 *(978-1-78035-452-1(5),* Fastprint Publishing) Upfront Publishing Ltd. GBR. Dist: Printondemand-worldwide.com.

Dahl, Michael. Bear Says Thank You, 1 vol. Vidal, Oriol, illus. 2011. (Hello Genius Ser.). (ENG.). 20p. (gr. 1-2). bds. 7.99 *(978-1-4048-6786-4(4))* Picture Window Bks.

—Big Bed for Giraffe. Vidal, Oriol, illus. 2015. (Hello Genius Ser.). (ENG.). 20p. (gr. 1-2). bds. 7.99 *(978-1-4795-5791-2(9))* Picture Window Bks.

—Bye-Bye Bottles, Zebra. Vidal, Oriol, illus. 2015. (Hello Genius Ser.). (ENG.). 20p. (gr. 1-2). bds. 7.99 *(978-1-4795-5792-9(7))* Picture Window Bks.

—Christmas. Ho, Jannie, illus. 2015. (Baby Face Ser.). (ENG.). 10p. (gr. -1 — 1). bds. 7.99 *(978-1-62370-292-2(5))* Capstone Young Readers of Coughlan Cos.

—Halloween. Ho, Jannie, illus. 2015. (Baby Face Ser.). (ENG.). 10p. (gr. -1 — 1). bds. 7.99 *(978-1-62370-293-9(3))* Capstone Young Readers of Coughlan Cos.

—Hello Genius, 4 vols., Set. Vidal, Oriol, illus. Incl. Bunny Eats Lunch. bds. 7.99 *(978-1-4048-5728-5(1));* Duck Goes Potty. bds. 7.99 *(978-1-4048-5726-1(5));* Pig Takes a Bath. bds. 7.99 *(978-1-4048-5729-2(X));* Pony Brushes His Teeth. bds. 7.99 *(978-1-4048-5727-8(3));* (gr. 1-2). 2010. (Hello Genius Ser.). (ENG., Illus.). 20p. 2009. Set bds. 31.96 *(978-1-4048-6198-5(X))* Picture Window Bks.

—Hippo Says "Excuse Me" Vidal, Oriol, illus. 2011. (Hello Genius Ser.). (ENG.). 20p. (gr. 1-2). bds. 7.99 *(978-1-4048-6787-1(2))* Picture Window Bks.

—Little Dinos Don't Bite, 1 vol. Record, Adam, illus. 2013. (Little Dinos Ser.). (ENG.). 20p. (gr. -1-k). bds. 7.99 *(978-1-4048-7536-4(0))* Picture Window Bks.

—Little Dinos Don't Hit, 1 vol. Record, Adam, illus. 2013. (Little Dinos Ser.). (ENG.). 20p. (gr. -1-k). bds. 7.99 *(978-1-4048-7533-3(6))* Picture Window Bks.

—Little Dinos Don't Push, 1 vol. Record, Adam, illus. 2013. (Little Dinos Ser.). (ENG.). 20p. (gr. -1-k). bds. 7.99 *(978-1-4048-7534-0(4))* Picture Window Bks.

—Little Dinos Don't Yell, 1 vol. Record, Adam, illus. 2013. (Little Dinos Ser.). (ENG.). 20p. (gr. -1-k). bds. 7.99 *(978-1-4048-7912-6(9))* Picture Window Bks.

—Little Elephant Listens, 1 vol. Vidal, Oriol, illus. 2014. (Hello Genius Ser.). (ENG.). 20p. (gr. 1-2). bds. 7.99 *(978-1-4795-2289-7(9))* Picture Window Bks.

—Little Lion Shares, 1 vol. Vidal, Oriol, illus. 2014. (Hello Genius Ser.). (ENG.). 20p. (gr. 1-2). bds. 7.99 *(978-1-4795-2287-3(2))* Picture Window Bks.

—Little Monkey Calms Down, 1 vol. Vidal, Oriol, illus. 2014. (Hello Genius Ser.). (ENG.). 20p. (gr. 1-2). bds. 7.99 *(978-1-4795-2286-6(4))* Picture Window Bks.

—Little Tiger Picks Up, 1 vol. Vidal, Oriol, illus. 2014. (Hello Genius Ser.). (ENG.). 20p. (gr. 1-2). bds. 7.99 *(978-1-4795-2288-0(0))* Picture Window Bks.

—Mouse Says Sorry, 1 vol. Vidal, Oriol, illus. 2011. (Hello Genius Ser.). (ENG.). 20p. (gr. 1-2). bds. 7.99 *(978-1-4048-6789-5(9))* Picture Window Bks.

—No More Pacifier, Duck. Vidal, Oriol, illus. 2015. (Hello Genius Ser.). (ENG.). 20p. (gr. 1-2). bds. 7.99 *(978-1-4795-5793-6(5))* Picture Window Bks.

—Penguin Misses Mom. Vidal, Oriol, illus. 2016. (Hello Genius Ser.). (ENG.). 20p. (gr. 1-2). bds. 7.99 *(978-1-4795-8739-1(7))* Picture Window Bks.

—Penguin Says Please, 1 vol. Vidal, Oriol, illus. 2011. (Hello Genius Ser.). (ENG.). 20p. (gr. 1-2). bds. 7.99 *(978-1-4048-6788-8(0))* Picture Window Bks.

—Pirate. Ho, Jannie, illus. 2015. (Baby Face Ser.). (ENG.). 10p. (gr. -1 — 1). bds. 9.99 *(978-1-62370-294-6(1))* Capstone Young Readers of Coughlan Cos.

—Princess. Ho, Jannie, illus. 2015. (Baby Face Ser.). (ENG.). 10p. (gr. -1 — 1). bds. 7.99 *(978-1-62370-295-3(X))* Capstone Young Readers of Coughlan Cos.

—Thumbs up, Brown Bear. Vidal, Oriol, illus. 2015. (Hello Genius Ser.). (ENG.). 20p. (gr. 1-2). bds. 7.99 *(978-1-4795-5794-3(3))* Picture Window Bks.

Dahlen, Noelle & Stickers. Glitter Candy Stickers. 2011. (Dover Little Activity Books Stickers Ser.). (ENG.). 2p. (J). (gr. 1-4). pap. 1.99 *(978-0-486-48282-8(0))* Dover Pubns., Inc.

Daisy Dinosaur's Opposites. 2015. (Illus.). (J). *(978-1-58865-881-4(3))* Kidsbooks, LLC.

Dale, Kim. What Am I? (Illus.). 32p. pap. *(978-0-7344-0125-0(6),* Lothian Children's Bks.) Hachette Australia.

Dale, Penny. Dinosaurs on the Go! Dale, Penny, illus. 2016. (ENG., Illus.). (J). (-k). bds. 19.99 *(978-0-7636-8936-0(X),* Nosy Crow) Candlewick Pr.

Daley, Michael J. Beach Socks, 1 vol. Corke, Estelle, illus. 2013. (ENG.). 10p. (J). bds. 6.99 *(978-1-59572-637-7(3))* Star Bright Bks., Inc.

Daley, Robert. What Color Are You? 2007. (Illus.). 34p. (J). pap. 8.75 *(978-0-9800839-1-0(5))* Daley, Robert.

Dalmatian Press Staff. Fuzzy Ducky's Birthday! 2008. (ENG.). 5p. bds. 4.95 *(978-1-58117-725-1(9),* Intervisual/Piggy Toes) Bendon, Inc.

—The Icky Sticky Anteater. 2008. (ENG.). 8p. bds. 4.95 *(978-1-58117-711-4(9),* Intervisual/Piggy Toes) Bendon, Inc.

—The Icky Sticky Frog. 2008. (ENG.). 8p. (J). bds. 4.95 *(978-1-58117-712-1(7),* Intervisual/Piggy Toes) Bendon, Inc.

—Maggie Can Count. 2008. (ENG.). 5p. (J). bds. 4.95 *(978-1-58117-728-2(3),* Intervisual/Piggy Toes) Bendon, Inc.

—On Top of Spaghetti. 2008. (ENG.). 6p. (J). bds. 4.95 *(978-1-58117-720-6(8),* Intervisual/Piggy Toes) Bendon, Inc.

—Pizza! Pizza! Pizza! 2008. (ENG.). 6p. (J). bds. 4.95 *(978-1-58117-721-3(6),* Intervisual/Piggy Toes) Bendon, Inc.

—Pop & Shine Colors. 2008. (ENG.). 12p. (J). bds. 10.95 *(978-1-58117-673-5(2),* Intervisual/Piggy Toes) Bendon, Inc.

—Pop & Shine Trucks. 2008. (ENG.). 12p. (J). 10.95 *(978-1-58117-672-8(4),* Intervisual/Piggy Toes) Bendon, Inc.

—Pop & Sniff Fruit. 2008. (ENG.). 12p. (J). 10.95 *(978-1-58117-676-6(7),* Intervisual/Piggy Toes) Bendon, Inc.

—Pop & Touch Baby Animals. 2008. (ENG.). 12p. (J). 10.95 *(978-1-58117-674-2(0),* Intervisual/Piggy Toes) Bendon, Inc.

—Say Moo! 2008. (ENG.). 5p. (J). bds. 4.95 *(978-1-58117-722-0(4),* Intervisual/Piggy Toes) Bendon, Inc.

—Thanks You, God: Board Book with Plush Toy. rev. ed. 2007. (ENG.). 7p. 12.99 *(978-1-4037-3074-9(1),* Spirit Pr.) Bendon, Inc.

Damon, Emma. Busytime. Damon, Emma, illus. 2010. (Pop-Up Flaps Ser.). (ENG., Illus.). 8p. (J). (gr. k-k). bds. 10.99 *(978-0-230-74454-7(0))* Macmillan Pubs., Ltd. GBR. Dist: Independent Pubs. Group.

D'Andrea, Deborah, creator. Words. 2006. (Picture Me Ser.). (Illus.). (J). *(978-1-57151-768-5(5))* Playhouse Publishing.

D'Andrea, Deborah & Borlasca, Hector. Pretend & Play Superhero. 2005. (Illus.). (J). *(978-1-57151-751-7(0))* Playhouse Publishing.

D'Angelo, Gus. New York ABCs. 2013. (ENG.). 30p. (J). (-k). bds. 9.95 *(978-0-615-70443-2(3))* DAngelo, Gus.

Daniel Goes to the Potty. 2014. (Daniel Tiger's Neighborhood Ser.). (ENG., Illus.). 14p. (J). (gr. -1 — 1). 8.99 *(978-1-4814-2048-8(8),* Simon Spotlight) Simon Spotlight.

Danson, Lesley, illus. Snow White. (Flip-Up Fairy Tales Ser.). (ENG.). 24p. (J). 2007. (gr. -1-2). audio compact disk *(978-1-84643-096-1(8))* 2006. (gr. 1-2). *(978-1-84643-023-7(2))* Child's Play International Ltd.

Dapre, Alan & Rooney, Ronnie. Brum Big Town Songs. 2004. (Illus.). 10p. (J). bds. *(978-0-7853-9898-1(8))* Publications International, Ltd.

David & Goliath Bible Sticker Book. 2003. (Illus.). 16p. (J). 2.98 *(978-1-4054-1554-5(1))* Parragon, Inc.

David, Juliet. The Busy Christmas Stable, 1 vol. Pitt, Sarah, illus. 2010. (Candle Peek-A-boo Ser.). (ENG.). 8p. (J). (gr. -1-2). bds. 11.99 *(978-1-85985-803-5(1),* Candle Bks.) Lion Hudson PLC GBR. Dist: Kregel Pubns.

—Candle Bible for Kids Board Book, 1 vol. Parry, Jo, illus. 2014. (ENG.). 42p. (J). bds. 9.99 *(978-1-78128-101-7(7),* Candle Bks.) Lion Hudson PLC GBR. Dist: Kregel Pubns.

—The Christmas Story, 1 vol. Ellis, Elina, illus. 2016. (ENG.). 24p. (J). 8.99 *(978-1-78128-282-3(X),* Candle Bks.) Lion Hudson PLC GBR. Dist: Kregel Pubns.

—Daniel & the Lions' Den, 1 vol. Denham, Gemma, illus. 2009. (Candle Playbook Ser.). 18p. (J). bds. 7.99 *(978-0-8254-7385-2(3),* Candle Bks.) Lion Hudson PLC GBR. Dist: Kregel Pubns.

—The Easter Story, 1 vol. Parry, Jo, illus. 2015. (ENG.). 12p. (J). bds. 3.99 *(978-1-85985-992-6(5),* Candle Bks.) Lion Hudson PLC GBR. Dist: Kregel Pubns.

—The First Christmas, 1 vol. Denham, Gemma, illus. 2008. (Candle Playbook Ser.). 18p. (J). bds. 7.99 *(978-0-8254-7377-7(2),* Candle Bks.) Lion Hudson PLC GBR. Dist: Kregel Pubns.

—God Helps Me, 1 vol. Byrne, Mike, illus. 2014. (ENG.). 10p. (J). bds. 7.99 *(978-1-78128-112-3(2),* Candle Bks.) Lion Hudson PLC GBR. Dist: Kregel Pubns.

—God Loves Me, 1 vol. Byrne, Mike, illus. 2014. (ENG.). 10p. (J). bds. 7.99 *(978-1-78128-114-7(9),* Candle Bks.) Lion Hudson PLC GBR. Dist: Kregel Pubns.

—The Great Flood, 1 vol. Parry, Jo, illus. 2014. (ENG.). 12p. (J). bds. 3.99 *(978-1-85985-991-9(7),* Candle Bks.) Lion Hudson PLC GBR. Dist: Kregel Pubns.

—Noah & His Boat, 1 vol. Denham, Gemma, illus. 2008. (Candle Playbook Ser.). 18p. (J). bds. 7.99 *(978-0-8254-7378-4(0),* Candle Bks.) Lion Hudson PLC GBR. Dist: Kregel Pubns.

—Puddle Pen Bible Stories, 1 vol. Martin, Stuart, illus. 2010. (Candle Puddle Pen Ser.). 10p. (J). (gr. -1). bds. 12.99 *(978-0-8254-7394-4(2),* Candle Bks.) Lion Hudson PLC GBR. Dist: Kregel Pubns.

—Puddle Pen Christmas, 1 vol. Poole, Helen, illus. 2010. (Candle Puddle Pen Ser.). (ENG.). 10p. (J). (gr. -1-k). bds. 12.99 *(978-1-85985-868-4(6),* Candle Bks.) Lion Hudson PLC GBR. Dist: Kregel Pubns.

—The Shepherds, 1 vol. Wood, Hannah, illus. 2009. (Christmas Trio Ser.). 18p. (J). bds. 4.99 *(978-0-8254-7406-4(X),* Candle Bks.) Lion Hudson PLC GBR. Dist: Kregel Pubns.

—A Stable in Bethlehem. Denham, Gemma & Scott, Richard, illus. 2007. 14p. (J). (gr. -1-3). 16.99 *(978-0-8254-7341-8(1),* Candle Bks.) Lion Hudson PLC GBR. Dist: Kregel Pubns.

—The Very First Christmas - Changing Pictures, 1 vol. Siewert, Pauline, illus. 2010. (ENG.). 14p. (J). 11.99 *(978-1-85985-870-7(8),* Candle Bks.) Lion Hudson PLC GBR. Dist: Kregel Pubns.

Davidson, Alice Joyce. Baby Blessings Christmas. 2009. (Baby Blessings Ser.). (ENG.). 18p. (J). (gr. -1-k). bds. 12.99 *(978-0-7847-2374-5(5),* B&H Kids) B&H Publishing Group.

Davidson, Carli, photos by. Heads & Tails. 2017. (ENG., Illus.). 20p. (J). bds. 8.99 *(978-1-4521-5137-3(7))* Chronicle Bks. LLC.

—Shake, Wiggle & Roll. 2017. (ENG., Illus.). 20p. (J). bds. 8.99 *(978-1-4521-5136-6(9))* Chronicle Bks. LLC.

Davidson, S. & Daynes, K. Princess Jewelry Kid Kit (Bag) 2008. (Kid Kits Ser.). 96p. (J). 15.99 *(978-1-60130-104-8(9),* Usborne) EDC Publishing.

—Princess Jewelry Kid Kit (Box) 2008. (Kid Kits Ser.). 96p. (J). 15.99 *(978-1-60130-115-4(4),* Usborne) EDC Publishing.

Davidson, Susanna. See Inside Fairyland. Ligi, Raffaella, illus. 2007. (See Inside Board Bks). 14p. (J). (gr. -1-k). bds. 12.99 *(978-0-7945-1570-6(3),* Usborne) EDC Publishing.

—That's Not My Puppy. 2009. (Touchy-Feely Board Bks). 10p. (J). bds. 8.99 *(978-0-7945-2511-8(3),* Usborne) EDC Publishing.

Davies, Becky. Bedtime Blessing. Macnaughton, Tina, illus. 2016. (ENG.). 24p. (J). (gr. -1-k). bds. 8.99 *(978-1-58925-205-9(5))* Tiger Tales.

—Peekaboo Pals Opposites. Lucas, Gareth, illus. 2016. (Peekaboo Pals Ser.). (ENG.). 20p. (J). (gr. -1). bds. 14.95 *(978-1-62686-522-8(1),* Silver Dolphin Bks.) Readerlink Distribution Services, LLC.

Davies, Caroline, illus. Duck. 2013. (Shake & Play Bath Bks.). (ENG.). 8p. (J). (gr. -1 — 1). 5.99 *(978-1-4380-7339-2(9))* Barron's Educational Series, Inc.

—Fish. 2013. (Shake & Play Bath Bks.). (ENG.). 8p. (J). (gr. -1 — 1). 5.99 *(978-1-4380-7340-8(2))* Barron's Educational Series, Inc.

—Turtle. 2013. (Shake & Play Bath Bks.). (ENG.). 8p. (J). (gr. -1 — 1). 5.99 *(978-1-4380-7341-5(0))* Barron's Educational Series, Inc.

—Whale. 2013. (Shake & Play Bath Bks.). (ENG.). 8p. (J). (gr. -1 — 1). 5.99 *(978-1-4380-7342-2(9))* Barron's Educational Series, Inc.

Davies, Gill. A Letter to Santa. Taylor, Ned, illus. 2015. (J). *(978-1-4351-6225-9(0))* Barnes & Noble, Inc.

Davies, Kate. See under the Sea. 2008. (See Inside Board Bks). 16p. (J). (gr. 2). bds. 12.99 *(978-0-7945-2238-4(6),* Usborne) EDC Publishing.

Davies, Kate, illus. Little Squeak School. 2014. (J). *(978-1-4351-5582-4(3))* Barnes & Noble, Inc.

—Welcome to the Mouse House. 2014. (J). *(978-1-4351-5583-1(1))* Barnes & Noble, Inc.

Davis, Caroline. First Abc. 2012. (ENG., Illus.). 10p. (J). (gr. k-1). bds. 7.99 *(978-1-84322-772-4(X))* Anness Publishing GBR. Dist: National Bk. Network.

—First Opposites. 2012. (ENG., Illus.). 10p. (J). (gr. -1-1). bds. 7.99 *(978-1-84322-844-8(0),* Armadillo) Anness Publishing GBR. Dist: National Bk. Network.

—First Pictures. 2012. (ENG., Illus.). 196p. bds. 7.99 *(978-1-84322-774-8(6),* Armadillo) Anness Publishing GBR. Dist: National Bk. Network.

—First Words. 2012. (ENG., Illus.). 196p. bds. 7.99 *(978-1-84322-842-4(4),* Armadillo) Anness Publishing GBR. Dist: National Bk. Network.

—Sparkly Farm. Davis, Caroline, illus. 2008. (Tiger Tales Ser.). (Illus.). 8p. (J). (gr. -1). bds. 6.95 *(978-1-58925-831-0(2))* Tiger Tales.

—Sparkly Ocean. Davis, Caroline, illus. 2008. (Tiger Tales Ser.). (Illus.). 8p. (J). (gr. -1). bds. 6.95 *(978-1-58925-832-7(0))* Tiger Tales.

Davis, Jacky. Ladybug Girl Ready for Snow. Soman, David, illus. 2014. (Ladybug Girl Ser.). (ENG.). 12p. (J). (gr. -1 — 1). bds. 5.99 *(978-0-8037-4137-9(5),* Dial Bks) Penguin Young Readers Group.

Davis, Jacky & Soman, David. Ladybug Girl & Her Mama. Soman, David, illus. 2013. (Ladybug Girl Ser.). (ENG., Illus.). 14p. (J). (gr. -1 — 1). bds. 5.99 *(978-0-8037-3891-1(9),* Dial Bks) Penguin Young Readers Group.

—Ladybug Girl Book & Doll Set. Soman, David, illus. 2011. (Ladybug Girl Ser.). (ENG., Illus.). 32p. (J). (gr. -1-k). 18.99 *(978-0-8037-3444-9(1),* Dial Bks) Penguin Young Readers Group.

—Ladybug Girl Feels Happy. Soman, David, illus. 2012. (Ladybug Girl Ser.). (ENG., Illus.). 12p. (J). (gr. -1 — 1). bds. 5.99 *(978-0-8037-3890-4(0),* Dial Bks) Penguin Young Readers Group.

—Ladybug Girl Plays. Soman, David, illus. 2013. (Ladybug Girl Ser.). (ENG., Illus.). 14p. (J). (gr. -1 — 1). bds. 5.99 *(978-0-8037-3892-8(7),* Dial Bks) Penguin Young Readers Group.

Davis, Jimmie. We Love to Sing Along! Church, Caroline Jayne, illus. 2016. (ENG.). 18p. (J). (gr. -1 — 1). bds. 8.99 *(978-0-545-90137-6(5),* Cartwheel Bks.) Scholastic, Inc.

Davis, Nancy. Halloween Faces. Davis, Nancy, illus. 2010. (ENG., Illus.). 18p. (J). (gr. k — 1). bds. 6.99 *(978-0-545-16586-0(5),* Cartwheel Bks.) Scholastic, Inc.

Davis, Nancy & Davis, Kathryn Lynn. The First Thanksgiving. Davis, Nancy & Davis, Kathryn Lynn, illus. 2010. (ENG., Illus.). 14p. (J). (gr. -1 — 1). bds. 5.99 *(978-1-4424-0807-4(3),* Little Simon) Little Simon.

Daynes, Katie. Flip Flap Airport. 2009. (Flip Flap Board Bks). 13p. (J). (gr. -1). bds. 14.99 *(978-0-7945-2401-2(X),* Usborne) EDC Publishing.

—Look Inside a Farm. rev. ed. 2012. (Look Inside Board Bks). 13p. (J). ring bd. 15.99 *(978-0-7945-3249-9(7),* Usborne) EDC Publishing.

—Questions & Answers. 2013. (Usborne Lift the Flap Bks.). (ENG., Illus.). 14p. (J). 14.99 *(978-0-7945-3207-9(1),* Usborne) EDC Publishing.

—See Inside Space. Allen, Peter, illus. 2009. (See Inside Board Bks). 16p. (J). (gr. 2). bds. 12.99 *(978-0-7945-2088-5(X),* Usborne) EDC Publishing.

—See Inside Your Body. King, Colin, illus. 2006. 15p. (J). (gr. -1-3). bds. 12.99 *(978-0-7945-1233-0(X),* Usborne) EDC Publishing.

Daynes, Katie & Allen, Peter. See Inside Planet Earth - Internet Referenced. 2008. (See Inside Board Bks). 16p. (J). bds. 12.99 *(978-0-7945-2070-0(7),* Usborne) EDC Publishing.

Daynes, Katie & King, Colin. Tu Cuerpo: Conoce Por Dentro. 2007. (Titles in Spanish Ser.). (Illus.). 15p. (J). (gr. -1). bds. 12.99 *(978-0-7460-8386-4(6),* Usborne) EDC Publishing.

Daynes, Katie & Watt, Fiona, eds. Baby Scrapbook. 2008. (Baby Scrapbook Ser.). (Illus.). 32p. (J). bds. 19.99 *(978-0-7945-1957-5(1),* Usborne) EDC Publishing.

DaySpring Greeting Card Staff & Jensen, Bonnie Rickner. Really Woolly Nighttime Lullabies, 1 vol. 2015. (Really Woolly Ser.). (ENG.). 40p. (J). bds. 9.99 *(978-0-7180-2295-2(5))* Nelson, Thomas Inc.

Daywalt, Drew. The Crayons' Book of Numbers. Jeffers, Oliver, illus. 2016. (ENG.). 18p. (J). (-k). bds. 8.99 *(978-0-451-53405-7(0),* Grosset & Dunlap) Penguin Young Readers Group.

de Brunhoff, Laurent & Rose, Phyllis. Babar & His Family. 2012. (ENG., Illus.). 24p. (J). (gr. -1 — 1). bds. 7.95 *(978-1-4197-0263-1(7),* Abrams Appleseed) Abrams, Inc.

de La Cour, Gary, et al, illus. Wheels on the Bus. rev. ed. 2007. (ENG.). 24p. (J). (gr. -1-3). 4.99 *(978-1-59069-562-3(3))* Studio Mouse LLC.

de Pavlova, Chrisi È. Animal Stories from Green Lane Estate: Series Four. 2012. (Illus.). 290p. pap. 22.00 *(978-1-78035-357-9(X),* Fastprint Publishing) Upfront Publishing Ltd. GBR. Dist: Printondemand-worldwide.com.

De Saint-Exupéry, Antoine. Le Petit Prince: Avec les dessins de l'auteur. (FRE., Illus.). 64p. (J). (gr. 1-7). audio, audio compact disk 12.95 *(978-2-921997-41-6(X))* Coffragants CAN. Dist: Penton Overseas, Inc.

—The Little Prince 70th Anniversary Gift Set (Book/CD/Downloadable Audio) Howard, Richard, tr. 2013. (Little Prince Ser.). (ENG., Illus.). 96p. (YA). (gr. 7). audio compact disk 24.99 *(978-0-547-97048-6(X))* Houghton Mifflin Harcourt Publishing Co.

—Meet the Little Prince (padded Board Book) 2015. (Little Prince Ser.). (ENG., Illus.). 10p. (J). (— 1). bds. 7.99 *(978-0-544-70902-7(0),* HMH Books For Young Readers) Houghton Mifflin Harcourt Publishing Co.

Dean, Kim & Dean, James. Big Easter Adventure. 2014. (Pete the Cat Ser.). (Illus.). (J). *(978-1-4844-1829-1(8))* HarperCollins Pubs.

D'Ecsery, Claire. Temples Dot the Earth. 2016. (ENG.). (J). bds. 9.99 *(978-1-4621-1842-7(9))* Cedar Fort, Inc./CFI Distribution.

Degen, Bruce. Jamberry Padded Board Book. Degen, Bruce, illus. 2017. (Illus.). 34p. (J). (gr. -1 — 1). bds. 9.99 *(978-0-06-264379-7(7),* HarperFestival) HarperCollins Pubs.

Del Moral, Susana. Como Me Siento. Zaidi, Nadeem, illus. 2005. (Baby Einstein: Libros de Carton Ser.). (SPA.). 14p. (J). (gr. -1). bds. *(978-970-718-308-7(X),* Silver Dolphin en Español) Advanced Marketing, S. de R. L. de C. V.

—El Juego de las Formas. Zaidi, Nadeem, illus. 2005. (Baby Einstein: Libros de Carton Ser.). (SPA.). 6p. (J). (gr. -1). bds. *(978-970-718-303-2(9),* Silver Dolphin en Español) Advanced Marketing, S. de R. L. de C. V.

—Las Rimas de Bard: Un Libro con Ventanas. Zaidi, Nadeem, illus. 2005. (Baby Einstein: Libros de Carton Ser.). (SPA.). 16p. (J). (gr. -1). bds. *(978-970-718-304-9(7),* Silver Dolphin en Español) Advanced Marketing, S. de R. L. de C. V.

del Risco, Eida, tr. What's in My Toybox? (Spanish/English) Un libro de formas/A Book of Shapes, 1 vol. 2009. (ENG & SPA., Illus.). 32p. (J). bds. 6.25 *(978-1-59572-179-2(7))* Star Bright Bks., Inc.

Deliso, Chris & Dorling Kindersley Publishing Staff. Playtime with Sophie. 2014. (ENG., Illus.). 14p. (J). (gr. -1 — 1). bds. 5.99 *(978-1-4654-2042-8(8),* DK Children) Dorling Kindersley Publishing, Inc.

Demarest, Chris L. Train. 2017. (ENG., Illus.). 16p. (J). (— 1). bds. 6.99 *(978-0-544-87608-8(3),* HMH Books For Young Readers) Houghton Mifflin Harcourt Publishing Co.

Denchfield, Nick. Charlie Chick Goes to School. Parker, Ant, illus. 2015. (Charlie Chick Ser.). (ENG.). 16p. (J). (-k). 12.99 *(978-1-4472-7718-7(X))* Pan Macmillan GBR. Dist: Independent Pubs. Group.

—Charlie Chick Learns to Fly. Parker, Ant, illus. 2016. (Charlie Chick Ser.: 3). (ENG.). 16p. (J). (gr. -1-k). 12.99 *(978-1-5098-0712-3(8))* Pan Macmillan GBR. Dist: Independent Pubs. Group.

—Frankie the Frog. Parker, Ant, illus. 2016. (Charlie Chick Ser.: 4). (ENG.). 16p. (J). (gr. -1-k). bds. 12.99 *(978-1-5098-1767-2(0))* Pan Macmillan GBR. Dist: Independent Pubs. Group.

—Penelope the Piglet. Parker, Ant, illus. 2008. (ENG.). 16p. (J). (gr. 2-5). bds. 13.95 *(978-0-230-01615-6(4),* Macmillan) Pan Macmillan GBR. Dist: Trans-Atlantic Pubns., Inc.

Deneux, Xavier. ABC: TouchThinkLearn. 2016. (ENG., Illus.). 32p. (J). (gr. -1-k). bds. 24.99 *(978-1-4521-4503-7(2))* Chronicle Bks. LLC.

—Baby Animals. 2016. (ENG., Illus.). 16p. (J). (gr. -1 — 1). bds. 14.99 *(978-1-4521-4519-8(9))* Chronicle Bks. LLC.

—Colours. 2013. (ENG.). 20p. (J). (gr. -1 — 1). bds. 14.99 *(978-1-4521-1726-3(8))* Chronicle Bks. LLC.

—Homes. 2016. (ENG., Illus.). 16p. (J). (gr. -1 — 1). bds. 14.99 *(978-1-4521-4518-1(0))* Chronicle Bks. LLC.

—Numbers. 2014. (ENG., Illus.). 22p. (J). (gr. -1 — 1). bds. 14.99 *(978-1-4521-1724-9(1))* Chronicle Bks. LLC.

—Opposites. 2013. (ENG., Illus.). 20p. (J). (gr. -1 — 1). bds. 14.99 *(978-1-4521-1725-6(X))* Chronicle Bks. LLC.

—Shapes. 2014. (ENG., Illus.). 20p. (J). (gr. -1 — 1). bds. 14.99 *(978-1-4521-1727-0(6))* Chronicle Bks. LLC.

—TouchThinkLearn: Farm. 2015. (ENG., Illus.). 22p. (J). (gr. -1 — 1). bds. 14.99 *(978-1-4521-4517-4(2))* Chronicle Bks. LLC.

—TouchThinkLearn: Fly! 2017. (ENG., Illus.). 14p. (J). bds. 17.99 *(978-1-4521-5922-5(X))* Chronicle Bks. LLC.

—TouchThinkLearn: Vehicles. 2015. (ENG., Illus.). 22p. (J). (gr. -1 — 1). bds. 14.99 *(978-1-4521-4516-7(4))* Chronicle Bks. LLC.

Depken, Kristen L. Merry Christmas, Pocoyo (Pocoyo) Random House, illus. 2013. (Glitter Board Book Ser.). (ENG.). 12p. (J). (— 1). bds. 6.99 *(978-0-449-81903-6(5)*, Random Hse. Bks. for Young Readers) Random Hse. Children's Bks.

—Where's Woody? (Disney/Pixar Toy Story) Random House Disney Staff, illus. 2012. (Pictureback(R) Ser.). (ENG.). 16p. (J). (gr. -1-2). pap. 4.99 *(978-0-7364-2850-7(X)*, RH/Disney) Random Hse. Children's Bks.

DePrisco, Dorothea. Apple. Taxali, Gary, illus. 2005. (Plush Learning Books Ser.). 10p. (J). bds. 6.95 *(978-1-58117-191-4(9)*, Intervisual/Piggy Toes) Bendon, Inc.

—Lemon. Taxali, Gary, illus. 2005. (Plush Learning Books Ser.). 10p. (J). bds. 6.95 *(978-1-58117-194-5(3)*, Intervisual/Piggy Toes) Bendon, Inc.

—Meet Gator: A Picture Clues Touch & Feel Book. Croft, James Lee, illus. 2005. (Learn to Read Ser.). 10p. (J). (gr. -1-18). 10.95 *(978-1-58117-123-5(4)*, Intervisual/Piggy Toes) Bendon, Inc.

—Pear. Taxali, Gary, illus. 2005. (Plush Learning Books Ser.). 10p. (J). bds. 6.95 *(978-1-58117-193-8(5)*, Intervisual/Piggy Toes) Bendon, Inc.

—Peek-A-Boooo Who? A Lift-the-Flap & Sound Book. Hedgecock, Lucie, illus. 2009. 12p. 8.95 *(978-1-58117-952-1(9)*, Intervisual/Piggy Toes) Bendon, Inc.

—Pig-a-Boo! A Farmyard Peekaboo Book. Runnells, Patricia & Runnells, Treesha, illus. 2009. (ENG.). 14p. (J). (gr. -1-k). 9.99 *(978-1-4169-7226-6(9)*, Little Simon) Little Simon.

—Tub-A-Tub. 2006. (Illus.). 10p. (J). (gr. -1-k). 9.95 *(978-1-58117-463-2(2)*, Intervisual/Piggy Toes) Bendon, Inc.

—Who's in the Jungle? Gilvan-Cartwright, Chris, illus. 2006. (ENG.). 10p. (J). bds. 4.95 *(978-1-58117-507-3(8)*, Intervisual/Piggy Toes) Bendon, Inc.

—Who's in the Ocean? Gilvan-Cartwright, Chris, illus. 2006. (ENG.). 10p. (gr. -1-k). bds. 4.95 *(978-1-58117-509-7(4)*, Intervisual/Piggy Toes) Bendon, Inc.

—Who's on the Farm? Gilvan-Cartwright, Chris, illus. 2006. (ENG.). 10p. (gr. -1-k). bds. 4.95 *(978-1-58117-508-0(6)*, Intervisual/Piggy Toes) Bendon, Inc.

Design Eye Publishing Staff, et al. Amazing Automata — Dinosaurs! 2013. (Dover Origami Papercraft Ser.). (ENG.). 24p. (J). (gr. 5). 14.99 *(978-0-486-49981-9(2))* Dover Pubns., Inc.

—Amazing Automata — Pirates! 2013. (Dover Origami Papercraft Ser.). (ENG.). 24p. (J). (gr. 5). 14.99 *(978-0-486-49980-2(4))* Dover Pubns., Inc.

DeVries, Catherine & Zondervan Staff. All Aboard with Noah!, 1 vol. Pulley, Kelly, illus. 2009. (Beginner's Bible Ser.). (ENG.). 12p. (J). bds. 7.99 *(978-0-310-71726-3(4))* Zonderkidz.

Dewdney, Anna. Llama Llama Easter Egg. Dewdney, Anna, illus. 2015. (Llama Llama Ser.). (ENG., Illus.). 14p. (J). (— 1). bds. 5.99 *(978-0-451-46982-3(8)*, Viking Books for Young Readers) Penguin Publishing Group.

—Llama Llama I Love You. 2014. (Llama Llama Ser.). (ENG., Illus.). 14p. (J). (gr. -1 — 1). bds. 5.99 *(978-0-451-46981-6(X)*, Viking Books for Young Readers) Penguin Young Readers Group.

—Llama Llama Jingle Bells. Dewdney, Anna, illus. 2014. (Llama Llama Ser.). (ENG., Illus.). 14p. (J). (— 1). bds. 5.99 *(978-0-451-46980-9(1)*, Viking Books for Young Readers) Penguin Young Readers Group.

—Llama Llama's Little Library. 2013. (Llama Llama Ser.). (ENG., Illus.). 56p. (J). (— 1). bds. 23.96 *(978-0-670-01648-8(9)*, Viking Books for Young Readers) Penguin Young Readers Group.

—Nobunny's Perfect. 2012. (ENG.). 32p. (J). (gr. -1-k). bds. 6.99 *(978-0-670-01408-8(7)*, Viking Books for Young Readers) Penguin Young Readers Group.

Dewin, Howard & Barba, M. J. Scooby-Doo! A to Z Ultimate Joke Book. 2011. (Illus.). 63p. (J). pap. *(978-0-545-37944-1(X))* Scholastic, Inc.

Diaz, James & Diaz, Francesca. Making Colors: A Pop-Up Book. 2014. (ENG.). 10p. (J). (gr. k). 19.95 *(978-1-85707-853-4(5))* Tango Bks. GBR. Dist: Independent Pubs. Group.

Diaz, James & Gerth, Melanie, illus. Numbers: Learning Fun for Little Ones! 2007. 10p. (J). reprint ed. *(978-1-4223-6683-7(9))* DIANE Publishing Co.

DiCicco, Sue. Funny Bunnies: Morning, Noon, & Night. 2015. (Illus.). 32p. (J). *(978-1-4844-4595-2(3))* Scholastic, Inc.

—1, 2, 3 in the Sea. DiCicco, Sue, illus. 2012. (ENG., Illus.). 10p. (J). (— 1). bds. 6.99 *(978-0-545-43238-2(3))* Scholastic, Inc.

—1, 2 at the Zoo. DiCicco, Sue, illus. 2012. (ENG., Illus.). 10p. (J). (— 1). bds. 6.99 *(978-0-545-43239-9(1))* Scholastic, Inc.

DiCicco, Sue, illus. Totally Monster: Manners. 2013. (Totally Monsters Ser.). (ENG.). 14p. (J). (gr. -1). 12.95 *(978-1-60710-645-6(0)*, Silver Dolphin Bks.) Readerlink Distribution Services, LLC.

Dickens, Rosie. My Very First Art Coloring Book with Stickers. 2012. (Art Ser.). 24p. (J). pap. 5.99 *(978-0-7945-3273-4(X)*, Usborne) EDC Publishing.

Dicmas, Courtney. Colours. Dicmas, Courtney, illus. 2017. (Wild! Concepts Ser.: 4). (ENG., Illus.). 14p. (J). bds. ***(978-1-84643-995-7(7))*** Child's Play International Ltd.

—Numbers. Dicmas, Courtney, illus. 2017. (Wild! Concepts Ser.: 4). (ENG., Illus.). 14p. (J). bds. ***(978-1-84643-993-3(0))*** Child's Play International Ltd.

—Opposites. Dicmas, Courtney, illus. 2017. (Wild! Concepts Ser.: 4). (ENG., Illus.). 14p. (J). bds. ***(978-1-84643-997-1(3))*** Child's Play International Ltd.

—Shapes. Dicmas, Courtney, illus. 2017. (Wild! Concepts Ser.: 4). (ENG., Illus.). 14p. (J). bds. ***(978-1-84643-994-0(9))*** Child's Play International Ltd.

—Wild Bath Time! 2014. (Wild! Ser.: 4). (ENG., Illus.). 14p. (J). (gr. k-k). bds. *(978-1-84643-686-4(9))* Child's Play International Ltd.

—Wild Bedtime! 2014. (Wild! Ser.: 4). (ENG., Illus.). 14p. (J). (gr. k-k). bds. *(978-1-84643-687-1(7))* Child's Play International Ltd.

—Wild Mealtime! 2014. (Wild! Ser.: 4). (ENG., Illus.). 14p. (J). (gr. k-k). bds. *(978-1-84643-684-0(2))* Child's Play International Ltd.

—WILD! Mealtime/¡QUÉ LOCURA! a la Hora de Comer. Dicmas, Courtney, illus. 2016. (Wild!/¡quÉ Locura! Ser.: 4). (ENG & SPA., Illus.). 14p. (J). bds. *(978-1-84643-905-6(1))* Child's Play International Ltd.

—Wild Playtime! 2014. (Wild! Ser.: 4). (ENG., Illus.). 14p. (J). (gr. k-k). bds. *(978-1-84643-685-7(0))* Child's Play International Ltd.

Diesen, Deborah. Happy Easter, Pout-Pout Fish. Hanna, Dan, illus. 2017. (Pout-Pout Fish Mini Adventure Ser.). (ENG.). 12p. (J). bds. 5.99 *(978-0-374-30400-3(9)*, 9780374304003, Farrar, Straus & Giroux (BYR)) Farrar, Straus & Giroux.

—Hide & Seek, Pout-Pout Fish. Hanna, Dan, illus. 2015. (Pout-Pout Fish Novelty Ser.). (ENG.). 18p. (J). (gr. -1 — 1). bds. 8.99 *(978-1-250-06011-2(7)*, 9781250060112) Square Fish.

—The Pout-Pout Fish Undersea Alphabet: Touch & Feel. Hanna, Dan, illus. 2016. (Pout-Pout Fish Novelty Ser.). (ENG.). 20p. (J). bds. 12.99 *(978-1-250-06392-2(2)*, 9781250063922, Farrar, Straus & Giroux (BYR)) Farrar, Straus & Giroux.

—Smile, Pout-Pout Fish. Hanna, Dan, illus. 2014. (Pout-Pout Fish Mini Adventure Ser.). (ENG.). 12p. (J). (gr. -1 — 1). bds. 5.99 *(978-0-374-37084-8(2)*, 9780374370848, Farrar, Straus & Giroux (BYR)) Farrar, Straus & Giroux.

DiPerna, Kaitlyn. Who's Hiding? in the Ocean. Capizzi, Giusi, illus. 2016. (Who's Hiding? Ser.). (ENG.). 16p. (J). (gr. -1). bds. 12.99 *(978-1-62686-745-1(3)*, Silver Dolphin Bks.) Readerlink Distribution Services, LLC.

—Who's Hiding? in the Wild. Capizzi, Giusi, illus. 2016. (Who's Hiding? Ser.). (ENG.). 16p. (J). (gr. -1). bds. 12.99 *(978-1-62686-747-5(X)*, Silver Dolphin Bks.) Readerlink Distribution Services, LLC.

Discovering Dinos. (Flip Flap Fun Book Ser.). 10p. (J). bds. *(978-2-7643-0137-1(5))* Phidal Publishing, Inc./Editions Phidal, Inc.

Disney. Disney Sofia the First: A Gift of Friendship. 2014. (ENG.). 16p. (J). (gr. -1-1). bds. 8.99 *(978-0-7944-3200-3(X))* Reader's Digest Assn., Inc., The.

Disney & Scollon, Bill. Disney*Pixar Finding Dory - Follow Me. 2016. (ENG.). 10p. (J). (gr. -1-k). bds. 9.99 *(978-0-7944-3669-8(2))* Studio Fun International.

Disney Book Group. Disney Baby My First Colors. Disney Storybook Art Team, illus. 2016. (ENG.). 10p. (J). (gr. -1 — 1). bds. 6.99 *(978-1-4847-2943-4(9))* Disney Pr.

—Disney Baby My First Halloween. Disney Storybook Art Team, illus. 2017. (ENG.). 12p. (J). (gr. -1 — 1). bds. 8.99 ***(978-1-4847-9936-9(4))*** Disney Pr.

—Disney Baby My First Words. Disney Storybook Art Team, illus. 2016. (ENG.). 24p. (J). (gr. -1 — 1). bds. 7.99 *(978-1-4847-5261-6(9))* Disney Pr.

—Disney Baby Shapes All Around. Disney Storybook Art Team, illus. 2017. (ENG.). 18p. (J). (gr. -1 — 1). bds. 8.99 *(978-1-368-00079-6(7))* Disney Pr.

—Disney*Pixar Board Book & CD Treasury Box. Disney Storybook Art Team, illus. 2017. (Board Book & CD Treasury Box Ser.). (ENG.). 18p. (J). (gr. -1-k). 12.99 ***(978-1-368-00323-0(0))*** Disney Pr.

—Finding Dory Novelty. 2016. (ENG.). 10p. (J). (gr. -1-k). bds. 9.99 *(978-1-4847-2592-4(1))* Disney Pr.

—The Lion Guard Join the Lion Guard! Disney Storybook Art Team, illus. 2016. (ENG.). 10p. (J). (gr. -1-k). bds. 7.99 *(978-1-4847-4678-3(3))* Disney Pr.

—Lion Guard Meet the New Guard. Disney Storybook Art Team, illus. 2016. (ENG.). 10p. (J). (gr. -1-k). bds. 8.99 *(978-1-4847-1914-5(X))* Disney Pr.

—Lion Guard, the Lion Guard, Defend! Book & Magnetic Playset. Disney Storybook Art Team, illus. 2016. (Book & Magnetic Play Set Ser.). (ENG.). 32p. (J). (gr. -1-k). 15.99 *(978-1-4847-1913-8(1))* Disney Pr.

—M Is for Mickey. Disney Storybook Art Team, illus. 2017. (ENG.). 26p. (J). (gr. -1-k). bds. 12.99 *(978-1-4847-8221-7(6))* Disney Pr.

—Puppy Dog Pals Design-A-Dog. Disney Storybook Art Team & Premise Entertainment Staff, illus. 2017. (ENG.). 24p. (J). (gr. -1-k). pap. 4.99 ***(978-1-368-00418-3(0))*** Disney Pr.

—Star Wars Bounty Hunt: Lift-The-Flap Book. 2017. (ENG.). 18p. (J). (gr. 1-3). 12.99 ***(978-1-368-00305-6(2)***, Disney Lucasfilm Press) Disney Publishing Worldwide.

Disney Book Group Staff. Color Our World. Disney Storybook Artists Staff, illus. 2013. (ENG.). 14p. (J). (gr. -1-k). bds. 7.99 *(978-1-4231-6009-0(6))* Disney Pr.

—Fly-and-Drive Read-Along Storybook. Disney Storybook Artists Staff & Disney Storybook Art Team, illus. 2014. (Read-Along Storybook & CD Ser.). (ENG.). 136p. (J). (gr. 1-3). 12.99 *(978-1-4847-0656-5(0))* Disney Pr.

—Guess Who! Disney Storybook Artists Staff, illus. 2012. (ENG.). 14p. (J). (gr. -1-k). bds. 6.99 *(978-1-4231-6008-3(8))* Disney Pr.

—Haunted Clubhouse. 2010. (ENG., Illus.). 12p. (J). (gr. -1-k). bds. 6.99 *(978-1-4231-2832-8(X))* Disney Pr.

—Mickey Mouse Clubhouse Choo Choo Express. 2009. (ENG.). 16p. (J). (gr. -1-k). pap. 4.99 *(978-1-4231-2230-2(5))* Disney Pr.

—Nursery Rhymes. 2011. (Read-Along Storybook & CD Ser.). (ENG.). 32p. (J). (gr. -1-k). bds. 10.99 *(978-1-4231-3743-6(4))* Disney Pr.

—Sofia the First Royal Prep Academy. Disney Storybook Artists Staff & Disney Storybook Art Team, illus. 2014. (ENG.). 14p. (J). (gr. -1-k). bds. 8.99 *(978-1-4847-0760-9(5))* Disney Pr.

Disney Book Group Staff & Higginson, Sheila Sweeny. Doc Mcstuffins Bunny in a Basket. Disney Storybook Art Team, illus. 2015. (ENG.). 12p. (J). (gr. -1-k). bds. 7.99 *(978-1-4847-0679-4(X))* Disney Pr.

—Doc Mcstuffins Doc's Big Book of Boo-Boos. Disney Storybook Artists Staff, illus. 2014. (ENG.). 64p. (J). (gr. -1-k). 10.99 *(978-1-4231-8483-6(1))* Disney Pr.

—Henry Hugglemonster Daddo in Charge. Disney Storybook Art Team, illus. 2015. (ENG.). 12p. (J). (gr. -1-k). bds. 7.99 *(978-1-4847-0642-8(0))* Disney Pr.

Disney Book Group Staff, et al. Doc Mcstuffins Boo to You! Disney Storybook Artists Staff, illus. 2014. (ENG.). 12p. (J). (gr. -1-k). bds. 7.99 *(978-1-4231-8388-4(6))* Disney Pr.

Disney Frozen Let It Go! 2014. (ENG.). 12p. (J). (gr. -1-k). bds. 10.99 *(978-0-7944-3267-6(0)*, Reader's Digest Children's Bks.) Studio Fun International.

Disney Frozen Melt My Heart. 2014. (Hugs Book Ser.). (ENG.). 10p. (J). (gr. -1-k). bds. 10.99 *(978-0-7944-3266-9(2)*, Reader's Digest Children's Bks.) Studio Fun International.

Disney Inside Out, Disney Inside. So Many Feelings: Riley's World Inside & Out. 2015. (ENG.). 64p. (J). (gr. 1-3). 11.99 *(978-0-7944-3387-1(1)*, Reader's Digest Children's Bks.) Studio Fun International.

Disney Junior Staff & Higginson, Sheila Sweeny. Disney Doc McStuffins Carryalong Play Book. Hall, Susan, illus. 2014. (CarryAlong Book Ser.). (ENG.). 14p. (J). (gr. -1-k). bds. 14.99 *(978-0-7944-3178-5(X))* Reader's Digest Assn., Inc., The.

Disney Pixar Staff. Big Monsters on Campus. 2013. (Picture Viewer Ser.: 1). (ENG.). 32p. (J). (gr. k-2). 15.99 *(978-0-7944-2743-6(X))* Reader's Digest Assn., Inc., The.

Disney Planes, Disney. Disney Planes Fire & Rescue to the Rescue: Build 6 Planes That Really Fly! 2014. (Build It Ser.: 3). (ENG.). 24p. (J). (gr. -1-1). 14.99 *(978-0-7944-3139-6(9))* Reader's Digest Assn., Inc., The.

Disney Press Staff & Disney Book Group Staff. Furry Friends! Disney Storybook Artists Staff, illus. 2011. (Touch-And-feel Book Ser.). (ENG.). 16p. (J). (gr. -1-k). bds. 7.99 *(978-1-4231-4183-9(0))* Disney Pr.

—Road Trip. Disney Storybook Art Team, illus. 2011. (ENG.). 10p. (J). (gr. -1-k). bds. 8.99 *(978-1-4231-4416-8(3))* Disney Pr.

Disney Press Staff, et al. Hello, World! Disney Storybook Artists Staff, illus. 2011. (ENG.). 14p. (J). (gr. -1-k). bds. 5.99 *(978-1-4231-4140-2(7))* Disney Pr.

Disney Princess, Disney. Disney Princess - Bibbity-Bobbity-Boo! 2015. (ENG.). 12p. (J). (gr. -1-k). bds. 10.99 *(978-0-7944-3375-8(8)*, Reader's Digest Children's Bks.) Studio Fun International.

Disney Princess Staff, et al. Disney Princess Carry along Treasury. 2009. (Carry along Treasury Ser.). (ENG., Illus.). 22p. (J). (gr. -1-3). bds. 14.99 *(978-0-7944-1891-5(0)*, Reader's Digest Children's Bks.) Studio Fun International.

Disney, Princesses, ed. Snow White, My Best Friends Audio Tales: Disney. 2009. 32p. 8.99 *(978-1-59069-772-6(3))* Studio Mouse LLC.

Disney Publishing Staff & Studiomouse Staff. Panda Cub Explores. 2011. (ENG.). 20p. (J). *(978-1-59069-944-7(0))* Studio Mouse LLC.

Disney, Sofia the First. Disney Guess Who, Sofia! 2014. (Guess Who Ser.: 1). (ENG.). 10p. (J). (gr. -1-k). 10.99 *(978-0-7944-3074-0(0)*, Reader's Digest Children's Bks.) Studio Fun International.

Disney Sofia the First, Disney Sofia. Disney Sofia the First: Where Is My Tiara? 2014. (Open Door Book Ser.: 2). (ENG.). 16p. (J). (gr. -1 — 1). bds. 10.99 *(978-0-7944-3109-9(7)*, Reader's Digest Children's Bks.) Studio Fun International.

Disney Staff, contrib. by. Write, Slide & Learn Disney Mickey Mouse Clubhouse: Colors & Shapes. 2011. (Disney Write, Slide & Learn Ser.). 12p. (J). 9.99 *(978-1-74183-850-3(9))* Hinkler Bks. Pty, Ltd. AUS. Dist: Ideals Pubns.

—Write, Slide & Learn Disney Pixar Cars: Numbers. 2011. (Disney Write, Slide & Learn Ser.). 12p. (J). 9.99 *(978-1-74183-851-0(7))* Hinkler Bks. Pty, Ltd. AUS. Dist: Ideals Pubns.

—Write, Slide & Learn Disney Princess: Spelling. 2011. (Disney Write, Slide & Learn Ser.). 12p. (J). 9.99 *(978-1-74183-852-7(5))* Hinkler Bks. Pty, Ltd. AUS. Dist: Ideals Pubns.

—Write, Slide & Learn Disney Winnie the Pooh: ABC. 2011. (Disney Write, Slide & Learn Ser.). 12p. (J). bds. 9.99 *(978-1-74183-853-4(3))* Hinkler Bks. Pty, Ltd. AUS. Dist: Ideals Pubns.

Disney Storybook Art Team, illus. Monsters, Inc. 2012. (Read-Along Storybook & CD Ser.). (ENG.). 32p. (J). (gr. -1 — 1). pap. 6.99 *(978-1-4231-4259-1(4))* Disney Pr.

Disney Storybook Artists Staff, contrib. by. Princess Songs. 2011. (Illus.). 12p. (J). bds. *(978-1-4508-2074-5(3)*, 1450820743) Publications International, Ltd.

Disney Storybook Artists Staff, et al, illus. Disney's the Lion King. 2007. (Play-A-Sound Ser.). 16p. (J). (gr. -1-3). 16.98 *(978-1-4127-8776-5(9))* Publications International, Ltd.

Disney Storybook Artists Staff, illus. Finding Nemo. 2007. (Play-A-Sound Ser.). 15p. (J). (gr. -1-3). 15.98 *(978-1-4127-8754-3(8))* Publications International, Ltd.

Division Mastery w/Audio CD: Kit with Book, Wrap-up & CD. 2004. (ENG.). (J). 19.99 *(978-0-943343-98-3(4))* Learning Wrap-Ups, Inc.

Dodd, Emma. Counting. 2017. (ENG., Illus.). 12p. (J). (gr. -1-12). bds. 9.99 ***(978-1-86147-839-9(9)***, Armadillo) Anness Publishing GBR. Dist: National Bk. Network.

—On the Farm. 2017. (ENG., Illus.). 12p. (J). (gr. -1-12). bds. 9.99 ***(978-1-86147-838-2(0)***, Armadillo) Anness Publishing GBR. Dist: National Bk. Network.

Dodd, Emma, illus. Dog & Friends: Birthday. 2017. (ENG.). 12p. (J). (gr. -1-12). bds. 9.99 ***(978-1-86147-836-8(4)***, Armadillo) Anness Publishing GBR. Dist: National Bk. Network.

—Dog & Friends: Busy Day. 2017. (ENG.). 12p. (J). (gr. -1-12). bds. 9.99 ***(978-1-86147-835-1(6)***, Armadillo) Anness Publishing GBR. Dist: National Bk. Network.

—Dog's 123: A Canine Counting Adventure! 2016. (ENG.). 14p. bds. 14.99 *(978-1-86147-698-2(1)*, Armadillo) Anness Publishing GBR. Dist: National Bk. Network.

—Dog's ABC: An Alphabet Adventure! 2016. (ENG.). 14p. bds. 14.99 *(978-1-86147-699-9(X)*, Armadillo) Anness Publishing GBR. Dist: National Bk. Network.

—Tick Tock Dog: A Tell the Time Book - with a Special Movable Clock! 2016. (ENG.). 12p. (J). (gr. -1-12). bds. 14.99 *(978-1-86147-718-7(X)*, Armadillo) Anness Publishing GBR. Dist: National Bk. Network.

Dods, Emma. The Zoo. Daubney, Kate, illus. 2015. (I Explore Ser.). (ENG.). 12p. (J). (gr. -1-k). bds. 6.95 *(978-1-4549-1503-4(X))* Sterling Publishing Co., Inc.

Donaghy, Thomas J. Angels All Around Us. 2004. (Illus.). (J). *(978-0-89942-717-1(0))* Catholic Bk. Publishing Corp.

—Celebrating Mass. 2009. (St. Joseph Board Bks.). (Illus.). 12p. bds. 5.95 *(978-0-89942-662-4(X))* Catholic Bk. Publishing Corp.

—Joyful Prayers. 2009. (St. Joseph Board Bks.). (Illus.). 12p. bds. 5.95 *(978-0-89942-663-1(8))* Catholic Bk. Publishing Corp.

Donaher, D F. & Bibleco. Daniel & the Lions. 2004. (Illus.). (J). bds. *(978-0-9746058-2-1(4)*, Biblemania) Bibleco, Inc.

Donahue, Peter & Whelon, Chuck. 3-D Mazes — Robots. 2012. (Dover 3-D Mazes Ser.). (ENG.). 32p. (J). (gr. 1-6). 5.99 *(978-0-486-49017-5(3))* Dover Pubns., Inc.

Donaldson, Julia. Animal Music. Sharratt, Nick, illus. 2015. (ENG.). 20p. (J). (-k). bds. 10.99 *(978-1-4472-7679-1(5))* Pan Macmillan GBR. Dist: Independent Pubs. Group.

—Chocolate Mousse for Greedy Goose. Sharratt, Nick, illus. 2015. (ENG.). 18p. (J). (-k). bds. 9.99 *(978-1-4472-8788-9(6))* Pan Macmillan GBR. Dist: Independent Pubs. Group.

—Goat Goes to Playgroup. Sharratt, Nick, illus. (ENG.). (J). (-k). 2015. 24p. bds. 9.99 *(978-1-4472-8791-9(6))* 2014. 26p. bds. 9.99 *(978-1-4472-5484-3(8))* Pan Macmillan GBR. Dist: Independent Pubs. Group.

—The Gruffalo Theatre, 1. Scheffler, Axel, illus. 2008. (ENG.). 18p. (gr. 2-5). 34.95 *(978-0-230-53179-6(2)*, Macmillan) Pan Macmillan GBR. Dist: Trans-Atlantic Pubns., Inc.

—Jack & the Flumflum Tree. Roberts, David, illus. 2016. (ENG.). 30p. (J). (gr. -1-k). bds. 9.99 *(978-1-4472-8549-6(2))* Pan Macmillan GBR. Dist: Independent Pubs. Group.

—One Mole Digging A Hole. Sharratt, Nick, illus. 2015. (ENG.). 22p. (J). (-k). bds. 9.99 *(978-1-4472-8790-2(8))* Pan Macmillan GBR. Dist: Independent Pubs. Group.

—One Ted Falls Out of Bed. Currey, Anna, illus. 2014. (ENG.). 12p. (J). (gr. -1 — 1). bds. 8.99 *(978-1-4472-0995-9(8))* Pan Macmillan GBR. Dist: Independent Pubs. Group.

—Room on the Broom Board Book. Sheffler, Axel, illus. 2012. (ENG.). 24p. (J). (— 1). bds. 6.99 *(978-0-8037-3841-6(2)*, Dial Bks) Penguin Young Readers Group.

—Toddle Waddle. Sharratt, Nick, illus. (ENG.). (J). (-k). 2015. 24p. bds. 10.99 *(978-1-4472-8792-6(4))* 2012. 32p. bds. 8.99 *(978-0-230-75751-6(0))* Pan Macmillan GBR. Dist: Independent Pubs. Group.

Donna, Gelsinger, ed. In My Father's Garden. 2007. (ENG.). 10p. (J). bds. 6.99 *(978-1-4037-3625-3(1)*, Spirit Pr.) Bendon, Inc.

Donoghue, Stella. Lift & Learn 123. Snaith, Andy, photos by. 2006. (Illus.). 24p. (gr. -1). per., bds. *(978-1-84610-030-7(5))* Make Believe Ideas.

Don't Stick Sticks up Your Nose! Don't Stuff Stuff in Your Ears! 2013. (Don't Stick Sticks up Your Nose! Don't Stuff Stuff in Your Ears! Ser.). (ENG.). 22p. bds. 5.99 *(978-0-9888861-0-0(3)*, 9780988886100) Dontstickdontstuff.

Doodler, Todd H. Peas on Earth. 2012. (ENG., Illus.). 20p. (J). (gr. k — 1). bds. 6.99 *(978-0-307-93088-0(2)*, Robin Corey Bks.) Random Hse. Children's Bks.

Dora the Explorer Publishing Staff. Dora the Explorer Dora Loves Easter! 2014. (Hugs Book Ser.: 2). (ENG.). 10p. (J). (gr. -1-k). bds. 10.99 *(978-0-7944-3032-0(5))* Reader's Digest Assn., Inc., The.

Dorling Kindersley Publishing Staff. ABC Games. 2016. (Skills for Starting School Ser.). (ENG.). 52p. (J). (gr. -1-k). 9.99 *(978-1-4654-4455-4(6)*, DK Children) Dorling Kindersley Publishing, Inc.

—Animal Colors. (ENG., (J). (gr. -1-k). 2015. Illus.). 14p. bds. 7.99 *(978-1-4654-2946-9(8))* 2012. 12p. bds. 6.99 *(978-1-4654-0164-9(4))* Dorling Kindersley Publishing, Inc. (DK Children).

—Animals. Quasha, Jennifer, ed. 2008. (Baby Touch & Feel Ser.). (ENG., Illus.). 14p. (J). (gr. -1 — 1). bds. 5.99 *(978-0-7566-3468-1(7)*, DK Children) Dorling Kindersley Publishing, Inc.

—Baby - Hide & Seek! 2012. (ENG.). 16p. (J). (gr. -1 — 1). bds. 6.99 *(978-0-7566-8999-5(6)*, DK Children) Dorling Kindersley Publishing, Inc.

—Baby - Tractor! 2012. (ENG.). 16p. (J). (gr. -1 — 1). bds. 6.99 *(978-0-7566-8998-8(8)*, DK Children) Dorling Kindersley Publishing, Inc.

—Baby Animals. (Touch & Feel Ser.). (ENG.). (J). (gr. -1-k). 2011. 12p. bds. 6.99 *(978-0-7566-8991-9(0))* 2009. 14p. bds. 5.99 *(978-0-7566-4301-0(5))* Dorling Kindersley Publishing, Inc. (DK Children).

—Baby Baa Baa! 2009. (ENG.). 16p. (J). (gr. -1 — 1). bds. 6.99 *(978-0-7566-5802-1(0)*, DK Children) Dorling Kindersley Publishing, Inc.

—Baby Cheep! Cheep! 2015. (ENG.). 14p. (J). (gr. -1 — 1). bds. 5.99 *(978-1-4654-3184-4(5)*, DK Children) Dorling Kindersley Publishing, Inc.

—Baby Faces. 2016. (ENG., Illus.). 14p. (J). (— 1). bds. 5.99 *(978-1-4654-4466-0(1)*, DK Children) Dorling Kindersley Publishing, Inc.

—Baby Faces! 2011. (ENG.). 16p. (J). (gr. -1 — 1). bds. 6.99 *(978-0-7566-7175-4(2)*, DK Children) Dorling Kindersley Publishing, Inc.

—Baby First Words! 2013. (ENG.). 16p. (J). (gr. -1 — 1). bds. 6.99 *(978-1-4654-0168-7(7)*, DK Children) Dorling Kindersley Publishing, Inc.

—Baby Loves Peekaboo! Quasha, Jennifer, ed. King, Dave, photos by. 2008. (ENG., Illus.). 12p. (J). (gr. -1-k). bds. 6.99 *(978-0-7566-3486-5(5)*, DK Children) Dorling Kindersley Publishing, Inc.

—Baby Night-Night. 2016. (ENG., Illus.). 14p. (J). (— 1). bds. 5.99 *(978-1-4654-4389-2(4)*, DK Children) Dorling Kindersley Publishing, Inc.

—Baby Peekaboo! 2011. (ENG.). 16p. (J). (gr. -1 — 1). bds. 6.99 *(978-0-7566-7165-5(5)*, DK Children) Dorling Kindersley Publishing, Inc.

—Baby Talk: 6 Giant Flasp for Baby to Flip. 2005. (Fun Flaps Ser.). (ENG., Illus.). 14p. (J). (gr. -1-k). bds. 4.99

(978-0-7566-0986-3(0), DK Children) Dorling Kindersley Publishing, Inc.

—Baby Touch & Feel: Halloween. 2017. (Baby Touch & Feel Ser.). (ENG., Illus.). 14p. (J). (— 1). bds. 5.99 ***(978-1-4654-6235-0(X)***, DK Children) Dorling Kindersley Publishing, Inc.

—Baby Touch & Feel: Kittens. 2017. (Baby Touch & Feel Ser.). (ENG.). 14p. (J). (— 1). bds. 5.99 *(978-1-4654-5622-9(8)*, DK Children) Dorling Kindersley Publishing, Inc.

—Baby Touch & Feel: Puppies. 2017. (Baby Touch & Feel Ser.). (ENG., Illus.). 14p. (J). (— 1). bds. 5.99 *(978-1-4654-5621-2(X)*, DK Children) Dorling Kindersley Publishing, Inc.

—Baby What's That? 2015. (ENG.). 14p. (J). (gr. -1 — 1). bds. 5.99 *(978-1-4654-3181-3(0)*, DK Children) Dorling Kindersley Publishing, Inc.

—Baby's First Thanksgiving. 2017. (ENG.). 14p. (J). (— 1). bds. 5.99 ***(978-1-4654-6349-4(6)***, DK Children) Dorling Kindersley Publishing, Inc.

—Bathtime. 2009. (Baby Touch & Feel Ser.). (ENG., Illus.). 14p. (J). (gr. -1 — 1). bds. 5.99 *(978-0-7566-5149-7(2)*, DK Children) Dorling Kindersley Publishing, Inc.

—Bathtime Peekaboo! 2005. (ENG., Illus.). 12p. (J). (gr. -1-k). bds. 6.99 *(978-0-7566-1145-3(8)*, DK Children) Dorling Kindersley Publishing, Inc.

—Bedtime. 2008. (Baby Touch & Feel Ser.). (ENG.). 14p. (J). (gr. -1 — 1). bds. 5.99 *(978-0-7566-4511-3(5)*, DK Children) Dorling Kindersley Publishing, Inc.

—Beep! Beep! 2012. (Baby Touch & Feel Ser.). (ENG., Illus.). 14p. (J). (gr. -1 — 1). bds. 5.99 *(978-0-7566-9785-3(9)*, DK Children) Dorling Kindersley Publishing, Inc.

—Big Dump Truck. 2003. (Wheelie Bks.). (ENG., Illus.). 12p. (J). (gr. -1-k). bds. 6.99 *(978-0-7894-9714-7(X)*, DK Children) Dorling Kindersley Publishing, Inc.

—Big Red Barn. 2017. (ENG.). 12p. (J). (— 1). bds. 14.99 ***(978-1-4654-6313-5(5)***, DK Children) Dorling Kindersley Publishing, Inc.

—Birthday. 2014. (Touch & Feel Ser.). (ENG.). 12p. (J). (gr. -1-k). bds. 6.99 *(978-1-4654-1694-0(3)*, DK Children) Dorling Kindersley Publishing, Inc.

—Boys' Potty Time. 2010. (ENG., Illus.). 14p. (J). (gr. -1-k). bds. 7.99 *(978-0-7566-5884-7(5)*, DK Children) Dorling Kindersley Publishing, Inc.

—Build Your Own Adventure. 2015. (ENG.). 80p. (J). (gr. 2-5). 24.99 *(978-1-4654-3590-3(5)*, DK Children) Dorling Kindersley Publishing, Inc.

—Bunny. 2011. (Baby Touch & Feel Ser.). (ENG.). 14p. (J). (gr. -1 — 1). bds. 5.99 *(978-0-7566-8987-2(2)*, DK Children) Dorling Kindersley Publishing, Inc.

—Christmas Peekaboo! 2008. (ENG.). 12p. (J). (gr. -1-k). bds. 9.99 *(978-0-7566-4022-4(9)*, DK Children) Dorling Kindersley Publishing, Inc.

—Colors. 2013. (ENG.). 16p. (J). (gr. -1 — 1). bds. 6.99 *(978-1-4654-0959-1(9)*, DK Children) Dorling Kindersley Publishing, Inc.

—Cuddly Animals. 2011. (Baby Touch & Feel Ser.). (ENG.). 14p. (J). (gr. -1 — 1). bds. 5.99 *(978-0-7566-8688-8(1)*, DK Children) Dorling Kindersley Publishing, Inc.

—Dinosaur. 2016. (ENG., Illus.). 36p. (J). bds. *(978-0-241-23758-8(0))* Dorling Kindersley Publishing, Inc.

—Dinosaurs. 2012. (Touch & Feel Ser.). (ENG.). 12p. (J). (gr. -1-k). bds. 6.99 *(978-0-7566-9288-9(1)*, DK Children) Dorling Kindersley Publishing, Inc.

—Eyes, Nose, Toes Peekaboo! 2008. (ENG.). 12p. (J). (gr. -1-k). bds. 6.99 *(978-0-7566-3759-0(7)*, DK Children) Dorling Kindersley Publishing, Inc.

—Farm. (ENG., (J). (gr. -1 — 1). 2014. Illus.). 10p. bds. 6.99 *(978-1-4654-1687-2(0))* 2011. 12p. bds. 6.99 *(978-0-7566-8989-6(9))* 2011. (Illus.). 12p. bds. 9.99 *(978-0-7566-7172-3(8))* Dorling Kindersley Publishing, Inc. (DK Children).

—Farm - Little Hide & Seek. 2013. (ENG.). 14p. (J). (gr. -1 — 1). bds. 7.99 *(978-1-4654-0932-4(7)*, DK Children) Dorling Kindersley Publishing, Inc.

—Farm Animals. 2011. (Baby Touch & Feel Ser.). (ENG.). 14p. (J). (gr. -1 — 1). bds. 5.99 *(978-0-7566-8986-5(4)*, DK Children) Dorling Kindersley Publishing, Inc.

—Farm Friends. 2013. (Baby Touch & Feel Ser.). (ENG., Illus.). 14p. (J). (gr. -1 — 1). bds. 5.99 *(978-1-4654-1672-8(2)*, DK Children) Dorling Kindersley Publishing, Inc.

—Farm Tractor. 2003. (Wheelie Bks.). (ENG., Illus.). 12p. (J). (gr. -1-k). bds. 6.99 *(978-0-7894-9713-0(1)*, DK Children) Dorling Kindersley Publishing, Inc.

—Fire Engine. 2011. (Touch & Feel Ser.). (ENG.). 12p. (J). (gr. -1-k). bds. 6.99 *(978-0-7566-8992-6(9)*, DK Children) Dorling Kindersley Publishing, Inc.

—Fire Truck. 2009. (ENG.). 10p. (J). (gr. -1-k). bds. 7.99 *(978-0-7566-5228-9(6)*, DK Children) Dorling Kindersley Publishing, Inc.

—Fluffy Animals. 2012. (Baby Touch & Feel Ser.). (ENG.). 14p. (J). (gr. -1 — 1). bds. 5.99 *(978-0-7566-9786-0(7)*, DK Children) Dorling Kindersley Publishing, Inc.

—Follow the Trail: Trucks. 2016. (ENG., Illus.). 14p. (J). (-k). bds. 9.99 *(978-1-4654-5126-2(9)*, DK Children) Dorling Kindersley Publishing, Inc.

—Follow the Trail: Winter Wonderland. 2017. (Follow the Trail Ser.). (ENG.). 14p. (J). (-k). bds. 9.99 ***(978-1-4654-6136-0(1)***, DK Children) Dorling Kindersley Publishing, Inc.

—Good Night Sophie - A Touch & Feel Book. 2017. (ENG.). 12p. (J). (— 1). bds. 5.99 *(978-1-4654-5625-0(2)*, DK Children) Dorling Kindersley Publishing, Inc.

—Heroes Unite! 2014. (Ultimate Sticker Collections). (ENG.). 96p. (J). (gr. 1-4). pap. 12.99 *(978-1-4654-1684-1(6)*, DK Children) Dorling Kindersley Publishing, Inc.

—Hoppity Hop Peekaboo! 2010. (ENG.). 12p. (J). (gr. -1 — 1). bds. 9.99 *(978-0-7566-5861-8(6)*, DK Children) Dorling Kindersley Publishing, Inc.

—Jungle Animals. 2012. (Touch & Feel Ser.). (ENG.). 12p. (J). (gr. -1-k). bds. 6.99 *(978-0-7566-9289-6(X)*, DK Children) Dorling Kindersley Publishing, Inc.

—Kitten. 2011. (Touch & Feel Ser.). (ENG.). 12p. (J). (gr. -1-k). bds. 6.99 *(978-0-7566-9165-3(6)*, DK Children) Dorling Kindersley Publishing, Inc.

—LEGO(r) Star Wars Minifigures Ultimate Sticker Collection. 2012. (ENG.). 96p. pap. *(978-1-4053-9826-8(4))* Dorling Kindersley.

—Let's Get Counting! 2013. (My First Bks.). (ENG.). 36p. (J). (gr. -1 — 1). bds. 5.99 *(978-1-4654-0958-4(0)*, DK Children) Dorling Kindersley Publishing, Inc.

—Little Hide & Seek Animals. 2012. (ENG.). 16p. (J). (gr. -1 — 1). bds. 7.99 *(978-0-7566-9273-5(3)*, DK Children) Dorling Kindersley Publishing, Inc.

—Little Hide & Seek Words. 2012. (ENG.). 16p. (J). (gr. -1 — 1). bds. 7.99 *(978-0-7566-9274-2(1)*, DK Children) Dorling Kindersley Publishing, Inc.

—My Best Pop-Up Space Book. 2015. (ENG., Illus.). 18p. (J). (-k). bds. 14.99 *(978-1-4654-3914-7(5)*, DK Children) Dorling Kindersley Publishing, Inc.

—My First 123. 2015. (My First Bks.). (ENG.). 36p. (J). (gr. -1 — 1). bds. 5.99 *(978-1-4654-2903-2(4)*, DK Children) Dorling Kindersley Publishing, Inc.

—My First Animals. 2015. (My First Bks.). (ENG.). 36p. (J). (gr. -1 — 1). bds. 5.99 *(978-1-4654-2901-8(8)*, DK Children) Dorling Kindersley Publishing, Inc.

—My First Body. 2016. (ENG., Illus.). 36p. (J). (— 1). bds. 5.99 *(978-1-4654-4492-9(0)*, DK Children) Dorling Kindersley Publishing, Inc.

—My First Colors: Let's Learn Them All! 2010. (Tab Board Bks.). (ENG.). 28p. (J). (gr. -1 — 1). bds. 9.99 *(978-0-7566-7141-9(8)*, DK Children) Dorling Kindersley Publishing, Inc.

—My First Dinosaur. 2016. (ENG., Illus.). 36p. (J). (— 1). bds. 5.99 *(978-1-4654-4491-2(2)*, DK Children) Dorling Kindersley Publishing, Inc.

—My First Farm. 2016. (ENG., Illus.). 36p. (J). (— 1). bds. 5.99 *(978-1-4654-4487-5(4)*, DK Children) Dorling Kindersley Publishing, Inc.

—My First Opposites. 2017. (My First Bks.). (ENG.). 36p. (J). (— 1). bds. 5.99 ***(978-1-4654-6141-4(8)***, DK Children) Dorling Kindersley Publishing, Inc.

—My First Out & About. 2017. (My First Bks.). (ENG.). 36p. (J). (— 1). bds. 5.99 ***(978-1-4654-6083-7(7)***, DK Children) Dorling Kindersley Publishing, Inc.

—My First Pets. 2016. (ENG., Illus.). 36p. (J). (— 1). bds. 5.99 *(978-1-4654-4489-9(0)*, DK Children) Dorling Kindersley Publishing, Inc.

—My First Shapes. 2017. (My First Bks.). (ENG., Illus.). 36p. (J). (— 1). bds. 5.99 ***(978-1-4654-6082-0(9)***, DK Children) Dorling Kindersley Publishing, Inc.

—My First Things That Go. 2016. (ENG., Illus.). 36p. (J). (— 1). bds. 5.99 *(978-1-4654-4490-5(4)*, DK Children) Dorling Kindersley Publishing, Inc.

—My First Things That Go: Let's Get Moving! 2009. (Tab Board Bks.). (ENG.). 28p. (J). (gr. -1-k). bds. 9.99 *(978-0-7566-4502-1(6)*, DK Children) Dorling Kindersley Publishing, Inc.

—My First Tractor. 2016. (ENG., Illus.). 36p. (J). (— 1). bds. 5.99 *(978-1-4654-4390-8(8)*, DK Children) Dorling Kindersley Publishing, Inc.

—My First Trucks & Diggers. 2013. (Tab Board Bks.). (ENG.). 28p. (J). (gr. -1 — 1). bds. 9.99 *(978-1-4654-1673-5(0)*, DK Children) Dorling Kindersley Publishing, Inc.

—Noisy Animal Peekaboo! 2015. (ENG., Illus.). 12p. (J). (gr. -1 — 1). bds. 12.99 *(978-1-4654-3182-0(9)*, DK Children) Dorling Kindersley Publishing, Inc.

—Noisy Baby Peekaboo! 2015. (ENG.). 12p. (J). (— 1). bds. 12.99 *(978-1-4654-3821-8(1)*, DK Children) Dorling Kindersley Publishing, Inc.

—Noisy Digger Peekaboo! 2015. (ENG., Illus.). 12p. (J). (gr. -1 — 1). bds. 12.99 *(978-1-4654-3183-7(7)*, DK Children) Dorling Kindersley Publishing, Inc.

—Noisy Farm Peekaboo! 2015. (ENG., Illus.). 12p. (J). (— 1). bds. 12.99 *(978-1-4654-3820-1(3)*, DK Children) Dorling Kindersley Publishing, Inc.

—Noisy Peekaboo! Baa! Baa! 2009. (ENG.). 12p. (J). (gr. -1 — 1). bds. 12.99 *(978-0-7566-4299-0(X)*, DK Children) Dorling Kindersley Publishing, Inc.

—Noisy Toys Peekaboo! 2016. (ENG., Illus.). 12p. (J). (— 1). bds. 12.99 *(978-1-4654-5423-2(3)*, DK Children) Dorling Kindersley Publishing, Inc.

—Park. 2010. (Baby Touch & Feel Ser.). (ENG.). 14p. (J). (gr. -1 — 1). bds. 5.99 *(978-0-7566-7131-0(0)*, DK Children) Dorling Kindersley Publishing, Inc.

—Pets. 2010. (Baby Touch & Feel Ser.). (ENG., Illus.). 14p. (J). (gr. -1 — 1). bds. 5.99 *(978-0-7566-6684-2(8)*, DK Children) Dorling Kindersley Publishing, Inc.

—Pirate Glow-in-the-Dark. 2004. (Ultimate Sticker Bks.). (ENG.). 16p. (J). (gr. k-3). pap. 6.99 *(978-0-7566-0219-2(X)*, DK Children) Dorling Kindersley Publishing, Inc.

—Playtime. (My First Bks.). (ENG.). (J). 2017. 36p. (— 1). bds. 5.99 *(978-1-4654-5677-9(5))* 2012. 12p. (gr. -1-k). bds. 6.99 *(978-1-4654-0166-3(0))* Dorling Kindersley Publishing, Inc. (DK Children).

—Playtime Peekaboo! 2005. (ENG., Illus.). 12p. (J). (gr. -1-k). bds. 6.99 *(978-0-7566-1144-6(X)*, DK Children) Dorling Kindersley Publishing, Inc.

—Please & Thank You. 2017. (Skills for Starting School Ser.). (ENG.). 18p. (J). (— 1). bds. 5.99 *(978-1-4654-5679-3(1)*, DK Children) Dorling Kindersley Publishing, Inc.

—Ponies. 2013. (Touch & Feel Ser.). (ENG.). 12p. (J). (gr. -1-k). bds. 6.99 *(978-1-4654-0919-5(X)*, DK Children) Dorling Kindersley Publishing, Inc.

—Pop-Up Peekaboo! - Meow! 2012. (ENG., Illus.). 12p. (J). (gr. -1 — 1). bds. 9.99 *(978-0-7566-9309-1(8)*, DK Children) Dorling Kindersley Publishing, Inc.

—Pop-Up Peekaboo! - Playtime. 2011. (ENG.). 12p. (J). (gr. -1 — 1). bds. 9.99 *(978-0-7566-7171-6(X)*, DK Children) Dorling Kindersley Publishing, Inc.

—Pop-Up Peekaboo Pumpkin. 2017. (ENG.). 12p. (J). (— 1). bds. 9.99 *(978-1-4654-5276-4(1)*, DK Children) Dorling Kindersley Publishing, Inc.

—Pull the Tab: Numbers. 2015. (ENG., Illus.). 10p. (J). (— 1). bds. 6.99 *(978-1-4654-3857-7(2)*, DK Children) Dorling Kindersley Publishing, Inc.

—Puppies & Kittens. 2008. (Baby Touch & Feel Ser.). (ENG., Illus.). 14p. (J). (gr. -1 — 1). bds. 5.99 *(978-0-7566-3835-1(6)*, DK Children) Dorling Kindersley Publishing, Inc.

—Puppy. 2011. (Touch & Feel Ser.). (ENG.). 12p. (J). (gr. -1-k). bds. 6.99 *(978-0-7566-9166-0(4)*, DK Children) Dorling Kindersley Publishing, Inc.

—Rainbow Colors Peekaboo! 2008. (ENG.). 12p. (J). (gr. -1-k). bds. 6.99 *(978-0-7566-3760-6(0)*, DK Children) Dorling Kindersley Publishing, Inc.

—Really Feely: Baby Animals. 2017. (ENG., Illus.). 12p. (J). (— 1). bds. 6.99 *(978-1-4654-5697-7(X)*, DK Children) Dorling Kindersley Publishing, Inc.

—Shapes. 2013. (Touch & Feel Ser.). (ENG.). 12p. (J). (gr. -1-k). bds. 6.99 *(978-1-4654-0920-1(3)*, DK Children) Dorling Kindersley Publishing, Inc.

—Sophie la Girafe: ABC Flashcards. 2017. (ENG.). 26p. (J). (— 1). bds. 9.99 *(978-1-4654-5702-8(X)*, DK Children) Dorling Kindersley Publishing, Inc.

—Sophie la Girafe: Hide & Seek. 2016. (ENG., Illus.). 16p. (J). (— 1). bds. 6.99 *(978-1-4654-4461-5(0)*, DK Children) Dorling Kindersley Publishing, Inc.

—Sophie la Girafe: on the Move. 2016. (Baby Touch & Feel Ser.). (ENG., Illus.). 14p. (J). (— 1). bds. 5.99 *(978-1-4654-4395-3(9)*, DK Children) Dorling Kindersley Publishing, Inc.

—Sophie la Girafe: Sophie's Big Beep Beep Book! 2016. (ENG., Illus.). 12p. (J). (— 1). bds. 14.99 *(978-1-4654-5375-4(X)*, DK Children) Dorling Kindersley Publishing, Inc.

—Sophie la Girafe: Sophie's Big First Word Book. 2016. (ENG., Illus.). 18p. (J). (gr. -1 — 1). bds. 9.99 *(978-1-4654-4494-3(7)*, DK Children) Dorling Kindersley Publishing, Inc.

—Sophie la Girafe: Sophie's Pull the Tab Play Book. 2016. (ENG., Illus.). 10p. (J). (gr. -1 — 1). bds. 6.99 *(978-1-4654-4467-7(X)*, DK Children) Dorling Kindersley Publishing, Inc.

—Sophie's Busy Day. 2013. (Baby Touch & Feel Ser.). (ENG.). 14p. (J). (gr. -1 — 1). bds. 5.99 *(978-1-4654-0967-6(X)*, DK Children) Dorling Kindersley Publishing, Inc.

—Sports Car. 2003. (Wheelie Bks.). (ENG., Illus.). 12p. (J). (gr. -1-k). bds. 6.99 *(978-0-7894-9711-6(5)*, DK Children) Dorling Kindersley Publishing, Inc.

—Stars & Planets: Glow in the Dark. 2014. (ENG.). 24p. (J). (gr. k-4). 19.99 *(978-1-4654-1420-5(7)*, DK Children) Dorling Kindersley Publishing, Inc.

—Story Time. 2016. (Skills for Starting School Ser.). (ENG.). 18p. (J). (-k). 13.99 *(978-1-4654-5134-7(X)*, DK Children) Dorling Kindersley Publishing, Inc.

—Tabbed Board Books: My First Zoo: Let's Meet the Animals! 2016. (Tab Board Bks.). (ENG., Illus.). 28p. (J). (— 1). bds. 9.99 *(978-1-4654-4883-5(7)*, DK Children) Dorling Kindersley Publishing, Inc.

—Tangled. 2010. (Ultimate Sticker Bks.). (ENG.). 16p. (J). (gr. k-3). pap. 6.99 *(978-0-7566-6687-3(2)*, DK Children) Dorling Kindersley Publishing, Inc.

—Things That Go. 2012. (ENG., Illus.). 12p. (J). (gr. -1 — 1). bds. 9.99 *(978-0-7566-9009-0(9)*, DK Children) Dorling Kindersley Publishing, Inc.

—Touch & Feel 123. 2013. (Touch & Feel Ser.). (ENG.). 12p. (J). (gr. -1-k). bds. 6.99 *(978-1-4654-0917-1(3)*, DK Children) Dorling Kindersley Publishing, Inc.

—Touch & Feel: Animal Library: Animal Library. 2014. (Touch & Feel Ser.). (ENG., Illus.). 36p. (J). (gr. -1-k). bds. 19.99 *(978-1-4654-2766-3(X)*, DK Children) Dorling Kindersley Publishing, Inc.

—Touch & Feel Christmas. 2014. (Touch & Feel Ser.). (ENG., Illus.). 12p. (J). (gr. -1-k). bds. 6.99 *(978-1-4654-2036-7(3)*, DK Children) Dorling Kindersley Publishing, Inc.

—Touch & Feel Pets. 2012. (Touch & Feel Ser.). (ENG.). 12p. (J). (gr. -1-k). bds. 6.99 *(978-0-7566-8990-2(2)*, DK Children) Dorling Kindersley Publishing, Inc.

—Tractor. 2010. (Baby Touch & Feel Ser.). (ENG.). (J). (gr. -1 — 1). 14p. bds. 5.99 *(978-0-7566-7132-7(9))*; (Illus.). 10p. bds. 8.99 *(978-0-7566-6302-5(4))* Dorling Kindersley Publishing, Inc. (DK Children).

—Wheelie Baby: Truck & Friends. 2012. (Wheelie Bks.). (ENG.). 10p. (J). (gr. -1 — 1). bds. 6.99 *(978-0-7566-9291-9(1)*, DK Children) Dorling Kindersley Publishing, Inc.

—Who Am I? Baby Animals. 2012. (ENG.). 28p. (J). (gr. -1 — 1). bds. 6.99 *(978-0-7566-9018-2(8)*, DK Children) Dorling Kindersley Publishing, Inc.

—Who Am I? Farm Animals. 2012. (ENG.). 28p. (J). (gr. -1 — 1). bds. 6.99 *(978-0-7566-9017-5(X)*, DK Children) Dorling Kindersley Publishing, Inc.

—Wild Animals. (ENG., Illus.). 14p. (J). 2016. (-k). bds. 9.99 *(978-1-4654-5125-5(0))* 2009. (gr. -1 — 1). bds. 5.99 *(978-0-7566-5150-3(6))* Dorling Kindersley Publishing, Inc. (DK Children).

—Woof! Woof! (ENG., 12p. (J). (gr. -1 — 1). 2013. Illus.). bds. 9.99 *(978-1-4654-0929-4(7))* 2009. bds. 12.99 *(978-0-7566-5236-4(7))* Dorling Kindersley Publishing, Inc. (DK Children).

Dorling Kindersley Publishing Staff, creator. Bedtime Peekaboo! 2006. (ENG., Illus.). 12p. (J). (gr. -1-k). bds. 6.99 *(978-0-7566-1622-9(0)*, DK Children) Dorling Kindersley Publishing, Inc.

—Dog. 2005. (Ultimate Sticker Bks.). (ENG., Illus.). 16p. (J). (gr. k-3). pap. 6.99 *(978-0-7566-1457-7(0)*, DK Children) Dorling Kindersley Publishing, Inc.

Dorling Kindersley Publishing Staff, ed. Digger. 2009. (ENG.). 10p. (J). (gr. -1-k). bds. 8.99 *(978-0-7566-5229-6(4)*, DK Children) Dorling Kindersley Publishing, Inc.

—Noisy Farm. 2005. (Fun Flaps Ser.). (ENG., Illus.). 14p. (J). (gr. -1-k). bds. 4.99 *(978-0-7566-0987-0(9)*, DK Children) Dorling Kindersley Publishing, Inc.

Dorling Kindersley Publishing Staff & Pearson, Nicole. My First Halloween Board Book. 2012. (My First Bks.). (ENG.). 36p. (J). (gr. -1-k). bds. 5.99 *(978-0-7566-9856-0(1)*, DK Children) Dorling Kindersley Publishing, Inc.

Douglas, Lisa Jo. Active Animals A Thru Z. 2008. (ENG., Illus.). 30p. (J). per. 12.99 *(978-1-59879-311-6(X)*, Lifevest) Lifevest Publishing, Inc.

Dowley, Tim. Bible Animal Stencil Book, 1 vol. 2008. 6p. (J). bds. 11.99 *(978-0-8254-7365-4(9)*, Candle Bks.) Lion Hudson PLC GBR. Dist: Kregel Pubns.

—Noah's Ark Pop-Up. Martin, Stuart, illus. 2007. 6p. (J). bds. 14.99 *(978-0-8254-7330-2(6)*, Candle Bks.) Lion Hudson PLC GBR. Dist: Kregel Pubns.

Downing, Julie, illus. All the Ways I Love You (bilingual Edition) 2005. (SPA & ENG.). 10p. (J). 8.95 *(978-1-58117-335-2(0)*, Intervisual/Piggy Toes) Bendon, Inc.

Downing, Sue. Cheep, Cheep! Baby Animal Sounds. 2016. (ENG., Illus.). 10p. (J). bds. 7.99 *(978-1-61963-833-4(9)*, 9781619638334, Bloomsbury USA Childrens) Bloomsbury Publishing USA.

—Look, Look! Baby Animal Friends. 2016. (ENG., Illus.). 10p. (J). bds. 7.99 *(978-1-61963-832-7(0)*, 9781619638327, Bloomsbury USA Childrens) Bloomsbury Publishing USA.

Dowswell, P. Secret Agent Spy. 2009. (Kid Kits Ser.). 144p. (J). 16.99 *(978-1-60130-152-9(9))*; 16.99 *(978-1-60130-153-6(7))* EDC Publishing. (Usborne).

Doxey, Heidi. Jesus Was Just Like Me. 2017. (ENG.). (J). bds. 10.99 ***(978-1-4621-1925-7(5))*** Cedar Fort, Inc./CFI Distribution.

The Dragon & the Knight. 2014. (ENG., Illus.). 22p. (J). (gr. k). 29.99 *(978-1-4169-6081-2(3)*, Little Simon) Little Simon.

Dragonwagon, Crescent. All the Awake Animals Are Almost Asleep. McPhail, David, illus. 2016. (ENG.). 30p. (J). (gr. -1 — 1). bds. 7.99 *(978-0-316-33627-7(0))* Little, Brown Bks. for Young Readers.

Drake, Ernest. Dragonology: The Complete Book of Dragons. Steer, Dugald A., ed. 2003. (Ologies Ser.). (ENG., Illus.). 32p. (J). (gr. 3-7). 24.99 *(978-0-7636-2329-6(6))* Candlewick Pr.

Drescher, Daniela. What's Hiding in There? 2008. Orig. Title: Was Raschelt Denn Da? (ENG., Illus.). 16p. (J). *(978-0-86315-634-2(7))* Floris Bks.

Drescher, Henrik. Pat the Beastie: A Pull-and-Poke Book. Drescher, Henrik, illus. 2009. (ENG., Illus.). 11p. (J). (gr. -1-3). bds. 11.95 *(978-0-7611-5610-9(0)*, 15610) Workman Publishing Co., Inc.

Driscoll, Laura. Thumper Goes A-Thumpin' Tyminski, Lori, illus. 2015. (ENG.). 12p. (J). (gr. -1 — 1). bds. 6.99 *(978-1-4847-0960-3(8))* Disney Pr.

Drummond, Karona. Along Came You, 1 vol. 2014. (ENG.). 24p. (J). bds. 7.99 *(978-0-310-72859-7(2))* Zonderkidz.

Dubois, Liz Goulet. What Does a Seed Need? 2011. (ENG.). 18p. (J). (gr. -1-k). 7.99 *(978-0-8431-9901-7(6)*, Price Stern Sloan) Penguin Young Readers Group.

Ducatteau, Florence. A Day at the Museum. Peten, Chantal, illus. 2013. (Want to Know Ser.). (ENG.). 32p. (J). (gr. k-2). 16.95 *(978-1-60537-142-9(4))* Cobblestone Publishing Co.

Duksta, Laura. I Love You More. Keesler, Karen, illus. 2009. (ENG.). 24p. (J). bds. 6.99 *(978-1-4022-2460-7(5)*, Sourcebooks Jabberwocky) Sourcebooks, Inc.

—I Love You More Padded Board Book. Keesler, Karen, illus. 2013. (ENG.). 24p. (J). bds. 8.99 *(978-1-4022-9250-7(3)*, Sourcebooks Jabberwocky) Sourcebooks, Inc.

—Te Quiero Más. Keesler, Karen, illus. 2013. (ENG & SPA.). 24p. (J). bds. 6.99 *(978-1-4022-8177-8(3)*, Sourcebooks Jabberwocky) Sourcebooks, Inc.

Dunn, Judy. The Little Duck. Dunn, Phoebe, photos by. 2014. (ENG., Illus.). 14p. (J). (— 1). bds. 6.99 *(978-0-385-38521-3(8)*, Random Hse. Bks. for Young Readers) Random Hse. Children's Bks.

Dunn, Phoebe. The Little Kitten. 2015. (ENG., Illus.). 14p. (J). (— 1). bds. 6.99 *(978-0-553-51138-3(6)*, Random Hse. Bks. for Young Readers) Random Hse. Children's Bks.

Dunn, Phoebe & Dunn, Judy. The Little Puppy. 2015. (ENG., Illus.). 14p. (J). (— 1). bds. 6.99 *(978-0-553-51139-0(4)*, Random Hse. Bks. for Young Readers) Random Hse. Children's Bks.

Dunrea, Olivier. Gossie & Friends: A First Flap Book. Dunrea, Olivier, illus. 2006. (Gossie & Friends Ser.). (ENG., Illus.). 8p. (J). (gr. -1 — 1). 11.99 *(978-0-618-70786-7(7))* Houghton Mifflin Harcourt Publishing Co.

—Jasper & Joop: A Perfect Pair: One Tidy, One Messy. 2014. (Gossie & Friends Ser.). (ENG., Illus.). 32p. (J). (— 1). bds. 6.99 *(978-0-544-17320-0(1)*, HMH Books For Young Readers) Houghton Mifflin Harcourt Publishing Co.

—Ollie's Halloween. 2013. (Gossie & Friends Ser.). (ENG., Illus.). 30p. (J). (gr. -1 — 1). bds. 6.99 *(978-0-544-05720-3(1))* Houghton Mifflin Harcourt Publishing Co.

Durant, Alan. If You Go Walking in Tiger Wood. Boon, Debbie, illus. 2005. (ENG.). 100p. (J). (gr. -1-k). pap. 9.99 *(978-0-00-710390-4(5)*, HarperSport) HarperCollins Pubs. Ltd. GBR. Dist: Independent Pubs. Group.

Dynamo. Googly Eyes: Flipper the Seal Makes a Discovery! 2014. (ENG., Illus.). 12p. (J). (gr. -1-2). bds. 6.99 *(978-1-84322-905-6(6)*, Armadillo) Anness Publishing GBR. Dist: National Bk. Network.

—Googly Eyes: Fluffy Kitten Goes Exploring! 2014. (ENG., Illus.). 12p. (J). (gr. 3-2). bds. 6.99 *(978-1-84322-880-6(7)*, Armadillo) Anness Publishing GBR. Dist: National Bk. Network.

—Googly Eyes: Goodnight, Benjy Bunny! 2014. (ENG., Illus.). 12p. (J). (gr. -1-12). bds. 6.99 *(978-1-84322-879-0(3)*, Armadillo) Anness Publishing GBR. Dist: National Bk. Network.

—Googly Eyes: Leo Lion's Noisy Roar! 2014. (ENG., Illus.). 12p. (J). (gr. -1-2). bds. 6.99 *(978-1-84322-906-3(4)*, Armadillo) Anness Publishing GBR. Dist: National Bk. Network.

East, Jacqueline, illus. Princess Palace: A Three-Demensional Playset. 2006. 8p. (J). (gr. -1-3). 22.95 *(978-1-58117-492-2(6)*, Intervisual/Piggy Toes) Bendon, Inc.

Eastman, P. D. Are You My Mother? 2015. (Big Bright & Early Board Book Ser.). (ENG., Illus.). 24p. (J). (— 1). bds. 6.99 *(978-0-553-49680-2(8)*, Random Hse. Bks. for Young Readers) Random Hse. Children's Bks.

—Go, Dog. Go! 2015. (Big Bright & Early Board Book Ser.). (ENG., Illus.). 24p. (J). (gr. -1-2). bds. 6.99 *(978-0-553-52109-2(8)*, Random Hse. Bks. for Young Readers) Random Hse. Children's Bks.

Eastman, P. D. & Frith, Michael. The Little Red Box of Bright & Early Board Books. 2014. (Bright & Early Board Books(TM) Ser.). (ENG., Illus.). 24p. (J). (— 1). bds. 19.96 *(978-0-385-39207-5(9)*, Random Hse. Bks. for Young Readers) Random Hse. Children's Bks.

Eastman, Peter. Fred & Ted Like to Fly. 2011. (Bright & Early Board Books Ser.). (ENG., Illus.). 24p. (J). (— 1). bds. 4.99 *(978-0-375-86802-3(X)*, Random Hse. Bks. for Young Readers) Random Hse. Children's Bks.

Eaton, Kait. I Want to Be A... Fairy. Enright, Amanda, illus. 2014. (J). *(978-1-4351-5499-5(1))* Barnes & Noble, Inc.
Ebbeler, Jeffrey, illus. Jingle Bells - Musical. 2009. (ENG.). 20p. (J). (gr. -1-k). bds. 12.99 *(978-0-8249-1829-3(0))*, Ideal Pubns.) Worthy Publishing.
Echeverria, Jessica. Dora y el Día lluvioso. Savitsky, Steven, illus. 2009. (Dora la Exploradora Ser.). Orig. Title: Dora & the Rainy Day. (SPA.). 26p. (J). (gr. -1). bds. 5.99 *(978-1-4169-7186-3(6)*, Libros Para Ninos) Libros Para Ninos.
Edgson, Alison, illus. The Emperor's New Clothes. (Flip-Up Fairy Tales Ser.). (ENG.). 24p. (J). 2007. (gr. -1-2). audio compact disk *(978-1-84643-093-0(3))* 2006. (gr. 2-2). *(978-1-84643-020-6(8))* Child's Play International Ltd.
—The Magician's Apprentice. 2011. (Flip-Up Fairy Tales Ser.). (ENG.). 24p. (J). audio compact disk *(978-1-84643-409-9(2))* Child's Play International Ltd.
—Three Billy Goats Gruff. (Flip-Up Fairy Tales Ser.). (ENG.). 24p. (J). 2007. (gr. -1-2). audio compact disk *(978-1-84643-089-3(5))* 2006. (gr. 1-2). *(978-1-904550-72-3(X))* Child's Play International Ltd.
Edgson, Alison & Stockham, Jessica. Hansel & Gretel. Petrlik, Andrea, illus. 2006. (Flip-Up Fairy Tales Ser.). (ENG.). 24p. (J). (gr. 1-2). *(978-1-904550-73-0(8))* Child's Play International Ltd.
Editions Phidal Staff. Radical Rides Super Sticker Book. (Illus.). 64p. (J). pap. *(978-2-7643-0024-4(7))* Phidal Publishing, Inc./Editions Phidal, Inc.
Editors of Kingfisher. Who's That? Playing. 2013. (Who's That? Ser.). (ENG.). 14p. (J). (gr. -1-k). bds. 5.99 *(978-0-7534-7071-8(3)*, 9780753470718, Kingfisher) Roaring Brook Pr.
Editors of Publications, ed. Baby Einstein My First Look & Find. 2014. 16p. (J). bds. 7.98 *(978-1-4508-8374-0(5)*, 1450883745) Phoenix International Publications, Inc.
Edwards, Amelia. Name That Dinosaur. Jirankova-Limbrick, Martina, illus. 2009. (ENG.). 40p. (J). (gr. -1-3). 17.99 *(978-0-7636-3473-5(5))* Candlewick Pr.
Edwards, Josh. Christmas, 1 vol. Embleton-Hall, Chris, illus. 2014. (ENG.). 10p. (J). bds. 11.99 ***(978-1-85985-999-5(2)***, Lion Children's) Lion Hudson PLC GBR. Dist: Kregel Pubns.
—Pull-Out David & Goliath, 1 vol. Embleton Hall, Chris, illus. 2014. (ENG.). 10p. (J). bds. 11.99 *(978-1-85985-997-1(6)*, Candle Bks.) Lion Hudson PLC GBR. Dist: Kregel Pubns.
—Pull-Out Jonah & the Big Fish, 1 vol. Embleton-Hall, Chris, illus. 2014. (ENG.). 10p. (J). bds. 11.99 *(978-1-85985-998-8(4)*, Candle Bks.) Lion Hudson PLC GBR. Dist: Kregel Pubns.
Edwards, Pamela Duncan. Teddy Bear Hide-and-Seek. Birkett, Georgie, illus. 2008. (ENG.). 20p. (J). (gr. 2-5). 14.95 *(978-0-230-01442-8(9)*, Macmillan) Pan Macmillan GBR. Dist: Trans-Atlantic Pubns., Inc.
Egielski, Richard. Itsy Bitsy Spider. Egielski, Richard, illus. 2012. (ENG., Illus.). 12p. (J). (gr. -1-1). 19.99 *(978-1-4169-9895-2(0)*, Atheneum Bks. for Young Readers) Simon & Schuster Children's Publishing.
Egmont UK, Egmont. Peekaboo! Sea. 2014. (Animaru Ser.). (ENG., Illus.). 12p. (J). (— 1). bds. 9.99 *(978-1-4052-6778-6(X))* Egmont Bks., Ltd. GBR. Dist: Independent Pubs. Group.
—Peekaboo! Snow. 2014. (Animaru Ser.). (ENG., Illus.). 12p. (J). (— 1). bds. 9.99 *(978-1-4052-6775-5(5))* Egmont Bks., Ltd. GBR. Dist: Independent Pubs. Group.
Ehlert, Lois. Hands: Growing up to Be an Artist. 2004. (ENG., Illus.). 48p. (J). (gr. -1-3). 16.99 *(978-0-15-205107-5(4))* Houghton Mifflin Harcourt Publishing Co.
—Leaf Man. 2014. (ENG., Illus.). 40p. (J). (gr. -1-3). 26.99 *(978-0-544-33916-3(9)*, HMH Books For Young Readers) Houghton Mifflin Harcourt Publishing Co.
—Planting a Rainbow: Lap-Sized Board Book. 2008. (ENG., Illus.). 32p. (J). (gr. -1 — 1). bds. 11.99 *(978-0-15-206304-7(8))* Houghton Mifflin Harcourt Publishing Co.
Eight Jolly Reindeer. 2014. (ENG., Illus.). 16p. (J). (gr. -1 — 1). bds. 6.99 *(978-0-545-65145-5(X)*, Cartwheel Bks.) Scholastic, Inc.
Electric Confetti. Neon Baby: Numbers. 2017. (Neon Baby Ser.). (ENG., Illus.). 20p. (J). (— 1). bds. 12.99 ***(978-1-76012-931-6(3))*** Hardie Grant Egmont Pty, Ltd. AUS. Dist: Independent Pubs. Group.
—Neon Baby: Words. 2017. (Neon Baby Ser.). (ENG., Illus.). 20p. (J). (— 1). bds. 12.99 ***(978-1-76012-906-4(2))*** Hardie Grant Egmont Pty, Ltd. AUS. Dist: Independent Pubs. Group.
Elgar, Rebecca. Where's My Dinner? 2003. (ENG., Illus.). 12p. (J). bds. 9.99 *(978-1-4052-0451-4(6))* Egmont Bks., Ltd. GBR. Dist: Trafalgar Square Publishing.
Eliot, Hannah. If Everything Were Blue. Lalalimola, illus. 2015. (ENG.). 16p. (J). (gr. -1-k). bds. 8.99 *(978-1-4814-3539-0(6)*, Little Simon) Little Simon.
—If Everything Were Pink. Lalalimola, illus. 2015. (ENG.). 16p. (J). (gr. -1-k). bds. 8.99 *(978-1-4814-3538-3(8)*, Little Simon) Little Simon.
Eliot, T. S., et al. Macavity's Not There! A Lift-the-Flap Book. Robins, Arthur, illus. 2017. (Old Possum Picture Bks.). (ENG.). 16p. (-k). 14.95 *(978-0-571-32863-5(6))* Faber & Faber, Inc.
Elliott, Rebecca. God Bless This Starry Night. Elliott, Rebecca, illus. 2016. (ENG., Illus.). 5p. (J). (— 1). bds. 7.99 *(978-0-7459-6558-1(X))* Lion Hudson PLC GBR. Dist: Independent Pubs. Group.
—God Loves Little Me. Elliott, Rebecca, illus. 2016. (ENG., Illus.). 10p. (J). (— 1). bds. 7.99 *(978-0-7459-6559-8(8))* Lion Hudson PLC GBR. Dist: Independent Pubs. Group.
—Noah's Noisy Animals. Elliott, Rebecca, illus. 2016. (ENG., Illus.). 5p. (J). (— 1). bds. 7.99 *(978-0-7459-6561-1(X))* Lion Hudson PLC GBR. Dist: Independent Pubs. Group.
Ellis, Belinda. Tractor. 2007. (Pull-Alongs Ser.). (Illus.). 12p. (gr. -1). per. *(978-1-84610-443-5(2))* Make Believe Ideas.
Ellis, Greg & BeachHouse Publishing. Baby's First 1-2-3 in Hawaii. 2008. (ENG.). 20p. (J). (gr. -1-1). bds. 7.95 *(978-1-933067-24-7(1))* Beachhouse Publishing, LLC.
Ellis, Gwen. The First Christmas, 1 vol. Pichon, Liz, illus. 2007. 10p. (J). bds. 15.99 *(978-0-8254-5538-4(3))* Kregel Pubns.
Ellis, Paula. Yellowstone & Grand Teton Activity Book. Nitzsche, Shane, illus. 2011. (Color & Learn Ser.). (ENG.). 64p. (J). (gr. 1-3). pap. 5.95 *(978-1-59193-356-4(0))* Adventure Pubns.
Elmquist, Laurie. Beach Baby, 1 vol. MacKay, Elly, illus. 2016. (ENG.). 24p. (J). (gr. -1-k). bds. 9.95 *(978-1-4598-0954-3(8))* Orca Bk. Pubs. USA.
Emberley, Ed. Bye-Bye, Big Bad Bullybug! Emberley, Ed, illus. 2007. (ENG., Illus.). 32p. (J). (gr. -1-3). 14.99 *(978-0-316-01762-6(0))* Little, Brown Bks. for Young Readers.
Emma Treehouse Ltd. My Babies. Davis, Caroline, illus. 2007. (Easy Flaps Ser.). 10p. (J). (gr. -1). bds. 6.95 *(978-1-58925-822-8(3))* Tiger Tales.
—My Friends. Davis, Caroline, illus. 2007. (Easy Flaps Ser.). 10p. (J). (gr. -1). bds. 6.95 *(978-1-58925-823-5(1))* Tiger Tales.
—My Pets. Davis, Caroline, illus. 2007. (Easy Flaps Ser.). 10p. (J). (gr. -1). bds. 6.95 *(978-1-58925-824-2(X))* Tiger Tales.
—My Toys. Davis, Caroline, illus. 2007. (Easy Flaps Ser.). 10p. (J). (gr. -1). bds. 6.95 *(978-1-58925-825-9(8))* Tiger Tales.
Endle, Kate. What Is Green? A Colors Book by Kate Endle. 2010. (ENG., Illus.). 18p. (J). (gr. k-k). bds. 9.99 *(978-1-57061-648-8(5)*, Little Bigfoot) Sasquatch Bks.
—Who Hoo Are You? An Animals Book by Kate Endle. 2010. (ENG., Illus.). 10p. (J). (gr. k-k). bds. 10.99 *(978-1-57061-647-1(7)*, Little Bigfoot) Sasquatch Bks.
Engel, Christiane. Little Green Helpers Grow! 2011. (Little Green Helpers Ser.). (ENG., Illus.). 10p. (J). (gr. -1-k). bds. 7.99 *(978-0-230-74356-4(0))* Pan Macmillan GBR. Dist: Independent Pubs. Group.
English Heritage Staff. My Life as a Knight. 2005. (Illus.). 32p. pap. 19.95 *(978-1-85074-985-1(X))* Historic England Publishing GBR. Dist: Casemate Academic.
—My Life as a Princess. 2005. (Illus.). 32p. pap. 19.95 *(978-1-85074-984-4(1))* Historic England Publishing GBR. Dist: Casemate Academic.
Epstein, Brad M. Army 101: My First Text-Board-Book. l.t. ed. 2007. (101 — My First Text-Board Books). (Illus.). 20p. (J). bds. *(978-1-932530-42-1(8)*, 101 Bk.) Michaelson Entertainment.
—Atlanta Braves 101: My First Team-Board-Book. l.t. ed. 2007. (Illus.). 22p. (J). bds. *(978-1-932530-74-2(6)*, 101 Bk.) Michaelson Entertainment.
—Boston 101. l.t. ed. 2009. (My First City Ser.). (Illus.). 24p. (J). (gr. -1-k). bds. *(978-1-60730-000-7(1)*, 101 Bk.) Michaelson Entertainment.
—Chicago 101: My First City-Board-book. l.t. ed. 2009. (101 — My First Text-Board Books). (Illus.). 24p. (J). *(978-1-60730-001-4(X)*, 101 Bk.) Michaelson Entertainment.
—Kansas State Univ 101: My First Text-Board-Book. l.t. ed. 2007. (101 — My First Text-Board Books). (Illus.). 20p. (J). bds. *(978-1-932530-57-5(6)*, 101 Bk.) Michaelson Entertainment.
—Los Angeles 101: My First City-Board-book. l.t. ed. 2009. (Illus.). 24p. (J). *(978-1-60730-002-1(8)*, 101 Bk.) Michaelson Entertainment.
—Milwaukee Brewers 101: My First Team-Board-Book. l.t. ed. 2007. (101 — My First Text-Board Books). (Illus.). 22p. (J). *(978-1-932530-75-9(4)*, 101 Bk.) Michaelson Entertainment.
—New York 101. l.t. ed. 2009. (My First City Ser.). (Illus.). 24p. (J). (gr. -1-k). bds. *(978-1-60730-003-8(6)*, 101 Bk.) Michaelson Entertainment.
—Stanford 101. 2013. (My First Text-Board-Book Ser.). (ENG., Illus.). 20p. (J). (gr. -1). bds. *(978-1-60730-066-3(4)*, 101 Bk.) Michaelson Entertainment.
—University of Kansas 101: My First Text-Board-Book. 2006. (101 — My First Text-Board Books). (ENG., Illus.). 20p. (J). bds. *(978-1-932530-40-7(1)*, 101 Bk.) Michaelson Entertainment.
—University of Nebraska 101: My First Text-Board-book. 2013. (My First Text-Board-Book Ser.). (ENG., Illus.). 20p. (J). bds. *(978-1-60730-063-2(X))* Michaelson Entertainment.
—University of Washington 101. 2013. (My First Text-Board-Book Ser.). (ENG., Illus.). 20p. (J). (gr. -1). bds. *(978-1-60730-068-7(0)*, 101 Bk.) Michaelson Entertainment.
—Washington D. C. 101: My First City-Board-book. l.t. ed. 2009. (ENG., Illus.). 24p. (J). 9.95 *(978-1-60730-004-5(4)*, 101 Bk.) Michaelson Entertainment.
epstein, brad M. & lee-Epstein, michael. Pittsburgh Steelers Doodle Playbook: For Kids & Fans. 2012. (ENG., Illus.). 200p. (J). pap. *(978-1-60730-324-4(8))* Michaelson Entertainment.
Ericsson, Annie Beth & Christian, Cheryl. ¿Que hay en mi Jardin? (Spanish/English) Un libro de colores/A Book of Colors. del Risco, Eida, tr. 2009. (ENG & SPA., Illus.). 16p. (J). bds. 6.25 *(978-1-59572-181-5(9))* Star Bright Bks., Inc.
Ernst, Lisa Campbell. The Turn-Around, Upside-Down Alphabet Book. Ernst, Lisa Campbell, illus. 2004. (ENG., Illus.). 32p. (J). (gr. -1-3). 17.99 *(978-0-689-85685-3(7)*, Simon & Schuster Bks. For Young Readers) Simon & Schuster Bks. For Young Readers.
Esquinaldo, Virginia. What Did Baby Jesus Do? Esquinaldo, Virginia, illus. 2006. (Illus.). 12p. (J). bds. 6.95 *(978-0-8198-8310-0(7))* Pauline Bks. & Media.
Eubank, Patricia Reeder. Countdown to Christmas. 2003. (ENG., Illus.). 14p. (J). (gr. -1-k). bds. 9.95 *(978-0-8249-6505-1(1)*, Ideal Pubns.) Worthy Publishing.
—Halloween 123s. Eubank, Patricia Reeder, illus. 2011. (Illus.). 22p. (J). bds. 6.99 *(978-0-8249-1868-2(1)*, Ideal Pubns.) Worthy Publishing.
Eubank, Patti Reeder. Count Your Blessings! 2004. (ENG., Illus.). 14p. (J). bds. 9.95 *(978-0-8249-6544-0(2)*, Ideal Pubns.) Worthy Publishing.
Evans, Hestia. The Mythology Handbook: An Introduction to the Greek Myths. Steer, Dugald A., ed. 2009. (Ologies Ser.). (ENG., Illus.). 80p. (J). (gr. 4-7). 12.99 *(978-0-7636-4291-4(6))* Candlewick Pr.
Evanson, Ashley. London: A Book of Opposites. Evanson, Ashley, illus. 2015. (Hello, World Ser.). (ENG., Illus.). 14p. (J). (— 1). bds. 6.99 *(978-0-448-48916-2(3)*, Grosset & Dunlap) Penguin Young Readers Group.
—Paris: A Book of Shapes. Evanson, Ashley, illus. 2015. (Hello, World Ser.). (ENG., Illus.). 14p. (J). (— 1). bds. 6.99 *(978-0-448-48915-5(5)*, Grosset & Dunlap) Penguin Young Readers Group.
—San Francisco: A Book of Numbers. Evanson, Ashley, illus. 2015. (Hello, World Ser.). (ENG., Illus.). 14p. (J). (— 1). bds. 6.99 *(978-0-448-48914-8(7)*, Grosset & Dunlap) Penguin Young Readers Group.
Everett, Melissa. I Wish I Was a Little. Paiva, Johannah Gilman, ed. Manning, Mary, illus. 2014. (ENG.). 20p. (J). 8.99 *(978-1-77093-844-1(3))* Flowerpot Children's Pr. Inc. CAN. Dist: Cardinal Pubs. Group.
—Jack & Jill. Paiva, Johannah Gilman, ed. Imodraj, illus. 2014. (ENG.). 20p. (J). (gr. -1-1). 8.99 *(978-1-77093-843-4(5))* Flowerpot Children's Pr. Inc. CAN. Dist: Cardinal Pubs. Group.
—Pat-A-Cake. Kummer, Mark, illus. 2013. (ENG.). 20p. (J). (gr. -1-1). 8.99 *(978-1-77093-521-1(5))* Flowerpot Children's Pr. Inc. CAN. Dist: Cardinal Pubs. Group.
Evert, Lori. The Brave Little Puppy. Breiehagen, Per, illus. 2016. (ENG.). 28p. (J). (-k). bds. 8.99 *(978-0-399-54945-8(5)*, Random Hse. Bks. for Young Readers) Random Hse. Children's Bks.
Faces. Date not set. (Illus.). 40p. (J). 3.98 *(978-1-4054-0174-6(5))* Parragon, Inc.
Fact Families Staff. LP-Fact Families: Level 1 Math. 2004. (ENG.). (J). 9.99 *(978-1-59204-016-2(0))* Learning Wrap-Ups, Inc.
Fairley, Melissa. Ding! Dong! Harland, Jackie, illus. 2011. (ENG.). 12p. (J). (gr. -1-k). 15.95 *(978-1-84898-362-5(X)*, TickTock Books) Octopus Publishing Group GBR. Dist: Independent Pubs. Group.
Fairy Tale- Cinderella. 2005. (J). bds. *(978-1-4194-0039-1(8))* Paradise Pr., Inc.
Falconer, Ian. Olivia Cuenta. 2006. (Olivia Ser.).Tr. of Olivia Counts. (SPA.). (J). (gr. -1-k). bds. 6.99 *(978-1-930332-89-8(0)*, LC33420) Lectorum Pubns., Inc.
—Olivia Helps with Christmas. Falconer, Ian, illus. 2013. (Classic Board Bks.). (ENG., Illus.). 40p. (J). (gr. -1-2). bds. 7.99 *(978-1-4424-9446-6(8)*, Atheneum Bks. for Young Readers) Simon & Schuster Children's Publishing.
Falken, Linda & The Metropolitan Museum of Art, The Metropolitan. Puzzling Cats. 2015. (ENG., Illus.). 16p. (J). (gr. -1-1). 16.95 *(978-1-4197-1363-7(9)*, Abrams Bks. for Young Readers) Abrams, Inc.
—Puzzling Dogs. 2015. (ENG., Illus.). 16p. (J). (gr. -1-1). 16.95 *(978-1-4197-1362-0(0)*, Abrams Bks. for Young Readers) Abrams, Inc.
Familius Staff & Miles, David. Slide-N-Seek: Earth. 2017. (ENG., Illus.). 10p. (J). 15.95 *(978-1-944822-45-3(3))* Familius LLC.
—Slide-N-Seek: Ocean. 2017. (ENG., Illus.). 10p. (J). 15.95 *(978-1-944822-46-0(1))* Familius LLC.
Farm Animals. (My Sticker Activity Ser.). (Illus.). 12p. (J). *(978-1-4054-1181-3(3))* Parragon, Inc.
Farnsworth, Lauren. Clever Babies Love Art - Wild Animals. 2016. (Clever Babies Love Art Ser.). (ENG., Illus.). 14p. (J). (— 1). bds. 7.99 *(978-1-78055-397-9(8))* O'Mara, Michael Bks., Ltd. GBR. Dist: Independent Pubs. Group.
Farshtey, Greg. Way of the Ninja. 2012. (Lego Ninjago Ser.). (ENG.). 32p. (J). (gr. -1-3). pap. 3.99 *(978-0-545-40113-5(5))* Scholastic, Inc.
Fascinating Firefly. 2004. (Illus.). 10p. (J). *(978-1-59340-144-3(2))* Grandreams Bks., Inc.
Fashion Fun Sticker Book. (Girlfriend Gang Ser.). 16p. (J). *(978-2-7643-0018-3(2))* Phidal Publishing, Inc./Editions Phidal, Inc.
Fashion Pixiez Sticker Scene. (Bratz Sticker Scene Books Ser.). 12p. pap. *(978-1-4054-8734-4(8))* Parragon, Inc.
Faulkner, Keith. Charlie Chimp's Christmas: A Pop-up Extravaganza of Festive Friends. Lambert, Jonathan, illus. 2006. 12p. (J). (gr. -1-3). reprint ed. 10.00 *(978-1-4223-5446-9(6))* DIANE Publishing Co.
—Flip-Flap Math: Flip the Flaps to Check Your Answers! Irish, Martin, illus. 2005. 12 p.p. (J). *(978-0-439-78578-5(2))* Scholastic, Inc.
—Maths Machine: A Fun New Way to Do Maths! Tyger, Rory, illus. 2004. (J). *(978-0-439-72174-5(1))* Scholastic, Inc.
Faulkner, Keith & Holmes, Stephen. Animal ? Math. Faulkner, Keith & Holmes, Stephen, illus. 2003. (Illus.). (J). *(978-0-439-62755-9(9))* Scholastic, Inc.
Faulkner, Keith & Tyger, Rory. Time's Up! Faulkner, Keith & Tyger, Rory, illus. Lambert, Jonathan, illus. 2003. (J). *(978-0-439-56155-6(8))* Scholastic, Inc.
Feder, Jane. A Little Kitty. Schwartz, Amy, illus. 2009. (ENG.). 14p. (J). (— 1). bds. 4.99 *(978-0-7636-2650-1(3))* Candlewick Pr.
Feldman, Thea. ASPCA Mix & Match Pets: A Colors & Counting Book. 2015. (Mix & Match Ser.: 1). (ENG.). 12p. (J). (gr. -1-k). 8.99 *(978-0-7944-3299-7(9)*, Reader's Digest Children's Bks.) Studio Fun International.
—Hello, Farm! 2015. (Flap Book Ser.: 3). (ENG.). 14p. (J). (gr. -1-k). 8.99 *(978-0-7944-3298-0(0)*, Reader's Digest Children's Bks.) Studio Fun International.
Félix, Lucie. Apples & Robins. 2016. (ENG., Illus.). 56p. (J). (gr. k-3). 16.99 *(978-1-4521-3264-8(X))* Chronicle Bks. LLC.
—Give & Take. Félix, Lucie, illus. 2016. (ENG., Illus.). 16p. (J). (gr. -1-2). bds. 19.99 *(978-0-7636-9011-3(2))* Candlewick Pr.
Fennell, Clare, illus. Noisy Jungle. 2017. (Push & Pull Ser.). (ENG.). 8p. (J). (gr. -1 — 1). bds. 5.99 *(978-0-7641-6889-5(4))* Barron's Educational Series, Inc.
—Playtime Pond. 2017. (Push & Pull Ser.). (ENG.). 8p. (J). (gr. -1 — 1). bds. 5.99 *(978-0-7641-6890-1(8))* Barron's Educational Series, Inc.
Fernandes, Eugenie. Kitten's Summer. Fernandes, Eugenie, illus. 2013. (ENG., Illus.). 24p. (J). (gr. -1 — 1). bds. 7.95 *(978-1-55453-721-1(5))* Kids Can Pr., Ltd. CAN. Dist: Hachette Bk. Group.
Fernandez, Rajiv. Baby to Brooklyn. 2017. (ENG., Illus.). 32p. (J). (— 1). bds. 6.99 *(978-1-57687-785-2(X)*, powerHouse Bks.) powerHouse Cultural Entertainment, Inc.
Ferrero, Mar, illus. My Sunflower: A Pop-Up Book from Seed to Sunflower. 2016. (Grow with Me! Ser.). (ENG.). 16p. (J). (gr. -1-3). 16.95 *(978-1-63322-084-3(2))* Quarto Publishing Group USA.
Ferri, Francesca. Hello Teddy. 2016. (Cuddly Book Set Ser.). (ENG.). 8p. (J). (gr. -1 — 1). bds. 12.99 *(978-1-4380-7756-7(4))* Barron's Educational Series, Inc.
—Peek-A-Boo Sea. 2014. (ENG., Illus.). 12p. (J). (gr. -1 — 1). 8.99 *(978-0-7641-6724-9(3))* Barron's Educational Series, Inc.
Ferrie, Chris. General Relativity for Babies. 2017. (Baby University Ser.: 0). (ENG., Illus.). 24p. (J). bds. 9.99 ***(978-1-4926-5626-5(7)***, Sourcebooks Jabberwocky) Sourcebooks, Inc.
—Quantum Physics for Babies. 2017. (Baby University Ser.: 0). (ENG., Illus.). 24p. (J). bds. 9.99 ***(978-1-4926-5622-7(4)***, Sourcebooks Jabberwocky) Sourcebooks, Inc.
Field, Rachel. Oración para los Niños. Romay, Alexis, tr. Jones, Elizabeth Orton, illus. 2011.Tr. of Prayer for a Child. (SPA.). 32p. (J). (gr. -1-2). bds. 6.99 *(978-1-4424-1350-4(6)*, Libros Para Ninos) Libros Para Ninos.
Fielding, Beth. Animal Colors. 2010. (ENG., Illus.). 24p. (J). (— 1). bds. 7.99 *(978-0-9797455-6-0(X))* EarlyLight Bks., Inc.
Filigenzi, Courtney & Bersani, Shennen. Let My Colors Out. Bersani, Shennen, illus. 2009. (ENG., Illus.). 16p. (J). (gr. -1-k). pap. 11.95 *(978-1-60443-011-0(7)*, 1604430117) American Cancer Society, Inc.
Filipek, Nina. Colors. O'Toole, Jeanette, illus. 2009. (Bright Basics Ser.). 12p. (J). (gr. -1-k). bds. 11.40 *(978-1-60754-687-0(6))* Windmill Bks.
—Counting. O'Toole, Jeanette, illus. 2009. (Bright Basics Ser.). 12p. (J). (gr. -1-k). bds. 11.40 *(978-1-60754-686-3(8))* Windmill Bks.
Finch, Keith. Poppy Cat's Garden. Jones, Lara, illus. 2008. (ENG.). 8p. (J). (gr. 3-6). bds. 16.95 *(978-0-230-01715-3(0)*, Macmillan) Pan Macmillan GBR. Dist: Trans-Atlantic Pubns., Inc.
Fincher, Kathy, illus. Baby's First Christmas. 2006. 8p. (gr. -1-k). bds. 7.95 *(978-0-88271-705-0(7))* Regina Pr., Malhame & Co.
Finn, Rebecca. Sammy the Snowman! 2013. (Sparkly Christmas Ser.). (ENG., Illus.). 12p. (J). (gr. -1-k). bds. 5.99 *(978-0-230-76062-2(7))* Pan Macmillan GBR. Dist: Independent Pubs. Group.
Finn, Rebecca, illus. Busy Beach. 2016. (Busy Bks.). (ENG.). 10p. (J). (gr. -1). bds. 8.95 *(978-1-4549-1941-4(8))* Sterling Publishing Co., Inc.
—Busy Fire Station. 2016. (Busy Bks.). (ENG.). 10p. (J). (gr. -1). bds. 8.95 *(978-1-4549-1942-1(6))* Sterling Publishing Co., Inc.
—Busy Park. 2016. (Busy Bks.). (ENG.). 10p. (J). (gr. -1). bds. 8.95 *(978-1-4549-1943-8(4))* Sterling Publishing Co., Inc.
—Little Bunny. (Cuddly Cuffstm Ser.). 6p. (J). 6.95 *(978-1-58925-767-2(7))* Tiger Tales.
—Little Ducky. (Cuddly Cuffstm Ser.). 6p. (J). 6.95 *(978-1-58925-766-5(9))* Tiger Tales.
The First Christmas. (Illus.). 12p. (J). 4.95 *(978-1-58989-102-9(3))* Thurman Hse., LLC.
First Words. 2014. (ENG.). 16p. (J). (gr. -1 — 1). bds. 6.99 *(978-1-4654-1832-6(6)*, DK Children) Dorling Kindersley Publishing, Inc.
Fisher-Price. Fisher-Price Little People: Trick or Treat! 2016. (ENG.). 12p. (J). (gr. -1-k). bds. 5.99 *(978-0-7944-3757-2(5)*, Reader's Digest Children's Bks.) Studio Fun International.
Fisher-Price Little People, Fisher-Price Little. Fisher-Price Little People Planes, Cars, Trucks & Trains! 2015. (Lift-The-Flap Ser.: 24). (ENG.). 10p. (J). (gr. -1-k). bds. 9.99 *(978-0-7944-3468-7(1))* Reader's Digest Assn., Inc., The.
Fisher-Price Little People Lift the Flap Library 2. 2014. (ENG.). 50p. bds. 49.95 *(978-0-7944-2979-9(3))* Studio Fun International.
Fitch, Sheree. Kisses Kisses Baby-O!, 1 vol. Rose, Hilda, illus. 2008. (ENG.). 10p. (J). (gr. -1-2). bds. 6.50 *(978-1-55109-646-9(3))* Nimbus Publishing, Ltd. CAN. Dist: Orca Bk. Pubs. USA.
Fleming, Maria. Mini-Book of the Week: 40 Easy-to-Read Mini-Books on Fiction & Nonfiction Topics for Every Week of the School Year. 2005. (ENG.). 96p. (gr. k-2). pap. 14.99 *(978-0-439-05921-3(6)*, Teaching Resources) Scholastic, Inc.
Fletcher, Corina. Playbook Farm. Teckentrup, Britta, illus. 2012. (ENG.). 12p. (J). (gr. -1-2). 24.00 *(978-0-7636-6165-6(1)*, Nosy Crow) Candlewick Pr.
—Small Smaller Smallest. Marshall, Natalie, illus. 2015. (ENG.). 12p. (J). (— 1). bds. 8.95 *(978-1-4549-1559-1(5))* Sterling Publishing Co., Inc.
—Up down Across. Marshall, Natalie, illus. 2015. (ENG.). 12p. (J). (— 1). bds. 8.95 *(978-1-4549-1562-1(5))* Sterling Publishing Co., Inc.
Fletcher, Corina, et al. The Little Christmas Tree. 2016. (ENG., Illus.). 16p. (J). (gr. -1-k). 19.99 *(978-1-4052-7566-8(9))* Egmont Bks., Ltd. GBR. Dist: Independent Pubs. Group.
Flintham, Thomas. Animal Numbers. Flintham, Thomas, illus. 2016. (ENG., Illus.). 24p. (J). (gr. -1 — 1). bds. 7.99 *(978-1-4814-6937-1(1)*, Little Simon) Little Simon.
Florian, Douglas. Once I Was a Pollywog. Bakos, Barbara, illus. 2016. (Animals Play Ser.). (ENG.). 18p. (J). (gr. -1-1). bds. 6.99 *(978-1-4998-0141-5(6))* Little Bee Books Inc.
Flowerpot Children's Press Staff, contrib. by. My Animal Buddies: With Duck, Pig, & Frog. 2015. (Illus.). (J). *(978-1-4351-6023-1(1))* Barnes & Noble, Inc.
Flowerpot Press, contrib. by. Sockheadz: 5 Little Sockheadz. 2013. (ENG., Illus.). 20p. (J). (gr. -1-k). 8.99 *(978-1-77093-618-8(1))* Flowerpot Children's Pr. Inc. CAN. Dist: Cardinal Pubs. Group.
—Sockheadz: Hide & Seek. 2013. (Illus.). 20p. (J). (gr. -1-k). 8.99 *(978-1-77093-619-5(X))* Flowerpot Children's Pr. Inc. CAN. Dist: Cardinal Pubs. Group.
Flowerpot Press Staff. A Child's Book of Prayers: Good Morning, Dear God. Paiva, Johannah Gilman, ed. 2013. (ENG., Illus.). 20p. (J). 8.99 *(978-1-77093-635-5(1))* Flowerpot Children's Pr. Inc. CAN. Dist: Cardinal Pubs. Group.
—A Child's Book of Prayers: Good Night, Dear God. 2013. (ENG., Illus.). 20p. (J). 8.99 *(978-1-77093-636-2(X))* Flowerpot Children's Pr. Inc. CAN. Dist: Cardinal Pubs. Group.
Flowerpot Press Staff, contrib. by. Sockheadz: Counting. 2013. (ENG., Illus.). 20p. (J). (gr. -1-k). 6.99 *(978-1-77093-594-5(0))* Flowerpot Children's Pr. Inc. CAN. Dist: Cardinal Pubs. Group.
—Sockheadz: First Words. 2013. (ENG., Illus.). 20p. (J). (gr. -1-k). 6.99 *(978-1-77093-595-2(9))* Flowerpot Children's Pr. Inc. CAN. Dist: Cardinal Pubs. Group.
—Sockheadz: Shapes. 2013. (ENG., Illus.). 20p. (J). (gr. -1-k). 6.99 *(978-1-77093-596-9(7))* Flowerpot Children's Pr. Inc. CAN. Dist: Cardinal Pubs. Group.
Flying Frog Pub, creator. ABC Fun with Elmo & Friends. 2011. (Sesame Street (Publications International) Ser.). (ENG.,

Illus.). 14p. (J). (gr. -1). bds. 3.99 *(978-1-60745-030-6(5))* Flying Frog Publishing.

—Big & Small Fun with Elmo & Friends. 2011. (ENG., Illus.). 14p. (gr. -1-k). bds. 3.99 *(978-1-60745-033-7(X))* Flying Frog Publishing.

—Color Fun with Elmo & Friends. 2011. (ENG., Illus.). 14p. (gr. -1-k). bds. 3.99 *(978-1-60745-031-3(3))* Flying Frog Publishing.

—Counting Fun with Elmo & Friends. 2011. (Sesame Street (Publications International) Ser.). (ENG., Illus.). 14p. (J). (gr. -1). bds. 3.99 *(978-1-60745-032-0(1))* Flying Frog Publishing.

Foley, Tim. American Presidents Sticker Book. 2011. (Dover Sticker Bks.). (ENG., Illus.). 4p. (J). (gr. 1-5). 6.99 *(978-0-486-47879-1(3))* Dover Pubns., Inc.

Folgueira, Rodrigo. Ribbit! Bernatene, Poly, illus. 2016. (ENG.). 34p. (J). (-k). bds. 8.99 *(978-0-553-53721-5(0),* Knopf Bks. for Young Readers) Random Hse. Children's Bks.

Ford, Emily. Ten Little Bluebirds. Julian, Russell, illus. 2016. (ENG.). 22p. (J). (gr. -1-k). bds. 10.99 *(978-0-545-79441-1(2),* Cartwheel Bks.) Scholastic, Inc.

Fordham, Kate. Me & My Kitten. 2006. (Illus.). 80p. (J). *(978-0-439-89293-3(7))* Scholastic, Inc.

Foster James, Helen. Little America. 2011. (My Little State Ser.). (ENG., Illus.). 22p. (J). 7.95 *(978-1-58536-179-3(8))* Sleeping Bear Pr.

Foster, Jane. Jane Foster's 123. 2015. (Jane Foster Bks.). (ENG., Illus.). 24p. (J). (gr. -1 — 1). bds. 7.99 *(978-1-4998-0073-9(8))* Little Bee Books Inc.

—Jane Foster's ABC. 2015. (Jane Foster Bks.). (ENG., Illus.). 26p. (J). (gr. -1 — 1). bds. 8.99 *(978-1-4998-0074-6(6))* Little Bee Books Inc.

—Jane Foster's Black & White. 2016. (ENG., Illus.). 26p. (J). (gr. -1 — 1). bds. 8.99 *(978-1-4998-0255-9(2))* Little Bee Books Inc.

—Jane Foster's Colors. 2016. (ENG., Illus.). 26p. (J). (gr. -1 — 1). bds. 7.99 *(978-1-4998-0256-6(0))* Little Bee Books Inc.

—Jane Foster's First Words. 2016. (ENG., Illus.). 26p. (J). (gr. -1 — 1). bds. 7.99 *(978-1-4998-0284-9(6))* Little Bee Books Inc.

Foster, Kate, ed. Nice & Pretty. 2013. (Look at Me! Ser.). (ENG., Illus.). 10p. (J). (-k). bds. 10.95 *(978-1-61889-392-5(0))* AZ Bks. LLC.

Fox, Mem. Time for Bed. Dyer, Jane, illus. 2010. (ENG.). 28p. (J). (gr. k — 1). bds. 8.99 *(978-0-547-40856-9(0))* Houghton Mifflin Harcourt Publishing Co.

—Time for Bed (Es Hora de Dormir) Dyer, Jane, illus. 2012. (ENG & SPA.). 28p. (J). (gr. k — 1). bds. 6.99 *(978-0-547-71907-8(8))* Houghton Mifflin Harcourt Publishing Co.

Fractions Cards Staff. LP-Fractions: Level 2 Math. 2004. (ENG.). (J). 9.99 *(978-1-59204-020-9(9))* Learning Wrap-Ups, Inc.

Franceschelli, Christopher. Alphablock. Peskimo, illus. 2013. (Alphablock Ser.). (ENG.). 104p. (J). (gr. -1 — 1). bds. 16.95 *(978-1-4197-0936-4(4),* Abrams Appleseed) Abrams, Inc.

—Oliver. 2011. (ENG., Illus.). 16p. (J). (gr. -1). 12.95 *(978-1-935954-01-9(6),* 9781935954019) Lemniscaat USA.

Francia, Giada. Alex & Penny's Italy Jigsaw Book. Colombo, Angelo, illus. 2007. (ENG.). 14p. (gr. 1-3). pap. 14.95 *(978-88-544-0242-3(7),* White Star) Rizzoli International Pubns., Inc.

Frankel, Alona. Once upon a Potty Sound Book for Girls. Publications International Ltd. Staff, ed. 2010. 8p. (J). bds. 7.98 *(978-1-4508-0828-6(X))* Publications International, Ltd.

Frantz, Jennifer. Color & Iron-Ons Book. Middleton, Gayle, illus. 2005. (My Little Pony Ser.). 32p. (J). (gr. -1-1). 3.99 *(978-0-06-074441-0(3),* HarperFestival) HarperCollins Pubs.

Freeman, Anna Harber. Love You More Than Anything. Henry, Jed, illus. 2016. (Snuggle Time Stories Ser.). (ENG.). 24p. (J). (— 1). bds. 6.95 *(978-1-4549-1490-7(4))* Sterling Publishing Co., Inc.

Freeman, Don. Corduroy. (Corduroy Ser.). (ENG., (J). (gr. -1 — 1). 2014. Illus.). 32p. bds. 7.99 *(978-0-451-47079-9(6))* 2011. 28p. bds. 11.99 *(978-0-670-01311-1(0))* Penguin Young Readers Group. (Viking Books for Young Readers).

—A Pocket for Corduroy. 2015. (Corduroy Ser.). (ENG.). 32p. (J). (— 1). bds. 7.99 *(978-0-451-47113-0(X),* Viking Books for Young Readers) Penguin Young Readers Group.

Freeman, Tor. Benji Bear's Busy Day. Freeman, Tor, illus. 2015. (ENG., Illus.). 18p. (J). (-k). bds. 17.99 *(978-1-5098-0111-4(1))* Pan Macmillan GBR. Dist: Independent Pubs. Group.

French, Jackie. Pete the Sheep. Whatley, Bruce, illus. 2008. 30p. (J). bds. *(978-0-7322-8794-8(4))* HarperCollins Pubs. Australia.

French, Jess. Fluttering Minibeast Adventures. Woodward, Jonathan, illus. 2016. (ENG.). 32p. (J). (gr. -1-k). 10.99 *(978-1-4052-7755-6(6))* Egmont Bks., Ltd. GBR. Dist: Independent Pubs. Group.

Friden, Chris. Bathtime with Bubbles. Zapater Oliva, Carlos & Depew, Robert, illus. 2008. (J). *(978-0-9801849-2-1(4))* Haydenburri Lane.

—Bedtime Safari. 2008. (Illus.). 27p. (J). bds. 14.99 *(978-0-9758785-4-5(9))* Haydenburri Lane.

—Bedtime Safari. Otoshi, Kathryn & Ciccarelli, Gary, illus. 2007. (J). *(978-0-9758785-3-8(0))* Haydenburri Lane.

—Pajamatime with P.J. Zapater Oliva, Carlos & Glazier, Garth, illus. 2008. (J). *(978-0-9801849-5-2(9));* *(978-0-9758785-9-0(X))* Haydenburri Lane.

—Sleepytime with Rory. Zapater Oliva, Carlos & Glazier, Garth, illus. 2008. (J). *(978-0-9801849-1-4(6))* Haydenburri Lane.

—Toothtime with Chomper. Rodriguez Braojos, Alberto et al, illus. 2008. (J). *(978-0-9801849-3-8(2))* Haydenburri Lane.

Friden, Chris & Rodriguez Braojos, Alberto. Storytime with Paige. Jaraiz, David, illus. 2008. (J). *(978-0-9801849-4-5(0));* *(978-0-9758785-8-3(1))* Haydenburri Lane.

Friedman, Becky. What Is Daniel Wearing? Fruchter, Jason, illus. 2015. (Daniel Tiger's Neighborhood Ser.). (ENG.). 14p. (J). (gr. -1 — 1). 8.99 *(978-1-4814-2899-6(3),* Simon Spotlight) Simon Spotlight.

Friedman, Maya. Three Falafels in My Pita. Mack, Steve, illus. 2015. (ENG.). 12p. (J). (gr. -1 — 1). bds. 5.95 *(978-1-4677-3472-1(1),* Kar-Ben Publishing) Lerner Publishing Group.

Friel, Helen, des. Midnight Creatures: A Pop-Up Shadow Search Book. 2016. (ENG., Illus.). 10p. (J). (gr. -1-1). 24.95 *(978-1-78067-822-1(3))* King, Laurence Publishing GBR. Dist: Hachette Bk. Group.

Friester, Paul. Owl Howl Board Book. Goossens, Philippe, illus. 2nd rev. ed. 2016. (ENG.). 26p. (J). bds. 8.95 *(978-0-7358-4234-2(5))* North-South Bks., Inc.

Frith, Alex. Lift the Flap Picture Atlas. 2010. (Atlases Ser.). (Illus.). 16p. (J). bds. 15.99 *(978-0-7945-2402-9(8),* Usborne) EDC Publishing.

—See Inside Science. 2007. 16p. (J). bds. 12.99 *(978-0-7945-1549-2(5),* Usborne) EDC Publishing.

—See Inside the World of Dinosaurs. Scott, Peter, illus. 2007. 16p. (J). bds. 13.99 *(978-0-7945-1436-5(7),* Usborne) EDC Publishing.

Frith, Alex & King, Colin. See Inside Inventions IR. 2012. (See Inside Board Bks). 16p. (J). ring bd. 13.99 *(978-0-7945-3239-0(X),* Usborne) EDC Publishing.

—See Inside Your Head. 2008. (Usborne Lift the Flap Bks.). 15p. (J). (gr. 4-7). bds. 12.99 *(978-0-7945-1948-3(2),* Usborne) EDC Publishing.

—See under the Ground. 2007. (See Inside Science Ser.). (Illus.). 15p. (J). bds. 12.99 *(978-0-7945-1600-0(9),* Usborne) EDC Publishing.

Frith, Alex & Lacey, Minna. See Inside Math - Internet Referenced. 2008. (See Inside Board Bks). 16p. (J). bds. 12.99 *(978-0-7945-2093-9(6),* Usborne) EDC Publishing.

Fritz, Greg. God Made You Special! Reed, Lisa, illus. 2015. (J). *(978-0-8249-1947-4(5),* Ideal Pubns.) Worthy Publishing.

Froeb, Lori. Disney Princess: to Be a Princess. 2016. (ENG.). 12p. (J). (gr. -1-k). 15.99 *(978-0-7944-3507-3(6),* Reader's Digest Children's Bks.) Studio Fun International.

—Fisher-Price Little People Christmastime Is Here! 2015. (Fisher Price Lift the Flap Ser.). (ENG., Illus.). 10p. (J). (gr. -1-k). bds. 9.99 *(978-0-7944-3534-9(3))* Reader's Digest Assn., Inc., The.

Froeb, Lori & Mitter, Matt. Fisher-Price Little People Valentine's Day Is Here! 2015. (Fisher Price Lift the Flap Ser.). (ENG.). 10p. (J). (gr. -1-k). bds. 9.99 *(978-0-7944-3535-6(1))* Reader's Digest Assn., Inc., The.

Froeb, Lori C. Disney Princess: Part of Your World. 2015. (Spin Arounds Ser.: 2). (ENG.). 12p. (J). (gr. -1-k). bds. 10.99 *(978-0-7944-3291-1(3),* Reader's Digest Children's Bks.) Studio Fun International.

—Fisher-Price Little People Easter Is Here! 2016. (Lift-The-Flap Ser.). (ENG.). 10p. (J). (gr. -1-k). bds. 9.99 *(978-0-7944-3580-6(7),* Reader's Digest Children's Bks.) Studio Fun International.

—Fisher-Price Little People Noah & the Animals. 2016. (Lift-The-Flap Ser.: 18). (ENG.). 10p. (J). (gr. -1-k). bds. 9.99 *(978-0-7944-3667-4(6))* Studio Fun International.

—Noah & the Animals. Corke, Estelle, illus. 2015. (Open Door Book Ser.: 3). (ENG.). 16p. (J). (gr. -1 — 1). bds. 9.99 *(978-0-7944-3342-0(1))* Studio Fun International.

—Noah's Ark, 1 vol. Rinaldo, Luana, illus. 2008. 12p. (J). bds. 7.99 *(978-0-8254-5546-9(4))* Kregel Pubns.

Froeb, Lori C., ed. My First Bedtime Bible Stories. Jones, Anna, illus. 2015. (ENG.). 10p. (J). (gr. -1-k). bds. 8.99 *(978-0-7944-3474-8(6))* Studio Fun International.

Fromental, Jean-Luc. Rapido's Next Stop. Jolivet, Joëlle, illus. 2012. (ENG.). 20p. (J). (gr. k-2). 17.95 *(978-1-4197-0195-5(9),* Abrams Bks. for Young Readers) Abrams, Inc.

Fronis, Aly. If You're Spooky & You Know It. Ho, Jannie, illus. 2016. (ENG.). 16p. (J). (gr. -1-k). bds. 5.99 *(978-1-4998-0165-1(3))* Little Bee Books Inc.

Frost, Lulu. The Moonlight Tooth Fairy. Brown, Loma, illus. 2013. (J). *(978-1-4351-4919-9(X))* Barnes & Noble, Inc.

Fruchter, Jason, illus. A Duckling for Daniel. 2016. (Daniel Tiger's Neighborhood Ser.). (ENG.). 14p. (J). (gr. -1-k). bds. 5.99 *(978-1-4814-5781-1(0),* Simon Spotlight) Simon Spotlight.

—How Is Daniel Feeling? 2015. (Daniel Tiger's Neighborhood Ser.). (ENG.). 14p. (J). (gr. -1-k). bds. 10.99 *(978-1-4814-3856-8(5),* Simon Spotlight) Simon Spotlight.

—What Time Is It, Daniel Tiger? 2016. (Daniel Tiger's Neighborhood Ser.). (ENG.). 14p. (J). (gr. -1-k). bds. 10.99 *(978-1-4814-6934-0(7),* Simon Spotlight) Simon Spotlight.

—You're Still You! 2016. (Daniel Tiger's Neighborhood Ser.). (ENG.). 12p. (J). (gr. -1-k). bds. 5.99 *(978-1-4814-6743-8(3),* Simon Spotlight) Simon Spotlight.

Fry, Sonali. I'm a Little Vampire. Rescek, Sanja, illus. 2014. (ENG.). 16p. (J). (gr. -1 — 1). bds. 5.99 *(978-1-4814-0504-1(7),* Little Simon) Little Simon.

—The Itsy Bitsy Pumpkin. Rescek, Sanja, illus. 2014. (Itsy Bitsy Ser.). (ENG.). 16p. (J). (gr. -1 — 1). bds. 5.99 *(978-1-4814-0505-8(5),* Little Simon) Little Simon.

—Where Are You, Blue? Clifton-Brown, Holly, illus. 2015. (Dot Town Ser.). (ENG.). 32p. (J). (gr. -1 — 1). bds. 8.99 *(978-1-4814-3589-5(2),* Little Simon) Little Simon.

Fujikawa, Gyo, illus. Sleepy Time. 2011. (ENG.). 20p. (J). (gr. k-k). bds. 5.95 *(978-1-4027-6820-0(6))* Sterling Publishing Co., Inc.

Fuller, Rachel. All Kinds of Festivals. 2012. (All Kinds Of Ser.). (ENG., Illus.). 16p. (J). (gr. -1-k). 12.99 *(978-1-85707-801-5(2))* Tango Bks. GBR. Dist: Independent Pubs. Group.

Fuller, Rachel, illus. Look at Me! 2009. (New Baby Ser.). (ENG.). 12p. (J). (gr. -1). bds. *(978-1-84643-278-1(2))* Child's Play International Ltd.

Furlong, Frank, illus. Pop Pop's Magic Chair. 2010. 24p. pap. 12.95 *(978-1-60844-658-2(1))* Dog Ear Publishing, LLC.

Furman, Eric. Sesame Street: Elmo (Giant First Play-a-Sound) 2010. 10p. (J). bds. 17.98 *(978-1-60553-546-3(X))* Publications International, Ltd.

Furukawa, Masumi, illus. The Ugly Duckling. (Flip-Up Fairy Tales Ser.). (ENG.). 24p. (J). 2007. (gr. -1-2). audio compact disk *(978-1-84643-095-4(X))* 2006. (gr. 2-2). pap. *(978-1-84643-022-0(4))* Child's Play International Ltd.

G., Ashley. Critter Colors. G., Ashley, illus. 2015. (ENG., Illus.). 28p. (J). (gr. -1-k). bds. 7.99 *(978-1-4814-4218-3(X),* Little Simon) Little Simon.

Gaffney, Michael. Time-Life Programa de Aprendizaje Infantil (Time-Life Early Learning Program), 10 bks. Incl. Cuantos Hipopotamos Hay? 1963. 16.95 *(978-0-7835-3512-8(0));* Cuentos para un Dia de Tormenta (Takes for a Stormy Day) 1996. 16.95 *(978-0-7835-3533-3(3));* Dia en la Vida del Sr. Atolondron. 1996. 16.95 *(978-0-7835-3525-8(2));* Relojes Magicos del Abuelo Roberto (Roberto's Magical Clocks) 1996. 16.95 *(978-0-7835-3504-3(X));* Secretos del Bosque (The Secret Forest) 1996. 16.95 *(978-0-7835-3500-5(7));* Tania y Sus Amigos (Tanya Thinker & the Gizmo Gang) 1996. 16.95 *(978-0-7835-3516-6(3));* Tomasol, el Mago del Color (Balderdash the Brilliant) 1996. 16.95 *(978-0-7835-3529-6(5));* Viaje de los "Micronautas" (Voyage of the Micronauts) 1996. 16.95 *(978-0-7835-3537-1(6));* (Illus.). 64p. (J). (gr. k-2). 144.08 *(978-0-7835-3541-8(4))* Time-Life, Inc.

Gaiman, Neil. Chu's Day Board Book. Rex, Adam, illus. 2014. (ENG.). 36p. (J). (gr. -1 — 1). bds. 7.99 *(978-0-06-234746-6(2),* HarperFestival) HarperCollins Pubs.

Gaines, Isabel & Milne, A. A. Pooh's Leaf Pile. Rigol, Francesc, illus. 2012. (J). *(978-1-4351-4190-2(3))* Disney Pr.

Galbraith, Kathryn O. Boo, Bunny! Board Book. Mack, Jeff, illus. 2012. (ENG.). 32p. (J). (gr. -1 — 1). bds. 5.99 *(978-0-547-81850-4(5))* Houghton Mifflin Harcourt Publishing Co.

Gall, Chris. Dinotrux. 2015. (Dinotrux Ser.: 1). (ENG., Illus.). 28p. (J). (gr. -1 — 1). bds. 7.99 *(978-0-316-40584-3(1))* Little, Brown Bks. for Young Readers.

—Revenge of the Dinotrux. 2015. (Dinotrux Ser.: 2). (ENG., Illus.). 28p. (J). (gr. -1 — 1). bds. 6.99 *(978-0-316-40635-2(X))* Little, Brown Bks. for Young Readers.

Gallo, Tina. Cinderella: A Wheel-Y Silly Fairy Tale. Scott, Kimberley, illus. 2011. (Little Simon Sillies Ser.). (ENG.). 14p. (J). (gr. -1-1). lib. bdg. 5.99 *(978-1-4424-2106-6(1),* Little Simon) Little Simon.

—Lettuce In! And Other Knock-Knock Jokes. Chollat, Emilie, illus. 2011. (Little Simon Sillies Ser.). (ENG.). 20p. (J). (gr. -1-1). 5.99 *(978-1-4424-1404-4(9),* Little Simon) Little Simon.

—The Three Little Pigs: A Wheel-Y Silly Fairy Tale. Bryne, Kelly, illus. 2011. (Little Simon Sillies Ser.). (ENG.). 14p. (J). (gr. -1-1). 5.99 *(978-1-4424-2107-3(X),* Little Simon) Little Simon.

—Where's My Valentine? 2013. (Yo Gabba Gabba! Ser.). (ENG., Illus.). 12p. (J). (gr. -1-1). bds. 5.99 *(978-1-4424-8647-8(3),* Simon Spotlight) Simon Spotlight.

Galvin, Laura G. & Galvin, Laura. I Love My Mommy (with Download) 2011. (ENG.). 16p. (J). *(978-1-60727-345-5(4))* Soundprints.

Galvin, Laura Gates. Baby Dolphins Busy Day. 2011. (Baby Animals (Soundprints) Ser.). (ENG., Illus.). 16p. (gr. -1-k). 15.95 *(978-1-60727-329-5(2))* Soundprints.

—Fawn & Her Family. 2011. (Baby Animals (Soundprints) Ser.). (ENG., Illus.). 16p. (J). (gr. -1-k). 6.95 *(978-1-60727-283-0(0))* Soundprints.

—First Look at Aircraft. Eaddy, Susan, illus. 2008. (ENG.). 16p. (J). (gr. -1-k). 6.95 *(978-1-59249-862-8(0))* Soundprints.

—First Look at Dinosaurs. Pindroh, Paula, illus. 2011. (First Look At... (Soundprints) Ser.). (ENG.). 16p. 6.95 *(978-1-60727-285-4(7))* Soundprints.

—First Look at Rescue Vehicles. Eaddy, Susan, illus. 2009. (ENG.). 16p. (J). (gr. -1-k). 6.95 *(978-1-60727-106-2(0));* bds. 6.95 *(978-1-60727-093-5(5))* Soundprints.

—First Look at Trucks. Eaddy, Susan, illus. 2008. (ENG.). 16p. (J). (gr. -1-k). 6.95 *(978-1-59249-861-1(2))* Soundprints.

—I Love My Family. 2011. (ENG.). 16p. (J). *(978-1-60727-621-0(6))* Soundprints.

—I Love My Sister. Oughton, Taylor et al, illus. 2011. (I Love My... Ser.). (ENG.). 16p. (gr. -1-k). 6.95 *(978-1-60727-311-0(4))* Soundprints.

—If I Were a Bird. 2014. (Illus.). (J). *(978-1-58865-787-9(6))* Kidsbooks, LLC.

Galvin, Laura Gates & Odierno, Lisa. Puppy Explores. 2008. (ENG.). 16p. (J). (gr. -1-k). 13.95 *(978-1-59249-864-2(7))* Soundprints.

Galvin, Laura Gates & Studio Mouse Editorial. Cinderella: Dreams Do Come True. 2008. (Illus.). 36p. (J). (gr. -1). 7.99 *(978-1-59069-436-7(8))* Studio Mouse LLC.

Galvin, Laura Gates & Studio Mouse Staff. Write-with-Me Alphabet. Giblin, Brian E., ed. (Write-with-Me Ser.). (Illus.). 28p. (J). 2011. 15.99 *(978-1-59069-921-8(1))* 2008. (ENG., 14.99 *(978-1-59069-618-7(2))* Studio Mouse LLC.

Gamble, Adam. Buenas Noches, California. Kelly, Cooper, illus. 2012. (Buenas Noches Ser.). (SPA & ENG.). 24p. (J). (gr. k — 1). bds. 9.95 *(978-1-60219-070-2(4))* Good Night Bks.

—Buenas Noches, Estados Unidos. Chan, Suwin, illus. 2012. (Buenas Noches Ser.). (ENG.). 28p. (J). (gr. k — 1). bds. 9.95 *(978-1-60219-069-6(0))* Good Night Bks.

—Buenas Noches, Nueva York. Veno, Joe & Jasper, Mark, illus. 2013. (Buenas Noches Ser.). (SPA & ENG.). 24p. (J). (— 1). bds. 9.95 *(978-1-60219-091-7(7))* Good Night Bks.

—Good Night Baby Jesus. 2010. (Good Night Our World Ser.). (ENG.). 20p. (J). (gr. k — 1). bds. 9.95 *(978-1-60219-049-8(6))* Good Night Bks.

—Good Night Country Store. Rosen, Anne & Jasper, Mark, illus. 2010. (Good Night Our World Ser.). (ENG.). 20p. (J). (gr. k — 1). bds. 9.95 *(978-1-60219-044-3(5))* Good Night Bks.

—Good Night Michigan. Rosen, Anne, illus. 2011. (Good Night Our World Ser.). (ENG.). 20p. (J). (gr. k — 1). bds. 9.95 *(978-1-60219-054-2(2))* Good Night Bks.

—Good Night Montana. 2013. (Good Night Our World Ser.). (ENG., Illus.). 20p. (J). (— 1). bds. 9.95 *(978-1-60219-080-1(1))* Good Night Bks.

—Good Night North Pole. Jasper, Mark, illus. 2012. (Good Night Our World Ser.). (ENG.). 20p. (J). (gr. k — 1). bds. 9.95 *(978-1-60219-071-9(2),* 1350772) Good Night Bks.

—Good Night Ohio. Jasper, Mark, illus. 2013. (Good Night Our World Ser.). (ENG.). 20p. (J). (— 1). bds. 9.95 *(978-1-60219-076-4(3))* Good Night Bks.

—Good Night Texas. Veno, Joe & Kelly, Cooper, illus. 2nd ed. 2011. (Good Night Our World Ser.). (ENG.). 20p. (J). (gr. k — 1). bds. 9.95 *(978-1-60219-053-5(4))* Good Night Bks.

—Good Night World. Kelly, Cooper, illus. 2009. (Good Night Our World Ser.). (ENG.). 28p. (J). (gr. k — 1). bds. 9.95 *(978-1-60219-030-6(5))* Good Night Bks.

Gamble, Adam & Adams, David J. Good Night Canada. Kelly, Cooper, illus. 2010. (Good Night Our World Ser.). (ENG.). 28p. (J). (gr. k — 1). bds. 9.95 *(978-1-60219-038-2(0))* Good Night Bks.

Gamble, Adam & Jasper, Mark. Buenas Noches, Florida. 2013. (Buenas Noches Ser.). (SPA & ENG., Illus.). 20p. (J). (— 1). bds. 9.95 *(978-1-60219-092-4(5))* Good Night Bks.

—Buenas Noches, Texas. 2013. (Buenas Noches Ser.). (SPA & ENG., Illus.). 20p. (J). (— 1). bds. 9.95 *(978-1-60219-093-1(3))* Good Night Bks.

—Count to Sleep America. Veno, Joe, illus. 2015. (Count to Sleep Ser.). (ENG.). 20p. (J). (— 1). bds. 7.95 *(978-1-60219-231-7(6))* Good Night Bks.

—Count to Sleep California. Veno, Joe, illus. 2014. (Count to Sleep Ser.). (ENG.). 20p. (J). (— 1). bds. 7.95 *(978-1-60219-200-3(6))* Good Night Bks.

—Count to Sleep Florida. Veno, Joe, illus. 2014. (Count to Sleep Ser.). (ENG.). 20p. (J). (— 1). bds. 7.95 *(978-1-60219-202-7(2))* Good Night Bks.

—Count to Sleep Michigan. Veno, Joe, illus. 2014. (Count to Sleep Ser.). (ENG.). 20p. (J). (— 1). bds. 7.95 *(978-1-60219-327-7(4))* Good Night Bks.

—Count to Sleep Minnesota. Veno, Joe, illus. 2014. (Count to Sleep Ser.). (ENG.). 20p. (J). (— 1). bds. 7.95 *(978-1-60219-205-8(7))* Good Night Bks.

—Count to Sleep Wisconsin. Veno, Joe, illus. 2014. (Count to Sleep Ser.). (ENG.). 20p. (J). (— 1). bds. 7.95 *(978-1-60219-328-4(2))* Good Night Bks.

—Good Night Baby Animals. Chan, Suwin, illus. 2016. (Good Night Our World Ser.). (ENG.). 20p. (J). (— 1). bds. 9.95 *(978-1-60219-499-1(8))* Good Night Bks.

—Good Night Boats. Veno, Joe, illus. 2016. (Good Night Our World Ser.). (ENG.). 20p. (J). (— 1). bds. 9.95 *(978-1-60219-500-4(5))* Good Night Bks.

—Good Night Books. Chan, Suwin, illus. 2017. (Good Night Our World Ser.). (ENG.). 20p. (J). (— 1). bds. 9.95 ***(978-1-60219-470-0(X))*** Good Night Bks.

—Good Night Broadway. Veno, Joe, illus. 2017. (Good Night Our World Ser.). (ENG.). 20p. (J). (gr. -1 — 1). bds. 9.95 *(978-1-60219-436-6(X))* Good Night Bks.

—Good Night Brooklyn. 2013. (Good Night Our World Ser.). (ENG., Illus.). 20p. (J). (— 1). bds. 9.95 *(978-1-60219-094-8(1))* Good Night Bks.

—Good Night Central Park. Palmer, Ruth, illus. 2013. (Good Night Our World Ser.). (ENG.). 20p. (J). (— 1). bds. 9.95 *(978-1-60219-082-5(8))* Good Night Bks.

—Good Night Daddy. Kelly, Cooper, illus. 2015. (Good Night Our World Ser.). (ENG.). 20p. (J). (— 1). bds. 9.95 *(978-1-60219-229-4(4))* Good Night Bks.

—Good Night Delaware. Jasper, Mark, illus. 2012. (Good Night Our World Ser.). (ENG., Illus.). 20p. (J). (gr. k — 1). bds. 9.95 *(978-1-60219-066-5(6))* Good Night Bks.

—Good Night Dump Truck. Kelly, Cooper, illus. 2014. (Good Night Our World Ser.). (ENG.). 26p. (J). (— 1). bds. 9.95 *(978-1-60219-189-1(1))* Good Night Bks.

—Good Night Families. Kelly, Cooper, illus. 2017. (Good Night Our World Ser.). (ENG.). 20p. (J). (— 1). bds. 9.95 ***(978-1-60219-465-6(3))*** Good Night Bks.

—Good Night Florida. Veno, Joe & Hansen, Red, illus. 2nd ed. 2010. (Good Night Our World Ser.). (ENG.). 20p. (J). (gr. k — 1). bds. 9.95 *(978-1-60219-045-0(3))* Good Night Bks.

—Good Night Grandma. Kelly, Cooper, illus. 2016. (ENG.). 20p. (J). (— 1). bds. 9.95 *(978-1-60219-409-0(2))* Good Night Bks.

—Good Night Illinois. 2013. (Good Night Our World Ser.). (ENG., Illus.). 20p. (J). (— 1). bds. 9.95 *(978-1-60219-086-3(0))* Good Night Bks.

—Good Night Indiana. 2013. (Good Night Our World Ser.). (ENG., Illus.). 20p. (J). (— 1). bds. 9.95 *(978-1-60219-075-7(5))* Good Night Bks.

—Good Night Iowa. 2013. (Good Night Our World Ser.). (ENG., Illus.). 20p. (J). (— 1). bds. 9.95 *(978-1-60219-085-6(2))* Good Night Bks.

—Good Night Little Brother. Kelly, Cooper, illus. 2016. (Good Night Our World Ser.). (ENG.). 20p. (J). (— 1). bds. 9.95 *(978-1-60219-505-9(6))* Good Night Bks.

—Good Night Little Monsters. Kelly, Cooper, illus. 2017. (Good Night Our World Ser.). (ENG.). 20p. (J). (gr. -1 — 1). bds. 9.95 ***(978-1-60219-489-2(0))*** Good Night Bks.

—Good Night Little Sister. Kelly, Cooper, illus. 2016. (Good Night Our World Ser.). (ENG.). 20p. (J). (— 1). bds. 9.95 *(978-1-60219-506-6(4))* Good Night Bks.

—Good Night Maryland. Veno, Joe et al, illus. 2011. (Good Night Our World Ser.). (ENG.). 20p. (J). (gr. k — 1). bds. 9.95 *(978-1-60219-046-7(1))* Good Night Bks.

—Good Night Massachusetts. 2013. (Good Night Our World Ser.). (ENG., Illus.). 20p. (J). (— 1). bds. 9.95 *(978-1-60219-084-9(4))* Good Night Bks.

—Good Night Mermaids. Chan, Suwin, illus. 2015. (Good Night Our World Ser.). (ENG.). 20p. (J). (— 1). bds. 9.95 *(978-1-60219-226-3(X))* Good Night Bks.

—Good Night Mississippi. Veno, Joe, illus. 2015. (Good Night Our World Ser.). (ENG.). 20p. (J). (— 1). bds. 9.95 *(978-1-60219-221-8(9))* Good Night Bks.

—Good Night Missouri. Veno, Joe, illus. 2013. (Good Night Our World Ser.). (ENG.). 20p. (J). (— 1). bds. 9.95 *(978-1-60219-077-1(1))* Good Night Bks.

—Good Night Nebraska. 2015. (Good Night Our World Ser.). (ENG., Illus.). 20p. (J). (— 1). bds. 9.95 *(978-1-60219-087-0(9))* Good Night Bks.

—Good Night Nevada. Rosen, Anne & Veno, Joe, illus. 2012. (Good Night Our World Ser.). (ENG.). 20p. (J). (gr. k — 1). bds. 9.95 *(978-1-60219-060-3(7))* Good Night Bks.

—Good Night New Mexico. Palmer, Ruth, illus. 2014. (Good Night Our World Ser.). (ENG.). 20p. (J). (— 1). bds. 9.95 *(978-1-60219-088-7(7))* Good Night Bks.

—Good Night Pennsylvania. 2013. (Good Night Our World Ser.). (ENG., Illus.). 20p. (J). (— 1). bds. 9.95 *(978-1-60219-074-0(7))* Good Night Bks.

—Good Night Pirate Ship. Kelly, Cooper, illus. 2015. (Good Night Our World Ser.). (ENG.). 26p. (J). (— 1). bds. 9.95 *(978-1-60219-217-1(0))* Good Night Bks.

—Good Night Pittsburgh. Palmer, Ruth, illus. 2012. (Good Night Our World Ser.). (ENG.). 20p. (J). (gr. k — 1). bds. 9.95 *(978-1-60219-073-3(9))* Good Night Bks.

—Good Night Planes. Kelly, Cooper, illus. 2015. (Good Night Our World Ser.). (ENG.). 26p. (J). (— 1). bds. 9.95 *(978-1-60219-218-8(9))* Good Night Bks.

—Good Night Princesses. Gardner, Louise, illus. 2016. (Good Night Our World Ser.). (ENG.). 20p. (J). (— 1). bds. 9.95 *(978-1-60219-225-6(1))* Good Night Bks.

—Good Night Snow. 2016. (Good Night Our World Ser.). (ENG., Illus.). 20p. (J). (— 1). bds. 9.95 *(978-1-60219-412-0(2))* Good Night Bks.
—Good Night Statue of Liberty. Kelly, Cooper, illus. 2017. (Good Night Our World Ser.). (ENG.). 20p. (J). (gr. -1 — 1). bds. 9.95 ***(978-1-60219-429-8(7))*** Good Night Bks.
—Good Night Summer. Blackmore, Katherine, illus. 2017. (Good Night Our World Ser.). (ENG.). 20p. (J). (— 1). bds. 9.95 *(978-1-60219-440-3(8))* Good Night Bks.
—Good Night Toronto. Veno, Joe & Kelly, Cooper, illus. 2011. (Good Night Our World Ser.). (ENG.). 20p. (J). (gr. k — 1). bds. 9.95 *(978-1-60219-048-1(8))* Good Night Bks.
—Good Night Utah. Rosen, Anne & Hart, Jason, illus. 2012. (Good Night Our World Ser.). (ENG.). 20p. (J). (gr. k — 1). bds. 9.95 *(978-1-60219-059-7(3))* Good Night Bks.
—Good Night Washington State. Veno, Joe & Kelly, Cooper, illus. 2012. (Good Night Our World Ser.). (ENG.). 20p. (J). (gr. k — 1). bds. 9.95 *(978-1-60219-072-6(0))* Good Night Bks.
—Good Night Yosemite. McDonnell, Janet & Chan, Suwin, illus. 2016. (Good Night Our World Ser.). (ENG.). 20p. (J). (— 1). bds. 9.95 *(978-1-60219-389-5(4))* Good Night Bks.
Gamble, Adam & Mackey, Bill. Good Night Colorado. Rosen, Anne, illus. 2012. (Good Night Our World Ser.). (ENG.). 20p. (J). (gr. k — 1). bds. 9.95 *(978-1-60219-055-9(0))* Good Night Bks.
Gamble, Adam, et al. Good Night Kentucky. 2014. (Good Night Our World Ser.). (ENG., Illus.). 20p. (J). (— 1). bds. 9.95 *(978-1-60219-089-4(5))* Good Night Bks.
—Good Night Mountains. 2013. (Good Night Our World Ser.). (ENG., Illus.). 26p. (J). (— 1). bds. 9.95 *(978-1-60219-090-0(9))* Good Night Bks.
—Good Night New Baby. 2014. (Good Night Our World Ser.). (ENG., Illus.). 20p. (J). (— 1). bds. 9.95 *(978-1-60219-188-4(3))* Good Night Bks.
—Good Night New Orleans. Kelly, Cooper, illus. 2012. (Good Night Our World Ser.). (ENG.). 20p. (J). (gr. k — 1). bds. 9.95 *(978-1-60219-061-0(5))* Good Night Bks.
—Good Night South Carolina. 2014. (Good Night Our World Ser.). (ENG.). 20p. (J). (— 1). bds. 9.95 *(978-1-60219-190-7(5))* Good Night Bks.
Gamble, Jasper, et al. Good Night New York State. Jasper, Mark, illus. 2012. (Good Night Our World Ser.). (ENG.). 20p. (J). (gr. k — 1). bds. 9.95 *(978-1-60219-063-4(1))* Good Night Bks.
—Good Night Wisconsin. Jasper, Mark & Kelly, Cooper, illus. 2012. (Good Night Our World Ser.). (ENG.). 20p. (J). (gr. k — 1). bds. 9.95 *(978-1-60219-064-1(X))* Good Night Bks.
Ganeri, Anita. My Pop-Up World Atlas. Waterhouse, Stephen, illus. 2012. (ENG.). 16p. (J). (gr. k-3). 19.99 *(978-0-7636-6094-9(9),* Templar) Candlewick Pr.
—Volcanes y terremotos/Earthquakes & Volcanoes. 2011. 16p. pap. *(978-607-404-319-8(1),* Silver Dolphin en Español) Advanced Marketing, S. de R. L. de C. V.
Gardiner, Lisa. Things That Work. Flowerpot Press, ed. 2012. (Illus.). 20p. (J). *(978-1-926988-03-0(5))* Flowerpot Children's Pr. Inc.
Gardner, Louise, illus. Five Little Easter Eggs. (ENG.). 10p. (J). 2009. (gr. -1). 5.95 *(978-1-58117-849-4(2))* 2008. 9.95 *(978-1-58117-682-7(1))* Bendon, Inc. (Intervisual/Piggy Toes).
Garralon, Claire. Black Cat & White Cat. 2016. (ENG.). 30p. (J). bds. 7.99 *(978-1-4926-3781-3(5),* 9781492637813, Sourcebooks Jabberwocky) Sourcebooks, Inc.
Garton, Michael. Countdown by the Sea. 2012. (ENG.). 20p. (J). bds. *(978-1-60727-701-9(8))* Soundprints.
Garton, Sam. I Am Otter. Garton, Sam, illus. 2016. (Illus.). 34p. (J). (gr. -1 — 1). bds. 7.99 *(978-0-06-240908-9(5))* HarperCollins Pubs.
Gates Galvin, Laura. First Look at Insects. Oh, Charlotte, illus. 2011. (ENG.). 16p. (J). *(978-1-60727-223-6(7))* Soundprints.
Gay, Susana. Jonah & the Big Fish. 2017. (Illus.). 16p. (J). ***(978-0-8249-1666-4(2))*** Worthy Publishing.
Géhin, Élisa. One & All. 2016. (ENG., Illus.). 42p. (J). (gr. -1-k). 14.95 *(978-1-4197-1904-2(1),* Abrams Appleseed) Abrams, Inc.
Géhin, Élisa & Duisit, Bernard. Can You Keep a Straight Face? 2017. (Flip Flap Pop-Up Ser.: 0). (ENG., Illus.). 16p. (gr. -1-1). 14.95 *(978-0-500-65091-2(8),* 565091) Thames & Hudson.
Gehl, Laura. Peep & Egg: I'm Not Trick-Or-Treating. Wan, Joyce, illus. 2017. (Peep & Egg Ser.). (ENG.). 32p. (J). bds. 7.99 *(978-0-374-30543-7(9),* 9780374305437, Farrar, Straus & Giroux (BYR)) Farrar, Straus & Giroux.
Geis Conti, Patricia. Alexander Calder. 2010. (¡Mira Qué Artista! Ser.). (SPA.). 18p. (J). (gr. 2-4). 21.95 *(978-84-9825-375-7(6))* Combel Editorial, S.A. ESP. Dist: Independent Pubs. Group.
—Andy Warhol. 2010. (¡Mira Qué Artista! Ser.). (SPA.). 18p. (J). (gr. 2-4). 21.95 *(978-84-9825-485-3(X))* Combel Editorial, S.A. ESP. Dist: Independent Pubs. Group.
Geis, Patricia. Alexander Calder. 2014. (Meet the Artist Ser.). (ENG., Illus.). 18p. (J). (gr. 2-7). 24.95 *(978-1-61689-225-8(0))* Princeton Architectural Pr.
—Good-bye Pacifier! Folch, Sergio, illus. 2009. (Good Habits with Coco & Tula Ser.). 16p. (J). (gr. -1-k). bds. 11.40 *(978-1-60754-405-0(9))* Windmill Bks.
—Henri Matisse: Meet the Artist! 2014. (Meet the Artist Ser.). (ENG., Illus.). 16p. (J). (gr. 2-7). 24.95 *(978-1-61689-282-1(X))* Princeton Architectural Pr.
—Let's Get Well! Folch, Sergio, illus. 2009. (Good Habits with Coco & Tula Ser.). 16p. (J). (gr. -1-k). bds. 11.40 *(978-1-60754-407-4(5))* Windmill Bks.
—Let's Wash Up! Folch, Sergio, illus. 2009. (Good Habits with Coco & Tula Ser.). 16p. (J). (gr. -1-k). bds. 11.40 *(978-1-60754-410-4(5))* Windmill Bks.
—Pablo Picasso. 2014. (Meet the Artist Ser.). (ENG., Illus.). 18p. (J). (gr. 2-7). 24.95 *(978-1-61689-251-7(X))* Princeton Architectural Pr.
Geller, Amy. My First Words OUTSIDE. 1 vol. 2013. (ENG., Illus.). 20p. (J). bds. 6.99 *(978-1-59572-332-1(3))* Star Bright Bks., Inc.
George, Bobby & George, June. Montessori - Shape Work. Nassner, Alyssa, illus. 2013. (Montessori Ser.). (ENG.). 18p. (J). (gr. -1-k). bds. 9.95 *(978-1-4197-0935-7(6),* Abrams Appleseed) Abrams, Inc.
—Montessori: Number Work. Nassner, Alyssa, illus. 2012. (Montessori Ser.). (ENG.). 24p. (J). (gr. -1-k). bds., bds. 9.95 *(978-1-4197-0412-3(5),* Abrams Appleseed) Abrams, Inc.
Gershator, Phillis. Who's in the Farmyard? McDonald, Jill, illus. 2012. (ENG.). 24p. (J). (gr. -1-k). bds. 14.99 *(978-1-84686-574-9(3))* Barefoot Bks., Inc.
—Who's in the Garden? McDonald, Jill, illus. 2010. (ENG.). 24p. (J). (gr. -1-k). 14.99 *(978-1-84686-403-2(8))* Barefoot Bks., Inc.
Gershator, Phillis & Green, Mim. Time for a Hug. Walker, David, illus. 2013. (Snuggle Time Stories Ser.). (ENG.). 22p. (J). (gr. -1-k). bds. 6.95 *(978-1-4549-0856-2(4))* Sterling Publishing Co., Inc.
Gerstein, Sherry. Imagination Vacation: A Color-Foil Shapes Book. Bennett, Andy, illus. 2006. 14p. (J). (gr. -1-3). bds. 6.95 *(978-1-57791-261-3(6))* Brighter Minds Children's Publishing.
—Moo, Moo Who Are You? Bennett, Andy, illus. 2006. 14p. (J). (gr. -1-k). bds. 7.95 *(978-1-57791-258-3(6))* Brighter Minds Children's Publishing.
Gervais, Ricky. Flanimals Pop-Up. Steen, Rob, illus. 2010. (ENG.). 14p. (J). (gr. k-4). 19.99 *(978-0-7636-4781-0(0))* Candlewick Pr.
Gerver, Jane E. Christmas Shapes. Davis, Nancy & Davis, Kathryn Lynn, illus. 2010. (ENG.). 14p. (J). (gr. -1 — 1). bds. 6.99 *(978-1-4169-9759-7(8),* Little Simon) Little Simon.
—I Love You. Brown, Jo, illus. 2015. (ENG.). 14p. (J). (— 1). bds. 4.99 *(978-1-62979-416-7(3),* Highlights) Boyds Mills Pr.
—Who's at Home? Davis, Nancy & Davis, Kathryn Lynn, illus. 2010. (ENG.). 14p. (J). (gr. -1 — 1). bds. 6.99 *(978-1-4169-9758-0(X),* Little Simon) Little Simon.
Get a Grip on Life: What Every Teen Must Know to Have a Great Life. 2004. 240p. (YA). per. 14.00 *(978-0-9748994-0-4(2))* Youth Quest Institute.
Gevry, Claudine, illus. One Little Penguin & His Friends: A Pushing, Turning, Counting Book. 2012. (ENG.). 10p. (J). bds. *(978-1-84956-027-6(7))* Top That! Publishing PLC.
Ghigna, Charles. Hail to Spring! Watson, Laura, illus. 2015. (Springtime Weather Wonders Ser.). (ENG.). 20p. (gr. -1-2). bds. 7.99 *(978-1-4795-6041-7(3))* Picture Window Bks.
—Sunshine Brightens Springtime. Watson, Laura, illus. 2015. (Springtime Weather Wonders Ser.). (ENG.). 20p. (gr. -1-2). bds. 7.99 *(978-1-4795-6043-1(X))* Picture Window Bks.
Gibbs, Edward. I Spy under the Sea. Gibbs, Edward, illus. 2012. (ENG., Illus.). 32p. (J). (gr. k-k). 14.99 *(978-0-7636-5952-3(5),* Templar) Candlewick Pr.
Gifford, Clive. Robots. 2011. 48p. 11.99 *(978-84-96252-41-7(8))* Edilupa Ediciones, S.L. ESP. Dist: Lectorum Pubns., Inc.
—100 Facts Around Town. Kearney, Brendan, illus. 2015. (ENG.). 14p. (J). (gr. -1-1). 12.99 *(978-1-4052-7171-4(X))* Egmont Bks., Ltd. GBR. Dist: Independent Pubs. Group.
Giles, Mike, illus. Spring Showers Bring Flowers. 2014. (Yo Gabba Gabba! Ser.). (ENG.). 12p. (J). (gr. -1-k). bds. 5.99 *(978-1-4424-9572-2(3),* Simon Spotlight) Simon Spotlight.
Gili, Phillida. Cinderella: A Pop-up Book. Gili, Phillida, illus. 2007. (Illus.). 12p. (J). 25.00 *(978-1-4223-9031-3(4))* DIANE Publishing Co.
Gillingham, Sara. Cozy Christmas: A Touch-and-Feel Book. 2016. (Sago Mini Ser.). (ENG., Illus.). 14p. (J). (gr. -1 — 1). bds. 6.99 *(978-1-4998-0324-2(9))* Little Bee Books Inc.
—In My Barn. Siminovich, Lorena, illus. 2012. (ENG.). 12p. (J). (gr. -1 — 1). bds. 8.99 *(978-1-4521-0641-0(X))* Chronicle Bks. LLC.
—In My Forest. Siminovich, Lorena, illus. 2010. (ENG.). 12p. (J). (gr. -1 — 1). bds. 8.99 *(978-0-8118-7566-0(0))* Chronicle Bks. LLC.
—In My Pond. Siminovich, Lorena, illus. 2009. (ENG.). 12p. (J). (gr. -1 — 1). bds. 8.99 *(978-0-8118-6556-2(8))* Chronicle Bks. LLC.
—My Little Stocking. 2011. (ENG.). 12p. (J). (gr. -1 — 1). 9.99 *(978-1-4521-0225-2(2))* Chronicle Bks. LLC.
—My Little Sweetheart. 2011. (ENG.). 12p. (J). (gr. -1 — 1). 9.99 *(978-1-4521-0226-9(0))* Chronicle Bks. LLC.
—On My Beach. Siminovich, Lorena, illus. 2015. (ENG.). 12p. (J). (gr. -1 — 1). bds. 8.99 *(978-1-4521-0640-3(1))* Chronicle Bks. LLC.
—On My Leaf. Siminovich, Lorena, illus. 2012. (ENG.). 12p. (J). (gr. -1 — 1). bds. 8.99 *(978-1-4521-0813-1(7))* Chronicle Bks. LLC.
Gillingham, Sara, illus. Snuggle the Baby. 2014. (ENG.). 12p. (J). (gr. -1 — 1). bds. 12.99 *(978-1-4197-1124-4(5),* Abrams Appleseed) Abrams, Inc.
Gillingham, Sara & Chronicle Books Staff. In My Flower. Siminovich, Lorena, illus. 2009. (ENG.). 12p. (J). (gr. -1 — 1). bds. 8.99 *(978-0-8118-7339-0(0))* Chronicle Bks. LLC.
—In My Meadow. Siminovich, Lorena, illus. 2009. (ENG.). 12p. (J). (gr. -1 — 1). bds. 8.99 *(978-0-8118-7338-3(2))* Chronicle Bks. LLC.
Girard, Alexander. Alexander Girard Color. 2011. (ENG., Illus.). 58p. (J). bds. 14.95 *(978-1-934429-77-8(5))* AMMO Bks., LLC.
Girard, Alexander, illus. Alexander Girard Coloring Book. 2014. (ENG.). 30p. pap. 9.95 *(978-1-934429-86-0(4))* AMMO Bks., LLC.
Girl Friends Super Sticker Book. (Illus.). 64p. (J). pap. *(978-2-7643-0026-8(3))* Phidal Publishing, Inc./Editions Phidal, Inc.
Glaser, Rebecca. Bunnies Hop. 2017. (Amicus Ink Board Bks.). (ENG., Illus.). 14p. (J). (gr. -1 — 1). bds. 7.99 ***(978-1-68152-199-2(7))*** Amicus.
—Fish Swim. 2017. (Amicus Ink Board Bks.). (ENG., Illus.). 14p. (J). (gr. -1 — 1). bds. 7.99 ***(978-1-68152-198-5(9))*** Amicus.
—Kittens Pounce. 2017. (Amicus Ink Board Bks.). (ENG., Illus.). 14p. (J). (gr. -1 — 1). bds. 7.99 ***(978-1-68152-197-8(0))*** Amicus.
—Puppies Chase. 2017. (Amicus Ink Board Bks.). (ENG., Illus.). 14p. (J). (gr. -1 — 1). bds. 7.99 ***(978-1-68152-196-1(2))*** Amicus.
Glaser, Rebecca Stromstad. Cars Zoom. 2016. (ENG., Illus.). 14p. (J). (gr. -1 — 1). bds. 7.99 *(978-1-68152-121-3(0))* Amicus.
—Dolphins Play. 2016. (ENG., Illus.). 16p. (J). (gr. -1 — 1). bds. 7.99 *(978-1-68152-067-4(2))* Amicus.
—Ducks Quack. 2016. (ENG., Illus.). 14p. (J). (gr. -1 — 1). bds. 7.99 *(978-1-68152-127-5(X))* Amicus.
—Elephants Spray. 2016. (ENG., Illus.). 16p. (J). (gr. -1 — 1). bds. 7.99 *(978-1-68152-068-1(0))* Amicus.
—Giraffes Stretch. 2016. (ENG., Illus.). 16p. (J). (gr. -1 — 1). bds. 7.99 *(978-1-68152-069-8(9))* Amicus.
—Horses Neigh. 2016. (ENG., Illus.). 14p. (J). (gr. -1 — 1). bds. 7.99 *(978-1-68152-126-8(1))* Amicus.
—Lions Roar. 2016. (ENG., Illus.). 16p. (J). (gr. -1 — 1). bds. 7.99 *(978-1-68152-071-1(0))* Amicus.
—Penguins Waddle. 2016. (ENG., Illus.). 16p. (J). (gr. -1 — 1). bds. 7.99 *(978-1-68152-070-4(2))* Amicus.
—Pigs Oink. 2016. (ENG., Illus.). 14p. (J). (gr. -1 — 1). bds. 7.99 *(978-1-68152-128-2(8))* Amicus.
—Planes Soar. 2016. (ENG., Illus.). 14p. (J). (gr. -1 — 1). bds. 7.99 *(978-1-68152-122-0(9))* Amicus.
—Tractors Pull. 2016. (ENG., Illus.). 14p. (J). (gr. -1 — 1). bds. 7.99 *(978-1-68152-123-7(7))* Amicus.
—Trucks Haul. 2016. (ENG., Illus.). 14p. (J). (gr. -1 — 1). bds. 7.99 *(978-1-68152-124-4(5))* Amicus.
Glass, Calliope. Disney Tails Figaro's Halloween Surprise. Disney Storybook Art Team, illus. 2015. (Disney Tails Ser.). (ENG.). 10p. (J). (gr. -1 — 1). bds. 6.99 *(978-1-4847-1372-3(9),* 1392357) Disney Pr.
—Disney Tails We Love Marie. Disney Storybook Art Team, illus. 2015. (Disney Tails Ser.). (ENG.). 10p. (J). (gr. -1 — 1). bds. 6.99 *(978-1-4847-1373-0(7))* Disney Pr.
Glori, Debi. No Matter What. 2012. (ENG., Illus.). 24p. (J). (gr. -1 — 1). bds. 12.99 *(978-0-547-71905-4(1))* Houghton Mifflin Harcourt Publishing Co.
Global Fund for Children Staff. American Babies. 2010. (ENG., Illus.). 16p. (J). (gr. -1 — 1). bds. 6.95 *(978-1-58089-280-3(9))* Charlesbridge Publishing, Inc.
Glow in the Dark Advent Sticker Book. (Illus.). 16p. (J). (gr. -1-5). 6.99 *(978-0-8254-7233-6(4))* Kregel Pubns.
Going Shopping! Sticker Book. (Girlfriend Gang Ser.). 16p. (J). *(978-2-7643-0020-6(4))* Phidal Publishing, Inc./Editions Phidal, Inc.
Gold, Gina. Disney Palace Pets Guess Who Castle Cuties. 2014. (Guess Who Ser.). (ENG.). 10p. (J). (gr. -1-k). 10.99 *(978-0-7944-3192-1(5),* Reader's Digest Children's Bks.) Studio Fun International.
Goldberg, Ella, ed. Farm Life. 2013. (Matching Pictures Ser.). (ENG.). 20p. (J). (gr. -1-k). bds. 5.95 *(978-1-61889-309-3(2))* AZ Bks. LLC.
—Simple Shapes. 2013. (Matching Pictures Ser.). (ENG.). 20p. (J). (gr. -1-k). bds. 5.95 *(978-1-61889-311-6(4))* AZ Bks. LLC.
Goldberg, Malky. What Else Do I Say? A Lift the Flap Book. Argoff, Patti, illus. 2007. (J). (gr. -1-k). bds. 9.95 *(978-1-929628-34-6(X))* Hachai Publishing.
Golden Books. The Fire Engine Book. Gergely, Tibor, illus. 2015. (Little Golden Board Book Ser.). (ENG.). 26p. (J). (-k). bds. 7.99 *(978-0-553-52224-2(8),* Golden Bks.) Random Hse. Children's Bks.
—Good Morning, Bunny/Good Night, Bunny. 2015. (ENG., Illus.). 26p. (J). (— 1). bds. 10.99 *(978-0-553-51057-7(6),* Golden Bks.) Random Hse. Children's Bks.
—The Little Red Hen. Miller, J. P., illus. 2015. (ENG.). 26p. (J). (-k). bds. 7.99 *(978-0-385-39094-1(7),* Golden Bks.) Random Hse. Children's Bks.
—Love Is in the Hair! Golden Books, illus. 2016. (4 Color Plus Stkrs & Cards Ser.). (ENG., Illus.). 48p. (J). (gr. -1-2). pap. 7.99 *(978-0-399-55892-4(6),* Golden Bks.) Random Hse. Children's Bks.
—Pat the Pet (Pat the Bunny) Vilela, Luiz, illus. 2014. (Lift-The-Flap Ser.). (ENG.). 16p. (J). (— 1). 14.99 *(978-0-385-37673-0(1),* Golden Bks.) Random Hse. Children's Bks.
—Pat the Zoo (Pat the Bunny) LV Studio, illus. 2012. (Touch-And-Feel Ser.). (ENG.). 16p. (J). (gr. k — 1). 14.99 *(978-0-307-97797-7(8),* Golden Bks.) Random Hse. Children's Bks.
—Teenage Mutant Ninja Turtles. Golden Books, illus. 2014. (Magnetic Play Book Ser.). (ENG., Illus.). 8p. (J). (gr. -1-2). bds. 8.99 *(978-0-385-37522-1(0),* Golden Bks.) Random Hse. Children's Bks.
—Trains, Cranes & Troublesome Trucks (Thomas & Friends) 2015. (Big Bright & Early Board Book Ser.). (ENG., Illus.). 24p. (J). (— 1). bds. 6.99 *(978-0-385-37393-7(7),* Random Hse. Bks. for Young Readers) Random Hse. Children's Bks.
Golden Books Staff. Bunny Business. Aikins, Dave, illus. 2011. (Color Plus Flocked Stickers Ser.). (ENG.). 64p. (J). (gr. -1-2). pap. 4.99 *(978-0-375-86818-4(6),* Golden Bks.) Random Hse. Children's Bks.
—Bunny's Garden. Golden Books Staff, illus. 2010. (Shaped Board Book Ser.). (ENG., Illus.). 12p. (J). (gr. -1 — 1). bds. 7.99 *(978-0-375-85788-1(5),* Golden Bks.) Random Hse. Children's Bks.
—Christmas Is Coming! (Dora the Explorer) McGee, Warner, illus. 2011. (Glitter Sticker Book Ser.). (ENG.). 64p. (J). (gr. -1-2). pap. 4.99 *(978-0-375-87393-5(7),* Golden Bks.) Random Hse. Children's Bks.
—Pat the Bunny: At the Apple Orchard. Vilela, Luiz, illus. 2015. (ENG.). 24p. (J). (— 1). bds. 6.99 *(978-0-553-51205-2(6),* Golden Bks.) Random Hse. Children's Bks.
—A Very Krabby Christmas (SpongeBob SquarePants) Aikins, Dave, illus. 2011. (Glitter Sticker Book Ser.). (ENG.). 64p. (J). (gr. -1-2). pap. 4.99 *(978-0-375-87392-8(9),* Golden Bks.) Random Hse. Children's Bks.
The Golden Key. 2013. (Illus.). (J). *(978-1-4351-4948-9(3))* Disney Pr.
Goldhawk, Emma. Cuddly Koala. Lambert, Jonathan, illus. 2015. (Snuggle Puppet Ser.). (ENG.). 10p. bds. 14.95 *(978-1-62686-328-6(8),* Silver Dolphin Bks.) Readerlink Distribution Services, LLC.
Golding, Elizabeth. Moonlight Animals. Lodge, Ali, illus. 2011. (ENG.). 12p. (J). (gr. -1-3). 12.95 *(978-0-7624-4316-1(2))* Running Pr. Bk. Pubs.
—Moonlight Ocean. Lodge, Ali, illus. 2012. (ENG.). 12p. (J). (gr. -1-3). 12.95 *(978-0-7624-4486-1(X))* Running Pr. Bk. Pubs.
Goldsack, Gaby. Fairies Die Cut. (Die-Cut Kids Ser.). 10p. bds. *(978-1-4054-6966-1(8))* Parragon, Inc.
—Fire Engine. Lawson, Peter, illus. 2009. (Turn the Wheel Ser.). (ENG.). 10p. (J). (gr. -1-k). bds. 5.95 *(978-0-7892-1022-7(3),* Abbeville Kids) Abbeville Pr., Inc.
—Fishing Boat. Lawson, Peter, illus. 2009. (Turn the Wheel Ser.). (ENG.). 10p. (J). (gr. -1-k). bds. 5.95 *(978-0-7892-1025-8(8),* Abbeville Kids) Abbeville Pr., Inc.
Goldsmith, Mike. Dinosaurs. Abbott, Simon, illus. 2011. (Flip Flap Science Ser.). (ENG.). 10p. (J). (gr. -1-k). 9.95 *(978-1-84898-365-6(4),* TickTock Books) Octopus Publishing Group GBR. Dist: Independent Pubs. Group.
—Flip the Flaps: Planet Earth. Palin, Nicki, illus. 2012. (Flip the Flaps Ser.). (ENG.). 32p. (J). (gr. -1-1). pap. 6.99 *(978-0-7534-6860-9(3),* 9780753468609, Kingfisher) Roaring Brook Pr.
—Space Adventure. Abbott, Simon, illus. 2011. (Flip Flap Science Ser.). (ENG.). 10p. (J). (gr. -1-k). 9.95 *(978-1-84898-364-9(6),* TickTock Books) Octopus Publishing Group GBR. Dist: Independent Pubs. Group.
Gomi, Taro. Hide & Seek. 2013. (ENG., Illus.). 22p. (J). (gr. -1 — 1). bds. 6.99 *(978-1-4521-0840-7(4))* Chronicle Bks. LLC.
—Peekaboo! 2013. (ENG., Illus.). 16p. (J). (gr. -1 — 1). bds. 6.99 *(978-1-4521-0835-3(8))* Chronicle Bks. LLC.
—Presents Through the Window. 2016. (ENG., Illus.). 36p. (J). (gr. -1-k). 15.99 *(978-1-4521-5138-0(5))* Chronicle Bks. LLC.
—Wiggle! 2013. (ENG., Illus.). 16p. (J). (gr. -1 — 1). bds. 6.99 *(978-1-4521-0836-0(6))* Chronicle Bks. LLC.
Gompper, Gail. Every Day by the Bay. Gompper, Gail, illus. 2011. (ENG., Illus.). 24p. (J). bds. 9.95 *(978-0-9726487-7-6(1))* Puddle Jump Pr., Ltd.
Gondek, Heather. Who's in the Jungle? Lift-the-Flap 'n' Learn. Gilvan-Cartwright, Chris, illus. 2005. (Fun with Animals Ser.). 10p. (J). 9.95 *(978-1-58117-075-7(0),* Intervisual/Piggy Toes) Bendon, Inc.
Gondek, Heather J. Who's on the Farm? Lift-the-Flap 'n' Learn Book. Gilvan-Cartwright, Chris, illus. 2005. (Fun with Animals Ser.). 10p. (J). (gr. -1-k). act. bk. ed. 9.95 *(978-1-58117-143-3(9),* Intervisual/Piggy Toes) Bendon, Inc.
Gonyea, Mark. Monkey Suit. 2015. (ENG., Illus.). 28p. (J). (-k). bds. 10.95 *(978-1-57687-772-2(8),* powerHouse Bks.) powerHouse Cultural Entertainment, Inc.
—The Spooky Box. Gonyea, Mark, illus. 2013. (ENG., Illus.). 32p. (J). (gr. -1-3). 15.99 *(978-0-8050-8813-7(X),* 9780805088137, Holt, Henry & Co. Bks. For Young Readers) Holt, Henry & Co.
Goodhart, Pippa. Little Monster & the Spooky Party. Sharratt, Nick, illus. 2016. (ENG.). 16p. (J). (gr. -1-k). 12.99 ***(978-1-4052-7742-6(4))*** Egmont Bks., Ltd. GBR. Dist: Independent Pubs. Group.
Goodings, Christina. Guess Who? Noah's Ark: A Flip-The-Flap Book. Muss, Angela, illus. 2014. (ENG.). 6p. (J). (— 1). bds. 9.99 *(978-0-7459-6496-6(6))* Lion Hudson PLC GBR. Dist: Independent Pubs. Group.
—My Big Bright Bible Board Book. Barker, Stephen, illus. 2014. (ENG.). 10p. (J). (— 1). bds. 9.99 *(978-0-7459-6525-3(3))* Lion Hudson PLC GBR. Dist: Independent Pubs. Group.
—My Carry-Along Nativity: Activity Book with Stickers. Hughes, Cathy, illus. 2016. (ENG.). 32p. (J). (gr. -1-2). pap. 9.99 *(978-0-7459-6511-6(3))* Lion Hudson PLC GBR. Dist: Independent Pubs. Group.
Goodings, Christina & Hudson, Annabel. Bible Stories. 2009. (ENG., Illus.). 24p. (J). (gr. -1-k). 12.95 *(978-0-7459-6091-3(X))* Lion Hudson PLC GBR. Dist: Independent Pubs. Group.
Goodman, Sarah & Sorkin, Louis N. Bugs - Fandex Family Field Guides. 2009. (ENG., Illus.). 50p. (J). (gr. 4-12). 12.95 *(978-0-7611-5414-3(0),* 15414) Workman Publishing Co., Inc.
Gooly & Campbell Books Staff. Happy Families. Hyun, Kim, illus. 2015. (Chat About Ser.). (ENG.). 22p. (J). (— 1). bds. 9.99 ***(978-1-4472-7729-3(5))*** Pan Macmillan GBR. Dist: Independent Pubs. Group.
Gooly, Gooly, et al. Best Friends. Hyun, Kim, illus. 2015. (Chat About Ser.). (ENG.). 22p. (J). (— 1). bds. 9.99 ***(978-1-4472-7730-9(9))*** Pan Macmillan GBR. Dist: Independent Pubs. Group.
Gorbachev, Valeri. Two Little Chicks Go to School. 2011. (ENG., Illus.). 28p. (J). (gr. -1-3). 6.95 *(978-0-7358-4027-0(X))* North-South Bks., Inc.
Gordon, Bob. Carry-Me ABC. 2009. (Carry-Me Ser.). (ENG., Illus.). 12p. (gr. -1-k). 7.99 *(978-1-84610-873-0(X))* Make Believe Ideas GBR. Dist: Nelson, Thomas Inc.
—Lift & Learn Colors. Snaith, Andy, photos by. 2006. (Illus.). 24p. (gr. -1 — 1). per., bds. *(978-1-84610-028-4(3))* Make Believe Ideas.
Gordon, Gordon Coyle. Do Princesses Wear Hiking Boots? 2016. (ENG., Illus.). 32p. (J). (gr. -1-1). bds. 7.95 *(978-1-63076-164-6(8))* Taylor Trade Publishing.
Gore, Leonid. Mommy, Where Are You? Gore, Leonid, illus. 2009. (ENG., Illus.). 32p. (J). (gr. -1-2). 16.99 *(978-1-4169-5505-4(4),* Atheneum Bks. for Young Readers) Simon & Schuster Children's Publishing.
Gormley, Greg. Daddy's Day at Work. 2007. (Fantastic Phones Ser.). (ENG., Illus.). 12p. (J). (gr. k-k). bds. 9.99 *(978-0-7475-8378-3(1))* Bloomsbury Publishing Plc GBR. Dist: Independent Pubs. Group.
Goscinny, René. Asterix on the Warpath: Pop-Up. 2015. (ENG., Illus.). 14p. (J). (gr. 4-6). 35.00 *(978-1-5101-0042-8(3),* Asterix) Hachette Children's Group GBR. Dist: Hachette Bk. Group.
Govan, Nina & Olive and Moss Staff. Margot & Mo. 2014. (Olive & Moss Ser.). (ENG., Illus.). 10p. (J). (— 1). bds. 8.99 *(978-1-4052-6002-2(5))* Egmont Bks., Ltd. GBR. Dist: Independent Pubs. Group.
—Michael the Monkey. 2014. (Olive & Moss Ser.). (ENG., Illus.). 10p. (J). (— 1). bds. 8.99 *(978-1-4052-6001-5(7))* Egmont Bks., Ltd. GBR. Dist: Independent Pubs. Group.
Gowan, Barbara. Little Arizona. 2012. (My Little State Ser.). (ENG., Illus.). 20p. (J). (gr. k-3). 9.95 *(978-1-58536-208-0(5))* Sleeping Bear Pr.
Graire, Virginie, illus. Shapes. 2016. (ENG.). 12p. (J). (gr. -1 — 1). bds. 6.99 *(978-1-4998-0294-8(3))* Little Bee Books Inc.
—Snowman. 2016. (ENG.). 12p. (J). (gr. -1 — 1). bds. 6.99 *(978-1-4998-0344-0(3))* Little Bee Books Inc.
—123. 2016. (ENG.). 12p. (J). (gr. -1 — 1). bds. 6.99 *(978-1-4998-0295-5(1))* Little Bee Books Inc.
Grant, Callie. Mud Puddle Hunting Day. Magee, Melanie, illus. 2013. (ENG.). 20p. (J). bds. 8.99 *(978-0-9854090-0-5(2))* Blanchard, Graham.

TUV

Graux, Amélie. I Love to Eat. Graux, Amélie, illus. deluxe ed. 2012. (ENG, SPA & FRE., Illus.). 12p. (J). (gr. k — 1). bds. 9.99 (978-0-547-84842-6(0)) Houghton Mifflin Harcourt Publishing Co.

Graux, Amélie, et al. I Love to Sleep. Graux, Amélie, illus. deluxe ed. 2012. (ENG, SPA & FRE., Illus.). 12p. (J). (gr. k — 1). bds. 9.99 (978-0-547-84843-3(9)) Houghton Mifflin Harcourt Publishing Co.

Graves, Keith. The Monsterator. 2014. (ENG., Illus.). 40p. (J). (gr. 2-5). 17.99 (978-1-59643-855-2(X), 9781596438552) Roaring Brook Pr.

Gravett, Emily. Little Mouse's Big Book of Fears. Gravett, Emily, illus. 2nd rev. ed. 2007. (ENG., Illus.). 32p. (J). (gr. k-4). (978-1-4050-8948-7(2), Macmillan Children's Bks.) Pan Macmillan.

—Little Mouse's Big Book of Fears. Gravett, Emily, illus. 2008. (ENG., Illus.). 32p. (J). (gr. -1-3). 19.99 (978-1-4169-5930-4(0), Simon & Schuster Bks. For Young Readers) Simon & Schuster Bks. For Young Readers.

—Meerkat Mail. Gravett, Emily, illus. 2007. (ENG., Illus.). 32p. (J). (gr. -1-3). 17.99 (978-1-4169-3473-8(1), Simon & Schuster Bks. For Young Readers) Simon & Schuster Bks. For Young Readers.

—The Rabbit Problem. Gravett, Emily, illus. 2010. (ENG., Illus.). 32p. (J). (gr. -1-3). 17.99 (978-1-4424-1255-2(0), Simon & Schuster Bks. For Young Readers) Simon & Schuster Bks. For Young Readers.

Gray, Amy & Holland, Lucy E. Myths, Angels, & Masquerades: Exploring European Art. 2017. (ENG., Illus.). 104p. 18.95 (978-0-692-39101-3(0)) Marquand Bks., Inc.

Gray, Kes. Nuddy Ned's Christmas. Parsons, Garry, illus. 2016. (ENG.). 32p. (J). 20.99 (978-1-4088-6598-9(X), 9781408865989, Bloomsbury USA Childrens) Bloomsbury Publishing USA.

Green, Jen. Barron's Amazing Fact-Packed, Fold-Out Atlas of the World: With Awesome Pop-Up Map! Engel, Christiane, illus. 2014. (ENG.). 56p. (J). (gr. 3-6). 18.99 (978-0-7641-6746-1(4)) Barron's Educational Series, Inc.

Green, John. Horses Tattoos. 2003. (Dover Tattoos Ser.). (ENG., Illus.). 2p. (J). (gr. 1-4). pap. 1.99 (978-0-486-43029-4(4)) Dover Pubns., Inc.

Green, John, illus. Who Lives on the Farm? 2004. (Who Lives... Ser.). 12p. (J). bds. 4.99 (978-1-85854-647-6(8)) Brimax Books Ltd. GBR. Dist: Byeway Bks.

Greene, Melanie W., et al. Goodnight, Boone. Marlowe, Susan B., illus. 2012. (J). (978-1-933251-80-6(8)) Parkway Pubs., Inc.

Greene, Rhonda Gowler. Push! Dig! Scoop! A Construction Counting Rhyme. Kirk, Daniel, illus. 2017. (ENG.). 26p. (J). bds. 7.99 (978-1-68119-085-3(0), 9781681190853, Bloomsbury USA Childrens) Bloomsbury Publishing USA.

Greene, Sefton. Space Painters. 2003. 18p. bds. (978-1-904502-30-2(X)) MediaWorld/BestBooks.

Greenway, Bethany. Waikiki Lullaby. America, illus. 2009. (ENG.). 20p. (J). (gr. -1-1). bds. 7.95 (978-1-933067-30-8(6)) Beachhouse Publishing, LLC.

Greenwell, Jessica. First Colors Sticker Book. 2015. (Get Ready for School Sticker Bks.). (ENG.). 24+8p. (J). pap. 7.99 (978-0-7945-3600-8(X), Usborne) EDC Publishing.

—First Sticker Book Easter. 2012. (First Sticker Bks). 16p. (J). pap. 8.99 (978-0-7945-3266-6(7), Usborne) EDC Publishing.

—Noisy Body Book. 2012. (Noisy Bks). 10p. (J). ring bd. 18.99 (978-0-7945-3133-1(4), Usborne) EDC Publishing.

—This Is My Car. 2009. (Touchy-Feely Board Bks). 10p. (J). bds. 16.99 (978-0-7945-2545-3(8), Usborne) EDC Publishing.

—This Is My Digger. 2009. (Noisy Touchy-Feely Board Bks). 10p. (J). bds. 16.99 (978-0-7945-2520-0(2), Usborne) EDC Publishing.

Greenwell, Jessical. Farm Animals Lift & Look. 2010. (Lift & Look Board Bks). 12p. (J). bds. 9.99 (978-0-7945-2612-2(8), Usborne) EDC Publishing.

Gregory, Lorraine NAR NEEDED. One, Two, Tie Your Shoes! Carlson, Nancy Gayle, illus. 2010. (J). (978-0-545-26482-2(0)) Scholastic, Inc.

Grieser, Jeanne K. Touch & Feel Petting Zoo. Pedler, Caroline, illus. 2010. (ENG.). 20p. (J). (gr. k — 1). bds. 9.95 (978-1-4027-6524-7(X)) Sterling Publishing Co., Inc.

Griffin, Keith. Carry-Me 123. 2009. (Carry-Me Ser.). (ENG., Illus.). 12p. (J). (gr. -1-k). 7.99 (978-1-84610-872-3(1)) Make Believe Ideas GBR. Dist: Nelson, Thomas Inc.

Grimaldi, Catherine. It's Raining! A Pop-Up Book with Patterns. Grimaldi, Catherine, illus. 2005. (ENG., Illus.). 18p. (J). (gr. -1-k). act. bk. ed. 16.99 (978-1-85707-666-0(4)) Tango Bks. GBR. Dist: Independent Pubs. Group.

Grimm, Jacob & Grimm, Wilhelm. Little Red Riding Hood. Sourdais, Clémentine, illus. 2014. (ENG.). 28p. (J). (gr. -1-3). 16.95 (978-3-89955-723-7(9)) Die Gestalten Verlag DEU. Dist: Penguin Random Hse. LLC.

Grindley, Sally. Help! 2016. (ENG., Illus.). 32p. (J). (gr. -1-k). pap. 9.99 (978-1-4449-2474-9(5)) Hachette Children's Group GBR. Dist: Hachette Bk. Group.

—Help! Utton, Peter, illus. 2015. (Kipper Ser.). (ENG.). 32p. (J). (gr. -1-k). 14.99 (978-1-4449-2473-2(7)) Hodder & Stoughton GBR. Dist: Hachette Bk. Group.

—Shhh! 2008. (ENG.). 32p. (J). (gr. -1-3). 16.95 (978-1-933718-19-4(6)) Tanglewood Pr.

Grogan, John. Marley Looks for Love. Cowdrey, Richard, illus. 2010. (Marley Ser.). (ENG.). 16p. (J). (gr. -1-1). pap. 6.99 (978-0-06-185590-0(1), HarperFestival) HarperCollins Pubs.

Gross, Sandra & Busch, Leah. Toast to Counting: Toast to Baby. Hutton, John, ed. 2012. (Toast to Baby Ser.). (ENG., Illus.). 14p. (J). (— 1). bds. 7.99 (978-1-936669-09-7(9)) Blue Manatee Press.

Grossblatt, Ben. Keep Out! Door Alarm: Build Your Own Key-Card Security System! 2004. (Illus.). 24p. (J). (978-0-439-66835-4(2)) Scholastic, Inc.

Grossman, Rena. Carry Me (Spanish/English), 1 vol. Fiol, Maria A., tr. 2010. (Babies Everywhere Ser.). (ENG & SPA., Illus.). 16p. (J). (gr. -1). bds. 6.95 (978-1-59572-199-0(1)) Star Bright Bks., Inc.

Grover, Lorie Ann. Big Hug for Little Cub. Kightley, Rosalinda, illus. 2014. (ENG.). 18p. (J). (— 1). bds. 7.99 (978-0-545-53091-0(1), Cartwheel Bks.) Scholastic, Inc.

Gruelle, Johnny. Raggedy Ann & Andy & the Camel with the Wrinkled Knees. Moerbeek, Kees, illus. collector's ed. 2003. (Raggedy Ann Ser.). (ENG.). 14p. (J). (gr. -1-2). 29.99 (978-0-689-85775-1(6), Little Simon) Little Simon.

Guess Who? Christmas: A Flip-The-Flap Book. 2015. (ENG., Illus.). 6p. (J). (— 1). bds. 9.99 (978-0-7459-6408-9(7)) Lion Hudson PLC GBR. Dist: Independent Pubs. Group.

Guess Who, Elmo! Adivina Quién! 2014. (Guess Who Ser.). (ENG., Illus.). 10p. (J). (gr. -1-k). 10.99 (978-0-7944-3212-6(3)) Reader's Digest Assn., Inc., The.

Guest, Elissa Haden. Who's My Cupcake? Fedotova, Marina, illus. 2011. (ENG.). 16p. (J). (gr. -1 — 1). bds. 6.99 (978-1-4424-2051-9(0), Little Simon) Little Simon.

Guettier, Bénédicte. At the Circus. 2011. (Funny Faces Ser.). (Illus.). 14p. bds. (978-1-84089-678-7(7)) Zero to Ten, Ltd.

—Dinosaur Dinners. 2011. (Funny Faces Ser.). (Illus.). 14p. bds. (978-1-84089-677-0(9)) Zero to Ten, Ltd.

—In the Jungle. 2010. (Funny Faces Ser.). (Illus.). 14p. bds. (978-1-84089-645-9(0)) Zero to Ten, Ltd.

—On the Farm. 2010. (Funny Faces Ser.). (Illus.). 14p. bds. (978-1-84089-646-6(9)) Zero to Ten, Ltd.

Guicciardini, Desideria & McNicholas, Shelagh, illus. Hop, Skip & Jump. 2008. (Usborne Baby Board Bks.). 8p. (J). (gr. -1). bds. 15.99 incl. audio compact disk (978-0-7945-1914-8(8), Usborne) EDC Publishing.

Guillain, Adam & Guillain, Charlotte. School Gremlins. Chatterton, Chris, illus. 2017. (ENG.). 18p. (J). (gr. -1-k). pap. 10.99 (978-1-4052-7714-3(9)) Egmont Bks., Ltd. GBR. Dist: Independent Pubs. Group.

Guillain, Adam & Guillain, Charlotte. Supermarket Gremlins. Chatterton, Chris, illus. 2016. (ENG.). 18p. (J). (gr. -1-k). pap. 11.99 (978-1-4052-7713-6(0)) Egmont Bks., Ltd. GBR. Dist: Independent Pubs. Group.

Gulbis, Stephen, illus. Old MacDonald Had a Barn. 2003. 22p. (YA). (978-1-85602-453-2(9), Pavilion Children's Books) Pavilion Bks.

Gulliver, Amanda, illus. Colors. 2011. (Baby Rattle Bks.). 12p. (J). (gr. -1-k). 5.99 (978-0-7641-6391-3(4)) Barron's Educational Series, Inc.

Gunzi, Christiane. My Favourite Things. 2013. (ENG., Illus.). 6p. (J). bds. 7.95 (978-1-907604-37-9(5)) Award Pubns. Ltd. GBR. Dist: Parkwest Pubns., Inc.

—My Lovely Day. 2013. (ENG., Illus.). 6p. (J). bds. 7.95 (978-1-907604-36-2(7)) Award Pubns. Ltd. GBR. Dist: Parkwest Pubns., Inc.

Gunzi, Christiane. Colours. 2015. (ENG., Illus.). 6p. (J). 7.99 (978-1-907604-95-9(2)) Award Pubns. Ltd. GBR. Dist: Parkwest Pubns., Inc.

—Furry Kittens. 2005. (Feels Real Bks.). (ENG., Illus.). 10p. (J). bds. 6.99 (978-0-7641-5854-4(6)) Barron's Educational Series, Inc.

—Little Ponies: A Feels Real Book to Touch & Share. 2015. (ENG., Illus.). 8p. (J). 9.99 (978-1-909763-10-4(1)) Award Pubns. Ltd. GBR. Dist: Parkwest Pubns., Inc.

—Numbers. 2015. (ENG., Illus.). 6p. (J). 7.99 (978-1-907604-94-2(4)) Award Pubns. Ltd. GBR. Dist: Parkwest Pubns., Inc.

—On the Farm. 2015. (ENG., Illus.). 8p. (J). 9.99 (978-1-909763-09-8(8)) Award Pubns. Ltd. GBR. Dist: Parkwest Pubns., Inc.

Guttiere, Benedicte. When Christmas Comes. 2011. (Funny Faces Ser.). (Illus.). 14p. bds. (978-1-84089-710-4(4)) Zero to Ten, Ltd.

Guy, Ginger Foglesong & Guy, Ginger F. Siesta Board Book. Moreno, Rene King, illus. 2009. (SPA & ENG.). 34p. (J). (gr. -1 — 1). bds. 7.99 (978-0-06-168884-3(3), Greenwillow Bks.) HarperCollins Pubs.

Gynux, illus. Jesus Loves Me, 1 vol. 2017. (Sing-Along Book Ser.). (ENG.). 20p. (J). bds. 8.99 (978-0-310-75894-5(7)) Zonderkidz.

H & T Imaginations Unlimited, Inc. Kid's Sand Box Fun with Professor Woodpecker: Good Old Fashion Wholesome Fun Children's Story. 2008. 12p. pap. 8.49 (978-1-4389-1116-8(5)) AuthorHouse.

Hachler, Bruno. I Am Who I Am. Wolferman, Iris, illus. 2010. (ENG.). 16p. (J). (gr. -1 — 1). bds. 8.95 (978-0-7358-2299-3(9)) North-South Bks., Inc.

Hacohen, Dean. Tuck Me In! Scharschmidt, Sherry, illus. 2010. (ENG.). 40p. (J). (gr. -1 — 1). 9.99 (978-0-7636-4728-5(4)) Candlewick Pr.

Hacohen, Dean & Scharschmidt, Sherry. Tuck Me In! 2010. (Illus.). (J). (978-0-7636-5363-7(2)) Candlewick Pr.

Haft, Sheryl. I Love You, Blankie. Massey, Jane, illus. 2015. (ENG.). 22p. (J). (gr. -1 — 1). bds. 8.99 (978-0-316-28356-4(8)) Little, Brown Bks. for Young Readers.

Hahn, Blair. My Purple Kisses. Nation, Tate, illus. 2011. (My Purple Toes Ser.). 26p. (J). bds. 10.99 (978-0-9844556-7-6(1)) My Purple Toes, LLC.

Haines, Genny, illus. Five Cute Kittens. 2016. (ENG.). 10p. (J). (gr. -1 — 1). bds. 8.99 (978-1-4998-0218-4(8)) Little Bee Books Inc.

—Five Little Ducks. 2016. (ENG.). 10p. (J). (gr. -1 — 1). bds. 8.99 (978-1-4998-0217-7(X)) Little Bee Books Inc.

Hale, Kate. Little Massachusetts. Brett, Jeannie, illus. 2016. (Little State Ser.). (ENG.). 20p. (J). (gr. -1-k). 9.95 (978-1-58536-949-2(7), 204035) Sleeping Bear Pr.

Hale, Ohara. Who Did It? Who Farted? Who Burped? Who Pooped? Who Peed? Who Sneezed?, 5 vols. 2014. (ENG., Illus.). 50p. (J). (-k). 14.95 (978-1-57687-681-7(0), powerHouse Bks.) powerHouse Cultural Entertainment, Inc.

Hale, Rachael. Baby Colors. 2009. (ENG., Illus.). 20p. (J). (gr. -1 — 1). bds. 6.99 (978-0-316-04452-3(0)) Little Brown & Co.

—Somebunny Loves You. 2009. (Paw Pals Ser.). (ENG., Illus.). 20p. (J). (gr. -1 — 1). bds. 6.99 (978-0-316-11370-0(0)) Little, Brown Bks. for Young Readers.

Hall, Hannah C. God Bless My Boo Boo, 1 vol. Whitlow, Steve, illus. 2015. (God Bless Book Ser.). (ENG.). 20p. (J). bds. 9.99 (978-0-7180-3051-3(6)) Nelson, Thomas Inc.

—God Bless Our Fall, 1 vol. Whitlow, Steve, illus. 2015. (God Bless Book Ser.). (ENG.). 20p. (J). bds. 9.99 (978-0-529-12333-6(9)) Nelson, Thomas Inc.

Hall, Michael. It's an Orange Aardvark! Hall, Michael, illus. 2014. (ENG., Illus.). 40p. (J). (gr. -1-3). 17.99 (978-0-06-225206-7(2), Greenwillow Bks.) HarperCollins Pubs.

Hall, Pamela. ELEMENOPEE, the Day I, M, N, O & P Left the Abc's. Williamson, James, illus. 2005. 16p. (J). 12.95 (978-1-58117-209-6(5), Intervisual/Piggy Toes) Bendon, Inc.

Hallensleben, Georg & Gutman, Anne. Mommy & Daddy Boxed Set, 4 vols. 2009. (ENG., Illus.). 56p. (J). (gr. -1 — 1). bds. 19.99 (978-0-8118-7055-9(3)) Chronicle Bks. LLC.

Hallinan, P. K. Let's Share. Hallinan, P. K., illus. 2009. (ENG., Illus.). 24p. (J). (gr. -1-2). 8.99 (978-0-8249-5610-3(9), Ideal Pubns.) Worthy Publishing.

—Sisters Forever. Hallinan, P. K., illus. 2014. (Illus.). 22p. (J). bds. 7.99 (978-0-8249-1921-4(1), Ideal Pubns.) Worthy Publishing.

Hamilton, Kersten. Blue Boat. Petrone, Valeria, illus. 2016. (ENG.). 26p. (J). (-k). bds. 7.99 (978-1-101-99853-3(9), Viking Books for Young Readers) Penguin Young Readers Group.

Hamilton, Libby. The Fairy Tale Handbook. Tomic, Tomislav, illus. 2014. (ENG.). 20p. (J). (gr. k-4). 22.99 (978-0-7636-7130-3(4), Templar) Candlewick Pr.

Hamilton, Libby & Haworth, Katie. Around the World. Shuttlewood, Craig, illus. 2015. (ENG.). 10p. (J). (gr. -1 — 1). bds. 6.99 (978-1-4998-0075-3(4)) Little Bee Books Inc.

—Through the Town. Shuttlewood, Craig, illus. 2015. (ENG.). 10p. (J). (gr. -1 — 1). bds. 6.99 (978-1-4998-0076-0(2)) Little Bee Books Inc.

Hamilton, Tisha. Mickey Mouse Clubhouse. Disney Storybook Artists Staff, illus. 2008. (Carry along Treasury Ser.). (ENG.). 14p. (J). (gr. -1-1). bds. 14.99 (978-0-7944-1481-8(8)) Reader's Digest Assn., Inc., The.

Hanby, Benjamin Russell. Up on the Housetop. Snyder, Robert, illus. 2007. (ENG.). 26p. (J). (gr. -1-3). bds. 12.99 (978-0-8249-6714-7(3), Ideal Pubns.) Worthy Publishing.

Hanna, Virginie. The Secret Life of Princesses. Delanssay, Cathy, illus. 2009. 26p. (J). (gr. -1-3). 17.99 (978-0-8437-1476-0(X)) Hammond World Atlas Corp.

Hannigan, Paula. Hugs for You. Brown, Heather, illus. 2012. (J). (-k). (ENG.). 10p. bds. 7.99 (978-1-4494-2192-2(X)); (978-1-4351-5022-5(8)) Andrews McMeel Publishing.

—Under Construction. Brown, Heather, illus. 2013. (ENG.). 18p. (J). bds. 5.99 (978-1-4494-3556-1(4)) Andrews McMeel Publishing.

Hannigan, Paula & Accord Publishing Staff. Music Star. Slade, Christian, illus. 2011. (ENG.). 16p. (J). (gr. -1-3). 14.99 (978-1-4494-0173-3(2)) Andrews McMeel Publishing.

Hansel, Karen & Ham, Ken. Charlie & Trike Grand Canyon Adventure. 2010. (Illus.). 24p. (J). spiral bd. 15.99 (978-0-89051-569-3(7)) Master Bks.

Hanson, Faye. Cinderella's Secret Diary. Hanson, Faye, illus. 2013. (ENG., Illus.). 24p. (J). (gr. 1-3). 19.99 (978-0-230-74204-8(1)) Pan Macmillan GBR. Dist: Independent Pubs. Group.

Hanson, P. H. My Granny's Purse. 2013. (ENG., Illus.). 16p. (J). (gr. -1-1). bds. 14.95 (978-0-7611-7742-5(6), 17742) Workman Publishing Co., Inc.

—My Mommy's Tote. 2013. (ENG.). 16p. (J). (gr. -1-1). 14.95 (978-0-7611-7740-1(X), 17740) Workman Publishing Co., Inc.

Hanton, Sophie. Colors by the Sea. 2009. (Mag-NUT-Tics! Ser.). (Illus.). (J). bds. 9.99 (978-1-934650-73-8(0)) Just For Kids Pr., LLC.

Hapka, Catherine, pseud. Disney Sofia the First - Sweet Dreams, Sofia! Cardona, Jose, illus. 2015. (ENG.). 12p. (J). (gr. -1-k). 12.99 (978-0-7944-3383-3(9)) Studio Fun International.

Hapka, Cathy, pseud. Dancing. 2006. (Illus.). (J). (978-1-57151-775-3(8)) Playhouse Publishing.

—Pretend & Play Kitty: With Real Crown You Can Wear! Borlasca, Hector, illus. 2004. (Role Play Ser.). 10p. (J). (gr. -1-18). bds. 6.99 (978-1-57151-742-5(1)) Playhouse Publishing.

Happpy Books. A Day at the Farm. 2012. (Day at ... Bks.). (ENG., Illus.). 8p. (J). bds. 6.99 (978-0-7641-6532-0(1)) Barron's Educational Series, Inc.

Happy Books. A Day at the Circus. 2012. (Day at ... Bks.). (ENG., Illus.). 8p. (J). bds. 7.99 (978-0-7641-6531-3(3)) Barron's Educational Series, Inc.

—Little Frog. 2013. (Mini-Creatures Ser.). (ENG., Illus.). 10p. (J). (gr. -1 — 1). bds. 4.99 (978-0-7641-6597-9(6)) Barron's Educational Series, Inc.

—Little Ladybug. 2013. (Mini-Creatures Ser.). (ENG., Illus.). 8p. (J). (gr. -1 — 1). bds. 4.99 (978-0-7641-6595-5(X)) Barron's Educational Series, Inc.

Harbo, Christopher L. Humpty Dumpty Flip-Side Rhymes. Chatzikonstantinou, Danny, illus. 2015. (Flip-Side Nursery Rhymes Ser.). (ENG.). 24p. (gr. -1-2). lib. bdg. 27.32 (978-1-4795-5986-2(5)) Picture Window Bks.

—Jack & Jill Flip-Side Rhymes. Jack, Colin, illus. 2015. (Flip-Side Nursery Rhymes Ser.). (ENG.). 24p. (gr. -1-2). lib. bdg. 27.32 (978-1-4795-5988-6(1)) Picture Window Bks.

—Little Bo Peep Flip-Side Rhymes. Chatzikonstantinou, Danny, illus. 2015. (Flip-Side Nursery Rhymes Ser.). (ENG.). 24p. (gr. -1-2). lib. bdg. 27.32 (978-1-4795-5989-3(X)) Picture Window Bks.

—Little Miss Muffet Flip-Side Rhymes. Jack, Colin, illus. 2015. (Flip-Side Nursery Rhymes Ser.). (ENG.). 24p. (gr. -1-2). lib. bdg. 27.32 (978-1-4795-5987-9(3)) Picture Window Bks.

Hargreaves, Roger. Little Miss Giggles. 2011. (Mr. Men & Little Miss Ser.). (ENG.). 32p. (J). (gr. -1-2). mass mkt. 4.99 (978-0-8431-9890-4(7), Price Stern Sloan) Penguin Young Readers Group.

Harper, Charise Mericle. Go! Go! Go! Stop! 2015. (ENG.). 32p. (J). (-k). bds. 7.99 (978-0-553-53391-0(6), Knopf Bks. for Young Readers) Random Hse. Children's Bks.

Harper, Charley. ABC's. 2008. (ENG., Illus.). 62p. (J). (gr. -1-3). bds. 14.95 (978-1-934429-07-5(4)) AMMO Bks., LLC.

—123's. Harper, Charley, illus. 2008. (ENG., Illus.). 20p. (J). (gr. -1-3). bds. 9.95 (978-1-934429-22-8(8)) AMMO Bks., LLC.

Harrast, Tracy. My Giant Fold-Out Book: Christmas. Doherty, Paula, illus. 2008. 10p. (J). (gr. -1). bds. 13.49 (978-0-7586-1425-4(X)) Concordia Publishing Hse.

Harris, John. Pop-Up Aesop. Brown, Calef, illus. 2005. (ENG.). 10p. (J). (gr. -1-7). 19.95 (978-0-89236-814-3(4)) Oxford Univ. Pr., Inc.

Harris, Marian & Harris, Jim. Ten Little Kittens. 2011. (ENG., Illus.). 26p. (J). (gr. -1-k). bds. 9.99 (978-1-4494-0175-7(9)) Andrews McMeel Publishing.

Harrison, Kenny. Hide & Seek Harry on the Farm. Harrison, Kenny, illus. 2015. (ENG., Illus.). 20p. (J). (-k). bds. 6.99 (978-0-7636-7370-3(6)) Candlewick Pr.

Harrod-Eagles, Cynthia. I Love You to the Moon. Poh, Jennie, illus. 2014. (ENG.). 22p. (J). (gr. -1). bds. 8.95 (978-1-58925-642-2(5)) Tiger Tales.

—It's Spring Time! Baccala, Gladys, illus. 2013. (ENG.). 16p. (gr. -1). bds. 8.95 (978-1-58925-639-2(5)) Tiger Tales.

Hart, Caryl. There's a Monster in My Fridge: With Fun Split Pages. Allwright, Deborah, illus. 2016. (ENG.). 24p. (J). (gr. -1-2). pap. 7.99 (978-1-4380-0824-0(4)) Barron's Educational Series, Inc.

Harter, Debbie. Cha-Cha-Cha en la Selva. Canetti, Yanitzia, tr. Harter, Debbie, illus. 2003.Tr. of Animal Boogie. (SPA., Illus.). 32p. (J). pap. 6.99 (978-1-84148-265-1(X)) Barefoot Bks., Inc.

Hasbro. My Little Pony: Make Your Own Pop-Up Book. 2016. (ENG.). 36p. (J). (gr. 1-3). 14.99 (978-0-7944-3666-7(8), Reader's Digest Children's Bks.) Studio Fun International.

Hashimoto, Meika & Tillworth, Mary. I Am Buzz Lightyear (Disney/Pixar Toy Story) Random House Disney Staff, illus. 2011. (Shaped Board Book Ser.). (ENG.). 12p. (J). (— 1). bds. 4.99 (978-0-7364-2821-7(6), Golden/Disney) Random Hse. Children's Bks.

Haskamp, Steven, illus. Five Silly Monkeys. 2006. (ENG.). 12p. (J). (gr. -1-k). 12.95 (978-1-58117-460-1(8), Intervisual/Piggy Toes) Bendon, Inc.

Haughom, Lisa, illus. People, Places & Things. 2010. (J). (978-1-58865-541-7(5)) Kidsbooks, LLC.

—Things That Go! 2010. 16p. (J). (978-1-58865-542-4(3)) Kidsbooks, LLC.

Haughton, Chris. Goodnight Everyone. Haughton, Chris, illus. 2016. (ENG., Illus.). 32p. (J). (-k). 15.99 (978-0-7636-9079-3(1)) Candlewick Pr.

—Oh No, George! Haughton, Chris, illus. 2015. (ENG., Illus.). 32p. (J). (-k). bds. 7.99 (978-0-7636-7652-0(7)) Candlewick Pr.

Hawcock, David. Dinosaurs! Pop-Up Paper Designs. Hawcock, David, illus. 2015. (ENG., Illus.). 16p. (J). (gr. -1-k). 14.99 (978-1-85707-804-6(7)) Tango Bks. GBR. Dist: Independent Pubs. Group.

Hawcock, David & Kentley, Eric. The Pop-Up Book of Ships. 2011. (ENG.). 6p. (J). (gr. k-4). 14.98 (978-0-7893-2408-5(3), Rizzoli Universe Promotional Bks.) Rizzoli International Pubns., Inc.

Hawk, Benjamin. Meadow Mystery. 2008. (Illus.). (J). (978-1-4127-8875-5(7)) Publications International, Ltd.

Hawkins, Colin. Mr. Wolf's Week. 2005. (ENG., Illus.). 12p. (J). pap. 8.99 (978-1-4052-0708-9(6)) Egmont Bks., Ltd. GBR. Dist: Trafalgar Square Publishing.

—Pirate Ship: A Pop-up Adventure. Hawkins, Colin et al, illus. 2006. 28p. (J). (gr. 4-8). reprint ed. 20.00 (978-0-7567-9827-7(2)) DIANE Publishing Co.

—What's the Time,Mr. Wolf? Mini Pop-Up. 2005. (Illus.). 14p. (J). bds. 8.99 (978-1-4052-0707-2(8)) Egmont Bks., Ltd. GBR. Dist: Trafalgar Square Publishing.

Hawkins, Emily. Good Night, Little Bunny: A Changing-Picture Book. Butler, John, illus. 2011. (ENG.). 14p. (J). (gr. -1-2). 12.99 (978-0-7636-5263-0(6), Templar) Candlewick Pr.

Hawksley, Gerald, illus. Danny Dog's Car: Press Out Parts Make a Car Carrying Danny Dog! 2009. (Toddler Make & Play Ser.). 10p. (J). bds. 6.95 (978-1-59496-184-7(0)) Teora USA LLC.

—Patty Cow's Tractor: Press Out Parts Make a Tractor Carrying Patty Cow. 2009. (Toddler Make & Play Ser.). 10p. bds. 6.95 (978-1-59496-182-3(4)) Teora USA LLC.

—Quacky Duck's Plane: Press Out Parts Make an Airplane Carrying Quacky Duck! 2009. (Toddler Make & Play Ser.). 10p. bds. 6.95 (978-1-59496-185-4(9)) Teora USA LLC.

—Splashy Dolphin's Boat: Press Out Parts Make a Boat Carrying Splashy Dolphin. 2009. (Toddler Make & Play Ser.). 10p. bds. 6.95 (978-1-59496-183-0(2)) Teora USA LLC.

Hawthorn, Philip & Tyler, Jenny. Who's Making That Mess? Cartwright, Stephen, illus. 2008. (Luxury Flap Bks). (gr. -1-k). 9.99 (978-0-7945-1694-9(7)) EDC Publishing.

Hawthorn, Phillip & Tyler, Jenny. There's A Monster in My House. 2007. 16p. (J). 9.99 (978-0-7945-1567-6(3), Usborne) EDC Publishing.

Hawthorne, Philip & Tyler, Jenny. Who's Making That Noise? Cartwright, Stephen, illus. 2005. (Flap Books Ser.). 16p. (J). (gr. 1-18). pap. 7.95 (978-0-7945-0432-8(9), Usborne) EDC Publishing.

Hay DeSimone, Corkey. Mammal Animal Board Book 2nd Edition. Hay DeSimone, Corkey, illus. 2007. (Illus.). 24p. (J). 7.95 (978-0-9777394-2-4(2)) Gentle Giraffe Pr.

Head, Vivian. Times Tables. 2013. (ENG., Illus.). 14p. (J). (gr. 1-5). 9.99 (978-1-84322-936-0(6), Armadillo) Anness Publishing GBR. Dist: National Bk. Network.

Hearn, Sam. Busy Builders. Hearn, Sam, illus. 2016. (ENG., Illus.). 16p. (J). (— 1). bds. 10.99 (978-0-545-79957-7(0), Cartwheel Bks.) Scholastic, Inc.

Heath, Beverly C. A Bedtime Lullaby. Floyd, John, Jr., illus. 2006. 9p. (J). (gr. -1). bds. 5.95 (978-0-9752860-1-2(3)) OurRainbow Pr., LLC.

—Counting with Colors. Floyd, John, Jr., illus. 2005. 8p. (J). (gr. -1). bds. 5.95 (978-0-9752860-0-5(5)) OurRainbow Pr., LLC.

—My Parts Equal Me! Floyd, John, Jr., illus. 2005. 15p. (J). (gr. -1). bds. 5.95 (978-0-9752860-2-9(1)) OurRainbow Pr., LLC.

—Opposites. Floyd, John, Jr., illus. 2006. 8p. (J). (gr. -1). bds. 5.95 (978-0-9752860-3-6(X)) OurRainbow Pr., LLC.

Hegarty, Pat. If I Were a... Ballerina. Pope, Liz & Pope, Kate, illus. 2008. (If I Were A Ser.). 10p. (J). (gr. -1-k). bds. 6.95 (978-1-58925-834-1(7)) Tiger Tales.

—If I Were a... Soccer Star. Pope, Liz & Pope, Kate, illus. 2008. (If I Were A Ser.). 10p. (J). (gr. -1-k). bds. 6.95 (978-1-58925-835-8(5)) Tiger Tales.

Hegarty, Patricia. Five Black Cats. Woolf, Julia, illus. (ENG.). 22p. (J). (gr. -1-k). 2016. bds. 6.99 (978-1-58925-239-4(X)) 2013. bds. 8.95 (978-1-58925-611-8(5)) Tiger Tales.

—Five Little Ghosts. Woolf, Julia, illus. 2014. (ENG.). 22p. (J). (gr. -1-k). bds. 8.99 (978-1-58925-587-6(9)) Tiger Tales.

—Who's There? Beware! 2015. (Amazing Changing Pictures! Ser.). (ENG.). 14p. (J). (gr. -1-3). 12.99 (978-1-68010-000-6(9)) Tiger Tales.

Heinze, Monica Bacon. A Day with Shapes. Dow, S. B., illus. 2004. (J). (978-0-9761710-0-3(7)) Paisley Publishing.

Hellen, Nancy. My Magic House. 2003. (Illus.). 11p. (J). 9.99 (978-0-333-66000-3(5)) Macmillan Pubs., Ltd. GBR. Dist: Trafalgar Square Publishing.
Heller, Alyson. Raggedy Ann's Beach Bag. Thomas, Laura, illus. 2009. (Raggedy Ann & Me! Ser.). (ENG.). 10p. (J). (gr. -1-k). bds. 5.99 (978-1-4169-5546-7(1), Little Simon) Little Simon.
Heller, Sarah. Tinker Bell My Music MP3 Player: Storybook & Personal Music Player. 2008. (RD Innovative Book & Player Format Ser.). (ENG.). 36p. (YA). bds. 24.99 (978-0-7944-1673-7(X)) Reader's Digest Assn., Inc., The.
Heller, Sarah & Reader's Digest Staff. Disney Fairies Music Player. 2008. (RD Innovative Book & Player Format Ser.). (ENG.). 36p. (J). 24.99 (978-0-7944-1300-2(5)) Reader's Digest Assn., Inc., The.
Hellier, Catherine. Baby's World of Colors. Ferri, Francesca, illus. 2010. (Baby's Bks.). (ENG.). 6p. (J). (gr. -1-k). 12.99 (978-0-7641-4539-1(8)) Barron's Educational Series, Inc.
Helman, Andrea. O Is for Orca. Wolfe, Art, photos by. 2016. (ENG., Illus.). 20p. (J). (— 1). bds. 9.99 (978-1-63217-033-0(7), Little Bigfoot) Sasquatch Bks.
—1, 2, 3 Moose. Wolfe, Art, photos by. 2016. (ENG., Illus.). 20p. (J). (— 1). bds. 9.99 (978-1-63217-032-3(9), Little Bigfoot) Sasquatch Bks.
Helmore, Jim & Wall, Karen. Stripy Horse - Off We Go! 2014. (Stripy Horse Ser.). (ENG., Illus.). 12p. (J). (gr. -1). bds. 7.99 (978-1-4052-5746-6(6)) Egmont Bks., Ltd. GBR. Dist: Independent Pubs. Group.
Helmore Wall Staff & Helmore, Jim. Oh No, Monster Tomato! Wall, Karen, illus. 2009. (ENG.). 32p. (J). (gr. -1). 16.99 (978-1-4052-4740-5(1)) Egmont Bks., Ltd. GBR. Dist: Independent Pubs. Group.
Hendry, Diana. The Very Snowy Christmas. Chapman, Jane, illus. 2013. (ENG.). 16p. (J). (gr. -1). bds. 8.95 (978-1-58925-617-0(4)) Tiger Tales.
Henkes, Kevin. A Good Day Board Book. Henkes, Kevin, illus. 2010. (ENG., Illus.). 28p. (J). (gr. -1 — 1). bds. 7.99 (978-0-06-185778-2(5), Greenwillow Bks.) HarperCollins Pubs.
—Kitten's First Full Moon. Henkes, Kevin, illus. 2015. (ENG., Illus.). 34p. (J). (gr. -1 — 1). bds. 8.99 (978-0-06-241710-7(X), Greenwillow Bks.) HarperCollins Pubs.
Henley, Claire. Baby Jesus & the Noisy Stable. 2009. (All Join In Ser.). (ENG., Illus.). 16p. (J). (gr. k — 1). bds. 6.99 (978-0-7459-6068-5(5)) Lion Hudson PLC GBR. Dist: Independent Pubs. Group.
—Jonah & the Big Fish. 2009. (All Join In Ser.). (ENG.). 16p. (J). (gr. k — 1). bds. 6.99 (978-0-7459-6075-3(8)) Lion Hudson PLC GBR. Dist: Independent Pubs. Group.
—Lost Sheep & the Scary Day. 2009. (All Join In Ser.). (ENG.). 16p. (J). (gr. k — 1). bds. 6.95 (978-0-7459-6070-8(7)) Lion Hudson PLC GBR. Dist: Independent Pubs. Group.
—Noah & the Flood. 2009. (All Join In Ser.). (ENG.). 16p. (J). (gr. k — 1). bds. 6.99 (978-0-7459-6071-5(5)) Lion Hudson PLC GBR. Dist: Independent Pubs. Group.
Henning, Heather. Christmas. Bull, Nicola, ed. Chapman, Gillian, illus. 2007. (Touch & Feel Ser.). 14p. (J). (gr. -1-3). bds. 10.49 (978-0-7586-1383-7(0)) Concordia Publishing Hse.
—Creation. Bull, Nicola, ed. Chapman, Gillian, illus. 2007. (Touch & Feel Ser.). 14p. (J). (gr. -1-3). bds. 10.49 (978-0-7586-1384-4(9)) Concordia Publishing Hse.
Heo, Yumi. Red Light, Green Light. Heo, Yumi, illus. 2015. (ENG., Illus.). 20p. (J). (gr. -1-k). bds. 6.99 (978-0-545-74463-8(6), Cartwheel Bks.) Scholastic, Inc.
Herbauts, Anne, creator. What Color Is the Wind? 2016. (ENG., Illus.). 48p. (J). (gr. k). pap. 19.95 (978-1-59270-221-3(X)) Enchanted Lion Bks., LLC.
Hergé. On a Marche sur la Lune. (Tintin Ser.).Tr. of Explorers on the Moon. (FRE.). (J). pap. 21.95 (978-2-203-00116-9(X)) Casterman, Editions FRA. Dist: Distribooks, Inc.
—On a Marche sur la Lune.Tr. of Explorers on the Moon. (FRE., Illus.). (J). (gr. 7-9). ring bd. 19.95 (978-0-8288-5053-7(4)) French & European Pubns., Inc.
Hewitt, Angie. First Numbers: Touch-And-Trace Early Learning Fun! 2017. (Little Groovers Ser.). (ENG., Illus.). 12p. (J). (— 1). bds. 7.99 (978-1-5107-0838-9(3), Sky Pony Pr.) Skyhorse Publishing Co., Inc.
Hewitt, Sally. Face to Face Safari. Gilvan-Cartwright, Chris, illus. 2011. (ENG.). 12p. (J). (gr. -1-1). 15.95 (978-0-8109-4261-5(5)) Abrams, Inc.
—Happy Dresser. Cameron, Craig, illus. 2003. 14p. (J). pap. 10.95 (978-1-57145-733-2(X), Silver Dolphin Bks.) Readerlink Distribution Services, LLC.
Higginson, Sheila Sweeny. You're Getting a Baby Brother! Williams, Sam, illus. 2012. (ENG.). 24p. (J). (gr. -1-k). bds. 7.99 (978-1-4424-2021-2(9), Little Simon) Little Simon.
—You're Getting a Baby Sister! Williams, Sam, illus. 2012. (ENG.). 24p. (J). (gr. -1-k). bds. 7.99 (978-1-4424-2050-2(2), Little Simon) Little Simon.
Higginson, Sheila Sweeny & Disney Book Group Staff. Whose Birthday Is It? Disney Storybook Artists Staff, illus. 2007. (ENG.). 16p. (J). (gr. -1-k). 4.99 (978-1-4231-0652-4(0)) Disney Pr.
Highlights, creator. The Jumbo Book of Things to Find & Color. 2017. (Highlights(tm) Jumbo Books & Pads Ser.). (ENG.). 256p. (J). (gr. -1-k). pap. 12.99 (978-1-62979-779-3(0), Highlights) Boyds Mills Pr.
Highlights for Children Editorial Staff, creator. Farm Fun. 2016. (Highlights(tm) Carry-And-Play Board Bks.). (ENG., Illus.). 24p. (J). (gr. -1-k). bds. 8.99 (978-1-62979-709-0(X), Highlights) Boyds Mills Pr.
—Find It! at Bedtime. 2016. (Highlights(tm) Find It! Padded Board Bks.). (ENG., Illus.). 14p. (J). (— 1). bds. 8.99 (978-1-62979-704-5(9), Highlights) Boyds Mills Pr.
Highlights for Children, Highlights for & Jordan, Karen. Things That Go. Meisel, Paul, illus. 2015. (Highlights(tm) Find It! Padded Board Bks.). (ENG.). 14p. (J). (— 1). bds. 7.99 (978-1-62979-414-3(7), Highlights) Boyds Mills Pr.
Highlights Staff, compiled by. Find It! First Words. 2016. (Find It! Lift-The-Flap Board Bks.). (ENG.). 14p. (J). (— 1). 7.99 (978-1-62979-536-2(4), Highlights) Boyds Mills Pr.
Hill, Eric. Spot Bakes a Cake. Hill, Eric, illus. 2005. (Spot Ser.). (ENG., Illus.). 20p. (J). (gr. k — 1). 6.99 (978-0-14-240329-7(6), Warne) Penguin Young Readers Group.
—Spot Can Count. 2009. (Spot (Chinese) Ser.). (CHI., Illus.). 22p. (J). (978-957-762-468-0(5)) Hsin Yi Pubns.
—Spot Can Count. Hill, Eric, illus. 2005. (ENG., Illus.). 22p. (J). (gr. -1-1). bds. 7.99 (978-0-399-24361-5(5)) Penguin Publishing Group.
—Spot Goes to School. Hill, Eric, illus. 2004. (Spot Ser.). (ENG., Illus.). 24p. (J). (gr. -1-k). 6.99 (978-0-14-240167-5(6), Warne) Penguin Young Readers Group.
—Spot Goes to the Farm. Hill, Eric, illus. 2003. (Spot Ser.). (ENG., Illus.). 24p. (J). (gr. -1-k). 7.99 (978-0-14-250123-8(9), Warne) Penguin Young Readers Group.
—Spot Goes to the Farm. 2003. (Spot Ser.). (gr. -1-2). lib. bdg. 18.40 (978-0-613-86708-5(4), Turtleback) Turtleback Bks.
—Spot Goes to the Park. Hill, Eric, illus. 2005. (Spot Ser.). (ENG., Illus.). 24p. (J). (gr. -1 — 1). bds. 7.99 (978-0-399-24363-9(1), Warne) Penguin Young Readers Group.
—Spot Loves His Daddy. Hill, Eric, illus. 2005. (Spot Ser.). (ENG., Illus.). 14p. (J). (gr. -1 — 1). bds. 5.99 (978-0-399-24351-6(8), Warne) Penguin Young Readers Group.
—Spot Loves School. Hill, Eric, illus. 2015. (Spot Ser.). (ENG., Illus.). 10p. (J). (gr. -1-k). bds. 5.99 (978-0-14-135654-9(5), Warne) Penguin Publishing Group.
—Spot Says Please. Hill, Eric, illus. 2013. (Spot Ser.). (ENG., Illus.). 14p. (J). (gr. -1-k). bds. 5.99 (978-0-7232-7832-0(6), Warne) Penguin Young Readers Group.
—Spot's Favorite Things. Hill, Eric, illus. 2012. (Spot Ser.). (ENG., Illus.). 12p. (J). (gr. -1 — 1). bds. 8.99 (978-0-399-25758-2(6), Warne) Penguin Young Readers Group.
—Spot's First Walk. Hill, Eric, illus. 2005. (Spot Ser.). (ENG., Illus.). 24p. (J). (gr. -1 — 1). bds. 7.99 (978-0-399-24482-7(4), Warne) Penguin Young Readers Group.
—Spot's Peekaboo. Hill, Eric, illus. 2015. (Spot Ser.). (ENG., Illus.). 12p. (J). (-k). bds. 9.99 (978-0-14-136170-3(0), Warne) Penguin Young Readers Group.
—Where's Spot? Hill, Eric, illus. 2003. (Spot Ser.). (Illus.). (J). (gr. -1 — 1). (SPA & ENG.). 12p. bds. 7.99 (978-0-399-24046-1(2), 53517281); (ENG., 24p. 7.99 (978-0-14-250126-9(3)) Penguin Young Readers Group. (Warne).
—Where's Spot? Hill, Eric, illus. 2007. (Spot Ser.). (ENG., Illus.). 18.00 (978-0-7569-7965-2(X)) Perfection Learning Corp.
—Where's Spot? 2003. (Spot Ser.). 18.40 (978-1-4176-3889-5(3), Turtleback) Turtleback Bks.
Hill, Susanna Leonard. Airplane Flight! Larrañaga, Ana Martín, illus. 2009. (ENG.). 12p. (J). (gr. -1-k). bds. 7.99 (978-1-4169-7832-9(1), Little Simon) Little Simon.
—Freight Train Trip! A Lift-the-Flap Adventure. Larrañaga, Ana Martín, illus. 2009. (ENG.). 12p. (J). (gr. -1-k). bds. 7.99 (978-1-4169-7833-6(X), Little Simon) Little Simon.
Hills, Laila, illus. Squirty Bath Books - Duck. 2014. (Squirty Bath Bks.). (ENG.). 8p. (J). (— 1). 8.99 (978-1-4472-6816-1(4)) Pan Macmillan GBR. Dist: Independent Pubs. Group.
Hills, Tad. Duck & Goose, Goose Needs a Hug. Hills, Tad, illus. 2012. (Duck & Goose Ser.). (ENG., Illus.). 22p. (J). (-k). bds. 6.99 (978-0-307-98293-3(9), Schwartz & Wade Bks.) Random Hse. Children's Bks.
—Duck & Goose, Here Comes the Easter Bunny! Hills, Tad, illus. 2012. (Duck & Goose Ser.). (ENG., Illus.). 22p. (J). (gr. k-k). bds. 7.99 (978-0-375-87280-8(9), Schwartz & Wade Bks.) Random Hse. Children's Bks.
—Duck & Goose, How Are You Feeling? Hills, Tad, illus. 2009. (Duck & Goose Ser.). (ENG., Illus.). 22p. (J). (gr. -1 — 1). bds. 7.99 (978-0-375-84629-8(8), Schwartz & Wade Bks.) Random Hse. Children's Bks.
—Find a Pumpkin. Hills, Tad, illus. 2012. (Duck & Goose Ser.). (ENG., Illus.). 22p. (J). (gr. k-k). bds. 10.99 (978-0-307-98155-4(X), Schwartz & Wade Bks.) Random Hse. Children's Bks.
—It's Time for Christmas! Hills, Tad, illus. (Duck & Goose Ser.). (ENG., Illus.). 22p. (J). 2011. (gr. -1 — 1). bds. 10.99 (978-0-375-87112-2(8)) 2010. (gr. k — 1). bds. 7.99 (978-0-375-86484-1(9)) Random Hse. Children's Bks. (Schwartz & Wade Bks.).
—Rocket's Mighty Words. 2015. (ENG., Illus.). 22p. (J). (-k). bds. 7.99 (978-0-553-53866-3(7), Schwartz & Wade Bks.) Random Hse. Children's Bks.
Hilton, Jennifer Sue & McCurry, Kristen. El Mundo Maravilloso de Dios. Rimmington, Natasha, illus. 2016. (SPA.). (J). (978-1-5064-2094-3(X)) Augsburg Fortress, Pubs.
—Ora a Dios. Garton, Michael, illus. 2016. (SPA.). (J). (978-1-5064-2093-6(1)) Augsburg Fortress, Pubs.
Hinkler Books, creator. 101 First Words. 2011. (101 First Words Ser.). (Illus.). 16p. (J). (gr. -1). bds. 7.99 (978-1-74184-816-8(4)) Hinkler Bks. Pty, Ltd. AUS. Dist: Ideals Pubns.
—101 First Words: Animals. 2011. (101 First Words Ser.). (Illus.). 16p. (J). (gr. -1). bds. 7.99 (978-1-74184-817-5(2)) Hinkler Bks. Pty, Ltd. AUS. Dist: Ideals Pubns.
—101 First Words: At Home. 2011. (101 First Words Ser.). (Illus.). 16p. (J). (gr. -1). bds. 7.99 (978-1-74184-819-9(9)) Hinkler Bks. Pty, Ltd. AUS. Dist: Ideals Pubns.
—101 First Words: Things That Go. 2011. (101 First Words Ser.). (Illus.). 16p. (J). (gr. -1). bds. 7.99 (978-1-74184-818-2(0)) Hinkler Bks. Pty, Ltd. AUS. Dist: Ideals Pubns.
Hinkler Books Staff. My Cool Box of Dress-up Dolls. 2012. 16p. (J). 9.99 (978-1-74184-277-7(8)) Hinkler Bks. Pty, Ltd. AUS. Dist: Ideals Pubns.
Hinkler Books Staff, ed. Spelling. 2009. (ENG.). 24p. (J). 9.99 (978-0-8249-1402-8(3), Ideal Pubns.) Worthy Publishing.
Hinkler Studios Staff., ed. Baby's First Christmas. 2011. (Baby's First Ser.). 12p. (J). bds. 5.99 (978-1-74184-699-7(4)) Hinkler Bks. Pty, Ltd. AUS. Dist: Ideals Pubns.
—Baby's First Halloween. 2011. (Baby's First Ser.). 12p. (J). bds. 5.99 (978-1-74184-700-0(1)) Hinkler Bks. Pty, Ltd. AUS. Dist: Ideals Pubns.
—Little Red Riding Hood. 2011. (Fairytale Pop-Ups Ser.). 12p. (J). 12.99 (978-1-74185-088-8(6)) Hinkler Bks. Pty, Ltd. AUS. Dist: Ideals Pubns.
Hinkler Studios Staff, ed. Snow White. 2011. (Fairytale Pop-Ups Ser.). 12p. (J). 12.99 (978-1-74185-089-5(4)) Hinkler Bks. Pty, Ltd. AUS. Dist: Ideals Pubns.
Hinkler Studios Staff., ed. Three Little Pigs. 2011. (Fairytale Pop-Ups Ser.). 12p. (J). 12.99 (978-1-74185-086-4(X)) Hinkler Bks. Pty, Ltd. AUS. Dist: Ideals Pubns.
Hinton, Steph. Let's Learn First Words with Stickers. 2015. (Illus.). (J). (978-1-4351-5921-1(7)) Barnes & Noble, Inc.
Hinton, Stephanie, illus. Busy Book for Boys: 550 Things to Find. 2014. (J). (978-1-4351-5358-5(8)) Barnes & Noble, Inc.
—Muddle & Match: Adventure. 2014. 16p. (J). bds. 8.99 (978-1-61067-288-7(7)) Kane Miller.
—Muddle & Match: Imagine. 2014. 16p. (J). bds. 8.99 (978-1-61067-289-4(5)) Kane Miller.
—Muddle & Match Jungle Animals. 2015. (ENG.). 16p. (J). bds. 8.00 (978-1-61067-401-0(4)) Kane Miller.
—Muddle & Match Monsters. 2015. (ENG.). 16p. (J). bds. (978-1-61067-423-2(5)) Kane Miller.
Hirschi, Ron. Winter Is for Whales: A Book of Hawaiian Seasons. Green, Yuko, illus. 2007. (ENG.). 36p. (J). (gr. -1-3). (978-1-59700-504-3(5)) Island Heritage Publishing.
Hirschmann, Kris. Blast Off. 2006. (Illus.). 63p. (J). (978-0-439-55092-5(0)) Scholastic, Inc.
Hnatov, Catherine. Up & Down, 1 vol. Hnatov, Catherine, illus. 2014. (ENG., Illus.). 32p. (J). bds. 5.99 (978-1-59572-340-6(4)) Star Bright Bks., Inc.
—Yum, Yum (Spanish/English), 1 vol. 2011. (ENG., Illus.). 32p. (J). bds. 5.95 (978-1-59572-276-8(9)) Star Bright Bks., Inc.
Ho, Jannie. The Great Matzoh Hunt. Ho, Jannie, illus. 2010. (ENG., Illus.). 12p. (J). (gr. -1-k). 6.99 (978-0-8431-8969-8(X), Price Stern Sloan) Penguin Young Readers Group.
—Guess Who? Ho, Jannie, illus. 2013. (ENG., Illus.). 8p. (J). (gr. -1 — 1). bds. 7.99 (978-0-545-49331-4(5), Cartwheel Bks.) Scholastic, Inc.
Hoban, Tana. Black & White. Hoban, Tana, illus. 2007. (ENG., Illus.). 16p. (J). (gr. -1 — 1). bds. 7.99 (978-0-06-117211-3(1), Greenwillow Bks.) HarperCollins Pubs.
—Black White. Hoban, Tana, illus. 2017. (Illus.). 36p. (J). (gr. -1 — 1). pap. 8.99 (978-0-06-265690-2(2), Greenwillow Bks.) HarperCollins Pubs.
Hodgman, Ann. Do Touch! Don't Touch! Barnard, Lucy, illus. 2012. (ENG.). 18p. (J). bds. (978-1-58925-867-9(3)) Tiger Tales.
—Monsters Dance. Wood, Hannah, illus. 2013. (ENG.). 16p. (J). (gr. -1). bds. 8.95 (978-1-58925-627-9(1)) Tiger Tales.
—That's My Mommy! Logan, Laura, illus. 2013. (ENG.). 22p. bds. (978-1-58925-645-3(X)) Tiger Tales.
Hodson, Sarah E. Wh- Questions. 2012. (Illus.). (J). (978-0-7606-1382-5(6)) LinguiSystems, Inc.
Hoffmann, E. T. A. & Ventura, Paola Fratalocchi. The Nutcracker. 2010. (ENG., Illus.). 32p. (J). 14.99 (978-0-7944-2044-4(3)) Reader's Digest Assn., Inc., The.
Hogan, Martina, illus. Dinosaur Big, Dinosaur Small. 2016. (Early Birds Ser.). (ENG.). 12p. (J). (gr. -1 — 1). bds. 6.99 (978-1-4998-0184-2(X)) Little Bee Books Inc.
—Rainbow Zoo. 2016. (Early Birds Ser.). (ENG.). 12p. (J). (gr. -1 — 1). bds. 6.99 (978-1-4998-0209-2(9)) Little Bee Books Inc.
—Roar! Shh! 2016. (Early Birds Ser.). (ENG.). 12p. (J). (gr. -1 — 1). bds. 6.99 (978-1-4998-0183-5(1)) Little Bee Books Inc.
—123 under the Sea. 2016. (Early Birds Ser.). (ENG.). 12p. (J). (gr. -1 — 1). bds. 6.99 (978-1-4998-0208-5(0)) Little Bee Books Inc.
Holcroft, John & Candlewick Press Staff. Space Exploration: Panorama Pops. Holcroft, John, illus. 2015. (ENG., Illus.). 30p. (J). (gr. k-4). 8.99 (978-0-7636-7699-5(3)) Candlewick Pr.
Holmen, Lene. Lift & Learn Opposites. Snaith, Andy, photos by. 2006. (Illus.). 24p. (gr. -1 — 1). per., bds. (978-1-84610-031-4(3)) Make Believe Ideas.
Holtfreter, Nastja, illus. Push Puzzles: in the Woods. 2016. (ENG.). 10p. (J). (gr. -1 — 1). bds. 7.99 (978-1-4998-0349-5(4)) Little Bee Books Inc.
—Push Puzzles: on the Farm. 2016. (ENG.). 10p. (J). (gr. -1 — 1). bds. 7.99 (978-1-4998-0348-8(6)) Little Bee Books Inc.
Holub, Joan. Dragon Dance: A Chinese New Year. Huang, Benrei, illus. 2003. (Lift-The-Flap, Puffin Ser.). (ENG.). 16p. (J). (gr. -1-k). pap. 6.99 (978-0-14-240000-5(9), Puffin Books) Penguin Young Readers Group.
—This Little Explorer: A Pioneer Primer. Roode, Daniel, illus. 2016. (This Little Ser.). (ENG.). 26p. (J). (gr. -1-k). bds. 7.99 (978-1-4814-7175-6(9), Little Simon) Little Simon.
—This Little President: A Presidential Primer. Roode, Daniel, illus. 2016. (This Little Ser.). (ENG.). 26p. (J). (gr. -1-k). bds. 7.99 (978-1-4814-5850-4(7), Little Simon) Little Simon.
Holzwarth, Werner. The Story of the Little Mole Who Knew It Was None of His Business. Erlbruch, Wolf, illus. 2012. (ENG.). 24p. (J). (gr. -1-2). bds. 17.99 (978-1-84365-132-1(7), Pavilion Children's Books) Pavilion Bks. GBR. Dist: Independent Pubs. Group.
Honda, Liana. Kou Lima. Kukahiko, Puni, illus. 2010. 22p. 8.00 (978-0-87336-236-8(5)) Kamehameha Publishing.
—Kou Wawae. Kukahiko, Puni, illus. 2010. 22p. 8.00 (978-0-87336-237-5(3)) Kamehameha Publishing.
Honey, Alison. My Ashmolean Discovery Book. 2010. (ENG., Illus.). 24p. (J). (gr. -1-3). pap. 9.95 (978-1-85444-242-0(2)) Ashmolean Museum GBR. Dist: National Bk. Network.
Hood, Susan. Caterpillar Spring, Butterfly Summer: 10th Anniversary Edition. Gevry, Claudine, illus. 2014. (ENG.). 12p. (J). (gr. -1-k). 12.99 (978-0-7944-3038-2(4)) Reader's Digest Assn., Inc., The.
—Tickly Toes. Barroux, Stéphane, illus. 2014. (ENG.). 24p. (J). (gr. -1 — 1). bds. 9.95 (978-1-894786-52-2(1)) Kids Can Pr., Ltd. CAN. Dist: Hachette Bk. Group.
Hooks, Bell. Happy to Be Nappy (Board Book) Happy to Be Nappy. Raschka, Chris, illus. 2017. (ENG.). 32p. (J). (gr. -1 — 1). bds. 7.99 (978-1-4847-8841-7(9), Jump at the Sun) Hyperion Bks. for Children.
Hooper, Ruth. Santa's Factory. Charbonnel, Olivier & Mostyn, David, illus. 2004. 6p. (J). (gr. k-4). reprint ed. 16.00 (978-0-7567-7585-8(X)) DIANE Publishing Co.
Hopgood, Sally. A Day on the Farm: A Pull-The-Tab Book. Hinton, Stephanie, illus. 2014. (J). (978-1-4351-5688-3(9)) Barnes & Noble, Inc.
—In the Forest: A Pull-The-Tab Book. Hinton, Stephanie, illus. 2014. (J). (978-1-4351-5689-0(7)) Barnes & Noble, Inc.
—A Trip to Busy Town: A Pull-The-Tab Book. Hinton, Stephanie, illus. 2014. (J). (978-1-4351-5690-6(0)) Barnes & Noble, Inc.
Horácek, Petr. Honk, Honk! Baa, Baa! Horácek, Petr, illus. 2014. (ENG., Illus.). 16p. (J). (— 1). bds. 7.99 (978-0-7636-6780-1(3)) Candlewick Pr.
—Silly Suzy Goose. Horácek, Petr, illus. 2009. (ENG., Illus.). 32p. (J). (— 1). bds. 7.99 (978-0-7636-4141-2(3)) Candlewick Pr.
—A Surprise for Tiny Mouse. Horácek, Petr, illus. 2015. (ENG., Illus.). 16p. (J). (— 1). bds. 8.99 (978-0-7636-7967-5(4)) Candlewick Pr.
—Time for Bed. Horácek, Petr, illus. 2014. (ENG., Illus.). 16p. (J). (— 1). bds. 7.99 (978-0-7636-6779-5(X)) Candlewick Pr.
Horne, Jane. Busy Baby Noisy Book. 2007. (Busy Baby Ser.). (Illus.). 12p. (gr. -1). per., bds. (978-1-84610-434-3(3)) Make Believe Ideas.
—Busy Baby Sparklies 4 Volume Boxed Set: Baby's First Box of Books. 2007. (Illus.). 12p. (gr. -1-k). bds., bds. (978-1-84610-565-4(X)) Make Believe Ideas.
—Flip & Find 123. 2008. (Illus.). 12p. (J). (gr. -1-3). bds. (978-1-84610-731-3(8)) Make Believe Ideas.
—Flip & Find Abc. 2008. (Illus.). 12p. (J). (gr. -1-3). bds. (978-1-84610-730-6(X)) Make Believe Ideas.
—Rough & Tough: Tractors & Trucks/Cars/Diggers & Dumpers/Emergency. 2007. (Illus.). 12p. (gr. -1-k). (978-1-84610-559-3(5)) Make Believe Ideas.
—Sparklies Colors. 2008. (Illus.). 12p. (gr. -1-k). bds. (978-1-84610-608-8(7)) Make Believe Ideas.
Horne, Jane & Page, Claire. I Really Like Puppies. 2010. (ENG., Illus.). 12p. (J). (gr. -1-k). bds. 9.99 (978-1-84610-963-8(9)) Make Believe Ideas GBR. Dist: Nelson, Thomas Inc.
Horne, Jane, et al. Five Noisy Ducks: An Action-Packed Counting Book. 2014. (Illus.). (J). (978-1-4351-6034-7(7)) Barnes & Noble, Inc.
Houbre, Gilbert. Vegetables. Houbre, Gilbert, illus. 2012. (ENG., Illus.). 36p. (J). (gr. -1-k). 12.99 (978-1-85103-402-4(1)) Moonlight Publishing, Ltd. GBR. Dist: Independent Pubs. Group.
Houghton Mifflin Harcourt Publishing Company Staff & Nouvian, Judith. Shapes. 2015. (Picture This Ser.). (ENG., Illus.). 40p. (J). (gr. -1-3). bds. 7.99 (978-0-544-51830-8(6), HMH Books For Young Readers) Houghton Mifflin Harcourt Publishing Co.
Houle, Kelly. Gracie's Gallery: A Magic Mirror Book. 2008. (ENG., Illus.). 28p. (J). (gr. -1). 14.95 (978-1-58117-784-8(4), Intervisual/Piggy Toes) Bendon, Inc.
Howarth, Jill, illus. Jingle Bells. 2015. (ENG.). 8p. (J). (gr. -1-17). bds. 10.95 (978-0-7624-5842-4(9), Running Pr. Kids) Running Pr. Bk. Pubs.
Howell, Gail L. Sarah & the Blue Sled: Sarah's World (Series) 2010. 32p. pap. 12.99 (978-1-4389-7597-9(X)) AuthorHouse.
Howie, Vickie & MacLean, Moira. Easter Surprise: A Lift-the-Flap Board Book. 2006. (Illus.). 32p. (J). (gr. -1-k). bds. 9.49 (978-0-7586-1148-2(X)) Concordia Publishing Hse.
Hruby, Patrick. ABC Is for Circus: Hardcover Popular Edition. 2017. (ENG., Illus.). 56p. 9.95 (978-1-62326-107-8(4)) AMMO Bks., LLC.
Hruby, Patrick & Hruby, Emily. Counting in the Garden. 2011. (ENG., Illus.). 58p. (J). bds. 14.95 (978-1-934429-70-9(8)) AMMO Bks., LLC.
Huang, Yu-Hsuan. Let's Play... Ice Skating. 2014. (Let's Play Ser.). (ENG.). 10p. (J). (gr. -1 — 1). 15.99 (978-1-4472-7644-9(2)) Pan Macmillan GBR. Dist: Independent Pubs. Group.
Huang, Yu-Hsuan, illus. Baby Bear: Finger Puppet Book. 2016. (ENG.). 12p. (J). (gr. -1 — 1). bds. 6.99 (978-1-4521-4235-7(1)) Chronicle Bks. LLC.
—Baby Bunny: Finger Puppet Book. 2017. (ENG.). 12p. (J). bds. 6.99 (978-1-4521-5609-5(3)) Chronicle Bks. LLC.
—Baby Chipmunk: Finger Puppet Book. 2017. (ENG.). 12p. (J). (gr. -1 — 1). bds. 6.99 (978-1-4521-5612-5(3)) Chronicle Bks. LLC.
—Baby Elephant: Finger Puppet Book. 2016. (ENG.). 12p. (J). (gr. -1 — 1). 6.99 (978-1-4521-4237-1(8)) Chronicle Bks. LLC.
—Baby Fish: Finger Puppet Book. 2017. (ENG.). 12p. (J). bds. 6.99 (978-1-4521-5610-1(7)) Chronicle Bks. LLC.
—Baby Giraffe: Finger Puppet Book. 2017. (ENG.). 12p. (J). (gr. -1 — 1). bds. 6.99 (978-1-4521-5611-8(5)) Chronicle Bks. LLC.
—Baby Reindeer. 2016. (ENG.). 12p. (J). (gr. -1 — 1). 6.99 (978-1-4521-4661-4(6)) Chronicle Bks. LLC.
—Baby Tiger: Finger Puppet Book. 2016. (ENG.). 12p. (J). (gr. -1 — 1). bds. 6.99 (978-1-4521-4236-4(X)) Chronicle Bks. LLC.
—Let's Play Aliens in Space. 2016. (Let's Play Ser.). (ENG.). 10p. (J). (gr. -1-k). bds. 16.99 (978-1-4472-8653-0(7)) Pan Macmillan GBR. Dist: Independent Pubs. Group.
—Let's Play Fairy Homes. 2016. (Let's Play Ser.). (ENG.). 12p. (J). (gr. -1-k). bds. 16.99 (978-1-4472-7723-1(6)) Pan Macmillan GBR. Dist: Independent Pubs. Group.
Hubbard, Ben. My Very Own Kitten. Guile, Gill, illus. 2014. (ENG.). 12p. (J). (gr. -1). (978-1-78244-602-6(8)) Top That! Publishing PLC.
—My Very Own Puppy. Guile, Gill, illus. 2014. (ENG.). 12p. (gr. -1). (978-1-78244-603-3(6)) Top That! Publishing PLC.
Hudson, Cheryl Willis. Hands Can. 2013. lib. bdg. 14.75 (978-0-606-31602-6(7), Turtleback) Turtleback Bks.
Hudson, Sue. I Love You. Watanabe, Kaori, illus. 2004. (My First Taggies Book Ser.). (ENG.). 3p. (J). (gr. k — 1). 12.99 (978-0-439-64947-6(1), Cartwheel Bks.) Scholastic, Inc.
Hughes, John Ceiriog. All Through the Night. Boulton, Harold, tr. from WEL. Alizadeh, Kate, illus. 2013. (ENG.). 24p. (J). (gr. -1-2). bds. 12.95 (978-1-927018-09-5(9)) Simply Read Bks. CAN. Dist: Ingram Publisher Services.
Hughes, Laura. We're Going on an Egg Hunt. Hughes, Laura, illus. 2017. (ENG., Illus.). 24p. (J). 17.99 (978-1-68119-314-4(0), 9781681193144, Bloomsbury USA Childrens) Bloomsbury Publishing USA.
Hulme, Joy N. Eerie Feary Feeling: A Hairy Scary Pop-up Book. Ely, Paul & Dudley, Dick, illus. 2006. 12p. (J). (gr. k-4). reprint ed. 14.00 (978-1-4223-5171-0(8)) DIANE Publishing Co.

Huneck, Stephen. Sally in the Snow. 2014. (Sally Board Bks.). (ENG., Illus.). 20p. (J). (gr. -1 — 1). bds. 7.95 *(978-1-4197-1227-2(6)*, Abrams Appleseed) Abrams, Inc.

Hung, Yating. Where Is Mama? A Pop-Up Story. 2013. (ENG., Illus.). 24p. (J). (gr. -1-k). 19.95 *(978-1-4197-0718-6(3)*, Abrams Appleseed) Abrams, Inc.

Hurry, Helen. Peepo! Boo! Who Are You? 2014. (ENG., Illus.). 12p. (J). 17.00 *(978-0-85707-679-3(5)*, Simon & Schuster Children's) Simon & Schuster, Ltd. GBR. Dist: Simon & Schuster, Inc.

Hurt-Newton, Tania. Yee-Ha Harvey. 2007. (ENG., Illus.). 14p. (J). (gr. k — 1). 14.95 *(978-0-00-724414-0(2))* HarperCollins Pubs. Ltd. GBR. Dist: Independent Pubs. Group.

Husar, Lisa & Husar, Mike. Grand Canyon Babies. 2011. 26p. 8.95 *(978-1-56037-507-4(8))* Farcountry Pr.

Hutchings, Tony, illus. A Week at the Seaside. 2014. (J). *(978-1-4351-5464-3(9))* Barnes & Noble, Inc.

Hutchinson McMullen, Angela. I Like Me. 2013. 24p. pap. *(978-1-926831-01-5(2))* Navarone Bks.

Hutton, John. Blocks: Baby Unplugged. Hutton, John, ed. Kang, Andrea, illus. 2013. (Baby Unplugged Ser.). (ENG.). 14p. (J). (— 1). bds. 7.99 *(978-1-936669-13-4(7))* Blue Manatee Press.

—Box: Baby Unplugged. Kang, Andrea, illus. 2012. (Baby Unplugged Ser.). (ENG.). 14p. (J). (— 1). bds. 7.99 *(978-1-936669-08-0(0))* Blue Manatee Press.

—Pets: Baby Unplugged. Kang, Andrea, illus. 2011. (Baby Unplugged Ser.). (ENG.). 14p. (J). (— 1). bds. 7.99 *(978-1-936669-02-8(1))* Blue Manatee Press.

Huven, Kim. The Birthday Bears. Padron, Alicia, illus. 2010. 10p. bds. 10.95 *(978-1-60747-774-7(2)*, Pickwick Pr.) Phoenix Bks., Inc.

Huws, Emily & Gomer, Gwasg. CAE Berllan. 2005. (WEL.). 28p. 5.99 *(978-1-85902-998-5(1))* Gomer Pr. GBR. Dist: Gomer Pr.

Hvass & Hannibal. Technicolor Treasure Hunt: Learn to Count with Nature. 2016. (ENG.). 14p. (J). (gr. -1-k). bds. 12.99 *(978-1-84780-780-9(1)*, Wide Eyed Editions) Quarto Publishing Group UK GBR. Dist: Hachette Bk. Group.

Hvass, Nan Na & Hannibal, Sofie, illus. Technicolour Treasure Hunt: Learn to Count with Nature. 2016. (ENG.). 14p. (J). bds. 12.99 *(978-1-84780-744-1(5)*, Wide Eyed Editions) Quarto Publishing Group UK GBR. Dist: Littlehampton Bk Services, Ltd.

Hyde, Margaret. Mo Smells Green: A Scentsational Journey. Giacomini, Amanda, illus. 2009. (Mo's Nose Ser.). (ENG.). 16p. (J). (gr. k-k). 17.95 *(978-0-9816255-2-2(5))* Mo's Nose, LLC.

—Mo Smells the Holidays: A Scentsational Journey. Giacomini, Amanda, illus. 2009. (Mo's Nose Ser.). (ENG.). 24p. (J). (gr. k-k). 17.95 *(978-0-9816255-3-9(3))* Mo's Nose, LLC.

Hyun, Kim. Come & Play: A Book about Playing, with Tabs for Older Babies. 2016. (Chat About Ser.). (ENG., Illus.). 22p. (J). bds. 9.99 ***(978-1-5098-0458-0(7))*** Pan Macmillan GBR. Dist: Independent Pubs. Group.

I Want to be a Ballerina. 2008. (Magnetic Board Books Ser.). 7p. bds. *(978-1-4075-1414-7(8))* Parragon, Inc.

I Want to Be a Cowboy. 2008. (Magnetic Board Books Ser.). 7p. bds. *(978-1-4075-1416-1(4))* Parragon, Inc.

I Want to Be a Mermaid. 2008. (Magnetic Board Books Ser.). 7p. bds. *(978-1-4075-1417-8(2))* Parragon, Inc.

Ideals Publications Inc. Staff. Thomas & Friends Write, Slide & Learn: Numbers. 2011. (Write, Slide & Learn Ser.). 14p. (J). pap. *(978-1-74184-161-9(5))* Hinkler Bks. Pty. Ltd.

Idle, Molly. Flora & the Chicks. 2017. (ENG., Illus.). 20p. (J). bds. 9.99 *(978-1-4521-4657-7(8))* Chronicle Bks. LLC.

—Flora & the Ostrich: An Opposites Book. 2017. (ENG., Illus.). 20p. (J). (gr. -1 — 1). bds. 9.99 *(978-1-4521-4658-4(6))* Chronicle Bks. LLC.

—Flora & the Peacocks. 2016. (ENG., Illus.). 40p. (J). (gr. -1-k). 17.99 *(978-1-4521-3816-9(8))* Chronicle Bks. LLC.

—Flora & the Penguin. 2014. (ENG., Illus.). 40p. (J). (gr. -1-k). 16.99 *(978-1-4521-2891-7(X))* Chronicle Bks. LLC.

Ikids Staff. Animals Everywhere. Phillips, Jillian, illus. 2010. (ENG.). 20p. (J). (gr. -1-17). 6.99 *(978-1-60169-006-7(1))* Innovative Kids.

—Little Turtles. Larranaga, Ana, illus. 2008. (iBaby Float-Alongs Ser.). (ENG.). 6p. (J). (gr. -1). 12.99 *(978-1-58476-808-1(8))* Innovative Kids.

Ikids Staff & Francis, Guy. Pets. 2009. (ENG., Illus.). 10p. (J). (gr. -1-1). 15.99 *(978-1-58476-940-8(8))* Innovative Kids.

I'm Going to be the Best Astronaut Ever! 2008. (I'm Going to be Storybooks... Ser.). 32p. *(978-1-4075-1705-6(8))* Parragon, Inc.

I'm Going to be the Best Ballerina Ever! 2008. (I'm Going to be Storybooks... Ser.). 32p. *(978-1-4075-1706-3(6))* Parragon, Inc.

I'm Going to be the Best Princess Ever! 2008. (I'm Going to be Storybooks... Ser.). 32p. *(978-1-4075-1584-7(5))* Parragon, Inc.

I'm Going to be the Best Superhero Ever! 2008. (I'm Going to be Storybooks... Ser.). 32p. *(978-1-4075-1585-4(3))* Parragon, Inc.

Image Books Staff. Little Chick: Finger Puppet Book. Put, Klaartje van der, illus. 2015. (ENG.). 12p. (J). (gr. -1 — 1). bds. 6.99 *(978-1-4521-2917-4(7))* Chronicle Bks. LLC.

—Little Chicken. Put, Klaartje van der, illus. 2012. (Little Finger Puppet Board Bks.: FING). (ENG.). 12p. (J). (gr. -1 — 1). bds. 6.99 *(978-1-4521-0811-7(0))* Chronicle Bks. LLC.

—Little Dolphin. Put, Klaartje van der, illus. 2012. (Little Finger Puppet Board Bks.: FING). (ENG.). 12p. (J). (gr. -1 — 1). bds. 6.99 *(978-1-4521-0816-2(1))* Chronicle Bks. LLC.

—Little Seal: Finger Puppet Book. Put, Klaartje van der, illus. 2012. (Little Finger Puppet Board Bks.: FING). (ENG.). 12p. (J). (gr. -1 — 1). bds. 6.99 *(978-1-4521-0812-4(9))* Chronicle Bks. LLC.

Image Books Staff & Chronicle Books Staff. Little Bunny. van der Put, Klaartje, illus. 2006. (Little Finger Puppet Board Bks.: FING). (ENG.). 12p. (J). (gr. -1 — 1). bds. 6.99 *(978-0-8118-5644-7(5))* Chronicle Bks. LLC.

—Little Butterfly. van der Put, Klaartje, illus. 2006. (Little Finger Puppet Board Bks.: FING). (ENG.). 12p. (J). (gr. -1 — 1). bds. 6.99 *(978-0-8118-5645-4(3))* Chronicle Bks. LLC.

—Little Pig. Put, Klaartje van der, illus. 2012. (Little Finger Puppet Board Bks.). (ENG.). 12p. (J). (gr. -1 — 1). bds. 6.99 *(978-1-4521-0817-9(X))* Chronicle Bks. LLC.

ImageBooks Staff. Little Cow. 2007. (Little Finger Puppet Board Bks.: FING). (ENG., Illus.). 12p. (J). (gr. -1 — 1). bds. 6.95 *(978-0-8118-6109-0(0))* Chronicle Bks. LLC.

—Little Dog: Finger Puppet Book. 2014. (Little Finger Puppet Board Bks.). (ENG.). 12p. (J). (gr. -1 — 1). bds. 6.99 *(978-1-4521-2915-0(0))* Chronicle Bks. LLC.

—Little Horse: Finger Puppet Book. Put, Klaartje van der, illus. 2013. (Little Finger Puppet Board Bks.). (ENG.). 12p. (J). (gr. -1 — 1). bds. 6.99 *(978-1-4521-1249-7(5))* Chronicle Bks. LLC.

—Little Monkey. Put, Klaartje van der, illus. 2013. (Little Finger Puppet Board Bks.). (ENG.). 12p. (J). (gr. -1 — 1). bds. 6.99 *(978-1-4521-1250-3(9))* Chronicle Bks. LLC.

—Little Mouse. 2007. (Little Finger Puppet Board Bks.: FING). (ENG., Illus.). 12p. (J). (gr. -1 — 1). bds. 6.99 *(978-0-8118-6110-6(4))* Chronicle Bks. LLC.

—Little Owl Finger Puppet Book. 2011. (Little Finger Puppet Board Bks.). (ENG.). 12p. (J). (gr. -1 — 1). bds. 6.99 *(978-1-4521-0221-4(X))* Chronicle Bks. LLC.

—Little Sea Turtle: Finger Puppet Book. 2014. (Little Finger Puppet Board Bks.). (ENG.). 12p. (J). (gr. -1 — 1). bds. 6.99 *(978-1-4521-2913-6(4))* Chronicle Bks. LLC.

—Little Shark: Finger Puppet Book. Put, Klaartje van der, illus. 2013. (Little Finger Puppet Board Bks.). (ENG.). 12p. (J). (gr. -1 — 1). bds. 6.99 *(978-1-4521-1251-0(7))* Chronicle Bks. LLC.

—Little Zebra. Put, Klaartje van der, illus. 2013. (Little Finger Puppet Board Bks.). (ENG.). 12p. (J). (gr. -1 — 1). bds. 6.99 *(978-1-4521-1252-7(5))* Chronicle Bks. LLC.

—Snow Baby Finger Puppet Book. 2011. (Little Finger Puppet Board Bks.). (ENG.). 12p. (J). (gr. -1 — 1). bds. 6.99 *(978-1-4521-0220-7(1))* Chronicle Bks. LLC.

ImageBooks Staff & Chronicle Books Staff. Little Crab Finger Puppet Book. 2010. (Little Finger Puppet Board Bks.). (ENG., Illus.). 12p. (J). (gr. -1 — 1). bds. 6.99 *(978-0-8118-7340-6(4))* Chronicle Bks. LLC.

—Little Fish Finger Puppet Book. 2010. (Little Finger Puppet Board Bks.). (ENG., Illus.). 12p. (J). (gr. -1 — 1). bds. 6.99 *(978-0-8118-7344-4(7))* Chronicle Bks. LLC.

—Little Fox: Finger Puppet Book. Put, Klaartje van der, illus. 2015. (ENG.). 12p. (J). (gr. -1 — 1). bds. 6.99 *(978-1-4521-4230-2(0))* Chronicle Bks. LLC.

—Little Spider Finger Puppet Book. van der Put, Klaartje, illus. 2007. (Little Finger Puppet Board Bks.: FING). (ENG.). 12p. (J). (gr. -1 — 1). bds. 6.99 *(978-0-8118-6104-5(X))* Chronicle Bks. LLC.

ImageBooks Staff & Mulligan, Lenz. Little Panda Finger Puppet Book. 2009. (Little Finger Puppet Board Bks.: FING). (ENG., Illus.). 12p. (J). (gr. -1 — 1). bds. 6.99 *(978-0-8118-6999-7(7))* Chronicle Bks. LLC.

ImageBooks Staff, et al. Little Snowman. 2008. (Little Finger Puppet Board Bks.). (ENG., Illus.). 12p. (J). (gr. -1 — 1). bds. 6.99 *(978-0-8118-6356-8(5))* Chronicle Bks. LLC.

Imperato, Teresa. Colors All Around: A Turn & Pop Book. Petrone, Valeria, illus. 2005. (Turn & Pop Book Ser.). 10p. (J). bds. 5.95 *(978-1-58117-277-5(X)*, Intervisual/Piggy Toes) Bendon, Inc.

—Fiona's Fairy Magic. Huang, Benrei, illus. 2005. 14p. (J). 10.95 *(978-1-58117-322-2(9)*, Intervisual/Piggy Toes) Bendon, Inc.

—Good Morning, Good Night! Mitchell, Melanie, illus. 2006. (ENG.). 12p. (J). (gr. -1-18). 9.95 *(978-1-58117-279-9(6)*, Intervisual/Piggy Toes) Bendon, Inc.

—How Many Ducks in a Row? A Turn & Pop Book. Petrone, Valeria, illus. 2005. 10p. (J). bds. 5.95 *(978-1-58117-278-2(8)*, Intervisual/Piggy Toes) Bendon, Inc.

—On the Farm: A Barnyard Book. Rayner, Olivia, illus. 2005. 10p. (J). 7.95 *(978-1-58117-270-6(2)*, Intervisual/Piggy Toes) Bendon, Inc.

—On the Go! A Transportation Book. Rayner, Olivia, illus. 2005. 10p. (J). 7.95 *(978-1-58117-271-3(0)*, Intervisual/Piggy Toes) Bendon, Inc.

—Ten Christmas Lights: Count the Lights from One to Ten! Parry, Jo, illus. 2005. (ENG.). 20p. (J). 10.95 *(978-1-58117-321-5(0)*, Intervisual/Piggy Toes) Bendon, Inc.

—This Little Piggy. Haskamp, Steve, illus. 2006. (ENG.). 22p. (J). 9.95 *(978-1-58117-281-2(8)*, Intervisual/Piggy Toes) Bendon, Inc.

Inkpen, Mick. Kipper: Kipper's Christmas Eve. 2016. (Kipper Ser.). (ENG., Illus.). 26p. (J). (gr. -1-k). bds. 8.99 *(978-1-4449-3029-0(X))* Hachette Children's Group GBR. Dist: Hachette Bk. Group.

—Lullabyhullaballoo! Inkpen, Mick, illus. 2007. (ENG., Illus.). 32p. (gr. 13-17). pap. 10.99 *(978-0-340-93108-0(6))* Hodder & Stoughton GBR. Dist: Hachette Bk. Group.

Intrater, Roberta Grobel. Peek-a-Boo, You! Intrater, Roberta Grobel, photos by. 2nd rev. l.t. ed. 2005. (Illus.). 14p. (J). 14.99 *(978-0-9764985-0-6(2))* 1212 Pr.

Iossa, Federica, illus. Peekaboo Bunny. 2016. (Peekaboo Bks.). (ENG.). 8p. (J). (gr. -1 — 1). bds. 7.99 *(978-0-7641-6861-1(4))* Barron's Educational Series, Inc.

—Peekaboo Teddy. 2016. (Peekaboo Bks.). (ENG.). 8p. (J). (gr. -1 — 1). bds. 7.99 *(978-0-7641-6862-8(2))* Barron's Educational Series, Inc.

Ipcar, Dahlov. Dahlov Ipcar's Farmyard Alphabet, 1 vol. 2010. (ENG., Illus.). 18p. (J). bds. 10.95 *(978-1-934031-43-8(7)*, 322cba51-66de-4792-9574-ca10ba745057) Islandport Pr., Inc.

—Dahlov Ipcar's Maine Alphabet. 2012. (ENG., Illus.). 24p. (J). bds. 10.95 *(978-1-934031-87-2(9)*, e93823ef-f4cd-45da-bc3f-2f7da4f8dc56) Islandport Pr., Inc.

Iriyama, Satoshi. Good Night, Chirp. 2015. (Chirp the Chick Ser.). (ENG., Illus.). 36p. (J). (— 1). 8.99 *(978-0-544-35994-9(1)*, HMH Books For Young Readers) Houghton Mifflin Harcourt Publishing Co.

—Happy Spring, Chirp! 2015. (Chirp the Chick Ser.). (ENG., Illus.). 32p. (J). (— 1). 8.99 *(978-0-544-36150-8(4)*, HMH Books For Young Readers) Houghton Mifflin Harcourt Publishing Co.

Ishida, Jui, illus. Who Says Moo? A Touch & Feel Board Book. 2005. 16p. (J). bds. 6.95 *(978-1-58117-178-5(1)*, Intervisual/Piggy Toes) Bendon, Inc.

Ismail, Yasmeen, illus. Inside, Outside, Upside Down: Draw & Discover. 2017. (ENG.). 56p. (J). (gr. -1-2). pap. 9.99 *(978-1-78067-929-7(7))* King, Laurence Publishing GBR. Dist: Hachette Bk. Group.

—Push, Pull, Empty, Full: Draw & Discover. 2017. (ENG.). 56p. (J). (gr. -1-2). pap. 9.99 *(978-1-78067-931-0(9))* King, Laurence Publishing GBR. Dist: Hachette Bk. Group.

Itoïz, Mayana. Search & Find: Fairy Tales as Children Have Never Seen Them Before! 2012. (ENG., Illus.). 24p. (J). (gr. k). 12.95 *(978-2-7338-1983-8(6))* Auzou, Philippe Editions FRA. Dist: Consortium Bk. Sales & Distribution.

Jackson, Antonia & Nagy, Krisztina Kallai. My Advent Calendar Christmas Book. 2014. (ENG., Illus.). 32p. (J). (-2). 9.99 *(978-0-7459-6392-1(7))* Lion Hudson PLC GBR. Dist: Independent Pubs. Group.

Jackson, Richard. Have a Look, Says Book. Hawkes, Kevin, illus. 2016. (ENG.). 48p. (J). (gr. -1-2). 17.99 *(978-1-4814-2105-8(0))* Simon & Schuster Children's Publishing.

Jaeger, Elizabeth. It's Halloween, Little Pumpkin! Boyer, Robin, illus. 2014. 16p. (J). bds. 12.99 *(978-0-8249-1942-9(4)*, Ideal Pubns.) Worthy Publishing.

Jake's Big Adventure. 2008. (Jake Flocked Board Ser.). 8p. bds. *(978-1-4075-1818-3(6))* Parragon, Inc.

Jake's Perfect Day. 2008. (Jake Flocked Board Ser.). 8p. bds. *(978-1-4075-1817-6(8))* Parragon, Inc.

James, Annabelle. Jack & the Beanstalk Story in a Box. Ackerman, Michele L., illus. 2003. (Story in a Box Ser.). 12p. (J). bds. 8.99 *(978-1-883043-42-1(5))* Straight Edge Pr., The.

James, Brian. Eight Spinning Planets. Benfanti, Russell, illus. 2010. (ENG.). 16p. (J). (gr. k — 1). 12.99 *(978-0-545-23517-4(0)*, Cartwheel Bks.) Scholastic, Inc.

Jameson, Louise. Christmas in Gabba Land. Style Guide Staff, illus. 2009. (Yo Gabba Gabba! Ser.). (ENG.). 12p. (J). (gr. -1-k). bds. 7.99 *(978-1-4169-9167-0(0)*, Simon Spotlight) Simon Spotlight.

Jansson, Tove. Lift-the-Flap Hide & Seek. 2011. (Moomins Ser.). (ENG., Illus.). 24p. (J). (gr. -1 — 1). 8.99 *(978-0-374-35051-2(5)*, 9780374350512, Farrar, Straus & Giroux (BYR)) Farrar, Straus & Giroux.

—Moomin's Little Book of Words. 2011. (Moomins Ser.). (ENG., Illus.). 16p. (J). (gr. -1 — 1). 7.99 *(978-0-374-35048-2(5)*, 9780374350482, Farrar, Straus & Giroux (BYR)) Farrar, Straus & Giroux.

Jarvis, illus. Who Is Happy? 2016. (ENG.). 22p. (J). 16.99 *(978-1-84780-722-9(4)*, Frances Lincoln Children's Bks.) Quarto Publishing Group UK GBR. Dist: Littlehampton Bk Services, Ltd.

Jasper, Mark. Good Night Israel. Rosen, Anne, illus. 2010. (Good Night Our World Ser.). (ENG.). 24p. (J). (gr. k — 1). bds. 9.95 *(978-1-60219-043-6(7))* Good Night Bks.

Jasper, Mark & Gamble, Adam. Good Night Galaxy. Kelly, Cooper, illus. 2012. (Good Night Our World Ser.). (ENG.). 20p. (J). (gr. k — 1). bds. 9.95 *(978-1-60219-065-8(8))* Good Night Bks.

Jatkowska, Ag, illus. The Christmas Treasure Hunt. 2014. (ENG.). 10p. (J). (gr. -1-k). 15.99 *(978-0-230-76863-5(6))* Pan Macmillan GBR. Dist: Independent Pubs. Group.

Jenkins, Steve. The Animal Book: A Collection of the Fastest, Fiercest, Toughest, Cleverest, Shyest - And Most Surprising - Animals on Earth. Jenkins, Steve, illus. 2013. (ENG., Illus.). 208p. (J). (gr. 1-4). 24.99 *(978-0-547-55799-1(X))* Houghton Mifflin Harcourt Publishing Co.

Jennings, Sarah, illus. My Feelings. 2017. (ENG.). 14p. (J). bds. 9.99 *(978-1-68119-539-1(9)*, 9781681195391, Bloomsbury Activity Bks.) Bloomsbury Publishing USA.

Jewitt, Kathryn. 3D Theater: Oceans. Dogi, Fiametta, illus. 2011. (3D Theater Ser.). (ENG.). 20p. (J). (gr. -1-3). 19.99 *(978-0-7534-6466-3(7)*, 9780753464663, Kingfisher) Roaring Brook Pr.

Jewitt, Kathryn & Dogi, Fiametta. 3D Theater: Rainforest. 2011. (3D Theater Ser.). (ENG., Illus.). 20p. (J). (gr. -1-3). 19.99 *(978-0-7534-6467-0(5)*, 9780753464670, Kingfisher) Roaring Brook Pr.

Jiggly Giraffe Book & Soft Rattle. 2014. (Illus.). (J). *(978-1-4723-3976-8(2))* Parragon Bk. Service Ltd.

Jin, Susie Lee, illus. It's Bedtime for Little Monkeys. 2010. (ENG.). 5p. (J). bds. 5.99 *(978-0-7369-2832-8(4))* Harvest Hse. Pubs.

Jobling, Curtis. Old MacDonald Had a Zoo. McLaughlin, Tom, illus. 2014. (ENG.). 32p. (J). (gr. -1-k). pap. 10.99 *(978-1-4052-6712-0(7))* Egmont Bks., Ltd. GBR. Dist: Independent Pubs. Group.

Johnson, Crockett. Harold & the Purple Crayon Board Book. Johnson, Crockett, illus. 2015. (ENG., Illus.). 34p. (J). (gr. -1-3). bds. 7.99 *(978-0-06-208652-5(9)*, HarperFestival) HarperCollins Pubs.

—Harold & the Purple Crayon Lap Edition. Johnson, Crockett, illus. 2016. (Illus.). 34p. (J). (gr. -1 — 1). pap. 12.99 *(978-0-06-242730-4(X)*, HarperFestival) HarperCollins Pubs.

Johnson, Richard, illus. Three Little Pigs. (Flip-Up Fairy Tales Ser.). (ENG.). 24p. (J). 2007. (gr. -1-2). audio compact disk *(978-1-84643-087-9(9))* 2005. pap. *(978-1-904550-21-1(5))* Child's Play International Ltd.

Johnson, Shane, illus. OLIVIA Paints a Mural. 2011. (Olivia TV Tie-In Ser.). (ENG.). 12p. (J). (gr. -1-1). bds. 5.99 *(978-1-4424-1674-1(2)*, Simon Spotlight) Simon Spotlight.

Johnson, Shane L., illus. Princess for a Day: A Pop-Up Storybook. 2011. (Olivia TV Tie-In Ser.). (ENG.). 12p. (J). (gr. -1-1). 17.99 *(978-1-4424-3141-6(5)*, Simon Spotlight) Simon Spotlight.

Johnson, Stephen T. My Little Pink Princess Purse. Johnson, Stephen T., illus. 2010. (ENG., Illus.). 16p. (J). (gr. -1-3). 19.99 *(978-1-4169-7979-1(4)*, Simon & Schuster/Paula Wiseman Bks.) Simon & Schuster/Paula Wiseman Bks.

Jonah Bible Sticker Book. 2003. (Illus.). 16p. (J). 2.98 *(978-1-4054-1555-2(X))* Parragon, Inc.

Jonath, Leslie & Christy, Jana. In Your Dreams. (ENG.). (J). 2013. 14p. bds. 5.99 *(978-1-4494-2858-7(4))* 2011. (Illus.). 12p. 9.99 *(978-1-4494-0332-4(8))* Andrews McMeel Publishing.

Jones, Bryony. Very Tasty Vegetables. 2011. (ENG., Illus.). 14p. (J). (gr. -1-k). bds. *(978-1-84089-615-2(9))* Zero to Ten, Ltd.

Jones, Christianne C. Camping in Green, 1 vol. Ouren, Todd, illus. 2007. (Know Your Colors Ser.). (ENG.). 24p. (gr. -1-1). lib. bdg. 26.65 *(978-1-4048-3107-0(X)*, 1265677) Picture Window Bks.

—The Elf Boogie. Randall, Emma, illus. 2015. (Holiday Jingles Ser.). (ENG.). 20p. (gr. -1 — 1). bds. 5.99 *(978-1-4795-6493-4(1))* Picture Window Bks.

—The Reindeer Dance. Randall, Emma, illus. 2015. (Holiday Jingles Ser.). (ENG.). 20p. (gr. -1 — 1). bds. 5.99 *(978-1-4795-6496-5(6))* Picture Window Bks.

—The Santa Shimmy. Randall, Emma, illus. 2015. (Holiday Jingles Ser.). (ENG.). 20p. (gr. -1 — 1). bds. 5.99 *(978-1-4795-6494-1(X))* Picture Window Bks.

—The Snowman Shuffle. Randall, Emma, illus. 2015. (Holiday Jingles Ser.). (ENG.). 20p. (gr. -1 — 1). bds. 5.99 *(978-1-4795-6495-8(8))* Picture Window Bks.

Jones, Dennis, illus. Read with Me Bible for Little Ones, 1 vol. 2016. (ENG.). 32p. (J). bds. 9.99 *(978-0-310-75386-5(4))* Zonderkidz.

Jones, Francesca & Jones, Frankie. Where's the Pumpkin? Galloway, Fhiona, illus. 2015. (ENG.). 16p. (J). (gr. -1 — 1). bds. 5.99 *(978-1-4998-0097-5(5))* Little Bee Books Inc.

Jones, Frankie. Bedtime: Trace the Trails with Your Finger to Get to Bed! Galloway, Fhiona, illus. 2016. (ENG.). 10p. (J). (gr. -1 — 1). bds. 7.99 *(978-1-4998-0267-2(6))* Little Bee Books Inc.

—Counting. Max & Sid, Max &, illus. 2016. (What Can You Spot? Ser.). (ENG.). 18p. (J). (gr. -1 — 1). bds. 7.99 *(978-1-4998-0269-6(2))* Little Bee Books Inc.

—Faces: A Follow-the-Trail Book. Galloway, Fhiona, illus. 2016. (ENG.). 10p. (J). (gr. -1 — 1). bds. 7.99 *(978-1-4998-0268-9(4))* Little Bee Books Inc.

—Fall Is Here! Galloway, Fhiona, illus. 2015. (ENG.). 16p. (J). (gr. -1-k). bds. 5.99 *(978-1-4998-0110-1(6))* Little Bee Books Inc.

—In the Wild. 2015. (What Can You Spot? Ser.). (ENG., Illus.). 18p. (J). (gr. -1 — 1). bds. 6.99 *(978-1-4998-0055-5(X))* Little Bee Books Inc.

—Muddle & Match Jobs. Hinton, Stephanie, illus. 2016. 16p. (J). bds. 8.99 *(978-1-61067-491-1(X))* Kane Miller.

Jones, Karl. Day of the Dead Activity Book. Simpson, Steve, illus. 2013. (ENG.). 16p. (J). (gr. 1-4). 9.99 *(978-0-8431-7300-0(9)*, Price Stern Sloan) Penguin Young Readers Group.

Jones, Lara. All Aboard! 2015. (Poppy Cat Ser.). (ENG., Illus.). 18p. (J). (gr. -1-k). bds. 7.99 *(978-0-230-75400-3(7))* Pan Macmillan GBR. Dist: Independent Pubs. Group.

—Blast Off! 2015. (Poppy Cat Ser.). (ENG., Illus.). 18p. (J). (gr. -1-k). bds. 7.99 *(978-0-230-75399-0(X))* Pan Macmillan GBR. Dist: Independent Pubs. Group.

Jones, Rob Lloyd. Flip Flap Cars. 2010. (Flip Flap Board Bks). 14p. (J). (gr. 1). bds. 14.99 *(978-0-7945-2554-5(7)*, Usborne) EDC Publishing.

—Look Inside an Airport. rev. ed. 2012. (Look Inside Board Bks). 14p. (J). ring bd. 15.99 *(978-0-7945-3234-5(9)*, Usborne) EDC Publishing.

—Look Inside Space. 2012. (Look Inside Board Bks). 14p. (J). bds. 14.99 *(978-0-7945-3282-6(9)*, Usborne) EDC Publishing.

—See Inside Famous Buildings. Ablett, Barry, illus. 2009. (See Inside Board Bks). 16p. (J). (gr. 2). bds. 13.99 *(978-0-7945-2350-3(1)*, Usborne) EDC Publishing.

—See Inside the Second World War. Pritelli, Maria Cristina, illus. 2012. (See Inside Board Bks). 16p. (J). ring bd. 13.99 *(978-0-7945-3085-3(0)*, Usborne) EDC Publishing.

Jones, Sally Lloyd. Lift-the-Flap Bible. Moroney, Tracey, illus. 2011. (Lift-The-Flap Ser.). (ENG.). 20p. (J). (gr. -1-k). bds. 10.99 *(978-0-7944-2278-3(0)*, Reader's Digest Children's Bks.) Studio Fun International.

Jordan, Karen. On the Farm. Steuerwald, Joy, illus. 2015. (Highlights(tm) Find It! Padded Board Bks.). (ENG.). 14p. (J). (— 1). bds. 7.99 *(978-1-62979-413-6(9)*, Highlights) Boyds Mills Pr.

Joseph Bible Sticker Book. 2003. (Illus.). 16p. (J). 2.98 *(978-1-4054-1556-9(8))* Parragon, Inc.

Josephs, Mary. All Aboard Noah's Ark! Bratun, Katy, illus. 2007. (Chunky Book Ser.). (ENG.). 22p. (J). (— 1). bds. 3.99 *(978-0-679-86054-9(1)*, Golden Inspirational) Random Hse. Children's Bks.

Joyce, Bridget & Furman, Eric. Tonka Rescue Trucks! Dean Kleven Studios & Finley, Shawn, illus. 2007. (Fold & Go Vehicles Ser.). 15.98 *(978-1-4127-2981-9(5))* Publications International, Ltd.

J.s., Monroe-Daley. A Is for Arizona. 2009. (J). 14.95 *(978-1-934878-65-1(0))* Mascot Bks., Inc.

Jugran, Jan. Baby Dolphins. Larranaga, Ana Martin, illus. 2006. (ENG.). 6p. (J). (gr. -1 — 1). 14.99 *(978-1-58476-490-8(2)*, IKIDS) Innovative Kids.

—Goodnight Faces: A Book of Masks. Larranaga, Ana Martin, illus. 2007. (ENG.). 12p. (J). (gr. -1 — 1). bds. 6.99 *(978-1-58476-672-8(7)*, IKIDS) Innovative Kids.

—Hugs. Larranaga, Ana Martin, illus. 2007. (ENG.). 12p. (J). (gr. -1 — 1). 9.99 *(978-1-58476-620-9(4)*, IKIDS) Innovative Kids.

—Three Little Duckies. Parsons, Jackie & Larranaga, Ana Martin, illus. 2006. (ENG.). 6p. (J). (gr. -1 — 1). 14.99 *(978-1-58476-352-9(3)*, IKIDS) Innovative Kids.

Julian, Russell. Busy Dog. 2005. (Farm Board Book Ser.). (ENG., Illus.). 12p. (J). bds. 9.99 *(978-1-4052-1031-7(1))* Egmont Bks., Ltd. GBR. Dist: Trafalgar Square Publishing.

—Happy Cockerel. 2005. (Farm Board Book Ser.). (ENG., Illus.). 12p. (J). bds. 9.99 *(978-1-4052-1030-0(3))* Egmont Bks., Ltd. GBR. Dist: Trafalgar Square Publishing.

Jullien, Jean. Before & After. 2017. (ENG., Illus.). 40p. (gr. -1 — 1). bds. 12.95 ***(978-0-7148-7408-1(6))*** Phaidon Pr., Inc.

Jumbo's Jungle: Colors. 2011. (Illus.). (J). *(978-1-58865-893-7(7))* Kidsbooks, LLC.

Junor, Amy. My Giant Fold-Out Bright Bugs. 2014. (My Giant Fold-Outs Ser.). (ENG.). 10p. (J). (gr. -1 — 1). 6.99 *(978-0-7641-6668-6(9))* Barron's Educational Series, Inc.

—My Giant Fold-Out Wild Animals. 2014. (My Giant Fold-Outs Ser.). (ENG.). 10p. (J). (gr. -1 — 1). 6.99 *(978-0-7641-6669-3(7))* Barron's Educational Series, Inc.

Just for Boys. 2008. (Amazing Body Growing Up Ser.). 96p. *(978-1-4075-1570-0(5))* Parragon, Inc.

Kanzler, John. Rock-a -Bye Baby. Tiger Tales Staff, ed. Kanzler, John, illus. 2011. (ENG., Illus.). 24p. (J). (gr. -1-k). bds. 8.95 *(978-1-58925-853-2(3))* Tiger Tales.

Karr, Lily. Five Bouncing Bunnies. Rogers, Jacqueline, illus. 2013. (ENG.). 10p. (J). (gr. -1 — 1). bds. 6.99 *(978-0-545-45825-2(0)*, Cartwheel Bks.) Scholastic, Inc.

—Noah's Ark. Berg, Michelle, illus. 2007. (ENG.). 6p. (J). (gr. -1). bds. 12.99 *(978-0-439-86396-4(1))* Scholastic, Inc.

Kasso, Martin. Sharks. Jeffirs, Matt, illus. 2008. (ENG.). 24p. (J). (gr. 3-18). 19.95 *(978-1-58117-797-8(6)*, Intervisual/Piggy Toes) Bendon, Inc.

Kate, Maggie, ed. Glitter Roses Stickers. 2004. (Dover Stickers Ser.). (ENG., Illus.). 2p. (J). (gr. -1-5). 1.99 *(978-0-486-43534-3(2))* Dover Pubns., Inc.

Katschke, Judy. Shrek the Third. 2007. (Illus.). (J). *(978-0-696-23949-6(3))* Meredith Bks.

Katz, David. DC Super Heroes Colors, Shapes & More! 2012. (DC Super Heroes Ser.). (ENG.). 20p. (J). (gr. -1 — 1). bds. 9.99 *(978-1-935703-73-0(0))* Downtown Bookworks.

Katz, David Bar. My First Wonder Woman Book: Touch & Feel. 2011. (DC Super Heroes Ser.). (ENG.). 12p. (J). (gr. -1). bds. 11.99 *(978-1-935703-13-6(7))* Downtown Bookworks.

Katz, Julie & Merberg, Julie. Turn the Key: Who Do You See? McQueen, Lucinda, illus. 2011. (ENG.). 12p. (J). (gr. -1). bds. 11.99 *(978-1-935703-11-2(0))* Downtown Bookworks.

Katz, Karen. Baby at the Farm. Katz, Karen, illus. 2009. (ENG., Illus.). 12p. (J). (gr. -1 — 1). bds. 7.99 *(978-1-4169-8568-6(9)*, Little Simon) Little Simon.

—Baby Loves Fall! A Karen Katz Lift-The-Flap Book. Katz, Karen, illus. 2013. (ENG., Illus.). 14p. (J). (gr. -1 — 1). bds. 6.99 *(978-1-4424-5209-1(9)*, Little Simon) Little Simon.

—Baby Loves Spring! Katz, Karen, illus. 2012. (ENG., Illus.). 14p. (J). (gr. -1 — 1). bds. 6.99 *(978-1-4424-2745-7(0)*, Little Simon) Little Simon.

—Baby Loves Summer! Katz, Karen, illus. 2012. (ENG., Illus.). 14p. (J). (gr. -1 — 1). bds. 6.99 *(978-1-4424-2746-4(9)*, Little Simon) Little Simon.

—Baby Loves Winter! A Karen Katz Lift-The-Flap Book. Katz, Karen, illus. 2013. (ENG., Illus.). 14p. (J). (gr. -1 — 1). bds. 6.99 *(978-1-4424-5213-8(7)*, Little Simon) Little Simon.

—Baby's Colors. Katz, Karen, illus. 2010. (ENG., Illus.). 14p. (J). (gr. -1 — 1). bds. 6.99 *(978-1-4169-9821-1(7)*, Little Simon) Little Simon.

—Baby's Numbers. Katz, Karen, illus. 2010. (ENG., Illus.). 14p. (J). (gr. -1 — 1). bds. 5.99 *(978-1-4424-0627-8(8)*, Little Simon) Little Simon.

—Baby's Shapes. Katz, Karen, illus. 2010. (ENG., Illus.). 14p. (J). (gr. -1 — 1). bds. 7.99 *(978-1-4169-9824-2(1)*, Little Simon) Little Simon.

—Beddy-Bye, Baby. Katz, Karen, illus. 2009. (ENG., Illus.). 12p. (J). (gr. -1 — 1). bds. 7.99 *(978-1-4169-8048-3(2)*, Little Simon) Little Simon.

—Buzz, Buzz, Baby! Katz, Karen, illus. 2014. (ENG., Illus.). 14p. (J). (gr. -1 — 1). bds. 6.99 *(978-1-4424-9313-1(5)*, Little Simon) Little Simon.

—¡Cu-Cú, Bebé! Katz, Karen, illus. 2009. (SPA., Illus.). 14p. (J). (gr. -1 — 1). bds. 7.99 *(978-1-4169-7938-8(7)*, Libros Para Ninos) Libros Para Ninos.

—¿Dónde Está el Ombliguito? Ziegler, Argentina Palacios, tr. Katz, Karen, illus. 2004. (SPA., Illus.). 14p. (J). (gr. -1-1). bds. 6.99 *(978-0-689-86977-8(0)*, Libros Para Ninos) Libros Para Ninos.

—Grandpa & Me. Katz, Karen, illus. 2004. (ENG., Illus.). 14p. (J). (gr. -1-k). bds. 6.99 *(978-0-689-86644-9(5)*, Little Simon) Little Simon.

—How Does Baby Feel? A Karen Katz Lift-The-Flap Book. Katz, Karen, illus. 2013. (ENG., Illus.). 14p. (J). (gr. -1 — 1). bds. 6.99 *(978-1-4424-5204-6(8)*, Little Simon) Little Simon.

—I Can Share! 2011. (ENG.). 24p. (J). (gr. -1-k). mass mkt. 4.99 *(978-0-448-45592-1(7)*, Grosset & Dunlap) Penguin Young Readers Group.

—Kiss Baby's Boo-Boo. Katz, Karen, illus. 2016. (ENG., Illus.). 14p. (J). (gr. -1 — 1). bds. 6.99 *(978-1-4814-4208-4(2)*, Little Simon) Little Simon.

—Mommy Hugs: Lap Edition. Katz, Karen, illus. 2010. (ENG., Illus.). 26p. (J). (gr. -1 — 1). bds. 12.99 *(978-1-4424-0791-6(3)*, Little Simon) Little Simon.

—My Big Boy Undies. 2012. (ENG.). 14p. (J). (gr. -1-k). bds. 7.99 *(978-0-448-45705-5(9)*, Grosset & Dunlap) Penguin Young Readers Group.

—My Big Girl Undies. 2012. (ENG.). 14p. (J). (gr. -1-k). bds. 7.99 *(978-0-448-45703-1(2)*, Grosset & Dunlap) Penguin Young Readers Group.

—No Biting! 2011. (ENG.). 24p. (J). (gr. -1-k). mass mkt. 4.99 *(978-0-448-45581-5(1)*, Grosset & Dunlap) Penguin Young Readers Group.

—No Hitting! 2011. (ENG.). 24p. (J). (gr. -1-k). mass mkt. 4.99 *(978-0-448-45596-9(X)*, Grosset & Dunlap) Penguin Young Readers Group.

—No Hitting! Katz, Karen, illus. 2004. (ENG., Illus.). 14p. (J). (gr. -1-k). 5.99 *(978-0-448-43612-8(4)*, Grosset & Dunlap) Penguin Young Readers Group.

—Peek-a-Baby. Katz, Karen, illus. (ENG., Illus.). 14p. (J). (gr. -1 — 1). 2010. 11.99 *(978-1-4424-0790-9(5))* 2007. bds. 6.99 *(978-1-4169-3622-0(X))* Little Simon. (Little Simon).

—Princess Baby. Katz, Karen, illus. 2012. (Princess Baby Ser.). (ENG., Illus.). 30p. (J). (gr. k-k). bds. 7.99 *(978-0-307-93146-7(3)*, Schwartz & Wade Bks.) Random Hse. Children's Bks.

—Princess Baby, Night-Night. Katz, Karen, illus. 2014. (Princess Baby Ser.). (ENG., Illus.). 28p. (J). (— 1). bds. 7.99 *(978-0-385-37848-2(3)*, Schwartz & Wade Bks.) Random Hse. Children's Bks.

—Roar, Roar, Baby! Katz, Karen, illus. 2015. (ENG., Illus.). 14p. (J). (gr. -1 — 1). bds. 6.99 *(978-1-4814-1788-4(6)*, Little Simon) Little Simon.

—Shake It up, Baby! Katz, Karen, illus. 2009. (ENG., Illus.). 14p. (J). (gr. -1 — 1). bds. 7.99 *(978-1-4169-6737-8(0)*, Little Simon) Little Simon.

—Splish, Splash, Baby! Katz, Karen, illus. 2015. (ENG., Illus.). 14p. (J). (gr. -1 — 1). bds. 6.99 *(978-1-4814-1789-1(4)*, Little Simon) Little Simon.

—Ten Tiny Babies. Katz, Karen, illus. 2011. (Classic Board Bks.). (ENG., Illus.). 32p. (J). (gr. -1-k). bds. 7.99 *(978-1-4424-1394-8(8)*, Little Simon) Little Simon.

—Ten Tiny Tickles. Katz, Karen, illus. 2008. (Classic Board Bks.). (ACE & ENG., Illus.). 32p. (J). (gr. -1-k). bds. 7.99 *(978-1-4169-5101-8(6)*, Little Simon) Little Simon.

—Vroom, Vroom, Trucks! Katz, Karen, illus. 2016. (ENG., Illus.). 14p. (J). (gr. -1 — 1). bds. 6.99 *(978-1-4814-4209-1(0)*, Little Simon) Little Simon.

—Where Is Baby's Beach Ball? Katz, Karen, illus. 2009. (ENG., Illus.). 14p. (J). (gr. -1 — 1). bds. 6.99 *(978-1-4169-4962-6(3)*, Little Simon) Little Simon.

—Where Is Baby's Belly Button? Katz, Karen, illus. anniv. ed. 2009. (ENG., Illus.). 14p. (J). (gr. -1 — 1). bds. 12.99 *(978-1-4169-8733-8(9)*, Little Simon) Little Simon.

—Where Is Baby's Belly Button? 2005. (CHI.). 12p. (J). 6.95 *(978-986-7517-72-2(5))* Shan Jen Publishing Co., Ltd. TWN. Dist: Chinasprout, Inc.

—Where Is Baby's Birthday Cake? Katz, Karen, illus. 2008. (ENG., Illus.). 14p. (J). (gr. -1 — 1). bds. 6.99 *(978-1-4169-5817-8(7)*, Little Simon) Little Simon.

—Where Is Baby's Christmas Present? Katz, Karen, illus. 2009. (ENG., Illus.). 14p. (J). (gr. -1 — 1). bds. 7.99 *(978-1-4169-7145-0(9)*, Little Simon) Little Simon.

—Where Is Baby's Puppy? Katz, Karen, illus. 2011. (ENG., Illus.). 14p. (J). (gr. -1 — 1). bds. 6.99 *(978-1-4169-8684-3(7)*, Little Simon) Little Simon.

—Where Is Baby's Valentine? Katz, Karen, illus. 2006. (ENG., Illus.). 14p. (J). (gr. -1 — 1). bds. 7.99 *(978-1-4169-0971-2(0)*, Little Simon) Little Simon.

—Where Is Baby's Yummy Tummy? Katz, Karen, illus. 2011. (ENG., Illus.). 14p. (J). (gr. -1 — 1). bds. 6.99 *(978-1-4424-2165-3(7)*, Little Simon) Little Simon.

—Wiggle Your Toes: A Karen Katz Book to Pull, Fluff, & Wiggle. Katz, Karen, illus. 2006. (ENG., Illus.). 14p. (J). (gr. -1-k). bds. 11.99 *(978-1-4169-0365-9(8)*, Little Simon) Little Simon.

—Zoom, Zoom, Baby! A Karen Katz Lift-The-Flap Book. Katz, Karen, illus. 2014. (ENG., Illus.). 14p. (J). (gr. -1 — 1). bds. 6.99 *(978-1-4424-9314-8(3)*, Little Simon) Little Simon.

Katz, Karen & Bauer, Marion Dane. Baby's Box of Fun! A Karen Katz Lift-the-Flap Gift Set - Where Is Baby's Bellybutton? - Where Is Baby's Mommy? - Toes, Ears, & Nose! Katz, Karen, illus. gif. ed. 2004. (ENG., Illus.). 44p. (J). (gr. -1 — 1). bds. 17.99 *(978-0-689-03862-4(3)*, Little Simon) Little Simon.

Kavanaugh, Missy & Gurman, Sarah, texts. Puppies. 2009. (Illus.). 8p. (J). **(978-1-4351-1783-9(2))** Barnes & Noble, Inc.

Kavanaugh, Missy & Gurman, Sarah, texts. Sea Creatures. 2009. (Illus.). (J). *(978-1-4351-1785-3(9))* Barnes & Noble, Inc.

Kawamura, Yayo. A Day with Pepe & Milli. Kawamura, Yayo, illus. 2017. (Pepe & Millie Ser.). (ENG., Illus.). 16p. (J). (gr. -1 — 1). bds. 9.99 **(978-0-8075-6481-3(8))** Whitman, Albert & Co.

Keast, Jennifer H. Dora the Explorer (Giant First Play-a-Sound) 2010. 10p. (J). bds. 17.98 *(978-1-60553-544-9(3))* Publications International, Ltd.

—Mickey Mouse Clubhouse (Giant First Play-a-Sound) 2010. 10p. (J). bds. 17.98 *(978-1-60553-545-6(1))* Phoenix International Publications, Inc.

Keith, Donna. I Love You Even When, 1 vol. Edgson, Allison, illus. 2015. (ENG.). 20p. (J). bds. 9.99 *(978-0-7180-3644-7(1))* Nelson, Thomas Inc.

Kelly, Cooper, et al. Good Night Christmas. 2015. (Good Night Our World Ser.). (ENG., Illus.). 20p. (J). (— 1). bds. 9.95 *(978-1-60219-197-6(2))* Good Night Bks.

Kelman, Marcy & Disney Book Group Staff. Hoppy Clubhouse Easter. Disney Storybook Art Team, illus. 2011. (ENG.). 12p. (J). (gr. -1-k). bds. 6.99 *(978-1-4231-3910-2(0))* Disney Pr.

Kenison, Misti, illus. Egypt - The Tiny Traveler: A Book of Shapes. 2015. (ENG.). 24p. (J). (— 1). bds. 5.95 *(978-1-62914-607-2(2)*, Sky Pony Pr.) Skyhorse Publishing Co., Inc.

—France - The Tiny Traveler: A Book of Colors. 2015. (ENG.). 24p. (J). (— 1). bds. 5.95 *(978-1-62914-609-6(9)*, Sky Pony Pr.) Skyhorse Publishing Co., Inc.

Kennedy, Jimmy. The Teddy Bears' Picnic. Day, Alexandra, illus. 2015. (Classic Board Bks.). (ENG.). 34p. (J). (gr. -1-k). bds. 7.99 *(978-1-4814-2274-1(X)*, Little Simon) Little Simon.

Kennelly, Sean & Carpenter, Dan. Amazing America: An Adventure into American History. Gilman, Thomas W. & Paiva, Johannah Gilman, eds. 2014. (ENG., Illus.). 48p. (J). (gr. 4). 8.99 *(978-1-4867-0255-8(4))* Flowerpot Children's Pr. Inc. CAN. Dist: Cardinal Pubs. Group.

Kenney, Sean. Amazing ABC: An Alphabet Book of Lego Creations. Kenney, Sean, illus. 2012. (ENG., Illus.). 30p. (J). (gr. -1-k). bds. 7.99 *(978-0-8050-9464-0(4)*, 9780805094640, Holt, Henry & Co. Bks. For Young Readers) Holt, Henry & Co.

Kent, Lorna, illus. Baby's First Board Books: On the Move; Animals; My Home; Playtime. 2004. (Baby's First Board Books Gift Set Ser.). 12p. (J). bds. 12.99 *(978-1-85854-694-0(X))* Brimax Books Ltd. GBR. Dist: Byeway Bks.

Kerley, Barbara. Portland Baby. Cleland, Josh, illus. 2017. (Local Baby Ser.). (ENG.). 22p. (J). (gr. -1-k). bds. 8.95 **(978-1-946064-05-9(X))** Duo Pr. LLC.

Kertell, Lynn Maslen. Alphabet. Maslen, John R. & Hendra, Sue, illus. 2008. (Bob Bks.). (ENG.). 144p. (J). (gr. -1-3). pap. 16.99 *(978-0-545-01921-7(4)*, Cartwheel Bks.) Scholastic, Inc.

Khan, Sarah. Pets Lift-the-Flap. 2005. (Luxury Lift-the-Flap Learners Ser.). 16p. (J). (gr. 1-18). 11.95 *(978-0-7945-0914-9(2)*, Usborne) EDC Publishing.

Kiely, Orla. Colors. Kiely, Orla, illus. 2012. (ENG., Illus.). 20p. (J). (gr. -1 — 1). bds. 12.99 *(978-0-8050-9491-6(1)*, 9780805094916, Holt, Henry & Co. Bks. For Young Readers) Holt, Henry & Co.

—Numbers. Kiely, Orla, illus. 2012. (ENG., Illus.). 20p. (J). (gr. -1 — 1). bds. 12.99 *(978-0-8050-9492-3(X)*, 9780805094923, Holt, Henry & Co. Bks. For Young Readers) Holt, Henry & Co.

Killen, Nicola. Animal Opposites. 2014. (Nicola Killen Animals Ser.). (ENG., Illus.). 10p. (J). (— 1). bds. 9.99 *(978-1-4052-6286-6(9))* Egmont Bks., Ltd. GBR. Dist: Independent Pubs. Group.

—Things That Go. 2014. (My Pop-Up World Ser.). (ENG., Illus.). 14p. (J). (gr. -1). 12.99 *(978-1-4052-6861-5(1))* Egmont Bks., Ltd. GBR. Dist: Independent Pubs. Group.

Kilpatrick, Irene. Foofa's Happy Book. (Yo Gabba Gabba! Ser.). (ENG.). 12p. (J). (gr. -1-1). 2012. bds. 5.99 *(978-1-4424-5444-6(X))* 2009. bds. 6.99 *(978-1-4169-7855-8(0))* Simon Spotlight. (Simon Spotlight).

—Welcome to Gabba Land! 2009. (Yo Gabba Gabba! Ser.). (ENG.). 14p. (J). (gr. -1-k). 8.99 *(978-1-4169-7096-5(7)*, Simon Spotlight) Simon Spotlight.

Kim, Melissa. A Little Brown Bat Story, 1 vol. Fitch, Jada, illus. 2015. (ENG.). 24p. (J). bds. 10.95 *(978-1-939017-70-3(X)*, 7f78678a-9b76-46c9-94f1-ff6d96df81bf) Islandport Pr., Inc.

Kimmelman, Leslie. Do You Know Noses? 2016. (Rookie Toddler(tm) Ser.). (ENG., Illus.). 12p. (J). bds. 6.95 *(978-0-531-22618-6(2)*, Children's Pr.) Scholastic Library Publishing.

Kingfisher Editors. Baby Animals in the Forest. 2011. (Baby Animals Ser.). (ENG., Illus.). 14p. (J). (gr. -1-k). bds. 5.99 *(978-0-7534-6566-0(3)*, 9780753465660, Kingfisher) Roaring Brook Pr.

—Baby Animals in the Jungle. 2011. (Baby Animals Ser.). (ENG., Illus.). 14p. (J). (gr. -1-k). bds. 5.99 *(978-0-7534-6491-5(8)*, 9780753464915, Kingfisher) Roaring Brook Pr.

—In Grasslands. 2011. (Baby Animals Ser.). (ENG., Illus.). 14p. (J). (gr. -1-k). bds. 5.99 *(978-0-7534-6492-2(6)*, 9780753464922, Kingfisher) Roaring Brook Pr.

—Who's That? Eating. 2013. (Who's That? Ser.). (ENG.). 14p. (J). (gr. -1-k). bds. 5.99 *(978-0-7534-7070-1(5)*, 9780753470701, Kingfisher) Roaring Brook Pr.

—Who's That? Jumping. 2013. (Who's That? Ser.). (ENG., Illus.). 14p. (J). (gr. -1-k). bds. 5.99 *(978-0-7534-6971-2(5)*, 9780753469712, Kingfisher) Roaring Brook Pr.

—Who's That? Roaring. 2013. (Who's That? Ser.). (ENG., Illus.). 14p. (J). (gr. -1-k). bds. 5.99 *(978-0-7534-6970-5(7)*, 9780753469705, Kingfisher) Roaring Brook Pr.

Kingfisher Editors, ed. Puzzling Puzzles: What Shape Is This? Book + 2004. (J). pap. 7.95 *(978-0-7534-5644-6(3))* Kingfisher Bks.

Kirk, Daniel. Honk Honk! Beep Beep! Kirk, Daniel, illus. 2014. (ENG., Illus.). 32p. (J). (gr. -1-k). bds. 6.99 *(978-1-4231-8041-8(0))* Hyperion Bks. for Children.

Kirkova, Milena & Hannigan, Paula. When I'm Big. 2010. (ENG.). 12p. (J). (gr. -1-1). bds. 14.99 *(978-0-7407-9727-9(1))* Andrews McMeel Publishing.

Kirwan, Wednesday. Baby Loves to Boogie! Kirwan, Wednesday, illus. 2014. (ENG., Illus.). 30p. (J). (gr. -1 — 1). bds. 5.99 *(978-1-4814-0383-2(4)*, Little Simon) Little Simon.

—Baby Loves to Rock! Kirwan, Wednesday, illus. 2013. (ENG., Illus.). 28p. (J). (gr. -1 — 1). bds. 5.99 *(978-1-4424-5989-2(1)*, Little Simon) Little Simon.

—Baby Loves to Rock! & Baby Loves to Boogie! 2-Pack. Kirwan, Wednesday, illus. 2014. (ENG., Illus.). 58p. (J). (gr. -1 — 1). bds. 11.98 *(978-1-4814-2924-5(8)*, Little Simon) Little Simon.

Klausmeier, Jesse. Open This Little Book. Lee, Suzy, illus. 2013. (ENG.). 40p. (J). (gr. -1-3). 16.99 *(978-0-8118-6783-2(8))* Chronicle Bks. LLC.

Kleinberg, Naomi. Elmo's Book of Friends (Sesame Street) 2016. (ENG., Illus.). 16p. (J). (-k). bds. 7.99 *(978-0-399-55211-3(1)*, Random Hse. Bks. for Young Readers) Random Hse. Children's Bks.

—Elmo's Christmas Snowman (Sesame Street) Brannon, Tom, illus. 2013. (ENG.). 12p. (J). (— 1). bds. 6.99 *(978-0-449-81257-0(X)*, Random Hse. Bks. for Young Readers) Random Hse. Children's Bks.

Klutz Editors, ed. Little Letters, Set. 2006. (Chicken Socks Ser.). (ENG., Illus.). 14p. (J). (gr. -1-3). 9.95 *(978-1-59174-244-9(7)*, Chicken Socks) Klutz.

Kneen, Maggie. The First Christmas: An Angel Came to Nazareth. 2010. (ENG., Illus.). 24p. (J). (gr. -1-1). 9.99 *(978-0-8118-7662-9(4))* Chronicle Bks. LLC.

Knowlton, Laurie Lazzaro. My Valentine for Jesus, 1 vol. Erdogan, Buket, illus. 2009. (ENG.). 10p. (J). bds. 4.99 *(978-0-310-71333-3(1))* Zonderkidz.

Kober, Shahar, illus. Dreidel, Dreidel, Dreidel. 2014. (ENG.). 12p. (J). (gr. -1 — 1). bds. 4.99 *(978-0-545-53364-5(3)*, Cartwheel Bks.) Scholastic, Inc.

Koeppel, Ruth. In the Wild. McBee, Scott, illus. 2009. (ENG.). 10p. (J). (gr. -1-1). 15.99 *(978-1-58476-816-6(9))* Innovative Kids.

Kolanovic, Dubravka. Wipe-Clean Colours. Kolanovic, Dubravka, illus. 2009. (Honey Hill Ser.). (ENG., Illus.). 12p. (J). (gr. -1-k). bds. 9.99 *(978-0-230-70915-7(X))* Macmillan Pubs., Ltd. GBR. Dist: Independent Pubs. Group.

Korman, Justine. The Poky Little Puppy's First Christmas. Korman, Justine, illus. 2014. (Little Golden Board Book Ser.). (ENG., Illus.). 26p. (J). (-k). bds. 7.99 *(978-0-385-38473-5(4)*, Golden Bks.) Random Hse. Children's Bks.

Korngold, Jamie S. Mazel Tov! It's a Boy: Mazel Tov! It's a Girl. Finkelstein, Jeff, illus. Finkelstein, Jeff, photos by. 2015. (J). 6.99 *(978-1-4677-6206-9(7)*, Kar-Ben Publishing) Lerner Publishing Group.

Kovacs, Victoria. Elijah/John the Baptist Flip-Over Book. Ryley, David, illus. 2016. (Little Bible Heroes(tm) Ser.). (ENG.). 32p. (J). (gr. k-2). pap. 3.99 *(978-1-4336-4324-8(3)*, B&H Kids) B&H Publishing Group.

—The Little Giver/Zacchaeus Flip-Over Book. Ryley, David, illus. 2016. (Little Bible Heroes(tm) Ser.). (ENG.). 32p. (J). (gr. k-2). pap. 3.99 *(978-1-4336-4326-2(X)*, B&H Kids) B&H Publishing Group.

—Peter/Paul Flip-Over Book. Ryley, David, illus. 2016. (Little Bible Heroes(tm) Ser.). (ENG.). 32p. (J). (gr. k-2). pap. 3.99 *(978-1-4336-4327-9(8)*, B&H Kids) B&H Publishing Group.

Kraft, Ellen Christiansen. Fiesta! Stickers. 2011. (Dover Little Activity Books Stickers Ser.). (ENG.). 4p. (J). (gr. -1-5). pap. 1.50 *(978-0-486-48120-3(4))* Dover Pubns., Inc.

Krensky, Stephen. Now I Am Big! Gillingham, Sara, illus. 2012. (Empowerment Ser.). (ENG.). 12p. (J). (gr. -1 — 1). bds. 6.95 *(978-1-4197-0416-1(8)*, Abrams Appleseed) Abrams, Inc.

—What Do You See? A Lift-the-Flap Book about Endangered Animals. Schimler, Amy, illus. 2009. (Little Green Bks.). (ENG.). 16p. (J). (gr. -1-k). 6.99 *(978-1-4169-7123-8(8)*, Little Simon) Little Simon.

Krinsky, Rivkah. Touch of Shabbat: A Touch & Feel Book. Becker, Boruch, illus. 2011. (J). bds. 9.95 *(978-0-8266-0019-6(0))* Kehot Pubn. Society.

Kroll, Steven. The Biggest Pumpkin Surprise Ever. Bassett, Jeni, illus. 2012. (ENG.). 10p. (J). (gr. -1-k). bds. 6.99 *(978-0-545-40285-9(9)*, Cartwheel Bks.) Scholastic, Inc.

Krutop, Lee, creator. Go Out to Play. 2008. (Illus.). 10p. (J). (gr. -1-1). bds. *(978-1-74178-572-2(3))* Brimax Books Ltd.

Kubler, Annie. Dinosaur Diner. 2008. (Finger Puppet Bks.). (ENG., Illus.). 24p. (J). (gr. -1-1). *(978-1-84643-183-8(2))* Child's Play International Ltd.

—See You Later, Alligator! 2004. (Finger Puppet Bks.). (ENG., Illus.). 24p. (J). (gr. 1-2). *(978-1-904550-05-1(3))* Child's Play International Ltd.

Kubler, Annie, illus. Dress Up! 2012. (Mix & Match Babies Ser.). (ENG.). 12p. (J). bds. *(978-1-84643-485-3(8))* Child's Play International Ltd.

—Head, Shoulders, Knees & Toes.../Cabeza, Hombros, Piernas, Pies... 2009. (Baby Board Bks.). (SPA & ENG.). 12p. (J). bds. *(978-1-84643-311-5(8))* Child's Play International Ltd.

—Ride On! 2012. (Mix & Match Babies Ser.). (ENG.). 12p. (J). bds. *(978-1-84643-483-9(1))* Child's Play International Ltd.

—What Can I Feel? 2011. (Small Senses Ser.). (ENG.). 12p. (J). bds. *(978-1-84643-374-0(6))* Child's Play International Ltd.

—What Can I Hear? 2011. (Small Senses Ser.). (ENG.). 12p. (J). bds. *(978-1-84643-377-1(0))* Child's Play International Ltd.

—What Can I See? 2011. (Small Senses Ser.). (ENG.). 12p. (J). bds. *(978-1-84643-378-8(9))* Child's Play International Ltd.

—What Can I Smell? 2011. (Small Senses Ser.). (ENG.). 12p. (J). bds. *(978-1-84643-376-4(2))* Child's Play International Ltd.

—What Can I Taste? 2011. (Small Senses Ser.). (ENG.). 12p. (J). bds. *(978-1-84643-375-7(4))* Child's Play International Ltd.

—Work Out! 2012. (Mix & Match Babies Ser.). (ENG.). 12p. (J). bds. *(978-1-84643-484-6(X))* Child's Play International Ltd.

Kumon. What Does Baby See? 2008. (Illus.). 12p. (J). bds. *(978-1-934618-27-1(6))* Begin Smart LLC.

Kunhardt, Dorothy. Pat the Bunny. Golden Books Staff, illus. collector's deluxe ed. 2011. (Touch-And-Feel Ser.). (ENG.). 24p. (J). (gr. -1-2). 14.99 *(978-0-307-20047-1(7)*, Golden Bks.) Random Hse. Children's Bks.

—Pat the Bunny: First Books for Baby, 3 vols. 2015. (Touch-And-Feel Ser.). (ENG., Illus.). 20p. (J). (— 1). pap. 29.99 *(978-0-553-50838-3(5)*, Golden Bks.) Random Hse. Children's Bks.

Kurtz, John, illus. Disney Princess: Look & Find. 2004. (Disney Princess Ser.). 24p. (J). 7.98 *(978-0-7853-7918-8(5)*, 7179200) Phoenix International Publications, Inc.

Kwiat, Ernie, illus. Sesame Street Boo! Guess Who, Elmo! 2015. (Guess Who! Book Ser.). (ENG.). 10p. (J). (gr. -1-k). bds. 10.99 *(978-0-7944-3475-5(4))* Reader's Digest Assn., Inc., The.

La Coccinella. Here Comes Leo Lion. 2015. (Pull & Play Ser.). (ENG., Illus.). 12p. (J). (gr. -1-k). bds. 7.95 *(978-1-4549-1582-9(X))* Sterling Publishing Co., Inc.

—Little Star. 2014. (Look & See! Ser.). (ENG., Illus.). 24p. (J). (gr. -1 — 1). bds. 6.95 *(978-1-4549-0599-8(9))* Sterling Publishing Co., Inc.

—Look & See: Mommy, Where Are You? 2014. (Look & See! Ser.). (ENG., Illus.). 24p. (J). (gr. -1 — 1). bds. 6.95 *(978-1-4549-0615-5(4))* Sterling Publishing Co., Inc.

—Look & See: Wheels on the Go! 2008. (Look & See! Ser.). (ENG., Illus.). 24p. (J). (gr. -1-1). bds. 6.95 *(978-1-4027-5826-3(X))* Sterling Publishing Co., Inc.

—Look at Me. 2015. (Peekaboo! Ser.). (ENG., Illus.). 26p. (J). (gr. -1-k). bds. 6.95 *(978-1-4549-1584-3(6))* Sterling Publishing Co., Inc.

Lacey, Minna. Look Inside Science. 2011. (Look Inside Board Bks). 13p. (J). ring bd. 15.99 *(978-0-7945-2946-8(1)*, Usborne) EDC Publishing.

Laden, Nina. Peek-A Boo! 2015. (ENG., Illus.). 22p. (J). (gr. -1 — 1). bds. 6.99 *(978-1-4521-3396-6(4))* Chronicle Bks. LLC.

—Peek-A Choo-Choo! 2016. (ENG., Illus.). 22p. (J). (gr. -1 — 1). bds. 6.99 *(978-1-4521-5473-2(2))* Chronicle Bks. LLC.

—Peek-A Moo! 2017. (ENG., Illus.). 22p. (J). (gr. -1 — 1). bds. 6.99 **(978-1-4521-5474-9(0))** Chronicle Bks. LLC.

—Peek-A Zoo! 2014. (ENG., Illus.). 22p. (J). (gr. -1 — 1). bds. 6.99 *(978-1-4521-1175-9(8))* Chronicle Bks. LLC.

—Who Loves You, Baby? 2007. (ENG., Illus.). 18p. (J). (gr. -1 — 1). bds. 6.95 *(978-0-8118-5724-6(7))* Chronicle Bks. LLC.

Ladybird. On the Farm. 2016. (Read It Yourself with Ladybird Ser.). (ENG., Illus.). 32p. (J). (gr. 2-4). 5.99 *(978-0-241-23731-1(9))* Penguin Bks., Ltd. GBR. Dist: Independent Pubs. Group.

Lake Press Ltd. Baby Friends. 2016. (Little Grabbers Ser.). (ENG., Illus.). 6p. (J). (gr. -1 — 1). bds. 5.99 *(978-0-7641-6833-8(9))* Barron's Educational Series, Inc.

—Farm Friends. 2016. (Little Grabbers Ser.). (ENG., Illus.). 6p. (J). (gr. -1 — 1). bds. 5.99 *(978-0-7641-6834-5(7))* Barron's Educational Series, Inc.

—Fun at Home. 2016. (Little Grabbers Ser.). (ENG., Illus.). 6p. (J). (gr. -1 — 1). bds. 5.99 *(978-0-7641-6835-2(5))* Barron's Educational Series, Inc.

—Hug Me Tight. 2016. (ENG., Illus.). 10p. (J). (gr. -1 — 1). bds. 6.99 *(978-0-7641-6838-3(X))* Barron's Educational Series, Inc.

Lamb, Anne. Beat Bugs: Rain. 2017. (Beat Bugs Ser.). 16p. (J). (gr. -1 — 1). bds. 6.99 *(978-0-06-264073-4(9)*, HarperFestival) HarperCollins Pubs.

Lamb, Stacey, illus. Wipe-Clean Doodles. 2013. (Wipe-Clean Bks). 20p. (J). pap. 7.99 *(978-0-7945-3312-0(4)*, Usborne) EDC Publishing.

—123 Sticker Book. 2009. (Sticker Bks). 24p. (J). pap. 6.99 *(978-0-7945-2361-9(7)*, Usborne) EDC Publishing.

Lambert, Lydia. Scrub-A-Dub Gingerbread Man: Splash & Play with Gingerbread Man. Jones, Anna, illus. 2016. (Scrub-A-Dub Bath Mitt & Bath Book Sets Ser.). (ENG.). 8p. (J). (gr. -1 — 1). 9.99 *(978-1-4380-7741-3(6))* Barron's Educational Series, Inc.

Lamere, Jill. Upside Down. Lamere, Jill, illus. 2005. (Illus.). (J). bds. 12.95 *(978-0-9772320-0-0(X))* Minikin Pr.

Land of Milk & Honey, 2 vols. 2008. (LMH Ser.). (Illus.). (J). Bk. 5. bds. 6.99 *(978-0-7814-4529-0(9))*Bk. 6. bds. 6.99 *(978-0-7814-4530-6(2))* Cook, David C.

Landers, Ace. Lego Star Wars: The Yoda Chronicles Trilogy. 2014. (LEGO Star Wars Chapter Bks.). lib. bdg. 18.40 *(978-0-606-35414-1(X))* Turtleback Bks.

Landers, Ace & Cartwheel Editors. I Am a Garbage Truck. Scholastic, Inc. Staff, ed. 2008. (ENG.). 8p. (J). (gr. -1 — 1). bds. 4.99 *(978-0-545-07963-1(2)*, Cartwheel Bks.) Scholastic, Inc.

TUV

Landers, Ace & Doodle Pictures Studio Staff. Save the Galaxy! Hyland, Greg, illus. 2011. (Lego Star Wars Ser.). (ENG.). 7p. (J). (gr. -1-3). bds. 9.99 (978-0-545-30101-5(7)) Scholastic, Inc.

Landwehr, Neil. Listen & Learn with Love. 2016. (ENG., Illus.). 26p. (J). pap. 7.99 (978-1-61984-465-0(6), BlogIntoBook.com) Price World Publishing.

Langen, Annette. Letters from Felix: A Little Rabbit on a World Tour. Droop, Constanza, illus. 2003. 47p. (J). 14.99 (978-1-59384-034-1(9)) Parklane Publishing.

Langlois, Florence. The Extraordinary Gift. Goodman, John, tr. from FRE. Langlois, Florence, illus. 2005. (Illus.). 48p. (J). (gr. -1-2). reprint ed. 15.00 (978-0-7567-8942-8(7)) DIANE Publishing Co.

LaPadula, Thomas, illus. My Giant Tractor. 2014. (ENG.). 12p. (J). (gr. -1 — 1). bds. 10.99 (978-0-7944-3012-2(0), Reader's Digest Children's Bks.) Studio Fun International.

Larkin, Susan. All the Ways I Love You. Trotter, Stuart, illus. 2012. 16p. (J). (978-1-4351-3857-5(0)) Barnes & Noble, Inc.

Larranaga, Ana M. Noisy Home. 2014. (Rattle Buggy Buddies Ser.). (ENG., Illus.). 10p. (J). (— 1). bds. 7.99 (978-1-4472-6798-0(2)) Pan Macmillan GBR. Dist: Independent Pubs. Group.

—Pull & Play - Opposites. Martín, Ana I., illus. 2013. (Pull & Play Ser.). (ENG.). 10p. (J). (— 1). bds. 7.99 (978-0-230-75040-1(0)) Pan Macmillan GBR. Dist: Independent Pubs. Group.

Larranaga, Ana Martin. Noisy Home. Larranaga, Ana Martin, illus. 2011. (Rattle Buggy Buddies Ser.). (ENG., Illus.). 12p. (J). (gr. k — 1). bds. 7.99 (978-0-230-70621-7(5)) Macmillan Pubs., Ltd. GBR. Dist: Independent Pubs. Group.

Larranaga, Ana Martin, illus. Counting. 2013. (Pull & Play Ser.). (ENG.). 10p. (J). (— 1). bds. 7.99 (978-0-230-75038-8(9)) Pan Macmillan GBR. Dist: Independent Pubs. Group.

Larrañaga, Martin & Innovative Kids Staff. I Love You, Little One. 2009. (ENG., Illus.). 12p. (J). (gr. -1 — 1). bds. 9.99 (978-1-58476-791-6(X)) Innovative Kids.

Larsen, Carolyn. My 123 Bible Storybook. Turk, Caron, illus. 2008. (My Bible Storybooks Ser.). 30p. (J). (gr. -1-3). bds. (978-1-86920-925-4(7)) Christian Art Pubs.

—My ABC Bible Storybook. Turk, Caron, illus. 2008. (My Bible Storybooks Ser.). 30p. (J). (gr. -1-3). bds. (978-1-86920-926-1(5)) Christian Art Pubs.

Larson, Beverly. Toca y Siente las Historias de la Biblia. Pineda, Nancy, tr. Dillard, Sarah, illus. 2003. (Touch & Feel Ser.). (SPA.). (J). (gr. -1-k). bds. 8.99 (978-0-7899-1088-2(8)) Editorial Unilit.

Lathey, Nicola & Blake, Tracey. Small Talk/Going to the Park Board Book: A First Experience Book for Babies. Busby, Ailie, illus. 2016. (ENG.). 24p. (J). (— 1). bds. 10.99 **(978-1-4472-7693-7(0))** Pan Macmillan GBR. Dist: Independent Pubs. Group.

—Small Talk/It's Bedtime Board Book. Busby, Ailie, illus. 2016. (ENG.). 24p. (J). bds., bds. 11.99 **(978-1-4472-7692-0(2))** Pan Macmillan GBR. Dist: Independent Pubs. Group.

Latimer, Mariam. Choose to Reuse. 2009. (Touch & Feel Ser.). (ENG.). 10p. (J). (gr. -1). 7.95 (978-1-58117-869-2(7), Intervisual/Piggy Toes) Bendon, Inc.

Latimer, Miriam. Little Red Riding Hood. 2013. (Classic Fairy Tale Pop-Ups Ser.). (ENG.). 12p. (J). (gr. -1-1). 12.99 (978-0-7641-6598-6(4)) Barron's Educational Series, Inc.

Laverde, Arlene. Alaska's Three Little Pigs. Dwyer, Mindy, illus. 2015. (Paws IV Ser.). (ENG.). 20p. (J). (— 1). bds. 8.99 (978-1-57061-974-8(3), Little Bigfoot) Sasquatch Bks.

Lawler, Janet. If Kisses Were Colors. Jay, Alison, illus. 2010. (ENG.). 22p. (J). (gr. -1 — 1). bds. 6.99 (978-0-8037-3530-9(8), Dial Bks) Penguin Young Readers Group.

Lawrence, Trisha. A Princess's Crown: A Magnetic Storybook. Barnard, Lucy, illus. 2008. 6p. (J). (gr. -1-1). bds. 10.99 (978-2-7641-2186-3(5)) Gardner Pubns.

Lawson-Miller, Barb. I Love Daddy Because... 2004. (Illus.). 14p. bds. (978-0-9688553-0-0(X)) Barbamel Bks., Inc.

—I Love Mommy Because... 2004. (Illus.). 14p. bds. (978-0-9688553-1-7(8)) Barbamel Bks., Inc.

Lawson, Peter. Tractor. 2009. (Turn the Wheel Ser.). (ENG., Illus.). 10p. (J). (gr. -1-k). bds. 5.95 (978-0-7892-1023-4(1), Abbeville Kids) Abbeville Pr., Inc.

Lawson, Peter & Smith, Kathryn. Animal Ambulance. 2009. (Turn the Wheel Ser.). (ENG., Illus.). 10p. (J). (gr. -1-k). bds. 5.95 (978-0-7892-1026-5(6), Abbeville Kids) Abbeville Pr., Inc.

Layton, Neal. The Story of Things: From the Stone Age to the Modern Age in 10 Pop-Up Spreads. 2010. (ENG., Illus.). 24p. (J). (gr. k-2). 15.99 (978-0-340-94532-2(X), Hodder Children's Books) Hachette Children's Group GBR. Dist: Hachette Bk. Group.

Leapfrog Learners - Pirates. (Awesome Adventures Ser.). 16p. (J). (978-2-7643-0117-3(0)) Phidal Publishing, Inc./Editions Phidal, Inc.

Learn As You Grow. God Loves You So Much... Reuben, Borgen & Jenny, Lindley, photos by. 2010. (ENG., Illus.). 24p. (J). 12.95 (978-0-9824652-3-3(8)) Learn As You Grow, L.L.C.

Learn Your Numbers. 2003. (Illus.). 10p. (J). bds. (978-1-74047-003-2(6)) Book Co. Publishing Pty, Ltd., The.

Learning Wrap Ups Palette Base. 2004. (ENG.). (J). 14.99 (978-1-59204-000-1(4)) Learning Wrap-Ups, Inc.

Leblond, Michaël & Bertrand, Frédérique. Pyjamarama: Carnival. 2017. (ENG., Illus.). 22p. (gr. k-4). pap. 16.95 **(978-0-500-65125-4(6)**, 565125) Thames & Hudson.

Lee, Brian, illus. A Construction Site. 2005. (What's Inside Ser.). (J). (978-0-7607-6570-8(7)) backpackbook.

—A Pirate Ship. 2005. (What's Inside? Ser.). (978-0-7607-6809-9(9)) backpackbook.

—The World of Dinosaurs. 2005. (J). (978-0-7607-6569-2(3)) backpackbook.

Lee, Dennis. Zoomberry Board Book. Petricic, Dusan, illus. 2016. 26p. (J). bds. 10.50 (978-1-4434-1166-0(3)) HarperCollins Pubs.

Lee, Howard. A Day at the Zoo. Reasoner, Charles, illus. 2009. (Inside Outside Board Bks.). 10p. (J). bds. 10.99 (978-1-934650-55-4(2)) Just For Kids Pr., LLC.

Lee, Mark. Veinte Camiones Grandes en Medio de la Calle. Cyrus, Kurt, illus. 2015. (ENG & SPA.). 30p. (J). (-k). bds. 7.99 (978-0-7636-7651-3(9)) Candlewick Pr.

Lee, Maxine, illus. Hippo's Hiccups. 2015. (Pardon Me! Ser.: 4). (ENG.). 14p. (J). (978-1-84643-751-9(2)) Child's Play International Ltd.

—Zebra's Sneeze. 2015. (Pardon Me! Ser.: 4). (ENG.). 14p. (J). (978-1-84643-753-3(9)) Child's Play International Ltd.

Leeson, Tom and Pat, et al, photos by. Cascade Babies. 2013. (Illus.). 26p. (J). 8.95 (978-1-56037-330-8(X)) Farcountry Pr.

Leithauser, Jessica & National Geographic Learning Staff. Maps Show Us the Way. 2012. (ENG., Illus.). 12p. (C). (gr. 1-2). pap. 9.95 (978-0-8239-6357-7(8)) National Geographic School Publishing, Inc.

LeLeu, Lisa. Diggity the Dog Puppet Show Play Set. 2004. (Lisa Leleu Puppet Show Books Ser.). (J). 19.95 (978-0-9710537-2-4(3), LeLeu, Lisa Puppet Show Bks.) LeLeu, Lisa Studios! Inc.

—Percilla the Gorilla Gift Set: Puppet Book Gift Set with 2 Books. 2004. (J). bds. 19.99 (978-0-9710537-3-1(1)) LeLeu, Lisa Studios! Inc.

Lemke, Donald. Book-O-Beards. Lentz, Bob, illus. 2015. (Wearable Bks.). (ENG.). 12p. (gr. -1-1). bds. 7.99 (978-1-62370-183-3(X), Wear-A-Book) Capstone Young Readers of Coughlan Cos.

—Book-O-Hats. Lentz, Bob, illus. 2015. (Wearable Bks.). (ENG.). 12p. (gr. -1-1). bds. 7.99 (978-1-62370-184-0(8), Wear-A-Book) Capstone Young Readers of Coughlan Cos.

—Book-O-Masks. Lentz, Bob, illus. 2015. (Wearable Bks.). (ENG.). 12p. (gr. -1-1). bds. 7.99 (978-1-62370-185-7(6), Wear-A-Book) Capstone Young Readers of Coughlan Cos.

Lemke, Donald B. Book-O-Teeth. Lentz, Bob, illus. 2015. (Wearable Bks.). (ENG.). 12p. (gr. -1-1). bds. 7.99 (978-1-62370-186-4(4), Wear-A-Book) Capstone Young Readers of Coughlan Cos.

—Superman. Ku, Min Sung, illus. 2014. (DC Super Friends Word Adventures Ser.). (ENG.). 12p. (gr. -1 — 1). bds. 6.99 (978-1-4795-5243-6(7)) Picture Window Bks.

—Wonder Woman. Ku, Min Sung, illus. 2014. (DC Super Friends Word Adventures Ser.). (ENG.). 12p. (gr. -1 — 1). bds. 6.99 (978-1-4795-5244-3(5)) Picture Window Bks.

Lemmens, Riske. A Box Full of Monsters. 2004. (Illus.). 26p. (J). (978-1-85269-847-8(0)); (978-1-85269-842-3(X)); (978-1-85269-837-9(3)); (978-1-85269-827-0(6)); (978-1-85269-852-2(7)) Mantra Lingua.

Lemmens, Riske & Dutta, Kunal, texts. A Box Full of Monsters: Kutia Plot Me Monstra. 2004. (Illus.). 25p. (J). (978-1-85269-822-5(5)) Mantra Lingua.

Lendroth, Susan & Endle, Kate. Old Manhattan Has Some Farms: (E-I-E-I-Grow!) 2017. (ENG., Illus.). 28p. (J). (— 1). bds. 7.99 (978-1-58089-573-6(5)) Charlesbridge Publishing, Inc.

Lenz Mulligan Rights and Co. Staff & Chronicle Books Staff. Little Dino. 2008. (Little Finger Puppet Board Bks.: FING). (ENG., Illus.). 12p. (J). (gr. -1 — 1). bds. 6.99 (978-0-8118-6353-7(0)) Chronicle Bks. LLC.

Lenz Mulligan Rights and Co. Staff, et al. Little Penguin. 2008. (Little Finger Puppet Board Bks.: FING). (ENG., Illus.). 12p. (J). (gr. -1 — 1). bds. 6.99 (978-0-8118-6355-1(7)) Chronicle Bks. LLC.

Lerner, Sharon. DC Board Books. 2013. (DC Board Bks.). (ENG.). 16p. (gr. -1 — 1). bds. 15.98 (978-1-4795-4707-4(7)) Picture Window Bks.

—DC Board Books (Small), 1 vol. 2014. (DC Board Bks.). (ENG.). 20p. (gr. -1 — 1). bds. 17.97 (978-1-4795-6234-3(3)) Picture Window Bks.

Lester, Anna. Stories of Fairies. Gower, Teri, illus. 2006. (Young Reading Series 1 Gift Bks.). 47p. (J). (gr. 2-5). 8.99 (978-0-7945-1326-9(3), Usborne) EDC Publishing.

Let's Look at Boats. 2009. (Let's Go! Ser.). (Illus.). 18p. (J). (gr. -1-k). bds. 12.75 (978-1-60754-417-3(2)) Windmill Bks.

Let's Look at Planes. 2009. (Let's Go! Ser.). (Illus.). 18p. (J). (gr. -1-k). bds. 12.75 (978-1-60754-416-6(4)) Windmill Bks.

Let's Say Our Numbers. 2007. (Simple First Words Ser.). (Illus.). 14p. (J). (978-1-84332-520-8(9)) Priddy Bks.

Levine, Julia Pimsleur. Little Pim: Animals. 2012. (ENG.). 10p. (J). (gr. -1-k). bds. 8.95 (978-1-4197-0174-0(6)) Abrams, Inc.

—Little Pim: Numbers. 2012. (ENG.). 10p. (J). (gr. -1-k). bds. 8.95 (978-1-4197-0175-7(4)) Abrams, Inc.

Levison, Jesse. U Is for Underwear. 2014. (ENG., Illus.). 28p. (J). (-k). bds. 9.95 (978-1-57687-690-9(X), powerHouse Bks.) powerHouse Cultural Entertainment, Inc.

Lewis, Anthony, illus. Carrots or Peas? 2008. (Pick & Choose Ser.). (ENG.). 12p. (J). (gr. -1). bds. (978-1-84643-242-2(1)) Child's Play International Ltd.

—Little Ocean Explorers. 2007. (Little Explorers Ser.). (ENG.). 14p. (J). (gr. 1-1). bds. (978-1-84643-039-8(9)) Child's Play International Ltd.

—Little Snow Explorers. 2007. (Little Explorers Ser.). (ENG.). 14p. (J). (gr. -1-k). bds. (978-1-84643-037-4(2)) Child's Play International Ltd.

—Teddy or Train? 2008. (Pick & Choose Ser.). (ENG.). 12p. (J). (gr. -1). bds. (978-1-84643-241-5(3)) Child's Play International Ltd.

—Wind or Rain? 2008. (Pick & Choose Ser.). (ENG.). 12p. (J). (gr. -1). bds. (978-1-84643-240-8(5)) Child's Play International Ltd.

Lewis, Edwina. Who Eats? Parker, Ant, illus. 2003. (Who... Ser.). 16p. (YA). (978-1-85602-470-9(9), Pavilion Children's Books) Pavilion Bks.

—Who Jumps? Parker, Ant, illus. 2003. (Who... Ser.). 16p. (YA). (978-1-85602-447-1(4), Pavilion Children's Books) Pavilion Bks.

—Who Plays? Parker, Ant, illus. 2003. (Who... Ser.). 16p. (J). (978-1-85602-469-3(5), Pavilion Children's Books) Pavilion Bks.

—Who Swims? Parker, Ant, illus. 2003. (Who... Ser.). 16p. (YA). (978-1-85602-448-8(2), Pavilion Children's Books) Pavilion Bks.

Lewis, J. Patrick & Lewis, Leigh. It's Not the Baby. Frost, Maddie, illus. 2017. (ENG.). 14p. (J). (gr. -1 — 1). bds. 9.99 **(978-1-68152-194-7(6))** Amicus.

Lewis, Jan. Baby's First Book of Prayers. 2013. (ENG., Illus.). 24p. (J). (gr. -1-12). bds. 6.99 (978-1-86147-340-0(0), Armadillo) Anness Publishing GBR. Dist: National Bk. Network.

—Baby's First Stories of Jesus. 2015. (ENG., Illus.). 24p. (J). (gr. -1-2). bds. 6.99 (978-1-86147-415-5(6), Armadillo) Anness Publishing GBR. Dist: National Bk. Network.

—Best-Ever Rhymes. 2015. (ENG., Illus.). 24p. bds. 6.99 (978-1-86147-499-5(7), Armadillo) Anness Publishing GBR. Dist: National Bk. Network.

—Farm. 2015. (ENG., Illus.). 24p. bds. 6.99 (978-1-86147-635-7(3), Armadillo) Anness Publishing GBR. Dist: National Bk. Network.

—First Fairy Tales: Puss in Boots. 2015. (ENG., Illus.). 24p. bds. 6.99 (978-1-86147-626-5(4), Armadillo) Anness Publishing GBR. Dist: National Bk. Network.

—First Fairy Tales Aladdin & the Lamp. 2013. (ENG., Illus.). 24p. (J). (gr. -1-12). bds. 6.99 (978-1-86147-337-0(0), Armadillo) Anness Publishing GBR. Dist: National Bk. Network.

—First Fairy Tales Goldilocks & the Three Bears. 2013. (ENG., Illus.). 24p. (J). (gr. -1-12). bds. 6.99 (978-1-86147-332-5(X), Armadillo) Anness Publishing GBR. Dist: National Bk. Network.

—First Fairy Tales Little Red Riding Hood. 2013. (ENG., Illus.). 24p. (J). (gr. -1-12). bds. 6.99 (978-1-86147-336-3(2), Armadillo) Anness Publishing GBR. Dist: National Bk. Network.

—First Fairy Tales Snow White. 2013. (ENG., Illus.). 24p. (J). (gr. -1-12). bds. 6.99 (978-1-86147-335-6(4), Armadillo) Anness Publishing GBR. Dist: National Bk. Network.

—Look & Learn with Little Dino: Colour Fun. Lewis, Jan, illus. 2014. (ENG., Illus.). 24p. (J). (gr. -1-2). bds. 6.99 (978-1-86147-380-6(X), Armadillo) Anness Publishing GBR. Dist: National Bk. Network.

—Mother Goose Nursery Rhymes. 2015. (ENG., Illus.). 48p. bds. 9.99 (978-1-86147-649-4(3), Armadillo) Anness Publishing GBR. Dist: National Bk. Network.

—My First Words. 2015. (ENG., Illus.). 24p. bds. 6.99 (978-1-86147-498-8(9), Armadillo) Anness Publishing GBR. Dist: National Bk. Network.

—Princess Fairy Tales: Cinderella, the Princess & the Pea, Sleeping Beauty, the Little Mermaid. Lewis, Jan, illus. 2015. (ENG., Illus.). 48p. bds. 9.99 (978-1-86147-423-0(7), Armadillo) Anness Publishing GBR. Dist: National Bk. Network.

Lewis, Jan, illus. ABC: Turn the Wheels; Find the Words. 2016. (ENG.). 10p. bds. 14.99 (978-1-86147-712-5(0), Armadillo) Anness Publishing GBR. Dist: National Bk. Network.

—Animals: Turn the Wheels Find the Pictures. 2016. (ENG.). 10p. bds. 14.99 (978-1-86147-713-2(9), Armadillo) Anness Publishing GBR. Dist: National Bk. Network.

—The Emperor's New Clothes. 2015. (ENG.). 24p. (J). (gr. -1-2). bds. 6.99 (978-1-86147-413-1(X), Armadillo) Anness Publishing GBR. Dist: National Bk. Network.

—Fairy Palace: You Are Invited to a Party in the Fairy Palace! 2015. (ENG.). 10p. (J). (gr. k-3). bds. 7.99 (978-1-86147-315-8(X), Armadillo) Anness Publishing GBR. Dist: National Bk. Network.

—First Fairy Tales: Cinderella. 2013. (ENG.). 24p. (J). (gr. -1-k). bds. 6.99 (978-1-86147-334-9(6), Armadillo) Anness Publishing GBR. Dist: National Bk. Network.

—First Fairy Tales: Sleeping Beauty. 2013. (ENG.). 24p. (J). (gr. -1-k). bds. 6.99 (978-1-86147-338-7(9), Armadillo) Anness Publishing GBR. Dist: National Bk. Network.

—First Fairy Tales: The Ugly Duckling. 2013. (ENG.). 24p. (J). (gr. -1-k). bds. 6.99 (978-1-86147-333-2(8), Armadillo) Anness Publishing GBR. Dist: National Bk. Network.

—First Fairy Tales: Three Little Pigs. 2013. (ENG.). 24p. (J). (gr. -1-k). bds. 6.99 (978-1-86147-331-8(1), Armadillo) Anness Publishing GBR. Dist: National Bk. Network.

—First Prayers for Little Ones: Prayers for Every Day, Special Occasions & the Family. 2016. (ENG.). 48p. (J). (gr. -1-12). 9.99 (978-1-86147-716-3(3), Armadillo) Anness Publishing GBR. Dist: National Bk. Network.

—Lift-The-Flap Word House: 200 Things to Find, See & Say. 2016. (ENG.). 10p. (J). (gr. -1-12). bds. 7.99 (978-1-86147-778-1(3), Armadillo) Anness Publishing GBR. Dist: National Bk. Network.

—Look & Learn with Little Dino: Action Words. 2014. (ENG.). 24p. (J). (gr. k-2). bds. 6.99 (978-1-86147-382-0(6), Armadillo) Anness Publishing GBR. Dist: National Bk. Network.

—Look & Learn with Little Dino: Busy Day. 2014. (ENG.). 24p. (J). (gr. k-2). bds. 6.99 (978-1-86147-379-0(6), Armadillo) Anness Publishing GBR. Dist: National Bk. Network.

—Look & Learn with Little Dino: Count 123. 2014. (ENG.). 24p. (J). (gr. -1-1). bds. 6.99 (978-1-86147-381-3(8), Armadillo) Anness Publishing GBR. Dist: National Bk. Network.

—Love from Santa, 6 vols. 2013. (ENG.). 60p. (J). (gr. -1-2). bds. 7.99 (978-1-86147-313-4(3), Armadillo) Anness Publishing GBR. Dist: National Bk. Network.

—Magical Fairy Tales: Aladdin & the Lamp; the Ugly Duckling; the Emperor's New Clothes; Puss in Boots. 2016. (ENG.). 48p. bds. 9.99 (978-1-86147-700-2(7), Armadillo) Anness Publishing GBR. Dist: National Bk. Network.

—Mother Goose Rhymes: One, Two, Buckle My Shoe. 2015. (ENG.). 24p. bds. 6.99 (978-1-86147-637-1(X), Armadillo) Anness Publishing GBR. Dist: National Bk. Network.

—My First 123. 2014. (ENG.). 24p. (J). (gr. -1-k). bds. 6.99 (978-1-86147-371-4(0), Armadillo) Anness Publishing GBR. Dist: National Bk. Network.

—My First 123: Learn to Count from 1 To 100! 2015. (ENG.). 48p. pap. 9.99 (978-1-86147-425-4(3), Armadillo) Anness Publishing GBR. Dist: National Bk. Network.

—My First ABC. 2014. (ENG.). 24p. (J). (gr. -1-k). bds. 6.99 (978-1-86147-372-1(9), Armadillo) Anness Publishing GBR. Dist: National Bk. Network.

—My First Animals. 2014. (ENG.). 24p. (J). (gr. -1-k). bds. 6.99 (978-1-86147-373-8(7), Armadillo) Anness Publishing GBR. Dist: National Bk. Network.

—My First Colours. 2014. (ENG.). 24p. (J). (gr. -1-k). bds. 6.99 (978-1-86147-374-5(5), Armadillo) Anness Publishing GBR. Dist: National Bk. Network.

—My First Learning Library: 3 Great Books: First Abc First 123 First Words, 3 vols. 2014. (ENG.). 72p. (J). (gr. -1-1). bds., bds., bds. 9.99 (978-1-86147-387-5(7), Armadillo) Anness Publishing GBR. Dist: National Bk. Network.

—My First Words: Over 300 Everyday Words & Pictures. 2015. (ENG.). 48p. bds. 9.99 (978-1-86147-627-2(2), Armadillo) Anness Publishing GBR. Dist: National Bk. Network.

—My Little Nursery Rhymes. 2015. (ENG.). 24p. bds. 6.99 (978-1-86147-469-8(5), Armadillo) Anness Publishing GBR. Dist: National Bk. Network.

—Old Macdonald Had a Farm. 2015. (ENG.). 24p. bds. 6.99 (978-1-86147-468-1(7), Armadillo) Anness Publishing GBR. Dist: National Bk. Network.

—On the Farm: A Friendly Story with Flaps to Lift. 2016. (ENG.). 10p. (J). (gr. -1-12). bds. 7.99 (978-1-86147-779-8(1), Armadillo) Anness Publishing GBR. Dist: National Bk. Network.

—Pirate Ship: Lift the Flaps to Follow the Clues & Discover the Fabulous Treasure. 2016. (ENG.). 10p. (J). (gr. -1-12). 7.99 (978-1-86147-767-5(8), Armadillo) Anness Publishing GBR. Dist: National Bk. Network.

—Round & Round the Garden. 2015. (ENG.). 24p. bds. 6.99 (978-1-86147-636-4(1), Armadillo) Anness Publishing GBR. Dist: National Bk. Network.

—Santa's Workshop: The Inside Story! 2015. (ENG.). 10p. (J). (gr. k-4). bds. 7.99 (978-1-86147-314-1(1), Armadillo) Anness Publishing GBR. Dist: National Bk. Network.

—The Princess & the Pea. 2015. (ENG.). 24p. bds. 6.99 (978-1-86147-467-4(9), Armadillo) Anness Publishing GBR. Dist: National Bk. Network.

—Words: Turn the Wheels, Find the Pictures. 2015. (ENG.). 10p. bds. 14.99 (978-1-86147-660-9(4), Armadillo) Anness Publishing GBR. Dist: National Bk. Network.

—123: Turn the Wheels - Learn to Count! 2015. (ENG.). 10p. (J). (gr. -1-12). bds. 14.99 (978-1-86147-661-6(2), Armadillo) Anness Publishing GBR. Dist: National Bk. Network.

Lhomme, Sandrine & Piu, Amandine. Sammy the Snail's Amazing Day, 1 vol. Lhomme, Sandrine, illus. 2012. (My Baby Stories Ser.). (ENG., Illus.). 24p. (J). (gr. -1). bds. 9.95 (978-2-7338-1981-4(X)) Auzou, Philippe Editions FRA. Dist: Consortium Bk. Sales & Distribution.

Lift & See 123. (Baby Goldstars Lift Out Eva Ser.). 5p. (978-1-4054-9312-3(7)) Parragon, Inc.

Lift & See Colors. (Baby Goldstars Lift Out Eva Ser.). 5p. (978-1-4054-9313-0(5)) Parragon, Inc.

Lift-The-Flap Fractions & Decimals IR. 2017. (Advanced Lift-The-Flap BDs* Ser.). (ENG.). (J). bds. 14.99 **(978-0-7945-3727-2(8)**, Usborne) EDC Publishing.

Lift-The-Flap Questions & Answers about Food IR. 2017. (Lift-The-Flap Questions & Answers Ser.). (ENG.). (J). bds. 14.99 **(978-0-7945-3927-6(0)**, Usborne) EDC Publishing.

Lift-The-Flap Questions & Answers about Science IR. 2017. (Lift-The-Flap Questions & Answers Ser.). (ENG.). (J). bds. 14.99 **(978-0-7945-3940-5(8)**, Usborne) EDC Publishing.

Lift-The-Flap Telling the Time. 2017. (Advanced Lift-The-Flap BDs* Ser.). (ENG.). (J). bds. 14.99 **(978-0-7945-3865-1(7)**, Usborne) EDC Publishing.

Light, Steve. Boats Go. 2015. (ENG., Illus.). 16p. (J). (gr. -1 — 1). bds. 9.99 (978-1-4521-2900-6(2)) Chronicle Bks. LLC.

—Planes Go. 2014. (ENG., Illus.). 16p. (J). (gr. -1 — 1). bds. 9.99 (978-1-4521-2899-3(5)) Chronicle Bks. LLC.

—Trains Go. 2012. (ENG., Illus.). 16p. (J). (gr. -1 — 1). bds. 9.99 (978-0-8118-7942-2(9)) Chronicle Bks. LLC.

Lightfoot, Martha, illus. The Lion's Share. 2009. (Finger Puppet Bks.). (ENG.). 24p. (J). (gr. -1-1). (978-1-84643-248-4(0)) Child's Play International Ltd.

Lindert, Reyna & Anthony, Michelle. My First Signs. 2009. (Signing Smart Ser.). (ENG.). 14p. (J). (gr. k — 1). 7.99 (978-0-545-10924-6(8), Cartwheel Bks.) Scholastic, Inc.

Lindman, Maj. Flicka, Ricka, Dicka & the New Dotted Dresses. Lindman, Maj, illus. 2012. (Flicka, Ricka, Dicka Ser.). (ENG., Illus.). 32p. (J). (gr. k-3). 9.99 (978-0-8075-2484-8(0)) Whitman, Albert & Co.

Lindner, Brooke. Dance with Brobee! 2012. (Yo Gabba Gabba! Ser.). (ENG.). 12p. (J). (gr. -1-1). bds. 5.99 (978-1-4424-5445-3(8), Simon Spotlight) Simon Spotlight.

Linenthal, Peter. Look Look Outside! 2012. (ENG.). 16p. (J). (gr. -1 — 1). bds. 6.99 (978-0-8037-3729-7(7), Dial Bks) Penguin Young Readers Group.

Linke, Uwe. Knights of the Castle. Muller, Daniel, illus. 2008. (ENG.). 24p. (J). (gr. -1-3). 11.95 (978-0-7358-2201-6(8)) North-South Bks., Inc.

Lionni, Leo. What? 2014. (ENG., Illus.). 16p. (J). (— 1). bds. 5.99 (978-0-385-75406-4(X), Knopf Bks. for Young Readers) Random Hse. Children's Bks.

—When? 2014. (ENG., Illus.). 16p. (J). (— 1). bds. 5.99 (978-0-385-75408-8(6), Knopf Bks. for Young Readers) Random Hse. Children's Bks.

—Where? 2014. (ENG., Illus.). 16p. (J). (— 1). bds. 5.99 (978-0-385-75407-1(8), Knopf Bks. for Young Readers) Random Hse. Children's Bks.

—Who? 2014. (ENG., Illus.). 16p. (J). (— 1). bds. 5.99 (978-0-385-75405-7(1), Knopf Bks. for Young Readers) Random Hse. Children's Bks.

Lippman, Peter. Mini Express. (J). 119.40 (978-0-7611-2876-2(X), 22876); (ENG.). bds. 79.60 (978-0-7611-2883-0(2), 22883) Workman Publishing Co., Inc.

Litchfield, Jo. At Home. rev. ed. 2013. (First Words Board Bks). 12p. (J). ring bd. 6.99 (978-0-7945-2617-7(9), Usborne) EDC Publishing.

—Usborne Lift-The-Flap Nitivity. Allman, Howard, photos by. 2004. (Illus.). (J). (978-0-439-68683-9(0)) Scholastic, Inc.

—Very First ABC. 2010. (Very First Words Board Bks). 10p. (J). bds. 6.99 (978-0-7945-2709-9(4), Usborne) EDC Publishing.

—Weather. Maynard, Marc, illus. 2008. (Usborne Look & Say Ser.). 12p. (J). (gr. -1-3). bds. 7.99 (978-0-7945-1989-6(X), Usborne) EDC Publishing.

Litchfield, Jo, illus. Baby Brother Look & Say. 2008. (Look & Say Board Bks). 12p. (J). bds. 7.99 (978-0-7945-2101-1(0), Usborne) EDC Publishing.

Litten, Kristyna. Rome: a 3D Keepsake Cityscape. Litten, Kristyna, illus. 2013. (Panorama Pops Ser.). (ENG., Illus.). 15p. (J). (gr. k-12). 8.99 (978-0-7636-6415-2(4)) Candlewick Pr.

little bee books, little bee. A Day with Cinderella. 2015. (ENG., Illus.). 16p. (J). (gr. -1-1). 8.99 (978-1-4998-0061-6(4)) Little Bee Books Inc.

—Dive into the Sea! Llewhellin, Gareth, illus. 2016. (ENG.). 12p. (J). (gr. -1 — 1). bds. 7.99 (978-1-4998-0297-9(8)) Little Bee Books Inc.

little bee books, little bee & Blake, Carly. Baby's First ABC. Max and Sid Staff, illus. 2015. (Baby's First Ser.). (ENG.).

12p. (J). (gr. -1 — 1). bds. 4.99 *(978-1-4998-0052-4(5))* Little Bee Books Inc.
—Baby's First Shapes. Max and Sid Staff, illus. 2015. (Baby's First Ser.). (ENG.). 12p. (J). (gr. -1 — 1). bds. 4.99 *(978-1-4998-0053-1(3))* Little Bee Books Inc.
little bee books, little bee & Llewhellin, Gareth. Jump into Fall! 2016. (ENG., Illus.). 12p. (J). (gr. -1 — 1). bds. 6.99 *(978-1-4998-0298-6(6))* Little Bee Books Inc.
little bee books, little bee & Powell, Richard. If You See a Cow. Martin Larranaga, Ana, illus. 2015. (ENG.). 12p. (J). (gr. -1-k). 4.99 *(978-1-4998-0112-5(2))* Little Bee Books Inc.
—If You See a Tiger. Larranaga, Ana Martin, illus. 2015. (ENG.). 12p. (J). (gr. -1-k). 4.99 *(978-1-4998-0113-2(0))* Little Bee Books Inc.
little bee books, little bee & Seal, Julia. Jungle. 2016. (ENG., Illus.). 12p. (J). (gr. -1 — 1). bds. 6.99 *(978-1-4998-0259-7(5))* Little Bee Books Inc.
Little Bee Books Staff. My Santa Book. 2015. (ENG., Illus.). 12p. (J). (gr. -1 — 1). bds. 5.99 *(978-1-4998-0129-3(7))* Little Bee Books Inc.
—On the Move: A Touch-and-Feel Book. 2015. (ENG.). 12p. (J). (gr. -1 — 1). bds. 6.99 *(978-1-4998-0013-5(4))* Little Bee Books Inc.
—Our Christmas Stockings: A Touch-and-Feel Book. 2015. (ENG., Illus.). 12p. (J). (gr. -1-1). 6.99 *(978-1-4998-0144-6(0))* Little Bee Books Inc.
—Snowflake. Graire, Virginie, illus. 2015. (ENG.). 12p. (J). (gr. -1 — 1). 6.99 *(978-1-4998-0148-4(3))* Little Bee Books Inc.
—Who's Hiding? Baruzzi, Agnese, illus. 2015. (ENG.). 16p. (J). (gr. -1-1). 9.99 *(978-1-4998-0168-2(8))* Little Bee Books Inc.
Little Bee Books Staff & Blake, Carly. Baby's First 123. Max and Sid Staff, illus. 2015. (Baby's First Ser.). (ENG.). 12p. (J). (gr. -1 — 1). bds. 4.99 *(978-1-4998-0051-7(7))* Little Bee Books Inc.
Little Bee Books Staff & Brook-Piper, Holly. Animal Homes. Max and Sid Staff, illus. 2015. (Tiny Touch Ser.). (ENG.). 12p. (J). (gr. -1 — 1). bds. 4.99 *(978-1-4998-0023-4(1))* Little Bee Books Inc.
—Fun with Colors. Max and Sid Staff, illus. 2015. (Tiny Touch Ser.). (ENG.). 12p. (J). (gr. -1 — 1). bds. 4.99 *(978-1-4998-0001-2(0))* Little Bee Books Inc.
Little Dragon & the Magic Wagon. 2008. (Little Dragon Storybooks Ser.). 32p. *(978-1-4075-1289-1(7))* Parragon, Inc.
Little Dragon Catches Colors. 2008. (Little Dragon Tab Board Book Ser.). 6p. bds. *(978-1-4075-2666-9(9))* Parragon, Inc.
Little Dragon Counts 1, 2, 3, 4, 5. 2008. (Little Dragon Flying Board Ser.). 7p. bds. *(978-1-4075-2665-2(0))* Parragon, Inc.
Little Dragon Makes Friends. 2008. (Little Dragon Storybooks Ser.). 32p. *(978-1-4075-1288-4(9))* Parragon, Inc.
Little Elephant & Friends. (Flocked Soft-to-Touch Board Ser.). 5p. bds. *(978-1-4054-9445-8(X))* Parragon, Inc.
Little Mermaid. 2009. (Disney Glitter Board Book Ser.). 5p. *(978-1-4054-9825-8(0))* Parragon, Inc.
Little Mole Boxed Book & Toy Set. 2013. (ENG., Illus.). 24p. (J). (gr. -1-2). 22.99 *(978-1-84365-217-5(X)*, Pavilion) Pavilion Bks. GBR. Dist: Independent Pubs. Group.
Little Monkey & Friends. (Flocked Soft-to-Touch Board Ser.). 5p. bds. *(978-1-4054-9504-2(9))* Parragon, Inc.
Little Penguin & Friends. (Flocked Soft-to-Touch Board Ser.). 5p. bds. *(978-1-4054-9446-5(8))* Parragon, Inc.
Little Pony's Secret. (Glitter Books... Ser.). 24p. *(978-1-4054-9471-7(9))* Parragon, Inc.
Litton, Jonathan. Cock-A-doodle-moo! Cunliffe, Ian, illus. 2016. (My First Ser.). (ENG.). 12p. (J). (gr. -1-k). bds. 12.99 *(978-1-58925-232-5(2))* Tiger Tales.
—Hello World. L'Atelier Cartographik, illus. 2016. (360 Degrees Ser.). (ENG.). 16p. (J). (gr. 3-6). 19.99 *(978-1-944530-00-6(2)*, 360 Degrees) Tiger Tales.
—Mouse in the Haunted House. Anderson, Nicola, illus. 2015. (Planet Pop-Up Ser.). (ENG.). 12p. (J). (gr. -1). 12.95 *(978-1-62686-485-6(3)*, Silver Dolphin Bks.) Readerlink Distribution Services, LLC.
—Noisy Dinosaurs. 2015. (My First Ser.). (ENG.). 12p. (J). (gr. -1-3). bds. 12.99 *(978-1-58925-207-3(1))* Tiger Tales.
—Noisy Noisy Digger. Galloway, Fiona, illus. 2017. (My Little World Ser.). (ENG.). 10p. (J). (gr. -1-2). bds. 12.99 ***(978-1-58925-242-4(X))*** Tiger Tales.
—One, Two, Baa, Moo: A Pop-Up Book of Counting. Verrall, Lisa, illus. 2015. (My Little World Ser.). (ENG.). 12p. (J). bds. 8.99 *(978-1-68010-507-0(8))* Tiger Tales.
—Peek-Through Forest. Nowowiejska, Kasia, illus. 2015. (Little Snappers Ser.). (ENG.). 12p. (J). (gr. -1-2). bds. 9.99 *(978-1-68010-508-7(6))* Tiger Tales.
—Peek-Through Jungle. Nowowiejska, Kasia, illus. 2015. (Little Snappers Ser.). (ENG.). 12p. (J). (gr. -1-2). bds. 9.99 *(978-1-68010-504-9(3))* Tiger Tales.
—Planet Pop-Up: Shark Makes a Splash! Anderson, Nicola, illus. 2015. (Planet Pop-Up Ser.). (ENG.). 12p. (J). (gr. -1). 12.95 *(978-1-62686-353-8(9)*, Silver Dolphin Bks.) Readerlink Distribution Services, LLC.
—Planet Pop-Up: Tiger Takes Off. Anderson, Nicola, illus. 2015. (Planet Pop-Up Ser.). (ENG.). 12p. (J). (gr. -1). 12.95 *(978-1-62686-373-6(3)*, Silver Dolphin Bks.) Readerlink Distribution Services, LLC.
—Red Car, Blue Car. Verrall, Lisa, illus. 2015. (My Little World Ser.). (ENG.). 12p. (J). (gr. -1-2). bds. 8.99 *(978-1-68010-506-3(X))* Tiger Tales.
—Roar: A Big-Mouthed Book of Sounds! Galloway, Fiona, illus. 2014. (ENG.). 16p. (J). bds. 7.99 *(978-1-58925-593-7(3))* Tiger Tales.
—Snap: A Peek-Through Book of Shapes. Galloway, Fiona, illus. 2014. (My Little World Ser.). (ENG.). 16p. (J). (gr. -1-k). bds. 7.99 *(978-1-58925-566-1(6))* Tiger Tales.
—Snip Snap: Pop-Up Fun. Nowowiejska, Kasia, illus. 2015. (Little Snappers Ser.). (ENG.). 10p. (J). 9.99 *(978-1-58925-548-7(8))* Tiger Tales.
—Splish Splash: Pop-Up Fun. Galloway, Fiona, illus. 2016. (Little Snappers Ser.). (ENG.). 10p. (J). (gr. -1-k). 9.99 *(978-1-58925-259-2(4))* Tiger Tales.
—Surprise: A Book of Christmas Shapes. Galloway, Fiona, illus. 2014. (ENG.). 16p. (J). (gr. -1-k). bds. 7.99 *(978-1-58925-567-8(4))* Tiger Tales.
—Touch & Feel Colors. Galloway, Fiona, illus. 2017. (My Little World Ser.). (ENG.). 10p. (J). (gr. -1-k). bds. 8.99 ***(978-1-68010-510-0(8))*** Tiger Tales.
Litton, Jonathan. Touch & Trace Farm. Rumiz, Susanna, illus. 2016. (ENG.). 26p. (J). (gr. -1-k). bds. 8.99 *(978-1-58925-220-2(9))* Tiger Tales.
Ljungkvist, Laura. A Line Can Be ... 2015. (ENG., Illus.). 24p. (J). (-k). bds. 9.95 *(978-1-57687-753-1(1)*, powerHouse Bks.) powerHouse Cultural Entertainment, Inc.
Llenas, Anna. The Color Monster: A Pop-Up Book of Feelings. 2015. (ENG., Illus.). 20p. (J). (gr. -1-2). 19.95 *(978-1-4549-1729-8(6))* Sterling Publishing Co., Inc.
Lloyd-Jones, Sally. Song of the Stars, 1 vol. Jay, Alison, illus. 2015. (ENG.). 32p. (J). bds. 7.99 *(978-0-310-73630-1(7))* Zonderkidz.
—Tiny Bear's Bible, 1 vol. Oleynikov, Igor, illus. 2015. (ENG.). 22p. (J). bds. 15.99 *(978-0-310-74787-1(2))* Zonderkidz.
—Tiny Bear's Bible, 1 vol. Oleynikov, Igor, illus. 2009. (Furry Bible Stories Ser.). 22p. (J). (gr. -1-k). pap. 14.99 *(978-0-310-71818-5(X))* Zonderkidz.
Lloyd, Sam. Grumpy Gertie. 2013. (ENG., Illus.). 24p. (J). (gr. -1-k). 12.99 *(978-1-84365-228-1(5)*, Pavilion) Pavilion Bks. GBR. Dist: Independent Pubs. Group.
—Shape Sorters - Numbers, 2. Lloyd, Sam, illus. 2011. (Shape Sorters Ser.). (ENG., Illus.). 12p. (J). (gr. k-k). bds. 7.99 *(978-0-230-70962-1(1))* Macmillan Pubs., Ltd. GBR. Dist: Independent Pubs. Group.
—What's in Your Tummy Mummy? Lloyd, Sam, illus. 2007. (ENG., Illus.). 24p. (J). (gr. -1-k). pap. 13.95 *(978-1-84365-091-1(6)*, Pavilion) Pavilion Bks. GBR. Dist: Independent Pubs. Group.
Lluch, Alex A. Animal Alphabet: Slide & Seek the ABCs. Defenbaugh, David, illus. 2013. (ENG.). 13p. (J). (-k). bds. 12.99 *(978-1-61351-041-4(1))* WS Publishing.
—Animal Alphabet: Slide & Seek the ABCs. 2011. (Animal Alphabet Ser.). (ENG.). 13p. (J). (gr. -1-k). bds. 7.95 *(978-1-936061-49-5(X))* WS Publishing.
—Animal Numbers: Slide & Seek Counting. 2012. (ENG.). 14p. (J). bds. 7.95 *(978-1-936061-90-7(2))* WS Publishing.
—I Like to Learn Alphabet: Zoo Clues. 2011. (ENG.). 32p. (J). (gr. -1-k). bds. 4.95 *(978-1-934386-00-2(6))* WS Publishing.
—I Like to Learn Colors: Curious Penguin. 2011. (ENG.). 32p. (J). (gr. -1-k). bds. 4.95 *(978-1-934386-02-6(2))* WS Publishing.
—I Like to Learn Numbers: Hungry Chameleon. 2011. (ENG.). 32p. (J). (gr. -1-k). bds. 4.95 *(978-1-934386-01-9(4))* WS Publishing.
—I Like to Learn Opposites: Amazing Bugs. 2011. (ENG.). 32p. (J). (gr. -1-k). bds. 4.95 *(978-1-934386-03-3(0))* WS Publishing.
—Touch the Red Button. 2014. (ENG.). 60p. (J). (gr. -1-k). 9.99 *(978-1-61351-094-0(2))* WS Publishing.
Lo Monaco, Gérard. A Sea Voyage. 2016. (ENG., Illus.). 8p. (J). (gr. k-2). 29.95 *(978-0-500-65088-2(8)*, 565088) Thames & Hudson.
Lobo, Julia. Eek! That's Creepy! Look & Find. Cavallini, Linda, illus. 2010. 24p. (J). 7.98 *(978-1-60553-898-3(1))* Publications International, Ltd.
Lodge, Jo. Bump! Little Owl. 2014. (Push, Pull, POP! Bks.). (ENG., Illus.). 10p. (J). (gr. -1 — 1). 6.99 *(978-0-7641-6667-9(0))* Barron's Educational Series, Inc.
—Dig! Little Puppy. Lodge, Jo, illus. 2017. (Little Movers Ser.). (ENG., Illus.). 10p. (J). (gr. -1-k). bds. 9.99 ***(978-1-5098-0668-3(7))*** Pan Macmillan GBR. Dist: Independent Pubs. Group.
—Farm. 2014. (Touch & Feel Buggy Buddies Ser.). (ENG., Illus.). 10p. (J). (— 1). bds. 7.99 *(978-1-4472-6800-0(8))* Pan Macmillan GBR. Dist: Independent Pubs. Group.
—Little Roar's Red Boots. 2013. (ENG., Illus.). 20p. (J). (gr. -1-k). 8.99 *(978-1-4449-0482-6(5))* Hodder & Stoughton GBR. Dist: Hachette Bk. Group.
—Little Roar's Round Balloon. 2013. (ENG., Illus.). 20p. (J). (gr. -1-k). 5.99 *(978-1-4449-0483-3(3))* Hodder & Stoughton GBR. Dist: Hachette Bk. Group.
—Oops! Little Chick. 2013. (Push, Pull, Pop! Bks.). (ENG., Illus.). 10p. (J). (gr. -1 — 1). 6.99 *(978-0-7641-6633-4(6))* Barron's Educational Series, Inc.
—Peekaboo Little Roar. 2013. (ENG., Illus.). 12p. (J). (gr. -1-k). 10.99 *(978-1-4449-0478-9(7))* Hodder & Stoughton GBR. Dist: Hachette Bk. Group.
—Pets. 2014. (Touch & Feel Buggy Buddies Ser.). (ENG., Illus.). 12p. (J). (— 1). bds. 7.99 *(978-1-4472-6801-7(6))* Pan Macmillan GBR. Dist: Independent Pubs. Group.
—Stomp! Little Dinosaur. 2013. (Push, Pull, Pop! Bks.). (ENG., Illus.). 10p. (J). (gr. -1 — 1). 6.99 *(978-0-7641-6632-7(8))* Barron's Educational Series, Inc.
Lodge, Jo, illus. Pounce! Little Kitten. 2017. (Little Movers Ser.). (ENG.). 10p. (J). (gr. -1-k). bds. 9.99 ***(978-1-5098-0669-0(5))*** Pan Macmillan GBR. Dist: Independent Pubs. Group.
Lodge, Yvette. Noah's Ark: Baby's First Pop-up! Lodge, Ali, illus. gif. ed. 2006. 8p. (J). 19.95 *(978-1-57791-217-0(9))* Brighter Minds Children's Publishing.
Logan, Bob. Rocket Town. 2011. (ENG., Illus.). 24p. (J). (gr. -1-k). bds. 7.99 *(978-1-4022-4186-4(0)*, Sourcebooks Jabberwocky) Sourcebooks, Inc.
Logan, Laura, illus. Jesus Loves Me. 2008. (ENG.). 20p. (J). (gr. -1). bds. 12.99 *(978-0-8249-6730-7(5)*, Ideal Pubns.) Worthy Publishing.
Lombardi, Kristine. Barbie What Shall I Be? Mattel, illus. 2010. (Vinyl Shaped Purse Ser.). (ENG.). 72p. (J). (gr. -1-k). bds. 14.99 *(978-0-7944-2034-5(6))* Reader's Digest Assn., Inc., The.
Lombardi, Kristine & Disney Storybook Artists Staff. Disney Cars Carry along Treasury. 2010. (Carry along Bks.). (ENG., Illus.). 20p. (J). (gr. -1). bds. 14.99 *(978-0-7944-1947-9(X))* Reader's Digest Assn., Inc., The.
Lonely Planet & Mansfield, Andy. POP-UP LONDON, 1 vol. 2016. (Lonely Planet Kids Ser.). (ENG., Illus.). 16p. (J). 9.99 *(978-1-76034-339-2(0)*, 5339) Lonely Planet Pubns.
—POP-UP PARIS, 1 vol. 2016. (Lonely Planet Kids Ser.). (ENG., Illus.). 16p. (J). 9.99 *(978-1-76034-335-4(8)*, 5335) Lonely Planet Pubns.
Lonely Planet Publications Staff. Adventures in Smelly Places: Packed Full of Activities & over 250 Stickers, 1 vol. 2015. (Lonely Planet Kids Ser.). (ENG.). 48p. (J). pap. 9.99 *(978-1-74360-781-7(4)*, 4984) Lonely Planet Pubns.
—World Search - Amazing Jobs, 1 vol. 2014. (Lonely Planet Kids Ser.). (ENG., Illus.). 16p. (J). 14.99 *(978-1-74321-920-1(2)*, 4640) Lonely Planet Pubns.
—World Search - Incredible Animals, 1 vol. 2014. (Lonely Planet Kids Ser.). (ENG., Illus.). 16p. (J). 14.99 *(978-1-74321-922-5(9)*, 4643) Lonely Planet Pubns.
Long, Ethan. Thank You! 2016. (Animal Sounds Ser.). (ENG., Illus.). 20p. (J). (gr. -1 — 1). bds. 7.95 *(978-1-4197-1364-4(7))* Abrams, Inc.
Long, Sylvia, illus. Sylvia Long's Mother Goose: Four Classic Board Books. 2016. (ENG.). 48p. (J). (gr. -1 — 1). bds. 14.99 *(978-1-4521-3818-3(4))* Chronicle Bks. LLC.
López, Oscar J., illus. Sing along with Abuelita Rosa: Hispanic Lullabies = Canciones de Cuna. 2006. (ENG & SPA.). 13p. (J). *(978-0-9788379-0-7(8))* Baby Abuelita Productions, Inc.
Lord, Jill Roman. If Jesus Walked Beside Me. Wummer, Amy, illus. 2014. (If Jesus Ser.). 22p. (J). bds. 6.99 *(978-0-8249-1920-7(3)*, Ideal Pubns.) Worthy Publishing.
Lorini, Andrea. Bunny's Easter Surprise. 2015. (ENG., Illus.). 8p. (J). (gr. -1 — 1). bds. 6.99 *(978-0-7641-6782-9(0))* Barron's Educational Series, Inc.
—Easter Egg Party. Rigo, Laura, illus. 2014. (ENG.). 8p. (J). (gr. -1 — 1). bds. 6.99 *(978-0-7641-6716-4(2))* Barron's Educational Series, Inc.
—Spooky Castle. 2014. (ENG.). 8p. (J). (gr. -1-k). bds. 6.99 *(978-0-7641-6734-8(0))* Barron's Educational Series, Inc.
—Trick or Treat. 2015. (ENG., Illus.). 8p. (J). (gr. -1-k). bds. 6.99 *(978-0-7641-6783-6(9))* Barron's Educational Series, Inc.
The Lost Treasure of Skull Island. 2012. (Illus.). (J). *(978-1-4351-4328-9(0))* Barnes & Noble, Inc.
Lovasik, Lawrence G. A Child's Prayer Treasury. 2004. (Illus.). (J). *(978-0-89942-719-5(7))* Catholic Bk. Publishing Corp.
Love, Maryann Cusimano. You Are My I Love You. Ichikawa, Satomi, illus. 2010. (ENG.). 30p. (J). (gr. -1 — 1). bds. 6.99 *(978-0-399-24395-0(X)*, Philomel Bks.) Penguin Young Readers Group.
—You Are My I Love You / Tú Eres Mi Te Quiero. Ichikawa, Satomi, illus. 2012. (SPA & ENG.). 28p. (J). (gr. -1 — 1). bds. 6.99 *(978-0-399-24396-7(8)*, Philomel Bks.) Penguin Young Readers Group.
Lovitt, Chip. My Big Dump Truck. LaPadula, Thomas, illus. 2011. (Diecut Vehicles Ser.). (ENG.). 12p. (J). (gr. -1-1). bds. 5.99 *(978-0-7944-2272-1(1)*, Reader's Digest Children's Bks.) Studio Fun International.
Low, Susan. Just Draw! 2006. (Illus.). 24p. *(978-2-7643-0295-8(9))* Phidal Publishing, Inc./Editions Phidal, Inc.
LP-Addition: Level 2 Math. 2004. (ENG.). (J). 9.99 *(978-1-59204-018-6(7))* Learning Wrap-Ups, Inc.
LP-Blends & Digraphs: Level 1 Reading. 2004. (ENG.). (J). 9.99 *(978-1-59204-005-6(5))* Learning Wrap-Ups, Inc.
LP-Capitalization & Punctuation: Level 2 Reading. 2004. (ENG.). (J). 9.99 *(978-1-59204-009-4(8))* Learning Wrap-Ups, Inc.
LP-Place Value: Level 2 Math. 2004. (ENG.). (J). 9.99 *(978-1-59204-017-9(9))* Learning Wrap-Ups, Inc.
LP-Reading Comprehension: Level 2 Reading. 2004. (ENG.). (J). 9.99 *(978-1-59204-011-7(X))* Learning Wrap-Ups, Inc.
LP-Subtraction: Level 2 Math. 2004. (ENG.). (J). 9.99 *(978-1-59204-019-3(5))* Learning Wrap-Ups, Inc.
Lubber, William. Pirateology: The Pirate Hunter's Companion. Steer, Dugald A., ed. 2006. (Ologies Ser.). (ENG., Illus.). 32p. (J). (gr. 3-7). 21.99 *(978-0-7636-3143-7(4))* Candlewick Pr.
Lucas, Gareth, illus. Dinos on Deck! 2017. (Gareth Lucas Noisy Bks.). (ENG.). 12p. (J). (gr. -1). bds. 14.99 *(978-1-62686-938-7(3)*, Silver Dolphin Bks.) Readerlink Distribution Services, LLC.
Ludwig, Ashley. You Tickle My Heart: and other ways you make me laugh. 2008. (Illus.). 18p. (J). (gr. k-1). bds. 11.50 *(978-0-9800630-0-4(0))* Beachcomber Press.com.
Luiz, Fernando, illus. How to Be a Princess: A Girly Girl Book. 2009. 12p. (J). bds. 6.95 *(978-1-58117-850-0(6)*, Intervisual/Piggy Toes) Bendon, Inc.
Lund, Deb. All Aboard the Dinotrain. Fine, Howard, illus. 2011. (ENG.). 30p. (J). (gr. -1 — 1). bds. 7.99 *(978-0-547-55415-0(X))* Houghton Mifflin Harcourt Publishing Co.
Lyons, P. J. Thank You, Lord, for Everything, 1 vol. Warnes, Tim, illus. 2015. (ENG.). 16p. (J). bds. 9.99 *(978-0-310-74812-0(7))* Zonderkidz.
Mac Killian, Caroline. Travels of the Zephyr: An Interactive Journey Around the World. 2010. (ENG., Illus.). 88p. (J). (gr. 3-7). 24.95 *(978-0-8109-8974-0(3)*, Abrams Bks. for Young Readers) Abrams, Inc.
Macaulay, David. How Machines Work: Zoo Break! 2015. (ENG., Illus.). 32p. (J). (gr. 2-5). 19.99 *(978-1-4654-4012-9(7)*, DK Children) Dorling Kindersley Publishing, Inc.
Maccarone, Grace. The Gingerbread Family: A Scratch-and-Sniff Book. Gardner, Louise, illus. 2010. (ENG.). 14p. (J). (gr. -1-k). bds. 7.99 *(978-1-4424-0678-0(X)*, Little Simon) Little Simon.
Macdonald, Fiona. The Medieval Chronicles: Vikings, Knights, & Castles. Antram, David, illus. 2013. 92p. (J). *(978-1-4351-5067-6(8))* Barnes & Noble, Inc.
Mack, Dinah. Daddy, Look What I Can Do! 2013. (Look What I Can Do Ser.). (ENG.). 14p. (J). (— 1). bds. 10.95 *(978-1-60537-170-2(X))* Cobblestone Publishing Co.
—Mommy, Look What I Can Do! 2013. (Look What I Can Do Ser.). (ENG.). 14p. (J). (— 1). bds. 10.95 *(978-1-60537-169-6(6))* Cobblestone Publishing Co.
Mack, Tracy, et al. Cinderella: Les Petits Fairytales. Lake, Oliver, illus. 2012. (Petits Fairytales Ser.). (ENG.). 24p. (J). (gr. -1 — 1). bds. 7.99 *(978-0-8050-9624-8(8)*, 9780805096248, Holt, Henry & Co. Bks. For Young Readers) Holt, Henry & Co.
—Snow White: Les Petits Fairytales. Lake, Oliver, illus. 2012. (Petits Fairytales Ser.). (ENG.). 26p. (J). (gr. -1 — 1). bds. 7.99 *(978-0-8050-9623-1(X)*, 9780805096231, Holt, Henry & Co. Bks. For Young Readers) Holt, Henry & Co.
Mackenzie, Catherine. I Can Say to God, Please. 2015. (Prayer (Board Books) Ser.). (ENG.). 10p. (J). bds. 3.99 *(978-1-85792-691-0(9)*, 4a46cdd3-be1d-48a9-bbee-7f9ad59ca112) Christian Focus Pubns. GBR. Dist: Bookmasters Distribution.
MacKenzie, Lachlan. The Duke's Daughter: A Story of Faith & Love. Anderson, Jeff, illus. 2008. (Story Time Ser.). (ENG.). 24p. (J). (gr. -1-3). 7.99 *(978-1-84550-326-0(0)*, de5339b0-1f9f-400d-8814-ce3da22de27c) Christian Focus Pubns. GBR. Dist: Bookmasters Distribution.
MacLaine, James. The Usborne Little Children's Travel Activity Book. Watt, Fiona, ed. Harrison, Erica et al, illus. 2013. (Activity Books for Little Children Ser.). (ENG.). 63p. (J). pap. 9.99 *(978-0-7945-3127-0(X)*, Usborne) EDC Publishing.
MacLean, Kerry Lee. Just Me & My Mind. 2014. (ENG., Illus.). 16p. (J). (gr. -1-1). 18.95 *(978-1-61429-124-4(1))* Wisdom Pubns.
Macmillan, Sue. Happy, Hoppy Bunny. Ward, Sarah, illus. 2014. (Cheery Chasers Ser.). (ENG.). 8p. (J). (gr. -1 — 1). bds. 4.99 *(978-0-7641-6699-0(9))* Barron's Educational Series, Inc.
Macnair, Patricia. Sensational Senses. Watson, Richard, illus. 2016. (ENG.). 14p. (J). (gr. k-2). 14.99 *(978-1-4052-7163-9(9))* Egmont Bks., Ltd. GBR. Dist: Independent Pubs. Group.
Maddox, Jake. Striker Assist, 1 vol. Tiffany, Sean, illus. 2012. (Jake Maddox Sports Stories Ser.). (ENG.). 72p. (gr. 2-3). pap. 5.95 *(978-1-4342-4208-2(0))* Stone Arch Bks.
Madema, Victoria & Stickers. Woodland Music Stickers. 2011. (Dover Little Activity Books Stickers Ser.). (ENG.). 4p. (J). (gr. k-3). pap. 1.50 *(978-0-486-48332-0(0))* Dover Pubns., Inc.
Magsamen, Sandra. Are You My Cuddle Bunny? 2017. (Heart-Felt Bks.: 4). (ENG.). 12p. (J). (— 1). 7.99 *(978-0-545-92797-0(8)*, Cartwheel Bks.) Scholastic, Inc.
—Beecause I Love You. 2014. (ENG., Illus.). 14p. (J). (gr. -1 — 1). bds. 7.99 *(978-0-316-25519-6(X))* Little, Brown Bks. for Young Readers.
—Boo, Boo, I Love You! 2015. (ENG., Illus.). 10p. (J). (gr. -1 — 1). bds. 7.99 *(978-0-316-25514-1(9))* Little, Brown Bks. for Young Readers.
—Go to Sleepy, Little Sheepy. 2015. (ENG., Illus.). 10p. (J). (gr. -1 — 1). bds. 7.99 *(978-0-316-25515-8(7))* Little, Brown Bks. for Young Readers.
—I Love Hugs & Kisses. 2016. (Heart-Felt Bks.). (ENG.). 12p. (J). (gr. -1-k). 7.99 *(978-0-545-92796-3(X)*, Cartwheel Bks.) Scholastic, Inc.
—I Love You, Honey Bunny. Magsamen, Sandra, illus. 2016. (ENG., Illus.). 12p. (J). (— 1). bds. 7.99 *(978-1-338-11084-5(5)*, Cartwheel Bks.) Scholastic, Inc.
—I Love You Snow Much. Magsamen, Sandra, illus. 2015. (ENG., Illus.). 10p. (J). (gr. -1 — 1). bds. 7.99 *(978-0-316-37876-5(3))* Little, Brown Bks. for Young Readers.
—I'M Wild about You! Magsamen, Sandra, illus. 2016. (Heart-Felt Bks.). (ENG., Illus.). 10p. (J). (— 1). 7.99 *(978-0-545-46839-8(6)*, Cartwheel Bks.) Scholastic, Inc.
—Itsy-Bitsy I Love You! Magsamen, Sandra, illus. 2016. (Heart-Felt Bks.). (ENG., Illus.). 10p. (J). (— 1). 7.99 *(978-0-545-46841-1(8)*, Cartwheel Bks.) Scholastic, Inc.
—Love Bug. rev. ed. 2007. (Board Books with Plush Toys Ser.). (ENG., Illus.). 20p. (J). (gr. -1 — 1). 8.99 *(978-0-316-06596-2(X))* Little, Brown Bks. for Young Readers.
—Merry Christmas, Little One! 2010. (Padded Cloth Covers with Lift-The-Flaps Ser.). (ENG., Illus.). 10p. (J). (gr. -1-17). bds. 7.99 *(978-0-316-07003-4(3))* Little, Brown Bks. for Young Readers.
—Our Little Deer (Made with Love) Magsamen, Sandra, illus. 2016. (ENG., Illus.). 12p. (J). bds. 7.99 *(978-1-338-11081-4(0)*, Cartwheel Bks.) Scholastic, Inc.
—Twinkle, Twinkle, You're My Star. 2010. (ENG., Illus.). 10p. (J). (gr. -1 — 1). bds. 7.99 *(978-0-316-04142-3(4))* Little, Brown Bks. for Young Readers.
—You're My Little Chickadee. 2016. (ENG., Illus.). 10p. (J). (gr. -1 — 1). bds. 7.99 *(978-0-316-37879-6(8))* Little, Brown Bks. for Young Readers.
—You're Purrfect to Me. 2013. (Earesistables Ser.). (ENG., Illus.). 20p. (J). (gr. -1-17). bds. 7.99 *(978-0-316-13352-4(3))* Little, Brown Bks. for Young Readers.
—You're Tutu Cute! 2014. (ENG., Illus.). 10p. (J). (gr. -1 — 1). bds. 7.99 *(978-0-316-25517-2(3))* Little, Brown Bks. for Young Readers.
Mahoney, Daniel J., illus. I See a Monster. 2008. (ENG.). 12p. (J). bds. 5.95 *(978-1-58117-729-9(1)*, Intervisual/Piggy Toes) Bendon, Inc.
Mahoney, Jean. Swan Lake Ballet Theatre. Seddon, Viola Anne, illus. 2009. (ENG.). 16p. (J). (gr. 1-4). 24.99 *(978-0-7636-4396-6(3))* Candlewick Pr.
Maizels, Jennie. Pop-Up New York. Maizels, Jennie, illus. 2014. (ENG., Illus.). 12p. (J). (gr. k-4). 19.99 *(978-0-7636-7162-4(2))* Candlewick Pr.
Make Believe Ideas. Even Pirates Poop. 2014. (ENG.). 12p. (J). bds. 9.99 *(978-1-78393-113-2(2))* Make Believe Ideas GBR. Dist: Nelson, Thomas Inc.
—Even Princesses Poop. 2014. (ENG.). 12p. (J). bds. 9.99 *(978-1-78393-112-5(4))* Make Believe Ideas GBR. Dist: Nelson, Thomas Inc.
—Flower Friends Daisy's First Words. 2013. (ENG.). 10p. (J). bds. 6.99 *(978-1-78235-604-2(5))* Make Believe Ideas GBR. Dist: Nelson, Thomas Inc.
—Flower Friends Poppy's Shapes. 2013. (ENG.). 10p. (J). bds. 6.99 *(978-1-78235-603-5(7))* Make Believe Ideas GBR. Dist: Nelson, Thomas Inc.
—Flower Friends Primrose's Counting. 2013. (ENG.). 10p. (J). bds. 6.99 *(978-1-78235-602-8(9))* Make Believe Ideas GBR. Dist: Nelson, Thomas Inc.
—Flower Friends Rosie's Colors. 2013. (ENG.). 10p. (J). bds. 6.99 *(978-1-78235-605-9(3))* Make Believe Ideas GBR. Dist: Nelson, Thomas Inc.
—Little Red Riding Hood. 2015. (ENG.). 24p. (J). bds. 7.99 *(978-1-78393-536-9(7))* Make Believe Ideas GBR. Dist: Nelson, Thomas Inc.
Make Believe Ideas, creator. Alphabet Book. 2014. (ENG., Illus.). 20p. (J). (gr. -1). bds. 9.99 *(978-1-78235-969-2(9))* Make Believe Ideas GBR. Dist: Nelson, Thomas Inc.
—Busy Baby: First 100 Things That Go. 2008. (Busy Baby Ser.). (Illus.). 26p. (J). (gr. -1-k). bds. *(978-1-84610-774-0(1))* Make Believe Ideas.
—Touch & Learn 123 Casebound. 2007. per. *(978-1-84610-507-4(2))* Make Believe Ideas.
—Touch & Learn ABC. 2007. (Illus.). (gr. -1). per. *(978-1-84610-506-7(4))* Make Believe Ideas.
—Touch & Learn Baby Animals Casebound. 2007. per. *(978-1-84610-508-1(0))* Make Believe Ideas.

TUV

—Touch & Learn Tractors & Trucks Casebound. 2007. per. (978-1-84610-509-8(9)) Make Believe Ideas.

Make Believe Ideas, Ltd., creator. Pets & Puppies Pack. 2007. (Touch & Sparkle Ser.). (Illus.). (gr. -1-k). per., bds. (978-1-84610-692-7(3)) Make Believe Ideas.

Malepart, Celine, illus. When Pigs Fly: A Piggy Pop-up Book! 2008. (ENG.). 12p. 16.95 (978-1-58117-671-1(6), Intervisual/Piggy Toes) Bendon, Inc.

Man-Kong, Mary. My Fabulous Friends! Golden Books Staff, illus. 2009. (Pictureback(R) Ser.). (ENG.). 16p. (J). (gr. -1-2). pap. 3.99 (978-0-375-85789-8(3), Random Hse. Bks. for Young Readers) Random Hse. Children's Bks.

Mandy and Ness Staff, et al. George's Garden. 2005. (Senses Ser.). (URD, ENG, VIE, CHI & BEN., Illus.). 16p. (J). pap. 9.95 (978-1-84059-168-2(4)) Milet Publishing.

—Peter's Party. 2005. (Senses Ser.). (URD, ENG, VIE, CHI & BEN., Illus.). 16p. (J). pap. 9.95 (978-1-84059-150-7(1)) Milet Publishing.

—Rosie's Room. 2005. (Senses Ser.). (URD, ENG, TUR, VIE & CHI., Illus.). 16p. (J). (gr. -1-1). pap. 9.95 (978-1-84059-162-0(5)) Milet Publishing.

Mangual, Cynthia Ines. 3 Super Hero Tales (DC Super Friends) Random House & Doescher, Erik, illus. 2017. (Padded Board Book Ser.). (ENG.). 30p. (J). (— 1). bds. 11.99 **(978-1-5247-1714-8(2)**, Random Hse. Bks. for Young Readers) Random Hse. Children's Bks.

Manolessou, Katherina. Mummy & Me. 2017. (ENG., Illus.). 24p. (J). (— 1). bds. 10.99 **(978-1-4472-8877-0(7))** Pan Macmillan GBR. Dist: Independent Pubs. Group.

Mansfield, Andy. Fish Food. Lohlein, Henning, illus. 2015. (ENG.). 14p. (J). (gr. -1-k). 9.99 (978-1-4998-0044-9(4)) Little Bee Books Inc.

—Journey to the Moon. 2015. (ENG., Illus.). 14p. (J). (gr. -1-2). 12.99 (978-1-4998-0072-2(X)) Little Bee Books Inc.

Manson, Beverlie, illus. Stories to Share: The Twelve Dancing Princesses. 2017. (ENG.). 24p. (J). (gr. -1-12). pap. 7.99 **(978-1-86147-829-0(1)**, Armadillo) Anness Publishing GBR. Dist: National Bk. Network.

Mara, Nichole. All Aboard! Let's Ride a Train. Kolb, Andrew, illus. 2017. (ENG.). 10p. (J). (gr. -1 — 1). bds. 9.95 **(978-1-4197-2567-8(X)**, Abrams Appleseed) Abrams, Inc.

Mara, Nichole. So Many Feet. Vidal, Alexander & Santillanes, Alexander Vidal, illus. 2017. (ENG.). 34p. (J). (gr. -1 — 1). bds. 12.95 (978-1-4197-2318-6(9)) Abrams, Inc.

Marceau, Fani. Panorama: A Foldout Book. Jolivet, Joëlle, illus. 2009. (ENG.). 32p. (J). (gr. -1-k). 21.95 (978-0-8109-8332-8(X), Abrams Bks. for Young Readers) Abrams, Inc.

Marchesi, Stephen, illus. Glow-In-The-Dark Constellations. 2006. (J). (978-1-59412-171-5(0)) Mud Puddle, Inc.

Marchon, Benoit. Good Night! Bravi, Soledad, illus. 2013. (ENG.). 40p. (J). (gr. k — 1). bds. 7.99 (978-0-547-89314-3(0)) Houghton Mifflin Harcourt Publishing Co.

Markes, Julie. Thanks for Thanksgiving Board Book. Barrette, Doris, illus. 2017. 32p. (J). (gr. -1 — 1). bds. 7.99 **(978-0-06-264331-5(2)**, HarperFestival) HarperCollins Pubs.

Marks, Burton. Tanya Tinker & the Gizmo Gang. Smath, Jerry, illus. 2003. 20p. (J). (gr. -1-3). reprint ed. 22.00 (978-0-7567-6760-0(1)) DIANE Publishing Co.

Marley, Cedella & Marley, Bob. Every Little Thing: Based on the Song 'Three Little Birds' by Bob Marley. Brantley-Newton, Vanessa, illus. 2015. (ENG.). 24p. (J). (gr. -1-k). bds. 7.99 (978-1-4521-4290-6(4)) Chronicle Bks. LLC.

Marqina, Mignon. Shapes & Me: A Flip & Learn Book. I.t. ed. 2006. (Illus.). 32p. (J). lib. bdg. (978-1-934190-05-0(5)) Ocean Front Bk. Publishing, Inc.

Marsh, Carole. Alaska Wheel of Fortune: Game Book. (Orig.). pap. 9.95 (978-0-7933-9621-4(2)) Gallopade International.

Marshall, Linda Elovitz. Shh... Shh... Shabbat. Golubeva, Evgenia, illus. 2016. (ENG.). 12p. (gr. -1 — 1). 5.99 (978-1-4677-5873-4(6), Kar-Ben Publishing) Lerner Publishing Group.

Marshall, Natalie. Five Little Ducks. 2017. (Fingers & Toes Nursery Rhymes Ser.). (ENG.). 12p. (J). (— 1). bds. 6.99 (978-1-338-09116-8(6), Cartwheel Bks.) Scholastic, Inc.

—Millie-Mae: In Winter. 2014. (Illus.). (J). (978-1-4351-5613-5(7)) Barnes & Noble, Inc.

Marshall, Natalie, illus. Millie-Mae: In Autumn. 2014. (J). (978-1-4351-5612-8(9)) Barnes & Noble, Inc.

—Seaside Sandcastle! 2014. (J). (978-1-4351-5505-3(X)) Barnes & Noble, Inc.

—Tiny Creatures: Touch & Feel Book. 2015. (J). (978-1-4351-5935-8(7)) Barnes & Noble, Inc.

—Zoo Fun: A Lift the Flap Guessing Book. 2013. (J). (978-1-4351-4930-4(0)) Barnes & Noble, Inc.

Marshall, Rita. Taste the Clouds. Domeniconi, Paolo, illus. 2016. (ENG.). 14p. (J). (gr. -1-k). bds. 8.99 (978-1-56846-285-1(9), Creative Editions) Creative Co., The.

—Wake up, Weather! Felix, Monique, illus. 2016. (ENG.). 14p. (J). (gr. -1-k). bds. 8.99 (978-1-56846-286-8(7), Creative Editions) Creative Co., The.

Marsoli, Lisa Ann. Harold Takes a Trip: Harold & the Purple Crayon. Chiang, Andy, illus. 2005. 10p. (J). 7.95 (978-1-58117-262-1(1), Intervisual/Piggy Toes) Bendon, Inc.

—Rudolph the Red-Nosed Reindeer Pop-Up Book. Finch, Keith Andrew, illus. 2014. (ENG.). 12p. (J). (gr. -1). 19.95 (978-1-62686-197-8(8), Silver Dolphin Bks.) Readerlink Distribution Services, LLC.

Martin, Bill, Jr. Baby Bear, Baby Bear, What Do You See? Carle, Eric, illus. 2014. (Brown Bear & Friends Ser.). (ENG.). 28p. (J). (gr. -1-k). bds. 12.99 (978-0-8050-9949-2(2), 9780805099492, Holt, Henry & Co. Bks. For Young Readers) Holt, Henry & Co.

—Brown Bear, Brown Bear, What Do You See? Carle, Eric, illus. 2010. (ENG.). 22p. (J). (-1). bds. 12.99 (978-0-312-50926-2(X), 9780312509262, Priddy Bks.) St. Martin's Pr.

Martin, Bill, Jr. Brown Bear, Brown Bear, What Do You See? / Oso Pardo, Oso Pardo, ¿qué Ves Ahí? (Bilingual Board Book - Spanish Edition) Carle, Eric, illus. 2017. (ENG.). 28p. (J). bds. 9.99 **(978-1-250-15232-9(1)**, 9781250152329, Holt, Henry & Co. Bks. For Young Readers) Holt, Henry & Co.

Martin, Bill, Jr. & Archambault, John. Chica Chica Bum Bum ABC. Ehlert, Lois, illus. 2011. (SPA.). 16p. (J). (gr. -1-1): bds. 7.99 (978-1-4424-2292-6(0), Libros Para Ninos) Libros Para Ninos.

—Chicka Chicka ABC. Ehlert, Lois, illus. 2009. (Chicka Chicka Book Ser.). (ENG.). 16p. (J). (gr. -1-1). bds. 10.99 (978-1-4169-8447-4(X), Little Simon) Little Simon.

Martin, Bill, Jr & Sampson, Michael. Chicka Chicka 1, 2, 3. Ehlert, Lois, illus. 2014. (Chicka Chicka Book Ser.). (ENG.). 36p. (J). (gr. -1 — 1). bds. 7.99 (978-1-4814-0056-5(8), Little Simon) Little Simon.

Martin, David Lozell. Christmas Tree. Sweet, Melissa, illus. 2009. (ENG.). 26p. (J). (— 1). bds. 5.99 (978-0-7636-3030-0(6)) Candlewick Pr.

—Hanukkah Lights. Sweet, Melissa, illus. 2009. (ENG.). 26p. (J). (gr. -1 — 1). bds. 5.99 (978-0-7636-3029-4(2)) Candlewick Pr.

Martin, Emily Winfield. Day Dreamers: A Journey of Imagination. 2016. (ENG., Illus.). 32p. (J). (— 1). bds. 8.99 (978-1-101-93522-4(7), Random Hse. Bks. for Young Readers) Random Hse. Children's Bks.

—Dream Animals: A Bedtime Journey. 2015. (ENG., Illus.). 34p. (J). (— 1). bds. 8.99 (978-0-553-52190-0(X), Random Hse. Bks. for Young Readers) Random Hse. Children's Bks.

Martin, Ruth. Little Explorers: My Amazing Body. Sanders, Allan, illus. 2015. (Little Explorers Ser.). (ENG.). 18p. (J). (gr. -1-3). 9.99 (978-1-4998-0040-1(1)) Little Bee Books Inc.

—Little Explorers: Outer Space. Sanders, Allan, illus. 2016. (Little Explorers Ser.). (ENG.). 18p. (J). (gr. -1-3). 9.99 (978-1-4998-0250-4(1)) Little Bee Books Inc.

—Little Explorers: the Animal World. Sanders, Allan, illus. 2016. (Little Explorers Ser.). (ENG.). 18p. (J). (gr. -1-3). 9.99 (978-1-4998-0249-8(8)) Little Bee Books Inc.

—Noisy Nature: in the Jungle. Pledger, Maurice, illus. 2015. (ENG.). 12p. (J). (gr. -1). 16.95 (978-1-62686-104-6(8), Silver Dolphin Bks.) Readerlink Distribution Services, LLC.

—Noisy Nature: on the Farm. Pledger, Maurice, illus. 2015. (ENG.). 12p. (J). (gr. -1). 16.95 (978-1-62686-103-9(X), Silver Dolphin Bks.) Readerlink Distribution Services, LLC.

Martinez, Lisa Bolivar, et al. Good Night Miami. 2011. (Good Night Our World Ser.). (ENG.). 20p. (J). (gr. k — 1). bds. 9.95 (978-1-60219-051-1(8)) Good Night Bks.

Mason, Conrad. See Inside How Things Work. 2010. (See Inside Board Bks). 16p. (J). bds. 12.99 (978-0-7945-2406-7(0), Usborne) EDC Publishing.

—See Inside Ships. King, Colin, illus. 2011. (See Inside Board Books Ser.). 16p. (J). rng bd. 12.99 (978-0-7945-3005-1(2), Usborne) EDC Publishing.

Mason, Tom & Danko, Dan. A Christmas Surprise. Shannon, David et al, illus. 2011. (Jon Scieszka's Trucktown Ser.). (ENG.). 12p. (J). (gr. -1-k). 7.99 (978-1-4169-4193-4(2), Simon & Schuster Bks. For Young Readers) Simon & Schuster Bks. For Young Readers.

Mason, Tom, et al. Who's That Truck? Shannon, David et al, illus. 2008. (Jon Scieszka's Trucktown Ser.). (ENG.). 14p. (J). (gr. -1-1). bds. 7.99 (978-1-4169-4175-0(4), Little Simon) Little Simon.

Massironi, Daniela, illus. Frankie the Frog. 2014. (J). (978-1-4351-5573-2(4)) Barnes & Noble, Inc.

—Freddie the Fish. 2014. (J). (978-1-4351-5574-9(2)) Barnes & Noble, Inc.

Matheson, Christie. Tap the Magic Tree. Matheson, Christie, illus. 2013. (ENG., Illus.). 40p. (J). (gr. -1-3). 16.99 (978-0-06-227445-8(7), Greenwillow Bks.) HarperCollins Pubs.

—Tap the Magic Tree Board Book. Matheson, Christie, illus. 2016. (Illus.). 42p. (J). (gr. -1-3). bds. 7.99 (978-0-06-227446-5(5), Greenwillow Bks.) HarperCollins Pubs.

Mathy, Vincent, illus. Who's Hiding with Penguin? 2016. (ENG.). 10p. (J). (gr. -1 — 1). bds. 8.99 (978-1-4521-5661-3(1)) Chronicle Bks. LLC.

—Who's Hiding with Tiger? 2016. (ENG.). 10p. (J). (gr. -1 — 1). bds. 8.99 (978-1-4521-5662-0(X)) Chronicle Bks. LLC.

Mattel Inc. Staff, illus. Barbie Always in Style. 2011. (Storybook & Playset Ser.). (ENG.). 24p. (J). (gr. -1-1). 19.99 (978-0-7944-2316-2(7)) Reader's Digest Assn., Inc., The.

Matthews, Derek. Animales de la Granja. 2005. (Escucha y Aprende Ser.). (SPA., Illus.). 10p. (J). (gr. -1-1). (978-970-718-300-1(4), Silver Dolphin en Español) Advanced Marketing, S. de R. L. de C. V.

—Animales de la Selva. 2005. (Escucha y Aprende Ser.). (SPA., Illus.). 10p. (J). (gr. -1-1). (978-970-718-298-1(9), Silver Dolphin en Español) Advanced Marketing, S. de R. L. de C. V.

—Escucha y Aprende - Mascotas. 2005. (Escucha y Aprende Ser.). (SPA., Illus.). 10p. (J). (gr. -1-k). (978-970-718-299-8(7), Silver Dolphin en Español) Advanced Marketing, S. de R. L. de C. V.

—Tráfico: Con Graciosos Sonidos de vehículos. 2005. (Escucha y Aprende Ser.). (SPA., Illus.). 10p. (J). (gr. -1-1). (978-970-718-297-4(0), Silver Dolphin en Español) Advanced Marketing, S. de R. L. de C. V.

Mawhinney, Art & Disney Storybook Artists Staff, illus. Fairies. 2007. (Look & Find Ser.). 7.98 (978-1-4127-7423-9(3)) Publications International, Ltd.

Max and Sid Staff, illus. My First Animals. 2016. (My First Ser.). (ENG.). 12p. (J). (gr. -1 — 1). bds. 5.99 (978-1-4998-0185-9(8)) Little Bee Books Inc.

Maxwell-Hyslop, Miranda. Fish Go Woof! 2005. (Illus.). 36p. (J). (978-0-340-87338-0(8)) Hodder & Stoughton.

May, Darcy. Glitter Fairies Stickers. 2004. (Dover Little Activity Books Stickers Ser.). (ENG., Illus.). 2p. (J). (gr. 1-4). pap. 1.99 (978-0-486-43530-5(X)) Dover Pubns., Inc.

Mayer, Helena. The Lost Riolu: Pokémon Academy. 2009. (Pokémon Ser.). (Illus.). 62p. (J). pap. (978-0-545-20050-9(4)) Scholastic, Inc.

Mayer, Mercer. To the Rescue! Mayer, Mercer, illus. 2008. (My First I Can Read Bks.). (ENG., Illus.). 32p. (J). (gr. -1-3). 16.99 (978-0-06-083548-4(6)); pap. 3.99 (978-0-06-083547-7(8)) HarperCollins Pubs.

Mayo, Margaret. Mini Tab: Dig Dig Digging. Ayliffe, Alex, illus. 2017. (ENG.). 14p. (J). bds. 6.99 (978-1-62779-714-6(9), 9781627797146, Holt, Henry & Co. Bks. For Young Readers) Holt, Henry & Co.

McBratney, Sam. Guess How Much I Love You. Jeram, Anita, illus. (Guess How Much I Love You Ser.). (ENG.). (J). 2014. 30p. (gr. k-4). 9.99 (978-0-7636-7446-5(X)) 2011. 16p. (gr. -1-2). 19.99 (978-0-7636-5378-1(0)) Candlewick Pr.

—Guess How Much I Love You Lap-Size Board Book. Jeram, Anita, illus. 2013. (Guess How Much I Love You Ser.). (ENG.). 24p. (J). (— 1). bds. 12.99 (978-0-7636-7006-1(5)) Candlewick Pr.

—Guess How Much I Love You: Look What I Can Do: A First Concepts Book. Jeram, Anita, illus. 2014. (Guess How Much I Love You Ser.). (ENG.). 16p. (J). (— 1). bds. 9.99 (978-0-7636-7064-1(2)) Candlewick Pr.

—Guess How Much I Love You: One More Tickle! Jeram, Anita, illus. 2016. (Guess How Much I Love You Ser.). (ENG.). (J). (gr. k-k). bds. 17.99 (978-0-7636-8819-6(3)) Candlewick Pr.

—Let's Play in the Snow. Jeram, Anita, illus. 2012. (Guess How Much I Love You Ser.). (ENG.). 24p. (J). (gr. k — 1). bds. 4.99 (978-0-7636-6121-2(X)) Candlewick Pr.

—There, There. Bates, Ivan, illus. 2015. (ENG.). 32p. (J). (-k). bds. 7.99 (978-0-7636-7565-3(2), Templar) Candlewick Pr.

McCarthy, Dan & Rosen, Anne. Good Night Oregon. Veno, Joe, illus. 2010. (Good Night Our World Ser.). (ENG.). 20p. (J). (gr. k — 1). bds. 9.95 (978-1-60219-041-2(0)) Good Night Bks.

McCombs, Margi. Dios es Bueno Todo el Tiempo. Ivanov, Aleksey & Ivanov, Olga, illus. 2012. (SPA.). 20p. (J). (gr. -1-k). bds. 9.99 (978-0-545-45618-0(5), Scholastic en Espanol) Scholastic, Inc.

McCourt, Lisa. It's Time for School. Moore, Cyd, illus. 2017. (Stinky Face Ser.). (ENG.). 32p. (J). (— 1). bds. 6.99 **(978-1-338-13582-4(1)**, Cartwheel Bks.) Scholastic, Inc.

—Merry Christmas, Stinky Face. Moore, Cyd, illus. 2008. (ENG.). 32p. (J). (gr. k — 1). bds. 6.99 (978-0-439-73123-2(2), Cartwheel Bks.) Scholastic, Inc.

—You Can Do It, Stinky Face! Moore, Cyd, illus. 2016. (ENG.). 32p. (J). (— 1). bds. 6.99 (978-0-545-80648-0(8), Cartwheel Bks.) Scholastic, Inc.

McCue, Lisa. The Animals' Advent. 2010. (ENG., Illus.). 14p. (J). (gr. k — 1). 5.99 (978-0-375-85815-4(6), Random Hse. Bks. for Young Readers) Random Hse. Children's Bks.

McCue, Lisa, illus. Busy Bunnies. 2014. (ENG.). 14p. (J). (gr. -1 — 1). bds. 5.99 (978-0-7944-3039-9(2)) Reader's Digest Assn., Inc., The.

—Corduroy's Thanksgiving. 2006. (Corduroy Ser.). (ENG.). 16p. (J). (gr. -1 — 1). bds. 5.99 (978-0-670-06108-2(5), Viking Books for Young Readers) Penguin Young Readers Group.

—Time for Bed! A Cozy Counting Bedtime Book. 2015. (ENG.). 20p. (J). (gr. -1 — 1). bds. 12.99 (978-0-7944-3337-6(5)) Reader's Digest Assn., Inc., The.

McCurry, Kristen & Hilton, Jennifer. Dios No Creo Todos. Garton, Michael, illus. 2016. (SPA.). (J). **(978-1-5064-2092-9(3))** Augsburg Fortress, Pubs.

—Good Morning, World. Rimmington, Natasha, illus. 2017. (J). 6.99 **(978-1-5064-1785-1(X)**, Sparkhouse Family) Augsburg Fortress, Pubs.

McDonnell, Patrick. The Little Gift of Nothing. 2016. (ENG., Illus.). 30p. (J). (gr. -1 — 1). bds. 7.99 (978-0-316-39473-4(4)) Little, Brown Bks. for Young Readers.

McDoogle, Farrah, adapted by. A Party for Brobee! 2010. (Yo Gabba Gabba! Ser.). (ENG.). 14p. (J). (gr. -1-k). bds. 5.99 (978-1-4169-9934-8(5), Simon Spotlight) Simon Spotlight.

McDougall, Carol & LaRamee-Jones, Shanda. Baby Look, 1 vol. 2013. (Baby Steps Ser.). (ENG., Illus.). 16p. (J). (gr. -1-k). bds. 8.95 (978-1-55109-937-8(3)) Nimbus Publishing, Ltd. CAN. Dist: Orca Bk. Pubs. USA.

McElligott, Matthew. Even Monsters Need Haircuts. McElligott, Matthew, illus. 2015. (ENG., Illus.). 30p. (J). (gr. -1-2). bds. 6.99 (978-0-8027-3839-4(7), 9780802738394, Bloomsbury USA Childrens) Bloomsbury Publishing USA.

McElroy, Jean. Baby's Colorful World. 2011. (ENG.). 14p. (J). (gr. -1 — 1). 4.99 (978-1-4424-1197-5(X), Little Simon) Little Simon.

McFadden, Patricia. Oh No, Woolly Bear!, 1 vol. Coxon, Michele, illus. 2008. (ENG.). 32p. (J). (gr. -1-3). 6.50 (978-1-59572-149-5(5)) Star Bright Bks., Inc.

McGrath, Barbara Barbieri. Birthday Counting. Tagel, Peggy, illus. 2017. (First Celebrations Ser.). (ENG.). 12p. (J). (— 1). bds. 6.99 (978-1-58089-537-8(9)) Charlesbridge Publishing, Inc.

—Easter Counting. Tagel, Peggy, illus. 2017. (First Celebrations Ser.). (ENG.). 12p. (J). (— 1). bds. 6.99 (978-1-58089-535-4(2)) Charlesbridge Publishing, Inc.

—Halloween Colors. Tagel, Peggy, illus. 2016. (First Celebrations Ser.). (ENG.). 12p. (J). (— 1). bds. 6.95 (978-1-58089-533-0(6)) Charlesbridge Publishing, Inc.

McGrath, Barbara Barbieri & Tagel, Peggy. Parade Colors. 2017. (First Celebrations Ser.). (ENG., Illus.). 12p. (J). (— 1). bds. 6.99 (978-1-58089-536-1(0)) Charlesbridge Publishing, Inc.

—Thanksgiving Counting. 2016. (First Celebrations Ser.). (ENG., Illus.). 12p. (J). (— 1). bds. 6.95 (978-1-58089-534-7(4)) Charlesbridge Publishing, Inc.

—Valentine's Shapes. 2016. (First Celebrations Ser.). (ENG., Illus.). 12p. (J). (— 1). bds. 6.95 (978-1-58089-532-3(8)) Charlesbridge Publishing, Inc.

McGuinness, Elle J. & Caron, Romi. Baby Turtle's Tale. 2011. (ENG.). 12p. (J). 9.99 (978-1-4494-0354-6(9)) Andrews McMeel Publishing.

McGuirk, Leslie. Ho, Ho, Ho, Tucker! McGuirk, Leslie, illus. 2010. (Candlewick Storybook Animations Ser.). (ENG., Illus.). 32p. (J). (-k). 8.99 (978-0-7636-5043-8(9)) Candlewick Pr.

—Tucker's Spooky Halloween. McGuirk, Leslie. illus. 2011. (Candlewick Storybook Animations Ser.). (ENG., Illus.). 32p. (J). (gr. k-k). 8.99 (978-0-7636-5113-8(3)) Candlewick Pr.

McKee, David. Elmer Board Book. McKee, David, illus. 2014. (Illus.). 32p. (J). (gr. -1 — 1). bds. 7.99 (978-0-06-232405-4(5), HarperFestival) HarperCollins Pubs.

—Elmer's First Counting Book. McKee, David, ed. 2012. (Andersen Press Board Bks). (ENG., Illus.). 10p. (J). (gr. -1-2). bds. 7.95 (978-0-7613-8999-6(7)) Lerner Publishing Group.

McKendry, Sam. Are You Ticklish?/Tienes Cosquillas? Mitchell, Melanie, illus. 2005. (ENG.). 12p. (gr. -1-k). 10.95 (978-1-58117-472-4(1), Intervisual/Piggy Toes) Bendon, Inc.

—Bless Everyone. 2006. (ENG., Illus.). 12p. (J). (gr. -1-k). 8.95 (978-1-58117-445-8(4), Intervisual/Piggy Toes) Bendon, Inc.

—Curious Kitties: A Colors Book. Mitchell, Melanie, illus. 2005. (ENG.). 16p. (J). bds. 9.95 (978-1-58117-417-5(9), Intervisual/Piggy Toes) Bendon, Inc.

McMahon, Kara. Dress up Dora! Aikins, Dave, illus. 2009. (Dora the Explorer Ser.). (ENG.). 12p. (J). 8.99 (978-1-4169-6067-6(8), Simon Spotlight/Nickelodeon) Simon Spotlight/Nickelodeon.

McMahon, Kara & Jordan, Apple. My Growing-Up Library. 2010. (ENG., Illus.). 12p. (J). (gr. k — 1). bds. 10.99 (978-0-375-85984-7(5), Random Hse. Bks. for Young Readers) Random Hse. Children's Bks.

McMaster, Juliet & Cote, Patricia. Where Are You Little Red Ball?, 1 vol. Reva, Maria, tr. from FRE. Yayo, illus. 2016. (ENG.). 12p. (J). (gr. k-1). bds. 8.95 (978-1-926890-12-8(4)) Tradewind Bks. CAN. Dist: Orca Bk. Pubs. USA.

McMenemy, Sarah. Washington D. C. A 3D Keepsake Cityscape. McMenemy, Sarah, illus. 2012. (Panorama Pops Ser.). (ENG., Illus.). 20p. (J). (gr. k-12). 8.99 (978-0-7636-5935-6(5)) Candlewick Pr.

McMullan, Kate. Supercat to the Rescue. Lemaître, Pascal, illus. (ENG.). 1p. (J). bds. 55.60 (978-0-7611-3234-9(1), 23234) Workman Publishing Co., Inc.

McNamara, Connie. My First Wisconsin Words Go Badgers. 2012. (ENG.). 16p. 10.99 (978-0-06-219606-4(5)) HarperCollins Pubs.

McNaughton, Colin. Dracula's Tomb. McNaughton, Colin, illus. 2009. (ENG., Illus.). 24p. (J). (gr. k-4). 14.99 (978-0-7636-4488-8(9)) Candlewick Pr.

McNeil, Kelli. Sleepy Toes. Doerrfeld, Cori, illus. 2017. (ENG.). 26p. (J). (gr. -1 — 1). bds. 8.99 (978-1-338-03072-3(8), Cartwheel Bks.) Scholastic, Inc.

McNicholas, Shelagh, illus. This Little Light of Mine. 2013. (ENG.). 12p. (J). (gr. -1-k). bds. 6.99 (978-0-545-47768-0(9), Little Shepherd) Scholastic, Inc.

McPhail, David. Baby Pig Pig Talks. McPhail, David, illus. 2014. (ENG., Illus.). 14p. (J). (— 1). bds. 6.95 (978-1-58089-597-2(2)) Charlesbridge Publishing, Inc.

—Baby Pig Pig Walks. McPhail, David, illus. 2014. (ENG., Illus.). 14p. (J). (— 1). bds. 6.95 (978-1-58089-596-5(4)) Charlesbridge Publishing, Inc.

—Hermanos Brothers. Calvo, Carlos, tr. 2017. (ENG & SPA., Illus.). 28p. (J). (— 1). bds. 4.99 (978-0-544-91586-2(0), HMH Books For Young Readers) Houghton Mifflin Harcourt Publishing Co.

—I Get Dressed. 2015. (ENG., Illus.). 12p. (J). (gr. -1 — 1). bds. 5.99 (978-1-62672-147-0(5), 9781626721470) Roaring Brook Pr.

—I Play. 2015. (ENG., Illus.). 12p. (J). (gr. -1 — 1). bds. 5.99 (978-1-62672-148-7(3), 9781626721487) Roaring Brook Pr.

—Olivia Loves Owl. 2016. (ENG., Illus.). 20p. (J). (gr. -1 — 1). bds. 8.95 (978-1-4197-2127-4(5), Abrams Appleseed) Abrams, Inc.

—Peter Loves Penguin. 2014. (David Mcphail's Love Ser.). (ENG., Illus.). 22p. (J). (gr. -1 — 1). bds. 8.95 (978-1-4197-1337-8(X), Abrams Appleseed) Abrams, Inc.

McQuinn, Anna. Wanda's Washing Machine. McCafferty, Jan, illus. 2005. 20p. (J). (gr. -1-2). 12.95 (978-1-58925-768-9(5)) Tiger Tales.

Mead, David & Berry, Ron. Who's at the Door? 2010. (Illus.). 12p. (J). (gr. -1-1). 10.99 (978-0-8249-1431-8(7), Ideal Pubns.) Worthy Publishing.

Meadows, Daisy & Scholastic, Inc. Staff. The Jewel Fairies Collection, Vol. 1. 2008. (Jewel Fairies Ser.: Bks. 1-4). (ENG., Illus.). 288p. (J). (gr. -1-3). pap. 6.99 (978-0-545-08838-1(0), Scholastic Paperbacks) Scholastic, Inc.

Meeuwissen, Tony. Remarkable Animals: Mix & Match to Create 100 Crazy Creatures. Meeuwissen, Tony, illus. rev. ed. 2016. (ENG., Illus.). 24p. (J). (gr. -1-k). 7.99 (978-1-84780-762-5(3), Frances Lincoln Children's Bks.) Quarto Publishing Group UK GBR. Dist: Hachette Bk. Group.

Meister, Cari & Ritchey, Kate. Happy Doodling! 2014. (Mr. Men & Little Miss Ser.). (ENG., Illus.). 128p. (J). (gr. -1-2). 12.99 (978-0-8431-8043-5(9), Price Stern Sloan) Penguin Young Readers Group.

Melcher, Mary, illus. Puppies Count. 2010. (J). (978-1-58865-596-7(2)) Kidsbooks, LLC.

Mellor, Corinne & Ericksson, Ashe. Snowlies Find a Letter. 2007. 22p. (J). (978-1-84666-410-6(1), Tide Mill Pr.) Top That! Publishing PLC.

Melvin, Alice, illus. Grandma's House. 2015. (ENG.). 32p. (J). (gr. -1-3). 19.95 (978-1-84976-222-9(8)) Tate Publishing, Ltd. GBR. Dist: Abrams, Inc.

Merberg, Julie. My Favorite Shoes: A Touch-and-Feel Shoe-Stravaganza! Bove, Neysa & Rucker, Georgia, illus. 2013. (ENG.). 16p. (J). (gr. -1 — 1). bds. 12.99 (978-1-935703-64-8(1)) Downtown Bookworks.

—Turn the Key: Around Town: Look & See! McQueen, Lucinda, illus. 2012. (ENG.). 12p. (J). (gr. -1 — 1). bds. 11.99 (978-1-935703-44-0(7)) Downtown Bookworks.

Meredith, Samantha. Flip & Find Builders. 2016. (Flip & Find Ser.). (ENG., Illus.). 10p. (J). (— 1). bds. 7.99 (978-1-4472-7714-9(7)) Pan Macmillan GBR. Dist: Independent Pubs. Group.

—Flip & Find Farmers Board Book. 2016. (Flip & Find Ser.). (ENG., Illus.). 10p. (J). (— 1). bds. 7.99 (978-1-4472-7715-6(5)) Pan Macmillan GBR. Dist: Independent Pubs. Group.

—Flip & Find Pilots: A Guess Who/Where Flap Book about a Pilot. Meredith, Samantha, illus. 2016. (Flip & Find Ser.). (ENG., Illus.). 12p. (J). (— 1). bds. 7.99 (978-1-4472-7717-0(1)) Pan Macmillan GBR. Dist: Independent Pubs. Group.

Merer, Laura, illus. Fuzzy Ducky's Birthday: A Touch-and-Feel Pop-up Book. 2005. 10p. (J). 8.95 (978-1-58117-324-6(5), Intervisual/Piggy Toes) Bendon, Inc.

Merlin, Christophe. Under the Hood. 2011. (ENG., Illus.). 14p. (J). (gr. -1-2). 14.99 (978-0-7636-5535-8(X)) Candlewick Pr.

Metcalf, Paula. Mouse's Sock Tree. Mitchell, Susan, illus. 2014. (ENG.). 12p. (J). (— 1). bds. 7.99 (978-0-230-76475-0(4)) Pan Macmillan GBR. Dist: Independent Pubs. Group.

—My Mummy. Barnard, Lucy, illus. 2015. (ENG.). 24p. (J). (-1). bds. 9.99 (978-1-4472-7699-9(X)) Pan Macmillan GBR. Dist: Independent Pubs. Group.

—Rabbits Don't Lay Eggs! Johnson-Isaacs, Cally, illus. 2016. (ENG.). 24p. (J). (gr. -1-k). bds. 9.99 (978-1-4472-8277-8(9)) Pan Macmillan GBR. Dist: Independent Pubs. Group.

Metsola, Aino-Maija. Colors. 2016. (Learning Garden Ser.). (ENG.). 16p. (J). (gr. -1-k). bds. 9.99 *(978-1-84780-705-2(4),* Wide Eyed Editions) Quarto Publishing Group UK GBR. Dist: Hachette Bk. Group.
—Colours: With Lift-Flap Surprises on Every Page. 2015. (Learning Garden Ser.). (ENG., Illus.). 14p. (J). bds. 9.99 *(978-1-84780-609-3(0),* Wide Eyed Editions) Quarto Publishing Group UK GBR. Dist: Littlehampton Bk Services, Ltd.
—Counting. (Learning Garden Ser.). (ENG.). 14p. (J). 2016. (gr. -1-k). bds. 9.99 *(978-1-84780-706-9(2))* 2015. (Illus.). bds. 9.99 *(978-1-84780-610-9(4))* Quarto Publishing Group UK GBR. (Wide Eyed Editions). Dist: Hachette Bk. Group, Littlehampton Bk Services, Ltd.
—Traffic Jam: Puzzle Book. 2016. (Learning Garden Ser.). (ENG., Illus.). 14p. (J). bds. 14.99 *(978-1-84780-746-5(1),* Wide Eyed Editions) Quarto Publishing Group UK GBR. Dist: Littlehampton Bk Services, Ltd.
Mettler, René. Birds. Mettler, René, illus. 2012. (My First Discoveries Ser.: 15). (ENG., Illus.). 38p. (J). (gr. -1-k). spiral bd. 12.99 *(978-1-85103-397-3(1))* Moonlight Publishing, Ltd. GBR. Dist: Independent Pubs. Group.
Metzger, Steve. I Love You All Year Long. Keay, Claire, illus. 2009. 20p. (J). (gr. -1-k). 8.95 *(978-1-58925-847-1(9))* Tiger Tales.
Meyers, Haily & Meyers, Kevin. All Aboard California, 1 vol. Meyers, Haily, illus. 2015. (ENG., Illus.). 22p. (J). bds. 9.99 *(978-1-4236-4080-6(2))* Gibbs Smith, Publisher.
—Gotta Go, Buffalo: The Goodbye Book, 1 vol. 2017. (ENG., Illus.). 20p. (J). 12.99 *(978-1-4236-4598-6(7))* Gibbs Smith, Publisher.
Meyers, Susan. Everywhere Babies. Frazee, Marla, illus. (ENG.). 30p. (J). 2016. (— 1). bds. 8.99 *(978-0-544-79120-6(7),* HMH Books For Young Readers) 2011. (gr. -1 — 1). bds. 11.99 *(978-0-547-51074-3(8))* Houghton Mifflin Harcourt Publishing Co.
Miesen, Christina & Novick, Mary. Colours & Shapes: With Flip the Flap Pages. 2013. (Mini Marvels Ser.). (ENG., Illus.). 10p. (J). (gr. -1-k). 9.99 *(978-1-921049-62-0(6))* Little Hare Bks. AUS. Dist: Independent Pubs. Group.
Milbourne, Anna. Peek Inside Animal Homes. Dimitri, Simona, illus. 2014. (Peek Inside Board Bks.). (ENG.). 14p. (gr. -1). bds. 11.99 *(978-0-7945-2549-1(0),* Usborne) EDC Publishing.
Miles, David, illus. Wild about the Bible Sticker & Activity Book, 1 vol. 2016. (Adventure Bible Ser.). (ENG.). 32p. (J). pap. 6.99 *(978-0-310-75405-3(4))* Zonderkidz.
Miles Kelly Staff. Mix-Ups. 2003. (Illus.). 14p. 9.95 *(978-1-902947-83-9(5))* Miles Kelly Publishing, Ltd. GBR. Dist: Independent Pubs. Group.
—Noises: Let's Learn. Nilsen, Anna, ed. 2003. (Let's Learn Ser.). (Illus.). 20p. (J). 7.95 *(978-1-84236-139-9(2))* Miles Kelly Publishing, Ltd. GBR. Dist: Independent Pubs. Group.
—Opposites: Let's Learn. Nilsen, Anna, ed. 2003. (Let's Learn Ser.). (Illus.). 20p. (J). 7.95 *(978-1-84236-138-2(4))* Miles Kelly Publishing, Ltd. GBR. Dist: Independent Pubs. Group.
—Sizes: Let's Learn. Nilsen, Anna, ed. 2003. (Let's Learn Ser.). (Illus.). 20p. (J). 7.95 *(978-1-84236-140-5(6))* Miles Kelly Publishing, Ltd. GBR. Dist: Independent Pubs. Group.
Miles Kelly Staff & Nilsen, Anna. Actions: Let's Learn. 2003. (Let's Learn Ser.). (Illus.). 20p. (J). 7.95 *(978-1-84236-137-5(6))* Miles Kelly Publishing, Ltd. GBR. Dist: Independent Pubs. Group.
—Numbers: Let's Learn. 2003. (Let's Learn Ser.). (Illus.). 20p. (J). 7.95 *(978-1-84236-018-7(3))* Miles Kelly Publishing, Ltd. GBR. Dist: Independent Pubs. Group.
—Shapes: Let's Learn. 2003. (Let's Learn Ser.). (Illus.). 20p. (J). 7.95 *(978-1-84236-016-3(7))* Miles Kelly Publishing, Ltd. GBR. Dist: Independent Pubs. Group.
Milet Publishing Staff. Animals. 2011. (My First Bilingual Book Ser.). (Illus.). 24p. (J). (gr. k — 1). (FRE & ENG.). bds. 8.99 *(978-1-84059-612-0(0));* (ENG., bds. 7.99 *(978-1-84059-622-9(8));* (ENG., bds. 8.99 *(978-1-84059-613-7(9));* (ENG., bds. 8.99 *(978-1-84059-615-1(5))* Milet Publishing.
—Animals - My First Bilingual Book. 2011. (My First Bilingual Book Ser.). (ENG., Illus.). 24p. (J). (gr. k — 1). bds. 7.99 *(978-1-84059-608-3(2));* bds. 7.99 *(978-1-84059-618-2(X));* bds. 8.99 *(978-1-84059-623-6(6))* Milet Publishing.
—Clothes. 2014. (My First Bilingual Book Ser.). (Illus.). 20p. (J). (— 1). (SPA & ENG.). bds. 7.99 *(978-1-84059-870-4(0));* (ENG & KOR., bds. 7.99 *(978-1-84059-865-0(4))* Milet Publishing.
—Clothes - My First Bilingual Book. 2014. (My First Bilingual Book Ser.). (Illus.). 20p. (J). (— 1). (POR & ENG.). bds. 7.99 *(978-1-84059-867-4(0));* (ENG & VIE., bds. 7.99 *(978-1-84059-873-5(5));* (ENG & CHI., bds. 7.99 *(978-1-84059-860-5(3));* (ENG & ITA., bds. 7.99 *(978-1-84059-864-3(6))* Milet Publishing.
—Colors. (My First Bilingual Book Ser.). 24p. (J). (gr. k — 1). 2011. (ENG.). bds. 7.99 *(978-1-84059-606-9(6))* 2011. (ENG.). bds. 8.99 *(978-1-84059-597-0(3))* 2010. (SPA & ENG., Illus.). bds. 7.99 *(978-1-84059-539-0(6))* Milet Publishing.
—Colors - My First Bilingual Book. 2011. (My First Bilingual Book Ser.). (ENG.). 24p. (J). (gr. k — 1). bds. 7.99 *(978-1-84059-601-4(5));* bds. 7.99 *(978-1-84059-599-4(X))* Milet Publishing.
—Colours. 2010. (My First Bilingual Book Ser.). (Illus.). 24p. (J). (gr. k — 1). (VIE & ENG.). bds. 7.99 *(978-1-84059-569-7(8));* (KOR & ENG., bds. 7.99 *(978-1-84059-564-2(7));* (ENG & JPN., bds. 7.99 *(978-1-84059-563-5(9))* Milet Publishing.
—Colours - My First Bilingual Book. 2010. (My First Bilingual Book Ser.). (Illus.). 24p. (J). (gr. k — 1). (URD & ENG.). bds. 7.99 *(978-1-84059-568-0(X));* (SOM & ENG., bds. 7.99 *(978-1-84059-567-3(1));* (RUS & ENG., bds. 7.99 *(978-1-84059-566-6(3));* (ARA & ENG., bds. 7.99 *(978-1-84059-560-4(4));* (PER & ENG., bds. 7.99 *(978-1-84059-562-8(0));* (POR & ENG., bds. 7.99 *(978-1-84059-565-9(5));* (ENG & POL., bds. 8.99 *(978-1-84059-538-3(8));* (ENG & GER., bds. 8.99 *(978-1-84059-536-9(1));* (ENG & ITA., bds. 8.99 *(978-1-84059-537-6(X))* Milet Publishing.
—Fruit. 2011. (My First Bilingual Book Ser.). (ENG., Illus.). 24p. (J). (gr. k — 1). bds. 7.99 *(978-1-84059-625-0(2))* Milet Publishing.
—Fruit - My First Bilingual Book. 2011. (My First Bilingual Book Ser.). (ENG., Illus.). 24p. (J). (gr. k — 1). bds. 7.99 *(978-1-84059-637-3(6));* bds. 7.99 *(978-1-84059-624-3(4));* bds. 7.99 *(978-1-84059-632-8(5));* bds. 7.99 *(978-1-84059-634-2(1));* bds. 8.99 *(978-1-84059-630-4(9))* Milet Publishing.
—Fruit (English-French) 2011. (My First Bilingual Book Ser.). (FRE & ENG., Illus.). 24p. (J). (gr. k — 1). bds. 7.99 *(978-1-84059-628-1(7))* Milet Publishing.
—Home. 2011. (My First Bilingual Book Ser.). (ENG., Illus.). 24p. (J). (gr. k — 1). bds. 7.99 *(978-1-84059-642-7(2));* bds. 7.99 *(978-1-84059-646-5(5))* Milet Publishing.
—Home - My First Bilingual Book. 2011. (My First Bilingual Book Ser.). (ENG., Illus.). 24p. (J). (gr. k — 1). bds. 7.99 *(978-1-84059-641-0(4));* bds. 8.99 *(978-1-84059-645-8(7))* Milet Publishing.
—Home (English-Arabic) 2011. (My First Bilingual Book Ser.). (ENG., Illus.). 24p. (J). (gr. k — 1). bds. 7.99 *(978-1-84059-640-3(6))* Milet Publishing.
—Home (English-French) 2011. (My First Bilingual Book Ser.). (FRE & ENG., Illus.). 24p. (J). (gr. k — 1). bds. 8.99 *(978-1-84059-644-1(9))* Milet Publishing.
—Home (English-Polish) 2011. (My First Bilingual Book Ser.). (ENG & POR., Illus.). 24p. (J). (gr. k — 1). bds. 7.99 *(978-1-84059-648-9(1))* Milet Publishing.
—Home (English-Portuguese) 2011. (My First Bilingual Book Ser.). (ENG., Illus.). 24p. (J). (gr. k — 1). bds. 7.99 *(978-1-84059-649-6(X))* Milet Publishing.
—Jobs Profesiones. 2012. (My First Bilingual Book Ser.). (SPA & ENG., Illus.). 24p. (J). (gr. k — 1). bds. 7.99 *(978-1-84059-712-7(7))* Milet Publishing.
—Music. 2012. (My First Bilingual Book Ser.). (ENG, POL & POR., Illus.). 24p. (J). (gr. k — 1). bds. 7.99 *(978-1-84059-724-0(0))* Milet Publishing.
—Music - My First Bilingual Book. 2012. (My First Bilingual Book Ser.). (ENG & POR., Illus.). 24p. (J). (gr. k — 1). bds. 7.99 *(978-1-84059-725-7(9))* Milet Publishing.
—My First Bilingual Book - Animals. 2011. (My First Bilingual Book Ser.). (ENG., Illus.). 24p. (J). (gr. k — 1). bds. 7.99 *(978-1-84059-611-3(2));* bds. 7.99 *(978-1-84059-609-0(0));* bds. 7.99 *(978-1-84059-621-2(X))* Milet Publishing.
—My First Bilingual Book - Animals (English-Somali) 2011. (My First Bilingual Book Ser.). (ENG., Illus.). 24p. (J). (gr. k — 1). bds. 8.99 *(978-1-84059-619-9(8))* Milet Publishing.
—My First Bilingual Book - Clothes. 2014. (My First Bilingual Book Ser.). (Illus.). 20p. (J). (— 1). (ENG & RUS.). bds. 7.99 *(978-1-84059-868-1(9));* (FRE & ENG., bds. 7.99 *(978-1-84059-862-9(X));* (ENG & TUR., bds. 7.99 *(978-1-84059-871-1(9));* (ENG, POL & POR., bds. 7.99 *(978-1-84059-866-7(2));* (ENG & ARA., bds. 7.99 *(978-1-84059-858-2(1));* (ENG & URD., bds. 7.99 *(978-1-84059-872-8(7));* (ENG & BEN., bds. 7.99 *(978-1-84059-859-9(X));* (ENG & PER., bds. 7.99 *(978-1-84059-861-2(1));* (ENG & GER., bds. 7.99 *(978-1-84059-863-6(8));* (ENG & SOM., bds. 7.99 *(978-1-84059-869-8(7))* Milet Publishing.
—My First Bilingual Book - Colors. 2011. (My First Bilingual Book Ser.). (ENG.). 24p. (J). (gr. k — 1). bds. 7.99 *(978-1-84059-604-5(X));* bds. 7.99 *(978-1-84059-600-7(7));* bds. 7.99 *(978-1-84059-598-7(1));* bds. 7.99 *(978-1-84059-602-1(3));* bds. 7.99 *(978-1-84059-603-8(1))* Milet Publishing.
—My First Bilingual Book - Colors (English-Urdu) 2011. (My First Bilingual Book Ser.). (ENG.). 24p. (J). (gr. k — 1). bds. 7.99 *(978-1-84059-605-2(8))* Milet Publishing.
—My First Bilingual Book - Colours. 2010. (My First Bilingual Book Ser.). (Illus.). 24p. (J). (gr. k — 1). (ENG & TUR.). bds. 7.99 *(978-1-84059-540-6(X));* (FRE & ENG., bds. 8.99 *(978-1-84059-535-2(3))* Milet Publishing.
—My First Bilingual Book - Fruit. 2011. (My First Bilingual Book Ser.). (ENG., Illus.). 24p. (J). (gr. k — 1). bds. 8.99 *(978-1-84059-626-7(0));* bds. 7.99 *(978-1-84059-627-4(9));* bds. 7.99 *(978-1-84059-631-1(7));* bds. 8.99 *(978-1-84059-633-5(3));* bds. 7.99 *(978-1-84059-629-8(5))* Milet Publishing.
—My First Bilingual Book - Home. 2011. (My First Bilingual Book Ser.). (ENG., Illus.). 24p. (J). (gr. k — 1). bds. 7.99 *(978-1-84059-643-4(0));* bds. 7.99 *(978-1-84059-647-2(3))* Milet Publishing.
—My First Bilingual Book - Numbers. (My First Bilingual Book Ser.). (Illus.). 24p. (J). (gr. k — 1). 2011. (CHI & ENG.). bds. 8.99 *(978-1-84059-571-0(X))* 2011. (PER & ENG., bds. 7.99 *(978-1-84059-572-7(8))* 2011. (VIE & ENG., bds. 8.99 *(978-1-84059-579-6(5))* 2011. (KOR & ENG., bds. 7.99 *(978-1-84059-574-1(4))* 2011. (POR & ENG., bds. 7.99 *(978-1-84059-575-8(2))* 2011. (URD, ENG & RUS., bds. 8.99 *(978-1-84059-578-9(7))* 2011. (JPN & ENG., bds. 7.99 *(978-1-84059-573-4(6))* 2010. (ENG & TUR., bds. 7.99 *(978-1-84059-546-8(9))* 2010. (SPA & ENG., bds. 8.99 *(978-1-84059-545-1(0))* Milet Publishing.
—My First Bilingual Book - Plants. 2014. (My First Bilingual Book Ser.). (Illus.). 20p. (J). (— 1). (ENG & TUR.). bds. 7.99 *(978-1-84059-887-2(5));* (ENG & CHI., bds. 7.99 *(978-1-84059-876-6(X));* (ENG & SOM., bds. 7.99 *(978-1-84059-885-8(9));* (POR & ENG., bds. 7.99 *(978-1-84059-883-4(2));* (ENG & ARA., bds. 7.99 *(978-1-84059-874-2(3))* Milet Publishing.
—My First Bilingual Book - Plants (English-Farsi) 2014. (My First Bilingual Book Ser.). (ENG & PER., Illus.). 20p. (J). (— 1). bds. 7.99 *(978-1-84059-877-3(8))* Milet Publishing.
—My First Bilingual Book - Plants (English-Korean) 2014. (My First Bilingual Book Ser.). (ENG & KOR., Illus.). 20p. (J). (— 1). bds. 7.99 *(978-1-84059-881-0(6))* Milet Publishing.
—My First Bilingual Book - School. 2014. (My First Bilingual Book Ser.). (Illus.). 20p. (J). (— 1). (ENG & BEN.). bds. 7.99 *(978-1-84059-891-9(3));* (ENG & GER., bds. 7.99 *(978-1-84059-895-7(6));* (POR & ENG., bds. 7.99 *(978-1-84059-899-5(9));* (ENG & CHI., bds. 7.99 *(978-1-84059-892-6(1));* (ENG & VIE., bds. 7.99 *(978-1-84059-905-3(7));* (ENG & TUR., bds. 7.99 *(978-1-84059-903-9(0))* Milet Publishing.
—My First Bilingual Book - School (English-Korean) 2014. (My First Bilingual Book Ser.). (ENG & KOR., Illus.). 20p. (J). (— 1). bds. 7.99 *(978-1-84059-897-1(2))* Milet Publishing.
—My First Bilingual Book - School (English-Somali) 2014. (My First Bilingual Book Ser.). (ENG & SOM., Illus.). 20p. (J). (— 1). bds. 7.99 *(978-1-84059-901-5(4))* Milet Publishing.
—My First Bilingual Book - Tools. 2014. (My First Bilingual Book Ser.). (Illus.). 20p. (J). (— 1). (ENG & BEN.). bds. 7.99 *(978-1-84059-907-7(3));* (ENG & ARA., bds. 7.99 *(978-1-84059-906-0(5));* (ENG & URD., bds. 7.99 *(978-1-84059-920-6(0));* (ENG, POL & POR., bds. 7.99 *(978-1-84059-914-5(6));* (ENG & GER., bds. 7.99 *(978-1-84059-911-4(1));* (SPA & ENG., bds. 7.99 *(978-1-84059-918-3(9));* (ENG & TUR., bds. 7.99 *(978-1-84059-919-0(7));* (ENG & RUS., bds. 7.99 *(978-1-84059-916-9(2))* Milet Publishing.
—My First Bilingual Book - Tools - English. 2014. (My First Bilingual Book Ser.). (ENG & VIE., Illus.). 20p. (J). (— 1). bds. 7.99 *(978-1-84059-921-3(9))* Milet Publishing.
—My First Bilingual Book - Tools - Ferramentas. 2014. (My First Bilingual Book Ser.). (POR & ENG., Illus.). 20p. (J). (— 1). bds. 7.99 *(978-1-84059-915-2(4))* Milet Publishing.
—My First Bilingual Book - Tools (English-Somali) 2014. (My First Bilingual Book Ser.). (ENG & SOM., Illus.). 20p. (J). (— 1). bds. 7.99 *(978-1-84059-917-6(0))* Milet Publishing.
—My First Bilingual Book - Vehicles. 2014. (My First Bilingual Book Ser.). (ENG & KOR., Illus.). 20p. (J). (— 1). bds. 7.99 *(978-1-84059-929-9(4));* bds. 7.99 *(978-1-84059-924-4(3));* bds. 7.99 *(978-1-84059-935-0(9));* bds. 7.99 *(978-1-84059-925-1(1));* bds. 7.99 *(978-1-84059-937-4(5));* bds. 7.99 *(978-1-84059-933-6(2))* Milet Publishing.
—My First Bilingual Book - Vehicles (English-Russian) 2014. (My First Bilingual Book Ser.). (ENG & RUS., Illus.). 20p. (J). (— 1). bds. 7.99 *(978-1-84059-932-9(4))* Milet Publishing.
—My First Bilingual Book-Fruit (English-Somali) 2011. (My First Bilingual Book Ser.). (ENG., Illus.). 24p. (J). (gr. k — 1). bds. 7.99 *(978-1-84059-635-9(X))* Milet Publishing.
—My First Bilingual Book-Fruit (English-Spanish) 2011. (My First Bilingual Book Ser.). (SPA & ENG., Illus.). 24p. (J). (gr. k — 1). bds. 7.99 *(978-1-84059-636-6(8))* Milet Publishing.
—My First Bilingual Book-Fruit (English-Urdu) 2011. (My First Bilingual Book Ser.). (ENG., Illus.). 24p. (J). (gr. k — 1). bds. 7.99 *(978-1-84059-638-0(4))* Milet Publishing.
—My First Bilingual Book-Home (English-Russian) 2011. (My First Bilingual Book Ser.). (ENG., Illus.). 24p. (J). (gr. k — 1). bds. 7.99 *(978-1-84059-650-2(3))* Milet Publishing.
—My First Bilingual Book-Jobs. 2012. (My First Bilingual Book Ser.). (ENG & ARA., Illus.). 24p. (J). (gr. k — 1). bds. 7.99 *(978-1-84059-700-4(3))* Milet Publishing.
—My First Bilingual Book-Jobs (English-Korean) 2012. (My First Bilingual Book Ser.). (ENG & KOR., Illus.). 24p. (J). (gr. k — 1). bds. 7.99 *(978-1-84059-707-3(0))* Milet Publishing.
—My First Bilingual Book-Music (English-Russian) 2012. (My First Bilingual Book Ser.). (ENG & RUS., Illus.). 24p. (J). (gr. k — 1). bds. 7.99 *(978-1-84059-726-4(7))* Milet Publishing.
—My First Bilingual Book-Music (English-Somali) 2012. (My First Bilingual Book Ser.). (ENG & SOM., Illus.). 24p. (J). (gr. k — 1). bds. 7.99 *(978-1-84059-727-1(5))* Milet Publishing.
—My First Bilingual Book-Opposites. 2012. (My First Bilingual Book Ser.). (ENG & CHI., Illus.). 24p. (J). (gr. k — 1). bds. 7.99 *(978-1-84059-734-9(8))* Milet Publishing.
—Numbers. 2011. (My First Bilingual Book Ser.). (Illus.). 24p. (J). (gr. k — 1). (ARA & ENG.). bds. 7.99 *(978-1-84059-570-3(1));* (SOM & ENG., bds. 8.99 *(978-1-84059-577-2(9))* Milet Publishing.
—Numbers - My First Bilingual Book. (My First Bilingual Book Ser.). (Illus.). 24p. (J). (gr. k — 1). 2011. (RUS & ENG.). bds. 7.99 *(978-1-84059-576-5(0))* 2010. (FRE & ENG., bds. 7.99 *(978-1-84059-541-3(8))* 2010. (ENG & ITA., bds. 7.99 *(978-1-84059-543-7(4))* 2010. (ENG & POL., bds. 8.99 *(978-1-84059-544-4(2))* Milet Publishing.
—Opposites. 2012. (My First Bilingual Book Ser.). (ENG & PER., Illus.). 24p. (J). (gr. k — 1). bds. 7.99 *(978-1-84059-735-6(6))* Milet Publishing.
—Plants - My First Bilingual Book. 2014. (My First Bilingual Book Ser.). (Illus.). 20p. (J). (— 1). (ENG & ITA.). bds. 7.99 *(978-1-84059-880-3(8));* (ENG & BEN., bds. 7.99 *(978-1-84059-875-9(1));* (ENG, POL & POR., bds. 7.99 *(978-1-84059-882-7(4));* (SPA & ENG., bds. 7.99 *(978-1-84059-886-5(7));* (ENG & VIE., bds. 7.99 *(978-1-84059-889-6(1));* (FRE & ENG., bds. 7.99 *(978-1-84059-878-0(6));* (ENG & URD., bds. 7.99 *(978-1-84059-888-9(3));* (ENG & RUS., bds. 7.99 *(978-1-84059-884-1(0))* Milet Publishing.
—School. 2014. (My First Bilingual Book Ser.). (ENG & ITA., Illus.). 20p. (J). (— 1). bds. 7.99 *(978-1-84059-896-4(4))* Milet Publishing.
—School - My First Bilingual Book. 2014. (My First Bilingual Book Ser.). (Illus.). 20p. (J). (— 1). (ENG & RUS.). bds. 7.99 *(978-1-84059-900-8(6));* (ENG & URD., bds. 7.99 *(978-1-84059-904-6(9));* (SPA & ENG., bds. 7.99 *(978-1-84059-902-2(2));* (ENG & ARA., bds. 7.99 *(978-1-84059-890-2(5))* Milet Publishing.
—School - My First Bilingual Book (Szkola) 2014. (My First Bilingual Book Ser.). (ENG, POL & POR., Illus.). 20p. (J). (— 1). bds. 7.99 *(978-1-84059-898-8(0))* Milet Publishing.
—Sports. 2012. (My First Bilingual Book Ser.). (ENG & POR., Illus.). 24p. (J). (gr. k — 1). bds. 7.99 *(978-1-84059-757-8(7))* Milet Publishing.
—Sports - My First Bilingual Book. 2012. (My First Bilingual Book Ser.). (ENG & SOM., Illus.). 24p. (J). (gr. k — 1). bds. 7.99 *(978-1-84059-759-2(3))* Milet Publishing.
—Tools. 2014. (My First Bilingual Book Ser.). (ENG & ITA., Illus.). 20p. (J). (— 1). bds. 7.99 *(978-1-84059-912-1(X))* Milet Publishing.
—Tools - My First Bilingual Book. 2014. (My First Bilingual Book Ser.). (ENG & CHI., Illus.). 20p. (J). (— 1). bds. 7.99 *(978-1-84059-908-4(1));* bds. 7.99 *(978-1-84059-913-8(8));* bds. 7.99 *(978-1-84059-909-1(X))* Milet Publishing.
—Tools (English-French) 2014. (My First Bilingual Book Ser.). (FRE & ENG., Illus.). 20p. (J). (— 1). bds. 7.99 *(978-1-84059-910-7(3))* Milet Publishing.
—Vehicles. 2014. (My First Bilingual Book Ser.). (Illus.). 20p. (J). (— 1). (ENG & ARA.). bds. 7.99 *(978-1-84059-922-0(7));* (ENG & ITA., bds. 7.99 *(978-1-84059-928-2(6));* (SPA & ENG., bds. 7.99 *(978-1-84059-934-3(0))* Milet Publishing.
—Vehicles - My First Bilingual Book. 2014. (My First Bilingual Book Ser.). (Illus.). 20p. (J). (— 1). (ENG & URD.). bds. 7.99 *(978-1-84059-936-7(7));* (FRE & ENG., bds. 7.99 *(978-1-84059-926-8(X));* (POR & ENG., bds. 7.99 *(978-1-84059-931-2(6));* (ENG & BEN., bds. 7.99 *(978-1-84059-923-7(5));* (ENG, POL & POR., bds. 7.99 *(978-1-84059-930-5(8))* Milet Publishing.
—Vehicles (English-German) 2014. (My First Bilingual Book Ser.). (ENG & GER., Illus.). 20p. (J). (— 1). bds. 7.99 *(978-1-84059-927-5(8))* Milet Publishing.
Milich, Zoran. City 123, 0 vols. 2014. (ENG., Illus.). 32p. (J). (gr. -1-k). bds. 12.95 *(978-1-77138-120-8(5))* Kids Can Pr., Ltd. CAN. Dist: Hachette Bk. Group.
Miller, Bryan. Dinosaur Fun: With Letters. 2008. (Illus.). 24p. (J). (gr. -1). bds. 11.99 *(978-0-89051-488-7(7))* Master Bks.
Miller, Jocelyn. My Carry-Along Angel Activity Book: Christmas Fun with Stickers. Hughes, Cathy, illus. 2013. (ENG.). 32p. (J). (gr. k-2). pap. 9.99 *(978-0-7459-6418-8(4))* Lion Hudson PLC GBR. Dist: Independent Pubs. Group.
—My Carry-Along Santa Activity Book: Christmas Fun with Stickers. Hughes, Cathy, illus. 2013. (ENG.). 32p. (J). (gr. k-2). pap. 9.99 *(978-0-7459-6419-5(2))* Lion Hudson PLC GBR. Dist: Independent Pubs. Group.
Miller, Jonathan, illus. When I Grow Up. 2011. 16p. (J). *(978-1-58865-637-7(3))* Kidsbooks, LLC.
—Winter, Spring, Summer, Fall. 2010. 16p. (J). *(978-1-58865-578-3(4))* Kidsbooks, LLC.
Milne, A. A. Giant. Shepard, Ernest H., illus. 2009. (Winnie-The-Pooh Ser.). (ENG.). 12p. (J). (gr. -1-k). bds. 9.99 *(978-0-525-42088-0(6),* Dutton Books for Young Readers) Penguin Young Readers Group.
Mischel, Jenny Ann. Animal Alphabet. Bell-Myers, Darcy, illus. 2006. (J). bds. *(978-0-9769239-0-9(4))* Perfect 4 Preschool.
Mitchell, Melanie, illus. Good Morning. 2008. (ENG.). 10p. (J). bds. 5.95 *(978-1-58117-708-4(9),* Intervisual/Piggy Toes) Bendon, Inc.
—Good Morning, Good Night! 2007. (Touch & Feel Ser.). 13p. 15.95 *(978-1-58117-572-1(8),* Intervisual/Piggy Toes) Bendon, Inc.
—Good Morning, Good Night! A Touch & Feel Bedtime Book. 2006. 12p. (J). (gr. -1-k). 12.95 *(978-1-58117-461-8(6),* Intervisual/Piggy Toes) Bendon, Inc.
—Good Night. 2008. (ENG.). 6p. (J). bds. 5.95 *(978-1-58117-709-1(7),* Intervisual/Piggy Toes) Bendon, Inc.
—Wake up Little Ones. 2009. (ENG.). 12p. 10.95 *(978-1-58117-927-9(8),* Intervisual/Piggy Toes) Bendon, Inc.
—Who Do You Love? 2008. (ENG.). 6p. (J). bds. 5.95 *(978-1-58117-707-7(0),* Intervisual/Piggy Toes) Bendon, Inc.
Mitter, Matt. Fisher-Price Little People Let's Imagine at the Zoo / Imaginemos el Zoologico. Pixel Mouse House, Pixel Mouse, illus. 2015. (Lift-The-Flap Ser.: 31). (ENG.). 10p. (J). (gr. -1-k). bds. 9.99 *(978-0-7944-3559-2(9))* Reader's Digest Assn., Inc., The.
Mitter, Matt & Rudko, Che. Ready, Set, Brush! Brannon, Tom, illus. 2008. (Pop-Up Book Ser.). (ENG.). 12p. (J). (gr. -1-k). bds. 12.99 *(978-0-7944-1445-0(1),* Reader's Digest Children's Bks.) Studio Fun International.
Mitton, Tony. Dinosaurumpus! (a StoryPlay Book) Parker-Rees, Guy, illus. 2016. (ENG.). 40p. (J). (gr. -1-k). 5.99 *(978-1-338-11536-9(7),* Cartwheel Bks.) Scholastic, Inc.
Mitton, Tony & Parker, Ant. Rainforest Romp. 2009. (Amazing Animals Ser.). (ENG., Illus.). 24p. (J). (gr. -1-1). 9.99 *(978-0-7534-6298-0(2),* 9780753462980, Kingfisher) Roaring Brook Pr.
Miura, Taro. Bum, Bum. Miura, Taro, illus. 2016. (ENG., Illus.). 24p. (J). (— 1). bds. 8.99 *(978-0-7636-8784-7(7))* Candlewick Pr.
—There, There. Miura, Taro, illus. 2016. (ENG., Illus.). 22p. (J). (— 1). bds. 8.99 *(978-0-7636-8785-4(5))* Candlewick Pr.
Mizielinska, Aleksandra & Mizielinski, Daniel. Maps Activity Book. 2015. (ENG., Illus.). 72p. (J). (gr. 2-5). 14.99 *(978-0-7636-7771-8(X),* Big Picture Press) Candlewick Pr.
Mlawer, Teresa, tr. Feeling Great!/Sentirse Bien! Stockham, Jess, illus. 2013. (Just Like Me! Ser.). (ENG & SPA.). 12p. (J). (gr. -1). bds. *(978-1-84643-561-4(7))* Child's Play International Ltd.
—Looking Good!/Lucir Bien! Stockham, Jess, illus. 2013. (Just Like Me! Ser.). (ENG & SPA.). 12p. (J). (gr. -1). bds. *(978-1-84643-560-7(9))* Child's Play International Ltd.
—On the Go!/a Moverse! Stockham, Jess, illus. 2013. (Just Like Me! Ser.). (ENG & SPA.). 12p. (J). (gr. -1). bds. *(978-1-84643-563-8(3))* Child's Play International Ltd.
MMStudios & Allman, Howard, photos by. Big & Little: A Book about Opposites. 2007. (Usborne Look & Say Ser.). (Illus.). 18p. (J). (gr. -1-3). bds. 14.99 *(978-0-7945-1884-4(2),* Usborne) EDC Publishing.
Modern Publishing Staff. Look at Me! 2007. (Illus.). (J). (gr. -1-3). bds. 4.99 *(978-0-7666-2607-2(5))* Modern Publishing.
—When I Grow Up: Giant Wall Art Flash Cards. 2007. (Illus.). (J). (gr. -1-k). bds. 12.99 *(978-0-7666-2700-0(4))* Modern Publishing.
Moerbeck, Kees, illus. & des. Cinderella. Moerbeck, Kees, des. 2006. (Roly Poly Box Bks.). (ENG.). 24p. (J). *(978-1-84643-019-0(4))* Child's Play International Ltd.
Monckeberg, Paulina. Pascualina 2006. 2005. (Pascualina Family of Products Ser.). (ENG., Illus.). 272p. (J). spiral bd. 16.99 *(978-956-8222-28-4(6))* Pascualina Producciones S.A.
—Rosamunda Della Calabazza 2006 Agenda & Stationary 2006: The Youngest & Most Dangerous Sister of Pascualina. 2005. (Pascualina Family of Products Ser.). (ENG., Illus.). 228p. (J). spiral bd. 11.99 *(978-956-8222-21-5(9))* Pascualina Producciones S.A.
Monks, Lydia. Mungo Monkey Goes on a Train. 2015. (ENG., Illus.). 14p. (J). (gr. -1-k). 13.99 *(978-1-4052-6910-0(3))* Egmont Bks., Ltd. GBR. Dist: Independent Pubs. Group.
—Mungo Monkey Goes to School. 2014. (ENG., Illus.). 14p. (J). (gr. -1-k). 13.99 *(978-1-4052-6909-4(X))* Egmont Bks., Ltd. GBR. Dist: Independent Pubs. Group.
—Mungo Monkey to the Rescue. 2016. (ENG., Illus.). 14p. (J). (gr. -1-k). 10.99 *(978-1-4052-7818-8(8))* Egmont Bks., Ltd. GBR. Dist: Independent Pubs. Group.
Monks, Lydia, illus. Mungo Monkey Has a Birthday Party. 2014. (ENG.). 14p. (J). (gr. -1). 12.99 *(978-1-4052-6866-0(2))* Egmont Bks., Ltd. GBR. Dist: Independent Pubs. Group.
Moon, Jo, illus. Buggy Buddies. 2014. (Wipe-Clean Buggy Buddies Ser.). (ENG.). 10p. (J). (-k). 9.99 *(978-1-4472-6778-2(8))* Pan Macmillan GBR. Dist: Independent Pubs. Group.

—Counting. 2014. (Wipe-Clean Buggy Buddies Ser.). (ENG.). 10p. (J). (— 1). 9.99 *(978-1-4472-6779-9(6))* Pan Macmillan GBR. Dist: Independent Pubs. Group.

Moore, Clement C. My First Night Before Christmas. Newsom, Tom, illus. 2008. (ENG.). 12p. (J). 9.95 *(978-1-58117-808-1(5)*, Intervisual/Piggy Toes) Bendon, Inc.

—The Night Before Christmas. Newsom, Tom, illus. 2007. (ENG.). 18p. (J). (gr. -1-3). 19.95 *(978-1-4037-2947-7(6)*, Intervisual/Piggy Toes) Bendon, Inc.

—The Night Before Christmas. 2007. (ENG., Illus.). 26p. (gr. -1-17). bds. 5.95 *(978-0-7624-3014-7(1))* Running Pr. Bk. Pubs.

—The Night Before Christmas: The Classic Rhyme with Flaps to Lift & Sparkling Surprises! Downer, Maggie, illus. 2015. (ENG.). 10p. (J). (gr. k-3). bds. 7.99 *(978-1-86147-293-9(5)*, Armadillo) Anness Publishing GBR. Dist: National Bk. Network.

—Night Before Christmas Board Book: The Classic Edition. Santore, Charles, illus. 2013. (ENG.). 26p. (J). bds. 8.95 *(978-1-60433-438-8(X)*, Applesauce Pr.) Cider Mill Pr. Bk. Pubs., LLC.

Moore, Clement C., ed. & illus. The Night Before Christmas. Moore, Clement C., illus. Porfirio, Guy, illus. 2004. 20p. (J). 9.95 *(978-0-8249-6553-2(1)*, Ideal Pubns.) Worthy Publishing.

Moore, Lilian. My First Counting Book. Williams, Garth, illus. 2015. (Little Golden Board Book Ser.). (ENG.). 26p. (J). (-k). bds. 7.99 *(978-0-553-52223-5(X)*, Golden Bks.) Random Hse. Children's Bks.

Moroney, Trace. Bathtime: Baxter Bear Chubby. Moroney, Trace, illus. 2008. (Baxter Bear Collection). (Illus.). 10p. (J). (gr. -1-1). bds. *(978-1-86463-175-3(9))* Brimax Books Ltd.

—Things I Love about Bedtime. Moroney, Trace, illus. 2012. (ENG., Illus.). 16p. (J). (gr. -1-k). bds. 8.99 *(978-0-545-29016-6(3)*, Cartwheel Bks.) Scholastic, Inc.

Moroney, Trace, creator. Baa, Baa, Black Sheep. 2008. (Illus.). 10p. (gr. -1-1). bds. 4.99 *(978-1-74178-526-5(X))* Gardner Pubns.

—The Owl & the Pussy Cat. 2008. (Illus.). 10p. (gr. -1-1). bds. 4.99 *(978-1-74178-515-9(4))* Gardner Pubns.

Morris, Jennifer E. May I Please Have a Cookie? Morris, Jennifer E., illus. 2015. (ENG., Illus.). 30p. (J). (— 1). bds. 6.99 *(978-0-545-81502-4(9)*, Cartwheel Bks.) Scholastic, Inc.

Moses Bible Sticker Book. 2003. (Illus.). 16p. (J). 2.98 *(978-1-4054-1557-6(6))* Parragon, Inc.

Muldrow, Diane. Frosty the Snowman. Golden Books, illus. 2013. (Big Golden Board Book Ser.). (ENG.). 22p. (J). (-k). bds. 10.99 *(978-0-385-37870-3(X)*, Golden Bks.) Random Hse. Children's Bks.

Mullen, Amy. Colors of New England. 2017. (Naturally Local Ser.). (ENG., Illus.). 20p. (J). (gr. -1-k). bds. 8.95 ***(978-1-938093-99-9(2))*** Duo Pr. LLC.

—Colors of the Pacific Northwest. 2017. (Naturally Local Ser.). (ENG., Illus.). 20p. (J). (gr. -1 — 1). bds. 8.95 ***(978-1-938093-80-7(1)***, Duo Pr. Llc (US)) Duo Pr. LLC.

Mullins, Amy. I'm Reverent When- Bagley, Val Chadwick, illus. 2005. ("Move-About" Book Ser.). (J). *(978-1-59156-951-0(6))* Covenant Communications.

Multiplication Mastery W/CD: Multiplication Mastery with Audio CD. 2004. (ENG.). (J). 19.99 *(978-0-943343-00-6(3))* Learning Wrap-Ups, Inc.

Mumme, Sarah. Guess Who's under the Sea. Samuel, Janet, illus. 2015. (Guess Who's... Bks.). (ENG.). 10p. (J). (gr. -1 — 1). 5.99 *(978-0-7641-6803-1(7))* Barron's Educational Series, Inc.

Mummy Sticker Book. 2003. (Illus.). 16p. (J). 2.98 *(978-1-84273-122-2(X))* Parragon, Inc.

Munro, Fiona & Phillipson, Fiona. Whose Nose? Moon, Jo, illus. 2011. (ENG.). 10p. (J). (gr. -1-k). bds. 6.99 *(978-0-8431-9811-9(7)*, Price Stern Sloan) Penguin Young Readers Group.

—Whose Stripes? Garden, Jo, illus. 2011. (ENG.). 10p. (J). (gr. -1-k). bds. 6.99 *(978-0-8431-9812-6(5)*, Price Stern Sloan) Penguin Young Readers Group.

Munsch, Robert. Angela's Airplane. Martchenko, Michael, illus. 2016. (ENG.). 24p. (J). (-k). bds. 7.99 *(978-1-55451-829-6(6))* Annick Pr., Ltd. CAN. Dist: Publishers Group West (PGW).

—The Fire Station. Martchenko, Michael, illus. 5th ed. 2012. (ENG.). 24p. (J). (gr. -1-k). bds. 7.99 *(978-1-55451-423-6(1)*, 9781554514236) Annick Pr., Ltd. CAN. Dist: Publishers Group West (PGW).

—I Have to Go! Martchenko, Michael, illus. 8th ed. 2010. (ENG.). 24p. (J). (gr. -1-k). bds. 7.99 *(978-1-55451-253-9(0)*, 9781554512539) Annick Pr., Ltd. CAN. Dist: Publishers Group West (PGW).

—Love You Forever Pop-Up Edition. McGraw, Sheila, illus. 2017. (ENG.). 14p. (J). (gr. -1-1). 24.95 ***(978-1-77085-965-4(9)***, 9781770859654) Firefly Bks., Ltd.

—Murmel, Murmel, Murmel. Martchenko, Michael, illus. 2014. (ENG.). 26p. (J). (gr. -1 — 1). bds. 7.99 *(978-1-55451-656-8(0)*, 9781554516568) Annick Pr., Ltd. CAN. Dist: Publishers Group West (PGW).

—The Paper Bag Princess. Martchenko, Michael, illus. 10th ed. 2009. (ENG.). 28p. (J). (gr. -1-2). bds. 7.99 *(978-1-55451-211-9(5)*, 9781554512119) Annick Pr., Ltd. CAN. Dist: Publishers Group West (PGW).

—Pigs. Martchenko, Michael, illus. 2014. (ENG.). 26p. (J). (gr. -1-k). bds. 7.99 *(978-1-55451-628-5(5)*, 9781554516285) Annick Pr., Ltd. CAN. Dist: Publishers Group West (PGW).

—Thomas' Snowsuit. Martchenko, Michael, illus. 6th ed. 2011. (ENG.). 22p. (J). (gr. -1 — 1). bds. 7.99 *(978-1-55451-363-5(4)*, 9781554513635) Annick Pr., Ltd. CAN. Dist: Publishers Group West (PGW).

—50 below Zero. Martchenko, Michael, illus. 3rd ed. 2013. (Munsch for Kids Ser.). (ENG.). 22p. (J). (gr. -1-k). bds. 7.99 *(978-1-55451-532-5(7)*, 9781554515325) Annick Pr., Ltd. CAN. Dist: Publishers Group West (PGW).

Muntean, Michaela. Elmo Can... Taste! Touch! Smell! See! Hear! (Sesame Street) Swanson, Maggie, illus. 2013. (Big Bird's Favorites Board Bks.). (ENG.). 24p. (J). (— 1). bds. 4.99 *(978-0-307-98078-6(2)*, Random Hse. Bks. for Young Readers) Random Hse. Children's Bks.

Munton, Gill. Who Ate All the Lettuce? Top That Publishing Staff, ed. Elliott, Rebecca, illus. 2007. 12p. (gr. -1-k). bds. *(978-1-84666-177-8(3)*, Tide Mill Pr.) Top That! Publishing PLC.

Murphy, Harriet. Diego in Action! Follow the Reader Level 2. 2007. (Go, Diego, Go! Ser.). (ENG., Illus.). 24p. (J). (gr. -1-2). 24.99 *(978-1-4169-4993-0(3)*, Simon Scribbles) Simon Scribbles.

Murphy, Mary. Crocopotamus: Mix & Match the Wild Animals! 2016. (ENG., Illus.). 12p. (J). (— 1). bds. 8.99 *(978-0-7636-8102-9(4))* Candlewick Pr.

—Good Night Like This. Murphy, Mary, illus. 2016. (ENG., Illus.). 32p. (J). (gr. -1-k). 12.99 *(978-0-7636-7970-5(4))* Candlewick Pr.

—Let's Go! 2005. (ENG., Illus.). 16p. (J). bds. 14.99 *(978-1-4052-1115-4(6))* Egmont Bks., Ltd. GBR. Dist: Trafalgar Square Publishing.

Murray, Diana. Doris the Bookasaurus. Chen, Yuyi, illus. 2017. (ENG.). 40p. (J). 17.99 *(978-1-250-11676-5(7)*, 9781250116765) Imprint IND. Dist: Macmillan.

Musgrave, Susan. Love You More, 1 vol. Melo, Esperança, illus. 2014. (ENG.). 24p. (J). (gr. -1-k). bds. 9.95 *(978-1-4598-0240-7(3))* Orca Bk. Pubs. USA.

Musical Robot. If You're a Robot & You Know It. Carter, David A., illus. 2015. (ENG.). 14p. (J). (gr. -1-k). bds. 16.99 *(978-0-545-81980-0(6)*, Cartwheel Bks.) Scholastic, Inc.

My Day. 2011.Tr. of Mi dia. (Illus.). (J). *(978-1-4508-1610-6(X))* Publications International, Ltd.

My Friends Around the World: Sticker Book. (Girlfriend Gang Ser.). 16p. (J). *(978-2-7643-0016-9(6))* Phidal Publishing, Inc./Editions Phidal, Inc.

My Little Library of Baby Animals. 2008. (Pocket Libraries Ser.). 5p. bds. *(978-1-4075-3191-5(3))* Parragon, Inc.

My Little Library of Things That do. 2008. (Pocket Libraries Ser.). 5p. bds. *(978-1-4075-3192-2(1))* Parragon, Inc.

My Super Activity Book. (Bumper Photographic Sticker Ser.). 72p. pap. *(978-1-4054-8212-7(5))* Parragon, Inc.

Na, Il Sung. A Book of Sleep. 2011. (ENG.). 24p. (J). (gr. k — 1). bds. 6.99 *(978-0-375-86618-0(3)*, Knopf Bks. for Young Readers) Random Hse. Children's Bks.

Nagara, Innosanto. Counting on Community. 2015. (ENG., Illus.). 24p. (J). (gr. -1-2). bds. 9.99 *(978-1-60980-632-3(8)*, Triangle Square) Seven Stories Pr.

—A Is for Activist. 2016. (ENG., Illus.). 32p. (J). (gr. -1-2). 17.95 *(978-1-60980-693-4(X)*, Triangle Square) Seven Stories Pr.

Napier, Matt. Little Canada. 2012. (Little Country Ser.). (ENG., Illus.). 22p. (J). (gr. k-3). 9.95 *(978-1-58536-178-6(X))* Sleeping Bear Pr.

National Geographic Kids Staff. Baby Animal Pop! With 5 Incredible, Life-Size Fold-Outs. 2011. (ENG., Illus.). 20p. (J). (gr. -1-k). 14.95 *(978-1-4263-0765-2(9)*, National Geographic Children's Bks.) National Geographic Society.

—Bugs. 2015. (Look & Learn Ser.). (ENG., Illus.). 24p. (J). (-k). bds. 6.99 *(978-1-4263-1876-4(6)*, National Geographic Children's Bks.) National Geographic Society.

—Colors! 2012. (ENG., Illus.). 24p. (J). (gr. k-k). bds. 6.99 *(978-1-4263-0929-8(5)*, National Geographic Children's Bks.) National Geographic Society.

—Dig. 2015. (Look & Learn Ser.). (ENG., Illus.). 24p. (J). (-k). bds. 6.99 *(978-1-4263-2062-0(0)*, National Geographic Children's Bks.) National Geographic Society.

—Ocean Creatures. 2015. (Look & Learn Ser.). (ENG., Illus.). 24p. (J). (-k). bds. 6.99 *(978-1-4263-2063-7(9)*, National Geographic Children's Bks.) National Geographic Society.

—Opposites! 2012. (Look & Learn Ser.). (ENG., Illus.). 24p. (J). (gr. k-k). bds. 6.99 *(978-1-4263-1043-0(9)*, National Geographic Children's Bks.) National Geographic Society.

—Patterns! 2013. (Look & Learn Ser.). (ENG.). 24p. (J). (-k). bds. 6.99 *(978-1-4263-1123-9(0)*, National Geographic Children's Bks.) National Geographic Society.

—People! 2013. (Look & Learn Ser.). (ENG.). 24p. (J). (-k). bds. 6.99 *(978-1-4263-1122-2(2)*, National Geographic Children's Bks.) National Geographic Society.

—Same & Different. 2012. (ENG., Illus.). 24p. (J). (gr. k-k). bds. 6.99 *(978-1-4263-0928-1(7)*, National Geographic Children's Bks.) National Geographic Society.

—Shapes! 2012. (Look & Learn Ser.). (ENG., Illus.). 24p. (J). (gr. k-k). bds. 6.99 *(978-1-4263-1042-3(0)*, National Geographic Children's Bks.) National Geographic Society.

National Geographic Society (U.S.) Staff, contrib. by. Shapes! 2013. (Illus.). (J). *(978-0-545-62212-7(3))* Scholastic, Inc.

National Wildlife Federation Staff. My First Book of Funny Animals. 2015. (ENG., Illus.). 22p. (J). (— 1). bds. 6.95 *(978-1-62354-051-7(8))* Charlesbridge Publishing, Inc.

Neis, Izzy. I Want to Potty. Shakir, Susie, illus. 2005. 10p. (J). 9.95 *(978-1-58117-422-9(5)*, Intervisual/Piggy Toes) Bendon, Inc.

Nellist, Glenys. Christmas Love Letters from God: Bible Stories, 1 vol. Clowes, Rachel, illus. 2016. (Love Letters from God Ser.). (ENG.). 32p. (J). 16.99 *(978-0-310-74824-3(0))* Zonderkidz.

—Little Love Letters from God: Bible Stories, 1 vol. Allsopp, Sophie, illus. 2015. (Love Letters from God Ser.). (ENG.). 18p. (J). bds. 9.99 *(978-0-310-75047-5(4))* Zonderkidz.

Nelson-Schmidt, Michelle. Cats, Cats! Nelson-Schmidt, Michelle, illus. 2011. (ENG., Illus.). 32p. (J). pap. 5.99 *(978-1-61067-042-5(6))* Kane Miller.

—Dogs, Dogs! Nelson-Schmidt, Michelle, illus. 2011. (ENG., Illus.). 32p. (J). pap. 5.99 *(978-1-61067-041-8(8))* Kane Miller.

Nelson, Steve & Rollins, Jack. Here Comes Peter Cottontail! 2014. (Illus.). 16p. (J). bds. 12.99 *(978-0-8249-1927-6(0)*, Ideal Pubns.) Worthy Publishing.

—Here Comes Peter Cottontail! Levy, Pamela R., illus. 2011. 16p. (J). bds. 10.99 *(978-0-8249-1843-9(6)*, Ideal Pubns.) Worthy Publishing.

Neubecker, Robert. Too Many Monsters! A Halloween Counting Book. Neubecker, Robert, illus. 2010. (ENG., Illus.). 26p. (J). (gr. -1-k). bds. 7.99 *(978-1-4424-0172-3(9)*, Little Simon) Little Simon.

Newcome, Zita. This Royal Baby. Newcome, Zita, illus. 2013. (ENG., Illus.). 12p. (J). (— 1). bds. 14.99 *(978-0-230-77284-7(6))* Pan Macmillan GBR. Dist: Independent Pubs. Group.

Newman, Tracy. Passover Is Coming! Garófoli, Viviana, illus. 2016. (ENG.). 12p. (J). (gr. -1 — 1). 5.99 *(978-1-4677-5242-8(8)*, Kar-Ben Publishing) Lerner Publishing Group.

—Passover Is Coming! Garofoli, Viviana, illus. 2016. (ENG.). 12p. (gr. -1 — 1). 23.99 *(978-1-4677-9610-1(7)*, Kar-Ben Publishing) Lerner Publishing Group.

—Purim Is Coming! Garófoli, Viviana, illus. 2017. (ENG.). 12p. (gr. -1 — 1). 5.99 *(978-1-5124-0827-0(1)*, Kar-Ben Publishing) Lerner Publishing Group.

—Purim Is Coming! Garofoli, Viviana, illus. 2017. (Purim Ser.). (ENG.). 12p. (gr. -1 — 1). 23.99 ***(978-1-5124-2725-7(X)***, Kar-Ben Publishing) Lerner Publishing Group.

Newman, Tracy. Rosh Hashanah Is Coming! Garofoli, Viviana, illus. 2016. (ENG.). 12p. (J). (gr. -1 — 1). 5.99 *(978-1-4677-7988-3(1)*, Kar-Ben Publishing) Lerner Publishing Group.

Newsom, Tom, illus. The First Noel. 2006. 14p. (J). (gr. k-4). reprint ed. 8.00 *(978-1-4223-5413-1(X))* DIANE Publishing Co.

Nex, Anthony, photos by. Little Feet Love. 2009. (Illus.). 12p. 7.95 *(978-1-58117-881-4(6)*, Intervisual/Piggy Toes) Bendon, Inc.

Nicely, Adam. Bedtime for Tad. 2009. (ENG., Illus.). 28p. (J). (gr. k — 1). bds. 7.95 *(978-1-894965-84-2(1))* Simply Read Bks. CAN. Dist: Ingram Publisher Services.

Nicholls, Paul, illus. I Want to Be A... Pirate. 2014. (J). *(978-1-4351-5500-8(9))* Barnes & Noble, Inc.

Nicholson, Sue. All about Me. (All about Me Ser.). *(978-1-4054-6547-2(6))* Parragon, Inc.

Nickelodeon. PAW Patrol: Pawsome Teamwork. 2016. (ENG.). 12p. (J). (gr. -1-k). bds. 9.99 *(978-0-7944-3759-6(1))* Studio Fun International.

Nickelodeon Dora the Explorer Staff. Say Boo! 2013. (Guess Who! Book Ser.: 1). (ENG.). 10p. (J). (gr. -1-1). bds. 10.99 *(978-0-7944-2857-0(6))* Reader's Digest Assn., Inc., The.

Nickelodeon Staff, ed. Words - Dora the Explorer. 2010. (Write, Slide & Learn Ser.). 14p. (J). (gr. -1-1). 9.99 *(978-1-74184-519-8(X)*, Ideal Pubns.) Worthy Publishing.

Nieminen, Lotta. Pancakes! An Interactive Recipe Book. 2016. (Cook in a Book Ser.). (ENG., Illus.). 16p. (gr. -1 — 1). 14.95 *(978-0-7148-7283-4(0))* Phaidon Pr., Inc.

Night & Day Studios. Peekaboo Presents. Lunn, Corey, illus. 2015. (Peekaboo Ser.). (ENG.). 20p. (J). (— 1). bds. 7.99 *(978-0-7636-7567-7(9)*, Candlewick Entertainment) Candlewick Pr.

Niland, Kilmeny. The Gingerbread Man. 2006. (Illus.). 16p. *(978-1-921049-49-1(9))* Little Hare Bks. AUS. Dist: HarperCollins Pubs. Australia.

Nilsen, Anna. Bella's Butterfly Ball. Partis, Joanne, illus. 2012. (ENG.). 20p. (J). (gr. -1-1). pap. 9.99 *(978-1-84365-194-9(7)*, Pavilion Children's Books) Pavilion Bks. GBR. Dist: Independent Pubs. Group.

—Bella's Midsummer Secret. Partis, Joanne, illus. 2005. (ENG.). 18p. (J). (gr. -1-1). pap. 9.99 *(978-1-84458-338-6(4)*, Pavilion Children's Books) Pavilion Bks. GBR. Dist: Independent Pubs. Group.

Nippert-Eng, Christena. What Is Baby Gorilla Doing? Dominski, John & Martinez, Miguel, illus. 2017. (ENG.). 22p. (J). bds. 7.99 *(978-1-62779-479-4(4)*, 9781627794794, Holt, Henry & Co. Bks. For Young Readers) Holt, Henry & Co.

Nister, Ernest, illus. Merry Magic-Go-Round: An Antique Book of Changing Pictures. 2005. 14p. (J). (gr. k-4). reprint ed. 19.00 *(978-0-7567-9156-8(1))* DIANE Publishing Co.

Noah's Ark Bible Sticker Book. 2003. (Illus.). 16p. (J). 2.98 *(978-1-4054-1558-3(4))* Parragon, Inc.

Noble, Trinka Hakes. Little New Jersey. Brett, Jeannie, illus. 2012. (My Little State Ser.). (ENG.). 20p. (J). bds. 9.95 *(978-1-58536-786-3(9))* Sleeping Bear Pr.

—Little Pennsylvania Board Book. Brett, Jeannie, illus. 2010. (My Little State Ser.). (ENG.). 22p. (J). 9.95 *(978-1-58536-506-7(8))* Sleeping Bear Pr.

Nolan, Allia Zobel. Animal Parade. Maddocks, Maria, illus. 2011. (ENG.). 10p. (J). (gr. -1 — 1). 12.99 *(978-0-547-55867-7(8))* Houghton Mifflin Harcourt Publishing Co.

—God's Oak Tree. Chung, Chi, illus. 2007. 16p. (J). (gr. -1). 12.99 *(978-0-8254-5536-0(7))* Kregel Pubns.

—God's Winter Wonderland. Mitchell, Melanie, illus. 2006. 10p. (J). bds. 8.99 *(978-0-8254-5526-1(X))* Kregel Pubns.

Norman, Kim. If It's Snowy & You Know It, Clap Your Paws! Woodruff, Liza, illus. abr. ed. 2015. (ENG.). 26p. (J). (— 1). bds. 6.95 *(978-1-4549-1692-5(3))* Sterling Publishing Co., Inc.

Norris, Eryl. What's That in the Water? Mansfield, Andy, illus. 2015. (ENG.). 18p. (J). (gr. -1-1). 9.99 *(978-1-4998-0139-2(4))* Little Bee Books Inc.

—Who's Who in the Woods? Mansfield, Andy, illus. 2015. (ENG.). 18p. (J). (gr. -1-1). 9.99 *(978-1-4998-0140-8(8))* Little Bee Books Inc.

Norris, Jeannine Q. Tonight You Are My Baby: Mary's Christmas Gift. Ladwig, Tim, illus. 2010. (HarperBlessings Ser.). (ENG.). 30p. (J). (gr. -1-k). bds. 7.99 *(978-0-06-147999-1(3)*, HarperFestival) HarperCollins Pubs.

North, Dawn. Pull-Alongs: Digger. 2007. 12p. (gr. -1). per. *(978-1-84610-446-6(7))* Make Believe Ideas.

North, Merry. My Grandma & Me: A Picture, Play & Tote Book. 2004. 10p. (J). (gr. -1-18). bds. 5.99 *(978-1-57151-724-1(3))* Playhouse Publishing.

—Squeaky Clean. 2005. 9p. *(978-1-57151-752-4(9))* Playhouse Publishing.

Nosy Crow Staff. Bizzy Bear: Deep-Sea Diver. Davies, Benji, illus. 2016. (Bizzy Bear Ser.). (ENG.). 8p. (J). (— 1). bds. 6.99 *(978-0-7636-8647-5(6)*, Nosy Crow) Candlewick Pr.

—Bizzy Bear: Fun on the Farm. Davies, Benji, illus. 2011. (Bizzy Bear Ser.). (ENG.). 8p. (J). (gr. k — 1). bds. 6.99 *(978-0-7636-5879-3(0)*, Nosy Crow) Candlewick Pr.

—Bizzy Bear: Knights' Castle. Davies, Benji, illus. 2015. (Bizzy Bear Ser.). (ENG.). 8p. (J). (— 1). bds. 6.99 *(978-0-7636-7602-5(0)*, Nosy Crow) Candlewick Pr.

—Bizzy Bear: off We Go! Davies, Benji, illus. 2012. (Bizzy Bear Ser.). (ENG.). 8p. (J). (gr. k — 1). bds. 6.99 *(978-0-7636-5900-4(2)*, Nosy Crow) Candlewick Pr.

—Bizzy Bear: Zookeeper. Davies, Benji, illus. 2015. (Bizzy Bear Ser.). (ENG.). 8p. (J). (— 1). bds. 6.99 *(978-0-7636-7603-2(9)*, Nosy Crow) Candlewick Pr.

—Can You Say It, Too? Arf! Arf! Braun, Sebastien, illus. 2015. (Can You Say It, Too? Ser.). (ENG.). 10p. (J). (— 1). bds. 8.99 *(978-0-7636-7894-4(5)*, Nosy Crow) Candlewick Pr.

—Can You Say It, Too? Growl! Growl! Braun, Sebastien, illus. 2014. (Can You Say It, Too? Ser.). (ENG.). 10p. (J). (— 1). bds. 8.99 *(978-0-7636-7396-3(X)*, Nosy Crow) Candlewick Pr.

—Can You Say It, Too? Hoot! Hoot! Braun, Sebastien, illus. 2015. (Can You Say It, Too? Ser.). (ENG.). 10p. (J). (— 1). bds. 8.99 *(978-0-7636-7588-2(1)*, Nosy Crow) Candlewick Pr.

—Can You Say It, Too? Quack! Quack! Braun, Sebastien, illus. 2015. (Can You Say It, Too? Ser.). (ENG.). 10p. (J). (— 1). bds. 8.99 *(978-0-7636-7589-9(X)*, Nosy Crow) Candlewick Pr.

—Can You Say It, Too? Roar! Roar! Braun, Sebastien, illus. 2014. (Can You Say It, Too? Ser.). (ENG.). 10p. (J). (— 1). bds. 8.99 *(978-0-7636-7397-0(8)*, Nosy Crow) Candlewick Pr.

—Cuddly Cow: A Farm Friends Sound Book. Scheffler, Axel, illus. 2017. (Farm Friends Sound Book Ser.). (ENG.). 12p. (J). (— 1). bds. 9.99 *(978-0-7636-9325-1(1)*, Nosy Crow) Candlewick Pr.

—Cutie Pie Looks for the Easter Bunny: A Tiny Tab Book. Ho, Jannie, illus. 2015. (Tiny Tab Ser.). (ENG.). 8p. (J). (— 1). bds. 7.99 *(978-0-7636-7599-8(7)*, Nosy Crow) Candlewick Pr.

—Flip Flap Safari. Scheffler, Axel, illus. 2015. (ENG.). 28p. (J). (gr. -1-2). 11.99 *(978-0-7636-7605-6(5)*, Nosy Crow) Candlewick Pr.

—Higgly Hen: A Farm Friends Sound Book. Scheffler, Axel, illus. 2017. (Farm Friends Sound Book Ser.). (ENG.). 12p. (J). (— 1). bds. 9.99 *(978-0-7636-9324-4(3)*, Nosy Crow) Candlewick Pr.

—Little Bubba Looks for His Elephant. Ho, Jannie, illus. 2014. (ENG.). 8p. (J). (— 1). bds. 7.99 *(978-0-7636-7401-4(X)*, Nosy Crow) Candlewick Pr.

—Noodle Loves the Beach. Billet, Marion, illus. 2012. (Noodle Ser.). (ENG.). 10p. (J). (gr. k — 1). bds. 8.99 *(978-0-7636-5898-4(7)*, Nosy Crow) Candlewick Pr.

—Pookie Pop Plays Hide-And-Seek: A Tiny Tab Book. Ho, Jannie, illus. 2015. (Tiny Tab Ser.). (ENG.). 8p. (J). (— 1). bds. 7.99 *(978-0-7636-7600-1(4)*, Nosy Crow) Candlewick Pr.

—Press-Out & Color: Butterflies. Ingram, Zoe, illus. 2017. (ENG.). 20p. (J). (gr. 5). 15.99 *(978-0-7636-9506-4(8)*, Nosy Crow) Candlewick Pr.

—Row, Row, Row Your Boat: Sing along with Me! Huang, Yu-Hsuan, illus. 2017. (Sing along with Me! Ser.). (ENG.). 10p. (J). (-k). bds. 8.99 *(978-0-7636-9240-7(9)*, Nosy Crow) Candlewick Pr.

—Twinkle, Twinkle, Little Star: Sing along with Me! Huang, Yu-Hsuan, illus. 2017. (Sing along with Me! Ser.). (ENG.). 10p. (J). (-k). bds. 8.99 *(978-0-7636-9241-4(7)*, Nosy Crow) Candlewick Pr.

—The Wheels on the Bus: Sing along with Me! Huang, Yu-Hsuan, illus. 2016. (Sing along with Me! Ser.). (ENG.). (J). (-k). bds. 8.99 *(978-0-7636-8648-2(4)*, Nosy Crow) Candlewick Pr.

Novesky, Amy. Love Is a Tutu. Gillingham, Sara, illus. 2016. (Love Is Ser.). (ENG.). 24p. (J). (-k). 12.95 *(978-1-937359-81-2(6))* Cameron & Co., Inc.

Novick, Mary. The Big Book of Animals & Bugs. Hale, Jenny, illus. (Double Delights Ser.). 32p. (J). pap. *(978-1-877003-38-7(7))* Little Hare Bks. AUS. Dist: HarperCollins Pubs. Australia.

—Bugs. Hale, Jenny, illus. 2003. 16p. (Orig.). pap. *(978-1-877003-32-5(8))* Little Hare Bks. AUS. Dist: HarperCollins Pubs. Australia.

—Double Delight - Nursery Rhymes. Hale, Jenny, illus. 2011. (Double Delight Ser.). (ENG.). 16p. (J). (gr. -1 — 1). pap. 8.99 *(978-1-877003-06-6(9))* Little Hare Bks. AUS. Dist: Independent Pubs. Group.

—Nursery Songs. Hale, Jenny, illus. 2003. 16p. (Orig.). pap. *(978-1-877003-33-2(6))* Little Hare Bks. AUS. Dist: HarperCollins Pubs. Australia.

Novick, Mary & Hale, Jenny. Farm & Zoo. 2006. (Illus.). 32p. *(978-1-921049-26-2(X))* Little Hare Bks. AUS. Dist: HarperCollins Pubs. Australia.

Novick, Mary, et al. Alphabet. Hale, Jenny, illus. 2006. (Princess Poppets Ser.). (ENG.). 16p. (J). (gr. k-k). 10.95 *(978-1-921049-03-3(0))* Little Hare Bks. AUS. Dist: Independent Pubs. Group.

Numeroff, Laura Joffe. Happy Birthday, Mouse! Bond, Felicia, illus. 2012. (If You Give... Ser.). (ENG.). 24p. (J). (gr. -1 — 1). bds. 6.99 *(978-0-694-01425-5(7))* HarperCollins Pubs.

—Happy Valentine's Day, Mouse! Lap Edition. Bond, Felicia, illus. 2015. (If You Give... Ser.). (ENG.). 24p. (J). (gr. -1-3). bds. 12.99 *(978-0-06-242740-3(7))* HarperCollins Pubs.

—What Brothers Do Best. Munsinger, Lynn, illus. 2012. (ENG.). 20p. (J). (gr. -1 — 1). bds. 7.99 *(978-1-4521-1073-8(5))* Chronicle Bks. LLC.

—What Sisters Do Best. Munsinger, Lynn, illus. (ENG.). (J). (gr. -1 — 1). 2012. 20p. bds. 6.99 *(978-1-4521-1074-5(3))* 2009. 44p. 15.99 *(978-0-8118-6545-6(2))* Chronicle Bks. LLC.

Nunn, Daniel. Eddie & Ellie's Opposites. 2013. (Eddie & Ellie's Opposites Ser.). (ENG.). 24p. (gr. -1-k). pap. 27.80 *(978-1-4109-5349-0(1))*; lib. bdg. 90.60 *(978-1-4109-5344-5(0))* Heinemann-Raintree. (NA-r).

—Farm Animals, 1 vol. 2013. (True or False? Ser.). (ENG.). 20p. (gr. -1-1). bds. 7.99 *(978-1-4109-5084-0(0)*, NA-r) Heinemann-Raintree.

Nussbaum, Ben. Take Me Out to the Ballgame. Studio Mouse Staff, ed. rev. ed. 2007. (ENG.). 24p. 4.99 *(978-1-59069-603-3(4))* Studio Mouse LLC.

O'Brien, Anne Sibley. Abracadabra, It's Spring! Gal, Susan, illus. 2016. (Seasonal Magic Ser.). (ENG.). 24p. (J). (gr. -1-k). 14.95 *(978-1-4197-1891-5(6)*, Abrams Appleseed) Abrams, Inc.

—Hocus Pocus, It's Fall! Gal, Susan, illus. 2016. (ENG.). 24p. (J). (gr. -1-k). 12.95 *(978-1-4197-2125-0(9)*, Abrams Appleseed) Abrams, Inc.

O'Brien, Joan. Fashion Accessories Stickers. 2003. (Dover Little Activity Bks.). (ENG., Illus.). 4p. 1.50 *(978-0-486-43071-3(5))* Dover Pubns., Inc.

—Littlest Angels Stickers. 2003. (Dover Little Activity Books Stickers Ser.). (ENG., Illus.). 4p. (J). (gr. -1-5). pap. 1.50 *(978-0-486-43007-2(3))* Dover Pubns., Inc.

—Lucky Ladybug Stickers. 2004. (Dover Little Activity Books Stickers Ser.). (ENG., Illus.). 4p. (J). (gr. k-3). pap. 1.99 *(978-0-486-43008-9(1))* Dover Pubns., Inc.

O'Brien, Kristen. Little Red Riding Hood Story in a Box. Winter, Janet, illus. 2003. (Story in a Box Ser.). 12p. (J). (gr. -1-1). bds. 8.99 *(978-1-883043-41-4(7))* Straight Edge Pr., The.

O'Brien, Melanie. My Belly Button. 2009. 12p. 9.95 *(978-1-58117-917-0(0)*, Intervisual/Piggy Toes) Bendon, Inc.
—No More Pacifiers! With Disappearing Pacifiers! Enright, Amanda, illus. 2008. (ENG.). 18p. (J). (gr. -1-k). 10.95 *(978-1-58117-684-1(8)*, Intervisual/Piggy Toes) Bendon, Inc.
O'Connell, Rebecca. The Baby Goes Beep. Wilson-Max, Ken, illus. 2010. (ENG.). 16p. (J). (gr. -1 — 1). bds. 7.99 *(978-0-8075-0508-3(0))* Whitman, Albert & Co.
O'Connor, Jane. Fancy Nancy's Marvelous Mother's Day Brunch. Glasser, Robin Preiss, illus. 2011. (Fancy Nancy Ser.). (ENG.). 16p. (J). (gr. -1-3). pap. 6.99 *(978-0-06-170380-5(X)*, HarperFestival) HarperCollins Pubs.
O'Dare, Helen. Love. O'Byrne, Nicola, illus. 2016. (ENG.). 26p. (J). bds. 6.99 *(978-1-62686-677-5(5)*, Silver Dolphin Bks.) Readerlink Distribution Services, LLC.
Odierno, Lisa. Bunny Hide-and-Seek. 2009. (Smithsonian Baby Animals Ser.). (ENG., Illus.). 16p. (J). (gr. -1-k). 6.95 *(978-1-60727-092-8(7))* Soundprints.
Odierno, Lisa & Soundprints Staff. Bunny Hide-and-Seek. 2009. (Smithsonian Baby Animals Ser.). (ENG., Illus.). 16p. (J). (gr. -1-k). 6.95 *(978-1-60727-105-5(2))* Soundprints.
Ohrt, Kate. The Rainbow Book. 2011. (ENG.). 18p. (J). (gr. -1-1). pap. 9.99 *(978-1-4494-0171-9(6))* Andrews McMeel Publishing.
O'Leary, Sara & Opal, Paola. Zingy. Morstad, Julie, illus. 2013. (Simply Small Ser.: 10). (ENG.). 24p. (J). (gr. k — 1). bds. 7.95 *(978-1-897476-75-8(2))* Simply Read Bks. CAN. Dist: Ingram Publisher Services.
Olesen, Cecilie. My First Handy Bible. Mazali, Gustavo, illus. 2006. (ENG.). 64p. (gr. -1-k). bds. 12.99 *(978-1-59052-608-8(2)*, Multnomah) Doubleday Religious Publishing Group, The.
Opal, Paola. Dotty. 2010. (Simply Small Ser.). (ENG., Illus.). 24p. (J). (gr. -1 — 1). bds. 7.95 *(978-1-897476-54-3(X))* Simply Read Bks. CAN. Dist: Ingram Publisher Services.
—Emma. 2014. (Simply Small Ser.: 12). (ENG., Illus.). 24p. (J). (gr. -1-k). bds. 7.95 *(978-1-897476-93-2(0)*, 9781897476932) Simply Read Bks. CAN. Dist: Ingram Publisher Services.
—Pippy. 2013. (Simply Small Ser.: 12). (ENG., Illus.). 24p. (J). bds. 7.95 *(978-1-897476-92-5(2))* Simply Read Bks. CAN. Dist: Ingram Publisher Services.
—Totty. 2009. (Simply Small Ser.). (ENG., Illus.). 24p. (J). (gr. -1 — 1). bds. 7.95 *(978-1-897476-06-2(X))* Simply Read Bks. CAN. Dist: Ingram Publisher Services.
Opal, Paola, illus. Saffy & Ollie. 2012. (Simply Small Ser.). (ENG.). 24p. (J). (gr. -1 — 1). bds. 7.95 *(978-1-897476-69-7(8))* Simply Read Bks. CAN. Dist: Ingram Publisher Services.
Osteen, Victoria. My Happy Heart Books, Set. Day, Betsy, illus. 2009. (ENG.). 66p. (J). (gr. -1-k). bds. 19.99 *(978-1-4169-5549-8(6)*, Little Simon Inspirations) Little Simon Inspirations.
O'Toole, Janet. On the Farm: Lift the Flaps to Find Out about Farms! Adams, Ben, illus. 2013. (ENG.). 16p. bds. 6.99 *(978-1-84322-794-6(0)*, Armadillo) Anness Publishing GBR. Dist: National Bk. Network.
O'Toole, Janet & Anness Publishing Staff. First Words: Lift the Flaps to Find Out about Words! Adams, Ben, illus. 2013. (ENG.). 16p. bds. 6.99 *(978-1-84322-795-3(9)*, Armadillo) Anness Publishing GBR. Dist: National Bk. Network.
—Vehicles: Lift the Flaps to Find Out about Vehicles! Adams, Ben, illus. 2013. (ENG.). 16p. bds. 6.99 *(978-1-84322-728-1(2)*, Armadillo) Anness Publishing GBR. Dist: National Bk. Network.
Ottersley, Martha T. Guess Who Loves Christmas! Hall, Susan, illus. 2014. (Guess Who Ser.). (ENG.). 10p. (J). (gr. -1-k). 10.99 *(978-0-7944-3210-2(7))* Reader's Digest Assn., Inc., The.
Oud, Pauline. Eating with Lily & Milo. Oud, Pauline, illus. 2010. (Lily & Milo Ser.). (ENG., Illus.). 30p. (J). (gr. k — 1). 12.95 *(978-1-60537-055-2(X))* Cobblestone Publishing Co.
Owl's Forest Numbers. 2015. (Illus.). (J). *(978-1-58865-882-1(1))* Kidsbooks, LLC.
Oxenbury, Helen. Baby Love Set: All Fall down - Clap Hands - Say Goodnight - Tickle, Tickle. Oxenbury, Helen, illus. gif. ed. 2009. (ENG., Illus.). 40p. (J). (gr. -1 — 1). bds. 8.99 *(978-1-4169-9546-3(3)*, Little Simon) Little Simon.
Packard, Mary. The Storyteller. Land Eagle, illus. 2009. 196p. (J). *(978-1-4351-1557-6(0))* Metro Bks.
Pacovská, Kveta. The Sun Is Yellow. 2012. (ENG., Illus.). 32p. (J). 24.95 *(978-1-84976-064-5(0))* Tate Publishing, Ltd. GBR. Dist: Abrams, Inc.
Paes, Rob, illus. Mighty Machines. 2003. 12p. (J). (gr. k-3). 20.00 *(978-0-7567-6652-8(4))* DIANE Publishing Co.
Page, Claire. Carry-Me Pets. 2008. (Carry-Me Ser.). (Illus.). 10p. (J). (gr. -1). bds. *(978-1-84610-878-5(0))* Make Believe Ideas.
—Five Noisy Ducks: An Action-Packed Counting Book. 2008. (Illus.). 18p. (J). (gr. -1-k). bds. *(978-1-84610-587-6(0))* Make Believe Ideas.
—Hide & Seek Vehicles. 2008. (Hide & Seek Ser.). (Illus.). 20p. (gr. -1). bds. *(978-1-84610-586-9(2))* Make Believe Ideas.
—I Really Like Trucks. 2010. (ENG., Illus.). 12p. (gr. -1-k). bds. 9.99 *(978-1-84610-962-1(0))* Make Believe Ideas GBR. Dist: Nelson, Thomas Inc.
Page, Nick. Touch & Feel Noisy Dinosaurs. 2007. (Touch & Feel Ser.). (Illus.). 12p. (gr. -1). per., bds. *(978-1-84610-444-2(0))* Make Believe Ideas.
Page, Nick & Page, Claire. Finger Puppet Books Christmas Story. 2008. (Illus.). 12p. (gr. -1-k). bds. *(978-1-84610-821-1(7))* Make Believe Ideas.
—Finger Puppet Books Christmas Story. 2009. (Finger Puppet Bks.). (Illus.). 12p. (gr. -1-k). bds. 12.99 *(978-1-84610-573-9(0))* Make Believe Ideas GBR. Dist: Nelson, Thomas Inc.
—Funny Faces: Baby Animals. 2006. (Funny Faces Ser.). (Illus.). 10p. (gr. -1-k). per., bds. *(978-1-84610-118-2(2))* Make Believe Ideas.
—Funny Faces Farm Animals. 2006. (Funny Faces Ser.). (Illus.). 10p. (gr. -1-k). bds. *(978-1-84610-117-5(4))* Make Believe Ideas.
Pagnoni, Roberta, illus. It's Easter Time. 2010. (ENG.). 10p. (J). (gr. -1-k). bds. 6.99 *(978-0-7641-6334-0(5))* Barron's Educational Series, Inc.
Pagnoni, Roberta & Rigo, Laura, illus. My Easter Basket. 2016. (ENG.). 10p. (J). (gr. -1 — 1). bds. 6.99 *(978-0-7641-6822-2(3))* Barron's Educational Series, Inc.
—The Twelve Days of Christmas. 2013. (ENG.). 24p. (J). (gr. -1 — 1). bds. 10.99 *(978-0-7641-6622-8(0))* Barron's Educational Series, Inc.
Paiva, Johannah Gilman, ed. A Child's Book of Prayers: Please. 2013. (ENG., Illus.). 20p. (J). 8.99 *(978-1-77093-637-9(8))* Flowerpot Children's Pr. Inc. CAN. Dist: Cardinal Pubs. Group.
—A Child's Book of Prayers: Thank You. 2013. (ENG., Illus.). 20p. (J). 8.99 *(978-1-77093-638-6(6))* Flowerpot Children's Pr. Inc. CAN. Dist: Cardinal Pubs. Group.
—Crazy Critters. Gardiner, Lisa M., illus. 2013. (Big Padded Lift-The-Flap Ser.). (ENG.). 20p. (J). (gr. -1-2). 8.99 *(978-1-77093-630-0(0))* Flowerpot Children's Pr. Inc. CAN. Dist: Cardinal Pubs. Group.
—Farm Find. Gardiner, Lisa M., illus. 2013. 20p. (J). (gr. -1-1). 8.99 *(978-1-77093-688-1(2))* Flowerpot Children's Pr. Inc. CAN. Dist: Cardinal Pubs. Group.
—Zoo Friends. 2013. (Illus.). 20p. (J). bds. 8.99 *(978-1-77093-629-4(7))* Flowerpot Children's Pr. Inc. CAN. Dist: Cardinal Pubs. Group.
Pallotta, Jerry & Newton, Joy. The Very Berry Counting Book. 2017. (ENG., Illus.). 10p. (J). (— 1). bds. 6.99 *(978-1-58089-784-6(3))* Charlesbridge Publishing, Inc.
Pampered Pupz Sticker Scene. (Bratz Sticker Scene Books Ser.). 12p. pap. *(978-1-4054-8870-9(0))* Parragon, Inc.
Pan Macmillan, Pan. Christmas Stories: Baby's First Storybook: Follow the Finger Trails. 2015. (ENG., Illus.). 10p. (J). bds. 12.99 ***(978-1-4472-8700-1(2))*** Pan Macmillan GBR. Dist: Independent Pubs. Group.
Pan MacMillan Staff & Books, Campbell. Playtime Stories. Rinaldo, Luana, illus. 2016. (ENG.). 12p. (J). bds. 12.99 ***(978-1-4472-7705-7(8))*** Pan Macmillan GBR. Dist: Independent Pubs. Group.
PAN Macmillan UK, P. A. N. Macmillan & Books, Campbell. Bedtime Stories. Rinaldo, Luana, illus. 2015. (ENG.). 12p. (J). bds. 11.99 ***(978-1-4472-7704-0(X))*** Pan Macmillan GBR. Dist: Independent Pubs. Group.
Pankova, Yuliya, ed. Veggies - Guess What? 2013. (Guess What? Ser.). (ENG.). 10p. (J). (— 1). bds. 5.95 *(978-1-61889-319-2(X))* AZ Bks. LLC.
Pantone, Inc Staff, contrib. by. Pantone - Box of Colour: 6 Mini Board Books!, 6 vols. 2012. (ENG., Illus.). 60p. (J). (gr. -1 — 1). 12.95 *(978-1-4197-0515-1(6))* Abrams, Inc.
Paprocki, Greg, illus. M Is for Monocle - Victorian Alphabet, 1 vol. 2016. (ENG.). 32p. (J). bds. 9.99 *(978-1-4236-4284-8(8))* Gibbs Smith, Publisher.
Paquette, Ammi-Joan. Ghost in the House. Record, Adam, illus. 2015. (ENG.). 20p. (J). (gr. -1-2). 9.99 *(978-0-7636-7622-3(5))* Candlewick Pr.
Paradis, Anne. Caillou, My House: Includes 4 Chunky Board Books. Brignaud, Pierre, illus. 2015. (ENG.). 40p. (J). (gr. -1-k). 16.99 *(978-2-89718-224-3(5))* Caillouet, Gerry.
Parisi, Anthony. First Look at Space. Pindroh, Paula, illus. 2011. (ENG.). 16p. (J). *(978-1-60727-225-0(3)*, Blackbirch Pr., Inc.) Soundprints.
Parker, Amy. How Big Is Love? 2016. (Faith, Hope, Love Ser.). (ENG.). 24p. (J). (gr. -1-k). bds. 9.99 *(978-1-4336-9042-6(X)*, B&H Kids) B&H Publishing Group.
—How Far Is Faith? (padded Board Book) 2016. (Faith, Hope, Love Ser.). (ENG.). 24p. (J). (gr. -1-k). bds. 9.99 *(978-1-4336-9040-2(3)*, B&H Kids) B&H Publishing Group.
—How High Is Hope? (padded Board Book) 2016. (Faith, Hope, Love Ser.). (ENG.). 24p. (J). (gr. -1-k). bds. 9.99 *(978-1-4336-9041-9(1)*, B&H Kids) B&H Publishing Group.
—Night Night, Farm, 1 vol. Allyn, Virginia, illus. 2016. (Night Night Ser.). (ENG.). 20p. (J). bds. 8.99 *(978-0-7180-8831-6(X))* Nelson, Thomas Inc.
—A Night Night Prayer, 1 vol. Pedler, Caroline, illus. 2014. (Night Night Ser.). (ENG.). 20p. (J). bds. 9.99 *(978-1-4003-2431-6(9))* Nelson, Thomas Inc.
Parker, Amy & Walsh, Sarah. Tiny Blessings: for Bedtime. Running Press Staff, ed. 2016. (ENG., Illus.). 10p. (J). (gr. -1-17). bds. 7.95 *(978-0-7624-5990-2(5)*, Running Pr. Kids) Running Pr. Bk. Pubs.
—Tiny Blessings: for Giving Thanks. Running Press Staff, ed. 2016. (ENG., Illus.). 10p. (J). (gr. -1-17). bds. 7.95 *(978-0-7624-5989-6(1)*, Running Pr. Kids) Running Pr. Bk. Pubs.
Parker, Ant, illus. Amazing Machines First Concepts: Colors. 2015. (ENG.). 12p. (J). (gr. -1-1). bds. 5.99 *(978-0-7534-7233-0(3)*, 9780753472330, Kingfisher) Roaring Brook Pr.
—Amazing Machines First Concepts: Numbers. 2015. (ENG.). 12p. (J). (gr. -1-1). bds. 5.99 *(978-0-7534-7231-6(7)*, 9780753472316, Kingfisher) Roaring Brook Pr.
—Amazing Machines First Concepts: Opposites. 2015. (ENG.). 12p. (J). (gr. -1-1). bds. 5.99 *(978-0-7534-7234-7(1)*, 9780753472347, Kingfisher) Roaring Brook Pr.
Parker, Ant & Denchfield, Nick. Charlie Chick Wants to Play. Parker, Ant, illus. 2017. (Charlie Chick Ser.: 6). (ENG., Illus.). 10p. (J). (-k). bds. 9.99 ***(978-1-5098-2900-2(8))*** Pan Macmillan GBR. Dist: Independent Pubs. Group.
Parker-Rees, Guy. Party Time with Littlebob & Plum: Lots of Lift-the-Flap Fun. Parker-Rees, Guy, illus. 2012. (ENG., Illus.). 20p. (J). (gr. k-2). 12.99 *(978-1-4083-0443-3(0))* Hodder & Stoughton GBR. Dist: Hachette Bk. Group.
Parmley, Dave & Ruffing, Eric. Alternative ABCs. 2010. (Illus.). 58p. bds. 14.95 *(978-1-934429-39-6(2))* AMMO Bks., LLC.
Parot, Annelore. Kimonos. 2011. (ENG.). 36p. (J). (gr. k-17). 17.99 *(978-1-4521-0493-5(X))* Chronicle Bks. LLC.
Parr, Todd. The Daddy Book. 2015. (ENG., Illus.). 20p. (J). (gr. -1 — 1). bds. 6.99 *(978-0-316-25784-8(2))* Little, Brown Bks. for Young Readers.
Parr, Todd & Chronicle Books Staff. Save the Blue. 2009. (ENG.). 160p. (J). (gr. -1-3). 9.99 *(978-0-8118-7153-2(3))* Chronicle Bks. LLC.
Parragon, creator. Growl with the Animals! 2014. (Discovery Kids 10 Button Ser.). (ENG., Illus.). (J). (gr. -1). bds. *(978-1-4723-6108-0(3))* Parragon Bk. Service Ltd.
Parragon Publishing Staff. Busy Day at the Airport. (Busy Books Large Ser.). *(978-1-4054-7873-1(X))* Parragon, Inc.
Parrish, Emma. Little Owl Says Goodnight. 2016. (Slide-And-Seek Ser.). (ENG., Illus.). 10p. (J). (gr. -1-k). bds. 8.99 *(978-1-4998-0406-5(7))* Little Bee Books Inc.
Parrott, Leslie. God Made You Nose to Toes, 1 vol. Corke, Estelle, illus. 2017. (ENG.). 18p. (J). bds. 9.99 *(978-0-310-75740-5(1))* Zonderkidz.
Parry, Jo. Blast Off! 2009. (Wow! Bks.). (Illus.). (J). bds. 12.99 *(978-1-934650-26-4(9))* Just For Kids Pr., LLC.
Parry, Rosanne. Daddy's Home! Leonard, David, illus. 2009. (ENG.). 20p. (J). bds. 6.99 *(978-0-8249-1823-1(1)*, Ideal Pubns.) Worthy Publishing.
Pasquali, Elena. Santa's Midnight Sleighride. Vagnozzi, Barbara, illus. 2013. (Finger-Trail Animal Tales Ser.). (ENG.). 10p. (J). (gr. -1-k). bds. 9.99 *(978-0-7459-6242-9(4))* Lion Hudson PLC GBR. Dist: Independent Pubs. Group.
Patchett, F. Plane Fun. 2009. (Kid Kits Ser.). 32p. (J). 11.99 *(978-1-60130-162-8(6)*, Usborne) EDC Publishing.
Patricelli, Leslie. Big Little. Patricelli, Leslie, illus. 2003. (Leslie Patricelli Board Bks.). (ENG., Illus.). 24p. (J). (— 1). bds. 6.99 *(978-0-7636-1951-0(5))* Candlewick Pr.
—The Birthday Box. Patricelli, Leslie, illus. 2009. (Leslie Patricelli Board Bks.). (ENG., Illus.). 26p. (J). (gr. k — 1). bds. 6.99 *(978-0-7636-4449-9(8))* Candlewick Pr.
—Blankie/Mantita. Patricelli, Leslie, illus. 2016. (Leslie Patricelli Board Bks.). (ENG & SPA., Illus.). 24p. (J). (— 1). bds. 6.99 *(978-0-7636-8897-4(5))* Candlewick Pr.
—Fa la La. Patricelli, Leslie, illus. 2012. (Leslie Patricelli Board Bks.). (ENG., Illus.). 26p. (J). (gr. k — 1). bds. 6.99 *(978-0-7636-3247-2(3))* Candlewick Pr.
—Higher! Higher! Patricelli, Leslie, illus. 2010. (Leslie Patricelli Board Bks.). (ENG., Illus.). 30p. (J). (-k). bds. 6.99 *(978-0-7636-4433-8(1))* Candlewick Pr.
—Hop! Hop! Patricelli, Leslie, illus. 2015. (Leslie Patricelli Board Bks.). (ENG., Illus.). 26p. (J). (— 1). bds. 6.99 *(978-0-7636-6319-3(0))* Candlewick Pr.
—Huggy Kissy. Patricelli, Leslie, illus. 2012. (Leslie Patricelli Board Bks.). (ENG., Illus.). 26p. (J). (gr. k — 1). bds. 6.99 *(978-0-7636-3246-5(5))* Candlewick Pr.
—Potty/Bacinica. Patricelli, Leslie, illus. 2016. (Leslie Patricelli Board Bks.). (ENG & SPA., Illus.). (J). (— 1). bds. 6.99 *(978-0-7636-8777-9(4))* Candlewick Pr.
—Tickle. Patricelli, Leslie, illus. 2014. (Leslie Patricelli Board Bks.). (ENG., Illus.). 26p. (J). (— 1). bds. 6.99 *(978-0-7636-6322-3(0))* Candlewick Pr.
—Toot. Patricelli, Leslie, illus. 2014. (Leslie Patricelli Board Bks.). (ENG., Illus.). 24p. (J). (— 1). bds. 6.99 *(978-0-7636-6321-6(2))* Candlewick Pr.
—Tubby / Bañito. Patricelli, Leslie, illus. 2017. (Leslie Patricelli Board Bks.). (ENG & SPA., Illus.). 28p. (J). (— 1). bds. 6.99 *(978-0-7636-9316-9(2))* Candlewick Pr.
—Yummy Yucky. Patricelli, Leslie, illus. 2003. (Leslie Patricelli Board Bks.). (ENG., Illus.). 24p. (J). (gr. k — 1). bds. 6.99 *(978-0-7636-1950-3(7))* Candlewick Pr.
Patterson, Sandra Jean. Crabby Crab. 2006. bds. 12.95 *(978-1-59700-246-2(1))* Island Heritage Publishing.
Paul, Cinco & Daurio, Ken. Sleepy Kittens. Guillon, Eric, illus. 2010. (Despicable Me Ser.). (ENG.). 10p. (J). (gr. -1 — 1). bds. 8.99 *(978-0-316-08381-2(X)*, L.B Kids) Hachette Bk. Group.
Paul Frank Industries. Let's Dance with Julius & Friends. 2012. (ENG., Illus.). 14p. (J). (gr. -1 — 1). bds. 8.99 *(978-1-4521-0637-3(1))* Chronicle Bks. LLC.
Paul Frank Industries & Gillingham, Sara. I Love Color: A Paul Frank Book. 2011. (ENG.). 10p. (J). (gr. -1 — 1). bds. 8.99 *(978-1-4521-0222-1(8))* Chronicle Bks. LLC.
Paul Frank Industries Staff & Chronicle Books Staff. High Five with Julius! & Friends. 2010. (ENG., Illus.). 10p. (J). (gr. -1 — 1). bds. 8.99 *(978-0-8118-7147-1(9))* Chronicle Bks. LLC.
PAW Patrol on the Roll! 2016. (Illus.). (J). ***(978-1-5182-2638-0(8))*** Random House Children's Books.
Paw Patrol, Paw. Paw Patrol: Pups Save the Day - A Slide Surprise Book. 2015. (Sliding Surprise Ser.: 4). (ENG.). 12p. (J). (gr. -1-k). bds. 10.99 *(978-0-7944-3558-5(0)*, Reader's Digest Children's Bks.) Studio Fun International.
Peanuckle. Mrs. Peanuckle's Vegetable Alphabet. Ford, Jessie, illus. 2017. (Mrs. Peanuckle's Alphabet Library: 1). (ENG.). 28p. (J). bds. 7.99 ***(978-1-62336-870-8(7)***, 9781623368708, Rodale Kids) Rodale Pr., Inc.
Pearlman, Bobby. Passover Is Here! Desmoinaux, Christel, illus. 2005. (ENG.). 16p. (J). (gr. k-2). pap. 6.99 *(978-0-689-86587-9(2)*, Little Simon) Little Simon.
A Pebble Story. 2014. (ENG., Illus.). 26p. (J). (gr. -1 — 1). bds. 6.95 *(978-1-55451-654-4(4)*, 9781554516544) Annick Pr., Ltd. CAN. Dist: Publishers Group West (PGW).
Pedigree Books. Turbo Annual 2014. 2013. 80p. (J). 12.99 *(978-1-907602-93-1(3))* Pedigree Bks., Ltd. GBR. Dist: Diamond Bk. Distributors.
Pelham, David. Here Comes Santa: A Mini Holiday Pop-Up. Pelham, David, illus. 2008. (ENG., Illus.). 18p. (J). 11.99 *(978-1-4169-5440-8(6)*, Little Simon) Little Simon.
—Sam's Sandwich. Pelham, David, illus. 2015. (ENG., Illus.). 24p. (J). (gr. -1-2). 9.99 *(978-0-7636-7808-1(2))* Candlewick Pr.
Penn, Audrey. A Color Game for Chester Raccoon. Gibson, Barbara Leonard, illus. 2012. (Kissing Hand Ser.). (ENG.). 14p. (J). (gr. -1-k). bds. 7.95 *(978-1-933718-58-3(7))* Tanglewood Pr.
People. Date not set. (I Can Draw Ser.). 32p. (J). 4.98 *(978-1-4054-0020-6(X))* Parragon, Inc.
Percival, Tom. Herman's Letter. 2014. (ENG., Illus.). 32p. (J). (gr. -1-1). 17.99 *(978-1-61963-423-7(6)*, 9781619634237, Bloomsbury USA Childrens) Bloomsbury Publishing USA.
Perez, Jessica. Under Construction: A Moving Track Book. Schneider, Christine, illus. 2005. (ENG.). 12p. (J). 12.95 *(978-1-58117-272-0(9)*, Intervisual/Piggy Toes) Bendon, Inc.
—Who's Hiding Inside? Dinosaurs. Lensch, Chris, illus. 2005. (Who's Hiding Inside Ser.). 12p. (J). bds. 7.95 *(978-1-58117-246-1(X)*, Intervisual/Piggy Toes) Bendon, Inc.
Perkins, Al. The Nose Book. Mathieu, Joe, illus. 2017. (Big Bright & Early Board Book Ser.). (ENG.). 24p. (J). (— 1). bds. 6.99 *(978-0-553-53863-2(2)*, Random Hse. Bks. for Young Readers) Random Hse. Children's Bks.
Perrin, Martine. Look Who's There! Martens, Marianne, tr. from FRE. Perrin, Martine, illus. 2011. (ENG., Illus.). 16p. (J). (gr. -1-k). bds. 8.99 *(978-0-8075-7676-2(X))* Whitman, Albert & Co.
—What Do You See? Perrin, Martine, illus. 2011. (ENG., Illus.). 16p. (J). (gr. -1-k). bds. 8.99 *(978-0-8075-6712-8(4))* Whitman, Albert & Co.
Peter Pauper Press Staff & Zschock, Heather. Princess Bella: An Art Activity Story Book for Princesses of All Ages. Barbas, Kerren, illus. 2005. (Activity Journal Ser.). 64p. (J). (gr. -1-7). 14.99 *(978-1-59359-972-0(2))* Peter Pauper Pr. Inc.
Peters, Elizabeth Anne. Worms Like to Wiggle. Yerbey, Lindsey Blake, illus. 2007. (J). *(978-0-9769737-1-3(5))* Creative Minds Pubns.
Peters, Rob, illus. Kansas City Chiefs ABCs And 1-2-3s. 2015. (ENG.). 26p. (J). bds. 18.95 *(978-0-9961944-0-2(1))* Ascend Bks., LLC.
Petricic, Dusan & Suomalainen, Sami, illus. Mud Puddle. 2012. (ENG.). 26p. (J). (gr. -1 — 1). bds. 7.99 *(978-1-55451-754-1(0)*, 9781554517541) Annick Pr., Ltd. CAN. Dist: Publishers Group West (PGW).
Petrlik, Andrea, illus. Hansel & Gretel. 2007. (Flip-Up Fairy Tales Ser.). (ENG.). 24p. (J). (gr. -1-2). audio compact disk *(978-1-84643-090-9(9))* Child's Play International Ltd.
Petruccio, Steven James. Cowboy Tattoos. 2003. (Dover Tattoos Ser.). (ENG., Illus.). 2p. (J). (gr. 1-4). pap. 1.99 *(978-0-486-43028-7(6))* Dover Pubns., Inc.
Peyo. All about Brainy Smurf! 2013. (Smurfs Classic Ser.). (ENG.). 12p. (J). (gr. -1-k). bds. 5.99 *(978-1-4424-7264-8(2)*, Simon Spotlight) Simon Spotlight.
—Papa Smurf's Favorite Things. Peyo, illus. 2013. (Smurfs Classic Ser.). (ENG., Illus.). 12p. (J). (gr. -1-k). bds. 5.99 *(978-1-4424-6167-3(5)*, Simon Spotlight) Simon Spotlight.
—Smurfs Mini Library: Rise & Shine; Happy Smurfdays; Fun & Games; Making Music; Whatever the Weather. Peyo, illus. 2014. (Smurfs Classic Ser.). (ENG., Illus.). 70p. (J). (gr. -1-2). bds. 6.99 *(978-1-4424-9543-2(X)*, Simon Spotlight) Simon Spotlight.
—Who's That Smurf? Peyo, illus. 2013. (Smurfs Classic Ser.). (ENG., Illus.). 18p. (J). (gr. -1-1). bds. 5.99 *(978-1-4424-7235-8(9)*, Simon Spotlight) Simon Spotlight.
Pezzimenti, Grace. Busy Families: Learning to Tell Time by the Hour. (Math for the Real World: Early Emergent Ser.). (ENG., Illus.). 8p. (gr. k-1). 2009. pap. 5.15 *(978-0-8239-8912-6(7))* 2004. 29.95 *(978-0-8239-7627-0(0))* Rosen Publishing Group, Inc., The.
Pfeffer, Wendy. Sounds All Around. Chernyshova, Anna, illus. 2016. (Let's-Read-And-Find-Out Science 1 Ser.). 40p. (J). (gr. -1-3). pap. 6.99 *(978-0-06-238669-4(7))* HarperCollins Pubs.
Pfister, Marcus. Good Night, Little Rainbow Fish. 2017. (Rainbow Fish Ser.: 1). (ENG., Illus.). 12p. (J). (gr. -1-k). bds. 9.95 ***(978-0-7358-4285-4(X))*** North-South Bks., Inc.
—Milo & the Magical Stones. Pfister, Marcus, illus. 2010. (Milo Ser.). (ENG., Illus.). 32p. (J). (gr. k-3). 17.95 *(978-0-7358-2253-5(0))* North-South Bks., Inc.
—Questions, Questions. 2014. (ENG & GER., Illus.). 32p. (J). (gr. -1 — 1). bds. 8.95 *(978-0-7358-4170-3(5)*, 9780735841703) North-South Bks., Inc.
—Rainbow Fish Deep Sea Adventure Sticker & Coloring Storybook. 2010. (Rainbow Fish Ser.). (ENG.). 24p. (gr. -1-2). 5.95 *(978-0-7358-2318-1(9))* North-South Bks., Inc.
—Rainbow Fish Opposites. 2013. (Rainbow Fish Ser.). (ENG., Illus.). 12p. (J). (gr. 1-1). bds. 7.95 *(978-0-7358-4146-8(2))* North-South Bks., Inc.
—Rainbow Fish Puzzle Book. 2012. (Rainbow Fish Ser.). (ENG., Illus.). 16p. (J). (gr. -1-3). bds. 9.95 *(978-0-7358-4096-6(2))* North-South Bks., Inc.
Phaidon Editors & Matisse, Henri. Blue & Other Colors. 2016. (ENG., Illus.). 30p. (gr. -1 — 1). bds. 9.95 *(978-0-7148-7142-4(7))* Phaidon Pr., Inc.
Phidal Publishing Staff, ed. Totally Girls: Super Sticker Book. (Illus.). 64p. (J). pap. *(978-2-7643-0190-6(1))* Phidal Publishing, Inc./Editions Phidal, Inc.
Phillips, Dee. Baby's Day. 2009. (Flip Flap Fun Bks.). (ENG.). 5p. (J). (gr. -1-k). bds. 5.95 *(978-1-84696-087-1(8)*, TickTock Books) Octopus Publishing Group GBR. Dist: Independent Pubs. Group.
—Big Zoo. 2009. (Flip Flap Fun Bks.). (ENG.). 5p. (J). (gr. -1-k). bds. 5.95 *(978-1-84696-086-4(X)*, TickTock Books) Octopus Publishing Group GBR. Dist: Independent Pubs. Group.
—Colors. 2009. (Christmas Lift the Flap Ser.). (ENG.). 10p. (J). (gr. -1-k). bds. 5.95 *(978-1-84696-966-9(2)*, TickTock Books) Octopus Publishing Group GBR. Dist: Independent Pubs. Group.
—First Addition. 2009. (Christmas Lift the Flap Ser.). (ENG.). 10p. (J). (gr. -1-k). bds. 5.95 *(978-1-84696-967-6(0)*, TickTock Books) Octopus Publishing Group GBR. Dist: Independent Pubs. Group.
—First Words. 2009. (Christmas Lift the Flap Ser.). (ENG.). 10p. (J). (gr. -1-k). bds. 5.95 *(978-1-84696-968-3(9)*, TickTock Books) Octopus Publishing Group GBR. Dist: Independent Pubs. Group.
—Numbers. 2009. (Christmas Lift the Flap Ser.). (ENG.). 10p. (J). (gr. -1-k). bds. 5.95 *(978-1-84696-969-0(7)*, TickTock Books) Octopus Publishing Group GBR. Dist: Independent Pubs. Group.
Phillips, Karen. Lettering in Crazy, Cool, Quirky Style. 2006. (ENG., Illus.). 56p. (J). (gr. 3-7). 18.95 *(978-1-57054-428-6(X))* Klutz.
Phillips, Sara & Running Press Staff. Animals. 2003. (Illus.). 8p. (J). pap. 4.95 *(978-0-7624-1650-9(5))* Running Pr. Bk. Pubs.
Phillips, Sarah. Flip, Flap, Match Noisy Farm. 2013. (ENG.). 12p. (J). bds. 7.99 *(978-1-78235-570-0(7))* Make Believe Ideas GBR. Dist: Nelson, Thomas Inc.
—Lift & Learn ABC. Snaith, Andy, photos by. 2006. (Illus.). 24p. (gr. -1). per., bds. *(978-1-84610-029-1(1))* Make Believe Ideas.
—Touch & Learn: ABC. 2007. (Touch & Learn (Make Believe Ideas) Ser.). (Illus.). 12p. (gr. -1). per., bds. *(978-1-84610-461-9(0))* Make Believe Ideas.
Phoenix International Staff, illus. Doc Mcstuffins the Doc Is in. 2014. 10p. (J). bds. 17.98 *(978-1-4508-8186-9(6)*, 1450881866) Phoenix International Publications, Inc.
—Let's Go to the Doctor. 2014. 12p. (J). bds. 9.98 *(978-1-4508-6805-1(3)*, 3dabf932-f542-41b5-a62a-7268d1f15970) Phoenix International Publications, Inc.
—Thomas & Friends(r) - Thomas' Piano Book. deluxe ed. 2014. 12p. (J). bds. 17.98 *(978-1-4127-4552-9(7)*, 1412745527) Phoenix International Publications, Inc.

T
U
V

Picthall, Chez. Flip Flaps Zoo. 2015. (ENG., Illus.). 18p. (J). 9.99 *(978-1-907604-53-9(7))* Award Pubns. Ltd. GBR. Dist: Parkwest Pubns., Inc.

—Puppies. 2015. (ENG., Illus.). 10p. (J). 7.99 *(978-1-905503-77-3(6))* Award Pubns. Ltd. GBR. Dist: Parkwest Pubns., Inc.

Picthall, Chez, creator. Flip Flap Colours: A Turn-the-Flap Book! 2014. (ENG., Illus.). 36p. pap. 10.00 *(978-1-906572-79-2(8))* Award Pubns. Ltd. GBR. Dist: Parkwest Pubns., Inc.

—Flip Flaps Shapes. 2014. (ENG., Illus.). 32p. bds. 10.00 *(978-1-906572-80-8(1))* Award Pubns. Ltd. GBR. Dist: Parkwest Pubns., Inc.

Picthall, Chez, des. Flowers. 2015. (ENG., Illus.). 10p. (J). 9.99 *(978-1-907604-76-8(6))* Award Pubns. Ltd. GBR. Dist: Parkwest Pubns., Inc.

—Hearts & Stars. 2015. (ENG., Illus.). 10p. (J). 9.99 *(978-1-909763-05-0(5))* Award Pubns. Ltd. GBR. Dist: Parkwest Pubns., Inc.

—Spots & Dots. 2015. (ENG., Illus.). 10p. (J). 9.99 *(978-1-909763-02-9(0))* Award Pubns. Ltd. GBR. Dist: Parkwest Pubns., Inc.

Pidgeon, Jean, illus. Brush Your Teeth, Please: A Pop-Up Book. 2013. (Pop-Up Book Ser.: 2). (ENG.). 12p. (J). (gr. -1-k). 14.99 *(978-0-7944-3040-5(6)*, Reader's Digest Children's Bks.) Studio Fun International.

Pienkowski, Jan. The First Noel: A Christmas Carousel. Pienkowski, Jan et al, illus. 2004. (ENG.). 1p. (J). (gr. k-12). 14.99 *(978-0-7636-2190-2(0))* Candlewick Pr.

Piercy, Helen. Animation Studio. 2013. (ENG., Illus.). 32p. (J). (gr. 3-7). 19.99 *(978-0-7636-6701-6(3))* Candlewick Pr.

Pierpont, James Lord. Jingle Bells: A Magical Cut-Paper Edition. Puttapipat, Niroot, illus. 2015. (ENG.). 12p. (J). (gr. -1-3). 19.99 *(978-0-7636-7821-0(X))* Candlewick Pr.

Pierre Brignaud, Pierre, illus. Baby Caillou: My Farm Friends: A Finger Fun Book. 2015. (Baby Caillou Ser.). (ENG.). 16p. (J). (— 1). bds. 6.99 *(978-2-89718-177-2(X))* Caillouet, Gerry.

Piggy Toes Press. Our Ballet Recital. Maddocks, Maria, illus. 2005. (ENG.). 12p. (J). (gr. -1-3). 12.95 *(978-1-58117-425-0(X)*, Intervisual/Piggy Toes) Bendon, Inc.

Piggy Toes Press, creator. Crayola Sea Life: Counting Sea Life. 2011. (Crayola (Piggy Toes Press) Ser.). (ENG., Illus.). 6p. (gr. -1). bds. 5.95 *(978-1-61524-289-4(9)*, Intervisual/Piggy Toes) Bendon, Inc.

—Five Little Kisses. 2007. (ENG., Illus.). 10p. (J). (gr. -1-3). 9.95 *(978-1-58117-683-4(X)*, Intervisual/Piggy Toes) Bendon, Inc.

—Pop & Touch Kittens. 2008. (ENG., Illus.). 12p. (J). 10.95 *(978-1-58117-675-9(9)*, Intervisual/Piggy Toes) Bendon, Inc.

Pilkey, Dav. Big Dog & Little Dog Getting in Trouble (Reader) 2015. (Green Light Readers Level 1 Ser.). (ENG., Illus.). 24p. (J). (gr. -1-3). pap. 3.99 *(978-0-544-53095-9(0)*, HMH Books For Young Readers) Houghton Mifflin Harcourt Publishing Co.

—Big Dog & Little Dog Wearing Sweaters (Reader) 2015. (Green Light Readers Level 1 Ser.). (ENG., Illus.). 24p. (J). (gr. -1-3). 12.99 *(978-0-544-53097-3(7)*, HMH Books For Young Readers) Houghton Mifflin Harcourt Publishing Co.

—Super-Silly Sticker Studio. Klutz Editors, ed. 2013. (ENG.). 42p. (J). (gr. 1). act. bk. ed. 16.99 *(978-0-545-61522-8(4))* Klutz.

Pingry, Patricia A. The Easter Story. Utt, Mary Ann, illus. 2008. (ENG.). 26p. (J). (gr. -1-3). bds. 12.99 *(978-0-8249-6731-4(3)*, Ideal Pubns.) Worthy Publishing.

—The Story of the Star-Spangled Banner. Munger, Nancy, illus. 2014. (Story of Ser.). 24p. (J). bds. 6.99 *(978-0-8249-1930-6(0)*, Ideal Pubns.) Worthy Publishing.

Pinky's Farm: Moms & Babies. 2011. (Illus.). (J). *(978-1-58865-894-4(5))* Kidsbooks, LLC.

Pipe, Jim. Lift, Look & Learn Castle: Uncover the Secrets of a Medieval Fortress. Taylor, Maria, illus. 2014. (ENG.). 24p. (J). (gr. 1). 19.95 *(978-1-78312-081-9(9))* Carlton Bks., Ltd. GBR. Dist: Sterling Publishing Co., Inc.

—Lift, Look & Learn Doll's House: Uncover the Secrets of a Victorian Home. Taylor, Maria, illus. 2014. (ENG.). 24p. (J). (gr. 1). 19.95 *(978-1-78312-082-6(7))* Carlton Bks., Ltd. GBR. Dist: Sterling Publishing Co., Inc.

Piper, Sophie. Baby's First Bible. Maddocks, Maria, illus. 2014. (ENG.). 40p. (J). (— 1). bds. 9.99 *(978-0-7459-6411-9(7))* Lion Hudson PLC GBR. Dist: Independent Pubs. Group.

—From the Day You Were Born. Stephenson, Kristina, illus. 2014. (ENG.). 24p. (J). (— 1). bds. 6.99 *(978-0-7459-6237-5(8))* Lion Hudson PLC GBR. Dist: Independent Pubs. Group.

Piper, Sophie, et al. God Bless. 2nd ed. 2013. (Prayers for Little Hands Ser.). (ENG., Illus.). 8p. (J). (— 1). 8.99 *(978-0-7459-6375-4(7))* Lion Hudson PLC GBR. Dist: Independent Pubs. Group.

Piper, Watty. The Little Engine That Could. Long, Loren, illus. 2005. (Little Engine That Could Ser.). (ENG.). 48p. (J). (gr. -1-2). 17.99 *(978-0-399-24467-4(0)*, Philomel Bks.) Penguin Young Readers Group.

Piper, Watty & dePaola, Tomie. The Little Engine That Could. Hauman, George and Doris & Hauman, Doris, illus. 2015. (Little Engine That Could Ser.). (ENG.). 26p. (J). (gr. -1 — 1). bds. 11.99 *(978-0-448-48731-1(4)*, Grosset & Dunlap) Penguin Young Readers Group.

Piper, Watty, et al. My First Library, 3 vols. 2014. (ENG.). 96p. (J). (gr. -1-2). bds. 23.00 *(978-0-448-48288-0(6)*, Grosset & Dunlap) Penguin Young Readers Group.

Pitt, Sarah. Peek a Boo! Farm. 2009. (Little Peek a Boo Bks.). (Illus.). (J). bds. 9.99 *(978-1-934650-59-2(5))* Just For Kids Pr., LLC.

Pitzer, Marjorie. Animal Fun for Everyone! 2014. (ENG., Illus.). 14p. (J). pap. *(978-1-60613-188-6(5))* Woodbine Hse.

Pixton, Kaaren. Jungle, Rumble! Hey Baby! Look at These Wild Animals! 2010. (Indestructibles Ser.). (ENG., Illus.). 12p. (J). (gr. k — 1). pap. 5.95 *(978-0-7611-5858-5(8)*, 15858) Workman Publishing Co., Inc.

—Mama & Baby! 2010. (Indestructibles Ser.). (ENG., Illus.). 12p. (J). (gr. k — 1). pap. 5.95 *(978-0-7611-5859-2(6)*, 15859) Workman Publishing Co., Inc.

—Plip, Plop, Pond! Hey Baby! Look at These Animals in the Pond! 2010. (Indestructibles Ser.). (ENG., Illus.). 12p. (J). (gr. k — 1). pap. 5.95 *(978-0-7611-5857-8(X)*, 15857) Workman Publishing Co., Inc.

Pizzoli, Greg. The Watermelon Seed. Pizzoli, Greg, illus. 2016. (ENG., Illus.). 30p. (J). (gr. -1 — 1). bds. 7.99 *(978-1-4847-1236-8(6))* Hyperion Bks. for Children.

Platt, Richard. Halloween. Watson, Richard, illus. 2017. (Flip Flap Journeys Ser.). (ENG.). 14p. (J). (gr. k-2). 12.99 ***(978-1-4052-7659-7(2))*** Egmont Bks., Ltd. GBR. Dist: Independent Pubs. Group.

Play, Laugh, & Learn All Year Long. 2007. (ENG., Illus.). 28p. (J). (gr. -1-1). 16.99 *(978-1-59069-503-6(8)*, 1P1000) Studio Mouse LLC.

Pledger, Maurice. Bobby Bear & the Honeybees. Pledger, Maurice, illus. 2014. (Friendship Tales Ser.). (ENG., Illus.). 16p. (J). (gr. -1). bds. 10.95 *(978-1-62686-189-3(7)*, Silver Dolphin Bks.) Readerlink Distribution Services, LLC.

Pledger, Maurice, illus. Daisy Duckling's Adventure. 2014. (ENG.). 16p. (J). (gr. -1). bds. 10.95 *(978-1-62686-015-5(7)*, Silver Dolphin Bks.) Readerlink Distribution Services, LLC.

—Dottie Dolphin Plays Hide-And-Seek. 2015. (Friendship Tales Ser.). (ENG.). 16p. (gr. -1). bds. 10.95 *(978-1-62686-344-6(X)*, Silver Dolphin Bks.) Readerlink Distribution Services, LLC.

—Ping-Ping Panda's Bamboo Journey. 2015. (Friendship Tales Ser.). (ENG.). 16p. (J). (gr. -1). bds. 10.95 *(978-1-62686-345-3(8)*, Silver Dolphin Bks.) Readerlink Distribution Services, LLC.

Poitier, Anton. Flippy Floppy Farm Animals. Touliatou, Sophia, illus. 2014. 10p. (J). 12.99 *(978-1-61067-310-5(7))* Kane Miller.

—Flippy Floppy Ocean Animals. Touliatou, Sophia, illus. 2015. 10p. (J). 12.99 *(978-1-61067-346-4(8))* Kane Miller.

Poitier, Anton, illus. Colors: Match the Words & Colors. 2014. (Twisters Ser.). (ENG.). 10p. (J). (gr. -1 — 1). bds. 7.99 *(978-0-7641-6687-7(5))* Barron's Educational Series, Inc.

Poleahla, Anita. Celebrate My Hopi Name. James, Eric, illus. 2013. (CAI & ENG.). (J). *(978-1-893354-65-4(2))* Salina Bookshelf Inc.

Pop-Up Dinosaurs. 2017. (Pop-Up Bks.). (ENG.). (J). 14.99 ***(978-0-7945-3862-0(2)***, Usborne) EDC Publishing.

Porter, Jen. I Am Brave. Saunders, Katie, illus. 2016. (ENG.). 16p. (J). (-3). bds. 7.99 *(978-1-4926-4165-0(0)*, 9781492641650, Sourcebooks Jabberwocky) Sourcebooks, Inc.

—I Am Good. Saunders, Katie, illus. 2016. (ENG.). 16p. (J). (-3). bds. 7.99 *(978-1-4926-4167-4(7)*, 9781492641674, Sourcebooks Jabberwocky) Sourcebooks, Inc.

—I Am Kind. Saunders, Katie, illus. 2016. (ENG.). 16p. (J). (-3). bds. 7.99 *(978-1-4926-4169-8(3)*, 9781492641698, Sourcebooks Jabberwocky) Sourcebooks, Inc.

—I Am Tidy. Saunders, Katie, illus. 2016. (ENG.). 16p. (J). (-3). bds. 7.99 *(978-1-4926-4171-1(5)*, 9781492641711, Sourcebooks Jabberwocky) Sourcebooks, Inc.

Porter, Matthew. Flowers. 2010. (ENG., Illus.). 28p. (J). (gr. -1-k). bds. 8.95 *(978-1-897476-13-0(2))* Simply Read Bks. CAN. Dist: Ingram Publisher Services.

—Tails Chasing Tails. 2013. (ENG., Illus.). 20p. (J). (— 1). bds. 9.99 *(978-1-57061-852-9(6)*, Little Bigfoot) Sasquatch Bks.

Portis, Antoinette. Not a Box Board Book. Portis, Antoinette, illus. 2011. (ENG., Illus.). 28p. (J). (gr. -1 — 1). bds. 7.99 *(978-0-06-199442-5(1)*, HarperFestival) HarperCollins Pubs.

Poskitt, Kjartan & Watson, Richard. Maths Adventure. 2016. (ENG., Illus.). 14p. (J). (gr. k-2). 14.99 *(978-1-4052-7661-0(4))* Egmont Bks., Ltd. GBR. Dist: Independent Pubs. Group.

Posner-Sanchez, Andrea. Ariel's Dolphin Adventure - Snow White's New Friend, 2 bks. in 1. Random House Disney Staff, illus. 2010. (Pictureback(R) Ser.). (ENG.). 32p. (J). (gr. -1-2). pap. 4.99 *(978-0-7364-2654-1(X)*, RH/Disney) Random Hse. Children's Bks.

—Bath Time with Ariel (Disney Princess) DiCicco, Sue, illus. 2015. (Board Book Ser.). (ENG.). 24p. (J). (— 1). bds. 6.99 *(978-0-7364-3310-5(4)*, RH/Disney) Random Hse. Children's Bks.

—A Frozen Christmas (Disney Frozen) Random House Disney Staff, illus. 2015. (Glitter Board Book Ser.). (ENG.). 12p. (J). (gr. -1 — 1). bds. 8.99 *(978-0-7364-3479-9(8)*, RH/Disney) Random Hse. Children's Bks.

—Good Night, Princess! (Disney Princess) Legramandi, Francesco & Matta, Gabriella, illus. 2012. (Pictureback(R) Ser.). (ENG.). 16p. (J). (gr. -1-2). pap. 4.99 *(978-0-7364-2851-4(8)*, RH/Disney) Random Hse. Children's Bks.

—Sleepy Time with Aurora (Disney Princess) RH Disney Staff & DiCicco, Sue, illus. 2015. (Board Book Ser.). (ENG.). 24p. (J). (— 1). bds. 6.99 *(978-0-7364-3311-2(2)*, RH/Disney) Random Hse. Children's Bks.

—Tidy-Up Time with Cinderella (Disney Princess) DiCicco, Sue, illus. 2015. (Board Book Ser.). (ENG.). 24p. (J). (-k). bds. 6.99 *(978-0-7364-3408-9(9)*, RH/Disney) Random Hse. Children's Bks.

Post, Jim. Frog in the Kitchen Sink. Vasconcellos, Daniel, illus. 2015. (ENG.). 26p. (J). bds. 9.99 *(978-1-4494-6709-8(1))* Andrews McMeel Publishing.

Potter, Beatrix. The Classic Tale of Mr. Jeremy Fisher. Santore, Charles, illus. 2015. (ENG.). 22p. (J). bds. 8.95 *(978-1-60433-548-4(3)*, Applesauce Pr.) Cider Mill Pr. Bk. Pubs., LLC.

—The Classic Tale of the Flopsy Bunnies. Santore, Charles, illus. 2015. (ENG.). 22p. (J). bds. 8.95 *(978-1-60433-551-4(3)*, Applesauce Pr.) Cider Mill Pr. Bk. Pubs., LLC.

—Hello, Jemima! 2012. (Peter Rabbit Ser.). (ENG.). 10p. (J). (gr. -1-k). bds. 5.99 *(978-0-7232-6749-2(9)*, Warne) Penguin Young Readers Group.

—Hello, Peter! 2012. (Peter Rabbit Ser.). (ENG.). 10p. (J). (gr. -1-k). bds. 6.99 *(978-0-7232-6744-7(8)*, Warne) Penguin Young Readers Group.

—Munch! 2009. (Peter Rabbit Naturally Better Ser.). (ENG.). 10p. (J). (gr. -1 — 1). bds. 7.99 *(978-0-7232-6390-6(6)*, Warne) Penguin Young Readers Group.

—Peekaboo! 2009. (Peter Rabbit Naturally Better Ser.). (ENG.). 10p. (J). (gr. -1 — 1). bds. 6.99 *(978-0-7232-6350-0(7)*, Warne) Penguin Young Readers Group.

—Peter Rabbit. 2008. (Peter Rabbit Ser.). (ENG., Illus.). 12p. (J). (gr. -1 — 1). bds. 8.99 *(978-0-7232-5956-5(9)*, Warne) Penguin Young Readers Group.

—Peter Rabbit 1 2 3. 2013. (Peter Rabbit Ser.). (ENG., Illus.). 24p. (J). (gr. -1-k). bds. 6.99 *(978-0-7232-6867-3(3)*, Warne) Penguin Young Readers Group.

—Peter Rabbit Book & Toy. 2006. (Peter Rabbit Ser.). (ENG., Illus.). 70p. (J). (gr. -1 — 1). 16.99 *(978-0-7232-5356-3(0)*, Warne) Penguin Young Readers Group.

—Peter Rabbit Finger Puppet Book. 2011. (Peter Rabbit Ser.). (ENG., Illus.). 14p. (J). (gr. -1-k). bds. 12.99 *(978-0-7232-6639-6(5)*, Warne) Penguin Young Readers Group.

—The Peter Rabbit Gift Set: Including a Classic Board Book & Peter Rabbit Plush. Santore, Charles, illus. 2017. (ENG.). 8p. (J). bds. 16.95 *(978-1-60433-685-6(4)*, Applesauce Pr.) Cider Mill Pr. Bk. Pubs., LLC.

—Peter Rabbit Lift-the-Flap Words, Colors, & Numbers. 2007. (Potter Ser.). (ENG., Illus.). 12p. (J). (gr. -1-18). 14.99 *(978-0-7232-5828-5(7)*, Warne) Penguin Publishing Group.

—Tickle, Tickle, Peter! 2012. (Peter Rabbit Ser.). (ENG.). 10p. (J). (gr. -1-k). bds. 9.99 *(978-0-7232-6750-8(2)*, Warne) Penguin Young Readers Group.

—Where's Peter? 2011. (Peter Rabbit Ser.). (ENG.). 12p. (J). (gr. -1-k). bds. 10.99 *(978-0-7232-6636-5(0)*, Warne) Penguin Young Readers Group.

Pountney, Beth. My Books of Animal Fun Slipcase. 2007. (Illus.). 12p. (gr. -1-k). per. *(978-1-84610-563-0(3))* Make Believe Ideas.

Powell, Debbie. Make It Grow. 2016. (ENG., Illus.). 16p. (J). (gr. -1-2). 14.99 *(978-1-84780-789-2(5)*, Frances Lincoln Children's Bks.) Quarto Publishing Group UK GBR. Dist: Hachette Bk. Group.

Powell, Richard. Quiet as a Mouse: A Moving Picture Storybook. Hendra, Sue, illus. 2003. 16p. (J). 7.95 *(978-1-58925-678-1(6))* Tiger Tales.

—Whose Hat Is That? Martín Larrañaga, Ana, illus. 2004. (Ana's Mini Movers Ser.). 12p. (J). 5.95 *(978-1-58925-740-5(5))* Tiger Tales.

Powell, Richard & Davis, Caroline. A Book for Baby for Every Time of Day, 3 vols. 2003. (Illus.). (J). *(978-0-7641-5644-1(6))*; *(978-0-7641-2472-3(2))*; *(978-0-7641-2471-6(4))* Barron's Educational Series, Inc.

Powell-Tuck, Maudie. Pumpkin Party! Guile, Gill, illus. 2015. (ENG.). 22p. (J). (gr. -1-2). bds. 8.99 *(978-1-58925-206-6(3))* Tiger Tales.

—A Very Merry Christmas. Guile, Gill, illus. 2014. (ENG.). 22p. (J). (gr. -1-k). bds. 8.99 *(978-1-58925-560-9(7))* Tiger Tales.

Prasadam-halls, Smriti. Have You Seen Duck? Berg, Michelle, illus. 2012. (ENG.). 12p. (J). (gr. -1-k). 7.99 *(978-1-4083-1500-2(9))* Hodder & Stoughton GBR. Dist: Hachette Bk. Group.

Prasadam-Halls, Smriti. In the Garden. Scobie, Lorna, illus. 2017. (Pairs Ser.). (ENG.). 12p. (J). (gr. -1-k). bds. 9.99 *(978-1-84780-883-7(2)*, Frances Lincoln Children's Bks.) Quarto Publishing Group UK GBR. Dist: Hachette Bk. Group.

Prasadam-halls, Smriti. Noisy Farm. Scheffler, Axel, illus. 2014. (ENG.). 10p. (J). (gr. -1-k). 19.99 *(978-0-230-76680-8(3))* Pan Macmillan GBR. Dist: Independent Pubs. Group.

Prasadam, Smriti. Hello, Animals! Bolam, Emily, illus. 2010. (Black & White Sparklers Ser.). (ENG.). 10p. (J). (gr. -1). bds. 6.99 *(978-1-58925-861-7(4))* Tiger Tales.

—Hello, Bugs! Bolam, Emily, illus. 2010. (Black & White Sparklers Ser.). (ENG.). 10p. (J). (gr. -1). bds. 6.99 *(978-1-58925-862-4(2))* Tiger Tales.

Prasadam, Smriti & Mitchell, Melanie. Peepo Paw Printes. 2008. (ENG., Illus.). 14p. (J). bds. 13.95 *(978-0-7475-9535-9(6))* Bloomsbury Publishing Plc GBR. Dist: Independent Pubs. Group.

Pratt, Leonie. Sticker Dolly Dressing Ballerinas. Baggott, Stella & Leyhane, Vici, illus. 2007. (Usborne Activities Ser.). 24p. (J). (gr. -1-3). pap. 8.99 *(978-0-7945-1392-4(1)*, Usborne) EDC Publishing.

—Sticker Dolly Dressing Fairies. Baggott, Stella & Leyhane, Vici, illus. 2007. (Usborne Activities Ser.). 24p. (J). (gr. -1-3). pap. 8.99 *(978-0-7945-1391-7(3)*, Usborne) EDC Publishing.

Precious Moments, Precious. Precious Moments: Happy Harvest, 1 vol. 2016. (ENG., Illus.). 32p. (J). bds. 9.99 *(978-0-7180-3241-8(1))* Nelson, Thomas Inc.

Press, Pikachu. Super Pokemon Pop-Up! - White Kyurem. 2013. (ENG.). 5p. (J). (gr. 3-6). 9.99 *(978-1-60438-180-1(9))* Pokemon, USA, Inc.

Preston-Gannon, Frann. Deep Deep Sea. 2015. (ENG., Illus.). 14p. (J). (— 1). bds. 7.99 *(978-1-84365-268-7(4)*, Pavilion) Pavilion Bks. GBR. Dist: Independent Pubs. Group.

—Hot Dog, Cold Dog. 2014. (ENG., Illus.). 20p. (J). (gr. -1-2). bds. 12.95 *(978-1-57687-679-4(9)*, powerHouse Bks.) powerHouse Cultural Entertainment, Inc.

—What a Hoot! 2015. (ENG., Illus.). 20p. (J). (-k). bds. 12.95 *(978-1-57687-758-6(2)*, powerHouse Bks.) powerHouse Cultural Entertainment, Inc.

Price, Denise D. Freedom Trail Pop up Book of Boston. 2015. (ENG., Illus.). 17p. (J). 29.99 *(978-0-9907781-0-3(X))* White Dharma Ltd.

Price, Mathew. Cachorro. Goldman, Judy, tr. Kemp, Moira, illus. 2010. (SPA & ENG.). 10p. bds. 5.99 *(978-1-935021-64-3(8))* Price, Mathew Ltd.

—Gatito. Goldman, Judy, tr. Kemp, Moira, illus. 2010. (SPA & ENG.). 10p. bds. 5.99 *(978-1-935021-99-5(0))* Price, Mathew Ltd.

Price, Olivia. All Aboard Noah's Ark: A Touch & Feel Book. Mitchell, Melanie, illus. 2008. (ENG.). 12p. (J). (gr. -1). 12.95 *(978-1-58117-778-7(X)*, Intervisual/Piggy Toes) Bendon, Inc.

—Bible Stories: A Touch & Feel Book. Mitchell, Melanie, illus. 2008. (ENG.). 12p. (J). (gr. -1). 12.95 *(978-1-58117-802-9(6)*, Intervisual/Piggy Toes) Bendon, Inc.

Priddy Books Staff & Priddy, Roger. My Big Animal Book. 2011. (ENG.). 14p. (J). bds. *(978-0-312-51365-8(8)*, Priddy Bks.) St. Martin's Pr.

Priddy, Roger. Airport. rev. ed. 2016. (ENG., Illus.). 14p. (J). bds. 9.99 *(978-0-312-52170-7(7)*, 9780312521707, Priddy Bks.) St. Martin's Pr.

—Alphaprints: ABC. 2013. (Alphaprints Ser.). (ENG.). 28p. (J). (gr. -1 — 1). bds. 9.99 *(978-0-312-51646-8(0)*, 9780312516468, Priddy Bks.) St. Martin's Pr.

—Alphaprints Fun in the Sun! 2017. (Alphaprints Ser.). (ENG., Illus.). 10p. (J). bds. 7.99 *(978-0-312-52518-7(4)*, 9780312525187, Priddy Bks.) St. Martin's Pr.

—Alphaprints: Gobble Gobble. 2016. (Alphaprints Ser.). (ENG.). 10p. (J). bds. 7.99 *(978-0-312-52057-1(3)*, 9780312520571, Priddy Bks.) St. Martin's Pr.

—Alphaprints: Sweet Heart. 2015. (Alphaprints Ser.). (ENG., Illus.). 12p. (J). (gr. -1 — 1). bds. 7.99 *(978-0-312-51913-1(3)*, 9780312519131, Priddy Bks.) St. Martin's Pr.

—Animals. 2005. (ENG.). 12p. (J). bds. 0.97 *(978-0-312-49610-4(9)*, Priddy Bks.) St. Martin's Pr.

—At the Zoo. 2006. (Bright Baby Touch & Feel Ser.). (ENG., Illus.). 10p. (J). (gr. -1 — 1). bds. 4.95 *(978-0-312-49857-3(8)*, 9780312498573, Priddy Bks.) St. Martin's Pr.

—Baby Animals. 2006. (Bright Baby Touch & Feel Ser.). (ENG., Illus.). 10p. (J). (gr. -1 — 1). bds. 4.95 *(978-0-312-49858-0(6)*, 9780312498580, Priddy Bks.) St. Martin's Pr.

—Baby Basics Animals. 2013. (Baby Basics Ser.). (ENG., Illus.). 10p. (J). (gr. -1 — 1). bds. 4.99 *(978-0-312-51553-9(7)*, 9780312515539, Priddy Bks.) St. Martin's Pr.

—Baby Hugs Gift Set. 2013. (ENG.). (J). (— 1). 19.99 *(978-0-312-51642-0(8)*, 9780312516420, Priddy Bks.) St. Martin's Pr.

—Baby Shaker Teethers Animals. 2012. (ENG., Illus.). 22p. (J). (gr. -1 — 1). bds. 5.99 *(978-0-312-51465-5(4)*, 9780312514655, Priddy Bks.) St. Martin's Pr.

—Baby Touch & Feel Baby Bunny. 2009. (Baby Touch & Feel Ser.). (ENG.). 12p. (J). (gr. -1 — 1). bds. 8.95 *(978-0-312-50606-3(6)*, 9780312506063, Priddy Bks.) St. Martin's Pr.

—Baby's First 123. 2016. (Baby's First Ser.). (ENG., Illus.). 8p. (J). bds. 7.99 *(978-0-312-51951-3(6)*, 9780312519513, Priddy Bks.) St. Martin's Pr.

—Baby's First Animals. 2016. (Baby's First Ser.). (ENG., Illus.). 8p. (J). bds. 7.99 *(978-0-312-51952-0(4)*, 9780312519520, Priddy Bks.) St. Martin's Pr.

—Baby's First Colors. 2016. (Baby's First Ser.). (ENG., Illus.). 8p. (J). bds. 7.99 *(978-0-312-51949-0(4)*, 9780312519490, Priddy Bks.) St. Martin's Pr.

—Barnyard Fun! 2015. (Little Friends Ser.). (ENG., Illus.). 12p. (J). (gr. -1 — 1). bds. 8.99 *(978-0-312-51841-7(2)*, 9780312518417, Priddy Bks.) St. Martin's Pr.

—Best Friends: We Are a Family. 2015. (Best Friends Ser.). (ENG., Illus.). 20p. (J). (gr. -1-1). bds. 9.99 *(978-0-312-51923-0(0)*, 9780312519230, Priddy Bks.) St. Martin's Pr.

—Best Friends: We Are Best Friends. 2015. (Best Friends Ser.). (ENG.). 20p. (J). (gr. -1-1). bds. 9.99 *(978-0-312-51922-3(2)*, 9780312519223, Priddy Bks.) St. Martin's Pr.

—Bible Stories. 2011. (ENG., Illus.). 30p. (J). (gr. -1-1). bds. 12.95 *(978-0-312-51089-3(6)*, 9780312510893, Priddy Bks.) St. Martin's Pr.

—Big & Small. 2015. (Little Friends Ser.). (ENG., Illus.). 12p. (J). (gr. -1 — 1). bds. 8.99 *(978-0-312-51778-6(5)*, 9780312517786, Priddy Bks.) St. Martin's Pr.

—Bright Baby Touch & Feel Easter. 2012. (Bright Baby Touch & Feel Ser.). (ENG., Illus.). 12p. (J). (gr. -1 — 1). bds. 4.95 *(978-0-312-51375-7(5)*, 9780312513757, Priddy Bks.) St. Martin's Pr.

—Bright Baby Touch & Feel Hanukkah. 2011. (Bright Baby Touch & Feel Ser.). (ENG., Illus.). 12p. (J). (gr. -1 — 1). bds. 4.95 *(978-0-312-51338-2(0)*, 9780312513382, Priddy Bks.) St. Martin's Pr.

—Bright Baby Touch & Feel Hugs & Kisses. 2009. (Bright Baby Touch & Feel Ser.). (ENG.). 12p. (J). (gr. -1 — 1). bds. 4.95 *(978-0-312-50827-2(1)*, 9780312508272, Priddy Bks.) St. Martin's Pr.

—Bright Baby Touch & Feel Numbers. 2008. (Bright Baby Touch & Feel Ser.). (ENG.). 12p. (J). (gr. -1 — 1). bds. 4.95 *(978-0-312-50423-6(3)*, 9780312504236, Priddy Bks.) St. Martin's Pr.

—Bright Baby Touch & Feel Winter. 2011. (Bright Baby Touch & Feel Ser.). (ENG., Illus.). 12p. (J). (gr. -1 — 1). bds. 4.95 *(978-0-312-50976-7(6)*, 9780312509767, Priddy Bks.) St. Martin's Pr.

—Builders Tool Kit. 2009. (Let's Pretend Ser.). (ENG.). 10p. (J). (gr. -1 — 1). 14.95 *(978-0-312-50490-8(X)*, Priddy Bks.) St. Martin's Pr.

—Christmas. 2016. (Mini Tab Ser.). (ENG.). 16p. (J). bds. 5.99 *(978-0-312-52051-9(4)*, 9780312520519, Priddy Bks.) St. Martin's Pr.

—Colors. (Little Friends Ser.). (ENG.). (J). 2016. 12p. bds. 14.99 *(978-0-312-52005-2(0)*, 9780312520052) 2013. (Illus.). 10p. (gr. -1 — 1). bds. 7.99 *(978-0-312-51606-2(1)*, 9780312516062) 2013. (Illus.). 10p. (gr. -1 — 1). bds. 4.99 *(978-0-312-51514-0(6)*, 9780312515140) 2008. 14p. (gr. -1 — 1). bds. 4.95 *(978-0-312-50425-0(X)*, 9780312504250) St. Martin's Pr. (Priddy Bks.).

—Counting Colors. 2007. (ENG., Illus.). 20p. (J). (gr. -1-1). 8.95 *(978-0-312-50137-2(4)*, 9780312501372, Priddy Bks.) St. Martin's Pr.

—Cow - Animal Buddies. 2015. (Animal Buddies Ser.). (ENG.). 8p. (J). (gr. -1 — 1). bds. 5.99 *(978-0-312-51854-7(4)*, 9780312518547, Priddy Bks.) St. Martin's Pr.

—Dinosaurs. 2012. (ENG., Illus.). 10p. (J). (gr. -1-k). 9.99 *(978-0-312-51511-9(1)*, 9780312515119, Priddy Bks.) St. Martin's Pr.

—Doll's House. 2013. (Lift-The-Flap Tab Bks.). (ENG.). 16p. (J). (gr. -1 — 1). bds. 8.99 *(978-0-312-51657-4(6)*, 9780312516574, Priddy Bks.) St. Martin's Pr.

—Easter Surprise. 2011. (ENG., Illus.). (J). (gr. -1-k). bds. 9.99 *(978-0-312-51002-2(0)*, 9780312510022, Priddy Bks.) St. Martin's Pr.

—Farm. 2016. (Playtown Ser.). (ENG., Illus.). 12p. (J). bds. 9.99 *(978-0-312-51959-9(1)*, 9780312519599, Priddy Bks.) St. Martin's Pr.

—Farm: A Noisy Animal Book. 2017. (Baby's First Ser.). (ENG., Illus.). 8p. (J). bds. 8.99 *(978-0-312-52164-6(2)*, 9780312521646, Priddy Bks.) St. Martin's Pr.

—Farm Friends. 2013. (My Carry-Along Sound Bks.). (ENG.). 10p. (J). (gr. -1 — 1). bds. 9.99 *(978-0-312-51645-1(2)*, 9780312516451, Priddy Bks.) St. Martin's Pr.

—First 100 Animals. 2011. (First 100 Ser.). (ENG., Illus.). 26p. (J). (gr. -1 — 1). bds. 5.99 *(978-0-312-51079-4(9)*, 9780312510794, Priddy Bks.) St. Martin's Pr.

—First 100 Animals Lift-The-Flap. 2014. (First 100 Ser.). (ENG., Illus.). 14p. (J). (gr. -1 — 1). bds. 9.99 *(978-0-312-51752-6(1))*, 9780312517526, Priddy Bks.) St. Martin's Pr.
—First 100 Board Books First 100 Numbers. 2012. (First 100 Ser.). (ENG., Illus.). 14p. (J). (gr. -1 — 1). bds. 8.95 *(978-0-312-51376-4(3))*, 9780312513764, Priddy Bks.) St. Martin's Pr.
—First 100 Numbers. 2017. (First 100 Ser.). (ENG.). 24p. (J). bds. 5.99 *(978-0-312-52282-7(7))*, 9780312522827, Priddy Bks.) St. Martin's Pr.
—First 100 Trucks. 2011. (First 100 Ser.). (ENG., Illus.). 26p. (J). (gr. -1 — 1). bds. 5.99 *(978-0-312-51080-0(2))*, 9780312510800, Priddy Bks.) St. Martin's Pr.
—First 100 Trucks & Things That Go Lift-The-Flap. 2015. (First 100 Ser.). (ENG., Illus.). 14p. (J). (gr. -1 — 1). bds. 9.99 *(978-0-312-51782-3(3))*, 9780312517823, Priddy Bks.) St. Martin's Pr.
—First 100 Words. 2011. (First 100 Ser.). (ENG., Illus.). 26p. (J). (— 1). bds. 5.99 *(978-0-312-51078-7(0))*, 9780312510787, Priddy Bks.) St. Martin's Pr.
—First Words / Primeras Palabras. 2007. (Bright Baby Ser.). (ENG & SPA., Illus.). 12p. (J). (gr. -1 — 1). bds. 4.95 *(978-0-312-50300-0(8))*, 9780312503000, Priddy Bks.) St. Martin's Pr.
—Fluffy Chick & Friends. 2015. (Touch & Feel Cloth Bks.). (ENG.). 6p. (J). (gr. -1 — 1). 12.99 *(978-0-312-51892-9(7))*, 9780312518929, Priddy Bks.) St. Martin's Pr.
—Funny Faces: Easter Parade. 2015. (Funny Faces Ser.). (ENG.). 10p. (J). (gr. -1-1). bds. 8.99 *(978-0-312-51785-4(8))*, 9780312517854, Priddy Bks.) St. Martin's Pr.
—Funny Faces Halloween Jack. 2012. (Funny Faces Ser.). (ENG., Illus.). 10p. (J). (gr. -1-1). bds. 8.99 *(978-0-312-51554-6(5))*, 9780312515546, Priddy Bks.) St. Martin's Pr.
—Funny Faces Haunted House. 2012. (Funny Faces Ser.). (ENG., Illus.). 10p. (J). (gr. -1-1). bds. 8.99 *(978-0-312-51557-7(X))*, 9780312515577, Priddy Bks.) St. Martin's Pr.
—The Great Turkey Race. 2014. (Shaped Board Bks.). (ENG., Illus.). 6p. (J). (gr. -1-k). bds. 6.99 *(978-0-312-51719-9(X))*, 9780312517199, Priddy Bks.) St. Martin's Pr.
—Happy Birthday: A Touch-and-Feel Book. 2014. (Little Friends Ser.). (ENG.). 10p. (J). (gr. -1 — 1). bds. 6.99 *(978-0-312-51680-2(0))*, 9780312516802, Priddy Bks.) St. Martin's Pr.
—Hello Baby, Set. 2013. (Hello Baby Ser.). (ENG.). (J). (gr. -1 — 1). 19.99 *(978-0-312-51641-3(X))*, 9780312516413, Priddy Bks.) St. Martin's Pr.
—Hello Baby - A High Contrast Book. 2012. (Hello Baby Ser.). (ENG., Illus.). 6p. (J). (gr. -1 — 1). bds. 5.99 *(978-0-312-51505-8(7))*, 9780312515058, Priddy Bks.) St. Martin's Pr.
—Hello Kitty - My Home. 2014. (Lift-The-Flap Tab Bks.). (ENG.). 16p. (J). (gr. -1-1). bds. 8.99 *(978-0-312-51768-7(8))*, 9780312517687, Priddy Bks.) St. Martin's Pr.
—Hello Kitty: Wipe Clean Activity Fun. 2015. (Hello Kitty Ser.). (ENG.). 24p. (J). (gr. -1-1). bds. 8.99 *(978-0-312-51873-8(0))*, 9780312518738, Priddy Bks.) St. Martin's Pr.
—Hide & Seek Bunnies. 2015. (Lift-The-Flap Tab Bks.). (ENG., Illus.). 16p. (J). (gr. -1 — 1). bds. 8.99 *(978-0-312-51784-7(X))*, 9780312517847, Priddy Bks.) St. Martin's Pr.
—Ho! Ho! Ho! 2015. (Alphaprints Ser.). (ENG., Illus.). 10p. (J). (gr. -1 — 1). bds. 7.99 *(978-0-312-51896-7(X))*, 9780312518967, Priddy Bks.) St. Martin's Pr.
—Home Sweet Home. 2014. (Little Friends Ser.). (ENG.). 10p. (J). (gr. -1 — 1). bds. 6.99 *(978-0-312-51679-6(7))*, 9780312516796, Priddy Bks.) St. Martin's Pr.
—I Love You. 2015. (Mini Tab Ser.). (ENG.). 16p. (J). (gr. -1 — 1). bds. 5.99 *(978-0-312-51919-3(2))*, 9780312519193, Priddy Bks.) St. Martin's Pr.
—Learn to Write Your First Words - Cat. 2012. (Wipe Clean Ser.). (ENG., Illus.). 24p. (J). (gr. -1-1). bds. 8.95 *(978-0-312-51393-1(3))*, 9780312513931, Priddy Bks.) St. Martin's Pr.
—Let's Pretend: My Pirate Ship Sticker Activity Book. 2015. (Let's Pretend Ser.). (ENG.). 72p. (J). (gr. -1-1). pap. 5.99 *(978-0-312-51843-1(9))*, 9780312518431, Priddy Bks.) St. Martin's Pr.
—Lift the Flap - Fairy Tales. 2016. (Can You Find Me? Ser.). (ENG.). 16p. (J). bds. 9.99 *(978-0-312-52059-5(X))*, 9780312520595, Priddy Bks.) St. Martin's Pr.
—Lift-the-Flap Tab - Farm. 2014. (Lift-The-Flap Tab Bks.). (ENG.). 16p. (J). (gr. -1 — 1). bds. 8.99 *(978-0-312-51753-3(X))*, 9780312517533, Priddy Bks.) St. Martin's Pr.
—Lift-The-Flap Tab: on the Go. 2014. (Lift-The-Flap Tab Bks.). (ENG., Illus.). 16p. (J). (gr. -1 — 1). bds. 8.99 *(978-0-312-51731-1(9))*, 9780312517311, Priddy Bks.) St. Martin's Pr.
—Lift-The-Flap Tab: Santa's Workshop. 2015. (Lift-The-Flap Tab Bks.). (ENG., Illus.). 16p. (J). (gr. -1 — 1). bds. 8.99 *(978-0-312-51898-1(6))*, 9780312518981, Priddy Bks.) St. Martin's Pr.
—Lift-The-Tab: Easter. 2017. (ENG., Illus.). 18p. (J). bds. 8.99 *(978-0-312-52158-5(8))*, 9780312521585, Priddy Bks.) St. Martin's Pr.
—Little Alphaprints: Animals. 2015. (Alphaprints Ser.). (ENG., Illus.). 10p. (J). (gr. -1 — 1). bds. 5.99 *(978-0-312-51828-8(5))*, 9780312518288, Priddy Bks.) St. Martin's Pr.
—Little Alphaprints: Colors. 2015. (Alphaprints Ser.). (ENG., Illus.). 10p. (J). (gr. -1 — 1). bds. 5.99 *(978-0-312-51829-5(3))*, 9780312518295, Priddy Bks.) St. Martin's Pr.
—Little Friends: Big Adventure. 2015. (Little Friends Ser.). (ENG., Illus.). 12p. (J). (gr. -1 — 1). bds. 14.99 *(978-0-312-51869-1(2))*, 9780312518691, Priddy Bks.) St. Martin's Pr.
—Little Friends Gift Set. 2014. (Little Friends Ser.). (ENG.). (J). (gr. -1 — 1). 19.99 *(978-0-312-51777-9(7))*, 9780312517779, Priddy Bks.) St. Martin's Pr.
—Little Friends: Let's Play. 2014. (Little Friends Ser.). (ENG., Illus.). 8p. (J). (gr. -1 — 1). bds. 8.99 *(978-0-312-51683-3(5))*, 9780312516833, Priddy Bks.) St. Martin's Pr.
—Little Friends: Sleepy Time. 2014. (Little Friends Ser.). (ENG.). 6p. (J). (gr. -1 — 1). 9.99 *(978-0-312-51681-9(9))*, 9780312516819, Priddy Bks.) St. Martin's Pr.
—Little Penguin. 2014. (Baby Touch & Feel Ser.). (ENG.). 12p. (J). (gr. -1 — 1). bds. 8.99 *(978-0-312-51718-2(1))*, 9780312517182, Priddy Bks.) St. Martin's Pr.
—Love You Always. 2016. (Shiny Shapes Ser.). (ENG.). 10p. (J). bds. 7.99 *(978-0-312-52053-3(0))*, 9780312520533, Priddy Bks.) St. Martin's Pr.
—Match It! 2015. (Early Learning Fun Ser.). (ENG.). 56p. (J). (gr. k-3). spiral bd. 12.99 *(978-0-312-51802-8(1))*, 9780312518028, Priddy Bks.) St. Martin's Pr.
—Mealtime - A High Contrast High Chair Book. 2013. (Hello Baby Ser.). (ENG., Illus.). 8p. (J). (gr. -1 — 1). bds. 5.99 *(978-0-312-51602-4(9))*, 9780312516024, Priddy Bks.) St. Martin's Pr.
—Merry Christmas. 2009. (Bright Baby Touch & Feel Ser.). (ENG.). 12p. (J). (gr. -1 — 1). bds. 4.95 *(978-0-312-50652-0(X))*, 9780312506520, Priddy Bks.) St. Martin's Pr.
—Mini Tab: Easter. 2017. (Mini Tab Ser.). (ENG., Illus.). 16p. (J). bds. 5.99 *(978-0-312-52157-8(X))*, 9780312521578, Priddy Bks.) St. Martin's Pr.
—Mix & Match: Halloween. 2016. (Mix & Match Ser.). (ENG., Illus.). 14p. (J). bds. 5.99 *(978-0-312-52021-2(2))*, 9780312520212, Priddy Bks.) St. Martin's Pr.
—Mo Chéad Foclóir. Ó Murchadha, Niall, tr. 2013. (GLE & IRI.). 10p. (J). 19.00 *(978-0-7171-5807-2(1))* M.H. Gill & Co. U. C. IRL. Dist: Dufour Editions, Inc.
—My Big Animal Book. 2011. (My Big Board Bks.). (ENG., Illus.). 12p. (J). (gr. -1 — 1). bds. 7.99 *(978-0-312-51107-4(8))*, 9780312511074, Priddy Bks.) St. Martin's Pr.
—My Big Train Book. 2015. (My Big Board Bks.). (ENG.). 10p. (J). (gr. -1 — 1). bds. 7.99 *(978-0-312-51943-8(5))*, 9780312519438, Priddy Bks.) St. Martin's Pr.
—My Big Truck Book. 2011. (My Big Board Bks.). (ENG., Illus.). 12p. (J). (gr. -1 — 1). bds. 7.99 *(978-0-312-51106-7(X))*, 9780312511067, Priddy Bks.) St. Martin's Pr.
—My Carry-Along Sound Book: Perfect Pets. 2014. (My Carry-Along Sound Bks.). (ENG.). 10p. (J). (— 1). bds. 9.99 *(978-0-312-51720-5(3))*, 9780312517205, Priddy Bks.) St. Martin's Pr.
—My Fold Out Books I Love You. 2011. (ENG., Illus.). 12p. (J). (gr. -1 — 1). bds. 6.99 *(978-0-312-51334-4(8))*, 9780312513344, Priddy Bks.) St. Martin's Pr.
—My Little Numbers Book. 2012. (My Little Bks.). (ENG., Illus.). 24p. (J). (gr. -1-k). bds. 8.99 *(978-0-312-51463-1(8))*, 9780312514631, Priddy Bks.) St. Martin's Pr.
—My Press-Out Tea Set, Set. 2009. (Let's Pretend Ser.). (ENG.). 10p. (J). (gr. -1 — 1). 14.95 *(978-0-312-50491-5(8))*, Priddy Bks.) St. Martin's Pr.
—My Super Duper Sticker Activity Book. 2015. (ENG.). 308p. (J). (gr. -1-1). pap. 12.99 *(978-0-312-51820-2(X))*, 9780312518202, Priddy Bks.) St. Martin's Pr.
—My World. 2015. (Hello Kitty Ser.). (ENG.). 16p. (J). (gr. -1-1). bds. 12.99 *(978-0-312-51817-2(X))*, 9780312518172, Priddy Bks.) St. Martin's Pr.
—Noisy Peekaboo: Moo. 2016. (Noisy Peekaboo Ser.). (ENG.). 8p. (J). bds. 9.99 *(978-0-312-52062-5(X))*, 9780312520625, Priddy Bks.) St. Martin's Pr.
—Numbers Colors Shapes. 2011. (First 100 Ser.). (ENG., Illus.). 26p. (J). (gr. -1 — 1). bds. 5.99 *(978-0-312-51081-7(0))*, 9780312510817, Priddy Bks.) St. Martin's Pr.
—Numbers (Números) English-Spanish Bilingual. 2008. (Bright Baby Touch & Feel Ser.). (ENG & SPA., Illus.). 12p. (J). (gr. -1 — 1). bds. 4.95 *(978-0-312-50215-7(X))*, 9780312502157, Priddy Bks.) St. Martin's Pr.
—On the Farm. 2006. (Bright Baby Touch & Feel Ser.). (ENG., Illus.). 10p. (J). (gr. -1 — 1). bds. 4.95 *(978-0-312-49859-7(4))*, 9780312498597, Priddy Bks.) St. Martin's Pr.
—Perfect Pets. 2006. (Bright Baby Touch & Feel Ser.). (ENG., Illus.). 10p. (J). (gr. -1 — 1). bds. 4.95 *(978-0-312-49860-3(8))*, 9780312498603, Priddy Bks.) St. Martin's Pr.
—Picture Fit Board Books: a Parade of Animals (Large) A Counting Book. 2017. (Picture Fit Ser.). (ENG., Illus.). 14p. (J). bds. 12.99 *(978-0-312-52174-5(X))*, 9780312521745, Priddy Bks.) St. Martin's Pr.
—Picture Fit Board Books: a Stampede of Dinosaurs: An Opposites Book. 2017. (Picture Fit Ser.). (ENG., Illus.). 14p. (J). bds. 8.99 *(978-0-312-52298-8(3))*, 9780312522988, Priddy Bks.) St. Martin's Pr.
—Picture Fit Board Books: a Stampede of Dinosaurs (Large) An Opposites Book. 2017. (Picture Fit Ser.). (ENG., Illus.). 14p. (J). bds. 12.99 *(978-0-312-52524-8(9))*, 9780312525248, Priddy Bks.) St. Martin's Pr.
—Picture Fit Board Books: a Traffic Jam of Trucks: A Colors Book. 2017. (Picture Fit Ser.). (ENG., Illus.). 14p. (J). bds. 8.99 *(978-0-312-52160-8(X))*, 9780312521608, Priddy Bks.) St. Martin's Pr.
—Picture Fit Board Books: a Traffic Jam of Trucks (Large) A Colors Book. 2017. (Picture Fit Ser.). (ENG., Illus.). 14p. (J). bds. 12.99 *(978-0-312-52172-1(3))*, 9780312521721, Priddy Bks.) St. Martin's Pr.
—Picture Play: Mealtime. 2016. (Picture Play Ser.). (ENG., Illus.). 10p. (J). bds. 5.99 *(978-0-312-51961-2(3))*, 9780312519612, Priddy Bks.) St. Martin's Pr.
—Picture Play: Playtime. 2016. (Picture Play Ser.). (ENG., Illus.). 10p. (J). bds. 5.99 *(978-0-312-51960-5(5))*, 9780312519605, Priddy Bks.) St. Martin's Pr.
—Play & Learn: Colors. 2014. (Play & Learn Ser.). (ENG.). 10p. (J). (gr. -1-k). bds. 12.99 *(978-0-312-51751-9(3))*, 9780312517519, Priddy Bks.) St. Martin's Pr.
—Playtime. 2013. (Hello Baby Ser.). (ENG., Illus.). 12p. (J). (gr. -1 — 1). bds. 14.99 *(978-0-312-51603-1(7))*, 9780312516031, Priddy Bks.) St. Martin's Pr.
—Playtown. 2014. (Playtown Ser.). (ENG.). 16p. (J). (gr. -1-k). bds. 12.99 *(978-0-312-51737-3(8))*, 9780312517373, Priddy Bks.) St. Martin's Pr.
—Playtown Chunky Pack: Construction. 2017. (Playtown Ser.). (ENG., Illus.). 10p. (J). bds. 7.99 *(978-0-312-52196-7(0))*, 9780312521967, Priddy Bks.) St. Martin's Pr.
—Playtown: Emergency. 2016. (ENG.). 14p. (J). bds. 9.99 *(978-0-312-52009-0(3))*, 9780312520090, Priddy Bks.) St. Martin's Pr.
—Playtown Emergency, Pack. 2016. (Chunky 3 Pack Ser.). (ENG.). 10p. (J). bds. 7.99 *(978-0-312-52076-2(X))*, 9780312520762, Priddy Bks.) St. Martin's Pr.
—Pop-Up Surprise Haunted House. 2012. (ENG., Illus.). 10p. (J). (gr. -1-1). 7.99 *(978-0-312-51471-6(9))*, 9780312514716, Priddy Bks.) St. Martin's Pr.
—Pull the Tab: Colors. 2016. (Pull the Tab Ser.). (ENG.). 10p. (J). bds. 8.99 *(978-0-312-52069-4(7))*, 9780312520694, Priddy Bks.) St. Martin's Pr.
—Pull the Tab: Trucks. 2016. (Pull the Tab Ser.). (ENG.). 10p. (J). bds. 8.99 *(978-0-312-52068-7(9))*, 9780312520687, Priddy Bks.) St. Martin's Pr.
—Puppy. 2015. (Animal Buddies Ser.). (ENG., Illus.). 8p. (J). (gr. -1 — 1). bds. 5.99 *(978-0-312-51867-7(6))*, 9780312518677, Priddy Bks.) St. Martin's Pr.
—Rudolph the Red-Nosed Reindeer Lift-the-Flap Tab. 2014. (Lift-The-Flap Tab Bks.). (ENG., Illus.). 16p. (J). (gr. -1 — 1). bds. 8.99 *(978-0-312-51749-6(1))*, 9780312517496, Priddy Bks.) St. Martin's Pr.
—Santa Claus. 2012. (Funny Faces Ser.). (ENG., Illus.). 10p. (J). (gr. -1-1). bds. 8.99 *(978-0-312-51558-4(8))*, 9780312515584, Priddy Bks.) St. Martin's Pr.
—Santa Express. 2013. (Shaped Board Bks.). (ENG., Illus.). 6p. (J). (gr. -1-k). bds. 6.99 *(978-0-312-51619-2(3))*, 9780312516192, Priddy Bks.) St. Martin's Pr.
—Seaside. 2014. (Toddler Town Ser.). (ENG.). 10p. (J). (gr. -1 — 1). bds. 7.99 *(978-0-312-51670-3(3))*, 9780312516703, Priddy Bks.) St. Martin's Pr.
—Shiny Shapes: Easter Surprise. 2017. (Shiny Shapes Ser.). (ENG., Illus.). 10p. (J). bds. 7.99 *(978-0-312-52159-2(6))*, 9780312521592, Priddy Bks.) St. Martin's Pr.
—Simple First Words Let's Talk. 2011. (Simple First Words Ser.). (ENG.). 12p. (J). (gr. -1 — 1). bds. 14.95 *(978-0-312-51421-1(2))*, 9780312514211, Priddy Bks.) St. Martin's Pr.
—Slide & Find Christmas. 2010. (Slide & Find Ser.). (ENG., Illus.). 10p. (J). (gr. -1 — 1). bds. 7.95 *(978-0-312-50969-9(3))*, 9780312509699, Priddy Bks.) St. Martin's Pr.
—Slide & Find Easter. 2011. (Slide & Find Ser.). (ENG., Illus.). 8p. (J). (gr. -1 — 1). bds. 8.99 *(978-0-312-51001-5(2))*, 9780312510015, Priddy Bks.) St. Martin's Pr.
—Slide & Find Spooky. 2011. (ENG., Illus.). 8p. (J). (— 1). bds. 8.99 *(978-0-312-51095-4(0))*, 9780312510954, Priddy Bks.) St. Martin's Pr.
—Slide & Surprise Alphabet. 2010. (ENG., Illus.). 16p. (J). (gr. -1-k). bds. 6.99 *(978-0-312-50948-4(0))*, 9780312509484, Priddy Bks.) St. Martin's Pr.
—Spring: Bright Baby Touch & Feel. 2011. (Bright Baby Touch & Feel Ser.). (ENG., Illus.). 12p. (J). (gr. -1 — 1). bds. 4.95 *(978-0-312-51006-0(3))*, 9780312510060, Priddy Bks.) St. Martin's Pr.
—Squishy Turtle Cloth Book. 2015. (Touch & Feel Cloth Bks.). (ENG.). 6p. (J). (gr. -1 — 1). 12.99 *(978-0-312-51890-5(0))*, 9780312518905, Priddy Bks.) St. Martin's Pr.
—Ten Barnyard Babies. 2009. (ENG.). 10p. (J). (gr. -1-k). bds. 15.99 *(978-0-312-50584-4(1))*, 9780312505844, Priddy Bks.) St. Martin's Pr.
—Tiger - Animal Buddies. 2015. (Animal Buddies Ser.). (ENG., Illus.). 8p. (J). (gr. -1 — 1). bds. 5.99 *(978-0-312-51865-3(X))*, 9780312518653, Priddy Bks.) St. Martin's Pr.
—Toddler Town - City. 2014. (Toddler Town Ser.). (ENG.). 10p. (J). (gr. -1 — 1). bds. 7.99 *(978-0-312-51673-4(8))*, 9780312516734, Priddy Bks.) St. Martin's Pr.
—Toddler Town - Zoo. 2014. (Toddler Town Ser.). (ENG.). 10p. (J). (gr. -1 — 1). bds. 7.99 *(978-0-312-51672-7(X))*, 9780312516727, Priddy Bks.) St. Martin's Pr.
—Toddler Town: Farm. 2014. (Toddler Town Ser.). (ENG.). 10p. (J). (gr. -1 — 1). bds. 7.99 *(978-0-312-51671-0(1))*, 9780312516710, Priddy Bks.) St. Martin's Pr.
—Trucks. 2007. (Bright Baby Ser.). (ENG & SPA., Illus.). 12p. (J). (gr. -1 — 1). bds. 4.95 *(978-0-312-50299-7(0))*, 9780312502997, Priddy Bks.) St. Martin's Pr.
—Tweet! Tweet! 2015. (Alphaprints Ser.). (ENG.). 10p. (J). (gr. -1 — 1). bds. 7.99 *(978-0-312-51781-6(5))*, 9780312517816, Priddy Bks.) St. Martin's Pr.
—We Are a Family. 2015. (ENG.). 20p. (J). bds. 7.99 *(978-0-312-52033-5(6))*, 9780312520335, Priddy Bks.) St. Martin's Pr.
—Wipe Clean: Starting School. 2015. (Wipe Clean Ser.). (ENG.). 24p. (J). (gr. -1-1). bds. 8.99 *(978-0-312-51790-8(4))*, 9780312517908, Priddy Bks.) St. Martin's Pr.
—Words. 2008. (Bright Baby Touch & Feel Ser.). (ENG.). 12p. (J). (gr. -1 — 1). bds. 4.95 *(978-0-312-50424-3(1))*, 9780312504243); (Illus.). bds. 4.95 *(978-0-312-50216-4(8))*, 9780312502164) St. Martin's Pr. (Priddy Bks.).
—Words: A High Contrast Board Book. 2013. (Hello Baby Ser.). (ENG., Illus.). 16p. (J). (gr. -1 — 1). bds. 4.99 *(978-0-312-51598-0(7))*, 9780312515980, Priddy Bks.) St. Martin's Pr.
—Words Palabras. 2009. (Slide & Find Ser.). (ENG.). 10p. (J). (gr. -1 — 1). bds. 4.95 *(978-0-312-50729-9(1))*, 9780312507299, Priddy Bks.) St. Martin's Pr.
—Zoo: A Noisy Animal Book. 2017. (Baby's First Ser.). (ENG., Illus.). 8p. (J). bds. 8.99 *(978-0-312-52165-3(0))*, 9780312521653, Priddy Bks.) St. Martin's Pr.
Priddy, Roger & Crimi-Trent, Ellen. My School Day. 2013. (Schoolies Ser.). (ENG., Illus.). 32p. (J). (gr. -1-1). 14.99 *(978-0-312-51607-9(X))*, 9780312516079, Priddy Bks.) St. Martin's Pr.
—School House. 2013. (Schoolies Ser.). (ENG., Illus.). 14p. (J). (gr. -1-1). 14.99 *(978-0-312-51613-0(4))*, 9780312516130, Priddy Bks.) St. Martin's Pr.
Prince, April Jones. Dig In! Berg, Michelle, illus. 2013. (ENG.). 14p. (J). (gr. -1 — 1). bds. 7.95 *(978-1-4197-0522-9(9))* Abrams, Inc.
—Dive In! Berg, Michelle, illus. 2013. (ENG.). 14p. (J). (gr. -1 — 1). bds. 7.95 *(978-1-4197-0523-6(7))* Abrams, Inc.
Princess Activities & Stickers. 160p. pap. *(978-1-4054-8476-3(4))* Parragon, Inc.
Princess Teatime, 5 vols. 2005. (Illus.). (J). *(978-0-7868-3667-3(9))*; *(978-0-7868-3668-0(7))*; *(978-0-7868-3663-5(6))*; *(978-0-7868-3665-9(2))*; *(978-0-7868-3664-2(4))* Disney Pr.
Pristash, Nicole. Purple. 2010. (My Colorful World Ser.). (ENG., Illus.). 16p. (J). bds. 11.95 *(978-1-4358-9318-4(2))*, PowerKids Pr.) Rosen Publishing Group, Inc., The.
Pritchett, Susan & Wetterwald, Florence. Sardine Goes Fishing (a Blabla Book) 2017. (ENG., Illus.). 24p. (J). (— 1). bds. 7.99 ***(978-0-553-52052-1(0))***, Random Hse. Bks. for Young Readers) Random Hse. Children's Bks.
Proudfoot, Peter R., et al, illus. Creepy Critters: A Pop-Up Book of Creatures That Jump, Crawl, & Fly. 2012. (ENG.). 14p. (J). (gr. k-3). 15.95 *(978-0-8109-8942-9(5))*, Abrams Bks. for Young Readers) Abrams, Inc.
Pruett, Jason. Seek & Find: Book of Mormon Stories (Board Book) 2017. (ENG., Illus.). (gr. -1). bds. 12.99 ***(978-1-4621-2099-4(7))*** Cedar Fort, Inc./CFI Distribution.
Prunier, James. Dinosaurs. Galeron, Henri, illus. 2012. (My First Discoveries Ser.: 3). (ENG.). 36p. (J). (gr. -1-k). 12.99 *(978-1-85103-379-9(3))* Moonlight Publishing, Ltd. GBR. Dist: Independent Pubs. Group.
Publications International Ltd. Staff. Baby's Day. 2010. 8p. (J). bds. 9.98 *(978-1-60553-401-5(3))*, PIL Kids) Publications International, Ltd.
—BK & Plush Mickey Mouse Club House. 2010. (J). 12.98 *(978-1-4127-8864-9(1))* Phoenix International Publications, Inc.
—Chuggington Little Lift & Listen. 2011. 12p. (J). bds. 10.98 *(978-1-4508-0504-9(3))* Phoenix International Publications, Inc.
—Disney Adventure Look & Find. 2013. (gr. 1-3). 7.98 *(978-1-4127-7146-7(3)*, 1412771463) Phoenix International Publications, Inc.
—Disney Princess PNO BK. 2010. 10p. (J). 16.98 *(978-1-4127-8997-4(4))* Phoenix International Publications, Inc.
—Disney Princess Songs. 2013. 12p. (J). (gr. k-4). bds. 21.99 *(978-1-4127-8016-2(0)*, fdc578c6-8169-40c1-acde-e3e9449607c7) Phoenix International Publications, Inc.
—Dora PNO BK Follow Music. 2008. 10p. (J). 16.98 *(978-1-4127-8996-7(6))*, PIL Kids) Publications International, Ltd.
—Dora the Explorer My First Look & Find. 2006. 18p. (J). 9.98 *(978-1-4127-3909-2(8))* Phoenix International Publications, Inc.
—Elmo PNO BK. 2008. 10p. (J). 16.98 *(978-1-4127-8995-0(8))* Phoenix International Publications, Inc.
—First Look & Find Wonder Pets. 2008. 16p. (J). bds. 9.98 *(978-1-4127-9394-0(7))*, PIL Kids) Publications International, Ltd.
—For the Love of Hockey BK Brick. 2008. 320p. 12.98 *(978-1-4127-1535-5(0))*, PIL Kids) Publications International, Ltd.
—Giant Look & Find Disney Pixar Cars. 2008. 24p. (J). 15.98 *(978-1-4127-8967-7(2))*, PIL Kids) Publications International, Ltd.
—Giant Look & Find Elmo. 2008. 24p. (J). 15.98 *(978-1-4127-8975-2(3))*, PIL Kids) Publications International, Ltd.
—Interactive Sound Surfs Up. 2007. 24p. (J). 16.98 *(978-1-4127-6829-0(2))*, PIL Kids) Publications International, Ltd.
—Interactive Sound Transformers. 2007. 24p. (J). 16.98 *(978-1-4127-6797-2(0))*, PIL Kids) Publications International, Ltd.
—Little English Spanish Sound Diego. 2007. 12p. (J). 10.98 *(978-1-4127-6738-5(5))* Publications International, Ltd.
—Little Lift & Listen Sound Dora Go to School. 2007. 12p. (J). 10.98 *(978-1-4127-8575-4(8))*, PIL Kids) Publications International, Ltd.
—Little Sound Barbie Fairytopia. 2007. 12p. (J). 10.98 *(978-1-4127-6770-5(9))*, PIL Kids) Publications International, Ltd.
—Little Sound Mickey Mouse Club. 2007. 10p. (J). 10.98 *(978-1-4127-6711-8(3))* Phoenix International Publications, Inc.
—Look & Find Ratatouille. 2007. 24p. (J). 7.10 *(978-1-4127-6837-5(3))*, PIL Kids) Publications International, Ltd.
—Look & Find Transformers. 2007. 24p. (J). 7.10 *(978-1-4127-6817-7(9))*, PIL Kids) Publications International, Ltd.
—Mickey Mouse Club First Look & Find. 2008. 18p. (J). bds. 9.98 *(978-1-4127-7455-0(1))* Phoenix International Publications, Inc.
—Mickey Mouse Club House Little Pop up Sd. 2008. 8p. (J). 10.50 *(978-1-4127-8869-4(2))* Phoenix International Publications, Inc.
—My 1St Libraries Baby Enstein. 2011. 12p. 12.98 *(978-1-4508-1572-7(3))* Phoenix International Publications, Inc.
—My 1St Libraries Disney Baby Animals. 2011. 12p. 12.98 *(978-1-4508-1571-0(5))* Phoenix International Publications, Inc.
—My 1St Libraries Disney Princess. 2011. 12p. 12.98 *(978-1-4508-1303-7(8))* Publications International, Ltd.
—My 1St Libraries Winnie the Pooh. 2011. 10p. (J). bds. 13.98 *(978-1-4508-0870-5(0))* Phoenix International Publications, Inc.
—My Little Pony Magic Friendship Songs. 2013. 10p. (J). (gr. k-4). bds. 10.99 *(978-1-4508-6352-0(3)*, e11c6844-0b70-40b4-a490-b56ef2e7ed9f) Phoenix International Publications, Inc.
—Nemo First Look & Find. 2007. 18p. (J). 9.98 *(978-1-4127-6838-2(1))* Phoenix International Publications, Inc.
—Open Season Little Sound Bk. 2006. 12p. (J). 10.50 *(978-1-4127-6378-3(9))*, PIL Kids) Publications International, Ltd.
—Sound Pooh Clues. 2007. 14p. (J). 16.98 *(978-1-4127-6201-4(4))* Publications International, Ltd.
—Steering Wheel Sound Cars. 2007. 12p. (J). 17.98 *(978-1-4127-5884-0(X))* Phoenix International Publications, Inc.
—Steering Wheel Sound Elmo Away We Go. 2008. 12p. (J). bds. 17.98 *(978-1-4127-8948-6(6))*, PIL Kids) Publications International, Ltd.

—Teenage Mutant Ninja Turtles - Ninja Heroes: Flashlight Adventure Sound Book. 2013. 14p. (J). (gr. 1-3). bds. 17.98 *(978-1-4127-5339-5(2),* 0c51eeb7-c20f-4b72-a87f-c492bcc6f86f) Phoenix International Publications, Inc.

—Thomas & Friends: First Look & Find. 2010. 18p. 7.98 *(978-1-4508-1139-2(6))* Phoenix International Publications, Inc.

—Wall E Large Sound BK. 2008. 24p. (J). 17.98 *(978-1-4127-8991-2(5),* PIL Kids) Publications International, Ltd.

Publications International Ltd. Staff, creator. Disney Pixar Cars Tour the Town. 2007. (Steering Wheel Sound Ser.). (Illus.). (gr. -1-k). 16.98 *(978-1-4127-8804-5(8))* Publications International, Ltd.

—Disney Princess: Musical Pop-up Treasury. 2007. (Disney Princess Ser.). (Illus.). (J). (gr. -1-3). 15.98 *(978-1-4127-7431-4(4))* Publications International, Ltd.

—Dora the Explorer Laugh-along Sing-along. 2007. (Play-A-Song Ser.). (Illus.). bds. 15.98 *(978-1-4127-7417-8(9))* Publications International, Ltd.

—Dora the Explorer Learn to Write. 2007. (Play-A-Sound Bks.). (Illus.). (J). (gr. -1-3). 19.98 *(978-1-4127-6659-3(1))* Publications International, Ltd.

—Get Ready for Fun! 2007. (Sesame Street Music Works). (Illus.). 6p. (J). bds. 9.98 *(978-1-4127-8746-8(7))* Publications International, Ltd.

—Hello Elmo! 2007. (Sesame Street Ser.). (Illus.). 10p. (J). (gr. -1-3). bds. 19.98 *(978-1-4127-8724-6(6))* Publications International, Ltd.

—Help along Sing a Song. 2007. (Play-A-Song Ser.). (Illus.). bds. 15.98 *(978-1-4127-7419-2(5))* Publications International, Ltd.

—Magic Songs. 2007. (Play-A-Song Ser.). (Illus.). (gr. -1-k). bds. 15.98 *(978-1-4127-8813-7(7))* Publications International, Ltd.

—Pooh Surprise Sing-along. 2007. (Surprise Mirror Book Ser.). (Illus.). (gr. -1-k). 15.98 *(978-1-4127-7418-5(7))* Publications International, Ltd.

Publications International Ltd. Staff, ed. Baby Animals (Listen & Learn Sound Book) 2011. 19p. (J). bds. 11.98 *(978-1-4508-1440-9(9))* Phoenix International Publications, Inc.

—Baby Einstein. 2007. (J). 5.98 *(978-1-4127-8481-8(6))*; 18p. bds. *(978-1-4127-8436-8(0),* 1412784360) Phoenix International Publications, Inc.

—Baby Einstein. 2007. (J). 10.98 *(978-1-4127-7467-3(5))* Publications International, Ltd.

—Baby Faces. 2011. 10p. (J). bds. 12.98 *(978-1-4508-1404-1(2))* Phoenix International Publications, Inc.

—A Baby Is Born. 2011. 22p. (J). bds. 6.98 *(978-1-4508-1865-0(X))* Phoenix International Publications, Inc.

—Baby's 123. 2010. 18p. (J). bds. 7.98 *(978-1-60553-960-7(0))* Publications International, Ltd.

—Baby's ABC. 2010. 18p. (J). bds. 7.98 *(978-1-60553-961-4(9))* Publications International, Ltd.

—Baby's Shapes. 2010. 18p. (J). bds. 7.98 *(978-1-60553-963-8(5))*; (Illus.). bds. 7.98 *(978-1-60553-965-2(1))* Phoenix International Publications, Inc.

—Barney: I Love You Songs. 2011. 14p. (J). bds. 22.98 *(978-1-4508-1249-8(X))* Publications International, Ltd.

—Barney: Let's Play Together. 2011. 10p. (J). bds. 8.98 *(978-1-4508-0859-0(X))* Publications International, Ltd.

—Barney: Music All Around. 2008. (J). bds. 10.98 *(978-1-4127-9990-4(2))* Publications International, Ltd.

—Barney & Friends Book Box & Plush. 2011. 8p. (J). 14.98 *(978-1-4508-0854-5(9))* Publications International, Ltd.

—The Big Fix-It Day. 2010. 14p. (J). 19.98 *(978-1-60553-110-6(3),* PIL Kids) Publications International, Ltd.

—Book Block(tm) Thomas & Friends (tm) 12 Board Books. 2015. 10p. (J). 12.98 *(978-1-4508-9373-2(2),* 1450893732) Publications International, Ltd.

—Busy Little Monster. 2010. 14p. (J). bds. 10.98 *(978-1-60553-125-0(1),* PIL Kids) Publications International, Ltd.

—Cars: Fun with Friends. 2010. (J). bds. 5.98 *(978-1-60553-038-3(7))* Phoenix International Publications, Inc.

—Cars (Musical Treasury) 2011. 40p. (J). bds. 15.98 *(978-1-4508-1085-2(3))* Publications International, Ltd.

—Cars My First Look & Find. 2014. 16p. (J). bds. *(978-1-4508-8210-1(2),* 1450882102) Phoenix International Publications, Inc.

—Chuggington Little Music Note Sound: Traintastic Tunes. 2011. 12p. (J). (gr. k-3). bds. 10.99 *(978-1-4508-1141-5(8),* dd98fbb4-eb4f-47f8-80b4-3d7a907afc5f) Phoenix International Publications, Inc.

—Come along, Sing a Song! 2010. 12p. (J). bds. 12.98 *(978-1-60553-438-1(2),* PIL Kids) Publications International, Ltd.

—Custom Cool. 2008. (Illus.). 8p. (J). bds. 11.98 *(978-1-4127-7503-8(5))* Phoenix International Publications, Inc.

—Dance Mat Sound Book Dora Lets Dance. 2007. (J). 17.98 *(978-1-4127-8305-7(4))* Publications International, Ltd.

—A Day with Hello Kitty: Play-A-Sound. 2013. 10p. (J). bds. 7.98 *(978-1-4508-6154-0(7),* 1450861547) Phoenix International Publications, Inc.

—Diego What a Team. 2007. (J). 10.98 *(978-1-4127-6744-6(X))* Publications International, Ltd.

—Dinosaur Train All Aboard! 2011. 10p. (J). bds. 10.98 *(978-1-4508-1140-8(X))* Publications International, Ltd.

—Discover the Day. 2010. 12p. (J). bds. 9.98 *(978-1-4127-6747-7(4))* Phoenix International Publications, Inc.

—Disney Classics Shaped Books. 2011. 8p. (J). bds. 4.98 *(978-1-4508-0909-2(X))* Publications International, Ltd.

—Disney(r) Doc Mcstuffins I Can Brush My Teeth! Lift-A-Flap Sound Book. 2015. 12p. (J). bds. *(978-1-4508-8991-9(3),* 1450889913) Publications International, Ltd.

—Disney Fairies: Bienvenuda Tinker Bell! 2011. 12p. (J). bds. 10.98 *(978-1-4508-1402-7(6))* Publications International, Ltd.

—Disney Fairies: Wellcome Tinker Bell: (Lenticular Play-a-Sound Book) 2010. 14p. (J). bds. 17.98 *(978-1-60553-606-4(7))* Phoenix International Publications, Inc.

—Disney(r) Frozen Sing-Along Songs! Features Do You Want to Build a Snowman? 2014. 12p. (J). bds. *(978-1-4508-9139-4(X),* 145089139X) Publications International, Ltd.

—Disney Jr. Minnie's Big Day. 2012. (Illus.). 8p. (J). bds. 7.98 *(978-1-4508-6139-7(3),* 80290db9-6224-4b01-bd50-c2f0c4be4093) Phoenix International Publications, Inc.

—Disney Little First Look & Find Pack. 2010. 18p. (J). 14.98 *(978-1-4508-0334-2(2))* Phoenix International Publications, Inc.

—Disney Pixar: School Memory Keeper. 2011. 48p. (J). spiral bd. 16.98 *(978-1-4508-1137-8(X))* Phoenix International Publications, Inc.

—Disney Pixar ABC Board Books. 2010. 10p. (J). 23.98 *(978-1-4508-0370-0(9))* Phoenix International Publications, Inc.

—Disney Pixar (book Block) 2010. (J). 10.98 *(978-1-4508-0674-9(0))* Publications International, Ltd.

—Disney Pixar Cars: Cuentos de Miedo (Little English Spanish Sound Book) 2011. 12p. (J). bds. 10.98 *(978-1-4508-1401-0(8))* Phoenix International Publications, Inc.

—Disney Pixar Cars: First Look & Find & Shaped Puzzle Box Set. 2010. (J). 22.98 *(978-1-4508-0136-2(6))* Publications International, Ltd.

—Disney Pixar Cars: Road Trip Adventure. 2010. (J). 10.98 *(978-1-4508-0387-8(3))* Phoenix International Publications, Inc.

—Disney Pixar Cars: (Stereo Play-a-Sound) 2010. 24p. (J). 19.98 *(978-1-60553-857-0(4))* Publications International, Ltd.

—Disney Pixar Cars: Story Reader 2. 0 3 Storybook Library. 2011. (J). 19.98 *(978-1-4508-0606-0(6))* Publications International, Ltd.

—Disney Pixar Cars 2 - World Tour. 2011. 14p. (J). 17.98 *(978-1-4508-1473-7(5))* Phoenix International Publications, Inc.

—Disney Pixar Cars 2 (Look & Find Soft Cover) 2011. 20p. (J). pap. 5.98 *(978-1-4508-1457-7(3))* Publications International, Ltd.

—Disney Pixar Cars (book Block) 2010. (J). 10.98 *(978-1-4508-0671-8(6))* Phoenix International Publications, Inc.

—Disney Pixar Cars; Cruising' Cool. 2011. 12p. (J). bds. 10.98 *(978-1-4508-0915-3(4))* Publications International, Ltd.

—Disney Pixar Cars My First Look & Find & Shaped Puzzle. 2010. (J). 22.98 *(978-1-4508-0801-9(8))* Phoenix International Publications, Inc.

—Disney Pixar Cars Ride-along Songs. 2010. 14p. (J). bds. 19.98 *(978-1-4127-5368-5(6))* Phoenix International Publications, Inc.

—Disney Pixar Cars Story Reader 2. 0 Unit. 2011. (J). 30.98 *(978-1-4508-0588-9(4))* Publications International, Ltd.

—Disney Pixar Little First Look & Find 4 pack in carry Case. 2010. 18p. (J). 14.98 *(978-1-4508-0333-5(4))* Phoenix International Publications, Inc.

—Disney Pixar School Memories. 2011. 24p. (J). spiral bd. 10.98 *(978-1-4508-1136-1(1))* Publications International, Ltd.

—Disney Pixar Shaped Books. 2011. (J). bds. 4.98 *(978-1-4508-0826-2(3))* Publications International, Ltd.

—Disney Princess. 2008. (J). 3.98 *(978-1-4127-9248-6(7))* Phoenix International Publications, Inc.

—Disney Princess: 26 Stories of Virtue. 2010. 12p. (J). 25.98 *(978-1-60553-692-7(X))* Phoenix International Publications, Inc.

—Disney Princess: Canciones the Princesas. 2011. 24p. (J). 17.98 *(978-1-4508-1615-1(0))* Publications International, Ltd.

—Disney Princess: Dreams Come True (Talking Look & Find) 2010. 16p. (J). bds. 12.98 *(978-1-60553-538-8(9))* Publications International, Ltd.

—Disney Princess: Enchanted Dreams. 2010. 40p. (J). bds. 14.98 *(978-1-60553-685-9(7))* Publications International, Ltd.

—Disney Princess: Enchanted Stables (Look & Find) 2010. 24p. (J). 7.98 *(978-1-60553-633-0(4))* Phoenix International Publications, Inc.

—Disney Princess: Follow Your Dreams. 2010. 24p. (J). 19.98 *(978-1-4127-5357-9(0),* PIL Kids) Publications International, Ltd.

—Disney Princess: Magical Princess Songs. 2011. 14p. (J). bds. 17.98 *(978-1-4508-1132-3(9))* Publications International, Ltd.

—Disney Princess: Princess Jewels (Little First Look & Find) 2010. 18p. (J). bds. *(978-1-4508-0279-6(6),* 1450802796) Phoenix International Publications, Inc.

—Disney Princess: Royal Recital. 2011. 14p. (J). bds. 17.98 *(978-1-4508-1006-7(3))* Phoenix International Publications, Inc.

—Disney Princess: Stories of Virtue. 2010. 10p. (J). bds. 12.98 *(978-1-4508-0164-5(1))* Phoenix International Publications, Inc.

—Disney Princess (book Block) 2010. (J). 10.98 *(978-1-4508-0672-5(4))* Phoenix International Publications, Inc.

—Disney Princess First Look & Find & Giant Puzzle. 2010. (J). 22.98 *(978-1-4508-0135-5(8))* Publications International, Ltd.

—Disney Princess Jewels First Look & Find & Shaped Puzzle. 2010. 18p. (J). 22.98 *(978-1-4508-0802-6(6))* Phoenix International Publications, Inc.

—Disney Princess (Musical Treasury) 2011. 40p. (J). bds. 15.98 *(978-1-4508-1082-1(9))* Publications International, Ltd.

—Disney Princess Storybook & Magic Bracelet. 2010. 12p. (J). bds. 12.98 *(978-1-4127-9912-6(0))* Phoenix International Publications, Inc.

—Disney Princess under the Starry Sky. 2013. 8p. (J). bds. *(978-1-4508-7130-3(5),* 1450871305) Phoenix International Publications, Inc.

—Disney(r) Sofia the First the Perfect Party: A Flashlight Adventure Sound Book. 2014. 14p. (J). 16.98 *(978-1-4508-7476-2(2),* 31bc99fe-fde1-4d89-9e76-09c40bd0ccb5) Phoenix International Publications, Inc.

—Disney Tinkerbell Book Box Plush. 2011. 8p. (J). bds. 7.04 net. *(978-1-4508-0576-6(0),* 1450805760) Publications International, Ltd.

—Doodles for Kids. 2011. 100p. (J). spiral bd. 13.98 *(978-1-4508-0991-7(X))* Publications International, Ltd.

—Doodles to Go: Razzle Dazzle Doodles. 2011. 146p. (J). spiral bd. 8.98 *(978-1-4508-1662-5(2))* Publications International, Ltd.

—Doodles to Go: Super Duper Doodles. 2011. 146p. (J). spiral bd. *(978-1-4508-1603-8(7))* Publications International, Ltd.

—Dora Little Stars, Big Adventure. 2013. 14p. (J). bds. 16.98 *(978-1-4127-8950-9(8),* 1412789508) Phoenix International Publications, Inc.

—Dora Says Good Night. 2011. 12p. (J). bds. 11.98 *(978-1-4508-0764-7(X))* Phoenix International Publications, Inc.

—Dora the Explorer. (J). 2010. 128p. pap. 12.98 *(978-1-60553-793-1(4))* 2007. (Illus.). 4.00 *(978-1-4127-8442-9(5))* Phoenix International Publications, Inc.

—Dora the Explorer: Island Adventure (Talking Look & Find) 2010. 16p. (J). bds. 12.98 *(978-1-60553-471-8(4))* Publications International, Ltd.

—Dora the Explorer: Little Star's Big Adventure. 2010. (J). 10.98 *(978-1-4508-0391-5(1))* Phoenix International Publications, Inc.

—Dora the Explorer: Little Star's Big Adventure (Flashlight Adventure Book & Dora Plush) 2010. (J). 24.98 *(978-1-4508-0129-4(3))* Publications International, Ltd.

—Dora the Explorer: Scavenger Hunt (Little Look & Find) 2010. 24p. (J). 2.98 *(978-1-4127-7113-9(7))* Phoenix International Publications, Inc.

—Dora the Explorer: Sounds All Around! 2011. 24p. (J). 20.98 *(978-1-4508-0011-2(4))* Phoenix International Publications, Inc.

—Dora the Explorer: We Did It! 2010. 10p. (J). bds. 14.98 *(978-1-4508-0384-7(9))* Phoenix International Publications, Inc.

—Dora the Explorer, Ding Dong! It's Dora! 2009. 12p. (J). bds. 11.98 *(978-1-4127-7598-4(1))* Phoenix International Publications, Inc.

—Dragon Boat Festival. 2009. 9p. (J). bds. 10.98 *(978-1-4127-7782-7(8),* PIL Kids) Publications International, Ltd.

—Electronic Time for Learning: Music. 2011. 120p. (J). *(978-1-4508-0260-4(5))* Publications International, Ltd.

—Electronic Time for Learning: The Human Body. 2010. 120p. 18.98 *(978-1-4127-9854-9(X),* PIL Kids) Publications International, Ltd.

—Elmo. 2007. (J). 9.98 *(978-1-4127-8301-9(1))* Phoenix International Publications, Inc.

—The Enchanted Forest. 2011. 14p. (J). 17.98 *(978-1-4508-0565-0(5))* Phoenix International Publications, Inc.

—Finding Nemo. 2007. (J). 9.98 *(978-1-4127-6516-9(1))* Publications International, Ltd.

—Finding Nemo: A Party for Nemo. 2009. 9p. (J). bds. 4.50 *(978-1-4127-2926-0(2),* PIL Kids) Publications International, Ltd.

—Fire Truck: (Play-a-Sound Book) 2010. 12p. (J). bds. 12.98 *(978-1-4508-0110-2(2))* Phoenix International Publications, Inc.

—First Look & Find Hello Kitty. 2013. (gr. -1-1). bds. 7.98 *(978-1-4508-6378-0(7),* 900f7270-d27c-4dbf-8614-52373c31c3df) Phoenix International Publications, Inc.

—First Look & Find Little Elf. 2013. 18p. (J). bds. *(978-1-4508-7093-1(7),* 1450870937) Phoenix International Publications, Inc.

—First Words (Listen & Learn Sound Book) 2011. 19p. (J). bds. 11.98 *(978-1-4508-1441-6(7))* Phoenix International Publications, Inc.

—Halloween Is Coming! 2010. 14p. (J). bds. 10.98 *(978-1-60553-691-0(1),* PIL Kids) Publications International, Ltd.

—Handy Manny: Fiesta Fun. 2008. (J). bds. 10.98 *(978-1-4127-8867-0(6))* Publications International, Ltd.

—Happy Baby. 2011. 8p. (J). bds. 7.98 *(978-1-4508-1243-6(0))* Publications International, Ltd.

—Head to Toe! Go! Go! Go! 2009. 24p. (J). 17.98 *(978-0-7853-1321-2(4),* PIL Kids) Publications International, Ltd.

—Hello Kitty: My Friend Hello Kitty: Play-A-Sound Book & Cuddly Hello Kitty. 2013. (J). (gr. -1-4). bds. 13.99 *(978-1-4508-1181-1(7),* 21ea0785-0317-4c86-b812-bf2727f2df16) Phoenix International Publications, Inc.

—Hello Kitty Sweet Songs: Play-A-Sound. 2013. 12p. (J). bds. 9.98 *(978-1-4508-6167-0(9),* 1450861679) Phoenix International Publications, Inc.

—I Love You. 2010. 14p. (J). bds. 10.98 *(978-1-4127-4504-8(7),* PIL Kids) Publications International, Ltd.

—Interactive Play a Sound Thomas the Tank. 2009. 24p. (J). 17.98 *(978-0-7853-1360-1(5),* PIL Kids) Publications International, Ltd.

—It's Riddle Time! 2009. 10p. (J). bds. 11.98 *(978-1-4127-1689-5(6),* PIL Kids) Publications International, Ltd.

—Jake & the Neverland Pirates. 2014. 8p. (J). bds. *(978-1-4508-7763-3(X),* e168afdc-4d1e-411f-b3c5-d4e40b1ae222) Phoenix International Publications, Inc.

—Jake & the Neverland Pirates: What Do You See? Pop up Book & Flashlight Set. 2013. 8p. (J). (gr. k-4). bds. 10.99 *(978-1-4508-6836-5(3),* 2baa77ff-d973-4d57-acdb-676cb1d56b2d) Phoenix International Publications, Inc.

—Jesus Loves Me. 2010. 14p. (J). bds. 10.98 *(978-1-4127-4471-3(7),* PIL Kids) Publications International, Ltd.

—Let's Have a Race, Surprises, Little Engines. 2010. 14p. (J). 12.98 *(978-1-4127-4716-5(3))* Phoenix International Publications, Inc.

—Lights & Music. 2008. 160p. (J). bds. 17.98 *(978-1-4127-8500-6(6),* PIL Kids) Publications International, Ltd.

—Lights & Music Treasury. 2010. 160p. (J). bds. 16.98 *(978-1-4127-7911-1(1))* Phoenix International Publications, Inc.

—Lights & Music Treasury 10Led Spa Disney Classics. 2009. 160p. 15.98 *(978-1-4127-5454-5(2))* Phoenix International Publications, Inc.

—Lights, Music, & Me! Love Sparkles. 2010. 14p. (J). bds. 10.98 *(978-1-4127-1884-4(8),* PIL Kids) Publications International, Ltd.

—Little Carry Case Spa Cars 8 Bks. 2009. 8p. 9.98 *(978-1-4127-6434-6(3),* PIL Kids) Publications International, Ltd.

—Little Lift & Listen Sound Mickey Mouse Clubhouse. 2007. (J). 10.98 *(978-1-4127-8457-3(3))* Phoenix International Publications, Inc.

—Little Sound the Princess & the Frog. 2009. 24p. (J). bds. 10.98 *(978-1-4127-6446-9(7))* Publications International, Ltd.

—Look & Find - My First Look & Find Barney. 2011. 18p. (J). bds. 3.75 net. *(978-1-4508-1892-6(7),* 1450818927) Publications International, Ltd.

—Marvel Heroes. 2007. (J). 9.98 *(978-1-4127-8449-8(2))* Phoenix International Publications, Inc.

—Marvel Heroes. 2007. (J). 7.10 *(978-1-4127-6665-4(6))* Publications International, Ltd.

—Marvel: Spider-Man: Spectacular Spider Powers! 2014. 12p. (J). bds. *(978-1-4508-6830-3(4),* 4081a6bc-7da7-4aa0-ac34-16d92600c8f0) Phoenix International Publications, Inc.

—Mater Saves the Day. 2011. 12p. (J). bds. 10.98 *(978-1-4508-0695-4(3))* Phoenix International Publications, Inc.

—Me Reader Jr(tm) Old MacDonald's Farm: Electronic Reader & 8-Book Library. 2015. (J). 22.98 *(978-1-4508-9401-2(1),* 1450894011) Publications International, Ltd.

—Los Mejores Amigos. 2009.Tr. of Toy Story Best Friends. 12p. (J). bds. 10.98 *(978-1-4127-0269-0(0))* Phoenix International Publications, Inc.

—Mickey Mouse Clubhouse: Doctor Kit Book & Mickey Plush. 2010. (J). 24.98 *(978-1-4508-0124-9(2))* Publications International, Ltd.

—Mickey Mouse Clubhouse: Mickey's Silly Shadow Book. 2011. 14p. (J). bds. 8.45 net. *(978-1-4508-0564-3(7))* Phoenix International Publications, Inc.

—Mickey Mouse Clubhouse: Play Day Songs. 2011. (Illus.). 12p. (J). bds. 15.98 *(978-1-4508-0925-2(1))* Publications International, Ltd.

—Mickey Mouse Clubhouse - Who's Not Sleepy? 2011. 12p. (J). bds. *(978-1-4508-0398-4(9))* Publications International, Ltd.

—Mickey Mouse Clubhouse: Colors: Sing & Learn. 2010. 12p. (J). bds. 10.98 *(978-1-4127-1729-8(9))* Publications International, Ltd.

—Mickey Mouse Clubhouse: Mickey's Surprise! 2013. 14p. (J). (gr. k-3). bds. 16.99 *(978-1-4508-2188-9(X),* 87b7723a-b11c-4ce1-8b21-522e3e8ff7e2) Phoenix International Publications, Inc.

—Mickey Mouse Clubhouse: Sing-along Christmas Songs: Holiday Play-a-Song Book. 2010. 10p. (J). bds. 12.98 *(978-1-4127-7862-6(X))* Publications International, Ltd.

—Mickey's Adventure. 2010. 24p. (J). bds. 16.98 *(978-1-4127-4599-4(3))* Phoenix International Publications, Inc.

—Mickey's Clubhouse Drum Song Sound. 2011. 14p. (J). bds. 20.98 *(978-1-4508-1240-5(6))* Phoenix International Publications, Inc.

—Mickey's Piano Songs Play & Learn. 2010. 24p. (J). 12.98 *(978-1-4508-0114-0(5))* Phoenix International Publications, Inc.

—Move to the Music. 2011. 14p. (J). bds. 20.98 *(978-1-4508-1242-9(2))* Phoenix International Publications, Inc.

—Musical Pop up Disney Princess. 2008. (SPA.). (J). 15.98 *(978-1-4127-8980-6(X))* Publications International, Ltd.

—My 1st Libraries Disney Classics. 2011. 10p. (J). bds. 13.98 *(978-1-4508-1029-6(2))* Phoenix International Publications, Inc.

—My First Book Block - First Words. 2011. 12p. (J). bds. 3.75 net. *(978-1-4508-1666-3(5),* 1450816665) Publications International, Ltd.

—My First Book Block Set Animals. 2011. 12p. (J). bds. 14.98 *(978-1-4508-1244-3(9))* Publications International, Ltd.

—My First Book Block Set Disey Princess. 2011. 5p. (J). bds. 14.98 *(978-1-4508-1630-4(4))* Phoenix International Publications, Inc.

—My First Story Reader Dora the Explorer. 2011. (J). 31.98 *(978-1-4508-0618-3(X))* Phoenix International Publications, Inc.

—My First Story Reader Sesame Street, 3 vols. 2007. (Illus.). (J). 31.98 *(978-1-4127-8989-9(3))* Phoenix International Publications, Inc.

—My Shapes Book. 2011. 32p. (J). bds. *(978-1-4508-1023-4(3))* Publications International, Ltd.

—Nickelodeon Dora the Explorer: Cook with Dora: Abuela's Birthday Fiesta. 2010. 14p. (J). bds. 16.98 *(978-1-4508-0842-2(5))* Phoenix International Publications, Inc.

—Numbers (Listen & Learn Sound Book) 2011. 19p. (J). bds. 11.98 *(978-1-4508-1705-9(X))* Phoenix International Publications, Inc.

—Old MacDonald Had a Farm. 2010. 12p. (J). bds. 3.98 *(978-1-60553-146-5(4))* Publications International, Ltd.

—On Sesame Street. 2010. 10p. (J). bds. 14.98 *(978-1-4127-4610-6(8))* Publications International, Ltd.

—Once upon a Potty Sound Book for Boys. 2010. 8p. (J). bds. 7.98 *(978-1-4508-0829-3(8))* Phoenix International Publications, Inc.

—Out & About. 2010. 18p. (J). bds. 12.98 *(978-1-4127-4466-9(0),* PIL Kids) Publications International, Ltd.

—Phineas & Ferb Time for Fun Play-A-Sound. 2013. (Illus.). 24p. (J). (gr. 1-3). 12.98 *(978-1-4508-6604-0(2),* fea3b34e-591a-41e6-a62a-78ca59cb997d) Publications International, Ltd.

—Pirate. 2008. (J). bds. 9.98 *(978-1-4127-9357-5(2))* Publications International, Ltd.

—Planes up, up & Away! 2013. (Illus.). 10p. (J). bds. **(978-1-4508-6284-4(5))** Publications International, Ltd.
—Play-a-Puzzle Book: Halloween. 2010. 12p. (J). bds. 10.98 *(978-1-60553-736-8(5))* Publications International, Ltd.
—Play-a-Puzzle trade; Book: Alphabet. 2010. 12p. (J). bds. 10.98 *(978-1-60553-799-3(3))* Publications International, Ltd.
—Play & Learn Piano Dora. 2011. 24p. (J). 17.98 *(978-1-4508-1165-1(5))* Phoenix International Publications, Inc.
—Play & Learn Piano Elmo. 2011. 24p. (J). 17.98 *(978-1-4508-0871-2(9))* Phoenix International Publications, Inc.
—Pooh's Pop-up Stories. 2010. (J). 8.98 *(978-1-60553-497-8(8))* Phoenix International Publications, Inc.
—Pooh's Pop-up Stories 2. 2010. (J). 8.98 *(978-1-60553-838-9(8))* Phoenix International Publications, Inc.
—Popping up on Sesame Street. 2010. 14p. (J). 19.98 *(978-1-4127-4512-3(8))* Phoenix International Publications, Inc.
—Potty Time for Monsters. 2011. 14p. (J). bds. 17.98 *(978-1-4508-0572-8(8))* Phoenix International Publications, Inc.
—Potty Time with Big Sister Dora. 2011. 12p. (J). bds. 11.98 *(978-1-4508-1438-6(7))* Phoenix International Publications, Inc.
—Potty Time with Elmo. 2011. 12p. (J). 4.69 net. *(978-1-4508-1353-2(4)*, 1450813534) Phoenix International Publications, Inc.
—Potty Time with Tiger: Boy. 2010. (J). bds. 5.98 *(978-1-4127-6915-0(9))* Publications International, Ltd.
—Potty Time with Tiger: Girl. 2010. (SPA.). (J). bds. 5.98 *(978-1-4127-6916-7(7))* Publications International, Ltd.
—Prince Elmo & the Pea. 2007. (J). 10.98 *(978-1-4127-6745-3(8))* Publications International, Ltd.
—The Princess & the Frog. 2009. 24p. (J). 16.98 *(978-1-4127-6421-6(1))* Publications International, Ltd.
—Princess Magic. 2010. (My First Look & Find Ser.). (Illus.). 12p. (gr. -1). bds. 7.98 *(978-1-4127-3074-7(0)*, 7227000) Phoenix International Publications, Inc.
—Race Car. 2013. 12p. (J). bds. 9.98 *(978-1-4508-0112-6(9)*, 1450801129) Phoenix International Publications, Inc.
—Race Day. 2010. 10p. (J). bds. 11.98 *(978-1-4127-4931-2(X)*, PIL Kids) Publications International, Ltd.
—Really Useful Engines. 2010. 40p. (J). bds. 14.98 *(978-1-60553-744-3(6))* Phoenix International Publications, Inc.
—Record A Story: My Grandma Is Special. 2011. 20p. (J). bds. 19.99 *(978-1-4508-1352-5(6))* Phoenix International Publications, Inc.
—Record a Story: My Grandpa Is Special. 2011. 20p. (J). bds. 25.98 *(978-1-4508-1381-5(X))* Phoenix International Publications, Inc.
—Record a Story: 'Twas the Night Before Christmas. 2010. 20p. (J). (gr. k-3). bds. 19.99 *(978-1-4508-0201-7(X)*, 145080201X) Phoenix International Publications, Inc.
—Ring-a-Ling! A Friend Is Here. 2010. 12p. (J). 9.98 *(978-1-4127-7939-5(1))* Phoenix International Publications, Inc.
—A Ring-A-Ling Day! 2009. 12p. (J). bds. 11.98 *(978-1-4127-9614-9(8)*, PIL Kids) Publications International, Ltd.
—Rock & Roll with Elmo. 2010. 24p. (J). bds. 19.98 *(978-1-4127-4475-1(X)*, PIL Kids) Publications International, Ltd.
—Rockin' on the Railway. 2010. 24p. (J). 17.98 *(978-1-60553-339-1(4)*, PIL Kids) Publications International, Ltd.
—Rudolph the Red-Nosed Reindeer(r): A Flashlight Adventure Sound Book. 2014. 14p. (J). *(978-1-4508-9047-2(4)*, 1450890474) Publications International, Ltd.
—Rudolph the Red-Nosed Reindeer (Book & Plush) 2011. 8p. (J). bds. 11.98 *(978-1-4508-2170-4(7))* Publications International, Ltd.
—Sesame Street: Good Night Stories. 2010. 40p. (J). bds. 14.98 *(978-1-60553-861-7(2))* Phoenix International Publications, Inc.
—Sesame Street: Merry Christmas, Elmo! 2010. 8p. (J). bds. 5.98 *(978-1-60553-980-5(5))* Phoenix International Publications, Inc.
—Sesame Street: Merry Christmas, Elmo! (Book & Plush) 2011. 8p. (J). bds. 11.98 *(978-1-4508-2169-8(3))* Publications International, Ltd.
—Sesame Street: Potty Time Songs. 12p. (J). 2011. bds. *(978-1-4508-0401-1(2))* 2010. bds. 9.98 *(978-1-4508-0365-6(2))* Phoenix International Publications, Inc.
—Sesame Street: Sing with Elmo, Let's Sing! & Wake up, Elmo! 2011. (J). bds. 14.98 *(978-1-4508-0627-5(9))* Phoenix International Publications, Inc.
—Sesame Street: The Itsy Bitsy Spider. 2011. 10p. (J). bds. 7.98 *(978-1-4508-0858-3(1)*, 6461bf3e-ab03-4ebc-81c6-091daf4fbc8e) Phoenix International Publications, Inc.
—Sesame Street: Trick or Treat with Elmo. 2009. 12p. (J). bds. *(978-1-4127-7896-1(4)*, 1412778964) Phoenix International Publications, Inc.
—Sesame Street (Musical Treasury) 2011. 40p. (J). bds. 15.98 *(978-1-4508-1081-4(0))* Publications International, Ltd.
—Sesame Street, Ding Dong, Elmo's Here! 2009. 12p. (J). bds. 11.98 *(978-1-4127-9613-2(X))* Phoenix International Publications, Inc.
—Sesame Street: Find a Friend: A Busy Box Book. 2010. 14p. (J). bds. 16.98 *(978-1-60553-622-4(9))* Phoenix International Publications, Inc.
—Sesame Street(r) Happy Easter, Elmo! 2014. 12p. (J). bds. *(978-1-4508-3302-8(0)*, c726526e-0586-4bbf-a70d-c1093f5cc14b) Phoenix International Publications, Inc.
—Sesame Street(r) Listen & Learn in Your Neighborhood. 2014. 19p. (J). bds. *(978-1-4508-7519-6(X)*, 145087519X) Publications International, Ltd.
—Sesame Street: Sing & Play Guitar Songs. 2014. 12p. (J). *(978-1-4508-7988-0(8)*, d11d1f4c-d61d-46f5-a30f-cd01ce8a740a) Phoenix International Publications, Inc.
—Sesame Street(r) Where Is Elmo's Friend? Play-A-Sound(r) Lift-a-Flap Sound Book. 2014. 10p. (J). bds. *(978-1-4508-8976-6(X)*, 145088976X) Publications International, Ltd.
—Sesame Write & Erase Board Book. 2014. 28p. (J). bds. 9.98 *(978-1-4508-8130-2(0)*, 1450881300) Phoenix International Publications, Inc.
—Shapes Wipe off Learning Board. 2011. 1p. (J). bds. *(978-1-4508-1432-4(8))* Publications International, Ltd.
—The Smurfs Large Play a Sound. 2011. 24p. (J). 14.98 *(978-1-60553-403-9(X))* Phoenix International Publications, Inc.
—Sofia the First: Princess in Training: Play-A-Sound Book. 2013. 12p. (J). (gr. k-3). bds. 10.99 *(978-1-4508-6278-3(0)*, 8d870699-8d28-476c-b7fd-49589bc268a4) Phoenix International Publications, Inc.
—Soft! Furry! Bumpy! A Touch, Hear, & Learn with Elmo Book. 2010. 10p. (J). bds. 11.98 *(978-1-4127-5805-5(X)*, PIL Kids) Publications International, Ltd.
—Spider Sense Spider-Man: Super Villain Showdown. 2010. 12p. (J). bds. 12.98 *(978-1-4127-9911-9(2))* Phoenix International Publications, Inc.
—Spooky Stories. 2008. (J). 12.98 *(978-1-4127-9384-1(X))* Publications International, Ltd.
—Steering Wheel Spa Cars. 2009. 14p. 16.98 *(978-1-4127-9241-7(X))* Phoenix International Publications, Inc.
—Stories to Grow on Spa Disney Classics. 2009. 40p. 9.98 *(978-1-4127-1109-8(6))* Phoenix International Publications, Inc.
—Stories to Grow on Spa Mickey Mouse Clubhous. 2009. 40p. 9.98 *(978-1-4127-1127-2(4)*, PIL Kids) Publications International, Ltd.
—A Surprise for Belle. 2010. 12p. (J). bds. 9.98 *(978-1-4127-4454-6(7))* Phoenix International Publications, Inc.
—Teenage Ninja Turtles: Skateboard Heroes! 2014. 12p. (J). bds. 12.98 *(978-1-4508-8453-2(9)*, 5b3a6351-f0d0-4a36-b0d1-c89677f0352a) Phoenix International Publications, Inc.
—Things That Go Board Book. 2014. (Illus.). 22p. (J). bds. 4.98 *(978-1-4508-8581-2(0)*, 1450885810) Phoenix International Publications, Inc.
—Thomas & Friends: Engine Roll Call. 2011. 8p. (J). bds. 7.98 *(978-1-4508-1435-5(2))* Publications International, Ltd.
—Thomas & Friends: Let's Go, Thomas! 2010. 14p. (J). 17.98 *(978-1-4508-0212-3(5))* Phoenix International Publications, Inc.
—Thomas & Friends: Play-a-Tune Puzzle Book. 2010. 10p. (J). bds. 13.98 *(978-1-60553-756-6(X))* Publications International, Ltd.
—Thomas & Friends: Sodor Snapshots. 2010. 14p. (J). bds. 19.98 *(978-1-4127-1918-6(6))* Publications International, Ltd.
—Thomas & Friends(tm) Super Look & Find(r) Activity Pad: Spot the Find 'ems, Find the Differences! Giant Play Scene! More Than 50 Stickers! 2014. 64p. (J). *(978-1-4508-8559-1(4)*, 1450885594) Publications International, Ltd.
—Thomas Celebration Pop Up Sound. 2010. 14p. 19.98 *(978-1-4127-4513-0(6))* Publications International, Ltd.
—Thomas Great to be Engine Little Sound. 2011. 12p. 9.98 *(978-1-4508-0872-9(7))* Phoenix International Publications, Inc.
—Thomas Songs Play & Learn. 2010. 24p. (J). 12.98 *(978-1-4508-0115-7(3))* Phoenix International Publications, Inc.
—Thomas the Tank Good Morning Engines. 12p. (J). bds. *(978-0-7853-8282-9(8)*, 0785382828) Phoenix International Publications, Inc.
—Tinker Bell. 2010. 10p. (J). 11.98 *(978-1-4127-4472-0(5)*, PIL Kids) Publications International, Ltd.
—Tinker Bell: Songs from Pixie Hollow. 2010. 12p. (J). bds. 9.98 *(978-1-4508-0366-3(0))* Phoenix International Publications, Inc.
—Tinker Bell -Tink's Magical Day. 2011. 8p. (J). bds. *(978-1-4508-0910-8(3))* Publications International, Ltd.
—Tinker Bell (Book & Plush) 2011. 8p. (J). bds. 11.98 *(978-1-4508-2171-1(5))* Publications International, Ltd.
—Touch & Hear Adventure. 2010. 10p. (J). 11.98 *(978-1-4127-4932-9(8)*, PIL Kids) Publications International, Ltd.
—Toy Story 3: New Friends. 2010. 12p. (J). bds. 10.98 *(978-1-4127-4584-0(5)*, PIL Kids) Publications International, Ltd.
—Toys to the Rescue. 2010. 14p. (J). 16.98 *(978-1-4127-4585-7(3)*, PIL Kids) Publications International, Ltd.
—Trains. 2011. 12p. (J). bds. 13.98 *(978-1-4508-1138-5(8))* Publications International, Ltd.
—Treasure Hunt. 2010. 12p. (J). bds. 9.98 *(978-1-4127-9885-3(X))* Phoenix International Publications, Inc.
—Up & down! Play-a-Sound Book & Huggable Kai-lan. 2010. (J). 14.98 *(978-1-4127-5591-7(3))* Publications International, Ltd.
—Vampires & Other Scary Creatures(Look & Find) 2010. 24p. (J). 7.98 *(978-1-60553-839-6(6))* Publications International, Ltd.
—Video Play a Sound Dora. 2010. 24p. (J). 19.98 *(978-1-4127-9210-3(X)*, PIL Kids) Publications International, Ltd.
—What Do You See? 2012. (Illus.). 14p. (J). (gr. 2-4). 17.98 *(978-1-4508-4545-8(2)*, 23956fd6-2821-435f-aef0-d47191d0621e) Phoenix International Publications, Inc.
—What's Different. 2009. 24p. (J). 7.98 *(978-1-4127-1725-0(6)*, PIL Kids) Publications International, Ltd.
—What's Different Finding Nemo. 2009. 24p. (J). 9.98 *(978-1-4127-7769-8(0)*, PIL Kids) Publications International, Ltd.
—Winnie the Pooh. 2007. (J). 15.98 *(978-1-4127-8351-4(8))* Publications International, Ltd.
—Winnie the Pooh Drum Sound. 2011. 14p. (J). bds. 20.98 *(978-1-4508-0911-5(1))* Phoenix International Publications, Inc.
—Winnie the Pooh (Find-A-Friend Book) 2011. 14p. (J). bds. 17.98 *(978-1-4508-0694-7(5))* Phoenix International Publications, Inc.
—Wonder Pets: Save the Baby Kitten. 2008. (J). bds. 10.98 *(978-1-4127-9198-4(7))* Publications International, Ltd.
—The World of Eric Carle - Baby Animals. 2011. 10p. (J). bds. 7.98 *(978-1-4508-0508-7(6))* Phoenix International Publications, Inc.
—The World of Eric Carle(tm) Hear Bear Roar. 2014. 24p. (J). bds. 16.98 *(978-1-4508-7477-9(0)*, 1450874770) Phoenix International Publications, Inc.
—Write-And-Erase Look & Find(r) Disney Minnie: Packed with 'find 'ems & Picture Puzzles! Look, Circle, Wipe Clean, & Play Again! 2014. 28p. (J). bds. 9.98 *(978-1-4508-7918-7(7)*, 1450879187) Phoenix International Publications, Inc.
—Writing Skills Wipe off Leaning Board. 2011. 1p. (J). bds. *(978-1-4508-1433-1(6))* Publications International, Ltd.
—Zoom! 2010. 14p. (J). bds. 17.98 *(978-1-4127-4594-9(2))* Phoenix International Publications, Inc.
Publications International Ltd. Staff & Red Giraffe, Ltd Staff, eds. The Big Race - Stories Come to Life, 3Bks. 2011. (J). *(978-1-4508-0586-5(8))* Phoenix International Publications, Inc.
Publishing, Arcturus. Farm. 2016. (ENG.). 10p. (J). 9.95 *(978-1-78599-101-1(9)*, 9781785991011) Arcturus Publishing GBR. Dist: Bookmasters Distribution.
—Jungle. 2016. (ENG.). 10p. (J). 9.95 *(978-1-78599-102-8(7)*, 9781785991028) Arcturus Publishing GBR. Dist: Bookmasters Distribution.
Publishing, Sterling. Daddy & Me. 2008. (Illus.). 12p. (J). bds. *(978-1-934618-44-8(6))* Begin Smart LLC.
—Hello, Baby! 2008. (Illus.). 10p. (J). bds. *(978-1-934618-26-4(8))* Begin Smart LLC.
—Look at Me! 2008. (Illus.). 10p. (J). bds. *(978-1-934618-41-7(1))* Begin Smart LLC.
—Woof. 2008. (Books for Brainy Babies). (Illus.). 12p. (J). bds. *(978-1-934618-33-2(0))* Begin Smart LLC.
Puck. My Foodie ABC: A Little Gourmet's Guide. Lemay, Violet, illus. 2010. (ENG.). 22p. (J). (gr. -1-k). bds. 8.95 *(978-0-9825295-2-2(X))* Duo Pr. LLC.
—123 Chicago. Somers, Kevin, illus. 2009. (Cool Counting Bks.). (ENG.). 22p. (J). (gr. k — 1). bds. 8.95 *(978-0-9796213-5-2(6))* Duo Pr. LLC.
—123 San Francisco. Somers, Kevin, illus. 2009. (Cool Counting Bks.). (ENG.). 22p. (J). (gr. k — 1). bds. 8.95 *(978-0-9796213-8-3(0))* Duo Pr. LLC.
—123 Texas. Somers, Kevin, illus. 2009. (Cool Counting Bks.). (ENG.). 22p. (J). (gr. k — 1). bds. 8.95 *(978-0-9796213-6-9(4))* Duo Pr. LLC.
Puppy. 2004. (J). per. *(978-1-57657-397-6(4))* Paradise Pr., Inc.
Puppy. (Buggy Buddies Ser.). (Illus.). (J). (gr. -1). bds. *(978-1-56021-351-2(5)*, 202) W.J. Fantasy, Inc.
Putumayo Kids Staff, creator. African Sticker Collection. 2010. (J). 11.95 *(978-1-58759-273-7(8))* Putumayo World Music & Crafts.
Quinton, Sasha, text. Ears. 2010. (Illus.). 10p. (J). *(978-1-936199-15-0(7))* Book Shop, Ltd., The.
—Noses. 2010. (Illus.). 10p. (J). *(978-1-936199-17-4(3))* Book Shop, Ltd., The.
—Paws. 2010. (Illus.). 10p. (J). *(978-1-936199-16-7(5))* Book Shop, Ltd., The.
—Tails. 2010. (Illus.). 10p. (J). *(978-1-936199-14-3(9))* Book Shop, Ltd., The.
Rabe, Tish. Hello, My Baby (Dr. Seuss/Cat in the Hat) Mathieu, Joe & Ruiz, Aristides, illus. 2013. (Nifty Lift-And-Look Ser.). (ENG.). 12p. (J). (— 1). bds. 5.99 *(978-0-449-81434-5(3)*, Random Hse. Bks. for Young Readers) Random Hse. Children's Bks.
—Love You, Hug You, Read to You! Endersby, Frank, illus. 2015. (ENG.). 32p. (J). (gr. -1 — 1). bds. 7.99 *(978-1-101-93655-9(X)*, Random Hse. Bks. for Young Readers) Random Hse. Children's Bks.
Rader, Mark. Dinosaur. Sanborn, Casey, illus. 2008. (J). *(978-1-4127-9359-9(9))* Publications International, Ltd.
Radford, Tracey. Animal Fun! Count to 10: Lift the Flaps & Find the Number! 2016. (ENG., Illus.). 10p. (J). (gr. 1-4). 6.95 *(978-1-78249-400-3(6)*, 1782494006, CICO Books) Ryland Peters & Small GBR. Dist: WIPRO.
—Animal Fun! Touch & Feel: Stroke the Animals! 2016. (ENG., Illus.). 10p. (J). (gr. 1-4). 6.95 *(978-1-78249-401-0(4)*, 1782494014, CICO Books) Ryland Peters & Small GBR. Dist: WIPRO.
—Animal Fun! What Sound Do I Make? Press the Button! 2016. (ENG., Illus.). 10p. (J). (gr. 1-4). 6.95 *(978-1-78249-398-3(0)*, 1782493980, CICO Books) Ryland Peters & Small GBR. Dist: WIPRO.
—Animal Fun Where Do I Live? 2016. (ENG., Illus.). 10p. (J). (gr. 1-4). 6.95 *(978-1-78249-399-0(9)*, 1782493999, CICO Books) Ryland Peters & Small GBR. Dist: WIPRO.
Radtke, Becky J. Princess Activity Book. 2009. (Dover Little Activity Bks.). (ENG., Illus.). 64p. (J). (gr. k-3). pap. 1.50 *(978-0-486-47034-4(2))* Dover Pubns., Inc.
Ramljak, Marijan. Are You My Friend? 2009. (Look for Me Bks.). (Illus.). (J). bds. 9.99 *(978-1-934650-67-7(6))* Just For Kids Pr., LLC.
—Are You My Mommy? 2009. (Look for Me Bks.). (Illus.). (J). bds. 9.99 *(978-1-934650-65-3(X))* Just For Kids Pr., LLC.
Randall, Ronne. Snuggle up, Little Penguin! Church, Caroline Jayne, illus. 2003. (Little Friends Ser.). 14p. (J). 12.95 *(978-1-57145-919-0(7)*, Silver Dolphin Bks.) Readerlink Distribution Services, LLC.
Random House. Ash & Pikachu: Alola Region/Team Rocket. Random House, illus. 2017. (Pictureback(R) Ser.). (ENG., Illus.). 32p. (J). (gr. -1-2). pap. 5.99 **(978-1-5247-7008-2(6)**, Random Hse. Bks. for Young Readers) Random Hse. Children's Bks.
—Big Fish, Little Fish: a Book of Opposites (Bubble Guppies) Random House, illus. 2015. (Board Book Ser.). (ENG., Illus.). 24p. (J). (-k). bds. 4.99 *(978-0-385-38442-1(4)*, Random Hse. Bks. for Young Readers) Random Hse. Children's Bks.
—Follow That Egg! (Team Umizoomi) Aikins, David, illus. 2014. (Glitter Board Book Ser.). (ENG.). 12p. (J). (-k). bds. 6.99 *(978-0-385-37518-4(2)*, Random Hse. Bks. for Young Readers) Random Hse. Children's Bks.
—Here Comes Peter Cottontail. Random House, illus. 2015. (Board Book Ser.). (ENG., Illus.). 24p. (J). (-k). bds. 4.99 *(978-0-553-50975-5(6)*, Random Hse. Bks. for Young Readers) Random Hse. Children's Bks.
—Hide-And-Go-Swim! (Bubble Guppies) MJ Illustrations, illus. 2014. (Nifty Lift-And-Look Ser.). (ENG.). 12p. (J). (— 1). bds. 5.99 *(978-0-385-38515-2(3)*, Random Hse. Bks. for Young Readers) Random Hse. Children's Bks.
—Isa's Flower Garden (Dora the Explorer) Miller, Victoria, illus. 2014. (Glitter Board Book Ser.). (ENG.). 12p. (J). (— 1). bds. 6.99 *(978-0-385-37621-1(9)*, Random Hse. Bks. for Young Readers) Random Hse. Children's Bks.
—Let's Find Adventure! (Paw Patrol) Jackson, Mike, illus. 2015. (Nifty Lift-And-Look Ser.). (ENG.). 12p. (J). (-k). bds. 5.99 *(978-0-553-51027-0(4)*, Random Hse. Bks. for Young Readers) Random Hse. Children's Bks.
—Open the Barn Door... Santoro, Christopher, illus. 2016. (ENG.). 22p. (J). (— 1). bds. 6.99 *(978-0-399-54948-9(X)*, Random Hse. Bks. for Young Readers) Random Hse. Children's Bks.
—Patrol Pals (Paw Patrol) Random House, illus. 2015. (Friendship Box Ser.). (ENG., Illus.). 48p. (J). (— 1). bds. 10.99 *(978-0-553-50796-6(6)*, Random Hse. Bks. for Young Readers) Random Hse. Children's Bks.
—PAW Patrol Big Lift-And-Look Board Book (PAW Patrol) Moore, Harry, illus. 2017. (Big Lift-And-Look Book Ser.). (ENG.). 12p. (J). (— 1). bds. 11.99 **(978-1-5247-1722-3(3)**, Random Hse. Bks. for Young Readers) Random Hse. Children's Bks.
—A Paw Patrol Treasury (PAW Patrol) Random House, illus. 2016. (Padded Board Book Ser.). (ENG., Illus.). 30p. (J). (— 1). bds. 11.99 *(978-1-101-93957-4(5)*, Random Hse. Bks. for Young Readers) Random Hse. Children's Bks.
—Peter Cottontail: the Great Easter Egg Hunt (Peter Cottontail) Random House, illus. 2016. (Lift-The-Flap Ser.). (ENG., Illus.). 12p. (J). (gr. -1-k). bds. 6.99 *(978-1-101-93169-1(8)*, Random Hse. Bks. for Young Readers) Random Hse. Children's Bks.
—The Pups Save the Bunnies (Paw Patrol) Jackson, Mike, illus. 2016. (Pictureback(R) Ser.). (ENG.). 16p. (J). (gr. -1-1). 4.99 *(978-1-101-93168-4(X)*, Random Hse. Bks. for Young Readers) Random Hse. Children's Bks.
—Red Alert! (Teenage Mutant Ninja Turtles) Spaziante, Patrick, illus. 2015. (Pictureback(R) Ser.). (ENG.). 16p. (J). (gr. -1-2). 4.99 *(978-0-553-50901-4(2)*, Random Hse. Bks. for Young Readers) Random Hse. Children's Bks.
—Rough-And-Tumble Turtles! (Teenage Mutant Ninja Turtles: Half-Shell Heroes) Spaziante, Patrick, illus. 2016. (Touch-And-Feel Ser.). (ENG.). 10p. (J). (— 1). bds. 12.99 *(978-1-101-94029-7(8)*, Random Hse. Bks. for Young Readers) Random Hse. Children's Bks.
—Shape Patrol! (Paw Patrol) MJ Illustrations, illus. 2016. (ENG.). 24p. (J). (— 1). bds. 6.99 *(978-1-101-93695-5(9)*, Random Hse. Bks. for Young Readers) Random Hse. Children's Bks.
—Super Pup Heroes! (PAW Patrol) Random House, illus. 2016. (Tabbed Board Book Ser.). (ENG., Illus.). 16p. (J). (— 1). bds. 7.99 *(978-0-399-55313-4(4)*, Random Hse. Bks. for Young Readers) Random Hse. Children's Bks.
—Team Colors (Paw Patrol) Random House, illus. 2015. (Board Book Ser.). (ENG., Illus.). 24p. (J). (— 1). bds. 6.99 *(978-0-553-49771-7(5)*, Random Hse. Bks. for Young Readers) Random Hse. Children's Bks.
—Thomas Counts on Christmas (Thomas & Friends) 2016. (ENG., Illus.). 12p. (J). (— 1). bds. 6.99 *(978-0-385-37390-6(2)*, Random Hse. Bks. for Young Readers) Random Hse. Children's Bks.
—1 2 3 Blaze! (Blaze & the Monster Machines) Pixel Mouse House LLC, illus. 2016. (ENG.). 24p. (J). (— 1). bds. 6.99 *(978-1-101-93679-5(7)*, Random Hse. Bks. for Young Readers) Random Hse. Children's Bks.
Random House Disney Staff. Taking the Lead. Random House Disney Staff, illus. 2011. (Puzzle Book Ser.). (ENG., Illus.). 8p. (J). (gr. -1-2). 7.99 *(978-0-7364-2822-4(4)*, RH/Disney) Random Hse. Children's Bks.
Random House Editors & Posner-Sanchez, Andrea. I Am Cinderella. Random House Editors & Disney Storybook Artists Staff, illus. 2011. (Shaped Board Book Ser.). (ENG.). 12p. (J). (— 1). bds. 4.99 *(978-0-7364-2769-2(4)*, Golden/Disney) Random Hse. Children's Bks.
Random House Editors & RH Disney Staff. Aurora & the Helpful Dragon/Tiana & Her Furry Friend. Disney Storybook Artists Staff & Studio Iboix Staff, illus. 2011. (Pictureback(R) Ser.). (ENG.). 32p. (J). (gr. -1-2). pap. 4.99 *(978-0-7364-2757-9(0)*, RH/Disney) Random Hse. Children's Bks.
Random House Staff. Colors Everywhere! (Bubble Guppies) Random House Staff, illus. 2013. (Board Book Ser.). (ENG., Illus.). 24p. (J). (-k). bds. 4.99 *(978-0-449-81782-7(2)*, Random Hse. Bks. for Young Readers) Random Hse. Children's Bks.
—I Love Colors (Dora the Explorer) Random House Staff, illus. 2013. (ENG., Illus.). 24p. (J). (-k). bds. 4.99 *(978-0-449-81481-9(5)*, Random Hse. Bks. for Young Readers) Random Hse. Children's Bks.
Random, Melanie, des. The Alphabet Song Book. 2006. (ENG., Illus.). 16p. (J). (gr. -1-3). 12.95 *(978-1-58117-444-1(6)*, Intervisual/Piggy Toes) Bendon, Inc.
Ranson, Erin. A Bright New Star: With Color-Changing Star Light. Crisp, Dan, illus. 2007. (Story Book Ser.). 16p. (J). (gr. -1-3). bds. *(978-1-84666-161-7(7)*, Tide Mill Pr.) Top That! Publishing PLC.
—Let's Build. Green, Barry, illus. 2007. (Magnetic Story & Play Scene Ser.). (ENG.). 8p. (J). (gr. -1). 9.99 *(978-1-84666-091-7(2))* Top That! Publishing PLC GBR. Dist: Independent Pubs. Group.
—Ocean Wonders. Top That! Staff, ed. Mahoney, Daniel & Wood, Hannah, illus. 2007. (Sparkling Slide Nature Bks.). (ENG.). 12p. (J). (gr. -1). 9.99 *(978-1-84666-167-9(6))* Top That! Publishing PLC GBR. Dist: Independent Pubs. Group.
—One Little Bear & Her Friends. Gévry, Claudine, illus. 2007. 10p. (J). (gr. -1-k). bds. *(978-1-84666-354-3(7)*, Tide Mill Pr.) Top That! Publishing PLC.
—Rainforest Wonders. Wood, Hannah & Mahoney, Daniel J., illus. 2007. (Sparkling Slide Nature Bks.). (ENG.). 12p. (J).

(gr. -1-k). 9.99 (978-1-84666-356-7(3), Tide Mill Pr.) Top That! Publishing PLC GBR. Dist: Independent Pubs. Group.

—The Story of Noah's Ark. Petrlik, Andrea, illus. 2007. (Interactive Magnetic Book Ser.). 10p. (J). (gr. -1). (978-1-84666-359-8(8), Tide Mill Pr.) Top That! Publishing PLC.

—Wild Animals. Green, Barry, illus. 2007. (Magnetic Story & Play Scene Ser.). (ENG.). 8p. (J). (gr. -1-1). 9.99 (978-1-84666-093-1(9)) Top That! Publishing PLC GBR. Dist: Independent Pubs. Group.

—Woodland Fairies. Top That Publishing Staff, ed. Richards, Kirsten, illus. 2008. (Magnetic Story & Play Scene Ser.). 9p. (J). (gr. -1). bds. (978-1-84666-440-3(3), Tide Mill Pr.) Top That! Publishing PLC.

Rao, Lisa. Don't Bite Your Friends! 2009. (Yo Gabba Gabba! Ser.). (ENG.). 10p. (J). (gr. -1-2). 8.99 (978-1-4169-9014-7(3), Simon Spotlight) Simon Spotlight.

Raposo, Joe. Sing. Lichtenheld, Tom, illus. 2016. (ENG.). 32p. (J). bds. 8.99 (978-1-62779-502-9(2), 9781627795029, Holt, Henry & Co. Bks. For Young Readers) Holt, Henry & Co.

Raschka, Chris. Farmy Farm. Raschka, Chris, illus. 2011. (ENG., Illus.). 8p. (J). (gr. -1 — 1). bds. 8.99 (978-0-545-21981-5(7), Orchard Bks.) Scholastic, Inc.

Rasmussen, Jason. The House of the Lord: A Pop-Up Book. 2011. 32p. (J). 29.99 (978-1-60641-939-7(0)) Deseret Bk. Co.

Ratnett, Michael. Dracula Steps Out. Goulding, June & Smyth, Iain, illus. 2005. 12p. (J). (gr. k-4). reprint ed. 16.00 (978-0-7567-8585-7(5)) DIANE Publishing Co.

Ravera, Giuseppe. My Ballet Bag. Pagnoni, Roberta et al, illus. 2015. (ENG.). 8p. (J). (gr. -1-k). bds. 6.99 (978-0-7641-6786-7(3)) Barron's Educational Series, Inc.

Rayner, Catherine. Ernest, the Moose Who Doesn't Fit. Rayner, Catherine, illus. 2010. (ENG., Illus.). 32p. (J). (gr. -1-1). 18.99 (978-0-374-32217-5(1), 9780374322175, Farrar, Straus & Giroux (BYR)) Farrar, Straus & Giroux.

—Smelly Louie. Rayner, Catherine, illus. 2016. (ENG., Illus.). 24p. (J). (gr. -1-k). bds. 10.99 (978-1-5098-0344-6(0)) Pan Macmillan GBR. Dist: Independent Pubs. Group.

Rayner, Katy. Trucks. 2014. (ENG., Illus.). 22p. pap. 8.95 (978-1-906572-11-2(9)) Award Pubns. Ltd. GBR. Dist: Parkwest Pubns., Inc.

Read Together Books Inc Staff & Shoule, Michael. My Daddy Loves Boston College Football. 2010. (ENG.). 20p. (J). bds. 11.95 (978-0-9822615-0-7(0), 9780982261507) Read Together Bks.

Reader's Digest Editors, et al. Music Player. Brannon, Tom, illus. 40th anniv. collector's ed. 2009. (Music Player Storybook Ser.). (ENG.). 40p. (J). (gr. -1). 19.99 (978-0-7944-1913-4(5)) Reader's Digest Assn., Inc., The.

Reader's Digest Staff. Baby's First Bible. MacLean, Colin & MacLean, Moira, illus. 2009. (ENG.). 20p. (J). (gr. -1 — 1). bds. 14.99 (978-0-7944-1942-4(9), Reader's Digest Children's Bks.) Studio Fun International.

—Busy Day Bunnies: A Carry along Treasury. McCue, Lisa, illus. 2011. (Carry along Bks.). (ENG.). 20p. (J). (gr. -1-k). 14.99 (978-0-7944-2168-7(7)) Reader's Digest Assn., Inc., The.

—Thomas & Friends Movie Theater. HIT Entertainment Staff, illus. 2010. (Movie Theater Ser.). (ENG.). 48p. (J). (gr. -1-2). bds. 19.99 (978-0-7944-2002-4(8)) Reader's Digest Assn., Inc., The.

—Tractor Trouble Drive Through Storybook. Pitt, Sarah, illus. 2011. (Drive-Through Storybooks Ser.). (ENG.). 10p. (J). (gr. -1-1). bds. 12.99 (978-0-7944-2169-4(5)) Reader's Digest Assn., Inc., The.

Reader's Digest Staff & Mitter, Matt. Me Love Cookies! Brannon, Tom, illus. 2010. (Hugs Book Ser.). (ENG.). 12p. (J). (— 1). bds. 10.99 (978-0-7944-2176-2(8)) Reader's Digest Assn., Inc., The.

Reader's Digest Staff & Roe, David. How to Train Your Dragon Mix & Match. 2010. (Mix & Match Ser.). (ENG., Illus.). 12p. (J). (gr. -1-1). bds. 14.99 (978-0-7944-1938-7(0), Reader's Digest Children's Bks.) Studio Fun International.

Reader's Digest Staff & Shepherd, Jodie. Guess Who Baby Animals. Ovresat, Laura, illus. 2011. (Guess Who Ser.). (ENG.). 10p. (J). (gr. -1-k). bds. 7.99 (978-0-7944-2196-0(2)) Reader's Digest Assn., Inc., The.

Reasoner, Charles. Animal Friends on the Farm. Pitt, Sarah, illus. 2009. (3D Board Bks.). 12p. (J). (gr. -1-k). bds. 9.99 (978-1-934650-35-6(8)) Just For Kids Pr., LLC.

—Animals in the Jungle. Pitt, Sarah, illus. 2009. (3D Board Bks.). 12p. (J). (gr. -1-k). bds. 9.99 (978-1-934650-38-7(2)) Just For Kids Pr., LLC.

—Brrr! 2009. (Lift & Learn Ser.). (Illus.). 10p. (J). (gr. -1-k). 10.99 (978-1-934650-09-7(9)) Just For Kids Pr., LLC.

—Bug Babies. Devaney, Adam, illus. 2009. (Baby Animal Board Bks.). 12p. (J). (gr. -1-k). bds. 7.99 (978-1-934650-51-6(X)) Just For Kids Pr., LLC.

—Charles Reasoner Peek-a-Book Books. 2013. (Charles Reasoner Peek-A-Boo Bks.). (ENG., Illus.). 10p. (gr. -1 — 1). bds. 19.98 (978-1-4795-4699-2(2)) Picture Window Bks.

—Color Crunch! 2009. (Bite Bks.). (Illus.). (J). bds. 7.99 (978-1-934650-15-8(3)) Just For Kids Pr., LLC.

—Colors in the Garden. Pitt, Sarah, illus. 2009. (3D Board Bks.). 12p. (J). (gr. -1-k). bds. 9.99 (978-1-934650-40-0(4)) Just For Kids Pr., LLC.

—A Day Around Town. 2009. (Inside Outside Board Bks.). (Illus.). (J). bds. 10.99 (978-1-934650-53-0(6)) Just For Kids Pr., LLC.

—A Day at School. 2009. (Inside Outside Board Bks.). (Illus.). (J). bds. 10.99 (978-1-934650-56-1(0)) Just For Kids Pr., LLC.

—A Day at the Farm. 2009. (Inside Outside Board Bks.). (Illus.). 10p. (J). bds. 10.99 (978-1-934650-54-7(4)) Just For Kids Pr., LLC.

—Dinosaur Babies. Devaney, Adam, illus. 2009. (Baby Animal Board Bks.). 12p. (J). (gr. -1-k). bds. 7.99 (978-1-934650-49-3(8)) Just For Kids Pr., LLC.

—Dinosaurs. Doherty, Paula, illus. 2009. (Little Big Flap Bks.). 10p. (J). (gr. -1-k). 9.99 (978-1-934650-24-0(2)) Just For Kids Pr., LLC.

—Farm Babies. Devaney, Adam, illus. 2009. (Baby Animal Board Bks.). 12p. (J). (gr. -1-k). bds. 7.99 (978-1-934650-52-3(8)) Just For Kids Pr., LLC.

—Halloween Ghost, 1 vol. 2014. (Charles Reasoner Halloween Bks.). (ENG.). 12p. (gr. -1 — 1). bds. 5.99 (978-1-4795-5971-8(7)) Picture Window Bks.

—Hey, Diddle, Diddle, 1 vol. Le Ray, Marina, illus. 2014. (Charles Reasoner Nursery Rhymes Ser.). (ENG.). 10p. (gr. -1 — 1). bds. 4.99 (978-1-4795-3807-2(8)) Picture Window Bks.

—Hickory, Dickory, Dock. Le Ray, Marina, illus. 2014. (Charles Reasoner Nursery Rhymes Ser.). (ENG.). 10p. (gr. -1 — 1). bds. 4.99 (978-1-4795-3805-8(1)) Picture Window Bks.

—I'm Just a Bird. 2008. (978-1-84666-153-2(6)) Top That! Publishing PLC.

—I'm Just a Bird. Reasoner, Charles, illus. 2007. (I'm Just Book Ser.). (Illus.). 12p. (J). (gr. -1). bds. (978-1-84666-289-8(3), Tide Mill Pr.) Top That! Publishing PLC.

—I'M Just a Crab! Reasoner, Charles, illus. 2007. (Large Googley-Eye Bks.). (ENG., Illus.). 12p. (J). (gr. -1). 9.99 (978-1-84666-291-1(5), Tide Mill Pr.) Top That! Publishing PLC GBR. Dist: Independent Pubs. Group.

—I'm Just a Fish. 2008. (Googley-Eye Bks.). (ENG.). 12p. (J). (gr. -1). 7.99 (978-1-84666-155-6(2)) Top That! Publishing PLC GBR. Dist: Independent Pubs. Group.

—I'm Just a Frog. 2008. (978-1-84666-159-4(5)) Top That! Publishing PLC.

—Inside Jolly Rodger's Pirate Ship. 2014. (Illus.). (J). (978-1-4351-5466-7(5)) Barnes & Noble, Inc.

—Inside Old MacDonald's Barn. 2014. (Illus.). (J). (978-1-4351-5467-4(3)) Barnes & Noble, Inc.

—Inside Old Mcdonald's Barn. Reasoner, Charles, illus. 2007. (Story Book Ser.). (Illus.). 12p. (J). (gr. k). bds. (978-1-84666-287-4(7), Tide Mill Pr.) Top That! Publishing PLC.

—Inside Santa's Toy Shop. Reasoner, Charles, illus. 2007. (Story Book Ser.). (Illus.). 12p. (J). (gr. k-3). bds. (978-1-84666-151-8(X), Tide Mill Pr.) Top That! Publishing PLC.

—Itsy Bitsy Spider, 1 vol. Le Ray, Marina, illus. 2013. (Charles Reasoner Nursery Rhymes Ser.). (ENG.). 10p. (gr. -1 — 1). bds. 4.99 (978-1-4795-1691-9(0)) Picture Window Bks.

—Jack & Jill, 1 vol. Le Ray, Marina, illus. 2014. (Charles Reasoner Nursery Rhymes Ser.). (ENG.). 10p. (gr. -1 — 1). bds. 4.99 (978-1-4795-3806-5(X)) Picture Window Bks.

—Jungle Animals. Doherty, Paula, illus. 2009. (Little Big Flap Bks.). 10p. (J). (gr. -1-k). 9.99 (978-1-934650-22-6(6)) Just For Kids Pr., LLC.

—Let It Snow. Jones, Anna, illus. 2013. (Charles Reasoner Holiday Bks.). (ENG.). 10p. (gr. -1 — 1). bds. 9.99 (978-1-4048-8147-1(6)) Picture Window Bks.

—Little Bo Peep, 1 vol. Le Ray, Marina, illus. 2014. (Charles Reasoner Nursery Rhymes Ser.). (ENG.). 10p. (gr. -1 — 1). bds. 4.99 (978-1-4795-3804-1(3)) Picture Window Bks.

—Ooink! 2009. (Lift & Learn Ser.). (Illus.). 10p. (J). (gr. -1-k). 10.99 (978-1-934650-12-7(9)) Just For Kids Pr., LLC.

—Peek-a-Boo Fairies. Le Ray, Marina, illus. 2013. (Charles Reasoner Peek-A-Boo Bks.). (ENG.). 10p. (gr. -1 — 1). bds. 9.99 (978-1-4795-2173-9(6)) Picture Window Bks.

—Peek-A-Boo Ghosts. Le Ray, Marina & Jones, Anna, illus. 2013. (Charles Reasoner Peek-A-Boo Bks.). (ENG.). 10p. (gr. -1 — 1). bds. 9.99 (978-1-4795-2359-7(3)); bds. 4.99 (978-1-4795-2360-3(7)) Picture Window Bks.

—Pumpkin Shapes. 2015. (Charles Reasoner Halloween Bks.). (ENG., Illus.). 12p. (gr. -1 — 1). bds. 5.99 (978-1-4795-8499-4(1)) Picture Window Bks.

—Twinkle, Twinkle, Little Star, 1 vol. Le Ray, Marina, illus. 2013. (Charles Reasoner Nursery Rhymes Ser.). (ENG.). 10p. (gr. -1 — 1). bds. 4.99 (978-1-4795-1693-3(7)) Picture Window Bks.

—Whooo? 2009. (Lift & Learn Ser.). (Illus.). 10p. (J). (gr. -1-k). 10.99 (978-1-934650-11-0(0)) Just For Kids Pr., LLC.

—Winter Friends, 1 vol. Reasoner, Charles & Jones, Anna, illus. 2013. (Charles Reasoner Holiday Bks.). (ENG.). 10p. (gr. -1 — 1). bds. 4.99 (978-1-4048-8156-3(5)) Picture Window Bks.

—The 3 Blind Mice Inside the Spooky Scary & Creepy Haunted House. Reasoner, Charles, illus. 2007. (Story Book Ser.). (Illus.). 10p. (J). (gr. -1-3). bds. (978-1-84666-381-9(4), Tide Mill Pr.) Top That! Publishing PLC.

Reasoner, Charles, illus. Bear Hugs. 2015. (J). (978-1-4795-5944-2(X)) Picture Window Bks.

—Honey Bunny. 2015. (J). (978-1-4795-5945-9(8)) Picture Window Bks.

—Peep! Peep! 2015. (J). (978-1-4795-5943-5(1)) Picture Window Bks.

—Puppy Love. 2015. (J). (978-1-4795-5946-6(6)) Picture Window Bks.

Reasoner, Charles & Wood, Hannah. Peek-A-Boo Reindeer, 1 vol. Reasoner, Charles, illus. 2014. (Charles Reasoner Peek-A-Boo Bks.). (ENG., Illus.). 10p. (gr. -1 — 1). bds. 12.99 (978-1-4795-5179-8(1)) Picture Window Bks.

—Peek-A-Boo Snowman, 1 vol. Reasoner, Charles, illus. 2014. (Charles Reasoner Peek-A-Boo Bks.). (ENG., Illus.). 10p. (gr. -1 — 1). bds. 12.99 (978-1-4795-5181-1(3)) Picture Window Bks.

Reasoner, Charles & Wood, Steven. Little Monster. 2015. (Charles Reasoner Halloween Bks.). (ENG., Illus.). 12p. (gr. -1 — 1). bds. 5.99 (978-1-4795-8502-1(5)) Picture Window Bks.

—Owl's Halloween. 2015. (Charles Reasoner Halloween Bks.). (ENG., Illus.). 12p. (gr. -1 — 1). bds. 5.99 (978-1-4795-8500-7(9)) Picture Window Bks.

—Scaredy Cat. 2015. (Charles Reasoner Halloween Bks.). (ENG., Illus.). 12p. (gr. -1 — 1). bds. 5.99 (978-1-4795-8501-4(7)) Picture Window Bks.

Redenbaugh, Vicki. Skar's Picnic ... A Bear's Tale. Redenbaugh, Vicki, illus. 2005. (Illus.). (J). 14.95 (978-1-59091-034-4(6)) Eastern National.

Reed, Jonathan. Christmas Surprise. Hale, Jenny, illus. 2011. (ENG.). 16p. (J). (gr. -1-k). 14.99 (978-1-921714-88-7(3)) Little Hare Bks. AUS. Dist: Independent Pubs. Group.

Reed, Jonathan & Hale, Jenny. Christmas Surprise. 2007. (Illus.). 16p. (978-1-921049-59-0(6)) Little Hare Bks. AUS. Dist: HarperCollins Pubs. Australia.

Reeve, Tim. Action Robots: A Pop-up Book Showing How They Work. MacLeod, Gavin, illus. 2004. 14p. (YA). (gr. 4-10). reprint ed. 17.00 (978-0-7567-7284-0(2)) DIANE Publishing Co.

Regan, Patricia, illus. Musical Christmas Tree. 2017. (ENG.). 16p. (J). (gr. -1-1). bds. 10.99 **(978-0-7641-6899-4(1))** Barron's Educational Series, Inc.

Regan, Patrick. The Nutcracker. Kuricheva, Natasha, illus. 2016. (ENG.). 26p. (J). bds. 9.99 (978-1-4494-5586-6(7)) Andrews McMeel Publishing.

Reich, Kass. Hooray for Hamsters! A Two-Book Set, 2 vols. 2015. (ENG.). 48p. (J). (gr. -1-k). bds. 15.95 (978-1-4598-1100-3(3)) Orca Bk. Pubs. USA.

Reid, Camilla. Lulu & the Noisy Baby. Busby, Ailie, illus. 2016. (Lulu Ser.). (ENG.). 20p. (J). (gr. -1-k). 12.99 (978-1-4088-2818-2(9), 9781408828182, Bloomsbury USA Childrens) Bloomsbury Publishing USA.

—Lulu Loves Colours. Busby, Ailie, illus. 2015. (ENG.). 12p. (J). (gr. -1-k). bds. 8.99 (978-1-4088-4964-4(X), 9781408849644, Bloomsbury USA Childrens) Bloomsbury Publishing USA.

—Lulu Loves Noises. Busby, Ailie, illus. 2015. (ENG.). 12p. (J). (gr. -1-k). bds. 8.99 (978-1-4088-4963-7(1), 9781408849637, Bloomsbury USA Childrens) Bloomsbury Publishing USA.

—Lulu Loves Numbers. Busby, Ailie, illus. 2015. (ENG.). 12p. (J). (gr. -1-1). bds. 8.99 (978-1-4088-4957-6(7), 9781408849576, Bloomsbury USA Childrens) Bloomsbury Publishing USA.

—Lulu Loves Shapes. Busby, Ailie, illus. 2015. (ENG.). 12p. (J). (gr. -1-1). bds. 8.99 (978-1-4088-4958-3(5), 9781408849583, Bloomsbury USA Childrens) Bloomsbury Publishing USA.

Reid, Hunter. Beach Day! Hinton, Stephanie, illus. 2016. (Fluorescent Pop! Ser.). (ENG.). 14p. (J). (gr. -1-k). bds. 5.99 (978-1-4998-0219-1(6)) Little Bee Books Inc.

—Let's Have a Picnic! Hinton, Stephanie, illus. 2016. (Fluorescent Pop! Ser.). (ENG.). 14p. (J). (gr. -1-k). bds. 5.99 (978-1-4998-0220-7(X)) Little Bee Books Inc.

Reid, Stephanie. My Body, 1 vol. 2011. (Early Childhood Themes Ser.). (ENG.). 16p. (J). (gr. -1-2). pap. 19.99 (978-1-4333-2368-3(0)) Teacher Created Materials, Inc.

—My Country, 1 vol. 2011. (Early Childhood Themes Ser.). (ENG.). 16p. (J). (gr. -1-2). pap. 19.99 (978-1-4333-2361-4(3)) Teacher Created Materials, Inc.

—School, 1 vol. 2011. (Early Childhood Themes Ser.). (ENG.). 16p. (J). (gr. -1-2). pap. 19.99 (978-1-4333-2354-6(0)) Teacher Created Materials, Inc.

Reinhart, Matthew. The Ark: A Pop-up Book. Reinhart, Matthew, illus. 2006. (Illus.). 12p. (J). (gr. k-4). reprint ed. 17.00 (978-1-4223-5673-9(6)) DIANE Publishing Co.

—Cinderella: A Pop-Up Fairy Tale. Reinhart, Matthew, illus. 2005. (ENG., Illus.). 12p. (J). (gr. -1-3). 34.99 (978-1-4169-0501-1(4), Little Simon) Little Simon.

—Frozen. Reinhart, Matthew, illus. 2016. (ENG., Illus.). 12p. (YA). (gr. 7-12). 40.00 (978-1-4847-3780-4(6), Disney Editions) Disney Pr.

—Frozen Frozen Pop-Up. Reinhart, Matthew, illus. ltd. ed. 2016. (ENG., Illus.). 12p. (YA). (gr. 7-12). 250.00 (978-1-4847-9837-9(6), Disney Editions) Disney Pr.

—The Jungle Book: A Pop-Up Adventure. Reinhart, Matthew, illus. 2006. (ENG., Illus.). 12p. (J). 34.99 (978-1-4169-1824-0(8), Little Simon) Little Simon.

—LEGO Pop-Up. 2016. (ENG., Illus.). 10p. (J). (gr. 2-5). 29.99 (978-0-545-88104-3(8)) Scholastic, Inc.

—Marvel's the Avengers - Age of Ultron: A Pop-Up Book. Reinhart, Matthew, illus. 2015. (ENG., Illus.). 10p. (J). (gr. 1-17). 14.99 (978-0-316-34086-1(3)) Little, Brown Bks. for Young Readers.

—My Little Pony: the Castles of Equestria: An Enchanted My Little Pony Pop-Up Book. 2015. (ENG., Illus.). 10p. (J). (gr. 1-17). 24.99 (978-0-316-18832-6(8)) Little, Brown Bks. for Young Readers.

—A Pop-Up Book of Nursery Rhymes. Reinhart, Matthew, illus. 2009. (ENG., Illus.). 12p. (J). (gr. -1-3). 29.99 (978-1-4169-1825-7(6), Little Simon) Little Simon.

Reinhart, Matthew & Lucasfilm Ltd. Staff. A Galactic Pop-Up Adventure. 2012. (Star Wars Ser.). (ENG.). 5p. (J). (gr. 2-5). 36.99 (978-0-545-17616-3(6), Orchard Bks.) Scholastic, Inc.

Reinhart, Matthew & Sabuda, Robert. Dragons & Monsters. Reinhart, Matthew & Sabuda, Robert, illus. 2011. (Encyclopedia Mythologica Ser.). (ENG., Illus.). 12p. (J). (gr. k-4). 250.00 (978-0-7636-3476-6(X)) Candlewick Pr.

—Encyclopedia Prehistorica Dinosaurs. Reinhart, Matthew & Sabuda, Robert, illus. 2005. (Encyclopedia Prehistorica Ser.: 1). (ENG., Illus.). 12p. (J). (gr. k-4). 34.99 (978-0-7636-2228-2(1)) Candlewick Pr.

—Gods & Heroes. Reinhart, Matthew & Sabuda, Robert, illus. 2010. (Encyclopedia Mythologica Ser.: 2). (ENG., Illus.). 12p. (J). (gr. k-4). 29.99 (978-0-7636-3171-0(X)) Candlewick Pr.

Reisch, J. A. Mi Primera Biblia. Rimmington, Natasha, illus. 2016. (SPA.). (J). (978-1-5064-2103-2(2)) Augsburg Fortress, Pubs.

Rescek, Sanja. Buggy Buddies Fairy Moonbeam. Rescek, Sanja, illus. 2015. (Buggy Buddies Ser.). (ENG., Illus.). 8p. (J). (-k). bds. 8.99 (978-1-4472-7614-2(0)) Pan Macmillan GBR. Dist: Independent Pubs. Group.

—Buggy Buddies Fairy Sunshine. Rescek, Sanja, illus. 2015. (Buggy Buddies Ser.). (ENG., Illus.). 8p. (J). (-k). bds. 8.99 (978-1-4472-7612-8(4)) Pan Macmillan GBR. Dist: Independent Pubs. Group.

Rescek, Sanja, illus. A Bedtime Prayer. 2013. (ENG.). 24p. (gr. -1). bds. 8.95 (978-1-58925-606-4(9)) Tiger Tales.

Rescue Vehicles. (Illus.). 24p. (J). 1.99 (978-1-59445-057-0(9)) Dogs in Hats Children's Publishing Co.

Rescue Vehicles. (Radical Rides Ser.). 16p. (J). (978-2-7643-0014-5(X)) Phidal Publishing, Inc./Editions Phidal, Inc.

Rettore. Elephant & Friends. 2014. (Friends Cloth Bks.). (ENG.). 8p. (J). (gr. -1 — 1). 9.99 (978-1-4380-0527-0(X)) Barron's Educational Series, Inc.

—Giraffe & Friends. 2014. (Friends Cloth Bks.). (ENG.). 8p. (J). (gr. -1 — 1). 9.99 (978-1-4380-0528-7(8)) Barron's Educational Series, Inc.

Rey, H. A. Awake-Asleep Cloth Book & Door Hanger. 2010. (Curious Baby Curious George Ser.). (ENG., Illus.). 4p. (J). (gr. -1 — 1). 8.99 (978-0-547-23897-5(5)) Houghton Mifflin Harcourt Publishing Co.

—Curious about Christmas. 2011. (Curious Baby Curious George Ser.). (ENG., Illus.). 12p. (J). (gr. k — 1). bds. 8.99 (978-0-547-58841-4(0)) Houghton Mifflin Harcourt Publishing Co.

—Curious George Neighborhood Friends. 2010. (Curious George Ser.). (ENG., Illus.). 12p. (J). (gr. -1 — 1). bds. 6.99 (978-0-547-23875-3(4)) Houghton Mifflin Harcourt Publishing Co.

—Curious George Parade Day. 2011. (Curious George Ser.). (ENG., Illus.). 14p. (J). (gr. -1 — 1). bds. 7.99 (978-0-547-47282-9(X)) Houghton Mifflin Harcourt Publishing Co.

—Curious George's Fire Truck. 2014. (Curious George Ser.). (ENG., Illus.). 12p. (J). (— 1). bds. 8.99 (978-0-544-14709-6(X), HMH Books For Young Readers) Houghton Mifflin Harcourt Publishing Co.

—Curious George's Train (mini Movers Shaped Board Books) 2014. (Curious George Ser.). (ENG., Illus.). 12p. (J). (— 1). bds. 8.99 (978-0-544-32074-1(3), HMH Books For Young Readers) Houghton Mifflin Harcourt Publishing Co.

—Day at the Farm. 2017. (Curious George Ser.). (ENG., Illus.). 16p. (J). (— 1). bds. 8.99 **(978-0-544-98874-3(4)**, HMH Books For Young Readers) Houghton Mifflin Harcourt Publishing Co.

—Happy Halloween. 2008. (Curious George Ser.). (ENG., Illus.). 14p. (J). (gr. -1 — 1). bds. 7.99 (978-0-618-91952-9(X)) Houghton Mifflin Harcourt Publishing Co.

—Happy St. Patrick's Day. 2014. (Curious George Ser.). (ENG., Illus.). 14p. (J). (— 1). bds. 7.99 (978-0-544-08888-7(3)) Houghton Mifflin Harcourt Publishing Co.

—Happy Thanksgiving. 2010. (Curious George Ser.). (ENG., Illus.). 14p. (J). (gr. -1 — 1). bds. 7.99 (978-0-547-13106-1(2)) Houghton Mifflin Harcourt Publishing Co.

—Happy Valentine's Day. Young, Mary O'Keefe, illus. 2011. (Curious George Ser.). (ENG.). 14p. (J). (gr. -1-3). 8.99 (978-0-547-13107-8(0)) Houghton Mifflin Harcourt Publishing Co.

—Music Play. 2009. (Curious Baby Curious George Ser.). (ENG., Illus.). 10p. (J). (gr. -1 — 1). bds. 8.99 (978-0-547-23876-0(2)) Houghton Mifflin Harcourt Publishing Co.

—My Curious World. 2009. (Curious Baby Curious George Ser.). (ENG., Illus.). 10p. (J). (gr. -1 — 1). 14.99 (978-0-547-21520-4(7)) Houghton Mifflin Harcourt Publishing Co.

—My Favorite Things. 2011. (Curious Baby Curious George Ser.). (ENG., Illus.). 14p. (J). (gr. -1 — 1). bds. 8.99 (978-0-547-42893-2(6)) Houghton Mifflin Harcourt Publishing Co.

—My First Words at the Farm, Set. gif. ed. 2010. (Curious Baby Curious George Ser.). (ENG., Illus.). 12p. (J). (gr. k — 1). 14.99 (978-0-547-24306-1(5)) Houghton Mifflin Harcourt Publishing Co.

—My Little Boat. 2009. (Curious Baby Curious George Ser.). (ENG., Illus.). 8p. (J). (gr. -1 — 1). 12.99 (978-0-547-21541-9(X)) Houghton Mifflin Harcourt Publishing Co.

—On the Go! 2011. (Curious George Ser.). (ENG., Illus.). 10p. (J). (gr. -1 — 1). bds. 6.99 (978-0-547-55151-7(7)) Houghton Mifflin Harcourt Publishing Co.

Rey, H. A. & Houghton Mifflin Company Staff. Bigger & Smaller. 2007. (Curious George Ser.). (ENG., Illus.). 12p. (J). (gr. -1 — 1). bds. 6.99 (978-0-618-73760-4(X)) Houghton Mifflin Harcourt Publishing Co.

Rey, H. A. & Rey, Margret. Before & After. 2007. (Curious George Ser.). (ENG., Illus.). 12p. (J). (gr. -1 — 1). bds. 6.99 (978-0-618-72399-7(4)) Houghton Mifflin Harcourt Publishing Co.

—Curious Baby My Growing World. 2011. (Curious Baby Curious George Ser.). (ENG., Illus.). 14p. (J). (gr. k — 1). bds. 9.99 (978-0-547-27939-8(6)) Houghton Mifflin Harcourt Publishing Co.

—Curious George Hide-and-Seek. 2008. (Curious George Ser.). (ENG., Illus.). 10p. (J). (gr. -1 — 1). bds. 6.99 (978-0-618-89199-3(4)) Houghton Mifflin Harcourt Publishing Co.

—My First Words at the Zoo, Set. gif. ed. 2010. (Curious Baby Curious George Ser.). (ENG., Illus.). 12p. (J). (gr. -1 — 1). 14.99 (978-0-618-99953-8(1)) Houghton Mifflin Harcourt Publishing Co.

—Seasons. 2008. (Curious George Ser.). (ENG., Illus.). 10p. (J). (gr. -1 — 1). bds. 6.99 (978-0-618-99848-7(9)) Houghton Mifflin Harcourt Publishing Co.

Rey, H. A. & Young, Mary OKeefe. Ready for School. 2017. (Curious George Ser.). (ENG., Illus.). 14p. (J). (— 1). bds. 7.99 (978-0-544-93120-6(3), HMH Books For Young Readers) Houghton Mifflin Harcourt Publishing Co.

Rey, H. A., et al. Curious George Discovery Day. 2007. (Curious George Ser.). (ENG., Illus.). 14p. (J). (gr. k — 1). bds. 13.95 (978-0-618-73761-1(8)) Houghton Mifflin Harcourt Publishing Co.

—Curious George the Movie. movie tie-in ed. 2006. (Curious George Ser.). (ENG., Illus.). 10p. (J). (gr. -1 — 1). bds. 6.99 (978-0-618-60587-3(8)) Houghton Mifflin Harcourt Publishing Co.

Reynolds, Alison. Let's Grow a Garden. Hopgood, Andrew, illus. 2009. (Save Our Planet! Ser.). 12p. (J). (gr. -1-3). bds. 11.40 (978-1-60754-412-8(1)) Windmill Bks.

—Let's Save Water. Hopgood, Andrew, illus. 2009. (Save Our Planet! Ser.). 12p. (J). (gr. -1-3). bds. 11.40 (978-1-60754-413-5(X)) Windmill Bks.

—Let's Turn It Off. Hopgood, Andrew, illus. 2009. (Save Our Planet! Ser.). 12p. (J). (gr. -1-3). bds. 11.40 (978-1-60754-414-2(8)) Windmill Bks.

—Let's Use It Again. Hopgood, Andrew, illus. 2009. (Save Our Planet! Ser.). 12p. (J). (gr. -1-3). bds. 11.40 (978-1-60754-415-9(6)) Windmill Bks.

RH Disney. Gus Loves Cinderella (Disney Princess) RH Disney, illus. 2016. (Padded Board Book Ser.). (ENG., Illus.). 26p. (J). (gr. -1-1). bds. 9.99 (978-0-7364-3706-6(1), RH/Disney) Random Hse. Children's Bks.

—Hello, Dory! RH Disney, illus. 2016. (Tabbed Board Book Ser.). (ENG., Illus.). 16p. (J). (— 1). bds. 7.99 (978-0-7364-3625-0(1), RH/Disney) Random Hse. Children's Bks.

—An Ocean Adventure. RH Disney, illus. 2016. (Magnetic Play Book Ser.). (ENG., Illus.). 8p. (J). (-k). bds. 9.99

(978-0-7364-3626-7(X), Random Hse. Bks. for Young Readers) Random Hse. Children's Bks.

RH Disney Staff. Olaf's 1-2-3. RH Disney Staff, illus. 2013. (Glitter Board Book Ser.). (ENG., Illus.). 12p. (J). (— 1). bds. 6.99 *(978-0-7364-3064-7(4)*, Golden/Disney) Random Hse. Children's Bks.

Rice, Dona. What Kind of Weather?, 1 vol. 2009. (Early Childhood Themes Ser.). (ENG., Illus.). 16p. (J). (gr. -1-2). pap. 19.99 *(978-1-4333-1459-9(2))* Shell Educational Publishing.

Rice, Dona Herweck. American Through & Through Lap Book, 1 vol. 2011. (Early Childhood Themes Ser.). (ENG.). 16p. (J). (gr. -1-2). pap. 19.99 *(978-1-4333-2363-8(X))* Teacher Created Materials, Inc.

—Big Kid School, 1 vol. 2011. (Early Childhood Themes Ser.). (ENG.). 16p. (J). (gr. -1-2). pap. 19.99 *(978-1-4333-2356-0(7))* Teacher Created Materials, Inc.

—Delicious & Nutritious, 1 vol. 2011. (Early Childhood Themes Ser.). (ENG.). 16p. (J). (gr. -1-2). pap. 19.99 *(978-1-4333-2370-6(2))* Teacher Created Materials, Inc.

Richards, Mark, et al. Tractors. 2009. (Carry-Me Ser.). (ENG., Illus.). 12p. (gr. -1-k). 7.99 *(978-1-84610-868-6(3))* Make Believe Ideas GBR. Dist: Nelson, Thomas Inc.

Richmond, Marianne. Friendly Floppy Fishie, What Do Wish For? 2009. (Beginner Boards Ser.). (ENG., Illus.). 14p. (gr. -1-k). bds. 7.95 *(978-1-934082-52-2(X)*, Marianne Richmond Studios, Inc.) Sourcebooks, Inc.

—Grandma Loves Me! 2nd ed. 2015. (Marianne Richmond Ser.: 0). (ENG., Illus.). 24p. (J). (-2). bds. 7.99 *(978-1-4926-2295-6(8)*, Sourcebooks Jabberwocky) Sourcebooks, Inc.

—Grandpa Loves Me! 2nd ed. 2015. (Marianne Richmond Ser.: 0). (ENG., Illus.). 24p. (J). (-2). bds. 7.99 *(978-1-4926-2298-7(2)*, Sourcebooks Jabberwocky) Sourcebooks, Inc.

—The Night Night Book. Richmond, Marianne, illus. 2011. (Marianne Richmond Ser.: 0). (ENG., Illus.). 24p. (J). (gr. -1-3). bds. 7.95 *(978-1-934082-90-4(2)*, Sourcebooks Jabberwocky) Sourcebooks, Inc.

—Si Pudiera Conservarte Pequeño... 2014. (SPA & ENG., Illus.). 24p. (J). bds. 6.99 *(978-1-4926-0369-6(4)*, Sourcebooks Jabberwocky) Sourcebooks, Inc.

Richter, Bernd & Richter, Susan. Listen to Alaskas Animals. Richter, Bernd, illus. (Illus.). 12p. 2006. (J). act. bk. ed. 12.95 *(978-1-931353-25-0(5))* 2003. bds. 12.95 *(978-1-931353-12-0(3))* Saddle Pal Creations, Inc.

Riegelman, Rianna & Accord Publishing Staff. Safari: A Build & Play Story. Chandler, Shannon, illus. 2012. (ENG.). 10p. (J). (gr. -1-1). bds. 15.99 *(978-1-4494-2191-5(1))* Andrews McMeel Publishing.

Rigaud, Louis & Boisrobert, Anouck. That's My Hat! 2016. (ENG., Illus.). 26p. (J). (gr. -1-1). 24.95 *(978-0-500-65057-8(8)*, 565057) Thames & Hudson.

Riggs, Kate. Colors of Nature. Domeniconi, Paolo, illus. 2017. (ENG.). 14p. (J). (gr. -1 — 1). bds. 8.99 *(978-1-56846-299-8(9)*, Creative Education) Creative Co., The.

—Counting on Birds. Van der Linde, Jori, illus. 2017. (ENG.). 14p. (J). (gr. -1 — 1). bds. 8.99 *(978-1-56846-300-1(6)*, Creative Education) Creative Co., The.

—Crowds of Creatures. Dogi, Fiammetta, illus. 2017. (ENG.). 14p. (J). (gr. -1 — 1). bds. 7.99 *(978-1-56846-301-8(4)*, Creative Education) Creative Co., The.

—Under the Sea. Leonard, Tom, illus. 2017. (ENG.). 14p. (J). (gr. -1 — 1). bds. 7.99 *(978-1-56846-302-5(2)*, Creative Editions) Creative Co., The.

Rights, Lenz-Mulligan, et al. Little Ladybug. 2005. (Little Finger Puppet Board Bks.: FING). (ENG., Illus.). 12p. (J). (gr. -1 — 1). bds. 6.99 *(978-0-8118-4848-0(5))* Chronicle Bks. LLC.

Rigo, L. Little Cow. 2011. (Look at Me Bks.). (ENG., Illus.). 10p. (J). bds. 7.99 *(978-0-7641-6446-0(5))* Barron's Educational Series, Inc.

—Little Kitten. 2012. (Look at Me Bks.). (ENG., Illus.). 10p. (J). bds. 7.99 *(978-0-7641-6523-8(2))* Barron's Educational Series, Inc.

—Little Lion. 2012. (Look at Me Bks.). (ENG., Illus.). 10p. (J). bds. 7.99 *(978-0-7641-6525-2(9))* Barron's Educational Series, Inc.

—Little Owl. 2011. (Look at Me Bks.). (ENG., Illus.). 10p. (J). bds. 8.99 *(978-0-7641-6447-7(3))* Barron's Educational Series, Inc.

—Little Penguin. Rigo, L., illus. 2014. (Mini Look at Me Bks.). (ENG., Illus.). 10p. (J). (gr. -1 — 1). bds. 4.99 *(978-0-7641-6731-7(6))* Barron's Educational Series, Inc.

—Little Pony. 2011. (Look at Me Bks.). (ENG., Illus.). 10p. (J). bds. 8.99 *(978-0-7641-6448-4(1))* Barron's Educational Series, Inc.

—Little Reindeer. 2011. (Look at Me Bks.). (ENG., Illus.). 10p. (J). bds. 7.99 *(978-0-7641-6450-7(3))* Barron's Educational Series, Inc.

Rigo, L., illus. Little Bunny. 2012. (Mini Look at Me Bks.). (ENG.). 10p. (J). bds. 4.99 *(978-0-7641-6509-2(7))* Barron's Educational Series, Inc.

—Little Dinosaur. 2010. (Look at Me Bks.). (ENG.). 10p. (J). (gr. -1-k). bds. 8.99 *(978-0-7641-6356-2(6))* Barron's Educational Series, Inc.

—Little Duckling. (Mini Look at Me Bks.). 10p. (J). 2012. (ENG.). bds. 4.99 *(978-0-7641-6510-8(0))* 2011. bds. 7.99 *(978-0-7641-6425-5(2))* Barron's Educational Series, Inc.

—Little Elephant. 2011. (Look at Me Bks.). 10p. (J). bds. 8.99 *(978-0-7641-6426-2(0))* Barron's Educational Series, Inc.

—Little Lamb. (Mini Look at Me Bks.). 10p. (J). 2012. (ENG.). bds. 4.99 *(978-0-7641-6511-5(9))* 2011. (gr. -1). bds. 7.99 *(978-0-7641-6427-9(9))* Barron's Educational Series, Inc.

—Little Monkey. 2011. (Look at Me Bks.). 10p. (J). bds. 7.99 *(978-0-7641-6428-6(7))* Barron's Educational Series, Inc.

—Little Panda. 2010. (Look at Me Bks.). (ENG.). 10p. (J). (gr. -1-k). 8.99 *(978-0-7641-6339-5(6))* Barron's Educational Series, Inc.

—Little Panda Bear. 2014. (Mini Look at Me Bks.). (ENG.). 10p. (J). (gr. -1 — 1). bds. 4.99 *(978-0-7641-6739-3(1))* Barron's Educational Series, Inc.

—Little Penguin. 2010. (Look at Me Bks.). (ENG.). 10p. (J). (gr. -1-k). bds. 8.99 *(978-0-7641-6353-1(1))* Barron's Educational Series, Inc.

—Little Pig. 2010. (Look at Me Bks.). (ENG.). 10p. (J). (gr. -1-k). bds. 7.99 *(978-0-7641-6355-5(8))* Barron's Educational Series, Inc.

—Little Polar Bear. 2010. (Look at Me Bks.). (ENG.). 10p. (J). (gr. -1-k). bds. 8.99 *(978-0-7641-6325-8(6))* Barron's Educational Series, Inc.

—Little Pony. 2014. (Mini Look at Me Bks.). (ENG.). 10p. (J). (gr. -1 — 1). bds. 4.99 *(978-0-7641-6733-1(2))* Barron's Educational Series, Inc.

—Little Puppy. 2012. (Mini Look at Me Bks.). (ENG.). 10p. (J). bds. 4.99 *(978-0-7641-6512-2(7))* Barron's Educational Series, Inc.

Rigo, L. & Caviezel, Giovanni, illus. Little Bunny. 2010. (Look at Me Bks.). (ENG.). 10p. (J). (gr. -1-k). bds. 7.99 *(978-0-7641-6322-7(1))* Barron's Educational Series, Inc.

—Little Puppy. 2010. (Look at Me Bks.). (ENG.). 10p. (J). (gr. -1-k). bds. 8.99 *(978-0-7641-6324-1(8))* Barron's Educational Series, Inc.

—Little Tiger. 2010. (Look at Me Bks.). (ENG.). 10p. (J). (gr. -1-k). bds. 8.99 *(978-0-7641-6326-5(4))* Barron's Educational Series, Inc.

Rigo, L. & Pagnoni, Roberta, illus. Little Elf. 2010. (ENG.). 10p. (J). (gr. -1-2). bds. 7.99 *(978-0-7641-6380-7(9))* Barron's Educational Series, Inc.

Rigo, Laura, illus. Little Chimp. 2017. (Mini Look at Me Bks.). (ENG.). 10p. (J). (gr. -1 — 1). bds. 4.99 *(978-0-7641-6878-9(9))* Barron's Educational Series, Inc.

—Little Elephant. 2017. (Mini Look at Me Bks.). (ENG.). 10p. (J). (gr. -1 — 1). bds. 4.99 *(978-0-7641-6879-6(7))* Barron's Educational Series, Inc.

—Little Polar Bear. 2017. (Mini Look at Me Bks.). (ENG.). 10p. (J). (gr. -1 — 1). bds. 4.99 *(978-0-7641-6880-2(0))* Barron's Educational Series, Inc.

—Little Tiger. 2017. (Mini Look at Me Bks.). (ENG.). 10p. (J). (gr. -1 — 1). bds. 4.99 *(978-0-7641-6881-9(9))* Barron's Educational Series, Inc.

Riley, Cooper. Absolutely Awesome Island Animals. 2009. 24p. pap. 9.95 *(978-0-9740582-4-5(6))* Tiki Tales.

Riley, Kellee, illus. Happy Halloween, Kai-lan! A Lift-the-Flap Story. 2010. (Ni Hao, Kai-Lan Ser.). (ENG.). 16p. (J). pap. 6.99 *(978-1-4424-0178-5(8)*, Simon Spotlight/Nickelodeon) Simon Spotlight/Nickelodeon.

Rimmington, Natasha, illus. The Wolf & the Seven Little Kids. 2014. (Flip-Up Fairy Tales Ser.). (ENG.). 24p. (J). *(978-1-84643-656-7(7))* Child's Play International Ltd.

Rinaldo, Luana. Beep Beep Stories. 2016. (ENG., Illus.). 12p. (J). bds. 12.99 ***(978-1-5098-0899-1(X))*** Pan Macmillan GBR. Dist: Independent Pubs. Group.

—Farm Stories. 2016. (ENG., Illus.). 12p. (J). bds. 12.99 ***(978-1-5098-0900-4(7))*** Pan Macmillan GBR. Dist: Independent Pubs. Group.

Rinaldo, Luana & Prasadam-halls, Smriti. Who Am I? This Is My Mouth. 2012. (ENG., Illus.). 12p. (J). (gr. -1-k). 7.99 *(978-1-4083-1509-5(2))* Hodder & Stoughton GBR. Dist: Hachette Bk. Group.

—Who Am I? This Is My Tail. 2012. (ENG., Illus.). 12p. (J). (gr. -1-k). 7.99 *(978-1-4083-1510-1(6))* Hodder & Stoughton GBR. Dist: Hachette Bk. Group.

Ring, Susan. Body: An Interactive & 3-D Exploration. Graham, Michele, illus. 2008. (ENG.). 20p. (J). (gr. 2). 19.95 *(978-1-58117-801-2(8)*, Intervisual/Piggy Toes) Bendon, Inc.

—On the Farm. Melmon, Deborah, illus. 2008. (ENG.). 10p. (J). (gr. 3-17). 12.99 *(978-1-58476-729-9(4))* Innovative Kids.

Rinkel, Ken, illus. Giant Machines. 2003. 12p. (J). (gr. k-3). 20.00 *(978-0-7567-6653-5(2))* DIANE Publishing Co.

Rinker, Sherri Duskey. Goodnight, Goodnight, Construction Site: Let's Go! Lichtenheld, Tom, illus. 2017. (ENG.). 10p. (J). (gr. -1 — 1). bds. 8.99 ***(978-1-4521-6476-2(2))*** Chronicle Bks. LLC.

Ripley's Believe It Or Not! Staff, compiled by. Oddphabet. 2017. (Little Bks.: 2). (ENG.). 26p. (J). bds. 6.99 *(978-1-60991-170-6(9))* Ripley Entertainment, Inc.

—Wacky 1, 2, 3: Ripley's Believe It or Not! 2017. (Little Bks.: 1). (ENG.). 26p. (J). bds. 6.99 *(978-1-60991-181-2(4))* Ripley Entertainment, Inc.

Rissman, Rebecca. A Cat's Day, 1 vol. Moor, Becka, illus. 2014. (ENG.). 32p. (gr. 1-2). 26.65 *(978-1-4846-0396-3(6))* Heinemann-Raintree.

Ristuccia, Christine & Ristuccia, James. The Entire World of WH? Questions. 2004. (J). 39.99 *(978-0-9723457-9-8(5))* Say It Right.

—The Entire World of WH? Questions Flip Book. 2004. (Illus.). 9p. (J). spiral bd. 14.99 *(978-0-9723457-8-1(7))* Say It Right.

Ritchie, Alison. The Tortoise & the Hare. Noj, Nahta, illus. 2015. (ENG.). 32p. (J). (-k). 15.99 *(978-0-7636-7601-8(2)*, Templar) Candlewick Pr.

Ritchie, Joseph R. Baby Looney Tunes Visit a Haunted House. Halverson, Lydia, illus. 2005. (Baby Looney Tunes Ser.). 14p. (J). (gr. -1-3). bds. 9.95 *(978-0-8249-6609-6(0)*, Ideal Pubns.) Worthy Publishing.

—Peek-a-Boo! Halverson, Lydia, illus. 2004. (ENG.). 14p. (J). bds. 7.95 *(978-0-8249-6550-1(7)*, Ideal Pubns.) Worthy Publishing.

—Peter Cottontail's Busy Day. Halverson, Lydia, illus. (J). 2009. 14p. (gr. -1-k). bds. 6.99 *(978-0-8249-1842-2(8))* 2006. (ENG.). 26p. (gr. -1-k). 12.95 *(978-0-8249-6652-2(X))* 2005. (ENG.). 16p. bds. 9.95 *(978-0-8249-6571-6(X))* Worthy Publishing. (Ideal Pubns.).

—Peter Cottontail's Easter Egg Hunt. Thornburgh, Rebecca McKillip, illus. 2004. (ENG.). 12p. (J). (gr. -1-k). bds. 9.95 *(978-0-8249-6522-8(1)*, Ideal Pubns.) Worthy Publishing.

—Peter Cottontail's Easter Surprise. Halverson, Lydia, illus. 2006. (ENG.). 18p. (J). (gr. -1-k). bds. 9.95 *(978-0-8249-6627-0(9)*, Ideal Pubns.) Worthy Publishing.

—Peter Cottontaol's Easter Egg Hunt. Thornburgh, Rebecca, illus. 2006. (ENG.). 26p. (J). (gr. -1-k). 12.95 *(978-0-8249-6653-9(8)*, Ideal Pubns.) Worthy Publishing.

—Where's Santa? Halverson, Lydia, illus. 2006. (ENG.). 14p. (J). (gr. -1-k). bds. 7.95 *(978-0-8249-6673-7(2)*, Ideal Pubns.) Worthy Publishing.

Rivers-Moore, Debbie. Five Christmas Reindeer. Everitt-Stewart, Andrew, illus. 2015. (ENG.). 10p. (J). (gr. -1 — 1). bds. 8.99 *(978-1-4998-0169-9(6))* Little Bee Books Inc.

—Five Little Snowmen. Everitt-Stewart, Andrew, illus. 2015. (ENG.). 10p. (J). (gr. -1 — 1). bds. 8.99 *(978-1-4998-0170-5(X))* Little Bee Books Inc.

—God Made the World, 1 vol. Haines, Emma, illus. 2017. 4p. 11.99 ***(978-0-8254-4520-0(5))*** Kregel Pubns.

—Lamb Loves Springtime. Fox, Lisa, illus. 2012. (Springtime Shakers Ser.). (ENG.). 8p. (J). bds. 5.99 *(978-0-7641-6487-3(2))* Barron's Educational Series, Inc.

—Let's Go - Tractor! Backhouse, Carolyn, illus. 2011. (Let's Go Bath Bks.). (ENG.). 8p. (J). (gr. -1-k). 6.99 *(978-1-4380-7117-6(5))* Barron's Educational Series, Inc.

—Little Bunny's Butterflies. Fox, Lisa, illus. 2012. (Springtime Shakers Ser.). (ENG.). 8p. (J). bds. 5.99 *(978-0-7641-6488-0(0))* Barron's Educational Series, Inc.

—Pig. Larranaga, Ana Martin, illus. 2012. (Come Out & Play Bks.). (ENG.). 10p. (J). bds. 2.99 *(978-0-7641-6519-1(4))* Barron's Educational Series, Inc.

—Pony. Larranaga, Ana Martin, illus. 2012. (Come Out & Play Bks.). (ENG.). 10p. (J). bds. 2.99 *(978-0-7641-6520-7(8))* Barron's Educational Series, Inc.

—Puppy. Larranaga, Ana Martin, illus. 2012. (Come Out & Play Bks.). (ENG.). 10p. (J). bds. 2.99 *(978-0-7641-6521-4(6))* Barron's Educational Series, Inc.

Rizzi, Kathleen. What's in My Dresser?, 1 vol. Riggs, Jenna, illus. 2013. (ENG.). 32p. (J). bds. 7.99 *(978-1-59572-165-5(7))* Star Bright Bks., Inc.

—Who Lives Here?, 1 vol. 2013. (Photoflap Board Books Ser.). (ENG., Illus.). 16p. (J). bds. 5.99 *(978-1-59572-354-3(4))* Star Bright Bks., Inc.

Robaard, Jedda. The Little Bear Who Lost Her Way. 2015. (ENG., Illus.). 10p. (J). (gr. -1-k). 7.99 *(978-1-4998-0092-0(4))* Little Bee Books Inc.

—The Little Bird Who Lost His Song. 2015. (ENG., Illus.). 10p. (J). (gr. -1-k). 7.99 *(978-1-4998-0093-7(2))* Little Bee Books Inc.

—The Little Lion Who Lost Her Roar. 2014. (Illus.). 9p. (J). *(978-1-4351-5391-2(X))* Barnes & Noble, Inc.

—The Little Mouse Who Lost Her Squeak. 2015. (ENG., Illus.). 12p. (J). (gr. -1-k). 7.99 *(978-1-4998-0002-9(9))* Little Bee Books Inc.

—The Little Zebra Who Lost His Stripes. 2013. (Illus.). (J). *(978-1-4351-5392-9(8))* Barnes & Noble, Inc.

Roberts, Bethany. Valentine Mice! Cushman, Doug, illus. 2016. (Green Light Readers Level 1 Ser.). (ENG.). 32p. (J). (gr. -1-3). 12.99 *(978-0-544-80897-3(5)*, HMH Books For Young Readers) Houghton Mifflin Harcourt Publishing Co.

—Valentine Mice! Board Book. Cushman, Doug, illus. 2011. (ENG.). 28p. (J). (gr. k — 1). bds. 5.99 *(978-0-547-37144-3(6))* Houghton Mifflin Harcourt Publishing Co.

Roberts, Victoria. Best Pet Ever. Allwright, Deborah, illus. 2011. (ENG.). 32p. pap. 7.95 *(978-1-58925-432-9(5))* Tiger Tales.

Robertson, James. Katie's A tae Z: An Alphabet for Wee Folk. Sutherland, Karen, illus. 2014. (ENG.). 20p. (J). (-k). bds. 12.99 *(978-1-84502-754-4(X))* Black and White Publishing Ltd. GBR. Dist: Independent Pubs. Group.

Roche, Maite. My First Pictures of Easter. 2012. 14p. 6.99 *(978-1-58617-653-2(6))* Ignatius Pr.

Rock, Lois. Goodnight. 2nd ed. 2013. (Prayers for Little Hands Ser.). (ENG., Illus.). 8p. (J). (— 1). 8.99 *(978-0-7459-6376-1(5))* Lion Hudson PLC GBR. Dist: Independent Pubs. Group.

—Here I Am. Widdowson, Kay, illus. 2nd ed. 2013. (Prayers for Little Hands Ser.). (ENG.). 8p. (J). (— 1). 8.99 *(978-0-7459-6374-7(9))* Lion Hudson PLC GBR. Dist: Independent Pubs. Group.

—Look Inside Bible Times. Lewis, Anthony, illus. 2016. (ENG.). 64p. (J). (gr. k-2). 16.99 *(978-0-7459-7614-3(X))* Lion Hudson PLC GBR. Dist: Independent Pubs. Group.

—Look Inside the Time of Jesus. Orlandi, Lorenzo, illus. 2014. (ENG.). 8p. (J). (gr. k-2). bds. 14.99 *(978-0-7459-6398-3(6))* Lion Hudson PLC GBR. Dist: Independent Pubs. Group.

—Now We Have a Baby. Massey, Jane, illus. 2014. (ENG.). 24p. (J). (gr. -1-k). bds. 7.99 *(978-0-7459-6345-7(5))* Lion Hudson PLC GBR. Dist: Independent Pubs. Group.

—Thank You, God. Widdowson, Kay, illus. 2nd ed. 2013. (Prayers for Little Hands Ser.). (ENG.). 8p. (J). (— 1). 8.99 *(978-0-7459-6377-8(3))* Lion Hudson PLC GBR. Dist: Independent Pubs. Group.

Roe, David & Reader's Digest Editors. Mix & Match. Milne, Alex & Ruffolo, Rob, illus. 2007. (ENG.). 12p. (J). (gr. -1-1). bds. 14.99 *(978-0-7944-1286-9(6))* Reader's Digest Assn., Inc., The.

Rogers, Alan. En Forme de Bateau. 2003. (Little Giants Ser.). (FRE., Illus.). 16p. (J). (gr. -1-k). 5.95 *(978-1-58728-177-8(5)*, Two-Can Publishing) T&N Children's Publishing.

—Higher & Higher. 2004. (Little Giants Ser.). (Illus.). 16p. (J). (gr. -1-k). 5.95 *(978-1-58728-153-2(8)*, Two-Can Publishing) T&N Children's Publishing.

Rohmann, Eric. A Kitten Tale. 2015. (ENG., Illus.). 32p. (J). (gr. -1-2). bds. 6.99 *(978-0-553-49831-8(2)*, Knopf Bks. for Young Readers) Random Hse. Children's Bks.

Rollins, Jack & Nelson, Steve. Frosty the Snowman. Reed, Lisa, illus. 2014. 22p. (J). bds. 6.99 *(978-0-8249-1935-1(1)*, Ideal Pubns.) Worthy Publishing.

Ron, Berry. Daddy Do You Love Me. 2009. (ENG.). 20p. bds. 5.99 *(978-0-8249-1423-3(6)*, Ideal Pubns.) Worthy Publishing.

Rookie Toddler(r) (Fall 2014 Set Of 4) 2014. (Rookie Toddler(r) Ser.). (J). bds. 27.80 *(978-0-531-24361-9(3))* Scholastic Library Publishing.

Rooney, Anne. Wallace & Gromit's World of Mysteries. 2004. (Illus.). 30p. (gr. 5-9). reprint ed. 30.00 *(978-0-7567-7410-3(1))* DIANE Publishing Co.

Roop, Connie, et al. Our Solar System. 2016. (Science for Toddlers Ser.: 1). (ENG., Illus.). 26p. (J). (gr. -1 — 1). bds. 7.95 *(978-1-4549-1418-1(1)*, 1404673) Sterling Publishing Co., Inc.

Root, Phyllis. The House That Jill Built: A Pop-up Book. Durand, Delphine, illus. 2007. 18p. (J). reprint ed. 16.00 *(978-1-4223-6756-8(8))* DIANE Publishing Co.

—Ten Sleepy Sheep. Gaber, Susan, illus. 2009. (ENG.). 12p. (J). (-k). bds. 7.99 *(978-0-7636-4142-9(1))* Candlewick Pr.

Roper, Robert. Dora Goes to the Doctor. 2013. (Dora the Explorer 8X8 Ser.). lib. bdg. 14.75 *(978-0-606-32216-4(7)*, Turtleback) Turtleback Bks.

Rosa-Mendoza, Gladys. I Live Here!/Yo Vivo Aqui! Gonzalez, Margarita E. & Weber, Amy, eds. Burnett, Lindy, illus. 2007. (# 1 Bilingual Board Book Ser.). (ENG & SPA.). 20p. (J). (gr. -1-k). bds. 6.95 *(978-1-931398-19-0(4))* Me+Mi Publishing.

Rosario, Sherwin, illus. Meet the Letters. 2005. 26p. (J). 9.99 *(978-0-9767008-0-7(8))* Preschool Prep Co.

—Meet the Numbers Lift the Flap Book. 2005. 12p. (J). bds. 9.99 *(978-0-9767008-1-4(6))* Preschool Prep Co.

Rose, Alexa. The Prankster Handbook. 2014. (PACKtivities Ser.: 4). (ENG.). 48p. (J). 11.99 *(978-1-935703-45-7(5))* Downtown Bookworks.

Rosen, Michael J. Chanukah Lights. Sabuda, Robert, illus. 2011. (ENG.). 16p. (J). (gr. k-4). 34.99 *(978-0-7636-5533-4(3))* Candlewick Pr.

Rosenbaum, Andria Warmflash. A Grandma Like Yours: A Grandpa Like Yours. Bjornson, Barbara, illus. 2006. 32p. (J). 16.95 *(978-1-58013-167-4(0)*, Kar-Ben Publishing) Lerner Publishing Group.

Rosenberg, Amye. A Surprise in the Mail! Salanitro, Robert, illus. 2009. (Discovery Ser.). (ENG.). 12p. (J). 7.99 *(978-1-60436-018-9(6))* Educational Publishing LLC.

Rosenthal, Amy Krouse. Little Hoot. Corace, Jen, illus. (ENG.). (J). (gr. -1-k). 2016. 28p. bds. 7.99 *(978-1-4521-5207-3(1))* 2007. 36p. 15.99 *(978-0-8118-6023-9(X))* Chronicle Bks. LLC.

—Little Oink. Corace, Jen, illus. 2017. (ENG.). 24p. (J). bds. 7.99 *(978-1-4521-5319-3(1))* Chronicle Bks. LLC.

Rosenthal, Marc. Big Bot, Small Bot: A Book of Robot Opposites. 2015. (ENG., Illus.). 20p. (J). (-k). 17.95 *(978-1-57687-750-0(7)*, powerHouse Bks.) powerHouse Cultural Entertainment, Inc.

—One Robot Lost His Head. 2015. (ENG., Illus.). 16p. (J). (-k). 17.95 *(978-1-57687-749-4(3)*, powerHouse Bks.) powerHouse Cultural Entertainment, Inc.

Rosewarne, Graham, illus. My First Dinosaur Book. 2015. (ENG.). 48p. bds. 9.99 *(978-1-86147-424-7(5)*, Armadillo) Anness Publishing GBR. Dist: National Bk. Network.

Ross, Tony. Goldilocks & the Three Bears. 2016. (ENG., Illus.). 10p. (J). (-k). ring bd. 9.99 *(978-1-78344-409-0(6))* Andersen Pr. GBR. Dist: Independent Pubs. Group.

—Jack & the Beanstalk. 2016. (ENG., Illus.). 10p. (J). (-k). ring bd. 9.99 *(978-1-78344-410-6(X))* Andersen Pr. GBR. Dist: Independent Pubs. Group.

Rossetti-Shustak, Bernadette. I Love You Through & Through (Te Quiero, Yo Te Quiero) Church, Caroline Jayne, illus. 2013. (Caroline Jayne Church Ser.). (ENG & SPA.). 24p. (J). (— 1). bds. 8.95 *(978-0-545-58416-6(7))* Scholastic, Inc.

Roth, Megan. Bright Books: Baby Bear's Busy Day. Hayashi, Emiri, illus. 2016. (Bright Bks.). (ENG.). 12p. (J). bds. 14.99 *(978-1-62686-717-8(8)*, Silver Dolphin Bks.) Readerlink Distribution Services, LLC.

Rouss, Sylvia A. A Sammy Spider Passover. Kahn, Katherine & Kahn, Katherine Janus, illus. 2017. (ENG.). 12p. (gr. -1 — 1). 5.99 *(978-1-4677-7970-8(9)*, Kar-Ben Publishing) Lerner Publishing Group.

Rowe, Helen, illus. Fun with Pets: A Pop-Up Book. 2016. (ENG.). 12p. (J). (gr. -1 — 1). bds. 8.99 *(978-1-4998-0300-6(1))* Little Bee Books Inc.

Rowe, Jeanette. First 1, 2, 3. 2016. (I Spy with My Little Eye... Bks.). (ENG.). 16p. (J). (gr. -1-k). bds. 9.99 *(978-0-7641-6815-4(0))* Barron's Educational Series, Inc.

—First Words. 2016. (I Spy with My Little Eye... Bks.). (ENG.). 16p. (J). (gr. -1-k). bds. 9.99 *(978-0-7641-6816-1(9))* Barron's Educational Series, Inc.

Roxbee-Cox, Phil. Ted's Shed. 2004. (Easy Words to Read Ser.). (ENG., Illus.). 1p. (J). (gr. 1-18). pap. 6.95 *(978-0-7460-4210-6(8))* EDC Publishing.

Rozelaar, Angie, illus. Hello School. 2016. (Hello! Ser.). (ENG.). 10p. (J). (gr. -1-k). 15.99 *(978-1-4472-6693-8(5))* Pan Macmillan GBR. Dist: Independent Pubs. Group.

Rubin, Susan Goldman. Jacob Lawrence in the City. 2009. (ENG., Illus.). 24p. (J). (gr. -1 — 1). bds. 7.99 *(978-0-8118-6582-1(7))* Chronicle Bks. LLC.

Rudi, Julie A. That's How Much I Love You. Beeke, Tiphanie, illus. 2013. (ENG.). 20p. (gr. -1). bds. 8.95 *(978-1-58925-644-6(1))* Tiger Tales.

Rudolph. 2012. (Illus.). (J). *(978-1-4351-4386-9(8))* Barnes & Noble, Inc.

Rueda, Claudia. Bunny Slopes. 2016. (ENG., Illus.). 60p. (J). (gr. -1-k). 15.99 *(978-1-4521-4197-8(5))* Chronicle Bks. LLC.

—Huff & Puff: Can You Blow down the Houses of the Three Little Pigs? 2012. (ENG., Illus.). 32p. (J). (gr. -1-k). 15.95 *(978-1-4197-0170-2(3)*, Abrams Appleseed) Abrams, Inc.

Rueda, Claudia, illus. I Know an Old Lady Who Swallowed a Fly. 2005. 14p. (J). 12.95 *(978-1-58117-267-6(2)*, Intervisual/Piggy Toes) Bendon, Inc.

Rumbaugh, Melinda. The Great Easter Egg Hunt. Reed, Lisa, illus. 2014. (VeggieTales Bk Ser.). 16p. (J). 12.99 *(978-0-8249-1928-3(9)*, Ideal Pubns.) Worthy Publishing.

—Somebunny Loves You! Biscoe, Cee, illus. 2015. (ENG.). 16p. (J). 12.99 *(978-0-8249-1950-4(5)*, Ideal Pubns.) Worthy Publishing.

Runnells, Treesha. Forest Friends: A Fold-Out Fun Book. Runnells, Treesha, illus. 2005. (Fold-Out Fun Ser.). (Illus.). 10p. (J). 4.95 *(978-1-58117-275-1(3)*, Intervisual/Piggy Toes) Bendon, Inc.

Running Press Staff, ed. Peanuts Finger Puppet Theater: Starring Charlie Brown & Snoopy! 2013. (Miniature Editions Ser.). (ENG., Illus.). 32p. 9.95 *(978-0-7624-4789-3(3)*, Running Pr. Minature Editions) Running Pr. Bk. Pubs.

Running Press Staff & Hello Kitty Staff. Hello Kitty: A Little Book of Happiness. 2009. (Miniature Editions Ser.). (ENG.). 96p. 5.95 *(978-0-7624-3594-4(1))* Running Pr. Bk. Pubs.

Running Press Staff & Parker, Amy. Tiny Blessings: for a Merry Christmas. Walsh, Sarah, illus. 2016. (ENG.). 10p. (J). (gr. -1-17). bds. 7.95 *(978-0-7624-6095-3(4)*, Running Pr. Kids) Running Pr. Bk. Pubs.

—Tiny Blessings: for Mealtime. Walsh, Sarah, illus. 2016. (ENG.). 10p. (J). (gr. -1-17). bds. 7.95 *(978-0-7624-6096-0(2)*, Running Pr. Kids) Running Pr. Bk. Pubs.

Rutherford, Peter, illus. Noah's Ark. 2015. (ENG.). 24p. bds. 6.99 *(978-1-86147-644-9(2)*, Armadillo) Anness Publishing GBR. Dist: National Bk. Network.

Sabuda, Robert. America the Beautiful. Sabuda, Robert, illus. 2004. (ENG., Illus.). 16p. (J). (gr. -1-3). 35.00 *(978-0-689-84744-8(0)*, Little Simon) Little Simon.

—Beauty & the Beast: A Pop-Up Adaptation of the Classic Tale. Sabuda, Robert, illus. 2010. (ENG., Illus.). 12p. (J). (gr. -1-2). 34.99 *(978-1-4169-6079-9(1)*, Little Simon) Little Simon.

—The Christmas Story. 2016. (ENG.). 12p. (J). (gr. k-3). 35.00 *(978-0-7636-8326-9(4))* Candlewick Pr.
—Winter in White: A Mini Pop-Up Treat. Sabuda, Robert, illus. 2007. (ENG., Illus.). 18p. (J). (gr. -1-3). 17.99 *(978-0-689-85365-4(3)*, Little Simon) Little Simon.
—Winter's Tale: An Original Pop-Up Journey. 2005. (ENG., Illus.). 12p. (J). (gr. -1-3). 39.99 *(978-0-689-85363-0(7)*, Little Simon) Little Simon.
—The 12 Days of Christmas. Sabuda, Robert, illus. 10th anniv. ed. 2006. (ENG., Illus.). 14p. (J). (gr. -1-3). 34.99 *(978-1-4169-2792-1(1)*, Little Simon) Little Simon.
Safran, Sheri. All Kinds of Babies. Damon, Emma, illus. 2007. (All Kinds Of... Ser.). (ENG.). 16p. (J). (gr. -1-k). 12.99 *(978-1-85707-679-0(6))* Tango Bks. GBR. Dist: Independent Pubs. Group.
—All Kinds of Festivals. Fuller, Rachel, illus. 2012. (ENG.). 12p. (J). (gr. -1). 12.99 *(978-1-60887-162-9(2))* Insight Editions.
—Let's Dress! Fuller, Rachel, illus. 2011. (ENG.). 20p. (J). (gr. -1-2). 18.99 *(978-1-85707-725-4(3))* Tango Bks. GBR. Dist: Independent Pubs. Group.
—The Magic Carousel: A Book & Removable 3-D Play Carousel. Safran, Sheri, illus. 2011. (ENG., Illus.). 6p. (J). (gr. -1-k). 24.99 *(978-1-85707-800-8(4))* Tango Bks. GBR. Dist: Independent Pubs. Group.
Sago & Sago Mini. Jinja's Surprise! 2016. (Sago Mini Ser.). (ENG., Illus.). 14p. (J). (gr. -1 — 1). bds. 7.99 *(978-1-4998-0323-5(0))* Little Bee Books Inc.
Sajnani, Surya. Can You Find Me? Sajnani, Surya, illus. 2017. (Animosaic Ser.). (ENG., Illus.). 20p. (J). (gr. -1 — 1). bds. 12.95 ***(978-1-68297-146-8(5)***, Words & Pictures) Quarto Publishing Group UK GBR. Dist: Hachette Bk. Group.
Salmon, Michael. Dinosaur. 2006. (Illus.). 32p. (J). *(978-1-74178-213-4(9))* Bonnier Publishing Australia.
Saltzberg, Barney. Arlo Needs Glasses. 2012. (ENG., Illus.). 24p. (gr. k-1). 17.95 *(978-0-7611-6879-9(6)*, 16879) Workman Publishing Co., Inc.
—Beautiful Oops! 2010. (ENG., Illus.). 28p. (J). (gr. -1-2). 15.95 *(978-0-7611-5728-1(X)*, 15728) Workman Publishing Co., Inc.
—My Book of Beautiful Oops! A Scribble It, Smear It, Fold It, Tear It Journal for Young Artists. 2017. (ENG., Illus.). 52p. (J). (gr. -1-1). 15.95 *(978-0-7611-8950-3(5))* Workman Publishing Co., Inc.
—Redbird: Friends Come in Different Sizes. 2015. (ENG., Illus.). 22p. (J). bds. 5.95 *(978-0-7611-8190-3(3))* Workman Publishing Co., Inc.
—Redbird: Colors, Colors, Everywhere! 2015. (ENG., Illus.). 22p. (J). bds. 5.95 *(978-0-7611-8185-9(7))* Workman Publishing Co., Inc.
Salyards, Jeffrey. Dino Thunder. 2004. (Illus.). (J). *(978-1-4127-0493-9(6))* Publications International, Ltd.
Salzano, Tammi. One Rainy Day. Wood, Hannah, illus. 2011. (ENG.). 24p. (J). (gr. -1-k). bds. 8.95 *(978-1-58925-860-0(6))* Tiger Tales.
—One Sunny Day. 2013. pap. *(978-0-545-53655-4(3))* Scholastic, Inc.
—Truck Party. Wood, Hannah, illus. 2011. (ENG.). 20p. bds. 7.95 *(978-1-58925-865-5(7))* Tiger Tales.
Sambar, Syma. This Is Olivia. Spaziante, Patrick, illus. 2009. (Olivia TV Tie-In Ser.). (ENG.). 12p. (J). (gr. -1-2). 7.99 *(978-1-4169-8709-3(6)*, Simon Spotlight) Simon Spotlight.
SAMi. Flip-a-Face: Colors. (J). bds. 8.95 *(978-1-59354-137-8(6))* Blue Apple Bks.
—Let's Learn Colors & Shapes. 2012. (Illus.). (J). *(978-1-60905-243-0(9))* Handprint Bks.
Samoun, Abigail. How Iguana Says I Love You! Watts, Sarah, illus. 2016. (Little Traveler Ser.). (ENG & MUL.). 22p. (J). (gr. -1-k). bds. 6.95 *(978-1-4549-1813-4(6))* Sterling Publishing Co., Inc.
—How Monkey Says My Name Is! Watts, Sarah, illus. 2016. (Little Traveler Ser.). (ENG & MUL.). 22p. (J). (gr. -1-k). bds. 6.95 *(978-1-4549-1814-1(4))* Sterling Publishing Co., Inc.
—How Penguin Says Please! Watts, Sarah, illus. 2015. (Little Traveler Ser.). (ENG & MUL.). 24p. (J). (gr. -1-k). bds. 6.95 *(978-1-4549-1496-9(3))* Sterling Publishing Co., Inc.
—How Tiger Says Thank You! Watts, Sarah, illus. 2015. (Little Traveler Ser.). (ENG & MUL.). 22p. (J). (gr. -1-k). bds. 6.95 *(978-1-4549-1497-6(1))* Sterling Publishing Co., Inc.
—What's in Your Purse? Dion, Nathalie, illus. 2014. (ENG.). 12p. (J). (gr. -1-17). 17.99 *(978-1-4521-1701-0(2))* Chronicle Bks. LLC.
Sams, Carl R., II. Stranger in the Woods. 2004. (ENG.). 14.95 *(978-0-9671748-7-7(2))* Sams, II, Carl R. Photography, Inc.
Sams, Carl R., II & Stoick, Jean. Happy Bird Day! Sams, Carl R., II & Stoick, Jean, photos by. 2012. (ENG., Illus.). 14p. (J). bds. 7.95 *(978-0-9827625-2-3(6))* Sams, II, Carl R. Photography, Inc.
Sams II, Carl R. & Stoick, Jean, photos by. When Snowflakes Fall. 2009. (ENG., Illus.). 14p. bds. 7.95 *(978-0-9770108-9-9(9))* Sams, II, Carl R. Photography, Inc.
Samuel, Anna. Glitter Butterflies Stickers. 2004. (Dover Stickers Ser.). (ENG., Illus.). 2p. (gr. -1). 1.50 *(978-0-486-43537-4(7))* Dover Pubns., Inc.
Samuel, Janet, illus. One Sneaky Sheep: The Sheep Who Didn't Want to Get Sheared. 2009. (ENG.). 20p. (J). 9.95 *(978-1-58117-841-8(7)*, Intervisual/Piggy Toes) Bendon, Inc.
San Antonio Museum of Art Staff & Budnick, Madeleine. Colores Everywhere! Colors in English & Spanish. 2013. (ArteKids Ser.). (ENG & SPA., Illus.). 16p. (J). (gr. k-k). bds. 7.95 *(978-1-59534-139-6(0))* Trinity Univ. Pr.
Sander, Sonia. Easter Egg Dash! A Lift-The-Flap Book with Stickers. Shannon, David et al, illus. 2010. (Jon Scieszka's Trucktown Ser.). (ENG.). 12p. (J). (gr. -1-k). bds. 7.99 *(978-1-4169-4183-5(5)*, Little Simon) Little Simon.
Sanders, Jane. Nighttime Slumber, 1 vol. 2017. (ENG., Illus.). 22p. (J). bds. 9.99 *(978-1-4236-4714-0(9))* Gibbs Smith, Publisher.
—Seashore Stroll, 1 vol. 2017. (ENG., Illus.). 22p. (J). bds. 9.99 *(978-1-4236-4712-6(2))* Gibbs Smith, Publisher.
Sands, Emily. Egyptology: Search for the Tomb of Osiris. Steer, Dugald A., ed. Andrew, Ian et al, illus. 2004. (Ologies Ser.). (ENG.). 32p. (J). (gr. 3-7). 24.99 *(978-0-7636-2638-9(4))* Candlewick Pr.
Sandviks HOP, Inc. Staff, contrib. by. My Colors Wipe-off Board Book with DVD. DVD 10.99 *(978-1-60143-896-6(6))* HOP, LLC.
Sanfilippo, Simona, illus. Rapunzel. 2009. (Flip-Up Fairy Tales Ser.). (ENG.). 24p. (J). (gr. -1-2). pap. *(978-1-84643-249-1(9))*; audio compact disk *(978-1-84643-292-7(8))* Child's Play International Ltd.
Sanrio. Merry Christmas, Hello Kitty! 2014. (ENG., Illus.). 24p. (J). (gr. k-2). 6.95 *(978-1-4197-1376-7(0)*, Abrams Bks. for Young Readers) Abrams, Inc.
Sanrio Company, LTD. Hello Kitty, Hello Winter! Hirashima, Jean, illus. 2013. (ENG.). 14p. (J). (gr. -1 — 1). bds. 7.95 *(978-1-4197-0797-1(3)*, Abrams Appleseed) Abrams, Inc.
Sanrio Company, Ltd. Staff. Hello Kitty, Hello Fall! Hirashima, Jean, illus. 2013. (ENG.). 14p. (J). (gr. -1 — 1). bds. 7.95 *(978-1-4197-0799-5(X)*, Abrams Appleseed) Abrams, Inc.
—Hello Kitty, Hello New York! Hirashima, Jean, illus. 2014. (ENG.). 16p. (J). (gr. -1 — 1). bds. 7.95 *(978-1-4197-1096-4(6)*, Abrams Appleseed) Abrams, Inc.
—Hello Kitty, Hello Spring! Hirashima, Jean, illus. 2013. (ENG.). 14p. (J). (gr. -1 — 1). bds. 7.95 *(978-1-4197-0668-2(8)*, Abrams Appleseed) Abrams, Inc.
—Hello Kitty, Hello Summer! Hirashima, Jean, illus. 2013. (ENG.). 14p. (J). (gr. -1 — 1). bds. 7.95 *(978-1-4197-0687-5(X)*, Abrams Appleseed) Abrams, Inc.
Sanschagrin, Joceline. Caillou at the Doctor. Brignaud, Pierre, illus. 3rd ed. 2013. (Step by Step Ser.). (ENG.). 24p. (J). (gr. -1-k). bds. 5.99 *(978-2-89718-058-4(7))* Caillouet, Gerry.
Santomero, Angela C. Big Brother Daniel. Fruchter, Jason, illus. 2015. (Daniel Tiger's Neighborhood Ser.). (ENG.). 14p. (J). (gr. -1-k). bds. 5.99 *(978-1-4814-3172-9(2)*, Simon Spotlight) Simon Spotlight.
—Happy Halloween, Daniel Tiger! Style Guide Staff & Fruchter, Jason, illus. 2014. (Daniel Tiger's Neighborhood Ser.). (ENG.). 14p. (J). (gr. -1-2). bds. 6.99 *(978-1-4814-0429-7(6)*, Simon Spotlight) Simon Spotlight.
Santore, Charles & Potter, Beatrix. Peter Rabbit Board Book. Encarnacion, Elizabeth, ed. 2014. (ENG., Illus.). 22p. (J). bds. 8.95 *(978-1-60433-511-8(4)*, Applesauce Pr.) Cider Mill Pr. Bk. Pubs., LLC.
Santoro, Christopher. It's Haunted! 2015. (ENG., Illus.). 12p. (J). (— 1). 7.99 *(978-0-553-52370-6(8)*, Random Hse. Bks. for Young Readers) Random Hse. Children's Bks.
Santoro, Lucio & Santoro, Meera. Wild Oceans: A Pop-Up Book with Revolutionary Technology. 2010. (ENG.). 12p. (J). (gr. 1-5). 29.99 *(978-1-4169-8467-2(4)*, Little Simon) Little Simon.
Sapp, Karen, illus. Ellie's Christmas. 2013. (J). *(978-1-4351-4835-2(5))* Barnes & Noble, Inc.
Sassi, Laura. Goodnight, Ark, 1 vol. Chapman, Jane, illus. 2015. (ENG.). 24p. (J). bds. 8.99 *(978-0-310-74938-7(7))* Zonderkidz.
Sattler, Jennifer. Frankie the Blankie. 2016. (ENG., Illus.). 32p. (J). 16.99 *(978-1-61963-675-0(1)*, 9781619636750, Bloomsbury USA Childrens) Bloomsbury Publishing USA.
Sattler, Jennifer. My Friend Moe. 2017. (ENG., Illus.). 22p. (J). (gr. -1 — 1). bds. 7.99 ***(978-0-7641-6897-0(5))*** Barron's Educational Series, Inc.
Sauer, Tammi. Cowboy Camp. Reed, Mike, illus. 2015. (ENG.). 24p. (J). (gr. -1-k). bds. 6.95 *(978-1-4549-1389-4(4))* Sterling Publishing Co., Inc.
Saunders, Katie. Toddler Time Teddy Hunt. 2014. (Toddler Bks.). (ENG.). 12p. (J). (gr. -1 — 1). bds. 10.99 *(978-0-7641-6722-5(7))* Barron's Educational Series, Inc.
Saunders, Katie, illus. Let's Learn Opposites. 2013. 10p. (J). ***(978-1-4351-4940-3(8))*** Barnes & Noble, Inc.
Saunders, Katie, illus. Little Reindeer. 2012. 10p. (J). *(978-1-4351-4314-2(0))* Barnes & Noble, Inc.
Saunders, Katie & Little Bee Books Staff. Color Fun! An Abacus Book. Saunders, Katie, illus. 2015. (Baby Steps Ser.). (ENG., Illus.). 14p. (J). (gr. -1 — 1). bds. 7.99 *(978-1-4998-0006-7(1))* Little Bee Books Inc.
—Counting Fun! An Abacus Book. Saunders, Katie, illus. 2015. (Baby Steps Ser.). (ENG., Illus.). 14p. (J). (gr. -1 — 1). bds. 7.99 *(978-1-4998-0005-0(3))* Little Bee Books Inc.
Savage, Stephen. Little Tug. Savage, Stephen, illus. 2015. (ENG., Illus.). 34p. (J). (gr. -1-1). bds. 7.99 *(978-1-62672-124-1(6)*, 9781626721241) Roaring Brook Pr.
—Seven Orange Pumpkins Board Book. 2015. (ENG., Illus.). 28p. (J). (gr. -1 — 1). bds. 6.99 *(978-0-8037-4138-6(3)*, Dial Bks) Penguin Young Readers Group.
Sayre, April Pulley. Rah, Rah, Radishes! A Vegetable Chant. Sayre, April Pulley, photos by. 2014. (Classic Board Bks.). (ENG., Illus.). 34p. (J). (gr. -1 — 1). bds. 7.99 *(978-1-4424-9927-0(3)*, Little Simon) Little Simon.
Scarry, Patsy. The Bunny Book. Scarry, Richard, illus. 2016. (Little Golden Board Book Ser.). (ENG.). 26p. (J). (— 1). bds. 7.99 *(978-0-553-53587-7(0)*, Random Hse. Bks. for Young Readers) Random Hse. Children's Bks.
Scarry, Richard. Egg in the Hole. Golden Books Staff, illus. 2011. (Shaped Board Book Ser.). (ENG.). 20p. (J). (gr. k — 1). bds. 8.99 *(978-0-375-86291-5(9)*, Golden Bks.) Random Hse. Children's Bks.
—My School Backpack. 2012. (ENG., Illus.). 56p. (J). (gr. -1-k). bds. 9.99 *(978-1-4380-7295-1(3))* Barron's Educational Series, Inc.
—Richard Scarry Mr. Paint Pig's ABC's. Random House Staff, illus. 2013. (ENG.). 12p. (J). (-k). bds. 5.99 *(978-0-449-81902-9(7)*, Golden Bks.) Random Hse. Children's Bks.
—Richard Scarry's All the Colors of Busytown. 2013. (Richard Scarry's Concept Bks.). (ENG.). 18p. (J). (gr. -1 — 1). bds. 7.99 *(978-0-7641-6601-3(8))* Barron's Educational Series, Inc.
—Richard Scarry's Best Little Books Ever, 4 vols. 2011. (My Mini Book Collection). (ENG., Illus.). 48p. (J). (gr. -1 — 1). 6.95 *(978-1-4027-8565-8(8))* Sterling Publishing Co., Inc.
—Richard Scarry's Boats. Scarry, Richard, illus. 2015. (ENG., Illus.). 24p. (J). (— 1). bds. 4.99 *(978-0-385-39269-3(9)*, Golden Bks.) Random Hse. Children's Bks.
—Richard Scarry's Bunnies. Scarry, Richard, illus. 2014. (ENG., Illus.). 26p. (J). (-k). bds. 8.99 *(978-0-385-38518-3(8)*, Golden Bks.) Random Hse. Children's Bks.
—Richard Scarry's Busytown on the Go! 2015. (ENG., Illus.). 18p. (J). (gr. -1-k). bds. 7.99 *(978-0-7641-6776-8(6))* Barron's Educational Series, Inc.
—Richard Scarry's Cars & Trucks. 2013. (ENG., Illus.). 18p. (J). (gr. -1 — 1). bds. 6.95 *(978-1-4549-0535-6(2))* Sterling Publishing Co., Inc.
—Richard Scarry's Cars & Trucks. Scarry, Richard, illus. 2017. (Little Golden Book Ser.). (ENG., Illus.). 24p. (J). (-k). 4.99 ***(978-1-101-93927-7(3)***, Golden Bks.) Random Hse. Children's Bks.
—Richard Scarry's Christmas Tales, 4 vols. 2011. (My Mini Book Collection). (ENG., Illus.). 48p. (J). (gr. -1 — 1). 6.95 *(978-1-4027-8567-2(4))* Sterling Publishing Co., Inc.
—Richard Scarry's Good Morning, Busytown! 2015. (ENG., Illus.). 18p. (J). (gr. -1-k). bds. 7.99 *(978-0-7641-6777-5(4))* Barron's Educational Series, Inc.
—Richard Scarry's Huckle's Hide & Seek! Lift-The-Flap Book. 2015. (ENG., Illus.). 10p. (J). (gr. -1 — 1). bds. 7.99 *(978-0-7641-6812-3(6))* Barron's Educational Series, Inc.
—Richard Scarry's Just Right Word Book! Scarry, Richard, illus. 2015. (ENG., Illus.). 26p. (J). (— 1). bds. 7.99 *(978-0-553-50902-1(0)*, Golden Bks.) Random Hse. Children's Bks.
—Richard Scarry's Let's Count with Lowly. 2013. (Richard Scarry's Concept Bks.). (ENG.). 18p. (J). (gr. -1 — 1). bds. 7.99 *(978-0-7641-6600-6(X))* Barron's Educational Series, Inc.
—Richard Scarry's Planes. Scarry, Richard, illus. 2015. (ENG., Illus.). 24p. (J). (— 1). bds. 4.99 *(978-0-385-39270-9(2)*, Golden Bks.) Random Hse. Children's Bks.
—Richard Scarry's the Rooster Struts. 2015. (ENG., Illus.). 26p. (J). (— 1). bds. 7.99 *(978-0-553-50852-9(0)*, Golden Bks.) Random Hse. Children's Bks.
—School Bus Box Set. 2014. (Illus.). (J). *(978-0-7641-6690-7(5))* Barron's Educational Series, Inc.
Schaefer, Lola M. Boo Who? A Foldout Halloween Adventure. Frost, Michael, photos by. 2009. (ENG., Illus.). 12p. (J). (gr. -1-k). bds. 7.99 *(978-1-4169-5911-3(4)*, Little Simon) Little Simon.
Schaefer, Lola M. & McCue, Lisa. Easter Surprises. 2009. (ENG., Illus.). 18p. (J). (gr. -1-1). 7.99 *(978-1-4169-6476-6(2)*, Little Simon) Little Simon.
Schaefer, Peggy. Bob & Larry's Book of Prayers. Reed, Lisa, illus. 2014. (VeggieTales Bk Ser.). 32p. (J). bds. 10.99 *(978-0-8249-1929-0(7)*, Ideal Pubns.) Worthy Publishing.
—Trick or Treat! Halverson, Lydia, illus. 2009. (ENG.). 16p. (J). (gr. -1-k). bds. 12.99 *(978-0-8249-1828-6(2)*, Ideal Pubns.) Worthy Publishing.
Scharer, Niko. Emily's House, 1 vol. Fitzgerald, Joanne, illus. 2010. (ENG.). 22p. (J). (gr. k — 1). bds. 7.95 *(978-0-88899-831-6(7))* Groundwood Bks. CAN. Dist: Publishers Group West (PGW).
Scheffler, Axel. Treasury of Rhyming Stories. Scheffler, Axel, illus. 2015. (ENG., Illus.). 22p. (J). (-k). bds. 13.99 *(978-1-4472-7725-5(2))* Pan Macmillan GBR. Dist: Independent Pubs. Group.
Scheffler, Axel, illus. Axel Scheffler's Noisy Jungle. 2014. (ENG.). 10p. (J). (gr. -1-k). 19.99 *(978-1-4472-4634-3(9))* Pan Macmillan GBR. Dist: Independent Pubs. Group.
—Freddy the Frog. 2015. (Buggy Buddies Ser.). (ENG.). 12p. (J). (— 1). bds. 7.99 *(978-0-230-75614-4(X))* Pan Macmillan GBR. Dist: Independent Pubs. Group.
—Katie the Kitten. 2015. (Buggy Buddies Ser.). (ENG.). 12p. (J). (— 1). bds. 7.99 *(978-0-230-75615-1(8))* Pan Macmillan GBR. Dist: Independent Pubs. Group.
—Lizzy the Lamb. 2015. (Buggy Buddies Ser.). (ENG.). 12p. (J). (— 1). bds. 7.99 *(978-0-230-75616-8(6))* Pan Macmillan GBR. Dist: Independent Pubs. Group.
—Pip the Puppy. 2015. (Buggy Buddies Ser.). (ENG.). 12p. (J). (— 1). bds. 7.99 *(978-0-230-75617-5(4))* Pan Macmillan GBR. Dist: Independent Pubs. Group.
—Rhyming Stories: Pip the Dog & Freddy the Frog. 2015. (ENG.). 20p. (J). (— 1). bds. 9.99 *(978-1-4472-6824-6(5))* Pan Macmillan GBR. Dist: Independent Pubs. Group.
—Rhyming Stories Bk. 2: Katie the Kitten; Lizzy the Lamb. 2015. (ENG.). 20p. (J). (— 1). bds. 9.99 *(978-1-4472-6828-4(8))* Pan Macmillan GBR. Dist: Independent Pubs. Group.
Schertle, Alice. El Camioncito Azul. McElmurry, Jill, illus. 2013. (Little Blue Truck Ser.).Tr. of Little Blue Truck. (SPA & ENG.). 30p. (J). (— 1). bds. 7.99 *(978-0-547-98397-4(2))* Houghton Mifflin Harcourt Publishing Co.
—Little Blue Truck. McElmurry, Jill, illus. 2015. (Little Blue Truck Ser.). (ENG.). 30p. (J). (— 1). bds. 12.99 *(978-0-544-05685-5(X)*, HMH Books For Young Readers) Houghton Mifflin Harcourt Publishing Co.
Schiller, Pam. Five Little Ducks. Newsom, Carol, illus. 2014. 19p. (J). ***(978-1-60128-879-0(4))*** Frog Street Pr.
Schimler, Amy. Splish Splash! A Touch & Hear Book. Schimler, Amy, illus. 2011. (ENG., Illus.). 14p. (J). (gr. -1 — 1). bds. 6.99 *(978-1-4424-1354-2(9)*, Little Simon) Little Simon.
Schindel, John. Busy Pandas. Husar, Lisa & Husar, Mike, photos by. 2008. (Busy Book Ser.). (ENG., Illus.). 20p. (J). (gr. k — 1). bds. 6.99 *(978-1-58246-259-2(3)*, Knopf Bks. for Young Readers) Random Hse. Children's Bks.
Schindel, John & Woodward, Molly. The Babies & Doggies Book. 2015. (ENG., Illus.). 26p. (J). (— 1). bds. 7.99 *(978-0-544-44477-5(9)*, HMH Books For Young Readers) Houghton Mifflin Harcourt Publishing Co.
Schneider, Judy. But Not Quite. Weeks, Mary, illus. 2004. (J). 19.95 *(978-1-59404-005-4(2))* Peanut Butter Publishing.
Schnetzler, Pattie. Ten Little Dinosaurs. Harris, Jim, illus. 2015. (ENG.). 24p. (J). bds. 9.99 *(978-1-4494-6491-2(2))* Andrews McMeel Publishing.
Scholastic. Touch, Slide, & Lift Busy Farm (Scholastic Early Learners) 2016. (Scholastic Early Learners Ser.). (ENG.). 26p. (J). (— 1). bds. 12.99 *(978-1-338-11662-5(2)*, Cartwheel Bks.) Scholastic, Inc.
Scholastic Inc, contrib. by. Touch & Feel Trucks. 2016. (Scholastic Early Learners Ser.). (ENG.). 14p. (J). (— 1). bds. 6.99 *(978-1-338-11663-2(0)*, Cartwheel Bks.) Scholastic, Inc.
Scholastic, Inc. Staff. First 100 Things That Go. 2016. (Scholastic Early Learners Ser.). (ENG.). 12p. (J). (gr. -1 — 1). bds. 6.99 *(978-0-545-90343-1(2))* Scholastic, Inc.
—Learn to Write. 2016. (Scholastic Early Learners Ser.). (ENG.). 28p. (J). (gr. -1-k). pap. 8.99 *(978-0-545-90345-5(9))* Scholastic, Inc.
—Lightsabers: A Guide to Weapons of the Force. 2010. (Star Wars Ser.). (ENG., Illus.). 64p. (J). pap., instr.'s gde. ed. 8.99 *(978-0-545-27177-6(0))* Scholastic, Inc.
—Peek-a-Who? Are You My Mom? 2015. (Scholastic Early Learners Ser.). (ENG.). 12p. (J). (gr. -1 — 1). bds. 9.99 *(978-0-545-90338-7(6))* Scholastic, Inc.
—Sight Word Tales Interactive E-Storybooks: 25 e-Books with Engaging Interactive Whiteboard Activities That Teach the Top 100 High-Frequency Words. 2014. (ENG., Illus.). 144p. (-2). 129.99 *(978-0-545-64707-6(X)*, Teaching Resources) Scholastic, Inc.
—Slide & Find ABC Animals. 2016. (Scholastic Early Learners Ser.). (ENG.). 10p. (J). (gr. -1 — 1). bds. 9.99 *(978-0-545-90344-8(0))* Scholastic, Inc.
—Woof! 2016. (Scholastic Early Learners Ser.). (ENG.). 12p. (J). (gr. -1-k). bds. 9.99 *(978-0-545-90340-0(8))* Scholastic, Inc.
Scholastic, Inc. Staff, contrib. by. ABC. 2013. (Rookie Toddler(r) Ser.). (ENG.). 12p. (J). bds. 6.95 *(978-0-531-21576-0(8)*, Children's Pr.) Scholastic Library Publishing.
—Baby Animals. 2013. (Rookie Toddler(r) Ser.). (ENG.). 12p. (J). bds. 6.95 *(978-0-531-21577-7(6)*, Children's Pr.) Scholastic Library Publishing.
—Big & Little: Things That Go. 2013. (ENG.). 12p. (J). bds. 6.95 *(978-0-531-27253-4(2))* Scholastic Library Publishing.
—Collector's Sticker Book. 2011. (Lego Ninjago Ser.). (ENG.). 16p. (J). (gr. 2-5). pap. 6.99 *(978-0-545-35630-5(X))* Scholastic, Inc.
—Counting 1 to 10. 2012. (Rookie Toddler Ser.). (ENG., Illus.). 12p. (J). bds. 6.95 *(978-0-531-20851-9(6)*, Children's Pr.) Scholastic Library Publishing.
—Counting Machines. 2015. (Rookie Toddler(tm) Ser.). (ENG., Illus.). 12p. (J). bds. 6.95 *(978-0-531-21268-4(8)*, Children's Pr.) Scholastic Library Publishing.
—Eat Your Colors. 2016. (Rookie Toddler(tm) Ser.). (ENG., Illus.). 12p. (J). bds. 6.95 *(978-0-531-22619-3(0)*, Children's Pr.) Scholastic Library Publishing.
—Hot Dog, Cold Dog. 2016. (Rookie Toddler(tm) Ser.). (ENG.). 12p. (J). bds. 6.95 *(978-0-531-22620-9(4)*, Children's Pr.) Scholastic Library Publishing.
—If I Were a Doctor. 2015. (Rookie Toddler(tm) Ser.). (ENG., Illus.). 12p. (J). bds. 6.95 *(978-0-531-21264-6(5)*, Children's Pr.) Scholastic Library Publishing.
—Let's Go to the Firehouse. 2015. (ENG.). 20p. (J). (gr. -1 — 1). pap. 12.99 *(978-0-545-76634-0(6)*, Cartwheel Bks.) Scholastic, Inc.
—Look Inside. 2016. (Rookie Toddlers Ser.). (ENG.). 12p. (J). bds. 6.95 *(978-0-531-22455-7(4)*, Children's Pr.) Scholastic Library Publishing.
—Meet My Feet! 2016. (Rookie Toddler(tm) Ser.). (ENG., Illus.). 12p. (J). bds. 6.95 *(978-0-531-22621-6(2)*, Children's Pr.) Scholastic Library Publishing.
—More or Less. 2015. (Rookie Toddler(r) Ser.). (ENG.). 12p. (J). bds. 6.95 *(978-0-531-20571-6(1))* Scholastic Library Publishing.
—My Favorite Color Is... 2016. (Rookie Toddlers Ser.). (ENG., Illus.). 12p. (J). bds. 6.95 *(978-0-531-22456-4(2)*, Children's Pr.) Scholastic Library Publishing.
—Red Truck, Yellow Bus: A Book of Colors. 2012. (Rookie Toddler Ser.). (ENG., Illus.). 12p. (J). bds. 6.95 *(978-0-531-20852-6(4)*, Children's Pr.) Scholastic Library Publishing.
—Shapes. 2013. (Rookie Toddler(r) Ser.). (ENG., Illus.). 12p. (J). bds. 6.95 *(978-0-531-21579-1(2)*, Children's Pr.) Scholastic Library Publishing.
—Shapes at Home. 2015. (Rookie Toddler(r) Ser.). (ENG.). 12p. (J). bds. 6.95 *(978-0-531-20573-0(8))* Scholastic Library Publishing.
—Shapes in the Sky. 2016. (Rookie Toddlers Ser.). (ENG.). 12p. (J). bds. 6.95 *(978-0-531-22457-1(0)*, Children's Pr.) Scholastic Library Publishing.
—Where Is Your Nose? 2015. (Rookie Toddler(tm) Ser.). (ENG., Illus.). 12p. (J). bds. 6.95 *(978-0-531-21263-9(7)*, Children's Pr.) Scholastic Library Publishing.
Scholastic, Inc. Staff & DreamWorks Animation Staff, contrib. by. Over the Hedge: Animal Antics. 2006. (Illus.). 16p. (J). *(978-1-4156-7542-7(2))* Scholastic, Inc.
School Zone. Animal Alphabet. 2008. (ENG.). 26p. (J). 5.99 *(978-1-58947-932-6(7))* School Zone Publishing Co.
School Zone Publishing Company Staff. Numbers & Shapes. 2008. (ENG.). (J). 5.99 *(978-1-60159-102-9(0))* School Zone Publishing Co.
—3D Think & Blink Alphabet. 2007. (ENG.). (J). 7.99 *(978-1-60159-101-2(2))* School Zone Publishing Co.
School Zone Staff. My First Smart Art Alphabet. 2009. pap. 2.99 *(978-1-60159-250-7(7))* School Zone Publishing Co.
Schories, Pat, illus. Biscuit Visits the Farm. 2012. (J). *(978-1-4351-4383-8(3)*, HarperFestival) HarperCollins Pubs.
—Biscuit's Fourth of July. 2005. (J). *(978-1-4156-0311-6(1)*, HarperFestival) HarperCollins Pubs.
—Biscuit's Graduation Day. 2005. (J). *(978-1-4155-9660-9(3)*, HarperFestival) HarperCollins Pubs.
—Jack Wants a Snack. 2015. (Jack Bks.). (ENG.). 32p. (J). (— 1). bds. 7.99 *(978-1-62979-406-8(6))* Boyds Mills Pr.
Schrader, Missy Wolgemuth & Schrader, Missy W. Hooray! I Obeyed!, 1 vol. Nuffer, Bruce, ed. 2008. (ENG., Illus.). 12p. (J). (gr. -1). bds. 3.99 *(978-0-310-71396-8(X))* Zondervan.
Schulman, Janet. 10 Easter Egg Hunters. 2015. lib. bdg. 14.75 *(978-0-606-36379-2(3))* Turtleback Bks.
—10 Trim-the-Tree'ers. Davick, Linda, illus. 2011. (ENG.). 32p. (J). (gr. -1 — 1). bds. 6.99 *(978-0-375-87302-7(3)*, Knopf Bks. for Young Readers) Random Hse. Children's Bks.
Schulz, Charles & Schulz, Charles M. It's the Great Pumpkin, Charlie Brown: with Sound & Music. 2012. (ENG., Illus.). 48p. (J). (gr. -1-3). 19.95 *(978-0-7624-4606-3(4)*, Running Pr. Kids) Running Pr. Bk. Pubs.
Schulz, Charles M. It's the Easter Beagle, Charlie Brown: with Sound & Music. 2013. (ENG., Illus.). 48p. (J). (gr. -1-17). 19.95 *(978-0-7624-4608-7(0)*, Running Pr. Kids) Running Pr. Bk. Pubs.
Schwartz, Betty & Seresin, Lynn. Puppies, Puppies, Everywhere! A Back-And-Forth Opposites Book. Powell, Luciana Navarro, illus. 2015. (J). *(978-1-62370-236-6(4))* Capstone Young Readers of Coughlan Cos.
—Ten Playful Tigers: A Touch-And-Feel Counting Book. Powell, Luciana Navarro, illus. 2015. (Back-And-Forth Bks.). (ENG.). 22p. (gr. -1 — 1). bds. 9.99 *(978-1-62370-233-5(X))* Capstone Young Readers of Coughlan Cos.

—You're It, Little Red Fish! A Back-And-Forth Color Book. Powell, Luciana Navarro, illus. 2015. (J). (978-1-62370-235-9(6)) Capstone Young Readers of Coughlan Cos.

Schwartz, Betty Ann. One to Ten... & Back Again. Shakir, Susie, illus. 2009. 24p. bds. 12.99 (978-0-8249-1436-3(8), Ideal Pubns.) Worthy Publishing.

—What Makes a Rainbow? Turner, Dona, illus. 2006. (Magic Ribbon Books). (ENG.). 14p. (J). 4.95 (978-1-58117-220-1(6), Intervisual/Piggy Toes) Bendon, Inc.

Schwartz, Betty Ann & Seresin, Lynn. My Barnyard! A Read & Play Book! Bendall-Brunello, John, illus. 2015. (ENG.). 10p. (J). (gr. -1-k). bds. 7.99 (978-0-545-69077-5(3), Cartwheel Bks.) Scholastic, Inc.

—Run, Run Piglet. Ng, Neiko, illus. 2015. (Follow-Along Book Ser.). (ENG.). 10p. (J). (gr. -1 — 1). bds. 9.99 (978-1-4521-2467-4(1)) Chronicle Bks. LLC.

Scoggins, Terry. Electric Ellie & Lightning Lucy: Firefly Friends Forever. 2008. 16p. pap. 8.99 (978-1-4389-1254-7(4)) AuthorHouse.

Scott, MaryJo. Corduroy's Colors. McCue, Lisa, illus. 2016. (Corduroy Ser.). (ENG.). 14p. (J). (— 1). bds. 5.99 (978-0-451-47247-2(0), Viking Books for Young Readers) Penguin Young Readers Group.

—Corduroy's Seasons. McCue, Lisa, illus. 2016. (Corduroy Ser.). (ENG.). 14p. (J). (— 1). bds. 5.99 (978-0-451-47249-6(7), Viking Books for Young Readers) Penguin Young Readers Group.

—Corduroy's Shapes. McCue, Lisa, illus. 2016. (Corduroy Ser.). (ENG.). 14p. (J). (— 1). bds. 5.99 (978-0-451-47250-2(0), Viking Books for Young Readers) Penguin Young Readers Group.

Scotton, Rob. Splat the Cat Board Book. Scotton, Rob, illus. 2016. (Splat the Cat Ser.). (Illus.). 34p. (J). (gr. -1 — 1). bds. 7.99 (978-0-06-229436-4(9), HarperFestival) HarperCollins Pubs.

—Splish, Splash, Splat! Board Book. Scotton, Rob, illus. 2016. (Splat the Cat Ser.). (Illus.). 36p. (J). (gr. -1 — 1). bds. 7.99 (978-0-06-229438-8(5), HarperFestival) HarperCollins Pubs.

Scrimshire, Hazel. Big Crash. 2005. (Shaped Board Bks.). (ENG., Illus.). 8p. (J). (gr. -1-k). bds. 3.99 (978-1-85792-085-7(6), 7135c229-921e-450e-96c9-d1a972dafc2a, Christian Focus) Christian Focus Pubns. GBR. Dist: Bookmasters Distribution.

Seal, Julia. Three Little Pigs. 2013. (Classic Fairy Tale Pop-Ups Ser.). (ENG.). 12p. (J). (gr. -1-1). 12.99 (978-0-7641-6599-3(2)) Barron's Educational Series, Inc.

Seal, Kerry. Five Silly Pumpkins: A Pop-up Halloween Book. Smith, Jane, illus. 2009. 10p. (J). 5.95 (978-1-58117-908-8(1), Intervisual/Piggy Toes) Bendon, Inc.

Seder, Rufus Butler. ¡Al Galope! Un Libro de Scanimation. 2009. (Scanimation Ser.). (SPA., Illus.). 12p. (J). (gr. -1-3). 12.95 (978-0-7611-5415-0(9), 15415) Workman Publishing Co., Inc.

—Gallop! Cards: 8 Scanimation Gift Cards. 2008. (Scanimation Ser.). (ENG., Illus.). 18p. (J). (gr. -1-12). 16.00 (978-0-7611-5239-2(3), 15239) Workman Publishing Co., Inc.

—Santa! A Scanimation Picture Book. 2013. (Scanimation Ser.). (ENG., Illus.). 24p. (gr. k-12). 14.95 (978-0-7611-7725-8(6), 17725) Workman Publishing Co., Inc.

—Star Wars: A Scanimation Book - 11 Iconic Scenes from a Galaxy Far, Far Away... 2010. (Scanimation Ser.). (ENG., Illus.). 13p. (gr. k-12). 14.95 (978-0-7611-5846-2(4), 15846) Workman Publishing Co., Inc.

—Swing! 2008. (Scanimation Ser.). (ENG., Illus.). 12p. (J). (gr. -1-3). 12.95 (978-0-7611-5127-2(3), 15127) Workman Publishing Co., Inc.

—Waddle! 2009. (Scanimation Ser.). (ENG., Illus.). 12p. (gr. -1-2). 13.95 (978-0-7611-5112-8(5), 15112) Workman Publishing Co., Inc.

Segal, Nechamy. The Torah Book of Opposites. Lumer, Marc, illus. 2012. 12p. (J). pap. 7.95 (978-1-929628-67-4(6)) Hachai Publishing.

Seibold, J. Otto. Count, Dagmar! 2011. (ENG.). 20p. (J). (gr. -1 — 1). 8.99 (978-0-8118-7773-2(6)) Chronicle Bks. LLC.

Seiss, Ellie. Best Friends: A Chock-a-Block Book. Scanlon, Michael, illus. 2010. (Yo Gabba Gabba! Ser.). (ENG.). 12p. (J). 5.99 (978-1-4424-0970-5(3), Simon Spotlight) Simon Spotlight.

Seiss, Ellie, adapted by. It's Okay, Try Again! 2011. (Yo Gabba Gabba! Ser.). (ENG.). 14p. (J). (gr. -1-k). bds. 5.99 (978-1-4424-2900-0(3), Simon Spotlight) Simon Spotlight.

Sellier, Marie. Renoir's Colors. 2010. (ENG., Illus.). 40p. (J). (gr. -1-k). 16.95 (978-1-60606-003-2(1)) Getty Pubns.

Sendak, Maurice. Alligators All Around Board Book: An Alphabet. Sendak, Maurice, illus. 2017. (Illus.). 32p. (J). (gr. -1-3). bds. 7.95 (978-0-06-266807-3(2)) HarperCollins Pubs.

—Chicken Soup with Rice Board Book: A Book of Months. Sendak, Maurice, illus. 2017. (Illus.). 32p. (J). (gr. -1 — 1). bds. 7.95 (978-0-06-266808-0(0)) HarperCollins Pubs.

—One Was Johnny Board Book: A Counting Book. Sendak, Maurice, illus. 2017. (Illus.). 46p. (J). (gr. -1-3). bds. 7.95 (978-0-06-266809-7(9)) HarperCollins Pubs.

—Pierre Board Book: A Cautionary Tale in Five Chapters & a Prologue. Sendak, Maurice, illus. 2017. (Illus.). 38p. (J). (gr. -1-3). bds. 7.95 (978-0-06-266810-3(2)) HarperCollins Pubs.

Senior, Suzy. Teddy Bear Says Goodnight. Mitchell, Melanie, illus. 2014. (Teddy Bear Says Ser.). (ENG.). 12p. (J). (— 1). bds. 7.99 (978-0-7459-6436-2(2)) Lion Hudson PLC GBR. Dist: Independent Pubs. Group.

—Teddy Bear Says I Love You. Mitchell, Melanie, illus. 2014. (Teddy Bear Says Ser.). (ENG.). 12p. (J). (— 1). bds. 7.99 (978-0-7459-6437-9(0)) Lion Hudson PLC GBR. Dist: Independent Pubs. Group.

—Teddy Bear Says Let's Hug. Mitchell, Melanie, illus. 2014. (Teddy Bear Says Ser.). (ENG.). 12p. (J). (— 1). bds. 7.99 (978-0-7459-6439-3(7)) Lion Hudson PLC GBR. Dist: Independent Pubs. Group.

—Teddy Bear Says Wake Up! Mitchell, Melanie, illus. 2014. (Teddy Bear Says Ser.). (ENG.). 12p. (J). (— 1). bds. 7.99 (978-0-7459-6438-6(9)) Lion Hudson PLC GBR. Dist: Independent Pubs. Group.

Seresin, Lynn & Schwartz, Betty Ann. Hop, Hop Bunny. Ng, Neiko, illus. 2015. (Follow-Along Book Ser.). (ENG.). 10p. (J). (gr. -1 — 1). bds. 9.99 (978-1-4521-2464-3(7)) Chronicle Bks. LLC.

Serrano, Francisco. Our Lady of Guadalupe, 1 vol. Davalos, Felipe, illus. 2nd ed. 2011. (ENG.). 12p. (gr. -1). 22.95 (978-1-55498-074-1(7)) Groundwood Bks. CAN. Dist: Publishers Group West (PGW).

Sesame Street, Sesame. Sesame Street Elmo's 1 2 3. 2015. (Lift-The-Flap Ser.). (ENG.). 10p. (J). (gr. -1-k). bds. 11.99 (978-0-7944-3476-2(2)) Studio Fun International.

—Sesame Street: Happy Like Elmo/Grouchy Like Oscar. 2016. (ENG.). 20p. (J). (gr. -1-k). bds. 10.99 (978-0-7944-3803-6(2)) Studio Fun International.

Sesame Street, Sesame & Kimmelmen, Leslie. Sesame Street - Celebrate You! Celebrate Me! A Peek & Touch Book. 2017. (ENG., Illus.). 10p. (J). (gr. -1-k). 10.99 (978-0-7944-3871-5(7), Reader's Digest Children's Bks.) Studio Fun International.

Sesame Street Staff. Fairly Furry 2 bk Big Red Riding Hood 3 Little Grouches. 2007. 15.99 (978-1-59069-625-5(5)) Studio Mouse LLC.

—Fairly Furry 2 bk Rhyming Rapunzel Rosita & Beanstalk. 2007. 15.99 (978-1-59069-624-8(7)) Studio Mouse LLC.

—Fairly Furry Fairy Tales 3 bk Pack. 2007. 19.99 (978-1-59069-623-1(9)) Studio Mouse LLC.

—Sesame Street Hide & Seek, Elmo! 2014. (ENG.). 12p. (J). (gr. -1-k). bds. 10.99 (978-0-7944-3037-5(6)) Reader's Digest Assn., Inc., The.

Sesame Street Staff, creator. Sesame Street: Early Learning Boxed Set. 2011. 72p. (J). bds. 12.99 (978-1-60745-237-9(5)) Flying Frog Pubs.

—Sesame Street: Elmo & Me! Boxed Set. 2011. 40p. (J). bds. 12.99 (978-1-60745-166-2(2)) Flying Frog Pubs.

—Sesame Street: My First Manners Boxed Set. 2011. 72p. (J). bds. 12.99 (978-1-60745-238-6(3)) Flying Frog Pubs.

Sesame Street Staff & Studio Mouse Staff. Learning Fun. 2008. (ENG.). 60p. (J). 4.99 (978-1-59069-671-2(9)) Studio Mouse LLC.

Seuss, Dr. All Aboard the Circus McGurkus. 2004. (Dr. Seuss Nursery Collection). (ENG., Illus.). 10p. (J). (— 1). bds. 7.99 (978-0-375-83011-2(1), Random Hse. Bks. for Young Readers) Random Hse. Children's Bks.

—The Big Box of Bright & Early Board Books about Me. 2015. (Big Bright & Early Board Book Ser.). (ENG., Illus.). 24p. (J). (gr. -1-3). bds. 27.96 (978-0-553-53629-4(X), Random Hse. Bks. for Young Readers) Random Hse. Children's Bks.

—Dr. Seuss's ABC: An Amazing Alphabet Book! 2014. (Big Bright & Early Board Book Ser.). (ENG., Illus.). 24p. (J). (— 1). bds. 6.99 (978-0-385-37516-0(6), Random Hse. Bks. for Young Readers) Random Hse. Children's Bks.

—Fox in Socks. 2015. (Big Bright & Early Board Book Ser.). (ENG., Illus.). 24p. (J). (— 1). bds. 6.99 (978-0-553-51336-3(2), Random Hse. Bks. for Young Readers) Random Hse. Children's Bks.

—Fox in Socks, Bricks & Blocks. Gerardi, Jan, illus. 2011. (Dr. Seuss Nursery Collection). (ENG.). 14p. (J). (gr. -1 — 1). 7.99 (978-0-375-87209-9(4), Random Hse. Bks. for Young Readers) Random Hse. Children's Bks.

—The Grinch's Great Big Flap Book. 2014. (Great Big Board Book Ser.). (ENG.). 12p. (J). (-k). bds. 12.99 (978-0-385-38494-0(7), Random Hse. Bks. for Young Readers) Random Hse. Children's Bks.

—Hop on Pop. 2015. (Big Bright & Early Board Book Ser.). (ENG., Illus.). 24p. (J). (— 1). bds. 6.99 (978-0-553-49679-6(4), Random Hse. Bks. for Young Readers) Random Hse. Children's Bks.

—The Little Blue Box of Bright & Early Board Books by Dr. Seuss. 2012. (Bright & Early Board Books(TM) Ser.). (ENG., Illus.). 24p. (J). (— 1). bds. 19.96 (978-0-307-97586-7(X), Random Hse. Bks. for Young Readers) Random Hse. Children's Bks.

—What Was I Scared Of? A Glow-in-the-Dark Encounter. 2009. (Classic Seuss Ser.). (ENG., Illus.). 32p. (J). (gr. k-4). 12.99 (978-0-375-85342-5(1), Random Hse. Bks. for Young Readers) Random Hse. Children's Bks.

—Would You Rather Be a Bullfrog? 2014. (Big Bright & Early Board Book Ser.). (ENG., Illus.). 24p. (J). (— 1). bds. 6.99 (978-0-385-37515-3(8), Random Hse. Bks. for Young Readers) Random Hse. Children's Bks.

Seven, John. Happy, Sad, Silly, Mad. Christy, Jana, illus. 2012. (ENG.). 26p. (J). (-k). bds. 6.99 (978-1-4494-2229-5(2)) Andrews McMeel Publishing.

Seven, John & Christy, Jana. Happy Punks 1 2 3: A Counting Story. 2013. (ENG., Illus.). 32p. (gr. -1). bds. 15.95 (978-1-933149-67-7(1)) Manic D Pr.

Sévigny, Eric, illus. Caillou Around Town. 2nd ed. 2013. (Coloring & Activity Book Ser.). (ENG.). 16p. (J). (gr. -1-1). bds. 9.99 (978-2-89718-045-4(5)) Caillouet, Gerry.

—Caillou: Family Fun Story Box, 4 vols. 2014. (Boxset Ser.). (ENG.). 40p. (J). (gr. -1-k). bds. 12.99 (978-2-89718-123-9(0)) Caillouet, Gerry.

Seymour, Arlene. The Moon Book: A Lunar Pop-up Celebration. Seymour, Arlene, illus. 2004. (Illus.). 14p. (YA). (gr. k-4). reprint ed. 22.00 (978-0-7567-7645-9(7)) DIANE Publishing Co.

Shaffer, Christy. Glitter Unicorns Stickers. 2004. (Dover Little Activity Books Stickers Ser.). (ENG., Illus.). 2p. (J). (gr. 1-4). pap. 1.99 (978-0-486-43538-1(5)) Dover Pubns., Inc.

Shand, Jennifer. Why Do Tractors Have Such Big Tires? Paiva, Johannah Gilman, ed. Fabbri, Daniele, illus. 2014. (ENG.). 20p. (J). (gr. k-4). 8.99 (978-1-4867-0382-1(8)) Flowerpot Children's Pr. Inc. CAN. Dist: Cardinal Pubs. Group.

—Why Do Tractors Have Such Big Tires? 2015. (Why Do... ? Ser.). lib. bdg. 19.65 (978-1-4867-0624-2(X)) Turtleback Bks.

Shand, Jennifer & Fabbri, Daniele. Why Do Rainbows Have So Many Colors? Paiva, Johannah Gilman, ed. 2014. (ENG., Illus.). 20p. (J). (gr. k-4). 8.99 (978-1-4867-0383-8(6)) Flowerpot Children's Pr. Inc. CAN. Dist: Cardinal Pubs. Group.

Shanklin, Sandra, told to. Tales of Cat Canyon. 2005. (Illus.). 143p. pap. 12.95 (978-0-9632459-2-2(9)) Great Plains Pr.

Sharp, N. L. The Flower Girl / the Ring Bear. Hantula, Timothy James, illus. 2009. 40p. (J). 19.95 (978-0-9759829-3-8(1)) Prairieland Pr.

Sharratt, Nick. What's in the Witch's Kitchen? Sharratt, Nick, illus. 2011. (ENG., Illus.). 20p. (J). (gr. -1-2). 12.99 (978-0-7636-5224-1(5)) Candlewick Pr.

Sharratt, Nick & Tucker, Stephen. The Three Little Pigs, 2 vols. Sharratt, Nick, illus. 2016. (Lift-The-Flap Fairy Tales Ser.). (ENG., Illus.). 24p. (J). (gr. -1-k). bds. 11.99 (978-1-5098-1713-9(1)) Pan Macmillan GBR. Dist: Independent Pubs. Group.

Shaw, Nancy E. Sheep in a Jeep. Apple, Margot, illus. (ENG.). (J). (gr. -1-3). 2013. 32p. 26.99 (978-0-547-99383-6(8)) 2009. 26p. bds. 12.99 (978-0-547-23775-6(8)) Houghton Mifflin Harcourt Publishing Co.

Shaw, Nancy E. Sheep in a Shop (board Book) Apple, Margot, illus. 2017. (ENG.). 28p. (J). (— 1). bds. 7.99 **(978-1-328-70286-9(3)**, HMH Books For Young Readers) Houghton Mifflin Harcourt Publishing Co.

Shaw, Natalie. Be Careful, Friend! Craig, Karen, illus. 2010. (Yo Gabba Gabba! Ser.). (ENG.). 26p. (J). (gr. -1 — 1). bds. 5.99 (978-1-4169-9534-0(X), Simon Spotlight) Simon Spotlight.

—A Guide to Life. Spaziante, Patrick, illus. 2015. (Olivia TV Tie-In Ser.). (ENG.). 16p. (J). (gr. -1-2). 5.99 (978-1-4814-2788-3(1), Simon Spotlight) Simon Spotlight.

—I'm Feeling Happy. Fruchter, Jason, illus. 2016. (Daniel Tiger's Neighborhood Ser.). (ENG.). 14p. (J). (gr. -1 — 1). bds. 5.99 (978-1-4814-6178-8(8), Simon Spotlight) Simon Spotlight.

—I'm Feeling Mad. Fruchter, Jason, illus. 2016. (Daniel Tiger's Neighborhood Ser.). (ENG.). 14p. (J). (gr. -1 — 1). bds. 5.99 (978-1-4814-6176-4(1), Simon Spotlight) Simon Spotlight.

—I'M Feeling Silly. Fruchter, Jason, illus. 2016. (Daniel Tiger's Neighborhood Ser.). (ENG.). 14p. (J). (gr. -1 — 1). bds. 5.99 (978-1-4814-6815-2(4), Simon Spotlight) Simon Spotlight.

—Meet the Neighbors! Style Guide Staff, illus. 2014. (Daniel Tiger's Neighborhood Ser.). (ENG.). 16p. (J). (gr. -1-k). bds. 7.99 (978-1-4424-9837-2(4), Simon Spotlight) Simon Spotlight.

Shaw-Russell, Susan. Animal ABC. 2011. (Dover Sticker Bks.). (ENG., Illus.). 4p. (J). (gr. 1-5). 7.99 (978-0-486-48396-2(7)) Dover Pubns., Inc.

Shea, Bob. Dinosaur vs. Bedtime. Shea, Bob, illus. 2011. (Dinosaur vs. Book Ser.). (ENG., Illus.). 30p. (J). (gr. -1-k). bds. 6.99 (978-1-4231-3788-7(4)) Hyperion Pr.

—Dinosaur vs. Mommy Board Book. Shea, Bob, illus. 2017. (Dinosaur vs. Book Ser.). (ENG., Illus.). 32p. (J). (gr. -1-k). bds. 7.99 (978-1-4231-6315-2(X)) Hyperion Bks. for Children.

Shea, Kevin. H Is for Hockey. 2013. (ENG.). (J). pap. (978-1-58536-891-4(1)) Sleeping Bear Pr.

Shealy, Dennis. Joker's Joyride - Built for Speed. Random House Editors, illus. 2010. (Pictureback(R) Ser.). (ENG.). 32p. (J). (gr. -1-2). pap. 4.99 (978-0-375-85967-0(5), Random Hse. Bks. for Young Readers) Random Hse. Children's Bks.

Sheehan, Monica. Be Happy! Sheehan, Monica, illus. 2014. (ENG., Illus.). 68p. (J). (gr. -1-3). 14.99 (978-1-4424-9857-0(9), Little Simon) Little Simon.

—Love Is You & Me. Sheehan, Monica, illus. 2010. (ENG., Illus.). 38p. (J). (gr. -1-k). bds. 7.99 (978-1-4424-0765-7(4), Little Simon) Little Simon.

Sheehy, Shawn. Welcome to the Neighborwood. Sheehy, Shawn, illus. 2015. (ENG., Illus.). 18p. (J). (gr. -1-3). 29.99 (978-0-7636-6594-4(0)) Candlewick Pr.

Sheikh-Miller, Jonathan. Sharks. 2009. (Discovery Nature Ser.). 64p. (YA). (gr. 3-18). 8.99 (978-0-7945-2241-4(6), Usborne) EDC Publishing.

Shepherd, Jodie. Ocean Friends. Ovresat, Laura, illus. 2007. (Guess Who Ser.). (ENG.). 12p. (J). (gr. -1-k). bds. 8.99 (978-0-7944-1122-0(3), Reader's Digest Children's Bks.) Studio Fun International.

—Presidents of the United States of America. 2015. (Illus.). 50p. (J). (978-1-4351-6156-6(4)) Barnes & Noble, Inc.

Sherry, Kevin. I'm the Biggest Thing in the Ocean! 2010. (ENG.). 28p. (J). (gr. k — 1). bds. 6.99 (978-0-8037-3529-3(4), Dial Bks) Penguin Young Readers Group.

Shoulders, Michael. Say Daddy! Weidner, Teri, illus. 2013. (ENG.). 26p. (J). (gr. -1-k). 8.99 (978-1-58536-863-1(6), 202383) Sleeping Bear Pr.

Shubuck, Sheila. I Love You All Year Round. Padron, Alicia, illus. 2008. (ENG.). 16p. (J). (gr. -1). 10.95 (978-1-58117-786-2(0), Intervisual/Piggy Toes) Bendon, Inc.

Shulman, Mark. Big Cat. Chambers, Sally, illus. 2004. 8p. (J). bds. 6.95 (978-1-58925-737-5(5)) Tiger Tales.

—Foxy Fox. Chambers, Sally, illus. 2004. 8p. (J). bds. 6.95 (978-1-58925-738-2(3)) Tiger Tales.

Siede Preis Photography (Firm) Staff & Brian Warling Photography (Firm) Staff, contrib. by. First Words. 2003. (Lift-A-Flap Ser.). (Illus.). 12p. (J). bds. 12.98 (978-0-7853-8624-7(6), 7188400) Publications International, Ltd.

Sight Words/ESL Intro Klt. 2004. (ENG.). (J). 44.99 (978-0-943343-75-4(5)) Learning Wrap-Ups, Inc.

Silberg, Francis Barry. The Story of Chanukah. Levy, Pamela R., illus. 2017. 24p. (J). **(978-0-8249-1665-7(4))** Worthy Publishing.

Silver Dolphin. Sleepyhead. Chang, Flora, illus. 2017. (ENG.). 10p. (J). bds. 7.99 (978-1-62686-874-8(3), Silver Dolphin Bks.) Readerlink Distribution Services, LLC.

Silver Dolphin & Lebrun, Maxime. Up, up, up in the Tree. 2017. (Lift-And-Learn Peek-Through Book Ser.). (ENG., Illus.). 12p. (J). (gr. -1). 9.99 (978-1-62686-907-3(3), Silver Dolphin Bks.) Readerlink Distribution Services, LLC.

Silver Dolphin en Español Editors. Seqorita Cmrculo: Miss Circle, Spanish-Language Edition. 2005. (Mis figuras Geometricas Ser.). (SPA., Illus.). 6p. (J). (978-970-718-293-6(8), Silver Dolphin en Español) Advanced Marketing, S. de R. L. de C. V.

Silver Dolphin en Español Staff, creator. Mis Figuras Geometricas, Srita Estrella. 2005. (Mis figuras Geometricas Ser.). (SPA., Illus.). 6p. (J). (gr. -1-k). (978-970-718-295-0(4), Silver Dolphin en Español) Advanced Marketing, S. de R. L. de C. V.

Silver Dolphin Staff. Cuerpo humano/Human Body. 2011. 16p. (978-607-404-318-1(3), Silver Dolphin en Español) Advanced Marketing, S. de R. L. de C. V.

Silver Dolphin Staff, ed. Peek-A-Boo Sliders: Baby Animals. Choux, Nathalie, illus. 2016. (Peek-A-Boo Sliders Ser.). (ENG.). 10p. (J). bds. 8.99 (978-1-62686-731-4(3), Silver Dolphin Bks.) Readerlink Distribution Services, LLC.

Sim, David. Jump Freddy, Jump! Sim, David, illus. 2007. (ENG., Illus.). 12p. (J). (gr. -1-k). 12.99 (978-1-85707-659-2(1)) Tango Bks. GBR. Dist: Independent Pubs. Group.

Simi, Gillingham & Gillingham, Sara. In My Patch. Siminovich, Lorena, illus. 2010. (ENG.). 12p. (J). (gr. -1 — 1). bds. 8.99 (978-0-8118-7567-7(9)) Chronicle Bks. LLC.

Siminovich, Lorena. I Like Toys. Siminovich, Lorena, illus. 2011. (Petit Collage Ser.). (ENG., Illus.). 10p. (J). (— 1). bds. 6.99 (978-0-7636-5074-2(9), Templar) Candlewick Pr.

Siminovich, Lorena, illus. You Are My Baby - Farm. 2013. (ENG.). 10p. (J). (gr. -1 — 1). bds. 8.99 (978-1-4521-0643-4(6)) Chronicle Bks. LLC.

—You Are My Baby - Safari. 2013. (ENG.). 10p. (J). (gr. -1 — 1). bds. 8.99 (978-1-4521-0642-7(8)) Chronicle Bks. LLC.

—You Are My Baby: Garden. 2014. (ENG.). 10p. (J). (gr. -1 — 1). bds. 8.99 (978-1-4521-2649-4(6)) Chronicle Bks. LLC.

—You Are My Baby: Meadow. 2015. (ENG.). 10p. (J). (gr. -1 — 1). bds. 8.99 (978-1-4521-4011-7(1)) Chronicle Bks. LLC.

—You Are My Baby: Ocean. 2014. (ENG.). 10p. (J). (gr. -1 — 1). bds. 8.99 (978-1-4521-2650-0(X)) Chronicle Bks. LLC.

—You Are My Baby: Woodland. 2014. (ENG.). 10p. (J). (gr. -1 — 1). bds. 8.99 (978-1-4521-3431-4(6)) Chronicle Bks. LLC.

Simon, Jenne. Tell the Time! Hino, Sachiho, illus. 2015. (J). (978-0-545-74720-2(1)) Scholastic, Inc.

Simon, Mary Manz. God Made the Moon. Walkley, Lizzie, illus. 2016. (J). (978-0-8249-1981-8(5), Ideal Pubns.) Worthy Publishing.

—God Made the Sun. Walkley, Lizzie, illus. 2016. (J). (978-0-8249-1980-1(7), Ideal Pubns.) Worthy Publishing.

Sims, Lesley. Illustrated Classics for Girls. Mason, Conrad, illus. 2009. (Illustrated Stories Ser.). 384p. (YA). (gr. 3-18). 19.99 (978-0-7945-2419-7(2), Usborne) EDC Publishing.

Sims, Nat. Peekaboo Barn. Tabor, Nathan, illus. 2014. (Peekaboo Ser.). (ENG.). 20p. (J). (— 1). bds. 7.99 (978-0-7636-7557-8(1), Candlewick Entertainment) Candlewick Pr.

—¿Quién Está en el Granero? Tabor, Nathan, illus. 2017. (ENG & SPA.). 20p. (J). (— 1). bds. 7.99 (978-0-7636-9315-2(4), Candlewick Entertainment) Candlewick Pr.

Singer, Marilyn. Fun with Animals Friendship Box. Zaidi, Nadeem, illus. 2009. (J). (978-1-4231-2799-4(4)); (978-1-4231-2797-0(8)); (978-1-4231-2798-7(6)) Disney Pr.

Singh, Lee. ABC & Do. Wall, Karen, illus. 2013. (ENG.). 24p. (J). (gr. -1-k). 19.99 (978-1-4052-6532-4(9)) Egmont Bks., Ltd. GBR. Dist: Independent Pubs. Group.

Sirett, Dawn & Dorling Kindersley Publishing Staff. All about Me! 6 Fun Flaps to Flap. 2008. (Fun Flaps Ser.). (ENG., Illus.). 14p. (J). (gr. -1-k). bds. 4.99 (978-0-7566-3438-4(5), DK Children) Dorling Kindersley Publishing, Inc.

—Beep! Beep! Peekaboo! Quasha, Jennifer, ed. King, Dave, photos by. 2008. (ENG., Illus.). 12p. (J). (gr. -1-k). bds. 6.99 (978-0-7566-3487-2(3), DK Children) Dorling Kindersley Publishing, Inc.

Sisler, Celeste. Disney Fairies: Love, Tinker Bell. 2014. (ENG., Illus.). 10p. (J). (gr. -1 — 1). bds. 6.99 (978-0-316-28347-2(9)) Little, Brown Bks. for Young Readers.

—Disney Fairies: the Perfect Pumpkin. 2015. (ENG., Illus.). 10p. (J). (gr. -1 — 1). bds. 6.99 (978-0-316-37854-3(2)) Little, Brown Bks. for Young Readers.

Skeffington, Miranda. My Little Pony: Mini Pony Collector's Guide with Exclusive Figure. 2013. (ENG., Illus.). 240p. (J). (gr. 1-17). 19.00 (978-0-316-24907-2(6)) Little, Brown Bks. for Young Readers.

Skeleton Sticker Book. 2003. (Illus.). 16p. (J). 2.98 (978-1-84273-121-5(1), Exclusive Editions) Parragon, Inc.

Skewes, John. Larry Loves Boston! 2016. (Larry Gets Lost Ser.). (ENG., Illus.). 20p. (J). (— 1). pap. 9.99 (978-1-63217-047-7(7), Little Bigfoot) Sasquatch Bks.

—Larry Loves San Francisco! Skewes, John, illus. 2014. (Larry Gets Lost Ser.). (ENG., Illus.). 20p. (J). (— 1). bds. 9.99 (978-1-57061-912-0(3), Little Bigfoot) Sasquatch Bks.

—Larry Loves Washington, DC! 2016. (Larry Gets Lost Ser.). (ENG., Illus.). 20p. (J). (— 1). pap. 9.99 (978-1-63217-048-4(5), Little Bigfoot) Sasquatch Bks.

Skewes, John & Ode, Eric. Larry Gets Lost in Seattle: 10th Anniversary Edition. 10th ed. 2017. (Larry Gets Lost Ser.). (ENG., Illus.). 32p. (J). (gr. -1-2). 17.99 (978-1-63217-092-7(2), Little Bigfoot) Sasquatch Bks.

Sklansky, Amy E. You Are My Little Pumpkin Pie. 2013. (ENG., Illus.). 16p. (J). (gr. -1 — 1). bds. 6.99 (978-0-316-20714-0(4)) Little, Brown Bks. for Young Readers.

Slater, Jean M. At the Fire Station: An Interactive Book. 2nd ed. 2003. (Illus.). 13p. (J). bds. (978-0-9743149-0-7(0)) Slater Software, Inc.

Slater, Nicola, illus. We're Bored. 2005. 12p. (J). 12.95 (978-1-58117-384-0(9), Intervisual/Piggy Toes) Bendon, Inc.

Slee, Natasha. Design Line: History of Women's Fashion. Mander, Sanna, illus. 2015. (ENG.). 16p. (J). (gr. 5). 17.99 (978-0-7636-7962-0(3), Big Picture Press) Candlewick Pr.

Sleeping Bear Press. Little Dance. Benoit, Renné, illus. 2013. (ENG.). 20p. (J). (gr. -1-k). 8.99 (978-1-58536-884-6(9), 202899) Sleeping Bear Pr.

Slegers, Liesbet. Eating. 2010. (Clavis Toddler: Daily Life Ser.). (ENG.). 12p. (J). (gr. k — 1). bds. 5.95 (978-1-60537-067-5(3)) Cobblestone Publishing Co.

—Fall Leaves. 2012. (Clavis Toddler: Daily Life Ser.). (ENG.). 12p. (J). (gr. k — 1). bds. 5.95 (978-1-60537-122-1(X)) Cobblestone Publishing Co.

—Funny Tails. 2011. (Funny Board Bks.). (ENG.). 16p. (J). (gr. k — 1). bds. 9.95 (978-1-60537-090-3(8)) Cobblestone Publishing Co.

—Guess Where I Am. 2008. (Guess Ser.). (ENG.). 26p. (J). (gr. k — 1). 7.95 (978-1-60537-001-9(0)) Clavis Publishing.

—Guess Who I Am. 2008. (Guess Ser.). (ENG.). 26p. (J). (gr. k — 1). 7.95 (978-1-60537-000-2(2)) Clavis Publishing.

—Move! 2012. (ENG.). 12p. (J). (gr. k — 1). bds. 7.95 (978-1-60537-118-4(1)) Cobblestone Publishing Co.

—Que Veo?/ What Do I See? 2008. 24p. bds. 11.95 (978-84-263-6705-1(4)) Vives, Luis Editorial (Edelvives) ESP. Dist: Baker & Taylor Bks.

—Sleeping. 2010. (Clavis Toddler: Daily Life Ser.). (ENG.). 12p. (J). (gr. k — 1). bds. 5.95 (978-1-60537-068-2(1)) Cobblestone Publishing Co.

—Surprise! 2012. (ENG.). 12p. (J). (gr. k — 1). bds. 7.95 (978-1-60537-117-7(3)) Cobblestone Publishing Co.

—Winter Snow. 2012. (Clavis Toddler: the World Ser.). (ENG.). 12p. (J). (gr. k — 1). bds. 5.95 (978-1-60537-123-8(8)) Cobblestone Publishing Co.

Slier, Debby. Babies on the Go!, 1 vol. 2013. (ENG., Illus.). 32p. (J). bds. 5.99 (978-1-59572-173-0(8)) Star Bright Bks., Inc.

—Loving Me, 1 vol. 2013. (ENG., Illus.). 32p. (J). bds. 5.99 (978-1-59572-334-5(X)) Star Bright Bks., Inc.

Slobodkina, Esphyr. Caps for Sale. Slobodkina, Esphyr, illus. 75th ed. 2015. (Reading Rainbow Bks.). (ENG., Illus.). 32p. (J). (gr. -1-3). bds. 8.99 (978-0-06-147453-8(3), HarperFestival) HarperCollins Pubs.

Smallman, Steve, et al. My First Santa's Coming to My House. Dunn, Robert, illus. 2015. (ENG.). 18p. (J). bds. 9.99 (978-1-4926-2885-9(9), Sourcebooks Jabberwocky) Sourcebooks, Inc.

Smart Kidz, creator. The ABC's of How I Love You: You're My Alphabet of Love! 2013. (Parent Love Letters Ser.). (ENG., Illus.). 12p. (gr. -1). bds. 12.99 (978-1-891100-30-7(0), Smart Kids) Penton Overseas, Inc.

—I'm a Little Teapot. 2013. (Sing N Play Songs Ser.). (ENG., Illus.). 12p. (J). bds. 12.99 (978-1-891100-07-9(6), Smart Kids) Penton Overseas, Inc.

—It's Potty Time for Boys. 2013. (ENG., Illus.). 12p. (J). bds. 12.99 (978-1-891100-05-5(X), Smart Kids) Penton Overseas, Inc.

—Jingle Bells. 2013. (ENG., Illus.). 12p. (gr. -1). bds. 12.99 (978-1-939658-03-6(9), Smart Kids) Penton Overseas, Inc.

—The 123s of How I Love You. 2013. (Parent Love Letters Ser.). (ENG., Illus.). 12p. (gr. -1). bds. 12.99 (978-1-891100-31-4(9), Smart Kids) Penton Overseas, Inc.

Smart Kidz Media, creator. O Christmas Tree! 2013. (ENG., Illus.). 12p. (J). bds. 12.99 (978-1-939658-05-0(5), Smart Kids) Penton Overseas, Inc.

—Silent Night. 2013. (ENG., Illus.). 12p. (J). bds. 12.99 (978-1-939658-01-2(2), Smart Kids) Penton Overseas, Inc.

—Up on the Housetop! 2013. (ENG., Illus.). 12p. (J). bds. 12.99 (978-1-939658-04-3(7), Smart Kids) Penton Overseas, Inc.

Smart Kidz Media Studios Staff, ed. It's Bedtime! 2011. 16p. 7.99 (978-1-891100-78-9(5), Smart Kids) Penton Overseas, Inc.

SMARTLAB Creative Team. Space Exploration. 2010. 10p. mass mkt. 39.99 (978-1-60380-050-1(6)) becker&mayer! books.

Smith, A. & Tatchell, J. How are Babies Made? How do Your Senses Work? What Happens to Your Food? rev. ed. 2004. (Flip Flaps Ser.). 48p. (J). (gr. 2-18). 14.95 (978-0-7945-0618-6(6), Usborne) EDC Publishing.

Smith, Alastair. Baby Animals. 2004. (Lift-the-Flap Learners Ser.). (SPA & ENG., Illus.). 1p. (J). (gr. 1-18). pap. 8.95 (978-0-7945-0133-4(8), Usborne) EDC Publishing.

—Nighttime Lift-the-flap. Butler, John, illus. 2005. 16p. (J). (gr. 1-18). 11.95 (978-0-7945-0967-5(3), Usborne) EDC Publishing.

—On the Farm Lift-the-Flap. Torode, Justine, illus. 2004. (Luxury Lift-the-Flap Ser.). 16p. (J). (gr. 1-18). 11.95 (978-0-7945-0508-0(2), Usborne) EDC Publishing.

Smith, Alastair, ed. Homes & Houses Then & Now. 2004. (Then & Now Flip Flaps Ser.). (SPA & ENG., Illus.). 1p. (J). (gr. 2-18). pap. 7.95 (978-0-7460-3100-1(9)) EDC Publishing.

—Travel & Transport Then & Now. 2004. (Then & Now Flip Flaps Ser.). (ENG., Illus.). 1p. (J). (gr. 2-18). pap. 7.95 (978-0-7460-3102-5(5)) EDC Publishing.

Smith, Alastair & Howell, Laura. On the Beach. 2004. (Lift-the-Flap Learners Ser.). (Illus.). 16p. (J). (gr. 1-18). pap. 8.95 (978-0-7945-0213-3(X), Usborne) EDC Publishing.

Smith, Alastair & Tachell, Judy. Under the Sea. Scott, Peter David, illus. 2007. (J). (978-0-545-03305-3(5)) Scholastic, Inc.

Smith, Alastair & Tatchell, Judy. Dinosaurs. 2004. (Jumbo Lift-the-Flap Learners Ser.). (Illus.). 16p. (J). (gr. 1-18). 11.99 (978-0-7945-0418-2(3), Usborne) EDC Publishing.

—Dinosaurs. Scott, Peter David, illus. 2005. (J). (978-0-439-68903-8(1)) Scholastic, Inc.

Smith Bresciani, Cathleen & Eldredge, Richard. Sassafrass Jones & the Search for a Forever Home. 2013. 54p. 24.99 (978-0-578-12084-3(4)) Misfit Mouse.

Smith, Iain. Angel Fish: A Pull & Lift Book. Smith, Iain, illus. 2005. (Stories to Share Ser.). (Illus.). 12p. (J). 10.95 (978-1-58117-084-9(X), Intervisual/Piggy Toes) Bendon, Inc.

Smith, Jodene Lynn & Rice, Dona Herweck. If I Were a Tree, 1 vol. 2010. (Early Childhood Themes Ser.). (ENG., Illus.). 16p. (J). (gr. -1-2). pap. 19.99 (978-1-4333-1488-9(6)) Shell Educational Publishing.

Smith, Jodene Lynn & Thompson, Chad. Baa, Baa, Black Sheep, 1 vol. 2010. (Early Childhood Themes Ser.). (ENG., Illus.). 16p. (J). (gr. -1-2). pap. 19.99 (978-1-4333-1484-1(3)) Shell Educational Publishing.

—Beh, Beh, Borreguito Negro, 1 vol. rev. ed. 2010. (Early Childhood Themes Ser.). (SPA., Illus.). 16p. (J). (gr. -1-2). pap. 19.99 (978-1-4333-2095-8(9)) Shell Educational Publishing.

Smith, Lane. It's a Little Book. 2011. (ENG., Illus.). 24p. (J). (— 1). bds. 7.99 (978-1-59643-758-6(8), 9781596437586) Roaring Brook Pr.

Smith, Maggie. One Naked Baby. 2015. (ENG., Illus.). 34p. (J). (— 1). bds. 6.99 (978-0-553-49889-9(4), Knopf Bks. for Young Readers) Random Hse. Children's Bks.

Smith, Mike. Catch the Cuddle. 2015. (ENG., Illus.). 18p. (J). (gr. -1-k). pap. 11.99 (978-1-4052-7190-5(6)) Egmont Bks., Ltd. GBR. Dist: Independent Pubs. Group.

Snape, Emily. Motor Mix Emergency: Invent Your Own Mix-And-Match Vehicles! Alexander, Rilla, illus. 2017. (ENG.). 16p. (J). (gr. -1 — 1). bds. 9.99 (978-1-4521-4838-0(4)) Chronicle Bks. LLC.

—Motor Mix, Flight: Invent Your Own Mix-And-Match Vehicles! Alexander, Rilla, illus. 2017. (ENG.). 16p. (J). (gr. -1 — 1). bds. 9.99 (978-1-4521-4839-7(2)) Chronicle Bks. LLC.

Snow, Todd. You Are Beautiful. Strong, Melodee, illus. 2007. (You Are Important Ser.). (ENG.). 24p. (J). (gr. -1-k). bds. 7.99 (978-1-934277-10-2(X)) Mam Green Publishing, Inc.

—You Are Brave. Strong, Melodee, illus. 2007. (ENG.). 24p. (J). bds. 7.99 (978-1-934277-08-9(8)) Mam Green Publishing, Inc.

—You Are Creative. Strong, Melodee, illus. 2007. (ENG.). 24p. (J). bds. 7.99 (978-1-934277-07-2(X)) Mam Green Publishing, Inc.

—You Are Friendly. Strong, Melodee, illus. 2007. (You Are Important Ser.). (ENG.). 24p. (J). (gr. -1-k). bds. 7.99 (978-1-934277-09-6(6)) Mam Green Publishing, Inc.

—You Are Important. Strong, Melodee, illus. 2007. (You Are Important Ser.). (ENG.). 24p. (J). (gr. -1-k). bds. 7.99 (978-1-934277-06-5(1)) Mam Green Publishing, Inc.

Snowflake Day! 2014. (Daniel Tiger's Neighborhood Ser.). (ENG., Illus.). 14p. (J). (gr. -1-k). bds. 5.99 (978-1-4814-1771-6(1), Simon Spotlight) Simon Spotlight.

Snyder, Betsy E. Bulldozer. 2015. (Illus.). (J). (978-1-62885-064-2(7)) Kidsbooks, LLC.

—Fire Engine. 2015. (Illus.). (J). (978-1-62885-065-9(5)) Kidsbooks, LLC.

—Train. 2015. (Illus.). (J). (978-1-62885-066-6(3)) Kidsbooks, LLC.

Snyder, Betsy E., illus. I Can Dance. 2015. (ENG.). 14p. (J). (gr. -1 — 1). bds. 8.99 (978-1-4521-2929-7(0)) Chronicle Bks. LLC.

—I Can Play. 2015. (ENG.). 14p. (J). (gr. -1 — 1). bds. 8.99 (978-1-4521-2905-1(3)) Chronicle Bks. LLC.

Sobel, June. The Goodnight Train (lap Board Book) Huliska-Beith, Laura, illus. 2017. (ENG.). 30p. (J). (— 1). bds. 12.99 **(978-1-328-76438-6(9)**, HMH Books For Young Readers) Houghton Mifflin Harcourt Publishing Co.

Sokol, Dawn DeVries. Leapin' Lizards - Pet Palooza: A Lizards Primer, 1 vol. 2017. (ENG.). 22p. (J). bds. 9.99 **(978-1-4236-4737-9(8))** Gibbs Smith, Publisher.

Sollinger, Emily. This Is Our World: A Story about Taking Care of the Earth. Brown, Jo, illus. 2010. (Little Green Bks.). (ENG.). 12p. (J). (gr. -1-1). bds. 7.99 (978-1-4169-7821-3(6), Little Simon) Little Simon.

Soman, David & Davis, Jacky. Little Box of Ladybug Girl, 4 vols. Soman, David, illus. 2013. (Ladybug Girl Ser.). (ENG., Illus.). 14p. (J). (gr. -1-k). bds. 23.96 (978-0-8037-4102-7(2), Dial Bks) Penguin Young Readers Group.

—Play All Day with Ladybug Girl. Soman, David, illus. 2013. (Ladybug Girl Ser.). (ENG., Illus.). 16p. (J). (gr. -1-k). 6.99 (978-0-448-46686-6(4), Grosset & Dunlap) Penguin Young Readers Group.

Sophie & Friends. 2014. (ENG.). 12p. (J). (gr. -1 — 1). bds. 6.99 (978-1-4654-1815-9(6), DK Children) Dorling Kindersley Publishing, Inc.

Soundprints, creator. Orang Utan's Playtime. 2011. (Let's Go to the Zoo! Ser.). (ENG., Illus.). 16p. (gr. -1). 5.95 (978-1-60727-456-8(6)) Soundprints.

Soundprints Staff & Galvin, Laura Gates. First Look at Aircraft. 2009. (ENG.). 16p. (J). 6.95 (978-1-60727-118-5(4)) Soundprints.

Spafford, Suzy. Witzy's Fall Collection. 2010. (Illus.). (J). (978-1-4037-9599-1(1)) Creative Edge.

Spanish Intro Kit. 2004. (ENG & SPA.). (J). 44.99 (978-0-943343-76-1(3)) Learning Wrap-Ups, Inc.

Spanyol, Jessica. Clive Is a Librarian. Spanyol, Jessica, illus. 2017. (Clive's Jobs Ser.: 4). (ENG., Illus.). 14p. (J). bds. **(978-1-84643-989-6(2))** Child's Play International Ltd.

—Clive Is a Nurse. Spanyol, Jessica, illus. 2017. (Clive's Jobs Ser.: 4). (ENG., Illus.). 14p. (J). bds. **(978-1-84643-991-9(4))** Child's Play International Ltd.

—Clive Is a Teacher. Spanyol, Jessica, illus. 2017. (Clive's Jobs Ser.: 4). (ENG., Illus.). 14p. (J). bds. **(978-1-84643-990-2(6))** Child's Play International Ltd.

—Clive Is a Waiter. Spanyol, Jessica, illus. 2017. (Clive's Jobs Ser.: 4). (ENG., Illus.). 14p. (J). bds. **(978-1-84643-992-6(2))** Child's Play International Ltd.

Spelman, Cornelia Maude. When I Feel Scared. Parkinson, Kathy, illus. 2010. (ENG.). 16p. (J). (gr. -1 — 1). bds. 7.99 (978-0-8075-8905-2(5)) Whitman, Albert & Co.

Spence, Ann. Elmo's Play Day. 2010. (Illus.). 6p. (J). bds. 12.98 (978-0-7853-8441-0(3), 7186300) Phoenix International Publications, Inc.

Sper, Emily. The Kids' Fun Book of Jewish Time. Sper, Emily, illus. 2006. (HEB & ENG., Illus.). 24p. (J). (gr. -1-1). 16.99 (978-1-58023-311-8(2), 1260461, Jewish Lights Publishing) LongHill Partners, Inc.

Sperring, Mark. The Shape of My Heart. Paterson, Alys, illus. 2015. (ENG.). 32p. (J). (gr. -1-1). bds. 7.99 (978-1-68119-017-4(6), 9781681190174, Bloomsbury USA Childrens) Bloomsbury Publishing USA.

Spinelli, Eileen. Love My Shoes! 2011. 18p. (J). (gr. -1-k). bds. 7.99 (978-0-8249-1853-8(3), Ideal Pubns.) Worthy Publishing.

—Two to Cuddle. Logan, Laura, illus. 2009. (ENG.). 20p. (J). bds. 6.99 (978-0-8249-1824-8(X), Ideal Pubns.) Worthy Publishing.

Spinner, Cala. A Busy Day in the Neighborhood. Fruchter, Jason, illus. 2017. (Daniel Tiger's Neighborhood Ser.). (ENG.). 12p. (J). (gr. -1-k). bds. 14.99 (978-1-4814-8583-8(0), Simon Spotlight) Simon Spotlight.

Spiro, Ruth & Chan, Irene. Baby Loves Aerospace Engineering! 2016. (Baby Loves Science Ser.). (ENG., Illus.). 20p. (J). (— 1). bds. 8.95 (978-1-58089-541-5(7)) Charlesbridge Publishing, Inc.

Spurr, Elizabeth. Happy Sparkling Hanukkah. Madden, Colleen, illus. 2011. (J). (978-1-4027-9660-9(9)) Sterling Publishing Co., Inc.

—In the Wind, 1 vol. Oliphant, Manelle, illus. 2016. (In the Weather Ser.). (ENG.). 22p. (J). (gr. -1-k). bds. 6.95 (978-1-56145-854-7(6)) Peachtree Pubs.

Squillace, Elisa, illus. Aladdin. 2007. (Flip-Up Fairy Tales Ser.). (ENG.). 24p. (J). (gr. 2-2). (978-1-84643-113-5(1)) Child's Play International Ltd.

—Down in the Jungle. 2005. (Classic Books with Holes Board Book Ser.). (ENG.). 14p. (J). (gr. -1-1). bds. (978-1-904550-61-7(4)) Child's Play International Ltd.

Srinivasan, Divya. Little Owl's Colors. Srinivasan, Divya, illus. 2015. (ENG., Illus.). 18p. (J). (— 1). 5.99 (978-0-451-47456-8(2), Viking Books for Young Readers) Penguin Young Readers Group.

Stahl, Stephanie. The Best Snowman Ever! Vasylenko, Veronica, illus. 2013. (ENG.). 16p. (J). (gr. -1-k). bds. 8.95 (978-1-58925-605-7(0)) Tiger Tales.

Star Bright Books. Carry Me (Portuguese/English), 1 vol. Icibaci, Neusa, tr. 2009. (Babies Everywhere Ser.). (ENG & POR., Illus.). 20p. (J). (gr. -1). 6.95 (978-1-59572-200-3(9)) Star Bright Bks., Inc.

Star Wars Villains. 2011. (Illus.). (J). (978-0-545-28664-0(6)) Scholastic, Inc.

Steadman, Barbara. Little Flower Girls Sticker Paper Dolls. 2003. (Dover Little Activity Books Paper Dolls Ser.). (ENG., Illus.). 4p. (J). (gr. k-3). pap. 1.99 (978-0-486-43019-5(7)) Dover Pubns., Inc.

Steele, Philip. A Knight's City: With Amazing Pop-Ups & an Interactive Tour of Life in a Medieval City! 2008. (ENG.). 32p. (J). (gr. 1-5). 18.99 (978-1-4169-6124-6(0), Little Simon) Little Simon.

Steer, Dugald A. Snappy Little Halloween. Matthews, Derek, illus. 2004. 20p. (J). (gr. k-4). reprint ed. 13.00 (978-0-7567-7403-5(9)) DIANE Publishing Co.

Steers, Billy. Lift-The-Flap Tab: Tractor Mac: Friends on the Farm. 2015. (Lift-The-Flap Tab Bks.). (ENG., Illus.). 16p. (J). (gr. -1-k). bds. 8.99 (978-0-374-30168-2(9), 9780374301682) Square Fish.

—Tractor Mac Countdown to Christmas. 2016. (Tractor Mac Ser.). (ENG., Illus.). 16p. (J). bds. 6.99 (978-0-374-30120-0(4), 9780374301200, Farrar, Straus & Giroux (BYR)) Farrar, Straus & Giroux.

—Tractor Mac Farm Days. 2016. (Tractor Mac Ser.). (ENG., Illus.). 16p. (J). bds. 5.99 (978-0-374-30117-0(4), 9780374301170, Farrar, Straus & Giroux (BYR)) Farrar, Straus & Giroux.

Steers, Billy. Tractor Mac Plane Jane's Journey. Steers, Billy, illus. 2017. (Tractor Mac Ser.). (ENG., Illus.). 16p. (J). bds. 5.99 **(978-0-374-30634-2(6)**, 9780374306342, Farrar, Straus & Giroux (BYR)) Farrar, Straus & Giroux.

Steigemeyer, Julie. My Little Easter Book. Regan, Dana, illus. 2008. 20p. (J). (gr. -1-k). bds. 6.49 (978-0-7586-1444-5(6)) Concordia Publishing Hse.

Sterling Children's Staff. My Mommy's the Bestest. 2016. (ENG., Illus.). 22p. (J). (— 1). bds. 6.95 (978-1-4549-1876-9(4)) Sterling Publishing Co., Inc.

Sterling Children's, Sterling. Begin Smart(tm) Moo! Moo! What Are You? Kreloff, Elliot, illus. 2017. (Begin Smart(tm) Ser.). (ENG.). 14p. (J). (— 1). bds. 8.95 (978-1-4549-2084-7(X)) Sterling Publishing Co., Inc.

—Begin Smart(tm) Peek-A-Boo What? Kreloff, Elliot, illus. 2017. (Begin Smart(tm) Ser.). (ENG.). 18p. (J). (— 1). bds. 8.95 (978-1-4549-2086-1(6)) Sterling Publishing Co., Inc.

—Builders. Finn, Rebecca, illus. 2015. (Busy Bks.). (ENG.). 10p. (J). (— 1). bds. 8.95 (978-1-4549-1733-5(4)) Sterling Publishing Co., Inc.

—Clothes/la Ropa. 2016. (Say & Play Ser.). (ENG., Illus.). 28p. (J). (— 1). bds. 4.95 (978-1-4549-1997-1(3)) Sterling Publishing Co., Inc.

—Food/Los Alimentos. 2016. (Say & Play Ser.). (ENG., Illus.). 28p. (J). (— 1). bds. 4.95 (978-1-4549-1998-8(1)) Sterling Publishing Co., Inc.

—Meow, Moo, Cock-A-Doodle-Doo: A Book of Animals. 2016. (ENG., Illus.). 28p. (J). (— 1). bds. 6.95 (978-1-4114-7586-1(0), Spark Publishing Group) Sterling Publishing Co., Inc.

—Move It! 2017. (ENG., Illus.). 22p. (J). (— 1). bds. 6.95 (978-1-4549-2311-4(3)) Sterling Publishing Co., Inc.

—Things That Go Vroom: A Book of Vehicles. 2016. (ENG., Illus.). 28p. (J). (— 1). bds. 6.95 (978-1-4114-7589-2(5), Spark Publishing Group) Sterling Publishing Co., Inc.

Sterling Children's, Sterling, ed. Sleepy Kitty. 2015. (ENG., Illus.). 22p. (J). (— 1). bds. 6.95 (978-1-4549-1464-8(5)) Sterling Publishing Co., Inc.

—Sleepy Puppy. 2015. (ENG., Illus.). 22p. (J). (— 1). bds. 6.95 (978-1-4549-1465-5(3)) Sterling Publishing Co., Inc.

Sterling Publishing Co., Inc. Begin Smart(tm) Look at Me! 2016. (Begin Smart(tm) Ser.). (ENG., Illus.). 10p. (J). (— 1). bds. 8.95 (978-1-4549-1755-7(5)) Sterling Publishing Co., Inc.

—Begin Smart(tm) Meow. 2016. (Begin Smart(tm) Ser.). (ENG., Illus.). 14p. (J). (— 1). bds. 8.95 (978-1-4549-1877-6(2)) Sterling Publishing Co., Inc.

—Begin Smart(tm) What Does Baby Do? A First Lift-The-Flap Book. 2016. (Begin Smart(tm) Ser.). (ENG., Illus.). 16p. (J). (— 1). bds. 8.95 (978-1-4549-1879-0(9)) Sterling Publishing Co., Inc.

—Begin Smart(tm) What Does Baby Say? A First Lift-The-Flap Book. 2016. (Begin Smart(tm) Ser.). (ENG., Illus.). 16p. (J). (— 1). bds. 8.95 (978-1-4549-1880-6(2)) Sterling Publishing Co., Inc.

—Begin Smart(tm) Who Am I? 2016. (Begin Smart(tm) Ser.). (ENG., Illus.). 10p. (J). (— 1). bds. 8.95 (978-1-4549-1756-4(3)) Sterling Publishing Co., Inc.

—Begin Smart(tm) Woof. 2016. (Begin Smart(tm) Ser.). (ENG., Illus.). 14p. (J). (— 1). bds. 8.95 (978-1-4549-1878-3(0)) Sterling Publishing Co., Inc.

—Clothes. 2016. (Say & Play Ser.). (ENG., Illus.). 28p. (J). (— 1). bds. 4.95 (978-1-4549-1971-1(X)) Sterling Publishing Co., Inc.

—Food. 2016. (Say & Play Ser.). (ENG., Illus.). 28p. (J). (— 1). bds. 4.95 (978-1-4549-1973-5(6)) Sterling Publishing Co., Inc.

—My First Hockey Book. 2016. (First Sports Ser.). (ENG., Illus.). 22p. (J). (— 1). bds. 6.95 (978-1-4549-1974-2(4)) Sterling Publishing Co., Inc.

—My First Tennis Book. 2016. (First Sports Ser.). (ENG., Illus.). 22p. (J). (— 1). bds. 6.95 (978-1-4549-1975-9(2)) Sterling Publishing Co., Inc.

Sterling Publishing Co., Inc. Staff. Garage. Finn, Rebecca, illus. 2015. (Busy Bks.). (ENG.). 10p. (J). (— 1). bds. 8.95 (978-1-4549-1734-2(2)) Sterling Publishing Co., Inc.

Stern, Ariella. Chanukah Guess Who? A Lift the Flap Book. Argoff, Patti, illus. 2012. (ENG.). 32p. (J). 9.95 (978-1-929628-68-1(4)) Hachai Publishing.

Steven, Kenneth C. The Biggest Thing in the World. Mitchell, Melanie, illus. 2013. (ENG.). 32p. (J). (gr. -1-k). 6.99 (978-0-7459-6402-7(8)) Lion Hudson PLC GBR. Dist: Independent Pubs. Group.

Stevenson, Peter, illus. Baby's First Nativity. 2016. (ENG.). 20p. (J). (gr. -1-k). bds. 9.99 (978-0-7944-3850-0(4)) Studio Fun International.

—Baby's First Nativity: A CarryAlong Treasury. 2016. (Carry along Treasury Ser.: 1). (ENG.). 20p. (J). (gr. -1-k). bds. 14.99 (978-0-7944-3836-4(9)) Studio Fun International.

Stewart, Melissa & American Museum of Natural History. Caterpillar to Butterfly. 2016. (Science for Toddlers Ser.). (ENG., Illus.). 24p. (J). (gr. -1 — 1). bds. 7.95 (978-1-4549-1406-8(8)) Sterling Publishing Co., Inc.

Stileman, Kali. Roly Poly Egg. 2011. (ENG.). 26p. (J). (gr. -1-k). 12.95 (978-1-58925-852-5(5)) Tiger Tales.

Stiles, Dan. Baby's First Bloox: Colors, Shapes, & Patterns. 2014. (ENG., Illus.). 22p. (J). (— 1). bds. 16.95 (978-1-57687-684-8(5), powerHouse Bks.) powerHouse Cultural Entertainment, Inc.

—Put on Your Shoes! 2013. (ENG., Illus.). 16p. (J). (-k). 9.95 (978-1-57687-646-6(2), powerHouse Bks.) powerHouse Cultural Entertainment, Inc.

—Today I'm Going to Wear ... 2014. (ENG., Illus.). 16p. (J). (gr. -1-2). bds. 9.95 (978-1-57687-718-0(3), powerHouse Bks.) powerHouse Cultural Entertainment, Inc.

Stine, R. L. Lizard of Oz. 2016. (Goosebumps: Most Wanted Ser.: 10). (ENG.). 160p. (J). (gr. 3-7). pap. 6.99 (978-0-545-82549-8(0), Scholastic Paperbacks) Scholastic, Inc.

Stinson, Kathy. Big or Little? Bell, Jennifer & Goffe, Toni, illus. 2nd ed. 2014. (ENG.). 24p. (J). (gr. -1 — 1). bds. 6.95 (978-1-55451-610-0(2), 9781554516100) Annick Pr., Ltd. CAN. Dist: Publishers Group West (PGW).

—Red Is Best. Lewis, Robin Baird, illus. 6th ed. 2011. (ENG.). 26p. (J). (gr. -1 — 1). bds. 7.99 (978-1-55451-364-2(2), 9781554513642) Annick Pr., Ltd. CAN. Dist: Publishers Group West (PGW).

Stockham, Jess. Cinderella. 2006. (Flip-Up Fairy Tales Ser.). (ENG., Illus.). 24p. (J). (gr. 2-2). (978-1-904550-74-7(6)) Child's Play International Ltd.

Stockham, Jess, illus. Beauty & the Beast. 2007. (Flip-Up Fairy Tales Ser.). (ENG.). 24p. (J). (gr. 2-2). (978-1-84643-114-2(X)) Child's Play International Ltd.

—Cinderella. 2007. (Flip-Up Fairy Tales Ser.). (ENG.). 24p. (J). (gr. -1-2). audio compact disk (978-1-84643-091-6(7)) Child's Play International Ltd.

—The Cockerel, the Mouse & the Little Red Hen. (Flip-Up Fairy Tales Ser.). (ENG.). 24p. (J). 2007. (gr. -1-2). audio compact disk (978-1-84643-092-3(5)) 2006. (gr. 2-2). (978-1-904550-75-4(4)) Child's Play International Ltd.

—Down by the Station. 2003. (Classic Books with Holes 8x8 Ser.). (ENG.). 16p. (J). (978-0-85953-132-0(5)) Child's Play International Ltd.

—Having Fun! 2008. (Just Like Us! Ser.). (ENG.). 12p. (J). (gr. -1). bds. (978-1-84643-178-4(6)) Child's Play International Ltd.

—Little Red Riding Hood. (Classic Fairy Tales Ser.). (ENG.). 24p. (J). 2011. audio compact disk (978-1-84643-458-7(0)) 2007. (gr. -1-2). audio compact disk (978-1-84643-088-6(7)) Child's Play International Ltd.

—Making Friends! 2008. (Just Like Us! Ser.). (ENG.). 12p. (J). (gr. -1). bds. (978-1-84643-180-7(8)) Child's Play International Ltd.

—The Princess & the Pea. 2010. (Flip-Up Fairy Tales Ser.). (ENG.). 24p. (J). (gr. -1-2). audio compact disk (978-1-84643-332-0(0)) Child's Play International Ltd.

—The Steadfast Tin Soldier. 2012. (Flip-Up Fairy Tales Ser.). (ENG.). 24p. (J). audio compact disk (978-1-84643-516-4(1)); (978-1-84643-477-8(7)) Child's Play International Ltd.

—Stone Soup. (Flip-Up Fairy Tales Ser.). (ENG.). 24p. (J). 2007. (gr. -1-2). audio compact disk (978-1-84643-094-7(1)) 2006. (gr. 2-2). pap. (978-1-84643-021-3(6)) Child's Play International Ltd.

Stockham, Jessica. Taking It Easy! 2008. (Just Like Us! Ser.). (ENG., Illus.). 12p. (J). (gr. -1). bds. (978-1-84643-181-4(6)) Child's Play International Ltd.

Stockham, Jessica, illus. Little Red Riding Hood. 2005. (Flip-Up Fairy Tales Ser.). (ENG.). 24p. (J). pap. (978-1-904550-22-8(3)) Child's Play International Ltd.

Stone, Jamie, ed. Danny Dino Ventures Out. 2013. (Pop-Up: Play & Listen Ser.). (ENG., Illus.). 10p. (J). (gr. -1-k). bds. 16.95 (978-1-61889-034-4(4)) AZ Bks. LLC.

Stone, Jon. Another Monster at the End of This Book (Sesame Street) Smollin, Michael, illus. 2016. (Little Golden Board Book Ser.). (ENG.). 26p. (J). (-k). bds. 7.99 (978-1-101-93137-0(X), Golden Bks.) Random Hse. Children's Bks.

—The Monster at the End of This Book. Smollin, Michael, illus. 2015. (Little Golden Board Book Ser.). (ENG.). 26p. (J). (— 1). bds. 7.99 (978-0-553-50873-4(3), Golden Bks.) Random Hse. Children's Bks.

Stone, Judith. Billie the Buffalo Goes to Town. 2008. 20p. pap. 12.95 (978-1-4389-2877-7(7)) AuthorHouse.

Stone, Kate. Happy Birthday, Mouse! (ENG.). 16p. (J). 2014. bds. 5.99 (978-1-4494-4387-0(7)) 2012. (Illus.). bds. 10.99 (978-1-4494-0838-1(9)) Andrews McMeel Publishing.

Stone, Kate, illus. ABC Train. 2013. (ENG.). 20p. (J). bds. 10.99 (978-1-4494-3157-0(7)) Andrews McMeel Publishing.

—Heads & Tails. 2013. (ENG.). 20p. (J). bds. 10.99 (978-1-4494-3246-1(8)) Andrews McMeel Publishing.

Stortz, Diane M. Baby, Baby! Busby, Ailie, illus. 2016. (J). (978-0-8249-1988-7(2), Ideal Pubns.) Worthy Publishing.

The Story of Christmas. 2014. (Boardbooks - Board Book Ser.). (ENG.). 10p. (J). (gr. -1-k). bds. 6.99 (978-0-7944-3198-3(4), Reader's Digest Children's Bks.) Studio Fun International.

Stott, Dorothy, illus. Ten in the Bed. 2010. (Padded Board Book W/CD Ser.). 8p. (J). (gr. k-2). bds. 10.99 incl. audio compact disk (978-1-59922-578-4(6)) Twin Sisters IP, LLC.

Stowell, Louie. Look Inside Your Body. (Look Inside Board Bks). (J). 2011. 13p. ring bd. 15.99 (978-0-7945-2996-3(8)) 2013. 10p. ring bd. 14.99 (978-0-7945-3311-3(6)) EDC Publishing. (Usborne).

—Wind-Up Pirate Ship. Fox, Christyan, illus. 2010. (Wind-up Bks). 13p. (J). bds. 29.99 (978-0-7945-2835-5(X), Usborne) EDC Publishing.

Strauss, Linda Leopold. Best Friends Pretend. Munsinger, Lynn, illus. 2014. (ENG.). 14p. (J). (gr. -1 — 1). bds. 6.99 (978-0-545-45171-0(X), Cartwheel Bks.) Scholastic, Inc.

Strawberry Shortcake Paint n' Play with Sticker Rolls. 2005. (J). spiral bd. (978-1-59487-146-7(9)) Artist Studios, Ltd.

Strawberry Shortcake Secret Diary with Pendant. 2005. (J). *(978-1-59487-155-9(8))* Artist Studios, Ltd.
Stren, Ariella. Bracha Do You Know? Argoff, Patti, illus. 2015. 28p. (J). 9.95 *(978-1-929628-76-6(5))* Hachai Publishing.
Strong, Belinda. Hold & Touch Bedtime. 2015. (Hold & Touch Ser.). (ENG., Illus.). (J). bds. *(978-1-74363-413-4(7))* Hinkler Bks. Pty, Ltd.
Studio Mouse. Princess Colors & Shapes Pack. 2003. (ENG., Illus.). 36p. (J). (gr. -1-3). 12.99 *(978-1-59069-366-7(3)*, 1A501) Studio Mouse LLC.
Studio Mouse, creator. Get Your Grouchies Out! A Vocabulary of Feelings. rev. ed. 2007. (ENG., Illus.). (J). 12.99 *(978-1-59069-610-1(7))* Studio Mouse LLC.
—Kindness Counts. rev. ed. 2008. (Learn-Aloud Bks.). (ENG., Illus.). (J). 12.99 *(978-1-59069-627-9(1))* Studio Mouse LLC.
—Rhymes on the Go! rev. ed. 2008. (ENG., Illus.). 36p. (J). 12.99 *(978-1-59069-614-9(X))* Studio Mouse LLC.
Studio Mouse, ed. Disney Preincess Best Friends: Flat Learn & Carry 4 Board Books & CD. rev. ed. 2008. 80p. (J). 12.99 *(978-1-59069-553-1(4))* Studio Mouse LLC.
—Disney Time to Learn with Pooh: Flat Learn & Carry 4 Board Books & CD. rev. ed. 2007. (ENG.). 12.99 *(978-1-59069-626-2(3))* Studio Mouse LLC.
—Jojo's Circus Get up & Move! Flat Learn & Carry 4 Board Books & CD. rev. ed. 2007. (ENG.). 12.99 *(978-1-59069-548-7(8))* Studio Mouse LLC.
Studio Mouse Editorial. Ariel: The Brave Little Mermaid. 2008. (ENG., Illus.). 36p. (gr. -1-k). 7.99 *(978-1-59069-434-3(1))* Studio Mouse LLC.
—Belle: The Power of Love. 2008. (ENG., Illus.). 36p. (gr. -1-k). 7.99 *(978-1-59069-435-0(X))* Studio Mouse LLC.
Studio Mouse Staff. Cars on the Road to Learning: Flat Learn & Carry 4 Board Books & CD. rev. ed. 2007. (ENG.). 80p. 12.99 *(978-1-59069-549-4(6))* Studio Mouse LLC.
—Five Little Monkeys: And Other Counting Rhymes. Elliott, Rebecca et al, illus. rev. ed. 2007. (ENG.). 24p. (J). (gr. -1-k). 4.99 *(978-1-59069-608-8(5))* Studio Mouse LLC.
—Let's Move: Nursery Rhymes for Moving & Learning. 2008. (ENG., Illus.). 36p. (gr. -1-k). 7.99 *(978-1-59249-796-6(9))* Studio Mouse LLC.
—Mickey Mouse Clubhouse Count Along. rev. ed. 2007. (ENG.). 36p. 12.99 *(978-1-59069-613-2(1))* Studio Mouse LLC.
—Musical Fun: Colors & Patterns. rev. ed. 2008. (ENG., Illus.). 24p. (J). 4.99 *(978-1-59069-605-7(0))* Studio Mouse LLC.
—Pet Friends. rev. ed. 2008. (ENG.). 12p. (J). 12.99 *(978-1-59069-611-8(5))* Studio Mouse LLC.
—Pooh & Friends ABCs & 123s: First Concepts. rev. ed. 2007. (ENG., Illus.). 24p. (J). (gr. -1-3). 4.99 *(978-1-59069-606-4(9))* Studio Mouse LLC.
—Sesame Street Bert & Ernie Work Together. rev. ed. 2008. (ENG.). 24p. 4.99 *(978-1-59069-620-0(4))* Studio Mouse LLC.
—Sesame Street Rosita Reads a Recipe. rev. ed. 2008. (ENG.). 24p. 4.99 *(978-1-59069-619-4(0))* Studio Mouse LLC.
—Space Adventure. rev. ed. 2008. (ENG., Illus.). (J). 12.99 *(978-1-59069-609-5(3))* Studio Mouse LLC.
—Spelling Fun. 2011. (Cars Ser.). (Illus.). 28p. (J). 15.99 *(978-1-59069-938-6(6))* Studio Mouse LLC.
—Time to Learn!, 4 vols. rev. ed. 2007. (ENG., Illus.). 4x20p. (J). (gr. -1-k). 14.99 *(978-1-59069-564-7(X))* Studio Mouse LLC.
—Walt Disney Bambi Learning Library. rev. ed. 2007. (ENG.). 60p. 12.99 *(978-1-59069-612-5(3))* Studio Mouse LLC.
—Wedding Countdown. 2008. 36p. (J). (gr. -1). 12.99 *(978-1-59069-740-5(5))* Studio Mouse LLC.
—Winnie Pooh y sus amigos Ejercicios: Puffy Book with CD. rev. ed. 2007. (ESP & ENG.). 36p. (J). 14.99 *(978-1-59069-528-9(3))* Studio Mouse LLC.
Style Guide Staff, illus. I'm Thankful for You! 2014. (Yo Gabba Gabba! Ser.). (ENG.). 12p. (J). (gr. -1-k). bds. 5.99 *(978-1-4814-1723-5(1)*, Simon Spotlight) Simon Spotlight.
—SpongeBob's Backpack Book. 2003. (SpongeBob SquarePants Ser.). (ENG.). 16p. (J). bds. 6.99 *(978-0-689-85648-8(2)*, Simon Spotlight/Nickelodeon) Simon Spotlight/Nickelodeon.
Style Guide Staff & Style Guide, illus. Patricks Backpack Book. 2003. (SpongeBob SquarePants Ser.). (ENG.). 16p. (J). bds. 6.99 *(978-0-689-85649-5(0)*, Simon Spotlight/Nickelodeon) Simon Spotlight/Nickelodeon.
Subtraction Mastery w/Audio CD: Kit with Book, Wrap-up & CD. 2004. (ENG.). (J). 19.99 *(978-0-943343-99-0(2))* Learning Wrap-Ups, Inc.
Sulgit, Nicole. Caillou Leads the Parade. Poupart, Jean-Sébastien, illus. 2004. (J). *(978-0-7853-9949-0(6))* Publications International, Ltd.
Sullivan, Mary. Ball. 2016. (ENG., Illus.). 32p. (J). (— 1). bds. 12.99 *(978-0-544-81901-6(2)*, HMH Books For Young Readers) Houghton Mifflin Harcourt Publishing Co.
Sully, Katherine. Baby Goldstars Rainbow Peekaboo! (Baby Goldstars Changing Faces Ser.). 10p. bds. *(978-1-4054-9309-3(7))* Parragon, Inc.
—Night-Night California. Kolanovic, Dubravka & Poole, Helen, illus. 2016. (ENG.). 20p. (J). (-1). bds. 9.99 *(978-1-4926-3939-8(7)*, 9781492639398, Sourcebooks Jabberwocky) Sourcebooks, Inc.
—Night-Night Chicago. Kolanovic, Dubravka & Poole, Helen, illus. 2016. (ENG.). 20p. (J). (-1). bds. 9.99 *(978-1-4926-3935-0(4)*, 9781492639350, Sourcebooks Jabberwocky) Sourcebooks, Inc.
—Night-Night Colorado. Kolanovic, Dubravka & Poole, Helen, illus. 2016. (ENG.). 20p. (J). (-1). bds. 9.99 *(978-1-4926-3938-1(9)*, 9781492639381, Sourcebooks Jabberwocky) Sourcebooks, Inc.
—Night-Night Florida. Kolanovic, Dubravka & Poole, Helen, illus. 2016. (ENG.). 20p. (J). (-1). bds. 9.99 *(978-1-4926-4218-3(5)*, 9781492642183, Sourcebooks Jabberwocky) Sourcebooks, Inc.
—Night-Night Georgia. Kolanovic, Dubravka & Poole, Helen, illus. 2016. (ENG.). 20p. (J). (-1). bds. 9.99 *(978-1-4926-4216-9(9)*, 9781492642169, Sourcebooks Jabberwocky) Sourcebooks, Inc.
—Night-Night Kansas. Kolanovic, Dubravka & Poole, Helen, illus. 2016. (ENG.). 20p. (J). (-1). bds. 9.99 *(978-1-4926-3941-1(9)*, 9781492639411, Sourcebooks Jabberwocky) Sourcebooks, Inc.
—Night-Night Michigan. Kolanovic, Dubravka & Poole, Helen, illus. 2016. (ENG.). 20p. (J). (-1). bds. 9.99 *(978-1-4926-3934-3(6)*, 9781492639343, Sourcebooks Jabberwocky) Sourcebooks, Inc.
—Night-Night Minnesota. Kolanovic, Dubravka & Poole, Helen, illus. 2016. (ENG.). 20p. (J). (-1). bds. 9.99 *(978-1-4926-3940-4(0)*, 9781492639404, Sourcebooks Jabberwocky) Sourcebooks, Inc.
—Night-Night New Jersey. Kolanovic, Dubravka & Poole, Helen, illus. 2016. (ENG.). 20p. (J). (-1). bds. 9.99 *(978-1-4926-3933-6(8)*, 9781492639336, Sourcebooks Jabberwocky) Sourcebooks, Inc.
—Night-Night New York City. Kolanovic, Dubravka & Poole, Helen, illus. 2016. (ENG.). 20p. (J). (-1). bds. 9.99 *(978-1-4926-3932-9(X)*, 9781492639329, Sourcebooks Jabberwocky) Sourcebooks, Inc.
—Night-Night Ohio. Kolanovic, Dubravka & Poole, Helen, illus. 2016. (ENG.). 20p. (J). (-1). bds. 9.99 *(978-1-4926-4220-6(7)*, 9781492642206, Sourcebooks Jabberwocky) Sourcebooks, Inc.
—Night-Night Pennsylvania. Kolanovic, Dubravka & Poole, Helen, illus. 2016. (ENG.). 20p. (J). (-1). bds. 9.99 *(978-1-4926-4219-0(3)*, 9781492642190, Sourcebooks Jabberwocky) Sourcebooks, Inc.
—Night-Night Texas. Kolanovic, Dubravka & Poole, Helen, illus. 2016. (ENG.). 20p. (J). (-1). bds. 9.99 *(978-1-4926-3936-7(2)*, 9781492639367, Sourcebooks Jabberwocky) Sourcebooks, Inc.
—Night-Night Wisconsin. Kolanovic, Dubravka & Poole, Helen, illus. 2016. (ENG.). 20p. (J). (-1). bds. 9.99 *(978-1-4926-4217-6(7)*, 9781492642176, Sourcebooks Jabberwocky) Sourcebooks, Inc.
Surovec, Yasmine. I See Kitty. Surovec, Yasmine, illus. 2015. (ENG., Illus.). 34p. (J). (gr. -1-1). bds. 7.99 *(978-1-62672-093-0(2)*, 9781626720930) Roaring Brook Pr.
Sutton, Sally. Construction Board Book Boxed Set. Lovelock, Brian, illus. 2016. (ENG.). (J). (-k). bds. 19.99 *(978-0-7636-9260-5(3))* Candlewick Pr.
—Construir una Carretera (Roadwork) Lovelock, Brian, illus. 2013. (SPA.). 28p. (J). (-k). bds. 6.99 *(978-0-7636-6494-7(4))* Candlewick Pr.
—Construyendo. Lovelock, Brian, illus. 2015. (ENG & SPA.). 32p. (J). (gr. -1-2). bds. 6.99 *(978-0-7636-7976-7(3))* Candlewick Pr.
—Demolicion. Lovelock, Brian, illus. 2014. (SPA.). 22p. (J). (-k). bds. 6.99 *(978-0-7636-7031-3(6))* Candlewick Pr.
—Demolition. Lovelock, Brian, illus. 2014. (ENG.). 22p. (J). (-k). bds. 6.99 *(978-0-7636-6493-0(6))* Candlewick Pr.
Sweeney, Monica & Yelvington, Lauren. Can You Snore Like a Dinosaur? A Help-Your-Child-To-Sleep Book. Watkins, Laura, illus. 2017. (ENG.). 32p. (J). 15.99 *(978-1-250-11868-4(9)*, 9781250118684) St. Martin's Pr.
Sweet Dreams, Pout-Pout Fish. 2015. (Pout-Pout Fish Mini Adventure Ser.). (ENG., Illus.). 12p. (J). (gr. -1 — 1). bds. 5.99 *(978-0-374-38010-6(4)*, 9780374380106, Farrar, Straus & Giroux (BYR)) Farrar, Straus & Giroux.
Swenson, Jamie A. Big Rig [Board Book]. Young, Ned, illus. 2016. (ENG.). 32p. (J). (gr. -1 — 1). bds. 6.99 *(978-1-4231-9252-7(4))* Hyperion Bks. for Children.
Swift, Ginger. Little Blue Boat. Persico, Zoe, illus. 2016. (ENG.). 10p. (J). bds. 0.00 *(978-1-68052-077-4(6))* Cottage Door Pr.
—Little Red Barn. Pavon, David, illus. 2016. (ENG.). 10p. (J). bds. 0.00 *(978-1-68052-055-2(5))* Cottage Door Pr.
Symes, Sally. Whose Toes Are Those? Sharratt, Nick, illus. 2012. (ENG.). 22p. (J). (gr. k-12). bds. 7.99 *(978-0-7636-6274-5(7))* Candlewick Pr.
Syswerda, Jean E. My Bedtime Story Bible for Little Ones, 1 vol. Howarth, Daniel, illus. 2016. (ENG.). 32p. (J). bds. 9.99 *(978-0-310-75330-8(9))* Zonderkidz.
Taback, Simms. Joseph Had a Little Overcoat. Taback, Simms, illus. (Illus.). pap. incl. audio compact disk *(978-1-59112-608-9(8))* Live Oak Media.
Tabby's Pet Pals: Shapes. 2011. (Illus.). (J). *(978-1-58865-895-1(3))* Kidsbooks, LLC.
Tagel, Peggy, illus. On the Go. 2003. (Squishy Shapes Ser.). 10p. (J). 12.95 *(978-1-57145-739-4(9)*, Silver Dolphin Bks.) Readerlink Distribution Services, LLC.
Tai, Elise See. Farm Animal Counting. 2014. (Lumpy Bumpy Ser.). (ENG., Illus.). 10p. (J). (gr. -1 — 1). 5.99 *(978-0-7641-6708-9(1))* Barron's Educational Series, Inc.
—Wild Animal Alphabet. 2014. (Lumpy Bumpy Ser.). (ENG., Illus.). 10p. (J). (gr. -1 — 1). 5.99 *(978-0-7641-6709-6(X))* Barron's Educational Series, Inc.
Takken, Sylvia, illus. Cancer. 2014. (Zodiac Sign Bks.). (ENG.). 12p. (J). (gr. -1 — 1). bds. 3.99 *(978-0-7641-6681-5(6))* Barron's Educational Series, Inc.
—Capricorn: December 22-January 20. 2014. (Zodiac Sign Bks.). (ENG.). 12p. (J). (gr. -1 — 1). bds. 3.99 *(978-0-7641-6675-4(1))* Barron's Educational Series, Inc.
Tangerine Designs Ltd. Sleep Tight Bunny: A Soft & Snuggly Pillow Book. 2014. (Sleepy Cuddle Pillow Bks.). (ENG.). 8p. (J). (gr. -1 — 1). 11.99 *(978-1-4380-0440-2(0))* Barron's Educational Series, Inc.
Tango Books. Book of Greek Gods Pop-Up Board Games. Maddison, Kevin, illus. 2007. (Pop-Up Board Games Ser.). (ENG.). 10p. (J). (gr. -1-2). 24.99 *(978-1-85707-689-9(3))* Tango Bks. GBR. Dist: Independent Pubs. Group.
—Tractor: A Lift-the-Flap & Stand-Up. Burton, Terry, illus. 2011. (Mini Trucks Ser.). (ENG.). 12p. (J). (gr. -1-k). 5.99 *(978-1-85707-753-7(9))* Tango Bks. GBR. Dist: Independent Pubs. Group.
Tango Books Staff. Armour. Moulder, Bob, illus. 2011. (3-Dimensional Exploration Bks.). (ENG.). 20p. (J). (gr. -1-2). 22.95 *(978-1-85707-664-6(8))* Tango Bks. GBR. Dist: Independent Pubs. Group.
—The Book of Dragon Myths. Wade, Gini, illus. 2011. (Pop-Up Board Games Ser.). (ENG.). 10p. (J). (gr. -1-2). 29.99 *(978-1-85707-720-9(2))* Tango Bks. GBR. Dist: Independent Pubs. Group.
—Digger: A Lift-the-Flap & Stand Up. Burton, Terry, illus. 2011. (Mini Trucks Ser.). (ENG.). 12p. (J). (gr. -1-k). 5.99 *(978-1-85707-751-3(2))* Tango Bks. GBR. Dist: Independent Pubs. Group.
—Noisy Pops - Fire Engine. Abbott, Simon, illus. 2011. (Noisy Pops! Ser.). (ENG.). 10p. (J). (gr. -1-k). bds. 11.99 *(978-1-85707-710-0(5))* Tango Bks. GBR. Dist: Independent Pubs. Group.
Taplin, Sam. Baby Animals. 2014. (Usborne Flap Book Ser.). (ENG., Illus.). 10p. (gr. -1). bds. 7.99 *(978-0-7945-2105-9(3)*, Usborne) EDC Publishing.
—Easter Bunny Flap Book. 2012. (Flap Bks). 10p. (J). ring bd. 7.99 *(978-0-7945-3256-7(X)*, Usborne) EDC Publishing.
—Little Stories for Bedtime. Chiara, Francesca De, illus. 2010. (Bedtime Stories Ser.). 12p. (J). bds. 12.99 *(978-0-7945-2673-3(X)*, Usborne) EDC Publishing.
—Noisy Building Site Board Book. 2008. (Busy Sounds Board Bks). 10p. (J). bds. 18.99 *(978-0-7945-2076-2(6)*, Usborne) EDC Publishing.
—Noisy Diggers. 2012. (Noisy Bks). 10p. (J). bds. 18.99 *(978-0-7945-3264-2(0)*, Usborne) EDC Publishing.
—Pop-Up Haunted House. 2015. (Pop-Up Bks.). (ENG.). 10p. (J). 29.99 *(978-0-7945-2185-1(1)*, Usborne) EDC Publishing.
—Sleeping Beauty. 2008. (First Fairytales Look & Say Ser.). 12p. (J). (gr. -1). bds. 9.99 *(978-0-7945-2200-1(9)*, Usborne) EDC Publishing.
—Sleepytime Stories. Chaira, Francesca di, illus. 2011. (Baby Board Books Ser.). 12p. (J). ring bd. 12.99 *(978-0-7945-3006-8(0)*, Usborne) EDC Publishing.
—This Is My Dinosaur. 2009. (Noisy Touchy-Feely Board Bks). (Illus.). 10p. (J). bds. 16.99 *(978-0-7945-2366-4(8)*, Usborne) EDC Publishing.
—This Is My Monster. Furukawa, Masumi, illus. 2008. (Noisy Touchy-Feely Board Bks). 10p. (J). bds. 16.99 *(978-0-7945-2353-4(6)*, Usborne) EDC Publishing.
Tatchell, Judy. Dragons. Scott, Peter David & Furnival, Keith, illus. 2006. (J). *(978-0-439-82790-4(6))* Scholastic, Inc.
—Dragons Lift-the-flap. Scott, Peter, illus. 2005. 16p. (J). (gr. 1-18). 11.99 *(978-0-7945-0968-2(1)*, Usborne) EDC Publishing.
Tatcheva, Eva. Witch Zelda's Birthday Cake: A Wild & Wicked Pop-up, Pull-the-Tab Book. Tatcheva, Eva, illus. 2004. (Illus.). 12p. (J). (gr. k-3). reprint ed. 18.00 *(978-0-7567-7225-3(7))* DIANE Publishing Co.
Tawa, Renee. Tink's Magical Day. 2011. (Illus.). (J). *(978-1-4508-1707-3(6))* Publications International, Ltd.
Taylor, Dereen. Alien Adventure: Peek Inside the Pop-Up Windows! Hutchinson, Tim, illus. 2015. (ENG.). 12p. 16.99 *(978-1-86147-487-2(3)*, Armadillo) Anness Publishing GBR. Dist: National Bk. Network.
—The Dragon's Magic Wish. Hutchinson, Tim, illus. 2012. (ENG.). 12p. (J). (gr. 1-6). 16.99 *(978-1-84322-856-1(4))* Anness Publishing GBR. Dist: National Bk. Network.
—The Fairy Midnight Surprise Party. Stone, Lyn, illus. 2012. (ENG.). 12p. (J). (gr. 1-6). 16.99 *(978-1-84322-763-2(0))* Anness Publishing GBR. Dist: National Bk. Network.
—Journey to the World of the Dinosaurs: Peek Inside the Pop-Up Windows! Kavanagh, Peter, illus. 2014. (ENG.). 12p. (J). (gr. 2-7). 16.99 *(978-1-86147-319-6(2)*, Armadillo) Anness Publishing GBR. Dist: National Bk. Network.
—The Knight's First Tournament. Kavanagh, Peter, illus. 2012. (ENG.). 12p. (J). (gr. 1-6). 16.99 *(978-1-84322-760-1(6))* Anness Publishing GBR. Dist: National Bk. Network.
—The Lost Treasure of the Jungle Temple: Peek Inside the 3D Windows! Hutchinson, Tim, illus. 2013. (ENG.). 12p. (J). (gr. 1-8). 16.99 *(978-1-84322-822-6(X)*, Armadillo) Anness Publishing GBR. Dist: National Bk. Network.
—The Mermaid's Treasure Hunt. East, Jacqueline, illus. 2012. (ENG.). 12p. (J). (gr. -1-12). 16.99 *(978-1-84322-762-5(2))* Anness Publishing GBR. Dist: National Bk. Network.
—The Mystery of the Vampire Boy: Dare You Peek Through the Pop-Up Windows? Spoor, Mike, illus. 2014. (ENG.). 12p. (J). (gr. k-5). 16.99 *(978-1-86147-410-0(5)*, Armadillo) Anness Publishing GBR. Dist: National Bk. Network.
—Paulo & the Football Thieves: Peek Inside the Pop-Up Windows! Hutchinson, Tim, illus. 2014. (ENG.). 12p. 16.99 *(978-1-86147-409-4(1)*, Armadillo) Anness Publishing GBR. Dist: National Bk. Network.
—Robo-Pup to the Rescue! Hutchinson, Tim, illus. 2013. (ENG.). 12p. (J). (gr. 1-8). 16.99 *(978-1-84322-821-9(1)*, Armadillo) Anness Publishing GBR. Dist: National Bk. Network.
—Rosie Rides to the Rescue: Peek Inside the Pop-Up Windows! Stone, Lyn, illus. 2015. (ENG.). 12p. 16.99 *(978-1-86147-488-9(1)*, Armadillo) Anness Publishing GBR. Dist: National Bk. Network.
—Trapped in the Witch's Lair: Peek Inside the Pop-Up Windows! Catchpole, Diana, illus. 2014. (ENG.). 12p. (J). (gr. 2-7). 16.99 *(978-1-86147-320-2(6)*, Armadillo) Anness Publishing GBR. Dist: National Bk. Network.
Taylor, Jon, illus. Tower of Babel. 2007. 24p. (J). (gr. 4-7). 14.99 *(978-0-89051-487-0(9))* Master Bks.
Taylor, Mark A. One Tiny Baby. Burroughs, Scott, illus. 2014. (Happy Day Ser.). (ENG.). 16p. (J). pap. 2.49 *(978-1-4143-9478-7(0))* Tyndale Hse. Pubs.
Taylor, Martin. The Lost Treasure of the Sunken City. Catling, Andy, illus. 2012. (J). *(978-1-4351-4330-2(2))* Barnes & Noble, Inc.
Taylor, W. Y. I'm Not too Little to Help the Earth. 2009. 14p. 9.95 *(978-1-58117-913-2(8)*, Intervisual/Piggy Toes) Bendon, Inc.
—This Little Piggy Goes Green. 2009. (ENG.). 12p. bds. 3.95 *(978-1-58117-925-5(1)*, Intervisual/Piggy Toes) Bendon, Inc.
Teckentrup, Britta. Find the Circle. 2016. (Find the Shape Ser.). (ENG., Illus.). 24p. (J). (— 1). bds. 6.95 *(978-1-4549-1759-5(8))* Sterling Publishing Co., Inc.
—Find the Line. 2016. (Find the Shape Ser.). (ENG., Illus.). 24p. (J). (— 1). bds. 6.95 *(978-1-4549-1760-1(1))* Sterling Publishing Co., Inc.
—Find the Square. 2016. (Find the Shape Ser.). (ENG., Illus.). 24p. (J). (— 1). bds. 6.95 *(978-1-4549-1761-8(X))* Sterling Publishing Co., Inc.
—Find the Triangle. 2016. (Find the Shape Ser.). (ENG., Illus.). 24p. (J). (— 1). bds. 6.95 *(978-1-4549-1762-5(8))* Sterling Publishing Co., Inc.
—Tree: A Peek-Through Picture Book. 2016. (ENG.). 32p. (J). (gr. -1-2). 14.99 *(978-1-101-93242-1(2)*, Doubleday Bks. for Young Readers) Random Hse. Children's Bks.
—Up & Down. Teckentrup, Britta, illus. 2014. (ENG., Illus.). 28p. (J). (-k). 17.99 *(978-0-7636-7129-7(0)*, Templar) Candlewick Pr.
Teckentrup, Britta, illus. Big & Small. 2013. (ENG.). 14p. (J). (gr. -1-k). bds. 6.99 *(978-1-84686-951-8(X))* Barefoot Bks., Inc.
—Fast & Slow. 2013. (ENG.). 14p. (J). (gr. -1-k). bds. 6.99 *(978-1-84686-952-5(8))* Barefoot Bks., Inc.
Tegen, Katherine. The Story of the Easter Bunny Board Book. Lambert, Sally Anne, illus. 2017. 32p. (J). (gr. -1-3). bds. 7.99 *(978-0-06-238155-2(5)*, HarperFestival) HarperCollins Pubs.
Teitelbaum, Michael. Steer the Wheel! Shannon, David et al, illus. 2011. (Jon Scieszka's Trucktown Ser.). (ENG.). 12p. (J). (gr. -1-1). bds. 7.99 *(978-1-4169-4185-9(1)*, Simon & Schuster Bks. For Young Readers) Simon & Schuster Bks. For Young Readers.
Teitelbaum, Michael & Scieszka, Jon. On the Move! Shannon, David et al, illus. 2009. (Jon Scieszka's Trucktown Ser.). (ENG.). 10p. (J). (gr. -1-k). bds. 6.99 *(978-1-4169-4178-1(9)*, Little Simon) Little Simon.
Tekiela, Stan. Critter Litter. 2016. (ENG., Illus.). 26p. (J). (-k). 12.95 *(978-1-59193-590-2(3))* Adventure Pubns.
—Floppers & Loppers, 1 vol. 2013. (Adventure Boardbook Ser.). (ENG.). 22p. (J). (gr. -1-k). bds. 6.95 *(978-1-59193-424-0(9))* Adventure Pubns.
—Paws & Claws, 1 vol. 2013. (Adventure Boardbook Ser.). (ENG.). 22p. (J). (gr. -1-k). bds. 6.95 *(978-1-59193-425-7(7))* Adventure Pubns.
—Peepers & Peekers, 1 vol. 2013. (Adventure Boardbook Ser.). (ENG.). 22p. (J). (gr. -1-k). bds. 6.95 *(978-1-59193-423-3(0))* Adventure Pubns.
Terada, Junzo. Animal Friends: Barnyard Jamboree! 2017. (ENG., Illus.). 10p. (J). bds. 9.99 *(978-1-4521-5189-2(X))* Chronicle Bks. LLC.
—Animal Friends: Swimming Hole Party! 2017. (ENG., Illus.). 10p. (J). bds. 9.99 *(978-1-4521-4983-7(6))* Chronicle Bks. LLC.
Terry, Michael, illus. Who Lives Here? 2012. (ENG.). 12p. (J). (gr. -1-k). 14.99 *(978-1-4088-1943-2(0)*, 9781408819432, Bloomsbury USA Childrens) Bloomsbury Publishing USA.
Testa, Maggie. Friends Are the Best! Style Guide, Style & Fruchter, Jason, illus. 2014. (Daniel Tiger's Neighborhood Ser.). (ENG.). 12p. (J). (gr. -1-k). bds. 5.99 *(978-1-4424-9547-0(2)*, Simon Spotlight) Simon Spotlight.
—Happy Halloween, Brobee! 2013. (Yo Gabba Gabba! Ser.). (ENG., Illus.). 12p. (J). (gr. -1-k). bds. 5.99 *(978-1-4424-7407-9(6)*, Simon Spotlight) Simon Spotlight.
—Meet the Heroes ... & the Villains, Too! Style Guide, Style, illus. 2016. (PJ Masks Ser.). (ENG.). 14p. (J). (gr. -1-k). bds. 7.99 *(978-1-4814-8650-7(0)*, Simon Spotlight) Simon Spotlight.
—OLIVIA & Her Favorite Things. Spaziante, Patrick, illus. 2013. (Olivia TV Tie-In Ser.). (ENG.). 12p. (J). (gr. -1-1). bds. 5.99 *(978-1-4424-6587-9(5)*, Simon Spotlight) Simon Spotlight.
—Play with Plex. Zdanowicz, Paul, illus. 2010. (Yo Gabba Gabba! Ser.). (ENG.). 14p. (J). (gr. -1-1). bds. 8.99 *(978-1-4169-9740-5(7)*, Simon Spotlight) Simon Spotlight.
—A Ride Through the Neighborhood. Style Guide Staff, illus. 2014. (Daniel Tiger's Neighborhood Ser.). (ENG.). 12p. (J). (gr. -1-1). bds. 6.99 *(978-1-4424-9839-6(0)*, Simon Spotlight) Simon Spotlight.
Teves, Miles, illus. The Dragon Hunter's Handbook. 2008. (J). *(978-1-4351-0204-0(5))* Metro Bks.
That's Not My Badger. 2017. (Touchy-Feely BDs Ser.). (ENG.). (J). bds. 9.99 ***(978-0-7945-3808-8(8)***, Usborne) EDC Publishing.
That's Not My... Puppy & Kitten Box Set. 2017. (Touchy-Feely BDs Ser.). (ENG.). (J). bds. 14.99 ***(978-0-7945-3978-8(5)***, Usborne) EDC Publishing.
The Book Company, prod. Noah's Ark 3-D Pop-ups. 2016. (ENG.). 10p. (J). bds. 19.99 *(978-1-4964-0454-1(8))* Tyndale Hse. Pubs.
The Library Fairy. The Magical Tree & Musical Wind. Faust, Laurie A., illus. 2008. 32p. pap. 16.95 *(978-1-59858-604-6(1))* Dog Ear Publishing, LLC.
Things People Do. (Push & Pop Ser.). 5p. bds. *(978-1-4054-6873-2(4))* Parragon, Inc.
Things That Go! (Flip Flap Fun Book Ser.). 10p. (J). bds. *(978-2-89393-933-9(3))* Phidal Publishing, Inc./Editions Phidal, Inc.
Thomas: It's Great to Be an Engine. 2004. (Little Music Note Ser.). (Illus.). 10p. (J). bds. *(978-0-7853-9950-6(X)*, 7209400) Phoenix International Publications, Inc.
Thomas & Friends, Thomas &. Thomas & Friends: Thomas Speeds Along. 2015. (Lift-The-Flap Ser.: 1). (ENG.). 10p. (J). (gr. -1-k). 11.99 *(978-0-7944-3480-9(0)*, Reader's Digest Children's Bks.) Studio Fun International.
Thomas, Jan. The Doghouse. 2015. (ENG., Illus.). 36p. (J). (— 1). bds. 7.99 *(978-0-544-43063-1(8)*, HMH Books For Young Readers) Houghton Mifflin Harcourt Publishing Co.
Thomas Nelson. Babytown Noisy Farm. 2015. (ENG., Illus.). 14p. (gr. -1). bds. *(978-1-78393-875-9(7))* Make Believe Ideas.
—Fit & Feel Vroom. 2015. (ENG.). 12p. (gr. -1). bds. *(978-1-78393-437-9(9))* Make Believe Ideas.
—Flip Flap Fun Animals. 2015. (ENG.). 62p. (J). (gr. -1-7). *(978-1-78393-711-0(4))* Make Believe Ideas.
—Touch & Feel Never Touch a Monster. 2016. (ENG.). 12p. (gr. -1). bds. *(978-1-78598-395-5(4))* Make Believe Ideas.
—Touch & Feel Robbie Reindeer's Snowy Adventure. 2016. (ENG.). 12p. (gr. -1). bds. *(978-1-78598-437-2(3))* Make Believe Ideas.
—Touch & Sparkle Farm Animals. 2016. (ENG.). 12p. (gr. -1). bds. *(978-1-78598-133-3(1))* Make Believe Ideas.
—Touch & Sparkle Pets. 2016. (ENG.). 12p. (gr. -1). bds. *(978-1-78598-131-9(5))* Make Believe Ideas.
—Touch & Sparkle Wild Animals. 2016. (ENG.). 12p. (gr. -1). bds. *(978-1-78598-134-0(X))* Make Believe Ideas.
Thomas Nelson Community College Staff. God's Love in My Heart, 1 vol. 2014. (ENG.). 24p. bds. 9.99 *(978-0-529-11141-8(1))* Nelson, Thomas Inc.
Thomas Nelson Publishing Staff. Daddy Loves You So Much, 1 vol. Parry, Jo, illus. 2015. (ENG.). 20p. (J). bds. 9.99 *(978-0-529-12335-0(5))* Nelson, Thomas Inc.
—Grandma Kisses, 1 vol. 2015. (ENG., Illus.). 20p. (J). bds. 9.99 *(978-0-7180-3659-1(X))* Nelson, Thomas Inc.
—Mommy Loves You So Much, 1 vol. Parry, Jo, illus. 2015. (ENG.). 20p. (J). bds. 9.99 *(978-0-529-12338-1(X))* Nelson, Thomas Inc.

Thomas Nelson, Thomas. Good Night, Little Love, 1 vol. 2015. (ENG., Illus.). 24p. (J). bds. 8.99 *(978-0-7180-3467-2(8))* Nelson, Thomas Inc.

—My Give Thanks Bible, 1 vol. Masse, Josée, illus. 2015. (ENG.). 32p. (J). bds. 9.99 *(978-0-310-74942-4(5))* Zonderkidz.

—Starter Bible, 1 vol. 2016. (ENG.). 40p. (J). bds. 9.99 *(978-0-7180-9005-0(5))* Nelson, Thomas Inc.

Thompson, Carol. Dance. Thompson, Carol, illus. 2017. (Amazing Me! Ser.: 4). (ENG., Illus.). 12p. (J). (gr. k-k). bds. ***(978-1-84643-959-9(0))*** Child's Play International Ltd.

—Dressing Up. Thompson, Carol, illus. 2017. (Amazing Me! Ser.: 4). (ENG., Illus.). 12p. (J). (gr. k-k). bds. ***(978-1-84643-960-5(4))*** Child's Play International Ltd.

—Mockingbird Song. 2011. (ENG., Illus.). 24p. (J). *(978-1-84643-446-4(7))* Child's Play International Ltd.

—Music. Thompson, Carol, illus. 2017. (Amazing Me! Ser.: 4). (ENG., Illus.). 12p. (J). (gr. k-k). bds. ***(978-1-84643-961-2(2))*** Child's Play International Ltd.

—Rain! 2014. (Whatever the Weather Ser.: 4). (ENG., Illus.). 12p. (J). (gr. k-k). bds. *(978-1-84643-683-3(4))* Child's Play International Ltd.

—Sing. Thompson, Carol, illus. 2017. (Amazing Me! Ser.: 4). (ENG., Illus.). 12p. (J). (gr. k-k). bds. ***(978-1-84643-962-9(0))*** Child's Play International Ltd.

—Snow! 2014. (Whatever the Weather Ser.). (ENG., Illus.). 12p. (J). (gr. k-k). bds. *(978-1-84643-681-9(8))* Child's Play International Ltd.

—Sun! 2014. (Whatever the Weather Ser.). (ENG., Illus.). 12p. (J). (gr. k-k). bds. *(978-1-84643-680-2(X))* Child's Play International Ltd.

—Wind! 2014. (Whatever the Weather Ser.). (ENG., Illus.). 12p. (J). (gr. k-k). bds. *(978-1-84643-682-6(6))* Child's Play International Ltd.

Thompson, Chad. The Itsy Bitsy Spider, 1 vol. 2009. (Early Childhood Themes Ser.). (ENG., Illus.). 16p. (J). (gr. -1-2). pap. 19.99 *(978-1-4333-1455-1(X))* Shell Educational Publishing.

—Yankee Doodle, 1 vol. 2011. (Early Childhood Themes Ser.). (ENG.). 16p. (J). (gr. -1-2). pap. 19.99 *(978-1-4333-2365-2(6))* Teacher Created Materials, Inc.

Thompson, Kate. I Can Tell the Time. Green, Barry, illus. 2014. (I Can Bks.). (ENG.). 12p. (J). (gr. -1). 7.99 *(978-1-78244-825-9(X))* Top That! Publishing PLC GBR. Dist: Independent Pubs. Group.

Thompson, Kim Mitzo. Old MacDonald Had a Farm. Girouard, Patrick, illus. 2010. (Padded Board Book W/CD Ser.). 8p. (J). (gr. k-2). bds. 10.99 incl. audio compact disk *(978-1-59922-579-1(4))* Twin Sisters IP, LLC.

Thompson, Lauren. Cuaquito (Little Quack) Anderson, Derek, illus. 2010. (SPA.). 34p. (J). (gr. -1-1). bds. 7.99 *(978-1-4169-9894-5(2),* Libros Para Ninos) Libros Para Ninos.

—Little Quack Counts. Anderson, Derek, illus. 2009. (Super Chubbies Ser.). (ENG.). 26p. (J). (gr. -1 — 1). bds. 5.99 *(978-1-4169-6093-5(7),* Little Simon) Little Simon.

—Little Quack Loves Colors. Anderson, Derek, illus. 2009. (Super Chubbies Ser.). (ENG.). 26p. (J). (gr. -1 — 1). bds. 5.99 *(978-1-4169-6094-2(5),* Little Simon) Little Simon.

—Little Quack's ABC's. Anderson, Derek, illus. 2010. (Super Chubbies Ser.). (ENG.). 26p. (J). (gr. -1 — 1). bds. 5.99 *(978-1-4169-6091-1(0),* Little Simon) Little Simon.

—Little Quack's Bath Book. Anderson, Derek, illus. 2006. (ENG.). 8p. (J). (gr. -1 — 1). 8.99 *(978-1-4169-0803-6(X),* Little Simon) Little Simon.

—Little Quack's Opposites. Anderson, Derek, illus. 2010. (Super Chubbies Ser.). (ENG.). 26p. (J). (gr. -1 — 1). bds. 5.99 *(978-1-4169-6092-8(9),* Little Simon) Little Simon.

—Mouse's First Spring. Erdogan, Buket, illus. 2012. (Classic Board Bks.). (ENG.). 34p. (J). (gr. -1-3). bds. 7.99 *(978-1-4424-3431-8(7),* Little Simon) Little Simon.

—Mouse's First Summer. Erdogan, Buket, illus. 2014. (J). *(978-1-4351-5506-0(8))* Simon & Schuster.

Thoms, Susan Collins. Jonah & the Big Fish. Stoop, Naoko, illus. 2016. (ENG.). 22p. (J). (— 1). bds. 6.95 *(978-1-4549-1493-8(9),* 1402423) Sterling Publishing Co., Inc.

Thornley, Rebecca Gundersen. I Know He Is There: A Lift-A-Flap Book about Faith. Dorman, Brandon, illus. 2006. (J). *(978-1-59038-550-0(0))* Deseret Bk. Co.

Thuillier, Eléonore, illus. Wolf, Are You There? Learn How to Get Dressed with the Little Wolf. 2012. (ENG.). 14p. (J). (gr. -1). bds. 14.99 *(978-2-7338-1952-4(6))* Auzou, Philippe Editions FRA. Dist: Consortium Bk. Sales & Distribution.

Tickle, Jack. Fish on a Dish! Tickle, Jack, illus. 2015. (ENG., Illus.). 24p. (J). (gr. -1-3). 16.99 *(978-1-58925-191-5(1))* Tiger Tales.

Tickle, Jessica Courtney, illus. Four Seasons in One Day. 2016. (Story Orchestra Ser.). (ENG.). 24p. (J). (gr. 1-4). 22.99 *(978-1-84780-877-6(8),* Frances Lincoln Children's Bks.) Quarto Publishing Group UK GBR. Dist: Hachette Bk. Group.

Ticktock Media, Ltd. Staff. At the Beach with the Snappy Little Crab. 2009. (Touch & Feel Fun Ser.). (ENG.). 10p. (J). (gr. k — 1). bds. 5.95 *(978-1-84696-809-9(7),* TickTock Books) Octopus Publishing Group GBR. Dist: Independent Pubs. Group.

—Birthday Party. 2009. (Busy Tots Ser.). (ENG.). 10p. (J). (gr. -1-k). bds. 6.95 *(978-1-84696-801-3(1),* TickTock Books) Octopus Publishing Group GBR. Dist: Independent Pubs. Group.

—Dinosaurs. 2009. (Animal Fun Touch & Feel Ser.). (ENG.). 10p. (J). (gr. -1-k). bds. 4.95 *(978-1-84696-829-7(1),* TickTock Books) Octopus Publishing Group GBR. Dist: Independent Pubs. Group.

—Farm. 2009. (Animal Fun Touch & Feel Ser.). (ENG.). 10p. (J). (gr. -1-k). bds. 4.95 *(978-1-84696-827-3(5),* TickTock Books) Octopus Publishing Group GBR. Dist: Independent Pubs. Group.

—Favorite Foods: Colors & Shapes. 2008. (Tab Bks.). (ENG.). 10p. (J). (gr. -1-k). bds. 4.95 *(978-1-84696-821-1(6),* TickTock Books) Octopus Publishing Group GBR. Dist: Independent Pubs. Group.

—Guess What? Everyday Things. 2008. (Mini Flap Ser.). (ENG.). 10p. (J). (gr. k — 1). bds. 5.95 *(978-1-84696-818-1(6),* TickTock Books) Octopus Publishing Group GBR. Dist: Independent Pubs. Group.

—Guess What? Things That Go. 2008. (Mini Flap Ser.). (ENG.). 10p. (J). (gr. k — 1). bds. 5.95 *(978-1-84696-819-8(4),* TickTock Books) Octopus Publishing Group GBR. Dist: Independent Pubs. Group.

—Hungry Dinosaurs. 2009. (Dinosaur Shape Bks.). (ENG.). 10p. (J). (gr. -1-k). bds. 5.95 *(978-1-84696-834-1(8),* TickTock Books) Octopus Publishing Group GBR. Dist: Independent Pubs. Group.

—In the Garden with the Hungry Little Snail. 2009. (Touch & Feel Fun Ser.). (ENG.). 10p. (J). (gr. k — 1). bds. 5.95 *(978-1-84696-810-5(0),* TickTock Books) Octopus Publishing Group GBR. Dist: Independent Pubs. Group.

—Itsy Bitsy Spider. 2011. (Sing-Along Songs Ser.). (ENG.). 10p. (J). (gr. k — 1). bds. 6.95 *(978-1-84898-170-6(8),* TickTock Books) Octopus Publishing Group GBR. Dist: Independent Pubs. Group.

—Jungle. 2009. (Animal Fun Touch & Feel Ser.). (ENG.). 10p. (J). (gr. -1-k). bds. 4.95 *(978-1-84696-828-0(3),* TickTock Books) Octopus Publishing Group GBR. Dist: Independent Pubs. Group.

—Kittens & Puppies: Counting. 2008. (Tab Bks.). (ENG.). 10p. (J). (gr. -1-k). bds. 4.95 *(978-1-84696-822-8(4),* TickTock Books) Octopus Publishing Group GBR. Dist: Independent Pubs. Group.

—Little Helper. 2009. (Busy Tots Ser.). (ENG.). 10p. (J). (gr. -1-k). bds. 6.95 *(978-1-84696-798-6(8),* TickTock Books) Octopus Publishing Group GBR. Dist: Independent Pubs. Group.

—Living Planet: Uncovering the Wonders of the Natural World. 2008. (ENG.). 128p. (J). (gr. 4-7). pap. 12.95 *(978-1-84696-816-7(X),* TickTock Books) Octopus Publishing Group GBR. Dist: Independent Pubs. Group.

—My Fairy Garden. 2008. (Sparkle Bks.). (ENG.). 10p. (J). (gr. -1-k). bds. 6.95 *(978-1-84696-802-0(X),* TickTock Books) Octopus Publishing Group GBR. Dist: Independent Pubs. Group.

—My Night-Time Animals. 2008. (Sparkle Bks.). (ENG.). 10p. (J). (gr. -1-k). bds. 6.95 *(978-1-84696-803-7(8),* TickTock Books) Octopus Publishing Group GBR. Dist: Independent Pubs. Group.

—My Ocean Creatures. 2008. (Sparkle Bks.). (ENG.). 10p. (J). (gr. -1-k). bds. 6.95 *(978-1-84696-804-4(6),* TickTock Books) Octopus Publishing Group GBR. Dist: Independent Pubs. Group.

—My Space Adventure. 2008. (Sparkle Bks.). (ENG.). 10p. (J). (gr. -1-k). bds. 6.95 *(978-1-84696-805-1(4),* TickTock Books) Octopus Publishing Group GBR. Dist: Independent Pubs. Group.

—My World: Opposites. 2008. (Tab Bks.). (ENG.). 10p. (J). (gr. -1-k). bds. 4.95 *(978-1-84696-823-5(2),* TickTock Books) Octopus Publishing Group GBR. Dist: Independent Pubs. Group.

—Ocean. 2009. (Animal Fun Touch & Feel Ser.). (ENG.). 10p. (J). (gr. -1-k). bds. 4.95 *(978-1-84696-830-3(5),* TickTock Books) Octopus Publishing Group GBR. Dist: Independent Pubs. Group.

—Scary Dinosaurs. 2009. (Dinosaur Shape Bks.). (ENG.). 10p. (J). (gr. -1-k). bds. 5.95 *(978-1-84696-835-8(6),* TickTock Books) Octopus Publishing Group GBR. Dist: Independent Pubs. Group.

—Shopping Day. 2009. (Busy Tots Ser.). (ENG.). 10p. (J). (gr. -1-k). bds. 6.95 *(978-1-84696-799-3(6),* TickTock Books) Octopus Publishing Group GBR. Dist: Independent Pubs. Group.

—Summer Vacation. 2009. (Busy Tots Ser.). (ENG.). 10p. (J). (gr. -1-k). bds. 6.95 *(978-1-84696-800-6(3),* TickTock Books) Octopus Publishing Group GBR. Dist: Independent Pubs. Group.

—Under the Ocean with the Little Yellow Submarine. 2009. (Touch & Feel Fun Ser.). (ENG.). 10p. (J). (gr. k — 1). bds. 5.95 *(978-1-84696-811-2(9),* TickTock Books) Octopus Publishing Group GBR. Dist: Independent Pubs. Group.

—What Am I? Animal Moms & Babies. 2008. (Mini Flap Ser.). (ENG.). 10p. (J). (gr. k — 1). bds. 5.95 *(978-1-84696-817-4(8),* TickTock Books) Octopus Publishing Group GBR. Dist: Independent Pubs. Group.

—What Do Cows Do? 2008. (What Do Animals Do? Ser.). (ENG.). 10p. (J). (gr. k — 1). bds. 4.95 *(978-1-84696-796-2(1),* TickTock Books) Octopus Publishing Group GBR. Dist: Independent Pubs. Group.

—What Do Hippos Do? 2008. (What Do Animals Do? Ser.). (ENG.). 10p. (J). (gr. k — 1). bds. 4.95 *(978-1-84696-791-7(0),* TickTock Books) Octopus Publishing Group GBR. Dist: Independent Pubs. Group.

—What Do Penguins Do? 2008. (What Do Animals Do? Ser.). (ENG.). 10p. (J). (gr. k — 1). bds. 4.95 *(978-1-84696-792-4(9),* TickTock Books) Octopus Publishing Group GBR. Dist: Independent Pubs. Group.

—What Do Sheep Do? 2008. (What Do Animals Do? Ser.). (ENG.). 10p. (J). (gr. k — 1). bds. 4.95 *(978-1-84696-793-1(7),* TickTock Books) Octopus Publishing Group GBR. Dist: Independent Pubs. Group.

—What Do Tigers Do? 2008. (What Do Animals Do? Ser.). (ENG.). 10p. (J). (gr. k — 1). bds. 4.95 *(978-1-84696-794-8(5),* TickTock Books) Octopus Publishing Group GBR. Dist: Independent Pubs. Group.

—What Do Zebras Do? 2008. (What Do Animals Do? Ser.). (ENG.). 10p. (J). (gr. k — 1). bds. 4.95 *(978-1-84696-795-5(3),* TickTock Books) Octopus Publishing Group GBR. Dist: Independent Pubs. Group.

—Zoom into Space with the Shiny Red Rocket. 2009. (Touch & Feel Fun Ser.). (ENG.). 10p. (J). (gr. k — 1). bds. 5.95 *(978-1-84696-812-9(7),* TickTock Books) Octopus Publishing Group GBR. Dist: Independent Pubs. Group.

Tidholm, Anna-Clara. Knock! Knock! Bradley, MaryChris, tr. 2009. (Illus.). 32p. (J). (gr. -1). 9.95 *(978-0-9815761-6-9(8))* Mackenzie Smiles, LLC.

Tiger, Tales, ed. Baby's First Bear. Ward, Sarah, illus. 2016. (To Baby with Love Ser.). (ENG.). 10p. (J). (gr. -1-k). 14.99 *(978-1-58925-214-1(4))* Tiger Tales.

Tiger Tales, ed. A Christmas Prayer. Rescek, Sanja, illus. 2014. (ENG.). 22p. (J). (gr. -1-k). bds. 8.95 *(978-1-58925-596-8(8))* Tiger Tales.

—A Is for Apple. Birkett, Georgie, illus. 2011. (ENG.). 26p. (J). bds. 7.95 *(978-1-58925-872-3(X))* Tiger Tales.

—Ten Twinkly Stars. Julian, Russell, illus. 2016. (ENG.). 28p. (J). (gr. -1-k). mass mkt. 3.99 *(978-1-58925-475-6(9))* Tiger Tales.

—1 2 3 Count with Me. Birkett, Georgie, illus. 2011. (ENG.). 26p. (J). bds. 7.95 *(978-1-58925-873-0(8))* Tiger Tales.

Tiger Tales, ed. & compiled by. Baby Animals. Tiger Tales, compiled by. 2014. (My First Lift & Learn Ser.). (ENG.). 10p. (J). (gr. -1 — 1). bds. 7.99 *(978-1-58925-624-8(7))* Tiger Tales.

—Christmas Surprise. Tiger Tales, compiled by. 2014. (My First Lift & Learn Ser.). (ENG.). 10p. (J). (gr. -1 — 1). bds. 7.99 *(978-1-58925-577-7(1))* Tiger Tales.

—First Words. Tiger Tales, compiled by. 2014. (My First Lift & Learn Ser.). (ENG.). 10p. (J). (gr. -1 — 1). bds. 7.99 *(978-1-58925-623-1(9))* Tiger Tales.

—Halloween Surprise. Tiger Tales, compiled by. 2014. (My First Lift & Learn Ser.). (ENG.). 10p. (J). (gr. -1 — 1). bds. 7.99 *(978-1-58925-571-5(2))* Tiger Tales.

—Kittens. Tiger Tales, compiled by. 2014. (My First Touch & Feel Ser.). (ENG.). 10p. (J). (gr. -1 — 1). bds. 8.99 *(978-1-58925-563-0(1))* Tiger Tales.

—Puppies. Tiger Tales, compiled by. 2014. (My First Touch & Feel Ser.). (ENG.). 10p. (J). (gr. -1 — 1). bds. 8.99 *(978-1-58925-564-7(X))* Tiger Tales.

Tiger Tales Staff. Christmas Holiday Fun. 2014. (My First Touch & Feel Ser.). (ENG.). 24p. (J). (gr. -1 — 1). bds. 12.99 *(978-1-58925-562-3(3))* Tiger Tales.

—Hug! Mantle, Ben, illus. 2013. (ENG.). 16p. (J). bds. *(978-1-58925-637-8(9))* Tiger Tales.

—Lift & See Animals. 2013. (My First Matching Book Ser.). (ENG.). 10p. bds. 7.99 *(978-1-58925-613-2(1))* Tiger Tales Pubns.

—My First Book of Things to See. 2013. (ENG.). 12p. bds. *(978-1-58925-629-3(8))* Tiger Tales.

—Peek-A-Boo! Mantle, Ben, illus. 2013. (ENG.). 16p. (J). bds. *(978-1-58925-636-1(0))* Tiger Tales.

Tiger Tales Staff, creator. Count 123. 2013. (My First Touch & Trace Ser.). (ENG., Illus.). 26p. (gr. -1). bds. 7.99 *(978-1-58925-625-5(5))* Tiger Tales.

—Things That Go. 2014. (My First Jumbo Tab Bks.). (ENG., Illus.). 12p. (J). (gr. -1). bds. 8.99 *(978-1-58925-589-0(5))* Tiger Tales.

—100 First Animals. 2013. (My Big Book of Lift & Learn Ser.). (ENG., Illus.). 12p. (gr. -1). bds. 9.99 *(978-1-58925-608-8(5))* Tiger Tales.

—100 First Words. 2013. (My Big Book of Lift & Learn Ser.). (ENG., Illus.). 12p. (gr. -1). bds. 9.99 *(978-1-58925-607-1(7))* Tiger Tales.

—123 Counting Fun. 2014. (My First Touch & Feel Bks.). (ENG., Illus.). 22p. (J). bds. 12.99 *(978-1-58925-591-3(7))* Tiger Tales.

Tiger Tales Staff, ed. Animals Go. Emily, Bolam, illus. 2010. (Touch, Look, & Learn! Ser.). (ENG.). 10p. (J). (gr. -1). bds. 5.95 *(978-1-58925-854-9(1))* Tiger Tales.

—Animals Talk. Emily, Bolam, illus. 2010. (Touch, Look, & Learn! Ser.). (ENG.). 10p. (J). (gr. -1). bds. 5.95 *(978-1-58925-855-6(X))* Tiger Tales.

—Easter Surprise: My First Lift & Learn. 2014. (ENG.). 10p. (J). bds. 7.99 *(978-1-58925-580-7(1))* Tiger Tales.

—This Little Piggy. Hannah, Wood, illus. 2010. (ENG.). 24p. (J). (gr. -1-k). bds. 8.95 *(978-1-58925-849-5(5))* Tiger Tales.

Tiger Tales Staff & Mantle, Ben. Five Little Pumpkins. Tiger Tales Staff, ed. 2010. (ENG., Illus.). 24p. (J). (gr. -1-k). bds. 8.95 *(978-1-58925-856-3(8))* Tiger Tales.

Tiger Tales, Tiger, ed. Love You, Baby! Ward, Sarah, illus. 2017. (To Baby with Love Ser.). (ENG.). 12p. (J). (gr. -1 — 1). bds. 9.99 ***(978-1-68010-517-9(5))*** Tiger Tales.

Tiger's Tail. Date not set. (Touch & Feel Ser.). (J). 4.98 *(978-0-7525-9570-2(9))* Parragon, Inc.

Tildes, Phyllis Limbacher. Baby Animals Day & Night. Tildes, Phyllis Limbacher, illus. 2016. (ENG., Illus.). 10p. (J). (— 1). bds. 6.95 *(978-1-58089-609-2(X))* Charlesbridge Publishing, Inc.

—Baby's First Book of Birds & Colors. Tildes, Phyllis Limbacher, illus. 2017. (ENG., Illus.). 18p. (J). (— 1). bds. 7.99 *(978-1-58089-742-6(8))* Charlesbridge Publishing, Inc.

—Eye Guess: A Foldout Guessing Game. Tildes, Phyllis Limbacher, illus. 2005. (ENG., Illus.). 36p. (J). (gr. -1-2). 11.95 *(978-1-57091-650-2(0))* Charlesbridge Publishing, Inc.

Tillman, Nancy. Tumford the Terrible. Tillman, Nancy, illus. 2015. (Tumford Ser.). (ENG., Illus.). 32p. (J). (gr. -1-1). bds. 7.99 *(978-1-250-03364-2(0),* 9781250033642) Feiwel & Friends.

Tillworth, Mary. Color Fiesta! (Dora & Friends) Random House, illus. 2016. (ENG.). 24p. (J). (gr. -1 — 1). bds. 6.99 *(978-0-553-53839-7(X),* Random Hse. Bks. for Young Readers) Random Hse. Children's Bks.

Time for Toys! (Flip Flap Fun Book Ser.). 10p. (J). bds. *(978-2-7643-0040-4(9))* Phidal Publishing, Inc./Editions Phidal, Inc.

Tolkien, J. R. R. Letters from Father Christmas. Tolkien, Baillie, ed. 2004. (ENG., Illus.). 128p. pap. 23.99 *(978-0-618-51265-2(9))* Houghton Mifflin Harcourt Publishing Co.

Tomaselli, Doris. My Little People Farm (Mi Pequena Granja) Thompson Brothers Staff, illus. 2003. (Lift-The-Flap Ser.). (ENG & SPA.). 5p. (J). (gr. -1-k). bds. 8.99 *(978-0-7944-0213-6(5))* Reader's Digest Assn., Inc., The.

Tomlinson, Jill. The Owl Who Was Afraid of the Dark. Howard, Paul, illus. 2017. (ENG.). 28p. (J). (gr. -1-k). bds. 9.99 ***(978-1-4052-8336-6(X))*** Egmont Bks., Ltd. GBR. Dist: Independent Pubs. Group.

Toms, Kate. The Bear Who Dares. 2008. (Kate Toms Ser.). (Illus.). 26p. (gr. -1-k). bds. 7.99 *(978-1-84610-819-8(5))* Make Believe Ideas GBR. Dist: Nelson, Thomas Inc.

—The Bear Who Dares Book & Plush. 2008. (Illus.). 26p. (gr. -1-k). bds. *(978-1-84610-855-6(1))* Make Believe Ideas.

—Duckie Duck. 2009. (Kate Toms Ser.). (Illus.). 26p. (gr. -1-k). bds. 7.99 *(978-1-84610-726-9(1))* Make Believe Ideas GBR. Dist: Nelson, Thomas Inc.

—Duckie Duck Boxed Set. 2008. (Illus.). 26p. (gr. -1-k). bds. *(978-1-84610-740-5(7))* Make Believe Ideas.

—I Udderly Love You! 2007. (Illus.). 25p. (gr. -1). *(978-1-84610-680-4(X))* Make Believe Ideas.

TONKA. TONKA Busy Trucks: A Lift-The-Flap Book. 2014. (Lift-The-Flap Ser.: 3). (ENG.). 10p. (J). (gr. -1-k). bds. 9.99 *(978-0-7944-3031-3(7),* Reader's Digest Children's Bks.) Studio Fun International.

Top That. Let's Stencil Things That Go. 2008. *(978-1-84666-584-4(1))* Top That! Publishing PLC.

—Press Out & Play Magic Castle. 2008. *(978-1-84666-600-1(7))* Top That! Publishing PLC.

Top That, ed. Let's Play Magnetic Play Scene Trains. 2008. *(978-1-84666-557-8(4))* Top That! Publishing PLC.

—Sammy the Snake. 2008. (Story Book Ser.). 18p. (J). (gr. -1). *(978-1-84666-541-7(8),* Tide Mill Pr.) Top That! Publishing PLC.

Top That Publishing. Writing My First Sums. 2007. (Early Days Ser.). (Illus.). 10p. bds. *(978-1-84666-338-3(5))* Top That! Publishing PLC.

Top That Publishing, creator. Writing My First Words: Early Days Magic Writing Book. 2007. (Illus.). 8p. (gr. -1-k). bds. *(978-1-84666-340-6(7))* Top That! Publishing PLC.

Top That Publishing Staff, ed. Alphabet Farm. Parry, Jo, illus. 2007. (Magnetic - Alphabet Ser.). 10p. (J). (gr. -1). bds. *(978-1-84666-272-0(9),* Tide Mill Pr.) Top That! Publishing PLC.

—Counting on the Farm. Sapp, Karen, illus. 2007. (Magnetic Fun Ser.). 16p. (J). (gr. -1). *(978-1-84666-270-6(2),* Tide Mill Pr.) Top That! Publishing PLC.

—Jungle Numbers. Parry, Jo, illus. 2007. (Magnetic - Numbers Ser.). 10p. (J). (gr. -1). bds. *(978-1-84666-163-1(3),* Tide Mill Pr.) Top That! Publishing PLC.

—The Midnight Fairies. Atkins, Alison, illus. 2007. (Sparkling Jigsaw Book Ser.). 10p. (J). (gr. -1). bds. *(978-1-84666-278-2(8),* Tide Mill Pr.) Top That! Publishing PLC.

—There Were Ten Bears in a Bed: A Count-and-Feel Book. Atkins, Alison, illus. 2007. (Story Book Ser.). 22p. (J). (gr. -1). bds. *(978-1-84666-130-3(7),* Tide Mill Pr.) Top That! Publishing PLC.

Top That! Jungle Numbers (large Version) Parry, Jo, illus. 2007. 10p. (J). (gr. -1). *(978-1-84666-552-3(3),* Tide Mill Pr.) Top That! Publishing PLC.

—Playtime Shapes (large Version) Parry, Jo, illus. 2007. 10p. (J). (gr. -1). *(978-1-84666-555-4(8),* Tide Mill Pr.) Top That! Publishing PLC.

Top That!, creator. ABC Train. 2007. (Jigsaw Book Ser.). (Illus.). 18p. (J). (gr. -1-3). bds. *(978-1-84666-095-5(5))* Top That! Publishing PLC.

—Shapes with Penny the Penguin. 2012. (Learn with Magnets Ser.). (ENG., Illus.). 10p. (J). (gr. -1). *(978-1-84956-671-1(2))* Top That! Publishing PLC.

—123 Train. 2007. (Jigsaw Book Ser.). (Illus.). 18p. (J). (gr. -1-3). bds. *(978-1-84666-097-9(1))* Top That! Publishing PLC.

Top That! Kids, creator. Things That Go. 2008. (Magnetic Play & Learn Ser.). (ENG., Illus.). 12p. (J). (gr. -1-k). *(978-1-84510-726-0(8))* Top That! Publishing PLC.

Torres, J. Checkers & Dot at the Beach. Lum, J., illus. 2013. (J). E-Book *(978-1-77049-448-0(0))* Tundra Bks.

—Checkers & Dot at the Beach. Lum, J., illus. 2013. (Checkers & Dot Ser.). (ENG.). 16p. (J). (— 1). bds. 7.95 *(978-1-77049-444-2(8),* Tundra Bks.) Tundra Bks. CAN. Dist: Penguin Random Hse. LLC.

—Checkers & Dot at the Zoo. Lum, J., illus. 2012. (Checkers & Dot Ser.). (ENG.). 16p. (J). (gr. k — 1). bds. 7.95 *(978-1-77049-442-8(1),* Tundra Bks.) Tundra Bks. CAN. Dist: Penguin Random Hse. LLC.

—Checkers & Dot on the Farm. Lum, J., illus. 2013. (Checkers & Dot Ser.). (ENG.). 16p. (J). (— 1). bds. 7.95 *(978-1-77049-443-5(X),* Tundra Bks.) Tundra Bks. CAN. Dist: Penguin Random Hse. LLC.

Touch & Feel Playtime. braille ed. 2004. (J). (gr. -1-18). bds. *(978-0-616-14614-9(0))* Canadian National Institute for the Blind/Institut National Canadien pour les Aveugles.

Toufexis, George. Extreme Lions & Tigers Tattoos. 2011. (Dover Tattoos Ser.). (ENG.). 4p. (J). (gr. 1-4). pap. 1.50 *(978-0-486-48184-5(0))* Dover Pubns., Inc.

Tractors & Trucks Sticker Activity Book. (My Sticker Activity Ser.). (Illus.). 12p. (J). *(978-1-4054-1182-0(1))* Parragon, Inc.

Traditional. Away in a Manger. Reed, Lisa & Bennett, Randle Paul, illus. 2012. (VeggieTales Bk Ser.). 16p. (J). 12.99 *(978-0-8249-1882-8(7),* Ideal Pubns.) Worthy Publishing.

Trasler, Janee. Bedtime for Chickies. Trasler, Janee, illus. 2014. (Chickies Ser.). (ENG., Illus.). 24p. (J). (gr. -1 — 1). bds. 8.99 *(978-0-06-227468-7(6),* HarperFestival) HarperCollins Pubs.

—Big Chickie, Little Chickie. Trasler, Janee, illus. 2016. (Illus.). 24p. (J). (gr. -1 — 1). bds. 8.99 *(978-0-06-234231-7(2),* HarperFestival) HarperCollins Pubs.

—Dinnertime for Chickies. Trasler, Janee, illus. 2014. (Chickies Ser.). (ENG., Illus.). 24p. (J). (gr. -1 — 1). bds. 8.99 *(978-0-06-227470-0(8),* HarperFestival) HarperCollins Pubs.

Trent, Shanda. Giddy-Up Buckaroos! Knight, Tom, illus. 2016. (ENG.). 32p. (J). (gr. -1-2). 16.99 *(978-1-68010-008-2(4))* Tiger Tales.

Trimble, Irene. Snow Princesses (Disney Princess) RH Disney Staff, illus. 2012. (Glitter Board Book Ser.). (ENG.). 12p. (J). (gr. -1 — 1). bds. 6.99 *(978-0-7364-3004-3(0),* RH/Disney) Random Hse. Children's Bks.

Trithart, Emma, illus. Crocodile's Burp. 2015. (Pardon Me! Ser.: 4). (ENG.). 14p. (J). *(978-1-84643-750-2(4))* Child's Play International Ltd.

—Leopard's Snore. 2015. (Pardon Me! Ser.: 4). (ENG.). 14p. (J). *(978-1-84643-752-6(0))* Child's Play International Ltd.

Trivizas, Eugene. The Three Little Wolves & the Big Bad Pig. Oxenbury, Helen, illus. 2004. (ENG.). 16p. (J). 24.95 *(978-1-4052-0669-3(1))* Egmont Bks., Ltd. GBR. Dist: Trafalgar Square Publishing.

Trukhan, Ekaterina, illus. Five Little Ducks. 2012. (J). *(978-1-58865-854-8(6))* Kidsbooks, LLC.

Tse, Brian. This Is the Greatest Place! A Palace Inspired by the World of Small Animals. Steinhardt, Nancy S., ed. Wang, Ben, tr. from CHI. Mak, Alice, illus. rev. ed. 2014. (ENG.). 44p. (J). (gr. -1-3). 12.95 *(978-0-9893776-2-1(8))* China Institute Gallery, China Institute in America.

Tucker, Stephen. Goldilocks, 2 vols. Sharratt, Nick, illus. 2017. (Lift-The-Flap Fairy Tales Ser.). (ENG.). 24p. (J). (gr. -1-k). 10.99 ***(978-1-5098-2818-0(4))*** Pan Macmillan GBR. Dist: Independent Pubs. Group.

—Jack & the Beanstalk, 2 vols. Sharratt, Nick, illus. 2016. (Lift-The-Flap Fairy Tales Ser.). (ENG.). 24p. (J). (gr. -1-k).

bds. 12.99 *(978-1-5098-1714-6(X))* Pan Macmillan GBR. Dist: Independent Pubs. Group.

Tucker, Stephen. Little Red Riding Hood, 2 vols. Sharratt, Nick, illus. 2017. (Lift-The-Flap Fairy Tales Ser.). (ENG.). 24p. (J). (gr. -1-1). 10.99 ***(978-1-5098-2815-9(X))*** Pan Macmillan GBR. Dist: Independent Pubs. Group.

Tudor, Tasha. A Tale for Easter. Tudor, Tasha, illus. 2014. (Classic Board Bks.). (ENG., Illus.). 34p. (J). (gr. -1 — 1). bds. 7.99 *(978-1-4424-8857-1(3)*, Little Simon) Little Simon.

Tulip, Jenny, illus. Who's Hiding in the Jungle? A Mystery Touch-and-Feel Flap Book! 2008. 10p. (gr. -1-k). bds. 6.99 *(978-1-57755-784-5(0))* Flying Frog Publishing.

Tullet, Hervé. The Ball Game. 2014. (ENG., Illus.). 14p. 12.95 *(978-0-7148-6688-8(1))* Phaidon Pr., Inc.

—The Countryside Game. 2013. (ENG., Illus.). 14p. 12.95 *(978-0-7148-6074-9(3))* Phaidon Pr., Inc.

—The Eyes Game. 2014. (ENG., Illus.). 14p. 12.95 *(978-0-7148-6689-5(X))* Phaidon Pr., Inc.

—The Finger Circus Game. Oceano Editorial Staff, ed. 2013. (ENG., Illus.). 14p. 12.95 *(978-0-7148-6531-7(1))* Phaidon Pr., Inc.

—The Finger Travel Game. 2015. (ENG., Illus.). 14p. (gr. -1 — 1). 12.95 *(978-0-7148-6977-3(5))* Phaidon Pr., Inc.

—The Fnger Sport Game. 2015. (ENG., Illus.). 14p. (gr. -1 — 1). 12.95 *(978-0-7148-6979-7(1))* Phaidon Pr., Inc.

—The Game in the Dark. 2012. (Tullet Game Ser.). (ENG., Illus.). 14p. (gr. -1-1). 12.95 *(978-0-7148-6485-3(4))* Phaidon Pr., Inc.

—The Game of Let's Go! Edicare Staff, ed. 2011. (ENG., Illus.). 14p. (gr. -1 — 1). 9.95 *(978-0-7148-6075-6(1))* Phaidon Pr., Inc.

—The Game of Light. Children's Publication Company Staff, ed. 2011. (ENG., Illus.). 14p. (gr. -1 — 1). 12.95 *(978-0-7148-6189-0(8))* Phaidon Pr., Inc.

—The Game of Lines. 2015. (ENG., Illus.). 14p. (gr. -1-17). 12.95 *(978-0-7148-6873-8(6))* Phaidon Pr., Inc.

—The Game of Mirrors. 2014. (ENG., Illus.). 14p. (gr. -1-17). 12.95 *(978-0-7148-6687-1(3))* Phaidon Pr., Inc.

—The Game of Mix & Match. Edicare, ed. 2011. (ENG., Illus.). 14p. (gr. -1 — 1). 9.95 *(978-0-7148-6073-2(5))* Phaidon Pr., Inc.

—The Game of Mix-Up Art. 2011. (ENG.). 14p. (gr. -1 — 1). 12.95 *(978-0-7148-6188-3(X))* Phaidon Pr., Inc.

—The Game of Patterns. 2011. (ENG., Illus.). 14p. (gr. -1 — 1). 8.95 *(978-0-7148-6187-6(1))* Phaidon Pr., Inc.

—The Game of Shadows. 2013. (ENG., Illus.). 14p. 12.95 *(978-0-7148-6532-4(X))* Phaidon Pr., Inc.

—The Game of Shapes. 2015. (ENG., Illus.). 14p. (gr. -1 — 1). 12.95 *(978-0-7148-6975-9(9))* Phaidon Pr., Inc.

—The Game of Tops & Tails. 2015. (ENG., Illus.). 14p. (gr. -1-17). 12.95 *(978-0-7148-6874-5(4))* Phaidon Pr., Inc.

—The Good Morning Game. 2015. (ENG., Illus.). 14p. (gr. -1-17). 12.95 *(978-0-7148-6875-2(2))* Phaidon Pr., Inc.

—Press Here. 2011. (ENG., Illus.). 56p. (J). (gr. -1-17). 15.99 *(978-0-8118-7954-5(2))* Chronicle Bks. LLC.

—The Trail Game. 2015. (ENG., Illus.). 14p. (gr. -1-17). 12.95 *(978-0-7148-6876-9(0))* Phaidon Pr., Inc.

Tullet, Hervé & Perez, Peter L. Presiona Aqui. Perez, Peter L., illus. 2012. (SPA & ENG., Illus.). 56p. (J). (gr. -1-3). 15.99 *(978-1-4521-1287-9(8))* Chronicle Bks. LLC.

Turn-the-Wheel, 4 bks., Set. Incl. Animal Ambulance. Lawson, Peter & Smith, Kathryn. bds. 5.95 *(978-0-7892-1026-5(6))*; Fire Engine. Goldsack, Gaby. Lawson, Peter, illus. bds. 5.95 *(978-0-7892-1022-7(3))*; Fishing Boat. Goldsack, Gaby. Lawson, Peter, illus. bds. 5.95 *(978-0-7892-1025-8(8))*; Tractor. Lawson, Peter. bds. 5.95 *(978-0-7892-1023-4(1))*; 10p. (J). (gr. -1-k). (Turn the Wheel Ser.). (ENG., Illus.). 40p. 2009. Set bds. 22.95 *(978-0-7892-1027-2(4)*, Abbeville Kids) Abbeville Pr., Inc.

Tumbull, Stephanie. Trains. 2009. (Discovery History Ser.). 48p. (YA). (gr. 3-18). 8.99 *(978-0-7945-2246-9(7)*, Usborne) EDC Publishing.

Turner, Marie B. God Made the Animals. Romero, Naomi, illus. 2017. (J). 6.99 ***(978-1-5064-2185-8(7)***, Sparkhouse Family) Augsburg Fortress, Pubs.

TUXWORTH NICOLA. Animals. 2014. (ENG., Illus.). 20p. (J). (gr. -1-k). bds. 6.99 *(978-1-84322-859-2(9)*, Armadillo) Anness Publishing GBR. Dist: National Bk. Network.

Tuxworth, Nicola. Baby Animals. 2015. (ENG., Illus.). 20p. (J). (gr. -1-12). bds. 6.99 *(978-1-86147-357-8(5)*, Armadillo) Anness Publishing GBR. Dist: National Bk. Network.

TUXWORTH NICOLA. Bodies. 2014. (ENG., Illus.). 20p. (J). (gr. k-2). bds. 6.99 *(978-1-84322-860-8(2)*, Armadillo) Anness Publishing GBR. Dist: National Bk. Network.

Tuxworth, Nicola. Clothes. 2014. (ENG., Illus.). 20p. (J). (gr. -1 — 1). bds. 6.99 *(978-1-84322-861-5(0)*, Armadillo) Anness Publishing GBR. Dist: National Bk. Network.

—Colours. 2014. (ENG., Illus.). 20p. (J). (gr. -1-12). bds. 6.99 *(978-1-84322-749-6(5)*, Armadillo) Anness Publishing GBR. Dist: National Bk. Network.

—Farm Animals. 2016. (ENG., Illus.). 20p. bds. 6.99 *(978-1-86147-476-6(8)*, Armadillo) Anness Publishing GBR. Dist: National Bk. Network.

—Messy. 2016. (ENG., Illus.). 20p. (J). (gr. -1-k). bds. 6.99 *(978-1-86147-690-6(6)*, Armadillo) Anness Publishing GBR. Dist: National Bk. Network.

—Pets. 2015. (ENG., Illus.). 20p. bds. 6.99 *(978-1-86147-647-0(7)*, Armadillo) Anness Publishing GBR. Dist: National Bk. Network.

—Puppies. 2016. (ENG., Illus.). 20p. bds. 6.99 *(978-1-86147-631-9(0)*, Armadillo) Anness Publishing GBR. Dist: National Bk. Network.

—Shapes. 2015. (ENG., Illus.). 20p. bds. 6.99 *(978-1-86147-648-7(5)*, Armadillo) Anness Publishing GBR. Dist: National Bk. Network.

—Sizes. 2016. (ENG., Illus.). 20p. bds. 6.99 *(978-1-84322-751-9(7)*, Armadillo) Anness Publishing GBR. Dist: National Bk. Network.

—Things That Go. 2016. (ENG., Illus.). 20p. bds. 6.99 *(978-1-84322-752-6(5)*, Armadillo) Anness Publishing GBR. Dist: National Bk. Network.

Tuxworth, Nicole. Kittens. 2015. (ENG., Illus.). 20p. (J). (gr. -1 — 1). bds. 6.99 *(978-1-86147-384-4(2)*, Armadillo) Anness Publishing GBR. Dist: National Bk. Network.

Twin Sisters(r), et al. Christmas Joy Black & White Board Book. 2016. (Tell Me about God Board Bks.). (ENG.). 8p. (J). bds. 4.99 *(978-1-63409-802-1(1))* Barbour Publishing, Inc.

—Where Is Baby Jesus? a Lift-The-Flap Book. 2016. (ENG.). 10p. (J). bds. 9.99 *(978-1-63409-806-9(4))* Barbour Publishing, Inc.

Twin Sisters(r) Staff. B-i-n-g-o. 2010. (J). (gr. k-1). 14.99 *(978-1-59922-630-9(8))* Twin Sisters IP, LLC.

Twin Sisters(r) Staff, et al, adapted by. B-i-n-g-o. 2010. (J). (gr. k-1). 14.99 *(978-1-59922-422-0(4))* Twin Sisters IP, LLC.

Twin Sisters(r) Staff, et al. David & Goliath Padded Board Book & CD, 1 vol. 2014. (Let's Share a Story Ser.). 16p. (J). (-5). bds. 9.99 incl. audio compact disk *(978-1-63058-784-0(2))* Barbour Publishing, Inc.

—Five Little Bunnies. 2010. (J). (gr. k-1). 14.99 *(978-1-59922-421-3(6))*; 14.99 *(978-1-59922-629-3(4))* Twin Sisters IP, LLC.

—I Thank God for You. 2010. (J). (gr. k-2). pap. 4.99 *(978-1-59922-497-8(6))* Twin Sisters IP, LLC.

—Jesus Loves Me More Than... 2015. (Let's Share a Story Ser.). (ENG., Illus.). 10p. (J). (gr. -1-k). bds. 9.99 *(978-1-63058-896-0(2))* Barbour Publishing, Inc.

—My First Bible Stories for Girls with CD. 2015. (ENG., Illus.). 24p. (J). (-k). 12.99 *(978-1-63409-095-7(0))* Barbour Publishing, Inc.

Twinn, A. Down by the Station. Stockham, Jess, illus. 2007. (Classic Books with Holes 8x8 with CD Ser.). (ENG.). 16p. (J). (gr. -1-1). pap. incl. audio compact disk *(978-1-904550-68-6(1))* Child's Play International Ltd.

—Ten Little Monkeys: Jumping on the Bed. Freeman, Tina, illus. 2007. (Classic Books with Holes 8x8 with CD Ser.). (ENG.). 16p. (J). (gr. -1-1). pap. incl. audio compact disk *(978-1-904550-67-9(3))* Child's Play International Ltd.

Twinn, M. Metamorphoses: Butterfly. 2006. (Metamorphoses Ser.). (ENG., Illus.). 16p. (J). (gr. 1-5). bds. *(978-1-84643-013-8(5))* Child's Play International Ltd.

—Metamorphoses: Egg, Tadpole, Frog. 2006. (Metamorphoses Ser.). (ENG., Illus.). 16p. (J). (gr. 1-5). bds. *(978-1-84643-012-1(7))* Child's Play International Ltd.

—Old MacDonald Had a Farm. Adams, Pam, illus. 2007. (Classic Books with Holes 8x8 with CD Ser.). (ENG.). 16p. (J). (gr. -1-1). pap. incl. audio compact disk *(978-1-904550-64-8(9))* Child's Play International Ltd.

—There Was an Old Lady Who Swallowed a Fly. Adams, Pam, illus. 2007. (Classic Books with Holes 8x8 with CD Ser.). (ENG.). 16p. (J). (gr. -1-1). pap. incl. audio compact disk *(978-1-904550-62-4(2))* Child's Play International Ltd.

Tyler, Jenny & Hawthorn, P. There's a Monster in My House. 2004. (Illus.). 16p. (J). (gr. 1-18). pap. 7.95 *(978-0-7945-0624-7(0))* EDC Publishing.

—Who's Making That Mess? rev. ed. 2004. (Illus.). 16p. (J). (gr. 1-18). pap. 7.99 *(978-0-7945-0431-1(0))* EDC Publishing.

—Who's Making That Smell? rev. ed. 2004. (Illus.). 16p. (J). (gr. 1-18). pap. 7.95 *(978-0-7945-0523-3(6))* EDC Publishing.

Tyler, Jenny & Hawthorn, Phillip. Who's Making That Noise? 2008. (Luxury Flap Bks). 16p. (J). 9.99 *(978-0-7945-1695-6(5)*, Usborne) EDC Publishing.

—Who's Making That Smell? Cartwright, Stephen, illus. 2007. (Luxury Flap Bks). 16p. (J). (gr. -1-3). 9.99 *(978-0-7945-1696-3(3)*, Usborne) EDC Publishing.

UG, Philippe. Funny Birds. 2013. (ENG., Illus.). 18p. (J). (gr. -1-3). 19.95 *(978-3-7913-7147-4(9))* Prestel Verlag GmbH & Co KG. DEU. Dist: Penguin Random Hse. LLC.

—In the Butterfly Garden. 2015. (ENG., Illus.). 16p. (J). (gr. -1-3). 19.95 *(978-3-7913-7207-5(6))* Prestel Verlag GmbH & Co KG. DEU. Dist: Penguin Random Hse. LLC.

—Robots: Watch Out, Water About! 2014. (ENG., Illus.). 16p. (J). (gr. -1-3). 19.95 *(978-3-7913-7198-6(3))* Prestel Verlag GmbH & Co KG. DEU. Dist: Penguin Random Hse. LLC.

Ultimate Boats Sticker Book. (Radical Rides Ser.). 16p. (J). *(978-2-7643-0012-1(3))* Phidal Publishing, Inc./Editions Phidal, Inc.

Ultimate Cars Sticker Book. (Radical Rides Ser.). 16p. (J). *(978-2-7643-0010-7(7))* Phidal Publishing, Inc./Editions Phidal, Inc.

Ultimate Planes Sticker Book, 4 vols. (Radical Rides Ser.). (Illus.). 16p. (J). *(978-2-7643-0008-4(5))* Phidal Publishing, Inc./Editions Phidal, Inc.

Ultman, Suzy, illus. Masha & Her Sisters. 2017. (ENG.). 10p. (J). bds. 9.99 *(978-1-4521-5159-5(8))* Chronicle Bks. LLC.

Underwood, Deborah. The Loud Book! Padded Board Book. Liwska, Renata, illus. 2015. (ENG.). 32p. (J). (— 1). bds. 8.99 *(978-0-544-43064-8(6)*, HMH Books For Young Readers) Houghton Mifflin Harcourt Publishing Co.

University Games Staff. Very Hungrey Caterpillar. 2006. 24p. (J). *(978-1-57528-891-8(5))* Univ. Games.

Unknown & Grosset and Dunlap Staff. Let's Count! A First Book of Numbers. Aikins, Dave, illus. 2014. (Sassy Ser.). (ENG.). 10p. (J). (gr. -1 — 1). bds. 6.99 *(978-0-448-48012-1(3)*, Grosset & Dunlap) Penguin Young Readers Group.

Urban, Chieu Anh. Hooray for Spring! Urban, Chieu Anh, illus. 2016. (Color Wonder Ser.). (ENG., Illus.). 14p. (J). (gr. -1 — 1). bds. 7.99 *(978-1-4814-8720-7(5)*, Little Simon) Little Simon.

Vagnozzi, Barbara. The Musicians of Bremen. 2007. (Flip-Up Fairy Tales Ser.). (ENG., Illus.). 24p. (J). (gr. 1-2). *(978-1-84643-115-9(8))* Child's Play International Ltd.

Vagnozzi, Barbara, illus. Jack & the Beanstalk. (Classic Fairy Tales Ser.). (ENG.). 24p. (J). 2011. audio compact disk *(978-1-84643-456-3(4))* 2007. (gr. -1-2). audio compact disk *(978-1-84643-086-2(0))* Child's Play International Ltd.

Valat, Pierre-Marie. Water. Valat, Pierre-Marie, illus. 2012. (ENG., Illus.). 36p. (J). (gr. -1-k). spiral bd. 14.99 *(978-1-85103-403-1(X))* Moonlight Publishing, Ltd. GBR. Dist: Independent Pubs. Group.

Vampire Sticker Book. 2003. (Illus.). 16p. (J). 2.98 *(978-1-84273-119-2(X)*, Exclusive Editions) Parragon, Inc.

Van Buren, David. I Love You As Big As the World. Warnes, Tim, illus. 2013. (ENG.). 22p. (J). bds. *(978-1-58925-603-3(4))* Tiger Tales.

Van Camp, Richard. Little You, 1 vol. Flett, Julie, illus. 2013. (ENG.). 24p. (J). (gr. -1-k). bds. 9.95 *(978-1-4598-0248-3(9))* Orca Bk. Pubs. USA.

van der Meulen, Majel, illus. My London: Color, Draw, Explore. 2017. (ENG.). 40p. (J). (gr. 1-4). pap. 12.99 *(978-1-78067-912-9(2))* King, Laurence Publishing GBR. Dist: Hachette Bk. Group.

—My New York: Color, Draw, Explore. 2017. (ENG.). 40p. (J). (gr. 1-4). pap. 12.99 *(978-1-78067-962-4(9))* King, Laurence Publishing GBR. Dist: Hachette Bk. Group.

van der Put, Klaartje, et al. Little Duck: Finger Puppet. 2005. (Little Finger Puppet Board Bks.: FING). (ENG., Illus.). 12p. (J). (gr. -1 — 1). bds. 6.99 *(978-0-8118-4847-3(7))* Chronicle Bks. LLC.

—Little Lamb. 2006. (Little Finger Puppet Board Bks.: FING). (ENG., Illus.). 12p. (J). (gr. -1-7). bds. 6.99 *(978-0-8118-5235-7(0))* Chronicle Bks. LLC.

Van Fleet, Mara. Little Color Fairies. Van Fleet, Mara, illus. 2012. (ENG., Illus.). 16p. (J). (gr. -1-1). 14.99 *(978-1-4424-3434-9(1)*, Simon & Schuster/Paula Wiseman Bks.) Simon & Schuster/Paula Wiseman Bks.

—Night-Night, Princess. Van Fleet, Mara. illus. 2014. (ENG., Illus.). 16p. (J). (gr. -1-1). 14.99 *(978-1-4424-8646-1(5)*, Simon & Schuster/Paula Wiseman Bks.) Simon & Schuster/Paula Wiseman Bks.

Van Fleet, Mara & Wade, Sarah. The Very Mixed-Up Princess. 2009. (Mix & Match Ser.). (ENG., Illus.). 14p. (J). (gr. -1-3). bds. 8.99 *(978-0-7944-1775-8(2))* Reader's Digest Assn., Inc., The.

Van Fleet, Matthew. Color Dog. Stanton, Brian, illus. Stanton, Brian, photos by. 2015. (ENG.). 22p. (J). (gr. -1-k). 19.99 *(978-1-4814-4986-1(9)*, Simon & Schuster Bks. For Young Readers) Simon & Schuster Bks. For Young Readers.

—Dance. Van Fleet, Matthew, illus. 2017. (ENG., Illus.). 16p. (J). (gr. -1). 19.99 *(978-1-4814-8707-8(8)*, Simon & Schuster/Paula Wiseman Bks.) Simon & Schuster/Paula Wiseman Bks.

—Lick! Van Fleet, Matthew, illus. 2013. (ENG., Illus.). 14p. (J). (gr. -1-1). 9.99 *(978-1-4424-6049-2(0)*, Simon & Schuster/Paula Wiseman Bks.) Simon & Schuster/Paula Wiseman Bks.

—Monday the Bullfrog. Van Fleet, Matthew, illus. 2010. (ENG., Illus.). 20p. (J). (gr. -1). 24.99 *(978-1-4424-0958-3(4)*, Simon & Schuster/Paula Wiseman Bks.) Simon & Schuster/Paula Wiseman Bks.

—Moo. Stanton, Brian, photos by. 2011. (ENG., Illus.). 18p. (J). (gr. -1-1). 18.99 *(978-1-4424-3503-2(8)*, Simon & Schuster/Paula Wiseman Bks.) Simon & Schuster/Paula Wiseman Bks.

Van Fleet, Matthew. Tails. 2017. (ENG., Illus.). 20p. (J). (— 1). 14.99 ***(978-1-328-88685-9(9)***, HMH Books For Young Readers) Houghton Mifflin Harcourt Publishing Co.

van Genechten, Guido. Big & Small. 2013. (Odd One Out Ser.). (ENG.). 18p. (J). (gr. -1-k). bds. 12.95 *(978-1-60537-149-8(1))* Cobblestone Publishing Co.

—The Big Baby Book. 2011. (ENG.). 22p. (J). (gr. k — 1). bds. 12.95 *(978-1-60537-079-8(7))* Cobblestone Publishing Co.

—The Big Potty Book. 2009. (ENG.). 20p. (J). (gr. k — 1). bds. 12.95 *(978-1-60537-031-6(2))* Cobblestone Publishing Co.

—Guess What? 2012. (Guess Along Ser.). (ENG.). 16p. (J). (gr. k — 1). 9.95 *(978-1-60537-116-0(5))* Cobblestone Publishing Co.

—Guess Where? 2012. (Guess Along Ser.). (ENG.). 16p. (J). (gr. k — 1). 9.95 *(978-1-60537-115-3(7))* Cobblestone Publishing Co.

—Guess Who? van Genechten, Guido, illus. 2010. (ENG., Illus.). 28p. (J). (gr. k — 1). 8.95 *(978-1-60537-061-3(4))* Cobblestone Publishing Co.

—Mommies & Their Babies. 2012. (Black & White Ser.). (ENG.). 20p. (J). (gr. k — 1). bds. 9.95 *(978-1-60537-109-2(2))* Cobblestone Publishing Co.

—Moon Is Sad. 2010. (ENG.). 12p. (J). (gr. k — 1). bds. 8.95 *(978-1-60537-048-4(7))* Clavis Publishing.

van Genechten, Guido & Frippiat, Stéphanie. In, Out & All Around. 2013. (Odd One Out Ser.). (ENG.). 18p. (J). (gr. -1-k). bds. 12.95 *(978-1-60537-150-4(5))* Cobblestone Publishing Co.

van Genechten, Guido & Paradise, Susan. My Daddy. 2011. (ENG.). 20p. (J). (gr. k — 1). bds. 12.95 *(978-1-60537-098-9(3))* Cobblestone Publishing Co.

Van Hoven, Constance. The Twelve Days of Christmas in Minnesota. Wohnoutka, Mike, illus. 2016. (Twelve Days of Christmas in America Ser.). (ENG.). 22p. (J). (— 1). bds. 7.95 *(978-1-4549-2057-1(2))* Sterling Publishing Co., Inc.

Vanden-Heuvel, John C., Sr. & Ostrovsky, Andrey. ABCs of the Web. Holmes, Tom, illus. 2016. (ENG.). 28p. (J). (gr. -1-3). bds. 8.99 *(978-1-4998-0312-9(5))* Little Bee Books Inc.

Vander Klipp, Michael. God Made Animals, 1 vol. 2008. (God Made... Ser.). 14p. (J). bds. 3.99 *(978-0-8254-3911-7(6))* Kregel Pubns.

—God Made My Body, 1 vol. 2008. (God Made... Ser.). 14p. (J). bds. 3.99 *(978-0-8254-3912-4(4))* Kregel Pubns.

—God Made the World, 1 vol. 2008. (God Made... Ser.). 14p. (J). bds. 3.99 *(978-0-8254-3914-8(0))* Kregel Pubns.

Vasquez, Natalia, illus. The Pied Piper of Hamelin. 2012. (Flip-Up Fairy Tales Ser.). (ENG.). 24p. (J). *(978-1-84643-480-8(7))* Child's Play International Ltd.

Vasylenko, Veronica. Deck the Halls. Tiger Tales Staff, ed. 2011. (ENG., Illus.). 20p. bds. 8.95 *(978-1-58925-868-6(1))* Tiger Tales.

—Jingle Bells. Tiger Tales Staff, ed. 2011. (ENG., Illus.). 20p. bds. 8.95 *(978-1-58925-869-3(X))* Tiger Tales.

Veggie Tales, Veggie. VeggieTales: Bob Is a Buddy! A Story about Friends. 2015. (Googly Eyes Ser.: 1). (ENG.). 10p. (J). (gr. -1 — 1). bds. 8.99 *(978-0-7944-3465-6(7)*, Reader's Digest Children's Bks.) Studio Fun International.

Veitch, Catherine. Animal Babies. 2013. (Animal Babies Ser.). (ENG.). 24p. (gr. -1-1). pap. 35.94 *(978-1-4329-8422-9(5))*; pap. 215.64 *(978-1-4329-8429-8(2))*; lib. bdg. 135.90 *(978-1-4329-7497-8(1))* Heinemann-Raintree. (Acorn).

Velthuijs, Max. Where Is Frog? 2017. (ENG., Illus.). 14p. (J). (gr. -1-k). bds. 8.95 ***(978-0-2281-0002-7(X)***, 9780228100027) Firefly Bks., Ltd.

Venturini, Claudia, illus. Ali Baba & the Forty Thieves. 2009. (Flip-Up Fairy Tales Ser.). (ENG.). 24p. (J). (gr. -1-2). pap. *(978-1-84643-251-4(0))*; audio compact disk *(978-1-84643-294-1(4))* Child's Play International Ltd.

Verdick, Elizabeth. Bye-Bye Time. Heinlen, Marieka, illus. 2008. (Toddler Tools Ser.). (ENG.). 24p. (J). (gr. k — 1). bds. 7.95 *(978-1-57542-299-2(9))* Free Spirit Publishing, Inc.

—Bye-Bye Time/Momento de la Despedida. Heinlen, Marieka, illus. 2017. (Toddler Tools Ser.). (ENG, SPA & MUL.). 24p. (J). bds. 7.95 ***(978-1-63198-151-7(X))*** Free Spirit Publishing, Inc.

—Clean-Up Time. Heinlen, Marieka, illus. 2008. (Toddler Tools Ser.). (ENG.). 24p. (J). (gr. k — 1). bds. 7.95 *(978-1-57542-298-5(0))* Free Spirit Publishing, Inc.

—Manners Time / Los Buenos Modales. Heinlen, Marieka, illus. 2016. (Toddler Tools Ser.). (ENG & SPA.). 24p. (J). bds. 7.95 *(978-1-63198-120-3(X))* Free Spirit Publishing, Inc.

Verdick, Elizabeth & Heinlen, Marieka. Listening Time / Momento para Escuchar. 2016. (Toddler Tools Ser.). (ENG & SPA., Illus.). 24p. (J). bds. 7.95 *(978-1-63198-117-3(X))* Free Spirit Publishing, Inc.

Verdick, Elizabeth & Lisovskis, Marjorie. Cuddle. 2013. (Happy Healthy Baby Ser.). (ENG., Illus.). 22p. (J). bds. 6.99 *(978-1-57542-423-1(1))* Free Spirit Publishing, Inc.

—Move. 2013. (Happy Healthy Baby Ser.). (ENG., Illus.). 22p. (J). bds. 6.99 *(978-1-57542-422-4(3))* Free Spirit Publishing, Inc.

Vere, Ed. Everyone's Hungry. 2003. (ENG., Illus.). 12p. (J). 6.95 *(978-0-333-78041-1(8))* Macmillan Pubs., Ltd. GBR. Dist: Trafalgar Square Publishing.

—Everyone's Little. 2003. (ENG., Illus.). 12p. (J). bds. 6.95 *(978-0-333-78039-8(6))* Macmillan Pubs., Ltd. GBR. Dist: Trafalgar Square Publishing.

—Everyone's Noisy. 2003. (ENG., Illus.). 14p. (J). 8.99 *(978-0-333-78040-4(X))* Macmillan Pubs., Ltd. GBR. Dist: Trafalgar Square Publishing.

—Everyone's Sleepy. 2003. (ENG., Illus.). 12p. (J). 8.99 *(978-0-333-78038-1(8))* Macmillan Pubs., Ltd. GBR. Dist: Trafalgar Square Publishing.

Verhille, Alexandre & Tavernier, Sarah. Legendary Routes of the World. 2015. (ENG., Illus.). 18p. (J). (gr. k-4). 29.99 *(978-3-89955-759-6(X))* Die Gestalten Verlag DEU. Dist: Penguin Random Hse. LLC.

Vermeulen, Mariska. Anton & Boris Finger Puppet Book. van de Liejgraaf, Deborah, illus. 2016. (My Best Friend & Me Ser.). (ENG.). 10p. (J). (gr. -1-k). bds., bds. 6.99 *(978-0-7641-6831-4(2))* Barron's Educational Series, Inc.

—Bella & Clara Finger Puppet Book. van de Liejgraaf, Deborah, illus. 2016. (My Best Friend & Me Ser.). (ENG.). 10p. (J). (gr. -1-k). bds. 6.99 *(978-0-7641-6829-1(0))* Barron's Educational Series, Inc.

—Kaila & Kahuna Finger Puppet Book. van de Liejgraaf, Deborah, illus. 2016. (My Best Friend & Me Ser.). (ENG.). 10p. (J). (gr. -1-k). bds. 6.99 *(978-0-7641-6832-1(0))* Barron's Educational Series, Inc.

Vernick, Shirley & La Forest, Courtney. Boston Baby: A Local Baby Book. 2016. (Local Baby Bks.). (ENG., Illus.). 22p. (J). (-k). bds. 8.95 *(978-1-938093-69-2(0))* Duo Pr. LLC.

Vilcoq, Marianne. Espero un Hermanito. (SPA.). 24p. (J). *(978-84-8470-013-5(5))* Corimbo, Editorial S.L. ESP. Dist: Lectorum Pubns., Inc.

Vischer, Phil. I Thank God for This Day! Reed, Lisa, illus. 2016. (J). *(978-0-8249-1966-5(1)*, Ideal Pubns.) Worthy Publishing.

Vize, Dania. Lift, Stick & Learn Baby Animals. 2006. (Illus.). 24p. (J). (gr. -1-k). pap. *(978-1-84610-032-1(1))* Make Believe Ideas.

Vocabulary Flip Chart. 2004. (Scott Foresman Reading Ser.). (gr. 1-18). suppl. ed. 109.15 *(978-0-673-62166-5(9))*; (gr. 2-18). suppl. ed. 109.15 *(978-0-673-62167-2(7))* Addison-Wesley Educational Pubs., Inc.

Voce, Karma. Forever Inspired Coloring Book: Tokyo Fashions. 2016. (ENG., Illus.). 96p. (J). (gr. 3-7). pap. 7.99 *(978-1-944686-61-1(4)*, Racehorse Publishing) Skyhorse Publishing Co., Inc.

Volker, Kerstin. Suzie Goes to Sleep. 2003. (Funny Friends Lift-and-Learn Bks.). (Illus.). 14p. (J). 5.99 *(978-1-59384-024-2(1))* Parklane Publishing.

Wagner, Veronica. Disney Mickey Mouse Clubhouse: 3 Book Play-A-Sound Set, 3 vols. 2011. (Illus.). (J). bds. *(978-1-4508-1724-0(6)*, 1450817246) Phoenix International Publications, Inc.

Wakeham, Kate. Moby-Dick, 1 vol. Tempest, Annabel, illus. 2017. (ENG.). 30p. 12.99 ***(978-1-4236-4784-3(X))*** Gibbs Smith, Publisher.

Walden, Libby. Bear Hugs. Riley, Vicky, illus. 2017. (ENG.). 18p. (J). (gr. -1-1). bds. 7.99 ***(978-1-68010-519-3(1))*** Tiger Tales.

—Finding First Animals & More! Galloway, Fhiona, illus. 2016. (My Little World Ser.). (ENG.). 12p. (J). (gr. -1-k). bds. 12.99 *(978-1-58925-229-5(2))* Tiger Tales.

—Finding First Words & More! Galloway, Fhiona, illus. 2016. (My Little World Ser.). (ENG.). 12p. (J). (gr. -1-k). bds. 12.99 *(978-1-58925-218-9(7))* Tiger Tales.

—Noisy Touch & Feel: Cow Says Moo. Enright, Amanda, illus. 2016. (Noisy Touch & Feel Ser.). (ENG.). 12p. (J). bds. 14.99 *(978-1-62686-575-4(2)*, Silver Dolphin Bks.) Readerlink Distribution Services, LLC.

—Noisy Touch & Feel: Owl Says Hoot. Enright, Amanda, illus. 2016. (Noisy Touch & Feel Ser.). (ENG.). 12p. (J). bds. 14.99 *(978-1-62686-576-1(0)*, Silver Dolphin Bks.) Readerlink Distribution Services, LLC.

Walden, Libby. Touch & Feel First Words. Galloway, Fhiona, illus. 2017. (My Little World Ser.). (ENG.). 10p. (J). (gr. -1-k). bds. 8.99 ***(978-1-68010-521-6(3))*** Tiger Tales.

Walker, John, illus. The Story of Christmas: The Birth of Jesus. 2008. (ENG.). 24p. (J). (gr. 2). 19.95 *(978-1-58117-793-0(3)*, Intervisual/Piggy Toes) Bendon, Inc.

Walker, Joni, illus. Jesus Hears Me. 2008. 20p. (J). (gr. -1). bds. 6.49 *(978-0-7586-1508-4(6))* Concordia Publishing Hse.

Walker, Rob. Baby Animals. 2009. (Chunkie Hunkies Ser.). (ENG.). 18p. (J). (gr. -1). bds. 4.99 *(978-0-7641-6212-1(8))* Barron's Educational Series, Inc.

Wall, Laura. Goose on the Farm Board Book. Wall, Laura, illus. 2017. (Illus.). 36p. (J). (gr. -1 — 1). bds. 7.99 *(978-0-06-232440-5(3)*, HarperFestival) HarperCollins Pubs.

Wallace, B. My Books of Colors Slipcase. 2007. (Illus.). 12p. (gr. -1-k). pap., per. *(978-1-84610-561-6(7))* Make Believe Ideas.

Wallace, Karen. Flip the Flaps: Farm Animals. Palin, Nicki, illus. 2012. (Flip the Flaps Ser.). (ENG.). 32p. (J). (gr. -1-1). pap. 6.99 *(978-0-7534-6738-1(0)*, 9780753467381, Kingfisher) Roaring Brook Pr.

—I Wonder Why Flip the Flaps Farm Animals. 2009. *(978-0-7534-6222-5(2)*, Kingfisher) Roaring Brook Pr.

Wallin, Betsy. My First Farm Friends, 4 vols. 2011. (ENG., Illus.). 20p. (J). (gr. -1 — 1). bds. 18.95 *(978-1-60342-991-7(3)*, 62991) Storey Publishing, LLC.

Walsh, Ellen Stoll. Mouse Paint - Pintura de Ratón. 2010. (ENG & SPA., Illus.). 30p. (J). (gr. k — 1). bds. 4.99 *(978-0-547-33332-8(3))* Houghton Mifflin Harcourt Publishing Co.

Walsh, Melanie. Living with Mom & Living with Dad. Walsh, Melanie, illus. 2012. (ENG., Illus.). 40p. (J). (gr. -1-2). 15.99 *(978-0-7636-5869-4(3))* Candlewick Pr.

Walt Disney Company Staff & Phidal Publishing Staff, contrib. by. Cars. 2006. (Illus.). 24p. *(978-2-7643-0261-3(4))* Phidal Publishing, Inc./Editions Phidal, Inc.

Walton, Rick. Mini Mysteries 2: 20 More Tricky Tales to Untangle. Scheuer, Lauren, illus. 2006. 87p. (J). *(978-1-4156-6869-6(8))*, American Girl) American Girl Publishing, Inc.

—Mini Mysteries 3: 20 More Tricky Tales to Untangle. Scheuer, Lauren, illus. 2007. (ENG.). 80p. (gr. 4-7). pap. 7.95 *(978-1-59369-281-0(1))* American Girl Publishing, Inc.

Wan, Joyce. Are You My Mommy? 2014. (ENG.). 18p. (J). (gr. -1 — 1). bds. 6.99 *(978-0-545-54047-6(X))*, Cartwheel Bks.) Scholastic, Inc.

—My Lucky Little Dragon. Wan, Joyce, illus. 2014. (ENG., Illus.). 14p. (J). (— 1). bds. 6.99 *(978-0-545-54046-9(1))*, Cartwheel Bks.) Scholastic, Inc.

—Peek-A-Boo Farm. 2015. (ENG., Illus.). 14p. (J). (— 1). bds. 6.99 *(978-0-545-75045-5(8))*, Cartwheel Bks.) Scholastic, Inc.

—Peek-A-Boo Zoo. 2015. (ENG., Illus.). 14p. (J). (— 1). bds. 6.99 *(978-0-545-75042-4(3))*, Cartwheel Bks.) Scholastic, Inc.

—You Are My Cupcake: a Cloth Book. 2016. (ENG.). 6p. (J). (— 1). 12.99 *(978-1-338-02921-5(5))*, Cartwheel Bks.) Scholastic, Inc.

—You Are My Merry Little Christmas. Wan, Joyce, illus. 2016. (ENG., Illus.). 14p. (J). (— 1). 6.99 *(978-0-545-88093-0(9))*, Cartwheel Bks.) Scholastic, Inc.

Wang, Dorothea DePrisco & Imperato, Teresa. All the Ways I Love You. Downing, Julie, illus. 2005. (ENG.). 10p. (J). bds. 8.95 *(978-1-58117-190-7(0))*, Intervisual/Piggy Toes) Bendon, Inc.

Wang, Dorthea Deprisco. Five Minutes until Bed. Vaux, Patricia, illus. 2012. (ENG.). 14p. (J). (-k). bds. 5.99 *(978-1-4494-2244-8(6))* Andrews McMeel Publishing.

Wang, Holman & Wang, Jack. Charles Dickens's Great Expectations. 2016. (ENG., Illus.). 24p. (J). (gr. -1 — 1). bds. 9.95 *(978-1-4521-5243-1(8))* Chronicle Bks. LLC.

Wang, Margaret. I Love You, Every Little Bit. Butler, John, illus. 2006. (ENG.). 10p. (gr. -1-k). bds. 9.95 *(978-1-58117-482-3(9))*, Intervisual/Piggy Toes) Bendon, Inc.

—Who Do You Love? A Touch & Feel Book. Mitchell, Melanie, illus. 2007. (gr. -1-k). 15.95 *(978-1-58117-570-7(1))*, Intervisual/Piggy Toes) Bendon, Inc.

Wang, Margaret C. When I Grow Up: A Touch & Feel Book. Gévry, Claudine, illus. 2005. (ENG.). 12p. (J). bds. 10.95 *(978-1-58117-423-6(3))*, Intervisual/Piggy Toes) Bendon, Inc.

Ward, Sarah, illus. Carry & Learn Opposites. 2016. (ENG.). 10p. (J). (— 1). bds. 7.99 *(978-0-545-79789-4(6))*, Cartwheel Bks.) Scholastic, Inc.

Wargin, Kathy-jo. Little Minnesota. Urban, Helle, illus. 2011. (My Little State Ser.). (ENG.). 22p. (J). 9.95 *(978-1-58536-174-8(7))* Sleeping Bear Pr.

—Little Wisconsin. 2012. (My Little State Ser.). (ENG., Illus.). 20p. (J). (gr. k-3). 9.95 *(978-1-58536-209-7(3))* Sleeping Bear Pr.

Washburn, Kim. Lots of Love, 1 vol. East, Jacqueline, illus. 2016. (ENG.). 18p. (J). bds. 8.99 *(978-0-310-75861-7(0))* Zonderkidz.

Watt, F. & Wells, R. That's Not My Dinosaur... It's Body Is Too Squashy. 2004. (Touchy-Feely Board Bks.). (SPA & ENG., Illus.). 1p. (J). (gr. -1-18). bds. 7.95 *(978-0-7945-0129-7(X))*, Usborne) EDC Publishing.

—That's Not My Lion. 2004. (Touchy-Feely Board Bks.). (SPA.). 10p. (J). 7.99 *(978-0-7945-0047-4(1))*, Usborne) EDC Publishing.

Watt, Fiona. ABC. Elkerton, Andy, illus. 2009. (Luxury Touchy-Feely Board Bks). 10p. (J). (gr. -1). bds. 15.99 *(978-0-7945-2094-6(4))*, Usborne) EDC Publishing.

—Baby's Very First Book of Little Babies. 2011. (Baby's Very First Board Bks). 10p. (J). ring bd. 6.99 *(978-0-7945-3109-6(1))*, Usborne) EDC Publishing.

—Baby's Very First Noisy Book Jungle. 2017. (Picture Bks.). (ENG.). 10p. (J). 15.99 ***(978-0-7945-3986-3(6))***, Usborne) EDC Publishing.

—Baby's Very First Slide & See Animals. 2015. (Baby's Very First Slide & See Board Bks.). (ENG.). 10p. (J). 14.99 *(978-0-7945-3479-0(1))*, Usborne) EDC Publishing.

—Baby's Very First Slide & See under the Sea. 2015. (Baby's Very First Slide & See Board Bks.). (ENG.). 10p. (J). 14.99 *(978-0-7945-3482-0(1))*, Usborne) EDC Publishing.

—Big Doodling Book. 2012. (Activity Bks). 96p. (J). bds. 11.99 *(978-0-7945-3269-7(1))*, Usborne) EDC Publishing.

—Busy Bug Book. Mantle, Ben, illus. 2011. (Pull-Back Books Ser.). 10p. (J). ring bd. 24.99 *(978-0-7945-2941-3(0))*, Usborne) EDC Publishing.

—Busy Helicopter Book. 2012. (Pull-Back Bks). 10p. (J). ring bd. 24.99 *(978-0-7945-3203-1(9))*, Usborne) EDC Publishing.

—Busy Santa Book. 2011. (Pull-Back Bks). 10p. (J). ring bd. 24.99 *(978-0-7945-3178-2(4))*, Usborne) EDC Publishing.

—Cars. 2011. (Luxury Touchy-Feely Board Books Ser.). 10p. (J). ring bd. 15.99 *(978-0-7945-2568-2(7))*, Usborne) EDC Publishing.

—Christmas Eve. Wells, Rachel, illus. 2007. (Luxury Touchy-Feely Board Bks). 10p. (J). (gr. -1-k). bds. 11.99 *(978-0-7945-1478-5(2))*, Usborne) EDC Publishing.

—Este No Es Mi Tren. rev. ed. 2004. (Titles in Spanish Ser.).Tr. of That's Not My Train. 32p. (J). 12.99 *(978-1-58086-585-2(2))* EDC Publishing.

—Fairies. Cartwright, Stephen & Bird, Glen, illus. 2004. 10p. (J). (gr. -1 — 1). per. 15.95 *(978-0-7945-0811-1(1))*, Usborne) EDC Publishing.

—Farm. Wells, Rachel, illus. 2008. (Usborne Touchy-Feely Board Bks.). 8p. (J). (gr. -1-k). bds. 15.99 *(978-0-7945-1959-9(8))*, Usborne) EDC Publishing.

—Go to Sleep Little Baby. Watt, Fiona, illus. 2009. (Baby Board Books w/CD Ser.). (Illus.). 12p. (J). (gr. -1). bds. 15.99 *(978-0-7945-1936-0(9))*, Usborne) EDC Publishing.

—Jungle. Elkerton, Andy, illus. 2009. (Luxury Touchy-Feely Board Bks). 10p. (J). (gr. -1). bds. 15.99 *(978-0-7945-2433-3(8))*, Usborne) EDC Publishing.

—The Nativity. Wells, Rachel, illus. 2005. (Usborne Touchy-Feely Board Bks.). 10p. (J). (gr. -1-k). bds. 15.95 *(978-0-7945-1172-2(4))*, Usborne) EDC Publishing.

—Nursery Rhymes Touchy-Feely Board Book. Meyer, Kerry, illus. 2010. (Luxury Touchy-Feely Board Bks). 10p. (J). bds. 15.99 *(978-0-7945-2662-7(4))*, Usborne) EDC Publishing.

—Penguins Luxury Touchy-Feely Board Book. 2010. (Luxury Touchy-Feely Board Bks). 10p. (J). bds. 15.99 *(978-0-7945-2586-6(5))*, Usborne) EDC Publishing.

—Polar Bears. Chiara, Francesca De, illus. 2010. (Luxury Touchy-Feely Board Bks). 10p. (J). bds. 15.99 *(978-0-7945-2544-6(X))*, Usborne) EDC Publishing.

—Pull-Back Busy Train. Field, Jim, illus. 2013. (Pull-Back Bks). 10p. (J). ring bd. 24.99 *(978-0-7945-3333-5(7))*, Usborne) EDC Publishing.

—Quack, Quack, Quack. 2008. (Bath Bks). 8p. (J). 14.99 *(978-0-7945-2304-6(8))*, Usborne) EDC Publishing.

—Sleepy Baby. MacKinnon, Catherine-Anne, illus. 2006. (Snuggletime Board Bks.). 10p. (J). (gr. -1). bds. 8.99 *(978-0-7945-1071-8(X))*, Usborne) EDC Publishing.

—Sticker Dolly Dressing Back to School. 2012. (Sticker Dolly Dressing Ser.). 34p. (J). pap. 8.99 *(978-0-7945-3303-8(5))*, Usborne) EDC Publishing.

—Sticker Dolly Dressing Ballerinas & Dolls (Combined Volume) 2008. (Sticker Dolly Dressing Ser.). (Illus.). 48p. (J). pap. 14.99 *(978-0-7945-2382-4(X))*, Usborne) EDC Publishing.

—Sticker Dolly Dressing Dancers. Baggott, Stella, illus. 2011. (Sticker Dolly Dressing Ser.). 24p. (J). pap. 8.99 *(978-0-7945-2931-4(3))*, Usborne) EDC Publishing.

—Sticker Dolly Dressing Dolls. Leyhane, Vici & Baggott, Stella, illus. 2006. (Usborne Activities Ser.). 23p. (J). pap. 8.99 *(978-0-7945-1389-4(1))*, Usborne) EDC Publishing.

—Sticker Dolly Dressing Princesses. Leyhane, Vici & Baggott, Stella, illus. 2007. (Sticker Dolly Dressing Ser.). 32p. (J). pap. 8.99 *(978-0-7945-1390-0(5))*, Usborne) EDC Publishing.

—Sticker Dolly Dressing Princesses & Fairies (Combined Volume) 2008. (Sticker Dolly Dressing Ser.). (Illus.). 48p. (J). pap. 14.99 *(978-0-7945-2418-0(4))*, Usborne) EDC Publishing.

—Sticker Dolly Dressing Shopping Girls. 2012. (Sticker Dolly Dressing Ser.). 24p. (J). pap. 8.99 *(978-0-7945-3254-3(3))*, Usborne) EDC Publishing.

—Sticker Dolly Dressing Sportsgirls. 2011. (Sticker Dolly Dressing Ser.). 24p. (J). pap. 8.99 *(978-0-7945-3003-7(6))*, Usborne) EDC Publishing.

—Sticker Dolly Dressing Travel. 2012. (Sticker Dolly Dressing Ser.). 34p. (J). pap. 8.99 *(978-0-7945-3313-7(2))*, Usborne) EDC Publishing.

—Sticker Dolly Dressing Weddings. Baggott, Stella, illus. 2011. (Usborne Activities Ser.). 24p. (J). 8.99 *(978-0-7945-3105-8(9))*, Usborne) EDC Publishing.

—That's Not My Angel. 2009. (Touchy-Feely Board Bks). 10p. (J). bds. 9.99 *(978-0-7945-2428-9(1))*, Usborne) EDC Publishing.

—That's Not My Baby (Boy) 2010. (Touchy Feely Board Book Ser.). 43p. (J). bds. 8.99 *(978-0-7945-2604-7(7))*, Usborne) EDC Publishing.

—That's Not My Baby (Girl) 2010. (Touchy Feely Board Book Ser.). 43p. (J). bds. 8.99 *(978-0-7945-2603-0(9))*, Usborne) EDC Publishing.

—That's Not My Cow. 2015. (Touchy-Feely Board Bks.). (ENG.). 10p. (J). 9.99 *(978-0-7945-3544-5(5))*, Usborne) EDC Publishing.

—That's Not My Dolly. rev. ed. 2012. (Touchy-Feely Board Bks). 10p. (J). bds. 8.99 *(978-0-7945-3308-3(6))*, Usborne) EDC Publishing.

—That's Not My Donkey. Wells, Rachel, illus. 2011. (Touchy-Feely Board Books Ser.). 10p. (J). ring bd. 8.99 *(978-0-7945-3012-9(5))*, Usborne) EDC Publishing.

—That's Not My Duck... Wells, Rachel, illus. 2014. (ENG.). (gr. -1). bds. 9.99 *(978-0-7945-3193-5(8))*, Usborne) EDC Publishing.

—That's Not My Elephant. Wells, Rachel, illus. 2012. (Touchy-Feely Board Bks). 10p. (J). ring bd. 8.99 *(978-0-7945-3167-6(9))*, Usborne) EDC Publishing.

—That's Not My Frog. Wells, Rachel, illus. 2009. (Touchy-Feely Board Bks). 10p. (J). bds. 8.99 *(978-0-7945-2505-7(9))*, Usborne) EDC Publishing.

—That's Not My Hamster. 2012. (Touchy-Feely Board Bks). 10p. (J). bds. 8.99 *(978-0-7945-3277-2(2))*, Usborne) EDC Publishing.

—That's Not My Meerkat. 2015. (Touchy-Feely Board Bks.). (ENG.). 10p. (J). 9.99 *(978-0-7945-3599-5(2))*, Usborne) EDC Publishing.

—That's Not My Mermaid. rev. ed. 2012. (Touchy-Feely Board Bks). 10p. (J). bds. 9.99 *(978-0-7945-3307-6(8))*, Usborne) EDC Publishing.

—That's Not My Monkey. 2008. (Touchy-Feely Board Bks). 10p. (J). bds. 7.99 *(978-0-7945-2178-3(9))*, Usborne) EDC Publishing.

—That's Not My Monster. Wells, Rachel, illus. 2004. 10p. (J). 7.99 *(978-0-7945-0818-0(9))*, Usborne) EDC Publishing.

—That's Not My Penguin. Wells, Rachel, illus. 2007. (Usborne Touchy-Feely Board Bks.). 8p. (gr. -1-k). bds. 7.99 *(978-0-7945-1810-3(9))*, Usborne) EDC Publishing.

—That's Not My Pig... Its Nose Is Too Fuzzy. Wells, Rachel, illus. 2014. (Usborne Touchy-Feely Board Bks.). (ENG.). 10p. (gr. -1). bds. 9.99 *(978-0-7945-2666-5(7))*, Usborne) EDC Publishing.

—That's Not My Pirate. Wells, Rachel, illus. 2007. (Touchy-Feely Board Bks). 10p. (J). (gr. -1-k). bds. 8.99 *(978-0-7945-1702-1(1))*, Usborne) EDC Publishing.

—That's Not My Plane. rev. ed. 2012. (Touchy-Feely Board Bks). 10p. (J). bds. 8.99 *(978-0-7945-3294-9(2))*, Usborne) EDC Publishing.

—That's Not My Polar Bear. 2009. (Touchy-Feely Board Bks). 10p. (J). bds. 8.99 *(978-0-7945-2551-4(2))*, Usborne) EDC Publishing.

—That's Not My Prince. Wells, Rachel, illus. 2013. (Usborne Touchy-Feely Board Bks.). (ENG.). 10p. (J). 9.99 *(978-0-7945-2838-6(4))*, Usborne) EDC Publishing.

—That's Not My Princess. Wells, Rachel, illus. 2006. (Usborne Touchy-Feely Board Bks.). 10p. (J). (gr. -1). bds. 9.99 *(978-0-7945-1325-2(5))*, Usborne) EDC Publishing.

—That's Not My Reindeer... Wells, Rachel, illus. 2014. (Usborne Touchy-Feely Bks.). (ENG.). 10p. (gr. -1). bds. 9.99 *(978-0-7945-3390-8(6))*, Usborne) EDC Publishing.

—That's Not My Reindeer: Its Body Is Too Furry. Wells, Rachel, illus. 2008. (Usborne Touchy-Feely Board Bks.). 10p. (J). (gr. -1-k). bds. 9.99 *(978-0-7945-1890-5(7))*, Usborne) EDC Publishing.

—That's Not My Santa. rev. ed. 2012. (Touchy-Feely Board Bks). 10p. (J). bds. 8.99 *(978-0-7945-3310-6(8))*, Usborne) EDC Publishing.

—That's Not My Teddy... Wells, Rachel, illus. 2008. (Usborne Touchy-Feely Board Bks.). 8p. (J). (gr. -1). bds. 7.99 *(978-0-7945-2026-7(X))*, Usborne) EDC Publishing.

—That's Not My Truck. 2009. (Touchy-Feely Board Bks). 10p. (J). bds. 8.99 *(978-0-7945-2188-2(6))*, Usborne) EDC Publishing.

—Tie-a-Bow Book. 2008. (Tie-a-Bow Book Ser.). 10p. (J). bds. 9.99 *(978-0-7945-1528-7(2))*, Usborne) EDC Publishing.

—Tractors. King, Sue, illus. 2009. (Luxury Touchy-Feely Board Bks). 10p. (J). bds. 15.99 *(978-0-7945-2432-6(X))*, Usborne) EDC Publishing.

—Under the Sea Baby Jigsaw Book. 2010. (Baby Jigsaw Bks.). (Illus.). 10p. (J). bds. 9.99 *(978-0-7945-1314-6(X))*, Usborne) EDC Publishing.

—Water Baby. 2011. (Snuggletime Board Books Ser.). 10p. (J). ring bd. 8.99 *(978-0-7945-2038-0(3))*, Usborne) EDC Publishing.

Watt, Fiona, des. Sticker Dolly Dressing Princess Kit. 2011. (Activity Kit Ser.). 24p. (J). pap. 15.99 *(978-1-60130-278-6(9))*, Usborne) EDC Publishing.

Watt, Fiona & Cartwright, Stephen. Tie-a-Bow Book. 2004. (Treasury of Farmyard Tales Ser.). (Illus.). 10p. (J). 7.95 *(978-0-7945-0330-7(6))*, Usborne) EDC Publishing.

Watt, Fiona & Wells, Rachel. Anifeiliaid y Fferm. 2005. (WEL., Illus.). 10p. *(978-1-84512-000-9(0))* Cymdeithas Lyfrau Ceredigion.

—That's Not My Tractor. 2004. (Touchy-Feely Board Bks.). (SPA & ENG., Illus.). 1p. (J). bds. 7.99 *(978-0-7945-0011-5(0))*, Usborne) EDC Publishing.

Watts, Frances. Goodnight, Mice! Watson, Judy, illus. 2017. 24p. bds. 6.99 *(978-0-7333-3530-3(6))* ABC Bks. AUS. Dist: HarperCollins Pubs.

Wax, Wendy. Look Who's Buzzing. 2009. 12p. 9.95 *(978-1-58117-911-8(1))*, Intervisual/Piggy Toes) Bendon, Inc.

Wax, Wendy A. Musica en Casa: Libro de Cuentos. de Alba, Arlette, tr. 2005. (Disney Princess Ser.). (SPA., Illus.). 38p. (J). (gr. -1-7). incl. audio compact disk *(978-970-718-289-9(X))*, Silver Dolphin en Español) Advanced Marketing, S. de R. L. de C. V.

Wax, Wendy A. & Wax, Naomi. Even Princesses Go to the Potty. Carabelli, Francesca, illus. 2014. (ENG.). 22p. (J). (gr. -1 — 1). 7.99 *(978-1-4424-8886-1(7))*, Little Simon) Little Simon.

We Go to Mass. 2004. (Illus.). (J). *(978-0-89942-716-4(2))* Catholic Bk. Publishing Corp.

Weakland, Mark. Football ABC, 1 vol. 2013. (SI Kids Rookie Bks.). (ENG.). 20p. (gr. 1-2). bds. 7.95 *(978-1-4296-9965-5(5))* Capstone Press of Coughlan Cos.

—Football Colors, 1 vol. 2013. (SI Kids Rookie Bks.). (ENG.). 20p. (gr. 1-2). bds. 7.95 *(978-1-4296-9966-2(3))* Capstone Press of Coughlan Cos.

—Football Opposites, 1 vol. 2013. (SI Kids Rookie Bks.). (ENG., Illus.). 20p. (gr. 1-2). bds. 7.95 *(978-1-4296-9967-9(1))* Capstone Press of Coughlan Cos.

Weeks, Sarah. Who's under That Hat? A Lift-the-Flap Pop-up Adventure. Carter, David A., illus. 2006. 14p. (J). (gr. -1-2). 14.00 *(978-1-4223-5440-7(7))* DIANE Publishing Co.

Wegman, William. 3... 2... 1... Circus! 2014. (ENG., Illus.). 24p. (J). (— 1). bds. 6.99 *(978-0-8037-3934-5(6))*, Dial Bks) Penguin Young Readers Group.

Wehr, Paul. The Animated Bunny's Tail. Wehr, Julian, illus. 2005. 20p. (J). 18.95 *(978-0-9748093-1-1(4))* Wehr Animations.

Wehrmeijer, Annelien. Anik & Yukon. van de Liejgraaf, Deborah, illus. 2015. (My Best Friend & Me Ser.). (ENG.). 10p. (J). (gr. -1-k). bds. 6.99 *(978-0-7641-6763-8(4))* Barron's Educational Series, Inc.

—Jacob & Rex. van de Liejgraaf, Deborah, illus. 2014. (My Best Friend & Me Ser.). (ENG.). 10p. (J). (gr. -1 — 1). bds. 7.99 *(978-0-7641-6663-1(8))* Barron's Educational Series, Inc.

—Kato & Simba. van de Liejgraaf, Deborah, illus. 2015. (My Best Friend & Me Ser.). (ENG.). 10p. (J). (gr. -1-k). bds. 6.99 *(978-0-7641-6762-1(6))* Barron's Educational Series, Inc.

—Mimi & Ling. van de Liejgraaf, Deborah, illus. 2015. (My Best Friend & Me Ser.). (ENG.). 10p. (J). (gr. -1-k). bds. 6.99 *(978-0-7641-6765-2(0))* Barron's Educational Series, Inc.

—Sophie & Daisy. van de Liejgraaf, Deborah, illus. 2014. (My Best Friend & Me Ser.). (ENG.). 10p. (J). (gr. -1 — 1). bds. 7.99 *(978-0-7641-6664-8(6))* Barron's Educational Series, Inc.

—Tariq & Mika. van de Liejgraaf, Deborah, illus. 2015. (My Best Friend & Me Ser.). (ENG.). 10p. (J). (gr. -1-k). bds. 6.99 *(978-0-7641-6764-5(2))* Barron's Educational Series, Inc.

Weimer, Heidi. I Love You More Than... . 2006. (Ideals Interactive Ser.). (ENG., Illus.). 16p. (J). (gr. -1-k). bds. 12.99 *(978-0-8249-6679-9(1))*, Ideal Pubns.) Worthy Publishing.

—You're My Little Love Bug! 2013. (ENG., Illus.). 12p. (gr. -1). bds. 12.99 *(978-1-891100-29-1(7))*, Smart Kids) Penton Overseas, Inc.

Weimer, Heidi R. Happy Birthday to You! 2007. (ENG., Illus.). 14p. (gr. -1-k). bds. 12.99 *(978-0-8249-6699-7(6))*, Ideal Pubns.) Worthy Publishing.

—How Do I Kiss You? Sharp, Chris, illus. 2008. (ENG.). 18p. (J). (gr. -1-k). bds. 12.99 *(978-0-8249-1814-9(2))*, Ideal Pubns.) Worthy Publishing.

Weinberger, Kimberly. Spring Is Here, Hello Kitty! (Hello Kitty) Hino, Sachiho, illus. 2016. (Hello Kitty Ser.). (ENG.). 32p. (J). (gr. k-2). pap. 3.99 *(978-1-338-11364-8(X))* Scholastic, Inc.

Weir, Patricia. My Kitty & Me. 2008. 20p. per. 24.95 *(978-1-60441-908-5(3))* America Star Bks.

Weiss, Ellen & Nelson, Marybeth. Dinosaur Rescue. Weiss, Ellen & Nelson, Marybeth, illus. 2009. (Illus.). (J). *(978-1-59292-359-5(3))* SoftPlay, Inc.

—Elmo's Beautiful Day. Weiss, Ellen & Nelson, Marybeth, illus. 2009. (Illus.). (J). *(978-1-59292-358-8(5))* SoftPlay, Inc.

Wejrmeijer, Annelien. Dan & Max. van de Liejgraaf, Deborah, illus. 2013. (My Best Friend & Me Ser.). (ENG.). 10p. (J). (gr. -1 — 1). bds. 6.99 *(978-0-7641-6634-1(4))* Barron's Educational Series, Inc.

—Emma & Bo. van de Liejgraaf, Deborah, illus. 2013. (My Best Friend & Me Ser.). (ENG.). 10p. (J). (gr. -1 — 1). bds. 6.99 *(978-0-7641-6635-8(2))* Barron's Educational Series, Inc.

—Lily & Dolly. van de Liejgraaf, Deborah, illus. 2013. (My Best Friend & Me Ser.). (ENG.). 10p. (J). (gr. -1 — 1). bds. 6.99 *(978-0-7641-6636-5(0))* Barron's Educational Series, Inc.

—Mason & Buddy. van de Liejgraaf, Deborah, illus. 2013. (My Best Friend & Me Ser.). (ENG.). 10p. (J). (gr. -1 — 1). bds. 6.99 *(978-0-7641-6637-2(9))* Barron's Educational Series, Inc.

Wellington, Monica. Apple Farmer Annie Board Book. Wellington, Monica, illus. 2012. (ENG., Illus.). 24p. (J). (gr. -1 — 1). bds. 5.99 *(978-0-8037-3888-1(9))*, Dial Bks) Penguin Young Readers Group.

—Firefighter Frank. 2011. (ENG.). 26p. (J). (gr. -1 — 1). bds. 5.99 *(978-0-525-42373-7(7))*, Dutton Books for Young Readers) Penguin Young Readers Group.

Wells, Rosemary. Bunny Mail. Wells, Rosemary, illus. 2004. (Max & Ruby Ser.). (ENG., Illus.). 32p. (J). (gr. -1-k). 15.99 *(978-0-670-03630-1(7))*, Viking Books for Young Readers) Penguin Young Readers Group.

—Max & Ruby's Preschool Pranks. 2016. (Max & Ruby Ser.). (ENG., Illus.). 40p. (J). (-k). 17.99 *(978-0-670-78462-2(1))*, Viking Books for Young Readers) Penguin Young Readers Group.

—Max & Ruby's Show-and-Tell. 2006. (Max & Ruby Ser.). (ENG., Illus.). 32p. (J). (gr. -1-k). mass mkt. 3.99 *(978-0-448-43952-5(2))*, Grosset & Dunlap) Penguin Young Readers Group.

—Time-Out for Sophie. Wells, Rosemary, illus. 2015. (ENG., Illus.). 26p. (J). (gr. -1). bds. 6.99 *(978-0-451-47766-8(9))*, Viking Books for Young Readers) Penguin Young Readers Group.

Wen, Dref. Fy Llyfr Geiriau Croes Cyntaf. 2005.Tr. of My First Opposites. (WEL., Illus.). 34p. *(978-1-85596-671-0(9))* Dref Wen.

—Traeth Prysur. 2005.Tr. of Busy Beach. (WEL., Illus.). 12p. *(978-1-85596-661-1(1))* Dref Wen.

We're Going on a Bear Hunt: Lap Edition. 2014. (ENG., Illus.). 36p. (J). (gr. -1-k). bds. 12.99 *(978-1-4814-1924-6(2))*, Little Simon) Little Simon.

Werner Watson, Jane. The Fuzzy Duckling. Provensen, Alice & Provensen, Martin, illus. 2012. (Golden Baby Ser.). (ENG.). 24p. (J). (gr. k — 1). bds. 6.99 *(978-0-307-92966-2(3))*, Golden Bks.) Random Hse. Children's Bks.

Weston Woods Staff, creator. Joseph Had a Little Overcoat. 2004. 29.95 *(978-1-55592-109-5(4))* Weston Woods Studios, Inc.

Wetterwald, Florence. Peekaboo, Pierre (a Blabla Book) Wetterwald, Florence, illus. 2016. (ENG., Illus.). 24p. (J). (— 1). bds. 7.99 *(978-0-553-51347-9(8))*, Random Hse. Bks. for Young Readers) Random Hse. Children's Bks.

Wharton, Ellie. Preschool Pirates. Enright, Amanda & Lee, Maxine, illus. 2013. (ENG.). 10p. (J). (gr. -1-k). 9.99 *(978-1-78244-875-4(6))* Top That! Publishing PLC GBR. Dist: Independent Pubs. Group.

What Does Baby Love? 2014. (ENG., Illus.). 14p. (J). (gr. -1 — 1). bds. 6.99 *(978-1-4814-0521-8(7))*, Little Simon) Little Simon.

What Will I Be?, 4 vols. (Girlfriend Gang Ser.). (Illus.). 16p. (J). *(978-2-7643-0022-0(0))* Phidal Publishing, Inc./Editions Phidal, Inc.

Whatley, Bruce & Beatrice, Chris, illus. Aesop's Fables: A Pop-Up Book of Classic Tales. 2011. (ENG.). 14p. (J). (gr. -1-3). 27.99 *(978-1-4169-7146-7(7))*, Little Simon) Little Simon.

What's the Time Fairy Princess? 2014. (Illus.). (J). *(978-1-4351-5497-1(5))* Barnes & Noble, Inc.

Whelon, Chuck. 3-D Mazes — Treasure Hunters. 2012. (Dover 3-D Mazes Ser.). (ENG.). 32p. (J). (gr. 1-6). 5.99 *(978-0-486-49018-2(1))* Dover Pubns., Inc.

Where Do I Live? (Peek A Boo Pockets Ser.). 12p. (J). bds. *(978-2-7643-0108-1(1))* Phidal Publishing, Inc./Editions Phidal, Inc.

Where Is Baby's Christmas Present? A Lift-The-Flap Book/Lap Edition. 2014. (ENG., Illus.). 14p. (J). (gr. -1 — 1). bds. 12.99 *(978-1-4424-0363-5(2))*, Little Simon) Little Simon.

Where's My Mommy? 2015. (J). *(978-1-4351-5982-2(9))* Barnes & Noble, Inc.

White, George. Halloween at the Zoo: A Pop-up Trick of Treat Experience. 2007. (Illus.). 16p. (J). 16.99 *(978-0-9795441-0-1(6))* Jumping Jack Pr.

—Kirby the Easter Dog: A Pop-up Easter Egg Hunt. 2008. (Illus.). 14p. (J). 14.99 *(978-0-9795441-2-5(2))* Jumping Jack Pr.

Whitehill, Simcha. Now You See It! Watch Pokémon Evolve — Right Before Your Eyes! 2012. (Illus.). 63p. (J). pap. *(978-0-545-45356-1(9))* Scholastic, Inc.

Whitlow, Steve, illus. Old MacDonald & Other Stories. 2011. (J). *(978-1-4508-2628-0(8))* Phoenix International Publications, Inc.

Who Lives in the Garden? 2004. (Who Lives... Ser.). 12p. (J). bds. 4.99 *(978-1-85854-643-8(5))* Brimax Books Ltd. GBR. Dist: Byeway Bks.

Who's Coming to Stay?, 1 vol. 2014. 12p. (J). bds. 5.99 *(978-0-8254-4206-3(0))* Kregel Pubns.

Whybrow, Ian. The Bedtime Bear. Scheffler, Axel, illus. 2016. (ENG.). 12p. (J). (gr. -1-2). pap. 9.99 *(978-1-5098-0695-9(4))* Pan Macmillan GBR. Dist: Independent Pubs. Group.

—The Christmas Bear. Scheffler, Axel, illus. 2016. (ENG.). 10p. (J). (gr. -1-2). bds. 8.99 *(978-1-5098-0696-6(2))* Pan Macmillan GBR. Dist: Independent Pubs. Group.

—The Tickle Book. Scheffler, Axel, illus. (ENG.). 12p. (J). (gr. -1-k). 2016. pap. 8.99 *(978-1-5098-0697-3(0))* 3rd ed. 2006. pap. 13.99 *(978-1-4050-5363-1(1))* Pan Macmillan GBR. Dist: Independent Pubs. Group.

Whybrow, Ian, et al. Owain A'r Cloc. 2005. (WEL., Illus.). 20p. 6.99 *(978-1-84323-366-4(5))* Gomer Pr. GBR. Dist: Gomer Pr.

Whyman, Jennifer E., text. Heavenly Blessings: Baby's Book of Bible Blessing/Baby's Book of Bible Promises. 2008.

(Land of Milk & Honey Ser.). (Illus.). 32p. (J). (gr. -1-k). bds. 9.99 *(978-1-4347-9945-6(X))* Cook, David C.

Wick, Walter. Christmas Board Book (Can You See What I See?) 2015. (Can You See What I See? Ser.). (ENG.). 24p. (J). (gr. -1-k). bds. 6.99 *(978-0-545-83183-3(0)*, Cartwheel Bks.) Scholastic, Inc.

—Trucks & Cars. Wick, Walter, photos by. 2007. (Can You See What I See? Ser.). (ENG., Illus.). 16p. (J). (gr. k — 1). bds. 5.99 *(978-0-439-86230-1(2)*, Cartwheel Bks.) Scholastic, Inc.

Wick, Walter, photos by. I Spy: Interactive Sound Book of Picture Riddles. 2003. (Illus.). 30p. (J). 15.98 *(978-0-7853-8424-3(3))* Publications International, Ltd.

Widdowson, Kay, illus. Please, Mr. Crocodile. 2006. (Lift-the-Flap Books (Child's Play) Ser.). (ENG.). 24p. (J). (gr. -1-1). *(978-1-84643-025-1(9))* Child's Play International Ltd.

Wight, Karol. Paperweight Pals. 2012. (Illus.). 22p. (J). *(978-0-87290-191-9(2))* Corning Museum of Glass.

Wild Animals Sticker Activity Book. (My Sticker Activity Ser.). (Illus.). 12p. (J). *(978-1-4054-1183-7(X))* Parragon, Inc.

Wildlife Education, compiled by. Frogs. 2007. (ENG., Illus.). 12p. (J). 5.99 *(978-1-932396-37-9(3)*, Critters Up Close) Wildlife Education, Ltd.

—Turtles. 2007. (Illus.). 12p. (J). 5.99 *(978-1-932396-40-9(3)*, Critters Up Close) Wildlife Education, Ltd.

Willems, Mo. Who Says That, Cat the Cat? Willems, Mo, illus. 2014. (ENG., Illus.). 22p. (J). (gr. -1 — 1). bds. 6.99 *(978-0-06-230654-8(5))* HarperCollins Pubs.

—Who Sleeps, Cat the Cat? Willems, Mo, illus. 2014. (ENG., Illus.). 22p. (J). (gr. -1 — 1). bds. 6.99 *(978-0-06-230655-5(3))* HarperCollins Pubs.

Williams, Becky. Good Night Little Piggy. Howarth, Daniel, illus. 2007. (Night Light Book Ser.). 10p. (gr. -1-k). bds. *(978-1-84666-129-7(3)*, Tide Mill Pr.) Top That! Publishing PLC.

—Ten Little Mermaids. East, Jacqueline, illus. 2007. (Story Book Ser.). 22p. (J). (gr. -1). bds. *(978-1-84666-375-8(X)*, Tide Mill Pr.) Top That! Publishing PLC.

Williams, Garth. Baby's First Book. Williams, Garth, illus. 2011. (Golden Baby Ser.). (ENG., Illus.). 24p. (J). (— 1). bds. 6.99 *(978-0-375-85905-2(5)*, Golden Bks.) Random Hse. Children's Bks.

Williamson, Karen. Bible Sliders, 1 vol. Selbert, Kathryn, illus. 2015. (ENG.). 10p. (J). bds. 9.99 *(978-1-78128-224-3(2)*, Candle Bks.) Lion Hudson PLC GBR. Dist: Kregel Pubns.

—The Christmas Story, 1 vol. Barnard, Lucy, illus. 2016. (Bible Mini-Pops Ser.). (ENG.). 10p. (J). 9.99 *(978-1-78128-284-7(6)*, Candle Bks.) Lion Hudson PLC GBR. Dist: Kregel Pubns.

—Easter, 1 vol. Embleton-Hall, Chris, illus. 2015. (Candle Tabs Ser.). (ENG.). 12p. (J). bds. 7.99 *(978-1-78128-157-4(2)*, Candle Bks.) Lion Hudson PLC GBR. Dist: Kregel Pubns.

—Lift the Flap Bible, 1 vol. Anglicas, Louise, illus. 2014. (ENG.). 16p. (J). bds. 12.99 *(978-1-78128-130-7(0)*, Candle Bks.) Lion Hudson PLC GBR. Dist: Kregel Pubns.

—Lost Sheep & Other Stories, 1 vol. Barnard, Lucy, illus. 2015. (Bible Mini-Pops Ser.). (ENG.). 10p. (J). bds. 9.99 *(978-1-78128-150-5(5)*, Candle Bks.) Lion Hudson PLC GBR. Dist: Kregel Pubns.

—More Bible Sliders, 1 vol. Selbert, Kathryn, illus. 2016. (Candle Tiny Tots Ser.). (ENG.). 10p. (J). bds. 9.99 *(978-1-78128-273-1(0)*, Candle Bks.) Lion Hudson PLC GBR. Dist: Kregel Pubns.

—Noah, 1 vol. Embleton-Hall, Chris, illus. 2015. (Candle Tabs Ser.). (ENG.). 12p. (J). bds. 7.99 *(978-1-78128-156-7(4)*, Candle Bks.) Lion Hudson PLC GBR. Dist: Kregel Pubns.

—Noah & Other Stories, 1 vol. Barnard, Lucy, illus. 2015. (Bible Mini-Pops Ser.). (ENG.). 10p. (J). 9.99 *(978-1-78128-149-9(1)*, Candle Bks.) Lion Hudson PLC GBR. Dist: Kregel Pubns.

—Play-Time Noah, 1 vol. Anglicas, Louise, illus. 2014. (ENG.). 8p. (J). bds. 9.99 *(978-1-78128-111-6(4)*, Candle Bks.) Lion Hudson PLC GBR. Dist: Kregel Pubns.

Williamson, Sarah, illus. Where Are You? 2017. (ENG.). 32p. (J). (— 1). 16.99 *(978-1-5247-0063-8(0)*, Knopf Bks. for Young Readers) Random Hse. Children's Bks.

Willis, Jeanne. We're Going to a Party! Ross, Tony, illus. (ENG.). 16p. (J). 2015. (-k). pap. 14.99 *(978-1-84939-456-7(3))* 2013. (gr. -1-k). 12.99 *(978-1-84939-122-1(X))* Andersen Pr. GBR. Dist: Independent Pubs. Group.

—Who's in the Loo? Reynolds, Adrian, illus. 10th ed. 2016. (ENG.). 16p. (J). (— 1). bds. 9.99 *(978-1-78344-420-5(7))* Andersen Pr. GBR. Dist: Independent Pubs. Group.

Wilson, Anne, illus. My First Box of Books: 1 2 3 Colours Animals, 3 vols. 2016. (ENG.). 72p. (J). (gr. -1-2). bds. 9.99 *(978-1-86147-416-2(4)*, Armadillo) Anness Publishing GBR. Dist: National Bk. Network.

Wilson, Hannah. Flip the Flaps: Jungle Animals. Palin, Nicki, illus. 2012. (Flip the Flaps Ser.). (ENG.). 32p. (J). (gr. -1-1). pap. 6.99 *(978-0-7534-6859-3(X)*, 9780753468593, Kingfisher) Roaring Brook Pr.

Wilson, Hannah & Parrish, Emma. Flutterby Butterfly: A Hide-and-Seek Book. 2015. (Slide-And-Seek Ser.). (ENG., Illus.). 10p. (J). (gr. -1-k). bds. 8.99 *(978-1-4998-0029-6(0))* Little Bee Books Inc.

—Hoppity Frog: A Hide-and-Seek Book. 2015. (Slide-And-Seek Ser.). (ENG., Illus.). 10p. (J). (gr. -1-k). 8.99 *(978-1-4998-0030-2(4))* Little Bee Books Inc.

Wilson, Karma. Baby, I Love You. Williams, Sam, illus. 2009. (ENG.). 30p. (J). (gr. -1 — 1). bds., bds. 7.99 *(978-1-4169-1910-0(4)*, Little Simon) Little Simon.

—Beautiful Babies. Wilson, Karma, photos by. 2009. (ENG., Illus.). 14p. (J). (gr. -1 — 1). bds. 6.99 *(978-1-4169-1908-7(2)*, Little Simon) Little Simon.

—Trick or Treat, Calico! Erdogan, Buket, illus. 2014. (J). *(978-1-4351-5610-4(2)*, Little Simon) Little Simon.

Wilson, Kris E. & Maurer, Toby. How Putter Learned His ABC's: An alphabet Book for Your Littlest Golfer. 2010. 17.00 *(978-0-578-05153-6(2))* Sandy Putter Pr.

Wilson-Max, Ken. Big Red Fire Engine. 2013. (ENG., Illus.). 12p. (J). (— 1). 11.99 *(978-1-84365-168-0(8)*, Pavilion) Pavilion Bks. GBR. Dist: Independent Pubs. Group.

Windmill Books & Windmill Books. Let's Look at Trains. 2009. (Let's Go! Ser.). (Illus.). 18p. (J). (gr. -1-k). bds. 12.75 *(978-1-60754-419-7(9))* Windmill Bks.

Winkler, Jude. Noah & the Flood. 2004. (Illus.). (J). *(978-0-89942-718-8(9))* Catholic Bk. Publishing Corp.

Winnie the Pooh. The Close-up Day. 2010. 16p. 5.99 *(978-1-4231-3096-3(0))* Disney Pr.

—Goodbye, Honeypot! 2010. 12p. 6.99 *(978-1-4231-3098-7(7))* Disney Pr.

Winters, Kay. Whooo's That? Winston, Jeannie, illus. 2009. (ENG.). 14p. (J). (gr. -1 — 1). 9.99 *(978-0-15-206480-8(X))* Houghton Mifflin Harcourt Publishing Co.

Witch Sticker Book. 2003. (Illus.). 16p. (J). 2.98 *(978-1-84273-117-8(3)*, Exclusive Editions) Parragon, Inc.

Witek, Jo. All My Treasures: A Book of Joy. Roussey, Christine, illus. 2016. (Growing Hearts Ser.). (ENG.). 32p. (J). (gr. -1 — 1). bds. 16.95 *(978-1-4197-2204-2(2)*, Abrams Appleseed) Abrams, Inc.

Witkowski, Teri. Bitty Bear & the Bugs. Ackley, Peggy Jo, illus. 2008. (J). *(978-1-59369-383-1(4)*, American Girl) American Girl Publishing, Inc.

—Bitty Bear, Flower Girl. Ackley, Peggy Jo, illus. 2009. (J). *(978-1-59369-564-4(0)*, American Girl) American Girl Publishing, Inc.

—Bitty Bear's Birthday Treats. Ackley, Peggy Jo, illus. 2008. (J). *(978-1-59369-384-8(2)*, American Girl) American Girl Publishing, Inc.

—Bitty Bear's New Friend. Ackley, Peggy Jo, illus. 2005. (J). *(978-1-59369-021-2(5))* American Girl Publishing, Inc.

—Bitty Bear's Snowflake Dreams. Ackley, Peggy Jo, illus. 2006. (J). *(978-1-59369-166-0(1))* American Girl Publishing, Inc.

—Bitty Bear's Valentines. Ackley, Peggy Jo, illus. 2004. (J). *(978-1-58485-837-9(0))* American Girl Publishing, Inc.

—Bitty Bear's Walk in the Woods. Ackley, Peggy Jo, illus. 2006. (J). *(978-1-59369-156-1(4))* American Girl Publishing, Inc.

—The Bitty Bunch Bath Book. Ackley, Peggy Jo, illus. 2006. (J). *(978-1-59369-080-9(0))* American Girl Publishing, Inc.

—Bitty Bunny's Bedtime. Ackley, Peggy Jo, illus. 2004. (J). *(978-1-58485-921-5(0))* American Girl Publishing, Inc.

—Bitty Bunny's Slipper Search. Ackley, Peggy Jo, illus. 2009. (J). *(978-1-59369-586-6(1)*, American Girl) American Girl Publishing, Inc.

—Bunny & Piggy at the Beach. Ackley, Peggy Jo, illus. 2005. (J). *(978-1-58485-961-1(X))* American Girl Publishing, Inc.

—Happy Birthday, Bitty Bear! Ackley, Peggy Jo, illus. 2005. (J). *(978-1-58485-959-8(8))* American Girl Publishing, Inc.

—It's Spring, Bitty Bear! Ackley, Peggy Jo, illus. 2007. (J). *(978-1-59369-242-1(0))* American Girl Publishing, Inc.

—Time for Bed, Bitty Bunch. Ackley, Peggy Jo, illus. 2008. (J). *(978-1-59369-380-0(X))* American Girl Publishing, Inc.

—Wait Your Turn, Bitty Froggy! Ackley, Peggy Jo, illus. 2008. (J). *(978-1-59369-285-8(4))* American Girl Publishing, Inc.

Wizard Sticker Book. (Creepy Sticker Ser.). (Illus.). 16p. (J). *(978-1-84273-118-5(1)*, Exclusive Editions) Parragon, Inc.

Wolf, Jackie, et al. My Sparkle Egg Book. 2005. (Illus.). (J). *(978-1-57151-750-0(2))* Playhouse Publishing.

Wolf, Sallie. Truck Stuck. Davies, Andy Robert, illus. 2017. (ENG.). 28p. (J). (— 1). bds. 7.99 *(978-1-58089-781-5(9))* Charlesbridge Publishing, Inc.

Wolfe, Jane. Cheeky Frog. Benham, Tors, illus. 2016. (ENG.). 8p. (J). (gr. -1-12). bds. 6.99 *(978-1-84322-718-2(5)*, Armadillo) Anness Publishing GBR. Dist: National Bk. Network.

—Crazy Cow. Benham, Tors, illus. 2013. (ENG.). 8p. (J). (gr. -1-k). bds. 6.99 *(978-1-84322-775-5(4)*, Armadillo) Anness Publishing GBR. Dist: National Bk. Network.

—Dizzy Duck. Benham, Tors, illus. 2016. (ENG.). 8p. (J). (gr. -1-12). bds. 6.99 *(978-1-84322-719-9(3)*, Armadillo) Anness Publishing GBR. Dist: National Bk. Network.

—Happy Cat. Benham, Tors, illus. 2016. (ENG.). 8p. bds. 6.99 *(978-1-84322-720-5(7)*, Armadillo) Anness Publishing GBR. Dist: National Bk. Network.

—Hungry Horse. Benham, Tors, illus. 2016. (ENG.). 8p. bds. 6.99 *(978-1-84322-721-2(5)*, Armadillo) Anness Publishing GBR. Dist: National Bk. Network.

—Messy Pig. Benham, Tors, illus. 2013. (ENG.). 8p. (J). (gr. -1-k). bds. 6.99 *(978-1-84322-777-9(0)*, Armadillo) Anness Publishing GBR. Dist: National Bk. Network.

—Noisy Dog. Benham, Tors, illus. 2013. (ENG.). 8p. (J). (gr. -1-k). bds. 6.99 *(978-1-84322-779-3(7)*, Armadillo) Anness Publishing GBR. Dist: National Bk. Network.

—Pull the Lever: Who Are You? The Toy Box, illus. 2014. (ENG.). 8p. (J). (gr. -1-2). bds. 6.99 *(978-1-86147-391-2(5)*, Armadillo) Anness Publishing GBR. Dist: National Bk. Network.

—Pull the Lever: Who Does What? Benham, Tors, illus. 2014. (ENG.). 8p. (J). (gr. -1-2). bds. 6.99 *(978-1-86147-392-9(3)*, Armadillo) Anness Publishing GBR. Dist: National Bk. Network.

—Pull the Lever: Who's in Here? Benham, Tors, illus. 2014. (ENG.). 8p. (J). (gr. -1-2). bds. 6.99 *(978-1-86147-394-3(X)*, Armadillo) Anness Publishing GBR. Dist: National Bk. Network.

—Sleepy Sheep. Benham, Tors, illus. 2013. (ENG.). 8p. (J). (gr. -1-k). bds. 6.99 *(978-1-84322-778-6(9)*, Armadillo) Anness Publishing GBR. Dist: National Bk. Network.

Wood, A. J. Slide & Play: Busy Bunny. Pledger, Maurice, illus. 2016. (Slide & Play Ser.). (ENG.). 16p. (J). (gr. -1). bds. 14.99 *(978-1-62686-573-0(6)*, Silver Dolphin Bks.) Readerlink Distribution Services, LLC.

—Slide & Play: Curious Kitten. Pledger, Maurice, illus. 2016. (Slide & Play Ser.). (ENG.). 16p. (J). (gr. -1). bds. 14.99 *(978-1-62686-574-7(4)*, Silver Dolphin Bks.) Readerlink Distribution Services, LLC.

—Slide & Play: Playful Puppy. Pledger, Maurice, illus. 2016. (Slide & Play Ser.). (ENG.). 16p. (J). (gr. -1). bds. 14.99 *(978-1-62686-572-3(8)*, Silver Dolphin Bks.) Readerlink Distribution Services, LLC.

Wood, Amanda. Amazing Baby Touch & Play! 2005. (Illus.). 12p. (J). 15.95 *(978-1-59223-529-2(8)*, Silver Dolphin Bks.) Readerlink Distribution Services, LLC.

Wood, Audrey. The Napping House. Wood, Don, illus. 2010. (ENG.). 34p. (J). (gr. k — 1). bds. 8.99 *(978-0-547-48147-0(0))* Houghton Mifflin Harcourt Publishing Co.

—The Napping House Board Book. Wood, Don, illus. 2015. (ENG.). 32p. (J). (— 1). bds. 7.99 *(978-0-544-60225-0(0)*, HMH Books For Young Readers) Houghton Mifflin Harcourt Publishing Co.

Wood, Hannah, illus. Dino Pop-up Faces: A Let's Pretend Pop-up Book. 2007. (ENG.). 12p. (J). (gr. -1-3). 14.95 *(978-1-58117-596-7(5)*, Intervisual/Piggy Toes) Bendon, Inc.

Woodworth, Viki & Whelon, Chuck. 3-D Mazes — Maze Mania. 2012. (Dover 3-D Mazes Ser.). (ENG.). 32p. (J). (gr. 1-6). 5.99 *(978-0-486-49016-8(5))* Dover Pubns., Inc.

Woolf, Julia, illus. Gingerbread Joy. 2008. (ENG.). 10p. (J). bds. 4.95 *(978-1-58117-814-2(X)*, Intervisual/Piggy Toes) Bendon, Inc.

—Reindeer Run. 2008. (ENG.). 10p. (J). bds. 4.95 *(978-1-58117-813-5(1)*, Intervisual/Piggy Toes) Bendon, Inc.

—Snowman Surprise. 2008. (ENG.). 10p. (J). bds. 4.95 *(978-1-58117-812-8(3)*, Intervisual/Piggy Toes) Bendon, Inc.

—Special Star. 2008. (ENG.). 10p. (J). bds. 4.95 *(978-1-58117-815-9(8)*, Intervisual/Piggy Toes) Bendon, Inc.

Worms, Penny. Dinosaurs. 2016. (ENG., Illus.). 24p. (J). (gr. 1). pap. 11.95 *(978-1-78312-109-0(2))* Carlton Kids GBR. Dist: Sterling Publishing Co., Inc.

Worthington, Leonie & Bedford, David. Bums. 2004. (ENG., Illus.). 16p. (J). (gr. -1-k). 10.95 *(978-1-877003-71-4(9))* Little Hare Bks. AUS. Dist: Independent Pubs. Group.

Wren, Jenny, illus. In the Jungle. 2017. (First Explorers Ser.). (ENG.). 10p. (J). (— 1). bds. 8.95 ***(978-1-4549-2656-6(2))*** Sterling Publishing Co., Inc.

—Night Animals. 2017. (First Explorers Ser.). (ENG.). 10p. (J). (— 1). bds. 8.95 ***(978-1-4549-2657-3(0))*** Sterling Publishing Co., Inc.

Wright, Dee. The Peanut Butter Finger Mystery. 2013. (Little Ruth Ser.). (ENG., Illus.). 38p. (J). pap. *(978-1-59684-606-7(2))* Penman Publishers.

Yang, Belle. A Nest in Springtime: A Bilingual Book of Numbers. Yang, Belle, illus. 2012. (CHI & ENG., Illus.). 24p. (J). (gr. k — 1). bds. 6.99 *(978-0-7636-5279-1(2))* Candlewick Pr.

Yarlett, Emma, illus. Nibbles: The Book Monster. 2016. (J). *(978-1-61067-467-6(7))* Kane Miller.

Yarrow, Peter & Lipton, Lenny. Puff, the Magic Dragon Pop-Up. Puybaret, Eric, illus. 2011. (ENG.). 14p. (J). (gr. 1). 26.95 *(978-1-4027-8711-9(1))* Sterling Publishing Co., Inc.

Yates, Gene. The Chameleon Colors Book. 2004. (Illus.). (J). *(978-1-58865-182-2(7))* Kidsbooks, LLC.

Yates, Gene, illus. The Chameleon Colors Book. 2006. (J). *(978-1-58865-361-1(7))* Kidsbooks, LLC.

—The Giraffe Numbers Book. 2006. (J). *(978-1-58865-364-2(1))* Kidsbooks, LLC.

Yates, Gene & Frank, Thomas. What Can Simon Be? Yates, Gene, illus. 2006. (Illus.). (J). *(978-1-58865-366-6(8))* Kidsbooks, LLC.

Yeretskaya, Yevgeniya, illus. The Snow Queen: A Pop-Up Adaption of a Classic Fairytale. 2013. (ENG.). 7p. 29.95 *(978-1-60580-955-7(1)*, 9781605809557) Jumping Jack Pr.

Ying, Jonathan. Lost & Found, What's That Sound? Ying, Victoria, illus. 2017. 32p. (J). (gr. -1-3). 14.99 *(978-0-06-238068-5(0))* HarperCollins Pubs.

Yonezu, Yusuke, illus. We Love Each Other. 2013. (Yonezu Board Book Ser.). (ENG.). 28p. (J). (— 1). bds. 9.95 *(978-988-8240-56-2(0))* Neugebauer, Michael (Publishing) Limited HKG. Dist: Independent Pubs. Group.

Yoon, Salina. At the Beach. 2011. (ENG., Illus.). 12p. (J). (gr. -1 — 1). bds. 6.99 *(978-0-312-66303-2(X)*, 9780312663032) Feiwel & Friends.

—At the Park. 2011. (ENG., Illus.). 12p. (J). (gr. -1 — 1). bds. 5.99 *(978-0-312-66298-1(X)*, 9780312662981) Feiwel & Friends.

—Bug Hunt. 2017. (Lift-The-Flap Adventures Ser.). (ENG., Illus.). 14p. (J). (gr. -1-2). bds. 8.95 *(978-1-4549-2108-0(0))* Sterling Publishing Co., Inc.

—Deep Sea Dive. 2012. (Lift-The-Flap Adventures Ser.). (ENG., Illus.). 12p. (J). (gr. -1-2). bds. 8.95 *(978-1-4027-8525-2(9))* Sterling Publishing Co., Inc.

—Dinosaur Discovery. 2017. (Lift-The-Flap Adventures Ser.). (ENG., Illus.). 14p. (J). (gr. -1-2). bds. 8.95 *(978-1-4549-2087-8(4))* Sterling Publishing Co., Inc.

—Five Trick-or-Treaters. 2010. 10p. bds. 5.95 *(978-1-60747-745-7(9)*, Pickwick Pr.) Phoenix Bks., Inc.

—Kaleidoscope. 2012. (ENG.). 18p. (J). (gr. -1-17). bds. 12.99 *(978-0-316-18641-4(4))* Little, Brown Bks. for Young Readers.

—My Chanukah Playbook. Yoon, Salina, illus. 2009. (ENG., Illus.). 10p. (J). (gr. -1-k). 10.99 *(978-1-4169-8957-8(9)*, Little Simon) Little Simon.

—Opposnakes: A Lift-the-Flap Book about Opposites. Yoon, Salina, illus. 2009. (ENG., Illus.). 16p. (J). (gr. -1-1). 12.99 *(978-1-4169-7875-6(5)*, Little Simon) Little Simon.

—Penguin Gets Dressed! Yoon, Salina, illus. 2010. (Illus.). 10p. bds. 7.95 *(978-1-60747-750-1(5)*, Pickwick Pr.) Phoenix Bks., Inc.

—Penguin Gets Ready for Bed! Yoon, Salina, illus. 2010. (Illus.). 10p. bds. 7.95 *(978-1-60747-751-8(3)*, Pickwick Pr.) Phoenix Bks., Inc.

—Penguin Goes to the Farm! Yoon, Salina, illus. 2010. (Illus.). 10p. bds. 7.95 *(978-1-60747-752-5(1)*, Pickwick Pr.) Phoenix Bks., Inc.

—Penguin's Christmas Wish. 2017. (Penguin Ser.). (ENG.). 32p. (J). bds. 7.99 ***(978-1-68119-573-5(9)***, 9781681195735, Bloomsbury USA Childrens) Bloomsbury Publishing USA.

—Where's Boo? 2013. (ENG., Illus.). 18p. (J). (— 1). bds. 6.99 *(978-0-307-97808-0(7)*, Random Hse. Bks. for Young Readers) Random Hse. Children's Bks.

—Where's Ellie? 2012. (ENG., Illus.). 18p. (J). (gr. k — 1). bds. 6.99 *(978-0-307-97806-6(0)*, Random Hse. Bks. for Young Readers) Random Hse. Children's Bks.

—Wings: A Book to Touch & Feel. Yoon, Salina, illus. 2010. (ENG., Illus.). 14p. (J). (gr. -1 — 1). bds. 8.99 *(978-1-4169-8958-5(7)*, Little Simon) Little Simon.

Yoon, Salina, creator. Sea Creatures: A Sparkling Little Colors Book, 4 vols. 2005. (ENG., Illus.). 12p. (J). bds. 5.95 *(978-1-58117-169-3(2)*, Intervisual/Piggy Toes) Bendon, Inc.

Yoon, Salina, illus. Peek-a-Boo Farm Animals. 2005. (Peek-a-Boo Guess Who Book Ser.: Vol. 2). 10p. (J). 7.95 *(978-1-58117-158-7(7)*, Intervisual/Piggy Toes) Bendon, Inc.

—Peek-a-Boo Wild Animals. 2005. (Peek-a-Boo Guess Who Book Ser.: Vol. 1). 10p. (J). (gr. -1-k). 7.95 *(978-1-58117-157-0(9)*, Intervisual/Piggy Toes) Bendon, Inc.

Yost-Filgate, Susan. A Good Day for Abbey. Filgate, Leonard, illus. 2009. (ENG.). 12p. (J). (gr. -1-12). 6.99 *(978-1-934960-45-5(4)*, Raven Tree Pr.,Csi) Continental Sales, Inc.

Young, Cybèle. Out the Window, 1 vol. 2014. (ENG., Illus.). 30p. (J). (-k). bds. 12.95 *(978-1-55498-370-4(3))* Groundwood Bks. CAN. Dist: Publishers Group West (PGW).

Young, Ed. Seven Blind Mice. Young, Ed, illus. 2012. (ENG., Illus.). 36p. (J). (gr. -1 — 1). bds. 8.99 *(978-0-399-25742-1(X)*, Philomel Bks.) Penguin Young Readers Group.

Young, Jay. Magic World of Learning. Tucker, Sian, illus. 2003. 32p. *(978-1-903174-42-5(2)*, Pavilion Children's Books) Pavilion Bks.

Young, Judy & Wargin, Kathy-jo. Little Missouri. Urban, Helle, illus. 2012. (My Little State Ser.). (ENG.). 20p. (J). bds. 9.95 *(978-1-58536-206-6(9))* Sleeping Bear Pr.

Young, Laurie. I See a Monster! Mahoney, Daniel J., illus. 2007. (Touch & Feel Ser.). 12p. (gr. -1-k). 15.95 *(978-1-58117-574-5(4)*, Intervisual/Piggy Toes) Bendon, Inc.

Young, Rebecca & Accord Publishing Staff. Hop, Pop, & Play: A Mini Animotion Book. 2011. (ENG.). 12p. (J). 9.99 *(978-1-4494-0177-1(5))* Andrews McMeel Publishing.

Young, Sarah. Jesus Calling for Little Ones, 1 vol. Woodward, Antonia, illus. 2015. (ENG.). 26p. (J). bds. 7.99 *(978-0-7180-3384-2(1))* Nelson, Thomas Inc.

Yoyo Books, creator. Vroom. 2011. (Baby's First Library). (ENG., Illus.). 38p. (gr. -1-k). bds. *(978-90-8622-910-9(7))* YoYo Bks.

Yoyo Books Staff. Bedtime: Learning Words Series. 2004. 12p. bds. *(978-90-5843-607-8(1))* YoYo Bks.

—On the Farm: Learning Words Series. 2005. 12p. bds. *(978-90-5843-605-4(5))* YoYo Bks.

Yuly, Toni. Cat Nap. 2017. (ENG., Illus.). 32p. (J). bds. 7.99 *(978-1-250-11261-3(3)*, 9781250112613) Feiwel & Friends.

—Early Bird. Yuly, Toni, illus. 2015. (ENG., Illus.). 16p. (J). (— 1). bds. 7.99 *(978-1-250-05706-8(X)*, 9781250057068) Feiwel & Friends.

—Night Owl. Yuly, Toni, illus. 2015. (ENG., Illus.). 40p. (J). (— 1). 15.99 *(978-1-250-05457-9(5)*, 9781250054579) Feiwel & Friends.

Zabini, Eleni & Livanios, Eleni. Best Grandma in the World! Lütje, Susanne, illus. 2015. (ENG.). 16p. (J). bds. 7.95 *(978-0-7358-4225-0(6))* North-South Bks., Inc.

—Best Grandpa in the World! Lütje, Susanne, illus. 2015. (ENG.). 16p. (J). bds. 7.95 *(978-0-7358-4237-3(X))* North-South Bks., Inc.

Zadrozny, Alicia & Church, Caroline Jayne. The Wild Little Jungle: A Mix-and-Match Flap Book. 2008. (ENG.). 10p. (J). bds. 12.99 *(978-0-7944-1605-8(5))* Reader's Digest Assn., Inc., The.

Zakarin, Debra Mostow. First Fairytales. Fiore, Rob, illus. 2010. 10p. 9.95 *(978-1-60747-746-4(7)*, Pickwick Pr.) Phoenix Bks., Inc.

Zakiyyah & Zakiyyah. Chatterworld My Numbers in Spanish/My Numbers in French: MIS Numeros en Espanol/Mes Mombres en Francais. 2006. (Illus.). 40p. (J). (gr. -1-3). 14.99 *(978-0-9777085-0-5(0))* Little Linguists Press.

Zapp, et al. Baby Bear's Read-Along Goldilocks & the Three Bears. (Illus.). *(978-2-7641-0516-0(9))* Tormont Pubns.

Zebra's Stripes. Date not set. (Touch & Feel Ser.). (Illus.). (J). 4.98 *(978-0-7525-9571-9(7))* Parragon, Inc.

Zerkin, Becca, et al. The Walking Dead: the Pop-Up Book. Jackson, Sally Elizabeth, illus. 2015. (ENG.). 5p. 65.00 *(978-1-60887-444-6(3))* Insight Editions.

Ziefert, Harriet. The Best Smelling Christmas Book Ever: 9 Scents to Scratch & Sniff! Rader, Laura, illus. 2004. 18p. (J). (gr. k-4). reprint ed. 13.00 *(978-0-7567-7600-8(7))* DIANE Publishing Co.

—Monkey's Noisy Jungle. Newton, Jill, illus. 2007. bds. 7.95 *(978-1-59354-598-7(3))* Blue Apple Bks.

—Two Little Witches: A Halloween Counting Story. Taback, Simms, illus. 2007. (ENG.). 32p. (J). (gr. k-k). pap. 3.99 *(978-0-7636-3309-7(7))* Candlewick Pr.

Ziegler-Sullivan, Ursula. The Pups Save the Bunnies. 2016. (Illus.). (J). *(978-1-5182-1575-9(0))* Random Hse., Inc.

Zimmerman, Andrea & Clemesha, David. Train Man. Zimmerman, Andrea & Clemesha, David, illus. 2017. (ENG., Illus.). 32p. (J). bds. 8.99 *(978-1-62779-504-3(9)*, 9781627795043, Holt, Henry & Co. Bks. For Young Readers) Holt, Henry & Co.

Zinsmeister, Elke, illus. Ten Fat Sausages. 2005. (Classic Books with Holes Board Book Ser.). (ENG.). 14p. (J). (gr. -1-1). bds. *(978-1-904550-59-4(2))* Child's Play International Ltd.

Zobel-Nolan, Allia. Animal Parade. Maddocks, Maria, illus. 2008. 10p. (J). (gr. -1). 12.95 *(978-1-932915-63-1(X))* Sandvik Innovations, LLC.

—Hugs for Baby! Mitchell, Susan, illus. 2008. (Lift-the-Flap Hear-the-Sound Ser.). 10p. (J). (gr. -1). 12.95 *(978-1-932915-64-8(8))* Sandvik Innovations, LLC.

—Lift-the-Flap Nativity. Moroney, Trace, illus. 2015. (Lift-The Flap Ser.). (ENG.). 20p. (J). (gr. -1-k). 10.99 *(978-0-7944-3527-1(0)*, Reader's Digest Children's Bks.) Studio Fun International.

—What I Like about Me! Sakamoto, Miki, illus. 2009. (What I Like about Me Ser.). (ENG.). 14p. (J). (gr. -1-2). 6.99 *(978-0-7944-1945-5(3)*, Reader's Digest Children's Bks.) Studio Fun International.

Zolan, Donald, illus. My Favorite Farm Animal Friends. 2010. (ENG.). 5p. (J). bds. 5.99 *(978-0-7369-2663-8(1))* Harvest Hse. Pubs.

Zondervan. The Beginner's Bible Activity Book, 1 vol. 2017. (Beginner's Bible Ser.). (ENG.). 64p. (J). pap. 4.99 *(978-0-310-75979-9(X))* Zonderkidz.

—Ready, Set, Find Christmas, 1 vol. 2016. (Ready, Set, Find Ser.). (ENG.). 12p. (J). bds. 8.99 *(978-0-310-75766-5(5))* Zonderkidz.

—Ready, Set, Find Easter, 1 vol. 2017. (Ready, Set, Find Ser.). (ENG.). 12p. (J). bds. 8.99 *(978-0-310-75769-6(X))* Zonderkidz.

Zondervan Staff. All Aboard the Ark, 1 vol. 2016. (ENG., Illus.). 24p. (J). bds. 6.99 *(978-0-310-75377-3(5))* Zonderkidz.

Zondervan Staff & Walburg, Lori. The Legend of the Candy Cane, 1 vol. Cowdrey, Richard, illus. 2014. (ENG.). 30p. (J). bds. 9.99 *(978-0-310-74672-0(8))* Zonderkidz.

Zoo-Zológico Bilingual Board Book. 2008. (ENG & SPA., Illus.). (J). pap. 5.99 (978-0-9727886-8-7(9)) Osmosis, LLC.

Zschock, Martha Day. Hello, New Orleans! 2011. (Hello! Ser.). (ENG., Illus.). 16p. (J). (gr. -1-k). bds. 9.95 (978-1-933212-63-0(2), Commonwealth Editions) Applewood Bks.

—Hello, Philadelphia! 2011. (Hello! Ser.). (ENG., Illus.). 16p. (J). (gr. -1-k). bds. 9.95 (978-1-933212-64-7(0), Commonwealth Editions) Applewood Bks.

—Hello, San Francisco! 2012. (Hello! Ser.). (ENG., Illus.). 16p. (J). (gr. -1-k). bds. 9.95 (978-1-933212-65-4(9), Commonwealth Editions) Applewood Bks.

—Hello Williamsburg! 2013. (ENG., Illus.). 16p. (J). (gr. -1-k). bds. 9.95 (978-1-933212-03-6(9), Commonwealth Editions) Applewood Bks.

Zschock, Martha Day & Zschock, Martha. Hello, Cape Cod! 2009. (Hello! Ser.). (ENG., Illus.). 16p. (gr. -1-k). bds. 9.95 (978-0-9819430-1-5(2), Commonwealth Editions) Applewood Bks.

Zuckerman, Andrew, photos by. Creature Colors. 2014. (ENG., Illus.). 20p. (J). (gr. -1 — 1). bds. 7.99 (978-1-4521-1668-6(7)) Chronicle Bks. LLC.

Zuravicky, Orli. C Is for City: An Alphabet Book. Castellano, Giuseppe, illus. 2011. (Mister Doodle Ser.). (ENG.). 40p. (J). (gr. -1-k). bds. 7.99 (978-1-4424-2049-6(9), Little Simon) Little Simon.

123. 2004. (Illus.). (J). (978-1-59060-333-8(8)) Waldman Publishing Corp.

TOY MAKING

Aaseng, Nathan. Business Builders in Toys. 2003. (Business Builders Ser.). (Illus.). 160p. (gr. 5-18). lib. bdg. 22.95 (978-1-881508-81-6(1)) Oliver Pr., Inc.

Balmer, Alden J. Mousetrap Racers: The Complete Builder's Manual - Science Secrets You'll Need to Win. 2008. (ENG., Illus.). 144p. (gr. 7-18). pap. 14.95 (978-1-56523-359-1(X), 3591D) Fox Chapel Publishing Co., Inc.

Brodman, Larisa. Pom-Pom Pets. Magruder, Trula, ed. 2006. (ENG., Illus.). 48p. (gr. -1-3). 17.95 (978-1-59369-151-6(3), American Girl) American Girl Publishing, Inc.

Cunningham, Kevin. Toys. 2008. (21st Century Skills Library: Global Products Ser.). (ENG., Illus.). 32p. (gr. 4-8). 28.50 (978-1-60279-252-4(6), 200119) Cherry Lake Publishing.

Doney, Meryl. Toys. 2004. (Crafts from Many Cultures Ser.). (Illus.). 32p. (gr. 2-5). lib. bdg. 26.00 (978-0-8368-4048-3(8), Gareth Stevens Learning Library) Stevens, Gareth Publishing LLLP.

Elton, Richard & Elton, Candice. Every Kid Needs a Rubber Band Launcher. 2007. (J). (978-1-4236-0268-2(4)) Gibbs Smith, Publisher.

Felix, Rebecca. Cool Action Figures & Dolls: Crafting Creative Toys & Amazing Games, 1 vol. 2016. (Cool Toys & Games Ser.). (ENG., Illus.). 32p. (J). (gr. 3-6). 28.50 (978-1-68078-045-1(X)) ABDO Publishing Co.

Fryer, Jane Eayre. The Mary Frances Sewing Book 100th Anniversary Edition: A Childrens Story-Instruction Sewing Book with Doll Clothes Patterns for American Girl & Other 18-Inch Dolls. 2011. (ENG., Illus.). 284p. (J). pap. 19.95 (978-1-937564-01-8(0), Classic Bookwrights) Lindaloo Enterprises.

Giacobello, John. Choosing a Career in the Toy Industry. (World of Work Ser.). 64p. 2009. (gr. 5-5). 58.50 (978-1-60854-341-0(2)) 2005. (Illus.). (YA). (gr. 7-12). lib. bdg. 31.95 (978-0-8239-3438-6(1)) Rosen Publishing Group, Inc., The.

Harbo, Christopher L. Easy Origami Toys, 1 vol. 2010. (Easy Origami Ser.). (ENG.). 24p. (gr. 1-2). lib. bdg. 25.32 (978-1-4296-5386-2(8), First Facts) Capstone Press of Coughlan Cos.

Heller, D. M. Let's Make a Bike with Everyday Materials. (Let's Do Arts & Crafts Ser.). 24p. 2009. (gr. 2-2). 42.50 (978-1-61514-196-8(0), PowerKids Pr.) 2006. (Illus.). (J). lib. bdg. 22.60 (978-1-4042-3064-4(5)) Rosen Publishing Group, Inc., The.

Hinkler Books Staff. Balloon Animals. 2004. (ENG., Illus.). 48p. (J). 6.95 (978-1-86515-644-6(2)) Hinkler Bks. Pty, Ltd. AUS. Dist: Penton Overseas, Inc.

Irvine, Joan. How to Make Super Pop-Ups. Hendry, Linda, illus. 2008. (Dover Origami Papercraft Ser.). (ENG.). 96p. (gr. 3-7). per. 8.95 (978-0-486-46589-0(6)) Dover Pubns., Inc.

Maderna, Victoria. Make Your Own Plush Pals. 2010. (ENG., Illus.). 96p. (gr. 6). pap. 9.95 (978-0-486-47674-2(X)) Dover Pubns., Inc.

Nichols, Kaitlyn. Felted Friends: Create Your Own Soft, Fuzzy Animals. 2014. (ENG.). 56p. (J). (gr. 5). 19.99 (978-0-545-64796-0(7)) Klutz.

Owen, Ruth. Ready, Aim, Fire!, 1 vol., 1. 2014. (DIY for Boys Ser.). (ENG.). 32p. (J). (gr. 3-6). 27.50 (978-1-4777-6286-8(8), PowerKids Pr.) Rosen Publishing Group, Inc., The.

Oxlade, Chris. Toys Through Time: How Toys Were Designed, Developed, & Made. 2004. (Illus.). 45p. (J). (gr. 4-8). reprint ed. (978-0-7567-7848-4(4)) DIANE Publishing Co.

Pohl, Kathleen. What Happens at a Toy Factory?/¿Qué Pasa en una Fábrica de Juguetes? 2006. (Where People Work/Dónde Trabaja la Gente? Ser.). (Illus.). 24p. (gr. -1-3). (SPA & ENG.). (J). lib. bdg. 22.00 (978-0-8368-7390-0(4)); (ENG & SPA., pap. 8.15 (978-0-8368-7397-9(1)) Stevens, Gareth Publishing LLLP. (Weekly Reader Leveled Readers).

Roytman, Arkady & Paper Dolls for Grownups Staff. Glow-in-the-Dark Ghouls Paper Action Figures. 2011. (Dover Paper Dolls Ser.). (ENG.). 32p. (J). (gr. 3-5). pap. 9.99 (978-0-486-48364-1(9)) Dover Pubns., Inc.

Scott-Waters, Marilyn, creator. The Toymaker: Paper Toys That You Can Make Yourself, 1. 2004. (Illus.). 20p. (YA). 12.95 (978-0-9759884-0-4(9)) Scott-Waters, Marilyn.

Storey, Rita. Make Your Own Toys. 2010. (Do It Yourself Projects! Ser.). (Illus.). 24p. (J). (gr. 4-6). lib. bdg. 25.25 (978-1-61532-592-4(1), PowerKids Pr.) Rosen Publishing Group, Inc., The.

Wilson, Donna. Creative Creatures: A Step-by-Step Guide to Making Your Own Creations. Wilson, Donna, illus. 2013. (ENG., Illus.). 48p. (J). (gr. 3-9). 15.99 (978-0-7534-6947-7(2), 9780753469477, Kingfisher) Roaring Brook Pr.

TOYS

see also Dollhouses; Dolls

Ackelsberg, Amy. Ultimate Collector's Guide. 2013. (Lalaloopsy Ser.). (ENG.). 128p. (J). (gr. -1-3). pap. 8.99 (978-0-545-47770-3(0)) Scholastic, Inc.

Adams, Linda. Make & Learn Bible Toys. 2004. (Illus.). 96p. (J). (gr. -1-k). pap. 11.95 (978-1-885358-39-4(3), RB36722) Rainbow Pubs. & Legacy Pr.

Aebersold, Carol V. & Bell, Chanda. The Elf on the Shelf: Spanish Boy Dark Elf. Steinwart, Coe, illus. 2012. 32p. (J). lib. bdg. 15.00 net. (978-0-9769907-5-8(X)) CCA & B, LLC.

Animales Bebes. 2005. (Collection Abre Tus Ojos, Collection Eye Openers Ser.).Tr. of Animal Babies. (SPA.). (J). (gr. k-2). 6.95 (978-950-11-0964-1(X)) Sigmar ARG. Dist: Iaconi, Mariuccia Bk. Imports.

Arlon, Penelope & Gordon-Harris, Tory. Planets: A LEGO Adventure in the Real World. 2016. (Illus.). 64p. (J). **(978-1-4844-8522-4(X))** Scholastic, Inc.

AZ Books Staff. Where's My Toy? Sisoj, Natalja, ed. 2012. (Peek-A-Boo Ser.). (ENG.). 10p. (J). (— 1). bds. 10.95 (978-1-61889-116-7(2)) AZ Bks. LLC.

Baby's First Toys. 2004. 10p. (J). bds. 4.99 (978-1-85854-922-4(1)) Brimax Books Ltd. GBR. Dist: Byeway Bks.

Baggott, Stella, illus. Baby's Very First Toys Book. 2009. (Baby Board Bks). 10p. (J). bds. 6.99 (978-0-7945-2466-1(4), Usborne) EDC Publishing.

Baier, Harry. Yo-Yo World Trick Book. 2014. (ENG., Illus.). 96p. (J). (gr. 3). pap. 5.99 (978-0-486-49488-3(8)) Dover Pubns., Inc.

Balaban, Mariah. The Ultimate Handbook. 2007. (Littlest Pet Shop Ser.). (Illus.). 64p. (J). pap. (978-0-545-07697-5(8)) Scholastic, Inc.

Beaton, Clare, illus. Toys: Los Juguetes. 2003. (Bilingual First Books/English-Spanish Ser.). (ENG & SPA.). 24p. (J). pap. 4.95 (978-0-7641-2611-6(3)) Barron's Educational Series, Inc.

Beecroft, Simon & Fry, Jason. The Visual Dictionary. rev. exp. ed. 2014. (ENG.). 144p. (J). (gr. 3-7). lib. bdg. 21.99 (978-1-4654-2136-4(X), DK Children) Dorling Kindersley Publishing, Inc.

Beswick, Clare. 30 Fun Ways to Learn about Blocks & Boxes. 2011. (30 Fun Ways to Learn Ser.). (ENG.). 80p. (gr. -1-k). pap. 12.95 (978-0-87659-369-1(4), Gryphon House Inc) Gryphon Hse., Inc.

Bidder, Jane. Inventions We Use for Play. 2006. (Everyday Inventions Ser.). (Illus.). 32p. (gr. 1-4). lib. bdg. 26.00 (978-0-8368-6900-2(1), Gareth Stevens Learning Library) Stevens, Gareth Publishing LLLP.

Bolitho, Mark. Fold Your Own Origami Air Force. 2013. 32p. (J). (gr. 3-6). 26.50 (978-1-4777-1319-8(0)); pap. 11.75 (978-1-4777-1469-0(3)) Rosen Publishing Group, Inc., The. (PowerKids Pr.).

—Fold Your Own Origami Army. 2013. 32p. (J). (gr. 3-6). 26.50 (978-1-4777-1317-4(4)); pap. 11.75 (978-1-4777-1465-2(0)) Rosen Publishing Group, Inc., The. (PowerKids Pr.).

—Fold Your Own Origami Navy. 2013. 32p. (J). (gr. 3-6). 26.50 (978-1-4777-1318-1(2)); pap. 11.75 (978-1-4777-1467-6(7)) Rosen Publishing Group, Inc., The. (PowerKids Pr.).

—Fold Your Own Origami Weapons. 2013. 32p. (J). (gr. 3-6). 26.50 (978-1-4777-1320-4(4)); pap. 11.75 (978-1-4777-1471-3(5)) Rosen Publishing Group, Inc., The. (PowerKids Pr.).

Boothroyd, Jennifer. From Marbles to Video Games: How Toys Have Changed. 2011. (Comparing Past & Present Ser.). pap. 7.95 (978-0-7613-7841-9(3)); pap. 45.32 (978-0-7613-8391-8(3)); (ENG., Illus.). 32p. lib. bdg. 26.60 (978-0-7613-6746-8(2)) Lerner Publishing Group.

Brack, Amanda. Big Book of Brick Trucks. 2015. (ENG., Illus.). 32p. (J). (-k). 14.99 (978-1-63220-598-8(X), Sky Pony Pr.) Skyhorse Publishing Co., Inc.

Burton, Margie, et al. My Models. 2011. (Early Connections Ser.). (J). (978-1-61672-301-9(7)) Benchmark Education Co.

Butterfield, Moira. Toys & Games Around the World. 2016. (Children Like Us Ser.). (ENG., Illus.). 32p. (J). (gr. 3-3). pap. 10.58 (978-1-5026-0850-5(2), 1399892) Cavendish Square Publishing.

La Casa. 2005. (Coleccion Primeras Imagenes). (SPA., Illus.). 86p. (J). (gr. -1-18). pap. 7.95 (978-950-11-0990-0(9), SGM9909) Sigmar ARG. Dist: Continental Bk. Co., Inc.

Castleforte, Brian. Papertoy Monsters: 50 Cool Papertoys You Can Make Yourself! 2010. (ENG., Illus.). 124p. (J). pap. 18.95 (978-0-7611-5882-0(0), 15882) Workman Publishing Co., Inc.

Christian, Cheryl. What's in My Toybox: A Book of Shapes, 1 vol. Ericsson, Annie Beth, illus. 2009. (ENG.). 32p. (J). (gr. -1). bds. 6.25 (978-1-59572-164-8(9)) Star Bright Bks., Inc.

Chronicle Books Staff & Museum of Modern Art (New York, N.Y.) Staff. String-Along Books. 2010. (ENG., Illus.). 10p. (J). (gr. -1-17). 18.99 (978-0-8118-7342-0(0)) Chronicle Bks. LLC.

Cohn, Jessica. 10 Fascinating Facts about Toys. 2016. (Rookie Star — Fact Finder Ser.). (ENG., Illus.). 32p. (J). lib. bdg. 25.00 (978-0-531-22818-0(5), Children's Pr.) Scholastic Library Publishing.

Cole, Jeff & Stone, Kate. Stick to It - Toys: A Magnetic Puzzle Book. 2011. (ENG., Illus.). 14p. (J). bds. 16.99 (978-1-4494-0499-4(5)) Andrews McMeel Publishing.

Cook, Deanna F. Teddy Bear Doctor: Fix the Boo-Boos & Heal the Ouchies of Your Favorite Stuffed Animals. 2015. (ENG., Illus.). 64p. (J). (gr. -1). pap. 10.95 (978-1-61212-402-5(X), 622402) Storey Publishing, LLC.

Cunningham, Kevin. Toys: From Concept to Consumer. 2013. (Calling All Innovators). (ENG.). 64p. (J). 30.00 (978-0-531-26522-2(6)); pap. 8.95 (978-0-531-22010-8(9)) Scholastic Library Publishing.

Dale, Jay. My Little Toys, 1 vol. 2012. (Engage Literacy Magenta Ser.). (ENG.). 32p. (gr. k-2). pap. 5.99 (978-1-4296-8876-5(9), Engage Literacy) Capstone Press of Coughlan Cos.

—My Toy Box, 1 vol. Kreinberg, Sylvia, photos by. 2012. (Engage Literacy Magenta Ser.). (ENG., Illus.). 32p. (gr. k-2). pap. 5.99 (978-1-4296-8860-4(2), Engage Literacy) Capstone Press of Coughlan Cos.

De Compreas. 2005. (Coleccion Primeras Imagenes). (SPA., Illus.). 86p. (J). (gr. -1-18). pap. 7.95 (978-950-11-0985-6(2), SGM9852) Sigmar ARG. Dist: Continental Bk. Co., Inc.

del Risco, Eida, tr. What's in My Toybox? (Spanish/English) Un libro de formas/A Book of Shapes, 1 vol. 2009. (ENG & SPA., Illus.). 32p. (J). bds. 6.25 (978-1-59572-179-2(7)) Star Bright Bks., Inc.

Dolan, Hannah. Ninjago the Visual Dictionary. 2014. (ENG., Illus.). 96p. (J). (gr. 4-7). 21.99 (978-1-4654-2299-6(4), DK Children) Dorling Kindersley Publishing, Inc.

Doney, Meryl. Toys. 2004. (Crafts from Many Cultures Ser.). (Illus.). 32p. (gr. 2-5). lib. bdg. 26.00 (978-0-8368-4048-3(8), Gareth Stevens Learning Library) Stevens, Gareth Publishing LLLP.

Dorling Kindersley Publishing Staff. The Adventure Guide. 2015. (ENG., Illus.). 96p. (J). (gr. k-4). lib. bdg. 16.99 (978-1-4654-3623-8(5), DK Children) Dorling Kindersley Publishing, Inc.

—The Amazing Book of LEGO Star Wars. 2017. (ENG.). 48p. (J). (gr. 1-4). 14.99 (978-1-4654-5541-3(8), DK Children) Dorling Kindersley Publishing, Inc.

—Build Your Own Adventure. 2015. (ENG.). 80p. (J). (gr. k-4). 24.99 (978-1-4654-3589-7(1), DK Children) Dorling Kindersley Publishing, Inc.

—I Love That Minifigure. 2015. (ENG.). 208p. (J). (gr. k-4). lib. bdg. 18.99 (978-1-4654-3970-3(6), DK Children) Dorling Kindersley Publishing, Inc.

—I Want That Minifigure! 2015. (ENG.). 208p. (J). (gr. k-4). 18.99 (978-1-4654-3683-2(9), DK Children) Dorling Kindersley Publishing, Inc.

—LEGO Absolutely Everything You Need to Know. 2017. (ENG.). 240p. (J). (gr. 2-5). 19.99 **(978-1-4654-6411-8(5)**, DK Children) Dorling Kindersley Publishing, Inc.

—Lego Nexo Knights Character Encyclopedia. 2017. (ENG.). 176p. (J). (gr. 1-4). lib. bdg. 19.99 **(978-1-4654-6554-2(5)**, DK Children) Dorling Kindersley Publishing, Inc.

—LEGO Ninjago: Character Encyclopedia. 2012. (ENG., Illus.). 176p. (978-1-4093-7597-5(8)) Penguin Bks., Ltd.

—LEGO NINJAGO Character Encyclopedia, Updated Edition. 2016. (ENG., Illus.). 224p. (J). (gr. 1-4). lib. bdg. 18.99 (978-1-4654-5093-7(9), DK Children) Dorling Kindersley Publishing, Inc.

—The LEGO NINJAGO MOVIE. 2017. (ENG.). 64p. (J). (gr. 2-5). 12.99 **(978-1-4654-6117-9(5)**, DK Children) Dorling Kindersley Publishing, Inc.

—LEGO Star Wars Character Encyclopedia: Updated & Expanded: Updated & Expanded. 2015. (ENG., Illus.). 288p. (J). (gr. 3-7). 18.99 (978-1-4654-3550-7(6), DK Children) Dorling Kindersley Publishing, Inc.

—Lego Star Wars in 100 Scenes. 2015. (ENG.). 216p. (J). (gr. 3-7). 18.99 (978-1-4654-3437-1(2), DK Children) Dorling Kindersley Publishing, Inc.

—LEGOÂ(r) City Factivity Fun READERLINK. 2015. (ENG.). 96p. (J). (gr. 1-4). pap. 16.99 (978-1-4654-4184-3(0)) Dorling Kindersley Publishing, Inc.

—Noisy Peekaboo! Vroom! Vroom! 2009. (ENG.). 12p. (J). (gr. -1 — 1). bds. 12.99 (978-0-7566-4298-3(1), DK Children) Dorling Kindersley Publishing, Inc.

—Noisy Peekabook - Toot! Toot! 2013. (ENG., Illus.). 12p. (J). (gr. -1 — 1). bds. 12.99 (978-1-4654-1068-9(6), DK Children) Dorling Kindersley Publishing, Inc.

—Toys. 2014. (Touch & Feel Ser.). (ENG.). 12p. (J). (gr. -1-k). bds. 6.99 (978-1-4654-2037-4(1), DK Children) Dorling Kindersley Publishing, Inc.

—Ultimate Factivity Collection: LEGO City: LEGO City. 2014. (ENG.). 96p. (J). (gr. 2-4). pap. 12.99 (978-1-4654-1667-4(6), DK Children) Dorling Kindersley Publishing, Inc.

—Ultimate Factivity Collection: LEGO Star Wars. 2016. (ENG.). 96p. (J). (gr. 1-4). pap. 12.99 (978-1-4654-4980-1(9), DK Children) Dorling Kindersley Publishing, Inc.

—Ultimate Factivity Collection: My Little Pony. 2016. (ENG.). 96p. (J). (gr. 1-4). pap. 12.99 (978-1-4654-4459-2(9), DK Children) Dorling Kindersley Publishing, Inc.

—Ultimate Sticker Collection: LEGO Star Wars: Mighty Minifigures: LEGO Star Wars: Mighty Minifigures. 2015. (Ultimate Sticker Collections). (ENG.). 96p. (J). (gr. 1-4). pap. 12.99 (978-1-4654-3551-4(4), DK Children) Dorling Kindersley Publishing, Inc.

Dorling Kindersley Publishing Staff & Hugo, Simon. LEGO NEXO KNIGHTS Build Your Own Adventure. 2017. (ENG.). 80p. (J). (gr. 1-4). 24.99 **(978-1-4654-6087-5(X)**, DK Children) Dorling Kindersley Publishing, Inc.

Dorling Kindersley Publishing Staff & Lipkowitz, Daniel. Character Encyclopedia. 2013. (ENG.). 208p. (J). (gr. k-4). 18.99 (978-1-4654-0172-4(5), DK Children) Dorling Kindersley Publishing, Inc.

—LEGO DC Comics Super Heroes Build Your Own Adventure. 2017. (ENG.). 80p. (J). (gr. 1-4). 24.99 **(978-1-4654-6089-9(6)**, DK Children) Dorling Kindersley Publishing, Inc.

—LEGO Ideas Book. 2011. (ENG.). 200p. (J). (gr. 2-5). 24.99 (978-0-7566-8606-2(7), DK Children) Dorling Kindersley Publishing, Inc.

—LEGO Star Wars: Build Your Own Adventure. 2016. (ENG.). 80p. (J). (gr. 3-4). 24.99 (978-1-4654-5045-6(9), DK Children) Dorling Kindersley Publishing, Inc.

—Yoda Chronicles. 2013. (ENG.). 64p. (J). (gr. 1-4). 18.99 (978-1-4654-0868-6(1), DK Children) Dorling Kindersley Publishing, Inc.

Dorling Kindersley Publishing Staff & March, Julia. LEGO NEXO KNIGHTS: the Book of Knights. 2016. (ENG.). 80p. (J). (gr. 1-4). 19.99 (978-1-4654-5400-3(4), DK Children) Dorling Kindersley Publishing, Inc.

Dorling Kindersley Publishing Staff & Taylor, Victoria. Super-Villains Level 2. 2013. (DK Readers Ser.). (ENG., Illus.). 32p. (J). (gr. 1-3). pap. 3.99 (978-1-4654-0176-2(8), DK Children) Dorling Kindersley Publishing, Inc.

Dorling Kindersley Publishing Staff, et al. LEGO Star Wars: Chronicles of the Force. 2016. (ENG., Illus.). 96p. (J). (gr. 1-4). 16.99 (978-1-4654-4967-2(1)); lib. bdg. 16.99 (978-1-4654-5165-1(X)) Dorling Kindersley Publishing, Inc. (DK Children).

—The Visual Dictionary. rev. exp. ed. 2014. (ENG.). 144p. (J). (gr. 3-7). 21.99 (978-1-4654-1921-7(7), DK Children) Dorling Kindersley Publishing, Inc.

Eck, Kristin. Hide-and-Seek Toys. 2004. (Hide-And-Seek Books). (Illus.). (J). lib. bdg. 21.25 (978-1-4042-2704-0(0), PowerKids Pr.) Rosen Publishing Group, Inc., The.

—Hide & Seek Toys. 2009. (Tough Toddler Bks). 16p. (gr. k-k). 42.50 (978-1-60854-573-5(3), PowerKids Pr.) Rosen Publishing Group, Inc., The.

Elsmore, Warren. Brick History: A Brick History of the World in LEGO(r). 2016. (ENG., Illus.). 256p. pap. 18.99 (978-1-4380-0754-0(X)) Barron's Educational Series, Inc.

Farshtey, Greg. Lego Ninjago Official Guide. 2011. (Illus.). 128p. (J). pap. (978-0-545-38285-4(8)) Scholastic, Inc.

Farshtey, Greg & Lipkowitz, Daniel. LEGO(r) Minifigure Year by Year: A Visual History. 2013. (ENG., Illus.). 256p. (J). 40.00 (978-1-4654-1411-3(8), DK Children) Dorling Kindersley Publishing, Inc.

Felix, Rebecca. Cool Construction & Building Blocks: Crafting Creative Toys & Amazing Games, 1 vol. 2016. (Cool Toys & Games Ser.). (ENG., Illus.). 32p. (J). (gr. 3-6). lib. bdg. 28.50 (978-1-68078-047-5(6), Checkerboard Library) ABDO Publishing Co.

—Cool Doughs, Putties, Slimes, & Goops: Crafting Creative Toys & Amazing Games, 1 vol. 2016. (Cool Toys & Games Ser.). (ENG., Illus.). 32p. (J). (gr. 3-6). lib. bdg. 28.50 (978-1-68078-049-9(2), Checkerboard Library) ABDO Publishing Co.

Fold Your Own Origami Air Force. 2013. (Origami Army Ser.). 32p. (J). (gr. 3-6). pap. 70.50 (978-1-4777-1470-6(7), PowerKids Pr.) Rosen Publishing Group, Inc., The.

Fold Your Own Origami Army. 2013. (Origami Army Ser.). 32p. (J). (gr. 3-6). pap. 70.50 (978-1-4777-1466-9(9), PowerKids Pr.) Rosen Publishing Group, Inc., The.

Fold Your Own Origami Navy. 2013. (Origami Army Ser.). 32p. (J). (gr. 3-6). pap. 70.50 (978-1-4777-1468-3(5), PowerKids Pr.) Rosen Publishing Group, Inc., The.

Fold Your Own Origami Weapons. 2013. (Origami Army Ser.). 32p. (J). (gr. 3-6). pap. 70.50 (978-1-4777-1472-0(3), PowerKids Pr.) Rosen Publishing Group, Inc., The.

Fontichiaro, Kristin & Thomas, AnnMarie P. Squishy Circuits. 2014. (21st Century Skills Innovation Library: Makers As Innovators Ser.). (ENG., Illus.). 32p. (J). (gr. 4-8). 28.50 (978-1-63137-775-4(2), 205343) Cherry Lake Publishing.

Forgione, Len. Pocket Book of Powers. 2017. (LEGO NEXO Knights Ser.). (ENG.). 192p. (J). (gr. 2-5). pap. 7.99 (978-1-338-11810-0(2)) Scholastic, Inc.

Foy, Debbie. Toys, Play, Tidy Away! 2016. (All by Myself Ser.). (ENG., Illus.). 20p. (J). (gr. -1-k). pap. 6.99 (978-0-7502-9616-8(X), Wayland) Hachette Children's Group GBR. Dist: Hachette Bk. Group.

Fuller, Jill. Toy Box Subtraction. 2004. (Rookie Read-About Math Ser.). (J). 20.50 (978-0-516-24423-5(X), Children's Pr.) Scholastic Library Publishing.

Gardner, Robert. Ace Your Science Project Using Chemistry Magic & Toys: Great Science Fair Ideas. 2009. (Ace Your Science Project Ser.). (Illus.). 128p. (J). (gr. 5-9). lib. bdg. 33.27 (978-0-7660-3226-2(4)) Enslow Pubs., Inc.

—The Physics of Toys & Games Science Projects. 2013. (Exploring Hands-On Science Projects Ser.). 128p. (J). (gr. 5-12). pap. 10.95 (978-1-4644-0219-7(1)); lib. bdg. 27.94 (978-0-7660-4143-1(3)) Enslow Pubs., Inc.

Glenn, Lexi & Nia. My Invention: How Lexi Glenn, a fourth grader, came up with an idea & got it in toy stores all over the world. A story of how you must first believe in Yourself. 2011. 32p. 12.99 (978-1-4389-3949-0(3)) AuthorHouse.

Greathouse, Lisa. Cómo Funcionan los Juguetes, 1 vol. rev. ed. 2010. (Science Readers: a Closer Look Ser.). (SPA., Illus.). 32p. (J). (gr. 2-3). pap. 8.99 (978-1-4333-2148-1(3)) Shell Educational Publishing.

Green, Sara. Lego. (Lego Ser.). 24p. (J). (gr. 3-8). 2017. pap. 7.99 **(978-1-61891-249-7(6))** 2015. (ENG., Illus.). lib. bdg. 25.95 (978-1-62617-208-1(0)) Bellwether Media. (Pilot Bks.).

Green, Sara. Nerf. 2016. (Brands We Know Ser.). (ENG., Illus.). 24p. (J). (gr. 3-8). lib. bdg. 25.95 (978-1-62617-349-1(4), Pilot Bks.) Bellwether Media.

Group/McGraw-Hill, Wright. Toys, Then & Now: Level E, 6 vols. (Take Twostm Ser.). 16p. 29.95 (978-0-322-08950-1(6)) Wright Group/McGraw-Hill.

Grupos. 2005. (Coleccion Primeras Imagenes). (SPA., Illus.). 86p. (J). (gr. -1-18). pap. 7.95 (978-950-11-0986-3(0), SGM9860) Sigmar ARG. Dist: Continental Bk. Co., Inc., Lectorum Pubns., Inc.

Hagar, Erin. The Inventors of Lego(r) Toys. Hagar, Erin, illus. 2016. (Awesome Minds Ser.). (ENG., Illus.). 48p. (J). (gr. 1-7). 14.99 (978-1-938093-53-1(4)) Duo Pr. LLC.

Harper, Sandy. Educational Toys for Kids of All Ages. 2013. 56p. pap. 12.55 (978-1-63022-577-3(0)) Speedy Publishing LLC.

Harris, Patricia. Understanding Coding with Lego Wedo(tm), 01 vols., 1. 2016. (Kids Can Code Ser.). (ENG., Illus.). 24p. (J). pap. 11.75 (978-1-5081-4466-3(4), PowerKids Pr.) Rosen Publishing Group, Inc., The.

Henderson, Meryl, illus. Things to Play With. (Picture Bks.: No. S8817-5). 28p. (J). (gr. -1). pap. 3.95 (978-0-7214-5144-2(6), Dutton Juvenile) Penguin Publishing Group.

Herrold, Karen L. The Ice Cream Truck. 2012. (ENG.). pap. (978-1-4675-3466-6(8)) Independent Pub.

Hirschmann, Kris. LEGO Toys. 2008. (Great Idea Ser.). (Illus.). 48p. (J). (gr. 4-6). lib. bdg. 26.60 (978-1-59953-194-6(1)) Norwood Hse. Pr.

Hixon, Rena. Mindstorms: Level 1. 2016. (21st Century Skills Innovation Library: Unofficial Guides). (ENG., Illus.). 32p. (J). (gr. 4-8). 29.93 (978-1-63470-524-0(6), 207827) Cherry Lake Publishing.

—Mindstorms: Level 2. 2016. (21st Century Skills Innovation Library: Unofficial Guides). (ENG., Illus.). 32p. (J). (gr. 4-8). 29.93 (978-1-63470-525-7(4), 207831) Cherry Lake Publishing.

—Mindstorms: Level 3. 2016. (21st Century Skills Innovation Library: Unofficial Guides). (ENG., Illus.). 32p. (J). (gr. 4-8). 29.93 (978-1-63470-526-4(2), 207835) Cherry Lake Publishing.

—Mindstorms: Level 4. 2016. (21st Century Skills Innovation Library: Unofficial Guides). (ENG., Illus.). 32p. (J). (gr. 4-8). 29.93 (978-1-63470-527-1(0), 207839) Cherry Lake Publishing.

Holden, Pam. Toys That Can Go, 6 pack. 2009. (Red Rocket Readers Ser.). (ENG., Illus.). 16p. (gr. -1-1). pap. (978-1-877435-93-5(7)) Flying Start Bks.

La Hora. 2005. (Coleccion Primeras Imagenes). (SPA., Illus.). 86p. (J). (gr. -1-18). pap. 7.95 (978-950-11-0987-0(9), SGM9879) Sigmar ARG. Dist: Continental Bk. Co., Inc.

Hudson, Amanda. This Is My Bear. 2008. (Our Toys Ser.). (Illus.). 16p. (gr. -1-2). (J). lib. bdg. 19.00 *(978-0-8368-9253-6(4))*; pap. 5.30 *(978-0-8368-9352-6(2))* Stevens, Gareth Publishing LLLP. (Weekly Reader Leveled Readers).

Hugo, Simon. 365 Things to Do with LEGO Bricks. 2016. (ENG.). 256p. (J). (gr. 1-4). 24.99 *(978-1-4654-5302-0(4))*, DK Children) Dorling Kindersley Publishing, Inc.

Kalman, Bobbie. Toys & Games Then & Now. 2013. (ENG., Illus.). 24p. (J). *(978-0-7787-0128-6(X))*; pap. *(978-0-7787-0210-8(3))* Crabtree Publishing Co.

Kenney, Sean. Cool Cars & Trucks. Kenney, Sean, illus. Barrett, John E., photos by. 2009. (ENG., Illus.). 32p. (J). (gr. -1-3). 12.99 *(978-0-8050-8761-1(3))*, 9780805087611, Holt, Henry & Co. Bks. For Young Readers) Holt, Henry & Co.

—Cool Castles. 2012. (ENG., Illus.). 32p. (J). (gr. -1-3). 12.99 *(978-0-8050-9539-5(X))*, 9780805095395, Holt, Henry & Co. Bks. For Young Readers) Holt, Henry & Co.

—Cool City. Kenney, Sean, illus. 2011. (ENG., Illus.). 32p. (J). (gr. -1-3). 12.99 *(978-0-8050-8762-8(1))*, 9780805087628, Holt, Henry & Co. Bks. For Young Readers) Holt, Henry & Co.

—Cool Creations in 101 Pieces. Kenney, Sean, illus. 2014. (ENG., Illus.). 32p. (J). (gr. -1-4). 14.99 *(978-1-62779-017-8(9))*, 9781627790178, Holt, Henry & Co. Bks. For Young Readers) Holt, Henry & Co.

—Totally Cool Creations. Kenney, Sean, illus. 2013. (ENG., Illus.). 128p. (J). (gr. -1-3). pap. 19.99 *(978-1-250-03110-5(9))*, 9781250031105) Square Fish.

Kent, Lorna, illus. Baby's First Toys Book. 2004. 10p. (J). bds. 7.99 *(978-1-85854-882-1(9))* Brimax Books Ltd. GBR. Dist: Byeway Bks.

Lake Press Ltd. Time to Play. 2016. (Little Grabbers Ser.). (ENG., Illus.). 6p. (J). (gr. -1 — 1). bds. 5.99 *(978-0-7641-6836-9(3))* Barron's Educational Series, Inc.

Larranaga, Ana Martin. Noisy Home. Larranaga, Ana Martin, illus. 2011. (Rattle Buggy Buddies Ser.). (ENG., Illus.). 12p. (J). (gr. k — 1). bds. 7.99 *(978-0-230-70621-7(5))* Macmillan Pubs., Ltd. GBR. Dist: Independent Pubs. Group.

Lawrence, Ellen. Time to Play. 2015. (My World Your World Ser.). (ENG.). 24p. (J). (gr. -1-3). lib. bdg. 23.93 *(978-1-910549-06-3(1))* Bearport Publishing Co., Inc.

Lim, Annalees. Fun with Fabric. 2013. (Clever Crafts Ser.). (ENG., Illus.). 24p. (gr. k-3). 25.25 *(978-1-4777-0180-5(X))*; pap. 10.60 *(978-1-4777-0188-1(5))* Windmill Bks.

Lipkowitz, Daniel. Dark Side. 2014. (ENG.). 96p. (J). (gr. 1-4). 16.99 *(978-1-4654-1897-5(0))*, DK Children) Dorling Kindersley Publishing, Inc.

—The LEGO Book. rev. ed. 2012. (ENG.). 256p. (J). (gr. 3-7). 24.99 *(978-0-7566-6693-4(7))*, DK Children) Dorling Kindersley Publishing, Inc.

Lipkowitz, Daniel & Dorling Kindersley Publishing Staff. LEGO Ideas Book. 2011. (ENG., Illus.). 200p. *(978-1-4053-5067-9(9))* Dorling Kindersley.

Lipkowitz, Daniel & Farshtey, Greg. Lego Play Book. 2013. (ENG., Illus.). 200p. (J). (gr. 2-10). 24.99 *(978-1-4654-1412-0(6))*, DK Children) Dorling Kindersley Publishing, Inc.

Littlewood, Peter. Rain Forest Destruction. 2012. (Mapping Global Issues Ser.). 48p. (J). (gr. 7-9). lib. bdg. 34.25 *(978-1-59920-512-0(2))* Black Rabbit Bks.

Lyles, Brian & Lyles, Jason. The LEGO Neighborhood Book: Build Your Own Town! 2014. (ENG., Illus.). 204p. (J). (gr. 5). 19.95 *(978-1-59327-571-6(4))* No Starch Pr., Inc.

MacDonald, Margaret. Toys Long Ago. 2011. (Learn-Abouts: Level 10 Ser.). (Illus.). 16p. (J). pap. 7.95 *(978-1-59920-597-7(1))* Black Rabbit Bks.

Macdonald, Margaret. What Things Did Your Parents Play With? 2014. (Little Books of Answers: Level e Ser.). (Illus.). 16p. (gr. k-2). pap. 7.95 *(978-1-927136-41-6(5))* Three Crows Media NZL. Dist: RiverStream Publishing.

Macken, JoAnn Early. Toys. 2010. (Everyday Science Ser.). 24p. (J). (gr. k-3). 25.65 *(978-1-60753-017-6(1))* Amicus Publishing.

Malam, John. Grow Your Own Cat Toy, 1 vol. 2011. (Grow It Yourself! Ser.). (ENG.). 32p. (gr. k-2). 27.32 *(978-1-4329-5110-8(6))*, Heinemann First Library) Heinemann-Raintree.

—Journey of a Toy, 1 vol. 2012. (Journey of A... Ser.). (ENG.). 32p. (gr. 1-3). pap. 8.29 *(978-1-4329-6612-6(X))*, Heinemann First Library) Heinemann-Raintree.

Marks, Jennifer L. Clasificar Juguetes/Sorting Toys, 1 vol. 2012. (Vamos a Ordenar / Sorting Ser.). (ENG, SPA & MUL.). 32p. (gr. 1-2). lib. bdg. 27.32 *(978-1-4296-8254-1(X))*, A+ Bilingue/Bilingual) Capstone Press of Coughlan Cos.

Marunas, Nathaniel. NERF: Ultimate Blaster Book. 2013. (ENG., Illus.). 96p. (J). (gr. 3-7). 21.95 *(978-1-57687-641-1(1))*, powerHouse Bks.) powerHouse Cultural Entertainment, Inc.

McDonnell, Rory. Matemáticas con Juguetes / Math with Toys. de la Vega, Eida, tr. 2016. (¡Matemáticas en Todas Partes! / Math Is Everywhere! Ser.). (ENG & SPA.). 24p. (gr. k-k). lib. bdg. 22.60 *(978-1-4824-5214-3(6))* Stevens, Gareth Publishing LLLP.

Meachen Rau, Dana. Juegos y Diversiones en la Historia de América. 2006. (Como era la vida en America (How People Lived in America) Ser.). (SPA., Illus.). 24p. (gr. 1-4). lib. bdg. 22.00 *(978-0-8368-7429-7(3))*, Weekly Reader Leveled Readers) Stevens, Gareth Publishing LLLP.

—Juegos y diversiones en la historia de America (Toys, Games, & Fun in American History) 2006. (Como era la vida en America (How People Lived in America) Ser.). (SPA.). 24p. (gr. 1-4). pap. 8.15 *(978-0-8368-7436-5(6))*, Weekly Reader Leveled Readers) Stevens, Gareth Publishing LLLP.

—Toys, Games, & Fun in American History. 2006. (How People Lived in America Ser.). (Illus.). 24p. (gr. 1-4). pap. 8.15 *(978-0-8368-7216-3(9))*; lib. bdg. 22.00 *(978-0-8368-7209-5(6))* Stevens, Gareth Publishing LLLP. (Weekly Reader Leveled Readers).

Modern Publishing Staff, ed. First to the Finish Line. 2005. 12p. pap. 3.99 *(978-0-7666-1911-1(7))* Modern Publishing.

—Lean Mean Screamin Machines. 2005. 12p. pap. 3.99 *(978-0-7666-1910-4(9))* Modern Publishing.

Moore, Elizabeth. Toys from the Past. 2011. (Wonder Readers Emergent Level Ser.). (ENG.). 8p. (gr. -1-1). pap. 35.94 *(978-1-4296-8236-7(1))*, Wonder Readers) Capstone Press of Coughlan Cos.

—Toys in the Past, 1 vol. 2011. (Wonder Readers Emergent Level Ser.). (ENG.). 32p. (gr. -1-1). pap. 5.99 *(978-1-4296-7850-6(X))*, Wonder Readers) Capstone Press of Coughlan Cos.

Morey, Allan. Miniature Pinschers. 2016. (Tiny Dogs Ser.). (ENG., Illus.). 24p. (gr. k-1). lib. bdg. 26.65 *(978-1-5157-1968-7(5))*, Pebble Plus) Capstone Press of Coughlan Cos.

—Pomeranians. 2016. (Tiny Dogs Ser.). (ENG., Illus.). 24p. (gr. k-1). lib. bdg. 26.65 *(978-1-5157-1967-0(7))*, Pebble Plus) Capstone Press of Coughlan Cos.

—Yorkshire Terriers. 2016. (Tiny Dogs Ser.). (ENG., Illus.). 24p. (gr. k-1). lib. bdg. 26.65 *(978-1-5157-1966-3(9))*, Pebble Plus) Capstone Press of Coughlan Cos.

Murphy, Stuart J. Jack the Builder. Rex, Michael, illus. 2006. (MathStart 1 Ser.). (ENG.). 40p. (J). (gr. -1-3). pap. 5.99 *(978-0-06-055775-1(3))* HarperCollins Pubs.

Murphy, Stuart J. & Rex, Michael. Jack the Builder. 2006. (Mathstart Ser.). (Illus.). 33p. (gr. -1-3). 16.00 *(978-0-7569-6667-6(1))* Perfection Learning Corp.

My Little Firehouse. (Illus.). 12p. (J). (gr. -1-k). bds. *(978-1-56021-354-3(X))*, 205) W.J. Fantasy, Inc.

Opuestos. (Coleccion Libritos Acordeon). (SPA., Illus.). (J). 10p. pap. 5.50 *(978-950-11-0826-2(0))*, SGM260); 2005. 86p. (gr. -1-18). pap. 7.95 *(978-950-11-0906-1(2))*, SGM9062) Sigmar ARG. Dist: Continental Bk. Co., Inc.

Owen, Ruth. Chugs. 2014. (Designer Dogs Ser.). (Illus.). 32p. (J). (gr. k-5). lib. bdg. 26.25 *(978-1-4777-7047-4(X))*, PowerKids Pr.) Rosen Publishing Group, Inc., The.

—Malshis. 2014. (Designer Dogs Ser.). (Illus.). 32p. (J). (gr. k-5). lib. bdg. 26.25 *(978-1-4777-7027-6(5))*, PowerKids Pr.) Rosen Publishing Group, Inc., The.

—Peekapoos. 2014. (Designer Dogs Ser.). (Illus.). 32p. (J). (gr. k-5). lib. bdg. 26.25 *(978-1-4777-7031-3(3))*, PowerKids Pr.) Rosen Publishing Group, Inc., The.

—Ready, Aim, Fire!, 1 vol., 1. 2014. (DIY for Boys Ser.). (ENG.). 32p. (J). (gr. 3-6). 27.50 *(978-1-4777-6286-8(8))*, PowerKids Pr.) Rosen Publishing Group, Inc., The.

—Yochons. 2014. (Designer Dogs Ser.). (Illus.). 32p. (J). (gr. k-5). lib. bdg. 26.25 *(978-1-4777-7043-6(7))*, PowerKids Pr.) Rosen Publishing Group, Inc., The.

—Yorkipoos. 2014. (Designer Dogs Ser.). (Illus.). 32p. (J). (gr. k-5). lib. bdg. 26.25 *(978-1-4777-7035-1(6))*, PowerKids Pr.) Rosen Publishing Group, Inc., The.

Oxlade, Chris. Gadgets & Games, 1 vol. 2013. (Design & Engineering for STEM Ser.). (ENG., Illus.). 56p. (gr. 6-8). pap. 9.99 *(978-1-4329-7036-9(4))*, NA-h); lib. bdg. 34.65 *(978-1-4329-7031-4(3))* Heinemann-Raintree.

Pack, Linda Hager. Appalachian Toys & Games from a to Z. Banks, Pat, illus. 2013. (ENG.). 56p. 17.95 *(978-0-8131-4104-6(4))* Univ. Pr. of Kentucky.

Parker, Steve. Robots for Work & Fun. 2010. (Robot World Ser.). 32p. (J). 28.50 *(978-1-60753-071-8(6))* Amicus Publishing.

—Robots in Dangerous Places. 2010. (Robot World Ser.). 32p. (J). 28.50 *(978-1-60753-072-5(4))* Amicus Publishing.

Powell Smith, Brendan. David & Goliath: The Brick Bible for Kids. 2013. (ENG., Illus.). 32p. (J). (gr. -1-1). 12.95 *(978-1-62087-982-5(4))*, 620982, Sky Pony Pr.) Skyhorse Publishing Co., Inc.

—Jonah & the Whale: The Brick Bible for Kids. 2014. (Brick Bible for Kids Ser.). (ENG., Illus.). 32p. (J). (gr. -1-k). 12.95 *(978-1-62873-589-5(9))*, Sky Pony Pr.) Skyhorse Publishing Co., Inc.

Priddy, Roger. It's Time to Play. 2013. (Bright Baby Ser.). (ENG.). 8p. (J). (gr. -1 — 1). bds. 4.99 *(978-0-312-51636-9(3))*, 9780312516369, Priddy Bks.) St. Martin's Pr.

Random House. Ultimate Fidget Spinner Guide. 2017. (ENG., Illus.). 96p. (J). (gr. 3-7). pap. 6.99 ***(978-0-525-57934-2(6))***, Random Hse. Bks. for Young Readers) Random Hse. Children's Bks.

Reinhart, Matthew. LEGO Pop-Up. 2016. (ENG., Illus.). 10p. (J). (gr. 2-5). 29.99 *(978-0-545-88104-3(8))* Scholastic, Inc.

Rigsby, Mike. Amazing Rubber Band Cars: Easy-to-build Wind-up Racers, Models, & Toys. 2007. (ENG., Illus.). 136p. (J). (gr. 4-18). pap. 14.95 *(978-1-55652-736-4(5))* Chicago Review Pr., Inc.

La Ropa. 2005. (Coleccion Primeras Imagenes). (SPA., Illus.). 86p. (J). (gr. -1-18). pap. 7.95 *(978-950-11-0988-7(7))*, SGM9887) Sigmar ARG. Dist: Continental Bk. Co., Inc.

Rosen, Michael J. Balls! Margeson, John, illus. 2006. 72p. (J). (gr. 4-8). 18.95 *(978-1-58196-030-3(1))*, Darby Creek) Lerner Publishing Group.

Rosie Raccoon & her Messy Room. 2004. (Play Pals Ser.). (Illus.). 12p. (J). bds. *(978-1-84229-650-9(7))* Top That! Publishing PLC.

Ross, Stewart. Toys. 2013. (Start-Up Connections Ser.). (ENG., Illus.). 32p. (J). pap. 12.99 *(978-0-237-54365-5(6))* Evans Brothers, Ltd. GBR. Dist: Independent Pubs. Group.

Rothrock, Megan H. The Lego Adventure, Vol. 3. 2015. (ENG., Illus.). 192p. (gr. 5). 24.95 *(978-1-59327-610-2(9))* No Starch Pr., Inc.

—The LEGO Adventure Book Vol. 2: Spaceships, Pirates, Dragons & More! 2013. (ENG., Illus.). 196p. (gr. 5). 24.95 *(978-1-59327-512-9(9))*, 9781593275129) No Starch Pr., Inc.

Salzmann, Mary Elizabeth. Know Your Numbers: Toys, 1 vol. 2014. (Numbers 1-20 Ser.). (ENG.). 24p. (J). (gr. k-3). lib. bdg. 24.21 *(978-1-62403-269-1(9))*, SandCastle) ABDO Publishing Co.

—Money for Toys, 1 vol. 2010. (Your Piggy Bank: A Guide to Spending & Saving for Kids! Ser.). (ENG.). 24p. (J). (gr. k-3). 27.07 *(978-1-61641-032-2(9))* Magic Wagon.

Saunders, Catherine. Character Encyclopedia. 2014. (ENG.). 176p. (J). (gr. k-4). 18.99 *(978-1-4654-2135-7(1))*, DK Children) Dorling Kindersley Publishing, Inc.

—LEGO Friends Character Encyclopedia. 2014. (ENG.). 176p. (J). (gr. k-4). 18.99 *(978-1-4654-1894-4(6))*, DK Children) Dorling Kindersley Publishing, Inc.

Scholastic. Shopkins Berry Special Poster Book. 2016. (Shopkins Ser.). (ENG.). 24p. (J). (gr. -1-3). pap. 4.99 *(978-1-338-11126-2(4))* Scholastic, Inc.

—The Updated Ultimate Collector's Guide. Scholastic, illus. rev. collector's ed. 2016. (Shopkins Ser.). (ENG., Illus.). 112p. (J). (gr. -1-3). pap. 7.99 *(978-0-545-90497-1(8))* Scholastic, Inc.

Scholastic, Inc. Staff. World of Ninjago. 2015. (LEGO Ninjago Ser.). (ENG., Illus.). 128p. (J). (gr. 2-5). 12.99 *(978-0-545-80801-9(4))* Scholastic, Inc.

Scholastic, Inc. Staff, contrib. by. Collectable Poster Book. 2015. (Shopkins Ser.). (ENG.). 24p. (J). (gr. 1-6). pap. 4.99 *(978-0-545-91229-7(6))* Scholastic, Inc.

Sévigny, Eric, illus. Caillou Puts Away His Toys. 3rd ed. 2012. (Clubhouse Ser.). (ENG.). 24p. (J). (gr. -1-1). pap. 3.99 *(978-2-89450-938-8(3))* Caillouet, Gerry.

Shaughnessy, Mara. LEGO Man in Space: A True Story. 2013. (ENG., Illus.). 32p. (J). (gr. -1-3). 14.95 *(978-1-62087-544-5(6))*, 620544, Sky Pony Pr.) Skyhorse Publishing Co., Inc.

Shores, Lori. How to Build Flipsticks, 1 vol. 2011. (Hands-On Science Fun Ser.). (ENG., Illus.). 24p. (gr. k-1). pap. 7.29 *(978-1-4296-6213-0(1))*, Pebble Plus) Capstone Press of Coughlan Cos.

Simon, Jenne. Shopkins: The Ultimate Collector's Guide. 2015. (Shopkins Ser.). (ENG., Illus.). 64p. (J). (gr. -1-3). pap. 5.99 *(978-0-545-83602-9(6))* Scholastic, Inc.

Slater, Lee. Lego Manufacturers: The Kristiansen Family, 1 vol. 2016. (Toy Trailblazers Ser.). (ENG., Illus.). 32p. (J). (gr. 3-6). lib. bdg. 27.07 *(978-1-62403-977-5(4))*, Checkerboard Library) ABDO Publishing Co.

—Play-Doh Pioneer: Joseph Mcvicker, 1 vol. 2016. (Toy Trailblazers Ser.). (ENG., Illus.). 32p. (J). (gr. 3-6). lib. bdg. 27.07 *(978-1-62403-978-2(2))*, Checkerboard Library) ABDO Publishing Co.

—Slinky Innovators: The James Family, 1 vol. 2016. (Toy Trailblazers Ser.). (ENG., Illus.). 32p. (J). (gr. 3-6). lib. bdg. 27.07 *(978-1-62403-979-9(0))*, Checkerboard Library) ABDO Publishing Co.

—Toy Trailblazers. 2016. (Toy Trailblazers Ser.: 6). (ENG.). 32p. (J). (gr. 3-6). lib. bdg. 162.42 *(978-1-62403-973-7(1))*, Checkerboard Library) ABDO Publishing Co.

Smith, Brendan Powell. Assassination! The Brick Chronicle of Attempts on the Lives of Twelve US Presidents. 2013. (ENG., Illus.). 272p. 19.95 *(978-1-62087-998-6(0))*, 620998) Skyhorse Publishing Co., Inc.

—The Brick Bible, Set. 2013. (ENG., Illus.). 576p. 29.95 *(978-1-62636-177-5(0))*, 263177) Skyhorse Publishing Co., Inc.

—The Complete Brick Bible for Kids: Six Classic Bible Stories. 2015. (ENG., Illus.). 192p. (J). (gr. -1-k). 15.99 *(978-1-63450-209-2(4))*, Sky Pony Pr.) Skyhorse Publishing Co., Inc.

—Noah's Ark: The Brick Bible for Kids. 2015. (Brick Bible for Kids Ser.). (ENG., Illus.). 32p. (J). (gr. -1-k). 3.99 *(978-1-63450-054-8(7))*, Sky Pony Pr.) Skyhorse Publishing Co., Inc.

Smith, Sian. Levers, 1 vol. 2012. (How Toys Work Ser.). (ENG.). 24p. (gr. -1-1). pap. 6.29 *(978-1-4329-6586-0(7))*; lib. bdg. 22.65 *(978-1-4329-6579-2(4))* Heinemann-Raintree. (Acorn).

—Pulleys, 1 vol. 2012. (How Toys Work Ser.). (ENG.). 24p. (gr. -1-1). pap. 6.29 *(978-1-4329-6587-7(5))*; lib. bdg. 22.65 *(978-1-4329-6580-8(8))* Heinemann-Raintree. (Acorn).

—Ramps & Wedges, 1 vol. 2012. (How Toys Work Ser.). (ENG.). 24p. (gr. -1-1). pap. 6.29 *(978-1-4329-6588-4(3))*; lib. bdg. 22.65 *(978-1-4329-6581-5(6))* Heinemann-Raintree. (Acorn).

—Screws, Nuts, & Bolts, 1 vol. 2012. (How Toys Work Ser.). (ENG.). 24p. (gr. -1-1). pap. 6.29 *(978-1-4329-6589-1(1))*; lib. bdg. 22.65 *(978-1-4329-6582-2(4))* Heinemann-Raintree. (Acorn).

—Springs, 1 vol. 2012. (How Toys Work Ser.). (ENG.). 24p. (gr. -1-1). pap. 6.29 *(978-1-4329-6590-7(5))*; lib. bdg. 22.65 *(978-1-4329-6583-9(2))* Heinemann-Raintree. (Acorn).

—Wheels & Axles, 1 vol. 2012. (How Toys Work Ser.). (ENG.). 24p. (gr. -1-1). pap. 6.29 *(978-1-4329-6591-4(3))*; lib. bdg. 22.65 *(978-1-4329-6584-6(0))* Heinemann-Raintree. (Acorn).

Sohn, Emily. Experiments in Forces & Motion with Toys & Everyday Stuff. 2015. (Fun Science Ser.). (ENG., Illus.). 24p. (gr. 1-2). lib. bdg. 25.32 *(978-1-4914-5032-1(0))* Capstone Press of Coughlan Cos.

Spinning Top: Level L, 6 vols. (Wonder Worldtm Ser.). 16p. 34.95 *(978-0-7802-2908-2(8))* Wright Group/McGraw-Hill.

Taylor, Dereen. Toys. 2017. (Popcorn: in the Past Ser.). (ENG., Illus.). 24p. (J). (gr. k-2). pap. 10.99 ***(978-0-7502-6423-5(3))***, Wayland) Hachette Children's Group GBR. Dist: Hachette Bk. Group.

Tietjens, Harold. Cybertronian Transformers Index. Tietjens, Harold, photos by. 2003. (ENG., Illus.). 128p. (YA). pap. 29.95 *(978-0-9663588-3-4(X))*, 9780966358834) Antarctic Pr., Inc.

Time for Toys! (Flip Flap Fun Book Ser.). 10p. (J). bds. *(978-2-7643-0040-4(9))* Phidal Publishing, Inc./Editions Phidal, Inc.

Tocando. (Coleccion Mil Preguntas). (SPA., Illus.). (J). 24p. pap. 5.50 *(978-950-11-0657-2(8))*, SGM625); 2005. 86p. (gr. -1-18). pap. 7.95 *(978-950-11-0902-3(X))*, SGM902X) Sigmar ARG. Dist: Continental Bk. Co., Inc.

Toys with Wheels: Individual Title Six-Packs. (gr. -1-2). 23.00 *(978-0-7635-9006-2(1))* Rigby Education.

The True Cost of Toys. 2014. (ENG., Illus.). 48p. (J). *(978-0-7787-0486-7(6))* Crabtree Publishing Co.

Unglick, Richard. Journey Around the World. 2016. (Playmobil Ser.). (ENG., Illus.). 64p. (J). (gr. 1-7). 19.95 *(978-1-63322-079-9(6))*, Walter Foster Jr) Quarto Publishing Group USA.

Weekly Reader Early Learning Library Staff. Las Cosas con las Que Juego. 2006. (Things in My World/ Las cosas de mi mundo Ser.). (ENG & SPA., Illus.). 16p. (gr. -1-2). lib. bdg. 19.00 *(978-0-8368-7223-1(1))*, Weekly Reader Leveled Readers) Stevens, Gareth Publishing LLLP.

—Things I Play With. 2006. (Things in My World Ser.). (Illus.). 16p. (gr. -1-2). lib. bdg. 19.00 *(978-0-8368-6811-1(0))*, Weekly Reader Leveled Readers) Stevens, Gareth Publishing LLLP.

Weekly Reader Editorial Staff. Things I Play With/Las Cosas con las Que Juego. 2006. (Things in My World/ Las cosas de mi mundo Ser.). (ENG & SPA.). 16p. (gr. -1-2). pap. 5.30 *(978-0-8368-7230-9(4))*, Weekly Reader Leveled Readers) Stevens, Gareth Publishing LLLP.

West, Tracey. World of Ninjago Official Guide. 2015. (Illus.). 128p. (J). pap. ***(978-0-545-80813-2(8))*** Scholastic, Inc.

Which Toys? Individual Title Six-Packs. (gr. -1-2). 23.00 *(978-0-7635-9007-9(X))* Rigby Education.

Wick, Walter. Toyland Express: Picture Puzzles to Search & Solve. Wick, Walter, photos by. 2011. (Can You See What I See? Ser.). (ENG., Illus.). 40p. (J). 13.99 *(978-0-545-24483-1(8))* Scholastic, Inc.

Wolf, Laurie Goldrich. The Lonely Sock Club: One Sock, Tons of Cool Projects! 2011. (Green & Groovy Ser.: 1). (ENG.). 64p. (J). (gr. 3). 16.99 *(978-1-935703-06-8(4))* Downtown Bookworks.

Wulffson, Don. Toys! Keller, Laurie, illus. 2014. (ENG.). 208p. (J). (gr. 3-7). pap. 9.99 *(978-1-250-03409-0(4))*, 9781250034090) Square Fish.

TOYS—FICTION

ABDO Publishing Company Staff. Little Whistle - 4 Titles. Bowers, Tim, illus. 2007. (Little Whistle Ser.). (ENG.). 32p. 96.84 *(978-1-59961-252-2(6))* Spotlight.

Abruzzo, Nancy. Pop Flop's Great Balloon Ride. Chilton, Noel, illus. 2005. (ENG.). 32p. (J). (gr. k-17). bds. 12.95 *(978-0-89013-475-7(8))* Museum of New Mexico Pr.

Adams, Colleen. At the Toy Store. 2006. (Neighborhood Readers Ser.). (ENG.). 8p. (gr. -1-3). pap. 5.15 *(978-1-4042-5732-0(2))*, Rosen Classroom) Rosen Publishing Group, Inc., The.

Adan, Jennifer. I Don't See Heaven. 2013. 24p. pap. 10.99 *(978-1-4808-0307-7(3))* Archway Publishing.

Adderson, Caroline. Jasper John Dooley: Lost & Found. Shiell, Mike, illus. 2015. (Jasper John Dooley Ser.). (ENG.). 128p. (J). (gr. 2-5). 15.95 *(978-1-77138-014-0(4))* Kids Can Pr., Ltd. CAN. Dist: Hachette Bk. Group.

Addino, Victoria. Sadie's Wish: Three Little Elves. Garafalo, Beatrice, illus. 2012. 32p. (-18). pap. 24.95 *(978-1-4626-9907-0(3))* America Star Bks.

Akins, David. Tyler's Toys & the Bully. 2010. 28p. 13.99 *(978-1-4520-0304-7(1))* AuthorHouse.

Alfau, Georgette. Alfred & Alex & the Toy Eating Monster. 2009. 16p. 18.95 *(978-0-557-15276-6(3))* Lulu Pr., Inc.

Allison, Teresa J. Bobble Stories: The Bobbleup Pup. Allison, Charles T., illus. 2013. 42p. pap. 12.99 *(978-0-9887612-2-3(X))* Tawnsy Publishing.

Ameet Studio Staff. The Book of Monsters. 2016. (LEGO NEXO Knights Ser.). (ENG.). 96p. (J). (gr. 2-5). 12.99 *(978-1-338-03488-2(X))* Scholastic, Inc.

—These Aren't the Droids You're Looking For: A Search & Find Book. Ameet Studio Staff, illus. 2014. (LEGO Star Wars Ser.). (ENG., Illus.). 32p. (J). (gr. -1-3). pap. 6.99 *(978-0-545-60804-6(X))* Scholastic, Inc.

—Where's the Pizza Boy? 2013. (LEGO City Ser.). (ENG.). 64p. (J). (gr. -1-3). pap. 6.99 *(978-0-545-60805-3(8))* Scholastic, Inc.

Ameet Studio Staff, illus. The Piece of Resistance. 2013. (ENG.). 32p. (J). (gr. 2-5). pap., act. bk. ed. 8.99 *(978-0-545-62461-9(4))* Scholastic, Inc.

Andersen, Hans Christian. The Steadfast Tin Soldier, 1 vol. Jorgensen, David, illus. 2005. (Rabbit Ears: A Classic Tale Ser.).Tr. of Standhaftige Tinsoldat. (ENG.). 40p. (gr. -1-3). 25.65 *(978-1-59679-346-0(5))* Spotlight.

Applegate, Katherine. Never Swipe a Bully's Bear. Biggs, Brian, illus. 2008. (Roscoe Riley Rules Ser.: 2). (ENG.). 96p. (J). (gr. 1-5). 15.99 *(978-0-06-114884-2(9))*; pap. 4.99 *(978-0-06-114883-5(0))* HarperCollins Pubs.

Arnold, Shauna. Baa. Hines, Irene, illus. 2004. 19p. (J). (gr. -1-3). 12.00 *(978-0-9743669-0-6(0))* Trinity Bks.

Baby's Box of Toys. 2008. (Baby Gold Stars Fabric Ser.). 6p. bds. *(978-1-4075-2520-4(4))* Parragon, Inc.

Ballou, Kathy. The Tracks Out Back. I.t. ed. 2005. (Illus.). 24p. (J). per. 10.00 *(978-1-932338-50-8(0))* Lifevest Publishing, Inc.

Baltazar, Art & Aureliani, Franco. Attack of the Toyman!, 1 vol. 2014. (Superman Family Adventures Ser.). (ENG., Illus.). 32p. (gr. 1-2). 22.60 *(978-1-4342-6476-3(9))* Stone Arch Bks.

Banks, Kate. Max's Castle. Kulikov, Boris, illus. 2011. (Max's Words Ser.: 3). (ENG.). 40p. (J). (gr. -1-3). 18.99 *(978-0-374-39919-1(0))*, 9780374399191, Farrar, Straus & Giroux (BYR)) Farrar, Straus & Giroux.

Banks, Lynne Reid. The Indian in the Cupboard. 2011. 9.14 *(978-0-7848-3449-7(0))*, Everbind) Marco Bk. Co.

—The Indian in the Cupboard. 2010. (Indian in the Cupboard Ser.). (ENG.). 240p. (J). (gr. 3-7). 6.99 *(978-0-375-84753-0(7))*, Yearling) Random Hse. Children's Bks.

—The Mystery of the Cupboard. Newsom, Tom, illus. 2004. (Indian in the Cupboard Ser.: No. 4). (ENG.). 256p. (J). (gr. 4-18). pap. 6.99 *(978-0-380-72013-2(2))* HarperCollins Pubs.

—The Return of the Indian. 2010. (Indian in the Cupboard Ser.). (ENG.). 208p. (J). (gr. 3-7). 6.99 *(978-0-375-85523-8(8))*, Yearling) Random Hse. Children's Bks.

—The Secret of the Indian. 2010. (Indian in the Cupboard Ser.). (ENG.). 192p. (J). (gr. 3-7). 6.99 *(978-0-375-85524-5(6))*, Yearling) Random Hse. Children's Bks.

—Secret of the Indian. 2003. (ENG., Illus.). 160p. pap. *(978-0-00-714900-1(X))*, Collins) HarperCollins Pubs. Ltd.

Banks, Lynne Reid & Banks, L. The Return of the Indian. 2010. (Indian in the Cupboard Ser.: 2). (gr. 3-6). lib. bdg. 17.20 *(978-0-8335-0902-4(0))*, Turtleback) Turtleback Bks.

Banks, Steven. The Song That Never Ends. DePorter, Vince, illus. 2004. (Spongebob Squarepants Ser.). 32p. (J). (gr. k-2). 11.65 *(978-0-7569-5374-4(X))* Perfection Learning Corp.

—Special Delivery. DePorter, Vince, illus. 2005. (Ready-to-Read Ser.). 32p. (J). lib. bdg. 15.00 *(978-1-59054-986-5(4))* Fitzgerald Bks.

Barchers, Suzanne I. Get to Bed, Ren!, 1 vol. 2011. (Targeted Phonics Ser.). (ENG.). 16p. (J). (gr. k-2). pap. 5.99 *(978-1-4333-2416-1(4))* Teacher Created Materials, Inc.

Barradel, Isabel. Toyshop Tales. 2006. 275p. pap. 27.95 *(978-1-4241-2798-6(X))* PublishAmerica, Inc.

Barradell, Isabel. Even More Tales from the Toyshop. 2008. 380p. pap. 29.95 *(978-1-60474-508-5(8))* America Star Bks.

Bass, L. G. & Geringer, Laura. Boom Boom Go Away! Ibatoulline, Bagram, illus. 2010. (ENG.). 40p. (J). (gr. -1-1). 15.99 *(978-0-689-85093-6(X))*, Atheneum Bks. for Young Readers) Simon & Schuster Children's Publishing.

Baxter, Nicola. Tales from the Toy Box. Press, Jenny, illus. 2012. (ENG.). 80p. (J). (gr. k-4). pap. 9.99 *(978-1-84322-951-3(X))* Anness Publishing GBR. Dist: National Bk. Network.

TUV

Bell, Cece. Sock Monkey Boogie-Woogie. Bell, Cece, illus. 2015. (ENG., Illus.). 32p. (J). (gr. -1-3). 14.00 *(978-0-7636-7758-9(2))* Candlewick Pr.

—Sock Monkey Takes a Bath. Bell, Cece, illus. 2015. (ENG., Illus.). 32p. (J). (gr. -1-3). 14.00 *(978-0-7636-7759-6(0))* Candlewick Pr.

Bell, Tom. Where the Lost Things Go. 2012. (ENG., Illus.). 48p. (J). 15.00 *(978-1-84135-874-1(6))*; pap. 9.95 *(978-1-84135-892-5(4))* Award Pubns. Ltd. GBR. Dist: Parkwest Pubns., Inc.

Bellisario, Gina. Super Fluffy to the Rescue. Von Innerebner, Jessika, illus. 2016. (Ellie Ultra Ser.). (ENG.). 128p. (gr. 2-3). lib. bdg. 25.99 *(978-1-4965-3142-1(6))* Stone Arch Bks.

Benedictus, David. Return to the Hundred Acre Wood. Burgess, Mark, illus. 2009. (Winnie-The-Pooh Ser.). (ENG.). 216p. (J). (gr. 3-7). 19.99 *(978-0-525-42160-3(2)*, Dutton Books for Young Readers) Penguin Young Readers Group.

Bentley, Jonathan, illus. Where Is Bear? 2017. (ENG.). 32p. (J). (gr. -1-2). 16.99 *(978-0-399-55593-0(5)*, Doubleday Bks. for Young Readers) Random Hse. Children's Bks.

Bernstein, Susan H. N. E. Pominonous Epstein Minds His Mind. (E. Pominonous Epstein Ser.). 18p. (J). (gr. -1-3). pap. 8.95 *(978-0-9706596-0-6(1))* Bernstein, Susan.

Bianco, Margery Williams. Poor Cecco. Rackham, Arthur, illus. 2013. (ENG.). 160p. (J). (gr. 3-12). pap. 9.99 *(978-0-486-49226-1(5))* Dover Pubns., Inc.

—The Velveteen Rabbit, or, How Toys Become Real. Nicholson, William, illus. 2015. iii, 27p. (J). pap. *(978-1-4677-9307-0(8)*, First Avenue Editions) Lerner Publishing Group.

Birchall, Mark. Rabbit's Birthday Surprise. Birchall, Mark, illus. 2003. (Illus.). 32p. (J). (gr. -1-3). 15.95 *(978-0-87614-910-2(7)*, Carolrhoda Bks.) Lerner Publishing Group.

—Rabbit's Wooly Sweater. Birchall, Mark, illus. 2003. (Picture Bks.). (Illus.). 32p. (J). (gr. -1-3). 15.95 *(978-1-57505-465-0(5)*, Carolrhoda Bks.) Lerner Publishing Group.

Birkett, Georgie, illus. Fix It!/¡A Reparar! 2009. (Helping Hands English/Spanish Edition Ser.). (ENG & SPA.). 24p. (J). (gr. -1-k). pap. *(978-1-84643-571-3(4))* Child's Play International Ltd.

Birney, Betty G. Humphrey's Really Wheely Racing Day. Burris, Priscilla, illus. 2014. (Humphrey's Tiny Tales Ser.: 1). (ENG.). 96p. (J). (gr. k-3). pap. 4.99 *(978-0-14-751485-1(1)*, Puffin Books) Penguin Young Readers Group.

Blanquet, Stephane. Toys in the Basement. 2010. (ENG., Illus.). 32p. 14.99 *(978-1-60699-402-3(6)*, 699402) Fantagraphics Bks.

Blizzard on Moose Mountain. 2007. (J). pap. *(978-0-9794542-0-2(4))* Battat, Inc.

Blyton, Enid. The Little Toy Engine & Other Stories. 2013. (ENG., Illus.). 192p. (J). 9.95 *(978-1-84135-460-6(0))* Award Pubns. Ltd. GBR. Dist: Parkwest Pubns., Inc.

Bolger, Kevin. Zombiekins 2. Blecha, Aaron, illus. 2011. (J). 10.99 *(978-1-59514-432-4(3)*, Razorbill) Penguin Publishing Group.

Bostrom, Kathleen Long. Rufus & Ryan Celebrate Easter! Thornburgh, Rebecca, illus. 2014. (Rufus & Ryan Ser.). 20p. (J). bds. 7.99 *(978-0-8249-1919-1(X)*, Ideal Pubns.) Worthy Publishing.

Breece, Beverly. The Curwood Acorns. DeWeese, Susan, illus. 2012. 40p. pap. 24.95 *(978-1-4626-8202-7(2))* America Star Bks.

Brezenoff, Steve. Curses for Sale, 1 vol. Percival, Tom, illus. 2012. (Ravens Pass Ser.). (ENG.). 96p. (gr. 2-3). pap. 6.15 *(978-1-4342-4209-9(9))*; lib. bdg. 25.32 *(978-1-4342-3763-7(X))* Stone Arch Bks.

Bright, J. E. Escape from Prison Island. 2016. (LEGO City 8X8 Ser.). lib. bdg. 13.55 *(978-0-606-38828-3(1))* Turtleback Bks.

—Reader. Lee, Paul, illus. 2016. (Lego City Ser.). (ENG.). 32p. (J). (gr. -1-3). pap. 3.99 *(978-0-545-91386-7(1))* Scholastic, Inc.

Brinkley, Lonnie. I Believe: Lost at the North Pole. 2008. (Illus.). 450p. (J). 29.95 *(978-0-9801215-3-7(1))* Big Bear Publishing U.S.

Brooke, Samantha. Fire in the Forest! Kiernan, Kenny, illus. 2012. 31p. (J). *(978-1-4242-5340-1(3))* Scholastic, Inc.

—Fire in the Forest! 2012. (LEGO City Scholastic Readers Level 1 Ser.). (Illus.). 31p. (J). lib. bdg. 13.55 *(978-0-606-23730-7(5)*, Turtleback) Turtleback Bks.

Brown, Alan James. Love-a-Duck. Chessa, Francesca, illus. 2010. (ENG.). 32p. (J). (gr. -1-1). pap. 16.95 *(978-0-8234-2263-0(1))* Holiday Hse., Inc.

Brown, Gwen. Clifford & His Bear. 2006. (Illus.). 48p. pap. *(978-1-84401-650-1(1))* Athena Pr.

Buell, Janet. Sail Away, Little Boat. Ishida, Jui, illus. 2006. 32p. (J). 15.95 *(978-1-57505-821-4(9)*, Carolrhoda Bks.) Lerner Publishing Group.

Bunting, Eve. Ducky. Wisniewski, David, illus. 2004. (ENG.). 32p. (J). (gr. k — 1). 6.99 *(978-0-618-43240-0(X))* Houghton Mifflin Harcourt Publishing Co.

—Reggie. Burkett, D. Brent, illus. 2006. (ENG.). 112p. (J). (gr. 1-4). 16.95 *(978-0-8126-2746-6(6))* Cricket Bks.

Butterworth, Nick. Albert the Bear to the Rescue. 2008. (J). 16.99 *(978-0-06-147046-2(5))* HarperCollins Pubs.

Byrd, B. N. My Favorite Toy. 2011. 40p. pap. 21.99 *(978-1-4500-5290-0(8))* Xlibris Corp.

Calhoun, Terry. The Muggwapps. 2007. (J). pap. 8.00 *(978-0-8059-7223-8(4))* Dorrance Publishing Co., Inc.

Cameron, Sharon. The Dark Unwinding. (ENG.). 336p. (J). (gr. 7). 2013. pap. 9.99 *(978-0-545-32787-9(3)*, Scholastic Paperbacks) 2012. 17.99 *(978-0-545-32786-2(5)*, Scholastic Pr.) Scholastic, Inc.

Carle, Eric. 10 Little Rubber Ducks. Carle, Eric, illus. 2005. (ENG., Illus.). 36p. (J). (gr. -1-1). 21.99 *(978-0-06-074075-7(2))* HarperCollins Pubs.

—10 Little Rubber Ducks Board Book. Carle, Eric, illus. 2010. (ENG., Illus.). 34p. (J). (gr. -1-k). bds. 7.99 *(978-0-06-196428-2(X)*, HarperFestival) HarperCollins Pubs.

Carsey, Alice, illus. Pinocchio. 2005.Tr. of Avventure di Pinocchio. (ENG.). 136p. (J). (gr. 2-5). 19.95 *(978-1-933327-00-6(6))* Purple Bear Bks., Inc.

Casado, Dami. Como Comes Tu? (SPA.). 8p. 9.95 *(978-84-272-8325-1(3))* Molino, Editorial ESP. Dist: Distribooks, Inc.

—Como Te Lavas? (SPA.). 8p. 9.95 *(978-84-272-8326-8(1))* Molino, Editorial ESP. Dist: Distribooks, Inc.

—Como Te Vistes? (SPA.). 8p. 9.95 *(978-84-272-8328-2(8))* Molino, Editorial ESP. Dist: Distribooks, Inc.

Castillo, Lauren. The Troublemaker. 2014. (ENG., Illus.). 48p. (J). (gr. -1-3). 16.99 *(978-0-547-72991-6(X))* Houghton Mifflin Harcourt Publishing Co.

Charles Santore & Williams, Margery. The Velveteen Rabbit Set: Or How Toys Become Real. gif. ed. 2014. (ENG.). 48p. (J). 24.95 *(978-1-60433-335-0(9)*, Applesauce Pr.) Cider Mill Pr. Bk. Pubs., LLC.

Chester, Malcolm. Elysia: The World in Children's Dreams. 2012. 320p. 29.11 *(978-1-4669-4812-9(4))*; pap. 19.11 *(978-1-4669-4810-5(8))* Trafford Publishing.

Choldenko, Gennifer. Dad & the Dinosaur. Santat, Dan, illus. 2017. (ENG.). 40p. (J). (gr. k-3). 17.99 *(978-0-399-24353-0(4)*, G.P. Putnam's Sons Books for Young Readers) Penguin Young Readers Group.

Chou, Yih-fen. Mimi Tidies Up. Chen, Zhiyuan, illus. 2011. (J). *(978-0-9845523-6-8(7))* Heryin Publishing Corp.

Clark, Harriet. Davy Asks His Dad. Clark, Tim, photos by. 2012. (Illus.). 32p. pap. *(978-1-77097-977-2(8))* FriesenPress.

CleverKits, creator. Safari Adventure. 2006. (J). (gr. -1-2). audio compact disk 19.95 *(978-0-9778771-1-9(6))* CleverKits,LLC.

—Under the Sea. 2006. (J). (gr. -1-2). audio compact disk 19.95 *(978-0-9778771-0-2(8))* CleverKits,LLC.

Cole, Henry. The Somewhat True Adventures of Sammy Shine, 1 vol. Cole, Henry, illus. 2016. (ENG., Illus.). 272p. (J). (gr. 3-6). 16.95 *(978-1-56145-866-0(X))* Peachtree Pubs.

Collingridge, Richard. Lionheart. 2016. (ENG., Illus.). 32p. (J). (gr. -1-k). 17.99 *(978-0-545-83321-9(3))* Scholastic, Inc.

Collins, Heather, illus. Hey Diddle Diddle. 2003. (Traditional Nursery Rhymes Ser.). (ENG.). 12p. (J). (gr. -1 — 1). bds. 3.95 *(978-1-55337-078-9(3))* Kids Can Pr., Ltd. CAN. Dist: Hachette Bk. Group.

—Jack & Jill. 2003. (Traditional Nursery Rhymes Ser.). (ENG.). 12p. (J). (gr. -1 — 1). bds. 3.95 *(978-1-55337-075-8(9))* Kids Can Pr., Ltd. CAN. Dist: Hachette Bk. Group.

—Little Miss Muffet. 2003. (Traditional Nursery Rhymes Ser.). (ENG.). 12p. (J). (gr. -1 — 1). bds. 3.95 *(978-1-55337-076-5(7))* Kids Can Pr., Ltd. CAN. Dist: Hachette Bk. Group.

—Pat-a-Cake. 2003. (Traditional Nursery Rhymes Ser.). (ENG.). 12p. (J). (gr. -1 — 1). bds. 3.95 *(978-1-55337-077-2(5))* Kids Can Pr., Ltd. CAN. Dist: Hachette Bk. Group.

Cook, Melissa. Anna & the Garden Fairy: Anna's Little Black Bear. 2009. (ENG., Illus.). 20p. (J). 14.95 *(978-1-57197-501-0(2)*, Ivy House Publishing Group) Pentland Pr., Inc.

Cooper, Helen S. Historias de Juguetes. (SPA., Illus.). 80p. (J). (gr. k-2). 23.95 *(978-84-261-3127-0(1)*, JV1108) Juventud, Editorial ESP. Dist: Lectorum Pubns., Inc.

—Tatty-Ratty. Cooper, Helen S., illus. 2004. (Illus.). 28p. (J). (gr. k-3). reprint ed. 19.00 *(978-0-7567-7214-7(1))* DIANE Publishing Co.

Corderoy, Tracey. It's Potty Time! Pedler, Caroline, illus. 2014. (ENG.). 22p. (J). (gr. -1-k). bds. 8.99 *(978-1-58925-574-6(7))* Tiger Tales.

Las Cosas Del Cuarto de Baño. (SPA.). 24p. 7.95 *(978-84-488-1110-5(0))* Beascoa, Ediciones S.A. ESP. Dist: Distribooks, Inc.

Cotton, Katie. Dear Bunny... Gomez, Bianca, illus. 2016. (ENG.). 24p. (J). (gr. -1-2). 15.99 *(978-1-84780-846-2(8)*, Frances Lincoln Children's Bks.) Quarto Publishing Group UK GBR. Dist: Hachette Bk. Group.

Cousins, Lucy. Los Juguetes de Maisy. Cousins, Lucy, illus. 2009. (Maisy Ser.). (SPA & ENG., Illus.). 16p. (J). (gr. -1-2). bds. 5.99 *(978-0-7636-4520-5(6))* Candlewick Pr.

Cowell, Cressida. That Rabbit Belongs to Emily Brown. Layton, Neal, illus. 2007. (ENG.). 40p. (gr. -1-3). 16.99 *(978-1-4231-0645-6(8))* Hyperion Pr.

Cowley, Joy. Miss Doll & Friends: A Surprise for Miss Doll. Bordicchia, Gaia, illus. 2014. (ENG.). 8p. pap. *(978-0-927244-52-7(7)*, Joy Cowley Club) Flying Start Bks.

—Miss Doll & Friends: Old Jokes. Bordicchia, Gaia, illus. 2014. (ENG.). 8p. pap. *(978-0-927244-60-2(8)*, Joy Cowley Club) Flying Start Bks.

—Miss Doll & Friends: Red Lipstick. Bordicchia, Gaia, illus. 2014. (ENG.). 8p. pap. *(978-0-927244-78-7(0)*, Joy Cowley Club) Flying Start Bks.

—Miss Doll & Friends: Rocking Race. Bordicchia, Gaia, illus. 2014. (ENG.). 8p. pap. *(978-0-927244-64-0(0)*, Joy Cowley Club) Flying Start Bks.

—Miss Doll & Friends: The Rainbow Bird. Bordicchia, Gaia, illus. 2014. (ENG.). 8p. pap. *(978-0-927244-65-7(9)*, Joy Cowley Club) Flying Start Bks.

—Miss Doll & Friends: Tin Clown. Bordicchia, Gaia, illus. 2014. (ENG.). 8p. pap. *(978-0-927244-55-8(1)*, Joy Cowley Club) Flying Start Bks.

—Miss Doll & Friends: Tin Clown¿s Hat. Bordicchia, Gaia, illus. 2014. (ENG.). 8p. pap. *(978-0-927244-79-4(9)*, Joy Cowley Club) Flying Start Bks.

—Miss Doll & Friends: Toy Music. Bordicchia, Gaia, illus. 2014. (ENG.). 8p. pap. *(978-0-927244-59-6(4)*, Joy Cowley Club) Flying Start Bks.

—Miss Doll & Friends: Where Is Fire Engine? Bordicchia, Gaia, illus. 2014. (ENG.). 8p. pap. *(978-0-927244-57-2(8)*, Joy Cowley Club) Flying Start Bks.

—Miss Doll & Friends: Yellow Duck. Bordicchia, Gaia, illus. 2014. (ENG.). 8p. pap. *(978-0-927244-62-6(4)*, Joy Cowley Club) Flying Start Bks.

Cox, Katherine. The Missing Fox. Brantley-Newton, Vanessa, illus. 2015. 32p. (J). *(978-1-4806-8800-1(2))* Scholastic, Inc.

—The Missing Fox (Scholastic Reader, Level 2: Katie Fry, Private Eye #2) Newton, Vanessa Brantley, illus. 2015. (Scholastic Reader, Level 2 Ser.). (ENG.). 32p. (J). (gr. 1-3). pap. 3.99 *(978-0-545-66675-6(9))* Scholastic, Inc.

Crimi, Carolyn. There Might Be Lobsters. Molk, Laurel, illus. 2017. (ENG.). 32p. (J). (gr. -1-2). 16.99 *(978-0-7636-7542-4(3))* Candlewick Pr.

Crow, Nosy. Pip & Posy: the Bedtime Frog. Scheffler, Axel, illus. 2014. (Pip & Posy Ser.). (ENG.). 32p. (J). (-k). 12.99 *(978-0-7636-7068-9(5)*, Nosy Crow) Candlewick Pr.

Crum, Shutta. Mine! Barton, Patrice, illus. 2011. (ENG.). 32p. (J). (gr. -1-2). 16.99 *(978-0-375-86711-8(2)*, Knopf Bks. for Young Readers) Random Hse. Children's Bks.

Custer, Jason. Everyday Monsters. 2005. (J). lib. bdg. 19.95 *(978-0-9754728-3-5(6))* Big Ransom Studio.

Daley, Laurie & Panckridge, Michael. Live Action. 2007. 224p. *(978-0-207-20053-3(X))* HarperCollins Pubs. Australia.

DANOWSKI, Sonja. Night Cat. 2016. (ENG., Illus.). 48p. 19.95 *(978-0-7358-4266-3(3))* North-South Bks., Inc.

Davidson, Susanna. Nutcracker with Music. 2012. (Picture Books with Music Ser.). 24p. (J). bds. 18.99 *(978-0-7945-2646-7(2)*, Usborne) EDC Publishing.

Davis, Jacky. Ladybug Girl & the Best Ever Playdate. Soman, David, illus. 2015. (Ladybug Girl Ser.). (ENG.). 40p. (J). (gr. -1-k). 17.99 *(978-0-8037-4030-3(1)*, Dial Bks) Penguin Young Readers Group.

de Sève, Randall. A Fire Truck Named Red. Staake, Bob, illus. 2016. (ENG.). 40p. (J). 16.99 *(978-0-374-30073-9(9)*, 9780374300739, Farrar, Straus & Giroux (BYR)) Farrar, Straus & Giroux.

—Toy Boat. Long, Loren, illus. (ENG.). (J). (gr. -1 — 1). 2014. 30p. bds. 7.99 *(978-0-399-16797-3(8))* 2007. 40p. 17.99 *(978-0-399-24374-5(7))* Penguin Young Readers Group. (Philomel Bks.).

de Vries, Anke. Raf. Dematons, Charlotte, illus. 2009. (ENG.). 32p. (J). (gr. k-3). 16.95 *(978-1-59078-749-6(8)*, Lemniscaat) Boyds Mills Pr.

Deedman, Heidi. Too Many Toys! Deedman, Heidi, illus. 2015. (ENG., Illus.). 32p. (J). (gr. -1-1). 15.99 *(978-0-7636-7861-6(9))* Candlewick Pr.

deGroat, Diane. Happy Birthday to You, You Belong in a Zoo. deGroat, Diane, illus. 2007. (Gilbert & Friends Ser.). (Illus.). (gr. -1-3). 17.00 *(978-0-7569-8108-2(5))* Perfection Learning Corp.

Dempster, Al. Santa's Toy Shop (Disney) RH Disney Staff, illus. 2015. (Little Golden Book Ser.). (ENG.). 24p. (J). (-k). 4.99 *(978-0-7364-3401-0(1)*, Golden/Disney) Random Hse. Children's Bks.

Depken, Kristen L. Merry Christmas, Woody. 2013. lib. bdg. 13.55 *(978-0-606-32213-3(2)*, Turtleback) Turtleback Bks.

—Merry Christmas, Woody (Disney/Pixar Toy Story) RH Disney Staff, illus. 2013. (Pictureback Ser.). (ENG.). 16p. (J). (gr. -1-2). 3.99 *(978-0-7364-3070-8(9)*, RH/Disney) Random Hse. Children's Bks.

—A Roaring Adventure (Disney/Pixar Toy Story) RH Disney Staff & Holtsclaw, Josh, illus. 2012. (Little Golden Book Ser.). (ENG.). 24p. (J). (gr. k-k). 4.99 *(978-0-7364-2907-8(7)*, Golden/Disney) Random Hse. Children's Bks.

—Scuffy the Tugboat. 2017. (Step into Reading Ser.). (ENG., Illus.). 32p. (J). (gr. -1-1). 3.99 *(978-1-101-93929-1(X)*, Random Hse. Bks. for Young Readers) Random Hse. Children's Bks.

—Where's Woody? (Disney/Pixar Toy Story) Random House Disney Staff, illus. 2012. (Pictureback(R) Ser.). (ENG.). 16p. (J). (gr. -1-2). pap. 4.99 *(978-0-7364-2850-7(X)*, RH/Disney) Random Hse. Children's Bks.

Devargas, Casey Anthony. The Kindergarten Treasure. 2012. 44p. pap. 7.00 *(978-0-9859042-0-3(8))* CD Publishing.

deVet, L. J. Teddy's Christmas Wish. Zabarylo-Duma, Ewa, illus. 2013. 46p. (J). pap. *(978-0-9873686-5-2(6))* Print-Rite Publishers.

DiCamillo, Kate. The Miraculous Journey of Edward Tulane. Ibatoulline, Bagram, illus. (ENG.). (J). 2015. 240p. (gr. 2-5). pap. 7.99 *(978-0-7636-8090-9(7))* 2009. 228p. (gr. 2-5). pap. 11.99 *(978-0-7636-4783-4(7))* 2006. 228p. (gr. 1-4). 19.99 *(978-0-7636-2589-4(2))* Candlewick Pr.

—The Miraculous Journey of Edward Tulane. 2012. 22.00 *(978-1-61383-813-6(1))* Perfection Learning Corp.

—The Miraculous Journey of Edward Tulane. 2015. lib. bdg. 17.20 *(978-0-606-37892-5(8))* Turtleback Bks.

—The Miraculous Journey of Edward Tulane. Ibatoulline, Bagram, illus. 2009. 198p. (gr. 8-12). 23.30 *(978-1-4178-0763-5(6)*, Turtleback) Turtleback Bks.

Dickens, Ned. By a Thread, 1 vol. Ross, Graham, illus. 2005. (ENG.). 32p. (J). (gr. -1-3). 16.95 *(978-1-55143-325-7(7))* Orca Bk. Pubs. USA.

Disney Book Group. Doc McStuffins: Awesome Guy to the Rescue! - Bella's Big Break, 2 bks. in 1. Disney Storybook Art Team, illus. 2015. (ENG.). 48p. (J). (gr. -1-k). pap. 5.99 *(978-1-4847-0695-4(1))* Disney Pr.

—Doc McStuffins a Baby Doll for Doc. Disney Storybook Art Team, illus. 2016. (ENG.). 14p. (J). (gr. -1-k). 10.99 *(978-1-4847-4187-0(0))* Disney Pr.

—Doc Mcstuffins a Day with Doc. Disney Storybook Art Team, illus. 2016. (ENG.). 24p. (J). (gr. -1-k). 8.99 *(978-1-4847-4156-6(0))* Disney Pr.

Disney Book Group Staff. Doc Mcstuffins Dad's Favorite Toy. Disney Storybook Art Team, illus. 2015. (ENG.). 24p. (J). (gr. -1-k). pap. 4.99 *(978-1-4847-2164-3(0))* Disney Pr.

—Doc Mcstuffins Helping Hands. Disney Storybook Artists Staff & Disney Storybook Art Team, illus. 2014. (Sneak-A-Peek Ser.). (ENG.). 14p. (J). (gr. -1-k). bds. 8.99 *(978-1-4847-0766-1(4))* Disney Pr.

—Doc on Call. Disney Storybook Art Team, illus. 2015. (ENG.). 40p. (J). (gr. -1-k). 10.99 *(978-1-4847-2187-2(X))* Disney Pr.

—The Easter Egg Hunt. 2010. (Read-Along Storybook & CD Ser.). (ENG.). 32p. (J). (gr. -1-2). pap. 6.99 *(978-1-4231-2087-2(6))* Disney Pr.

—Toy Story. 2010. (Read-Along Storybook & CD Ser.). (ENG.). 32p. (J). (gr. -1 — 1). pap. 6.99 *(978-1-4231-3349-0(8))* Disney Pr.

Disney Book Group Staff & Higginson, Sheila Sweeny. Doc Mcstuffins Doctor's Helper: Purchase Includes Disney EBook! Disney Storybook Artists Staff, illus. 2014. (ENG.). 40p. (J). (gr. -1-k). 16.99 *(978-1-4231-8390-7(8))* Disney Pr.

—My Huggy Valentine. Disney Storybook Art Team, illus. 2013. (ENG.). 24p. (J). (gr. -1-k). pap. 5.99 *(978-1-4847-0425-7(8))* Disney Pr.

Disney Editors. Disney Zootopia Cinestory. 2016. (J). lib. bdg. 26.95 *(978-0-606-38728-6(5))* Turtleback Bks.

Disney Junior Staff. Disney Doc Mcstuffins: All Better! 2014. (ENG.). 32p. (J). (gr. -1-1). 17.99 *(978-0-7944-3230-0(1)*, Reader's Digest Children's Bks.) Studio Fun International.

Disney Junior Staff & Higginson, Sheila Sweeny. Disney Doc McStuffins Carryalong Play Book. Hall, Susan, illus. 2014. (CarryAlong Book Ser.). (ENG.). 14p. (J). (gr. -1-k). bds. 14.99 *(978-0-7944-3178-5(X))* Reader's Digest Assn., Inc., The.

Disney Press Editors. Dad's Favorite Toy. 2015. (Doc Mcstuffins 8X8 Ser.). (J). lib. bdg. 14.75 *(978-0-606-36898-8(1))* Turtleback Bks.

—Training Army Al. 2014. (Doc Mcstuffins 8X8 Ser.). (J). lib. bdg. 13.55 *(978-0-606-35910-8(9))* Turtleback Bks.

Disney Staff. Disney Doc Mcstuffins Happy to Be Healthy! 2014. (Dress-Up Ser.: 4). (ENG.). 24p. (J). (gr. -1-1). 11.99 *(978-0-7944-3019-1(8)*, Reader's Digest Children's Bks.) Studio Fun International.

Disney/Pixar 6. 2010. bds. 12.99 *(978-1-4231-2789-5(7))* Disney Pr.

Dixon, Bob. Holiday Bunny. 2009. 28p. pap. 13.99 *(978-1-4490-0436-1(9))* AuthorHouse.

d'Lacey, Chris. Frankin's Bear. Taylor, Thomas, illus. 2005. (Red Go Bananas Ser.). (ENG.). 48p. (J). (gr. 2-3). *(978-0-7787-2696-8(7))* Crabtree Publishing Co.

Docherty, Thomas. Wash-A-Bye Bear. Docherty, Thomas, illus. 2013. (ENG., Illus.). 32p. (J). (gr. -1-2). 14.99 *(978-0-7636-6486-2(3)*, Templar) Candlewick Pr.

Dodd, Emma & Nosy Crow Staff. Baby & Me. Dodd, Emma, illus. 2013. (ENG., Illus.). 16p. (J). (gr. -1-2). 14.99 *(978-0-7636-6544-9(4)*, Nosy Crow) Candlewick Pr.

Don, Freeman. Corduroy. 2014. (Corduroy Ser.). (ENG.). 32p. (J). (gr. k-12). 11.24 *(978-1-63245-291-7(X))* Lectorum Pubns., Inc.

Dorling Kindersley Publishing Staff. Attack of the Clones. 2013. (LEGO Star Wars DK Reader Ser.). lib. bdg. 13.55 *(978-0-606-32111-2(X)*, Turtleback) Turtleback Bks.

—Baby Peekaboo! 2011. (ENG.). 16p. (J). (gr. -1 — 1). bds. 6.99 *(978-0-7566-7165-5(5)*, DK Children) Dorling Kindersley Publishing, Inc.

—Baby What's That? 2015. (ENG.). 14p. (J). (gr. -1 — 1). bds. 5.99 *(978-1-4654-3181-3(0)*, DK Children) Dorling Kindersley Publishing, Inc.

—Batman's Missions. 2015. (DK Readers Ser.). (ENG.). 64p. (J). (gr. 2-4). pap. 3.99 *(978-1-4654-3014-4(8)*, DK Children) Dorling Kindersley Publishing, Inc.

—Lego Friends: The Adventure Guide. 2015. (ENG., Illus.). 96p. (J). (gr. k-4). 16.99 *(978-1-4654-3549-1(2)*, DK Children) Dorling Kindersley Publishing, Inc.

—Pop-Up Peekaboo! - Playtime. 2011. (ENG.). 12p. (J). (gr. -1 — 1). bds. 9.99 *(978-0-7566-7171-6(X)*, DK Children) Dorling Kindersley Publishing, Inc.

—Revenge of the Sith. 2013. (LEGO Star Wars DK Reader Ser.). lib. bdg. 13.55 *(978-0-606-32112-9(8)*, Turtleback) Turtleback Bks.

—Secret Ninja Force. 2017. (DK Readers Ser.). (ENG.). 48p. (J). (gr. k-2). pap. 3.99 ***(978-1-4654-6195-7(7)***, DK Children) Dorling Kindersley Publishing, Inc.

—Shark Attack! 2017. (DK Readers Ser.). (ENG.). 24p. (J). (-k). pap. 3.99 ***(978-1-4654-6193-3(0)***, DK Children) Dorling Kindersley Publishing, Inc.

Dorling Kindersley Publishing Staff & Taylor, Victoria. Ready for Action! 2013. (DK Readers Ser.). (ENG., Illus.). 32p. (J). (gr. k-4). pap. 3.99 *(978-1-4654-0174-8(1)*, DK Children) Dorling Kindersley Publishing, Inc.

Drake, R. C. Let's Find a Toy for Moo Moo the Mutdog. 2011. 24p. pap. 24.95 *(978-1-4560-0881-9(1))* America Star Bks.

Drinnon, Sheila. Cuddles. 2008. 24p. pap. 24.95 *(978-1-60474-857-4(5))* America Star Bks.

Driscoll, Laura. A Mousy Mess. Melmon, Deborah, illus. 2014. (Mouse Math (r) Ser.). 32p. (J). (gr. -1-1). 22.60 *(978-1-57565-646-5(9))* Kane Press, Inc.

—Real Heroes Don't Wear Capes. 2008. pap. 34.95 *(978-1-58013-764-5(4))* Kane Press, Inc.

Dumesnil, Phil & Sanchez, Asa. The Woollyhoodwinks: Vs. the Dark Patch. Root, Jeff & Runcorn, Scott, illus. 2008. (ENG.). 36p. (J). (gr. -1-3). 15.95 *(978-1-59702-012-1(5))* Immedium.

Dunrea, Olivier. Gideon & Otto. 2012. (Gossie & Friends Ser.). (ENG., Illus.). 32p. (J). (gr. k — 1). 9.99 *(978-0-618-43662-0(6))* Houghton Mifflin Harcourt Publishing Co.

—Gideon & Otto: Best Friends, Lost & Found. 2013. (Gossie & Friends Ser.). (ENG., Illus.). 32p. (J). (— 1). bds. 6.99 *(978-0-547-98398-1(0))* Houghton Mifflin Harcourt Publishing Co.

Easton, Marilyn. New Girl in Town. 2013. (ENG., Illus.). 64p. (J). (gr. 2-5). pap. 4.99 *(978-0-545-54762-8(8))* Math Solutions.

—New Girl in Town. 2013. (LEGO Friends Chapter Bks.: 1). lib. bdg. 14.75 *(978-0-606-31548-7(9)*, Turtleback) Turtleback Bks.

Elizabeth, Julie & Elizabeth, Annelise. Take Care of Our Friend, Baby Dog. 2012. 24p. pap. 13.95 *(978-1-61493-115-7(1))* Peppertree Pr., The.

Emma Treehouse Ltd. My Toys. Davis, Caroline, illus. 2007. (Easy Flaps Ser.). 10p. (J). (gr. -1). bds. 6.95 *(978-1-58925-825-9(8))* Tiger Tales.

Engler, Michael. Elephantastic! Tourlonias, Joëlle, illus. 2014. (ENG.). 32p. (J). 16.99 *(978-1-4413-0841-2(5)*, 9781441308412) Peter Pauper Pr. Inc.

Eshed, Tina. The Adventures of Bunzy: The Beginning. 2009. 60p. pap. 24.49 *(978-1-4389-2673-5(1))* AuthorHouse.

Everett, Clare. Henrietta - a Rabbit's Tale of Summer Time Fun. 2012. 116p. pap. *(978-1-84914-296-0(3))* CompletelyNovel.com.

Fagan, Cary. Thing-Thing. Debon, Nicolas, illus. 2008. (ENG.). 32p. (J). (gr. -1-1). 18.95 *(978-0-88776-839-2(3)*, Tundra Bks.) Tundra Bks. CAN. Dist: Penguin Random Hse. LLC.

Falconer, Ian. Olivia... & the Missing Toy. Falconer, Ian, illus. 2003. (ENG., Illus.). 42p. (J). (gr. -1-3). 18.99 *(978-0-689-85291-6(6)*, Atheneum Bks. for Young Readers) Simon & Schuster Children's Publishing.

—Olivia y el Juguete Desaparecido. Mlawer, Teresa, tr. from ENG. Falconer, Ian, illus. 2004. (Olivia Ser.).Tr. of Olivia & the Missing Toy. (SPA., Illus.). 30p. (J). 16.95 *(978-1-930332-71-3(8))* Lectorum Pubns., Inc.

Farshtey, Greg. The Doom Box. 2012. (LEGO Hero Factory Ser.: 1). lib. bdg. 16.00 *(978-0-606-26768-7(9)*, Turtleback) Turtleback Bks.

—Fire & Ice. 2014. (LEGO Legends of Chima Chapter Bks.: 6). lib. bdg. 14.75 *(978-0-606-36069-2(7))* Turtleback Bks.

—Handbook. 2015. (LEGO DC Super Heroes Ser.). (ENG.). 144p. (J). (gr. -1-3). pap. 9.99 *(978-0-545-86800-6(9))* Scholastic, Inc.

—Lego DC Super Heroes. 2013. (LEGO DC Super Heroes Ser.). lib. bdg. 19.65 *(978-0-606-32019-1(9),* Turtleback) Turtleback Bks.
—Mirror World. 2013. (LEGO Hero Factory Ser.: 5). lib. bdg. 16.00 *(978-0-606-32020-7(2),* Turtleback) Turtleback Bks.
Farshtey, Greg, et al. Night of the Nindroids. 2014. (Illus.). 63p. (J). *(978-1-4844-1967-0(7))* Papercutz.
Feldman, Jody. The Gollywhopper Games. Jamieson, Victoria, illus. 2008. (Gollywhopper Games Ser.: 1). (ENG.). 320p. (J). (gr. 3-7). 16.99 *(978-0-06-121450-9(7),* Greenwillow Bks.) HarperCollins Pubs.
Fellers, Tina. Toby & the Alien: In the Adventures of the Unusual Toys, 1 vol. Fellers, Cody, illus. 2009. 28p. pap. 24.95 *(978-1-60672-195-7(X))* America Star Bks.
Fentiman, David. The Lego Movie. 2013. (DK Reader Level 3 Ser.). lib. bdg. 13.55 *(978-0-606-35322-9(4))* Turtleback Bks.
Fieber, Valerie. Three Caterpillars & a Lost Toy. 2012. 24p. pap. 14.93 *(978-1-4669-5573-8(2))* Trafford Publishing.
Field, Elaine. Toys (Cuddly Cuffs W/Hang Tag) Finn, Rebecca, illus. (Cuddly Cuffs Ser.). 12p. (J). tchr. ed. 5.95 *(978-1-58925-709-2(X))* Tiger Tales.
Fine, Anne. Jamie & Angus Together. Dale, Penny, illus. 2007. (ENG.). 112p. (J). (gr. -1-1). 15.99 *(978-0-7636-3374-5(7))* Candlewick Pr.
Finnegan, Evelyn M. My Little Friend Goes to a Baseball Game. Houghton, Diane R., illus. 2006. 32p. (J). (gr. -1-3). reprint ed. pap. 7.00 *(978-1-4223-5403-2(2))* DIANE Publishing Co.
Fitzgerald, Caroline. Animal Kingdom Goes to New York. 2011. 48p. pap. 18.46 *(978-1-4520-9966-8(9))* AuthorHouse.
Fleischman, Paul. Whirligig. 2010. (ENG.). 144p. (YA). (gr. 7-12). pap. 7.99 *(978-0-312-62911-3(7),* 9780312629113) Square Fish.
Flory, Jane & dePaola, Tomie. The Too Little Fire Engine. Flory, Jane, illus. 2015. (G&d Vintage Ser.). (ENG., Illus.). 24p. (J). (gr. -1-k). bds. 7.99 *(978-0-448-48217-0(7),* Grosset & Dunlap) Penguin Young Readers Group.
Fontes, Justine. Toy Trouble. Hefferan, Rob, illus. 2003. 24p. (J). pap. *(978-1-59034-447-7(2));* 14.95 *(978-1-59034-446-0(4))* Mondo Publishing.
Foreman, Michael. Scraps. (Illus.). 32p. (J). pap. 8.99 *(978-1-84270-003-7(0))* Andersen Pr. GBR. Dist: Trafalgar Square Publishing.
Fox, Mem. Tell Me about Your Day Today. Stringer, Lauren, illus. 2012. (ENG.). 40p. (J). (gr. -1-3). 17.99 *(978-1-4169-9006-2(2),* Beach Lane Bks.) Beach Lane Bks.
Freedman, Claire. Night-Night, Emily! Massey, Jane, illus. 2005. 32p. (J). 6.95 *(978-1-58925-390-2(6))* Tiger Tales.
—Night-Night, Emily! Massey, Jane, tr. Massey, Jane, illus. 2003. 32p. (J). (gr. -1-1). tchr. ed. 15.95 *(978-1-58925-032-1(X))* Tiger Tales.
Freeman, Don. Corduroy. 2011. (Corduroy Ser.). (ENG.). 28p. (J). (gr. -1 — 1). bds. 11.99 *(978-0-670-01311-1(0),* Viking Books for Young Readers) Penguin Young Readers Group.
—Corduroy Book & Bear. 2008. (Corduroy Ser.). (ENG.). 32p. (J). (gr. -1-k). 17.99 *(978-0-670-06342-0(8),* Viking Books for Young Readers) Penguin Young Readers Group.
—A Pocket for Corduroy, 1 vol. 2008. (Corduroy Ser.). (ENG., Illus.). 32p. (J). (gr. -1-k). 10.99 *(978-0-14-241040-0(3),* Puffin Books) Penguin Young Readers Group.
—A Pocket for Corduroy. 2015. (Corduroy Ser.). (ENG.). 32p. (J). (— 1). bds. 7.99 *(978-0-451-47113-0(X),* Viking Books for Young Readers) Penguin Young Readers Group.
Gall, Chris. Awesome Dawson. 2013. (ENG., Illus.). 40p. (J). (gr. -1-3). 17.99 *(978-0-316-21330-1(6))* Little, Brown Bks. for Young Readers.
Garza, Xavier, illus. The Great & Mighty Nikko. 2015. (ENG.). 32p. (J). pap. 7.95 *(978-1-935955-83-2(7));* (gr. -1-4). 16.95 *(978-1-935955-82-5(9))* Cinco Puntos Pr.
Gorbachev, Valeri. Doctor Nice. (ENG.). 32p. (J). (gr. -1-3). 2016. 6.99 *(978-0-8234-3690-3(X))* 2015. (Illus.). 16.95 *(978-0-8234-3203-5(3))* Holiday Hse., Inc.
Goss, Matt. Bear Crimbo. 2010. (ENG., Illus.). 72p. (J). 17.95 *(978-0-9815381-3-6(4))* Hilton Publishing Co.
Gould, Lorraine. Warren the Watchdog. 2010. 48p. pap. 19.49 *(978-1-4490-6845-5(6))* AuthorHouse.
Grange, Emma. Empire Strikes Back. 2014. (DK Readers Ser.). (ENG.). 32p. (J). (gr. 1-3). 14.99 *(978-1-4654-2028-2(2),* DK Children) Dorling Kindersley Publishing, Inc.
—The Empire Strikes Back. 2014. (LEGO Star Wars DK Reader Ser.). lib. bdg. 13.55 *(978-0-606-35734-0(3))* Turtleback Bks.
—Lego Star Wars: The Return of the Jedi. 2014. (LEGO Star Wars DK Reader Ser.). lib. bdg. 13.55 *(978-0-606-35735-7(1))* Turtleback Bks.
—A New Hope. 2014. (DK Readers Ser.). (ENG.). 32p. (J). (gr. k-4). 14.99 *(978-1-4654-2026-8(6),* DK Children) Dorling Kindersley Publishing, Inc.
—A New Hope. 2014. (LEGO Star Wars DK Reader Ser.). lib. bdg. 13.55 *(978-0-606-35733-3(5))* Turtleback Bks.
Graves, Annie. The Wolfling's Bite. McElhinney, Glenn, illus. 2015. (Nightmare Club Ser.: 6). (ENG.). 64p. (J). (gr. 2-5). pap. 6.99 *(978-1-4677-6048-5(X),* Darby Creek); lib. bdg. 25.32 *(978-1-4677-4353-2(4))* Lerner Publishing Group.
Gravett, Emily. Monkey & Me. Gravett, Emily, illus. 2008. (ENG., Illus.). 32p. (J). (gr. -1-3). 17.99 *(978-1-4169-5457-6(0),* Simon & Schuster Bks. For Young Readers) Simon & Schuster Bks. For Young Readers.
Greene, Stephanie. Princess Posey & the Tiny Treasure. Sisson, Stéphanie Roth, illus. 2013. (Princess Posey, First Grader Ser.: 5). (ENG.). 96p. (J). (gr. k-3). pap. 5.99 *(978-0-14-242415-5(3),* Puffin Books) Penguin Young Readers Group.
Grey, Mini. Toys in Space. 2013. (ENG.). 32p. (J). (gr. k-3). 16.99 *(978-0-307-97812-7(5),* Knopf Bks. for Young Readers) Random Hse. Children's Bks.
—Traction Man & the Beach Odyssey. 2012. (ENG., Illus.). 32p. (J). (gr. k-3). 16.99 *(978-0-375-86952-5(2),* Knopf Bks. for Young Readers) Random Hse. Children's Bks.
—Traction Man Is Here! 2012. (ENG.). 32p. (J). (gr. -1-3). pap. 7.99 *(978-0-307-93111-5(0),* Dragonfly Bks.) Random Hse. Children's Bks.
Gurewitz, Samantha & Polay, Ellyn. Marvin Mcgunk & All of His Junk. 2012. (ENG.). 27p. (J). pap. 12.95 *(978-1-4327-9705-8(0))* Outskirts Pr., Inc.
H & T Imaginations Unlimited, Inc. Toy Trains with Professor Woodpecker. 2009. 12p. pap. 8.49 *(978-1-4389-5927-6(3))* AuthorHouse.
Hall, Tamony. The Rick Brick & the Quest to Save Brickport. 2015. (ENG.). 112p. (J). (gr. 1). pap. 7.99 *(978-1-63450-149-1(7),* Sky Pony Pr.) Skyhorse Publishing Co., Inc.
Hancock, Chris. Starting Playschool- Mini-Pals Go, Too. 2013. 28p. pap. 16.09 *(978-1-4669-7906-2(2))* Trafford Publishing.
Hansen, Sue. Little Bitty Bella in a Big, Big World. 2012. 24p. pap. 10.99 *(978-1-4624-0272-4(0),* Inspiring Voices) Author Solutions, Inc.
Harper, Benjamin. Hot Wheels: To the Extreme. Wisinski, Ed & White, Dave, illus. 2007. (Scholastic Reader Ser.). 30p. (J). pap. *(978-0-545-02019-0(0))* Scholastic, Inc.
Harris, Robie H. Turtle & Me. Freeman, Tor, illus. 2015. (ENG.). 40p. (J). (gr. -1-3). 16.99 *(978-1-4998-0046-3(0))* Little Bee Books Inc.
Hatton, Libby. Pete Puffin's Wild Ride Cruising Alaska's Currents. Hatton, Libby, illus. 2008. (Illus.). (J). pap. 16.95 *(978-0-930931-92-6(0))* Alaska Geographic Assn.
Havill, Juanita. Jamaica's Find. O'Brien, Anne Sibley, illus. 2009. (ENG.). 32p. (J). (gr. -1-3). audio compact disk 10.99 *(978-0-547-11961-8(5))* Houghton Mifflin Harcourt Publishing Co.
Hawksley, Gerald. Good Puppy. Stanley, Mandy, illus. 2005. (J). *(978-1-890647-14-8(4))* TOMY International, Inc.
Heap, Sue. Mine! Heap, Sue, illus. 2014. (ENG., Illus.). 32p. (J). (-k). 15.99 *(978-0-7636-6888-4(5))* Candlewick Pr.
Helmore, Jim & Wall, Karen. Stripy Horse - Off We Go! 2014. (Stripy Horse Ser.). (ENG., Illus.). 12p. (J). (gr. -1-k). bds. 7.99 *(978-1-4052-5746-6(6))* Egmont Bks., Ltd. GBR. Dist: Independent Pubs. Group.
Henkes, Kevin. Waiting. Henkes, Kevin, illus. 2015. (Illus.). 32p. (J). (gr. -1-3). (ENG.). 17.99 *(978-0-06-236843-0(5),* Collins Design); lib. bdg. 18.89 *(978-0-06-236844-7(3),* Greenwillow Bks.) HarperCollins Pubs.
Hennessy, B. G. Claire & the Unicorn Happy Ever After. Mitchell, Susan, illus. 2006. (ENG.). 32p. (J). (gr. -1-3). 17.99 *(978-1-4169-0815-9(3),* Simon & Schuster Bks. For Young Readers) Simon & Schuster Bks. For Young Readers.
Hester, Beth Landis. Ninjago: Secret World of the Ninja. 2015. (ENG.). 96p. (J). (gr. 2-5). 16.99 *(978-1-4654-2137-1(8),* DK Children) Dorling Kindersley Publishing, Inc.
Hester, Beth Landis & Dorling Kindersley Publishing Staff. Secret World of the Ninja. 2015. (ENG., Illus.). 96p. (J). (gr. 2-5). 16.99 *(978-1-4654-2078-7(9),* DK Children) Dorling Kindersley Publishing, Inc.
Hicer, Nancy. The Missing Block. 2015. (Rosen REAL Readers: STEM & STEAM Collection). (ENG.). 8p. pap. 5.46 *(978-1-4994-9554-6(4),* Rosen Classroom) Rosen Publishing Group, Inc., The.
Higgins, Jim. The Enchanted Nursery: Nessie's Friends. 2008. 24p. pap. 11.49 *(978-1-4343-8993-0(6))* AuthorHouse.
Higginson, Sheila Sweeny. Chilly Catches a Cold. 2013. (Doc Mcstuffins 8X8 Ser.). (J). lib. bdg. 13.55 *(978-0-606-35109-6(4),* Turtleback) Turtleback Bks.
—Jingle Bell Doc. Disney Book Group Staff et al, illus. 2013. (ENG.). 12p. (J). (gr. -1-k). bds. 6.99 *(978-1-4231-8386-0(X))* Disney Pr.
—Leilani's Luau. Disney Storybook Artists Staff, illus. 2014. (ENG.). 32p. (J). (gr. -1-k). pap. 4.99 *(978-1-4231-9417-0(9))* Disney Pr.
—A Very McStuffins Christmas. 2014. (Doc Mcstuffins 8X8 Ser.). (J). lib. bdg. 16.00 *(978-0-606-35908-5(7))* Turtleback Bks.
Higginson, Sheila Sweeny & Disney Book Group Staff. Brontosaurus Breath. Disney Storybook Art Team, illus. 2013. (World of Reading Ser.). (ENG.). 32p. (J). (gr. -1-k). pap. 3.99 *(978-1-4231-6894-2(1))* Disney Pr.
—Loud Louie. Disney Storybook Artists Staff, illus. 2013. (World of Reading Ser.). (ENG.). 32p. (J). (gr. -1-k). pap. 3.99 *(978-1-4231-6456-2(3))* Disney Pr.
—The Mermaid Dives In. Disney Storybook Art Team, illus. 2013. (ENG.). 24p. (J). (gr. -1-k). pap. 4.99 *(978-1-4231-7132-4(2))* Disney Pr.
Higginson, Sheila Sweeny, et al. Chilly Catches a Cold. 2013. (Illus.). 24p. (J). *(978-1-4844-1108-7(0))* Disney Pr.
Hill, Eric. Buenas Noches Spot. (SPA.). pap. 4.95 *(978-950-07-1964-3(9))* Editorial Sudamericana S.A. ARG. Dist: Distribooks, Inc.
—A Jugar Con Spot. (SPA.). pap. 4.95 *(978-950-07-1961-2(4))* Editorial Sudamericana S.A. ARG. Dist: Distribooks, Inc.
—Spot's Favorite Things. Hill, Eric, illus. 2012. (Spot Ser.). (ENG., Illus.). 12p. (J). (gr. -1 — 1). bds. 8.99 *(978-0-399-25758-2(6),* Warne) Penguin Young Readers Group.
Hillert, Margaret. The Birthday Car. Girouard, Patrick, illus. 2016. (BeginningtoRead Ser.). (ENG.). 32p. (J). (gr. k-2). 22.60 *(978-1-59953-795-5(8))* Norwood Hse. Pr.
—The Purple Pussycat. Cosgrove, Kate, illus. 2016. (BeginningtoRead Ser.). (ENG.). 32p. (J). (gr. -1-2). pap. 11.94 *(978-1-60357-944-5(3));* 21st ed. (gr. k-2). 22.60 *(978-1-59953-803-7(2))* Norwood Hse. Pr.
—The Yellow Boat. Baird, Roberta, illus. 2016. (BeginningtoRead Ser.). (ENG.). 32p. (J). (gr. -1-2). 22.60 *(978-1-59953-811-2(3))* Norwood Hse. Pr.
Hinbest, Wendy. Frizzy Tizzy Cleans Up. 2011. 20p. pap. 11.95 *(978-1-4583-5828-8(3))* Lulu Pr., Inc.
Hissey, Jane. Old Bear. 2013. (ENG., Illus.). 36p. (J). (gr. -1-1). 17.95 *(978-1-77049-481-7(2),* Tundra Bks.) Tundra Bks. CAN. Dist: Penguin Random Hse. LLC.
Holechek, Max. Edsel Mcfarlan's New Car. Toland, Darrell, illus. 2010. 52p. (J). *(978-1-935359-40-1(1))* Book Pubs. Network.
Holmes, Anna. Wyldstyle: The Search for the Special. 2014. lib. bdg. 13.55 *(978-0-606-36366-2(1))* Turtleback Bks.
Holmes, Janet A. Have You Seen Duck? Bentley, Jonathan, illus. 2011. (ENG.). 24p. (J). (gr. -1-3). 8.99 *(978-0-545-22488-8(8),* Cartwheel Bks.) Scholastic, Inc.
Holst, Jerome Alphonse. Gretchen & the Gremlins. Krajenbrink Hulin, Yvonne, illus. 2012. 48p. pap. 15.95 *(978-0-9794133-5-3(4))* TV Acres Bks.
Hood, Sue. Monkey Business. Chapman, Susan, illus. 2005. (J). bds. *(978-1-890647-17-9(9))* TOMY International, Inc.
Hope, Laura. The Story of a Plush Bear. 2005. pap. 9.95 *(978-1-55742-463-1(2))* Wildside Pr., LLC.
Hope, Laura Lee. The Story of a Nodding Donkey. rev. ed. 2006. 108p. 25.95 *(978-1-4218-1794-1(2));* pap. 10.95 *(978-1-4218-1894-8(9))* 1st World Publishing, Inc. (1st World Library - Literary Society).
Hopper, Bobby E. Bleep the Purple Bear. Hopper, Andy Lee, illus. 2009. 36p. pap. 18.99 *(978-1-4389-1908-9(5))* AuthorHouse.
Horse, Harry. Little Rabbit Goes to School. Horse, Harry, illus. (Little Rabbit Ser.). (Illus.). 32p. (J). 2011. (gr. -1-1). pap. 7.95 *(978-1-56145-574-4(1))* 2004. (ENG., (gr. k-1). 15.95 *(978-1-56145-320-7(X))* Peachtree Pubs.
Howard, Kate. The Lego Movie. movie tie-in ed. 2013. (ENG.). 144p. (J). (gr. 2-5). pap. 5.99 *(978-0-545-62464-0(9))* Scholastic, Inc.
—Ninja vs. Ninja. 2015. (Lego Ninjago Ser.: 12). (ENG., Illus.). 32p. (J). (gr. 1-3). pap. 3.99 *(978-0-545-82552-8(0))* Scholastic, Inc.
—The Rescue Mission. 2015. (Lego Ninjago Ser.: 11). (ENG., Illus.). 32p. (J). (gr. -1-3). pap. 3.99 *(978-0-545-74639-7(6))* Scholastic, Inc.
—The Search for Zane. 2015. (Lego Ninjago Ser.: 7). (ENG.). 80p. (J). (gr. 2-5). pap. 4.99 *(978-0-545-75054-7(7))* Scholastic, Inc.
—Techno Strike! 2014. (Ninjago Readers Ser.: 9). lib. bdg. 13.55 *(978-0-606-35860-6(9))* Turtleback Bks.
Howard, Kate, adapted by. Spy vs. Spy. 2015. (Illus.). 32p. (J). *(978-1-4806-9048-6(1))* Scholastic, Inc.
Howe, James. It Came from Beneath the Bed! 2004. (Tales from the House of Bunnicula Ser.). 112p. (J). (gr. 3-6). pap. 17.00 incl. audio *(978-1-4000-8632-0(9),* Listening Library) Random Hse. Audio Publishing Group.
Hughes, Shirley. Bobbo Goes to School. Hughes, Shirley, illus. 2013. (ENG., Illus.). 32p. (J). (gr. -1-2). 16.99 *(978-0-7636-6524-1(X))* Candlewick Pr.
—Dogger. Hughes, Shirley, illus. ltd. ed. 2010. (ENG., Illus.). 32p. (J). (gr. k-k). pap. 12.99 *(978-1-86230-805-3(5),* Red Fox) Random House Children's Books GBR. Dist: Independent Pubs. Group.
—Jonadab & Rita. Hughes, Shirley, illus. 2010. (Alfie Ser.). (ENG., Illus.). 32p. (J). (gr. -1-k). pap. 11.99 *(978-1-86230-313-3(4),* Red Fox) Random House Children's Books GBR. Dist: Independent Pubs. Group.
Hunter, Sally. Humphrey's Playtime. 2013. (Illus.). (J). *(978-1-4351-4766-9(9))* Barnes & Noble, Inc.
Hunter, Todd H. Elf Night: A Christmas Story. Gavrilovskiy, Olga, illus. 2006. 52p. (J). (gr. -1-7). 16.95 *(978-0-9788085-0-1(9))* Tetoca Pr.
Huxman, K. D. Dragon Talk. 2007. (Illus.). 24p. (J). per. 11.99 *(978-0-9797574-9-5(5))* Dragonfly Publishing, Inc.
—Dragon Talk. Farrington, Teresa, illus. l.t. ed. 2006. 24p. (J). pap. 14.99 *(978-0-9765786-7-3(0))* Dragonfly Publishing, Inc.
Huxman, Karin (K. D.). Dragon Talk. 2006. (Illus.). 24p. (J). lib. bdg. 24.95 *(978-0-9778651-7-8(7))* Dragonfly Publishing, Inc.
I Can Say- Toys. 2005. (J). bds. *(978-1-4194-0033-9(9))* Paradise Pr., Inc.
The Indian in the Cupboard. 2004. (J). *(978-1-59564-280-6(3))* Steps To Literacy, LLC.
Inkpen, Mick. Kipper's Toybox. (Illus.). 25p. (J). (CHI, ENG, URD, VIE & FRE.). *(978-1-85430-350-9(3),* 93452); (ENG, FRE, URD, VIE & CHI., *(978-1-85430-351-6(1),* 93453) Little Tiger Pr. Group.
Inkpen, Mick & Butterworth, Nick. Just Like Jasper! 2008. (ENG., Illus.). 32p. (J). (gr. -1-k). pap. 9.99 *(978-0-340-94510-0(9))* Hodder & Stoughton GBR. Dist: Hachette Bk. Group.
Jay, Alison. Alice's Adventures in Wonderland Board Book. 2015. (ENG.). 22p. (J). (— 1). bds. 6.99 *(978-0-525-42979-1(4),* Dial Bks) Penguin Young Readers Group.
Jeffers, Susan. The Nutcracker. Jeffers, Susan, illus. 2007. (Illus.). 40p. (J). (gr. -1-3). 17.89 *(978-0-06-074387-1(5));* (ENG., 17.99 *(978-0-06-074386-4(7))* HarperCollins Pubs.
Jenkins, Emily. Toy Dance Party. Zelinsky, Paul O., illus. 2010. (Toys Go Out Ser.). (ENG.). 176p. (J). (gr. 1-4). 6.99 *(978-0-375-85525-2(4),* Yearling) Random Hse. Children's Bks.
—Toy Dance Party: Being the Further Adventures of a Bossyboots Stingray, a Courageous Buffalo, & a Hopeful Round Someone Called Plastic. Zelinsky, Paul O., illus. 2008. (Toys Go Out Ser.). (ENG.). 176p. (J). (gr. 1-4). 16.99 *(978-0-375-83935-1(6),* Schwartz & Wade Bks.) Random Hse. Children's Bks.
—Toys Come Home: Being the Early Experiences of an Intelligent Stingray, a Brave Buffalo, & a Brand-New Someone Called Plastic. Zelinsky, Paul O., illus. 2011. (Toys Go Out Ser.). (ENG.). 144p. (J). (gr. 1-4). 16.99 *(978-0-375-86200-7(5),* Schwartz & Wade Bks.) Random Hse. Children's Bks.
—Toys Go Out: Being the Adventures of a Knowledgeable Stingray, a Toughy Little Buffalo, & Someone Called Plastic. Zelinsky, Paul O., illus. (Toys Go Out Ser.). (ENG.). (J). (gr. 1-4). 2008. 144p. 6.99 *(978-0-385-73661-9(4),* Yearling) 2006. 128p. 16.95 *(978-0-375-83604-6(7),* Schwartz & Wade Bks.) Random Hse. Children's Bks.
—Toys Meet Snow. Zelinsky, Paul O., illus. 2015. (ENG.). 40p. (J). (gr. -1-2). 17.99 *(978-0-385-37330-2(9),* Schwartz & Wade Bks.) Random Hse. Children's Bks.
Jennings, Linda. Duna y Dan. Chapman, Jane, illus. (SPA.). 28p. (J). (gr. k-1). *(978-84-8418-027-2(1),* ZZ4481) Zendrera Zariquiey, Editorial ESP. Dist: Lectorum Pubns., Inc.
Jesset, Aurore. Loopy. Jesset, Aurore & Korthues, Barbara, illus. 2009. (ENG.). 32p. (J). (gr. -1-3). 7.95 *(978-0-7358-2261-0(1))* North-South Bks., Inc.
Jordan, Apple. The Bunny Surprise. 2012. (Step into Reading Level 1 Ser.). lib. bdg. 13.55 *(978-0-606-23723-9(2),* Turtleback) Turtleback Bks.
—A Spooky Adventure (Disney/Pixar Toy Story) Random House Disney Staff, illus. 2011. (Step into Reading Ser.). (ENG.). 32p. (J). (gr. k-3). pap. 3.99 *(978-0-7364-2777-7(5),* RH/Disney) Random Hse. Children's Bks.
Joyce, William. Ollie's Odyssey. Joyce, William, illus. 2017. (ENG., Illus.). 304p. (J). (gr. 2-6). pap. 9.99 *(978-1-4424-7356-0(8))* Simon & Schuster, Inc.
Kamon, Playtoon & the Antpod. Krit, Joey, illus. 2012. 28p. pap. 24.95 *(978-1-4626-7346-9(5))* PublishAmerica, Inc.
Kao, Sleepless. Monchan's Bag. 2010. (ENG., Illus.). 36p. (J). (gr. -1-3). 16.95 *(978-1-897476-32-1(9))* Simply Read Bks. CAN. Dist: Ingram Publisher Services.
Katschke, Judy. Karate Kangaroos (Disney Junior: Doc Mcstuffins) Random House Disney Staff & Martinez, Heather, illus. 2016. (Little Golden Book Ser.). (ENG.). 24p. (J). (gr. -1-k). 4.99 *(978-0-7364-3382-2(1),* Golden/Disney) Random Hse. Children's Bks.
Kehoe, Tim. The Unusual Mind of Vincent Shadow. Francis, Guy & Wohnoutka, Mike, illus. 2009. (Vincent Shadow Ser.: 1). (ENG.). 192p. (J). (gr. 3-7). 9.99 *(978-0-316-05665-6(0))* Little, Brown Bks. for Young Readers.
—Vincent Shadow: Toy Inventor. Francis, Guy & Wohnoutka, Mike, illus. 2011. (Vincent Shadow Ser.: 1). (ENG.). 224p. (J). (gr. 3-7). pap. 6.99 *(978-0-316-05666-3(9))* Little, Brown Bks. for Young Readers.
Kelly, Katherine, text. Albert Bear & the Big Celebration. 2005. (J). 12.95 *(978-0-9773481-0-7(5))* Kelly, Katherine.
Kelly, Mij. Lion's Lullaby. Clifton-Brown, Holly, illus. 2016. (ENG.). 32p. (J). (gr. -1 — 1). 16.99 *(978-1-4847-2526-9(3))* Disney Pr.
Kelman, Marcy. Doc Mcstuffins Doc's Mobile Clinic. Disney Storybook Artists Staff, illus. 2014. (ENG.). 12p. (J). (gr. -1-k). bds. 7.99 *(978-1-4231-9420-0(9))* Disney Pr.
Kelman, Marcy & Disney Book Group Staff. Out of the Box. Disney Storybook Art Team, illus. 2014. (Flap 'n Tab Ser.). (ENG.). 10p. (J). (gr. -1-k). bds. 6.99 *(978-1-4231-8092-0(5))* Disney Pr.
Kenah, Katharine. Scholastic Reader Level 1: the Saturday Triplets #3: Teacher Trouble! Lyon, Tammie, illus. 2013. (Scholastic Reader Level 1 Ser.). (ENG.). 32p. (J). (gr. -1-2). pap. 3.99 *(978-0-545-48145-8(7))* Scholastic, Inc.
Kiernan, Kenny, illus. Save the Day! 2013. (J). *(978-1-4844-0146-0(8))* Scholastic, Inc.
Kilgore, Mary & Kilgore, Mitchell. Where Is My Mommy? Coping When a Parent Leaves (and Doesn't Come Back) Pillo, Cary, illus. 2010. (ENG.). 32p. (J). (gr. -1-4). pap. 12.95 *(978-1-884734-46-5(4))* Parenting Pr., Inc.
Kim, YeShil. We Are Proud of You. The Pope Twins, illus. rev. ed. 2014. (MySELF Bookshelf Ser.). (ENG.). 32p. (J). (gr. k-2). pap. 11.94 *(978-1-60357-651-2(7));* lib. bdg. 25.27 *(978-1-59953-642-2(0))* Norwood Hse. Pr.
King-Cargile, Gillian. The Toy & the Twister. Krull, Kevin, illus. 2015. (Stuffed Bunny Science Adventure Ser.). (ENG.). 36p. (J). (gr. k-3). 18.99 *(978-0-87580-496-5(9))* Northern Illinois Univ. Pr.
King, Trey. Detective Chase McCain- Save That Cargo! Primeau, Chuck, illus. 2013. (Lego City Ser.). (ENG.). 24p. (J). (gr. -1-3). 3.99 *(978-0-545-51573-3(4))* Scholastic, Inc.
—Friends & Foes! Wang, Sean, illus. 2015. (LEGO DC Super Heroes Ser.: 1). (ENG.). 24p. (J). (gr. -1-3). pap. 3.99 *(978-0-545-78504-4(9))* Scholastic, Inc.
—The Legend Begins. 2013. (LEGO Legends of Chima: Comic Reader Ser.: 1). lib. bdg. 13.55 *(978-0-606-32012-2(1),* Turtleback) Turtleback Bks.
—Mystery on the LEGO Express. Wang, Sean, illus. 2014. 24p. (J). *(978-1-4242-6168-0(6))* Scholastic, Inc.
—Mystery on the Lego Express. 2014. (LEGO City 8X8 Ser.). (Illus.). 24p. (J). lib. bdg. 13.55 *(978-0-606-36068-5(9))* Turtleback Bks.
—Sidekick Showdown! Wang, Sean, illus. 2016. (LEGO DC Super Heroes Ser.). (ENG.). 24p. (J). (gr. -1-3). pap. 3.99 *(978-1-338-04742-4(6))* Scholastic, Inc.
King, Trey & Kiernan, Kenny. Cops, Crocs, & Crooks! 2015. (LEGO City 8X8 Ser.). lib. bdg. 13.55 *(978-0-606-36360-0(2))* Turtleback Bks.
Kinra, Richa, illus. The Princess Panda Tea Party: A Cerebral Palsy Fairy Tale. 2014. 45p. (J). pap. 14.95 *(978-1-61599-219-5(7))* Loving Healing Pr., Inc.
Kirk, Daniel. You Are Not My Friend, but I Miss You. 2014. (ENG., Illus.). 32p. (J). (gr. k-2). 16.95 *(978-1-4197-1236-4(5),* Abrams Bks. for Young Readers) Abrams, Inc.
Kirkland, Kim M. Car Cars Go Zoom Zoom Zoom. 2012. 24p. pap. 24.95 *(978-1-4626-6926-4(3))* America Star Bks.
Kleinberg, Naomi. Naptime/Cuddlies (Sesame Street) Moroney, Christopher, illus. 2017. (ENG.). 24p. (J). (— 1). bds. 8.99 ***(978-1-5247-1636-3(7),*** Random Hse. Bks. for Young Readers) Random Hse. Children's Bks.
Korda, Lerryn. It's Vacation Time. Korda, Lerryn, illus. 2010. (Playtime with Little Nye Ser.). (ENG., Illus.). 26p. (J). (— 1). 8.99 *(978-0-7636-4813-8(2))* Candlewick Pr.
Korngold, Jamie. Sadie, Ori, & Nuggles Go to Camp. Fortenberry, Julie, illus. 2014. (ENG.). 24p. (J). (gr. -1-1). 17.95 *(978-1-4677-0424-3(5),* Kar-Ben Publishing) Lerner Publishing Group.
Kreloff, Elliot, illus. Counting Duckies. 2010. 16p. (J). bds. *(978-1-60906-007-7(5))* Begin Smart LLC.
Kulick Triscila, Verne. Joel & the Magic Toy Tree. 2005. 36p. (J). 11.99 *(978-1-4116-6985-7(1))* Lulu Pr., Inc.
Lagonegro, Melissa & Redbank, Tennant. Five Toy Tales. 2012. (Step into Reading Level 1 Ser.). lib. bdg. 18.40 *(978-0-606-23853-3(0),* Turtleback) Turtleback Bks.
Landers, Ace. Arctic Blast. White, Dave, illus. 2012. 32p. (J). *(978-0-545-33455-6(1))* Scholastic, Inc.
—Emmet's Guide to Being Awesome. Scholastic, Inc. Staff, illus. 2014. (LEGO: the LEGO Movie Ser.). (ENG.). 128p. (J). (gr. 2-5). 9.99 *(978-0-545-79532-6(X))* Scholastic, Inc.
—The Empire Strikes Out. 2013. (Lego Star Wars Ser.). (ENG., Illus.). 48p. (J). (gr. 2-5). pap. 4.99 *(978-0-545-55224-0(9))* Math Solutions.
—Empire Strikes Out. 2013. (LEGO Star Wars Chapter Bks.). lib. bdg. 14.75 *(978-0-606-31554-8(3),* Turtleback) Turtleback Bks.
—The Lego Official Movie Handbook. 2013. lib. bdg. 16.00 *(978-0-606-35405-9(0))* Turtleback Bks.
—Lego Star Wars: The Yoda Chronicles Trilogy. 2014. (LEGO Star Wars Chapter Bks.). lib. bdg. 18.40 *(978-0-606-35414-1(X))* Turtleback Bks.
—A New Hope. 2015. (Lego Star Wars Ser.). (ENG.). 24p. (J). (gr. -1-3). pap. 3.99 *(978-0-545-80135-5(4))* Scholastic, Inc.
—The Padawan Menace. 2012. lib. bdg. 13.55 *(978-0-606-23975-2(8),* Turtleback) Turtleback Bks.
—Revenge of the Sith. 2015. (LEGO Star Wars 8X8 Ser.). lib. bdg. 13.55 *(978-0-606-37767-6(0))* Turtleback Bks.

—Shark Attack. 2013. (Scholastic Reader Level 1 Ser.). lib. bdg. 13.55 *(978-0-606-32391-8(0),* Turtleback) Turtleback Bks.

—Start Your Engines. White, Dave, illus. 2007. (Scholastic Reader Ser.). (J). pap. *(978-0-545-02017-6(4))* Scholastic, Inc.

—Tales of the Rebellion. Ameet Studio Staff, illus. 2016. (Lego Star Wars Ser.: 3). (ENG.). 64p. (J). (gr. 2-5). pap. 4.99 *(978-0-545-87326-0(6))* Scholastic, Inc.

—Vader's Secret Missions. Ameet Studio Staff, illus. 2015. (Lego Star Wars Ser.: 2). (ENG.). 64p. (J). (gr. 2-5). pap. 4.99 *(978-0-545-83557-2(7))* Scholastic, Inc.

—The Yoda Chronicles Trilogy. 2014. (Lego Star Wars Ser.). (ENG.). 96p. (J). (gr. -1-3). 7.99 *(978-0-545-62901-0(2))* Scholastic, Inc.

—Yoda's Secret Missions. 2014. (LEGO Star Wars Chapter Bks.: 1). lib. bdg. 14.75 *(978-0-606-36070-8(0))* Turtleback Bks.

Lansley, Oliver. Holly & Ivan's Christmas Adventure. 2012. (ENG., Illus.). 96p. (J). (gr. k-5). pap. 16.95 *(978-1-84943-136-1(1))* Oberon Bks., Ltd. GBR. Dist: Consortium Bk. Sales & Distribution.

LaReau, Kara. Rocko & Spanky Call It Quits. LaReau, Jenna, illus. 2008. (Rocko & Spanky Ser.). 40p. (J). 16.00 *(978-0-15-216611-3(4))* Harcourt Children's Bks.

Larson, Melissa J. It's Your Ball after All. Larson, Caleb A., illus. 2007. 20p. per. 24.95 *(978-1-4241-9046-1(0))* America Star Bks.

Last, Shari. Meet the Mixels. 2014. (DK Reader Level 1 Ser.). lib. bdg. 13.55 *(978-0-606-36276-4(2))* Turtleback Bks.

Lee Green Pope. The Enchanted Toy Shop. 2009. 32p. pap. 16.49 *(978-1-4389-7320-3(9))* AuthorHouse.

Lee, Ingrid. George Most Wanted. Denis, Stephane, illus. 2005. 62p. (J). lib. bdg. 20.00 *(978-1-4242-1253-8(7))* Fitzgerald Bks.

—George, the Best of All!, 1 vol. Denis, Stephane, illus. 2006. (Orca Echoes Ser.). (ENG.). 64p. (J). (gr. 2-3). per. 4.99 *(978-1-55143-623-4(X))* Orca Bk. Pubs. USA.

—The True Story of George. Denis, Stephane, illus. 2004. 62p. (J). lib. bdg. 20.00 *(978-1-4242-1262-0(6))* Fitzgerald Bks.

Lego, et al. Fire Truck to the Rescue!, No. 1. 2009. (Lego City Ser.). (ENG.). 32p. (J). (gr. -1-k). pap. 3.99 *(978-0-545-11543-8(4))* Scholastic, Inc.

Lehman, Barbara. Trainstop. 2008. (ENG., Illus.). 32p. (J). (gr. -1-3). 16.99 *(978-0-618-75640-7(X))* Houghton Mifflin Harcourt Publishing Co.

LeLeu, Lisa. Miss Moo-Moo the Cow: Puppet Show Play Set with 2 books & Crayons. 2004. (Lisa Leleu Puppet Show Books Ser.). 30p. 19.95 *(978-0-9710537-4-8(X))* LeLeu, Lisa Studios! Inc.

Leonard, Barry, ed. The Little Tin Soldier. 2003. (Illus.). 12p. (J). (gr. k-4). reprint ed. 17.00 *(978-0-7567-6867-6(5))* DIANE Publishing Co.

Let's Pretend: Individual Title Six-Packs. (gr. -1-2). 23.00 *(978-0-7635-9001-7(0))* Rigby Education.

Lewis, Kim. Hooray for Harry. 2006. (Illus.). (J). *(978-1-4156-7111-5(7))* Candlewick Pr.

Lewis, Michael G. The Great Pirate Christmas Battle, 1 vol. Jaskiel, Stan, illus. 2014. (ENG.). 32p. (J). (gr. k-3). 16.99 *(978-1-4556-1934-4(5))* Pelican Publishing Co., Inc.

Linforth, Veda. More Toy Shop Tales. 2009. 124p. pap. 10.99 *(978-1-4389-0795-6(8))* AuthorHouse.

Long, Loren. The Drummer Boy. Long, Loren, illus. 2008. (ENG., Illus.). 40p. (J). (gr. -1-k). 18.99 *(978-0-399-25174-0(X),* Philomel Bks.) Penguin Young Readers Group.

—Drummer Boy. Long, Loren, illus. 2012. (ENG., Illus.). 40p. (J). (gr. -1-k). mass mkt. 7.99 *(978-0-14-242341-7(6),* Puffin Books) Penguin Young Readers Group.

Lovell, Patty. Have Fun, Molly Lou Melon. Lovell, Patty & Catrow, David, illus. 2012. (ENG.). 32p. (J). (gr. k-3). 16.99 *(978-0-399-25406-2(4),* G.P. Putnam's Sons Books for Young Readers) Penguin Young Readers Group.

Lucado, Max. You Are Special. Martinez, Sergio, illus. rev. ed. 2007. 32p. (J). (gr. -1-3). 19.99 *(978-1-58134-894-1(0))* Crossway.

LUCAS, David. Christmas at the Toy Museum. LUCAS, David, illus. 2012. (ENG., Illus.). 32p. (J). (gr. -1-2). 15.99 *(978-0-7636-5868-7(5))* Candlewick Pr.

Luster, Bonnie. The Adventures of Mrs. Tibbles & Her Toys: Spots. 2012. 28p. pap. 16.95 *(978-1-4497-6929-1(2),* WestBow Pr.) Author Solutions, Inc.

Lynn, Sarah. 1-2-3 Va-Va-Vroom! A Counting Book, 0 vols. Griffo, Daniel, illus. 2012. (ENG.). 32p. (J). (gr. -1-3). 16.99 *(978-0-7614-6162-3(0),* 9780761461623, Amazon Children's Publishing) Amazon Publishing.

Making Waves. 2004. (J). per. *(978-1-57657-460-7(1))* Paradise Pr., Inc.

Malone, Sydney. Lost & Hound (Shopkins) 2017. (Shopkins Ser.). (ENG.). 32p. (J). (gr. -1-3). pap. 4.99 ***(978-1-338-13554-1(6))*** Scholastic, Inc.

Marcellino, Fred, illus. The Steadfast Tin Soldier. 2017.Tr. of Standhaftige Tinsoldat. (ENG.). 32p. (J). (gr. -1-3). 17.99 ***(978-1-4814-7662-1(9),*** Atheneum/Caitlyn Dlouhy Books) Simon & Schuster Children's Publishing.

March, Julia. DK Readers L2: LEGO NEXO KNIGHTS: Meet the Knights. 2016. (DK Readers Ser.). (ENG.). 48p. (J). (gr. 1-3). 14.99 *(978-1-4654-4473-8(4),* DK Children) Dorling Kindersley Publishing, Inc.

—DK Readers L3: LEGO NEXO KNIGHTS: Monster Battles. 2016. (DK Readers Ser.). (ENG.). 64p. (J). (gr. 2-4). 14.99 *(978-1-4654-4475-2(0),* DK Children) Dorling Kindersley Publishing, Inc.

—Power Up! 2015. (DK Reader Level 3 Ser.). lib. bdg. 13.55 *(978-0-606-36691-5(1))* Turtleback Bks.

Marsoli, Lisa Ann. Let's Go to the Zoo. Smitherton, Jeb, illus. 2005. (J). bds. 14.99 *(978-0-9767325-4-9(8))* Toy Quest.

Marvel Comics, text. Toy Story: Tales from the Toy Chest. 2012. (ENG., Illus.). 96p. (J). (gr. -1-17). pap. 9.99 *(978-0-7851-6506-4(1))* Marvel Worldwide, Inc.

Marzollo, Jean. I Spy Animals. 2012. (I Spy — Scholastic Ser.). lib. bdg. 13.55 *(978-0-606-23968-4(5),* Turtleback) Turtleback Bks.

—I Spy Little Toys. Wick, Walter, illus. Wick, Walter, photos by. 2011. (I Spy Ser.). (ENG.). 26p. (J). (gr. -1-k). bds. 6.99 *(978-0-545-22096-5(3))* Scholastic, Inc.

Masterson, Josephine. Toy Box Trouble. 2015. (Rosen REAL Readers: STEM & STEAM Collection). (ENG.). 8p. pap. 5.46 *(978-1-4994-9599-7(4),* Rosen Classroom) Rosen Publishing Group, Inc., The.

Mayfield, Sue. The Four Franks. 2005. (Blue Go Bananas Ser.). (ENG., Illus.). 48p. (J). (gr. 1-2). lib. bdg. *(978-0-7787-2629-6(0))* Crabtree Publishing Co.

—The Four Franks. Parsons, Garry, illus. 2005. (Blue Go Bananas Ser.). (ENG.). 48p. (J). (gr. 1-2). *(978-0-7787-2651-7(7))* Crabtree Publishing Co.

McCallum, Ann. Beanstalk: The Measure of a Giant. Balkovek, James, illus. 2006. (Math Adventures Ser.). (ENG.). 32p. (J). (gr. 2-5). per. 7.95 *(978-1-57091-894-0(5))* Charlesbridge Publishing, Inc.

McCarthy, Rebecca. Save This Christmas! May, Jason J., illus. 2012. (Lego City Ser.). (ENG.). 24p. (J). (gr. -1-3). pap. 3.99 *(978-0-545-45727-9(0))* Scholastic, Inc.

Mccarthy, Rebecca L. Save This Christmas! 2012. (LEGO City 8X8 Ser.). lib. bdg. 13.55 *(978-0-606-26767-0(0),* Turtleback) Turtleback Bks.

McClure, Brian D. The Bubble. 2006. (Illus.). 64p. (J). 14.95 *(978-1-933426-05-1(5))* Universal Flag Publishing.

McCue, Lisa, illus. Corduroy's Thanksgiving. 2006. (Corduroy Ser.). (ENG.). 16p. (J). (gr. -1 — 1). bds. 5.99 *(978-0-670-06108-2(5),* Viking Books for Young Readers) Penguin Young Readers Group.

McGougan, Kathy. Buddy's Toys. 2007. (J). pap. 5.00 *(978-0-9799980-2-7(6))* Buddy Bks. Publishing.

McNease, Mitzy. Chester's Presents. Cox, Kim, illus. 2006. 28p. (J). 10.95 *(978-0-9779488-0-2(3))* Blancmange Publishing LLC.

McPhail, David. Bella Loves Bunny. Brukoff, Barry, photos by. 2013. (David Mcphail's Love Ser.). (ENG., Illus.). 22p. (J). (gr. -1 — 1). bds. 8.95 *(978-1-4197-0543-4(1),* Abrams Appleseed) Abrams, Inc.

—Olivia Loves Owl. 2016. (ENG., Illus.). 20p. (J). (gr. -1 — 1). bds. 8.95 *(978-1-4197-2127-4(5),* Abrams Appleseed) Abrams, Inc.

—Peter Loves Penguin. 2014. (David Mcphail's Love Ser.). (ENG., Illus.). 22p. (J). (gr. -1 — 1). bds. 8.95 *(978-1-4197-1337-8(X),* Abrams Appleseed) Abrams, Inc.

Meddaugh, Susan. Toy Trouble. 2010. (Martha Speaks Ser.). (ENG., Illus.). 24p. (J). (gr. -1-3). pap. 3.99 *(978-0-547-21078-0(7))* Houghton Mifflin Harcourt Publishing Co.

Meet the GiggleWings. 2005. (J). bds. 14.99 *(978-1-890647-13-1(6))* TOMY International, Inc.

Meyer, Susan. Matthew & Tall Rabbit Go Camping. Huntington, Amy, illus. 2008. (ENG.). 32p. (J). (gr. -1-3). 15.95 *(978-0-89272-769-8(1))* Down East Bks.

Michael, Melanie. Nerfnerd. Alderton, John, illus. 2011. (J). *(978-0-938467-07-6(7))* Headline Bks., Inc.

Miller, Toby. The Magic Word. 2011. (Illus.). 24p. pap. 14.09 *(978-1-4567-7793-7(9))* AuthorHouse.

Milne, A. A. The House at Pooh Corner. Shepard, Ernest H., illus. deluxe ed. 2009. (Winnie-The-Pooh Ser.). (ENG.). 192p. (J). (gr. 3-7). 19.99 *(978-0-525-47856-0(6),* Dutton Books for Young Readers) Penguin Young Readers Group.

—Tigger Tales. Shepard, Ernest H., illus. 2006. 36p. (J). (gr. k-4). reprint ed. 15.00 *(978-1-4223-5453-7(9))* DIANE Publishing Co.

—Winnie Ille Pu. Lenardo, Alexandro, tr. from ENG. 2015.Tr. of Winnie-the-Pooh. (LAT., Illus.). 170p. (J). pap. 19.95 *(978-4-87187-394-9(3))* Ishi Pr. International.

Mitchell, Colleen. A Dinosaur under My Bed. Daly, Karen Anne, illus. 2013. 24p. (J). pap. 7.49 *(978-0-9853600-2-3(X))* Thistlewood Publishing.

Mitchell, Lee Ann. Milo the Mighty Protector. 2010. 32p. pap. 12.99 *(978-1-4490-5447-2(1))* AuthorHouse.

Miyares, Daniel. Float. Miyares, Daniel, illus. 2015. (ENG., Illus.). 48p. (J). (gr. -1-3). 17.99 *(978-1-4814-1524-8(7),* Simon & Schuster Bks. For Young Readers) Simon & Schuster Bks. For Young Readers.

Moon, Jo. Toys. Fordham, John & Moon, Jo, illus. 2011. (ENG.). 8p. (J). (gr. k — 1). pap. 8.99 *(978-0-230-74595-7(4))* Pan Macmillan GBR. Dist: Independent Pubs. Group.

Morgan, Allen. Matthew & the Midnight Wrecker. 2004. (Illus.). (J). (gr. k-3). spiral bd. *(978-0-616-11123-9(1))* Canadian National Institute for the Blind/Institut National Canadien pour les Aveugles.

Muir, Sally. Patch's Grand Dog Show. Osborne, Joanna, illus. 2016. (ENG.). 32p. (J). (gr. -1-1). 12.99 *(978-1-84365-298-4(6),* Pavilion) Pavilion Bks. GBR. Dist: Independent Pubs. Group.

Mullican, Judy. My Toys. Bicking, Judith, illus. l.t. ed. 2005. (HRL Board Book Ser.). (J). (gr. -1-k). pap. 10.95 *(978-1-57332-307-9(1),* HighReach Learning, Incorporated) Carson-Dellosa Publishing, LLC.

Murray, Helen. The Lego Movie. 2013. (DK Reader Level 2 Ser.). lib. bdg. 13.55 *(978-0-606-35321-2(6))* Turtleback Bks.

My Yo-Yo. Date not set. pap. 3.95 *(978-0-89868-294-6(0))* ARO Publishing Co.

Nash, Sarah. Scaredy Bear. Everitt-Stewart, Andy, illus. 2009. (Stories to Grow with Ser.). 24p. (J). (gr. -1-2). 22.60 *(978-1-60754-472-2(5))* Windmill Bks.

Nash, Scott. Tuff Fluff: The Case of Duckie's Missing Brain. Nash, Scott, illus. 2004. (Illus.). (J). 101.94 *(978-0-7636-2503-0(5));* (ENG., 40p. (gr. 1-4). 16.99 *(978-0-7636-1882-7(9))* Candlewick Pr.

Naylor, Phyllis Reynolds. Please Do Feed the Bears. Escriva, Ana Lopez, illus. 2007. (ENG.). 40p. (J). (gr. -1-2). 11.99 *(978-1-4169-6750-7(8),* Simon & Schuster/Paula Wiseman Bks.) Simon & Schuster/Paula Wiseman Bks.

Newman, Vivian. Ella's Trip to Israel. Nathan, Cheryl & Gutierrez, Akemia, illus. 2011. (Israel Ser.). (ENG.). 24p. (J). (gr. -1 — 1). pap. 8.95 *(978-0-7613-6029-2(8),* Kar-Ben Publishing) Lerner Publishing Group.

Nicholas, Christopher. Toy Story 2, Vol. 2. Butcher, Ben, illus. 2006. (Little Golden Book Ser.). (ENG.). 24p. (J). (gr. -1-2). 3.99 *(978-0-7364-2394-6(X),* Golden/Disney) Random Hse. Children's Bks.

Niddrie, June. Pom, the Pomegranate Pixie. 2010. 32p. pap. 16.10 *(978-0-557-31875-9(0))* Lulu Pr., Inc.

Nielsen-Fernlund, Susin. The Magic Beads. Cote, Genevieve, illus. 2007. (ENG.). 32p. (J). (gr. -1-3). 16.95 *(978-1-894965-47-7(7))* Simply Read Bks. CAN. Dist: Ingram Publisher Services.

Niland, Kilmeny. Two Tough Teddies. Niland, Kilmeny, illus. 2008. (ENG., Illus.). 24p. (J). (gr. -1-k). 14.95 *(978-1-921272-05-9(8))* Little Hare Bks. AUS. Dist: Independent Pubs. Group.

Noisy Toys: Individual Title Six-Packs. (gr. -1-2). 23.00 *(978-0-7635-9002-4(9))* Rigby Education.

Odierno, Lisa. Bunny Hide-and-Seek. 2009. (Smithsonian Baby Animals Ser.). (ENG., Illus.). 16p. (J). (gr. -1-k). 6.95 *(978-1-60727-092-8(7))* Soundprints.

Odierno, Lisa & Soundprints Staff. Bunny Hide-and-Seek. 2009. (Smithsonian Baby Animals Ser.). (ENG., Illus.). 16p. (J). (gr. -1-k). 6.95 *(978-1-60727-105-5(2))* Soundprints.

Ogilvy, Ian. Measle & the Dragodon. 2006. 344p. (J). (gr. 3-8). per. 6.99 *(978-0-06-058690-4(7),* Harper Trophy) HarperCollins Pubs.

Ohi, Ruth. Chicken, Pig, Cow. Ohi, Ruth, illus. 2008. (ENG., Illus.). 32p. (J). (gr. -1-k). 2nd ed. 19.95 *(978-1-55451-157-0(7),* 9781554511570) 6th ed. pap. 6.95 *(978-1-55451-156-3(9),* 9781554511563) Annick Pr., Ltd. CAN. Dist: Publishers Group West (PGW).

Olmstead, Kathleen & Andersen, Hans Christian. The Steadfast Tin Soldier. Calo, Marcos, illus. 2013. (Silver Penny Stories Ser.). (ENG.). 48p. (J). (gr. -1-1). 4.95 *(978-1-4027-8351-7(5))* Sterling Publishing Co., Inc.

The Ooshes A Wish Comes True. 2005. (J). *(978-1-932233-05-6(9))* Aurora Libris Corp.

The Ooshes the Night Before Christmas. 2004. (J). mass mkt. *(978-1-932233-03-2(2))* Aurora Libris Corp.

O'Reilly, Sean. The Toy Snatcher, 1 vol. Arcana Studio Staff, illus. 2012. (Mighty Mighty Monsters Ser.). (ENG.). 48p. (gr. 2-3). pap. 6.10 *(978-1-4342-4612-7(4))* Stone Arch Bks.

—The Toy Snatcher, 1 vol. 2011. (Mighty Mighty Monsters Ser.). (ENG.). 48p. (J). (gr. 2-3). lib. bdg. 23.99 *(978-1-4342-3221-2(2))* Stone Arch Bks.

Orman, Roscoe, illus. Ricky & Mobo. 2007. (J). 14.95 *(978-1-59299-255-3(2))* Inkwater Pr.

Ottenbreit, Sharon. Only One Toy Allowed. 2010. 32p. pap. 15.99 *(978-0-557-36426-8(4))* Lulu Pr., Inc.

Paradine, Mike. King of Toys. 2006. 83p. pap. 19.95 *(978-1-4241-2694-1(0))* America Star Bks.

Parker, Danny. Lola's Toy Box: Party at Cuddleton Castl. 2017. (Lola's Toy Box Ser.: 6). (ENG.). 96p. (J). (gr. k-2). pap. 6.99 ***(978-1-76012-685-8(3))*** Hardie Grant Egmont Pty, Ltd. AUS. Dist: Independent Pubs. Group.

—Lola's Toybox: on the Story Sea. 2017. (Lola's Toy Box Ser.: 2). (ENG.). 96p. (J). (gr. k-2). pap. 6.99 *(978-1-76012-437-3(0))* Hardie Grant Egmont Pty, Ltd. AUS. Dist: Independent Pubs. Group.

—Lola's Toybox: the Patchwork Picnic. 2017. (Lola's Toy Box Ser.: 1). (ENG.). 96p. (J). (gr. k-2). pap. 6.99 ***(978-1-76012-436-6(2))*** Hardie Grant Egmont Pty, Ltd. AUS. Dist: Independent Pubs. Group.

—Lola's Toybox: the Plastic Palace. Shield, Guy, illus. 2017. (Lola's Toy Box Ser.: 4). (ENG.). 96p. (J). (gr. k-2). pap. 6.99 ***(978-1-76012-439-7(7))*** Hardie Grant Egmont Pty, Ltd. AUS. Dist: Independent Pubs. Group.

—Lola's Toybox: the Treasure Trove. 2017. (Lola's Toy Box Ser.: 3). (ENG.). 96p. (J). (gr. k-2). pap. 6.99 ***(978-1-76012-438-0(9))*** Hardie Grant Egmont Pty, Ltd. AUS. Dist: Independent Pubs. Group.

—The Silk Lakes Rescue. Shield, Guy, illus. 2017. (Lola's Toy Box Ser.: 7). (ENG.). 96p. (J). (gr. k-2). pap. 9.99 ***(978-1-76012-686-5(1))*** Hardie Grant Egmont Pty, Ltd. AUS. Dist: Independent Pubs. Group.

—The Timberfield Talent Show. Shield, Guy, illus. 2017. (Lola's Toy Box Ser.: 5). (ENG.). 96p. (J). (gr. k-2). pap. 6.99 ***(978-1-76012-674-2(8))*** Hardie Grant Egmont Pty, Ltd. AUS. Dist: Independent Pubs. Group.

Parker, Theron J. June Bug & the Homemade Toys. 2013. 24p. 24.95 *(978-1-62709-397-2(4));* pap. 24.95 *(978-1-62709-158-9(0))* America Star Bks.

Parragon Staff. Celebrate the Year with Winnie the Pooh. 2010. (Disney Diecut Classics). 72p. (J). (gr. -1-1). *(978-1-4075-8902-2(4))* Parragon, Inc.

—Disney Toy Story 3: Toy Stars. 2010. (Disney Twinkly Lights Board Bks.). 6p. (J). (gr. -1-k). bds. *(978-1-4075-9341-8(2))* Parragon, Inc.

Paxton, Tom. The Marvelous Toy. Cox, Steve, illus. 2014. (ENG.). 22p. (J). (gr. -1-2). bds. 7.95 *(978-1-62354-043-2(7))* Charlesbridge Publishing, Inc.

Pegg, Laura Wittman. The Patch Quilt Pony. 2006. 17.00 *(978-0-8059-7346-4(X))* Dorrance Publishing Co., Inc.

Pett, Mark. The Boy & the Airplane. Pett, Mark, illus. 2013. (ENG., Illus.). 40p. (J). 15.99 *(978-1-4424-5123-0(8),* Simon & Schuster Bks. For Young Readers) Simon & Schuster Bks. For Young Readers.

Pierce, Ricky. Bouncing Billy. 2008. 24p. per. 10.95 *(978-1-4327-1696-7(4))* Outskirts Pr., Inc.

Piggy Toes Press. Our Ballet Recital. Maddocks, Maria, illus. 2005. (ENG.). 12p. (J). (gr. -1-3). 12.95 *(978-1-58117-425-0(X),* Intervisual/Piggy Toes) Bendon, Inc.

Piggy Toes Press, creator. Toy Story 3. 2011. (Splish-Splash Stories Ser.). (ENG., Illus.). (J). (gr. -1-k). 5.95 *(978-1-61524-419-5(0),* Intervisual/Piggy Toes) Bendon, Inc.

Pilutti, Deb. Ten Rules of Being a Superhero. Pilutti, Deb, illus. 2014. (ENG., Illus.). 32p. (J). (gr. -1-2). 17.99 *(978-0-8050-9759-7(7),* 9780805097597, Holt, Henry & Co. Bks. For Young Readers) Holt, Henry & Co.

Piper, Watty. The Little Engine That Could. Long, Loren, illus. 2005. (Little Engine That Could Ser.). (ENG.). 48p. (J). (gr. -1-2). 17.99 *(978-0-399-24467-4(0),* Philomel Bks.) Penguin Young Readers Group.

—The Little Engine That Could. Hauman, George & Hauman, Doris, illus. deluxe ed. 2009. (Little Engine That Could Ser.). (ENG.). 48p. (J). (gr. -1-2). 17.99 *(978-0-448-45257-9(X),* Grosset & Dunlap) Penguin Young Readers Group.

Piper, Watty & Penguin / LeapFrog. The Little Engine That Could. Long, Loren, illus. 2008. (J). 13.99 *(978-1-59319-938-8(4))* LeapFrog Enterprises, Inc.

Polacco, Patricia. Bun Bun Button. Polacco, Patricia, illus. 2011. (ENG., Illus.). 36p. (J). (gr. -1-k). 17.99 *(978-0-399-25472-7(2),* G.P. Putnam's Sons Books for Young Readers) Penguin Young Readers Group.

Posner-Sanchez, Andrea. As Big As a Whale (Disney Junior: Doc Mcstuffins) RH Disney Staff, illus. 2014. (Little Golden Book Ser.). (ENG.). 24p. (J). (-k). 4.99 *(978-0-7364-3087-6(3),* Golden/Disney) Random Hse. Children's Bks.

—Bubble-Rific! RH Disney Staff, illus. 2014. (Little Golden Book Ser.). (ENG.). 24p. (J). (-k). 4.99 *(978-0-7364-3236-8(1),* Golden/Disney) Random Hse. Children's Bks.

—Doc Is the Best Medicine! (Disney Junior: Doc Mcstuffins) Wall, Mike, illus. 2014. (Big Golden Book Ser.). (ENG.). 64p. (J). (gr. -1-2). 9.99 *(978-0-7364-3264-1(7),* Golden/Disney) Random Hse. Children's Bks.

—A Knight in Sticky Armor (Disney Junior: Doc Mcstuffins) Random House Disney Staff, illus. 2012. (Little Golden Book Ser.). (ENG.). 24p. (J). (-k). 4.99 *(978-0-7364-3030-2(X),* Golden/Disney) Random Hse. Children's Bks.

Posner-Sanchez, Andrea & Random House Staff. Snowman Surprise (Disney Junior: Doc Mcstuffins) Golden Books Staff, illus. 2013. (Little Golden Book Ser.). (ENG.). 24p. (J). (-k). 4.99 *(978-0-7364-3142-2(X),* Golden/Disney) Random Hse. Children's Bks.

Poydar, Nancy. Bus Driver. Poydar, Nancy, illus. 2012. (ENG., Illus.). 32p. (J). 15.95 *(978-0-8234-2411-5(1))* Holiday Hse., Inc.

Poyner, James R. Toy-Maker's Apprentice. 2006. 67p. per. 12.00 *(978-1-60002-282-1(0),* 4145) Mountain Valley Publishing, LLC.

Price, John. Quest. 2005. 37p. pap. 15.00 *(978-1-4116-5649-9(0))* Lulu Pr., Inc.

Price, Mathew. Tic, Tac Toc. (SPA.). pap. 3.95 *(978-950-07-2059-5(0))* Editorial Sudamericana S.A. ARG. Dist: Distribooks, Inc.

Price, Michael & Howard, Kate. Droid Tales. 2015. (Lego Star Wars Ser.). (ENG.). 96p. (J). (gr. 2-5). pap. 7.99 *(978-0-545-87328-4(2))* Scholastic, Inc.

Publications International Ltd. Staff. My 1St Look & Find Disney Pixar Friends & Heroes. 2007. 18p. (J). 9.98 *(978-1-4127-6848-1(9),* PIL Kids) Publications International, Ltd.

—Steering Wheel Sound Cars. 2007. 12p. (J). 17.98 *(978-1-4127-5884-0(X))* Phoenix International Publications, Inc.

Publications International Ltd. Staff, ed. Los Mejores Amigos. 2009.Tr. of Toy Story Best Friends. 12p. (J). bds. 10.98 *(978-1-4127-0269-0(0))* Phoenix International Publications, Inc.

—Sesame Street(r) Where Is Elmo's Friend? Play-A-Sound(r) Lift-a-Flap Sound Book. 2014. 10p. (J). bds. *(978-1-4508-8976-6(X),* 145088976X) Publications International, Ltd.

Publishing, Chouette & Paradis, Anne. Caillou, Sweet Dreams: Nightlight Book. Dupuis, Karina & Kary, illus. 2016. (ENG.). 14p. (J). (gr. -1-k). 12.99 *(978-2-89718-336-3(5))* Caillouet, Gerry.

Pulford, Elizabeth. Finding Monkey Moon. Wilkinson, Kate, illus. 2015. (ENG.). 32p. (J). (gr. -1-2). 15.99 *(978-0-7636-6777-1(3))* Candlewick Pr.

R., Charlie. The Christmas Mama Santa Delivered the Toys. 2012. 36p. 19.95 *(978-1-4626-6824-3(0))* PublishAmerica, Inc.

Rack, Charlene. The Adventures of Delaware Bear & Young George Washington. 2011. 24p. (gr. 1-2). pap. 12.79 *(978-1-4567-5681-9(8))* AuthorHouse.

Rainey, L. E. Sad Sam, Glad Sam. 2006. (Illus.). 32p. (J). 16.95 *(978-0-9785521-0-7(5))* Shoetree Publishers, Inc.

Raitman, Ira. Amanda's Bunny. 2010. 16p. 8.99 *(978-1-4520-2021-1(3))* AuthorHouse.

Raley, Hugh W. Erin the Excellent Elf. 2013. 20p. pap. 12.95 *(978-1-4908-0533-7(8),* WestBow Pr.) Author Solutions, Inc.

Randall, Chuck. Curley's Wish Comes True. 2013. 28p. pap. 24.95 *(978-1-4626-9795-3(X))* America Star Bks.

Reasoner, Charles. Inside Santa's Toy Shop. Reasoner, Charles, illus. 2007. (Story Book Ser.). (Illus.). 12p. (J). (gr. k-3). bds. *(978-1-84666-151-8(X),* Tide Mill Pr.) Top That! Publishing PLC.

Rees, Susan A. P. The Pine Cone Wishing Tree. 2008. (Illus.). 20p. pap. 10.49 *(978-1-4343-7155-3(7))* AuthorHouse.

Rey, H. A. Car Wash. 2013. (Curious George Ser.). (ENG., Illus.). 24p. (J). (gr. -1-3). pap. 3.99 *(978-0-547-94086-1(6))* Houghton Mifflin Harcourt Publishing Co.

—Curious George Car Wash. 2013. (Curious George Ser.). (ENG., Illus.). 24p. (J). (gr. -1-3). 12.99 *(978-0-544-03251-4(9))* Houghton Mifflin Harcourt Publishing Co.

—Curious George Saves His Pennies. 2013. (Curious George Ser.). (ENG., Illus.). 32p. (J). (gr. -1-3). 12.99 *(978-0-547-63231-5(2))* Houghton Mifflin Harcourt Publishing Co.

—Curious George Tool Time (CGTV Board Book) 2013. (Curious George Ser.). (ENG., Illus.). 12p. (J). (gr. -1 — 1). bds. 6.99 *(978-0-547-96818-6(3))* Houghton Mifflin Harcourt Publishing Co.

—My Favorite Things. 2011. (Curious Baby Curious George Ser.). (ENG., Illus.). 14p. (J). (gr. -1 — 1). bds. 8.99 *(978-0-547-42893-2(6))* Houghton Mifflin Harcourt Publishing Co.

Rey, H. A. & Rey, Margret. Curious George Saves His Pennies. 2014. (Curious George Ser.). (ENG., Illus.). 24p. (J). (gr. -1-3). pap. 4.99 *(978-0-547-81853-5(X))* Houghton Mifflin Harcourt Publishing Co.

—Takes a Trip. 2007. (Curious George Ser.). (ENG., Illus.). 24p. (J). (gr. -1-3). pap. 3.99 *(978-0-618-88403-2(3))* Houghton Mifflin Harcourt Publishing Co.

RH Disney Staff. Toy Story. RH Disney Staff, illus. 2009. (Little Golden Book Ser.). (ENG., Illus.). 24p. (J). (gr. -1-2). 4.99 *(978-0-7364-2596-4(9),* Golden/Disney) Random Hse. Children's Bks.

RH Disney Staff & Auerbach, Annie. Toy Story 3. RH Disney Staff & Molina, Adrian H., illus. 2010. (Little Golden Book Ser.). (ENG.). 24p. (J). (gr. -1-2). 4.99 *(978-0-7364-2668-8(X),* Golden/Disney) Random Hse. Children's Bks.

RH Disney Staff & Depken, Kristen L. The Pet Problem (Disney/Pixar Toy Story) RH Disney Staff & Egan, Caroline, illus. 2011. (Little Golden Book Ser.). (ENG.). 24p. (J). (gr. -1-2). 3.99 *(978-0-7364-2698-5(1),* Golden/Disney) Random Hse. Children's Bks.

RH Disney Staff & Redbank, Tennant. Toy to Toy. RH Disney Staff et al, illus. 2010. (Step into Reading Ser.). (ENG.). 32p. (J). (gr. k-3). pap. 3.99 *(978-0-7364-2665-7(5)*, RH/Disney) Random Hse. Children's Bks.

RH Disney Staff & Weingartner, Amy. Toy Box Trouble! RH Disney Staff & Laguna, Fabio, illus. 2015. (Stepping Stone Book Ser.). (ENG.). 80p. (J). (gr. 1-4). 4.99 *(978-0-7364-3326-6(0)*, RH/Disney) Random Hse. Children's Bks.

Rickards, Lynne. Jack's Bed. Beardshaw, Rosalind, illus. 2006. (Green Bananas Ser.). (ENG.). 48p. (J). (gr. -1-k). *(978-0-7787-1044-8(0))* Crabtree Publishing Co.

Rillo, Lori-Anne. Lorelei Finds a Home. 2010. 32p. pap. 13.49 *(978-1-4490-5890-6(6))* AuthorHouse.

Rinker, Gary W. The Very Best Toy. Rangel, Rawderson, illus. 2010. 28p. (J). (gr. -1). pap. 5.99 *(978-1-59188-881-9(6))* Maverick Bks., Inc.

Robertson, Si & Nelson, Ashley Howard. Uncle Si, the Christmas Elf: Work Hard, Nap Hard. Gilpin, Stephen, illus. 2014. (ENG.). 48p. (J). (gr. -1-3). 29.99 *(978-1-4814-1821-8(1)*, Simon & Schuster Bks. For Young Readers) Simon & Schuster Bks. For Young Readers.

Robinson, Marquita E. Teddy's Bear, 1 vol. Roscoe Robinson, illus. 2009. 15p. pap. 24.95 *(978-1-60749-249-8(0))* America Star Bks.

Rogers, Kenny & Junkerman, Kelly. Kenny Rogers Presents the Toy Shoppe. 2004. (Illus.). 30p. (J). (gr. 4-8). reprint ed. 16.00 *(978-0-7567-7758-6(5))* DIANE Publishing Co.

Roques, Dominique. Anna Banana & the Chocolate Explosion. Dormal, Alexis, illus. 2015. (Anna Banana Ser.). (ENG.). 28p. (J). (gr. k-2). 15.99 *(978-1-62672-020-6(7)*, 9781626720206, First Second Bks.) Roaring Brook Pr.

—Sleep Tight, Anna Banana! Dormal, Alexis, illus. 2014. (Anna Banana Ser.). (ENG.). 28p. (J). (gr. -1-2). 15.99 *(978-1-62672-019-0(3)*, 9781626720190, First Second Bks.) Roaring Brook Pr.

Rosen, Michael. Red Ted & the Lost Things. Stewart, Joel, illus. 2009. (ENG.). 40p. (J). (gr. -1-2). pap. 8.99 *(978-0-7636-4624-0(5))* Candlewick Pr.

Rosenberg, Aaron. Case of the Topsy-Turvy Toy. Harrington, David, illus. 2011. (Pete & Penny's Pizza Puzzles Ser.: 2). (ENG.). 64p. (J). (gr. 1-3). pap. 3.99 *(978-0-8431-9929-1(6)*, Price Stern Sloan) Penguin Young Readers Group.

Rosenthal, Amy Krouse. I Scream! Ice Cream! A Book of Wordles. Bloch, Serge, illus. 2013. (ENG.). 40p. (J). (gr. -1-17). 16.99 *(978-1-4521-0004-3(7))* Chronicle Bks. LLC.

Rosenthal, Eileen. Bobo the Sailor Man! Rosenthal, Marc, illus. 2013. (ENG.). 40p. (J). (gr. -1-1). 15.99 *(978-1-4424-4443-0(6))* Simon & Schuster Children's Publishing.

—I Must Have Bobo! Rosenthal, Marc, illus. 2011. (ENG.). 40p. (J). (gr. -1-1). 14.99 *(978-1-4424-0377-2(2)*, Atheneum Bks. for Young Readers) Simon & Schuster Children's Publishing.

Ross, Dev. We Both Read Bilingual Edition-Frank & the Tiger/Sapi y el Tigre. Canetti, Yanitzia, tr. from ENG. Reinhart, Larry, illus. 2014. (We Both Read - Level K-1 (Quality) Ser.). (ENG & SPA.). 44p. (J). (gr. k-1). pap. 4.99 *(978-1-60115-058-5(X))* Treasure Bay, Inc.

—We Both Read-Frank & the Tiger. Reinhart, Larry, illus. 2011. 44p. (J). 9.95 *(978-1-60115-259-6(0))* Treasure Bay, Inc.

Rusu, Meredith. Legend of the Brown Ninja. 2016. (LEGO Ninjago Ser.). (ENG.). 80p. (J). (gr. 2-5). pap. 4.99 *(978-1-338-04466-9(4))* Scholastic, Inc.

—Police Pursuit! (LEGO City) Lee, Paul, illus. 2017. (Lego City Ser.). (ENG.). 24p. (J). (gr. -1-3). pap. 3.99 *(978-1-338-11750-9(5))* Scholastic, Inc.

Ryherd, Tim. My Hurricane Book. 2006. (Illus.). (J). 12.95 *(978-0-9749974-1-4(2))* Ryherd, Tim Publishing.

Rylant, Cynthia. Little Whistle. Bowers, Tim, illus. 2007. (Little Whistle Ser.). 32p. (gr. -1-3). 24.21 *(978-1-59961-253-9(4))* Spotlight.

—Little Whistle's Dinner Party. Bowers, Tim, illus. 2007. (Little Whistle Ser.). 32p. (gr. -1-3). 24.21 *(978-1-59961-255-3(0))* Spotlight.

—Little Whistle's Medicine. Bowers, Tim, illus. 2007. (Little Whistle Ser.). 32p. (gr. -1-2). 24.21 *(978-1-59961-256-0(9))* Spotlight.

Rylant, Cynthia & Andersen, Hans Christian. The Steadfast Tin Soldier. Corace, Jen, illus. 2013. (ENG.). 32p. (J). (gr. k-2). 18.95 *(978-1-4197-0432-1(X)*, Abrams Bks. for Young Readers) Abrams, Inc.

Sakai, Komako, creator. The Velveteen Rabbit. 2012. (ENG., Illus.). 40p. (J). (gr. -1). 17.95 *(978-1-59270-128-5(0))* Enchanted Lion Bks., LLC.

Salane, Jeffrey. The Lego Movie. Kiernan, Kenny, illus. 2013. (ENG.). 64p. (J). (gr. 2-5). pap. 5.99 *(978-0-545-62462-6(2))* Scholastic, Inc.

Salzmann, Mary Elizabeth. Here Are Toys!, 1 vol. (First Words Ser.). (Illus.). (J). (gr. k-3). 2006. (ENG.). 24p. lib. bdg. 24.21 *(978-1-59679-374-3(0)*, SandCastle) 2005. 23p. pap. 48.42 *(978-1-59679-375-0(9))* ABDO Publishing Co.

Samarrippas, Gloria. In Search for Lucky's Lost Toys. 2006. 17.00 *(978-0-8059-7329-7(X))* Dorrance Publishing Co., Inc.

Samuels, Barbara. The Trucker. Samuels, Barbara, illus. 2010. (ENG., Illus.). 40p. (J). (gr. -1-1). 16.99 *(978-0-374-37804-2(5)*, 9780374378042, Farrar, Straus & Giroux (BYR)) Farrar, Straus & Giroux.

Samworth, Kate. Aviary Wonders Inc. Spring Catalog & Instruction Manual. 2014. (ENG., Illus.). 32p. (J). (gr. 5-7). 17.99 *(978-0-547-97899-4(5))* Houghton Mifflin Harcourt Publishing Co.

San Souci, Robert D. Zigzag. Czernecki, Stefan, illus. 2005. (ENG.). 32p. (J). (gr. -1-2). 16.95 *(978-0-87483-764-3(2))* August Hse. Pubs., Inc.

Sander, Sonia. Help Is on the Way! 2009. (LEGO City Adventures Scholastic Readers Level 1 Ser.: 2). lib. bdg. 13.55 *(978-0-606-07119-2(9)*, Turtleback) Turtleback Bks.

—LEGO City Reader Collection: LEGO City Emergency. 2012. (Illus.). 127p. (J). *(978-1-4351-3985-5(2))* Scholastic, Inc.

Sanschagrin, Joceline. Caillou: It's Mine! Brignaud, Pierre, illus. 3rd ed. 2013. (Step by Step Ser.). (ENG.). 24p. (J). (gr. -1-k). bds. 5.99 *(978-2-89718-059-1(5))* Caillouet, Gerry.

—El Osito de Peluche. 2004. (Caillou Ser.).Tr. of Where's Teddy? (SPA & ENG., Illus.). 24p. (J). (gr. -1-17). bds. 5.95 *(978-1-58728-404-5(9))* Cooper Square Publishing Llc.

Sansone, V. K. WANTED: Children for Toys. 2009. 32p. pap. 14.98 *(978-0-557-16717-3(5))* Lulu Pr., Inc.

Santillo, LuAnn. The Ball. Santillo, LuAnn, ed. 2003. (Half-Pint Kids Readers Ser.). (Illus.). 7p. (J). (gr. -1-1). pap. 1.00 *(978-1-59256-081-3(4))* Half-Pint Kids, Inc.

Saunders, Catherine. DK Readers L4: LEGO NINJAGO: Team Ninja. 2016. (ENG., Illus.). 96p. (J). (gr. 3-7). pap. 3.99 *(978-1-4654-5191-0(9)*, DK Children) Dorling Kindersley Publishing, Inc.

—Team Ninja. 2016. (DK Reader Level 4 Ser.). lib. bdg. 13.55 *(978-0-606-38712-5(9))* Turtleback Bks.

Schaefer, Elizabeth. The Force Awakens. White, Dave, illus. 2016. (Lego Star Wars Ser.). (ENG.). 24p. (J). (gr. -1-3). pap. 3.99 *(978-0-545-94072-6(9))* Scholastic, Inc.

Scholastic. Battle of the Books! 2016. (LEGO NEXO Knights Ser.). (ENG.). 32p. (J). (gr. 2-5). pap., act. bk. ed. 8.99 *(978-1-338-03801-9(X))* Scholastic, Inc.

Scholastic & Howard, Kate. Fright Knight!, Bk. 2. 2016. (LEGO NEXO Knights Ser.). (ENG.). 80p. (J). (gr. 2-5). pap. 4.99 *(978-0-545-92555-6(X))* Scholastic, Inc.

Scholastic & Schmidt, Rebecca L. Movie Magic. Scholastic, Inc. Staff, illus. 2016. (LEGO NEXO Knights Ser.). (ENG.). 32p. (J). (gr. 2-5). pap. 3.99 *(978-1-338-03802-6(8))* Scholastic, Inc.

Scholastic Editors. Stop That Heist! 2013. (LEGO City Scholastic Readers Level 1 Ser.). lib. bdg. 13.55 *(978-0-606-31540-1(3)*, Turtleback) Turtleback Bks.

Scholastic Editors, ed. Last Laugh! 2013. (LEGO DC Super Heroes Ser.). lib. bdg. 13.55 *(978-0-606-32018-4(0)*, Turtleback) Turtleback Bks.

Scholastic Inc, contrib. by. Baby-Sitting Blues. 2015. (Shopkins Ser.). (ENG., Illus.). 32p. (J). (gr. -1-3). pap. 4.99 *(978-0-545-90495-7(1))* Scholastic, Inc.

Scholastic, Inc. Staff. Merry Christmas, Lego City! 2012. (Lego City Ser.). (ENG.). 16p. (J). (gr. -1-k). pap. 6.99 *(978-0-545-42396-0(1))* Scholastic, Inc.

—The New Ninja, Bk. 9. 2015. (Lego Ninjago Ser.). (ENG., Illus.). 80p. (J). (gr. 2-5). pap. 4.99 *(978-0-545-90588-6(5))* Scholastic, Inc.

—Ready for Takeoff! 2010. (LEGO City Adventures Scholastic Readers Level 1 Ser.: 5). lib. bdg. 13.55 *(978-0-606-15057-6(9)*, Turtleback) Turtleback Bks.

—Space Justice! 2015. (LEGO DC Super Heroes Ser.). (ENG., Illus.). 32p. (J). (gr. -1-3). pap. 3.99 *(978-0-545-82556-6(3))* Scholastic, Inc.

Scholastic, Inc. Staff, contrib. by. Adventures in LEGO City, Set. 2nd ed. 2015. (Lego City Ser.). (ENG.). (J). (gr. -1-3). pap. 24.99 *(978-0-545-80861-3(8))* Scholastic, Inc.

Scholastic, Inc. Staff, ed. Save the Day. 2013. (LEGO DC Super Heroes Ser.). lib. bdg. 13.55 *(978-0-606-32017-7(2)*, Turtleback) Turtleback Bks.

Scholastic, Inc. Staff & Farshtey, Greg. Lego Ninjago. 2011. (Lego Ninjago Ser.). (ENG., Illus.). 112p. (J). (gr. 2-5). pap. 7.99 *(978-0-545-36258-0(X))* Scholastic, Inc.

Scholastic, Inc. Staff & King, Trey. Deep Sea Treasure Dive. Hyland, Greg, illus. 2016. (Lego City Ser.). (ENG.). 24p. (J). (gr. 2-5). pap. 3.99 *(978-0-545-90591-6(5))* Scholastic, Inc.

Scholastic, Inc. Staff & Simon, Jenne. Welcome to Shopville. Scholastic, Inc. Staff, illus. 2015. (Shopkins Ser.). (ENG., Illus.). 24p. (J). (gr. -1-3). pap. 3.99 *(978-0-545-84228-0(X))* Scholastic, Inc.

Scholastic, Inc. Staff & Steele, Michael Anthony. Fix That Truck! Dynamo Limited Staff, illus. 2012. (Lego City Ser.). (ENG.). 24p. (J). (gr. -1-3). pap. 3.99 *(978-0-545-47061-2(7))* Scholastic, Inc.

Scholastic, Inc. Staff & West, Tracey. Graduation Day, Bk. 1. 2016. (LEGO NEXO Knights Ser.). (ENG.). 80p. (J). (gr. 2-5). pap. 4.99 *(978-0-545-92554-9(1))* Scholastic, Inc.

Scholastic, Inc. Staff & West, Tracy. Nexo Knights. 2016. (LEGO NEXO Knights Ser.). (ENG., Illus.). 64p. (J). (gr. 2-5). pap., instr.'s hndbk. ed. 5.99 *(978-0-545-90586-2(9))* Scholastic, Inc.

Scholastic, Inc. Staff, et al. Attack of the Legion of Doom! 2016. (LEGO DC Super Heroes Ser.). (ENG.). 64p. (J). (gr. 2-5). pap. 4.99 *(978-0-545-86799-3(1))* Scholastic, Inc.

Schories, Pat. Jack & the Missing Piece. 2004. (Jacks Ser.). (ENG., Illus.). 32p. (J). 13.95 *(978-1-932425-17-8(9)*, Lemniscaat) Boyds Mills Pr.

Schorr, Loretta Jean. Sash: The Life of a Little Toy Poodle. 2009. 32p. pap. 16.49 *(978-1-4490-0142-1(4))* AuthorHouse.

Schwartz, Amy & Marcus, Leonard S. Oscar: The Big Adventure of a Little Sock Monkey. Schwartz, Amy, illus. 2006. (Illus.). 32p. (J). (gr. -1-2). 16.99 *(978-0-06-072622-5(9)*, Tegen, Katherine Bks) HarperCollins Pubs.

Scollon, Bill & Nee, Chris. Engine Nine, Feelin' Fine! 2013. (Illus.). 24p. (J). *(978-1-4844-0835-3(7))* Disney Pr.

Scraper, Katherine. Tag Sale Today. 2005. (J). pap. *(978-1-4108-4210-7(X))* Benchmark Education Co.

Seabrook, Heather. Lego Chima - Heroes' Quest. 2014. (DK Reader Level 3 Ser.). lib. bdg. 13.55 *(978-0-606-35732-6(7))* Turtleback Bks.

Searl, Duncan. The Jamie & Angus Stories: A Study Guide. Friedland, Joyce & Kessler, Rikki, eds. 2008. (Novel-Ties Ser.). (Illus.). 23p. pap. 16.95 *(978-0-7675-1485-9(8))* Learning Links Inc.

The Secrets of Eastcliff-By-the-Sea: The Story of Annaliese Easterling & Throckmorton, Her Simply Remarkable Sock Monkey. 2014. (ENG., Illus.). 288p. (J). (gr. 3-7). 16.99 *(978-1-4424-9840-2(4)*, Beach Lane Bks.) Beach Lane Bks.

Shannon, David. Too Many Toys. Shannon, David, illus. 2008. (ENG., Illus.). 32p. (J). (gr. -1-3). 16.99 *(978-0-439-49029-0(4))* Scholastic, Inc.

—Uh-Oh, David! A David Sticker Book. Shannon, David, illus. 2013. (ENG., Illus.). 16p. (J). (gr. -1-k). 6.99 *(978-0-545-43768-4(7)*, Cartwheel Bks.) Scholastic, Inc.

Shay, Kenley. Marsha Mellow Goes Missing: An Unofficial Story for Shopkins Collectors. 2015. (Unofficial Shopkins Collectors Ser.). (ENG.). 112p. (J). (gr. 1-7). pap. 7.99 *(978-1-5107-0251-6(2)*, Sky Pony Pr.) Skyhorse Publishing Co., Inc.

—Prommy Meets Her Match: An Unofficial Story for Shopkins Collectors. 2015. (Unofficial Shopkins Collectors Ser.). (ENG.). 112p. (J). (gr. 1-7). pap. 7.99 *(978-1-5107-0374-2(8)*, Sky Pony Pr.) Skyhorse Publishing Co., Inc.

Sheninger, Rick. Buddy the Duck Gets Lost. 2012. 20p. pap. 15.99 *(978-1-4685-8371-7(9))* AuthorHouse.

Shepherd, Jodie. Merry Christmas, Rarity! Fletcher, Lyn, illus. 2006. (My Little Pony Ser.). 32p. (J). (gr. -1-1). pap., act. bk. ed. 3.99 *(978-0-06-079472-9(0)*, HarperFestival) HarperCollins Pubs.

Shumate, Robert O. Snuffley. Sutherland, Nicholas, illus. 2008. 28p. pap. 24.95 *(978-1-60610-707-2(0))* America Star Bks.

Sills, Kathy & Sills, Karen. Feelings, Feelings, Feelings. 2012. 19p. 19.00 *(978-1-4349-8743-3(4)*, RoseDog Bks.) Dorrance Publishing Co., Inc.

Silver Dolphin en Español Editors. Figuras Magicas: Disney Princesses Magical Magnets. 2005. (SPA., Illus.). 8p. (J). bds. *(978-970-718-241-7(5)*, Silver Dolphin en Español) Advanced Marketing, S. de R. L. de C. V.

—Figuras Magicas: Disney Winnie the Pooh Magical Magnets. 2005. (SPA., Illus.). 8p. (J). bds. *(978-970-718-243-1(1)*, Silver Dolphin en Español) Advanced Marketing, S. de R. L. de C. V.

Simonson, Audrey. Where Is Your Mousey? 2006. (ENG.). 40p. per. 22.65 *(978-1-4134-0270-4(4))* Xlibris Corp.

Slegers, Liesbet. Playing. 2011. (Clavis Toddler: Daily Life Ser.). (ENG.). 12p. (J). (gr. k — 1). bds. 5.95 *(978-1-60537-091-0(6))* Cobblestone Publishing Co.

Slonim, David. Oh, Ducky! A Chocolate Calamity. Slonim, David, illus. 2006. (Illus.). 28p. (J). (gr. k-4). 16.00 *(978-1-4223-5259-5(5))* DIANE Publishing Co.

Smallman, Steve. Bumbletum. Warnes, Tim, illus. 2006. 24p. (J). (gr. -1-3). 15.95 *(978-1-58925-060-4(5))* Tiger Tales.

—A Very Special Hug. Warnes, Tim, illus. 2008. 32p. pap. 6.95 *(978-1-58925-410-7(4))* Tiger Tales.

Smith, Joel D. Santa's Secret Deal: Who Else Signed It, & Where You Can Find Proof of the Deal in Your Room Right Now. 2012. 30p. pap. 14.25 *(978-1-4575-1458-6(3))* Dog Ear Publishing, LLC.

Smith, John A. A Special Christmas for Oscar, 1 vol. 2010. 32p. 24.95 *(978-1-4512-0999-0(1))* PublishAmerica, Inc.

Smith, Maggie. My Blue Bunny, Bubbit. 2014. (ENG., Illus.). 40p. (J). (gr. -1-3). 16.99 *(978-0-547-55861-5(9))* Houghton Mifflin Harcourt Publishing Co.

Smith, Michael. My Ducky Buddy. Oliva, Octavio, illus. 2011. 23p. (J). *(978-0-9821675-4-0(7))* East West Discovery Pr.

—My Ducky Buddy/Mi Amigo el Pato. Oliva, Octavio, illus. 2011. (ENG & SPA.). 24p. (J). (gr. -1-3). 12.95 *(978-0-9821675-5-7(5))* East West Discovery Pr.

Smith, Michael & Wang, Emily. My Ducky Buddy. Oliva, Octavio, illus. 2011. (CHI & ENG.). 23p. (J). *(978-0-9821675-7-1(1))* East West Discovery Pr.

Snellenberger, Tracy. Tyler the Toddler Feeds the Cows. 2010. 28p. 13.99 *(978-1-4520-5169-7(0))* AuthorHouse.

Snider, Jesse Blaze. Return of Buzz Lightyear, Vol. 2. Watson, Nathan, illus. 2010. (Toy Story Ser.). (ENG.). 112p. (J). pap. 9.99 *(978-1-60886-557-4(6))* Boom! Studios.

—Return of Buzz Lightyear Vol. 2. Watson, Nathan, illus. 2010. (Toy Story Ser.). (ENG.). 112p. (J). 24.99 *(978-1-60886-558-1(4))* Boom! Studios.

—Toy Story: Some Assembly Required. Watson, Nathan, illus. 2010. (Toy Story Ser.). 112p. (J). pap. 9.99 *(978-1-60886-570-3(3))* Boom! Studios.

—Toy Story: Toy Overboard. Watson, Nathan, illus. 2011. 128p. (J). pap. 9.99 *(978-1-60886-605-2(X))* Boom! Studios.

Sowder, G. Wesley & Sowder, Joseph, told to. Hunter-Lee & the Toy Monster: Book One. 2008. 48p. pap. 16.95 *(978-1-60703-137-6(X))* America Star Bks.

Spiegelman, Art. Jack & the Box, 1 vol. 2013. (Toon Bks). (ENG.). 36p. (J). (gr. k-1). lib. bdg. 27.07 *(978-1-61479-151-5(1))* Spotlight.

—Jack & the Box. Hayes, Geoffrey, illus. 2008. (ENG.). 32p. (J). (gr. -1-3). 12.95 *(978-0-9799238-3-8(2))* TOON Books / RAW Junior, LLC.

Spinelli, Eileen & Spinelli. Bath Time, 1 vol. Pedersen, Janet, illus. 2003. (ENG.). 32p. (J). 14.95 *(978-0-7614-5117-4(X))* Marshall Cavendish Corp.

Springstubb, Tricia. Phoebe & Digger. Newman, Jeff, illus. (ENG.). 32p. (J). (gr. -1-2). 2016. 7.99 *(978-0-7636-8894-3(0))* 2013. 16.99 *(978-0-7636-5281-4(4))* Candlewick Pr.

Steele, Michael Anthony. Catch That Crook! Wang, Sean, illus. 2012. 23p. (J). *(978-1-4242-5333-3(0))* Scholastic, Inc.

—Catch That Crook! 2012. (LEGO City 8X8 Ser.). (Illus.). 23p. (J). lib. bdg. 13.55 *(978-0-606-23960-8(X)*, Turtleback) Turtleback Bks.

—Fix That Truck! 2012. (LEGO City 8X8 Ser.). lib. bdg. 13.55 *(978-0-606-26773-1(5)*, Turtleback) Turtleback Bks.

—LEGO City: Catch That Crook! 2012. (Lego City Ser.). (ENG., Illus.). 24p. (J). (gr. -1-3). pap. 3.99 *(978-0-545-36991-6(6))* Scholastic, Inc.

—Look Out Below! Kiernan, Kenny, illus. 2012. (Lego City Ser.). (ENG.). 32p. (J). (gr. -1-3). pap. 3.99 *(978-0-545-41555-2(1))* Scholastic, Inc.

—Work This Farm! 2011. (Lego City Ser.). (ENG.). 24p. (J). (gr. -1-k). pap. 3.99 *(978-0-545-29857-5(1))* Scholastic, Inc.

Stein, Peter. Toys Galore. Staake, Bob, illus. 2013. (ENG.). 32p. (J). (gr. -1-3). 15.99 *(978-0-7636-6254-7(2))* Candlewick Pr.

Stevenson, James. Night after Christmas. 2003. (ENG.). 32p. (J). pap. 2.95 *(978-0-590-41600-9(6))* Scholastic, Inc.

Stierle, Cynthia. Together Forever. 2010. (Playbox Ser.). (ENG., Illus.). 32p. (J). bds. 19.99 *(978-0-7944-2026-0(5))* Reader's Digest Assn., Inc., The.

Stock, Lisa. Perfect Pets. 2014. (DK Reader Level 2 Ser.). lib. bdg. 13.55 *(978-0-606-35731-9(9))* Turtleback Bks.

Suen, Anastasia. Un Premio Adentro. Heck, Claudia M., tr. from ENG. Laughead, Mike, illus. 2012. (Robot y Rico/Robot & Rico Ser.).Tr. of Prize Inside. (MUL, SPA & ENG.). 32p. (gr. 1-2). pap. 5.05 *(978-1-4342-3919-8(5))*; lib. bdg. 22.65 *(978-1-4342-3780-4(X))* Stone Arch Bks. (Bilingual Stone Arch Readers).

—A Prize Inside: A Robot & Rico Story, 1 vol. Laughead, Mike, illus. 2009. (Robot & Rico Ser.). (ENG.). 32p. (gr. 1-2). 22.65 *(978-1-4342-1627-4(6))* Stone Arch Bks.

—Test Drive: A Robot & Rico Story. Laughead, Mike, illus. 2010. (Robot & Rico Ser.). (ENG.). 32p. (gr. 1-2). pap. 6.25 *(978-1-4342-2303-6(5))* Stone Arch Bks.

Taylor, Sean. The World Champion of Staying Awake. Liao, Jimmy, illus. 2011. (ENG.). 32p. (J). (gr. -1-2). 15.99 *(978-0-7636-4957-9(0))* Candlewick Pr.

Terada, Junzo. A Good Home for Max. 2014. (ENG., Illus.). 40p. (J). (gr. -1-k). 16.99 *(978-1-4521-2702-6(6))* Chronicle Bks. LLC.

Thompson, Don. Bunny World: Kindness Is the Key to Happiness. 2009. 28p. pap. 14.99 *(978-1-4389-5475-2(1))* AuthorHouse.

Thornburgh, Rebecca McKillip, illus. Rufus & Ryan Give Thanks. 2014. (Rufus & Ryan Ser.). 20p. (J). bds. 7.99 *(978-0-8249-1936-8(X)*, Ideal Pubns.) Worthy Publishing.

Tidhar, Lavie. Central Station, 1 vol. unabr. ed. 2017. (ENG.). 9.99 ***(978-1-5436-2453-3(7)***, 9781543624533) Brilliance Publishing, Inc.

Tillworth, Mary. Dump Truck Trouble/Let's Build a Doghouse! (Bubble Guppies) Random House Beginners Books Staff & MJ Illustrations Staff, illus. 2014. (Pictureback(R) Ser.). (ENG.). 32p. (J). (gr. -1-2). 4.99 *(978-0-385-37526-9(3)*, Random Hse. Bks. for Young Readers) Random Hse. Children's Bks.

Tolley, Diane Stringam. Kris Kringle's Magic. 2012. 169p. (J). 14.99 *(978-1-4621-1105-3(X))* Cedar Fort, Inc./CFI Distribution.

Tootin' Around Town. (Magnets on the Move Ser.). 8p. (J). bds. *(978-2-7643-0101-2(4))* Phidal Publishing, Inc./Editions Phidal, Inc.

Tosten, S. Kennedy. Troy's Amazing Universe Bk. 2: T for Toy. 2004. (Illus.). 149p. (YA). (gr. 2-18). pap. 13.95 *(978-0-9743185-1-6(5))* Brite Pr.

Toy Box Innovations, creator. Disney/Pixar: Volume 2. abr. ed. 2006. (Disney's Read along Collection Ser.). (ENG.). 24p. (J). (gr. -1-3). pap. *(978-0-7634-2181-6(2))* Walt Disney Records.

Toy Town: Individual Title Six-Packs. (gr. -1-2). 23.00 *(978-0-7635-9003-1(7))* Rigby Education.

ToyBox Innovations, creator. Disney Pixar's Toy Story: Read-along. 2006. (Disney's Read Along Ser.). (ENG., Illus.). 24p. (J). (gr. -1-3). pap. *(978-0-7634-2179-3(0))* Walt Disney Records.

Tuma, Refe & Tuma, Susan. What the Dinosaurs Did Last Night: A Very Messy Adventure. 2015. (What the Dinosaurs Did Ser.: 1). (ENG., Illus.). 40p. (J). (gr. -1-1). 17.00 *(978-0-316-33562-1(2))* Little Brown & Co.

Unglick, Richard. Sherlock Holmes: the Hound of the Baskervilles. 2016. (Playmobil Ser.). (ENG.). 96p. (J). (gr. 1-7). 19.95 *(978-0-63322-078-2(8)*, Walter Foster Jr) Quarto Publishing Group USA.

V, Vasanthi. The Toy-Gobbling Monster. Lee, Anais, illus. 2013. (ENG.). (J). 14.95 *(978-1-62086-330-5(8))* Mascot Bks., Inc.

Vaitonis, Steven. Edison the Christmas Elf & the Imperfect Perfect Toy. Blue, Melissa, illus. 2014. 32p. (J). (gr. -1-1). pap. 12.95 *(978-1-939930-33-0(2)*, Belle Isle Bks.) Brandylane Pubs., Inc.

Valente, Shannon. Trucks, Trains & Worm Brains. 2009. 16p. pap. 10.79 *(978-1-4389-5411-0(5))* AuthorHouse.

Valentine, Madeline. The Bad Birthday Idea. 2013. (ENG., Illus.). 40p. (J). (gr. -1-2). 17.99 *(978-0-449-81331-7(2)*, Knopf Bks. for Young Readers) Random Hse. Children's Bks.

Varicak, Rebecca. The Journey of a Toys for Tots Toy! 2012. 24p. pap. 15.99 *(978-1-4772-8601-2(2))* AuthorHouse.

Vaughan, Richard & Crews, Marcia. Three Bears of the Pacific Northwest. Trammell, Jeremiah, illus. 2016. (ENG.). 20p. (J). (— 1). bds. 9.99 *(978-1-63217-076-7(0)*, Little Bigfoot) Sasquatch Bks.

Velasquez, Eric. Looking for Bongo. 2017. (ENG.). 32p. (J). (gr. -1-1). 6.99 *(978-0-8234-3767-2(1))* Holiday Hse., Inc.

—Looking for Bongo. Velasquez, Eric, illus. 2016. (ENG., Illus.). 32p. (J). (gr. -1-1). 16.95 *(978-0-8234-3565-4(2))* Holiday Hse., Inc.

Verrett, Michael. Cozmo the Elf. 2010. 86p. pap. 32.00 *(978-0-557-25717-1(4))* Lulu Pr., Inc.

Vestal, Julie Cheek. Gracie's Lullaby Land. 2011. 24p. pap. 15.99 *(978-1-4568-9014-8(X))* Xlibris Corp.

Vogel, Vin. Bedtime for Yeti. 2016. (ENG., Illus.). 32p. (J). (-k). 16.99 *(978-1-101-99431-3(2)*, Dial Bks) Penguin Young Readers Group.

Voigt, Cynthia. Teddy & Co. Zakimi, Paola, illus. 2016. (ENG.). 192p. (J). (gr. 2-5). 16.99 *(978-0-553-51160-4(2)*, Knopf Bks. for Young Readers) Random Hse. Children's Bks.

Voigtsberger, Sandra A. Jack's Pockets. 2008. 17p. pap. 24.95 *(978-1-60563-546-0(4))* America Star Bks.

Waldman, Debby & Feutl, Rita. Room Enough for Daisy, 1 vol. Revell, Cindy, illus. 2011. (ENG.). 32p. (J). (gr. -1-3). 19.95 *(978-1-55469-255-2(5))* Orca Bk. Pubs. USA.

Walker, Anna. Alfie's Lost Sharkie. 2016. (ENG., Illus.). 24p. (J). (gr. -1-3). 14.99 *(978-0-544-58656-7(5)*, Houghton Mifflin Harcourt Publishing Co.

Wallace, William H. Santa's Magic Key. 2010. 20p. (J). 10.49 *(978-1-4490-8924-5(0))* AuthorHouse.

Wang, Adria. My World: My Playtimes Toys. Nicholls, Paul, illus. 2005. 10p. (J). 4.95 *(978-1-58117-250-8(8)*, Intervisual/Piggy Toes) Bendon, Inc.

Ward, Helen. Twenty-five December Lane. Anderson, Wayne, illus. 2007. 17p. (J). *(978-1-74178-722-1(X))* Bonnier Publishing Australia.

Warnock, Chris. Toys Overboard!, 1 vol. 2009. (ENG.). 48p. 24.95 *(978-1-60672-197-1(6))* America Star Bks.

Watt, F. & Wells, R. That's Not My Dolly. 2004. 10p. (J). 7.95 *(978-0-7945-0635-3(6))* EDC Publishing.

Weinberg, Jennifer Liberts. Christmas Toys. 2012. (Step into Reading Level 2 Ser.). lib. bdg. 13.55 *(978-0-606-26796-0(4)*, Turtleback) Turtleback Bks.

Weinberger, David J. Answers to a Christmas Question. 2012. (ENG.). (J). pap. *(978-1-4675-2381-3(X))* Independent Pub.

—Answers to a Christmas Question Coloring Book. 2012. (ENG.). (J). pap. *(978-1-4675-2380-6(1))* Independent Pub.

Weisner, David. Mr. Wuffles! Weisner, David, illus. 2013. (Illus.). 49.99 *(978-0-9777098-7-8(6))*; 14.99 *(978-0-9777098-8-5(4))* Dreamscape Media, LLC.

Wells, Rosemary. Bunny Party. 2003. (Max & Ruby Ser.). (ENG., Illus.). 32p. (J). (gr. -1-k). pap. 6.99 *(978-0-14-250162-7(X)*, Puffin Books) Penguin Young Readers Group.

West, Tracey. Chronicles of Ninjago. 2014. (Lego Ninjago Ser.). (ENG.). 64p. (J). (gr. 2-5). pap. 5.99 *(978-0-545-74638-0(8))* Scholastic, Inc.

—The Golden Weapons. 2012. (Ninjago Readers Ser.: 3). lib. bdg. 13.55 *(978-0-606-26555-3(4)*, Turtleback) Turtleback Bks.

—The Green Ninja. 2013. (Lego Ninjago Ser.). (ENG.). 32p. (J). (gr. -1-3). pap. 3.99 *(978-0-545-60798-8(1))* Scholastic, Inc.

—The Green Ninja. 2013. (Ninjago Readers Ser.: 7). lib. bdg. 13.55 *(978-0-606-32027-6(X)*, Turtleback) Turtleback Bks.

—Masters of Spinjitzu. 2012. (Lego Ninjago Ser.). (ENG.). 32p. (J). (gr. -1-3). pap. 3.99 *(978-0-545-40114-2(3))* Scholastic, Inc.

—Masters of Spinjitzu. 2012. (Ninjago Readers Ser.: 2). lib. bdg. 13.55 *(978-0-606-23978-3(2)*, Turtleback) Turtleback Bks.

—More Monsters, More Problems. 2016. (LEGO NEXO Knights Ser.). (ENG.). 80p. (J). (gr. 2-5). pap. 4.99 *(978-1-338-03804-0(4))* Scholastic, Inc.

—A Ninja's Path. 2012. (Lego Ninjago Ser.). (ENG.). 32p. (J). (gr. -1-3). pap. 3.99 *(978-0-545-43593-2(5))* Scholastic, Inc.

—Pirates vs. Ninja. 2013. (Ninjago Readers Ser.: 6). lib. bdg. 13.55 *(978-0-606-32026-9(1)*, Turtleback) Turtleback Bks.

—Rise of the Snakes. 2012. (Lego Ninjago Ser.). (ENG.). 32p. (J). (gr. -1-3). pap. 3.99 *(978-0-545-43592-5(7))* Scholastic, Inc.

—Snake Attack!, Bk. 5. 2012. (Lego Ninjago Ser.). (ENG.). 80p. (J). (gr. 2-5). pap. 4.99 *(978-0-545-46518-2(4))* Scholastic, Inc.

—A Team Divided. 2014. (LEGO Ninjago Chapter Bks.: 6). lib. bdg. 14.75 *(978-0-606-36367-9(X))* Turtleback Bks.

West, Tracey & Howard, Kate. Attack of the Nindroids. 2014. (Lego Ninjago Ser.). (ENG.). 32p. (J). (gr. -1-3). pap. 3.99 *(978-0-545-64390-0(2))* Scholastic, Inc.

—Techno Strike! 2014. (Lego Ninjago Ser.). (ENG.). 32p. (J). (gr. -1-3). pap. 3.99 *(978-0-545-66384-7(9))* Scholastic, Inc.

Weston Woods Staff, creator. Too Many Toys! 2011. 29.95 *(978-0-545-37421-7(9))* Weston Woods Studios, Inc.

Whybrow, Ian. Harry & the Bucketful of Dinosaurs. Reynolds, Adrian, illus. 2010. (Harry & the Dinosaurs Ser.). (ENG.). 32p. (J). (gr. -1-2). pap. 7.99 *(978-0-375-85119-3(4)*, Dragonfly Bks.) Random Hse. Children's Bks.

Wiesner, David. Mr. Wuffles! 2013. (CHI.). 40p. (J). *(978-986-189-418-8(7))* Grimm Cultural Ent., Co., Ltd.

—Mr. Wuffles! 2013. (ENG., Illus.). 32p. (J). (gr. -1-3). 17.99 *(978-0-618-75661-2(2)*, Clarion Bks.) Houghton Mifflin Harcourt Publishing Co.

Wilburn, Mary Lynne. Sam's Toy Museum. 2012. 24p. pap. 15.99 *(978-1-4653-4029-0(7))* Xlibris Corp.

Willems, Mo. A Cautionary Tale. Willems, Mo, illus. 2011. (Illus.). 40p. (gr. -1-1). 19.99 *(978-1-4231-4449-6(X))* Hyperion Pr.

—El Conejito Knuffle: Un Cuento Aleccionador. Willems, Mo, illus. rev. ed. 2007. (Knuffle Bunny Ser.). (ENG & SPA., Illus.). 40p. (J). (gr. -1-k). pap. 7.99 *(978-1-4231-0567-1(2))* Hyperion Pr.

—Hooray for Amanda & Her Alligator! Willems, Mo, illus. 2011. (ENG., Illus.). 72p. (J). (gr. -1-3). 17.99 *(978-0-06-200400-0(X))* HarperCollins Pubs.

—I Love My New Toy! Willems, Mo, illus. 2008. (Elephant & Piggie Book Ser.). (ENG., Illus.). 64p. (J). (gr. -1-k). 9.99 *(978-1-4231-0961-7(9))* Hyperion Pr.

—Knuffle Bunny. 2014. 36p. pap. 8.00 *(978-1-61003-228-5(4))* Center for the Collaborative Classroom.

—Knuffle Bunny: A Cautionary Tale. Willems, Mo, illus. unabr. ed. 2006. (Illus.). (J). (gr. -1-1). 29.95 *(978-0-439-90583-1(4))* Weston Woods Studios, Inc.

—Knuffle Bunny Free: An Unexpected Diversion. Willems, Mo, illus. 2010. (Illus.). 52p. (J). (gr. -1-3). (ENG.). 17.99 *(978-0-06-192957-1(3))*; lib. bdg. 18.89 *(978-0-06-192958-8(1))* HarperCollins Pubs.

—Knuffle Bunny Free: An Unexpected Diversion. 2012. *(978-0-545-44810-9(7))* Scholastic, Inc.

—Knuffle Bunny Too: A Case of Mistaken Identity. Willems, Mo, illus. rev. ed. 2007. (Knuffle Bunny Ser.). (ENG., Illus.). 48p. (J). (gr. -1-k). 17.99 *(978-1-4231-0299-1(1))* Hyperion Pr.

Willems, Mo & Willems, Trixie, narrated by. Knuffle Bunny Too: A Case of Mistaken Identity. 2011. (J). (gr. -1-2). 29.95 *(978-0-545-13456-9(0))* Weston Woods Studios, Inc.

William H. Sadlier Staff. Tina's Toys: Big Book. 2005. (Emergent Library: Vol. 1). (gr. -1-1). 24.00 net. *(978-0-8215-8903-8(2))* Sadlier, William H. Inc.

Williams, Karen Lynn. Galimoto. Stock, Catherine, illus. 2015. 32p. pap. 7.00 *(978-1-61003-604-7(2))* Center for the Collaborative Classroom.

Williams, Margery. The Velveteen Rabbit, 0 vols. Spirin, Gennady, illus. 2011. (ENG.). 48p. (gr. 3-7). 17.99 *(978-0-7614-5848-7(4)*, 9780761458487, Amazon Children's Publishing) Amazon Publishing.

—The Velveteen Rabbit. Felix, Monique, illus. 40p. 2013. (ENG.). (J). (gr. 1-3). pap. 9.99 *(978-0-89812-831-4(5)*, Creative Paperbacks) 2005. pap. 8.95 *(978-0-89812-383-8(6))* Creative Co., The.

—The Velveteen Rabbit. Nicholson, William, illus. 2011. (Dover Children's Classics Ser.). (ENG.). 48p. (J). (gr. k-5). pap. 8.99 *(978-0-486-48606-2(0))* Dover Pubns., Inc.

—The Velveteen Rabbit. 2003. (J). 9.99 *(978-0-9740847-3-2(5))* GiGi Bks.

—The Velveteen Rabbit. Kliros, Thea, illus. 2004. (ENG.). 22p. (J). (gr. -1-1). bds. 6.99 *(978-0-06-052746-4(3)*, HarperFestival) HarperCollins Pubs.

—The Velveteen Rabbit. 2010. (CHI., Illus.). (J). *(978-957-762-476-5(6))* Hsin Yi Pubns.

—The Velveteen Rabbit. Nicholson, William, illus. 44p. (J). (gr. 2-3). pap. 3.50 *(978-0-8072-1346-9(2)*, Listening Library) Random Hse. Audio Publishing Group.

—The Velveteen Rabbit. Nicholson, William, illus. 2014. (ENG.). 48p. (J). (gr. -1-2). 19.99 *(978-0-385-37566-5(2)*, Doubleday Bks. for Young Readers) Random Hse. Children's Bks.

—The Velveteen Rabbit, 1 vol. Jorgensen, David, illus. 2005. (Rabbit Ears: A Classic Tale Ser.). (ENG.). 40p. (gr. 2-7). 25.65 *(978-1-59197-757-5(6))* Spotlight.

—The Velveteen Rabbit. Hague, Michael, illus. 2008. (ENG.). 48p. (J). (gr. -1-2). per. 7.99 *(978-0-312-37750-2(9)*, 9780312377502) Square Fish.

—The Velveteen Rabbit. Wilson, Katherine, illus. 2006. (ENG.). 32p. (J). (gr. -1-1). per. 3.95 *(978-0-8249-5530-4(7)*, Ideal Pubns.) Worthy Publishing.

—The Velveteen Rabbit. Daily, Don, illus. 2007. (ENG.). 28p. (J). (gr. -1-17). bds. 5.95 *(978-0-7624-2935-6(6)*, Running Pr. Kids) Running Pr. Bk. Pubs.

—The Velveteen Rabbit: Or How Toys Become Real. Santore, Charles, illus. 2013. (Classic Edition Ser.). (ENG.). 48p. (J). 17.95 *(978-1-60433-277-3(8)*, Applesauce Pr.) Cider Mill Pr. Bk. Pubs., LLC.

—The Velveteen Rabbit: Or, How Toys Become Real. Encarnacion, Liz, ed. Santore, Charles, illus. 2014. (ENG.). 24p. (J). bds. 8.95 *(978-1-60433-461-6(4)*, Applesauce Pr.) Cider Mill Pr. Bk. Pubs., LLC.

Williams, Margery & Bianco, Margery Williams. The Velveteen Rabbit. Felix, Monique, illus. 2004. (ENG.). 40p. (J). (gr. 1-3). 19.99 *(978-1-56846-217-2(4)*, Creative Editions) Creative Co., The.

Williams, Sam. Santa's Toys. Gill, Tim, illus. 2003. 14p. bds. *(978-1-85602-274-3(9)*, Pavilion Children's Books) Pavilion Bks.

Wilson, Karma. Princess Me. Unzner, Christa, illus. 2007. (ENG.). 32p. (J). (gr. -1-3). 16.99 *(978-1-4169-4098-2(7)*, McElderry, Margaret K. Bks.) McElderry, Margaret K. Bks.

Windham, Ryder. LEGO(r) Bionicle. Scholastic, illus. 2016. (LEGO Bionicle Ser.: 3). (ENG.). 128p. (J). (gr. 2-5). pap. 5.99 *(978-0-545-92540-2(1))* Scholastic, Inc.

Winnie the Pooh & a Day for Eeyore (Read-Along Ser.). (J). 7.99 incl. audio *(978-1-55723-176-5(1))* Walt Disney Records.

Wojtowycz, David, illus. Whatever the Weather, Clavde! 2004. 10p. (J). (gr. -1-2). reprint ed. 8.00 *(978-0-7567-8257-3(0))* DIANE Publishing Co.

Wolfe, Frances. The Little Toy Shop. Wolfe, Frances, illus. 2008. (ENG., Illus.). 32p. (J). (gr. -1-2). 19.95 *(978-0-88776-865-1(2)*, Tundra Bks.) Tundra Bks. CAN. Dist: Penguin Random Hse. LLC.

Wood, Courtney. Just the Way It Was. 2013. 28p. pap. 19.99 *(978-1-4817-0734-3(5))* AuthorHouse.

Wooten, Arthur. Wise Bear William: A New Beginning. Santora, Bud, illus. 2012. 44p. pap. 12.99 *(978-0-9850529-1-1(0))* Galaxias Productions.

Wrate, Richard. Din-o-mite in Aarons Closet. 2009. 28p. (J). 14.99 *(978-0-615-19210-9(6))* Show n' Tell Publishing.

Xiong, Kim, illus. The Clay General. 2008. (J). 18.95 *(978-1-60603-002-8(7))* Better Chinese LLC.

—Paper Horse. 2008. (ENG & CHI.). 37p. (J). 18.95 *(978-1-60603-003-5(5))* Better Chinese LLC.

Yaccarino, Dan. Class Pet Squad: Journey to the Center of Town. 2016. (ENG., Illus.). 144p. (J). 13.99 *(978-1-250-02462-6(5)*, 9781250024626) Feiwel & Friends.

Yaccarino, Dan. Journey to the Center of Town. 2017. (Class Pet Squad Ser.: 1). (J). lib. bdg. 17.20 ***(978-0-606-39943-2(7))*** Turtleback Bks.

Yoon, Salina. Bear's Big Day. 2017. (ENG., Illus.). 32p. (J). bds. 7.99 *(978-1-68119-436-3(8)*, 9781681194363, Bloomsbury USA Childrens) Bloomsbury Publishing USA.

—Found. Yoon, Salina, illus. 2014. (ENG., Illus.). 40p. (J). (gr. -1-1). 14.99 *(978-0-8027-3559-1(2)*, 9780802735591, Bloomsbury USA Childrens) Bloomsbury Publishing USA.

Yorinks, Arthur. Harry & Lulu. braille ed. 2004. (Illus.). (J). (gr. k-3). spiral bd. *(978-0-616-07250-9(3))*; spiral bd. *(978-0-616-07249-3(X))* Canadian National Institute for the Blind/Institut National Canadien pour les Aveugles.

—Harry & Lulu. Matje, Martin, illus. 32p. (J). pap. 4.99 *(978-0-7868-1221-9(4))* Hyperion Paperbacks for Children.

Yuen, Dan. Charlie the Chopper & the Greatest Toymaker. Davis, Tim, illus. 2010. 26p. (J). *(978-0-88144-480-3(4))* Yorkshire Publishing Group.

Zagarenski, Pamela. Henry & Leo. 2016. (ENG., Illus.). 40p. (J). (gr. -1-3). 17.99 *(978-0-544-64811-1(0)*, HMH Books For Young Readers) Houghton Mifflin Harcourt Publishing Co.

Zak, Faith. Naptime Adventures: Train. 2012. 24p. 24.95 *(978-1-4626-5000-2(7))* America Star Bks.

Zolotow, Charlotte. Growing up Stories for 5-6 Year Olds. 114p. (J). (gr. -1-17). 19.99 *(978-0-7868-0519-8(6))* Disney Pr.

Zuber, Diane C. The Broken Doll. Firtl, Mary Meehan, illus. 2006. (ENG.). 32p. (J). (gr. -1-3). incl. audio compact disk *(978-0-9785551-1-5(2))* Zuber Publishing.

TOYS—POETRY

Bolocan, D. Stephie Learns about Animals: Funny Rhymes for Children about Toys & Animals. 2010. (Illus.). 56p. pap. 21.99 *(978-1-4490-9045-6(1))* AuthorHouse.

Evans, Olive. The Thrift Store Bears. Woolley, Patricia, illus. 2004. (ENG.). 41p. (J). 18.97 *(978-0-9748954-0-6(7))* Teddy Traveler Co.

Tanner, Suzy-Jane, illus. Nursery Rhymes. 2012. (ENG.). 24p. (J). pap. 9.95 *(978-1-84135-743-0(X))* Award Pubns. Ltd. GBR. Dist: Parkwest Pubns., Inc.

TRACK AND FIELD

see also Walking

Amstutz, Lisa J. The Science Behind Track & Field. 2016. (Science of the Summer Olympics Ser.). (ENG., Illus.). 32p. (gr. 3-4). lib. bdg. 27.99 *(978-1-4914-8158-5(7)*, Edge Bks.) Capstone Press of Coughlan Cos.

Belval, Brian. Olympic Track & Field. 2007. (Illus.). 52p. (gr. 3-7). pap. 26.50 *(978-1-4358-3779-9(7))* Rosen Publishing Group, Inc., The.

Bodden, Valerie. Running. 2009. (Active Sports Ser.). 24p. (J). (gr. 1-5). lib. bdg. 24.25 *(978-1-58341-700-3(1)*, Creative Education) Creative Co., The.

Clarke, Zoë. The Modern Pentathlon. 2012. (Collins Big Cat Progress Ser.). (ENG., Illus.). 48p. (J). (gr. 4-5). pap. 6.99 *(978-0-00-742884-7(7))* HarperCollins Pubs. Ltd. GBR. Dist: Independent Pubs. Group.

Cohn, Jessica. Free Running. 2013. (Incredibly Insane Sports Ser.). (Illus.). 48p. (J). (gr. 4-6). 31.95 *(978-1-4339-8826-4(7))*; pap. 14.05 *(978-1-4339-8827-1(5))* Stevens, Gareth Publishing LLLP. (Gareth Stevens Learning Library).

Conklin, Wendy. No Way! Jolting Jumps (Grade 7) 2017. (TIME for KIDS(r) Nonfiction Readers Ser.). (Illus.). 48p. (J). (gr. 7-7). pap. 9.99 ***(978-1-4938-3610-9(2))*** Teacher Created Materials, Inc.

Crabtree Staff & Johnson, Robin. Take off Track & Field. 2012. (ENG., Illus.). 32p. (J). pap. *(978-0-7787-3181-8(2))* Crabtree Publishing Co.

Crossingham, John & Kalman, Bobbie. Track Events in Action. 2004. (Sports in Action Ser.). (ENG., Illus.). 32p. (J). pap. *(978-0-7787-0359-4(2))* Crabtree Publishing Co.

Doeden, Matt. Track & Field. 2015. (Summer Olympic Sports Ser.). (ENG., Illus.). 32p. (J). (gr. 2-4). 19.95 *(978-1-60753-810-3(5))* Amicus Publishing.

Douglas, Peter. Track & Field: Conditioning for Greatness. 2017. (Preparing for Game Day Ser.: Vol. 10). (ENG.). (YA). (gr. 7-12). 24.95 ***(978-1-4222-3920-9(9))*** Mason Crest.

Fleming, Sally. Rapid Runners. Underwood, Kay Povelite, illus. 2004. (It's Nature! Ser.). 32p. (J). (gr. 3-6). pap. 7.95 *(978-1-55971-789-2(0)*, NorthWord Bks. for Young Readers) T&N Children's Publishing.

Foster, John. Marathon. 2006. (Collins Big Cat Ser.). (ENG., Illus.). 24p. (J). (gr. 2-2). pap. 6.99 *(978-0-00-718689-1(4))* HarperCollins Pubs. Ltd. GBR. Dist: Independent Pubs. Group.

Frederick, Shane. Track & Field. 2012. (Illus.). 48p. (J). 35.65 *(978-1-60818-212-1(6)*, Creative Education) Creative Co., The.

Gifford, Clive. Athletics. 2016. (ENG., Illus.). 32p. (J). (gr. 4-6). pap. 11.99 *(978-1-4451-4960-8(5)*, Franklin Watts) Hachette Children's Group GBR. Dist: Hachette Bk. Group.

—Baseball. 2009. (Tell Me about Sports Ser.). 32p. (gr. 3-5). 28.50 *(978-0-7614-4453-4(X))* Marshall Cavendish Corp.

—The Inside Story of Track & Field. 2011. (Sports World Ser.). (YA). (gr. 5-9). lib. bdg. 29.25 *(978-1-4488-4846-1(6))* Rosen Publishing Group, Inc., The.

—Running. 2009. (Tell Me about Sports Ser.). 32p. (gr. 3-5). 28.50 *(978-0-7614-4459-6(9))* Marshall Cavendish Corp.

—Track & Field. 2011. (ENG., Illus.). 32p. (J). pap. 10.95 *(978-1-77092-040-8(4))* Saunders Bk. Co. CAN. Dist: RiverStream Publishing.

Glass, Maya. The Running Book / Correr. 2009. (Let's Get Moving / Diviértete en movimiento Ser.). (ENG & SPA.). 24p. (gr. k-1). 42.50 *(978-1-61514-236-1(3)*, Editorial Buenas Letras) Rosen Publishing Group, Inc., The.

Goodrow, Carol. Kids Running: Have Fun, Get Faster, & Go Farther. 2008. (ENG., Illus.). 88p. (J). (gr. 1-6). per. 10.95 *(978-1-891369-76-6(8))* Breakaway Bks.

Greek, Joe. Parkour. 2015. (Sports to the Extreme Ser.). (ENG., Illus.). 48p. (J). (gr. 5-6). 30.25 *(978-1-4994-3553-5(3)*, Rosen Central) Rosen Publishing Group, Inc., The.

—Zombie Runs, 01 vols., 1. 2016. (Role-Playing for Fun & Profit Ser.). (ENG.). 48p. (J). pap. 11.75 *(978-1-4994-3736-2(6)*, Rosen Central) Rosen Publishing Group, Inc., The.

Griffis, Molly Levite. Great American Bunion Derby. 2003. (Illus.). viii, 87p. (J). 15.95 *(978-1-57168-801-9(3)*, Eakin Pr.) Eakin Pr.

Hayhurst, Chris. Ultra Marathon Running. 2009. (Ultra Sports Ser.). 64p. (gr. 5-8). 58.50 *(978-1-60854-609-1(8)*, Rosen Reference) Rosen Publishing Group, Inc., The.

Jackson, Demi. Parkour. 2015. (Daredevil Sports Ser.). (ENG., Illus.). 32p. (J). (gr. 1-1). pap. 10.50 *(978-1-4824-2993-0(4))* Stevens, Gareth Publishing LLLP.

Johnson, Robin. Take off Track & Field. 2012. (ENG., Illus.). 32p. (J). lib. bdg. *(978-0-7787-3154-2(5))* Crabtree Publishing Co.

Kalman, Bobbie. Field Events in Action. 2004. (Sports in Action Ser.). (ENG., Illus.). 32p. (J). pap. *(978-0-7787-0360-0(6))* Crabtree Publishing Co.

—Field Events in Action. Crabtree, Marc & Rouse, Bonna, illus. Crabtree, Marc, photos by. 2004. (Sports in Action Ser.). (ENG.). 32p. (J). lib. bdg. *(978-0-7787-0340-2(1))* Crabtree Publishing Co.

Kortemeier, Todd. 12 Reasons to Love Track & Field. 2018. (ENG.). 32p. (gr. 3-6). 31.35 ***(978-1-63235-431-0(4)***, 12-Story Library) Pr. Room Editions LLC.

Lang, Heather. Fearless Flyer: Ruth Law & Her Flying Machine. Colón, Raúl, illus. 2016. (ENG.). 40p. (J). (gr. k-3). 16.95 *(978-1-62091-650-6(9))* Boyds Mills Pr.

Loh-Hagan, Virginia. Extreme Ultra Running. 2016. (Illus.). 32p. *(978-1-63470-484-7(3))* Cherry Lake Publishing.

Luke, Andrew. Track & Field, Vol. 13. 2016. (Inside the World of Sports Ser.: Vol. 13). (ENG., Illus.). 80p. (J). (gr. 7-12). 24.95 *(978-1-4222-3467-9(3))* Mason Crest.

MacKay, Jennifer, ed. Track & Field. 2012. (Science Behind Sports Ser.). (Illus.). 128p. (YA). (gr. 7-12). lib. bdg. 34.45 *(978-1-4205-0707-2(9))* Cengage Gale.

Malaspina, Ann. Vivian & Victor Learn about Verbs. Prater, Linda, illus. 2014. (Language Builders Ser.). (ENG.). 32p. (J). (gr. 2-4). lib. bdg. 25.27 *(978-1-59953-667-5(6))* Norwood Hse. Pr.

Manley, Claudia B. Competitive Track & Field for Girls. 2005. (SportsGirl Ser.). (Illus.). 64p. (YA). (gr. 5-9). lib. bdg. 31.95 *(978-0-8239-3408-9(X))* Rosen Publishing Group, Inc., The.

Marsico, Katie, et al. Running. 2008. (21st Century Skills Library: Real World Math Ser.). (ENG., Illus.). 32p. (gr. 4-8). lib. bdg. 28.50 *(978-1-60279-249-4(6)*, 200032) Cherry Lake Publishing.

Mason, Paul & Eason, Sarah. Free Running. 2011. (On the Radar: Sports Ser.). (ENG., Illus.). 32p. (gr. 4-8). lib. bdg. 26.60 *(978-0-7613-7759-7(X))* Lerner Publishing Group.

McDougall, Chros. Girls Play to Win Track & Field. 2011. (Girls Play to Win Ser.). 64p. (J). (gr. 3-6). lib. bdg. 27.93 *(978-1-59953-467-1(3))* Norwood Hse. Pr.

Nitz, Kristin Wolden. Play-by-Play Field Events. King, Andy, illus. King, Andy, photos by. 2004. (Play-by-Play Ser.). 80p. (J). (gr. 4-8). lib. bdg. 23.93 *(978-0-8225-3933-9(0))* Lerner Publishing Group.

Payment, Simone. What Happens to Your Body When You Run. 2009. (How & Why of Exercise Ser.). (Illus.). 48p. (YA). (gr. 5-9). 29.25 *(978-1-4358-5306-5(7))* Rosen Publishing Group, Inc., The.

A Robbie Reader-Extreme Sports, 4 vols., Set. Incl. Extreme Cycling with Dale Holmes. Hinman, Bonnie. lib. bdg. 25.70 *(978-1-58415-487-7(X))*; Extreme Skateboarding with Paul Rodriquez JR. Kjelle, Marylou Morano. lib. bdg. 25.70 *(978-1-58415-489-1(6))*; Ride the Giant Waves with Garrett Mcnamara. Smalley, Carol Parenzan. lib. bdg. 25.70 *(978-1-58415-486-0(1))*; Ultra Running with Scott Jurek. Whiting, Jim. lib. bdg. 25.70 *(978-1-58415-484-6(5))*; 32p. (J). (gr. 1-4). 2006. (Robbie Reader Ser.). (Illus.). 2006. lib. bdg. *(978-1-58415-485-3(3))* Mitchell Lane Pubs., Inc.

Rosen, Karen. Great Moments in Olympic Track & Field, 1 vol. 2014. (Great Moments in Olympic Sports Ser.). (ENG.). 64p. (gr. 10-14). lib. bdg. 32.79 *(978-1-62403-400-8(4)*, SportsZone) ABDO Publishing Co.

Royston, Angela. Why Do I Run? 2012. (My Body Ser.). (ENG., Illus.). 24p. (gr. k-4). pap. 7.95 *(978-1-77092-000-2(5))* Saunders Bk. Co. CAN. Dist: RiverStream Publishing.

Running, 6 vols. (Multicultural Programs Ser.). 16p. (gr. 1-3). 24.95 *(978-0-7802-9215-4(4))* Wright Group/McGraw-Hill.

Schraff, Anne. Wilma Rudolph: The Greatest Woman Sprinter in History. 2004. (African-American Biographies Ser.). (Illus.). 112p. (J). lib. bdg. 26.60 *(978-0-7660-2291-1(9))* Enslow Pubs., Inc.

Sisk, Siobhan. Would You Dare Run a Marathon? 2016. (Would You Dare? Ser.). 00032p. (J). pap. 10.50 *(978-1-4824-5822-0(5))* Stevens, Gareth Publishing LLLP.

Speno, Andrew. The Great American Foot Race: Ballyhoo for the Bunion Derby! 2017. (ENG.). 176p. (J). (gr. 3). 17.95 *(978-1-62979-602-4(6)*, Calkins Creek) Boyds Mills Pr.

Teller, Jackson. Free Running. 2012. (Adrenaline Rush Ser.). (Illus.). 32p. (gr. 4-7). lib. bdg. 31.35 *(978-1-59920-682-0(X))* Black Rabbit Bks.

Thom, Kara Douglass. See Mom Run. Golden, Lilly, illus. 2003. (ENG.). 32p. (J). 15.00 *(978-1-891369-40-7(7))* Breakaway Bks.

Tuminelly, Nancy. Super Simple Walk & Run: Healthy & Fun Activities to Move Your Body, 1 vol. 2011. (Super Simple Exercise Ser.). (ENG., Illus.). 32p. (J). (gr. k-3). 27.07 *(978-1-61714-964-1(0))* ABDO Publishing Co.

Vanderhoof, Gabrielle. Track & Field. 2010. (Getting the Edge Ser.). 96p. (YA). lib. bdg. 24.95 *(978-1-4222-1740-5(X))* Mason Crest.

Wade, Alison. The Female Distance Runner's Training Log. 2003. 6.00 *(978-0-9701566-3-1(4))* Idea, Inc.

Way, Jennifer. The Running Book. (Let's Get Moving Ser.). 24p. (gr. k-k). 2009. 42.50 *(978-1-61514-230-9(4))* 2004. (Illus.). (J). lib. bdg. 22.60 *(978-1-4042-2512-1(9))* Rosen Publishing Group, Inc., The. (PowerKids Pr.).

—The Running Book: Correr. 2004. (Let's Get Moving / Diviértete en Movimiento Ser.). (ENG & SPA., Illus.). 24p. (J). (gr. -1-1). lib. bdg. 22.60 *(978-1-4042-7512-6(6)*, Editorial Buenas Letras) Rosen Publishing Group, Inc., The.

TRACK AND FIELD—FICTION

Almond, David. Harry Miller's Run. Rubbino, Salvatore, illus. 2017. (ENG.). 64p. (J). (gr. 2-4). 16.99 *(978-0-7636-8975-9(0))* Candlewick Pr.

Bar, Ellen. Jumping Jenny. Macia, Raquel Garcia, illus. 2011. (ENG.). 32p. (J). (gr. k-3). pap. 7.95 *(978-0-7613-5143-6(4)*, Kar-Ben Publishing) Lerner Publishing Group.

—Jumping Jenny. Maciá, Raquel García, illus. 2011. (Kar-Ben Favorites Ser.). (ENG.). 32p. (J). (gr. k-3). lib. bdg. 17.95 *(978-0-7613-5141-2(8)*, Kar-Ben Publishing) Lerner Publishing Group.

Bergeron, Alain M. Abby's Fabulous Season, 1 vol. 2014. (ENG.). 200p. (J). (gr. 4-6). pap. 10.95 *(978-1-927583-47-0(0))* Second Story Pr. CAN. Dist: Orca Bk. Pubs. USA.

Bridwell, Norman. Clifford's Field Day. 2012. (Scholastic Reader Level 1 Ser.). (ENG.). 32p. (J). (gr. -1-3). pap. 3.99 *(978-0-545-22325-6(3)*, Cartwheel Bks.) Scholastic, Inc.

Cartier, Wesley. Marco's Run. Ruffins, Reynold, illus. 2003. (Green Light Readers Level 2 Ser.). (ENG.). 24p. (J). (gr. -1-3). pap. 3.95 *(978-0-15-204828-0(6))* Houghton Mifflin Harcourt Publishing Co.

Coniglio, Rebecca Perlman. Lily's Little Life Lessons: Lily's Laces. Mundy, Jen, illus. 2013. (ENG.). 24p. (J). (gr. -1-3). 14.95 *(978-1-62086-408-1(8))* Mascot Bks., Inc.

Cotler, Steve. Cheesie Mack Is Running Like Crazy! Holgate, Douglas, illus. (Cheesie Mack Ser.). (ENG.). (J). (gr. 3-7). 2014. 256p. pap. 6.99 *(978-0-307-97716-8(1)*, Yearling) 2013. 240p. 15.99 *(978-0-307-97713-7(7)*, Random Hse. Bks. for Young Readers) Random Hse. Children's Bks.

Cross-country Race: Individual Title Six-Packs. (gr. 1-2). 22.00 *(978-0-7635-9169-4(6))* Rigby Education.

DelleCava, Karen. A Closer Look. 2011. 304p. (YA). (gr. 9-18). 16.95 *(978-1-934813-49-2(4))* Westside Bks.

Driscoll, Laura. Slow down, Sara! O'Rourke, Page Eastburn, illus. 2003. (Science Solves It! Ser.). 32p. (J). pap. 5.95 *(978-1-57565-125-5(4))* Kane Press, Inc.

Fehlbaum, Beth. Hope in Patience. 2010. 312p. (YA). (gr. 8-18). 16.95 *(978-1-934813-41-6(9))* Westside Bks.

Fry, Erin. Losing It, 0 vols. 2014. (ENG.). 274p. (J). (gr. 5-7). pap. 9.99 *(978-1-4778-1668-4(2)*, 9781477816684, Amazon Children's Publishing) Amazon Publishing.

Geary, Cailean McCarrick. Kelsey Shining Bright. 2012. 198p. pap. 12.95 *(978-1-934074-76-3(4))* Apprentice Hse.

Harkness, Karen. Coralee's Best Run Yet. 2007. (Illus.). 40p. (J). per. 7.99 net. *(978-0-9800934-0-7(6))* H&W Publishing Inc.

Hengel, Katherine. The Handoff, 1 vol. unabr. ed. 2011. (District 13 Ser.). (ENG.). 48p. (YA). (gr. 9-12). 7.95 *(978-1-61651-583-6(X))* Saddleback Educational Publishing, Inc.

—No Easy Race, 1 vol. unabr. ed. 2011. (District 13 Ser.). (ENG.). 47p. (YA). (gr. 9-12). pap. 7.95 *(978-1-61651-277-4(6))* Saddleback Educational Publishing, Inc.

Kim, JiYu. Zippy the Runner. Seon, JeongHyeon, illus. rev. ed. 2014. (MySELF Bookshelf Ser.). (ENG.). 32p. (J). (gr. k-2). pap. 11.94 *(978-1-60357-656-7(8))*; lib. bdg. 25.27 *(978-1-59953-647-7(1))* Norwood Hse. Pr.

Kuskowski, Alex. Line Up, 1 vol. unabr. ed. 2011. (District 13 Ser.). (ENG.). 48p. (YA). (gr. 9-12). pap. 7.95 *(978-1-61651-279-8(2))* Saddleback Educational Publishing, Inc.

Maddox, Jake. Record Run, 1 vol. Tiffany, Sean, illus. 2009. (Jake Maddox Sports Stories Ser.). (ENG.). 72p. (gr. 2-3). 25.32 *(978-1-4342-1598-7(9))* Stone Arch Bks.

—Track & Field Takedown, 1 vol. Garcia, Eduardo, illus. 2012. (Jake Maddox Sports Stories Ser.). (ENG.). 72p. (gr. 2-3). pap. 5.95 *(978-1-4342-3901-3(2))*; lib. bdg. 25.32 *(978-1-4342-3287-8(5))* Stone Arch Bks.

Maddox, Jake & Anderson, Josh. Second Shot. Aburtov, Jesus Aburto, illus. 2016. (Jake Maddox Sports Stories Ser.). (ENG.). 72p. (gr. 2-3). lib. bdg. 25.32 *(978-1-4965-3052-3(7))* Stone Arch Bks.

Malaspina, Ann. Touch the Sky: Alice Coachman, Olympic High Jumper. Velasquez, Eric, illus. 2012. (ENG.). 32p. (J). (gr. 1-3). 16.99 *(978-0-8075-8035-6(X))* Whitman, Albert & Co.

Molokie, Tom. Introducing Willy Mcspry. 2011. 36p. pap. 15.65 *(978-1-4634-3697-1(1))* AuthorHouse.

Montgomery, R. A. Track Star! 2009. (Choose Your Own Adventure Ser.: No. 31). (Illus.). 144p. (J). (gr. 2-7). pap. 6.99 *(978-1-933390-31-4(X))* Chooseco LLC.

O'Connor, Jane. Fancy Nancy & the Mean Girl. Glasser, Robin Preiss, illus. 2011. (I Can Read Level 1 Ser.). (ENG.). 32p. (J). (gr. -1-3). 16.99 *(978-0-06-200178-8(7))*; pap. 3.99 *(978-0-06-200177-1(9))* HarperCollins Pubs.

Peters, Stephanie True & Cano, Fernando M. Track Team Titans, 1 vol. Aburto, Jesus et al, illus. 2011. (Sports Illustrated Kids Graphic Novels Ser.). (ENG.). 56p. (gr. 2-3). pap. 7.19 *(978-1-4342-3072-0(4))*; lib. bdg. 26.65 *(978-1-4342-2224-4(1))* Stone Arch Bks.

Powell, Jillian. Fun Run. Gulliver, Amanda, illus. 2013. (Start Reading Ser.). (ENG.). 24p. (J). (gr. k-1). pap. 41.94 *(978-1-4765-3210-3(9))*; pap. 7.95 *(978-1-4765-3189-2(7))* Capstone Press of Coughlan Cos.

Reynolds, Jason. Ghost. (Track Ser.: bk.1). (ENG., Illus.). (J). (gr. 5). 2017. 208p. pap. 6.99 *(978-1-4814-5016-4(6))* 2016. 192p. 17.99 *(978-1-4814-5015-7(8)*, Atheneum/Caitlyn Dlouhy Books) Simon & Schuster Children's Publishing.

—Ghost. 2017. (Track Ser.: bk.1). (ENG.). (J). lib. bdg. 17.20 ***(978-0-606-40160-9(1))*** Turtleback Bks.

—Patina. 2017. (J). pap. ***(978-1-4814-5019-5(0))***; (Track Ser.: 2). (ENG., Illus.). 240p. (gr. 5). 16.99 ***(978-1-4814-5018-8(2)***, Atheneum/Caitlyn Dlouhy Books) Simon & Schuster Children's Publishing.

Richards, Katherine. My Favorite Run. Fieldhouse, Vicky, illus. 2013. (ENG.). 32p. (J). 16.99 *(978-0-9895095-2-7(4))* Fit Kids Publishing.

Robins, Eleanor. The Fastest Runner, 1 vol. unabr. ed. 2011. (Carter High Chronicles Ser.). (ENG.). 52p. (YA). (gr. 9-12). pap. 7.95 *(978-1-61651-308-5(X))* Saddleback Educational Publishing, Inc.

Schraff, Anne. A Boy Called Twister, 1 vol. unabr. ed. 2010. (Urban Underground Ser.). (ENG.). 180p. (YA). (gr. 9-12). pap. 9.95 *(978-1-61651-002-2(1))* Saddleback Educational Publishing, Inc.

—A Boy Called Twister. 2010. (Urban Underground — Harriet Tubman High School Ser.). (YA). lib. bdg. 20.80 *(978-0-606-14271-7(1)*, Turtleback) Turtleback Bks.

Scudamore, Beverly. Ready to Run, 1 vol. 2006. (Lorimer Sports Stories Ser.). (ENG.). 96p. (J). (gr. 4-8). 16.95 *(978-1-55028-915-2(2)*, 9781550289152); 8.95 *(978-1-55028-914-5(4)*, 9781550289145) Lorimer, James & Co., Ltd., Pubs. CAN. Dist: Casemate Pubs. & Bk. Distributors, LLC.

Sommer, Carl. The Great Royal Race. 2003. (Another Sommer-Time Story Ser.). (Illus.). 48p. (J). (gr. k-4). lib. bdg. 23.95 incl. audio *(978-1-57537-758-2(6))* Advance Publishing, Inc.

—The Great Royal Race. Westbrook, Dick, illus. 2003. (Another Sommer-Time Story Ser.). 48p. (J). (gr. k-4). lib. bdg. 23.95 incl. audio compact disk *(978-1-57537-708-7(X))* Advance Publishing, Inc.

—The Great Royal Race. 2003. (Another Sommer-Time Story Ser.). (Illus.). 48p. (J). (gr. 1-4). 16.95 incl. audio *(978-1-57537-557-1(5))* Advance Publishing, Inc.

—The Great Royal Race. Westbrook, Dick, illus. 2003. (Another Sommer-Time Story Ser.). 48p. (J). (gr. 1-4). 16.95 incl. audio compact disk *(978-1-57537-508-3(7))* Advance Publishing, Inc.

—The Great Royal Race(La Gran Carrera Real) Westbrook, Dick, illus. 2009. (Another Sommer-Time Story Bilingual Ser.). (SPA & ENG.). 48p. (J). lib. bdg. 16.95 *(978-1-57537-152-8(9))* Advance Publishing, Inc.

Terrell, Brandon. Valor & Victory. Max, Iman, illus. 2016. (Time Machine Magazine Ser.). (ENG.). 128p. (gr. 3-4). lib. bdg. 22.65 *(978-1-4965-2594-9(9))* Capstone Press of Coughlan Cos.

Voigt, Cynthia. The Runner. 2012. (Tillerman Cycle Ser.: 4). (ENG., Illus.). 240p. (YA). (gr. 7). 18.99 *(978-1-4424-5066-0(5))*; pap. 7.99 *(978-1-4424-2881-2(3))* Simon & Schuster Children's Publishing. (Atheneum Bks. for Young Readers).

Wallace, Rich. Chasing the Baton, 1 vol. Heitz, Tim, illus. 2016. (Game Face Ser.). (ENG.). 112p. (J). (gr. 3-7). 27.07 *(978-1-62402-133-6(6))* Magic Wagon.

TRACK AND FIELD ATHLETES

Baer, Peter. Wilma Rudolph: Gold-Medal Winner. 2013. (InfoMax Readers Ser.). (ENG.). 24p. (J). (gr. 2-3). pap. 49.50 *(978-1-4777-2383-8(8))*; pap. 8.25 *(978-1-4777-2381-4(1))* Rosen Publishing Group, Inc., The. (Rosen Classroom).

Baer, Peter & Castle, Grace. Olympic Champion: Wilma Rudolph. 2013. (Rosen Readers Ser.). (ENG.). 24p. (J). (gr. 2-3). pap. 8.25 *(978-1-4777-2385-2(4))*; pap. 49.50 *(978-1-4777-2386-9(2))* Rosen Publishing Group, Inc., The. (Rosen Classroom).

Benge, Janet & Benge, Geoff. Louis Zamperini: Redemption. 2014. (ENG.). 218p. (YA). pap. 9.99 *(978-1-62486-049-2(4))* Emerald Bks.

Buckley, James. Who Was Jesse Owens? 2015. (Who Was... ? Ser.). lib. bdg. 16.00 *(978-0-606-36754-7(3))* Turtleback Bks.

Burlingame, Jeff. Jesse Owens: I Always Loved Running. 2011. (African-American Biography Library). (Illus.). 128p. (J). (gr. 7-12). lib. bdg. 33.27 *(978-0-7660-3497-6(6))* Enslow Pubs., Inc.

Calkhoven, Laurie. Jesse Owens. Vukovic, Elizabet, illus. 2017. (You Should Meet Ser.). (ENG.). 48p. (J). (gr. 1-3). pap. 3.99 *(978-1-4814-8095-6(2)*, Simon Spotlight) Simon Spotlight.

Frederick, Shane. Track & Field. 2012. (Illus.). 48p. (J). 35.65 *(978-1-60818-212-1(6)*, Creative Education) Creative Co., The.

Krull, Kathleen. Wilma Unlimited. Diaz, David, illus. 2015. 44p. pap. 7.00 *(978-1-61003-502-6(X))* Center for the Collaborative Classroom.

Lang, Heather. Queen of the Track: Alice Coachman, Olympic High-Jump Champion. Cooper, Floyd, illus. 2012. (ENG.). 40p. (J). (gr. k). 16.95 *(978-1-59078-850-9(8))* Boyds Mills Pr.

McDougall, Chros. Jesse Owens: Trailblazing Sprinter, 1 vol. 2011. (Legendary Athletes Ser.). (ENG., Illus.). 112p. (YA). (gr. 7-12). 34.22 *(978-1-61714-758-6(3))* ABDO Publishing Co.

McKissack, Patricia C. & McKissack, Fredrick L. Jesse Owens: Legendary Track Star. 2013. (Famous African Americans Ser.). 24p. (J). (gr. k-3). pap. 7.95 *(978-1-4644-0199-2(3)*, Enslow Elementary); (Illus.). 22.60 *(978-0-7660-4104-2(2))* Enslow Pubs., Inc.

Mooney, Carla. Caitlyn Jenner. 2016. (Transgender Pioneers Ser.). 112p. (J). (gr. 6-6). 37.10 *(978-1-5081-7158-4(0))* Rosen Publishing Group, Inc., The.

Offutt, Jason. Helen Stephens: The Fulton Flash. Hare, John, illus. 2014. (ENG.). 48p. (J). lib. bdg. 24.00 *(978-1-61248-114-2(0))* Truman State Univ. Pr.

Patrick, Jean L. S. & Gustavson, Adam. Long-Armed Ludy & the First Women's Olympics: Based on the True Story of Lucile Ellerbe Godbold. 2017. (ENG., Illus.). 32p. (J). (gr. 1-4). lib. bdg. 16.99 *(978-1-58089-546-0(8))* Charlesbridge Publishing, Inc.

Stanmyer, Jackie F. Jesse Owens: Facing down Hitler. 2016. (Game-Changing Athletes Ser.). (ENG., Illus.). 112p. (J). (gr. 9-9). lib. bdg. 42.79 *(978-1-5026-1049-2(3))* Cavendish Square Publishing.

TRACK ATHLETICS

see Track and Field

TRACKING AND TRAILING

Arnosky, Jim. Wild Tracks! A Guide to Nature's Footprints. 2008. (ENG., Illus.). 32p. (J). (gr. 1-5). 14.95 *(978-1-4027-3985-9(0))* Sterling Publishing Co., Inc.

Engel, Steve. Tracks Count: A Guide to Counting Animal Prints. Petersen, Alexander, illus. 2014. (Little Naturalist Ser.). (ENG.). 32p. (J). (gr. -1-k). 17.99 *(978-1-940052-07-6(6))* Craigmore Creations.

Graubart, Norman D. How to Track a Deer, 1 vol. 2015. (ENG., Illus.). 24p. (J). lib. bdg. 23.60 *(978-1-4777-5415-3(6)*, Windmill Bks.) Rosen Publishing Group, Inc., The.

—How to Track a Rabbit, 1 vol. 2015. (ENG., Illus.). 24p. (J). lib. bdg. 23.60 *(978-1-4777-5434-4(2)*, Windmill Bks.) Rosen Publishing Group, Inc., The.

—How to Track a Turkey, 1 vol. 2015. (ENG., Illus.). 24p. (J). lib. bdg. 23.60 *(978-1-4777-5414-6(8)*, Windmill Bks.) Rosen Publishing Group, Inc., The.

Jackson, Tom. Tracking Animal Movement. 2015. (Animal Trackers Ser.). (ENG., Illus.). 32p. (gr. 3-4). lib. bdg. 27.32 *(978-1-4914-6985-9(4)*, Fact Finders) Capstone Press of Coughlan Cos.

—Tracking Animal Numbers. 2015. (Animal Trackers Ser.). (ENG., Illus.). 32p. (gr. 3-4). lib. bdg. 27.32 *(978-1-4914-6967-3(0)*, Fact Finders) Capstone Press of Coughlan Cos.

Johnson, Jinny. Animal Tracks & Signs: Track over 400 Animals from Big Cats to Backyard Birds. 2008. (ENG., Illus.). 192p. (J). (gr. 5-9). 24.95 *(978-1-4263-0253-4(3))*; lib. bdg. 32.90 *(978-1-4263-0254-1(1))* National Geographic Society. (National Geographic Children's Bks.).

Johnson, Rebecca L. & National Geographic Learning Staff. Tracking Animal Migrators. 2007. (Reading Expeditions Ser.). (ENG., Illus.). 32p. (J). pap. 17.95 *(978-0-7922-8449-9(6))* CENGAGE Learning.

Mauro, Paul & Melton, H. Keith. Tracking & Surveillance. 2004. (Detective Academy Ser.). (Illus.). 48p. (J). *(978-0-439-57180-7(4))* Scholastic, Inc.

Maynard, Charles W. Going to the Great Smoky Mountains National Park. 2008. (Farcountry Explorer Bks.). (Illus.). 48p. (J). (gr. 3-7). per. 14.95 *(978-1-56037-477-0(2))* Farcountry Pr.

National Geographic Staff. Animal Pop! With 5 Incredible, Life Size Fold-Outs. 2010. (In Your Face Ser.). (ENG., Illus.). 20p. (J). (gr. 2-5). 14.95 *(978-1-4263-0716-4(0)*, National Geographic Children's Bks.) National Geographic Society.

Oxlade, Chris. Be a Tracker. Sassin, Eva, illus. 2015. (Go Wild Ser.). (ENG.). 32p. (J). (gr. 3-6). pap. 7.99 *(978-1-4677-7650-9(5)*, Lerner Pubns.) Lerner Publishing Group.

—Be an Explorer. Sassin, Eva, illus. 2015. (Go Wild Ser.). (ENG.). 32p. (gr. 3-6). (J). lib. bdg. 26.65 *(978-1-4677-6358-5(6))*; 26.65 *(978-1-4677-7223-5(2))* Lerner Publishing Group.

Patterson, Caroline. Who Pooped in the Zoo? Exploring the Weirdest, Wackiest, Grossest, & Most Surprising Facts about Zoo Poop. Rath, Robert, illus. 2011. 40p. (J). 14.95 *(978-1-56037-504-3(3))* Farcountry Pr.

Posada, Mia. Who Was Here? Discovering Wild Animal Tracks. Posada, Mia, illus. 2014. (ENG., Illus.). 32p. (J). (gr. k-3). 16.95 *(978-1-4677-1871-4(8)*, Millbrook Pr.) Lerner Publishing Group.

Robson, Gary D. Who Pooped in the Northwoods? 2008. (Illus.). 48p. (J). pap. 11.95 *(978-1-56037-434-3(9))* Farcountry Pr.

—Who Pooped in the Park? Yellowstone. 2004. (Illus.). 48p. (J). pap. 11.95 *(978-1-56037-273-8(7))* Farcountry Pr.

—Who Pooped in the Park? Red Rock Canyon National Conservation Area: Scats & Tracks for Kids. Rath, Robert, illus. 2005. (Who Pooped in the Park? Ser.). 48p. (J). (gr. -1-3). pap. 9.95 *(978-1-56037-371-1(7))* Farcountry Pr.

—Who Pooped in the Park? Shenandoah National Park: Scats & Tracks for Kids. Rath, Robert, illus. 2006. (Who Pooped in the Park? Ser.). 48p. (J). (gr. -1-3). pap. *(978-1-56037-339-1(3))* Farcountry Pr.

—Who Pooped in the Sonoran Desert? Scats & Tracks for Kids. Rath, Robert, illus. 2006. (Who Pooped in the Park? Ser.). 48p. (J). (gr. -1-3). pap. 11.95 *(978-1-56037-349-0(0))* Farcountry Pr.

—Who Pooped on the Colorado Plateau? Scat & Tracks for Kids. Rath, Robert, illus. 2008. (Who Pooped in the Park? Ser.). 48p. (J). (gr. 1-7). pap. 11.95 *(978-1-56037-430-5(6))* Farcountry Pr.

Robson, Gary D. & Rath, Robert. Who Pooped in the Park? Olympic National Park. 2006. (Illus.). 48p. (J). pap. 11.95 *(978-1-56037-337-7(7))* Farcountry Pr.

TRACTION ENGINES

see Tractors

TRACTORS

Addison, D. R. Tractors at Work. 2009. (Big Trucks Ser.). 24p. (Illus.). (J). (gr. k-2). pap. 8.25 *(978-1-4358-3090-5(3)*, PowerKids Pr.); (gr. 1-1). 42.50 *(978-1-61511-588-4(9)*, PowerKids Pr.); (Illus.). (J). lib. bdg. 22.60 *(978-1-4358-2704-2(X))* Rosen Publishing Group, Inc., The.

Alphabet Soup (Firm) Staff, contrib. by. Let's Look at Tractors. 2009. (Let's Go! Ser.). (Illus.). 18p. (J). (gr. -1-k). bds. 12.75 *(978-1-60754-418-0(0))* Windmill Bks.

Becker, Ann. Tractors. 2009. (Amazing Machines Ser.). 32p. (gr. 2). 28.50 *(978-0-7614-4406-0(8))* Marshall Cavendish GBR. Dist: Marshall Cavendish Corp.

Bell, Samantha. Four-Track Tractor. 2016. (21st Century Basic Skills Library: Welcome to the Farm Ser.). (ENG.). 24p. (J). (gr. k-3). 24.21 *(978-1-63471-033-6(9)*, 208212) Cherry Lake Publishing.

—Four-Wheel Drive Utility Tractor. 2016. (21st Century Basic Skills Library: Welcome to the Farm Ser.). (ENG.). 24p. (J). (gr. k-3). 24.21 *(978-1-63471-038-1(X)*, 208232) Cherry Lake Publishing.

Bender, Lionel. Diggers & Tractors. 2006. (J). *(978-1-59389-267-8(5))* Chrysalis Education.

Bowman, Chris. Monster Tractors. 2014. (Monster Machines Ser.). (ENG., Illus.). 24p. (J). (gr. k-3). lib. bdg. 25.95 *(978-1-62617-055-1(X)*, Blastoff! Readers) Bellwether Media.

Brady, Peter. Tractors in Action. 2012. (Transportation Zone Ser.). (ENG.). 24p. (gr. 1-2). pap. 41.70 *(978-1-4296-8397-5(X))*; (Illus.). lib. bdg. 25.32 *(978-1-4296-7693-9(0))* Capstone Press of Coughlan Cos. (First Facts).

Brooks, Felicity. Build a Picture Tractors Sticker Book. Lovell, Katie, illus. 2013. (Build a Picture Sticker Bks). 24p. (J). pap. 6.99 *(978-0-7945-3319-9(1)*, Usborne) EDC Publishing.

—Usborne Lift & Look Tractors. Van Wyk, Hanri, illus. 2007. (Lift & Look Board Bks.). 10p. (J). (gr. -1-k). bds. 9.99 *(978-0-7945-1597-3(5)*, Usborne) EDC Publishing.

Burch, Lynda S. Wicky Wacky Things that Go! Tractors. Burch, Lynda S., photos by. 2004. (Illus.). 28p. (J). E-Book 9.95 incl. cd-rom *(978-1-933090-09-2(X))* Guardian Angel Publishing, Inc.

Dayton, Connor. Tractors. 2012. (Illus.). 24p. (J). 49.50 *(978-1-4488-5043-3(6)*, 1329062); pap. 8.25 *(978-1-4488-5042-6(8)*, 1329062); lib. bdg. 22.60 *(978-1-4488-4946-8(2)*, 1329062) Rosen Publishing Group, Inc., The. (PowerKids Pr.).

Dieker, Wendy. Tractors. 2012. (ENG., Illus.). 24p. (J). lib. bdg. 25.65 *(978-1-62031-023-6(6))* Jump! Inc.

Disney, et al. The World of Cars: Tractor Tipping. 2008. (J). 13.99 *(978-1-59319-930-2(9))* LeapFrog Enterprises, Inc.

Dorling Kindersley Publishing Staff. Chug Chug Tractor. 2013. (ENG.). 12p. (J). (gr. -1 — 1). bds. 14.99 *(978-1-4654-1426-7(6)*, DK Children) Dorling Kindersley Publishing, Inc.

—Farm Tractor. 2003. (Wheelie Bks.). (ENG., Illus.). 12p. (J). (gr. -1-k). bds. 6.99 *(978-0-7894-9713-0(1)*, DK Children) Dorling Kindersley Publishing, Inc.

—My First Tractor. 2016. (ENG., Illus.). 36p. (J). (— 1). bds. 5.99 *(978-1-4654-4390-8(8)*, DK Children) Dorling Kindersley Publishing, Inc.

—Total Tractor! 2015. (ENG., Illus.). 144p. (J). (gr. 2-5). 14.99 *(978-1-4654-2942-1(5)*, DK Children) Dorling Kindersley Publishing, Inc.

—Tractor. (Touch & Feel Ser.). (ENG., (J). (gr. -1-k). 2011. Illus.). 12p. bds. 6.99 *(978-0-7566-9167-7(2))* 2010. 14p. bds. 5.99 *(978-0-7566-7132-7(9))* 2010. (Illus.). 10p. bds. 8.99 *(978-0-7566-6302-5(4))* Dorling Kindersley Publishing, Inc. (DK Children).

Editors of Kingfisher. Tough Tractors. 2016. (It's All About... Ser.). (ENG.). 32p. pap. 5.99 *(978-0-7534-7285-9(6)*, 9780753472859, Kingfisher) Roaring Brook Pr.

Ellis, Belinda. Tractor. 2007. (Pull-Alongs Ser.). (Illus.). 12p. (gr. -1). per. *(978-1-84610-443-5(2))* Make Believe Ideas.

Gifford, Clive. Tractors. 2013. (ENG.). 24p. (J). *(978-0-7787-1001-1(7))*; pap. *(978-0-7787-1005-9(X))* Crabtree Publishing Co.

Gilpin, Rebecca. Trucks & Tractors. 2005. (ENG.). 32p. (J). pap. 8.95 *(978-0-7945-1134-0(1)*, Usborne) EDC Publishing.

Glaser, Rebecca Stromstad. Tractors Pull. 2016. (ENG., Illus.). 14p. (J). (gr. -1 — 1). bds. 7.99 *(978-1-68152-123-7(7))* Amicus.

Glover, David & Glover, Penny. Tractors in Action. 2008. (On the Go Ser.). (Illus.). 24p. (J). (gr. 3-7). lib. bdg. 22.60 *(978-1-4042-4309-5(7)*, PowerKids Pr.) Rosen Publishing Group, Inc., The.

Gregory, Josh. What Does It Do? Tractor. 2011. (Community Connections: What Does It Do? Ser.). (ENG.). 24p. (gr. 2-5). lib. bdg. 25.64 *(978-1-60279-970-7(9)*, 200960) Cherry Lake Publishing.

Gunzi, Christiane. Big Noisy Tractors. 2015. (ENG., Illus.). 10p. (J). 9.99 *(978-1-904618-89-8(8))* Award Pubns. Ltd. GBR. Dist: Parkwest Pubns., Inc.

Hayes, Amy. Big Tractors. 2015. (Machines That Work Ser.). (ENG., Illus.). 24p. (J). (gr. 1-1). 24.21 *(978-1-5026-0401-9(9))* Cavendish Square Publishing.

Kawa, Katie. Tractors. 2011. (Big Machines Ser.). (Illus.). 24p. (gr. k-2). (J). pap. 8.15 *(978-1-4339-5572-3(5))*; (J). 22.60 *(978-1-4339-5570-9(9))*; 69.20 *(978-1-4339-6891-4(6))* Stevens, Gareth Publishing LLLP.

—Tractors / Tractores. 2011. (Big Machines / Grandes MáQuinas Ser.). (SPA & ENG., Illus.). 24p. (J). (gr. k-3). 22.60 *(978-1-4339-5584-6(9))* Stevens, Gareth Publishing LLLP.

LaPadula, Thomas, illus. My Giant Tractor. 2014. (ENG.). 12p. (J). (gr. -1 — 1). bds. 10.99 *(978-0-7944-3012-2(0)*, Reader's Digest Children's Bks.) Studio Fun International.

Lindeen, Mary. Tractors. 2007. (Mighty Machines Ser.). (ENG., Illus.). 24p. (J). (gr. k-3). lib. bdg. 25.95 *(978-1-60014-061-7(0))* Bellwether Media.

Litchfield, Jo & Brooks, F. Tractors. 2004. (ENG., Illus.). 10p. (J). bds. 4.95 *(978-0-7945-0588-2(0))* EDC Publishing.

Make Believe Ideas, creator. Touch & Learn Tractors & Trucks Casebound. 2007. per. *(978-1-84610-509-8(9))* Make Believe Ideas.

Manolis, Kay. Big Rigs. 2008. (Mighty Machines Ser.). (ENG., Illus.). 24p. (J). (gr. k-3). lib. bdg. 25.95 *(978-1-60014-177-5(3))* Bellwether Media.

Mead, Sue. Monster Trucks & Tractors. rev. collector's ed. 2005. (Race Car Legends Ser.). (Illus.). 80p. (YA). (gr. 5-9). lib. bdg. 25.00 *(978-0-7910-8689-6(5))* Facts On File, Inc.

Mezzanotte, Jim. Giant Tractors. 2005. (Giant Vehicles Ser.). (Illus.). 24p. (J). (gr. 1-4). pap. 8.15 *(978-0-8368-4922-6(1))*; lib. bdg. 23.00 *(978-0-8368-4915-8(9))* Stevens, Gareth Publishing LLLP. (Gareth Stevens Learning Library).

—Tractores (Giant Tractors) 2005. (Vehículos Gigantes (Giant Vehicles) Ser.). (SPA.). 24p. (gr. 1-4). lib. bdg. 23.00 *(978-0-8368-5986-7(3)*, Gareth Stevens Learning Library) Stevens, Gareth Publishing LLLP.

Nelson, Kristin. Tractores Agrícolas. Translations.com Staff, tr. 2006. (Libros para Avanzar-Potencia en Movimiento (Pull Ahead Books-Mighty Movers) Ser.). Tr. of Farm Tractors. (SPA.). 32p. (gr. k-3). pap. 7.95 *(978-0-8225-6645-8(1)*, Ediciones Lerner) Lerner Publishing Group.

Nelson, Kristin L. Farm Tractors on the Move. 2011. (Lightning Bolt Books Vroom-Vroom Ser.). 32p. pap. 45.32 *(978-0-7613-7617-0(8))*; (ENG.). pap. 7.95 *(978-0-7613-7111-3(7))* Lerner Publishing Group.

—Tractores Agrícolas. Translations.com Staff, tr. from ENG. 2006. (Libros para Avanzar-Potencia en Movimiento (Pull Ahead Books-Mighty Movers) Ser.). (SPA., Illus.). 32p. (gr. k-3). lib. bdg. 22.60 *(978-0-8225-6231-3(6)*, Ediciones Lerner) Lerner Publishing Group.

Nixon, James. Tractors. 2010. (Machines on the Move Ser.). 32p. (J). 28.50 *(978-1-60753-063-3(5))* Amicus Publishing.

—Tractors. 2012. (Illus.). 32p. (gr. 1-3). pap. 8.95 *(978-1-926722-73-3(6))* Saunders Bk. Co. CAN. Dist: RiverStream Publishing.

Oachs, Emily Rose. Tractors. 2017. (Mighty Machines in Action Ser.). (ENG., Illus.). 24p. (J). (gr. k-3). lib. bdg. 25.95 *(978-1-62617-609-6(4)*, Blastoff! Readers) Bellwether Media.

Oxlade, Chris. This Is My Tractor. Lalla, Christine, photos by. 2008. (Mega Machine Drivers Ser.). (Illus.). 30p. (J). (gr. k). lib. bdg. 28.50 *(978-1-59771-106-7(3))* Sea-To-Sea Pubns.

Pearcey, Alice. Usborne Tractors & Trucks Stencil Book. Milbourne, Anna, ed. Tudor, Andy, illus. 2006. 10p. (J). bds. 12.99 *(978-0-7945-1139-5(2)*, Usborne) EDC Publishing.

Peppas, Lynn. Les Tracteurs. 2013. (FRE.). 32p. (J). pap. 9.95 *(978-2-89579-489-9(8))* Bayard Canada Livres CAN. Dist: Crabtree Publishing Co.

—Tractors at Work. 2010. (Vehicles on the Move Ser.). (ENG.). 32p. (J). (gr. k-3). pap. *(978-0-7787-3064-4(6))* Crabtree Publishing Co.

Pritchard, Louise & Gunzi, Christiane. Mega Tractors: Amazing Tractors & Other Tough Farm Machines. 2016. (Mega Vehicles Ser.). (ENG.). 32p. (J). (gr. -1-2). pap. 6.99 *(978-1-4380-0917-9(8))* Barron's Educational Series, Inc.

Publications International Ltd. Staff. John Deere Classics. 2008. (Illus.). 128p. 10.98 *(978-1-4127-1603-1(9)*, PIL Kids) Publications International, Ltd.

Publications International Ltd. Staff & Pripps, Robert N. John Deere: Yesterday & Today. 2010. 192p. 24.95 *(978-1-60553-486-2(2))* Publications International, Ltd.

Ransom, Candice. Camiones Grandes. Translations.com Staff, tr. from ENG. 2006. (Libros para Avanzar-Potencia en Movimiento (Pull Ahead Books-Mighty Movers) Ser.).Tr. of Big Rigs. (ENG & SPA., Illus.). 32p. (gr. k-3). lib. bdg. 22.60 *(978-0-8225-6500-0(5)*, Ediciones Lerner) Lerner Publishing Group.

Richards, Mark, et al. Tractors. 2009. (Carry-Me Ser.). (ENG., Illus.). 12p. (gr. -1-k). 7.99 *(978-1-84610-868-6(3))* Make Believe Ideas GBR. Dist: Nelson, Thomas Inc.

Rogers, Hal. Tractors. 2014. (Big Machines at Work Ser.). (ENG.). 24p. (J). (gr. -1-2). 25.64 *(978-1-62323-971-8(0)*, 206746) Child's World, Inc., The.

Ross, Paula Kovacs, et al. Tractors & Trucks: An Exciting Mechanical & Educational Experience Awaits You When You Meet Tractors & Trucks. 2013. (Kids Meet Ser.: 1). (ENG., Illus.). 96p. (J). 12.95 *(978-1-60433-326-8(X)*, Applesauce Pr.) Cider Mill Pr. Bk. Pubs., LLC.

Santos, Penelope. All about Tractors. 2015. (Rosen REAL Readers: STEM & STEAM Collection). (ENG.). 8p. pap. 5.46 *(978-1-4994-9690-1(7)*, Rosen Classroom) Rosen Publishing Group, Inc., The.

Schuh, Mari C. The Tractor Race. 2016. (Let's Race Ser.). (ENG., Illus.). 16p. (J). (gr. k-3). 17.95 *(978-1-60753-916-2(0))* Amicus Publishing.

Scollen, Chris. Busy Kids Tractors & Trucks Sticker Activity Book. 2008. (Busy Kids Ser.). (Illus.). 20p. (J). (gr. -1-3). 4.99 *(978-1-84610-634-7(6))* Make Believe Ideas GBR. Dist: Nelson, Thomas Inc.

Small World Creations Ltd., illus. Zippy Wheels: Tractors. 2016. (Zippy Wheels Ser.). (ENG.). 10p. (J). (gr. -1-k). bds. 8.99 *(978-0-7641-6828-4(2))* Barron's Educational Series, Inc.

Spaight, Anne J. Big Rigs on the Go. 2016. (Bumba Books (tm) — Machines That Go Ser.). (ENG.). 24p. (J). (gr. -1-1). lib. bdg. 25.32 *(978-1-5124-1450-9(6))* Lerner Publishing Group.

Spaight, Anne J. & Granat, Annette. Tractocamiones en Acción. 2017. (Bumba Books (tm) en Español — Máquinas en Acción (Machines That Go) Ser.). (SPA., Illus.). 24p. (J). (gr. -1-1). 25.32 *(978-1-5124-2877-3(9))* Lerner Publishing Group.

Storey, Rita. Tractors & Trucks. 2013. (Have Fun with Arts & Crafts Ser.). (Illus.). 32p. (gr. 4-7). lib. bdg. 31.35 *(978-1-59920-901-2(2))* Black Rabbit Bks.

Tango Books. Tractor: A Lift-the-Flap & Stand-Up. Burton, Terry, illus. 2011. (Mini Trucks Ser.). (ENG.). 12p. (J). (gr. -1-k). 5.99 *(978-1-85707-753-7(9))* Tango Bks. GBR. Dist: Independent Pubs. Group.

Tourville, Amanda Doering. Tractors, 1 vol. Trover, Zachary, illus. 2009. (Mighty Machines Ser.). (ENG.). 32p. (J). (gr. -1-3). 28.50 *(978-1-60270-626-2(3))* Magic Wagon.

Tractors & Diggers. 2003. (Illus.). 32p. 12.98 *(978-1-4054-2005-1(7))* Parragon, Inc.

Tractors & Trucks Sticker Activity Book. (My Sticker Activity Ser.). (Illus.). 12p. (J). *(978-1-4054-1182-0(1))* Parragon, Inc.

Watt, Fiona. Tractors. King, Sue, illus. 2009. (Luxury Touchy-Feely Board Bks). 10p. (J). bds. 15.99 *(978-0-7945-2432-6(X)*, Usborne) EDC Publishing.

Weingarten, E. T. Tractors. 2016. (Fantastic Farm Machines Ser.). 24p. (gr. 2-1). 22.60 *(978-1-4824-4586-2(7))* Stevens, Gareth Publishing LLLP.

Williams, Michael. Power Tractors. 2006. (Cool Wheels Ser.). (Illus.). 32p. (gr. 2-6). lib. bdg. 26.00 *(978-0-8368-6828-9(5)*,

TUV

Gareth Stevens Learning Library) Stevens, Gareth Publishing LLLP.

Wiseman, Blaine. Tough Tractors. 2010. (World of Wonder Ser.). 24p. (J). (gr. 2-4). lib. bdg. 25.70 (978-1-61690-148-6(9)) Weigl Pubs., Inc.

—Tractors: WOW: Big Machines. 2010. (J). pap. 9.95 (978-1-61690-149-3(7)) Weigl Pubs., Inc.

Young, Caroline. Tractors. Lyon, Chris & Gower, Teri, illus. 2004. (Young MacHines Ser.). 32p. (J). (gr. k). lib. bdg. 14.95 (978-1-58086-616-3(6), Usborne) EDC Publishing.

Young, Charles A. Tractors. rev. ed. 2004. (Young MacHines Ser.). (ENG., Illus.). 32p. (J). pap. 6.95 (978-0-7945-0632-2(1)) EDC Publishing.

TRACTORS—FICTION

Amery, Heather. Red Tractor Board Book. Cartwright, Stephen, illus. 2004. (Young Farmyard Tales Board Books Ser.). 10p. (J). bds. 3.95 (978-0-7945-0469-4(8), Usborne) EDC Publishing.

Amery, Heather & Doherty, Gillian. Wind-Up Tractor Book. 2007. (Wind-up Tractor Book Ser.). 14p. (J). bds. 25.99 (978-0-7945-1861-5(3), Usborne) EDC Publishing.

Aumann, Jane & Ladage, Cindy. The Christmas Tractor. Freitag, Charles, Illus. 2003. 30p. (J). (gr. k-4). pap. 8.95 (978-0-9703319-2-2(4)) Roots & Wings.

Ayers, Sanda. Tommy Tractor Goes to the City, 1 vol. Young, Sue, illus. 2009. 29p. pap. 19.95 (978-1-61582-054-2(X)) PublishAmerica, Inc.

Baxter, Nicola. Stop That Tractor! Glover, Peter, illus. 2016. (ENG.). 24p. (J). (gr. -1-12). pap. 6.99 (978-1-86147-758-3(9), Armadillo) Anness Publishing GBR. Dist: National Bk. Network.

—The Trouble with Tractors. Ball, Geoff, illus. 2012. (ENG.). 24p. pap. 6.99 (978-1-84322-784-7(3), Armadillo) Anness Publishing GBR. Dist: National Bk. Network.

Berrios, Frank. Tractor Trouble (Disney/Pixar Cars) RH Disney Staff, illus. 2011. (Little Golden Book Ser.). (ENG.). 24p. (J). (gr. -1-2). 4.99 (978-0-7364-2831-6(3), Golden/Disney) Random Hse. Children's Bks.

Brooks, Felicity. This Is My Tractor. Dimitri, Simona, illus. 2009. (Noisy Touchy-Feely Board Bks). 10p. (J). bds. 16.99 (978-0-7945-2473-9(7), Usborne) EDC Publishing.

Bryant, Ann. Hurry Up! 2011. (Tadpoles Ser.). (ENG., Illus.). 24p. (J). (gr. k-2). (978-0-7787-0580-2(3)); pap. (978-0-7787-0591-8(9)) Crabtree Publishing Co.

Burton, Virginia Lee. Katy & the Big Snow. (ENG., Illus.). (J). 2010. 38p. (gr. k — 1). bds. 7.99 (978-0-547-37145-0(4)) 2009. 40p. (gr. -1-3). audio compact disk 10.99 (978-0-547-25264-3(1)) Houghton Mifflin Harcourt Publishing Co.

—Katy & the Big Snow Lap Board Book. 2014. (ENG., Illus.). 38p. (J). (— 1). bds. 11.99 (978-0-544-31717-8(3), HMH Books For Young Readers) Houghton Mifflin Harcourt Publishing Co.

Clement, Nathan, illus. Big Tractor. 2015. (ENG.). 32p. (J). (gr. k-3). 16.95 (978-1-62091-790-9(4)) Boyds Mills Pr.

Cousins, Lucy. Maisy's Tractor. Cousins, Lucy, illus. 2015. (Maisy Ser.). (ENG., Illus.). 18p. (J). (— 1). bds. 5.99 (978-0-7636-7305-5(6)) Candlewick Pr.

Crow, Melinda Melton. Brave Fire Truck, 1 vol. Thompson, Chad, illus. 2011. (Wonder Wheels Ser.). (ENG.). 32p. (gr. -1-1). pap. 6.25 (978-1-4342-3384-4(7)); lib. bdg. 22.65 (978-1-4342-3029-4(5)) Stone Arch Bks.

—Busy, Busy Train, 1 vol. Thompson, Chad, illus. 2011. (Wonder Wheels Ser.). (ENG.). 32p. (gr. -1-1). pap. 6.25 (978-1-4342-3383-7(9)); lib. bdg. 22.65 (978-1-4342-3028-7(7)) Stone Arch Bks.

—Helpful Tractor, 1 vol. Thompson, Chad, illus. 2011. (Wonder Wheels Ser.). (ENG.). 32p. (gr. -1-1). pap. 6.25 (978-1-4342-3382-0(0)); lib. bdg. 22.65 (978-1-4342-3027-0(9)) Stone Arch Bks.

Dobbins, Jan. Driving My Tractor. Sim, David, illus. 2009. (ENG.). 32p. (J). (gr. -1-3). 16.99 incl. audio compact disk (978-1-84686-358-5(9)) Barefoot Bks., Inc.

—Driving My Tractor Puzzle. Sim, David, illus. 2011. (ENG.). (J). (gr. -1-1). 14.99 (978-1-84686-573-2(5)) Barefoot Bks., Inc.

Dorling Kindersley Publishing Staff. Baby - Tractor! 2012. (ENG.). 16p. (J). (gr. -1 — 1). bds. 6.99 (978-0-7566-8998-8(8), DK Children) Dorling Kindersley Publishing, Inc.

Gabel, Stacey. The New Blue Tractor. Neuman, Richard, illus. 2007. 24p. per. 13.95 (978-1-59858-424-0(3)) Dog Ear Publishing, LLC.

Garland, Michael. Grandpa's Tractor. Garland, Michael, illus. 2011. (ENG., Illus.). 32p. (J). (gr. k-1). 16.95 (978-1-59078-762-5(5)) Boyds Mills Pr.

Gould, Robert. Tractors. 2004. (Big Stuff Ser.). (ENG., Illus.). 16p. (J). bds. 7.95 (978-1-929945-44-3(2)) Big Guy Bks., Inc.

Harris, Carrie. Sally Slick & the Steel Syndicate. Valentine, Amanda, ed. 2014. (Illus.). 200p. (YA). pap. 15.00 (978-1-61317-063-2(7)) Evil Hat Productions LLC.

Hawksley, Gerald, illus. Patty Cow's Tractor: Press Out Parts Make a Tractor Carrying Patty Cow. 2009. (Toddler Make & Play Ser.). 10p. bds. 6.95 (978-1-59496-182-3(4)) Teora USA LLC.

Hillenbrand, Will. Down by the Barn, 0 vols. 2014. (ENG.). 32p. (J). (gr. -1-k). 16.99 (978-1-4778-4731-2(6), 9781477847312, Amazon Children's Publishing) Amazon Publishing.

Ladage, Cindy & Aumann, Jane. My Name Is Huber. (Illus.). (J). 2013. (ENG.). 24p. pap. 10.00 (978-1-61009-054-4(3)) 2012. (978-1-61009-050-6(0)) Oak Tree Publishing. (Acorn).

Long, Loren. Otis. Long, Loren, illus. (Otis Ser.). (Illus.). (J). (gr. -1-k). 2013. (SPA & ENG.). 40p. 7.99 (978-0-14-751124-9(0), Puffin Books) 2011. (ENG., 32p. bds. 8.99 (978-0-399-25600-4(8), Philomel Bks.) 2009. (ENG., 40p. 17.99 (978-0-399-25248-8(7), Philomel Bks.) Penguin Young Readers Group.

—Otis & the Kittens. Long, Loren, illus. 2016. (Otis Ser.). (ENG., Illus.). 40p. (J). (gr. -1-3). 17.99 (978-0-399-16398-2(0), Philomel Bks.) Penguin Young Readers Group.

—Otis & the Puppy. Long, Loren, illus. (Otis Ser.: 3). (ENG., Illus.). (J). (gr. -1-k). 2014. 38p. bds. 8.99 (978-0-399-17196-3(7)) 2013. 40p. 17.99 (978-0-399-25469-7(2)) Penguin Young Readers Group. (Philomel Bks.).

—Otis & the Scarecrow. Long, Loren, illus. 2014. (Otis Ser.). (ENG., Illus.). 40p. (J). (gr. k-3). 17.99 (978-0-399-16396-8(4), Philomel Bks.) Penguin Publishing Group.

—Otis & the Tornado. Long, Loren, illus. 2011. (Otis Ser.: 2). (ENG., Illus.). 40p. (J). (gr. -1-2). 17.99 (978-0-399-25477-2(3), Philomel Bks.) Penguin Young Readers Group.

—An Otis Christmas. Long, Loren, illus. 2013. (Otis Ser.: Bk. 4). (ENG., Illus.). 40p. (J). (gr. -1-2). 17.99 (978-0-399-16395-1(6), Philomel Bks.) Penguin Publishing Group.

—An Otis Christmas. Long, Loren, illus. 2016. (Otis Ser.). (ENG., Illus.). 38p. (J). (gr. -1-2). bds. 8.99 (978-0-399-54811-6(4), Philomel Bks.) Penguin Young Readers Group.

—Otis's Busy Day. Long, Loren, illus. 2014. (Otis Ser.). (ENG., Illus.). 32p. (J). (gr. k-1). pap. 3.99 (978-0-448-48130-2(8), Penguin Young Readers) Penguin Young Readers Group.

Menges, Thais D. Granny & the Tractor. King, Joseph, illus. 2012. 36p. pap. 10.95 (978-1-60920-047-3(0)) Ajoyin Publishing, Inc.

Mitton, Tony & Parker, Ant. Tremendous Tractors. 2005. (Amazing Machines Ser.). (ENG., Illus.). 24p. (J). (gr. -1-k). 4.99 (978-0-7534-5918-8(3), 9780753459188, Kingfisher) Roaring Brook Pr.

Oliver, Merlin. John Laughinghouse. 2007. 20.00 (978-0-8059-7333-4(8)) Dorrance Publishing Co., Inc.

Pavón, Mar. A Very, Very Noisy Tractor. 2013. (ENG., Illus.). 28p. (J). (gr. -1-k). 16.95 (978-84-15619-65-9(0)) Eastern National.

Publications International Ltd. Staff, ed. Tractor. 2010. 12p. (J). bds. 13.98 (978-1-4508-0125-6(0)) Phoenix International Publications, Inc.

Rand, Johnathan. Freddie Fernortner #11: Tadpole Trouble. 2010. 95p. (J). pap. 4.99 (978-1-893699-29-8(3)) AudioCraft Publishing, Inc.

Reader's Digest Staff. Tractor Trouble Drive Through Storybook. Pitt, Sarah, illus. 2011. (Drive-Through Storybooks Ser.). (ENG.). 10p. (J). (gr. -1-1). bds. 12.99 (978-0-7944-2169-4(5)) Reader's Digest Assn., Inc., The.

Rivers-Moore, Debbie. Let's Go - Tractor! Backhouse, Carolyn, illus. 2011. (Let's Go Bath Bks.). (ENG.). 8p. (J). (gr. -1-k). 6.99 (978-1-4380-7117-6(5)) Barron's Educational Series, Inc.

Roberts, Margiad & Owen, Carys Eurwen. Tecwyn a Ffergi Lwyd. 2005. (WEL., Illus.). 35p. pap. (978-0-86381-495-2(6)) Gwasg Carreg Gwalch.

—Tecwyn A'r Combein. 2005. (WEL., Illus.). 36p. pap. (978-0-86381-368-9(2)) Gwasg Carreg Gwalch.

—Tecwyn A'r Moto-Beic. 2005. (WEL., Illus.). 36p. pap. (978-0-86381-437-2(9)) Gwasg Carreg Gwalch.

—Tecwyn Yn Plannu Tatws. 2005. (WEL., Illus.). 36p. pap. (978-0-86381-408-2(5)) Gwasg Carreg Gwalch.

—Tecwyn Yn Teilo. 2005. (WEL., Illus.). 36p. pap. (978-0-86381-328-3(3)) Gwasg Carreg Gwalch.

Robinson, Michelle. Goodnight Tractor: The Perfect Bedtime Book! 2015. (Goodnight Ser.). (ENG., Illus.). 32p. (J). (gr. -1 — 1). pap. 7.99 (978-1-4380-0664-2(0)) Barron's Educational Series, Inc.

Rucker, Mike. Terry & the Beaver Dam Fiasco. 2003. (Terry the Tractor Ser.: Vol. 11). (Illus.). 63p. (J). (gr. -1-5). pap. 4.95 (978-0-9711659-2-2(0)) Univ. Editions.

—Terry & the Earthquake. 2006. (Terry the Tractor Ser.: Vol. 14). 72p. (J). (gr. k-4). pap. 4.95 (978-0-9711659-5-3(5)) Univ. Editions.

—Terry & the Elephant. pap. (978-1-56002-746-1(0)) Univ. Editions.

—Terry & The South Pole Breakdown. pap. (978-0-615-11379-1(6)) Univ. Editions.

—Terry & the Super Powerful Fuel. (978-1-56002-673-0(1)) Univ. Editions.

Session, Garry. Odessa Bluegill - Out Shovels a Yellow Tractor. Warren, Pamela, ed. Redel, Nicole, illus. Gorman, Suzy, photos by. 2003. 42p. (J). pap. 9.95 (978-0-9658006-2-4(8)) Session Family.

Shannon, David. Duck on a Tractor. 2017. 59.95 (978-1-338-16188-5(1)) 2016. (ENG.). 40p. (J). (gr. -1-3). 16.99 (978-0-545-61941-7(6), Blue Sky Pr., The) Scholastic, Inc.

Shannon, David. Un Pato en Tractor (Duck on a Tractor) 2016. (ENG & SPA.). 32p. (J). (gr. -1-3). 17.20 (978-0-606-39157-3(6)) Turtleback Bks.

Silcox, Beth Douglass. Little Rumely Man. Peters, Darcy, illus. 2012. 36p. pap. 12.99 (978-0-9832514-2-2(8)) Gypsy Heart Pr.

Spinelli, Jami. David's Tractor. Margolis, Lois, illus. l.t. ed. 2006. (J). 32p. 20.99 (978-1-59879-242-3(3)); 27p. (gr. -1-3). per. 11.99 (978-1-59879-241-6(5)) Lifevest Publishing, Inc.

Steers, Billy. Lift-The-Flap Tab: Tractor Mac: Friends on the Farm. 2015. (Lift-The-Flap Tab Bks.). (ENG., Illus.). 16p. (J). (gr. -1-k). bds. 8.99 (978-0-374-30168-2(9), 9780374301682) Square Fish.

—Tractor Mac Arrives at the Farm. (Tractor Mac Ser.). (ENG., Illus.). (J). 2016. 24p. pap. 4.99 (978-0-374-30536-9(6), 9780374305369) 2015. 32p. (gr. -1-k). 8.99 (978-0-374-30102-6(6), 9780374301026) Farrar, Straus & Giroux. (Farrar, Straus & Giroux (BYR)).

—Tractor Mac Builds a Barn. 2015. (Tractor Mac Ser.). (ENG., Illus.). 32p. (J). (gr. -1-2). 8.99 (978-0-374-30105-7(0), 9780374301057, Farrar, Straus & Giroux (BYR)) Farrar, Straus & Giroux.

—Tractor Mac Countdown to Christmas. 2016. (Tractor Mac Ser.). (ENG., Illus.). 16p. (J). bds. 6.99 (978-0-374-30120-0(4), 9780374301200, Farrar, Straus & Giroux (BYR)) Farrar, Straus & Giroux.

—Tractor Mac Family Reunion. 2015. (Tractor Mac Ser.). (ENG., Illus.). 32p. (J). (gr. -1-k). 8.99 (978-0-374-30109-5(3), 9780374301095, Farrar, Straus & Giroux (BYR)) Farrar, Straus & Giroux.

—Tractor Mac Farm Days. 2016. (Tractor Mac Ser.). (ENG., Illus.). 16p. (J). bds. 5.99 (978-0-374-30117-0(4), 9780374301170, Farrar, Straus & Giroux (BYR)) Farrar, Straus & Giroux.

—Tractor Mac Farmers' Market. 2015. (Tractor Mac Ser.). (ENG., Illus.). 32p. (J). (gr. -1-k). 8.99 (978-0-374-30107-1(7), 9780374301071, Farrar, Straus & Giroux (BYR)) Farrar, Straus & Giroux.

—Tractor Mac Farmers Market: Farmer's Market: Steers, Billy, illus. 2009. (ENG., Illus.). (J). 7.95 (978-0-9826870-1-7(X)) Tractor Mac Inc.

—Tractor Mac Harvest Time. (Tractor Mac Ser.). (ENG., Illus.). (J). 2017. 24p. pap. 4.99 (978-0-374-30600-7(1), 9780374306007) 2015. 32p. (gr. -1-2). 8.99 (978-0-374-30111-8(5), 9780374301118) Farrar, Straus & Giroux. (Farrar, Straus & Giroux (BYR)).

—Tractor Mac Learns to Fly. (Tractor Mac Ser.). (ENG., Illus.). (J). 2016. 24p. pap. 4.99 (978-0-374-30537-6(4), 9780374305376) 2015. 32p. (gr. -1-2). 8.99 (978-0-374-30103-3(4), 9780374301033) Farrar, Straus & Giroux. (Farrar, Straus & Giroux (BYR)).

—Tractor Mac Learns to Fly. 2016. (Tractor Mac Ser.). (J). lib. bdg. 14.75 (978-0-606-39558-8(X)) Turtleback Bks.

—Tractor Mac New Friend. 2015. (Tractor Mac Ser.). (ENG., Illus.). 32p. (J). (gr. -1-k). 8.99 (978-0-374-30110-1(7), 9780374301101, Farrar, Straus & Giroux (BYR)) Farrar, Straus & Giroux.

—Tractor Mac Parade's Best. (Tractor Mac Ser.). (ENG.). (J). 2017. 24p. pap. 4.99 (978-0-374-30599-4(4), 9780374305994) 2015. (Illus.). 32p. (gr. -1-k). 8.99 (978-0-374-30106-4(9), 9780374301064) Farrar, Straus & Giroux. (Farrar, Straus & Giroux (BYR)).

—Tractor Mac Saves Christmas. 2015. (Tractor Mac Ser.). (ENG., Illus.). 32p. (J). (gr. -1-2). 8.99 (978-0-374-30112-5(3), 9780374301125, Farrar, Straus & Giroux (BYR)) Farrar, Straus & Giroux.

—Tractor Mac Teamwork. 2016. (Tractor Mac Ser.). (ENG., Illus.). 32p. (J). 8.99 (978-0-374-30113-2(1), 9780374301132, Farrar, Straus & Giroux (BYR)) Farrar, Straus & Giroux.

—Tractor Mac Tune-Up. 2015. (Tractor Mac Ser.). (ENG., Illus.). 32p. (J). (gr. -1-2). 8.99 (978-0-374-30108-8(5), 9780374301088, Farrar, Straus & Giroux (BYR)) Farrar, Straus & Giroux.

—Tractor Mac Worth the Wait. 2017. (Tractor Mac Ser.). (ENG., Illus.). 32p. (J). 8.99 (978-0-374-30115-6(8), 9780374301156, Farrar, Straus & Giroux (BYR)) Farrar, Straus & Giroux.

—Tractor Mac You're a Winner. (Tractor Mac Ser.). (ENG., Illus.). (J). 2016. 24p. pap. 4.99 (978-0-374-30538-3(2), 9780374305383) 2015. 32p. (gr. -1-k). 8.99 (978-0-374-30104-0(2), 9780374301040) Farrar, Straus & Giroux. (Farrar, Straus & Giroux (BYR)).

—You're a Winner. 2016. (Tractor Mac Ser.). (ENG.). 24p. (J). (gr. -1-k). 14.75 (978-0-606-39283-9(1)) Turtleback Bks.

Steers, Billy, illus. Tractor Mac Learns to Fly. 2007. (J). 7.95 (978-0-9788496-2-7(0)) Tractor Mac Inc.

Steggall, Susan. Following the Tractor. 2015. (ENG., Illus.). 32p. (J). pap. 8.99 (978-1-84780-657-4(0), Frances Lincoln) Quarto Publishing Group UK GBR. Dist: Littlehampton Bk Services, Ltd.

Stoddard, Jeffery. Skid & the Too Tiny Tunnel: A Story of Courage Based on Deuteronomy 31:6. Fogle, Robin & Rhodes, Karen, eds. Stoddard, Jeffery, illus. 2009. (ENG., Illus.). 32p. (J). (gr. -1-2). 12.99 (978-1-59317-355-5(5)) Warner Pr., Inc.

Stone, Connie. A Tractor Green Day. Barnes, Garry, illus. 2008. 36p. pap. 24.95 (978-1-60474-948-9(2)) PublishAmerica, Inc.

Sutton, Sally. Farmer John's Tractor. Belton, Robyn, illus. 2013. (ENG.). 32p. (J). (gr. -1-2). 15.99 (978-0-7636-6430-5(8)) Candlewick Pr.

Terry & the Ecological Disaster. pap. (978-1-56002-792-8(4)) Univ. Editions.

Watt, Fiona & Wells, Rachel. That's Not My Tractor. 2004. (Touchy-Feely Board Bks.). (SPA & ENG., Illus.). 1p. (J). bds. 7.99 (978-0-7945-0011-5(0), Usborne) EDC Publishing.

Wellington, Monica. Truck Driver Tom. 2007. (ENG., Illus.). 32p. (J). (gr. -1-k). 16.99 (978-0-525-47831-7(0), Dutton Books for Young Readers) Penguin Young Readers Group.

TRADE FAIRS

see Fairs

TRADE-MARKS

see Trademarks

TRADE ROUTES

Ceceri, Kathy. The Silk Road: Explore the World's Most Famous Trade Route with 20 Projects. Ceceri, Kathy, illus. 2011. (Build It Yourself Ser.). (ENG., Illus.). 128p. (J). (gr. 3-7). pap. 15.95 (978-1-934670-62-0(6)) Open City Bks.

Heing, Bridey. Phoenician Trade Routes. 2017. (J). **(978-1-5026-2861-9(9))** Cavendish Square Publishing.

—Trade Routes to India. 2017. (J). **(978-1-5026-2694-3(2))** Cavendish Square Publishing.

Keranen, Rachel. The Northwest Passage. 2017. (J). **(978-1-5026-2695-0(0))** Cavendish Square Publishing.

Levy, Janey. The Silk Road: Using a Map Scale to Measure Distances. 2009. (PowerMath Ser.). (ENG., Illus.). 32p. (gr. 5-6). pap. 10.00 (978-1-4042-5140-3(5)) Rosen Publishing Group, Inc., The.

—The Silk Road: Using A Map Scale to Measure Distances. 2005. (PowerMath Ser.). (Illus.). 32p. (J). (gr. 3-6). lib. bdg. 23.95 (978-1-4042-2938-9(8), PowerKids Pr.) Rosen Publishing Group, Inc., The.

TRADE SCHOOLS

see Technical Education

TRADE UNIONS

see Labor Unions

TRADE-UNIONS

see Labor Unions

TRADE WASTE

see Waste Products

TRADEMARKS

Skinner, Tina & Palecko-Schuck, Jenna. Trademarks of The 1950s, 1 vol. 2003. (ENG., Illus.). 160p. (gr. 10-13). pap. 29.95 (978-0-7643-1828-3(4), 9780764318283) Schiffer Publishing, Ltd.

TRADITIONS

see Folklore; Legends; Superstition

TRAFFIC ACCIDENTS

Berry, Joy. Trauma. 2009. (ENG.). 52p. (J). (gr. k-7). pap. 7.95 (978-1-60577-501-2(0)) Berry, Joy Enterprises.

Graham, Ian. Forces & Motion: Investigating a Car Crash, 1 vol. Stayte, James, illus. 2013. (Anatomy of an Investigation Ser.). (ENG.). 56p. (gr. 7-8). pap. 9.95 (978-1-4329-7608-8(7)) Heinemann-Raintree.

Grosshandler, Janet. Drugs & Driving. 2009. (Drug Abuse Prevention Library). 64p. (gr. 5-5). 58.50 (978-1-60853-429-6(4)) Rosen Publishing Group, Inc., The.

Mendralla, Valerie & Grosshandler, Janet. Drinking & Driving, Now What? 2011. (Teen Life 411 Ser.). (Illus.). 120p. (YA). (gr. 7-12). lib. bdg. 34.60 (978-1-4488-4654-2(4)) Rosen Publishing Group, Inc., The.

Walker, Niki. Transportation Disaster Alert! 2005. (Disaster Alert! Ser.). (ENG., Illus.). 32p. (J). (gr. 4-7). lib. bdg. (978-0-7787-1584-9(1)) Crabtree Publishing Co.

TRAFFIC ACCIDENTS—FICTION

Atwater-Rhodes, Amelia. Token of Darkness. 2011. (ENG.). 208p. (YA). (gr. 7). pap. 8.99 (978-0-385-73751-7(3), Ember) Random Hse. Children's Bks.

Bruchac, Joseph. Whisper in the Dark. Comport, Sally Wern, illus. 2009. (ENG.). 192p. (J). (gr. 5). pap. 6.99 (978-0-06-058089-6(5)) HarperCollins Pubs.

Danticat, Edwidge. Untwine: A Novel. 2015. (ENG.). 320p. (J). (gr. 7). 16.99 (978-0-545-42303-8(1), Scholastic Pr.) Scholastic, Inc.

Delacre, Lulu. Alicia Afterimage. 2008. (ENG.). 144p. (YA). (gr. 7-18). 19.95 (978-1-60060-242-9(8)) Lee & Low Bks., Inc.

Downes, Patrick. Ten Miles One Way. 2017. (ENG.). 208p. (YA). (gr. 9). 17.99 (978-0-399-54499-6(2), Philomel Bks.) Penguin Young Readers Group.

Easton, Kelly. Aftershock. 2007. (ENG.). 176p. (YA). (gr. 7-12). pap. 6.99 (978-1-4169-0053-5(5), McElderry, Margaret K. Bks.) McElderry, Margaret K. Bks.

Frank, E. R. Wrecked. (ENG., (YA). 2015. Illus.). 336p. (gr. 9). pap. 10.99 (978-1-4814-5137-6(5)) 2007. 256p. (gr. 7-12). pap. 9.99 (978-0-689-87384-3(0)) Simon & Schuster Children's Publishing. (Atheneum Bks. for Young Readers).

Grabenstein, Chris. The Crossroads. 2009. (Haunted Mystery Ser.: 1). (ENG.). 352p. (J). (gr. 3-7). 7.99 (978-0-375-84698-4(0), Yearling) Random Hse. Children's Bks.

Grant, Michael & Applegate, Katherine. Eve & Adam. 2013. (ENG.). 304p. (YA). (gr. 8-12). pap. 9.99 (978-1-250-03419-9(1), 9781250034199) Square Fish.

Green, Tim. Lost Boy. 2015. (ENG.). 304p. (J). (gr. 3-7). 16.99 (978-0-06-231708-7(3)) HarperCollins Pubs.

Griffin, Adele. Loud Awake & Lost. (ENG.). 304p. (YA). (gr. 7). 2015. pap. 9.99 (978-0-385-75275-6(X), Ember) 2013. lib. bdg. 19.99 (978-0-385-75273-2(3), Knopf Bks. for Young Readers) Random Hse. Children's Bks.

Grover, Lorie Ann. Hit, 1 vol. 2015. (ENG.). 224p. (YA). pap. 8.99 (978-0-310-72938-9(6)) Blink.

Guest, Jacqueline. Racing Fear, 1 vol. 2004. (Lorimer SideStreets Ser.). (ENG.). 160p. (YA). (gr. 9-12). 9.95 (978-1-55028-838-4(5), 9781550288384); 16.95 (978-1-55028-839-1(3), 9781550288391) Lorimer, James & Co., Ltd., Pubs. CAN. Dist: Casemate Pubs. & Bk. Distributors, LLC.

Jocelyn, Marthe. Would You. 2008. (ENG.). 176p. (YA). (gr. 4-7). 19.99 (978-0-88776-816-3(4), Tundra Bks.) Tundra Bks. CAN. Dist: Penguin Random Hse. LLC.

Johnson, Terry Lynn. Falcon Wild. 2017. (ENG.). 176p. (J). (gr. 5). lib. bdg. 16.99 **(978-1-58089-788-4(6))** Charlesbridge Publishing, Inc.

Koertge, Ronald. Strays. 2007. (ENG.). 176p. (YA). (gr. 9-12). 16.99 (978-0-7636-2705-8(4)) Candlewick Pr.

Lerangis, Peter. Wtf. (ENG., (YA). (gr. 9). 2013. Illus.). 288p. 17.99 (978-1-4424-9369-8(0)) 2013. (Illus.). 288p. pap. 9.99 (978-1-4424-9368-1(2)) 2009. 272p. pap. 8.99 (978-1-4169-1360-3(2)) Simon Pulse. (Simon Pulse).

Mankell, Henning. Shadows in the Twilight. 2010. (Joel Gustafson Stories Ser.: No. 2). (ENG.). 208p. (YA). (gr. 7). pap. 7.99 (978-0-440-24043-3(3), Delacorte Bks. for Young Readers) Random Hse. Children's Bks.

Mcghee, Alison. All Rivers Flow to the Sea. 2005. (ENG.). 176p. (YA). (gr. 9-12). 15.99 (978-0-7636-2591-7(4)) Candlewick Pr.

Messer, Celeste M. Three Miracles. 2004. (Adventures of Andi O'Malley Ser.). (Illus.). 82-92p. (J). (gr. 4-7). 4.95 (978-0-9702171-4-1(5)) AshleyAlan Enterprises.

Meyers, Ann Marie. Up in the Air. 2013. 244p. (J). 22.99 (978-1-939967-03-9(1), Jolly Fish Pr.) North Star Editions.

Mitchard, Jacquelyn. All We Know of Heaven. 2008. (ENG.). 320p. (YA). (gr. 8-18). 16.99 (978-0-06-134578-4(4), HarperTeen) HarperCollins Pubs.

Phillips, Dee. Joyride, 1 vol. unabr. ed. 2011. (Right Now! Ser.). (ENG., Illus.). 45p. (YA). (gr. 9-12). pap. 8.95 (978-1-61651-251-4(2)) Saddleback Educational Publishing, Inc.

Rice, Luanne. The Secret Language of Sisters. 2016. (ENG.). 352p. (J). (gr. 7). 18.99 (978-0-545-83955-6(6)) Scholastic, Inc.

Scieszka, Jon. Garage Tales. Gordon, David et al, illus. 2010. (Jon Scieszka's Trucktown Ser.). (ENG.). 80p. (J). (gr. -1-3). 12.99 (978-1-4424-1196-8(1), Simon & Schuster Bks. For Young Readers) Simon & Schuster Bks. For Young Readers.

—Race from A to Z, No. 4. Gordon, David et al, illus. 2014. (Jon Scieszka's Trucktown Ser.). (ENG.). 48p. (J). (gr. -1-3). 17.99 (978-1-4169-4136-1(3), Simon & Schuster Bks. For Young Readers) Simon & Schuster Bks. For Young Readers.

—Uh-Oh, Max. Shannon, David et al, illus. 2009. (Jon Scieszka's Trucktown Ser.). (ENG.). 24p. (J). (gr. -1-1). pap. 3.99 (978-1-4169-4141-5(X), Simon Spotlight) Simon Spotlight.

Scrimger, Richard. Me & Death: An Afterlife Adventure. 2010. (ENG.). 192p. (YA). (gr. 5). pap. 12.95 (978-0-88776-796-8(6), Tundra Bks.) Tundra Bks. CAN. Dist: Penguin Random Hse. LLC.

Shusterman, Neal. Everlost. (Skinjacker Trilogy Ser.: 1). (ENG.). (YA). (gr. 7). 2009. 336p. pap. 11.99 (978-1-4169-9749-8(0)) 2006. 320p. 19.99 (978-0-689-87237-2(2)) Simon & Schuster Bks. For Young Readers. (Simon & Schuster Bks. For Young Readers).

The check digit for ISBN-10 appears in parentheses after the full ISBN-13

Sonnebom, Scott. Meet the South Police. Lozano, Omar, illus. 2015. (North Police Ser.). (ENG.). 32p. (gr. k-2). lib. bdg. 21.32 *(978-1-4795-6486-6(9))* Picture Window Bks.
Thompson, Michelle. Taming the Wind. 2010. 176p. pap. 12.99 *(978-1-59955-379-5(1))* Cedar Fort, Inc./CFI Distribution.
Walters, Eric. Overdrive. 2004. (Orca Soundings Ser.). 102p. (gr. 8-12). 19.95 *(978-0-7569-4320-2(5))* Perfection Learning Corp.
—A Toda Velocidad. 1 vol. 2008. (Spanish Soundings Ser.). (SPA.). 112p. (YA). (gr. 8-12). pap. 9.95 *(978-1-55469-055-8(2))* Orca Bk. Pubs. USA.
Webber, Katherine. The Heartbeats of Wing Jones. 2017. (ENG.). 336p. (YA). (gr. 7). 17.99 *(978-0-399-55502-2(1),* Delacorte Pr.) Random Hse. Children's Bks.
Weyn, Suzanne. Bionic. 2016. (ENG.). 240p. (YA). (gr. 7). 17.99 *(978-0-545-90677-7(6),* Scholastic Pr.) Scholastic, Inc.

TRAFFIC REGULATIONS
see also Traffic Accidents

Beaver, Simon. Traffic Jams: the Road Ahead Beginning Book with Online Access. 2014. (ENG., Illus.). 24p. (J). pap. 9.50 *(978-1-107-67468-4(9))* Cambridge Univ. Pr.
Brezina, Corona. I've Gotten a DWI/DUI, Now What? 2015. (Teen Life 411 Ser.). (ENG., Illus.). 112p. (J). (gr. 6-7). 35.60 *(978-1-4994-6146-6(1),* Rosen Young Adult) Rosen Publishing Group, Inc., The.
Crossing the Street: Individual Title Six-Packs. (gr. -1-2). 27.00 *(978-0-7635-9443-5(1))* Rigby Education.
Hemstock, Whitney M. The ABC's of Traffic Safety. 2010. 34p. pap. 16.95 *(978-0-557-28733-8(2))* Lulu Pr., Inc.
Herrington, Lisa M. Car Safety. 2012. (Rookie Read-About(tm) Safety Ser.). (ENG., Illus.). 32p. (J). lib. bdg. 25.00 *(978-0-531-28969-3(9))* Scholastic Library Publishing.
Jackson, Joann. Green Light, Red Light, Go! 2008. 20p. per. 24.95 *(978-1-60441-778-4(1))* America Star Bks.
McCaughtry, Keith. All about Street Signs & Laws. 2012. 16p. pap. 15.99 *(978-1-4772-5981-8(3))* AuthorHouse.
Moore, Elizabeth. Watch Out! 2011. (Wonder Readers Emergent Level Ser.). (ENG.). 8p. (gr. -1-1). pap. 35.94 *(978-1-4296-8237-4(X),* Wonder Readers) Capstone Press of Coughlan Cos.
Suseata Publishing, Inc. Circulación Vial: Un Juego de Niños. 2010. (Juegolibros Ser.). (SPA., Illus.). 16p. (J). (gr. k-2). bds. 27.95 *(978-84-8426-991-5(4))* Susaeta Ediciones, S.A. ESP. Dist: Independent Pubs. Group.

TRAFFIC REGULATIONS—FICTION

Diggle, David Mark. Douglas: Pays the Price for Not Paying Attention. Preuss, Sarah Louise, illus. 2011. 24p. (J). pap. *(978-0-9871658-5-5(2))* Diggle de Doo Productions Pty, Ltd.
Harper, Charise Mericle. Go, Go, Go, Stop! 2014. (ENG.). 32p. (J). (-k). 16.99 *(978-0-375-86924-2(7),* Knopf Bks. for Young Readers) Random Hse. Children's Bks.
Judith Mader. I Went to Safety Town! 2009. 40p. pap. 16.99 *(978-1-4389-0129-9(1))* AuthorHouse.
McGovan, Michael. The Bobby Dazzlers. 2011. (Illus.). 28p. pap. 14.11 *(978-1-4567-8862-9(0))* AuthorHouse.
Molyneux, Caroline. Red for Stop. Green for Go. Yellow for Be Careful. 2010. 32p. 14.49 *(978-1-4490-5824-1(8))* AuthorHouse.
Scieszka, Jon. Pete's Party. Gordon, David et al, illus. 2008. (Jon Scieszka's Trucktown Ser.). (ENG.). 24p. (J). (gr. -1-k). lib. bdg. 13.89 *(978-1-4169-4149-1(5));* pap. 3.99 *(978-1-4169-4138-5(X))* Simon Spotlight. (Simon Spotlight).

TRAILERS
see Automobiles—Trailers

TRAILING
see Tracking and Trailing

TRAINING OF ANIMALS
see Animals—Training

TRAINING OF CHILDREN
see Child Rearing

TRAINING OF EMPLOYEES
see Employees—Training of

TRAINS, RAILROAD
see Railroads

TRAMPS—FICTION

Cory, Kim Delmar. Tending Ben's Garden. 2009. (J). pap. *(978-0-88092-778-9(X))* Royal Fireworks Publishing Co.
Guest, Jacqueline. Secret Signs, 1 vol. 2006. (Orca Young Readers Ser.). (ENG., Illus.). 144p. (J). (gr. 3-6). per. 7.95 *(978-1-55143-599-2(3))* Orca Bk. Pubs. USA.
Hoban, Russell. Charlie the Tramp. Hoban, Lillian, illus. 2016. (ENG.). 48p. (J). 16.00 *(978-0-87486-780-0(0))* Plough Publishing Hse.
Hope, Laura Lee. The Outdoor Girls of Deepdale: Or Camping & Tramping for Fun & Health. 2007. (ENG.). 136p. pap. 18.99 *(978-1-4346-2152-8(9));* 150p. pap. 19.99 *(978-1-4346-2212-9(6))* Creative Media Partners, LLC.
Lindren, Astrid. Rasmus & the Vagabond. Bothmer, Gerry, tr. from SWE. Palmquist, Eric, illus. 2014. (ENG.). 180p. pap. 9.95 *(978-0-87486-597-4(2))* Plough Publishing Hse.
Mackall, Dandi Daley. Rudy Rides the Rails: A Depression Era Story. Ellison, Chris, illus. rev. ed. 2007. (Tales of Young Americans Ser.). (ENG.). 32p. (J). (gr. -1-3). 17.95 *(978-1-58536-286-8(7))* Sleeping Bear Pr.

TRANSATLANTIC FLIGHTS
see Aeronautics—Flights

TRANSCONTINENTAL JOURNEYS
see Overland Journeys to the Pacific

TRANSFORMERS (FICTITIOUS CHARACTERS)—FICTION

Auerbach, Annie. Transformers: Rescue Bots: Meet Boulder the Construction-Bot. 2013. (Passport to Reading Level 1 Ser.). (ENG., Illus.). 32p. (J). (gr. -1-3). 4.99 *(978-0-316-22831-2(1))* Little, Brown Bks. for Young Readers.
Ball, Georgia. Transformers Robots in Disguise Animated. 2016. lib. bdg. 26.95 *(978-0-606-38026-3(4))* Turtleback Bks.
Barber, John. Transformers: Official Movie Adaptation: Vol 1, 1 vol. Moreno, Jorge Jimenez, illus. 2012. (Transformers: Dark of the Moon Official Movie Adaptation Ser.). (ENG.). 24p. (J). 24.21 *(978-1-59961-966-8(0),* Graphic Novels) Spotlight.
—Transformers: Official Movie Adaptation: Vol 2, 1 vol. Moreno, Jorge Jimenez, illus. 2012. (Transformers: Dark of the Moon Official Movie Adaptation Ser.). (ENG.). 24p. (J). 24.21 *(978-1-59961-967-5(9),* Graphic Novels) Spotlight.
—Transformers: Official Movie Adaptation: Vol 4, 1 vol. Moreno, Jorge Jimenez, illus. 2012. (Transformers: Dark of the Moon Official Movie Adaptation Ser.). (ENG.). 24p. (J). 24.21 *(978-1-59961-969-9(5),* Graphic Novels) Spotlight.
—Transformers: Official Movie Adaption: Vol 3, 1 vol. Moreno, Jorge Jimenez, illus. 2012. (Transformers: Dark of the Moon Official Movie Adaptation Ser.). (ENG.). 24p. (J). 24.21 *(978-1-59961-968-2(7),* Graphic Novels) Spotlight.
Burroughs, Caleb. Transformers. Mawhinney, Art, illus. 2007. (Look & Find (Publications International) Ser.). 16p. (J). (gr. -1-3). 7.98 *(978-1-4127-8673-7(8))* Publications International, Ltd.
Elson, Maya Mackowiak. The Mystery of the Pirate Bell. 2013. (Transformers 8x8 Ser.). (J). lib. bdg. 13.55 *(978-0-606-32273-7(6),* Turtleback) Turtleback Bks.
Fox, Jennifer. Meet Optimus Prime. 2015. (Passport to Reading Level 1 Ser.). (ENG., Illus.). 32p. (J). (gr. -1-3). pap. 3.99 *(978-0-316-40558-4(2))* Little, Brown Bks. for Young Readers.
—Team of Heroes. 2014. (Transformers Passport to Reading Ser.). (J). lib. bdg. 13.55 *(978-0-606-35936-8(2))* Turtleback Bks.
Foxe, Steve. Race to the Rescue. 2016. (Transformers 8x8 Ser.). (J). lib. bdg. 13.55 *(978-0-606-39192-4(4))* Turtleback Bks.
—Transformers Robots in Disguise: a New Adventure. 2016. (Passport to Reading Level 2 Ser.). (ENG.). 32p. (J). (gr. -1-3). pap. 4.99 *(978-0-316-27432-6(1))* Little, Brown Bks. for Young Readers.
Habro Transformers Staff. Transformers Rescue Bots Roll to the Rescue! A Lift-the-Flap Book. 2013. (Lift-The-Flap Ser.: 1). (ENG.). 10p. (J). (gr. -1-k). bds. 9.99 *(978-0-7944-2849-5(5),* Reader's Digest Children's Bks.) Studio Fun International.
Hasbro. Meet Griffin Rock Rescue - Character Guide. 2016. (ENG., Illus.). 24p. (J). (gr. -1-3). pap. 5.99 *(978-0-316-38978-5(1))* Little, Brown Bks. for Young Readers.
—Roll Out & Read Adventures. 2014. (Transformers Passport to Reading Ser.). (J). lib. bdg. 18.40 *(978-0-606-35294-9(5))* Turtleback Bks.
—Transformers Rescue Bots: Reading Adventures: Passport to Reading Level 1. 2015. (Passport to Reading Level 1 Ser.). (ENG., Illus.). 192p. (J). (gr. -1-1). pap. 7.99 *(978-0-316-28627-5(3))* Little, Brown Bks. for Young Readers.
—Transformers Rescue Bots: Storybook Collection. 2016. (ENG., Illus.). 192p. (J). (gr. -1-3). 11.99 *(978-0-316-41091-5(8))* Little, Brown Bks. for Young Readers.
—Transformers Rescuebots: Robots to the Rescue! 2016. (ENG.). 12p. (J). (gr. -1-1). bds. 10.99 *(978-0-7944-3685-8(4))* Studio Fun International.
—Transformers Robots in Disguise: Chapter Book Bind-Up. 2016. (ENG.). 416p. (J). (gr. 3-7). pap. 12.99 *(978-0-316-39618-9(4))* Little, Brown Bks. for Young Readers.
Hasbro & King, Trey. Transformers Rescue Bots. 2015. (ENG., Illus.). 12p. (J). (gr. -1-1). pap. 6.99 *(978-0-316-40560-7(4))* Little, Brown Bks. for Young Readers.
Hasbro & Shea, Lisa. Transformers: Rescue Bots: Meet Chase the Police-Bot. 2013. (Passport to Reading Level 1 Ser.). (ENG.). 32p. (J). (gr. -1-3). 3.99 *(978-0-316-22829-9(X))* Little, Brown Bks. for Young Readers.
Hasbro Industries Incorporated Staff & King, Trey. Transformers Rescue Bots: Training Academy: Dinosaurs! 2016. (Passport to Reading Level 2 Ser.). (ENG., Illus.). 32p. (J). (gr. -1-3). pap. 3.99 *(978-0-316-39377-5(0))* Little, Brown Bks. for Young Readers.
Jakobs, D. Meet Blades the Copter-Bot. 2014. (Transformers Passport to Reading Ser.). (J). lib. bdg. 14.75 *(978-0-606-35295-6(3))* Turtleback Bks.
—Transformers Rescue Bots: Meet Blades the Copter-Bot. 2014. (Passport to Reading Level 1 Ser.). (ENG., Illus.). 32p. (J). (gr. -1-1). 4.99 *(978-0-316-18870-8(0))* Little, Brown Bks. for Young Readers.
Johnson, Mike & Scott, Mairghread. Transformers Prime: Rage of the Dinobots: Rage of the Dinobots. Padilla, Agustin, illus. 2013. (Transformers Ser.). (ENG.). 104p. pap. 17.99 *(978-1-61377-606-3(3),* 9781613776063) Idea & Design Works, LLC.
Mackowiak Elson, Maya. Transformers: Rescue Bots: the Mystery of the Pirate Bell. 2013. (Transformers Rescue Bots Ser.). (ENG., Illus.). 24p. (J). (gr. -1-3). 3.99 *(978-0-316-22833-6(8))* Little, Brown Bks. for Young Readers.
Mairghread, Scott. Transformers: Distant Stars: Distant Stars. Howell, Corin & Pitre-Durocher, Sara, illus. 2016. (Transformers Ser.). (ENG.). 120p. pap. 19.99 *(978-1-63140-600-3(0),* 9781631406003) Idea & Design Works, LLC.
Metzen, Chris, et al. Transformers: IDW Collection Phase Two Volume 2: IDW Collection Phase Two Volume 2. Ramondelli, Livio, illus. 2015. (Transformers Ser.: 2). (ENG.). 332p. 49.99 *(978-1-63140-364-4(8),* 9781631403644) Idea & Design Works, LLC.
Publications International Ltd. Staff. Interactive Sound Transformers. 2007. 24p. (J). 16.98 *(978-1-4127-6797-2(0),* PIL Kids) Publications International, Ltd.
—Look & Find Transformers. 2007. 24p. (J). 7.10 *(978-1-4127-6817-7(9),* PIL Kids) Publications International, Ltd.
Rau, Zachary. Autobots Versus Zombies. 2012. (Transformers 8x8 Ser.). (J). lib. bdg. 13.55 *(978-0-606-26687-1(9),* Turtleback) Turtleback Bks.
Roche, Nick, et al. Transformers: IDW Collection Phase Two Volume 3: IDW Collection Phase Two Volume 3. Milne, Alex & Salgado, Jimbo, illus. 2016. (Transformers Ser.: 3). (ENG.). 332p. 49.99 *(978-1-63140-540-2(3),* 9781631405402) Idea & Design Works, LLC.
Roe, David & Reader's Digest Editors. Mix & Match. Milne, Alex & Ruffolo, Rob, illus. 2007. (ENG.). 12p. (J). (gr. -1-1). bds. 14.99 *(978-0-7944-1286-9(6))* Reader's Digest Assn., Inc., The.
Sarracini, Chris & Furman, Simon. Transformers: Armada Omnibus: Armada Omnibus. Raiz, James et al, illus. 2016. (Transformers Ser.). (ENG.). 416p. pap. 29.99 *(978-1-63140-563-1(2),* 9781631405631) Idea & Design Works, LLC.
Sazaklis, John. The Ghosts of Griffin Rock. 2014. (Transformers 8x8 Ser.). (J). lib. bdg. 13.55 *(978-0-606-35935-1(4))* Turtleback Bks.
—Optimus Prime Versus Predaking. 2013. (Transformers 8x8 Ser.). (J). lib. bdg. 13.55 *(978-0-606-32272-0(8),* Turtleback) Turtleback Bks.
—Transformers: Rescue Bots: the Ghosts of Griffin Rock. 2014. (ENG., Illus.). 24p. (J). (gr. -1-3). pap. 3.99 *(978-0-316-27704-4(5))* Little, Brown Bks. for Young Readers.
Shea, Lisa. Meet Heatwave the Fire-Bot. 2013. (Transformers Passport to Reading Ser.). (J). lib. bdg. 14.75 *(978-0-606-31737-5(6),* Turtleback) Turtleback Bks.
—Transformers: Rescue Bots: Meet Heatwave the Fire-Bot. 2013. (Passport to Reading Level 1 Ser.). (ENG., Illus.). 32p. (J). (gr. -1-1). 4.99 *(978-0-316-22830-5(3))* Little, Brown Bks. for Young Readers.
Snider, Brandon T. Transformers Rescue Bots: Ghost in the Machine. 2017. (ENG., Illus.). 24p. (J). (gr. -1-3). pap. 4.99 ***(978-0-316-31880-8(9))*** Little, Brown Bks. for Young Readers.
Transformers: Rescue Bots: Team of Heroes. 2014. (Passport to Reading Level 1 Ser.). (ENG., Illus.). 32p. (J). (gr. -1-3). pap. 3.99 *(978-0-316-40557-7(4))* Little, Brown Bks. for Young Readers.

TRANSISTORS

MacCarald, Clara. The Invention of the Transistor. 2017. (Engineering That Made America Ser.). (ENG.). 32p. (J). (gr. 3-6). lib. bdg. 28.50 *(978-1-5038-1638-1(9),* 211159) Child's World, Inc., The.
Roland, James. How Transistors Work. 2016. (Connect with Electricity Ser.). (ENG., Illus.). 40p. (J). (gr. 4-6). lib. bdg. 30.65 *(978-1-5124-0783-9(6));* 46.65 *(978-1-5124-1011-2(X),* Lerner Pubns.) Lerner Publishing Group.

TRANSMISSION OF POWER
see Electric Lines

TRANSPLANTATION OF ORGANS, TISSUES, ETC.

Abramovitz, Melissa. Transplants. 2012. (Hot Topics Ser.). (ENG., Illus.). 128p. (gr. 7-10). lib. bdg. 39.40 *(978-1-4205-0816-1(4),* Lucent Bks.) Cengage Gale.
Ballard, Carol. Organ Transplants. 2007. (Cutting Edge Medicine Ser.). (Illus.). 64p. (gr. 6-12). lib. bdg. 34.00 *(978-0-8368-7868-4(X),* Gareth Stevens Secondary Library) Stevens, Gareth Publishing LLLP.
Campbell, Andrew. Cosmetic Surgery. 2010. (J). 34.25 *(978-1-59920-322-5(7))* Black Rabbit Bks.
—Organ Transplants. 2010. (Illus.). 45p. (J). 34.25 *(978-1-59920-321-8(9))* Black Rabbit Bks.
Claybourne, Anna. What Are the Limits of Organ Transplants?, 1 vol. 2012. (Sci-Hi: Science Issues Ser.). (ENG., Illus.). 48p. (gr. 4-4). pap. 8.99 *(978-1-4109-4473-3(5));* lib. bdg. 33.32 *(978-1-4109-4466-5(2))* Heinemann-Raintree. (Sci-Hi).
Egendorf, Laura K. Organ Donation. (Opposing Viewpoints Ser.). (ENG., Illus.). (gr. 10-12). 2013. 224p. lib. bdg. 48.80 *(978-0-7377-6332-4(9))* 2009. 240p. (YA). 29.45 *(978-0-7377-4221-3(6),* LML02109-243142) 2009. 240p. (YA). pap. 42.95 *(978-0-7377-4220-6(8),* LML02109-243109) Cengage Gale. (Greenhaven Pr., Inc.).
Fisanick, Christina. Is Selling Body Parts Ethical? 2009. (At Issue Ser.). (ENG.). 128p. (gr. 10-12). pap. 24.45 *(978-0-7377-4305-0(0));* pap. 34.45 *(978-0-7377-4306-7(9))* Cengage Gale. (Greenhaven Pr., Inc.).
Foran, Racquel. Organ Transplants, 1 vol. 2013. (Medical Marvels Ser.). (ENG., Illus.). 112p. (YA). (gr. 6-12). lib. bdg. 35.64 *(978-1-61783-904-7(3),* Essential Library) ABDO Publishing Co.
Gray, Susan H. Transplants. 2008. (21st Century Skills Innovation Library: Innovation in Medicine Ser.). (ENG., Illus.). 32p. (gr. 4-8). lib. bdg. 28.50 *(978-1-60279-225-8(9),* 200156) Cherry Lake Publishing.
Hunnicutt, Susan. Organ Transplants. 2007. (At Issue Ser.). (ENG., Illus.). 128p. (J). (gr. 10-12). 22.50 *(978-0-7377-3692-2(5),* Greenhaven Pr., Inc.); 123p. (YA). (gr. 9-12). pap. 31.80 *(978-0-7377-3691-5(7))* Cengage Gale.
Kovacs, Vic. Organ Transplants. 2016. (Miracles of Medicine Ser.). 00048p. (J). pap. 14.05 ***(978-1-4824-6100-8(5))*** Stevens, Gareth Publishing LLLP.
McClellan, Marilyn. Organ & Tissue Transplants: Medical Miracles & Challenges. 2003. (Issues in Focus Ser.). (Illus.). 128p. (J). (gr. 6-12). lib. bdg. 27.94 *(978-0-7660-1943-0(8))* Enslow Pubs., Inc.
Stearman, Kaye. The Debate about Cosmetic Surgery. 2010. (Ethical Debates Ser.). (ENG.). 48p. (YA). lib. bdg. 29.25 *(978-1-4358-9650-5(5),* Rosen Reference) Rosen Publishing Group, Inc., The.
UNOS (Organization) Staff, contrib. by. Organ Transplants: What Every Kid Needs to Know. 2003. (Illus.). (J). *(978-1-886651-43-2(4))* United Network for Organ Sharing.
Wood, Ramona. Now Caitlin Can: A Donated Organ Helps a Child Get Well. 2004. (Illus.). 32p. (J). 16.00 *(978-0-9758622-0-9(0))* ABC Pr.
Wouk, Henry. Organ Transplants. 2013. (Advances in Medicine Ser.). 64p. (J). (gr. 6-9). pap. 15.28 *(978-1-62712-010-4(6));* (Illus.). 34.21 *(978-1-60870-467-5(X))* Cavendish Square Publishing.

TRANSPORTATION
see also Aeronautics, Commercial; Automobiles; Bridges; Buses; Canals; Commerce; Freight and Freightage; Harbors; Postal Service; Railroads; Roads; Steamboats; Streets; Subways; Trade Routes; Traffic Regulations; Trucks; Waterways

ABDO Publishing Company Staff & Murray, Julie. Transportation. 2014. (Transportation Ser.: 6). (ENG.). 24p. (J). (gr. 4-8). lib. bdg. 171.00 *(978-1-62970-077-9(0))* ABDO Publishing Co.
Aboff, Marcie. A Transportation Time Line from Feet to Cars & Beyond. 2016. (Spring Forward Ser.). (J). (gr. 1). *(978-1-4900-9407-6(5))* Benchmark Education Co.
Abramson, Beverley. Off We Go! 2006. (ENG., Illus.). 24p. (J). (gr. -1-k). 15.95 *(978-0-88776-728-9(1),* Tundra Bks.) Tundra Bks. CAN. Dist: Penguin Random Hse. LLC.
Amstutz, L. J. & Amstutz, Lisa J. How Can We Reduce Transportation Pollution? 2016. (Searchlight Books — What Can We Do about Pollution? Ser.). (ENG., Illus.). 40p. (J). (gr. 3-5). lib. bdg. 30.65 *(978-1-4677-9515-9(1))* Lerner Publishing Group.
Animals at Work: Individual Title Six-Packs. (gr. k-1). 23.00 *(978-0-7635-9060-4(6))* Rigby Education.
Appleby, Alex. Dinosaurs on the Go. 2013. (Dinosaur School Ser.). 24p. (J). (gr. k-1). pap. 48.90 *(978-1-4339-9063-2(6));* pap. 8.15 *(978-1-4339-9062-5(8));* (ENG., Illus.). lib. bdg. 22.60 *(978-1-4339-9061-8(X))* Stevens, Gareth Publishing LLLP.
Ard, Catherine. Origami on the Move. 2015. (Amazing Origami Ser.). (ENG.). 32p. (J). (gr. 2-3). 26.60 *(978-1-4824-2202-3(6))* Stevens, Gareth Publishing LLLP.
Baer, Edith. This Is the Way We Go to School. 2014. 17.00 *(978-1-63419-734-2(8))* Perfection Learning Corp.
Ball, Jacqueline A. Traveling Green. (Going Green Ser.). 32p. 2016. (ENG.). (J). (gr. 2-7). pap. 8.95 *(978-1-944998-67-7(5))* 2009. (Illus.). (YA). (gr. 3-6). lib. bdg. 25.27 *(978-1-59716-964-6(1))* Bearport Publishing Co., Inc.
Barraclough, Sue. On the Move. 2009. (Me & My World Ser.). (Illus.). 24p. (J). (gr. -1-2). pap. 8.15 *(978-1-60754-064-9(9));* lib. bdg. 22.60 *(978-1-60754-058-8(4))* Windmill Bks.
Barraclough, Sue, et al. Be an Eco Hero on the Move. 2013. (Be an Eco Hero Ser.). (Illus.). 24p. (J). (gr. 2-4). lib. bdg. 25.65 *(978-1-59771-380-1(5))* Sea-To-Sea Pubns.
Benchmark Education Company, LLC Staff, compiled by. Transportation. 2006. (J). 91.00 *(978-1-4108-7043-8(X))* Benchmark Education Co.
Bethea, Nikole Brooks. High-Tech Highways & Super Skyways: The Next 100 Years of Transportation. Pota, Giovanni et al, illus. 2016. (Our World: the Next 100 Years Ser.). (ENG.). 32p. (gr. 3-4). lib. bdg. 30.65 *(978-1-4914-8266-7(4),* Graphic Library) Capstone Press of Coughlan Cos.
Beylon, Cathy. Color Your Own Things That Go Stickers. 2006. (Dover Sticker Bks.). (ENG., Illus.). 2p. (J). (gr. 3-3). 2.95 *(978-0-486-44898-5(3))* Dover Pubns., Inc.
Bicknell, Joanna. Emergency. 2005. (Shimmer & Shine Bks.). 12p. (gr. -1-k). per., bds. *(978-1-905051-32-8(8))* Make Believe Ideas.
—My Digger Book. 2005. (Shimmer & Shine Books Ser.). 12p. (gr. -1-k). per., bds. *(978-1-905051-30-4(1))* Make Believe Ideas.
Biggs, Brian. Blue Bus, Red Balloon: A Book of Colors. Biggs, Brian, illus. 2013. (ENG., Illus.). 24p. (J). (gr. -1 — 1). bds. 7.99 *(978-0-06-195814-4(X))* HarperCollins Pubs.
Birch, Beverley. Transport. (Illus.). 128p. pap. 8.99 *(978-0-340-65698-3(0))* Hodder & Stoughton GBR. Dist: Trafalgar Square Publishing.
Bird, Nicola. Go! Go! Go! Land, Fiona, illus. 2012. (ENG.). 10p. (J). (— 1). bds. 10.99 *(978-0-545-42545-2(X))* Scholastic, Inc.
Bodden, Valerie. National Transportation Safety Board: Agents of Government. 2016. (Agents of Government Ser.). (ENG.). 48p. (J). (gr. 5-9). pap. 12.00 *(978-1-62832-149-4(0),* Creative Paperbacks) Creative Co., The.
Boothroyd, Jennifer. From the Model T to Hybrid Cars: How Transportation Has Changed. 2011. (Comparing Past & Present Ser.). pap. 7.95 *(978-0-7613-7837-2(5));* pap. 45.32 *(978-0-7613-8392-5(1));* (ENG., Illus.). 32p. lib. bdg. 26.60 *(978-0-7613-6743-7(8))* Lerner Publishing Group.
—Transportation. 2006. (First Step Nonfiction - We Are Alike & Different Ser.). (ENG., Illus.). 8p. (J). (gr. -1-1). pap. 4.95 *(978-0-8225-5730-2(4),* Lerner Pubns.) Lerner Publishing Group.
Brady, Peter. Transportation Zone. 2012. (Transportation Zone Ser.). (ENG.). 24p. (gr. 1-2). pap. 250.20 *(978-1-4296-8399-9(6));* lib. bdg. 151.92 *(978-1-4296-8156-8(X));* lib. bdg. 278.52 *(978-1-4296-8157-5(8))* Capstone Press of Coughlan Cos. (First Facts).
Broyles, Matthew. U. S. Air Marshals. (Extreme Careers Ser.). 64p. 2009. (gr. 5-5). 58.50 *(978-1-61512-416-9(0),* Rosen Reference) 2007. (Illus.). (J). (gr. 3-7). lib. bdg. 31.95 *(978-1-4042-0942-8(5))* Rosen Publishing Group, Inc., The.
Buckley, James. Things That Go! 2013. (Illus.). 32p. *(978-0-545-62399-5(5))* Scholastic, Inc.
Bull, Peter, illus. Transport. (Music about Us Ser.). 64p. 9.95 *(978-1-85909-294-1(2),* Warner Bros. Pubns.) Alfred Publishing Co., Inc.
Burton, Margie, et al. Going Places. 2011. (Early Connections Ser.). (J). *(978-1-61672-490-0(0))* Benchmark Education Co.
Butterfield, Moira. Transportation Around the World. 2016. (Children Like Us Ser.). (ENG., Illus.). 32p. (J). (gr. 3-3). pap. 10.58 *(978-1-5026-0854-3(5))* Cavendish Square Publishing.
Carle, Eric. My Very First Book of Motion. Carle, Eric, illus. 2007. (ENG., Illus.). 18p. (J). (gr. -1 — 1). bds. 5.99 *(978-0-399-24748-4(3),* Philomel Bks.) Penguin Young Readers Group.
Catala, Ellen. How Do You Move? 2005. (Yellow Umbrella Fluent Level Ser.). (ENG., Illus.). 16p. (gr. k-1). pap. 35.70 *(978-0-7368-5295-1(6),* Yellow Umbrella Bks.) Capstone Press of Coughlan Cos.
Cates, David & Armstrong, Margalynne. Plessy v. Ferguson: Segregation & the Separate but Equal Policy, 1 vol. 2012. (Landmark Supreme Court Cases Ser.). (ENG., Illus.). 160p. (J). (gr. 6-12). 37.07 *(978-1-61783-475-2(0))* ABDO Publishing Co.
Channing, Margot. On the Go. Claude, Jean, illus. 2017. (First Words & Pictures Ser.). (ENG.). 14p. (J). (gr. -1 — 1). bds. 9.99 *(978-1-68152-201-2(2))* Amicus.
Chappell, Jackie. When I Ride the Bus. 2006. (My Day at School (Rourke) Ser.). (Illus.). 8p. (J). (gr. 3-7). pap. 5.95 *(978-1-59515-939-7(8))* Rourke Educational Media.
Chmielewski, Gary. Let's Go in the Funny Zone: Jokes, Riddles, Tongue Twisters & Daffynitions. Caputo, Jim, illus. rev. ed. 2007. (Funny Zone Ser.). (ENG.). 24p. (J). (gr. 2-4). lib. bdg. 22.60 *(978-1-59953-182-3(8))* Norwood Hse. Pr.
Clark, Willow. Transportation Station, 6 vols., Sect. Incl. Bikes on the Move. lib. bdg. 22.60 *(978-1-4358-9334-4(4));* Boats on the Move. lib. bdg. 22.60 *(978-1-4358-9336-8(0));* Cars on

the Move. lib. bdg. 22.60 (978-1-4358-9333-7(6)); Motorcycles on the Move. lib. bdg. 22.60 (978-1-4358-9335-1(2)); Planes on the Move. lib. bdg. 22.60 (978-1-4358-9332-0(8)); Trains on the Move. lib. bdg. 22.60 (978-1-4358-9331-3(X)); (J). (gr. 2-5). (Illus.). 24p. 2010. Set lib. bdg. 127.50 (978-1-4358-9404-4(9), PowerKids Pr.) Rosen Publishing Group, Inc., The.

Close, Edward. Wheels, Wings, & Motors, 1 vol., 1. 2014. (Discovery Education: How It Works). (ENG.). 32p. (gr. 3-6). 26.25 (978-1-4777-6313-1(9), PowerKids Pr.) Rosen Publishing Group, Inc., The.

Coleman, Miriam. Earth-Friendly Transportation. 2011. (How to Be Earth Friendly Ser.). (Illus.). 32p. (gr. 3-4). (J). pap. 10.00 (978-1-4488-2769-5(8), PowerKids Pr.); (YA). lib. bdg. 25.25 (978-1-4488-2590-5(3)) Rosen Publishing Group, Inc., The.

de Seve, Karen. National Geographic Little Kids First Big Book of Things That Go. 2017. (National Geographic Little Kids First Big Bks.). (ENG.). 128p. (J). (gr. -1-3). lib. bdg. 24.90 **(978-1-4263-2805-3(2)**, National Geographic Children's Bks.) National Geographic Society.

de Seve, Karen & National Geographic Kids Staff. Little Kids First Big Book of Things That Go. 2017. (National Geographic Little Kids First Big Bks.). (ENG.). 128p. (J). (gr. -1-3). 14.99 **(978-1-4263-2804-6(4)**, National Geographic Children's Bks.) National Geographic Society.

DeGezelle, Terri, et al. Mighty Machines: Construction (6 book Set) [NASCO]. 2012. (Mighty Machines Ser.). (ENG.). 24p. (gr. k-1). pap. 41.70 (978-1-62065-474-3(1), Pebble Plus) Capstone Press of Coughlan Cos.

Demarest, Chris L. & Mayer, Bill. All Aboard! A Traveling Alphabet. 2008. (ENG., Illus.). 40p. (J). (gr. -1-2). 17.99 (978-0-689-85249-7(5), McElderry, Margaret K. Bks.) McElderry, Margaret K. Bks.

Depue, Anne. All Kinds of Transportation. 2016. (Spring Forward Ser.). (J). (gr. 1). (978-1-4900-6022-4(7)) Benchmark Education Co.

DiSiena, Laura Lyn & Eliot, Hannah. Trains Can Float: And Other Fun Facts. Oswald, Pete & Spurgeon, Aaron, illus. 2014. (Did You Know? Ser.). (ENG.). 32p. (J). (gr. -1-3). 17.99 (978-1-4814-0281-1(1), Little Simon) Little Simon.

Dittmer, Lori. The Future of Transportation. 2012. (What's Next? Ser.). (Illus.). 48p. (J). (gr. 5-12). 23.95 (978-1-60818-224-4(X), Creative Education) Creative Co., The.

Doering Tourville, Amanda. Transportation in the City, 1 vol. Thompson, Jeffrey, illus. 2011. (First Graphics: My Community Ser.). (ENG.). 24p. (gr. 1-2). pap. 6.29 (978-1-4296-6233-8(6)); pap. 35.70 (978-1-4296-6403-5(7)) Capstone Press of Coughlan Cos.

Dorman, Mary Kate. Big Military Machines. 2011. (All about Big Machines Ser.). (Illus.). 24p. (J). (gr. -1-18). pap. 7.95 (978-1-59845-243-3(6), Enslow Elementary) Enslow Pubs., Inc.

Dorling Kindersley Publishing Staff. Baby Go! Go! Go! 2015. (ENG.). 14p. (J). (gr. -1 — 1). bds. 5.99 (978-1-4654-3553-8(0), DK Children) Dorling Kindersley Publishing, Inc.

—Beep! Beep! 2012. (Baby Touch & Feel Ser.). (ENG., Illus.). 14p. (J). (gr. -1 — 1). bds. 5.99 (978-0-7566-9785-3(9), DK Children) Dorling Kindersley Publishing, Inc.

—Cars, Trains, Ships, & Planes. 2015. (ENG., Illus.). 256p. (J). (gr. 3-7). 24.99 (978-1-4654-3805-8(X), DK Children) Dorling Kindersley Publishing, Inc.

—My First Things That Go. 2016. (ENG., Illus.). 36p. (J). (— 1). bds. 5.99 (978-1-4654-4490-5(4), DK Children) Dorling Kindersley Publishing, Inc.

—My First Things That Go: Let's Get Moving! 2009. (Tab Board Bks.). (ENG.). 28p. (J). (gr. -1-k). bds. 9.99 (978-0-7566-4502-1(6), DK Children) Dorling Kindersley Publishing, Inc.

—Squeaky Baby Bath: Things That Go. 2017. (ENG.). 8p. (J). (— 1). 5.99 (978-1-4654-5601-4(5), DK Children) Dorling Kindersley Publishing, Inc.

—Things That Go. 2012. (ENG., Illus.). 12p. (J). (gr. -1 — 1). bds. 9.99 (978-0-7566-9009-0(9), DK Children) Dorling Kindersley Publishing, Inc.

Dunn, Karen Lewit. Visiting Grandma. 2008. (Discovering & Exploring Science Ser.). (Illus.). 16p. (J). (gr. -1-3). lib. bdg. 12.95 (978-0-7569-8434-2(3)) Perfection Learning Corp.

Eboch, M. M. The 12 Biggest Breakthroughs in Transportation Technology. 2014. (ENG.). 32p. (J). (978-1-63235-017-6(3)) Pr. Room Editions LLC.

Encyclopaedia Britannica, Inc. Staff, compiled by. Discover English with Ben & Bella: Series 2: Going Places. 2010. 180.00 (978-1-61535-349-1(6)) Encyclopaedia Britannica, Inc.

Falk, Laine. This Is the Way We Go to School. 2009. (Scholastic News Nonfiction Readers Ser.). (ENG.). 24p. (J). (gr. 1-2). pap. 6.95 (978-0-531-21440-4(0), Children's Pr.); lib. bdg. 22.00 (978-0-531-21341-4(2)) Scholastic Library Publishing.

Finn, Denny Von. Snowmobiles. 2009. (Cool Rides Ser.). (ENG., Illus.). 24p. (J). (gr. 3-7). lib. bdg. 25.95 (978-1-60014-256-7(7)) Bellwether Media.

Fireside, Harvey & Rauf, Don. Separate but Equal: Plessy V. Ferguson. 2016. (US Supreme Court Landmark Cases Ser.). (Illus.). 128p. (J). 37.27 (978-0-7660-8434-6(5)) Enslow Pubs., Inc.

Flounders, Anne. Getting from Here to There. 2014. (Our Green Earth Ser.). (Illus.). 32p. (gr. 2-4). pap. 8.95 (978-1-939656-30-8(3)) Red Chair Pr.

Freudenthal. Ways to Go. 3rd ed. 2003. (Math in Context Ser.). (Illus.). 8.33 (978-0-03-071614-0(4)) Holt McDougal.

Fridell, Ron. Seven Wonders of Transportation. 2010. (Seven Wonders Ser.). (Illus.). 80p. (J). (gr. 5-9). lib. bdg. 33.26 (978-0-7613-4238-0(9)) Twenty First Century Bks.

Furgang, Kathy. On the Move: Green Transportation. 2009. (Your Carbon Footprint Ser.). 48p. (gr. 5-5). 53.00 (978-1-60854-909-2(7), Rosen Reference) Rosen Publishing Group, Inc., The.

Furgang, Kathy & Furgang, Adam. On the Move: Green Transportation. 2008. (Your Carbon Footprint Ser.). (Illus.). 48p. (YA). (gr. 5-9). lib. bdg. 29.25 (978-1-4042-1773-7(8)) Rosen Publishing Group, Inc., The.

Gaarder-Juntti, Oona. What in the World Is Green Transportation?, 1 vol. 2010. (Super SandCastle Ser.). (ENG.). 24p. 25.65 (978-1-61613-193-7(4), Super SandCastle) ABDO Publishing Co.

Galloway, Fhiona. Look Through: Things That Go. 2016. (Look Through Ser.). (ENG., Illus.). 10p. (J). bds. 8.99 (978-1-62686-579-2(5), Silver Dolphin Bks.) Readerlink Distribution Services, LLC.

Ganeri, Anita. Flip the Flaps: Things That Go! Humphries, Tudor, illus. 2014. (Flip the Flaps Ser.). (ENG.). 32p. (J). (gr. -1-1). pap. 6.99 (978-0-7534-7133-3(7), 9780753471333, Kingfisher) Roaring Brook Pr.

Gardner, Jane P. Travel Science, Vol. 11. Lewin, Russ, ed. 2015. (Science 24/7 Ser.). (Illus.). 48p. (J). (gr. 5). 20.95 (978-1-4222-3415-0(0)) Mason Crest.

Gibbons, Gail. Transportation: How People Get Around. 2017. (ENG., Illus.). 32p. (J). (gr. -1-3). 17.95 (978-0-8234-3425-1(7)) Holiday Hse., Inc.

Gillett, Jack & Gillett, Meg. Transportation-Network Maps. 2012. (Maps of the Environmental World Ser.). (ENG., Illus.). 32p. (J). (gr. 4-6). 26.50 (978-1-4488-8613-5(9)); pap. 10.60 (978-1-4488-8619-7(8)) Rosen Publishing Group, Inc., The. (PowerKids Pr.).

Goldish, Meish & Parkhurst, Anthony. Horses, Donkeys, & Mules in the Marines. 2012. (America's Animal Soldiers Ser.). 24p. (J). (gr. 1-6). lib. bdg. 23.93 (978-1-61772-453-4(X)) Bearport Publishing Co., Inc.

Goldsworthy, Steve. Travel Green. 2010. (Being Green Ser.). (Illus.). 32p. (YA). (gr. 3-6). lib. bdg. 27.13 (978-1-61690-085-4(7)); (J). (gr. 4-6). pap. 12.95 (978-1-61690-086-1(5)) Weigl Pubs., Inc.

Goldsworthy, Steve. Travelling Green. 2016. (J). **(978-1-5105-2223-7(9))** SmartBook Media, Inc.

Goodman, Polly. Transportation for the Future. 2011. (Earth Alert! Ser.). 32p. (YA). (gr. 3-6). lib. bdg. 26.60 (978-1-4339-6011-6(7)) Stevens, Gareth Publishing LLLP.

Gordon, Bob. Touch & Sparkle Emergency. 2005. (Illus.). 12p. (gr. -1). bds. (978-1-905051-58-8(1)) Make Believe Ideas.

Graham, Buck. My First Big Book of Questions & Answers: Things That Go. 2005. (Illus.). 10p. bds. 9.98 (978-0-7853-7227-1(X), 7171500) Publications International, Ltd.

Graham, Ian, et al. Firefly Encyclopedia of Transportation: A Comprehensive Look at the World of Transportation. Green, Oliver, ed. 2017. (ENG., Illus.). 160p. (J). (gr. 4-7). pap. 14.95 **(978-1-77085-931-9(4)**, 9781770859319) Firefly Bks., Ltd.

Greek, Joe. Solving Real World Problems with Transportation Engineering, 01 vols., 1. 2016. (Let's Find Out! Ser.). (ENG., Illus.). 32p. (J). pap. 12.90 (978-1-5081-0071-3(3), Britannica Educational Publishing) Rosen Publishing Group, Inc., The.

Gregory, Helen. Getting There. 2011. (Wonder Readers Early Level Ser.). (ENG.). (gr. -1-1). 16p. pap. 35.94 (978-1-4296-8091-2(1)); 32p. pap. 5.99 (978-1-4296-7805-6(4)) Capstone Press of Coughlan Cos. (Wonder Readers).

Grossbard, H. A. Driving in Florida: The Politically Incorrect Guide to Surviving the Roadways of the Sunshine State. 2011. 40p. (gr. -1). pap. 16.99 (978-1-4520-9741-1(0)) AuthorHouse.

Grossman, Rena. Carry Me, 1 vol. 2009. (Babies Everywhere Ser.). (ENG.). 32p. (J). (gr. -1). bds. 6.95 (978-1-59572-180-8(0)) Star Bright Bks., Inc.

Guin, Valerie. On the Move. 2005. (One World (Smart Apple Media) Ser.). (Illus.). 30p. (J). (gr. 3-6). lib. bdg. 27.10 (978-1-58340-699-1(9)) Black Rabbit Bks.

Halle. Brunnert und Partners, Flughafen Leipzig/Halle: Opus 52. 2004. (GER & ENG., Illus.). 72p. 39.00 (978-3-930698-52-3(8)) Edition Axel Menges GmbH DEU. Dist: National Bk. Network.

Harrier Jump Jet. 2004. (Press-Out & Build Ser.). (Illus.). 24p. (J). per. (978-1-84229-725-4(2)) Top That! Publishing PLC.

Harrison, Paul. On the Move. 2011. (Window on the World Ser.). (Illus.). 32p. (978-1-84089-660-2(4)) Zero to Ten, Ltd.

—Speed Machines. (Up Close Ser.). 24p. 2009. (gr. 3-3). 47.90 (978-1-60854-705-0(1)) 2008. (Illus.). (J). (gr. 4-7). lib. bdg. 25.25 (978-1-4042-4222-7(8)) Rosen Publishing Group, Inc., The. (PowerKids Pr.).

Hergé. Tintín: Descubro Los Transportes. 2004. (SPA., Illus.). 24p. 19.95 (978-1-59497-064-1(5)) Public Square Bks.

Hewitt, Sally. Transportation. 2010. (Starting Geography Ser.). 32p. (J). (gr. 2-5). 28.50 (978-1-60753-129-6(1)) Amicus Publishing.

—Transportation. 2012. (Map Smart Ser.). 32p. (gr. 2-6). lib. bdg. 27.10 (978-1-59920-415-4(0)) Black Rabbit Bks.

Highlights for Children Editorial Staff, compiled by. All about Transportation. 2016. (Highlights(tm) All about Activity Bks.). (ENG.). 32p. (J). (gr. -1-k). pap. 4.99 (978-1-62979-540-9(2), Highlights) Boyds Mills Pr.

Hinkler Books, creator. 101 First Words: Things That Go. 2011. (101 First Words Ser.). (Illus.). 16p. (J). (gr. -1). bds. 7.99 (978-1-74184-818-2(0)) Hinkler Bks. Pty, Ltd. AUS. Dist: Ideals Pubns.

HOP, LLC. Hooked on Trains, Planes, & Cars Super Activity Kit. 2006. (J). (gr. -1). 9.99 (978-1-933863-21-4(8)) HOP, LLC.

—Super Activity 3-pack - Hooked on Things That Go. 2006. (J). (gr. -1). 24.99 (978-1-933863-96-2(X)) HOP, LLC.

Ieda, Hitoshi, ed. Sustainable Urban Transport in an Asian Context, 1 vol. 2010. (CSUR-UT Series: Library for Sustainable Urban Regeneration Ser.: 9). (ENG., Illus.). xviii, 422p. 209.00 (978-4-431-93953-5(9), 9784431939535) Springer.

Imperato, Teresa. On the Go! A Transportation Book. Rayner, Olivia, illus. 2005. 10p. (J). 7.95 (978-1-58117-271-3(0), Intervisual/Piggy Toes) Bendon, Inc.

—Speed Machines: A Pop-up Book with Moving Gears. Robinson, Keith, illus. 2005. 8p. (J). 14.95 (978-1-58117-323-9(7), Intervisual/Piggy Toes) Bendon, Inc.

Ipcizade, Catherine. H Is for Honk! A Transportation Alphabet, 1 vol. 2010. (Alphabet Fun Ser.). (ENG.). 32p. (gr. 1-2). lib. bdg. 27.32 (978-1-4296-4464-8(8), Aplus Bks.) Capstone Press of Coughlan Cos.

Iyer, Rani. Green Transport: Exploring Eco-Friendly Travel for a Better Tomorrow. 2016. (ENG.). 120p. (gr. 8-12). (978-81-7993-444-9(6)) Energy and Resources Institute, The IND. Dist: Motilal (UK) Bks. of India.

Kalman, Bobbie. Animals Move Like This. 2011. (ENG.). 24p. (J). (978-0-7787-9564-3(0)); pap. (978-0-7787-9589-6(6)) Crabtree Publishing Co.

—I Like Riding. 2011. (ENG.). 16p. (J). (978-0-7787-9550-6(0)); (My World Ser.: No. 52). pap. (978-0-7787-9575-9(6)) Crabtree Publishing Co.

—Travel Then & Now. 2013. (ENG., Illus.). 24p. (J). (978-0-7787-0129-3(8)); pap. (978-0-7787-0211-5(1)) Crabtree Publishing Co.

Kawa, Katie. My First Trip on an Airplane. 2012. (My First Adventures Ser.). (Illus.). 24p. (J). (gr. k-2). pap. 8.15 (978-1-4339-7297-3(2)); lib. bdg. 22.60 (978-1-4339-7296-6(4)) Stevens, Gareth Publishing LLLP.

Kemp, Kristin. Amazing Americans: Rosa Parks, 1 vol. rev. ed. 2014. (Primary Source Readers Content & Literacy Ser.). (ENG., Illus.). 32p. (gr. 3-3). pap. 8.99 (978-1-4333-7375-6(0)) Teacher Created Materials, Inc.

Kent, Lorna, illus. On the Move. 2004. 8p. (J). pap. 3.99 (978-1-85854-089-4(5)) Brimax Books Ltd. GBR. Dist: Byeway Bks.

Kroll, Jennifer. A la Vanguardia: Adelantos en Tecnología. 2016. (TIME for Kids en Español - Level 5 Ser.). (SPA.). 64p. (gr. 5-5). lib. bdg. 31.99 (978-1-5157-2927-3(3)) Time for Kids Inc AUS. Dist: Capstone Pub.

Lanz, Helen. How Shall We Travel? 2012. (Go Green Ser.). (Illus.). 32p. (gr. 3-6). lib. bdg. 28.50 (978-1-59771-302-3(3)) Sea-To-Sea Pubns.

Laval, Thierry. Look & Find Transportation. 2016. (Look & Find Ser.). (ENG., Illus.). 14p. (J). 18.99 (978-0-531-22237-9(3), Children's Pr.) Scholastic Library Publishing.

Leitten, Amanda. Transportation Then & Now. 2009. (Real Life Readers Ser.). 12p. (gr. 1-2). pap. 5.90 (978-1-4042-7903-2(2), Rosen Classroom) Rosen Publishing Group, Inc., The.

Lerner Publishing Group Staff. Lightning Bolt Books: Vroom-Vroom, 6 vols., Set. 2011. (J). (gr. k-2). lib. bdg. 151.56 (978-0-7613-7481-7(7)) Lerner Publishing Group.

Let's Find Out! Transportation. 2016. (Let's Find Out! Ser.). 32p. (gr. 3-2). 195.60 (978-1-5081-0217-5(1)); pap. 103.20 (978-1-68048-598-1(9)) Rosen Publishing Group, Inc., The. (Britannica Educational Publishing).

Light, Steve. Trucks Go. 2008. (ENG., Illus.). 16p. (J). (gr. -1 — 1). bds. 9.99 (978-0-8118-6542-5(8)) Chronicle Bks. LLC.

Lomberg, Michelle. Avoiding Gridlock. Schwartzenberger, Tina, ed. 2004. (Understanding Global Issues). (Illus.). 56p. (J). (gr. 10-12). lib. bdg. 28.50 (978-1-58340-357-0(4)) Weigl Pubs., Inc.

Lyons, Shelly. Transportation in My Neighborhood. 2013. (My Neighborhood Ser.). (ENG.). 24p. (gr. k-1). pap. 41.70 (978-1-62065-892-5(5)); (Illus.). pap. 7.29 (978-1-62065-891-8(7)); (Illus.). lib. bdg. 26.65 (978-1-62065-101-8(7)) Capstone Press of Coughlan Cos. (Pebble Plus).

Manolis, Kay. Big Rigs. 2008. (Mighty Machines Ser.). (ENG., Illus.). 24p. (J). (gr. k-3). lib. bdg. 25.95 (978-1-60014-177-5(3)) Bellwether Media.

Marks, Aaron. Transportation: Then & Now. 2008. (Discovering & Exploring Science Ser.). (Illus.). 16p. (J). (gr. -1-3). lib. bdg. 12.95 (978-0-7569-8420-5(3)) Perfection Learning Corp.

Mason, Paul. How Big Is Your Travel Footprint? 2009. (Environmental Footprints Ser.). 32p. (gr. 4). 28.50 (978-0-7614-4415-2(7)) Marshall Cavendish Corp.

Mattern, Joanne. Staying Safe in the Car. 2007. (Safety First Ser.). (Illus.). 24p. (gr. k-3). pap. 8.15 (978-0-8368-7800-4(0)); lib. bdg. 22.00 (978-0-8368-7793-9(4)) Stevens, Gareth Publishing LLLP. (Weekly Reader Leveled Readers).

—Staying Safe in the Car (la Seguridad en el Auto) 2007. (Safety First / la Seguridad Es lo Primero Ser.). (ENG & SPA., Illus.). 24p. (gr. k-3). lib. bdg. 22.00 (978-0-8368-8058-8(7), Weekly Reader Leveled Readers) Stevens, Gareth Publishing LLLP.

—Staying Safe in the Car (la Seguridad en el Auto) 2007. (Safety First / la Seguridad Es lo Primero Ser.). (ENG & SPA.). 24p. (gr. k-3). pap. 8.15 (978-0-8368-8065-6(X), Weekly Reader Leveled Readers) Stevens, Gareth Publishing LLLP.

Maynard, Christopher. I Wonder Why Planes Have Wings: And Other Questions about Transportation. 2012. (I Wonder Why Ser.). (ENG., Illus.). 32p. (J). (gr. k-3). pap. 6.99 (978-0-7534-6703-9(8), 9780753467039, Kingfisher) Roaring Brook Pr.

McGill, Jordan. Medios de Transporte. 2012. (SPA.). (J). (978-1-61913-213-9(3)) Weigl Pubs., Inc.

—Transportation. 2011. (J). (978-1-61690-598-9(0)); lib. bdg. 27.13 (978-1-61690-952-9(8)) Weigl Pubs., Inc.

McIntosh, Kenneth. Buggies, Bicycles & Iron Horses: Transportation in the 1800s. 2009. (Daily Life in America in the 1800s Ser.). 64p. (YA). (gr. 7-18). pap. 9.95 (978-1-4222-1849-5(X)); lib. bdg. 22.95 (978-1-4222-1776-4(0)) Mason Crest.

Meachen Rau, Dana. Safety on the Go. 2009. (Bookworms: Safe Kids Ser.). (SPA & ENG.). 32p. (gr. k-2). 15.95 (978-0-7614-4085-7(2)) Marshall Cavendish GBR. Dist: Marshall Cavendish Corp.

—Travel in American History. 2006. (How People Lived in America Ser.). (Illus.). 24p. (gr. 1-4). lib. bdg. 22.00 (978-0-8368-7210-1(X), Weekly Reader Leveled Readers) Stevens, Gareth Publishing LLLP.

Mitten, Ellen. Moving People, Moving Stuff. 2011. (ENG., Illus.). 24p. (gr. k-2). pap. 8.95 (978-1-61741-994-2(X)) Rourke Educational Media.

Mitton, Tony & Parker, Ant. Cool Cars. 2014. (Amazing Machines Ser.). (ENG., Illus.). 24p. (J). (gr. -1-k). 4.99 (978-0-7534-7207-1(4), 9780753472071, Kingfisher) Roaring Brook Pr.

—Cool Cars. 2014. (Amazing Machines Ser.). (J). lib. bdg. 14.75 (978-0-606-36132-3(4)) Turtleback Bks.

Moore, Andrew. Traveling in New York City. 2011. (My Community Ser.). (ENG., Illus.). 12p. (gr. 2-2). pap. 6.95 (978-1-4488-5719-7(8), Rosen Classroom) Rosen Publishing Group, Inc., The.

Morris, Ann. On the Go. Heyman, Ken, photos by. 2015. (Illus.). 32p. pap. 7.00 (978-1-61003-611-5(5)) Center for the Collaborative Classroom.

Morrison, Heather S. Inventors of Transportation Technology. 2015. (Designing Engineering Solutions Ser.). (ENG.). 144p. (J). (gr. 8-8). lib. bdg. 42.79 (978-1-5026-0662-4(3)) Cavendish Square Publishing.

Nakata, Ritsuko & Hanson, Anders. Let's Go. 2008. (Let's Go Ser.: 12). (ENG.). 24p. (J). (gr. k-3). lib. bdg. 290.52 (978-1-59928-892-5(3), SandCastle) ABDO Publishing Co.

Nardo, Don. Roman Roads & Aqueducts. 2014. (History's Great Structures). (ENG., Illus.). 80p. (J). lib. bdg. (978-1-60152-634-2(2)) ReferencePoint Pr., Inc.

National Geographic. Things That Go! Collection. 2015. (Readers Ser.). (ENG., Illus.). 120p. (J). (gr. k-3). lib. bdg. 16.90 (978-1-4263-1973-0(8), National Geographic Children's Bks.) National Geographic Society.

National Geographic Staff. Things That Go Collection: Readers That Grow With You. 2015. (Readers Ser.). (ENG.). 120p. (J). (gr. k-3). pap. 7.99 (978-1-4263-1972-3(X), National Geographic Children's Bks.) National Geographic Society.

Nous Vous. Show + Tell - Transportation Activities. 2017. (ENG.). 18p. (J). (gr. -1-k). pap. 9.99 (978-1-84780-776-2(3), Wide Eyed Editions) Quarto Publishing Group UK GBR. Dist: Hachette Bk. Group.

Nunn, Daniel. The Transportation. 2013. (True or False? Ser.). (ENG.). 24p. (gr. -1-1). pap. 6.29 (978-1-4109-5075-8(1)); lib. bdg. 22.65 (978-1-4109-5069-7(7)) Heinemann-Raintree. (NA-r).

O'Connell, Eleanor. Transportation Around the World. 2016. (Adventures in Culture Ser.). 00024p. (J). pap. 8.15 **(978-1-4824-5593-9(5))** Stevens, Gareth Publishing LLLP.

Orr, Tamra B. The Department of Transportation. 2005. (This Is Your Government Ser.). (Illus.). 64p. (J). (gr. k-3). lib. bdg. 31.95 (978-1-4042-0211-5(0)) Rosen Publishing Group, Inc., The.

Owens, Tom. Traveling on the Freedom Machines of the Transportation Age. 2003. (Reading Essentials in Social Studies). (Illus.). 40p. pap. 8.00 (978-0-7891-5873-4(6)) Perfection Learning Corp.

Oxlade, Chris. Hands-on Science Projects: Transport. 2008. (ENG., Illus.). 64p. (J). (gr. 4-7). pap. 7.99 (978-1-84476-533-1(4)) Anness Publishing GBR. Dist: National Bk. Network.

—Transportation Around the World: How Do We Get Where We're Going?, 8 bks. (Illus.). (gr. k-2). Set. lib. bdg. 170.88 (978-1-57572-310-5(7))Set 1. (J). lib. bdg. 85.44 (978-1-57572-304-4(2))Set 2. lib. bdg. 85.44 (978-1-57572-309-9(3)) Heinemann-Raintree.

Oxlade, Chris, et al. The Big Illustrated Book of Transport: All about Ships, Trains, Cars & Flight with Photographs, Artworks & 40 Step-by-Step Projects & Experiments! 2009. (ENG., Illus.). 256p. (J). (gr. 4-7). pap. 24.99 (978-1-84476-552-2(0)) Anness Publishing GBR. Dist: National Bk. Network.

Pebble Books: Transportation: Who, Where, & What. 2005. (YA). (gr. k-3). 475.20 (978-0-7368-4216-7(0), Pebble Bks.) Capstone Press of Coughlan Cos.

Perritano, John. Revolution in Transportation. 2009. (It Works! Ser.). 32p. (gr. 3). 28.50 (978-0-7614-4379-7(7)) Marshall Cavendish Corp.

—Stem in Current Events: Transportation, Vol. 10. 2016. (Stem in Current Events Ser.: Vol. 10). (ENG., Illus.). 64p. (J). (gr. 7-12). 23.95 (978-1-4222-3596-6(3)) Mason Crest.

Peters, Elisa. Let's Ride the City Bus! 2014. (Public Transportation Ser.). 24p. (J). (gr. k-2). 23.60 (978-1-4777-6482-4(8), PowerKids Pr.) Rosen Publishing Group, Inc., The.

—Let's Ride the Streetcar! 2014. (Public Transportation Ser.). 24p. (J). (gr. k-2). pap. 49.50 (978-1-4777-6513-5(1), PowerKids Pr.) Rosen Publishing Group, Inc., The.

—Let's Take the Train! 2014. (Public Transportation Ser.). (Illus.). 24p. (J). (gr. k-2). pap. 49.50 (978-1-4777-6514-2(X), PowerKids Pr.) Rosen Publishing Group, Inc., The.

—¡Vamos a Tomar el Autobús! / Let's Ride the City Bus! de la Vega, Eida, ed. 2014. (Transporte Público / Public Transportation Ser.). (SPA & ENG.). 24p. (J). (gr. k-2). 23.60 (978-1-4777-6777-1(0), PowerKids Pr.) Rosen Publishing Group, Inc., The.

—¡Vamos a Tomar el Tranvía! / Let's Ride the Streetcar! de la Vega, Eida, ed. 2014. (Transporte Público / Public Transportation Ser.). (SPA & ENG.). 24p. (J). (gr. k-2). 23.60 (978-1-4777-6779-5(7), PowerKids Pr.) Rosen Publishing Group, Inc., The.

—¡Vamos a Tomar el Tren! / Let's Take the Train! de la Vega, Eida, ed. 2014. (Transporte Público / Public Transportation Ser.). (SPA & ENG.). 24p. (J). (gr. k-2). 23.60 (978-1-4777-6781-8(9), PowerKids Pr.) Rosen Publishing Group, Inc., The.

Picthall, Chez. On the Move. Gunzi, Christiane, ed. 2015. (ENG., Illus.). 16p. (J). pap. 7.99 (978-1-907604-81-2(2)) Award Pubns. Ltd. GBR. Dist: Parkwest Pubns., Inc.

Priddy, Roger. Lift-The-Flap Tab: on the Go. 2014. (Lift-The-Flap Tab Bks.). (ENG., Illus.). 16p. (J). (gr. -1 — 1). bds. 8.99 (978-0-312-51731-1(9), 9780312517311, Priddy Bks.) St. Martin's Pr.

Public Transportation. 2014. (Public Transportation Ser.). 24p. (J). (gr. k-2). 141.60 (978-1-4777-6478-7(X)); pap. 49.50 (978-1-4777-7238-6(3)) Rosen Publishing Group, Inc., The. (PowerKids Pr.).

Rau, Dana Meachen. Bookworms We Go!, 6 vols., Set. Incl. Boats. 15.95 (978-0-7614-4076-5(3)); Buses. 15.95 (978-0-7614-4077-2(1)); Cars. 15.95 (978-0-7614-4078-9(X)); Planes. 15.95 (978-0-7614-4080-2(1)); Trains. 15.95 (978-0-7614-4081-9(X)); Trucks. 15.95 (978-0-7614-4083-3(6)); 24p. (gr. k-1). (Bookworms: We Go! Ser.). 2009. Set lib. bdg. 95.70 o.p. (978-0-7614-4075-8(5)) Marshall Cavendish Corp.

—Safety on the Go: Seguridad en el Viaje. 2009. (Bookworms — Bilingual Editions: Safe Kids/Ninos Seguros Ser.). (SPA & ENG.). 32p. (gr. k-2). lib. bdg. 15.95 (978-0-7614-4776-4(8)) Marshall Cavendish Corp.

Raum, Elizabeth. The Scoop on Clothes, Homes, & Daily Life in Colonial America. 2017. (Life in the American Colonies Ser.). (ENG.). 32p. (gr. 3-4). pap. 8.10 **(978-1-5157-9746-3(5)**, Fact Finders) Capstone Press of Coughlan Cos.

Raum, Elizabeth. Transportation: From Walking to High Speed Rail. 2010. (Timeline History Ser.). (ENG., Illus.). 32p. (gr. 3-5). 29.99 (978-1-4329-3804-8(5), NA-h) Heinemann-Raintree.

Reich, Kass, illus. Hamsters on the Go, 1 vol. 2016. (ENG.). 24p. (J). (gr. -1-k). bds. 9.95 *(978-1-4598-1016-7(3))* Orca Bk. Pubs. USA.

Reis, Ronald A. The New York City Subway System. 2009. (Building America Ser.). (Illus.). 144p. (J). (gr. 5-8). 35.00 *(978-1-60413-046-1(6),* Chelsea Hse.) Facts On File, Inc.

Rice, Dona Herweck. On the Go, 1 vol. 2nd rev. ed. 2013. (Nonfiction Readers Ser.). (ENG., Illus.). 12p. (J). (gr. 1-1). pap. 15.96 *(978-1-4807-1010-8(5))* Shell Educational Publishing.

Richard, John. Big Book of Transport. Leeks, David, illus. 2004. 48p. (J). 7.99 *(978-1-85854-550-9(1))* Brimax Books Ltd. GBR. Dist: Byeway Bks.

Richards, Jon. Transportation. 2005. (How Things Have Changed Ser.). (Illus.). 32p. (J). (gr. 3-7). lib. bdg. 27.10 *(978-1-59389-196-1(2))* Chrysalis Education.

RIGBY. Transportation: Then & Now: Third Grade Big Books. 2003. (Rigby on Our Way to English Ser.). (ENG.). 24p. (gr. 3-3). pap. 50.70 *(978-0-7578-4209-2(7))* Rigby Education.

Riggs, Kate. How Fast Can You Go? Williams, Nate, illus. 2014. (ENG.). 14p. (J). (gr. -1-k). bds. 7.99 *(978-1-56846-253-0(0),* Creative Editions) Creative Co., The.

Ripley Entertainment. Life in the Fast Lane. 2010. (Ripley's Believe It or Not Ser.). 36p. (YA). (gr. 3-18). lib. bdg. 19.95 *(978-1-4222-1538-8(5))* Mason Crest.

Roberts, Sheena. We All Go Traveling By. Bell, Siobhan, illus. 2003. (ENG.). 24p. (J). 17.99 *(978-1-84148-168-5(8))* Barefoot Bks., Inc.

Rosen, Michael J. & Kassoy, Ben. Bizarre Vehicles. Sandy, J. P., illus. 2013. (No Way! Ser.). (ENG.). 32p. (gr. 3-5). lib. bdg. 26.60 *(978-0-7613-8985-9(7),* Millbrook Pr.) Lerner Publishing Group.

Rosenberg, Aaron. Kick Scooters: Techniques & Tricks. 2005. (Rad Sports: Techniques & Tricks Ser.). (Illus.). 48p. (YA). (gr. 5-8). lib. bdg. 29.25 *(978-0-8239-3846-9(8))* Rosen Publishing Group, Inc., The.

Roy, Jennifer Rozines & Roy, Gregory. Shapes in Transportation. (Math All Around Ser.). (Illus.). 31p. (J). 2007. (gr. 4-7). pap. 6.99 *(978-0-7614-3387-3(2))* 2006. (gr. 3-7). lib. bdg. 29.93 *(978-0-7614-2265-5(X))* Marshall Cavendish Corp. (Benchmark Bks.).

Roza, Greg. Gross Things on Buses, Trains, & Planes. 2012. (That's Gross! Ser.). (Illus.). 24p. (J). (gr. 2-5). 22.60 *(978-1-4339-7127-3(5))*; pap. 8.15 *(978-1-4339-7128-0(3))* Stevens, Gareth Publishing LLLP. (Gareth Stevens Learning Library).

Rustad, Martha E. H. Across the Country 18, 19, 20: A Transportation Counting to 20 Book. 2017. (1, 2, 3 Count with Me Ser.). (ENG., Illus.). 24p. (J). (gr. k-2). pap. 8.99 *(978-1-68152-110-7(5))* Amicus.

—Across the Country 18, 19, 20: A Transportation Counting to 20 Book. 2016. (1, 2, 3 Count with Me Ser.). (ENG., Illus.). 24p. (J). (gr. k-3). 20.95 *(978-1-60753-919-3(5))* Amicus Publishing.

—Transportation in Many Cultures. 2016. (Life Around the World Ser.). (ENG.). 24p. (gr. k-1). pap. 7.29 *(978-1-5157-4241-8(5),* Pebble Plus) Capstone Press of Coughlan Cos.

Rutherford, Peter. Let's Look on the Move. Spong, Clive, illus. 2015. (ENG.). 24p. (J). (gr. -1-2). bds. 6.99 *(978-1-86147-414-8(8),* Armadillo) Anness Publishing GBR. Dist: National Bk. Network.

Salazar, Julia. Spanish Words on the Road, Vol. 1. 2014. (Learn My Language! Spanish Ser.). (ENG & SPA., Illus.). 24p. (J). (gr. 1-2). 22.60 *(978-1-4824-0365-7(X))* Stevens, Gareth Publishing LLLP.

Scarry, Richard. Richard Scarry's Hop Aboard! Here We Go! 2012. (ENG., Illus.). 48p. (J). (gr. -1-2). 12.95 *(978-1-4027-7222-1(X))* Sterling Publishing Co., Inc.

Scholastic, Inc. Staff. First 100 Things That Go. 2016. (Scholastic Early Learners Ser.). (ENG.). 12p. (J). (gr. -1 — 1). bds. 6.99 *(978-0-545-90343-1(2))* Scholastic, Inc.

Schuh, Mari. Show Me Transportation: My First Picture Encyclopedia, 1 vol. 2013. (My First Picture Encyclopedias Ser.). (ENG., Illus.). 32p. (gr. 1-2). 7.95 *(978-1-62065-931-1(X),* Aplus Bks.) Capstone Press of Coughlan Cos.

Sebastiani, Laura, creator. Penny & Drew's Penciltips: Transportation. 2006. 80p. (J). 4.95 *(978-0-9766793-3-2(7))* ThoughtRockets, Inc.

Sévigny, Eric, illus. The School Bus. 2003. (Clubhouse Ser.). (ENG.). 24p. (J). (gr. -1-1). pap. 3.99 *(978-2-89450-421-5(7))* Caillouet, Gerry.

Shackleton, Caroline. Down to Earth Intermediate Book with Online Access. 2014. (ENG., Illus.). 28p. pap. 9.50 *(978-1-107-66117-2(X))* Cambridge Univ. Pr.

Sheen, Barbara. Cutting Edge Transportation Technology. 2016. (ENG.). 80p. (J). (gr. 5-12). lib. bdg. *(978-1-68282-046-9(7))* ReferencePoint Pr., Inc.

Simons, Lisa M. Bolt, et al. Long Ago & Today, 1 vol. 2014. (Long Ago & Today Ser.). (ENG.). 24p. (gr. 1-2). 101.28 *(978-1-4914-0311-2(X),* First Facts) Capstone Press of Coughlan Cos.

Sirett, Dawn & Dorling Kindersley Publishing Staff. Beep! Beep! Peekaboo! Quasha, Jennifer, ed. King, Dave, photos by. 2008. (ENG., Illus.). 12p. (J). (gr. -1-k). bds. 6.99 *(978-0-7566-3487-2(3),* DK Children) Dorling Kindersley Publishing, Inc.

Smith, Alastair, ed. Travel & Transport Then & Now. 2004. (Then & Now Flip Flaps Ser.). (ENG., Illus.). 1p. (J). (gr. 2-18). pap. 7.95 *(978-0-7460-3102-5(5))* EDC Publishing.

Smith, Paula. Transportation in Different Places. 2015. (Learning about Our Global Community Ser.). (ENG., Illus.). 24p. (J). *(978-0-7787-2014-0(4))* Crabtree Publishing Co.

Smith, Robin Wayne. If You Got It, a Truck Brought It. Smith, Robin Wayne, illus. 2012. (Illus.). 20p. pap. 6.00 *(978-0-615-63721-1(3))* Bright Tyke Creations LLC.

Solway, Andrew. Transportation, 1 vol. 2012. (Impact of Environmentalism Ser.). (ENG.). 64p. (gr. 6-10). lib. bdg. 35.99 *(978-1-4329-6520-4(4))* Heinemann-Raintree.

Souter, Janet. Air Marshal: And Careers in Transportation Security. 2006. (Homeland Security & Counterterrorism Careers Ser.). (Illus.). 128p. (J). (gr. 6). lib. bdg. 33.27 *(978-0-7660-2647-6(7))* Enslow Pubs., Inc.

Starke, John. Speed Machines: Mission Xtreme 3D. 2004. (Mission Xtreme 3D Ser.). (Illus.). 18p. (J). pap. 5.95 *(978-1-902626-50-5(8))* Red Bird Publishing GBR. Dist: Weatherhill, Inc.

Sterling Publishing Co., Inc. Things That Go/Cosas Que Se Mueven. 2013. (Say & Play Ser.). (ENG & SPA., Illus.). 28p. (J). (— 1). bds. 4.95 *(978-1-4549-1042-8(9))* Sterling Publishing Co., Inc.

Summers, Alex. School Bus. 2017. (Transportation & Me! Ser.). (ENG.). (J). (gr. k-1). 28.51 ***(978-1-68342-160-3(4))*** Rourke Educational Media.

—Taxi Cab. 2017. (Transportation & Me! Ser.). (ENG.). (J). (gr. k-1). 28.51 ***(978-1-68342-161-0(2))*** Rourke Educational Media.

Sundance/Newbridge LLC Staff. On the Move! 2004. (Reading PowerWorks Ser.). (gr. 1-3). 37.50 *(978-0-7608-8928-2(7))*; pap. 6.10 *(978-0-7608-8929-9(5))* Sundance/Newbridge Educational Publishing.

Teckentrup, Britta, illus. Fast & Slow. 2013. (ENG.). 14p. (J). (gr. -1-k). bds. 6.99 *(978-1-84686-952-5(8))* Barefoot Bks., Inc.

—Fast & Slow Spanish. 2013. (ENG & SPA.). 14p. (J). (gr. -1-k). bds. 6.99 *(978-1-78285-035-9(X))* Barefoot Bks., Inc.

Things That Go. (Push & Pop Ser.). 5p. bds. *(978-1-4054-6893-0(9))* Parragon, Inc.

Ticktock Media, Ltd. Staff. Guess What? Things That Go. 2008. (Mini Flap Ser.). (ENG.). 10p. (J). (gr. k — 1). bds. 5.95 *(978-1-84696-819-8(4),* TickTock Books) Octopus Publishing Group GBR. Dist: Independent Pubs. Group.

Top That! Kids, creator. Things That Go. 2008. (Magnetic Play & Learn Ser.). (ENG., Illus.). 12p. (J). (gr. -1-k). *(978-1-84510-726-0(8))* Top That! Publishing PLC.

Transportation. 2010. (Mighty Machines Ser.). 24p. 191.92 *(978-1-4296-5197-4(0),* Pebble Plus) Capstone Press of Coughlan Cos.

Transportation. (Butterfly Bks.). (Illus.). 15p. (J). 11.95 *(978-0-86685-613-3(7))* International Bk. Ctr., Inc.

Transportation & Communication. (J). (gr. k-1). *(978-84-342-2418-6(6),* PR30572) Parramon Ediciones S.A. ESP. Dist: Lectorum Pubns., Inc.

Transportation & Communication Series, 14 bks., Set. Incl. Bridges. Farbman, Melinda. 48p. lib. bdg. 23.93 *(978-0-7660-1647-7(1))*; Cars. Flammang, James M. 48p. lib. bdg. 23.93 *(978-0-7660-1646-0(3))*; Fire Engines. Molzahn, Arlene Bourgeois. 48p. lib. bdg. 23.93 *(978-0-7660-1643-9(9))*; Motorcycles. Stuart, Dee. 48p. lib. bdg. 23.93 *(978-0-7660-1648-4(X))*; Television. Feeney, Kathy. 48p. lib. bdg. 23.93 *(978-0-7660-1644-6(7))*; Trains. Perry, Phyllis J. 46p. lib. bdg. 23.93 *(978-0-7660-1645-3(5))*; (J). (gr. 1-4). 2001. (Illus.). Set lib. bdg. 284.25 *(978-0-7660-1804-4(0))* Enslow Pubs., Inc.

Transportation Technology Systems. 2nd rev. ed. 2004. 55p. pap. *(978-0-86657-514-0(6))* Lab-Volt Systems, Inc.

Varonka, Steve. Hard Coal Times Vol. 3: Early Coal Transportation. 2004. (Illus.). 24p. (YA). 4.72 *(978-0-9709630-5-5(X))* Coal Hole Productions.

Vehiculos de Alta Tecnologia Series, 6 bks., Set. 2003. (Vehiculos de Alta Tecnologia Ser.). (SPA & ENG., Illus.). (J). lib. bdg. 103.50 *(978-0-8239-6919-7(3),* Editorial Buenas Letras) Rosen Publishing Group, Inc., The.

Veitch, Catherine. Big Machines Drive!, 1 vol. 2014. (Big Machines Ser.). (ENG.). 24p. (gr. k-1). 23.32 *(978-1-4846-0585-1(3),* Heinemann Read & Learn) Heinemann-Raintree.

Verstraete, Larry. Innovations in Transportation. 2016. (Problem Solved! Your Turn to Think Big Ser.). (ENG., Illus.). 32p. (J). (gr. 3-6). *(978-0-7787-2680-7(0))* Crabtree Publishing Co.

Vous, Nous. Show & Tell: Transport Activities. 2017. (ENG., Illus.). 10p. (J). pap. 9.99 *(978-1-84780-731-1(3),* Wide Eyed Editions) Quarto Publishing Group UK GBR. Dist: Littlehampton Bk Services, Ltd.

Walker, Niki. Transportation Disaster Alert! 2005. (Disaster Alert! Ser.). (ENG., Illus.). 32p. (J). (gr. 4-7). lib. bdg. *(978-0-7787-1584-9(1))* Crabtree Publishing Co.

Walker, Robert. Transportation Inventions. 2013. (ENG., Illus.). 48p. (J). pap. *(978-0-7787-0240-5(5))* Crabtree Publishing Co.

—Transportation Inventions: Moving Our World Forward. 2013. (ENG., Illus.). 48p. (J). *(978-0-7787-0223-8(5))* Crabtree Publishing Co.

Waxman, Laura Hamilton. Ambulances. 2004. (Pull Ahead Bks.). (Illus.). 32p. (J). (gr. k-2). lib. bdg. 22.60 *(978-0-8225-0769-7(2))* Lerner Publishing Group.

—Terrific Transportation Inventions. 2013. (Awesome Inventions You Use Every Day Ser.). (ENG., Illus.). 32p. (gr. 3-6). lib. bdg. 26.60 *(978-1-4677-1096-1(2),* Lerner Pubns.) Lerner Publishing Group.

Waxman, Laura Hamilton & Levine, Michelle. Ambulances. 2004. (Pull Ahead Bks.). (Illus.). 32p. (J). (gr. k-2). pap. 6.95 *(978-0-8225-9923-4(6))* Lerner Publishing Group.

Way, Steve & Bailey, Gerry. Land Transportation. 2008. (Simply Science Ser.). (Illus.). 32p. (YA). (gr. 3-6). lib. bdg. 26.00 *(978-0-8368-9228-4(3))* Stevens, Gareth Publishing LLLP.

Welvaert, Scott R. Follow That Crop: From the Farmer's Field to Our Grocery Store. 2003. (From Here to There Ser.). (J). *(978-1-58417-194-2(4))*; pap. *(978-1-58417-195-9(2))* Lake Street Pubs.

West, Tracey & dePaola, Tomie. No Way ... Way! Road Trip. 2015. (Smithsonian Ser.). (ENG., Illus.). 208p. (J). (gr. 3-7). bds. 9.99 *(978-0-448-48211-8(8),* Grosset & Dunlap) Penguin Young Readers Group.

Wheels & Rockets. (J). (gr. 4). 42.95 *(978-0-673-72657-5(6),* Scott Foresman) Addison Wesley Schl.

Will, Sandra. Transportation Inventions: From Subways to Submarines. 2006. (Which Came First? Ser.). (Illus.). 32p. (YA). (gr. 3-6). lib. bdg. 25.27 *(978-1-59716-133-6(0))* Bearport Publishing Co., Inc.

Williams, Brian. Transport Technology. 2010. (New Technology Ser.). (ENG., Illus.). 48p. (J). 23.99 *(978-0-237-53429-5(0))* Evans Brothers, Ltd. GBR. Dist: Independent Pubs. Group.

Wooldridge, Connie Nordhielm. Just Fine the Way They Are: From Dirt Roads to Rail Roads to Interstates. Walz, Richard, illus. 2011. (ENG.). 32p. (J). (gr. 3-18). 17.95 *(978-1-59078-710-6(2),* Calkins Creek) Boyds Mills Pr.

World Book, Inc Staff, contrib. by. On the Move. 2007. *(978-0-7166-7728-4(8))* World Bk., Inc.

A World of Wheels, 8 vols., Set. (Illus.). 104,132p. (gr. 7-18). lib. bdg. *(978-1-59084-483-0(1))* Mason Crest.

Yaun, Katherine. Getting a Job in the Transportation Industry. 2016. (Job Basics: Getting the Job You Need Ser.). 80p. (J). (gr. 8-8). 35.75 *(978-1-4777-8568-3(X))* Rosen Publishing Group, Inc., The.

Yomtov, Nel. Troop Transport. 2016. (Military Missions Ser.). (ENG., Illus.). 24p. (J). (gr. 3-7). 25.95 *(978-1-62617-440-5(7),* Epic Bks.) Bellwether Media.

Yoyo Books, creator. Vroom. 2011. (Baby's First Library). (ENG., Illus.). 38p. (gr. -1-k). bds. *(978-90-8622-910-9(7))* YoYo Bks.

Zobel, Derek. Blastoff! Readers - Mighty Machines, 4 vols., Set. Incl. Bucket Trucks. 20.00 *(978-0-531-21707-8(8))*; Diggers. 20.00 *(978-0-531-21708-5(6))*; Pickup Trucks. 20.00 *(978-0-531-21709-2(4))*; Wheel Loaders. 20.00 *(978-0-531-21710-8(8))*; (Illus.). 24p. (J). (gr. k-3). 2009. 2009. Set lib. bdg. 80.00 *(978-0-531-26127-9(1),* Children's Pr.) Scholastic Library Publishing.

TRANSPORTATION, AUTOMOTIVE

see also Automobiles; Buses; Trucks

Bozzo, Linda & Library. Getting Around in the Past, Present, & Future. 2010. (Imagining the Future Ser.). (Illus.). 24p. (J). lib. bdg. 22.60 *(978-0-7660-3437-2(2),* Enslow Elementary) Enslow Pubs., Inc.

Doeden, Matt. Lowriders. 2009. pap. 8.95 *(978-0-8225-6664-9(8))* Lerner Publishing Group.

Dorling Kindersley Publishing Staff. Cars. 2014. (Eye Wonder Ser.). (ENG.). 56p. (J). (gr. k-4). 10.99 *(978-1-4654-1692-6(7),* DK Children) Dorling Kindersley Publishing, Inc.

Edwards, Pamela Duncan. The Bus Ride That Changed History: The Story of Rosa Parks. Shanahan, Danny, illus. 2009. (ENG.). 32p. (J). (gr. -1-3). pap. 6.99 *(978-0-547-07674-4(6))* Houghton Mifflin Harcourt Publishing Co.

Flounders, Anne. Cars. 2013. (Machines in Motion Ser.). 48p. (J). (gr. 3-5). pap. 84.30 *(978-1-4339-9598-9(0))*; (ENG., Illus.). lib. bdg. 31.95 *(978-1-4339-9596-5(4))* Stevens, Gareth Publishing LLLP.

Gilpin, Daniel & Pang, Alex. Record Breakers. 2010. (Machines Close-Up Ser.). 32p. (J). (gr. 4-7). 28.50 *(978-1-60870-113-1(1))* Marshall Cavendish Corp.

—Rescue Vehicles. 2010. (Machines Close-Up Ser.). 32p. (J). (gr. 4-7). 28.50 *(978-1-60870-111-7(5))* Marshall Cavendish Corp.

Gustaitis, Joseph Alan. Arctic Trucker. 2010. (Benchmark Rockets: Dirty & Dangerous Jobs Ser.). 32p. (J). (gr. 3-6). 28.50 *(978-1-60870-169-8(7))* Marshall Cavendish Corp.

Hemstock, Whitney M. The ABC's of Traffic Safety. 2010. 34p. pap. 16.95 *(978-0-557-28733-8(2))* Lulu Pr., Inc.

Jackson, Tom. Land & Water Transportation. 2012. (FAYFT: Invention & Technology Ser.). 64p. (gr. 4-10). lib. bdg. 39.95 *(978-1-936333-42-4(2))* Brown Bear Bks.

Mean Machines Series, 4 bks., Set 2. 2004. (Illus.). (J). pap. 32.20 *(978-1-4109-1200-8(0))* Harcourt Schl. Pubs.

Moore, Elizabeth. Watch Out!, 1 vol. 2011. (Wonder Readers Emergent Level Ser.). (ENG.). 32p. (gr. -1-1). pap. 5.99 *(978-1-4296-7852-0(6),* Wonder Readers) Capstone Press of Coughlan Cos.

Scott, Lee, et al. Where Is It Going. 2007. (Windows on Literacy Ser.). (ENG., Illus.). 12p. (J). pap. 10.95 *(978-0-7922-8476-5(3))* National Geographic School Publishing, Inc.

Stephens, Ronald, ed. Road Safety. 2014. (Safety First Ser.: 11). 48p. (J). (gr. 5-18). 20.95 *(978-1-4222-3052-7(X))* Mason Crest.

Tugeau, Jeremy, illus. Cars, Trucks, & Planes. 2010. (My World Ser.). (ENG.). 24p. (J). (gr. -1-1). pap. 8.15 *(978-1-61533-031-7(3))*; lib. bdg. 22.60 *(978-1-60754-949-9(2))* Windmill Bks.

Winget, Mary. Taxis. 2007. (Pull Ahead Books-Mighty Movers Ser.). (ENG., Illus.). 32p. (gr. k-3). lib. bdg. 22.60 *(978-0-8225-6419-5(X),* Lerner Pubns.) Lerner Publishing Group.

Woods, Bob. Wild Racers. 2009. (Racing Mania Ser.). 48p. (gr. 4-18). lib. bdg. 31.36 *(978-0-7614-4389-6(4))* Marshall Cavendish Corp.

TRANSPORTATION, AUTOMOTIVE—FICTION

Alexander, Jenny. The Rugged Off-Roader. 2010. (ENG., Illus.). 64p. (J). *(978-0-340-98150-4(4),* Hodder Children's Books) Hachette Children's Group GBR. Dist: Hachette Bk. Group.

Dale, Penny. Dinosaur Zoom! Dale, Penny, illus. 2013. (ENG., Illus.). 32p. (J). (-k). 15.99 *(978-0-7636-6448-0(0),* Nosy Crow) Candlewick Pr.

Gutman, Dan. Mission Unstoppable. 2011. (Genius Files Ser.: 1). (ENG.). 304p. (J). (gr. 3-7). pap. 6.99 *(978-0-06-182766-2(5))*; (Illus.). 16.99 *(978-0-06-182764-8(9))* HarperCollins Pubs.

—Mission Unstoppable. 2011. (Genius Files Ser.: 1). (J). lib. bdg. 17.20 *(978-0-606-23559-4(0),* Turtleback) Turtleback Bks.

—Never Say Genius. 2012. (Genius Files Ser.: 2). 288p. (J). (gr. 3-7). (ENG.). 16.99 *(978-0-06-182767-9(3))*; lib. bdg. 17.89 *(978-0-06-182768-6(1))* HarperCollins Pubs.

TRANSPORTATION—FICTION

Angleberger, Tom. McToad Mows Tiny Island. Hendrix, John, illus. 2015. (ENG.). 40p. (J). (gr. -1-3). 16.95 *(978-1-4197-1650-8(6),* Abrams Bks. for Young Readers) Abrams, Inc.

Arnold, Tedd. Ride, Fly Guy, Ride! 2012. (Fly Guy Ser.: 11). (ENG., Illus.). 32p. (J). (gr. -1-3). 6.99 *(978-0-545-22276-1(1),* Cartwheel Bks.) Scholastic, Inc.

—Ride, Fly Guy, Ride! 2012. (Fly Guy Ser.: 11). lib. bdg. 17.20 *(978-0-606-23904-2(9),* Turtleback) Turtleback Bks.

Awdry, W. Blue Mountain Mystery. Golden Books, illus. 2012. (Little Golden Book Ser.). (ENG.). 24p. (J). (gr. k-k). 4.99 *(978-0-307-97590-4(8),* Golden Bks.) Random Hse. Children's Bks.

—Thomas & Percy & the Dragon. Courtney, Richard, illus. 2003. (Step into Reading Ser.). (ENG.). 32p. (J). (gr. -1-1). pap. 3.99 *(978-0-375-82230-8(5),* Random Hse. Bks. for Young Readers) Random Hse. Children's Bks.

Awdry, Wilbert V. Blue Mountain Mystery. Stubbs, Tommy, illus. 2012. (Big Golden Book Ser.). (ENG.). 48p. (J). (gr. -1-2). 9.99 *(978-0-307-93149-8(8),* Golden Bks.) Random Hse. Children's Bks.

Awdry, Wilbert V. & Terrill, Elizabeth. Go, Train, Go! Stubbs, Tommy, illus. 2005. (Beginner Books(R) Ser.). (ENG.). 48p. (J). (gr. -1-1). 9.99 *(978-0-375-83177-5(0),* Random Hse. Bks. for Young Readers) Random Hse. Children's Bks.

AZ Books Staff. Fast Vehicles Moving & Talking. Harko, Lubov, ed. 2012. (Funny Trails Ser.). (ENG.). 10p. (J). (gr. -1-k). bds. 9.95 *(978-1-61889-177-8(4))* AZ Bks. LLC.

Barton, Byron. My Bus Board Book. Barton, Byron, illus. 2015. (ENG., Illus.). 38p. (J). (gr. -1 — 1). bds. 7.99 *(978-0-06-228738-0(9),* Greenwillow Bks.) HarperCollins Pubs.

Bianchini, Bob. Charlie Rides: Planes, Trains, Bikes, & More! 2017. (ENG., Illus.). 20p. (J). (gr. -1-k). bds. 8.95 *(978-1-4197-2292-9(1),* Abrams Appleseed) Abrams, Inc.

Biggs, Brian. Everything Goes: On Land. Biggs, Brian, illus. 2011. (ENG., Illus.). 56p. (J). (gr. -1-3). 14.99 *(978-0-06-195809-0(3))* HarperCollins Pubs.

—In the Air. Biggs, Brian, illus. 2012. (ENG., Illus.). 56p. (J). (gr. -1-3). 14.99 *(978-0-06-195810-6(7))* HarperCollins Pubs.

—Stop! Go! Biggs, Brian, illus. 2012. (ENG., Illus.). 24p. (J). (gr. -1 — 1). bds. 7.99 *(978-0-06-195813-7(1))* HarperCollins Pubs.

—123 Beep Beep Beep! Biggs, Brian, illus. 2012. (ENG., Illus.). 24p. (J). (gr. -1 — 1). bds. 7.99 *(978-0-06-195812-0(3))* HarperCollins Pubs.

Blackstone, Stella & Barefoot Books. Bear on a Bike (Oso en Bicicleta) Harter, Debbie, illus. 2014. (ENG & SPA.). 32p. (J). (gr. -1-1). pap. 6.99 *(978-1-78285-079-3(1))* Barefoot Bks., Inc.

Blathwayt, Benedict. Dougal the Digger. Blathwayt, Benedict, illus. 2009. (ENG., Illus.). 24p. (J). (gr. -1-k). pap. 12.99 *(978-1-86230-625-7(7))* Transworld Publishers Ltd. GBR. Dist: Independent Pubs. Group.

Blechman, Nicholas. Night Light. 2013. (ENG.). 48p. (J). (gr. -1-k). 16.99 *(978-0-545-46263-1(0))* Scholastic, Inc.

Book Company Staff. Beep Beep. 2003. (Novelty Bks.). (Illus.). (J). 15.95 *(978-1-74047-232-6(2))* Book Co. Publishing Pty, Ltd., The AUS. Dist: Penton Overseas, Inc.

Boyd, Bentley. Moving & Grooving. 2009. (Chester Comix Ser.). (Illus.). 24p. pap. 6.95 *(978-1-933122-36-6(6))* Chester Comix, LLC.

Burleigh, Robert. Zoom! Zoom! Sounds of Things That Go in the City. Carpenter, Tad, illus. 2014. (ENG.). 32p. (J). (gr. -1-3). 17.99 *(978-1-4424-8315-6(6),* Simon & Schuster Bks. For Young Readers) Simon & Schuster Bks. For Young Readers.

Calmenson, Stephanie. Late for School! Yoshikawa, Sachiko, illus. 2008. (ENG.). 32p. (J). (gr. -1-2). lib. bdg. 16.95 *(978-1-57505-935-8(5))* Lerner Publishing Group.

Carpenter, Tad. On the Go. 2015. (Who's That? Ser.). (ENG., Illus.). 16p. (J). (— 1). bds. 7.95 *(978-1-4549-1225-5(1))* Sterling Publishing Co., Inc.

Chapman, Allen. Bart Stirling's Road to Success; or, the Young Express Agent. 2007. 112p. per. *(978-1-4068-4512-9(4))* Echo Library.

Collicutt, Paul. Murder on the Robot City Express. Collicutt, Paul, illus. 2010. (Robot City Ser.: 4). (ENG., Illus.). 48p. (J). (gr. 3-7). pap. 8.99 *(978-0-7636-5015-5(3),* Templar) Candlewick Pr.

Cordsen, Carol Foskett. The Milkman. Jones, Douglas B., illus. 2007. (gr. -1-3). 17.00 *(978-0-7569-8148-8(4))* Perfection Learning Corp.

Crampton, Gertrude. Tootle: Classic Edition. Gergely, Tibor, illus. Date not set. 21p. (J). (gr. -1-1). *(978-1-929566-53-2(0))* Cronies.

Crisp, Dan. Trabajo/ Work. 2007. 14p. 10.95 *(978-84-263-6452-4(7))* Vives, Luis Editorial (Edelvives) ESP. Dist: Baker & Taylor Bks.

Dale, Jay. I Go up & Down. Dybing, Michelle, illus. 2012. (Wonder Words Ser.). (ENG.). 32p. (gr. k-2). pap. 5.99 *(978-1-4296-8894-9(7),* Engage Literacy) Capstone Press of Coughlan Cos.

DeLand, M. Maitland. Baby Santa's Worldwide Christmas Adventure. Wilson, Phil, illus. 2010. 32p. (J). 14.95 *(978-1-60832-062-2(6))* Greenleaf Book Group.

Derubertis, Barbara. Walter Warthog's Wonderful Wagon. Alley, R. W., illus. 2011. (Animal Antics A to Z Set III Ser.). pap. 45.32 *(978-0-7613-8432-8(4))* Kane Press, Inc.

Dorling Kindersley Publishing Staff. Cars 2. 2011. (Ultimate Sticker Bks.). (ENG.). 16p. (J). (gr. k-4). pap. 6.99 *(978-0-7566-7787-9(4),* DK Children) Dorling Kindersley Publishing, Inc.

Durango, Julia. Go-Go Gorillas. Taylor, Eleanor, illus. 2010. (ENG.). 32p. (J). (gr. -1-1). 15.99 *(978-1-4169-3779-1(X),* Simon & Schuster Bks. For Young Readers) Simon & Schuster Bks. For Young Readers.

Eastman, P. D. Ve, Perro, Ve! Perdomo, Adolfo Perez, tr. 2003. (Bright & Early Board Books(TM) Ser.).Tr. of Go, Dog, Go! (SPA & ENG., Illus.). 24p. (J). (— 1). bds. 4.99 *(978-0-375-82361-9(1),* Random House Para Ninos) Random Hse. Children's Bks.

Franco, Betsy. Going to Grandma's Farm. 2004. (Rookie Reader Español Ser.). (ENG., Illus.). 24p. (J). (gr. k-2). pap. 4.95 *(978-0-516-27787-5(1),* Children's Pr.) Scholastic Library Publishing.

Friday, Stormy. Signal's Airport Adventure. Saroff, Phyllis, illus. 2006. (J). 14.95 *(978-0-9717047-5-6(9))* Bay Media, Inc.

Gergely, Tibor, illus. Tootle. Golden Books Staff, photos by. deluxe ed. Date not set. (J). (gr. -1-2). reprint ed. *(978-1-929566-58-7(1))* Cronies.

Hajdusiewicz, Babs Bell. The Bridge Is Up! Hefferan, Rob, illus. 2006. (J). pap. 7.99 *(978-0-15-365089-5(3))* Houghton Mifflin Harcourt School Pubs.

Harper, Benjamin & Scieszka, Jon. All Around Trucktown. Shannon, David et al, illus. 2008. (Jon Scieszka's Trucktown Ser.). (ENG.). 32p. (J). (gr. -1-1). 3.99 *(978-1-4169-4194-1(0),* Simon Scribbles) Simon Scribbles.

Heo, Yumi. Red Light, Green Light. Heo, Yumi, illus. 2015. (ENG., Illus.). 20p. (J). (gr. -1-k). bds. 6.99 *(978-0-545-74463-8(6),* Cartwheel Bks.) Scholastic, Inc.

Hit Entertainment. Lost at Sea! Stubbs, Tommy, illus. 2010. (Pictureback(R) Ser.). (ENG.). 24p. (J). (gr. -1-2). pap. 3.99 *(978-0-375-84754-7(5),* Random Hse. Bks. for Young Readers) Random Hse. Children's Bks.

TUV

Holden, Pam. See Me Ride, 6 pack. East, Jacqueline, illus. 2009. (Red Rocket Readers Ser.). (ENG.). 16p. (gr. -1-1). pap. *(978-1-877363-30-6(8)*, Red Rocket Readers) Flying Start Bks.

Hopgood, Sally. A Trip to Busy Town: A Pull-The-Tab Book. Hinton, Stephanie, illus. 2014. (J). *(978-1-4351-5690-6(0))* Barnes & Noble, Inc.

Konrad, Marla Stewart. Getting There. 2009. (Early Reader Ser.). (ENG., Illus.). 24p. (J). (gr. -1-2). 12.95 *(978-0-88776-867-5(9)*, Tundra Bks.) Tundra Bks. CAN. Dist: Penguin Random Hse. LLC.

Let's Go Downtown: Individual Title Six-Packs. (gr. -1-2). 27.00 *(978-0-7635-9458-9(X))* Rigby Education.

Liwska, Renata. Red Wagon. Liwska, Renata, illus. 2013. (ENG., Illus.). 32p. (J). (gr. -1 — 1). 6.99 *(978-0-399-16239-8(9)*, Philomel Bks.) Penguin Young Readers Group.

Lord, Janet. Here Comes Grandma! Paschkis, Julie, illus. rev. ed. 2005. (ENG.). 32p. (J). (gr. -1-k). 16.99 *(978-0-8050-7666-0(2)*, 9780805076660, Holt, Henry & Co. Bks. For Young Readers) Holt, Henry & Co.

Maccarone, Grace. Bunny Race! Long, Ethan, illus. 2009. (J). *(978-0-545-11290-1(7))* Scholastic, Inc.

Mayo, Margaret. Choo Choo Clickety-Clack! Ayliffe, Alex, illus. 2005. (ENG.). 32p. (J). (gr. k-3). 16.95 *(978-1-57505-819-1(7))* Lerner Publishing Group.

McOmber, Rachel B., ed. McOmber Phonics Storybooks: The Tan Cab. rev. ed. (Illus.). (J). *(978-0-944991-04-6(1))* Swift Learning Resources.

Meachen Rau, Dana. Riding. 2006. (On the Move Ser.). (Illus.). 24p. (gr. k-1). lib. bdg. 15.95 *(978-0-7614-2317-1(6))* Marshall Cavendish Corp.

Meshon, Aaron. Delivery! Meshon, Aaron, illus. 2017. (ENG., Illus.). 48p. (J). (gr. -1-3). 17.99 *(978-1-4814-4175-9(2))* Simon & Schuster Children's Publishing.

Mok, Carmen. Ride the Big Machines Across Canada. 2015. (My Big Machines Ser.). (ENG.). 14p. (J). bds. 10.50 *(978-1-4434-3810-0(3))* HarperCollins Pubs.

My Big Book of Beginner Books about Me. 2011. (Beginner Books(R) Ser.). (ENG., Illus.). 208p. (J). (gr. -1-2). 16.99 *(978-0-307-93183-2(8)*, Random Hse. Bks. for Young Readers) Random Hse. Children's Bks.

Nosy Crow Staff. Bizzy Bear: off We Go! Davies, Benji, illus. 2012. (Bizzy Bear Ser.). (ENG.). 8p. (J). (gr. k — 1). bds. 6.99 *(978-0-7636-5900-4(2)*, Nosy Crow) Candlewick Pr.

Pallotta, Jerry. How Will I Get to School This Year? Biedrzycki, David, illus. 2011. (J). *(978-0-545-26659-8(9))* Scholastic, Inc.

Parker, Emma. How Shall I Get to School Today? 2010. (Illus.). pap. *(978-1-877547-84-3(0))* First Edition Ltd.

PAW Patrol on the Roll! 2016. (Illus.). (J). ***(978-1-5182-2638-0(8))*** Random House Children's Books.

Perlman, Rhea. Water Balloon Doom. Santat, Dan, illus. 2006. (Otto Undercover Ser.: No. 3). 124p. (J). (gr. 2-6). 14.99 *(978-0-06-075500-3(8)*, Tegen, Katherine Bks) HarperCollins Pubs.

Priddy, Roger. On the Go. 2013. (Hello Baby Ser.). (ENG., Illus.). 16p. (J). (gr. -1 — 1). bds. 4.99 *(978-0-312-51599-7(5)*, 9780312515997, Priddy Bks.) St. Martin's Pr.

Random House. PAW Patrol on the Roll! (PAW Patrol) Random House, illus. 2016. (Pictureback(R) Ser.). (ENG., Illus.). 16p. (J). (gr. -1-2). 4.99 *(978-1-101-93867-6(6)*, Random Hse. Bks. for Young Readers) Random Hse. Children's Bks.

Rey, H. A. On the Go! 2011. (Curious George Ser.). (ENG., Illus.). 10p. (J). (gr. -1 — 1). bds. 6.99 *(978-0-547-55151-7(7))* Houghton Mifflin Harcourt Publishing Co.

Reynolds, Aaron. Back of the Bus. Cooper, Floyd, illus. 2010. (ENG.). 32p. (J). (gr. 1-3). 16.99 *(978-0-399-25091-0(3)*, Philomel Bks.) Penguin Young Readers Group.

Rosa-Mendoza, Gladys. Cars, Trucks & Planes/Carros, Camiones y Aviones. Tugeau, Jeremy, illus. 2004. (English-Spanish Foundations Ser.). (SPA & ENG.). 20p. (J). (gr. -1). bds. 6.95 *(978-1-931398-14-5(3))* Me+Mi Publishing.

Rosen, Michael. The Bus Is for Us. Tyler, Gillian, illus. 2015. (ENG.). 32p. (J). (-k). 16.99 *(978-0-7636-6983-6(0))* Candlewick Pr.

Samuel, Quentin. Where's Everybody Going? Corr, Christopher, illus. 2003. 24p. (J). *(978-1-84089-218-5(8))* Zero to Ten, Ltd.

—Why Is Everybody So Excited. Corr, Christopher, illus. 2003. 24p. (J). *(978-1-84089-219-2(6))* Zero to Ten, Ltd.

Sander, Sonia. All Aboard! 2010. (Lego City Ser.). (ENG.). 32p. (J). (gr. -1-k). pap. 3.99 *(978-0-545-17764-1(2))* Scholastic, Inc.

Scarry, Richard. Cosas Que Se Mueven.Tr. of Things That Move. (SPA., Illus.). (J). pap. 6.95 *(978-950-04-1042-7(7))* Emecé Editores S.A. ARG. Dist: Planeta Publishing Corp.

—Cosas Que Se Mueven. 2003. (Richard Scarry Ser.).Tr. of Things That Move. (SPA.). (J). pap. *(978-970-690-847-6(1))* Planeta Mexicana Editorial S. A. de C. V.

—Richard Scarry's Mixed-Up Cars & Trucks. 2014. (ENG., Illus.). 34p. (J). (gr. -1-2). 12.95 *(978-1-4027-7220-7(3))* Sterling Publishing Co., Inc.

Schertle, Alice. Little Blue Truck Leads the Way. McElmurry, Jill, illus. 2009. (Little Blue Truck Ser.). (ENG.). 40p. (J). (gr. -1-3). 17.99 *(978-0-15-206389-4(7))* Houghton Mifflin Harcourt Publishing Co.

Schwartz, Amy. What James Likes Best. Schwartz, Amy, illus. 2014. (ENG., Illus.). 32p. (J). (gr. -1-k). 16.99 *(978-1-4814-2536-0(6)*, Atheneum Bks. for Young Readers) Simon & Schuster Children's Publishing.

Sharpe, Jeannie w. Once There Was an Orange Truck. 2005. 37p. (J). 15.95 *(978-0-9763117-0-6(4))* Sharpe, Jeannie W.

Siy, Alexandra. One Tractor. Rogers, Jacqueline, illus. 2009. (ENG.). 32p. (J). (gr. -1-k). pap. 6.95 *(978-0-8234-2188-6(0))* Holiday Hse., Inc.

Tibo, Gilles & Vaillancourt, François. El Senor Patapum. (Barril Sin Fondo Ser.). (SPA.). (J). (gr. 3-5). pap. *(978-968-6465-58-7(8))* Casa de Estudios de Literatura y Talleres Artisticos Amaquemecan A.C. MEX. Dist: Lectorum Pubns., Inc.

Ticktock Media, Ltd. Staff. Under the Ocean with the Little Yellow Submarine. 2009. (Touch & Feel Fun Ser.). (ENG.). 10p. (J). (gr. k — 1). bds. 5.95 *(978-1-84696-811-2(9)*, TickTock Books) Octopus Publishing Group GBR. Dist: Independent Pubs. Group.

Transportation Board Books 800618, 4. 2005. (J). bds. *(978-1-59794-035-1(6))* Environments, Inc.

Upton, Elizabeth. Maxi the Little Taxi. Cole, Henry, illus. 2016. (ENG.). 32p. (J). (gr. -1-k). 17.99 *(978-0-545-79860-0(4)*, Scholastic Pr.) Scholastic, Inc.

Wellington, Monica. Truck Driver Tom. 2007. (ENG., Illus.). 32p. (J). (gr. -1-k). 16.99 *(978-0-525-47831-7(0)*, Dutton Books for Young Readers) Penguin Young Readers Group.

Wells, Rosemary. Max Drives Away. 2003. (Max & Ruby Ser.). (ENG., Illus.). 12p. (J). (gr. -1 — 1). bds. 6.99 *(978-0-670-03651-6(X)*, Viking Books for Young Readers) Penguin Young Readers Group.

TRANSPORTATION, HIGHWAY

see Transportation, Automotive

TRANSPORTATION—HISTORY

Edison, Erin. Rosa Parks, 1 vol. 2013. (Great Women in History Ser.). (ENG.). 24p. (gr. k-1). pap. 6.29 *(978-1-62065-863-5(1))*; pap. 35.70 *(978-1-62065-864-2(X))* Capstone Press of Coughlan Cos. (Pebble Bks.).

From There to Here: a Transportation Time Line: Individual Title Six-Packs. (Discovery World Ser.). 24p. (gr. 1-2). 33.00 *(978-0-7635-8484-9(3))* Rigby Education.

Harris, Joseph. Transportation: The Impact of Science & Technology. 2009. (Pros & Cons Ser.). (ENG.). 64p. (YA). (gr. 5-9). lib. bdg. 35.00 *(978-1-4339-1990-9(7))* Stevens, Gareth Publishing LLLP.

Harris, Tim. Transportation Technology. 2015. (Science Q & A Ser.). (ENG., Illus.). 32p. (J). (gr. 5-5). pap. 10.58 *(978-1-5026-0627-3(5)*, 1389984) Cavendish Square Publishing.

Jackson, Tom. Land & Water Transportation. 2012. (FAYFT: Invention & Technology Ser.). 64p. (gr. 4-10). lib. bdg. 39.95 *(978-1-936333-42-4(2))* Brown Bear Bks.

Meachen Rau, Dana. Travel in American History. 2006. (How People Lived in America Ser.). (Illus.). 24p. (gr. 1-4). pap. 8.15 *(978-0-8368-7217-0(7)*, Weekly Reader Leveled Readers) Stevens, Gareth Publishing LLLP.

—Los Viajes en la Historia de América. 2006. (Como era la vida en America (How People Lived in America) Ser.). (SPA., Illus.). 24p. (gr. 1-4). pap. 8.15 *(978-0-8368-7441-9(2)*, Weekly Reader Leveled Readers) Stevens, Gareth Publishing LLLP.

—Los Viajes en la Historia de America. 2006. (Como era la vida en America (How People Lived in America) Ser.). (SPA., Illus.). 24p. (gr. 1-4). lib. bdg. 22.00 *(978-0-8368-7434-1(X)*, Weekly Reader Leveled Readers) Stevens, Gareth Publishing LLLP.

Murdico, Suzanne J. Railroads & Steamships: Important Developments in American Transportation. (America's Industrial Society in the 19th Century Ser.). 32p. 2009. (gr. 4-4). 47.90 *(978-1-61511-340-8(1))* 2004. (ENG., Illus.). (J). (gr. 5-8). pap. 10.00 *(978-0-8239-4278-7(3))* Rosen Publishing Group, Inc., The.

Newquist, H. P. From Here to There: The Story of How We Transport Ourselves & Our Stuff. 2017. (Smithsonian: Invention & Impact Ser.: 2). (ENG., Illus.). 128p. (J). (gr. 5). 18.99 ***(978-0-451-47645-6(X)***, Viking Books for Young Readers) Penguin Young Readers Group.

Orme, David. Speed. 2009. (Fact to Fiction Grafx Ser.). (Illus.). 36p. (J). pap. 6.95 *(978-0-7891-7906-7(7))* Perfection Learning Corp.

Orr, Tamra. The Department of Transportation. 2009. (This Is Your Government Ser.). 64p. (gr. 5-6). 58.50 *(978-1-60854-377-9(3)*, Rosen Reference) Rosen Publishing Group, Inc., The.

Orr, Tamra B. The Department of Transportation. 2006. (This Is Your Government Ser.). (ENG., Illus.). 64p. (gr. 4-8). per. 12.95 *(978-1-4042-0664-9(7))* Rosen Publishing Group, Inc., The.

Oxlade, Chris. The History of Transportation. 2017. (History of Technology Ser.). (ENG.). 32p. (gr. 2-5). lib. bdg. 27.32 ***(978-1-4846-4038-8(1)***, Heinemann First Library) Heinemann-Raintree.

Petersen, Christine. The Wheelwright. 2013. (Colonial People 3 Ser.). 48p. (J). (gr. 4-8). pap. 12.93 *(978-1-62712-049-4(1))* Cavendish Square Publishing.

Raum, Elizabeth. The Scoop on Clothes, Homes, & Daily Life in Colonial America, 1 vol. 2011. (Life in the American Colonies Ser.). (ENG.). 32p. (gr. 3-4). 27.32 *(978-1-4296-6138-6(0))*; pap. 47.70 *(978-1-4296-7214-6(5))* Capstone Press of Coughlan Cos. (Fact Finders).

Ray, Kurt. New Roads, Canals, & Railroads in Early 19th-Century America: The Transportation Revolution. (Life in the New American Nation Ser.). 32p. 2009. (gr. 4-4). 47.90 *(978-1-61514-281-1(9))* 2004. (ENG., Illus.). (gr. 5-8). pap. 10.00 *(978-0-8239-4254-1(6))* Rosen Publishing Group, Inc., The.

Ruiz, Rachel. When Rosa Parks Went Fishing. Fedele, Chiara, illus. 2017. (Leaders Doing Headstands Ser.). (ENG.). 32p. (gr. 2-3). lib. bdg. 27.99 ***(978-1-5158-1574-7(9))*** Picture Window Bks.

Simons, Lisa M. Bolt. Transportation Long Ago & Today, 1 vol. 2014. (Long Ago & Today Ser.). (ENG., Illus.). 24p. (gr. 1-2). 25.32 *(978-1-4914-0298-6(9)*, First Facts) Capstone Press of Coughlan Cos.

Spengler, Kremena T. An Illustrated Timeline of Transportation, 1 vol. Doty, Eldon, illus. 2011. (Visual Timelines in History Ser.). (ENG.). 32p. (gr. 3-4). pap. 7.49 *(978-1-4048-7019-2(9))*; lib. bdg. 28.65 *(978-1-4048-6661-4(2))* Picture Window Bks.

Stott, Colin. Victorian Transport. (Illus.). 32p. pap. *(978-0-7502-3752-9(X)*, Wayland) Hachette Children's Group.

Suen, Anastasia. Finding a Way: Six Historic U.S. Routes. 2004. (ENG., Illus.). 32p. (J). (gr. 5-5). pap. 13.05 *(978-0-7652-5239-5(2)*, Celebration Pr.) Pearson Schl.

Tracy, Kathleen. The Life & Times of Rosa Parks. 2008. (Illus.). 48p. (J). (gr. 4-8). lib. bdg. 29.95 *(978-1-58415-666-6(X))* Mitchell Lane Pubs., Inc.

El Transporte Ayer y Hoy Series, 6 bks., Set. 2003. (Transporte Ayer y Hoy Ser.). (SPA & ENG., Illus.). (J). lib. bdg. 103.50 *(978-0-8239-6916-6(9)*, Editorial Buenas Letras) Rosen Publishing Group, Inc., The.

Turner, Matt. Genius Transportation Inventions: From the Wheel to Spacecraft. Conner, Sarah, illus. 2017. (Incredible Inventions Ser.). (ENG.). 32p. (J). (gr. 3-6). 26.65 ***(978-1-5124-3209-1(1))*** Lerner Publishing Group.

Wirkner, Linda. Learning about America's Industrial Growth with Graphic Organizers. 2005. (Graphic Organizers in Social Studies). (Illus.). 24p. (J). (gr. 3-5). lib. bdg. 22.60 *(978-1-4042-2812-2(8)*, PowerKids Pr.) Rosen Publishing Group, Inc., The.

Woods, Michael & Woods, Mary B. Ancient Transportation: From Camels to Canals. 2005. (Ancient Technology Ser.). (Illus.). 96p. (gr. 6-12). 25.26 *(978-0-8225-2993-4(9))* Lerner Publishing Group.

World Book, Inc Staff, contrib. by. Transportation. 2009. (J). *(978-0-7166-0381-8(0))* World Bk., Inc.

TRANSPORTATION—POETRY

Scieszka, Jon. Truckery Rhymes. 2009. (Jon Scieszka's Trucktown Ser.). (ENG., Illus.). 24p. (J). (gr. k). pap. 6.25 *(978-0-328-50050-5(X)*, Scott Foresman) Addison Wesley Schl.

—Truckery Rhymes. Gordon, David et al, illus. 2009. (Jon Scieszka's Trucktown Ser.). (ENG.). 64p. (J). (gr. -1-3). 17.99 *(978-1-4169-4135-4(5)*, Simon & Schuster Bks. For Young Readers) Simon & Schuster Bks. For Young Readers.

TRANSPORTATION—VOCATIONAL GUIDANCE

Cohn, Jessica. Great Careers with a High School Diploma: Manufacturing & Transportation. 2008. (Great Careers with a High School Diploma Ser.). 127p. (C). (gr. 9). 32.95 *(978-0-8160-7050-3(4)*, Ferguson Publishing Co.) Facts On File, Inc.

Dakers, Diane. Green Ways of Getting Around: Careers in Transportation. 2011. (ENG., Illus.). 64p. (J). pap. *(978-0-7787-4867-0(7)*, 1331598); (gr. 5-9). *(978-0-7787-4856-4(1)*, 1331596) Crabtree Publishing Co.

Facts on File, Inc. Staff. Transportation. 2010. (New Discovering Careers for Your Future Ser.). (Illus.). 128p. (gr. 4-9). 24.95 *(978-0-8160-8048-9(8)*, Ferguson Publishing Co.) Facts On File, Inc.

Ferguson, creator. Transportation. 3rd rev. ed. 2007. (Careers in Focus Ser.). (Illus.). 192p. (gr. 6-12). 32.95 *(978-0-8160-6595-0(0)*, Ferguson Publishing Co.) Facts On File, Inc.

Miller, Malinda. Tomorrow's Transportation: Green Solutions for Air, Land & Sea. 2010. (New Careers for the 21st Century Ser.). 64p. (YA). (gr. 7-18). lib. bdg. 22.95 *(978-1-4222-1824-2(4))* Mason Crest.

—Tomorrow's Transportation: Green Solutions for Air, Land, & Sea. 2010. (New Careers for the 21st Century Ser.). 64p. (YA). (gr. 7-18). pap. 9.95 *(978-1-4222-2045-0(1))* Mason Crest.

Reeves, Diane Lindsey. Transportation. 2017. (Bright Futures Press: World of Work Ser.). (ENG., Illus.). 32p. (J). (gr. 4-7). lib. bdg. 29.93 *(978-1-63472-629-0(4)*, 209550) Cherry Lake Publishing.

Yomtov, Nel. Transportation Planner. 2013. (21st Century Skills Library: Cool STEM Careers Ser.). (ENG.). 32p. (J). (gr. 4-8). 28.50 *(978-1-62431-008-9(7)*, 202483); pap. 14.21 *(978-1-62431-032-4(X)*, 202485) Cherry Lake Publishing.

TRANSVAAL WAR, 1899-1902

see South African War, 1899-1902

TRAPP FAMILY SINGERS

Anderson, William. V Is for Von Trapp: A Musical Family Alphabet. Graves, Linda, illus. 2010. (ENG.). 32p. (J). (gr. 1-4). 16.95 *(978-1-58536-531-9(9)*, 202214) Sleeping Bear Pr.

Ransom, Candice. Maria von Trapp: Beyond the Sound of Music. 2005. (Trailblazers Biographies Ser.). (Illus.). 112p. (J). (gr. 5-9). lib. bdg. 27.93 *(978-1-57505-444-5(2))* Lerner Publishing Group.

TRAPPING

see also Fur Trade; Game and Game Birds; Hunting

Gilsvik, Bob. The Complete Book of Trapping. Gilsvik, David, illus. 172p. (J). (gr. 7). reprint ed. 14.95 *(978-0-936622-29-3(6))* A.R. Harding Publishing Co.

TRAPPING—FICTION

Anderson, Laurie Halse. Trapped. 2009. (Vet Volunteers Ser.: 8). (ENG.). 144p. (J). (gr. 3-7). 6.99 *(978-0-14-241223-7(6)*, Puffin Books) Penguin Young Readers Group.

Dalton, Matthew. The Next Steve Erwin, 1 vol. Cavanaugh, Stacy, illus. 2009. 16p. pap. 24.95 *(978-1-60836-635-4(9))* America Star Bks.

Kehret, Peg & the Cat, Pete. Trapped! 2008. (Pete the Cat Ser.). (ENG.). 192p. (J). (gr. 3-7). 5.99 *(978-0-14-241189-6(2)*, Puffin Books) Penguin Young Readers Group.

Kjelgaard, Jim. Big Red. 2011. (ENG., Illus.). 254p. (J). pap. 8.95 *(978-0-8234-2391-0(3))* Holiday Hse., Inc.

Lindsey, Stephanie. Crabs in a Bucket. 2013. 28p. pap. 24.95 *(978-1-63000-538-2(X))* America Star Bks.

Smelcer, John. The Trap. 2007. (ENG.). 176p. (YA). (gr. 7-9). per. 9.99 *(978-0-312-37755-7(X)*, 9780312377557) Square Fish.

TRAVEL

see also Automobile Travel; Games for Travelers; Tourism; Voyages and Travels; Voyages around the World

also names of countries, states, etc. with the subdivision Description and Travel, e.g. United States—Description and travel

AA Publishing. My Travel Journal: Snap, Stick, Write & Draw Your Holiday Memories. 2017. (ENG.). 96p. (J). (gr. k-2). spiral bd. 12.99 ***(978-0-7495-7821-3(1))*** Automobile Assn. GBR. Dist: Independent Pubs. Group.

Aguilera, Rich. Passport to Adventure: Daily Devotions for Juniors. 2016. 369p. (J). pap. *(978-0-8163-6189-2(4))* Pacific Pr. Publishing Assn.

Anderson, Jill, ed. Let's Go!/Vamos a Viajar! Evrard, Gaetan, illus. 2005. (Word Play/Juegos con Pala Ser.). (ENG & SPA.). 20p. (J). (gr. -1-17). bds. 6.95 *(978-1-58728-513-4(4))* Cooper Square Publishing Llc.

Awal, Pia. Travel Math. 2008. (Math Alive! Ser.). 32p. (gr. 4-18). lib. bdg. 28.50 *(978-0-7614-3217-3(5)*, Benchmark Bks.) Marshall Cavendish Corp.

Ball, Jacqueline A. Traveling Green. (Going Green Ser.). 32p. 2016. (ENG.). (J). (gr. 2-7). pap. 8.95 *(978-1-944998-67-7(5))* 2009. (Illus.). (YA). (gr. 3-6). lib. bdg. 25.27 *(978-1-59716-964-6(1))* Bearport Publishing Co., Inc.

Barbas, Keri, des. Travel Scratch & Sketch. 2005. (Activity Journal Ser.). (J). 12.99 *(978-0-88088-486-0(X))* Peter Pauper Pr. Inc.

Bardswich, Elizabeth & Bardswich, Miriam. Out There - Travel. 2007. (Steck-Vaughn BOLDPRINT Anthologies Ser.). (ENG., Illus.). 48p. (gr. 8-10). pap. 16.90 *(978-1-4190-4030-6(8))* Houghton Mifflin Harcourt Publishing Co.

Barnham, Kay. Journeys. 2004. (Starters Ser.). (Illus.). 24p. (J). lib. bdg. 22.80 *(978-1-58340-566-6(6))* Black Rabbit Bks.

Bernardo, Kat. Stem: The Science of Travel: Multiplication (Grade 3) 2017. (Mathematics Readers Ser.). (Illus.). 32p. (J). (gr. 3-3). pap. 8.99 ***(978-1-4807-5797-4(7))*** Teacher Created Materials, Inc.

Bree, Loris & Bree, Marlin. Kid's Trip Diary: Kids! Write about Your Own Adventures & Experiences! 4th ed. 2007. (Kid's Travel Ser.). (ENG., Illus.). 96p. (J). (gr. 2-4). per. 7.99 *(978-1-892147-14-1(9))* Marlor Pr., Inc.

Calfee, Susan. St. Augustine a to Z: A Young Reader's Guide to America's Oldest City. Senn, Oscar, illus. 2016. (ENG.). (J). pap. 12.95 *(978-0-9895487-1-7(6))* Wordwhittler Bks.

Cargile, Phillip & Miss Cheryl. The Wagon Man: The Untold Story of the Go-Bum Kids. 2009. 54p. pap. 16.95 *(978-1-60703-939-6(7))* America Star Bks.

Daniels, Jimmy. The Dusty Road. 2008. (ENG.). 26p. pap. 11.00 *(978-1-4196-2664-7(7))* CreateSpace Independent Publishing Platform.

Demarest, Chris L. & Mayer, Bill. All Aboard! A Traveling Alphabet. 2008. (ENG., Illus.). 40p. (J). (gr. -1-2). 17.99 *(978-0-689-85249-7(5)*, McElderry, Margaret K. Bks.) McElderry, Margaret K. Bks.

Doering Tourville, Amanda. Manners on the School Bus. Lensch, Chris, illus. 2009. (Way to Be!: Manners Ser.). 24p. (gr. -1-2). pap. 2.76 *(978-1-4048-6052-0(5)*, Nonfiction Picture Bks.) Picture Window Bks.

Dyan, Penelope. I Remember Still, a Kid's Guide to Seville, Spain. Weigand, John D., photos by. 2012. (Illus.). 34p. pap. 11.95 *(978-1-61477-034-3(4))* Bellissima Publishing, LLC.

—Turkish Delight — A Kid's Guide to Istanbul, Turkey. Weigand, John D., photos by. 2011. (Illus.). 44p. pap. 12.95 *(978-1-935630-54-8(7))* Bellissima Publishing, LLC.

Enchantment of the World, Second Series (Fall 2014 Set Of 6) 2014. (Enchantment of the World, Second Ser.). (J). lib. bdg. 240.00 *(978-0-531-24351-0(6))* Scholastic Library Publishing.

Givens, David, ed. For the Kids! A Family-Friendly Guide to Outings & Activities. 2003. (ENG., Illus.). 220p. pap. 24.95 *(978-1-904148-27-2(1))* Liffey Pr., The IRL. Dist: Dufour Editions, Inc.

Going Out: KinderWords Individual Title Six-Packs. (Kinderstarters Ser.). 8p. (gr. -1-1). 21.00 *(978-0-7635-8696-6(X))* Rigby Education.

Goldsworthy, Steve. Travelling Green. 2016. (J). ***(978-1-5105-2223-7(9))*** SmartBook Media, Inc.

Hamilton, Robert M. On a Bus. 2012. (Going Places Ser.). (ENG.). 24p. (J). (gr. k-2). pap. 8.15 *(978-1-4339-6275-2(6))*; lib. bdg. 22.60 *(978-1-4339-6273-8(X))* Stevens, Gareth Publishing LLLP.

—On a Plane. 2012. (Going Places Ser.). (ENG.). 24p. (J). (gr. k-2). pap. 8.15 *(978-1-4339-6279-0(9))*; lib. bdg. 22.60 *(978-1-4339-6277-6(2))* Stevens, Gareth Publishing LLLP.

—On a Train. 2012. (Going Places Ser.). (ENG.). 24p. (J). (gr. k-2). pap. 8.15 *(978-1-4339-6283-7(7))*; lib. bdg. 22.60 *(978-1-4339-6281-3(0))* Stevens, Gareth Publishing LLLP.

Hammond World Atlas Corporation Staff, ed. World Passport: Atlas & Travelmate. 2nd rev. ed. 2008. 128p. 6.95 *(978-0-8437-1350-3(X))* Hammond World Atlas Corp.

Hawkins, Emily. Atlas of Miniature Adventures: A Pocket-Sized Collection of Small-scale Wonders - Because Bigger Isn't Always Better. Letherland, Lucy, illus. (Atlas Of Ser.). (ENG.). 64p. (J). 2017. (gr. 1-4). 9.99 *(978-1-84780-910-0(3))* 2016. 9.99 *(978-1-84780-909-4(X))* Quarto Publishing Group UK GBR. (Wide Eyed Editions). Dist: Hachette Bk. Group, Littlehampton Bk Services, Ltd.

Heuer, Steve. Spectacular Experiments & Mad Science Kids Love: Science That Dazzles @ Home, School or on the Go! 2010. 204p. pap. 19.99 *(978-1-4490-7041-0(8))* AuthorHouse.

Hewitt, Sally. Transportation. 2010. (Starting Geography Ser.). 32p. (J). (gr. 2-5). 28.50 *(978-1-60753-129-6(1))* Amicus Publishing.

—Transportation. 2012. (Map Smart Ser.). 32p. (gr. 2-6). lib. bdg. 27.10 *(978-1-59920-415-4(0))* Black Rabbit Bks.

Higgins, Melissa. A Traveler's Guide to a Smooth Roadtrip. 2017. (Go-To Guides). (ENG., Illus.). 32p. (gr. 3-4). lib. bdg. 27.99 *(978-1-5157-3661-5(X)*, Snap Bks.) Capstone Press of Coughlan Cos.

Hood, Karen Jean Matsko. Adventure Travel: A Daily Journal, Vol. 1. Whispering Pine Press International, Inc. Staff, ed. Artistic Design Services Staff, illus. 2014. (Hood Journal Ser.). (ENG.). 130p. (J). 19.95 *(978-1-59210-428-4(2))*; per. 13.95 *(978-1-59210-134-4(8)*, 1-59210-134-8) Whispering Pine Pr. International, Inc.

—Adventure Travel Activity & Coloring Book. Whispering Pine Press International, ed. Hatakeyama, Hiroshi, tr. Hatakeyama, Hiroshi, illus. 2014. (Hood Activity & Coloring Book Ser.). (ENG & JPN.). 160p. (J). spiral bd. 19.95 *(978-1-59649-334-6(8))*; per. 19.95 *(978-1-59210-590-8(4))* Whispering Pine Pr. International, Inc.

—Adventure Travel Activity & Coloring Book: Activity & Coloring Book Series. 2006. (Educational Activity & Coloring Book Ser.). (Illus.). (J). 17.95 *(978-1-930948-58-7(1))* Whispering Pine Pr. International, Inc.

James, Trisha. I Know Things That Go. 2017. (What I Know Ser.). 24p. (J). (gr. k-k). pap. 8.15 ***(978-1-4824-6309-5(1))*** Stevens, Gareth Publishing LLLP.

Jocelyn, Marthe. Which Way? Slaughter, Tom, illus. 2010. (ENG.). 24p. (J). (gr. k-k). 15.95 *(978-0-88776-970-2(5)*, Tundra Bks.) Tundra Bks. CAN. Dist: Penguin Random Hse. LLC.

Johnson, Allen L. Kayaking Around Iceland: Adventures with Grandchildren. 2003. (Illus.). 196p. 15.00 *(978-1-880675-07-6(2))* Creative Enterprises.

Juarez, Christine. Countries, 1 vol. 2014. (Countries Ser.). (ENG.). 24p. (gr. k-1). pap. 23.80 *(978-1-4765-7044-0(2)*, Pebble Bks.) Capstone Press of Coughlan Cos.

Krebs, Laurie & Corr, Christopher. Off We Go to Mexico! An Adventure in the Sun. 2008. (ENG., Illus.). 32p. (J). (gr. k-5). 8.99 *(978-1-84686-159-8(4))* Barefoot Bks., Inc.
Lanz, Helen. How Shall We Travel? 2012. (Go Green Ser.). (Illus.). 32p. (gr. 3-6). lib. bdg. 28.50 *(978-1-59771-302-3(3))* Sea-To-Sea Pubns.
Ledieux, Jack. The Worst Trip EVER! 2017. (Text Connections Guided Close Reading Ser.). (J). (gr. 2). *(978-1-4900-1853-9(0))* Benchmark Education Co.
Lewin, Ted & Lewin, Betsy. How to Babysit a Leopard: And Other True Stories from Our Travels Across Six Continents. 2015. (ENG., Illus.). 144p. (J). (gr. 4-7). 22.99 *(978-1-59643-616-9(6)*, 9781596436169) Roaring Brook Pr.
Lonely Planet, et al. MY TRAVEL JOURNAL, 1 vol. 2016. (Lonely Planet Kids Ser.). (ENG., Illus.). 72p. (J). 12.99 *(978-1-76034-100-8(2)*, 5184) Lonely Planet Pubns.
Lonely Planet Publications Staff. Adventures in Noisy Places: Packed Full of Activities & over 250 Stickers, 1 vol. 2015. (Lonely Planet Kids Ser.). (ENG., Illus.). 48p. (J). pap. 9.99 *(978-1-74360-780-0(6)*, 4982) Lonely Planet Pubns.
—Adventures in Smelly Places: Packed Full of Activities & over 250 Stickers, 1 vol. 2015. (Lonely Planet Kids Ser.). (ENG.). 48p. (J). pap. 9.99 *(978-1-74360-781-7(4)*, 4984) Lonely Planet Pubns.
—Not for Parents China: Everything You Ever Wanted to Know, 1 vol. 2012. (Lonely Planet Kids Ser.). (ENG., Illus.). 96p. (J). pap. 14.99 *(978-1-74321-427-5(8)*, 4358) Lonely Planet Pubns.
—The Travel Book: A Journey Through Every Country in the World, 1 vol. 2015. (Lonely Planet Kids Ser.). (ENG., Illus.). 212p. (J). 19.99 *(978-1-74360-774-9(1)*, 4980) Lonely Planet Pubns.
MacDonald, Fiona. Travel & Trade in the Middle Ages. 2005. (World Almanac Library of the Middle Ages). (Illus.). 48p. (gr. 5-12). pap. 14.05 *(978-0-8368-5908-9(1))*; lib. bdg. 31.00 *(978-0-8368-5899-0(9))* Stevens, Gareth Publishing LLLP. (Gareth Stevens Secondary Library).
MacLaine, James. The Usborne Little Children's Travel Activity Book. Watt, Fiona, ed. Harrison, Erica et al, illus. 2013. (Activity Books for Little Children Ser.). (ENG.). 63p. (J). pap. 9.99 *(978-0-7945-3127-0(X)*, Usborne) EDC Publishing.
Maloney, Brenna. This Is Mouse - An Adventure in Sewing: Make Mouse & Friends * Travel with Them from Africa to Outer Space. 2015. (ENG., Illus.). 112p. pap. 16.95 *(978-1-60705-977-6(0)*, FunStitch Studio) C & T Publishing.
Mason, Paul. How Big Is Your Travel Footprint? 2009. (Environmental Footprints Ser.). 32p. (gr. 4). 28.50 *(978-0-7614-4415-2(7))* Marshall Cavendish Corp.
Mattern, Joanne. I Use Math on a Trip. 2005. (I Use Math Ser.). (Illus.). 24p. (gr. k-3). pap. 8.15 *(978-0-8368-4866-3(7))*; lib. bdg. 22.00 *(978-0-8368-4859-5(4))* Stevens, Gareth Publishing LLLP. (Weekly Reader Leveled Readers).
Mayo Clinic Staff, contrib. by. Healthy Traveler: Answers on Staying Well While Away from Home. 2004. (Mayo Clinic on Health Ser.). (Illus.). 36,52p. (YA). (gr. 8-18). lib. bdg. 15.95 *(978-1-59084-253-9(7))* Mason Crest.
Meachen Rau, Dana. Travel in American History. 2006. (How People Lived in America Ser.). (Illus.). 24p. (gr. 1-4). lib. bdg. 22.00 *(978-0-8368-7210-1(X)*, Weekly Reader Leveled Readers) Stevens, Gareth Publishing LLLP.
—Los Viajes en la Historia de América. 2006. (Como era la vida en America (How People Lived in America) Ser.). (SPA., Illus.). 24p. (gr. 1-4). pap. 8.15 *(978-0-8368-7441-9(2)*, Weekly Reader Leveled Readers) Stevens, Gareth Publishing LLLP.
—Los Viajes en la Historia de America. 2006. (Como era la vida en America (How People Lived in America) Ser.). (SPA., Illus.). 24p. (gr. 1-4). lib. bdg. 22.00 *(978-0-8368-7434-1(X)*, Weekly Reader Leveled Readers) Stevens, Gareth Publishing LLLP.
Michel, June, illus. Going Places: True Tales from Young Travelers. 2003. 160p. (J). (gr. 4-12). pap. *(978-1-58270-070-0(2))* Beyond Words Publishing, Inc.
Newman-D'Amico, Fran. Fun on the Go. 2005. (Dover Little Activity Bks.). (ENG., Illus.). 64p. (J). (gr. k-3). per., act. bk. ed. 1.99 *(978-0-486-44456-7(2))* Dover Pubns., Inc.
—Travel Fun. 2004. (Dover Little Activity Bks.). (ENG., Illus.). 64p. (J). (gr. k-3). pap., act. bk. ed. 1.99 *(978-0-486-43532-9(6))* Dover Pubns., Inc.
Ortiz, Rafael. Road Trip Across America. 2017. (Text Connections Guided Close Reading Ser.). (J). (gr. 2). *(978-1-4900-1841-6(7))* Benchmark Education Co.
Otowa, Rebecca. My Awesome Japan Adventure: A Diary about the Best 4 Months Ever! 2013. (ENG., Illus.). 48p. (J). (gr. 2-6). 14.95 *(978-4-8053-1216-2(5))* Tuttle Publishing.
Peters, Scott. How I Go. 2011. (Early Connections Ser.). (J). *(978-1-61672-322-4(X))* Benchmark Education Co.
Quan, Elizabeth. Once upon a Full Moon. 2007. (ENG., Illus.). 48p. (J). (gr. 1-4). 19.95 *(978-0-88776-813-2(X)*, Tundra Bks.) Tundra Bks. CAN. Dist: Penguin Random Hse. LLC.
Rice, Dona Herweck. Places to Go, 1 vol. 2nd rev. ed. 2013. (Nonfiction Readers Ser.). (ENG., Illus.). 12p. (J). (gr. 1-1). pap. 15.96 *(978-1-4807-1012-2(1))* Shell Educational Publishing.
—Places to Go, 1 vol. 2nd rev. ed. 2011. (Nonfiction Readers Ser.). (ENG.). 12p. (J). (gr. 1-1). pap. 4.99 *(978-1-4333-3573-0(5))* Teacher Created Materials, Inc.
Rissman, Rebecca. Taking a Trip: Comparing Past & Present, 1 vol. 2014. (Comparing Past & Present Ser.). (ENG.). 24p. (gr. -1-1). lib. bdg. 22.65 *(978-1-4329-8994-1(4)*, Acorn) Heinemann-Raintree.
Road Trip: Famous Routes. 2016. (Road Trip Ser.). 24p. (gr. 3-2). pap. 48.90 *(978-1-4824-5300-3(2))*; lib. bdg. 135.60 *(978-1-4824-4603-6(0))* Stevens, Gareth Publishing LLLP.
Sánchez, Gervasio. Cinco Anos Despues: Vidas Minadas. 2004. (SPA & ENG., Illus.). 80p. pap. 24.95 *(978-84-95939-33-3(9))* Blume ESP. Dist: Independent Pubs. Group.
Sasek, Miroslav. This Is the World: A Global Treasury. 2014. (ENG., Illus.). 234p. (J). (gr. 5). 35.00 *(978-0-8478-4396-1(3))* Universe Publishing.
Scillian, Devin. P Is for Passport: A World Alphabet. Rose, Melanie, illus. 2003. (Discover the World Ser.). (ENG.). 48p. (J). (gr. 1-3). 19.95 *(978-1-58536-157-1(7)*, 202017) Sleeping Bear Pr.
Smith, Aimee & Johnston, Deon. My Hometown Is the Best Place to Visit. 2017. (Text Connections Guided Close Reading Ser.). (J). (gr. 1). *(978-1-4900-1824-9(7))* Benchmark Education Co.
Spenser & Mom. Spenser Goes to Portland. Jacobsen, Amie, illus. 2008. 32p. 14.95 *(978-0-9817598-0-7(7))* Simple Fish Bk. Co., LLC.
Suen, Anastasia. Finding a Way: Six Historic U.S. Routes. 2004. (ENG., Illus.). 32p. (J). (gr. 5-5). pap. 13.05 *(978-0-7652-5239-5(2)*, Celebration Pr.) Pearson Schl.
Thomson, Ruth. Countries, 4 vols., Set. Incl. France. lib. bdg. 22.60 *(978-1-4488-3275-0(6))*; India. lib. bdg. 22.60 *(978-1-4488-3276-7(4))*; Poland. lib. bdg. 22.60 *(978-1-4488-3277-4(2))*; Spain. lib. bdg. 22.60 *(978-1-4488-3278-1(0))*; (J). (gr. k-3). (Countries Ser.). (Illus.). 24p. 2011. Set lib. bdg. 85.00 *(978-1-4488-3304-7(3)*, PowerKids Pr.) Rosen Publishing Group, Inc., The.
Tweh, Steven R. Traveling Abroad: How to Proceed & Succeed. 2011. 132p. (gr. -1). pap. 10.99 *(978-1-4343-3933-1(5))* AuthorHouse.
Unglick, Richard. Journey Around the World. 2016. (Playmobil Ser.). (ENG., Illus.). 64p. (J). (gr. 1-7). 19.95 *(978-1-63322-079-9(6)*, Walter Foster Jr) Quarto Publishing Group USA.
Williams, Rachel. Atlas of Adventures: A Collection of Natural Wonders, Exciting Experiences & Fun Festivities from the Four Corners of the Globe. Letherland, Lucy, illus. 2015. (Atlas Of Ser.). (ENG.). 96p. (J). (gr. 2-5). 30.00 *(978-1-84780-695-6(3)*, Wide Eyed Editions) Quarto Publishing Group UK GBR. Dist: Hachette Bk. Group.
Wood, Anita. Travel Doodles for Kids, 1 vol. 2012. (ENG., Illus.). 272p. (J). pap. 9.99 *(978-1-4236-2454-7(8))* Gibbs Smith, Publisher.
Woods, Michael & Woods, Mary B. Ancient Transportation Technology: From Oars to Elephants. 2011. (Technology in Ancient Cultures Ser.). (ENG., Illus.). 96p. (J). (gr. 6-12). lib. bdg. 31.93 *(978-0-7613-6524-2(9))* Lerner Publishing Group.
Zannos, Susan. The Life & Times of Marco Polo. 2004. (Biography from Ancient Civilizations Ser.). (Illus.). 48p. (J). (gr. 4-8). lib. bdg. 29.95 *(978-1-58415-264-4(8))* Mitchell Lane Pubs., Inc.

TRAVEL—FICTION

Abbott, Jacob. Aunt Margaret; or, How John True Kept His Resolutions. 2013. 160p. pap. 19.95 *(978-1-4455-2937-0(8))* Research Pr.
—Rollo in Holland. 2008. 108p. 23.95 *(978-1-60664-820-9(9))*; pap. 9.95 *(978-1-60664-065-4(8))* Aegypan.
—Rollo in London. 2008. 124p. 23.95 *(978-1-60664-942-8(6))*; pap. 10.95 *(978-1-60312-492-8(6))* Aegypan.
—Rollo in Naples. 2008. 108p. 23.95 *(978-1-60664-821-6(7))*; pap. 9.95 *(978-1-60664-066-1(6))* Aegypan.
—Rollo in Paris. 2008. 116p. 22.95 *(978-1-60664-943-5(4))*; pap. 9.95 *(978-1-60312-493-5(4))* Aegypan.
Abraham, Ametta. Miss Robbie's House. 2009. 64p. pap. 23.49 *(978-1-4490-4571-5(5))* AuthorHouse.
Abshier, Stan. Teddy's Journal: Cruise to Japan, China, & Singapore. 2012. 96p. pap. 31.99 *(978-1-4685-2319-5(8))* AuthorHouse.
Ahern, Carolyn L. Tino Turtle Travels to Beijing, China. Burt-Sullivan, Neallia, illus. 2011. (ENG.). 56p. (J). (gr. -1-4). 19.95 incl. audio compact disk *(978-0-9793158-4-8(0))* Tino Turtle Travels, LLC.
—Tino Turtle Travels to Kenya - the Great Safari. Burt Sullivan, Neallia, illus. 2009. (ENG & SWA.). 32p. (J). (gr. -1-4). 19.95 incl. audio compact disk *(978-0-9793158-3-1(2))* Tino Turtle Travels, LLC.
—Tino Turtle Travels to London, England. Burt Sullivan, Neallia, illus. (J). 2007. 36p. 17.95 incl. audio compact disk *(978-0-9793158-0-0(8))* 2008. (ENG.). 32p. 19.95 incl. audio compact disk *(978-0-9816297-0-4(9))* Tino Turtle Travels, LLC.
—Tino Turtle Travels to Mexico City, Mexico. Burt Sullivan, Neallia, illus. 2008. (ENG & SPA.). 32p. (J). (gr. -1-4). 19.95 incl. audio compact disk *(978-0-9793158-2-4(4))* Tino Turtle Travels, LLC.
—Tino Turtle Travels to Paris, France. Burt Sullivan, Neallia, illus. 2007. 36p. (J). (gr. -1-4). 17.95 incl. audio compact disk *(978-0-9793158-1-7(6))* Tino Turtle Travels, LLC.
Alonso, Manuel L. Rumbo Sur. 2005. *(978-84-263-5948-3(5))* Vives, Luis Editorial (Edelvives).
Alter, Anna. Sprout Street Neighbors: Bon Voyage. 2017. (Sprout Street Neighbors Ser.: 3). (ENG., Illus.). 96p. (J). (gr. 1-4). pap. 6.99 ***(978-1-5247-0053-9(3)***, Yearling) Random Hse. Children's Bks.
Anderson, Nancy. Jeff's Trip to Holland. 2016. (Rosen REAL Readers: STEM & STEAM Collection). 12p. (gr. 1-k). pap. 6.33 *(978-1-5081-2679-9(8)*, Rosen Classroom) Rosen Publishing Group, Inc., The.
Angleberger, Tom. Emperor Pickletine Rides the Bus. 2014. (Origami Yoda Ser.). (ENG., Illus.). 224p. (J). (gr. 3-7). 13.95 *(978-1-4197-0933-3(X)*, Amulet Bks.) Abrams, Inc.
Asher, Penny & Booker, Ricki. Mommy & Daddy Are Going on a Trip. Kassab, Selena, illus. 2006. 32p. (J). 12.95 *(978-0-9755902-1-8(9))* Change Is Strange, Inc.
Auerbach, Annie. My Race into Space! A Water Wonder Book. Garofoli, Viviana, illus. 2005. 18p. (J). 9.95 *(978-1-58117-351-2(2)*, Intervisual/Piggy Toes) Bendon, Inc.
AZ Books, creator. Tyler Turtle Travels to Australia. 2013. (Pop-Up: Play & Listen Ser.). (ENG., Illus.). 10p. (J). (gr. -1-k). bds. 16.95 *(978-1-61889-036-8(0))* AZ Bks. LLC.
Barchers, Suzanne I. Pack a Bag!, 1 vol. 2011. (Targeted Phonics Ser.). (ENG.). 16p. (J). (gr. k-2). pap. 5.99 *(978-1-4333-2409-3(1))* Teacher Created Materials, Inc.
Barton, Bob. Trouble on the Voyage. 2010. (ENG., Illus.). 240p. (J). (gr. 4-7). pap. 10.95 *(978-1-926607-10-8(4)*, Napoleon & Co.) Dundurn CAN. Dist: Ingram Publisher Services.
Benchimol, Brigitte. Jadyn & the Magic Bubble: I Met Gandhi. Adams, Mark Wayne, illus. 2008. (J). 24.95 *(978-0-9799339-7-4(8))* East West Discovery Pr.
Benchmark Education Co., LLC. A Trip to Washington, D. C. A Capital Idea Teacher's Guide. 2013. (Reader's Theater Word Plays Ser.). *(978-1-4509-9037-0(1))* Benchmark Education Co.
Bennett, Holly. Redwing, 1 vol. 2012. (ENG.). 208p. (YA). (gr. 8-12). pap. 12.95 *(978-1-4598-0038-0(9))* Orca Bk. Pubs. USA.
Bidziiya, Kristin. Two Girls Dreams Come True. 2007. 64p. per. 9.95 *(978-1-934246-87-0(5))* Peppertree Pr., The.
Bilbrey, Heather. The Cookie Man. Green, Megan, illus. 2008. 20p. pap. 24.95 *(978-1-60703-328-8(3))* America Star Bks.
Bilik-Franklin, MidiAna & Griffith, Indigo, photos by. The Carseat Tourist. 2006. (Illus.). (J). bds. 7.95 *(978-0-9772825-0-0(3))* Critter Camp Inc.
Blake, Christine & Lopez, Jill. Signs, Signs, Everywhere Signs. 2008. 32p. pap. 15.95 *(978-1-4327-2523-5(8))* Outskirts Pr., Inc.
Bond, Michael. Love from Paddington. Fortnum, Peggy & Alley, R. W., illus. 2016. (Paddington Ser.). 144p. (J). (gr. 3-7). pap. 5.99 *(978-0-06-242526-3(9))* HarperCollins Pubs.
Bowater, Alan. A Pig Called Pete. Pascoe, Pete, illus. 2009. (Pig Called Pete Ser.). 32p. (J). (gr. -1-2). 22.60 *(978-1-60754-558-3(6))*; pap. 10.55 *(978-1-60754-559-0(4))* Windmill Bks.
Bradbury, Jennifer. Shift. (ENG., Illus.). (YA). (gr. 7). 2012. 272p. pap. 10.99 *(978-1-4424-0852-4(9))* 2008. 256p. 17.99 *(978-1-4169-4732-5(9))* Simon & Schuster Children's Publishing. (Atheneum Bks. for Young Readers).
Brannon, Tom, illus. Sesame Street All Aboard! 2015. (ENG.). 10p. (J). (gr. -1-k). bds. 10.99 *(978-0-7944-3329-1(4))* Reader's Digest Assn., Inc., The.
Bridwell, Norman. Clifford Takes a Trip. Bridwell, Norman, illus. 2011. (Clifford Ser.). (ENG., Illus.). 32p. (J). (gr. -1-k). pap. 3.99 *(978-0-545-21591-6(9)*, Cartwheel Bks.) Scholastic, Inc.
—Clifford's Class Trip. Bridwell, Norman, illus. 2011. (Scholastic Reader Level 1 Ser.). (ENG., Illus.). 32p. (J). (gr. -1-2). pap. 3.99 *(978-0-545-22319-5(9)*, Cartwheel Bks.) Scholastic, Inc.
Brooks, Walter R. Freddy & the North Pole. Wiese, Kurt, illus. 2013. (ENG.). 322p. (gr. 4-13). pap. 10.99 *(978-1-4683-0320-9(1)*, 460320) Overlook Pr., The.
—Freddy Goes to Florida. Wiese, Kurt, illus. 2012. (ENG.). 224p. (gr. 4-13). 10.99 *(978-1-59020-741-3(6)*, 902741) Overlook Pr., The.
Broom, Jenny. Walk This World. Nieminen, Lotta, illus. 2013. (ENG.). 24p. (J). (gr. k-3). 18.99 *(978-0-7636-6895-2(8)*, Big Picture Press) Candlewick Pr.
Brown, Amanda C. Flying Courage. Archeval, Jose, illus. 2012. (ENG.). 26p. (J). pap. 9.99 *(978-1-62006-121-3(X))* Sunbury Press, Inc.
Brown, Margaret Wise. Around the World We Go! 2013. (Illus.). (J). *(978-1-4351-4720-1(0))* Barnes & Noble, Inc.
Brown, Rosie L. Zach & Rob's Journey: The Lost Eggs. 2007. 24p. per. 24.95 *(978-1-4241-8401-9(0))* America Star Bks.
Bunting, Eve. The Man with the Red Bag. 2007. 230p. (J). (gr. 5-9). 15.99 *(978-0-06-081828-9(X)*, Cotler, Joanna Books) HarperCollins Pubs.
Burleigh, Robert. Hit the Road, Jack. MacDonald, Ross, illus. 2012. (ENG.). 48p. (J). (gr. k-2). 17.95 *(978-1-4197-0399-7(4)*, Abrams Bks. for Young Readers) Abrams, Inc.
Butler, Ethel And Steven, creator. Callie the Kangie Traveling America. 2012. 32p. pap. 15.99 *(978-1-4685-6197-5(9))* AuthorHouse.
Cameron, Thomas "Tom". Freddy's Adventure on the Safari River. 2012. 36p. pap. 24.95 *(978-1-4626-7436-7(4))* America Star Bks.
Campbell, Aileen. The Wee Scot Travels. 2003. 32p. pap. 7.95 *(978-1-56554-873-2(6))* Pelican Publishing Co., Inc.
Caravan. 2007. (Choose Your Own Adventure - Dragonlarks Ser.). (Illus.). 64p. (J). (gr. 4-7). pap. 7.99 *(978-1-933390-54-3(9))* Chooseco LLC.
Carbonell, Paula. BUTTERFLY TRIP. 2007. (ENG., Illus.). 48p. (J). 18.95 *(978-84-96788-85-5(7))* OQO, Editora ESP. Dist: Baker & Taylor Bks.
Carlon, Mick. Riding on Duke's Train. 2011. (LeapKids Ser.). (ENG.). 160p. (J). (gr. k-7). pap. 9.95 *(978-1-935248-06-4(5))* Leapfrog Pr.
Chalifoux, Lisa M. Spotty & Eddie Visit Percé. 2010. 24p. pap. 14.95 *(978-1-4269-2660-0(X))* Trafford Publishing.
Chapman, Nancy Kapp & Chapman, Nancy. Tripper's Travels: An International Scrapbook, 1 vol. Chapman, Lee, illus. 2005. (ENG.). 32p. (J). (gr. 1-5). 16.95 *(978-0-7614-5240-9(0))* Marshall Cavendish Corp.
Chesne, Sabrina. Lillie's Treasures/Los tesoros de Lili. Capasso, Diana, tr. Patagonia School, illus. 2004. (ENG & SPA.). 32p. per. 15.00 *(978-0-9630310-9-9(0))* Will Hall Bks.
Christelow, Eileen. Five Little Monkeys Travel Activity Kit. 2010. (Five Little Monkeys Story Ser.). (ENG., Illus.). 64p. (J). (gr. -1-3). 12.99 *(978-0-547-25879-9(8))* Houghton Mifflin Harcourt Publishing Co.
Chronicle Books Editors & Player, Micah. Lately Lily ABC Travel Flash Cards. 2014. (ENG., Illus.). 26p. (J). (gr. -1-17). 14.99 *(978-1-4521-1524-5(9))* Chronicle Bks. LLC.
Church, Anna. Hug-A-Bug Travels to Peru. Church, Anna & Taylor, Nicole, illus. 2013. 44p. pap. 12.00 *(978-0-9831449-4-6(X))* Mighty Lion Ventures.
Clark, Ruth E. Airport Mouse Becomes a VIP/VIM World Traveler. Jones, Phil, illus. 2009. 32p. (J). 15.95 *(978-0-9792963-5-2(8))* Kimball, Jane A.
Cohen, Deborah Bodin. Engineer Ari & the Rosh Hashanah Ride. Kober, Shahar, illus. 2008. (ENG.). 32p. (J). (gr. k-3). pap. 7.95 *(978-0-8225-8650-0(9)*, Kar-Ben Publishing) Lerner Publishing Group.
Cole, Dina. Are There Alligators at the Equator? An Eddie the Equator Adventure. 2012. 40p. pap. 20.99 *(978-1-4772-6819-3(7))* AuthorHouse.
Conklin, Wendy. Dos Amigos Planos Viajan por el Mundo, 1 vol. rev. ed. 2007. (Building Fluency Through Reader's Theater Ser.).Tr. of Two Flat Friends Travel the World. (SPA.). 24p. (J). (gr. 3-4). pap. 6.99 *(978-1-4333-0022-6(2))* Teacher Created Materials, Inc.
Cousins, Lucy. Maisy Goes to London. Cousins, Lucy, illus. 2016. (Maisy Ser.). (ENG., Illus.). 32p. (J). (-k). 15.99 *(978-0-7636-8399-3(X))* Candlewick Pr.
Cowan, Sarah & Kitchen. A Trip to the Beach. 2009. 60p. pap. *(978-1-84923-198-5(2))* YouWriteOn.
Crawford, Laura. Postcards from Chicago/Postales Desde Chicago. de La Vega, Eida, tr. Adamson, Bonnie, illus. 2008. (Traveling with Anna Ser.). (ENG.). 32p. (J). (gr. 4-7). 16.95 *(978-0-9795477-4-4(1)*, Raven Tree Pr.,Csi) Continental Sales, Inc.
—Postcards from New York City/Postales Desde New York City. de La Vega, Eida, tr. Adamson, Bonnie, illus. 2008. (Traveling with Anna Ser.). (ENG.). 32p. (J). (gr. 4-7). 16.95 *(978-0-9795477-2-0(5))*; per. 7.95 *(978-0-9795477-3-7(3))* Continental Sales, Inc. (Raven Tree Pr.,Csi).
—Postcards from Washington D. C./Postales Desde Washington D. C. de La Vega, Eida, tr. Adamson, Bonnie, illus. 2008. (Traveling with Anna Ser.). (ENG.). 32p. (J). (gr. 4-7). 16.95 *(978-0-9795477-0-6(9))*; per. 7.95 *(978-0-9795477-1-3(7))* Continental Sales, Inc. (Raven Tree Pr.,Csi).
Crawford, Quinton. Moochie the Soochie - Visits the Peace People. 2009. 42p. pap. 17.98 *(978-0-557-07714-4(1))* Lulu Pr., Inc.
Creek, Silent. All the Ice of Afric. 2009. 160p. 22.95 *(978-1-4401-2118-0(4))* iUniverse, Inc.
Crimi-Trent, Ellen & Priddy, Roger. The Field Trip. 2014. (Schoolies Ser.). (ENG.). 28p. (J). (gr. -1-1). 4.99 *(978-0-312-51662-8(2)*, 9780312516628, Priddy Bks.) St. Martin's Pr.
Cunningham, Mary. The Missing Locket. 2005. (Cynthia's Attic Ser.). 152p. (J). (gr. 5). per. 9.99 *(978-1-59080-441-4(4))* Echelon Press Publishing.
Czerw, Nancy Carpenter. Itty & Bitty - On the Road. Berlin, Rose Mary, illus. 2008. (Itty & Bitty Ser.: 3). (ENG.). 32p. (J). (gr. -1-3). 16.95 *(978-0-9755618-4-3(7))* McWitty Pr., Inc.
Darrington, Rebecca. Doodletoot- a Happy Little Basset Hound Dog. 2012. 24p. pap. 17.99 *(978-1-61996-337-5(X))* Salem Author Services.
Davies, Lewis. Tai, Troll & the Black & White Cow. 2009. (ENG., Illus.). 30p. (J). pap. 7.95 *(978-1-905762-64-4(X))* Parthian Bks. GBR. Dist: Independent Pubs. Group.
Davis, Pat. Estelle & the Escape from Mars: A Children's Novel By. 2009. 136p. pap. 10.99 *(978-1-4389-5432-5(8))* AuthorHouse.
De Haven, Amanda. Queen Elizabeth's Travel. 2012. 24p. pap. 15.99 *(978-1-4691-6388-8(8))* Xlibris Corp.
DeLand, M. Maitland. Baby Santa's Worldwide Christmas Adventure. Wilson, Phil, illus. 2010. 32p. (J). 14.95 *(978-1-60832-062-2(6))* Greenleaf Book Group.
Demi. Marco Polo, 0 vols. 2008. (ENG., Illus.). 56p. (J). (gr. 4-7). 19.99 *(978-0-7614-5433-5(0)*, 9780761454335, Amazon Children's Publishing) Amazon Publishing.
DeMico, Judy. The Bus Trip, 1 vol. Johnson, Catherine LeAnn, illus. 2010. 26p. pap. 24.95 *(978-1-4489-2767-8(6))* PublishAmerica, Inc.
Denofsky, Howard. Sillyishis, Beanie & the Hobblebobs. 2012. 32p. 24.95 *(978-1-4626-6211-1(0))* America Star Bks.
DeNucci, Sharon. Ava Goes to Africa. DeNucci, Corinne, illus. 2010. 32p. pap. 16.99 *(978-1-4520-4091-2(5))* AuthorHouse.
Diesen, Deborah. The Pout-Pout Fish, Far, Far from Home. Hanna, Dan, illus. 2017. (Pout-Pout Fish Adventure Ser.). (ENG.). 32p. (J). 16.99 *(978-0-374-30194-1(8)*, 9780374301941, Farrar, Straus & Giroux (BYR)) Farrar, Straus & Giroux.
Docherty, Thomas. To the Beach. Docherty, Thomas, illus. 2009. (ENG., Illus.). 40p. (J). (gr. -1-2). 15.99 *(978-0-7636-4429-1(3)*, Templar) Candlewick Pr.
Dodson, Shon. All I Need. 2010. 36p. 15.99 *(978-1-4520-1053-3(6))* AuthorHouse.
Donaki & Rosenberry, Donald. Spectacular Journey. Rosenberry, Akiko & Rosenberry, Susan, illus. 2006. (J). per. 20.00 *(978-0-9771482-6-4(2)*, Ithaca Pr.) Authors & Artists Publishers of New York, Inc.
Dotlich, Rebecca Kai. The Knowing Book. Cordell, Matthew, illus. 2016. (ENG.). 32p. (J). (gr. k). 16.95 *(978-1-59078-926-1(1))* Boyds Mills Pr.
Downey, Tika. Tracks in the Snow. 2006. (Neighborhood Readers Ser.). (ENG.). 16p. (gr. 1-3). pap. 6.50 *(978-1-4042-7180-7(5)*, Rosen Classroom) Rosen Publishing Group, Inc., The.
Dream Catchers - Evaluation Guide: Evaluation Guide. 2006. (J). *(978-1-55942-403-5(6))* Witcher Productions.
du Bois, William Pène. Twenty-One Balloons. du Bois, William Pène, illus. 2005. (Illus.). 180p. (J). lib. bdg. 15.00 *(978-1-4242-2270-4(2))* Fitzgerald Bks.
Dubyn, Bj. The Thrilling & Dynamic Adventures of Barbara Ann, Her Kid Brother, Billy, Jr , & Manfred the Magnificent, Their Parrot. 2008. 104p. pap. 15.99 *(978-1-4363-2652-0(4))* Xlibris Corp.
DuPrau, Jeanne. Car Trouble. 2005. 288p. (J). 15.99 *(978-0-06-073672-9(0))*; lib. bdg. 16.89 *(978-0-06-073674-3(7))* HarperCollins Pubs.
Duthaluru, Vidhya. Michael's Field Trip. 2007. (Illus.). 18p. (J). 3.99 *(978-0-9797657-0-4(6))* Duthaluru, Vidhya.
Earp-Bridgmon, Krista D. The Adventures of Jim-Bob: A Bearography. 2013. 24p. pap. 10.99 *(978-1-4582-1005-0(7)*, Abbott Pr.) Author Solutions, Inc.
Eastman, P. D. Ve, Perro, Ve! Perdomo, Adolfo Perez, tr. 2003. (Bright & Early Board Books(TM) Ser.).Tr. of Go, Dog, Go! (SPA & ENG., Illus.). 24p. (J). (— 1). bds. 4.99 *(978-0-375-82361-9(1)*, Random House Para Ninos) Random Hse. Children's Bks.
Edman Lamote, Lisa. A Day Out for Opus. Wilson, Alisha, illus. 2006. (Bookmann Family Presents Ser.). 32p. (J). (gr. k-3). 15.99 *(978-1-933673-03-5(6)*, BookMann Pr.) Mann Publishing Group.
Edwards, Wallace. Uncle Wally's Old Brown Shoe, 1 vol. 2012. (ENG., Illus.). 32p. (J). (gr. -1-3). 19.95 *(978-1-4598-0154-7(7))* Orca Bk. Pubs. USA.
Eller, Sylvia Klope. The Squirrel Who Hitchhiked to Atlanta. 2007. (Illus.). 32p. (J). pap. 8.00 *(978-0-8059-7596-3(9))* Dorrance Publishing Co., Inc.
Elya, Susan Middleton. Oh No, Gotta Go! Karas, G. Brian, illus. 2003. (SPA & ENG.). 32p. (J). (gr. -1-2). 15.99 *(978-0-399-23493-4(4)*, G.P. Putnam's Sons Books for Young Readers) Penguin Young Readers Group.
Errico, Jessica / C. Grandpa's Magical Accordion. Star, Brenda, illus. 2007. 28p. (J). pap. 17.95 incl. cd-rom *(978-0-9800577-0-6(1))* Three Part Harmony LLC.
Evans, Douglas. MVP. Shelley, John, illus. 2004. (ENG.). 232p. (J). (gr. 4-6). 16.95 *(978-1-932425-13-0(6)*, Lemniscaat) Boyds Mills Pr.
Fath, Teresa. The Train Track Trolley & the Bell Dogs. 2009. 32p. pap. 21.99 *(978-1-4415-4350-9(3))* Xlibris Corp.
Fenn, George. Yussuf the Guide or the Mountain Bandits: Being the Strange Story of the Travels in Asia Minor of Burne the Lawyer, Preston the Professor, & Lawren.

Schönberg, John, illus. 2007. 424p. 26.95 *(978-0-9776786-6-2(0))* Salem Ridge Press LLC.
Figorito, Marcus. Tara Takes the Train. 2006. (Neighborhood Readers Ser.). (ENG.). 16p. (gr. 1-3). pap. 6.50 *(978-1-4042-7208-8(9)*, Rosen Classroom) Rosen Publishing Group, Inc., The.
Finley, Martha. Elsie's Winter Trip, Vol. 26. 320p. (gr. 4-7). pap. 5.95 *(978-1-58182-181-9(6)*, Cumberland Hse.) Sourcebooks, Inc.
Flack, Annie. Mysteries of the Lake. 2009. 92p. pap. 10.49 *(978-1-4389-6264-1(9))* AuthorHouse.
Florence, Leigh Anne. Mr. Dogwood Goes to Washington. Asher, James, illus. 2008. (Woody the Kentucky Wiener Ser.). 56p. (J). (gr. 2-8). pap. 12.95 *(978-0-9741417-5-6(5))* HotDiggetyDog Pr.
Floyd, Belinda D. Going to America. 2005. 28p. per. 25.49 *(978-1-4208-8693-1(2))* AuthorHouse.
Fosberry, Jennifer. Isabella: Girl on the Go. Litwin, Mike, illus. 2012. (ENG.). 32p. (J). (gr. k-3). 16.99 *(978-1-4022-6648-5(0)*, Sourcebooks Jabberwocky) Sourcebooks, Inc.
Foster, Tim & Foster, Tina. Abap the Ambulance in Happy to Help! 2008. 28p. 18.95 *(978-0-9556910-0-3(1))* Eclipse Solutions (UK) Ltd. GBR. Dist: Lulu Pr., Inc.
Francia, Giada. In the Wild West on MacKenzie's Trail. McCloskey, Erin, ed. Howard, Catherine, tr. 2007. (Alex & Penny Ser.). (ENG., Illus.). 80p. (gr. 2-5). pap. 14.95 *(978-88-544-0245-4(1))* White Star ITA. Dist: Random Hse., Inc.
Franco, Betsy. Going to Grandma's Farm. 2004. (Rookie Reader Español Ser.). (ENG., Illus.). 24p. (J). (gr. k-2). pap. 4.95 *(978-0-516-27787-5(1)*, Children's Pr.) Scholastic Library Publishing.
George, Audra. Vagabonding. George, Audra, illus. 2006. (Illus.). 32p. (J). (gr. -1-3). 17.95 *(978-1-60108-010-3(7))* Red Cygnet Pr.
George, Sandy. Anika's Travel Diaries: The Lava Island Trip. 2012. 28p. pap. 17.99 *(978-1-4772-9297-6(7))* AuthorHouse.
Gill, Heidi. Egypt. Carter, Kris, illus. 2012. (2 Kurious Kids Ser.: Vol. 5). (ENG.). 24p. (J). (gr. -1-5). 14.95 *(978-1-936319-93-0(4))* Mascot Bks., Inc.
—2 Kurious Kids: France. Carter, Kris, illus. 2012. 38p. (J). 14.95 *(978-1-936319-90-9(X))* Mascot Bks., Inc.
—2 Kurious Kids: India. Carter, Kris, illus. 2012. 38p. (J). 14.95 *(978-1-936319-92-3(6))* Mascot Bks., Inc.
Gill, Heidi & Carter, Kris. 2 Kurious Kids: Mexico. 2012. (Illus.). 38p. (J). 14.95 *(978-1-936319-91-6(8))* Mascot Bks., Inc.
Ginn, Jennifer. My Father Flies, 1 vol. Kramer, David, illus. 2013. (ENG.). 32p. (J). 16.99 *(978-0-7643-4385-8(8)*, 9780764343858) Schiffer Publishing, Ltd.
Golden Books Staff. Travel with Thomas. Santanach, Tino, illus. 2007. (Deluxe Coloring Book Ser.). (ENG.). 96p. (J). (gr. -1-2). pap. 3.99 *(978-0-375-83953-5(4)*, Golden Bks.) Random Hse. Children's Bks.
Grant, Natalie. Light up New York, 1 vol. 2017. (Faithgirlz / Glimmer Girls Ser.). (ENG.). 208p. (J). pap. 8.99 *(978-0-310-75274-5(4))* Zonderkidz.
Greene, Reggie. The Adventures of Swami Somewhere- the Supermarket. Graham, Michael, illus. 2011. 32p. (J). 14.95 *(978-1-60131-095-8(1))* Big Tent Bks.
Gregerson, Lajuan. A Child's Tour of the Holy Land. 2008. 73p. pap. 19.95 *(978-1-60610-367-8(9))* America Star Bks.
Grindley, Sally. Danger in the Dust. 2013. (ENG.). 128p. (YA). (gr. 3-6). pap. 10.99 *(978-1-4088-1946-3(5)*, 9781408819463, Bloomsbury USA Childrens) Bloomsbury Publishing USA.
—Feathers in the Wind. 2012. (ENG.). 128p. (YA). (gr. 5-7). pap. 10.99 *(978-1-4088-1947-0(3)*, 9781408819470) Bloomsbury Publishing USA.
Haddix, Margaret Peterson. Takeoffs & Landings. 2004. 201p. (gr. 5-9). 17.00 *(978-0-7569-4255-7(1))* Perfection Learning Corp.
Haidar, Hanna. Earl's Big Adventure in Costa Rica. Hutcheson, Meredith, ed. Newton, Kimberly, illus. 2007. 22p. (J). per. 7.99 *(978-0-9800975-0-4(9))* Old Silver Pr.
Harley, Bill. The Amazing Flight of Darius Frobisher, 1 vol. 2009. (ENG.). 160p. (J). pap. 7.95 *(978-1-56145-494-5(X))* Peachtree Pubs.
Harrington, Jane. Four Things My Geeky-Jock-of-a-Best-Friend Must Do in Europe. 2006. (ENG.). 160p. (J). (gr. 6-9). 15.95 *(978-1-58196-041-9(7)*, Darby Creek) Lerner Publishing Group.
Harrison, Troon. Poetry & Potatoes. Hellard, Susan, illus. 2003. 32p. (YA). *(978-1-84365-020-1(7)*, Pavilion Children's Books) Pavilion Bks.
Hathorn, Sarah Alexandra. Teenagents: World Challenge. 2012. 240p. pap. 12.99 *(978-2-9700738-2-6(X))* Simon & Schuster, Inc.
Henisz, Jerzy E. SOPHIE in PARIS & other Stories. 2009. 99p. pap. 9.46 *(978-0-557-09520-9(4))* Lulu Pr., Inc.
Henisz, Jerzy E. & Henisz, Sophie, illustrator. TEDDY BEAR who went on a Trip around the World & other Stories. 2007. 88p. (J). pap. 30.40 *(978-0-615-13851-0(9))* Henisz, Jerzy E.
Hersh, Kristin. Toby Snax. 2016. (ENG., Illus.). 40p. (J). 14.95 *(978-1-4773-1127-1(0))* Univ. of Texas Pr.
Hill, Eveline. Hugo & Oscar Go Travelling: Continuing the Adventures of Hugo & Oscar. 2012. (Illus.). 52p. pap. 27.45 *(978-1-4772-2733-6(4))* AuthorHouse.
Hirota, Denise. Little Zippy Duffelbag Goes to France. 2012. 24p. pap. 12.45 *(978-1-4624-0443-8(X)*, Inspiring Voices) Author Solutions, Inc.
Hobbie, Holly. Toot & Puddle. 2010. (Toot & Puddle Ser.: 1). (ENG., Illus.). 32p. (J). (gr. -1-3). pap. 7.99 *(978-0-316-08080-4(2))* Little, Brown Bks. for Young Readers.
—Toot & Puddle. Hobbie, Holly, illus. 2007. (Toot & Puddle Ser.: 1). (ENG., Illus.). 32p. (J). (gr. -1-3). 17.99 *(978-0-316-16702-4(9))* Little, Brown Bks. for Young Readers.
—Top of the World. 2008. (Toot & Puddle Ser.: 6). (ENG.). 32p. (gr. -1-3). pap. 7.99 *(978-0-316-03384-8(7))* Little, Brown Bks. for Young Readers.
Hobbs, Leigh. Mr Chicken Arriva a Roma. 2017. (Mr Chicken Ser.). (ENG.). 32p. (J). (gr. -1-3). 17.99 ***(978-1-925266-77-1(X))*** Allen & Unwin AUS. Dist: Independent Pubs. Group.
Hobbs, Will. Changes in Latitudes. 2004. (ENG.). 176p. (YA). (gr. 7). pap. 9.95 *(978-0-689-87069-9(8)*, Simon Pulse) Simon Pulse.
Hoffman, Amalia. Klezmer Bunch. 2009. 36p. 15.95 *(978-965-229-447-0(0))* Gefen Publishing Hse., Ltd ISR. Dist: Strauss Consultants.
Hoffman, Mary Ann. Elbert Takes a Trip. 2006. (Neighborhood Readers Ser.). (ENG., Illus.). 12p. (gr. 1-3). pap. 5.90 *(978-1-4042-6847-0(2)*, Rosen Classroom) Rosen Publishing Group, Inc., The.
Hofmeister, Alan, et al. A Trip. (Reading for All Learners Ser.). (Illus.). (J). pap. *(978-1-56861-130-3(7))* Swift Learning Resources.
Hooray for Boys & Girls! 2006. (J). 15.95 *(978-0-9776837-0-3(2))* West Woods Pr.
Horácek, Petr. Suzy Goose & the Christmas Star. Horácek, Petr, illus. 2009. (ENG., Illus.). 32p. (J). (gr. -1-2). 15.99 *(978-0-7636-4487-1(0))* Candlewick Pr.
Horowitz, Dave. Duck Duck Moose. Horowitz, Dave, illus. 2009. (ENG., Illus.). 32p. (J). (gr. k-3). 16.99 *(978-0-399-24782-8(3)*, G.P. Putnam's Sons Books for Young Readers) Penguin Young Readers Group.
Hubbard, Kirsten. Wanderlove. (ENG.). 352p. (YA). (gr. 9). 2013. pap. 9.99 *(978-0-385-73938-2(9)*, Ember) 2012. 17.99 *(978-0-385-73937-5(0)*, Delacorte Bks. for Young Readers) Random Hse. Children's Bks.
Hunter, K. N. Hollow: N2 the Hollow World. 2008. 62p. pap. 16.95 *(978-1-4241-0220-4(0))* PublishAmerica, Inc.
I Am A Dog. 2008. (Illus.). 26p. 24.95 *(978-0-9801054-0-7(4))* Teahouse of Danger.
Inzer, Christine Mari. Diary of a Tokyo Teen. 2016. (ENG., Illus.). 128p. (J). (gr. 6-12). pap. 14.99 *(978-4-8053-1396-1(X))* Tuttle Publishing.
Islam, M. N. Hamza's Journey of a Lifetime. 2012. 124p. pap. *(978-1-909395-70-1(6))* Legend Pr.
Jackson, Clandress. Chloe the Jumbo Jet: A Problem of Olympic Proportions. 2012. 26p. (-18). pap. 8.99 *(978-1-61286-131-9(8))* Avid Readers Publishing Group.
Jacquemain, Patti. Journey of the Great Bear: Through California's Golden Past. Jacquemain, Patti, illus. 2006. (Illus.). (J). *(978-0-929702-10-0(7))* Mission Creek Studios.
Jebiwool Art Museum Staff. Destination Blackbeard: Destinations in Time, Book 2, 1 vol. 2009. 101p. pap. 19.95 *(978-1-60749-626-7(7))* America Star Bks.
Jofre, Paola. Lilliput Blasts Off! 2010. 36p. 17.50 *(978-1-4490-7450-0(2))* AuthorHouse.
Johnston-Thomas, Lee Ann. The Hidden Treasure of the Forgotten Pharaoh. 2008. 136p. 21.95 *(978-0-595-71157-4(X))*; pap. 11.95 *(978-0-595-47552-0(3))* iUniverse, Inc.
Jones, V. C. Anna Banana Goes to Louisiana. 2010. 16p. 8.49 *(978-1-4490-8390-8(0))* AuthorHouse.
Joy, Brenda. Kaweah's Journey to New Mexico. 2005. 57p. pap. 16.95 *(978-1-4137-9549-3(8))* America Star Bks.
Jules. Bubble's World: Book Four Enchanted England. 2010. 40p. 16.99 *(978-1-4520-5407-0(X))* AuthorHouse.
Keene, Carolyn. Nancy Drew Diaries 3-Books-In-1! Curse of the Arctic Star; Strangers on a Train; Mystery of the Midnight Rider. 2016. (Nancy Drew Diaries). (ENG., Illus.). 592p. (J). (gr. 3-7). pap. 8.99 *(978-1-4814-8554-8(7)*, Aladdin) Simon & Schuster Children's Publishing.
Kent, Elizabeth. The Enchanted Adventures of the Caroline Kemps. 2007. 148p. pap. 24.95 *(978-1-4241-9915-0(8))* America Star Bks.
Kincaid, Tracy. The Adventures of Casey the Lost Suitcase. 2007. (Illus.). 32p. (J). (gr. -1-3). 16.95 *(978-0-929915-67-8(4))* Headline Bks., Inc.
King, Philip. Bluey, the Little Drip. King, Janet, illus. 2011. 40p. pap. 14.95 *(978-1-60976-661-0(X)*, Eloquent Bks.) Strategic Book Publishing & Rights Agency (SBPRA).
Klepeis, Alicia. From Pizza to Pisa. 2015. (ENG.). 96p. (gr. 3-6). 31.36 *(978-1-63430-399-6(7))* Rourke Educational Media.
—Mountains, Monsoons, & Mules. 2015. (ENG.). 96p. (gr. 3-6). 31.36 *(978-1-63430-398-9(9))* Rourke Educational Media.
Knight, Grover. Ahzar's Travels & Life Lessons - Meet Ahzar: Book One. 2003. (Illus.). 40p. (J). 16.95 *(978-0-9746130-0-0(2))* Ahzar's Bk. Co. Publishing.
Kovacs, Deborah. Catie Copley's Great Escape. Williams, Jared T., illus. 2009. (J). 17.95 *(978-1-56792-382-7(8))*; (ENG.). 32p. (gr. -1-3). 17.95 *(978-1-56792-379-7(8))* Godine, David R. Pub.
Kurchinski, Alessandra. Disney Story. 2010. 36p. pap. 17.30 *(978-0-557-25447-7(7))* Lulu Pr., Inc.
Laberje, Reji. Max Explores Chicago. Fenech, Liza, illus. 2014. (Max Explores Ser.). (ENG.). 20p. (J). (— 1). bds. 9.95 *(978-1-62937-003-3(7))* Triumph Bks.
—Max Explores New York. Fenech, Liza, illus. 2014. (Max Explores Ser.). (ENG.). 20p. (J). (— 1). bds. 9.95 *(978-1-62937-004-0(5))* Triumph Bks.
—Max Explores San Francisco. Fenech, Liza, illus. 2014. (Max Explores Ser.). (ENG.). 20p. (J). (— 1). bds. 9.95 *(978-1-62937-005-7(3))* Triumph Bks.
Lagonegro, Melissa. Travel Like a Princess. 2014. (Disney Princess Step into Reading Ser.). lib. bdg. 13.55 *(978-0-606-35554-4(5))* Turtleback Bks.
—Travel Like a Princess (Disney Princess) RH Disney Staff et al, illus. 2014. (Step into Reading Ser.). (ENG.). 24p. (J). (gr. -1-1). 3.99 *(978-0-7364-3089-0(X)*, RH/Disney) Random Hse. Children's Bks.
Lainez, René Colato. My Shoes & I. Broeck, Fabricio Vanden, illus. 2010. (ENG.). 32p. (J). (gr. 2-4). 16.95 *(978-1-59078-385-6(9))* Boyds Mills Pr.
Langen, Annette. Felix Explores Planet Earth. Droop, Constanza, illus. 2004. (Perfect for Earth Day Promotions! Ser.). 47p. (J). 14.99 *(978-1-59384-030-3(6))* Parklane Publishing.
Lay, Kathryn. Book 1: Time & Space. 2016. (Time Twisters Ser.). (ENG.). (J). (gr. 2-6). lib. bdg. 27.07 ***(978-1-62402-177-0(8))*** ABDO Publishing Co.
—Book 2: Haunted Time. 2016. (Time Twisters Ser.). (ENG.). (J). (gr. 2-6). lib. bdg. 27.07 ***(978-1-62402-178-7(6))*** ABDO Publishing Co.
—Book 3: the Curse of Time. 2016. (Time Twisters Ser.). (ENG.). (J). (gr. 2-6). lib. bdg. 27.07 ***(978-1-62402-179-4(4))*** ABDO Publishing Co.
Le Guin, Ursula K. Tom Mouse. 2004. (Illus.). (J). (gr. k-3). spiral bd. *(978-0-616-14584-5(5))* Canadian National Institute for the Blind/Institut National Canadien pour les Aveugles.
Learning Company Books Staff, ed. Westward Bound! 2004. (Oregon Trail Adventures Ser.). (Illus.). 96p. (J). pap. *(978-0-7630-7724-2(0))* Magma.
Leckey, Carl. Pop up & Go. 2012. (Illus.). 176p. (gr. -1). 30.51 *(978-1-4685-7851-5(0))*; pap. 18.24 *(978-1-4685-7852-2(9))* AuthorHouse.
Lewis, J. Patrick & Zappitello, Beth. First Dog. Bowers, Tim, illus. 2009. (ENG.). 32p. (J). (gr. k-6). 15.95 *(978-1-58536-467-1(3))* Sleeping Bear Pr.
Lewis, K. s. & Lewis, K. S. Happiness: A Charlie Travel Adventure Story. 2009. 28p. pap. 21.20 *(978-0-557-12094-9(2))* Lulu Pr., Inc.
Loesch, Joe. The Tuskegee Airmen: Raiders of the Skies with Buffalo Biff & Farley's Raiders. Hutchinson, Cheryl, ed. 2004. (Backyard Adventure Ser.). (Illus.). 56p. (J). bds. 16.95 incl. audio compact disk *(978-1-932332-27-8(8))* Toy Box Productions.
London, Olivia. Welcome to Equestria! 2013. (My Little Pony 8X8 Picture Bks.). (J). lib. bdg. 13.55 *(978-0-606-31731-3(7)*, Turtleback) Turtleback Bks.
Look, Lenore. Alvin Ho: Allergic to the Great Wall, the Forbidden Palace, & Other Tourist Attractions. Pham, LeUyen, illus. 2014. (Alvin Ho Ser.). (ENG.). 176p. (J). (gr. 1-4). 15.99 *(978-0-385-36972-5(7)*, Schwartz & Wade Bks.) Random Hse. Children's Bks.
Lopez, Sixto. Snarloff Duwaki's Adventures. 2011. 24p. pap. 24.95 *(978-1-4626-2557-4(6))* America Star Bks.
Lorraine. The Adventures of Ruthy: Ruthy Gets Lost. 2012. 32p. pap. 19.99 *(978-1-4772-6000-5(5))* AuthorHouse.
Luedtke, Courtney. Baby Boo: The Happy Beginning. 2009. (Illus.). 72p. pap. 27.49 *(978-1-4389-2696-4(0))* AuthorHouse.
Lund, Celia. Square Sails & Dragons. 2006. 284p. per. 19.95 *(978-1-4120-5758-5(2))* Trafford Publishing.
Lund, Deb. All Aboard the Dinotrain. Fine, Howard, illus. (ENG.). (J). (gr. -1 — 1). 2011. 30p. bds. 7.99 *(978-0-547-55415-0(X))* 2009. 40p. pap. 7.99 *(978-0-547-24825-7(3))* Houghton Mifflin Harcourt Publishing Co.
Malone, Jen. Wanderlost. 2016. 352p. (YA). (gr. 9). pap. 9.99 *(978-0-06-238015-9(X)*, HarperTeen) HarperCollins Pubs.
Mancuso, Jackie Clark. Paris-Chien: Adventures of an Ex-Pat Dog. 2013. (ENG., Illus.). 32p. (J). (gr. k-2). 17.95 *(978-0-615-54542-4(4))* La Librairie Parisienne.
Manzano, Sonia & Muth, Jon J. No Dogs Allowed! Muth, Jon J., illus. 2004. (ENG., Illus.). 32p. (J). (gr. -1-2). 17.99 *(978-0-689-83088-4(2)*, Atheneum Bks. for Young Readers) Simon & Schuster Children's Publishing.
Marceau, Fani. Panorama: A Foldout Book. Jolivet, Joëlle, illus. 2009. (ENG.). 32p. (J). (gr. -1-k). 21.95 *(978-0-8109-8332-8(X)*, Abrams Bks. for Young Readers) Abrams, Inc.
Marsh, Carole. The Curse of the Ancient Acropolis: Athens, Greece. 2008. (Carole Marsh Mysteries Ser.). 133p. (J). (gr. 3-5). per. 7.99 *(978-0-635-06470-7(7)*, Marsh, Carole Bks.) Gallopade International.
—The Rip-Roaring Mystery on the African Safari. 2009. (Around the World in 80 Mysteries Ser.). (Illus.). 133p. (J). (gr. 4-7). pap. 7.99 *(978-0-635-06829-3(X)*, Marsh, Carole Bks.) Gallopade International.
—The Wild Water Mystery of Niagra Falls. 2009. (Real Kids, Real Places Ser.). (Illus.). 146p. (J). (gr. 4-7). pap. 7.99 *(978-0-635-06825-5(7)*, Marsh, Carole Bks.) Gallopade International.
Martin, Lance. The Little Hermit. 2008. 56p. pap. 14.95 *(978-0-9815573-1-1(7))* Highland Pr.
Mayer, Mercer & Mayer, Gina. On the Go. 2013. (Big Little Critter Ser.: 4). (ENG., Illus.). 96p. (J). 12.95 *(978-1-60746-983-4(9)*, Premiere) FastPencil, Inc.
McCue, Lisa. My First Mother Goose. 2009. (Carry along Bks.). (ENG., Illus.). 20p. (J). (gr. -1-k). bds. 14.99 *(978-0-7944-1931-8(3)*, Reader's Digest Children's Bks.) Studio Fun International.
McGovern, DeeDee Jean. The Heartland of Home: Tight Quarters in the City. 2008. 58p. pap. 16.95 *(978-1-60610-058-5(0))* America Star Bks.
McKennon, Tony. You're Moving Where?! 2008. 40p. pap. 18.55 *(978-1-4389-1397-1(4))* AuthorHouse.
Mcleod-Stecy, Tracey. The Stone Guardian. 2011. 144p. (gr. 4-6). pap. 11.95 *(978-1-4620-3954-8(5))* iUniverse, Inc.
McMiller, Theresa R. Bessie Goes All over the World. 2012. 28p. pap. 24.95 *(978-1-4626-9464-8(0))* America Star Bks.
McPherson, Missie & O'Neill, Elizabeth. Alfred Visits Washington, D. C. 2005. (ENG., Illus.). 24p. (J). (gr. -1-3). pap. 12.00 *(978-0-9771836-1-6(0))* Lipp, G. Douglas & Assocs.
Medina, Sylvia M. & Ballock-Dixon, Saige J. Jade Elephant. Eagle, Joy, illus. 2012. 36p. pap. 11.49 *(978-0-9836602-4-8(7))* Green Kids Club, Inc.
Mims-Word, Marsha. The Great Vacation. 2011. 36p. pap. 21.99 *(978-1-4568-9675-1(X))* Xlibris Corp.
Miner, Deb. I get Around. Miner, Deb, illus. 2007. (ENG., Illus.). 32p. (J). bds. 11.00 *(978-0-9794262-0-9(0))* do be you.
Mitchell, Jack. The Ancient Ocean Blues. 2008. (ENG.). 200p. (YA). (gr. 5-8). pap. 9.95 *(978-0-88776-832-3(6)*, Tundra Bks.) Tundra Bks. CAN. Dist: Penguin Random Hse. LLC.
Mitchell, Julie & Rinkel, Ken. Slow down, Mrs. Brown! 2008. (Rigby Focus Forward: Level F Ser.). (Illus.). 24p. (J). (gr. 4-7). pap. *(978-1-4190-3700-9(5)*, Rigby) Pearson Education Australia.
Mitchell, Trish. Noah Pals: Journey to the Apple Tree. 2011. 32p. pap. 16.99 *(978-1-4567-9939-7(8))* AuthorHouse.
Mizielinska, Aleksandra & Mizielinski, Daniel. Welcome to Mamoko. 2013. (ENG., Illus.). 16p. (J). (gr. k-3). 17.99 *(978-0-7636-6891-4(5)*, Big Picture Press) Candlewick Pr.
Montague, Chester. Timmy's Vacation. 2008. 40p. pap. 24.95 *(978-1-60441-225-3(9))* America Star Bks.
Montes, Marisa. Get Ready for Gabi No. 5: All in the Familia. Cepeda, Joe, illus. 2004. (ENG.). 112p. (J). (gr. 2-5). pap. *(978-0-439-66156-0(0)*, Scholastic Paperbacks) Scholastic, Inc.
Morrill, Lauren. Meant to Be. (ENG.). 304p. (YA). (gr. 7). 2014. pap. 9.99 *(978-0-385-74178-1(2)*, Ember) 2012. 17.99 *(978-0-385-74177-4(4)*, Delacorte Pr.) 2012. E-Book *(978-0-375-98711-3(8)*, Delacorte Pr.) Random Hse. Children's Bks.
Mullican, Judy. Let's Take a Ride. Gillen, Lisa P., illus. l.t. ed. 2004. (HRL Little Book Ser.). (J). (gr. -1-k). pap. 10.95 *(978-1-57332-319-2(5))*; pap. 10.95 *(978-1-57332-318-5(7))* Carson-Dellosa Publishing, LLC. (HighReach Learning, Incorporated).
Murray, Scott. Granny's Christmas Blunder. 2012. 28p. pap. 18.00 *(978-1-4772-0990-5(5))* AuthorHouse.
Newcomb, Kristene. Molly Q's Trash Travels Through the Water Cycle. Paschall, Patricia, ed. Newcomb, Kristene, illus. 2007. (Illus.). 32p. (J). per. 8.00 *(978-0-9760790-9-5(7))* Folsom Fallies Pr.
North, Merry. My Vacation: Picture, Play, & Tote. 2003. (Picture, Play & Tote-Book Ser.). (Illus.). 10p. (J). (gr. -1-18). bds. 5.99 *(978-1-57151-720-3(0))* Playhouse Publishing.
O'Connor, Jane. Girl on the Go: A Doodle & Draw Book. Glasser, Robin Preiss et al, illus. 2012. (Fancy Nancy Ser.). (ENG.). 64p. (J). (gr. -1-3). pap. 6.99 *(978-0-06-188282-1(8)*, HarperFestival) HarperCollins Pubs.
O'Dell, Kathryn L. From Wagon to Train. Chalik, Chris, illus. 2017. (Text Connections Guided Close Reading Ser.). (J). (gr. 2). *(978-1-4900-1854-6(9))* Benchmark Education Co.
Ofanansky, Allison. What's the Buzz? Honey for a Sweet New Year. Alpern, Eliyahu, photos by. 2014. (ENG., Illus.). 32p. (J). (gr. -1-5). 8.95 *(978-1-4677-5706-5(3)*, Kar-Ben Publishing) Lerner Publishing Group.
O'Neill, Elizabeth. Alfred Visits Georgia. 2007. (Illus.). 24p. (gr. -1-3). pap. 12.00 *(978-0-9799121-0-8(5))* Global Business Information Strategies, Inc.
—Alfred Visits Hawaii. 2009. 24p. (J). pap. 12.00 *(978-0-9822288-5-2(6))* Global Business Information Strategies, Inc.
—Alfred Visits Maine. 2008. (Illus.). 24p. (J). pap. 12.00 *(978-0-9799121-3-9(X))* Funny Bone Bks.
—Alfred Visits Minnesota. 2007. (Illus.). 24p. (J). pap. 12.00 *(978-0-9799121-2-2(1))* Global Business Information Strategies, Inc.
—Alfred Visits Missouri. 2008. 24p. (J). pap. 12.00 *(978-0-9799121-4-6(8))* Global Business Information Strategies, Inc.
—Alfred Visits Montana. 2009. 24p. pap. 12.00 *(978-0-9822288-6-9(4))* Global Business Information Strategies, Inc.
—Alfred Visits Nevada. 2007. (ENG., Illus.). 24p. (J). pap. 12.00 *(978-0-9799121-1-5(3))* Global Business Information Strategies, Inc.
—Alfred Visits New Jersey. 2007. 24p. (J). pap. 12.00 *(978-0-9790240-7-8(2))* Global Business Information Strategies, Inc.
—Alfred Visits Rhode Island. 2007. (Illus.). 24p. (J). pap. 12.00 *(978-0-9790240-6-1(4))* Global Business Information Strategies, Inc.
—Alfred Visits Texas. 2007. 24p. (J). pap. 12.00 *(978-0-9790240-9-2(9))* Global Business Information Strategies, Inc.
—Alfred Visits Utah. 2009. 24p. (J). pap. 12.00 *(978-0-9822288-3-8(X))* Global Business Information Strategies, Inc.
—Alfred Visits Washington State. 2009. 24p. (J). pap. 12.00 *(978-0-9822288-4-5(8))* Global Business Information Strategies, Inc.
Oneill, Elizabeth. Alfred Visits West Virginia. 2009. 24p. (J). pap. 12.00 *(978-0-9822288-2-1(1))* Global Business Information Strategies, Inc.
—Alfred Visits Wyoming. 2008. 24p. (J). pap. 12.00 *(978-0-9822288-1-4(3))* Global Business Information Strategies, Inc.
O'Neill, Sean. Rocket Robinson & the Secret of the Saint. 2016. (Rocket Robinson Ser.). (ENG.). 240p. (J). (gr. 4-7). pap. 19.95 *(978-0-9893655-2-9(2))* Independent Pubs. Group.
O'Reilly, Basha. Count Pompeii - Stallion of the Steppes. 2005. (Illus.). pap. 9.99 *(978-1-59048-007-6(4))* Long Riders' Guild Pr., The.
Otis, James. Ruth of Boston: A story of the Massachusetts Bay Colony. 2007. 140p. per. 9.95 *(978-0-9790876-3-9(5))* Living Bks. Pr.
Owens, L. L. The Longest Car Ride Ever. Tolson, Scott, illus. 2004. 28p. *(978-1-57021-032-7(2))* Comprehensive Health Education Foundation.
Page, Cecelia Frances. Phenomenal Experiences. 2007. 144p. per. 11.95 *(978-0-595-46360-2(6))* iUniverse, Inc.
Parker, Sandy. What Month Is It? Hofner, Cathy, illus. l.t. ed. 2004. 32p. 15.95 *(978-0-9643462-5-3(7)*, Just Think Bks.) Canary Connect Pubns.
Pati, Geeta. Finny's Voyage Through the Universe: The. 2005. (ENG.). 64p. per. 10.95 *(978-1-59526-019-2(6))* Aeon Publishing Inc.
Pattison, Darcy. The Journey of Oliver K. Woodman. Cepeda, Joe, illus. 2009. (ENG.). 52p. (J). (gr. -1-3). pap. 7.99 *(978-0-15-206118-0(5))* Houghton Mifflin Harcourt Publishing Co.
Paulsen, Gary. The Car. 2006. (ENG., Illus.). 192p. (YA). (gr. 7-12). pap. 7.99 *(978-0-15-205827-2(3))* Houghton Mifflin Harcourt Publishing Co.
—The Car. 2006. 182p. (gr. 7-12). 17.00 *(978-0-7569-6685-0(X))* Perfection Learning Corp.
Payne, Rachel. Summer of Circles & Sapphires: Iggy Colvin Adventure Series. 2003. 194p. 23.95 *(978-0-595-74705-4(1))*; pap. 13.95 *(978-0-595-27915-9(5))* iUniverse, Inc.
Penn, Linda M. Is Kentucky in the Sky? 2012. 36p. pap. 9.95 *(978-0-9852488-0-2(7))* Racing to Joy Pr. LLC.
Perry, Shelly. Duckling's First Adventure. Loebel, Bonnie, illus. 2006. (ENG.). 56p. (J). per. 9.95 *(978-0-9787740-3-5(5))* Peppertree Pr., The.
Peterson, Doug & Kenney, Cindy. Lost in Place: A Lesson in Overcoming Fear, 1 vol. Big Idea Productions Staff, illus. 2005. (Big Idea Books / VeggieTown Values Ser.: Bk. 4). (ENG.). 32p. (J). pap. 3.99 *(978-0-310-70629-8(7))* Zonderkidz.
Pla, Sally J. The Someday Birds. McLaughlin, Julie, illus. 2017. 336p. (J). (gr. 3-7). 16.99 *(978-0-06-244576-6(6))* HarperCollins Pubs.

Ponnay, Brenda & Ponnay, Brenda. Secret Agent Josephine in Paris. 2013. 32p. pap. 9.99 (978-1-62395-552-6(1)) Xist Publishing.
Potter, Ellen. Going Places. Leng, Qin, illus. 2017. 108p. (J). (978-1-101-93961-1(3)) Knopf, Alfred A. Inc.
—Piper Green & the Fairy Tree: Going Places. Leng, Qin, illus. 2017. (Piper Green & the Fairy Tree Ser.). (ENG.). (J). (gr. 2-4). 20.95 **(978-1-4301-2680-5(9))** Live Oak Media.
Potter, Ellen. Piper Green & the Fairy Tree: Going Places. Leng, Qin, illus. 2017. (Piper Green & the Fairy Tree Ser.). (ENG.). 128p. (J). (gr. 2-4). lib. bdg. 17.99 (978-1-101-93962-8(1), Knopf Bks. for Young Readers) Random Hse. Children's Bks.
Powell, Gail. The Adventures of Harold J. Kat. 2008. 40p. pap. 16.99 (978-1-4259-6334-7(X)) AuthorHouse.
Priceman, Marjorie. How to Make a Cherry Pie & See the U. S. A. Priceman, Marjorie, illus. 2013. (ENG., Illus.). 40p. (J). (gr. k-3). 7.99 (978-0-385-75293-0(8), Dragonfly Bks.) Random Hse. Children's Bks.
Rabley, Stephen. The Twins & the Time Machine/Les Jumeaux et la Machine du Temps. Bougard, Marie-Therese, tr. Eudes-Pascal, Elisabeth, illus. 2008. (Let's Read! Bks.). (ENG & FRE.). 32p. (J). (gr. 3-7). pap. 5.99 (978-0-7641-4048-8(5)) Barron's Educational Series, Inc.
Rangel, Graciela. Anthony's Christmas Journey. 2006. (ENG.). 80p. pap. 9.95 (978-1-59526-650-7(X), Llumina Christian Bks.) Aeon Publishing Inc.
Raphael, Akili & Lewis, Harriet. Malik & the Malaria-Carrying Mosquito. 2012. 32p. pap. 19.99 (978-1-4772-8813-9(9)) AuthorHouse.
—Malik Says, Turn off the Water! 2012. 36p. pap. 20.99 (978-1-4772-9541-0(0)) AuthorHouse.
Rapoport, Cindy. The Adventures of Poca & Flea Bert. 2008. 64p. pap. 19.95 (978-1-60672-901-4(2)) America Star Bks.
Ready Reader Staff. Mr. Fins' Trip: Short I, Level A. 2003. (J). (gr. -1-3). 24.50 (978-0-8136-1959-0(9)) Modern Curriculum Pr.
Reece, Eva. The Boinking Bubble MacHine. Davis, Shelley L. A., illus. 2013. 24p. pap. 12.99 (978-0-9886360-2-6(6)) Kids At Heart Publishing, LLC.
Rey, H. A. Curious George Travel Activity Kit. 2010. (Curious George Ser.). (ENG., Illus.). 64p. (J). (gr. -1-3). 12.99 (978-0-547-25875-1(5)) Houghton Mifflin Harcourt Publishing Co.
Rigby Education Staff. The Island of Wingo. (Sails Literacy Ser.). (Illus.). 16p. (gr. 2-3). 27.00 (978-0-7635-9946-1(8), 699468C99) Rigby Education.
Riordan, Betty J. The Imaginary Journeys of Bj & Dobbin. 2008. 108p. pap. 11.99 (978-1-60647-432-7(4)) Salem Author Services.
Ripley's Believe It Or Not! Staff. The Lost Island. 2010. (Rbi Ser.: 8). (ENG.). 128p. (J). pap. 4.99 (978-1-893951-59-4(6)) Ripley Entertainment, Inc.
—Shock Horror. 2010. (Rbi Ser.: 7). (ENG.). 128p. (J). pap. 4.99 (978-1-893951-58-7(8)) Ripley Entertainment, Inc.
Roberts, Sheena. We All Go Traveling By. Bell, Siobhan, illus. 2004. (ENG.). 24p. (J). pap. 9.99 (978-1-84148-410-5(5)) Barefoot Bks., Inc.
Roberts, Willo Davis. What Could Go Wrong? 2012. (ENG., Illus.). 176p. (J). (gr. 3-7). reprint ed. pap. 9.99 (978-0-689-71690-4(7), Simon & Schuster/Paula Wiseman Bks.) Simon & Schuster/Paula Wiseman Bks.
Robertson, Barry & Smith, Jeff. Pirates of the "I Don't Care" -Ibbean: A Kids' Musical about Storing up Treasures in Heaven. 2007. (ENG.). 104p. pap. 7.99 (978-0-8341-7595-2(9), 0834175959) Lillenas Publishing Co.
Robertson, J. Jean. Everyone Travels. 2015. (ENG.). 24p. (gr. k-3). 28.50 (978-1-63430-366-8(0)) Rourke Educational Media.
Rogers, Carol J. The Adventures of Buttonballs' Trails. 2012. 28p. pap. 19.99 (978-1-4772-4481-4(6)) AuthorHouse.
Ruellan, Susan. The Lost Treasure of Finistere. 2008. (ENG & FRE., Illus.). 83p. (J). (gr. 4-7). pap. 9.95 (978-1-933916-24-8(9)) Nelson Publishing & Marketing.
Runholt, Susan. The Mystery of the Third Lucretia. 2009. (Kari & Lucas Mystery Ser.). (ENG.). 304p. (J). (gr. 5-18). pap. 6.99 (978-0-14-241338-8(0), Puffin Books) Penguin Young Readers Group.
Saha, Tulika. 'Kosho & Sid on the Rainbow' 2014. 22p. pap. 13.99 (978-1-4828-1762-1(4)) Partridge Pub.
Samoun, Abigail. How Hippo Says Hello! Watts, Sarah, illus. 2014. (Little Traveler Ser.). (ENG.). 22p. (J). (gr. -1-k). bds. 6.95 (978-1-4549-0820-3(3)) Sterling Publishing Co., Inc.
—How Penguin Says Please! Watts, Sarah, illus. 2015. (Little Traveler Ser.). (ENG & MUL.). 24p. (J). (gr. -1-k). bds. 6.95 (978-1-4549-1496-9(3)) Sterling Publishing Co., Inc.
Santillo, LuAnn. The Trip. Santillo, LuAnn, ed. 2003. (Half-Pint Kids Readers Ser.). (Illus.). 7p. (J). (gr. -1-1). pap. 1.00 (978-1-59256-057-8(1)) Half-Pint Kids, Inc.
Sayle, Stephen. Cam & Zara the Travel Bugs. 2012. 20p. pap. 11.70 (978-1-105-42214-0(3)) Lulu Pr., Inc.
—Cam & Zara the Travel Bugs: Egypt. 2011. 36p. pap. 15.25 (978-1-4567-6978-9(2)) AuthorHouse.
Scala, Vincent. Beep Beep Goes the Bus Driver, 1 vol. 2013. (ENG., Illus.). 32p. (J). 16.99 (978-0-7643-4493-0(5), 9780764344930) Schiffer Publishing, Ltd.
Scherer, Catherine W. Simon & Barklee in China, Book 2 - the Mountains. 2008. (Another Country Calling Ser.). (J). per. 15.00 (978-0-9714502-7-1(7), Explorer Media) Simon & Barklee, Inc./ExplorerMedia.
—Simon & Barklee in China, Book 3 - the North. 2008. (Another Country Calling Ser.). (J). per. 15.00 (978-0-9714502-8-8(5), Explorer Media) Simon & Barklee, Inc./ExplorerMedia.
Schomer-Wendel, Gretchen & Schomer, Adam Anthony. Becka Goes to the North Pole. 2009. (Becka & the Big Bubble Ser.). (Illus.). 32p. (J). (gr. -1-3). pap. 10.55 (978-1-60754-117-2(3)) Windmill Bks.
Scott, Shirley A. The Adventures of Jack & Dobbie: Traveling Buddies. 2012. 30p. pap. 18.99 (978-1-4772-7851-2(6)) AuthorHouse.
Seerattan, Tanya. Uncle Noel's Journey to Americ. 2011. 28p. pap. 15.99 (978-1-4568-3065-6(1)) Xlibris Corp.
Seidler, Tor. Gully's Travels. Cole, Brock, illus. 2008. (ENG.). 192p. (J). (gr. -1-3). 17.95 (978-0-545-02506-5(0), Di Capua, Michael) Scholastic, Inc.
Sempe, Goscinny. Las Vacaciones del Pequeno Nicolas. 2003. (SPA., Illus.). 150p. (J). (gr. 5-8). pap. 9.95 (978-84-204-4813-8(3)) Santillana USA Publishing Co., Inc.
Shea, Therese. A Trip to the White House. 2006. (Neighborhood Readers Ser.). (ENG.). 16p. (gr. 1-3). pap. 6.50 (978-1-4042-7204-0(6), Rosen Classroom) Rosen Publishing Group, Inc., The.
Shirley Russak Wachtel. Howie Rocket — World Traveler-Detective: The Search for the Lovely Precious. 2010. 100p. pap. 9.95 (978-1-4401-9993-6(0)) iUniverse, Inc.
Shreeve, Elizabeth. Hector Finds a Fortune. Levy, Pamela R., illus. 2004. 68p. (J). lib. bdg. 15.00 (978-1-4242-0903-3(X)) Fitzgerald Bks.
—Hector Finds a Fortune. Levy, Pamela R., illus. 2004. (Adventures of Hector Fuller Ser.). 68p. (J). (gr. 1-4). 11.65 (978-0-7569-5527-4(0)) Perfection Learning Corp.
Shrum, Brianna. How to Make Out. 2016. (ENG.). 284p. (J). (gr. 6). 16.99 (978-1-5107-0167-0(2), Sky Pony Pr.) Skyhorse Publishing Co., Inc.
Simpson, Wanda. Sammy, the Earth Traveling Turtle, 1 vol. 2010. 16p. pap. 24.95 (978-1-4489-9844-9(1)) PublishAmerica, Inc.
Smith, Jennifer E. The Statistical Probability of Love at First Sight. 2012. (ENG.). 256p. (YA). (gr. 7-17). 17.99 (978-0-316-12238-2(6)) Little Brown & Co.
Smith, Vicki. Jamaican Adventure with Tori & Paul. 2012. (ENG., Illus.). 24p. (J). pap. 13.95 (978-1-4327-8578-9(8)) Outskirts Pr., Inc.
Southall, Donna. The Bubble Trailer. 2004. (J). 15.00 (978-0-8059-6585-8(8)) Dorrance Publishing Co., Inc.
Stanek, Robert, pseud. Journey Beyond the Beyond. 2007. (ENG., Illus.). 156p. (J). 18.95 (978-1-57545-133-6(6)) RP Media.
Stern, Leonard. The Mad Libs Worst-Case Scenario Survival Handbook. 2004. (Mad Libs Ser.). (ENG., Illus.). 48p. (J). (gr. 3-7). 4.99 (978-0-8431-1033-3(3), Mad Libs) Penguin Young Readers Group.
Stewart, Dianne C. Longitude - Zero Degrees. 2009. (ENG.). 200p. pap. 8.95 (978-0-9667359-4-9(3), BeanPole Bks.) Harren Communications, LLC.
Still, Cynthia W. Gypsy Travels the World. 2012. 48p. pap. 21.99 (978-1-4685-5839-5(0)) AuthorHouse.
Stilton, Geronimo. The Race Across America. 2009. (Geronimo Stilton Ser.: 37). lib. bdg. 18.40 (978-0-606-00228-8(6), Turtleback) Turtleback Bks.
Stilton, Geronimo & Stilton, Thea. Thea Stilton & the Ghost of the Shipwreck. 2010. (Thea Stilton Ser.: 3). (ENG., Illus.). 176p. (J). (gr. 2-5). mass mkt. 8.99 (978-0-545-15059-0(0), Scholastic Paperbacks) Scholastic, Inc.
Stilton, Thea. Thea Stilton & the Frozen Fiasco: a Geronimo Stilton Adventure (Thea Stilton #25) 2017. (Thea Stilton Ser.: 25). (ENG.). 176p. (J). (gr. 2-5). pap. 8.99 **(978-1-338-08786-4(X)**, Scholastic Paperbacks) Scholastic, Inc.
Stockdale, Stephanie. Sidney Visits Australi. 2009. 44p. pap. 18.99 (978-1-4389-8698-2(X)) AuthorHouse.
Sundstrom, Dainel H. The Return of Oz. 2007. pap. 10.00 (978-0-8059-8944-1(7)) Dorrance Publishing Co., Inc.
Szymanski, Lois K. The True Story of Sea Feather, 1 vol. 2010. (ENG., Illus.). 48p. (J). pap. 14.99 (978-0-7643-3609-6(6), 9780764336096) Schiffer Publishing, Ltd.
Takara, Kathryn Waddell. Timmy Turtle Teaches. Driver, Audrey, illus. 2012. 54p. pap. 29.95 (978-0-9840204-3-0(8)) Pacific Raven Pr.
Taylor, Pearl Fleming. Snowbird Weenie, 1 vol. 2009. 59p. pap. 16.95 (978-1-60836-745-0(2)) America Star Bks.
Taylor, Thomas. Haunters. 2013. (ENG.). 336p. (J). (gr. 5-9). 17.99 (978-0-545-49644-5(6)) Scholastic, Inc.
Tillis, Doris. Rudy the Rabbit. Tillis, Carrie, illus. 2005. 32p. per. 17.95 (978-1-58961-410-9(0)) PageFree Publishing, Inc.
Time, Nicholas O. Stay a Spell. 2016. (In Due Time Ser.: 2). lib. bdg. 17.20 (978-0-606-38986-0(5)) Turtleback Bks.
Tolan, Stephanie S. & Tolan, R. J. Applewhites Coast to Coast. 2017. 320p. (J). (gr. 3-7). 16.99 **(978-0-06-213320-5(9))** HarperCollins Pubs.
Turnage, Cyndy. A Trip to Washington, D. C. A Capital Idea. Fagan, Martin, illus. 2013. (Reader's Theater Word Plays Ser.). (J). (gr. 1-2). (978-1-4509-8941-1(1)) Benchmark Education Co.
Uncle Markie. Piglettè & Bobo in Berkeley. 2003. (YA). ring bd. 9.95 (978-1-933129-07-5(7)) Studio 403.
—Piglettè & Bobo in Kansas City. 2003. (YA). ring bd. 9.95 (978-1-933129-08-2(5)) Studio 403.
—Piglettè & Bobo in Sud Africa. 2003. (YA). ring bd. 9.95 (978-1-933129-15-0(8)) Studio 403.
—Piglettè & Bobo Join the Manscouts. 2003. (YA). ring bd. 9.95 (978-1-933129-05-1(0)) Studio 403.
—Piglettè & Bobo on Safari. 2003. (YA). ring bd. 9.95 (978-1-933129-16-7(6)) Studio 403.
—Piglettè & Bobo Winter in Zagreb. 2003. (YA). ring bd. 9.95 (978-1-933129-11-2(5)) Studio 403.
—Piglettè & BoBoTrash Orange County. 2003. (YA). ring bd. 9.95 (978-1-933129-09-9(3)) Studio 403.
Van Straaten, Harmen. TIM & the FLYING MACHINE. 2008. (ENG.). 28p. (J). (gr. 1-7). 12.95 (978-1-60136-003-8(7)) Audio Holdings, LLC.
Vancil, Marybelle. Adventures with Macy & the Sneezy, Sneezy Dog: First Adventure: We Visit Indians. 2010. (Illus.). 43p. (J). pap. 23.95 (978-1-4327-5038-1(0)) Outskirts Pr., Inc.
Vasquez, Elisa Irene. My Little Piggy: A Bilingual English-Spanish Children's Book. 2010. 28p. 14.95 (978-1-4490-8716-6(7)) AuthorHouse.
Verdick, Elizabeth. On-the-Go Time. Heinlen, Marieka, illus. 2011. (Toddler Tools Ser.). (ENG.). 24p. (J). 7.95 (978-1-57542-379-1(0), 1331978) Free Spirit Publishing, Inc.
Verne, Jules. The Adventures of a Special Correspondent. 2009. 180p. pap. 13.95 (978-1-60664-377-8(0)) Rodgers, Alan Bks.
Verne, Jules, ed. Cinco Semanas en Globo.Tr. of Around the World in Eighty Days. (SPA., Illus.). 142p. (YA). 14.95 (978-84-7281-102-7(6), AF1102) Auriga, Ediciones S.A. ESP. Dist: Continental Bk. Co., Inc.
—Cinco Semanas en Globo. 2003. (Advanced Reading Ser.).Tr. of Around the World in Eighty Days. (SPA., Illus.). 240p. (J). 11.95 (978-84-239-5898-6(1)) Espasa Calpe, S.A. ESP. Dist: Planeta Publishing Corp.
Waldron, Douglas E. Cody Sackett of Montana: Tales of Adventure. 2008. 188p. per. 24.95 (978-1-4241-9781-1(3)) America Star Bks.
Wamack, Rhonda. Kelsey's Candy World Adventure. 2009. 48p. pap. 17.49 (978-1-4490-4438-1(7)) AuthorHouse.
Watt, Fiona. Complete Book of First Experiences. rev. ed. 2011. (First Experiences Ser.). 144p. (J). ring bd. 19.99 (978-0-7945-2948-2(8), Usborne) EDC Publishing.
Watts, Tammy E. From Libya to Namibi. 2012. 24p. 24.95 (978-1-4626-5928-9(4)) America Star Bks.
Webster, Frank V. The Boy from the Ranch: Or, Roy Bradner's City Experiences. 2007. (ENG.). 132p. pap. 18.99 (978-1-4346-4347-6(6)); 148p. pap. 19.99 (978-1-4346-4348-3(4)) Creative Media Partners, LLC.
Wendel, Gretchen Schomer & Schomer, Adam Anthony. Becka Goes to San Diego. Renthrope, Damon, illus. 2008. (ENG.). 32p. (J). (gr. -1-3). 11.99 (978-1-933754-51-2(6)) Waterside Publishing.
Wendel, Gretchen Schomer & Schomer, Adam Anthony. Becka Goes to Chicago. Renthrope, Damon, illus. 2008. (ENG.). 36p. (J). (gr. -1-3). 11.99 (978-1-933754-52-9(4)) Waterside Publishing.
Weston Woods Staff, creator. Henry Hikes to Fitchburg. 2011. 38.75 (978-0-439-90698-2(9)); 18.95 (978-0-439-90696-8(2)) Weston Woods Studios, Inc.
Wheelie, P. Tommy's Triumph: The tales of Tommy the tortoise & Friends. 2009. (Illus.). 28p. pap. 12.49 (978-1-4389-2718-3(5)) AuthorHouse.
Whint, Ana Lee. Espalemit. 2003. (ENG.). 112p. pap. 9.95 (978-0-595-26259-5(7), Writers Club Pr.) iUniverse, Inc.
White-Adams, Beverly. The Adventures of Rusty: Rusty Goes to Maine Vol. 3. 2012. 40p. pap. 19.57 (978-1-4669-5442-7(6)) Trafford Publishing.
Wightman, Jillian C. The Adventures of Erin Mctavitt. 2008. 68p. pap. 19.95 (978-1-4327-3164-9(5)) Outskirts Pr., Inc.
Wilhelm, Kj. Grandma Cooooonutts Goes to Boston. 2009. 28p. pap. 15.99 (978-1-4363-9933-3(5)) Xlibris Corp.
Willett, Edward. Twist of the Blade, 1 vol. 2014. (Shards of Excalibur Ser.: 2). (ENG.). 232p. (YA). (gr. 7-10). pap. 14.95 (978-1-55050-599-3(8)) Coteau Bks. CAN. Dist: Orca Bk. Pubs. USA.
Williams, M. J. Alora & the Howling Guff. 2010. 132p. pap. 10.68 (978-1-4520-3207-8(6)) AuthorHouse.
Williams, Rozanne Lanczak. Captain Jack's Journal. Grayson, Rick, illus. 2006. (Learn to Write Ser.). 16p. (J). (gr. k-2). pap. 2.99 (978-1-59198-303-3(7), 6197) Creative Teaching Pr., Inc.
—Captain Jack's Journal. Maio, Barbara, ed. Grayson, Rick, illus. 2006. (J). per. 8.99 (978-1-59198-361-3(4)) Creative Teaching Pr., Inc.
—Postcards from Barney Bear. Maio, Barbara & Faulkner, Stacey, eds. Thelen, Mary, illus. 2006. (Learn to Write Ser.). 8p. (J). pap. 3.49 (978-1-59198-287-6(1), 6181) Creative Teaching Pr., Inc.
Willis Hudson, Cheryl. Sights I Love to See. 2009. 24p. 3.99 (978-1-60349-009-2(4), Marimba Bks.) Hudson Publishing Group, The.
Wolff, Tracy. Book 1: Crisis. 2016. (Mars Bound Ser.). (ENG.). (J). (gr. 2-8). lib. bdg. 28.50 **(978-1-62402-197-8(2))** ABDO Publishing Co.
Worcester, Daryl D. The Story of the Famous Traves Travislot. 2006. 48p. pap. 16.95 (978-1-4241-2417-6(4)) America Star Bks.
Yansky, Brian. My Road Trip to the Pretty Girl Capital of the World. 2003. (ENG.). 160p. (J). 16.95 (978-0-8126-2691-9(5)) Cricket Bks.
Zachary, Ken. Missions of Big Zach. Waytula, Brian, illus. 2005. 36p. (J). (gr. -1-3). per. 9.95 (978-1-59879-061-0(7)) Lifevest Publishing, Inc.
Zschock, Martha Day. Hello, San Francisco! 2012. (Hello! Ser.). (ENG., Illus.). 16p. (J). (gr. -1-k). bds. 9.95 (978-1-933212-65-4(9), Commonwealth Editions) Applewood Bks.

TRAVEL GAMES

see Games for Travelers

TRAVELERS

see also Explorers

A Yusuf, Ali. Three Travellers to India. 2006. 108p. per. (978-1-4067-3192-7(7), Hesperides Pr.) Read Bks.
Comerciantes Y Viajeros, 6 vols., Vol. 2. (Explorers. Exploradores Nonfiction Sets Ser.). (SPA.). 32p. (gr. 3-6). 44.95 (978-0-7699-0647-8(8)) Shortland Pubns. (U. S. A.) Inc.
Harmon, Daniel E. Ibn Battuta: The Medieval World's Greatest Traveler Throughout Africa, Asia, the Middle East, & Europe. 2016. (Silk Road's Greatest Travelers Ser.). 112p. (J). (gr. 6-6). 37.10 (978-1-5081-7150-8(5)) Rosen Publishing Group, Inc., The.
McLean, Jacqueline. Women of Adventure. 2003. (Profiles Ser.). (Illus.). 160p. (gr. 5-18). lib. bdg. 19.95 (978-1-881508-73-1(0)) Oliver Pr., Inc.
Porterfield, Jason. Marco Polo. 2016. (Silk Road's Greatest Travelers Ser.). 112p. (gr. 6-6). 37.10 (978-1-5081-7152-2(1)) Rosen Publishing Group, Inc., The.
Toth, Henrietta. Ibn Battuta: The Greatest Traveler of the Muslim World. 2017. (Spotlight on Explorers & Colonization Ser.). 48p. (gr. 10-11). pap. 11.75 **(978-1-5081-7499-8(7)**, Rosen Young Adult) Rosen Publishing Group, Inc., The.
Twist, Clint. Marco Polo: History's Great Adventurer. 2011. (Historical Notebooks Ser.). (ENG., Illus.). 30p. (J). (gr. 3-7). 19.99 (978-0-7636-5286-9(5), Templar) Candlewick Pr.

TRAVELERS—FICTION

Aesop. Two Travelers & a Bear. 2012. (J). (978-1-61913-102-6(1)) Weigl Pubs., Inc.
Curtis, Jamie Lee. This Is Me: A Story of Who We Are & Where We Came From. Cornell, Laura, illus. 2016. (ENG.). 32p. (J). (gr. -1-3). 17.89 (978-1-5235-0005-5(0)); 16.95 (978-0-7611-8011-1(7)) Workman Publishing Co., Inc.
Fenn, George Manville. Yussuf the Guide or the Mountain Bandits: Being the Strange Story of the Travels in Asia Minor of Burne the Lawyer, Preston the Professor, & Lawrenc. Schönberg, John, illus. 2008. 432p. pap. 16.95 (978-1-934671-20-7(7)) Salem Ridge Press LLC.
Friedman, J. S. Casablanca. Beatrice, Chris, illus. 2013. (Maurice's Valises: Moral Tails in an Immoral World Ser.: Vol. 3). (ENG.). 45p. (J). (gr. k-4). pap. (978-94-91613-09-8(X)) Mouse Prints Pr.
Garis, Howard Roger. Uncle Wiggily's Travels. Date not set. 192p. (J). 20.95 (978-0-8488-2278-1(1)) Amereon Ltd.
Gentile, Joe. Mysterious Traveler. 2003. (ENG., Illus.). 48p. (gr. 12-18). pap. 5.50 (978-0-9721668-5-0(8), 9780972166850) Moonstone.
Hunsaker, Joan. A Dagger in Time - the Web of Spies. 2010. 200p. 25.99 (978-1-58930-247-1(8)); pap. 15.99 (978-1-58930-248-8(6)) Selah Publishing Group, LLC.
Hunt, Wayne. Zack & the Validators: Good As Gold. 2011. 138p. pap. 19.99 (978-1-4653-5816-5(1)) Xlibris Corp.
Jackson, Lyn D. The Perilous Journey Home. 2009. 200p. pap. 14.49 (978-1-4389-4651-1(1)) AuthorHouse.
Joan, Marler. Secrets of the Wind. 2006. pap. (978-1-888251-37-1(9)) Voice & Vision Pubns.
Lang, Andrew, ed. & compiled by. The Orange Fairy Book. Lang, Andrew, compiled by. 2011. 234p. 27.95 (978-1-4638-9520-4(8)) Rodgers, Alan Bks.
Mahy, Margaret. Maddigan's Fantasia. 2005. 320p. (978-1-86950-561-5(1)) HarperCollins Pubs. Australia.
Ranade, Soumitra. Tak-Tak! Suleman, Shilo Shiv, illus. 2013. (ENG.). 32p. (J). (gr. k). pap. 9.95 (978-81-8190-183-5(5)) Karadi Tales Co. Pvt. Ltd. IND. Dist: Consortium Bk. Sales & Distribution.
Stokes, Katherine. Motor Maids in Fair Japan. 2006. pap. (978-1-4068-3090-3(9)) Echo Library.
Webster, Jean. Jerry. 2008. 108p. 22.95 (978-1-60664-939-8(6)) Aegypan.
Wiggin, Kate Douglas. Penelope Travels Abroad. 2008. 460p. 34.95 (978-1-60664-818-6(7)) Aegypan.

TRAVELERS—POETRY

Capildeo, Vahni. No Traveller Returns. 2004. (Salt Modern Poets). (ENG.). 184p. pap. (978-1-876857-88-2(9)) Salt Publishing.

TRAVELS

see Overland Journeys to the Pacific; Scientific Expeditions; Voyages and Travels; Voyages around the World

TRAVESTIES

see Parodies

TRAY GARDENS

see Gardens, Miniature

TREASURE ISLAND (IMAGINARY PLACE)—FICTION

Blum, Alex A., et al. Treasure Island. 2015. (Classics Illustrated Ser.: 21). (ENG., Illus.). 48p. pap. 9.95 (978-1-906814-47-2(3)) Classic Comic Store, Ltd. GBR. Dist: Casemate Pubs. & Bk. Distributors, LLC.
Cole, Bob. Power Reading: Classics/Treasure Island. Lee, Joe, illus. 2004. 94p. (J). (gr. 5-6). vinyl bd. 39.95 (978-1-883186-59-3(5), PPCL3) National Reading Styles Institute, Inc.
Dennis, Peter & Rawson, Christopher. Treasure Island. 2004. (Young Reading Ser.). (Illus.). 64p. (J). (gr. 2-18). pap. 5.95 (978-0-7945-0411-3(6), Usborne) EDC Publishing.
Francis, Pauline, retold by. Treasure Island. 2010. (Essential Classics - Adventure Ser.). (Illus.). 48p. pap. (978-0-237-54085-2(1)) Evans Brothers, Ltd.
Fuerst, Jeffrey B. & Benchmark Education Co., LLC. Robert Louis Stevenson's Treasure Island: My Sea Adventure Israel Hands. Hondru, Ovi, illus. 2014. (Text Connections Ser.). (J). (gr. 3). (978-1-4509-9652-5(3)) Benchmark Education Co.
Publications International Ltd. Staff, ed. Treasure Hunt. 2010. 12p. (J). bds. 9.98 (978-1-4127-9885-3(X)) Phoenix International Publications, Inc.
Stevenson, Robert Louis. Treasure Island. 2003. (More for Teens Ser.). 64p. (Orig.). (YA). (gr. 6-12). pap. 6.00 (978-0-88734-412-1(7)) Players Pr., Inc.
—Treasure Island. McKowen, Scott, illus. 2004. (Sterling Unabridged Classics Ser.). (ENG.). 232p. (J). (gr. 5). 9.95 (978-1-4027-1457-3(2)) Sterling Publishing Co., Inc.
—Treasure Island. 2009. (Foundation Classics Ser.). (Illus.). 56p. (J). (gr. 5-9). lib. bdg. 27.95 (978-1-60754-543-9(8)) Windmill Bks.
—Treasure Island. (Young Collector's Illustrated Classics Ser.). (Illus.). 192p. (J). (gr. 3-7). 9.95 (978-1-56156-456-9(7)) Kidsbooks, LLC.
—Treasure Island. Todd, Justin, illus. unabr. ed. 2003. (Chrysalis Childrens Classics Ser.). 208p. (YA). pap. (978-1-84365-037-9(1), Pavilion Children's Books) Pavilion Bks.
—Treasure Island: A Classic Story about Responsibility. 2003. (Illus.). 32p. per. 3.95 (978-0-9747133-4-2(1), Values to Live By Classic Stories) Thomas, Frederic Inc.
—Treasure Island: With Story of the Treasure of Normon Island. Date not set. (J). (gr. 5-6). reprint ed. lib. bdg. 22.95 (978-0-89190-236-2(8), American Reprint Co.) Amereon Ltd.
Stevenson, Robert Louis & Wyeth, N. C. Treasure Island. abr. ed. 2003. (Scribner Storybook Classics Ser.). (ENG., Illus.). 64p. (J). (gr. 3-7). 19.99 (978-0-689-85468-2(4), Atheneum Bks. for Young Readers) Simon & Schuster Children's Publishing.
Stilton, Geronimo. El Misterio Del Ojo Esmeralda. (SPA., Illus.). 128p. (J). (gr. 3-5). pap. 7.95 (978-1-59437-453-1(8)) Santillana USA Publishing Co., Inc.
Stratemeyer, Edward. The Rover Boys on Treasure Isle. 2007. 268p. 27.95 (978-1-4218-4148-9(7)); per. 12.95 (978-1-4218-4246-2(7)) 1st World Publishing, Inc. (1st World Library - Literary Society).

TREASURE TROVES

see Buried Treasure

TREE HOUSES—FICTION

Adams, Jennifer. Edgar & the Tree House of Usher: Inspired by Edgar Allan Poe's the Fall of the House of Usher, 1 vol. Stucki, Ron, illus. 2016. (ENG.). 22p. (J). bds. 9.99 (978-1-4236-4493-4(X)) Gibbs Smith, Publisher.
—Edgar & the Treehouse of Usher: A BabyLit First Steps Book, 1 vol. Stucki, Ron, illus. 2015. (ENG.). 32p. (J). 16.99 (978-1-4236-4043-1(8)) Gibbs Smith, Publisher.
Apted, Violet. Tommy & Jacqui: Laughing with Kookaburras. 2011. 32p. pap. 13.00 (978-1-61204-118-6(3), Eloquent Bks.) Strategic Book Publishing & Rights Agency (SBPRA).

T U V

Arena, Felice & Kettle, Phil. The Tree House. Vane, Mitch, illus. 2004. (J). pap. (978-1-59336-357-4(5)) Mondo Publishing.
Atwood, Margaret. Up in the Tree, 1 vol. 2010. (ENG., Illus.). 32p. (J). (gr. k-k). 19.95 (978-1-55498-080-2(1)) Groundwood Bks. CAN. Dist: Publishers Group West (PGW).
Baltazar, Art & Aureliani, Franco. Welcome to the Treehouse, 1 vol. Baltazar, Art & Aureliani, Franco, illus. 2013. (Tiny Titans Ser.). (ENG., Illus.). 32p. (gr. 1-2). lib. bdg. 22.60 (978-1-4342-4697-4(3)) Stone Arch Bks.
Banning, Gail. Out on a Limb. 2008. (ENG.). 256p. (YA). (gr. 6-9). (978-1-55470-012-7(4)) Me to We.
Bauer, Carole. The Tree House Kids. 2013. 40p. pap. 15.95 (978-1-4624-0849-8(4), Inspiring Voices) Author Solutions, Inc.
Bishop, Clive. Trophy Trouble. 2009. 74p. pap. 9.99 (978-1-60860-547-7(7), Strategic Bk. Publishing) Strategic Book Publishing & Rights Agency (SBPRA).
Blyton, Enid. Hollow Tree House. 160p. (J). (gr. k-6). pap. 5.95 (978-0-09-947220-9(1)) Random Hse. GBR. Dist: Trafalgar Square Publishing.
Bowlin, Serina. Wandering Sam. Thrasher, Brian, illus. 2011. 20p. pap. 9.97 (978-1-61204-280-0(5), Eloquent Bks.) Strategic Book Publishing & Rights Agency (SBPRA).
Brown, Marc. Arthur's Tree House. 2007. (ENG., Illus.). 24p. (J). (gr. -1-1). pap. 3.99 (978-0-316-05776-9(2)) Little, Brown Bks. for Young Readers.
Burk, Rachelle. Tree House in a Storm. Schneider, Rex, illus. 2009. 42p. (J). (gr. k-4). 16.95 (978-0-916144-23-4(2)) Stemmer Hse. Pubs.
Dahlstrom, Halene. Raven Cove Mystery: A Rennie of Alaska Mystery. 2003. (YA). pap. 12.95 (978-1-59433-001-8(8)) Publication Consultants.
Dean, James. Pete the Cat & the Tip-Top Tree House. Dean, James, illus. 2017. (My First I Can Read Ser.). (Illus.). 32p. (J). (gr. -1-3). pap. 3.99 (978-0-06-240431-2(8)) HarperCollins Pubs.
Dixon, Joyce Ann. Katie's Tree House. 2009. 48p. pap. 16.95 (978-1-60836-626-2(X)) America Star Bks.
Donahue, Peter & Coloring Books Staff. Robot Buddies Stained Glass Coloring Book. 2012. (Dover Stained Glass Coloring Book Ser.). (ENG., Illus.). 32p. (J). (gr. k-5). pap. 6.99 (978-0-486-48673-4(7)) Dover Pubns., Inc.
Durbin, Amanda. Tree Houses & Treasures. 2013. 24p. pap. 24.95 (978-1-63004-353-7(2)) America Star Bks.
Edwards, Jean E. Adventure Tales: For Kids Who Want to Become Better Readers. 2012. 102p. 24.99 (978-1-4771-4118-2(9)) Xlibris Corp.
Edwards, Pamela Duncan. Jack & Jill's Treehouse. Cole, Henry & Bond, Felicia, illus. 2008. 24p. (J). (gr. -1-2). lib. bdg. 17.89 (978-0-06-009078-4(2), Tegen, Katherine Bks) HarperCollins Pubs.
Eliot, Ethel Cook. The House above the Trees. 2003. (Illus.). 140p. (J). 20.00 (978-0-9615961-7-0(1)); 2nd ed. pap. 12.00 (978-0-9615961-6-3(3)) Raven Rocks Pr.
Foster, Marilyn. Moon Tricks. Vega, Alison, illus. 2012. 48p. pap. (978-1-77097-960-4(3)) FriesenPress.
Garant, Andre J. Jake's Tree House. 2010. 128p. pap. 10.99 (978-1-4490-8369-4(2)) AuthorHouse.
Graff, Lisa. The Great Treehouse War. 2017. (ENG.). 288p. (J). (gr. 3-7). 16.99 (978-0-399-17500-8(8), Philomel Bks.) Penguin Young Readers Group.
Griffiths, Andy. The 13-Story Treehouse. Denton, Terry, illus. 2013. (Treehouse Bks.: 1). (ENG.). 256p. (J). (gr. 1-5). 13.99 (978-1-250-02690-3(3), 9781250026903) Feiwel & Friends.
—The 13-Story Treehouse. Denton, Terry, illus. 2015. (Treehouse Bks.: 1). (ENG.). 272p. (J). (gr. 1-5). pap. 6.99 (978-1-250-07065-4(1), 9781250070654) Square Fish.
—The 26-Story Treehouse. Denton, Terry, illus. 2014. (Treehouse Bks.: 2). (ENG.). 352p. (J). (gr. 1-5). 13.99 (978-1-250-02691-0(1), 9781250026910) Feiwel & Friends.
—The 39-Story Treehouse. Denton, Terry, illus. 2015. (Treehouse Bks.). (ENG.). 352p. (J). (gr. 1-5). 13.99 (978-1-250-02692-7(X), 9781250026927) Feiwel & Friends.
—The 39-Story Treehouse. Barcellona, Christine, ed. Denton, Terry, illus. 2016. (Treehouse Bks.: 3). (ENG.). 368p. (J). pap. 6.99 (978-1-250-07511-6(4), 9781250075116) Square Fish.
—The 52-Story Treehouse. Denton, Terry, illus. 2016. (Treehouse Bks.: 4). (ENG.). 336p. (J). (gr. 2-5). 13.99 (978-1-250-02693-4(8), 9781250026934) Feiwel & Friends.
—The 52-Story Treehouse. Denton, Terry, illus. 2017. (Treehouse Bks.). (ENG.). 352p. (J). pap. 6.99 (978-1-250-10379-6(7), 9781250103796) Square Fish.
—The 52-Story Treehouse. 2017. (Treehouse Adventures Ser.: 4). (J). lib. bdg. 17.20 (978-0-606-40350-4(7)) Turtleback Bks.
Guest, Elissa Haden. Iris & Walter. Davenier, Christine, illus. alt. ed. 2012. (Green Light Readers Level 3 Ser.). (ENG.). 44p. (J). (gr. 1-4). pap. 3.99 (978-0-547-74555-8(9)) Houghton Mifflin Harcourt Publishing Co.
Hibbeler, Stephen Paul. A Wonderful, Magical World. 2006. 48p. pap. 16.95 (978-1-4241-2631-6(2)) PublishAmerica, Inc.
Hoenecke, Karen. Tree House. Graves, Dennis, illus. 2005. (ENG.). 12p. (gr. k-1). pap. 7.95 (978-1-57874-090-1(8), Kaeden Bks.) Kaeden Corp.
Hughes, Jenny. Audrey's Tree House. Bentley, Jonathan, illus. 2015. (J). pap. (978-0-545-81405-8(7)); (ENG.). 32p. (gr. -1-k). 17.99 (978-0-545-81327-3(1)) Scholastic, Inc. (Scholastic Pr.).
Kreidler, Shannon. The Adventures of Sally the Squirrel: Interactive... Educational & Earn Gold Stars. 2013. 28p. pap. 15.99 (978-1-4797-7674-0(2)) Xlibris Corp.
Lee, Shell. Teenie's Treehouse Adventures: The Magic Begins. 2004. 37p. pap. 24.95 (978-1-4137-2879-8(0)) PublishAmerica, Inc.
London, Jonathan. Froggy Builds a Tree House. 2013. (Froggy Ser.). (ENG.). 32p. (J). (-k). pap. 6.99 (978-0-14-242533-6(8), Puffin Books) Penguin Young Readers Group.
—Froggy Builds a Tree House. 2013. (Froggy Ser.). lib. bdg. 17.20 (978-0-606-30518-1(1), Turtleback) Turtleback Bks.
McPhail, David. Boy, Bird, & Dog. McPhail, David, illus. (I Like to Read(r) Ser.). (ENG., Illus.). 24p. (J). (gr. -1-2). 2012. pap. 6.99 (978-0-8234-2639-3(4)) 2011. 14.95 (978-0-8234-2346-0(8)) Holiday Hse., Inc.
Mercer, M. J. O'No It's Henry. 2010. 24p. 12.99 (978-1-4520-2125-6(2)) AuthorHouse.
Milton, Elizabeth. Bob the Builder. 2016. (ENG.). 24p. (J). (gr. -1-3). pap. 3.99 (978-0-316-27294-0(9)) Little, Brown Bks. for Young Readers.
Miyares, Daniel. That Neighbor Kid. Miyares, Daniel, illus. 2017. (ENG., Illus.). 32p. (J). (gr. -1-3). 17.99 (978-1-4814-4979-3(6), Simon & Schuster Bks. For Young Readers) Simon & Schuster Bks. For Young Readers.
Moore, Natascha. Lost Verloren. 2013. 28p. pap. 19.99 (978-1-4817-0664-3(0)) AuthorHouse.
Munoz, Norma. Los Cuentos de la Casa del Arbol. Olson, John & Olson, Johan, illus. rev. ed. 2005. (Castillo de la Lectura Blanca Ser.). (SPA & ENG.). 72p. (J). (gr. -1-3). pap. 6.95 (978-970-20-0124-9(2)) Castillo, Ediciones, S. A. de C. V. MEX. Dist: Macmillan.
O'Hagan, William. Anything Else but Me. 2008. 36p. pap. 24.95 (978-1-60563-701-3(7)) America Star Bks.
Osborne, Mary Pope. Abe Lincoln at Last! Murdocca, Sal, illus. 2011. (Magic Tree House Merlin Mission Ser.: No. 19). (ENG.). 128p. (J). (gr. 2-5). 12.99 (978-0-375-86825-2(9), Random Hse. Bks. for Young Readers) Random Hse. Children's Bks.
—Balto of the Blue Dawn. Murdocca, Sal, illus. 2016. (Magic Tree House Merlin Missions Ser.: No. 26). (ENG.). 128p. (J). (gr. 2-5). 13.99 (978-0-553-51085-0(1), Random Hse. Bks. for Young Readers) Random Hse. Children's Bks.
—Barcos Vikingos Al Amanecer. Brovelli, Marcela, tr. from ENG. Murdocca, Sal, illus. 2007. (Casa del Arbol Ser.: 15). (SPA.). 73p. (J). per. 5.99 (978-1-933032-21-4(9)) Lectorum Pubns., Inc.
—A Big Day for Baseball. Murdocca, Sal, illus. 2017. (Magic Tree House Ser.: 29). (ENG.). (J). (gr. 1-4). 80p. 13.99 (978-1-5247-1308-9(2)); 96p. lib. bdg. 16.99 (978-1-5247-1309-6(0)) Random Hse. Children's Bks. (Random Hse. Bks. for Young Readers).
—Blizzard of the Blue Moon. Murdocca, Sal, illus. 2007. (Magic Tree House Merlin Mission Ser.: 8). (ENG.). 144p. (J). (gr. 2-5). 5.99 (978-0-375-83038-9(3), Random Hse. Bks. for Young Readers) Random Hse. Children's Bks.
—Buffalo Before Breakfast. 2004. (Magic Tree House Ser.: No. 18). 72p. (J). (gr. k-3). pap. 17.00 incl. audio (978-0-8072-0927-1(9), Listening Library) Random Hse. Audio Publishing Group.
—El Caballero Del Alba. 2004. (Casa del Arbol Ser.: 2). (SPA.). (J). pap. 5.99 (978-1-930332-50-8(5)) Lectorum Pubns., Inc.
—Carnival at Candlelight. Murdocca, Sal, illus. 2006. (Magic Tree House Merlin Mission Ser.: 5). (ENG.). 144p. (J). (gr. 2-5). 5.99 (978-0-375-83034-1(0), Random Hse. Bks. for Young Readers) Random Hse. Children's Bks.
—Un Castillo Embrujado en la Noche de Halloween. 2015. (Casa De árbol Ser.: 30). (SPA., Illus.). 144p. (J). (gr. 2-4). pap. 5.99 (978-1-63245-533-8(1)) Lectorum Pubns., Inc.
—Christmas in Camelot. Murdocca, Sal, illus. 2009. (Magic Tree House Merlin Mission Ser.: 1). (ENG.). 144p. (J). (gr. 2-5). 5.99 (978-0-375-85812-3(1), Random Hse. Bks. for Young Readers) Random Hse. Children's Bks.
—Christmas in Camelot. 2009. (Magic Tree House Merlin Missions Ser.: 1). lib. bdg. 16.00 (978-0-606-06386-9(2), Turtleback) Turtleback Bks.
—Civil War on Sunday. unabr. ed. 2004. (Magic Tree House Ser.: No. 21). 76p. (J). (gr. k-3). pap. 17.00 incl. audio (978-0-8072-0930-1(9), S FTR 253 SP, Listening Library) Random Hse. Audio Publishing Group.
—A Crazy Day with Cobras. Murdocca, Sal, illus. (ENG.). (J). 2012. (Magic Tree House Merlin Missions Ser.: No. 17). 144p. (gr. 1-4). 5.99 (978-0-375-86795-8(3)) 2011. (Magic Tree House Merlin Mission Ser.: 45). 128p. (gr. 2-5). 12.99 (978-0-375-86823-8(2)) Random Hse. Children's Bks. (Random Hse. Bks. for Young Readers).
—A Crazy Day with Cobras. 2012. (Magic Tree House Merlin Missions Ser.: 17). lib. bdg. 16.00 (978-0-606-26997-1(5), Turtleback) Turtleback Bks.
—Dark Day in the Deep Sea. 2009. (Magic Tree House Merlin Missions Ser.: 11). lib. bdg. 16.00 (978-0-606-01778-7(X), Turtleback) Turtleback Bks.
—Das magische Baumhaus 09. Der Ruf der Delfine. 18.95 (978-3-7855-4185-2(6)) Loewe Verlag GmbH DEU. Dist: Distribooks, Inc.
—Day of the Dragon King. unabr. ed. 2004. (Magic Tree House Ser.: No. 14). 68p. (J). (gr. k-3). pap. 17.00 incl. audio (978-0-8072-0783-3(7), S FTR 242 SP, Listening Library) Random Hse. Audio Publishing Group.
—Dinosaurs Before Dark. unabr. ed. 2004. (Magic Tree House Ser.: No. 1). 68p. (J). (gr. k-5). pap. 17.00 incl. audio (978-0-8072-0330-9(0), FTR208SP, Listening Library) Random Hse. Audio Publishing Group.
—Dinosaurs Before Dark. Murdocca, Sal, illus. 20th anniv. ed. 2012. (Magic Tree House Ser.: 1). (ENG.). 96p. (J). (gr. k-3). 14.99 (978-0-375-86988-4(3), Random Hse. Bks. for Young Readers) Random Hse. Children's Bks.
—Earthquake in the Early Morning. unabr. ed. 2004. (Magic Tree House Ser.: No. 24). 71p. (J). (gr. k-3). pap. 17.00 incl. audio (978-0-8072-0933-2(3), S FTR 256 SP, Listening Library) Random Hse. Audio Publishing Group.
—Eve of the Emperor Penguin. Murdocca, Sal, illus. 2009. (Magic Tree House Merlin Mission Ser.: No. 12). (ENG.). 144p. (J). (gr. 2-5). 5.99 (978-0-375-83734-0(5), Random Hse. Bks. for Young Readers) Random Hse. Children's Bks.
—Ghost Town at Sundown. unabr. ed. 2004. (Magic Tree House Ser.: No. 10). 73p. (J). (gr. k-3). pap. 17.00 incl. audio (978-0-8072-0535-8(4), Listening Library) Random Hse. Audio Publishing Group.
—Haunted Castle on Hallows Eve. Murdocca, Sal, illus. 2010. (Magic Tree House Merlin Mission Ser.: 2). (ENG.). 144p. (J). (gr. 2-5). pap. 5.99 (978-0-375-86090-4(8), Random Hse. Bks. for Young Readers) Random Hse. Children's Bks.
—Haunted Castle on Hallows Eve. 2010. (Magic Tree House Merlin Missions Ser.: 2). lib. bdg. 16.00 (978-0-606-13992-2(3), Turtleback) Turtleback Bks.
—High Tide in Hawaii. Murdocca, Sal, illus. 2003. (Magic Tree House (R) Ser.: 28). (ENG.). 96p. (J). (gr. 1-4). pap. 5.99 (978-0-375-80616-2(4), Random Hse. Bks. for Young Readers) Random Hse. Children's Bks.
—High Tide in Hawaii. 2003. (Magic Tree House Ser.: 28). (gr. k-3). lib. bdg. 16.00 (978-0-613-62386-5(X), Turtleback) Turtleback Bks.
—High Time for Heroes. Murdocca, Sal, illus. 2016. (Magic Tree House Merlin Mission Ser.: 23). (ENG.). 144p. (J). (gr. 2-5). 5.99 (978-0-307-98052-6(9), Random Hse. Bks. for Young Readers) Random Hse. Children's Bks.
—La Hora de Los Juegos Olimpicos. Brovelli, Marcela, tr. Murdocca, Sal, illus. 2007. (Casa del Arbol Ser.: 16).Tr. of Hour of the Olympics Games. (ENG & SPA.). 68p. (J). per. 5.99 (978-1-933032-22-1(7)) Lectorum Pubns., Inc.
—Hour of the Olympics. unabr. ed. 2004. (Magic Tree House Ser.: No. 16). 70p. (J). (gr. k-3). pap. 17.00 incl. audio (978-0-8072-0785-7(3), LFTR 244 SP, Listening Library) Random Hse. Audio Publishing Group.
—Hurry up, Houdini! Murdocca, Sal, illus. (Magic Tree House Merlin Mission Ser.: No. 22). (ENG.). (J). (gr. 2-5). 2015. 144p. 5.99 (978-0-307-98048-9(0)) 2013. 128p. 12.99 (978-0-307-98045-8(6)) Random Hse. Children's Bks. (Random Hse. Bks. for Young Readers).
—The Knight at Dawn. unabr. ed. 2004. (Magic Tree House Ser.: No. 2). 66p. (J). (gr. k-3). pap. 17.00 incl. audio (978-0-8072-0331-6(9), Listening Library) Random Hse. Audio Publishing Group.
—The Knight at Dawn. Murdocca, Sal, illus. 20th anniv. ed. 2013. (Magic Tree House Ser.). (ENG.). 96p. (J). (gr. 1-4). 14.99 (978-0-449-81822-0(5), Random Hse. Bks. for Young Readers) Random Hse. Children's Bks.
—Leprechaun in Late Winter. Murdocca, Sal, illus. (Magic Tree House Merlin Mission Ser.: No. 15). (ENG.). 128p. (J). (gr. 2-5). 2012. 5.99 (978-0-375-85651-8(X)) 2010. 12.99 (978-0-375-85650-1(1)) Random Hse. Children's Bks. (Random Hse. Bks. for Young Readers).
—Leprechaun in Late Winter. 2012. (Magic Tree House Merlin Missions Ser.: 15). lib. bdg. 16.00 (978-0-606-23860-1(3), Turtleback) Turtleback Bks.
—Una Momia Al Amanecer. 2004. (Casa del Arbol Ser.: 3). (SPA.). (J). pap. 5.99 (978-1-930332-51-5(3)) Lectorum Pubns., Inc.
—Una Momia en la Manana. 2003. (Magic Tree House Ser.: 3). (SPA.). (gr. 3-6). lib. bdg. 16.00 (978-0-613-64609-3(6), Turtleback) Turtleback Bks.
—Navidad en Camelot. 2015. (Casa De árbol Ser.: 29). (SPA., Illus.). 144p. (J). (gr. 2-4). pap. 5.99 (978-1-63245-532-1(3)) Lectorum Pubns., Inc.
—Night of the Ninth Dragon. Murdocca, Sal, illus. 2016. (Magic Tree House Merlin Missions Ser.: No. 27). (ENG.). 144p. (J). (gr. 2-5). 13.99 (978-0-553-51089-8(4), Random Hse. Bks. for Young Readers) Random Hse. Children's Bks.
—Osos Polares Despues de la Medianoche. 2005. (Casa del Arbol Ser.: 12).Tr. of Polar Bears Past Bedtime. (SPA.). (J). pap. 5.99 (978-1-930332-99-7(8)) Lectorum Pubns., Inc.
—Piratas Despues Del Mediodia. 2004. (Casa del Arbol Ser.: 4). (SPA.). (J). pap. 5.99 (978-1-930332-52-2(1)) Lectorum Pubns., Inc.
—Revolutionary War on Wednesday. unabr. ed. 2004. (Magic Tree House Ser.: No. 22). 69p. (J). (gr. k-3). pap. 17.00 incl. audio (978-0-8072-0931-8(7), S FTR 254 SP, Listening Library) Random Hse. Audio Publishing Group.
—Summer of the Sea Serpent. Murdocca, Sal, illus. 2011. (Magic Tree House Merlin Mission Ser.: No. 3). (ENG.). 144p. (J). (gr. 2-5). 5.99 (978-0-375-86491-9(1), Random Hse. Bks. for Young Readers) Random Hse. Children's Bks.
—Twister on Tuesday. 2004. (Magic Tree House Ser.: No. 23). 70p. (J). (gr. k-3). pap. 17.00 incl. audio (978-0-8072-9932-6(4), Listening Library) Random Hse. Audio Publishing Group.
—Vacaciones Al Pie de un Volcan. Brovelli, Marcela, tr. from ENG. Murdocca, Sal, illus. 2007. (Casa del Arbol Ser.: 13).Tr. of Vacation under the Colcano. (SPA.). 74p. (J). per. 5.99 (978-1-933032-19-1(7)) Lectorum Pubns., Inc.
—Vacation under the Volcano. unabr. ed. 2004. (Magic Tree House Ser.: No. 13). 74p. (J). (gr. k-3). pap. 17.00 incl. audio (978-0-8072-0782-6(9), LFTR 241 SP, Listening Library) Random Hse. Audio Publishing Group.
—Viking Ships at Sunrise. unabr. ed. 2004. (Magic Tree House Ser.: No. 15). 71p. (J). (gr. k-3). pap. 17.00 incl. audio (978-0-8072-0784-0(5), LFTR 243 SP, Listening Library) Random Hse. Audio Publishing Group.
—Winter of the Ice Wizard. Murdocca, Sal, illus. 2011. (Magic Tree House Merlin Mission Ser.: 4). (ENG.). 144p. (J). (gr. 2-5). 5.99 (978-0-375-87395-9(3), Random Hse. Bks. for Young Readers) Random Hse. Children's Bks.
Osborne, Mary Pope & Osborne, Magic Tree. Dark Day in the Deep Sea. Murdocca, Sal, illus. 2009. (Magic Tree House Merlin Mission Ser.: 11). (ENG.). 144p. (J). (gr. 2-5). 5.99 (978-0-375-83732-6(9), Random Hse. Bks. for Young Readers) Random Hse. Children's Bks.
Osborne, Mary Pope & PLC Editors Staff. Carnival at Candlelight. Murdocca, Sal, illus. 2006. (Magic Tree House Merlin Missions Ser.: No. 5). 105p. (gr. 2-6). 15.00 (978-0-7569-6690-4(6)) Perfection Learning Corp.
Osborne, Mary Pope, et al. Buenos Días, Gorilas. Murdocca, Sal, illus. 2014. 26. (SPA.). 88p. (J). (gr. 2-4). pap. 5.99 (978-1-933032-93-1(6)) Lectorum Pubns., Inc.
—Búfalos Antes Del Desayuno. Murdocca, Sal, illus. 2008. (Casa del Arbol Ser.: 18).Tr. of Buffalo Before Breakfast. (SPA.). (J). (gr. 2-4). pap. 5.99 (978-1-933032-48-1(0)) Lectorum Pubns., Inc.
—Carnaval a Media Luz. Murdocca, Sal, illus. 2016. (SPA.). (J). (gr. 2-4). pap. 5.99 (978-1-63245-643-4(5)) Lectorum Pubns., Inc.
—Maremoto en Hawái. Murdocca, Sal, illus. 2014. 28. (SPA.). 88p. (J). (gr. 2-4). pap. 5.99 (978-1-933032-95-5(2)) Lectorum Pubns., Inc.
—Miedo Escénico en una Noche de Verano. Murdocca, Sal, illus. 2014. 25. (SPA.). 86p. (J). (gr. 2-4). pap. 5.99 (978-1-933032-92-4(8)) Lectorum Pubns., Inc.
—Tigres Al Anochecer. Murdocca, Sal, illus. 2008. (Casa del Arbol Ser.: 19).Tr. of Tigers at Twilight. (SPA.). (J). (gr. 2-4). pap. 5.99 (978-1-933032-49-8(9)) Lectorum Pubns., Inc.
Osborne, Mary Pope, et al. Tormenta de Nieve en Luna Azul. Murdocca, Sal, illus. 2016. (SPA.). (J). (gr. 2-4). pap. 5.99 (978-1-63245-646-5(X)) Lectorum Pubns., Inc.
Parish, Herman. Amelia Bedelia Chapter Book #6: Amelia Bedelia Cleans Up (POB) Avril, Lynne, illus. 2015. (Amelia Bedelia Ser.). (ENG.). 160p. (J). (gr. 1-5). 9.99 (978-0-06-233403-9(4), Greenwillow Bks.) HarperCollins Pubs.
—Amelia Bedelia Cleans Up. Avril, Lynne, illus. 2015. (Amelia Bedelia Ser.). (ENG.). 160p. (J). (gr. 1-5). pap. 4.99 (978-0-06-233400-8(X), Greenwillow Bks.) HarperCollins Pubs.
Pittar, Gill. Milly, Molly & the Tree Hut (book W/dolls) 2006. 28p. pap. (978-1-86972-096-4(2)) Milly Molly Bks.
Plume, Ken, et al. There's a Zombie in My Treehouse! 2010. 52p. pap. 10.00 (978-0-557-28932-5(7)) Lulu Pr., Inc.
Rey, H. A. Builds a Tree House. 2017. (Curious George Ser.). (SPA & ENG., Illus.). 24p. (J). (gr. -1-3). 12.99 (978-0-544-97461-6(1), HMH Books For Young Readers) Houghton Mifflin Harcourt Publishing Co.
Rouillard, Wendy W. Barnaby's Tree House. 2005. (Illus.). 30p. (J). (978-0-9651070-4-4(3)) Barnaby & Co.
Rylant, Cynthia. Henry & Mudge & the Tall Tree House. Bracken, Carolyn, illus. 2003. (Henry & Mudge Ser.). (ENG.). 40p. (J). (gr. k-2). pap. 3.99 (978-0-689-83445-5(4), Simon Spotlight) Simon Spotlight.
—Henry & Mudge & the Tall Tree House. 2003. (Henry & Mudge Ready-To-Read Ser.: 21). (gr. k-3). lib. bdg. 13.55 (978-0-613-90605-0(5), Turtleback) Turtleback Bks.
Shoesmith-Bateman, Amanda. The Magic Tree House, 1 vol. Beitz-Grant, Heather, illus. 2010. 22p. 24.95 (978-1-4489-3866-7(X)) PublishAmerica, Inc.
Simon, Nadine. Flickers of True Destiny. 2010. 58p. pap. 11.95 (978-1-60860-948-2(0), Eloquent Bks.) Strategic Book Publishing & Rights Agency (SBPRA).
Soman, David. The Monster Next Door. 2016. (ENG., Illus.). 40p. (J). (-k). 17.99 (978-0-525-42783-4(X), Dial Bks) Penguin Young Readers Group.
Steinkraus, Kyla. La Casita Del Arbol. 2012. (SPA & ENG.). 24p. (gr. 2-3). pap. 8.95 (978-1-61810-539-4(6)) Rourke Educational Media.
—The Tree Fort. Reese, Bob, illus. 2011. (ENG.). 24p. (gr. 2-3). pap. 8.95 (978-1-61236-038-6(6)) Rourke Educational Media.
Stine, R. L. Stay Away from the Tree House & Eye of the Fortuneteller: Twice Terrifying Tales. 2009. (R. L. Stine's Ghosts of Fear Street Ser.). (ENG., Illus.). 224p. (J). (gr. 3-7). pap. 7.99 (978-1-4169-9137-3(9), Aladdin) Simon & Schuster Children's Publishing.
The Tree House Lab. 2003. (J). per. (978-1-57657-826-1(7)) Paradise Pr., Inc.
The Treehouse Club: Individual Title Six-Packs. (gr. -1-2). 23.00 (978-0-7635-8821-2(0)) Rigby Education.
Verburg, Bonnie. The Tree House That Jack Built. Teague, Mark, illus. 2014. (ENG.). 40p. (J). (gr. -1-k). 17.99 (978-0-439-85338-5(9), Orchard Bks.) Scholastic, Inc.
Volker, Kerstin. Henry Builds a Tree House. 2003. (Funny Friends Lift-and-Learn Bks.). (Illus.). 14p. (J). 5.99 (978-1-59384-023-5(3)) Parklane Publishing.
Weitzman, Jacqueline Preiss. Superhero Joe & the Creature Next Door. Barrett, Ron, illus. 2013. (ENG.). 32p. (J). (gr. -1-3). 16.99 (978-1-4424-1268-2(2), Simon & Schuster Bks. For Young Readers) Simon & Schuster Bks. For Young Readers.
Wolfe, Bradley W. Upside Downside Up. 2009. 144p. 27.99 (978-0-557-11670-6(8)) Lulu Pr., Inc.

TREE PLANTING

see also Trees

Ayers, Patricia. A Kid's Guide to How Trees Grow. 2003. (Digging in the Dirt Ser.). (Illus.). 24p. (J). (gr. -1-3). lib. bdg. 22.60 (978-0-8239-5463-6(3), PowerKids Pr.) Rosen Publishing Group, Inc., The.
Johnson, Jen Cullerton. Seeds of Change. Sadler, Sonia Lynn, illus. 2013. (ENG.). 40p. (J). (gr. 1-6). 18.95 (978-1-60060-367-9(X)) Lee & Low Bks., Inc.
Sévigny, Eric, illus. Caillou Plants a Tree. 2012. (Ecology Club Ser.). (ENG.). 24p. (J). (gr. -1-1). pap. 5.99 (978-2-89450-834-3(4)) Caillouet, Gerry.
Stamper, Judith Bauer. Growing Trees. Lowe, Wesley, illus. 2010. (J). (978-1-60617-127-1(5)) Teaching Strategies, LLC.

TREES

see also Forests and Forestry; Fruit Culture; Landscape Gardening; Leaves; Lumber and Lumbering; Nuts; Shrubs; Tree Planting; Wood

Aldrich, William & Williamson, Don. Tree & Shrub Gardening for Illinois, 1 vol., Vol. 1. rev. ed. 2004. (ENG., Illus.). 352p. (gr. 4). pap. 18.95 (978-1-55105-404-9(3), 1551054043) Lone Pine Publishing USA.
Allison, R. Bruce. If Trees Could Talk: Stories about Wisconsin Trees. 2009. (ENG., Illus.). 80p. (J). (gr. 1-5). pap. 15.95 (978-0-87020-419-7(X)) Wisconsin Historical Society.
Andrews, Alexa. In the Forest. Keimig, Candice, illus. 2013. (Penguin Young Readers, Level 1 Ser.). (ENG.). 32p. (J). (gr. k-1). pap. 3.99 (978-0-448-46719-1(4), Penguin Young Readers) Penguin Young Readers Group.
Ashley, Michele. When Do Trees Look Different? 2014. (Little Books of Answers: Level d Ser.). (Illus.). 16p. (gr. k-2). pap. 7.95 (978-1-927136-38-6(5)) Three Crows Media NZL. Dist: RiverStream Publishing.
Bachmann, Elaine Rice. While a Tree Grew: The Story of Maryland's Wye Oak, 1 vol. Harrell, Kim, illus. 2009. (ENG.). 30p. (gr. -1-3). 10.50 (978-0-87033-577-8(4), 9780870335778, Cornell Maritime Pr./Tidewater Pubs.) Schiffer Publishing, Ltd.
Baumbusch, Brigitte. Trees in Art. 2005. (What Makes a Masterpiece? Ser.). (Illus.). 32p. (gr. 1-4). lib. bdg. 23.00 (978-0-8368-4449-8(1), Gareth Stevens Learning Library) Stevens, Gareth Publishing LLLP.
Berne, Emma. From Cone to Pine Tree. 2017. (Start to Finish, Second Ser.). (ENG.). (J). (gr. k-3). pap. 6.99 (978-1-5124-5622-6(5)) Lerner Publishing Group.
Berne, Emma Carlson. From Cone to Pine Tree. 2017. (Start to Finish, Second Ser.). (ENG.). 24p. (J). (gr. k-3). 23.99 (978-1-5124-3444-6(2)) Lerner Publishing Group.
Bernhard, Durga Yael. Just Like Me, Climbing a Tree: Exploring Trees Around the World, Vol. 2015. (ENG., Illus.). 32p. (J). (gr. k-2). 16.95 (978-1-937786-34-2(X), Wisdom Tales) World Wisdom, Inc.
Boothroyd, Jennifer. In a Tree. 2006. (First Step Nonfiction - Animal Homes Ser.). (ENG., Illus.). 8p. (gr. -1-1). pap. 4.95 (978-0-8225-5663-3(4), Lerner Pubns.) Lerner Publishing Group.
Bowman, Debbie. The Happy Tree. 2013. 20p. pap. 8.99 (978-1-62509-760-6(3)) Salem Author Services.

Bredeson, Carmen & Cousins, Lindsey. Can You Find These Trees? 2012. (All about Nature Ser.). 24p. (J). (gr. -1-1). (Illus.). pap. 7.95 *(978-1-4644-0070-4(9)*, Enslow Elementary); 22.60 *(978-0-7660-3981-0(1))* Enslow Pubs., Inc.

Broutin, Chistian, illus. Trees. 2012. (ENG.). 38p. (J). (gr. -1-k). spiral bd. 12.99 *(978-1-85103-401-7(3))* Moonlight Publishing, Ltd. GBR. Dist: Independent Pubs. Group.

Broutin, Christian & de Bourgoing, Pascale. El Arbol. (Coleccion Mundo Maravilloso). (SPA., Illus.). 40p. (J). (gr. 2-4). *(978-84-348-4056-0(1)*, AR9290) SM Ediciones.

Brown, Carron. Secrets of the Apple Tree. Nassner, Alyssa, illus. 2014. (ENG.). 36p. (J). 12.99 *(978-1-61067-243-6(7))* Kane Miller.

Buckley, Arabella B. Trees & Shrubs. 2008. (Illus.). 88p. pap. 11.95 *(978-1-59915-275-2(4))* Yesterday's Classics.

Bullard, Lisa. The Redwood Forests. 2010. (Lightning Bolt Books (tm) — Famous Places Ser.). (ENG.). 32p. (gr. k-2). lib. bdg. 26.60 *(978-0-7613-4452-0(7)*, Lerner Pubns.) Lerner Publishing Group.

Burnie, David. DK Eyewitness Books: Tree. 2015. (DK Eyewitness Bks.). (ENG., Illus.). 72p. (J). (gr. 3-7). pap. 9.99 *(978-1-4654-3847-8(5)*, DK Children) Dorling Kindersley Publishing, Inc.

Cain, Marie Mowery. Tremendous Trees. 2013. (Big Books, Red Ser.). (ENG & SPA., Illus.). 16p. pap. 33.00 *(978-1-59246-219-3(7))* Big Books, by George!

Cardenas, Ernesto A. Wood or Paper? 2009. 23.95 *(978-1-60698-059-0(9))*; pap. 4.95 *(978-1-60698-057-6(2))* Milo Educational Bks. & Resources.

Chapman. Seasons & Woodman. 2010. (ENG.). 88p. pap. 35.99 *(978-0-521-14142-0(7))* Cambridge Univ. Pr.

Claybourne, Anna. I Love This Tree: Discover the Life, Beauty & Importance of Trees. 2017. (ENG., Illus.). 64p. (J). (gr. 4-6). pap. 12.99 *(978-1-4451-5265-3(7)*, Franklin Watts) Hachette Children's Group GBR. Dist: Hachette Bk. Group.

Colby, Jennifer. Trees. 2014. (21st Century Junior Library: Plants Ser.). (ENG.). 24p. (J). (gr. 2-5). 25.64 *(978-1-63188-041-4(1)*, 205571) Cherry Lake Publishing.

Collinson, Clare. British Trees & Flowers. 2017. (Nature in Your Neighbourhood Ser.). (ENG., Illus.). 32p. (J). (gr. 2-4). 17.99 *(978-1-4451-3641-7(4)*, Franklin Watts) Hachette Children's Group GBR. Dist: Hachette Bk. Group.

Conroy, Jim & Alexander, Basia. Messages from Trees Set 1: A Coloring Book for the Young & Young-At-Heart. 2013. (ENG., Illus.). 32p. (J). pap. 8.00 *(978-0-9834114-5-1(X))* Plant Kingdom Communications.

Cornell, Kari. Big Trees. 2016. (Illus.). 24p. (J). *(978-0-87659-702-6(9))* Gryphon Hse., Inc.

Dawson, Emily C. Birds & Trees. 2010. (Our Animal World Ser.). 24p. (J). 25.65 *(978-1-60753-010-7(4))* Amicus Publishing.

Delano, Marfe Ferguson. Explore My World a Tree Grows Up. 2016. (Explore My World Ser.). (ENG., Illus.). 32p. (J). (gr. -1-2). pap. 4.99 *(978-1-4263-2429-1(4)*, National Geographic Children's Bks.) National Geographic Society.

DePalma, Mary Newell. A Grand Old Tree. 2005. (ENG., Illus.). 32p. (J). (gr. -1-3). 17.99 *(978-0-439-62334-6(0)*, Levine, Arthur A. Bks.) Scholastic, Inc.

Dreyer, Ellen. Grow, Tree, Grow! Swanson, Maggie, tr. Swanson, Maggie, illus. 2003. (Hello Reader! Ser.). (J). *(978-0-439-43964-0(7))* Scholastic, Inc.

Edwards, Nicola. Trees. 2007. (See How Plants Grow Ser.). (Illus.). 24p. (J). (gr. 3-7). lib. bdg. 22.60 *(978-1-4042-3571-7(X))* Rosen Publishing Group, Inc., The.

Fletcher, Patricia. Bristlecone Pines Are Ancient! 2016. (World's Weirdest Plants Ser.). 00024p. (J). pap. 8.15 *(978-1-4824-5599-1(4))* Stevens, Gareth Publishing LLLP.

Flounders, Anne. Healthy Trees, Healthy Planet. 2014. (Our Green Earth Ser.). (Illus.). 32p. (gr. 2-4). pap. 8.95 *(978-1-939656-32-2(X))* Red Chair Pr.

Fredericks, Anthony D. Around One Log: Chipmunks, Spiders, & Creepy Insiders, 1 vol. DiRubbio, Jennifer, illus. 2011. 32p. (J). (gr. -1-5). (ENG.). 16.95 *(978-1-58469-137-2(9))*; pap. 8.95 *(978-1-58469-138-9(7))* Dawn Pubns.

Fretland VanVoorst, Jenny. Los árboles en la Primavera. 2015.Tr. of Trees in Spring. (SPA., Illus.). 24p. (J). lib. bdg. *(978-1-62031-251-3(4)*, Bullfrog Bks.) Jump! Inc.

—Trees in Spring. 2015. (Illus.). 24p. (J). lib. bdg. *(978-1-62031-237-7(9)*, Bullfrog Bks.) Jump! Inc.

Gardner, Robert. Temperate Forest Experiments: 8 Science Experiments in One Hour or Less. 2014. (Last Minute Science Projects with Biomes Ser.). 48p. (J). (gr. 5-12). 25.27 *(978-0-7660-5922-1(7))* Enslow Pubs., Inc.

—Temperate Forest Experiments: 8 Science Experiments in One Hour or Less. 2014. (Last Minute Science Projects with Biomes Ser.). (Illus.). 48p. (YA). (gr. 5-12). pap. 8.95 *(978-0-7660-5923-8(5)*, Enslow Elementary) Enslow Pubs., Inc.

Gerber, Carole. Leaf Jumpers. Evans, Leslie, illus. (ENG.). (J). 2017. 28p. (— 1). bds. 7.99 *(978-1-58089-782-2(7))* 2006. 32p. (gr. -1-2). per. 7.95 *(978-1-57091-498-0(2))* Charlesbridge Publishing, Inc.

Gillespie, Lisa. Trees. 2009. (Beginners Nature Ser.). 32p. (J). (gr. 1). 4.99 *(978-0-7945-2156-1(8)*, Usborne) EDC Publishing.

Gleisner, Jenna Lee. Trees in Fall. 2017. (Welcome, Fall! Ser.). (ENG.). 24p. (J). (gr. -1-2). lib. bdg. 27.07 *(978-1-5038-1663-3(X)*, 211500) Child's World, Inc., The.

Gould, Margee. Giant Plants. 2012. (Strangest Plants on Earth Ser.). (Illus.). 24p. (J). lib. bdg. 22.60 *(978-1-4488-4990-1(X))* Rosen Publishing Group, Inc., The.

Gregoire, Maryellen. Trees. 2011. (Wonder Readers Early Level Ser.). (ENG.). (gr. -1-1). 16p. pap. 35.94 *(978-1-4296-8196-4(9))*; 32p. pap. 5.99 *(978-1-4296-7830-8(5))* Capstone Press of Coughlan Cos. (Wonder Readers).

Gregory, Cam. Where Do Tall Trees Grow? 2014. (Little Books of Answers: Level C Ser.). (Illus.). 16p. (gr. k-2). pap. 7.95 *(978-1-927136-28-7(8))* Three Crows Media NZL. Dist: RiverStream Publishing.

Gregson, Margaret M. The Story of Our Trees: In Twenty-Four Lessons. 2013. (ENG., Illus.). 174p. pap. 35.99 *(978-1-107-66278-0(6))* Cambridge Univ. Pr.

Hall, Katharine. Árboles: Un Libro de Comparación y Contraste, 1 vol. 2015. (SPA.). 32p. (J). (gr. k-3). pap. 9.95 *(978-1-62855-469-4(X))* Arbordale Publishing.

Halter, Loretta. A Voice for the Redwoods. Bartczak, Peter, illus. 2010. (ENG.). 64p. (J). 18.95 *(978-0-9822942-0-8(4))* Nature's Hopes & Heroes.

Hawk, Fran. Count down to Fall, 1 vol. Neidigh, Sherry, illus. 2009. (ENG.). 32p. (J). (gr. -1-3). 16.95 *(978-1-934359-94-5(7))* Arbordale Publishing.

Henderson, Dave, illus. A Story of Three Trees: And the miracle of Prayer. 2005. (ENG.). 12p. (J). bds. 5.99 *(978-1-4037-1197-7(6)*, Spirit Pr.) Bendon, Inc.

Heos, Bridget. So You Want to Grow a Pie? Fabbri, Daniele, illus. 2015. (Grow Your Food Ser.). (ENG.). 24p. (gr. 1-3). 19.95 *(978-1-60753-739-7(7))* Amicus Publishing.

Hibbert, Clare. Trees, 01 vols., 1. 2016. (Adventures in Nature Ser.). (ENG.). 32p. (J). pap. 10.00 *(978-1-5081-4591-2(1)*, PowerKids Pr.) Rosen Publishing Group, Inc., The.

Hipp, Andrew. El Árbol del Olivo: Por Dentro y Por fuera. 2004. (Explora la Naturaleza (Getting into Nature) Ser.). (SPA., Illus.). 32p. lib. bdg. 25.25 *(978-1-4042-2865-8(9))* Rosen Publishing Group, Inc., The.

—Oak. 2004. (Getting into Nature Ser.). (Illus.). 32p. (J). lib. bdg. 25.25 *(978-0-8239-4206-0(6))* Rosen Publishing Group, Inc., The.

—Olive Tree. 2004. (Getting into Nature Ser.). (Illus.). 32p. (J). lib. bdg. 25.25 *(978-0-8239-4207-7(4))* Rosen Publishing Group, Inc., The.

—Olive Trees: Inside & Out. 2009. (Getting into Nature Ser.). 32p. (gr. 3-4). 47.90 *(978-1-61512-723-8(2)*, PowerKids Pr.) Rosen Publishing Group, Inc., The.

—El Roble: Por Dentro y Por Fuera. Gonzalez, Tomas, tr. from ENG. Dogi, Fiammetta, illus. 2004. (Explora la Naturaleza (Getting into Nature) Ser.). (SPA.). 27p. (J). (gr. 3-7). lib. bdg. 25.25 *(978-1-4042-2864-1(0))* Rosen Publishing Group, Inc., The.

Hiscock, Bruce. The Big Tree. Hiscock, Bruce, illus. 2003. (ENG., Illus.). 32p. (J). (gr. 2-4). pap. 9.95 *(978-1-56397-810-4(5))* Boyds Mills Pr.

Holden, Pam. Good Things from Trees. 2015. (ENG., Illus.). 16p. (-1). pap. *(978-1-77654-079-2(4)*, Red Rocket Readers) Flying Start Bks.

Holland, Trish. Trees: Count. 2010. (J). *(978-1-60617-128-8(3))* Teaching Strategies, LLC.

Howse, Jennifer. Trees. 2010. pap. 9.95 *(978-1-60596-917-6(6))*; 24p. (J). (gr. 2-4). lib. bdg. 25.70 *(978-1-60596-916-9(8))* Weigl Pubs., Inc.

Hubbell, Patricia. Every Orchard Tree. Broxon, Janet, illus. 2008. (J). *(978-1-55971-986-5(9)*, NorthWord Bks. for Young Readers) T&N Children's Publishing.

Hughes, Meredith Sayles. Hard to Crack: Nut Trees. 2005. (Plants We Eat Ser.). (Illus.). 104p. (gr. 6-9). 26.60 *(978-0-8225-2838-8(X))* Lerner Publishing Group.

—Tall & Tasty: Fruit Trees. 2005. (Plants We Eat Ser.). (Illus.). 104p. (gr. 6-9). 26.60 *(978-0-8225-2837-1(1))* Lerner Publishing Group.

Ingoglia, Gina. The Tree Book for Kids & Their Grown-Ups. 2013. (ENG., Illus.). 96p. (J). 15.95 *(978-1-889538-86-0(8))* Brooklyn Botanic Garden.

Kalman, Bobbie. El Ciclo de Vida del Árbol. 2005. (Serie Ciclos de Vida Ser.). (SPA., Illus.). 32p. (J). lib. bdg. *(978-0-7787-8665-8(X))* Crabtree Publishing Co.

Kalman, Bobbie, et al. Les Arbres. 2005. (Petit Monde Vivant Ser.). (FRE., Illus.). 32p. (J). pap. 9.95 *(978-2-89579-052-5(3))* Bayard Canada Livres CAN. Dist: Crabtree Publishing Co.

Kavanagh, James. Hawaii Trees & Wildflowers: A Folding Pocket Guide to Familiar Species. Leung, Raymond, illus. 2010. (Pocket Naturalist Guide Ser.). (ENG.). 1p. 6.95 *(978-1-58355-509-5(9))* Western National Parks Assn.

Kim, Tae-yeon. Mango Trees: Philippines. Cowley, Joy, ed. Muhn, Gu-seon, illus. 2015. (Global Kids Storybooks Ser.). (ENG.). 32p. (gr. 1-4). 7.99 *(978-1-925246-59-9(0))*; 26.65 *(978-1-925246-07-0(8))*; 26.65 *(978-1-925246-33-9(7))* ChoiceMaker Pty. Ltd., The AUS. (Big and SMALL). Dist: Lerner Publishing Group.

—Mango Trees: Philippines. Cowley, Joy, ed. Muhn, Gu-seon, illus. 2015. (Global Kids Storybooks Ser.). (ENG.). 32p. (J). (gr. 1-4). pap. 7.99 *(978-1-925233-46-9(4))* Lerner Publishing Group.

Klepeis, Alicia. Deciduous Trees & Coniferous Trees Explained. 2016. (Distinctions in Nature Ser.). (Illus.). 32p. (J). (gr. 3-3). 28.50 *(978-1-5026-1743-9(9))* Cavendish Square Publishing.

Lawley, Lacy. The Life Cycle of a Tree. 2013. (Rosen Readers Ser.). (ENG.). 24p. (J). (gr. 3-4). pap. 8.25 *(978-1-4777-2565-8(2))*; pap. 49.50 *(978-1-4777-2566-5(0))* Rosen Publishing Group, Inc., The. (Rosen Classroom).

Lawrence, Ellen. Extreme Trees. 2015. (Illus.). 24p. (J). lib. bdg. *(978-1-62724-306-3(2))* Bearport Publishing Co., Inc.

Lemniscates. Trees. Lemniscates, illus. 2017. (ENG., Illus.). 40p. (J). (-k). 14.99 *(978-0-7636-9001-4(5))* Candlewick Pr.

Lowery, Lawrence F. The Tree by Diane's House. 2015. (I Wonder Why Ser.). (ENG., Illus.). 36p. (J). (gr. k-3). pap. 11.95 *(978-1-941316-25-2(5))* National Science Teachers Assn.

MacDonald, Margaret. Deciduous & Evergreen Trees. 2011. (Learn-Abouts: Level 10 Ser.). (Illus.). 16p. (J). pap. 7.95 *(978-1-59920-603-5(X))* Black Rabbit Bks.

Macdonald, Margaret. When Does This Tree Grow Best? 2014. (Little Books of Answers: Level a Ser.). (Illus.). 16p. (gr. k-2). pap. 7.95 *(978-1-927136-04-1(0))* Three Crows Media NZL. Dist: RiverStream Publishing.

Marsico, Katie. The Oldest & the Newest. 2015. (True Book(tm) — Extreme Places Ser.). (ENG., Illus.). 48p. (J). pap. 6.95 *(978-0-531-21785-6(X)*, Children's Pr.) Scholastic Library Publishing.

Matinkhah, Sue Ann. Plant a Tree & Watch It Grow. 2013. 28p. pap. 16.95 *(978-1-4624-0676-0(9)*, Inspiring Voices) Author Solutions, Inc.

Mattern, Joanne. How Pine Trees Grow. 2006. (How Plants Grow Ser.). (Illus.). 24p. (gr. k-2). pap. 8.15 *(978-0-8368-6340-6(2))*; lib. bdg. 22.00 *(978-0-8368-6333-8(X))* Stevens, Gareth Publishing LLLP. (Weekly Reader Leveled Readers).

—How Pine Trees Grow (Cómo crecen los Pinos) Cómo Crecen los Pinos. 2006. (How Plants Grow/ Como crecen las plantas Ser.). (ENG & SPA., Illus.). 24p. (gr. k-3). pap. 8.15 *(978-0-8368-6471-7(9)*, Weekly Reader Leveled Readers) Stevens, Gareth Publishing LLLP.

—How Pine Trees Grow/Cómo crecen los Pinos. 2006. (How Plants Grow/ Como crecen las plantas Ser.). (ENG & SPA., Illus.). 24p. (gr. k-3). lib. bdg. 22.00 *(978-0-8368-6464-9(6)*, Weekly Reader Leveled Readers) Stevens, Gareth Publishing LLLP.

McGinlay, Richard. My First Encyclopedia of Trees: A Great Big Book of Amazing Plants to Discover. 2017. (ENG., Illus.). 24p. (J). (gr. -1-12). pap. 7.99 ***(978-1-86147-825-2(9)***, Armadillo) Anness Publishing GBR. Dist: National Bk. Network.

Meierhenry, Mark V. & Volk, David. The Mystery of the Tree Rings. Folkerts, Jason, illus. 2008. 44p. (J). 13.95 *(978-0-9798940-0-8(X)*, South Dakota State Historical Society Pr.) South Dakota State Historical Society Pr.

Mellet, Peter. Find Out about Trees: With 18 Projects & More Than 250 Pictures. 2013. (ENG., Illus.). 64p. (J). (gr. 3-7). 9.99 *(978-1-84322-897-4(1))* Anness Publishing GBR. Dist: National Bk. Network.

Miller, Debbie S. Are Trees Alive? Schuett, Stacey, illus. 2003. (ENG.). 32p. (J). (gr. -1-3). 17.99 *(978-0-8027-8801-6(7)*, 9780802788016, Bloomsbury USA Childrens) Bloomsbury Publishing USA.

Mitchell, Melanie S. Oak Trees. (First Step Nonfiction Ser.). (Illus.). (gr. k-2). 2005. 24p. lib. bdg. 17.27 *(978-0-8225-4610-8(8))* 2003. 23p. (J). pap. 5.95 *(978-0-8225-4611-5(6)*, Lerner Pubns.) Lerner Publishing Group.

Moore, David. Expl on Your Own Trees Seeds & Leaves. 2009. (Explore on Your Own Ser.). (ENG.). (C). pap. 7.95 *(978-0-7362-5563-9(X))* National Geographic School Publishing, Inc.

Munson, Victoria. British Trees. 2016. (Nature Detective Ser.). (ENG., Illus.). 64p. (J). (gr. 2-4). pap. 9.99 *(978-0-7502-9325-9(X)*, Wayland) Hachette Children's Group GBR. Dist: Hachette Bk. Group.

Owen, Ruth. Science & Craft Projects with Trees & Leaves. 2013. (Get Crafty Outdoors Ser.). (ENG., Illus.). 32p. (J). (gr. k-3). 26.50 *(978-1-4777-0248-2(2))*; pap. 11.75 *(978-1-4777-0259-8(8))* Rosen Publishing Group, Inc., The. (PowerKids Pr.).

Pallotta, Jerry. Who Will Plant a Tree? Leonard, Tom, illus. 2010. (ENG.). 32p. (J). (gr. -1-2). 15.95 *(978-1-58536-502-9(5))* Sleeping Bear Pr.

Patton, Christopher. Jack Pine, 1 vol. Young, Cybèle, illus. 2007. (ENG.). 32p. (J). (gr. 1-7). 18.95 *(978-0-88899-780-7(9))* Groundwood Bks. CAN. Dist: Publishers Group West (PGW).

Payne, Kimberley J. Trees of the Book: Learning from God's Creation. 2013. 28p. pap. *(978-1-896213-73-6(1))* Praise Publishing.

Pearson Learning Staff, creator. Trees & Leaves. 2005. (IOpeners Ser.). (J). pap. 7.56 *(978-0-7652-5136-7(1))* Celebration Pr.

Petersen, Christine. Trees. 2008. (21st Century Junior Library: Plants Ser.). (ENG.). 24p. (gr. 2-5). lib. bdg. 25.64 *(978-1-60279-274-6(7)*, 200179) Cherry Lake Publishing.

Pipe, Jim. You Wouldn't Want to Live Without Trees! 2016. (You Wouldn't Want to Live Without Ser.). lib. bdg. 20.80 *(978-0-606-38720-0(X))* Turtleback Bks.

Pourquié, Bernadette & Gambini, Cécile. Strange Trees: And the Stories Behind Their Names. Broad, Yolanda Stern, tr. from FRE. 2016. (ENG., Illus.). 40p. (J). (gr. 3-6). 16.95 *(978-1-61689-459-7(8))* Princeton Architectural Pr.

Preus, Margi. Celebritrees: Historic & Famous Trees of the World. Gibbon, Rebecca, illus. 2011. (ENG.). 40p. (J). (gr. 2-4). 16.99 *(978-0-8050-7829-9(0)*, 9780805078299, Holt, Henry & Co. Bks. For Young Readers) Holt, Henry & Co.

Pugliano-Martin, Carol. Discover the Life Cycle of Pine Trees. 2006. (English Explorers Ser.). (J). pap. *(978-1-4108-6473-4(1))* Benchmark Education Co.

—The Life Cycle of Pine Trees. 2006. (English Explorers Ser.). (J). pap. *(978-1-4108-6470-3(7))* Benchmark Education Co.

Rechenbaeume-Terme-Texte. (Duden-Schuelerhilfen Ser.). (GER.). 96p. (J). (gr. 5-6). *(978-3-411-02621-0(9))* Bibliographisches Institut & F. A. Brockhaus AG DEU. Dist: International Bk. Import Service, Inc.

Richardson, Joy. Trees. 2005. (Variety of Life Ser.). (Illus.). 32p. (gr. 1-4). lib. bdg. 26.00 *(978-0-8368-4509-9(9)*, Gareth Stevens Learning Library) Stevens, Gareth Publishing LLLP.

Rushworth, Gary. The Life Cycle of Trees: Set Of 6. 2011. (Navigators Ser.). (J). pap. 44.00 net. *(978-1-4108-6223-5(2))* Benchmark Education Co.

—The Life Cycle of Trees: Text Pairs. 2008. (Bridges/Navigators Ser.). (J). (gr. 3). 94.00 *(978-1-4108-8364-3(7))* Benchmark Education Co.

Russo, Monica. Treecology: 30 Activities & Observations for Exploring the World of Trees & Forests. Byron, Kevin, photos by. 2016. (Young Naturalists Ser.). (ENG., Illus.). 144p. (J). (gr. 2). pap. 15.99 *(978-1-61373-396-7(8))* Chicago Review Pr., Inc.

Rustad, Martha E. H. What's in a Tree? 2015. (What's in There? Ser.). (ENG., Illus.). 24p. (gr. k-1). lib. bdg. 21.99 *(978-1-4914-6011-5(3)*, Pebble Bks.) Capstone Press of Coughlan Cos.

Saunders, Gary L. My Life with Trees: A Sylvan Journey. 2015. (ENG.). 256p. pap. *(978-1-55447-151-5(6))* Gaspereau Pr.

Schuh, Mari. Apples Grow on a Tree. 2011. (How Fruits & Vegetables Grow Ser.). (ENG.). 24p. (gr. k-1). pap. 35.70 *(978-1-4296-6182-9(8)*, Pebble Bks.) Capstone Press of Coughlan Cos.

Shapiro, Sara. What Do You See? A Book about the Seasons. 2009. (Illus.). 16p. (J). pap. *(978-0-545-16154-1(1))* Scholastic, Inc.

Sharp, Zoe, et al. In the Tree. 2007. (Windows on Literacy Ser.). (ENG., Illus.). 12p. (J). pap. 10.95 *(978-0-7922-8461-1(5))* CENGAGE Learning.

Shea, Therese. Watch Pine Trees Grow. 2011. (Watch Plants Grow! Ser.). (Illus.). 24p. (J). (gr. k-2). pap. 8.15 *(978-1-4339-4840-4(0))*; lib. bdg. 22.60 *(978-1-4339-4839-8(7))* Stevens, Gareth Publishing LLLP.

Singley, Judith M. A B C Trees. 2012. 32p. pap. 17.25 *(978-1-4669-4640-8(7))* Trafford Publishing.

Snow, Wesley. A Tree's Life. 2013. (InfoMax Readers Ser.). (ENG.). 24p. (J). (gr. 3-4). pap. 49.50 *(978-1-4777-2629-7(2)*, Rosen Classroom) Rosen Publishing Group, Inc., The.

Sohn, Emily & Rothbardt, Karen. Trees: Worlds Within Leaves. 2011. (IScience Readers Ser.). 24p. (J). (gr. k-2). lib. bdg. 21.27 *(978-1-59953-411-4(8))* Norwood Hse. Pr.

Spilsbury, Richard. Tree. Hanna, Gary, illus. 2013. (Look Inside Ser.). (ENG.). 32p. (gr. 1-3). 27.32 *(978-1-4329-7198-4(0))*; pap. 8.29 *(978-1-4329-7205-9(7))* Heinemann-Raintree. (Heinemann First Library).

Stamper, Judith Bauer. Growing Trees. Lowe, Wesley, illus. 2010. (J). *(978-1-60617-127-1(5))* Teaching Strategies, LLC.

—A Tree Is For- 2010. (J). *(978-1-60617-126-4(7))* Teaching Strategies, LLC.

Stevens, Kathryn. Christmas Trees. 2015. (Our Holiday Symbols Ser.). (ENG.). 24p. (J). (gr. 1-4). 25.64 *(978-1-63143-742-7(9)*, 208551) Child's World, Inc., The.

Stockland, Patricia M. Look at a Birch Tree. 2012. (First Step Nonfiction - Look at Trees Ser.). (ENG., Illus.). 8p. (gr. -1-1). pap. 4.95 *(978-1-4677-0524-0(1)*, Lerner Pubns.) Lerner Publishing Group.

—Look at a Palm Tree. 2012. (First Step Nonfiction - Look at Trees Ser.). (ENG., Illus.). 8p. (gr. -1-1). pap. 4.95 *(978-1-4677-0523-3(3)*, Lerner Pubns.) Lerner Publishing Group.

—Look at a Pine Tree. 2012. (First Step Nonfiction - Look at Trees Ser.). (ENG., Illus.). 8p. (gr. -1-1). pap. 4.95 *(978-1-4677-0520-2(9)*, Lerner Pubns.) Lerner Publishing Group.

Sundance/Newbridge LLC Staff. Life in a Tree. 2007. (Early Science Ser.). (gr. k-3). 18.95 *(978-1-4007-6459-4(9))*; pap. 6.10 *(978-1-4007-6455-6(6))* Sundance/Newbridge Educational Publishing.

Tanem, Bob & Williamson, Don. Tree & Shrub Gardening for Northern California, 1 vol. rev. ed. 2003. (ENG., Illus.). 360p. (gr. 4). pap. 18.95 *(978-1-55105-275-5(X)*, 155105275X) Lone Pine Publishing USA.

Tate, Nikki. Deep Roots: How Trees Sustain Our Planet, 1 vol. 2016. (Orca Footprints Ser.). (ENG., Illus.). 48p. (J). (gr. 3-7). 19.95 *(978-1-4598-0582-8(8))* Orca Bk. Pubs. USA.

Tree. 2005. (J). *(978-0-9767139-0-6(X))* Britt Allcroft Productions.

Trees, Please! Level M, 6 vols. 128p. (gr. 2-3). 40.50 *(978-0-7699-1034-5(3))* Shortland Pubns. (U. S. A.) Inc.

Udry, Janice May & Udry, Janice M. Un Arbol es Hermoso, 1 vol. Fiol, Maria A., tr. Simont, Marc, illus. 2006.Tr. of Tree Is Nice. (SPA.). 32p. (J). (gr. -1-3). pap. 7.99 *(978-0-06-088708-7(7))* HarperCollins Pubs.

Veitch, Catherine. Learning about Trees, 1 vol. 2013. (Natural World Ser.). (ENG., Illus.). 24p. (J). (gr. -1-1). 22.65 *(978-1-4109-5402-2(1))*; pap. 6.95 *(978-1-4109-5407-7(2))* Heinemann-Raintree. (NA-r).

Voake, Charlotte, et al. A Little Guide to Trees. 2011. (ENG., Illus.). 80p. (J). (gr. -1-2). pap. 16.99 *(978-1-903919-82-8(7))* Transworld Publishers Ltd. GBR. Dist: Independent Pubs. Group.

Webb, Barbara & Webb, Barbara L. Trees: Earth's Lungs. 2010. (ENG., Illus.). 24p. (gr. k-2). pap. 8.95 *(978-1-61590-543-0(X))* Rourke Educational Media.

Weiss, Ellen. From Pinecone to Pine Tree. 2007. (Scholastic News Nonfiction Readers Ser.). (ENG., Illus.). 24p. (J). (gr. 1-2). 22.00 *(978-0-531-18537-7(0))* Scholastic Library Publishing.

—From Pit to Peach Tree. 2007. (Scholastic News Nonfiction Readers Ser.). (ENG., Illus.). 24p. (J). (gr. 1-2). pap. 6.95 *(978-0-531-18791-3(8))* Scholastic Library Publishing.

Whelan, Piper. Trees. (Illus.). 24p. (J). 2017. ***(978-1-5105-1408-9(2))*** 2016. *(978-1-5105-1411-9(2))* SmartBook Media, Inc.

Williams, Nancy Noel. Don't Lose It, Reuse It. 2010. *(978-1-60617-130-1(5))* Teaching Strategies, LLC.

Williams, Rachel. Little Pear Tree. Bowers, Jenny, illus. 2014. (ENG.). 12p. (J). (-k). bds. 14.99 *(978-0-7636-7126-6(6)*, Big Picture Press) Candlewick Pr.

Wood, Timothy D. & Beck, Alison. Tree & Shrub Gardening for Michigan, 1 vol. rev. ed. 2003. (ENG., Illus.). 352p. (gr. 4). pap. 18.95 *(978-1-55105-347-9(0)*, 1551053470) Lone Pine Publishing USA.

World Book, Inc. Staff, contrib. by. Trees of the United States & Canada. 2004. (World Book's Science & Nature Guides Ser.). (Illus.). 80p. (J). *(978-0-7166-4219-0(0))* World Bk., Inc.

Worth, Bonnie. I Can Name 50 Trees Today! All about Trees. Ruiz, Aristides & Mathieu, Joe, illus. 2006. (Cat in the Hat's Learning Library). (ENG.). 48p. (J). (gr. -1-3). 9.99 *(978-0-375-82277-3(1)*, Random Hse. Bks. for Young Readers) Random Hse. Children's Bks.

TREES—FICTION

Abel, Melanie. Kitten up a Tree. Lederhos, Anne, illus. 2008. 24p. (J). pap. 15.95 *(978-0-9791606-4-6(2))* E & E Publishing.

Adams, Lacole Sessions. Maggie & Her Tree. 2011. 28p. (gr. -1). pap. 15.29 *(978-1-4567-2416-0(9))* AuthorHouse.

Alexander, Carol. The Bean Trees. Friedland, Joyce & Kessler, Rikki, eds. 2007. (Novel-Ties Ser.). (Illus.). 35p. pap. 16.95 *(978-0-7675-3554-0(5))* Learning Links Inc.

Allamand, Maite. Alamito el Largo. (SPA.). (J). (gr. 2-3). pap. *(978-956-13-1428-3(2)*, AB3840) Bello, Andres CHL. Dist: Lectorum Pubns., Inc.

Alonso, Fernando. El Arbol de los Suenos. Urberuaga, Emilio, illus. 2005. (Alfaguara Juvenil Ser.).Tr. of Dream Trees. (SPA.). 124p. (J). (gr. 5-8). pap. 10.95 *(978-968-19-0978-9(X))* Santillana USA Publishing Co., Inc.

—El Arbol Que No Tenia Hojas (The Tree Without Leaves) (Superbks./Superlibros). (J). (gr. k-1). (SPA.). pap. 6.95 *(978-0-88272-469-0(X))*;Big Book. 21.95 *(978-0-88272-460-7(6))*;Big Book. (SPA.). 21.95 *(978-0-88272-459-1(2))* Santillana USA Publishing Co., Inc.

—The Tree Without Leaves. (Superbks./Superlibros). (Illus.). 16p. (J). (gr. k-3). pap. 6.95 *(978-0-88272-470-6(3))* Santillana USA Publishing Co., Inc.

Amo, Montserrat del. Montes, Pájaros y Amigos. 2007. (SPA.). 104p. (gr. 5-8). pap. 13.99 *(978-84-207-2788-2(1)*, GS6293) Grupo Anaya, S.A. ESP. Dist: Lectorum Pubns., Inc.

Ann. My Name Is Oak... Daytona Oak. 2013. 28p. pap. 24.95 *(978-1-63004-172-4(6))* America Star Bks.

Anna. The Magic Money Tree. 2009. (Illus.). 20p. pap. 15.49 *(978-1-4389-0472-6(X))* AuthorHouse.

Anna's Tree: Individual Title Six-Packs. (gr. 1-2). 25.00 *(978-0-7635-9134-2(3))* Rigby Education.

TUV

Applegate, Katherine. Wishtree. 2017. (ENG., Illus.). 224p. (J). 16.99 **(978-1-250-04322-1(0)**, 9781250043221) Feiwel & Friends.

Araque, Ana. My little Seed. 2009. 36p. pap. 21.99 *(978-1-4415-8537-0(0))* Xlibris Corp.

Arnold, Tedd. Dirty Gert. Arnold, Tedd, illus. (ENG., Illus.). (J). (gr. 2-5). 2014. 32p. 6.99 *(978-0-8234-3054-3(5))* 2013. 40p. 16.95 *(978-0-8234-2404-7(9))* Holiday Hse., Inc.

Arrington, Linda. Ugly Trees. Arrington, Linda, photos by. 2012. (Illus.). 24p. pap. 24.95 *(978-1-4626-8925-5(6))* America Star Bks.

Atwood, Margaret. Up in the Tree, 1 vol. (ENG., Illus.). 32p. (J). 2010. (gr. k-k). 19.95 *(978-1-55498-080-2(1))* 2006. (gr. -1-k). 14.95 *(978-0-88899-729-6(9))* Groundwood Bks. CAN. Dist: Publishers Group West (PGW).

Babel, Ann. Little Tree. 2011. 32p. pap. 12.99 *(978-1-4520-8781-8(4))* AuthorHouse.

Babin, Claire. Gus Is a Tree. Tallec, Olivier & Sorman, Joy, illus. 2009. (ENG.). 32p. (J). (gr. -1-2). 14.95 *(978-1-59270-078-3(0))* Enchanted Lion Bks., LLC.

Bailey, David J. The Storm. 2016. (ENG.). 190p. (J). pap. 11.95 *(978-1-78554-826-0(3),* 5b2b8f35-3768-4ec6-b355-c37d9c3384a8) Austin, Stan AUS. Dist: Bookmasters Distribution.

Bailey, Dawn Wentz. Joey & the Mighty Oak. 2008. 20p. pap. 24.95 *(978-1-60813-377-2(X))* PublishAmerica, Inc.

Bang, Molly. When Sophie's Feelings Are Really, Really Hurt. 2015. (ENG., Illus.). 40p. (J). (gr. -1-3). 17.99 *(978-0-545-78831-1(5),* Blue Sky Pr., The) Scholastic, Inc.

Barchers, Suzanne. The Brothers & the Star Fruit Tree: A Tale from Vietnam. Tablason, Jamie, illus. 2015. (Tales of Honor Ser.). (ENG.). 32p. (gr. 1-3). lib. bdg. 26.60 *(978-1-939656-83-4(4))* Red Chair Pr.

Barr, Carolyn Mims. The Waiting Tree. 2012. 20p. pap. 13.77 *(978-1-4669-5538-7(4))* Trafford Publishing.

Barron, T. A. Tree Girl. 2013. (ENG.). 144p. (J). (gr. 3-7). pap. 7.99 *(978-0-14-242708-8(X),* Puffin Books) Penguin Young Readers Group.

Beamish, Diane. The Treefellows. 2006. 35p. (J). pap. 14.28 *(978-1-4116-5967-4(8))* Lulu Pr., Inc.

Beard, Darleen Bailey & Malone, Heather Harms. Annie Glover Is Not a Tree Lover. Malone, Heather Harms, illus. 2009. (ENG., Illus.). 128p. (J). (gr. 2-5). 15.99 *(978-0-374-30351-8(7),* 9780374303518, Farrar, Straus & Giroux (BYR)) Farrar, Straus & Giroux.

Benedis-Grab, Daphne. The Angel Tree. 2014. (ENG.). 256p. (J). (gr. 3-7). 16.99 *(978-0-545-61378-1(7),* Scholastic Pr.) Scholastic, Inc.

Bennett, Earl. The Legend of Bucky the Beaver. 2009. 44p. pap. 12.95 *(978-1-4269-1669-4(8))* Trafford Publishing.

Bennett-Minnerly, Denise. The Color Tree. Bennett-Minnerly, Denise, illus. 2005. (Illus.). (J). 14.95 *(978-1-56290-328-2(4))* Crystal Productions.

Berger, Carin. The Little Yellow Leaf. Berger, Carin, illus. 2008. (ENG., Illus.). 40p. (J). (gr. -1-3). 16.99 *(978-0-06-145223-9(8),* Greenwillow Bks.) HarperCollins Pubs.

Berkes, Marianne. El árbol Que Trepó el Oso, 1 vol. Rietz, Kathleen, illus. 2012. (SPA.). 32p. (J). (gr. -1-3). 17.95 *(978-1-60718-679-3(9))* Arbordale Publishing.

—The Tree That Bear Climbed, 1 vol. Rietz, Kathleen, illus. 2012. 32p. (J). (gr. -1-3). (ENG & SPA.). 17.95 *(978-1-60718-528-4(8));* (ENG & SPA.). pap. 9.95 *(978-1-60718-537-6(7));* (SPA.). pap. 9.95 *(978-1-62855-426-7(6))* Arbordale Publishing.

Bishop, Helena Edwards. Simon & the Money Tree. 2012. (Illus.). 40p. pap. 18.95 *(978-1-4709-9783-0(5))* Lulu Pr., Inc.

Blackdog, J. M. Loni Talltree: The world's greatest tree Climber. 2012. 24p. pap. 14.99 *(978-1-4685-5319-2(4))* AuthorHouse.

Blyton, Enid. Up the Faraway Tree. (Illus.). 96p. (J). pap. 5.95 *(978-0-09-942720-9(6))* Random Hse. GBR. Dist: Trafalgar Square Publishing.

Boger-Bass, Vallerie. The Mustard Seed: A Christian Promise. Boger-Bass, Vallerie, illus. 2003. (Illus.). 40p. pap. 10.00 *(978-0-8059-5640-5(9))* Dorrance Publishing Co., Inc.

Brallier, Jess M. Tess's Tree. Reynolds, Peter H., illus. 2010. (JPN.). 28p. (J). *(978-4-07-269392-6(8))* Shufunotomo Company, Limited.

Brodsky, Kathy. My Bent Tree. Bennett, Cameron, illus. 2008. (ENG.). 44p. (J). 19.95 *(978-0-615-16066-5(2))* Helpingwords.

Brooke, Samantha. Apple-Picking Day! Durk, Jim, illus. 2007. (Clifford's Puppy Days Ser.). (J). *(978-0-545-02841-7(8))* Scholastic, Inc.

Brown, Margaret Wise. The Little Fir Tree. LaMarche, Jim, illus. 32p. (J). (gr. -1-1). 2005. lib. bdg. 16.89 *(978-0-06-028190-8(1))* 2005. (ENG.). 15.99 *(978-0-06-028189-2(8))* Vol. 2009. (ENG.). pap. 6.99 *(978-0-06-443529-1(6))* HarperCollins Pubs.

Brown, Palmer. The Silver Nutmeg. Brown, Palmer, illus. 2012. (ENG., Illus.). 152p. (J). (gr. k-4). 15.95 *(978-1-59017-500-2(X),* NYR Children's Collection) New York Review of Bks., Inc., The.

Bryant, Clorinda. Imaginary World: The Stone of Amajara. 2012. 252p. 30.50 *(978-0-557-54922-1(1))* Lulu Pr., Inc.

Buckingham, Royce. The Dead Boys. 2010. (ENG.). 208p. (J). (gr. 5-18). 16.99 *(978-0-399-25222-8(3),* G.P. Putnam's Sons Books for Young Readers) Penguin Young Readers Group.

Burgess, Thornton W. Blacky the Crow. 2011. 132p. 25.95 *(978-1-4638-9575-4(5))* Rodgers, Alan Bks.

—Happy Jack. 2011. 140p. 25.95 *(978-1-4638-9558-7(5))* Rodgers, Alan Bks.

Bushweller, Ellie. The Tree with A Hundred Hands. 2008. 40p. 18.50 *(978-0-615-24478-5(5))* Bushweller, Ellie.

Cabral, Jeane. Tree Hugs. 2009. (Jeane Cabral Bks.). (Illus.). (J). bds. 12.99 *(978-1-934650-08-0(0))* Just For Kids Pr., LLC.

Candy, Wolf. The Tree, the House & the Hurricane. I.t. ed. 2005. (Illus.). 24p. (J). 7.00 *(978-0-9762292-3-0(4))* New Global Publishing.

Cannon, K. L. Mr. Mortimer: The Grapevine That Wouldn't Die. 2005. (J). 4.95 *(978-0-9675594-2-1(1))* Cannon, K. L.

Cano, Carles & Cano Peiró, Carles. El Árbol de las Hojas Din A-4. (SPA., Illus.). 28p. (J). (gr. k-2). *(978-84-8464-027-1(2),* KA30310) Kalandraka Editora, S.L. ESP. Dist: Lectorum Pubns., Inc.

Cardin, Beth W. Little Red Leaf. 2010. 24p. 12.99 *(978-1-4520-7414-6(3))* AuthorHouse.

Caron, Susie. Twee' Eckstein, Joe, illus. 2013. 24p. (J). pap. 12.99 *(978-0-9889113-0-7(2))* Coda Grove Publishing.

Carr, Lawrence. Under the Peach Tree. 2006. pap. 8.00 *(978-0-8059-7019-7(3))* Dorrance Publishing Co., Inc.

Carrasco, Jose Manuel, illus. El viaje de las semillas. 2008. 48p. *(978-84-95225-83-2(2))* Saure, Jean-Francois Editor.

Carver, David. Leafy Leafs Where Is Lester?, 1 vol. Carver, Erin, illus. 2009. 34p. pap. 19.95 *(978-1-4489-2203-1(8))* PublishAmerica, Inc.

—Lester Returns Home with His New Friend La'doo, 1 vol. Carver, Erin, illus. 2010. 28p. 24.95 *(978-1-4489-6340-9(0))* PublishAmerica, Inc.

Cerimele, Ron. Winup. 2012. 28p. pap. 21.99 *(978-1-4771-1144-4(1))* Xlibris Corp.

Charley, Grace. The Trouble with Benny Bubble. 2007. (Illus.). 72p. per. 9.76 *(978-1-4251-0147-3(X))* Trafford Publishing.

Chase, et al. Angel in a Gum Tree. (Illus.). 32p. pap. 13.95 *(978-1-86368-222-0(8))* Fremantle Pr. AUS. Dist: Independent Pubs. Group.

Chering, Don. The Acorn That Doubted. 2008. 32p. pap. 14.49 *(978-1-4389-0493-1(2))* AuthorHouse.

Christmas Book - Christmas Tree. 2005. (J). bds. *(978-1-4194-0073-5(8))* Paradise Pr., Inc.

Church, Bryan. The Dreamcatcher Bowl. 2009. 54p. pap. 9.99 *(978-0-557-07517-1(3))* Lulu Pr., Inc.

Clauson, Marilyn & Drake, Lana. Woody Acorn. Drake, Lana, illus. 2012. (Illus.). 48p. 24.95 *(978-1-4626-9647-5(3))* America Star Bks.

Coffey, Joe. Lynnie Leonardson & the Weeping Willow. Selby, Shannon, illus. 2011. 44p. pap. 24.95 *(978-1-4560-6487-7(8))* America Star Bks.

Cole, Henry. The Littlest Evergreen. Cole, Henry, illus. 2011. (ENG., Illus.). 32p. (J). (gr. -1-2). 16.99 *(978-0-06-114619-0(6),* Tegen, Katherine Bks) HarperCollins Pubs.

—The Littlest Evergreen. 2010. (J). lib. bdg. 18.89 *(978-0-06-114620-6(X))* HarperCollins Pubs.

Colfer, Chris. The Curvy Tree. Dorman, Brandon, illus. 2015. (ENG.). 32p. (J). (gr. -1-3). 17.00 *(978-0-316-40685-7(6))* Little Brown & Co.

Coll-Seck, Jayden. A Tree's Tale, 01 vols., 1. 2016. (Rosen REAL Readers: STEM & STEAM Collection). (ENG.). 8p. (J). pap. 5.46 *(978-1-5081-1397-3(1),* Rosen Classroom) Rosen Publishing Group, Inc., The.

Corley, Sandra J. The Scrawny Little Tree. 2011. 28p. pap. 16.95 *(978-1-4497-1274-7(6),* WestBow Pr.) Author Solutions, Inc.

Costa, Nicoletta. The Little Tree That Would Not Share. Costa, Nicoletta, illus. 2016. (ENG., Illus.). 32p. (J). 16.95 *(978-0-8234-3549-4(0))* Holiday Hse., Inc.

Coulton, Mia. Danny's Special Tree. Coulton, Mia, photos by. 2008. (ENG., Illus.). pap. 6.95 *(978-1-933624-25-9(6))* Maryruth Bks., Inc.

Coutin, Gustavo. When I climb a Tree. 2011. 20p. 12.00 *(978-1-4567-4303-1(1))* AuthorHouse.

Cruikshank, Fran. The Tale of the Not-So-Perfect Christmas Tree. Olson, Tom, illus. 2005. 17p. (J). 9.95 *(978-1-59971-055-6(2))* Aardvark Global Publishing.

Cuccia, Louis J. The Bottle Tree. 2003. (Illus.). 106p. (J). per. *(978-0-9727415-1-4(8))* Cuccia, Louis.

Cuniffe, April. Willy the Weeping Willow. 2008. 36p. pap. 24.95 *(978-1-60441-613-8(0))* America Star Bks.

Curry, Kenneth. The Legend of the Dancing Trees: An African American Folk Tale. 2007. 111p. (J). per. 14.95 *(978-0-9798364-0-4(9))* Curry Brothers Publishing Group.

Curry, Kenneth, et al. The Legend of the Dancing Tees Teachers Resource: The Legend of the Dancing Trees. 2007.Tr. of Teachers Resource. per. 19.95 *(978-0-9798364-1-1(7))* Curry Brothers Publishing Group.

Curto Family, The & Fischer, Rusty. One Little Christmas Tree. 2012. 26p. pap. 9.99 *(978-0-9840338-1-2(5))* Good Times at Home LLC.

Cyr, Joe. Magical Trees & Crayons: Great Stories. 2006. (Illus.). pap. 9.95 *(978-0-9778525-6-7(3))* Peppertree Pr., The.

Darling, Pollyanna. Heartwood. Chalmers, Kirsty, illus. 2013. 66p. (J). pap. *(978-0-9871164-4-4(4))* Imaginaria.

Daugherty, Doug. Boxy: A Tree of the Prairie. Gasal, Ben, illus. 2008. 24p. pap. 24.95 *(978-1-60610-808-6(5))* PublishAmerica, Inc.

Davenport, Kelly. Do Hotdogs Grow on Trees? 2010. 32p. pap. 17.99 *(978-1-4520-6636-3(1))* AuthorHouse.

Davis, Lynda S. & Weisel, Kaitlyn E. Christopher James Mcabee & the Wonderful Tree. Trone, Melody Kams, illus. 2013. 54p. pap. 6.99 *(978-0-9889907-0-8(9))* Sruvis Publishing.

Dawson, Jennifer. Silly Sally Sue. 2013. 24p. pap. 24.95 *(978-1-62709-938-7(7))* America Star Bks.

De Fombelle, Timothée. Toby Alone. Ardizzone, Sarah, tr. from FRE. Place, Francois, illus. 2009. (ENG.). 400p. (J). (gr. 4-7). 17.99 *(978-0-7636-4181-8(2))* Candlewick Pr.

—Toby & the Secrets of the Tree. Ardizzone, Sarah, tr. from FRE. Place, Francois, illus. 2010. (ENG.). 432p. (J). (gr. 4-7). 16.99 *(978-0-7636-4655-4(5))* Candlewick Pr.

de Lint, Charles. The Cats of Tanglewood Forest. 2014. (J). lib. bdg. 22.10 *(978-0-606-36532-1(X))* Turtleback Bks.

Decola, Diane. Butterfly. 2008. 180p. pap. 15.99 *(978-1-4389-0715-4(X))* AuthorHouse.

Dee, Carolyn. The Tree Who Couldn't Choose. 2008. 36p. pap. 15.49 *(978-1-4389-2950-7(1))* AuthorHouse.

Deluna, Alicia C. Tippy Gets a Friend. 2012. 20p. pap. 17.99 *(978-1-4685-5513-4(8))* AuthorHouse.

Derrick, Patricia. Farley the Ferret of Farkleberry Farm. Martinez, J-P Loppo, illus. 2007. 32p. (J). (gr. -1-3). 18.95 incl. audio compact disk *(978-1-933818-12-2(3))* Animalations.

Desrochers, Diane O. The Little Tree That Would Be Great. Boucher, Julie, illus. 2009. 36p. pap. 14.95 *(978-0-9819727-7-0(2))* Fiction Publishing, Inc.

Dixon, Bob. Rooty the Tree Troll. 2009. 28p. pap. 13.99 *(978-1-4389-9129-0(0))* AuthorHouse.

Doman, Dave. Tree Talkers: A Christmas Story, 1 vol. Swope, Brenda, illus. 2009. 32p. pap. 24.95 *(978-1-61546-180-6(9))* America Star Bks.

Drane, John Wanzer. Sassafras & Chicory. 2012. 32p. pap. 13.00 *(978-0-578-10633-5(7))* Drane, John Wanzer.

Duvall, John. The Great Spruce. Gibbon, Rebecca, illus. 2016. (ENG.). 40p. (J). (gr. k-3). 17.99 *(978-0-399-16084-4(1),* G.P. Putnam's Sons Books for Young Readers) Penguin Young Readers Group.

Edgren, Elizabeth. Little Tree's Mightiest Deed. Penk, Kathryn, illus. 2009. 36p. pap. 12.95 *(978-1-59858-825-5(7))* Dog Ear Publishing, LLC.

Ehlert, Lois. Pie in the Sky. 2004. (ENG., Illus.). 40p. (J). (gr. -1-3). 17.99 *(978-0-15-216584-0(3))* Houghton Mifflin Harcourt Publishing Co.

Ellen, Connie. Marvel Mansion Gang. 2012. 114p. 22.19 *(978-1-4269-6666-8(0))* Trafford Publishing.

Ellis, Leanne Statland. Tree Huggers. 2010. (J). pap. *(978-0-88092-521-1(3))* Royal Fireworks Publishing Co.

Emerson, Carl. The Cold Winter Day, 1 vol. Doerrfeld, Cori, illus. 2008. (Read-It! Readers: Science Ser.). (ENG.). 32p. (gr. k-2). lib. bdg. 21.32 *(978-1-4048-2627-4(0),* Easy Readers) Picture Window Bks.

Emma's Problem, 6, Pack. (Literatura 2000 Ser.). (gr. 1-2). 28.00 *(978-0-7635-0131-0(X))* Rigby Education.

Erickson, Patricia. The Little Christmas Tree. 2012. 24p. (-18). pap. 17.99 *(978-1-4772-8610-4(1))* AuthorHouse.

Evert, Jeffrey. The Tree That Didn't Want to Be. 2004. pap. 9.00 *(978-0-8059-6189-8(5))* Dorrance Publishing Co., Inc.

Félix, Lucie. Apples & Robins. 2016. (ENG., Illus.). 56p. (J). (gr. k-3). 16.99 *(978-1-4521-3264-8(X))* Chronicle Bks. LLC.

Fields, Trisha A. Eggbert, the Hero. 2012. 44p. pap. 21.99 *(978-1-4771-3548-8(0))* Xlibris Corp.

Fischer, Lavanya Regunathan. One Tree, One King & the Open Road. 2015. 212p. 14.99 *(978-93-5177-028-2(1))* HarperCollins Pubs.

Fisher, Phyllis Mae Richardson. Twiglet the Little Christmas Tree. Fisher, Phyllis Mae Richardson & Fisher, Douglas W., illus. 2003. (J). 30.00 *(978-0-9745615-1-6(7),* Twiglet The Little Christmas Tree); 186p. 12.00 *(978-0-9745615-4-7(1))* PJs Corner.

Fitzgerald, J. Rupert, the Sturdy Oak Tree: Who thought he was a little better than the other Trees. 2010. 16p. (J). pap. 14.95 *(978-1-4327-5734-2(2))* Outskirts Pr., Inc.

Fitzmartin, Elisa D. God's Silent Soldier. 2012. 32p. pap. 13.99 *(978-1-4497-3913-3(X),* WestBow Pr.) Author Solutions, Inc.

Fleischman, Paul. The Birthday Tree. Root, Barry, illus. 2008. (ENG.). 40p. (J). (gr. -1-3). 16.99 *(978-0-7636-2604-4(X))* Candlewick Pr.

Fleming, Chula. Spooky Old Tree, 1 vol. 2010. 26p. pap. 24.95 *(978-1-4489-9166-2(8))* PublishAmerica, Inc.

Forbes, Chris. El Tronco de Arbol, Level 1. Flor Ada, Alma, tr. Sullivan, Don, illus. 2003. (Dejame Leer Ser.). (SPA.). 8p. (J). (gr. -1-k). 6.50 *(978-0-673-36300-8(7),* Good Year Bks.) Celebration Pr.

Ford, RoShawn T. Marty & the Magical Christmas Tree. 2012. 24p. pap. 17.99 *(978-1-4772-3719-9(4))* AuthorHouse.

Formento, Alison. This Tree Counts!, 1 vol. Snow, Sarah, illus. 2010. (These Things Count! Ser.). (ENG.). 32p. (J). (gr. -1-3). 16.99 *(978-0-8075-7890-2(8))* Whitman, Albert & Co.

Fortuna, Lorna. When God Spoke to Trees. 2006. 17.00 *(978-0-8059-9884-9(5))* Dorrance Publishing Co., Inc.

Fowles, Shelley. Climbing Rosa. 2009. (ENG., Illus.). 32p. (J). (gr. -1-2). pap. 7.95 *(978-1-84507-595-8(1),* Frances Lincoln) Quarto Publishing Group UK GBR. Dist: Hachette Bk. Group.

Freedman, Georgene. The Olive Tree. 2nd num. ed. 2006. (J). per. 12.95 *(978-0-9771322-1-8(8))* Simpatico Bks.

French, Joyce. The Popcorn Tree. Hansen, Paisley, illus. 2012. 22p. 15.95 *(978-1-60414-639-4(7))* Fideli Publishing, Inc.

French, S. Terrell. Operation Redwood. 2011. (ENG.). 368p. (J). (gr. 3-7). pap. 9.95 *(978-0-8109-9720-2(7),* Amulet Bks.) Abrams, Inc.

French, Vivian. Morris in the Apple Tree. Villet, Olivia, illus. 2011. (ENG.). 64p. (J). pap. 5.99 *(978-0-00-718027-1(6))* HarperCollins Pubs. Ltd. GBR. Dist: HarperCollins Pubs.

Frisch, Aaron. The Lonely Pine. Delessert, Etienne, illus. 2011. (ENG.). 32p. (J). (gr. 1-3). 17.99 *(978-1-56846-214-1(X),* Creative Editions) Creative Co., The.

Fuggle, Debbie. The Two Little Fir Trees. 2012. 28p. pap. 32.70 *(978-1-4691-3253-2(2))* Xlibris Corp.

Galbraith, Kathryn O. Arbor Day Square, 1 vol. Moore, Cyd, illus. 2016. (ENG.). 32p. (J). (gr. -1-3). pap. 7.95 *(978-1-56145-922-3(4))* Peachtree Pubs.

Galbraith, Kathryn Osebold. Arbor Day Square, 1 vol. Moore, Cyd, illus. 2010. (ENG.). 32p. (J). (gr. -1-3). 16.95 *(978-1-56145-517-1(2))* Peachtree Pubs.

Galjanic, Lisa. When Leaves Die. Hope, Michelle, illus. 2007. (J). 9.95 *(978-1-933532-00-4(9))* LSG Pubns.

Gardner, Sally. The Little Nut Tree. Gardner, Sally, illus. 2014. (ENG., Illus.). 64p. (J). (gr. -1-k). pap. 7.99 *(978-1-4440-1027-5(1),* Orion Children's Bks.) Hachette Children's Group GBR. Dist: Hachette Bk. Group.

Gardner, Yvonne. Scrawny the Tree. 2005. 12p. 11.33 *(978-1-4116-6413-5(2))* Lulu Pr., Inc.

Gates, Pat. The Apple Tree's Secret, 1 vol. Hosselkus, Devin, illus. 2009. 47p. pap. 24.95 *(978-1-60836-637-8(5))* America Star Bks.

Gault, Linda Fulford. The Chosen Tree. 2011. 28p. pap. 12.95 *(978-1-4567-1561-8(5))* AuthorHouse.

Gentner, Norma L. & Young, Steve. Save a Tree for Me. (Song Box Ser.). (Illus.). 16p. (gr. 1-2). 31.50 *(978-0-7802-2264-9(4))* Wright Group/McGraw-Hill.

George, Lynn. The Leaf Pile. 2006. (Neighborhood Readers Ser.). (ENG.). 16p. (gr. 1-3). pap. 6.50 *(978-1-4042-7120-3(1),* Rosen Classroom) Rosen Publishing Group, Inc., The.

George, Olivia. The Weather. Fletcher, Rusty, illus. 2005. (My First Reader Ser.). (ENG.). 32p. (J). (gr. k-1). lib. bdg. 18.50 *(978-0-516-24880-6(4),* Children's Pr.) Scholastic Library Publishing.

Gettman, Cheryl. Molly Magee & the Jelly Bean Tree. 2011. 24p. pap. 12.99 *(978-1-4634-3770-1(6))* AuthorHouse.

Gibbs, D. Renee. The Special Little Christmas Tree. 2003. (Illus.). (J). bds. 14.95 *(978-0-9741406-0-5(0))* Cranberry Quill Publishing Co.

Gile, John. El Primer Bosque. Kohen-Klieman, Clarita, tr. 2006.Tr. of First Forest. (SPA., Illus.). 40p. per. 9.95 *(978-0-910941-15-0(7))* JGC/United Publishing Corps.

Gillen, Lisa P. Spring Time. Gillen, Lisa P., illus. I.t. ed. 2006. (Illus.). 12p. (J). (gr. -1-k). pap. 10.95 *(978-1-57332-351-2(9),* HighReach Learning, Incorporated) Carson-Dellosa Publishing, LLC.

Gillingham, Sara & Siminovich, Lorena. In My Tree. 2009. (ENG., Illus.). 12p. (J). (gr. -1 — 1). bds. 8.99 *(978-0-8118-7052-8(9))* Chronicle Bks. LLC.

Gilman, Phoebe. The Balloon Tree. 2011. (ENG., Illus.). 32p. (J). (gr. -1-k). 16.95 *(978-1-61608-454-7(5),* 608454, Sky Pony Pr.) Skyhorse Publishing Co., Inc.

Givens, Ed. Molly Maple: The Wishing Star. 2004. (Illus.). 32p. (J). bds. 14.95 *(978-1-59094-053-2(9),* Jawbreakers for Kids) Jawbone Publishing Corp.

Goebel, Kelly. Adventures in the Weeping Willow Tree. Murfield, Anna, illus. 2013. 26p. pap. 9.99 *(978-1-937165-49-9(3))* Orange Hat Publishing.

Goertzen, Angelina. Tinsel the Christmas Tree. 2009. 32p. pap. 12.49 *(978-1-4389-8569-5(X))* AuthorHouse.

Gold-Vukson, Marji. Grandpa & Me on Tu B'Shevat. Evans, Leslie, illus. 2004. (ENG.). 32p. (J). (gr. -1-3). pap. 6.95 *(978-1-58013-122-3(0),* Kar-Ben Publishing) Lerner Publishing Group.

Golden Books Staff. A Tree for Me! Gerardi, Jan, illus. 2012. (Stickerific Ser.). (ENG.). 48p. (J). (gr. k — 1). pap. 3.99 *(978-0-307-92981-5(7),* Golden Bks.) Random Hse. Children's Bks.

Goldstyn, Jacques. Bertolt. 2017. (ENG.). 80p. (J). (gr. -1-4). 15.95 *(978-1-59270-229-9(5))* Enchanted Lion Bks., LLC.

Gordon, Amy. Painting the Rainbow. Tuschman, Richard, illus. 2014. (ENG.). 176p. (J). (gr. 3-7). 16.95 *(978-0-8234-2525-9(8))* Holiday Hse., Inc.

Gordon, Leslie M. The Homeless Christmas Tree. Bailey, Court, illus. 2008. (ENG.). 42p. (J). 19.95 *(978-0-87565-384-6(7))* Texas Christian Univ. Pr.

Gosline, Andrea Alban. The Happiness Tree: Celebrating the Gifts of Trees We Treasure. Bossi, Lisa Burnett, illus. 2008. (ENG.). 40p. (J). (gr. k-3). 17.99 *(978-0-312-37017-6(2),* 9780312370176) Feiwel & Friends.

Gottesfeld, Jeff. The Tree in the Courtyard: Looking Through Anne Frank's Window. McCarty, Peter, illus. 2016. (ENG.). 40p. (J). (gr. k-3). 17.99 *(978-0-385-75397-5(7));* lib. bdg. 20.99 *(978-0-385-75398-2(5))* Random Hse. Children's Bks. (Knopf Bks. for Young Readers).

Gove, Doris. My Mother Talks to Trees, 1 vol. Mallory, Marilynn H., illus. 2005. (ENG.). 32p. (J). (gr. k-3). pap. 7.95 *(978-1-56145-336-8(6),* Q31285) Peachtree Pubs.

Graham, Brandon. Perverts of the Unknown. Graham, Brandon, illus. 2003. (ENG., Illus.). 56p. pap. 10.99 *(978-1-56163-374-6(7))* NBM Publishing Co.

Grandfather Pine & His Special Place: Book One - Spring. 2013. 48p. *(978-1-4602-2520-2(1))* FriesenPress.

Grant, Carolyn E. Christmas in Maggie's Neighborhood. 2009. 24p. pap. 12.99 *(978-1-4490-0633-4(7))* AuthorHouse.

Greathouse, Lisa. Johnny Appleseed, 1 vol. 2009. (Building Fluency Through Reader's Theater Ser.). (ENG.). 24p. (J). (gr. 2-4). pap. 6.99 *(978-1-4333-0990-8(4))* Teacher Created Materials, Inc.

Green, M. L. Underneath My Favorite Tree. 2008. 20p. pap. 24.95 *(978-1-60474-858-1(3))* America Star Bks.

Greenwood, Chris. Tanya Talia Plants A Tree. 2007. (Illus.). 32p. (J). 12.95 *(978-0-9799540-1-6(0))* E Innovative Ideas.

—Tanya Talia Plats a Tree. 2007. (Illus.). 32p. (J). pap. 10.95 *(978-0-9799540-0-9(2))* E Innovative Ideas.

Griffin, Saundra J. Which Should I Be? 2004. 21p. pap. 24.95 *(978-1-4137-3167-5(8))* PublishAmerica, Inc.

Grime, L. L. Little Tree. 2007. 48p. pap. 22.95 *(978-1-4357-0092-5(9))* Lulu Pr., Inc.

Guarneri, Cristina. The Magic Tree. 2005. 50p. pap. 10.95 *(978-0-7414-2336-8(7))* Infinity Publishing.

Gurney, Stella. Not so Silly Sausage. Million, Liz, illus. 2011. 32p. pap. *(978-1-84089-707-4(4))* Zero to Ten, Ltd.

Haen, Teri R. Treasure to Love. 2012. 74p. pap. 27.95 *(978-1-4497-4207-2(6),* WestBow Pr.) Author Solutions, Inc.

Hahn, Molly. Under the Sneep Tree: The Wamboozling of a Village. 2009. pap. *(978-1-61623-907-7(7))* Independent Pub.

Hale, Shannon. Forest Born. (Books of Bayern Ser.). (ENG.). (YA). 2017. 400p. pap. 9.99 *(978-1-68119-319-9(1),* 9781681193199) 2011. 400p. (gr. 7). pap. 9.99 *(978-1-59990-692-8(9),* 9781599906928) 2009. (Illus.). 400p. (gr. 7-18). 18.99 *(978-1-59990-167-1(6),* 9781599901671) 2011. 416p. (gr. 7-12). 19.99 *(978-1-59990-691-1(0),* 9781599906911) Bloomsbury Publishing USA. (Bloomsbury USA Childrens).

Hall, Michael. Wonderfall. Hall, Michael, illus. 2016. (Illus.). 40p. (J). (gr. -1-3). 17.99 *(978-0-06-238298-6(5),* Greenwillow Bks.) HarperCollins Pubs.

Hannah, Helen Elizabeth. Let's Help Little Polka Dot Find His Way Home. 2011. 32p. pap. 21.99 *(978-1-4568-5194-1(2))* Xlibris Corp.

Harman, Ian. The Adventures of Terry Tool Bench: Book 1 Terry Is Born. 2009. 36p. pap. 16.99 *(978-1-4490-0048-6(7))* AuthorHouse.

Harman, Michael. Parrot & the Fig Tree. 2nd ed. 2009. (Jataka Tales Ser.). (ENG., Illus.). 32p. (J). (gr. -1-3). pap. 8.95 *(978-0-89800-430-4(6))* Dharma Publishing.

Harris, Odis Clinton. Wee Willie & the Lonely Pine. 2008. 23p. pap. 24.95 *(978-1-60563-741-9(6))* America Star Bks.

Harrison, Francesca. Obus the Eucalyptus Tree Fairy. 2012. 26p. pap. *(978-1-909381-03-2(9))* Foote, Douglas.

Hartwell, Dana S. The Angry Tree. 2011. 24p. pap. 24.95 *(978-1-4626-3671-6(3))* America Star Bks.

Haxhia, Miranda. Andy's Cherry Tree. Deisadze, Zaur, illus. 2007. (POL & ENG.). 32p. (J). pap. 12.95 *(978-1-60195-094-9(2))* International Step by Step Assn.

Haynes, Anne S. Little Tree Makes a New Year's Resolution. 2013. 28p. pap. 24.95 *(978-1-4241-0479-6(3))* America Star Bks.

Henderson, Brandon. The Legend of the Kukui Nut. 2008. 32p. (J). 15.99 *(978-1-59955-119-7(5))* Cedar Fort, Inc./CFI Distribution.

Higgs, Liz Curtis. The Pine Tree Parable. 2005. (Parable Ser.). 32p. (J). pap. 3.99 *(978-1-4003-0685-5(X))* Nelson, Thomas Inc.

Hoedl, Lee. Jesse the Wait of the Wood. Hoedl, Lee, photos by. 2006. (Illus.). 30p. (J). per. 12.95 *(978-1-59879-139-6(7))* Lifevest Publishing, Inc.
Hoffman, Mary Ann. The Maple Tree Mystery. (Neighborhood Readers Ser.). (ENG.). 16p. 2007. 37.95 *(978-1-4042-7342-9(5))* 2006. (gr. 1-3). pap. 6.50 *(978-1-4042-7220-0(8))* Rosen Publishing Group, Inc., The. (Rosen Classroom).
—El misterio en el árbol (the Maple Tree Mystery) 2007. (Lecturas del barrio (Neighborhood Readers) Ser.). (SPA.). 16p. 37.95 *(978-1-4042-7343-6(3)*, Rosen Classroom) Rosen Publishing Group, Inc., The.
Hofmeister, Alan, et al. Bud & the Tree. (Reading for All Learners Ser.). (Illus.). (J). pap. *(978-1-56861-135-8(8))* Swift Learning Resources.
Holm, M. S. The Arborist. Sayles, Susana, illus. 2007. (ENG.). 104p. (J). 16.95 *(978-0-9796199-1-5(2))*; pap. 11.95 *(978-0-9796199-3-9(9))* Great West Publishing. (Sentry Bks.).
Holston-Holloway, Angela M. The Apple Pie Kids. 2006. (J). pap. 8.00 *(978-0-8059-6899-6(7))* Dorrance Publishing Co., Inc.
Hopkins, Leslie. A World Apart. 2012. 20p. pap. 17.99 *(978-1-4772-6783-7(2))* AuthorHouse.
Hopkinson, Deborah. Apples to Oregon. 2014. 17.00 *(978-1-63419-642-0(2))* Perfection Learning Corp.
—Apples to Oregon: Being the (Slightly) True Narrative of How a Brave Pioneer Father Brought Apples, Peaches, Pears, Plums, Grapes, & Cherries (and Children) Across the Plains. Carpenter, Nancy, illus. 2008. (ENG.). 40p. (J). (gr. -1-3). 7.99 *(978-1-4169-6746-0(X)*, Aladdin) Simon & Schuster Children's Publishing.
Hopkinson, Deborah & Carpenter, Nancy. Apples to Oregon: Being the (Slightly) True Narrative of How a Brave Pioneer Father Brought Apples, Peaches, Pears, Plums, Grapes, & Cherries (and Children) Across the Plains. 2004. (ENG., Illus.). 40p. (J). (gr. -1-3). 17.99 *(978-0-689-84769-1(6)*, Atheneum Bks. for Young Readers) Simon & Schuster Children's Publishing.
Horman, Marnie. Carrie's Silver Christmas Tree. 2007. 32p. per. 12.95 *(978-1-4327-1615-8(8))* Outskirts Pr., Inc.
Horowitz, Ruth. Are We Still Friends? Gomez, Blanca, illus. 2017. (ENG.). 40p. (J). (gr. -1-3). 16.99 *(978-0-545-64521-8(2)*, Scholastic Pr.) Scholastic, Inc.
Howard, Chris. Rootless. 2012. (ENG.). 336p. (J). (gr. 9). 17.99 *(978-0-545-38789-7(2))* Scholastic, Inc.
Howell, Julie Ann. The Pepper Tree, How the Seeds Were Planted! LaGrange, Tiffany, illus. 2008. 28p. pap. 12.95 *(978-0-9820479-0-3(8))* Peppertree Pr., The.
—The Pepper Tree, How the Seeds Were Planted. LaGrange, Tiffany, illus. 2012. 28p. 24.95 *(978-1-61493-059-4(7))* Peppertree Pr., The.
Hughes, David Pierce & Perot, Richard. The One Tree. 2006. (Illus.). 48p. (J). pap. 7.99 *(978-1-905470-18-1(5))* SeaSquirt Pubns. GBR. Dist: Basic Distribution, Inc.
Hunt, Angela Elwell. Los Tres Árboles: Cento Tradicional. Jonke, Tim, illus. 2010. Orig. Title: The Tale of Three Trees - A Traditional Folktale. (SPA & ENG.). 32p. (J). 5.99 *(978-1-4143-3737-1(X))* Tyndale Hse. Pubs.
Hunt, Zoe. Azarels Christmas Wish. 2007. (J). per. 10.95 *(978-1-934345-20-7(2))* SouthWest Pubns.
Hunt, Zoe Paton. Azrael's Magical Moment. 2008. 24p. pap. 18.95 *(978-1-60693-070-0(2)*, Strategic Bk. Publishing) Strategic Book Publishing & Rights Agency (SBPRA).
I Am Twee' 2013. (Illus.). 24p. (J). pap. 12.99 *(978-0-9889113-2-1(9))* Coda Grove Publishing.
Ikeda, Daisaku. The Cherry Tree. McCraughrean, Geraldine, tr. from JPN. Wildsmith, Brian, illus. 2013. 6.95 *(978-1-935523-57-4(0))* World Tribune Pr.
Irene's Wish. 2014. (ENG., Illus.). 32p. (J). (gr. k-4). 17.99 *(978-0-689-86300-4(4)*, Simon & Schuster/Paula Wiseman Bks.) Simon & Schuster/Paula Wiseman Bks.
Irish, Terry. Tree Secrets. 2012. (ENG.). (J). pap. *(978-1-4675-4341-5(1))* Independent Pub.
Iverson, Diane. My Favorite Tree: Terrific Trees of North America. 2004. (Sharing Nature with Children Book Ser.). (Illus.). 64p. (YA). (gr. -1-3). pap. 9.95 *(978-1-883220-93-8(9))* Dawn Pubns.
Ives, Suzanne Lintz. Bob, the Tree who Became a Star. 2010. 16p. (J). pap. 14.95 *(978-1-4327-2748-2(6))* Outskirts Pr., Inc.
Jackson, Tyrone. Save Our Home. 2006. (ENG.). 88p. per. 16.95 *(978-1-4241-0875-6(6))* PublishAmerica, Inc.
Jamieson, Mark. Ico Island. 2007. (J). pap. 11.95 *(978-0-9792518-0-1(X))* Gequalsa.
Jeanfield, Twinkle, a Christmas Story. 2009. 36p. pap. 13.95 *(978-1-60693-745-7(6)*, Eloquent Bks.) Strategic Book Publishing & Rights Agency (SBPRA).
Jeffers, Oliver. The Great Paper Caper. Jeffers, Oliver, illus. 2009. (ENG., Illus.). 40p. (J). (gr. -1-k). 17.99 *(978-0-399-25097-2(2)*, Philomel Bks.) Penguin Young Readers Group.
Jo-Marie. Adi's World. 2013. 198p. 33.99 *(978-1-4497-9417-0(3))*; pap. 17.99 *(978-1-4497-9416-3(5))* Author Solutions, Inc. (WestBow Pr.).
Johns, Eric. The Giraffe Tree & Other Tall Stories. 2012. 180p. (-18). pap. 12.95 *(978-1-291-03279-6(7))* Lulu Pr., Inc.
Johnson-Carrigan, Ettarose. Old Rugged: How the Tree Became the Cross. 2008. 24p. pap. 11.99 *(978-1-4389-2781-7(9))* AuthorHouse.
Johnson, Dennis. The Tree That Went Sailing. 2009. (J). pap. *(978-1-61623-539-0(X))* Independent Pub.
Johnson, Donna. The Story of the Little Red Leaf. Johnson, Emily, illus. l.t. ed. 2006. (ENG.). 22p. (J). 25.00 *(978-0-9778774-0-9(X))* Choice Point Editions.
Johnson, Grant. Big Tree Bob. 2012. 20p. pap. 12.50 *(978-1-61897-208-8(1)*, Strategic Bk. Publishing) Strategic Book Publishing & Rights Agency (SBPRA).
Johnson, Lafayette, Jr. & Liberty, Dendron. Tyler's Wise Old Tree. 2012. (Illus.). 65p. (J). pap. 12.99 *(978-0-9817448-1-0(8))* MaMbabooks.com.
Johnson, William C. Little Tree. 2007. pap. 9.00 *(978-0-8059-8486-6(0))* Dorrance Publishing Co., Inc.
Johnston, Tony. Isabel's House of Butterflies. Guevara, Susan, illus. 2005. 32p. pap. 6.95 *(978-1-58685-844-5(0))* Gibbs Smith, Publisher.
Jones, Andrea Koehle. The Wish Trees. 2008. (Illus.). 24p. pap. 12.99 *(978-1-4343-9205-3(8))* AuthorHouse.
Karas, G. Brian. As an Oak Tree Grows. Karas, G. Brian, illus. 2014. (ENG., Illus.). 32p. (J). (gr. k-3). 17.99 *(978-0-399-25233-4(9)*, Nancy Paulsen Books) Penguin Young Readers Group.
Karwoski, Gail & Gootman, Marilyn E. Thank You, Trees! Balouch, Kristen, illus. 2013. (Tu B'Shevat Ser.). (ENG.). 12p. (J). (gr. -1 — 1). pap. 5.95 *(978-1-58013-973-1(6)*, Kar-Ben Publishing) Lerner Publishing Group.
Kauble, Christa. The Little Acorn. Natural Resources Conservation Service (U.S.), ed. Tannehill, Mary Jo, illus. 2008. (ENG.). 24p. (gr. -1-4). pap. 5.00 *(978-0-16-081701-4(3)*, Forest Service) United States Government Printing Office.
Kayler, Ralph. The Tea Party in the Tree Tops. 2009. 48p. pap. 19.49 *(978-1-4389-8000-3(0))* AuthorHouse.
Kellis, Michael. The Grubkins. 2008. 36p. pap. 17.49 *(978-1-4343-8708-0(9))* AuthorHouse.
Kelly, Karen. Angel Tree. 2012. (Illus.). 24p. pap. 19.82 *(978-1-4678-9637-5(3))* AuthorHouse.
Kelso, Mary Jean. One Family's Christmas. Snider, K. C., illus. 2012. 24p. 19.95 *(978-1-61633-308-9(1))* Guardian Angel Publishing, Inc.
Kendall, Jack. The Magic Apple Tree. Bostrom, Sally, illus. l.t. ed. 2006. (ENG.). 48p. (J). per. 9.95 *(978-0-9787740-4-2(3))* Peppertree Pr., The.
King, Jo. A Flight of Fancy. 2011. 58p. 24.99 *(978-1-4691-3665-3(1))*; pap. 15.99 *(978-1-4653-9298-5(X))* Xlibris Corp.
Kirk, Janice. The Christmas Redwood. Kirk, Janice, illus. 2007. (Illus.). 56p. per. 18.95 *(978-1-60290-147-6(3))* OakTara Publishing Group LLC.
Kisson, Nisha. Leah - the Fairy of the Lime Tree. KecskTs, Anna, illus. 2008. 36p. pap. *(978-1-904312-39-0(X))* MX Publishing, Ltd.
Klise, Kate & Klise, M. Sarah. Regarding the Trees: A Splintered Saga Rooted in Secrets. 2007. (Regarding The ... Ser.: Bk. 3). (ENG., Illus.). 160p. (J). (gr. 2-5). pap. 7.99 *(978-0-15-206090-9(1))* Houghton Mifflin Harcourt Publishing Co.
Knights, David. Stumpy the Tree. 2013. 28p. pap. 24.95 *(978-1-62709-375-0(3))* America Star Bks.
Korten, Gerri. The Parakeets & the Ginkgo Tree at Hide Park. l.t. ed. 2006. (Illus.). 36p. (J). 18.85 *(978-0-9785609-7-3(3))* New Global Publishing.
Koumjian, Gay Melanie. Mojo's Mojo. 2013. (ENG.). 23p. (J). pap. 12.95 *(978-1-4787-1623-5(1))* Outskirts Pr., Inc.
Krensky, Stephen. Once upon a Time in the Woods. Shortley, Michele, illus. 2011. (J). pap. *(978-0-7680-3488-2(4))* SAE Intl.
Krishnaswami, Uma. Out of the Way! Out of the Way!, 1 vol. Krishnaswamy, Uma, illus. 2012. (ENG.). 28p. (J). (gr. -1-2). 17.95 *(978-1-55498-130-4(1))* Groundwood Bks. CAN. Dist: Publishers Group West (PGW).
Kruusval, Catarina. Ellen's Apple Tree. Sandin, Joan, tr. from SWE. 2008. (Illus.). 32p. (J). (gr. -1-3). 16.00 *(978-91-29-66905-3(7))* R & S Bks. SWE. Dist: Macmillan.
Laing, Amy Wilson. Ginger Helps Spikey. 2011. (Illus.). 28p. pap. 15.99 *(978-1-4568-5912-1(9))* Xlibris Corp.
Langton, Jane. The Dragon Tree. 2008. (Hall Family Chronicles). 176p. (J). (gr. 3-7). lib. bdg. 16.89 *(978-0-06-082342-9(9))* HarperCollins Pubs.
Lanqcaon, Jeff. Grandpa's Magic Banyan Tree. 2005. 32p. (J). 12.95 *(978-1-56647-740-6(9))* Mutual Publishing LLC.
Lasky, Kathryn. The Golden Tree. 2007. (Guardians of Ga'Hoole Ser.: 12). (Illus.). 192p. lib. bdg. 17.20 *(978-1-4177-8260-4(9)*, Turtleback) Turtleback Bks.
—The River of Wind. 2007. (Guardians of Ga'hoole Ser.: 13). (ENG., Illus.). 224p. (J). (gr. 3-7). 6.99 *(978-0-439-88807-3(7))* Scholastic, Inc.
—The Shattering. 2004. (Guardians of Ga'hoole Ser.: 5). (ENG., Illus.). 192p. (J). (gr. 3-7). 6.99 *(978-0-439-40561-4(0)*, Scholastic Paperbacks) Scholastic, Inc.
—The Siege. 2004. (Guardians of Ga'hoole Ser.: 4). (ENG., Illus.). 224p. (J). (gr. 3-7). mass mkt. 6.99 *(978-0-439-40560-7(2)*, Scholastic Paperbacks) Scholastic, Inc.
Lawless, Mary Ann. The Proud Christmas Tree. McCool, Arlene, illus. 2006. (J). 12.95 *(978-0-9772795-0-0(2))* Tuesday's Child.
Layton, Neal. The Tree. Layton, Neal, illus. 2017. (ENG., Illus.). 40p. (J). (-k). 16.99 *(978-0-7636-8952-0(1))* Candlewick Pr.
Leavey, Peggy Dymond. The Path Through the Trees. 2005. (ENG., Illus.). 136p. (J). pap. 8.95 *(978-1-894917-21-6(9)*, Napoleon & Co.) Dundurn CAN. Dist: Ingram Publisher Services.
Lee, Glenda. Alexander's Tree. 2012. 28p. pap. 24.95 *(978-1-4626-9734-2(8))* America Star Bks.
Leigh, Autumn. The Apple Tree. (Neighborhood Readers Ser.). (ENG.). 16p. 2007. 33.50 *(978-1-4042-7328-3(X))* 2006. (gr. 1-3). pap. 6.50 *(978-1-4042-7128-9(7))* Rosen Publishing Group, Inc., The. (Rosen Classroom).
—El manzano (the Apple Tree) 2007. (Lecturas del barrio (Neighborhood Readers) Ser.). (SPA.). 16p. 33.50 *(978-1-4042-7329-0(8)*, Rosen Classroom) Rosen Publishing Group, Inc., The.
Leon, Georgina Lazaro & León, Georgina Lázaro. El Flamboyan Amarillo. Delacre, Lulu, illus. 2nd ed. 2016.Tr. of Yellow Flame Tree. (SPA.). 32p. (J). 14.99 *(978-1-930332-55-3(6))* Lectorum Pubns., Inc.
Lester, Julius. The Girl Who Saved Yesterday. Angel, Carl, illus. 2016. (ENG.). 32p. (J). (gr. -1-4). 16.99 *(978-1-939547-24-8(5))* Creston Bks.
Lindquist, Jennie D. The Crystal Tree. Chalmers, Mary, illus. 2008. (J). (gr. 2-6). 25.00 *(978-0-8446-6287-9(9))* Smith, Peter Pub., Inc.
Linsley, Sonja Paschal. The Conifer Court Competition. Linsley, Paul, illus. 2006. 26p. (J). 18.95 *(978-0-9766062-1-5(6)*, HGP 2005-2) Higher Ground Pr.
Little Tree. Date not set. *(978-0-517-80134-5(5))* Random Hse. Value Publishing.
The Littlest Christmas Tree. 2005. 45.00 *(978-0-916773-85-4(X))* Book Peddlers.
Long, Loren. Little Tree. Long, Loren, illus. 2015. (ENG., Illus.). 40p. (J). (gr. k-3). 17.99 *(978-0-399-16397-5(2)*, Philomel Bks.) Penguin Young Readers Group.
Lucado, Max. Best of All. Martinez, Sergio, illus. 2003. (Max Lucado's Wemmicks Ser.: 4). 32p. (J). 16.99 *(978-1-58134-501-8(1))* Crossway.
Lucken, Eve M. The Tree, the Crazy Leaf, & Me. 2012. 64p. pap. 20.99 *(978-1-4525-5016-9(6))* Balboa Pr.
Lynn, Michelle. Fall Leaves. 2008. 17p. pap. 24.95 *(978-1-60672-027-1(9))* America Star Bks.
MacKay, Elly. If You Hold a Seed. MacKay, Elly, illus. 2013. (ENG., Illus.). 32p. (J). (gr. -1-17). 16.95 *(978-0-7624-4721-3(4)*, Running Pr. Kids) Running Pr. Bk. Pubs.
Macor, Jim. Frazier Fir, A Christmas Fable. Macor, Jim, illus. 2007. (Illus.). 32p. (J). 17.95 *(978-0-9785551-3-9(9))* Zuber Publishing.
Maddock-Cowart, Donna. The Anhinga Tree. Mann, William A., illus. 2012. 74p. pap. 9.95 *(978-0-9836484-3-7(3))* Miglior Pr.
Madhu, Kailash. The Wise Tree & Meu: Mind & Spirit. 2012. 108p. pap. 40.81 *(978-1-4669-2744-5(5))* Trafford Publishing.
Mahon, Matthew. The Defenders of All Thats Fall. 2008. 56p. pap. 24.95 *(978-1-4327-3169-4(6))* Outskirts Pr., Inc.
Maner, Dee. Artie: The First Artificial Christmas Tree. 2016. (ENG.). 32p. (J). 19.95 *(978-1-942945-28-4(0)*, 9781942945284) Bright Sky Pr.
Markarian, Marianne. The Pesky Bird Wasielewski, Margaret M., illus. l.t. ed. 2005. 32p. (J). 16.00 *(978-0-9767377-0-4(1))* Pomegranate Publishing.
Marshall, Jane Garrett. The Christmas Tree That Cried. Tomasek, Dean, illus. 2013. 106p. pap. 24.99 *(978-0-9896247-0-1(6))* WRB Pub.
Marston, Elsa. The Olive Tree. Ewart, Claire, illus. 2014. (ENG.). 32p. (J). (gr. -1-2). 16.95 *(978-1-937786-29-8(3)*, Wisdom Tales) World Wisdom, Inc.
Martin, Bill, Jr. & Archambault, John. Chicka Chicka ABC. Ehlert, Lois, illus. 2009. (Chicka Chicka Book Ser.). (ENG.). 16p. (J). (gr. -1-1). bds. 10.99 *(978-1-4169-8447-4(X)*, Little Simon) Little Simon.
—Chicka Chicka Boom Boom. Ehlert, Lois, illus. 2006. (Chicka Chicka Book Ser.). (ENG.). 40p. (J). (gr. -1-3). 10.99 *(978-1-4169-2718-1(2)*, Little Simon) Little Simon.
Martin, David Lozell. Christmas Tree. Sweet, Melissa, illus. 2009. (ENG.). 26p. (J). (— 1). bds. 5.99 *(978-0-7636-3030-0(6))* Candlewick Pr.
Martin, Jayme. Skinny Little Tree. 2013. (ENG.). 28p. (J). 18.95 *(978-1-4787-0813-1(1))*; pap. 13.95 *(978-1-4787-0870-4(0))* Outskirts Pr., Inc.
Martin, T. J. Why Do the Leaves Fall? 2008. (ENG.). 20p. 12.49 *(978-1-4389-4329-6(6))* AuthorHouse.
Marvelous Marty. 2008. (J). *(978-0-9778113-4-2(4))*; pap. *(978-0-9778113-5-9(2))* HeartFelt Stories LLC.
Mason, Charlene. Mr Wilson's Tree. 2012. 28p. pap. 24.95 *(978-1-4626-7975-1(7))* America Star Bks.
Matheson, Christie. Tap the Magic Tree. Matheson, Christie, illus. 2013. (ENG., Illus.). 40p. (J). (gr. -1-3). 16.99 *(978-0-06-227445-8(7)*, Greenwillow Bks.) HarperCollins Pubs.
Matsuura, Richard & Matsuura, Ruth. Fruit, the Tree & the Flower. (J). 8.95 *(978-1-887916-02-8(4))* Orchid Isle Publishing Co.
Maylin, Grace B. There Will Come Another: A Lesson from the Trees. Maylin, Grace B., photos by. 2007. (Illus.). per. *(978-0-9792384-0-6(4))* Maylin, Grace.
Mazzola, Lori. Tales of the Tree People to Tree... or. 2006. 48p. pap. 16.95 *(978-1-4241-5065-6(5))* PublishAmerica, Inc.
McAllister, Ava. The Honor Tree. 2011. 24p. 15.00 *(978-1-4567-3524-1(1))* AuthorHouse.
McEvoy, Grace. The Tiniest Tepee. 2005. 9.00 *(978-0-8059-8040-0(7))* Dorrance Publishing Co., Inc.
McLeod, Rona. Big Daddy Chinaberry: Love Given - Love Returned. McLeod, Herbert, illus. 2012. 24p. pap. 24.95 *(978-1-4626-7700-9(2))* America Star Bks.
McPhail, David. The Searcher & Old Tree. McPhail, David, illus. 2011. (ENG., Illus.). 32p. (J). (gr. -1-2). pap. 7.95 *(978-1-58089-224-7(8))* Charlesbridge Publishing, Inc.
McVay, Elizabeth. Baby Bun & the Littlest Tree. 2004. (Illus.). 31p. (J). pap. 9.95 *(978-0-9759621-0-7(8))* Koenisha Pubns.
Meister, Cari. I Love Trees. Sirrell, Terry, illus. 2011. (Rookie Ready to Learn Ser.). 40p. (J). pap. 5.95 *(978-0-531-26733-2(4))*; (gr. -1-k). lib. bdg. 23.00 *(978-0-531-26501-7(3))* Scholastic Library Publishing. (Children's Pr.).
Meister, Cari & Sirrell, Terry. Me Fascinan Los Arboles. Sirrell, Terry, illus. 2005. (Rookie Reader Español Ser.). (ENG & SPA., Illus.). 32p. (J). (gr. k-2). 19.50 *(978-0-516-25253-7(4)*, Children's Pr.) Scholastic Library Publishing.
—Me Fascinan Los árboles. Sirrell, Terry, illus. 2011. (Rookie Ready to Learn Español Ser.). (SPA., Illus.). 40p. (J). lib. bdg. 23.00 *(978-0-531-26118-7(2)*, Children's Pr.) Scholastic Library Publishing.
—Me Fascinan los Árboles. Sirrell, Terry, illus. 2011. (Rookie Ready to Learn Español Ser.). (SPA., Illus.). 40p. (J). pap. 5.95 *(978-0-531-26786-8(5)*, Children's Pr.) Scholastic Library Publishing.
Mellon, Nancy. The Knottles. Lieberherr, Ruth, illus. 2012. 32p. (J). pap. 11.95 *(978-1-62148-003-7(8))* SteinerBooks, Inc.
Mercer, Steven A. Florence the Fir Tree: (and the Angels of the Forest) 2012. 36p. 24.95 *(978-1-4560-6659-8(5))* America Star Bks.
Meron, Renato Mas. Why Mangrove Roots Float. 2013. 20p. pap. 24.95 *(978-1-63000-427-9(8))* America Star Bks.
Mesibere, Ellen. The Curse of the Laulau Tree. Manasau, Amos, illus. 2012. 34p. pap. *(978-9980-945-67-9(2))* University of Papua New Guinea Press.
Messier, Mireille. The Branch. Pratt, Pierre, illus. 2016. (ENG.). 32p. (J). (gr. -1-2). 16.95 *(978-1-77138-564-0(2))* Kids Can Pr., Ltd. CAN. Dist: Hachette Bk. Group.
Messner, Kate. The Brilliant Fall of Gianna Z. (ENG.). 224p. 2017. (J). pap. 8.99 ***(978-1-68119-547-6(X)***, 9781681195476) 2010. (YA). (gr. 3-6). pap. 8.99 *(978-0-8027-2173-0(7)*, 9780802721730) Bloomsbury Publishing USA. (Bloomsbury USA Childrens).
—The Brilliant Fall of Gianna Z. 2017. (J). lib. bdg. 19.65 ***(978-0-606-40595-9(X))*** Turtleback Bks.
Metcalf, Paula. Mouse's Sock Tree. Mitchell, Susan, illus. 2014. (ENG.). 12p. (J). (— 1). bds. 7.99 *(978-0-230-76475-0(4))* Pan Macmillan GBR. Dist: Independent Pubs. Group.
Metzger, Steve. Under the Apple Tree. Girasole, Alessia, illus. 2009. (J). *(978-0-545-14200-7(8))* Scholastic, Inc.
Micklos, John. One Leaf, Two Leaves, Count with Me! McFarland, Clive, illus. 2017. (ENG.). 32p. (J). (— 1). 16.99 ***(978-0-399-54471-2(2)***, Nancy Paulsen Books) Penguin Young Readers Group.
Migliore, R. Elizabeth. Stanley, 1 vol. 2009. 13p. pap. 24.95 *(978-1-61546-829-4(3))* America Star Bks.
Mill, Lynda. Let's Climb the Apple Tree. 2012. 44p. pap. 17.45 *(978-1-4669-6871-4(0))* Trafford Publishing.
Miller, Sibley & Lenhard, Elizabeth. Horse Happy. Chang, Tara Larsen & Gershman, Jo, illus. 2008. (Wind Dancers Ser.: 2). (ENG.). 80p. (J). (gr. 1-4). pap. 7.99 *(978-0-312-38281-0(2)*, 9780312382810) Feiwel & Friends.
Mills, Joyce C. Gentle Willow: A Story for Children about Dying. Pillo, Cary, illus. 2nd ed. 2003. 32p. (J). 14.95 *(978-1-59147-071-7(4))*; pap. 9.95 *(978-1-59147-072-4(2))* American Psychological Assn. (Magination Pr.).
—Little Tree: A Story for Children with Serious Medical Illness. Sebern, Brian, illus. 2nd ed. 2003. 32p. (J). pap. 9.95 *(978-1-59147-042-7(0))*; 14.95 *(978-1-59147-041-0(2))* American Psychological Assn. (Magination Pr.).
Mills, Patricia Anne. Stevie's First Christmas. 2009. 28p. pap. 12.49 *(978-1-4490-3452-8(7))* AuthorHouse.
Milson, Matthew R. Young Arcan & the Garden of Loc. 2007. (Tales from Emberthel Ser.). 221p. (J). (gr. 3-7). per. 14.95 *(978-1-933770-03-1(1))* Avari Pr.
Mitchell, Trish. Noah Pals: Journey to the Apple Tree. 2011. 32p. pap. 16.99 *(978-1-4567-9939-7(8))* AuthorHouse.
Mohler, Marie. Hearts of Trees. 2008. 32p. pap. 18.95 *(978-1-4357-4614-5(7))* Lulu Pr., Inc.
Mollis Lindquist, Melody Rose. Oak Tree. 2009. 16p. pap. 10.99 *(978-1-4490-0859-8(3))* AuthorHouse.
Monaghan, Joseph. The Boy Who Loved Trees. 2013. (Illus.). 24p. pap. 19.82 *(978-1-4817-8225-8(8))* AuthorHouse.
Moore, Sandra. The Peace Tree from Hiroshima: A Little Japanese Bonsai with a Big Story. Wilds, Kazumi, illus. 2015. (ENG.). 32p. (J). (gr. 2-6). 14.95 *(978-4-8053-1347-3(1))* Tuttle Publishing.
Moran, Kelly. The Tiny Caterpillar & the Great Big Tree. 2009. 50p. pap. 19.50 *(978-0-557-09498-1(4))* Lulu Pr., Inc.
Morgan, Melissa. The Tip Trip. 2008. 36p. pap. 24.95 *(978-1-4241-9226-7(9))* America Star Bks.
Morse, Rose. The Everlasting Evergreen. 2009. 32p. pap. 18.01 *(978-0-557-21209-5(X))* Lulu Pr., Inc.
Moulton, Mark Kimball. Miss Sadie Mcgee Who Lived in a Tree. Good, Karen H., illus. 2008. (ENG.). 32p. (J). (gr. k-3). 16.95 *(978-0-8249-5152-8(2)*, Ideal Pubns.) Worthy Publishing.
Munoz, R. C. In Honor of the Oak Tree. 2012. 20p. pap. 24.95 *(978-1-4626-6454-2(7))* America Star Bks.
Munsch, Robert. Up, up, Down. 2004. (Illus.). (J). (gr. k-3). spiral bd. *(978-0-616-11127-7(4))*; spiral bd. *(978-0-616-11126-0(6))* Canadian National Institute for the Blind/Institut National Canadien pour les Aveugles.
Murphy, Susan White. D. J. 's Special Tree. 2012. 50p. (-18). pap. 8.95 *(978-1-4759-5983-3(4))* iUniverse, Inc.
Musariri, Blessing. Going Home: A Tree's Story. 2005. (Illus.). 29p. pap. *(978-1-77922-042-4(1))* Weaver Pr. ZWE. Dist: Michigan State Univ. Pr.
My Apple Tree. 2003. (J). per. *(978-1-57657-899-5(2))* Paradise Pr., Inc.
Nan, Carol. Nana the Baby Pine Tree. 2012. 24p. pap. 24.95 *(978-1-4626-8944-6(2))* America Star Bks.
Navarro, Cece P. My Cherry Tree House. 2008. 16p. pap. 24.95 *(978-1-60474-415-6(4))* America Star Bks.
Neff, Fred. The Memory Tree. Montmeat, Jack, illus. 2008. 36p. pap. 14.99 *(978-1-59858-854-5(0))* Dog Ear Publishing, LLC.
Neimark, Jill. The Hugging Tree: A Story about Resilience. Wong, Nicole, illus. 2015. (J). *(978-1-4338-1907-0(4)*, Magination Pr.) American Psychological Assn.
Nelson, Holly. Ig's Apples. l.t. ed. 2003. (Illus.). (J). 28p. lib. bdg. 14.95 *(978-1-932338-32-4(2))*; 15p. per. 9.99 *(978-1-932338-17-1(9))* Lifevest Publishing, Inc.
The Nevergreen. 2003. (J). 15.99 *(978-0-9744565-9-1(4))* Heart-to-Heart Pubns.
Newman, C. Edward. The Enchanted Bat. 2007. pap. 0.01 net. *(978-1-60402-471-5(2))* Independent Pub.
Nichols, Lori. Maple. Nichols, Lori, illus. 2014. (ENG., Illus.). 32p. (J). (gr. -1-k). 16.99 *(978-0-399-16085-1(X)*, Nancy Paulsen Books) Penguin Young Readers Group.
Niddrie, June. Pom, the Pomegranate Pixie. 2010. 32p. pap. 16.10 *(978-0-557-31875-9(0))* Lulu Pr., Inc.
Noble, Trinka Hakes. Apple Tree Christmas. Noble, Trinka Hakes, illus. 2005. (Holiday Ser.). (ENG., Illus.). 32p. (J). (gr. -1-3). 16.95 *(978-1-58536-270-7(0))* Sleeping Bear Pr.
Nolan, Allia Zobel. God's Oak Tree. Chung, Chi, illus. 2007. 16p. (J). (gr. -1). 12.99 *(978-0-8254-5536-0(7))* Kregel Pubns.
Nunnery, Donna. The Leaf That Was Afraid to Fall, 1 vol. Scardina, Tom, illus. 2010. 26p. 24.95 *(978-1-4489-5927-3(6))* PublishAmerica, Inc.
Nye, Donna Kight. Sammi & the Tree. 2011. 12p. pap. 8.32 *(978-1-4634-4659-8(4))* AuthorHouse.
Obed, Ellen Bryan. Who Would Like a Christmas Tree? A Tree for All Seasons. Hunter, Anne, illus. 2009. (ENG.). 32p. (J). (gr. -1-3). 16.00 *(978-0-547-04625-9(1))* Houghton Mifflin Harcourt Publishing Co.
O'Connor, Jane. Fancy Nancy: Poison Ivy Expert. Glasser, Robin Preiss & Enik, Ted, illus. 2008. (I Can Read Level 1 Ser.). (ENG.). 32p. (J). (gr. -1-3). 16.99 *(978-0-06-123614-3(4))*; pap. 3.99 *(978-0-06-123613-6(6))* HarperCollins Pubs.
Orliac, Catherine. Te Tumu o Rapa Nui: El Arbolito de Rapa Nui. the Little Tree of Rapa Nui. le Petit Arbre de Rapa Nui. Haoa Cardinali, Viki et al, trs. Willemin, Veronique, illus. 2005. (FRE, SPA & ENG.). 40p. (J). spiral bd. 12.00 *(978-1-880636-02-2(6))* Easter Island Foundation.
Our Shinning Christmas Tree. 2003. (J). per. *(978-1-57657-911-4(5))* Paradise Pr., Inc.
Ozment, Jones. The Tree. 2012. (ENG.). pap. *(978-1-4675-2966-2(4))* Independent Pub.

TUV

Page, Lawana. The Weeping Willow Tree. Amaya, Laura, tr. Heaton, Layce, illus. 2006. (SPA.). 32p. 10.95 *(978-0-9761128-2-2(5))* KB Bks. & More.

Pappas, Charles. The Tree That Loved the Eagle. Schlueter, Rachel, illus. 2013. 56p. (J). 19.95 *(978-1-58790-175-1(7))* Regent Pr.

Parent, Nancy. A Tree for Me, 15 vols. Harchy, Atelier Philippe, illus. 2003. (It's Fun to Learn Ser.). 32p. (J). (gr. -1-3). 3.99 *(978-1-57973-138-0(4))* Advance Pubs. LLC.

Parish, Alex. Peter & the Flying Sergeant. 2009. 30p. 21.50 *(978-0-9561613-0-7(8))* Parish, Alex GBR. Dist: Lulu Pr., Inc.

Park, Barbara & Wotherspoon, John. The Adventures of Lily Leaf. 2011. (Illus.). 28p. pap. 11.36 *(978-1-4567-8648-9(2))* AuthorHouse.

Parker, Emma. The Spaghetti Tree. 2010. (Illus.). pap. *(978-1-877561-02-3(9))* First Edition Ltd.

Patterson, Jim. Lisa B's Cookie Tree. 2011. 36p. pap. 24.95 *(978-1-4560-3599-0(1))* America Star Bks.

peddi, radhika. Kichkide. 2010. 44p. pap. 19.70 *(978-0-557-16435-6(4))* Lulu Pr., Inc.

Penson, Mary. Billy Bardin & the Witness Tree. 2004. (Chaparral Bks.). (ENG.). 146p. (J). pap. 11.95 *(978-0-87565-283-2(2))* Texas Christian Univ. Pr.

Peters, Andrew. Ravenwood. 2011. (ENG.). 368p. (J). (gr. 5-9). 16.99 *(978-0-545-30550-1(0)*, Chicken Hse., The) Scholastic, Inc.

Pfitsch, Patricia Curtis. Riding the Flume. 2004. (Aladdin Historical Fiction Ser.). 232p. (gr. 5-9). 15.00 *(978-0-7569-2938-1(5))* Perfection Learning Corp.

Phillips, Dixie & Phillips, Sharon. Once upon an Empty Tomb. 2013. 24p. pap. 7.95 *(978-1-61633-380-5(4))* Guardian Angel Publishing, Inc.

Pitt, Tamina & Terri, Janke. What Makes a Tree Smile? Francine Ngardab, Riches, illus. 2003. (Uupababa Ser.). 24p. (J). pap. *(978-1-875641-80-2(7))* Magabala Bks.

Poehler, S. Applecheeks & the Pop E. Tree. 2012. 12p. pap. 15.99 *(978-1-4772-8180-2(0))* AuthorHouse.

Postma, Carryl. The Tree That Could Be Green. 2009. 20p. pap. 14.99 *(978-1-4389-5842-2(0))* AuthorHouse.

Potter, Dawn. Isobel's Tree. 2010. 16p. pap. 9.99 *(978-1-60860-966-6(9)*, Eloquent Bks.) Strategic Book Publishing & Rights Agency (SBPRA).

Power, Eloise. The Apple Tree Inside of Me. 2012. 36p. pap. 16.95 *(978-1-4525-5522-5(2))* Balboa Pr.

Price, Cheryl. The Golden Aspen. 2009. 36p. pap. 15.95 *(978-1-4490-2855-8(1))* AuthorHouse.

Pugliano-Martin, Carol. Ready for Fall! 2006. (Early Explorers Ser.). (J). pap. *(978-1-4108-6103-0(1))* Benchmark Education Co.

Rabe, Tish. The Tree Doctor. 2013. (Step into Reading Level 2 Ser.). lib. bdg. 13.55 *(978-0-606-26965-0(7)*, Turtleback) Turtleback Bks.

Ramsey, Byra L. Little Stick. 2009. 28p. pap. 13.99 *(978-1-4490-3371-2(7))* AuthorHouse.

Randolph, Joanne. Greenley: A Tree's Story. 2009. (Nature Stories Ser.). (Illus.). 24p. (J). (gr. -1-2). pap. 8.15 *(978-1-60754-090-8(8))*; lib. bdg. 22.60 *(978-1-60754-089-2(4))* Windmill Bks.

Ranganathan, Babu G. The Selfish Apple Tree. 2010. 12p. 7.95 *(978-1-4497-0312-7(7)*, WestBow Pr.) Author Solutions, Inc.

Ransburg, Ashley B. Evie Finds Her Family Tree. 2006. (Illus.). 34p. (J). (gr. -1-3). 14.95 *(978-0-87195-187-8(8))* Indiana Historical Society.

Rawlinson, Julia. Fletcher & the Falling Leaves. Beeke, Tiphanie, illus. 2008. (ENG.). 32p. (J). (gr. -1-2). pap. 7.99 *(978-0-06-157397-2(3)*, Greenwillow Bks.) HarperCollins Pubs.

—Fletcher & the Falling Leaves. 2011. (J). (gr. -1-2). 29.95 *(978-0-545-19699-4(X))*; 18.95 *(978-0-545-19705-2(8))* Weston Woods Studios, Inc.

Rawlinson, Julia & Rawlinson. Fletcher & the Falling Leaves. Beeke, Tiphanie, illus. 2006. (ENG.). 32p. (J). (gr. -1-2). 16.99 *(978-0-06-113401-2(5)*, Greenwillow Bks.) HarperCollins Pubs.

Ray, Mary Lyn. Christmas Farm. Root, Barry, illus. alt. ed. 2013. (ENG.). 40p. (J). (gr. -1-3). 6.99 *(978-0-544-10509-6(5))* Houghton Mifflin Harcourt Publishing Co.

Razilov, Evelyn. The Little Ant & the Apple Tree. 2013. 24p. pap. 12.56 *(978-1-4669-7729-7(9))* Trafford Publishing.

Reardon, John. The South Overlook Oaks. Youngbluth, Chris, illus. 2006. 119p. (J). (gr. 4-7). 16.95 *(978-1-931643-91-7(1))* Seven Locks Pr.

Redwine, Connie. A Story from Graandfather Tree. Keithline, Brian, illus. 2005. 25p. (J). (gr. k-2). pap. 7.95 *(978-0-88100-135-8(X))* National Writers Pr., The.

Reed, Jennifer. The Falling Flowers. Cole, Dick, illus. 2005. (Falling Flowers Ser.). 32p. (J). (gr. -1-3). 16.95 *(978-1-885008-28-2(7)*, Shen's Bks.) Lee & Low Bks., Inc.

Reid, Barbara. Picture a Tree. Reid, Barbara, illus. 2013. (ENG., Illus.). 32p. (J). (gr. -1-3). 16.99 *(978-0-8075-6526-1(1))* Whitman, Albert & Co.

Reilly, Carmel & Wallace-Mitchell, Jane. Mercury & the Woodcutter. 2008. (Rigby Focus Forward: Level J Ser.). (Illus.). 24p. (J). (gr. 4-7). pap. *(978-1-4190-3765-8(X)*, Rigby) Pearson Education Australia.

Reinertson, Bob. The Mysterious Visitor. 2012. 28p. pap. 21.99 *(978-1-4771-0006-6(7))* Xlibris Corp.

Rey, H. A. Curious George at the Park. Meyer, Emily, ed. 2010. (Curious George Ser.). (ENG., Illus.). 10p. (J). (gr. -1 — 1). bds. 6.99 *(978-0-547-24300-9(6))* Houghton Mifflin Harcourt Publishing Co.

—Curious George Plants a Tree. Wilcox, Mary, ed. 2010. (Curious George Ser.). (ENG., Illus.). 24p. (J). (gr. -1-3). pap. 4.99 *(978-0-547-29776-7(9))* Houghton Mifflin Harcourt Publishing Co.

—Curious George Plants a Tree. 2009. (Curious George Ser.). (ENG., Illus.). 32p. (J). (gr. -1-3). 14.99 *(978-0-547-15087-1(3))* Houghton Mifflin Harcourt Publishing Co.

Rhiger, Tenna. The Story about How the Spotted Wobblepig Got Its Spots. 2012. 40p. pap. *(978-1-84903-152-3(5))* Schiel & Denver Publishing Ltd.

Rhode, Paul. Presents for Phoebe: Growing Independent. Margolis, Al, illus. 2011. 24p. (YA). pap. 9.95 *(978-1-935706-05-2(5))* Wiggles Pr.

Rice, June K. The Little Blue Tree. 2009. 20p. pap. 10.99 *(978-1-4389-4806-5(9))* AuthorHouse.

Rie, Jannie. The Community Food Tree. 2012. (ENG.). (J). pap. *(978-1-4675-5240-0(2))* Independent Pub.

Ringgold, Robyn. My Mom Hugs Trees. Vasudevan, Vidya, illus. 2006. 24p. (J). per. 15.95 *(978-0-9785326-1-1(9))* Solar Publishing LLC.

Ripton, Kyle. The Mourning Tree. 2012. 74p. pap. 9.97 *(978-1-300-31829-3(5))* Lulu Pr., Inc.

Robinson, Cindy. Baby Baobab. Robinson, Cindy, illus. 2010. (ENG., Illus.). 32p. (J). (gr. k-2). pap. 9.00 *(978-1-77009-671-4(X))* Jacana Media ZAF. Dist: Independent Pubs. Group.

Rocklin, Joanne. One Day & One Amazing Morning on Orange Street. 2012. (ENG., Illus.). 240p. (J). (gr. 3-7). pap. 8.95 *(978-1-4197-0181-8(9)*, Amulet Bks.) Abrams, Inc.

Rodhe, Paul & Wallas Reidy, Sarah. The Little Plum Tree. Margolis, Al & Young, Bill, illus. 2010. 24p. (J). pap. 9.95 *(978-1-935706-06-9(3))* Wiggles Pr.

Rodman, Mary Ann. A Tree for Emmy, 1 vol. Mai-Wyss, Tatjana, illus. 2009. (ENG.). 32p. (J). (gr. -1-3). 15.95 *(978-1-56145-475-4(3))* Peachtree Pubs.

Roman, Celso. El Arbol de Los Tucanes. 2012. 44p. (J). (gr. 2-4). pap. 12.99 *(978-958-30-3662-0(5))* Panamericana Editorial COL. Dist: Lectorum Pubns., Inc.

Rosenberg, Madelyn. Happy Birthday, Tree! A Tu B'Shevat Story. Christy, Jana, illus. 2012. (ENG.). 24p. (J). (gr. -1-3). 15.99 *(978-0-8075-3151-8(0))* Whitman, Albert & Co.

Rothman, Lorne. Southcrop Forest. 2008. 184p. pap. 13.95 *(978-0-595-49588-7(5))* iUniverse, Inc.

Rouss, Sylvia. The Littlest Tree. Binus, Ari, illus. 2005. 32p. (J). 16.95 *(978-1-932687-25-5(4)*, Devora Publishing) Simcha Media Group.

Roy, Alene Adele. The Legend of Dragonfly Pond: Coloring Book. 2008. 56p. pap. 11.99 *(978-1-4343-4628-5(5))* AuthorHouse.

Ruben, Pamela. Lessons from the Bubbe & Zayde Tree. 2004. (Illus.). 33p. (J). 12.95 *(978-0-9764813-2-4(4))* Peppery Pr.

—Lessons from the Grandma & Grandpa Tree. 2004. (J). 12.95 *(978-0-9764813-3-1(2))* Peppery Pr.

Rucker, David. The Valley of the Christmas Trees: A Legend. Laster, Brenda, illus. 2007. 41p. (J). (gr. -1-3). 14.95 *(978-1-931643-94-8(6))* Seven Locks Pr.

Ruiz-Flores, Lupe. The Woodcutter's Gift/el Regalo del Lenador. Ventura, Gabriela Baeza, tr. from ENG. Jerome, Elaine, illus. 2007. (SPA & ENG.). 32p. (J). (gr. -1-2). 16.95 *(978-1-55885-489-5(4)*, Piñata Books) Arte Publico Pr.

Ryan, Mary C., illus. & text. Twitcher Mcgee & the Wonderful Tree. Ryan, Mary C., text. 2008. 12p. (J). 4.95 *(978-0-9678115-3-6(8))* Dragonseed Pr.

Saito, Ryusuke & Takidaira, Jiro. The Tree of Courage. Laughlin, Sako, tr. 2008. (Illus.). 32p. (J). 14.95 incl. audio compact disk *(978-1-74126-442-5(1))* R.I.C. Pubns. AUS. Dist: SCB Distributors.

Salib Salibi, Nuha. The Palm Tree & the Fir. 2009. 24p. pap. 11.49 *(978-1-4389-9419-2(2))* AuthorHouse.

San Giacomo, Renee. Herbie's Star. 2012. 24p. pap. 24.95 *(978-1-4626-7596-8(4))* America Star Bks.

Santillan, Suzanne. Grandma's Pear Tree. Pernisco, Atilio, illus. 2010. (ENG.). 32p. (J). (gr. 4-7). 16.95 *(978-1-934960-82-0(9)*, Raven Tree Pr.,Csi) Continental Sales, Inc.

—Grandma's Pear Tree/El Peral de Abuela. Pernisco, Atilio, illus. 2010. (ENG & SPA.). 32p. (J). (gr. 4-7). 16.95 *(978-1-934960-80-6(2)*, Raven Tree Pr.,Csi) Continental Sales, Inc.

Scali, Jacob, et al. Sprucy: The Tallest Christmas Tree. Carrier, Jason, illus. 2011. (ENG.). 32p. (J). (gr. k-4). 14.99 *(978-1-4634-2468-8(X)*, 9781463424688) AuthorHouse.

Scanlon, Liz Garton. Another Way to Climb a Tree. Hooper, Hadley, illus. 2017. (ENG.). 40p. (J). 17.99 *(978-1-62672-352-8(4)*, 9781626723528) Roaring Brook Pr.

Schneider, Richard H. Why Christmas Trees Aren't Perfect. 2016. (ENG.). 32p. 12.99 *(978-1-5018-2583-5(6)*, Cokesbury) Abingdon Pr.

Schorr, Titus. Tony's Tree, 01 vols., 1. 2016. (Rosen REAL Readers: Social Studies Nonfiction / Fiction: Family, Community, & the World Ser.). (ENG.). 12p. (J). pap. 6.33 *(978-1-5081-2000-1(5)*, Rosen Classroom) Rosen Publishing Group, Inc., The.

Schouest, Stacey. The Very 1st Christmas Tree. 2011. 44p. pap. 16.95 *(978-1-4497-2528-0(7)*, WestBow Pr.) Author Solutions, Inc.

Schram, Peninnah & Davis, Rachayl Eckstein. The Apple Tree's Discovery. Lee, Wendy W., illus. 2012. (Kar-Ben Favorites Ser.). (ENG.). 24p. (J). (gr. -1-2). pap. 7.95 *(978-0-7613-5132-0(9))*; lib. bdg. 16.95 *(978-0-7613-5130-6(2))* Lerner Publishing Group. (Kar-Ben Publishing).

Schultz, Agnes Szenozicska. The Little Tree. 2007. 32p. (J). 14.00 *(978-0-8059-7211-5(0))* Dorrance Publishing Co., Inc.

Schwartz, Suzanne & Schwartz, Robert. The Christmas Palm Tree: A Storybook to Color. Schwartz, Suzanne & Schwartz, Robert, illus. l.t. ed. 2005. (Illus.). 22p. (J). spiral bd. 3.99 *(978-0-9764152-3-7(2))* Seascay Productions.

Scott-Branagan, Brownen. The Pandanuspeople. 2009. 32p. pap. 13.75 *(978-1-60860-006-9(8)*, Strategic Bk. Publishing) Strategic Book Publishing & Rights Agency (SBPRA).

Scott, Earnestine E. Little Mike's Family: A Novel for Second & Third Graders. 2012. 30p. 24.95 *(978-1-4626-6018-6(5))* America Star Bks.

Scott, Leah. Tincup & the Tornado. 2012. (ENG.). 34p. (J). pap. 12.95 *(978-1-4327-8695-3(4))*; pap. 18.95 *(978-1-4327-8826-1(4))* Outskirts Pr., Inc.

Sera, Lucia. Another Tree in the Yard. Lonergan Iorio, John, illus. 2004. 32p. (J). per. 16.95 *(978-1-932653-36-6(8))* Vocalis, Ltd.

Seredy, Kate. A Tree for Peter. Seredy, Kate, illus. 2004. (Illus.). 112p. (J). reprint ed. 19.95 *(978-1-930900-26-4(0))* Purple Hse. Pr.

Sevonna. Simon, the Christmas Tree Fle. 2012. 32p. pap. 21.99 *(978-1-4771-3105-3(1))* Xlibris Corp.

Shankman, Ed. Champ & Me by the Maple Tree. O'Neill, Dave, illus. 2010. (Shankman & O'Neill Ser.). (ENG.). 32p. (gr. -1-3). 14.95 *(978-0-9819430-5-3(5)*, Commonwealth Editions) Applewood Bks.

Shannon, Terry Miller. George & the Cherry Tree. 2016. (Spring Forward Ser.). (J). (gr. 1). *(978-1-4900-9408-3(3))* Benchmark Education Co.

Shapiro, Lindy. Moon Mangoes. Peterson, Kathleen, illus. 2011. (ENG.). 36p. (J). (gr. -1-2). 14.95 *(978-1-933067-42-1(X))* Beachhouse Publishing, LLC.

Sharp, Euan. Diggedy Dozer in Treetop Troubles. 2008. 34p. 15.95 *(978-1-4357-0982-9(9))* Lulu Pr., Inc.

Shelby, Anne. The Man Who Lived in a Hollow Tree. Hazelaar, Cor, illus. 2009. (ENG.). 40p. (J). (gr. -1-2). 17.99 *(978-0-689-86169-7(9)*, Atheneum/Richard Jackson Bks.) Simon & Schuster Children's Publishing.

Shoen, Melinda. Invisible Me: A Walking Stick's Wish. 2009. 24p. pap. 11.79 *(978-1-4389-4851-5(4))* AuthorHouse.

Shuff, Chrissi. The Dancing Tree & other Stories. 2010. (Illus.). 80p. pap. 28.99 *(978-1-4520-0054-1(9))* AuthorHouse.

Silber, Jere. Tree Story. 2008. 44p. pap. 19.95 *(978-1-4343-9682-2(7))* AuthorHouse.

Silverstein, Shel. The Giving Tree. (Illus.). 95.94 *(978-0-06-056897-9(6))* HarperCollins Pubs.

—The Giving Tree. Silverstein, Shel, illus. (Illus.). 64p. 2003. (J). (gr. -1-3). lib. bdg. 17.89 *(978-0-06-025666-1(4))* anniv. ed. 2014. (ENG., (J). (gr. -1-3). 19.99 *(978-0-06-058675-1(3))* gif. ed. 2007. 16.99 *(978-0-06-124001-0(X))* 50th anniv. ed. 2014. (ENG., (J). (gr. -1-3). 17.99 *(978-0-06-025665-4(6)*, HC5567) HarperCollins Pubs.

Simmons, Mary Louise. The Little Fir Tree Who Wanted a Friend. 2008. 28p. per. 24.95 *(978-1-60441-391-5(3))* America Star Bks.

Simon, Jenne. Let's Pick Apples. Hill, Prescott, illus. 2013. (Lalaloopsy Ser.). (ENG.). 32p. (J). (gr. -1-3). pap. 3.99 *(978-0-545-53182-5(9))* Scholastic, Inc.

Simpson, Lesley. Yuvi's Candy Tree. Porter, Janice Lee, illus. 2011. (ENG.). 32p. (J). (gr. k-3). pap. 7.95 *(978-0-7613-5652-3(5))*; lib. bdg. 17.95 *(978-0-7613-5651-6(7))* Lerner Publishing Group. (Kar-Ben Publishing).

Smith, Jodene Lynn & Rice, Dona Herweck. If I Were a Tree, 1 vol. 2010. (Early Childhood Themes Ser.). (ENG., Illus.). 16p. (J). (gr. -1-2). pap. 6.99 *(978-1-4333-1487-2(8))*; pap. 19.99 *(978-1-4333-1488-9(6))* Shell Educational Publishing.

Smith, Linda. The Inside Tree. Brown, Kathryn, illus. Date not set. 32p. (J). (gr. -1-3). 5.99 *(978-0-06-443542-0(3))* HarperCollins Pubs.

Smith, Roy. Louphole Forest Tells Its Tale of Enchantment. Magpie, ed. Burnell Walsh, Avenda, illus. 2012. 38p. *(978-1-908000-18-7(X))* Pyjama Pr.

Smucker, Shawn. The Day the Angels Fell. 2017. (ENG.). 320p. (YA). 17.99 ***(978-0-8007-2849-6(1))*** Revell.

Spalding, Andrea. Solomon's Tree, 1 vol. Wilson, Janet, illus. 2005. (ENG.). 32p. (J). (gr. -1-3). 10.95 *(978-1-55143-380-6(X))* Orca Bk. Pubs. USA.

Speed, Bryan W. Little Bent Cedar. Todd, Sheri, illus. 2007. (ENG.). 24p. (J). (gr. 2-4). per. *(978-1-933255-38-5(2))* DNA Pr.

Stack, Kevin W. The Great Oak Tree. 2008. (Illus.). 32p. pap. 12.99 *(978-1-4389-1856-3(9))* AuthorHouse.

Standiford, Natalie. The Secret Tree. (J). 2014. (ENG.). 256p. (gr. 3-7). pap. 6.99 *(978-0-545-33480-8(2)*, Scholastic Paperbacks) 2012. 245p. pap. *(978-0-545-48976-8(8)*, Scholastic Pr.) Scholastic, Inc.

Starks-Johnson, Annie. Dottie Meets Gilda the Old Oak Tree. 2009. 28p. pap. 12.49 *(978-1-4389-5361-8(5))* AuthorHouse.

Stewart, Joel. Tree Soup. 2011. (Stanley Wells Mystery Ser.: 2). (ENG., Illus.). 180p. (J). (gr. 2-4). pap. 9.99 *(978-0-440-86717-3(7))* Transworld Publishers Ltd. GBR. Dist: Independent Pubs. Group.

Strange, J. R. The Tree & the Light. Massivebrain.com, illus. 2013. 48p. pap. 11.99 *(978-0-9887214-0-1(6))* Firesidenook.

Strathie, Chae. The Tickle Tree. Bernatene, Poly, illus. 2008. 24p. (J). (gr. -1-1). *(978-1-84539-344-1(9))*; *(978-1-84539-345-8(7))* Meadowside Children's Bks.

Stuart & McArthur, Amanda. Humphry & the Tree. 2012. 24p. pap. 15.99 *(978-1-4691-5082-6(4))* Xlibris Corp.

Suchy, Julianne. Leaf Me Alone. 2009. 36p. pap. 13.95 *(978-1-60693-300-8(0)*, Eloquent Bks.) Strategic Book Publishing & Rights Agency (SBPRA).

Summers, Gillian. Shadows of the Redwood Bk. 1, Bk. 1. 2010. (Faire Folk Saga Ser.: 4). (ENG.). 336p. (YA). (gr. 7-18). pap. 9.95 *(978-0-7387-1552-0(2)*, Flux) North Star Editions.

The Talking Christmas Tree. 2003. (J). per. *(978-1-57657-925-1(5))* Paradise Pr., Inc.

Tara, Stephanie Lisa. Eliza's Forever Trees. Walton, Alex, illus. 2012. 290p. (J). pap. 9.99 net. *(978-1-61254-067-2(8))* Brown Books Publishing Group.

Tatsuyama, Sayuri. Happy Happy Clover, Vol. 4. Tatsuyama, Sayuri, illus. 2010. (ENG., Illus.). 192p. (J). pap. 7.99 *(978-1-4215-2735-2(9))* Viz Media.

Taylor, Mildred D. Song of the Trees. Pinkney, Jerry, illus. 2003. (ENG.). 80p. (J). (gr. 5-7). 7.99 *(978-0-14-250075-0(5)*, Puffin Books) Penguin Young Readers Group.

Teckentrup, Britta. Tree: A Peek-Through Picture Book. 2016. (ENG.). 32p. (J). (gr. -1-2). 14.99 *(978-1-101-93242-1(2)*, Doubleday Bks. for Young Readers) Random Hse. Children's Bks.

The Library Fairy. The Magical Tree & Musical Wind. Faust, Laurie A., illus. 2008. 32p. pap. 16.95 *(978-1-59858-604-6(1))* Dog Ear Publishing, LLC.

Thomas, John & Rowe, Susan. Mynydd y Brain. 2005. (WEL., Illus.). 32p. pap. *(978-1-85596-221-7(7))* Dref Wen.

Thompson, Lauren. The Apple Pie That Papa Baked. Bean, Jonathan, illus. 2007. (ENG.). 32p. (J). (gr. k-3). 17.99 *(978-1-4169-1240-8(1)*, Simon & Schuster Bks. For Young Readers) Simon & Schuster Bks. For Young Readers.

Tim Todd. The Town of Ill. 2009. 36p. pap. 18.99 *(978-1-4389-2778-7(9))* AuthorHouse.

Toombs, Tom. The Mysterious Money Tree: Little Tommy Learns a Lesson in Giving. Smith, Abby, illus. 2012. 28p. (J). pap. 12.95 *(978-1-61314-033-8(9)*, Innovo Pr.) Innovo Publishing, LLC.

Torrance-Matthews, Armer, et al. Miss Bertha, the Talking Tree: A Delightful Story of a Talking Tree. 2010. 36p. pap. 18.95 *(978-1-4269-2051-6(2))* Trafford Publishing.

Trembley, Skip & Ochs, Susan A. You'll See, Little Tree. Hollis, Michael, illus. 2003. (J). pap. 7.95 *(978-0-9643452-2-5(6))* Graphics North.

Trinco, Trish. The Leaf That Wouldn't Leave. Langdo, Bryan, illus. 2008. (ENG.). 32p. (J). 16.95 *(978-0-931674-90-7(5)*, Waldman House Pr.) TRISTAN Publishing, Inc.

Trites, Judy. Charlie's Challenge. 2011. 24p. pap. 15.99 *(978-1-4628-4568-2(1))* Xlibris Corp.

Tu, Tzu Hui. Traveling Tree. 2012. 36p. pap. 20.99 *(978-1-4685-9594-9(6))* AuthorHouse.

Tukel, Onur. Little Friends, 0 vols. 2012. (ENG.). 64p. (J). (gr. 1-4). 14.99 *(978-0-7614-6260-6(0)*, 9780761462606, Amazon Children's Publishing) Amazon Publishing.

Tunbridge, J. L. The Jellybean Tree. 2012. 40p. pap. 15.95 *(978-1-4525-0813-9(5))* Balboa Pr.

Uncle Chuck. The Monkey Puzzle Tree. 2011. 32p. pap. 24.95 *(978-1-4560-6992-6(6))* America Star Bks.

Van, Muon. The Little Tree. Adinolfi, JoAnn, illus. 2015. (ENG.). 32p. (J). (gr. -1). 16.95 *(978-1-939547-19-4(9))* Creston Bks.

Vance, L. K. Jennadi. 2006. 73p. pap. 16.95 *(978-1-4241-1574-7(4))* PublishAmerica, Inc.

VanDerlinden, Jean A. The Family Tree: The Secret Door. 2013. 64p. pap. 24.99 *(978-1-4772-7941-0(5))* AuthorHouse.

Verrett, Michael. Galid's Christmas Wish. 2010. 44p. pap. 22.90 *(978-0-557-29109-0(7))* Lulu Pr., Inc.

Violet Mackerel's Pocket Protest. 2014. (Violet Mackerel Ser.). (ENG., Illus.). 128p. (J). (gr. 1-5). 17.99 *(978-1-4424-9458-9(1)*, Atheneum Bks. for Young Readers) Simon & Schuster Children's Publishing.

Vos, Sharon. Neddy the Nutty Acorn. Rosenfelder, Cheryl, illus. 2008. 40p. per. 24.95 *(978-1-60441-232-1(1))* America Star Bks.

Wahl, Charis. Rosario's Fig Tree, 1 vol. Melanson, Luc, illus. 2015. (ENG.). 32p. (J). (gr. -1-2). 18.95 *(978-1-55498-341-4(X))* Groundwood Bks. CAN. Dist: Publishers Group West (PGW).

Wales, Amy S. Fiona & the Fiddle Tree. 2012. 32p. pap. 21.99 *(978-1-4691-5485-5(4))* Xlibris Corp.

Walker, Crystal. Maceys Magic Tree. 2009. 28p. pap. 12.49 *(978-1-4490-4916-4(8))* AuthorHouse.

Walker, Mary. The Flower Tree. 2010. (Illus.). 50p. pap. 12.95 *(978-1-4327-3588-3(8))* Outskirts Pr., Inc.

Walsh, Ann. Flower Power, 1 vol. 2005. (Orca Currents Ser.). (ENG.). 128p. (J). (gr. 5-9). per. 9.95 *(978-1-55143-386-8(9))* Orca Bk. Pubs. USA.

Ward, Jennifer. The Busy Tree, 0 vols. Falkenstern, Lisa, illus. 2009. (ENG.). 32p. (J). (gr. k-3). 17.99 *(978-0-7614-5550-9(7)*, 9780761455509, Amazon Children's Publishing) Amazon Publishing.

Waszak, Madonna. Mason's Mashed Potato Tree. Johnston, Lisa Harp, illus. 2011. 34p. pap. 14.95 *(978-1-4575-0159-3(7))* Dog Ear Publishing, LLC.

Watkins, Albert. The Brothers Three. l.t. ed. 2004. (Illus.). 48p. (J). pap. 22.95 *(978-0-9629124-4-3(1))* Floppinfish Publishing Co., Ltd.

Watkins, Samuel R. Precious Palm Tree. 2011. 32p. (gr. -1). pap. 17.25 *(978-1-4269-5267-8(8))* Trafford Publishing.

Weber, Rivka Doba. Dear Tree. Rosenfeld, D. L., ed. Saroff, Phyllis, illus. 2010. 24p. (YA). 10.95 *(978-1-929628-48-3(X))* Hachai Publishing.

Weinberger, David J. Answers to a Christmas Question. 2012. (ENG.). (J). pap. *(978-1-4675-2381-3(X))* Independent Pub.

—Answers to a Christmas Question Coloring Book. 2012. (ENG.). (J). pap. *(978-1-4675-2380-6(1))* Independent Pub.

Wellington, Monica. My Leaf Book. 2015. (ENG., Illus.). 32p. (J). (gr. -1-k). 16.99 *(978-0-8037-4141-6(3)*, Dial Bks) Penguin Young Readers Group.

Wells, Rita. Janie Plants a Tree. 2013. 26p. pap. 16.95 *(978-1-4497-8903-9(X)*, WestBow Pr.) Author Solutions, Inc.

Wells, Rosemary. Ruby's Falling Leaves. 2007. (Max & Ruby Ser.). lib. bdg. 13.55 *(978-1-4177-9651-9(0)*, Turtleback) Turtleback Bks.

Welsh, Kenneth Wilbur. The Oak Brothers. 2011. 16p. 12.00 *(978-1-4520-6079-8(7))* AuthorHouse.

Weston Woods Staff, creator. Fletcher & the Falling Leaves. 2011. 38.75 *(978-0-545-19710-6(4))* Weston Woods Studios, Inc.

The Whispering Sycamore. 2012. (Illus.). 24p. pap. 8.99 *(978-1-938768-02-6(7))* Gypsy Pubns.

Williams, Karen Lynn. Circles of Hope. Saport, Linda, illus. 2005. (ENG.). 32p. (J). 16.00 *(978-0-8028-5276-2(9))* Eerdmans, William B. Publishing Co.

Williams, Mercedes. The Little Tree. 2011. 16p. pap. 18.95 *(978-0-557-84137-0(2))* Lulu Pr., Inc.

Wilson, Melissa Anne. Nalyn & the Indigo Pearl. 2008. (Illus.). 24p. (J). pap. 8.00 *(978-0-8059-7409-6(1))* Dorrance Publishing Co., Inc.

Wilson, N. D. The Door Before (100 Cupboards Prequel) 2017. (ENG.). 240p. (J). (gr. 3-7). lib. bdg. 19.99 *(978-0-449-81678-3(8)*, Random Hse. Bks. for Young Readers) Random Hse. Children's Bks.

Wilson, Wendy. The First Book of Red. 2005. 99p. pap. 19.95 *(978-1-4137-5570-1(4))* America Star Bks.

Woebkenberg, Valerie. The Story the Little Christmas Tree Told. 2013. 26.95 *(978-0-7414-8367-6(X))* Infinity Publishing.

Woebkenberg, Valerie & Ingels, Diane. The Story the Little Christmas Tree Told. 2012. pap. 11.95 *(978-0-7414-8095-8(6))* Infinity Publishing.

Youngs, Puma Wun. Dreamtime. 2010. 28p. pap. 13.99 *(978-1-4490-8378-6(1))* AuthorHouse.

Zhou, Carmen. A Tree's Dream. 2012. 24p. pap. 15.99 *(978-1-4691-8958-1(5))* Xlibris Corp.

Ziskind, Hélio & Duchesne, Christiane. Le Géant de la Forêt: Un Voyage Musical. Pratt, Pierre, illus. 2014. (FRE.). 48p. (J). (gr. k-2). 16.95 *(978-2-923163-36-9(2))* La Montagne Secrete CAN. Dist: Independent Pubs. Group.

Zito, Ann R. Rock, Stream, Tree. Matheny, Melody, illus. 2010. 52p. pap. 11.00 *(978-1-4520-7822-9(X))* AuthorHouse.

Zweibel, Alan. Our Tree Named Steve. Catrow, David & David, Catrow, illus. 2007. (ENG.). 32p. (J). (gr. -1-k). pap. 5.99 *(978-0-14-240743-1(7)*, Puffin Books) Penguin Young Readers Group.

—Our Tree Named Steve. 2007. 16.00 *(978-1-4177-6974-2(2)*, Turtleback) Turtleback Bks.

TREES—POETRY

Florian, Douglas. Poetrees. Florian, Douglas, illus. 2010. (ENG., Illus.). 48p. (J). (gr. 1-5). 17.99 *(978-1-4169-8672-0(3)*, Beach Lane Bks.) Beach Lane Bks.

George, Kristine O'Connell. Old Elm Speaks. Kiesler, Kate, illus. 2007. (ENG.). 48p. (J). (gr. -1-3). 6.99 *(978-0-618-75242-3(0))* Houghton Mifflin Harcourt Publishing Co.

Johnston, Tony. Sequoia. Minor, Wendell, illus. 2014. (ENG.). 40p. (J). (gr. -1-3). 18.99 *(978-1-59643-727-2(8)*, 9781596437272) Roaring Brook Pr.

Mervyn, Catherine Antolino. A Lesson from a Tree. Carr, Tabatha, illus. 2008. 32p. pap. 12.95 *(978-0-9821153-2-9(6))* Living Waters Publishing Co.

Singh, Rina. A Forest of Stories: Magical Tree Tales from Around the World. Cann, Helen, illus. 2003. 64p. (J). 19.99 *(978-1-84148-963-6(8))* Barefoot Bks., Inc.

TRENTON (N.J.)

Waldman, Scott P. The Battle of Trenton. 2003. (Atlas of Famous Battles of the American Revolution Ser.). (Illus.). 24p. (J). lib. bdg. 22.60 *(978-0-8239-6333-1(0)*, PowerKids Pr.) Rosen Publishing Group, Inc., The.

TRIAL BY JURY

see Jury

TRIALS

Blohm, Craig E. The O. J. Simpson Case. 2008. (Crime Scene Investigations Ser.). (ENG., Illus.). 104p. (YA). (gr. 7-10). lib. bdg. 35.45 *(978-1-4205-0038-7(4)*, LML02109-240025, Lucent Bks.) Cengage Gale.

Cates, David. The Scottsboro Boys, 1 vol. 2012. (Essential Events Set 8 Ser.). (ENG.). 112p. (J). (gr. 6-12). lib. bdg. 35.64 *(978-1-61783-310-6(X))* ABDO Publishing Co.

Coleman, Wim & Perrin, Pat. Racism on Trial: From the Medgar Evers Murder Case to Ghosts of Mississippi. 2009. (Famous Court Cases That Became Movies Ser.). (Illus.). 112p. (J). (gr. 7-12). lib. bdg. 33.27 *(978-0-7660-3059-6(8))* Enslow Pubs., Inc.

Crewe, Sabrina & Uschan, Michael V. The Scottsboro Case. 2004. (Events That Shaped America Ser.). (Illus.). 32p. (gr. 3-6). lib. bdg. 26.00 *(978-0-8368-3407-9(0)*, Gareth Stevens Learning Library) Stevens, Gareth Publishing LLLP.

Currie, Stephen. The Struggle for Equality: Landmark Court Cases. 2009. (Lucent Library of Black History Ser.). (ENG., Illus.). 128p. (gr. 7-10). 39.40 *(978-1-4205-0122-3(4)*, Lucent Bks.) Cengage Gale.

D'Costa, Jasmine. Real Justice: Branded a Baby Killer: The Story of Tammy Marquardt. 2015. (Lorimer Real Justice Ser.). (ENG., Illus.). 120p. (YA). (gr. 9-12). pap. 12.95 *(978-1-4594-0993-4(0))* Lorimer, James & Co., Ltd., Pubs. CAN. Dist: Casemate Pubs. & Bk. Distributors, LLC.

D'Costa, Jasmine Anita Yvette. Branded a Baby Killer: The Story of Tammy Marquardt. 2016. (Lorimer Real Justice Ser.). (ENG.). 120p. (YA). (gr. 9-12). lib. bdg. 27.99 *(978-1-4594-0994-1(9)*, 9781459409941) Lorimer, James & Co., Ltd., Pubs. CAN. Dist: Casemate Pubs. & Bk. Distributors, LLC.

Doeden, Matt. The Salem Witch Trials: An Interactive History Adventure. (You Choose: History Ser.). (ENG.). 112p. (gr. 3-4). 2011. pap. 41.70 *(978-1-4296-6440-0(1))* 2010. 31.99 *(978-1-4296-5478-4(3))* Capstone Press of Coughlan Cos. (You Choose Bks.).

Don Nardo. The Trial of Galileo. 2003. (Famous Trials Ser.). (ENG., Illus.). 112p. (J). 29.95 *(978-1-59018-423-3(8))* Cengage Gale.

Donnelly, Karen J. Cruzan v. Missouri: The Right to Die. 2004. (Supreme Court Cases Through Primary Sources Ser.). (Illus.). 64p. (YA). (gr. 5-9). lib. bdg. 31.95 *(978-0-8239-4014-1(4))* Rosen Publishing Group, Inc., The.

Ferguson, Amanda. The Attack Against the U. S. Embassies in Kenya & Tanzania. (Terrorist Attacks Ser.). 64p. 2009. (gr. 5-5). 58.50 *(978-1-60853-309-1(3))* 2005. (Illus.). (J). (gr. 7-12). lib. bdg. 31.95 *(978-0-8239-3652-6(X))* Rosen Publishing Group, Inc., The.

Fireside, Bryna J. The Trial of the Police Officers in the Shooting Death of Amadou Diallo: A Headline Court Case. 2004. (Headline Court Cases Ser.). (Illus.). 128p. (J). lib. bdg. 27.94 *(978-0-7660-2166-2(1))* Enslow Pubs., Inc.

Gold, Susan Dudley. Clear & Present Danger: Schenck V. United States. 2014. (J). lib. bdg. *(978-1-62712-387-7(3))* Cavendish Square Publishing.

Gourley, Catherine. The Horrors of Andersonville: Life & Death Inside a Civil War Prison. 2010. (ENG.). 192p. (gr. 9-12). lib. bdg. 38.60 *(978-0-7613-4212-0(5))* Lerner Publishing Group.

Graves, Renee. The Scopes Trial. 2003. (Cornerstones of Freedom Ser.). (ENG., Illus.). 48p. (YA). (gr. 4-7). 26.00 *(978-0-516-24221-7(0))* Scholastic Library Publishing.

Headline Court Cases, 21 bks., Set. Incl. Alger Hiss Communist Spy Trial: A Headline Court Case. Alonso, Karen. 128p. (J). 2001. lib. bdg. 27.94 *(978-0-7660-1483-1(5))*; Andersonville Prison Civil War Crimes Trial: A Headline Court Case. Banfield, Susan. 112p. (J). 2000. lib. bdg. 26.60 *(978-0-7660-1386-5(3))*; Court-Martial Trial of West Point Cadet Johnson Whittaker: A Headline Court Case. Gray, Valerie A. 104p. (J). 2001. lib. bdg. 26.60 *(978-0-7660-1485-5(1))*; John Brown Slavery Revolt Trial: A Headline Court Case. DeVillers, David. 104p. (YA). 2000. lib. bdg. 26.60 *(978-0-7660-1385-8(5))*; Lindbergh Baby Kidnapping Trial: A Headline Court Case. Monroe, Judy. 128p. (YA). 2000. lib. bdg. 26.60 *(978-0-7660-1389-6(8))*; Lizzie Borden "Axe Murder" Trial: A Headline Court Case. Axelrod-Contrada, Joan. 128p. (J). 2000. lib. bdg. 26.60 *(978-0-7660-1422-0(3))*; Mary Surratt "Lincoln Assassination" Trial: A Headline Court Case. Fireside, Bryna J. 128p. (J). 2001. lib. bdg. 26.60 *(978-0-7660-1481-7(9))*; Nuremberg Nazi War Crimes Trials: A Headline Court Case. Fireside, Harvey. 128p. (J). 2000. lib. bdg. 27.94 *(978-0-7660-1384-1(7))*; O. J. Simpson Murder Trial: A Headline Court Case. Pellowski, Michael J. 104p. (J). 2001. lib. bdg. 26.60 *(978-0-7660-1480-0(0))*; Rosenberg Cold War Spy Trial: A Headline Court Case. Monroe, Judy. 128p. (J). 2001. lib. bdg. 20.95 *(978-0-7660-1479-4(7))*; Sacco & Vanzetti Controversial Murder Trial: A Headline Court Case. Monroe, Judy. 112p. (YA). 2000. lib. bdg. 26.60 *(978-0-7660-1387-2(1))*; Salem Witchcraft Trials: A Headline Court Case. Woods, Geraldine. 104p. (YA). 2000. lib. bdg. 26.60 *(978-0-7660-1383-4(9))*; Scopes Monkey Trial: A Headline Court Case. Hanson, Freya Ottem. 128p. (YA). 2000. lib. bdg. 26.60 *(978-0-7660-1388-9(X))*; Teapot Dome Scandal: A Headline Court Case. Thorndike, Jonathan L. 104p. (J). 2001. lib. bdg. 26.60 *(978-0-7660-1484-8(3))*; Trial of Gangster Al Capone: A Headline Court Case. Trespacz, Karen L. 112p. (J). 2001. lib. bdg. 26.60 *(978-0-7660-1482-4(7))*; (gr. 6-12). (Illus.). Set lib. bdg. 439.95 *(978-0-7660-1603-3(X))* Enslow Pubs., Inc.

Herda, D. J. Fighting Censorship: New York Times V. United States. 2016. (US Supreme Court Landmark Cases Ser.). (Illus.). 128p. (J). 37.27 *(978-0-7660-8432-2(9))* Enslow Pubs., Inc.

—A Woman's Right to an Abortion: Roe V. Wade. 2016. (US Supreme Court Landmark Cases Ser.). (Illus.). 128p. (J). 37.27 *(978-0-7660-8424-7(8))* Enslow Pubs., Inc.

Hinds, Maurene J. Witchcraft on Trial: From the Salem Witch Hunts to the Crucible. 2009. (Famous Court Cases That Became Movies Ser.). (Illus.). 104p. (J). (gr. 7-12). lib. bdg. 33.27 *(978-0-7660-3055-8(5))* Enslow Pubs., Inc.

Hinton, Kerry. The Trial of Sacco & Vanzetti: A Primary Source Account. (Great Trials of the Twentieth Century Ser.). 64p. (gr. 5-8). 2009. 58.50 *(978-1-61513-220-1(1))* 2004. (Illus.). lib. bdg. 31.95 *(978-0-8239-3973-2(1)*, Rosen Reference) Rosen Publishing Group, Inc., The.

Hitchcock, Susan Tyler. Roe V. Wade: Protecting a Woman's Right to Choose. 2006. (Great Supreme Court Decisions Ser.). (Illus.). 128p. (J). (gr. 5-9). lib. bdg. 32.95 *(978-0-7910-9239-2(9))* Facts On File, Inc.

Knudsen, Shannon. Alice Ray & the Salem Witch Trials. Palmer, Ruth, illus. 2011. (History Speaks: Picture Books Plus Reader's Theater Ser.). (ENG., Illus.). 48p. (gr. 2-4). 27.93 *(978-0-7613-5879-4(X)*, Millbrook Pr.) Lerner Publishing Group.

Landau, Elaine. Sacco & Vanzetti. 2004. (Cornerstones of Freedom Ser.). (ENG., Illus.). 48p. (YA). (gr. 4-7). 26.00 *(978-0-516-24237-8(7))* Scholastic Library Publishing.

Lawrence, Sandra. Twisted History - Trials & Treachery. 2016. (Hideous History Ser.). (ENG., Illus.). 64p. (J). (gr. 5-9). 11.99 *(978-1-4998-0081-4(9))* Little Bee Books Inc.

Lock, Joan. Famous Trials. 2004. (Crime & Detection Ser.). (Illus.). 96p. (YA). (gr. 7-18). lib. bdg. 22.95 *(978-1-59084-381-9(9))* Mason Crest.

Lowery, Zoe & MacBain, Jenny. A Primary Source Investigation of the Salem Witch Trials. 2015. (Uncovering American History Ser.). (ENG., Illus.). 64p. (J). (gr. 5-6). 32.95 *(978-1-4994-3513-9(4)*, Rosen Central) Rosen Publishing Group, Inc., The.

Lucas, Eileen. The Aaron Burr Treason Trial. 2003. (Headline Court Cases Ser.). (Illus.). 112p. (J). (gr. 6-12). lib. bdg. 27.94 *(978-0-7660-1765-8(6))* Enslow Pubs., Inc.

MacBain, Jenny. The Salem Witch Trials: A Primary Source History of the Witchcraft Trials in Salem, Massachusetts. 2003. (Primary Sources in American History Ser.). (Illus.). 64p. (gr. 5-8). lib. bdg. 31.95 *(978-0-8239-3683-0(X)*, Rosen Reference) Rosen Publishing Group, Inc., The.

Malaspina, Ann. Heart on Fire: Susan B. Anthony Votes for President. James, Steven, illus. 2012. (ENG.). 32p. (J). (gr. 1-3). 16.99 *(978-0-8075-3188-4(X))* Whitman, Albert & Co.

Midland, C. J. Found Guilty. 2011. (J). pap. *(978-0-531-22555-4(0))* Scholastic, Inc.

Miller, Sarah. The Borden Murders: Lizzie Borden & the Trial of the Century. 2016. (ENG., Illus.). 304p. (J). (gr. 5). 17.99 *(978-0-553-49808-0(8)*, Schwartz & Wade Bks.) Random Hse. Children's Bks.

Morrison, Toni. Remember: The Journey to School Integration. 2004. (ENG., Illus.). 80p. (J). (gr. -1-3). tchr. ed. 19.99 *(978-0-618-39740-2(X))* Houghton Mifflin Harcourt Publishing Co.

Morse, Scott. Visitations. 2003. (ENG., Illus.). 96p. (YA). (gr. 8-18). pap. 8.95 *(978-1-929998-34-0(1)*, 9781929998340) Oni Pr., Inc.

Pellowski, Michael J. The Charles Manson Murder Trial: A Headline Court Case. 2004. (Headline Court Cases Ser.). (Illus.). 128p. (J). lib. bdg. 26.60 *(978-0-7660-2167-9(X))* Enslow Pubs., Inc.

Perl, Lila. Cruzan V. Missouri: The Right to Die. 2007. (Supreme Court Milestones Ser.). (Illus.). 128p. (gr. 7-7). lib. bdg. 42.79 *(978-0-7614-2581-6(0)*, Benchmark Bks.) Marshall Cavendish Corp.

Pettifor, Bonnie & Petit, Charles E. McCulloch V. Maryland: When State & Federal Powers Conflict. 2004. (Landmark Supreme Court Cases Ser.). (Illus.). 128p. (J). lib. bdg. 27.94 *(978-0-7660-1887-7(3))* Enslow Pubs., Inc.

Randolph, Ryan P. Marbury V. Madison: The New Supreme Court Gets More Power. 2004. (Life in the New American Nation Ser.). (ENG., Illus.). 32p. (gr. 5-8). pap. 10.00 *(978-0-8239-4252-7(X))* Rosen Publishing Group, Inc., The.

Roensch, Greg. The Lindbergh Baby Kidnapping Trial: A Primary Source Account. 2004. (Great Trials of the Twentieth Century Ser.). (Illus.). 64p. (gr. 5-8). lib. bdg. 31.95 *(978-0-8239-3971-8(5)*, Rosen Reference) Rosen Publishing Group, Inc., The.

Slavicek, Louise Chipley. The Salem Witch Trial: Hysteria in Colonial America. 2011. (Milestones in American History Ser.). (Illus.). 124p. (gr. 6-12). 35.00 *(978-1-60413-763-7(0)*, Chelsea Hse.) Facts On File, Inc.

Smith, Andrea P. The Salem Witch Trials. 2012. (Illus.). 24p. 63.60 *(978-1-4488-5215-4(3))*; pap. 10.60 *(978-1-4488-5214-7(5))*; lib. bdg. 25.25 *(978-1-4488-5188-1(2))* Rosen Publishing Group, Inc., The. (PowerKids Pr.).

Toth, Henrietta. The Murder of Emmett Till. 2017. pap. ***(978-1-5383-8054-3(4))*** Rosen Publishing Group, Inc., The.

Uschan, Michael V. The Salem Witch Trials. 2004. (Landmark Events in American History Ser.). (Illus.). 48p. (gr. 5-12). pap. 14.05 *(978-0-8368-5415-2(2))*; lib. bdg. 31.00 *(978-0-8368-5387-2(3))* Stevens, Gareth Publishing LLLP. (Gareth Stevens Secondary Library).

—The Scottsboro Case. 2004. (Landmark Events in American History Ser.). (Illus.). 48p. (gr. 5-12). lib. bdg. 31.00 *(978-0-8368-5388-9(1)*, Gareth Stevens Secondary Library) Stevens, Gareth Publishing LLLP.

Van Meter, Larry A. Miranda V. Arizona: The Rights of the Accused. 2006. (Great Supreme Court Decisions Ser.). (Illus.). 112p. (YA). (gr. 5-9). 32.95 *(978-0-7910-9259-0(3))* Facts On File, Inc.

von Zumbusch, Amelie. The True Story of the Salem Witch Hunts. 2009. (What Really Happened? Ser.). 24p. (gr. 2-3). 42.50 *(978-1-60854-770-8(1)*, PowerKids Pr.) Rosen Publishing Group, Inc., The.

TRIALS—FICTION

Basye, Dale E. Snivel: the Fifth Circle of Heck. Dob, Bob, illus. 2013. (Heck Ser.). (ENG.). 448p. (J). (gr. 4-7). 8.99 *(978-0-375-86806-1(2)*, Yearling) Random Hse. Children's Bks.

Bolte, Marissa. Arrested for Witchcraft! Nickolas Flux & the Salem Witch Trials, 1 vol. Ginevra, Dante, illus. 2014. (Nickolas Flux History Chronicles Ser.). (ENG.). (gr. 3-4). 40p. pap. 7.95 *(978-1-4765-5151-7(0))*; 32p. lib. bdg. 30.65 *(978-1-4765-3947-8(2))* Capstone Press of Coughlan Cos. (Graphic Library).

Bond, Douglas. Hand of Vengeance. 2012. (J). pap. *(978-1-59638-215-2(5))* P & R Publishing.

Bryant, Jennifer. The Trial. 2005. (ENG., Illus.). 176p. (J). (gr. 3-7). 5.99 *(978-0-440-41986-0(7)*, Yearling) Random Hse. Children's Bks.

Davies, Jacqueline. The Lemonade Crime. 2011. (Lemonade War Ser.: 2). (ENG., Illus.). 160p. (J). (gr. 2-5). 15.99 *(978-0-547-27967-1(1))* Houghton Mifflin Harcourt Publishing Co.

—The Lemonade Crime. 2012. (Lemonade War Ser.: 2). lib. bdg. 18.40 *(978-0-606-24518-0(9)*, Turtleback) Turtleback Bks.

Gilbert, Kelly Loy. Conviction. 2015. (ENG.). 352p. (YA). (gr. 7-12). 17.99 *(978-1-4231-9738-6(0))* Hyperion Bks. for Children.

Grisham, John. The Accused. (Theodore Boone Ser.: 3). (ENG.). (J). (gr. 3-7). 2013. 304p. pap. 8.99 *(978-0-14-242613-5(X)*, Puffin Books) 2012. 288p. 16.99 *(978-0-525-42576-2(4)*, Dutton Books for Young Readers) Penguin Young Readers Group.

—The Accused. 2013. (Theodore Boone Ser.: 3). lib. bdg. 18.40 *(978-0-606-31696-5(5)*, Turtleback) Turtleback Bks.

—Kid Lawyer. (Theodore Boone Ser.: 1). (ENG.). (J). (gr. 3-7). 2011. 288p. 8.99 *(978-0-14-241722-5(X)*, Puffin Books) 2010. 272p. 16.99 *(978-0-525-42384-3(2)*, Dutton Books for Young Readers) Penguin Young Readers Group.

—Kid Lawyer. l.t. ed. 2010. (Theodore Boone Ser.: Bk. 1). (ENG.). 278p. (J). 24.99 *(978-1-4104-3050-2(2))* Thorndike Pr.

—Kid Lawyer. 2011. (Theodore Boone Ser.: 1). lib. bdg. 19.65 *(978-0-606-23071-1(8)*, Turtleback) Turtleback Bks.

Lee, J. A. The Trials of Edward Finlay. 2010. 223p. pap. 15.99 *(978-0-557-36757-3(3))* Lulu Pr., Inc.

Mackall, Dandi Daley. The Silence of Murder. 2011. (ENG.). 336p. (YA). (gr. 9). 16.99 *(978-0-375-86896-2(8)*, Knopf Bks. for Young Readers) Random Hse. Children's Bks.

Miller, Marvin. You Be the Jury: Courtroom Collection. Roper, Bob, illus. 2005. 361p. pap. *(978-0-439-77480-2(2))* Scholastic, Inc.

Montgomery, Lewis B. The Case of the Locked Box. Wummer, Amy, illus. 2013. (ENG.). (J). (gr. 2-4). (Milo & Jazz Mysteries (r) Ser.: 11). 112p. pap. 6.95 *(978-1-57565-626-7(4))*; (Milo & Jazz Mysteries Ser.: Vol. 11). 106p. lib. bdg. 22.60 *(978-1-57565-625-0(6))* Kane Press, Inc.

Myers, Walter Dean. Monster. Myers, Christopher, illus. 2004. (Monster Ser.). (ENG.). 304p. (YA). (gr. 8). reprint ed. pap. 9.99 *(978-0-06-440731-1(4)*, Amistad) HarperCollins Pubs.

Pearsall, Shelley. Crooked River. 2007. (ENG.). 272p. (J). (gr. 3-7). 7.99 *(978-0-440-42101-6(2)*, Yearling) Random Hse. Children's Bks.

Smith-Ready, Jeri. Shade. (ENG.). (YA). (gr. 9). 2011. 336p. pap. 9.99 *(978-1-4169-9407-7(6))* 2010. 320p. 17.99 *(978-1-4169-9406-0(8))* Simon Pulse. (Simon Pulse).

Thompson, Paul B. The Devil's Door: A Salem Witchcraft Story. 2010. (Historical Fiction Adventures (HFA) Ser.). (Illus.). 160p. (J). (gr. 3-6). 29.27 *(978-0-7660-3387-0(2))* Enslow Pubs., Inc.

TRIBES

Gachot, Lynn. June-Ah-Vee's Blessing. 2010. 24p. 14.50 *(978-1-4520-7747-5(9))* AuthorHouse.

TRIBES AND TRIBAL SYSTEM

see Tribes

TRICKS

see also Card Tricks; Magic

Amazing Tricks: Level L, 6 vols. 128p. (gr. 2-3). 40.50 *(978-0-7699-0996-7(5))* Shortland Pubns. (U. S. A.) Inc.

Barnhart, Norm. Fantastically Funny Tricks, 1 vol. 2013. (Magic Manuals Ser.). (ENG.). 32p. (gr. 3-4). 27.99 *(978-1-4765-0136-9(X)*, Edge Bks.) Capstone Press of Coughlan Cos.

—Marvelous Money Tricks, 1 vol. 2013. (Magic Manuals Ser.). (ENG.). 32p. (gr. 3-4). 27.99 *(978-1-4765-0134-5(3)*, Edge Bks.) Capstone Press of Coughlan Cos.

—Stunning Stage Tricks, 1 vol. 2013. (Magic Manuals Ser.). (ENG.). 32p. (gr. 3-4). 27.99 *(978-1-4765-0135-2(1)*, Edge Bks.) Capstone Press of Coughlan Cos.

Brunelle, Lynn. Mama's Little Book of Tricks: Keep the Kids Entertained! Eckel, Jessie & Mount, Arthur, illus. 2007. (ENG.). 144p. (gr. 8-17). pap. 12.95 *(978-0-8118-5571-6(6))* Chronicle Bks. LLC.

Charney, Steve. Awesome Coin Tricks, 1 vol. 2010. (Easy Magic Tricks Ser.). (ENG.). 24p. (gr. 1-2). lib. bdg. 25.32 *(978-1-4296-4514-0(8)*, First Facts) Capstone Press of Coughlan Cos.

Cooke, Tim. Magic & Illusions. 2015. (ENG., Illus.). 32p. (J). *(978-0-7787-8072-4(4))* Crabtree Publishing Co.

Crompton, Richmal. Just William's Tricks. 2003. (ENG., Illus.). 64p. (J). pap. 2.95 *(978-0-333-62679-5(6))* Macmillan Pubs., Ltd. GBR. Dist: Trafalgar Square Publishing.

Fullman, Joe. Coin & Rope Tricks. 2009. (Magic Handbook Ser.). (ENG., Illus.). 32p. (J). (gr. 3-12). pap. 6.95 *(978-1-55407-570-6(X)*, 9781554075706) Firefly Bks., Ltd.

Hamilton, S. L. Daredevil. 2015. 32p. E-Book 27.07 *(978-1-62403-757-3(7))* ABDO Publishing Co.

Hunter, Nick. Silly Circus Tricks, 1 vol. 2013. (Try This at Home! Ser.). (ENG., Illus.). 32p. (gr. 1-2). pap. 8.29 *(978-1-4109-5010-9(7))*; lib. bdg. 29.99 *(978-1-4109-5003-1(4))* Heinemann-Raintree. (Read Me!).

Labrecque, Ellen. Amazing Bike Tricks, 1 vol. 2013. (Try This at Home! Ser.). (ENG.). 32p. (gr. 1-2). pap. 8.29 *(978-1-4109-5008-6(5))*; lib. bdg. 29.99 *(978-1-4109-5001-7(8))* Heinemann-Raintree. (Read Me!).

Labrecque, Ellen & Hunter, Nick. Try This at Home! 2013. (Try This at Home! Ser.). (ENG.). 32p. (gr. 1-2). pap. 39.95 *(978-1-4109-5014-7(X))*; lib. bdg. 149.95 *(978-1-4109-5007-9(7))* Heinemann-Raintree. (Read Me!).

Leet, Karen M. Gross Pranks, 1 vol. 2013. (Gross Guides). (ENG., Illus.). 32p. (gr. 3-4). 27.99 *(978-1-4296-9922-8(1))* Capstone Press of Coughlan Cos.

Mason, Tom, et al. Funny Magic: How to Do Tricks That Make People Laugh! 2007. (Illus.). 48p. (J). pap. *(978-0-439-90714-9(4))* Scholastic, Inc.

Moore, Gareth. Not So Ordinary. 2015. (Brain Benders Ser.). (ENG., Illus.). 32p. (J). (gr. 3-6). pap. 7.99 *(978-1-4677-7199-3(6)*, Lerner Pubns.) Lerner Publishing Group.

Owen, Ruth. Pranks, Tricks, & Practical Jokes, 1 vol., 1. 2014. (DIY for Boys Ser.). (ENG.). 32p. (J). (gr. 3-6). 27.50 *(978-1-4777-6294-3(9)*, PowerKids Pr.) Rosen Publishing Group, Inc., The.

Ransford, Sandy. Jokes & Pranks, 3 vols. 2003. (Wicked Wallets Ser.). (Illus.). 24p. (YA). *(978-1-84347-040-3(3)*, Pavilion Children's Books) Pavilion Bks.

Roff, Don. Holiday Magic. 2012. (Illus.). 32p. (J). *(978-0-545-52106-2(8))* Scholastic, Inc.

Stephens, Sarah Hines & Mann, Bethany. Do It Now! Tricks: Rad Stunts & Sneaky Pranks. 2012. (ENG.). 80p. (J). pap. 6.99 *(978-1-61628-391-9(2))* Weldon Owen, Inc.

Turnbull, Stephanie. Easy Coin Tricks. 2014. (Beginner Magic Ser.). (Illus.). 24p. (gr. 3-6). 28.50 *(978-1-62588-007-9(3))* Black Rabbit Bks.

—Easy Scarf & Rope Tricks. 2014. (Beginner Magic Ser.). 24p. (gr. 3-6). 28.50 *(978-1-62588-008-6(1))* Black Rabbit Bks.

Zenon, Paul. Gimmicks & Card Tricks: Illusions for the Intermediate Magician. 2008. (Amazing Magic Ser.). (ENG., Illus.). 64p. (gr. 5-8). pap. 14.05 *(978-1-4042-1758-4(4)*, Rosen Reference) Rosen Publishing Group, Inc., The.

TRICYCLES

see Bicycles and Bicycling

TRIGONOMETRY

Accelerated Math West Virginia State Tagged Pre-Calculus Library. 2004. cd-rom 1199.00 *(978-1-59455-116-1(2))* Renaissance Learning, Inc.

Algebra & Trigonometry: Complete Solutions Guide. 6th ed. 2004. (gr. 11-12). *(978-0-618-31785-1(6)*, 3-32723) CENGAGE Learning.

Algebra & Trigonometry: Learning Tools. 6th ed. 2004. (gr. 11-12). stu. ed. incl. cd-rom *(978-0-618-31794-3(5)*, 3-32732) CENGAGE Learning.

Algebra & Trigonometry: Test Item File. 6th ed. 2004. (gr. 11-12). *(978-0-618-31786-8(4)*, 3-32724) CENGAGE Learning.

Faulkner, Nicholas & Hosch, William L. Algebra & Trigonometry. 2017. (J). lib. bdg. ***(978-1-68048-774-9(4))*** Rosen Publishing Group, Inc., The.

Holt, Rinehart and Winston Staff. Precalculus: A Graphing Approach. 4th ed. 2004. (Holt Precalculus: a Graphing Approach Ser.). (ENG.). 1184p. (gr. 9-9). 114.05 *(978-0-03-069608-4(9))* Houghton Mifflin Harcourt Publishing Co.

Hostetler, Robert P. & Larson, Ron. Trigonometry. 6th ed. 2003. (ENG.). (C). 156.95 *(978-0-618-37393-2(4)*, 332774) Brooks/Cole.

Hungerford, Thomas W. Contemporary College Algebra & Trigonometry: A Graphing Approach. 2nd ed. 2004. (ENG.). 496p. (C). pap. 111.95 *(978-0-534-46792-0(X))* Brooks/Cole.

Larson, Ron. Precalculus. 6th ed. 2003. (ENG.). 184p. (C). (gr. 11-12). pap., stu. ed. 18.95 *(978-0-618-31440-9(7)*, 332746) CENGAGE Learning.

—Study & Solutions Guide: Used with ... Larson-Precalculus. 6th ed. 2003. (YA). (gr. 11-12). stu. ed. 54.36 *(978-0-618-31437-9(7)*, 332743) CENGAGE Learning.

—Trigonometry Advanced Placement Version. 6th ed. 2003. (YA). (gr. 11-12). 137.96 *(978-0-618-31797-4(X)*, 332762) CENGAGE Learning.

—Trigonometry Computer Solutions. (J). 7.00 *(978-0-669-12001-1(4))* Houghton Mifflin Harcourt School Pubs.

—Trigonometry IG. (J). 2.00 *(978-0-669-08612-6(6))* Houghton Mifflin Harcourt School Pubs.

Larson, Ron, et al. Precalculus with Limits: A Graphing Approach. 4th ed. 2004. (ENG.). 1104p. (C). 199.95 *(978-0-618-39478-4(8)*, 333050) CENGAGE Learning.

Precalculus: Complete Solutions Guide. 6th ed. 2004. (gr. 11-12). *(978-0-618-31438-6(5)*, 3-32744) CENGAGE Learning.

Precalculus: HM MathSpace Technology Package. 3rd ed. 2004. (gr. 6-12). tchr. ed. *(978-0-618-35699-7(1)*, 3-02981) Holt McDougal.

Precalculus with Limits: a Graphing Approach: Learning Tools. 6th ed. 2004. (gr. 11-12). stu. ed. incl. cd-rom *(978-0-618-31447-8(4)*, 3-32754) CENGAGE Learning.

Reeves, Brian & Robinson, Craig. Pre-Calculus Student Activity Book. Matthews, Douglas L., ed. 2003. (Illus.). stu. ed., per., wbk. ed. *(978-1-931680-24-0(8)*, Expert Systems for Teachers) Teaching Point, Inc.

Ssm Precalc: Func/Graphs. 10th ed. 2005. (C). pap. 37.95 *(978-0-534-99995-7(6))* Brooks/Cole.

Trigonometrie. 2nd ed. (Duden-Schuelerhilfen Ser.). (GER.). 112p. (YA). (gr. 10). *(978-3-411-70892-5(1))* Bibliographisches Institut & F. A. Brockhaus AG DEU. Dist: International Bk. Import Service, Inc.

Wingard-Nelson, Rebecca. Trigonometry. 2004. (Math Success Ser.). (Illus.). 64p. (J). lib. bdg. 23.94 *(978-0-7660-2568-4(3))* Enslow Pubs., Inc.

TRINIDAD AND TOBAGO

Benjamin, Floella. Coming to England. 2016. (ENG., Illus.). 144p. (J). (gr. 4-6). 14.99 ***(978-1-5098-3548-5(2))*** Pan Macmillan GBR. Dist: Independent Pubs. Group.

Frederick, Malcolm. Kamal Goes to Trinidad. Das, Prodeepta, illus. 2008. (Children Return to Their Roots Ser.). (ENG.). 40p. (J). (gr. 1-4). 16.95 *(978-1-84507-702-0(4)*, Frances Lincoln Children's Bks.) Quarto Publishing Group UK GBR. Dist: Hachette Bk. Group.

Greenwood, Mark & Lessac, Frané. Drummer Boy of John John. 2006. (ENG., Illus.). 40p. (J). 18.95 (978-1-60060-652-6(0)) Lee & Low Bks., Inc.

Hernandez, Romel. Trinidad & Tobago. 2010. (Caribbean Today Ser.). (Illus.). 64p. (YA). (gr. 9-12). 21.95 (978-1-4222-0629-4(7)) Mason Crest.

—Trinidad & Tobago, Vol. 11. Henderson, James D., ed. 2015. (Discovering the Caribbean: History, Politics, & Culture Ser.). (Illus.). 64p. (J). (gr. 7). lib. bdg. 22.95 (978-1-4222-3317-7(0)) Mason Crest.

Sheehan, Sean & Yong, Jui Lin. Trinidad & Tobago. 2nd rev. ed. 2010. (Cultures of the World 22 Ser.). 144p. (gr. 6). 42.79 (978-1-60870-456-9(4)) Marshall Cavendish GBR. Dist: Marshall Cavendish Corp.

TRINIDAD AND TOBAGO—FICTION

Baptiste, Tracey. Angel's Grace. 2009. (ENG.). 176p. (YA). (gr. 7). pap. 9.99 (978-1-4169-9537-1(4), Simon & Schuster/Paula Wiseman Bks.) Simon & Schuster/Paula Wiseman Bks.

Benjamin, Floella. My Two Grannies. Chamberlain, Margaret, illus. 2009. (ENG.). 32p. (J). (gr. k-3). pap. 7.95 (978-1-84780-034-3(3), Frances Lincoln Children's Bks.) Quarto Publishing Group UK GBR. Dist: Hachette Bk. Group.

Binch, Caroline. Gregory Cool. 2012. (ENG., Illus.). 32p. (J). (gr. k-3). pap. 8.99 (978-1-84780-258-3(3), Frances Lincoln) Quarto Publishing Group UK GBR. Dist: Hachette Bk. Group.

Bootman, Colin. Fish for the Grand Lady. Bootman, Colin, illus. 2006. (ENG., Illus.). 32p. (J). (gr. -1-3). 16.95 (978-0-8234-1898-5(7)) Holiday Hse., Inc.

Rahaman, Vashanti. Divali Rose. Akib, Jamel, illus. 2008. (ENG.). 32p. (J). (gr. 2-4). 16.95 (978-1-59078-524-9(X)) Boyds Mills Pr.

Wiggins, Thalia. Greg & the Cheat Sheets, 1 vol. Tate, Don, illus. 2012. (Making Choices: the Mcnair Cousins Ser.). (ENG.). 64p. 27.07 (978-1-61641-630-0(0), Calico Chapter Bks) Magic Wagon.

—Greg & the Mural, 1 vol. Tate, Don, illus. 2012. (Making Choices: the Mcnair Cousins Ser.). (ENG.). 64p. 27.07 (978-1-61641-631-7(9), Calico Chapter Bks) Magic Wagon.

—Greg's Game Dilemma, 1 vol. Tate, Don, illus. 2012. (Making Choices: the Mcnair Cousins Ser.). (ENG.). 64p. 27.07 (978-1-61641-632-4(7), Calico Chapter Bks) Magic Wagon.

—James Cheats!, 1 vol. Tate, Don, illus. 2012. (Making Choices: the Mcnair Cousins Ser.). (ENG.). 64p. 27.07 (978-1-61641-633-1(5), Calico Chapter Bks) Magic Wagon.

—James Makes a Choice, 1 vol. Tate, Don, illus. 2012. (Making Choices: the Mcnair Cousins Ser.). (ENG.). 64p. 27.07 (978-1-61641-634-8(3), Calico Chapter Bks) Magic Wagon.

—James the Rock's Boys, 1 vol. Tate, Don, illus. 2012. (Making Choices: the Mcnair Cousins Ser.). (ENG.). 64p. 27.07 (978-1-61641-635-5(1), Calico Chapter Bks) Magic Wagon.

TRIPLETS—FICTION

Bennett, Paul. Freddie, Bill & Irving. Shannon, Kate, illus. 2009. 112p. (gr. 2-2). pap. 25.16 (978-1-4251-7692-1(5)) Trafford Publishing.

Blackthorn, J. D. & Rinehart, J. D. Crown of Three. 2015. (Crown of Three Ser.: 1). (ENG.). 416p. (J). (gr. 4-8). 17.99 (978-1-4814-2443-1(2), Aladdin) Simon & Schuster Children's Publishing.

Carpenter, Donna. A Triple Treat. 2007. (Illus.). 20p. (J). 14.95 (978-0-9793987-0-4(3)) DFC Pubs.

Childs, Tera Lynn. Sweet Legacy. 2013. (Sweet Venom Ser.: 3). (ENG.). 384p. (YA). (gr. 8). 17.99 (978-0-06-200185-6(X), Tegen, Katherine Bks) HarperCollins Pubs.

—Sweet Shadows. (Sweet Venom Ser.: 2). (ENG.). (YA). (gr. 8). 2013. 352p. pap. 9.99 (978-0-06-200184-9(1)) 2012. 336p. 17.99 (978-0-06-200183-2(3)) HarperCollins Pubs. (Tegen, Katherine Bks).

Cooney, Caroline B. Three Black Swans. 2012. (ENG.). 288p. (YA). (gr. 7). pap. 9.99 (978-0-385-73868-2(4), Ember) Random Hse. Children's Bks.

DeVillers, Julia & Roy, Jennifer. Triple Trouble. 2014. (Mix Ser.). (ENG., Illus.). 240p. (J). (gr. 4-8). pap. 7.99 (978-1-4424-3406-6(6), Aladdin) Simon & Schuster Children's Publishing.

Fishbone, Greg. The Penguins of Doom. 2007. (From the Desk of Septina Nash Ser.). (ENG., Illus.). 182p. (J). (gr. 2-7). 13.95 (978-1-933831-03-9(0)) Blooming Tree Pr.

Goldberg, Whoopi. Perfectly Prima, No. 3. Roos, Maryn, illus. 2010. (ENG.). 160p. (J). (gr. 1-17). pap. 4.99 (978-0-7868-5262-8(3), Jump at the Sun) Hyperion Bks. for Children.

—Sugar Plum to the Rescue! Roos, Maryn, illus. 2011. (ENG.). 160p. (J). (gr. 1-5). pap. 4.99 (978-0-7868-5264-2(X), Jump at the Sun) Hyperion Bks. for Children.

Goulbourne, Nathaniel. The Aliens Zoo. 2013. (Illus.). 28p. pap. 21.35 (978-1-4817-8198-5(7)) AuthorHouse.

Horse, Harry. Little Rabbit's New Baby, 1 vol. Horse, Harry, illus. (Little Rabbit Ser.). (Illus.). 32p. (J). 2016. (ENG.). (gr. -1-k). pap. 7.95 (978-1-56145-915-5(1)) 2008. (gr. k-1). 16.95 (978-1-56145-431-0(1)) Peachtree Pubs.

—Little Rabbit's New Baby / Book & Doll Package. 2008. (Illus.). 32p. (J). (gr. k-1). pap., pap. 22.90 (978-1-56145-453-2(2)) Peachtree Pubs.

Huelin, Jodi. Alvin & the Chipmunks: Alvin's Easter Break. Artful Doodlers Limited Staff & Carzon, Walter, illus. 2014. (ENG.). 24p. (J). (gr. -1-3). pap. 3.99 (978-0-06-225222-7(4), HarperFestival) HarperCollins Pubs.

Kenah, Katharine. Scholastic Reader Level 1: the Saturday Triplets #2: the Pumpkin Fair Problem. Lyon, Tammie, illus. 2013. (Scholastic Reader Level 1 Ser.). (ENG.). 32p. (J). (gr. -1-2). pap. 3.99 (978-0-545-48144-1(9)) Scholastic, Inc.

—Scholastic Reader Level 1: the Saturday Triplets #3: Teacher Trouble! Lyon, Tammie, illus. 2013. (Scholastic Reader Level 1 Ser.). (ENG.). 32p. (J). (gr. -1-2). pap. 3.99 (978-0-545-48145-8(7)) Scholastic, Inc.

Landis, Mary M. Winter Days with the Treelo Triplets. 2012. (Illus.). 218p. (J). (978-0-7399-2447-1(8)) Rod & Staff Pubs., Inc.

Lindman. Flicka, Ricka, Dicka & the Little Dog. Lindman, illus. 2013. (Flicka, Ricka, Dicka Ser.). (ENG., Illus.). 32p. (J). (gr. k-3). 9.99 (978-0-8075-2509-8(X)) Whitman, Albert & Co.

—Flicka, Ricka, Dicka & the Strawberries. Lindman, illus. 2013. (Flicka, Ricka, Dicka Ser.). (ENG., Illus.). 32p. (J). (gr. k-3). 9.99 (978-0-8075-2512-8(X)) Whitman, Albert & Co.

—Flicka, Ricka, Dicka & the Three Kittens. Lindman, illus. 2013. (Flicka, Ricka, Dicka Ser.). (ENG., Illus.). 32p. (J). (gr. k-3). 9.99 (978-0-8075-2515-9(4)) Whitman, Albert & Co.

—Flicka, Ricka, Dicka & Their New Skates: Updated Edition with Paperdolls. Lindman, illus. 2011. (Flicka, Ricka, Dicka Ser.). (ENG., Illus.). 32p. (J). (gr. k-3). 9.99 (978-0-8075-2496-1(4)) Whitman, Albert & Co.

—Flicka, Ricka, Dicka Bake a Cake. Lindman, illus. 2013. (Flicka, Ricka, Dicka Ser.). (ENG., Illus.). 32p. (J). (gr. k-3). 9.99 (978-0-8075-2506-7(5)) Whitman, Albert & Co.

Lindman, Maj. Flicka, Ricka, Dicka & the New Dotted Dresses. 2012. (J). (978-0-8075-2495-4(6)) Whitman, Albert & Co.

—Flicka, Ricka, Dicka & the New Dotted Dresses. Lindman, Maj, illus. 2012. (Flicka, Ricka, Dicka Ser.). (ENG., Illus.). 32p. (J). (gr. k-3). 9.99 (978-0-8075-2484-8(0)) Whitman, Albert & Co.

—Flicka, Ricka, Dicka & Their New Skates. Lindman, Maj, illus. 2011. (ENG., Illus.). 32p. (J). (gr. k-3). 9.99 (978-0-8075-2491-6(3)) Whitman, Albert & Co.

—Flicka, Ricka, Dicka Go to Market. Lindman, Maj, illus. 2012. (ENG., Illus.). 32p. (J). (gr. -1-3). 9.99 (978-0-8075-2478-7(6)); (gr. k-3). 9.99 (978-0-8075-2479-4(4)) Whitman, Albert & Co.

May, Maggie. Times Three. L, Joe, illus. 2011. 36p. pap. 24.95 (978-1-4626-2504-8(5)) America Star Bks.

Moore, Stephanie Perry. Enjoying True Peace, 1 vol. 2010. (Yasmin Peace Ser.: 5). (ENG.). 176p. pap. 6.99 (978-0-8024-8606-6(1), Lift Every Voice) Moody Pubs.

—Experiencing the Joy, 1 vol. 2009. (Yasmin Peace Ser.: 3). (ENG.). 160p. (gr. 7-10). pap. 7.99 (978-0-8024-8604-2(5), Lift Every Voice) Moody Pubs.

Moore, Stephanie Perry & Moody Publishing Staff. Believing in Hope. 2009. (Yasmin Peace Ser.: 2). (ENG.). 176p. (gr. 7-10). pap. 7.99 (978-0-8024-8603-5(7), Lift Every Voice) Moody Pubs.

—Finding Your Faith 2009. (Yasmin Peace Ser.: 1). (ENG.). 176p. (gr. 7-10). pap. 7.99 (978-0-8024-8602-8(9), Lift Every Voice) Moody Pubs.

Novak, Ali. The Heartbreakers. 2015. (Heartbreak Chronicles Ser.: 1). (ENG.). 336p. (YA). (gr. 6-12). pap. 10.99 (978-1-4926-1256-8(1), 9781492612568) Sourcebooks, Inc.

Pearce, Jackson. Fathomless. 2013. (Fairy Tale Retelling Ser.). (ENG.). 320p. (YA). (gr. 10-17). pap. 8.99 (978-0-316-20777-5(2)) Little, Brown Bks. for Young Readers.

Poploff, Michelle. Where Triplets Go, Trouble Follows. Jamieson, Victoria, illus. 2015. (ENG.). 96p. (J). (gr. 2-6). 16.95 (978-0-8234-3289-9(0)) Holiday Hse., Inc.

Rhoton, Lesa. Angus & the Triplets. Switzer, Bobby, illus. 2006. 28p. (J). (gr. -1-3). per. 13.95 (978-1-58939-852-8(1)) Virtualbookworm.com Publishing, Inc.

Rinehart, J. D. Crown of Three. 2016. (Crown of Three Ser.: 1). (ENG., Illus.). 432p. (J). (gr. 4-8). pap. 7.99 (978-1-4814-2444-8(0), Aladdin) Simon & Schuster Children's Publishing.

—The Lost Realm. 2016. (Crown of Three Ser.: 2). (ENG., Illus.). 496p. (J). (gr. 4-8). 17.99 (978-1-4814-2446-2(7), Aladdin) Simon & Schuster Children's Publishing.

The T-Shirt Triplets: Individual Title Six-Packs. (Literatura 2000 Ser.). (gr. 2-3). 33.00 (978-0-7635-0187-7(5)) Rigby Education.

Ziegler, Jennifer. Revenge of the Flower Girls. 2014. (ENG.). 240p. (J). (gr. 3-7). 16.99 (978-0-545-56141-9(8), Scholastic Pr.) Scholastic, Inc.

Zirkind, Chaya Sara. Bas Mitzvah X 3. 2008. 156p. (J). (978-1-56871-448-6(3)) Targum Pr., Inc.

TROJAN WAR

Black Ships Before Troy. 2011. 8.80 (978-0-7848-3649-1(3), Everbind) Marco Bk. Co.

Bowman, Patrick. Tom from Troy. 2011. (ENG., Illus.). 200p. (YA). (gr. 5-18). pap. 11.95 (978-1-55380-110-8(5)) Ronsdale Pr. CAN. Dist: SPD-Small Pr. Distribution.

Capaldi, Mario, illus. Odysseus & the Wooden Horse: A Greek Legend. 2003. (Dominie Collection of Myths & Legends). (SPA.). 20p. (J). lib. bdg. (978-0-7685-2425-3(3)) Dominie Pr., Inc.

—Odysseus & the Wooden Horse: A Greek Legend. 2004. (SPA & ENG.). 20p. (J). (gr. 3-3). pap. 6.47 net. (978-0-7685-2128-3(9), Dominie Elementary) Pearson Schl.

Chandler, Matt, retold by. The Trojan War: A Graphic Retelling. 2015. (Ancient Myths Ser.). (ENG.). 32p. (gr. 3-4). lib. bdg. 30.65 (978-1-4914-2074-4(X), Graphic Library) Capstone Press of Coughlan Cos.

Church, Alfred John. The Story of the Iliad. 2005. reprint ed. pap. 31.95 (978-1-4191-5466-9(4)) Kessinger Publishing, LLC.

Clarke, M. The Story of Troy. 2007. (Illus.). 184p. per. (978-1-4065-1381-3(4)) Dodo Pr.

Clarke, Michael. The Story of Troy. 2007. 192p. 25.95 (978-1-4218-4207-3(6)); per. 10.95 (978-1-4218-4305-6(6)) 1st World Publishing, Inc. (1st World Library - Literary Society).

—The Story of Troy. l.t. ed. 2007. (ENG.). 202p. pap. 22.99 (978-1-4346-0682-2(1)) Creative Media Partners, LLC.

—The Story of Troy: The Story of Troy. 2007. (ENG.). 178p. pap. 19.99 (978-1-4346-0607-5(4)) Creative Media Partners, LLC.

Claybourne, A. & Khanduri, K. Greek Myths: Ulysses & the Trojan War: Mini-Edition. 2004. (Spotter's Guides). 160p. (J). 8.95 (978-0-7945-0535-6(X)) EDC Publishing.

Cline, Eric H. & Rubalcaba, Jill. Digging for Troy: From Homer to Hisarlik. Brannen, Sarah S., illus. 2011. (ENG.). 80p. (J). (gr. 4-7). 17.95 (978-1-58089-326-8(0)); pap. 9.95 (978-1-58089-327-5(9)) Charlesbridge Publishing, Inc.

Colum, Padraic. The Adventures of Odysseus & the Tale of Troy. Pogány, Willy, illus. 2004. (Dover Children's Classics Ser.). (ENG.). 176p. (J). (gr. 3-8). pap. 6.95 (978-0-486-43455-1(9)) Dover Pubns., Inc.

—The Adventures of Odysseus & the Tale of Troy. Pogány, Willy, illus. 2008. 164p. pap. (978-1-4068-2730-9(4)) Echo Library.

—The Adventures of Odysseus & the Tales of Troy. 2007. (ENG.). 200p. pap. 19.99 (978-1-4346-0573-3(6)); 220p. pap. 22.99 (978-1-4346-0648-8(1)) Creative Media Partners, LLC.

—The Children's Homer: The Adventures of Odysseus & the Tale of Troy. Pogány, Willy, illus. 2004. (ENG.). 256p. (J). (gr. 5-9). pap. 9.99 (978-0-689-86883-2(9), Aladdin) Simon & Schuster Children's Publishing.

—The Children's Homer: The Adventures of Odysseus & the Tale of Troy. 2011. 144p. pap. 7.95 (978-1-61382-004-9(6)) Simon & Brown.

Ferrell, David L. Achilles & the Trojan War, 1 vol., 1. 2014. (Jr. Graphic Myths: Greek Heroes Ser.). (ENG.). 24p. (J). (gr. 3-6). 26.25 (978-1-4777-6240-0(X), PowerKids Pr.) Rosen Publishing Group, Inc., The.

Green, Roger Lancelyn. Tales of the Greek Heroes. 2015. (Puffin Pixels Ser.). (ENG., Illus.). 304p. (J). 11.99 (978-0-14-751715-9(X), Puffin Books) Penguin Young Readers Group.

Hoena, Blake. The Trojan War: An Interactive Mythological Adventure. Takvorian, Nadine, illus. 2017. (You Choose: Ancient Greek Myths Ser.). (ENG.). 112p. (gr. 3-4). lib. bdg. 31.99 (978-1-5157-4822-9(7), You Choose Bks.) Capstone Press of Coughlan Cos.

Holub, Joan. Surprise, Trojans! The Story of the Trojan Horse. Jones, Dani, illus. 2014. (Ready-To-Reads Ser.). (ENG.). 32p. (J). (gr. k-2). 16.99 (978-1-4814-2087-7(9)); pap. 3.99 (978-1-4814-2086-0(0)) Simon Spotlight. (Simon Spotlight).

Jeffrey, Gary. Achilles & the Trojan War. 2012. (Graphic Mythical Heroes Ser.). (Illus.). 24p. (J). (gr. 3-5). pap. 8.15 (978-1-4339-7508-0(4)); lib. bdg. 23.95 (978-1-4339-7507-3(6)) Stevens, Gareth Publishing LLLP.

Lang, Andrew. Tales of Troy: Ulysses the Sacker of Cities. 2004. reprint ed. pap. 1.99 (978-1-4192-5072-9(8)) Kessinger Publishing, LLC.

—Tales of Troy & Greece. Ford, H. J., illus. 2006. (Dover Children's Classics Ser.). (ENG.). 336p. (gr. 9-12). per. 9.95 (978-0-486-44917-3(3)) Dover Pubns., Inc.

McCarty, Nick. Troy: The Myth & Reality Behind the Epic Legend. 2008. (Prime Time History Ser.). (Illus.). 122p. (YA). (gr. 9-12). lib. bdg. 42.60 (978-1-4042-1365-4(1)) Rosen Publishing Group, Inc., The.

O'Connor, George. Ares. O'Connor, George, illus. 2015. (Olympians Ser.: 7). (ENG., Illus.). 80p. (J). (gr. 4-9). pap. 10.99 (978-1-62672-013-8(4), 9781626720138, First Second Bks.) Roaring Brook Pr.

Rosemary, Sutcliff. Black Ships Before Troy: The Story of the Iliad. 2014. (ENG.). 160p. (YA). 11.24 (978-1-63245-187-3(5)) Lectorum Pubns., Inc.

Sheppard, Si. Heroes of the Trojan War. 2015. (Heroes & Legends Ser.). (ENG., Illus.). 80p. (J). (gr. 7-8). 35.60 (978-1-4994-6172-5(0), Rosen Young Adult) Rosen Publishing Group, Inc., The.

Spies, Karen Bornemann. Mythology of the Iliad & the Odyssey. 2014. (Mythology, Myths, & Legends Ser.). 96p. (J). (gr. 6-12). 27.94 (978-0-7660-6172-9(8)) Enslow Pubs., Inc.

Sutcliff, Rosemary. Black Ships Before Troy: The Story of the Iliad. 2005. (ENG.). 176p. (YA). (gr. 7). mass mkt. 7.99 (978-0-553-49483-9(X), Laurel Leaf) Random Hse. Children's Bks.

Tracy, Kathleen. The Life & Times of Homer. 2004. (Biography from Ancient Civilizations Ser.). (Illus.). 48p. (J). (gr. 4-8). lib. bdg. 29.95 (978-1-58415-260-6(5)) Mitchell Lane Pubs., Inc.

—Odysseus. 2008. (Profiles in Greek & Roman Mythology Ser.). (Illus.). 48p. (J). (gr. 4-7). lib. bdg. 29.95 (978-1-58415-705-2(4)) Mitchell Lane Pubs., Inc.

World Book, Inc Staff, contrib. by. The Mysteries of the Trojan War. 2014. (J). (978-0-7166-2668-8(3)) World Bk., Inc.

TROLLS

see Fairies

TROPICAL RAIN FOREST ECOLOGY

see Rain Forest Ecology

TROPICAL RAIN FORESTS

see Rain Forests

TROPICS

Baker, Stuart. In the Tropics. 2009. (Climate Change Ser.). 32p. (gr. 4). 28.50 (978-0-7614-4440-4(8)) Marshall Cavendish Corp.

Benduhn, Tea. Living in Tropical Rain Forests. 2007. (Life on the Edge Ser.). (Illus.). 24p. (gr. 1-4). pap. 8.15 (978-0-8368-8349-7(7)); lib. bdg. 22.00 (978-0-8368-8344-2(6)) Stevens, Gareth Publishing LLLP. (Weekly Reader Leveled Readers).

Besel, Jennifer M. The Hottest Places on Earth. 2010. (Extreme Planet Ser.). (ENG.). 24p. (gr. 1-2). lib. bdg. 25.32 (978-1-4296-3964-4(4), First Facts) Capstone Press of Coughlan Cos.

Bradley, Timothy J. Terror in the Tropics, 1 vol. 2nd rev. ed. 2013. (TIME for KIDS(r) Nonfiction Readers Ser.). (ENG.). 64p. (J). (gr. 5-5). pap. 10.99 (978-1-4333-4898-3(5)) Teacher Created Materials, Inc.

First Discovery Staff & Mettler, René. Jungle. Mettler, René, illus. 2006. (ENG., Illus.). 36p. (J). (gr. k-3). pap. 11.99 (978-1-85103-183-2(9)) Moonlight Publishing, Ltd. GBR. Dist: Independent Pubs. Group.

Gritzner, Charles F. The Tropics. 2007. (Geography of Extreme Environments Ser.). (Illus.). 100p. (YA). (gr. 7-12). lib. bdg. 30.00 (978-0-7910-9233-0(X)) Facts On File, Inc.

Lazor, Stephanie. Life on the Equator. 2004. (Life in Extreme Environments Ser.). (Illus.). 64p. (gr. 5-8). lib. bdg. 31.95 (978-0-8239-3986-2(3), Rosen Reference) Rosen Publishing Group, Inc., The.

Rustad, Martha E. H. The Wettest Places on Earth, 1 vol. 2010. (Extreme Planet Ser.). (ENG.). 24p. (gr. 1-2). lib. bdg. 25.32 (978-1-4296-3966-8(0), First Facts) Capstone Press of Coughlan Cos.

Senker, Cath. Tropical Climates. 2017. (Focus on Climate Zones Ser.). (ENG., Illus.). 48p. (gr. 4-6). pap. 4.95 (978-1-4846-3787-6(9)); lib. bdg. 33.32 (978-1-4846-3783-8(6)) Heinemann-Raintree. (Heinemann InfoSearch).

Soll, Karen. Hottest Places on the Planet. 2016. (Extreme Earth Ser.). (ENG., Illus.). 24p. (gr. k-1). lib. bdg. 26.65 (978-1-4914-8341-1(5), Pebble Plus) Capstone Press of Coughlan Cos.

TROPICS—FICTION

Billups, Ruth A. No Place for a Horse. 2008. 48p. pap. 16.95 (978-1-60703-118-5(3)) America Star Bks.

Collins, Pat Lowery. The Fattening Hut. 2005. (ENG.). 192p. (YA). (gr. 7). pap. 12.95 (978-0-618-55209-2(X)) Houghton Mifflin Harcourt Publishing Co.

Payne, M. D. Fartsunami. Dockery, Amanda, illus. 2013. (Monster Juice Ser.: 2). (ENG.). 192p. (J). (gr. 3-7). pap. 5.99 (978-0-448-46227-1(3), Grosset & Dunlap) Penguin Young Readers Group.

TROUT

Coldiron, Deborah. Trout, 1 vol. 2008. (Underwater World Set II Ser.). (ENG.). 32p. (gr. k-4). 27.07 (978-1-60453-139-8(8), Buddy Bks.) ABDO Publishing Co.

TROY (EXTINCT CITY)

Capaldi, Mario, illus. Odysseus & the Wooden Horse: A Greek Legend. 2003. (Dominie Collection of Myths & Legends). (SPA.). 20p. (J). lib. bdg. (978-0-7685-2425-3(3)) Dominie Pr., Inc.

—Odysseus & the Wooden Horse: A Greek Legend. 2004. (SPA & ENG.). 20p. (J). (gr. 3-3). pap. 6.47 net. (978-0-7685-2128-3(9), Dominie Elementary) Pearson Schl.

Clarke, Michael. The Story of Troy. 2007. 192p. 25.95 (978-1-4218-4207-3(6)); per. 10.95 (978-1-4218-4305-6(6)) 1st World Publishing, Inc. (1st World Library - Literary Society).

Cline, Eric H. & Rubalcaba, Jill. Digging for Troy: From Homer to Hisarlik. Brannen, Sarah S., illus. 2011. (ENG.). 80p. (J). (gr. 4-7). 17.95 (978-1-58089-326-8(0)); pap. 9.95 (978-1-58089-327-5(9)) Charlesbridge Publishing, Inc.

Crompton, Samuel Willard. Troy. 2012. (Lost Worlds & Mysterious Civilizations Ser.). (Illus.). 104p. (gr. 6-12). 35.00 (978-1-60413-974-7(9), Chelsea Hse.) Facts On File, Inc.

Kerns, Ann. Troy. 2008. (Unearthing Ancient Worlds Ser.). (ENG.). 80p. (gr. 5-8). lib. bdg. 30.60 (978-0-8225-7582-5(5)) Lerner Publishing Group.

McCarty, Nick. Troy: The Myth & Reality Behind the Epic Legend. 2008. (Prime Time History Ser.). (Illus.). 122p. (YA). (gr. 9-12). lib. bdg. 42.60 (978-1-4042-1365-4(1)) Rosen Publishing Group, Inc., The.

Schlitz, Laura Amy. The Hero Schliemann: The Dreamer Who Dug up Troy. Byrd, Robert, illus. 2006. (ENG.). 80p. (J). (gr. 4-7). lib. bdg. 17.99 (978-0-7636-2283-1(4)) Candlewick Pr.

TROY (EXTINCT CITY)—FICTION

Alexander, Lloyd. The Xanadu Adventure. 2007. (Vesper Holly Ser.). (ENG.). 160p. (J). (gr. 5-18). 5.99 (978-0-14-240786-8(0), Puffin Books) Penguin Young Readers Group.

Bowler, Bill. Troy. 2nd ed. 2013. (ENG., Illus.). 40p. pap. 9.38 **(978-0-19-424970-6(0))** Oxford Univ. Pr., Inc.

Cross, Gillian. The Iliad. Packer, Neil, illus. 2015. (ENG.). 160p. (J). (gr. 3-7). 19.99 (978-0-7636-7832-6(5)) Candlewick Pr.

Gabrielson, Ernest & Gabrielson, Brian. Home in Ithaca: A novel of Ancient Greece & Troy. 2004. 120p. (YA). pap. 10.95 (978-0-595-30889-7(9)) iUniverse, Inc.

Geras, Adèle. Troy. 2004. 368p. (J). (gr. 8-18). pap. 48.00 incl. audio (978-0-8072-2288-1(7), Listening Library) Random Hse. Audio Publishing Group.

—Troy. Gillain, Dominique, illus. 2017. (ENG.). 368p. (YA). (gr. 9). pap. 9.99 (978-0-544-92546-5(7), HMH Books For Young Readers) Houghton Mifflin Harcourt Publishing Co.

McLaren, Clemence. Inside the Walls of Troy. 2004. (ENG., Illus.). 208p. (YA). (gr. 7-12). mass mkt. 7.99 (978-0-689-87397-3(2), Simon Pulse) Simon Pulse.

Peacock, L. A. Terror at Troy. Hale, Nathan, illus. 2012. 90p. (J). (978-0-545-34063-2(2)) Scholastic, Inc.

TRUANCY (SCHOOLS)

see School Attendance

TRUCK DRIVERS

Barrington, Richard. Careers in Trucking. 2013. (Essential Careers Ser.). (ENG., Illus.). 80p. (YA). (gr. 7-12). lib. bdg. 33.25 (978-1-4488-9473-4(5), Rosen Classroom) Rosen Publishing Group, Inc., The.

Gustaitis, Joseph Alan. Arctic Trucker. 2010. (Benchmark Rockets: Dirty & Dangerous Jobs Ser.). 32p. (J). (gr. 3-6). 28.50 (978-1-60870-169-8(7)) Marshall Cavendish Corp.

Mara, Wil. Motor Transport Operator. 2012. (21st Century Skills Library: Cool Military Careers Ser.). (ENG.). 32p. (gr. 4-8). 28.50 (978-1-61080-450-9(3), 202060); pap. 14.21 (978-1-61080-624-4(7), 202234) Cherry Lake Publishing.

Syrewicz, Connor. Truck Driver. 2013. (Earning $50,000 - $100,000 with a High School Diploma or Less Ser.: 14). 64p. (J). (gr. 7-18). 22.95 (978-1-4222-2900-2(9)) Mason Crest.

Thomas, William David. Truck Driver. 2009. (Cool Careers: on the Go Ser.). 32p. (gr. 5-8). pap. 10.50 (978-1-4339-0169-0(2)); (YA). lib. bdg. 26.00 (978-1-4339-0005-1(X)) Stevens, Gareth Publishing LLLP.

Trumbauer, Lisa. What Does a Truck Driver Do? 2006. (What Does a Community Helper Do? Ser.). (Illus.). 24p. (J). (gr. 1-3). lib. bdg. 22.60 (978-0-7660-2324-6(9), Enslow Elementary) Enslow Pubs., Inc.

TRUCK DRIVERS—FICTION

Iverson, Gregory. Tyler's Big Blue Truck. Fritz, Siegfried, illus. 2006. 40p. (J). (978-0-9755184-0-3(2)) Sandbox Bks.

London, Jonathan. My Big Rig, 0 vols. Garofoli, Viviana, illus. 2013. (ENG.). 32p. (J). (gr. -1-3). pap. 9.99 (978-1-4778-1673-8(9), 9781477816738, Amazon Children's Publishing) Amazon Publishing.

Royston, Angela. Truck Trouble, Level 1. 2013. (DK Readers Ser.). (ENG.). 32p. (J). (gr. k-4). pap. 3.99 (978-1-4654-0243-1(8), DK Children) Dorling Kindersley Publishing, Inc.

Venning, Edward W. The Truck & a Boy: The Truck with a big Heart. 2007. 48p. (YA). per. 15.95 (978-1-4327-0738-5(8)) Outskirts Pr., Inc.

Wellington, Monica. Truck Driver Tom. 2007. (ENG., Illus.). 32p. (J). (gr. -1-k). 16.99 (978-0-525-47831-7(0), Dutton Books for Young Readers) Penguin Young Readers Group.

TRUCK FARMING

see Vegetable Gardening

TRUCKS

Abbot, Henry. I Want to Drive a Snowplow. 2016. (At the Wheel Ser.). 00024p. (J). (gr. 1-1). pap. 8.25 (978-1-4994-2666-3(6), PowerKids Pr.) Rosen Publishing Group, Inc., The.

ABDO Publishing Company Staff. Mighty Movers. 2005. (Mighty Movers Ser.). (gr. k-4). 153.90 *(978-1-59197-824-4(6),* Buddy Bks.) ABDO Publishing Co.

Abramovitz, Melissa. Military Trucks. 2012. (Military Machines Ser.). (ENG.). 24p. (gr. k-1). pap. 41.70 *(978-1-4296-8317-3(1));* lib. bdg. 26.65 *(978-1-4296-7570-3(5))* Capstone Press of Coughlan Cos. (Pebble Plus).

Addison, D. R. Garbage Trucks at Work. 2009. (Big Trucks Ser.). (Illus.). 24p. (J). (gr. k-2). pap. 8.25 *(978-1-4358-3085-1(7),* PowerKids Pr.) Rosen Publishing Group, Inc., The.

Alinas, Marv. Garbage Trucks. 2014. (Big Machines at Work Ser.). (ENG.). 24p. (J). (gr. -1-2). 25.64 *(978-1-62323-969-5(9),* 206744) Child's World, Inc., The.

Aloian, Molly. Fire Trucks: Racing to the Scene. 2010. (Vehicles on the Move Ser.). (ENG.). 32p. (J). (gr. k-3). pap. *(978-0-7787-3060-6(3))* Crabtree Publishing Co.

Amoroso, Cynthia. Dump Trucks. 2014. (Big Machines at Work Ser.). (ENG.). 24p. (J). (gr. -1-2). 25.64 *(978-1-62323-967-1(2),* 206742) Child's World, Inc., The.

—Tow Trucks. 2014. (Big Machines at Work Ser.). (ENG.). 24p. (J). (gr. -1-2). 25.64 *(978-1-62323-970-1(2),* 206745) Child's World, Inc., The.

Anderson, Jill, ed. Let's Get to Work!/Vamos a Trabajar! Evrard, Gaetan, illus. 2005. (Word Play/Juegos con Pala Ser.). (ENG & SPA.). 20p. (J). (gr. -1-17). bds. 6.95 *(978-1-58728-512-7(6))* Cooper Square Publishing Llc.

Ardagh, Philip. All at Sea. (Mighty Machines Ser.). (Illus.). 32p. (J). lib. bdg. 24.25 *(978-1-931983-04-4(6))* Chrysalis Education.

—On the Farm. (Mighty Machines Ser.). (Illus.). 32p. lib. bdg. 24.25 *(978-1-931983-05-1(4))* Chrysalis Education.

Arnold, Quinn M. Seedlings: Garbage Trucks. 2017. (Seedlings Ser.). (ENG., Illus.). 24p. (J). (gr. -1-1). pap. 7.99 ***(978-1-62832-386-3(8),*** Creative Paperbacks) Creative Co., The.

—Seedlings: Monster Trucks. 2017. (Seedlings Ser.). (ENG., Illus.). 24p. (J). (gr. -1-1). pap. 7.99 ***(978-1-62832-387-0(6),*** Creative Paperbacks) Creative Co., The.

Award, Anna. Picture the World of Working Trucks. 2012. (ENG., Illus.). 16p. (J). pap. 3.95 *(978-0-86163-969-4(3))* Award Pubns. Ltd. GBR. Dist: Parkwest Pubns., Inc.

Bach, Rachel. The Monster Truck Race. 2017. (Let's Race Ser.). (ENG.). 16p. (J). (gr. -1-1). pap. 7.99 *(978-1-68152-134-3(2))* Amicus.

—The Monster Truck Race. 2016. (Let's Race Ser.). (ENG.). 16p. (J). (gr. k-3). 17.95 *(978-1-60753-917-9(9))* Amicus Publishing.

Baker, Theo. Hard Hat Zone. 2014. (Penguin Core Concepts Ser.). (ENG., Illus.). 32p. (J). (gr. -1-k). 3.99 *(978-0-448-47923-1(0),* Grosset & Dunlap) Penguin Young Readers Group.

Becker, Ann. Monster Trucks. 2009. (Illus.). 24p. (J). pap. 7.95 *(978-1-60694-838-5(5))* Rourke Educational Media.

Benchmark Education Co., LLC. Big Trucks Big Book. 2014. (Shared Reading Foundations Ser.). (J). (gr. -1). *(978-1-4509-9445-3(8))* Benchmark Education Co.

Bender, Lionel. Trucks & Trailers. 2006. (J). *(978-1-59389-270-8(5))* Chrysalis Education.

Bowman, Chris. Monster Bulldozers. 2014. (Monster Machines Ser.). (ENG., Illus.). 24p. (J). (gr. k-3). lib. bdg. 25.95 *(978-1-62617-053-7(3),* Blastoff! Readers) Bellwether Media.

—Monster Tractors. 2014. (Monster Machines Ser.). (ENG., Illus.). 24p. (J). (gr. k-3). lib. bdg. 25.95 *(978-1-62617-055-1(X),* Blastoff! Readers) Bellwether Media.

—Monster Trucks. 2017. (Mighty Machines in Action Ser.). (ENG., Illus.). 24p. (J). (gr. k-3). lib. bdg. 25.95 *(978-1-62617-606-5(X),* Blastoff! Readers) Bellwether Media.

Brack, Amanda. Big Book of Brick Trucks. 2015. (ENG., Illus.). 32p. (J). (-k). 14.99 *(978-1-63220-598-8(X),* Sky Pony Pr.) Skyhorse Publishing Co., Inc.

Bradley, Michael. Escalade. 2009. (Cars 2 Ser.). 32p. (gr. 3). 28.50 *(978-0-7614-4101-4(8))* Marshall Cavendish GBR. Dist: Marshall Cavendish Corp.

—The Hummer. 2008. (Cars Ser.). (Illus.). 32p. (J). (gr. 3-18). lib. bdg. 28.50 *(978-0-7614-2981-4(6),* Benchmark Bks.) Marshall Cavendish Corp.

Bridges, Sarah. Yo Manejo un Camión de Volteo. Alderman, Derrick & Shea, Denise, illus. 2010. (Vehículos de Trabajo/Working Wheels Ser.).Tr. of I Drive a Dump Truck. (MUL & SPA.). 24p. (gr. -1-2). lib. bdg. 26.65 *(978-1-4048-6301-9(X))* Picture Window Bks.

Brill, Marlene Targ. Garbage Trucks. 2004. (Pull Ahead Books-Mighty Movers Ser.). (ENG., Illus.). 32p. (gr. k-3). pap. 7.95 *(978-0-8225-2381-9(7));* lib. bdg. 22.60 *(978-0-8225-1539-5(3))* Lerner Publishing Group.

Brooks, Felicity, des. Build a Picture Trucks Sticker Book. 2012. (Build a Picture Sticker Bks). 24p. (J). pap. 6.99 *(978-0-7945-3248-2(9),* Usborne) EDC Publishing.

Brooks, Felicity & Durber, Matt. Trucks & Diggers. Mazali, Gustavo, illus. 2008. (Magnet Bks.). 10p. (J). (gr. -1-3). bds. 19.99 *(978-0-7945-1907-0(5),* Usborne) EDC Publishing.

Burch, Lynda S. Wicky Wacky Things That Go! Trucks. Burch, Lynda S., photos by. 2004. (Illus.). 28p. (J). E-Book 9.95 incl. cd-rom *(978-1-933090-11-5(1))* Guardian Angel Publishing, Inc.

Buzzeo, Toni. Whose Truck? Datz, Jim, illus. 2015. (Whose Tools? Ser.). (ENG.). 16p. (J). (gr. -1 — 1). bds. 9.95 *(978-1-4197-1612-6(3))* Abrams, Inc.

Byerly, Robbie. Trucks in the City. 2016. (1-3Y Getting Around Ser.). (ENG., Illus.). 16p. (J). pap. 5.99 ***(978-1-63437-719-5(2))*** American Reading Co.

Calver, Paul & Gunzi, Christiane. Trucks. Warren Photographic Staff, photos by. 2012. (Little Noisy Bks.). (ENG., Illus.). 12p. (J). bds. 5.99 *(978-0-7641-6504-7(6))* Barron's Educational Series, Inc.

Camionetas Gigantes (Monster Trucks) 2006. (J). pap. 6.95 *(978-0-8225-6646-5(X),* Ediciones Lerner) Lerner Publishing Group.

Carr, Aaron. Semi Trucks. 2014. (Illus.). 24p. (J). *(978-1-4896-3232-6(8))* Weigl Pubs., Inc.

Cars & Trucks. Date not set. (Illus.). (J). bds. 9.98 *(978-0-7525-9892-5(9))* Parragon, Inc.

Castor, Harriet. Trucks. Lyon, Chris, illus. 2006. (Big MacHines Ser.). 32p. (J). (gr. k). lib. bdg. 14.95 *(978-1-58086-847-1(9))* EDC Publishing.

—Trucks. Lyon, Chris et al, illus. rev. ed. 2004. (Usborne Big Machines Ser.). 31p. (J). (gr. -1). per. 6.95 *(978-0-7945-0839-5(1),* Usborne) EDC Publishing.

Clay, Kathryn. Dump Trucks. 2016. (Construction Vehicles at Work Ser.). (ENG.). 24p. (gr. k-1). lib. bdg. 21.99 *(978-1-5157-2526-8(X))* Capstone Press of Coughlan Cos.

Cohn, Jessica. Trucks. 2013. 48p. (J). (gr. 3-5). 31.95 *(978-1-4339-9616-0(2));* pap. 14.05 *(978-1-4339-9617-7(0));* pap. 84.30 *(978-1-4339-9618-4(9))* Stevens, Gareth Publishing LLLP.

Colson, Rob Scott. Trucks. 2013. (Ultimate Machines Ser.). (ENG., Illus.). 24p. (J). (gr. 3-6). pap. 8.25 *(978-1-4777-0121-8(4));* lib. bdg. 22.60 *(978-1-4777-0068-6(4))* Rosen Publishing Group, Inc., The. (PowerKids Pr.).

Construction Trucks. 2004. (Mega MacHines Ser.). (Illus.). 16p. (J). *(978-2-7643-0198-2(7))* Phidal Publishing, Inc./Editions Phidal, Inc.

Coppendale, Jean. Trucks. 2010. (Mighty Machines Ser.). (ENG., Illus.). 24p. (J). (gr. -1-2). pap. 5.95 *(978-1-55407-619-2(6),* 9781554076192) Firefly Bks., Ltd.

Cox, Katie, des. Little Hands Trucks. 2009. (Little Hands (Make Believe Ideas) Ser.). (Illus.). 24p. (gr. -1-k). 6.99 *(978-1-84610-983-6(3))* Make Believe Ideas GBR. Dist: Nelson, Thomas Inc.

Dalmatian Press Staff. Pop & Shine Trucks. 2008. (ENG.). 12p. (J). 10.95 *(978-1-58117-672-8(4),* Intervisual/Piggy Toes) Bendon, Inc.

David, Jack. Torque: Humvees. 2009. (Torque Ser.). 24p. (J). (gr. 3-7). 20.00 *(978-0-531-21734-4(5),* Children's Pr.) Scholastic Library Publishing.

Daynes, Katie. Trucks. 2004. (Beginners Ser.). 32p. (J). (gr. 1-18). (ENG.). pap. 4.95 *(978-0-7945-0365-9(9));* lib. bdg. 12.95 *(978-1-58086-511-1(9))* EDC Publishing.

Dickason, Chris. The Diggers & Trucks Colouring Book. Dickason, Chris, illus. 2017. (ENG., Illus.). 64p. (J). (gr. k-2). pap. 6.99 ***(978-1-78055-250-7(5))*** O'Mara, Michael Bks., Ltd. GBR. Dist: Independent Pubs. Group.

Dinmont, Kerry. Monster Trucks on the Go. 2016. (Bumba Books (tm) — Machines That Go Ser.). (ENG., Illus.). 24p. (J). (gr. -1-1). lib. bdg. 25.32 *(978-1-5124-1445-5(X))* Lerner Publishing Group.

Dinmont, Kerry & Granat, Annette. Camiones Monstruo en Acción. 2017. (Bumba Books (tm) en Español — Máquinas en Acción (Machines That Go) Ser.). (SPA., Illus.). 24p. (J). (gr. -1-1). 25.32 *(978-1-5124-2878-0(7))* Lerner Publishing Group.

Doeden, Matt. Monster Trucks. 2007. (J). lib. bdg. 26.60 *(978-0-8225-6567-3(6),* Lerner Pubns.) Lerner Publishing Group.

Doman, Mary Kate. Big Trucks. 2011. (All about Big Machines Ser.). (Illus.). 24p. (J). (gr. -1-18). pap. 7.95 *(978-1-59845-241-9(X),* Enslow Elementary); (gr. k-3). lib. bdg. 22.60 *(978-0-7660-3929-2(3))* Enslow Pubs., Inc.

Donahue, Peter. Cars & Trucks Stained Glass Coloring Book. 2010. (Dover Stained Glass Coloring Book Ser.). (ENG., Illus.). 32p. (J). (gr. -1-5). pap. 6.99 *(978-0-486-47706-0(1))* Dover Pubns., Inc.

Dorling Kindersley Publishing Staff. Big Dump Truck. 2003. (Wheelie Bks.). (ENG., Illus.). 12p. (J). (gr. -1-k). bds. 6.99 *(978-0-7894-9714-7(X),* DK Children) Dorling Kindersley Publishing, Inc.

—Follow the Trail: Trucks. 2016. (ENG., Illus.). 14p. (J). (-k). bds. 9.99 *(978-1-4654-5126-2(9),* DK Children) Dorling Kindersley Publishing, Inc.

—My First Trucks. 2015. (My First Bks.). (ENG.). 36p. (J). (gr. -1 — 1). bds. 5.99 *(978-1-4654-2904-9(2),* DK Children) Dorling Kindersley Publishing, Inc.

—My First Trucks & Diggers. 2013. (Tab Board Bks.). (ENG.). 28p. (J). (gr. -1 — 1). bds. 9.99 *(978-1-4654-1673-5(0),* DK Children) Dorling Kindersley Publishing, Inc.

—Tractor. 2010. (Baby Touch & Feel Ser.). (ENG.). 14p. (J). (gr. -1 — 1). bds. 5.99 *(978-0-7566-7132-7(9),* DK Children) Dorling Kindersley Publishing, Inc.

—Trucks. 2008. (Baby Touch & Feel Ser.). (ENG., Illus.). 14p. (J). (gr. -1 — 1). bds. 5.99 *(978-0-7566-3465-0(2),* DK Children) Dorling Kindersley Publishing, Inc.

—What Am I? Truck. 2013. (ENG.). 28p. (J). (gr. -1 — 1). bds. 6.99 *(978-1-4654-1429-8(0),* DK Children) Dorling Kindersley Publishing, Inc.

—Wheelie Baby: Truck & Friends. 2012. (Wheelie Bks.). (ENG.). 10p. (J). (gr. -1 — 1). bds. 6.99 *(978-0-7566-9291-9(1),* DK Children) Dorling Kindersley Publishing, Inc.

Dorling Kindersley Publishing Staff, ed. Trucks. 2004. (Ultimate Sticker Bks.). (ENG.). 16p. (J). (gr. k-3). pap. 6.99 *(978-0-7566-0239-0(4),* DK Children) Dorling Kindersley Publishing, Inc.

Dos Santos, Julie. Trucks. 2009. (Amazing Machines Ser.). 32p. (gr. 2). 28.50 *(978-0-7614-4407-7(6))* Marshall Cavendish Corp.

Editors of Kingfisher. Mighty Trucks. 2016. (It's All About... Ser.). (ENG.). 32p. pap. 5.99 *(978-0-7534-7288-0(0),* 9780753472880, Kingfisher) Roaring Brook Pr.

Ellis, Catherine. Cars & Trucks. 2009. (Mega Military Machines Ser.). 24p. (gr. 1-1). 42.50 *(978-1-61514-634-5(2),* PowerKids Pr.) Rosen Publishing Group, Inc., The.

—Cars & Trucks/Autos y Camiones. 2009. (Mega Military Machines/Megamaquinas militares Ser.). (ENG & SPA.). 24p. (gr. 1-1). 42.50 *(978-1-61514-639-0(3),* Editorial Buenas Letras) Rosen Publishing Group, Inc., The.

Emberley, Ed. Ed Emberley's Drawing Book of Trucks & Trains. Emberley, Ed, illus. 2005. (ENG., Illus.). 32p. (J). (gr. 2-17). pap. 6.99 *(978-0-316-78967-7(4))* Little, Brown Bks. for Young Readers.

Farndon, John. Megafast Trucks. Edwards, Mat & Pyke, Jeremy, illus. 2016. (Megafast Ser.). (ENG.). 32p. (J). (gr. 3-6). lib. bdg. 26.65 *(978-1-4677-9366-7(3))* Lerner Publishing Group.

Feldman, Thea & Stones, Brenda. Trucks. 2013. (Kingfisher Readers Ser.). (ENG., Illus.). 32p. (J). (gr. k-3). 12.99 *(978-0-7534-6960-6(X),* 9780753469606); pap. 3.99 *(978-0-7534-6927-9(8),* 9780753469279) Roaring Brook Pr. (Kingfisher).

Finn, Denny Von. Humvees. 2013. (Military Vehicles Ser.). (ENG., Illus.). 24p. (J). (gr. 3-7). lib. bdg. 25.95 *(978-1-60014-886-6(7),* Epic Bks.) Bellwether Media.

Frisch, Aaron. Dump Trucks. 2013. 24p. 20.57 *(978-1-60818-341-8(6))* Creative Co., The.

—Seedlings: Dump Trucks. 2014. (Seedlings Ser.). (ENG.). 24p. (J). (gr. -1-k). pap. 7.99 *(978-0-89812-886-4(2),* Creative Paperbacks) Creative Co., The.

Galvin, Laura Gates. First Look at Trucks. Eaddy, Susan, illus. 2008. (ENG.). 16p. (J). (gr. -1-k). 6.95 *(978-1-59249-861-1(2))* Soundprints.

Gibbs, Lynne. Mega Book of Trucks: Discover the Most Amazing Trucks on Earth! 2003. (Illus.). 32p. (YA). pap. *(978-1-904516-21-7(1),* Pavilion Children's Books) Pavilion Bks.

Gifford, Clive. Trucks. 2012. (ENG.). 24p. (J). lib. bdg. *(978-0-7787-7477-8(5));* (Illus.). pap. *(978-0-7787-7482-2(1))* Crabtree Publishing Co.

Gigliotti, Jim. Monster Trucks. 2009. (Racing Mania Ser.). 48p. (gr. 4-18). lib. bdg. 31.36 *(978-0-7614-4385-8(1))* Marshall Cavendish Corp.

Gilbert, Sara. Dump Trucks: Machines That Build. 2011. (Machines That Build Ser.). (ENG.). 24p. (J). (gr. 1-17). pap. 7.99 *(978-1-897563-75-5(2),* Creative Paperbacks) Creative Co., The.

Gilpin, Rebecca. Trucks & Tractors. 2005. (ENG.). 32p. (J). pap. 8.95 *(978-0-7945-1134-0(1),* Usborne) EDC Publishing.

Glaser, Rebecca. Dump Truck. 2012. (ENG., Illus.). 24p. (J). lib. bdg. 25.65 *(978-1-62031-019-9(8))* Jump! Inc.

Glaser, Rebecca Stromstad. Trucks Haul. 2016. (ENG., Illus.). 14p. (J). (gr. -1 — 1). bds. 7.99 *(978-1-68152-124-4(5))* Amicus.

Glover, David & Glover, Penny. Trucks in Action. 2008. (On the Go Ser.). (Illus.). 24p. (J). (gr. 3-7). lib. bdg. 22.60 *(978-1-4042-4310-1(0),* PowerKids Pr.) Rosen Publishing Group, Inc., The.

Goldish, Meish. Titanic Trucks. 2009. (World's Biggest Ser.). (Illus.). 24p. (J). (gr. 1-6). lib. bdg. 22.61 *(978-1-59716-957-8(9))* Bearport Publishing Co., Inc.

Goodman, Susan E. Monster Trucks! Doolittle, Michael, illus. 2010. (Step into Reading Ser.). (ENG.). 48p. (J). (gr. k-3). pap. 3.99 *(978-0-375-86208-3(0),* Random Hse. Bks. for Young Readers) Random Hse. Children's Bks.

Gordon, Nick. Monster Trucks. 2013. (Monster Machines Ser.). (ENG., Illus.). 24p. (J). (gr. k-3). lib. bdg. 25.95 *(978-1-60014-940-5(5),* Blastoff! Readers) Bellwether Media.

Graham, Ian. Dump Trucks & Other Big Machines. 2016. (Mighty Machines Ser.). (ENG., Illus.). 24p. (J). (gr. -1-2). pap. 5.95 *(978-1-77085-850-3(4),* 9781770858503) Firefly Bks., Ltd.

—Monster Trucks. 2016. (Mighty Machines Ser.). (Illus.). 24p. (J). (ENG.). (gr. -1-2). pap. 5.95 *(978-1-77085-851-0(2),* 9781770858510); ***(978-1-4844-9477-6(6))*** Firefly Bks., Ltd.

—Super Trucks. Bergin, Mark & Hewetson, N. J., illus. 2014. (Time Shift Speed Ser.). 32p. (gr. 3-6). 31.35 ***(978-1-908973-97-9(8))*** Book Hse. GBR. Dist: Black Rabbit Bks.

Graham, Ian. Trucks. 2007. (Extreme Machines/Watts Ser.). (Illus.). 32p. (YA). (gr. 4-7). lib. bdg. 28.50 *(978-1-59920-043-9(0))* Black Rabbit Bks.

Graubart, Norman D. Tractor-Trailers, 1 vol. 2015. (ENG.). 24p. (J). lib. bdg. 23.60 *(978-1-4994-0219-3(8),* PowerKids Pr.) Rosen Publishing Group, Inc., The.

Greve, Meg & Robertson, J. Jean. Camiones: Trucks. 2008. (Mis Primeros Descubrimientos = My First Discovery Ser.). (ENG & SPA., Illus.). 24p. (J). (gr. k-2). 19.44 *(978-1-60472-504-9(4))* Rourke Educational Media.

Gunzi, Christiane. Big Noisy Trucks. 2015. (ENG., Illus.). 10p. (J). 9.99 *(978-1-904618-88-1(X))* Award Pubns. Ltd. GBR. Dist: Parkwest Pubns., Inc.

Hamilton, John. Humvees. 2011. (Military Vehicles Ser.). (Illus.). 32p. (YA). (gr. 4-7). 27.07 *(978-1-61783-076-1(3))* ABDO Publishing Co.

Hankin, Rosie. Cut & Paste Trucks, Trains, & Big Machines. 2007. (Cut, Paste, & Create Ser.). (Illus.). 32p. (gr. k-3). lib. bdg. 26.00 *(978-0-8368-7721-2(7),* Gareth Stevens Learning Library) Stevens, Gareth Publishing LLLP.

Hanson, Anders. Let's Go by Truck, 1 vol. 2008. (Let's Go Ser.). (ENG., Illus.). 24p. (J). (gr. k-3). lib. bdg. 24.21 *(978-1-59928-904-5(0),* SandCastle) ABDO Publishing Co.

Harrison, Paul. Monster Trucks. (Up Close Ser.). 24p. (gr. 3-3). 2009. 47.90 *(978-1-60854-697-8(7))* 2008. (Illus.). (J). lib. bdg. 25.25 *(978-1-4042-4223-4(6))* Rosen Publishing Group, Inc., The. (PowerKids Pr.).

—Supertrucks. 2013. (Illus.). 32p. (J). *(978-1-84858-566-9(7))* Arcturus Pubs., Inc.

Hayes, Amy. Dump Trucks Are Big Trucks. 2015. (Machines That Work Ser.). (ENG., Illus.). 24p. (J). (gr. 1-1). pap. 8.22 *(978-1-5026-0394-4(2))* Cavendish Square Publishing.

Helbrough, Emma & Brooks, Felicity. First Picture Trucks. Van Wyk, Hanri & Newell, Keith, illus. MMStudios, photos by. 2007. (First Picture Board Bks.). 16p. (J). (gr. -1-k). bds. 11.99 *(978-0-7945-1454-9(5),* Usborne) EDC Publishing.

HOP, LLC. Hooked on Trucks Super Activity Kit. 2006. (J). (gr. -1). 9.99 *(978-1-933863-18-4(8))* HOP, LLC.

Howell, Brian. Monster Trucks: Tearing It Up. 2014. (Dirt & Destruction Sports Zone Ser.). (ENG., Illus.). 32p. (gr. 4-8). lib. bdg. 26.60 *(978-1-4677-2120-2(4),* Lerner Pubns.) Lerner Publishing Group.

Hudson, Amanda. This Is My Truck. 2008. (Our Toys Ser.). (Illus.). 16p. (gr. -1-2). (J). lib. bdg. 19.00 *(978-0-8368-9255-0(0));* pap. 5.30 *(978-0-8368-9354-0(9))* Stevens, Gareth Publishing LLLP. (Weekly Reader Leveled Readers).

—This Is My Truck (Éste es mi Camión) 2008. (Our Toys/Nuestros Juguetes Ser.). (SPA.). 16p. (gr. -1-2). pap. 5.30 *(978-0-8368-9358-8(1),* Weekly Reader Leveled Readers) Stevens, Gareth Publishing LLLP.

—This Is My Truck/Éste Es Mi Camión. 2008. (Our Toys/Nuestros Juguetes Ser.). (ENG & SPA., Illus.). 16p. (J). (gr. -1-2). lib. bdg. 19.00 *(978-0-8368-9259-8(3),* Weekly Reader Leveled Readers) Stevens, Gareth Publishing LLLP.

Ikids Staff. Soft Shapes: Trucks (Baby's First Book + Puzzle) Ski, Jenn, illus. 2010. (ENG.). 8p. (J). (gr. -1 — 1). 10.99 *(978-1-60169-044-9(4))* Innovative Kids.

—Trucks. Larranaga, Ana Martin, illus. 2009. (ENG.). 12p. (J). (gr. -1 — 1). bds. 5.99 *(978-1-58476-936-1(X))* Innovative Kids.

Ipcizade, Catherine. BIG Trucks. 2016. (Big Ser.). (ENG.). 24p. pap. 6.95 *(978-1-5157-6202-7(5),* Pebble Plus) Capstone Press of Coughlan Cos.

Jango-Cohen, Judith. Dump Trucks on the Move. 2011. (Lightning Bolt Books Vroom-Vroom Ser.). (ENG.). 32p. (gr. k-2). lib. bdg. 26.60 *(978-0-7613-3917-5(5))* Lerner Publishing Group.

—Fire Trucks on the Move. 2010. (Lightning Bolt Books Vroom-Vroom Ser.). (ENG.). 32p. (gr. k-2). pap. 7.95 *(978-0-7613-6119-0(7))* Lerner Publishing Group.

—Volquetes. Translations.com Staff, tr. from ENG. 2006. (Libros para Avanzar-Potencia en Movimiento (Pull Ahead Books-Mighty Movers) Ser.). (SPA., Illus.). 32p. (gr. k-3). lib. bdg. 22.60 *(978-0-8225-6228-3(6),* Ediciones Lerner) Lerner Publishing Group.

—Volquetes (Dump Trucks) Translations.com Staff, tr. 2006. (Libros para Avanzar-Potencia en Movimiento (Pull Ahead Books-Mighty Movers) Ser.). (SPA.). 32p. (gr. k-3). pap. 7.95 *(978-0-8225-6643-4(5),* Ediciones Lerner) Lerner Publishing Group.

Jennings, Terry. Trucks. 2009. (J). 28.50 *(978-1-59920-291-4(3))* Black Rabbit Bks.

—Trucks. 2009. (How Machines Work Ser.). (Illus.). 32p. (J). (gr. 3-7). pap. *(978-1-897563-45-8(0))* Saunders Bk. Co.

Johansen, Heidi Leigh. My Book of Trucks. 2005. (Early Learning Collections Ser.). (Illus.). (J). 8.95 *(978-1-4042-2800-9(4),* PowerKids Pr.) Rosen Publishing Group, Inc., The.

Johnson, Earl L. & Hawkins, Grace. The World's Greatest Working Trucks Vol. 5: The Best of the Northeast. 2003. 100p. (Orig.). (YA). (gr. 8-12). pap. 19.95 *(978-0-9649645-1-8(1))* Johnson, Earl Photography.

Johnstone, Michael. Monster Trucks. 2005. (Need for Speed Ser.). (Illus.). 32p. (gr. 3-5). lib. bdg. 23.93 *(978-0-8225-0388-0(3))* Lerner Publishing Group.

Kalman, Bobbie. Camiones Robustos. 2007. (Vehículos en Acción Ser.). (SPA & ENG., Illus.). 32p. (J). (gr. 4-7). pap. *(978-0-7787-8316-9(2));* lib. bdg. *(978-0-7787-8306-0(5))* Crabtree Publishing Co.

—Tough Trucks. 2007. (Vehicles on the Move Ser.). (ENG., Illus.). 32p. (J). (gr. 3-7). lib. bdg. *(978-0-7787-3044-6(1));* (gr. 1-5). pap. *(978-0-7787-3058-3(1))* Crabtree Publishing Co.

Kane, Tim. Monster Mega Trucks: ... & Other Four-Wheeled Creatures. 2014. (ENG.). 48p. (J). (gr. 4-7). pap. 5.99 *(978-1-62937-035-4(5))* Triumph Bks.

Kawa, Katie. Dump Trucks. 2011. (Big Machines Ser.). (Illus.). 24p. (gr. k-2). (J). pap. 8.15 *(978-1-4339-5564-8(4));* (J). lib. bdg. 22.60 *(978-1-4339-5562-4(8));* 69.20 *(978-1-4339-6889-1(4))* Stevens, Gareth Publishing LLLP.

—Dump Trucks: Camiones de Volteo. 2011. (Big Machines / Grandes MáQuinas Ser.). (SPA., Illus.). 24p. (J). (gr. k-3). lib. bdg. 22.60 *(978-1-4339-5580-8(6))* Stevens, Gareth Publishing LLLP.

Kiland, Taylor Baldwin & Teitelbaum, Michael. Military Humvees: Armored Mobility. 2015. (Military Engineering in Action Ser.). (ENG., Illus.). 48p. (J). (gr. 6-6). 27.93 *(978-0-7660-6914-5(1))* Enslow Pubs., Inc.

Kilby, Don. At a Construction Site. Kilby, Don, illus. 2006. (Wheels at Work Ser.). (ENG., Illus.). 24p. (J). (gr. -1-2). 6.95 *(978-1-55337-987-4(X))* Kids Can Pr., Ltd. CAN. Dist: Hachette Bk. Group.

—On the Road. 2003. (Wheels at Work Ser.). (Illus.). 24p. (J). (gr. -1-k). *(978-1-55337-043-7(0))* Kids Can Pr., Ltd.

—On the Road. Kilby, Don, illus. 2006. (Wheels at Work Ser.). (ENG., Illus.). 24p. (J). (gr. -1-2). 5.95 *(978-1-55337-986-7(1))* Kids Can Pr., Ltd. CAN. Dist: Hachette Bk. Group.

LaFontaine, Bruce. History of Trucks. 2013. (Dover History Coloring Book Ser.). (ENG., Illus.). 48p. (J). (gr. 3-12). pap. 4.99 *(978-0-486-29278-6(9))* Dover Pubns., Inc.

Landers, Ace & Cartwheel Editors. I Am a Garbage Truck. Scholastic, Inc. Staff, ed. 2008. (ENG.). 8p. (J). (gr. -1 — 1). bds. 4.99 *(978-0-545-07963-1(2),* Cartwheel Bks.) Scholastic, Inc.

Latham, Donna. Superfast Trucks. 2006. (Ultimate Speed Ser.). (Illus.). 32p. (J). (gr. 3-6). lib. bdg. 25.27 *(978-1-59716-253-1(1))* Bearport Publishing Co., Inc.

Lennie, Charles. Dump Trucks, 1 vol. 2014. (Construction Machines Ser.). (ENG.). 24p. (J). (gr. 4-8). lib. bdg. 28.50 *(978-1-62970-018-2(5))* ABDO Publishing Co.

Leonard, Barry, ed. Drawing Trucks & Diggers: A Book of 10 Stencils. 2004. (Illus.). 34p. (J). (gr. k-4). reprint ed. ring bd. 10.00 *(978-0-7567-8505-5(7))* DIANE Publishing Co.

Let's Make a Dump Truck with Everyday Materials. 2006. (Let's Do Arts & Crafts Ser.). (Illus.). 24p. (J). (gr. -1-3). lib. bdg. 22.60 *(978-1-4042-3059-0(9))* Rosen Publishing Group, Inc., The.

Levete. Monster Trucks 6-Pack. 2004. (Mean Machines Ser.). (Illus.). (J). pap. 48.30 *(978-1-4109-1202-2(7))* Harcourt Schl. Pubs.

Light, Steve. Trucks Go. 2008. (ENG., Illus.). 16p. (J). (gr. -1 — 1). bds. 9.99 *(978-0-8118-6542-5(8))* Chronicle Bks. LLC.

Lindeen, Mary. Garbage Trucks. 2007. (Mighty Machines Ser.). (ENG., Illus.). 24p. (J). (gr. k-3). lib. bdg. 25.95 *(978-1-60014-117-1(X))* Bellwether Media.

—Trucks. 2007. (Mighty Machines Ser.). (ENG., Illus.). 24p. (J). (gr. k-3). lib. bdg. 25.95 *(978-1-60014-063-1(7))* Bellwether Media.

Litchfield, Jo & Brooks, F. Trucks. 2004. (Chunky Board Bks.). (ENG., Illus.). 6p. (J). bds. 4.95 *(978-0-7945-0349-9(7),* Usborne) EDC Publishing.

Llewellyn, Claire. Trucks. 2015. (Wonderwise Ser.). (Illus.). 32p. (gr. 2-6). 31.35 *(978-1-62588-363-6(3))* Black Rabbit Bks.

Lock, Deborah. Big Trucks. 2013. (DK Reader Pre Level Ser.). lib. bdg. 13.55 *(978-0-606-32459-5(3),* Turtleback) Turtleback Bks.

Lock, Deborah & Dorling Kindersley Publishing Staff. Big Trucks. 2013. (DK Readers Ser.). (ENG.). 32p. (J). (gr. -1-1). pap. 3.99 *(978-1-4654-0890-7(8),* DK Children) Dorling Kindersley Publishing, Inc.

Lovitt, Chip. My Big Dump Truck. LaPadula, Thomas, illus. 2011. (Diecut Vehicles Ser.). (ENG.). 12p. (J). (gr. -1-1). bds.

5.99 (978-0-7944-2272-1(1), Reader's Digest Children's Bks.) Studio Fun International.

Make Believe Ideas, creator. Touch & Learn Tractors & Trucks Casebound. 2007. per. (978-1-84610-509-8(9)) Make Believe Ideas.

Manolis, Kay. Big Rigs. 2008. (Mighty Machines Ser.). (ENG., Illus.). 24p. (J). (gr. k-3). lib. bdg. 25.95 (978-1-60014-177-5(3)) Bellwether Media.

—Monster Trucks. 2008. (Mighty Machines Ser.). (ENG., Illus.). 24p. (J). (gr. k-3). lib. bdg. 25.95 (978-1-60014-178-2(1)) Bellwether Media.

—Tow Trucks. 2008. (Mighty Machines Ser.). (ENG., Illus.). 24p. (J). (gr. k-3). lib. bdg. 25.95 (978-1-60014-182-9(X)) Bellwether Media.

Mara, Wil. Trucks! 2009. (Readers Ser.). (ENG., Illus.). 32p. (J). (gr. -1-1). 13.90 (978-1-4263-0527-6(3)); pap. 3.99 (978-1-4263-0526-9(5)) National Geographic Society. (National Geographic Children's Bks.).

Marshall, Jane. Trucks & Diggers. 2013. (Wild Rides Ser.). 32p. (J). (gr. k-2). (978-1-84898-623-7(8), TickTock Books) Octopus Publishing Group.

Marsico, Katie. Giant Trucks. 2016. (True Book(tm) — Engineering Wonders Ser.). (ENG., Illus.). 48p. (J). pap. 6.95 (978-0-531-22271-3(3), Children's Pr.) Scholastic Library Publishing.

Mason, Paul. Monster Trucks. 2010. (Motorsports Ser.). 32p. (J). (gr. 3-6). 28.50 (978-1-60753-120-3(8)) Amicus Publishing.

Masters, Neil. Trucks Coloring Book. 2013. (ENG.). 32p. 12.48 (978-1-62884-654-6(2), Baby Professor (Education Kids)) Speedy Publishing LLC.

Matthies, Janna. Monster Trucks. Barretta, Gene, illus. 2009. (ENG.). 14p. (J). (gr. -1-k). 9.95 (978-1-58117-853-1(0), Intervisual/Piggy Toes) Bendon, Inc.

Maurer, Tracy Nelson. Land Rover. 2006. (Full Throttle Ser.). (Illus.). 32p. (J). (gr. -1-3). lib. bdg. 28.50 (978-1-60044-225-4(0)) Rourke Educational Media.

Mead, Sue. Monster Trucks & Tractors. rev. collector's ed. 2005. (Race Car Legends Ser.). (Illus.). 80p. (YA). (gr. 5-9). lib. bdg. 25.00 (978-0-7910-8689-6(5)) Facts On File, Inc.

Mezzanotte, Jim. Camiones Basculantes. 2005. (Vehiculos Gigantes (Giant Vehicles) Ser.). (SPA.). 24p. (gr. 1-4). lib. bdg. 23.00 (978-0-8368-5985-0(5), Gareth Stevens Learning Library) Stevens, Gareth Publishing LLLP.

—Giant Dump Trucks. 2005. (Giant Vehicles Ser.). (Illus.). 24p. (gr. 1-4). pap. 8.15 (978-0-8368-4919-6(1)); lib. bdg. 23.00 (978-0-8368-4912-7(4)) Stevens, Gareth Publishing LLLP. (Gareth Stevens Learning Library).

Molzahn, Arlene Bourgeois. Trucks & Big Rigs. 2003. (Transportation & Communication Ser.). (Illus.). 48p. (J). lib. bdg. 25.27 (978-0-7660-2024-5(X)) Enslow Pubs., Inc.

Morganelli, Adrianna. Trucks: Pickups to Big Rigs. 2007. (Automania! Ser.). (ENG., Illus.). 32p. (J). (gr. 3-7). lib. bdg. (978-0-7787-3015-6(8)); (gr. 2-9). pap. (978-0-7787-3037-8(9)) Crabtree Publishing Co.

Mullins, Matt. Trucks. 2008. (21st Century Skills Innovation Library: Innovation in Transportation Ser.). (ENG., Illus.). 32p. (gr. 4-8). lib. bdg. 28.50 (978-1-60279-237-1(2), 200167) Cherry Lake Publishing.

Murray, Julie. Trucks, 1 vol. 2014. (Transportation Ser.). (ENG.). 24p. (J). (gr. 4-8). lib. bdg. 28.50 (978-1-62970-083-0(5)) ABDO Publishing Co.

Murray, Julie, et al. Camiones. 2015. (Medios de Transporte Ser.). (SPA.). 24p. (gr. k-1). pap. 7.95 (978-1-4966-0489-7(X)) Capstone Classroom.

My First Book of Trucks. 2004. (Illus.). 18p. (J). bds. 5.99 (978-1-85854-431-1(9)) Brimax Books Ltd. GBR. Dist: Byeway Bks.

National Geographic. Things That Go! Collection. 2015. (Readers Ser.). (ENG., Illus.). 120p. (J). (gr. k-3). lib. bdg. 16.90 (978-1-4263-1973-0(8), National Geographic Children's Bks.) National Geographic Society.

Nelson, Kristin L. Camionetas Gigantes. Translations.com Staff, tr. from ENG. 2006. (Libros para Avanzar-Potencia en Movimiento (Pull Ahead Books-Mighty Movers) Ser.). (SPA., Illus.). 32p. (gr. k-3). lib. bdg. 22.60 (978-0-8225-6227-6(8), Ediciones Lerner) Lerner Publishing Group.

—Monster Trucks on the Move. 2010. pap. 45.32 (978-0-7613-6939-4(2)); (ENG.). 32p. pap. 7.95 (978-0-7613-6120-6(0)); (ENG., Illus.). 32p. (J). lib. bdg. 26.60 (978-0-7613-6022-3(0)) Lerner Publishing Group.

Nixon, James. Trucks. 2010. (Machines on the Move Ser.). 32p. 28.50 (978-1-60753-064-0(3)) Amicus Publishing.

—Trucks. 2012. (Illus.). 32p. (gr. 1-3). pap. 8.95 (978-1-926722-74-0(4)) Saunders Bk. Co. CAN. Dist: RiverStream Publishing.

Noble, Marty. Fun with Fire Trucks Stencils. 2008. (Dover Stencils Ser.). (ENG., Illus.). 6p. (J). (gr. -1-5). pap. 1.50 (978-0-486-46686-6(8)) Dover Pubns., Inc.

Oachs, Emily Rose. Dump Trucks. 2017. (Mighty Machines in Action Ser.). (ENG., Illus.). 24p. (J). (gr. k-3). lib. bdg. 25.95 (978-1-62617-603-4(5), Blastoff! Readers) Bellwether Media.

Osier, Dan. Dump Trucks, 1 vol., 1. 2014. (Construction Site Ser.). (ENG.). 24p. (J). (gr. k-2). 23.60 (978-1-4777-2862-8(7), PowerKids Pr.) Rosen Publishing Group, Inc., The.

—Forklifts, 1 vol., 1. 2014. (Construction Site Ser.). (ENG.). 24p. (J). (gr. k-2). pap. 8.25 (978-1-4777-2956-4(9), PowerKids Pr.) Rosen Publishing Group, Inc., The.

Oxlade, Chris. This Is My Dump Truck. Crawford, Andy, photos by. 2008. (Mega Machine Drivers Ser.). (Illus.). 30p. (J). (gr. k). lib. bdg. 28.50 (978-1-59771-105-0(5)) Sea-To-Sea Pubns.

—Trucks. 2009. (Mighty Machines Ser.). (Illus.). 31p. (J). (gr. 4-7). pap. 7.95 (978-1-59920-256-3(5)) Black Rabbit Bks.

—Trucks Inside & Out. 2009. (Machines Inside Out Ser.). (ENG.). 32p. (J). (gr. 4-6). pap. 10.00 (978-1-4358-2940-4(9), PowerKids Pr.); (YA). (gr. 3-6). lib. bdg. 25.25 (978-1-4358-2862-9(3)) Rosen Publishing Group, Inc., The.

Page, Josephine. I Am a Dump Truck. Migliari, Paola, illus. 2007. (ENG.). 4p. (J). (gr. -1 — 1). bds. 4.99 (978-0-439-91617-2(8), Cartwheel Bks.) Scholastic, Inc.

Parker, Steve. Cars Trucks & Bikes. 2010. (How It Works Ser.). (Illus.). 40p. (J). (gr. 3-18). lib. bdg. 19.95 (978-1-4222-1792-4(2), 1317905) Mason Crest.

—Giant Machines. 2010. (How It Works Ser.). 40p. (J). (gr. 3-18). lib. bdg. 19.95 (978-1-4222-1796-2(5)) Mason Crest.

Pearcey, Alice. Usborne Tractors & Trucks Stencil Book. Milbourne, Anna, ed. Tudor, Andy, illus. 2006. 10p. (J). bds. 12.99 (978-0-7945-1139-5(2), Usborne) EDC Publishing.

Peppas, Lynn. Monster Trucks. 2012. (ENG., Illus.). 32p. (J). (978-0-7787-3019-4(0)); pap. (978-0-7787-3024-8(7)) Crabtree Publishing Co.

Perez, Jessica. Under Construction: A Moving Track Book. Schneider, Christine, illus. 2005. (ENG.). 12p. (J). 12.95 (978-1-58117-272-0(9), Intervisual/Piggy Toes) Bendon, Inc.

Petruccio, Steven James. BOOST Trucks Coloring Book. 2013. (BOOST Educational Ser.). (ENG.). 32p. (J). (gr. 1-2). pap. 4.99 (978-0-486-49411-1(X)) Dover Pubns., Inc.

—Create Your Own Construction Truck Sticker Activity Book. 2011. (Dover Little Activity Books Stickers Ser.). (ENG., Illus.). 4p. (J). (gr. k-3). 1.99 (978-0-486-47232-4(9)) Dover Pubns., Inc.

—Create Your Own Fire Truck. 2010. (Dover Little Activity Books Stickers Ser.). (ENG., Illus.). 4p. (J). (gr. 1-4). pap. 1.50 (978-0-486-47548-6(4)) Dover Pubns., Inc.

Pettiford, Rebecca. Big Rigs. 2017. (Mighty Machines in Action Ser.). (ENG., Illus.). 24p. (J). (gr. k-3). lib. bdg. 25.95 **(978-1-62617-629-4(9)**, Blastoff! Readers) Bellwether Media.

Picthall, Chez. My Favourite Trucks Sticker Book. Rayner, Katy, ed. 2015. (ENG., Illus.). 20p. (J). pap. 7.99 (978-1-906572-83-9(6)) Award Pubns. Ltd. GBR. Dist: Parkwest Pubns., Inc.

Piehl, Janet. Humvees. 2005. (Pull Ahead Books-Mighty Movers Ser.). (ENG., Illus.). 32p. (gr. k-3). per. 7.95 (978-0-8225-2874-6(6), Lerner Pubns.) Lerner Publishing Group.

Poolos, J. Monster Trucks/Camionetas Gigantes. Alaman, Eduardo, tr. 2007. (Wild Rides / Autos de Locura Ser.). (SPA., Illus.). 24p. (YA). (gr. 2-5). lib. bdg. 22.60 (978-1-4042-7640-6(8)) Rosen Publishing Group, Inc., The.

—Wild about Monster Trucks. (Wild Rides Ser.). 24p. (gr. 2-3). 2009. 42.50 (978-1-60854-801-9(5), PowerKids Pr.) 2007. (Illus.). (J). lib. bdg. 22.60 (978-1-4042-3791-9(7)) Rosen Publishing Group, Inc., The.

—Wild about Monster Trucks/Camionetas Gigantes. 2009. (Wild Rides/Autos de locura Ser.). 24p. (gr. 2-3). 42.50 (978-1-60854-808-8(2), Editorial Buenas Letras) Rosen Publishing Group, Inc., The.

Powell, Debbie. Trucks. Powell, Debbie, illus. 2012. (ENG., Illus.). 16p. (J). (gr. -1 — 1). bds. 5.99 (978-0-7636-5934-9(7)) Candlewick Pr.

Priddy, Roger. First 100 Trucks. 2011. (First 100 Ser.). (ENG., Illus.). 26p. (J). (gr. -1 — 1). bds. 5.99 (978-0-312-51080-0(2), 9780312510800, Priddy Bks.) St. Martin's Pr.

—First 100 Trucks & Things That Go. 2016. (First 100 Ser.). (ENG.). 80p. (J). pap. 9.99 (978-0-312-52145-5(6), 9780312521455, Priddy Bks.) St. Martin's Pr.

—First 100 Trucks & Things That Go Lift-The-Flap. 2015. (First 100 Ser.). (ENG., Illus.). 14p. (J). (gr. -1 — 1). bds. 9.99 (978-0-312-51782-3(3), 9780312517823, Priddy Bks.) St. Martin's Pr.

—Let's Go Learning: I Love Trucks. 2013. (Let's Go Learning Ser.). (ENG.). 104p. (J). (gr. -1-1). pap. 6.99 (978-0-312-51071-8(3), 9780312510718, Priddy Bks.) St. Martin's Pr.

—My Big Truck Book. 2011. (My Big Board Bks.). (ENG., Illus.). 12p. (J). (gr. -1 — 1). bds. 7.99 (978-0-312-51106-7(X), 9780312511067, Priddy Bks.) St. Martin's Pr.

—Pull the Tab: Trucks. 2016. (Pull the Tab Ser.). (ENG.). 10p. (J). bds. 8.99 (978-0-312-52068-7(9), 9780312520687, Priddy Bks.) St. Martin's Pr.

—T Is for Truck. 2014. (ABC Bks.). (ENG.). 24p. (J). (gr. -1 — 1). bds. 12.99 (978-0-312-51734-2(3), 9780312517342, Priddy Bks.) St. Martin's Pr.

—Trucks. 2013. (Lift-The-Flap Tab Bks.). (ENG., Illus.). 16p. (J). (gr. -1 — 1). bds. 8.99 (978-0-312-51582-9(0), 9780312515829, Priddy Bks.) St. Martin's Pr.

—Trucks. 2007. (Slide & Find Ser.). (ENG., Illus.). 8p. (J). (gr. -1 — 1). bds. 7.99 (978-0-312-49909-9(4), 9780312499099, Priddy Bks.) St. Martin's Pr.

—Trucks. (Bright Baby Ser.). (ENG & SPA., Illus.). (J). (gr. -1 — 1). 2007. 12p. bds. 4.95 (978-0-312-50299-7(0), 9780312502997) 2004. 26p. bds. 4.99 (978-0-312-49389-9(4), 9780312493899) St. Martin's Pr. (Priddy Bks.).

Pritchard, Louise & Gunzi, Christiane. Mega Trucks: The Biggest, Toughest Trucks in the World! 2016. (Mega Vehicles Ser.). (ENG.). 32p. (J). (gr. -1-2). pap. 6.99 (978-1-4380-0918-6(6)) Barron's Educational Series, Inc.

Racing Mania, 6 bks., Set. Incl. Drag Racing. Kelley, K. C. lib. bdg. 31.36 (978-0-7614-4384-1(3)); Monster Trucks. Gigliotti, Jim. lib. bdg. 31.36 (978-0-7614-4385-8(1)); Motorcross. Stealey, Bryan. lib. bdg. 31.36 (978-0-7614-4386-5(X)); NASCAR. Kelley, K. C. lib. bdg. 31.36 (978-0-7614-4387-2(8)); Off-Road Racing. Gigliotti, Jim. lib. bdg. 31.36 (978-0-7614-4388-9(6)); Wild Racers. Woods, Bob. lib. bdg. 31.36 (978-0-7614-4389-6(4)); 48p. (gr. 4-18). (Racing Mania Ser.). 2009. Set lib. bdg. 188.16 o.p. (978-0-7614-4380-3(0)) Marshall Cavendish Corp.

Randolph, Joanne. Concrete Mixers. 2009. (Road Machines Ser.). 24p. (gr. k-1). 37.50 (978-1-60852-461-7(2), PowerKids Pr.) Rosen Publishing Group, Inc., The.

—Tow Trucks. 2009. (To the Rescue! Ser.). 24p. (gr. 1-1). 42.50 (978-1-60854-399-1(4), PowerKids Pr.) Rosen Publishing Group, Inc., The.

—Tow Trucks/Gruas. 2009. (To the Rescue! / ¡Al rescate! Ser.). (ENG & SPA.). 24p. (gr. 1-1). 42.50 (978-1-60854-405-9(2), Editorial Buenas Letras) Rosen Publishing Group, Inc., The.

Ransom, Candice. Big Rigs on the Move. 2010. pap. 45.32 (978-0-7613-6937-0(6)); (ENG.). 32p. pap. 7.95 (978-0-7613-6115-2(4)); (ENG., Illus.). 32p. lib. bdg. 26.60 (978-0-7613-3919-9(1)) Lerner Publishing Group.

—Camiones Grandes (Big Rigs) Translations.com Staff, tr. 2006. (Libros para Avanzar-Potencia en Movimiento (Pull Ahead Books-Mighty Movers) Ser.). (SPA.). 32p. (gr. k-3). pap. 7.95 (978-0-8225-6647-2(8), Ediciones Lerner) Lerner Publishing Group.

Rau, Dana Meachen. Trucks. 2009. (Bookworms Ser.). 24p. (gr. k-1). 15.95 (978-0-7614-4083-3(6)) Marshall Cavendish Corp.

—Trucks/En Camiones. 2009. (Bookworms Ser.). (SPA & ENG.). 24p. (gr. k-1). lib. bdg. 15.95 (978-0-7614-4774-0(1)) Marshall Cavendish Corp.

Rayner, Katy. Trucks. 2014. (ENG., Illus.). 22p. pap. 8.95 (978-1-906572-11-2(9)) Award Pubns. Ltd. GBR. Dist: Parkwest Pubns., Inc.

Rea, Amy C. Ice Road Truckers in Action. 2017. (Dangerous Jobs in Action Ser.). (ENG.). 32p. (J). (gr. 3-6). lib. bdg. 27.07 (978-1-5038-1630-5(3), 211146) Child's World, Inc., The.

Reinke, Beth Bence. Dump Trucks Haul! 2017. (Bumba Books (tm) — Construction Zone Ser.). (ENG.). 24p. (J). (gr. -1-1). 25.32 **(978-1-5124-3359-3(4))** Lerner Publishing Group.

Richards, M. & Creese, S. Carry Me Rough N Tough - Trucks. 2009. 12p. pap. (978-1-84610-871-6(3)) Make Believe Ideas.

Rigg, Jo, et al. I Love Trucks. 2007. (I Love Ser.). (ENG., Illus.). 20p. (J). (gr. -1-k). pap. 4.99 (978-0-312-49961-7(2), 9780312499617, Priddy Bks.) St. Martin's Pr.

Riggs, Kate. Seedlings: Pickup Trucks. 2017. (Seedlings Ser.). (ENG., Illus.). 24p. (J). (gr. -1-1). pap. 7.99 **(978-1-62832-388-7(4)**, Creative Paperbacks) Creative Co., The.

—Seedlings: Tanker Trucks. 2017. (Seedlings Ser.). (ENG., Illus.). 24p. (J). (gr. -1-1). pap. 7.99 **(978-1-62832-389-4(2)**, Creative Paperbacks) Creative Co., The.

—Seedlings: Tow Trucks. 2017. (Seedlings Ser.). (ENG., Illus.). 24p. (J). (gr. -1-1). pap. 7.99 **(978-1-62832-390-0(6)**, Creative Paperbacks) Creative Co., The.

Robbins, Ken. Trucks: Giants of the Highway. Robbins, Ken, illus. 2013. (ENG., Illus.). 32p. (J). (gr. -1-3). pap. 16.99 (978-1-4814-0164-7(5), Atheneum Bks. for Young Readers) Simon & Schuster Children's Publishing.

Rosen Publishing Staff. Giants on the Road, 1 vol. 2015. (Giants on the Road Ser.). (ENG.). 24p. (J). 141.60 (978-1-4777-5744-4(9), PowerKids Pr.) Rosen Publishing Group, Inc., The.

Ross, Paula Kovacs, et al. Tractors & Trucks: An Exciting Mechanical & Educational Experience Awaits You When You Meet Tractors & Trucks. 2013. (Kids Meet Ser.: 1). (ENG., Illus.). 96p. (J). 12.95 (978-1-60433-326-8(X), Applesauce Pr.) Cider Mill Pr. Bk. Pubs., LLC.

Ruck, Colleen. Trucks. 2011. (My Favorite Machines Ser.). 24p. (gr. 2-5). 28.50 (978-1-59920-680-6(3)) Black Rabbit Bks.

Sautter, Aaron. How to Draw Monster Trucks, 1 vol. Whigham, Rod, illus. 2007. (Drawing Cool Stuff Ser.). (ENG.). 32p. (gr. 3-4). 27.99 (978-1-4296-0079-8(9), Edge Bks.) Capstone Press of Coughlan Cos.

Savage, Jeff. Monster Trucks, 1 vol. 2010. (Full Throttle Ser.). (ENG.). 32p. (gr. 3-4). lib. bdg. 27.99 (978-1-4296-3943-9(1), Edge Bks.) Capstone Press of Coughlan Cos.

Schaefer, Lola M. Semitrucks in Action, 1 vol. 2011. (Transportation Zone Ser.). (ENG.). 24p. (gr. 1-2). lib. bdg. 25.32 (978-1-4296-6826-2(1), First Facts) Capstone Press of Coughlan Cos.

Schmauss, Judy Kentor. A Truck Can Help. 2006. (Reader's Clubhouse Level 1 Reader Ser.). (ENG., Illus.). 24p. (J). (gr. 1-4). pap. 4.99 (978-0-7641-3290-2(3)) Barron's Educational Series, Inc.

Scholastic, Inc. Staff, contrib. by. Counting Cars & Trucks. 2016. (Rookie Toddlers Ser.). (ENG.). 12p. (J). bds. 6.95 (978-0-531-22453-3(8), Children's Pr.) Scholastic Library Publishing.

Schuh, Mari. Los Camiones Volquetes (Dump Trucks) 2017. (Spot Mighty Machines Ser.). (ENG & SPA.). 16p. (J). (gr. k-3). 17.95 **(978-1-68151-268-6(8)**, Amicus Readers) Amicus Publishing.

—Trucks. 2017. (Transportation Ser.). (ENG.). 24p. (gr. k-1). lib. bdg. 21.99 **(978-1-5157-7300-9(0)**, Pebble Bks.) Capstone Press of Coughlan Cos.

Schuh, Mari C. Dump Trucks. 2017. (Spot Mighty Machines Ser.). (ENG.). 16p. (J). (gr. k-3). 17.95 **(978-1-68151-102-3(9))** Amicus Publishing.

Scollen, Chris. Busy Kids Tractors & Trucks Sticker Activity Book. 2008. (Busy Kids Ser.). (Illus.). 20p. (J). (gr. -1-3). 4.99 (978-1-84610-634-7(6)) Make Believe Ideas GBR. Dist: Nelson, Thomas Inc.

Shealy, Dennis. I'm a Truck. Staake, Bob, illus. 2006. (Little Golden Book Ser.). (ENG.). 24p. (J). (gr. -1-2). 4.99 (978-0-375-83263-5(7), Golden Bks.) Random Hse. Children's Bks.

Shelly, Jeff. Cars & Trucks: Step by Step Instructions for 28 Different Vehicles. 2004. (Learn to Draw Ser.). (ENG., Illus.). 40p. (J). (gr. 1-3). per. 4.95 (978-1-56010-819-1(3), 1560108193) Quarto Publishing Group USA.

Silverman, Buffy. How Do Big Rigs Work? 2016. (Lightning Bolt Books (tm) — How Vehicles Work Ser.). (ENG.). 32p. (J). (gr. 1-3). 26.65 (978-1-4677-9501-2(1), Lerner Pubns.) Lerner Publishing Group.

—How Do Monster Trucks Work? 2016. (Lightning Bolt Books (tm) — How Vehicles Work Ser.). (ENG., Illus.). 32p. (J). (gr. 1-3). lib. bdg. 26.65 (978-1-4677-9499-2(6)) Lerner Publishing Group.

Small World Creations Ltd., illus. Zippy Wheels: Diggers. 2016. (Zippy Wheels Ser.). (ENG.). 10p. (J). (gr. -1-k). bds. 8.99 (978-0-7641-6825-3(8)) Barron's Educational Series, Inc.

—Zippy Wheels: Dump Trucks. 2016. (Zippy Wheels Ser.). (ENG.). 10p. (J). (gr. -1-k). bds. 8.99 (978-0-7641-6826-0(6)) Barron's Educational Series, Inc.

—Zippy Wheels: Firetrucks. 2016. (Zippy Wheels Ser.). (ENG.). 10p. (J). (gr. -1-k). bds. 8.99 (978-0-7641-6827-7(4)) Barron's Educational Series, Inc.

Storey, Rita. Tractors & Trucks. 2013. (Have Fun with Arts & Crafts Ser.). (Illus.). 32p. (gr. 4-7). lib. bdg. 31.35 (978-1-59920-901-2(2)) Black Rabbit Bks.

Sturges, Philemon. I Love Trucks! Halpern, Shari, illus. 2003. (ENG.). 34p. (J). (gr. -1-3). bds. 7.99 (978-0-06-052666-5(1), HarperFestival) HarperCollins Pubs.

Super Explorers. Big Trucks, 1 vol. 2016. (Super Explorers Ser.). (ENG., Illus.). 64p. (J). pap. 6.99 **(978-1-926700-64-9(3)**, 9781926700649) Blue Bike Bks. CAN. Dist: Lone Pine Publishing USA.

Sutton, Sally. Roadwork. Lovelock, Brian, illus. 2011. (ENG.). 28p. (J). (gr. k-k). bds. 6.99 (978-0-7636-4653-0(9)) Candlewick Pr.

Tatge, Cathy. Trucks. 2007. (My First Look at: Vehicles Ser.). (Illus.). 24p. (J). (gr. -1-3). lib. bdg. 24.25 (978-1-58341-530-6(0), Creative Education) Creative Co., The.

Taylor, Trace. The Tree Truck. Taylor, Trace, illus. 2008. (1-3Y Jobs & Careers Ser.). (ENG., Illus.). 24p. (J). (gr. k-2). pap. 5.99 (978-1-59301-463-6(5)) American Reading Co.

Teitelbaum, Michael. Humvees: High Mobility in the Field. Nelson, Scott, photos by. 2006. (Mighty Military Machines Ser.). (Illus.). 48p. (J). (gr. 4-7). lib. bdg. 25.27 (978-0-7660-2661-2(2)) Enslow Pubs., Inc.

Tiner, John Hudson. Trucks. (Illus.). 32p. 2004. pap. 8.95 (978-0-89812-392-0(5), Creative Paperbacks) 2003. (J). lib. bdg. 18.95 (978-1-58341-259-6(X), Creative Education) Creative Co., The.

Tourville, Amanda Doering. Dump Trucks, 1 vol. Trover, Zachary, illus. 2009. (Mighty Machines Ser.). (ENG.). 32p. (J). (gr. -1-3). 28.50 (978-1-60270-623-1(9)) Magic Wagon.

—Garbage Trucks, 1 vol. Trover, Zachary, illus. 2009. (Mighty Machines Ser.). (ENG.). 32p. (J). (gr. -1-3). 28.50 (978-1-60270-625-5(5)) Magic Wagon.

Tractors & Trucks Sticker Activity Book. (My Sticker Activity Ser.). (Illus.). 12p. (J). (978-1-4054-1182-0(1)) Parragon, Inc.

Trucks & Cars. 2003. 32p. 12.98 (978-1-4054-2006-8(5)) Parragon, Inc.

Tuxworth, Nicola. Diggers & Dumpers. 2015. (ENG., Illus.). 20p. (J). (gr. -1 — 1). bds. 6.99 (978-1-86147-383-7(4), Armadillo) Anness Publishing GBR. Dist: National Bk. Network.

Vamos, Samantha R. Alphabet Trucks. O'Rourke, Ryan, illus. 2016. (J). (978-1-58089-740-2(1)) Charlesbridge Publishing, Inc.

Von Finn, Denny. Torque: 4X4 Trucks. 2009. (Torque Ser.). (ENG.). 24p. (J). (gr. 3-7). 20.00 (978-0-531-21741-2(8), Children's Pr.) Scholastic Library Publishing.

Watt, Fiona. That's Not My Truck. 2009. (Touchy-Feely Board Bks). 10p. (J). bds. 8.99 (978-0-7945-2188-2(6), Usborne) EDC Publishing.

Watt, Fiona & Wells, Rachel. Trucks. 2004. (Ultimate Touchy-Feely Ser.). (ENG., Illus.). 12p. (J). bds. 15.95 (978-0-7945-0228-7(8), Usborne) EDC Publishing.

Wilson, CeCe. My Dad's Truck. 2015. (Rosen REAL Readers: STEM & STEAM Collection). (ENG.). 8p. pap. 5.46 (978-1-4994-9672-7(9), Rosen Classroom) Rosen Publishing Group, Inc., The.

Winget, Mary & Winget, W. Bryan. Tow Trucks. 2006. (Pull Ahead Books-Mighty Movers Ser.). (ENG., Illus.). 32p. (gr. k-3). per. 7.95 (978-0-8225-5894-1(7), First Avenue Editions) Lerner Publishing Group.

Wiseman, Blaine. Dump Trucks. 2010. (World of Wonder Ser.). (Illus.). 24p. (J). (gr. 2-4). lib. bdg. 25.70 (978-1-61690-145-5(4), 1315074) Weigl Pubs., Inc.

—Dump Trucks: WOW: Big Machines. 2010. (Illus.). 24p. (J). pap. 9.95 (978-1-61690-146-2(2), 1315074) Weigl Pubs., Inc.

—Monster Trucks. 2010. (World of Wonder Ser.). 24p. (J). (gr. 2-4). lib. bdg. 25.70 (978-1-61690-139-4(X)) Weigl Pubs., Inc.

—Monster Trucks: WOW: Big Machines. 2010. (J). pap. 9.95 (978-1-61690-140-0(3)) Weigl Pubs., Inc.

World Book, Inc Staff, contrib. by. Tough Trucks. 2007. (J). (978-0-7166-7730-7(X)) World Bk., Inc.

Worms, Penny. Trucks. 2016. (Motormania Ser.). 32p. (gr. 2-7). 31.35 (978-1-59920-997-5(7), Smart Apple Media) Black Rabbit Bks.

Young, Jeff C. Trucks: The Ins & Outs of Monster Trucks, Semis, Pickups, & Other Trucks. 2010. (Rpm Ser.). (ENG.). 48p. (gr. 3-4). pap. 59.70 (978-1-4296-5129-5(6)) Capstone Press of Coughlan Cos.

Yoyo Books, creator. Vroom. 2011. (Baby's First Library). (ENG., Illus.). 38p. (gr. -1-k). bds. (978-90-8622-910-9(7)) YoYo Bks.

Zeiger, Jennifer. What Does It Do? Dump Truck. 2011. (Community Connections: What Does It Do? Ser.). (ENG.). 24p. (gr. 2-5). lib. bdg. 25.64 (978-1-60279-974-5(1), 200962) Cherry Lake Publishing.

Zobel, Derek. Bucket Trucks. 2009. (Mighty Machines Ser.). (ENG., Illus.). 24p. (J). (gr. k-3). lib. bdg. 25.95 (978-1-60014-234-5(6)) Bellwether Media.

—Bucket Trucks. 2009. (Blastoff! Readers Ser.). (ENG., Illus.). 24p. (J). (gr. k-3). 20.00 (978-0-531-21707-8(8), Children's Pr.) Scholastic Library Publishing.

—Diggers. 2009. (Mighty Machines Ser.). (ENG., Illus.). 24p. (J). (gr. k-3). lib. bdg. 25.95 (978-1-60014-235-2(4)) Bellwether Media.

—Pickup Trucks. 2009. (Mighty Machines Ser.). (ENG., Illus.). 24p. (J). (gr. k-3). lib. bdg. 25.95 (978-1-60014-236-9(2)) Bellwether Media.

—Pickup Trucks. 2009. (Blastoff! Readers Ser.). (ENG., Illus.). 24p. (J). (gr. k-3). 20.00 (978-0-531-21709-2(4), Children's Pr.) Scholastic Library Publishing.

—Wheel Loaders. 2009. (Mighty Machines Ser.). (ENG., Illus.). 24p. (J). (gr. k-3). lib. bdg. 25.95 (978-1-60014-237-6(0)) Bellwether Media.

Zuehlke, Jeffrey. Camionetas. Translations.com Staff, tr. from ENG. 2006. (Libros para Avanzar-Potencia en Movimiento (Pull Ahead Books-Mighty Movers) Ser.). (ENG & SPA., Illus.). 32p. (gr. k-3). lib. bdg. 22.60 (978-0-8225-6499-7(8), Ediciones Lerner) Lerner Publishing Group.

—Camionetas (Pickup Trucks) Translations.com Staff, tr. 2006. (Libros para Avanzar-Potencia en Movimiento (Pull Ahead Books-Mighty Movers) Ser.). (SPA.). 32p. (gr. k-3). pap. 7.95 (978-0-8225-6642-7(7), Ediciones Lerner) Lerner Publishing Group.

—Forklifts. 2006. (Pull Ahead Bks.). (Illus.). 32p. (J). (gr. 3-7). (ENG.). pap. 6.95 (978-0-8225-5896-5(3), First Avenue Editions); lib. bdg. 22.60 (978-0-8225-6008-1(9), Lerner Pubns.) Lerner Publishing Group.

—Pickup Trucks. Mueller, Mike, photos by. 2007. (Motor Mania Ser.). (ENG., Illus.). 48p. (J). (gr. 4-7). lib. bdg. 26.60 (978-0-8225-6564-2(1)) Lerner Publishing Group.

—Pickup Trucks. 2004. (Pull Ahead Books-Mighty Movers Ser.). (ENG., Illus.). 32p. (gr. k-3). pap. 7.95

(978-0-8225-2384-0(1)); lib. bdg. 22.60 (978-0-8225-1542-5(3)) Lerner Publishing Group.

—Pickup Trucks on the Move. 2010. pap. 45.32 (978-0-7613-6941-7(4)); (ENG.). 32p. pap. 7.95 (978-0-7613-6118-3(9)); (ENG., Illus.). 32p. lib. bdg. 26.60 (978-0-7613-6024-7(7)) Lerner Publishing Group.

TRUCKS—FICTION

Accord Publishing Staff. Trucks: A Mini Animotion Book. (ENG.). (J). 2013. 14p. bds. 5.99 (978-1-4494-3558-5(0)) 2010. (Illus.). 12p. (gr. -1). 9.99 (978-0-7407-9200-7(8)) Andrews McMeel Publishing.

Allen, Francesca & Brooks, Felicity. Busy Truck. Crisp, Dan, illus. 2007. (Usborne Play Bks.). 10p. (J). (gr. -1-k). bds. 10.99 (978-0-7945-1453-2(7), Usborne) EDC Publishing.

Anderson, Peggy Perry. Chuck's Truck. 2017. (Green Light Readers Level 1 Ser.). (ENG., Illus.). 32p. (J). (gr. -1-3). 12.99 (978-0-544-92618-9(8), HMH Books For Young Readers) Houghton Mifflin Harcourt Publishing Co.

Andrews, Julie. Dumpy's Apple Shop. Walton, Tony, illus. 2004. (My First I Can Read Bks.). 32p. (J). (gr. -1-18). lib. bdg. 15.89 (978-0-06-052693-1(9)) HarperCollins Pubs.

—Dumpy's Happy Holiday. Walton, Tony, illus. 2005. (Julie Andrews Collection). 32p. (J). lib. bdg. 16.89 (978-0-06-052685-6(8), Julie Andrews Collection) HarperCollins Pubs.

Andrews, Julie & Hamilton, Emma Walton. Dumpy & the Firefighters. Walton, Tony, illus. 2003. (Julie Andrews Collection). (ENG.). 32p. (J). (gr. -1-2). 15.99 (978-0-06-052681-8(5), Julie Andrews Collection) HarperCollins Pubs.

—Dumpy to the Rescue! Walton, Tony, illus. 2004. 24p. (J). lib. bdg. 13.85 (978-1-4242-0707-7(X)) Fitzgerald Bks.

Arnold, Janet. The Special Number. 2011. 28p. pap. 15.99 (978-1-4568-8982-1(6)) Xlibris Corp.

Awdry, Wilbert V. The Close Shave. Courtney, Richard H., illus. 2008. (Step into Reading Ser.). (ENG.). 32p. (J). (gr. -1-1). pap. 3.99 (978-0-375-85180-3(1), Random Hse. Bks. for Young Readers) Random Hse. Children's Bks.

Back-Canevaro, Vanessa. The Other Side of Yesterday. 2006. (J). per. 12.00 (978-0-9769132-8-3(3)) Capri Publishing.

Barton, Chris. Mighty Truck. Cummings, Troy, illus. 2016. 32p. (J). (gr. -1-3). 17.99 (978-0-06-234478-6(1)) HarperCollins Pubs.

—Muddymania! Cummings, Troy, illus. 2017. 32p. (J). (gr. -1-3). 17.99 (978-0-06-234479-3(X)) HarperCollins Pubs.

Baxter, Nicola. The Trouble with Trucks. Ball, Geoff, illus. 2012. (ENG.). 24p. (J). (gr. -1-k). pap. 6.99 (978-1-84322-786-1(X), Armadillo) Anness Publishing GBR. Dist: National Bk. Network.

Bedford, David. Tipper, Tipper! Watson, Judy, illus. 2008. 9p. bds. (978-1-921272-26-4(0)) Little Hare Bks. AUS. Dist: HarperCollins Pubs. Australia.

Beil, Karen Magnuson. Jack's House. Wohnoutka, Mike, illus. 2009. (ENG.). 32p. (J). (gr. -1-3). pap. 7.99 (978-0-8234-2242-5(9)) Holiday Hse., Inc.

Beinstein, Phoebe. Dora & the Stuck Truck. Roper, Robert, illus. 2008. (Dora the Explorer Ser.: 25). (ENG.). 24p. (J). (gr. -1-2). pap. 3.99 (978-1-4169-4799-8(X), Simon Spotlight/Nickelodeon) Simon Spotlight/Nickelodeon.

Berenstain, Jan & Berenstain, Mike. The Berenstain Bears - We Love Trucks! Berenstain, Jan & Berenstain, Mike, illus. 2013. (I Can Read Level 1 Ser.). (ENG., Illus.). 32p. (J). (gr. -1-3). pap. 3.99 (978-0-06-207535-2(7)) HarperCollins Pubs.

—We Love Trucks! Berenstain, Jan & Berenstain, Mike, illus. 2013. (I Can Read Level 1 Ser.). (ENG., Illus.). 32p. (J). (gr. -1-3). 16.99 (978-0-06-207536-9(5)) HarperCollins Pubs.

—We Love Trucks! 2013. (Berenstain Bears: I Can Read! Ser.). (J). lib. bdg. 13.55 (978-0-606-27159-2(7), Turtleback) Turtleback Bks.

Bergen, Lara. Let's Dig It! Shannon, David et al, illus. 2010. (Jon Scieszka's Trucktown Ser.). (ENG.). 12p. (J). (gr. -1-k). bds. 5.99 (978-1-4169-4190-3(8), Little Simon) Little Simon.

Berneger, Marcia. Buster the Little Garbage Truck. Zimmer, Kevin, illus. 2015. (ENG.). 32p. (J). (gr. -1-1). 14.99 (978-1-58536-894-5(6), 203814) Sleeping Bear Pr.

Berrios, Frank. The Easter Buggy. 2014. lib. bdg. 14.75 (978-0-606-35543-8(X)) Turtleback Bks.

—The Easter Buggy (Disney/Pixar Cars) Random House Disney Staff, illus. 2014. (Pictureback(R) Ser.). (ENG.). 16p. (J). (gr. -1-2). 4.99 (978-0-7364-3139-2(X), RH/Disney) Random Hse. Children's Bks.

—Lights Out!; Tow Truck Trouble. RH Disney Staff, illus. 2010. (Pictureback(R) Ser.). (ENG.). 32p. (J). (gr. -1-2). pap. 4.99 (978-0-7364-2713-5(9), RH/Disney) Random Hse. Children's Bks.

—Mater to the Rescue! (Disney/Pixar Cars) Random House Disney Staff, illus. 2012. (Pictureback(R) Ser.). (ENG.). 16p. (J). (gr. -1-2). pap. 4.99 (978-0-7364-2863-7(1), RH/Disney) Random Hse. Children's Bks.

Biggs, Brian. Good Night, Trucks: A Bedtime Book. Biggs, Brian, illus. 2013. (ENG., Illus.). 24p. (J). (gr. -1 — 1). bds. 7.99 (978-0-06-195815-1(8)) HarperCollins Pubs.

Billet, Marion. My First Truck. 2016. (Whizzy Wheels Ser.: 12). (ENG., Illus.). 10p. (J). (— 1). bds. 11.99 (978-1-5098-0427-6(7)) Pan Macmillan GBR. Dist: Independent Pubs. Group.

Bleck, Linda. What's in My Truck? Bleck, Linda, illus. 2014. (ENG., Illus.). 10p. (J). (gr. -1 — 1). bds. 6.99 (978-0-545-53525-0(5), Cartwheel Bks.) Scholastic, Inc.

Bourgeois, Paulette. Police Workers. LaFave, Kim, illus. 2004. 32p. (J). lib. bdg. 15.38 (978-1-4242-1191-3(3)) Fitzgerald Bks.

Bowser, Ken. Bobbi's Big Brake. Bowser, Ken, illus. 2016. (Funny Bone Readers: Truck Pals on the Job Ser.). (ENG., Illus.). 24p. (gr. k-2). lib. bdg. 19.99 (978-1-63440-062-6(3)) Red Chair Pr.

—Bobbi's Big Brake: Self-Confidence. Bowser, Ken, illus. 2016. (Funny Bone Readers: Truck Pals on the Job Ser.). (ENG., Illus.). 24p. (gr. k-2). 30.65 (978-1-63440-064-0(X)) Red Chair Pr.

—Hal & Al. Bowser, Ken, illus. 2016. (Funny Bone Readers: Truck Pals on the Job Ser.). (ENG., Illus.). 24p. (gr. k-2). lib. bdg. 19.99 (978-1-63440-068-8(2)) Red Chair Pr.

—Hal & Al: Self-Esteem. Bowser, Ken, illus. 2016. (Funny Bone Readers: Truck Pals on the Job Ser.). (ENG., Illus.). 24p. (gr. k-2). 30.65 (978-1-63440-070-1(4)) Red Chair Pr.

—Hitch Takes Off. Bowser, Ken, illus. 2016. (Funny Bone Readers: Truck Pals on the Job Ser.). (ENG., Illus.). 24p. (gr. k-2). lib. bdg. 19.99 (978-1-63440-071-8(2), 1401368) Red Chair Pr.

—Hitch Takes Off: Perseverance. Bowser, Ken, illus. 2016. (Funny Bone Readers: Truck Pals on the Job Ser.). (ENG., Illus.). 24p. (gr. k-2). 30.65 (978-1-63440-073-2(9)) Red Chair Pr.

—Lawni Takes the Field. Bowser, Ken, illus. 2016. (Funny Bone Readers: Truck Pals on the Job Ser.). (ENG., Illus.). 24p. (gr. k-2). lib. bdg. 19.99 (978-1-63440-074-9(7), 1401369) Red Chair Pr.

—Lawni Takes the Field: Teamwork. Bowser, Ken, illus. 2016. (Funny Bone Readers: Truck Pals on the Job Ser.). (ENG., Illus.). 24p. (gr. k-2). 30.65 (978-1-63440-076-3(3)) Red Chair Pr.

—One Wrong Turn. Bowser, Ken, illus. 2016. (Funny Bone Readers: Truck Pals on the Job Ser.). (ENG., Illus.). 24p. (gr. k-2). lib. bdg. 19.99 (978-1-63440-077-0(1), 1401370) Red Chair Pr.

—One Wrong Turn: Helping Those in Need. Bowser, Ken, illus. 2016. (Funny Bone Readers: Truck Pals on the Job Ser.). (ENG., Illus.). 24p. (gr. k-2). 30.65 (978-1-63440-079-4(8)) Red Chair Pr.

Bryant, Megan E. Dump Truck Duck. de Ruiter, Jo, illus. 2016. (ENG.). 32p. (J). (gr. -1-3). 16.99 (978-0-8075-1736-9(4)) Whitman, Albert & Co.

Burton, Jeffrey. Food Trucks! A Lift-The-Flap Meal on Wheels! Cooper, Jay, illus. 2016. (ENG.). 12p. (J). (gr. -1). bds. 7.99 (978-1-4814-6521-2(X), Little Simon) Little Simon.

Calder, C. J. Busy Truck, 1 vol. Rooney, Ronnie & Peterson, Shauna, illus. 2012. (Truck Buddies Ser.). (ENG.). 16p. (gr. -1-k). bds. 7.95 (978-1-4342-4388-1(5)) Stone Arch Bks.

—Fast Truck. Rooney, Ronnie & Peterson, Shauna, illus. 2012. (Truck Buddies Ser.). (ENG.). 16p. (gr. -1-k). bds. 7.95 (978-1-4342-4389-8(3)) Stone Arch Bks.

—Muddy Truck, 1 vol. Rooney, Ronnie & Peterson, Shauna, illus. 2012. (Truck Buddies Ser.). (ENG.). 16p. (gr. -1-k). bds. 7.95 (978-1-4342-4390-4(7)) Stone Arch Bks.

Cammy Fox Riley. Truckee's Adventures: Book One. 2009. 24p. pap. 11.49 (978-1-4389-4023-6(8)) AuthorHouse.

Cassidy, Colette, DIVCO, the Little Milk Truck. 2007. (Illus.). 28p. (J). pap. 7.99 (978-0-615-17346-7(2)) Redcay Publishing.

Clement, Nathan. Drive. Clement, Nathan, illus. (ENG., Illus.). 32p. (J). 2013. (gr. k-2). pap. 6.95 (978-1-62091-030-6(6)) 2008. (gr. -1-3). 16.95 (978-1-59078-517-1(7)) Boyds Mills Pr.

Clement, Nathan, illus. Drive. 2016. (ENG.). 32p. (J). (— 1). bds. 7.99 (978-1-62979-692-5(1)) Boyds Mills Pr.

Cochran, Jean M. Farmer Brown & His Little Red Truck. Enos, Daryl, illus. 2009. (ENG.). 32p. (J). (gr. -1-k). 16.95 (978-0-9792035-0-3(3)) Pleasant St. Pr.

Crisp, Dan. Trabajo/ Work. 2007. 14p. 10.95 (978-84-263-6452-4(7)) Vives, Luis Editorial (Edelvives) ESP. Dist: Baker & Taylor Bks.

Crooks, Andrea Syvrud. Little Truck Without a Load. 2013. 40p. pap. 16.95 (978-1-4497-9737-9(7), WestBow Pr.) Author Solutions, Inc.

Crow, Melinda Melton. Camiones Amigos/Truck Buddies, 1 vol. Heck, Claudia M., tr. from ENG. Rooney, Ronnie, illus. 2012. (Camiones Amigos/Truck Buddies Ser.). (ENG, SPA & MUL.). 32p. (gr. -1-1). pap. 5.05 (978-1-4342-3913-6(6)); lib. bdg. 22.65 (978-1-4342-3774-3(5)) Stone Arch Bks. (Bilingual Stone Arch Readers).

—Carrera en la Carretera. Heck, Claudia M., tr. Rooney, Ronnie, illus. 2012. (Camiones Amigos/Truck Buddies Ser.).Tr. of Road Race. (ENG, SPA & MUL.). 32p. (gr. -1-1). pap. 5.05 (978-1-4342-3915-0(2), Bilingual Stone Arch Readers) Stone Arch Bks.

—Drive Along, 1 vol. Girouard, Patrick, illus. 2010. (Truck Buddies Ser.). (ENG.). 32p. (gr. -1-1). pap. 6.25 (978-1-4342-2296-1(9)); lib. bdg. 22.65 (978-1-4342-1866-7(X)) Stone Arch Bks.

—Líos en el Lodo. Heck, Claudia M., tr. from ENG. Rooney, Ronnie, illus. 2012. (Camiones Amigos/Truck Buddies Ser.).Tr. of Mud Mess. (MUL & SPA.). 32p. (gr. -1-1). pap. 5.05 (978-1-4342-3916-7(0)); lib. bdg. 22.65 (978-1-4342-3777-4(X)) Stone Arch Bks. (Bilingual Stone Arch Readers).

—Líos en la Nieve. Heck, Claudia M., tr. from ENG. Rooney, Ronnie, illus. 2012. (Camiones Amigos/Truck Buddies Ser.).Tr. of Snow Trouble. (MUL, SPA & ENG.). 32p. (gr. -1-1). pap. 5.05 (978-1-4342-3914-3(4), Bilingual Stone Arch Readers) Stone Arch Bks.

—Little Wheels, 1 vol. Girouard, Patrick, illus. 2010. (Truck Buddies Ser.). (ENG.). 32p. (gr. -1-1). pap. 6.25 (978-1-4342-2297-8(7)); lib. bdg. 22.65 (978-1-4342-1865-0(1)) Stone Arch Bks.

—Mud Mess, 1 vol. Rooney, Ronnie, illus. 2009. (Truck Buddies Ser.). (ENG.). 32p. (gr. -1-1). pap. 6.25 (978-1-4342-1753-0(1)) Stone Arch Bks.

—Ride & Seek, 1 vol. Girouard, Patrick, illus. 2010. (Truck Buddies Ser.). (ENG.). 32p. (gr. -1-1). pap. 6.25 (978-1-4342-2298-5(5)) Stone Arch Bks.

—Road Race, 1 vol. Rooney, Ronnie, illus. 2009. (Truck Buddies Ser.). (ENG.). 32p. (gr. -1-1). 22.65 (978-1-4342-1623-6(3)); pap. 6.25 (978-1-4342-1754-7(X)) Stone Arch Bks.

—Snow Trouble, 1 vol. Rooney, Ronnie, illus. 2009. (Truck Buddies Ser.). (ENG.). 32p. (gr. -1-1). 22.65 (978-1-4342-1624-3(1)); pap. 6.25 (978-1-4342-1755-4(8)) Stone Arch Bks.

—Tired Trucks, 1 vol. Girouard, Patrick, illus. 2010. (Truck Buddies Ser.). (ENG.). 32p. (gr. -1-1). pap. 6.25 (978-1-4342-2299-2(3)); lib. bdg. 22.65 (978-1-4342-1864-3(3)) Stone Arch Bks.

—Truck Buddies, 1 vol. Rooney, Ronnie, illus. 2009. (Truck Buddies Ser.). (ENG.). 32p. (gr. -1-1). 22.65 (978-1-4342-1625-0(X)); pap. 6.25 (978-1-4342-1756-1(6)) Stone Arch Bks.

—Truck Parade, 1 vol. Thompson, Chad, illus. 2012. (Wonder Wheels Ser.). (ENG.). 32p. (gr. -1-1). pap. 6.25 (978-1-4342-4240-2(4)); lib. bdg. 22.65 (978-1-4342-4017-0(7)) Stone Arch Bks.

Curry, Peter, illus. Cars & Trucks. 2016. (ENG.). 12p. (J). (gr. -1 — 1). bds. 4.99 (978-1-4998-0199-6(8)) Little Bee Books Inc.

Cuyler, Margery. The Little Dump Truck. Kolar, Bob, illus. 2014. (Little Vehicles Ser.). (ENG.). 24p. (J). (gr. -1-1). bds. 7.99 (978-0-8050-9990-4(5), 9780805099904, Holt, Henry & Co. Bks. For Young Readers) Holt, Henry & Co.

Delco, Bobby. Lil Mack Jr. 2009. 108p. pap. 11.99 (978-1-4389-0473-3(8)) AuthorHouse.

Diaz, T. Richard. Little Growler, Big Heart. l.t. ed. 2003. (Illus.). 12p. (J). lib. bdg. 11.95 (978-1-932338-21-8(7)); per. 8.95 (978-1-932338-15-7(2)) Lifevest Publishing, Inc.

Docherty, Thomas. To the Beach. Docherty, Thomas, illus. 2009. (ENG., Illus.). 40p. (J). (gr. -1-2). 15.99 (978-0-7636-4429-1(3), Templar) Candlewick Pr.

DreamWorks. Dinotrux: Team Dinotrux! 2016. (ENG., Illus.). 32p. (J). (gr. -1-3). 12.99 (978-0-316-26074-9(6)) Little, Brown Bks. for Young Readers.

Dronsfield, Paul, illus. The Bulldozer. 2009. (My Shiny Little Truck Bks.). (ENG.). 10p. (J). bds. 3.95 (978-1-58117-858-6(1), Intervisual/Piggy Toes) Bendon, Inc.

—The Concrete Mixer. 2009. (My Shiny Little Truck Bks.). (ENG.). 10p. (J). bds. 3.95 (978-1-58117-859-3(X), Intervisual/Piggy Toes) Bendon, Inc.

—The Digger. 2009. (My Shiny Little Truck Bks.). (ENG.). 10p. (J). bds. 3.95 (978-1-58117-860-9(3), Intervisual/Piggy Toes) Bendon, Inc.

—The Dump Truck. 2009. (My Shiny Little Truck Bks.). (ENG.). 10p. (J). bds. 3.95 (978-1-58117-861-6(1), Intervisual/Piggy Toes) Bendon, Inc.

Eaton, Jason Carter. How to Track a Truck. Rocco, John, illus. 2016. (ENG.). 32p. (J). (gr. -1-3). 16.99 (978-0-7636-8065-7(6)) Candlewick Pr.

Fliess, Sue. Tons of Trucks. Snyder, Betsy E., illus. 2012. (ENG.). 18p. (J). (gr. k — 1). 13.99 (978-0-547-44927-2(5)) Houghton Mifflin Harcourt Publishing Co.

Floca, Brian. Five Trucks. Floca, Brian, illus. 2014. (ENG., Illus.). 32p. (J). (gr. -1-3). 17.99 (978-1-4814-0593-5(4), Atheneum Bks. for Young Readers) Simon & Schuster Children's Publishing.

Friend, David. With Any Luck, I'll Drive a Truck. Rex, Michael, illus. 2016. (ENG.). 32p. (J). (-k). 16.99 (978-0-399-16956-4(3), Nancy Paulsen Books) Penguin Young Readers Group.

Gall, Chris. Dinotrux. Gall, Chris, illus. 2009. (Dinotrux Ser.: 1). (ENG., Illus.). 32p. (gr. -1-3). 16.99 (978-0-316-02777-9(4)) Little Brown & Co.

—Dinotrux. 2012. (J). lib. bdg. 17.20 (978-0-606-26144-9(3), Turtleback) Turtleback Bks.

—Dinotrux Dig the Beach. 2015. (Dinotrux Ser.: 3). (ENG., Illus.). 32p. (J). (gr. -1-3). 17.00 (978-0-316-37553-5(5)) Little Brown & Co.

—Dinotrux Go to School. 2014. (Passport to Reading Level 1 Ser.). (ENG., Illus.). 32p. (J). (gr. -1-3). 3.99 (978-0-316-40061-9(0)) Little, Brown Bks. for Young Readers.

—Revenge of the Dinotrux. 2012. (Dinotrux Ser.: 2). (ENG., Illus.). 32p. (J). (gr. -1-3). 16.99 (978-0-316-13288-6(8)) Little Brown & Co.

Gamble, Adam & Jasper, Mark. Good Night Dump Truck. Kelly, Cooper, illus. 2014. (Good Night Our World Ser.). (ENG.). 26p. (J). (— 1). bds. 9.95 (978-1-60219-189-1(1)) Good Night Bks.

Goebel, Jenny. Foreman Farley Has a Backhoe. Van Doninck, Sebastiaan, illus. 2014. (Penguin Core Concepts Ser.). (ENG.). 32p. (J). (gr. -1-k). 3.99 (978-0-448-46398-8(9), Grosset & Dunlap) Penguin Young Readers Group.

Goetz, Steve. Old MacDonald Had a Truck. Kaban, Eda, illus. 2016. (ENG.). 40p. (J). (gr. -1-k). 16.99 (978-1-4521-3260-0(7)) Chronicle Bks. LLC.

Golden Books. To the Limit! (Blaze & the Monster Machines) Hechtenkopf, Omar, illus. 2015. (Deluxe Paint Box Book Ser.). (ENG.). 128p. (J). (gr. -1-2). pap. 7.99 (978-0-553-52459-8(3), Golden Bks.) Random Hse. Children's Bks.

—Wind Power! (Blaze & the Monster Machines) Burch, Benjamin, illus. 2016. (Little Golden Book Ser.). (ENG.). 24p. (J). (-k). 4.99 (978-1-101-93682-5(7), Golden Bks.) Random Hse. Children's Bks.

Golden Books & Chlebowski, Rachel. Monster in the Forest! (Blaze & the Monster Machines) Golden Books & Pixel Mouse House Staff, illus. 2016. (Holographic Sticker Book Ser.). (ENG.). 64p. (J). (gr. -1-2). pap. 4.99 (978-1-101-93700-6(9), Golden Bks.) Random Hse. Children's Bks.

Golden Books Staff. Mighty Monster Machines (Blaze & the Monster Machines) Golden Books Staff & Lambe, Steve, illus. 2015. (Little Golden Book Ser.). (ENG.). 24p. (J). (-k). 4.99 (978-0-553-52456-7(9), Golden Bks.) Random Hse. Children's Bks.

Gordon, David. The Three Little Rigs. Gordon, David, illus. 2005. (ENG., Illus.). 32p. (J). (gr. -1-3). 17.99 (978-0-06-058118-3(2)) HarperCollins Pubs.

—The Ugly Truckling. Gordon, David, illus. 2004. (Illus.). 32p. (J). (gr. -1-2). lib. bdg. 16.89 (978-0-06-054601-4(8), Geringer, Laura Book) HarperCollins Pubs.

Gould, Robert. Monster Trucks. 2004. (Big Stuff Ser.). (ENG., Illus.). 16p. (J). bds. 7.95 (978-1-929945-43-6(4)) Big Guy Bks., Inc.

Green, Margaret. Dinotrux: It Takes Teamwork! 2016. (ENG., Illus.). 24p. (J). (gr. -1-3). pap. 4.99 (978-0-316-26077-0(0)) Little, Brown Bks. for Young Readers.

—Dinotrux: Night Repair. 2016. (ENG.). 12p. (J). (gr. -1 — 1). bds. 9.99 (978-0-316-27266-7(3)) Little, Brown Bks. for Young Readers.

—Dinotrux: Ty Finds a New Home. 2017. (ENG., Illus.). 24p. (J). (gr. -1-3). pap. 4.99 (978-0-316-26075-6(4)) Little, Brown Bks. for Young Readers.

Greene, Rhonda Gowler. Push! Dig! Scoop! A Construction Counting Rhyme. Kirk, Daniel, illus. (ENG.). (J). 2017. 26p. bds. 7.99 (978-1-68119-085-3(0), 9781681190853) 2016. 32p. 16.99 (978-0-8027-3506-5(1), 9780802735065) Bloomsbury Publishing USA. (Bloomsbury USA Childrens).

H & T Imaginations Unlimited, Inc. Kid's Sand Box Fun with Professor Woodpecker: Good Old Fashion Wholesome Fun Children's Story. 2008. 12p. pap. 8.49 (978-1-4389-1116-8(5)) AuthorHouse.

Hamilton, Kersten. Red Truck. Petrone, Valeria, illus. 2012. (ENG.). 24p. (J). (gr. -1-k). bds. 6.99 (978-0-670-01467-5(2), Viking Books for Young Readers) Penguin Young Readers Group.

Hardyment, Christina. Arthur Ransome & Captain Flint's Trunk. (Illus.). 224p. (J). (978-0-224-02989-6(4)) Random Hse.

Harper, Benjamin & Scieszka, Jon. All Around Trucktown. Shannon, David et al, illus. 2008. (Jon Scieszka's Trucktown Ser.). (ENG.). 32p. (J). (gr. -1-1). 3.99 (978-1-4169-4194-1(0), Simon Scribbles) Simon Scribbles.

Hegarty, Patricia. Bear's Truck Is Stuck! 2015. (Amazing Changing Pictures! Ser.). (ENG.). 14p. (J). (gr. -1-3). 12.99 (978-1-68010-001-3(7)) Tiger Tales.

Holmes, Andy. Building God's Kingdom - Diggit Saves the Day, 1 vol. de Giorgi, Sergio, illus. 2014. (ENG.). 22p. (J). bds. 9.99 (978-0-529-11100-5(4)) Nelson, Thomas Inc.

—Tipper Tells a Lie, 1 vol. de Giorgi, Sergio, illus. 2014. (ENG.). 22p. (J). bds. 9.99 (978-0-529-11213-2(2)) Nelson, Thomas Inc.

Holub, Joan. Mighty Dads. Dean, James, illus. 2014. (ENG.). 40p. (J). (gr. -1-k). 16.99 (978-0-545-60968-5(2), Scholastic Pr.) Scholastic, Inc.

Houghton Mifflin Company Staff. Fire Truck Fun with Curious George. 2005. (J). (gr. -1-k). pap. (978-0-618-70499-6(X)) Houghton Mifflin Harcourt Trade & Reference Pubs.

Houghton Mifflin Harcourt Publishing Company Staff & Rey, H. A. Start Your Engines 5-Minute Stories. 2014. (5-Minute Stories Ser.). (ENG., Illus.). 224p. (J). (gr. -1-3). 12.99 (978-0-544-15881-8(4), HMH Books For Young Readers) Houghton Mifflin Harcourt Publishing Co.

Hubbell, Patricia. Trucks: Whizz! Zoom! Rumble!, 0 vols. Halsey, Megan, illus. 2006. (ENG.). 32p. (J). (gr. -1-1). per. 9.99 (978-0-7614-5328-4(8), 9780761453284, Amazon Children's Publishing) Amazon Publishing.

Hurt, Laurie. Jay & the Old Big Blue Truck. 2009. 48p. pap. 21.99 (978-1-4363-5487-5(0)) Xlibris Corp.

The ice cream Truck. 2004. (J). per. 15.95 (978-0-9778937-4-4(X)) Priceless Ink Publishing Co., Inc.

Iverson, Gregory. Tyler's Big Blue Truck. Fritz, Siegfried, illus. 2006. 40p. (J). (978-0-9755184-0-3(2)) Sandbox Bks.

James, Martin. William Is Going Green. 2008. 38p. 14.95 (978-0-9799465-1-6(4)) Martin, James Jr.

Jon Scieszkas Trucktown, et al. Take a Trip with Trucktown! Gordon, David et al, illus. 2011. (Jon Scieszka's Trucktown Ser.). (ENG.). 24p. (J). (gr. -1-3). pap. 3.99 (978-1-4169-4181-1(9), Simon & Schuster Bks. For Young Readers) Simon & Schuster Bks. For Young Readers.

Katz, Karen. Vroom, Vroom, Trucks! Katz, Karen, illus. 2016. (ENG., Illus.). 14p. (J). (gr. -1 — 1). bds. 6.99 (978-1-4814-4209-1(0), Little Simon) Little Simon.

Keller, Joy. Monster Trucks. Saburi, Misa, illus. 2017. (ENG.). 32p. (J). 16.99 (978-1-62779-617-0(7), 9781627796170, Holt, Henry & Co. Bks. For Young Readers) Holt, Henry & Co.

Kirk, David. Truckeroo School. Kirk, David, illus. 2017. (ENG., Illus.). 40p. (J). 17.99 (978-1-250-01690-4(8), 9781250016904) Feiwel & Friends.

Krensky, Stephen. Trucks. Lola & Ivanke, illus. 2009. (Ready-To-Reads Ser.). (ENG.). 32p. (J). (gr. -1-1). pap. 3.99 (978-1-4169-0236-2(8), Simon Spotlight) Simon Spotlight.

Lagonegro, Melissa. Mater's Birthday Surprise. 2012. (Cars Step into Reading Ser.). lib. bdg. 13.55 (978-0-606-23724-6(0), Turtleback) Turtleback Bks.

—Mater's Birthday Surprise (Disney/Pixar Cars) Random House Disney Staff, illus. 2012. (Step into Reading Ser.). (ENG.). 32p. (J). (gr. -1-1). pap. 3.99 (978-0-7364-2858-3(5), RH/Disney) Random Hse. Children's Bks.

Lee, Mark. Twenty Big Trucks in the Middle of the Street. Cyrus, Kurt, illus. (ENG.). (J). 2015. 30p. (-k). bds. 7.99 (978-0-7636-7650-6(0)) 2013. 32p. (gr. -1-2). 15.99 (978-0-7636-5809-0(X)) Candlewick Pr.

Lewis, Kevin & Kirk, Daniel. My Truck Is Stuck! Kirk, Daniel, illus. 2006. (ENG., Illus.). 30p. (J). (gr. -1 — 1). bds. 7.99 (978-0-7868-3739-7(X)) Hyperion Pr.

Liberts, Jennifer. Go, Go, Trucks! Yamada, Mike, illus. 2017. (Step into Reading Ser.). (ENG.). 32p. (J). (gr. -1-1). 3.99 **(978-0-399-54951-9(X))**; lib. bdg. 12.99 **(978-0-399-54952-6(8))** Random Hse. Children's Bks. (Random Hse. Bks. for Young Readers).

London, Jonathan. I'm a Truck Driver. Parkins, David, illus. 2010. (ENG.). 32p. (J). (gr. -1-2). 15.99 (978-0-8050-7989-0(0), 9780805079890, Holt, Henry & Co. Bks. For Young Readers) Holt, Henry & Co.

Lyon, George Ella. Trucks Roll! Frazier, Craig, illus. 2007. (ENG.). 40p. (J). (gr. -1-2). 18.99 (978-1-4169-2435-7(3), Atheneum/Richard Jackson Bks.) Simon & Schuster Children's Publishing.

Maddox, Jake. Striker Assist, 1 vol. Tiffany, Sean, illus. 2012. (Jake Maddox Sports Stories Ser.). (ENG.). 72p. (gr. 2-3). pap. 5.95 (978-1-4342-4208-2(0)) Stone Arch Bks.

Marshall, Amelia. Big Truck's Road Adventure. 2016. (Big Machines Ser.). 32p. (gr. 2-1). pap. 10.00 (978-1-4994-8099-3(7), Windmill Bks.) Rosen Publishing Group, Inc., The.

Mason, Tom & Danko, Dan. A Christmas Surprise. Shannon, David et al, illus. 2011. (Jon Scieszka's Trucktown Ser.). (ENG.). 12p. (J). (gr. -1-k). 7.99 (978-1-4169-4193-4(2), Simon & Schuster Bks. For Young Readers) Simon & Schuster Bks. For Young Readers.

Mason, Tom, et al. Honk That Horn! Shannon, David et al, illus. 2011. (Jon Scieszka's Trucktown Ser.). (ENG.). 24p. (J). (gr. -1-k). pap. 3.99 (978-1-4169-4184-2(3), Simon & Schuster Bks. For Young Readers) Simon & Schuster Bks. For Young Readers.

—Who's That Truck? Shannon, David et al, illus. 2008. (Jon Scieszka's Trucktown Ser.). (ENG.). 14p. (J). (gr. -1-1). bds. 7.99 (978-1-4169-4175-0(4), Little Simon) Little Simon.

Masterson, Josephine. Toy Box Trouble. 2015. (Rosen REAL Readers: STEM & STEAM Collection). (ENG.). 8p. pap. 5.4 (978-1-4994-9599-7(4), Rosen Classroom) Rosen Publishing Group, Inc., The.

Mattel. Bob the Builder: Lofty & the Giraffe. 2016. (Passport Reading Level 1 Ser.). (ENG., Illus.). 32p. (J). (gr. -1-3). p 3.99 (978-0-316-35682-4(4)) Little, Brown Bks. for Youn Readers.

McKown, Hunter. Meet Jack Truck! Shannon, David et a 2008. (Jon Scieszka's Trucktown Ser.). (ENG.). 14p. (-1-1). bds. 5.99 (978-1-4169-4173-6(8), Little Simon) Simon.

TUV

—Sand Castle Bash: Counting from 1 To 10. Shannon, David et al, illus. 2009. (Jon Scieszka's Trucktown Ser.). (ENG.). 26p. (J). (gr. -1-k). bds. 5.99 (978-1-4169-4179-8(7), Little Simon) Little Simon.

McMullan, Kate. I'm Brave! McMullan, Jim, illus. 2014. (ENG.). 40p. (J). (gr. -1-3). 16.99 (978-0-06-220318-2(5)) HarperCollins Pubs.

—I'm Dirty! 2015. (J). lib. bdg. 17.20 (978-0-606-36466-9(8)) Turtleback Bks.

Meister, Cari. Dump Truck Day, 1 vol. Emmerson, Michael, illus. (My First Graphic Novel Ser.). (ENG.). 32p. (gr. k-2). 2010. pap. 6.25 (978-1-4342-2288-6(8)) 2009. 24.65 (978-1-4342-1621-2(7)) Stone Arch Bks. (My First Graphic Novel).

Mellor, Colleen Kelly. Grandpa & the Truck Book 2. Irwin, Dana M., illus. 2012. 34p. pap. 9.99 (978-0-9856770-2-2(3)) truckerkidzPr.

—Grandpa & the Truck Book One. Irwin, Dana, illus. 2012. 34p. pap. 9.99 (978-0-9856770-0-8(7)) truckerkidzPr.

Meltzer, Lynn. The Construction Crew. Eko-Burgess, Carrie, illus. (ENG.). (J). 2017. 32p. bds. 7.99 (978-1-250-11267-5(2), 9781250112675) 2011. 40p. (gr. -1-k). 15.99 (978-0-8050-8884-7(9), 9780805088847) Holt, Henry & Co. (Holt, Henry & Co. Bks. For Young Readers).

Merrill, Jean. The Pushcart War. Solbert, Ronni, illus. 50th anniv. ed. 2014. (ENG.). 232p. (J). (gr. 3-7). 15.95 (978-1-59017-819-5(X), NYR Children's Collection) New York Review of Bks., Inc., The.

—The Pushcart War. 2006. (J). 1.25 (978-1-4193-8348-9(5)) Recorded Bks., Inc.

Miller, Cindy M. The Little Green Truck: The Adventures of a 1998 Ford Ranger & Its Owner. 2012. 20p. pap. 15.00 (978-1-4772-0319-4(2)) AuthorHouse.

Milton, Elizabeth. Rolling with the Rollodons! 2017. (Dinotrux 8X8 Ser.). (J). lib. bdg. 14.75 **(978-0-606-39909-8(7))** Turtleback Bks.

Mitton, Tony. Truckload of Fun, 10 bks., Set. Parker, Ant, illus. 2007. (Amazing Machines Ser.). (ENG.). 24p. (J). (gr. -1-k). 24.99 (978-0-7534-6154-9(4), 9780753461549, Kingfisher) Roaring Brook Pr.

Mitton, Tony & Parker, Ant. Tough Trucks. 2005. (Amazing Machines Ser.). (ENG., Illus.). 24p. (J). (gr. -1-k). 4.99 (978-0-7534-5917-1(5), 9780753459171, Kingfisher) Roaring Brook Pr.

Mok, Carmen. Ride the Big Machines Across Canada. 2015. (My Big Machines Ser.). (ENG.). 14p. (J). bds. 10.50 (978-1-4434-3810-0(3)) HarperCollins Pubs.

Mr. Cheesehead Goes for a Ride... 2nd rev. ed. 2005. (Illus.). 32p. (J). 12.99 (978-0-9764463-1-6(6)) Vertigo Publishing.

Nelson, Suzanne. You're Bacon Me Crazy. 2014. 248p. (J). pap. (978-0-545-65268-1(5)) Scholastic, Inc.

Ode, Eric. Busy Trucks on the Go. Culotta, Kent, illus. 2014. (ENG.). 32p. (J). pap. 6.99 (978-1-61067-287-0(9)) Kane Miller.

—Busy Trucks on the Go. 2014. (ENG.). 32p. (J). 11.99 (978-1-61067-313-6(1)) Kane Miller.

Odgers, Sally. Good Night, Truck. McKenzie, Heath, illus. 2016. (ENG.). 32p. (J). 16.99 (978-1-250-07019-7(8), 9781250070197) Feiwel & Friends.

Page, Claire. I Really Like Trucks. 2010. (ENG., Illus.). 12p. (gr. -1-k). bds. 9.99 (978-1-84610-962-1(0)) Make Believe Ideas GBR. Dist: Nelson, Thomas Inc.

Petrie, Catherine. Joshua James Likes Trucks. Snyder, Joel, illus. 2011. (Rookie Ready to Learn — Out & about: in My Community Ser.). 32p. (J). (gr. -1-k). lib. bdg. 25.00 (978-0-531-27177-3(3)); (ENG.). pap. 5.95 (978-0-531-26827-8(6)) Scholastic Library Publishing. (Children's Pr.).

Random House. Big Truck Show! (Bubble Guppies) Random House, illus. 2016. (Step into Reading Ser.). (ENG., Illus.). 24p. (J). (gr. -1-1). 4.99 (978-1-101-93887-4(0), Random Hse. Bks. for Young Readers) Random Hse. Children's Bks.

—Driving Force! (Blaze & the Monster Machines) Garcia, Segundo, illus. 2016. (Pictureback(R) Ser.). (ENG.). 24p. (J). (gr. -1-2). 4.99 (978-0-553-53889-2(6), Random Hse. Bks. for Young Readers) Random Hse. Children's Bks.

—Pop the Hood! (Blaze & the Monster Machines) Hechtenkopf, Omar, illus. 2016. (Lift-The-Flap Ser.). (ENG.). 12p. (J). (gr. -1 — 1). bds. 6.99 (978-0-553-53893-9(4), Random Hse. Bks. for Young Readers) Random Hse. Children's Bks.

—Racing Colors! (Blaze & the Monster Machines) Random House, illus. 2016. (ENG., Illus.). 24p. (J). (gr. -1 — 1). bds. 6.99 (978-0-553-53892-2(6), Random Hse. Bks. for Young Readers) Random Hse. Children's Bks.

—Ready to Race! (Blaze & the Monster Machines) Kobasic, Kevin, illus. 2015. (Step into Reading Ser.). (ENG.). 24p. (J). (gr. -1-1). 4.99 (978-0-553-52460-4(7), Random Hse. Bks. for Young Readers) Random Hse. Children's Bks.

—Speed Lights! (Blaze & the Monster Machines) Random House & Dynamo Limited Staff, illus. 2016. (Step into Reading Ser.). (ENG.). 24p. (J). (gr. -1-1). pap. 4.99 (978-0-399-55692-0(3), Random Hse. Bks. for Young Readers) Random Hse. Children's Bks.

Random House Staff. Big Truck Show! Jackson, Mike, illus. 2013. (Step into Reading Ser.). (ENG.). 32p. (J). (gr. -1-1). 3.99 (978-0-449-81896-1(9), Random Hse. Bks. for Young Readers) Random Hse. Children's Bks.

—Blaze of Glory (Blaze & the Monster Machines) Foley, Niki, illus. 2015. (Pictureback(R) Ser.). (ENG.). 16p. (J). (gr. -1-2). 4.99 (978-0-553-52457-4(7), Random Hse. Bks. for Young Readers) Random Hse. Children's Bks.

Random House Staff & Disney Editors. Five Tales from the Road. 2013. (Cars Step into Reading Ser.). lib. bdg. 18.40 (978-0-606-32198-3(5), Turtleback) Turtleback Bks.

Rao, Lisa. Blaze & the Monster Machines: We're Movin' 2016. (ENG.). 10p. (J). (gr. -1-k). bds. 10.99 (978-0-7944-3762-6(1), Reader's Digest Children's Bks.) Studio Fun International.

—Playtime in Trucktown. Shannon, David et al, illus. 2008. (Jon Scieszka's Trucktown Ser.). (ENG.). 24p. (J). (gr. -1-1). 5.99 (978-1-4169-4197-2(5), Simon Scribbles) Simon Scribbles.

RH Disney. Can You Find Dory? RH Disney, illus. 2016. (Lift-The-Flap Ser.). (ENG., Illus.). 12p. (J). (— 1). bds. 9.99 (978-0-7364-3561-1(1), RH/Disney) Random Hse. Children's Bks.

Riley, J. D. Axel the Truck: Beach Race. Dorman, Brandon, illus. 2013. (My First I Can Read Ser.). (ENG.). 32p. (J). (gr. -1-3). 16.99 (978-0-06-222230-5(9)); pap. 3.99 (978-0-06-222229-9(5)) HarperCollins Pubs. (Greenwillow Bks.).

—Axel the Truck: Beach Race. 2013. (My First I Can Read Ser.). (J). lib. bdg. 13.55 (978-0-606-31812-9(7), Turtleback) Turtleback Bks.

—Axel the Truck: Rocky Road. Dorman, Brandon, illus. 2013. (My First I Can Read Ser.). (ENG.). 32p. (J). (gr. -1-3). pap. 3.99 (978-0-06-222231-2(7), Greenwillow Bks.) HarperCollins Pubs.

—Axel the Truck: Rocky Road. 2013. (My First I Can Read Ser.). (J). lib. bdg. 13.55 (978-0-606-32163-1(2), Turtleback) Turtleback Bks.

—Rocky Road. Dorman, Brandon, illus. 2013. (My First I Can Read Ser.). (ENG.). 32p. (J). (gr. -1-3). 16.99 (978-0-06-222232-9(5), Greenwillow Bks.) HarperCollins Pubs.

Rinker, Sherri Duskey. Goodnight, Goodnight, Construction Site. Lichtenheld, Tom, illus. (ENG.). (J). 2017. 30p. bds. 7.99 (978-1-4521-1173-5(1)) 2016. 32p. (gr. -1 — 1). 18.99 (978-1-4521-5215-8(2)) 2016. 20p. (gr. -1-7). 12.99 (978-1-4521-5463-3(5)) 2015. 66p. (gr. -1 — 1). 15.99 (978-1-4521-4698-0(5)) 2011. 32p. (gr. -1-1). 16.99 (978-0-8118-7782-4(5)) Chronicle Bks. LLC.

—Goodnight, Goodnight Construction Site Sound Book. Lichtenheld, Tom, illus. 2014. (ENG.). 12p. (J). (gr. -1 — 1). 12.99 (978-1-4521-2824-5(3)) Chronicle Bks. LLC.

—Mighty, Mighty Construction Site. Lichtenheld, Tom, illus. 2017. (ENG.). 40p. (J). 16.99 (978-1-4521-5216-5(0)) Chronicle Bks. LLC.

Rinker, Sherri Duskey & Lichtenheld, Tom. Goodnight, Goodnight, Construction Site. 2012. 12.95 (978-0-545-50222-1(5)) Scholastic, Inc.

Robertson, Ruth. The Truck That Wouldn't! 2004. pap. 9.00 (978-0-8059-6316-8(2)) Dorrance Publishing Co., Inc.

Royston, Angela. Truck Trouble, Level 1. 2013. (DK Readers Ser.). (ENG.). 32p. (J). (gr. k-4). pap. 3.99 (978-1-4654-0243-1(8), DK Children) Dorling Kindersley Publishing, Inc.

Salzano, Tammi. Truck Party. Wood, Hannah, illus. 2011. (ENG.). 20p. bds. 7.95 (978-1-58925-865-5(7)) Tiger Tales.

Samuels, Barbara. The Trucker. Samuels, Barbara, illus. 2010. (ENG., Illus.). 40p. (J). (gr. -1-1). 16.99 (978-0-374-37804-2(5), 9780374378042, Farrar, Straus & Giroux (BYR)) Farrar, Straus & Giroux.

Sander, Sonia. Easter Egg Dash! A Lift-The-Flap Book with Stickers. Shannon, David et al, illus. 2010. (Jon Scieszka's Trucktown Ser.). (ENG.). 12p. (J). (gr. -1-k). bds. 7.99 (978-1-4169-4183-5(5), Little Simon) Little Simon.

Sander, Sonia & Scieszka, Jon. Smash That Trash! Shannon, David et al, illus. 2009. (Jon Scieszka's Trucktown Ser.). (ENG.). 14p. (J). (gr. -1-k). 7.99 (978-1-4169-4180-4(0), Little Simon) Little Simon.

Sauer, Tammi. Truck, Truck, Goose! Waring, Zoe, illus. 2017. 40p. (J). (gr. -1-3). 14.99 **(978-0-06-242153-1(0))** HarperCollins Pubs.

Savage, Stephen. The Mixed-Up Truck. 2016. (ENG., Illus.). 32p. (J). 16.99 (978-1-62672-153-1(X), 9781626721531) Roaring Brook Pr.

—Supertruck. Savage, Stephen, illus. 2015. (ENG., Illus.). 32p. (J). (gr. -1-1). 12.99 (978-1-59643-821-7(5), 9781596438217) Roaring Brook Pr.

Sayres, Brianna Caplan. Where Do Diggers Sleep at Night? Slade, Christian, illus. (ENG.). (J). (-k). 2014. 26p. bds. 7.99 (978-0-385-37415-6(1)) 2012. 32p. 16.99 (978-0-375-86848-1(8)) Random Hse. Children's Bks. (Random Hse. Bks. for Young Readers).

Scarry, Richard. Richard Scarry's Trucks. 2015. (ENG., Illus.). 24p. (J). (— 1). bds. 4.99 (978-0-385-38925-9(6), Golden Bks.) Random Hse. Children's Bks.

Schertle, Alice. El Camioncito Azul. McElmurry, Jill, illus. 2013. (Little Blue Truck Ser.).Tr. of Little Blue Truck. (SPA & ENG.). 30p. (J). (— 1). bds. 7.99 (978-0-547-98397-4(2)) Houghton Mifflin Harcourt Publishing Co.

—Little Blue Truck. McElmurry, Jill, illus. (Little Blue Truck Ser.). (ENG.). (J). 2010. 32p. (gr. -1-3). 26.99 (978-0-547-48248-4(5)) 2008. 32p. (gr. -1-3). 17.99 (978-0-15-205661-2(0)) 2015. 30p. (— 1). bds. 7.99 (978-0-544-56803-7(6), HMH Books For Young Readers) Houghton Mifflin Harcourt Publishing Co.

—Little Blue Truck Leads the Way. McElmurry, Jill, illus. (Little Blue Truck Ser.). (ENG.). (J). 2016. 38p. (— 1). bds. 12.99 (978-0-544-70899-0(7), HMH Books For Young Readers) 2012. 40p. (gr. -1-3). 26.99 (978-0-547-85060-3(3)) 2009. 40p. (gr. -1-3). 17.99 (978-0-15-206389-4(7)) 2015. 38p. (— 1). bds. 7.99 (978-0-544-56805-1(2), HMH Books For Young Readers) Houghton Mifflin Harcourt Publishing Co.

—Little Blue Truck's Christmas. McElmurry, Jill, illus. 2014. (Little Blue Truck Ser.). (ENG.). 24p. (J). (— 1). 14.99 (978-0-544-32041-3(7), HMH Books For Young Readers) Houghton Mifflin Harcourt Publishing Co.

—Little Blue Truck's Halloween. McElmurry, Jill, illus. 2016. (Little Blue Truck Ser.). (ENG.). 16p. (J). (— 1). bds. 12.99 (978-0-544-77253-3(9), HMH Books For Young Readers) Houghton Mifflin Harcourt Publishing Co.

Schertle, Alice & McElmurry, Jill. Little Blue Truck's Beep-Along Book. McElmurry, Jill, illus. 2015. (Little Blue Truck Ser.). (ENG., Illus.). 8p. (J). (— 1). bds. 12.99 (978-0-544-56812-9(5), HMH Books For Young Readers) Houghton Mifflin Harcourt Publishing Co.

Scholastic, Inc. Staff. A Construir la Ciudad! 2011. (Lego City Ser.). (SPA.). 24p. (J). (gr. -1-3). pap. 3.99 (978-0-545-34464-7(6), Scholastic en Espanol) Scholastic, Inc.

Scholastic, Inc. Staff, contrib. by. Build This City! 2010. (LEGO City Ser.). (ENG.). 24p. (J). (gr. -1-3). pap. 3.99 (978-0-545-17765-8(0)) Scholastic, Inc.

—Trucks Around the City. 2011. (Lego City Ser.). (ENG.). 14p. (J). (gr. -1-k). bds. 7.99 (978-0-545-35629-9(6)) Scholastic, Inc.

Schorr, Titus. The Truck Parade, 01 vols., 1. 2016. (Rosen REAL Readers: STEM & STEAM Collection). (ENG.). 8p. (J). pap. 5.46 (978-1-5081-1401-7(3), Rosen Classroom) Rosen Publishing Group, Inc., The.

Schotter, Roni. Go, Little Green Truck! Kuo, Julia, illus. 2016. (ENG.). 32p. (J). 16.99 (978-0-374-30070-8(4), 9780374300708, Farrar, Straus & Giroux (BYR)) Farrar, Straus & Giroux.

Scieszka, Jon. Dizzy Izzy. Shannon, David et al, illus. 2014. (Jon Scieszka's Trucktown Ser.). (ENG.). 24p. (J). (gr. -1-1). 16.99 (978-1-4814-1460-9(7), Simon Spotlight) Simon Spotlight.

—Dizzy Izzy. Gordon, David et al, illus. 2010. (Jon Scieszka's Trucktown Ser.). (ENG.). 24p. (J). (gr. -1-1). pap. 3.99 (978-1-4169-4145-3(2), Simon Spotlight) Simon Spotlight.

—Dizzy Izzy. Shannon, David et al, illus. 2010. (Jon Scieszka's Trucktown Ser.). (ENG.). 24p. (J). (gr. -1-1). lib. bdg. 14.99 (978-1-4169-4156-9(8), Simon Spotlight) Simon Spotlight.

—Garage Tales. Gordon, David et al, illus. 2010. (Jon Scieszka's Trucktown Ser.). (ENG.). 80p. (J). (gr. -1-3). 12.99 (978-1-4424-1196-8(1), Simon & Schuster Bks. For Young Readers) Simon & Schuster Bks. For Young Readers.

—The Great Truck Rescue. Shannon, David et al, illus. 2010. (Jon Scieszka's Trucktown Ser.). (ENG.). 40p. (J). (gr. -1-3). pap. 3.99 (978-1-4424-0932-3(0), Simon & Schuster Bks. For Young Readers) Simon & Schuster Bks. For Young Readers.

—Kat's Maps. Shannon, David et al, illus. 2011. (Jon Scieszka's Trucktown Ser.). (ENG.). 24p. (J). (gr. -1-1). pap. 3.99 (978-1-4169-4148-4(7), Simon Spotlight) Simon Spotlight.

—Kat's Mystery Gift. Gordon, David et al, illus. 2009. (Jon Scieszka's Trucktown Ser.). (ENG.). 24p. (J). (gr. -1-1). pap. 3.99 (978-1-4169-4143-9(6), Simon Spotlight) Simon Spotlight.

—Kat's Mystery Gift. Shannon, David et al, illus. 2009. (Jon Scieszka's Trucktown Ser.). (ENG.). 24p. (J). (gr. -1-1). lib. bdg. 14.99 (978-1-4169-4154-5(1), Simon Spotlight) Simon Spotlight.

—Melvin Might? Gordon, David et al, illus. 2008. (Jon Scieszka's Trucktown Ser.). (ENG.). 44p. (J). (gr. -1-3). 16.99 (978-1-4169-4134-7(7), Simon & Schuster Bks. For Young Readers) Simon & Schuster Bks. For Young Readers.

—Melvin's Valentine. Shannon, David et al, illus. (Jon Scieszka's Trucktown Ser.). (ENG.). 24p. (J). (gr. -1-1). 2014. 16.99 (978-1-4814-1458-6(5)) 2009. pap. 3.99 (978-1-4169-4144-6(4)) 2009. lib. bdg. 15.99 (978-1-4169-4155-2(X)) Simon Spotlight. (Simon Spotlight).

—Pete's Party. Gordon, David et al, illus. 2008. (Jon Scieszka's Trucktown Ser.). (ENG.). 24p. (J). (gr. -1-k). lib. bdg. 13.89 (978-1-4169-4149-1(5)); pap. 3.99 (978-1-4169-4138-5(X)) Simon Spotlight. (Simon Spotlight).

—Race from A to Z, No. 4. Gordon, David et al, illus. 2014. (Jon Scieszka's Trucktown Ser.). (ENG.). 48p. (J). (gr. -1-3). 17.99 (978-1-4169-4136-1(3), Simon & Schuster Bks. For Young Readers) Simon & Schuster Bks. For Young Readers.

—Smash! Crash! Shannon, David et al, illus. 2008. (Jon Scieszka's Trucktown Ser.). (ENG.). 42p. (J). (gr. -1-3). 17.99 (978-1-4169-4133-0(9), Simon & Schuster Bks. For Young Readers) Simon & Schuster Bks. For Young Readers.

—Snow Trucking! Gordon, David et al, illus. 2008. (Jon Scieszka's Trucktown Ser.). (ENG.). 24p. (J). (gr. -1-1). pap. 3.99 (978-1-4169-4140-8(1), Simon Spotlight) Simon Spotlight.

—The Spooky Tire. Shannon, David et al, illus. 2009. (Jon Scieszka's Trucktown Ser.). (ENG.). 24p. (J). (gr. -1-k). lib. bdg. 15.99 (978-1-4169-4153-8(3)); pap. 3.99 (978-1-4169-4142-2(8)) Simon Spotlight. (Simon Spotlight).

—Trucks Line Up. Shannon, David et al, illus. 2011. (Jon Scieszka's Trucktown Ser.). (ENG.). 24p. (J). (gr. -1-1). 16.99 (978-1-4169-4158-3(4), Simon Spotlight) Simon Spotlight.

—Trucks Line Up. Gordon, David et al, illus. 2011. (Jon Scieszka's Trucktown Ser.). (ENG.). 24p. (J). (gr. -1-1). pap. 3.99 (978-1-4169-4147-7(9), Simon Spotlight) Simon Spotlight.

—Trucksgiving. Shannon, David et al, illus. 2010. (Jon Scieszka's Trucktown Ser.). (ENG.). 24p. (J). (gr. -1-1). 16.99 (978-1-4169-4157-6(6)); pap. 3.99 (978-1-4169-4146-0(0)) Simon Spotlight. (Simon Spotlight).

—Uh-Oh, Max. Shannon, David et al, illus. (Jon Scieszka's Trucktown Ser.). (ENG.). 24p. (J). (gr. -1-1). 2014. 16.99 (978-1-4814-1461-6(5)) 2009. pap. 3.99 (978-1-4169-4141-5(X)) Simon Spotlight. (Simon Spotlight).

—Welcome to Trucktown! Shannon, David et al, illus. 2010. (Jon Scieszka's Trucktown Ser.). (ENG.). 40p. (J). (gr. -1-3). pap. 3.99 (978-1-4424-1271-2(2), Simon & Schuster Bks. For Young Readers) Simon & Schuster Bks. For Young Readers.

—Zoom! Boom! Bully. Shannon, David et al, illus. 2008. (Jon Scieszka's Trucktown Ser.). (ENG.). 24p. (J). (gr. -1-1). pap. 3.99 (978-1-4169-4139-2(8), Simon Spotlight) Simon Spotlight.

Shea, Christine. Las Aventuras de Max, el Camión Volteador: El Mejor Día de Nieve! = the Adventures of Max the Dump Truck: The Greatest Snow Day Ever! Chase, Michelle B. & Chase, Tanor R., illus. 2007. (ENG & SPA.). (J). (978-1-933002-01-9(8)) PublishingWorks.

Shealy, Dennis. I'm a Monster Truck. Staake, Bob, illus. 2016. (Little Golden Board Book Ser.). (ENG.). 26p. (J). (gr. -1-k). bds. 7.99 (978-0-553-53586-0(2), Random Hse. Bks. for Young Readers) Random Hse. Children's Bks.

—I'm a Truck. 2014. (Little Golden Board Book Ser.). (ENG., Illus.). 26p. (J). (-k). bds. 7.99 (978-0-385-38923-5(X), Random Hse. Bks. for Young Readers) Random Hse. Children's Bks.

Shealy, Dennis & Little Golden Books Staff. I'm a Monster Truck. Staake, Bob, illus. 2011. (Little Golden Book Ser.). (ENG.). 24p. (J). (gr. -1-2). 4.99 (978-0-375-86132-1(7), Golden Bks.) Random Hse. Children's Bks.

Shealy, Dennis & Miryam. Favorites: I'm a Truck/The Happy Man & His Dump Truck/I'm a Monster Truck. Staake, Bob et al, illus. 2011. (Little Golden Book Favorites Ser.). (ENG.). 80p. (J). (gr. -1-2). 7.99 (978-0-375-86549-7(7), Golden Bks.) Random Hse. Children's Bks.

Shulevitz, Uri. Troto & the Trucks. 2015. (ENG., Illus.). 32p. (J). (gr. -1-1). 17.99 (978-0-374-30080-7(1), 9780374300807, Farrar, Straus & Giroux (BYR)) Farrar, Straus & Giroux.

Silver Dolphin en Español Editors. Tonka Vehiculos Robustos y Sensacionales. 2006. (Tonka Board Bks.). (Illus.). 22p. (J). (gr. -1). bds. (978-970-718-362-9(4), Silver Dolphin en Español) Advanced Marketing, S. de R. L. de C. V.

Silver Dolphin en Español Staff, creator. Camiones a la Obra! 2006. (Tonka Figuras Magicas Ser.). (Illus.). 8p. (J). (gr. -1). (978-970-718-360-5(8), Silver Dolphin en Español) Advanced Marketing, S. de R. L. de C. V.

Sís, Peter. Trucks Trucks Trucks. Sís, Peter, illus. 2004. (ENG., Illus.). 28p. (J). (gr. -1-1). bds. 7.99 (978-0-06-056258-8(7), Greenwillow Bks.) HarperCollins Pubs.

Slack, Michael H. & Slack, Mike. Monkey Truck. Slack, Michael H. & Slack, Mike, illus. 2011. (ENG., Illus.). 32p. (J). (gr. -1 — 1). 12.99 (978-0-8050-8878-6(4), 9780805088786, Holt, Henry & Co. Bks. For Young Readers) Holt, Henry & Co.

Sollinger, Emily. Dare to Repair! 2016. (Dinotrux 8X8 Ser.). (J). lib. bdg. 13.55 (978-0-606-38318-9(2)) Turtleback Bks.

—Dinotrux: Dare to Repair! 2016. (ENG., Illus.). 24p. (J). (gr. -1-3). pap. 3.99 (978-0-316-26082-4(7)) Little, Brown Bks. for Young Readers.

—Dinotrux: Dinotrux to the Rescue! 2016. (Passport to Reading Level 1 Ser.). (ENG., Illus.). 32p. (J). (gr. -1-3). pap. 3.99 (978-0-316-26078-7(9)) Little, Brown Bks. for Young Readers.

—Dinotrux: Just Hatched! 2016. (ENG., Illus.). 10p. (J). (gr. -1 — 1). bds. 6.99 (978-0-316-26080-0(0)) Little, Brown Bks. for Young Readers.

—Dinotrux to the Rescue! 2016. (Dinotrux Passport Reading Level 1 Ser.). (J). lib. bdg. 13.55 (978-0-606-38320-2(4)) Turtleback Bks.

Staunton, Ted. Morgan on Ice, 1 vol. Slavin, Bill, illus. 2013. (Formac First Novels Ser.). (ENG.). 56p. (J). (gr. 2-3). 14.95 (978-1-4595-0289-5(2), 9781459502895); pap. 5.95 (978-1-4595-0290-1(6), 9781459502901) Formac Publishing Co., Ltd. CAN. Dist: Casemate Pubs. & Bk. Distributors, LLC.

Steele, Michael Anthony. Fix That Truck! 2012. (LEGO City 8X8 Ser.). lib. bdg. 13.55 (978-0-606-26773-1(5), Turtleback) Turtleback Bks.

Stoddard, Jeffery. Pete & Pillar: A Story of Friendship Based on John 15:13: the Big Rain. Stoddard, Jeffery, illus. 2007. (Pete & Pillar Ser.). (ENG., Illus.). 32p. (J). (gr. -1-2). 12.99 (978-1-59317-203-9(6)) Warner Pr., Inc.

Sweeney, Kathleen. Matty Monster Truck. 2008. 14p. pap. 24.95 (978-1-60672-865-9(2)) America Star Bks.

Swenson, Jamie A. Big Rig. Young, Ned, illus. 2014. (ENG.). 32p. (J). (gr. -1-k). 16.99 (978-1-4231-6330-5(3)) Hyperion Bks. for Children.

—Big Rig [Board Book]. Young, Ned, illus. 2016. (ENG.). 32p. (J). (gr. -1 — 1). bds. 6.99 (978-1-4231-9252-7(4)) Hyperion Bks. for Children.

Taborn, Debbie. When a Feather Fell. 2012. 32p. pap. 16.99 (978-1-4685-4150-2(1)) AuthorHouse.

Teitelbaum, Michael. Steer the Wheel! Shannon, David et al, illus. 2011. (Jon Scieszka's Trucktown Ser.). (ENG.). 12p. (J). (gr. -1-1). bds. 7.99 (978-1-4169-4185-9(1), Simon & Schuster Bks. For Young Readers) Simon & Schuster Bks. For Young Readers.

Teitelbaum, Michael & Scieszka, Jon. On the Move! Shannon, David et al, illus. 2009. (Jon Scieszka's Trucktown Ser.). (ENG.). 10p. (J). (gr. -1-k). bds. 6.99 (978-1-4169-4178-1(9), Little Simon) Little Simon.

Tillworth, Mary. Blaze Loves to Race! (Blaze & the Monster Machines) Kobasic, Kevin, illus. 2016. (Step into Reading Ser.). (ENG.). 24p. (J). (gr. -1-1). pap. 4.99 (978-0-399-55888-7(8), Random Hse. Bks. for Young Readers) Random Hse. Children's Bks.

—Bouncy Tires! (Blaze & the Monster Machines) Burch, Benjamin, illus. 2016. (Little Golden Book Ser.). (ENG.). 24p. (J). (gr. -1-k). 4.99 (978-0-553-53891-5(8), Golden Bks.) Random Hse. Children's Bks.

—Nickelodeon 5-Minute Stories Collection. Random House, illus. 2016. (5-Minute Story Collection). (ENG.). 160p. (J). (gr. -1-2). 12.99 (978-0-399-55314-1(2), Random Hse. Bks. for Young Readers) Random Hse. Children's Bks.

—Stuntmania! (Blaze & the Monster Machines) Hechtenkopf, Omar, illus. 2016. (Pictureback Ser.). (ENG.). 16p. (J). (gr. -1-2). 4.99 (978-1-101-93868-3(4), Random Hse. Bks. for Young Readers) Random Hse. Children's Bks.

Tillworth, Mary. Zeg & the Egg. Foley, Niki, illus. 2016. 18p. (J). **(978-1-4806-9878-9(4))** Random Hse., Inc.

Todd, Mark. Food Trucks! 2014. (ENG., Illus.). 32p. (J). (gr. -1-3). 16.99 (978-0-544-15784-2(2), HMH Books For Young Readers) Houghton Mifflin Harcourt Publishing Co.

TONKA. TONKA Busy Trucks: A Lift-The-Flap Book. 2014. (Lift-The-Flap Ser.: 3). (ENG.). 10p. (J). (gr. -1-k). bds. 9.99 (978-0-7944-3031-3(7), Reader's Digest Children's Bks.) Studio Fun International.

Torres, Jennifer. Stef Soto, Taco Queen. 2017. (ENG.). 176p. (J). (gr. 3-7). 16.99 (978-0-316-30686-7(X)) Little Brown & Co.

Truck Buddies. 2013. (Truck Buddies Ser.). (ENG.). 32p. (gr. -1-1). 135.90 (978-1-4342-8839-4(0)) Stone Arch Bks.

The Truck Is Stuck. (Little Book Practice Reader). (J). (978-0-8136-5379-2(7)) Modern Curriculum Pr.

Venning, Edward W. The Story of Pete & Ralph. 2008. 56p. pap. 16.95 (978-1-4327-2237-1(9)) Outskirts Pr., Inc.

Weldon, Stayton. Whitey on the Ranch. Anderson-Shorter, Susan, illus. 2010. 52p. pap. 12.95 (978-1-4490-5474-8(9)) AuthorHouse.

Wheeler, Lisa. Farmer Dale's Red Pickup Truck. Bates, Ivan, illus. 2014. (ENG.). 32p. (J). (— 1). bds. 7.99 (978-0-544-24765-9(5), HMH Books For Young Readers) Houghton Mifflin Harcourt Publishing Co.

Wildman, Dale. Big Rig Daddy: A Ride in the Truck of All Trucks. Dickson, Bill, illus. 2006. 24p. (J). per. 2.99 (978-1-59958-007-4(1)) Journey Stone Creations, LLC.

Williamson, Jennifer. Timmy the Tow Truck, 6 vols. Williamson, Alan, 8th, illus. 2005. 28p. (J). pap. (978-0-9771678-1-4(X)) Theee Hole Punch Publishing.

Wolf, Sallie. Peter's Trucks. 2013. 26p. 26.95 (978-1-62352-033-5(9)) IntoPrint Publishing LLC.

—Truck Stuck. Davies, Andy Robert, illus. (ENG.). (J). (— 1). 2017. 28p. bds. 7.99 (978-1-58089-781-5(9)) 2009. 32p. pap. 7.95 (978-1-58089-257-5(4)) Charlesbridge Publishing, Inc.

Wyre, Yvonne. The Adventures of Cuthbert the Coal Lorry. 2005. 160p. pap. (978-1-84401-500-9(9)) Athena Pr.

Zandman, Herm. It's Not a Truck! It's a B-Double! 2012. 40p. pap. 32.70 (978-1-4797-0543-6(8)) Xlibris Corp.

TRUMAN, HARRY S., 1884-1972

Blake, Kevin. Harry S. Truman: The 33rd President. 2016. (First Look at America's Presidents Ser.). (ENG., Illus.). 24p. (J). (gr. -1-3). lib. bdg. 17.95 (978-1-943553-29-7(7)) Bearport Publishing Co., Inc.

Elston, Heidi. Harry S. Truman, 1 vol. 2016. (ENG., Illus.). 40p. (J). (978-1-68078-119-9(7)) ABDO Publishing Co.

Elston, Heidi M. D. Harry S. Truman, 1 vol. 2009. (United States Presidents Ser.). (ENG., Illus.). 40p. (YA). (gr. 3-6). 27.07 (978-1-60453-476-4(1)) ABDO Publishing Co.

Etingoff, Kim. Harry Truman: From Farmer to President. 2012. (J). pap. (978-1-4222-2485-4(6)); 64p. (gr. 7-8). 22.95 (978-1-4222-2482-3(1)) Mason Crest.

Geller, Kevin. Harry S. Truman. 2017. (Pivotal Presidents: Profiles in Leadership Ser.). 80p. (gr. 12-13). lib. bdg. 33.90 **(978-1-68048-633-9(0)**, Britannica Educational Publishing) Rosen Publishing Group, Inc., The.

Lazo, Caroline Evensen. Harry S. Truman. 2003. (Presidential Biography Ser.). (Illus.). 112p. (J). (gr. 6-12). lib. bdg. 29.27 (978-0-8225-0096-4(5)) Lerner Publishing Group.

Mara, Wil. Harry Truman. 2011. (Presidents & Their Times 5 Ser.). (Illus.). 96p. (J). (gr. 6). 34.21 (978-1-60870-185-8(9)) Marshall Cavendish Corp.

Parker, Lewis. How to Draw the Life & Times of Harry S. Truman. 2009. (Kid's Guide to Drawing the Presidents of the United States of America Ser.). 32p. (gr. 4-4). 50.50 (978-1-61511-143-5(3), PowerKids Pr.) Rosen Publishing Group, Inc., The.

Parker, Lewis K. How to Draw the Life & Times of Harry S. Truman. 2005. (Kid's Guide to Drawing the Presidents of the United States of America Ser.). (Illus.). 32p. (YA). (gr. 2-5). lib. bdg. 26.50 (978-1-4042-3009-5(2)) Rosen Publishing Group, Inc., The.

Saffer, Barbara. Harry S. Truman. 2004. (Childhoods of the Presidents Ser.). (Illus.). 48p. (J). (gr. 4-18). lib. bdg. 17.95 (978-1-59084-282-9(0)) Mason Crest.

Schuman, Michael A. Harry S. Truman. rev. ed. 2003. (United States Presidents Ser.). (Illus.). 112p. (J). (gr. 5-12). lib. bdg. 26.60 (978-0-7660-2010-8(X)) Enslow Pubs., Inc.

Stanley, George E. Harry S. Truman: Thirty-Third President of the United States. Henderson, Meryl, illus. 2004. (Childhood of Famous Americans Ser.). (ENG.). 256p. (J). (gr. 3-7). pap. 12.99 (978-0-689-86247-2(4), Aladdin) Simon & Schuster Children's Publishing.

Uhl, Xina M. Harry S. Truman. 2016. (Premier Presidents Ser.). (ENG.). 24p. (J). (gr. 1-4). 27.07 (978-1-5038-0858-4(0), 210708) Child's World, Inc., The.

Venezia, Mike. Harry S. Truman: Thirty-Third President. Venezia, Mike, illus. 2007. (Getting to Know the U. S. Presidents Ser.). (Illus.). 32p. (J). (gr. 3-4). 28.00 (978-0-516-22637-8(1), Children's Pr.) Scholastic Library Publishing.

TRUMBULL, JOHN, 1756-1843

Murray, Stuart A. P. John Trumbull: Painter of the Revolutionary War. 2008. (ENG., Illus.). 83p. (C). (gr. 6-18). lib. bdg. 158.00 (978-0-7656-8150-8(1), Y182501) Routledge.

TRUMP, DONALD, 1946-

Marsh, Carole. Donald Trump: Presidential Coloring & Activity Book. 2017. (Here & Now Ser.). (ENG., Illus.). (J). (gr. 3-7). 5.99 **(978-0-635-12561-3(7))** Gallopade International.

—I'm Reading about Donald Trump: America's 45th President. 2017. (I'm Reading About Ser.). (ENG., Illus.). (J). lib. bdg. 24.99 **(978-0-635-12565-1(X))** Gallopade International.

Mattern, Joanne. President Donald Trump. 2017. (Rookie Biographies(tm) Ser.). (ENG., Illus.). 32p. (J). lib. bdg. 25.00 **(978-0-531-23226-2(3)**, Children's Pr.) Scholastic Library Publishing.

—Rookie Biographies: President Donald Trump. 2017. (Rookie Biographies Ser.). (ENG., Illus.). 32p. (J). pap. 5.95 **(978-0-531-23860-8(1)**, Children's Pr.) Scholastic Library Publishing.

—A True Book: President Donald Trump. 2017. (True Book(tm), A — Biographies Ser.). (ENG.). 48p. (J). 31.00 **(978-0-531-22718-3(9))**; pap. 7.95 **(978-0-531-23014-5(7))** Scholastic Library Publishing. (Children's Pr.).

Robison, Nick. Donald Trump. 2017. (Pebble Plus Ser.). (ENG., Illus.). 32p. (gr. k-1). lib. bdg. 26.65 **(978-1-5157-7895-0(9)**, Pebble Plus) Capstone Press of Coughlan Cos.

Santos, Rita. Donald Trump: Businessman & President. 2017. (Junior Biographies Ser.). 24p. (gr. 3-4). lib. bdg. 22.60 **(978-0-7660-8666-1(6))** Enslow Pubs., Inc.

Wheeler, Jill C. Donald Trump. 2016. (United States Presidents Ser.). (ENG.). (J). (gr. 3-6). lib. bdg. 27.07 **(978-1-68078-363-6(7))** ABDO Publishing Co.

Wooten, Sara McIntosh. Donald Trump: Real Estate Mogul & President. 2017. (Influential Lives Ser.). 128p. (J). (gr. 7-8). lib. bdg. 37.27 **(978-0-7660-8499-5(X))** Enslow Pubs., Inc.

TRUMPET—FICTION

Acampora, Paul. Rachel Spinelli Punched Me in the Face. 2013. (ENG.). 192p. (J). (gr. 3-7). pap. 8.99 (978-1-250-01669-0(X), 9781250016690) Square Fish.

Dorie & Me. 2003. (YA). per. (978-1-59431-071-3(8), Ebks. On The Net) Write Words, Inc.

Hopgood, Tim. Here Comes Frankie! 2008. (ENG., Illus.). 32p. (J). (gr. 2-6). 23.95 (978-1-4050-9271-5(8), Macmillan) Pan Macmillan GBR. Dist: Trans-Atlantic Pubns., Inc.

Kehoe, Stasia Ward. The Sound of Letting Go. 2014. (ENG.). 400p. (YA). (gr. 7). 17.99 (978-0-670-01553-5(9), Viking Books for Young Readers) Penguin Young Readers Group.

Lipsyte, Robert. Yellow Flag. 2009. (ENG.). 256p. (YA). (gr. 8). pap. 9.99 (978-0-06-055709-6(5), Tegen, Katherine Bks) HarperCollins Pubs.

Polizzotto, Carolyn & Spinks, Sarah. Trumpet's Kittens. Duke, Marion, illus. 2003. 32p. (YA). 22.50 (978-1-86368-331-9(3)) Fremantle Pr. AUS. Dist: Independent Pubs. Group.

Redbank, Tennant. Lily: Tiana's Helpful Kitten (Disney Princess: Palace Pets) Random House Disney Staff & Matta, Gabriella, illus. 2016. (Stepping Stone Book(TM) Ser.). (ENG.). 64p. (J). (gr. 1-4). 5.99 (978-0-7364-3393-8(7), RH/Disney) Random Hse. Children's Bks.

Ritter, John H. Under the Baseball Moon. 2008. (ENG., Illus.). 320p. (J). (gr. 5-18). 9.99 (978-0-14-241090-5(X), Puffin Books) Penguin Young Readers Group.

—Under the Baseball Moon. 2008. (Illus.). 283p. (gr. 8-12). 17.00 (978-0-7569-8934-7(5)) Perfection Learning Corp.

Torres, Jos A. & Torres, Jose A. Joey Kanga Roo: Plays the Trumpet. 2009. 36p. pap. 15.99 (978-1-4389-7434-7(5)) AuthorHouse.

Townsend, Daniel. Trumpet. 2008. 24p. pap. 24.95 (978-1-4241-9387-5(7)) America Star Bks.

Willems, Mo. Listen to My Trumpet! Willems, Mo, illus. 2012. (Elephant & Piggie Book Ser.). (ENG., Illus.). 64p. (J). (gr. -1-k). 9.99 (978-1-4231-5404-4(5)) Hyperion Pr.

TRUST IN GOD

see Faith

TRUTH, SOJOURNER, 1799-1883

Butler, Mary. Sojourner Truth: From Slave to Activist for Freedom. 2009. (Library of American Lives & Times Ser.). 112p. (gr. 5-5). 69.20 (978-1-60853-505-7(3)) Rosen Publishing Group, Inc., The.

Butler, Mary G. Sojourner Truth: From Slave to Activist for Freedom. 2005. (Library of American Lives & Times). (Illus.). 112p. (YA). (gr. 4-8). lib. bdg. 34.60 (978-0-8239-5736-1(5)) Rosen Publishing Group, Inc., The.

Clinton, Catherine. When Harriet Met Sojourner. Evans, Shane W., illus. 2007. (ENG.). 32p. (J). (gr. k-2). 16.99 (978-0-06-050425-0(0), Tegen, Katherine Bks) HarperCollins Pubs.

Collins, Kathleen. Sojourner Truth: Defensora de los derechos Civiles. 2004. (Grandes personajes en la historia de los Estados Unidos Ser.). (SPA.). 32p. (gr. 3-6). pap. 10.00 (978-0-8239-4239-8(2), Rosen Classroom) Rosen Publishing Group, Inc., The.

—Sojourner Truth: Defensora de los derechos civiles (Sojourner Truth: Equal Rights Advocate) 2009. (Grandes personajes en la historia de los Estados Unidos (Famous People in American History) Ser.). (SPA.). 32p. (gr. 2-3). 47.90 (978-1-61512-808-2(5), Editorial Buenas Letras) Rosen Publishing Group, Inc., The.

—Sojourner Truth: Equal Rights Advocate. (Primary Sources of Famous People in American History Ser.). 32p. 2009. (gr. 2-3). 47.90 (978-1-60851-727-5(6)) 2004. (ENG., Illus.). (gr. 4-8). pap. 10.00 (978-0-8239-4193-3(0)) Rosen Publishing Group, Inc., The.

—Sojourner Truth: Equal Rights Advocate / Defensora de los derechos Civiles. 2009. (Famous People in American History/Grandes personajes en la historia de los Estados Unidos Ser.). (ENG & SPA.). 32p. (gr. 2-3). 47.90 (978-1-61512-556-2(6), Editorial Buenas Letras) Rosen Publishing Group, Inc., The.

Krass. Sojourner Truth. 2004. (Black Americans of Achievement Ser.). (Illus.). 112p. (gr. 6-12). 35.00 (978-0-7910-8165-5(6), Chelsea Hse.) Facts On File, Inc.

Kudlinski, Kathleen. Sojourner Truth: Voice for Freedom. Wooden, Lenny, illus. 2003. (Childhood of Famous Americans Ser.). (ENG.). 160p. (Orig.). (J). (gr. 3-7). mass mkt. 7.99 (978-0-689-85274-9(6), Simon & Schuster/Paula Wiseman Bks.) Simon & Schuster/Paula Wiseman Bks.

Lantier, Patricia & Michael Horn, Geoffrey. Sojourner Truth: Speaking up for Freedom. 2009. (Voices for Freedom Ser.). (ENG.). 64p. (J). (gr. 5-8). pap. (978-0-7787-4840-3(5)); lib. bdg. (978-0-7787-4824-3(3)) Crabtree Publishing Co.

Marsh, Carole. Sojourner Truth. 2003. 12p. (gr. k-4). 2.95 (978-0-635-02355-1(5)) Gallopade International.

Mattern, Joanne. Sojourner Truth: Early Abolitionist. (Women Who Shaped History Ser.). 24p. 2009. (gr. 2-3). 42.50 (978-1-60854-821-7(X)) 2003. (Illus.). (J). lib. bdg. 22.60 (978-0-8239-6502-1(3)) Rosen Publishing Group, Inc., The. (PowerKids Pr.).

Mcdonough, Yona Zeldis. Who Was Sojourner Truth? 2015. (Who Was... ? Ser.). lib. bdg. 16.00 (978-0-606-37560-3(0)) Turtleback Bks.

McDonough, Yona Zeldis & dePaola, Tomie. Who Was Sojourner Truth? Eldridge, Jim, illus. 2015. (Who Was? Ser.). (ENG.). 112p. (J). (gr. 3-7). 5.99 (978-0-448-48678-9(4), Grosset & Dunlap) Penguin Young Readers Group.

McKissack, Patricia C. & McKissack, Fredrick, Jr. Sojourner Truth: Ain't I a Woman? 2003. (Illus.). 186p. (gr. 4-7). 17.20 (978-0-7857-2515-2(6), Turtleback) Turtleback Bks.

Moore, Barbara R. Sojourner Truth. 2005. (Illus.). 16p. (J). (978-0-618-56039-4(4)) Houghton Mifflin Harcourt Publishing Co.

Ruffin, Frances E. Her Story, Her Words: The Narrative of Sojourner Truth. (Great Moments in American History Ser.). 32p. 2009. (gr. 3-3). 47.90 (978-1-61513-144-0(2)) 2004. (Illus.). (gr. 4-8). lib. bdg. 22.50 (978-0-8239-4387-6(9), Rosen Reference) Rosen Publishing Group, Inc., The.

—Sojourner Truth: Early Abolitionist. 2009. (American Legends Ser.). 24p. (gr. 3-3). 42.50 (978-1-61511-387-3(8), PowerKids Pr.) Rosen Publishing Group, Inc., The.

Swain, Gwenyth. Sojourner Truth. Archambault, Matthew, illus. 2005. (On My Own Biography Ser.). 48p. (J). (gr. 1-3). pap. 6.95 (978-1-57505-827-6(8)) Lerner Publishing Group.

—Sojourner Truth. 2005. (On My Own Biography Ser.). (Illus.). 48p. (J). 25.26 (978-1-57505-651-7(8), Carolrhoda Bks.) Lerner Publishing Group.

Taylor, Charlotte. Sojourner Truth: Abolitionist & Activist. 2016. (Exceptional African Americans Ser.). (ENG.). 24p. (J). (gr. 3-3). pap. 9.35 (978-0-7660-7370-8(X)); (Illus.). 22.60 (978-0-7660-7372-2(6)) Enslow Pubs., Inc.

Waxman, Laura Hamilton. Sojourner Truth. 2008. pap. 52.95 (978-0-8225-9396-6(3)); (ENG., Illus.). 48p. (gr. 3-6). lib. bdg. 27.93 (978-0-8225-7172-8(2), Lerner Pubns.) Lerner Publishing Group.

TRUTHFULNESS AND FALSEHOOD

see also Honesty

Amos, Janine & Spenceley, Annabel. Let's Own Up. 2009. (Best Behavior Ser.). (Illus.). 32p. (J). (gr. -1-2). 22.60 (978-1-60754-503-3(9)); pap. 10.55 (978-1-60754-505-7(5)) Windmill Bks.

Beeson, Sam. White Lies. 2009. 9.99 (978-1-59955-343-6(0)) Cedar Fort, Inc./CFI Distribution.

Berry, Joy. Help Me Be Good about Lying. 2009. (Help Me Be Good Ser.). 32p. pap. 7.95 (978-1-60577-113-7(9)) Berry, Joy Enterprises.

Berry, Joy Wilt. A Book about Cheating. 2005. (Illus.). (J). (978-0-7172-8583-9(9)) Scholastic, Inc.

—A Book about Lying. 2005. (Illus.). (J). (978-0-7172-8576-1(6)) Scholastic, Inc.

Gerber, Larry. The Distortion of Facts in the Digital Age. 2012. (Digital & Information Literacy Ser.). (ENG., Illus.). 48p. (YA). (gr. 5-8). 29.25 (978-1-4488-8357-8(1)); pap. 11.75 (978-1-4488-8368-4(7)) Rosen Publishing Group, Inc., The. (Rosen Reference).

Graves, Sue & Guicciardini, Desideria. I Didn't Do It! 2013. (Our Emotions & Behavior Ser.). (ENG., Illus.). 32p. (J). (gr. -1-3). 12.99 (978-1-57542-445-3(2)) Free Spirit Publishing, Inc.

Kiesbye, Stefan. Cheating. 2010. (Social Issues Firsthand Ser.). (ENG.). 192p. (gr. 10-12). 38.30 (978-0-7377-5009-6(X), Greenhaven Pr., Inc.) Cengage Gale.

Larsen, Carolyn. Telling the Truth: A Book about Lying. O'Connor, Tim, illus. 2016. (Growing God's Kids Ser.). (ENG.). 32p. (J). pap. 4.99 (978-0-8010-0926-6(X)) Baker Bks.

Lynette, Rachel. How to Deal with Lying. 2009. (Let's Work It Out Ser.). 24p. (gr. 2-3). 42.50 (978-1-61514-265-1(7), PowerKids Pr.); (Illus.). (J). lib. bdg. 22.60 (978-1-4042-4517-4(0), 1284659) Rosen Publishing Group, Inc., The.

Miller, Connie Colwell. You're in Trouble: Fib or Truth? Victoria Assanelli, illus. 2017. (Making Good Choices Ser.). (ENG.). 24p. (J). (gr. 1-4). 20.95 **(978-1-68151-163-4(0)**, Amicus Illustrated) Amicus Publishing.

Rondina, Catherine. Lying: Deal with It Straight Up, 1 vol. Workman, Dan, illus. 2006. (Lorimer Deal with It Ser.). (ENG.). 32p. (J). (gr. 4-6). pap. 12.95 (978-1-55028-906-0(3), 9781550289060) Lorimer, James & Co., Ltd., Pubs. CAN. Dist: Casemate Pubs. & Bk. Distributors, LLC.

Rothschild, Jennifer. Me, Myself, & Lies for Young Women: What to Say When You Talk to Yourself. 2017. (ENG.). 192p. (J). pap. 12.99 (978-0-7369-6421-0(5)) Harvest Hse. Pubs.

Vermond, Kira & Hanmer, Clayton. Half-Truths & Brazen Lies: An Honest Look at Lying. 2016. (ENG., Illus.). 48p. (J). (gr. 3-7). 16.95 (978-1-77147-146-6(8), Owlkids) Owlkids Bks. Inc. CAN. Dist: Publishers Group West (PGW).

Vranich, Belisa & Eagleson, Holly. Boys Lie: How Not to Get Played. 2010. (ENG.). 264p. (YA). (gr. 13-18). pap. 12.95 (978-0-7573-1364-6(7), HCI Teens) Health Communications, Inc.

Wittrock, Jeni. How Honest Are You?, 1 vol. 2011. (Friendship Quizzes Ser.). (ENG.). 32p. (gr. 3-4). lib. bdg. 27.99 (978-1-4296-6542-1(4), Snap Bks.) Capstone Press of Coughlan Cos.

TRUTHFULNESS AND FALSEHOOD—FICTION

Alexan, Julie. Nolia Fasolia: Read-Along Book: Arabic & English. El-Ahraf, Amer, ed. Ceasar, Fady, illus. 2011. (ARA & ENG.). 48p. pap. 5.99 (978-0-9844310-1-4(2)) BigKids Bilingual Bks.

Atwood, Megan. Olive Spins a Tale (and It's a Doozy!) Fleming, Lucy, illus. 2016. (Dear Molly, Dear Olive Ser.). (ENG.). 96p. (gr. 1-3). lib. bdg. 21.99 (978-1-4795-8695-0(1)) Picture Window Bks.

Banning, Gail. Out on a Limb. 2008. (ENG.). 256p. (YA). (gr. 6-9). (978-1-55470-012-7(4)) Me to We.

Beifus, Ruth. Shlavim Classics 2-in-1 Vol. 1: The Best Reward & the Taste of Truth. 2009. 32p. 14.99 (978-1-59826-329-9(3)) Feldheim Pubs.

Bodeen, S. A. The Compound. 2008. (Compound Ser.: 1). (ENG.). 256p. (YA). (gr. 7-12). 18.99 (978-0-312-37015-2(6), 9780312370152) Feiwel & Friends.

—The Compound. 2009. (Compound Ser.: 1). (ENG.). 272p. (YA). (gr. 7-12). pap. 9.99 (978-0-312-57860-2(1), 9780312578602) Square Fish.

Bogart, Jo Ellen. The White Cat & the Monk: A Retelling of the Poem Pangur Bán, 1 vol. Smith, Sydney, illus. 2016. (ENG.). 32p. (J). (gr. -1-3). 18.95 (978-1-55498-780-1(6)) Groundwood Bks. CAN. Dist: Publishers Group West (PGW).

Braxton-Smith, Ananda. Merrow. 2016. (ENG.). 240p. (YA). (gr. 9). 16.99 (978-0-7636-7924-8(0)) Candlewick Pr.

Carlson, Melody. Grover Tells a Whopper: A Scoozie Tale about Honesty. Fincher, Kathryn Andrews, illus. Date not set. 32p. (J). 9.99 (978-0-7369-0733-0(5)) Harvest Hse. Pubs.

Cook, Julia. Well, I Can Top That! Dufalla, Anita, illus. 2014. (ENG.). 32p. (J). pap. 10.95 (978-1-934490-57-0(1)) Boys Town Pr.

Curry, Kenneth. Chuka & the Drum. 2007. (Illus.). 22p. (J). 10.95 (978-0-9798364-4-2(1)) Curry Brothers Publishing Group.

Denman, K. L. Agent Angus, 1 vol. 2012. (Orca Currents Ser.). (ENG.). 128p. (J). (gr. 5-9). 16.95 (978-1-4598-0104-2(0)); pap. 9.95 (978-1-4598-0103-5(2)) Orca Bk. Pubs. USA.

Dimplechin, Lord Reginald. McKenzie Was Here. 2012. 24p. pap. 24.95 (978-1-4626-8674-2(5)) America Star Bks.

Dyan, Penelope. I Did It, & I Hid It! a Book about Taking Responsibility. Dyan, Penelope, illus. 2009. (Illus.). 44p. pap. 11.95 (978-1-935118-68-8(4)) Bellissima Publishing, LLC.

Eason, Sarah. Come Clean, Carlos: Tell the Truth. 2013. (You Choose Ser.). 32p. (J). (gr. k-3). pap. 7.95 (978-1-4644-0557-0(3), Enslow Elementary) Enslow Pubs., Inc.

Fields, Jan. Meri Mercer Doesn't Lie, Mostly, 1 vol. 2014. (Meri's Mirror Ser.). (ENG., Illus.). 80p. (J). (gr. 2-5). lib. bdg. 27.07 (978-1-62402-009-4(7), Calico Chapter Bks) Magic Wagon.

Garrelts, Christopher. Squarey Head Tells a Lie. Mayabb, Darrell, ed. 2003. (Adventures of Squarey Head Ser.: Bk. 1). (Illus.). 30p. (J). (gr. k-6). 4.95 (978-0-9742003-0-9(1)) Squarey Head, Inc.

Gewirtz, Adina Rishe. Zebra Forest. (ENG., 208p. (J). (gr. 4-7). 2014. Illus.). pap. 7.99 (978-0-7636-7166-2(5)) 2013. 15.99 (978-0-7636-6041-3(8)) Candlewick Pr.

Hall, Kirsten. Little Lies: All about Math. Luedecke, Bev, illus. 2004. (Beastieville Ser.). (ENG.). 32p. (J). (gr. k-1). pap. 3.95 (978-0-516-24656-7(9), Children's Pr.) Scholastic Library Publishing.

Hamilton, Martha & Weiss, Mitch. The Well of Truth: A Folktale from Egypt. Wrenn, Tom, illus. 2008. (Story Cove Ser.). (ENG.). 32p. (J). (gr. -1-3). pap. 4.95 (978-0-87483-880-0(0)) August Hse. Pubs., Inc.

Hennessy, B. G. The Boy Who Cried Wolf. Kulikov, Boris, illus. 2006. (ENG.). 40p. (J). (gr. -1-3). 17.99 (978-0-689-87433-8(2), Simon & Schuster Bks. For Young Readers) Simon & Schuster Bks. For Young Readers.

—The Boy Who Cried Wolf. Kulikov, Boris, illus. 2011. (J). (gr. -1-2). 29.95 (978-0-545-09452-8(6)) Weston Woods Studios, Inc.

Hopkins, Cathy. The Princess of Pop. 2012. (Truth or Dare Ser.). (ENG.). 224p. (YA). (gr. 7). pap. 10.99 (978-1-4424-6057-7(1), Simon Pulse) Simon Pulse.

Hughes, Huw John, tr. from ENG. Cadi Deud Celwydd. 2005. (Storiau Crefyddol Religious Stories Ser.). (WEL., Illus.). 24p. pap. (978-1-85994-517-9(1)) Cyhoeddiadau'r Gair.

Ivey, Lisa. The Christmas Tree That Didn't Get Picked. 2007. 64p. per. 19.95 (978-1-4241-8276-3(X)) America Star Bks.

Jeffrey, Sarah. Me & My Invisible Guy, 0 vols. 2013. (ENG.). 256p. (YA). (gr. 7-11). 15.99 (978-1-4778-1636-3(4), 9781477816363, Amazon Children's Publishing) Amazon Publishing.

Juby, Susan & Wells, Rosemary. The Truth Commission. 2015. (ENG., Illus.). 320p. (YA). (gr. 9). bds. 18.99 (978-0-451-46877-2(5), Viking Books for Young Readers) Penguin Young Readers Group.

Keplinger, Kody. Lying Out Loud: A Companion to the DUFF. 2015. (ENG.). 288p. (J). (gr. 9). 17.99 (978-0-545-83109-3(1)) Scholastic, Inc.

—Lying Out Loud: a Companion to the DUFF. 2016. (ENG.). 304p. (J). (gr. 9). pap. 9.99 (978-0-545-83110-9(5), Scholastic Paperbacks) Scholastic, Inc.

Knudsen, Shannon. Testing the Truth. 2015. (ENG.). 104p. (YA). (gr. 6-12). 27.99 (978-1-4677-5708-9(X)) Lerner Publishing Group.

Kropp, Paul. Winner! (978-1-897039-31-1(X)) High Interest Publishing (HIP).

Kulick Triscila, Verne. Joel & the Magic Toy Tree. 2005. 36p. (J). 11.99 (978-1-4116-6985-7(1)) Lulu Pr., Inc.

Kyi, Tanya Lloyd. Truth. 2004. (Orca Soundings Ser.). 108p. 19.95 (978-0-7569-4346-2(9)) Perfection Learning Corp.

Lamb, Lenny. The Truth about Lying: Greener Grass Volume 3. 2012. 48p. 24.95 (978-1-4626-5046-0(5)) America Star Bks.

Mackinnon, Mairi. The Boy Who Cried Wolf. 2009. (First Reading Level 3 Ser.). 48p. (J). 6.99 (978-0-7945-2472-2(9), Usborne) EDC Publishing.

Mathieu, Jennifer. The Truth about Alice. 2014. (ENG.). 208p. (YA). (gr. 7). 16.99 (978-1-59643-909-2(2), 9781596439092) Roaring Brook Pr.

McClintock, Norah. Tell. 2007. (Orca Soundings Ser.). 100p. (gr. 4-7). 19.95 (978-0-7569-8069-6(0)) Perfection Learning Corp.

McConnaughhay, JoDee H. Tell the Truth, Tyler. Urbanovic, Jackie, illus. 2014. (Happy Day Ser.). (ENG.). 16p. (J). pap. 2.49 (978-1-4143-9468-8(3)) Tyndale Hse. Pubs.

Moranville, Sharelle Byars. 27 Magic Words. 2016. (ENG.). 208p. (J). (gr. 3-7). 16.95 (978-0-8234-3657-6(8)) Holiday Hse., Inc.

O'Dell, Patrick Timothy Wayne. Elvin. 2009. 58p. pap. 16.95 (978-1-61546-576-7(6)) America Star Bks.

Penn, Tony. The Misadventures of Michael Mcmichaels: The Creepy Campers, vol. 3. Martin, Brian, illus. 2017. (Michael Mcmichaels Ser.: 3). (ENG.). 84p. (J). pap. 7.95 **(978-1-944882-10-5(3))** Boys Town Pr.

Petrucci, Lou. Heart of the Hide. 2008. 320p. 22.95 (978-1-4401-0102-1(7), iUniverse Star) iUniverse, Inc.

Picou, Lin. Who's Right. Dufalla, Anita, illus. 2012. (ENG.). 24p. (gr. 2-3). pap. 8.95 (978-1-61810-323-9(7)) Rourke Educational Media.

Pincus, Gregory K. The 14 Fibs of Gregory K. 2013. (J). pap. (978-0-439-91300-3(4)); (ENG.). 240p. (gr. 3-7). 17.99 (978-0-439-91299-0(7)) Scholastic, Inc. (Levine, Arthur A. Bks.).

Rayner, Robert. Suspended, 1 vol. 2004. (Lorimer Sports Stories Ser.). (ENG.). 112p. (J). (gr. 4-8). 16.95 (978-1-55028-861-2(X), 9781550288612) Lorimer, James & Co., Ltd., Pubs. CAN. Dist: Casemate Pubs. & Bk. Distributors, LLC.

Reynolds, Betty. Little Lies. 2012. 102p. pap. 7.99 (978-0-9856724-0-9(4)) Personal.

Rippin, Sally. The Little Lie. Fukuoka, Aki, illus. 2014. 43p. (J). (978-1-61067-291-7(7)) Kane Miller.

Robins, Eleanor. No Limits, 1 vol. unabr. ed. 2011. (Choices Ser.). (ENG.). 52p. (YA). (gr. 9-12). 7.95 (978-1-61651-598-0(8)) Saddleback Educational Publishing, Inc.

Ross, Jill. What's the Matter, Mr. Ticklebritches? Pruitt, Gwendolyn, illus. 2010. (ENG.). 70p. (J). (gr. 3-7). pap. 9.95 (978-1-59825-948-3(2)) Shenanigans Series.

Sargeant, Glen. Finders Keepers, 1 vol. 2009. 142p. pap. 24.95 (978-1-61582-202-7(X)) America Star Bks.

Seal, Vickie Di-Ann. Edgar Tells the Truth. 2012. 26p. 24.95 (978-1-4626-0976-5(7)) America Star Bks.

Shepard, Sara. Ali's Pretty Little Lies. 2013. (Pretty Little Liars Companion Novel Ser.). (ENG.). (gr. 9). 320p. (YA). pap. 9.99 (978-0-06-223337-0(8)); 304p. (J). 17.99 (978-0-06-223336-3(X)) HarperCollins Pubs. (HarperTeen).

—Ali's Pretty Little Lies. 2013. (Pretty Little Liars Ser.). (YA). lib. bdg. 20.85 (978-0-606-35048-8(9), Turtleback) Turtleback Bks.

Simon, Mary Manz. Piglet Tells the Truth. Stott, Dorothy, illus. 2006. (First Virtues for Toddlers Ser.). 20p. (J). 5.99 (978-0-7847-1407-2(X), 04035) Standard Publishing.

Sommer, Carl. No One Will Ever Know. Westbrook, Dick, illus. 2003. (Another Sommer-Time Story Ser.). (ENG.). 48p. (J). (gr. 1-4). 16.95 incl. audio compact disk (978-1-57537-506-9(0)) Advance Publishing, Inc.

—Tied up in Knots. Budwine, Greg, illus. 2003. (Another Sommer-Time Story Ser.). (ENG.). 48p. (J). 16.95 incl. audio compact disk (978-1-57537-503-8(6)) Advance Publishing, Inc.

—Tied up in Knots. 2003. (Another Sommer-Time Story Ser.). (Illus.). 48p. (J). (gr. 1-4). 16.95 incl. audio (978-1-57537-552-6(4)) Advance Publishing, Inc.

Staunton, Ted. Morgan & the Money. Slavin, Bill, illus. 2008. (First Novel Ser.). (ENG.). 64p. (J). (gr. 1-5). (978-0-88780-776-3(3)) Formac Publishing Co., Ltd.

—Morgan & the Money, 1 vol. Shannon, Ben, illus. 2008. (Formac First Novels Ser.). (ENG.). 64p. (gr. 1-5). 4.95 (978-0-88780-774-9(7), 9780887807749) Formac Publishing Co., Ltd. CAN. Dist: Casemate Pubs. & Bk. Distributors, LLC.

Undercuffler, Gary, illus. The Boy Who Cried Wolf: A Tale about Telling the Truth. 2006. (Famous Fables Ser.). (J). 6.99 (978-1-59939-026-0(4)) Cornerstone Pr.

Weigl Publishers, creator. The Shoemaker & His Medicine: Why Should You Tell the Truth? 2013. (AV2 Animated Storytime Ser.: Vol. 18). (ENG., Illus.). 32p. (J). (gr. -1-3). lib. bdg. 29.99 (978-1-62127-922-8(7), AV2 by Weigl) Weigl Pubs., Inc.

TUAREGS

Reynolds, Jan. Sahara, 1 vol. 2007. (Vanishing Cultures Ser.). (ENG., Illus.). 32p. (978-1-60060-146-0(4)); (J). (gr. 4-7). 10.95 (978-1-60060-131-6(6)) Lee & Low Bks., Inc.

TUBA—FICTION

Bartlett, T. C. Tuba Lessons. Felix, Monique, illus. (ENG.). 32p. (J). (gr. 1-17). 2011. pap. 9.95 (978-0-89812-522-1(7), Creative Paperbacks) 2009. 17.95 (978-1-56846-209-7(3)) Creative Co., The.

Tripp, Paul. Tubby the Tuba. Cole, Henry, illus. 2006. (ENG.). 32p. (J). (gr. -1-3). 16.99 (978-0-525-47717-4(9), Dutton Books for Young Readers) Penguin Young Readers Group.

Zeppa, Talaylin. Teddy the Tub. 2011. 32p. pap. 32.70 (978-1-4568-6908-3(6)) Xlibris Corp.

TUBMAN, HARRIET, 1820?-1913

Abnett, Dan. Harriet Tubman & the Underground Railroad. (Jr. Graphic Biographies Ser.). (ENG.). 24p. 2009. (J). (gr. 2-3). 47.90 (978-1-61513-816-6(1), PowerKids Pr.) 2007. (Illus.). (J). (gr. 2-5). lib. bdg. 25.25 (978-1-4042-3393-5(8)) 2007. (Illus.). (gr. 3-8). pap. 10.60 (978-1-4042-2146-8(8), PowerKids Pr.) Rosen Publishing Group, Inc., The.

—Harriet Tubman y el Ferrocarril Clandestino. 2009. (Historietas Juveniles: Biografías (Jr. Graphic Biographies) Ser.). (SPA., Illus.). 24p. (J). (gr. 2-5). 25.25 (978-1-4358-8563-9(5)); (gr. 3-8). pap. 10.60 (978-1-4358-3320-3(1)) Rosen Publishing Group, Inc., The.

Adler, David A. Harriet Tubman & the Underground Railroad. 2012. (ENG.). 144p. (J). 18.95 (978-0-8234-2365-1(4)) Holiday Hse., Inc.

—A Picture Book of Harriet Tubman. Byrd, Samuel, illus. unabr. ed. 2005. (Picture Book Readalong Ser.). (J). (gr. k-4). 28.95 incl. audio compact disk (978-1-59519-385-8(5)); 25.95 incl. audio (978-1-59519-381-0(2));Set. pap. 37.95 incl. audio (978-1-59519-382-7(0));Set. pap. 39.95 incl. audio compact disk (978-1-59519-386-5(3)) Live Oak Media.

Allen, Thomas B. Harriet Tubman, Secret Agent: How Daring Slaves & Free Blacks Spied for the Union During the Civil War. 2008. (ENG., Illus.). 192p. (J). (gr. 5). 5.95 (978-1-4263-0401-9(3), National Geographic Children's Bks.) National Geographic Society.

—Harriet Tubman, Secret Agent: How Daring Slaves & Free Blacks Spied for the Union During the Civil War. Bauer, Carla, illus. 2006. (National Geographic Ser.). (ENG.). 192p. (gr. 5-8). 16.95 (978-0-7922-7889-4(5)); lib. bdg. 25.90 (978-0-7922-7890-0(9)) National Geographic Society. (National Geographic Children's Bks.).

Anderson, Jane. Harriet Tubman & the Underground Railroad. 2005. (J). pap. (978-1-4108-4202-2(9)) Benchmark Education Co.

Auch, Allison. Women Who Dared & Mujeres que se Atrevieron: 6 English, 6 Spanish Adaptations. 2011. (ENG & SPA.). (J). 97.00 net. (978-1-4108-5692-0(5)) Benchmark Education Co.

Baumann, Susan K. Harriet Tubman. 2013. (Jr. Graphic African American History Ser.). 24p. (J). (gr. 3-6). 25.25 (978-1-4777-1312-9(3)); pap. 10.60 (978-1-4777-1449-2(9)) Rosen Publishing Group, Inc., The. (PowerKids Pr.).

—Harriet Tubman: Conductor of the Underground Railroad. 2013. (Jr. Graphic African American History Ser.). 24p. (J). (gr. 3-6). pap. 63.60 (978-1-4777-1450-8(2), PowerKids Pr.) Rosen Publishing Group, Inc., The.

Blue, Rose, et al. Harriet Tubman: Riding the Freedom Train. 2003. (Gateway Biographies Ser.: 4). (ENG., Illus.). 48p. (gr. 4-8). lib. bdg. 26.60 (978-0-7613-2571-0(9), Millbrook Pr.) Lerner Publishing Group.

Clinton, Catherine. When Harriet Met Sojourner. Evans, Shane W., illus. 2007. (ENG.). 32p. (J). (gr. k-2). 16.99 (978-0-06-050425-0(0), Tegen, Katherine Bks) HarperCollins Pubs.

Connors, Kathleen. The Life of Harriet Tubman, Vol. 1. 2014. (Famous Lives Ser.). (ENG.). 24p. (J). (gr. 1-2). 22.60 (978-1-4824-0412-8(5)) Stevens, Gareth Publishing LLLP.

Cosson, M. J. Harriet Tubman, 1 vol. 2007. (Essential Lives Set 1 Ser.). (ENG., Illus.). 112p. (J). (gr. 6-12). lib. bdg. 35.64 (978-1-59928-842-0(7)) ABDO Publishing Co.

DeFord, Diane. Harriet Tubman. 2009. pap. 13.25 (978-1-60559-061-5(4)) Hameray Publishing Group, Inc.

Doak, Robin S. Harriet Tubman. 2015. (ENG., Illus.). 48p. (J). pap. 6.95 (978-0-531-21757-3(4)); lib. bdg. (978-0-531-21595-1(4)) Scholastic, Inc. (Orchard Bks.).

Edison, Erin. Harriet Tubman. 2013. (Great Women in History Ser.). (ENG.). 24p. (gr. k-1). pap. 35.70 (978-1-62065-860-4(7)); pap. 6.29 (978-1-62065-859-8(3)) Capstone Press of Coughlan Cos. (Pebble Bks.).

Feinstein, Stephen. Read about Harriet Tubman. 2005. (I Like Biographies! Ser.). (Illus.). 24p. (J). lib. bdg. 22.60 (978-0-7660-2591-2(8), Enslow Elementary) Enslow Pubs., Inc.

Findley, Violet. Easy Reader Biographies: Harriet Tubman: Follow the North Star. 2007. (ENG.). 16p. pap. 2.99 (978-0-439-92330-9(1), Teaching Resources) Scholastic, Inc.

Ganeri, Anita. Harriet Tubman: The Life of an African-American Abolitionist. Shone, Rob, illus. 2005. (Graphic Biographies Ser.). (ENG.). 48p. (gr. 5-8). pap. 14.05 (978-1-4042-5172-4(3)) Rosen Publishing Group, Inc., The.

Gayle, Sharon. Harriet Tubman & the Freedom Train. Marshall, Felicia, illus. 2005. (Ready-to-Read Ser.). 32p. (J). lib. bdg. 15.00 (978-1-59054-960-5(0)) Fitzgerald Bks.

—Harriet Tubman & the Freedom Train. Marshall, Felicia, illus. 2003. (Ready-To-read SOFA Ser.). (ENG.). 32p. (J). (gr. 1-3). pap. 3.99 (978-0-689-85480-4(3), Simon Spotlight) Simon Spotlight.

Gold, Susan Dudley. Harriet Tubman & the Underground Railroad. 2015. (Primary Sources of the Abolitionist Movement Ser.). (ENG., Illus.). 64p. (J). (gr. 6-6). 34.21 (978-1-5026-0522-1(8)) Cavendish Square Publishing.

Gosman, Gillian. Harriet Tubman. 2011. (Life Stories Ser.). (Illus.). 24p. (J). pap. 8.25 (978-1-4488-2761-9(2), PowerKids Pr.); (ENG & SPA., (gr. 1-4). lib. bdg. 22.60 (978-1-4488-3220-0(9)); (gr. 1-4). lib. bdg. 22.60 (978-1-4488-2586-8(5), PowerKids Pr.) Rosen Publishing Group, Inc., The.

Hale, Nathan. The Underground Abductor. 2015. (Nathan Hale's Hazardous Tales Ser.). (ENG., Illus.). 128p. (J). (gr. 3-9). 12.95 (978-1-4197-1536-5(4), Amulet Bks.) Abrams, Inc.

—The Underground Abductor. 2017. (Nathan Hale's Hazardous Tales Ser.). (J). lib. bdg. 24.45 **(978-0-606-40708-3(1))** Turtleback Bks.

Kernan, Elizabeth. Harriet Tubman: A Lesson in Bravery. 2009. (Reading Room Collection 2 Ser.). 24p. (gr. 3-4). 42.50 (978-1-60851-966-8(X), PowerKids Pr.) Rosen Publishing Group, Inc., The.

Lantier, Patricia. Harriet Tubman: Conductor on the Underground Railroad. 2009. (Voices for Freedom Ser.). (ENG., Illus.). 64p. (J). (gr. 5-8). pap. (978-0-7787-4838-0(3)); lib. bdg. (978-0-7787-4822-9(7)) Crabtree Publishing Co.

Leavitt, Amie Jane. Harriet Tubman. 2007. (What's So Great About... ? Ser.). (Illus.). 32p. (J). (gr. 2-4). lib. bdg. 25.70 (978-1-58415-577-5(9)) Mitchell Lane Pubs., Inc.

Malaspina, Ann. Harriet Tubman. 2009. (Leaders of the Civil War Era Ser.). (Illus.). 120p. (gr. 6-12). 35.00 (978-1-60413-303-5(1), Chelsea Hse.) Facts On File, Inc.

Maloof, Torrey. Harriet Tubman: Leading Others to Liberty. 2017. (Primary Source Readers Ser.). (Illus.). 32p. (J). (gr. 4-5). pap. 8.99 (978-1-4938-3802-8(4)) Teacher Created Materials, Inc.

Mara, Wil. Harriet Tubman. 2013. (ENG.). 32p. (C). pap. 9.95 (978-0-531-24703-7(1)) National Geographic School Publishing, Inc.

—Harriet Tubman. 2013. (Rookie Biographies(r) Ser.). (ENG.). 32p. (J). lib. bdg. 23.00 (978-0-531-24737-2(6)) Scholastic Library Publishing.

Martin, Michael & Martin, Michael J. Harriet Tubman & the Underground Railroad, 1 vol. Hoover, Dave & Anderson, Bill, illus. 2005. (Graphic History Ser.). (ENG.). 32p. (gr. 3-4). 30.65 (978-0-7368-3829-0(5), Graphic Library) Capstone Press of Coughlan Cos.

Martin, Michael J. Harriet Tubman & the Underground Railroad, 1 vol. Hoover, Dave & Anderson, Bill, illus. 2005. (Graphic History Ser.). (ENG.). 32p. (gr. 3-4). per. 8.10 (978-0-7368-5245-6(X), Graphic Library) Capstone Press of Coughlan Cos.

McDonnell, Julia. Harriet Tubman in Her Own Words. 2016. (Eyewitness to History Ser.). (ENG., Illus.). 32p. (J). (gr. 4-5). pap. 10.50 (978-1-4824-4066-9(0)) Stevens, Gareth Publishing LLLP.

McDonough, Yona Zeldis. Who Was Harriet Tubman? Harrison, Nancy, illus. 2003. (Who Was... ? Ser.). 106p. (gr. 4-7). 15.00 (978-0-7569-1590-2(2)) Perfection Learning Corp.

Norwich, Grace. I Am #6: Harriet Tubman. 2013. (I Am Ser.: 6). (ENG.). 128p. (J). (gr. 2-5). pap. 5.99 (978-0-545-48436-7(7), Scholastic Paperbacks) Scholastic, Inc.

—I Am Harriet Tubman. Simon, Ute, illus. 2013. 127p. (J). (978-0-545-61344-6(2)) Scholastic, Inc.

Pace, Lorenzo. Harriet Tubman & My Grandmother's Quilts, 1 vol. 2015. (African American Quartet Ser.). (ENG., Illus.). 48p. (J). 30.25 (978-1-4777-9289-6(9), Windmill Bks.) Rosen Publishing Group, Inc., The.

Patterson, Marie. Harriet Tubman, 1 vol. 2005. (Primary Source Readers Ser.). (SPA & ENG.). 24p. (J). (gr. 4-4). pap. 8.99 (978-0-7439-8912-1(0)) Shell Educational Publishing.

Petry, Ann & Reynolds, Jason. Harriet Tubman: Conductor on the Underground Railroad. 2007. (ENG.). 256p. (J). (gr. 3-7). pap. 7.99 (978-0-06-446181-8(5), Amistad) HarperCollins Pubs.

Rausch, Monica. Harriet Tubman. 2007. (Great Americans Ser.). (Illus.). 24p. (gr. 1-4). lib. bdg. 22.00 (978-0-8368-7686-4(5), Weekly Reader Leveled Readers) Stevens, Gareth Publishing LLLP.

Rausch, Monica L. Harriet Tubman. 2007. (Grandes personajes (Great Americans) Ser.). (ENG & SPA., Illus.). 24p. (gr. 1-4). lib. bdg. 22.00 (978-0-8368-7985-8(6), Weekly Reader Leveled Readers) Stevens, Gareth Publishing LLLP.

Sawyer, Kem Knapp. Harriet Tubman - A Photographic Story of a Life. 2010. (DK Biography Ser.). (ENG.). 128p. (J). (gr. 5-12). 6.99 (978-0-7566-5806-9(3), DK Children) Dorling Kindersley Publishing, Inc.

Schraff, Anne. The Life of Harriet Tubman: Moses of the Underground Railroad. 2014. (Legendary African Americans Ser.). (Illus.). 96p. (J). (gr. 6-12). 27.94 (978-0-7660-6137-8(X)) Enslow Pubs., Inc.

Shone, Rob. Harriet Tubman: The Life of an African-American Abolitionist. 2009. (Graphic Nonfiction Biographies Ser.). (ENG.). 48p. (YA). (gr. 4-5). 58.50 (978-1-61513-018-4(7), Rosen Reference) Rosen Publishing Group, Inc., The.

Shone, Rob & Ganeri, Anita. Harriet Tubman: The Life of an African-American Abolitionist. 2005. (Graphic Nonfiction Biographies Ser.). (ENG., Illus.). 48p. (J). (gr. 4-7). lib. bdg. 31.95 (978-1-4042-0245-0(5)) Rosen Publishing Group, Inc., The.

Skelton, Renee. Harriet Tubman A Woman of Courage. 2005. 2005p. (J). lib. bdg. 15.00 (978-1-4242-0849-4(1)) Fitzgerald Bks.

—A Woman of Courage. 2005. (Time for Kids Ser.). (ENG., Illus.). 48p. (J). (gr. 2-4). pap. 3.99 (978-0-06-057607-3(3)) HarperCollins Pubs.

Skelton, Renee & Time for Kids Editors. Time for Kids: A Woman of Courage. 2005. (Time for Kids Ser.). (ENG., Illus.). 48p. (J). 16.99 (978-0-06-057608-0(1)) HarperCollins Pubs.

Slavicek, Louise Chipley. Harriet Tubman & the Underground Railroad. 2006. (Lucent Library of Black History). (ENG., Illus.). 104p. (J). (gr. 3-7). lib. bdg. 34.80 (978-1-59018-927-6(2), Lucent Bks.) Cengage Gale.

Stearns, Dan. Harriet Tubman & the Underground Railroad. 2006. (In the Footsteps of American Heroes Ser.). (Illus.). 64p. (gr. 5-12). pap. 14.05 (978-0-8368-6433-5(6)); lib. bdg. 34.00 (978-0-8368-6428-1(X)) Stevens, Gareth Publishing LLLP. (Gareth Stevens Secondary Library).

Stein, R. Conrad. Harriet Tubman: On My Underground Railroad I Never Ran My Train off the Track. 2010. (Americans—the Spirit of a Nation Ser.). (Illus.). 128p. (J). lib. bdg. 33.27 (978-0-7660-3481-5(X)) Enslow Pubs., Inc.

Taylor, Charlotte & Feinstein, Stephen. Harriet Tubman: Hero of the Underground Railroad. 2015. (Exceptional African Americans Ser.). (ENG.). 24p. (J). (gr. 3-4). pap. 9.35 (978-0-7660-7126-1(X)) Enslow Pubs., Inc.

Taylor, Marian. Harriet Tubman. 2004. (Black Americans of Achievement Ser.). (Illus.). 112p. (gr. 6-12). 35.00 (978-0-7910-8166-2(4), Chelsea Hse.) Facts On File, Inc.

Turner, Glennette Tilley. An Apple for Harriet Tubman. Keeter, Susan, illus. 2016. (ENG.). 24p. (J). (gr. -1-3). pap. 6.99 (978-0-8075-0396-6(7)) Whitman, Albert & Co.

Waxman, Laura Hamilton. How Did Slaves Find a Route to Freedom? And Other Questions about the Underground Railroad. 2011. (Six Questions of American History Ser.). (ENG.). 48p. (gr. 4-6). pap. 56.72 (978-0-7613-7641-5(0)); pap. 9.95 (978-0-7613-7129-8(X)); lib. bdg. 30.60 (978-0-7613-5229-7(5)) Lerner Publishing Group.

Weatherford, Carole Boston. Moses: When Harriet Tubman Led Her People to Freedom. Nelson, Kadir, illus. 2006. (ENG.). 48p. (J). (gr. 1-3). 15.99 (978-0-7868-5175-1(9), Jump at the Sun) Hyperion Bks. for Children.

Weidt, Maryann N. Harriet Tubman. 2003. (History Maker Bios Ser.). (Illus.). 47p. (J). 26.60 (978-0-8225-4676-4(0), Lerner Pubns.) Lerner Publishing Group.

Wheeler, Jill C. Harriet Tubman. 2003. (Breaking Barriers Ser.). (Illus.). 64p. (gr. 3-8). 27.07 (978-1-57765-908-2(2), Abdo & Daughters) ABDO Publishing Co.

TUBMAN, HARRIET, 1820?-1913—FICTION

Grimes, Nikki. Chasing Freedom: The Life Journeys of Harriet Tubman & Susan B. Anthony, Inspired by Historical Facts. Wood, Michele, illus. 2015. (ENG.). 56p. (J). (gr. 2-5). 18.99 (978-0-439-79338-4(6), Orchard Bks.) Scholastic, Inc.

Hedstrom-Page, Deborah. From Slavery to Freedom with Harriet Tubman. Martinez, Sergio, illus. 2007. (My American Journey Ser.). 84p. (J). (gr. 3-9). 9.99 (978-0-8054-3268-8(X)) B&H Publishing Group.

Steinkraus, Kyla. Sundaes with Harriet Tubman. 2016. (Time Hop Sweets Shop Ser.). (ENG.). 32p. (gr. k-3). 25.65 (978-1-68191-371-1(2)) Rourke Educational Media.

TUGBOATS

Garland, Michael. Tugboat. Garland, Michael, illus. 2014. (ENG., Illus.). 32p. (J). (gr. -1-3). 16.95 (978-0-8234-2866-3(4)) Holiday Hse., Inc.

TUGBOATS—FICTION

Braun, Sebastien. Toot & Pop! Braun, Sebastien, illus. 2012. (Illus.). 32p. (J). (gr. -1-2). 12.99 (978-0-06-207750-9(3)) HarperCollins Pubs.

Depken, Kristen L. Scuffy the Tugboat. 2017. (Step into Reading Ser.). (ENG., Illus.). 32p. (J). (gr. -1-1). 3.99 (978-1-101-93929-1(X), Random Hse. Bks. for Young Readers) Random Hse. Children's Bks.

Donaldson, Leo. Toby's Big Surprise. 2009. (Illus.). 52p. pap. 20.49 (978-1-4389-4739-6(9)) AuthorHouse.

Edgar, Robert. Tom Tuff to the Rescue. Sharp, Todd, illus. 2013. 26p. pap. (978-0-9874832-0-1(X)) MoshPit Publishing.

Gramatky, Hardie. Little Toot. Gramatky, Hardie, illus. 2007. (ENG., Illus.). 104p. (J). (gr. -1-2). 17.99 (978-0-399-24713-2(0), G.P. Putnam's Sons Books for Young Readers) Penguin Young Readers Group.

Hamilton, Kersten. Blue Boat. Petrone, Valeria, illus. 2016. (ENG.). 32p. (J). (-k). 16.99 (978-0-451-47141-3(5), Viking Books for Young Readers) Penguin Young Readers Group.

Harris-Davies, Dafydd, et al. Caleb a Tyg. 2005. (WEL., Illus.). 24p. pap. (978-0-86381-854-7(4)) Gwasg Carreg Gwalch.

McMullan, Kate. I'm Mighty! McMullan, Jim, illus. 2003. (ENG.). 40p. (J). (gr. -1-3). 17.99 (978-0-06-009290-0(4)) HarperCollins Pubs.

Savage, Stephen. Little Tug. 2012. (ENG., Illus.). 32p. (J). (gr. -1-1). 14.99 (978-1-59643-648-0(4), 9781596436480) Roaring Brook Pr.

Watts, Kevin Bradley. Ben & the Mysterious Sound: Series: the Adventures of Tug Boat Ben. 2007. (Illus.). 32p. (J). (978-0-9782625-2-5(2)); pap. (978-0-9782625-1-8(4)) Alderney Publishing, Inc.

TUMBLING

Mullarkey, Lisa. Cheerleading Stunts & Tumbling. 2010. (Ready, Set, Cheer! Ser.). (Illus.). 48p. (J). pap. 8.95 (978-1-59845-200-6(2)) Enslow Pubs., Inc.

Mullarkey, Lisa & Library. Cheerleading Stunts & Tumbling. 2010. (Ready, Set, Cheer! Ser.). (Illus.). 48p. (J). lib. bdg. 25.27 (978-0-7660-3537-9(9)) Enslow Pubs., Inc.

TUNISIA

Brown, Roslind Varghese & Spilling, Michael. Tunisia. 2nd rev. ed. 2008. (Cultures of the World Ser.). (Illus.). 144p. (J). (gr. 6-18). lib. bdg. 42.79 (978-0-7614-3037-7(7), Benchmark Bks.) Marshall Cavendish Corp.

Carew-Miller, Anna. Tunisia. 2010. (Major Muslim Nations Ser.). 120p. (YA). (gr. 5-18). lib. bdg. 25.95 (978-1-4222-1393-3(5)) Mason Crest.

Grolier Educational Staff, contrib. by. Argentina. 2003. (Illus.). 32p. (J). 309.00 (978-0-7172-5788-1(6), Grolier) Scholastic Library Publishing.

Newsome, Joel. Hannibal. 2017. (J). **(978-1-5026-2869-5(4))** Cavendish Square Publishing.

Price, Sean. Hannibal of Carthage, 1 vol. 2013. (Hero Journals). (ENG., Illus.). 48p. (gr. 4-6). 33.32 (978-1-4109-5359-9(9)); pap. 9.95 (978-1-4109-5366-7(1)) Heinemann-Raintree. (NA-r).

TUNISIA—FICTION

Colfer, Eoin. Benny & Omar. 2003. 240p. (YA). (gr. 5-18). pap. 7.95 (978-0-86278-567-3(7)) O'Brien Pr., Ltd., The IRL. Dist: Independent Pubs. Group.

TUNNELS

see also Excavation; Subways

Borchelt, Kelly L. The Longest Tunnel. 2004. (Extreme Places Ser.). (ENG., Illus.). 48p. (J). 27.50 (978-0-7377-1882-9(X), Greenhaven Pr., Inc.) Cengage Gale.

Crowther, Robert. Deep down under Ground: A Pop-up Book of Amazing Facts & Feats. Crowther, Robert, illus. 2004. (Illus.). 18p. (J). (gr. 3-8). reprint ed. pap. 22.00 (978-0-7567-7179-9(X)) DIANE Publishing Co.

Donovan, Sandy. The Channel Tunnel. 2003. (Great Building Feats Ser.). (Illus.). 96p. (J). (gr. 5-9). 27.93 (978-0-8225-4692-4(2)) Lerner Publishing Group.

Fine, Jil. The Chunnel: The Building of a 200-Year-Old Dream. 2004. (High Interest Bks.). (ENG.). 48p. (J). (gr. 7-12). pap. 6.95 (978-0-516-25906-2(7), Children's Pr.) Scholastic Library Publishing.

Franchino, Vicky. How Did They Build That? Tunnel. 2009. (Community Connections: How Did They Build That? Ser.). (ENG.). 24p. (gr. 2-5). lib. bdg. 25.64 (978-1-60279-484-9(7), 200260) Cherry Lake Publishing.

Graham, Ian. Tremendous Tunnels. 2010. (Superstructures Ser.). 32p. (YA). (gr. 4-7). 28.50 (978-1-60753-134-0(8)) Amicus Publishing.

—Tremendous Tunnels. 2012. (What's in My Food Ser.). 32p. (gr. 1-4). lib. bdg. 27.10 (978-1-59920-420-8(7)) Black Rabbit Bks.

Hardyman, Robyn. Tunnels. 2016. (Engineering Eurekas Ser.). 00032p. (J). (gr. 3-4). pap. 10.00 (978-1-4994-3109-4(0), PowerKids Pr.) Rosen Publishing Group, Inc., The.

Latham, Donna. Bridges & Tunnels: Investigate Feats of Engineering with 25 Projects. Vaughn, Jen, illus. 2012. (Build It Yourself Ser.). (ENG.). 128p. (J). (gr. 3-7). 21.95 (978-1-936749-52-2(1)) Open City Bks.

Loh-Hagan, Virginia. Tunnels. 2017. (21st Century Junior Library: Extraordinary Engineering Ser.). (ENG., Illus.). 24p. (J). (gr. 2-5). lib. bdg. 27.07 (978-1-63472-167-7(5), 209240) Cherry Lake Publishing.

MacLeod, Elizabeth. Secrets Underground: North America's Buried Past. 2014. (ENG., Illus.). 96p. (YA). (gr. 5-12). 24.95 (978-1-55451-631-5(5), 9781554516315); pap. 14.95 (978-1-55451-630-8(7), 9781554516308) Annick Pr., Ltd. CAN. Dist: Publishers Group West (PGW).

Mattern, Joanne. Tunnels. 2015. (ENG.). 48p. (gr. 3-6). 35.64 (978-1-63430-420-7(9)) Rourke Educational Media.

Mitchell, Susan K. The Longest Tunnels. 2007. (Megastructures Ser.). (Illus.). 32p. (gr. 5-8). lib. bdg. 26.00 (978-0-8368-8365-7(9)) Stevens, Gareth Publishing LLLP.

Pettiford, Rebecca. Tunnels. 2015. (Illus.). 24p. (J). lib. bdg. 25.65 (978-1-62031-212-4(3)) Jump! Inc.

Reilly, Kevin. Zoom in on Tunnels. 2017. (Zoom in on Engineering Ser.). 24p. (J). (gr. 2-2). lib. bdg. 22.60 **(978-0-7660-8712-5(3))** Enslow Pubs., Inc.

Sikkens, Crystal. A Tunnel Runs Through. 2017. 24p. (J). **(978-0-7787-2903-7(6))** Crabtree Publishing Co.

Stefoff, Rebecca. Building Tunnels. 2015. (Great Engineering Ser.). (ENG.). 32p. (J). (gr. 3-4). pap. 10.58 (978-1-5026-0600-6(3)) Cavendish Square Publishing.

Tan, Richard. The Bridges & Tunnels of New York City. 2011. (My Community Ser.). (ENG., Illus.). 12p. (gr. 2-2). pap. 6.95 (978-1-4488-5717-3(1), Rosen Classroom) Rosen Publishing Group, Inc., The.

Thomas, Mark. The Seikan Railroad Tunnel: World's Longest Tunnel. 2009. (Record-Breaking Structures Ser.). 24p. (gr. 1-2). 42.50 (978-1-60852-458-7(2), PowerKids Pr.) Rosen Publishing Group, Inc., The.

—El Tunel Ferroviario Seikan: El Tunel Mas Largo Del Mundo. 2004. (Estructuras extraordinarias (Record-Breaking Structures) Ser.). (SPA & ENG., Illus.). 24p. (J). (gr. 3-6). lib. bdg. 22.60 (978-0-8239-6867-1(7), Editorial Buenas Letras) Rosen Publishing Group, Inc., The.

—El túnel ferroviario Seikan: El túnel más largo del mundo (the Seikan Railroad Tunnel: World's Longest Tunnel) 2009. (Estructuras extraordinarias (Record-Breaking Structures) Ser.). (SPA.). 24p. (gr. 1-2). 42.50 (978-1-61512-312-4(1), Editorial Buenas Letras) Rosen Publishing Group, Inc., The.

Tunnels: Early Level Satellite Individual Title Six-Packs. (Sails Literacy Ser.). 16p. (gr. 1-2). 27.00 (978-0-7578-2942-0(2)) Rigby Education.

Wolny, Philip. High Risk Construction Work: Life Building Skyscrapers, Bridges, & Tunnels. 2008. (Extreme Careers Ser.). (Illus.). 64p. (YA). (gr. 5-9). lib. bdg. 31.95 (978-1-4042-1789-8(4)) Rosen Publishing Group, Inc., The.

—High-Risk Construction Work: Life Building Skyscrapers, Bridges, & Tunnels. 2009. (Extreme Careers Ser.). 64p. (gr. 5-5). 58.50 (978-1-61512-397-1(0), Rosen Reference) Rosen Publishing Group, Inc., The.

TURKEY

Blomquist, Christopher. A Primary Source Guide to Turkey. (Countries of the World). 24p. 2009. (gr. 2-3). 42.50 (978-1-61512-048-2(3)) 2005. (Illus.). (J). (gr. -1-3). lib. bdg. 22.60 (978-1-4042-2759-0(8)) Rosen Publishing Group, Inc., The. (PowerKids Pr.).

Canino, Kate. Turkey Hunting. 2011. (Hunting: Pursuing Wild Game! Ser.). 64p. (YA). (ENG.). pap. 12.95 (978-1-4488-2274-4(2), Rosen Reference); (Illus.). (gr. 5-9). lib. bdg. 31.95 (978-1-4488-1244-8(5)) Rosen Publishing Group, Inc., The.

Cornell, Kari & Turkoglu, Nurcay. Cooking the Turkish Way. 2nd rev. ed. 2004. (Easy Menu Ethnic Cookbooks 2nd Edition Ser.). (ENG., Illus.). 72p. (gr. 5-12). 25.26 (978-0-8225-4123-3(8), Carolrhoda Bks.) Lerner Publishing Group.

Donaldson, Madeline. Turkey. 2011. (Country Explorers Ser.). 48p. pap. 51.02 (978-0-7613-7628-6(3)); (ENG.). (gr. 2-4). 29.27 (978-0-7613-6409-2(9)); (ENG.). (gr. 2-4). pap. 9.95 (978-0-7613-7085-7(4)) Lerner Publishing Group.

Dyan, Penelope. A Step in Time — A Kid's Guide to Ephesus, Turkey. Weigand, John D., photos by. 2011. (Illus.). 40p. pap. 12.95 (978-1-935630-57-9(1)) Bellissima Publishing, LLC.

—Turkish Delight — A Kid's Guide to Istanbul, Turkey. Weigand, John D., photos by. 2011. (Illus.). 44p. pap. 12.95 (978-1-935630-54-8(7)) Bellissima Publishing, LLC.

Franchino, Vicky. It's Cool to Learn about Countries: Turkey. 2012. (Explorer Library: Social Studies Explorer Ser.). (ENG.). 48p. (gr. 4-8). 31.36 (978-1-61080-442-4(2), 202052); pap. 15.64 (978-1-61080-616-9(6), 202226) Cherry Lake Publishing.

Ganeri, Anita. Focus on Turkey. 2007. (World in Focus Ser.). 64p. (gr. 5-12). pap. 14.05 (978-0-8368-6760-2(2)); (Illus.).

lib. bdg. 34.00 *(978-0-8368-6753-4(X))* Stevens, Gareth Publishing LLLP. (Gareth Stevens Secondary Library).
Harmon, Daniel E. Turkey. rev. ed. 2010. (Major Muslim Nations Ser.). (Illus.). 119p. (J). (gr. 4-8). 25.95 *(978-1-4222-1399-5(4))* Mason Crest.
Jackson, Elaine. Discover Turkey. 2012. (Discover Countries Ser.). (Illus.). 32p. (YA). (gr. 4-7). lib. bdg. 26.50 *(978-1-4488-5272-7(2))* Rosen Publishing Group, Inc., The.
Klepeis, Alicia. Understanding Turkey Today. 2014. (Illus.). 63p. (J). (gr. 3-6). 33.95 *(978-1-61228-649-5(6))* Mitchell Lane Pubs., Inc.
McNeil, Niki, et al. HOCPP 1117 Turkey Time. 2006. spiral bd. 14.00 *(978-1-60308-117-7(8))* In the Hands of a Child.
Pavlovic, Zoran. Turkey. 2004. (Modern World Nations Ser.). (Illus.). 120p. (gr. 6-12). 35.00 *(978-0-7910-7916-4(3),* Chelsea Hse.) Facts On File, Inc.
Stefoff, Rebecca. Asian Empires. 2004. (Illus.). 48p. (J). 31.36 *(978-0-7614-1643-2(9),* Benchmark Bks.) Marshall Cavendish Corp.
Zocchi, Judy. In Turkey. Brodie, Neale, illus. 2005. (Global Adventures II Ser.). 32p. (J). per. 10.95 *(978-1-59646-153-6(5))* Dingles & Co.
—In Turkey/en Turquia. Brodie, Neale, illus. 2005. (Global Adventures II Ser.).Tr. of En Turquia. (ENG & SPA.). 32p. (J). per. 10.95 *(978-1-59646-155-0(1))* Dingles & Co.

TURKEY—BIOGRAPHY

Lashnits, Tom. Recep Tayyip Erdogan: Prime Minister ofTurkey. Schlesinger, Arthur M., Jr., ed. 2005. (Major World Leaders Ser.). (Illus.). 144p. (gr. 6-12). 30.00 *(978-0-7910-8263-8(6),* Chelsea Hse.) Facts On File, Inc.
Samanci, Özge. Dare to Disappoint: Growing up in Turkey. 2015. (ENG., Illus.). 200p. (YA). (gr. 9). pap. 16.99 *(978-0-374-31698-3(8),* 9780374316983, Farrar, Straus & Giroux (BYR)) Farrar, Straus & Giroux.
Stefoff, Rebecca. Redbeard. 2015. (J). lib. bdg. *(978-1-62713-533-7(2));* (ENG.). 48p. (gr. 3-3). 31.36 *(978-1-5026-0199-5(0))* Cavendish Square Publishing.
Weintraub, Aileen. The Barbarossa Brothers: 16th-Century Pirates of the Barbary Coast. 2009. (Library of Pirates Ser.). 24p. (gr. 3-3). 42.50 *(978-1-60853-814-0(1),* PowerKids Pr.) Rosen Publishing Group, Inc., The.

TURKEY—FICTION

Alexander, Lloyd. The Xanadu Adventure. 2007. (Vesper Holly Ser.). (ENG.). 160p. (J). (gr. 5-18). 5.99 *(978-0-14-240786-8(0),* Puffin Books) Penguin Young Readers Group.
Anderson, Derek, et al. Over the River: A Turkey's Tale. 2005. (ENG., Illus.). 40p. (J). (gr. -1-3). 15.99 *(978-0-689-87635-6(1),* Simon & Schuster Bks. For Young Readers) Simon & Schuster Bks. For Young Readers.
Arnosky, Jim. I'm a Turkey! 2009. (Illus.). (J). *(978-0-545-22631-8(7),* Scholastic Pr.) Scholastic, Inc.
Cameron, Kristy. The Adventures of Herb the Wild Turkey - Herb Goes Camping. Shickle, Ian, illus. 2012. 38p. pap. *(978-0-9859790-0-3(3))* LP Publishing.
Duder, Tessa. Carpet of Dreams. Wilson, Mark, illus. 2008. 32p. pap. *(978-0-207-19991-2(4))* HarperCollins Pubs. Australia.
Durmush, F. Ayshe, an Anatolian Tale. 2007. (ENG.). 84p. per. *(978-1-84747-171-0(4))* Chipmunkapublishing.
Durston, George. Boy Scouts' Victory. 2005. pap. 26.95 *(978-1-885529-58-9(9))* Stevens Publishing.
Fenn, George. Yussuf the Guide or the Mountain Bandits: Being the Strange Story of the Travels in Asia Minor of Burne the Lawyer, Preston the Professor, & Lawren. Schönberg, John, illus. 2007. 424p. 26.95 *(978-0-9776786-6-2(0))* Salem Ridge Press LLC.
Fenn, George Manville. Yussuf the Guide or the Mountain Bandits: Being the Strange Story of the Travels in Asia Minor of Burne the Lawyer, Preston the Professor, & Lawrenc. Schönberg, John, illus. 2008. 432p. pap. 16.95 *(978-1-934671-20-7(7))* Salem Ridge Press LLC.
Letria, Andre, illus. A Donkey Reads, 1 vol. 2011. (ENG.). 32p. (J). (gr. k-3). 16.95 *(978-1-59572-255-3(6));* pap. 6.95 *(978-1-59572-256-0(4))* Star Bright Bks., Inc.
Mein eigenes Auto. 2005. (GER.). 4.95 net. *(978-0-929724-89-8(5))* Command Performance Language Institute.
Petrucha, Stefan & Kinney, Sarah. City under the Basement. Murase, Sho, illus. 2009. (Nancy Drew Graphic Novels: Girl Detective Ser.: 18). (ENG.). 96p. (J). (gr. 3-7). pap. 7.95 *(978-1-59707-154-3(4),* 9781597071543); 18th ed. 12.95 *(978-1-59707-155-0(2),* 9781597071550) Papercutz.
—Night of the Living Chatchke. 2009. (Nancy Drew Graphic Novels: Girl Detective Ser.). (ENG., Illus.). 96p. (J). (gr. 3-7). pap. 7.95 *(978-1-59707-143-7(9),* 9781597071437) Papercutz.
—Night of the Living Chatchke. Murase, Sho, illus. 17th ed. 2009. (Nancy Drew Graphic Novels: Girl Detective Ser.: 17). (ENG.). 96p. (J). (gr. 3-7). 12.95 *(978-1-59707-144-4(7),* 9781597071444) Papercutz.
Priddy, Roger. The Great Turkey Race. 2014. (Shaped Board Bks.). (ENG., Illus.). 6p. (J). (gr. -1-k). bds. 6.99 *(978-0-312-51719-9(X),* 9780312517199, Priddy Bks.) St. Martin's Pr.
Rains, Deborah Jane. Cuddles & Snuggles. 2011. 24p. pap. 24.95 *(978-1-4489-3917-6(8))* America Star Bks.
Renn, Diana. Blue Voyage. 2015. (ENG.). 464p. (YA). (gr. 7). 18.99 *(978-0-670-01559-7(8),* Viking Books for Young Readers) Penguin Young Readers Group.
Sargent, Dave & Sargent, David, Jr. Tom Turkey: Don't Bully, 19, 20. Lenoir, Jane, illus. 2003. (Feather Tales Ser.: 20). 42p. (J). pap. 6.95 *(978-1-56763-758-8(2))* Ozark Publishing.
Shady, Justin & Shady, Bethany. I Beg Your Pardon. 2009. 32p. (J). 12.99 *(978-1-60706-136-6(8))* Image Comics.
Thompson, Emma. The Christmas Tale of Peter Rabbit. Taylor, Eleanor, illus. 2013. (Peter Rabbit Ser.). (ENG.). 72p. (J). (gr. -1-2). 20.00 *(978-0-7232-7694-4(3),* Warne) Penguin Young Readers Group.
Whelan, Gloria. Parade of Shadows. 2007. 304p. (J). (gr. 5-18). lib. bdg. 16.89 *(978-0-06-089029-2(0))* HarperCollins Pubs.
Winter, Barbara. Trapped in Gallipoli. 2007. (Illus.). 48p. (YA). lib. bdg. 15.00 *(978-1-4242-1643-7(5))* Dingles & Co.

TURKEY—HISTORY

Bower, Gary. A Patch on the Peak of Ararat. Chotiner, Barbara, illus. 2017. (Faith That God Built Book Ser.). (ENG.). 32p. (J). 14.99 *(978-1-4964-1744-2(5),* Tyndale Kids) Tyndale Hse. Pubs.
Cline, Bev. Turkey. 2014. (J). *(978-1-4896-3070-4(8))* Weigl Pubs., Inc.
Freedman, Jeri. The Armenian Genocide. 2009. (Genocide in Modern Times Ser.). 64p. (gr. 6-6). 58.50 *(978-1-61512-676-7(7))* Rosen Publishing Group, Inc., The.
Galat, Joan Marie. Cultural Traditions in Turkey. 2017. 32p. (J). ***(978-0-7787-8100-4(3))*** Crabtree Publishing Co.
Greenwood, Mark. The Donkey of Gallipoli: A True Story of Courage in World War I. Lessac, Frané, illus. 2008. (ENG.). 32p. (J). (gr. 1-4). 16.99 *(978-0-7636-3913-6(3))* Candlewick Pr.
Harmon, Daniel E. Turkey, Vol. 13. 2015. (Major Nations of the Modern Middle East Ser.). (Illus.). 120p. (J). (gr. 7). lib. bdg. 25.95 *(978-1-4222-3452-5(5))* Mason Crest.
Hawker, Frances & Alicavusoglu, Leyla. Islam in Turkey. Campbell, Bruce, photos by. 2009. (ENG., Illus.). 32p. (J). (gr. 3-6). *(978-0-7787-5009-3(4))* Crabtree Publishing Co.
Jeffrey, Gary. Gallipoli & the Southern Theaters. 2013. (ENG., Illus.). 48p. (J). pap. *(978-0-7787-0917-6(5))* Crabtree Publishing Co.
Kalman, Bobbie & Jeffrey, Gary. Gallipoli & the Southern Theaters. 2013. (ENG.). 48p. (J). *(978-0-7787-0911-4(6))* Crabtree Publishing Co.
Kneib, Martha. Turkey: A Primary Source Cultural Guide. 2009. (Primary Sources of World Cultures Ser.). 128p. (gr. 4-5). 79.90 *(978-1-60851-931-6(7))* Rosen Publishing Group, Inc., The.
Kohler, Christine. Turkey in the News: Past, Present, & Future. 2006. (Middle East Nations in the News Ser.). (Illus.). 128p. (J). (gr. 5-9). lib. bdg. 34.60 *(978-1-59845-024-8(7),* MyReportLinks.com Bks.) Enslow Pubs., Inc.
LaRoche, Amelia. We Visit Turkey. 2011. (Your Land & My Land Ser.). (Illus.). 64p. (J). (gr. 4-7). lib. bdg. 33.95 *(978-1-58415-956-8(1))* Mitchell Lane Pubs., Inc.
Marsico, Katie. Turkey. 2011. (21st Century Junior Library: Farm Animals Ser.). (ENG.). 24p. (gr. 2-4). lib. bdg. 25.64 *(978-1-60279-976-9(8),* 200942) Cherry Lake Publishing.
Murray, Julie. Turkey, 1 vol. 2014. (Explore the Countries Set 2 Ser.). (ENG.). 40p. (gr. 7-11). lib. bdg. 29.93 *(978-1-62403-348-3(2),* Big Buddy Bks.) ABDO Publishing Co.
Orr, Tamra B. Turkey. 2014. (ENG.). 144p. (J). lib. bdg. 40.00 *(978-0-531-20792-5(7))* Scholastic Library Publishing.
Owings, Lisa. Turkey. 2011. (Exploring Countries Ser.). (ENG., Illus.). 32p. (J). (gr. 3-7). lib. bdg. 26.95 *(978-1-60014-625-1(2),* Blastoff! Readers) Bellwether Media.
Robbins, Gerald. The Ottoman & Qajar Empires in the Age of Reform. 2009. (Making of the Middle East Ser.). (Illus.). 80p. (YA). (gr. 7-18). lib. bdg. 22.95 *(978-1-4222-0167-1(8))* Mason Crest.
Robinson, Joanna J. Turkey. 2015. (One World, Many Countries Ser.). (ENG.). 32p. (J). (gr. 1-4). 28.50 *(978-1-63407-058-4(5),* 208894) Child's World, Inc., The.
Steele, Philip. Turkey. 2015. (Emerging Nations Ser.). (ENG., Illus.). 48p. (J). (gr. 4-9). 37.10 *(978-1-59920-991-3(8))* Black Rabbit Bks.
World Book, Inc Staff, contrib. by. Carved by Time. 2017. (J). ***(978-0-7166-3365-5(5))*** World Bk.-Childcraft International.
World Book, Inc Staff, contrib. by. The Mysteries of the Trojan War. 2014. (J). *(978-0-7166-2668-8(3))* World Bk., Inc.
Zocchi, Judy. In Turkey. Brodie, Neale, illus. 2005. (Global Adventures I Ser.). 32p. (J). pap. 10.95 *(978-1-59646-152-9(7));* lib. bdg. 21.65 *(978-1-59646-031-7(8))* Dingles & Co.
—In Turkey/en Turquia. Brodie, Neale, illus. 2005. (Global Adventures I Ser.).Tr. of En Turquia. (ENG & SPA.). 32p. (J). pap. 10.95 *(978-1-59646-154-3(3));* lib. bdg. 21.65 *(978-1-59646-032-4(6))* Dingles & Co.

TURKEYS

Carr, Aaron. Turkey. 2014. (Illus.). 24p. (J). *(978-1-62127-233-5(8))* Weigl Pubs., Inc.
Carter, Denzel T. All about Turkeys. 2015. (Rosen REAL Readers: STEM & STEAM Collection). (ENG.). 8p. pap. 5.46 *(978-1-4994-9692-5(3),* Rosen Classroom) Rosen Publishing Group, Inc., The.
Chandler, Matt, et al. Into the Great Outdoors. 2012. (Into the Great Outdoors Ser.). (ENG.). 32p. (gr. 3-4). 167.94 *(978-1-4296-9144-4(1),* Edge Bks.) Capstone Press of Coughlan Cos.
Coffelt, Soraya Diase. It's Not about You Mrs. Turkey: A Love Letter about the True Meaning of Thanksgiving. 2015. (Love Letters Book Ser.). (ENG., Illus.). 32p. (J). pap. 8.99 *(978-1-63047-636-6(6))* Morgan James Publishing.
Dicker, Katie. Turkeys. 2014. (Farm Animals Ser.). (Illus.). 24p. (gr. 2-5). 28.50 *(978-1-62588-025-3(1))* Black Rabbit Bks.
Dieker, Wendy. Turkeys. 2012. (Illus.). 24p. (J). lib. bdg. 25.65 *(978-1-62031-007-6(4))* Jump! Inc.
Endres, Hollie. Turkeys. 2007. (Farm Animals Ser.). (ENG., Illus.). 24p. (J). (gr. k-3). lib. bdg. 25.95 *(978-1-60014-086-0(6))* Bellwether Media.
Graubart, Norman D. How to Track a Turkey, 1 vol. 2015. (ENG., Illus.). 24p. (J). lib. bdg. 23.60 *(978-1-4777-5414-6(8),* Windmill Bks.) Rosen Publishing Group, Inc., The.
Howard, Melanie A., et al. Into the Great Outdoors. 2012. (Into the Great Outdoors Ser.). (ENG.). 32p. (gr. 3-4). pap. 39.75 *(978-1-4296-9271-7(5),* Edge Bks.) Capstone Press of Coughlan Cos.
Magby, Meryl. Wild Turkeys. 2013. (American Animals Ser.). 24p. (J). (gr. k-5). 22.60 *(978-1-4777-0787-6(5));* pap. 49.50 *(978-1-4777-0947-4(9));* pap. 8.25 *(978-1-4777-0946-7(0))* Rosen Publishing Group, Inc., The. (PowerKids Pr.).
Merrick, Patrick. Thanksgiving Turkeys. 2015. (Our Holiday Symbols Ser.). (ENG.). 24p. (J). (gr. 1-4). 25.64 *(978-1-63143-747-2(X),* 208556) Child's World, Inc., The.
Murray, Julie. Turkeys, 1 vol. 2005. (Animal Kingdom Set Ii Ser.). (ENG., Illus.). 24p. (gr. k-4). 25.65 *(978-1-59197-337-9(6),* Buddy Bks.) ABDO Publishing Co.
Schuetz, Kristin. Wild Turkeys. 2014. (Backyard Wildlife Ser.). (ENG.). 24p. (J). (gr. k-3). lib. bdg. 25.95 *(978-1-60014-972-6(3),* Blastoff! Readers) Bellwether Media.
Stiefel, Chana. Turkeys on the Family Farm. 2013. (Animals on the Family Farm Ser.). 24p. (J). (gr. k-3). pap. 7.95 *(978-1-4644-0357-6(0),* Enslow Elementary); lib. bdg. 22.60 *(978-0-7660-4207-0(3))* Enslow Pubs., Inc.
Stockland, Patricia M. In the Turkey Pen, 1 vol. Ouren, Todd, illus. 2009. (Barnyard Buddies Set 2 Ser.). (ENG.). 24p. (gr. -1-2). 27.07 *(978-1-60270-646-0(8),* Looking Glass Library-Nonfiction) Magic Wagon.

TURKEYS—FICTION

Allen, Christina. A Micro-Chip on my Shoulder: A True Story of a Little Poult. 2010. 28p. pap. 13.99 *(978-1-4490-6681-9(X))* AuthorHouse.
Auch, Mary Jane. Beauty & the Beaks: A Turkey's Cautionary Tale. Auch, Herm & Auch, Mary Jane, illus. 2007. (ENG.). 32p. (J). (gr. -1-3). 17.95 *(978-0-8234-1990-6(8))* Holiday Hse., Inc.
Balian, Lorna. Sometimes It's Turkey, Sometimes It's Feathers, 1 vol. 2003. (ENG., Illus.). 32p. (J). 14.95 *(978-1-932065-33-6(4));* pap. 5.95 *(978-1-932065-41-1(5))* Star Bright Bks., Inc.
Bateman, Teresa. A Plump & Perky Turkey, 0 vols. Shelly, Jeff, illus. 2013. (ENG.). 32p. (J). (gr. k-4). pap. 9.99 *(978-0-7614-5188-4(9),* 9780761451884, Amazon Children's Publishing) Amazon Publishing.
Berenstain, Mike, et al. The Berenstain Bears Give Thanks, 1 vol. Berenstain, Stan, illus. 2009. (Berenstain Bears/Living Lights Ser.). (ENG.). 32p. (J). (gr. -1-2). pap. 3.99 *(978-0-310-71251-0(3))* Zonderkidz.
Bishop, Rhonda. Felix's Fabulous Feathers, 1 vol. Roberts, Gaylia, illus. 2009. 23p. pap. 24.95 *(978-1-60836-890-7(4))* America Star Bks.
Cazet, Denys. Bob & Tom. Cazet, Denys, illus. 2017. (ENG., Illus.). 40p. (J). (gr. -1-3). 17.99 ***(978-1-4814-6140-5(0),*** Atheneum/Richard Jackson Bks.) Simon & Schuster Children's Publishing.
Colandro, Lucille. There Was an Old Lady Who Swallowed a Turkey! Lee, Jared D., illus. 2016. (There Was an Old Lad Ser.). (ENG.). 32p. (J). (gr. -1-1). 6.99 *(978-0-545-93190-8(8),* Cartwheel Bks.) Scholastic, Inc.
Cole, Brock. The Money We'll Save. Cole, Brock, illus. 2011. (ENG., Illus.). 40p. (J). (gr. -1-3). 16.99 *(978-0-374-35011-6(6),* 9780374350116, Farrar, Straus & Giroux (BYR)) Farrar, Straus & Giroux.
Crissey, Brian L. The Loneliest Christmas Tree. Crissey, Noah, illus. 2004. (J). *(978-1-930724-13-6(6));* *(978-1-930724-12-9(8))* Granite Publishing, LLC.
Cumming, Wendy. How to Soar Like an Eagle When You Are Standing with the Turkeys. 2012. 32p. pap. 21.99 *(978-1-4797-2934-0(5))* Xlibris Corp.
Falwell, Cathryn. Gobble, Gobble, 1 vol. Falwell, Cathryn, illus. 2011. (ENG., Illus.). 32p. (J). 16.95 *(978-1-58469-148-8(4));* pap. 8.95 *(978-1-58469-149-5(2))* Dawn Pubns.
Goodspeed, Jjdy. Perky Turkey's 4th of July Adventure. 2008. (Illus.). 24p. (J). per. *(978-0-9801376-1-3(6))* Dragonfly Publishing, Inc.
Goodspeed, Judy. Perky Turkey Finds a Friend. (Illus.). 24p. (J). 2007. per. 11.99 *(978-0-9797574-2-6(8))* 2006. lib. bdg. 24.95 *(978-0-9778651-2-3(6))* Dragonfly Publishing, Inc.
—Perky Turkey's 4th of July Adventure. 2008. (Illus.). 24p. (J). lib. bdg. *(978-0-9801376-0-6(8))* Dragonfly Publishing, Inc.
—Perky Turkey's Perfect Plan. (Illus.). 22p. (J). 2007. per. 11.99 *(978-0-9797574-3-3(6))* 2006. lib. bdg. 24.95 *(978-0-9778651-1-6(8))* Dragonfly Publishing, Inc.
—Perky Turkey's Perfect Plan. Taylor, Chet, illus. 2005. 22p. (J). 18.99 *(978-0-9765786-0-4(3))* Dragonfly Publishing, Inc.
Griechen, Jane M. Theodore B a Turkey. 2008. 68p. pap. 41.99 *(978-1-4363-2703-9(2))* Xlibris Corp.
Halverson, Barbara. Farm Friends Forever: Everyone Needs Friends. 2013. (ENG.). 27p. (J). pap. 13.95 *(978-1-4787-1380-7(1))* Outskirts Pr., Inc.
Harris, Nikki. Adventures in Friendship for Benji Butterfly & Tom Turkey. 2013. 24p. pap. 24.95 *(978-1-63004-741-2(4))* America Star Bks.
Honeycutt, Scarlet. Turkeys in Disguise. Aarvig, Cindy, illus. 2007. 48p. per. 24.95 *(978-1-4137-4035-6(9))* America Star Bks.
Hubble, Miles & Bryant, Justin. Bob & the Fowl War: Book One in the Poultry Series. 2008. 140p. pap. 11.95 *(978-1-4401-0857-0(9))* iUniverse, Inc.
Isbell, Tessa J. Animal Adventures: Goosey & Beauty Take a Mystery Magic Carpet Ride to Jamaica. 2013. 48p. pap. 21.99 *(978-1-4669-7217-9(3))* Trafford Publishing.
Johnston, Tony. 10 Fat Turkeys. Deas, Rich, illus. 2009. (ENG.). 28p. (J). (gr. -1-k). bds. 6.99 *(978-0-545-16469-6(9),* Cartwheel Bks.) Scholastic, Inc.
—10 Fat Turkeys. Deas, Richard F., illus. 2004. (ENG.). 32p. (J). (gr. -1-k). pap. 3.99 *(978-0-439-45948-8(6),* Cartwheel Bks.) Scholastic, Inc.
Kane, Bob. Sandwich Day & Our Family Album. Nguyen, Dustin, illus. 2015. (Batman: Li'l Gotham Ser.). (ENG.). 32p. (gr. 2-3). lib. bdg. 22.60 *(978-1-4342-9737-2(3))* Stone Arch Bks.
Karr, Kathleen. The Great Turkey Walk. 2004. 199p. (gr. 4-7). 18.00 *(978-0-7569-4124-6(5))* Perfection Learning Corp.
Kenah, Katharine. The Very Stuffed Turkey. Talib, Binny, illus. 2015. (ENG.). 32p. (J). (gr. -1-k). pap. 6.99 *(978-0-545-76109-3(3),* Cartwheel Bks.) Scholastic, Inc.
King, Lisa. Lurkey the Proud Turkey. 2013. 24p. pap. 24.95 *(978-1-63004-113-7(0))* America Star Bks.
Langlois, Annie. L' Evasion d'Alfred le Dindon. Beaulieu, Jimmey, illus. 2004. (Roman Jeunesse Ser.). (FRE.). 96p. (J). (gr. 4-7). pap. *(978-2-89021-687-7(X))* Diffusion du livre Mirabel (DLM).
—Mia, Matt & the Turkey Chase, 1 vol. Cummins, Sarah, tr. from FRE. Beaulieu, Jimmy, illus. 2008. (Formac First Novels Ser.). (ENG.). 64p. (J). (gr. 2-5). 5.95 *(978-0-88780-763-3(1),* 9780887807633) Formac Publishing Co., Ltd. CAN. Dist: Casemate Pubs. & Bk. Distributors, LLC.
Langlois, Suzanne. Mia, Matt & the Turkey Chase. Cummins, Sarah, tr. from FRE. Beaulieu, Jimmy, illus. 2008. (Formac First Novels Ser.). (ENG.). 64p. (J). (gr. 2-5). 14.95 *(978-0-88780-765-7(8),* 9780887807657) Formac Publishing Co., Ltd. CAN. Dist: Casemate Pubs. & Bk. Distributors, LLC.
Lonsdale, Cathy. Bill the Brush Turkey. 2008. 24p. 13.95 *(978-1-4092-0414-5(6))* Lulu Pr., Inc.
Maccarone, Grace. Turkey Day. Manders, John, illus. 2010. (Scholastic Reader Level 1 Ser.). (ENG.). 32p. (J). (gr. -1-3). pap. 3.99 *(978-0-545-12001-2(2),* Cartwheel Bks.) Scholastic, Inc.
Masterson, Hoss. Wild Receiver. Alves, Josh, illus. 2017. (Animal All-Stars Ser.). (ENG.). 56p. (gr. 1-3). lib. bdg. 25.32 *(978-1-4965-4307-3(6))* Stone Arch Bks.
Mayr, Diane. Run, Turkey, Run! Rader, Laura, illus. 2009. (ENG.). 32p. (J). (gr. -1-2). pap. 7.99 *(978-0-8027-8481-0(X),* 9780802784810, Bloomsbury USA Childrens) Bloomsbury Publishing USA.
McDoogle, Farrah. OLIVIA Talks Turkey. Osterhold, Jared, illus. 2011. (Olivia TV Tie-In Ser.). (ENG.). 16p. (J). (gr. -1-1). pap. 5.99 *(978-1-4424-3061-7(3),* Simon Spotlight) Simon Spotlight.
Metzger, Steve. The Great Turkey Race. Paillot, Jim, illus. 2006. (J). *(978-0-439-85930-1(1))* Scholastic, Inc.
—The Turkey Train. Paillot, Jim, illus. 2013. (ENG.). 32p. (J). (gr. -1-k). 6.99 *(978-0-545-49229-4(7),* Cartwheel Bks.) Scholastic, Inc.
Neimark, Jill & Weiner, Marcella Bakur. Toodles & Teeny: A Story about Friendship. 2012. (J). pap. 9.95 *(978-1-4338-1199-9(5));* (Illus.). 14.95 *(978-1-4338-1198-2(7))* American Psychological Assn. (Magination Pr.).
Nielsen, Gwyn English. Torey the Turkey Goes Skiing. 2003. (Illus.). 24p. (Orig.). (gr. -1-4). pap. 5.99 *(978-0-9660726-0-0(X))* C.G.S. Pr.
Park, Barbara. Turkeys We Have Loved & Eaten (And Other Thankful Stuff) Brunkus, Denise, illus. 2014. (Junie B. Jones Ser.). (ENG.). 144p. (J). (gr. 1-4). 4.99 *(978-0-375-87115-3(2),* Random Hse. Bks. for Young Readers) Random Hse. Children's Bks.
Parnell, Declan. Tina & the Turkeys, 01 vols., 1. 2016. (Rosen REAL Readers: STEM & STEAM Collection). (ENG.). 8p. (J). pap. 5.46 *(978-1-5081-1458-1(7),* Rosen Classroom) Rosen Publishing Group, Inc., The.
Phillips, Tikera M. Thanksgiving Turkey. 2012. 16p. pap. 12.70 *(978-1-4669-4053-6(0))* Trafford Publishing.
Roesser, Griffin. Who Ate the Turkey? 2006. (Neighborhood Readers Ser.). (ENG.). 12p. (gr. -1-3). pap. 5.90 *(978-1-4042-6457-1(4),* Rosen Classroom) Rosen Publishing Group, Inc., The.
Ross, Patrick. Runt River Rat's Wild Ride, 1 vol. Burcham, David, illus. 2010. 24p. 24.95 *(978-1-4512-0067-6(6))* PublishAmerica, Inc.
Roy, Ronald. Turkey Trouble on the National Mall. Bush, Timothy, illus. 2012. (Capital Mysteries Ser.: 14). (ENG.). 96p. (J). (gr. 1-4). 4.99 *(978-0-307-93220-4(6),* Random Hse. Bks. for Young Readers) Random Hse. Children's Bks.
—Turkey Trouble on the National Mall. 2012. (Capital Mysteries Ser.: 14). lib. bdg. 14.75 *(978-0-606-26809-7(X),* Turtleback) Turtleback Bks.
Shannon, George. Turkey Tot. Mann, Jennifer K., illus. (ENG.). 32p. (J). (gr. -1-1). 2014. 6.99 *(978-0-8234-3175-5(4))* 2013. 16.95 *(978-0-8234-2379-8(4))* Holiday Hse., Inc.
Sharmat, Marjorie Weinman & Sharmat, Mitchell. Nate the Great Talks Turkey. Wheeler, Jody, illus. 2007. (Nate the Great Ser.: No. 25). (ENG.). 96p. (J). (gr. 1-4). per. 5.99 *(978-0-440-42126-9(8),* Yearling) Random Hse. Children's Bks.
—Nate the Great Talks Turkey: With Help from Olivia Sharp. Wheeler, Jody, illus. 2007. (Nate the Great Ser.). (gr. -1-3). lib. bdg. 16.00 *(978-1-4177-9248-1(5),* Turtleback) Turtleback Bks.
Silvano, Wendi. Turkey Trouble, 0 vols. 2009. (ENG., Illus.). 32p. (J). (gr. -1-2). 15.99 *(978-0-7614-5529-5(9),* 9780761455295, Two Lions) Amazon Publishing.
Silvano, Wendi J. Turkey Claus, 0 vols. Harper, Lee, illus. 2012. (ENG.). 40p. (J). (gr. -1-3). 16.99 *(978-0-7614-6239-2(2),* 9780761462392, Two Lions) Amazon Publishing.
Sommerset, Mark. Baa Baa Smart Sheep. Sommerset, Rowan, illus. 2016. (ENG.). 32p. (J). (gr. k-3). 14.00 *(978-0-7636-8066-4(4))* Candlewick Pr.
—I Love Lemonade. Sommerset, Rowan, illus. 2016. (ENG.). 32p. (J). (gr. k-3). 14.00 *(978-0-7636-8067-1(2))* Candlewick Pr.
Steinberg, Jessica. Not This Turkey! Pike, Amanda, illus. 2016. (ENG.). 32p. (J). (gr. -1-3). 16.99 *(978-0-8075-7908-4(4))* Whitman, Albert & Co.
Sturgis, Brenda Reeves. 10 Turkeys in the Road, 0 vols. Slonim, David, illus. 2011. (ENG.). 32p. (J). (gr. -1-1). 16.99 *(978-0-7614-5847-0(6),* 9780761458470, Amazon Children's Publishing) Amazon Publishing.
Suhay, Lisa. Pardon Me, It's Ham, Not Turkey. Barcita, Pamela, illus. 2007. (J). (gr. -1-3). 17.95 *(978-1-933982-01-4(2))* Bumble Bee Publishing.
Turkey in the Straw. (J). (gr. -1-1). pap. 7.50 *(978-0-932970-93-0(1))* Prinit Pr.
Waddell, Martin. Captain Small Pig, 1 vol. Varley, Susan, illus. 2010. (ENG.). 32p. (J). (gr. -1-3). 15.95 *(978-1-56145-519-5(9))* Peachtree Pubs.
Wallace, Carol. Turkeys Together. Rogers, Jaqueline & Rogers, Jacqueline, illus. 2005. (Holiday House Readers: Level 2 Ser.). (ENG.). 40p. (J). (gr. k-3). 15.95 *(978-0-8234-1895-4(2))* Holiday Hse., Inc.
Weiner, Marcella Bakur & Neimark, Jill. I Want Your Moo: A Story for Children about Self-Esteem. Adinolfi, JoAnn, illus. 2nd ed. 2009. 32p. (J). (gr. -1-3). 14.95 *(978-1-4338-0542-4(1));* pap. 9.95 *(978-1-4338-0552-3(9))* American Psychological Assn. (Magination Pr.).
Wheeler, Lisa. Turk & Runt: A Thanksgiving Comedy. Ansley, Frank, illus. 2005. (ENG.). 32p. (J). (gr. -1-2). 7.99 *(978-1-4169-0714-5(9),* Atheneum Bks. for Young Readers) Simon & Schuster Children's Publishing.
Wigden, Susan. I Want to Learn to Dance. Franzese, Nora Tapp, illus. 2012. 36p. pap. 11.99 *(978-1-60820-725-1(0))* MLR Pr., LLC.
Williams, Jacklyn. Feliz Dia de Gracias, Gus!, 1 vol. Abello, Patricia, tr. from ENG. Cushman, Doug, illus. 2006. (Read-It! Readers en Español: Gus el Erizo Ser.). (SPA.). 32p. (gr. k-3). lib. bdg. 19.99 *(978-1-4048-2690-8(4),* Easy Readers) Picture Window Bks.
Yoon, Salina. Five Silly Turkeys. Yoon, Salina, illus. 2005. (ENG., Illus.). 10p. (J). (gr. -1-k). bds. 7.99

T U V

(978-0-8431-1416-4(9), Price Stern Sloan) Penguin Young Readers Group.

TURNER, NAT, 1800?-1831

Bisson, Terry. Nat Turner: Slave Revolt Leader. 2004. (Black Americans of Achievement Ser.). (Illus.). 112p. (gr. 6-12). 35.00 (978-0-7910-8167-9(2), Chelsea Hse.) Facts On File, Inc.

Roxburgh, Ellis. Nat Turner's Slave Rebellion. 2017. (Rebellions, Revolts, & Uprisings Ser.). 48p. (gr. 5-5). pap. 84.30 **(978-1-5382-0753-6(2))** Stevens, Gareth Publishing LLLP.

Schmid, Katie Kelley. Nat Turner & Slave Life on a Southern Plantation. 2013. (Jr. Graphic African American History Ser.). 24p. (J). (gr. 3-6). pap. 63.60 (978-1-4777-1454-6(5)); (ENG., Illus.). pap. 10.60 (978-1-4777-1453-9(7)); (ENG., Illus.). lib. bdg. 25.25 (978-1-4777-1314-3(X)) Rosen Publishing Group, Inc., The. (PowerKids Pr.).

TURTLES

Allen, Kathy. Sea Turtles' Race to the Sea: A Cause & Effect Investigation, 1 vol. 2010. (Animals on the Edge Ser.). (ENG.). 32p. (gr. 3-4). lib. bdg. 27.32 (978-1-4296-5402-9(3), Fact Finders) Capstone Press of Coughlan Cos.

Arnold, Quinn M. & Riggs, Kate. Tortoises. 2017. (Seedlings Ser.). (ENG., Illus.). 24p. (J). (gr. k-2). pap. 7.99 (978-1-62832-336-8(1), Creative Paperbacks) Creative Co., The.

Arnosky, Jim. All about Turtles. Arnosky, Jim, illus. 2008. (All About Ser.). (ENG., Illus.). 32p. (J). (gr. -1-3). pap. 5.99 (978-0-590-69781-1(1)) Scholastic, Inc.

Ashton, Patricia. The Gopher Tortoise: A Life History. 2004. (Life History Ser.). (ENG., Illus.). 67p. (YA). 19.95 (978-1-56164-303-5(3)); pap. 14.95 (978-1-56164-301-1(7)) Pineapple Pr., Inc.

Barr, Catherine & Natural History Museum. 10 Reasons to Love a Turtle. Clulow, Hanako, illus. 2017. (10 Reasons to Love A... Ser.). (ENG.). 24p. (J). (gr. -1-1). 12.99 **(978-1-84780-941-4(3)**, Frances Lincoln Children's Bks.) Quarto Publishing Group UK GBR. Dist: Hachette Bk. Group.

Baxter, Bethany. Snapping Turtles. 2013. (Awesome Armored Animals Ser.). 24p. (J). (gr. k-5). pap. 8.25 (978-1-4777-0962-7(2)); pap. 49.50 (978-1-4777-0963-4(0)); lib. bdg. 22.60 (978-1-4777-0795-1(6)) Rosen Publishing Group, Inc., The. (PowerKids Pr.).

Becker, John E. Green Sea Turtles. 2003. (Returning Wildlife Ser.). (Illus.). 48p. (J). 26.20 (978-0-7377-1831-7(5), Greenhaven Pr., Inc.) Cengage Gale.

Bell, Samantha. Sea Turtles. 2014. (21st Century Skills Library: Exploring Our Oceans Ser.). (ENG., Illus.). 32p. (J). (gr. 3-6). 28.50 (978-1-62431-602-9(6), 203192) Cherry Lake Publishing.

Benrali. The turtle's dream & Keys. 2009. (Illus.). 32p. (YA). 19.99 net. (978-0-9763354-2-9(5)) ONLY1EARTH, LLC.

Best, B. J. Sea Turtles. 2016. (Migrating Animals Ser.). 24p. (J). pap. 8.22 (978-1-5026-2094-1(4)) Cavendish Square Publishing.

Biel, Timothy Levi. Turtles. rev. ed. 2003. (Illus.). 24p. (J). (gr. 1-7). 10.95 (978-1-888153-99-6(7), Zoo Bks.) Wildlife Education, Ltd.

Blomquist, Christopher. Desert Tortoises. (Library of Turtles & Tortoises Ser.). 24p. 2009. (gr. 3-3). 42.50 (978-1-60853-946-8(6), PowerKids Pr.) 2004. (Illus.). (YA). (gr. 2-5). lib. bdg. 22.60 (978-0-8239-6739-1(5)) Rosen Publishing Group, Inc., The.

—Gopher Tortoises. 2004. (Library of Turtles & Tortoises Ser.). (Illus.). 24p. (J). lib. bdg. 22.60 (978-0-8239-6740-7(9), PowerKids Pr.) Rosen Publishing Group, Inc., The.

—Snapping Turtles. (Library of Turtles & Tortoises Ser.). 24p. 2009. (gr. 3-3). 42.50 (978-1-60853-948-2(2)) 2004. (Illus.). (J). lib. bdg. 22.60 (978-0-8239-6736-0(0)) Rosen Publishing Group, Inc., The. (PowerKids Pr.).

—Spiny Soft Shell Turtles. 2004. (Library of Turtles & Tortoises Ser.). 24p. (J). lib. bdg. 22.60 (978-0-8239-6737-7(9), PowerKids Pr.) Rosen Publishing Group, Inc., The.

—Spiny Softshell Turtles. 2009. (Library of Turtles & Tortoises Ser.). 24p. (gr. 3-3). 42.50 (978-1-60853-949-9(0), PowerKids Pr.) Rosen Publishing Group, Inc., The.

Boothroyd, Jennifer. Shells. 2011. (First Step Nonfiction / Body Coverings Ser.). pap. 33.92 (978-0-7613-8610-0(6)); (ENG.). 24p. pap. 6.95 (978-0-7613-7830-3(8)); (ENG., Illus.). 24p. lib. bdg. 23.93 (978-0-7613-5788-9(2)) Lerner Publishing Group.

Borgert-Spaniol, Megan. Baby Turtles. 2016. (Super Cute! Ser.). (ENG., Illus.). 24p. (J). (gr. k-3). 25.95 (978-1-62617-390-3(7), Blastoff! Readers) Bellwether Media.

Box Turtle, Earth & Time. 2007. 34p. (YA). (978-0-9763354-3-6(3)) ONLY1EARTH, LLC.

Brannon, Cecelia H. Baby Turtles at the Zoo. 2016. (All about Baby Zoo Animals Ser.). (ENG.). 24p. (J). (gr. k-1). pap. 9.35 (978-0-7660-7158-2(8)); (Illus.). lib. bdg. 22.60 (978-0-7660-7160-5(X)) Enslow Pubs., Inc.

Bredeson, Carmen. Fun Facts about Turtles! 2007. (I Like Reptiles & Amphibians! Ser.). (Illus.). 24p. (J). (gr. 1-3). lib. bdg. 22.60 (978-0-7660-2785-5(6), Enslow Elementary) Enslow Pubs., Inc.

Bronson, Wilfrid S., illus. Turtles. 2008. 68p. (J). pap. 18.95 (978-0-86534-651-2(8)) Sunstone Pr.

Carr, Aaron. Sea Turtles. 2014. (Illus.). 24p. (J). (978-1-4896-3212-8(3)) Weigl Pubs., Inc.

Carraway, Rose. Terrific Turtles. 2012. (Pet Corner Ser.). (ENG., Illus.). 24p. (J). (gr. k-2). pap. 8.15 (978-1-4339-6311-7(6)); lib. bdg. 22.60 (978-1-4339-6309-4(4)) Stevens, Gareth Publishing LLLP.

—Terrific Turtles: Tortugas Asombrosas. 2012. (Pet Corner / RincóN de Las Mascotas Ser.). (SPA & ENG.). 24p. (J). (gr. k-3). lib. bdg. 22.60 (978-1-4339-6647-7(6)) Stevens, Gareth Publishing LLLP.

Carroll, D. Year of the Turtle. (Illus.). 160p. (J). 21.95 (978-0-8048-7036-8(5)) Tuttle Publishing.

Carstairs, Sue. Saving Turtles: A Kids' Guide to Helping Endangered Creatures. 2014. (ENG., Illus.). 64p. (J). (gr. 4-7). pap. 9.95 (978-1-77085-290-7(5), 9781770852907) Firefly Bks., Ltd.

Christopherson, Sara Cohen. Top 50 Reasons to Care about Marine Turtles: Animals in Peril. 2010. (Top 50 Reasons to Care about Endangered Animals Ser.). (Illus.). 104p. (J). (gr. 5-9). 33.27 (978-0-7660-3455-6(0)) Enslow Pubs., Inc.

Coleman, Miriam. Swimming with Sea Turtles. 2009. (Flippers & Fins Ser.). (Illus.). 24p. (J). (ENG.). pap. 8.25 (978-1-4358-3243-5(4), PowerKids Pr.); (gr. 1-3). lib. bdg. 22.60 (978-1-4042-8093-9(6)) Rosen Publishing Group, Inc., The.

Connors, Kathleen. Snapping Turtles. 2013. (Really Wild Reptiles Ser.). (Illus.). 24p. (gr. 2-5). 22.60 (978-1-4339-8384-9(2)); pap. 8.15 (978-1-4339-8385-6(0)) Stevens, Gareth Publishing LLLP. (Gareth Stevens Learning Library).

Cousteau, Philippe & Hopkinson, Deborah. Follow the Moon Home. So, Meilo, illus. 2016. (ENG.). 48p. (J). (gr. k-3). 16.99 (978-1-4521-1241-1(X)) Chronicle Bks. LLC.

Cunningham, Kevin. Sea Turtles & Yellow Tang Fish. 2016. (21st Century Junior Library: Better Together Ser.). (ENG., Illus.). 24p. (J). (gr. 2-5). 27.07 (978-1-63471-088-6(6), 208431) Cherry Lake Publishing.

Cussen, Sarah. Those Terrific Turtles. Weaver, Steve, illus. Dennis, David M., photos by. 2006. (Those Amazing Animals Ser.). (ENG.). 55p. (J). (gr. k-4). 14.95 (978-1-56164-363-9(7)); per. 9.95 (978-1-56164-364-6(5)) Pineapple Pr., Inc.

Dahlen, Kirsten. Wrong Way Peach Fuzz: A Turtle Tale. 2008. 108p. pap. 9.95 (978-1-4357-1273-7(0)) Lulu Pr., Inc.

Davies, Caroline, illus. Turtle. 2013. (Shake & Play Bath Bks.). (ENG.). 8p. (J). (gr. -1 — 1). 5.99 (978-1-4380-7341-5(0)) Barron's Educational Series, Inc.

Davies, Nicola. One Tiny Turtle: Read & Wonder. Chapman, Jane, illus. 2005. (Read & Wonder Ser.). (ENG.). 32p. (J). (gr. -1-3). reprint ed. pap. 6.99 (978-0-7636-2311-1(3)) Candlewick Pr.

Davis, Patricia. Turtles. 2008. (Nature's Children Ser.). (Illus.). 52p. (J). (978-0-7172-6288-5(X)) Grolier, Ltd.

Dennard, Deborah. Turtles. Dewey, Jennifer Owings, illus. 2003. (Our Wild World Ser.). (ENG.). 48p. (J). (gr. 2-5). pap. 7.95 (978-1-55971-861-5(7)) Cooper Square Publishing Llc.

Devers, Marie. Turtles. 2009. (Illus.). 112p. (J). 14.95 (978-1-932904-42-0(5)) Eldorado Ink.

Dickmann, Nancy. A Turtle's Life, 1 vol. 2010. (Watch It Grow Ser.). (ENG.). 24p. (gr. -1-1). 22.65 (978-1-4329-4231-1(X)); pap. 6.29 (978-1-4329-4234-2(4)) Heinemann-Raintree. (Acorn).

—La Vida de la Tortuga, 1 vol. 2011. (¡Mira Cómo Crece! Ser.). (ENG & SPA.). 24p. (gr. -1-1). pap. 6.29 (978-1-4329-5292-1(7), Bellota) Heinemann-Raintree.

Duhaime, Darla. Turtles. 2017. (Reptiles! Ser.). (ENG.). (J). (gr. k-1). 28.51 **(978-1-68342-157-3(4))** Rourke Educational Media.

Dunphy, Madeleine. At Home with the Gopher Tortoise: The Story of a Keystone Species. Rothman, Michael, illus. 2010. (ENG.). 32p. (J). (gr. k-4). 16.95 (978-0-9777539-6-3(4)); pap. 9.95 (978-0-9777539-5-6(6)) Web of Life Children's Bks.

Edwards, Roberta. Best Friends: The True Story of Owen & Mzee. Schwartz, Carol, illus. 2007. (Penguin Young Readers, Level 2 Ser.). (ENG.). 32p. (J). (gr. 1-2). mass mkt. 3.99 (978-0-448-44567-0(0), Penguin Young Readers) Penguin Young Readers Group.

—Best Friends: The True Story of Owen & Mzee. Schwartz, Carol, illus. 2007. (All Aboard Science Reader Ser.). 32p. (gr. -1-3). 14.00 (978-0-7569-8167-9(0)) Perfection Learning Corp.

Evans, Topper. 100-Year-Old Tortoises. 2016. (World's Longest-Living Animals Ser.). 00024p. (J). pap. 8.15 **(978-1-4824-5620-2(6))** Stevens, Gareth Publishing LLLP.

Findley, Violet. Sea Turtles. 2011. (Illus.). 16p. (J). pap. (978-0-545-24791-7(8)) Scholastic, Inc.

Franchino, Vicky. Sea Turtles. 2013. (Nature's Children Ser.). (ENG.). 48p. (J). 28.00 (978-0-531-20981-3(4)); pap. 6.95 (978-0-531-24307-7(9)) Scholastic Library Publishing. (Children's Pr.).

Franks, Katie. Turtles up Close. (Nature up Close Ser.). 24p. 2009. (gr. k-1). 42.50 (978-1-61514-830-1(2)) 2008. (SPA & ENG., Illus.). (J). (gr. -1-3). lib. bdg. 22.60 (978-1-4042-4139-8(6)) Rosen Publishing Group, Inc., The. (PowerKids Pr.).

—Turtles up Close / Las Tortugas. 2009. (Nature up Close / la naturaleza de cerca Ser.). (ENG & SPA.). 24p. (gr. k-1). 42.50 (978-1-61514-836-3(1), Editorial Buenas Letras) Rosen Publishing Group, Inc., The.

—Turtles up Close/Las Tortugas. Sanz, Pilar, tr. from ENG. 2008. (Nature up Close / la Naturaleza de Cerca Ser.). (Illus.). 24p. (J). (gr. 3-7). lib. bdg. 22.60 (978-1-4042-7681-9(5), Editorial Buenas Letras) Rosen Publishing Group, Inc., The.

Freeman, Debby. Turtle. 2017. (See Them Grow Ser.). (ENG., Illus.). 24p. (J). (gr. -1-3). 17.95 **(978-1-68402-041-6(7))** Bearport Publishing Co., Inc.

Furstinger, Nancy. Sea Turtles, 1 vol. 2014. (Amazing Reptiles Ser.). (ENG.). 48p. (gr. 8-12). lib. bdg. 32.79 (978-1-62403-375-9(X)) ABDO Publishing Co.

—Sea Turtles. 2015. (Endangered Animals Ser.). (ENG.). 24p. (J). (gr. 1-4). 27.07 (978-1-63143-973-5(1), 208808) Child's World, Inc., The.

Gareth Stevens Publishing Staff, contrib. by. Turtles. 2004. (All about Wild Animals Ser.). (Illus.). 32p. (gr. k-4). lib. bdg. 26.00 (978-0-8368-4123-7(9), Gareth Stevens Learning Library) Stevens, Gareth Publishing LLLP.

George, Jean Craighead. Galápagos George. Minor, Wendell, illus. 2014. (ENG.). 40p. (J). (gr. k-3). 15.99 (978-0-06-028793-1(4)) HarperCollins Pubs.

—Galapagos Picture Book. Minor, Wendell, illus. Date not set. 32p. (J). (gr. k-3). 5.99 (978-0-06-443648-9(9)) HarperCollins Pubs.

Gibson. Sail Yel Nf Out of the Egg. 2003. (Rigby Sails Early Ser.). (ENG.). 16p. (gr. 1-2). pap. 6.95 (978-0-7578-8892-2(5)) Rigby Education.

Gilkerson, Patricia. My Adventure with Sea Turtles. 2009. (ENG.). 44p. (J). 8.99 (978-1-59092-466-2(5)) Blue Forge Pr.

Gish, Melissa. Living Wild: Sea Turtles. 2015. (Living Wild Ser.). (ENG.). 48p. (J). (gr. 5-8). pap. 12.00 (978-1-62832-005-3(2), Creative Paperbacks) Creative Co., The.

—Living Wild: Tortoises. 2013. (Living Wild Ser.). (ENG., Illus.). 48p. (J). (gr. 4-7). pap. 12.00 (978-0-89812-777-5(7), Creative Paperbacks) Creative Co., The.

—Sea Turtles. 2014. 46p. (978-1-60818-419-4(6), Creative Education) Creative Co., The.

—Tortoises. 2012. (Living Wild Ser.). 48p. (gr. 5-12). 23.95 (978-1-60818-170-4(7), Creative Education) Creative Co., The.

Gordon, Sharon. Adivina Quien Se Esconde. 2006. (Bookworms Ser.). (SPA & ENG., Illus.). 32p. (gr. k-2). lib. bdg. 15.95 (978-0-7614-2385-0(0)) Marshall Cavendish Corp.

—Guess Who Hides/Adivina Quien Se Esconde. 2006. (Bookworms Ser.). (ENG & SPA., Illus.). 32p. (gr. k-2). lib. bdg. 15.95 (978-0-7614-2465-9(2)) Marshall Cavendish Corp.

—Hides. 2007. (J). pap. 6.99 (978-0-7614-3321-7(X)) Marshall Cavendish Corp.

Graubart, Norman D. Mi Tortuga / My Turtle, 1 vol., 1. Green, Christina, ed. 2014. (¡Las Mascotas Son Geniales! / Pets Are Awesome! Ser.). (SPA & BYN.). 24p. (J). (gr. k-2). 23.60 (978-1-4777-3316-5(7), PowerKids Pr.) Rosen Publishing Group, Inc., The.

—My Turtle, 1 vol., 1. 2014. (Pets Are Awesome! Ser.). (ENG.). 24p. (J). (gr. k-2). 23.60 (978-1-4777-2869-7(4), PowerKids Pr.) Rosen Publishing Group, Inc., The.

Green, Emily. Turtles. 2010. (Backyard Wildlife Ser.). (ENG., Illus.). 24p. (J). (gr. k-3). lib. bdg. 25.95 (978-1-60014-448-6(9), Blastoff! Readers) Bellwether Media.

Group/McGraw-Hill, Wright. The Turtle: Collection 2. (Storyteller Interactive Writing Cards Ser.). (gr. k-3). (978-0-322-09340-9(6)) Wright Group/McGraw-Hill.

—Turtles, Tortoises & Terrapins: Level M, 6 vols. (Summer Skies Ser.). 128p. (gr. 3-6). 36.95 (978-0-322-06723-3(5)) Wright Group/McGraw-Hill.

Guiberson, Brenda Z. Into the Sea. Berenzy, Alix, illus. 2014. 32p. pap. 9.00 (978-1-61003-227-8(6)) Center for the Collaborative Classroom.

Hall, Kirsten. Leatherback Turtle: The World's Heaviest Reptile. 2007. (SuperSized! Ser.). (Illus.). 24p. (J). (gr. k-3). lib. bdg. 21.28 (978-1-59716-393-4(7), 1265938) Bearport Publishing Co., Inc.

Hamilton, Lynn. Caring for Your Turtle. 2004. (Caring for Your Pet Ser.). (Illus.). 32p. (J). per. 9.95 (978-1-59036-153-5(9)) Weigl Pubs., Inc.

—Turtle. 2009. (My Pet Ser.). (Illus.). 32p. (J). (gr. 3-5). lib. bdg. 26.00 (978-1-60596-088-3(8)) Weigl Pubs., Inc.

—Turtle: My Pet. 2009. (Illus.). 32p. (J). pap. 9.95 (978-1-60596-089-0(6)) Weigl Pubs., Inc.

Hamilton, Lynn & Gillespie, Katie. Turtle. 2015. (J). (978-1-4896-2974-6(2)) Weigl Pubs., Inc.

Hamilton, Lynn A. Caring for Your Turtle. 2005. (Caring for Your Pet Ser.). (Illus.). 32p. (J). (gr. -1-3). lib. bdg. 26.00 (978-1-59036-118-4(0)) Weigl Pubs., Inc.

Haney, Johannah. Turtles. 2007. (Great Pets Ser.). (Illus.). 48p. (gr. 3). lib. bdg. 29.93 (978-0-7614-2709-4(0), Benchmark Bks.) Marshall Cavendish Corp.

Hansen, Grace. Turtles, 1 vol. 2014. (Reptiles Ser.). (ENG.). 24p. (J). (gr. 4-8). lib. bdg. 28.50 (978-1-62970-062-5(2)) ABDO Publishing Co.

Hansen, Grace, et al. Tortugas. 2015. (Reptiles Ser.). (SPA., Illus.). 24p. (gr. k-1). pap. 7.95 (978-1-4966-0509-2(8)) Capstone Classroom.

Hanson, Anders. Terrific Turtles, 1 vol. 2007. (Perfect Pets Ser.). (ENG., Illus.). 24p. (J). (gr. k-3). lib. bdg. 24.21 (978-1-59928-755-3(2), SandCastle) ABDO Publishing Co.

Hanson, Anders & Craig, Diane. Sea Turtle, 1 vol. 2014. (Giant Animals Ser.). (ENG., Illus.). 24p. (J). (gr. -1-3). 24.21 (978-1-62403-061-1(0)) ABDO Publishing Co.

Harris, Tim. Turtles. 2010. (Slimy, Scaly, Deadly Reptiles & Amphibians Ser.). (Illus.). 32p. (J). (gr. 2-6). pap. 10.50 (978-1-4339-3439-1(6)); lib. bdg. 26.00 (978-1-4339-3438-4(8)) Stevens, Gareth Publishing LLLP. (Gareth Stevens Learning Library).

Hatkoff, Craig, et al. Owen & Mzee: The Language of Friendship. Greste, Peter, photos by. 2007. (Owen & Mzee Ser.). (ENG., Illus.). 40p. (J). (gr. -1-3). 18.99 (978-0-439-89959-8(1), Scholastic Pr.) Scholastic, Inc.

—Owen & Mzee: The True Story of a Remarkable Friendship. Greste, Peter, illus. 2006. (Owen & Mzee Ser.). (ENG.). 40p. (J). (gr. -1-3). 17.99 (978-0-439-82973-1(9), Scholastic Pr.) Scholastic, Inc.

Heller, Ruth. Galapagos Means Tortoises. Heller, Ruth, illus. 2003. (ENG., Illus.). 48p. (J). (gr. k-4). reprint ed. pap. 7.95 (978-1-57805-101-4(0)) Gibbs Smith, Publisher.

Heos, Bridget. Do You Really Want a Turtle? Longhi, Katya, illus. 2015. (Do You Really Want a Pet? Ser.). (ENG.). 24p. (J). (gr. 1-3). 19.95 (978-1-60753-752-6(4)) Amicus Publishing.

Herriges, Ann. Sea Turtles. 2006. (Oceans Alive Ser.). (ENG., Illus.). 24p. (J). (gr. k-2). lib. bdg. 25.95 (978-1-60014-022-8(X)) Bellwether Media.

Herrington, Lisa M. Turtles & Tortoises. 2015. (Rookie Read-About(tm) Science: What's the Difference? Ser.). (ENG., Illus.). 32p. (J). lib. bdg. 25.00 (978-0-531-21482-4(6), Children's Pr.) Scholastic Library Publishing.

Hicer, Nancy. My Sister's Turtle. 2015. (Rosen REAL Readers: STEM & STEAM Collection). (ENG.). 8p. pap. 5.46 (978-1-4994-9675-8(3), Rosen Classroom) Rosen Publishing Group, Inc., The.

Hickman, Pamela. Turtle Rescue: Changing the Future for Endangered Wildlife. 2005. (Firefly Animal Rescue Ser.). (ENG., Illus.). 64p. (J). (gr. 5-12). 19.95 (978-1-55297-916-7(4), 9781552979167); pap. 9.95 (978-1-55297-915-0(6), 9781552979150) Firefly Bks., Ltd.

Hinman, Bonnie. Threat to the Leatherback Turtle. 2008. (On the Verge of Extinction Ser.). (Illus.). 32p. (YA). (gr. 2-5). lib. bdg. 25.70 (978-1-58415-690-1(2)) Mitchell Lane Pubs., Inc.

Hipp, Andrew. The Life Cycle of a Painted Turtle. 2009. (Life Cycles Library). 24p. (gr. 3-4). 42.50 (978-1-60853-996-3(2), PowerKids Pr.) Rosen Publishing Group, Inc., The.

Hirsch, Rebecca E. Galápagos Tortoises: Long-Lived Giant Reptiles. 2015. (ENG., Illus.). 32p. (J). (gr. 2-4). 26.65 (978-1-4677-7982-1(2), Lerner Pubns.) Lerner Publishing Group.

—Leatherback Sea Turtles: Ancient Swimming Reptiles. 2015. (ENG., Illus.). 32p. (J). (gr. 2-4). 26.65 (978-1-4677-7980-7(6), Lerner Pubns.) Lerner Publishing Group.

Hirschmann, Kris. Sea Turtles. 2005. (Creatures of the Sea Ser.). (ENG., Illus.). 48p. (J). (gr. 4-8). 29.15 (978-0-7377-3011-1(0), Greenhaven Pr., Inc.) Cengage Gale.

Houghton, Gillian. Tortugas: Por Dentro y Por Fuera. Gonzalez, Tomas, tr. Studio Stalio, illus. 2004. (Explora la Naturaleza (Getting into Nature) Ser.). (SPA.). 32p. (J). (gr. k-5). lib. bdg. 25.25 (978-1-4042-2869-6(1)) Rosen Publishing Group, Inc., The.

—Tortugas: Por dentro y por fuera (Turtles: Inside & Out) 2009. (Explora la Naturaleza (Getting into Nature) Ser.). (SPA.). 32p. (gr. 3-4). 47.90 (978-1-61512-339-1(3), Editorial Buenas Letras) Rosen Publishing Group, Inc., The.

—Turtle. 2004. (Getting into Nature Ser.). (Illus.). 32p. (J). lib. bdg. 25.25 (978-0-8239-4211-4(2)) Rosen Publishing Group, Inc., The.

—Turtles: Inside & Out. 2009. (Getting into Nature Ser.). 32p. (gr. 3-4). 47.90 (978-1-61512-727-6(5), PowerKids Pr.) Rosen Publishing Group, Inc., The.

Huelin, Jodi. Turtles. Gonzalez, Pedro Julio, illus. 2003. (Penguin Young Readers, Level 2 Ser.). (ENG.). 32p. (J). (gr. 1-2). mass mkt. 3.99 (978-0-448-43117-8(3), Penguin Young Readers) Penguin Young Readers Group.

Jacobs, Lee. Turtle. 2003. (Wild America Ser.). (Illus.). 24p. (J). 24.94 (978-1-56711-571-0(3), Blackbirch Pr., Inc.) Cengage Gale.

Johnson, Nancy Carole. Pierre, the Turtle Who Went to College. 2008. 24p. pap. 10.95 (978-1-4327-2614-0(5)) Outskirts Pr., Inc.

Kalman, Bobbie. Endangered Sea Turtles. 2004. (Earth's Endangered Animals Ser.). (ENG., Illus.). 32p. (J). pap. (978-0-7787-1899-4(9)) Crabtree Publishing Co.

—Les Tortues de Mer. Briere, Marie-Josee, tr. from ENG. 2007. (Petit Monde Vivant Ser.). (FRE., Illus.). 32p. (J). (gr. -1-3). pap. 9.95 (978-2-89579-164-5(3)) Bayard Canada Livres CAN. Dist: Crabtree Publishing Co.

Kingston, Anna. The Life Cycle of the Sea Turtle. 2011. (Nature's Life Cycles Ser.). (Illus.). 24p. (J). (gr. 2-5). pap. 8.15 (978-1-4339-4688-2(2)); lib. bdg. 22.60 (978-1-4339-4687-5(4)) Stevens, Gareth Publishing LLLP. (Gareth Stevens Learning Library).

Kishel, Ann-Marie. Turtles & Hatchlings. 2006. (First Step Nonfiction - Animal Families Ser.). (ENG., Illus.). 8p. (gr. -1-1). pap. 4.95 (978-0-8225-5647-3(2), Lerner Pubns.) Lerner Publishing Group.

Korman, Susan. Box Turtle at Silver Pond Lane. Marchesi, Stephen, illus. 2005. (Smithsonian's Backyard Ser.). (ENG.). 32p. (J). (gr. -1-2). 15.95 (978-1-56899-860-2(0), B5020) Soundprints.

Kuzio, Daisy Williams. All about Annie: (A True Story) 2006. 9.00 (978-0-8059-9118-5(2)) Dorrance Publishing Co., Inc.

Lasky, Kathryn. Interrupted Journey: Saving Endangered Sea Turtles. Knight, Christopher G., photos by. 2006. (ENG., Illus.). 48p. (J). (gr. 1-4). 6.99 (978-0-7636-2883-3(2)) Candlewick Pr.

Laughlin, Kara L. Sea Turtles. 2017. (In the Deep Blue Sea Ser.). (ENG.). 24p. (J). (gr. k-3). lib. bdg. 27.07 (978-1-5038-1690-9(7), 211523) Child's World, Inc., The.

Lawrence, Ellen. A Sea Turtle's Life. 2016. (Animal Diaries). (ENG.). 24p. (J). (gr. -1-3). lib. bdg. 17.95 (978-1-944102-48-7(5)) Bearport Publishing Co., Inc.

Lindeen, Carol K. & Lugtu, Carol J. Sea Turtles [Scholastic]. 2010. (Under the Sea Ser.). 24p. pap. 0.50 (978-1-4296-5067-0(2), Pebble Plus) Capstone Press of Coughlan Cos.

Loh-Hagan, Virginia. Discover Sea Turtles. 2015. (21st Century Basic Skills Library: Splash! Ser.). (ENG., Illus.). 24p. (J). (gr. 2-4). 24.21 (978-1-63362-607-2(5), 206612) Cherry Lake Publishing.

Machajewski, Sarah. Saving the Endangered Green Sea Turtle, 01 vols., 1. 2016. (Conservation of Endangered Species Ser.). (ENG., Illus.). 32p. (J). pap. 12.90 (978-1-5081-0056-0(X), Britannica Educational Publishing) Rosen Publishing Group, Inc., The.

Macheske, Felicia. Flying Flippers: Sea Turtle. 2016. (Guess What Ser.). (ENG.). 24p. (J). (gr. k-2). 28.50 (978-1-63470-716-9(8), 207575) Cherry Lake Publishing.

Marsh, Laura. National Geographic Readers: Sea Turtles. 2011. (Readers Ser.). (ENG., Illus.). 32p. (J). (gr. 1-4). lib. bdg. 13.90 (978-1-4263-0854-3(X), National Geographic Children's Bks.) National Geographic Society.

—Sea Turtles. 2011. (Readers Ser.). (ENG., Illus.). 32p. (J). (gr. 1-4). pap. 3.99 (978-1-4263-0853-6(1), National Geographic Children's Bks.) National Geographic Society.

Marsico, Katie. How Do We Live Together? Turtles. 2010. (Community Connections: How Do We Live Together? Ser.). (ENG.). 24p. (gr. 2-5). lib. bdg. 25.64 (978-1-60279-623-2(8), 200332) Cherry Lake Publishing.

Martin-James, Kathleen. Sturdy Turtles. 2003. (Pull Ahead Bks.). (ENG., Illus.). 32p. (J). (gr. k-2). pap. 5.95 (978-0-8225-3631-4(5)) Lerner Publishing Group.

Marx, Mandy R. Leatherback Turtles, 1 vol. 2012. (Reptiles Ser.). (ENG.). 24p. (gr. k-1). lib. bdg. 26.65 (978-1-4296-6646-6(3), Pebble Plus) Capstone Press of Coughlan Cos.

Mason, Janeen. Ocean Commotion: Sea Turtles, 1 vol. Mason, Janeen, illus. 2006. (ENG., Illus.). 32p. (J). (gr. k-3). 16.99 (978-1-58980-434-0(1)) Pelican Publishing Co., Inc.

McDonnell, Melissa. Tell Time with Turtles. 2011. (Animal Math Ser.). (Illus.). 24p. (J). (gr. 1-3). 22.60 (978-1-4339-5674-4(8)); pap. 8.15 (978-1-4339-5676-8(4)) Stevens, Gareth Publishing LLLP.

Meister, Cari. Sea Turtles. 2013. (ENG.). 24p. (J). lib. bdg. 25.65 (978-1-62031-034-2(1)) Jump! Inc.

—Snapping Turtles. 2015. (Illus.). 24p. (J). lib. bdg. (978-1-62031-199-8(2), Bullfrog Bks.) Jump! Inc.

—Turtles. 2014. (Illus.). 24p. (J). lib. bdg. 25.65 (978-1-62031-126-4(7), Bullfrog Bks.) Jump! Inc.

Miller, Mirella S. Sea Turtles Are Awesome. 2018. (ENG.). 32p. (gr. 3-6). 31.35 **(978-1-63235-437-2(3)**, 12-Story Library) Pr. Room Editions LLC.

Monroe, Mary Alice. Turtle Summer: A Journal for My Daughter, 1 vol. Bergwerf, Barbara J., illus. 2007. (ENG.). 32p. (J). (gr. k-4). 16.95 (978-0-9777423-5-6(0)) Arbordale Publishing.

Morgan, Sally. Turtles. 2006. (Animal Lives (QEB Publishing) Ser.). (Illus.). 32p. (J). (gr. 4-7). lib. bdg. 18.95 *(978-1-59566-206-4(5))* QEB Publishing Inc.

Morgan, Sally & Teacher Created Resources Staff. Tortoises & Turtles. 2007. (Animal Lives (QEB Publishing) Ser.). (ENG., Illus.). 32p. (gr. 2-9). pap. 7.99 *(978-1-4206-8110-9(9))* Teacher Created Resources, Inc.

Murray, Julie. Sea Turtles, 1 vol. 2007. (Life Cycles Ser.). (ENG., Illus.). 24p. (gr. 4-7). 25.65 *(978-1-59928-711-9(0),* Buddy Bks.) ABDO Publishing Co.

—Turtles, 1 vol. 2003. (Animal Kingdom Ser.). (ENG.). 24p. (gr. k-4). 25.65 *(978-1-57765-720-0(9),* Buddy Bks.) ABDO Publishing Co.

Nagelhout, Ryan. Turtles. 2013. (Underwater World Ser.). (Illus.). 24p. (J). (gr. k-2). pap. 8.15 *(978-1-4339-8579-9(9));* lib. bdg. 22.60 *(978-1-4339-8578-2(0))* Stevens, Gareth Publishing LLLP.

—Turtles: Tortugas. 2013. (Underwater World / el Mundo Submarino Ser.). (SPA., Illus.). 24p. (J). (gr. k-2). lib. bdg. 22.60 *(978-1-4339-8786-1(4))* Stevens, Gareth Publishing LLLP.

National Geographic Kids Staff & Marsh, Laura. Turtles. 2016. (Readers Ser.). (ENG., Illus.). 32p. (J). (gr. -1-1). pap. 3.99 *(978-1-4263-2293-8(3),* National Geographic Children's Bks.) National Geographic Society.

Newman, Aline Alexander. Lucky Leopards! 2014. (NGK Chapters Ser.). (ENG., Illus.). 112p. (J). (gr. 2-5). lib. bdg. 14.90 *(978-1-4263-1458-2(2),* National Geographic Children's Bks.) National Geographic Society.

Northeast Editing, Inc Staff, contrib. by. Turtles. 2008. (J). *(978-1-932904-34-5(4))* Eldorado Ink.

Oczkus, Lori. Turtles. 2015. (Close Reading with Paired Texts). (ENG., Illus.). 128p. (gr. 1-1). pap. 19.99 *(978-1-4258-1357-4(7))* Shell Educational Publishing.

Owen, Ruth. Sea Turtle Hatchlings. 2012. (Water Babies Ser.). 24p. (J). (gr. -1-3). lib. bdg. 21.32 *(978-1-61772-603-3(6))* Bearport Publishing Co., Inc.

Owings, Lisa. From Egg to Sea Turtle. 2016. (Start to Finish, Second Ser.). (ENG., Illus.). 24p. (J). (gr. k-3). 23.99 *(978-1-5124-1827-9(7))* Lerner Publishing Group.

Phillips, Dee. Desert Tortoise's Burrow. 2015. (Illus.). 24p. (J). lib. bdg. *(978-1-62724-308-7(9))* Bearport Publishing Co., Inc.

Pingry, Patricia A. Baby Sea Turtle. Rose, Drew, illus. 2006. (SeaWorld Library: Vol. 8). 26p. (J). (gr. -1-k). bds. 6.95 *(978-0-8249-6645-4(7),* Ideal Pubns.) Worthy Publishing.

Pohl, Kathleen. Sea Turtles. 2007. (Let's Read about Animals Ser.). (Illus.). 24p. (gr. k-3). pap. 8.15 *(978-0-8368-7827-1(2));* lib. bdg. 22.00 *(978-0-8368-7820-2(5))* Stevens, Gareth Publishing LLLP. (Weekly Reader Leveled Readers).

—Sea Turtles/Tortugas Marinas. 2007. (Let's Read about Animals/ Conozcamos a los animales Ser.). (SPA., Illus.). 24p. (gr. k-3). pap. 8.15 *(978-0-8368-8016-8(1));* lib. bdg. 22.00 *(978-0-8368-8009-0(9))* Stevens, Gareth Publishing LLLP. (Weekly Reader Leveled Readers).

Portman, Michael. Sea Turtles in Danger. 2011. (Animals at Risk Ser.). (Illus.). 24p. (J). (gr. 2-5). 22.60 *(978-1-4339-5802-1(3));* pap. 8.15 *(978-1-4339-5804-5(X))* Stevens, Gareth Publishing LLLP. (Gareth Stevens Learning Library).

Rake, Jody Sullivan. Leatherback Sea Turtles, 1 vol. 2012. (Endangered & Threatened Animals Ser.). (ENG., Illus.). 32p. (gr. 3-4). lib. bdg. 27.99 *(978-1-4296-8584-9(0),* Snap Bks.) Capstone Press of Coughlan Cos.

Randolph, Joanne. My Friend the Box Turtle. 2010. (Curious Pet Pals Ser.). (ENG.). 24p. (J). (gr. k-3). lib. bdg. 22.60 *(978-1-60754-979-6(4));* (Illus.). pap. 8.15 *(978-1-60754-989-5(1))* Windmill Bks.

—Turtles. (Classroom Pets Ser.). 24p. 2009. (gr. 2-3). 42.50 *(978-1-61511-863-2(2))* 2007. (Illus.). (J). (gr. 3-7). lib. bdg. 22.60 *(978-1-4042-3677-6(5),* 1266096) Rosen Publishing Group, Inc., The. (PowerKids Pr.).

Rathmell, Donna. Carolina's Story: Sea Turtles Get Sick Too!, 1 vol. Bergwerf, Barbara J., illus. 2005. (ENG.). 32p. (J). (gr. -1-3). 15.95 *(978-0-9764943-0-0(2))* Arbordale Publishing.

—Carolina's Story: Sea Turtles Get Sick Too!, 1 vol. Bergwerf, Barbara J., illus. Bergwerf, Barbara J., photos by. 2005. (ENG.). 32p. (J). (gr. -1-3). pap. 8.95 *(978-1-934359-00-6(9))* Arbordale Publishing.

Rebman, Renee C. Turtles & Tortoises. 2006. (Animals Animals Ser.). (Illus.). 48p. (gr. 3-7). lib. bdg. 29.93 *(978-0-7614-2239-6(0),* Benchmark Bks.) Marshall Cavendish Corp.

Reid, Siuna A. Reptiles Are Cool- Understanding My Tortoise. Lodge, Vivienne E., ed. 2013. (Illus.). 76p. pap. *(978-0-9576568-2-6(3))* Siuna A Reid.

Riggs, Kate. Amazing Animals: Sea Turtles. 2015. (Amazing Animals Ser.). (ENG.). 24p. (J). (gr. 1-3). pap. 8.99 *(978-1-62832-091-6(5),* Creative Paperbacks) Creative Co., The.

—Amazing Animals: Tortoises. 2014. (Amazing Animals Ser.). (ENG.). 24p. (J). (gr. 1-3). pap. 8.99 *(978-0-89812-929-8(X),* Creative Paperbacks) Creative Co., The.

—Sea Turtles. 2015. (J). *(978-1-60818-491-0(9),* Creative Education) Creative Co., The.

—Tortoises. (J). 2016. (Illus.). 24p. *(978-1-60818-740-9(3))* 2014. 25.65 *(978-1-60818-350-0(5))* Creative Co., The. (Creative Education).

Rodriguez, Cindy. Sea Turtles. 2009. (ENG., Illus.). 24p. (gr. 3-6). pap. 8.95 *(978-1-60694-844-6(X))* Rourke Educational Media.

Rudenko, Dennis. Sea Turtles, 01 vols., 1. 2016. (Ocean Friends Ser.). (ENG., Illus.). 24p. (J). pap. 8.25 *(978-1-5081-4185-3(1),* PowerKids Pr.) Rosen Publishing Group, Inc., The.

Rustad, Martha E. Sea Turtles [Scholastic]. 2009. (Ocean Life Ser.). 24p. (gr. k-1). pap. 2.99 *(978-1-4296-3676-6(9),* Pebble Bks.) Capstone Press of Coughlan Cos.

Ryndak, Rob. Turtle or Tortoise? 2015. (Animal Look-Alikes Ser.). (ENG., Illus.). 24p. (J). (gr. 1-2). pap. 8.15 *(978-1-4824-2728-8(1))* Stevens, Gareth Publishing LLLP.

Sánchez, Lucia M. & Cline, Gina. La Vida de la Tortuga de Mar. 2012. (2G Vida Marina Ser.). (SPA., Illus.). 32p. (J). pap. 6.99 *(978-1-61406-174-8(2))* American Reading Co.

Schreyer, Karmel. Turtles: Ancient Symbol/Modern Survivor Upper Intermediate Book with Online Access. 2014. (ENG.). 28p. (J). pap. 9.50 *(978-1-107-66057-1(2))* Cambridge Univ. Pr.

Schueler, Donald G. The Gopher Tortoise: A MyReportLinks.com Book. 2003. (Endangered & Threatened Animals Ser.). (Illus.). 48p. (J). (gr. 4-10). lib. bdg. 25.26 *(978-0-7660-5053-2(X),* MyReportLinks.com Bks.) Enslow Pubs., Inc.

Schuetz, Kari. Sea Turtles. 2016. (Ocean Life up Close Ser.). (ENG., Illus.). 24p. (J). (gr. k-3). 25.95 *(978-1-62617-422-1(9),* Blastoff! Readers) Bellwether Media.

Sexton, Colleen. Caring for Your Turtle. 2010. (Pet Care Library). (ENG., Illus.). 24p. (J). (gr. 2-5). lib. bdg. 25.95 *(978-1-60014-472-1(1),* Blastoff! Readers) Bellwether Media.

—The Life Cycle of a Turtle. 2010. (Life Cycles Ser.). (ENG., Illus.). 24p. (J). (gr. k-3). lib. bdg. 25.95 *(978-1-60014-452-3(7),* Blastoff! Readers) Bellwether Media.

Shaskan, Trisha Speed. What's the Difference Between a Turtle & a Tortoise?, 1 vol. Bandelin, Debra et al, illus. 2010. (What's the Difference? Ser.). (ENG.). 24p. (gr. k-3). lib. bdg. 26.65 *(978-1-4048-5546-5(7))* Picture Window Bks.

Spilsbury, Louise. Sea Turtle, 1 vol. 2010. (Day in the Life: Sea Animals Ser.). (ENG.). 24p. (J). (gr. k-2). pap. 6.79 *(978-1-4329-4008-9(2),* Heinemann Read & Learn) Heinemann-Raintree.

Steloff, Rebecca. Turtles. 2007. (Animalways Ser.). (Illus.). 104p. (gr. 6-3). lib. bdg. 24.95 *(978-0-7614-2539-7(X),* Benchmark Bks.) Marshall Cavendish Corp.

Stevens, Kathryn. Turtles. 2015. (Pet Care Ser.). (ENG.). 24p. (J). (gr. -1-2). 25.64 *(978-1-63143-731-1(3),* 208550) Child's World, Inc., The.

Stewart, Melissa. A Place for Turtles, 1 vol. Bond, Higgins, illus. 2013. (ENG.). 32p. (J). (gr. 1-5). pap. 16.95 *(978-1-56145-693-2(4))* Peachtree Pubs.

Stone, Lynn M. Box Turtles. Stone, Lynn M., photos by. 2007. (Nature Watch Ser.). (ENG., Illus.). 48p. (gr. 4-8). lib. bdg. 27.93 *(978-1-57505-869-6(3),* Lerner Pubns.) Lerner Publishing Group.

Storad, Conrad J. Galápagos Tortoises. 2009. (Early Bird Nature Bks.). (ENG.). 48p. (gr. 2-5). 26.60 *(978-0-8225-9431-4(5),* Lerner Pubns.) Lerner Publishing Group.

Swinburne, Stephen R. Sea Turtle Scientist. (Scientists in the Field Ser.). (ENG., Illus.). 80p. (J). (gr. 5-7). 2015. pap. 9.99 *(978-0-544-58240-8(3),* HMH Books For Young Readers) 2014. 18.99 *(978-0-547-36755-2(4))* Houghton Mifflin Harcourt Publishing Co.

Tara, Stephanie Lisa. I'll Follow the Moon. Fodi, Lee Edward, illus. 2011. 48p. (J). 12.99 *(978-1-61254-016-0(3))* Brown Books Publishing Group.

Taylor, Barbara. Turtles & Tortoises: An In-Depth Look at Chelonians, the Shelled Reptiles That Have Existed since the Time of the Dinosaurs. 2016. (ENG., Illus.). 64p. 12.99 *(978-1-86147-643-2(4),* Armadillo) Anness Publishing GBR. Dist: National Bk. Network.

Thivierge, Claude. BOOST the World of Turtles Coloring Book. 2013. (BOOST Educational Ser.). (ENG.). 32p. (J). (gr. 3-5). pap. 4.99 *(978-0-486-49442-5(X))* Dover Pubns., Inc.

—The World of Turtles. 2009. (Dover Nature Coloring Book Ser.). (ENG., Illus.). 32p. (J). (gr. 1-5). pap. 3.99 *(978-0-486-46854-9(2))* Dover Pubns., Inc.

Thomas, Elizabeth. Desert Tortoises, 1 vol. 2011. (Reptiles Ser.). (ENG.). 24p. (gr. k-1). lib. bdg. 26.65 *(978-1-4296-6645-9(5),* Pebble Plus) Capstone Press of Coughlan Cos.

—Eastern Box Turtles, 1 vol. 2011. (Reptiles Ser.). (ENG.). 24p. (gr. k-1). lib. bdg. 26.65 *(978-1-4296-6643-5(9),* Pebble Plus) Capstone Press of Coughlan Cos.

—Snapping Turtles, 1 vol. 2011. (Reptiles Ser.). (ENG.). 24p. (gr. k-1). lib. bdg. 26.65 *(978-1-4296-6644-2(7),* Pebble Plus) Capstone Press of Coughlan Cos.

Todino, Grace. Tina the Turtle. Keeble, Susan, illus. 2013. (ENG.). 58p. (J). (gr. k). 19.95 *(978-1-908531-00-1(2))* Gilgamesh Publishing GBR. Dist: Consortium Bk. Sales & Distribution.

Trifer, Jen. Turtles from Head to Tail. 2016. (Animals from Head to Tail Ser.). 24p. (J). (gr. k-k). lib. bdg. 22.60 *(978-1-4824-4540-4(9))* Stevens, Gareth Publishing LLLP.

Wang, Margaret. Turtles Take Their Time. 2007. 6p. 14.95 *(978-1-58117-601-8(5),* Intervisual/Piggy Toes) Bendon, Inc.

Watt, E. Melanie. Leatherback Turtles, with Code. 2012. (Animals on the Brink Ser.). (ENG., Illus.). 48p. (J). (gr. 3-7). pap. 14.95 *(978-1-61913-428-7(4),* AV2 by Weigl) Weigl Pubs., Inc.

Watt, Mélanie. Leatherback Turtles. 2013. (Illus.). 48p. *(978-1-61913-427-0(6))* Weigl Pubs., Inc.

Wearing, Judy. Sea Turtle: World of Wonder: Underwater Life. 2009. (Illus.). 24p. (J). pap. 8.95 *(978-1-60596-107-1(8))* Weigl Pubs., Inc.

—Sea Turtles. 2009. (World of Wonder Ser.). (Illus.). 24p. (J). (gr. 2-4). lib. bdg. 24.45 *(978-1-60596-106-4(X))* Weigl Pubs., Inc.

Weber, Valerie J. Sea Turtles. 2008. (Animals That Live in the Ocean Ser.). (Illus.). 24p. (gr. -1-3). pap. 8.15 *(978-0-8368-9343-4(3),* Weekly Reader Leveled Readers) Stevens, Gareth Publishing LLLP.

—Sea Turtles. 2008. (Animals That Live in the Ocean Ser.). (Illus.). 24p. (J). (gr. -1-3). lib. bdg. 22.60 *(978-0-8368-9244-4(5),* Weekly Reader Leveled Readers) Stevens, Gareth Publishing LLLP.

—Sea Turtles/Tortugas Marinas. 2008. (Animals That Live in the Ocean/Animales Que Viven en el Oceano Ser.). (SPA & ENG.). 24p. (gr. -1-3). (J). lib. bdg. 22.60 *(978-0-8368-9250-5(X));* pap. 8.15 *(978-0-8368-9349-6(2))* Stevens, Gareth Publishing LLLP. (Weekly Reader Leveled Readers).

Webster, Christine. Who on Earth Is Archie Carr? Protector of Sea Turtles. 2009. (Scientists Saving the Earth Ser.). (Illus.). 112p. (J). (gr. 5-9). lib. bdg. 33.27 *(978-1-59845-120-7(0))* Enslow Pubs., Inc.

Whitt, Stephen. The Turtle & the Universe. Hernandez, Stephanie, illus. 2008. (ENG.). 86p. (J). (gr. 3-7). pap. 14.99 *(978-1-59102-626-6(1))* Prometheus Bks., Pubs.

Wildlife Education, compiled by. Turtles. 2007. (Illus.). 12p. (J). 5.99 *(978-1-932396-40-9(3),* Critters Up Close) Wildlife Education, Ltd.

Wilsdon, Christina. Turtles. 2009. (Amazing Animals Ser.). (ENG.). 48p. (J). (gr. 2-6). pap. 10.50 *(978-1-4339-2127-8(8),* Gareth Stevens Learning Library); (YA). (gr. 3-6). lib. bdg. 28.00 *(978-0-8368-9123-2(6))* Stevens, Gareth Publishing LLLP.

—Turtles. 2007. (J). *(978-1-59939-112-0(0),* Reader's Digest Young Families, Inc.) Studio Fun International.

World Book, Inc. Box Turtles & Other Pond & Marsh Turtles. 2007. (World Book's Animals of the World Ser.). (Illus.). 64p. (J). *(978-0-7166-1326-8(3))* World Bk., Inc.

Young, Karen Romano. National Geographic Kids Mission: Sea Turtle Rescue: All about Sea Turtles & How to Save Them. 2015. (NG Kids Mission: Animal Rescue Ser.). (ENG., Illus.). 112p. (J). (gr. 5). lib. bdg. 21.90 *(978-1-4263-1894-8(4),* National Geographic Children's Bks.) National Geographic Society.

TURTLES—FICTION

Abbott, Monica. L T Makes New Friends. 2010. 24p. pap. 13.50 *(978-1-4520-6128-3(9))* AuthorHouse.

Abrahams, Marion. Thomas Goes to the Se. 2009. 24p. pap. 14.50 *(978-1-60693-831-7(2),* Eloquent Bks.) Strategic Book Publishing & Rights Agency (SBPRA).

Achrafi, Sherihan. Turtles' Day Out. 2017. (ENG., Illus.). 28p. (J). pap. 28.22 ***(978-1-5245-6081-2(2))*** AuthorHouse.

Adams, Alison. How the Turtle Cracked Its Shell: Classic Tales Edition. Greenhead, Bill, illus. 2011. (Classic Tales Ser.). (J). *(978-1-936258-58-1(7))* Benchmark Education Co.

Ahern, Carolyn L. Tino Turtle Travels to Beijing, China. Burt-Sullivan, Neallia, illus. 2011. (ENG.). 56p. (J). (gr. -1-4). 19.95 incl. audio compact disk *(978-0-9793158-4-8(0))* Tino Turtle Travels, LLC.

—Tino Turtle Travels to Kenya - the Great Safari. Burt Sullivan, Neallia, illus. 2009. (ENG & SWA.). 32p. (J). (gr. -1-4). 19.95 incl. audio compact disk *(978-0-9793158-3-1(2))* Tino Turtle Travels, LLC.

—Tino Turtle Travels to London, England. Burt Sullivan, Neallia, illus. (J). 2007. 36p. 17.95 incl. audio compact disk *(978-0-9793158-0-0(8))* 2008. (ENG.). 32p. 19.95 incl. audio compact disk *(978-0-9816297-0-4(9))* Tino Turtle Travels, LLC.

—Tino Turtle Travels to Mexico City, Mexico. Burt Sullivan, Neallia, illus. 2008. (ENG & SPA.). 32p. (J). (gr. -1-4). 19.95 incl. audio compact disk *(978-0-9793158-2-4(4))* Tino Turtle Travels, LLC.

—Tino Turtle Travels to Paris, France. Burt Sullivan, Neallia, illus. 2007. 36p. (J). (gr. -1-4). 17.95 incl. audio compact disk *(978-0-9793158-1-7(6))* Tino Turtle Travels, LLC.

Aina, Olaiya E. Ijapa, the Lion, & the Boar. 2010. 20p. 13.80 *(978-1-4269-3183-3(2))* Trafford Publishing.

Allen, Jean M. A Tangled Web. 2012. 26p. 24.95 *(978-1-4512-9475-0(1))* America Star Bks.

Amar, Cindy. Tommy's Discovery. 2012. 28p. pap. 16.99 *(978-1-4525-5399-3(8))* Balboa Pr.

Ananthanarayanan, Ashraya. Ring of Hope. 2011. pap. 10.95 *(978-0-7414-6492-7(6))* Infinity Publishing.

Anastasio, Dina. The Magic Turtle: Set Of 6. 2011. (Early Connections Ser.). (J). pap. 37.00 net. *(978-1-4108-1366-4(5))* Benchmark Education Co.

—The Magic Turtle & la tortuga Mágica: 6 English, 6 Spanish Adaptations. 2011. (ENG & SPA.). (J). 75.00 net. *(978-1-4108-5650-0(X))* Benchmark Education Co.

Arai, Shizuko. The Turtle & the Warrior. Maeda, Matsuo, illus. 2014. (J). 8.95 *(978-1-935523-69-7(4))* World Tribune Pr.

Armitage, Kimo. Limu: The Blue Turtle & His Hawaiian Garden. Kaneshiro, Scott, illus. 2004. 28p. (J). 11.95 *(978-0-931548-64-2(0))* Island Heritage Publishing.

Atkins, Jill. Tortoise Races Home. Blake, Beccy, illus. 2009. (Tadpoles Ser.). (ENG.). 24p. (J). (gr. -1-2). pap. *(978-0-7787-3902-9(3))* Crabtree Publishing Co.

Austin, K. B. Old Mother Turtle & the Three Frogs. 2005. (J). lib. bdg. *(978-0-9772027-0-6(4))* Dream Star Productions.

Award, Anna & Biro, Val. The Bear & the Travellers & the Ducks & the Tortoise. 2014. (ENG.). 24p. (J). pap. 6.95 *(978-1-84135-959-5(9))* Award Pubns. Ltd. GBR. Dist: Parkwest Pubns., Inc.

Award, Anna, et al. The Sick Lion & Hare & the Tortoise. 2014. (ENG.). 24p. (J). pap. 6.95 *(978-1-84135-954-0(8))* Award Pubns. Ltd. GBR. Dist: Parkwest Pubns., Inc.

AZ Books, creator. Tyler Turtle Travels to Australia. 2013. (Pop-Up: Play & Listen Ser.). (ENG., Illus.). 10p. (J). (gr. -1-k). bds. 16.95 *(978-1-61889-036-8(0))* AZ Bks. LLC.

Barker, Leslie. Bailey's Turtle. 2011. 20p. 12.49 *(978-1-4520-8762-7(8))* AuthorHouse.

Barnhouse Ms Ncc, Natalie. Shimmy Saves the Day: A Tale about Embracing Your Differences. 2012. 28p. pap. 19.99 *(978-1-4772-9933-3(5))* AuthorHouse.

Barr, Carolyn Mims. Blue Turtle. 2013. 24p. pap. 14.93 *(978-1-4669-8231-4(4))* Trafford Publishing.

Barsy, Kalman. Los Tres Naufragos. Perez-Moliere, Mamie, illus. 2004. (Orange Ser.). (SPA.). 40p. (J). (gr. 3-5). pap. 5.95 *(978-1-57581-469-8(2))* Santillana USA Publishing Co., Inc.

Bauer, Marion Dane. A Mama for Owen. Butler, John, illus. 2007. (ENG.). 32p. (J). (gr. -1-3). 17.99 *(978-0-689-85787-4(X),* Simon & Schuster Bks. For Young Readers) Simon & Schuster Bks. For Young Readers.

Bennett, Katrina. Pandora the Sea Turtle. 2012. 28p. pap. 21.99 *(978-1-4797-0537-5(3))* Xlibris Corp.

Benson, Donald. Tommy Turtle Turns Blue. 2007. 28p. (J). pap. 12.78 *(978-1-4251-2087-0(3))* Trafford Publishing.

Berkes, Marianne. The Tortoise & Hare's Amazing Race, 1 vol. Morrison, Cathy, illus. 2015. (ENG & SPA.). 32p. (J). (gr. k-3). 17.95 *(978-1-62855-635-3(8))* Arbordale Publishing.

Bernstein, Dan. The Tortoise & the Hare Race Again. Glass, Andrew, illus. 2006. (ENG.). (J). 36p. (gr. -1-3). 6.95 *(978-0-8234-2070-4(1));* 32p. (gr. 4-8). 16.95 *(978-0-8234-1867-1(7))* Holiday Hse., Inc.

Bernstein, Owen. My Turtle & Me. Thompson, Carol, illus. 2012. (ENG.). 10p. (J). (—1). bds. 9.99 *(978-0-545-43387-7(8))* Scholastic, Inc.

Best, Michael. Tommy the Turtle. 2011. 28p. pap. 15.99 *(978-1-4568-0354-4(9))* Xlibris Corp.

Best, Michael S. Tommy the Turtle. 2011. 24p. pap. 15.99 *(978-1-4628-8472-8(5))* Xlibris Corp.

Biachi, Kelvin K. Tortoise the King. 2010. 74p. pap. 21.50 *(978-1-60911-875-4(8),* Eloquent Bks.) Strategic Book Publishing & Rights Agency (SBPRA).

Biehn, Lesley. Humphrey & His Not So Lonely Shell. 2012. 20p. (-18). pap. 17.99 *(978-1-4772-8334-9(X))* AuthorHouse.

Birt, Michael. Kody the Conservation Pup: Helps Tori Cross the Road. Trammell, Brandon, illus. 2012. 58p. 27.95 *(978-0-578-11315-9(5));* pap. 19.95 *(978-0-578-11306-7(6))* Birt Hse. Publishing.

Blotnick, Elihu. Blue Turtle Moon Queen: The September Book. Robinson, Barbara J., illus. 2009. (ENG.). 114p. (J). (gr. 6-12). pap. 7.25 *(978-0-915090-20-4(1),* California Street) Firefall Editions.

Bodenstein, Dan. The Tale of Eartha the Sea Turtle. 2009. (Illus.). 36p. (J). pap. 12.99 *(978-0-9843228-0-0(9))* Totem Tales Publishing.

—The Tale of Eartha the Sea Turtle - Special Edition. 2011. (Illus.). 36p. (YA). pap. 12.99 *(978-0-9843228-1-7(7))* Totem Tales Publishing.

Bourgeois, Paulette. Benjamin et Sa Petite Soeur. 2004.Tr. of Franklin's Baby Sister. (FRE., Illus.). (J). (gr. k-3). spiral bd. *(978-0-616-14597-5(7))* Canadian National Institute for the Blind/Institut National Canadien pour les Aveugles.

—Franklin & the Bubble Gum. 2006. (Kids Can Read Ser.). (ENG., Illus.). 32p. (J). (gr. 1-2). 3.95 *(978-1-55337-817-4(2));* 14.95 *(978-1-55337-816-7(4))* Kids Can Pr., Ltd. CAN. Dist: Hachette Bk. Group.

—Franklin & the Computer. Clark, Brenda, illus. 2003. (Franklin Ser.: Bk. 16). 32p. (J). pap. 4.50 *(978-0-439-43121-7(2))* Scholastic, Inc.

—Franklin Es un Mandon. Varela, Alejandra López, tr. Clark, Brenda, illus.Tr. of Franklin Is Bossy. (SPA.). 10.95 *(978-1-930332-16-4(5),* LC6564) Lectorum Pubns., Inc.

—Franklin in the Dark. 2004. (Illus.). (J). (gr. -1-2). spiral bd. *(978-0-616-01574-2(7));* spiral bd. *(978-0-616-01575-9(5))* Canadian National Institute for the Blind/Institut National Canadien pour les Aveugles.

—Franklin Says I Love You. 2004. (Illus.). (J). (gr. k-3). spiral bd. *(978-0-616-14561-6(6));* spiral bd. *(978-0-616-14562-3(4))* Canadian National Institute for the Blind/Institut National Canadien pour les Aveugles.

—Franklin Wants a Badge. Clark, Brenda, illus. 2003. (Franklin TV Storybook Ser.). (ENG.). 32p. (J). (gr. -1-3). 4.95 *(978-1-55337-468-8(1));* 10.95 *(978-1-55337-467-1(3))* Kids Can Pr., Ltd. CAN. Dist: Hachette Bk. Group.

—Franklin's Baby Sister. Clark, Brenda, illus. (Franklin Ser.). (ENG.). 32p. (J). (gr. -1-3). *(978-1-55074-858-1(0))* Kids Can Pr., Ltd.

—Franklin's Family Treasury. Clark, Brenda, illus. 2003. (Franklin Ser.). (ENG.). 128p. (J). (gr. -1-3). 15.95 *(978-1-55337-479-4(7))* Kids Can Pr., Ltd. CAN. Dist: Hachette Bk. Group.

—Franklin's New Friend. Clark, Brenda, illus. (Franklin Ser.). (ENG.). 32p. (J). (gr. -1-3). *(978-1-55074-363-0(5))* Kids Can Pr., Ltd.

—Franklin's New Friend. 2004. (Illus.). (J). (gr. k-3). spiral bd. *(978-0-616-01590-2(9));* spiral bd. *(978-0-616-01591-9(7))* Canadian National Institute for the Blind/Institut National Canadien pour les Aveugles.

—Franklin's Soapbox Derby. 2006. (Kids Can Read Ser.). (ENG., Illus.). 32p. (J). (gr. 1-2). 3.95 *(978-1-55337-819-8(9));* 14.95 *(978-1-55337-818-1(0))* Kids Can Pr., Ltd. CAN. Dist: Hachette Bk. Group.

—Fun with Franklin: A Learning to Read Book. Clark, Brenda, illus. (Franklin Ser.). (J). (gr. -1-3). *(978-1-55074-646-4(4))* Kids Can Pr., Ltd.

—Neighborhood. 2004. (Illus.). (J). (gr. k-3). spiral bd. *(978-0-616-01589-6(5));* spiral bd. *(978-0-616-01588-9(7))* Canadian National Institute for the Blind/Institut National Canadien pour les Aveugles.

—Un Nouvel Ami pour Benjamin. 2004.Tr. of Franklin's New Friend. (FRE., Illus.). (J). (gr. -1-2). spiral bd. *(978-0-616-01828-6(2))* Canadian National Institute for the Blind/Institut National Canadien pour les Aveugles.

Bourgeois, Paulette & Clark, Brenda. Franklin & the Computer. 2003. (Franklin TV Storybook Ser.). (ENG., Illus.). 32p. (J). (gr. -1-3). 4.95 *(978-1-55337-363-6(4))* Kids Can Pr., Ltd. CAN. Dist: Hachette Bk. Group.

—Franklin & the Cookies. 2005. (Kids Can Read Ser.). (ENG., Illus.). 32p. (J). (gr. 1-2). 14.95 *(978-1-55337-716-0(8))* Kids Can Pr., Ltd. CAN. Dist: Hachette Bk. Group.

—Franklin & the New Teacher. 2004. (Franklin TV Storybook Ser.). (ENG., Illus.). 32p. (J). (gr. -1-3). 4.95 *(978-1-55337-500-5(9))* Kids Can Pr., Ltd. CAN. Dist: Hachette Bk. Group.

—Franklin Celebrates. 2005. (Franklin TV Storybook Ser.). (ENG., Illus.). 32p. (J). (gr. -1-3). 4.95 *(978-1-55337-502-9(5))* Kids Can Pr., Ltd. CAN. Dist: Hachette Bk. Group.

—Franklin Stays Up. Sinker, Alice, illus. 2003. (Kids Can Read Ser.). (ENG.). 32p. (J). (gr. 1-2). 3.95 *(978-1-55337-372-8(3));* 14.95 *(978-1-55337-371-1(5));* 14.95 *(978-1-55337-371-1(5))* Kids Can Pr., Ltd. CAN. Dist: Hachette Bk. Group.

—Franklin's Surprise. 2003. (Kids Can Read Ser.). (ENG., Illus.). 32p. (J). (gr. 1-2). 3.95 *(978-1-55337-466-4(5));* 14.95 *(978-1-55337-465-7(7))* Kids Can Pr., Ltd. CAN. Dist: Hachette Bk. Group.

Brett, Jan. Mossy. Brett, Jan, illus. 2012. (ENG., Illus.). 32p. (J). (gr. -1-k). 18.99 *(978-0-399-25782-7(9),* G.P. Putnam's Sons Books for Young Readers) Penguin Young Readers Group.

Briceno, Carole. Turtle's Journey, 1 vol. White, Tina Jorgenson, illus. 2009. 28p. pap. 24.95 *(978-1-60813-934-7(4))* America Star Bks.

Brightwood, Laura, illus. Anansi & the Turtle. Brightwood, Laura, . 2006. (J). *(978-0-9779290-0-9(0))* 3-C Institute for Social Development.

Bruchac, Joseph & Bruchac, James. Turtle's Race with Beaver. Aruego, Jose & Dewey, Ariane, illus. 2005. (ENG.). 32p. (J). (gr. k-3). pap. 5.99 *(978-0-14-240466-9(7),* Puffin Books) Penguin Young Readers Group.

Buckley, Richard. The Foolish Tortoise. Carle, Eric, illus. (World of Eric Carle Ser.). (ENG.). 24p. (J). (gr. -1-3). 2013. pap. 9.99 *(978-1-4424-6638-8(3))* 2009. bds. 7.99 *(978-1-4169-7916-6(6))* Little Simon. (Little Simon).

—The Foolish Tortoise. Carle, Eric, illus. 2015. (World of Eric Carle Ser.). (ENG.). 24p. (J). (gr. k-2). pap. 3.99 *(978-1-4814-3577-2(9),* Simon Spotlight) Simon Spotlight.

—The Foolish Tortoise: Lap Edition. Carle, Eric, illus. 2013. (World of Eric Carle Ser.). (ENG.). 24p. (J). (gr. -1-k). bds. 12.99 *(978-1-4424-8990-5(1),* Little Simon) Little Simon.

T U V

Bullock, Miranda. Mama Where Are You? 2008. 36p. pap. 16.99 *(978-1-4389-2962-0(5))* AuthorHouse.

Bumpsie the Red-Footed Tortoise. 2005. (J). bds. 5.99 *(978-0-9770957-0-4(3))* Turtle Time Bks.

Bumpsie's Neighborhood. 2006. (J). bds. 6.99 *(978-0-9770957-2-8(X))* Turtle Time Bks.

Bunting, Eve. Emma's Turtle. Winborn, Marsha, illus. (ENG.). 32p. (J). 2014. (gr. -1-2). pap. 6.95 *(978-1-62091-735-0(1))* 2007. (gr. 2-4). 15.95 *(978-1-59078-350-4(6))* Boyds Mills Pr.

—I Love You, Too! Sweet, Melissa, illus. 2015. (ENG.). 24p. (J). (— 1). bds. 7.99 *(978-0-545-81390-7(5),* Cartwheel Bks.) Scholastic, Inc.

Burgess, Thornton W. The Adventures of Jerry Muskrat. 2004. reprint ed. pap. 1.99 *(978-1-4192-5151-1(1));* pap. 15.95 *(978-1-4191-5151-4(7))* Kessinger Publishing, LLC.

Butler, Dori. The Tortoise & the Hare: An Aesop's Fable. 2006. (J). pap. *(978-1-4108-6167-2(8))* Benchmark Education Co.

Cain, Sheridan. La Pequena Tortuga y la Cancion del Mar. Burgin, Norma, illus. 2003. (SPA.). 24p. (J). (gr. k-2). *(978-84-8418-037-1(9),* ZZ30445) Zendrera Zariquiey, Editorial ESP. Dist: Lectorum Pubns., Inc.

Caplin, Daniel. Grandfather Turtle. 2003. pap. 14.95 *(978-0-9726781-0-0(7))* Evening Sun Pr.

Carle, Eric. Rooster Is off to See the World. 2013. (Eric Carle Ready-To-Read Ser.). lib. bdg. 13.55 *(978-0-606-32063-4(6),* Turtleback) Turtleback Bks.

Chaconas, Dori. Best Friends No. 1. McCue, Lisa, illus. 2010. (Cork & Fuzz Ser.: 1). (ENG.). 32p. (J). (gr. 1-2). mass mkt. 3.99 *(978-0-14-241593-1(6),* Penguin Young Readers) Penguin Young Readers Group.

Chalifoux, Lisa M. Spotty & Eddie Visit Percé. 2010. 24p. pap. 14.95 *(978-1-4269-2660-0(X))* Trafford Publishing.

Chanda, J-P. Turtle Rescue! Redondo, Jesus, illus. 2004. (Teenage Mutant Ninja Turtles Ser.). 32p. (J). (gr. 4-7). 11.65 *(978-0-7569-5371-3(5))* Perfection Learning Corp.

Cheek, Stephen. Catfish Cowboy & Mr. Turtle. 2008. 35p. pap. 21.80 *(978-0-557-02684-5(9))* Lulu Pr., Inc.

Chidebelu-Eze/Dove Publishing, Chibueze / Obi. The Tales of Tortoise: Inspirational Stories of Wisdom. Newborne, David / F., illus. 2005. (ENG.). 76p. (J). 16.00 *(978-0-9766578-0-4(5))* Dove Publishing, Inc.

Cockburn, Gerrie L. Why Turtles Have Shells. Cockburn, Ian, ed. Cockburn, Gerrie L., illus. (Friendship Ser.). (Illus.). 31p. (Orig.). (J). (gr. k-4). pap. 5.95 *(978-1-887461-00-9(0))* Cockburn Publishing.

Coll-Seck, Jayden. A Turtle for Malia. 01 vols., 1. 2016. (Rosen REAL Readers: STEM & STEAM Collection). (ENG.). 8p. (J). pap. 5.46 *(978-1-5081-1441-3(2),* Rosen Classroom) Rosen Publishing Group, Inc., The.

Collier, Kevin Scott. Esther's Channel. 2005. (Illus.). 160p. pap. 10.95 *(978-0-9752880-6-1(7))* Baker Trittin Pr.

Collier, Talina L. Jacob & the Turtle Race. 2012. 28p. pap. 24.95 *(978-1-4626-8045-0(3))* America Star Bks.

Conlin, Laura E. Winston's Wild Journeys: Live Outside Your Shell. 2011. 43p. (J). 18.95 *(978-1-4327-6885-0(9))* Outskirts Pr., Inc.

Conway, Aaron, illus. Alex the Sea Turtle. 2007. 26p. (J). *(978-0-9777923-0-6(7))* Shiloh Children's Bks.

Cook, Sherry & Johnson, Terri. Timothy Tornado. 26. Kuhn, Jesse, illus. l.t. ed. 2006. (Quirkles — Exploring Phonics through Science Ser.: 20). 32p. 7.99 *(978-1-933815-19-0(1),* Quirkles, The) Creative 3, LLC.

Corwin, Katherine A. R. Greg the Bearded Dragon & Thomas the Sea Turtle: A Tale of Adventure, Discovery, & Friendship. 2012. 28p. pap. 19.99 *(978-1-4685-7958-1(4))* AuthorHouse.

Cosgrove, Stephen. Tee-Tee. James, Robin, illus. 2015. (Serendipity Ser.: 17). (ENG.). 32p. (J). (gr. k-4). pap. 7.95 *(978-1-941437-36-0(2))* Heritage Builders, LLC.

Costello, Judi. Gertrude & the Creature. Bouthyette, Valerie, illus. 2008. 28p. pap. 24.95 *(978-1-60672-737-9(0))* America Star Bks.

Councilman, Janet H. Rocky & His Responsible Band of Cowboys, 1 vol. 2009. pap. 24.95 *(978-1-60749-384-6(5))* America Star Bks.

Courter, John. The Cheetah & the Turtle. 2011. 28p. pap. 15.99 *(978-1-4628-2952-1(X))* Xlibris Corp.

Courtney, Suzanne Gene. Ride to the Stars, a Story for Children about Life, Loss, & Love. 2009. 32p. pap. 16.50 *(978-1-60860-164-6(1),* Eloquent Bks.) Strategic Book Publishing & Rights Agency (SBPRA).

Cox, Janis. Tadeo Turtle. 2012. *(978-1-77069-695-2(4))* Word Alive Pr.

Crawford, Deborah. Tyler the Turtle Is Afraid of the Dark. Balzer, Jeremy, illus. 2006. 32p. (J). 14.95 *(978-0-9770516-1-8(7))* Laffin Minor Pr.

Crawford, Deborah & Crawford, Ryan. Pity's Porch. Ballard, Merry, illus. 2012. 24p. pap. 11.50 *(978-1-60976-796-9(9),* Strategic Bk. Publishing) Strategic Book Publishing & Rights Agency (SBPRA).

Crays, Lettie L. Timmy the Turtle Learns to Swim. Rollins, Joe, illus. 2011. 44p. (J). pap. 11.95 *(978-1-937089-06-1(1))* Truth Bk. Pubs.

Crowe, Ellie. Go to Sleep, Hide & Seek. Wu, Julie, illus. 2009. 10p. (J). bds. 11.95 *(978-1-59700-759-7(5))* Island Heritage Publishing.

Curriculum Corporation. Tai Hao Le! 2005. pap. 79.95 incl. audio compact disk *(978-1-86366-402-8(5))* Education Services Australia Ltd. AUS. Dist: Cheng & Tsui Co.

Curtis, Jennifer Keats. Turtles in My Sandbox, 1 vol. Schongut, Emanuel, illus. 2006. (ENG.). 32p. (J). (gr. 1-5). 16.95 *(978-0-9768823-7-4(X))* Arbordale Publishing.

Cyrus, Kurt. The Voyage of Turtle Rex. 2011. (ENG., Illus.). 40p. (J). (gr. -1-3). 16.99 *(978-0-547-42924-3(X))* Houghton Mifflin Harcourt Publishing Co.

Dadey, Debbie. Dream of the Blue Turtle. Avakyan, Tatevik, illus. 2014. (Mermaid Tales Ser.: 7). (ENG.). 128p. (J). (gr. 1-4). 16.99 *(978-1-4424-8264-7(8),* Aladdin) Simon & Schuster Children's Publishing.

Dahl, Roald. Esio Trot. 2009. 8.32 *(978-0-7848-2293-7(X),* Everbind) Marco Bk. Co.

—Esio Trot. Blake, Quentin, illus. 2009. (ENG.). 96p. (J). (gr. 3-7). 7.99 *(978-0-14-241382-1(8),* Puffin Books) Penguin Young Readers Group.

—Esio Trot. 2004. (CHI.). (J). pap. 11.70 *(978-957-574-477-9(2))* Youth Cultural Publishing Co. CHN. Dist: Chinasprout, Inc.

Davis, Laura. No! No! I Won't Be Slow! 2012. 24p. pap. 17.99 *(978-1-4772-5491-2(9))* AuthorHouse.

Demas, Corinne. Returning to Shore. 2014. 208p. (YA). (gr. 6-12). 17.95 *(978-1-4677-1328-3(7),* Carolrhoda Lab™) Lerner Publishing Group.

Dembicki, Carol & Dembicki, Matt. Mr. Big: A Tale of Pond Life. 2012. (ENG., Illus.). 160p. (J). (gr. 1-7). pap. 12.95 *(978-1-61608-967-2(9),* 608967, Sky Pony Pr.) Skyhorse Publishing Co., Inc.

Dillon-Butler, Marybeth. Myrtle the Hurdler: And Her Pink & Purple Polka-Dotted Girdle. Messing, David, illus. 2005. (ENG.). 32p. (J). (gr. -1-2). pap. 11.95 *(978-0-9785075-9-6(2),* Ferne Pr.) Nelson Publishing & Marketing.

Dixon, Kirstie. Pickles Helps a Friend. 2012. 16p. pap. 15.99 *(978-1-4772-6445-4(0))* AuthorHouse.

Doder, Joshua. Grk: Operation Tortoise. 2009. 219p. (J). pap. *(978-0-440-42152-8(7),* Delacorte Pr) Random House Publishing Group.

Doerr, Bonnie J. Stakeout. Edwards, Laurie J. & Britt, Joanna, illus. 2011. 310p. pap. 12.99 *(978-1-61603-007-0(0))* Leap Bks.

Dub-u-el. Zoom-Zoom & Slo-Poke. 2005. (J). pap. 15.00 *(978-0-8059-6808-8(3))* Dorrance Publishing Co., Inc.

Duncan, Tisha Admire. Myrtle the Blue Eyed Turtle: A My Dirty Cat Mutt Adventure. 2012. 28p. pap. 14.95 *(978-1-4497-5727-4(8),* WestBow Pr.) Author Solutions, Inc.

Dunkwu, Jude. The Tortoise Tales Niki the Tortoise & the Birds: Why the Tortoise's Shell Is Cracked. 2013. (Illus.). 54p. pap. *(978-0-9573727-2-6(8))* Sahara Media, Ltd.

Dunrea, Olivier. Gus. (Gossie & Friends Ser.). (ENG., Illus.). 32p. (J). 2017. (gr. -1-3). 12.99 *(978-0-544-93723-9(6))* 2015. (— 1). 9.99 *(978-0-547-86761-8(1))* Houghton Mifflin Harcourt Publishing Co. (HMH Books For Young Readers).

—Gus (board Book) 2016. (Gossie & Friends Ser.). (ENG., Illus.). 32p. (J). (— 1). bds. 6.99 *(978-0-544-64102-0(7),* HMH Books For Young Readers) Houghton Mifflin Harcourt Publishing Co.

Duracell and the National Center for Missing & Exploited Children (NCMEC), creator. The Great Tomato Adventure: A Story about Smart Safety Choices. 2007. 0.00 *(978-0-9795307-0-8(9))* Duracell & the National Ctr. for Missing & Exploited Children (NCMEC).

Durrell, Gerald. Toby the Tortoise. (Illus.). 32p. (J). 15.95 *(978-1-85479-032-3(3))* O'Mara, Michael Bks., Ltd. GBR. Dist: Trans-Atlantic Pubns., Inc.

Dutton, Maude Barrows. The Tortoise & the Geese & Other Fables of Bidpai. Smith, E. Boyd, illus. 2008. 104p. pap. 7.95 *(978-1-59915-249-3(5))* Yesterday's Classics.

Eggleton, Jill. Turtle's Trouble. Cammell, Sandra, illus. 2003. (Rigby Sails Early Ser.). (ENG.). 16p. (gr. 1-2). pap. 6.95 *(978-0-7578-8672-0(8))* Houghton Mifflin Harcourt Publishing Co.

Eke, Vincent. The Turtle's Shell. 2013. (Illus.). 46p. pap. *(978-1-909688-00-1(2))* Lionpen Publishing.

Elk, Ronit. A Surprise at Dancing Fields. 2009. 76p. pap. 10.49 *(978-1-4490-2064-4(X))* AuthorHouse.

Ende, Michael. Tranquila Tragaleguas: La Tortuga Cabezota. Asensio, Agusti, illus. 2003.Tr. of Tranquila Trampeltreu. (SPA.). 42p. (J). (gr. k-3). pap. 8.95 *(978-84-204-3709-5(3))* Santillana USA Publishing Co., Inc.

Fable, Aesop. The Tortoise & the Hare. 2012. (J). 29.99 *(978-1-61913-103-3(X))* Weigl Pubs., Inc.

Falwell, Cathryn. Turtle Splash! Countdown at the Pond. Falwell, Cathryn, illus. 2008. (ENG., Illus.). 32p. (J). (gr. -1-3). pap. 6.99 *(978-0-06-142927-9(9),* Greenwillow Bks.) HarperCollins Pubs.

Finally, Lil Rose. Slowpoke the Turtle & Company. Drape, Kaitlin, illus. 2005. (J). pap. 8.00 *(978-0-8059-6778-4(8))* Dorrance Publishing Co., Inc.

Finn, Ann-Marie. Captain Kieron. Finn, Ann-Marie, illus. 2013. (Illus.). 32p. pap. *(978-0-9874160-3-2(0))* Wybble Publishing.

Floyd, Lucy. Conejo y Tortuga van a la Escuela. Flor Ada, Alma & Campoy, F. Isabel, trs. from ENG. Denise, Christopher, illus. 2010. (Green Light Readers Level 1 Ser.).Tr. of Rabbit & Turtle Go to School. (SPA & ENG.). 28p. (J). (gr. -1-3). pap. 3.99 *(978-0-547-33898-9(8))* Houghton Mifflin Harcourt Publishing Co.

For the Love of Turtles: Six-Pack. (Greetings Ser.: Vol. 1). 24p. (gr. 2-3). 31.00 *(978-0-7635-9423-7(7))* Rigby Education.

Ford, Carole S. Timothy Turtle & Sammy Scallop. Edwin, Kimberly, illus. 30p. (J). (gr. -1-k). pap. 4.95 *(978-1-891533-02-0(9))* Calvin Partnership, LLC.

Fox, Laura. Stan the Timid Turtle: Helping Children Cope with Fears about School Violence. DuFalla, Anita, illus. 2014. (ENG.). 48p. (J). (gr. -1-2). 9.95 *(978-0-88282-466-6(X))* New Horizon Pr. Pubs., Inc.

Frances Holloway. The Turtle That Lived in the Sand. 2010. 28p. pap. 21.99 *(978-1-4535-4845-5(9))* Xlibris Corp.

Furrow, Eva & Napoli, Donna Jo. Take Your Time: A Tale of Harriet, the Galápagos Tortoise. Molk, Laurel, illus. 2017. (ENG.). 32p. (J). 16.99 *(978-0-8050-9521-0(7),* 9780805095210, Holt, Henry & Co. Bks. For Young Readers) Holt, Henry & Co.

Fusek Peters, Andrew. The Talkative Tortoise. 2011. (Traditional Tales with a Twist Ser.). (ENG., Illus.). 32p. (J). *(978-1-84643-418-1(1))* Child's Play International Ltd.

Fuson, Robin Densmore. Rosita Valdez: And the Giant Sea Turtle. 2012. 108p. 28.99 *(978-1-4497-6487-6(8));* pap. 11.99 *(978-1-4497-6486-9(X))* Author Solutions, Inc. (WestBow Pr.).

Gagnon, Céleste, et al, adapted by. Franklin & the Tin Flute. 2005. (Kids Can Read Ser.). (ENG., Illus.). 32p. (J). (gr. 1-2). 3.95 *(978-1-55337-801-3(6))* Kids Can Pr., Ltd. CAN. Dist: Hachette Bk. Group.

Galera Staff. La Liebre y la Tortuga. (SPA.). 24p. (J). 9.95 *(978-84-246-1555-0(7),* GL30396) La Galera, S.A. Editorial ESP. Dist: AIMS International Bks., Inc.

Gamlin, Jim. Lucky Nickel: The Story of Nickel the Sea Turtle. 2012. 44p. pap. 21.99 *(978-1-4691-9662-6(X))* Xlibris Corp.

Gaona, Gloria. Dominic & His Turtle Michael Angelo. 2003. 32p. (J). pap. 9.00 *(978-0-8059-5764-8(2))* Dorrance Publishing Co., Inc.

Garcia, R. M. The Steamer Trunk Adventures #1: The Trunk & the Tortoise. 2006. 76p. pap. 16.95 *(978-1-4241-0614-1(1))* PublishAmerica, Inc.

Gehl, Laura & Aesop. Hare & Tortoise Race Across Israel. Goodreau, Sarah, illus. 2015. (J). 6.99 *(978-1-4677-6202-1(4),* Kar-Ben Publishing) Lerner Publishing Group.

George, Lucy M. Back to School Tortoise. Eyckerman, Merel, illus. 2011. (ENG.). 24p. (J). (gr. -1-3). 15.99 *(978-0-8075-0510-6(2))* Whitman, Albert & Co.

Gerver, Jane E. The Santa Snatcher. Spaziante, Patrick, illus. 2004. 32p. (J). lib. bdg. 15.00 *(978-1-4242-0959-0(5))* Fitzgerald Bks.

Geyer, Clyde. The Awesome Adventures of Chuckie Chopper & Friends. 2012. 52p. pap. 15.95 *(978-1-4575-0741-0(2))* Dog Ear Publishing, LLC.

Gilbert, Matthew. Night of the T-Machines (Teenage Mutant Ninja Turtles) Spaziante, Patrick, illus. 2016. (Pictureback(R) Ser.). (ENG.). 16p. (J). (gr. -1-2). 4.99 *(978-1-101-93866-9(8),* Random Hse. Bks. for Young Readers) Random Hse. Children's Bks.

Gilland, Gary P. The Turtle Train Troop. 2011. 24p. pap. 24.95 *(978-1-4626-3210-7(6))* America Star Bks.

Gipson, Crash. Sheldon's Favorite Game. 2011. 36p. pap. 24.95 *(978-1-4626-4578-7(X))* America Star Bks.

Glick, Susan. Jemma's Got the Travel Bug, 1 vol. Nash, Kelli, illus. 2010. (ENG.). 32p. (J). 14.99 *(978-0-7643-3632-4(0),* 9780764336324) Schiffer Publishing, Ltd.

Golden Books. The Art of the Ninja (Teenage Mutant Ninja Turtles) Golden Books, illus. 2014. (Doodle Book Ser.). (ENG., Illus.). 128p. (J). (gr. -1-2). pap. 5.99 *(978-0-385-37851-2(3),* Golden Bks.) Random Hse. Children's Bks.

—The Big Book of Ninja Turtles (Teenage Mutant Ninja Turtles) Golden Books, illus. 2014. (Big Golden Book Ser.). (ENG., Illus.). 48p. (J). (gr. -1-2). 9.99 *(978-0-553-50769-0(9),* Golden Bks.) Random Hse. Children's Bks.

—Frog Fight! (Teenage Mutant Ninja Turtles) Lambe, Steve, illus. 2016. (Little Golden Book Ser.). (ENG.). 24p. (J). (-k). 4.99 *(978-0-553-53907-3(8),* Golden Bks.) Random Hse. Children's Bks.

—Let's Get Epic! (Teenage Mutant Ninja Turtles) Golden Books, illus. 2014. (Big Coloring Book Ser.). (ENG., Illus.). 48p. (J). (gr. -1-2). pap. 6.99 *(978-0-385-37849-9(1),* Golden Bks.) Random Hse. Children's Bks.

—Really Spaced Out! (Teenage Mutant Ninja Turtles) Golden Books, illus. 2016. (Little Golden Book Ser.). (ENG., Illus.). 24p. (J). (-k). 4.99 *(978-1-101-93694-8(0),* Golden Bks.) Random Hse. Children's Bks.

—Teenage Mutant Ninja Turtles. Golden Books, illus. 2014. (Magnetic Play Book Ser.). (ENG., Illus.). 8p. (J). (gr. -1-2). bds. 8.99 *(978-0-385-37522-1(0),* Golden Bks.) Random Hse. Children's Bks.

—Teenage Mutant Ninja Turtles: Out of the Shadows. Golden Books, illus. 2016. (Full-Color Activity Book with Stickers Ser.). (ENG., Illus.). 48p. (J). (gr. -1-2). pap. 4.99 *(978-1-101-94030-3(1),* Golden Bks.) Random Hse. Children's Bks.

—Teenage Mutant Ninja Turtles Holiday. Golden Books, illus. 2016. (Big Golden Book Ser.). (ENG., Illus.). 32p. (J). (gr. -1-2). 9.99 *(978-0-399-55119-2(0),* Golden Bks.) Random Hse. Children's Bks.

—Teenage Mutant Ninja Turtles Little Golden Book Favorites (Teenage Mutant Ninja Turtles) Golden Books, illus. 2016. (Little Golden Book Favorites Ser.). (ENG., Illus.). 80p. (J). (-k). 7.99 *(978-0-399-55359-2(2),* Golden Bks.) Random Hse. Children's Bks.

Golden Books & Berrios, Frank. Mutants Rule! (Teenage Mutant Ninja Turtles) Golden Books, illus. 2013. (Color & Paint Plus Stickers Ser.). (ENG., Illus.). 128p. (J). (gr. -1-2). pap. 9.99 *(978-0-449-81952-4(3),* Golden Bks.) Random Hse. Children's Bks.

Golden Books Staff. Follow the Ninja! Golden Books Staff & Lambe, Steve, illus. 2015. (Little Golden Book Ser.). (ENG.). 24p. (J). (-k). 4.99 *(978-0-553-51204-5(8),* Golden Bks.) Random Hse. Children's Bks.

Golden Books Staff & Random House Staff. Enter the Lair (Teenage Mutant Ninja Turtles) Golden Books Staff & Random House Staff, illus. 2013. (Pictureback(R) Ser.). (ENG., Illus.). 16p. (J). (gr. -1-2). pap. 4.99 *(978-0-449-81385-0(1),* Random Hse. Bks. for Young Readers) Random Hse. Children's Bks.

Gorbachev, Valeri. Ms. Turtle the Babysitter. Gorbachev, Valeri, illus. 2005. (I Can Read Bks.). (Illus.). 64p. (J). (gr. k-3). (ENG.). 15.99 *(978-0-06-058073-5(9));* lib. bdg. 16.89 *(978-0-06-058074-2(7))* HarperCollins Pubs.

—Whose Hat Is It? 2004. 30p. (J). lib. bdg. 13.85 *(978-1-4242-0713-8(4))* Fitzgerald Bks.

—Whose Hat Is It? Gorbachev, Valeri, illus. (My First I Can Read Ser.). (Illus.). 32p. (J). (gr. -1 — 1). 2005. (ENG.). pap. 3.99 *(978-0-06-053436-3(2))* 2004. (ENG.). 14.99 *(978-0-06-053434-9(6))* 2004. lib. bdg. 15.89 *(978-0-06-053435-6(4))* HarperCollins Pubs.

Greenberg, Penny. The Adventures of Toby the Turtle & Mighty Magoo. 2008. 16p. pap. 8.49 *(978-1-4389-1014-7(2))* AuthorHouse.

Grubnedor Press. Tuppy the Turtle Puppy. 2007. (Illus.). 32p. (J). 10.95 *(978-0-9795407-0-7(4))* Grubnedor Pr.

Guerra, Elisa Puricelli. The Night of the Blue Turtles. Zeni, Marco, tr. from ITA. Bernstein, Gabriel León, illus. 2015. (Minerva Mint Ser.). (ENG.). 160p. (gr. 2-4). lib. bdg. 25.32 *(978-1-4342-9672-6(5))* Stone Arch Bks.

Gumbs, Al-Tariq. The Turtle Who Bullied. 2012. (ENG.). pap. 10.00 *(978-1-4675-1785-0(2))* Independent Pub.

Haltigan, Susanne. Seymour the Sea Turtle Saves His Sea Friends. 2011. 28p. pap. 11.95 *(978-1-4567-6549-1(3))* AuthorHouse.

Hamilton, Linda. The Wise Old Turtle. 2005. (J). *(978-1-933248-06-6(8))* World Quest Learning.

Harder, Christopher. It's Tough to Nap on a Turtle. Harder, Rolf, illus. 2008. (ENG.). 11p. (J). (gr. -1). bds. 5.95 *(978-0-9726614-9-2(2))* Shenanigan Bks.

harkins, charles. Naptime Adventures of Luksi the Turtle. 2010. 174p. pap. 20.96 *(978-0-557-28695-9(6))* Lulu Pr., Inc.

Harris, Robie H. Turtle & Me. Freeman, Tor, illus. 2015. (ENG.). 40p. (J). (gr. -1-3). 16.99 *(978-1-4998-0046-3(0))* Little Bee Books Inc.

Hausman, Gerald. Timeswimmer. 2009. (Island Fiction Ser.). 187p. (J). (gr. 5-16). pap. *(978-1-4050-9898-4(8))* Macmillan Caribbean.

Heckt, Jackie. Tilly the Turtle. 2017. (Pet Tales! Ser.). 24p. (J). (gr. 4-6). pap. 8.25 ***(978-1-5081-5676-5(X),*** PowerKids Pr.) Rosen Publishing Group, Inc., The.

Helean, April K. Love Can Build a Bridge. 2012. 24p. pap. 15.99 *(978-1-4691-5621-7(0))* Xlibris Corp.

Henry, Kristina. The Turtle Tank, 1 vol. Ambler, Laura & Brown, Amanda, illus. 2011. (ENG.). 32p. (J). 16.99 *(978-0-7643-3843-4(9),* 9780764338434, Schiffer Publishing Ltd) Schiffer Publishing, Ltd.

Hensley, Terri Anne. Tobias Andrew Bartholomew. Hall, Norris, illus. 2007. 32p. per. 8.99 *(978-0-9789057-6-7(8))* Huntington Ludlow Media Group.

Hicks, Robert Z. Tommie Turtle's Secret. Rolseth, Ruthie, illus. 2007. (ENG.). 40p. (J). 16.95 *(978-0-9792031-0-7(4))* R.Z. Enterprises of Florida.

Himes, John. Everyone Is Special. 2012. 24p. pap. 24.95 *(978-1-4626-7462-6(3))* America Star Bks.

Himmelman, John. Tudley Didn't Know, 1 vol. Himmelman, John, illus. 2006. (ENG., Illus.). 32p. (J). (gr. -1-3). 15.95 *(978-0-9764943-6-2(1));* pap. 8.95 *(978-1-934359-04-4(1))* Arbordale Publishing.

Hixon, Mara Uman. Turtle's Way: Loggy, Greeny & Leather. Harris, Steve J., illus. 2004. 25p. (J). (gr. -1-3). 16.00 *(978-1-887774-20-8(3),* Wynden) Canmore Pr.

Holden, Pam. Turtle Is Lost. 2015. (ENG., Illus.). 16p. (-1). pap. *(978-1-77654-074-7(3),* Red Rocket Readers) Flying Start Bks.

Holyoak, Kathleen & Summers, Sherry. Flowers in Heaven. 2009. 32p. pap. 14.49 *(978-1-4389-4607-8(4))* AuthorHouse.

Hong, Catherine Thao. The Adventures of Miss Turtle. Pipe, Jasper, illus. 2012. 24p. (J). pap. *(978-0-9873790-0-9(3))* Icky Grass Books.

Hoobler, David. Zonk & the Secret Lagoon: The Further Adventures of Zonk the Dreaming Tortoise. Hoobler, David, illus. l.t. ed. 2005. (Illus.). 32p. (J). lib. bdg. 18.95 *(978-0-9706537-1-0(9))* Zonk Galleries and Pubns.

Hooray for Boys & Girls! 2006. (J). 15.95 *(978-0-9776837-0-3(2))* West Woods Pr.

Hopgood, Sally. See You Later, Alligator. Levey, Emma, illus. 2016. (ENG.). 32p. (J). (gr. -1-k). 16.99 *(978-1-5107-0484-8(1),* Sky Pony Pr.) Skyhorse Publishing Co., Inc.

Horn, Peter. The Best Father of All. James, J. Alison, tr. from GER. Kadmon, Cristina, illus. 2005. (ENG.). 32p. (J). (gr. -1). pap. 6.95 *(978-0-7358-1977-1(7))* North-South Bks., Inc.

—When I Grow Up... Kadmon, Cristina, illus. 2014. 32p. pap. 8.00 *(978-1-61003-370-1(1))* Center for the Collaborative Classroom.

Howell, Gill. Tortoise & the Baboon. Woody, illus. 2004. (ENG.). 16p. (J). lib. bdg. 23.65 *(978-1-59646-686-9(3))* Dingles & Co.

Hsia, Pei Chen. The Little Dumpling. 2012. 82p. pap. 19.95 *(978-1-4626-8041-2(0))* America Star Bks.

Hughes, John P. A Wish for Little Tommy Turtle. White, Tara B., illus. 2011. 48p. pap. 24.95 *(978-1-4626-0011-3(5))* America Star Bks.

Hunter, Sara Hoagland. Every Turtle Counts. Spellman, Susan, illus. 2014. (ENG.). 36p. (J). 16.95 *(978-1-931807-25-8(6))* Randall, Peter E. Pub.

I Am A Dog. 2008. (Illus.). 26p. 24.95 *(978-0-9801054-0-7(4))* Teahouse of Danger.

Ikids Staff. Little Turtles. Larranaga, Ana, illus. 2008. (iBaby Float-Alongs Ser.). (ENG.). 6p. (J). (gr. -1). 12.99 *(978-1-58476-808-1(8))* Innovative Kids.

Ikpe, Ernest & Madge. African Stories about the Tortoise. 2011. 32p. pap. 17.00 *(978-1-4634-2726-9(3))* AuthorHouse.

ImageBooks Staff. Little Sea Turtle: Finger Puppet Book. 2014. (Little Finger Puppet Board Bks.). (ENG.). 12p. (J). (gr. -1 — 1). bds. 6.99 *(978-1-4521-2913-6(4))* Chronicle Bks. LLC.

Ingram, Jacquelyn. Dakota's Doggie Tale. 2009. 32p. pap. 14.99 *(978-1-4490-1327-1(9))* AuthorHouse.

Irvin-Marston, Hope. My Little Book of Painted Turtles. Magdalena-Brown, Maria, illus. 2nd ed. 2004. 32p. (J). pap. 7.95 *(978-0-89317-055-4(0),* WW-0550, Windward Publishing) Finney Co., Inc.

Irwin, Bindi, et al. Surfing with Turtles: Bindi Wildlife Adventures. 2013. (Bindi's Wildlife Adventures Ser.: 8). (ENG.). 112p. (J). (gr. 3-6). pap. 4.99 *(978-1-4022-8094-8(7),* Sourcebooks Jabberwocky) Sourcebooks, Inc.

Itoh, Shimpei. Hyper Dolls, Vol. 5. 2003. (Illus.). 208p. pap. 15.95 *(978-1-929090-67-9(6))* International Comics & Entertainment L.L.C.

James, Hollis. Space Shark! (Teenage Mutant Ninja Turtles) Spaziante, Patrick, illus. 2016. (Step into Reading Ser.). (ENG.). 24p. (J). (gr. -1-1). 4.99 *(978-1-101-93708-2(4),* Random Hse. Bks. for Young Readers) Random Hse. Children's Bks.

Javernick, Ellen. The Birthday Pet, 0 vols. O'Malley, Kevin, illus. 2012. (ENG.). 34p. (J). (gr. k-3). pap. 7.99 *(978-0-7614-6238-5(4),* 9780761462385, Amazon Children's Publishing) Amazon Publishing.

Jay, Lorraine A. Sea Turtle Journey: The Story of a Loggerhead Turtle. Lee, Katie, illus. 2011. (Smithsonian Oceanic Collection Ser.). (ENG.). 32p. (J). (gr. -1-3). 19.95 *(978-1-60727-660-9(7))* Soundprints.

Jeffords, Stephanie & Branum, Anita. Jumpy the Turtle. May, Ashley, illus. 2012. 92p. pap. 20.00 *(978-1-936750-80-1(5))* Yorkshire Publishing Group.

Jenkins, Amanda. How the Turtle Cracked its Shell: A Tale from Guatemala. 2006. (J). pap. *(978-1-4108-6171-9(6))* Benchmark Education Co.

Jennings, Sharon. Franklin Stays Up. Jeffrey, Sean et al, illus. 2003. 32p. (J). pap. *(978-0-439-41815-7(1))* Scholastic, Inc.

Jennings, Sharon, et al, adapted by. Franklin & the Computer. 2003. (Franklin TV Storybook Ser.). (ENG., Illus.). 32p. (J). (gr. -1-3). 10.95 *(978-1-55337-362-9(6))* Kids Can Pr., Ltd. CAN. Dist: Hachette Bk. Group.

—Franklin & the Cookies. 2005. (Kids Can Read Ser.). (ENG., Illus.). 32p. (J). (gr. 1-2). 3.95 *(978-1-55337-717-7(6))* Kids Can Pr., Ltd. CAN. Dist: Hachette Bk. Group.

—Franklin & the Tin Flute. 2005. (Kids Can Read Ser.). (ENG., Illus.). 32p. (J). (gr. 1-2). 14.95 *(978-1-55337-800-6(8))* Kids Can Pr., Ltd. CAN. Dist: Hachette Bk. Group.

—Franklin's Pond Phantom. 2005. (Kids Can Read Ser.). (ENG., Illus.). 32p. (J). (gr. 1-2). 14.95 *(978-1-55337-718-4(4))* Kids Can Pr., Ltd. CAN. Dist: Hachette Bk. Group.

Jepson, Jeanette. The Adventures of Theodore Tortoise - Claude's Big Adventure: Claude's Big Adventure. 2011. 24p. pap. 15.99 *(978-1-4628-8646-3(9))* Xlibris Corp.

Johanson, Rhonda. The Great Tempo Race. 2011. 32p. pap. 21.99 *(978-1-4568-5363-1(5))* Xlibris Corp.

Johnson, Rebecca. Sea Turtle's Clever Plan. Parish, Steve, illus. 2005. (Animal Storybooks Ser.). 24p. (gr. k-3). lib. bdg. 22.00 *(978-0-8368-5975-1(8)*, Gareth Stevens Learning Library) Stevens, Gareth Publishing LLLP.

Jonas, Debbie Sue. The Key Lime Candies Clubt in Two Turtles' Tales. 2012. 44p. pap. 17.49 *(978-1-4691-5283-7(5))* Xlibris Corp.

Jones, Shelley V. & Sprick, Marilyn. Turtle in the Tuba: Read Well Level K Unit 8 Storybook. McDonnell, Kevin, illus. 2004. (Read Well Level K Ser.). 20p. *(978-1-57035-672-8(6))* Cambium Education, Inc.

Keane, Dave. Who Wants a Tortoise? Campbell, K. G., illus. 2016. (ENG.). 40p. (J). (gr. k-3). 17.99 *(978-0-385-75417-0(5)*, Knopf Bks. for Young Readers) Random Hse. Children's Bks.

Keane, Sarah. The Hare & the Tortoise: An Aesop's Fable Retold by Sarah Keane, 1 vol. 2013. (Fiction Readers Ser.). (ENG., Illus.). 28p. (J). (gr. 2-2). pap. 6.99 *(978-1-4333-5572-1(8))* Shell Educational Publishing.

Keith, Brooke. Chrissie's Shell. Bausman, Mary, illus. 2010. 32p. (J). 14.99 *(978-1-59317-398-2(9))* Warner Pr., Inc.

Kennedy, Geno. Tiny Takes a Trip. Engler, Lori, illus. 2011. 24p. pap. 24.95 *(978-1-4560-8523-0(9))* America Star Bks.

Kessler, Liz. Poppy the Pirate Dog & the Missing Treasure. Phillips, Mike, illus. (Candlewick Sparks Ser.). (ENG.). 64p. (J). (gr. k-4). 2016. pap. 3.99 *(978-0-7636-8772-4(3))* 2015. 14.99 *(978-0-7636-7497-7(4))* Candlewick Pr.

Kids Can Press Staff. Franklin's Picnic. 2006. (Kids Can Read Ser.). (ENG., Illus.). 32p. (J). (gr. 1-2). 3.95 *(978-1-55337-715-3(X))* Kids Can Pr., Ltd. CAN. Dist: Hachette Bk. Group.

Kids Can Read Staff, ed. Franklin's Pond Phantom. 2005. (Kids Can Read Ser.). (ENG., Illus.). 32p. (J). (gr. 1-2). 3.95 *(978-1-55337-719-1(2))* Kids Can Pr., Ltd. CAN. Dist: Hachette Bk. Group.

Kim, YeShil. Tortoise & Hare. Kheiriyeh, Rashin, illus. 2014. (MySELF Bookshelf Ser.). (ENG.). 32p. (J). (gr. k-2). pap. 11.94 *(978-1-60357-700-7(9))*; lib. bdg. 25.27 *(978-1-59953-665-1(X))* Norwood Hse. Pr.

Kimmel, Eric A. The Fisherman & the Turtle, 0 vols. 2013. (ENG.). 32p. (J). (gr. -1-3). pap. 9.99 *(978-1-4778-1672-1(0)*, 9781477816721, Amazon Children's Publishing) Amazon Publishing.

King, Jerry. Tommy the Turtle. 2009. 16p. pap. 9.95 *(978-1-4389-7551-1(1))* AuthorHouse.

Klassen, Jon. We Found a Hat. Klassen, Jon, illus. 2016. (ENG., Illus.). 56p. (J). (gr. -1-3). 17.99 *(978-0-7636-5600-3(3))* Candlewick Pr.

Kleemann, Linda. Larry the Turtle When Everyone Helps, Everyone Wins! Malkowski, Melissa, illus. 2005. (J). pap. 7.95 *(978-0-9776487-0-2(2))* Fencepost Communications Inc.

Klise, Kate. The Loch Ness Punster. Klise, M. Sarah, illus. 2016. (43 Old Cemetery Road Ser.: 7). (ENG.). 144p. (J). (gr. 2-5). pap. 6.99 *(978-0-544-81085-3(6)*, HMH Books For Young Readers) Houghton Mifflin Harcourt Publishing Co.

Korman, Susan. Box Turtle at Silver Pond Lane: Smithsonians Backyard. Marchesi, Stephen, illus. 2005. (Smithsonian's Backyard Ser.). (ENG.). 32p. (J). (gr. -1-2). pap. 6.95 *(978-1-56899-935-7(6)*, S5020) Soundprints.

Kreitz, Tina. Rocky the Sea Turtle. Triplett, Chris Harper, illus. 2013. (ENG.). (J). 14.95 *(978-1-62086-132-5(1))* Mascot Bks., Inc.

Kruse, Robyn A. Sammy the Sea Turtle, 1 vol. Litteral, Christopher, illus. 2010. 18p. 24.95 *(978-1-4489-4020-2(6))* PublishAmerica, Inc.

Kuperman, Marina. Turtle Feet, Surfer's Beat. 2007. 164p. (J). pap. 9.99 *(978-0-9801109-0-6(4))* Kuperman, Marina.

Labadie, Sally. Tanner's Turtle. Jeremiah, illus. 2012. 32p. pap. 12.95 *(978-1-61244-085-9(1))* Halo Publishing International.

Laing, Marilyn. Why the Turtle & the Snail Carried their Houses on Their Back. 2011. 24p. pap. 13.50 *(978-1-4567-3154-0(8))* AuthorHouse.

Lampley, David Gerald. Shorty's Dilemm. 2011. 74p. pap. 19.95 *(978-1-4560-4189-2(4))* America Star Bks.

Larsen, Alison. My Turtle. Larsen, Alison, illus. 2006. (Illus.). 24p. (J). (gr. -1-3). per. 11.95 *(978-1-60002-095-7(X)*, 3963) Mountain Valley Publishing, LLC.

—Thomas the Turtle. 2006. (Illus.). 21p. (J). per. 14.95 *(978-1-60002-097-1(6)*, 3961) Mountain Valley Publishing, LLC.

—Thomas the Turtle's Adventures. 2006. (Illus.). 23p. (J). per. 14.95 *(978-1-60002-096-4(8)*, 3962) Mountain Valley Publishing, LLC.

LeapFrog Staff. Pirates: The Treasure of Turtle Island. 2008. (J). 13.99 *(978-1-59319-927-2(9))* LeapFrog Enterprises, Inc.

Lee, Ginger. Tessa T's Treasures, 1 vol. 2010. 22p. 29.95 *(978-1-4489-4526-9(7))* America Star Bks.

León, Georgina Lázaro. ¡Viva la Tortuga! Torres, Walter, illus. (SPA.). 30p. (J). (gr. 3-5). 12.95 *(978-1-57581-605-0(9))* Santillana USA Publishing Co., Inc.

Lewman, David. Teenage Mutant Ninja Turtles: Out of the Shadows. Random House, illus. 2016. (Deluxe Junior Novel Ser.). (ENG.). 144p. (J). (gr. 3-7). 9.99 *(978-1-101-93919-2(2))*; 6.99 *(978-0-399-55694-4(X))* Random Hse. Children's Bks. (Random Hse. Bks. for Young Readers).

Libby, Lori Ann. The Adventures of Henry Hamper & the Flying Fish. Lee, Tricia Ting, illus. 2010. 34p. pap. 13.95 *(978-1-60911-493-0(0)*, Eloquent Bks.) Strategic Book Publishing & Rights Agency (SBPRA).

Lievre et la Tortue. pap. 5.95 *(978-88-8148-779-0(9))* EMC/Paradigm Publishing.

Limu the Blue Turtle. 2003. (J). 15.95 *(978-0-89610-549-2(0))* Island Heritage Publishing.

Lin, Joyce, tr. The frog in the Well. Caprio, Pattie, illus. 2008. (ENG & CHI.). 36p. (J). 14.95 *(978-0-9801305-1-5(4))* CE Bilingual Bks. LLC.

Lloyd, Sylvia. A Little Turtle's Tale. 2005. pap. *(978-1-932077-96-4(0))* Athena Pr.

Lockaby, Angie. Tad the Turtle It's Okay to Be Different. 2012. 28p. pap. 19.99 *(978-1-4772-7295-4(X))* AuthorHouse.

Lockard, Donna Lee. Sasha the Tortoise's Summer Vacation. 2013. (ENG.). 36p. (J). pap. 19.95 *(978-1-4787-0938-1(3))* Outskirts Pr., Inc.

The Long Legged Turtle. 2013. 44p. pap. 16.99 *(978-1-4808-0460-9(6))* Archway Publishing.

Lordon, Claire. Lorenzo, the Pizza-Loving Lobster. 2016. (ENG., Illus.). 32p. (J). (gr. -1-3). 16.99 *(978-1-4998-0228-3(5))* Little Bee Books Inc.

Lowe, Lana. The Three Little Girls & the Giant Sea Turtle. Beaumont, Peter, illus. 2006. (J). *(978-0-9777274-0-7(8))* Lone Star Publishing Co.

Lowell, Susan. The Tortoise & the Jackrabbit: La Tortuga y la Liebre. Harris, Jim, illus. 2004. (New Bilingual Picture Book Ser.). (ENG, SPA & MUL.). 32p. (J). (gr. -1-3). pap. 7.95 *(978-0-87358-869-0(X))* Cooper Square Publishing Llc.

Lowell, Susan, et al. The Tortoise & the Jackrabbit. Harris, Jim, illus. 2003. (Avenues Ser.). (ENG.). 32p. (C). (gr. -1-3). pap. 26.95 *(978-0-87358-586-6(0))* National Geographic School Publishing, Inc.

Lowery, Paul. Do You Know Where Sea Turtles Go? 2007. (J). 15.99 *(978-0-9792379-0-4(4))* PBL Stories LLC.

—Do You Know Where Sea Turtles Go? Thomas, Tim, illus. 2005. (J). lib. bdg. 15.99 *(978-0-9771059-9-1(7))* Thomas Expressions, LLC.

Lueders, Tamara Devitre. Hoagie, the Hockey Turtle. 2005. (ENG., Illus.). 33p. (J). per. 15.99 *(978-1-4257-0169-7(8))* Xlibris Corp.

Lynch, Stephen D. The Travels of Kui, the African Spurred Tortoise. Richard, Keisha Luana, illus. 2007. 36p. per. 24.95 *(978-1-4137-1602-7(7))* America Star Bks.

MacKinnon, Mairi, ed. The Hare & the Tortoise. Howarth, Daniel, illus. 2007. (First Reading Level 4 Ser.). 48p. (J). (gr. -1-3). 8.99 *(978-0-7945-1612-3(2)*, Usborne) EDC Publishing.

Malnor, Carol L. On Kiki's Reef, 1 vol. Hunner, Trina L., illus. 2014. (ENG.). 32p. (J). (gr. k-4). 16.95 *(978-1-58469-476-2(9))* Dawn Pubns.

Mangual, Cynthia Ines. Bug Battle! 2017. (Step into Reading Level 2 Ser.). lib. bdg. 14.75 ***(978-0-606-39863-3(5))*** Turtleback Bks.

March, Julia. Lego Ninjago - Ninja, Go! 2015. (DK Reader Level 2 Ser.). lib. bdg. 13.55 *(978-0-606-36924-4(4))* Turtleback Bks.

Marlow, Layn. Hurry up & Slow Down. 2009. (ENG., Illus.). 32p. (J). (gr. -1-3). 16.95 *(978-0-8234-2178-7(3))* Holiday Hse., Inc.

Martin, Candice J. Theo's Special Gift. Bonavita, Madison M., illus. l.t. ed. 2006. 12p. (J). per. 12.99 *(978-1-59879-190-7(7))* Lifevest Publishing, Inc.

Mason, Craig. Turtle Games. Mason, Bergetta, illus. 2003. 32p. (J). 4.99 *(978-0-9729153-0-4(3))* 1 Sleeve Publishing.

Matsumoto, Lisa. The Adventures of Gary & Harry: A Tale of Two Turtles. Furuya, Michael, illus. 2006. (J). 16.95 *(978-0-9647491-4-6(9))* Lehua, Inc.

Matter, Sandy. The Great Sea Chase. 2011. 20p. pap. 24.95 *(978-1-4626-2488-1(X))* America Star Bks.

Mau, Connie. Catch me if you Can. Lemus, Kristina, illus. l.t. ed. 2006. 28p. (J). 14.95 *(978-0-9778843-0-8(9))* Mau, C. Publishing Co.

May, Karen. Thelma the Tiny Sea Turtle. 2011. 26p. pap. *(978-1-908481-78-8(1))* YouWriteOn.

Mbe na Nkita: The Tortoise & the Dog. 2008. (YOR & ENG., Illus.). 36p. 16.00 *(978-0-9801243-1-6(X))* Blazing Ideas Ltd.

McCall, Val. Twelve Rabbits & a Turtle: Bilingual English French. 2012. 46p. pap. 9.95 *(978-1-938367-00-7(6))* Destinee Media.

McCune, Susan. Rabbit & Turtle, 01 vols., 1. 2016. (Rosen REAL Readers: STEM & STEAM Collection). (ENG.). 8p. (J). pap. 5.46 *(978-1-5081-1409-3(9)*, Rosen Classroom) Rosen Publishing Group, Inc., The.

McDermott, Gerald. Jabutí the Tortoise: A Trickster Tale from the Amazon. 2005. (ENG., Illus.). 32p. (J). (gr. -1-3). pap. 7.99 *(978-0-15-205374-1(3))* Houghton Mifflin Harcourt Publishing Co.

McGovern, Suzanne. Gator & Pete - More Alike Than It Seems. Bizjak, Donna, illus. 2007. (J). 13.99 *(978-0-9792558-0-9(5))* Hatch Ideas, Inc.

McGuinness, Elle J. & Caron, Romi. Baby Turtle's Tale. 2011. (ENG.). 12p. (J). 9.99 *(978-1-4494-0354-6(9))* Andrews McMeel Publishing.

McKelvie, Melissa, told to. Serena & the Turtle Eggs. 2007. (ENG.). 28p. pap. 15.99 *(978-1-4196-7780-9(2))* CreateSpace Independent Publishing Platform.

McMurtrie, Kevin. The Very Thoughtful Turtle. 2013. 20p. pap. 13.77 *(978-1-4907-0940-6(1))* Trafford Publishing.

McVicar, William E. Turtle Tries. 2008. 16p. pap. 24.95 *(978-1-60563-180-6(9))* America Star Bks.

Meadows, Daisy. Tess the Sea Turtle Fairy. 2011. (Illus.). 65p. (J). *(978-0-545-28874-3(6))* Scholastic, Inc.

Melancon, Lenell Levy. Tootles the Turtle Tells the Truth: An Interactive Tale about Secrets. 2013. 40p. pap. 15.99 *(978-1-4525-7900-9(8)*, Balboa Pr.) Author Solutions, Inc.

Meng, Cece. Always Remember. Jago, Alison, illus. 2016. (ENG.). 32p. (J). (gr. -1-2). 17.99 *(978-0-399-16809-3(5)*, Philomel Bks.) Penguin Young Readers Group.

Meredith, Amberley. Bessie Bump Gets a New Family. Lee, Nikita, illus. 2010. 26p. pap. 13.95 *(978-1-60911-901-0(0)*, Eloquent Bks.) Strategic Book Publishing & Rights Agency (SBPRA).

Michalak, Jamie. Joe & Sparky Get New Wheels. Remkiewicz, Frank, illus. 2013. (Candlewick Sparks Ser.). (ENG.). 48p. (J). (gr. k-4). pap. 3.99 *(978-0-7636-6641-5(6))* Candlewick Pr.

—Joe & Sparky Go to School. Remkiewicz, Frank, illus. 2014. (Candlewick Sparks Ser.). (ENG.). 48p. (J). (gr. k-4). pap. 3.99 *(978-0-7636-7181-5(9))* Candlewick Pr.

—Joe & Sparky, Superstars! Remkiewicz, Frank, illus. (Candlewick Sparks Ser.). (ENG.). 48p. (J). (gr. k-4). 2013. pap. 3.99 *(978-0-7636-6642-2(4))* 2011. 15.99 *(978-0-7636-4578-6(8))* Candlewick Pr.

Moore, Ginny. Fast. 2011. 28p. pap. 24.95 *(978-1-4626-2254-2(2))* America Star Bks.

Moran, Martin, V, ed. The Town Turtles of Sandy Springs: The Stories Behind the Turtles by the Children Who Saw Them. 2006. (Illus.). 64p. (J). 24.00 *(978-0-9742704-1-8(5))* Hardin Publishing, LLC.

Morrison, Toni & Morrison, Slade. The Tortoise or the Hare. Cepeda, Joe, illus. (ENG.). 32p. (J). (gr. -1-3). 2014. 7.99 *(978-1-4169-8335-4(X))* 2010. 17.99 *(978-1-4169-8334-7(1))* Simon & Schuster/Paula Wiseman Bks. (Simon & Schuster/Paula Wiseman Bks.).

Moses, Albert. The Hawk & the Turtles. Roberts, Pam, illus. 2011. 16p. pap. 24.95 *(978-1-4626-4261-8(6))* America Star Bks.

Moss, Deborah. Shelley, the Hyperactive Turtle. Schwartz, Carol, illus. 2nd ed. 2006. (ENG.). 20p. (J). (gr. -1-2). pap. *(978-1-890627-75-1(5))* Woodbine Hse.

Müller, Isabel. The Green Sea Turtle. 2014. (ENG., Illus.). 40p. (J). 18.95 *(978-0-7358-4189-5(6))* North-South Bks., Inc.

Murcray, Rod. Tuttle Stories. McDaniel, Rick, illus. 2012. 40p. pap. 14.95 *(978-1-61897-654-3(0)*, Strategic Bk. Publishing) Strategic Book Publishing & Rights Agency (SBPRA).

Murphy, Bobby. Ted the Turtle's Trip to the Moon. 2013. 24p. pap. 11.50 *(978-1-62212-431-2(6)*, Strategic Bk. Publishing) Strategic Book Publishing & Rights Agency (SBPRA).

Murphy, Steve & Murphy, Sonia. The Secret. Ostrom, Bob, illus. 2004. (Teenage Mutant Ninja Turtles Ser.). 32p. (J). (gr. k-2). 11.65 *(978-0-7569-5401-7(0))* Perfection Learning Corp.

Murray, Alison. Hare & Tortoise. Murray, Alison, illus. 2016. (ENG., Illus.). 32p. (J). (-k). 16.99 *(978-0-7636-8721-2(9))* Candlewick Pr.

Myracle, Lauren. Thirteen Plus One. 2011. (Winnie Years Ser.). (ENG.). 304p. (J). (gr. 5-18). 7.99 *(978-0-14-241901-4(X)*, Puffin Books) Penguin Young Readers Group.

Nelson, Sean. Bungles Loses His Marbles. 2008. 36p. pap. 16.95 *(978-1-59858-605-3(X))* Dog Ear Publishing, LLC.

Nieting, Sherry. Adventures in Hope Forest: Isabelle's Search for God. 2011. 24p. pap. 10.95 *(978-1-4497-2518-1(X)*, WestBow Pr.) Author Solutions, Inc.

Nnodim, Paul. The Tortoise & the Birds. Pierotti, Yvonne, illus. 32p. (J). 2012. 24.95 *(978-1-937622-09-1(6))* 2010. 14.95 *(978-0-9825842-9-3(6))* Africana Homestead Legacy Pubs., Inc. (Nefu Bks.).

Norfolk, Bobby & Norfolk, Sherry. Anansi & Turtle Go to Dinner. Hoffmire, Baird, illus. 2007. (Story Cove Ser.). (ENG.). 32p. (J). (gr. -1-3). pap. 4.95 *(978-0-87483-856-5(8))* August Hse. Pubs., Inc.

Nye, Naomi Shihab. The Turtle of Oman. 2014. (ENG.). 304p. (J). (gr. 3-7). 16.99 *(978-0-06-201972-1(4))* HarperCollins Pubs.

Nyirenda, Vukani G. The Wise Old Tortoise & the Monkey. 2011. 24p. pap. 15.99 *(978-1-4568-9133-6(2))* Xlibris Corp.

O Flatharta, Antoine. Hurry & the Monarch. So, Meilo, illus. 2009. (ENG.). 40p. (J). (gr. k-3). pap. 7.99 *(978-0-385-73719-7(X)*, Dragonfly Bks.) Random Hse. Children's Bks.

Oduwole, Ben. The Flying Tortoise. 2009. 182p. pap. 43.50 *(978-1-60693-611-5(5)*, Eloquent Bks.) Strategic Book Publishing & Rights Agency (SBPRA).

Oliver, Sheila. Tinky Turtle Finds the Word. McQuitty, LaVonia Corbin, illus. 2011. (ENG.). 16p. (J). 6.00 *(978-0-9801269-4-5(0))* Scribe's Closet Pubns., The.

Opal, Paola. Totty. 2009. (Simply Small Ser.). (ENG., Illus.). 24p. (J). (gr. -1 — 1). bds. 7.95 *(978-1-897476-06-2(X))* Simply Read Bks. CAN. Dist: Ingram Publisher Services.

Orr, Wendy. Nim's Island. Millard, Kerry, illus. 2008. (ENG.). 128p. (J). (gr. 3-7). 6.99 *(978-0-385-73606-0(1)*, Yearling) Random Hse. Children's Bks.

Ostrom, Bob, illus. Friends till the End! 2005. (Teenage Mutant Ninja Turtles Ser.: No. 3). 24p. (J). lib. bdg. 15.00 *(978-1-59054-833-2(7))* Fitzgerald Bks.

Otitoloju/Blazing Ideas Ltd, Ololade/Adewunmi, retold by. Kunkuru Da Kare: The Tortoise & the Dog. 2008. (YOR & ENG., Illus.). 36p. 16.00 *(978-0-9801243-6-1(0))* Blazing Ideas Ltd.

Otitoloju/Blazing Ideas ltd, Ololade/Adewunmi, retold by. Kunkuru, Jaba Da Kurege: The Tortoise, the Rat & the Squirrel. 2008. (YOR & ENG., Illus.). 36p. 16.00 *(978-0-9801243-7-8(9))* Blazing Ideas Ltd.

—Mbe, Nkapi na Osa. 2008. (YOR & ENG., Illus.). 36p. 16.00 *(978-0-9801243-3-0(6))* Blazing Ideas Ltd.

Paige, Nancy. Myrtle the Turtle, 1 vol. Green, Megan, illus. 2009. 19p. pap. 24.95 *(978-1-60836-085-7(7))* America Star Bks.

Parker, Beth. The Tale of Tom Turtle, 1 vol. 2009. 24p. pap. 24.95 *(978-1-61546-887-4(0))* America Star Bks.

—Tom Turtle Visits Grandma's Farm. 2011. 28p. pap. 24.95 *(978-1-4560-1000-3(X))* America Star Bks.

Pashilk, Meri. Pearl the Turtle. 2013. 32p. pap. 13.99 *(978-1-4525-6658-0(5))* Balboa Pr.

A Path of Clouds: The Book off Rhymes. 2013. 50p. pap. *(978-965-550-241-1(4))* Contento De Semrik.

Patton, Jack. The Turtle Invasion. 2016. (Battle Bugs Ser.: 10). (ENG.). 128p. (J). (gr. 2-5). pap. 4.99 *(978-0-545-94518-9(6)*, Scholastic Paperbacks) Scholastic, Inc.

Pellant, Terry. The Real Valentine's Story. 2004. 27p. (J). pap. 24.95 *(978-1-4137-2146-1(X))* PublishAmerica, Inc.

Pelton, Deena. My Turtle. 2012. 20p. pap. 24.95 *(978-1-4626-8210-2(3))* America Star Bks.

Peters, Andrew Fusek. Bear & Turtle & the Great Lake Race. Edgson, Alison, illus. 2005. (Traditional Tales with a Twist Ser.). (ENG.). 32p. (J). (gr. 2-2). per. *(978-1-904550-91-4(6))* Child's Play International Ltd.

Peters, Lou. The Owl & the Turtle. 2010. 32p. pap. 15.95 *(978-0-557-51727-5(3))* Lulu Pr., Inc.

Petersen, Pat. The Turtle Who Couldn't Swim. Pham, Xuan, illus. 2012. 28p. 24.95 *(978-1-4626-8615-5(X))*; pap. 24.95 *(978-1-4626-4847-4(9))* America Star Bks.

Peterson, Kay. Tillie the Turtle. 2012. 24p. pap. 15.99 *(978-1-4691-8414-2(1))* Xlibris Corp.

Peterson, Kevan. Turtle Takes the Bus. 2005. (Illus.). 32p. (J). 12.99 *(978-0-9767661-0-0(8))* Red Giant Publishing.

Peterson, Scott. Blackout! Spaziante, Patrick, illus. 2005. (Teenage Mutant Ninja Turtles Ser.: Garden & No. 6). 24p. (J). lib. bdg. 15.00 *(978-1-59054-831-8(0))* Fitzgerald Bks.

Petit, Denice. Twenty-Two Turtles. 2013. (ENG.). 34p. (J). pap. 15.95 *(978-1-4327-9875-8(8))* Outskirts Pr., Inc.

Piggy Toes Press Staff, creator. Little Feet Like: A Tiny Tootsie Touch & Feel Book. 2008. (ENG., Illus.). 12p. (gr. -1-k). 9.95 *(978-1-58117-692-6(9)*, Intervisual/Piggy Toes) Bendon, Inc.

Pinkney, Jerry. The Tortoise & the Hare. 2013. (ENG., Illus.). 40p. (J). (gr. -1-3). 18.00 *(978-0-316-18356-7(3))* Little, Brown Bks. for Young Readers.

Pinkwater, Daniel M. The Neddiad: How Neddie Took the Train, Went to Hollywood, & Saved Civilization. Brown, Calef, illus. 2009. (ENG.). 320p. (J). (gr. 5-7). pap. 8.99 *(978-0-547-13367-6(7))* Houghton Mifflin Harcourt Publishing Co.

Police, Gerard. Herbert the Frog Goes to the Store. 2008. 20p. pap. 13.50 *(978-1-60693-066-3(4)*, Eloquent Bks.) Strategic Book Publishing & Rights Agency (SBPRA).

Poling Kilough, Melissa. Titus the Turtle & the Hard Shell Story. 2009. 28p. pap. 13.99 *(978-1-4490-0962-5(X))* AuthorHouse.

Powell, Pamela. La Patrulla de las Tortugas. 2003. (SPA., Illus.). 190p. (YA). (gr. 5-8). *(978-84-236-3791-1(3)*, ED1183) Edebé ESP. Dist: Lectorum Pubns., Inc.

Pritchard, Gabby. Turtle Is a Hero Green Band. Di Baldo, Fabrizio, illus. 2016. (Cambridge Reading Adventures Ser.). (ENG.). 16p. pap. 6.56 *(978-1-107-55046-9(7))* Cambridge Univ. Pr.

Pugliano-Martin, Carol. The Earth on Turtles Back. 2011. (Early Connections Ser.). (J). *(978-1-61672-674-4(1))* Benchmark Education Co.

Puglisi, Salvatore. It's best to be Me. 2008. (ENG.). 36p. pap. 14.99 *(978-1-4196-8330-5(6))* CreateSpace Independent Publishing Platform.

Quail, Annette. Lucy & Coco. 2008. 44p. pap. 24.95 *(978-1-60441-854-5(0))* America Star Bks.

Random House. Ninja Dad! (Teenage Mutant Ninja Turtles) Johnson, Shane, illus. 2016. (Step into Reading Ser.). (ENG.). 24p. (J). (gr. -1-1). 4.99 *(978-0-553-53937-0(X)*, Random Hse. Bks. for Young Readers) Random Hse. Children's Bks.

—Pizza Party! (Teenage Mutant Ninja Turtles) Random House, illus. 2017. (Step into Reading Ser.). (ENG., Illus.). 24p. (J). (gr. -1-1). pap. 4.99 ***(978-1-5247-6982-6(7))***; lib. bdg. 12.99 ***(978-1-5247-6983-3(5))*** Random Hse. Children's Bks. (Random Hse. Bks. for Young Readers).

—Rough-And-Tumble Turtles! (Teenage Mutant Ninja Turtles: Half-Shell Heroes) Spaziante, Patrick, illus. 2016. (Touch-And-Feel Ser.). (ENG.). 10p. (J). (— 1). bds. 12.99 *(978-1-101-94029-7(8)*, Random Hse. Bks. for Young Readers) Random Hse. Children's Bks.

—Teenage Mutant Ninja Turtles. Villanelli, Paolo, illus. 2016. (Step into Reading Ser.). (ENG.). 24p. (J). (gr. -1-1). lib. bdg. 12.99 *(978-1-101-93856-0(0)*, Random Hse. Bks. for Young Readers) Random Hse. Children's Bks.

—Teenage Mutant Ninja Turtles: Out of the Shadows Pictureback. Random House, illus. 2016. (Pictureback(R) Ser.). (ENG., Illus.). 16p. (J). (gr. -1-2). 4.99 *(978-1-101-93858-4(7)*, Random Hse. Bks. for Young Readers) Random Hse. Children's Bks.

—Teenage Mutant Ninja Turtles: Out of the Shadows Step into Reading. Villanelli, Paolo, illus. 2016. (Step into Reading Ser.). (ENG.). 24p. (J). (gr. -1-1). 4.99 *(978-1-101-93855-3(2)*, Random Hse. Bks. for Young Readers) Random Hse. Children's Bks.

Random House Editors. Too Much Ooze! (Teenage Mutant Ninja Turtles) Random House Editors & Spaziante, Patrick, illus. 2015. (Step into Reading Ser.). (ENG.). 24p. (J). (gr. -1-1). 4.99 *(978-0-553-50866-6(0)*, Random Hse. Bks. for Young Readers) Random Hse. Children's Bks.

Random House Staff. Ooze Control. Navarra, Nino, illus. 2013. (Pictureback(R) Ser.). (ENG.). 16p. (J). (gr. -1-2). pap. 4.99 *(978-0-307-98229-2(7)*, Random Hse. Bks. for Young Readers) Random Hse. Children's Bks.

—Saved by the Shell! 2012. lib. bdg. 13.55 *(978-0-606-26800-4(6)*, Turtleback) Turtleback Bks.

—The T-Machine Turbo Guide. Random House Staff & Spaziante, Patrick, illus. 2015. (Pictureback(R) Ser.). (ENG.). 16p. (J). (gr. -1-2). 4.99 *(978-0-553-53867-0(5)*, Random Hse. Bks. for Young Readers) Random Hse. Children's Bks.

Random House Staff & Webster, Christy. Robot Rampage! (Teenage Mutant Ninja Turtles) Random House Staff & Spaziante, Patrick, illus. 2013. (Step into Reading Ser.). (ENG.). 48p. (J). (gr. k-3). pap. 3.99 *(978-0-307-98212-4(2)*, Random Hse. Bks. for Young Readers) Random Hse. Children's Bks.

Rao, Lisa. Diego & the Baby Sea Turtles. McGee, Warner, illus. 2008. (Go, Diego, Go! Ser.: 8). (ENG.). 24p. (J). pap. 3.99 *(978-1-4169-5450-7(3)*, Simon Spotlight/Nickelodeon) Simon Spotlight/Nickelodeon.

Raun, Robert L. Tales of the Clam Club: Turtle Soup. 2012. (ENG.). pap. *(978-1-4675-1923-6(5))* Independent Pub.

Reason, Diane. Travis the Traveling Turtle & the Beautiful Butterfly. 2011. 32p. pap. 14.98 *(978-1-4634-0206-8(6))* AuthorHouse.

Rebecca, Rebecca. The Turtle Who Did His Best. 2016. (ENG., Illus.). 26p. pap. 5.99 *(978-1-61984-471-1(0))* Price World Publishing.

Reis, Jason & Hurley, Meagan. The Adventures of Burt: Burt & the Big Race. 2012. 28p. pap. 19.99 *(978-1-4634-4126-5(6))* AuthorHouse.

Ricci, Christine. Diego's Sea Turtle Adventure. Maher, Alex, illus. 2006. 26p. (J). *(978-0-7172-9870-9(1))* Scholastic, Inc.

Rice, Dona Herwick. The Tortoise & the Hare, 1 vol. 2008. (Building Fluency Through Reader's Theater Ser.). (ENG.). 24p. (J). (gr. 1-3). pap. 6.99 *(978-1-4333-0290-9(X))* Teacher Created Materials, Inc.

Richard Scott Morris. Irving the Duck in the Tortoise Shell Suit. 2009. 36p. pap. 20.00 *(978-1-4389-5356-4(9))* AuthorHouse.

Rider, Cynthia. Chatterbox Turtle. Petrlik, Andrea, illus. 2004. (ENG.). 24p. (J). lib. bdg. 23.65 *(978-1-59646-696-8(0))* Dingles & Co.

Ridgell, Regina. Baby Loggerhead's Long Journey. 2008. 28p. pap. 15.99 *(978-1-4363-2087-0(9))* Xlibris Corp.

Rinck, Maranke. Hush Little Turtle. Van Der Linden, Martijn, illus. 2011. (ENG.). 24p. (J). (gr. -1). bds. 8.95 *(978-1-935954-06-4(7)*, 9781935954064) Lemniscaat USA.

Ritchie, Alison. The Tortoise & the Hare. Noj, Nahta, illus. 2015. (ENG.). 32p. (J). (-k). 15.99 *(978-0-7636-7601-8(2),* Templar) Candlewick Pr.
Robert, Quackenbush & Robert Quackenbush. Calling Doctor Quack. 2010. 68p. (J). (gr. k-4). pap. 8.95 *(978-1-4502-1379-0(0))* iUniverse, Inc.
Robertson, Allen. Timothy Tuttles Story Book. 2005. 27p. 11.58 *(978-1-4116-6352-7(7))* Lulu Pr., Inc.
—Timothy Tuttles Story Book 11. 2005. 32p. 13.83 *(978-1-4116-8045-6(6))* Lulu Pr., Inc.
Robertson, Jean. Team Captain. Dufalla, Anita, illus. 2012. (ENG.). 24p. (J). (gr. 1-2). pap. 8.95 *(978-1-61810-314-7(8))* Rourke Educational Media.
Rogers, Alan. En Forme de Bateau. 2003. (Little Giants Ser.). (FRE., Illus.). 16p. (J). (gr. -1-k). 5.95 *(978-1-58728-177-8(5),* Two-Can Publishing) T&N Children's Publishing.
Roh, Grace S. Booyoung & Sea Turtle's Adventure: God's Creatures' Adventures Series 1. Park, Mi-Ok, illus. 2013. 52p. pap. 17.50 *(978-1-62212-718-4(8),* Strategic Bk. Publishing) Strategic Book Publishing & Rights Agency (SBPRA).
Ron Cherney With Angel Logan. Coming Out of Her Shell. 2011. 72p. pap. 33.32 *(978-1-4568-7141-3(2))* Xlibris Corp.
Ross, Andrea. Turtles Go Slow. Ross, Andrea, illus. 2003. (Illus.). 25p. (J). (gr. 1-3). pap. 7.95 *(978-1-887683-45-6(3))* Storybook Pr. & Productions.
Russell, Bill. Bruno the Red Ear Slider. 2013. 24p. pap. 24.95 *(978-1-62709-547-1(0))* America Star Bks.
Rutt, Preston. Tortoise vs. Hare: The Rematch. Redlich, Ben, illus. 2015. (ENG.). 24p. (J). (gr. -1-3). 7.99 *(978-1-85733-722-8(0))* Lerner Publishing Group.
Rylant, Cynthia. The Turtle. McDaniels, Preston, illus. 2006. (Lighthouse Family Ser.). 47p. (J). (gr. -1-3). 11.65 *(978-0-7569-6611-9(6))* Perfection Learning Corp.
—The Turtle. McDaniels, Preston, illus. (Lighthouse Family Ser.: 4). (ENG.). 48p. (J). (gr. 1-5). 2006. pap. 5.99 *(978-0-689-86312-7(8))* 2005. 15.99 *(978-0-689-86244-1(X))* Simon & Schuster Bks. For Young Readers. (Simon & Schuster Bks. For Young Readers).
Salzmann, Mary Elizabeth. El Caracol de la Tortuga, 1 vol. Nobens, C. A., illus. 2007. (Cuentos de Animales Ser.). (SPA & ENG.). 24p. (J). (gr. k-3). lib. bdg. 24.21 *(978-1-59928-657-0(2),* SandCastle) ABDO Publishing Co.
—Turtle Shells, 1 vol. Nobens, Cheryl A., illus. 2006. (Animal Tales Ser.). (ENG.). 24p. (J). (gr. k-3). lib. bdg. 24.21 *(978-1-59679-969-1(2),* SandCastle) ABDO Publishing Co.
—Turtle Shells. Nobens, C. A., illus. 2006. (Fact & Fiction Ser.). 24p. (J). pap. 48.42 *(978-1-59679-970-7(6))* ABDO Publishing Co.
Sampson, Brent. One Wacky Wasp: The Perfect Children's Book for Kids Ages 3-6 Who Are Learning to Read. 2010. 24p. (J). 14.95 *(978-1-4327-6217-9(6));* pap. 9.95 *(978-1-4327-0465-0(6))* Outskirts Pr., Inc.
Samuel, Josiah C. Mr. Tortoise Funny Life, Bk. 1. 2013. 132p. pap. 45.07 *(978-1-4669-9904-6(7))* Trafford Publishing.
Sapre, Reshme. The Unfortunate Tale of Kachuva the Tortoise: As Told by Chukwa Sulcata. Robinson, Jayme, illus. 2012. (ENG.). 40p. 16.95 *(978-0-9829362-0-7(6))* Hathi Chiti Bks. for Kids.
Sargent, Dave & Sargent, Pat. Tunnel King: I Work Hard, 15 vols., Vol. 11. Huff, Jeane, illus. 2nd rev. ed. 2003. (Animal Pride Ser.: No. 11). 42p. (J). pap. 10.95 *(978-1-56763-780-9(9));* lib. bdg. 20.95 *(978-1-56763-779-3(5))* Ozark Publishing.
Sayre, April Pulley. Turtle, Turtle, Watch Out! Patterson, Annie, illus. 2010. (ENG.). 32p. (J). (gr. k-3). pap. 7.95 *(978-1-58089-149-3(7))* Charlesbridge Publishing, Inc.
Sazaklis, John. Salamander Smackdown. Baltazar, Art, illus. 2011. (DC Super-Pets Ser.). (ENG.). 56p. (gr. 2-2). pap. 4.95 *(978-1-4048-6844-1(5),* DC Super-Pets) Picture Window Bks.
—Salamander Smackdown!, 1 vol. Baltazar, Art, illus. 2011. (DC Super-Pets Ser.). (ENG.). 56p. (gr. 2-2). lib. bdg. 23.99 *(978-1-4048-6478-8(4),* DC Super-Pets) Picture Window Bks.
Schacht, Carol. Timmy Turtle's Journey to the Light. 2009. 20p. pap. 11.75 *(978-1-4490-0503-0(9))* AuthorHouse.
Scheunemann, Pam. Pelican's Pouch, 1 vol. 2007. (Critter Chronicles Ser.). (ENG., Illus.). 24p. (J). (gr. k-3). lib. bdg. 24.21 *(978-1-59928-462-0(6),* SandCastle) ABDO Publishing Co.
Scholastic Editors. The Rescue Mission. 2015. (Ninjago Readers Ser.: 11). lib. bdg. 13.55 *(978-0-606-36373-0(4))* Turtleback Bks.
Scholastic, Inc. Staff. Spy vs. Spy. 2015. (Ninjago Readers Ser.: 13). lib. bdg. 13.55 *(978-0-606-37080-6(3))* Turtleback Bks.
Seigel, Jonathan & Rother, Beverly S. Myrtle the Turtle & Popeye the Mouse: Learning about Our Solar System. 2012. 40p. pap. 24.95 *(978-1-4626-6587-7(X))* America Star Bks.
Senkungu, Dinah. How the Tortoise Got His Scars. 2011. 40p. pap. 18.66 *(978-1-4567-1811-4(8))* AuthorHouse.
Seyvos, Florence. Pockety: The Tortoise Who Lived As She Pleased. Provata-Carlone, Mika, tr. from FRE. Ponti, Claude, illus. 2014. (ENG.). 64p. (J). (gr. 2-4). pap. 9.99 *(978-1-78269-025-2(5),* Pushkin Press) Steerforth Pr.
Sheffer, Donnel Gloster. Seacil the Sea Turtle. 2003. (J). pap. 8.00 *(978-0-8059-5288-9(8))* Dorrance Publishing Co., Inc.
Sherry, Kevin. Turtle Island. 2014. (ENG.). 40p. (J). (gr. -1-k). 16.99 *(978-0-8037-3391-6(7),* Dial Bks) Penguin Young Readers Group.
Silvermetz, Marcia A. Gertrude the Albino Frog & Her Friend Rupert the Turtle. Doyel, Ginger, illus. 2003. 48p. (J). (gr. 2-3). 19.95 *(978-0-9718724-0-0(6))* Hiccup Cottage Pubns.
Simpson, Wanda. Sammy, the Earth Traveling Turtle, 1 vol. 2010. 16p. pap. 24.95 *(978-1-4489-9844-9(1))* PublishAmerica, Inc.
Slack, Michael. Turtle Tug to the Rescue. Slack, Michael, illus. 2017. (ENG., Illus.). 40p. (J). 16.99 *(978-1-62779-194-6(9),* 9781627791946, Holt, Henry & Co. Bks. For Young Readers) Holt, Henry & Co.
Smiley, Jeremy. Chester: Little Turtle, Big Adventure, 1 vol. 2009. 36p. pap. 24.95 *(978-1-60703-489-6(1))* America Star Bks.
Smith, Carrie. Tortoise & Hare Run a Race: Lap Book Edition. Berchtold, Lauren, illus. 2016. (My First Reader's Theater Tales Ser.). (J). (gr. k). *(978-1-5021-5509-2(5))* Benchmark Education Co.
—Tortoise & Hare Run a Race: Small Book Edition. Berchtold, Lauren, illus. 2016. (My First Reader's Theater Tales Ser.). (J). (gr. k). *(978-1-5021-5514-6(1))* Benchmark Education Co.
Smith, Geof. Know Your Shapes! (Teenage Mutant Ninja Turtles: Half-Shell Heroes) Linsley, Paul, illus. 2016. (ENG.). 24p. (J). (gr. -1-k). bds. 4.99 *(978-1-101-93497-5(2),* Random Hse. Bks. for Young Readers) Random Hse. Children's Bks.
Smith, James J. Mikey's Monster. 2013. (Step into Reading Level 4 Ser.). lib. bdg. 13.55 *(978-0-606-32223-2(X),* Turtleback) Turtleback Bks.
Smith, James J. & James, Hollis. Mikey's Monster (Teenage Mutant Ninja Turtles) Spaziante, Patrick, illus. 2013. (Step into Reading Ser.). (ENG.). 48p. (J). (gr. k-3). 3.99 *(978-0-449-81826-8(8),* Random Hse. Bks. for Young Readers) Random Hse. Children's Bks.
The Snappy Turtle. 2003. (J). per. *(978-1-57657-938-1(7))* Paradise Pr., Inc.
Soisson, Chelsea. Tate's Wayward Voyage. 2012. (ENG.). (J). pap. 17.99 *(978-1-4675-2651-7(7));* pap. 17.99 *(978-1-4675-2650-0(9))* Independent Pub.
Solis, Javier Rene. The Adventures of Tony the Turtle: La Familia the Family. 2008. 24p. pap. 14.99 *(978-1-4389-1421-3(0))* AuthorHouse.
Sparkes, Ali. Turtle Terror. Collins, Ross, illus. 2014. (S. W. I. T. C. H. Ser.: 11). (ENG.). 104p. (J). (gr. 2-5). lib. bdg. 27.93 *(978-1-4677-2114-1(X),* Darby Creek) Lerner Publishing Group.
Spaziante, Patrick. Too Much Ooze! 2015. (Step into Reading Level 2 Ser.). lib. bdg. 14.75 *(978-0-606-36399-0(8))* Turtleback Bks.
Spero, Mitch & Spero, Maria. Florida the Turtle: Who Thinks He's a Dog Finds His Feelings. 2012. 28p. pap. 21.99 *(978-1-4771-0184-1(5))* Xlibris Corp.
Spin & Match - Kings, Cookies, & Quakers: The Cookie Man, New Clothes for the King, the Ugly Baby Duck. 2006. (ENG.). 66p. (J). 9.99 *(978-1-59204-203-6(1))* Learning Wrap-Ups, Inc.
Spohn, Kate. Turtle & Snake's Day at the Beach. Spohn, Kate, illus. 2004. (Penguin Young Readers, Level 2 Ser.). (ENG., Illus.). 32p. (J). (gr. 1-2). mass mkt. 3.99 *(978-0-14-240157-6(9),* Penguin Young Readers) Penguin Young Readers Group.
—Turtle & Snake's Day at the Beach. Spohn, Kate, illus. 2004. (Puffin Easy-to-Read Ser.). (Illus.). 32p. (gr. k-3). 14.00 *(978-0-7569-2826-1(5))* Perfection Learning Corp.
—Turtle & Snake's Spooky Halloween. Spohn, Kate, illus. 2003. (Easy-to-Read Ser.). (Illus.). 32p. (J). (gr. -1-3). 11.65 *(978-0-7569-1949-8(5))* Perfection Learning Corp.
Sprick, Marilyn & Lemieux, Aurora, adapted by. The Race: Read Well Level K Unit 13 Storybook. 2003. (Read Well Level K Ser.). (Illus.). 20p. (J). *(978-1-57035-684-1(X),* 55538) Cambium Education, Inc.
Stamp, Jørgen & Buckley, William F., Jr. Flying High. 2009. (ENG., Illus.). 32p. (J). (gr. -1-2). 16.95 *(978-1-59270-089-9(6))* Enchanted Lion Bks., LLC.
Stark, Barbara. Blue Dinosaur's Friends. Lt. ed. 2006. (Illus.). 24p. (J). E-Book 9.95 incl. cd-rom *(978-1-933090-20-7(0))* Guardian Angel Publishing, Inc.
Stephens, Sarah Hines. Sleepy Time Crime, 1 vol. Baltazar, Art, illus. 2012. (DC Super-Pets Ser.). (ENG.). 56p. (gr. 2-2). pap. 4.95 *(978-1-4048-7215-8(9));* lib. bdg. 23.99 *(978-1-4048-6485-6(7))* Picture Window Bks. (DC Super-Pets).
Stewart, Chantal, illus. Tortoise Soup! 2009. 24p. pap. 10.67 *(978-1-4190-5523-2(2))* Rigby Education.
Stickler, John C. & Han, Soma. Maya & the Turtle: A Korean Fairy Tale. 2012. (ENG., Illus.). 32p. (J). (gr. -1-3). 14.95 *(978-0-8048-4277-8(9))* Tuttle Publishing.
Stone, Laura. Tulia Turtle Finds Her Talents. 2010. 33p. pap. 16.95 *(978-0-557-33227-4(3))* Lulu Pr., Inc.
Stone, Pam. Oscar's Adventures in the Woods: True story about a turtle that comes back every year to find his Friend. 2011. 15p. (J). pap. 14.95 *(978-1-4327-6382-4(2))* Outskirts Pr., Inc.
Stuart, Janet. Something New in Cloverville? 2010. 20p. 12.49 *(978-1-4520-7701-7(0))* AuthorHouse.
Syrstad, Suzi. Timmy the Tiny Troubled Turtle, 1 vol. Maki, Tab, illus. 2009. 13p. pap. 24.95 *(978-1-61546-455-5(7))* PublishAmerica, Inc.
Tagliere, Georgina. Turtle Tales - Book One: The Baby Turtle who Wanted to Fly. 2009. (Illus.). 60p. pap. *(978-1-84748-406-2(9))* Athena Pr.
Takara, Kathryn Waddell. Timmy Turtle Teaches. Driver, Audrey, illus. 2012. 54p. pap. 29.95 *(978-0-9840204-3-0(8))* Pacific Raven Pr.
Talbot, Amy. Deer & His Dear Friends: A Tale from India. 2006. (J). pap. *(978-1-4108-6173-3(2))* Benchmark Education Co.
Tate, Suzanne. Tammy Turtle: A Tale of Saving Sea Turtles. Melvin, James, illus. 2004. (Suzanne Tate's Nature Ser.: No. 11). 32p. (J). per. 10.95 *(978-1-878405-45-6(4))* Nags Head Art, Inc.
Tatro, MaryAnn. Milton the Square Shell Turtle. Lucas, Diane, illus. 2013. 24p. pap. 11.95 *(978-1-61244-106-1(8))* Halo Publishing International.
Taylor, Emma. Adventures of Bunting, the Turtle. 2011. 24p. pap. 15.99 *(978-1-4568-5911-4(0))* Xlibris Corp.
Teenage Mutant Ninja Turtles, Teenage Mutant. Teenage Mutant Ninja Turtles Green Team. 2014. (Flashlight Book Ser.: 3). (ENG.). 30p. (J). (gr. -1-3). 17.99 *(978-0-7944-3121-1(6),* Reader's Digest Children's Bks.) Studio Fun International.
Teitelbaum, Michael. Mutant Origin: Michelangelo/Raphael (Teenage Mutant Ninja Turtles) Random House Staff, illus. 2012. (Junior Novel Ser.). (ENG.). 128p. (J). (gr. 3-7). 4.99 *(978-0-449-80994-5(3),* Random Hse. Bks. for Young Readers) Random Hse. Children's Bks.
—Teenage Mutant Ninja Turtles Wheel Power Book & Skateboard. 2013. (ENG.). 48p. (J). 12.99 *(978-0-7944-2796-2(0))* Reader's Digest Assn., Inc., The.
Tewkesbury, Alexa. The Perfect Christmas Present. 2008. (ENG.). 32p. (J). *(978-1-85345-476-9(1))* Crusade for World Revival.
Tharp, Barbara, et al. Tillena Lou's Day in the Sun. Denk, James, ed. Lewis, T., illus. 2nd ed. 2013. (My World & Me Ser.). (ENG.). 32p. (J). (gr. k-2). pap. *(978-1-888997-44-6(3),* BioEd) Baylor College of Medicine.
Theval, Lio. Angela's Lost Turtle. 2007. 20p. 23.70 *(978-1-4357-0020-8(1))* Lulu Pr., Inc.
The Thirsty Turtle. 2003. 32p. (J). per. 14.95 *(978-1-59094-049-5(0))* Jawbone Publishing Corp.
Thomas, Jim. Comic Book Heroes. Ruiz, Aristides & Giles, Mike, illus. 2005. 32p. (J). lib. bdg. 15.00 *(978-1-59054-990-2(2))* Fitzgerald Bks.
Thwin, Soe Soe. The Story of Inle in the Galapagos. 2009. 44p. pap. 15.95 *(978-1-60860-361-9(X),* Strategic Bk. Publishing) Strategic Book Publishing & Rights Agency (SBPRA).
Tikki Turtle's Quest. (J). 8.95 *(978-0-9701528-0-0(9))* Ruwanga Trading.
Towle, Barbara E. How Timbo & Trevor Got Together. Spellman, Susan, illus. 2007. (ENG.). 38p. (J). (gr. -1-3). 19.95 *(978-1-933002-21-7(2))* PublishingWorks.
Tracy, Kathleen. The Turtle in Our Class. 2011. (Randy's Corner Ser.). (Illus.). (J). (gr. -1-2). lib. bdg. 25.70 *(978-1-58415-979-7(0))* Mitchell Lane Pubs., Inc.
Tucker, Sally A. Leo & Apollo: The Forbidden Land. 2012. 28p. pap. 15.00 *(978-1-105-60121-7(8))* Lulu Pr., Inc.
Turin, Adela. Arturo y Clementina. Bosnia, Nella, illus. (SPA.). 40p. (J). (gr. 3-5). *(978-84-264-3801-0(6))* Editorial Lumen ESP. Dist: Lectorum Pubns., Inc.
Turtellini the Turbo-Charged Turtle. 2011. (ENG., Illus.). 52p. (J). lib. bdg. 14.95 *(978-0-9654843-8-1(6))* MacGregor, Doug.
The Turtle Race. 2003. (J). per. *(978-1-57657-891-9(7))* Paradise Pr., Inc.
Turtles Z . up. 2006. (ENG., Illus.). 14p. (J). 7.95 *(978-0-9748884-5-3(1))* Little Thoughts For Little Ones Publishing, Inc.
Twohy, Mike. Poindexter Makes a Friend. Twohy, Mike, illus. 2011. (ENG., Illus.). 32p. (J). (gr. -1-3). 15.99 *(978-1-4424-0965-1(7),* Simon & Schuster/Paula Wiseman Bks.) Simon & Schuster/Paula Wiseman Bks.
Van Wemmer, Deby. Wishes & Walnuts. 2009. 28p. pap. 14.50 *(978-1-60860-723-5(2),* Eloquent Bks.) Strategic Book Publishing & Rights Agency (SBPRA).
Verrett, Michael. The White Alligator Crown Quatro. 2010. 147p. pap. 13.95 *(978-0-557-58121-4(4))* Lulu Pr., Inc.
—The White Alligator (paper Back) 2010. 116p. pap. 17.30 *(978-0-557-28042-1(7))* Lulu Pr., Inc.
—The White Alligator (paperback full Color) 2010. 116p. pap. 42.00 *(978-0-557-36924-9(X))* Lulu Pr., Inc.
Wacker, Eileen. Black Tortoise & the Dynasty Dragon. Low, Alan M., illus. 2012. (Fujimini Adventure Ser.: Vol. 5). (ENG.). 40p. (J). (gr. -1-3). 10.99 *(978-1-4675-1741-6(0))* Oncekids.
Ward, Helen. Hare & Tortoise. 2005. (Illus.). 32p. (J). (ALB & ENG.). pap. *(978-1-84444-779-4(0));* pap. *(978-1-84444-780-0(4));* pap. *(978-1-84444-781-7(2));* pap. *(978-1-84444-783-1(9));* (FRE & ENG., pap. *(978-1-84444-787-9(1));* pap. *(978-1-84444-789-3(8));* pap. *(978-1-84444-790-9(1));* pap. *(978-1-84444-793-0(6));* (POL & ENG., pap. *(978-1-84444-794-7(4));* (POR., pap. *(978-1-84444-795-4(2));* (ENG & RUM., pap. *(978-1-84444-796-1(0));* (RUS & ENG., pap. *(978-1-84444-797-8(9));* (SOM & ENG., pap. *(978-1-84444-799-2(5));* (SPA & ENG., pap. *(978-1-84444-800-5(2));* (ENG., pap. *(978-1-84444-801-2(0));* (TUR & ENG., pap. *(978-1-84444-803-6(7));* pap. *(978-1-84444-805-0(3));* (VIE & ENG., pap. *(978-1-84444-806-7(1));* pap. *(978-1-84444-786-2(3))* Mantra Lingua.
Ward, Helen & Aesop. Hare & Tortoise. 2005. (Illus.). 32p. (J). pap. *(978-1-84444-791-6(X));* pap. *(978-1-84444-788-6(X));* pap. *(978-1-84444-784-8(7))* Mantra Lingua.
Ward, Jean Elizabeth. A Barbara Anne Bushy Tale: Book #2 in a Series. 2007. 188p. per. 16.95 *(978-0-595-45726-7(6))* iUniverse, Inc.
Washer, Mark Gregory. Blue Bonnie Butterfly: Tale of Two Tails. 2013. 36p. pap. 18.41 *(978-1-4669-8434-9(1))* Trafford Publishing.
Wax, Wendy. Meet Leatherhead. Spaziante, Patrick, illus. 2005. 22p. (J). lib. bdg. 15.00 *(978-1-4242-0972-9(2))* Fitzgerald Bks.
Webster, Christy. Double-Team! (Teenage Mutant Ninja Turtles) Spaziante, Patrick, illus. 2014. (Step into Reading Ser.). (ENG.). 48p. (J). (gr. 2-4). 3.99 *(978-0-385-37434-7(8),* Random Hse. Bks. for Young Readers) Random Hse. Children's Bks.
—Green Team! 2012. (Step into Reading Level 4 Ser.). lib. bdg. 13.55 *(978-0-606-26801-1(4),* Turtleback) Turtleback Bks.
—Robot Rampage! 2013. (Step into Reading Level 4 Ser.). lib. bdg. 13.55 *(978-0-606-26985-8(1),* Turtleback) Turtleback Bks.
Weeks, Sarah. Follow the Moon. Duranceau, Suzanne, illus. 2003. (ENG.). 32p. (J). (gr. -1-3). 17.99 *(978-0-06-055744-7(3))* HarperCollins Pubs.
Weiss, Flo. Little Bit Is Big Enough. 2012. 28p. pap. 16.09 *(978-1-4669-4074-1(3))* Trafford Publishing.
Weller, Sadie Bedoka. Tsa Ch'ayah/How the Turtle Got Its Squares: A Traditional Caddo Indian Children's Story. Chafe, Wallace, tr. Montoya, Robin Michelle, illus. 2005. (CAD & ENG.). 40p. (J). (gr. 3-7). per. 16.99 *(978-1-4134-8836-4(6))* Xlibris Corp.
West, Tracey. Lego Ninjago: Breakout. 2015. (LEGO Ninjago Chapter Bks.: 8). lib. bdg. 14.75 *(978-0-606-37078-3(1))* Turtleback Bks.
—Lego Ninjago: Chronicles of Ninjago: an Official Handbook. 2014. lib. bdg. 16.00 *(978-0-606-36371-6(8))* Turtleback Bks.
—Titanium Ninja. 2014. (Ninjago Readers Ser.: 10). lib. bdg. 13.55 *(978-0-606-36372-3(6))* Turtleback Bks.
Westheimer, Ruth K. Leopold. (ENG., Illus.). 2017. 36p. pap. 11.99 **(978-1-68336-709-3(X))** 2015. 34p. (J). 23.99 *(978-1-63026-918-0(2))* Turner Publishing Co.
Wheelie, P. Tommy's Triumph: The tales of Tommy the tortoise & Friends. 2009. (Illus.). 28p. pap. 12.49 *(978-1-4389-2718-3(5))* AuthorHouse.
Whitfield, Peter. Up & Down. Bevington, Nancy, illus. 2005. (Zen Tails Ser.). (ENG.). 28p. (J). (gr. -1-3). 15.95 *(978-1-894965-22-4(1))* Simply Read Bks. CAN. Dist: Ingram Publisher Services.
Williams, Barbara A. Tilli's Tale. Lewis, Rebecca, illus. 2004. 48p. (J). per. *(978-1-932077-52-0(9))* Athena Pr.
Wilson, Angela. Tara the Terrified Turtle. Basta, Stormie, illus. 2012. 28p. pap. 24.95 *(978-1-4626-7454-1(2))* America Star Bks.
Winderman, Jay B. Thunder on the Desert. Becker, LuAnne E. & Becker, Lisa E., illus. 2005. 152p. (J). (gr. 3-7). per. 13.95 *(978-0-9761623-1-5(8))* Pill Bug Pr.
—Thunder on the Reservation. Becker, LuAnne E., illus. 2007. 147p. (J). (gr. 3-7). per. 13.95 *(978-0-9761623-2-2(6))* Pill Bug Pr.
Winn, Don M. The Tortoise & the Hairpiece. Hefflin, Toby, illus. 2009. 20p. pap. 7.99 *(978-0-88144-452-0(9))* Yorkshire Publishing Group.
Winningham, Barbara. The Turtle Pit. 2013. 36p. 24.95 *(978-1-62709-875-5(5));* pap. 24.95 *(978-1-62709-493-1(8))* America Star Bks.
Winship, Daniel, illus. The Tortoise & the Hare: The Tortoise & the Hare. 2012. (SGN, ARA, BOS, CHI & FRE.). 32p. (J). pap. 19.95 incl. DVD *(978-0-9818139-2-9(5))* ASL Tales.
Wise, Alicia. Myrtle's True Friend. Wise, Jesse D., illus. 2008. 15p. pap. 24.95 *(978-1-60610-626-6(0))* America Star Bks.
Wood, Douglas. Old Turtle: Questions of the Heart. Ruth, Greg, illus. 2017. (ENG.). 56p. (J). (gr. -1-3). 19.99 *(978-0-439-32111-2(5),* Scholastic Pr.) Scholastic, Inc.
Wright-McAdoo, Joyce & Wright-Mcadoo, Joyce. Zimb: Believe. 2009. (Illus.). 28p. pap. 15.99 *(978-1-4415-8051-1(4))* Xlibris Corp.
Wylie, Ruth G. The Adventures of George the Turtle. 2012. 16p. pap. 15.99 *(978-1-4772-5284-0(3))* AuthorHouse.
Yeoman, John. Quentin Blake's Amazing Animal Stories. Blake, Quentin, illus. 2012. (ENG.). 124p. (J). (gr. 2-4). 19.99 *(978-1-84365-195-6(5),* Pavilion Children's Books) Pavilion Bks. GBR. Dist: Independent Pubs. Group.
Yerger, Susan M. Mighty Little Samuel Seagull. 2013. 20p. pap. 24.95 *(978-1-4626-9941-4(3))* America Star Bks.
Young, Steve. Winchell Mink: The Misadventure Begins. 2004. 144p. (J). 16.89 *(978-0-06-053500-1(8))* HarperCollins Pubs.
Zagorski, Steve. The River of Wisdom. 2010. pap. 17.95 *(978-0-578-05364-6(0))* Zagorski, Steve.
Zambak Çucok Publishing Staff, ed. The Onion: Niloya 2. 2016. (J). pap. 4.99 *(978-1-4621-1863-2(1),* Horizon Pubs.) Cedar Fort, Inc./CFI Distribution.
—The Rainbow: Niloya 1. 2016. (J). pap. 4.99 *(978-1-4621-1862-5(3),* Horizon Pubs.) Cedar Fort, Inc./CFI Distribution.

TUSKEGEE INSTITUTE

Labrecque, Ellen. George Washington Carver, 1 vol. 2014. (Science Biographies Ser.). (ENG.). 32p. (gr. 2-4). lib. bdg. 30.65 *(978-1-4109-6240-9(7),* Raintree Perspectives) Heinemann-Raintree.

TUTANKHAMEN, KING OF EGYPT

Burgan, Michael. The Curse of King Tut's Tomb, 1 vol. Schulz, Barbara, illus. 2005. (Graphic History Ser.). (ENG.). 32p. (gr. 3-4). per. 8.10 *(978-0-7368-5244-9(1),* Graphic Library) Capstone Press of Coughlan Cos.
Burgan, Michael & Hoena, Blake A. The Curse of King Tut's Tomb, 1 vol. Lohse, Otha Zackariah Edward & Schulz, Barbara, illus. 2005. (Graphic History Ser.). (ENG.). 32p. (gr. 3-4). 30.65 *(978-0-7368-3833-7(3),* Graphic Library) Capstone Press of Coughlan Cos.
Chrisp, Peter. Explore 360° the Tomb of Tutankhamen: Be Transported Back in Time with a Breathtaking 3D Tour. 2016. (ENG., Illus.). 48p. (J). (gr. 3-9). 18.99 *(978-0-7641-6821-5(5))* Barron's Educational Series, Inc.
Conklin, Wendy. You Are There! Ancient Egypt 1535 BC. 2016. (TIME for KIDS(r) Nonfiction Readers Ser.). (Illus.). 32p. (J). (gr. 6-6). 8.99 *(978-1-4938-3602-4(1))* Teacher Created Materials, Inc.
Cottrell, Leonard. Land of the Pharaohs. Powers, Richard M., illus. 2012. 130p. 40.95 *(978-1-258-23853-7(5));* pap. 25.95 *(978-1-258-24652-5(X))* Literary Licensing, LLC.
Demi. Tutankhamun, 0 vols. 2009. (ENG., Illus.). 64p. (J). (gr. 2-3). 19.99 *(978-0-7614-5558-5(2),* 9780761455585, Amazon Children's Publishing) Amazon Publishing.
Harkins, Susan Sales & Harkins, William H. King Tut. 2008. (What's So Great About... ? Ser.). (Illus.). 32p. (YA). (gr. 2-4). lib. bdg. 25.70 *(978-1-58415-681-9(3))* Mitchell Lane Pubs., Inc.
Harvey, Gill. Tutankhamun. McNee, Ian, illus. 2006. (Usborne Young Reading Ser.). 64p. (J). (gr. 3-7). 8.99 *(978-0-7945-1271-2(2),* Usborne) EDC Publishing.
Hawass, Zahi A. Tutankhamun: The Mysteries of the Boy King. 2005. (ENG., Illus.). 64p. (J). (gr. 5-9). 27.90 *(978-0-7922-8355-3(4),* National Geographic Children's Bks.) National Geographic Society.
—Tutankhamun: The Mystery of the Boy King. 2005. (Crossroads America Ser.). (ENG., Illus.). 64p. (J). (gr. 5-9). 17.95 *(978-0-7922-8354-6(6),* National Geographic Children's Bks.) National Geographic Society.
Hyde, Natalie. King Tut. 2013. (ENG., Illus.). 48p. (J). *(978-0-7787-1172-8(2));* pap. *(978-0-7787-1181-0(1))* Crabtree Publishing Co.
Lace, William W. The Curse of King Tut. 2007. (Mysterious & Unknown Ser.). (Illus.). 104p. (YA). (gr. 7-12). lib. bdg. 25.95 *(978-1-60152-024-1(7))* ReferencePoint Pr., Inc.
Lunis, Natalie. Tut's Deadly Tomb. 2010. (HorrorScapes Ser.). 32p. (YA). (gr. 4-7). lib. bdg. 25.27 *(978-1-936087-98-3(7))* Bearport Publishing Co., Inc.
Málek, Jaromír. Tutankhamun: The Story of Egyptology's Greatest Discovery. 2013. (Illus.). 63p. (J). *(978-1-4351-4689-1(1))* Metro Bks.
Morley, Jacqueline. Inside the Tomb of Tutankhamun. James, John, illus. 2005. (ENG.). 48p. (J). (gr. 3-7). 19.95 *(978-1-59270-042-4(X))* Enchanted Lion Bks., LLC.
—You Wouldn't Want to Be Cursed by King Tut! Antram, David, illus. 2012. (You Wouldn't Want to... Ser.). (ENG.). 32p. (J). pap. 9.95 *(978-0-531-20949-3(0),* Watts, Franklin) Scholastic Library Publishing.
—You Wouldn't Want to Be Cursed by King Tut! A Mysterious Death You'd Rather Avoid. Antram, David, illus. 2012. (ENG.). 32p. (J). (gr. 3-12). lib. bdg. 29.00 *(978-0-531-20874-8(5))* Scholastic Library Publishing.
Stewart, David. Tutankhamen! A Mummy Who Really Got Meddled With. Antram, David, illus. 2007. (You Wouldn't

Want to... Ser.). (ENG.). 32p. (J). (gr. 2-5). 29.00 *(978-0-531-18725-8(X))* Scholastic Library Publishing.

—You Wouldn't Want to Be Tutankhamen! (Revised Edition) 2017. (You Wouldn't Want to... Ancient Civilizations Ser.). (ENG., Illus.). 32p. (J). lib. bdg. 29.00 *(978-0-531-23837-0(7),* Watts, Franklin) Scholastic Library Publishing.

The Treasures of Tutankhamun. (Butterfly Bks.). (ARA.). 48p. (YA). (gr. 5-8). 9.95 *(978-0-86685-485-6(1))* International Bk. Ctr., Inc.

Westphal, Jeremy. The Mummy's Curse. 2011. (Unexplained Ser.). (ENG., Illus.). 24p. (J). (gr. 3-7). lib. bdg. 25.95 *(978-1-60014-643-5(0),* Torque Bks.) Bellwether Media.

Woods, Michael & Woods, Mary B. The Tomb of King Tutankhamen. 2008. (Unearthing Ancient Worlds Ser.). (ENG., Illus.). 80p. (gr. 5-8). lib. bdg. 30.60 *(978-0-8225-7506-1(X))* Lerner Publishing Group.

World Book, Inc Staff, contrib. by. The Mystery of Tutankhamun. 2015. (Illus.). 48p. (J). *(978-0-7166-2678-7(0))* World Bk., Inc.

Wynne, Patricia J. King Tut Coloring Book. 2005. (Dover History Coloring Book Ser.). (ENG., Illus.). 32p. (J). (gr. 3-5). 3.99 *(978-0-486-44444-4(9))* Dover Pubns., Inc.

Zoehfeld, Kathleen Weidner. The Curse of King Tut's Mummy. Nelson, Jim, illus. 2007. (Totally True Adventures Ser.). (ENG.). 112p. (J). (gr. 2-5). per. 4.99 *(978-0-375-83862-0(7),* Random Hse. Bks. for Young Readers) Random Hse. Children's Bks.

TUTU, DESMOND, 1931-

Crompton, Samuel Willard. Desmond Tutu: Fighting Apartheid. 2007. (Modern Peacemakers Ser.). (Illus.). 112p. (YA). (gr. 9-12). lib. bdg. 30.00 *(978-0-7910-9221-7(6))* Facts On File, Inc.

TV

see Television

TWAIN, MARK, 1835-1910

Aller, Susan Bivin. Mark Twain. (Just the Facts Biographies Ser.). (Illus.). 112p. (J). 2006. 27.93 *(978-0-8225-3425-9(8),* Lerner Pubns.) 2006. (gr. 3-7). pap. 9.95 *(978-0-8225-5998-6(6),* Lerner Pubns.) 2003. (gr. 6-18). pap. 7.95 *(978-0-8225-9696-7(2))* Lerner Publishing Group.

Armentrout, David & Armentrout, Patricia. Mark Twain. 2003. (Discover the Life of an American Legend Ser.). (Illus.). 24p. (gr. 2-5). lib. bdg. *(978-1-58952-660-0(0))* Rourke Educational Media.

Ashmore, Wayne & Nault, Jennifer. The Adventurous World of Mark Twain. 2016. (J). ***(978-1-5105-1955-8(6))*** SmartBook Media, Inc.

Ashmore, Wayne & Nault, Jennifer. Mark Twain. 2008. (My Favorite Writer Ser.). (Illus.). 32p. (YA). (gr. 5-18). pap. 9.95 *(978-1-59036-931-9(9));* lib. bdg. 26.00 *(978-1-59036-930-2(0))* Weigl Pubs., Inc.

Bloom, Harold, ed. Mark Twain's the Adventures of Huckleberry Finn. 2nd rev. ed. 2007. (Bloom's Modern Critical Interpretations Ser.). 248p. (C). (gr. 9-18). lib. bdg. 45.00 *(978-0-7910-9426-6(X),* Chelsea Hse.) Facts On File, Inc.

Bodden, Valerie. Mark Twain, 1 vol. 2013. (Great American Authors Ser.). (ENG.). 48p. (J). (gr. 3-6). lib. bdg. 32.79 *(978-1-61783-719-7(9))* ABDO Publishing Co.

Burleigh, Robert. The Adventures of Mark Twain by Huckleberry Finn. Blitt, Barry, illus. 2011. (ENG.). 48p. (J). (gr. 2-5). 17.99 *(978-0-689-83041-9(6),* Atheneum Bks. for Young Readers) Simon & Schuster Children's Publishing.

Caravantes, Peggy. A Great & Sublime Fool: The Story of Mark Twain. 2010. (World Writers Ser.). (Illus.). 176p. (YA). (gr. 8-18). lib. bdg. 28.95 *(978-1-59935-088-2(2))* Reynolds, Morgan Inc.

Carew-Miller, Anna. Mark Twain. Di Gennaro, Andrea, illus. 2003. (Great Names Ser.). (J). 19.95 *(978-957-745-414-0(3))* Mason Crest.

—Mark Twain: Great American Fiction Writer. 2004. (Great Names Ser.). (Illus.). 32p. (J). (gr. 3-18). lib. bdg. 19.95 *(978-1-59084-158-7(1))* Mason Crest.

Diorio, Mary Ann L. A Student's Guide to Mark Twain. 2007. (Understanding Literature Ser.). (Illus.). 160p. (YA). (gr. 6-10). lib. bdg. 29.27 *(978-0-7660-2438-0(5))* Enslow Pubs., Inc.

Fleischman, Sid. The Trouble Begins at 8: A Life of Mark Twain in the Wild, Wild West. 2008. (Illus.). 224p. (J). (gr. 4-7). (ENG.). 18.99 *(978-0-06-134431-2(1));* lib. bdg. 19.89 *(978-0-06-134432-9(X))* HarperCollins Pubs. (Greenwillow Bks.).

Goldsmith, Howard. Mark Twain at Work! Habbas, Frank, illus. 2005. 32p. (J). lib. bdg. 15.00 *(978-1-59054-951-3(1))* Fitzgerald Bks.

—Mark Twain at Work! Habbas, Frank, illus. 2003. (Ready-To-read COFA Ser.). (ENG.). 32p. (J). (gr. k-2). pap. 3.99 *(978-0-689-85399-9(8),* Simon Spotlight) Simon Spotlight.

Heims, Neil. Reading the Adventures of Tom Sawyer. 2005. (Engaged Reader Ser.). (Illus.). 96p. (gr. 5-8). lib. bdg. 25.00 *(978-0-7910-8828-9(6),* Chelsea Hse.) Facts On File, Inc.

Hermann, Spring. Reading & Interpreting the Works of Mark Twain. 2017. (Lit Crit Guides). 160p. (J). (gr. 8-8). lib. bdg. 39.93 ***(978-0-7660-8493-3(0))*** Enslow Pubs., Inc.

Houle, Michelle M. Mark Twain: Banned, Challenged, & Censored. 2008. (Authors of Banned Bks.). (Illus.). 160p. (YA). (gr. 4-7). lib. bdg. 35.94 *(978-0-7660-2689-6(2))* Enslow Pubs., Inc.

Lacey, Saskia. The Prehistoric Masters of Literature: Discover Literary History with a Prehistoric Twist! 2016. (Jurassic Classics Ser.). (ENG., Illus.). 40p. (J). (gr. 2-6). 14.95 *(978-1-63322-098-0(2))* Quarto Publishing Group USA.

MacLeod, Elizabeth. Mark Twain: An American Star. 2008. (Snapshots: Images of People & Places in History Ser.). (ENG., Illus.). 32p. (J). (gr. 3-7). 14.95 *(978-1-55337-908-9(X));* pap. 6.95 *(978-1-55337-909-6(8))* Kids Can Pr., Ltd. CAN. Dist: Hachette Bk. Group.

Maloof, Torrey. Stepping into Mark Twain's World. 2017. (TIME for KIDS(r) Nonfiction Readers Ser.). 48p. (J). (gr. 7-7). pap. 9.99 ***(978-1-4938-3620-8(X))*** Teacher Created Materials, Inc.

—Stepping into Mark Twain's World. 2017. (Time for Kids Nonfiction Readers Ser.). lib. bdg. 20.85 ***(978-0-606-40285-9(3))*** Turtleback Bks.

Mark Twain. 2010. (Who Wrote That? Ser.). (Illus.). 128p. (YA). (gr. 6-12). 35.00 *(978-1-60413-728-6(2),* Chelsea Hse.) Facts On File, Inc.

North, Sterling. Mark Twain & the River. 2009. (ENG.). 192p. (J). (gr. 3-7). pap. 6.99 *(978-0-14-241235-0(X),* Puffin Books) Penguin Young Readers Group.

Prince, April Jones. Who Was Mark Twain? O'Brien, John A. & Harrison, Nancy, illus. 2004. (Who Was? Ser.). (ENG.). 112p. (J). (gr. 3-7). pap. 5.99 *(978-0-448-43319-6(2),* Grosset & Dunlap) Penguin Young Readers Group.

—Who Was Mark Twain? O'brien, John, illus. 2004. (Who Was... ? Ser.). 105p. (gr. 3-7). 16.00 *(978-0-7569-4590-9(9))* Perfection Learning Corp.

Rasmussen, R. Kent. Bloom's How to Write about Mark Twain. 2007. (Bloom's How to Write about Literature Ser.). 324p. (C). (gr. 9-12). 45.00 *(978-0-7910-9487-7(1),* Chelsea Hse.) Facts On File, Inc.

—Mark Twain for Kids: His Life & Times, 21 Activities. 2004. (For Kids Ser.). (ENG., Illus.). 160p. (J). (gr. 4). pap. 14.95 *(978-1-55652-527-8(3))* Chicago Review Pr., Inc.

Saddleback Educational Publishing Staff, ed. Adventures of Huckleberry Finn. 2011. (Timeless Classics Ser.). (ENG.). 48p. (YA). (gr. 9-12). pupil's gde. ed. 19.95 incl. cd-rom *(978-1-61651-125-8(7))* Saddleback Educational Publishing, Inc.

—Adventures of Tom Sawyer. 2011. (Timeless Classics Ser.). (ENG.). 48p. (YA). (gr. 9-12). pupil's gde. ed. 19.95 incl. cd-rom *(978-1-61651-126-5(5))* Saddleback Educational Publishing, Inc.

—Prince & the Pauper. 2011. (Timeless Classics Ser.). (ENG.). 48p. (YA). (gr. 9-12). pupil's gde. ed. 19.95 incl. cd-rom *(978-1-61651-147-0(8))* Saddleback Educational Publishing, Inc.

Sherman, Josepha. Mark Twain. 2005. (Classic Storytellers Ser.). (Illus.). 48p. (J). (gr. 4-8). lib. bdg. 29.95 *(978-1-58415-374-0(1))* Mitchell Lane Pubs., Inc.

Sickels, Amy. Mark Twain. 2nd rev. ed. 2006. (Bloom's Modern Critical Views Ser.). 300p. (C). (gr. 9). 45.00 *(978-0-7910-8569-1(4),* Chelsea Hse.) Facts On File, Inc.

Tieck, Sarah. Mark Twain, 1 vol. 2010. (First Biographies Set 6 Ser.). (ENG.). 32p. (J). (gr. 1-4). 27.07 *(978-1-60453-988-2(7))* ABDO Publishing Co.

Wilson, Douglas. Adventures of Huckleberry Finn. 2016. (J). pap. ***(978-1-944503-41-3(2))*** Canon Pr.

Youngblood, Wayne. Mark Twain along the Mississippi. 2006. (In the Footsteps of American Heroes Ser.). (Illus.). 64p. (gr. 5-12). pap. 14.05 *(978-0-8368-6435-9(2));* lib. bdg. 34.00 *(978-0-8368-6430-4(1))* Stevens, Gareth Publishing LLLP. (Gareth Stevens Secondary Library).

TWAIN, MARK, 1835-1910—FICTION

Buzbee, Lewis. Bridge of Time. 2013. (ENG.). 320p. (J). (gr. 5-9). pap. 14.99 *(978-1-250-02734-4(9),* 9781250027344) Square Fish.

Horender, Philip M. The Mighty Maximilian: Samuel Clemens's Traveling Companion, 1 vol. Wolek, Guy, illus. 2013. (Maximilian P. Mouse, Time Traveler Ser.). (ENG.). 112p. (J). (gr. 3-6). lib. bdg. 27.07 *(978-1-61641-960-8(1),* Calico Chapter Bks) Magic Wagon.

Howard, Joan. The Story of Mark Twain. Meadowcroft, Enid Lamonte, ed. McKay, Donald, illus. 2011. 186p. 42.95 *(978-1-258-05565-3(1))* Literary Licensing, LLC.

Kerley, Barbara. The Extraordinary Mark Twain (According to Susy) Fotheringham, Edwin, illus. 2010. (ENG.). 48p. (J). (gr. 2-5). 17.99 *(978-0-545-12508-6(1),* Scholastic Pr.) Scholastic, Inc.

—The "Extrodinary" Mark Twain (According to Susy) Fotheringham, Edwin, illus. 2010. (J). *(978-0-545-12509-3(X),* Scholastic Pr.) Scholastic, Inc.

Maltbie, P. I. Bambino & Mr. Twain. Miyares, Daniel, illus. 2012. (ENG.). 40p. (J). (gr. k-3). 15.95 *(978-1-58089-272-8(8))* Charlesbridge Publishing, Inc.

TWENTIETH CENTURY

Gardner, Faye, et al. Shopping in the 1940s. 2011. (When I Was Young Ser.). (ENG., Illus.). 32p. (J). pap. 10.99 *(978-0-237-54389-1(3))* Evans Brothers, Ltd. GBR. Dist: Independent Pubs. Group.

Golson Books, Ltd. Staff & Carlisle, Rodney P. The Thirties, 2 vols., Set. 2006. (Day by Day Ser.). 900p. (C). (gr. 9-18). 214.50 *(978-0-8160-6664-3(7))* Facts On File, Inc.

Hunter, Rebecca & Walker, Kathryn. Growing up in the Forties. 2003. (Illus.). 32p. pap. *(978-0-7502-3434-4(2),* Wayland) Hachette Children's Group.

—Growing up in the Thirties. 2003. (Illus.). 32p. pap. *(978-0-7502-3433-7(4),* Wayland) Hachette Children's Group.

Parker, Janice. 1980: Canadian Decades. 2011. 48p. (C). (gr. 4-6). pap. *(978-1-77071-729-9(3))* Weigl Educational Pubs. Ltd.

Ryan, James G. & Schlup, Leonard, eds. Historical Dictionary of The 1940s. 2006. (ENG., Illus.). 648p. (C). 158.00 *(978-0-7656-0440-8(X),* Y182788) Routledge.

Sharman, Margaret. 1950s. (Illus.). 47p. (J). pap. *(978-0-237-51664-2(0))* Evans Brothers, Ltd.

Thompson, Gare. The Roaring 20s: Voices from America's Past. 2007. (Reading Expeditions Ser.). (ENG., Illus.). 40p. (J). pap. 19.95 *(978-0-7922-4551-3(2))* National Geographic School Publishing, Inc.

World War I & the Roaring Twenties, 1914-1928. 2010. (Discovering U. S. History Ser.). (Illus.). 136p. (J). (gr. 5-8). 35.00 *(978-1-60413-356-1(2),* Chelsea Hse.) Facts On File, Inc.

1900s: Decades of the 20th Century, 10 vols. 2005. (Illus.). 64p. (YA). 29.95 *(978-1-932904-00-0(X))* Eldorado Ink.

1910s: Decades of the 20th Century, 10 vols. 2005. (Illus.). 64p. (YA). 29.95 *(978-1-932904-01-7(8))* Eldorado Ink.

1920s: Decades of the 20th Century, 10 vols. 2005. (Illus.). 64p. (YA). 29.95 *(978-1-932904-02-4(6))* Eldorado Ink.

1930s: Decades of the 20th Century, 10 vols. 2005. (Illus.). 64p. (YA). 29.95 *(978-1-932904-03-1(4))* Eldorado Ink.

1940s: Decades of the 20th Century, 10 vols. 2005. (Illus.). 64p. (YA). 29.95 *(978-1-932904-04-8(2))* Eldorado Ink.

1950s: Decades of the 20th Century, 10 vols. 2005. (Illus.). 64p. (YA). 29.95 *(978-1-932904-05-5(0))* Eldorado Ink.

1960s: Decades of the 20th Century, 10 vols. 2005. (Illus.). 64p. (YA). 29.95 *(978-1-932904-06-2(9))* Eldorado Ink.

1970s: Decades of the 20th Century, 10 vols. 2005. (Illus.). 64p. (YA). 29.95 *(978-1-932904-07-9(7))* Eldorado Ink.

1980s: Decades of the 20th Century, 10 vols. 2005. (Illus.). 64p. (YA). 29.95 *(978-1-932904-08-6(5))* Eldorado Ink.

1990s: Decades of the 20th Century, 10 vols. 2005. (Illus.). 64p. (YA). 29.95 *(978-1-932904-09-3(3))* Eldorado Ink.

TWINS

Cannon, Nick & Carey, Mariah. Roc & Roe's Twelve Days of Christmas. Ford, A. G., illus. 2014. (ENG.). 32p. (J). (gr. -1-k). 17.99 *(978-0-545-51950-2(0),* Orchard Bks.) Scholastic, Inc.

Kongyin. Sungrass. 2011. 344p. pap. *(978-0-9869858-5-0(6))* Kima Global Pubs.

Kor, Eva Mozes & Buccieri, Lisa Rojany. Surviving the Angel of Death: The True Story of a Mengele Twin in Auschwitz. 2012. (ENG.). 175p. (J). (gr. 6). pap. 8.95 *(978-1-933718-57-6(9))* Tanglewood Pr.

—Surviving the Angel of Death: The True Story of a Mengele Twin in Auschwitz. 2012. lib. bdg. 19.60 *(978-0-606-23838-0(7),* Turtleback) Turtleback Bks.

Kor, Eva Mozes, et al. Surviving the Angel of Death: The Story of a Mengele Twin in Auschwitz. 2009. (ENG., Illus.). 141p. (J). (gr. 6-18). 14.95 *(978-1-933718-28-6(5))* Tanglewood Pr.

Look A-Likes Don't Act A-Like. 2007. (Illus.). 40p. (J). 12.95 *(978-0-9776711-4-4(3),* Blue Marble Bks.) Sphinx Publishing.

Miller, Kerri. My Twin & Me - Fun with Twin Brothers & Sisters. 2013. (Illus.). 20p. pap. *(978-0-9576753-0-8(5))* Hot Tub Publishing, Ltd.

Olsen, Mary-Kate & Olsen, Ashley. The Ultimate Guide to Mary-Kate & Ashley. 2004. (Illus.). 93p. *(978-0-00-718136-0(1))* HarperCollins Pubs. Australia.

TWINS—FICTION

Abbott, E. F. Nettie & Nellie Crook: Orphan Train Sisters. 2016. (Based on a True Story Ser.). (ENG., Illus.). 176p. (J). 15.99 *(978-1-250-06835-4(5),* 9781250068354) Feiwel & Friends.

Abel, Cheyanne. It's Better by Far, When You Are Who You Are. 2012. 24p. pap. 17.99 *(978-1-4685-7492-0(2))* AuthorHouse.

Adventures with Kat & Dex: The search for the key to Golden Gate Park. l.t. ed. 2004. (Illus.). 32p. (J). lib. bdg. 22.95 *(978-0-9754853-0-9(X))* DeAngelis, Anthony.

Alexander, Kwame. The Crossover. 2014. (ENG.). (J). (gr. 4-7). E-Book 16.99 *(978-1-306-46985-2(6))* Harcourt Trade Pubs.

—The Crossover. 2014. (ENG.). 240p. (J). (gr. 4-7). 16.99 *(978-0-544-10771-7(3),* HMH Books For Young Readers) Houghton Mifflin Harcourt Publishing Co.

—The Crossover. 2014. lib. bdg. 29.40 *(978-0-606-37975-5(4))* Turtleback Bks.

Amato, Carol J. The Lost Treasure of the Golden Sun. 2005. 172p. (J). *(978-0-9713756-3-5(1))* Stargazer Publishing Co.

—The Secret of Blackhurst Manor. 2017. (ENG.). 232p. (J). pap. 9.95 *(978-1-933277-02-8(5))* Stargazer Publishing Co.

Amato, Mary. Sniff a Skunk!, Bk. 3. Jenkins, Ward, illus. 2015. (Good Crooks Ser.: Bk. 3). (ENG.). 128p. (gr. 2-4). 14.99 *(978-1-60684-598-1(5),* Darby Creek) Lerner Publishing Group.

Amirkhan, Michele. Princess Elian's Quest. 2008. 112p. 20.95 *(978-0-595-50870-9(7));* pap. 10.95 *(978-0-595-51400-7(6))* iUniverse, Inc.

Anderson, Laurie Halse. New Beginnings #13, 13 vols. 2012. (Vet Volunteers Ser.: 13). (ENG.). 192p. (J). (gr. 3-7). 6.99 *(978-0-14-241675-4(4),* Puffin Books) Penguin Young Readers Group.

Anderson, Patricia. It's Time for Kindergarten PJ & Parker. 2012. (Illus.). 26p. (J). 19.95 *(978-1-61863-379-8(1))* Bookstand Publishing.

Apte, Sunita. Ride the Whale: A Surfer Tall Tale. Reed, Kyle, illus. 2006. 16p. (J). pap. *(978-0-439-74638-0(8))* Scholastic, Inc.

Arcos, Carrie. There Will Come a Time. 2014. (ENG., Illus.). 320p. (YA). (gr. 9). 17.99 *(978-1-4424-9585-2(5),* Simon Pulse) Simon Pulse.

Armstrong, Kelley. Empire of Night. 2015. (Age of Legends Trilogy Ser.: 2). 432p. (YA). (gr. 8). 17.99 *(978-0-06-207127-9(0))* HarperCollins Pubs.

—Sea of Shadows. (gr. 8). 2015. (Age of Legends Trilogy Ser.: 1). 432p. (YA). pap. 9.99 *(978-0-06-207125-5(4))* 2014. (Age of Legends Trilogy: Bk. 1). 416p. (J). 17.99 *(978-0-06-207124-8(6))* HarperCollins Pubs.

—Sea of Shadows. 2015. (Age of Legends Ser.: 1). (YA). lib. bdg. 20.85 *(978-0-606-36511-6(7))* Turtleback Bks.

Atwood, Megan. Twin Dangers. 2013. (Dario Quincy Academy of Dance Ser.: 4). (ENG.). 112p. (gr. 6-12). (J). lib. bdg. 27.93 *(978-1-4677-0933-0(6));* (YA). pap. 7.95 *(978-1-4677-1486-0(0))* Lerner Publishing Group. (Darby Creek).

Auerbach, Annie. The Grosse Adventures Vol. 3: Trouble at Twilight Cave, 1 vol. Nicholas, Jamar, illus. 2009. (Tokyopop Ser.). (ENG.). 96p. (gr. 2-6). 25.65 *(978-1-59961-562-2(2))* Spotlight.

Auerbach, Annie & Mike, Norton. Grosse Adventures - The Good, the Bad & the Gassy, Vol. 1. 2006. (Illus.). 96p. pap. 4.99 *(978-1-59816-049-9(4))* TOKYOPOP, Inc.

Avery, Lara. A Million Miles Away. 2016. (ENG.). 336p. (YA). (gr. 10-17). pap. 9.99 *(978-0-316-28372-4(X),* Poppy) Little, Brown Bks. for Young Readers.

Avery, Tom. Not As We Know It. 2016. (ENG.). 176p. (J). (gr. 4-7). 16.99 *(978-0-553-53509-9(9),* Schwartz & Wade Bks.) Random Hse. Children's Bks.

Avi & Vail, Rachel. Never Mind! 2005. (Twin Novels Ser.). 200p. (gr. 5-9). 16.00 *(978-0-7569-5667-7(6))* Perfection Learning Corp.

Baier, Jeanne M. The Twins Jeffrey & Jeanne. 2012. 28p. pap. 16.00 *(978-1-4669-5194-5(X))* Trafford Publishing.

Bailey, Ethel M. T. Lily Pond Village, 1 vol. 2009. 57p. pap. 16.95 *(978-1-60703-379-0(8))* America Star Bks.

Bair, Sheila. Rock, Brock, & the Savings Shock. Gott, Barry, illus. (ENG.). (J). 2017. (gr. -1-3). pap. 7.99 ***(978-0-8075-7095-1(8))*** 2006. (gr. 1-3). 16.99 *(978-0-8075-7094-4(X))* Whitman, Albert & Co.

Balasubramanian, Lalitha. The Twins at the Ancient Villa, 1 vol. 2009. 48p. pap. 16.95 *(978-1-61582-601-8(7))* America Star Bks.

Banks, Jacqueline Turner & Turner Banks, Jacqueline. Egg-Drop Blues. 2003. (ENG.). 128p. (J). (gr. 5-7). pap. 10.95 *(978-0-618-25080-6(8))* Houghton Mifflin Harcourt Publishing Co.

Banks, Lynne Reid. Angela & Diabola. 163p. (J). (gr. 4-6). pap. 4.50 *(978-0-8072-1515-9(5),* Listening Library) Random Hse. Audio Publishing Group.

Baratz-Logsted, Lauren. The Twin's Daughter. (ENG.). (YA). 2014. 416p. (gr. 7-12). pap. 9.99 *(978-1-59990-661-4(9),* 9781599906614) 2010. 400p. (gr. 9-12). 16.99 *(978-1-59990-513-6(2),* 9781599905136) Bloomsbury Publishing USA. (Bloomsbury USA Childrens).

Barber, Ronde & Barber, Tiki. Go Long! 2011. (Barber Game Time Bks.). (ENG.). 160p. (J). (gr. 3-7). pap. 7.99 *(978-1-4169-8573-0(5),* Simon & Schuster/Paula Wiseman Bks.) Simon & Schuster/Paula Wiseman Bks.

Barber, Tiki & Barber, Ronde. End Zone. (Barber Game Time Bks.). (ENG., Illus.). (J). (gr. 3-7). 2014. 192p. pap. 7.99 *(978-1-4169-9098-7(4))* 2012. 176p. 15.99 *(978-1-4169-9097-0(6))* Simon & Schuster/Paula Wiseman Bks. (Simon & Schuster/Paula Wiseman Bks.).

—Extra Innings. 2014. (Barber Game Time Bks.). (ENG., Illus.). 160p. (J). (gr. 3-7). 16.99 *(978-1-4424-5726-3(0),* Simon & Schuster/Paula Wiseman Bks.) Simon & Schuster/Paula Wiseman Bks.

—Goal Line. (Barber Game Time Bks.). (ENG., Illus.). 176p. (J). (gr. 3-7). 2013. pap. 6.99 *(978-1-4169-9096-3(8))* 2011. 15.99 *(978-1-4169-9095-6(X))* Simon & Schuster/Paula Wiseman Bks. (Simon & Schuster/Paula Wiseman Bks.).

—Jump Shot. 2013. (Barber Game Time Bks.). (ENG., Illus.). 160p. (J). (gr. 3-7). 16.99 *(978-1-4424-5729-4(5),* Simon & Schuster/Paula Wiseman Bks.) Simon & Schuster/Paula Wiseman Bks.

—Red Zone. (Barber Game Time Bks.). (ENG., 176p. (J). (gr. 3-7). 2013. Illus.). pap. 7.99 *(978-1-4169-6861-0(X))* 2010. 15.99 *(978-1-4169-6860-3(1))* Simon & Schuster/Paula Wiseman Bks. (Simon & Schuster/Paula Wiseman Bks.).

—Wild Card. (Barber Game Time Bks.). (ENG.). 160p. (J). (gr. 3-7). 2012. pap. 7.99 *(978-1-4169-6859-7(8))* 2009. 15.99 *(978-1-4169-6858-0(X))* Simon & Schuster/Paula Wiseman Bks. (Simon & Schuster/Paula Wiseman Bks.).

Barker, Kathryn. In the Skin of a Monster. 2016. (ENG.). 304p. (YA). (gr. 10). pap. 12.99 *(978-1-76011-171-7(6))* Allen & Unwin AUS. Dist: Independent Pubs. Group.

Barnhill, Kelly. The Witch's Boy. 2014. (ENG.). 384p. (J). (gr. 4). 17.95 *(978-1-61620-351-1(X),* 73351) Algonquin Bks. of Chapel Hill.

Barrowman, John & Barrowman, Carole E. Bone Quill. 2014. (Hollow Earth Ser.). (ENG., Illus.). 304p. (J). (gr. 3-7). pap. 8.99 *(978-1-4424-8929-5(4),* Aladdin) Simon & Schuster Children's Publishing.

—Book of Beasts. 2016. (Hollow Earth Ser.). (ENG.). 336p. (J). (gr. 3-7). pap. 7.99 *(978-1-4814-4231-2(7),* Simon & Schuster/Paula Wiseman Bks.) Simon & Schuster/Paula Wiseman Bks.

—Conjuror. 2016. (Orion Chronicles Ser.). (ENG.). 320p. (YA). (gr. 7). 16.99 *(978-1-78185-637-6(0))* Head of Zeus GBR. Dist: Independent Pubs. Group.

—Hollow Earth. (Hollow Earth Ser.). (ENG., (J). (gr. 3-7). 2013. Illus.). 416p. pap. 7.99 *(978-1-4424-5853-6(4))* 2012. 400p. 16.99 *(978-1-4424-5852-9(6))* Simon & Schuster Children's Publishing. (Aladdin).

Barrows, Annie. The Magic Half. 2008. (ENG.). 224p. (YA). (gr. 3-7). 16.99 *(978-1-59990-132-9(3),* 9781599901329, Bloomsbury USA Childrens) Bloomsbury Publishing USA.

—Magic in the Mix. (ENG.). 288p. (YA). (gr. 3-6). 2015. pap. 7.99 *(978-1-61963-798-6(7),* 9781619637986) 2014. 16.99 *(978-1-61963-482-4(1),* 9781619634824) Bloomsbury Publishing USA. (Bloomsbury USA Childrens).

Bateman, Anya. The Makeover of James Orville Wickenbee. 2007. 262p. (J). pap. *(978-1-59038-707-8(4))* Deseret Bk. Co.

Bath, K. P. Flip Side. 2009. (YA). 16.99 *(978-0-316-03836-2(9))* Little Brown & Co.

Bauer, Deidre. Silver Mountain. 2008. 38p. pap. 8.00 *(978-0-8059-7672-4(8))* Dorrance Publishing Co., Inc.

Bavati, Robyn. Pirouette. 2013. (ENG.). 312p. (YA). pap. 9.99 *(978-0-7387-3481-1(0),* Flux) North Star Editions.

Baxter, David. The Tournesol Twins. 2006. 68p. pap. *(978-1-84401-901-4(2))* Athena Pr.

Beaty, Andrea. Attack of the Fluffy Bunnies. 2012. (Fluffy Bunnies Ser.). (ENG.). 192p. (YA). (gr. 2-8). pap. 7.95 *(978-1-4197-0519-9(9),* Amulet Bks.) Abrams, Inc.

—Fluffy Bunnies 2: The Schnoz of Doom. Santat, Dan, illus. (Fluffy Bunnies Ser.). (ENG.). (J). (gr. 3-7). 2016. 208p. pap. 7.95 *(978-1-4197-1942-4(4))* 2015. 192p. 12.95 *(978-1-4197-1051-3(6))* Abrams, Inc. (Amulet Bks.).

BEEBE, Diane. School's Out. 2006. (J). *(978-1-4276-0238-1(7))* Aardvark Global Publishing.

Bell, Michele Ashman. Dragon's Jaw: A Heart-Pounding Adventure. 2005. 241p. (J). *(978-1-59156-880-3(3))* Covenant Communications.

—Spyhunt: A Heart-Pounding Adventure: A Novel. 2004. 187p. (J). *(978-1-59156-457-7(3))* Covenant Communications.

Bellino, Sarah. The Little Miss Detectives: Case Number 1. 2012. 32p. pap. 14.51 *(978-1-4669-6867-7(2))* Trafford Publishing.

Bergen, Lara. Tutu Twins. Pastel, Elyse & Pastel, Elyse, illus. 2008. (ENG.). 24p. (J). (gr. k-17). per. 3.99 *(978-1-58476-615-5(8))* Innovative Kids.

Betancourt, Jeanne. Penny & Pepper. Riley, Kellee, illus. 2011. (Scholastic Reader Level 3 Ser.). (ENG.). 48p. (J). (gr. 1-4). pap. 3.99 *(978-0-545-11508-7(6),* Cartwheel Bks.) Scholastic, Inc.

Billingsley, Franny. Chime. 2011. (Playaway Young Adult Ser.). (YA). 59.99 *(978-1-61707-143-0(9))* Findaway World, LLC.

—Chime. 2012. (ENG.). 384p. (YA). (gr. 7-18). 8.99 *(978-0-14-242092-8(1),* Speak) Penguin Young Readers Group.

Bingham, Laura. Alvor. 2009. pap. 17.99 *(978-1-59955-272-9(8))* Cedar Fort, Inc./CFI Distribution.

—Wings of Light. 2011. 240p. pap. 15.99 *(978-1-59955-492-1(5),* Sweetwater Bks.) Cedar Fort, Inc./CFI Distribution.

Bitterman, Kevin. BD's Big Hit, 1 vol. 2009. (ENG.). 63p. pap. 19.95 *(978-1-60836-366-7(X))* America Star Bks.

Bjork, Linda. Salmon Cavern. 2006. 92p. pap. 10.95 *(978-1-59800-546-2(4))* Outskirts Pr., Inc.

Black, Holly & DiTerlizzi, Tony. The Ironwood Tree. DiTerlizzi, Tony, illus. 2013. (Spiderwick Chronicles Ser.: 4). (ENG.,

Illus.). (J). (gr. 1-5). 128p. 15.99 *(978-1-4424-8702-4(X))*; 144p. pap. 7.99 *(978-1-4424-8701-7(1))* Simon & Schuster Bks. For Young Readers. (Simon & Schuster Bks. For Young Readers).
—The Spiderwick. DiTerlizzi, Tony, illus. 2009. (Spiderwick Chronicles Ser.). (ENG., Illus.). 608p. (J). (gr. 3-7). 29.99 *(978-1-4169-8685-0(5)*, Simon & Schuster Bks. For Young Readers) Simon & Schuster Bks. For Young Readers.
Blade, Adam. Chasing Evil. (Chronicles of Avantia Ser.). (ENG.). 176p. (J). (gr. 3-7). 2013. pap. 5.99 *(978-0-545-36157-6(5)*, Scholastic Paperbacks) 2012. 15.99 *(978-0-545-36158-3(3)*, Scholastic Pr.) Scholastic, Inc.
—First Hero. 2012. (Chronicles of Avantia Ser.). (ENG.). 176p. (J). (gr. 3-7). 15.99 *(978-0-545-36160-6(5)*, Scholastic Pr.) Scholastic, Inc.
Blake-Garrett, Andrea. The Adventures of Izzy & Juju: Twin Detective Investigators (T. D. I.) 2012. 28p. pap. 19.99 *(978-1-4685-0683-9(8))* AuthorHouse.
—Las Aventuras de Izzy y Juju: Gemelos Detectives Investigadores (G. D. I.) 2012. 28p. pap. 19.99 *(978-1-4772-2523-3(4))* AuthorHouse.
Bliss, Bryan. No Parking at the End Times. 2015. (ENG.). 272p. (YA). (gr. 9). 17.99 *(978-0-06-227541-7(0)*, Greenwillow Bks.) HarperCollins Pubs.
Bloumis, Joy. An Adventure in Fairyland. 2013. 84p. pap. 10.50 *(978-1-62212-835-8(4)*, Strategic Bk. Publishing) Strategic Book Publishing & Rights Agency (SBPRA).
Blyton, Enid. House at the Corner: Family Adventure. 2013. (ENG.). 271p. (J). pap. 9.99 *(978-1-84135-647-1(6))* Award Pubns. Ltd. GBR. Dist: Parkwest Pubns., Inc.
Bo, Ben. Skullcrack. 2003. (ENG.). 168p. (YA). (gr. 5-12). pap. 6.95 *(978-0-8225-3311-5(1))* Lerner Publishing Group.
Bodeen, S. A. The Compound. 2008. (Compound Ser.: 1). (ENG.). 256p. (YA). (gr. 7-12). 18.99 *(978-0-312-37015-2(6)*, 9780312370152) Feiwel & Friends.
—The Compound. 2011. 9.46 *(978-0-7848-3490-9(3)*, Everbind) Marco Bk. Co.
—The Compound. 2009. (Compound Ser.: 1). (ENG.). 272p. (YA). (gr. 7-12). pap. 9.99 *(978-0-312-57860-2(1)*, 9780312578602) Square Fish.
Boeve, Eunice. Echoes of Kansas Past. Peterson-Shea, Julie, illus. 2012. 176p. pap. 10.99 *(978-0-9851196-9-0(1))* Rowe Publishing and Design.
Bogart, Jo Ellen. The Big Tree Gang, 1 vol. Griffiths, Dean, illus. 2005. (Orca Echoes Ser.). (ENG.). 64p. (J). (gr. 2-3). per. 6.95 *(978-1-55143-345-5(1))* Orca Bk. Pubs. USA.
Bogart, Mike. The Henderson Twins in Muckleball! 2006. 107p. pap. 16.95 *(978-1-4241-3050-4(6))* PublishAmerica, Inc.
—Ice Warriors, 1 vol. 2010. 72p. pap. 19.95 *(978-1-4489-3885-8(6))* America Star Bks.
Boling, Katharine. January 1905. 2006. (ENG., Illus.). 192p. (J). (gr. 5-7). pap. 6.99 *(978-0-15-205121-1(X))* Houghton Mifflin Harcourt Publishing Co.
Bollback, Anthony G. Capture of the Twin Dragon. 2012. 152p. pap. 8.99 *(978-0-9849359-1-8(6))* Finding the Cause, LLC.
—Hijacked. 2012. 176p. pap. 8.99 *(978-0-9849359-5-6(9))* Finding the Cause, LLC.
—Mystery of the Counterfeit Money. 2012. 170p. (gr. 4-7). pap. 8.99 *(978-0-9849359-2-5(4))* Finding the Cause, LLC.
—Rescue at Cripple Creek. 2012. 178p. pap. 8.99 *(978-0-9849359-3-2(2))* Finding the Cause, LLC.
—Smugglers in Hong Kong. 2012. 156p. pap. 8.99 *(978-0-9849359-0-1(8))* Finding the Cause, LLC.
—The Tiger Shark Strikes Again. 2012. 172p. pap. 8.99 *(978-0-9849359-4-9(0))* Finding the Cause, LLC.
Bosworth, Jennifer. The Killing Jar. 2016. (ENG.). 352p. (YA). 17.99 *(978-0-374-34137-4(0)*, 9780374341374, Farrar, Straus & Giroux (BYR)) Farrar, Straus & Giroux.
Boykin, Antonee. Alex & Tony Learn to Be Gentlemen. 2011. 31p. (J). pap. 13.95 *(978-1-4327-5255-2(3))* Outskirts Pr., Inc.
Bozarth, Jan. Lilu's Book. 2011. (Fairy Godmother Academy Ser.: No. 4). (ENG., Illus.). 192p. (J). (gr. 3-7). 6.99 *(978-0-375-85187-2(9)*, Yearling) Random Hse. Children's Bks.
Bradford, Chris. Hostage, Bk. 2. 2017. (Bodyguard Ser.). (ENG.). 224p. (J). (gr. 5). pap. 8.99 *(978-1-5247-3699-6(6)*, Philomel Bks.) Penguin Young Readers Group.
Brehm, David L. Willy Nilly Volume 1. Claerhout, Paul, illus. 2013. 94p. (J). pap. 19.95 *(978-0-9860669-0-0(7))* Blue Logic Publishing.
Brewer, Heather. The Cemetery Boys. 2015. (ENG.). 288p. (YA). (gr. 8). 17.99 *(978-0-06-230788-0(6)*, HarperTeen) HarperCollins Pubs.
—The Cemetery Boys. 2016. (YA). lib. bdg. 20.85 *(978-0-606-38741-5(2))* Turtleback Bks.
Bronte, Jules & Oapos, Jem, illus. The Castle Adventure. 2013. 171p. pap. *(978-1-908804-08-2(4))* Bingham Mayne & Smith, Ltd.
Brooks, Grace. The Asquinn Twins & Grant. 2010. 111p. pap. 9.94 *(978-0-557-26972-3(5))* Lulu Pr., Inc.
Brooks, Linda Grace. The Asquinn Twins & Where the Trail Forks. 2005. 119p. pap. 16.95 *(978-0-7414-2445-7(2))* Infinity Publishing.
Brown, Jim. The Foster Twins in the Mystery at Moore's Lake. 2005. 164p. 22.95 *(978-0-595-67087-1(3))* iUniverse, Inc.
Brown, Jim D. The Foster Twins in the Mystery of the House on Joiner Lane. 2003. 160p. pap. 11.95 *(978-0-595-26504-6(9)*, Writers Club Pr.) iUniverse, Inc.
Brown, Jim D. & Brown, Ina M. The Foster Twins in the Mystery of the House on Joiner Lane. 2003. (ENG.). 164p. 21.95 *(978-0-595-74653-8(5)*, Writers Club Pr.) iUniverse, Inc.
Brown, Lenoard. The Adventure of Paul & Page in Colorado: (Idennital Twins) l.t. ed. 2011. (ENG.). 32p. pap. 12.50 *(978-1-4635-6139-0(3))* CreateSpace Independent Publishing Platform.
—The Adventure of Paul & Page in Hawaii (the Big Island) (Identical Twins) l.t. ed. 2011. (ENG.). 50p. pap. 12.50 *(978-1-4635-6162-8(8))* CreateSpace Independent Publishing Platform.
Brunstetter, Wanda E. Humble Pie. Madden, Colleen, illus. 2014. (Double Trouble Ser.: 5). (ENG.). 160p. (J). pap. 5.99 *(978-1-62836-389-0(4)*, Barbour Bks.) Barbour Publishing, Inc.
—Humble Pie. Madden, Colleen M., illus. 2014. 158p. (J). *(978-1-63058-967-7(5))* Barbour Publishing, Inc.
Bruzon, Louise A. The Grimstone Galleries. 2010. 192p. pap. *(978-1-907652-17-2(5))* Grosvenor Hse. Publishing Ltd.
Burchett, Jan & Vogler, Sara. Avalanche Alert, 1 vol. Le Feyer, Diane, illus. (Wild Rescue Ser.). (ENG.). 152p. (gr. 3-6). 2013. 9.95 *(978-1-4342-4893-0(3))* 2012. 25.32 *(978-1-4342-3772-9(9))* Stone Arch Bks.
—Desert Danger, 1 vol. Le Feyer, Diane, illus. 2013. (Wild Rescue Ser.). (ENG.). 152p. (gr. 3-6). 9.95 *(978-1-4342-4892-3(5))* Stone Arch Bks.
—Desert Danger, 1 vol. Le Feyer, Diane & Kennedy, Sam, illus. 2012. (Wild Rescue Ser.). (ENG.). 152p. (gr. 3-6). lib. bdg. 25.32 *(978-1-4342-3773-6(7))* Stone Arch Bks.
—Earthquake Escape, 1 vol. Le Feyer, Diane, illus. 2012. (Wild Rescue Ser.). (ENG.). 152p. (gr. 3-6). lib. bdg. 25.32 *(978-1-4048-6891-5(7))* Picture Window Bks.
—Ocean S. O. S. Le Feyer, Diane, illus. 2013. (Wild Rescue Ser.). (ENG.). 152p. (gr. 3-6). 9.95 *(978-1-4342-4891-6(7))* Stone Arch Bks.
—Ocean S. O. S. Le Feyer, Diane & Kennedy, Sam, illus. 2012. (Wild Rescue Ser.). (ENG.). 152p. (gr. 3-6). lib. bdg. 25.32 *(978-1-4342-3771-2(0))* Stone Arch Bks.
—Poacher Panic, 1 vol. Le Feyer, Diane, illus. 2012. (Wild Rescue Ser.). (ENG.). 152p. (gr. 3-6). 9.95 *(978-1-4342-4593-9(4))*; lib. bdg. 25.32 *(978-1-4342-3286-1(7))* Stone Arch Bks.
—Polar Meltdown, 1 vol. Le Feyer, Diane, illus. 2012. (Wild Rescue Ser.). (ENG.). 152p. (gr. 3-6). 9.95 *(978-1-4342-4594-6(2))*; lib. bdg. 25.32 *(978-1-4342-3769-9(9))* Stone Arch Bks.
—Rainforest Rescue, 1 vol. Le Feyer, Diane, illus. 2012. (Wild Rescue Ser.). (ENG.). 152p. (gr. 3-6). 9.95 *(978-1-4342-4595-3(0))*; lib. bdg. 25.32 *(978-1-4342-3768-2(0))* Stone Arch Bks.
—Safari Survival, 1 vol. Le Feyer, Diane, illus. 2013. (Wild Rescue Ser.). (ENG.). 152p. (gr. 3-6). 9.95 *(978-1-4342-4890-9(9))* Stone Arch Bks.
—Safari Survival, 1 vol. Le Feyer, Diane & Kennedy, Sam, illus. 2012. (Wild Rescue Ser.). (ENG.). 152p. (gr. 3-6). lib. bdg. 25.32 *(978-1-4342-3770-5(2))* Stone Arch Bks.
Bush, Rosetta Bowman. The Coal Dust Twins. 2013. 36p. pap. 24.95 *(978-1-62709-920-2(4))* America Star Bks.
But... Why? 2006. (Illus.). 32p. (J). 14.95 *(978-0-9773651-0-4(7))* Coleman, CJ.
Butcher, Kristin. Zach & Zoe: Bully & the Beagle, 1 vol. 2009. (Lorimer Streetlights Ser.). (ENG.). 120p. (J). (gr. 2-4). 8.95 *(978-1-55277-427-4(9)*, 9781552774274) Lorimer, James & Co., Ltd., Pubs. CAN. Dist: Casemate Pubs. & Bk. Distributors, LLC.
—Zach & Zoe & the Bank Robber, 1 vol. 2008. (Lorimer Streetlights Ser.). (ENG.). 120p. (J). (gr. 2-4). 8.95 *(978-1-55277-015-3(X)*, 9781552770153) Lorimer, James & Co., Ltd., Pubs. CAN. Dist: Casemate Pubs. & Bk. Distributors, LLC.
Butcher, Nancy, et al. It's Snow Problem, 3 vols. 2003. (ENG., Illus.). 112p. *(978-0-00-714466-2(0)*, HarperCollins Children's Bks.) HarperCollins Pubs. Ltd.
—Two for the Road. 2003. (ENG., Illus.). 112p. *(978-0-00-714463-1(6)*, HarperCollins Children's Bks.) HarperCollins Pubs. Ltd.
Butler, Dori Hillestad. Yes, I Know Monkey Man, 1 vol. 2009. (ENG.). 224p. (YA). (gr. 5-9). 16.95 *(978-1-56145-479-2(6))* Peachtree Pubs.
Bybee, Linda & Lawless, Laura. Untwin. 2011. 32p. pap. 14.99 *(978-1-4567-5365-8(7))* AuthorHouse.
Byng, Georgia. Molly Moon, Micky Minus, & the Mind Machine. (Molly Moon Ser.: 4). (ENG.). (J). (gr. 3-7). 2008. 416p. pap. 7.99 *(978-0-06-075038-1(3))* 2007. 384p. 16.99 *(978-0-06-075036-7(7))* HarperCollins Pubs.
Calonita, Jen. Summer State of Mind. 2014. (ENG.). 256p. (YA). (gr. 7-17). pap. 10.00 *(978-0-316-09115-2(4)*, Poppy) Little, Brown Bks. for Young Readers.
Cameron, Sam. Mystery of the Tempest: A Fisher Key Adventure. 2011. (ENG.). 288p. (J). (gr. 7). pap. 13.95 *(978-1-60282-579-6(3))* Bold Strokes Bks.
Caring, Angela. Becoming Bryn. 2013. (ENG.). 297p. (YA). (gr. 7). pap. 11.95 *(978-1-935089-66-7(8))* Acacia Publishing, Inc.
Carmichael, Clay. Brother, Brother. 2013. (ENG.). 320p. (YA). (gr. 7). 17.99 *(978-1-59643-743-2(X))* Roaring Brook Pr.
Casella, Jody. Thin Space. 2013. (ENG.). 256p. (YA). (gr. 7). 16.99 *(978-1-58270-435-7(X))*; pap. 10.99 *(978-1-58270-392-3(2))* Simon Pulse. (Simon Pulse).
Casey, Carin Jayne. Granny Babysits: The Mischievous Five. 2012. 62p. 31.95 *(978-1-4582-0474-5(X)*, Abbott Pr.) Author Solutions, Inc.
Cassidy, Anne & Durant, Alan. Doing the Double. 2007. (Sharp Shades Ser.). (ENG., Illus.). 64p. (J). (gr. 6-8). pap. 8.99 *(978-0-237-53447-9(9))* Evans Brothers, Ltd. GBR. Dist: Independent Pubs. Group.
Cento, Nucci. Maverick & Miss Murphy at Rascal's Rescue Ranch. 2009. 48p. pap. 12.50 *(978-1-60860-388-6(1)*, Eloquent Bks.) Strategic Book Publishing & Rights Agency (SBPRA).
Chadwick, Jennie. The Peach Tree Kids: Circus Fleas. 2012. 96p. pap. 9.99 *(978-1-61897-455-6(6)*, Strategic Bk. Publishing) Strategic Book Publishing & Rights Agency (SBPRA).
Chan, Queenie. The Dreaming Collection. 2010. (ENG., Illus.). 576p. pap. 19.99 *(978-1-4278-1871-3(1))* TOKYOPOP, Inc.
Chankhamma, Shari. The Sisters' Luck. 2010. (ENG., Illus.). 144p. (YA). pap. 12.95 *(978-1-59362-190-2(6)*, 9781593621902) Slave Labor Bks.
Chapman, Allan W. Mr Wugidgem & the Darker Journey. 2012. 40p. pap. 7.99 *(978-0-9796780-3-5(X))* AC Writings.
—Mr. Wugidgem & the Phoenix Journey. 2012. 74p. pap. 7.99 *(978-0-9796780-4-2(8))* AC Writings.
Chapman, Elsie. Divided (Dualed Sequel) 2015. (ENG.). 336p. (YA). (gr. 7). pap. 9.99 *(978-0-449-81298-3(7)*, Ember) Random Hse. Children's Bks.
Choo, Choo, Choo, Me & You & You! 2005. (J). bds. *(978-0-9769910-5-2(5))* Terrific Twins LLC.
Christopher, Matt. The Great Quarterback Switch. 2008. (New Matt Christopher Sports Library). 144p. (J). (gr. 4-6). lib. bdg. 26.60 *(978-1-59953-216-5(6))* Norwood Hse. Pr.
Cicierega, Emmy. Gravity Falls Don't Color This Book! A Cursed Coloring Book. Ramirez, Stephanie, illus. 2017. (ENG.). 64p. pap. 12.99 ***(978-1-368-00899-0(2))*** Disney Pr.
Ciencin, Scott. Point-Blank Paintball, 1 vol. Aburtov, illus. 2010. (Sports Illustrated Kids Graphic Novels Ser.). (ENG.). 32p. pap. 1.00 *(978-1-4342-2137-7(7))* Stone Arch Bks.
Ciencin, Scott, et al. Point-Blank Paintball, 1 vol. Aburto, Jesus, illus. 2010. (Sports Illustrated Kids Graphic Novels Ser.). (ENG.). 56p. (gr. 2-3). pap. 7.19 *(978-1-4342-2293-0(4))*; 26.65 *(978-1-4342-1914-5(3))* Stone Arch Bks.
Clairmont, Patsy. 5 Cheesy Stories: About Friendship, Bravery, Bullying, & More, 1 vol. Oeltjenbruns, Joni, illus. 2007. (Tails from the Pantry Ser.). (ENG.). 144p. (gr. -1-2). 15.99 *(978-1-4003-1042-5(3))* Nelson, Thomas Inc.
Clare, Mimi St. The Fairbluffs of Pennington Island. 2013. 36p. pap. 12.99 *(978-1-935986-49-2(X))* Liberty University Press.
Clark-Elliott, Mary. The Day Ms. Qualbaum Came to Visit. 2013. 44p. pap. 20.72 *(978-1-4907-0921-5(5))* Trafford Publishing.
Clayton, Emma. The Roar. (ENG.). (J). (gr. 2-7). 2012. 512p. pap. 10.99 *(978-0-439-92785-7(4))* 2009. 496p. 17.99 *(978-0-439-92593-8(2))* Scholastic, Inc. (Chicken Hse., The).
—The Whisper. 2012. 309p. *(978-0-545-43365-5(7)*, Chicken Hse., The) Scholastic, Inc.
Cleary, Beverly. Two Times the Fun. Taylor, Thomas & Thompson, Carol, illus. 2005. (ENG.). 96p. (J). (gr. -1-2). 16.99 *(978-0-06-057921-0(8))* HarperCollins Pubs.
Clements, Andrew. Lost & Found. Elliott, Mark, illus. (ENG.). (J). (gr. 3-7). 2010. 192p. pap. 7.99 *(978-1-4169-0986-6(9))* 2008. 176p. 16.99 *(978-1-4169-0985-9(0))* Simon & Schuster Children's Publishing. (Atheneum Bks. for Young Readers).
Cleverly, Sophie. The Lost Twin. 2016. (Scarlet & Ivy Ser.: 1). (ENG.). 304p. (J). (gr. 5-8). 16.99 *(978-1-4926-3339-6(9)*, 9781492633396, Sourcebooks Jabberwocky) Sourcebooks, Inc.
Colfer, Chris. An Author's Odyssey. 2016. (Land of Stories Ser.: 5). (ENG.). (J). (gr. 3-7). 496p. pap. 11.99 *(978-0-316-27214-8(0))*; (Illus.). 464p. 19.99 *(978-0-316-38329-5(5))* Little, Brown Bks. for Young Readers.
—Beyond the Kingdoms. Dorman, Brandon, illus. 2015. (Land of Stories Ser.: Bk. 4). (ENG.). 432p. (J). (gr. 3-7). 19.99 *(978-0-316-40689-5(9))* Little, Brown Bks. for Young Readers.
—The Curvy Tree. Dorman, Brandon, illus. 2015. (ENG.). 32p. (J). (gr. -1-3). 17.00 *(978-0-316-40685-7(6))* Little Brown & Co.
—The Enchantress Returns. (Land of Stories Ser.: 2). (ENG.). (J). (gr. 3-7). 2014. 544p. pap. 9.99 *(978-0-316-20155-1(3))* 2013. (Illus.). 528p. 19.99 *(978-0-316-20154-4(5))* 2013. 832p. 43.99 *(978-0-316-24235-6(7))* Little, Brown Bks. for Young Readers.
—The Enchantress Returns. 2014. (Land of Stories Ser.: 2). (J). lib. bdg. 20.85 *(978-0-606-37229-9(6))* Turtleback Bks.
—A Grimm Warning. (Land of Stories Ser.: 3). (ENG.). (J). (gr. 3-7). 2015. 496p. pap. 9.99 *(978-0-316-40682-6(1))* 2014. 480p. 19.99 *(978-0-316-40681-9(3))* 2014. 768p. 32.99 *(978-0-316-40964-3(2))* Little, Brown Bks. for Young Readers.
—A Grimm Warning. 2015. (Land of Stories Ser.: 3). (J). lib. bdg. 20.85 *(978-0-606-37230-5(X))* Turtleback Bks.
—The Land of Stories: an Author's Odyssey. 2017. (Land of Stories Ser.: 5). (ENG., Illus.). 464p. (J). (gr. 3-7). pap. 9.99 ***(978-0-316-38321-9(X))*** Little, Brown Bks. for Young Readers.
Colfer, Chris. The Wishing Spell. 2013. (Land of Stories Ser.: Bk. 1). (ENG.). 464p. (J). (gr. 3-7). pap. 9.99 *(978-0-316-20156-8(1))* Little, Brown Bks. for Young Readers.
—The Wishing Spell. Dorman, Brandon, illus. 2012. (Land of Stories Ser.: 1). (ENG.). 448p. (J). (gr. 3-7). 19.99 *(978-0-316-20157-5(X))* Little, Brown Bks. for Young Readers.
—The Wishing Spell. l.t. ed. 2013. (Land of Stories Ser.: 1). (ENG.). 672p. (J). (gr. 3-7). pap. 10.00 *(978-0-316-24236-3(5))* Little, Brown Bks. for Young Readers.
—The Wishing Spell. 2013. (Land of Stories Ser.: 1). (J). lib. bdg. 20.85 *(978-0-606-31746-7(5)*, Turtleback) Turtleback Bks.
Colfer, Chris & Dorman, Brandon. The Land of Stories the Wishing Spell. 2013. pap. *(978-0-545-64793-9(2))* Scholastic, Inc.
Collins, Wendy Jane. The Adventure Door: Book 1 'How it all began' & Book 2 'Return to Courtney Bay' 2010. 112p. pap. 10.99 *(978-1-4520-4228-2(4))* AuthorHouse.
Common, Gabriel. The Demon of Basile High: The Return of Cassius. 2007. 132p. per. 11.95 *(978-1-4327-0664-7(0))* Outskirts Pr., Inc.
Condie, Ally. Atlantia. (ENG.). 320p. (gr. 7). 2015. (YA). pap. 10.99 *(978-0-14-751065-5(1)*, Speak) 2014. (J). 18.99 *(978-0-525-42644-8(2)*, Dutton Books for Young Readers) Penguin Young Readers Group.
—Atlantia. 2015. lib. bdg. 22.10 *(978-0-606-37576-4(7))* Turtleback Bks.
Cooney, Caroline B. Twins. 2016. (ENG.). 150p. (J). (gr. 7-12). pap. 11.99 *(978-1-5040-3559-0(3))* Open Road Integrated Media, Inc.
Corriveau, Art. 13 Hangmen. 2012. (ENG.). 352p. (J). (gr. 3-7). 17.95 *(978-1-4197-0159-7(2)*, Amulet Bks.) Abrams, Inc.
Covey, Sean. Sammy & the Pecan Pie. Curtis, Stacy, illus. 2013. (7 Habits of Happy Kids Ser.: 4). (ENG.). 32p. (J). (gr. -1-1). 7.99 *(978-1-4424-7647-9(8)*, Simon & Schuster Bks. For Young Readers) Simon & Schuster Bks. For Young Readers.
Creech, Sharon. Ruby Holler. 2012. (ENG.). 288p. (J). (gr. 3-7). pap. 6.99 *(978-0-06-056015-7(0))* HarperCollins Pubs.
—Ruby Holler. 2004. (Joanna Cotler Bks.). 310p. (gr. 3-7). 17.00 *(978-0-7569-1940-5(1))* Perfection Learning Corp.
—Ruby Holler. 2012. (J). (gr. 3-6). 17.20 *(978-0-613-86272-1(4)*, Turtleback) Turtleback Bks.
Creech, Sharon. Walk Two Moons: a Harper Classic. 2017. (Harper Classic Ser.). 288p. (J). (gr. 3-7). 16.99 ***(978-0-06-265877-7(8))*** HarperCollins Pubs.
Crossan, Sarah. One. 2015. (ENG.). 400p. (YA). (gr. 8). 17.99 *(978-0-06-211875-2(7)*, Greenwillow Bks.) HarperCollins Pubs.
Crowley, James. The Magic Hour. 2003. (Illus.). 280p. (J). pap. 17.95 *(978-1-55517-713-3(1)*, 77131) Cedar Fort, Inc./CFI Distribution.
Cry of the Falcon. 2006. 208p. (J). pap. 9.95 *(978-0-9788541-0-2(1))* m.d. hughes.
Cusack, Dale. Gwen & the Dragon. 2007. (Illus.). 114p. pap. 9.95 *(978-1-4303-1080-8(4))* Lulu Pr., Inc.
Cussler, Clive. The Adventures of Hotsy Totsy. 2011. (ENG., Illus.). 176p. (J). (gr. 3-7). 6.99 *(978-0-14-241873-4(0)*, Puffin Books) Penguin Young Readers Group.
Cuyler, Margery. Tick Tock Clock. Neubecker, Robert, illus. 2012. (My First I Can Read Ser.). (ENG.). 32p. (J). (gr. -1 — 1). 16.99 *(978-0-06-136309-2(X))*; pap. 3.99 *(978-0-06-136311-5(1))* HarperCollins Pubs.
Daddy! 2005. (J). bds. *(978-0-9769910-6-9(3))* Terrific Twins LLC.
Daily, Lorrie Ann. The Castlewood Twins, the Magic Begins. 2008. 196p. pap. 12.95 *(978-0-9820479-8-9(3))* Peppertree Pr., The.
Danna, Natasha. Any Two Can Be Twindollicious. Dye, Jerel, illus. 2013. 32p. (J). 17.95 *(978-1-60131-154-2(0)*, Castlebridge Bks.) Big Tent Bks.
Danticat, Edwidge. Untwine. 2017. (ENG.). 320p. (J). (gr. 7). pap. 9.99 *(978-0-545-42304-5(X))* Scholastic, Inc.
—Untwine: A Novel. 2015. (ENG.). 320p. (J). (gr. 7). 16.99 *(978-0-545-42303-8(1)*, Scholastic Pr.) Scholastic, Inc.
Darke, J. A. The Grin in the Dark. Evergreen, Nelson, illus. 2015. (Spine Shivers Ser.). (ENG.). 128p. (gr. 3-4). lib. bdg. 26.65 *(978-1-4965-0217-9(5))* Stone Arch Bks.
Darlison, Aleesah. Quinn's Riddles. Brailsford, Jill, illus. 2016. (Unicorn Riders Ser.). (ENG.). 112p. (gr. 3-5). lib. bdg. 22.65 *(978-1-4795-6544-3(X))* Picture Window Bks.
—Quinn's Truth Cancelled. Brailsford, Jill, illus. 2017. (Unicorn Riders Ser.). (ENG.). 112p. (gr. 3-5). pap. 5.95 *(978-1-4795-6556-6(3))* Picture Window Bks.
Darlison, Aleesha. Quinn's Riddles. Brailsford, Jill, illus. 2017. (Unicorn Riders Ser.). (ENG.). 112p. (gr. 3-5). pap. 5.95 *(978-1-4795-6552-8(0))* Picture Window Bks.
Dasilva, D. Mom Has Left & Gone to Vegas. Craig, Dan, illus. 2008. 32p. pap. 19.95 *(978-1-59858-603-9(3))* Dog Ear Publishing, LLC.
David, Jamie. Johann Sebastian Humpbach. David, Jamie, illus. 2009. (Illus.). 167p. pap. 14.95 *(978-0-615-31840-0(1))* Chai Yo Maui Pr.
Davis, Tanita S. Happy Families. (ENG.). 240p. (YA). (gr. 7). 2013. pap. 9.99 *(978-0-375-87170-2(5)*, Ember) 2012. 16.99 *(978-0-375-86966-2(2)*, Knopf Bks. for Young Readers) Random Hse. Children's Bks.
De la Cruz, Melissa. Double Eclipse. 2016. (Summer on East End Ser.). (ENG.). 336p. (YA). (gr. 7). 17.99 *(978-0-399-17356-1(0)*, G.P. Putnam's Sons Books for Young Readers) Penguin Young Readers Group.
Dearle, Anne Crofton. Ginger Cat. 2011. (Illus.). 92p. pap. 12.10 *(978-1-4567-7484-4(0))* AuthorHouse.
Deering, Leta. Patriotic Samaand the Mendez Twins at the Alamo. 2008. 112p. pap. 19.95 *(978-1-60610-689-1(9))* America Star Bks.
dePaola, Tomie. Meet the Barkers: Morgan & Moffat Go to School. dePaola, Tomie, illus. 2003. (Barker Twins Ser.). (ENG., Illus.). 32p. (J). (gr. -1-3). 6.99 *(978-0-14-250083-5(6)*, Puffin Books) Penguin Young Readers Group.
—Meet the Barkers: Morgan & Moffat Go to School. 2005. (J). (gr. k-3). pap. 17.95 incl. audio *(978-0-8045-6934-7(7)*, SAC6934) Spoken Arts, Inc.
—Strega Nona & the Twins. 2017. (Simon & Schuster Ready-To-Read Level 1 Ser.). lib. bdg. 13.55 ***(978-0-606-40215-6(2))*** Turtleback Bks.
dePaola, Tomie. Trouble in the Barkers' Class. dePaola, Tomie, illus. 2006. (Barker Twins Ser.). (ENG., Illus.). 32p. (J). (gr. -1-3). reprint ed. pap. 6.99 *(978-0-14-240585-7(X)*, Puffin Books) Penguin Young Readers Group.
DeVillers, Julia & Roy, Jennifer. Double Feature. 2012. (Mix Ser.). (ENG.). 288p. (J). (gr. 4-8). pap. 7.99 *(978-1-4424-3403-5(1)*, Aladdin) Simon & Schuster Children's Publishing.
—Triple Trouble. 2014. (Mix Ser.). (ENG., Illus.). 240p. (J). (gr. 4-8). pap. 7.99 *(978-1-4424-3406-6(6)*, Aladdin) Simon & Schuster Children's Publishing.
—Triple Trouble. 2013. (ENG.). 240p. (J). (gr. 4-8). 16.99 *(978-1-4424-3405-9(8)*, Simon & Schuster/Paula Wiseman Bks.) Simon & Schuster/Paula Wiseman Bks.
DeVillers, Julia & Roy, Jennifer Rozines. Double Feature. 2012. (ENG.). 272p. (J). (gr. 4-8). 16.99 *(978-1-4424-3402-8(3)*, Aladdin) Simon & Schuster Children's Publishing.
—Take Two. 2010. (Mix Ser.). (ENG.). 304p. (J). (gr. 4-8). pap. 7.99 *(978-1-4169-6731-6(1)*, Aladdin) Simon & Schuster Children's Publishing.
—Take Two. 2010. (ENG.). 240p. (J). (gr. 4-8). 16.99 *(978-1-4169-7533-5(0)*, Simon & Schuster/Paula Wiseman Bks.) Simon & Schuster/Paula Wiseman Bks.
—Times Squared. 2011. (Mix Ser.). (ENG.). (J). (gr. 4-8). 272p. pap. 7.99 *(978-1-4169-6732-3(X))*; 240p. 16.99 *(978-1-4169-7532-8(2))* Simon & Schuster Children's Publishing. (Aladdin).
—Trading Faces. 2008. (ENG.). 304p. (J). (gr. 4-8). 16.99 *(978-1-4169-7531-1(4)*, Simon & Schuster/Paula Wiseman Bks.) Simon & Schuster/Paula Wiseman Bks.
Diane, Rachel And Rebecca Sall. Mother Earth's Message. 2009. 28p. pap. 15.99 *(978-1-4363-8613-5(6))* Xlibris Corp.
Disney Book Group Staff, et al. Minnie Minnie's Winter Bow Show. Disney Storybook Artists Staff, illus. 2014. (ENG.). 24p. (J). (gr. -1-k). pap. 5.99 *(978-1-4231-8070-8(4))* Disney Pr.
DiTerlizzi, Tony & Black, Holly. The Ironwood Tree. DiTerlizzi, Tony, illus. 4th ed. 2004. (Spiderwick Chronicles Ser.: 4). (ENG., Illus.). 128p. (J). (gr. 2-6). 10.99 *(978-0-689-85939-7(2)*, Simon & Schuster Bks. For Young Readers) Simon & Schuster Bks. For Young Readers.
—The Ironwood Tree. l.t. ed. 2006. (Spiderwick Chronicles: Bk. 4). 90p. (YA). (gr. 2-18). 23.95 *(978-0-7862-8583-9(4))* Thorndike Pr.
Dixon, Franklin W. Double Down. 26th ed. 2008. (Hardy Boys (All New) Undercover Brothers Ser.: 26). (ENG.). 172p. (J). (gr. 3-7). pap. 5.99 *(978-1-4169-7446-8(6)*, Aladdin) Simon & Schuster Children's Publishing.

Dockter, Debra. Deadly Design. 2015. (ENG.). 368p. (YA). (gr. 7). 17.99 *(978-0-399-17105-5(3),* G.P. Putnam's Sons Books for Young Readers) Penguin Young Readers Group.

Dokey, Cameron. The World Above. 2010. (Once upon a Time Ser.). (ENG.). 208p. (YA). (gr. 7-18). pap. 6.99 *(978-1-4424-0337-6(3),* Simon Pulse) Simon Pulse.

Doktorski, Jennifer Salvato. The Summer after You & Me. 2015. (ENG.). 304p. (YA). (gr. 8-12). pap. 10.99 *(978-1-4926-1903-1(5))* Sourcebooks, Inc.

Double Deception, Bk. 3. 2009. (Hardy Boys (All New) Undercover Brothers Ser.: 27). (ENG.). 176p. (J). (gr. 3-7). pap. 5.99 *(978-1-4169-6766-8(4),* Aladdin) Simon & Schuster Children's Publishing.

Double or Nothing. 2014. (It Takes Two Ser.: 3). (ENG., Illus.). 160p. (J). (gr. 3-7). pap. 6.99 *(978-1-4814-1652-8(9),* Simon Spotlight) Simon Spotlight.

Driscoll, Laura. We Are Twins. Campion, Pascal, illus. 2012. (Penguin Young Readers, Level 1 Ser.). (ENG.). 32p. (J). (gr. k-1). mass mkt. 3.99 *(978-0-448-46157-1(9),* Penguin Young Readers) Penguin Young Readers Group.

—We Are Twins. 2012. (Penguin Young Readers Level 1 Ser.). lib. bdg. 13.55 *(978-0-606-26641-3(0),* Turtleback) Turtleback Bks.

Dudley, Blanche R. Siggy's Parade: Helping Kids with Disabilities Find Their Strengths. 2014. (ENG., Illus.). 48p. (J). (gr. -1-2). 9.95 *(978-0-88282-469-7(4))* New Horizon Pr. Pubs., Inc.

Dumas, Alexandre. The Man in the Iron Mask. Howell, Troy, illus. 2008. (Classic Starts(tm) Ser.). (ENG.). 160p. (J). (gr. 2-4). 6.95 *(978-1-4027-4579-9(6))* Sterling Publishing Co., Inc.

Duncan, Lois. Stranger with My Face. 2011. (ENG.). 320p. (YA). (gr. 7-17). pap., pap. 10.99 *(978-0-316-09904-2(X))* Little, Brown Bks. for Young Readers.

Durant, Alan. Doing the Double. 2004. (Shades Ser.). (ENG.). 64p. (J). pap. *(978-0-237-52846-1(0))* Evans Brothers, Ltd.

Durrant, Geraldine. Twinbane: an Appalling True History. 2010. 142p. pap. 16.95 *(978-1-4457-7998-0(6))* Lulu Pr., Inc.

Durst, Sarah Beth. Journey Across the Hidden Islands. 2017. (ENG., Illus.). 352p. (J). (gr. 5-7). 16.99 *(978-0-544-70679-8(X),* Clarion Bks.) Houghton Mifflin Harcourt Trade & Reference Pubs.

Dyan, Penelope. Mikey & Me & the Se. 2011. 36p. pap. 11.95 *(978-1-935630-63-0(6))* Bellissima Publishing, LLC.

Dyer, Heather. The Girl with the Broken Wing. Bailey, Peter, illus. 2005. 147p. (J). *(978-1-4156-3468-4(8))* Scholastic, Inc.

Dyer, Jonah Lisa & Dyer, Stephen. The Season. 2016. (ENG.). 352p. (YA). (gr. 9). 17.99 *(978-0-451-47634-0(4),* Viking Books for Young Readers) Penguin Young Readers Group.

Eaton, Jason Carter. The Facttracker. Constantin, Pascale, illus. 2008. 272p. (J). (gr. 3-7). 16.99 *(978-0-06-056434-6(2))* HarperCollins Pubs.

Echols, Jennifer. Such a Rush. 2012. (ENG.). 336p. pap. 20.99 *(978-1-4516-5802-6(8),* Gallery Bks.) Gallery Bks.

Eddy, Catherine J. Sandbox Sandshoes. Krupnek, Joann J., illus. 2009. 38p. pap. 10.95 *(978-0-9818488-5-3(0))* Ajoyin Publishing, Inc.

Edwards, Christine. The Charmed Enchanted Book. 2010. 24p. pap. 16.49 *(978-1-4490-7091-5(4))* AuthorHouse.

Ehrenhaft, Daniel. The After Life. 2006. (ENG.). 272p. (YA). (gr. 7-12). 8.99 *(978-1-59514-080-7(8),* Razorbill) Penguin Young Readers Group.

Ehrlich, Nikki. Twindergarten. Wagner, Zoey Abbott, illus. 2017. 32p. (J). (gr. -1-3). 15.99 *(978-0-06-256423-8(4))* HarperCollins Pubs.

Elizabeth's Story 1848. 2014. (Secrets of the Manor Ser.: 3). (ENG., Illus.). 160p. (J). (gr. 3-7). pap. 6.99 *(978-1-4814-1840-9(8),* Simon Spotlight) Simon Spotlight.

Emerson, Alice B. Ruth Fielding at Snow Camp or Lost in the Backwoods. 2005. reprint ed. pap. 24.95 *(978-1-4179-3132-3(9))* Kessinger Publishing, LLC.

Erickson, Mary Ellen. Who Jinxed the CG Ranch? 2009. 196p. 24.95 *(978-1-4401-4218-5(1));* pap. 14.95 *(978-1-4401-4216-1(5))* iUniverse, Inc.

Farnsworth, Frances Joyce. Tike & Tiny in the Tetons. 2007. (Illus.). 172p. (J). pap. 14.95 *(978-0-943972-79-4(5))* Homestead Publishing.

Farrant, Natasha. After Iris. 2013. (ENG.). 272p. (J). (gr. 5). 16.99 *(978-0-8037-3982-6(5),* Dial Bks) Penguin Young Readers Group.

Faust, Jon. Helicopter Harry & the Copter Kids. 2016. (ENG., Illus.). (J). pap. 9.95 ***(978-0-692-78184-5(6))*** Mother Lode Pr. LLC.

Fields, Jan. Terrible Twin Mania, 1 vol. 2014. (Meri's Mirror Ser.). (ENG.). 80p. (J). (gr. 2-5). lib. bdg. 27.07 *(978-1-62402-011-7(9),* Calico Chapter Bks) Magic Wagon.

Finch, Kate. Calling All Pets! 2013. (Pet Hotel Ser.: 1). lib. bdg. 14.75 *(978-0-606-31984-3(0),* Turtleback) Turtleback Bks.

—Pet Hotel #1: Calling All Pets! Gurney, John Steven & Jessell, Tim, illus. 2013. (Pet Hotel Ser.: 1). (ENG.). 96p. (J). (gr. 2-5). pap. 4.99 *(978-0-545-50180-4(6),* Scholastic Paperbacks) Scholastic, Inc.

Finkelstein, Ruth. The Thankyou Twins. Rubenstein, Reva, illus. 2006. 24p. (J). *(978-0-9628157-5-1(6))* Finkelstein, Ruth.

Fischel, Ana. The Twelve Quests - Book 2, a Dragon's Tooth. 2009. 158p. pap. *(978-1-84923-874-8(X))* YouWriteOn.

—The Twelve Quests - Book 3, the Pied Piper's Flute. 2009. 158p. pap. *(978-1-84923-875-5(8))* YouWriteOn.

—The Twelve Quests - Book 4, Rapunzel's Hair. 2009. 158p. pap. *(978-1-84923-876-2(6))* YouWriteOn.

—The Twelve Quests - Book 5, a Firebird's Feather. 2009. 158p. pap. *(978-1-84923-877-9(4))* YouWriteOn.

—The Twelve Quests - Book 6, the Enchanted Harp. 2009. 158p. pap. *(978-1-84923-878-6(2))* YouWriteOn.

Fisher, Catherine. Darkwater. 2012. (ENG.). 240p. (YA). (gr. 7). 16.99 *(978-0-8037-3818-8(8),* Dial Bks) Penguin Young Readers Group.

Fisher, Phyllis Mae Richardson. Twiglet the Little Christmas Tree. Fisher, Phyllis Mae Richardson & Fisher, Douglas W., illus. 2003. (J). 30.00 *(978-0-9745615-1-6(7),* Twiglet The Little Christmas Tree); 186p. 12.00 *(978-0-9745615-4-7(1))* PJs Corner.

Fontenot, Mary Alice & Fontenot Landry, Julie. Clovis Crawfish & the Twin Sister, 1 vol. Butler, Julie Dupre & Buckner, Julie Dupre, illus. 2007. (Clovis Crawfish Ser.). (ENG.). 32p. (J). (gr. k-3). 16.99 *(978-1-58980-467-8(8))* Pelican Publishing Co., Inc.

Foreman, Timothy. The Last Little Polar Bear: A Global Change Adventure Story. Laura Lee, Cundiff, illus. 2007. 60p. (J). per. 19.95 *(978-0-9776906-2-6(8))* Blueline Publishing.

Foster, Kia. Tom & Rondy. 2012. 24p. pap. 17.99 *(978-1-4772-0134-3(3))* AuthorHouse.

Francia, Giada. Alex & Penny in China Jigsaw Book. 2011. (ENG., Illus.). 14p. 14.95 *(978-88-544-0310-9(5))* White Star ITA. Dist: Random Hse., Inc.

—Alex & Penny in Egypt Jigsaw Book. 2011. (ENG., Illus.). 14p. 14.95 *(978-88-544-0240-9(0))* White Star ITA. Dist: Random Hse., Inc.

—In the Wild West on MacKenzie's Trail. McCloskey, Erin, ed. Howard, Catherine, tr. 2007. (Alex & Penny Ser.). (ENG., Illus.). 80p. (gr. 2-5). pap. 14.95 *(978-88-544-0245-4(1))* White Star ITA. Dist: Random Hse., Inc.

Francois, Rose Darlie. Little Miss Daring Evelynne. 2009. 47p. pap. 19.10 *(978-0-557-07136-4(4))* Lulu Pr., Inc.

Franklin, Shirley A. Emma's Fantastique Word Play. 2009. 80p. pap. 8.95 *(978-1-4401-3824-9(9))* iUniverse, Inc.

Fraustino, Lisa Rowe. The Hole in the Wall. 2011. (ENG.). 232p. (J). (gr. 2-8). pap. 8.00 *(978-1-57131-698-1(1))* Milkweed Editions.

Frazier, Sundee T. The Other Half of My Heart. 2011. (ENG.). 304p. (J). (gr. 3-7). 7.99 *(978-0-440-24006-8(9),* Yearling) Random Hse. Children's Bks.

Freeman, Martha. The Trouble with Twins. Smith, Cat Bowman, illus. 2007. (ENG.). 112p. (J). (gr. 2-6). 16.95 *(978-0-8234-2025-4(6))* Holiday Hse., Inc.

Friday, Anita. Twins. Branman, Liz, illus. 2013. 34p. pap. 11.99 *(978-0-9899544-0-2(4))* Two Chicks.

Fukui, Isamu. Truancy Origins. 2011. (Truancy Ser.: 2). (ENG.). 384p. (YA). (gr. 8-12). pap. 19.99 *(978-0-7653-2264-7(1),* 9780765322647, Tor Teen) Doherty, Tom Assocs., LLC.

Fuss, Kevin. The Brothers Geek. 2010. 180p. 24.99 *(978-1-4490-7366-4(2));* pap. 14.49 *(978-1-4490-7365-7(4))* AuthorHouse.

Gaffney, Linda. My Daddy Does GOOD Things, Too! Dabney, Undra & Goettling, Nickalas, illus. 2006. 55p. per. 10.99 *(978-0-9787501-0-7(1))* Gaffney, Linda.

Gallagher, Brian. Stormclouds: New Friends. Old Differences. 2014. (ENG.). 224p. (J). 13.95 *(978-1-84717-579-3(1))* O'Brien Pr., Ltd., The IRL. Dist: Dufour Editions, Inc.

Gallagher, Mary. Mulhern Twins. 2007. (ENG., Illus.). 126p. (J). pap. 11.95 *(978-1-905172-17-7(5))* Collins Pr., The IRL. Dist: Dufour Editions, Inc.

Gantos, Jack. The Love Curse of the Rumbaughs. 2008. (ENG.). 192p. (YA). (gr. 9-12). pap. 14.99 *(978-0-312-38052-6(6),* 9780312380526) Square Fish.

Garcia, Maria. Las Aventuras de Connie y Diego. 2004. (ENG & SPA., Illus.). (J). (gr. k-3). spiral bd. *(978-0-616-14605-7(1))* Canadian National Institute for the Blind/Institut National Canadien pour les Aveugles.

Gardner, Lyn. Fright in the Night. Asquith, Ros, illus. 2016. (Ghastly Mcnastys Ser.: 3). (ENG.). 192p. (J). (gr. k-3). pap. 9.99 *(978-1-84812-392-2(2))* Bonnier Publishing GBR. Dist: Independent Pubs. Group.

Gauthier, Bertrand. Abracadabra, les Jumeaux Sont La! 2003. (Premier Roman Ser.). (FRE.). 64p. (J). (gr. 2-5). pap. *(978-2-89021-144-5(4))* Diffusion du livre Mirabel (DLM).

Geist, Ken. Who's Who? Cole, Henry, illus. 2012. (ENG.). 28p. (J). (gr. -1 — 1). 16.99 *(978-0-312-64437-6(X),* 9780312644376) Feiwel & Friends.

Geraghty, Paul. Rotten & Rascal: The Two Terrible Pterosaur Twins. 2013. (ENG., Illus.). 32p. (J). (gr. k-2). pap. 9.99 *(978-1-84939-563-2(2))* Andersen Pr. GBR. Dist: Independent Pubs. Group.

Gibson, Jo. Afraid. 2014. (ENG.). 336p. (YA). (gr. 13). pap. 9.95 *(978-1-61773-242-3(7),* K-Teen) Kensington Publishing Corp.

Giff, Patricia Reilly. Hunter Moran Digs Deep. Sheban, Chris, illus. 2014. (ENG.). 160p. (J). (gr. 3-7). 16.95 *(978-0-8234-3165-6(7))* Holiday Hse., Inc.

—Hunter Moran Hangs Out. (ENG.). 144p. (J). (gr. 3-7). 2014. pap. 6.99 *(978-0-8234-3189-2(4))* 2013. (Illus.). 16.95 *(978-0-8234-2859-5(1))* Holiday Hse., Inc.

—Hunter Moran Saves the Universe. (ENG.). 128p. (J). (gr. 2-7). 2013. pap. 6.99 *(978-0-8234-2917-2(2))* 2012. 16.95 *(978-0-8234-1949-4(5))* Holiday Hse., Inc.

Gifford, Peggy. Moxy Maxwell Does Not Love Stuart Little. Fisher, Valorie, photos by. 2008. (Moxy Maxwell Ser.). (ENG., Illus.). 112p. (J). (gr. 2-5). 5.99 *(978-0-440-42230-3(2),* Yearling) Random Hse. Children's Bks.

—Moxy Maxwell Does Not Love Writing Thank-You Notes. Fisher, Valorie, illus. 2009. (Moxy Maxwell Ser.). (ENG.). 192p. (J). (gr. 2-5). 6.99 *(978-0-375-84343-3(4),* Yearling) Random Hse. Children's Bks.

Gilbert, Wendy June. Our Beds Are Cars. 2008. 44p. per. 24.95 *(978-1-60441-749-4(8))* America Star Bks.

Gill, Timothy. Flip & Fin: Super Sharks to the Rescue! Numberman, Neil, illus. 2016. 32p. (J). (gr. -1-3). 15.99 *(978-0-06-224301-0(2),* Greenwillow Bks.) HarperCollins Pubs.

—Flip & Fin: We Rule the School! Numberman, Neil, illus. 2014. (ENG.). 32p. (J). (gr. -1-3). 14.99 *(978-0-06-224300-3(4),* Greenwillow Bks.) HarperCollins Pubs.

Glewwe, Eleanor. Wildings. 2016. (ENG.). 336p. (J). (gr. 5). 16.99 *(978-0-451-46885-7(6),* Viking Books for Young Readers) Penguin Young Readers Group.

Go! Fight! Twin! 2014. (It Takes Two Ser.: 4). (ENG., Illus.). 160p. (J). (gr. 3-7). 17.99 *(978-1-4814-1656-6(1));* pap. 6.99 *(978-1-4814-1655-9(3))* Simon Spotlight. (Simon Spotlight).

Godby, Ron. The King of Imperial Hill. 2006. 76p. pap. 16.95 *(978-1-4241-1061-2(0))* PublishAmerica, Inc.

Golden Books. Shimmer & Shine Awesome Sticker Collection (Shimmer & Shine) Golden Books, illus. 2017. (4 Color Plus 1,000 Stickers Ser.). (ENG., Illus.). 64p. (J). (gr. -1-2). pap. 12.99 ***(978-1-5247-1680-6(4),*** Golden Bks.) Random Hse. Children's Bks.

—Shimmer & Shine Little Golden Book Favorites (Shimmer & Shine) Golden Books, illus. 2017. (Little Golden Book Favorites Ser.). (ENG., Illus.). 80p. (J). (gr. -1-2). 7.99 ***(978-1-5247-1720-9(7),*** Random Hse. Bks. for Young Readers) Random Hse. Children's Bks.

Goobie, Beth. Fixed, 1 vol. 2005. (ENG.). 294p. (YA). (gr. 8-12). 16.95 *(978-1-55143-374-5(5))* Orca Bk. Pubs. USA.

Gordon, Pauline C. The Adventures of the Droplet Twins. 2013. 136p. *(978-1-4602-1343-8(2));* pap. *(978-1-4602-1344-5(0))* FriesenPress.

Gormally, Eleanor. The Little Flower Bulb: Helping Children Bereaved by Suicide. Loki & Splink, illus. 2011. (ENG.). 32p. (J). (gr. -1-3). pap. 21.95 *(978-1-84730-260-1(2))* Veritas Pubns. IRL. Dist: Dufour Editions, Inc.

Gosling, Sharon. The Sapphire Cutlass. 2016. (Diamond Thief Ser.). (ENG.). 336p. (gr. 9-12). 16.95 *(978-1-63079-041-7(9))* Switch Pr.

Grace, Amanda. No One Needs to Know. 2014. (ENG.). 240p. (YA). pap. 9.99 *(978-0-7387-3625-9(2),* Flux) North Star Editions.

Grant, Michael. BZRK. (ENG.). 400p. (gr. 9). 2013. (J). pap. 9.99 *(978-1-60684-418-2(0))* 2012. 17.99 *(978-1-60684-312-3(5))* Lerner Publishing Group. (Carolrhoda Lab™).

—BZRK Apocalypse. 2014. (ENG.). 400p. (J). (gr. 9). 18.99 *(978-1-60684-408-3(3),* Carolrhoda Lab™) Lerner Publishing Group.

—BZRK Reloaded. (ENG.). 432p. (J). (gr. 9). 2014. pap. 9.99 *(978-1-60684-504-2(7))* 2013. 18.99 *(978-1-60684-394-9(X))* Lerner Publishing Group. (Carolrhoda Lab™).

Grant, Natalie. Light up New York, 1 vol. 2017. (Faithgirlz / Glimmer Girls Ser.). (ENG.). 208p. (J). pap. 8.99 *(978-0-310-75274-5(4))* Zonderkidz.

—The Miracle in Music City, 1 vol. 2016. (Faithgirlz / Glimmer Girls Ser.). (ENG.). 208p. (J). pap. 8.99 *(978-0-310-75250-9(7))* Zonderkidz.

Green, Paige. Family over Everything. 2013. (ENG., Illus.). 224p. pap. 15.99 *(978-1-59309-501-7(5),* Strebor Bks.) Strebor Bks.

Green, Tim. Pinch Hit. (ENG.). (J). (gr. 3-7). 2013. 336p. pap. 6.99 *(978-0-06-201247-0(9))* 2012. 320p. 16.99 *(978-0-06-201246-3(0))* HarperCollins Pubs.

Greenburg, Dan. Secrets of Dripping Fang: Attack of the Giant Octopus. Fischer, Scott M., illus. 2009. (Secrets of Dripping Fang Ser.). (ENG.). 160p. 25.65 *(978-1-59961-537-0(1))* Spotlight.

—Secrets of Dripping Fang: Fall of the House of Mandible. Fischer, Scott M., illus. 2009. (Secrets of Dripping Fang Ser.). (ENG.). 160p. 25.65 *(978-1-59961-535-6(5))* Spotlight.

—Secrets of Dripping Fang: Please Don't Eat the Children: Book 7: Book 7. Fischer, Scott M., illus. 2009. (Secrets of Dripping Fang Ser.). (ENG.). 160p. 25.65 *(978-1-59961-538-7(X))* Spotlight.

—Secrets of Dripping Fang: The Onts. Fischer, Scott M., illus. 2009. (Secrets of Dripping Fang Ser.). (ENG.). 144p. 25.65 *(978-1-59961-532-5(0))* Spotlight.

—Secrets of Dripping Fang: The Shluffmuffin Boy Is History. Fischer, Scott M., illus. 2009. (Secrets of Dripping Fang Ser.). (ENG.). 176p. 25.65 *(978-1-59961-536-3(3))* Spotlight.

—Secrets of Dripping Fang: The Vampire's Curse: Book 3: Book 3. Fischer, Scott M., illus. 2009. (Secrets of Dripping Fang Ser.). (ENG.). 144p. 25.65 *(978-1-59961-534-9(7))* Spotlight.

—Secrets of Dripping Fang: Treachery & Betrayal at Jolly Days. Fischer, Scott M., illus. 2009. (Secrets of Dripping Fang Ser.). (ENG.). 144p. 25.65 *(978-1-59961-533-2(9))* Spotlight.

—Secrets of Dripping Fang: When Bad Snakes Attack Good Children. Fischer, Scott M., illus. 2009. (Secrets of Dripping Fang Ser.). (ENG.). 144p. 25.65 *(978-1-59961-539-4(8))* Spotlight.

—Secrets of Dripping Fang, Book Eight: When Bad Snakes Attack Good Children. Fischer, Scott M., illus. 2007. (Secrets of Dripping Fang Ser.: Bk. 8). (ENG.). 144p. (J). (gr. 2-5). 11.99 *(978-0-15-206056-5(1))* Houghton Mifflin Harcourt Publishing Co.

—Secrets of Dripping Fang, Book Seven: Please Don't Eat the Children. Fischer, Scott M., illus. 2007. (Secrets of Dripping Fang Ser.: Bk. 7). (ENG.). 160p. (J). (gr. 2-5). 11.95 *(978-0-15-206047-3(2))* Houghton Mifflin Harcourt Publishing Co.

Greer, Hannah. The Lighthouse Summer Greer, Tica, illus. 2009. 156p. pap. 24.95 *(978-1-60813-493-9(8))* America Star Bks.

—The Velvet Bag Memoirs, Bk. 1. 2008. 132p. pap. 24.95 *(978-1-60672-190-2(9))* America Star Bks.

Griffin, Bethany. The Fall. 2014. (ENG.). 432p. (YA). (gr. 9). 17.99 *(978-0-06-210785-5(2),* Greenwillow Bks.) HarperCollins Pubs.

Grill-Merrill, Karen. The Muk & Tuk Tales. 2006. 65p. 20.00 *(978-1-4257-0795-8(5));* pap. 10.00 *(978-1-4257-0794-1(7))* Xlibris Corp.

Griner, Sophia Maria. Hooray for Saturday! 2013. 24p. pap. *(978-1-4602-1806-8(X))* FriesenPress.

Groth, Darren. Are You Seeing Me?, 1 vol. 2015. (ENG., Illus.). 288p. (YA). (gr. 8-12). 19.95 *(978-1-4598-1079-2(1))* Orca Bk. Pubs. USA.

Guillory, Sarah. Reclaimed. 2013. (ENG.). 296p. (YA). (gr. 7-9). pap. 9.95 *(978-1-937053-88-8(1),* Spencer Hill Contemporary) Spencer Hill Pr.

Gutman, Dan. From Texas with Love. 2014. (ENG.). (J). (gr. 3-7). (Genius Files Ser.: 4). 304p. pap. 6.99 *(978-0-06-182775-4(4));* (Genius Files Ser.: Bk. 4). (Illus.). 288p. 16.99 *(978-0-06-182773-0(8))* HarperCollins Pubs.

—From Texas with Love. 2014. (Genius Files Ser.: 4). (J). lib. bdg. 17.20 *(978-0-606-36462-1(5))* Turtleback Bks.

—The Genius Files #4: from Texas with Love. 2014. (Genius Files Ser.: 4). 288p. (J). (gr. 3-7). lib. bdg. 17.89 *(978-0-06-182774-7(6))* HarperCollins Pubs.

—Mission Unstoppable. 2011. (Genius Files Ser.: 1). (ENG.). 304p. (J). (gr. 3-7). pap. 6.99 *(978-0-06-182766-2(5));* (Illus.). 16.99 *(978-0-06-182764-8(9))* HarperCollins Pubs.

—Mission Unstoppable. 2011. (Genius Files Ser.: 1). (J). lib. bdg. 17.20 *(978-0-606-23559-4(0),* Turtleback) Turtleback Bks.

—Never Say Genius. 2012. (Genius Files Ser.: 2). (J). (gr. 3-7). (ENG.). 304p. pap. 6.99 *(978-0-06-182769-3(X));* (ENG.). 288p. 16.99 *(978-0-06-182767-9(3));* 288p. lib. bdg. 17.89 *(978-0-06-182768-6(1))* HarperCollins Pubs.

—Never Say Genius. 2012. (Genius Files Ser.: 2). (J). lib. bdg. 17.20 *(978-0-606-27128-8(7),* Turtleback) Turtleback Bks.

—You Only Die Twice. 2013. (Genius Files Ser.: 3). (J). (gr. 3-7). (ENG.). 320p. pap. 6.99 *(978-0-06-182772-3(X));* (ENG., Illus.). 304p. 16.99 *(978-0-06-182770-9(3));* (Illus.). 304p. lib. bdg. 17.89 *(978-0-06-182771-6(1))* HarperCollins Pubs.

—You Only Die Twice. 2013. (Genius Files Ser.: 3). (J). lib. bdg. 17.20 *(978-0-606-35043-3(8),* Turtleback) Turtleback Bks.

Haddix, Margaret Peterson. In over Their Heads. 2017. (Under Their Skin Ser.: 2). (ENG., Illus.). 320p. (J). (gr. 3-7). 16.99 *(978-1-4814-1761-7(4),* Simon & Schuster Bks. For Young Readers) Simon & Schuster Bks. For Young Readers.

—Redeemed. 2015. (Missing Ser.: 8). (ENG.). 416p. (J). (gr. 3-7). 17.99 *(978-1-4424-9756-6(4),* Simon & Schuster Bks. For Young Readers) Simon & Schuster Bks. For Young Readers.

—Redeemed. 2016. (Missing Ser.: 8). lib. bdg. 18.40 *(978-0-606-39234-1(3))* Turtleback Bks.

—Under Their Skin. 2016. (Under Their Skin Ser.: 1). (ENG.). 320p. (J). (gr. 3-7). 16.99 *(978-1-4814-1758-7(4),* Simon & Schuster Bks. For Young Readers) Simon & Schuster Bks. For Young Readers.

Hale, Bruce. Pirates of Underwhere. Hillman, Shane, illus. (Underwhere Ser.: 2). (J). (gr. 3-7). 2009. (ENG.). 176p. pap. 6.99 *(978-0-06-085129-3(5))* 2008. 164p. lib. bdg. 16.89 *(978-0-06-085128-6(7))* HarperCollins Pubs.

—Prince of Underwhere. Hillman, Shane, illus. 2009. (Underwhere Ser.: 1). (ENG.). 176p. (J). (gr. 3-7). pap. 5.99 *(978-0-06-085126-2(0))* HarperCollins Pubs.

Hall, Angela Marie. Priscilla Pennybrook: Hello World, I Have Arrived!, 1 vol. 2009. 55p. pap. 16.95 *(978-1-61582-899-9(0))* America Star Bks.

Hall, C. Aubrey. The Call of Eirian, 0 vols. 2012. (Faelin Chronicles Ser.: 2). (ENG.). 352p. (YA). (gr. 7-11). 17.99 *(978-0-7614-6262-0(7),* 9780761462620, Amazon Children's Publishing) Amazon Publishing.

Hamilton, Elizabeth L. Lost on Superstition Mountain. 2004. (Character Mystery Ser.: No. 3). (Illus.). 144p. (J). per. 9.95 *(978-0-9754629-5-9(4),* Character-in-Action) Quiet Impact, Inc.

—Mystery at Lake Cachuma. 2003. (Character Mystery Ser.: No. 1). (Illus.). 114p. (J). (gr. 3-6). per. 9.95 *(978-0-9713749-4-2(5),* Character-in-Action) Quiet Impact, Inc.

—Surprise at Pearl Harbor. 2004. (Character Mystery Ser.: No. 2). (Illus.). 144p. (J). per. 9.95 *(978-0-9754629-2-8(X),* Character-in-Action) Quiet Impact, Inc.

Harper, Meg. My Mum & the Gruesome Twosome. 2nd ed. (ENG.). 160p. pap. 9.99 *(978-0-7459-4829-4(4),* Lion Books) Lion Hudson PLC GBR. Dist: Trafalgar Square Publishing.

Harper, Suzanne. A Mischief of Mermaids. 2013. (Unseen World of Poppy Malone Ser.: 3). (ENG.). 288p. (J). (gr. 3-7). 16.99 *(978-0-06-199613-9(0),* Greenwillow Bks.) HarperCollins Pubs.

Harvey, Alyxandra. Whisper the Dead. 2014. (Lovegrove Legacy Ser.: Bk. 2). (ENG.). 408p. (YA). (gr. 7). 17.99 *(978-0-8027-3750-2(1),* 9780802737502, Bloomsbury USA Childrens) Bloomsbury Publishing USA.

Haspiel, Dean. Mo & Jo: Fighting Together Forever. Lynch, Jay, illus. 2013. (ENG.). 40p. (J). (gr. -1-3). pap. 4.99 *(978-1-935179-37-5(3))* TOON Books / RAW Junior, LLC.

Hassler, Kurt. Diva V Poe. 2006. (Illus.). 32p. (J). 16.95 *(978-1-933164-29-8(8))* Seven Seas Entertainment, LLC.

Hayes, Sadie. The Social Code. 2013. (Start-Up Ser.: 1). (ENG., Illus.). 320p. (YA). (gr. 7-12). pap. 9.99 *(978-1-250-03565-3(1),* 9781250035653, St. Martin's Griffin) St. Martin's Pr.

Hays, Sharon. The Tumbleweed Family. 2011. 28p. pap. 15.99 *(978-1-4568-6825-3(X))* Xlibris Corp.

Hayton, Althea. Two Little Birds. Schlitt, RaRa, illus. 2012. 38p. pap. *(978-0-9557808-1-3(0))* Wren Pubns.

Helland, Jenna. The August 5. 2015. (ENG., Illus.). 320p. (YA). (gr. 7). 16.99 *(978-0-374-38264-3(6),* 9780374382643, Farrar, Straus & Giroux (BYR)) Farrar, Straus & Giroux.

Heller, Andrew. A Fine Mess. 2003. (J). 7.99 *(978-0-9722038-6-9(9))* Mr Do It All, Inc.

Hendey, Lisa M. The Whisper in the Ruins. Bower, Jenn, illus. 2016. (Chime Travelers Ser.: 3). (ENG.). 128p. (gr. 2-5). pap. 6.99 *(978-1-63253-036-3(8),* Servant Bks.) Franciscan Media.

Higgins, B. T. The Master of Disaster. 2005. 103p. pap. 10.00 *(978-1-4116-3121-2(8))* Lulu Pr., Inc.

Higgins, Jack & Richards, Justin. Death Run. 2009. (Rich & Jade Ser.: Bk. 2). (ENG.). 288p. (YA). (gr. 7-18). 8.99 *(978-0-14-241475-0(1),* Speak) Penguin Young Readers Group.

—First Strike. 2011. (Rich & Jade Ser.: Bk. 4). (ENG.). 240p. (YA). (gr. 7-18). 8.99 *(978-0-14-241909-0(5),* Speak) Penguin Young Readers Group.

—Sharp Shot. 2010. (Rich & Jade Ser.: Bk. 3). (ENG.). 240p. (YA). (gr. 7-18). 8.99 *(978-0-14-241730-0(0),* Speak) Penguin Young Readers Group.

—Sure Fire. 2008. (Rich & Jade Ser.: Bk. 1). (ENG.). 272p. (YA). (gr. 7-18). 8.99 *(978-0-14-241213-8(9),* Speak) Penguin Young Readers Group.

Higgins, Lawrence. Demons & Dragons: Time, Space & Magic. 2010. (ENG., Illus.). 93p. pap. 20.99 *(978-1-906791-68-1(6))* Arena Bks. GBR. Dist: Lightning Source UK, Ltd.

Hill, C. J. Echo in Time. (YA). 2014. 387p. *(978-0-06-212395-4(5))* 2013. (Erasing Time Ser.: 2). (ENG.). 400p. (gr. 8). pap. 9.99 *(978-0-06-212396-1(3),* Tegen, Katherine Bks) HarperCollins Pubs.

—Erasing Time. 2012. (Erasing Time Ser.: 1). (ENG.). 368p. (YA). (gr. 8). 17.99 *(978-0-06-212392-3(0),* Tegen, Katherine Bks) HarperCollins Pubs.

Hill, Janet Muirhead. Kendall & Kyleah. Leonhard, Herb, illus. 2012. (J). pap. 13.00 *(978-1-937849-05-4(8))* Raven Publishing Inc. of Montana.

Hodgson, Mona. The Princess Twins & the Birthday Party, 1 vol. Olson, Julie, illus. 2016. (I Can Read! / Princess Twins Ser.). (ENG.). 32p. (J). pap. 3.99 *(978-0-310-75067-3(9))* Zonderkidz.

—The Princess Twins Collection, 1 vol. Olson, Julie, illus. 2017. (I Can Read! / Princess Twins Ser.). (ENG.). 128p. (J). 12.99 *(978-0-310-75319-3(8))* Zonderkidz.

Hodgson, Mona Gansberg. The Princess Twins & the Puppy, 1 vol. Hansen, Red, illus. 2011. (I Can Read! / Princess Twins Ser.). (ENG.). 32p. (J). pap. 3.99 *(978-0-310-72709-5(X))* Zonderkidz.

Hoffman, Mary. City of Ships. 2010. (Stravaganza Ser.). (ENG.). 368p. (YA). (gr. 7-18). 17.99 *(978-1-59990-491-7(8)*, 9781599904917, Bloomsbury USA Childrens) Bloomsbury Publishing USA.

—Stravaganza: City of Ships. 2012. (Stravaganza Ser.). (ENG.). 384p. (YA). (gr. 7). pap. 9.99 *(978-1-59990-832-8(8)*, 9781599908328, Bloomsbury USA Childrens) Bloomsbury Publishing USA.

Hole, Stian. Garmann's Secret. Hole, Stian, illus. 2011. (ENG., Illus.). 56p. (J). 17.00 *(978-0-8028-5400-1(1)*, Eerdmans Bks For Young Readers) Eerdmans, William B. Publishing Co.

Holm, H. R. Forever Santa. 2009. 14p. (J). pap. 2.99 *(978-1-59955-345-0(7))* Cedar Fort, Inc./CFI Distribution.

Holmes, Anna & Scholastic, Inc. Staff. Tickety Toc: Welcome to Tickety Town. 2014. (Tickety Toc Ser.). (ENG.). 24p. (J). (gr. -1-k). pap. 3.99 *(978-0-545-61472-6(4))* Scholastic, Inc.

Hood, Ann. Alexander Graham Bell: Master of Sound. Zilber, Denis, illus. 2013. (Treasure Chest Ser.: 7). (ENG.). 192p. (J). (gr. 3-7). 6.99 *(978-0-448-45730-7(X)*, Grosset & Dunlap) Penguin Young Readers Group.

—Anastasia Romanov: The Last Grand Duchess. Zilber, Denis, illus. 2014. (Treasure Chest Ser.: 10). (ENG.). 240p. (J). (gr. 3-7). 15.99 *(978-0-448-46770-2(4))*;No. 10. 6.99 *(978-0-448-46771-9(2))* Penguin Young Readers Group. (Grosset & Dunlap).

—Clara Barton: Angel of the Battlefield. Kwasney, Karl et al, illus. 2012. (Treasure Chest Ser.: 1). (ENG.). 208p. (J). (gr. 3-7). pap. 6.99 *(978-0-448-45467-2(X)*, Grosset & Dunlap) Penguin Young Readers Group.

—Crazy Horse: Brave Warrior. Altmann, Scott & Zilber, Denis, illus. 2013. (Treasure Chest Ser.: 5). (ENG.). 192p. (J). (gr. 3-7). pap. 6.99 *(978-0-448-45728-4(8)*, Grosset & Dunlap) Penguin Young Readers Group.

—Harry Houdini: Prince of Air. Altmann, Scott & Zilber, Denis, illus. 2012. (Treasure Chest Ser.: 4). (ENG.). 208p. (J). (gr. 3-7). pap. 6.99 *(978-0-448-45470-2(X)*, Grosset & Dunlap) Penguin Young Readers Group.

—Jewel of the East. Kwasny, Karl et al, illus. 2012. (Treasure Chest Ser.: 3). (ENG.). 208p. (J). (gr. 3-7). 15.99 *(978-0-448-45473-3(4))*; pap. 6.99 *(978-0-448-45469-6(6))* Penguin Young Readers Group. (Grosset & Dunlap).

—Leonardo Da Vinci No. 9: Renaissance Master. Zilber, Denis, illus. 2014. (Treasure Chest Ser.: 9). (ENG.). 224p. (J). (gr. 3-7). 15.99 *(978-0-448-46768-9(2)*, Grosset & Dunlap) Penguin Young Readers Group.

—Prince of Air, No. 4. Altmann, Scott & Zilber, Denis, illus. 2012. (Treasure Chest Ser.: 4). (ENG.). 208p. (J). (gr. 3-7). 15.99 *(978-0-448-45474-0(2)*, Grosset & Dunlap) Penguin Young Readers Group.

Hood, Ann & Altmann, Scott. Alexander Hamilton: Little Lion. Kwasney, Karl & Zilber, Denis, illus. 2012. (Treasure Chest Ser.: 2). (ENG.). 224p. (J). (gr. 3-7). pap. 6.99 *(978-0-448-45468-9(8)*, Grosset & Dunlap) Penguin Young Readers Group.

—Angel of the Battlefield. Kwasney, Karl & Zilber, Denis, illus. 2012. (Treasure Chest Ser.: 1). (ENG.). 240p. (J). (gr. 3-7). 15.99 *(978-0-448-45471-9(8)*, Grosset & Dunlap) Penguin Young Readers Group.

Hope, Laura. The Bobbsey Twins on Blueberry Island. 2007. 112p. (gr. 3-9). per. 11.95 *(978-1-4344-0033-8(6))* Wildside Pr., LLC.

Hope, Laura Lee. Bobbsey Twins. 2006. 25.95 *(978-1-4218-2978-4(9))*; pap. 10.95 *(978-1-4218-3078-0(7))* 1st World Publishing, Inc.

—The Bobbsey Twins: The First Fifteen Stories, Including Merry Days Indoors & Out, in the Country, at the Seashore, at School, at Snow Lodge, on A. 2013. 1080p. *(978-1-78139-372-7(9))* Benediction Classics.

—The Bobbsey Twins at Home. 2007. (ENG.). 134p. pap. 18.99 *(978-1-4264-5199-7(7))*; 152p. pap. 21.99 *(978-1-4264-5500-1(3))* Creative Media Partners, LLC.

—The Bobbsey Twins at Meadow Brook. 2005. 200p. 27.95 *(978-1-4218-0653-2(3)*, 1st World Library - Literary Society) 1st World Publishing, Inc.

—The Bobbsey Twins at Meadow Brook. 2007. (ENG.). 128p. pap. 18.99 *(978-1-4264-4949-9(6))*; 140p. pap. 19.99 *(978-1-4264-5250-5(0))* Creative Media Partners, LLC.

—The Bobbsey Twins at Snow Lodge. 2005. 26.95 *(978-1-4218-0973-1(7)*, 1st World Library - Literary Society) 1st World Publishing, Inc.

—The Bobbsey Twins at the County Fair. 2007. (ENG.). 120p. pap. 18.99 *(978-1-4346-0547-4(7))*; 132p. pap. 19.99 *(978-1-4346-0622-8(8))* Creative Media Partners, LLC.

—The Bobbsey Twins at the Seashore. 2005. 26.95 *(978-1-4218-1070-6(0))*; 176p. pap. 11.95 *(978-1-4218-1170-3(7))* 1st World Publishing, Inc. (1st World Library - Literary Society).

—The Bobbsey Twins in a Great City. 2005. 27.95 *(978-1-4218-1482-7(X))*; 204p. pap. 12.95 *(978-1-4218-1582-4(6))* 1st World Publishing, Inc. (1st World Library - Literary Society).

—The Bobbsey Twins in a Great City. 2007. (ENG.). 138p. pap. 18.99 *(978-1-4264-9426-0(2))*; 152p. pap. 21.99 *(978-1-4264-9807-7(1))* Creative Media Partners, LLC.

—The Bobbsey Twins in the Country. 2005. 208p. 27.95 *(978-1-4218-0655-6(X)*, 1st World Library - Literary Society) 1st World Publishing, Inc.

—The Bobbsey Twins in the Great West. 2005. 27.95 *(978-1-4218-0365-4(8)*, 1st World Library - Literary Society) 1st World Publishing, Inc.

—The Bobbsey Twins in Volcano Land. 2011. 190p. 42.95 *(978-1-258-04953-9(8))* Literary Licensing, LLC.

—The Bobbsey Twins in Washington. 2005. 27.95 *(978-1-4218-0974-8(5)*, 1st World Library - Literary Society) 1st World Publishing, Inc.

—The Bobbsey Twins in Washington. 2007. 256p. 29.95 *(978-1-4344-8591-5(9))*; per. 17.95 *(978-1-4344-8590-8(0))* Wildside Pr., LLC.

—The Bobbsey Twins on a House Boat. 2005. 204p. pap. 12.95 *(978-1-4218-1167-3(7)*, 1st World Library - Literary Society) 1st World Publishing, Inc.

—The Bobbsey Twins on A House Boat. 2005. 27.95 *(978-1-4218-1067-6(0)*, 1st World Library - Literary Society) 1st World Publishing, Inc.

—The Bobbsey Twins on Blueberry Island. 2007. (ENG.). 136p. pap. 18.99 *(978-1-4346-3610-2(0))*; 154p. pap. 21.99 *(978-1-4346-3611-9(9))* Creative Media Partners, LLC.

—Freddie & Flossie. Pyle, Chuck, illus. 2005. (Bobbsey Twins Ser.). (ENG.). 32p. (J). (gr. -1-k). pap. 3.99 *(978-1-4169-0270-6(8)*, Simon Spotlight) Simon Spotlight.

—Freddie & Flossie & Snap. Pyle, Chuck, illus. 2005. (Bobbsey Twins Ser.). (ENG.). 32p. (J). (gr. -1-k). pap. 13.99 *(978-1-4169-0267-6(8)*, Simon Spotlight) Simon Spotlight.

—Freddie & Flossie & the Train Ride. Pyle, Chuck, illus. 2005. (Bobbsey Twins Ser.). (ENG.). 32p. (J). (gr. -1-k). pap. 13.99 *(978-1-4169-0269-0(4)*, Simon Spotlight) Simon Spotlight.

—Freddie & Flossie at the Beach. Pyle, Chuck, illus. 2005. (Bobbsey Twins Ser.). (ENG.). 32p. (J). (gr. -1-k). pap. 13.99 *(978-1-4169-0268-3(6)*, Simon Spotlight) Simon Spotlight.

Hopkins, Ellen. Identical. (ENG.). (YA). (gr. 9-18). 2010. 592p. pap. 12.99 *(978-1-4169-5006-6(0))* 2008. 576p. 17.99 *(978-1-4169-5005-9(2))* McElderry, Margaret K. Bks. (McElderry, Margaret K. Bks.).

Horowitz, Anthony. Nightrise. 2008. (Gatekeepers Ser.: 3). (ENG.). 368p. (J). (gr. 3-7). pap. 8.99 *(978-0-439-68007-3(7)*, Scholastic Paperbacks) Scholastic, Inc.

—Oblivion. 2014. (Gatekeepers Ser.: 5). (ENG.). 592p. (J). (gr. 3-7). pap. 9.99 *(978-0-439-68005-9(0)*, Scholastic Paperbacks) Scholastic, Inc.

Howson, Imogen. Linked. 2013. (ENG., Illus.). 368p. (YA). (gr. 7). 16.99 *(978-1-4424-4656-4(0)*, Simon & Schuster Bks. For Young Readers) Simon & Schuster Bks. For Young Readers.

—Unravel. 2014. (ENG., Illus.). 480p. (YA). (gr. 7). 17.99 *(978-1-4424-4658-8(7)*, Simon & Schuster Bks. For Young Readers) Simon & Schuster Bks. For Young Readers.

Howson, Imogen & Smith, Ali. Linked. 2014. (ENG., Illus.). 384p. (YA). (gr. 7). pap. 9.99 *(978-1-4424-4660-1(9)*, Simon & Schuster Bks. For Young Readers) Simon & Schuster Bks. For Young Readers.

Hunt, Bonnie. Danger! Keep Out! The Grayson Twins Adventures. 2008. 96p. pap. 19.95 *(978-1-60563-202-5(3))* America Star Bks.

—The Missing Chimp: A Grayson Twins Adventures, 1 vol. 2009. 100p. pap. 19.95 *(978-1-60813-481-6(4))* America Star Bks.

Hurwitz, Johanna. Double or Nothing with the Two & Only Kelly Twins. Mourning, Tuesday, illus. 2017. (ENG.). 80p. (J). (gr. 1-4). 14.99 *(978-0-7636-8808-0(8))* Candlewick Pr.

—The Two & Only Kelly Twins. Mourning, Tuesday, illus. 2013. (ENG.). 96p. (J). (gr. 1-4). 14.99 *(978-0-7636-5602-7(X))* Candlewick Pr.

I'm Not a Rerun! 2005. (J). bds. *(978-0-9769910-4-5(7))* Terrific Twins LLC.

Imfeld, Robert. Baylor's Guide to the Other Side. 2016. (Beyond Baylor Ser.: 1). (ENG., Illus.). 320p. (J). (gr. 5-9). 16.99 *(978-1-4814-6636-3(4)*, Aladdin) Simon & Schuster Children's Publishing.

Irvin, William. The Adventures of Winston & Hazel: Episode 1: the Silver Medallion. 2006. 11.00 *(978-0-8059-8220-6(5))* Dorrance Publishing Co., Inc.

Isbell, Tom. The Capture. 2016. (Prey Trilogy Ser.: 2). 448p. (YA). (gr. 8). 17.99 *(978-0-06-221605-2(8)*, HarperTeen) HarperCollins Pubs.

—The Prey. 2015. (Prey Trilogy Ser.: 1). (ENG.). 416p. (YA). (gr. 8). 17.99 *(978-0-06-221601-4(5)*, HarperTeen) HarperCollins Pubs.

It's Dark! 2005. (J). bds. *(978-0-9769910-1-4(2))* Terrific Twins LLC.

Jean, Emiko. We'll Never Be Apart. 2015. (ENG.). 288p. (YA). (gr. 9). 17.99 *(978-0-544-48200-5(X)*, HMH Books For Young Readers) Houghton Mifflin Harcourt Publishing Co.

Jenkins, Jerry B. & Fabry, Chris. Canyon Echoes. 2005. (Red Rock Mysteries Ser.: 8). (ENG.). 234p. (YA). pap. 6.99 *(978-1-4143-0147-1(2)*, Tyndale Kids) Tyndale Hse. Pubs.

—Double Fault. 2005. (Red Rock Mysteries Ser.: 7). (ENG.). 272p. (YA). pap. 6.99 *(978-1-4143-0146-4(4)*, Tyndale Kids) Tyndale Hse. Pubs.

—Grave Shadows. 2005. (Red Rock Mysteries Ser.: 5). (ENG., Illus.). 240p. (YA). pap. 6.99 *(978-1-4143-0144-0(8)*, Tyndale Kids) Tyndale Hse. Pubs.

—Hollywood Holdup. 2006. (Red Rock Mysteries Ser.: 12). (ENG.). 224p. (YA). (gr. 8-12). per. 6.99 *(978-1-4143-0151-8(0)*, Tyndale Kids) Tyndale Hse. Pubs.

—Instant Menace. 2006. (Red Rock Mysteries Ser.: 9). (ENG.). 256p. (YA). (gr. 3-7). per. 6.99 *(978-1-4143-0148-8(0)*, Tyndale Kids) Tyndale Hse. Pubs.

—Phantom Writer. 2005. (Red Rock Mysteries Ser.: 6). (ENG.). 256p. (YA). pap. 5.99 *(978-1-4143-0145-7(6)*, Tyndale Kids) Tyndale Hse. Pubs.

—Stolen Secrets. 2005. (Red Rock Mysteries Ser.: 2). (ENG., Illus.). 224p. (YA). (gr. -1-7). pap. 6.99 *(978-1-4143-0141-9(3)*, Tyndale Kids) Tyndale Hse. Pubs.

—Wind Chill. 2006. (Red Rock Mysteries Ser.: 14). (ENG.). 240p. (YA). (gr. 3-7). per. 6.99 *(978-1-4143-0153-2(7)*, Tyndale Kids) Tyndale Hse. Pubs.

—Windy City Danger. 2006. (Red Rock Mysteries Ser.: 11). (ENG.). 246p. (YA). (gr. 8-12). per. 6.99 *(978-1-4143-0150-1(2)*, Tyndale Kids) Tyndale Hse. Pubs.

Jesus, Opal De. The Golden Apple Kingdom, 1 vol. 2009. 48p. pap. 16.95 *(978-1-60749-414-0(0))* America Star Bks.

Johnson, Allen, Jr. The Dead House. McMorris, Kelley, illus. 2014. (Blackwater Novels Ser.: Vol. 2). (ENG.). 212p. (J). (gr. 4-7). 14.99 *(978-1-933725-34-5(6))* Premium Pr. America.

—My Brother's Story. McMorris, Kelley, illus. 2014. (Blackwater Novels Ser.: Vol. 1). (ENG.). 191p. (J). (gr. 4-7). 14.99 *(978-1-933725-37-6(0))* Premium Pr. America.

Johnson, C. Homecoming. 2007. (Illus.). 64p. per. 10.00 *(978-1-4251-1358-2(3))* Trafford Publishing.

Jolley, Dan. The Hero Twins: Against the Lords of Death [A Mayan Myth]. Witt, David, illus. 2009. (Graphic Myths & Legends Ser.). (ENG.). 48p. (gr. 4-8). pap. 8.95 *(978-1-58013-892-5(6))* Lerner Publishing Group.

Jones, Jen. Maren's New Family. Franco, Paula, illus. 2015. (Sleepover Girls Ser.). (ENG.). 128p. (gr. 3-5). lib. bdg. 22.65 *(978-1-4965-0540-8(9))* Stone Arch Bks.

—Willow's Boy-Crazy Birthday. Franco, Paula, illus. 2014. (Sleepover Girls Ser.). (ENG.). 128p. (gr. 3-5). lib. bdg. 22.65 *(978-1-4342-9757-0(8))* Stone Arch Bks.

Jones, Sandra O. A Voice on the Wind: I Know about the Apple... do You? 2012. 24p. pap. 17.99 *(978-1-4567-3553-1(5))* AuthorHouse.

Jordan, Taylor. Movin' on In. Wummer, Amy, illus. 2005. (Social Studies Connects). 32p. (J). (gr. 1-3). pap. 5.95 *(978-1-57565-159-0(9))* Kane Press, Inc.

Jump Shot. 2014. (Barber Game Time Bks.). (ENG., Illus.). 160p. (J). (gr. 3-7). pap. 7.99 *(978-1-4424-5730-0(9)*, Simon & Schuster/Paula Wiseman Bks.) Simon & Schuster/Paula Wiseman Bks.

Kade, Stacey. For This Life Only. 2016. (ENG., Illus.). 320p. (YA). (gr. 9). 17.99 *(978-1-4814-3248-1(6)*, Simon & Schuster Bks. For Young Readers) Simon & Schuster Bks. For Young Readers.

Kassel, Roger de. Mr P & the Bully Birds. 2013. (Illus.). 12p. pap. 8.75 *(978-1-78035-677-8(3)*, Fastprint Publishing) Upfront Publishing Ltd. GBR. Dist: Printondemand-worldwide.com.

Kastner, Erich. Lisa & Lottie. 2015. (ENG.). 168p. (gr. 3). pap. 12.95 *(978-1-939601-33-9(9))* Ig Publishing, Inc.

Katherine's Story 1848. 2014. (Secrets of the Manor Ser.: 4). (ENG., Illus.). 160p. (J). (gr. 3-7). pap. 6.99 *(978-1-4814-1843-0(2)*, Simon Spotlight) Simon Spotlight.

Katschke, Judy. The Facts about Flirting. 2003. (Two of a Kind Ser.: Vol. 27). (Illus.). 112p. mass mkt. 4.99 *(978-0-06-009323-5(4)*, Harper Entertainment) HarperCollins Pubs.

Katschke, Judy, et al. Bye-Bye Boyfriend, 3 vols. 2003. (ENG., Illus.). 112p. *(978-0-00-714467-9(9)*, HarperCollins Children's Bks.) HarperCollins Pubs. Ltd.

Katz, Alan. The Day the Mustache Came Back. Easler, Kris, illus. 2016. (Mustache Ser.: 2). (ENG.). 224p. (J). 13.99 *(978-1-61963-560-9(7)*, 9781619635609, Bloomsbury USA Childrens) Bloomsbury Publishing USA.

—The Day the Mustache Took Over. Easler, Kris, illus. (Mustache Ser.: 1). (ENG.). 208p. 2016. (J). pap. 6.99 *(978-1-68119-148-5(2)*, 9781681191485) 2015. (YA). (gr. 2-4). 13.99 *(978-1-61963-558-6(5)*, 9781619635586) Bloomsbury Publishing USA. (Bloomsbury USA Childrens).

Keating, Jess. How to Outrun a Crocodile When Your Shoes Are Untied. 2014. (My Life Is a Zoo Ser.: 1). (ENG.). 288p. (J). (gr. 4-7). pap. 7.99 *(978-1-4022-9755-7(6)*, 9781402297557, Sourcebooks Jabberwocky) Sourcebooks, Inc.

—How to Outswim a Shark Without a Snorkel. 2015. (My Life Is a Zoo Ser.: 2). (ENG.). 304p. (J). (gr. 4-7). pap. 7.99 *(978-1-4022-9758-8(0)*, 9781402297588, Sourcebooks Jabberwocky) Sourcebooks, Inc.

Kehret, Peg. Runaway Twin. 2011. (ENG.). 208p. (J). (gr. 5-18). 6.99 *(978-0-14-241849-9(8)*, Puffin Books) Penguin Young Readers Group.

Kelley, Jane. The Girl Behind the Glass. 2012. (ENG.). 192p. (J). (gr. 4-7). pap. 6.99 *(978-0-375-86219-9(6)*, Yearling) Random Hse. Children's Bks.

Kelly, J. M. Speed of Life. 2016. (ENG.). 352p. (YA). (gr. 9). 17.99 *(978-0-544-74782-1(8)*, HMH Books For Young Readers) Houghton Mifflin Harcourt Publishing Co.

Kelly, Mark. Astrotwins — Project Rescue. 2016. (Astrotwins Ser.). (ENG., Illus.). 256p. (J). (gr. 3-7). 16.99 *(978-1-4814-2458-5(0)*, Simon & Schuster/Paula Wiseman Bks.) Simon & Schuster/Paula Wiseman Bks.

Kemnitz, Dianna. Meet Jack & His New Friend. 2011. 36p. pap. 24.95 *(978-1-4560-8776-0(2))* America Star Bks.

Kent, Jaden. #1: the Cave of Aaaaah! Doom! Bodnaruk, Iryna, illus. 2017. (Ella & Owen Ser.: 1). (ENG.). 112p. (J). (gr. 1-3). pap. 5.99 *(978-1-4998-0368-6(0))* Little Bee Books Inc.

—#2: Attack of the Stinky Fish Monster! Bodnaruk, Iryna, illus. 2017. (Ella & Owen Ser.: 2). (ENG.). 112p. (J). (gr. 1-3). pap. 5.99 *(978-1-4998-0369-3(9))* Little Bee Books Inc.

Kerr, P. B., pseud. The Day of the Djinn Warriors. 2008. (Children of the Lamp Ser.: 4). (ENG.). 400p. (J). (gr. 3-7). 7.99 *(978-0-439-93216-5(5)*, Scholastic Paperbacks) Scholastic, Inc.

—The Eye of the Forest. 2009. (Children of the Lamp Ser.: 5). (ENG.). 432p. (J). (gr. 3-7). 17.99 *(978-0-439-93215-8(7)*, Orchard Bks.) Scholastic, Inc.

—The Five Fakirs of Faizabad. 2011. (Children of the Lamp Ser.: Vol. 6). (ENG.). 448p. (J). (gr. 3-7). pap. 8.99 *(978-0-545-12659-5(2)*, Scholastic Paperbacks) Scholastic, Inc.

—The Grave Robbers of Genghis Khan. 2011. (Children of the Lamp Ser.: Vol. 7). (ENG.). 448p. (J). (gr. 3-7). 18.99 *(978-0-545-12660-1(6)*, Orchard Bks.) Scholastic, Inc.

Kiernan, Celine. Into the Grey. 2014. (ENG.). 304p. (YA). (gr. 7). 16.99 *(978-0-7636-7061-0(8))* Candlewick Pr.

Kimmel, Eric A. Scarlett & Sam: Escape from Egypt. Stevanovic, Ivica, illus. 2015. (J). 6.99 *(978-1-4677-6207-6(5))*; (ENG.). 168p. (gr. 1-3). lib. bdg. 15.95 *(978-1-4677-3850-7(6))* Lerner Publishing Group. (Kar-Ben Publishing).

Kleiman, Deanna M. My Twin Brother. Greenes, Shimra, illus. 2012. 24p. pap. 9.13 *(978-0-615-35370-8(3))* TwinsBooks.

Klein, Abby. April Fool's Surprise. McKinley, John, illus. 2012. (Double Trouble Ser.: Vol. 2). (ENG.). 96p. (J). (gr. -1-3). pap. 5.99 *(978-0-545-29495-9(9)*, Scholastic Paperbacks) Scholastic, Inc.

Klepeis, Alicia. Cairo, Camels, & Chaos. 2015. (ENG.). 96p. (gr. 3-6). 31.36 *(978-1-63430-397-2(0))* Rourke Educational Media.

—Mountains, Monsoons, & Mules. 2015. (ENG.). 96p. (gr. 3-6). 31.36 *(978-1-63430-398-9(9))* Rourke Educational Media.

Knutsson, Catherine. Shadows Cast by Stars. (ENG., Illus.). 464p. (YA). (gr. 7). 2013. pap. 11.99 *(978-1-4424-0192-1(3))* 2012. 17.99 *(978-1-4424-0191-4(5))* Simon & Schuster Children's Publishing. (Atheneum Bks. for Young Readers).

Kogler, Jennifer. The Otherworldlies. 2008. 400p. (J). lib. bdg. 17.89 *(978-0-06-073960-7(6))*; (ENG.). (gr. 5-18). 16.99 *(978-0-06-073959-1(2))* HarperCollins Pubs. (Eos).

Kogler, Jennifer Anne. The Siren's Cry. 2011. (ENG.). 384p. (YA). (gr. 8). 16.99 *(978-0-06-199443-2(X)*, HarperTeen) HarperCollins Pubs.

Kogler, Jennifer Anne & Kogler, Jennifer A. The Otherworldlies. 2009. (ENG.). 400p. (YA). (gr. 8). pap. 8.99 *(978-0-06-073961-4(4)*, HarperTeen) HarperCollins Pubs.

Kraft, Erik P. Lenny & Mel. Kraft, Erik P., illus. 2012. (Ready-for-Chapters Ser.). (ENG., Illus.). 64p. (J). (gr. 2-5). pap. 6.99 *(978-0-689-85891-8(4)*, Aladdin) Simon & Schuster Children's Publishing.

—Lenny & Mel after-School Confidential. Kraft, Erik P., illus. 2012. (Lenny & Mel Ser.). (ENG., Illus.). 64p. (J). (gr. 2-5). pap. 6.99 *(978-1-4424-6314-1(7)*, Simon & Schuster/Paula Wiseman Bks.) Simon & Schuster/Paula Wiseman Bks.

—Lenny & Mel's Summer Vacation. Kraft, Erik P., illus. 2012. (Ready-For-Chapters Ser.). (ENG., Illus.). 64p. (J). (gr. 2-5). pap. 6.99 *(978-0-689-86874-0(X)*, Simon & Schuster/Paula Wiseman Bks.) Simon & Schuster/Paula Wiseman Bks.

Kuhlman, Evan. Great Ball of Light. Holmes, Jeremy, illus. 2015. (ENG.). 304p. (J). (gr. 5-9). 16.99 *(978-1-4169-6461-2(4))* Simon & Schuster Children's Publishing.

Kuipers, Alice. The Best-Ever Bookworm Book. Murguia, Bethanie Deeney, illus. 2014. (ENG.). 40p. (J). (gr. -1-3). 17.00 *(978-0-316-21200-7(8))* Little, Brown Bks. for Young Readers.

—Violet & Victor Write the Most Fabulous Fairy Tale. 2016. (ENG., Illus.). 40p. (J). (gr. -1-3). 17.00 *(978-0-316-21202-1(4))* Little Brown & Co.

Lamb, Charles, et al. Tales from Shakespeare: "Twelfth Night" Strang, Kay, ed. rev. ed. 2005. (Illus.). 40p. pap. 4.95 *(978-0-9542905-7-3(7))* Capercaillie Bks., Ltd GBR. Dist: Wilson & Assocs.

Lambert, Clercina. The Indifferent Twin: Outside Beauty Will Fade Away but Inside Beauty Will Last for a Lifetime. 2012. 28p. (-18). pap. 15.99 *(978-1-4771-1647-0(8))* Xlibris Corp.

Lampman, Evelyn Sibley. The Shy Stegosaurus of Cricket Creek. Buel, Hubert, illus. 2007. 218p. (J). (gr. 4-7). per. 12.00 *(978-1-930900-37-0(6))* Purple Hse. Pr.

Langdale, Mark Roland. Professor Doppelganger & the Fantastical Cloud Factory. 2012. 106p. pap. *(978-1-78003-267-2(6))* Pen Pr. Pubs., Ltd.

Langlois, Annie. Mia, Matt & the Turkey Chase, 1 vol. Cummins, Sarah, tr. from FRE. Beaulieu, Jimmy, illus. 2008. (Formac First Novels Ser.). (ENG.). 64p. (J). (gr. 2-5). 5.95 *(978-0-88780-763-3(1)*, 9780887807633) Formac Publishing Co., Ltd. CAN. Dist: Casemate Pubs. & Bk. Distributors, LLC.

Langlois, Suzanne. Mia, Matt & the Turkey Chase. Cummins, Sarah, tr. from FRE. Beaulieu, Jimmy, illus. 2008. (Formac First Novels Ser.). (ENG.). 64p. (J). (gr. 2-5). 14.95 *(978-0-88780-765-7(8)*, 9780887807657) Formac Publishing Co., Ltd. CAN. Dist: Casemate Pubs. & Bk. Distributors, LLC.

Langrish, Katherine. Troll Fell. 2004. (Illus.). 272p. (J). (gr. 5-18). (ENG.). 16.99 *(978-0-06-058304-0(5))*; lib. bdg. 16.89 *(978-0-06-058305-7(3))* HarperCollins Pubs.

Larson, Hope. Compass South. Mock, Rebecca, illus. 2016. (Four Points Ser.: 1). (ENG.). 224p. (J). 17.99 *(978-0-374-30043-2(7)*, 9780374300432, Farrar, Straus & Giroux (BYR)) Farrar, Straus & Giroux.

—Compass South. 2017. (Four Points Ser.: 1). (J). lib. bdg. 24.50 ***(978-0-606-39953-1(4))*** Turtleback Bks.

Lasky, Kathryn. Double Trouble Squared. 2008. (ENG., Illus.). 240p. (J). (gr. 2-5). pap. 14.99 *(978-0-15-205878-4(8))* Houghton Mifflin Harcourt Publishing Co.

—Shadows in the Water. 2008. (ENG., Illus.). 224p. (J). (gr. 2-5). pap. 14.95 *(978-0-15-205874-6(5))* Houghton Mifflin Harcourt Publishing Co.

—A Voice in the Wind. 2008. (ENG., Illus.). 272p. (J). (gr. 2-5). pap. 15.95 *(978-0-15-205875-3(3))* Houghton Mifflin Harcourt Publishing Co.

Lathan, Betty Jean. Sierra, the Unwanted Cat. 2011. 28p. pap. 13.59 *(978-1-4567-3297-4(8))* AuthorHouse.

Lavoie, Jennifer. Andy Squared. 2012. (ENG.). 264p. (J). (gr. 7). pap. 11.95 *(978-1-60282-743-1(5))* Bold Strokes Bks.

Lawson, Jessica. Nooks & Crannies. Andrewson, Natalie, illus. 2015. (ENG.). 336p. (J). (gr. 3-7). 16.99 *(978-1-4814-1921-5(8)*, Simon & Schuster Bks. For Young Readers) Simon & Schuster Bks. For Young Readers.

Lay, Kathryn. The Substitutes: An Up2U Action Adventure, 1 vol. Calo, Marcos, illus. 2015. (ENG.). 80p. (J). *(978-1-62402-095-7(X))* Magic Wagon.

Leaver, Trisha. The Secrets We Keep. 2015. (ENG.). 304p. (YA). (gr. 7). 17.99 *(978-0-374-30046-3(1)*, Farrar, Straus & Giroux (BYR)) Farrar, Straus & Giroux.

Ledger, Kate. Twin Magic: School Bully, Beware! 2013. (Scholastic Reader Level 2 Ser.). (Illus.). 32p. (J). lib. bdg. 13.55 *(978-0-606-31972-0(7)*, Turtleback) Turtleback Bks.

Lee Hope, Laura. The Bobbsey Twins in the Great West. 2005. 200p. pap. 12.95 *(978-1-4218-0465-1(4)*, 1st World Library - Literary Society) 1st World Publishing, Inc.

—The Bobbsey Twins in the Great West. 2004. reprint ed. pap. 1.99 *(978-1-4192-5444-4(8))*; pap. 20.95 *(978-1-4191-5444-7(3))* Kessinger Publishing, LLC.

Lee, J. M. & dePaola, Tomie. Shadows of the Dark Crystal. Froud, Brian & Godbey, Cory, illus. 2016. (Jim Henson's the Dark Crystal Ser.: 1). (ENG.). 272p. (J). (gr. 7). bds. 17.99 *(978-0-448-48289-7(4)*, Grosset & Dunlap) Penguin Young Readers Group.

Lee, Shari. Mandie's & Mindie's Adventure under the Sea, 1 vol. 2009. 63p. pap. 19.95 *(978-1-4489-9977-4(4))* America Star Bks.

Lee, Wan, et al. A Fish Wish - Lunch for Patch - Squid Twins: BuildUp Unit 4 Lap Book. Moor, Beka et al, illus. 2015. (Build up Core Phonics Ser.). (J). (gr. 1). *(978-1-4900-2603-9(7))* Benchmark Education Co.

Leigh, Savanah-Rose. Trunks & Amelia. 2012. 48p. pap. 9.89 *(978-1-4669-3803-8(X))* Trafford Publishing.

L'Engle, Madeleine. Many Waters. 2007. (Wrinkle in Time Quintet Ser.: 3). (ENG.). 368p. (J). (gr. 5-9). per. 6.99 *(978-0-312-36857-9(7)*, 9780312368579) Square Fish.

Leonard, Marcia. Trae la Pelota, Tito. Handelman, Dorothy, photos by. 2005.Tr. of Get the Ball, Slim. (Illus.). 32p. (J). (ENG & SPA.). (gr. -1-1). pap. 4.99 *(978-0-8225-3293-4(X))*; (SPA., (gr. 1-1). per. 5.95 *(978-0-8225-3292-7(1)*, Ediciones Lerner) Lerner Publishing Group.

Leprechaun, Seamus T. The o'Shea Chronicles. 2013. 312p. pap. *(978-1-78407-190-5(0))* FeedARead.com.
Lerangis, Peter. The Code. 2004. (Spy X Ser.: No. 1). 139p. (Orig.). (J). *(978-0-439-70242-3(9))* Scholastic, Inc.
Let's Celebrate!, 10 bks. 2005. (Illus.). (J). bds. *(978-0-9769910-9-0(8))* Terrific Twins LLC.
Lewis. Want to Trade Two Brothers for a Cat? 2008. (ENG.). 112p. (YA). (gr. 7). pap. 7.95 *(978-1-4169-7538-0(1)*, Simon Pulse) Simon Pulse.
Lewison, Wendy Cheyette. Two Is for Twins. Nakata, Hiroe, illus. 2011. (ENG.). 28p. (J). (gr. -1 — 1). bds. 6.99 *(978-0-670-01310-4(2)*, Viking Books for Young Readers) Penguin Young Readers Group.
Liggett, Kim. Blood & Salt. 2015. (ENG.). 352p. (YA). (gr. 9-12). 17.99 *(978-0-399-16648-8(3)*, G.P. Putnam's Sons Books for Young Readers) Penguin Young Readers Group.
Lin, Grace. Ling & Ting: Not Exactly the Same! (Passport to Reading Level 3 Ser.). (ENG.). 48p. (J). (gr. 1-4). 2011. pap. 3.99 *(978-0-316-02453-2(8))* 2010. (Illus.). 14.99 *(978-0-316-02452-5(X))* Little, Brown Bks. for Young Readers.
—Ling & Ting: Together in All Weather. 2015. (ENG., Illus.). 48p. (J). (gr. 1-4). 16.00 *(978-0-316-33549-2(5))* Little Brown & Co.
—Ling & Ting: Together in All Weather. 2016. (Passport to Reading Level 3 Ser.). (J). lib. bdg. 14.75 *(978-0-606-39187-0(8))* Turtleback Bks.
—Ling & Ting Share a Birthday. (ENG.). 48p. (J). (gr. 1-4). 2014. pap. 4.99 *(978-0-316-18404-5(7))* 2013. (Illus.). 15.00 *(978-0-316-18405-2(5))* Little, Brown Bks. for Young Readers.
—Ling & Ting Share a Birthday. 2014. (Passport to Reading Level 3 Ser.). (J). lib. bdg. 14.75 *(978-0-606-35932-0(X))* Turtleback Bks.
—Ling & Ting: Together in All Weather. 2016. (ENG.). 48p. (J). (gr. 1-4). pap. 4.99 *(978-0-316-33548-5(7))* Little, Brown Bks. for Young Readers.
—Ling & Ting: Twice As Silly. 2014. (ENG., Illus.). 48p. (J). (gr. 1-4). 16.00 *(978-0-316-18402-1(0))* Little, Brown Bks. for Young Readers.
—Twice as Silly. 2015. (Passport to Reading Level 3 Ser.). (J). lib. bdg. 14.75 *(978-0-606-37464-4(7))* Turtleback Bks.
Lipsyte, Robert. The Twin Powers. 2014. (ENG.). 256p. (J). (gr. 5-7). 16.99 *(978-0-547-97335-7(7))* Houghton Mifflin Harcourt Publishing Co.
—The Twinning Project. (ENG.). (J). (gr. 5-7). 2014. 288p. pap. 6.99 *(978-0-544-22522-0(8)*, HMH Books For Young Readers) 2012. 272p. 16.99 *(978-0-547-64571-1(6))* Houghton Mifflin Harcourt Publishing Co.
Litz, Amanda. Sam & Pam Can & You Can Too! We Can Count. Garcia, Cynthia, illus. 2011. 32p. (J). pap. 3.99 *(978-0-9841496-3-6(5))* Traveler's Trunk Publishing LLC.
—Sam & Pam Can & You Can Too! We Can Help Our Mom. Garcia, Cynthia, illus. 2011. 32p. (J). pap. 3.99 *(978-0-9841496-1-2(9))* Traveler's Trunk Publishing LLC.
—Sam & Pam Can & You Can Too! We Can Ride Our Bikes. Garcia, Cynthia, illus. 2011. 32p. (J). pap. 3.99 *(978-0-9841496-2-9(7))* Traveler's Trunk Publishing LLC.
London, C. Alexander. We Are Not Eaten by Yaks. (Accidental Adventure Ser.: 1). (ENG.). (J). (gr. 3-7). 2013. 384p. pap. 7.99 *(978-0-14-242056-0(5)*, Puffin Books) 2011. 224p. 12.99 *(978-0-399-25487-1(0)*, Philomel Bks.) Penguin Young Readers Group.
—We Dine with Cannibals. 2013. (Accidental Adventure Ser.: 2). (ENG.). 384p. (J). (gr. 3-7). pap. 7.99 *(978-0-14-242474-2(9)*, Puffin Books) Penguin Young Readers Group.
—We Give a Squid a Wedgie. Duddle, Jonny, illus. 2013. (Accidental Adventure Ser.: 3). (ENG.). 400p. (J). (gr. 3-7). pap. 7.99 *(978-0-14-242475-9(7)*, Puffin Books) Penguin Young Readers Group.
Lord, Gabrielle. Black Ops Hunted: Conspiracy 365. 2014. 192p. (J). 10.99 *(978-1-61067-171-2(6))* Kane Miller.
Love, D. Anne. The Secret Prince. 2012. (ENG.). 240p. (J). (gr. 3-7). pap. 11.99 *(978-1-4424-5931-1(X)*, McElderry, Margaret K. Bks.) McElderry, Margaret K. Bks.
Lowell, Susan. The Great Grand Canyon Time Train. Shroades, John / W., illus. 2011. 32p. (J). 15.95 *(978-1-933855-63-9(0))* Rio Nuevo Pubs.
Luces-Tucker, Max. Bobby & Chrissy: One Gift. 2008. 36p. pap. 17.99 *(978-1-4343-8199-4(4))* AuthorHouse.
Lucy Fitch Perkins. The Dutch Twins. 2005. pap. *(978-1-905432-05-9(4))* Dodo Pr.
Lundquist, Jenny. The Opal Crown. 2014. (ENG.). 368p. (YA). (gr. 2-17). pap. 9.95 *(978-0-7624-5422-8(9)*, Running Pr. Kids) Running Pr. Bk. Pubs.
Lynch, Jay. Mo & Jo: Fighting Together Forever. Haspiel, Dean, illus. 2008. (ENG.). 40p. (J). (gr. -1-3). 12.95 *(978-0-9799238-5-2(9))* TOON Books / RAW Junior, LLC.
Lynch, Jay & Haspiel, Dean. Mo & Jo: Fighting Together Forever, 1 vol. 2013. (Toon Bks). (ENG.). 40p. (J). (gr. 2-3). lib. bdg. 27.07 *(978-1-61479-152-2(X))* Spotlight.
MacAndrew, Richard. A Little Trouble in California Level Starter/Beginner, 1 vol. 2011. (ENG.). 48p. pap. 11.00 *(978-84-8323-982-7(5))* Cambridge Univ. Pr.
—A Little Trouble in California Level Starter/Beginner American English Edition. 2012. (ENG., Illus.). 48p. pap. 9.50 *(978-1-107-68322-8(X))* Cambridge Univ. Pr.
—A Little Trouble in the Yorkshire Dales Level 3 Lower-Intermediate. 2009. (ENG.). 80p. pap. 12.75 *(978-84-8323-584-3(6))* Cambridge Univ. Pr.
Mack, W. C. Athlete vs. Mathlete. 2013. (Athlete vs. Mathlete Ser.). (ENG.). (YA). (gr. 3-6). 192p. 16.99 *(978-1-61963-129-8(6)*, 9781619631298); 192p. pap. 7.99 *(978-1-59990-938-7(3)*, 9781599909387); 208p. 16.99 *(978-1-59990-915-8(4)*, 9781599909158); (Illus.). 208p. pap. 7.99 *(978-1-59990-858-8(1)*, 9781599908588) Bloomsbury Publishing USA. (Bloomsbury USA Childrens).
—Time-Out. 2014. (Athlete vs. Mathlete Ser.). (ENG.). 208p. (YA). (gr. 3-6). 16.99 *(978-1-61963-301-8(9)*, 9781619633018, Bloomsbury USA Childrens) Bloomsbury Publishing USA.
Maddox, Jake. Speedway Switch. Tiffany, Sean, illus. 2007. (Jake Maddox Sports Stories Ser.). (ENG.). 72p. (gr. 2-3). pap. 5.95 *(978-1-59889-416-5(1))*; lib. bdg. 25.32 *(978-1-59889-321-2(1))* Stone Arch Bks.
Maddox, Jake & Berne, Emma Carlson. Rebound Time, 1 vol. Wood, Katie, illus. 2013. (Jake Maddox Girl Sports Stories Ser.). (ENG.). 72p. (gr. 2-3). pap. 5.95 *(978-1-4342-4202-0(1))*; lib. bdg. 25.32 *(978-1-4342-4013-2(4))* Stone Arch Bks.
Maguire, Gregory. Missing Sisters. 2009. 192p. (J). 16.99 *(978-0-06-123204-6(1))*; (ENG.). (gr. 3-7). pap. 6.99 *(978-0-06-123203-9(3))* HarperCollins Pubs.
Mahoney, Tammy. Eddie the Eagle Learns to Fly. 2012. 24p. pap. 19.99 *(978-1-4772-1747-4(9))* AuthorHouse.
Mak, D P. Invisible Pill. 2005. 44p. pap. *(978-1-84401-210-7(7))* Athena Pr.
Malouf, Juman. The Trilogy of Two. 2015. (ENG.). 416p. (J). (gr. 5-7). 17.99 *(978-0-399-17114-7(2)*, G.P. Putnam's Sons Books for Young Readers) Penguin Young Readers Group.
Mancusi, Mari. Shattered. (Scorched Ser.: 2). (ENG.). (YA). 2015. 416p. (gr. 8-12). pap. 9.99 *(978-1-4926-0869-1(6))* 2014. 400p. (gr. 7-12). 16.99 *(978-1-4022-8461-8(6)*, 9781402284618) Sourcebooks, Inc.
Manley, Francis G. Tellin Twins: The Great Art Scam. 2004. (Illus.). 132p. pap. *(978-1-84401-292-3(1))* Athena Pr.
Manson, Sheri. Bumpy & Boo Visits the Eye Doctor: Guess Who Needs Glasses? Cabrera, Marcela, illus. 2006. 32p. (J). 15.95 *(978-0-9744307-3-7(0))* Merry Lane Pr.
Margallo, Ramon. The MANGER, the CROSS, & the EMPTY TOMB Christian Apologetics for Young Readers: A Short Story. 2006. 108p. pap. 9.99 *(978-1-4116-5751-9(9))* Lulu Pr., Inc.
Margolis, Leslie. Girl's Best Friend. (Maggie Brooklyn Mystery Ser.). (ENG.). (YA). (gr. 3-12). 2011. 288p. pap. 7.99 *(978-1-59990-690-4(2)*, 9781599906904) 2010. 272p. 14.99 *(978-1-59990-525-9(6)*, 9781599905259) Bloomsbury Publishing USA. (Bloomsbury USA Childrens).
—The Secrets at the Chocolate Mansion. 2013. (Maggie Brooklyn Mystery Ser.). (ENG.). 256p. (YA). (gr. 3-6). 16.99 *(978-1-61963-036-9(2)*, 9781619630369, Bloomsbury USA Childrens) Bloomsbury Publishing USA.
—Secrets at the Chocolate Mansion. 2014. (Maggie Brooklyn Mystery Ser.). (ENG.). 272p. (YA). (gr. 3-6). pap. 7.99 *(978-1-61963-493-0(7)*, 9781619634930, Bloomsbury USA Childrens) Bloomsbury Publishing USA.
—Vanishing Acts. (Maggie Brooklyn Mystery Ser.). (ENG.). (YA). (gr. 3-6). 2013. 256p. pap. 6.99 *(978-1-59990-981-3(2)*, 9781599909813) 2012. 240p. 15.99 *(978-1-59990-536-5(1)*, 9781599905365) Bloomsbury Publishing USA. (Bloomsbury USA Childrens).
Martin, Ann M. The Long Way Home. 2013. (Family Tree Ser.: 2). (ENG.). 224p. (J). (gr. 3-7). 16.99 *(978-0-545-35943-6(0)*, Scholastic Pr.) Scholastic, Inc.
Martinez Jover, Carmen. The Twin Kangaroo Treasure Hunt, a Gay Parenting Story. Martinez, Rosemary, illus. 2013. 32p. pap. *(978-607-00-6545-3(X))* Martinez Jover, Maria del Carmen Dorotea.
Massie, Elizabeth. Ameri-Scares: New York. 2013. 148p. pap. 12.99 *(978-1-937530-55-6(8))* Crossroad Pr.
Matthews, L. S. Lexi. 2008. 200p. (J). pap. *(978-0-385-73575-9(8)*, Delacorte Pr) Random House Publishing Group.
Mawter, J. A. Launched! 2007. 256p. *(978-0-207-20073-1(4))* HarperCollins Pubs. Australia.
McAlpine, Gordon. Once upon a Midnight Eerie. Zuppardi, Sam, illus. 2015. (Misadventures of Edgar & Allan Poe Ser.: 2). (ENG.). 208p. (J). (gr. 3-7). 6.99 *(978-0-14-242349-3(1)*, Puffin Books) Penguin Young Readers Group.
—Once upon a Midnight Eerie: Book #2. Zuppardi, Sam, illus. 2014. (Misadventures of Edgar & Allan Poe Ser.: 2). (ENG.). 192p. (J). (gr. 3-7). 16.99 *(978-0-670-78493-6(1)*, Viking Books for Young Readers) Penguin Young Readers Group.
—The Tell-Tale Start. Zuppardi, Sam, illus. 2013. (Misadventures of Edgar & Allan Poe Ser.: 1). (ENG.). 208p. (J). (gr. 3-7). pap. 7.99 *(978-0-14-242346-2(7)*, Puffin Books) Penguin Young Readers Group.
McCafferty, Megan. Bumped. (Bumped Ser.: 1). (ENG.). (YA). (gr. 9). 2012. 352p. pap. 9.99 *(978-0-06-196275-2(9))* 2011. 336p. 16.99 *(978-0-06-196274-5(0))* HarperCollins Pubs.
—Thumped. 2013. (Bumped Ser.: 2). (ENG.). 304p. (YA). (gr. 8). pap. 8.99 *(978-0-06-196277-6(5))* HarperCollins Pubs.
McCall Smith, Alexander. School Ship Tobermory. 2016. (School Ship Tobermory Ser.). (ENG., Illus.). 224p. (J). (gr. 3-7). 15.99 *(978-0-399-55261-8(8)*, Delacorte Bks. for Young Readers) Random Hse. Children's Bks.
McClymer, Kelly. Must Love Black. 2008. (ENG.). 192p. (YA). (gr. 7-18). pap. 8.99 *(978-1-4169-4903-9(8)*, Simon Pulse) Simon Pulse.
McDonald, Kirsten. The Big Rain, 1 vol. Meza, Erika, illus. 2016. (Carlos & Carmen Ser.). (ENG.). 32p. (J). (gr. k-3). 27.07 *(978-1-62402-137-4(9))* Magic Wagon.
—The Costume Contest. 2016. (Carlos & Carmen Set 3 Ser.). (ENG.). (gr. -1-3). lib. bdg. 27.07 ***(978-1-62402-182-4(4))*** ABDO Publishing Co.
—The Green Surprise, 1 vol. Meza, Erika, illus. 2016. (Carlos & Carmen Ser.). (ENG.). 32p. (J). (gr. k-3). 27.07 *(978-1-62402-138-1(7))* Magic Wagon.
—The Nighttime Noise, 1 vol. Meza, Erika, illus. 2016. (Carlos & Carmen Ser.). (ENG.). 32p. (J). (gr. k-3). 27.07 *(978-1-62402-139-8(5))* Magic Wagon.
—The One-Tire House, 1 vol. Meza, Erika, illus. 2016. (Carlos & Carmen Ser.). (ENG.). 32p. (J). (gr. k-3). 27.07 *(978-1-62402-140-4(9))* Magic Wagon.
—The Perfect Piñatas. 2016. (Carlos & Carmen Set 3 Ser.). (ENG.). (gr. -1-3). lib. bdg. 27.07 ***(978-1-62402-183-1(2))*** ABDO Publishing Co.
—The Pet Show Problem. 2016. (Carlos & Carmen Set 3 Ser.). (ENG., Illus.). (J). (gr. -1-3). lib. bdg. 27.07 ***(978-1-62402-184-8(0))*** ABDO Publishing Co.
—The Sandy Weekend, 1 vol. Meza, Erika, illus. 2016. (ENG.). 32p. (J). 27.07 *(978-1-62402-142-8(5))* Magic Wagon.
—The Sparkly Night. 2016. (Carlos & Carmen Set 3 Ser.). (ENG., Illus.). (J). (gr. -1-3). lib. bdg. 27.07 ***(978-1-62402-185-5(9))*** ABDO Publishing Co.
—Tio Time, 1 vol. Meza, Erika, illus. 2016. (ENG.). 32p. (J). *(978-1-62402-143-5(3))* Magic Wagon.
—The Wobbly Wheels, 1 vol. Meza, Erika, illus. 2016. (ENG.). 32p. (J). *(978-1-62402-144-2(1))* Magic Wagon.
—The Yummy Mistake. Meza, Erika, illus. 2016. (ENG.). 32p. (J). *(978-1-62402-145-9(X))* Magic Wagon.
McKenzie, Precious. A Vacation in Ruins. 2015. (ENG.). 96p. (gr. 3-6). 31.36 *(978-1-63430-393-4(8))* Rourke Educational Media.
McMann, Lisa. Dragon Captives. 2017. (Unwanteds Quests Ser.: 1). (ENG., Illus.). 432p. (J). (gr. 3-7). 17.99 *(978-1-4814-5681-4(4)*, Simon & Schuster/Paula Wiseman Bks.) Simon & Schuster/Paula Wiseman Bks.
—Dragon Captives. 2018. (Unwanteds Quests Ser.: 1). lib. bdg. 18.40 ***(978-0-606-40846-2(0))*** Turtleback Bks.
—Island of Dragons. (Unwanteds Ser.: 7). (ENG., Illus.). 544p. (J). (gr. 3-7). 2017. pap. 8.99 *(978-1-4424-9338-4(0))* 2016. 17.99 *(978-1-4424-9337-7(2))* Simon & Schuster Children's Publishing. (Aladdin).
—Island of Fire. (Unwanteds Ser.: 3). (ENG., Illus.). (J). (gr. 3-7). 2014. 480p. pap. 8.99 *(978-1-4424-5846-8(1))* 2013. 464p. 19.99 *(978-1-4424-5845-1(3))* Simon & Schuster Children's Publishing. (Aladdin).
—Island of Fire. 2014. (Unwanteds Ser.: 3). lib. bdg. 19.65 *(978-0-606-35796-8(3))* Turtleback Bks.
—Island of Graves. (Unwanteds Ser.: 6). (ENG., Illus.). (J). (gr. 3-7). 2016. 560p. pap. 8.99 *(978-1-4424-9335-3(6))* 2015. 528p. 18.99 *(978-1-4424-9334-6(8))* Simon & Schuster Children's Publishing. (Aladdin).
—Island of Graves. 2016. (Unwanteds Ser.: 6). lib. bdg. 19.65 *(978-0-606-38497-1(9))* Turtleback Bks.
—Island of Shipwrecks. 2015. (Unwanteds Ser.: 5). (ENG., Illus.). 480p. (J). (gr. 3-7). pap. 8.99 *(978-1-4424-9332-2(1)*, Aladdin) Simon & Schuster Children's Publishing.
—Island of Silence. (Unwanteds Ser.: 2). (ENG., (J). (gr. 3-7). 2013. Illus.). 432p. pap. 8.99 *(978-1-4424-0772-5(7))* 2012. 416p. 18.99 *(978-1-4424-0771-8(9))* Simon & Schuster Children's Publishing. (Aladdin).
—Island of Silence. 2013. (Unwanteds Ser.: 2). lib. bdg. 18.40 *(978-0-606-32044-3(X)*, Turtleback) Turtleback Bks.
—The Unwanteds, 6 vols. 2011. (Unwanteds Ser.: Bk. 1). (J). 90.75 *(978-1-4618-4113-5(5))*; 88.75 *(978-1-4618-4117-3(8))*; 88.75 *(978-1-4618-4116-6(X))*; 245.75 *(978-1-4618-4114-2(3))*; 1.25 *(978-1-4640-2489-4(8))* Recorded Bks., Inc.
—The Unwanteds. (Unwanteds Ser.: 1). (ENG., Illus.). (J). (gr. 3-7). 2012. 416p. pap. 7.99 *(978-1-4424-0769-5(7))* 2011. 400p. 18.99 *(978-1-4424-0768-8(9))* Simon & Schuster Children's Publishing. (Aladdin).
—The Unwanteds. 2012. (Unwanteds Ser.: 1). lib. bdg. 18.40 *(978-0-606-26953-7(3)*, Turtleback) Turtleback Bks.
—The Unwanteds Set: The Unwanteds; Island of Silence; Island of Fire. 2013. (Unwanteds Ser.). (ENG.). 1280p. (J). (gr. 3-7). 51.99 *(978-1-4424-9450-3(6)*, Aladdin) Simon & Schuster Children's Publishing.
Meadows, Daisy. Annabelle the Drawing Fairy. 2015. (Magical Crafts Fairies Ser.: 2). (ENG., Illus.). 80p. (J). (gr. 2-5). pap. 4.99 *(978-0-545-70830-2(3)*, Scholastic Paperbacks) Scholastic, Inc.
—Josie the Jewelry Fairy. 2015. (Magical Crafts Fairies Ser.: 4). (ENG., Illus.). 80p. (J). (gr. 2-5). pap. 4.99 *(978-0-545-70832-6(X)*, Scholastic Paperbacks) Scholastic, Inc.
—Kayla the Pottery Fairy. 2015. (Magical Crafts Fairies Ser.: 1). (ENG., Illus.). 80p. (J). (gr. 2-5). pap. 4.99 *(978-0-545-70829-6(X)*, Scholastic Paperbacks) Scholastic, Inc.
—Lila & Myla, the Twins Fairies. 2015. (Rainbow Magic — Special Edition Ser.). lib. bdg. 17.20 *(978-0-606-36341-9(6))* Turtleback Bks.
—Rainbow Magic Special Edition: Lila & Myla the Twins Fairies. 2015. (Rainbow Magic Special Edition Ser.). (ENG., Illus.). 176p. (J). (gr. 2-5). pap. 6.99 *(978-0-545-70825-8(7)*, Scholastic Paperbacks) Scholastic, Inc.
—Roxie the Baking Fairy. 2015. (Magical Crafts Fairies Ser.: 7). (ENG., Illus.). 80p. (J). (gr. 2-5). pap. 4.99 *(978-0-545-70835-7(4)*, Scholastic Paperbacks) Scholastic, Inc.
—Violet the Painting Fairy. 2015. (Illus.). (J). (Magical Crafts Fairies Ser.: 5). (ENG.). 80p. (gr. 2-5). pap. 4.99 *(978-0-545-70833-3(8)*, Scholastic Paperbacks); 65p. *(978-0-545-72413-5(9))* Scholastic, Inc.
Mellon, David. Silent. 2017. (ENG.). 320p. (YA). (gr. 9-12). 17.99 *(978-1-5072-0168-8(0)*, Simon Pulse) Simon Pulse.
Mercer, Sienna. Cry Wolf!, Vol. 1. 2013. (My Brother the Werewolf Ser.: 1). (ENG.). 256p. (J). (gr. 4-6). pap. 9.99 *(978-1-4052-6438-9(1))* Egmont Bks., Ltd. GBR. Dist: Independent Pubs. Group.
—Date with Destiny. 2014. (My Sister the Vampire Ser.: 10). (ENG.). 224p. (J). (gr. 4-6). 6.99 *(978-1-4052-5985-9(X))* Egmont Bks., Ltd. GBR. Dist: Independent Pubs. Group.
—Fangs for the Memories. 2017. (My Sister the Vampire Ser.: 18). (ENG.). 208p. (J). (gr. 4-6). pap. 8.99 *(978-1-4052-7844-7(7))* Egmont Bks., Ltd. GBR. Dist: Independent Pubs. Group.
—Fangtastic! 2007. (My Sister the Vampire Ser.: 2). (ENG.). 208p. (J). (gr. 3-7). per. 6.99 *(978-0-06-087115-4(6))* HarperCollins Pubs.
—Fashion Frightmare! 2014. (My Sister the Vampire Ser.: 16). (ENG.). 240p. (J). (gr. 4-6). pap. 6.99 *(978-1-4052-6573-7(6))* Egmont Bks., Ltd. GBR. Dist: Independent Pubs. Group.
—Flipping Out ! 2014. (My Sister the Vampire Ser.: 14). (ENG.). 256p. (J). (gr. 4-6). pap. 6.99 *(978-1-4052-6571-3(X))* Egmont Bks., Ltd. GBR. Dist: Independent Pubs. Group.
—Love Bites. 2014. (My Sister the Vampire Ser.: 6). (ENG.). 256p. (J). (gr. 4-6). pap. 6.99 *(978-1-4052-5698-8(2))* Egmont Bks., Ltd. GBR. Dist: Independent Pubs. Group.
—Lucky Break. 2014. (My Sister the Vampire Ser.: 7). (ENG.). 256p. (J). (gr. 4-6). 6.99 *(978-1-4052-5699-5(0))* Egmont Bks., Ltd. GBR. Dist: Independent Pubs. Group.
—My Sister the Vampire - Twin Spins! 2014. (My Sister the Vampire Ser.: 9). (ENG.). 224p. (J). (gr. 4-6). pap. 6.99 *(978-1-4052-5984-2(1))* Egmont Bks., Ltd. GBR. Dist: Independent Pubs. Group.
—Secrets & Spies. 2014. (My Sister the Vampire Ser.: 15). (ENG.). 224p. (J). (gr. 4-6). pap. 8.99 *(978-1-4052-6572-0(8))* Egmont Bks., Ltd. GBR. Dist: Independent Pubs. Group.
—Star Style. 2014. (My Sister the Vampire Ser.: 8). (ENG.). 256p. (J). (gr. 4-6). pap. 6.99 *(978-1-4052-5700-8(8))* Egmont Bks., Ltd. GBR. Dist: Independent Pubs. Group.
—Vampalicious! 2008. (My Sister the Vampire Ser.: 4). (ENG.). 208p. (J). (gr. 3-7). per. 6.99 *(978-0-06-087121-5(0))* HarperCollins Pubs.
Mercer, Sienna & Miller, Sienna. Double Disaster! 2014. (My Sister the Vampire Ser.: 13). (ENG.). 256p. (J). (gr. 4-6). pap. 6.99 *(978-1-4052-6570-6(1))* Egmont Bks., Ltd. GBR. Dist: Independent Pubs. Group.
—Flying Solo. 2014. (My Sister the Vampire Ser.: 11). (ENG.). 224p. (J). (gr. 4-6). pap. 6.99 *(978-1-4052-5987-3(6))* Egmont Bks., Ltd. GBR. Dist: Independent Pubs. Group.
—Stake Out! 2014. (My Sister the Vampire Ser.: 12). (ENG.). 240p. (J). (gr. 4-6). pap. 6.99 *(978-1-4052-5988-0(4))* Egmont Bks., Ltd. GBR. Dist: Independent Pubs. Group.
Messer, Celeste M. The Ghost of Piper's Landing. Hoeffner, Deb, illus. 2004. 82-92p. 4.95 *(978-0-9702171-7-2(X))* AshleyAlan Enterprises.
Meyer, C. The Very First Unicorn. 2013. 24p. pap. 24.95 *(978-1-63004-317-9(6))* America Star Bks.
Michaels, Rune. Fix Me. 2011. (ENG., Illus.). 160p. (YA). (gr. 9). 16.99 *(978-1-4169-5772-0(3)*, Atheneum Bks. for Young Readers) Simon & Schuster Children's Publishing.
Miller, Gary & Miller, Lynda. The Adventures of Bob & Betty. 2006. (J). spiral bd. *(978-1-933594-92-7(6))* FBC Pubns. & Printing.
Mishica, C. Twins. 2007. (gr. k-3). pap. 5.50 *(978-0-8454-1692-1(8)*, Seedling Pubns.) Continental Pr., Inc.
Mitchard, Jacquelyn. Look Both Ways. 2010. (Midnight Twins Ser.: No. 2). (ENG.). 304p. (YA). (gr. 7-18). 8.99 *(978-1-59514-281-8(9)*, Razorbill) Penguin Young Readers Group.
Monson, Marianne. The Enchanted Tunnel Vol. 3: Journey to Jerusalem. Burr, Dan, illus. 2011. (J). (gr. 3-6). pap. 7.99 *(978-1-60908-068-6(8))* Deseret Bk. Co.
—The Enchanted Tunnel Vol. 4: Wandering in the Wilderness. Burr, Dan, illus. 2011. 85p. (YA). (gr. 3-6). pap. 7.99 *(978-1-60908-069-3(6))* Deseret Bk. Co.
—Pioneer Puzzle. 2010. (J). *(978-1-60641-669-3(3))* Deseret Bk. Co.
Moore, Karen. Everybody Counts. Reed, Lisa, illus. 2012. (Roma Downey's Little Angels Ser.). 24p. (J). bds. 7.99 *(978-0-8249-5643-1(5)*, Ideal Pubns.) Worthy Publishing.
Moore, Mykela. Meet the Super Sisters. Garrett, Myers, illus. 2013. (J). 9.99 *(978-0-9852746-9-6(7))* Hope of Vision Publishing.
Moore, Tessa. Dad & the Mad Cow Roundabout. 2007. (ENG.). 64p. (J). pap. 10.95 *(978-1-901737-54-7(3))* Anvil Bks., Ltd. IRL. Dist: Dufour Editions, Inc.
Morah, Chizoba. The Anderson Twins. 2007. 76p. per. 19.95 *(978-1-60441-015-0(9))* America Star Bks.
Morgan, C. M. Silver Doorway #1: A Gnome Away from Home. 2003. 104p. (J). pap. 6.99 *(978-0-9702189-2-6(3))* Sabledrake Enterprises.
—Silver Doorway #6: The Alchemist's Girl. 2008. 108p. pap. 6.99 *(978-0-9771005-2-1(9))* Sabledrake Enterprises.
Morgan, Melissa J. A Fair to Remember. 2007. (Camp Confidential Ser.: 13). (ENG.). 160p. (J). (gr. 3-7). pap. 4.99 *(978-0-448-44451-2(8)*, Grosset & Dunlap) Penguin Young Readers Group.
Morris, Chad. Cragbridge Hall, Book 2: The Avatar Battle. 2014. (Cragbridge Hall Ser.: 2). (ENG., Illus.). 360p. (J). (gr. 3-9). 17.99 *(978-1-60907-809-6(8)*, Shadow Mountain) Shadow Mountain Publishing.
—Cragbridge Hall, Book 3: The Impossible Race. 2015. (Cragbridge Hall Ser.: 3). (ENG., Illus.). 432p. (J). (gr. 3-9). 18.99 *(978-1-60907-979-6(5)*, Shadow Mountain) Shadow Mountain Publishing.
Morris, David. My Twins First Christmas. 2008. (Illus.). 24p. (J). pap. 14.95 *(978-0-9799885-0-9(0))* New Year Publishing.
Morris, Paris. My Twins First Halloween. 2008. (J). pap. 12.95 *(978-0-9760095-9-7(5))* New Year Publishing.
Morris, Paris & Florzak, Douglas. My Twins Are Coming Home. 2010. (ENG., Illus.). 24p. (J). pap. 12.95 *(978-0-9760095-5-9(2))* New Year Publishing.
—My Twins First Birthday. 2010. (ENG., Illus.). 24p. (J). pap. 12.95 *(978-0-9760095-8-0(7))* New Year Publishing.
Morris, Paris & Singer, Thom. I'm Having Twins, 1 vol. 2010. (ENG., Illus.). 24p. (J). pap. 12.95 *(978-0-9760095-4-2(4))* New Year Publishing.
Moses, Shelia P. The Baptism. (ENG., 144p. 2008. Illus.). (J). (gr. 5-9). pap. 5.99 *(978-1-4169-5833-8(9))* 2007. (YA). (gr. 7-12). 15.99 *(978-1-4169-0671-1(1))* McElderry, Margaret K. Bks. (McElderry, Margaret K. Bks.).
Moss, Christopher Hawthorne. Beloved Pilgrim. 2nd ed. 2016. (ENG., Illus.). (J). 29.99 ***(978-1-63477-939-5(8))*** 2014. 304p. pap. 17.99 *(978-1-62798-538-3(7))* Dreamspinner Pr. (Harmony Ink Pr.).
Mowry, Tia & Mowry, Tamera. Double Vision. 2015. (Twintuition Ser.: 1). (ENG.). 208p. (J). (gr. 3-7). 16.99 *(978-0-06-237286-4(6))* HarperCollins Pubs.
—Twintuition: Double Dare. 2017. (Twintuition Ser.: 3). 208p. (J). (gr. 3-7). 16.99 *(978-0-06-237292-5(0))* HarperCollins Pubs.
Moynihan, Lindsay. The Waiting Tree, 0 vols. 2013. (ENG.). 218p. (YA). (gr. 9-12). 17.99 *(978-1-4778-1634-9(8)*, 9781477816349, Amazon Children's Publishing) Amazon Publishing.
Mudrovich, Jane. Exorcising the Googie. 2012. 154p. pap. 14.97 *(978-1-61897-939-1(6)*, Strategic Bk. Publishing) Strategic Book Publishing & Rights Agency (SBPRA).
Muir, Suzanne. The Magic Tile. 2007. (Illus.). 48p. (J). lib. bdg. 15.00 *(978-1-4242-1619-2(2))* Dingles & Co.
Mukherjee, Sonya. Gemini. 2016. (ENG., Illus.). 336p. (YA). (gr. 9). 17.99 *(978-1-4814-5677-7(6)*, Simon & Schuster Bks. For Young Readers) Simon & Schuster Bks. For Young Readers.
Muldrow, Diane. Stirring It Up. Pollak, Barbara, illus. 2007. (Dish Ser.: 1). (ENG.). 160p. (J). (gr. 4-7). pap. 4.99 *(978-0-448-44526-7(3)*, Grosset & Dunlap) Penguin Young Readers Group.
—Turning up the Heat, No. 2. Pollak, Barbara, illus. 2nd ed. 2007. (Dish Ser.: 2). (ENG.). 160p. (J). (gr. 4-7). pap. 4.99 *(978-0-448-44527-4(1)*, Grosset & Dunlap) Penguin Young Readers Group.
Muller, Rachel Dunstan. The Solstice Cup, 1 vol. 2009. (ENG.). 176p. (J). (gr. 4-7). pap. 9.95 *(978-1-55469-017-6(X))* Orca Bk. Pubs. USA.

T U V

My Day! 2005. (J). bds. *(978-0-9769910-0-7(4))* Terrific Twins LLC.

Myers, Bill. Choices: A Truth Seekers Novel. 2014. (Truth Seekers Ser.). (ENG.). 224p. (J). (gr. 4-8). 10.99 *(978-1-4336-9081-5(0),* B&H Kids) B&H Publishing Group.

Myers, Kate Kae. The Vanishing Game. (ENG.). (YA). (gr. 7). 2014. 384p. pap. 9.99 *(978-1-61963-127-4(X),* 9781619631274) 2012. 368p. 17.99 *(978-1-59990-694-2(5),* 9781599906942) Bloomsbury Publishing USA. (Bloomsbury USA Childrens).

The Mystery of the Lion's Tail. 2014. (Greetings from Somewhere Ser.: 5). (ENG., Illus.). 128p. (J). (gr. -1-4). pap. 5.99 *(978-1-4814-1464-7(X),* Little Simon) Little Simon.

Natl Children's Book & Literacy Alliance. The Exquisite Corpse Adventure. 2011. (ENG., Illus.). 288p. (J). (gr. 4-7). pap. 7.99 *(978-0-7636-5773-4(5))* Candlewick Pr.

Neasi, Barbara J. Just Like Me. Hantel, Johanna, illus. 2011. (Rookie Ready to Learn — All about Me! Ser.). 40p. (J). (gr. -1-k). lib. bdg. 25.00 *(978-0-531-26371-6(1),* Children's Pr.); (ENG.). pap. 5.95 *(978-0-531-26676-2(1))* Scholastic Library Publishing.

Nelson, Jandy. I'll Give You the Sun. 2015. (CHI.). 384p. (YA). (gr. 9). pap. *(978-986-359-180-1(7))* Ecus Publishing Hse.

—I'll Give You the Sun. 2014. (ENG.). 384p. (YA). (gr. 9). 17.99 *(978-0-8037-3496-8(4),* Dial Bks) Penguin Publishing Group.

—I'll Give You the Sun. 2015. (ENG.). 400p. (YA). (gr. 9-12). pap. 10.99 *(978-0-14-242576-3(1),* Speak) Penguin Young Readers Group.

—I'll Give You the Sun. 2015. (ENG.). 400p. (YA). (gr. 9). 21.30 *(978-1-68065-512-4(4))* Perfection Learning Corp.

—I'll Give You the Sun. 2015. lib. bdg. 22.10 *(978-0-606-37572-6(4))* Turtleback Bks.

Neuschwander, Cindy. Pastry School in Paris: An Adventure in Capacity. Langdo, Bryan, illus. 2009. (ENG.). 32p. (J). (gr. 2-6). 18.99 *(978-0-8050-8314-9(6),* 9780805083149, Holt, Henry & Co. Bks. For Young Readers) Holt, Henry & Co.

Nickelodeon. Shimmer & Shine - Sleepover Wishes. 2016. (ENG.). 10p. (J). (gr. -1-2). bds. 9.99 *(978-0-7944-3827-2(X))* Studio Fun International.

Night, P. J. Together Forever. 2012. (You're Invited to a Creepover Ser.: 8). (ENG.). 160p. (J). (gr. 3-7). pap. 5.99 *(978-1-4424-5159-9(9),* Simon Spotlight) Simon Spotlight.

—Together Forever. 2012. (Creepover Ser.: 8). lib. bdg. 16.00 *(978-0-606-26339-9(X),* Turtleback) Turtleback Bks.

Nix, Garth & Williams, Sean. The Magic, Bk. 1. 2012. (Troubletwisters Ser.: 1). (ENG.). 304p. (J). (gr. 3-7). pap. 7.99 *(978-0-545-25903-3(7),* Scholastic Paperbacks) Scholastic, Inc.

—The Missing. 2014. (Troubletwisters Ser.: 4). (ENG.). 320p. (J). (gr. 3-7). 17.99 *(978-0-545-25900-2(2),* Scholastic Pr.) Scholastic, Inc.

—The Monster. (Troubletwisters Ser.: 2). (ENG.). 304p. (J). (gr. 3-7). 2013. pap. 6.99 *(978-0-545-25904-0(5),* Scholastic Paperbacks) 2012. 16.99 *(978-0-545-25898-2(7),* Scholastic Pr.) Scholastic, Inc.

—The Mystery. (Troubletwisters Ser.: 3). (ENG.). 304p. (J). (gr. 3-7). 2014. pap. 6.99 *(978-0-545-25905-7(3),* Scholastic Paperbacks) 2013. 16.99 *(978-0-545-25899-9(5))* Scholastic, Inc.

—Troubletwisters, Bk. 1. 2011. (Troubletwisters Ser.: 1). (ENG.). 304p. (J). (gr. 3-7). 16.99 *(978-0-545-25897-5(9),* Scholastic Pr.) Scholastic, Inc.

Nolan, Lea. Allure. 2013. (Hoodoo Apprentice Ser.: 2). (ENG.). 304p. (YA). (gr. 7-12). pap. 9.99 *(978-1-62266-022-3(6),* 9781622660223) Entangled Publishing, LLC.

Nolen, Jerdine. Block Party Surprise. Henninger, Michelle, illus. 2015. 41p. (J). *(978-1-4806-8574-1(7))* Harcourt.

—Bradford Street Buddies: Block Party Surprise. Henninger, Michelle, illus. 2015. (Green Light Readers Level 3 Ser.). (ENG.). 48p. (J). (gr. 1-4). pap. 3.99 *(978-0-544-35863-8(5),* HMH Books For Young Readers) Houghton Mifflin Harcourt Publishing Co.

Noonan, Rosalind, et al. The Love Factor. 2003. (ENG., Illus.). 128p. *(978-0-00-714454-9(7),* HarperCollins Children's Bks.) HarperCollins Pubs. Ltd.

Norris, Zack. The Secret of Skull Island. 2012. (Double Detectives Ser.). (ENG.). 144p. (J). (gr. 3-7). pap. 4.95 *(978-1-4027-7912-1(7))* Sterling Publishing Co., Inc.

Noyes, Deborah. Plague in the Mirror. 2013. (ENG.). 272p. (YA). (gr. 9). 16.99 *(978-0-7636-5980-6(0))* Candlewick Pr.

Nuri, Alya & Nuri, Alya. Amr's Adventure in Europe. 2013. 68p. pap. *(978-1-935948-29-2(6))* Roxby Media Ltd.

Odentz, Howard. Dead. 2013. 272p. pap. 14.95 *(978-1-61194-299-6(3),* Bell Bridge Bks.) BelleBks., Inc.

Odentz, Howard. Wicked Dead. 2016. (ENG., Illus.). (YA). pap. 15.95 ***(978-1-61194-712-0(X))*** BelleBks., Inc.

Ogden, Charles. Frost Bites. Carton, Rick, illus. 2008. (Edgar & Ellen Nodyssey Ser.: 2). (ENG.). 192p. (J). (gr. 3-7). 23.99 *(978-1-4169-5464-4(3),* Simon & Schuster/Paula Wiseman Bks.) Simon & Schuster/Paula Wiseman Bks.

—High Wire. Carton, Rick, illus. 2006. (Edgar & Ellen Ser.: 5). (ENG.). 208p. (J). (gr. 3-7). 24.99 *(978-1-4169-1500-3(1),* Simon & Schuster/Paula Wiseman Bks.) Simon & Schuster/Paula Wiseman Bks.

—Hot Air. Carton, Rick, illus. 2008. (Edgar & Ellen Nodyssey Ser.: 1). (ENG.). 192p. (J). (gr. 3-7). 9.99 *(978-1-4169-5465-1(1),* Aladdin) Simon & Schuster Children's Publishing.

—Nod's Limbs. Carton, Rick, illus. 2007. (Edgar & Ellen Ser.: 6). (ENG.). 224p. (J). (gr. 3-7). 24.99 *(978-1-4169-1501-0(X),* Simon & Schuster/Paula Wiseman Bks.) Simon & Schuster/Paula Wiseman Bks.

—Pet's Revenge. Carton, Rick, illus. 2006. (Edgar & Ellen Ser.: 4). (ENG.). 192p. (J). (gr. 3-7). 23.99 *(978-1-4169-1408-2(0),* Simon & Schuster/Paula Wiseman Bks.) Simon & Schuster/Paula Wiseman Bks.

O'Hair, Margaret. Twin to Twin. Courtin, Thierry, illus. 2003. (ENG.). 32p. (J). (gr. -1-3). 17.99 *(978-0-689-84494-2(8),* McElderry, Margaret K. Bks.) McElderry, Margaret K. Bks.

Oldfield, Jenny. Skye - The Champion, Bk. 13. (Illus.). 122p. (J). pap. 7.99 *(978-0-340-69985-0(X))* Hodder & Stoughton GBR. Dist: Trafalgar Square Publishing.

—Sorrel the Substitute, Bk. 12. (Illus.). 120p. (J). pap. 7.99 *(978-0-340-69984-3(1))* Hodder & Stoughton GBR. Dist: Trafalgar Square Publishing.

—Stanley the Troublemaker. (Illus.). 120p. (J). pap. 8.99 *(978-0-340-72675-4(X))* Hodder & Stoughton GBR. Dist: Trafalgar Square Publishing.

—Stevie the Rebel. (Home Farm Twins Ser.: Vol. 9). (Illus.). 128p. (J). pap. 7.99 *(978-0-340-68992-9(7))* Hodder & Stoughton GBR. Dist: Trafalgar Square Publishing.

—Sultan the Patient, Vol. 2. (Illus.). 119p. (J). pap. 7.99 *(978-0-340-69983-6(3))* Hodder & Stoughton GBR. Dist: Trafalgar Square Publishing.

—Sunny the Hero. (Home Farm Twins Ser.: No. 7). (Illus.). 120p. (J). pap. 7.99 *(978-0-340-68990-5(0))* Hodder & Stoughton GBR. Dist: Trafalgar Square Publishing.

Oliver, Lin. Almost Identical. 2012. (Almost Identical Ser.: 1). (ENG.). 224p. (J). (gr. 3-7). pap. 7.99 *(978-0-448-45191-6(3),* Grosset & Dunlap) Penguin Young Readers Group.

—Attack of the Growling Eyeballs. Gilpin, Stephen, illus. 2009. (Who Shrunk Daniel Funk? Ser.: 1). (ENG.). 160p. (J). (gr. 3-7). pap. 6.99 *(978-1-4169-0958-3(3),* Simon & Schuster Bks. For Young Readers) Simon & Schuster Bks. For Young Readers.

—Double-Crossed #3. 2013. (Almost Identical Ser.: 3). (ENG.). 224p. (J). (gr. 3-7). pap. 7.99 *(978-0-448-45193-0(X),* Grosset & Dunlap) Penguin Young Readers Group.

—Escape of the Mini-Mummy. Gilpin, Stephen, illus. 2009. (Who Shrunk Daniel Funk? Ser.: 2). (ENG.). 160p. (J). (gr. 3-7). pap. 8.99 *(978-1-4169-0960-6(5),* Simon & Schuster Bks. For Young Readers) Simon & Schuster Bks. For Young Readers.

—Revenge of the Itty-Bitty Brothers. Gilpin, Stephen, illus. (Who Shrunk Daniel Funk? Ser.: 3). (ENG.). 176p. (J). (gr. 3-7). 2010. pap. 6.99 *(978-1-4169-0962-0(1))* 2009. 14.99 *(978-1-4169-0961-3(3))* Simon & Schuster Bks. For Young Readers. (Simon & Schuster Bks. For Young Readers).

—Secret of the Super-Small Superstar. Gilpin, Stephen, illus. 2010. (Who Shrunk Daniel Funk? Ser.: 4). (ENG.). 160p. (J). (gr. 3-7). 14.99 *(978-1-4169-0963-7(X),* Simon & Schuster Bks. For Young Readers) Simon & Schuster Bks. For Young Readers.

—Twice as Nice. 2014. (Almost Identical Ser.: 4). (ENG.). 224p. (J). (gr. 3-7). 6.99 *(978-0-448-46447-3(0),* Grosset & Dunlap) Penguin Young Readers Group.

—Two-Faced, No. 2. 2012. (Almost Identical Ser.: 2). (ENG.). 224p. (J). (gr. 3-7). pap. 7.99 *(978-0-448-45192-3(1),* Grosset & Dunlap) Penguin Young Readers Group.

Olsen, Mary-Kate & Olsen, Ashley. Beach Collection, 3 vols. 2004. (ENG., Illus.). 320p. *(978-0-00-718443-9(3))* HarperCollins Pubs. Australia.

—The Cool Club. 2003. (ENG., Illus.). 112p. *(978-0-00-714469-3(5),* HarperCollins Children's Bks.) HarperCollins Pubs. Ltd.

—Dare to Scare. 2005. (ENG., Illus.). 112p. *(978-0-00-715887-4(4))* HarperCollins Pubs. Australia.

—Dating Game, 2 vols. 2003. (ENG., Illus.). 128p. *(978-0-00-714447-1(4),* HarperCollins Children's Bks.) HarperCollins Pubs. Ltd.

—The Facts about Flirting. 2005. (ENG., Illus.). 112p. *(978-0-00-715883-6(1),* HarperCollins Children's Bks.) HarperCollins Pubs. Ltd.

—A Girl's Guide to Guys. 2003. (ENG., Illus.). 128p. *(978-0-00-714455-6(5),* HarperCollins Children's Bks.) HarperCollins Pubs. Ltd.

—Let's Party, 3 vols. 2003. (ENG., Illus.). 112p. *(978-0-00-714473-0(3))* HarperCollins Pubs. Australia.

—Love, Set, Match. 2005. (ENG., Illus.). 112p. *(978-0-00-715885-0(8))* HarperCollins Pubs. Australia.

—P. S Wish You Were Here. 2003. (ENG., Illus.). 112p. *(978-0-00-714470-9(9),* HarperCollins Children's Bks.) HarperCollins Pubs. Ltd.

—Santa Girls, 3 vols. 2005. (ENG., Illus.). 112p. *(978-0-00-715888-1(2))* HarperCollins Pubs. Australia.

—Surf, Sand & Secrets. 2004. (ENG., Illus.). 112p. *(978-0-00-714459-4(8),* HarperCollins Children's Bks.) HarperCollins Pubs. Ltd.

—Tell Me about It. 2003. (ENG., Illus.). 128p. *(978-0-00-714451-8(2),* HarperCollins Children's Bks.) HarperCollins Pubs. Ltd.

—Two of a Kind Diaries: Winner Take All. 2003. (ENG., Illus.). 112p. *(978-0-00-714471-6(7),* HarperCollins Children's Bks.) HarperCollins Pubs. Ltd.

Omololu, C. J. The Third Twin. 2015. (ENG.). 336p. (YA). (gr. 7). 20.99 *(978-0-375-99171-4(9),* Delacorte Pr.) Random Hse. Children's Bks.

Oppel, Kenneth. Such Wicked Intent. (ENG., 320p. (YA). (gr. 7). 2012. Illus.). 16.99 *(978-1-4424-0318-5(7))*Bk. 2. 2013. pap. 9.99 *(978-1-4424-0319-2(5))* Simon & Schuster Bks. For Young Readers. (Simon & Schuster Bks. For Young Readers).

—This Dark Endeavor: The Apprenticeship of Victor Frankenstein. 2011. (Apprenticeship of Victor Frankenstein Ser.: Bk. 1). (ENG.). (YA). (gr. 7-12). 64.99 *(978-1-4558-2316-1(3))* Findaway World, LLC.

—This Dark Endeavor: The Apprenticeship of Victor Frankenstein. (ENG., (YA). (gr. 7). 2012. Illus.). 320p. pap. 10.99 *(978-1-4424-0316-1(0))* 2011. 304p. lib. bdg. 17.99 *(978-1-4424-0315-4(2))* Simon & Schuster Bks. For Young Readers. (Simon & Schuster Bks. For Young Readers).

Orr, Wendy. Mokie & Bik Go to Sea. Bean, Jonathan, illus. 2010. (ENG.). 80p. (J). (gr. 2-5). 15.99 *(978-0-8050-8174-9(7),* 9780805081749, Holt, Henry & Co. Bks. For Young Readers) Holt, Henry & Co.

O'Ryan, Ray. Operation Twin Trouble. Kraft, Jason, illus. 2015. (Galaxy Zack Ser.: 12). (ENG.). 128p. (J). (gr. k-4). pap. 5.99 *(978-1-4814-4399-9(2),* Little Simon) Little Simon.

Osbourne, Ozzy, pseud & Zink, Michelle. Guardian of the Gate. 2011. (Prophecy of the Sisters Trilogy Ser.: 2). (ENG.). 368p. (YA). (gr. 7-17). pap. 8.99 *(978-0-316-02740-3(5))* Little, Brown Bks. for Young Readers.

Owens, Bettina. Athena, Never A Bite. 2010. 32p. 18.99 *(978-1-4520-6381-2(8))* AuthorHouse.

Pandanas, Ms L. A. The Slinky Luminescence: Two Plus Who? 2013. 84p. pap. *(978-0-9870702-9-6(0))* Reed, Laura.

Papa's Gold. 2013. 196p. pap. 11.97 *(978-0-9851274-4-2(9))* Pen-L Publishing.

Paris, Harper. The Mystery Across the Secret Bridge. Calo, Marcos, illus. 2015. (Greetings from Somewhere Ser.: 7). (ENG.). 128p. (J). (gr. k-4). pap. 5.99 *(978-1-4814-2367-0(3),* Little Simon) Little Simon.

—The Mystery at the Coral Reef. Calo, Marcos, illus. 2015. (Greetings from Somewhere Ser.: 8). (ENG.). 128p. (J). (gr. k-4). pap. 5.99 *(978-1-4814-2370-0(3),* Little Simon) Little Simon.

—The Mystery in the Forbidden City. Calo, Marcos, illus. 2014. (Greetings from Somewhere Ser.: 4). (ENG.). 128p. (J). (gr. k-2). pap. 5.99 *(978-1-4814-0299-6(4),* Little Simon) Little Simon.

—The Mystery of the Gold Coin. Calo, Marcos, illus. 2014. (Greetings from Somewhere Ser.: 1). (ENG.). 128p. (J). (gr. k-4). pap. 5.99 *(978-1-4424-9718-4(1),* Little Simon) Little Simon.

—The Mystery of the Icy Paw Prints. Calo, Marcos, illus. 2015. (Greetings from Somewhere Ser.: 9). (ENG.). 128p. (J). (gr. k-4). pap. 5.99 *(978-1-4814-2373-1(8),* Little Simon) Little Simon.

—The Mystery of the Mosaic. Calo, Marcos, illus. 2014. (Greetings from Somewhere Ser.: 2). (ENG.). 128p. (J). (gr. k-2). pap. 5.99 *(978-1-4424-9721-4(1),* Little Simon) Little Simon.

—The Mystery of the Secret Society. Calo, Marcos, illus. 2016. (Greetings from Somewhere Ser.: 10). (ENG.). 128p. (J). (gr. k-4). pap. 5.99 *(978-1-4814-5171-0(5),* Little Simon) Little Simon.

—The Mystery of the Stolen Painting. Calo, Marcos, illus. 2014. (Greetings from Somewhere Ser.: 3). (ENG.). 128p. (J). (gr. k-2). pap. 5.99 *(978-1-4814-0296-5(X),* Little Simon) Little Simon.

—The Mystery of the Suspicious Spices. Calo, Marcos, illus. 2014. (Greetings from Somewhere Ser.: 6). (ENG.). 128p. (J). (gr. k-4). pap. 5.99 *(978-1-4814-1467-8(4),* Little Simon) Little Simon.

Pascal, Francine. Amigacho de Pluma del Amy. Orig. Title: Amy's Pen Pal. (SPA.). 144p. (YA). 6.95 *(978-84-272-3596-0(8))* Molino, Editorial ESP. Dist: AIMS International Bks., Inc.

—Centro de Atencion. (Gemelas de Sweet Valley Ser.: No. 18).Tr. of Center of Attention. (SPA.). (J). (gr. 3-7). 6.95 *(978-84-272-3788-9(X))* Molino, Editorial ESP. Dist: AIMS International Bks., Inc.

—Demasiado Perfecta.Tr. of Too Good to be True. (SPA.). 160p. (J). 7.95 *(978-84-272-3881-7(9))* Molino, Editorial ESP. Dist: AIMS International Bks., Inc.

—Esa Clase de Chica.Tr. of Wrong Kind of Girl. (SPA.). 168p. (J). 7.95 *(978-84-272-3880-0(0))* Molino, Editorial ESP. Dist: AIMS International Bks., Inc.

—Estrella del Rock. Orig. Title: Jessica the Rock Star. (SPA.). (J). 6.95 *(978-84-272-3595-3(X))* Molino, Editorial ESP. Dist: AIMS International Bks., Inc.

—Los Gemelos Consiguen Cogidos. Orig. Title: The Twins Get Caught. (SPA.). 136p. (J). 6.95 *(978-84-272-4641-6(2))* Molino, Editorial ESP. Dist: AIMS International Bks., Inc.

—Una Gran Luchadora. (Gemelas de Sweet Valley Ser.: No. 10).Tr. of One of the Gang. (SPA.). 128p. (J). (gr. 3-7). 6.95 *(978-84-272-3780-3(4))* Molino, Editorial ESP. Dist: AIMS International Bks., Inc.

—Una Larga Noche.Tr. of All Night Long. (SPA.). 128p. (J). 7.95 *(978-84-272-3875-6(4))* Molino, Editorial ESP. Dist: AIMS International Bks., Inc.

—Lo Que los Padres Ignoran.Tr. of What Your Parents Don't Know.... (SPA.). 224p. (J). 10.50 *(978-84-272-3163-4(6))* Molino, Editorial ESP. Dist: AIMS International Bks., Inc.

—Mala Idea de Jessica.Tr. of Jessica's Bad Idea. (SPA.). 112p. (J). 6.95 *(978-84-272-3593-9(3))* Molino, Editorial ESP. Dist: AIMS International Bks., Inc.

—Maria Falta. Orig. Title: Mary Is Missing. (SPA.). 128p. (YA). 6.95 *(978-84-272-3597-7(6))* Molino, Editorial ESP. Dist: AIMS International Bks., Inc.

—Peligrosa Tentacion.Tr. of Dangerous Love. (SPA., Illus.). 136p. (J). 7.95 *(978-84-272-3876-3(2))* Molino, Editorial ESP. Dist: AIMS International Bks., Inc.

—Querida Hermana.Tr. of Dear Sister. (SPA., Illus.). 168p. (J). 7.95 *(978-84-272-3877-0(0))* Molino, Editorial ESP. Dist: AIMS International Bks., Inc.

—Trabajo del Equipo. Orig. Title: Team Work. (SPA.). 120p. (J). 6.95 *(978-84-272-3797-1(9))* Molino, Editorial ESP. Dist: AIMS International Bks., Inc.

Pascal, Francine & Suzanne, Jamie. Señorita Jessica. (Sweet Valley Twins Ser.: No. 46). Orig. Title: Mademoiselle Jessica. (SPA.). 160p. (J). (gr. 3-7). 6.95 *(978-84-272-4646-1(3))* Molino, Editorial ESP. Dist: AIMS International Bks., Inc.

Paterson, Katherine. Jacob Have I Loved. 2003. (Trophy Bk.). (ENG.). 272p. (YA). (gr. 8-18). pap. 6.99 *(978-0-06-440368-9(8))* HarperCollins Pubs.

Patterson, James. Crazy House. 2017. (Crazy House Ser.: 1). (ENG.). 368p. (YA). (gr. 9-17). 17.99 ***(978-0-316-43131-6(1),*** Jimmy Patterson) Little Brown & Co.

Patterson, James & Grabenstein, Chris. Danger down the Nile. Neufeld, Juliana, illus. 2014. (Treasure Hunters Ser.). (ENG.). 480p. (J). (gr. 3-7). 14.99 *(978-0-316-37086-8(X),* Jimmy Patterson) Little Brown & Co.

—Peril at the Top of the World. Neufeld, Juliana, illus. 2016. (Treasure Hunters Ser.: 4). (ENG.). 384p. (J). (gr. 3-7). 14.99 *(978-0-316-34693-1(4),* Jimmy Patterson) Little Brown & Co.

—Secret of the Forbidden City. Neufeld, Juliana, illus. 2015. (Treasure Hunters Ser.: 3). (ENG.). 448p. (J). (gr. 3-7). 14.99 *(978-0-316-28480-6(7),* Jimmy Patterson) Little Brown & Co.

—Treasure Hunters. Neufeld, Juliana, illus. (Treasure Hunters Ser.: 1). (ENG.). 480p. (J). (gr. 3-7). 2015. pap. 8.00 *(978-0-316-20757-7(8))* 2013. 14.99 *(978-0-316-20756-0(X))* Little Brown & Co. (Jimmy Patterson).

—Treasure Hunters. 2015. (Treasure Hunters Ser.: 1). (J). lib. bdg. 18.45 *(978-0-606-37305-0(5))* Turtleback Bks.

Patterson, James & Paetro, Maxine. Confessions: The Paris Mysteries. 2014. (Confessions Ser.). (ENG.). 320p. (YA). (gr. 7-17). 18.00 *(978-0-316-37084-4(3),* Jimmy Patterson) Little Brown & Co.

—Confessions of a Murder Suspect. 2014. (Confessions Ser.: 1). (ENG.). 352p. (gr. 7-17). mass mkt. 8.00 *(978-1-4555-4774-6(3),* Jimmy Patterson) 2013. (ENG.). 400p. (J). (gr. 7-17). pap. 10.00 *(978-0-316-20700-3(4),* Jimmy Patterson) 2012. (Confessions Ser.: 1). (ENG.). 384p. (YA). (gr. 7-17). 19.99 *(978-0-316-20698-3(9),* Jimmy Patterson) 2012. 372p. (J). 11.99 *(978-0-316-22641-7(6))* 2012. (Confessions Ser.: 1). (ENG.). 400p. (YA). (gr. 7-17). 31.99 *(978-0-316-22418-5(9),* Jimmy Patterson) Little Brown & Co.

—Confessions of a Murder Suspect. 2013. (Confessions Ser.: 1). lib. bdg. 20.85 *(978-0-606-32278-2(7),* Turtleback) Turtleback Bks.

—Confessions: the Murder of an Angel. 2015. (Confessions Ser.: 4). (ENG.). 304p. (YA). (gr. 7-12). 18.00 *(978-0-316-30102-2(7),* Jimmy Patterson) Little Brown & Co.

—The Paris Mysteries. l.t. ed. 2014. (Confessions Ser.: 3). (ENG.). 352p. (YA). (gr. 7-17). 30.99 *(978-0-316-40963-6(4),* Jimmy Patterson) Little Brown & Co.

—The Paris Mysteries. 2015. (Confessions Ser.: 3). (YA). lib. bdg. 20.85 *(978-0-606-37526-9(0))* Turtleback Bks.

Patterson, James, et al. Treasure Hunters. Neufeld, Juliana, illus. 2013. 451p. (J). *(978-0-316-24262-2(4))* Little Brown & Co.

Paull, John W. The Great Stampede: A Jimmy James Story. 2010. 28p. 16.09 *(978-1-4269-4698-1(8))* Trafford Publishing.

Paulsen, Gary & Paulsen, Jim. Field Trip. 2015. (ENG.). 128p. (J). (gr. 5). 12.99 *(978-0-553-49674-1(3),* Lamb, Wendy Bks.) Random Hse. Children's Bks.

Payton, Belle. Are You Thinking What I'm Thinking? 2015. (It Takes Two Ser.: 8). (ENG., Illus.). 160p. (J). (gr. 3-7). pap. 6.99 *(978-1-4814-3137-8(4),* Simon Spotlight) Simon Spotlight.

—Even the Score. 2015. (It Takes Two Ser.: 5). (ENG., Illus.). 160p. (J). (gr. 3-7). pap. 6.99 *(978-1-4814-1951-2(X),* Simon Spotlight) Simon Spotlight.

—May the Best Twin Win. 2015. (It Takes Two Ser.: 7). (ENG., Illus.). 160p. (J). (gr. 3-7). pap. 6.99 *(978-1-4814-3134-7(X),* Simon Spotlight) Simon Spotlight.

—Two Cool for School. 2014. (It Takes Two Ser.: 2). (ENG., Illus.). 160p. (J). (gr. 3-7). 16.99 *(978-1-4814-0645-1(0),* Simon Spotlight) Simon Spotlight.

—Two Steps Back. 2015. (It Takes Two Ser.: 6). (ENG., Illus.). 160p. (J). (gr. 3-7). 17.99 *(978-1-4814-2519-3(6),* Simon Spotlight) Simon Spotlight.

—A Whole New Ball Game. 2014. (It Takes Two Ser.: 1). (ENG., Illus.). 160p. (J). (gr. 3-7). 16.99 *(978-1-4814-0642-0(6));* pap. 6.99 *(978-1-4814-0641-3(8))* Simon Spotlight. (Simon Spotlight).

Peacock, L. A. Panic in Pompeii. Hale, Nathan, illus. 2011. 92p. (J). pap. *(978-0-545-34062-5(4))* Scholastic, Inc.

—Terror at Troy. Hale, Nathan, illus. 2012. 90p. (J). *(978-0-545-34063-2(2))* Scholastic, Inc.

Pederson, Katie. The Point of No Return. 2006. 304p. pap. 29.95 *(978-1-4137-9945-3(0))* PublishAmerica, Inc.

Peete, Holly Robinson & Peete, Ryan Elizabeth. My Brother Charlie. Evans, Shane W., illus. 2010. (ENG.). 40p. (J). (gr. 2-5). 17.99 *(978-0-545-09466-5(6),* Scholastic Pr.) Scholastic, Inc.

Percival, Tom. The Magic Looking Glass. 2017. (Little Legends Ser.: 4). (ENG.). 192p. (J). (gr. 2-5). 14.99 ***(978-1-4926-4667-9(9))***; pap. 5.99 ***(978-1-4926-4259-6(2))*** Sourcebooks, Inc. (Sourcebooks Jabberwocky).

Perkins, Lucy Fitch. The Belgian Twins. 2004. reprint ed. pap. 1.99 *(978-1-4192-5388-1(3));* pap. 15.95 *(978-1-4191-5388-4(9))* Kessinger Publishing, LLC.

—The Dutch Twins. 2004. reprint ed. pap. 1.99 *(978-1-4192-6040-7(5))* Kessinger Publishing, LLC.

—The Eskimo Twins. 2004. reprint ed. pap. 1.99 *(978-1-4192-6126-8(6));* pap. 15.95 *(978-1-4191-6126-1(1))* Kessinger Publishing, LLC.

—The Eskimo Twins (Yesterday's Classics) 2006. (J). per. 9.95 *(978-1-59915-059-8(X))* Yesterday's Classics.

—The Japanese Twins. 2005. 26.95 *(978-1-4218-0369-2(0),* 1st World Library - Literary Society) 1st World Publishing, Inc.

—The Japanese Twins. 2004. reprint ed. pap. 1.99 *(978-1-4192-6781-9(7));* pap. 15.95 *(978-1-4191-6781-2(2))* Kessinger Publishing, LLC.

—The Japanese Twins (Yesterday's Classics) 2006. (J). per. 9.95 *(978-1-59915-058-1(1))* Yesterday's Classics.

—Rhe Japanese Twins. 2005. 96p. pap. 10.95 *(978-1-4218-0469-9(7),* 1st World Library - Literary Society) 1st World Publishing, Inc.

—The Scotch Twins. 2004. reprint ed. pap. 1.99 *(978-1-4192-8160-0(7));* pap. 15.95 *(978-1-4191-8160-3(2))* Kessinger Publishing, LLC.

—The Swiss Twins. 2004. reprint ed. pap. 1.99 *(978-1-4192-8467-0(3));* pap. 15.95 *(978-1-4191-8467-3(9))* Kessinger Publishing, LLC.

Peschke, Marci. Dead Man's Map, 1 vol. Smith, Tod G., illus. 2008. (Vortex Bks.). (ENG.). 112p. (gr. 2-3). pap. 7.19 *(978-1-59889-921-4(X),* 1271328, Vortex Bks.) Stone Arch Bks.

Peterson, Will. The Burning. 2009. (Triskellion Ser.: 2). (ENG., Illus.). 480p. (YA). (gr. 9-18). 16.99 *(978-0-7636-4223-5(1))* Candlewick Pr.

—The Gathering. 2010. (Triskellion Ser.: 3). (ENG., Illus.). 384p. (YA). (gr. 9-18). 16.99 *(978-0-7636-4847-3(7))* Candlewick Pr.

Petreman, Shan. Who Laid Those Eggs? 2013. 20p. pap. 11.59 *(978-1-4669-7633-7(0))* Trafford Publishing.

Phillips, Leigh Hope. Birthday Wishes. Fountain, John, illus. 2005. (J). pap. *(978-1-933156-10-1(4));* per. *(978-1-933156-03-3(1))* GSVQ Publishing. (VisionQuest Kids).

Pilkey, Dav. Captain Underpants & the Preposterous Plight of the Purple Potty People. Pilkey, Dav, illus. 2006. (Captain Underpants Ser.: 8). (ENG., Illus.). 176p. (J). (gr. 2-5). 5.99 *(978-0-439-37614-3(9));* 18.99 *(978-0-439-37613-6(0))* Scholastic, Inc.

Pollak, Dale. Velocity: From the Front Line to the Bottom Line. 2010. (ENG.). 144p. 29.95 *(978-0-9760095-7-3(9))* New Year Publishing.

Pollock, Tom. The Glass Republic. 2016. (Skyscraper Throne Ser.: 2). (ENG.). 448p. (YA). (gr. 7-9). pap. 14.99 *(978-1-68144-348-5(1),* Jo Fletcher Books) Quercus NA.

Pont, Beattie. Grandma, Tell Me More: Fishing with Grandpa. 2013. 80p. (gr. 2-4). pap. 19.95 *(978-1-4817-2073-1(2))* AuthorHouse.

Popovic, Lana. Wicked Like a Wildfire. 2017. 416p. (YA). (gr. 9). 17.99 *(978-0-06-243683-2(X),* Tegen, Katherine Bks) HarperCollins Pubs.

Power, Timothy. The Boy Who Howled. 2012. (ENG.). 272p. (YA). (gr. 3-12). pap. 7.99 *(978-1-59990-852-6(2),* 9781599908526, Bloomsbury USA Childrens) Bloomsbury Publishing USA.

Preller, James. Swamp Monster. Bruno, Iacopo, illus. 2015. (Scary Tales Ser.: 6). (ENG.). 96p. (J). (gr. 2-5). 15.99 *(978-1-250-04097-8(3),* 9781250040978) Feiwel & Friends.

Prime, Derek. Sarah & Paul Go Back to School Bk. 1: Discover about God & the Bible. 2006. (Sarah & Paul Ser.). (ENG., Illus.). 128p. (J). (gr. 2-5). per. 6.99 *(978-1-84550-157-0(8),* df1071c4-5480-4c1a-9480-a93d741bf494) Christian Focus Pubns. GBR. Dist: Bookmasters Distribution.

—Sarah & Paul Go on Holiday Again: Discover about Being a Christian. 2006. (Sarah & Paul Ser.). (ENG., Illus.). 128p. (J). per. 6.99 *(978-1-84550-162-4(4),* 94175d0d-6922-46f5-bc95-9e8edf2f526c) Christian Focus Pubns. GBR. Dist: Bookmasters Distribution.

—Sarah & Paul Go to the Museum: Discover about the Ten Commandments. 2006. (Sarah & Paul Ser.). (ENG., Illus.). 128p. (J). (gr. 2-5). per. 6.99 *(978-1-84550-161-7(6),* 4451dd6e-e239-4e8a-b092-b7a203a1a9fe) Christian Focus Pubns. GBR. Dist: Bookmasters Distribution.

—Sarah & Paul Go to the Seaside. 2006. (Sarah & Paul Ser.). (ENG., Illus.). 128p. (J). (gr. 2-5). per. 6.99 *(978-1-84550-159-4(4),* e21a5ea6-3d41-4387-977e-93990141367d) Christian Focus Pubns. GBR. Dist: Bookmasters Distribution.

—Sarah & Paul Have a Visitor: Discover about the Lord Jesus Christ. 2006. (Sarah & Paul Ser.). (ENG., Illus.). 128p. (J). (gr. 2-5). per. 6.99 *(978-1-84550-158-7(6),* 9fc8ce77-737f-45af-9bdb-cf0fca10e370) Christian Focus Pubns. GBR. Dist: Bookmasters Distribution.

—Sarah & Paul Make a Scrapbook. 2006. (Sarah & Paul Ser.). (ENG., Illus.). 128p. (J). (gr. 2-5). per. 6.99 *(978-1-84550-160-0(8),* a9643561-9103-4038-81fa-3bbc6a03ab7a) Christian Focus Pubns. GBR. Dist: Bookmasters Distribution.

Project Blastoff. 2015. (Astrotwins Ser.). (ENG., Illus.). 224p. (J). (gr. 3-7). 17.99 *(978-1-4814-1545-3(X),* Simon & Schuster/Paula Wiseman Bks.) Simon & Schuster/Paula Wiseman Bks.

The Promise. 2012. 218p. pap. *(978-1-78176-337-7(2))* FeedARead.com.

Pyles, Mary Kay. Rise & Shine Rosie. 2013. 134p. pap. 11.95 *(978-0-9887836-9-0(X))* Taylor and Seale Publishing, LLC.

Radford, Heather. The Asquinn Twins: Frontier Life. Oakley, Darlene, ed. 2012. 104p. *(978-1-77097-693-1(0));* pap. *(978-1-77097-694-8(9))* FriesenPress.

Raines, Jennifer. Alex & Andrew Swap Places. 2008. 32p. per. 24.95 *(978-1-4241-8938-0(1))* America Star Bks.

Ramos, Ramona J. A Summer with Kaitlyn & Lexi. 2011. 48p. pap. 16.95 *(978-1-4626-1890-3(1))* America Star Bks.

Random House. Make It Sparkle! (Shimmer & Shine) Random House, illus. 2016. (Glitter Board Book Ser.). (ENG., Illus.). 12p. (J). (— 1). bds. 8.99 *(978-1-5247-0159-8(9),* Random Hse. Bks. for Young Readers) Random Hse. Children's Bks.

—Meet Shimmer & Shine! (Shimmer & Shine) Cardona, Jose Maria, illus. 2016. (Step into Reading Ser.). (ENG.). 24p. (J). (gr. -1-1). 4.99 *(978-0-553-52203-7(5),* Random Hse. Bks. for Young Readers) Random Hse. Children's Bks.

Random House Disney Staff. Skate This Way! (Shimmer & Shine) Random House Disney Staff & Aikins, Dave, illus. 2016. (Book & CD Ser.). (ENG.). 24p. (J). (gr. -1-2). pap. 6.99 *(978-1-101-93870-6(6),* Random Hse. Bks. for Young Readers) Random Hse. Children's Bks.

Rettig, Liz. Jumping to Confusions. 2010. (ENG.). 320p. (YA). (gr. 7-18). pap. 8.99 *(978-0-552-55757-3(9))* Transworld Publishers Ltd. GBR. Dist: Independent Pubs. Group.

Rex, Adam. Cold Cereal. (Cold Cereal Saga Ser.: 1). (ENG.). (J). (gr. 3-7). 2013. 448p. pap. 7.99 *(978-0-06-206003-7(1))* 2012. 432p. 16.99 *(978-0-06-206002-0(3))* HarperCollins Pubs.

—Unlucky Charms. 2013. (Cold Cereal Saga Ser.: 2). (ENG., Illus.). 400p. (J). (gr. 3-7). 16.99 *(978-0-06-206005-1(8))* HarperCollins Pubs.

Reynolds, Paul A. Sydney & Simon: Going Green! Reynolds, Paul A. & Reynolds, Peter H., illus. 2015. (Sydney & Simon Ser.). (ENG.). 48p. (J). (gr. 1-4). lib. bdg. 12.95 *(978-1-58089-677-1(4))* Charlesbridge Publishing, Inc.

—Sydney & Simon: To the Moon & Beyond! Reynolds, Peter H., illus. 2017. (ENG.). 48p. (J). (gr. 1-4). lib. bdg. 12.99 *(978-1-58089-679-5(0))* Charlesbridge Publishing, Inc.

—Sydney & Simon: Full Steam Ahead! Reynolds, Peter H., illus. 2014. (Sydney & Simon Ser.). (ENG.). 48p. (J). (gr. 1-4). 12.95 *(978-1-58089-675-7(8))* Charlesbridge Publishing, Inc.

Richards, Stephen J. The Twins First Snow. 2010. 28p. pap. 13.99 *(978-1-4490-8853-8(8))* AuthorHouse.

Rivers, Karen. Finding Ruby Starling. 2014. (ENG.). 304p. (J). (gr. 4-7). 17.99 *(978-0-545-53479-6(8),* Levine, Arthur A. Bks.) Scholastic, Inc.

Roberts, Bethany. Double Trouble Groundhog Day. Cauley, Lorinda Bryan, illus. 2011. (ENG.). 40p. (J). (gr. -1-3). pap. 6.99 *(978-0-312-55350-0(1),* 9780312553500) Square Fish.

Roberts, Willo Davis. The One Left Behind. 2007. (ENG., Illus.). 144p. (J). (gr. 3-7). pap. 7.99 *(978-0-689-85083-7(2),* Aladdin) Simon & Schuster Children's Publishing.

Robinson, Jimmie. Evil & Malice - Save the World! 2009. (ENG., Illus.). 128p. (J). pap. 14.99 *(978-1-60706-091-8(4),* 9781607060918) Image Comics.

Robinson, Keith. Valley of Monsters. 2013. 212p. pap. *(978-0-9843906-6-3(9))* Roxby Media Ltd.

Rodkey, Geoff. The Tapper Twins Go to War (with Each Other) 2015. (Tapper Twins Ser.: 1). (ENG., Illus.). 240p. (J). (gr. 3-7). 13.99 *(978-0-316-29779-0(8))* Little Brown & Co.

—The Tapper Twins Go to War (with Each Other) 2016. (Tapper Twins Ser.: 1). (ENG., Illus.). 240p. (J). (gr. 3-7). pap. 5.99 *(978-0-316-31597-5(4))* Little, Brown Bks. for Young Readers.

—The Tapper Twins Go Viral. 2017. (Tapper Twins Ser.: 4). (ENG., Illus.). 256p. (J). (gr. 3-7). 13.99 *(978-0-316-29784-4(4))* Little Brown & Co.

—The Tapper Twins Run for President. 2016. (Tapper Twins Ser.: 3). (ENG., Illus.). 304p. (J). (gr. 3-7). 13.99 *(978-0-316-29785-1(2))* Little, Brown Bks. for Young Readers.

—The Tapper Twins Tear up New York. 2015. (Tapper Twins Ser.: 2). (ENG., Illus.). 288p. (J). (gr. 3-7). 13.99 *(978-0-316-29783-7(6))* Little Brown & Co.

—The Tapper Twins Tear up New York. 2016. (Tapper Twins Ser.: 2). (ENG., Illus.). 288p. (J). (gr. 3-7). pap. 5.99 *(978-0-316-31601-9(6))* Little, Brown Bks. for Young Readers.

Rogers, Blessing. Gabby & Ralph Meet Their New Teacher. 2010. 24p. 11.49 *(978-1-4520-5447-6(9))* AuthorHouse.

Roland, Timothy. Monkey Me & the Golden Monkey. Roland, Timothy, illus. 2014. (Monkey Me Ser.: 1). (ENG., Illus.). 96p. (J). (gr. 1-3). pap. 4.99 *(978-0-545-55976-8(6))* Scholastic, Inc.

—Monkey Me & the Golden Monkey. 2014. (Monkey Me Ser.: 1). lib. bdg. 14.75 *(978-0-606-35354-0(2))* Turtleback Bks.

—Monkey Me & the New Neighbor. Roland, Timothy, illus. 2014. (Monkey Me Ser.: 3). (ENG., Illus.). 96p. (J). (gr. 1-3). pap. 4.99 *(978-0-545-55984-3(7))* Scholastic, Inc.

—Monkey Me & the New Neighbor. 2014. (Monkey Me Ser.: 3). lib. bdg. 14.75 *(978-0-606-35360-1(7))* Turtleback Bks.

—Monkey Me & the Pet Show. 2014. (Monkey Me Ser.: 2). (ENG.). 96p. (J). (gr. 1-3). 15.99 *(978-0-545-55981-2(2))* Scholastic, Inc.

—Monkey Me & the Pet Show. 2014. (Monkey Me Ser.: 2). lib. bdg. 14.75 *(978-0-606-35359-5(3))* Turtleback Bks.

—Monkey Me & the School Ghost. 2014. (Monkey Me Ser.: 4). (ENG.). 96p. (J). (gr. 1-3). pap. 4.99 *(978-0-545-55989-8(8))* Scholastic, Inc.

—Monkey Me & the School Ghost. Roland, Timothy, illus. 2014. (Monkey Me Ser.: 4). (ENG., Illus.). 96p. (J). (gr. 1-3). 15.99 *(978-0-545-55990-4(1))* Scholastic, Inc.

—Monkey Me & the School Ghost. 2014. (Illus.). 90p. (J). *(978-1-4844-3840-4(X))* Scholastic, Inc.

—Monkey Me & the School Ghost. 2014. (Monkey Me Ser.: 4). lib. bdg. 14.75 *(978-0-606-36053-1(0))* Turtleback Bks.

—The Pet Show. 2014. (Monkey Me Ser.: 2). (ENG.). 96p. (J). (gr. 1-3). pap. 4.99 *(978-0-545-55980-5(4))* Scholastic, Inc.

Rose, Valerie. The Family Reunion Is Not A Real Vacation. 2003. 28p. (J). 9.95 *(978-0-9703489-2-0(4),* Little Petals) Roses Are READ Productions.

Rosenberg, Michael. The Little Lost Tune: More Adventures from Bendalot. 2010. 30p. pap. 13.00 *(978-1-60911-881-5(2),* Eloquent Bks.) Strategic Book Publishing & Rights Agency (SBPRA).

—The Story of Bendalot Part: The Return Home. 2009. (Illus.). 36p. pap. 15.49 *(978-1-4389-8294-6(1))* AuthorHouse.

Rovetch, Lissa & Rowe, Jeffrey. Gravity Falls Dipper & Mabel & the Curse of the Time Pirates' Treasure! I Don't Know, You Tell Me! Adventure! No New Art Needed et al, illus. 2016. (ENG.). 288p. (J). (gr. 3-7). 12.99 *(978-1-4847-4668-4(6))* Disney Pr.

Roy, Arundhati. Le Dieu des Petits Riens. pap. 19.95 *(978-2-07-041172-6(9))* Gallimard, Editions FRA. Dist: Distribooks, Inc.

Roy, Ron. April Adventure. Gurney, John Steven, illus. 2010. (Calendar Mysteries Ser.: 4). (ENG.). 80p. (J). (gr. 1-4). 4.99 *(978-0-375-86116-1(5),* Random Hse. Bks. for Young Readers) Random Hse. Children's Bks.

—April Adventure. 2010. (Calendar Mysteries Ser.: 4). lib. bdg. 14.75 *(978-0-606-12465-2(9),* Turtleback) Turtleback Bks.

—August Acrobat. Gurney, John Steven, illus. 2012. (Calendar Mysteries Ser.: 8). (ENG.). 80p. (J). (gr. 1-4). 4.99 *(978-0-375-86886-3(0));* lib. bdg. 12.99 *(978-0-375-96886-0(5))* Random Hse. Children's Bks. (Random Hse. Bks. for Young Readers).

—August Acrobat. 2012. (Calendar Mysteries Ser.: 8). lib. bdg. 14.75 *(978-0-606-26403-7(5),* Turtleback) Turtleback Bks.

—February Friend. Gurney, John Steven, illus. 2009. (Calendar Mysteries Ser.: 2). (ENG.). 80p. (J). (gr. 1-4). 4.99 *(978-0-375-85662-4(5),* Random Hse. Bks. for Young Readers) Random Hse. Children's Bks.

—January Joker. Gurney, John Steven, illus. 2009. (Calendar Mysteries Ser.: 1). (ENG.). 96p. (J). (gr. 1-4). 4.99 *(978-0-375-85661-7(7),* Random Hse. Bks. for Young Readers) Random Hse. Children's Bks.

—July Jitters. Gurney, John Steven, illus. 2012. (Calendar Mysteries Ser.: 7). (ENG.). 80p. (J). (gr. 1-4). 4.99 *(978-0-375-86882-5(8),* Random Hse. Bks. for Young Readers) Random Hse. Children's Bks.

—July Jitters. 2012. (Calendar Mysteries Ser.: 7). lib. bdg. 14.75 *(978-0-606-26402-0(7),* Turtleback) Turtleback Bks.

—June Jam. Gurney, John Steven, illus. 2011. (Calendar Mysteries Ser.: 6). (ENG.). 80p. (J). (gr. 1-4). 4.99 *(978-0-375-86112-3(2),* Random Hse. Bks. for Young Readers) Random Hse. Children's Bks.

—March Mischief. Gurney, John Steven, illus. 2010. (Calendar Mysteries Ser.: 3). (ENG.). 80p. (J). (gr. 1-4). 4.99 *(978-0-375-85663-1(3),* Random Hse. Bks. for Young Readers) Random Hse. Children's Bks.

—March Mischief. 2010. (Calendar Mysteries Ser.: 3). lib. bdg. 14.75 *(978-0-606-12460-7(8),* Turtleback) Turtleback Bks.

—May Magic. Gurney, John Steven, illus. 2011. (Calendar Mysteries Ser.: 5). (ENG.). 80p. (J). (gr. 1-4). 4.99 *(978-0-375-86111-6(4),* Random Hse. Bks. for Young Readers) Random Hse. Children's Bks.

—October Ogre. Gurney, John Steven, illus. 2013. (Calendar Mysteries Ser.: 10). (ENG.). 80p. (J). (gr. 1-4). 4.99 *(978-0-375-86888-7(7));* lib. bdg. 12.99 *(978-0-375-96888-4(1))* Random Hse. Children's Bks. (Random Hse. Bks. for Young Readers).

—October Ogre. 2013. (Calendar Mysteries Ser.: 10). lib. bdg. 14.75 *(978-0-606-32232-4(9),* Turtleback) Turtleback Bks.

—September Sneakers. Gurney, John Steven, illus. 2013. (Calendar Mysteries Ser.: 9). (ENG.). 80p. (J). (gr. 1-4). 4.99 *(978-0-375-86887-0(9),* Random Hse. Bks. for Young Readers) Random Hse. Children's Bks.

—September Sneakers. 2013. (Calendar Mysteries Ser.: 9). lib. bdg. 14.75 *(978-0-606-32231-7(0),* Turtleback) Turtleback Bks.

Roy, Ronald. November Night. Gurney, John Steven, illus. 2014. (Calendar Mysteries Ser.: 11). (ENG.). 80p. (J). (gr. 1-4). 4.99 *(978-0-385-37165-0(9),* Random Hse. Bks. for Young Readers) Random Hse. Children's Bks.

Royal, Stephen. The Journey Inside the Womb. 2012. (Illus.). 16p. pap. 18.30 *(978-1-4772-2604-9(4))* AuthorHouse.

Ryals, Lexi. Liv & Maddie: Double Trouble. 2015. (Liv & Maddie Junior Novel Ser.). (ENG.). 112p. (J). (gr. 3-7). pap. 5.99 *(978-1-4847-1694-6(9))* Disney Pr.

—Liv & Maddie: Sisters Forever. 2015. (Liv & Maddie Junior Novel Ser.). (ENG., Illus.). 112p. (J). (gr. 3-7). pap. 5.99 *(978-1-4847-1079-1(7))* Disney Pr.

Ryan, Patrick. Gemini Bites. 2011. (ENG.). 240p. (J). (gr. 7-8). 17.99 *(978-0-545-22128-3(5),* Scholastic Pr.) Scholastic, Inc.

Ryder, Michael Todd, illus. Twins. 2012. 32p. (J). pap. 12.00 *(978-0-9847836-0-1(1))* Celtic Cat Publishing.

S., Lisa Hamilton Ed. The Tale of the Talking Trees: The Tale of the Talking Trees a Story of Suspense & Surprise. 2012. 32p. pap. 21.99 *(978-1-4691-7846-2(X))* Xlibris Corp.

Saigeon, Lori. Fight for Justice, 1 vol. 2009. (ENG.). 128p. (J). (gr. 3-6). pap. 7.95 *(978-1-55050-405-7(3))* Coteau Bks. CAN. Dist: Orca Bk. Pubs. USA.

Salom, Susie. Kyle Finds Her Way. 2016. (ENG.). 256p. (J). (gr. 4-7). 16.99 *(978-0-545-85266-1(8),* Levine, Arthur A. Bks.) Scholastic, Inc.

Salzmann, Mary Elizabeth. Humming Hummingbird, 1 vol. 2007. (Critter Chronicles Ser.). (ENG., Illus.). 24p. (J). (gr. k-3). lib. bdg. 24.21 *(978-1-59928-442-2(1),* SandCastle) ABDO Publishing Co.

Same Day, Different Way! 2005. (J). pap. *(978-0-9769910-3-8(9))* Terrific Twins LLC.

Sansone, V. K. A Daunting Quest for Quincy & Quigley. 2009. 32p. pap. 8.98 *(978-0-557-03594-6(5))* Lulu Pr., Inc.

Sargeant, Theresa. The Drainpipe Gang - the Adventures of Chris & Andy Smy. 2011. 112p. pap. *(978-1-907256-80-6(6))* Abela Publishing.

Sateren, Shelley Swanson. Fearless Freddie. Melmon, Deborah, illus. 2015. (Adventures at Hound Hotel Ser.). (ENG.). 72p. (gr. 2-3). lib. bdg. 25.32 *(978-1-4795-5898-8(2),* Adventures at Hound Hotel) Picture Window Bks.

—Growling Gracie. Melmon, Deborah, illus. 2015. (Adventures at Hound Hotel Ser.). (ENG.). 72p. (gr. 2-3). lib. bdg. 25.32 *(978-1-4795-5899-5(0),* Adventures at Hound Hotel) Picture Window Bks.

—Homesick Herbie. Melmon, Deborah, illus. 2015. (Adventures at Hound Hotel Ser.). (ENG.). 72p. (gr. 2-3). lib. bdg. 25.32 *(978-1-4795-5897-1(4),* Adventures at Hound Hotel) Picture Window Bks.

—Mudball Molly. Melmon, Deborah, illus. 2015. (Adventures at Hound Hotel Ser.). (ENG.). 72p. (gr. 2-3). lib. bdg. 25.32 *(978-1-4795-5900-8(8),* Adventures at Hound Hotel) Picture Window Bks.

Saunders, Kate. The Curse of the Chocolate Phoenix: A Companion to the Whizz Pop Chocolate Shop. 2015. (ENG.). 272p. (J). (gr. 5). 19.99 *(978-0-375-99183-7(2),* Delacorte Bks. for Young Readers) Random Hse. Children's Bks.

—The Whizz Pop Chocolate Shop. (ENG.). 304p. (J). (gr. 5). 2014. 7.99 *(978-0-385-74302-0(5),* Yearling) 2013. 16.99 *(978-0-385-74301-3(7),* Delacorte Bks. for Young Readers) Random Hse. Children's Bks.

Schneider, Erin L. Summer of Sloane. (ENG.). 304p. (YA). (gr. 9-17). 2017. pap. 9.99 *(978-1-4847-2670-9(7))* 2016. (Illus.). 17.99 *(978-1-4847-2525-2(5))* Hyperion Bks. for Children.

Schuster, Judith A. No Place to Call Home: Book Two-the Eddie Brewster Adventures. 2008. 196p. pap. 24.95 *(978-1-60563-559-0(6))* PublishAmerica, Inc.

Schwartz, Corey Rosen. Twinderella, a Fractioned Fairy Tale. Marcero, Deborah, illus. 2017. (ENG.). 32p. (J). (gr. -1-3). 17.99 ***(978-0-399-17633-3(0),*** G.P. Putnam's Sons Books for Young Readers) Penguin Young Readers Group.

Schwarzkopf, Tom. Trouble Twins Save Christmas, 1 vol. 2007. (ENG.). 96p. (J). (gr. 3-7). pap. 10.95 *(978-1-55109-619-3(6))* Nimbus Publishing, Ltd. CAN. Dist: Orca Bk. Pubs. USA.

Sclafani, Terry. The Thompson Twins Cruise Adventure. 2007. 84p. per. 10.95 *(978-1-4327-1542-7(9))* Outskirts Pr., Inc.

—The Thompson Twins Western Adventure. 2009. 114p. pap. 11.95 *(978-1-4327-3783-2(X))* Outskirts Pr., Inc.

Scollon, Bill. Minnie: Case of the Missing Sparkle-Izer, 1 vol. Loter Inc. Staff, illus. 2014. (World of Reading Pre-1 Ser.). (ENG.). 32p. (J). (gr. 3-5). lib. bdg. 24.21 *(978-1-61479-248-2(8))* Spotlight.

Scollon, William. The Case of the Missing Sparkle-Izer. 2013. (Mickey & Friends World of Reading Ser.). (J). lib. bdg. 13.55 *(978-0-606-32292-8(2),* Turtleback) Turtleback Bks.

Scott, Michael. The Alchemyst. 2009. (ENG., Illus.). 375p. (gr. 6-10). 19.00 *(978-1-60686-514-9(5))* Perfection Learning Corp.

—The Alchemyst. (Secrets of the Immortal Nicholas Flamel Ser.: Bk. 1). (ENG.). 400p. (YA). (gr. 7). 2008. pap. 10.99 *(978-0-385-73600-8(2),* Ember) 2007. (Illus.). 16.99 *(978-0-385-73357-1(7),* Delacorte Bks. for Young Readers) Random Hse. Children's Bks.

—The Enchantress. 2012. (Secrets of the Immortal Nicholas Flamel Ser.). (ENG.). 528p. (YA). (gr. 7). 18.99 *(978-0-385-73535-3(9),* Delacorte Bks. for Young Readers) Random Hse. Children's Bks.

—The Enchantress. 2013. (Secrets of the Immortal Nicholas Flamel Ser.: 6). (ENG.). 528p. (YA). (gr. 7). pap. 10.99 *(978-0-385-73536-0(7),* Ember) Random Hse. Children's Bks.

—The Enchantress. 2013. (Secrets of the Immortal Nicholas Flamel Ser.: 6). lib. bdg. 22.10 *(978-0-606-31947-8(6),* Turtleback) Turtleback Bks.

—The Magician. 2009. (Secrets of the Immortal Nicholas Flamel Ser.: Bk. 2). (ENG.). 496p. (YA). (gr. 7). pap. 10.99 *(978-0-385-73728-9(9),* Ember) Random Hse. Children's Bks.

—The Necromancer. 2011. (Secrets of the Immortal Nicholas Flamel Ser.). (ENG.). 416p. (YA). (gr. 7). pap. 10.99 *(978-0-385-73532-2(4),* Ember) Random Hse. Children's Bks.

—The Necromancer the Secrets of the Immortal Nicholas Flamel. l.t. ed. 2010. (Secrets of the Immortal Nicholas Flamel Ser.). (ENG.). 492p. 23.99 *(978-1-4104-2851-6(6))* Thorndike Pr.

—The Sorceress. (Secrets of the Immortal Nicholas Flamel Ser.: 3). (ENG.). 512p. (YA). (gr. 7-18). 2010. pap. 10.99 *(978-0-385-73530-8(8),* Ember) 2009. 17.99 *(978-0-385-73529-2(4),* Delacorte Bks. for Young Readers) Random Hse. Children's Bks.

—The Sorceress. 2010. (Secrets of the Immortal Nicholas Flamel Ser.: 3). lib. bdg. 22.10 *(978-0-606-14133-8(2),* Turtleback) Turtleback Bks.

—The Sorceress the Secrets of the Immortal Nicholas Flamel. l.t. ed. 2009. (Secrets of the Immortal Nicholas Flamel Ser.). (ENG.). 614p. (YA). 23.95 *(978-1-4104-2092-3(2))* Thorndike Pr.

—The Warlock. (Secrets of the Immortal Nicholas Flamel Ser.: 5). (ENG.). 400p. (YA). (gr. 7). 2012. pap. 10.99 *(978-0-385-73534-6(0),* Ember) 2011. 18.99 *(978-0-385-73533-9(2),* Delacorte Bks. for Young Readers) Random Hse. Children's Bks.

—The Warlock. 2012. (Secrets of the Immortal Nicholas Flamel Ser.: 5). lib. bdg. 22.10 *(978-0-606-26411-2(6),* Turtleback) Turtleback Bks.

—The Warlock the Secrets of the Immortal Nicholas Flamel. l.t. ed. 2011. (Secrets of the Immortal Nicholas Flamel Ser.). (ENG.). 486p. 23.99 *(978-1-4104-4157-7(1))* Thorndike Pr.

Seeger, K R. Asa-Birdie Com. 2007. 244p. 26.95 *(978-0-595-69522-5(1));* per. 16.95 *(978-0-595-45553-9(0))* iUniverse, Inc.

Segal, Andrew. Clarissa the Clown. Scott, Peter & JessT, Grant, illus. 2007. 32p. per. *(978-1-905823-20-8(7))* Panoma Pr. Ltd.

Seif, Adam, creator. Tacos, Beans & Rice... the Episodes: From the Beginning. l.t. ed. 2006. (Illus.). 32p. (J). *(978-0-9719518-0-8(2))* Doodle Publishing.

Senior, Patricia. Mischief on Mumpit Mountain. 2009. 36p. pap. 14.75 *(978-1-60693-661-0(1),* Eloquent Bks.) Strategic Book Publishing & Rights Agency (SBPRA).

Sgarlato, Dawn. Big Sister. 2012. 24p. pap. 17.99 *(978-1-4685-9426-3(5))* AuthorHouse.

Shakespeare, William. Twelfth Night Paperback Book. 2006. (Shakespeare Classics Ser.). (Illus.). 94p. (J). (gr. 4-7). per. 7.95 *(978-1-56254-858-2(1))* Saddleback Educational Publishing, Inc.

—Twelfth Night Study Guide. 2006. (Shakespeare Classics Ser.). (Illus.). 48p. (J). (gr. 4-7). per. 17.95 *(978-1-56254-859-9(X))* Saddleback Educational Publishing, Inc.

Sharp, Lydia. Whenever I'm with You. 2017. (ENG.). 304p. (J). (gr. 7). 17.99 *(978-1-338-04749-3(3),* Scholastic Pr.) Scholastic, Inc.

Shaw, LaVerne. Mesa Magic. 2006. 184p. per. 19.95 *(978-1-59879-238-6(5))* Lifevest Publishing, Inc.

Shearer, Alex. Sea Legs. 2006. (ENG.). 320p. (J). (gr. 5-9). per. 17.99 *(978-0-689-87144-3(9),* Simon & Schuster/Paula Wiseman Bks.) Simon & Schuster/Paula Wiseman Bks.

Sheinmel, Courtney. Twinsanity. Bell, Jennifer A., illus. 2017. (Zacktastic Ser.). (ENG.). 272p. (J). (gr. 2-4). 11.99 ***(978-1-58536-936-2(5),*** 204319); pap. 6.99 ***(978-1-58536-937-9(3),*** 204333) Sleeping Bear Pr.

Sheinmel, Courtney. Zacktastic. 2015. (Zacktastic Ser.). (ENG.). 272p. (J). (gr. 2-5). 11.99 *(978-1-58536-934-8(9),* 203947) Sleeping Bear Pr.

Shepard, Sara. Cross My Heart, Hope to Die. 2013. (Lying Game Ser.: 5). (ENG.). 336p. (YA). (gr. 9). 17.99 *(978-0-06-212819-5(1),* HarperTeen) HarperCollins Pubs.

—Hide & Seek. (YA). 2013. (Lying Game Ser.: 4). (ENG.). 320p. (gr. 9). pap. 10.99 *(978-0-06-186977-8(5))* 2012. (Lying Game Ser.: 4). (ENG.). 304p. (gr. 9). 17.99 *(978-0-06-186976-1(7))* 2012. (Lying Game Ser.: Bk. 4). 289p. 9.99 *(978-0-06-219369-8(4))* HarperCollins Pubs. (HarperTeen).

—The Lying Game. (Lying Game Ser.: 1). (ENG.). (YA). (gr. 9-18). 2011. 336p. pap. 10.99 *(978-0-06-186971-6(6))* 2010. 320p. 16.99 *(978-0-06-186970-9(8))* 2011. 336p. 16.99 *(978-0-06-211416-7(6))* HarperCollins Pubs. (HarperTeen).

—The Lying Game. 2011. (Lying Game (Quality) Ser.: Vol. 1). (ENG.). (YA). (gr. 9). lib. bdg. 20.60 ***(978-1-61383-667-5(8))*** Perfection Learning Corp.

—Never Have I Ever. (Lying Game Ser.: 2). (ENG.). (YA). (gr. 9). 2012. 336p. pap. 9.99 *(978-0-06-186973-0(2))* 2011. 320p. 16.99 *(978-0-06-186972-3(4))* HarperCollins Pubs. (HarperTeen).

—Seven Minutes in Heaven. 2014. (Lying Game Ser.: 6). (ENG.). 400p. (YA). (gr. 9). pap. 10.99 *(978-0-06-212823-2(X),* HarperTeen) HarperCollins Pubs.

—Two Truths & a Lie. (Lying Game Ser.: 3). (ENG.). (YA). (gr. 9). 2013. 320p. pap. 9.99 *(978-0-06-186975-4(9))* 2012. 304p. 17.99 *(978-0-06-186974-7(0))* HarperCollins Pubs. (HarperTeen).

Shickman, Allan Richard. Dael & the Painted People. 2011. (Zan-Gah Ser.). 155p. (YA). pap. 9.95 *(978-0-9790357-6-0(7))* Earthshaker Bks.

—Zan-Gah & the Beautiful Country. 2009. 151p. pap. 9.95 *(978-0-9790357-1-5(6))* Earthshaker Bks.

Shimokawa, Melanie. A Family for Madison. 2008. 53p. pap. 16.95 *(978-1-60672-701-0(X))* America Star Bks.

Shusterman, Neal. Bruiser. 2010. (ENG.). 336p. (YA). (gr. 9-18). 17.99 *(978-0-06-113408-1(2),* HarperTeen) HarperCollins Pubs.

Siebel, Kathryn. The Trouble with Twins. 2016. (ENG., Illus.). 256p. (J). (gr. 3-7). 16.99 *(978-1-101-93273-5(2),* Knopf Bks. for Young Readers) Random Hse. Children's Bks.

Silvey, Diane. Spirit Quest. 2009. (ENG., Illus.). 64p. (J). (gr. 6). pap. 11.99 *(978-1-55002-831-7(6),* Sandcastle Bks.) Dundurn CAN. Dist: Ingram Publisher Services.

—Time of the Thunderbird. Mantha, John, illus. 2008. (ENG.). 88p. (J). (gr. 6-5). pap. 11.99 *(978-1-55002-792-1(1),* Sandcastle Bks.) Dundurn CAN. Dist: Ingram Publisher Services.

Skead, Robert A. & Skead, Robert J. Patriots, Redcoats & Spies, 1 vol. 2015. (American Revolutionary War Adventures Ser.). (ENG.). 192p. (J). 14.99 *(978-0-310-74841-0(0))* Zonderkidz.

Skelton, Vonda Skinner. Bitsy & the Mystery at Amelia Island. 2005. (Bitsy Burroughs Mysteries Ser.). 183p. (J). (gr. 3-7). per. 8.95 *(978-1-57072-307-0(9),* Silver Dagger Mysteries) Overmountain Pr.

Skurzynski, Gloria. Afterwar. 2011. (ENG., Illus.). 528p. (YA). (gr. 7). pap. 9.99 *(978-1-4424-1681-9(5),* Atheneum Bks. for Young Readers) Simon & Schuster Children's Publishing.

Skuse, C. J. Pretty Bad Things. 2011. (ENG.). 256p. (J). (gr. 7-7). 17.99 *(978-0-545-28973-3(4),* Chicken Hse., The) Scholastic, Inc.

Slater, David Michael. David Michael Slater: Missy Swiss & More, 6 vols., Set 2. Incl. Milo & the Monster. Ebbeler, Jeff, illus. 28.50 (978-1-60270-656-9(5)); Ned Breaks His Heart. Brooks, S. G., illus. 28.50 (978-1-60270-657-6(3)); Ned's Nose Is Running. Brooks, S. G., illus. 28.50 (978-1-60270-658-3(1)); (gr. -1-4). (David Michael Slater Set 2 Ser.). 32p. 2009. 171.00 (978-1-60270-654-5(9), Looking Glass Library) ABDO Publishing Co.

Smith, Greg Leitich. Chronal Engine. Henry, Blake, illus. 2013. (ENG.). 192p. (J). (gr. 5-7). pap. 6.99 (978-0-544-02277-5(7)) Houghton Mifflin Harcourt Publishing Co.

Smith, Jennifer E. The Storm Makers. Helquist, Brett, illus. 2013. (ENG.). 384p. (J). (gr. 3-7). pap. 8.00 (978-0-316-17959-1(0)) Little, Brown Bks. for Young Readers.

Smith, Roland. Cryptid Hunters. 2006. (ENG.). 352p. (J). (gr. 5-17). pap. 6.99 (978-0-7868-5162-1(7)) Hyperion Pr.

Snowe, Olivia. Hansen & Gracie, 1 vol. Lamoreaux, Michelle, illus. 2014. (Twicetold Tales Ser.). (ENG.). 128p. (gr. 3-4). pap. 5.95 (978-1-4342-9150-9(2)) Stone Arch Bks.

Snyder, Carol. One up, One Down. Chambliss, Maxie, illus. 2018. (ENG.). 32p. (J). (gr. -1-3). 16.99 (978-1-4814-2144-7(1), Atheneum Bks. for Young Readers) Simon & Schuster Children's Publishing.

Soderberg, Erin. The Quirks & the Quirkalicious Birthday. Light, Kelly, illus. 2015. (Quirks Ser.). (ENG.). 208p. (YA). (gr. 3-6). 13.99 (978-1-61963-370-4(1), 9781619633704, Bloomsbury USA Childrens) Bloomsbury Publishing USA.

Sommers, Jackie Lea. Truest. 2015. (ENG.). 384p. (YA). (gr. 8). 17.99 (978-0-06-234825-8(6), Tegen, Katherine Bks) HarperCollins Pubs.

Somper, Justin. Black Heart. 2010. (Vampirates Ser.: 4). (ENG.). 512p. (J). (gr. 3-7). pap. 8.99 (978-0-316-02088-6(5)) Little, Brown Bks. for Young Readers.

—Blood Captain. 2009. (Vampirates Ser.: 3). (ENG.). 592p. (J). (gr. 3-7). pap. 10.99 (978-0-316-02086-2(9)) Little Brown & Co.

—Demons of the Ocean. 2007. (Vampirates Ser.: 1). (ENG.). 352p. (J). (gr. 3-7). per. 8.99 (978-0-316-01444-1(3)) Little, Brown Bks. for Young Readers.

—Demons of the Ocean. 2006. 1.00 (978-1-4294-1974-1(1)) Recorded Bks., Inc.

—Demons of the Ocean. 2007. (Vampirates Ser.: 1). (Illus.). 330p. (J). 19.65 (978-1-4177-8287-1(0), Turtleback) Turtleback Bks.

—Empire of Night. 2011. (Vampirates Ser.: 5). (ENG.). 512p. (J). (gr. 3-7). pap. 10.99 (978-0-316-03323-7(5)) Little, Brown Bks. for Young Readers.

—Immortal War. 2013. (Vampirates Ser.: 6). (ENG.). 512p. (J). (gr. 3-7). pap. 10.99 (978-0-316-03325-1(1)) Little, Brown Bks. for Young Readers.

—Immortal War. 2013. (Vampirates Ser.: 6). (J). lib. bdg. 22.10 (978-0-606-26696-3(8), Turtleback) Turtleback Bks.

—Tide of Terror. 2008. (Vampirates Ser.: 2). (ENG.). 480p. (J). (gr. 3-7). pap. 10.99 (978-0-316-01445-8(1)) Little, Brown Bks. for Young Readers.

Sparkes, Ali. Alligator Action. Collins, Ross, illus. 2014. (S. W. I. T. C. H. Ser.: 14). (ENG.). 112p. (J). (gr. 2-5). lib. bdg. 27.93 (978-1-4677-2117-2(4), Darby Creek) Lerner Publishing Group.

—Anaconda Adventure. Collins, Ross, illus. 2014. (S. W. I. T. C. H. Ser.: 13). (ENG.). 104p. (J). (gr. 2-5). lib. bdg. 27.93 (978-1-4677-2116-5(6), Darby Creek) Lerner Publishing Group.

—Ant Attack. Collins, Ross, illus. 2013. (S. W. I. T. C. H. Ser.: 4). (ENG.). 104p. (J). (gr. 2-5). pap. 7.95 (978-1-4677-0713-8(9), Darby Creek) Lerner Publishing Group.

—Ant Attack. Collins, Ross, illus. 2013. (S. W. I. T. C. H. Ser.: 4). (ENG.). 104p. (J). (gr. 2-5). lib. bdg. 27.93 (978-0-7613-9202-6(5)) Lerner Publishing Group.

—Beetle Blast. Collins, Ross, illus. 2013. (S. W. I. T. C. H. Ser.: 6). (ENG.). 104p. (J). (gr. 2-5). pap. 7.95 (978-1-4677-0715-2(5), Darby Creek); lib. bdg. 27.93 (978-0-7613-9204-0(1)) Lerner Publishing Group.

—Crane Fly Crash. Collins, Ross, illus. 2013. (S. W. I. T. C. H. Ser.: 5). (ENG.). 104p. (J). (gr. 2-5). pap. 7.95 (978-1-4677-0714-5(7), Darby Creek); lib. bdg. 27.93 (978-0-7613-9203-3(3)) Lerner Publishing Group.

—Fly Frenzy. Collins, Ross, illus. 2013. (S. W. I. T. C. H. Ser.: 2). (ENG.). 104p. (J). (gr. 2-5). pap. 7.95 (978-1-4677-0711-4(2), Darby Creek) Lerner Publishing Group.

—Fly Frenzy. Collins, Ross, illus. 2013. (S. W. I. T. C. H. Ser.: 2). (ENG.). 104p. (J). (gr. 2-5). lib. bdg. 27.93 (978-0-7613-9200-2(9)) Lerner Publishing Group.

—Frog Freakout. Collins, Ross, illus. 2014. (S. W. I. T. C. H. Ser.: 7). (ENG.). 88p. (J). (gr. 2-5). lib. bdg. 27.93 (978-1-4677-2111-0(5), Darby Creek) Lerner Publishing Group.

—Gecko Gladiator. Collins, Ross, illus. 2014. (S. W. I. T. C. H. Ser.: 12). (ENG.). 104p. (J). (gr. 2-5). lib. bdg. 27.93 (978-1-4677-2115-8(8), Darby Creek) Lerner Publishing Group.

—Grasshopper Glitch. Collins, Ross, illus. 2013. (S. W. I. T. C. H. Ser.: 3). (ENG.). 104p. (J). (gr. 2-5). pap. 7.95 (978-1-4677-0712-1(0)) Lerner Publishing Group.

—Grasshopper Glitch. Collins, Ross, illus. 2013. (S. W. I. T. C. H. Ser.: 3). (ENG.). 104p. (J). (gr. 2-5). lib. bdg. 27.93 (978-0-7613-9201-9(7)) Lerner Publishing Group.

—Lizard Loopy. Collins, Ross, illus. 2014. (S. W. I. T. C. H. Ser.: 9). (ENG.). 104p. (J). (gr. 2-5). lib. bdg. 27.93 (978-1-4677-2112-7(3), Darby Creek) Lerner Publishing Group.

—Newt Nemesis. Collins, Ross, illus. 2014. (S. W. I. T. C. H. Ser.: 8). (ENG.). 88p. (J). (gr. 2-5). lib. bdg. 27.93 (978-1-4677-3233-8(8), Darby Creek) Lerner Publishing Group.

—Spider Stampede. Collins, Ross, illus. 2013. (S. W. I. T. C. H. Ser.: 1). (ENG.). 104p. (J). (gr. 2-5). pap. 7.95 (978-1-4677-0710-7(4)) Lerner Publishing Group.

—Spider Stampede. Collins, Ross, illus. 2013. (S. W. I. T. C. H. Ser.: 1). (ENG.). 104p. (J). (gr. 2-5). lib. bdg. 27.93 (978-0-7613-9199-9(1)) Lerner Publishing Group.

—Turtle Terror. Collins, Ross, illus. 2014. (S. W. I. T. C. H. Ser.: 11). (ENG.). 104p. (J). (gr. 2-5). lib. bdg. 27.93 (978-1-4677-2114-1(X), Darby Creek) Lerner Publishing Group.

Spears, Rick. Black Metal Volume 3: Darkness Enthroned: Darkness Enthroned. 2014. (ENG., Illus.). 160p. (YA). pap. 11.99 (978-1-934964-82-8(4), 9781934964828) Oni Pr., Inc.

Spinelli, Jerry. Jake & Lily. 2012. 352p. (J). (gr. 3-7). (ENG.). 16.99 (978-0-06-028135-9(9)); lib. bdg. 16.89 (978-0-06-028136-6(7)) HarperCollins Pubs.

Stadelmann, Amy Marie. The Not-So Itty-Bitty Spiders. 2015. (Olive & Beatrix Ser.: 1). (ENG., Illus.). 80p. (J). (gr. k-2). pap. 4.99 (978-0-545-81480-5(4)) Scholastic, Inc.

—The Super-Smelly Moldy Blob. Stadelmann, Amy Marie, illus. 2016. (Olive & Beatrix Ser.: 2). (ENG., Illus.). 80p. (J). (gr. k-2). 15.99 (978-0-545-81485-0(5)) Scholastic, Inc.

Stamper, Judith Bauer. Breakfast at Danny's Diner: A Book about Multiplication. Demarest, Chris L., illus. 2003. (All Aboard Math Reader Ser.). 48p. (J). (gr. 2-4). 11.65 (978-0-7569-1695-4(X)) Perfection Learning Corp.

Standish, Joyce, ed. The Adventures of Ryan Lincoln. Cooper, Nicole, illus. 2012. 46p. (J). pap. 10.00 (978-0-9716244-5-0(3)) TLS Publishing.

Starrenburg, Hasko. The Queen's Orb. 2012. (Illus.). 144p. pap. 8.00 (978-1-4349-8782-2(5), RoseDog Bks.) Dorrance Publishing Co., Inc.

Stein, A. K. EZEKIEL MAYHILL & the Crystal of God. 2007. 196p. pap. 16.96 (978-1-4303-2540-6(2)) Lulu Pr., Inc.

Stein, Tammar. Kindred. 2012. (ENG.). 276p. (YA). (gr. 7). pap. 8.99 (978-0-375-85349-4(9), Ember) Random Hse. Children's Bks.

Sterling, L. E. True North. 2017. (True Born Ser.: 2). (ENG.). 304p. (YA). 16.99 (978-1-63375-595-6(9), 9781633755956) Entangled Publishing, LLC.

Sternick, Michele J. The Charged up Twins. 2005. 29p. 9.98 (978-1-4116-3475-6(6)) Lulu Pr., Inc.

Stine, Megan, et al. Sealed with a Kiss. 2003. (ENG., Illus.). 112p. (978-0-00-714461-7(X), HarperCollins Children's Bks.) HarperCollins Pubs. Ltd.

—Surprise Surprise! 2003. (ENG., Illus.). 112p. (978-0-00-714462-4(8), HarperCollins Children's Bks.) HarperCollins Pubs. Ltd.

—War of the Wardrobes. 2003. (ENG., Illus.). 112p. (978-0-00-714468-6(7), HarperCollins Children's Bks.) HarperCollins Pubs. Ltd.

Stine, R. L. Bitten: Dangerous Girls & the Taste of Night. 2010. (ENG.). 496p. (YA). (gr. 9). pap. 9.99 (978-0-06-200739-1(4), HarperTeen) HarperCollins Pubs.

—Dangerous Girls. 2003. 256p. (J). 111.92 (978-0-06-056909-9(3)); 111.92 (978-0-06-056910-5(7)); (ENG., Illus.). (gr. 7-18). 13.99 (978-0-06-053080-8(4)) HarperCollins Pubs.

—First Evil. 2011. (Fear Street Cheerleaders Ser.: 1). (ENG.). 176p. (YA). (gr. 9). pap. 9.99 (978-1-4424-3086-0(9), Simon Pulse) Simon Pulse.

—Help! We Have Strange Powers! 2009. (Goosebumps Horrorland Ser.: 10). (ENG.). 160p. (J). (gr. 3-7). 6.99 (978-0-439-91878-7(2), Scholastic Paperbacks) Scholastic, Inc.

—Help! We Have Strange Powers! 2009. (Goosebumps HorrorLand Ser.: 10). lib. bdg. 17.20 (978-0-606-05347-1(6), Turtleback) Turtleback Bks.

—Night of the Living Dummy. 2008. (Classic Goosebumps Ser.: 1). (ENG.). 160p. (J). (gr. 3-7). 6.99 (978-0-545-03517-0(1), Scholastic Paperbacks) Scholastic, Inc.

—Night of the Puppet People. 2015. 136p. (J). (978-1-4806-9296-1(4)) Scholastic, Inc.

—Night of the Puppet People (Goosebumps Most Wanted #8) 2015. (Goosebumps: Most Wanted Ser.: 8). (ENG.). 160p. (J). (gr. 3-7). pap. 6.99 (978-0-545-62775-7(3), Scholastic Paperbacks) Scholastic, Inc.

—Weirdo Halloween. 2010. 240p. (J). (Goosebumps HorrorLand Ser.: No. 16). pap. (978-1-4071-1637-2(1)); (Goosebumps Horrorland Ser.: 16). (ENG.). (gr. 3-7). 7.99 (978-0-545-16197-8(5), Scholastic Paperbacks) Scholastic, Inc.

Stimkorb, Patricia. All about Me! Inspirational Version, 1. 2005. (Illus.). 12p. (J). bds. 12.99 (978-0-9758709-7-6(1), A.W.A. Gang) Journey Stone Creations, LLC.

Stone, Heather Duffy. This Is What I Want to Tell You. 2009. (ENG.). 240p. (YA). (gr. 7-18). pap. 9.95 (978-0-7387-1450-9(X), Flux) North Star Editions.

The Strange & Beautiful Sorrows of Ava Lavender. 2014. 320p. (J). (gr. 9). E-Book 8.99 (978-0-7636-7034-4(0)) Candlewick Pr.

Strasnick, Lauren. Her & Me & You. (ENG.). 208p. (YA). (gr. 9). 2011. pap. 9.99 (978-1-4169-8267-8(1)) 2010. 16.99 (978-1-4169-8266-1(3)) Simon Pulse. (Simon Pulse).

Street, Emily June. The Velocipede Races. 2016. (Bikes in Space Ser.). (ENG., Illus.). 256p. (J). (gr. 7). pap. 9.95 (978-1-62106-058-1(6), Elly Blue Publishing) Microcosm Publishing.

Streib, Sally. Octopus Encounter. 2007. (Illus.). 126p. (J). 6.97 (978-0-8163-2210-7(4)) Pacific Pr. Publishing Assn.

Swanson Sateren, Shelley. Adventures of Hound Hotel. Melmon, Deborah, illus. 2015. (Adventures at Hound Hotel Ser.). (ENG.). 72p. (gr. 2-3). 101.28 (978-1-4795-6291-6(2), Adventures at Hound Hotel) Picture Window Bks.

—Cool Crosby. Melmon, Deborah, illus. 2016. (Adventures at Hound Hotel Ser.). (ENG.). 72p. (gr. 2-3). lib. bdg. 25.32 (978-1-5158-0066-8(0), Adventures at Hound Hotel) Picture Window Bks.

—Drooling Dudley. Melmon, Deborah, illus. 2016. (Adventures at Hound Hotel Ser.). (ENG.). 72p. (gr. 2-3). lib. bdg. 25.32 (978-1-5158-0220-4(5), Adventures at Hound Hotel) Picture Window Bks.

—Mighty Murphy. Melmon, Deborah, illus. 2016. (Adventures at Hound Hotel Ser.). (ENG.). 72p. (gr. 2-3). lib. bdg. 25.32 (978-1-5158-0067-5(9), Adventures at Hound Hotel) Picture Window Bks.

—Stinky Stanley. Melmon, Deborah, illus. 2016. (Adventures at Hound Hotel Ser.). (ENG.). 72p. (gr. 2-3). lib. bdg. 25.32 (978-1-5158-0221-1(3), Adventures at Hound Hotel) Picture Window Bks.

Tagert-Paul, Kimberley. God's Ten Promises: Helping Children Understand the Ten Commandments. 2010. (J). 12.99 (978-0-8163-2379-1(8)) Pacific Pr. Publishing Assn.

Tashjian, Janet. Tru Confessions. 2007. (ENG., Illus.). 176p. (J). (gr. 4-7). per. 15.99 (978-0-312-37273-6(6), 9780312372736) Square Fish.

Taylor, G. P. The First Escape. 2008. (Dopple Ganger Chronicles Ser.: 1). (ENG., Illus.). 288p. (J). (gr. 3-7). 19.99 (978-1-4143-1947-6(9), SaltRiver) Tyndale Hse. Pubs.

—The Great Mogul Diamond. 2011. (Dopple Ganger Chronicles Ser.: 3). (ENG.). 304p. (J). (gr. 3-7). 19.99 (978-1-4143-1949-0(5), SaltRiver) Tyndale Hse. Pubs.

—The Secret of Indigo Moon. 2009. (Dopple Ganger Chronicles Ser.: 2). (ENG., Illus.). 304p. (J). (gr. 3-7). 19.99 (978-1-4143-1948-3(7), SaltRiver) Tyndale Hse. Pubs.

—The Tizzle Sisters & Erik. 2007. 188p. (978-1-905692-22-4(6)) Markosia Enterprises, Ltd.

Terrell, Brandon. The Cursed Stage. Epelbaum, Mariano, illus. 2017. (Snoops, Inc Ser.). (ENG.). 112p. (gr. 4-6). lib. bdg. 26.65 (978-1-4965-4346-2(7)) Stone Arch Bks.

—Mars for Humanity. Foti, Anthony J., illus. 2015. (Exploring Space & Beyond Ser.). (ENG.). 96p. (gr. 3-4). lib. bdg. 26.65 (978-1-4965-0502-6(6)) Stone Arch Bks.

—Phantom of the Library. Epelbaum, Mariano, illus. 2017. (Snoops, Inc Ser.). (ENG.). 112p. (gr. 4-6). lib. bdg. 26.65 (978-1-4965-5060-6(9)) Stone Arch Bks.

—Science Fair Sabotage. Epelbaum, Mariano, illus. 2017. (Snoops, Inc Ser.). (ENG.). 112p. (gr. 4-6). lib. bdg. 26.65 (978-1-4965-4347-9(5)) Stone Arch Bks.

—Tracking Champ. Epelbaum, Mariano, illus. 2017. (Snoops, Inc Ser.). (ENG.). 112p. (gr. 4-6). lib. bdg. 26.65 (978-1-4965-4348-6(3)) Stone Arch Bks.

—The Vanishing Treasure. Epelbaum, Mariano, illus. 2017. (Snoops, Inc Ser.). (ENG.). 112p. (gr. 4-6). lib. bdg. 26.65 (978-1-4965-4345-5(9)) Stone Arch Bks.

Terry, Gail Contreina. Twins. 2005. pap. 8.00 (978-0-8059-6818-7(0)) Dorrance Publishing Co., Inc.

Terry, Teri. The Book of Lies. 2017. (ENG.). 384p. (YA). (gr. 7). 17.99 (978-0-544-90048-6(0), Clarion Bks.) Houghton Mifflin Harcourt Trade & Reference Pubs.

Thomas, Dee. Silly, Silly, Eggleton Egg: Meet the Egg's of Eggville. 2012. 28p. pap. 21.99 (978-1-4771-5325-3(X)) Xlibris Corp.

Thompson, Colleen. Claudine & Claudette: A Bug Story. 2010. 12p. 8.49 (978-1-4520-7902-8(1)) AuthorHouse.

—Claudine & Claudette a Bug Story. 2011. 12p. pap. 8.32 (978-1-4634-2286-8(5)) AuthorHouse.

Tiernan, Cate. A Chalice of Wind - A Circle of Ashes - A Feather of Stone - A Necklace of Water. 2011. (Balefire Ser.). (ENG.). 976p. (YA). (gr. 7-18). 9.99 (978-1-59514-411-9(0), Razorbill) Penguin Young Readers Group.

Tillworth, Mary. All Bottled up! (Shimmer & Shine) Laviosa, Mattia Francesco, illus. 2017. (Pictureback(R) Ser.). (ENG.). 16p. (J). (gr. -1-2). pap. 5.99 (978-1-5247-1718-6(5), Random Hse. Bks. for Young Readers) Random Hse. Children's Bks.

—Leah's Dream Dollhouse (Shimmer & Shine) Yum, Heekyoung, illus. 2016. (Pictureback(R) Ser.). (ENG.). 16p. (J). (gr. -1-2). 4.99 (978-1-101-93249-0(X), Random Hse. Bks. for Young Readers) Random Hse. Children's Bks.

—Nickelodeon 5-Minute Stories Collection. Random House, illus. 2016. (5-Minute Story Collection). (ENG.). 160p. (J). (gr. -1-2). 12.99 (978-0-399-55314-1(2), Random Hse. Bks. for Young Readers) Random Hse. Children's Bks.

—The Sweetest Cupcake (Shimmer & Shine) Cartobaleno, illus. 2016. (Pictureback(R) Ser.). (ENG.). 16p. (J). (gr. -1-2). 4.99 (978-0-553-52201-3(9), Random Hse. Bks. for Young Readers) Random Hse. Children's Bks.

—Treasure Twins! (Shimmer & Shine) Cartobaleno, illus. 2017. (Little Golden Book Ser.). (ENG.). 24p. (J). (-k). 4.99 (978-0-399-55792-7(X), Golden Bks.) Random Hse. Children's Bks.

Tossell, David H. Charlie & Chippo Meet a Ghost. Pritchard, Louise, illus. 2012. 24p. pap. (978-1-908773-25-8(1)) Iponymous Publishing, Ltd.

Trees, Annie Mae. The Old Apartment Building: A Tale from the Trees. 2012. 24p. 24.95 (978-1-4626-6093-3(2)) America Star Bks.

Tremblay, Amanda. The Tornado Trial. 2010. 65p. pap. 12.00 (978-0-557-14051-0(X)) Lulu Pr., Inc.

Trevia, Rick & Benchmark Education Co., LLC Staff. Squid Twins. 2015. (BuildUp Ser.). (J). (gr. 1). (978-1-4900-0724-3(5)) Benchmark Education Co.

Troulis, Jennifer. Penelope & Priscilla: And the Enchanted House of Whispers. 2nd ed. 2004. (Illus.). 229p. per. 13.95 (978-0-9768602-0-4(1)) Twin Monkeys Pr.

—Penelope & Priscilla & the City of the Banished. 2007. (J). per. 14.95 (978-0-9768602-1-1(X)) Twin Monkeys Pr.

Troupe, Thomas Kingsley. Darling Doll. Faber, Rudy, illus. 2016. (Hauntiques Ser.). (ENG.). 128p. (gr. 4-6). lib. bdg. 25.32 (978-1-4965-3548-1(0)) Stone Arch Bks.

—Ghostly Goalie. Faber, Rudy, illus. 2016. (Hauntiques Ser.). (ENG.). 128p. (gr. 4-6). lib. bdg. 25.32 (978-1-4965-3544-3(8)) Stone Arch Bks.

—Phantom's Favorite. Faber, Rudy, illus. 2016. (Hauntiques Ser.). (ENG.). 128p. (gr. 4-6). lib. bdg. 25.32 (978-1-4965-3546-7(4)) Stone Arch Bks.

—Tornado: a Twisting Tale of Survival. Fagan, Kirbi, illus. 2016. (Survive! Ser.). (ENG.). 56p. (gr. 4-6). lib. bdg. 25.32 (978-1-4965-2556-7(6)) Stone Arch Bks.

—Wandering Wagon. Faber, Rudy, illus. 2016. (Hauntiques Ser.). (ENG.). 128p. (gr. 4-6). lib. bdg. 25.32 (978-1-4965-3547-4(2)) Stone Arch Bks.

Trueit, Trudi. Mom, There's a Dinosaur in Beeson's Lake. Paillot, Jim, illus. 2011. (Secrets of a Lab Rat Ser.). (ENG.). 160p. (J). (gr. 3-7). pap. 5.99 (978-1-4169-6112-3(7), Aladdin) Simon & Schuster Children's Publishing.

—No Girls Allowed (Dogs Okay) Paillot, Jim, illus. 2010. (Secrets of a Lab Rat Ser.). (ENG.). 144p. (J). (gr. 3-7). pap. 5.99 (978-1-4169-6111-6(9), Aladdin) Simon & Schuster Children's Publishing.

—No Girls Allowed (Dogs Okay) Paillot, Jim, illus. 2009. (Secrets of a Lab Rat Ser.). (ENG.). 128p. (J). (gr. 3-7). 14.99 (978-1-4169-7592-2(6), Simon & Schuster/Paula Wiseman Bks.) Simon & Schuster/Paula Wiseman Bks.

Trueit, Trudi Strain. Mom, There's a Dinosaur in Beeson's Lake. Paillot, Jim, illus. 2010. (Secrets of a Lab Rat Ser.). (ENG.). 160p. (J). (gr. 3-7). 14.99 (978-1-4169-7593-9(4), Simon & Schuster/Paula Wiseman Bks.) Simon & Schuster/Paula Wiseman Bks.

Trussell-Cullen, Alan. The Twin Competition. Hurst, Elise, illus. 2009. (Rigby PM Stars Bridge Bks.). (ENG.). 16p. (gr. 2-3). pap. 8.70 (978-1-4190-5510-2(0)) Rigby Education.

Tuck, Justin. Home-Field Advantage. Rodriguez, Leonardo, illus. 2011. (ENG.). 40p. (J). (gr. -1-3). 16.99 (978-1-4424-0369-7(1), Simon & Schuster Bks. For Young Readers) Simon & Schuster Bks. For Young Readers.

Two Peas in a Pod: 7. 2013. 68p. pap. 12.95 (978-1-4772-7082-0(5)) AuthorHouse.

Tym, Kate. Time to Share. 2008. (Manners Ser.). (Illus.). 24p. (J). (gr. -1-1). lib. bdg. 16.95 (978-1-59566-591-1(9)) QEB Publishing Inc.

Universal & Chesterfield, Sadie. Despicable Me 3: the Deluxe Junior Novel. 2017. (ENG.). 144p. (J). (gr. 3-7). 9.99 (978-0-316-50756-1(3)) Little, Brown Bks. for Young Readers.

Ure, Jean. Shrinking Violet. 2011. (ENG., Illus.). 176p. (J). (gr. 4-7). pap. 7.99 (978-0-00-714390-0(7), HarperCollins Children's Bks.) HarperCollins Pubs. Ltd. GBR. Dist: HarperCollins Pubs.

Vail, Rachel & Avi. Never Mind! 2005. (ENG.). 208p. (J). (gr. 5-18). reprint ed. pap. 6.99 (978-0-06-054316-7(7)) HarperCollins Pubs.

Van Stockum, Hilda. A Day on Skates: The Story of a Dutch Picnic. Van Stockum, Hilda, illus. 2007. (Illus.). 40p. (J). (gr. 1). 19.95 (978-1-932350-18-0(7)) Bethlehem Bks.

Van Wyk, Tasja. Twins: Meet the Doctor. 2011. (Illus.). 28p. pap. 13.78 (978-1-4567-7813-2(7)) AuthorHouse.

Venable, Alan. The Man in the Iron Mask. 2007. (Classic Adventures Ser.). pap. 9.95 (978-1-4105-0860-7(9)) Johnston, Don Inc.

Vick, Mamie Farrar. Someone's Near. 2012. 24p. pap. 17.99 (978-1-4670-4124-9(6)) AuthorHouse.

Vogiel, Eva. Facing the Music. 2003. 284p. 19.95 (978-1-880582-94-7(5)) Judaica Pr., Inc., The.

Walker, Lane. The Hunt for Scarface. 2014. (ENG.). 161p. (YA). (gr. 7-13). pap. 9.99 (978-1-58169-518-2(7), Evergreen Pr.) Genesis Communications, Inc.

Walters, Eric. Visions. 2011. (ENG.). 208p. (J). pap. (978-1-55455-122-4(6)) Fitzhenry & Whiteside, Ltd.

Walton, Leslye. The Strange & Beautiful Sorrows of Ava Lavender. (ENG.). 320p. (YA). (gr. 9). 2015. pap. 8.99 (978-0-7636-8027-5(3)) 2014. 17.99 (978-0-7636-6566-1(5)) Candlewick Pr.

—The Strange & Beautiful Sorrows of Ava Lavender. 2015. lib. bdg. 19.65 (978-0-606-36879-7(5)) Turtleback Bks.

Warman, Jessica. Beautiful Lies. 2014. (ENG.). 432p. (YA). (gr. 9). pap. 9.99 (978-0-8027-3543-0(6), 9780802735430, Bloomsbury USA Childrens) Bloomsbury Publishing USA.

Watson, Jude. Loot. (ENG.). 272p. (J). (gr. 3-7). 2015. pap. 6.99 (978-0-545-46803-9(5), Scholastic Paperbacks) 2014. 17.99 (978-0-545-46802-2(7), Scholastic Pr.) Scholastic, Inc.

—Sting. 2016. (ENG.). 272p. (J). (gr. 3-7). 16.99 (978-0-545-86346-9(5), Scholastic Pr.) Scholastic, Inc.

Watson, Renée. This Side of Home. 2015. (ENG.). 336p. (YA). (gr. 7). 17.99 (978-1-59990-668-3(6), 9781599906683, Bloomsbury USA Childrens) Bloomsbury Publishing USA.

Watts, Robin Queen. The Adventures of Beauty & Sam. 2009. 20p. pap. 10.50 (978-1-4269-1286-3(2)) Trafford Publishing.

Weidner, Teri. Always Twins. Weidner, Teri, illus. 2015. (ENG., Illus.). 32p. (J). (gr. -1-k). 16.95 (978-0-8234-3159-5(2)) Holiday Hse., Inc.

Weiner, Ellis. The Templeton Twins Have an Idea. Holmes, Jeremy, illus. 2012. (ENG.). 232p. (J). (gr. 4-7). 16.99 (978-0-8118-6679-8(3)) Chronicle Bks. LLC.

—The Templeton Twins Have an Idea: Book 1. Holmes, Jeremy, illus. 2013. (Templeton Twins Ser.). (ENG.). 240p. (J). (gr. 3-7). pap. 6.99 (978-1-4521-2704-0(2)) Chronicle Bks. LLC.

—The Templeton Twins Make a Scene: Book 2. Holmes, Jeremy, illus. 2014. (ENG.). 272p. (J). (gr. 3-7). pap. 6.99 (978-1-4521-2872-6(3)) Chronicle Bks. LLC.

Weiss, Ellen. Bathtime for Twins. Williams, Sam, illus. 2012. (ENG.). 30p. (J). (gr. -1 — 1). bds. 7.99 (978-1-4424-3026-6(5), Little Simon) Little Simon.

—Playtime for Twins. Williams, Sam, illus. 2012. (ENG.). 30p. (J). (gr. -1 — 1). bds. 7.99 (978-1-4424-3027-3(3), Little Simon) Little Simon.

—Twins in the Park. Williams, Sam, illus. 2003. (Ready-To-Reads Ser.). (ENG.). 24p. (J). (gr. -1-k). pap. 3.99 (978-0-689-85742-3(X), Simon Spotlight) Simon Spotlight.

We're a Team! 2005. (J). bds. (978-0-9769910-7-6(1)) Terrific Twins LLC.

Werlin, Nancy. Are You Alone on Purpose? 2007. (ENG.). 208p. (YA). (gr. 7-18). 7.99 (978-0-14-240777-6(1), Speak) Penguin Young Readers Group.

Wescott, Derek. Terry & Thomas the Tandem Twins. 2007. 160p. pap. (978-1-84401-875-8(X)) Athena Pr.

West, Steve, reader. Island of Legends. 2014. (Unwanteds Ser.: 4). (ENG., Illus.). 496p. (J). (gr. 3-7). 18.99 (978-1-4424-9328-5(3), Aladdin) Simon & Schuster Children's Publishing.

Weston, Paula. Shadows. 2013. (Rephaim Ser.). (ENG.). 400p. (YA). (gr. 9). 17.99 (978-1-77049-547-0(9), Tundra Bks.) Tundra Bks. CAN. Dist: Penguin Random Hse. LLC.

Weyn, Suzanne. Dr. Frankenstein's Daughters. 2013. (ENG.). 256p. (J). (gr. 7). 17.99 (978-0-545-42533-9(6), Scholastic Pr.) Scholastic, Inc.

Wiggin, Kate Douglas. Marm Lisa. 2004. reprint ed. pap. 1.99 (978-1-4192-3278-7(9)); pap. 15.95 (978-1-4191-3278-0(4)) Kessinger Publishing, LLC.

Wiggins, Bethany. Cured. 2015. (ENG.). 320p. (YA). (gr. 7). pap. 9.99 (978-0-8027-3787-8(0), 9780802737878, Bloomsbury USA Childrens) Bloomsbury Publishing USA.

Wilce, Colin. The Valley & Daffodils (Rabbit Brook T. 2007. 80p. pap. 11.34 (978-1-4116-8792-9(2)) Lulu Pr., Inc.

Wildavsky, Rachel. The Secret of Rover. Caparo, Antonio, illus. (ENG.). 368p. (J). (gr. 3-7). 2015. pap. 7.95 (978-1-4197-1968-4(8)) 2011. 17.95 (978-0-8109-9710-3(X)) Abrams, Inc. (Amulet Bks.).

Willard, Eliza, et al. Love Is in the Air. 2004. (ENG.). 128p. (978-0-00-718094-3(2)) HarperCollins Pubs. Australia.

Williams, Carol Lynch & Earl, Cheri Pray. Wizard of Menlo Park, New Jersey. Oliphant, Manelle, illus. 2014. (Just in

Time Ser.). (ENG.). 140p. (J). pap. 9.95 *(978-1-938301-77-3(3))* Familius LLC.

Williams, Geoffrey T. The Great White Red Alert. Artful Doodlers, illus. Campbell, Tom, photos by. 2008. (Save Our Seas Adventure Bks.). (ENG.). 64p. (J). (gr. 4-7). 8.95 *(978-0-9800444-0-9(5))* Save Our Seas, Ltd.

—The Hammerheads of Treasure Island. 2010. (ENG., Illus.). 64p. (J). (gr. 3-7). 8.95 *(978-0-9800444-2-3(1))* Save Our Seas, Ltd.

Williamson, Linda. Groundhog Breakfast, Soft Petals, & a Roof That Don't Leak Too Much, 1 vol. Mollett, Irene, illus. 2009. 23p. pap. 24.95 *(978-1-60749-618-2(6))* America Star Bks.

Winter, Ariel S. One of a Kind. Hitch, David, illus. 2012. (ENG.). 32p. (J). (gr. -1-2). 15.99 *(978-1-4424-2016-8(2)*, Aladdin) Simon & Schuster Children's Publishing.

Wood, Brian. The Cramp Twins: Lucien's Little. 2005. (Illus.). 112p. 13.95 *(978-1-904674-01-6(1))* Reynolds & Hearn GBR. Dist: Trafalgar Square Publishing.

Wylie, Sarah. All These Lives, 1 vol. 2012. (ENG.). 256p. (YA). (gr. 7-12). 24.99 *(978-0-374-30208-5(1)*, 9780374302085, Farrar, Straus & Giroux (BYR)) Farrar, Straus & Giroux.

Yang, Belle. Always Come Home to Me. Yang, Belle, illus. 2007. (ENG., Illus.). 32p. (J). (gr. -1-3). 16.99 *(978-0-7636-2899-4(9))* Candlewick Pr.

Yang, Belle & Williams, Marcia. Archie's War: My Scrapbook of the First World War. Williams, Marcia, illus. 2007. (ENG., Illus.). 48p. (J). (gr. 3-7). 18.99 *(978-0-7636-3532-9(4))* Candlewick Pr.

Young, Moira. Blood Red Road. (Dust Lands Ser.: 1). (ENG.). (YA). (gr. 9). 2012. 480p. pap. 10.99 *(978-1-4424-2999-4(2))* 2011. (Illus.). 464p. 17.99 *(978-1-4424-2998-7(4))* McElderry, Margaret K. Bks. (McElderry, Margaret K. Bks.).

—Blood Red Road, 9 vols. 2011. (YA). 122.75 *(978-1-4618-0629-5(1))*; 286.75 *(978-1-4618-0634-9(8))*; 120.75 *(978-1-4618-0630-1(5))*; 120.75 *(978-1-4618-0633-2(X))*; 1.25 *(978-1-4640-2632-4(7))* Recorded Bks., Inc.

—Raging Star. (Dust Lands Ser.: 3). (ENG., Illus.). 448p. (YA). (gr. 9). 2015. pap. 10.99 *(978-1-4424-3003-7(6))* 2014. 17.99 *(978-1-4424-3002-0(8))* McElderry, Margaret K. Bks. (McElderry, Margaret K. Bks.).

—Rebel Heart. 2013. (Dust Lands Ser.: 2). (ENG., Illus.). 448p. (YA). (gr. 9). pap. 11.99 *(978-1-4424-3001-3(X)*, McElderry, Margaret K. Bks.) McElderry, Margaret K. Bks.

Yum, Hyewon. The Twins' Blanket. Yum, Hyewon, illus. 2011. (ENG., Illus.). 40p. (J). (gr. -1-1). 17.99 *(978-0-374-37972-8(6)*, 9780374379728, Farrar, Straus & Giroux (BYR)) Farrar, Straus & Giroux.

—The Twins' Little Sister. Yum, Hyewon, illus. 2014. (ENG., Illus.). 40p. (J). (gr. -1-1). 17.99 *(978-0-374-37973-5(4)*, 9780374379735, Farrar, Straus & Giroux (BYR)) Farrar, Straus & Giroux.

Zafón, Carlos Ruiz. The Midnight Palace. 2012. (ENG.). 320p. (YA). (gr. 7-17). pap. 10.00 *(978-0-316-04474-5(1))* Little, Brown Bks. for Young Readers.

Zaugg, Sandra L. Hidden Notes & High Seas. 2005. (Illus.). 95p. (J). *(978-0-8163-2052-3(7))* Pacific Pr. Pubns.

—Secret of the Desert Lights: A Story about Following God's Laws. 2009. (J). pap. 9.99 *(978-0-8163-2294-7(5))* Pacific Pr. Publishing Assn.

Zink, Michelle. Circle of Fire. 2012. (Prophecy of the Sisters Trilogy Ser.: 3). (ENG.). 368p. (YA). (gr. 7-17). pap. 22.99 *(978-0-316-03446-3(0))* Little, Brown Bks. for Young Readers.

—Prophecy of the Sisters. 2010. (Prophecy of the Sisters Trilogy Ser.: 1). (ENG.). 368p. (YA). (gr. 7-17). pap. 8.99 *(978-0-316-02741-0(3))* Little, Brown Bks. for Young Readers.

1, 2, 3 Happy Family. 2005. (J). bds. *(978-0-9769910-2-1(0))* Terrific Twins LLC.

TWINS—POETRY

Lewis, J. Patrick & Yolen, Jane. Take Two! A Celebration of Twins. Blackall, Sophie, illus. 2012. (ENG.). 72p. (J). (gr. -1-3). 17.99 *(978-0-7636-3702-6(5))* Candlewick Pr.

TYLER, JOHN, 1790-1862

Gunderson, Megan M. John Tyler, 1 vol. 2009. (United States Presidents Ser.). (ENG., Illus.). 40p. (YA). (gr. 3-6). 27.07 *(978-1-60453-477-1(X))* ABDO Publishing Co.

Havelin, Kate. John Tyler. 2005. (Presidential Leaders Ser.). (Illus.). 112p. (J). (gr. 3-7). lib. bdg. 29.27 *(978-0-8225-1395-7(1))* Lerner Publishing Group.

Venezia, Mike. John Tyler: Tenth President, 1841-1845. Venezia, Mike, illus. 2005. (Getting to Know the U. S. Presidents Ser.). (ENG., Illus.). 32p. (J). (gr. 3-4). per. 7.95 *(978-0-516-27484-3(8))*; 28.00 *(978-0-516-22615-6(0))* Scholastic Library Publishing. (Children's Pr.).

Zamora, Dulce. How to Draw the Life & Times of John Tyler. (Kid's Guide to Drawing the Presidents of the United States of America Ser.). 2009. 32p. (gr. 4-4). 50.50 *(978-1-61511-153-4(0)*, PowerKids Pr.) 2006. (YA). (gr. 2-5). 26.50 *(978-1-4042-2987-7(6))* Rosen Publishing Group, Inc., The.

TYPEWRITERS—FICTION

Ackerman, Peter & Dalton, Max. The Lonely Typewriter. 2014. (Illus.). 32p. (J). 16.95 *(978-1-56792-518-0(9))* Godine, David R. Pub.

Cronin, Doreen. Click, Clack, Moo: Cows That Type. Lewin, Betsy, illus. (Click, Clack Book Ser.). (ENG.). (J). (gr. -1-3). 2011. 32p. pap. 9.99 *(978-1-4424-3370-0(1))* 2010. 34p. bds. 7.99 *(978-1-4424-0889-0(8))* Little Simon. (Little Simon).

—Click, Clack, Moo: Cows That Type. 2004. 29.95 *(978-1-55592-104-0(3))* Weston Woods Studios, Inc.

Cronin, Doreen & Lewin, Betsy. Click, Clack, Moo: Cows That Type. 2014. 32p. pap. 8.00 *(978-1-61003-342-8(6))* Center for the Collaborative Classroom.

Cronin, Doreen & Simon and Schuster/LeapFrog Staff. Click, Clack, Moo: Cows That Type. Lewin, Betsy, illus. 2008. (J). 13.99 *(978-1-59319-936-4(8))* LeapFrog Enterprises, Inc.

Dorie & Me. 2003. (YA). per. *(978-1-59431-071-3(8)*, Ebks. On The Net) Write Words, Inc.

TYPEWRITING

Scholastic, Inc. Staff. Brain Play 1st-3rd. 2008. (J). 29.99 *(978-0-545-05207-8(6))* Scholastic, Inc.

—Brain Play Preschool-1st. 2008. (J). 29.99 *(978-0-439-81350-1(6))* Scholastic, Inc.

TYPOGRAPHY

see Printing

TYROL (AUSTRIA)—FICTION

De La Ramee, Louise & Ouida. Bimbi. 2007. 152p. per. 13.95 *(978-1-60312-344-0(X))*; 24.95 *(978-1-60312-682-3(1))* Aegypan.

U

U BOATS

see Submarines (Ships)

UFOS

see Unidentified Flying Objects

U. N.

see United Nations

UGANDA

Barlas, Robert & Yong, Jui Lin. Uganda. 2nd rev. ed. 2009. (Cultures of the World 19 Ser.). 144p. (gr. 6). 42.79 *(978-0-7614-4859-4(4))* Marshall Cavendish GBR. Dist: Marshall Cavendish Corp.

Barter, James. Idi Amin. 2004. (Heroes & Villains Ser.). (ENG., Illus.). 112p. (J). (gr. 7-10). 32.10 *(978-1-59018-553-7(6)*, Lucent Bks.) Cengage Gale.

Blauer, Ettagale & Lauré, Jason. Uganda. 2nd rev. ed. 2009. (Enchantment of the World Ser.). (ENG.). 144p. (J). (gr. 5-9). 40.00 *(978-0-531-20655-3(6))* Scholastic Library Publishing.

Braun, Eric. Uganda in Pictures. 2nd ed. 2005. (Visual Geography Series, Second Ser.). (ENG., Illus.). 80p. (gr. 5-12). lib. bdg. 31.93 *(978-0-8225-2397-0(3))* Lerner Publishing Group.

Dougherty, Steve. Idi Amin. 2010. (Wicked History Ser.). 128p. (J). (gr. 6-12). pap. 5.95 *(978-0-531-22354-3(X)*, Watts, Franklin) Scholastic Library Publishing.

Dougherty, Steven. Idi Amin. 2010. (Wicked History Ser.). (ENG., Illus.). 128p. (J). (gr. 5-8). 31.00 *(978-0-531-20754-3(4))* Scholastic Library Publishing.

Immell, Myra, ed. Uganda. 2012. (Genocide & Persecution Ser.). (ENG., Illus.). 240p. (gr. 10-12). lib. bdg. 36.45 *(978-0-7377-6258-7(6)*, Greenhaven Pr., Inc.) Cengage Gale.

Kubuitsile, Lauri. Uganda. Rotberg, Robert I., ed. 2012. (Evolution of Africa's Major Nations Ser.). (Illus.). 80p. (J). (gr. 7). 22.95 *(978-1-4222-2187-7(3))* Mason Crest.

—Uganda. 2011. (J). pap. *(978-1-4222-2215-7(2))* 2006. (Illus.). 79p. (YA). lib. bdg. 21.95 *(978-1-59084-816-6(0))* Mason Crest.

Lewin, Betsy & Lewin, Ted, illus. Gorilla Walk Gorilla Walk, 1 vol. 2014. (Adventures Around the World Ser.). (ENG.). 48p. (J). pap. 11.95 *(978-1-62014-182-3(5))* Lee & Low Bks., Inc.

McCollum, Sean. Deadly Despot: Idi Amin Rains Terror on Uganda. 2011. (J). pap. *(978-0-545-32936-1(1))* Scholastic, Inc.

Oghojafor, Kingsley. Uganda. 2004. (Countries of the World Ser.). (Illus.). 96p. (gr. 5-12). lib. bdg. 31.00 *(978-0-8368-3112-2(8))* Stevens, Gareth Publishing LLLP.

Sawyer, Kem Knapp. Grace Akallo & the Pursuit of Justice for Child Soldiers. 2015. (J). *(978-1-59935-456-9(X))* Reynolds, Morgan Inc.

Sobol, Richard. Breakfast in the Rainforest: A Visit with Mountain Gorillas. Sobol, Richard, photos by. 2010. (Traveling Photographer Ser.). (ENG., Illus.). 48p. (J). (gr. 1-4). pap. 7.99 *(978-0-7636-5134-3(6))* Candlewick Pr.

—Growing Peace: A Story of Farming, Music, & Religious Harmony, 1 vol. 2016. (ENG., Illus.). 40p. (J). 18.95 *(978-1-60060-450-8(1))* Lee & Low Bks., Inc.

UKRAINE

Abrams, Dennis. Viktor Yushchenko. 2007. (Modern World Leaders Ser.). (Illus.). 120p. (YA). (gr. 7-12). lib. bdg. 30.00 *(978-0-7910-9266-8(6))* Facts On File, Inc.

Bassis, Volodymyr & Dhilawala, Sakina. Ukraine. 2nd rev. ed. 2007. (Cultures of the World Ser.). 144p. (gr. 6). lib. bdg. 42.79 *(978-0-7614-2090-3(8)*, Benchmark Bks.) Marshall Cavendish Corp.

Cooper, Catherine W. Ukraine. 2nd rev. ed. 2006. (Modern World Nations Ser.). (Illus.). 120p. (YA). (gr. 7-12). lib. bdg. 35.00 *(978-0-7910-9207-1(0))* Facts On File, Inc.

Cruise, Robin. The Nuclear Disaster at Chernobyl. Taylor, Marjorie, illus. rev. ed. 2003. (Take Ten Ser.). 46p. (J). (gr. 4-18). pap. 4.95 *(978-1-58659-022-2(7))* Artesian Pr.

Grimberg, Tina. Out of Line: Growing up Soviet. 2007. (ENG., Illus.). 128p. (J). (gr. 5-18). 22.95 *(978-0-88776-803-3(2)*, Tundra Bks.) Tundra Bks. CAN. Dist: Penguin Random Hse. LLC.

Johnson, Rebecca. Chernobyl's Wild Kingdom: Life in the Dead Zone. 2014. (Illus.). 64p. (J). (gr. 6-12). lib. bdg. 34.60 *(978-1-4677-1154-8(3)*, Twenty-First Century Bks.) Lerner Publishing Group.

Kent, Deborah. Ukraine. 2015. (ENG., Illus.). 144p. (J). lib. bdg. 40.00 *(978-0-531-21251-6(3)*, Orchard Bks.) Scholastic Library Publishing.

Owings, Lisa. Pripyat: The Chernobyl Ghost Town. 2017. (Abandoned Places Ser.). (ENG., Illus.). 24p. (J). (gr. 3-7). lib. bdg. 25.95 ***(978-1-62617-697-3(3)***, Torque Bks.) Bellwether Media.

Owings, Lisa & Borgert-Spaniol, Megan. Ukraine. 2014. (Exploring Countries Ser.). (ENG., Illus.). 32p. (J). (gr. 3-7). lib. bdg. 26.95 *(978-1-62617-071-1(1)*, Blastoff! Readers) Bellwether Media.

Rissman, Rebecca. Chernobyl Disaster, 1 vol. 2013. (History's Greatest Disasters Ser.). (ENG.). 48p. (J). (gr. 3-6). lib. bdg. 32.79 *(978-1-61783-955-9(8))* ABDO Publishing Co.

—Chernobyl Disaster Paperback. 2013. (J). pap. 15.64 *(978-1-62403-020-8(3)*, Core Library) ABDO Publishing Co.

Stewart, Gail B. Ukraine: Then & Now. 2014. (The Former Soviet Union: Then & Now). (ENG., Illus.). 80p. (J). lib. bdg. *(978-1-60152-708-0(X))* ReferencePoint Pr., Inc.

Taylor, Peter Lane. The Secret of Priest's Grotto: A Holocaust Survival Story. 2007. (Holocaust Ser.). (Illus.). 64p. (J). (gr. 3-7). lib. bdg. 18.95 *(978-1-58013-260-2(X)*, Kar-Ben Publishing) Lerner Publishing Group.

Taylor, Peter Lane & Nicola, Christos. The Secret of Priest's Grotto: A Holocaust Survival Story. 2007. (Holocaust Ser.). (ENG., Illus.). 64p. (YA). (gr. 5-12). per. 8.95 *(978-1-58013-261-9(8)*, Kar-Ben Publishing) Lerner Publishing Group.

Toll, Nelly S. Behind the Secret Window: A Memoir of a Hidden Childhood During World War II. 2003. (ENG.). 176p. (J). (gr. 3-7). 5.99 *(978-0-14-230241-5(4)*, Puffin Books) Penguin Young Readers Group.

Vasilyeva, Anastasiya. Ukraine. 2017. (Countries We Come From Ser.). (ENG., Illus.). 32p. (J). (gr. -1-3). 19.95 ***(978-1-68402-059-1(X))*** Bearport Publishing Co., Inc.

Weber, Valerie J. I Come from Ukraine. 2006. (This Is My Story Ser.). (Illus.). 24p. (gr. 1-4). pap. 8.15 *(978-0-8368-7245-3(2)*, Weekly Reader Leveled Readers) Stevens, Gareth Publishing LLLP.

—I Come from Ukraine. 2006. (This Is My Story Ser.). (Illus.). 24p. (gr. 1-4). lib. bdg. 22.00 *(978-0-8368-7238-5(X)*, Weekly Reader Leveled Readers) Stevens, Gareth Publishing LLLP.

Wolny, Philip. Holodomor: The Ukrainian Famine-Genocide. 2017. (J). ***(978-1-5081-7732-6(5)***, Rosen Young Adult) Rosen Publishing Group, Inc., The.

UKRAINE—FICTION

Kimmel, Eric A. Even Higher! A Rosh Hashanah Story by I. L. Peretz. Weber, Jill, illus. 2010. (ENG.). 32p. (J). (gr. -1-3). pap. 6.95 *(978-0-8234-2298-2(4))* Holiday Hse., Inc.

Landau, Natasha, illus. Misha Loves to Sing. 2004. (J). *(978-0-615-12595-4(6))* Tikva Corp.

Parker, Derek. Children of Zone. 2015. (ENG., Illus.). 142p. pap. *(978-1-925138-91-7(7))* Connor Court Publishing Pty Ltd.

Spradlin, Michael P. The Enemy Above. 2016. (ENG.). 240p. (J). (gr. 3-7). 16.99 *(978-0-545-85782-6(1)*, Scholastic Pr.) Scholastic, Inc.

Tal, Eve. Double Crossing: A Jewish Immigration Story. 2005. (ENG.). 216p. (J). (gr. 7-9). 16.95 *(978-0-938317-94-4(6))* Cinco Puntos Pr.

The Trail of the Wooden Horse. 2007. 32p. pap. 4.50 *(978-0-8341-2284-0(7)*, 083-412-2847) Beacon Hill Pr. of Kansas City.

Watts, Irene N. Touched by Fire. 2013. (ENG., Illus.). 202p. (YA). (gr. 5-9). 17.95 *(978-1-77049-524-1(X)*, Tundra Bks.) Tundra Bks. CAN. Dist: Penguin Random Hse. LLC.

White, Andrea. Radiant Girl. 2008. (J). *(978-1-933979-35-9(6))*; (ENG.). 256p. (gr. 4-7). 19.95 *(978-1-933979-23-6(2)*, 9781933979236) Bright Sky Pr.

The Winter Horses. 2014. (ENG., Illus.). 288p. (YA). (gr. 7). 16.99 *(978-0-385-75543-6(0)*, Knopf Bks. for Young Readers) Random Hse. Children's Bks.

Zemko Tetro, Maria, tr. from UKR. How the Animals Built their House & Other Stories. 2008. (Illus.). 40p. (J). 14.95 *(978-0-9797372-5-1(7))* Winter Light Bks., Inc.

ULTRASONIC WAVES

Jennings, Terry J. Sound. 2009. (J). 28.50 *(978-1-59920-275-4(1))* Black Rabbit Bks.

ULYSSES (GREEK MYTHOLOGY)

see Odysseus (Greek Mythology)

UMBRELLAS AND PARASOLS—FICTION

Baum, L. Frank. Sky Island. 2007. 144p. (gr. 4-7). per. 11.95 *(978-1-60312-253-5(2))* Aegypan.

Bennett, Marcia Allen. Umbrella Town. 2012. (ENG.). 33p. (J). pap. 15.95 *(978-1-4327-8439-3(0))* Outskirts Pr., Inc.

Blyton, Enid. The Strange Umbrella: And Other Stories. Gregory, Sally, illus. 2013. (ENG.). 192p. (J). 9.95 *(978-1-84135-461-3(9))* Award Pubns. Ltd. GBR. Dist: Parkwest Pubns., Inc.

Brett, Jan. The Umbrella. Brett, Jan, illus. 2004. (ENG., Illus.). 32p. (J). (gr. -1-3). 18.99 *(978-0-399-24215-1(5)*, G.P. Putnam's Sons Books for Young Readers) Penguin Young Readers Group.

—The Umbrella. 2005. (Illus.). (J). (gr. k-3). 27.95 incl. audio *(978-0-8045-6931-6(2)*, SAC6931) Spoken Arts, Inc.

Bridges, Shirin Yim. The Umbrella Queen. Yoo, Taeeun, illus. 2008. (ENG.). 40p. (J). (gr. k-3). 16.99 *(978-0-06-075040-4(5)*, Greenwillow Bks.) HarperCollins Pubs.

Carlton, Glenis. Four Snails & an Umbrella. 2016. (ENG.). 22p. (J). 23.95 *(978-1-78612-332-9(0)*, f4b5e8cc-5376-41df-9771-3c2f8cfc4526) Austin, Stan AUS. Dist: Bookmasters Distribution.

Dahl, Michael. The Penguin's Power Parasol. Vecchio, Luciano, illus. 2016. (Batman Tales of the Batcave Ser.). (ENG.). 40p. (gr. 1-3). lib. bdg. 24.65 *(978-1-4965-4012-6(3)*, DC Super Heroes) Stone Arch Bks.

Delcoglin, Gwen. Bella's Umbrella. Delcoglin, Nathan, illus. 2007. 28p. (J). (gr. -1-3). per. 10.99 *(978-1-59879-315-4(2))* Lifevest Publishing, Inc.

Derubertis, Barbara. Umma Ungka's Unusual Umbrella. Alley, R. W., illus. 2011. (Animal Antics A to Z Set III Ser.). pap. 45.32 *(978-0-7613-8430-4(8))* Kane Press, Inc.

deRubertis, Barbara. Umma Ungka's Unusual Umbrella. Alley, R. W., illus. 2011. (Animal Antics A to Z Ser.). pap. 7.95 *(978-1-57565-346-4(X))*; lib. bdg. 22.60 *(978-1-57565-354-9(0))* Kane Press, Inc.

deRubertis, Barbara & DeRubertis, Barbara. Umma Ungka's Unusual Umbrella. Alley, R. W., illus. 2012. (Animal Antics A to Z Ser.). 32p. (J). (gr. 2 — 1). cd-rom 7.95 *(978-1-57565-414-0(8))* Kane Press, Inc.

Grace, Elora. Umbrellas Everywhere! 2006. (Neighborhood Readers Ser.). (ENG.). 8p. (gr. 1-3). pap. 5.15 *(978-1-4042-6791-6(3)*, Rosen Classroom) Rosen Publishing Group, Inc., The.

Grimaldi, Catherine. It's Raining! A Pop-Up Book with Patterns. Grimaldi, Catherine, illus. 2005. (ENG., Illus.). 18p. (J). (gr. -1-k). act. bk. ed. 16.99 *(978-1-85707-666-0(4))* Tango Bks. GBR. Dist: Independent Pubs. Group.

Holden, Pam. Umbrellas Go Up. 2015. (ENG., Illus.). 16p. (-1). pap. *(978-1-77654-073-0(5)*, Red Rocket Readers) Flying Start Bks.

Kahanek, Kristine Elizabeth. Katie & the Magic Umbrella: A Stormy Adventure. 2008. (Katie & the Magic Umbrella Ser.). (Illus.). 44p. (J). (gr. -1-4). 14.95 *(978-0-9801423-0-3(X))* K.Co.Kids, LLC.

Levine, Rhoda. Harrison Loved His Umbrella. Kuskin, Karla, illus. 2016. (ENG.). 56p. (J). (-k). 14.95 *(978-1-59017-991-8(9)*, NYR Children's Collection) New York Review of Bks., Inc., The.

Lloyd, Jennifer. Ella's Umbrellas. Spires, Ashley, illus. 2010. (ENG.). 32p. (J). (gr. -1-3). 16.95 *(978-1-897476-23-9(X))* Simply Read Bks. CAN. Dist: Ingram Publisher Services.

Palmer, Judd. The Umbrella. 2012. (ENG., Illus.). 52p. (J). pap. 9.95 *(978-1-897411-34-6(0))* Bayeux Arts, Inc. CAN. Dist: Chicago Distribution Ctr.

Robertson, Charmaine. Nancy's Beach Umbrella. 2016. (Rosen REAL Readers: STEM & STEAM Collection). 12p. (gr. 1-k). pap. 6.33 *(978-1-5081-2658-4(5)*, Rosen Classroom) Rosen Publishing Group, Inc., The.

Robertson, Chris. My Yellow Umbrella. Robertson, Chris, illus. 2013. (Illus.). 32p. pap. 9.99 *(978-1-62395-543-4(2))* Xist Publishing.

Schubert, Dieter. The Umbrella Doodle Book. 2012. (ENG., Illus.). 48p. (J). (gr. -1). 7.95 *(978-1-935954-15-6(6)*, 9781935954156) Lemniscaat USA.

Schubert, Ingrid & Schubert, Dieter. The Umbrella. 2011. (ENG., Illus.). 40p. (J). (gr. -1). 16.95 *(978-1-935954-00-2(8)*, 9781935954002) Lemniscaat USA.

Stevens, Terry. Tommy, the Wizard & the Magic Umbrella. 2006. (Illus.). 60p. pap. *(978-1-84401-752-2(4))* Athena Pr.

Thomas, Gerry. The Umbrella Race. 2010. 25p. (J). pap. 25.95 *(978-1-4327-6006-9(8))* Outskirts Pr., Inc.

Tremblay, Carole. Floop's New Umbrella. Beshwaty, Steve, illus. 2009. (Floop Ser.). 24p. (J). (gr. -1-k). 22.60 *(978-1-60754-347-3(8))*; pap. 8.15 *(978-1-60754-348-0(6))* Windmill Bks.

Under the Big Green Umbrella. 2008. (J). spiral bd. *(978-0-9793930-4-4(3))* Dandelion Publishing.

Wilder, Vickie. The Umbrella. 2013. 24p. pap. 11.97 *(978-1-62212-534-0(7)*, Strategic Bk. Publishing) Strategic Book Publishing & Rights Agency (SBPRA).

UNDERGROUND, ANTI-COMMUNIST

see Anti-Communist Movements

UNDERGROUND MOVEMENTS (WORLD WAR, 1939-1945)

see World War, 1939-1945—Underground Movements

UNDERGROUND RAILROAD

see also Slavery—United States

Abnett, Dan. Harriet Tubman & the Underground Railroad. (Jr. Graphic Biographies Ser.). (ENG.). 24p. 2009. (J). (gr. 2-3). 47.90 *(978-1-61513-816-6(1)*, PowerKids Pr.) 2007. (Illus.). (J). (gr. 2-5). lib. bdg. 25.25 *(978-1-4042-3393-5(8))* 2007. (Illus.). (gr. 3-8). pap. 10.60 *(978-1-4042-2146-8(8)*, PowerKids Pr.) Rosen Publishing Group, Inc., The.

—Harriet Tubman y el Ferrocarril Clandestino. 2009. (Historietas Juveniles: Biografías (Jr. Graphic Biographies) Ser.). (SPA., Illus.). 24p. (J). (gr. 2-5). 25.25 *(978-1-4358-8563-9(5))*; (gr. 3-8). pap. 10.60 *(978-1-4358-3320-3(1))* Rosen Publishing Group, Inc., The.

Adler, David A. Harriet Tubman & the Underground Railroad. 2012. (ENG.). 144p. (J). 18.95 *(978-0-8234-2365-1(4))* Holiday Hse., Inc.

Allen, Nancy. The Underground Railroad. 2015. (ENG.). 32p. (gr. 3-6). 32.79 *(978-1-63430-043-8(2))* Rourke Educational Media.

Allen, Thomas B. Harriet Tubman, Secret Agent: How Daring Slaves & Free Blacks Spied for the Union During the Civil War. 2008. (ENG., Illus.). 192p. (J). (gr. 5). 5.95 *(978-1-4263-0401-9(3)*, National Geographic Children's Bks.) National Geographic Society.

Anderson, Jane. Harriet Tubman & the Underground Railroad. 2005. (J). pap. *(978-1-4108-4202-2(9))* Benchmark Education Co.

Arnéz, Lynda. My Journey on the Underground Railroad. 2016. (My Place in History Ser.). (ENG., Illus.). 24p. (J). (gr. 2-3). 22.60 *(978-1-4824-3997-7(2))*; pap. 8.15 *(978-1-4824-4010-2(5))* Stevens, Gareth Publishing LLLP.

Ashby, Ruth. The Underground Railroad. 2016. (Civil War Chronicles Ser.: Vol. 1). (ENG., Illus.). (J). (gr. 4-6). 23.95 ***(978-1-59687-515-9(1)***, ipicturebooks) ibooks, Inc.

Barton, Jen. What's Your Story, Harriet Tubman? 2015. (Cub Reporter Meets Famous Americans Ser.). (ENG., Illus.). 32p. (J). (gr. k-3). pap. 8.99 *(978-1-4677-8533-4(4)*, Lerner Pubns.) Lerner Publishing Group.

Baumann, Susan K. Harriet Tubman. 2013. (Jr. Graphic African American History Ser.). 24p. (J). (gr. 3-6). 25.25 *(978-1-4777-1312-9(3))*; pap. 10.60 *(978-1-4777-1449-2(9))* Rosen Publishing Group, Inc., The. (PowerKids Pr.).

—Harriet Tubman: Conductor of the Underground Railroad. 2013. (Jr. Graphic African American History Ser.). 24p. (J). (gr. 3-6). pap. 63.60 *(978-1-4777-1450-8(2)*, PowerKids Pr.) Rosen Publishing Group, Inc., The.

Blue, Rose, et al. Harriet Tubman: Riding the Freedom Train. 2003. (Gateway Biographies Ser.: 4). (ENG., Illus.). 48p. (gr. 4-8). lib. bdg. 26.60 *(978-0-7613-2571-0(9)*, Millbrook Pr.) Lerner Publishing Group.

Bolte, Mari. Flight to Freedom! Nickolas Flux & the Underground Railroad, 1 vol. Foster, Brad W. & Simmons, Mark, illus. 2014. (Nickolas Flux History Chronicles Ser.). (ENG.). 32p. (gr. 3-4). lib. bdg. 30.65 *(978-1-4914-0254-2(7)*, Graphic Library) Capstone Press of Coughlan Cos.

Brill, Marlene Targ. Allen Jay Y el Ferrocarril Subterraneo; Allen Jay & the Underground Railroad. 2008. pap. 40.95 *(978-0-8225-9679-0(2))* Lerner Publishing Group.

Burgan, Michael. The Underground Railroad. Schwarz, Philip, ed. 2006. (Slavery in the Americas Ser.). (Illus.). 112p. (gr. 5-8). 35.00 *(978-0-8160-6137-2(8))* Facts On File, Inc.

Carson, Mary Kay. The Underground Railroad for Kids: From Slavery to Freedom with 21 Activities. 2005. (For Kids Ser.). (ENG., Illus.). 176p. (J). (gr. 4). pap. 18.95 *(978-1-55652-554-4(0))* Chicago Review Pr., Inc.

—Which Way to Freedom? And Other Questions about the Underground Railroad. 2015. (Good Question! Ser.). (ENG., Illus.). 40p. (J). (gr. 2). 12.95 *(978-1-4549-0784-8(3))* Sterling Publishing Co., Inc.

Cary, Lorene. Free! Great Escapes from Slavery on the Underground Railroad. 2011. (J). pap. 15.00 *(978-0-9819560-3-9(3))*; 2nd ed. (ENG., Illus.). 86p. pap. 20.95 *(978-0-9819560-2-2(5))* New City Community Pr.

Conkling, Winifred. Passenger on the Pearl: The True Story of Emily Edmonson's Flight from Slavery. (ENG., 176p. (YA). (gr. 7-10). 2016. Illus.). pap. 10.95 *(978-1-61620-550-8(4))*

T U V

2015. 17.95 *(978-1-61620-196-8(7),* 73196) Algonquin Bks. of Chapel Hill.

Connors, Kathleen. The Life of Harriet Tubman, Vol. 1. 2014. (Famous Lives Ser.). (ENG.). 24p. (J). (gr. 1-2). 22.60 *(978-1-4824-0412-8(5))* Stevens, Gareth Publishing LLLP.

Cosson, M. J. Harriet Tubman, 1 vol. 2007. (Essential Lives Set 1 Ser.). (ENG., Illus.). 112p. (J). (gr. 6-12). lib. bdg. 35.64 *(978-1-59928-842-0(7))* ABDO Publishing Co.

DeFord, Diane. Harriet Tubman. 2009. pap. 13.25 *(978-1-60559-061-5(4))* Hameray Publishing Group, Inc.

Dendy, Christina. Underground Railroad: Defining Moments in Canadian History. 2011. (Illus.). 32p. (gr. 5-8). *(978-1-77071-691-9(2))* Weigl Educational Pubs. Ltd.

Doak, Robin S. Harriet Tubman. 2015. (ENG., Illus.). 48p. (J). pap. 6.95 *(978-0-531-21757-3(4));* lib. bdg. *(978-0-531-21595-1(4))* Scholastic, Inc. (Orchard Bks.).

Dunn, Joe. The Underground Railroad, 1 vol. 2007. (Graphic History Ser.). (ENG., Illus.). 32p. (gr. 3-7). 28.50 *(978-1-60270-080-2(X),* Graphic Planet- Nonfiction) ABDO Publishing Co.

Edison, Erin. Harriet Tubman. 2013. (Great Women in History Ser.). (ENG.). 24p. (gr. k-1). pap. 35.70 *(978-1-62065-860-4(7));* pap. 6.29 *(978-1-62065-859-8(3))* Capstone Press of Coughlan Cos. (Pebble Bks.).

Eskridge, Ann E. Slave Uprisings & Runaways: Fighting for Freedom & the Underground Railroad. 2004. (Slavery in American History Ser.). (Illus.). 128p. (J). lib. bdg. 27.94 *(978-0-7660-2154-9(8))* Enslow Pubs., Inc.

Evans, Shane W. Underground: Finding the Light to Freedom. Evans, Shane W., illus. 2011. (ENG., Illus.). 32p. (J). (gr. -1-3). 16.99 *(978-1-59643-538-4(0),* 9781596435384) Roaring Brook Pr.

Feinstein, Stephen. Read about Harriet Tubman. 2005. (I Like Biographies! Ser.). (Illus.). 24p. (J). lib. bdg. 22.60 *(978-0-7660-2591-2(8),* Enslow Elementary) Enslow Pubs., Inc.

Findley, Violet. Easy Reader Biographies: Harriet Tubman: Follow the North Star. 2007. (ENG.). 16p. pap. 2.99 *(978-0-439-92330-9(1),* Teaching Resources) Scholastic, Inc.

Flatt, Lizann. The Underground Railroad. 2015. (ENG.). 48p. (J). *(978-0-7787-1551-1(5))* Crabtree Publishing Co.

Ford, Carin T. Slavery & the Underground Railroad: Bound for Freedom. 2004. (Civil War Library). (Illus.). 48p. (J). lib. bdg. 25.27 *(978-0-7660-2251-5(X))* Enslow Pubs., Inc.

—The Underground Railroad & Slavery Through Primary Sources. 2013. (Civil War Through Primary Sources Ser.). 48p. (J). (gr. 4-10). pap. 8.95 *(978-1-4644-0185-5(3));* lib. bdg. 25.27 *(978-0-7660-4127-1(1))* Enslow Pubs., Inc.

Fradin, Dennis B. The Underground Railroad. 2011. (Great Escapes Ser.). 80p. (gr. 6). 34.21 *(978-1-60870-476-7(9))* Marshall Cavendish Corp.

Fradin, Dennis Brindell. The Underground Railroad. 2008. (Turning Points in U. S. History Ser.). 48p. (gr. 3-18). lib. bdg. 31.36 *(978-0-7614-3014-8(8),* Benchmark Bks.) Marshall Cavendish Corp.

Ganeri, Anita. Harriet Tubman: The Life of an African-American Abolitionist. Shone, Rob, illus. 2005. (Graphic Biographies Ser.). (ENG.). 48p. (gr. 5-8). pap. 14.05 *(978-1-4042-5172-4(3))* Rosen Publishing Group, Inc., The.

Gayle, Sharon. Harriet Tubman & the Freedom Train. Marshall, Felicia, illus. 2003. (Ready-To-read SOFA Ser.). (ENG.). 32p. (J). (gr. 1-3). pap. 3.99 *(978-0-689-85480-4(3),* Simon Spotlight) Simon Spotlight.

Glatzer, Jenna. Beacon to Freedom: The Story of a Conductor on the Underground Railroad. Glenn, Ebony, illus. 2017. (Encounter: Narrative Nonfiction Picture Bks.). (ENG.). 40p. (gr. 3-5). lib. bdg. 28.65 *(978-1-5157-3496-3(X))* Encounter Bks.

Gold, Susan Dudley. Harriet Tubman & the Underground Railroad. 2015. (Primary Sources of the Abolitionist Movement Ser.). (ENG., Illus.). 64p. (J). (gr. 6-6). 34.21 *(978-1-5026-0522-1(8))* Cavendish Square Publishing.

Hansen, Joyce & McGowan, Gary. Freedom Roads: Searching for the Underground Railroad. Ransome, James E., illus. 2003. (ENG.). 166p. (J). (gr. 5-9). 18.95 *(978-0-8126-2673-5(7))* Cricket Bks.

Hillstrom, Laurie Collier. The Underground Railroad. 2015. (Defining Moments Ser.). (Illus.). 240p. (J). lib. bdg. 55.00 *(978-0-7808-1346-5(4))* Omnigraphics, Inc.

Hudson, Wade. The Underground Railroad. 2005. (Cornerstones of Freedom Ser.). (ENG., Illus.). 48p. (J). (gr. 4-6). 26.00 *(978-0-516-23630-8(X),* Children's Pr.) Scholastic Library Publishing.

Huey, Lois Miner. American Archaeology Uncovers the Underground Railroad. 2009. (American Archaeology Ser.). 64p. (gr. 5-6). 31.36 *(978-0-7614-4267-7(7))* Marshall Cavendish Corp.

Jones, Viola & Wolny, Philip. A Primary Source Investigation of the Underground Railroad. 2015. (Uncovering American History Ser.). (ENG.). 64p. (J). (gr. 5-6). 32.95 *(978-1-4994-3517-7(7),* Rosen Central) Rosen Publishing Group, Inc., The.

Kennon, Caroline. Depots of the Underground Railroad. 2016. (Hidden History Ser.). 00032p. (J). pap. 10.50 *(978-1-4824-5794-0(6))* Stevens, Gareth Publishing LLLP.

Kernan, Elizabeth. Harriet Tubman: A Lesson in Bravery. 2009. (Reading Room Collection 2 Ser.). 24p. (gr. 3-4). 42.50 *(978-1-60851-966-8(X),* PowerKids Pr.) Rosen Publishing Group, Inc., The.

Krasner, Barbara. Harriet Tubman: Abolitionist & Conductor of the Underground Railroad. 2017. (Women Who Changed History Ser.). 48p. (gr. 10-12). lib. bdg. 26.85 ***(978-1-68048-659-9(4),*** Britannica Educational Publishing) Rosen Publishing Group, Inc., The.

Landau, Elaine. Fleeing to Freedom on the Underground Railroad: The Courageous Slaves, Agents, & Conductors. 2006. (People's History Ser.). (ENG., Illus.). 88p. (gr. 5-12). lib. bdg. 33.26 *(978-0-8225-3490-7(8))* Lerner Publishing Group.

—The Underground Railroad: Would You Help Them Escape? 2014. (What Would You Do? Ser.). (Illus.). 48p. (J). (gr. 3-4). 25.27 *(978-0-7660-4225-4(1))* Enslow Pubs., Inc.

Lantier, Patricia. Harriet Tubman: Conductor on the Underground Railroad. 2009. (Voices for Freedom Ser.). (ENG., Illus.). 64p. (J). (gr. 5-8). pap. *(978-0-7787-4838-0(3));* lib. bdg. *(978-0-7787-4822-9(7))* Crabtree Publishing Co.

Lassieur, Allison & Doeden, Matt. The Civil War Experience: An Interactive History Adventure, 1 vol. 2014. (You Choose: History Ser.). (ENG.). 328p. (gr. 3-4). pap. 14.95 *(978-1-4765-0839-9(9),* You Choose Bks.) Capstone Press of Coughlan Cos.

Leavitt, Amie Jane. Harriet Tubman. 2007. (What's So Great About... ? Ser.). (Illus.). 32p. (J). (gr. 2-4). lib. bdg. 25.70 *(978-1-58415-577-5(9))* Mitchell Lane Pubs., Inc.

Llanas, Sheila Griffin. The Underground Railroad: A History Perspectives Book. 2013. (Perspectives Library). (ENG., Illus.). 32p. (J). (gr. 4-8). 28.50 *(978-1-62431-423-0(6),* 202812); pap. 14.21 *(978-1-62431-499-5(6),* 202814) Cherry Lake Publishing.

Maloof, Torrey. Harriet Tubman: Leading Others to Liberty. 2017. (Primary Source Readers Ser.). (Illus.). 32p. (J). (gr. 4-5). pap. 8.99 *(978-1-4938-3802-8(4))* Teacher Created Materials, Inc.

Mara, Wil. Harriet Tubman. 2013. (ENG.). 32p. (C). pap. 9.95 *(978-0-531-24703-7(1))* National Geographic School Publishing, Inc.

—Harriet Tubman. 2013. (Rookie Biographies(r) Ser.). (ENG.). 32p. (J). lib. bdg. 23.00 *(978-0-531-24737-2(6))* Scholastic Library Publishing.

Marsh, Carole. Underground Railroad: Path to Freedom. 2006. 28p. pap. 5.95 *(978-0-635-06359-5(X))* Gallopade International.

Martin, Michael & Martin, Michael J. Harriet Tubman & the Underground Railroad, 1 vol. Hoover, Dave & Anderson, Bill, illus. 2005. (Graphic History Ser.). (ENG.). 32p. (gr. 3-4). 30.65 *(978-0-7368-3829-0(5),* Graphic Library) Capstone Press of Coughlan Cos.

McConaghy, Lorraine & Bentley, Judy. Free Boy: A True Story of Slave & Master. 2013. (V Ethel Willis White Bks.). (ENG., Illus.). 112p. pap. 18.95 *(978-0-295-99271-6(9))* Univ. of Washington Pr.

McDonnell, Julia. Harriet Tubman in Her Own Words. 2016. (Eyewitness to History Ser.). (ENG., Illus.). 32p. (J). (gr. 4-5). pap. 10.50 *(978-1-4824-4066-9(0))* Stevens, Gareth Publishing LLLP.

McDonough, Yona Zeldis. What Was the Underground Railroad? Mortimer, Lauren & Bennett, James, illus. 2013. (What Was? Ser.). (ENG.). 112p. (J). (gr. 3-7). 5.99 *(978-0-448-46712-2(7),* Penguin Workshop) Penguin Young Readers Group.

—What Was the Underground Railroad? 2013. (What Was... ? Ser.). lib. bdg. 16.00 *(978-0-606-32130-3(6),* Turtleback) Turtleback Bks.

—Who Was Harriet Tubman? Harrison, Nancy, illus. 2003. (Who Was... ? Ser.). 106p. (gr. 4-7). 15.00 *(978-0-7569-1590-2(2))* Perfection Learning Corp.

McGraw-Hill - Jamestown Education Staff. American History Ink Bk. 4: The Underground Railroad. 2007. (Jt Am Hist Graph Novel Ser.). (ENG.). 24p. (gr. 6-12). spiral bd. 12.72 *(978-0-07-878026-4(8),* 0078780268) McGraw-Hill Cos., The.

McNamara, Margaret. Discover the Underground Railroad. 2006. (J). pap. *(978-1-4108-6449-9(9))* Benchmark Education Co.

—The Underground Railroad. 2006. (J). pap. *(978-1-4108-6446-8(4))* Benchmark Education Co.

National Park Service Staff, ed. Discovering the Underground Railroad: Junior Ranger Activity Book. 2012. (ENG., Illus.). 20p. (gr. -1-6). pap. 6.00 *(978-0-16-090018-1(2))* National Park Service Div. of Pubns.

Norwich, Grace. I Am #6: Harriet Tubman. 2013. (I Am Ser.: 6). (ENG.). 128p. (J). (gr. 2-5). pap. 5.99 *(978-0-545-48436-7(7),* Scholastic Paperbacks) Scholastic, Inc.

—I Am Harriet Tubman. Simon, Ute, illus. 2013. 127p. (J). *(978-0-545-61344-6(2))* Scholastic, Inc.

Otfinoski, Steven. From Fugitive to Freedom: The Story of the Underground Railroad. 2017. (Tangled History Ser.). (ENG., Illus.). 112p. (gr. 3-4). lib. bdg. 31.99 *(978-1-5157-3604-2(0))* Capstone Press of Coughlan Cos.

Pace, Lorenzo. Harriet Tubman & My Grandmother's Quilts, 1 vol. 2015. (African American Quartet Ser.). (ENG., Illus.). 48p. (J). 30.25 *(978-1-4777-9289-6(9),* Windmill Bks.) Rosen Publishing Group, Inc., The.

Perrin, Pat & Coleman, Wim. The Mystery of the Vanishing Slaves. 2004. (Cover-To-Cover Books). (Illus.). 64p. pap. 9.00 *(978-0-7891-5874-1(4));* (J). (gr. 4-7). lib. bdg. 17.95 *(978-0-7569-1041-9(2))* Perfection Learning Corp.

Petry, Ann & Reynolds, Jason. Harriet Tubman: Conductor on the Underground Railroad. 2007. (ENG.). 256p. (J). (gr. 3-7). pap. 7.99 *(978-0-06-446181-8(5),* Amistad) HarperCollins Pubs.

Pferdehirt, Julia. Caroline Quarlls & the Underground Railroad. 2008. (Badger Biographies Ser.). (ENG., Illus.). 120p. (J). (gr. 3-7). per. 12.95 *(978-0-87020-388-6(6))* Wisconsin Historical Society.

—Freedom Train North: Stories of the Underground Railroad in Wisconsin. Butler, Jerry, illus. Date not set. (J). (gr. 3-8). pap. 10.00 *(978-0-9664925-0-7(1))* Living History Pr.

Pierce, Alan. Underground Railroad, 1 vol. 2005. (American Moments Ser.). (ENG., Illus.). 48p. (gr. 4-8). 27.07 *(978-1-59197-942-5(0),* Abdo & Daughters) ABDO Publishing Co.

Prince, Bryan. I Came As a Stranger: The Underground Railroad. 2004. (ENG., Illus.). 168p. (J). (gr. 5). pap. 15.95 *(978-0-88776-667-1(6),* Tundra Bks.) Tundra Bks. CAN. Dist: Penguin Random Hse. LLC.

Raatma, Lucia. The Underground Railroad. 2011. (Cornerstones of Freedom, Third Ser.). (Illus.). 64p. (J). (ENG.). pap. 8.95 *(978-0-531-26568-0(4));* lib. bdg. 30.00 *(978-0-531-25043-3(1))* Scholastic Library Publishing. (Children's Pr.).

Rajczak, Michael. The Underground Railroad, Vol. 1. 2014. (What You Didn't Know about History Ser.). (ENG.). 24p. (J). (gr. 2-3). 22.60 *(978-1-4824-0601-6(2))* Stevens, Gareth Publishing LLLP.

Rausch, Monica. Harriet Tubman. 2007. (Great Americans Ser.). (Illus.). 24p. (gr. 1-4). lib. bdg. 22.00 *(978-0-8368-7686-4(5),* Weekly Reader Leveled Readers) Stevens, Gareth Publishing LLLP.

Rausch, Monica L. Harriet Tubman. 2007. (Grandes personajes (Great Americans) Ser.). (ENG & SPA., Illus.). 24p. (gr. 1-4). lib. bdg. 22.00 *(978-0-8368-7985-8(6),* Weekly Reader Leveled Readers) Stevens, Gareth Publishing LLLP.

Roop, Peter & Roop, Connie. Who Conducted the Underground Railroad? And Other Questions about the Path to Freedom. 2008. (Illus.). 44p. (J). pap. *(978-0-439-02524-9(9))* Scholastic, Inc.

Sawyer, Kem Knapp. The Amazing Underground Railroad. 2012. (Stories in American History Ser.). (Illus.). 128p. (J). (gr. 5-18). 33.27 *(978-0-7660-3951-3(X)); (978-1-4645-0470-9(9)); (978-1-4646-0470-6(3))* Enslow Pubs., Inc.

—The Amazing Underground Railroad: Stories in American History. 2012. (Stories in American History Ser.). (Illus.). 128p. (J). (gr. 5-18). pap. 10.95 *(978-1-4644-0021-6(0))* Enslow Pubs., Inc.

—Harriet Tubman - A Photographic Story of a Life. 2010. (DK Biography Ser.). (ENG.). 128p. (J). (gr. 5-12). 6.99 *(978-0-7566-5806-9(3),* DK Children) Dorling Kindersley Publishing, Inc.

Schraff, Anne. The Life of Harriet Tubman: Moses of the Underground Railroad. 2014. (Legendary African Americans Ser.). (Illus.). 96p. (J). (gr. 6-12). 27.94 *(978-0-7660-6137-8(X))* Enslow Pubs., Inc.

Senker, Cath. Who Traveled the Underground Railroad?, 1 vol. 2014. (Primary Source Detectives Ser.). (ENG., Illus.). 64p. (gr. 7-8). lib. bdg. 35.99 *(978-1-4329-9603-1(7))* Heinemann-Raintree.

Shone, Rob. Harriet Tubman: The Life of an African-American Abolitionist. 2009. (Graphic Nonfiction Biographies Ser.). (ENG.). 48p. (YA). (gr. 4-5). 58.50 *(978-1-61513-018-4(7),* Rosen Reference) Rosen Publishing Group, Inc., The.

Shone, Rob & Ganeri, Anita. Harriet Tubman: The Life of an African-American Abolitionist. 2005. (Graphic Nonfiction Biographies Ser.). (ENG., Illus.). 48p. (J). (gr. 4-7). lib. bdg. 31.95 *(978-1-4042-0245-0(5))* Rosen Publishing Group, Inc., The.

Simon, Barbara Brooks. Escape to Freedom: The Underground Railroad Adventures of Callie & William. 2004. (I Am American Ser.). (ENG., Illus.). 40p. (J). (gr. 3-7). pap. 6.99 *(978-0-7922-6551-1(3),* National Geographic Children's Bks.) National Geographic Society.

—The Underground Railroad: Voices from America's Past. 2007. (Nonfiction Reading & Writing Workshops Ser.). (ENG., Illus.). 40p. (J). pap. 19.95 *(978-0-7922-4549-0(0))* National Geographic School Publishing, Inc.

Simons, Barbara Brooks. Escape to Freedom the Underground Railroad: Set Of 6. 2011. (Navigators Ser.). (J). pap. 48.00 net. *(978-1-4108-6261-7(5))* Benchmark Education Co.

—Escape to Freedom: the Underground Railroad: Text Pairs. 2008. (Bridges/Navigators Ser.). (J). (gr. 5). 81.00 *(978-1-4108-8415-2(5))* Benchmark Education Co.

Skelton, Renee. Harriet Tubman A Woman of Courage. 2005. 2005p. (J). lib. bdg. 15.00 *(978-1-4242-0849-4(1))* Fitzgerald Bks.

—A Woman of Courage. 2005. (Time for Kids Ser.). (ENG., Illus.). 48p. (J). (gr. 2-4). pap. 3.99 *(978-0-06-057607-3(3))* HarperCollins Pubs.

Skelton, Renee & Time for Kids Editors. Time for Kids: A Woman of Courage. 2005. (Time for Kids Ser.). (ENG., Illus.). 48p. (J). 16.99 *(978-0-06-057608-0(1))* HarperCollins Pubs.

Slavicek, Louise Chipley. Harriet Tubman & the Underground Railroad. 2006. (Lucent Library of Black History). (ENG., Illus.). 104p. (J). (gr. 3-7). lib. bdg. 34.80 *(978-1-59018-927-6(2),* Lucent Bks.) Cengage Gale.

Stearns, Dan. Harriet Tubman & the Underground Railroad. 2006. (In the Footsteps of American Heroes Ser.). (Illus.). 64p. (gr. 5-12). pap. 14.05 *(978-0-8368-6433-5(6));* lib. bdg. 34.00 *(978-0-8368-6428-1(X))* Stevens, Gareth Publishing LLLP. (Gareth Stevens Secondary Library).

Stein, R. Conrad. Escaping Slavery on the Underground Railroad. 2008. (From Many Cultures, One History Ser.). (Illus.). 128p. (J). (gr. 5-18). lib. bdg. 33.27 *(978-0-7660-2799-2(6))* Enslow Pubs., Inc.

—Harriet Tubman: On My Underground Railroad I Never Ran My Train off the Track. 2010. (Americans—the Spirit of a Nation Ser.). (Illus.). 128p. (J). lib. bdg. 33.27 *(978-0-7660-3481-5(X))* Enslow Pubs., Inc.

Taylor, Charlotte & Feinstein, Stephen. Harriet Tubman: Hero of the Underground Railroad. 2015. (Exceptional African Americans Ser.). (ENG.). 24p. (J). (gr. 3-4). pap. 9.35 *(978-0-7660-7126-1(X));* (Illus.). 22.60 *(978-0-7660-7128-5(6))* Enslow Pubs., Inc.

Taylor, Charlotte & Stein, R. Conrad. The Underground Railroad. 2015. (Our Shared History Ser.). (ENG., Illus.). 128p. (J). (gr. 7-7). lib. bdg. 37.27 *(978-0-7660-7014-1(X))* Enslow Pubs., Inc.

Taylor, Marian. Harriet Tubman. 2004. (Black Americans of Achievement Ser.). (Illus.). 112p. (gr. 6-12). 35.00 *(978-0-7910-8166-2(4),* Chelsea Hse.) Facts On File, Inc.

Troupe, Thomas Kingsley. Harriet Tubman's Escape: a Fly on the Wall History. Tejido, Jomike, illus. 2017. (Fly on the Wall History Ser.). (ENG.). 32p. (gr. 1-3). lib. bdg. 27.32 *(978-1-4795-9788-8(0))* Picture Window Bks.

The Underground Railroad: The Journey to Freedom. 2010. (Milestones in American History Ser.). (Illus.). 152p. (gr. 6-12). 35.00 *(978-1-60413-694-4(4),* Chelsea Hse.) Facts On File, Inc.

Waxman, Laura Hamilton. How Did Slaves Find a Route to Freedom? And Other Questions about the Underground Railroad. 2011. (Six Questions of American History Ser.). (ENG.). 48p. (gr. 4-6). pap. 56.72 *(978-0-7613-7641-5(0));* pap. 9.95 *(978-0-7613-7129-8(X));* lib. bdg. 30.60 *(978-0-7613-5229-7(5))* Lerner Publishing Group.

Weidt, Maryann N. Harriet Tubman. 2003. (History Maker Bios Ser.). (Illus.). 47p. (J). 26.60 *(978-0-8225-4676-4(0),* Lerner Pubns.) Lerner Publishing Group.

Weymouth Seguin, Marilyn. The Freedom Stairs: The Story of Adam Lowry Rankin, Underground Railroad Conductor. 2004. (Illus.). 93p. (J). (gr. 3-7). per. 12.95 net. *(978-0-8283-2084-9(5))* Branden Bks.

Wheeler, Jill C. Harriet Tubman. 2003. (Breaking Barriers Ser.). (Illus.). 64p. (gr. 3-8). 27.07 *(978-1-57765-908-2(2),* Abdo & Daughters) ABDO Publishing Co.

Wolny, Philip. The Underground Railroad: A Primary Source History of the Journey to Freedom. (Primary Sources in American History Ser.). 64p. (gr. 5-8). 2009. 58.50 *(978-1-60851-505-9(2))* 2004. (Illus.). (J). lib. bdg. 31.95 *(978-0-8239-4008-0(X),* Rosen Reference) Rosen Publishing Group, Inc., The.

UNDERGROUND RAILROAD—FICTION

Bradbury, Jennifer. River Runs Deep. 2015. (ENG., Illus.). 336p. (J). (gr. 4-8). 17.99 *(978-1-4424-6824-5(6),* Atheneum Bks. for Young Readers) Simon & Schuster Children's Publishing.

Brill, Marlene Targ. Allen Jay & the Underground Railroad, 4 bks., Set. Porter, Janice Lee, illus. 2007. (Readalongs for Beginning Readers Ser.). (J). (gr. 1-3). pap. 37.95 incl. audio *(978-1-59519-947-8(0))* Live Oak Media.

—Allen Jay y el Ferrocarril Subterraneo. Porter, Janice Lee, illus. 2007. (Yo Solo - Historia (on My Own - History) Ser.). 48p. (J). (gr. 4-7). per. 6.95 *(978-0-8225-7787-4(9))* Lerner Publishing Group.

—Allen Jay y el Ferrocarril Subtermeo. Translations.com Staff, tr. from ENG. Porter, Janice Lee, illus. 2007. (Yo Solo - Historia (on My Own - History) Ser.). (SPA.). 48p. (gr. 2-4). lib. bdg. 25.26 *(978-0-8225-7784-3(4))* Lerner Publishing Group.

—The Underground Railroad Adventure of Allen Jay, Antislavery Activist. Hammond, Ted & Carbajal, Richard Pimentel, illus. 2011. (History's Kid Heroes Set III Ser.). pap. 51.02 *(978-0-7613-8622-3(X));* (ENG.). 32p. (gr. 3-5). pap. 8.95 *(978-0-7613-7806-8(5))* Lerner Publishing Group. (Graphic Universe™).

—The Underground Railroad Adventure of Allen Jay, Antislavery Activist. Hammond, Ted & Carbajal, Richard, illus. 2011. (History's Kid Heroes Ser.). (ENG.). 32p. (gr. 3-5). lib. bdg. 26.60 *(978-0-7613-7804-4(9))* Lerner Publishing Group.

Capstone Press Staff. Follow the Drinking Gourd: An Underground Railroad Story, 1 vol. Squier, Robert, illus. 2012. (Night Sky Stories Ser.). (ENG.). 24p. (gr. 2-3). lib. bdg. 26.65 *(978-1-4048-7375-9(9))* Picture Window Bks.

Carbone, Elisa. Stealing Freedom. 2003. (EMC Masterpiece Series Access Editions). (Illus.). xix, 284p. (J). 12.99 *(978-0-8219-2507-2(5))* EMC/Paradigm Publishing.

Cole, Henry. Unspoken: A Story from the Underground Railroad. Cole, Henry, illus. 2012. (Unspoken Ser.). (ENG., Illus.). 40p. (J). (gr. -1-3). 17.99 *(978-0-545-39997-5(1),* Scholastic Pr.) Scholastic, Inc.

Dowell, Frances O'Roark. Trouble the Water. (ENG.). (J). (gr. 4-8). 2017. 304p. pap. 7.99 *(978-1-4814-2464-6(5))* 2016. (Illus.). 288p. 16.99 *(978-1-4814-2463-9(7))* Simon & Schuster Children's Publishing.

Draper, Sharon M. Lost in the Tunnel of Time. Watson, Jesse Joshua, illus. 2011. (Clubhouse Mysteries Ser.: 2). (ENG.). 112p. (J). (gr. 3-7). pap. 5.99 *(978-1-4424-2704-4(3),* Aladdin) Simon & Schuster Children's Publishing.

—Lost in the Tunnel of Time. Watson, Jesse Joshua, illus. 2011. (Clubhouse Mysteries Ser.: 2). (ENG.). 112p. (J). (gr. 3-7). lib. bdg. 15.99 *(978-1-4424-2703-7(5),* Simon & Schuster/Paula Wiseman Bks.) Simon & Schuster/Paula Wiseman Bks.

Evatt, Harriet. The Secret of the Old Coach Inn. Stone, David, illus. 2011. 190p. 42.95 *(978-1-258-08239-0(X))* Literary Licensing, LLC.

Falk, Elizabeth Sullivan. Lettie's North Star. Wolf, Elizabeth, illus. 2006. (J). *(978-1-59336-694-0(9))* Mondo Publishing.

Frazier, Jan. Prairie Points:: a Civil War Sanctuary. 2017. (ENG., Illus.). (J). pap. 12.95 ***(978-1-55571-864-0(7),*** Hellgate Pr.) L & R Publishing, LLC.

Gayle, Sharon Shavers. Emma's Escape: A Story of America's Underground Railroad. Velasquez, Eric, illus. 3rd ed. 2003. (Soundprints' Read-and-Discover Ser.). (ENG.). 48p. (J). (gr. -1-3). pap. 3.95 *(978-1-59249-021-9(2),* S2009) Soundprints.

Gilfert, Shirley Tankersley. The Other Side of Jordan: A Story of the Underground Railroad. 2007. 140p. 21.95 *(978-0-595-70289-3(9));* per. 11.95 *(978-0-595-46274-2(X))* iUniverse, Inc.

Griffiths, Robert. Adventures of Clive. 2005. 89p. pap. 8.81 *(978-1-4116-5191-3(X))* Lulu Pr., Inc.

Grimes, Nikki. Chasing Freedom: The Life Journeys of Harriet Tubman & Susan B. Anthony, Inspired by Historical Facts. Wood, Michele, illus. 2015. (ENG.). 56p. (J). (gr. 2-5). 18.99 *(978-0-439-79338-4(6),* Orchard Bks.) Scholastic, Inc.

Hamilton, Virginia. The House of Dies Drear. 8.97 *(978-0-13-437491-8(6))* Prentice Hall PTR.

—The House of Dies Drear. 2006. (ENG.). 256p. (J). (gr. 6-9). pap. 7.99 *(978-1-4169-1405-1(6),* Aladdin) Simon & Schuster Children's Publishing.

Hedstrom-Page, Deborah. From Slavery to Freedom with Harriet Tubman. Martinez, Sergio, illus. 2007. (My American Journey Ser.). 84p. (J). (gr. 3-9). 9.99 *(978-0-8054-3268-8(X))* B&H Publishing Group.

Hopkinson, Deborah. Under the Quilt of Night. Ransome, James E., illus. 2005. (gr. k-5). 18.00 *(978-0-7569-5077-4(5))* Perfection Learning Corp.

—Under the Quilt of Night. Ransome, James E., illus. 2005. (ENG.). 40p. (J). (gr. k-5). reprint ed. 7.99 *(978-0-689-87700-1(5),* Aladdin) Simon & Schuster Children's Publishing.

Hulme, Lucy V. Passages, 1 bk. Redpath, Dale, illus. 2005. 40p. (J). 7.95 *(978-0-9769854-0-2(3),* 001) Combs-Hulme Publishing.

Landau, Elaine. The Underground Railroad: Would You Help Them Escape? 2014. (What Would You Do? Ser.). (Illus.). 48p. (J). (gr. 3-4). pap. 8.95 *(978-1-4644-0393-4(7),* Enslow Elementary) Enslow Pubs., Inc.

LeSourd, Nancy. Escape on the Underground Railroad, 1 vol. 2008. (Liberty Letters Ser.). (ENG.). 224p. (J). pap. 7.99 *(978-0-310-71391-3(9))* Zonderkidz.

—Secrets of Civil War Spies, 1 vol. 2008. (Liberty Letters Ser.). (ENG.). 224p. (J). pap. 7.99 *(978-0-310-71390-6(0))* Zonderkidz.

Levine, Ellen. Henry's Freedom Box: A True Story from the Underground Railroad. Nelson, Kadir, illus. 2007. (ENG.). 40p. (J). (gr. -1-3). 17.99 *(978-0-439-77733-9(X),* Scholastic Pr.) Scholastic, Inc.

MacColl, Michaela. The Revelation of Louisa May. 2015. (ENG.). 272p. (J). (gr. 7-12). 16.99 *(978-1-4521-3357-7(3))* Chronicle Bks. LLC.

Marsh, Carole. The Mystery on the Underground Railroad. 2009. (Real Kids, Real Places Ser.). (Illus.). 146p. (J). lib. bdg. 18.99 *(978-0-635-06991-7(1)*, Marsh, Carole Mysteries) Gallopade International.

—The Mystery on the Underground Railroad (Hardcover) 2003. 160p. (gr. 2-8). 14.95 *(978-0-635-02110-6(2))* Gallopade International.

McKissack, Patricia C. A Picture of Freedom: The Diary of Clotee, a Slave Girl, Belmont Plantation, Virginia, 1859. 2011. (Dear America Ser.). (ENG.). 240p. (J). (gr. 3-7). 14.99 *(978-0-545-24253-0(3)*, Scholastic Pr.) Scholastic, Inc.

McMann, Lisa. The Trap Door. 2015. (Infinity Ring Ser.: 3). (ENG.). 192p. (J). (gr. 3-7). pap. 6.99 *(978-0-545-90109-3(X))* Scholastic, Inc.

—The Trap Door. 2015. (Infinity Ring Ser.: 3). lib. bdg. 17.20 *(978-0-606-37788-1(3))* Turtleback Bks.

Meltzer, Milton. Underground Man. 2006. (ENG.). 288p. (J). (gr. 5-7). pap. 8.99 *(978-0-15-205524-0(X))* Houghton Mifflin Harcourt Publishing Co.

Messner, Kate. Long Road to Freedom. McMorris, Kelley, illus. 2015. (Ranger in Time Ser.: 3). (ENG.). 160p. (J). (gr. 2-5). pap. 5.99 *(978-0-545-63920-0(4))* Scholastic, Inc.

Morrow, Barbara Olenyik. A Good Night for Freedom. Jenkins, Leonard, illus. 2003. (ENG.). 32p. (J). (gr. k-3). tchr. ed. 17.95 *(978-0-8234-1709-4(3))* Holiday Hse., Inc.

Nelson, Vaunda Micheaux. Almost to Freedom. Bootman, Colin, illus. 2003. (Carolrhoda Picture Books Ser.). (ENG.). 40p. (J). (gr. k-3). 16.95 *(978-1-57505-342-4(X))* Lerner Publishing Group.

Orzechowski, Shawneen. Midnight Journey: Running for Freedom on the Underground Railroad. 2006. 112p. (J). (gr. 3-7). per. 8.95 *(978-1-57249-379-7(8)*, White Mane Kids) White Mane Publishing Co., Inc.

Pearsall, Shelley. Trouble Don't Last. 2003. (ENG.). 256p. (J). (gr. 3-7). reprint ed. 6.99 *(978-0-440-41811-5(9)*, Yearling) Random Hse. Children's Bks.

Phillips, Dee. Runaway. 2014. (Yesterday's Voices Ser.). (YA). lib. bdg. 19.60 *(978-0-606-35584-1(7))* Turtleback Bks.

Plaxton, Judith & Second Story Press Staff. Morning Star, 1 vol. 2011. (ENG.). 180p. (J). (gr. 6-8). pap. 10.95 *(978-1-897187-97-5(1))* Second Story Pr. CAN. Dist: Orca Bk. Pubs. USA.

Polacco, Patricia. January's Sparrow. Polacco, Patricia, illus. 2009. (ENG., Illus.). 96p. (J). (gr. 3-7). 23.99 *(978-0-399-25077-4(8)*, Philomel Bks.) Penguin Young Readers Group.

Porter, Janice Lee, illus. Allen Jay & the Underground Railroad, 4 bks., Set. 2006. (Readalongs for Beginning Readers Ser.). (J). (gr. 2-5). pap. 39.95 incl. audio compact disk *(978-1-59519-951-5(9))* Live Oak Media.

Raven, Margot Theis. Night Boat to Freedom. Lewis, E. B., illus. 2008. (ENG.). 40p. (J). (gr. 1-4). pap. 8.99 *(978-0-312-55018-9(9)*, 9780312550189) Square Fish.

Reed, Stephanie. The Light Across the River, 1 vol. 2008. (Illus.). 216p. (J). (gr. 4-7). pap. 10.99 *(978-0-8254-3574-4(9))* Kregel Pubns.

Reese Martin, Faith. Ghost Train to Freedom: An Adventure on the Underground Railroad. Sachs, Barry, illus. 2012. (JMP Mystery Ser.: Bk. 3). (ENG.). 416p. (YA). pap. 14.99 *(978-1-60800-014-2(1)*, American Literary Publishing) LifeReloaded Specialty Publishing LLC.

Rinaldi, Ann. The Ever-After Bird. 2010. (ENG.). 240p. (J). (gr. 5-7). pap. 8.99 *(978-0-547-25854-6(2))* Houghton Mifflin Harcourt Publishing Co.

Robbins, Trina. Freedom Songs: A Tale of the Underground Railroad, 1 vol. Millet, Jason, illus. 2008. (Historical Fiction Ser.). (ENG.). 56p. (gr. 2-3). pap. 6.25 *(978-1-4342-0495-0(2)*, Graphic Flash) Stone Arch Bks.

Roop, Peter. Lead Us to Freedom, Harriet Tubman! 2006. (Illus.). 58p. (J). pap. *(978-0-439-79255-4(X))* Scholastic, Inc.

Russell, Krista. The Other Side of Free, 1 vol. 2013. (ENG.). 256p. (J). (gr. 5-9). 16.95 *(978-1-56145-710-6(8))* Peachtree Pubs.

Sargent, Dave & Sargent, Pat. Nubbin: (Linebacked Apricot Dun) Freedom, 30 vols., Vol. 43. Lenoir, Jane, illus. 2003. (Saddle up Ser.: Vol. 43). 42p. (J). pap. 10.95 *(978-1-56763-704-5(3))*; lib. bdg. 23.60 *(978-1-56763-703-8(5))* Ozark Publishing.

Squier, Robert, illus. Follow the Drinking Gourd: An Underground Railroad Story, 1 vol. 2012. (Night Sky Stories Ser.). (ENG.). 24p. (gr. 2-3). pap. 8.95 *(978-1-4048-7714-6(2))* Picture Window Bks.

Steenwyk, Elizabeth Van. Blacksmith's Song. Rich, Anna, illus. 2018. (ENG.). 32p. (J). (gr. 1-5). 17.95 *(978-1-56145-580-5(6))* Peachtree Pubs.

Steinkraus, Kyla. Sundaes with Harriet Tubman. 2016. (Time Hop Sweets Shop Ser.). (ENG.). 32p. (gr. k-3). 25.65 *(978-1-68191-371-1(2))* Rourke Educational Media.

Swain, Gwenyth. Voices for Freedom. Frankenhuyzen, Gijsbert van et al, illus. 2013. (American Adventures Ser.). (ENG.). 72p. (J). (gr. 3-6). 6.99 *(978-1-58536-886-0(5)*, 202900) Sleeping Bear Pr.

Tyre, Lisa Lewis & Airgood, Ellen. Last in a Long Line of Rebels. 2015. (ENG.). 288p. (J). (gr. 5). 16.99 *(978-0-399-16838-3(9)*, Nancy Paulsen Books) Penguin Young Readers Group.

Vande Velde, Vivian. There's a Dead Person Following My Sister Around. 2008. (ENG., Illus.). 160p. (J). (gr. 5-7). pap. 11.95 *(978-0-15-206467-9(2))* Houghton Mifflin Harcourt Publishing Co.

Walker, Sally M. Freedom Song: The Story of Henry "Box" Brown. Qualls, Sean, illus. 2012. (ENG.). 40p. (J). (gr. -1-3). 17.99 *(978-0-06-058310-1(X))* HarperCollins Pubs.

Warburton, Carol. Edge of Night: A Novel. 2004. (Illus.). 278p. pap. 14.95 *(978-1-59156-013-5(6))* Covenant Communications, Inc.

Weston Woods Staff, creator. Henry's Freedom Box. 2011. 18.95 *(978-0-545-31402-2(X))*; 38.75 *(978-0-545-31403-9(8))* Weston Woods Studios, Inc.

Winter, Jeanette. Follow the Drinking Gourd. Winter, Jeanette, illus. 2008. (ENG., Illus.). 48p. (J). (gr. -1-2). 17.99 *(978-0-394-89694-6(7)*, Knopf Bks. for Young Readers) Random Hse. Children's Bks.

Wishinsky, Frieda. Halifax Explodes! Lewis-MacDougall, Patricia Ann & Owlkids Books Inc. Staff, illus. 2011. (Canadian Flyer Adventures Ser.: 17). (ENG.). 96p. (J). (gr. 1-4). pap. 7.95 *(978-1-926818-98-6(9)*, Maple Tree Pr.) Owlkids Bks. Inc. CAN. Dist: Publishers Group West (PGW).

—Hurry, Freedom. Griffiths, Dean & Owlkids Books Inc. Staff, illus. 2008. (Canadian Flyer Adventures Ser.: 7). (ENG.). 96p. (J). (gr. 1-4). per. 9.95 *(978-1-897349-15-1(7)*, Maple Tree Pr.) Owlkids Bks. Inc. CAN. Dist: Publishers Group West (PGW).

Wyeth, Sharon Dennis. Message in the Sky Bk. 3: Corey's Underground Railroad Diary. 2003. (My America Ser.). (ENG.). 112p. (J). 10.95 *(978-0-439-37057-8(4)*, Scholastic Pr.) Scholastic, Inc.

UNDERGROUND RAILROADS

see Subways

UNDERSEA EXPLORATION

see Underwater Exploration

UNDERSEA TECHNOLOGY

see Oceanography

UNDERSTANDING

see Intellect; Knowledge, Theory of

UNDERWATER EXPLORATION

see also Marine Biology; Skin Diving

Bodden, Valerie. To the Ocean Deep. (Great Expeditions Ser.). 48p. (J). 2012. (ENG.). (gr. 4-7). pap. 12.00 *(978-0-89812-665-5(7)*, Creative Paperbacks) 2011. (Illus.). 35.65 *(978-1-60818-067-7(0)*, Creative Education) Creative Co., The.

Bradley, Timothy. Demonios de la Profundidad. 2016. (TIME for Kids en Español - Level 5 Ser.). (SPA.). 64p. (gr. 5-5). lib. bdg. 31.99 *(978-1-5157-2941-9(9))* Time for Kids Inc AUS. Dist: Capstone Pub.

Bradley, Timothy J. Demons of the Deep, 1 vol. 2nd rev. ed. 2013. (Nonfiction Readers Ser.). (ENG., Illus.). 64p. (J). (gr. 5-5). pap. 31.96 *(978-1-4333-7419-7(6))* Teacher Created Materials, Inc.

Chapman, Simon. Under the Sea. Chapman, Simon, illus. 2005. (Illus.). 112p. (J). lib. bdg. 20.00 *(978-1-4242-0631-5(6))* Fitzgerald Bks.

Dorling Kindersley Publishing Staff. Ocean. 2012. (Look Closer Ser.). (ENG., Illus.). 64p. (J). (gr. 1-4). 10.99 *(978-0-7566-9237-7(7)*, DK Children) Dorling Kindersley Publishing, Inc.

Dougherty, Terri. The Search for the Titanic: Finding the Ship's Watery Grave, 1 vol. 2014. (Titanic Perspectives Ser.). (ENG.). 48p. (gr. 3-4). 31.99 *(978-1-4914-0418-8(3))* Capstone Press of Coughlan Cos.

Fertig, Dennis. Sylvia Earle: Ocean Explorer, 1 vol. 2014. (Women in Conservation Ser.). (ENG., Illus.). 48p. (J). (gr. 3-6). 33.32 *(978-1-4846-0470-0(9))*; pap. 8.99 *(978-1-4846-0475-5(X))* Heinemann-Raintree. (Heinemann InfoSearch).

Graham, Ian. Be in the First Submarine! An Undersea Expedition You'D Rather Avoid. Antram, David, illus. 2008. (You Wouldn't Want to...: American History Ser.). (ENG.). 32p. (J). 29.00 *(978-0-531-20702-4(1)*, Watts, Franklin) Scholastic Library Publishing.

—You Wouldn't Want to Be in the First Submarine! An Undersea Expedition You'd Rather Avoid. Antram, David, illus. 2008. (You Wouldn't Want to...: American History Ser.). (ENG.). 32p. (J). (gr. 3-18). pap. 9.95 *(978-0-531-21912-6(7)*, Watts, Franklin) Scholastic Library Publishing.

Green, Barry & Linn, Susie. Under the Sea. 2017. (Scratch & Draw Ser.). (ENG.). 56p. (J). (gr. k-2). 12.99 *(978-1-78700-065-0(6))* Top That! Publishing PLC GBR. Dist: Independent Pubs. Group.

Hall, Kirsten. Deep Sea Adventures: A Chapter Book. 2003. (True Tales Ser.). (ENG., Illus.). 48p. (J). 22.50 *(978-0-516-22917-1(6)*, Children's Pr.) Scholastic Library Publishing.

Johnson, Rebecca L. & National Geographic Learning Staff. Robert Ballard: Discovering Underwater Treasures. 2007. (Rise & Shine Ser.). (ENG., Illus.). 32p. (J). pap. 17.95 *(978-0-7922-8881-7(5))* CENGAGE Learning.

Labrecque, Ellen. Sarah Mather & Underwater Telescopes. 2017. (21st Century Junior Library: Women Innovators Ser.). (ENG., Illus.). 24p. (J). (gr. 2-5). lib. bdg. 27.07 *(978-1-63472-181-3(0)*, 209296) Cherry Lake Publishing.

Mallory, Kenneth. Adventure Beneath the Sea: Living in an Underwater Science Station. Skerry, Brian, photos by. 2010. (ENG., Illus.). 48p. (J). (gr. 4-6). 18.95 *(978-1-59078-607-9(6))* Boyds Mills Pr.

Mara, Wil. Deep-Sea Exploration: Science, Technology, & Engineering. 2015. (ENG., Illus.). 64p. (J). pap. 8.95 *(978-0-531-21173-1(8)*, Orchard Bks.) Scholastic Library Publishing.

Marx, Christy. Life in the Ocean Depths. 2009. 64p. (gr. 5-8). (YA). pap. 12.95 *(978-1-4358-3265-7(5))*; 53.00 *(978-1-61514-272-9(X))* Rosen Publishing Group, Inc., The. (Rosen Reference).

Matsen, Bradford. An Extreme Dive under the Antarctic Ice. 2003. (Incredible Deep-Sea Adventures Ser.). (Illus.). 48p. (J). lib. bdg. 25.27 *(978-0-7660-2190-7(4))* Enslow Pubs., Inc.

—The Incredible Record-Setting Deep-Sea Dive of the Bathysphere. 2003. (Incredible Deep-Sea Adventures Ser.). (Illus.). 48p. (J). (gr. 4-10). lib. bdg. 25.27 *(978-0-7660-2188-4(2))* Enslow Pubs., Inc.

—The Incredible Submersible Alvin Discovers a Strange Deep-Sea World. 2003. (Incredible Deep-Sea Adventures Ser.). (Illus.). 48p. (J). (gr. 4-10). lib. bdg. 23.93 *(978-0-7660-2189-1(0))* Enslow Pubs., Inc.

Mizielinska, Aleksandra & Mizielinski, Daniel. Under Water, under Earth. 2016. (ENG., Illus.). 112p. (J). (gr. 2-4). 35.00 *(978-0-7636-8922-3(X)*, Big Picture Press) Candlewick Pr.

Orr, Tamra B. The Undersea World. 2016. (True Book(tm), a — Greatest Discoveries & Discoverers Ser.). (ENG., Illus.). 48p. (J). lib. bdg. 31.00 *(978-0-531-21859-4(7)*, Children's Pr.) Scholastic Library Publishing.

Paris, Stephanie. Drag! Friction & Resistance, 1 vol. 2nd rev. ed. 2013. (Nonfiction Readers Ser.). (ENG., Illus.). 64p. (J). (gr. 5-5). pap. 31.96 *(978-1-4333-7439-5(0))* Teacher Created Materials, Inc.

Reichard, Susan E. Who on Earth Is Sylvia Earle? Undersea Explorer of the Ocean. 2009. (Scientists Saving the Earth Ser.). (Illus.). 112p. (J). (gr. 5-9). lib. bdg. 33.27 *(978-1-59845-118-4(9))* Enslow Pubs., Inc.

Rhodes, Mary Jo & Hall, David. Undersea Encounters, 5 bks., Set. Hall, David, photos by. Incl. Seahorses & Sea Dragons. (Illus.). 48p. (J). (gr. 3-7). 2005. lib. bdg. 27.00 *(978-0-516-24393-1(4)*, Children's Pr.); (Illus.). 2005. 125.00 o.p. *(978-0-516-24439-6(6)*, Children's Pr.) Scholastic Library Publishing.

Rice, Racheal & Benchmark Education Co., LLC. Robert Ballard: Deepwater Explorer. 2014. (Text Connections Ser.). (J). (gr. 3). *(978-1-4509-9650-1(7))* Benchmark Education Co.

Sheehan, Robert. The Undersea Lab: Exploring the Oceans, 1 vol., 1. 2014. (Discovery Education: Earth & Space Science Ser.). (ENG.). 32p. (gr. 3-6). 26.25 *(978-1-4777-6166-3(7)*, PowerKids Pr.) Rosen Publishing Group, Inc., The.

Spilsbury, Richard. Deep Sea Exploration. 2010. (ENG.). 32p. (J). *(978-0-7787-9893-4(3))*; (gr. 3-6). pap. *(978-0-7787-9914-6(X))* Crabtree Publishing Co.

Tief im Meer. (GER.). 19.95 *(978-3-411-09271-0(8))* Bibliographisches Institut & F. A. Brockhaus AG DEU. Dist: Distribooks, Inc.

Vogel, Carole G. Underwater Exploration. 2003. (Restless Sea Ser.). (ENG., Illus.). 80p. (J). 30.50 *(978-0-531-12327-0(8)*, Watts, Franklin) Scholastic Library Publishing.

Westerskov, Kim, photos by. Diving in Antarctica. 2004. (Illus.). 32p. (J). *(978-0-7685-2384-3(2))* Dominie Pr., Inc.

White, Katherine. Sylvia Earle: Deep Sea Explorer & Ocean Activist. (Women Hall of Famers in Mathematics & Science Ser.). 112p. (gr. 5-8). 2009. 63.90 *(978-1-60854-814-9(7))* 2004. (Illus.). lib. bdg. 34.60 *(978-0-8239-3879-7(4))* Rosen Publishing Group, Inc., The. (Rosen Reference).

UNDERWATER EXPLORATION—FICTION

Bardhan-Quallen, Sudipta. Purrmaids #1: the Scaredy Cat. 2017. (Purrmaids Ser.: 1). (ENG.). 96p. (J). (gr. 1-4). lib. bdg. 12.99 ***(978-1-5247-0162-8(9))***; (Illus.). 4.99 ***(978-1-5247-0161-1(0))*** Random Hse. Children's Bks. (Random Hse. Bks. for Young Readers).

Belcher, Angie & Belcher, Andy. Swimming with Dolphins. 2005. (Big Cat Ser.). pap. 6.50 *(978-1-60457-102-8(0))* Pacific Learning, Inc.

Berardy, Lloyd, 1st. A Tropical Bear in Hawaii Goes Underwater. 2006. (J). 12.95 *(978-1-4276-0212-1(3))* Aardvark Global Publishing.

Bolam, Emily, illus. Under the Sea. 2013. (Peekabooks Ser.). (ENG.). 8p. (J). (gr. -1 — 1). bds. 5.99 *(978-0-7641-6630-3(1))* Barron's Educational Series, Inc.

Bonnell, Kris. Down in the Sea. 2006. (J). pap. 5.95 *(978-1-933727-38-7(1))* Reading Reading Bks., LLC.

Chiarello, Robin Taylor. The Clam Diggers Ball. Bohart, Lisa, illus. 2011. 40p. pap. 15.95 *(978-1-61493-013-6(9))* Peppertree Pr., The.

Cookson, Jan. Ant on the Run. 2003. 84p. pap. 8.95 *(978-0-595-29440-4(5))* iUniverse, Inc.

De Lesseps, Ferdinand Zoticus. Oceanology: The True Account of the Voyage of the Nautilus. Steer, Dugald A. & Hawkins, Emily, eds. 2009. (Ologies Ser.: 8). (ENG., Illus.). 32p. (J). (gr. 3-7). 24.99 *(978-0-7636-4290-7(8))* Candlewick Pr.

Dunmore, Helen. The Deep. 2009. (Ingo Ser.: 3). 336p. (YA). (gr. 5-18). 16.99 *(978-0-06-081858-6(1))* HarperCollins Pubs.

Fraioli, James O. Polar Ice Expedition: With Jean-Michel Cousteau. 2009. (J). (gr. 4-7). *(978-1-4236-0550-8(0))* Gibbs Smith, Publisher.

Greenburg, J. C. Under Water. Reed, Mike, illus. 2003. (Andrew Lost Ser.: 5). (ENG.). 96p. (J). (gr. 1-4). mass mkt. 3.99 *(978-0-375-82523-1(1)*, Random Hse. Bks. for Young Readers) Random Hse. Children's Bks.

Lee, Jihyeon. Pool. 2015. (ENG., Illus.). 56p. (J). (gr. -1-k). 16.99 *(978-1-4521-4294-4(7))* Chronicle Bks. LLC.

Meomi (Firm) Staff. The Octonauts & the Frown Fish. 2008. (Octonauts Ser.). (ENG., Illus.). 36p. (J). (gr. -1-3). 15.95 *(978-1-59702-014-5(1))* Immedium.

—The Octonauts & the Great Ghost Reef. 2009. (Octonauts Ser.). (ENG., Illus.). 36p. (J). (gr. -1-3). 15.95 *(978-1-59702-019-0(2))* Immedium.

—The Octonauts & the Sea of Shade. 2007. (Octonauts Ser.). (ENG., Illus.). 36p. (J). (gr. k-2). 15.95 *(978-1-59702-010-7(9))* Immedium.

Meomi (Firm) Staff, contrib. by. The Octonauts & the Only Lonely Monster. 2006. (Octonauts Ser.). (ENG., Illus.). 36p. (J). (gr. -1-3). 15.95 *(978-1-59702-005-3(2))* Immedium.

Miller, Jeff. The Nerdy Dozen #3: 20,000 Nerds under the Sea. 2016. (Nerdy Dozen Ser.: 3). 208p. (J). (gr. 3-7). pap. 6.99 *(978-0-06-227269-0(1))* HarperCollins Pubs.

Montgomery, R. A. Journey under the Sea. Sundaravej, Sittisan, illus. 2006. (Choose Your Own Adventure Ser.: No. 2). 144p. (J). (gr. 4-8). per. 6.99 *(978-1-933390-02-4(6)*, CHCL02) Chooseco LLC.

—Journey under the Sea. 2006. (Choose Your Own Adventure Ser.: 2). 17.20 *(978-1-4177-6410-5(4)*, Turtleback) Turtleback Bks.

—Return to Atlantis. 2005. (Choose Your Own Adventure Ser.). (Illus.). 119p. (gr. 4-8). pap. 5.50 *(978-0-7608-9706-5(9))* Sundance/Newbridge Educational Publishing.

Nosy Crow Staff. Bizzy Bear: Deep-Sea Diver. Davies, Benji, illus. 2016. (Bizzy Bear Ser.). (ENG.). 8p. (J). (— 1). bds. 6.99 *(978-0-7636-8647-5(6)*, Nosy Crow) Candlewick Pr.

Picard, Matthias. Jim Curious: A Voyage to the Heart of the Sea in 3-D Vision. 2014. (ENG., Illus.). 52p. (J). (gr. 1-4). 19.95 *(978-1-4197-1043-8(5)*, Abrams Bks. for Young Readers) Abrams, Inc.

Scholastic, Inc. Staff & King, Trey. Deep Sea Treasure Dive. Hyland, Greg, illus. 2016. (Lego City Ser.). (ENG.). 24p. (J). (gr. 2-5). pap. 3.99 *(978-0-545-90591-6(5))* Scholastic, Inc.

Scott, Jeff. The Discovery of Monkey Island. 2008. 64p. pap. 19.95 *(978-1-60610-921-2(9))* America Star Bks.

Sesso, Karen A. Off They Swam, 1 vol. 2009. 37p. pap. 19.95 *(978-1-61546-453-1(0))* PublishAmerica, Inc.

Stine, R. L. Espanto Marino. 2009. (Goosebumps Horrorland Ser.: 2). (SPA.). 160p. (J). (gr. 3-7). pap. 6.99 *(978-0-545-15408-6(1)*, Scholastic en Espanol) Scholastic, Inc.

Sundaravej, Sittisan & Thongmoon, Kriangsak, illus. Return to Atlantis. 2007. (Choose Your Own Adventure Ser.: No. 18). 119p. (J). (gr. 4-7). per. 6.99 *(978-1-933390-18-5(2)*, CHCL18) Chooseco LLC.

Treasures of the Barrier Reef. 2005. (J). audio, cd-rom 24.95 *(978-0-9771381-7-3(8))* Williams, Geoffrey T.

Trout, Richard. Devil's Breath Volcano, 1 vol. 2008. (MacGregor Family Adventure Ser.: 6). (ENG., Illus.). 208p. (YA). (gr. 6-10). 16.99 *(978-1-58980-558-3(5))* Pelican Publishing Co., Inc.

Verne, Jules. Twenty Thousand Leagues under the Sea. l.t. ed. 2006. 592p. pap. *(978-1-84702-222-6(7))* Echo Library.

—20,000 Leagues under the Sea. 2004. (Fast Track Classics Ser.). (Illus.). 48p. (J). pap. *(978-0-237-52688-7(3))* Evans Brothers, Ltd.

Zindel, Paul. Loch. 2005. 209p. (YA). (gr. 7-12). 13.65 *(978-0-7569-6001-8(0))* Perfection Learning Corp.

Zucker, Jonny. Mission 3: In Deep. Woodman, Ned, illus. 2013. (Max Flash Ser.: 3). (ENG.). 144p. (gr. 2-5). pap. 7.95 *(978-1-4677-1473-0(9))*; lib. bdg. 27.93 *(978-1-4677-1209-5(4))* Lerner Publishing Group. (Darby Creek).

UNDERWATER GEOLOGY

see Submarine Geology

UNDERWATER SWIMMING

see Skin Diving

UNDERWRITING

see Insurance

UNICEF

Bookmiller, Kirsten N. & Verloren, Ada. The United Nations Children's Fund (UNICEF) 2009. (Global Organizations Ser.). (Illus.). 128p. (YA). (gr. 7-12). 35.00 *(978-0-7910-9566-9(5))* Facts On File, Inc.

Connolly, Sean. UNICEF. 2009. 32.80 *(978-1-59920-303-4(0))* Black Rabbit Bks.

—Unicef. 2009. (Global Organizations Ser.). (Illus.). 46p. (J). (gr. 4-7). pap. *(978-1-897563-37-3(X))* Saunders Bk. Co.

Marsico, Katie. Unicef. 2014. (Community Connections: How Do They Help? Ser.). (ENG., Illus.). 24p. (J). (gr. 2-5). 25.64 *(978-1-63188-031-5(4)*, 205531) Cherry Lake Publishing.

Suen, Anastasia. UNICEF. 2004. (Organizaciones de Ayuda (Helping Organizations) Ser.). (SPA., Illus.). 24p. (J). (gr. 3-6). lib. bdg. 22.60 *(978-0-8239-6858-9(8)*, Editorial Buenas Letras) Rosen Publishing Group, Inc., The.

—Unicef. 2009. (Helping Organizations Ser.). 24p. (gr. 2-2). 42.50 *(978-1-61513-263-8(5)*, PowerKids Pr.) Rosen Publishing Group, Inc., The.

—Unicef (unicef) 2009. (Organizaciones de ayuda (Helping Organizations) Ser.). (SPA.). 24p. (gr. 2-2). 42.50 *(978-1-60851-148-8(0)*, Editorial Buenas Letras) Rosen Publishing Group, Inc., The.

UNICORNS

Accord Publishing Staff. Go Fun! Unicorns. 2014. (ENG.). 72p. (J). pap. 9.99 *(978-1-4494-3176-1(3))* Andrews McMeel Publishing.

Blaisdell, Molly. The Truth about Unicorns, 1 vol. Yilmaz, Necdet, illus. 2010. (Fairy-Tale Superstars Ser.). (ENG.). 32p. (gr. 1-3). lib. bdg. 27.32 *(978-1-4048-5748-3(6))* Picture Window Bks.

Dudley, William. Unicorns. 2008. (Mysterious & Unknown Ser.). (Illus.). 104p. (YA). (gr. 3-7). lib. bdg. *(978-1-60152-028-9(X))* ReferencePoint Pr., Inc.

Hamilton, John. Unicorns & Other Magical Creatures, 1 vol. 2004. (Fantasy & Folklore Ser.). (ENG., Illus.). 32p. (gr. 4-8). 27.07 *(978-1-59197-715-5(0)*, Abdo & Daughters) ABDO Publishing Co.

Hinds, Kathryn. Unicorns. 2013. (Creatures of Fantasy Ser.). 64p. (J). (gr. 4-8). pap. 15.28 *(978-1-62712-055-5(6))*; (Illus.). 34.21 *(978-0-7614-4928-7(0))* Cavendish Square Publishing.

Jeffrey, Gary. Unicorns. Verma, Dheeraj, illus. 2012. (Graphic Mythical Creatures Ser.). (ENG.). 24p. (J). (gr. 3-5). pap. 8.15 *(978-1-4339-6769-6(3))*; lib. bdg. 23.95 *(978-1-4339-6767-2(7))* Stevens, Gareth Publishing LLLP. (Gareth Stevens Learning Library).

Loh-Hagan, Virginia. Unicorns: Magic, Myth, & Mystery. 2016. (Magic, Myth, & Mystery Ser.). (ENG., Illus.). 32p. (J). (gr. 4-8). 29.93 *(978-1-63471-115-9(7)*, 208571, 45th Parallel Press) Cherry Lake Publishing.

More Unicorns. 2007. (Illus.). 20p. (J). 10.00 *(978-0-9795206-6-2(5))* Unseen Gallery.

Rau, Dana Meachen. Unicorns. 2010. (Bookworms Chapter Books: for Real? Ser.). 24p. (gr. 2-3). 22.79 *(978-0-7614-4864-8(0))* Marshall Cavendish Corp.

Renison, Jessica. The Secret History of Unicorns. 2008. (Illus.). 96p. *(978-1-904756-97-2(2))* Kandour Ltd.

Sautter, A. J. A Field Guide to Griffins, Unicorns, & Other Mythical Beasts, 1 vol. Juta, Jason, illus. 2014. (Fantasy Field Guides). (ENG.). 32p. (gr. 3-4). lib. bdg. 27.99 *(978-1-4914-0690-8(9))* Capstone Press of Coughlan Cos.

Shaffer, Christy. Glitter Unicorns Stickers. 2004. (Dover Little Activity Books Stickers Ser.). (ENG., Illus.). 2p. (J). (gr. 1-4). pap. 1.99 *(978-0-486-43538-1(5))* Dover Pubns., Inc.

—Magical Unicorns Stained Glass Coloring Book. 2004. (Dover Stained Glass Coloring Book Ser.). (ENG., Illus.). 32p. (gr. 3-8). pap. 6.99 *(978-0-486-43705-7(1))* Dover Pubns., Inc.

Summers, Portia & Rau, Dana Meachen. Are Unicorns Real? 2016. (I Want to Know Ser.). (Illus.). 32p. (J). pap. 10.52 *(978-0-7660-8248-9(2))* Enslow Pubs., Inc.

Wonderland Unicorns: Coloring book by Daria Hallmark. 2007. (Illus.). 20p. (YA). 10.00 *(978-0-9795206-1-7(4))* Unseen Gallery.

UNICORNS—FICTION

Augenstein, Marianne R. The Quest for Kair, 1 vol. 2009. 152p. pap. 24.95 *(978-1-60813-899-9(2))* America Star Bks.

Baker, E. D. Maggie & the Unicorn. 2017. (ENG., Illus.). 128p. (J). 16.99 ***(978-1-68119-145-4(8)***, 9781681191454, Bloomsbury USA Childrens) Bloomsbury Publishing USA.

—Magic Animal Rescue 3: Maggie & the Unicorn. 2017. (ENG., Illus.). 128p. (J). pap. 5.99 ***(978-1-68119-488-2(0)***, 9781681194882, Bloomsbury USA Childrens) Bloomsbury Publishing USA.

Bateman, Teresa. The Eyes of the Unicorn. Spalenka, Greg, illus. 2007. (ENG.). 32p. (J). (gr. 1-5). 17.95 *(978-0-8234-1728-5(X))* Holiday Hse., Inc.

Bateson, Maggie. Fairy Unicorn Riding Stables. Comfort, Louise, illus. 2012. (ENG.). 10p. (J). (gr. -1-k). 22.99 *(978-0-230-74331-1(5))* Macmillan Pubs., Ltd. GBR. Dist: Independent Pubs. Group.

T U V

Bell, Hilari. The Prophecy. 2006. (ENG., Illus.). 208p. (J). (gr. 5-9). 15.99 (978-0-06-059943-0(X)) HarperCollins Pubs.
Benz, Derek & Lewis, J. S. The Revenge of the Shadow King. 2006. (Grey Griffins Ser.: 1). (ENG.). (J). (gr. 3-7). audio compact disk 84.95 (978-0-439-87913-2(2)) Scholastic, Inc.
Bharadwaj, Meenakshi. Lonely Unicorn. 2004. (Illus.). 20p. (J). pap. (978-81-87649-89-2(5)) Katha.
Black, Holly. Zombies vs. Unicorns. 2012. lib. bdg. 22.10 (978-0-606-23686-7(4), Turtleback) Turtleback Bks.
Black, Holly & Larbalestier, Justine, eds. Zombies vs. Unicorns. (ENG.). 432p. (YA). (gr. 9). 2012. pap. 11.99 (978-1-4169-8954-7(4)) 2010. 18.99 (978-1-4169-8953-0(6)) McElderry, Margaret K. Bks. (McElderry, Margaret K. Bks.).
Bliss, Emily. Flash's Dash. Hanson, Sydney, illus. 2017. (Unicorn Princesses Ser.). (ENG.). 128p. (J). 15.99 (978-1-68119-329-8(9), 9781681193298, Bloomsbury USA Childrens) Bloomsbury Publishing USA.
—Sunbeam's Shine. Hanson, Sydney, illus. 2017. (Unicorn Princesses Ser.). (ENG.). 128p. (J). 15.99 (978-1-68119-325-0(6), 9781681193250, Bloomsbury USA Childrens) Bloomsbury Publishing USA.
Bohn, Kendall. Fantasy Adventure. 2008. (Kaleidoscopia Coloring Book Ser.). (Illus.). 56p. (J). (gr. -1-7). 8.95 (978-0-929636-83-2(X)) Syren Bk. Co.
Burkhart, Jessica. Bella's Birthday Unicorn. Ying, Victoria, illus. 2014. (Unicorn Magic Ser.: 1). (ENG.). 144p. (J). (gr. 1-4). 15.99 (978-1-4814-1105-9(5)); pap. 5.99 (978-1-4424-9822-8(6)) Simon & Schuster Children's Publishing. (Aladdin).
—The Hidden Treasure. Ying, Victoria, illus. 2015. (Unicorn Magic Ser.: 4). (ENG.). 112p. (J). (gr. 1-4). pap. 5.99 (978-1-4424-9829-7(3), Aladdin) Simon & Schuster Children's Publishing.
—Where's Glimmer? Ying, Victoria, illus. 2014. (Unicorn Magic Ser.: 2). (ENG.). 144p. (J). (gr. 1-4). pap. 5.99 (978-1-4424-9824-2(2), Aladdin) Simon & Schuster Children's Publishing.
Chapman, Linda. Flying High. Hull, Biz & Farley, Andrew, illus. 2004. (My Secret Unicorn Ser.). 118p. (J). (978-0-439-65273-5(1)) Scholastic, Inc.
—Starlight Surprise, Vol. 4. 4th ed. 2003. (ENG., Illus.). 144p. pap. (978-0-14-131344-3(7), Puffin) Penguin Bks., Ltd.
—Starlight Surprise. Hull, Biz, illus. 2003. (My Secret Unicorn Ser.). 130p. (J). (978-0-439-65275-9(8)) Scholastic, Inc.
—Twilight Magic. Kronheimer, Ann, illus. 2008. 149p. (J). pap. (978-0-545-03160-8(5)) Scholastic, Inc.
Clark, Isabelle. The Enchanted Forest of Hope. 2009. 44p. pap. 18.50 (978-1-4389-7781-2(6)) AuthorHouse.
Clark, Platte F. Bad Unicorn. 2013. (Bad Unicorn Trilogy Ser.: 1). (ENG., Illus.). 432p. (J). (gr. 3-7). 15.99 (978-1-4424-5012-7(6), Aladdin) Simon & Schuster Children's Publishing.
—Good Ogre. 2015. (Bad Unicorn Trilogy Ser.: 3). (ENG., Illus.). 384p. (J). (gr. 3-7). 17.99 (978-1-4424-5018-9(5), Aladdin) Simon & Schuster Children's Publishing.
Clarke, Phillip. Unicorns. Scott, Peter, illus. 2006. (Luxury Lift-the-Flap Learners Ser.). 16p. (J). (gr. -1-3). 11.99 (978-0-7945-1280-4(1), Usborne) EDC Publishing.
Clayton, Dallas. Lily the Unicorn. Clayton, Dallas, illus. 2014. (ENG., Illus.). 48p. (J). (gr. -1-3). 17.99 (978-0-06-211668-0(1)) HarperCollins Pubs.
Cole, Dina. Maggie's Magic Unicorn. 2012. 28p. pap. 19.99 (978-1-4685-7734-1(4)) AuthorHouse.
Cooper, Diana. Tara & the Talking Kitten Meet a Unicorn. Shannon, Kate, illus. 2011. (Tara & Ash-ting Ser.). (ENG.). 80p. (J). (gr. k-4). 8.95 (978-1-84409-557-5(6)) Innovation Pr., The.
Coville, Bruce. Into the Land of the Unicorns. 2008. (Unicorn Chronicles Ser.). (Illus.). 159p. (J). (gr. 4-7). 14.65 (978-0-7569-9061-9(0)) Perfection Learning Corp.
—The Unicorn Treasury: Stories, Poems, & Unicorn Lore. 2004. (ENG., Illus.). 224p. (J). (gr. 2-5). pap. 7.99 (978-0-15-205216-4(X)) Houghton Mifflin Harcourt Publishing Co.
Cross, Frances. Butternut Blobber & the Blue Jade. 2007. (Blobber Ser.). (ENG.). 84p. pap. (978-1-84167-561-9(X)) Ransom Publishing Ltd.
Currey, Anna. The Christmas Unicorn. 2013. (Illus.). (J). (978-1-4351-5017-1(1)) Barnes & Noble, Inc.
Darlison, Aleesah. Ellabeth's Light Cancelled. Brailsford, Jill, illus. 2017. (Unicorn Riders Ser.). (ENG.). 112p. (gr. 3-5). pap. 5.95 (978-1-4795-6559-7(8)) Picture Window Bks.
—Ellabeth's Test. Brailsford, Jill, illus. 2016. (Unicorn Riders Ser.). (ENG.). 112p. (gr. 3-5). lib. bdg. 22.65 (978-1-4795-6547-4(4)) Picture Window Bks.
—Ellabeth's Test Cancelled. Brailsford, Jill, illus. 2017. (Unicorn Riders Ser.). (ENG.). 112p. (gr. 3-5). pap. 5.95 (978-1-4795-6555-9(5)) Picture Window Bks.
—Krystal's Charge Cancelled. Brailsford, Jill, illus. 2017. (Unicorn Riders Ser.). (ENG.). 112p. (gr. 3-5). pap. 5.95 (978-1-4795-6558-0(X)) Picture Window Bks.
—Krystal's Choice. Brailsford, Jill, illus. 2016. (Unicorn Riders Ser.). (ENG.). 112p. (gr. 3-5). lib. bdg. 22.65 (978-1-4795-6546-7(6)) Picture Window Bks.
—Krystal's Choice Cancelled. Brailsford, Jill, illus. 2017. (Unicorn Riders Ser.). (ENG.). 112p. (gr. 3-5). pap. 5.95 (978-1-4795-6554-2(7)) Picture Window Bks.
—Quinn's Riddles. Brailsford, Jill, illus. 2016. (Unicorn Riders Ser.). (ENG.). 112p. (gr. 3-5). lib. bdg. 22.65 (978-1-4795-6544-3(X)) Picture Window Bks.
—Quinn's Truth Cancelled. Brailsford, Jill, illus. 2017. (Unicorn Riders Ser.). (ENG.). 112p. (gr. 3-5). pap. 5.95 (978-1-4795-6556-6(3)); lib. bdg. 22.65 (978-1-4795-6548-1(2)) Picture Window Bks.
—Unicorn Riders. Brailsford, Jill, illus. (Unicorn Riders Ser.). (ENG.). (gr. 3-5). 2017. 128p. pap. 23.80 **(978-1-4795-8544-1(0))** 2016. 112p. 90.60 (978-1-4795-7938-9(6)) Picture Window Bks.
—Willow's Challenge. Brailsford, Jill, illus. 2016. (Unicorn Riders Ser.). (ENG.). 112p. (gr. 3-5). lib. bdg. 22.65 (978-1-4795-6545-0(8)) Picture Window Bks.
—Willow's Victory Cancelled. Brailsford, Jill, illus. 2017. (Unicorn Riders Ser.). (ENG.). 112p. (gr. 3-5). pap. 5.95 (978-1-4795-6557-3(1)); lib. bdg. 22.65 (978-1-4795-6549-8(0)) Picture Window Bks.
Darlison, Aleesha. Quinn's Riddles. Brailsford, Jill, illus. 2017. (Unicorn Riders Ser.). (ENG.). 112p. (gr. 3-5). pap. 5.95 (978-1-4795-6552-8(0)) Picture Window Bks.
—Willow's Challenge. Brailsford, Jill, illus. 2017. (Unicorn Riders Ser.). (ENG.). 112p. (gr. 3-5). pap. 5.95 (978-1-4795-6553-5(9)) Picture Window Bks.
Diller, Kevin & Lowe, Justin. Hello, My Name Is Octicorn. Talib, Binny, illus. 2016. 48p. (J). (gr. -1-3). 17.99 (978-0-06-238793-6(6)) HarperCollins Pubs.
Drouhard, Brianne. Billie the Unicorn. 2011. (ENG., Illus.). 36p. (J). (gr. -1-3). 15.95 (978-1-59702-024-4(9)) Immedium.
Duey, Kathleen. Castle Avamir. Rayyan, Omar, illus. 2004. (Unicorn's Secret Ser.). 73p. (gr. 2-5). 15.00 (978-0-7569-3357-9(9)) Perfection Learning Corp.
—The Journey Home. Rayyan, Omar, illus. 2003. (Unicorn's Secret Ser.: 8). (ENG.). 80p. (J). (gr. 2-5). pap. 5.99 (978-0-689-85374-6(2), Aladdin) Simon & Schuster Children's Publishing.
—The Mountains of the Moon. Rayyan, Omar, illus. 2005. 76p. (J). lib. bdg. 15.00 (978-1-59054-907-0(4)) Fitzgerald Bks.
—The Silver Bracelet. Rayyan, Omar, illus. 2005. 90p. (J). lib. bdg. 15.00 (978-1-59054-917-9(1)) Fitzgerald Bks.
—True Heart. Rayyan, Omar, illus. 2004. (Unicorn's Secret Ser.). 75p. (gr. 2-5). 15.00 (978-0-7569-3385-2(4)) Perfection Learning Corp.
Duncan, Jasmin. The Unicorn Legacy. 2013. 100p. pap. (978-1-909402-11-9(7)); pap. (978-1-909402-12-6(5)) Vamptasy Publishing.
Durant, Sybrina, et al. Legend of the Blue Unicorn: Return of the Dragons, 3 vols. Johnson, Britt, ed. l.t. ed. 2003. (ENG., Illus.). 25p. (J). (gr. k-5). spiral bd. 8.99 (978-1-929063-93-2(8), 331) Moons & Stars Publishing For Children.
Dyckman, Ame. You Don't Want a Unicorn! Climo, Liz, illus. 2017. (ENG.). 40p. (J). (gr. -1-3). 16.99 (978-0-316-34347-3(1)) Little Brown & Co.
Dynyel. Windy the Winged Unicorn. 2004. 140p. 24.95 (978-1-4184-8615-0(9)) AuthorHouse.
Fabrizio, T. L. Natalie Bean. 2011. 28p. pap. 24.95 (978-1-4626-0645-0(8)) America Star Bks.
Fei, Kanara. Kalani's Wish. 2009. 44p. pap. 16.99 (978-1-4389-8118-5(X)) AuthorHouse.
Flor Ada, Alma. The Unicorn of the West. 2007.Tr. of El Unicornio del Oeste. (ENG.). 32p. (J). (gr. -1-3). 11.99 (978-1-4169-6843-6(1), Simon & Schuster/Paula Wiseman Bks.) Simon & Schuster/Paula Wiseman Bks.
—Unicorn of the West (Spanish Edition) 2007. (ENG.). 32p. (J). (gr. -1-3). 11.99 (978-1-4169-6844-3(X), Simon & Schuster/Paula Wiseman Bks.) Simon & Schuster/Paula Wiseman Bks.
Franklin, Cathy. Pinta & Polly Go to the Moon, 1 vol. Poole, Tracy, illus. 2009. 27p. pap. 24.95 (978-1-60813-861-6(5)) America Star Bks.
George, Joshua. Horses & Unicorns. Green, Barry, illus. 2017. (Scratch & Draw Ser.). (ENG.). 56p. (J). (gr. k-2). 12.99 **(978-1-78700-073-5(7))** Top That! Publishing PLC GBR. Dist: Independent Pubs. Group.
Green with Envy. 2014. (Unicorn Magic Ser.: 3). (ENG., Illus.). 144p. (J). (gr. 1-4). pap. 5.99 (978-1-4424-9826-6(9), Aladdin) Simon & Schuster Children's Publishing.
Grove, Malachai. Malachai Grove Plunt Solinatry: The Song of Malachai. 2010. 24p. 14.99 (978-1-4520-6441-3(5)) AuthorHouse.
Haesche, Richard, Sr. The Legend of the Unicorn. 2007. (ENG.). 61p. (J). 8.99 (978-0-9798536-9-2(9)) Kreative X-Pressions Pubns.
Hague, Michael. Michael Hague's Magical World of Unicorns. Hague, Michael, illus. 2012. (ENG., Illus.). 36p. (J). (gr. -1-3). pap. 17.99 (978-1-4424-6041-6(5), Simon & Schuster Bks. For Young Readers) Simon & Schuster Bks. For Young Readers.
Hale, Shannon & Hale, Dean. The Princess in Black & the Hungry Bunny Horde. Pham, LeUyen, illus. 2016. (Princess in Black Ser.: 3). (ENG.). (J). (gr. k-3). 96p. pap. 6.99 (978-0-7636-9089-2(9)); 85p. 14.99 (978-0-7636-6513-5(4)) Candlewick Pr.
—The Princess in Black & the Hungry Bunny Horde. Pham, LeUyen, illus. 2016. (Princess in Black Ser.: 3). (ENG.). 85p. (J). (gr. k-3). 17.20 (978-0-606-39109-2(6)) Turtleback Bks.
Hamilton, Rachel. Louie Lets Loose! (Unicorn in New York #1) 2017. (Unicorn in New York Ser.: 1). (ENG.). 128p. (J). (gr. 2-5). pap. 4.99 **(978-1-338-05508-5(9)**, Scholastic Paperbacks) Scholastic, Inc.
—Louie Takes the Stage! (Unicorn in New York #2) 2017. (Unicorn in New York Ser.: 2). (ENG.). 128p. (J). (gr. 2-5). pap. 4.99 **(978-1-338-05512-2(7)**, Scholastic Paperbacks) Scholastic, Inc.
Hasbro. Around Equestria! 2016. (ENG.). 160p. (J). (gr. -1-3). 11.99 (978-0-316-39529-8(3)) Little, Brown Bks. for Young Readers.
Hasbro & Finn, Perdita. My Little Pony: Friendship Is Magic. 2016. (Equestria Girls Ser.: 6). (ENG., Illus.). 208p. (J). (gr. 3-7). 9.99 (978-0-316-26699-4(X)) Little, Brown Bks. for Young Readers.
Hasbro Industries Incorporated Staff & Snider, Brandon T. Wonderbolts Academy Handbook. 2016. (ENG.). 192p. (J). (gr. 3-7). 17.99 (978-0-316-39499-4(8)) Little, Brown Bks. for Young Readers.
Hecker, Vera, illus. A Home for Rainbow. 2007. 32p. (J). (978-0-9799729-0-4(6)) Banta, Sandra.
Hegerhorst, Bethany. The Baseball Princess: Samantha's Summer & the Unicorn Flu. Abbott, Kristin, illus. 2012. 32p. (J). (978-0-9871281-5-7(9)) Murray Bks.
Hendrix, E. B. Angel & Evie: Catching a Unicorn. 2013. (Illus.). 42p. 19.99 (978-0-9857367-9-8(8)) Advanced Publishing LLC.
Hennessy, B. G. Claire & the Unicorn Happy Ever After. Mitchell, Susan, illus. 2006. (ENG.). 32p. (J). (gr. -1-3). 17.99 (978-1-4169-0815-9(3), Simon & Schuster Bks. For Young Readers) Simon & Schuster Bks. For Young Readers.
Heyman, Alissa. Twelve Dancing Unicorns. Gerard, Justin, illus. 2014. (ENG.). 32p. (J). (gr. -1-2). 14.95 (978-1-4027-8732-4(4)) Sterling Publishing Co., Inc.
Hicks, Angie, illus. Moonlight & the Mermaid. 2012. (ENG.). 24p. (J). 9.95 (978-1-84135-833-8(9)) Award Pubns. Ltd. GBR. Dist: Parkwest Pubns., Inc.
Howard, Cheryl L. Mikhael the Mighty: Be True to Who You Are & You Can Never Go Wrong. 2009. 52p. pap. 18.50 (978-1-60860-760-0(7), Strategic Bk. Publishing) Strategic Book Publishing & Rights Agency (SBPRA).
Hughes, Carol. The Princess & the Unicorn. 2010. (ENG.). 288p. (J). (gr. 3-7). 7.99 (978-0-375-85563-4(7), Bluefire) Random Hse. Children's Bks.
Hussey, Lorna. Little Lost Unicorn. 2009. (ENG., Illus.). 22p. (J). (gr. -1-2). 14.95 (978-1-4027-6861-3(3)) Sterling Publishing Co., Inc.
Johnson, Sandi, et al. Legend of the Blue Unicorn: Land of OSM. Johnson, Britt, ed. Krittendon, Kim & Johnson, Jim, illus. 2014. (Little Choo-Choo Bks.). (ENG.). 40p. (J). (gr. -1-6). 14.99 (978-1-929063-09-3(1), 109) Moons & Stars Publishing For Children.
Julius, Nicholas. The Mythfitz: Unee the Unicorn. 2012. (ENG., Illus.). 62p. 28.95 (978-1-4327-9868-0(5)); pap. 23.95 (978-1-4327-9365-4(9)) Outskirts Pr., Inc.
Kann, Victoria. Goldilicious. Kann, Victoria, illus. 2009. (Illus.). 40p. (J). (gr. k-3). (ENG.). 17.99 (978-0-06-124408-7(2)); lib. bdg. 18.89 (978-0-06-124409-4(0)) HarperCollins Pubs.
—Soccer Star. 2012. (Pinkalicious I Can Read Ser.). (J). lib. bdg. 13.55 (978-0-606-26280-4(6), Turtleback) Turtleback Bks.
King, Karen. Unicorn Magic. Hicks, Angie, illus. 2012. (ENG.). 24p. 9.95 (978-1-84135-832-1(0)) Award Pubns. Ltd. GBR. Dist: Parkwest Pubns., Inc.
K.M. Mohr, John Kelley and. Waking Dalifi. 2005. 72p. pap. 9.95 (978-1-4116-6364-0(0)) Lulu Pr., Inc.
Koch, Claus. The Three Little Wolves & the Big Bad Boar. 2011. 68p. pap. 9.99 (978-1-4520-5321-9(9)) AuthorHouse.
Kuenzler, Lou. The Dragon Dance. 2017. (Princess DisGrace Ser.). (ENG., Illus.). 272p. (J). (gr. 3-7). 15.99 (978-0-553-53781-9(4), Random Hse. Bks. for Young Readers) Random Hse. Children's Bks.
—Princess DisGrace: a Royal Disaster. 2016. (Princess DisGrace Ser.). (ENG., Illus.). 240p. (J). (gr. 3-7). 12.99 (978-0-553-53775-8(X), Random Hse. Bks. for Young Readers) Random Hse. Children's Bks.
Kurtz, John. Unicorn Fun Coloring Book. 2014. (ENG., Illus.). 32p. (J). (gr. k-5). pap. 3.99 (978-0-486-78196-9(8)) Dover Pubns., Inc.
LaFevers, R. L. The Unicorn's Tale. Murphy, Kelly, illus. 2012. (Nathaniel Fludd, Beastologist Ser.: 4). (ENG.). 160p. (J). (gr. 1-4). pap. 5.99 (978-0-547-85079-5(4)) Houghton Mifflin Harcourt Publishing Co.
Lee, Tanith. Black Unicorn. 2005. (ENG., Illus.). 144p. (J). (gr. -1-12). per. 12.00 (978-1-59687-162-5(8)) IBks., Inc.
LeGette, M. L. The Unicorn Girl. 2008. (ENG.). 416p. pap. 10.00 (978-1-4196-8696-2(8)) CreateSpace Independent Publishing Platform.
Lincoln, Jerri. The Little Unicorn Who Could Coloring Book. 2012. 34p. pap. 7.77 (978-1-938322-00-6(2)) Ralston Store Publishing.
Lincoln, Jerri Kay. Dancing with Unicorns. 2013. 254p. pap. 14.99 (978-1-938322-21-1(5)) Ralston Store Publishing.
Loehr, Mallory. Unicorn Wings. Silin-Palmer, Pamela, illus. 2006. (Step into Reading Ser.: Vol. 1). (ENG.). 32p. (J). (gr. -1-1). per. 3.99 (978-0-375-83117-1(7), Random Hse. Bks. for Young Readers) Random Hse. Children's Bks.
MacLean, Heather. The Moonicorn Fairies. 2011. 40p. pap. (978-1-77067-687-9(2)) FriesenPress.
—The Mousecat & the Moonicorns on Halloween Night. 2013. 40p. pap. 16.95 (978-1-4525-7617-6(3), Balboa Pr.) Author Solutions, Inc.
Matheis, Mickie. Sparkle Fest Showdown! (Nella the Princess Knight) Lew, Steph, illus. 2017. (Pictureback(R) Ser.). (ENG.). 24p. (J). (gr. -1-2). pap. 5.99 **(978-1-5247-1723-0(1)**, Random Hse. Bks. for Young Readers) Random Hse. Children's Bks.
McDonald, Ann-Eve. The Tale of the Black Square. 2004. (J). (978-0-9770158-2-5(3)) BeachWalk Bks. Inc.
Meadows, Daisy. Leona the Unicorn Fairy. 2012. (Illus.). 65p. (J). (978-0-545-42601-5(4)) Scholastic, Inc.
Miller, J. Cris. Stories to Read to Children: The Pony & the Unicorn & 3 other Stories, 8 vols., Vol. 1. 2007. (Illus.). 80p. (J). 19.95 (978-0-9725308-2-8(7)) Miller, J. Cris & Assocs.
Miller, Victoria, illus. Dora & the Unicorn King. 2011. (Dora the Explorer Ser.). (ENG.). 24p. (J). pap. 3.99 (978-1-4424-1312-2(3), Simon Spotlight/Nickelodeon) Simon Spotlight/Nickelodeon.
—Flowers for Mami Unicorn! 2010. (Dora the Explorer Ser.). (ENG.). 24p. (J). (gr. -1-2). pap. 3.99 (978-1-4169-9064-2(X), Simon Spotlight/Nickelodeon) Simon Spotlight/Nickelodeon.
Morehouse, Toni B. Junie's Unicorn Horn. 2012. 30p. pap. 19.99 (978-1-4772-9894-7(0)) AuthorHouse.
Nelson-Schmidt, Michelle. Bob Is a Unicorn. Nelson-Schmidt, Michelle, illus. 2014. (ENG., Illus.). 28p. (J). 14.99 (978-1-61067-155-2(4)) Kane Miller.
North, Poppy. The Ruby Stone. 2013. 52p. pap. 15.99 (978-1-4797-6920-9(7)) Xlibris Corp.
Oceanak, Karla. Goodnight Unicorn: A Magical Parody. Spanjer, Kendra, illus. 2016. (ENG.). 32p. (gr. -1-3). 16.95 (978-1-934649-63-3(5)) Bailiwick Pr.
Ogburn, Jacqueline. The Unicorn in the Barn. Green, Rebecca, illus. 2017. (ENG.). 304p. (J). (gr. 5-7). 16.99 (978-0-544-76112-4(X), HMH Books For Young Readers) Houghton Mifflin Harcourt Publishing Co.
Once upon a Time- Lost Unicorn. 2005. (J). bds. (978-1-4194-0097-1(5)) Paradise Pr., Inc.
Osborne, Mary Pope. Blizzard of the Blue Moon. Murdocca, Sal, illus. 2007. (Magic Tree House Merlin Mission Ser.: 8). (ENG.). 144p. (J). (gr. 2-5). 5.99 (978-0-375-83038-9(3), Random Hse. Bks. for Young Readers) Random Hse. Children's Bks.
Osborne, Mary Pope, et al. Tormenta de Nieve en Luna Azul. Murdocca, Sal, illus. 2016. (SPA.). (J). (gr. 2-4). pap. 5.99 **(978-1-63245-646-5(X))** Lectorum Pubns., Inc.
Perelman, Helen. A Valentine's Surprise. Waters, Erica-Jane, illus. 2011. (Candy Fairies Ser.: 7). (ENG.). 128p. (J). (gr. 2-5). pap. 5.99 (978-1-4424-2215-5(7), Aladdin) Simon & Schuster Children's Publishing.
Peterfreund, Diana. Ascendant. (ENG.). (YA). (gr. 9). 2012. 416p. pap. 8.99 (978-0-06-149005-7(9)) 2010. 400p. 17.99 (978-0-06-149002-6(4)) HarperCollins Pubs. (HarperTeen).
—Rampant. 2010. (ENG.). 432p. (YA). (gr. 9). pap. 8.99 (978-0-06-149004-0(0), HarperTeen) HarperCollins Pubs.
Pierce, Meredith Ann. The Birth of the Firebringer, Vol. 1. 2003. (ENG.). 208p. (YA). (gr. 7-18). pap. 7.99 (978-0-14-250053-8(4), Firebird) Penguin Young Readers Group.
—The Dark Moon. 2003. (ENG.). 256p. (YA). (gr. 7-11). 7.99 (978-0-14-250057-6(7), Firebird) Penguin Young Readers Group.
—The Son of Summer Stars, Vol. 3. 2003. (ENG.). 256p. (YA). (gr. 7-7). 7.99 (978-0-14-250074-3(7), Firebird) Penguin Young Readers Group.
Pigg, Theresa. Sunshine, the Golden Unicorn. Roberts, Rebecca, illus. 2011. 20p. pap. 24.95 (978-1-4626-0733-4(0)) America Star Bks.
Pilkey, Dav. Uranium Unicorns from Uranus., Bk. 7. 2015. (Ricky Ricotta Ser.: 7). (ENG., Illus.). 128p. (J). (gr. -1-3). pap. 5.99 (978-0-545-63015-3(0)) Scholastic, Inc.
Random House Staff. Dora & the Unicorn King (Dora the Explorer) Random House Staff, illus. 2013. (Step into Reading Ser.). (ENG., Illus.). 24p. (J). (gr. -1-1). pap. 3.99 (978-0-449-81437-6(8), Random Hse. Bks. for Young Readers) Random Hse. Children's Bks.
Rednose, Skiddles. Tale of the Land of Umble. 2013. 126p. pap. 18.99 (978-1-938487-14-9(1)) Big Country Publishing, LLC.
Reisner, Molly. Dora & the Unicorn King (Dora the Explorer) Aikins, David, illus. 2011. (Little Golden Book Ser.). (ENG.). 24p. (J). (gr. -1-2). 4.99 (978-0-375-87226-6(4), Golden Bks.) Random Hse. Children's Bks.
Ricci, Christine. Nella's Unicorn Rescue. Random House & Sorrentino, Alessandra, illus. 2017. (ENG.). 32p. (J). (gr. -1-2). 16.99 (978-1-5247-1875-6(0), Random Hse. Bks. for Young Readers) Random Hse. Children's Bks.
Rizzo, Cynthia Marie. Julie & the Unicorn. 2003. 49p. pap. 16.95 (978-1-4137-0785-4(8)) PublishAmerica, Inc.
Rodda, Emily. The Unicorn. Vitale, Raoul, illus. 2007. (Fairy Realm Ser.). 106p. (gr. 3-7). 25.65 (978-1-59961-328-4(X)) Spotlight.
Rosen, Lucy. My Little Pony: Cutie Map Quest: Punch Out & Play. 2016. (ENG., Illus.). 36p. (J). (gr. 1-5). pap. 12.99 (978-0-316-39293-8(6)) Little, Brown Bks. for Young Readers.
Rosenthal, Amy Krouse. Uni the Unicorn. Barrager, Brigette, illus. (ENG.). (J). 2017. 36p. (— 1). bds. 8.99 **(978-1-5247-6616-0(X))** 2014. 48p. (gr. -1-3). 17.99 (978-0-385-37555-9(7)) Random Hse. Children's Bks. (Random Hse. Bks. for Young Readers).
—Uni the Unicorn & the Dream Come True. Barrager, Brigette, illus. 2017. (ENG.). 40p. (J). (gr. -1-2). 17.99 **(978-1-101-93659-7(2))**; lib. bdg. 20.99 **(978-1-101-93660-3(6))** Random Hse. Children's Bks. (Random Hse. Bks. for Young Readers).
Rusu, Meredith. The Baby Unicorn (Little Charmers: 8x8) 2016. (Little Charmers Ser.). (ENG.). 24p. (J). (gr. -1-k). pap. 3.99 (978-1-338-11275-7(9)) Scholastic, Inc.
Ryder, Chloe. Princess Ponies 4: a Unicorn Adventure! 2014. (Princess Ponies Ser.). (ENG., Illus.). 128p. (J). (gr. 2-4). pap. 5.99 (978-1-61963-294-3(2), 9781619632943, Bloomsbury USA Childrens) Bloomsbury Publishing USA.
Saveley, Barb. Dusky: The Lost Unicorn. 2008. 24p. pap. 24.95 (978-1-60441-909-2(1)) America Star Bks.
Scalawag: (A Kathy Dubetz Production). Unicorns in the Mist: Books One & Two. 2011. 100p. pap. 19.95 (978-1-4560-5655-1(7)) America Star Bks.
Schemery, Beau. The Unlikely Hero [Library Edition]. 2013. 160p. pap. 14.99 (978-1-62380-920-1(7), Harmony Ink Pr.) Dreamspinner Pr.
Selfors, Suzanne. The Order of the Unicorn. Santat, Dan, illus. 2014. 197p. (J). (978-0-316-32339-0(X)) Little Brown & Co.
—The Order of the Unicorn: The Imaginary Veterinary. Santat, Dan, illus. 2014. (Imaginary Veterinary Ser.: 4). (ENG.). 208p. (J). (gr. 2-7). 16.00 (978-0-316-36406-5(1)) Little, Brown Bks. for Young Readers.
Sharma, Radhika. The Princess & the Unicorn Prince. 2007. 48p. pap. 19.96 (978-1-4357-0072-7(4)) Lulu Pr., Inc.
Shea, Bob. Unicorn Thinks He's Pretty Great. Shea, Bob, illus. 2013. (ENG., Illus.). 40p. (J). (gr. -1-k). 15.99 (978-1-4231-5952-0(7)) Hyperion Pr.
Sima, Jessie. Not Quite Narwhal. Sima, Jessie, illus. 2017. (ENG., Illus.). 40p. (J). (gr. -1-3). 17.99 (978-1-4814-6909-8(6), Simon & Schuster Bks. For Young Readers) Simon & Schuster Bks. For Young Readers.
Simpson, Dana. A Heavenly Nostrils Chronicle. 2014. (Phoebe & Her Unicorn Ser.: 1). (ENG., Illus.). 224p. (J). 9.99 (978-1-4494-4620-8(5)) Andrews McMeel Publishing.
—Phoebe & Her Unicorn: A Heavenly Nostrils Chronicle. 2014. (Phoebe & Her Unicorn Ser.: 1). (Illus.). 222p. (J). lib. bdg. 20.85 (978-0-606-36144-6(8)) Turtleback Bks.
—Razzle Dazzle Unicorn. 2016. (Phoebe & Her Unicorn Ser.: 4). (ENG.). 184p. (J). 13.99 (978-1-4494-8351-7(8)) Andrews McMeel Publishing.
—Razzle Dazzle Unicorn: Another Phoebe & Her Unicorn Adventure. 2016. (Phoebe & Her Unicorn Ser.: 4). (ENG., Illus.). 184p. (J). pap. 9.99 (978-1-4494-7791-2(7)) Andrews McMeel Publishing.
—Unicorn Crossing. 2017. (Phoebe & Her Unicorn Ser.: 5). lib. bdg. 20.85 **(978-0-606-39767-4(1))** Turtleback Bks.
—Unicorn Crossing: Another Phoebe & Her Unicorn Adventure. 2017. (Phoebe & Her Unicorn Ser.: 5). (ENG., Illus.). 176p. (J). pap. 9.99 (978-1-4494-8357-9(7)) Andrews McMeel Publishing.
—Unicorn on a Roll. 2016. (Phoebe & Her Unicorn Ser.: 2). (ENG.). 224p. (J). 13.99 (978-1-4494-8349-4(6)) Andrews McMeel Publishing.
—Unicorn on a Roll. 2015. (Phoebe & Her Unicorn Ser.: 2). lib. bdg. 20.85 (978-0-606-36985-5(6)) Turtleback Bks.
Smith, Cleveland W. Billabongo. 2008. 172p. pap. (978-1-84923-100-8(1)) YouWriteOn.
Smith, Sindy. Indy the Unicorn Prince. Smith, Sindy, illus. 2012. (Illus.). 46p. 29.95 (978-1-4626-9864-6(6)) America Star Bks.
—Indy the Unicorn Prince. 2012. 48p. pap. 24.95 (978-1-4626-7519-7(0)) America Star Bks.
Stiefvater, Maggie & Pearce, Jackson. Pip Bartlett's Guide to Unicorn Training. 2017. (Pip Bartlett Ser.: 2). (ENG.). 192p. (J). (gr. 3-7). 9.99 (978-0-545-70929-3(6), Scholastic Pr.) Scholastic, Inc.

The Strode Family. The Magical Land of Far, Far Away. 2011. 16p. pap. *(978-1-4269-5570-9(7))* Trafford Publishing (UK) Ltd.

Tillworth, Mary. Dragon in the School (Dora & Friends) Goddard, Brenda & Haskett, Dan, illus. 2015. (Little Golden Book Ser.). (ENG.). 24p. (J). (gr. -1-2). 4.99 *(978-0-553-52089-7(X)*, Golden Bks.) Random Hse. Children's Bks.

Universal. Agnes Loves Unicorns! 2017. (ENG., Illus.). 32p. (J). (gr. -1-3). 12.99 ***(978-0-316-50747-9(4))*** Little, Brown Bks. for Young Readers.

Vevers, Rachel. Quest for the Unicorn. 2012. 222p. pap. *(978-1-78176-316-2(X))* FeedARead.com.

Viknesh, R. My Fantasy Your Treat. 2012. 32p. pap. 28.55 *(978-1-4669-2733-9(X))* Trafford Publishing.

Warren, Cindy. The Unicorn's Horn. 2011. 98p. pap. 19.95 *(978-1-4560-6987-2(X))* America Star Bks.

Welch, Sheila Kelly. The Shadowed Unicorn. 2011. 192p. (gr. -1). pap. 12.95 *(978-1-4502-6991-9(5))* iUniverse, Inc.

Wreggelsworth, Irene. Liv's Search for the Last Unicorn. Anderson, Anya, illus. 2011. (ENG.). 112p. pap. 26.99 *(978-1-4538-9270-1(2))* CreateSpace Independent Publishing Platform.

Yolen, Jane. A Plague of Unicorns, 1 vol. 2016. (ENG.). 192p. (J). pap. 7.99 *(978-0-310-74611-9(6))* Zonderkidz.

—A Plague of Unicorns. 2015. (J). pap. *(978-0-310-74610-2(8))* Zondervan.

—Where Have the Unicorns Gone? Sanderson, Ruth, illus. 2003. (ENG.). 32p. (J). (gr. -1-3). 9.99 *(978-0-689-86359-2(4)*, Simon & Schuster/Paula Wiseman Bks.) Simon & Schuster Bks. For Young Readers.

Young, Amy. A New Friend for Sparkle. 2017. (ENG., Illus.). 40p. (J). 16.99 *(978-0-374-30553-6(6)*, 9780374305536, Farrar, Straus & Giroux (BYR)) Farrar, Straus & Giroux.

—A Unicorn Named Sparkle. Young, Amy, illus. 2016. (ENG., Illus.). 40p. (J). 16.99 *(978-0-374-30185-9(9)*, 9780374301859, Farrar, Straus & Giroux (BYR)) Farrar, Straus & Giroux.

UNIDENTIFIED FLYING OBJECTS

Aliens & UFOs: Famous UFO Sightings & Incidents. (Critical Reading Ser.). (YA). (gr. 6-12). pap. *(978-0-8092-1104-3(1))* Jamestown.

Asimov, Isaac & Hantula, Richard. UFOs. 2005. (Isaac Asimov's 21st Century Library of the Universe). (Illus.). 32p. (gr. 2-6). lib. bdg. 26.00 *(978-0-8368-3954-8(4)*, Gareth Stevens Learning Library) Stevens, Gareth Publishing LLLP.

Bringle, Jennifer. Alien Sightings in America. 2011. (America's Supernatural Secrets Ser.). (ENG.). 48p. (YA). (gr. 5-8). pap. 11.75 *(978-1-4488-5578-0(0))*; lib. bdg. 29.25 *(978-1-4488-5530-8(6))* Rosen Publishing Group, Inc., The.

Bullard, Lisa. I'm from Outer Space! Meet an Alien. Moran, Mike, illus. 2014. (Monster Buddies Ser.). (ENG.). 24p. (gr. k-2). lib. bdg. 23.93 *(978-0-7613-9193-7(2)*, Millbrook Pr.) Lerner Publishing Group.

Cheatham, Mark. Aliens! 2012. (Jr. Graphic Monster Stories Ser.). (ENG.). 24p. (J). (gr. 3-6). pap. 10.60 *(978-1-4488-6403-4(8))*; lib. bdg. 25.25 *(978-1-4488-6222-1(1))* Rosen Publishing Group, Inc., The. (PowerKids Pr.).

Coddington, Andrew. Aliens. 2016. (Creatures of Fantasy Ser.). 64p. (J). (gr. 6-6). 34.21 *(978-1-5026-1862-7(1))* Cavendish Square Publishing.

Coddington, Andrew. Aliens, UFOs, & Unexplained Encounters. 2017. (J). ***(978-1-5026-2845-9(7))*** Cavendish Square Publishing.

Dalley, Kirsten. Encounters with Ufos & Extraterrestrial Life. Pye, Michael, ed. 2012. (Mysteries Uncovered, Secrets Declassified Ser.). (ENG., Illus.). 224 &ndashp. (YA). (gr. 7-12). 37.25 *(978-1-4488-9252-5(X))* Rosen Publishing Group, Inc., The.

DeMolay, Jack. Ovnis: El Caso Roswell. Obregón, José María, tr. from ENG. 2008. (Historietas Juveniles: Misterios (Jr. Graphic Mysteries) Ser.). (SPA., Illus.). 24p. (J). (gr. 2-5). lib. bdg. 25.25 *(978-1-4358-2539-0(X))* Rosen Publishing Group, Inc., The.

—Ovnis: El caso Roswell (UFO: the Roswell Incidents) 2009. (Historietas Juveniles: Misterios (Jr. Graphic Mysteries) Ser.). (SPA.). 24p. (gr. 2-3). 47.90 *(978-1-61513-349-9(6)*, Editorial Buenas Letras) Rosen Publishing Group, Inc., The.

—UFOs: The Roswell Incident. (Jr. Graphic Mysteries Ser.). (ENG.). 24p. 2009. (J). (gr. 2-3). 47.90 *(978-1-61513-852-4(8)*, PowerKids Pr.) 2007. (Illus.). (J). (gr. 2-5). lib. bdg. 25.25 *(978-1-4042-3403-1(9))* 2007. (Illus.). (gr. 3-8). pap. 10.60 *(978-1-4042-2156-7(5)*, PowerKids Pr.) Rosen Publishing Group, Inc., The.

Dicker, Katie. Visitors from Space. 2015. (Mystery! Ser.). (Illus.). 24p. (gr. 3-6). 28.50 *(978-1-62588-206-6(8)*, 1381015) Black Rabbit Bks.

Diker, Katie. Visitors from Space. 2015. (ENG., Illus.). 24p. (J). pap. 8.95 *(978-1-77092-237-2(7))* RiverStream Publishing.

Dolan, Richard M. & Zabel, Bryce. Project Disclosure: Revealing Government Secrets & Breaking the Truth Embargo, 1 vol. 2015. (ENG.). 250p. (YA). 38.25 *(978-1-4777-8155-5(2)*, Rosen Young Adult) Rosen Publishing Group, Inc., The.

Duncan, John. UFOs. 2006. (Unexplained Ser.). (Illus.). 36p. (gr. 3-6). lib. bdg. 26.00 *(978-0-8368-6268-3(6)*, Gareth Stevens Learning Library) Stevens, Gareth Publishing LLLP.

Earth Cosmology: The Effects of the Giant Destroyer Comet. 2004. (UFO Fact Bks.). (YA). cd-rom 15.00 *(978-0-934269-41-4(6))* UFO Photo Archives.

Erickson, Justin. Alien Abductions. 2011. (Unexplained Ser.). (ENG., Illus.). 24p. (J). (gr. 3-7). lib. bdg. 25.95 *(978-1-60014-582-7(5)*, Torque Bks.) Bellwether Media.

Goldfarb, Ian M. & Silverstein, Janna. Searching for Close Encounters with Aliens. 2011. (J). 244.80 *(978-1-4488-4862-1(8)*, Rosen Reference) Rosen Publishing Group, Inc., The.

Grace, N. B. UFO Lands in USA! Was a Spacecraft Crash Covered Up? 2011. (J). pap. *(978-0-545-32947-7(7))* Scholastic, Inc.

—UFOs: What Scientists Say May Shock You! 2008. (24/7: Science Behind the Scenes Ser.). (ENG., Illus.). 64p. (J). (gr. 7-12). pap. 7.95 *(978-0-531-18741-8(1)*, Watts, Franklin) Scholastic Library Publishing.

—UFO's: What Scientists Say May Shock You! 2008. (24/7: Science Behind the Scenes Ser.). (ENG., Illus.). 64p. (J). (gr. 9-12). 29.00 *(978-0-531-12074-3(0)*, Watts, Franklin) Scholastic Library Publishing.

Greene, Janice. Strange but True, 1 vol., Bk. 5. unabr. ed. 2011. (Strange but True Ser.). (ENG.). 75p. (YA). (gr. 9-12). pap. 8.95 *(978-1-61651-769-4(7))* Saddleback Educational Publishing, Inc.

Halls, Kelly Milner. Alien Investigation: Searching for the Truth about UFOs & Aliens. Spears, Rick, C., illus. 2015. (ENG.). 64p. (gr. 5-12). 34.65 *(978-1-4677-5987-8(2)*, Lerner Digital) Lerner Publishing Group.

—Alien Investigation: Searching for the Truth about UFOs & Aliens. Spears, Rick, illus. 2012. (Single Titles Ser.). (ENG.). 64p. (gr. 5-12). lib. bdg. 20.95 *(978-0-7613-6204-3(5)*, Millbrook Pr.) Lerner Publishing Group.

Haney, Jill. Area 51. 2015. (Red Rhino Nonfiction Ser.). (J). lib. bdg. 20.80 *(978-0-606-37198-8(2))* Turtleback Bks.

Harrison, Benjamin. Aliens, Sasquatches, Flowers, & Plants. 2011. 56p. (gr. -1). pap. 15.99 *(978-1-4634-6011-2(2))* AuthorHouse.

—Aliens, Sasquatches, Flowers, & Plants: Volume I. 2011. 56p. (gr. -1). pap. 15.99 *(978-1-4634-6009-9(0))* AuthorHouse.

Hawkins, John. Aliens & UFOs. 2012. (Mystery Hunters Ser.). (ENG., Illus.). 32p. (J). (gr. 4-6). pap. 10.60 *(978-1-4488-6437-9(2))*; lib. bdg. 25.25 *(978-1-4488-6427-0(5))* Rosen Publishing Group, Inc., The. (PowerKids Pr.).

Henderson, Bonnie. UFOS: Out of the Black. 2004. (Illus.). 240p. pap. 15.95 *(978-0-910042-90-1(X))* Allegheny Pr.

Herbst, Judith. UFOs. (Unexplained Ser.). (ENG., Illus.). 48p. (gr. 5-12). 2005. pap. 8.95 *(978-0-8225-2409-0(0)*, Lerner Pubns.) 2004. lib. bdg. 26.60 *(978-0-8225-0961-5(X))* Lerner Publishing Group.

Higgins, Nadia. Area 51. 2014. (Unexplained Mysteries Ser.). (ENG., Illus.). 24p. (J). (gr. 3-7). lib. bdg. 25.95 *(978-1-62617-101-5(7)*, Epic Bks.) Bellwether Media.

—UFOs. 2014. (Unexplained Mysteries Ser.). (ENG., Illus.). 24p. (J). (gr. 3-7). lib. bdg. 25.95 *(978-1-62617-107-7(6)*, Epic Bks.) Bellwether Media.

Hile, Lori. Aliens & UFOs. King, Chris, illus. 2013. (Solving Mysteries with Science Ser.). (ENG.). 48p. (gr. 3-6). pap. 9.95 *(978-1-4109-5504-3(4))* Heinemann-Raintree.

—Aliens & UFOs. 2013. (Solving Mysteries with Science Ser.). (ENG.). 48p. (gr. 3-6). 29.99 *(978-1-4109-5498-5(6))* Heinemann-Raintree.

Hodge, Susie & Mason, Paul. Investigating UFOs & Aliens. 2010. (Extreme! Ser.). (ENG.). 32p. (gr. 3-4). pap. 47.70 *(978-1-4296-5115-8(6)*, Fact Finders) Capstone Press of Coughlan Cos.

Jeffrey, Gary. UFOs. 2006. (Graphic Mysteries Ser.). (ENG., Illus.). 48p. (gr. 5-8). pap. 14.05 *(978-1-4042-0808-7(9))* Rosen Publishing Group, Inc., The.

—UFOs: Alien Abduction & Close Encounters. (Graphic Mysteries Ser.). (ENG.). 48p. 2009. (YA). (gr. 5-5). 58.50 *(978-1-61512-973-7(1)*, Rosen Reference) 2006. (Illus.). (J). (gr. 4-7). lib. bdg. 31.95 *(978-1-4042-0797-4(X))* Rosen Publishing Group, Inc., The.

Karst, Ken. Area 51: Enduring Mysteries. 2014. (Illus.). 48p. (J). pap. *(978-1-60818-399-9(8))* Creative Co., The.

—Enduring Mysteries: Area 51. 2015. (Enduring Mysteries Ser.). (ENG.). 48p. (J). (gr. 5-8). pap. 12.00 *(978-1-62832-070-1(2)*, Creative Paperbacks) Creative Co., The.

Kenney, Karen Latchana. Mysterious UFOs & Aliens. 2017. (Searchlight Books (tm) — Fear Fest Ser.). (ENG., Illus.). 32p. (J). (gr. 3-5). 30.65 ***(978-1-5124-3406-4(X))***; pap. 9.99 ***(978-1-5124-5606-6(3))*** Lerner Publishing Group.

Kincade, Chris. Encountering Aliens: Eyewitness Accounts, 1 vol. Mallea, Cristian, illus. 2014. (Eyewitness to the Unexplained Ser.). (ENG.). 32p. (gr. 3-4). 30.65 *(978-1-4914-0244-3(X)*, Graphic Library) Capstone Press of Coughlan Cos.

King, Sharon. Junior Alien Zone: Creative Experiences for Hands of All Ages! 2009. (Illus.). 51p. pap. 14.95 *(978-1-4327-1162-7(8))* Outskirts Pr., Inc.

Levete, Sarah. Aliens & UFOs. 2016. (Mystery Hunters Ser.). 00048p. (J). pap. 14.05 ***(978-1-4824-5992-0(2))*** Stevens, Gareth Publishing LLLP.

Levy, Janey. UFOs. 2006. (Tony Stead Nonfiction Independent Reading Collection). (ENG.). 24p. (gr. 3-6). pap. 8.85 *(978-1-4042-5671-2(7))* Rosen Publishing Group, Inc., The.

Linde, Barbara M. What Happened at Area 51? 2015. (History's Mysteries Ser.). (ENG., Illus.). 32p. (J). (gr. 4-5). pap. 10.50 *(978-1-4824-2102-6(X))* Stevens, Gareth Publishing LLLP.

Lorimer, Janet. Strange but True Book 2, 1 vol. unabr. ed. 2011. (Strange but True Ser.). (ENG.). 75p. (YA). (gr. 9-12). pap. 8.95 *(978-1-61651-766-3(2))* Saddleback Educational Publishing, Inc.

—Strange but True Book 3, 1 vol. unabr. ed. 2011. (Strange but True Ser.). (ENG.). 76p. (YA). (gr. 9-12). pap. 8.95 *(978-1-61651-767-0(0))* Saddleback Educational Publishing, Inc.

—Strange but True Book 4, 1 vol. unabr. ed. 2011. (Strange but True Ser.). (ENG.). 76p. (YA). (gr. 9-12). pap. 8.95 *(978-1-61651-768-7(9))* Saddleback Educational Publishing, Inc.

Marden, Kathleen & Stoner, Denise. Making Contact: Alien Abduction Case Studies, 1 vol. 2015. (ENG., Illus.). 250p. (J). 38.25 *(978-1-4777-8159-3(5)*, Rosen Young Adult) Rosen Publishing Group, Inc., The.

Martin, Michael. Mystery of Alien Abductions. 2013. (Unexplained Mysteries Ser.). (ENG.). 24p. (gr. 1-2). 25.32 *(978-1-4765-3095-6(5)*, First Facts) Capstone Press of Coughlan Cos.

—The Unsolved Mystery of Alien Abductions. 2013. (Unexplained Mysteries Ser.). (ENG.). 24p. (gr. 1-2). pap. 7.95 *(978-1-4765-3440-4(3)*, First Facts) Capstone Press of Coughlan Cos.

Martin, Ted. Area 51. 2011. (Unexplained Ser.). (ENG., Illus.). 24p. (YA). (gr. 3-7). lib. bdg. 25.95 *(978-1-60014-642-8(2)*, Torque Bks.) Bellwether Media.

McClellan, Ray. Alien Abductions. 2014. (Unexplained Mysteries Ser.). (ENG., Illus.). 24p. (J). (gr. 3-7). lib. bdg. 25.95 *(978-1-62617-100-8(9)*, Epic Bks.) Bellwether Media.

McCollum, Sean. Handbook to UFOs, Crop Circles, & Alien Encounters. 2016. (Paranormal Handbooks Ser.). (ENG., Illus.). 32p. (gr. 3-4). lib. bdg. 27.99 *(978-1-5157-1309-8(1)*, Edge Bks.) Capstone Press of Coughlan Cos.

McEvoy, Paul. The Alien Files. 2003. (Real Deal Ser.). (Illus.). 32p. (J). pap. *(978-0-7608-6691-7(0))* Sundance/Newbridge Educational Publishing.

Messages from the Pleiades Vol. 1: The Contact Notes of Eduard Billy Meier. 2004. (UFO Fact Bks.). (YA). cd-rom 15.00 *(978-0-934269-49-0(1))* UFO Photo Archives.

The Mormon Gold Plates: Au Unusual Account. 2004. (YA). cd-rom 15.00 *(978-0-934269-57-5(2))* UFO Photo Archives.

Netzley, Patricia D. Alien Encounters. 2011. (Extraterrestrial Life Ser.). 80p. (YA). (gr. 7-12). lib. bdg. 27.95 *(978-1-60152-169-9(3))* ReferencePoint Pr., Inc.

Noll, Elizabeth. UFOs. 2017. (Strange ... but True? Ser.). (ENG.). 32p. (gr. 3-7). 31.35 ***(978-1-68072-027-3(9))*** Black Rabbit Bks.

O'Keefe, Emily. UFOs. 2015. (Unsolved Mysteries Ser.). (ENG.). 24p. (J). (gr. 1-4). 28.50 *(978-1-63407-075-1(5)*, 208910) Child's World, Inc., The.

O'Neill, Terry, ed. UFOs. 2003. (Opposing Viewpoints Ser.). (Illus.). 160p. (J). 27.45 *(978-0-7377-1070-0(5)*, Greenhaven Pr., Inc.) Cengage Gale.

Orme, David. UFOs - Are They Real? 2007. (Trailblazers Ser.). (ENG., Illus.). 36p. pap. *(978-1-84167-423-0(0))* Ransom Publishing Ltd.

Parks, Peggy J. Aliens. 2006. (Mysterious Encounters Ser.). (ENG., Illus.). 48p. (J). (gr. 3-7). lib. bdg. 27.50 *(978-0-7377-3518-5(X)*, Kidhaven) Cengage Gale.

Portman, Michael. Are UFOs Real? 2013. (Space Mysteries Ser.). (Illus.). 32p. (gr. 2-5). 25.25 *(978-1-4339-8262-0(5))*; pap. 10.50 *(978-1-4339-8263-7(3))* Stevens, Gareth Publishing LLLP. (Gareth Stevens Learning Library).

Rau, Dana Meachen. Aliens. 2010. (Bookworms Chapter Books: for Real? Ser.). 24p. (gr. 2-3). 22.79 *(978-0-7614-4861-7(6))* Marshall Cavendish Corp.

Redfern, Nick. True Stories of Space Exploration Conspiracies. 2014. (Off the Record! Ser.). 248p. (YA). (gr. 7-12). 38.25 *(978-1-4777-7833-3(0))* Rosen Publishing Group, Inc., The.

—True Stories of the Real Men in Black. 2014. (Off the Record! Ser.). (Illus.). 264p. (J). (gr. 7-12). 38.25 *(978-1-4777-7837-1(3))* Rosen Publishing Group, Inc., The.

Richards, Dillon H. & Stirling, Janet. Searching for UFOs. 2011. (J). pap. 12.95 *(978-1-4488-4766-2(4))*; lib. bdg. 31.95 *(978-1-4488-4765-5(6))* Rosen Publishing Group, Inc., The. (Rosen Reference).

Rivkin, Jennifer. Searching for UFOs. 2014. (Mysterious Monsters Ser.). 32p. (J). (gr. 3-6). lib. bdg. 26.25 *(978-1-4777-7109-9(3)*, PowerKids Pr.) Rosen Publishing Group, Inc., The.

Roberts, Steven. UFOs!, 1 vol., 1. 2014. (Jr. Graphic Monster Stories Ser.). (ENG.). 24p. (J). (gr. 3-6). 26.25 *(978-1-4777-6203-5(5)*, PowerKids Pr.) Rosen Publishing Group, Inc., The.

Roleff, Tamara L., ed. Alien Abductions. 2003. (Illus.). 160p. (J). lib. bdg. 32.45 *(978-0-7377-1589-7(8)*, Greenhaven Pr., Inc.) Cengage Gale.

Rooney, Anne. UFOs & Aliens. 2010. (Amazing Mysteries Ser.). (YA). (gr. 3-6). 28.50 *(978-1-59920-368-3(5))* Black Rabbit Bks.

Rutkowski, Chris A. I Saw It Too! Real UFO Sightings. 2009. (ENG., Illus.). 184p. (YA). (gr. 7-18). pap. 14.99 *(978-1-55488-448-3(9))* Dundurn CAN. Dist: Ingram Publisher Services.

Sautter, Aaron, et al. Searching for UFOs: An Isabel Soto Investigation. 2010. (Graphic Expeditions Ser.). (ENG.). 32p. (gr. 3-4). pap. 47.70 *(978-1-4296-5145-5(8))*; lib. bdg. 30.65 *(978-1-4296-3974-3(1))* Capstone Press of Coughlan Cos. (Graphic Library).

Shea, Therese. Investigating UFOs & Aliens, 1 vol. 2015. (ENG.). 48p. (YA). 25.85 *(978-1-62275-849-4(8)*, Britannica Educational Publishing) Rosen Publishing Group, Inc., The.

Sievert, Terri. The Unsolved Mystery of UFOs, 1 vol. 2013. (Unexplained Mysteries Ser.). (ENG.). 24p. (gr. 1-2). pap. 7.95 *(978-1-62065-812-3(7))*; pap. 41.70 *(978-1-62065-813-0(5)*, First Facts); lib. bdg. 25.32 *(978-1-62065-135-3(1))* Capstone Press of Coughlan Cos.

Silverstein, Janna. Close Encounters with Aliens. 2005. (Unsolved Mysteries: the Secret Files Ser.). (Illus.). 48p. (YA). (gr. 4-7). lib. bdg. 29.25 *(978-0-8239-3562-8(0))* Rosen Publishing Group, Inc., The.

Summers, Portia & Rau, Dana Meachen. Are Aliens Real? 2016. (I Want to Know Ser.). 32p. (J). pap. 10.52 *(978-0-7660-8228-1(8))* Enslow Pubs., Inc.

Terrell, Brandon. 12 Frightening Tales of Alien Encounters. 2017. (Scary & Spooky Ser.). (ENG., Illus.). 32p. (J). (gr. 3-6). 21.95 *(978-1-63235-293-4(1))* Pr. Room Editions LLC.

Tieck, Sarah. Aliens, 1 vol. 2015. (ENG., Illus.). 32p. (J). *(978-1-62403-763-4(1))* ABDO Publishing Co.

Troupe, Thomas Kingsley. The Legend of UFOs, 1 vol. Vignaga, Francesca Dafne, illus. 2012. (Legend Has It Ser.). (ENG.). 32p. (gr. 2-4). lib. bdg. 27.32 *(978-1-4048-6657-7(4))* Picture Window Bks.

UFO Abduction at Botucatu: A Preliminary Report. 2004. (UFO Fact Bks.). (YA). cd-rom 15.00 *(978-0-934269-36-0(X))* UFO Photo Archives.

UFO... Art: In Full Color. 2004. (UFO Fact Bks.). (YA). cd-rom 25.00 *(978-0-934269-54-4(8))* UFO Photo Archives.

UFO Capture of two f-14 Jets: Lost Navy Aircraft. 2004. (YA). cd-rom *(978-0-934269-56-8(4))* UFO Photo Archives.

UFO contact from beyond Rigel: A cherokee girl's Oddesy. 2004. (UFO Fact Bks.). (YA). cd-rom 15.00 *(978-0-934269-50-6(5))* UFO Photo Archives.

UFO Contact from COMA Berenesis. 2005. (YA). cd-rom *(978-0-934269-62-9(9))* UFO Photo Archives.

UFO Contact from Plamet Itibi-RA. 2003. (UFO Fact Bks.). (YA). cd-rom 15.00 *(978-0-934269-30-8(0))* UFO Photo Archives.

UFO Contact from Planet Acart: From Utopia to Reality. 2003. (UFO Fact Bks.). (YA). cd-rom 15.00 *(978-0-934269-32-2(7))* UFO Photo Archives.

UFO Contact from Planet Alcyone: Falling Bodies Theory. 2004. (UFO Fact Bks.). (YA). cd-rom 15.00 *(978-0-934269-47-6(5))* UFO Photo Archives.

UFO Contact from Planet Apu: 100 Hours with Extraterrestrials. 2004. (UFO Fact Bks.). (YA). cd-rom 15.00 *(978-0-934269-38-4(6))* UFO Photo Archives.

UFO Contact from Planet ARIAN. 2004. (YA). cd-rom 15.00 *(978-0-934269-33-9(5))* UFO Photo Archives.

UFO Contact from Planet Baavi: Proxima Centauri Group. 2004. (UFO Fact Bks.). (YA). cd-rom 15.00 *(978-0-934269-46-9(7))* UFO Photo Archives.

UFO Contact from Planet Klermer: Possibilities of the Infinite. 2004. (UFO Fact Bks.). (YA). cd-rom 15.00 *(978-0-934269-34-6(3))* UFO Photo Archives.

UFO Contact from Planet Korendor Vol. 1: Another Advanced Society. 2004. (YA). cd-rom 15.00 *(978-0-934269-63-6(7))* UFO Photo Archives.

UFO Contact from Planet Korendor, Vol. 2. 2005. (YA). cd-rom 15.00 *(978-0-934269-64-3(5))* UFO Photo Archives.

UFO Contact from Planet Nep-4: Earth Development. 2004. (UFO Fact Bks.). (YA). cd-rom 15.00 *(978-0-934269-40-7(8))* UFO Photo Archives.

UFO Contact from Planet Norca: The Shocking Truth. 2004. Orig. Title: The Shocking Truth. (YA). cd-rom 15.00 *(978-0-934269-59-9(9))* UFO Photo Archives.

UFO Contact from Planet Ummo, Vol. 3, Sesma: Daily Life on Ummo. 2004. (YA). cd-rom 15.00 *(978-0-934269-28-5(9))* UFO Photo Archives.

UFO Contact from Planet Venus: We Are Not Alone. 2004. (YA). cd-rom 15.00 *(978-0-934269-55-1(6))* UFO Photo Archives.

UFO Contact from Planet Zeti: Going Home? 2004. (UFO Fact Bks.). (YA). cd-rom 15.00 *(978-0-934269-39-1(4))* UFO Photo Archives.

UFO contact from the DAL Universe: With asket of the timmers Society. 2004. (UFO Fact Bks.). (YA). cd-rom 15.00 *(978-0-934269-48-3(3))* UFO Photo Archives.

UFO Contact of an Erotic Kind: The Assignment. 2003. (UFO Fact Bks.). (YA). cd-rom 15.00 *(978-0-934269-29-2(7))* UFO Photo Archives.

UFO Photographs Around the World, Vol. 3 of Series, Vol. 3. 2003. (UFO Fact Bks.). (YA). cd-rom 15.00 *(978-0-934269-35-3(1))* UFO Photo Archives.

UFO Photographs Around the World, Vol. 4 in Series, Vol. 4. 2003. (YA). cd-rom 15.00 *(978-0-934269-37-7(8))* UFO Photo Archives.

UFO, the DULCE Story: An Incredible Deception. 2004. (UFO Fact Bks.). (YA). cd-rom 15.00 *(978-0-934269-52-0(1))* UFO Photo Archives.

UmmoCat: The ummo Documents. 2004. (UFO Fact Bks.). (YA). cd-rom 25.00 *(978-0-934269-53-7(X))* UFO Photo Archives.

Webb, Stuart. UFOs. 2012. (Paranormal Files Ser.). (ENG., Illus.). 80p. (YA). (gr. 7-12). 33.25 *(978-1-4488-7176-6(X))* Rosen Publishing Group, Inc., The.

Wencel, Dave. UFOs. 2010. (Unexplained Ser.). (ENG., Illus.). 24p. (J). (gr. 3-7). lib. bdg. 25.95 *(978-1-60014-504-9(3)*, Torque Bks.) Bellwether Media.

Williams, Dinah. UFO Crash Sites. 2015. (Scary Places Ser.). (ENG.). 32p. (J). (gr. 4-8). lib. bdg. 26.60 *(978-1-62724-518-0(9))* Bearport Publishing Co., Inc.

63 Photographs in Color, Meier Vol. 5: The Meier Variation V. Photos. 2004. (UFO Fact Bks.). (YA). cd-rom 25.00 *(978-0-934269-51-3(3))* UFO Photo Archives.

76 UFO Photographs in Color, Vol 3: Clower Collection. 2004. (UFO Fact Bks.). (YA). cd-rom 25.00 *(978-0-934269-44-5(0))* UFO Photo Archives.

100 UFO Photographs in Color Vol, 2 Vol. 2 Series: Series in Sequence. 2004. (UFO Fact Bks.). (YA). cd-rom 25.00 *(978-0-934269-43-8(2))* UFO Photo Archives.

100 UFO Photographs in Color, Vol,1 Vol. 1: The Best of the Best. 2004. (UFO Fact Bks.). (YA). cd-rom 25.00 *(978-0-934269-42-1(4))* UFO Photo Archives.

135 UFO Photographs in Color, Vol. 4: Best of Meier Early UFO Photos. 2004. (UFO Fact Bks.). (YA). cd-rom 25.00 *(978-0-934269-45-2(9))* UFO Photo Archives.

UNIDENTIFIED FLYING OBJECTS—FICTION

Adler, David A. The Mystery of the U. F. O., 2 vols. Natti, Susanna, illus. 2004. (Cam Jansen Ser.: 2). (ENG.). 64p. (J). (gr. 2-5). 4.99 *(978-0-14-240011-1(4)*, Puffin Books) Penguin Young Readers Group.

Bramlett, Timothy A. A Visit to Skytropolis. 2012. 24p. pap. 17.99 *(978-1-4772-1173-1(X))* AuthorHouse.

Daly, Joseph M. Strange Town Volume One: The Woods Behind Trevor Malone's House. 2007. 265p. (YA). pap. 9.99 net. *(978-0-9779921-0-2(1))* Wolfs Corner Publishing.

Fontes, Justine & Fontes, Ron. Casebook: UFOs and/or Alien Encounter. 2009. (Top Secret Graphica Mysteries Ser.). (Illus.). 48p. (YA). (gr. 2-6). 29.25 *(978-1-60754-603-0(5))*; pap. 11.75 *(978-1-60754-604-7(3))* Windmill Bks.

Gutman, Dan. Mr. Cooper Is Super! Paillot, Jim, illus. 2015. (My Weirdest School Ser.: 1). (ENG.). 112p. (J). (gr. 1-5). pap. 4.99 *(978-0-06-228421-1(5))* HarperCollins Pubs.

—Mr. Cooper Is Super! Paillot, Jim, illus. 2015. (My Weirdest School Ser.: 1). (J). lib. bdg. 14.75 *(978-0-606-36482-9(X))* Turtleback Bks.

Higgins, B. T. The Master of Disaster. 2005. 103p. pap. 10.00 *(978-1-4116-3121-2(8))* Lulu Pr., Inc.

Kitamura, Satoshi. UFO Diary. Kitamura, Satoshi, illus. 2007. (ENG., Illus.). 32p. (J). (gr. k-2). 12.99 *(978-1-84270-591-9(1))* Andersen Pr. GBR. Dist: Independent Pubs. Group.

Ladbrooke, Sheree. Big Alien School. 2011. (Illus.). 20p. pap. 12.52 *(978-1-4567-8779-0(9))* AuthorHouse.

Lancaster, J. A. Joe Parker's Prophecy of Zargala. 2010. 392p. pap. 21.18 *(978-0-557-26685-2(8))* Lulu Pr., Inc.

Larsen, Kirsten. Whoa! Ufo! 2009. pap. 34.95 *(978-0-8225-4797-6(X))* Lerner Publishing Group.

—Whoa! UFO! Gott, Barry, illus. 2009. (Science Solves It! Ser.). 32p. (J). (gr. k-2). pap. 5.95 *(978-1-57565-280-1(3))* Kane Press, Inc.

Lyons, Fergus. Muckeen & the UFO. 2004. (Pandas Ser.: 28). (ENG., Illus.). 64p. (J). pap. 9.95 *(978-0-86278-832-2(3))* O'Brien Pr., Ltd., The IRL. Dist: Dufour Editions, Inc.

Magnin, Joyce. Jelly Bean Summer. 2017. (ENG.). 272p. (J). (gr. 3-7). 16.99 *(978-1-4926-4672-3(5)*, Sourcebooks Jabberwocky) Sourcebooks, Inc.

Marsh, Carole. The Mystery at Area 51. Friedlander, Randolyn, illus. 2011. (Carole Marsh Mysteries Ser.). 32p. pap. 7.99 *(978-0-635-07961-9(5)*, Marsh, Carole Mysteries) Gallopade International.

Metz, Melinda. S. M. A. R. T. S. & the Missing UFO. McKenzie, Heath, illus. 2015. (S. M. A. R. T. S. Ser.). (ENG.). 128p. (gr.

T
U
V

3-6). lib. bdg. 22.65 *(978-1-4965-0466-1(6))* S.M.A.R.T.S. Learning System.

Montgomery, R. A. Project UFO. Semionov, Vladimir & Cannella, Marco, illus. 2008. 144p. (J). (gr. 4-7). pap. 6.99 *(978-1-933390-27-7(1))* Chooseco LLC.

Parker, Neal. Lobsterman & the U. F. O. 2014. (ENG., Illus.). 66p. (J). (gr. 3-17). pap. 9.95 *(978-1-60893-350-1(4))* Down East Bks.

Passen, Lisa. The Attack of the 50-Foot Teacher. 2005. (Illus.). 28p. (J). (gr. k-4). reprint ed. 16.00 *(978-0-7567-9665-5(2))* DIANE Publishing Co.

Pelletier, Cathie. The Summer Experiment. 2014. (ENG.). 288p. (J). (gr. 4-7). 16.99 *(978-1-4022-8578-3(7),* 9781402285783, Sourcebooks Jabberwocky) Sourcebooks, Inc.

Pike, Christopher, pseud. Aliens in the Sky. 2014. (Spooksville Ser.: 4). (ENG., Illus.). 128p. (J). (gr. 3-7). pap. 6.99 *(978-1-4814-1058-8(X),* Aladdin) Simon & Schuster Children's Publishing.

Pilger, Seamus. Unidentified Farting Objects. Gilpin, Stephen, illus. 2016. (Fart Squad Ser.: 3). 112p. (J). (gr. 1-5). pap. 4.99 *(978-0-06-229049-6(5))* HarperCollins Pubs.

Santillo, LuAnn. The UFO. Santillo, LuAnn, ed. 2003. (Half-Pint Kids Readers Ser.). (Illus.). 7p. (J). (gr. -1-1). pap. 1.00 *(978-1-59256-045-5(8))* Half-Pint Kids, Inc.

Sutton, Laurie S. The Secret of the Flying Saucer. Neely, Scott, illus. 2015. (You Choose Stories: Scooby-Doo Ser.). (ENG.). 112p. (gr. 2-3). lib. bdg. 32.65 *(978-1-4965-0478-4(X))* Stone Arch Bks.

Walker, Kathryn. Unsolved! 2008. (J). (gr. 4-7). *(978-0-7787-4140-4(0))* Crabtree Publishing Co.

Ward, Ian. Bobby Blah Blah & the Mystery of the U F O in Sniggery Woods. 2009. (Illus.). 84p. pap. 10.49 *(978-1-4389-7963-2(0))* AuthorHouse.

Wells, Robison. Dark Energy. 2016. 288p. (YA). (gr. 8). 17.99 *(978-0-06-227505-9(4),* HarperTeen) HarperCollins Pubs.

Williams, Suzanna. Ninety-Five Percent Human. 2013. 270p. pap. *(978-0-9574662-2-7(6))* Beresford Publishing Hse.

UNIFORMS

see also Military Uniforms

McDonald, Fiona. Uniforms Through History. 2006. (Why Do We Wear? Ser.). (Illus.). 32p. (gr. 2-6). lib. bdg. 26.00 *(978-0-8368-6858-6(7),* Gareth Stevens Learning Library) Stevens, Gareth Publishing LLLP.

McNab, Chris. Everyday Dress. 2004. (Twentieth-Century Developments in Fashion & Costume Ser.). (Illus.). 64p. (YA). (gr. 7-18). lib. bdg. 19.95 *(978-1-59084-427-4(0))* Mason Crest.

UNIFORMS, MILITARY

see Military Uniforms

UNIFORMS, NAVAL

see Military Uniforms

UNION OF SOUTH AFRICA

see South Africa

UNION PACIFIC RAILROAD COMPANY

Halpern, Monica. Building the Transcontinental Railroad. 2007. (Reading Expeditions Ser.). (ENG., Illus.). 40p. (J). pap. 19.95 *(978-0-7922-8690-5(1))* CENGAGE Learning.

Lewis, Norma. Connecting the Coasts: The Race to Build the Transcontinental Railroad, 1 vol. 2014. (Adventures on the American Frontier Ser.). (ENG.). 32p. (gr. 3-4). lib. bdg. 27.32 *(978-1-4914-0186-6(9))* Capstone Press of Coughlan Cos.

Rajczak, Michael. The Transcontinental Railroad, Vol. 1. 2014. (What You Didn't Know about History Ser.). (Illus.). 24p. (J). (gr. 2-3). (ENG.). 22.60 *(978-1-4824-0600-9(4));* pap. 8.15 *(978-1-4824-0599-6(7))* Stevens, Gareth Publishing LLLP.

Renehan, Edward J., Jr. The Transcontinental Railroad: The Gateway to the West. 2007. (Milestones in American History Ser.). (Illus.). 120p. (YA). (gr. 7-12). lib. bdg. 35.00 *(978-0-7910-9351-1(4))* Facts On File, Inc.

Sandler, Martin W. Iron Rails, Iron Men, & the Race to Link the Nation: The Story of the Transcontinental Railroad. 2015. (ENG.). 224p. (J). (gr. 5). 22.99 *(978-0-7636-6527-2(4))* Candlewick Pr.

Shea, Therese. The Transcontinental Railroad: Using Proportions to Solve Problems. (Math for the Real World Ser.). 32p. 2009. (ENG., Illus.). (gr. 6-7). pap. 10.00 *(978-1-4042-6075-7(7))* 2009. (gr. 5-5). 47.90 *(978-1-60851-370-3(X),* PowerKids Pr.) 2006. (Illus.). (YA). (gr. 5-9). lib. bdg. 25.25 *(978-1-4042-3361-4(X))* Rosen Publishing Group, Inc., The.

Uschan, Michael V. & Crewe, Sabrina. The Transcontinental Railroad. 2004. (Events That Shaped America Ser.). (Illus.). 32p. (gr. 3-6). lib. bdg. 26.00 *(978-0-8368-3401-7(1),* Gareth Stevens Learning Library) Stevens, Gareth Publishing LLLP.

UNIONS, LABOR

see Labor Unions

UNITARIANISM

Baxter, Pam. A Cup of Light: All about the Flaming Chalice. 2010. (J). pap. 5.00 *(978-1-55896-575-1(0),* Skinner Hse. Bks.) Unitarian Universalist Assn.

Dant, Jennifer. Everybody Is Important: A Kids' Guide to Our Seven Principles. 2010. (J). pap. 6.00 *(978-1-55896-564-5(5),* Skinner Hse. Bks.) Unitarian Universalist Assn.

—Unitarian Universalism Is a Really Long Name. Carter, Anne, illus. 2008. (ENG.). 30p. (J). (gr. 3-7). 12.00 *(978-1-55896-508-9(4),* Skinner Hse. Bks.) Unitarian Universalist Assn.

UNITED KINGDOM

see Great Britain

UNITED NATIONS

Aldridge, Rebecca. Ban Ki-Moon: United Nations Secretary-General. 2009. (Modern World Leaders Ser.). 128p. (YA). (gr. 7-12). 30.00 *(978-1-60413-070-6(9))* Facts On File, Inc.

Bookmiller, Kirsten N. The United Nations. 2008. (Global Organizations Ser.). (Illus.). 144p. (YA). (gr. 7-12). 35.00 *(978-0-7910-9540-9(1))* Facts On File, Inc.

Byman, Jeremy. Madam Secretary: The Story of Madeleine Albright. rev. exp. ed. 2004. (Notable Americans Ser.). (Illus.). 128p. (YA). (gr. 6-12). 23.95 *(978-1-931798-34-1(6))* Reynolds, Morgan Inc.

Connolly, Sean. The United Nations. 2009. (Global Organizations Ser.). (Illus.). 46p. (J). (gr. 4-7). pap. *(978-1-897563-38-0(8))* Saunders Bk. Co.

Docalavich, Heather. Antiterrorism Policy & Fighting Fear, Vol. 10. Russett, Bruce, ed. 2015. (United Nations: Leadership & Challenges in a Global World Ser.). (Illus.). 88p. (J). (gr. 7). lib. bdg. 24.95 *(978-1-4222-3428-0(2))* Mason Crest.

—Economic Globalization & Sustainable Development, Vol. 10. Russett, Bruce, ed. 2015. (United Nations: Leadership & Challenges in a Global World Ser.). (Illus.). 88p. (J). (gr. 7). lib. bdg. 24.95 *(978-1-4222-3431-0(2))* Mason Crest.

—The History, Structure, & Reach of the Un, Vol. 10. Russett, Bruce, ed. 2015. (United Nations: Leadership & Challenges in a Global World Ser.). (Illus.). 88p. (J). (gr. 7). lib. bdg. 24.95 *(978-1-4222-3435-8(5))* Mason Crest.

Finley, Toiya Kristen. Russell Simmons. 2007. (Sharing the American Dream Ser.). 64p. (YA). (gr. 7-18). pap. 9.95 *(978-1-4222-0762-8(5))* Mason Crest.

Galé. Junior Worldmark Encyclopedia of the Nations, 10 vols. 6th ed. 2012. (Junior Worldmark Encyclopedia of the Nations Ser.). (ENG., Illus.). 3200p. lib. bdg. 819.00 *(978-1-4144-6313-1(8),* UXL) Cengage Gale.

Gunderson, Cory Gideon. U. N. Weapons Inspectors. 2003. (World in Conflict-the Middle East Ser.). 32p. (gr. 4-8). 27.07 *(978-1-59197-414-7(3),* Abdo & Daughters) ABDO Publishing Co.

Koestler-Grack, Rachel A. Kofi Annan: Guiding the United Nations. 2007. (Modern Peacemakers Ser.). (Illus.). 119p. (YA). (gr. 9-12). lib. bdg. 30.00 *(978-0-7910-8996-5(7))* Facts On File, Inc.

Nelson, Sheila. The Birth of the un, Decolonization & Building Strong Nations, Vol. 10. Russett, Bruce, ed. 2015. (United Nations: Leadership & Challenges in a Global World Ser.). (Illus.). 88p. (J). (gr. 7). lib. bdg. 24.95 *(978-1-4222-3430-3(4))* Mason Crest.

—Decolonization: Dismantling Empires & Building Independence. 2008. (United Nations Ser.). (Illus.). 88p. (YA). (gr. 5-18). lib. bdg. 21.95 *(978-1-4222-0066-7(3))* Mason Crest.

—International Law & Playing by the Rules, Vol. 10. Russett, Bruce, ed. 2015. (United Nations: Leadership & Challenges in a Global World Ser.). (Illus.). 88p. (J). (gr. 7). lib. bdg. 24.95 *(978-1-4222-3433-4(9))* Mason Crest.

O'Kelley, Jeff. A Visit to the United Nations. 2006. (Early Explorers Ser.). (J). pap. *(978-1-4108-6126-9(0))* Benchmark Education Co.

Rice, Liz. Bill Richardson. (Sharing the American Dream Ser.). 64p. (YA). (gr. 7-12). 2009. 22.95 *(978-1-4222-0589-1(4))* 2007. pap. 9.95 *(978-1-4222-0761-1(7))* Mason Crest.

Smith, Roger. Human Rights & Protecting Individuals, Vol. 10. Russett, Bruce, ed. 2015. (United Nations: Leadership & Challenges in a Global World Ser.). (Illus.). 88p. (J). (gr. 7). lib. bdg. 24.95 *(978-1-4222-3437-2(1))* Mason Crest.

—Humanitarian Relief & Lending a Hand, Vol. 10. Russett, Bruce, ed. 2015. (United Nations: Leadership & Challenges in a Global World Ser.). (Illus.). 88p. (J). (gr. 7). lib. bdg. 24.95 *(978-1-4222-3432-7(0))* Mason Crest.

Tor, Regina, et al. Growing Toward Peace. 2011. 90p. 38.95 *(978-1-258-02528-1(0))* Literary Licensing, LLC.

The United Nations: Global Leadership, 10 vols., Set. Incl. Decolonization: Dismantling Empires & Building Independence. Nelson, Sheila. (YA). lib. bdg. 21.95 *(978-1-4222-0066-7(3));* Humanitarian Relief Operations: Lending a Helping Hand. Smith, Roger. (YA). lib. bdg. 21.95 *(978-1-4222-0070-4(1));* un & the Global Marketplace: Economic Developments. Docalavich, Heather. (J). lib. bdg. 21.95 *(978-1-4222-0074-2(4),* 1260876); UNICEF & Other Human Rights Efforts: Protecting Individuals. Smith, Roger. (YA). lib. bdg. 21.95 *(978-1-4222-0069-8(8));* (gr. 5-18). 2008. (United Nations — Global Leadership Ser.). (Illus.). 88p. 2006. Set lib. bdg. 219.50 *(978-1-4222-0065-0(5),* 1260876) Mason Crest.

Walker, Ida. The un Security Council & the Center of Power, Vol. 10. Russett, Bruce, ed. 2015. (United Nations: Leadership & Challenges in a Global World Ser.). 88p. (J). (gr. 7). lib. bdg. 24.95 *(978-1-4222-3436-5(3))* Mason Crest.

UNITED NATIONS—ARMED FORCES

Beller, Susan Provost. Battling in the Pacific: Soldiering in World War II. 2007. (Soldiers on the Battlefront Ser.). (ENG., Illus.). 112p. (gr. 6-8). lib. bdg. 33.26 *(978-0-8225-6381-5(9))* Lerner Publishing Group.

UNITED NATIONS—CHILDREN'S FUND

see UNICEF

UNITED NATIONS—FICTION

Birmajer, Marcelo. Una Vida Más: Noticias Extranas IV. 2004. (SPA.). 111p. (J). pap. 9.95 *(978-958-04-7081-6(2))* Norma S.A. COL. Dist: Lectorum Pubns., Inc.

Bowen, Anne. How Did You Grow So Big, So Soon? Backer, Marni, illus. 2003. 32p. (J). (gr. -1-1). 15.95 *(978-0-87614-024-6(X),* Carolrhoda Bks.) Lerner Publishing Group.

Fidler, Mark. Blaze of the Great Cliff. 2003. 196p. pap. 14.95 *(978-0-595-28748-2(4))* iUniverse, Inc.

Zerfing, Robert A. The Silencer: A U. N. Conspiracy Novel. 2nd ed. 2003. 326p. (YA). per. 14.95 *(978-0-9747881-0-4(4))* Clawfoot Publishing.

UNITED NATIONS INTERNATIONAL CHILDREN'S EMERGENCY FUND

see UNICEF

UNITED STATES

see also names of regions of the U. S. and groups of states e.g. Atlantic States; Middle West; Mississippi valley; Northwest, Old; Northwest, Pacific; Southern States; Southwest, New; Southwest, Old; The West

Alabama to Wyoming: State Fact Cards. 2003rd ed. 2003. (Illus.). 105p. (J). ring bd. 39.00 *(978-1-884925-66-5(9))* Toucan Valley Pubns., Inc.

America the Beautiful. (Color & Learn Ser.). 36p. (J). (gr. 1-5). pap. *(978-1-882210-12-1(3))* Action Publishing, Inc.

America's 50 States. 2014. (Illus.). (J). *(978-1-4351-5773-6(7))* Barnes & Noble, Inc.

Anness Publishing. My First Book of the 50 States of America: With Maps, Dates & Fun Facts! 2015. (ENG., Illus.). 54p. bds. 9.99 *(978-1-86147-628-9(0),* Armadillo) Anness Publishing GBR. Dist: National Bk. Network.

Balkan, Gabrielle. The 50 States: Activity Book - Custom: Maps of the 50 States of the USA. Linero, Sol, illus. 2016. (ENG.). (J). (gr. 3-6). pap. 9.99 ***(978-1-84780-997-1(9),*** Wide Eyed Editions) Quarto Publishing Group UK GBR. Dist: Hachette Bk. Group.

Barlowe, Dot. America the Beautiful to Paint or Color. 2006. (Dover Art Coloring Book Ser.). (ENG., Illus.). 48p. (gr. 3-8). per. 5.99 *(978-0-486-44811-4(8))* Dover Pubns., Inc.

Benchmark Education Company, LLC Staff, compiled by. Regions of the U. S. 2006. spiral bd. 330.00 *(978-1-4108-7006-3(5))* 2005. (J). spiral bd. 265.00 *(978-1-4108-5769-9(7))* Benchmark Education Co.

—Regions of the U. S. Theme Set. 2006. (J). 259.00 *(978-1-4108-7111-4(8))* Benchmark Education Co.

—Social Studies Theme: Regions of the U. S. 2005. spiral bd. 115.00 *(978-1-4108-5330-1(6))* Benchmark Education Co.

Betances, Abigail. American Holidays. 2009. (Real Life Readers Ser.). 12p. (gr. 1-2). pap. 5.90 *(978-1-4042-7911-7(3),* Rosen Classroom) Rosen Publishing Group, Inc., The.

Boyd, Nicole. America's Many Regions. 2009. (Real Life Readers Ser.). 12p. (gr. 1-2). pap. 5.90 *(978-1-4042-7931-5(8),* Rosen Classroom) Rosen Publishing Group, Inc., The.

Brooks, Clare & Garrington, Sally. Focus on the United States. 2006. (World in Focus Ser.). (Illus.). 64p. (gr. 5-12). pap. 14.05 *(978-0-8368-6732-9(7),* Gareth Stevens Secondary Library) Stevens, Gareth Publishing LLLP.

Carr, Aaron. The Great Seal. 2013. (J). *(978-1-62127-204-5(4));* pap. *(978-1-62127-208-3(7))* Weigl Pubs., Inc.

Celebrate Freedom: Songs, Symbols, & Sayings of the United States. 2003. (Scott Foresman Social Study Ser.). (Illus.). 32p. (gr. k-2). *(978-0-328-03672-1(2));* 48p. (gr. 3-6). *(978-0-328-03674-5(9))* Addison-Wesley Educational Pubs., Inc. (Scott Foresman).

Celebrate the States - Group 5, 5 vols., Set. 2nd ed. Incl. Minnesota. Schwabacher, Martin & Kummer, Patricia K. 144p. (gr. 6). lib. bdg. 42.79 *(978-0-7614-2716-2(3));* Ohio. Sherrow, Victoria. (J). lib. bdg. 42.79 *(978-0-7614-2558-8(6));* Rhode Island. Klein, Ted. 144p. (gr. 6). lib. bdg. 42.79 *(978-0-7614-2560-1(8));* Washington. Stefoff, Rebecca. 144p. (gr. 6). lib. bdg. 42.79 *(978-0-7614-2561-8(6));* West Virginia. Hoffman, Nancy & Hart, Joyce. 144p. (gr. 6). lib. bdg. 42.79 *(978-0-7614-2562-5(4));* 2007. 2008. Set lib. bdg. 213.93 *(978-0-7614-2557-1(8),* Benchmark Bks.) Marshall Cavendish Corp.

Celebrate the States - Group 6, 5 vols., Set. 2nd rev. ed. Incl. Kentucky. Barrett, Tracy. lib. bdg. 42.79 *(978-0-7614-2715-5(5));* Mississippi. Shirley, David & Kummer, Patricia K. lib. bdg. 42.79 *(978-0-7614-2717-9(1));* New Hampshire. Otfinoski, Steven. lib. bdg. 42.79 *(978-0-7614-2718-6(X));* New Mexico. McDaniel, Melissa. lib. bdg. 42.79 *(978-0-7614-2719-3(8));* Wyoming. Baldwin, Guy & Hart, Joyce. lib. bdg. 42.79 *(978-0-7614-2563-2(2));* (gr. 6). (Celebrate the States 6 Ser.). 144p. 2007. Set lib. bdg. 213.93 *(978-0-7614-2714-8(7),* Benchmark Bks.) Marshall Cavendish Corp.

Celebrate the States Group 3, 5 bks., Set. 2nd rev. ed. Incl. Alaska. Stefoff, Rebecca. lib. bdg. 42.79 *(978-0-7614-2153-5(X));* Connecticut. Sherrow, Victoria. lib. bdg. 42.79 *(978-0-7614-2155-9(6));* South Dakota. McDaniel, Melissa. lib. bdg. 42.79 *(978-0-7614-2156-6(4));* Tennessee. Barrett, Tracy. lib. bdg. 42.79 *(978-0-7614-2151-1(3));* Wisconsin. Hart, Joyce & Zeinert, Karen. lib. bdg. 42.79 *(978-0-7614-2157-3(2));* (Illus.). (gr. 6-7). (Celebrate the States 3 Ser.). 144p. 2006. Set lib. bdg. 213.93 *(978-0-7614-2150-4(5),* Benchmark Bks.) Marshall Cavendish Corp.

Celebrate the States Group 4, 5 bks., Set. 2nd rev. ed. Incl. Florida. Hart, Joyce & Chang, Perry. lib. bdg. 42.79 *(978-0-7614-2348-5(6));* Hawai'i. Goldberg, Jake & Hart, Joyce. lib. bdg. 42.79 *(978-0-7614-2349-2(4));* Iowa. Morrice, Polly Alison & Hart, Joyce. lib. bdg. 42.79 *(978-0-7614-2350-8(8));* Michigan. Brill, Marlene Targ. lib. bdg. 42.79 *(978-0-7614-2351-5(6));* Washington, D. C. Elish, Dan. lib. bdg. 42.79 *(978-0-7614-2352-2(4));* (Illus.). (gr. 6-7). (Celebrate the States 4 Ser.). 144p. 2006. Set lib. bdg. 213.93 *(978-0-7614-2347-8(8),* Benchmark Bks.) Marshall Cavendish Corp.

Cohen, Stephanie. The Northeast: Text Pairs. 2008. (Bridges/Navigators Ser.). (J). (gr. 4). 89.00 *(978-1-4108-8394-0(9))* Benchmark Education Co.

Colonial America Complete Unit. (gr. 2-5). 286.95 *(978-0-7368-4487-1(2))* Red Brick Learning.

Coloring Fun of the U. S. States Images & Facts. 2003. (Illus.). 40p. (J). 3.95 *(978-0-9729026-3-2(5))* Midwest Cylinder Management, Inc.

CultureGrams 2005 World Edition - the Americas. 2004. (YA). per. 39.99 *(978-1-931694-89-6(3))* ProQuest LLC.

Davis, Kenneth C. Don't Know Much about the 50 States. Andriani, Renee, illus. 2004. (Don't Know Much About Ser.). (ENG.). 64p. (J). (gr. 1-4). pap. 7.99 *(978-0-06-446227-3(7))* HarperCollins Pubs.

DePietro, Frank. Latino American Cuisine. 2012. (Illus.). 64p. (J). pap. *(978-1-4222-2337-6(X))* Mason Crest.

—Latino American Cuisine. Limón, José E., ed. 2012. (Hispanic Americans: Major Minority Ser.). (Illus.). 64p. (J). (gr. 4). 22.95 *(978-1-4222-2320-8(5))* Mason Crest.

Dickmann, Nancy. The Complete Guide to the 50 States. 2016. (Illus.). 144p. (J). ***(978-1-4351-6358-4(3))*** Barnes & Noble, Inc.

Donovan, Sandy. Volunteering Smarts: How to Find Opportunities, Create a Positive Experience, & More. 2012. (USA TODAY Teen Wise Guides: Lifestyle Choices Ser.). (ENG., Illus.). 64p. (gr. 8-12). lib. bdg. 31.93 *(978-0-7613-7021-5(8))* Lerner Publishing Group.

Dyan, Penelope. A Step in Time — A Kid's Guide to Ephesus, Turkey. Weigand, John D., photos by. 2011. (Illus.). 40p. pap. 12.95 *(978-1-935630-57-9(1))* Bellissima Publishing, LLC.

Eldridge, Alison & Eldridge, Stephen. The Bald Eagle: An American Symbol. 2012. (All about American Symbols Ser.). 24p. (J). (gr. -1-16). 22.60 *(978-0-7660-4058-8(5),* Enslow Elementary) Enslow Pubs., Inc.

Espejo, Roman. Custody & Divorce. 2013. (Teen Rights & Freedoms Ser.). (ENG., Illus.). 176p. (gr. 10-12). lib. bdg. 42.00 *(978-0-7377-6400-0(7),* Greenhaven Pr., Inc.) Cengage Gale.

Estigarribia, Diana. Smithsonian National Zoological Park. 2009. (Great Zoos of the United States Ser.). 24p. (gr. 3-4). 42.50 *(978-1-61513-225-6(2),* PowerKids Pr.) Rosen Publishing Group, Inc., The.

Farseth, Erik. American Rock: Guitar Heroes, Punks, & Metalheads. 2012. (American Music Milestones Ser.). (ENG., Illus.). 64p. (gr. 5-12). lib. bdg. 30.60 *(978-0-7613-4503-9(5))* Lerner Publishing Group.

Franchino, Vicky. It's Cool to Learn about the United States Northeast. 2011. (Explorer Library: Social Studies Explorer Ser.). (ENG.). 48p. (gr. 4-8). pap. 15.64 *(978-1-61080-305-2(1),* 201201) Cherry Lake Publishing.

Gall, Timothy L. & Gall, Susan B. Junior Worldmark Encyclopedia of the States. 5th ed. 2007. (J). *(978-1-4144-1108-8(1)); (978-1-4144-1109-5(X)); (978-1-4144-1110-1(3)); (978-1-4144-1107-1(3));* Set. (ENG.). 307.00 *(978-1-4144-1106-4(5),* UXL) Cengage Gale.

Garrington, Sally. Focus on the United States. 2006. (World in Focus Ser.). (Illus.). 64p. (gr. 5-12). lib. bdg. 34.00 *(978-0-8368-6725-1(4),* Gareth Stevens Secondary Library) Stevens, Gareth Publishing LLLP.

Gillard, Arthur. Drug Abuse. 2013. (Issues That Concern You Ser.). (ENG., Illus.). 144p. (gr. 7-10). lib. bdg. 42.00 *(978-0-7377-6290-7(X),* Greenhaven Pr., Inc.) Cengage Gale.

Golden, Nancy. Exploring the United States with the Five Themes of Geography. 2005. (Library of the Western Hemisphere Ser.). (Illus.). 24p. (J). (gr. 5-7). lib. bdg. 22.60 *(978-1-4042-2670-8(2),* PowerKids Pr.); (ENG., (gr. 3-8). pap. 8.25 *(978-0-8239-4630-3(4))* Rosen Publishing Group, Inc., The.

Goodman, Susan E. Ultimate Field Trip #5: Blasting off to Space Academy. Doolittle, Michael J., illus. 2011. (ENG.). 48p. (J). (gr. 3-7). pap. 19.99 *(978-1-4424-4345-7(6),* Atheneum Bks. for Young Readers) Simon & Schuster Children's Publishing.

Gray, Leon. Horrible Jobs of the Industrial Revolution, Vol. 1. 2014. (History's Most Horrible Jobs Ser.). (ENG.). 48p. (J). (gr. 5-6). 31.95 *(978-1-4824-0343-5(9))* Stevens, Gareth Publishing LLLP.

Grayson, Robert. United States, 1 vol. 2013. (Countries of the World Set 2 Ser.). (ENG.). 144p. (J). (gr. 6-12). lib. bdg. 37.07 *(978-1-61783-640-4(0),* Essential Library) ABDO Publishing Co.

Green, Carl R. & Sanford, William R. Wyatt Earp. rev. ed. 2008. (Outlaws & Lawmen of the Wild West, Revised Edition Ser.). (Illus.). 48p. (J). (gr. 5-18). lib. bdg. 25.27 *(978-0-7660-3174-6(8))* Enslow Pubs., Inc.

Green, Jen. The USA. 2017. (Living In Ser.). (ENG., Illus.). 24p. (J). (gr. k-2). 16.99 *(978-1-4451-4871-7(4),* Franklin Watts) Hachette Children's Group GBR. Dist: Hachette Bk. Group.

Hamilton, John. United States Air Force. 2011. (Armed Forces Ser.). 32p. (YA). (gr. 3-6). 27.07 *(978-1-61783-068-6(2))* ABDO Publishing Co.

Hauser, Jill Frankel. Little Hands Celebrate America: Learning about the U. S. A. through Crafts & Activities. Kline, Michael, illus. 2012. (Little Hands! Book Ser.). 128p. (J). pap. 12.99 *(978-0-8249-6836-6(0),* Ideal Pubns.) Worthy Publishing.

—Little Hands Celebrate America! Learning about the U.S.A Through Crafts & Activities. 2004. (Williamson's Little Hands Book Ser.). (ENG., Illus.). 128p. (J). 14.29 *(978-1-885593-93-1(7),* Ideal Pubns.) Worthy Publishing.

Hetrick, Hans. Baseball's Record Breakers. 2017. (Record Breakers Ser.). (ENG., Illus.). 32p. (gr. 3-4). pap. 8.95 *(978-1-5157-3764-3(0))* Capstone Press of Coughlan Cos.

Higgins, Nadia. Logan Lerman: The Perks of Being of an Action Star. 2014. (Pop Culture Bios Ser.). (ENG., Illus.). 32p. (gr. 3-6). lib. bdg. 26.60 *(978-1-4677-1445-7(3),* Lerner Pubns.) Lerner Publishing Group.

Hill, Z. B. Tupac. 2012. (J). pap. *(978-1-4222-2556-1(9))* Mason Crest.

—Usher. 2012. (J). pap. *(978-1-4222-2557-8(7));* (Illus.). 48p. (gr. 3-4). 19.95 *(978-1-4222-2531-8(3))* Mason Crest.

Holden, Henry M. Danger in Space: Surviving the Apollo 13 Disaster. 2012. (American Space Missions — Astronauts, Exploration, & Discovery Ser.). (Illus.). 48p. (J). (gr. 5-18). 25.27 *(978-0-7660-4072-4(0))* Enslow Pubs., Inc.

Hudson, David L., Jr. Educational Standards. 2007. (Point/Counterpoint Ser.). (Illus.). 110p. (YA). (gr. 9-12). lib. bdg. 35.00 *(978-0-7910-9278-1(X))* Facts On File, Inc.

It's My State!, 18 vols., Set. 2nd rev. ed. Incl. California. Burgan, Michael & McGeveran, William. lib. bdg. 31.36 *(978-1-60870-045-5(3));* Colorado. Altman, Linda Jacobs & Fitzgerald, Stephanie. lib. bdg. 31.36 *(978-1-60870-046-2(1));* Connecticut. Burgan, Michael & Fitzgerald, Stephanie. lib. bdg. 31.36 *(978-1-60870-047-9(X));* Delaware. King, David C. & Fitzgerald, Brian. lib. bdg. 31.36 *(978-1-60870-048-6(8));* Florida. Hess, Debra & Wiesenfeld, Lori P. lib. bdg. 31.36 *(978-1-60870-049-3(6));* Illinois. Price-Groff, Claire & Kaplan, Elizabeth. lib. bdg. 31.36 *(978-1-60870-050-9(X));* Louisiana. Bjorklund, Ruth & Steinitz, Andy. lib. bdg. 31.36 *(978-1-60870-051-6(8));* Maryland. Otfinoski, Steven & Steinitz, Andy. lib. bdg. 31.36 *(978-1-60870-052-3(6));* Massachusetts. Bjorklund, Ruth & Fitzgerald, Stephanie. lib. bdg. 31.36 *(978-1-60870-053-0(4));* Minnesota. Brill, Marlene Targ & Kaplan, Elizabeth. lib. bdg. 31.36 *(978-1-60870-054-7(2));* New Jersey. King, David C. & McGeveran, William. lib. bdg. 31.36 *(978-1-60870-055-4(0));* New York. Elish, Dan & Fitzgerald, Stephanie. lib. bdg. 31.36 *(978-1-60870-056-1(9));* North Carolina. Gaines, Ann & Steinitz, Andy. lib. bdg. 31.36 *(978-1-60870-057-8(7));* Pennsylvania. Hart, Joyce & Hantula, Richard. lib. bdg. 31.36 *(978-1-60870-058-5(5));* Texas. Altman, Linda Jacobs & Benduhn, Tea. lib. bdg. 31.36 *(978-1-60870-059-2(3));* Virginia. King, David C. & Fitzgerald, Stephanie. lib. bdg. 31.36 *(978-1-60870-060-8(7));* Washington. Otfinoski, Steven & Benduhn, Tea. lib. bdg. 31.36 *(978-1-60870-061-5(5));* Wisconsin. Dornfeld, Margaret & Hantula, Richard. lib. bdg. 31.36 *(978-1-60870-062-2(3));* 80p. (gr. 3-18). (It's My State! Ser.). 2010. Set lib. bdg. 564.48 o.p. *(978-1-60870-044-8(5))* Marshall Cavendish Corp.

It's My State Group 8, 6 bks., Set. Incl. Alabama. Hart, Joyce. 2007. lib. bdg. 29.93 (978-0-7614-1925-9(X)); Hawaii. Gaines, Ann Graham. 2006. lib. bdg. 29.93 (978-0-7614-1926-6(8)); Indiana. Derzipilski, Kathleen. 2007. lib. bdg. 29.93 (978-0-7614-1927-3(6)); Iowa. King, David C. 2006. lib. bdg. 29.93 (978-0-7614-1928-0(4)); Washington, D. C. Hicks, Terry Allan. 2006. lib. bdg. 29.93 (978-0-7614-1929-7(2)); Wyoming. Petreycik, Rick. 2006. lib. bdg. 29.93 (978-0-7614-1930-3(6)); (Illus.). 80p. (J). (gr. 4-7). 2007. Set lib. bdg. 179.57 (978-0-7614-1924-2(1), Benchmark Bks.) Marshall Cavendish Corp.

It's My State! Series - Group 1, 6 bks., Set. 162.43 (978-0-7614-1417-9(7), Benchmark Bks.) Marshall Cavendish Corp.

Kaplan, Arie. American Pop: Hit Makers, Superstars, & Dance Revolutionaries. 2012. (American Music Milestones Ser.). (ENG., Illus.). 64p. (gr. 5-12). lib. bdg. 30.60 (978-0-7613-4504-6(3)) Lerner Publishing Group.

Kerrigan, Michael. Citizen Soldiers: The National Guard. 2017. (J). **(978-1-4222-3760-1(5))** Mason Crest.

Kiesbye, Stefan. Can Busy Teens Succeed Academically? 2009. (At Issue Ser.). (ENG., Illus.). 128p. (gr. 10-12). pap. 27.80 (978-0-7377-4285-5(2), Greenhaven Pr., Inc.) Cengage Gale.

Lange, Donna. On the Edge of Disaster: Youth in the Juvenile Court System. 2003. (Youth with Special Needs Ser.). (Illus.). 127p. (YA). (gr. 7). pap. 14.95 (978-1-4222-0428-3(6)) Mason Crest.

Latta, Sara L. & Anderson, Mary. The Woman Who Invented Windshield Wipers: Mary Anderson & Her Wonderful Invention. 2014. (Inventors at Work! Ser.). 48p. (J). 25.27 (978-0-7660-4203-2(0)) Enslow Pubs., Inc.

Lindeen, Mary. Welcome to North America, 1 vol. 2011. (Wonder Readers Fluent Level Ser.). (ENG.). 32p. (gr. -1-2). pap. 5.99 (978-1-4296-7974-9(3), Wonder Readers) Capstone Press of Coughlan Cos.

MacRae, Sloan. David Wright. 2012. (Sports Heroes Ser.). (ENG.). 24p. (J). (gr. 3-6). pap. 8.25 (978-1-4488-6286-3(8)); lib. bdg. 22.60 (978-1-4488-6164-4(0)) Rosen Publishing Group, Inc., The. (PowerKids Pr.).

—Evan Longoria. 2012. (Sports Heroes Ser.). (ENG.). 24p. (J). (gr. 3-6). pap. 8.25 (978-1-4488-6284-9(1)); lib. bdg. 22.60 (978-1-4488-6163-7(2)) Rosen Publishing Group, Inc., The. (PowerKids Pr.).

Marsico, Katie. United States. 2010. (Explorer Library: Social Studies Explorer Ser.). (ENG.). 48p. (gr. 4-8). lib. bdg. 31.36 (978-1-60279-825-0(7), 200516) Cherry Lake Publishing.

McClellam, Adam & Schifini, Alfredo. The Southwest: Its History & People. 2007. (Avenues Ser.). (ENG., Illus.). 32p. (J). pap. 17.95 (978-0-7922-8619-6(7)) CENGAGE Learning.

Micklos, John, Jr. People & Places of the Northeast. 2016. (United States by Region Ser.). (ENG., Illus.). 32p. (gr. 3-4). lib. bdg. 27.32 (978-1-5157-2444-5(1), Fact Finders) Capstone Press of Coughlan Cos.

Miller, Reagan & Hyde, Natalie. What's in the Southeast? 2011. (ENG.). 32p. (J). lib. bdg. (978-0-7787-1825-3(5)); (All Around the U.S. Ser.: No. 3). (gr. 3-6). pap. (978-0-7787-1831-4(X)) Crabtree Publishing Co.

Miller, Reagan & Peppas, Lynn. What's in the Southwest? 2011. (ENG.). 32p. (J). (978-0-7787-1826-0(3)) Crabtree Publishing Co.

Murphy, Maggie. Shia Labeouf. 2011. (Movie Superstars Ser.). (Illus.). 32p. (J). (gr. 4-6). 25.25 (978-1-4488-2563-9(6), PowerKids Pr.) Rosen Publishing Group, Inc., The.

My World of Neighbors. (YA). 22.00 (978-1-931555-46-3(X)) Our Lady of Victory Schl.

Nelson, Robin & National Geographic Learning Staff. Where Is My State? 2012. (ENG.). 24p. (C). (gr. k-2). pap. 10.95 (978-0-8225-1980-5(1)) National Geographic School Publishing, Inc.

Newman-D'Amico, Fran. All about America: Facts & Fun. 2008. (Dover Little Activity Bks.). (ENG., Illus.). 64p. (J). (gr. 1-4). pap. 1.99 (978-0-486-46573-9(X)) Dover Pubns., Inc.

Orr, Tamra B. It's Cool to Learn about the United States Southwest. 2011. (Explorer Library: Social Studies Explorer Ser.). (ENG.). 48p. (gr. 4-8). pap. 15.64 (978-1-61080-304-5(3), 201200) Cherry Lake Publishing.

Pearl, Norman. The Great Seal of the United States. Skeens, Matthew, illus. 2006. (American Symbols Ser.). (ENG.). 24p. (gr. 1-2). lib. bdg. 26.65 (978-1-4048-2214-6(3)) Picture Window Bks.

Peppas, Lynn. What's in the Northeast? Crabtree Publishing Staff, ed. 2011. (All Around the U.S. Ser.: No. 2). (ENG.). 32p. (J). pap. (978-0-7787-1830-7(1)) Crabtree Publishing Co.

Pink. 2011. (Megastars Ser.). (Illus.). 48p. (YA). pap. 11.75 (978-1-4488-2263-8(7), Rosen Reference) Rosen Publishing Group, Inc., The.

Popper, Garry. Billy Joe in the U. S. A. Johnson, Andi, illus. 2004. 36p. (gr. -1-7). 4.00 (978-1-84161-053-5(4)) Ravette Publishing, Ltd. GBR. Dist: Parkwest Pubns., Inc.

Rappaport, Doreen. In the Promised Land: Lives of Jewish Americans. Van Wright, Cornelius, illus. 2005. 32p. (J). (gr. k-4). lib. bdg. 16.89 (978-0-06-059395-7(4)) HarperCollins Pubs.

Ray, Liz. Coming to the United States, 6 vols., Set. 2004. (Phonics Readers Books 37-72 Ser.). (ENG.). 8p. (gr. k-1). pap. 35.70 (978-0-7368-4078-1(8), Phonics Readers) Capstone Press of Coughlan Cos.

Reid, Stephanie. My Country, 1 vol. 2011. (Early Childhood Themes Ser.). (ENG.). 16p. (J). (gr. -1-2). pap. 6.99 (978-1-4333-2360-7(5)); pap. 19.99 (978-1-4333-2361-4(3)) Teacher Created Materials, Inc.

Rossi, Ann. The Southeast: Text Pairs. 2008. (Bridges/Navigators Ser.). (J). (gr. 4). 89.00 (978-1-4108-8396-4(5)) Benchmark Education Co.

Rottman, Gordon L. The Most Daring Raid of the Civil War: The Great Locomotive Chase. 2011. (Most Daring Raids in History Ser.). (Illus.). 64p. (YA). (gr. 7-12). 31.95 (978-1-4488-1870-9(2)) Rosen Publishing Group, Inc., The.

Schroeder, Holly. The United States ABCs: A Book about the People & Places of the United States. Yesh, Jeff, illus. 2004. (Country ABCs Ser.). (ENG.). 32p. (gr. k-5). 27.99 (978-1-4048-0181-3(2), 1229509) Picture Window Bks.

Schulz, Christian Dahl. Professional Sports Organizations. 2012. (Career Launcher Ser.). 130p. (C). (gr. 9). 34.95 (978-0-8160-7964-3(1), Ferguson Publishing Co.) Facts On File, Inc.

Sherman, Patrice & Wood, Elaine. John James Audubon. 2011. (Conservation Heroes Ser.). (Illus.). 152p. (YA). (gr. 6-12). 35.00 (978-1-60413-953-2(6), Chelsea Hse.) Facts On File, Inc.

Sirota, Lyn. Pink. 2011. (Megastars Ser.). (Illus.). 48p. (YA). (gr. 5-8). 29.25 (978-1-4358-3577-1(8), Rosen Reference) Rosen Publishing Group, Inc., The.

Sís, Peter. The Train of States. 2007. (ENG., Illus.). 64p. (J). (gr. k-5). pap. 6.99 (978-0-06-057840-4(8), Greenwillow Bks.) HarperCollins Pubs.

—The Train of States. Sís, Peter, illus. 2004. (Illus.). 64p. (J). (gr. 1-18). 17.99 (978-0-06-057838-1(6)) HarperCollins Pubs.

Sleeping Bear Editor, ed. Diary of an American Kid. 2011. (Country Journal Ser.). (ENG.). 128p. (J). (gr. 4-8). pap. 9.95 (978-1-58536-171-7(2), 202262) Sleeping Bear Pr.

Solomon, Andrew. Far from the Tree. 2017. (J). pap. (978-1-4814-4091-2(8), Simon & Schuster Bks. For Young Readers) Simon & Schuster Bks. For Young Readers.

—Far from the Tree: Young Adult Edition. 2017. (ENG., Illus.). 464p. (YA). (gr. 9). 18.99 (978-1-4814-4090-5(X), Simon & Schuster Bks. For Young Readers) Simon & Schuster Bks. For Young Readers.

Talbott, Hudson. United Tweets of America: 50 State Birds Their Stories, Their Glories. Talbott, Hudson, illus. 2008. (ENG., Illus.). 64p. (J). (gr. 1-3). 17.99 (978-0-399-24520-6(0), G.P. Putnam's Sons Books for Young Readers) Penguin Young Readers Group.

Thompson, Gare & National Geographic Learning Staff. The Northeast: Its History & People. 2007. (Reading Expeditions Ser.). (ENG., Illus.). 32p. (J). pap. 17.95 (978-0-7922-8611-0(1)) CENGAGE Learning.

Troupe, Thomas Kingsley. Harriet Tubman's Escape: a Fly on the Wall History. Tejido, Jomike, illus. 2017. (Fly on the Wall History Ser.). (ENG.). 32p. (gr. 1-3). lib. bdg. 27.32 (978-1-4795-9788-8(0)) Picture Window Bks.

The United States, 52 vols., Set. Incl. Alabama. Smith, Rich. 27.07 (978-1-60453-636-2(5)); Alaska. Ollhoff, Jim. 27.07 (978-1-60453-637-9(3)); Arizona. Ollhoff, Jim. 27.07 (978-1-60453-638-6(1)); Arkansas. Smith, Rich. 27.07 (978-1-60453-639-3(X)); California. Smith, Rich. 27.07 (978-1-60453-640-9(3)); Colorado. Ollhoff, Jim. 27.07 (978-1-60453-641-6(1)); Connecticut. Ollhoff, Jim. 27.07 (978-1-60453-642-3(X)); Delaware. Ollhoff, Jim. 27.07 (978-1-60453-643-0(8)); Florida. Ollhoff, Jim. 27.07 (978-1-60453-644-7(6)); Georgia. Smith, Rich. 27.07 (978-1-60453-645-4(4)); Hawaii. Ollhoff, Jim. 27.07 (978-1-60453-646-1(2)); Idaho. Ollhoff, Jim. 27.07 (978-1-60453-647-8(0)); Illinois. Smith, Rich. 27.07 (978-1-60453-648-5(9)); Indiana. Smith, Rich. 27.07 (978-1-60453-649-2(7)); Iowa. Wheeler, Jill C. 27.07 (978-1-60453-650-8(0)); Kansas. Wheeler, Jill C. 27.07 (978-1-60453-651-5(9)); Kentucky. Smith, Rich. 27.07 (978-1-60453-652-2(7)); Louisiana. Smith, Rich. 27.07 (978-1-60453-653-9(5)); Maine. Jensen, Niels R. 27.07 (978-1-60453-654-6(3)); Maryland. Jensen, Niels R. 27.07 (978-1-60453-655-3(1)); Massachusetts. Smith, Rich. 27.07 (978-1-60453-656-0(X)); Michigan. Jensen, Niels R. 27.07 (978-1-60453-657-7(8)); Minnesota. Jensen, Niels R. 27.07 (978-1-60453-658-4(6)); Mississippi. Smith, Rich. 27.07 (978-1-60453-659-1(4)); Missouri. Ollhoff, Jim. 27.07 (978-1-60453-660-7(8)); Montana. Ollhoff, Jim. 27.07 (978-1-60453-661-4(6)); Nebraska. Ollhoff, Jim. 27.07 (978-1-60453-662-1(4)); Nevada. Ollhoff, Jim. 27.07 (978-1-60453-663-8(2)); New Hampshire. Jensen, Niels R. 27.07 (978-1-60453-664-5(0)); New Jersey. Wheeler, Jill C. 27.07 (978-1-60453-665-2(9)); New Mexico. Wheeler, Jill C. 27.07 (978-1-60453-666-9(7)); New York. Jensen, Niels R. 27.07 (978-1-60453-667-6(5)); North Carolina. Smith, Rich. 27.07 (978-1-60453-668-3(3)); North Dakota. Ollhoff, Jim. 27.07 (978-1-60453-669-0(1)); Ohio. Jensen, Niels R. 27.07 (978-1-60453-670-6(5)); Oklahoma. Smith, Rich. 27.07 (978-1-60453-671-3(3)); Oregon. Smith, Rich. 27.07 (978-1-60453-672-0(1)); Pennsylvania. Wheeler, Jill C. 27.07 (978-1-60453-673-7(X)); Puerto Rico. Ollhoff, Jim. 27.07 (978-1-60453-674-4(8)); Rhode Island. Jensen, Niels R. 27.07 (978-1-60453-675-1(6)); South Carolina. Ollhoff, Jim. 27.07 (978-1-60453-676-8(4)); South Dakota. Ollhoff, Jim. 27.07 (978-1-60453-677-5(2)); Tennessee. Ollhoff, Jim. 27.07 (978-1-60453-678-2(0)); Texas. Ollhoff, Jim. 27.07 (978-1-60453-679-9(9)); Utah. Ollhoff, Jim. 27.07 (978-1-60453-680-5(2)); Vermont. Jensen, Niels R. 27.07 (978-1-60453-681-2(0)); Virginia. Jensen, Niels R. 27.07 (978-1-60453-682-9(9)); Washington. Ollhoff, Jim. 27.07 (978-1-60453-683-6(7)); Washington, D. C. Ollhoff, Jim. 27.07 (978-1-60453-684-3(5)); West Virginia. Ollhoff, Jim. 27.07 (978-1-60453-685-0(3)); Wisconsin. Ollhoff, Jim. 27.07 (978-1-60453-686-7(1)); Wyoming. Ollhoff, Jim. 27.07 (978-1-60453-687-4(X)); (YA). (gr. 2-5). (United States Ser.). (Illus.). 48p. 2009. 1407.64 (978-1-60453-635-5(7), Checkerboard Library) ABDO Publishing Co.

Visca, Curt. How to Draw Cartoon Symbols of the United States. 2009. (Kid's Guide to Drawing Ser.). 24p. (gr. 3-3). 47.90 (978-1-61511-020-9(8), PowerKids Pr.) Rosen Publishing Group, Inc., The.

Wargin, Kathy-jo. The American Reader. Darnell, K. L., illus. 2006. (Readers Ser.). (ENG.). 96p. (J). (gr. 1-5). 12.95 (978-1-58536-095-6(3)) Sleeping Bear Pr.

Weatherford, Carole Boston. Dorothea Lange. Green, Sarah, illus. 2017. (ENG.). 32p. (J). (gr. -1-3). 16.99 (978-0-8075-1699-7(6)) Whitman, Albert & Co.

Wiseman, Blaine. The Northeast. 2016. (Illus.). 48p. (J). (978-1-5105-1138-5(5)) SmartBook Media, Inc.

Young, Laura. We Honor America. 2003. (Rosen Real Readers: Upper Emergent Ser.). (ENG., Illus.). 12p. (gr. 1-2). pap. 5.90 (978-0-8239-6367-6(5)) Rosen Publishing Group, Inc., The.

Zocchi, Judy. In the United States. Brodie, Neale, illus. 2005. (Global Adventures II Ser.). 32p. (J). per. 9.95 (978-1-59646-173-4(X)) Dingles & Co.

—In the United States/en los Estados Unidos. Brodie, Neale, illus. 2005. (Global Adventures II Ser.).Tr. of En los Estados Unidos. (ENG & SPA.). 32p. (J). per. 10.95 (978-1-59646-175-8(6)) Dingles & Co.

UNITED STATES—AIR FORCE

Braulick, Carrie A. U. S. Air Force Spy Planes [Scholastic]. 2011. (Military Vehicles Ser.). 32p. pap. 1.00 (978-1-4296-6482-0(7), Blazers) Capstone Press of Coughlan Cos.

—The U. S. Air Force Thunderbirds. 2005. (U. S. Armed Forces Ser.). (ENG., Illus.). 32p. (gr. 1-2). 25.99 (978-0-7368-4392-8(2), Blazers) Capstone Press of Coughlan Cos.

Burgan, Michael. Today's U. S. Air Force, 1 vol. 2013. (U. S. Armed Forces Ser.). (ENG.). 48p. (gr. 5-6). pap. 9.10 (978-0-7565-4633-5(8)); lib. bdg. 29.32 (978-0-7565-4620-5(6)) Compass Point Bks.

Camelo, Wilson. The U. S. Air Force & Military Careers. 2006. (U.S. Armed Forces & Military Careers Ser.). (Illus.). 128p. (J). (gr. 5). lib. bdg. 33.27 (978-0-7660-2524-0(1)) Enslow Pubs., Inc.

Caulkins, Sam. My Uncle Is in the Air Force, 01 vols., 1. 2016. (Military Families Ser.). (ENG., Illus.). 24p. (J). pap. 8.25 (978-1-5081-4455-7(9), PowerKids Pr.) Rosen Publishing Group, Inc., The.

David, Jack. Air Force Air Commandos. 2009. (Armed Forces Ser.). (ENG., Illus.). 24p. (J). (gr. 3-7). lib. bdg. 25.95 (978-1-60014-262-8(1)) Bellwether Media.

—B-1B Lancers. 2009. (Military Machines Ser.). (ENG., Illus.). 24p. (YA). (gr. 3-7). lib. bdg. 25.95 (978-1-60014-258-1(3)) Bellwether Media.

—B-52 Stratofortresses. 2009. (Military Machines Ser.). (ENG., Illus.). 24p. (YA). (gr. 3-7). lib. bdg. 25.95 (978-1-60014-259-8(1)) Bellwether Media.

Doeden, Matt. The U. S. Air Force [Scholastic]. 2010. (Military Branches Ser.). pap. 0.52 (978-1-4296-5069-4(9), Pebble Plus) Capstone Press of Coughlan Cos.

Doeden, Matt. The U.S. Air Force. 2017. (U. S. Military Branches Ser.). (ENG.). 24p. (gr. k-1). lib. bdg. 26.65 **(978-1-5157-6754-1(X))** Capstone Press of Coughlan Cos.

Dolan, Edward F. Military Service, 5 vols., Set. Incl. Careers in the U. S. Air Force. (YA). (gr. 7-9). 35.64 (978-0-7614-4205-9(7)); Careers in the U. S. Army. (YA). (gr. 7-9). 35.64 (978-0-7614-4206-6(5)); Careers in the U. S. Coast Guard. (gr. 7-9). 35.64 (978-0-7614-4207-3(3)); Careers in the U. S. Marine Corps. (YA). (gr. 8-18). 35.64 (978-0-7614-4209-7(X)); Careers in the U. S. Navy. (gr. 7-18). 35.64 (978-0-7614-4210-3(3)); 80p. 2009. 2010. Set lib. bdg. 178.21 o.p. (978-0-7614-4203-5(0)) Marshall Cavendish Corp.

Donovan, Sandy. The U. S. Air Force. 2005. (U. S. Armed Forces Ser.). (Illus.). 64p. (J). (gr. 4-7). lib. bdg. 26.60 (978-0-8225-1436-7(2)) Lerner Publishing Group.

Dougherty, Martin J. Air Warfare. 2010. (Modern Warfare Ser.). 32p. (YA). (gr. 2-5). lib. bdg. 26.00 (978-1-4339-2720-1(9)) Stevens, Gareth Publishing LLLP.

Freedman, Jeri. Special Ops: Air Commandos, 1 vol. 2015. (ENG.). 64p. (YA). 32.95 (978-1-4777-7993-4(0), Rosen Reference) Rosen Publishing Group, Inc., The.

—Your Career in the Air Force. 2011. (Call of Duty: Careers in the Armed Forces Ser.). (ENG.). 128p. (YA). (gr. 9-12). lib. bdg. 34.60 (978-1-4488-5513-1(6)) Rosen Publishing Group, Inc., The.

Goldish, Meish. Air Force: Civilian to Airman. 2010. (Becoming a Soldier Ser.). 24p. (YA). (gr. 3-6). lib. bdg. 22.61 (978-1-936088-10-2(X)) Bearport Publishing Co., Inc.

Gordon, Nick. Air Force Air Commandos. 2013. (U. S. Military Ser.). (ENG., Illus.). 24p. (J). (gr. 3-7). lib. bdg. 25.95 (978-1-60014-873-6(5), Epic Bks.) Bellwether Media.

—U. S. Air Force. 2012. (U. S. Military Ser.). (ENG., Illus.). 24p. (J). (gr. 3-7). lib. bdg. 25.95 (978-1-60014-826-2(3), Epic Bks.) Bellwether Media.

Grayson, Robert. US Air Force, 1 vol. 2014. (Essential Library of the US Military Ser.). (ENG.). 112p. (J). (gr. 6-12). lib. bdg. 35.64 (978-1-62403-432-9(2), Essential Library) ABDO Publishing Co.

Green, Michael. The United States Air Force, 1 vol. 2013. (U. S. Military Forces Ser.). (ENG.). 24p. (gr. 1-2). lib. bdg. 25.32 (978-1-4765-0071-3(1)) Capstone Press of Coughlan Cos.

Greene, Meg. Careers in the National Guards' Search & Rescue Units. (Careers in Search & Rescue Operations Ser.). 64p. (gr. 5-8). 2009. 58.50 (978-1-61511-812-0(8), Rosen Reference) 2005. (Illus.). (YA). lib. bdg. 31.95 (978-0-8239-3836-0(0)) Rosen Publishing Group, Inc., The.

Gregory, Josh. Avionics Technician. 2012. (21st Century Skills Library: Cool Military Careers Ser.). (ENG.). 32p. (gr. 4-8). 28.50 (978-1-61080-445-5(7), 202055); pap. 14.21 (978-1-61080-619-0(0), 202229) Cherry Lake Publishing.

Hand, Carol. Special Ops: Search & Rescue Operations, 1 vol. 2015. (ENG.). 64p. (J). 32.95 (978-1-4777-7997-2(3), Rosen Reference) Rosen Publishing Group, Inc., The.

Harasymiw, M. Alexander. Pararescuemen. 2012. (US Special Forces Ser.). (ENG., Illus.). 32p. (J). (gr. 3-6). pap. 10.50 (978-1-4339-6571-5(2)); lib. bdg. 26.60 (978-1-4339-6569-2(0)) Stevens, Gareth Publishing LLLP. (Gareth Stevens Learning Library).

Jordan, David. The U. S. Air Force. 2004. (America's Armed Forces Ser.). (Illus.). 48p. (gr. 5-12). lib. bdg. 31.00 (978-0-8368-5679-8(1), Gareth Stevens Secondary Library) Stevens, Gareth Publishing LLLP.

Keeter, Hunter. American Air Forces in the Vietnam War. 2005. (American Experience in Vietnam Ser.). (Illus.). 48p. (gr. 5-12). lib. bdg. 31.00 (978-0-8368-5773-3(9), Gareth Stevens Secondary Library) Stevens, Gareth Publishing LLLP.

Linde, Barbara. Heroes of the Us Air Force. 2012. (Heroes of the US Military Ser.). (Illus.). 32p. (gr. 3-6). 26.60 (978-1-4339-7232-4(8)); pap. 10.50 (978-1-4339-7233-1(6)) Stevens, Gareth Publishing LLLP. (Gareth Stevens Learning Library).

Loria, Laura. Air Force. 2011. (Us Military Forces Ser.). 32p. (gr. 3-6). (J). pap. 10.50 (978-1-4339-5844-1(9), Gareth Stevens Learning Library); (YA). lib. bdg. 26.60 (978-1-4339-5842-7(2)) Stevens, Gareth Publishing LLLP.

Loveless, Antony. Air War. 2008. (ENG., Illus.). 32p. (J). (gr. 6-10). lib. bdg. (978-0-7787-3812-1(4)) Crabtree Publishing Co.

Lusted, Marcia Amidon. Air Commandos: Elite Operations. 2013. (Military Special Ops Ser.). (ENG., Illus.). 32p. (gr. 3-8). lib. bdg. 26.60 (978-0-7613-9081-7(2), Lerner Pubns.) Lerner Publishing Group.

Marx, Mandy R. Amazing U. S. Air Force Facts. 2016. (Amazing Military Facts Ser.). (ENG., Illus.). 24p. (gr. k-1). lib. bdg. 26.65 (978-1-5157-0951-0(5), Pebble Plus) Capstone Press of Coughlan Cos.

Masters, Nancy Robinson. Pararescue Jumper. 2012. (21st Century Skills Library: Cool Military Careers Ser.). (ENG.). 32p. (gr. 4-8). 28.50 (978-1-61080-451-6(1), 202061); pap. 14.21 (978-1-61080-625-1(5), 202235) Cherry Lake Publishing.

McNab, Chris. The Air Force. 2017. (J). **(978-1-4222-3764-9(8))** Mason Crest.

—Protecting the Nation with the U. S. Air Force. 2004. (Rescue & Prevention Ser.). (Illus.). 96p. (YA). (gr. 7-18). lib. bdg. 22.95 (978-1-59084-416-8(5)) Mason Crest.

—Surviving Captivity. Carney, John, ed. 2014. (Extreme Survival in the Military Ser.: 12). 64p. (J). (gr. 7-18). lib. bdg. 23.95 (978-1-4222-3089-3(9)) Mason Crest.

Miller, Adam. U. S. Air Force True Stories: Tales of Bravery. 2014. (Courage under Fire Ser.). (ENG.). 32p. (gr. 3-4). lib. bdg. 27.99 (978-1-4765-9936-6(X)) Capstone Press of Coughlan Cos.

Mitchell, P. P. Join the Air Force. 2017. (U. S. Armed Forces Ser.). 32p. (gr. 1-2). pap. 63.00 **(978-1-5382-0540-2(8))** Stevens, Gareth Publishing LLLP.

Murray, Julie. United States Air Force, 1 vol. 2014. (U. S. Armed Forces Ser.). (ENG.). 24p. (J). (gr. 4-8). lib. bdg. 28.50 (978-1-62970-093-9(2)) ABDO Publishing Co.

Nardo, Don. Special Operations: Search & Rescue: Search & Rescue. 2012. (YA). 27.45 (978-1-59935-362-3(8)) Reynolds, Morgan Inc.

Porterfield, Jason. USAF Special Tactics Teams. (Inside Special Operations Ser.). 64p. 2009. (Illus.). (gr. 5-8). pap. 12.95 (978-1-4358-5131-3(5), Rosen Classroom) 2009. (gr. 6-6). 58.50 (978-1-61513-558-5(8), Rosen Reference) 2008. (Illus.). (J). lib. bdg. 31.95 (978-1-4042-1753-9(3)) Rosen Publishing Group, Inc., The.

Press, Applesauce & Entin, Cindy. My First Counting Book - Airforce: A Celebration of the United States Air Forces from 1 to 10! 2013. (ENG.). 10p. (J). bds. 5.99 (978-1-60433-320-6(0), Applesauce Pr.) Cider Mill Pr. Bk. Pubs., LLC.

Ray, Michael. The History of Air Forces Around the World, 1 vol., 1. Saxena, Shalini, ed. 2014. (World's Armed Forces Ser.). (ENG.). 144p. (YA). (gr. 7-12). 35.25 (978-1-62275-145-7(0)) Rosen Publishing Group, Inc., The.

Rice, Earle & Camelo, Wilson. Careers in the US Air Force. 2015. (Careers in the US Armed Forces Ser.). (ENG., Illus.). 128p. (J). (gr. 6-7). 37.27 (978-0-7660-6941-1(9)) Enslow Pubs., Inc.

Roberts, Jeremy. U. S. Air Force Special Operations. 2004. (U. S. Armed Forces Ser.). (ENG., Illus.). 64p. (gr. 4-8). lib. bdg. 26.60 (978-0-8225-1644-6(6)) Lerner Publishing Group.

Rose, Simon. Air Force. 2012. (J). (978-1-61913-292-4(3)); pap. (978-1-61913-295-5(8)) Weigl Pubs., Inc.

—Air Force Special Operations. 2014. (Illus.). 24p. (J). (978-1-62127-448-3(9)) Weigl Pubs., Inc.

Russo, Kristen J. Surprising Facts about Being an Air Force Airman. 2017. (What You Didn't Know about the U. S. Military Life Ser.). (ENG.). 32p. (gr. 3-4). lib. bdg. 27.99 **(978-1-5157-7428-0(7)**, Edge Bks.) Capstone Press of Coughlan Cos.

Ryan, Peter K. Black Ops & Other Special Missions of the U. S. Air Force Combat Control Team. 2012. (Inside Special Forces Ser.). (ENG., Illus.). 64p. (YA). (gr. 5-8). pap. 12.95 (978-1-4488-8389-9(X)); lib. bdg. 31.95 (978-1-4488-8382-0(2)) Rosen Publishing Group, Inc., The.

Sandler, Michael. Pararescuemen in Action. 2008. (Special Ops Ser.). (Illus.). 32p. (J). (gr. 3-6). lib. bdg. 25.27 (978-1-59716-633-1(2)) Bearport Publishing Co., Inc.

Schwartz, Heather E. Women of the U. S. Air Force: Aiming High, 1 vol. 2010. (Women in the U. S. Armed Forces Ser.). (ENG.). 32p. (gr. 3-4). lib. bdg. 27.99 (978-1-4296-5449-4(X), Snap Bks.) Capstone Press of Coughlan Cos.

Simons, Lisa M. Bolt. Airmen of the U. S. Air Force [Scholastic]. 2010. (People of the U. S. Armed Forces Ser.). (ENG.). 24p. pap. 0.49 (978-1-4296-5804-1(5), Pebble Plus) Capstone Press of Coughlan Cos.

—U. S. Air Force by the Numbers, 1 vol. 2014. (Military by the Numbers Ser.). (ENG.). 32p. (gr. 3-4). lib. bdg. 27.99 (978-1-4765-3920-1(0), Edge Bks.) Capstone Press of Coughlan Cos.

Slater, Lee. Pararescue Jumpers, 1 vol. 2016. (Special Ops Ser.). (ENG., Illus.). 32p. (J). (gr. 3-6). 27.07 (978-1-62403-972-0(3)) ABDO Publishing Co.

Terrell, Brandon. Guarding Air Force One. 2016. (Highly Guarded Places Ser.). (ENG.). 24p. (J). (gr. 2-5). 28.50 (978-1-5038-0808-9(4), 210643) Child's World, Inc., The.

Townsend, John. Air Force. 2016. (Action Force: World War II Ser.). 32p. (gr. 3-7). 31.35 (978-1-59920-985-2(3), Smart Apple Media) Black Rabbit Bks.

Tunnell, Michael O. Candy Bomber: The Story of the Berlin Airlift's Chocolate Pilot. 2010. (ENG., Illus.). 120p. (J). (gr. 4-7). pap. 9.95 (978-1-58089-337-4(6)) Charlesbridge Publishing, Inc.

Vanderhoof, Gabrielle. Air Force. 2010. (Special Forces Ser.). 64p. (YA). (gr. 7-18). lib. bdg. 22.95 (978-1-4222-1837-2(6)) Mason Crest.

Whiting, Jim. Air Force Special Operations Command. 2014. (J). (978-1-60818-460-6(9), Creative Education) Creative Co., The.

—U. S. Special Forces: Air Force Special Operations Command. 2015. (U. S. Special Forces Ser.). (ENG.). 48p. (J). (gr. 5-8). pap. 12.00 (978-1-62832-046-6(X), Creative Paperbacks) Creative Co., The.

Wood, Alix. Serving in the Air Force. 2013. (Protecting Our Country Ser.). 32p. (J). (gr. 3-6). pap. 60.00 (978-1-4777-1401-0(4)); pap. 10.00 (978-1-4777-1400-3(6)); lib. bdg. 25.25 (978-1-4777-1297-9(6)) Rosen Publishing Group, Inc., The. (PowerKids Pr.).

Zobel, Derek. United States Air Force. 2008. (Armed Forces Ser.). (ENG., Illus.). 24p. (YA). (gr. 3-7). lib. bdg. 25.95 (978-1-60014-161-4(7)) Bellwether Media.

UNITED STATES—AIR FORCE—BIOGRAPHY

Aronin, Miriam & Pushies, Fred J. Today's Air Force Heroes. 2012. (Acts of Courage: Inside America's Military Ser.). (Illus.). 32p. (J). (gr. 2-7). lib. bdg. 25.27 (978-1-61772-447-3(5)) Bearport Publishing Co., Inc.

Earl, Sari. Benjamin O. Davis, Jr: Air Force General & Tuskegee Airmen Leader, 1 vol. 2010. (Military Heroes Ser.). (ENG.). 112p. (J). (gr. 6-12). lib. bdg. 35.64 *(978-1-60453-961-5(5))* ABDO Publishing Co.

Fleischman, John. Black & White Airmen: Their True History. 2007. (ENG., Illus.). 160p. (gr. 5-12). 28.80 *(978-1-4287-3953-6(X),* Follettbound) Follett School Solutions.

Voices of War. 2010. (Voices of War Ser.). (ENG.). 32p. (gr. 3-4). pap. 31.80 *(978-1-4296-5704-4(9),* Edge Bks.) Capstone Press of Coughlan Cos.

UNITED STATES AIR FORCE ACADEMY—FICTION

Lynch, Chris. Casualties of War. 2013. (Vietnam Ser.: 4). (ENG.). 192p. (J). (gr. 5-9). pap. 7.99 *(978-0-545-27024-3(3),* Scholastic Pr.) Scholastic, Inc.

Weisleder, Stanley. Wings of the Panther. 2010. (ENG.). 224p. pap. 15.00 *(978-0-936783-38-3(9))* Merril Pr.

UNITED STATES—ANTIQUITIES

see also Indians of North America—Antiquities

Benson, Sonia & Baker, Deborah J. Almanac, Early Civilizations, 2 vols. 2005. (Early Civilizations in the Americas Ser.). (ENG., Illus.). 336p. (J). lib. bdg. 106.00 *(978-0-7876-7679-7(9),* UXL) Cengage Gale.

—Primary Sources, Early Americas, 2 vols. 2005. (Early Civilizations in the Americas Ser.). (ENG., Illus.). 368p. (J). lib. bdg. 106.00 *(978-0-7876-7681-0(0),* UXL) Cengage Gale.

Cunningham, Laura. The Bay Area Through Time. 2015. (Illus.). (J). *(978-1-59714-301-1(4))* Heyday.

Hansen, Joyce & McGowan, Gary. Freedom Roads: Searching for the Underground Railroad. Ransome, James E., illus. 2003. (ENG.). 166p. (J). (gr. 5-9). 18.95 *(978-0-8126-2673-5(7))* Cricket Bks.

Hawk, Frank. The Story of the H. L. Hunley & Queenie's Coin. Nance, Dan, illus. 2004. (ENG.). 40p. (J). (gr. k-6). 16.95 *(978-1-58536-218-9(2))* Sleeping Bear Pr.

Holliday, Diane & Malone, Bobbie. Digging & Discovery, Teachers Guide & Student Materials, 2nd Edition, on CD: Wisconsin Archaeology. 2011. (New Badger History Ser.). (ENG.). (J). cd-rom 49.95 *(978-0-87020-480-7(7))* Wisconsin Historical Society.

Huey, Lois Miner. Forgotten Bones: Uncovering a Slave Cemetery. 2015. (ENG., Illus.). 56p. (J). (gr. 4-8). lib. bdg. 30.65 *(978-1-4677-3393-9(8),* Millbrook Pr.) Lerner Publishing Group.

Manis, Shirley & Manis, Shirley. In a Scoop of Dirt: How Digging a Pond Changed North America's Prehistory. l.t. ed. 2011. (ENG., Illus.). 38p. pap. 17.95 *(978-0-9839286-0-7(6))* Manis, Shirley.

Walker, Sally M. Written in Bone: Buried Lives of Jamestown & Colonial Maryland. 2009. (Exceptional Social Studies Titles for Intermediate Grades). (ENG., Illus.). 144p. (J). (gr. 5-8). lib. bdg. 22.95 *(978-0-8225-7135-3(8))* Lerner Publishing Group.

Ward, Jill. Georgia's First People. 2010. (J). *(978-1-935077-74-9(0));* pap. *(978-1-935077-81-7(3))* State Standards Publishing, LLC.

UNITED STATES—ARMED FORCES

see also official names of branches of the Armed Forces, e.g. U. S. Army; U. S. Navy

ABDO Publishing Company Staff. Essential Library of the US Military. 2014. (Essential Library of the US Military Ser.: 6). (ENG.). 112p. (J). (gr. 6-12). lib. bdg. 213.84 *(978-1-62403-431-2(4),* Essential Library) ABDO Publishing Co.

ABDO Publishing Company Staff & Murray, Julie. U. S. Armed Forces. 2014. (U. S. Armed Forces Ser.: 6). (ENG.). 24p. (J). (gr. 4-8). lib. bdg. 171.00 *(978-1-62970-091-5(6))* ABDO Publishing Co.

Alpert, Barbara. U. S. Military Robots, 1 vol. 2012. (U. S. Military Technology Ser.). (ENG., Illus.). 32p. (gr. 1-2). lib. bdg. 26.65 *(978-1-4296-8438-5(0))* Capstone Press of Coughlan Cos.

Blackford, Cheryl. This Book Is Top Secret: A Collection of Awesome Military Trivia, 1 vol. 2012. (Super Trivia Collection). (ENG., Illus.). 32p. (gr. 3-4). lib. bdg. 27.99 *(978-1-4296-8591-7(3))* Capstone Press of Coughlan Cos.

Bowman, Chris. Special Forces Operator. 2014. (Dangerous Jobs Ser.). (ENG., Illus.). 24p. (J). (gr. 3-7). lib. bdg. 25.95 *(978-1-62617-114-5(9),* Torque Bks.) Bellwether Media.

Burgan, Michael, et al. The U. S. Armed Forces. 2013. (U. S. Armed Forces Ser.). (ENG.). 48p. (gr. 5-6). pap. 44.75 *(978-0-7565-4643-4(5),* CPB Grades 4-8) Compass Point Bks.

Campbell, Geoffrey A. Weapons of War. 2004. (American War Library). (Illus.). 112p. (J). (gr. 7-10). 30.85 *(978-1-59018-544-5(7),* Lucent Bks.) Cengage Gale.

Careers in the US Armed Forces. 2015. (Careers in the US Armed Forces Ser.). (ENG.). 128p. (J). (gr. 6-7). 186.35 *(978-0-7660-6694-6(0))* Enslow Pubs., Inc.

Collier, Peter. Choosing Courage: Inspiring Stories of What It Means to Be a Hero. 2015. (ENG., Illus.). 240p. (J). 18.95 *(978-1-57965-596-9(3))* Artisan.

David, Jack. M2A2 Bradleys. 2009. (Military Machines Ser.). (ENG., Illus.). 24p. (J). (gr. 3-7). lib. bdg. 25.95 *(978-1-60014-261-1(3))* Bellwether Media.

Dell, Pamela & Raatma, Lucia. The Science of Soldiers, 1 vol. 2012. (Science of War Ser.). (ENG.). 48p. (gr. 5-6). pap. 9.10 *(978-0-7565-4526-0(9));* lib. bdg. 33.99 *(978-0-7565-4460-7(2))* Compass Point Bks. (CPB Grades 4-8).

Demarest, Chris L. Alpha Bravo Charlie: The Military Alphabet. Demarest, Chris L., illus. 2005. (ENG., Illus.). 40p. (J). (gr. 1-5). 18.99 *(978-0-689-86928-0(2),* McElderry, Margaret K. Bks.) McElderry, Margaret K. Bks.

Dolan, Edward F. Military Service, 5 vols., Set. Incl. Careers in the U. S. Air Force. (YA). (gr. 7-9). 35.64 *(978-0-7614-4205-9(7));* Careers in the U. S. Army. (YA). (gr. 7-9). 35.64 *(978-0-7614-4206-6(5));* Careers in the U. S. Coast Guard. (gr. 7-9). 35.64 *(978-0-7614-4207-3(3));* Careers in the U. S. Marine Corps. (YA). (gr. 8-18). 35.64 *(978-0-7614-4209-7(X));* Careers in the U. S. Navy. (gr. 7-18). 35.64 *(978-0-7614-4210-3(3));* 80p. 2009. 2010. Set lib. bdg. 178.21 o.p. *(978-0-7614-4203-5(0))* Marshall Cavendish Corp.

Donovan, Sandy. Protecting America: A Look at the People Who Keep Our Country Safe. 2003. (How Government Works). (ENG., Illus.). 56p. (gr. 4-8). lib. bdg. 25.26 *(978-0-8225-1345-2(5))* Lerner Publishing Group.

Equipped for Battle: Weapons, Gear, & Uniforms of America's Wars. 2014. (Equipped for Battle Ser.). (ENG.). 176p. pap. 12.95 *(978-1-4765-7653-4(X),* Edge Bks.) Capstone Press of Coughlan Cos.

Fishkin, Rebecca Love. Vehicles of the Iraq War, 1 vol. 2013. (War Vehicles Ser.). (ENG.). 32p. (gr. 3-4). 27.99 *(978-1-4296-9914-3(0),* Edge Bks.) Capstone Press of Coughlan Cos.

Gente de las Fuerzas Armadas de EE. UU. 2010. (Gente de Las Fuerzas Armadas de EE. UU. /People of the Armed Forces Ser.).Tr. of People of the Armed Forces. (MUL.). 24p. (gr. k-1). 79.95 *(978-1-4296-6119-5(4))* Capstone Press of Coughlan Cos.

Gonzalez, Lissette. The U. S. Military: Defending the Nation. (Dangerous Jobs Ser.). 24p. 2009. (gr. 2-3). 42.50 *(978-1-61512-137-3(4),* PowerKids Pr.) 2007. (Illus.). (J). (gr. 3-7). lib. bdg. 22.60 *(978-1-4042-3777-3(1))* Rosen Publishing Group, Inc., The.

Green, Michael. U. S. Military Forces. 2013. (U. S. Military Forces Ser.). (ENG.). 24p. (gr. 1-2). lib. bdg. 101.28 *(978-1-4765-0073-7(8),* First Facts) Capstone Press of Coughlan Cos.

Gregory, Josh. Aircraft Pilot. 2012. (21st Century Skills Library: Cool Military Careers Ser.). (ENG.). 32p. (gr. 4-8). 28.50 *(978-1-61080-444-8(9),* 202054); pap. 14.21 *(978-1-61080-618-3(2),* 202228) Cherry Lake Publishing.

—Avionics Technician. 2012. (21st Century Skills Library: Cool Military Careers Ser.). (ENG.). 32p. (gr. 4-8). 28.50 *(978-1-61080-445-5(7),* 202055); pap. 14.21 *(978-1-61080-619-0(0),* 202229) Cherry Lake Publishing.

—Information Systems Technician. 2012. (21st Century Skills Library: Cool Military Careers Ser.). (ENG.). 32p. (gr. 4-8). 28.50 *(978-1-61080-447-9(3),* 202057); pap. 14.21 *(978-1-61080-621-3(2),* 202231) Cherry Lake Publishing.

—Special Ops. 2012. (21st Century Skills Library: Cool Military Careers Ser.). (ENG.). 32p. (gr. 4-8). 28.50 *(978-1-61080-446-2(5),* 202056); pap. 14.21 *(978-1-61080-620-6(4),* 202230) Cherry Lake Publishing.

Hamilton, John. America's Military. 2004. (War in Iraq Ser.). (Illus.). 48p. (gr. 4-8). 27.07 *(978-1-59197-492-5(5),* Abdo & Daughters) ABDO Publishing Co.

—Special Forces, 1 vol. 2007. (Defending the Nation Ser.). (ENG., Illus.). 32p. (gr. 4-7). 27.07 *(978-1-59679-759-8(2),* Checkerboard Library) ABDO Publishing Co.

—United States Armed Forces, 6 vols., Set. Incl. Green Berets. 27.07 *(978-1-61783-066-2(6));* Navy SEALs. 27.07 *(978-1-61783-067-9(4));* United States Air Force. 27.07 *(978-1-61783-068-6(2));* United States Army. 27.07 *(978-1-61783-069-3(0));* United States Marine Corps. 27.07 *(978-1-61783-070-9(4));* United States Navy. 27.07 *(978-1-61783-071-6(2));* (YA). (gr. 3-6). (Armed Forces Ser.). (Illus.). 32p. 2011. 162.42 *(978-1-61783-065-5(8),* A&D Xtreme) ABDO Publishing Co.

—Weapons of the Twenty-First Century. 2004. (War in Iraq Ser.). (Illus.). 48p. (gr. 4-8). 27.07 *(978-1-59197-501-4(8),* Abdo & Daughters) ABDO Publishing Co.

Hart, Joyce. Frequently Asked Questions about Being Part of a Military Family. 2009. (FAQ: Teen Life Ser.). (Illus.). 64p. (J). (gr. 5-6). lib. bdg. 31.95 *(978-1-4358-5328-7(8))* Rosen Publishing Group, Inc., The.

Libal, Joyce. Military & Elite Forces Officer. Riggs, Ernestine G. & Gholar, Cheryl, eds. 2013. (Careers with Character Ser.: 18). 96p. (J). (gr. 7-18). 22.95 *(978-1-4222-2760-2(X))* Mason Crest.

Lieurance, Suzanne. Weapons & Strategies of the Civil War: A MyReportLinks.com Book. 2004. (American Civil War Ser.). (Illus.). 48p. (J). lib. bdg. 25.26 *(978-0-7660-5185-0(4),* MyReportLinks.com Bks.) Enslow Pubs., Inc.

Lusted, Marcia Amidon. African Americans in the Military. 2012. (J). pap. *(978-1-4222-2392-5(2))* Mason Crest.

—African Americans in the Military. Hill, Marc Lamont, ed. 2012. (Major Black Contributions from Emancipation to Civil Rights Ser.). 64p. (J). (gr. 5). 22.95 *(978-1-4222-2379-6(5))* Mason Crest.

Mara, Wil. Helicopter Crew Chief. 2012. (21st Century Skills Library: Cool Military Careers Ser.). (ENG.). 32p. (gr. 4-8). 28.50 *(978-1-61080-449-3(X),* 202059); pap. 14.21 *(978-1-61080-623-7(9),* 202233) Cherry Lake Publishing.

—Motor Transport Operator. 2012. (21st Century Skills Library: Cool Military Careers Ser.). (ENG.). 32p. (gr. 4-8). 28.50 *(978-1-61080-450-9(3),* 202060); pap. 14.21 *(978-1-61080-624-4(7),* 202234) Cherry Lake Publishing.

Masters, Nancy Robinson. Drone Pilot. 2012. (21st Century Skills Library: Cool Military Careers Ser.). (ENG.). 32p. (gr. 4-8). 28.50 *(978-1-61080-448-6(1),* 202058); pap. 14.21 *(978-1-61080-622-0(0),* 202232) Cherry Lake Publishing.

Maxwell, Shannon. Our Daddy Is Invincible! Biggers, Liza, illus. 40p. (J). 2011. 15.95 *(978-1-61751-003-8(3))* 2010. pap. 9.95 *(978-1-61751-002-1(5))* Kurdyla, E L Publishing LLC. (4th Division Pr.).

McIntosh, J. S. Elite Forces Selection. 2010. (Special Forces Ser.). 64p. (YA). (gr. 7-18). lib. bdg. 22.95 *(978-1-4222-1839-6(2))* Mason Crest.

Mikaelian, Allen & Wallace, Mike. Medal of Honor: Profiles of America's Military Heroes from the Civil War to the Present. 2003. (ENG.). 336p. (gr. 8-17). pap. 20.99 *(978-0-7868-8576-3(9))* Hyperion Pr.

Miller, Adam, et al. Courage under Fire: Tales of Bravery, 1 vol. 2014. (Courage under Fire Ser.). (ENG.). 32p. (gr. 3-4). 111.96 *(978-1-4765-9939-7(4),* Edge Bks.) Capstone Press of Coughlan Cos.

—Courage under Fire: True Stories of Bravery from the U. S. Army, Navy, Air Force, & Marines, 1 vol. 2014. (Courage under Fire Ser.). (ENG., Illus.). 112p. (gr. 3-4). pap. 9.95 *(978-1-4914-1065-3(5))* Capstone Press of Coughlan Cos.

Montana, Jack. Parachute Regiment. 2010. (Special Forces Ser.). 64p. (YA). (gr. 7-18). lib. bdg. 22.95 *(978-1-4222-1845-7(7))* Mason Crest.

Mooney, Carla. Awesome Military Robots, 1 vol. 2014. (Ready for Military Action Ser.). (ENG.). 48p. (gr. 3-6). lib. bdg. 32.79 *(978-1-62403-649-1(X))* ABDO Publishing Co.

Morrison, Jessica. Military. 2016. (Illus.). 48p. (J). *(978-1-5105-1160-6(1))* SmartBook Media, Inc.

—Military. 2011. (J). (gr. 5-8). pap. 14.95 *(978-1-61690-665-8(0),* AV2 by Weigl); (Illus.). 48p. (YA). (gr. 1-4). 29.99 *(978-1-61690-661-0(8))* Weigl Pubs., Inc.

Page, Andrea. The Sioux Code Talkers of World War II, 1 vol. 2017. (Illus.). 136p. (J). (gr. 3-7). 14.95 *(978-1-4556-2243-6(5))* Pelican Publishing Co., Inc.

Piehl, Janet. Humvees. 2005. (Pull Ahead Books-Mighty Movers Ser.). (ENG., Illus.). 32p. (gr. k-3). per. 7.95 *(978-0-8225-2874-6(6),* Lerner Pubns.) Lerner Publishing Group.

Poole, H. W. Military Families, Vol. 12. 2016. (Families Today Ser.). (Illus.). 48p. (J). (gr. 5). 20.95 *(978-1-4222-3620-8(X))* Mason Crest.

Price, Sean Stewart. Amazing Military Robots. 2013. (Robots Ser.). (ENG.). 32p. (gr. 3-4). pap. 47.70 *(978-1-62065-777-5(5),* Edge Bks.); (Illus.). pap. 8.29 *(978-1-62065-776-8(7))* Capstone Press of Coughlan Cos.

—Amazing Military Robots, 1 vol. 2013. (Robots Ser.). (ENG.). 32p. (gr. 3-4). lib. bdg. 27.99 *(978-1-4296-9917-4(5))* Capstone Press of Coughlan Cos.

Rauf, Don, et al. Choose Your Own Career Adventure in the Military. 2016. (Bright Futures Press: Choose Your Own Career Adventure Ser.). (ENG., Illus.). 32p. (J). (gr. 4-6). 29.93 *(978-1-63471-912-4(3),* 208969) Cherry Lake Publishing.

Raum, Elizabeth, et al. True War Stories: Personal Accounts of History's Greatest Conflicts. Kinsella, Pat et al, illus. 2017. (J). *(978-1-4914-1965-6(2))* Capstone Press of Coughlan Cos.

Rice, Earle. Korea 1950: From Pusan to Chosin. 2003. (Great Battles Through the Ages Ser.). (Illus.). 112p. (gr. 6-12). 30.00 *(978-0-7910-7436-7(6),* Chelsea Hse.) Facts On File, Inc.

Roza, Greg. Careers in the Military. 2005. (World of Work Ser.). (Illus.). 64p. (YA). (gr. 7-12). lib. bdg. 31.95 *(978-0-8239-3331-0(8))* Rosen Publishing Group, Inc., The.

—Choosing a Career in the Military. 2009. (World of Work Ser.). 64p. (gr. 5-5). 58.50 *(978-1-60854-338-0(2))* Rosen Publishing Group, Inc., The.

Rudolph, Jessica. CIA Paramilitary Operatives in Action. 2013. (Special Ops II Ser.). 32p. (J). (gr. 2-7). lib. bdg. 26.60 *(978-1-61772-892-1(6))* Bearport Publishing Co., Inc.

Scillian, Devin. H Is for Honor: A Military Family Alphabet. Juhasz, Victor, illus. 2006. (ENG.). 40p. (J). (gr. k-6). 17.95 *(978-1-58536-292-9(1))* Sleeping Bear Pr.

Sheen, Barbara. Cutting Edge Military Technology. 2016. (ENG.). 80p. (J). (gr. 5-12). *(978-1-68282-044-5(0))* ReferencePoint Pr., Inc.

Simons, Lisa M. Bolt. The U. S. WASP: Trailblazing Women Pilots of World War II. 2017. (Women & War Ser.). (ENG.). 32p. (gr. 3-4). pap. 8.19 ***(978-1-5157-7944-5(0),*** Snap Bks.) Capstone Press of Coughlan Cos.

—Women in Combat: Bringing the Fight to the Front Lines. 2017. (Women & War Ser.). (ENG.). 32p. (gr. 3-4). lib. bdg. 27.99 ***(978-1-5157-7934-6(3),*** Snap Bks.) Capstone Press of Coughlan Cos.

Simons, Lisa M. Bolt, et al. U. S. Military by the Numbers, 1 vol. 2014. (ENG.). 112p. (gr. 3-4). pap. 9.95 *(978-1-62370-061-4(2))* Capstone Young Readers of Coughlan Cos.

A Soldier Comes Home. 2011. (ENG., Illus.). 32p. (J). pap. 9.99 *(978-0-578-06838-1(9))* Yari Publishing.

Stein, R. Conrad. World War II in the Pacific: From Pearl Harbor to Nagasaki. 2011. (United States at War Ser.). (Illus.). 128p. (J). (gr. 5-18). lib. bdg. 33.27 *(978-0-7660-3640-6(5))* Enslow Pubs., Inc.

Sterngass, Jon. John Brown. 2009. (Leaders of the Civil War Era Ser.). (Illus.). 144p. (gr. 6-12). 35.00 *(978-1-60413-305-9(8),* Chelsea Hse.) Facts On File, Inc.

Stout, Glenn. Soldier Athletes. 2011. (Good Sports Ser.). (ENG.). 112p. (J). (gr. 5-7). pap. 6.99 *(978-0-547-41729-5(2))* Houghton Mifflin Harcourt Publishing Co.

Sutherland, Adam. Armed Services. 2012. (On the Radar: Defend & Protect Ser.). (ENG., Illus.). 32p. (gr. 4-8). lib. bdg. 26.60 *(978-0-7613-7771-9(9),* Lerner Pubns.) Lerner Publishing Group.

Teitelbaum, Michael. Humvees: High Mobility in the Field. Nelson, Scott, photos by. 2006. (Mighty Military Machines Ser.). (Illus.). 48p. (J). (gr. 4-7). lib. bdg. 25.27 *(978-0-7660-2661-2(2))* Enslow Pubs., Inc.

U. S. Armed Forces. 2017. (U. S. Armed Forces Ser.). 32p. (gr. 1-2). pap. 63.00 ***(978-1-5382-0493-1(2));*** lib. bdg. 159.60 ***(978-1-5382-0479-5(7))*** Stevens, Gareth Publishing LLLP.

U. S. Armed Forces Pack [Scholastic]. 2010. (People of the U. S. Armed Forces Ser.). 24p. pap. 1.96 *(978-1-4296-5808-9(8),* Pebble Plus) Capstone Press of Coughlan Cos.

U. S. Military Branches & Careers, 5 bks., Set. Incl. Air Force in Action. Langley, Wanda. (J). lib. bdg. 27.94 *(978-0-7660-1636-1(6));* Army in Action. Sawyer, Susan. (J). lib. bdg. 27.94 *(978-0-7660-1635-4(8));* Coast Guard in Action. Gaines, Ann Graham. (J). lib. bdg. 27.94 *(978-0-7660-1634-7(X));* Marine Corps in Action. Aaseng, Nathan. (J). lib. bdg. 27.94 *(978-0-7660-1637-8(4));* Navy in Action. Gaines, Ann Graham. (YA). lib. bdg. 26.60 *(978-0-7660-1633-0(1));* 128p. (gr. 6-12). 2001. (Illus.). Set lib. bdg. 104.75 *(978-0-7660-1803-7(2))* Enslow Pubs., Inc.

Whiting, Jim. Green Berets. 2014. (U. S. Special Forces Ser.). (ENG., Illus.). 48p. (J). (gr. 5-8). lib. bdg. 35.65 *(978-1-60818-463-7(3),* Creative Education) Creative Co., The.

Williams, Brian. Special Forces, 1 vol. 2011. (War Stories Ser.). (ENG.). 32p. (gr. 3-6). 30.65 *(978-1-4329-4831-3(8),* NA-h) Heinemann-Raintree.

Wolny, Philip. American Troops in Afghanistan: Building a New Nation. (Frontline Coverage of Current Events Ser.). 48p. 2009. (gr. 5-5). 53.00 *(978-1-61512-653-8(8))* 2004. (Illus.). (J). lib. bdg. 29.25 *(978-1-4042-0343-3(5))* Rosen Publishing Group, Inc., The.

Yomtov, Nel. Patrolling. 2016. (Military Missions Ser.). (ENG., Illus.). 24p. (J). (gr. 3-7). 25.95 *(978-1-62617-435-1(0),* Epic Bks.) Bellwether Media.

—Rescue. 2016. (Military Missions Ser.). (ENG., Illus.). 24p. (J). (gr. 3-7). 25.95 *(978-1-62617-438-2(5),* Epic Bks.) Bellwether Media.

Zullo, Allan. World War I Heroes. 2014. 162p. (J). pap. ***(978-0-545-67533-8(2))*** Scholastic, Inc.

UNITED STATES—ARMED FORCES—FICTION

Andersen, C. B. The Secret Mission. 2008. (J). *(978-1-59038-906-5(9))* Deseret Bk. Co.

Cummings, Mary. And the Baker's Boy Went to Sea. 2006. (Illus.). 195p. (YA). 16.95 *(978-0-9774855-0-5(1))* Sparkling Pr.

Dowell, Frances O'Roark. Shooting the Moon. 2009. (ENG.). 192p. (J). (gr. 5-9). pap. 7.99 *(978-1-4169-7986-9(7),* Atheneum Bks. for Young Readers) Simon & Schuster Children's Publishing.

Duble, Kathleen Benner. Phantoms in the Snow. 2011. (ENG.). 240p. (J). (gr. 7-7). 17.99 *(978-0-545-19770-0(8),* Scholastic Pr.) Scholastic, Inc.

Ganzer, Diane & Swanson, Christopher. Called to Serve. 2008. 116p. pap. 9.99 *(978-1-935105-10-7(8))* Avid Readers Publishing Group.

Karr, Kathleen. Exiled: Memoirs of a Camel, 0 vols. 2006. (ENG.). 242p. (gr. 5-8). pap. 9.99 *(978-0-7614-5291-1(5),* 9780761452911, Amazon Children's Publishing) Amazon Publishing.

London, C. Alexander. Semper Fido. 2013. (Dog Tags Ser.: 1). (ENG.). 224p. (J). (gr. 5-9). pap. 5.99 *(978-0-545-47704-8(2))* Scholastic, Inc.

Mazer, Harry. Heroes Don't Run. 2007. (Aladdin Historical Fiction Ser.). 113p. (gr. 3-7). 16.00 *(978-0-7569-8111-2(5))* Perfection Learning Corp.

Myers, Walter Dean. Invasion. 2015. (ENG.). 224p. (J). (gr. 6). pap. 8.99 *(978-0-545-38429-2(X))* 2013. (YA). *(978-0-545-57659-8(8))* 2013. (ENG.). 224p. (J). (gr. 7). 17.99 *(978-0-545-38428-5(1))* Scholastic, Inc. (Scholastic Pr.).

Romoulous. Katalambano: 187 Warriors Killers. 2007. 15.00 *(978-0-9773064-4-2(5),* Romoulous) MIROGLYPHICS.

—Katalambano: The Strong Survive. 2005. 15.00 *(978-0-9773064-3-5(7))* MIROGLYPHICS.

Sherman, M. Zachary. Blood Brotherhood, 1 vol. Casas, Fritz, illus. 2011. (Bloodlines Ser.). (ENG.). 88p. (gr. 4-8). pap. 6.95 *(978-1-4342-3098-0(8));* 26.65 *(978-1-4342-2559-7(3))* Stone Arch Bks.

—The Heart of War. 2013. (Bloodlines Ser.). (ENG.). 240p. (gr. 4-8). pap. 7.95 *(978-1-62370-002-7(7))* Stone Arch Bks.

—A Time for War, 1 vol. Casas, Fritz, illus. 2011. (Bloodlines Ser.). (ENG.). 88p. (gr. 4-8). pap. 6.95 *(978-1-4342-3097-3(X));* 26.65 *(978-1-4342-2558-0(5))* Stone Arch Bks.

Sherman, M. Zachary & Lee, Raymund. Emergency Ops, 1 vol. Bermudez, Raymund, illus. 2012. (Bloodlines Ser.). (ENG.). 88p. (gr. 4-8). pap. 6.95 *(978-1-4342-3877-1(6));* lib. bdg. 26.65 *(978-1-4342-3766-8(4))* Stone Arch Bks.

Willink, Jocko. Way of the Warrior Kid: From Wimpy to Warrior the Navy SEAL Way. Bozak, Jon, illus. 2017. (Way of the Warrior Kid Ser.: 1). (ENG.). 192p. (J). 13.99 ***(978-1-250-15107-0(4),*** 9781250151070) Feiwel & Friends.

Zima, Marjorie H. Meghan's Military Family. 2008. 23p. pap. 24.95 *(978-1-60563-437-1(9))* America Star Bks.

UNITED STATES—ARMED FORCES—WOMEN

Coleman, Miriam. Women in the Military. 2015. (Women Groundbreakers Ser.). (ENG.). 32p. (J). (gr. 4-5). pap. 10.00 *(978-1-4994-1052-5(2),* PowerKids Pr.) Rosen Publishing Group, Inc., The.

Ferguson, Amanda. American Women of the Vietnam War. (American Women at War Ser.). 112p. 2009. (gr. 8-8). 63.90 *(978-1-61511-395-8(9))* 2004. (Illus.). (YA). (gr. 7-12). lib. bdg. 34.60 *(978-0-8239-4448-4(4))* Rosen Publishing Group, Inc., The.

Women in the U. S. Armed Forces. 2010. (Women in the U. S. Armed Forces Ser.). (ENG.). 32p. (gr. 3-4). lib. bdg. 111.96 *(978-1-4296-5451-7(1),* Snap Bks.) Capstone Press of Coughlan Cos.

Zeinert, Karen & Miller, Mary. The Brave Women of the Gulf Wars: Operation Desert Storm & Operation Iraqi Freedom. 2005. (Women at War Ser.). (ENG., Illus.). 96p. (gr. 7-12). 30.60 *(978-0-7613-2705-9(3),* Millbrook Pr.) Lerner Publishing Group.

UNITED STATES—ARMY

Allen, Thomas B. & Allen, Roger MacBride. Mr. Lincoln's High-Tech War: How the North Used the Telegraph, Railroads, Surveillance Balloons, Ironclads, High-Powered Weapons, & More to Win the Civil War. 2009. (ENG., Illus.). 144p. (J). (gr. 5-18). 18.95 *(978-1-4263-0379-1(3));* lib. bdg. 25.90 *(978-1-4263-0380-7(7))* National Geographic Society. (National Geographic Children's Bks.).

Aller, Susan Bivin. Ulysses S. Grant. 2006. (History Maker Bios Ser.). (Illus.). 48p. (J). (gr. 3-7). lib. bdg. 26.60 *(978-0-8225-2438-0(4),* Lerner Pubns.) Lerner Publishing Group.

Alvarez, Carlos. Army Delta Force. 2009. (Armed Forces Ser.). (ENG., Illus.). 24p. (J). (gr. 3-7). lib. bdg. 25.95 *(978-1-60014-290-1(7))* Bellwether Media.

—Army Night Stalkers. 2009. (Armed Forces Ser.). (ENG., Illus.). 24p. (J). (gr. 3-7). lib. bdg. 25.95 *(978-1-60014-280-2(X))* Bellwether Media.

Anderson, Dale. Soldiers & Sailors in the American Revolution. 2005. (World Almanac Library of the American Revolution Ser.). 48p. (gr. 5-12). pap. 14.05 *(978-0-8368-5938-6(3));* lib. bdg. 31.00 *(978-0-8368-5929-4(4))* Stevens, Gareth Publishing LLLP. (Gareth Stevens Secondary Library).

Anderson, Jane. My Name Is Deborah Samson. 2005. (J). pap. *(978-1-4108-4225-1(8))* Benchmark Education Co.

Archer, Jules. A House Divided: The Lives of Ulysses S. Grant & Robert E. Lee. rev. ed. 2015. (Jules Archer History for Young Readers Ser.). (ENG., Illus.). 176p. (J). (gr. 6). 16.99 *(978-1-63220-604-6(8),* Sky Pony Pr.) Skyhorse Publishing Co., Inc.

Aronson, Billy. Ulysses S. Grant. 2007. (Presidents & Their Times Ser.). (Illus.). 96p. (J). (gr. 3-7). lib. bdg. 34.21 *(978-0-7614-2430-7(X),* Benchmark Bks.) Marshall Cavendish Corp.

Avett, Harper. I See the Bald Eagle. 2016. (Symbols of Our Country Ser.). 00024p. (J). (gr. 1-1). pap. 8.25 *(978-1-4994-2763-9(8),* PowerKids Pr.) Rosen Publishing Group, Inc., The.

Bailey, Diane. General George Thomas: The Rock of Chickamauga. 2011. (J). *(978-1-59556-045-2(9));* pap. *(978-1-59556-051-3(3))* OTTN Publishing.

Baker, Brynn. Buffalo Soldiers: Heroes of the American West. 2015. (Military Heroes Ser.). (ENG., Illus.). 32p. (gr. 3-4). lib.

bdg. 27.32 *(978-1-4914-4838-0(5))* Capstone Press of Coughlan Cos.
—Roosevelt's Rough Riders: Fearless Cavalry of the Spanish-American War. 2015. (Military Heroes Ser.). (ENG., Illus.). 32p. (gr. 3-4). lib. bdg. 27.32 *(978-1-4914-4840-3(7))* Capstone Press of Coughlan Cos.
Barbier, Mary. The U. S. Army. 2004. (America's Armed Forces Ser.). (Illus.). 48p. (gr. 5-12). lib. bdg. 31.00 *(978-0-8368-5680-4(5),* Gareth Stevens Secondary Library) Stevens, Gareth Publishing LLLP.
Barnes, Pete. Richard Bong: World War II Flying Ace. 2009. (Badger Biographies Ser.). (ENG., Illus.). 128p. (J). (gr. 2-7). pap. 12.95 *(978-0-87020-434-0(3))* Wisconsin Historical Society.
Baumann, Susan K. Black Civil War Soldiers: The 54th Massachusetts Regiment. 2013. (Jr. Graphic African American History Ser.). (ENG., Illus.). 24p. (J). (gr. 3-6). pap. 10.60 *(978-1-4777-1457-7(X));* lib. bdg. 25.25 *(978-1-4777-1316-7(6))* Rosen Publishing Group, Inc., The. (PowerKids Pr.).
Beller, Susan Provost. Billy Yank & Johnny Reb: Soldiering in the Civil War. rev. ed. 2007. (Soldiers on the Battlefront Ser.). (ENG., Illus.). 112p. (gr. 6-8). lib. bdg. 33.26 *(978-0-8225-6803-2(9))* Lerner Publishing Group.
Benge, Janet & Benge, Geoff. Heroes of History - Douglas MacArthur: What Greater Honor. 2005. (ENG., Illus.). 205p. (YA). pap. 9.99 *(978-1-932096-15-6(9))* Emerald Bks.
Benson, Michael. The U. S. Army. 2005. (U. S. Armed Forces Ser.). (Illus.). 64p. (J). (gr. 4-7). lib. bdg. 26.60 *(978-0-8225-1645-3(4))* Lerner Publishing Group.
Besel, Jennifer M. The Army Rangers, 1 vol. 2010. (Elite Military Forces Ser.). (ENG.). 24p. (gr. 1-2). lib. bdg. 25.32 *(978-1-4296-5381-7(7),* First Facts) Capstone Press of Coughlan Cos.
—The Delta Force, 1 vol. 2010. (Elite Military Forces Ser.). (ENG.). 24p. (gr. 1-2). lib. bdg. 25.32 *(978-1-4296-5382-4(5),* First Facts) Capstone Press of Coughlan Cos.
—The Green Berets, 1 vol. 2010. (Elite Military Forces Ser.). (ENG.). 24p. (gr. 1-2). lib. bdg. 25.32 *(978-1-4296-5379-4(5),* First Facts) Capstone Press of Coughlan Cos.
Bircher, William. Diary of William Bircher: A Civil War Drummer, 1 vol. 2014. (First-Person Histories Ser.). (ENG.). 32p. (gr. 3-4). lib. bdg. 27.32 *(978-1-4765-4195-2(7),* Fact Finders) Capstone Press of Coughlan Cos.
Black Civil War Soldiers: The 54th Massachusetts Regiment. 2013. (Jr. Graphic African American History Ser.). 24p. (J). (gr. 3-6). pap. 63.60 *(978-1-4777-1458-4(8),* PowerKids Pr.) Rosen Publishing Group, Inc., The.
Bodie, Idella. Light-Horse Harry. 2004. (Illus.). 86p. (J). pap. 6.95 *(978-0-87844-172-3(7))* Sandlapper Publishing Co., Inc.
Boothroyd, Jennifer. Inside the US Air Force. 2017. (Lightning Bolt Books (tm) — US Armed Forces Ser.). (ENG.). (J). (gr. 1-3). 24p. lib. bdg. 25.32 *(978-1-5124-3392-0(6));* pap. 6.99 ***(978-1-5124-5599-1(7))*** Lerner Publishing Group.
Boothroyd, Jennifer. Inside the US Army. 2017. (Lightning Bolt Books (tm) — US Armed Forces Ser.). (ENG.). (J). (gr. 1-3). 24p. 25.32 *(978-1-5124-3391-3(8));* pap. 6.99 ***(978-1-5124-5600-4(4))*** Lerner Publishing Group.
Bozzo, Linda. Army Rangers. 2015. (Serving in the Military Ser.). (Illus.). 32p. (J). 28.50 *(978-1-60753-490-7(8))* Amicus Publishing.
—Delta Force. 2015. (Serving in the Military Ser.). (Illus.). 32p. (J). 28.50 *(978-1-60753-491-4(6))* Amicus Publishing.
—Green Berets. 2015. (Serving in the Military Ser.). (Illus.). 32p. (J). 28.50 *(978-1-60753-492-1(4))* Amicus Publishing.
Braun, Eric. Trapped Behind Enemy Lines: The Story of the U. S. Army Air Force 807th Medical Evacuation Squadron. 2016. (Encounter: Narrative Nonfiction Stories Ser.). (ENG.). 224p. (gr. 4-6). 14.95 *(978-1-62370-605-0(X));* (Illus.). lib. bdg. 32.65 *(978-1-4914-8042-7(4),* 1400082) Encounter Bks.
Brook, Henry. Special Forces. Frith, Alex, ed. Johnson, Staz, illus. 2014. (ENG.). 80p. (J). pap. 8.99 *(978-0-7945-3337-3(X),* Usborne) EDC Publishing.
Burgan, Michael. Benedict Arnold: American Hero & Traitor, 1 vol. Beatty, Terry, illus. 2007. (Graphic Biographies Ser.). (ENG.). 32p. (gr. 3-4). per. 8.10 *(978-0-7368-7906-4(4),* Graphic Library) Capstone Press of Coughlan Cos.
—Weapons, Gear, & Uniforms of the American Revolution, 1 vol. 2012. (Equipped for Battle Ser.). (ENG.). 32p. (gr. 3-4). lib. bdg. 27.99 *(978-1-4296-7647-2(7),* Edge Bks.) Capstone Press of Coughlan Cos.
Burgan, Michael, et al. The U. S. Armed Forces. 2013. (U. S. Armed Forces Ser.). (ENG.). 48p. (gr. 5-6). lib. bdg. 146.60 *(978-0-7565-4622-9(2),* CPB Grades 4-8) Compass Point Bks.
Burnett, Betty. Delta Force: Counterterrorism Unit of the U. S. Army. 2009. (Inside Special Operations Ser.). 64p. (gr. 6-6). 58.50 *(978-1-61513-554-7(5),* Rosen Reference) Rosen Publishing Group, Inc., The.
Burns, Heidi A., contrib. by. U. S. Army True Stories: Tales of Bravery. 2014. (Courage under Fire Ser.). (ENG.). 32p. (gr. 3-4). lib. bdg. 27.99 *(978-1-4765-9938-0(6))* Capstone Press of Coughlan Cos.
Caper, William. The U. S. Army Rangers: The Missions, 1 vol. 2012. (American Special Ops Ser.). (ENG., Illus.). 48p. (gr. 3-4). lib. bdg. 31.99 *(978-1-4296-8659-4(6))* Capstone Press of Coughlan Cos.
Catel, Patrick. Soldiers of the Revolutionary War, 1 vol. (Why We Fought: the Revolutionary War Ser.). (ENG.). 48p. (gr. 3-6). 2011. pap. 9.95 *(978-1-4329-3903-8(3))* 2010. 33.32 *(978-1-4329-3898-7(3))* Heinemann-Raintree. (Heinemann InfoSearch).
Chorlian, Meg & Hale, Sarah Elder, eds. Ulysses S. Grant: Confident Leader & Hero. 2005. (ENG., Illus.). 48p. (J). (gr. 3-9). 17.95 *(978-0-8126-7906-9(7))* Cobblestone Publishing Co.
Collins, Kathleen. El Marques de Lafayette: Heroe Frances de la Guerra de Independencia. 2004. (Grandes personajes en la historia de los Estados Unidos Ser.). (SPA.). 32p. (gr. 3-6). pap. 10.00 *(978-0-8239-4233-6(3),* Rosen Classroom) Rosen Publishing Group, Inc., The.
—Marquis de Lafayette: French Hero of the American Revolution. 2009. (Primary Sources of Famous People in American History Ser.). 32p. (gr. 2-3). 47.90 *(978-1-60851-703-9(9))* Rosen Publishing Group, Inc., The.
—Marquis de Lafayette / el Marques de Lafayette: French Hero of the American Revolution / Héroe francés de la Revolución Estadounidense. 2009. (Famous People in American History/Grandes personajes en la historia de los Estados Unidos Ser.). (ENG & SPA.). 32p. (gr. 2-3). 47.90 *(978-1-61512-550-0(7),* Editorial Buenas Letras) Rosen Publishing Group, Inc., The.
Conklin, Wendy. Civil War Leaders, 1 vol. 2005. (Primary Source Readers Ser.). (ENG.). 24p. (J). (gr. 5-5). pap. 8.99 *(978-0-7439-8917-6(1))* Shell Educational Publishing.
Cooke, Tim. US Airborne Forces. 2012. (Ultimate Special Forces Ser.). (ENG., Illus.). 48p. (J). (gr. 4-8). 27.95 *(978-1-4488-7882-6(9));* pap. 11.75 *(978-1-4488-7959-5(0))* Rosen Publishing Group, Inc., The. (PowerKids Pr.).
—US Army Rangers. 2012. (Ultimate Special Forces Ser.). (ENG., Illus.). 48p. (J). (gr. 4-8). 27.95 *(978-1-4488-7879-6(9));* pap. 11.75 *(978-1-4488-7956-4(6))* Rosen Publishing Group, Inc., The. (PowerKids Pr.).
—US Army Special Forces. 2012. (Ultimate Special Forces Ser.). (ENG., Illus.). 48p. (J). (gr. 4-8). 27.95 *(978-1-4488-7878-9(0));* pap. 11.75 *(978-1-4488-7955-7(8))* Rosen Publishing Group, Inc., The. (PowerKids Pr.).
—Weapons & Tactics. 2012. (American Civil War: the Right Answer Ser.). (Illus.). 48p. (J). (gr. 6-8). 31.95 *(978-1-4339-7551-6(3));* pap. 14.05 *(978-1-4339-7552-3(1))* Stevens, Gareth Publishing LLLP. (Gareth Stevens Secondary Library).
Corrigan, Jim. General George G. Meade: Victor at Gettysburg. 2011. (J). *(978-1-59556-044-5(0));* pap. *(978-1-59556-050-6(5))* OTTN Publishing.
Cox, Clinton. Undying Glory: The Story of the Massachusetts 54th Regiment. 2007. 196p. (YA). (gr. 4-7). per. 15.95 *(978-0-595-45116-6(0),* Backinprint.com) iUniverse, Inc.
Daniel Fernandez Memorial Center Projec. Man of Honor: The Story of Daniel Fernandez. 2009. 32p. pap. 15.49 *(978-1-4389-8338-7(7))* AuthorHouse.
Darby, Jean. Dwight D. Eisenhower. 2004. (Presidential Leaders Ser.). (Illus.). 112p. (J). (gr. 6-12). lib. bdg. 29.27 *(978-0-8225-0813-7(3))* Lerner Publishing Group.
David, Jack. Army Green Berets. 2009. (Armed Forces Ser.). (ENG., Illus.). 24p. (YA). (gr. 3-7). lib. bdg. 25.95 *(978-1-60014-263-5(X))* Bellwether Media.
—United States Army. 2008. (Armed Forces Ser.). (ENG., Illus.). 24p. (J). (gr. 3-7). lib. bdg. 25.95 *(978-1-60014-162-1(5))* Bellwether Media.
Davis, Graeme. The Weapons & Gear of the Revolutionary War. 2012. (Story of the American Revolution Ser.). (ENG.). 32p. (gr. 3-4). pap. 47.70 *(978-1-4296-9289-2(8),* Fact Finders) Capstone Press of Coughlan Cos.
Dell, Pamela. Memoir of Susie King Taylor: A Civil War Nurse. 2017. (First-Person Histories Ser.). (ENG., Illus.). 32p. (gr. 3-4). lib. bdg. 27.32 *(978-1-5157-3354-6(8),* Fact Finders) Capstone Press of Coughlan Cos.
Delmar, Pete. U. S. Army Green Berets: The Missions. 2013. (American Special Ops Ser.). (ENG.). 48p. (gr. 3-4). 31.99 *(978-1-4765-0113-0(0))* Capstone Press of Coughlan Cos.
Delmar, Pete & Grayson, Robert. American Special Ops. 2011. (American Special Ops Ser.). (ENG.). 48p. (gr. 3-4). lib. bdg. 191.94 *(978-1-62065-971-7(9))* Capstone Press of Coughlan Cos.
Doeden, Matt. The U. S. Army [Scholastic]. 2009. (Military Branches Ser.). (ENG.). 24p. pap. 0.52 *(978-1-4296-5070-0(2),* Pebble Plus) Capstone Press of Coughlan Cos.
—The U.S. Army. 2017. (U. S. Military Branches Ser.). (ENG.). 24p. (gr. k-1). lib. bdg. 26.65 ***(978-1-5157-6773-2(6))*** Capstone Press of Coughlan Cos.
—Weapons of the Revolutionary War. 2017. (Weapons of War Ser.). (ENG.). 32p. (gr. 2-3). lib. bdg. 26.65 ***(978-1-5157-7908-7(4))*** Capstone Press of Coughlan Cos.
Dolan, Edward F. Military Service, 5 vols., Set. Incl. Careers in the U. S. Air Force. (YA). (gr. 7-9). 35.64 *(978-0-7614-4205-9(7));* Careers in the U. S. Army. (YA). (gr. 7-9). 35.64 *(978-0-7614-4206-6(5));* Careers in the U. S. Coast Guard. (gr. 7-9). 35.64 *(978-0-7614-4207-3(3));* Careers in the U. S. Marine Corps. (YA). (gr. 8-18). 35.64 *(978-0-7614-4209-7(X));* Careers in the U. S. Navy. (gr. 7-18). 35.64 *(978-0-7614-4210-3(3));* 80p. 2009. 2010. Set lib. bdg. 178.21 o.p. *(978-0-7614-4203-5(0))* Marshall Cavendish Corp.
Dreyer, Ellen. A Band of Brave Men: The Story of the 54th Massachusetts Regiment. 2004. (ENG., Illus.). 31p. (J). (gr. 5-5). pap. 11.47 net. *(978-0-7652-5247-0(3),* Celebration Pr.) Pearson Schl.
Dugan, Christine. Marquis de Lafayette & the French (Alexander Hamilton) 2017. (Primary Source Readers Focus On Ser.). (Illus.). 32p. (J). (gr. 4-8). pap. 8.99 ***(978-1-4258-6353-1(1))*** Teacher Created Materials, Inc.
Dunn, Joeming & Espinosa De Santayana, Rodrigo De. Ulysses S. Grant: 18th U. S. President, 1 vol. 2011. (Presidents of the United States Bio-Graphics Ser.). (ENG., Illus.). 32p. (YA). (gr. 3-6). 28.50 *(978-1-61641-646-1(7))* Magic Wagon.
Earl, C. F. Green Berets. 2010. (Special Forces Ser.). 64p. (YA). (gr. 7-18). lib. bdg. 22.95 *(978-1-4222-1841-9(4))* Mason Crest.
Earl, Sari. George Washington: Revolutionary Leader & Founding Father, 1 vol. 2010. (Military Heroes Ser.). (ENG.). 112p. (J). (gr. 6-12). lib. bdg. 35.64 *(978-1-60453-967-7(4))* ABDO Publishing Co.
Edwards, Roberta. Who Was George Washington? Kelley, True & Harrison, Nancy, illus. 2009. (Who Was? Ser.). (ENG.). 112p. (J). (gr. 3-7). pap. 5.99 *(978-0-448-44892-3(0),* Grosset & Dunlap) Penguin Young Readers Group.
—Who Was George Washington? 2009. (Who Was... ? Ser.). lib. bdg. 16.00 *(978-0-606-04042-6(0),* Turtleback) Turtleback Bks.
Fein, Eric. Weapons, Gear, & Uniforms of the Civil War, 1 vol. 2012. (Equipped for Battle Ser.). (ENG.). 32p. (gr. 3-4). lib. bdg. 27.99 *(978-1-4296-7648-9(5),* Edge Bks.) Capstone Press of Coughlan Cos.
Feinstein, Stephen. Colin Powell. 2007. (African-American Heroes Ser.). (Illus.). 24p. (J). (gr. 1-3). lib. bdg. 22.60 *(978-0-7660-2761-9(9),* Enslow Elementary) Enslow Pubs., Inc.
Fleischman, John. Black & White Airmen: Their True History. 2007. (ENG., Illus.). 160p. (J). (gr. 5-7). 20.00 *(978-0-618-56297-8(4))* Houghton Mifflin Harcourt Publishing Co.
Garnett, Sammie & Pallotta, Jerry. U. S. Army Alphabet Book. 2012. (ENG., Illus.). (J). pap. 7.95 *(978-0-9852032-2-1(6))* Bald Eagle Bks.
Garstecki, Julia. Buffalo Soldiers. 2017. (All-American Fighting Forces Ser.). (ENG., Illus.). 32p. (J). (gr. 3-7). 31.35 ***(978-1-68072-000-6(7))*** Black Rabbit Bks.
Gimpel, Lee. Fighting Wars, Planning for Peace: The Story of George C. Marshall. 2005. (World Leaders Ser.). (Illus.). 176p. (J). (gr. 6-12). lib. bdg. 26.95 *(978-1-931798-66-2(4))* Reynolds, Morgan Inc.
Gitlin, Martin. George S. Patton: World War II General & Military Innovator, 1 vol. 2010. (Military Heroes Ser.). (ENG.). 112p. (J). (gr. 6-12). lib. bdg. 35.64 *(978-1-60453-964-6(X))* ABDO Publishing Co.
—Green Berets, 1 vol. 2013. (Great Warriors Ser.). 48p. (ENG.). (J). (gr. 3-6). lib. bdg. 32.79 *(978-1-61783-723-4(7));* (Illus.). pap. 32.79 *(978-1-61783-779-3(3))* ABDO Publishing Co.
Glaser, Jason. The Buffalo Soldiers & the American West. Smith, Tod G. et al, illus. 2005. (Graphic History Ser.). (ENG.). 32p. (gr. 3-4). 30.65 *(978-0-7368-4966-1(1),* Graphic Library) Capstone Press of Coughlan Cos.
Gordon, Nick. Army Delta Force. 2012. (U. S. Military Ser.). (ENG., Illus.). 24p. (J). (gr. 3-7). lib. bdg. 25.95 *(978-1-60014-822-4(0),* Epic Bks.) Bellwether Media.
—Army Green Berets. 2012. (U. S. Military Ser.). (ENG., Illus.). 24p. (J). (gr. 3-7). lib. bdg. 25.95 *(978-1-60014-823-1(9),* Epic Bks.) Bellwether Media.
—Army Night Stalkers. 2013. (U. S. Military Ser.). (ENG., Illus.). 24p. (J). (gr. 3-7). lib. bdg. 25.95 *(978-1-60014-874-3(3),* Epic Bks.) Bellwether Media.
—Army Rangers. 2012. (U. S. Military Ser.). (ENG., Illus.). 24p. (J). (gr. 3-7). lib. bdg. 25.95 *(978-1-60014-824-8(7),* Epic Bks.) Bellwether Media.
—U. S. Army. 2012. (U. S. Military Ser.). (ENG., Illus.). 24p. (J). (gr. 3-7). lib. bdg. 25.95 *(978-1-60014-827-9(1),* Epic Bks.) Bellwether Media.
Grayson, Robert & Delmar, Pete. American Special Ops. 2013. (American Special Ops Ser.). (ENG.). 48p. (gr. 3-4). lib. bdg. 63.98 *(978-1-62065-966-3(2))* Capstone Press of Coughlan Cos.
Green, Michael. The United States Army, 1 vol. 2013. (U. S. Military Forces Ser.). (ENG.). 24p. (gr. 1-2). lib. bdg. 25.32 *(978-1-4765-0069-0(X))* Capstone Press of Coughlan Cos.
Greene, Meg. Careers in the National Guards' Search & Rescue Units. (Careers in Search & Rescue Operations Ser.). 64p. (gr. 5-8). 2009. 58.50 *(978-1-61511-812-0(8),* Rosen Reference) 2005. (Illus.). (YA). lib. bdg. 31.95 *(978-0-8239-3836-0(0))* Rosen Publishing Group, Inc., The.
—The Hunt for Osama Bin Laden. 2004. (Frontline Coverage of Current Events Ser.). (Illus.). 48p. (J). lib. bdg. 29.25 *(978-1-4042-0279-5(X))* Rosen Publishing Group, Inc., The.
—The Hunt for Osama bin Laden. 2009. (Frontline Coverage of Current Events Ser.). 48p. (gr. 5-5). 53.00 *(978-1-61512-657-6(0))* Rosen Publishing Group, Inc., The.
Griffin, Margaret. Today's U. S. Army, 1 vol. 2013. (U. S. Armed Forces Ser.). (ENG.). 48p. (gr. 5-6). lib. bdg. 29.32 *(978-0-7565-4618-2(4))* Compass Point Bks.
Grove, Tim. First Flight Around the World: The Adventures of the American Fliers Who Won the Race. 2015. (ENG., Illus.). 96p. (J). (gr. 5-9). 21.95 *(978-1-4197-1482-5(1))* Abrams, Inc.
Gunderson, Jessica. Benedict Arnold: Battlefield Hero or Selfish Traitor?, 1 vol. 2013. (Perspectives on History Ser.). (ENG.). 32p. (gr. 3-4). 27.32 *(978-1-4765-0243-4(9));* pap. 7.95 *(978-1-4765-3407-7(1))* Capstone Press of Coughlan Cos. (Fact Finders).
Hamilton, John. The Army, 1 vol. 2007. (Defending the Nation Ser.). (ENG., Illus.). 32p. (gr. -1-5). 27.07 *(978-1-59679-754-3(1),* Checkerboard Library) ABDO Publishing Co.
—Green Berets. 2011. (Armed Forces Ser.). (Illus.). 32p. (YA). (gr. 3-6). 27.07 *(978-1-61783-066-2(6))* ABDO Publishing Co.
—United States Army. 2011. (Armed Forces Ser.). (Illus.). 32p. (YA). (gr. 3-6). 27.07 *(978-1-61783-069-3(0))* ABDO Publishing Co.
—Weapons of the American Revolution. 2013. (American Revolution Ser.). 32p. (J). (gr. 5-9). lib. bdg. 27.07 *(978-1-61783-683-1(4),* Abdo & Daughters) ABDO Publishing Co.
Harasymiw, Mark. Army. 2011. (Us Military Forces Ser.). 32p. (gr. 3-6). pap. 10.50 *(978-1-4339-5848-9(1),* Gareth Stevens Learning Library); (YA). lib. bdg. 26.60 *(978-1-4339-5846-5(5))* Stevens, Gareth Publishing LLLP.
—Rangers. 2012. (US Special Forces Ser.). (ENG., Illus.). 32p. (J). (gr. 3-6). pap. 10.50 *(978-1-4339-6575-3(5));* lib. bdg. 26.60 *(978-1-4339-6573-9(9))* Stevens, Gareth Publishing LLLP. (Gareth Stevens Learning Library).
Henningfeld, Diane Andrews. Should Women Be Allowed to Serve in Combat in the U. S. Armed Forces? 2007. (At Issue Ser.). (ENG., Illus.). 116p. (gr. 10-12). 24.45 *(978-0-7377-3939-8(8),* Greenhaven Pr., Inc.) Cengage Gale.
Honders, Christine. Buffalo Soldiers. 2015. (Heroes of Black History Ser.). (ENG., Illus.). 32p. (J). (gr. 3-4). pap. 10.50 *(978-1-4824-2900-8(4))* Stevens, Gareth Publishing LLLP.
Hoogenboom, Lynn. William Tecumseh Sherman: The Fight to Preserve the Union. 2009. (Library of American Lives & Times Ser.). 112p. (gr. 5-5). 69.20 *(978-1-60853-511-8(8))* Rosen Publishing Group, Inc., The.
Howse, Jennifer. The Civil War. 2008. (African American History Ser.). (Illus.). 48p. (YA). (gr. 5-8). pap. 10.95 *(978-1-59036-877-0(0));* lib. bdg. 29.05 *(978-1-59036-876-3(2))* Weigl Pubs., Inc.
—Civil War. 2013. (J). *(978-1-62127-191-8(9));* pap. *(978-1-62127-197-0(8))* Weigl Pubs., Inc.
Kajencki, AnnMarie Francis. Count Casimir Pulaski: From Poland to America, a Hero's Fight for Liberty. 2009. (Library of American Lives & Times Ser.). 112p. (gr. 5-5). 69.20 *(978-1-60853-475-3(8))* Rosen Publishing Group, Inc., The.
Knapp, Ron. Fighting U. S. Generals of World War II. 2013. (Inspiring Collective Biographies Ser.). 112p. (J). (gr. 5-12). pap. 10.95 *(978-1-4644-0249-4(3));* 33.27 *(978-0-7660-4164-6(6))* Enslow Pubs., Inc.
Koestler-Grack, Rachel A. William Tecumseh Sherman. 2009. (Leaders of the Civil War Era Ser.). (Illus.). 149p. (gr. 6-12). 35.00 *(978-1-60413-300-4(7),* Chelsea Hse.) Facts On File, Inc.
Kohl, Peter. My Dad Is in the Army, 01 vols., 1. 2016. (Military Families Ser.). (ENG., Illus.). 24p. (J). pap. 8.25 *(978-1-5081-4434-2(6),* PowerKids Pr.) Rosen Publishing Group, Inc., The.
Kupperberg, Paul. The Alaska Highway. 2009. (Building America Ser.). (Illus.). 144p. (gr. 5-8). 35.00 *(978-1-60413-074-4(1),* Chelsea Hse.) Facts On File, Inc.
Levete, Sarah. The Army. 2016. (Defend & Protect Ser.). (ENG.). 48p. (J). (gr. 4-5). pap. 14.05 *(978-1-4824-4119-2(5))* Stevens, Gareth Publishing LLLP.
Lewis, J. Patrick. Harlem Hellfighters. Kelley, Gary, illus. 2014. (ENG.). 32p. (J). (gr. 4-7). 19.99 *(978-1-56846-246-2(8),* Creative Editions) Creative Co., The.
Linde, Barbara M. Heroes of the US Army. 2012. (Heroes of the US Military Ser.). (Illus.). 32p. (J). (gr. 3-6). pap. 10.50 *(978-1-4339-7237-9(9));* lib. bdg. 26.60 *(978-1-4339-7236-2(0))* Stevens, Gareth Publishing LLLP.
Link, Theodore. George Armstrong Custer: General de la caballeria Estadounidense. 2004. (Grandes personajes en la historia de los Estados Unidos Ser.). (SPA.). 32p. (gr. 3-6). pap. 10.00 *(978-0-8239-4228-2(7),* Rosen Classroom) Rosen Publishing Group, Inc., The.
—George Armstrong Custer: General de la caballería estadounidense (George Armstrong Custer: General of the U. S. Cavalry) 2009. (Grandes personajes en la historia de los Estados Unidos (Famous People in American History) Ser.). (SPA.). 32p. (gr. 2-3). 47.90 *(978-1-61512-799-3(2),* Editorial Buenas Letras) Rosen Publishing Group, Inc., The.
—George Armstrong Custer: General of the U. S. Cavalry. 2009. (Primary Sources of Famous People in American History Ser.).Tr. of George Armstrong Custer: General de la Caballeria Estadounidense. 32p. (gr. 2-3). 47.90 *(978-1-60851-680-3(6))* Rosen Publishing Group, Inc., The.
—George Armstrong Custer: General of the U. S. Cavalry / General de la caballería Estadounidense. 2009. (Famous People in American History/Grandes personajes en la historia de los Estados Unidos Ser.). (ENG & SPA.). 32p. (gr. 2-3). 47.90 *(978-1-61512-545-6(0),* Editorial Buenas Letras) Rosen Publishing Group, Inc., The.
Llanas, Sheila Griffin. Women of the U. S. Army: Pushing Limits, 1 vol. 2010. (Women in the U. S. Armed Forces Ser.). (ENG.). 32p. (gr. 3-4). lib. bdg. 27.99 *(978-1-4296-5447-0(3),* Snap Bks.) Capstone Press of Coughlan Cos.
Loveless, Antony. Apache Helicoper Pilot. 2009. (World's Most Dangerous Jobs Ser.). (ENG., Illus.). 32p. (J). (gr. 3-6). pap. *(978-0-7787-5112-0(0))* Crabtree Publishing Co.
—Apache Helicoper Pilots. 2009. (World's Most Dangerous Jobs Ser.). (ENG., Illus.). 32p. (J). (gr. 3-6). lib. bdg. *(978-0-7787-5098-7(1))* Crabtree Publishing Co.
Lowe, Julian. My Aunt Is in the Army Reserve, 01 vols., 1. 2016. (Military Families Ser.). (ENG., Illus.). 24p. (J). pap. 8.25 *(978-1-5081-4426-7(5),* PowerKids Pr.) Rosen Publishing Group, Inc., The.
Lusted, Marcia Amidon. Army Delta Force: Elite Operations. 2013. (Military Special Ops Ser.). (ENG., Illus.). 32p. (gr. 3-8). lib. bdg. 26.60 *(978-0-7613-9077-0(4),* Lerner Pubns.) Lerner Publishing Group.
—Army Rangers: Elite Operations. 2013. (Military Special Ops Ser.). (ENG., Illus.). 32p. (gr. 3-8). lib. bdg. 26.60 *(978-0-7613-9078-7(2),* Lerner Pubns.) Lerner Publishing Group.
Margulies, Phillip. A Timeline of the Continental Army. 2009. (Timelines of American History Ser.). 32p. (gr. 4-4). 47.90 *(978-1-60854-383-0(8),* Rosen Reference) Rosen Publishing Group, Inc., The.
Markovics, Joyce L. & Pushies, Fred J. Today's Army Heroes. 2012. (Acts of Courage: Inside America's Military Ser.). 32p. (J). (gr. 2-7). lib. bdg. 25.27 *(978-1-61772-445-9(9))* Bearport Publishing Co., Inc.
Marx, Mandy R. Amazing U. S. Army Facts. 2016. (Amazing Military Facts Ser.). (ENG., Illus.). 24p. (gr. k-1). lib. bdg. 26.65 *(978-1-5157-0953-4(1),* Pebble Plus) Capstone Press of Coughlan Cos.
McCarthy, Pat. Famous Union Generals & Leaders of the North: A MyReportLinks. com Book. 2004. (American Civil War Ser.). (Illus.). 48p. (J). lib. bdg. 26.60 *(978-0-7660-5188-1(9),* MyReportLinks.com Bks.) Enslow Pubs., Inc.
McNab, Chris. Defending the Ground: The Army. 2017. (J). ***(978-1-4222-3762-5(1))*** Mason Crest.
McNab, Chris. Protecting the Nation with the U. S. Army. 2004. (Rescue & Prevention Ser.). (Illus.). 96p. (YA). (gr. 7-18). lib. bdg. 22.95 *(978-1-59084-414-4(9))* Mason Crest.
McPherson, Stephanie Sammartino. Douglas MacArthur. 2005. (History Maker Bios Ser.). (Illus.). 48p. (J). 26.60 *(978-0-8225-2434-2(1))* Lerner Publishing Group.
Micklos, John, Jr. Harlem Hellfighters: African-American Heroes of World War I. 2017. (Military Heroes Ser.). (ENG., Illus.). 32p. (gr. 3-4). lib. bdg. 27.32 *(978-1-5157-3348-5(3))* Capstone Press of Coughlan Cos.
Micklos, John. Washington's Crossing the Delaware & the Winter at Valley Forge: Through Primary Sources. 2013. (American Revolution Through Primary Sources Ser.). 48p. (J). (gr. 4-18). 25.27 *(978-0-7660-4132-5(8))* Enslow Pubs., Inc.
—Why We Won the American Revolution — Through Primary Sources. 2013. (American Revolution Through Primary Sources Ser.). 48p. (J). (gr. 4-18). 25.27 *(978-0-7660-4134-9(4))* Enslow Pubs., Inc.
Miller, Derek L. Minority Soldiers Fighting in the Korean War. 2017. (J). ***(978-1-5026-2665-3(9))*** Cavendish Square Publishing.
Miller, Reagan & Arthur, Martin. Great Leaders of the Civil War. 2011. (ENG.). 48p. (J). pap. *(978-0-7787-5359-9(X));* lib. bdg. *(978-0-7787-5342-1(5))* Crabtree Publishing Co.
Miller, Reagan & Claus, J. Matteson. Life on a Civil War Battlefield. 2011. (ENG.). 48p. (J). pap. *(978-0-7787-5357-5(3));* lib. bdg. *(978-0-7787-5340-7(9))* Crabtree Publishing Co.
Miller, Roger G. Billy Mitchell: Evangelist of Airpower. 2007. (Illus.). 152p. (J). (gr. 10-18). lib. bdg. 25.95 *(978-1-59556-025-4(4))* OTTN Publishing.

TUV

Mitchell, P. P. Join the Army. 2017. (U. S. Armed Forces Ser.). 32p. (gr. 1-2). 26.60 ***(978-1-5382-0536-5(X))*** Stevens, Gareth Publishing LLLP.

Murphy, Jim. The Crossing: How George Washington Saved the American Revolution. 2016. (ENG.). 96p. (J). (gr. 4-7). pap. 14.99 *(978-0-439-69187-1(7))* Scholastic, Inc.

Murray, Julie. United States Army, 1 vol. 2014. (U. S. Armed Forces Ser.). (ENG.). 24p. (J). (gr. 4-8). lib. bdg. 28.50 *(978-1-62970-094-6(0))* ABDO Publishing Co.

Murray, Stuart A. P. John Trumbull: Painter of the Revolutionary War. 2008. (ENG., Illus.). 83p. (C). (gr. 6-18). lib. bdg. 158.00 *(978-0-7656-8150-8(1)*, Y182501) Routledge.

Myers, Walter Dean & Miles, Bill. The Harlem Hellfighters: When Pride Met Courage. 2014. (ENG.). 160p. (J). (gr. 3-7). pap. 9.99 *(978-0-06-001138-3(6)*, Amistad) HarperCollins Pubs.

Myers, Walter Dean & William Miles. The Harlem Hellfighters: When Pride Met Courage. 2014. (J). lib. bdg. 20.85 *(978-0-606-35507-0(3))* Turtleback Bks.

Nagle, Jeanne. Delta Force. 2012. (US Special Forces Ser.). (ENG.). 32p. (J). (gr. 3-6). pap. 10.50 *(978-1-4339-6555-5(0))*; lib. bdg. 26.60 *(978-1-4339-6553-1(4))* Stevens, Gareth Publishing LLLP. (Gareth Stevens Learning Library).

Nardo, Don. The Civil War. 2009. (American History Ser.). pap. 24.10 *(978-1-4205-0302-9(2)*, Lucent Bks.) Cengage Gale.

Nelson, Drew. Green Berets. 2012. (US Special Forces Ser.). (ENG.). 32p. (J). (gr. 3-6). pap. 10.50 *(978-1-4339-6559-3(3))*; lib. bdg. 26.60 *(978-1-4339-6557-9(7))* Stevens, Gareth Publishing LLLP. (Gareth Stevens Learning Library).

Newman, Patricia. Army Special Forces: Elite Operations. 2013. (Military Special Ops Ser.). (ENG., Illus.). 32p. (gr. 3-8). lib. bdg. 26.60 *(978-0-7613-9076-3(6)*, Lerner Pubns.) Lerner Publishing Group.

Nobleman, Marc Tyler. Green Berets in Action. 2008. (Special Ops Ser.). (Illus.). 32p. (J). (gr. 3-6). lib. bdg. 25.27 *(978-1-59716-631-7(6))* Bearport Publishing Co., Inc.

Norfolk, Sherry & Norfolk, Bobby. The Virginia Giant: The True Story of Peter Francisco. Brennan, Cait, illus. 2014. (ENG.). 160p. (J). (gr. 4-7). 16.99 *(978-1-62619-117-4(4)*, History Pr., The) Arcadia Publishing.

Olesen, Andrew. George Washington: The First President of the United States. 2015. (Spotlight on American History Ser.). (ENG., Illus.). 24p. (J). (gr. 4-6). pap. 10.00 *(978-1-4994-1751-7(9)*, PowerKids Pr.) Rosen Publishing Group, Inc., The.

Ollhoff, Jim. The Civil War: Weapons, 1 vol. 2012. (Civil War Ser.). (ENG.). 32p. (J). (gr. 5-9). 27.07 *(978-1-61783-278-9(2))* ABDO Publishing Co.

Orr, Tamra. What's So Great about the Buffalo Soldiers. 2009. (What's So Great About... ? Ser.). 32p. (J). (gr. 2-4). lib. bdg. 25.70 *(978-1-58415-831-8(X))* Mitchell Lane Pubs., Inc.

—What's So Great about the Tuskegee Airmen. 2009. (What's So Great About... ? Ser.). 32p. (J). (gr. 2-4). lib. bdg. 25.70 *(978-1-58415-832-5(8))* Mitchell Lane Pubs., Inc.

Otfinoski, Steven. Pilots in Peril! The Untold Story of U. S. Pilots Who Braved the Hump in World War II. (Encounter: Narrative Nonfiction Stories Ser.). (ENG.). 232p. (gr. 3-4). 2016. pap. 9.95 *(978-1-4914-5166-3(1))* 2015. 16.95 *(978-1-62370-318-9(2))* Encounter Bks.

—Pilots in Peril! The Untold Story of U.S. Pilots Who Braved "The Hump" in World War II. 2015. (Encounter: Narrative Nonfiction Stories Ser.). (ENG., Illus.). 232p. (gr. 3-4). lib. bdg. 33.99 *(978-1-4914-5156-4(4))* Encounter Bks.

Pallotta, Jerry & Garnett, Sammie. U. S. Army Alphabet Book. 2012. (ENG., Illus.). 32p. (J). 16.95 *(978-0-9852032-3-8(4))* Bald Eagle Bks.

Person, Stephen. Army Night Stalkers in Action. 2013. (Special Ops II Ser.). 32p. (J). (gr. 2-7). lib. bdg. 26.60 *(978-1-61772-889-1(6))* Bearport Publishing Co., Inc.

Poolos, J. Army Rangers: Surveillance & Reconnaissance for the U. S. Army. (Inside Special Operations Ser.). 64p. 2009. (gr. 6-6). 58.50 *(978-1-61513-549-3(9))* 2003. (Illus.). (YA). (gr. 5-8). lib. bdg. 31.95 *(978-0-8239-3805-6(0))* Rosen Publishing Group, Inc., The. (Rosen Reference).

Porterfield, Jason. Your Career in the Army. 2011. (Call of Duty: Careers in the Armed Forces Ser.). (ENG.). 128p. (YA). (gr. 9-12). lib. bdg. 34.60 *(978-1-4488-5510-0(1))* Rosen Publishing Group, Inc., The.

Powell, Walter L. Benedict Arnold: Revolutionary War Hero & Traitor. (Library of American Lives & Timestm Ser.). 112p. (Illus.). (J). (gr. 4-8). lib. bdg. 31.95 *(978-1-4042-6627-8(5))*; 2009. (gr. 5-5). 69.20 *(978-1-60853-471-5(5))* Rosen Publishing Group, Inc., The.

Pratt, Mary K. US Army, 1 vol. 2014. (Essential Library of the US Military Ser.). (ENG.). 112p. (J). (gr. 6-12). lib. bdg. 35.64 *(978-1-62403-433-6(0)*, Essential Library) ABDO Publishing Co.

Press, Applesauce & Entin, Cindy. My First Counting Book - Army. 2013. (ENG.). 10p. (J). bds. 5.99 *(978-1-60433-321-3(9)*, Applesauce Pr.) Cider Mill Pr. Bk. Pubs., LLC.

Raabe, Emily. Buffalo Soldiers & the Western Frontier. (Westward Ho! Ser.). 24p. 2009. (gr. 2-3). 42.50 *(978-1-60854-759-3(0))* 2003. (Illus.). (J). lib. bdg. 22.60 *(978-0-8239-6495-6(7))* Rosen Publishing Group, Inc., The. (PowerKids Pr.).

Randolph, Joanne. The Call of Liberty: Marquis de Lafayette & the American Revolution. 2009. (Great Moments in American History Ser.). 32p. (gr. 3-3). 47.90 *(978-1-61513-152-5(3))* Rosen Publishing Group, Inc., The.

Ratliff, Thamas. Do You Want to Be a Revolutionary War Soldier? 2015. (Do You Want to Be... Ser.). (Illus.). 32p. (gr. 3-6). 28.50 *(978-1-909645-37-0(0))* Book Hse. GBR. Dist: Black Rabbit Bks.

Ratliff, Thomas. You Wouldn't Want to Be a Civil War Soldier! A War You'd Rather Not Fight. Antram, David, illus. 2013. (You Wouldn't Want to... Ser.). (ENG.). (J). 32p. 29.00 *(978-0-531-25947-4(1))*; 40p. pap. 9.95 *(978-0-531-24503-3(9))* Scholastic Library Publishing. (Watts, Franklin).

Rice, Earle. Careers in the US Army. 2015. (Careers in the US Armed Forces Ser.). (ENG., Illus.). 128p. (J). (gr. 6-7). 37.27 *(978-0-7660-6943-5(5))* Enslow Pubs., Inc.

—The Life & Times of the Brothers Custer: Galloping to Glory. 2008. (Profiles in American History Ser.). (Illus.). 48p. (J). (gr. 4-8). lib. bdg. 29.95 *(978-1-58415-665-9(1))* Mitchell Lane Pubs., Inc.

Rice, Earle, Jr. Robert E. Lee: First Soldier of the Confederacy. 2005. (Civil War Leaders Ser.). (Illus.). 176p. (gr. 6-12). 28.95 *(978-1-931798-47-1(8))* Reynolds, Morgan Inc.

Rice, Earle & Rice, Earle, Jr. The U. S. Army & Military Careers. 2006. (U.S. Armed Forces & Military Careers Ser.). (Illus.). 128p. (J). (gr. 5-9). lib. bdg. 33.27 *(978-0-7660-2699-5(X))* Enslow Pubs., Inc.

Riley, Gail Blasser. Delta Force in Action. 2008. (Special Ops Ser.). (Illus.). 32p. (YA). (gr. 3-6). lib. bdg. 25.27 *(978-1-59716-635-5(9))* Bearport Publishing Co., Inc.

Roberts, Jeremy. U. S. Army Special Operations Forces. 2004. (U. S. Armed Forces Ser.). (ENG., Illus.). 64p. (gr. 4-8). lib. bdg. 26.60 *(978-0-8225-1646-0(2))* Lerner Publishing Group.

Roche, Tim. Soldiers of the Civil War, 1 vol. (Why We Fought: the Civil War Ser.). (ENG.). 48p. (gr. 3-6). 2011. pap. 9.95 *(978-1-4329-3920-5(3))* 2010. 33.32 *(978-1-4329-3914-4(9))* Heinemann-Raintree. (Heinemann InfoSearch).

Rose, Simon. Army. 2012. (J). *(978-1-61913-291-7(5))*; pap. *(978-1-61913-296-2(6))* Weigl Pubs., Inc.

—Army Rangers. 2013. (J). *(978-1-62127-449-0(7))*; pap. *(978-1-62127-455-1(1))* Weigl Pubs., Inc.

—Delta Force. 2013. (J). *(978-1-62127-450-6(0))*; pap. *(978-1-62127-456-8(X))* Weigl Pubs., Inc.

—Green Berets. 2013. (J). *(978-1-62127-451-3(9))*; pap. *(978-1-62127-457-5(8))* Weigl Pubs., Inc.

Rumsch, BreAnn. Ulysses S. Grant, 1 vol. 2009. (United States Presidents Ser.). (ENG., Illus.). 40p. (YA). (gr. 3-6). 27.07 *(978-1-60453-453-5(2))* ABDO Publishing Co.

Sandler, Michael. Army Rangers in Action. 2008. (Special Ops Ser.). (Illus.). 32p. (YA). (gr. 3-6). lib. bdg. 25.27 *(978-1-59716-632-4(4))* Bearport Publishing Co., Inc.

Sapp, Richard. Ulysses S. Grant & the Road to Appomattox. 2006. (In the Footsteps of American Heroes Ser.). (Illus.). 64p. (gr. 5-12). pap. 14.05 *(978-0-8368-6436-6(0))*; lib. bdg. 34.00 *(978-0-8368-6431-1(X))* Stevens, Gareth Publishing LLLP. (Gareth Stevens Secondary Library).

Shea, John M. The Tuskegee Airmen. 2015. (Heroes of Black History Ser.). (ENG., Illus.). 32p. (J). (gr. 3-4). 26.60 *(978-1-4824-2918-3(7))* Stevens, Gareth Publishing LLLP.

Shea, Therese. Black Ops & Other Special Missions of the U. S. Army Green Berets. 2012. (Inside Special Forces Ser.). (ENG., Illus.). 64p. (YA). (gr. 5-8). pap. 12.95 *(978-1-4488-8387-5(3))*; lib. bdg. 31.95 *(978-1-4488-8381-3(4))* Rosen Publishing Group, Inc., The.

Sheinkin, Steve. The Notorious Benedict Arnold: A True Story of Adventure, Heroism & Treachery. 2013. (ENG., Illus.). 368p. (YA). (gr. 6-9). pap. 9.99 *(978-1-250-02460-2(9)*, 9781250024602) Square Fish.

Simons, Lisa M. Bolt. Soldados del Ejército de EE. UU. 2010. (Gente de Las Fuerzas Armadas de EE. UU. /People of the Armed Forces Ser.).Tr. of Soldiers of the U. S. Army. (MUL, SPA & ENG.). 24p. (gr. k-1). lib. bdg. 26.65 *(978-1-4296-6118-8(6))* Capstone Press of Coughlan Cos.

—Soldiers of the U. S. Army [Scholastic]. 2010. (People of the U. S. Armed Forces Ser.). (ENG.). 24p. pap. 0.49 *(978-1-4296-5807-2(X)*, Pebble Plus) Capstone Press of Coughlan Cos.

—Special Ops Mission Timelines. 2016. (Special Ops Mission Timelines Ser.). (ENG.). 32p. (gr. 1-2). 106.60 *(978-1-4914-8709-9(7)*, Blazers) Capstone Press of Coughlan Cos.

—U. S. Army by the Numbers, 1 vol. 2014. (Military by the Numbers Ser.). (ENG.). 32p. (gr. 3-4). lib. bdg. 27.99 *(978-1-4765-3917-1(0)*, Edge Bks.) Capstone Press of Coughlan Cos.

—U. S. Army Green Beret Missions: A Timeline. 2016. (Special Ops Mission Timelines Ser.). (ENG., Illus.). 32p. (gr. 1-2). lib. bdg. 26.65 *(978-1-4914-8702-0(X)*, Blazers) Capstone Press of Coughlan Cos.

—U. S. Army Ranger Missions: A Timeline. 2016. (Special Ops Mission Timelines Ser.). (ENG., Illus.). 32p. (gr. 1-2). lib. bdg. 26.65 *(978-1-4914-8701-3(1)*, Blazers) Capstone Press of Coughlan Cos.

Slater, Lee. Army Rangers, 1 vol. 2016. (Special Ops Ser.). (ENG., Illus.). 32p. (J). (gr. 3-6). 27.07 *(978-1-62403-967-6(7))* ABDO Publishing Co.

—Delta Force, 1 vol. 2016. (Special Ops Ser.). (ENG., Illus.). 32p. (J). (gr. 3-6). 27.07 *(978-1-62403-968-3(5))* ABDO Publishing Co.

—Green Berets, 1 vol. 2016. (Special Ops Ser.). (ENG., Illus.). 32p. (J). (gr. 3-6). 27.07 *(978-1-62403-969-0(3))* ABDO Publishing Co.

Small, Cathleen. Strategic Inventions of the Korean War. 2016. (Tech in the Trenches Ser.). 112p. (J). 42.79 *(978-1-5026-2345-4(5))* Cavendish Square Publishing.

Solomon, Sharon. Cathy Williams, Buffalo Soldier, 1 vol. Lorenzetti, Doreen, illus. 2010. (ENG.). 32p. (J). (gr. k-3). 16.99 *(978-1-58980-801-0(0))* Pelican Publishing Co., Inc.

Stanley, George E. George S. Patton: War Hero. Henderson, Meryl, illus. 2007. (Childhood of Famous Americans Ser.). (ENG.). 192p. (J). (gr. 3-7). pap. 6.99 *(978-1-4169-1547-8(8)*, Simon & Schuster/Paula Wiseman Bks.) Simon & Schuster/Paula Wiseman Bks.

Stewart, Gail B. Life of a Soldier in Washington's Army. 2003. (American War Library). (ENG., Illus.). 112p. (J). 30.85 *(978-1-59018-215-4(4)*, Lucent Bks.) Cengage Gale.

Stilwell, Alexander. Army Rangers. 2015. (J). lib. bdg. *(978-1-62713-457-6(3))*; (ENG.). 48p. (gr. 8-8). 31.36 *(978-1-5026-0166-7(4))* Cavendish Square Publishing.

Stine, Megan. Who Was Ulysses S. Grant? Harrison, Nancy & Geyer, Mark Edward, illus. 2014. (Who Was? Ser.). (ENG.). 112p. (J). (gr. 3-7). 5.99 *(978-0-448-47894-4(3)*, Grosset & Dunlap) Penguin Young Readers Group.

Stokes, Betty Southard. Postcards from George, 1763-1781: George Rogers Clark Writes Home to Virginia from the Kentucky Wilderness. Cable, Annette, illus. 2010. (J). *(978-1-935497-12-7(X))* Butler Bk. Publishing.

Stone, Tanya Lee. Courage Has No Color - The True Story of the Triple Nickles: America's First Black Paratroopers. 2013. (ENG., Illus.). 160p. (J). (gr. 5). pap. 17.99 *(978-0-7636-6548-7(7))*; 24.99 *(978-0-7636-5117-6(6))* Candlewick Pr.

Stotts, Stuart. Lucius Fairchild: Civil War Hero. 2011. (Badger Biographies Ser.). (ENG., Illus.). 112p. (J). pap. 12.95 *(978-0-87020-460-9(2))* Wisconsin Historical Society.

Sutcliffe, Jane. George S. Patton JR. 2006. (History Maker Bios Ser.). (Illus.). 48p. (J). (gr. 3-7). lib. bdg. 26.60 *(978-0-8225-2436-6(8)*, Lerner Pubns.) Lerner Publishing Group.

Today's U. S. Army, 1 vol. 2013. (U. S. Armed Forces Ser.). (ENG.). 48p. (gr. 5-6). pap. 9.10 *(978-0-7565-4635-9(4)*, CPB Grades 4-8) Compass Point Bks.

Townsend, John. Army. 2016. (Action Force: World War II Ser.). 32p. (gr. 3-7). 31.35 *(978-1-59920-982-1(9)*, Smart Apple Media) Black Rabbit Bks.

The U.S. Army in World War II. 2014. (ENG.). 48p. (J). lib. bdg. 29.00 *(978-0-531-20496-2(0))* Scholastic Library Publishing.

Vander Hook, Sue. Colin Powell: General & Statesman, 1 vol. 2010. (Military Heroes Ser.). (ENG.). 112p. (J). (gr. 6-12). lib. bdg. 35.64 *(978-1-60453-965-3(8))* ABDO Publishing Co.

Venezia, Mike. Ulysses S. Grant. Venezia, Mike, illus. 2005. (Getting to Know the U. S. Presidents Ser.). (ENG., Illus.). 32p. (J). (gr. 3-7). lib. bdg. 28.00 *(978-0-516-22623-1(1)*, Children's Pr.) Scholastic Library Publishing.

Vierow, Wendy. The Assault on Fort Wagner: Black Union Soldiers Make a Stand in South Carolina Battle. 2009. (Headlines from History Ser.). 24p. (gr. 3-3). 42.50 *(978-1-61513-240-9(6)*, PowerKids Pr.) Rosen Publishing Group, Inc., The.

Waxman, Laura Hamilton. Colin Powell. 2005. (History Maker Bios Ser.). 48p. (J). pap. 8.95 *(978-0-8225-5463-9(1))*; (ENG., Illus.). (gr. 3-6). lib. bdg. 27.93 *(978-0-8225-2433-5(3)*, Lerner Pubns.) Lerner Publishing Group.

Welch, Catherine A. George C. Marshall. (History Maker Bios Ser.). 48p. (J). 2006. (Illus.). (gr. 3-7). lib. bdg. 26.60 *(978-0-8225-2435-9(X)*, Lerner Pubns.) 2005. pap. 8.95 *(978-0-8225-5460-8(7))* Lerner Publishing Group.

Whiting, Jim. Delta Force. 2014. (J). *(978-1-60818-461-3(7)*, Creative Education) Creative Co., The.

—U. S. Special Forces: Delta Force. 2015. (U. S. Special Forces Ser.). (ENG.). 48p. (J). (gr. 5-8). pap. 12.00 *(978-1-62832-047-3(8)*, Creative Paperbacks) Creative Co., The.

—U. S. Special Forces: Green Berets. 2015. (U. S. Special Forces Ser.). (ENG.). 48p. (J). (gr. 5-8). pap. 12.00 *(978-1-62832-049-7(4)*, Creative Paperbacks) Creative Co., The.

Wilson, Patrick. Survival Equipment. Carney, John, ed. 2014. (Extreme Survival in the Military Ser.: 12). 64p. (J). (gr. 7-18). lib. bdg. 23.95 *(978-1-4222-3085-5(6))* Mason Crest.

Wood, Alix. Serving in the Army. 2013. 32p. (J). (gr. 3-6). 25.25 *(978-1-4777-1294-8(1))*; pap. 60.00 *(978-1-4777-1395-2(6))*; (ENG., Illus.). pap. 10.00 *(978-1-4777-1394-5(8))* Rosen Publishing Group, Inc., The. (PowerKids Pr.).

Yomtov, Nel. Combat. 2016. (Military Missions Ser.). (ENG., Illus.). 24p. (J). (gr. 3-7). 25.95 *(978-1-62617-433-7(4)*, Epic Bks.) Bellwether Media.

Young, Jeff C. Dwight D. Eisenhower: Soldier & President. 2004. (Notable Americans Ser.). (Illus.). 128p. (YA). (gr. 6-12). 23.95 *(978-1-883846-76-3(5)*, First Biographies) Reynolds, Morgan Inc.

Zaloga, Steven J. The Most Daring Raid of World War II: D-Day — Pointe-Du-Hoc. 2011. (Most Daring Raids in History Ser.). (Illus.). 64p. (YA). (gr. 7-12). lib. bdg. 31.95 *(978-1-4488-1867-9(2))* Rosen Publishing Group, Inc., The.

UNITED STATES—ARMY—MILITARY LIFE

Ammon, Richard. Valley Forge. Farnsworth, Bill, illus. 2004. (ENG.). 32p. (J). (gr. 4-6). tchr. ed. 17.95 *(978-0-8234-1746-9(8))* Holiday Hse., Inc.

Anderson, Dale. A Soldier's Life in the Civil War. 2004. (World Almanac Library of the Civil War). (Illus.). 48p. (gr. 5-12). pap. 14.05 *(978-0-8368-5595-1(7))*; lib. bdg. 31.00 *(978-0-8368-5586-9(8))* Stevens, Gareth Publishing LLLP. (Gareth Stevens Secondary Library).

Beller, Susan Provost. Yankee Doodle & the Redcoats: Soldiering in the Revolutionary War. rev. ed. 2007. (Soldiers on the Battlefront Ser.). (ENG., Illus.). 112p. (gr. 6-8). lib. bdg. 33.26 *(978-0-8225-6655-7(9))* Lerner Publishing Group.

Elite Military Forces. 2010. (Elite Military Forces Ser.). (ENG.). 24p. (gr. 1-2). lib. bdg. 101.28 *(978-1-4296-5383-1(3)*, First Facts) Capstone Press of Coughlan Cos.

Freedman, Russell. Washington at Valley Forge. 2008. (ENG., Illus.). 80p. (J). (gr. 4-7). 24.95 *(978-0-8234-2069-8(8))* Holiday Hse., Inc.

Frontline Families. 2015. (Frontline Families Ser.). (ENG.). 48p. (J). (gr. 5-6). pap., pap., pap. 505.80 *(978-1-4824-3471-2(7))* Stevens, Gareth Publishing LLLP.

Goldish, Meish. Army: Civilian to Soldier. 2010. (Becoming a Soldier Ser.). 24p. (YA). (gr. 3-6). lib. bdg. 22.61 *(978-1-936088-11-9(8))* Bearport Publishing Co., Inc.

—Baghdad Pups. 2011. (Dog Heroes Ser.). (Illus.). 32p. (J). (gr. 2-5). lib. bdg. 25.27 *(978-1-61772-150-2(6)*, 1321528) Bearport Publishing Co., Inc.

Hooker, Forrestine Cooper. Child of the Fighting Tenth: On the Frontier with the Buffalo Soldiers. Wilson, Steve, ed. 2011. (ENG., Illus.). 296p. pap. 19.95 *(978-0-8061-4080-3(1))* Univ. of Oklahoma Pr.

Jeffrey, Gary. George Washington & the Winter at Valley Forge. 2011. (Graphic Heroes of the American Revolution Ser.). 24p. (J). (gr. 3-8). pap. 8.15 *(978-1-4339-6014-7(1)*, Gareth Stevens Learning Library); (Illus.). lib. bdg. 23.95 *(978-1-4339-6174-8(1))* Stevens, Gareth Publishing LLLP.

Kohler, Dean Ellis & VanHecke, Susan. Rock 'n' Roll Soldier: A Memoir. 2009. (ENG.). 288p. (YA). (gr. 9-18). 17.99 *(978-0-06-124255-7(1)*, HarperTeen) HarperCollins Pubs.

Miller, Reagan & Claus, J. Matteson. Life on a Civil War Battlefield. 2011. (ENG.). 48p. (J). pap. *(978-0-7787-5357-5(3))*; lib. bdg. *(978-0-7787-5340-7(9))* Crabtree Publishing Co.

Price, Sean Stewart. Yanks in World War I: Americans in the Trenches, 1 vol. 2008. (American History Through Primary Sources Ser.). (ENG., Illus.). 32p. (gr. 2-2). 29.99 *(978-1-4109-3110-8(2)*, Raintree Fusion) Heinemann-Raintree.

Raum, Elizabeth. At Battle in the Revolutionary War: An Interactive Battlefield Adventure. 2015. (You Choose: Battlefields Ser.). (ENG., Illus.). 112p. (gr. 3-4). pap. 6.95 *(978-1-4914-2392-9(7)*, You Choose Bks.) Capstone Press of Coughlan Cos.

Roche, Tim. Soldiers of the Civil War, 1 vol. (Why We Fought: the Civil War Ser.). (ENG.). 48p. (gr. 3-6). 2011. pap. 9.95 *(978-1-4329-3920-5(3))* 2010. 33.32 *(978-1-4329-3914-4(9))* Heinemann-Raintree. (Heinemann InfoSearch).

Russo, Kristen J. Surprising Facts about Being an Army Soldier. 2017. (What You Didn't Know about the U. S. Military Life Ser.). (ENG.). 32p. (gr. 3-4). lib. bdg. 27.99 ***(978-1-5157-7429-7(5)***, Edge Bks.) Capstone Press of Coughlan Cos.

Shoup, Kate. Life As a Soldier in the Civil War. 2016. (Life As... Ser.). (ENG., Illus.). 32p. (J). (gr. 3-3). pap. 10.58 *(978-1-5026-1083-6(3))* Cavendish Square Publishing.

UNITED STATES—ARMY—UNIFORMS

Langellier, John P. & Loane, C. Paul. U. S. Army Headgear, 1812-1872, 1 vol. 2003. (ENG., Illus.). 160p. (gr. 10-13). 69.95 *(978-0-7643-1672-2(9)*, 9780764316722) Schiffer Publishing, Ltd.

UNITED STATES—ARTISTS

see Artists, American

UNITED STATES—AUTHORS

see Authors, American

UNITED STATES—BIOGRAPHY

Abbey, Cherie D., ed. Biography Today Annual Cumulation 2004: Profiles of People of Interest to Young Readers. 2004. (Biography Today General Ser.). 560p. lib. bdg. 73.00 *(978-0-7808-0686-3(7))* Omnigraphics, Inc.

ABDO Publishing Company Staff. Big Buddy Biographies Set 7, 1 vol. 2011. (Big Buddy Biographies Set 7 Ser.). (ENG., Illus.). 32p. 171.00 *(978-1-61783-016-7(X)*, Big Buddy Bks.) ABDO Publishing Co.

—Comic Book Creators. 2006. (Comic Book Creators Ser.). 32p. 162.42 *(978-1-59928-296-1(8)*, Abdo & Daughters) ABDO Publishing Co.

—First Biographies Set 5. 2006. (First Biographies Set 5 Ser.). 162.42 *(978-1-59679-784-0(3)*, Buddy Bks.) ABDO Publishing Co.

—Heroes of America. 2005. (Heroes of America Ser.). (gr. 3-8). 216.56 *(978-1-59679-254-8(X)*, Abdo & Daughters) ABDO Publishing Co.

Abnett, Dan. Abraham Lincoln y la Guerra Civil. 2009. (Historietas Juveniles: Biografías (Jr. Graphic Biographies) Ser.). (SPA., Illus.). 24p. (J). (gr. 2-5). 25.25 *(978-1-4358-8561-5(9))*; (gr. 3-8). pap. 10.60 *(978-1-4358-3316-6(3))* Rosen Publishing Group, Inc., The.

—George Washington y la Guerra de Independencia. 2009. (Historietas Juveniles: Biografías (Jr. Graphic Biographies) Ser.). (SPA & ENG., Illus.). 24p. (YA). (gr. 2-5). 25.25 *(978-1-4358-8564-6(3))*; (gr. 3-8). pap. 10.60 *(978-1-4358-3322-7(8))* Rosen Publishing Group, Inc., The.

Abrams, Dennis. America Ferrera. 2010. (Great Hispanic Heritage Ser.). (Illus.). 112p. (gr. 6-12). 35.00 *(978-1-60413-967-9(6)*, Chelsea Hse.) Facts On File, Inc.

—Gary Soto. 2008. (Who Wrote That? Ser.). (Illus.). 120p. (gr. 6-12). 35.00 *(978-0-7910-9529-4(0)*, Chelsea Hse.) Facts On File, Inc.

—Ty Cobb. 2007. (Baseball Superstars Ser.). (Illus.). 130p. (YA). (gr. 7-12). lib. bdg. 30.00 *(978-0-7910-9439-6(1))* Facts On File, Inc.

Adams, Colleen. Jake Gyllenhaal. 2006. (Stars in the Spotlight Ser.). (Illus.). 32p. (YA). (gr. 4-7). lib. bdg. 25.25 *(978-1-4042-3514-4(0))* Rosen Publishing Group, Inc., The.

—Johnny Depp. 2006. (Tony Stead Nonfiction Independent Reading Collection). (ENG.). 24p. (gr. 3-6). pap. 8.85 *(978-1-4042-5667-5(9))* Rosen Publishing Group, Inc., The.

Adams, Michelle. Cliff Lee. 2011. (Robbie Reader Ser.). (Illus.). 32p. (J). (gr. 2-5). lib. bdg. 25.70 *(978-1-61228-065-3(X))* Mitchell Lane Pubs., Inc.

—Katy Perry. 2011. (Blue Banner Biography Ser.). (Illus.). 32p. (YA). (gr. 4-7). lib. bdg. 25.70 *(978-1-61228-051-6(X))* Mitchell Lane Pubs., Inc.

Adler, David A. Honest Abe Lincoln: Easy-to-Read Stories about Abraham Lincoln. Wallner, John C., illus. 2009. (Holiday House Reader Level 2 Ser.). (ENG.). 32p. (J). (gr. k-3). 15.95 *(978-0-8234-2057-5(4))* Holiday Hse., Inc.

—A Picture Book of Benjamin Franklin. 2008. (J). (gr. k-3). pap. 39.95 incl. audio compact disk *(978-1-4301-0341-7(8))* Live Oak Media.

—A Picture Book of Patrick Henry. Wallner, John et al, illus. 2005. (ENG.). 32p. (J). (gr. k-3). pap. 6.95 *(978-0-8234-1678-3(X))* Holiday Hse., Inc.

Adler, Jack. Chinese Americans. (Successful Americans Ser.). 64p. (YA). 2009. (Illus.). (gr. 9-12). 22.95 *(978-1-4222-0520-4(7))* 2007. (gr. 7-18). pap. 9.95 *(978-1-4222-0855-7(9))* Mason Crest.

Aiwei, Daniel B. CM Punk: Pro Wrestling Superstar, 1 vol. 2014. (Pro Wrestling Superstars Ser.). (ENG.). 24p. (gr. 1-2). lib. bdg. 25.32 *(978-1-4765-4210-2(4)*, First Facts) Capstone Press of Coughlan Cos.

—John Cena: Pro Wrestling Superstar, 1 vol. 2014. (Pro Wrestling Superstars Ser.). (ENG.). 24p. (gr. 1-2). lib. bdg. 25.32 *(978-1-4765-4207-2(4)*, First Facts) Capstone Press of Coughlan Cos.

Alagna, Magdalena. Billie Holiday. 2009. (Rock & Roll Hall of Famers Ser.). 112p. (gr. 5-8). 63.90 *(978-1-60852-468-6(X)*, Rosen Reference) Rosen Publishing Group, Inc., The.

—Wyatt Earp: Lawman of the American West. 2009. (Primary Sources of Famous People in American History Ser.). 32p. (gr. 2-3). 47.90 *(978-1-60851-747-3(0))* Rosen Publishing Group, Inc., The.

—Wyatt Earp: Lawman of the American West / Sheriff del oeste Americano. 2009. (Famous People in American History/Grandes personajes en la historia de los Estados Unidos Ser.). (ENG & SPA.). 32p. (gr. 2-3). 47.90 *(978-1-61512-558-6(2)*, Editorial Buenas Letras) Rosen Publishing Group, Inc., The.

—Wyatt Earp: Sheriff del legano Oeste. 2004. (Grandes personajes en la historia de los Estados Unidos Ser.). (SPA.). 32p. (gr. 3-6). pap. 10.00 *(978-0-8239-4241-1(4)*, Rosen Classroom) Rosen Publishing Group, Inc., The.

—Wyatt Earp: Sheriff del oeste americano (Wyatt Earp: Lawman of the American West) 2009. (Grandes personajes en la historia de los Estados Unidos (Famous People in American History) Ser.). (SPA.). 32p. (gr. 2-3). 47.90

(978-1-61512-811-2(5), Editorial Buenas Letras) Rosen Publishing Group, Inc., The.
Aldridge, Rebecca. Apolo Anton Ohno. 2009. (Asian Americans of Achievement Ser.). (Illus.). 128p. (YA). (gr. 7-12). 35.00 (978-1-60413-565-7(4)) Facts On File, Inc.
Aldrin, Buzz. Reaching for the Moon. Minor, Wendell, illus. (ENG.). 40p. (J). (gr. 1-4). 2008. 6.99 (978-0-06-055447-7(9), Collins) 2005. 17.99 (978-0-06-055445-3(2)) HarperCollins Pubs.
—Reaching for the Moon. Minor, Wendell, illus. unabr. ed. 2005. (Picture Book Readalong Ser.). (gr. k-4). 28.95 incl. audio compact disk (978-1-59519-582-1(3)) Live Oak Media.
All-Star Players, 12 vols., Sets 1-2. Incl. Set. Rosen Publishing Group. 2007. lib. bdg. 143.70 (978-1-4042-3601-1(5)); Set 2. Edwards, Ethan. 2008. lib. bdg. 143.70 (978-1-4358-2564-2(0), PowerKids Pr.); (J). (gr. 4-6). 2008. Set lib. bdg. 287.40 (978-1-4358-2669-4(8)) Rosen Publishing Group, Inc., The.
Allen, Kathy. Drew Brees. 2013. (Football Stars up Close Ser.). 24p. (J). (gr. k-5). lib. bdg. 23.93 (978-1-61772-716-0(4)) Bearport Publishing Co., Inc.
—Tom Brady. 2013. (Football Stars up Close Ser.). 24p. (J). (gr. k-5). lib. bdg. 23.93 (978-1-61772-717-7(2)) Bearport Publishing Co., Inc.
—Tony Romo. 2013. (Football Stars up Close Ser.). 24p. (J). (gr. k-5). lib. bdg. 23.93 (978-1-61772-719-1(9)) Bearport Publishing Co., Inc.
Allen, Kenny. Kurt Busch. 2007. (NASCAR Champions Ser.). (Illus.). 24p. (J). (gr. 1-3). lib. bdg. 22.60 (978-1-4042-3457-4(8)) Rosen Publishing Group, Inc., The.
Allyson, Jackie. Chris Jesus Ferguson. 2007. (Superstars of Poker Ser.). (Illus.). 64p. (YA). pap. 7.95 (978-1-4222-0371-2(9)) Mason Crest.
—Doyle Texas Dolly Brunson. 2007. (Superstars of Poker Ser.). (Illus.). 64p. (YA). pap. 7.95 (978-1-4222-0368-2(9)) Mason Crest.
—Gus the Great Dane Hansen. 2007. (Superstars of Poker Ser.). (Illus.). 64p. (YA). pap. 7.95 (978-1-4222-0372-9(7)) Mason Crest.
—Howard the Professor Lederer. 2009. (Superstars of Poker Ser.). (Illus.). 64p. (YA). (gr. 3-7). lib. bdg. 22.95 (978-1-4222-0223-4(2)) Mason Crest.
—Phil Unabomber Laak. (Superstars of Poker Ser.). (Illus.). 64p. (YA). 2009. (gr. 3-7). lib. bdg. 22.95 (978-1-4222-0222-7(4)) 2007. pap. 7.95 (978-1-4222-0376-7(X)) Mason Crest.
Alter, Judy. Martín de León: Tejano Empresario. Messersmith, Patrick, illus. 2007. (Stars of Texas Ser.: 4). (ENG.). 72p. (gr. 4-7). 14.95 (978-1-933337-08-1(7)) State Hse. Pr.
Aluri, Rao. Backcountry Fury: A Sixteen-Year-Old Patriot in the Revolutionary War. 2010. (J). pap. 19.95 (978-1-59712-409-6(5)) Catawba Publishing Co.
Alyson, Jackie. Howard the Professor Lederer. 2007. (Superstars of Poker: Texas Hold'em Ser.). (Illus.). 64p. (YA). (gr. 3-7). pap. 7.95 (978-1-4222-0377-4(8)) Mason Crest.
Ambrosek, Renee. Shawn Fanning: The Founder of Napster. (Internet Career Biographies Ser.). 112p. 2009. (gr. 8-8). 63.90 (978-1-61513-600-1(2)) 2006. (Illus.). (YA). (gr. 7-12). lib. bdg. 34.60 (978-1-4042-0720-2(1)) Rosen Publishing Group, Inc., The.
American Biographies Set. 2005. (American Biographies Ser.). 464p. (C). (gr. 9). 130.00 (978-0-8160-6515-8(2)) Facts On File, Inc.
American Graphic. 2011. (American Graphic Ser.). (ENG.). 32p. (gr. 3-4). pap. 381.60 (978-1-4296-7344-0(3), Graphic Library) Capstone Press of Coughlan Cos.
American Graphic, 8 vols., Set. Incl. Bambino: The Story of Babe Ruth's Legendary 1927 Season. Yomtov, Nelson. Foley, Tim, illus. 2010. lib. bdg. 30.65 (978-1-4296-5473-9(2)); Biography of Malcolm X. Gunderson, Jessica. Hayden, Seitu, illus. 2010. lib. bdg. 30.65 (978-1-4296-5471-5(6)); Elvis: A Graphic Novel. Collins, Terry. Melcher, Michele, illus. 2010. lib. bdg. 30.65 (978-1-4296-5476-0(7)); Obama: The Historic Election of America's 44th President. Biskup, Agnieszka. Hayden, Seitu, illus. 2011. lib. bdg. 30.65 (978-1-4296-6016-7(3)); Robert E. Lee: The Story of the Great Confederate General. Collins, Terry. Mallea, Cristian, illus. 2010. lib. bdg. 30.65 (978-1-4296-5475-3(9)); Sarah Palin: Political Rebel. Yomtov, Nelson. D'Ottavi, Francesca, illus. 2011. lib. bdg. 30.65 (978-1-4296-6018-1(X)); Thunder Rolling down the Mountain: The Story of Chief Joseph & the Nez Perce. Biskup, Agnieszka. Zimmerman, Rusty, illus. 2010. lib. bdg. 30.65 (978-1-4296-5472-2(4)); (gr. 3-4). (American Graphic Ser.). (ENG.). 32p. 2011. Set lib. bdg. 214.55 (978-1-4296-6585-8(8), Graphic Library) Capstone Press of Coughlan Cos.
American Heroes, Group 2, 6 bks., Set. Incl. Booker T. Washington: Getting into the Schoolhouse. Brimner, Larry Dane. (YA). lib. bdg. 29.93 (978-0-7614-3063-6(6)); Chief Crazy Horse: Following a Vision. Brimner, Larry Dane. lib. bdg. 29.93 (978-0-7614-3061-2(X)); Eleanor Roosevelt: Making the World a Better Place. Collard, Sneed B., III. lib. bdg. 29.93 (978-0-7614-3069-8(5)); John Glenn: Hooked on Flying. Collard, Sneed B., III. (Illus.). (J). lib. bdg. 29.93 (978-0-7614-3066-7(0)); Pocahontas: Bridging Two Worlds. Brimner, Larry Dane. lib. bdg. 29.93 (978-0-7614-3065-0(2)); Thomas Jefferson: Let Freedom Ring! Collard, Sneed B., III. lib. bdg. 29.93 (978-0-7614-3067-4(9)); 48p. (gr. 3-18). 2008. Set lib. bdg. 179.57 (978-0-7614-3060-5(1), Benchmark Bks.) Marshall Cavendish Corp.
Anderson, Dale. Al Gore: A Wake-Up Call to Global Warming. 2009. (Voices for Green Choices Ser.). (ENG., Illus.). 48p. (J). (gr. 5-9). lib. bdg. (978-0-7787-4666-9(6)) Crabtree Publishing Co.
—Leaders of the American Revolution. 2005. (World Almanac Library of the American Revolution Ser.). 48p. (gr. 5-12). pap. 14.05 (978-0-8368-5940-9(5)); lib. bdg. 31.00 (978-0-8368-5931-7(6)) Stevens, Gareth Publishing LLLP. (Gareth Stevens Secondary Library).
Anderson, Michael. Biographies of the New World Power: Rutherford B. Hayes, Thomas Alva Edison, Margaret Sanger, & More. 2012. (Impact on America: Collective Biographies Ser.). (ENG., Illus.). 112p. (J). (gr. 7-12). 32.90 (978-1-61530-691-6(9)) Rosen Publishing Group, Inc., The.
Anderson, Michael, ed. Biographies of the New World: Leif Eriksson, Henry Hudson, Charles Darwin, & More. 2012. (Impact on America: Collective Biographies Ser.). (ENG., Illus.). 112p. (YA). (gr. 7-12). 65.80 (978-1-61530-803-3(2)) Rosen Publishing Group, Inc., The.
—Biographies of the New World Power: Rutherford B. Hayes, Thomas Alva Edison, Margaret Sanger, & More. 2012. (Impact on America: Collective Biographies Ser.). (ENG., Illus.). 112p. (YA). (gr. 7-12). 65.80 (978-1-61530-765-4(6)) Rosen Publishing Group, Inc., The.
Anderson, Sheila. America Ferrera: Latina Superstar. 2009. (Hot Celebrity Biographies Ser.). (Illus.). 48p. (J). (gr. 5-9). lib. bdg. 25.27 (978-0-7660-3210-1(8)) Enslow Pubs., Inc.
Anderson, Wayne A. Tony Stewart: NASCAR Driver. 2006. (Behind the Wheel Ser.). (Illus.). 48p. (YA). (gr. 5-9). lib. bdg. 29.25 (978-1-4042-0984-8(0)) Rosen Publishing Group, Inc., The.
Andre Norton. 2010. (Who Wrote That? Ser.). (Illus.). 128p. (gr. 6-12). 35.00 (978-1-60413-682-1(0), Chelsea Hse.) Facts On File, Inc.
Angel, Ann. Janis Joplin: Rise up Singing. 2010. (ENG., Illus.). 128p. (YA). (gr. 7-17). 24.95 (978-0-8109-8349-6(4), Amulet Bks.) Abrams, Inc.
Angst, Frank. Chad Johnson. 2009. (Superstars of Pro Football Ser.). (Illus.). 64p. (YA). (gr. 5-18). lib. bdg. 22.95 (978-1-4222-0556-3(8)) Mason Crest.
Arato, Rona. Working for Freedom: The Story of Josiah Henson. 2009. (Stories of Canada Ser.: 13). (ENG., Illus.). 88p. (J). (gr. 4-18). 18.95 (978-1-894917-50-6(2), Napoleon & Co.) Dundurn CAN. Dist: Ingram Publisher Services.
Aretha, David. Aaron Rodgers: Champion Football Star. 2017. (Sports Star Champions Ser.). 48p. (J). (gr. 5-6). lib. bdg. 27.93 **(978-0-7660-8716-3(6))** Enslow Pubs., Inc.
—José Altuve: Champion Baseball Star. 2017. (Sports Star Champions Ser.). 48p. (J). (gr. 5-6). lib. bdg. 27.93 **(978-0-7660-8690-6(9))** Enslow Pubs., Inc.
Armstrong, Jesse. Randy Orton. 2015. (Wrestling Superstars Ser.). (ENG., Illus.). 24p. (J). (gr. 3-7). lib. bdg. 25.95 (978-1-62617-182-4(3), Epic Bks.) Bellwether Media.
—Triple H. 2015. (Wrestling Superstars Ser.). (ENG., Illus.). 24p. (J). (gr. 3-7). lib. bdg. 25.95 (978-1-62617-183-1(1), Epic Bks.) Bellwether Media.
Armstrong, Linda. Henry Ford. 2009. pap. 13.25 (978-1-60559-062-2(0)) Hameray Publishing Group, Inc.
Artell, Mike. Drew Brees: Football Superstar, 1 vol. 2011. (Superstar Athletes Ser.). (ENG.). 24p. (gr. 1-2). pap. 7.29 (978-1-4296-7305-1(2)); pap. 41.70 (978-1-4296-7306-8(0)) Capstone Press of Coughlan Cos.
Auster, Michael A. They Led the Way. 2005. (Yellow Umbrella Fluent Level Ser.). (ENG.). 16p. (gr. k-1). pap. 35.70 (978-0-7368-5315-6(4), Yellow Umbrella Bks.) Capstone Press of Coughlan Cos.
Azzarelli, Ally. Selena Gomez: Latina TV & Music Star. 2011. (Hot Celebrity Biographies Ser.). (Illus.). 48p. (J). (gr. 5-9). lib. bdg. 25.27 (978-0-7660-3875-2(0)) Enslow Pubs., Inc.
—Taylor Lautner: Film Superstar. 2011. (Hot Celebrity Biographies Ser.). (Illus.). 48p. (J). (gr. 5-9). lib. bdg. 25.27 (978-0-7660-3874-5(2)) Enslow Pubs., Inc.
Bader, Bonnie. Who Was Alexander Graham Bell? Groff, David, illus. 2013. (Who Was? Ser.). (ENG.). 112p. (J). (gr. 3-7). 5.99 (978-0-448-46460-2(8), Grosset & Dunlap) Penguin Young Readers Group.
Bahadur, Gaiutra. Family Ties. 2011. (J). pap. (978-0-531-22554-7(2)) Scholastic, Inc.
Bailey, Diane. Miley Cyrus. 2011. (Megastars Ser.). (Illus.). 48p. (YA). (gr. 5-8). lib. bdg. 29.25 (978-1-4358-3573-3(5), Rosen Reference) Rosen Publishing Group, Inc., The.
Bailey, Tom. Jennifer Chandler: Olympic Champion Diver. 2005. (Alabama Roots Biography Ser.). (Illus.). 112p. (J). pap. (978-1-59421-014-3(4)) Seacoast Publishing, Inc.
Bair, Diane. Western Legends & Leyendas del Oeste: 6 English, 6 Spanish Adaptations. 2011. (ENG & SPA.). (J). 101.00 net. (978-1-4108-5735-4(2)) Benchmark Education Co.
Bair, Diane & Wright, Pamela. Western Legends: Set Of 6. 2011. (Navigators Ser.). (J). pap. 50.00 net. (978-1-4108-2577-3(9)) Benchmark Education Co.
Baldwin, James. Four Great Americans. 2006. pap. (978-1-4065-0509-2(9)) Dodo Pr.
Banting, Erinn. Angelina Jolie. 2008. (Remarkable People Ser.). (Illus.). 24p. (J). (gr. 4-6). pap. 8.95 (978-1-59036-987-6(4)); lib. bdg. 24.45 (978-1-59036-986-9(6)) Weigl Pubs., Inc.
—Katie Couric. 2007. (Remarkable People Ser.). (Illus.). 24p. (J). (gr. 4-6). pap. 8.95 (978-1-59036-644-8(1)); lib. bdg. 24.45 (978-1-59036-643-1(3)) Weigl Pubs., Inc.
Baptiste, Tracey. Jerry Spinelli. 2009. (Who Wrote That? Ser.). (Illus.). 128p. (gr. 6-12). 35.00 (978-0-7910-9572-0(X), Chelsea Hse.) Facts On File, Inc.
—Madeleine L'Engle. 2009. (Who Wrote That? Ser.). (Illus.). 128p. (gr. 6-12). 35.00 (978-0-7910-9573-7(8), Chelsea Hse.) Facts On File, Inc.
Barber, Tiki. Tiki: My Life in the Game & Beyond. 2008. (ENG.). 240p. pap. 15.99 (978-1-4169-5564-1(X), Gallery Bks.) Gallery Bks.
Baughan, Brian. Cesar Chavez. 2009. (Sharing the American Dream Ser.). (Illus.). 64p. (YA). (gr. 7-12). 22.95 (978-1-4222-0582-2(7)) Mason Crest.
Bednar, Chuck. Beyoncé. 2010. (Transcending Race in America Ser.). 64p. (YA). (gr. 4-8). lib. bdg. 22.95 (978-1-4222-1607-1(1)) Mason Crest.
—David Blaine: Illusionist & Endurance Artist. (Transcending Race in America: Biographies of Biracial Achievers Ser.). (Illus.). 64p. (YA). (gr. 5-18). 2010. lib. bdg. 22.95 (978-1-4222-1609-5(8)) 2009. pap. 9.95 (978-1-4222-1623-1(3)) Mason Crest.
—Kris Allen. 2009. (Dream Big: American Idol Superstars Ser.). 64p. (YA). (gr. 5-18). pap. 9.95 (978-1-4222-1596-8(2)); lib. bdg. 22.95 (978-1-4222-1515-9(6)) Mason Crest.
—Tim Duncan. 2007. (Role Model Athletes Ser.). (Illus.). 64p. (YA). pap. 9.95 (978-1-4222-0768-0(4)) Mason Crest.
Benchmark Education Company. Western Legends (Teacher Guide) 2004. (978-1-4108-2592-6(2)) Benchmark Education Co.
Benge, Janet & Benge, Geoff. D. L. Moody: Bringing Souls to Christ. 2011. (ENG.). (YA). pap. 9.99 (978-1-57658-552-8(2)) YWAM Publishing.
—Davy Crockett: Ever Westward. 2011. (ENG.). 192p. (YA). pap. 9.99 (978-1-932096-67-5(1)) Emerald Bks.
—Heroes of History - Daniel Boone: Frontiersman. 2004. (ENG.). 224p. (YA). pap. 9.99 (978-1-932096-09-5(4)) Emerald Bks.
—Ronald Reagan: Destiny at His Side. 2010. (ENG.). (YA). pap. 9.99 (978-1-932096-65-1(5)) Emerald Bks.
Bennett, Doraine & Scott, Clark C. Benjamin Franklin. 2012. (Illus.). 24p. (J). (978-1-935884-38-5(7)); pap. (978-1-935884-47-7(6)) State Standards Publishing, LLC.
Bentley, Karen. The Unsers. rev. collector's ed. 2005. (Race Car Legends Ser.). (Illus.). 72p. (YA). (gr. 5-9). lib. bdg. 25.00 (978-0-7910-8764-0(6)) Facts On File, Inc.
Berman, Ron. Future Stars of America. 2006. (Future Stars Ser.). (Illus.). 90p. (gr. 3-8). pap. 9.95 (978-0-9741997-4-0(5)) Scobre Pr. Corp.
Berne, Emma Carlson. Paris & Nicky Hilton. 2007. (Popular Culture: A View from the Paparazzi Ser.). (Illus.). 64p. (YA). (gr. 3-7). pap. 7.95 (978-1-4222-0358-3(1)) Mason Crest.
Berne, Stanley. Empire Sweets: How I Learned to Live & Love in the Greatest Empire on Earth. 2003. 160p. (YA). pap. 40.00 (978-0-913844-26-7(8)) Rising Tide Pr.
Bernstein, Ross. Shaquille O'Neal. rev. ed. 2009. (Amazing Athletes Ser.). (ENG.). 32p. (gr. 2-5). pap. 7.95 (978-0-7613-4489-6(6), First Avenue Editions) Lerner Publishing Group.
Bezdecheck, Bethany. Missy Elliott. 2009. (Library of Hip-Hop Biographies Ser.). 48p. (gr. 5-5). 53.00 (978-1-60853-697-9(1)) Rosen Publishing Group, Inc., The.
Biskup, Agnieszka. Houdini: The Life of the Great Escape Artist, 1 vol. Kinsella, Pat, illus. 2011. (American Graphic Ser.). (ENG.). 32p. (gr. 3-4). pap. 8.10 (978-1-4296-6268-0(9)); pap. 47.70 (978-1-4296-6435-6(5)) Capstone Press of Coughlan Cos. (Graphic Library).
Biskup, Agnieszka & Collins, Terry. American Graphic. Pope, Richie, illus. 2012. (American Graphic Ser.). (ENG.). 32p. (gr. 3-4). pap. 89.10 (978-1-4296-9338-7(X)); pap. 572.40 (978-1-4296-9339-4(8)); pap. 15.90 (978-1-4296-9494-0(7)) Capstone Press of Coughlan Cos. (Graphic Library).
Bjornlund, Lydia D. Angelina Jolie. 2010. (Modern Role Models Ser.). (Illus.). 64p. (YA). (gr. 7-12). 22.95 (978-1-4222-0504-4(5)) Mason Crest.
Blohm, Craig E. Great Cartoonists. 2016. (ENG.). 80p. (J). (gr. 5-12). (978-1-60152-996-1(1)) ReferencePoint Pr., Inc.
Bodden, Valerie & Gehry, Frank O. Frank Gehry. 2008. (Xtraordinary Artists Ser.). 48p. (J). (gr. 4-7). lib. bdg. 22.95 (978-1-58341-662-4(5), Creative Education) Creative Co., The.
Bodie, Idella. Heroes & Heroines of the American Revolution. 2004. (Illus.). 48p. (J). pap., instr.'s gde. ed. (978-0-87844-173-0(5)) Sandlapper Publishing Co., Inc.
Bolden, Tonya. The Champ: The Story of Muhammad Ali. Christie, R. Gregory, illus. 2007. (ENG.). 40p. (J). (gr. 1-4). pap. 7.99 (978-0-440-41782-8(1), Dragonfly Bks.) Random Hse. Children's Bks.
Boomhower, Ray E. The Soldier's Friend: A Life of Ernie Pyle. 2006. (Illus.). 134p. 17.95 (978-0-87195-200-4(9)) Indiana Historical Society.
Boone, Mary. Corbin Bleu. 2008. (Blue Banner Biography Ser.). (Illus.). 32p. (YA). (gr. 4-7). lib. bdg. 25.70 (978-1-58415-674-1(0)) Mitchell Lane Pubs., Inc.
—David Wright. 2010. (Blue Banner Biography Ser.). (Illus.). 32p. (YA). (gr. 4-7). lib. bdg. 25.70 (978-1-58415-910-0(3)) Mitchell Lane Pubs., Inc.
—Pink. 2009. (Blue Banner Biography Ser.). (Illus.). 32p. (YA). (gr. 4-7). lib. bdg. 25.70 (978-1-58415-767-0(4)) Mitchell Lane Pubs., Inc.
—Sue Bird. 2011. (Robbie Reader Ser.). (Illus.). 32p. (J). (gr. 2-5). lib. bdg. 25.70 (978-1-61228-062-2(5)) Mitchell Lane Pubs., Inc.
—Tim Lincecum. 2011. (Robbie Reader Ser.). (Illus.). 32p. (J). (gr. 2-5). lib. bdg. 25.70 (978-1-61228-058-5(7)) Mitchell Lane Pubs., Inc.
—Vanessa Anne Hudgens. 2008. (Blue Banner Biography Ser.). (Illus.). 32p. (YA). (gr. 4-7). lib. bdg. 25.70 (978-1-58415-672-7(4)) Mitchell Lane Pubs., Inc.
Boothroyd, Jennifer. Lou Gehrig. 2008. pap. 40.95 (978-0-8225-9473-4(0)) Lerner Publishing Group.
—Robert Fulton: A Life of Innovation. 2007. (Pull Ahead Bks.). (Illus.). 32p. (J). (gr. 3-7). lib. bdg. 22.60 (978-0-8225-6458-4(0), Lerner Pubns.) Lerner Publishing Group.
Bortz, Fred. The Big Bang Theory: Edwin Hubble & the Origins of the Universe. 2013. (Revolutionary Discoveries of Scientific Pioneers Ser.). (Illus.). 80p. (J). (gr. 7-12). 33.25 (978-1-4777-1803-2(6)) Rosen Publishing Group, Inc., The.
Bowe, Brian J. The Ramones: American Punk Rock Band. 2010. (Rebels of Rock Ser.). (Illus.). 128p. (J). (gr. 7-18). pap. 10.95 (978-1-59845-213-6(4)) Enslow Pubs., Inc.
Boyer, Marilyn. For you they Signed. 2010. (YA). lib. bdg. 34.99 (978-0-89051-598-3(0)) Master Bks.
Bradley, Michael. Pro Football's Underdogs: Players & Teams Who Shocked the Football World. 2017. (Sports Shockers! Ser.). (ENG.). 32p. (gr. 3-4). lib. bdg. 27.99 **(978-1-5157-8048-9(1))** Capstone Press of Coughlan Cos.
Braidich, Victoria. Dale Earnhardt. 2007. (NASCAR Champions Ser.). (Illus.). 24p. (J). (gr. 1-3). lib. bdg. 22.60 (978-1-4042-3512-0(4)) Rosen Publishing Group, Inc., The.
Branscomb, Leslie Wolf. Earl Warren. 2011. (Supreme Court Justices Ser.). (Illus.). 112p. 28.95 (978-1-59935-158-2(7)) Reynolds, Morgan Inc.
—Marc Jacobs. 2011. (Profiles in Fashion Ser.). (Illus.). 112p. 28.95 (978-1-59935-153-7(6), 1320457) Reynolds, Morgan Inc.
Braun, Eric. Pro Baseball's Underdogs: Players & Teams Who Shocked the Baseball World. 2017. (Sports Shockers! Ser.). (ENG.). 32p. (gr. 3-4). lib. bdg. 27.99 **(978-1-5157-8047-2(3))** Capstone Press of Coughlan Cos.
—Pro Basketball's Underdogs: Players & Teams Who Shocked the Basketball World. 2017. (Sports Shockers! Ser.). (ENG.). 32p. (gr. 3-4). lib. bdg. 27.99 **(978-1-5157-8046-5(5))** Capstone Press of Coughlan Cos.
Braun, Marta. Muybridge & the Riddle of Locomotion. 2013. (ENG., Illus.). 24p. (J). (gr. 4-12). 19.95 (978-1-77085-229-7(8), 9781770852297) Firefly Bks., Ltd.
Brennan, Kristine. Danica Patrick. 2010. (Role Model Athletes Ser.). (Illus.). 64p. (YA). (gr. 7-12). 22.95 (978-1-4222-0487-0(1)) Mason Crest.
—Indian Americans. (Successful Americans Ser.). 64p. (YA). 2009. (gr. 9-12). 22.95 (978-1-4222-0521-1(5)) 2007. (gr. 7-18). pap. 9.95 (978-1-4222-0862-5(1)) Mason Crest.
Brickweg, Jason. Christian. 2013. (Pro Wrestling Champions Ser.). (ENG., Illus.). 24p. (J). (gr. 3-7). lib. bdg. 25.95 (978-1-60014-903-0(0), Torque Bks.) Bellwether Media.
—Zack Ryder. 2013. (Pro Wrestling Champions Ser.). (ENG., Illus.). 24p. (J). (gr. 3-7). lib. bdg. 25.95 (978-1-60014-905-4(7), Torque Bks.) Bellwether Media.
Briggs, John. Pete Seeger the People's Singer. 2015. (ENG., Illus.). 112p. (J). pap. 6.99 (978-0-9905160-7-1(5)) Atombank Bks.
Brill, Marlene Targ. Michelle Obama. 2009. (Illus.). 48p. (J). pap. 8.95 (978-0-7613-5053-8(5)) Lerner Publishing Group.
—Michelle Obama: From Chicago's South Side to the White House. 2009. (Gateway Biographies Ser.). (ENG., Illus.). 48p. (gr. 4-8). 26.60 (978-0-7613-5033-0(0)) Lerner Publishing Group.
Brinster, Dick. Jeff Gordon. rev. ed. 2007. (Race Car Legends Ser.). (Illus.). 80p. (YA). (gr. 5-9). lib. bdg. 25.00 (978-0-7910-8760-2(3)) Facts On File, Inc.
Britton, Felicity. The Glee Cast: Inspiring Gleek Mania. 2012. (USA TODAY Lifeline Biographies Ser.). (ENG., Illus.). 112p. (gr. 6-12). lib. bdg. 34.60 (978-0-7613-8639-1(4)) Lerner Publishing Group.
Brooks, Aaron & Brown, Greg. Aaron Brooks: Rise Above. 2004. (Illus.). 48p. (J). 15.95 (978-0-9634650-9-2(0)) Positively for Kids, Inc.
Brown, Risa. Day by Day with Carrie Underwood. 2014. (ENG., Illus.). 32p. (J). (gr. -1-2). 25.70 (978-1-61228-631-0(3)) Mitchell Lane Pubs., Inc.
Brown, Terrell. Reverend Run (Run-D. M. C.) 2008. (Hip-Hop Ser.). (Illus.). 64p. (YA). (gr. 7-12). lib. bdg. 22.95 (978-1-4222-0127-5(9)) Mason Crest.
Bruccoli, Matthew J., et al. Student's Encyclopedia of American Literary Characters, 4 vols., Set. 2008. (Library of American Literature Ser.). 1600p. (C). (gr. 9-18). 340.00 (978-0-8160-6498-4(9)) Facts On File, Inc.
Bryant, Jennifer. A River of Words: The Story of William Carlos Williams. Sweet, Melissa, illus. 2008. (ENG.). 34p. (J). (gr. 4-7). 17.50 (978-0-8028-5302-8(1), Eerdmans Bks For Young Readers) Eerdmans, William B. Publishing Co.
Buckley, James. Who Were the Wright Brothers? 2014. (Who Was... ? Ser.). lib. bdg. 16.00 (978-0-606-35692-3(4)) Turtleback Bks.
Burgan, Michael. James Buchanan. 2010. (Presidents & Their Times 4 Ser.). 96p. (gr. 6). 34.21 (978-0-7614-4810-5(1)) Marshall Cavendish Corp.
—John F. Kennedy, 1 vol. HL Studios Staff, illus. 2013. (ENG.). 56p. (gr. 4-8). 33.32 (978-1-4329-8096-2(3)); pap. 10.95 (978-1-4329-8097-9(1)) Heinemann-Raintree. (NA-h).
Burlingame, Jeff. Jennifer! Film Star Jennifer Lawrence. 2013. (Sizzling Celebrities Ser.). 48p. (J). (gr. 4-9). pap. 8.95 (978-1-4644-0279-1(5)) Enslow Pubs., Inc.
—Jesse Owens: I Always Loved Running. 2011. (African-American Biography Library). (Illus.). 128p. (J). (gr. 7-12). lib. bdg. 33.27 (978-0-7660-3497-6(6)) Enslow Pubs., Inc.
—Malcolm X: "I Believe in the Brotherhood of Man, All Men" 2010. (American Rebels Ser.). 160p. (YA). (gr. 7-12). 35.94 (978-0-7660-3384-9(8)) Enslow Pubs., Inc.
—Taylor Swift: Music Superstar. 2011. (Hot Celebrity Biographies Ser.). (Illus.). 48p. (J). (gr. 5-9). lib. bdg. 25.27 (978-0-7660-3870-7(X)) Enslow Pubs., Inc.
Burns, Kylie. Carrie Underwood. 2013. (ENG., Illus.). 32p. (J). (978-0-7787-0024-1(0)); pap. (978-0-7787-0043-2(7)) Crabtree Publishing Co.
Business Leaders Set, vols. 13, vol. 13. Incl. Faces Behind Beauty. Langley, Wanda. (Illus.). 160p. lib. bdg. 28.95 (978-1-59935-097-4(1)); Michael Dell. Friedman, Lauri S. 128p. lib. bdg. 28.95 (978-1-59935-083-7(1)); Oprah Winfrey. Hasday, Judy L. (Illus.). 128p. lib. bdg. 28.95 (978-1-59935-096-7(3)); Ralph Lauren. Weatherly, Myra. 112p. lib. bdg. 28.95 (978-1-59935-084-4(X)); Russell Simmons. Baughan, Brain. 112p. lib. bdg. 28.95 (978-1-59935-075-2(0)); Steve Jobs. Corrigan, Jim. 128p. lib. bdg. 27.95 (978-1-59935-076-9(9)); Warren Buffett. Johnson, Anne Janette. 128p. lib. bdg. 28.95 (978-1-59935-080-6(7)); (YA). (gr. 7-12). 2008. 2008. Set lib. bdg. 376.35 (978-1-59935-094-3(7)) Reynolds, Morgan Inc.
Butts, Ellen R. & Schwartz, Joyce R. Carl Sagan. 2005. (Biography Ser.). (Illus.). 112p. (gr. 6-12). lib. bdg. 27.93 (978-0-8225-4986-4(7)) Lerner Publishing Group.
Callery, Sean. Victor Wouk: The Father of the Hybrid Car. 2009. (Voices for Green Choices Ser.). (ENG., Illus.). 48p. (J). (gr. 5-9). pap. (978-0-7787-4677-5(1)); lib. bdg. (978-0-7787-4664-5(X)) Crabtree Publishing Co.
Campbell, Marie L., illus. A Pocketful of Passage. 2007. (Great Lakes Books Ser.). (ENG.). 96p. (J). (gr. 3-7). per. 12.95 (978-0-8143-3341-9(9), 2078) Wayne State Univ. Pr.
Caravantes, Peggy. Writing Is My Business: The Story of O. Henry. 2006. (World Writers Ser.). (Illus.). 160p. (J). (gr. 3-7). lib. bdg. 27.95 (978-1-59935-031-8(9)) Reynolds, Morgan Inc.
Carlson-Berne, Emma. Snoop Dogg. 2008. (Hip-Hop Ser.). (Illus.). 64p. (YA). (gr. 7-12). lib. bdg. 22.95 (978-1-4222-0129-9(5)) Mason Crest.
Carlson, Cheryl. Dr. Seuss [Scholastic]. 2011. (First Biographies - Writers, Artists, & Athletes Ser.). 24p. pap. 0.50 (978-1-4296-6317-5(0), Pebble Bks.) Capstone Press of Coughlan Cos.
Carole Marsh. Patriotic Biographies. 2004. (Patriotic Favorites Ser.). lib. bdg. 29.95 (978-0-635-02225-7(7)); 32p. (gr. 3-8). pap. 7.95 (978-0-635-02224-0(9)) Gallopade International.
Carson, Mary Kay. Who Invented Home Video Games? — Ralph Baer. 2012. (I Like Inventors! Ser.). 24p. (J). (gr. k-3). 22.60 (978-0-7660-3975-9(7), Enslow Elementary) Enslow Pubs., Inc.
—Who Invented Television? — Philo Farnsworth. 2012. (I Like Inventors! Ser.). 24p. (J). (gr. k-3). 22.60 (978-0-7660-3974-2(9), Enslow Elementary) Enslow Pubs., Inc.

T
U
V

Casanova, Karen. Danica Patrick. 2010. (USA TODAY Lifeline Biographies Ser.). (ENG.). 112p. (gr. 6-12). lib. bdg. 34.60 (978-0-7613-5222-8(8)) Lerner Publishing Group.

Casapulla, Louise. Ashlee Simpson. 2005. (Pop People Ser.). (Illus.). 137p. (J). (978-0-439-76581-7(1)) Scholastic, Inc.

Casil, Amy Sterling. Tony Hawk: Skateboard Mogul. 2009. (Super Skateboarding Ser.). (Illus.). 48p. (J). (gr. 5-8). pap. 11.75 (978-1-4358-5391-1(1)); (YA). (gr. 4-7). lib. bdg. 29.25 (978-1-4358-5047-7(5)) Rosen Publishing Group, Inc., The.

Cefrey, Holly. From Slave to Cowboy: The Nat Love Story. 2009. (Great Moments in American History Ser.). 32p. (gr. 3-3). 47.90 (978-1-61513-142-6(6)) Rosen Publishing Group, Inc., The.

—The Inventions of Alexander Graham Bell: The Telephone. 2009. (19th Century American Inventors Ser.). 24p. (gr. 2-3). 42.50 (978-1-60854-949-8(6), PowerKids Pr.) Rosen Publishing Group, Inc., The.

—The Inventions of Eli Whitney: The Cotton Gin. 2009. (19th Century American Inventors Ser.). 24p. (gr. 2-3). 42.50 (978-1-60854-951-1(8), PowerKids Pr.) Rosen Publishing Group, Inc., The.

—The Inventions of Granville Woods: The Railroad Telegraph System & the Third Rail. 2009. (19th Century American Inventors Ser.). 24p. (gr. 2-3). 42.50 (978-1-60854-952-8(6), PowerKids Pr.) Rosen Publishing Group, Inc., The.

—The Inventions of Thomas Alva Edison: Father of the Light Bulb & the Motion Picture Camera. 2009. (19th Century American Inventors Ser.). 24p. (gr. 2-3). 42.50 (978-1-60854-954-2(2), PowerKids Pr.) Rosen Publishing Group, Inc., The.

Charlesworth, Eric. Easy Reader Biographies: Cesar Chavez: A Leader for Change. 2007. (ENG.). 16p. pap. 2.99 (978-0-439-77416-1(0), Teaching Resources) Scholastic, Inc.

Chatlien, Michael. Donovan McNabb. (Superstars of Pro Football Ser.). (Illus.). 64p. (YA). 2009. (gr. 7-12). lib. bdg. 22.95 (978-1-4222-0559-4(2)) 2007. (gr. 5-18). pap. 9.95 (978-1-4222-0829-8(X)) Mason Crest.

Ching, Jacqueline & Dorling Kindersley Publishing Staff. Thomas Jefferson. 2009. (DK Biography Ser.). (ENG.). 128p. (J). (gr. 5-12). 6.99 (978-0-7566-4506-9(9), DK Children) Dorling Kindersley Publishing, Inc.

Christopher, Matt. Dale Earnhardt Sr: Matt Christopher Legends in Sports. 2007. (ENG., Illus.). 128p. (J). (gr. 3-7). per. 15.99 (978-0-316-01114-3(2)) Little, Brown Bks. for Young Readers.

—On the Court with... Dwight Howard. 2010. (ENG., Illus.). 144p. (J). (gr. 3-7). pap. 5.99 (978-0-316-08480-2(8)) Little, Brown Bks. for Young Readers.

—On the Court with... Lebron James. 2008. (ENG., Illus.). 176p. (J). (gr. 3-7). pap. 6.99 (978-0-316-01630-8(6)) Little, Brown Bks. for Young Readers.

—On the Field With... Peyton & Eli Manning. 2008. (ENG.). 144p. (J). (gr. 3-7). pap. 5.99 (978-0-316-03696-2(X)) Little, Brown Bks. for Young Readers.

Clark, Travis. Alex Rodriguez. 2010. (Role Model Athletes Ser.). (Illus.). 64p. (YA). (gr. 7-12). 22.95 (978-1-4222-0488-7(X)) Mason Crest.

—Portland Trail Blazers, 1 vol. 2011. (Inside the NBA Ser.). (ENG., Illus.). 48p. (YA). (gr. 3-6). lib. bdg. 32.79 (978-1-61783-173-7(5)) ABDO Publishing Co.

Cline-Ransome, Lesa. Benny Goodman & Teddy Wilson: Taking the Stage As the First Black-and-White Jazz Band in History. Ransome, James E., illus. 2014. (ENG.). 32p. (J). (gr. 3-7). 16.95 (978-0-8234-2362-0(X)) Holiday Hse., Inc.

Coleman, Wim & Perrin, Pat. What Made the Wild West Wild. 2006. (Wild History of the American West Ser.). (Illus.). 128p. (J). (gr. 4-7). lib. bdg. 34.60 (978-1-59845-016-3(6), MyReportLinks.com Bks.) Enslow Pubs., Inc.

Collard, Sneed B., III. David Crockett: Fearless Frontiersman. 2006. (American Heroes Ser.). (Illus.). 40p. (J). (gr. 3-7). lib. bdg. 28.50 (978-0-7614-2160-3(2), Benchmark Bks.) Marshall Cavendish Corp.

Collins, Terry. Elvis: A Graphic Novel, 1 vol. Melcher, Michele, illus. (American Graphic Ser.). (ENG.). 32p. (gr. 3-4). 2011. pap. 8.10 (978-1-4296-6266-6(2)) 2011. pap. 47.70 (978-1-4296-6434-9(7)) 2010. lib. bdg. 30.65 (978-1-4296-5476-0(7)) Capstone Press of Coughlan Cos. (Graphic Library).

Collins, Terry, et al. American Graphic. Hayden, Seitu & Kinsella, Pat, illus. 2012. (American Graphic Ser.). (ENG.). 32p. (gr. 3-4). lib. bdg. 61.30 (978-1-4296-9162-8(X), Graphic Library) Capstone Press of Coughlan Cos.

Colonial Leaders. 2005. (Colonial Leaders Ser.). 80p. (gr. 5-8). 275.00 (978-0-7910-6279-1(1), Chelsea Hse.) Facts On File, Inc.

Conklin, Wendy. Robert E. Lee, 1 vol. 2005. (Primary Source Readers Ser.). (ENG.). 24p. (J). (gr. 4-4). pap. 8.99 (978-0-7439-8918-3(X)) Shell Educational Publishing.

Contro, Arturo. Landon Donovan. Benson, Megan, tr. 2008. (World Soccer Stars / Estrellas Del Fútbol Mundial Ser.). (SPA., Illus.). 24p. (J). (gr. 2-5). lib. bdg. 22.60 (978-1-4042-7666-6(1)) Rosen Publishing Group, Inc., The.

Cooper, Meghan. The Women's Suffrage Movement. 2017. (J). (978-1-5026-2711-7(6)) Cavendish Square Publishing.

Corbett, Sue. Jeff Kinney. 2013. 48p. (J). (gr. 5-8). 29.93 (978-1-60870-932-8(9)) Cavendish Square Publishing.

Corrick, James A. Dwayne "The Rock" Johnson. 2012. (Role Model Entertainers Ser.). 64p. (J). (gr. 7). 22.95 (978-1-4222-2716-9(2)) Mason Crest.

Corrigan, Jim. John Marshall: The Story of John Marshall. 2011. (Supreme Court Justices Ser.). (Illus.). 112p. (J). 28.95 (978-1-59935-159-9(5)) Reynolds, Morgan Inc.

Corwin, Jeff. A Wild Life: The Authorized Biography. 2009. (Jeff Corwin Ser.). (ENG.). 112p. (J). (gr. 3-7). 6.99 (978-0-14-241403-3(4), Puffin Books) Penguin Young Readers Group.

Cotts, Nat. Daddy Yankee. 2009. (Hip-Hop 2 Ser.). (Illus.). 64p. (YA). (gr. 7-12). lib. bdg. 22.95 (978-1-4222-0288-3(7)) Mason Crest.

—Don Omar. 2009. (Hip-Hop 2 Ser.). (Illus.). 64p. (YA). (gr. 7-12). lib. bdg. 22.95 (978-1-4222-0290-6(9)) Mason Crest.

—Pitbull. 2009. (Hip-Hop 2 Ser.). (Illus.). 64p. (YA). (gr. 7-12). lib. bdg. 22.95 (978-1-4222-0302-6(6)) Mason Crest.

—Young Jeezy. 2009. (Hip-Hop 2 Ser.). (Illus.). 64p. (YA). (gr. 7-12). lib. bdg. 22.95 (978-1-4222-0306-4(9)) Mason Crest.

Crain, Cynthia D. & Lee, Dwight R. Milton Friedman. 2009. (Profiles in Economics Ser.). (Illus.). 144p. (YA). lib. bdg. 28.95 (978-1-59935-108-7(0)) Reynolds, Morgan Inc.

Crawford, Laura. Benjamin Franklin from A to Z, 1 vol. Hierstein, Judith, illus. 2013. (ENG.). 32p. (J). (gr. k-3). 16.99 (978-1-4556-1713-5(X)) Pelican Publishing Co., Inc.

Crayton, Lisa A. Collective Biographies of Slave Resistance Heroes. 2016. (Slavery & Slave Resistance Ser.). 128p. (J). (gr. 6). 37.27 (978-0-7660-7555-9(9)) Enslow Pubs., Inc.

Crewe, Sabrina & Anderson, Dale. The Seneca Falls Women's Rights Convention. 2004. (Events That Shaped America Ser.). (Illus.). 32p. (J). (gr. 3-6). lib. bdg. 26.00 (978-0-8368-3408-6(9), Gareth Stevens Learning Library) Stevens, Gareth Publishing LLLP.

Crompton, Samuel Willard. John Elway. 2008. (Football Superstars Ser.). (Illus.). 152p. (J). (gr. 7-12). lib. bdg. 30.00 (978-0-7910-9604-8(1)) Facts On File, Inc.

—Thomas Paine & the Fight for Liberty. 2005. (Leaders of the American Revolution Ser.). (Illus.). 100p. (J). (gr. 5-8). lib. bdg. 30.00 (978-0-7910-8625-4(9)) Facts On File, Inc.

Crum, Anna-Maria. Trackers of Dynamic Earth & Rastreadores de nuestra dinámica Tierra: 6 English, 6 Spanish Adaptations. 2011. (ENG & SPA.). (J). 97.00 net. (978-1-4108-5718-7(2)) Benchmark Education Co.

Cuesta, Vivian. It Can Be Done: The Life & Legacy of César Chávez. 2003. (ENG., Illus.). 32p. (J). (gr. 6-8). pap. 8.47 net. (978-0-7652-3271-7(5), Celebration Pr.) Pearson Schl.

Dakers, Diane. Calvin Klein: Fashion Design Superstar. 2010. (Crabtree Groundbreaker Biographies Ser.). (ENG., Illus.). 112p. (J). (gr. 5-8). lib. bdg. (978-0-7787-2534-3(0)) Crabtree Publishing Co.

Daniel Fernandez Memorial Center Projec. Man of Honor: The Story of Daniel Fernandez. 2009. 32p. pap. 15.49 (978-1-4389-8338-7(7)) AuthorHouse.

Dann, Sarah. Beyonce. 2013. (ENG., Illus.). 32p. (J). pap. (978-0-7787-0039-5(9)) Crabtree Publishing Co.

—Lindsey Vonn. 2013. (ENG., Illus.). 32p. (J). (978-0-7787-0025-8(9)); pap. (978-0-7787-0067-8(4)) Crabtree Publishing Co.

Darraj, Susan Muaddi. Amy Tan. 2007. (Asian Americans of Achievement Ser.). 112p. (YA). (gr. 7-12). lib. bdg. 35.00 (978-0-7910-9269-9(0)) Facts On File, Inc.

De Capua, Sarah. Andrew Carnegie. 2007. (21st Century Skills Library: Life Skills Biographies Ser.). (ENG., Illus.). 48p. (gr. 4-8). lib. bdg. 31.36 (978-1-60279-067-4(1), 200038) Cherry Lake Publishing.

De Medeiros, James. Justin Timberlake. 2008. (Remarkable People Ser.). (Illus.). 24p. (J). (gr. 4-6). pap. 8.95 (978-1-59036-983-8(1)); lib. bdg. 24.45 (978-1-59036-982-1(3)) Weigl Pubs., Inc.

De Mille, Agnes. Dance to the Piper. 2015. (ENG., Illus.). 368p. pap. 17.95 (978-1-59017-908-6(0), NYRB Classics) New York Review of Bks., Inc., The.

DeCarolis, Lisa. Alexander Hamilton: Federalist & Founding Father. 2009. (Library of American Lives & Times Ser.). 112p. (gr. 5-5). 69.20 (978-1-60853-470-8(7)) Rosen Publishing Group, Inc., The.

DeGraw, Aleine. Alexander Hamilton: American Statesman. 2009. (Primary Sources of Famous People in American History Ser.). 32p. (gr. 2-3). 47.90 (978-1-60851-646-9(6)) Rosen Publishing Group, Inc., The.

—Alexander Hamilton: American Statesman / Estadista Estadounidense. 2009. (Famous People in American History/Grandes personajes en la historia de los Estados Unidos Ser.). (SPA.). 32p. (gr. 2-3). 47.90 (978-1-61512-536-4(1), Editorial Buenas Letras) Rosen Publishing Group, Inc., The.

—Alexander Hamilton: Estadista estadounidense (Alexander Hamilton: American Statesman) 2009. (Grandes personajes en la historia de los Estados Unidos (Famous People in American History) Ser.). 32p. (gr. 2-3). 47.90 (978-1-61512-788-7(7), Editorial Buenas Letras) Rosen Publishing Group, Inc., The.

Denenberg, Dennis & Roscoe, Lorraine. 50 American Heroes Every Kid Should Meet. rev. ed. 2005. (ENG., Illus.). 128p. (gr. 6-12). per. 14.95 (978-0-7613-9548-5(2), First Avenue Editions) Lerner Publishing Group.

—50 American Heroes Every Kid Should Meet (2nd Revised Edition) 2016. (ENG., Illus.). 120p. (J). (gr. 6-12). 53.32 (978-1-5124-1329-8(1), Millbrook Pr.) Lerner Publishing Group.

dePaola, Tomie. I'm Still Scared. 2007. (26 Fairmount Avenue Bks.). (Illus.). 83p. (gr. 2-5). 17.00 (978-0-7569-8150-1(6)) Perfection Learning Corp.

—Things Will Never Be the Same. dePaola, Tomie, illus. 2004. (26 Fairmount Avenue Bks.). (Illus.). 69p. (J). (gr. 3-7). 13.65 (978-0-7569-2951-0(2)) Perfection Learning Corp.

—What a Year: A 26 Fairmount Avenue Book, Vol. 4. 2004. (26 Fairmount Avenue Ser.). 75p. (J). (gr. 2-5). pap. 17.00 incl. audio (978-0-8072-0657-7(1), Listening Library) Random Hse. Audio Publishing Group.

Deprince, Michaela & DePrince, Elaine. Ballerina Dreams: From Orphan to Dancer. Morrison, Frank, illus. 2014. (Step into Reading Ser.). (ENG.). 48p. (J). (gr. 2-4). 3.99 (978-0-385-75515-3(5), Random Hse. Bks. for Young Readers) Random Hse. Children's Bks.

—Taking Flight: From War Orphan to Star Ballerina. 2014. (ENG.). 256p. (YA). (gr. 7). 16.99 (978-0-385-75511-5(2)); lib. bdg. 19.99 (978-0-385-75512-2(0)) Random Hse. Children's Bks. (Knopf Bks. for Young Readers).

Deutsch, Stacia & Cohon, Rhody. Carlos Mencia. 2009. (Sharing the American Dream Ser.). 64p. (YA). (gr. 7-12). 22.95 (978-1-4222-0578-5(9)) Mason Crest.

—Hot Pursuit: Murder in Mississippi. Orback, Craig, illus. 2010. (ENG.). 40p. (J). (gr. 3-5). pap. 7.95 (978-0-7613-3956-4(6)); lib. bdg. 17.95 (978-0-7613-3955-7(8)) Lerner Publishing Group. (Kar-Ben Publishing).

—Jermaine Dupri. (Sharing the American Dream Ser.). 64p. (YA). (gr. 7-12). 2009. 22.95 (978-1-4222-0581-5(9)) 2007. pap. 9.95 (978-1-4222-0744-4(7)) Mason Crest.

—Samuel L. Jackson. 2009. (Sharing the American Dream Ser.). (Illus.). 64p. (YA). (gr. 7-12). 22.95 (978-1-4222-0580-8(0)) Mason Crest.

DiConsiglio, John. Young Americans: Tales of Teenage Immigrants. 2005. (Illus.). 43p. (978-0-439-12405-8(0)) Scholastic, Inc.

DiPrimio, Pete. Drew Brees. 2010. (Blue Banner Biography Ser.). (Illus.). 32p. (YA). (gr. 4-7). lib. bdg. 25.70 (978-1-58415-911-7(1)) Mitchell Lane Pubs., Inc.

—Dwyane Wade. 2011. (Robbie Reader Ser.). 32p. (J). (gr. 2-5). lib. bdg. 25.70 (978-1-61228-063-9(3)) Mitchell Lane Pubs., Inc.

—Tom Brady. 2008. (Robbie Reader Ser.). (Illus.). 32p. (YA). (gr. 2-5). lib. bdg. 25.70 (978-1-58415-718-2(6)) Mitchell Lane Pubs., Inc.

Ditchfield, Christin. Condoleezza Rice: America's Leading Stateswoman. 2006. (Great Life Stories Ser.). (ENG., Illus.). 112p. (J). (gr. 6-8). lib. bdg. 30.50 (978-0-531-13874-8(7), Watts, Franklin) Scholastic Library Publishing.

Diver, Lucas. Zendaya: Disney Channel Actress, 1 vol. 2014. (Pop Bios Ser.). (ENG.). 24p. (J). (gr. 2-4). lib. bdg. 28.50 (978-1-62970-729-7(5)) ABDO Publishing Co.

Dixon-Engel, Tara & Jackson, Mike. Neil Armstrong: One Giant Leap for Mankind. 2008. (Sterling Biographies(r) Ser.). (ENG., Illus.). 128p. (J). (gr. 5). pap. 5.95 (978-1-4027-4496-9(X)) Sterling Publishing Co., Inc.

Doak, Robin S. Barack Obama. 2013. (True Book(tm), A — Biographies Ser.). (ENG., Illus.). 48p. (J). lib. bdg. 31.00 (978-0-531-21904-1(6)); pap. 6.95 (978-0-531-23875-2(X)) Scholastic Library Publishing.

Doeden, Matt. Lance Armstrong. 2006. (Sports Heroes & Legends Ser.). (ENG., Illus.). 120p. (gr. 5-12). lib. bdg. 30.60 (978-0-8225-5959-7(5)) Lerner Publishing Group.

—Miguel Cabrera: Baseball Superstar, 1 vol. 2014. (Superstar Athletes Ser.). (ENG.). 24p. (gr. 1-2). pap. 7.29 (978-1-4765-9431-6(7)); lib. bdg. 25.32 (978-1-4765-8602-1(0)) Capstone Press of Coughlan Cos.

—Peyton Manning. 2008. (Sports Heroes & Legends Ser.). (YA). (gr. 7-12). lib. bdg. 30.60 (978-0-8225-9041-5(7)) Twenty First Century Bks.

—Phil Kessel. 2015. (Hockey Superstars Ser.). (ENG., Illus.). 32p. (gr. 3-9). pap. 7.95 (978-1-4914-9022-8(5)); lib. bdg. 27.99 (978-1-4296-8278-7(7)) Capstone Press of Coughlan Cos.

—Shaun White. (Amazing Athletes Ser.). 32p. (gr. 2-5). 2006. (Illus.). (J). pap. 6.95 (978-0-8225-6841-4(1), First Avenue Editions) 2006. (Illus.). (J). lib. bdg. 23.93 (978-0-8225-6840-7(3), Lerner Pubns.) 2010. (ENG.). lib. bdg. 25.26 (978-0-7613-6859-5(0), Lerner Pubns.) Lerner Publishing Group.

—Will Smith. 2007. (Just the Facts Biographies Ser.). (ENG., Illus.). 112p. (gr. 5-12). lib. bdg. 27.93 (978-0-8225-6608-3(7), Lerner Pubns.) Lerner Publishing Group.

Doeden, Matt & Savage, Jeff. Eli Manning. 2009. (Sports Heroes & Legends Ser.). (ENG.). (gr. 5-12). pap. 56.72 (978-0-7613-4808-5(5)) Lerner Publishing Group.

Doeden, Matt & Stewart, Mark. Peyton Manning. 2009. (Sports Heroes & Legends Ser.). (ENG.). (gr. 5-12). pap. 56.72 (978-0-7613-4809-2(3)) Lerner Publishing Group.

Domblewski, Carol. Citizens Who Made a Difference: Text Pairs. 2008. (Bridges/Navigators Ser.). (J). (gr. 3). 81.00 (978-1-4108-8354-4(X)) Benchmark Education Co.

Donovan, Sandy. Derek Jeter. rev. ed. 2011. (Amazing Athletes Ser.). (ENG., Illus.). 32p. (gr. 2-5). lib. bdg. 25.26 (978-0-7613-7065-9(X)) Lerner Publishing Group.

Dorling Kindersley Publishing Staff. DK Readers L3: Real-Life Heroes. 2017. (DK Readers Ser.). (ENG.). 64p. (J). (gr. 2-4). 14.99 **(978-1-4654-6243-5(0))**; pap. 3.99 **(978-1-4654-6244-2(9))** Dorling Kindersley Publishing, Inc. (DK Children).

Dougherty, Terri. Ben Stiller. 2007. (People in the News Ser.). (ENG., Illus.). 128p. (J). (gr. 7-10). lib. bdg. 39.40 (978-1-59018-723-4(7), LML02109-221297) Cengage Gale.

—Tobey Maguire. 2010. (Modern Role Models Ser.). (Illus.). 64p. (YA). (gr. 7-12). 22.95 (978-1-4222-0505-1(3)) Mason Crest.

Down, Susan. Theodore Weld: Architect of Abolitionism. 2013. (ENG., Illus.). 64p. (J). (978-0-7787-1062-2(9)); pap. (978-0-7787-1065-3(3)) Crabtree Publishing Co.

Doyle, Bill H. Behind Enemy Lines. 2009. 135p. (J). pap. (978-0-545-14705-7(0)) Scholastic, Inc.

Dunn, Joe. The Wright Brothers, 1 vol. Dunn, Ben, illus. 2007. (Bio-Graphics Ser.). (ENG.). 32p. (gr. 3-6). 28.50 (978-1-60270-071-0(0), Graphic Planet- Nonfiction) ABDO Publishing Co.

Dunn, Joeming. Thomas Jefferson, 1 vol. Espinosa, Rod, illus. 2008. (Bio-Graphics Ser.). (ENG.). 32p. 28.50 (978-1-60270-174-8(1), Graphic Planet- Nonfiction) ABDO Publishing Co.

Dunn, Joeming W. Amelia Earhart, 1 vol. Dunn, Ben, illus. 2008. (Bio-Graphics Ser.). (ENG.). 32p. (gr. 3-5). 28.50 (978-1-60270-173-1(3), Graphic Planet- Nonfiction) ABDO Publishing Co.

—Booker T. Washington, 1 vol. Allen, Chris, illus. 2008. (Bio-Graphics Ser.). (ENG.). 32p. 28.50 (978-1-60270-177-9(6), Graphic Planet- Nonfiction) ABDO Publishing Co.

Dykstra, Danell. The Man Who Invented the Ferris Wheel: The Genius of George Ferris. 2013. (Genius Inventors & Their Great Ideas Ser.). (Illus.). 48p. (J). (gr. 3-18). 25.27 (978-0-7660-4136-3(0)) Enslow Pubs., Inc.

Earl, Sari. George Washington: Revolutionary Leader & Founding Father, 1 vol. 2010. (Military Heroes Ser.). (ENG.). 112p. (J). (gr. 6-12). lib. bdg. 35.64 (978-1-60453-967-7(4)) ABDO Publishing Co.

Edge, Laura B. Hilary Duff: Celebrity with Heart. 2010. (Celebrities with Heart Ser.). (Illus.). 128p. (J). pap. 10.95 (978-1-59845-205-1(3)) Enslow Pubs., Inc.

Edgers, Geoff. Who Is Stan Lee? 2014. (Who Is... ? Ser.). lib. bdg. 16.00 (978-0-606-36175-0(8)) Turtleback Bks.

Edwards, Ethan. All-Star Players, 6 bks., Set 2. Incl. Meet Albert Pujols: Baseball's Power Hitter. (YA). lib. bdg. 25.25 (978-1-4042-4487-0(5)); Meet Derek Jeter: Captain of the New York Yankees. (YA). lib. bdg. 25.25 (978-1-4042-4488-7(3)); Meet Kevin Garnett: Basketball's Big Ticket. (YA). lib. bdg. 25.25 (978-1-4042-4490-0(5)); Meet LaDainian Tomlinson: Football's Fastest Running Back. (YA). lib. bdg. 25.25 (978-1-4042-4491-7(3)); Meet Steve Nash: Basketball's Ultimate Team Player. (J). lib. bdg. 23.95 (978-1-4042-4489-4(1), PowerKids Pr.); Meet Tom Brady: Football's Famous Quarterback. (YA). lib. bdg. 25.25 (978-1-4042-4492-4(1)); (Illus.). 32p. (gr. 4-7). 2009. 2008. Set lib. bdg. 143.70 (978-1-4358-2564-2(0), PowerKids Pr.) Rosen Publishing Group, Inc., The.

Edwards, Karen. Christopher Reeve: A Real-Life Superhero. 2005. (Illus.). 32p. (J). (978-0-669-51411-7(X)) Great Source Education Group, Inc.

Egan, Jill. Hillary Rodham Clinton. 2009. (People We Should Know Ser.). (ENG., Illus.). 48p. (J). (gr. 3-5). pap. 10.50 (978-1-4339-2193-3(6)); lib. bdg. 31.00 (978-1-4339-2188-9(X)) Stevens, Gareth Publishing LLLP. (Gareth Stevens Learning Library).

Eggleston, Edward. Stories of Great Americans for Little Americans. 2008. 124p. 21.99 (978-0-554-39573-9(8)) 2007. 120p. per. 18.99 (978-1-4346-9703-5(7)) 2007. (ENG.). 122p. per. 19.99 (978-1-4346-9704-2(5)) Creative Media Partners, LLC.

—Stories of Great Americans for Little Americans. 2007. 120p. per. (978-1-4065-1784-2(4)) Dodo Pr.

—Stories of Great Americans for Little Americans. 2010. 162p. pap. 14.95 (978-1-60444-104-8(6)) IndoEuropeanPublishing.com.

—Stories of Great Americans for Little Americans. 2004. reprint ed. pap. 1.99 (978-1-4192-4958-7(4)); pap. 15.95 (978-1-4191-4958-0(X)) Kessinger Publishing, LLC.

—Stories of Great Americans for Little Americans (Yesterday's Classics) 2007. (ENG.). 172p. (J). per. 9.95 (978-1-59915-084-0(0)) Yesterday's Classics.

El Nabli, Dina. Danica Patrick. 2009. (People We Should Know Ser.). 32p. (J). (gr. 3-5). pap. 10.50 (978-1-4339-0158-4(7)); lib. bdg. 31.00 (978-1-4339-0018-1(1)) Stevens, Gareth Publishing LLLP. (Gareth Stevens Learning Library).

Eldridge, Stephen. Logan! Rising Star Logan Lerman. 2013. (Sizzling Celebrities Ser.). 48p. (J). (gr. 4-9). pap. 8.95 (978-1-4644-0281-4(7)) Enslow Pubs., Inc.

Eli Manning. 2009. (Amazing Athletes Ser.). (gr. 2-5). pap. 6.95 (978-0-7613-4137-6(4), First Avenue Editions) Lerner Publishing Group.

Elliot, Henry. Frederick Douglass: From Slavery to Statesman. 2009. (Voices for Freedom Ser.). (ENG., Illus.). 64p. (J). (gr. 5-8). pap. (978-0-7787-4836-6(7)); lib. bdg. (978-0-7787-4820-5(0)) Crabtree Publishing Co.

—John Muir: Protecting & Preserving the Environment. 2009. (Voices for Green Choices Ser.). (ENG., Illus.). 48p. (J). (gr. 5-9). pap. (978-0-7787-4681-2(X)); lib. bdg. (978-0-7787-4668-3(2)) Crabtree Publishing Co.

Espinosa, Rod. Benjamin Franklin, 1 vol. Espinosa, Rod, illus. 2007. (Bio-Graphics Ser.). (ENG., Illus.). 32p. (gr. 3-6). 28.50 (978-1-60270-066-6(4), Graphic Planet- Nonfiction) ABDO Publishing Co.

Esty, Amos. The Liberator: The Story of William Lloyd Garrison. 2011. (Civil Rights Leaders Ser.). 144p. 28.95 (978-1-59935-137-7(4)) Reynolds, Morgan Inc.

Etingoff, Kim. Jennifer Aniston. 2012. (Illus.). 64p. (J). pap. (978-1-4222-2483-0(X)) Mason Crest.

—Jennifer Aniston: From Friends to Films. 2012. (Extraordinary Success with a High School Diploma or Less Ser.). (Illus.). 64p. (J). (gr. 7-8). 22.95 (978-1-4222-2480-9(5)) Mason Crest.

—T. I. 2009. (Hip-Hop 2 Ser.). (Illus.). 64p. (YA). (gr. 7-12). lib. bdg. 22.95 (978-1-4222-0303-3(4)) Mason Crest.

Fandel, Jennifer & Milgrom, Al. George Eastman & the Kodak Camera, 1 vol. Purcell, Gordon & Milgrom, Al, illus. 2007. (Inventions & Discovery Ser.). (ENG.). 32p. (gr. 3-4). 30.65 (978-0-7368-6848-8(8), Graphic Library) Capstone Press of Coughlan Cos.

Fedorko, Jamie. Charles Barkley. (Sharing the American Dream Ser.). 64p. (YA). (gr. 7-12). 2009. 22.95 (978-1-4222-0576-1(2)) 2007. pap. 9.95 (978-1-4222-0737-6(4)) Mason Crest.

Fein, Eric. High Noon: Wild Bill Hickok & the Code of the Old West. 2009. (Great Moments in American History Ser.). 32p. (gr. 3-3). 47.90 (978-1-61513-145-7(0)) Rosen Publishing Group, Inc., The.

Feinstein, Stephen. Muhammad Ali. 2007. (African-American Heroes Ser.). (Illus.). 24p. (J). (gr. 1-3). lib. bdg. 22.60 (978-0-7660-2763-3(5), Enslow Elementary) Enslow Pubs., Inc.

—Read about Benjamin Franklin. 2006. (I Like Biographies! Ser.). (Illus.). 24p. (J). (gr. 1-3). lib. bdg. 22.60 (978-0-7660-2596-7(9), Enslow Elementary) Enslow Pubs., Inc.

Ferris, Jeri Chase. Noah Webster & His Words. Kirsch, Vincent X., illus. 2015. (ENG.). 32p. (J). (gr. -1-3). 6.99 (978-0-544-58242-2(X), HMH Books For Young Readers) Houghton Mifflin Harcourt Publishing Co.

Fighting the Monster. 2004. (YA). ring bd. 59.95 (978-0-9661256-2-7(2)) Youth Communication - New York Center.

Figley, Marty Rhodes. Prisoner for Liberty. Orback, Craig, illus. 2009. (On My Own History Ser.). (ENG.). 48p. (gr. 2-4). pap. 6.95 (978-0-8225-9022-4(0), First Avenue Editions) Lerner Publishing Group.

Finley, Toiya Kristen. Russell Simmons. 2009. (Sharing the American Dream Ser.). (Illus.). 64p. (YA). (gr. 7-12). 22.95 (978-1-4222-0584-6(3)) Mason Crest.

Fishman, Jon. Jose Altuve. 2017. (Sports All-Stars Ser.). (ENG.). (J). (gr. 2-5). 32p. pap. 8.99 **(978-1-5124-5615-8(2))**; (Illus.). lib. bdg. 26.65 **(978-1-5124-3923-6(1))** Lerner Publishing Group.

—Rob Gronkowski. 2017. (Sports All-Stars Ser.). (ENG.). (J). (gr. 2-5). 32p. pap. 8.99 **(978-1-5124-5619-6(5))**; (Illus.). lib. bdg. 26.65 **(978-1-5124-3924-3(X))** Lerner Publishing Group.

Fishman, Jon M. Miguel Cabrera. 2013. (Amazing Athletes Ser.). (ENG., Illus.). 32p. (gr. 2-5). lib. bdg. 25.26 (978-1-4677-1558-4(1), Lerner Pubns.) Lerner Publishing Group.

—Ronda Rousey. 2016. (Amazing Athletes Ser.). (ENG., Illus.). 32p. (J). (gr. 2-5). 26.65 (978-1-5124-1333-5(X)) Lerner Publishing Group.

Fleischman, Sid. Escape! The Story of the Great Houdini. 2006. (Illus.). (J). (ENG.). 224p. (gr. 3-7). 19.99 (978-0-06-085094-4(9), Greenwillow Bks.); 210p. (gr. 4-8). lib. bdg. 19.89 (978-0-06-085095-1(7)) HarperCollins Pubs.

Fleming, Candace. The Great & Only Barnum: The Tremendous, Stupendous Life of Showman P. T. Barnum. Fenwick, Ray, illus. 2009. (ENG.). 160p. (J). (gr. 3-7). 19.99

(978-0-375-84197-2(0), Schwartz & Wade Bks.) Random Hse. Children's Bks.
Flynn, Brendan. Miguel Cabrera: MVP & Triple Crown Winner. 2015. (Today's MVPs & Champions Ser.). (ENG.). 24p. (J). (gr. 2-5). 27.07 *(978-1-63143-736-6(4)*, 208572) Child's World, Inc., The.
Flynn, Jean. Henry B. Gonzalez: Rebel with a Cause. 2004. (Illus.). 140p. (J). (gr. 3-7). per. 16.95 *(978-1-57168-846-0(3))* Eakin Pr.
Ford, Carin T. Paul Robeson: I Want to Make Freedom Ring. 2007. (African-American Biography Library). (Illus.). 128p. (J). (gr. 3-7). lib. bdg. 33.27 *(978-0-7660-2703-9(1))* Enslow Pubs., Inc.
Fowler, Josh. Indiana Pacers, 1 vol. 2011. (Inside the NBA Ser.). (ENG., Illus.). 48p. (YA). (gr. 3-6). lib. bdg. 32.79 *(978-1-61783-159-1(X))* ABDO Publishing Co.
Franke, Aife. Miranda Lambert. 2010. (Country Music Stars Ser.). (ENG.). 32p. (J). (gr. 3-8). pap. 10.50 *(978-1-4339-3936-5(3))*; lib. bdg. 25.25 *(978-1-4339-3935-8(5))* Stevens, Gareth Publishing LLLP.
Franke, Livia. Kathleen Battle: American Soprano. 2010. (Inspiring Lives Ser.). (Illus.). 32p. (J). (gr. 5-8). pap. 10.50 *(978-1-4339-3635-7(6))*; lib. bdg. 25.25 *(978-1-4339-3634-0(8)*, 1309371) Stevens, Gareth Publishing LLLP.
Franks, Katie. Ashley Tisdale. 2009. (Kid Stars! Ser.). 24p. (gr. 2-3). 42.50 *(978-1-61513-876-0(5)*, PowerKids Pr.) Rosen Publishing Group, Inc., The.
—Drake Bell & Josh Peck. 2009. 24p. (gr. 1-6). pap. 9.40 *(978-1-4042-4534-1(0)*, Rosen Classroom); (gr. 2-3). 42.50 *(978-1-61513-879-1(X)*, PowerKids Pr.) Rosen Publishing Group, Inc., The.
—Kid Stars!, 6 vols., Set. Incl. Ashley Tisdale. lib. bdg. 22.60 *(978-1-4042-4468-9(9)*, 1284716); Drake Bell & Josh Peck. lib. bdg. 22.60 *(978-1-4042-4463-4(8))*; Dylan & Cole Sprouse. lib. bdg. 22.60 *(978-1-4042-4464-1(6))*; Miley Cyrus. lib. bdg. 22.60 *(978-1-4042-4467-2(0))*; Miranda Cosgrove. lib. bdg. 22.60 *(978-1-4042-4466-5(2))*; Zac Efron. lib. bdg. 22.60 *(978-1-4042-4465-8(4))*; (Illus.). 24p. (J). (gr. 1-6). 2009. 2008. Set lib. bdg. 127.50 *(978-1-4358-2550-5(0)*, PowerKids Pr.) Rosen Publishing Group, Inc., The.
—Zac Efron. 2009. (Kid Stars! Ser.). (Illus.). 24p. (J). (gr. 1-6). lib. bdg. 22.60 *(978-1-4042-4465-8(4)*, PowerKids Pr.) Rosen Publishing Group, Inc., The.
Frederick, Shane. John Tavares. 2015. (Hockey Superstars Ser.). (ENG., Illus.). 32p. (gr. 3-9). pap. 7.95 *(978-1-4914-9025-9(X))*; lib. bdg. 27.99 *(978-1-62065-158-2(0))* Capstone Press of Coughlan Cos.
Fredriksen, John C. Chronology of American History, 4 vols., Set. 2008. 2592p. (C). (gr. 9-18). 350.00 *(978-0-8160-6800-5(3))* Facts On File, Inc.
Freese, Susan M. Craigslist: The Company & Its Founder, 1 vol. 2011. (Technology Pioneers Set 1 Ser.). (ENG., Illus.). 112p. (J). (gr. 6-12). lib. bdg. 35.64 *(978-1-61714-806-4(7))* ABDO Publishing Co.
Friesen, Helen Lepp. Uncle Sam with Code. 2012. (AV2 American Icons Ser.). (ENG., Illus.). 24p. (J). (gr. -1-3). pap. 12.95 *(978-1-61913-304-4(0)*, AV2 by Weigl) Weigl Pubs., Inc.
Frisch, Aaron. Jesse James. 2005. (Legends of the West (Creative Education) Ser.). (Illus.). 48p. (J). (gr. 5-9). lib. bdg. 21.95 *(978-1-58341-338-8(3)*, Creative Education) Creative Co., The.
Fry, Erin. Arthur Ashe Against the Odds. 2005. (Voices Reading Ser.). (Illus.). 16p. (J). *(978-0-7367-2915-4(1))* Zaner-Bloser, Inc.
Furgang, Adam. Famous Immigrant Artists. 2017. (J). ***(978-0-7660-9245-7(3))*** Enslow Pubs., Inc.
Gagne, Tammy. Darius Rucker. 2014. (Illus.). 32p. (J). (gr. 1-4). 25.70 *(978-1-61228-639-6(9))* Mitchell Lane Pubs., Inc.
—Day by Day with Calvin Johnson. 2014. (Illus.). 32p. (J). (gr. -1-2). 25.70 *(978-1-61228-633-4(X))* Mitchell Lane Pubs., Inc.
—Day by Day with Elena Delle Donne. 2014. (Illus.). 32p. (J). (gr. -1-2). 25.70 *(978-1-61228-634-1(8))* Mitchell Lane Pubs., Inc.
—Day by Day with Shaun White. 2011. (Day by Day with... Ser.). (Illus.). 32p. (J). (gr. -1-2). lib. bdg. 25.70 *(978-1-58415-986-5(3))* Mitchell Lane Pubs., Inc.
—Derek Hough. 2017. lib. bdg. 25.70 ***(978-1-68020-118-5(2))*** Mitchell Lane Pubs., Inc.
—Hope Solo. 2014. (Illus.). 32p. (J). 25.70 *(978-1-61228-642-6(9))* Mitchell Lane Pubs., Inc.
—Kesha. 2011. (Blue Banner Biography Ser.). (Illus.). 32p. (YA). (gr. 4-7). lib. bdg. 25.70 *(978-1-61228-052-3(8))* Mitchell Lane Pubs., Inc.
—Roy Halladay. 2011. (Robbie Reader Ser.). (Illus.). 32p. (J). (gr. 2-5). lib. bdg. 25.70 *(978-1-61228-061-5(7))* Mitchell Lane Pubs., Inc.
—What It's Like to Be America Ferrara. de la Vega, Eida, tr. from ENG. 2010. (What It's Like to Be/Que se Siente al Ser Ser.). (ENG & SPA., Illus.). 32p. (J). (gr. -1-2). lib. bdg. 25.70 *(978-1-58415-854-7(9))* Mitchell Lane Pubs., Inc.
—What It's Like to Be Oscar de la Hoya. 2012. (Illus.). 32p. (J). lib. bdg. 25.70 *(978-1-61228-322-7(5))* Mitchell Lane Pubs., Inc.
—What Its Like to Be Sonia Sotomayor. de la Vega, Eida, tr. from SPA. 2010. (What It's Like to Be/Que se Siente al Ser Ser.). (ENG & SPA., Illus.). 32p. (J). (gr. -1-2). lib. bdg. 25.70 *(978-1-58415-853-0(0))* Mitchell Lane Pubs., Inc.
Gaines, Alison. Mary Edwards Walker. 2017. (J). ***(978-1-5026-2745-2(0))*** Cavendish Square Publishing.
Gallagher, Jim. Daniel Morgan: Fighting Frontiersman. 2006. (J). pap. *(978-1-59556-020-9(3))*; (Illus.). 88p. (gr. 5-11). lib. bdg. 23.95 *(978-1-59556-015-5(7))* OTTN Publishing.
Garcia, Tracy J. Eli Whitney. 2013. (Jr. Graphic American Inventors Ser.). (ENG., Illus.). 24p. (J). (gr. 3-6). lib. bdg. 25.25 *(978-1-4777-0075-4(7)*, PowerKids Pr.) Rosen Publishing Group, Inc., The.
—Thomas Edison. 2013. (Jr. Graphic American Inventors Ser.). (ENG., Illus.). 24p. (J). (gr. 3-6). pap. 10.60 *(978-1-4777-0137-9(0))*; lib. bdg. 25.25 *(978-1-4777-0076-1(5))* Rosen Publishing Group, Inc., The. (PowerKids Pr.).
Gaskill, Rachel. Agnes Demille. 2005. (Library of American Choreographers Ser.). (Illus.). 48p. (J). (gr. k-3). lib. bdg. 29.25 *(978-1-4042-0444-7(X))* Rosen Publishing Group, Inc., The.
Gaspar, Joe. Dustin Pedroia. 2010. (Reading Power: Baseball's MVPs Ser.). (Illus.). 24p. (J). pap. 8.85 *(978-1-4488-1784-9(6)*, PowerKids Pr.) Rosen Publishing Group, Inc., The.
—Jimmy Rollins. 2010. (Reading Power: Baseball's MVPs Ser.). (Illus.). 24p. (J). pap. 8.85 *(978-1-4488-1786-3(2)*, PowerKids Pr.) Rosen Publishing Group, Inc., The.
—Ryan Howard. 2010. (Baseball's MVPs Ser.). (ENG.). 24p. (J). (gr. 3-6). lib. bdg. 22.60 *(978-1-4488-0632-4(1))* Rosen Publishing Group, Inc., The.
Gateway Biographies: Spring 2012 New Releases. 2012. (Gateway Biographies Ser.). 48p. (gr. 4-8). lib. bdg. 53.20 *(978-0-8225-8564-0(2)*, Lerner Pubns.) Lerner Publishing Group.
Gatto, Kimberly. Kevin Garnett: A Basketball Star Who Cares. 2011. (Sports Stars Who Care Ser.). (Illus.). 48p. (J). (gr. 2-5). lib. bdg. 25.27 *(978-0-7660-3772-4(X))* Enslow Pubs., Inc.
Gazlay, Suzy. David Suzuki: Doing Battle with Climate Change. 2009. (Voices for Green Choices Ser.). (ENG., Illus.). 48p. (J). (gr. 5-9). pap. *(978-0-7787-4678-2(X))*; lib. bdg. *(978-0-7787-4665-2(8))* Crabtree Publishing Co.
Gibson, Karen. Adrian Peterson. 2011. (Robbie Reader Ser.). (Illus.). 32p. (J). (gr. 2-5). lib. bdg. 25.70 *(978-1-61228-060-8(9))* Mitchell Lane Pubs., Inc.
Giff, Patricia Reilly. Dias Sombrios.Tr. of Purple Climbing Days. (SPA.). (J). 3.95 *(978-0-922852-50-5(2))* AIMS International Bks., Inc.
Gigliotti, Jim. Linebackers. 2009. (Game Day: Football Ser.). (ENG.). 48p. (YA). (gr. 5-9). lib. bdg. 31.00 *(978-1-4339-1959-6(1))* Stevens, Gareth Publishing LLLP.
—Linemen. 2009. (Game Day: Football Ser.). (ENG.). 48p. (YA). (gr. 5-9). lib. bdg. 31.00 *(978-1-4339-1960-2(5))* Stevens, Gareth Publishing LLLP.
Gilbert, Sara. Annie Oakley. 2005. (Legends of the West (Creative Education) Ser.). (Illus.). 48p. (J). (gr. 5-9). lib. bdg. 21.95 *(978-1-58341-334-0(0)*, Creative Education) Creative Co., The.
Gilbreth, Frank B., Jr. & Carey, Ernestine Gilbreth. Cheaper by the Dozen. 188p. (YA). (gr. 7-18). reprint ed. lib. bdg. 24.95 *(978-0-88411-289-1(6))* Amereon Ltd.
—Cheaper by the Dozen. 180p. (YA). (gr. 7-18). pap. 5.50 *(978-0-8072-8308-0(8))*; 2004. (J). (gr. 4-7). pap. 38.00 incl. audio *(978-0-8072-8307-3(X)*, YA157SP) Random Hse. Audio Publishing Group. (Listening Library).
Gill, Shelley. Gabe. Scheff, Marc, illus. 2016. (ENG.). 64p. (J). (gr. 3-7). lib. bdg. 12.95 *(978-1-57091-354-9(4))* Charlesbridge Publishing, Inc.
Gillam, Scott. Andrew Carnegie: Industrial Giant & Philanthropist, 1 vol. 2009. (Essential Lives Set 3 Ser.). (ENG., Illus.). 112p. (J). (gr. 6-12). lib. bdg. 35.64 *(978-1-60453-521-1(0))* ABDO Publishing Co.
Gimpel, Lee. Fighting Wars, Planning for Peace: The Story of George C. Marshall. 2005. (World Leaders Ser.). (Illus.). 176p. (J). (gr. 6-12). lib. bdg. 26.95 *(978-1-931798-66-2(4))* Reynolds, Morgan Inc.
Giovanni, Nikki. Lincoln & Douglass: An American Friendship. Collier, Bryan, illus. 2008. (ENG.). 40p. (J). (gr. 2-6). 16.95 *(978-0-8050-8264-7(6)*, 9780805082647, Holt, Henry & Co. Bks. For Young Readers) Holt, Henry & Co.
Gitenstein, Judy. Alvin Ailey. 2009. (Library of American Choreographers Ser.). 48p. (gr. 5-8). 53.00 *(978-1-60853-455-5(3)*, Rosen Reference) Rosen Publishing Group, Inc., The.
Gitlin, Martin. Billie Jean King: Tennis Star & Social Activist, 1 vol. 2011. (Legendary Athletes Ser.). (ENG., Illus.). 112p. (YA). (gr. 7-12). 34.22 *(978-1-61714-757-9(5))* ABDO Publishing Co.
—EBay: The Company & Its Founder, 1 vol. 2011. (Technology Pioneers Set 1 Ser.). (ENG., Illus.). 112p. (J). (gr. 6-12). lib. bdg. 35.64 *(978-1-61714-807-1(5))* ABDO Publishing Co.
—Ed Reed. 2009. (Superstars of Pro Football Ser.). (Illus.). 64p. (YA). (gr. 7-12). lib. bdg. 22.95 *(978-1-4222-0558-7(4))* Mason Crest.
—George S. Patton: World War II General & Military Innovator, 1 vol. 2010. (Military Heroes Ser.). (ENG.). 112p. (J). (gr. 6-12). lib. bdg. 35.64 *(978-1-60453-964-6(X))* ABDO Publishing Co.
—Los Angeles Lakers, 1 vol. 2011. (Inside the NBA Ser.). (ENG., Illus.). 48p. (YA). (gr. 3-6). lib. bdg. 32.79 *(978-1-61783-161-4(1))* ABDO Publishing Co.
—Memphis Grizzlies, 1 vol. 2011. (Inside the NBA Ser.). (ENG., Illus.). 48p. (YA). (gr. 3-6). lib. bdg. 32.79 *(978-1-61783-162-1(X))* ABDO Publishing Co.
—Randy Orton: A Living Legacy, 1 vol. 2012. (Pro Wrestling Stars Ser.). (ENG.). 48p. (gr. 3-4). lib. bdg. 31.99 *(978-1-4296-8675-4(8))* Capstone Press of Coughlan Cos.
—Shaun White: Snow & Skateboard Champion. 2009. (Hot Celebrity Biographies Ser.). (Illus.). 48p. (J). (gr. 5-9). pap. 8.95 *(978-0-7660-3627-7(8))* Enslow Pubs., Inc.
—Walt Disney: Entertainment Visionary, 1 vol. 2009. (Essential Lives Set 4 Ser.). (ENG., Illus.). 112p. (J). (gr. 6-12). lib. bdg. 35.64 *(978-1-60453-700-0(0))* ABDO Publishing Co.
Glaser, Jason. Patrick Henry: Liberty or Death. McDonnell, Peter, illus. 2005. (Graphic Biographies Ser.). (ENG.). 32p. (gr. 3-4). 30.65 *(978-0-7368-4970-8(X)*, Graphic Library) Capstone Press of Coughlan Cos.
—Tim Lincecum. 2011. (Today's Sports Greats Ser.). (Illus.). 32p. (gr. 4-6). (J). pap. 10.50 *(978-1-4339-5880-9(5)*, Gareth Stevens Learning Library); (YA). lib. bdg. 26.60 *(978-1-4339-5878-6(3))* Stevens, Gareth Publishing LLLP.
—Tom Brady. 2011. (Today's Sports Greats Ser.). (Illus.). 32p. (gr. 4-6). (J). pap. 10.50 *(978-1-4339-5884-7(8)*, Gareth Stevens Learning Library); (YA). 26.60 *(978-1-4339-5882-3(1))* Stevens, Gareth Publishing LLLP.
Going, K. L. The Shape of the World: A Portrait of Frank Lloyd Wright. Stringer, Lauren, illus. 2017. (ENG.). 40p. (J). (gr. k-5). 17.99 ***(978-1-4424-7821-3(7))*** Beach Lane Bks.
Goldberg, Jan. Hernando de Soto: Trailblazer of the American Southeast. 2009. (Library of Explorers & Exploration Ser.). 112p. (gr. 5-8). 66.50 *(978-1-60853-607-8(6)*, Rosen Reference) Rosen Publishing Group, Inc., The.
Goldsworthy, Steve. Mark Zuckerberg. 2012. (J). *(978-1-61913-872-8(7))*; pap. *(978-1-61913-873-5(5))* Weigl Pubs., Inc.
Golus, Carrie. Biography Russell Simmons. 2007. (Biography Ser.). (Illus.). 112p. (J). (gr. -1). lib. bdg. *(978-0-8225-7158-2(7))* Twenty First Century Bks.
—Tupac Shakur. 2010. (USA TODAY Lifeline Biographies Ser.). (ENG., Illus.). 112p. (gr. 6-12). lib. bdg. 34.60 *(978-0-7613-5473-4(5))* Lerner Publishing Group.
Gondosch, Linda. Where Did Sacagawea Join the Corps of Discovery? And Other Questions about the Lewis & Clark Expedition. 2011. (Six Questions of American History Ser.). (ENG.). 48p. (gr. 4-6). lib. bdg. 30.60 *(978-0-7613-5226-6(0))* Lerner Publishing Group.
Goodman, Michael E. Buffalo Bill. 2005. (Legends of the West (Creative Education) Ser.). (Illus.). 48p. (J). (gr. 5-9). lib. bdg. 21.95 *(978-1-58341-336-4(7)*, Creative Education) Creative Co., The.
Gordon, Nick. Dolph Ziggler. 2012. (Pro Wrestling Champions Ser.). (ENG., Illus.). 24p. (J). (gr. 3-7). lib. bdg. 25.95 *(978-1-60014-783-8(6)*, Torque Bks.) Bellwether Media.
Gordon, Sherri Mabry. Josh! Leading Man Josh Hutcherson. 2013. (Sizzling Celebrities Ser.). 48p. (J). (gr. 4-9). pap. 8.95 *(978-1-4644-0343-9(0))* Enslow Pubs., Inc.
Gorman, Jacqueline Laks. Chris Rock. 2008. (Today's Superstars). 32p. (YA). (gr. 4-7). lib. bdg. 31.95 *(978-0-8368-9235-2(6))* Stevens, Gareth Publishing LLLP.
Gosman, Gillian. Benjamin Franklin. 2011. (Life Stories Ser.). (Illus.). 24p. (J). pap. 8.25 *(978-1-4488-2759-6(0))*; (gr. 1-4). lib. bdg. 22.60 *(978-1-4488-2585-1(7))* Rosen Publishing Group, Inc., The. (PowerKids Pr.).
—Jaden Smith. 2012. (Kid Stars! Ser.). (ENG., Illus.). 24p. (J). (gr. 1-6). pap. 8.25 *(978-1-4488-6341-9(4))*; lib. bdg. 22.60 *(978-1-4488-6191-0(8))* Rosen Publishing Group, Inc., The. (PowerKids Pr.).
Gotsch, Patrice. Cesar Chavez: Changing Lives. Arreola, Gil, illus. 2006. 19p. pap. 6.30 *(978-1-55501-780-4(0))* Ballard & Tighe Pubs.
Gould, Jane H. Benjamin Franklin. 2012. (Jr. Graphic Founding Fathers Ser.). (ENG., Illus.). 24p. (J). (gr. 3-6). pap. 10.60 *(978-1-4488-7990-8(6))*; lib. bdg. 25.25 *(978-1-4488-7896-3(9))* Rosen Publishing Group, Inc., The. (PowerKids Pr.).
—Steve Jobs. 2013. (Jr. Graphic American Inventors Ser.). (ENG., Illus.). 24p. (J). (gr. 3-6). pap. 10.60 *(978-1-4777-0145-4(1))*; lib. bdg. 25.25 *(978-1-4777-0080-8(3))* Rosen Publishing Group, Inc., The. (PowerKids Pr.).
Grabowski, John F. Americans of Central American Heritage. (Successful Americans Ser.). 64p. (YA). 2009. (gr. 9-12). 22.95 *(978-1-4222-0525-9(8))* 2007. (gr. 7-18). pap. 9.95 *(978-1-4222-0859-5(1))* Mason Crest.
—Vietnamese Americans. (Successful Americans Ser.). 64p. (YA). 2009. (gr. 9-12). 22.95 *(978-1-4222-0522-8(3))* 2007. (gr. 7-18). pap. 9.95 *(978-1-4222-0869-4(9))* Mason Crest.
Graham, Amy. Thomas Edison: Wizard of Light & Sound. 2007. (Inventors Who Changed the World Ser.). (Illus.). 128p. (J). (gr. 5-9). lib. bdg. 34.60 *(978-1-59845-052-1(2)*, MyReportLinks.com Bks.) Enslow Pubs., Inc.
Graves, Will. Best Hockey Players of All Time, 1 vol. 2014. (Sports' Best Ever Ser.). (ENG.). 64p. (gr. 3-6). lib. bdg. 32.79 *(978-1-62403-620-0(1)*, SportsZone) ABDO Publishing Co.
Gray, Peter Winslow. Who Was Who in America: Their Childhood Years, Vol. III. 2003. (Illus.). 54p. (J). spiral bd. 10.95 *(978-1-889639-07-9(9))* AMSC, Adventures in Math & Social Studies for Children.
—Who Was Who in America Volume II: Their Childhood Years. 2003. (Illus.). (J). spiral bd. 10.95 *(978-1-889639-02-4(8))* AMSC, Adventures in Math & Social Studies for Children.
Grayson, Robert. Ed Begley, Jr. Living Green. 2009. (Voices for Green Choices Ser.). (ENG., Illus.). 48p. (J). (gr. 5-9). pap. *(978-0-7787-4680-5(1))* Crabtree Publishing Co.
—John Cena. 2012. (Role Model Entertainers Ser.). 64p. (J). (gr. 7). 22.95 *(978-1-4222-2717-6(0))* Mason Crest.
—Plaxico Burress. 2009. (Superstars of Pro Football Ser.). (Illus.). 64p. (YA). (gr. 7-12). lib. bdg. 22.95 *(978-1-4222-0552-5(5))* Mason Crest.
Graziano, Jim. Johnny Depp. 2008. (Pop Culture Ser.). (Illus.). 64p. (YA). (gr. 3-7). lib. bdg. 22.95 *(978-1-4222-0200-5(3))* Mason Crest.
Great American Thinkers. 2016. (Great American Thinkers Ser.). 128p. (gr. 9-9). lib. bdg. 273.84 *(978-1-5026-1997-6(0))* Cavendish Square Publishing.
Green, Carl R. & Sanford, William R. Butch Cassidy. rev. ed. 2008. (Outlaws & Lawmen of the Wild West, Revised Edition Ser.). (Illus.). 48p. (J). (gr. 5-18). lib. bdg. 25.27 *(978-0-7660-3175-3(6))* Enslow Pubs., Inc.
—Jesse James. rev. ed. 2008. (Outlaws & Lawmen of the Wild West, Revised Edition Ser.). (Illus.). 48p. (J). (gr. 5-18). lib. bdg. 25.27 *(978-0-7660-3172-2(1))* Enslow Pubs., Inc.
Green, Sara. Elon Musk. 2014. (Tech Icons Ser.). (ENG., Illus.). 24p. (J). (gr. 3-8). lib. bdg. 25.95 *(978-1-60014-988-7(X)*, Pilot Bks.) Bellwether Media.
Greenberger, Robert. Gus Grissom. 2004. (Library of Astronaut Biographies Ser.). (Illus.). 112p. (gr. 5-8). lib. bdg. 34.60 *(978-0-8239-4458-3(1)*, Rosen Reference) Rosen Publishing Group, Inc., The.
—Will Eisner. 2009. (Library of Graphic Novelists Ser.). 112p. (gr. 7-12). 63.90 *(978-1-60853-656-6(4))* Rosen Publishing Group, Inc., The.
—Wilt Chamberlain. 2009. (Basketball Hall of Famers Ser.). 112p. (gr. 5-8). 63.90 *(978-1-61511-536-5(6)*, Rosen Reference) Rosen Publishing Group, Inc., The.
Gregory, Josh. Bill & Melinda Gates. 2013. (True Book(tm), A — Biographies Ser.). (ENG., Illus.). 48p. (J). lib. bdg. 31.00 *(978-0-531-21905-8(4))*; pap. 6.95 *(978-0-531-23876-9(8))* Scholastic Library Publishing.
—Steve Jobs. 2013. (True Book(tm), A — Biographies Ser.). (ENG., Illus.). (J). 48p. lib. bdg. 31.00 *(978-0-531-21907-2(0))*; 64p. pap. 8.95 *(978-0-531-21964-5(X))*; 48p. pap. 6.95 *(978-0-531-23878-3(4))*; 64p. lib. bdg. 30.00 *(978-0-531-23606-2(4))* Scholastic Library Publishing.
Grossi, Craig. Craig & Fred: the True Story of a Marine & His Dog. 2017. 256p. (J). (gr. 3). 16.99 ***(978-0-06-269335-8(2))*** HarperCollins Pubs.
Guzman, Lila & Guzman, Rick. Cesar Chavez: Fighting for Fairness. 2006. (Famous Latinos Ser.). (Illus.). 32p. (J). (gr. 3-7). lib. bdg. 22.60 *(978-0-7660-2370-3(2)*, Enslow Elementary) Enslow Pubs., Inc.
Guzmán, Lila & Guzmán, Rick. George Lopez: Comedian & TV Star. 2006. (Famous Latinos Ser.). (Illus.). 32p. (J). (gr. 3-4). lib. bdg. 23.94 *(978-0-7660-2644-5(2)*, Enslow Elementary) Enslow Pubs., Inc.
Habeeb, William Mark. Arab Americans. (Successful Americans Ser.). 64p. (YA). 2009. (Illus.). (gr. 9-12). 22.95 *(978-1-4222-0514-3(2))* 2007. (gr. 7-18). pap. 9.95 *(978-1-4222-0854-0(0))* Mason Crest.
Halfmann, Janet. Seven Miles to Freedom: The Robert Smalls Story. Smith, Duane, illus. 2008. 40p. (J). (gr. 1-6). 17.95 *(978-1-60060-232-0(0))* Lee & Low Bks., Inc.
Hamilton, John. B. J. Penn. 2010. (Xtreme UFC Ser.). 32p. (gr. 3-9). 27.07 *(978-1-61613-477-8(1)*, A&D Xtreme) ABDO Publishing Co.
—Forrest Griffin. 2010. (Xtreme UFC Ser.). 32p. (gr. 3-9). 27.07 *(978-1-61613-475-4(5)*, A&D Xtreme) ABDO Publishing Co.
Hamilton, Sue. Jack Kirby, 1 vol. 2006. (Comic Book Creators Ser.). (ENG.). 32p. (YA). (gr. 3-6). 27.07 *(978-1-59928-298-5(4))* ABDO Publishing Co.
—Joe Simon, 1 vol. 2006. (Comic Book Creators Ser.). (ENG.). 32p. (YA). (gr. 3-6). 27.07 *(978-1-59928-300-5(X))* ABDO Publishing Co.
—Joe Sinnott, 1 vol. 2006. (Comic Book Creators - 6 Titles Ser.). (ENG.). 32p. (YA). (gr. 3-6). 27.07 *(978-1-59928-299-2(2))* ABDO Publishing Co.
—John Buscema, 1 vol. 2006. (Comic Book Creators - 6 Titles Ser.). (ENG., Illus.). 32p. (YA). (gr. 3-6). 27.07 *(978-1-59928-297-8(6))* ABDO Publishing Co.
—John Romita, Sr, 1 vol. 2006. (Comic Book Creators - 6 Titles Ser.). (ENG.). 32p. (YA). (gr. 3-6). 27.07 *(978-1-59928-302-9(6))* ABDO Publishing Co.
Hamilton, Toby G. Dmx. 2009. (Hip Hop (Mason Crest Paperback) Ser.). (Illus.). 64p. (YA). (gr. 4-7). pap. 7.95 *(978-1-4222-0340-8(9))*; (gr. 7-12). lib. bdg. 22.95 *(978-1-4222-0289-0(5))* Mason Crest.
—Fat Joe. 2009. (Hip-Hop 2 Ser.). (Illus.). 64p. (YA). (gr. 7-12). lib. bdg. 22.95 *(978-1-4222-0291-3(7))* Mason Crest.
—Ice Cube. 2009. (Hip-Hop 2 Ser.). (Illus.). 64p. (YA). (gr. 7-12). lib. bdg. 22.95 *(978-1-4222-0294-4(1))* Mason Crest.
Hampton, Wilborn. Elvis Presley: A Twentieth Century Life. 2007. (ENG., Illus.). 192p. (YA). (gr. 7). 26.16 *(978-1-4287-4879-8(2))* Follett School Solutions.
Harbo, Christopher L. Bill Gates, 1 vol. 2014. (Business Leaders Ser.). (ENG.). 24p. (gr. k-1). lib. bdg. 21.99 *(978-1-4765-9641-9(7)*, Pebble Bks.) Capstone Press of Coughlan Cos.
Hardin, Travis. Called to Serve. 2007. (Young Writers Ser.). 95p. (YA). (gr. 8-14). per. 5.99 *(978-1-58158-108-9(4))* McDougal Publishing Co.
Harkins, Susan Sales & Harkins, William H. The Life & Times of Clara Barton. 2008. (Profiles in American History Ser.). (Illus.). 48p. (J). (gr. 4-8). lib. bdg. 29.95 *(978-1-58415-667-3(8))* Mitchell Lane Pubs., Inc.
—The Life & Times of Father Jacques Marquette. 2008. (Profiles in American History Ser.). (Illus.). 48p. (J). (gr. 4-8). lib. bdg. 29.95 *(978-1-58415-526-7(0))* Mitchell Lane Pubs., Inc.
Harmon, Daniel E. Al Gore & Global Warming. 2009. (Celebrity Activists Ser.). 112p. (gr. 8-8). 66.50 *(978-1-61511-826-7(8))* Rosen Publishing Group, Inc., The.
Harness, Cheryl. The Tragic Tale of Narcissa Whitman & a Faithful History of the Oregon Trail. Harness, Cheryl, illus. 2006. (Cheryl Harness Histories Ser.). (ENG., Illus.). 144p. (J). (gr. 5-9). 16.95 *(978-0-7922-5920-6(3)*, National Geographic Children's Bks.) National Geographic Society.
Harris, Laurie Lanzen. Presidents of the Uited States. 3rd ed. 2009. (J). lib. bdg. 55.00 *(978-1-931360-45-6(6))* Favorable Impressions.
Harrison, Kat. Lin-Manuel Miranda: Composer, Actor, & Creator of Hamilton. 2017. (Influential Lives Ser.). 128p. (J). (gr. 7-8). lib. bdg. 37.27 ***(978-0-7660-8505-3(8))*** Enslow Pubs., Inc.
Hasday, Judy & Hasday, Judy L. Americans of Eastern European Heritage. 2007. (Successful Americans Ser.). (Illus.). 64p. (YA). (gr. 5-18). pap. 9.95 *(978-1-4222-0860-1(5))* Mason Crest.
Hasday, Judy L. Americans of Eastern European Heritage. 2009. (Successful Americans Ser.). (Illus.). 64p. (YA). (gr. 9-12). 22.95 *(978-1-4222-0528-0(2))* Mason Crest.
—Japanese Americans. (Successful Americans Ser.). 64p. (YA). 2009. (gr. 9-12). 22.95 *(978-1-4222-0519-8(3))* 2007. (gr. 7-18). pap. 9.95 *(978-1-4222-0863-2(X))* Mason Crest.
Hasday, Judy L. & Crompton, Samuel Willard. Barry Sanders. 2008. (Football Superstars Ser.). (Illus.). 120p. (J). (gr. 7-12). 30.00 *(978-0-7910-9667-3(X))* Facts On File, Inc.
Haugen, Brenda. Johnathan Toews. 2015. (Hockey Superstars Ser.). (ENG., Illus.). 32p. (gr. 3-9). lib. bdg. 27.99 *(978-1-62065-157-5(2))* Capstone Press of Coughlan Cos.
—Jonathan Toews. 2015. (Hockey Superstars Ser.). (ENG.). 32p. (gr. 3-9). pap. 7.95 *(978-1-4914-9024-2(1))* Capstone Press of Coughlan Cos.
Hayes, Amy. Tim Cook: Industrial Engineer & CEO of Apple. 2017. (Breakout Biographies Ser.). 32p. (gr. 9-10). pap. 10.00 ***(978-1-5081-6074-8(0)***, PowerKids Pr.) Rosen Publishing Group, Inc., The.
Heitkamp, Kristina Lyn. Rachel Carson: Pioneering Environmental Activist. 2017. (J). ***(978-1-5383-8075-8(7))***; pap. ***(978-1-5383-8074-1(9))*** Rosen Publishing Group, Inc., The.
Heits, Rudolph T. DeMarcus Ware. 2010. (Superstars of Pro Football Ser.). 64p. (YA). (gr. 5-18). lib. bdg. 22.95 *(978-1-4222-1665-1(9))* Mason Crest.
Helenthal, Janet. Helen Keller. 2005. (Illus.). 16p. (J). *(978-0-7367-2853-9(8))* Zaner-Bloser, Inc.
Hemingway, Albert. Barack Obama. 2007. (Sharing the American Dream Ser.). 64p. (YA). (gr. 7-18). pap. 9.95 *(978-1-4222-0759-8(5))* Mason Crest.
—Chuck Norris. 2009. (Sharing the American Dream Ser.). 64p. (YA). (gr. 7-12). 22.95 *(978-1-4222-0591-4(6))* Mason Crest.

Henry, Nathan L. Good Behavior. 2011. 256p. pap. 9.99 *(978-1-59990-470-2(5),* Bloomsbury USA Childrens) Bloomsbury Publishing USA.

Heos, Bridget. Jay-Z. 2009. (Library of Hip-Hop Biographies Ser.). (ENG., Illus.). 48p. (J). (gr. 7-12). pap. 11.75 *(978-1-4358-5438-3(1))* Rosen Publishing Group, Inc., The.

—Kofi Kingston: Champ of Smackdown. 2011. (Slam! Stars of Wrestling Ser.). (ENG., Illus.). 48p. (YA). (gr. 5-8). pap. 11.75 *(978-1-4488-5595-7(0))*; lib. bdg. 29.25 *(978-1-4488-5535-3(7))* Rosen Publishing Group, Inc., The.

—Lady Gaga. 2011. (Megastars Ser.). (Illus.). 48p. (YA). (gr. 5-8). lib. bdg. 29.25 *(978-1-4358-3574-0(3))* Rosen Publishing Group, Inc., The.

—Rey Mysterio: Giant Killer. 2011. (Slam! Stars of Wrestling Ser.). (ENG.). 48p. (YA). (gr. 5-8). pap. 11.75 *(978-1-4488-5601-5(9))*; lib. bdg. 29.25 *(978-1-4488-5538-4(1))* Rosen Publishing Group, Inc., The.

—Ronde & Tiki Barber: Football Stars. 2010. (Sports Families Ser.). (Illus.). 48p. (ENG.). (J). pap. 11.75 *(978-1-4358-8510-3(4),* Rosen Reference); (YA). (gr. 4-7). lib. bdg. 29.25 *(978-1-4358-3553-5(0))* Rosen Publishing Group, Inc., The.

Herman, Gail. Who Was Davy Crockett? Squier, Robert & Harrison, Nancy, illus. 2013. (Who Was? Ser.). (ENG.). 112p. (J). (gr. 3-7). 5.99 *(978-0-448-46704-7(6),* Grosset & Dunlap) Penguin Young Readers Group.

Hermsen, Sarah, et al. American Reference Library. 2004. (Crime & Punishment in America Ser.). (ENG.). 39p. (J). 5.00 *(978-0-7876-9174-5(7),* UXL) Cengage Gale.

Hernandez, Daniel. They Call Me a Hero: A Memoir of My Youth. 2013. (ENG., Illus.). 240p. (YA). (gr. 7). 17.99 *(978-1-4424-6228-1(0),* Simon & Schuster Bks. For Young Readers) Simon & Schuster Bks. For Young Readers.

Herrera, Juan Felipe. El Canto de las Palomas/Calling the Doves. 2004. (Illus.). (J). (gr. 3-6). spiral bd. *(978-0-616-14607-1(8))* Canadian National Institute for the Blind/Institut National Canadien pour les Aveugles.

Herringshaw, DeAnn. Dorothy Dandridge: Singer & Actress, 1 vol. 2011. (Essential Lives Set 6 Ser.). (ENG., Illus.). 112p. (J). (gr. 6-12). lib. bdg. 35.64 *(978-1-61714-779-1(6),* Essential Library) ABDO Publishing Co.

Herweck, Don. Making It Go: The Life & Work of Robert Fulton, 1 vol. 2007. (Science Readers Ser.). (ENG.). 32p. (J). (gr. 3-3). pap. 8.99 *(978-0-7439-0578-7(4))* Shell Educational Publishing.

Herzog, Brad. Francis & Eddie: The True Story of America's Underdogs. Pullen, Zachary, illus. 2013. (ENG.). 32p. (J). (gr. 3-7). 17.95 *(978-0-9849919-2-1(1))* Why Not Bks.

Hicks, Kyra E. Martha Ann's Quilt for Queen Victoria. Fodi, Lee Edward, illus. 2006. 28p. (J). (gr. -1-3). 16.95 *(978-1-933285-59-7(1))* Brown Books Publishing Group.

Hicks, Peter. Lance Armstrong - Racing Hero. 2011. (Famous Lives Ser.). (Illus.). 32p. (YA). (gr. 3-6). lib. bdg. 26.50 *(978-1-4488-3289-7(6))* Rosen Publishing Group, Inc., The.

Hicks, Terry Allan. Uncle Sam. (Symbols of America Ser.). (Illus.). 40p. 2007. (J). (gr. -1-3). pap. 6.99 *(978-0-7614-3379-8(1),* Cavendish Children's Bks.) 2006. (gr. 3-7). lib. bdg. 20.95 *(978-0-7614-2137-5(8),* Benchmark Bks.) Marshall Cavendish Corp.

Hill, Anne E. Sasha Cohen. 2007. (Sports Heroes & Legends Ser.). (Illus.). 106p. (YA). (gr. 7-12). lib. bdg. 30.60 *(978-0-8225-7164-3(1))* Twenty First Century Bks.

Hill, Christine M. Lance Armstrong: Cycling, Surviving, Inspiring Hope. 2007. (People to Know Today Ser.). (Illus.). 128p. (J). (gr. 6). lib. bdg. 33.27 *(978-0-7660-2694-0(9))* Enslow Pubs., Inc.

Hill, Z. B. Tupac. 2012. (Superstars of Hip-Hop Ser.). (Illus.). 48p. (J). (gr. 3-4). 19.95 *(978-1-4222-2530-1(5))* Mason Crest.

Hiller, Sandra J. Annie Oakley. 2014. (Jr. Graphic American Legends Ser.). 24p. (J). (gr. 3-6). lib. bdg. 26.25 *(978-1-4777-7185-3(9),* PowerKids Pr.) Rosen Publishing Group, Inc., The.

Hillstrom, Kevin & Hillstrom, Laurie Collier. Dale Earnhardt, Jr. 2008. (People in the News Ser.). (ENG., Illus.). 128p. (gr. 7-12). lib. bdg. 39.40 *(978-1-4205-0088-2(0),* LML02109-242092) Cengage Gale.

Hillstrom, Laurie Collier. Jay-Z. 2009. (People in the News Ser.). (ENG., Illus.). 128p. (YA). (gr. 7-12). 33.95 *(978-1-4205-0158-2(5))* Cengage Gale.

Hinman, Bonnie. John Legend. 2009. (Blue Banner Biography Ser.). (Illus.). 32p. (YA). (gr. 4-7). lib. bdg. 25.70 *(978-1-58415-774-8(7))* Mitchell Lane Pubs., Inc.

Historical American Biographies, 53 bks., Set. (Illus.). (YA). (gr. 6-12). lib. bdg. 1111.35 *(978-0-89490-911-5(8))* Enslow Pubs., Inc.

Hoffman, Mary Ann. Alex Rodriguez: Baseball Star. 2009. (Sports Superstars Ser.). 24p. (gr. 1-1). 42.50 *(978-1-60853-173-8(2),* PowerKids Pr.) Rosen Publishing Group, Inc., The.

—Alex Rodriguez: Baseball Star/Estrella del Beisbol. 2009. (Amazing Athletes/Atletas increibles Ser.). (SPA.). 24p. (gr. 1-2). 42.50 *(978-1-61511-303-3(7),* Editorial Buenas Letras) Rosen Publishing Group, Inc., The.

—Dwayne Wade: Basketball Star. 2007. (Sports Superstars Ser.). (Illus.). 24p. (J). (gr. 1-3). lib. bdg. 22.60 *(978-1-4042-3536-6(1))* Rosen Publishing Group, Inc., The.

—Kyle Busch. 2010. (Superstars of NASCAR Ser.). (ENG.). 32p. (J). (gr. 3-8). pap. 10.50 *(978-1-4339-3963-1(0))*; lib. bdg. 25.25 *(978-1-4339-3962-4(2))* Stevens, Gareth Publishing LLLP.

—Lebron James: Basketball Star. 2007. (Sports Superstars Ser.). (Illus.). 24p. (J). (gr. 1-3). lib. bdg. 22.60 *(978-1-4042-3535-9(3))* Rosen Publishing Group, Inc., The.

—Peyton Manning: Football Star. 2007. (Sports Superstars Ser.). (Illus.). 24p. (J). (gr. 1-3). lib. bdg. 22.60 *(978-1-4042-3531-1(0))* Rosen Publishing Group, Inc., The.

—Scott Joplin: King of Ragtime. 2010. (Inspiring Lives Ser.). (Illus.). 32p. (J). (gr. 5-8). pap. 10.50 *(978-1-4339-3632-6(1))*; lib. bdg. 25.25 *(978-1-4339-3631-9(3),* 1309379) Stevens, Gareth Publishing LLLP.

—Shaun Alexander: Football Star. (Sports Superstars Ser.). 24p. (gr. 1-1). 2009. 42.50 *(978-1-60853-182-0(1),* PowerKids Pr.) 2007. (Illus.). (J). lib. bdg. 22.60 *(978-1-4042-3532-8(9))* Rosen Publishing Group, Inc., The.

—Shaun Alexander: Football Star/Estrella del futbol Americano. 2009. (Amazing Athletes/Atletas increibles Ser.). 24p. (gr. 1-2). 42.50 *(978-1-61511-308-8(8),* Editorial Buenas Letras) Rosen Publishing Group, Inc., The.

Hollow, Michele C. Grateful Dead: What a Long, Strange Trip It's Been. 2009. (Rebels of Rock Ser.). (Illus.). 104p. (J). (gr. 5-18). pap. 10.95 *(978-0-7660-3620-8(0))* Enslow Pubs., Inc.

Hoogenboom, Lynn. William Tecumseh Sherman: The Fight to Preserve the Union. 2009. (Library of American Lives & Times Ser.). 112p. (gr. 5-5). 69.20 *(978-1-60853-511-8(8))* Rosen Publishing Group, Inc., The.

Horn, Geoffrey M. Adam Sandler. 2005. (Today's Superstars). (Illus.). 32p. (gr. 5-8). lib. bdg. 31.95 *(978-0-8368-4234-0(0))* Stevens, Gareth Publishing LLLP.

—Alicia Keys. 2005. (Today's Superstars). (Illus.). 32p. (gr. 5-8). lib. bdg. 31.95 *(978-0-8368-4233-3(2))* Stevens, Gareth Publishing LLLP.

—Beyonce. 2005. (Today's Superstars). (Illus.). 32p. (gr. 5-8). lib. bdg. 31.95 *(978-0-8368-4230-2(8))* Stevens, Gareth Publishing LLLP.

—Cameron Diaz. 2005. (Today's Superstars). (Illus.). 32p. (gr. 5-8). lib. bdg. 31.95 *(978-0-8368-4231-9(6))* Stevens, Gareth Publishing LLLP.

—Jamie Foxx. 2005. (Today's Superstars). (Illus.). 32p. (gr. 5-8). lib. bdg. 31.95 *(978-0-8368-4232-6(4))* Stevens, Gareth Publishing LLLP.

Horn, Geoffrey Michael. John Brown: Putting Actions above Words. 2009. (Voices for Freedom Ser.). (ENG., Illus.). 64p. (J). (gr. 5-8). pap. *(978-0-7787-4839-7(1))*; lib. bdg. *(978-0-7787-4823-6(5))* Crabtree Publishing Co.

Houle, Michelle E. Lindsey Williams: Gardening for Impoverished Families. 2007. (Young Heroes Ser.). (ENG., Illus.). 48p. (J). (gr. 3-7). lib. bdg. 28.75 *(978-0-7377-3867-4(7),* Kidhaven) Cengage Gale.

Houts, Amy. Rachel Maddow, 1 vol. 2015. (ENG.). 112p. (YA). 35.60 *(978-1-4777-7891-3(8),* Rosen Young Adult) Rosen Publishing Group, Inc., The.

Howse, Jennifer. Miley Cyrus. 2008. (Remarkable People Ser.). (Illus.). 24p. (J). (gr. 4-6). pap. 8.95 *(978-1-59036-985-2(8))*; lib. bdg. 24.45 *(978-1-59036-984-5(X))* Weigl Pubs., Inc.

Hudak, Heather C. Oprah Winfrey. 2005. (Great African American Women for Kids Ser.). (Illus.). 24p. (J). (gr. 2-3). lib. bdg. 24.45 *(978-1-59036-335-5(3))*; (gr. 3-7). per. 8.95 *(978-1-59036-341-6(8))* Weigl Pubs., Inc.

Hudson, Amanda. Michelle Obama. 2009. (People We Should Know Ser.). (ENG.). 48p. (J). (gr. 3-5). pap. 10.50 *(978-1-4339-2192-6(8))*; lib. bdg. 31.00 *(978-1-4339-2187-2(1))* Stevens, Gareth Publishing LLLP. (Gareth Stevens Learning Library).

Huff, Richard. The Jarretts. rev. ed. 2007. (Race Car Legends Ser.). (Illus.). 80p. (YA). (gr. 5-9). lib. bdg. 25.00 *(978-0-7910-8762-6(X))* Facts On File, Inc.

Hurtig, Jennifer. Maurice Sendak. (My Favorite Writer Ser.). (Illus.). 32p. 2007. (YA). (gr. 5-18). pap. 9.95 *(978-1-59036-485-7(6))* 2006. (J). (gr. 3-7). lib. bdg. 9.95 *(978-1-59036-484-0(8))* Weigl Pubs., Inc.

Hyman, Trina Schart. Self-Portrait: Trina Schart Hyman. (ENG.). 100p. 12.95 *(978-0-201-09308-7(1))* HarperCollins Pubs.

Indovino, Shaina Carmel. Kobe Bryant. 2014. (Superstars in the World of Basketball Ser.: 10). 48p. (J). (gr. 5-18). 20.95 *(978-1-4222-3108-1(9))* Mason Crest.

James, Lincoln. Dale Jarrett. 2007. (NASCAR Champions Ser.). (Illus.). 24p. (J). (gr. 1-3). lib. bdg. 22.60 *(978-1-4042-3459-8(4))* Rosen Publishing Group, Inc., The.

Janic, Susan. Living the Dream: Hannah Montana & Miley Cyrus - The Unofficial Story. 2008. (ENG., Illus.). 144p. (J). (gr. 4-7). pap. *(978-1-55022-848-9(X))* Filmer Ltd.

Janic, Susan & Thomas, Scott. Jonas Brothers Forever: The Unofficial Story of Kevin, Joe & Nick. 2009. (ENG., Illus.). 158p. (J). (gr. 4-7). pap. *(978-1-55022-851-9(X))* Filmer Ltd.

Jarrow, Gail. The Amazing Harry Kellar: Great American Magician. 2012. (ENG., Illus.). 96p. (J). (gr. 3). 17.95 *(978-1-59078-865-3(6),* Calkins Creek) Boyds Mills Pr.

—Robert H. Jackson: New Deal Lawyer, Supreme Court Justice, Nuremberg Prosecutor. 2008. (ENG., Illus.). 104p. (J). (gr. 4-6). 18.95 *(978-1-59078-511-9(8),* Calkins Creek) Boyds Mills Pr.

Jeffery, Marika. Carrie Underwood. (Sharing the American Dream Ser.). 2009. 64p. (YA). (gr. 7-12). 22.95 *(978-1-4222-0599-0(1))* 2008. (J). pap. 9.95 *(978-1-4222-0764-2(1))* Mason Crest.

Jenson-Elliott, Cindy. Antsy Ansel: Ansel Adams, a Life in Nature. Hale, Christy, illus. 2016. (ENG.). 32p. (J). 17.99 *(978-1-62779-082-6(9),* 9781627790826, Holt, Henry & Co. Bks. For Young Readers) Holt, Henry & Co.

Jesse Owens. 2004. (Illus.). 112p. pap. 9.95 *(978-0-8225-5318-2(X))* Lerner Publishing Group.

Johns, Linda. A Rocket Boy Grows Up. 2005. (Illus.). 16p. (J). *(978-0-7367-2904-8(6))* Zaner-Bloser, Inc.

Johns, Michael-Anne. Hangin' with Lindsay Lohan. 2004. (Illus.). 48p. (J). *(978-0-439-72512-5(7))* Scholastic, Inc.

Jones, Charlotte Foltz. Westward Ho! Eleven Explorers of the American West. 2005. (ENG., Illus.). 240p. (J). (gr. 4-6). tchr. ed. 22.95 *(978-0-8234-1586-1(4))* Holiday Hse., Inc.

Jones, Natalya. George Washington Carver: Peanut Scientist. 2009. (Real Life Readers Ser.). 16p. (gr. 2-3). pap. 7.05 *(978-1-4358-0085-4(0),* Rosen Classroom) Rosen Publishing Group, Inc., The.

Josephson, Judith Pinkerton. Walt Disney: Genius of Entertainment. 2006. (People to Know Today Ser.). (Illus.). 128p. (J). (gr. 6). lib. bdg. 33.27 *(978-0-7660-2624-7(8))* Enslow Pubs., Inc.

Jurmain, Suzanne Tripp. George Did It. Day, Larry, illus. 2007. (gr. -1-3). 17.00 *(978-0-7569-8161-7(1))* Perfection Learning Corp.

Kallen, Stuart A. Elon Musk & Tesla. 2015. (ENG., Illus.). 80p. (J). lib. bdg. *(978-1-60152-870-4(1))* ReferencePoint Pr., Inc.

Kate Shelley & the Midnight Express. 9.95 *(978-1-59112-169-5(8))* Live Oak Media.

Keedle, Jayne. Jonas Brothers. 2009. (Today's Superstars Ser.). (ENG.). 48p. (J). (gr. 5-8). pap. 14.05 *(978-1-4339-2163-6(4))*; lib. bdg. 31.95 *(978-1-4339-1970-1(2))* Stevens, Gareth Publishing LLLP.

—Oprah Winfrey. 2008. (Today's Superstars). (Illus.). 32p. (J). (gr. 4-7). lib. bdg. 31.95 *(978-0-8368-9238-3(0))* Stevens, Gareth Publishing LLLP.

—Rachael Ray. 2009. (People We Should Know Ser.). (ENG., Illus.). 48p. (J). (gr. 3-5). pap. 10.50 *(978-1-4339-2149-0(9))*; lib. bdg. 31.00 *(978-1-4339-2189-6(8))* Stevens, Gareth Publishing LLLP. (Gareth Stevens Learning Library).

—Zac Efron. 2008. (Today's Superstars). (Illus.). 32p. (J). (gr. 4-7). lib. bdg. 31.95 *(978-0-8368-9239-0(9))* Stevens, Gareth Publishing LLLP.

Keenan, Sheila. Outstanding Americans. 2003. (ENG.). 256p. (J). 19.95 *(978-0-439-28358-8(2),* Scholastic Reference) Scholastic, Inc.

Keep the Lights Burning. 9.95 *(978-1-59112-293-7(7))* Live Oak Media.

Keller, Susanna. Alexander Hamilton: America's First Treasury Secretary. 2017. (J). pap. ***(978-1-68048-808-1(2))***; lib. bdg. ***(978-1-68048-809-8(0))*** Rosen Publishing Group, Inc., The. (Britannica Educational Publishing).

Kelley, K. C. Running Backs. 2009. (Game Day: Football Ser.). (ENG.). 48p. (J). (gr. 5-9). lib. bdg. 31.00 *(978-1-4339-1963-3(X))* Stevens, Gareth Publishing LLLP.

Kelly Slater. 2008. (Xtreme Athletes Ser.). (Illus.). 112p. (YA). (gr. 7-12). lib. bdg. 27.95 *(978-1-59935-078-3(5))* Reynolds, Morgan Inc.

Kennedy, Mike. Shaun White. 2009. (Today's Superstars Ser.). (ENG.). 48p. (J). (gr. 5-8). pap. 14.05 *(978-1-4339-2161-2(8))*; lib. bdg. 31.95 *(978-1-4339-1968-8(0))* Stevens, Gareth Publishing LLLP.

Kennelly, Sean & Carpenter, Dan. Great Americans. Paiva, Johannah Gilman, ed. 2014. (ENG., Illus.). 48p. (J). (gr. 4). 8.99 *(978-1-4867-0257-2(0))* Flowerpot Children's Pr. Inc. CAN. Dist: Cardinal Pubs. Group.

Kent, Zachary. Andrew Carnegie: Industrialist & Philanthropist. 2015. (Legendary American Biographies Ser.). 96p. (J). (gr. 6-12). 27.94 *(978-0-7660-6435-5(2))* Enslow Pubs., Inc.

Kerns, Ann. Martha Stewart. 2006. (Biography Ser.). (Illus.). 111p. (J). (gr. 3-7). lib. bdg. 29.27 *(978-0-8225-6613-7(3),* Twenty-First Century Bks.) Lerner Publishing Group.

Killcoyne, Hope Lourie. Key Figures of the Vietnam War. 2015. (Biographies of War Ser.). (ENG., Illus.). 112p. (J). (gr. 7-8). 32.90 *(978-1-68048-063-4(4),* Britannica Educational Publishing) Rosen Publishing Group, Inc., The.

Kimmich, Ian. Antonio Gates. 2009. (Superstars of Pro Football Ser.). (Illus.). 64p. (YA). (gr. 7-12). lib. bdg. 22.95 *(978-1-4222-0553-2(3))* Mason Crest.

King Farris, Christine. My Brother Martin: A Sister Remembers Growing up with the Rev. Dr. Martin Luther King Jr. Soentpiet, Chris K., illus. 2005. 35p. (J). (gr. 4-7). 15.65 *(978-0-7569-6552-5(7))* Perfection Learning Corp.

Kingsbury, Robert. The Assassination of James A. Garfield. 2009. (Library of Political Assassinations Ser.). 64p. (gr. 5-5). 58.50 *(978-1-60853-825-6(7))* Rosen Publishing Group, Inc., The.

Kirkpatrick, Rob. Alexi Lalas: Sensación del Fútbol Soccer (Soccer Sensation) 2009. (Grandes Idolos (Hot Shots) Ser.). 24p. (gr. 1-1). 42.50 *(978-1-61512-733-7(X),* Editorial Buenas Letras) Rosen Publishing Group, Inc., The.

—Alexi Lalas: Soccer Sensation / Sensación del Fútbol Soccer. 2009. (Hot Shots/Grandes idolos Ser.). (SPA.). 24p. (gr. 1-1). 42.50 *(978-1-61513-411-3(5),* Editorial Buenas Letras) Rosen Publishing Group, Inc., The.

—Evander Holyfield: Campeón de los Pesos Pesados (Heavyweight Champion) 2009. (Grandes Idolos (Hot Shots) Ser.). (SPA.). 24p. (gr. 1-1). 42.50 *(978-1-61512-736-8(4),* Editorial Buenas Letras) Rosen Publishing Group, Inc., The.

—Evander Holyfield: Heavyweight Champion / Campeón de los Pesos Pesados. 2009. (Hot Shots/Grandes idolos Ser.). (ENG & SPA.). 24p. (gr. 1-1). 42.50 *(978-1-61513-414-4(X),* Editorial Buenas Letras) Rosen Publishing Group, Inc., The.

—Terrell Davis: Corredor de Superbowl (Super Bowl Running Back) 2009. (Deportistas de Poder (Power Players) Ser.). 24p. (gr. 1-1). 42.50 *(978-1-61512-161-8(7),* Editorial Buenas Letras) Rosen Publishing Group, Inc., The.

Klein, Adam G. Norman Rockwell, 1 vol. 2007. (Great Artists Set 2 Ser.). (ENG., Illus.). 32p. (gr. -1-3). 27.07 *(978-1-59679-738-3(X),* Checkerboard Library) ABDO Publishing Co.

Klein, Adria F. Arnold Schwarzenegger. 2009. pap. 13.25 *(978-1-60559-054-7(1))* Hameray Publishing Group, Inc.

Klein, Dvora. Eleanor Roosevelt. 2009. pap. 13.25 *(978-1-60559-059-2(2))* Hameray Publishing Group, Inc.

Klimo, Kate. Walt Disney's Magic. Ivanov, O. & Ivanov, A., illus. 2017. (J). pap. *(978-0-399-55534-3(X))* Random Hse., Inc.

Koestler-Grack, Rachel A. Brett Favre. 2008. (Football Superstars Ser.). (Illus.). 144p. (gr. 6-12). lib. bdg. 30.00 *(978-0-7910-9690-1(4),* Chelsea Hse.) Facts On File, Inc.

—William Tecumseh Sherman. 2009. (Leaders of the Civil War Era Ser.). (Illus.). 149p. (gr. 6-12). 35.00 *(978-1-60413-300-4(7),* Chelsea Hse.) Facts On File, Inc.

Kortemeier, Todd. Unsung Heroes of U.S. History. 2017. (Unsung Heroes Ser.). (ENG., Illus.). 32p. (gr. 3-6). 21.95 *(978-1-63235-312-2(1))* Pr. Room Editions LLC.

Kramer, Barbara. Gloria Estefan: Never Give Up. 2005. (Awesome Values in Famous Lives Ser.). (Illus.). 48p. (J). (gr. 3-4). lib. bdg. 25.27 *(978-0-7660-2380-2(X),* Enslow Elementary) Enslow Pubs., Inc.

Kramer, Sydelle. Who Was Daniel Boone? Ulrich, George, illus. 2006. (Who Was? Ser.). (ENG.). 112p. (J). (gr. 3-7). pap. 5.99 *(978-0-448-43902-0(6),* Grosset & Dunlap) Penguin Young Readers Group.

Krensky, Stephen. Casey Jones. Schroder, Mark, illus. 2006. (On My Own Folklore Ser.). (ENG.). 48p. (J). (gr. 2-4). lib. bdg. 25.26 *(978-1-57505-890-0(1),* Millbrook Pr.) Lerner Publishing Group.

—Casey Jones. Schroder, Mark, illus. 2007. (On My Own Folklore Ser.). (ENG.). 48p. (gr. 2-4). per. 6.95 *(978-0-8225-6476-8(9),* First Avenue Editions) Lerner Publishing Group.

Krohn, Katherine. Biography Gwen Stefani. 2007. (Biography Ser.). (Illus.). 112p. (J). (gr. -1). lib. bdg. *(978-0-8225-7157-5(9))* Twenty First Century Bks.

Krohn, Katherine E. Michael Jackson: Ultimate Music Legend. 2010. (Gateway Biographies Ser.). (ENG., Illus.). 48p. (gr. 4-8). lib. bdg. 26.60 *(978-0-7613-5762-9(9),* Lerner Pubns.) Lerner Publishing Group.

Krull, Kathleen. The Boy on Fairfield Street: How Ted Geisel Grew up to Become Dr. Seuss. Johnson, Steve & Fancher, Lou, illus. 2010. (ENG.). 48p. (J). (gr. k-4). pap. 7.99 *(978-0-375-85550-4(5),* Dragonfly Bks.) Random Hse. Children's Bks.

—The Boy on Fairfield Street: How Ted Geisel Grew up to Become Dr. Seuss. 2010. lib. bdg. 18.40 *(978-0-606-12416-4(0),* Turtleback) Turtleback Bks.

—The Boy Who Invented TV: The Story of Philo Farnsworth. Couch, Greg, illus. 2014. (ENG.). 40p. (J). (gr. 1-4). 7.99 *(978-0-385-75557-3(0),* Dragonfly Bks.) Random Hse. Children's Bks.

Krumenauer, Heidi. Flo-Rida. 2010. (Blue Banner Biography Ser.). (Illus.). 32p. (YA). (gr. 4-7). lib. bdg. 25.70 *(978-1-58415-906-3(5))* Mitchell Lane Pubs., Inc.

—Jimmie Johnson. 2009. (Robbie Reader Ser.). (Illus.). 32p. (YA). (gr. 2-5). lib. bdg. 25.70 *(978-1-58415-756-4(9))* Mitchell Lane Pubs., Inc.

—Joe Flacco. 2009. (Blue Banner Biography Ser.). (Illus.). 32p. (YA). (gr. 4-7). lib. bdg. 25.70 *(978-1-58415-771-7(2))* Mitchell Lane Pubs., Inc.

—Lady Gaga. 2010. (Blue Banner Biography Ser.). (Illus.). 32p. (YA). (gr. 4-7). lib. bdg. 25.70 *(978-1-58415-904-9(9))* Mitchell Lane Pubs., Inc.

—Sean Kingston. 2008. (Blue Banner Biography Ser.). (Illus.). 32p. (YA). (gr. 4-7). lib. bdg. 25.70 *(978-1-58415-679-6(1))* Mitchell Lane Pubs., Inc.

Kudlinski, Kathleen. Dr. Seuss: Young Author & Artist. Henderson, Meryl, illus. 2005. (Childhood of Famous Americans Ser.). (ENG.). 192p. (J). (gr. 3-7). pap. 7.99 *(978-0-689-87347-8(6),* Simon & Schuster/Paula Wiseman Bks.) Simon & Schuster/Paula Wiseman Bks.

Kulling, Monica. In the Bag! Margaret Knight Wraps It Up. Parkins, David, illus. 2013. (Great Idea Ser.). (ENG.). 32p. (J). (gr. k-3). pap. 7.95 *(978-1-77049-515-9(0),* Tundra Bks.) Tundra Bks. CAN. Dist: Penguin Random Hse. LLC.

—It's a Snap! George Eastman's First Photograph. Slavin, Bill, illus. (Great Idea Ser.). (ENG.). 32p. (J). (gr. k-3). 2013. pap. 7.95 *(978-1-77049-513-5(4))* 2009. 17.95 *(978-0-88776-881-1(4))* Tundra Bks. CAN. (Tundra Bks.). Dist: Penguin Random Hse. LLC.

—Spic-and-Span! Lillian Gilbreth's Wonder Kitchen. 2014. (Great Idea Ser.). (ENG., Illus.). 32p. (J). (gr. k-3). 17.99 *(978-1-77049-380-3(8),* Tundra Bks.) Tundra Bks. CAN. Dist: Penguin Random Hse. LLC.

Kundiger, Marion S. Izzie of Fergus Falls: A Minnesota Childhood in The 1880s. Kundiger, Marion S., illus. 2008. (ENG., Illus.). 56p. (J). 29.95 *(978-0-9659712-8-7(7))* Ravenstone Pr.

Kupperberg, Paul. Jerry Yang. 2009. (Asian Americans of Achievement Ser.). (Illus.). 128p. (YA). (gr. 7-12). 35.00 *(978-1-60413-569-5(7))* Facts On File, Inc.

Kurtz, Jane. Jane Kurtz & YOU, 1 vol. 2007. (Author & YOU Ser.: No. 8). (Illus.). 204p. (C). per. 35.00 *(978-1-59158-295-3(4),* LU2954, Libraries Unlimited) ABC-CLIO, LLC.

La Bella, Laura. Kanye West. 2009. (Library of Hip-Hop Biographies Ser.). (ENG., Illus.). 48p. (J). (gr. 7-12). pap. 11.75 *(978-1-4358-5439-0(X))* Rosen Publishing Group, Inc., The.

Labrecque, Ellen. Gertrude B. Elion & Pharmacology. 2017. (21st Century Junior Library: Women Innovators Ser.). (ENG., Illus.). 24p. (J). (gr. 2-5). pap. 12.79 *(978-1-63472-314-5(7),* 209301) Cherry Lake Publishing.

—Magic Johnson. 2007. (21st Century Skills Library: Life Skills Biographies Ser.). (ENG.). 48p. (gr. 4-8). lib. bdg. 31.36 *(978-1-60279-071-1(X),* 200044) Cherry Lake Publishing.

Labrecque, Ellen & dePaola, Tomie. Who Was Frank Lloyd Wright? Copeland, Gregory & Harrison, Nancy, illus. 2015. (Who Was? Ser.). (ENG.). 112p. (J). (gr. 3-7). 5.99 *(978-0-448-48313-9(0),* Grosset & Dunlap) Penguin Young Readers Group.

Lace, William W. Benjamin Franklin. 2010. (Leaders of the Colonial Era Ser.). (Illus.). 120p. (gr. 5-8). 35.00 *(978-1-60413-737-8(1),* Chelsea Hse.) Facts On File, Inc.

—Nolan Ryan: Hall of Fame Baseball Superstar. 2013. (Hall of Fame Sports Greats Ser.). 64p. (J). (gr. 4-18). 15.95 *(978-1-62285-025-9(4))* Enslow Pubs., Inc.

Lady Gaga. 2011. (People in the News Ser.). 128p. lib. bdg. 33.95 *(978-1-4205-0426-2(6),* Lucent Bks.) Cengage Gale.

Lady Gaga. 2011. (Megastars Ser.). (ENG.). 48p. (YA). pap. 11.75 *(978-1-4488-2260-7(2))* Rosen Publishing Group, Inc., The.

Landau, Jennifer. Jeff Bezos & Amazon. 2012. (Internet Biographies Ser.). (ENG., Illus.). 128p. (J). (gr. 7-12). lib. bdg. 34.60 *(978-1-4488-6914-5(5))* Rosen Publishing Group, Inc., The.

Langston-George, Rebecca. The Booth Brothers: Drama, Fame, & the Death of President Lincoln. 2017. (Encounter: Narrative Nonfiction Stories Ser.). (ENG.). 112p. (gr. 3-5). lib. bdg. 30.65 ***(978-1-5157-7338-2(8))*** Encounter Bks.

Lantier, Patricia. Rachel Carson: Fighting Pesticides & Other Chemical Pollutants. 2009. (Voices for Green Choices Ser.). (ENG., Illus.). 48p. (J). (gr. 5-9). pap. *(978-0-7787-4676-8(3))*; lib. bdg. *(978-0-7787-4663-8(1))* Crabtree Publishing Co.

Larsen, Andrew. Andrew Carnegie: The Man Who Loved Libraries. Maurey, Katty, illus. 2017. (ENG.). 32p. (J). (gr. 1-5). 16.95 ***(978-1-77147-267-8(7))*** Owlkids Bks. Inc. CAN. Dist: Publishers Group West (PGW).

Latta, Sara L. Who Invented the Ferris Wheel? George Ferris. 2012. (I Like Inventors! Ser.). (Illus.). 24p. (J). (gr. k-3). 22.60 *(978-0-7660-3964-3(1),* Enslow Elementary) Enslow Pubs., Inc.

Lauren, Jill. That's Like Me!, 1 vol. 2009. (ENG.). 32p. (J). (gr. k-3). pap. 7.95 *(978-1-59572-208-9(4))* Star Bright Bks., Inc.

Leavitt, Amie. Miley Cyrus. 2007. (Robbie Reader Ser.). (Illus.). 32p. (J). (gr. 2-5). lib. bdg. 25.70 *(978-1-58415-590-4(6))* Mitchell Lane Pubs., Inc.

—Raven-Symone. 2007. (Robbie Reader Ser.). (Illus.). 32p. (YA). (gr. 2-5). lib. bdg. 25.70 *(978-1-58415-593-5(0))* Mitchell Lane Pubs., Inc.

Leavitt, Amie Jane. Abigail Breslin. 2009. (Robbie Reader Ser.). (Illus.). 32p. (YA). (gr. 2-5). lib. bdg. 25.70 *(978-1-58415-759-5(3))* Mitchell Lane Pubs., Inc.

—Day by Day with Miley Cyrus. 2010. (Randy's Corner Ser.). (Illus.). 32p. (J). (gr. -1-2). lib. bdg. 25.70 *(978-1-58415-856-1(5))* Mitchell Lane Pubs., Inc.

—Dylan & Cole Sprouse. 2007. (Robbie Reader Ser.). (Illus.). 32p. (YA). (gr. 2-5). lib. bdg. 25.70 *(978-1-58415-591-1(4))* Mitchell Lane Pubs., Inc.
—Miranda Cosgrove. 2008. (Robbie Reader Ser.). (Illus.). 32p. (YA). (gr. 2-5). lib. bdg. 25.70 *(978-1-58415-720-5(8))* Mitchell Lane Pubs., Inc.
—Taylor Lautner. 2010. (Robbie Reader Ser.). (Illus.). 32p. (YA). (gr. 2-5). lib. bdg. 25.70 *(978-1-58415-897-4(2))* Mitchell Lane Pubs., Inc.
Lee, Sally. Martha Washington, 1 vol. 2010. (First Ladies Ser.). (ENG.). 24p. (gr. k-1). lib. bdg. 26.65 *(978-1-4296-5011-3(7),* Pebble Plus) Capstone Press of Coughlan Cos.
—Sam Walton: Business Genius of Wal-Mart. 2007. (People to Know Today Ser.). (Illus.). 112p. (J). (gr. 3-7). lib. bdg. 33.27 *(978-0-7660-2692-6(2))* Enslow Pubs., Inc.
Lee, T. S. The Lincoln Story: The Boy Who Embraced a Nation. 4th ed. 2010. (Great Heroes Ser.). 184p. (J). pap. 14.95 *(978-0-9819542-3-3(5))* DASANBOOKS.
Lemmens, Mary Jo. Christina Aguilera. 2009. (Hip-Hop 2 Ser.). 64p. (YA). (gr. 7-12). lib. bdg. 22.95 *(978-1-4222-0285-2(2))* Mason Crest.
—Cypress Hill. 2009. (Hip Hop (Mason Crest Paperback) Ser.). (Illus.). 64p. (YA). (gr. 4-7). pap. 7.95 *(978-1-4222-0345-3(X))* Mason Crest.
Lemmens, Maryjo. Cypress Hill. 2009. (Hip-Hop 2 Ser.). (Illus.). 64p. (YA). (gr. 7-12). lib. bdg. 22.95 *(978-1-4222-0287-6(9))* Mason Crest.
—Jennifer Lopez. 2009. (Hip-Hop 2 Ser.). (Illus.). 64p. (YA). (gr. 7-12). lib. bdg. 22.95 *(978-1-4222-0296-8(8))* Mason Crest.
—Xzibit. 2009. (Hip-Hop 2 Ser.). (Illus.). 64p. (YA). (gr. 7-12). lib. bdg. 22.95 *(978-1-4222-0305-7(0))* Mason Crest.
Lenburg, Jeff. Genndy Tartakovsky. 2012. (Legends of Animation Ser.). (Illus.). 120p. (gr. 6-12). 34.95 *(978-1-60413-842-9(4),* Chelsea Hse.) Facts On File, Inc.
—John Lasseter. 2012. (Legends of Animation Ser.). (Illus.). 136p. (gr. 6-12). 34.95 *(978-1-60413-840-5(8),* Chelsea Hse.) Facts On File, Inc.
—Matt Groening. 2011. (Legends of Animation Ser.). (Illus.). 134p. (gr. 6-12). 34.95 *(978-1-60413-838-2(6),* Chelsea Hse.) Facts On File, Inc.
—Walter Lantz. 2012. (Legends of Animation Ser.). (Illus.). 136p. (gr. 6-12). 34.95 *(978-1-60413-839-9(4),* Chelsea Hse.) Facts On File, Inc.
—William Hanna & Joseph Barbera. 2011. (Legends of Animation Ser.). (Illus.). 168p. (gr. 6-12). 34.95 *(978-1-60413-837-5(8),* Chelsea Hse.) Facts On File, Inc.
Lesinski, Jeanne M. Bill Gates. 2007. (Illus.). 112p. (J). (gr. 6-9). per. 7.95 *(978-0-8225-7027-1(0),* Lerner Pubns.); lib. bdg. 29.27 *(978-0-8225-7363-0(6),* Twenty-First Century Bks.) Lerner Publishing Group.
LeTourneau, Anthony Alex, illus. Hanni & Beth: Safe & Sound. 2007. (J). (gr. k-3). 17.95 *(978-0-9792918-0-7(1))* Blue Marlin Pubns.
Leventhal, Josh. Linebackers. 2017. (Football's All-Time Greats Ser.). (ENG., Illus.). 32p. (J). (gr. 3-7). 31.35 ***(978-1-68072-040-2(6),*** Bolt) Black Rabbit Bks.
—Running Backs. 2017. (Football's All-Time Greats Ser.). (ENG., Illus.). 32p. (J). (gr. 3-7). 31.35 ***(978-1-68072-043-3(0),*** Bolt) Black Rabbit Bks.
Levin, Judith. Ichiro Suzuki. 2008. (Baseball Superstars Ser.). (Illus.). 144p. (gr. 6-12). pap. 11.95 *(978-0-7910-9849-3(4),* Checkmark Bks.) Facts On File, Inc.
Levy, Janey. Motocross Superstars. (Motocross Ser.). 32p. 2009. (gr. 4-5). 47.90 *(978-1-61514-667-3(9))* 2007. (Illus.). (J). (gr. 3-7). lib. bdg. 25.25 *(978-1-4042-3695-0(3))* Rosen Publishing Group, Inc., The. (PowerKids Pr.).
—William Penn: Shaping a Nation. 2009. (American History Milestones Ser.). 32p. (gr. 5-5). 47.90 *(978-1-61511-376-7(2),* PowerKids Pr.) Rosen Publishing Group, Inc., The.
Lies, Anne. Oprah Winfrey: Media Mogul, 1 vol. 2011. (Essential Lives Set 6 Ser.). (ENG., Illus.). 112p. (J). (gr. 6-12). lib. bdg. 35.64 *(978-1-61714-786-9(9),* Essential Library) ABDO Publishing Co.
Llanas, Sheila Griffin. Ettore Boiardi: Chef Boyardee Manufacturer, 1 vol. 2014. (Food Dudes Set 2 Ser.). (ENG.). 32p. (J). (gr. 8-12). lib. bdg. 27.07 *(978-1-62403-314-8(8),* Checkerboard Library) ABDO Publishing Co.
Lobb, Nancy. 16 Extraordinary Young Americans. 2nd ed. 2007. (16 Extraordinary Ser.). (Illus.). 127p. (gr. 6-12). tchr. ed., per. 25.00 *(978-0-8251-6283-1(1))* Walch Education.
Lommel, Cookie. Russell Simmons. 2007. (Hip-Hop Stars Ser.). (Illus.). 104p. (YA). (gr. 7-12). lib. bdg. 30.00 *(978-0-7910-9467-9(7))* Facts On File, Inc.
Lord, Raymond. Usher. 2008. (Hip-Hop Ser.). (Illus.). 64p. (YA). (gr. 7-12). lib. bdg. 22.95 *(978-1-4222-0131-2(7))* Mason Crest.
Louie, Ai-Ling. Vera Wang Queen of Fashion; Amazing Chinese American: Biographies of Amazing Asian Americans. 2007. (Biographies of Amazing Asian Americans Ser.). (ENG., Illus.). 48p. (J). pap. 12.99 *(978-0-9787465-3-7(8))* Dragoneagle Pr.
Lupo, Tamar. Warren Buffett. 2007. (Remarkable People Ser.). (Illus.). 24p. (J). (gr. 4-7). pap. 8.95 *(978-1-59036-652-3(2));* lib. bdg. 24.45 *(978-1-59036-651-6(4))* Weigl Pubs., Inc.
Lusted, Marcia Amidon. Mark Zuckerberg: Facebook Creator, 1 vol. 2011. (Essential Lives Set 7 Ser.). (ENG., Illus.). 112p. (J). (gr. 6-12). lib. bdg. 35.64 *(978-1-61783-008-2(9))* ABDO Publishing Co.
Lynch, Kelly Ann. He Said Yes: The Story of Father Mychal Judge. Oatman, M. Scott, illus. 2007. 32p. (J). (gr. -1-3). 12.95 *(978-0-8091-6740-1(9),* 6740-1) Paulist Pr.
Lynette, Rachel. Jennifer Aniston. 2010. (People in the News Ser.). (Illus.). 128p. (J). 33.95 *(978-1-4205-0235-0(2),* 1304724, Lucent Bks.) Cengage Gale.
Lynetter, Rachel. Ashley Shuyler: Founder of AfricAid. 2007. (Young Heroes Ser.). (ENG., Illus.). 48p. (J). (gr. 4-8). lib. bdg. 28.25 *(978-0-7377-3669-4(0),* Kidhaven) Cengage Gale.
MacCarry, Noel. Who Was Pete Seeger? Marchesi, Stephen, illus. 2017. (Who Was? Ser.). (ENG.). 112p. (J). (gr. 3-7). 5.99 *(978-0-448-48475-4(7),* Grosset & Dunlap) Penguin Young Readers Group.
MacDonald, James. Dale Earnhardt, Jr. Racing's Living Legacy. 2008. (Heroes of Racing Ser.). (Illus.). 128p. (J). (gr. 3-7). lib. bdg. 33.27 *(978-0-7660-2996-5(4))* Enslow Pubs., Inc.
—Dale Earnhardt, Sr. The Intimidator. 2009. (Heroes of Racing Ser.). (Illus.). 128p. (J). (gr. 5-9). lib. bdg. 33.27 *(978-0-7660-3297-2(3))* Enslow Pubs., Inc.
MacLeod, Elizabeth. Harry Houdini. Mantha, John, illus. 2009. (Kids Can Read Ser.). (ENG.). 32p. (J). (gr. 1-3). 3.95 *(978-1-55453-299-5(X));* 14.95 *(978-1-55453-298-8(1))* Kids Can Pr., Ltd. CAN. Dist: Hachette Bk. Group.
—Harry Houdini: A Magical Life. 2005. (Snapshots: Images of People & Places in History Ser.). (ENG., Illus.). 32p. (J). (gr. 3-7). 6.95 *(978-1-55337-770-2(2))* Kids Can Pr., Ltd. CAN. Dist: Hachette Bk. Group.
—Thomas Edison. Krystoforski, Andrej, illus. 2008. (ENG.). 32p. (J). (gr. 1-3). 14.95 *(978-1-55453-057-1(1))* Kids Can Pr., Ltd. CAN. Dist: Hachette Bk. Group.
Madison, Taylor. Boys We Love: Today's Top 30 Hottest Stars. 2005. (Illus.). (J). *(978-0-439-74864-3(X))* Scholastic, Inc.
Magid, Jennifer. Angelina Jolie. 2008. (Today's Superstars). 32p. (YA). (gr. 4-7). lib. bdg. 31.95 *(978-0-8368-9234-5(8))* Stevens, Gareth Publishing LLLP.
Mahaney, Ian F. Dave Mirra: Bicycle Stunt Champ. 2005. (Extreme Sports Biographies Ser.). (Illus.). 24p. (J). (gr. 2-5). 22.60 *(978-1-4042-2744-6(X))* Rosen Publishing Group, Inc., The.
Main, Mary. Dr. Phil: Self-Help Guru & TV Superstar. 2007. (People to Know Today Ser.). (Illus.). 128p. (J). (gr. 6-12). lib. bdg. 33.27 *(978-0-7660-2696-4(5))* Enslow Pubs., Inc.
Mallin, Jay. Al Sharpton: Community Activist. 2007. (Great Life Stories Ser.). (Illus.). 111p. (J). *(978-0-531-13672-0(8),* Franklin Watts) Hachette Children's Group.
Mara, Wil. Dwight Eisenhower. 2010. (Presidents & Their Times 4 Ser.). 96p. (gr. 6). 34.21 *(978-0-7614-4812-9(8))* Marshall Cavendish GBR. Dist: Marshall Cavendish Corp.
—George Washington. 2013. (Rookie Biographies(tm) Ser.). (ENG.). 32p. (J). lib. bdg. 25.00 *(978-0-531-24736-5(8));* pap. 5.95 *(978-0-531-24702-0(3))* Scholastic Library Publishing.
—Harriet Tubman. 2013. (ENG.). 32p. (C). pap. 9.95 *(978-0-531-24703-7(1))* National Geographic School Publishing, Inc.
—Harriet Tubman. 2013. (Rookie Biographies(r) Ser.). (ENG.). 32p. (J). lib. bdg. 23.00 *(978-0-531-24737-2(6))* Scholastic Library Publishing.
—Martin Luther King Jr. 2013. (Rookie Biographies(r) Ser.). (ENG.). 32p. (J). pap. 5.95 *(978-0-531-24704-4(X));* lib. bdg. 23.00 *(978-0-531-24738-9(4))* Scholastic Library Publishing.
—Ronald Reagan. 2010. (Presidents & Their Times 4 Ser.). 96p. (gr. 6). 34.21 *(978-0-7614-4814-3(4))* Marshall Cavendish Corp.
Marcovitz, Hal. Chris Daughtry. 2009. (Dream Big: American Idol Superstars Ser.). 64p. (YA). (gr. 5-18). 22.95 *(978-1-4222-1508-1(3));* pap. 9.95 *(978-1-4222-1595-1(4))* Mason Crest.
—Cuban Americans. (Successful Americans Ser.). 64p. (YA). 2009. (gr. 9-12). 22.95 *(978-1-4222-0523-5(1))* 2007. (gr. 7-18). pap. 9.95 *(978-1-4222-0856-4(7))* Mason Crest.
—Derek Jeter. 2010. (Modern Role Models Ser.). (Illus.). 64p. (YA). (gr. 7-12). lib. bdg. 22.95 *(978-1-4222-0482-5(0))* Mason Crest.
—Elliott Yamin. 2009. (Dream Big: American Idol Superstars Ser.). 64p. (YA). (gr. 5-18). 22.95 *(978-1-4222-1513-5(X));* pap. 9.95 *(978-1-4222-1599-9(7))* Mason Crest.
—Kellie Pickler. 2009. (Dream Big: American Idol Superstars Ser.). 64p. (YA). (gr. 5-18). pap. 9.95 *(978-1-4222-1603-3(9));* lib. bdg. 22.95 *(978-1-4222-1510-4(5))* Mason Crest.
—Lawrence Yep. 2008. (Who Wrote That? Ser.). (Illus.). 136p. (gr. 6-12). 35.00 *(978-0-7910-9527-0(4),* Chelsea Hse.) Facts On File, Inc.
—Madonna: Entertainer. 2010. (Women of Achievement Ser.). 128p. (gr. 6-12). 35.00 *(978-1-60413-859-7(9),* Chelsea Hse.) Facts On File, Inc.
—Maurice Sendak. 2006. (Who Wrote That? Ser.). (Illus.). 136p. (gr. 6-12). lib. bdg. 35.00 *(978-0-7910-8796-1(4),* Chelsea Hse.) Facts On File, Inc.
—Michelle. 2007. (Obamas Ser.). 64p. (YA). (gr. 3-6). pap. 9.95 *(978-1-4222-1485-5(0));* (gr. 4-7). lib. bdg. 19.95 *(978-1-4222-1478-7(8))* Mason Crest.
—Russian Americans. (Major American Immigration Ser.). (Illus.). 64p. (YA). (gr. 9-12). 2010. 22.95 *(978-1-4222-0617-1(3))* 2009. 22.95 *(978-1-4222-0513-6(4))* Mason Crest.
—Scott O'Dell. 2007. (Who Wrote That? Ser.). (Illus.). 128p. (gr. 6-12). lib. bdg. 35.00 *(978-0-7910-9526-3(6),* Chelsea Hse.) Facts On File, Inc.
—Uncle Sam: International Symbol of America. Moreno, Barry, ed. 2014. (Patriotic Symbols of America Ser.: 20). 48p. (J). (gr. 4-18). lib. bdg. 20.95 *(978-1-4222-3135-7(6))* Mason Crest.
Marsh, Carole. Dick Cheney: U. S. Vice President. 2004. (1000 Readers Ser.). (Illus.). 14p. (J). (gr. k-4). pap. 2.95 *(978-0-635-02670-5(8))* Gallopade International.
—Jefferson Davis, Civil War Hero. 2004. 12p. (gr. k-4). 2.95 *(978-0-635-02366-7(0))* Gallopade International.
—Jimmy Carter. 2003. 12p. (gr. k-4). 2.95 *(978-0-635-02126-7(9))* Gallopade International.
—John C. Fremont. 2004. 12p. (gr. k-4). 2.95 *(978-0-635-02380-3(6))* Gallopade International.
—John Edwards: Vice Presidential Hopeful. 2004. (Did You Know... ? Ser.). (Illus.). 12p. (J). (gr. k-4). pap. 2.95 *(978-0-635-02671-2(6))* Gallopade International.
—John F. Kennedy. 2003. 12p. (gr. k-4). 2.95 *(978-0-635-02127-4(7))* Gallopade International.
—Jonas Salk. 2004. 12p. (gr. k-4). 2.95 *(978-0-635-02377-3(6))* Gallopade International.
—Meriwether Lewis & William Clark: Explorers of the Uncharted West: Explorers of the Uncharted West. 2003. 12p. (gr. k-4). 2.95 *(978-0-635-02133-5(1))* Gallopade International.
—Roberto Clemente: Baseball Hero & Humanitarian: Baseball Hero & Humanitarian. 2003. 12p. (gr. k-4). 2.95 *(978-0-635-02140-3(4))* Gallopade International.
—Samuel Adams. 2003. 12p. (gr. k-4). 2.95 *(978-0-635-02367-4(9))* Gallopade International.
Marsico, Katie. Zora Neale Hurston, 1 vol. 2008. (Essential Lives Set 2 Ser.). (ENG., Illus.). 112p. (J). (gr. 6-12). lib. bdg. 35.64 *(978-1-60453-036-0(7))* ABDO Publishing Co.
Martin, Justin. Easy Reader Biographies: George Washington: George Washington. 2007. (ENG.). 16p. pap. 2.99 *(978-0-439-92331-6(X),* Teaching Resources) Scholastic, Inc.
Martin Luther King Jr. (Illus.). 112p. pap. 9.95 *(978-0-8225-5316-8(3))* Lerner Publishing Group.
Marvis, Barbara. Day by Day with Beyonce. 2010. (Randy's Corner Ser.). (Illus.). 32p. (J). (gr. -1-2). lib. bdg. 25.70 *(978-1-58415-859-2(X))* Mitchell Lane Pubs., Inc.
—Day by Day with Lebron James. 2010. (Randy's Corner Ser.). (Illus.). 32p. (YA). (gr. -1-2). lib. bdg. 25.70 *(978-1-58415-858-5(1))* Mitchell Lane Pubs., Inc.
Marzollo, Jean. The Little Plant Doctor: The Story of George Washington Carver. Wilson-Max, Ken, illus. 2011. (ENG.). 32p. (J). (gr. -1-3). 16.95 *(978-0-8234-2325-5(5))* Holiday Hse., Inc.
Mason, Paul. Extreme Sports Stars. 2012. (Celebrity Secrets Ser.). (ENG., Illus.). 24p. (J). (gr. 5-8). pap. 8.25 *(978-1-4488-7080-6(1));* lib. bdg. 22.60 *(978-1-4488-7035-6(6))* Rosen Publishing Group, Inc., The. (PowerKids Pr.).
Masters, Nancy Robinson. Extraordinary Patriots of the United States of America: Colonial Times to Pre-Civil War. 2005. (Extraordinary People Ser.). (ENG., Illus.). 288p. (J). (gr. 4-7). 40.00 *(978-0-516-24404-4(3),* Children's Pr.) Scholastic Library Publishing.
Mattern, Joanne. Barack Obama. 2013. (Rookie Biographies(r) Ser.). (ENG.). 32p. (J). pap. 5.95 *(978-0-531-24701-3(5));* lib. bdg. 23.00 *(978-0-531-24735-8(X))* Scholastic Library Publishing.
—Blake Lively. 2010. (Blue Banner Biography Ser.). (Illus.). 32p. (YA). (gr. 4-7). lib. bdg. 25.70 *(978-1-58415-909-4(X))* Mitchell Lane Pubs., Inc.
—Dak Prescott. 2017. lib. bdg. 25.70 ***(978-1-68020-127-7(1))*** Mitchell Lane Pubs., Inc.
—Dakota Fanning. 2006. (Robbie Reader Ser.). (Illus.). 32p. (J). (gr. 2-5). lib. bdg. 25.70 *(978-1-58415-519-5(1))* Mitchell Lane Pubs., Inc.
—Day by Day with Adam Jones. 2014. (Illus.). 32p. (J). (gr. -1-2). 25.70 *(978-1-61228-632-7(1))* Mitchell Lane Pubs., Inc.
—Derek Jeter: Baseball Superstar, 1 vol. 2011. (Superstar Athletes Ser.). (ENG.). 24p. (gr. 1-2). pap. 7.29 *(978-1-4296-7303-7(6));* pap. 41.70 *(978-1-4296-7304-4(4))* Capstone Press of Coughlan Cos.
—Dwight Howard: Basketball Superstar, 1 vol. 2011. (Superstar Athletes Ser.). (ENG.). 24p. (gr. 1-2). pap. 7.29 *(978-1-4296-7307-5(9));* pap. 41.70 *(978-1-4296-7308-2(7))* Capstone Press of Coughlan Cos.
—Jaden Smith. 2009. (Robbie Reader Ser.). (Illus.). 32p. (YA). (gr. 2-5). lib. bdg. 25.70 *(978-1-58415-757-1(7))* Mitchell Lane Pubs., Inc.
—James Harden. 2017. lib. bdg. 25.70 ***(978-1-68020-122-2(0))*** Mitchell Lane Pubs., Inc.
—Ludacris. 2011. (Blue Banner Biography Ser.). (Illus.). 32p. (YA). (gr. 4-7). lib. bdg. 25.70 *(978-1-61228-055-4(2))* Mitchell Lane Pubs., Inc.
—Ray Kroc: McDonald's Restaurants Builder, 1 vol. 2011. (Food Dudes Ser.). (ENG., Illus.). 32p. (J). (gr. 3-6). 27.07 *(978-1-61613-559-1(X))* ABDO Publishing Co.
—Steve Jobs. 2013. (Rookie Biographies(r) Ser.). (ENG.). 32p. (J). pap. 5.95 *(978-0-531-24705-1(8),* Children's Pr.); lib. bdg. 23.00 *(978-0-531-24739-6(2))* Scholastic Library Publishing.
Maurer, Tracy Nelson. Noah Webster's Fighting Words. Catusanu, Mircea, illus. 2017. (Millbrook Picture Bks.). (ENG.). 40p. (gr. 2-5). 30.65 ***(978-1-5124-2839-1(6),*** Millbrook Pr.) Lerner Publishing Group.
McCarthy, Meghan. Strong Man: The Story of Charles Atlas. 2015. (ENG., Illus.). 40p. (J). (gr. k-3). 7.99 *(978-0-553-11354-9(2),* Dragonfly Bks.) Random Hse. Children's Bks.
McCarthy, Pat. Famous Union Generals & Leaders of the North: A MyReportLinks. com Book. 2004. (American Civil War Ser.). (Illus.). 48p. (J). lib. bdg. 26.60 *(978-0-7660-5188-1(9),* MyReportLinks.com Bks.) Enslow Pubs., Inc.
McCarthy, Rose. Paul Revere: Jinete de la guerra de Independencia. 2004. (Grandes personajes en la historia de los Estados Unidos Ser.). (SPA.). 32p. (gr. 3-6). pap. 10.00 *(978-0-8239-4236-7(8),* Rosen Classroom) Rosen Publishing Group, Inc., The.
McCully, Emily Arnold. Ida M. Tarbell: The Woman Who Challenged Big Business-and Won! 2014. (ENG., Illus.). 288p. (YA). (gr. 7). 18.99 *(978-0-547-29092-8(6),* Clarion Bks.) Houghton Mifflin Harcourt Trade & Reference Pubs.
McDonnell, Peter. A Soldier in Disguise. Tormey, Carlotta, illus. 2005. 16p. (J). pap. *(978-0-7367-2909-3(7))* Zaner-Bloser, Inc.
McDougall, Chros. Arthur Ashe: Tennis Great & Civil Rights Leader, 1 vol. 2011. (Legendary Athletes Ser.). (ENG., Illus.). 112p. (YA). (gr. 7-12). 34.22 *(978-1-61714-753-1(2))* ABDO Publishing Co.
McElroy, Lisa Tucker. Nancy Pelosi: First Woman Speaker of the House. 2007. (Gateway Biographies Ser.). (ENG., Illus.). 48p. (gr. 4-8). lib. bdg. 26.60 *(978-0-8225-8685-2(1),* Lerner Pubns.) Lerner Publishing Group.
—Ted Kennedy: A Remarkable Life in the Senate. 2009. (Gateway Biographies Ser.). (ENG.). 48p. (gr. 4-8). 26.60 *(978-0-7613-4457-5(8))* Lerner Publishing Group.
McGowan, Joseph. Will Smith. 2009. (Today's Superstars Ser.). 48p. (J). (gr. 5-8). (ENG.). pap. 14.05 *(978-1-4339-2376-0(9));* lib. bdg. 31.95 *(978-1-4339-2380-7(7))* Stevens, Gareth Publishing LLLP.
McKinley, Fred B. Chinqua Where? The Spirit of Rural America, 1947-1955. Blassingame, Calvin, illus. 2003. 319p. 24.95 *(978-0-9729655-0-7(5))* Willow Creel Publishing Co.
McKissack, Patricia C. & McKissack, Fredrick L. Frederick Douglass: Fighter Against Slavery. 2013. (Famous African Americans Ser.). 24p. (J). (gr. k-3). pap. 7.95 *(978-1-4644-0196-1(9),* Enslow Elementary) Enslow Pubs., Inc.
—Marian Anderson: Amazing Opera Singer. 2013. (Famous African Americans Ser.). (Illus.). 24p. (J). (gr. k-3). pap. 7.95 *(978-1-4644-0202-9(7),* Enslow Elementary) Enslow Pubs., Inc.
—Paul Robeson: A Voice for Change. 2013. (Famous African Americans Ser.). 24p. (J). (gr. k-3). pap. 7.95 *(978-1-4644-0205-0(1));* (Illus.). 22.60 *(978-0-7660-4107-3(7))* Enslow Pubs., Inc. (Enslow Elementary).
McLeese, Don. Jonas Salk. 2005. (Rourke Discovery Library). (Illus.). 24p. (J). (gr. 2-5). lib. bdg. *(978-1-59515-436-1(1))* Rourke Educational Media.
—Robert Fulton. 2005. (Rourke Discovery Library). (Illus.). 24p. (J). (gr. 2-5). lib. bdg. *(978-1-59515-434-7(5),* 1244323) Rourke Educational Media.
McNeese, Tim. New Amsterdam. 2007. (Colonial Settlements in America Ser.). (Illus.). 109p. (YA). (gr. 5-9). lib. bdg. 30.00 *(978-0-7910-9334-4(4))* Facts On File, Inc.
McNeill, Allison & Hanes, Richard Clay. American Home Front in World War II Reference Library Cumulative Index. 2004. (American Homefront in World War II Reference Library). (ENG.). 32p. 5.00 *(978-0-7876-9125-7(9),* UXL) Cengage Gale.
McPherson, Stephanie Sammartino. Bill Clinton. 2008. (History Maker Biographies Ser.). (ENG.). 48p. (gr. 3-6). 27.93 *(978-0-8225-7986-1(3),* Lerner Pubns.) Lerner Publishing Group.
—Levi Strauss. 2007. (History Maker Bios Ser.). (Illus.). 48p. (J). (gr. 3-7). lib. bdg. 26.60 *(978-0-8225-6581-9(1),* Lerner Pubns.) Lerner Publishing Group.
—Susan B. Anthony. 2006. (History Maker Bios Ser.). (Illus.). 48p. (J). (gr. 3-7). lib. bdg. 26.60 *(978-0-8225-5938-2(2),* Lerner Pubns.) Lerner Publishing Group.
McVey, James. Martha Maxwell: Natural History Pioneer. 2005. (Now You Know Bio Ser.: 4). (Illus.). 84p. (J). pap. *(978-0-86541-075-6(5))* Filter Pr., LLC.
Mead, Wendy. William H. Taft. 2011. (Presidents & Their Times 5 Ser.). 96p. (gr. 6). 34.21 *(978-1-60870-186-5(7))* Marshall Cavendish Corp.
Meet NASA Inventor Masahiro Ono & His Team's Asteroid-Harpooning Hitcher. 2017. (J). ***(978-0-7166-6161-0(6))*** World Bk., Inc.
Meet NASA Inventor Robert Hoyt & His Team's Web-Spinning Space Spiders. 2017. (J). ***(978-0-7166-6157-3(8))*** World Bk., Inc.
Mello, Tara Baukus. Mark Martin. rev. ed. 2007. (Race Car Legends Ser.). (Illus.). 72p. (YA). (gr. 5-9). lib. bdg. 25.00 *(978-0-7910-8664-3(X))* Facts On File, Inc.
—Tony Stewart. rev. collector's ed. 2005. (Race Car Legends Ser.). (Illus.). 64p. (YA). (gr. 5-9). lib. bdg. 25.00 *(978-0-7910-8670-4(4))* Facts On File, Inc.
Meltzer, Milton. Henry David Thoreau: A Biography. 2007. (Literary Greats Ser.). (ENG., Illus.). 160p. (gr. 7-12). lib. bdg. 33.26 *(978-0-8225-5893-4(9),* Twenty-First Century Bks.) Lerner Publishing Group.
Meyer, Susan. Jimmy Wales & Wikipedia. 2012. (Internet Biographies Ser.). (ENG.). 128p. (YA). (gr. 7-12). lib. bdg. 34.60 *(978-1-4488-6912-1(9))* Rosen Publishing Group, Inc., The.
Mickle, Shelley Fraser. Barbaro: America's Horse. 2007. (ENG., Illus.). 160p. (J). (gr. 3-7). pap. 9.99 *(978-1-4169-4865-0(1),* Simon & Schuster/Paula Wiseman Bks.) Simon & Schuster/Paula Wiseman Bks.
Micklos, John, Jr. Jerry Spinelli: Master Teller of Teen Tales. 2007. (Authors Teens Love Ser.). (Illus.). 104p. (J). (gr. 8-12). lib. bdg. 33.27 *(978-0-7660-2718-3(X))* Enslow Pubs., Inc.
Miklowitz, Gloria. Cesar Chavez. 2009. pap. 13.25 *(978-1-60559-056-1(8))* Hameray Publishing Group, Inc.
Miley Cyrus. 2011. (Megastars Ser.). (ENG.). 48p. (YA). pap. 11.75 *(978-1-4488-2259-1(9),* Rosen Reference) Rosen Publishing Group, Inc., The.
Miller, Adam, et al. Courage under Fire: True Stories of Bravery from the U. S. Army, Navy, Air Force, & Marines, 1 vol. 2014. (Courage under Fire Ser.). (ENG., Illus.). 112p. (gr. 3-4). pap. 9.95 *(978-1-4914-1065-3(5))* Capstone Press of Coughlan Cos.
Miller, Barbara Kiely. John Muir. 2007. (Grandes Personajes (Great Americans) Ser.). 24p. (gr. 1-4). (SPA.). pap. 8.15 *(978-0-8368-8339-8(X));* (SPA.). lib. bdg. 22.00 *(978-0-8368-8332-9(2));* lib. bdg. 22.00 *(978-0-8368-8318-3(7))* Stevens, Gareth Publishing LLLP. (Weekly Reader Leveled Readers).
Miller, Brandon Marie. Women of the Frontier: 16 Tales of Trailblazing Homesteaders, Entrepreneurs, & Rabble-Rousers. 2013. (Women of Action Ser.). (ENG., Illus.). 256p. (J). (gr. 7). 19.95 *(978-1-883052-97-3(1))* Chicago Review Pr., Inc.
Miller, Calvin Craig. Roy Wilkins: Leader of the NAACP. 2005. (Civil Rights Leaders Ser.). (Illus.). 176p. (YA). (gr. 6-12). 26.95 *(978-1-931798-49-5(4))* Reynolds, Morgan Inc.
Miller, Connie Colwell. Rosa Parks & the Montgomery Bus Boycott, 1 vol. Kalal, Dan, illus. 2006. (Graphic History Ser.). (ENG.). 32p. (gr. 3-4). 30.65 *(978-0-7368-6495-4(4),* Graphic Library) Capstone Press of Coughlan Cos.
Miller, Kat. I Love Kristen Stewart. 2010. (Fan Club Ser.). (ENG.). 24p. (gr. 3-6). lib. bdg. 22.60 *(978-1-61533-060-7(7));* (Illus.). (J). pap. 8.15 *(978-1-61533-061-4(5))* Windmill Bks.
—I Love Miley Cyrus. 2010. (Fan Club Ser.). (ENG.). 24p. (J). (gr. 3-6). lib. bdg. 22.60 *(978-1-61533-045-4(3));* (Illus.). pap. 8.15 *(978-1-61533-046-1(1))* Windmill Bks.
—I Love the Jonas Brothers. 2010. (Fan Club Ser.). (ENG.). 24p. (J). (gr. 3-6). lib. bdg. 22.60 *(978-1-61533-048-5(8));* (Illus.). pap. 8.15 *(978-1-61533-049-2(6))* Windmill Bks.
Miller, Raymond H. Matt Groening. 2005. (Inventors & Creators Ser.). (ENG., Illus.). 48p. (gr. 4-8). 27.00 *(978-0-7377-3158-3(3),* Greenhaven Pr., Inc.) Cengage Gale.
Miller, Reagan & Arthur, Martin. Great Leaders of the Civil War. 2011. (ENG.). 48p. (J). pap. *(978-0-7787-5359-9(X));* lib. bdg. *(978-0-7787-5342-1(5))* Crabtree Publishing Co.
Mills, Cliff. Clayton Kershaw. 2014. (Illus.). 32p. (J). (gr. 1-4). 25.70 *(978-1-61228-636-5(4))* Mitchell Lane Pubs., Inc.
Mills, Clifford W. Ang Lee. 2009. (Asian Americans of Achievement Ser.). (Illus.). 120p. (J). (gr. 7-12). 35.00 *(978-1-60413-566-4(2))* Facts On File, Inc.
Mills, J. Elizabeth. Ken Griffey Sr. & Ken Griffey Jr: Baseball Heroes. 2010. (Sports Families Ser.). (ENG., Illus.). 48p. (J).

pap. 11.75 (978-1-4358-8514-1(7), Rosen Reference) Rosen Publishing Group, Inc., The.

—Ken Griffey Sr. & Ken Griffey Jr. Baseball Heroes. 2010. (Sports Families Ser.). (Illus.). 48p. (YA). (gr. 4-7). lib. bdg. 29.25 (978-1-4358-3554-2(9)) Rosen Publishing Group, Inc., The.

Mintzer, Richard. Latino Americans in Sports, Film, Music & Government: Trailblazers. 2007. (Hispanic Heritage Ser.). (Illus.). 112p. (YA). (gr. 4-7). lib. bdg. 22.95 (978-1-59084-936-1(1)) Mason Crest.

Mis, Melody S. Civil Rights Leaders, 6 vols., Set. Incl. Meet Al Sharpton. lib. bdg. 22.60 (978-1-4042-4213-5(9)); Meet Coretta Scott King. lib. bdg. 22.60 (978-1-4042-4211-1(2)); Meet Jesse Jackson. lib. bdg. 22.60 (978-1-4042-4212-8(0)); Meet Malcolm X. lib. bdg. 22.60 (978-1-4042-4214-2(7)); Meet Martin Luther King Jr. lib. bdg. 22.60 (978-1-4042-4209-8(0)); Meet Rosa Parks. lib. bdg. 22.60 (978-1-4042-4210-4(4)); (Illus.). 24p. (YA). (gr. 2-5). 2008. 2009. Set lib. bdg. 127.50 (978-1-4042-4240-1(6)) Rosen Publishing Group, Inc., The.

—Meet Al Sharpton. 2008. (Civil Rights Leaders Ser.). (Illus.). 24p. (YA). (gr. 2-5). lib. bdg. 22.60 (978-1-4042-4213-5(9)) Rosen Publishing Group, Inc., The.

Mitchell Lane Publishers Inc. Staff. Profiles in American History. 2007. (YA). lib. bdg. 460.90 (978-1-58415-532-4(9)) Mitchell Lane Pubs., Inc.

Mitchells, Brett. The Dixie Chicks. 2008. (Contemporary Musicians & Their Music Ser.). (Illus.). 48p. (J). lib. bdg. 29.25 (978-1-4042-1817-8(3)) Rosen Publishing Group, Inc., The.

—Dixie Chicks. 2009. (Contemporary Musicians & Their Music Ser.). 48p. (Illus.). (gr. 7-12). pap. 11.75 (978-1-4358-5125-2(0), Rosen Classroom); (gr. 6-6). 53.00 (978-1-61511-932-5(9)) Rosen Publishing Group, Inc., The.

Monroe, Tyler. Uncle Sam, 1 vol. 2013. (U. S. Symbols Ser.). (ENG.). 24p. (gr. k-1). 26.65 (978-1-4765-3086-4(6)); pap. 7.95 (978-1-4765-3535-7(3)) Capstone Press of Coughlan Cos. (Pebble Plus).

Montgomery, Sy. The Tarantula Scientist. Bishop, Nic, photos by. 2007. (Scientists in the Field Ser.). (ENG., Illus.). 80p. (J). (gr. 5-7). pap. 9.99 (978-0-618-91577-4(X)) Houghton Mifflin Harcourt Publishing Co.

Monumental Milestones: Great Events of Modern Times, 16 vols., Set. 2006. (J). (gr. 4-8). lib. bdg. 319.20 (978-1-58415-292-7(3)) Mitchell Lane Pubs., Inc.

Mooney, Carla. Asante Samuel. 2009. (Superstars of Pro Football Ser.). (Illus.). 64p. (YA). (gr. 7-12). lib. bdg. 22.95 (978-1-4222-0542-6(8)) Mason Crest.

—Vanessa Hudgens. 2007. (Sharing the American Dream Ser.). 64p. (YA). (gr. 7-18). pap. 9.95 (978-1-4222-0749-9(8)) Mason Crest.

—Vanessa Hudgens/Carla Mooney. 2009. (Sharing the American Dream Ser.). 64p. (YA). (gr. 7-12). 22.95 (978-1-4222-0583-9(5)) Mason Crest.

Mooney, Carla & Gale Editors. Jonas Brothers. 2009. (People in the News Ser.). (Illus.). 128p. (YA). (gr. 7-12). 33.95 (978-1-4205-0236-7(0)) Cengage Gale.

Moore, Barbara R. Sojourner Truth. 2005. (Illus.). 16p. (J). (978-0-618-56039-4(4)) Houghton Mifflin Harcourt Publishing Co.

Moore, Cathy. Ellen Craft's Escape from Slavery. Braught, Mark, illus. 2010. (History Speaks: Picture Books Plus Reader's Theater Ser.). (ENG.). 48p. (gr. 2-4). pap. 9.95 (978-0-7613-6672-0(5)); lib. bdg. 27.93 (978-0-7613-5875-6(7), Millbrook Pr.) Lerner Publishing Group.

Morgan, Kayla. Barnes & Noble: Groundbreaking Entrepreneurs, 1 vol. 2009. (Publishing Pioneers Ser.). (ENG., Illus.). 112p. (J). (gr. 6-12). lib. bdg. 35.64 (978-1-60453-758-1(2), Essential Library) ABDO Publishing Co.

Morganelli, Adrianna. Bruno Mars. 2013. (ENG., Illus.). 32p. (J). pap. (978-0-7787-0041-8(0)) Crabtree Publishing Co.

Morreale, Marie. Bethany Mota. 2016. (Real Bios Ser.). (ENG., Illus.). 48p. (J). lib. bdg. 29.00 (978-0-531-22378-9(7), Children's Pr.) Scholastic Library Publishing.

Morrison, Jessica. Hank Aaron: Home Run Hero. 2010. (Crabtree Groundbreaker Biographies Ser.). (ENG., Illus.). 112p. (J). (gr. 5-8). lib. bdg. (978-0-7787-2538-1(3)) Crabtree Publishing Co.

Moua, Mayhoua, et al. Mayhoua Moua: A Real-Life Story from a Hmong Story Cloth. 2014. (Text Connections Ser.). (J). (gr. 3). (978-1-4509-9647-1(7)) Benchmark Education Co.

Mour, Stanley I. Innovators of American Jazz. 2013. (Inspiring Collective Biographies Ser.). 112p. (J). (gr. 5-12). pap. 10.95 (978-1-4644-0271-5(X)) Enslow Pubs., Inc.

Mulhall, Jill K. James Madison, 1 vol. 2005. (Primary Source Readers Ser.). (ENG.). 24p. (J). (gr. 4-4). pap. 8.99 (978-0-7439-8908-4(2)) Shell Educational Publishing.

—Thomas Jefferson, 1 vol. 2004. (Primary Source Readers Ser.). (ENG.). 24p. (J). (gr. 4-4). pap. 8.99 (978-0-7439-8747-9(0)) Shell Educational Publishing.

Murphy, Maggie. The Jonas Brothers: Rock Stars. 2010. (Young & Famous Ser.). (ENG.). 24p. (J). (gr. 3-6). lib. bdg. 22.60 (978-1-4488-0646-1(1)) Rosen Publishing Group, Inc., The.

—Kristen Stewart: Twilight Star. 2010. (Reading Power). (Illus.). 24p. (J). pap. 8.85 (978-1-4488-1795-5(1), PowerKids Pr.) Rosen Publishing Group, Inc., The.

—Miley Cyrus: Rock Star. 2010. (Young & Famous Ser.). 24p. (J). (ENG.). (gr. 3-6). 22.60 (978-1-4488-0643-0(7)); (Illus.). pap. 8.85 (978-1-4488-1799-3(4), PowerKids Pr.) Rosen Publishing Group, Inc., The.

—Taylor Lautner: Twilight Star. 2010. (Young & Famous Ser.). (ENG.). 24p. (YA). (gr. 3-6). lib. bdg. 22.60 (978-1-4488-0642-3(9)) Rosen Publishing Group, Inc., The.

—Taylor Swift: Country Music Star. 2010. (Young & Famous Ser.). (ENG.). 24p. (J). (gr. 3-6). lib. bdg. 22.60 (978-1-4488-0645-4(3)) Rosen Publishing Group, Inc., The.

—Zac Efron: Movie Star. 2010. (Reading Power). (Illus.). 24p. (J). pap. 8.85 (978-1-4488-1801-3(X), PowerKids Pr.) Rosen Publishing Group, Inc., The.

Nagelhout, Ryan. Michael Phelps: Greatest Swimmer of All Time. 2017. (Breakout Biographies Ser.). 32p. (J). (gr. 9-10). pap. 10.00 **(978-1-5081-6066-3(X)**, PowerKids Pr.) Rosen Publishing Group, Inc., The.

Nagelhout, Ryan. Peyton Manning, Vol. 1. 2014. (Today's Great Quarterbacks Ser.). (ENG.). 32p. (J). (gr. 1-1). pap. 10.50 (978-1-4824-0480-7(X)) Stevens, Gareth Publishing LLLP.

Nardo, Don. Bernie Madoff. 2011. (People in the News Ser.). (ENG.). 128p. (gr. 10-10). lib. bdg. 39.40 (978-1-4205-0353-1(7)) Cengage Gale.

—Mathew Brady: The Camera Is the Eye of History. 2008. (Americans—the Spirit of a Nation Ser.). (Illus.). 128p. (J). (gr. k-5). lib. bdg. 33.27 (978-0-7660-3023-7(7)) Enslow Pubs., Inc.

Nault, Jennifer. The Insightful World of Judy Blume. 2016. (J). **(978-1-5105-1953-4(X))** SmartBook Media, Inc.

Nazario, Sonia. Enrique's Journey: The True Story of a Boys Determined to Reunite with His Mother. 2013. (ENG.). 288p. (YA). (gr. 7). 16.99 (978-0-385-74327-3(0), Delacorte Bks. for Young Readers) Random Hse. Children's Bks.

Neimark, Anne. There Ain't Nobody That Can Sing Like Me: The Life of Woody Guthrie. 2017. (ENG., Illus.). 128p. (J). (gr. 5-9). pap. 13.99 **(978-1-5344-0950-7(5)**, Atheneum Bks. for Young Readers) Simon & Schuster Children's Publishing.

Nelson, Maria. The Life of Paul Revere. 2012. (Famous Lives Ser.). (ENG.). 24p. (J). (gr. k-3). lib. bdg. 22.60 (978-1-4339-6353-7(1)); (gr. 1-4). pap. 8.15 (978-1-4339-6355-1(8)) Stevens, Gareth Publishing LLLP.

Nelson, Robin. George Washington Carver: A Life of Devotion. 2006. (Pull Ahead Bks.). (Illus.). 32p. (J). (gr. 3-7). lib. bdg. 22.60 (978-0-8225-6461-4(0), Lerner Pubns.) Lerner Publishing Group.

Nichols, Kaitlyn. Davey Crockett. 2009. pap. 13.25 (978-1-60559-057-8(6)) Hameray Publishing Group, Inc.

—Martin Luther King. 2009. pap. 13.25 (978-1-60559-065-3(7)) Hameray Publishing Group, Inc.

Northrup, Mary. Pioneering American Computer Geniuses. 2013. (Inspiring Collective Biographies Ser.). 112p. (J). (gr. 5-12). pap. 10.95 (978-1-4644-0273-9(6)) Enslow Pubs., Inc.

Noyes, Deborah. The Magician & the Spirits. 2017. (ENG., Illus.). 160p. (J). (gr. 5). 18.99 **(978-0-8037-4018-1(2)**, Viking Books for Young Readers) Penguin Young Readers Group.

Obama, Barack. Of Thee I Sing: A Letter to My Daughters. Long, Loren, illus. 2010. (ENG.). 40p. (J). (gr. k-12). 17.99 (978-0-375-83527-8(X), Knopf Bks. for Young Readers) Random Hse. Children's Bks.

O'Donnell, Jessica. Leontyne Price: First Lady of Opera. 2010. (Inspiring Lives Ser.). 32p. (J). (gr. 5-8). lib. bdg. 25.25 (978-1-4339-3628-9(3)) Stevens, Gareth Publishing LLLP.

O'Keefe, Sherry. Spin: The Story of Michael Jackson. 2011. (Modern Music Masters Ser.). (Illus.). 144p. (YA). (gr. 6-9). 28.95 (978-1-59935-134-6(X)) Reynolds, Morgan Inc.

Oliver-Miles, Zelda. Amelia Gayle Gorgas: First Woman of Position. 2005. (Alabama Roots Biography Ser.). (Illus.). 100p. (J). pap. (978-1-59421-017-4(9)) Seacoast Publishing, Inc.

O'Neal, Claire. Cole Hamels. 2009. (Blue Banner Biography Ser.). (Illus.). 32p. (YA). (gr. 4-7). lib. bdg. 25.70 (978-1-58415-776-2(3)) Mitchell Lane Pubs., Inc.

—T. I. 2009. (Blue Banner Biography Ser.). (Illus.). 32p. (YA). (gr. 4-7). lib. bdg. 25.70 (978-1-58415-769-4(0)) Mitchell Lane Pubs., Inc.

Oprah Winfrey. 2004. (Illus.). 112p. pap. 9.95 (978-0-8225-5320-5(1)) Lerner Publishing Group.

Orr, Tamara. Emily Osment. 2009. (Robbie Reader Ser.). (Illus.). 32p. (YA). (gr. 2-5). lib. bdg. 25.70 (978-1-58415-755-7(0)) Mitchell Lane Pubs., Inc.

Orr, Tamra. Alan Shepard: The First American in Space. 2009. (Library of Astronaut Biographies Ser.). 112p. (gr. 5-8). 63.90 (978-1-60853-518-7(5), Rosen Reference) Rosen Publishing Group, Inc., The.

—AnnaSophia Robb. 2010. (Robbie Reader Ser.). (Illus.). 32p. (YA). (gr. 2-5). lib. bdg. 25.70 (978-1-58415-898-1(0)) Mitchell Lane Pubs., Inc.

—Chris Johnson. 2011. (Robbie Reader Ser.). (Illus.). 32p. (J). (gr. 2-5). lib. bdg. 25.70 (978-1-61228-064-6(1)) Mitchell Lane Pubs., Inc.

—Day by Day with Selena Gomez. 2011. (Day by Day with... Ser.). (Illus.). 32p. (J). (gr. -1-2). lib. bdg. 25.70 (978-1-58415-987-2(1)) Mitchell Lane Pubs., Inc.

—Kristen Stewart. 2009. (Blue Banner Biography Ser.). (Illus.). 32p. (YA). (gr. 4-7). lib. bdg. 25.70 (978-1-58415-773-1(9)) Mitchell Lane Pubs., Inc.

—Shia Labeouf. 2010. (Blue Banner Biography Ser.). (Illus.). 32p. (YA). (gr. 4-7). lib. bdg. 25.70 (978-1-58415-908-7(1)) Mitchell Lane Pubs., Inc.

—Stephanie Meyer. 2010. (Blue Banner Biography Ser.). (Illus.). 32p. (YA). (gr. 4-7). lib. bdg. 25.70 (978-1-58415-907-0(3)) Mitchell Lane Pubs., Inc.

Orr, Tamra B. The Life & Times of Susan B. Anthony. 2006. (Profiles in American History Ser.). (Illus.). 48p. (J). (gr. 3-7). lib. bdg. 29.95 (978-1-58415-445-7(4)) Mitchell Lane Pubs., Inc.

Osborne, Mary Pope & Boyce, Natalie Pope. Abraham Lincoln: A Nonfiction Companion to Magic Tree House No. 47 - Abe Lincoln at Last! Murdocca, Sal, illus. 2011. (Magic Tree House - Fact Tracker Ser.: No. 25). (ENG.). 128p. (J). (gr. 2-5). 6.99 (978-0-375-87024-8(5), Random Hse. Bks. for Young Readers) Random Hse. Children's Bks.

Oscar de la Renta. 2010. (Great Hispanic Heritage Ser.). (Illus.). 128p. (gr. 6-12). 35.00 (978-1-60413-733-0(9), Chelsea Hse.) Facts On File, Inc.

O'Shei, Tim. Philo T. Farnsworth: Visionary Inventor of Television. 2008. (Inventors Who Changed the World Ser.). (Illus.). 128p. (J). (gr. 6-18). lib. bdg. 34.60 (978-1-59845-075-0(1), MyReportLinks.com Bks.) Enslow Pubs., Inc.

Osier, Dan. Dirk Nowitzki. 2011. (Basketball's MVPs Ser.). 24p. (J). (ENG.). pap. 8.85 (978-1-4488-2632-2(2)); (Illus.). (gr. 3-6). lib. bdg. 22.60 (978-1-4488-2524-0(5)) Rosen Publishing Group, Inc., The. (PowerKids Pr.).

Otfinoski, Steven. Grover Cleveland. 2010. (Presidents & Their Times 4 Ser.). 96p. (gr. 6). 34.21 (978-0-7614-4811-2(X)) Marshall Cavendish GBR. Dist: Marshall Cavendish Corp.

Owens, Jim. The Survivorship Net: A Parable for the Family, Friends, & Caregivers of People with Cancer. Cass, Bill, illus. 2010. (ENG.). 48p. (gr. 2). 14.95 (978-1-60443-018-9(4)) American Cancer Society, Inc.

Parker, Christi E. Abraham Lincoln, 1 vol. 2005. (Primary Source Readers Ser.). (ENG.). 24p. (J). (gr. 4-4). pap. 8.99 (978-0-7439-8916-9(3)) Shell Educational Publishing.

Pasachoff, Naomi E. Barbara Mcclintock: Genius of Genetics. 2006. (Great Minds of Science Ser.). (Illus.). 128p. (J). (gr. 4-10). lib. bdg. 33.27 (978-0-7660-2505-9(5)) Enslow Pubs., Inc.

Patrick, James. Legend of the Delta Blues. 2010. (Inspiring Lives Ser.). 32p. (J). (gr. 5-8). lib. bdg. 25.25 (978-1-4339-3619-7(4)); (Illus.). pap. 10.50 (978-1-4339-3620-3(8)) Stevens, Gareth Publishing LLLP.

Paulsen, Gary. Puppies, Dogs, & Blue Northers: Reflections on Being Raised by a Pack of Sled Dogs. 2007. (ENG., Illus.). 80p. (J). (gr. 5-7). pap. 5.95 (978-0-15-206103-6(7)) Houghton Mifflin Harcourt Publishing Co.

—Woodsong. 2007. (ENG., Illus.). 144p. (J). (gr. 5-9). pap. 7.99 (978-1-4169-3939-9(3), Simon & Schuster Bks. For Young Readers) Simon & Schuster Bks. For Young Readers.

Pawlak, Debra Ann. Bruce Lee. 2009. (Sharing the American Dream Ser.). 64p. (YA). (gr. 7-12). 22.95 (978-1-4222-0586-0(X)) Mason Crest.

Payan, Michael. In the Ring with Bret Hart. 2009. (World of Wrestling Ser.). 24p. (gr. 1-1). 42.50 (978-1-60854-342-7(0), PowerKids Pr.) Rosen Publishing Group, Inc., The.

—In the Ring with Diamond Dallas Page. 2009. (World of Wrestling Ser.). 24p. (gr. 1-1). 42.50 (978-1-60854-343-4(9), PowerKids Pr.) Rosen Publishing Group, Inc., The.

—In the Ring with Goldberg. 2009. (World of Wrestling Ser.). 24p. (gr. 1-1). 42.50 (978-1-60854-346-5(3), PowerKids Pr.) Rosen Publishing Group, Inc., The.

—In the Ring with Kevin Nash. 2009. (World of Wrestling Ser.). 24p. (gr. 1-1). 42.50 (978-1-60854-347-2(1), PowerKids Pr.) Rosen Publishing Group, Inc., The.

—In the Ring with Scott Steiner. 2009. (World of Wrestling Ser.). 24p. (gr. 1-1). 42.50 (978-1-60854-348-9(X), PowerKids Pr.) Rosen Publishing Group, Inc., The.

—In the Ring with Sting. 2009. (World of Wrestling Ser.). 24p. (gr. 1-1). 42.50 (978-1-60854-349-6(8), PowerKids Pr.) Rosen Publishing Group, Inc., The.

PC Treasures Staff, ed. Tony Stewart. 2009. (Nascar Drivers Coloring Book Ser.). (ENG., Illus.). 96p. (J). pap. 2.99 (978-1-60072-160-1(5)) PC Treasures, Inc.

Peacock, L. A. The Truth (and Myths) about American Heroes. Davis, Jon, illus. 2016. 96p. (J). **(978-0-545-83027-0(3))** Scholastic, Inc.

Peak, Doris-Jean. Wernher Von Braun: Alabama's Rocket Scientist. 2009. (Alabama Roots Biography Ser.). (Illus.). 112p. (J). (978-1-59421-044-0(6)) Seacoast Publishing, Inc.

Pearce, Q. L. Given Kachepa: Advocate for Human Trafficking Victims. 2007. (Young Heroes Ser.). (ENG., Illus.). 64p. (J). (gr. 4-8). lib. bdg. 35.70 (978-0-7377-3668-7(2), Kidhaven) Cengage Gale.

—Hannah Taylor: The Ladybug Foundation. 2008. (Young Heroes Ser.). (ENG., Illus.). 64p. (gr. 4-8). 35.70 (978-0-7377-4051-6(5), Kidhaven) Cengage Gale.

—James Quadrino: Wildlife Protector. 2006. (Young Heroes Ser.). (ENG., Illus.). 48p. (J). (gr. 3-7). lib. bdg. 28.75 (978-0-7377-3612-0(7), Kidhaven) Cengage Gale.

Peckham, Howard Henry. William Henry Harrison, Young Tippecanoe: Childhood of Famous Americans Series. Laune, Paul, illus. 2011. 190p. 42.95 (978-1-258-07766-2(3)) Literary Licensing, LLC.

Peerson, Marie Graham. Joseph Wheeler: The Fearless 'Fightin' Joe' 2003. (Alabama Roots Biography Ser.). (Illus.). 120p. (J). (978-1-878561-40-4(5)) Seacoast Publishing, Inc.

Pelleschi, Andrea. Samuel de Champlain. 2013. (Jr. Graphic Famous Explorers Ser.). (ENG., Illus.). 24p. (J). (gr. 3-6). pap. 10.60 (978-1-4777-0133-1(8)); lib. bdg. 25.25 (978-1-4777-0074-7(9)) Rosen Publishing Group, Inc., The. (PowerKids Pr.).

Peters, Gregory N. Muhammad Ali Boxing Legend, 1 vol. 2014. (Sports & Recreation Ser.). (ENG., Illus.). 48p. (gr. 4-12). 31.99 (978-1-4765-8439-3(7)) Capstone Press of Coughlan Cos.

Petrillo, Lisa. Isaac Mizrahi. 2011. (Profiles in Fashion Ser.). (Illus.). 111p. 28.95 (978-1-59935-152-0(8)) Reynolds, Morgan Inc.

Pfeffer, Wendy. Many Ways to Be a Soldier. Verstraete, Elaine, illus. 2008. (On My Own History Ser.). (ENG.). 48p. (gr. 2-4). lib. bdg. 25.26 (978-0-8225-7279-4(6), Millbrook Pr.) Lerner Publishing Group.

Pflueger, Lynda. Stonewall Jackson: General of the Confederate Army. 2015. (J). (978-0-7660-6495-9(6)) Enslow Pubs., Inc.

Phillips, Larissa. Wild Bill Hickok: Legend of the American Wild West / Leyenda del oeste Americano. 2009. (Famous People in American History/Grandes personajes en la historia de los Estados Unidos Ser.). (ENG & SPA.). 32p. (gr. 2-3). 47.90 (978-1-61512-557-9(4), Editorial Buenas Letras) Rosen Publishing Group, Inc., The.

—Wild Bill Hickok: Legend of the Wild West. 2009. (Primary Sources of Famous People in American History Ser.). 32p. (gr. 2-3). 47.90 (978-1-60851-740-4(3)) Rosen Publishing Group, Inc., The.

—Wild Bill Hickok: Leyenda del oeste Americano. 2004. (Grandes personajes en la historia de los Estados Unidos Ser.). (SPA.). 32p. (gr. 3-6). pap. 10.00 (978-0-8239-4240-4(6), Rosen Classroom) Rosen Publishing Group, Inc., The.

—Wild Bill Hickok: Leyenda del oeste americano (Wild Bill Hickok: Legend of the American Wild West) 2009. (Grandes personajes en la historia de los Estados Unidos (Famous People in American History) Ser.). (SPA.). 32p. (gr. 2-3). 47.90 (978-1-61512-810-5(7), Editorial Buenas Letras) Rosen Publishing Group, Inc., The.

Pingry, Patricia A. Meet Abraham Lincoln. Britt, Stephanie McFetridge, illus. 2009. (ENG.). 32p. (J). pap. 7.99 (978-0-8249-5613-4(3), Ideal Pubns.) Worthy Publishing.

—Meet George Washington. Britt, Stephanie McFetridge, illus. 2009. (ENG.). 32p. (J). pap. 7.99 (978-0-8249-5612-7(5), Ideal Pubns.) Worthy Publishing.

Pollack, Pamela & Belviso, Meg. Who Was Steve Jobs? 2012. (Who Was... ? Ser.). lib. bdg. 16.00 (978-0-606-26649-9(6), Turtleback) Turtleback Bks.

Poole, Rebecca. Jimi Hendrix. 2006. (Just the Facts Biographies Ser.). (Illus.). 112p. (J). (gr. 3-7). pap. 9.95 (978-0-8225-5994-8(3), Lerner Pubns.) Lerner Publishing Group.

Porterfield, Jason. Calvin Hill & Grant Hill: One Family's Legacy in Football & Basketball. 2010. (Sports Families Ser.). 48p. (YA). (gr. 5-8). lib. bdg., E-Book 53.00 (978-1-4488-0087-2(0)) Rosen Publishing Group, Inc., The.

Porterfield, Jason. Frederick Douglass: Abolitionist & Fighter for Equality. 2017. (J). **(978-1-5383-0019-0(2)**, Britannica Educational Publishing) Rosen Publishing Group, Inc., The.

Powell, Walter L. Benedict Arnold: Revolutionary War Hero & Traitor. 2009. (Library of American Lives & Times Ser.). 112p. (gr. 5-5). 69.20 (978-1-60853-471-5(5)) Rosen Publishing Group, Inc., The.

Pratt, Mary K. Michael Jackson: King of Pop. 2011. (Lives Cut Short Ser.). (YA). (gr. 7-12). 71.36 (978-1-61641-447-4(2), Essential Library) ABDO Publishing Co.

Prentzas, G. S. Mario Andretti. rev. ed. 2007. (Race Car Legends Ser.). (Illus.). 80p. (YA). (gr. 5-9). lib. bdg. 25.00 (978-0-7910-8755-8(7)) Facts On File, Inc.

Pringle, Laurence. American Slave, American Hero: York of the Lewis & Clark Expedition. Van Wright, Cornelius & Hu, Ying-Hwa, illus. 2006. (ENG.). 40p. (J). (gr. 3-3). 19.95 (978-1-59078-282-8(8)) Boyds Mills Pr.

Pristash, Nicole. Dale Earnhardt Jr. 2009. (NASCAR Champions Ser.). (Illus.). 24p. (gr. 1-6). pap. 8.25 (978-1-4042-4541-9(3), Rosen Classroom) Rosen Publishing Group, Inc., The.

—Jeff Gordon. 2009. (NASCAR Champions Ser.). (ENG., Illus.). 24p. (gr. 1-6). pap. 8.25 (978-1-4042-4542-6(1), PowerKids Pr.) Rosen Publishing Group, Inc., The.

—Jimmie Johnson. 2009. (NASCAR Champions Ser.). (ENG., Illus.). 24p. (gr. 1-6). pap. 8.25 (978-1-4042-4543-3(X), PowerKids Pr.) Rosen Publishing Group, Inc., The.

—Kevin Harvick. 2009. (NASCAR Champions Ser.). (ENG., Illus.). 24p. (J). (gr. 1-6). pap. 8.25 (978-1-4042-4544-0(8)) Rosen Publishing Group, Inc., The.

Profiles in American History, 18 vols., Set. Incl. Benjamin Franklin. Whiting, Jim. (gr. 3-7). 2006. lib. bdg. 29.95 (978-1-58415-435-8(7)); Betsy Ross. Harkins, Susan Sales & Harkins, William H. (gr. 3-7). 2006. lib. bdg. 29.95 (978-1-58415-446-4(2)); Eli Whitney. Gibson, Karen Bush. (gr. 3-7). 2006. lib. bdg. 29.95 (978-1-58415-434-1(9)); John Cabot. Rice, Earle, Jr. (gr. 3-7). 2006. lib. bdg. 29.95 (978-1-58415-451-8(9)); John Hancock. Kjelle, Marylou Morano. (gr. 3-7). 2006. lib. bdg. 29.95 (978-1-58415-443-3(8)); John Peter Zenger. Gibson, Karen Bush. (gr. 3-7). 2006. lib. bdg. 29.95 (978-1-58415-437-2(3)); Life & Times of Alexander Hamilton. Roberts, Russell. (gr. 3-7). 2006. lib. bdg. 29.95 (978-1-58415-436-5(5)); Life & Times of George Rogers Clark. Roberts, Russell. (gr. 3-7). 2006. lib. bdg. 29.95 (978-1-58415-448-8(9)); Life & Times of Hernando Cortes. Whiting, Jim. (gr. 3-7). 2006. lib. bdg. 29.95 (978-1-58415-449-5(7)); Life & Times of John Adams. Whiting, Jim. (gr. 3-7). 2006. lib. bdg. 29.95 (978-1-58415-442-6(X)); Life & Times of Patrick Henry. Harkins, Susan & Harkins, William H. (gr. 4-8). 2006. lib. bdg. 29.95 (978-1-58415-438-9(1)); Life & Times of Paul Revere. Whiting, Jim. (gr. 3-7). 2006. lib. bdg. 29.95 (978-1-58415-441-9(1)); Life & Times of Sir Walter Raleigh. Rice, Earle, Jr. (gr. 3-7). 2006. lib. bdg. 29.95 (978-1-58415-452-5(7)); Life & Times of Susan B. Anthony. Orr, Tamra B. (gr. 3-7). 2006. lib. bdg. 29.95 (978-1-58415-445-7(4)); Life & Times of William Penn. Hinman, Bonnie. (gr. 4-8). 2006. lib. bdg. 29.95 (978-1-58415-433-4(0), 1259521); Nathan Hale. Tracy, Kathleen. (gr. 3-7). 2006. lib. bdg. 29.95 (978-1-58415-447-1(0)); Samuel Adams. Gibson, Karen Bush. (gr. 3-7). 2006. lib. bdg. 20.95 (978-1-58415-440-2(3)); Thomas Jefferson: The Life & Times Of. Roberts, Russell. (gr. 3-7). 2007. lib. bdg. 29.95 (978-1-58415-439-6(X)); (Illus.). 48p. (J). 2006. Set lib. bdg. 359.10 (978-1-58415-287-3(7)) Mitchell Lane Pubs., Inc.

Publishers, Chelsea House, creator. Leaders of the Civil War Era Set, 10-Volumes. 2009. (Leaders of the Civil War Era Ser.). (gr. 6-12). 350.00 (978-1-60413-643-2(X), Chelsea Hse.) Facts On File, Inc.

Pulditor, Seth H. DeSean Jackson. 2010. (Superstars of Pro Football Ser.). 64p. (YA). (gr. 5-18). lib. bdg. 22.95 (978-1-4222-1663-7(2)) Mason Crest.

—Drew Brees. 2013. (J). (978-1-4222-2720-6(0)) Mason Crest.

Rajczak, Kristen. Demi Lovato. 2011. (Rising Stars Ser.). (Illus.). 32p. (J). (gr. 3-6). pap. 10.50 (978-1-4339-5888-5(0)); lib. bdg. 25.25 (978-1-4339-5886-1(4)) Stevens, Gareth Publishing LLLP.

Randolph, Ryan. Betsy Ross: The American Flag, & Life in a Young America. 2009. (Library of American Lives & Times Ser.). 112p. (gr. 5-5). 69.20 (978-1-60853-473-9(1)) Rosen Publishing Group, Inc., The.

Randolph, Ryan P. Wild West Lawmen & Outlaws. 2009. (Library of the Westward Expansion Ser.). 24p. (gr. 3-4). 42.50 (978-1-60853-944-4(X), PowerKids Pr.) Rosen Publishing Group, Inc., The.

Ransom, Candice. Daniel Boone. 2005. (History Maker Biographies Ser.). (ENG., Illus.). 48p. (gr. 3-6). lib. bdg. 27.93 (978-0-8225-2941-5(6), Lerner Pubns.) Lerner Publishing Group.

—Willie McLean & the Civil War Surrender. Reeves, Jeni, illus. 2004. (On My Own History Ser.). (ENG.). 48p. (gr. 2-4). 25.26 (978-1-57505-588-6(0)); pap. 6.95 (978-1-57505-698-2(4)) Lerner Publishing Group.

Rappoport, Ken. Basketball's Top 10 Slam Dunkers. 2010. (Top 10 Sports Stars Ser.). (Illus.). 48p. (J). (gr. 5-9). 25.27 (978-0-7660-3467-9(4)) Enslow Pubs., Inc.

—Dale Earnhardt, Jr: A Car Racer Who Cares. 2011. (Sports Stars Who Care Ser.). (Illus.). 48p. (J). (gr. 2-5). lib. bdg. 25.27 (978-0-7660-3777-9(0)) Enslow Pubs., Inc.

—Derek Jeter: Champion Baseball Star. 2012. (Sports Star Champions Ser.). (Illus.). 48p. (J). (gr. 5-18). 25.27 (978-0-7660-4025-0(9)) Enslow Pubs., Inc.

—Tim Tebow: A Football Star Who Cares. 2013. (Sports Stars Who Care Ser.). 48p. (J). 25.27 (978-0-7660-4297-1(9)) Enslow Pubs., Inc.

Rau, Dana Meachen. Bill & Melinda Gates. 2007. (21st Century Skills Library: Life Skills Biographies Ser.). (ENG., Illus.). 48p. (gr. 4-8). lib. bdg. 31.36 (978-1-60279-068-1(X), 200039) Cherry Lake Publishing.

Rauf, Don. Thomas Paine: Author of Common Sense. 2017. (J). ***(978-1-5383-8100-7(1))***; pap. ***(978-1-5383-8097-0(8))*** Rosen Publishing Group, Inc., The.

Raum, Elizabeth. Cam Newton. 2017. (Pro Sports Biographies Ser.). (ENG.). 24p. (J). (gr. 1-4). 20.95 ***(978-1-68151-137-5(1)***, Amicus High Interest) Amicus Publishing.

Rausch, Monica. Benjamin Franklin. 2007. (Great Americans Ser.). (Illus.). 24p. (gr. 1-4). pap. 8.15 *(978-0-8368-7689-5(X))*; lib. bdg. 22.00 *(978-0-8368-7682-6(2))* Stevens, Gareth Publishing LLLP. (Weekly Reader Leveled Readers).

Rausch, Monica L. Los Hermanos Wright y el Avion. 2007. (Inventores y sus descubrimientos (Inventors & Their Discoveries) Ser.). (SPA., Illus.). 24p. (gr. 1-4). pap. 8.15 *(978-0-8368-8001-4(3)*, Weekly Reader Leveled Readers) Stevens, Gareth Publishing LLLP.

—Thomas Edison y la bombilla Eléctrica. 2007. (Inventores y sus descubrimientos (Inventors & Their Discoveries) Ser.). (SPA., Illus.). 24p. (gr. 1-4). lib. bdg. 22.00 *(978-0-8368-7997-1(X)*, Weekly Reader Leveled Readers) Stevens, Gareth Publishing LLLP.

—Thomas Edison y la Bombilla Eléctrica. 2007. (Inventores y sus descubrimientos (Inventors & Their Discoveries) Ser.). (SPA., Illus.). 24p. (gr. 1-4). pap. 8.15 *(978-0-8368-8002-1(1)*, Weekly Reader Leveled Readers) Stevens, Gareth Publishing LLLP.

Rawson, Katherine. Abigail Breslin. (J). 2010. pap. 9.40 *(978-1-4358-3412-5(7))* 2009. (Illus.). 24p. lib. bdg. 22.60 *(978-1-4042-8146-2(0))* Rosen Publishing Group, Inc., The. (PowerKids Pr.).

—The Jonas Brothers. (J). 2010. pap. 9.40 *(978-1-4358-3402-6(X))* 2009. (Illus.). 24p. lib. bdg. 22.60 *(978-1-4042-8134-9(7))* Rosen Publishing Group, Inc., The.

—Taylor Swift. (J). 2010. pap. 9.40 *(978-1-4358-3410-1(0))* 2009. (Illus.). 24p. lib. bdg. 22.60 *(978-1-4042-8138-7(X))* Rosen Publishing Group, Inc., The. (PowerKids Pr.).

Regis, Frankye. A Voice from the Civil Rights Era, 1 vol. 2004. (Voices of Twentieth-Century Conflict Ser.). (Illus.). 184p. (C). 43.00 *(978-0-313-32998-2(2)*, GR2998, Greenwood) ABC-CLIO, LLC.

Reusser, Kayleen. Leona Lewis. 2009. (Blue Banner Biography Ser.). (Illus.). 32p. (YA). (gr. 4-7). lib. bdg. 25.70 *(978-1-58415-775-5(5))* Mitchell Lane Pubs., Inc.

—Selena Gomez. 2009. (Robbie Reader Ser.). (Illus.). 32p. (YA). (gr. 2-5). lib. bdg. 25.70 *(978-1-58415-752-6(6))* Mitchell Lane Pubs., Inc.

Rhodes-Courter, Ashley. Three Little Words: A Memoir. 2009. (ENG.). 336p. (YA). (gr. 9). pap. 12.99 *(978-1-4169-4807-0(4)*, Atheneum Bks. for Young Readers) Simon & Schuster Children's Publishing.

Rice, Condoleezza. Condoleezza Rice: A Memoir of My Extraordinary, Ordinary Family & Me. 2012. (ENG.). 336p. (J). (gr. 5). pap. 8.99 *(978-0-385-73880-4(3)*, Ember) Random Hse. Children's Bks.

Rice, Dona. 20th Century Superstar: Disney. 2017. (J). pap. *(978-1-4938-3632-1(3))* Teacher Created Materials, Inc.

Rice, Liz. Bill Richardson. 2009. (Sharing the American Dream Ser.). 64p. (YA). (gr. 7-12). 22.95 *(978-1-4222-0589-1(4))* Mason Crest.

Richards-Ross, Sanya. Run with Me: The Story of a U. S. Olympic Champion, 1 vol. 2017. (ENG.). 224p. (J). 16.99 ***(978-0-310-76121-1(2))*** Zondervan.

Riddle, Sharon Kay & Sanders, Nancy/Ida. Tony Loved to Learn. Mendoza, Megan Elizabeth, illus. 2007. 32p. (J). pap. 15.00 *(978-0-9761583-6-3(1))* Olive Leaf Pubns.

Ring, Susan. Elok. 2009. (J). *(978-1-60596-659-5(2))*; *(978-1-60596-660-1(6))* Weigl Pubs., Inc.

Rivera, Sheila. Rachel Carson: A Life of Responsibility. 2007. (Pull Ahead Bks.). (Illus.). 32p. (J). (gr. 3-7). lib. bdg. 22.60 *(978-0-8225-6462-1(9)*, Lerner Pubns.) Lerner Publishing Group.

Robb, Jackie. Miley Mania! Behind the Scenes with Miley Cyrus. 2008. (Star Scene Ser.). (ENG., Illus.). 48p. (J). (gr. 3-7). pap. 5.99 *(978-0-545-08565-6(9))* Scholastic, Inc.

Robbins, Trina. Hedy Lamarr & a Secret Communication System, 1 vol. Martin, Cynthia & Timmons, Anne, illus. 2006. (Inventions & Discovery Ser.). (ENG.). 32p. (gr. 3-4). 30.65 *(978-0-7368-6479-4(2)*, Graphic Library) Capstone Press of Coughlan Cos.

Roberts, Russell. C. C. Sabathia. 2011. (Blue Banner Biography Ser.). (Illus.). 32p. (YA). (gr. 4-7). lib. bdg. 25.70 *(978-1-61228-053-0(6))* Mitchell Lane Pubs., Inc.

—Larry Fitzgerald. 2010. (Robbie Reader Ser.). (Illus.). 32p. (J). (gr. 2-5). lib. bdg. 25.70 *(978-1-58415-899-8(9))* Mitchell Lane Pubs., Inc.

Roberts, Steven. Francisco Vasquez de Coronado. 2013. (Jr. Graphic Famous Explorers Ser.). (ENG., Illus.). 24p. (J). (gr. 3-6). pap. 10.60 *(978-1-4777-0125-6(7))*; lib. bdg. 25.25 *(978-1-4777-0070-9(6))* Rosen Publishing Group, Inc., The. (PowerKids Pr.).

—Henry Ford. 2013. (Jr. Graphic American Inventors Ser.). (ENG., Illus.). 24p. (J). (gr. 3-6). pap. 10.60 *(978-1-4777-0143-0(5))*; lib. bdg. 25.25 *(978-1-4777-0079-2(X))* Rosen Publishing Group, Inc., The. (PowerKids Pr.).

—John Cabot. 2013. (Jr. Graphic Famous Explorers Ser.). (ENG., Illus.). 24p. (J). (gr. 3-6). pap. 10.60 *(978-1-4777-0129-4(X))*; lib. bdg. 25.25 *(978-1-4777-0072-3(2))* Rosen Publishing Group, Inc., The. (PowerKids Pr.).

—Robert Fulton. 2013. (Jr. Graphic American Inventors Ser.). (ENG., Illus.). 24p. (J). (gr. 3-6). pap. 10.60 *(978-1-4777-0139-3(7))*; lib. bdg. 25.25 *(978-1-4777-0077-8(3))* Rosen Publishing Group, Inc., The. (PowerKids Pr.).

Robinson, Sharon. Jackie Robinson: American Hero. 2013. (ENG.). 48p. (J). (gr. -1-3). pap. 4.99 *(978-0-545-54006-3(2)*, Scholastic Paperbacks) Scholastic, Inc.

Robinson, Tom. Ben Roethlisberger: Gifted & Giving Football Star. 2010. (Sports Stars Who Give Back Ser.). (Illus.). 128p. (J). (gr. 5-9). lib. bdg. 33.27 *(978-0-7660-3590-4(5))* Enslow Pubs., Inc.

—John McCain: POW & Statesman, 1 vol. 2010. (Military Heroes Ser.). (ENG.). 112p. (J). (gr. 6-12). lib. bdg. 35.64 *(978-1-60453-963-9(1))* ABDO Publishing Co.

Robison, Ken. Apolo Ohno. 2012. (Xtreme Athletes Ser.). (Illus.). 112p. (J). (gr. 7-12). 28.95 *(978-1-59935-186-5(2))* Reynolds, Morgan Inc.

Robson, David. Chris Rock. 2010. (Modern Role Models Ser.). (Illus.). 64p. (YA). (gr. 7-12). 22.95 *(978-1-4222-0506-8(1))* Mason Crest.

—Miley Cyrus. 2010. (Role Model Entertainers Ser.). (Illus.). 64p. (YA). (gr. 7-12). 22.95 *(978-1-4222-0501-3(0))* Mason Crest.

Robson, David W. Brian Westbrook. 2009. (Superstars of Pro Football Ser.). (Illus.). 64p. (YA). (gr. 7-12). lib. bdg. 22.95 *(978-1-4222-0547-1(9))* Mason Crest.

Rockworth, Janice. Juelz Santana. 2009. (Hip-Hop 2 Ser.). (Illus.). 64p. (YA). (gr. 7-12). lib. bdg. 22.95 *(978-1-4222-0297-5(6))* Mason Crest.

—Nas. 2009. (Hip-Hop 2 Ser.). (Illus.). 64p. (YA). (gr. 7-12). lib. bdg. 22.95 *(978-1-4222-0300-2(X))* Mason Crest.

—Wu-Tang Clan. 2009. (Hip-Hop 2 Ser.). (Illus.). 64p. (YA). (gr. 7-12). lib. bdg. 22.95 *(978-1-4222-0304-0(2))* Mason Crest.

Rookie Biographies(r). 2013. (Rookie Biographies(r) Ser.). (J). 138.00 *(978-0-531-25114-0(4)*, Children's Pr.) Scholastic Library Publishing.

Roop, Peter & Roop, Connie. The Stormy Adventure of Abbie Burgess, Lighthouse Keeper. Trover, Zachary, illus. 2010. (History's Kid Heroes Ser.). (ENG.). 32p. (gr. 3-5). 26.60 *(978-0-7613-6172-5(3))* Lerner Publishing Group.

Roselius, J. Chris. Houston Rockets, 1 vol. 2011. (Inside the NBA Ser.). (ENG., Illus.). 48p. (YA). (gr. 3-6). lib. bdg. 32.79 *(978-1-61783-158-4(1))* ABDO Publishing Co.

—San Antonio Spurs, 1 vol. 2011. (Inside the NBA Ser.). (ENG., Illus.). 48p. (YA). (gr. 3-6). lib. bdg. 32.79 *(978-1-61783-175-1(1))* ABDO Publishing Co.

Ross, Harriet. Great American Heroes. (J). (gr. 4-9). lib. bdg. 12.95 *(978-0-87460-182-4(7))* Lion Bks.

Roycroft, Mitch. Chris Moneymaker. 2007. (Superstars of Poker Ser.). (Illus.). 64p. (YA). pap. 7.95 *(978-1-4222-0378-1(6))* Mason Crest.

—Jennifer Harman. 2007. (Superstars of Poker Ser.). (Illus.). 64p. (YA). pap. 7.95 *(978-1-4222-0373-6(5))* Mason Crest.

—Johnny Orient Express Chan. (Superstars of Poker Ser.). (Illus.). 64p. (YA). 2009. (gr. 4-7). lib. bdg. 22.95 *(978-1-4222-0224-1(0))* 2007. pap. 7.95 *(978-1-4222-0369-9(7))* Mason Crest.

—Phil the Poker Brat Hellmuth. (Superstars of Poker Ser.). 64p. (YA). 2009. (Illus.). (gr. 4-7). lib. bdg. 22.95 *(978-1-4222-0220-3(8))* 2007. pap. 7.95 *(978-1-4222-0374-3(3))* Mason Crest.

—Phil Tiger Woods of Poker Ivey. (Superstars of Poker Ser.). (Illus.). 64p. (YA). 2009. (gr. 4-7). lib. bdg. 22.95 *(978-1-4222-0221-0(6))* 2007. pap. 7.95 *(978-1-4222-0375-0(1))* Mason Crest.

Roza, Autumn & Roza, Greg. Miranda Cosgrove. 2010. (Today's Superstars Ser.). (ENG.). 48p. (J). (gr. 5-8). pap. 14.05 *(978-1-4339-3999-0(1))*; lib. bdg. 31.95 *(978-1-4339-3998-3(3))* Stevens, Gareth Publishing LLLP.

Roza, Greg. Henry Ford: Pioneer of Modern Industry. 2009. (Real Life Readers Ser.). 24p. (gr. 3-4). pap. 8.25 *(978-1-4358-0137-0(7)*, Rosen Classroom) Rosen Publishing Group, Inc., The.

—Kevin Harvick: NASCAR Driver. 2009. (Behind the Wheel Ser.). (ENG., Illus.). 48p. (J). (gr. 5-8). pap. 11.75 *(978-1-4358-5406-2(3))* Rosen Publishing Group, Inc., The.

—Terry Labonte. (NASCAR Champions Ser.). 24p. (gr. 1-2). 2009. 42.50 *(978-1-61514-787-8(X)*, PowerKids Pr.) 2007. (Illus.). (J). lib. bdg. 22.60 *(978-1-4042-3501-4(9))* Rosen Publishing Group, Inc., The.

—Venus & Serena Williams: The Sisters of Tennis. 2006. (Tony Stead Nonfiction Independent Reading Collection). (ENG.). 24p. (gr. 3-6). pap. 8.85 *(978-1-4042-5537-1(0))* Rosen Publishing Group, Inc., The.

Rubin, Susan Goldman. Whaam! The Art & Life of Roy Lichtenstein. 2008. (ENG., Illus.). 48p. (J). (gr. 3-7). 21.95 *(978-0-8109-9492-8(5)*, Abrams Bks. for Young Readers) Abrams, Inc.

Rudnicki, Richard. Cyrus Eaton, 1 vol. 2016. (ENG., Illus.). 40p. (J). (gr. 2-7). 19.95 *(978-1-77108-396-6(4))* Nimbus Publishing, Ltd. CAN. Dist: Orca Bk. Pubs. USA.

Ruffin, David C. The Duties & Responsibilities of the Secretary of State. 2005. (Your Government in Action Ser.). (Illus.). 32p. (J). (gr. 3-5). lib. bdg. 23.95 *(978-1-4042-2688-3(5)*, PowerKids Pr.) Rosen Publishing Group, Inc., The.

Ruiz, Rachel. When Hillary Rodham Clinton Played Ice Hockey. Doneva, Steliyana, illus. 2017. (Leaders Doing Headstands Ser.). (ENG.). 32p. (gr. 2-3). lib. bdg. 27.99 ***(978-1-5158-1573-0(0))*** Picture Window Bks.

Rusch, Elizabeth & Francis, Guy. The Planet Hunter: The Story Behind What Happened to Pluto. 2007. (ENG., Illus.). 32p. (J). (gr. -1-3). 15.95 *(978-0-87358-926-0(2))* Cooper Square Publishing Llc.

Sabin, Louis & Macken, JoAnn Early. Thomas Edison: Incredible Inventor. 2006. (Illus.). 52p. (J). *(978-0-439-88006-0(8))* Scholastic, Inc.

Saddleback Educational Publishing Staff. Pharrell Williams. 2015. (Hip-Hop Biographies (Saddleback Publishing) Ser.). (YA). lib. bdg. 23.25 *(978-0-606-36616-8(4))* Turtleback Bks.

Saddleback Educational Publishing Staff, ed. Amelia Earhart, 1 vol. unabr. ed. 2008. (Graphic Biographies Ser.). (ENG., Illus.). 25p. (YA). (gr. 9-12). pap. 7.95 *(978-1-59905-214-8(8))* Saddleback Educational Publishing, Inc.

—Babe Ruth, 1 vol. unabr. ed. 2008. (Graphic Biographies Ser.). (ENG., Illus.). 25p. (YA). (gr. 9-12). pap. 7.95 *(978-1-59905-215-1(6))* Saddleback Educational Publishing, Inc.

—Benjamin Franklin, 1 vol. unabr. ed. 2008. (Graphic Biographies Ser.). (ENG., Illus.). 25p. (YA). (gr. 9-12). pap. 7.95 *(978-1-59905-217-5(2))* Saddleback Educational Publishing, Inc.

Sammons, Sandra Wallus. Henry Flagler, Builder of Florida. 2010. (Pineapple Press Biography Ser.). (ENG.). 64p. (J). (gr. 4-7). pap. 8.95 *(978-1-56164-467-4(6))* Pineapple Pr., Inc.

—Marjory Stoneman Douglas & the Florida Everglades. 2010. (Pineapple Press Biography Ser.). (ENG.). 72p. (J). (gr. 4-7). pap. 7.95 *(978-1-56164-471-1(4))*; 11.95 *(978-1-56164-470-4(6))* Pineapple Pr., Inc.

Sandford, Chester M. Modern Americans: A Biographical School. 2005. reprint ed. pap. 26.95 *(978-1-4179-9549-3(1))* Kessinger Publishing, LLC.

Sandler, Michael. Bethany Hamilton: Follow Your Dreams! 2006. (Defining Moments Ser.). (Illus.). 32p. (J). (gr. 2-5). lib. bdg. 25.27 *(978-1-59716-270-8(1))* Bearport Publishing Co., Inc.

—Jean Driscoll: Dream Big, Work Hard! 2006. (Defining Moments Ser.). (Illus.). 32p. (J). (gr. 2-5). lib. bdg. 25.27 *(978-1-59716-268-5(X))* Bearport Publishing Co., Inc.

—Mark Sanchez. 2011. (Football Heroes Making a Difference Ser.). 24p. (YA). (gr. 2-5). lib. bdg. 22.61 *(978-1-61772-310-0(X))* Bearport Publishing Co., Inc.

Sandra Day O'Connor. 2005. 12p. (gr. k-4). 2.95 *(978-0-635-02621-7(X))* Gallopade International.

Sanford, William R. & Green, Carl R. Bill Pickett: Courageous African-American Cowboy. 2012. (Courageous Heroes of the American West Ser.). (Illus.). 48p. (J). (gr. 5-18). 22.60 *(978-0-7660-4001-4(1))* Enslow Pubs., Inc.

—Buffalo Bill Cody: Courageous Wild West Showman. 2012. (Courageous Heroes of the American West Ser.). (Illus.). 48p. (J). pap. 8.95 *(978-1-4644-0090-2(3))*; (gr. 5-18). 22.60 *(978-0-7660-4007-6(0))* Enslow Pubs., Inc.

—Calamity Jane: Courageous Wild West Woman. 2012. (Courageous Heroes of the American West Ser.). (Illus.). 48p. (J). pap. 8.95 *(978-1-4644-0093-3(8))*; (gr. 5-18). 22.60 *(978-0-7660-4010-6(0))* Enslow Pubs., Inc.

—Davy Crockett: Courageous Hero of the Alamo. 2012. (Courageous Heroes of the American West Ser.). (Illus.). 48p. (J). (gr. 5-18). 22.60 *(978-0-7660-4005-2(4))* Enslow Pubs., Inc.

—John C. Frémont: Courageous Pathfinder of the Wild West. 2012. (Courageous Heroes of the American West Ser.). (Illus.). 48p. (J). pap. 8.95 *(978-1-4644-0091-9(1))* Enslow Pubs., Inc.

Sanna, E. J. Lloyd Banks. 2009. (Hip-Hop 2 Ser.). (Illus.). 64p. (YA). (gr. 7-12). lib. bdg. 22.95 *(978-1-4222-0299-9(2))* Mason Crest.

Sanna, Lindsey. The Game. 2009. (Hip-Hop 2 Ser.). (Illus.). 64p. (YA). (gr. 7-12). lib. bdg. 22.95 *(978-1-4222-0292-0(5))* Mason Crest.

Santos, Rita. Donald Trump: Businessman & President. 2017. (Junior Biographies Ser.). 24p. (gr. 3-4). lib. bdg. 22.60 ***(978-0-7660-8666-1(6))*** Enslow Pubs., Inc.

Sapet, Kerrily. Jeff Gordon. 2012. (Role Model Athletes Ser.). 64p. (J). (gr. 7). 22.95 *(978-1-4222-2710-7(3))* Mason Crest.

—Mariah Carey: Singer, Songwriter, Record Producer, Actress. 2009. (Transcending Race in America: Biographies of Biracial Achievers Ser.). 64p. (YA). (gr. 5-18). pap. 9.95 *(978-1-4222-1627-9(6))* Mason Crest.

Savage, Jeff. Adrian Peterson. 2010. pap. 39.62 *(978-0-7613-6964-6(3))*; (ENG.). 32p. (gr. 2-5). 25.26 *(978-0-7613-5746-9(7))*; (ENG.). 32p. (gr. 2-5). pap. 7.95 *(978-0-7613-5758-2(0))* Lerner Publishing Group.

—Alex Ovechkin. 2011. (Amazing Athletes Ser.). (ENG.). 32p. (gr. 2-5). lib. bdg. 25.26 *(978-0-7613-7672-9(0))* Lerner Publishing Group.

—Brett Favre. 2010. pap. 39.62 *(978-0-7613-6965-3(1))*; (ENG.). 32p. (gr. 2-5). 25.26 *(978-0-7613-6651-5(2))*; (ENG.). 32p. (gr. 2-5). pap. 7.95 *(978-0-7613-6653-9(9))* Lerner Publishing Group.

—Brian Urlacher. 2009. (Amazing Athletes Ser.). (ENG.). 32p. (gr. 2-5). 25.26 *(978-0-8225-9991-3(0))* Lerner Publishing Group.

—Dave Mirra. 2007. (Amazing Athletes Ser.). (ENG., Illus.). 32p. (J). (gr. 2-5). 25.26 *(978-0-8225-6593-2(5))* Lerner Publishing Group.

—Drew Brees. 2010. (Amazing Athletes Ser.). 32p. (gr. 2-5). (J). 25.26 *(978-0-7613-6652-2(0))*; (ENG.). pap. 7.95 *(978-0-7613-6654-6(7))* Lerner Publishing Group.

—Dwight Howard. 2010. pap. 39.62 *(978-0-7613-6968-4(6))*; (ENG.). 32p. (gr. 2-5). pap. 7.95 *(978-0-7613-5756-8(4))*; (ENG.). 32p. (gr. 2-5). lib. bdg. 25.26 *(978-0-7613-5748-3(3))* Lerner Publishing Group.

—Dwyane Wade. 2006. (Amazing Athletes Ser.). (Illus.). 32p. (J). (gr. 4). pap. 6.95 *(978-0-8225-6013-5(5)*, First Avenue Editions) Lerner Publishing Group.

—Eli Manning. rev. ed. 2012. (Amazing Athletes Ser.). (ENG., Illus.). 32p. (gr. 2-5). lib. bdg. 25.26 *(978-1-4677-0873-9(9))* Lerner Publishing Group.

—Jeff Gordon. 2007. (Amazing Athletes Ser.). (J). pap. 6.95 *(978-0-8225-6802-5(0)*, Lerner Pubns.) Lerner Publishing Group.

—Josh Hamilton. 2009. pap. 40.95 *(978-0-7613-4782-8(8))* Lerner Publishing Group.

—Kevin Durant. 2011. (Amazing Athletes Ser.). (ENG., Illus.). 32p. (gr. 2-5). lib. bdg. 25.26 *(978-0-7613-7671-2(2))* Lerner Publishing Group.

—Kobe Bryant (Revised Edition) 2010. pap. 39.62 *(978-0-7613-6970-7(8))* Lerner Publishing Group.

—LaDainian Tomlinson. 2009. (Amazing Athletes Ser.). (ENG.). 32p. (gr. 2-5). 25.26 *(978-0-8225-9989-0(9))* Lerner Publishing Group.

—Stephen Strasburg. 2013. (Amazing Athletes Ser.). (ENG., Illus.). 32p. (gr. 2-5). lib. bdg. 25.26 *(978-1-4677-1100-5(4))* Lerner Publishing Group.

—Steve Nash. 2006. (Amazing Athletes Ser.). (ENG., Illus.). 32p. (gr. 2-5). pap. 7.95 *(978-0-8225-6014-2(3)*, First Avenue Editions) Lerner Publishing Group.

—Tiger Woods. (Amazing Athletes Ser.). 2007. (J). 23.93 *(978-0-8225-6889-6(6)*, Lerner Pubns.) 2nd rev. ed. 2009. (ENG.). 32p. (gr. 2-5). 25.26 *(978-0-7613-4921-1(9))* Lerner Publishing Group.

—Tony Romo. 2010. pap. 39.62 *(978-0-7613-6971-4(6))*; (ENG.). 32p. (gr. 2-5). 25.26 *(978-0-7613-5744-5(0))*; (ENG.). 32p. (gr. 2-5). pap. 7.95 *(978-0-7613-5754-4(8))* Lerner Publishing Group.

Scally, Robert. Jeff Bezos: Founder of Amazon & the Kindle. 2012. (Business Leaders Ser.). 112p. (YA). (gr. 7-12). 28.95 *(978-1-59935-178-0(1))* Reynolds, Morgan Inc.

Schanzer, Rosalyn. George vs. George: The Revolutionary War as Seen by Both Sides. 2004. (ENG., Illus.). 64p. (J). (gr. 4-7). 16.95 *(978-0-7922-7349-3(4)*, National Geographic Children's Bks.) National Geographic Society.

—John Smith Escapes Again! 2006. (ENG., Illus.). 64p. (J). (gr. 4-7). 16.95 *(978-0-7922-5930-5(0))*; lib. bdg. 25.90 *(978-0-7922-5931-2(9))* National Geographic Society. (National Geographic Children's Bks.).

Scher, Linda. The Texas City Disaster. 2007. (Code Red Ser.). (Illus.). 32p. (YA). (gr. 2-5). lib. bdg. 25.27 *(978-1-59716-363-7(5))* Bearport Publishing Co., Inc.

Scherer, Glenn & Fletcher, Marty. J. Robert Oppenheimer: The Brain Behind the Bomb. 2007. (Inventors Who Changed the World Ser.). (Illus.). 128p. (J). (gr. 5-9). lib. bdg. 34.60 *(978-1-59845-050-7(6)*, MyReportLinks.com Bks.) Enslow Pubs., Inc.

—Who on Earth Is Aldo Leopold? Father of Wildlife Ecology. 2009. (Scientists Saving the Earth Ser.). (Illus.). 112p. (J). (gr. 5-9). lib. bdg. 33.27 *(978-1-59845-115-3(4))* Enslow Pubs., Inc.

Schilling, Vincent. Native Athletes in Action: Sports Stars Past & Present. Peterson, Gary, illus. 2007. (Native Trailblazers Ser.). (ENG.). 128p. (YA). (gr. 3-11). pap. 9.95 *(978-0-9779183-0-0(0)*, 7th Generation) Book Publishing Co.

Scholl, Elizabeth. David Archuleta. 2009. (Robbie Reader Ser.). (Illus.). 32p. (YA). (gr. 2-5). lib. bdg. 25.70 *(978-1-58415-758-8(5))* Mitchell Lane Pubs., Inc.

Schubert, Barbara. George Washington. 2009. pap. 13.25 *(978-1-60559-060-8(6))* Hameray Publishing Group, Inc.

Schuette, Sarah L. Milton Hershey, 1 vol. 2014. (Business Leaders Ser.). (ENG.). 24p. (gr. k-1). lib. bdg. 21.99 *(978-1-4765-9640-2(9)*, Pebble Bks.) Capstone Press of Coughlan Cos.

Schuh, Mari. Troy Polamalu. 2013. (Football Stars up Close Ser.). 24p. (J). (gr. k-5). lib. bdg. 23.93 *(978-1-61772-715-3(6))* Bearport Publishing Co., Inc.

Schuh, Mari C. Stars of Stock Car Racing, 1 vol. 2014. (Sports Stars Ser.). (ENG.). 24p. (gr. k-1). 26.65 *(978-1-4914-0593-2(7)*, Pebble Plus) Capstone Press of Coughlan Cos.

Schulte, Mary. Dover Demon. 2009. (Mysterious Encounters Ser.). (ENG., Illus.). 48p. (J). 29.00 *(978-0-7377-4570-2(3)*, Greenhaven Pr., Inc.) Cengage Gale.

—Eva Longoria. (Sharing the American Dream Ser.). 64p. (YA). (gr. 7-12). 2009. 22.95 *(978-1-4222-0595-2(9))* 2007. pap. 9.95 *(978-1-4222-0754-3(4))* Mason Crest.

Schuman, Michael. Bob Dylan. 2017. (J). ***(978-0-7660-9206-8(2))*** Enslow Pubs., Inc.

—Charles Schulz. 2017. ***(978-0-7660-9209-9(7))*** Enslow Pubs., Inc.

Schuman, Michael A. Bill Gates: Computer Mogul & Philanthropist. 2007. (People to Know Today Ser.). (Illus.). 128p. (J). (gr. 3-7). lib. bdg. 33.27 *(978-0-7660-2693-3(0))* Enslow Pubs., Inc.

—Emma! Amazing Actress Emma Stone. 2013. (Sizzling Celebrities Ser.). 48p. (J). (gr. 4-9). pap. 8.95 *(978-1-4644-0175-6(6))* Enslow Pubs., Inc.

—Louis Armstrong: Jazz Is Played from the Heart. 2007. (African-American Biography Library). (Illus.). 128p. (J). (gr. 6-12). lib. bdg. 33.27 *(978-0-7660-2700-8(7))* Enslow Pubs., Inc.

Schwartz, Heather E. Gangsters, Bootleggers, & Bandits. 2013. (ShockZone (tm) — Villains Ser.). (ENG., Illus.). 32p. (gr. 5-8). pap. 8.95 *(978-1-4677-0895-1(X))* Lerner Publishing Group.

—Selena Gomez, 1 vol. 2012. (Star Biographies Ser.). (ENG., Illus.). 32p. (gr. 3-4). lib. bdg. 27.99 *(978-1-4296-4761-8(2)*, Snap Bks.) Capstone Press of Coughlan Cos.

—Zendaya: Capturing the Stage, Screen, & Modeling Scene. 2014. (Pop Culture Bios Ser.). (ENG., Illus.). 32p. (J). (gr. 3-6). lib. bdg. 26.60 *(978-1-4677-3673-2(2)*, Lerner Pubns.) Lerner Publishing Group.

Schweitzer, Karen. Americans of South American Heritage. (Successful Americans Ser.). 64p. (YA). 2009. (gr. 9-12). 22.95 *(978-1-4222-0526-6(6))* 2007. (gr. 7-18). pap. 9.95 *(978-1-4222-0861-8(3))* Mason Crest.

—Shaun White. 2010. (Modern Role Models Ser.). (Illus.). 64p. (YA). (gr. 7-12). lib. bdg. 22.95 *(978-1-4222-0493-1(6))* Mason Crest.

—Soulja Boy Tell 'Em. (Role Model Entertainers Ser.). (Illus.). 64p. (YA). 2010. (gr. 7-12). 22.95 *(978-1-4222-0509-9(6))* 2007. pap. 9.95 *(978-1-4222-0796-3(X))* Mason Crest.

Scott, Celicia. Mariah Carey. 2008. (Hip-Hop Ser.). (ENG., Illus.). 64p. (YA). (gr. 4-7). per. 7.95 *(978-1-4222-0265-4(8))* Mason Crest.

Seibert, Brian. George Balanchine. (Library of American Choreographers). (Illus.). 48p. 2006. (ENG.). (gr. 5-8). pap. 11.75 *(978-1-4042-0641-0(8)*, Rosen Reference) 2005. (J). (gr. k-3). lib. bdg. 29.25 *(978-1-4042-0447-8(4))* Rosen Publishing Group, Inc., The.

—Jerome Robbins. 2009. (Library of American Choreographers Ser.). 48p. (gr. 5-8). 53.00 *(978-1-60853-458-6(8)*, Rosen Reference) Rosen Publishing Group, Inc., The.

Seiple, Samantha. Lincoln's Spymaster: Allan Pinkerton, America's First Private Eye. 2015. (Illus.). 211p. (J). ***(978-0-545-90821-4(3))*** Scholastic, Inc.

Seiple, Samantha. Lincoln's Spymaster: Allan Pinkerton, America's First Private Eye. 2015. (ENG., Illus.). 224p. (J). (gr. 5-9). 17.99 *(978-0-545-70897-5(4)*, Scholastic Pr.) Scholastic, Inc.

Shea, Abigail. Victoria Justice. 2013. (Rising Stars Ser.). 32p. (J). (gr. 3-6). pap. 10.50 *(978-1-4339-8990-2(5))*; (ENG., Illus.). lib. bdg. 25.25 *(978-1-4339-8989-6(1))* Stevens, Gareth Publishing LLLP.

Shea, Pegi Deitz. Noah Webster: Weaver of Words. Vachula, Monica, illus. 2009. (ENG.). 40p. (J). (gr. 4-18). 18.95 *(978-1-59078-441-9(3)*, Calkins Creek) Boyds Mills Pr.

Shea, Therese. John Lee Hooker: King of the Blues. 2010. (Inspiring Lives Ser.). 32p. (J). (gr. 5-8). lib. bdg. 25.25 *(978-1-4339-3625-8(9))*; (Illus.). pap. 10.50 *(978-1-4339-3626-5(7))* Stevens, Gareth Publishing LLLP.

Shea, Therese M. Alexander Hamilton: Founding Father & Treasury Secretary. 2017. (J). pap. ***(978-0-7660-9045-3(0))*** Enslow Pubs., Inc.

Sherman, Patrice & Murica, Rebecca Thatcher. What It's Like to Be Ryan Howard: Como Es Ser Ryan Howard. de la Vega, Eida, tr. from ENG. Rasemas, Joe, illus. 2009. (What It's Like to Be Ser.). (SPA & ENG.). 32p. (J). (gr. -1-2). 25.70 *(978-1-58415-845-5(X))* Mitchell Lane Pubs., Inc.

Sherrard, Valerie. Vanessa Hudgens. 2010. (Superstars! Ser.). (ENG., Illus.). 32p. (J). (gr. 3-6). lib. bdg. (978-0-7787-7253-8(5)) Crabtree Publishing Co.

Sherrow, Victoria. Jonas Salk: Beyond the Microscope. 2nd rev. ed. 2008. (Makers of Modern Science Ser.). (Illus.). 146p. (gr. 6-12). 35.00 (978-0-8160-6180-8(7), Chelsea Hse.) Facts On File, Inc.

Shichtman, Sandra H. Colin Powell: Have a Vision. Be Demanding. 2005. (African-American Biography Library). (Illus.). 128p. (J). (gr. 6-12). lib. bdg. 33.27 (978-0-7660-2464-9(4)) Enslow Pubs., Inc.

—Michael Bloomberg. 2010. (Political Profiles Ser.). 112p. (J). 28.95 (978-1-59935-135-3(8)) Reynolds, Morgan Inc.

—Sonia Sotomayor. 2011. (Supreme Court Justices Ser.). (Illus.). 111p. 28.95 (978-1-59935-156-8(0)) Reynolds, Morgan Inc.

Shone, Rob. Muhammad Ali: The Life of a Boxing Hero. 2009. (Graphic Nonfiction Biographies Ser.). (ENG.). 48p. (YA). (gr. 4-5). 58.50 (978-1-61513-022-1(5), Rosen Reference) Rosen Publishing Group, Inc., The.

—Rosa Parks: The Life of a Civil Rights Heroine. Spender, Nik, illus. 2007. (Graphic Biographies Ser.). (ENG.). 48p. (gr. 5-8). pap. 14.05 (978-1-4042-0927-5(1)) Rosen Publishing Group, Inc., The.

Signature Lives - Reformation Era. 2006. (Signature Lives: Reformation Era Ser.). (ENG., Illus.). 112p. (gr. 6-7). 70.64 (978-0-7565-1712-0(5)) Compass Point Bks.

Signature Lives - Revolutionary War Era, 13 bks. 2006. (Signature Lives: Revolutionary War Era Ser.). (ENG., Illus.). 112p. (gr. 6-7). 176.60 (978-0-7565-1711-3(7)) Compass Point Bks.

Signature Lives: Colonial America. 2006. (Signature Lives: Colonial America Ser.). (ENG., Illus.). 112p. (gr. 6-7). 70.64 (978-0-7565-1710-6(9)) Compass Point Bks.

Silate, Jennifer. The Calhoun-Randolph Debate on the Eve of the War of 1812: A Primary Source Investigation. 2004. (Great Historic Debates & Speeches Ser.). (Illus.). 64p. (YA). (gr. 5-9). lib. bdg. 31.95 (978-1-4042-0150-7(5)) Rosen Publishing Group, Inc., The.

—The Calhoun-Randolph Debate on the Eve of the War Of 1812: A Primary Source Investigation. 2009. (Great Historic Debates & Speeches Ser.). 64p. (gr. 5-8). 58.50 (978-1-61513-124-2(8)) Rosen Publishing Group, Inc., The.

Simone, Jacquelyn. Ciara. 2009. (Hip-Hop Ser.). (Illus.). 64p. (YA). pap. 7.95 (978-1-4222-0334-7(4)); (gr. 7-12). lib. bdg. 22.95 (978-1-4222-0286-9(0)) Mason Crest.

—Outkast. 2009. (Hip-Hop 2 Ser.). (Illus.). 64p. (YA). (gr. 7-12). lib. bdg. 22.95 (978-1-4222-0301-9(8)) Mason Crest.

Simons, Rae. Bruce Springsteen. 2008. (Pop Rock Ser.). (Illus.). 64p. (YA). (gr. 4-7). lib. bdg. 22.95 (978-1-4222-0187-9(2)) Mason Crest.

Singer, Flora M. Flora - I Was but A Child. 2007. 180p. (J). pap. 26.50 (978-0-9760739-8-7(6)) Yad Vashem Pubns. ISR. Dist: Coronet Bks.

Sís, Peter. The Wall: Growing up Behind the Iron Curtain. Sís, Peter, illus. 2007. (ENG., Illus.). 56p. (J). (gr. 3-7). 19.99 (978-0-374-34701-7(8), 9780374347017, Farrar, Straus & Giroux (BYR)) Farrar, Straus & Giroux.

Skelton, Renee. A Woman of Courage. 2005. (Time for Kids Ser.). (ENG., Illus.). 48p. (J). (gr. 2-4). pap. 3.99 (978-0-06-057607-3(3)) HarperCollins Pubs.

Skelton, Renee & Time for Kids Editors. Time for Kids: A Woman of Courage. 2005. (Time for Kids Ser.). (ENG., Illus.). 48p. (J). 16.99 (978-0-06-057608-0(1)) HarperCollins Pubs.

Slavicek, Louise Chipley. I. M. Pei. 2009. (Asian Americans of Achievement Ser.). (Illus.). 120p. (YA). (gr. 7-12). 35.00 (978-1-60413-567-1(0)) Facts On File, Inc.

Sloate, Susan. Ray Charles: Find Another Way! 2006. (Defining Moments Ser.). (Illus.). 32p. (J). (gr. 2-5). lib. bdg. 25.27 (978-1-59716-267-8(1)) Bearport Publishing Co., Inc.

Small, Cathleen. Melinda Gates: Philanthropist & Education Advocate. 2017. (J). **(978-1-5026-2707-0(8))** Cavendish Square Publishing.

Smith, Charles R. What Makes Us Strong. 2017. (J). **(978-1-4926-2091-4(2))** Sourcebooks, Inc.

Smith, Pohla. Shaquille O'Neal: Superhero at Center. 2009. (Sports Illustrated for Kids Bks). 176p. (gr. 7-12). 63.90 (978-1-60853-153-0(8)) Rosen Publishing Group, Inc., The.

Smith, Terri Smith. Tony Hawk: Flying High. 2003. (J). pap. (978-1-932724-01-1(X), Bios for Kids) Panda Publishing, L.L.C.

Smith, Tom. Discovery of the Americas, 1492-1800. 2nd rev. ed. 2009. (Discovery & Exploration Ser.). (Illus.). 136p. (gr. 5-8). 35.00 (978-1-60413-195-6(0), Chelsea Hse.) Facts On File, Inc.

Sneed, Dani. Ferris Wheel! George Ferris & His Amazing Invention. 2008. (Genius at Work! Great Inventor Biographies Ser.). (Illus.). 32p. (J). (gr. 3-7). lib. bdg. 23.94 (978-0-7660-2834-0(8), Enslow Elementary) Enslow Pubs., Inc.

Snyder, Gail. Filipino Americans. (Successful Americans Ser.). 64p. (YA). 2009. (Illus.). (gr. 9-12). 22.95 (978-1-4222-0524-2(X)) 2007. (gr. 5-18). pap. 9.95 (978-1-4222-0857-1(5)) Mason Crest.

—Kelly Clarkson. 2009. (Dream Big: American Idol Superstars Ser.). 64p. (YA). (gr. 5-18). pap. 9.95 (978-1-4222-1604-0(7)); lib. bdg. 22.95 (978-1-4222-1506-7(7)) Mason Crest.

—Queen Latifah. 2008. (Hip-Hop Ser.). (Illus.). 64p. (YA). (ENG.). (gr. 3-7). per. 7.95 (978-1-4222-0276-0(3)); (gr. 7-12). lib. bdg. 22.95 (978-1-4222-0126-8(0)) Mason Crest.

Solomon, Sharon. Lewis Tewanima: Born to Run, 1 vol. Fields, Lisa, illus. 2014. (ENG.). 32p. (J). (gr. k-3). 16.99 (978-1-4556-1941-2(8)) Pelican Publishing Co., Inc.

Sonneborn, Liz. Harriet Beecher Stowe. 2009. (Leaders of the Civil War Era Ser.). (Illus.). 120p. (gr. 6-12). 35.00 (978-1-60413-302-8(3), Chelsea Hse.) Facts On File, Inc.

Sooner, Jeffrey. Rascal Flatts. 2010. (Country Music Stars Ser.). (Illus.). 32p. (J). (gr. 3-8). pap. 10.50 (978-1-4339-3617-3(8)); lib. bdg. 25.25 (978-1-4339-3616-6(X), 1309366) Stevens, Gareth Publishing LLLP.

Southwell, David. Unsolved Political Mysteries. 2009. (Mysteries & Conspiracies Ser.). 80p. (gr. 10-10). 61.20 (978-1-61514-747-2(0)) Rosen Publishing Group, Inc., The.

Spangenburg, Ray & Moser, Diane Kit. Barbara Mcclintock: Pioneering Geneticist. 2008. (Makers of Modern Science Ser.). (Illus.). 136p. (gr. 6-12). 35.00 (978-0-8160-6172-3(6), Chelsea Hse.) Facts On File, Inc.

—Wernher Von Braun: Out of the Fire, the Stars. 2nd rev. ed. 2008. (Makers of Modern Science Ser.). 192p. (gr. 6-12). 35.00 (978-0-8160-6179-2(3), Chelsea Hse.) Facts On File, Inc.

Spangenburg, Ray, et al. Robert Ballard. 2009. (Makers of Modern Science Ser.). (Illus.). 176p. (gr. 6-12). 35.00 (978-0-8160-6173-0(4), Chelsea Hse.) Facts On File, Inc.

Spencer, Eve. Stories of America, 25 bks., Set. (J). (gr. 1-8). lib. bdg. 483.50 (978-0-7398-3295-0(6)) Heinemann-Raintree.

Spencer, Liv. Taylor Swift: Every Day Is a Fairytale - The Unofficial Story. 2010. (ENG., Illus.). 155p. (YA). (gr. 7-18). pap. (978-1-55022-931-8(1)) Filmer Ltd.

Stanley, George E. Mr. Rogers: Young Friend & Neighbor. Henderson, Meryl, illus. 2004. (Childhood of Famous Americans Ser.). (ENG.). 208p. (J). (gr. 3-7). mass mkt. 10.99 (978-0-689-87186-3(4), Simon & Schuster/Paula Wiseman Bks.) Simon & Schuster/Paula Wiseman Bks.

Stansfield, John. Enos Mills: Rocky Mountain Naturalist. 2005. (Now You Know Bio Ser.). (Illus.). 103p. (J). pap. 8.95 (978-0-86541-072-5(0)) Filter Pr., LLC.

Star Biographies. 2010. (Star Biographies Ser.). 32p. lib. bdg. 213.20 (978-1-4296-5883-6(5), Snap Bks.) Capstone Press of Coughlan Cos.

Stefoff, Rebecca. Al Gore: Fighting for a Greener Planet. rev. ed. 2008. (Gateway Biographies Ser.). (ENG.). 48p. (gr. 4-8). 26.60 (978-1-57505-948-8(7)) Lerner Publishing Group.

—Stephen King. 2010. (Today's Writers & Their Works). 128p. (gr. 7-18). 42.79 (978-0-7614-4122-9(0)) Marshall Cavendish Corp.

Steinberg, Arnold. Whiplash! From JFK to Donald Trump, a Political Odyssey. 2017. (J). **(978-0-89803-180-5(X))** Jameson Bks., Inc.

Stewart, Whitney. Who Was Walt Disney? Harrison, Nancy, illus. 2009. (Who Was? Ser.). (ENG.). 112p. (J). (gr. 3-7). pap. 5.99 (978-0-448-45052-0(6), Grosset & Dunlap) Penguin Young Readers Group.

—Who Was Walt Disney? 2009. (Who Was... ? Ser.). lib. bdg. 16.00 (978-0-606-04160-7(5), Turtleback) Turtleback Bks.

Stine, Megan. Who Is Sonia Sotomayor? Putra, Dede & Harrison, Nancy, illus. 2017. (Who Was? Ser.). (ENG.). 112p. (J). (gr. 3-7). 5.99 (978-0-399-54192-6(6), Grosset & Dunlap) Penguin Young Readers Group.

—Who Was Sally Ride? 2013. (Who Was? Ser.). (ENG.). 112p. (J). (gr. 3-7). pap. 5.99 (978-0-448-46687-3(2), Grosset & Dunlap) Penguin Young Readers Group.

Stokes, Betty Southard. Postcards from George, 1763-1781: George Rogers Clark Writes Home to Virginia from the Kentucky Wilderness. Cable, Annette, illus. 2010. (J). (978-1-935497-12-7(X)) Butler Bk. Publishing.

Stone, Adam. The Big Show. 2011. (Pro Wrestling Champions Ser.). (ENG., Illus.). 24p. (J). (gr. 3-7). lib. bdg. 25.95 (978-1-60014-634-3(1), Torque Bks.) Bellwether Media.

—John Cena. 2011. (Pro Wrestling Champions Ser.). (ENG., Illus.). 24p. (J). (gr. 3-7). lib. bdg. 25.95 (978-1-60014-636-7(8), Torque Bks.) Bellwether Media.

Stone, Amy. Jim Carrey. 2007. (Today's Superstars). (Illus.). 32p. (gr. 5-8). lib. bdg. 31.95 (978-0-8368-8197-4(4)) Stevens, Gareth Publishing LLLP.

Stone, Tanya Lee. Elizabeth Leads the Way: Elizabeth Cady Stanton & the Right to Vote. Gibbon, Rebecca, illus. 2008. (ENG.). 32p. (J). (gr. 1-5). 18.99 (978-0-8050-7903-6(3), 9780805079036, Holt, Henry & Co. Bks. For Young Readers) Holt, Henry & Co.

—Elizabeth Leads the Way: Elizabeth Cady Stanton & the Right to Vote. Gibbon, Rebecca, illus. 2010. (ENG.). 32p. (J). (gr. 1-5). pap. 8.99 (978-0-312-60236-9(7), 9780312602369) Square Fish.

Stories of Great Americans for Little Americans. 2006. 164p. pap. 14.45 (978-1-59462-414-8(3), 450, Book Jungle) Standard Pubns., Inc.

Stotts, Stuart. Lucius Fairchild: Civil War Hero. 2011. (Badger Biographies Ser.). (ENG., Illus.). 112p. (J). pap. 12.95 (978-0-87020-460-9(2)) Wisconsin Historical Society.

Streissguth, Tom. Wilma Rudolph. 2007. (Illus.). 110p. (YA). pap. 9.95 (978-0-8225-6693-9(1)) Lerner Publishing Group.

Strom, Laura Layton. Racing on the Wind: Steve Fossett. 2007. (Shockwave: Life Stories Ser.). (ENG., Illus.). 36p. (J). (gr. 3-5). 25.00 (978-0-531-17774-7(2), Children's Pr.) Scholastic Library Publishing.

Strother, Ruth. Bill Gates, 1 vol. 2007. (Essential Lives Set 1 Ser.). (ENG., Illus.). 112p. (J). (gr. 6-12). lib. bdg. 35.64 (978-1-59928-841-3(9)) ABDO Publishing Co.

Sullivan, George. Helen Keller: Her Life in Pictures. 2007. (Helen Keller Ser.). (ENG., Illus.). 80p. (J). (gr. 2-5). 17.99 (978-0-439-91815-2(4), Scholastic Nonfiction) Scholastic, Inc.

Susi, Geraldine Lee. For My People: The Jennie Dean Story, 1. 2003. (Illus.). 128p. (J). per. 11.95 (978-1-886826-08-3(0)) Manassas Museum, The.

Sutcliffe, Jane. Barack Obama. 2010. (History Maker Biographies Ser.). (ENG.). 48p. (gr. 3-6). lib. bdg. 27.93 (978-0-7613-5205-1(8), Lerner Pubns.) Lerner Publishing Group.

—John Deere. 2006. (History Maker Biographies Ser.). (Illus.). 48p. (J). (gr. 3-7). lib. bdg. 26.60 (978-0-8225-6579-6(X), Lerner Pubns.) Lerner Publishing Group.

Swain, Gwenyth. Wanda Ga'G. 2005. (ENG., Illus.). 112p. (J). (gr. 3-7). per. 12.95 (978-0-87351-544-3(7), Borealis Bk.) Minnesota Historical Society Pr.

—Wanda Gag: Storybook Artist. 2005. (Illus.). 112p. (J). (gr. 3-7). 22.95 (978-0-87351-545-0(5), Borealis Bk.) Minnesota Historical Society Pr.

Tappan, Eva March. Heroes of Progress: Stories of Successful Americans. 2007. 240p. per. 11.95 (978-0-9790876-4-6(3)) Living Bks. Pr.

Taylor, Marian. Harriet Tubman. 2004. (Black Americans of Achievement Ser.). (Illus.). 112p. (gr. 6-12). 35.00 (978-0-7910-8166-2(4), Chelsea Hse.) Facts On File, Inc.

Teitelbaum, Michael. Jackie Robinson: Champion for Equality. 2010. (Sterling Biographies(r) Ser.). (ENG., Illus.). 128p. (J). (gr. 5-18). pap. 5.95 (978-1-4027-6362-5(X)) Sterling Publishing Co., Inc.

Thatcher Murcia, Rebecca. Thomas Edison: Great Inventor. 2004. (Uncharted, Unexplored, & Unexplained Ser.). (Illus.). 48p. (J). (gr. 4-8). lib. bdg. 29.95 (978-1-58415-306-1(7)) Mitchell Lane Pubs., Inc.

Thayer, William Makepeace. The Bobbin Boy: Or, How Nat Got His Learning. 2007. (ENG.). 210p. pap. 20.99 (978-1-4346-3420-7(5)); 228p. pap. 22.99 (978-1-4346-3421-4(3)) Creative Media Partners, LLC.

They Died Too Young. 2005. (They Died Too Young Ser.). (gr. 6-12). 109.75 (978-0-7910-9158-6(9), Chelsea Hse.) Facts On File, Inc.

Thomas, Paul. Olaudah Equiano: From Slavery to Freedom. Ambrus, Victor, illus. 2007. (Collins Big Cat Ser.). (ENG.). 48p. (J). (gr. 3-4). pap. 8.99 (978-0-00-723096-9(6)) HarperCollins Pubs. Ltd. GBR. Dist: Independent Pubs. Group.

Thornley, Stew. Kevin Garnett: Champion Basketball Star. 2012. (Sports Star Champions Ser.). (Illus.). 48p. (J). (gr. 5-18). 25.27 (978-0-7660-4028-1(3)) Enslow Pubs., Inc.

Tieck, Sarah. Abigail Breslin: Famous Actress, 1 vol. 2009. (Big Buddy Biographies Set 2 Ser.). (ENG., Illus.). 32p. (J). (gr. 2-5). 28.50 (978-1-60453-547-1(4)) ABDO Publishing Co.

—Barack Obama, 1 vol. 2010. (First Biographies Set 6 Ser.). (ENG.). 32p. (J). (gr. 1-4). 27.07 (978-1-60453-985-1(2)) ABDO Publishing Co.

—Beyonce: Famous Singer/Actress, 1 vol. 2008. (Big Buddy Biographies Ser.). (ENG.). 32p. (J). (gr. 2-5). 28.50 (978-1-60453-117-6(7)) ABDO Publishing Co.

—Carrie Underwood: American Idol Winner, 1 vol. 2008. (Big Buddy Biographies Ser.). (ENG.). 32p. (J). (gr. 2-5). 28.50 (978-1-60453-125-1(8)) ABDO Publishing Co.

—Drake Bell & Josh Peck: Famous Actors, 1 vol. 2009. (Big Buddy Biographies Set 2 Ser.). (ENG., Illus.). 32p. (J). (gr. 2-5). 28.50 (978-1-60453-546-4(6)) ABDO Publishing Co.

—Eleanor Roosevelt, 1 vol. 2010. (First Biographies Set 6 Ser.). (ENG., Illus.). 32p. (J). (gr. 1-4). 27.07 (978-1-60453-986-8(0)) ABDO Publishing Co.

—Jaden Smith: Talented Actor, 1 vol. 2011. (Big Buddy Biographies Set 6 Ser.). (ENG., Illus.). 32p. (J). (gr. 2-5). 28.50 (978-1-61714-707-4(9)) ABDO Publishing Co.

—Joe Mauer: Baseball Superstar, 1 vol. 2011. (Big Buddy Biographies Set 6 Ser.). (ENG., Illus.). 32p. (J). (gr. 2-5). 28.50 (978-1-61714-705-0(2)) ABDO Publishing Co.

—Katy Perry: Singing Sensation, 1 vol. 2011. (Big Buddy Biographies Set 7 Ser.). (ENG., Illus.). 32p. (J). (gr. 2-5). 28.50 (978-1-61783-021-1(6)) ABDO Publishing Co.

—Kristen Stewart: Twilight Star, 1 vol. 2010. (Big Buddy Bks.). (ENG.). 32p. (J). (gr. 2-5). 28.50 (978-1-61613-977-3(3)) ABDO Publishing Co.

—Kyle Massey: Talented Entertainer, 1 vol. 2011. (Big Buddy Biographies Set 7 Ser.). (ENG., Illus.). 32p. (J). (gr. 2-5). 28.50 (978-1-61783-019-8(4)) ABDO Publishing Co.

—Lady Gaga: Singing Sensation, 1 vol. 2011. (Big Buddy Biographies Set 7 Ser.). (ENG., Illus.). 32p. (J). (gr. 2-5). 28.50 (978-1-61783-017-4(8)) ABDO Publishing Co.

—Lea Michele: Star of Glee, 1 vol. 2011. (Big Buddy Biographies Set 6 Ser.). (ENG., Illus.). 32p. (J). (gr. 2-5). 28.50 (978-1-61714-706-7(0)) ABDO Publishing Co.

—Lindsey Vonn: Olympic Champion, 1 vol. 2010. (Big Buddy Bks.). (ENG., Illus.). 32p. (J). (gr. 2-5). 28.50 (978-1-61613-978-0(1)) ABDO Publishing Co.

—Michael Jackson: Music Legend, 1 vol. 2011. (Big Buddy Biographies Set 6 Ser.). (ENG., Illus.). 32p. (J). (gr. 2-5). 28.50 (978-1-61714-703-6(6)) ABDO Publishing Co.

—Miley Cyrus: Singer/Actress/ Star of Hannah Montana, 1 vol. 2008. (Big Buddy Biographies Ser.). (ENG.). 32p. (J). (gr. 2-5). 28.50 (978-1-60453-119-0(3)) ABDO Publishing Co.

—Miranda Lambert: Country Music Star, 1 vol. 2011. (Big Buddy Biographies Set 7 Ser.). (ENG., Illus.). 32p. (J). (gr. 2-5). 28.50 (978-1-61783-018-1(6)) ABDO Publishing Co.

—Nat & Alex Wolff: Stars of Nickelodeon's the Naked Brothers Band, 1 vol. 2008. (Big Buddy Biographies Ser.). (ENG.). 32p. (J). (gr. 2-5). 28.50 (978-1-60453-126-8(6)) ABDO Publishing Co.

—Rosa Parks, 1 vol. 2006. (Buddy Book Ser.). (ENG., Illus.). 32p. (gr. -1-3). 27.07 (978-1-59679-788-8(6), Buddy Bks.) ABDO Publishing Co.

—Shaun White: Olympic Champion, 1 vol. 2010. (Big Buddy Bks.). (ENG.). 32p. (J). (gr. 2-5). 28.50 (978-1-61613-979-7(X)) ABDO Publishing Co.

—Shia Labeouf: Movie Star, 1 vol. 2008. (Big Buddy Biographies Ser.). (ENG.). 32p. (J). (gr. 2-5). 28.50 (978-1-60453-123-7(1)) ABDO Publishing Co.

—Tiger Woods: Famous Golfer, 1 vol. 2008. (Big Buddy Biographies Ser.). (ENG.). 32p. (J). (gr. 2-5). 28.50 (978-1-60453-127-5(4)) ABDO Publishing Co.

—Tom Brady: Famous Quarterback, 1 vol. 2008. (Big Buddy Biographies Ser.). (ENG.). 32p. (J). (gr. 2-5). 28.50 (978-1-60453-118-3(5)) ABDO Publishing Co.

—Vanessa Hudgens: High School Musical Star, 1 vol. 2008. (Big Buddy Biographies Ser.). (ENG.). 32p. (J). (gr. 2-5). 28.50 (978-1-60453-121-3(5)) ABDO Publishing Co.

—Zac Efron: High School Musical Star, 1 vol. 2008. (Big Buddy Biographies Ser.). (ENG.). 32p. (J). (gr. 2-5). 28.50 (978-1-60453-120-6(7)) ABDO Publishing Co.

—Zac Efron CD & Book. 2010. (Big Buddy Biographies CD+Book Ser.). 32p. (gr. 2-5). audio compact disk 57.00 (978-1-61613-307-8(4), Big Buddy Bks.) ABDO Publishing Co.

—Zac Efron Site CD & Book. 2010. (Big Buddy Biographies Site CD+Book Ser.). 32p. (gr. 2-5). cd-rom 85.57 (978-1-61613-279-8(5), Big Buddy Bks.) ABDO Publishing Co.

The Bookazines Staff. Sports Illustrated: Brett Favre: The Tribute. 2008. (YA). pap. 14.95 (978-1-60320-549-8(7)) Time Inc. Bks.

Time for Kids Editors. Benjamin Franklin - A Man of Many Talents. 2005. (Time for Kids Ser.). (ENG., Illus.). 48p. (J). (gr. 2-4). pap. 3.99 (978-0-06-057609-7(X)) HarperCollins Pubs.

Timer: An American Story. 2003. 291p. (YA). per. (978-0-9740774-0-6(2)) J L Publishing Co.

Topinka, Joseph Baar. Just Judy: A Citizen & Leader for Illinois. 2017. (ENG.). (J). pap. 16.95 **(978-0-9983282-2-5(7))** Hilton Publishing Co.

Torres, John. Usher. 2005. (Blue Banner Biography Ser.). (Illus.). 32p. (J). (gr. 4-8). lib. bdg. 25.70 (978-1-58415-379-5(2)) Mitchell Lane Pubs., Inc.

Torres, John A. Lil Wayne. 2009. (Blue Banner Biography Ser.). (Illus.). 32p. (YA). (gr. 4-7). lib. bdg. 25.70 (978-1-58415-768-7(2)) Mitchell Lane Pubs., Inc.

Torres, John Albert. Clay Aiken. 2004. (Blue Banner Biography Ser.). (Illus.). 32p. (J). (gr. 3-8). lib. bdg. 25.70 (978-1-58415-316-0(4)) Mitchell Lane Pubs., Inc.

—Dwight Howard: A Basketball Star Who Cares. 2013. (Sports Stars Who Care Ser.). 48p. (J). 25.27 (978-0-7660-4294-0(4)) Enslow Pubs., Inc.

—Shaun White: A Snowboarder & Skateboarder Who Cares. 2013. (Sports Stars Who Care Ser.). 48p. (J). lib. bdg. 25.27 (978-0-7660-4295-7(2)); (gr. 3-4). pap. 8.95 (978-1-4644-0535-8(2)) Enslow Pubs., Inc. (Enslow Elementary).

Towle, Mike. Walter Payton: Football's Sweetest Superstar. 2005. (Great American Sports Legends Ser.). (ENG., Illus.). 225p. (gr. 3-7). per. 12.95 (978-1-58182-476-6(9), 1249190) Turner Publishing Co.

Tracy, Kathleen. Carrie Underwood. 2005. (Blue Banner Biography Ser.). (Illus.). 32p. (J). (gr. 4-8). lib. bdg. 25.70 (978-1-58415-425-9(X)) Mitchell Lane Pubs., Inc.

—Demi Lovato. 2009. (Robbie Reader Ser.). (Illus.). 32p. (YA). (gr. 2-5). lib. bdg. 25.70 (978-1-58415-754-0(2)) Mitchell Lane Pubs., Inc.

—Matt Christopher. 2008. (Classic Storytellers Ser.). (Illus.). 48p. (J). (gr. 4-7). lib. bdg. 29.95 (978-1-58415-535-5(3)) Mitchell Lane Pubs., Inc.

—Megan Fox. 2010. (Blue Banner Biography Ser.). (Illus.). 32p. (YA). (gr. 4-7). lib. bdg. 25.70 (978-1-58415-912-4(X)) Mitchell Lane Pubs., Inc.

Transcending Race in America: Biographies of Biracial Achievers, 13 vols., Set. Incl. Beyoncé. Bednar, Chuck. (YA). (gr. 4-8). lib. bdg. 22.95 (978-1-4222-1607-1(1)); Booker T. Washington. Whiting, Jim. (Illus.). (YA). (gr. 4-8). lib. bdg. 22.95 (978-1-4222-1608-8(X)); David Blaine: Illusionist & Endurance Artist. Bednar, Chuck. (Illus.). (YA). (gr. 5-18). lib. bdg. 22.95 (978-1-4222-1609-5(8)); Frederick Douglass. Whiting, Jim. (Illus.). (YA). (gr. 5-18). lib. bdg. 22.95 (978-1-4222-1611-8(X)); Halle Berry. Sapet, Kerrily. (Illus.). (J). (gr. 4-8). 22.95 (978-1-4222-1612-5(8)); Prince: Singer-Songwriter, Musician, & Record Producer. Robson, David. (Illus.). (YA). (gr. 4-8). lib. bdg. 22.95 (978-1-4222-1614-9(4)); Rosa Parks. Bednar, Chuck. (Illus.). (YA). (gr. 5-18). lib. bdg. 22.95 (978-1-4222-1615-6(2)); Salma Hayek. Sapet, Kerrily. (Illus.). (YA). (gr. 5-18). lib. bdg. 22.95 (978-1-4222-1616-3(0)); Soledad O'Brien. Robson, David. (Illus.). (J). (gr. 5-18). lib. bdg. 22.95 (978-1-4222-1617-0(9)); 64p. (Illus.). 2010. 298.35 (978-1-4222-1605-7(5)) Mason Crest.

Trent, Tererai. The Girl Who Buried Her Dreams in a Can. Gilchrist, Jan Spivey, illus. 2015. (ENG.). 34p. (J). (gr. 1-3). 17.99 (978-0-670-01654-9(3), Viking Books for Young Readers) Penguin Young Readers Group.

Tukan, Jaytoe Anthony, Sr. John Reid Edwards: The People's Senator. 2003. per. 19.95 (978-0-9665909-4-4(5)) Kalawantis Publishing Services, Inc.

Uphill All the Way. 2004. (Illus.). 170p. per. 12.95 (978-0-9748333-0-9(4)) Goldenrod Pr.

Urban, William. Wyatt Earp: The O. K. Corral & the Law of the American West. 2009. (Library of American Lives & Times Ser.). 112p. (gr. 5-5). 69.20 (978-1-60853-512-5(6)) Rosen Publishing Group, Inc., The.

USA TODAY(r) Health Reports: Diseases & Disorders: Spring 2012 New Releases. 2012. (USA TODAY Lifeline Biographies Ser.). 112p. (gr. 6-12). lib. bdg. 138.40 (978-0-7613-8912-5(1), Twenty-First Century Bks.) Lerner Publishing Group.

USA Today Lifeline Biographies, 8 vols., Set. Incl. Barack Obama: A Leader in a Time of Change. Sirvaitis, Karen. (gr. 6-12). 2009. lib. bdg. 34.60 (978-0-7613-4235-9(4)); Bill Gates: Entrepreneur & Philanthropist. Lesinski, Jeanne M. (YA). (gr. 7-12). 2008. lib. bdg. 33.26 (978-1-58013-570-2(6)); Hillary Rodham Clinton: Secretary of State. Guernsey, Joann Bren. (gr. 6-12). 2009. lib. bdg. 34.60 (978-0-7613-5122-1(1)); Oprah Winfrey: Global Media Leader. Krohn, Katherine E. (gr. 6-12). 2008. lib. bdg. 34.60 (978-1-58013-571-9(4)); Tiger Woods: Golf's Master. Roberts, Jeremy. (gr. 6-12). 2008. lib. bdg. 34.60 (978-1-58013-569-6(2)); Tim Berners-Lee: Inventor of the World Wide Web. McPherson, Stephanie Sammartino. (Illus.). (J). (gr. 6-12). 2009. lib. bdg. 34.60 (978-0-8225-7273-2(7)); Vera Wang: Enduring Style. Krohn, Katherine E. (gr. 6-12). 2008. lib. bdg. 34.60 (978-1-58013-572-6(2)); Will Smith: Box Office Superstar. Doeden, Matt. (Illus.). (J). (gr. 6-12). 2009. lib. bdg. 34.60 (978-0-7613-4265-6(6), 1299611); 112p. (USA TODAY Lifeline Biographies Ser.). (ENG.). 2008. Set lib. bdg. 934.20 (978-1-58013-568-9(4), Twenty-First Century Bks.) Lerner Publishing Group.

USA Today Lifeline Biographies, 4 vols., Set. Incl. Beatles: Music Revolutionaries. Roberts, Jeremy. (Illus.). lib. bdg. 34.60 (978-0-7613-6421-4(8)); Derek Jeter: Spectacular Shortstop. Greenberg, Keith Elliot. 34.60 (978-0-7613-6422-1(6)); Johnny Depp: Hollywood Rebel. Doeden, Matt. (Illus.). lib. bdg. 34.60 (978-0-7613-6420-7(X), 1322549); Tom Brady: Unlikely Champion. Doeden, Matt. lib. bdg. 34.60 (978-0-7613-6423-8(4)); 112p. (gr. 6-12). 2011. 2011. Set lib. bdg. 133.04 (978-0-7613-7472-5(8)) Lerner Publishing Group.

Uschan, Michael V. Brian Urlacher. (Superstars of Pro Football Ser.). 64p. (YA). (gr. 7-12). 2009. (Illus.). lib. bdg. 22.95 (978-1-4222-0555-6(X)) 2007. pap. 9.95 (978-1-4222-0838-0(9)) Mason Crest.

—50 Cent. 2007. (People in the News Ser.). (ENG., Illus.). 104p. (YA). (gr. 7-12). lib. bdg. 33.45 (978-1-4205-0011-0(2)) Cengage Gale.

Uschan, Michael V., ed. Tyler Perry. 2010. (People in the News Ser.). (ENG.). 96p. (YA). (gr. 7-12). 33.95 (978-1-4205-0309-8(X)) Cengage Gale.

Vallaly, Barbara Dean, compiled by. Life on East 76th Street: Stories of an American Family 2004. (Illus.). 194p. per. 18.50 (978-0-9755822-0-6(8)) Woodland Pr.

Van Steenwyk, Elizabeth. First Dog Fala, 1 vol. Montgomery, Michael G., illus. 2008. (ENG.). 32p. (J). (gr. k-3). 16.95 *(978-1-56145-411-2(7))* Peachtree Pubs.

Van Tol, Alex. Sonia Sotomayor: U. S. Supreme Court Justice. 2010. (Crabtree Groundbreaker Biographies Ser.). (ENG., Illus.). 112p. (J). (gr. 5-8). lib. bdg. *(978-0-7787-2537-4(5))* Crabtree Publishing Co.

Various, illus. Childhood of Famous Americans Ready-To-Read Value Pack: Abe Lincoln & the Muddy Pig; Albert Einstein; John Adams Speaks for Freedom; George Washington's First Victory; Ben Franklin & His First Kite; Thomas Jefferson & the Ghostriders. 2013. (Ready-To-read COFA Ser.). (ENG.). 208p. (J). (gr. k-2). pap. 15.96 *(978-1-4424-9440-4(9)*, Simon Spotlight) Simon Spotlight.

Venezia, Mike. Alexander Graham Bell: Setting the Tone for Communication. Venezia, Mike, illus. 2008. (Getting to Know the World's Greatest Inventors & Scientists Ser.). (ENG., Illus.). 32p. (J). (gr. 2-5). 28.00 *(978-0-531-14976-8(5))* Scholastic Library Publishing.

—Benjamin Franklin: Electrified the World with New Ideas. Venezia, Mike, illus. 2009. (Getting to Know the World's Greatest Inventors & Scientists Ser.). (ENG., Illus.). 32p. (J). (gr. 2-5). 28.00 *(978-0-531-23701-4(X))* Scholastic Library Publishing.

—Benjamin Harrison. Venezia, Mike, illus. 2006. (Getting to Know the U. S. Presidents Ser.). (ENG., Illus.). 32p. (J). (gr. 3-7). lib. bdg. 28.00 *(978-0-516-22628-6(2)*, Children's Pr.) Scholastic Library Publishing.

—Chester A. Arthur. Venezia, Mike, illus. 2006. (Getting to Know the U. S. Presidents Ser.). (ENG., Illus.). 32p. (J). (gr. 3-7). lib. bdg. 28.00 *(978-0-516-22626-2(6)*, Children's Pr.) Scholastic Library Publishing.

—Grover Cleveland: Twenty-Second & Twenty-Fourth President, 1885-1889, 1893-1897. Venezia, Mike, illus. 2006. (Getting to Know the U. S. Presidents Ser.). (ENG., Illus.). 32p. (J). (gr. 3-7). lib. bdg. 28.00 *(978-0-516-22627-9(4)*, Children's Pr.) Scholastic Library Publishing.

—Henry Ford: Big Wheel in the Auto Industry. Venezia, Mike, illus. 2009. (Getting to Know the World's Greatest Inventors & Scientists Ser.). (ENG., Illus.). 32p. (J). (gr. 2-5). 28.00 *(978-0-531-23726-7(5))* Scholastic Library Publishing.

—James A. Garfield. Venezia, Mike, illus. 2006. (Getting to Know the U. S. Presidents Ser.). (ENG., Illus.). 32p. (J). (gr. 3-7). lib. bdg. 28.00 *(978-0-516-22625-5(8)*, Children's Pr.) Scholastic Library Publishing.

—Lyndon B. Johnson: Thirty-Sixth President, 1963-1969. Venezia, Mike, illus. 2007. (Getting to Know the U. S. Presidents Ser.). (Illus.). 32p. (J). (gr. 3-4). 28.00 *(978-0-516-22640-8(1)*, Children's Pr.) Scholastic Library Publishing.

—Richard M. Nixon: Thirty-Seventh President, 1969-1974. Venezia, Mike, illus. 2007. (Getting to Know the U. S. Presidents Ser.). (Illus.). 32p. (J). (gr. 3-4). 28.00 *(978-0-516-22641-5(X)*, Children's Pr.) Scholastic Library Publishing.

—Thomas Edison: Inventor with a Lot of Bright Ideas. Venezia, Mike, illus. 2008. (Getting to Know the World's Greatest Inventors & Scientists Ser.). (ENG., Illus.). 32p. (J). (gr. 2-5). 28.00 *(978-0-531-14978-2(1))* Scholastic Library Publishing.

Vernick, Audrey. Brothers at Bat: The True Story of an Amazing All-Brother Baseball Team. Salerno, Steven, illus. 2012. (ENG.). 40p. (J). (gr. -1-3). 17.99 *(978-0-547-38557-0(9)*, Clarion Bks.) Houghton Mifflin Harcourt Trade & Reference Pubs.

Victoria Justice. 2013. (Rising Stars Ser.). 32p. (J). (gr. 3-6). pap. 63.00 *(978-1-4339-8991-9(3))* Stevens, Gareth Publishing LLLP.

Viegas, Jennifer. Pierre Omidyar: The Founder of Ebay. 2006. (Internet Career Biographies Ser.). (Illus.). 112p. (YA). (gr. 7-12). lib. bdg. 34.60 *(978-1-4042-0715-8(5))* Rosen Publishing Group, Inc., The.

—William James: American Philosopher, Psychologist, & Theologian. 2009. (Library of American Thinkers Ser.). 112p. (gr. 6-6). 66.50 *(978-1-60853-517-0(7)*, Rosen Reference) Rosen Publishing Group, Inc., The.

Vizzini, Ned. Teen Angst? Naaah... A Quasi-Autobiography. 2010. (ENG.). 272p. (YA). (gr. 7). pap. 9.99 *(978-0-385-73945-0(1)*, Ember) Random Hse. Children's Bks.

Wachtel, Alan. The FBI's Most Wanted. 2009. (FBI Story Ser.). 64p. (J). (gr. 4-7). lib. bdg. 22.95 *(978-1-4222-0562-4(2))* Mason Crest.

Wade, Mary Dodson. Amazing Champion of the Earth Rachel Carson. 2009. (Amazing Americans Ser.). (Illus.). 24p. (J). (gr. 1-3). lib. bdg. 22.60 *(978-0-7660-3283-5(3))* Enslow Pubs., Inc.

—Amazing Olympic Athlete Wilma Rudolph. 2009. (Amazing Americans Ser.). (Illus.). 24p. (J). (gr. 1-3). lib. bdg. 22.60 *(978-0-7660-3282-8(5))* Enslow Pubs., Inc.

—Stephen F. Austin: Keeping Promises. 2012. (Texas Heroes for Young Readers Ser.). 24p. (J). (gr. k-2). 16.95 *(978-1-933979-11-3(9))* Bright Sky Pr.

Waldman, Neil. A Land of Big Dreamers: Voices of Courage in America. Waldman, Neil, illus. 2011. (Single Titles Ser.). (ENG., Illus.). 32p. (gr. 3-5). lib. bdg. 16.95 *(978-0-8225-6810-0(1))* Lerner Publishing Group.

Wallmark, Laurie. Grace Hopper: Queen of Computer Code. Wu, Katy, illus. 2017. (ENG.). 48p. (J). (gr. k). 16.95 *(978-1-4549-2000-7(9))* Sterling Publishing Co., Inc.

Waters, Rosa. Ashanti. 2008. (Hip-Hop Ser.). (Illus.). 64p. (YA). (gr. 3-7). per. 7.95 *(978-1-4222-0263-0(1))* Mason Crest.

—Yung Joc. 2009. (Hip-Hop 2 Ser.). (Illus.). 64p. (YA). (gr. 7-12). lib. bdg. 22.95 *(978-1-4222-0307-1(7))* Mason Crest.

Watkins, Angela Farris. My Uncle Martin's Big Heart. Velasquez, Eric, illus. 2010. (ENG.). 32p. (J). (gr. k-2). 19.95 *(978-0-8109-8975-7(1)*, Abrams Bks. for Young Readers) Abrams, Inc.

Waxman, Laura Hamilton. Gerald R. Ford. 2008. (History Maker Biographies Ser.). (ENG.). 48p. (gr. 3-6). 27.93 *(978-0-8225-7985-4(5)*, Lerner Pubns.) Lerner Publishing Group.

—W. K. Kellogg. 2006. (History Maker Biographies Ser.). (Illus.). 48p. (J). (gr. 3-7). lib. bdg. 26.60 *(978-0-8225-6578-9(1)*, Lerner Pubns.) Lerner Publishing Group.

Weakland, Mark. When Neil Armstrong Built a Wind Tunnel. Lozano, Luciano, illus. 2017. (Leaders Doing Headstands Ser.). (ENG.). 32p. (gr. 2-3). lib. bdg. 27.99 ***(978-1-5158-1575-4(7))*** Picture Window Bks.

—When Walt Disney Rode a Pig. Pino, Pablo, illus. 2017. (Leaders Doing Headstands Ser.). (ENG.). 32p. (gr. 2-3). lib. bdg. 27.99 ***(978-1-5158-1576-1(5))*** Picture Window Bks.

Wearing, Judy. Abraham Lincoln. 2010. (My Life Ser.). 24p. (J). (gr. 2-4). lib. bdg. 25.70 *(978-1-61690-056-4(3))* Weigl Pubs., Inc.

—Abraham Lincoln: My Life. 2010. pap. 9.95 *(978-1-61690-057-1(1))* Weigl Pubs., Inc.

Wearing, Judy & Yasuda, Anita. Lebron James. 2011. (J). (gr. 4-6). pap. 12.95 *(978-1-61690-674-0(X)*, AV2 by Weigl); (Illus.). 24p. (YA). (gr. 3-6). 27.13 *(978-1-61690-669-6(3))* Weigl Pubs., Inc.

Weber, Terri Smith. Hilary Duff: Branching Out. 2003. (J). pap. *(978-1-932724-03-5(6))*; lib. bdg. *(978-1-932724-02-8(8)*, Bios for Kids) Panda Publishing, L.L.C.

—Jeff Gordon: Racing to Win. 2003. (J). pap. *(978-0-9740180-2-7(3))*; lib. bdg. *(978-0-9740180-0-3(7))* Panda Publishing, L.L.C. (Bios for Kids).

—Tony Hawk: Flying High. 2003. (J). lib. bdg. *(978-1-932724-00-4(1)*, Bios for Kids) Panda Publishing, L.L.C.

Weintraub, Aileen. Jean Lafitte: Pirate Hero of the War Of 1812. 2009. (Library of Pirates Ser.). 24p. (gr. 3-3). 42.50 *(978-1-60853-813-3(3)*, PowerKids Pr.) Rosen Publishing Group, Inc., The.

Welch, Catherine A. Eli Whitney: History Maker Bios Set. 2008. pap. 52.95 *(978-0-8225-9388-1(2))* Lerner Publishing Group.

—Farmland Innovator: A Story about Cyrus Mccormick. Jones, Jan Naimo, illus. 2007. (Creative Minds Biographies Ser.). (ENG.). 64p. (gr. 4-8). lib. bdg. 22.60 *(978-0-8225-5988-7(9))* Lerner Publishing Group.

—George H. W. Bush. 2008. (History Maker Biographies Ser.). (ENG.). 48p. (gr. 3-6). 27.93 *(978-0-8225-8895-5(1)*, Lerner Pubns.) Lerner Publishing Group.

Westen, Robin. Oprah Winfrey: A Biography of a Billionaire Talk Show Host. 2013. (African-American Icons Ser.). 104p. (J). (gr. 6-12). pap. 10.95 *(978-1-59845-394-2(7))* Enslow Pubs., Inc.

Weston, Michael R. Jerry Yang & David Filo: The Founders of Yahoo! 2006. (Internet Career Biographies Ser.). (Illus.). 112p. (YA). (gr. 7-12). lib. bdg. 34.60 *(978-1-4042-0718-9(X))* Rosen Publishing Group, Inc., The.

What It's Like to Be (Que Se Siente Al Ser), 8 vols., Set. Incl. What It's Like to Be America Ferrara. Gagne, Tammy. de la Vega, Eida, tr. 2010. lib. bdg. 25.70 *(978-1-58415-854-7(9))*; What Its Like to Be Marta Vieira. Thatcher Murcia, Rebecca. de la Vega, Eida, tr. 2010. lib. bdg. 25.70 *(978-1-58415-852-3(2))*; What It's Like to Be Miley Cyrus. Leavitt, Amie Jane. Vega, Eida de la, tr. 2009. lib. bdg. 25.70 *(978-1-58415-841-7(7))*; What It's Like to Be President Barack Obama? Sherman, Patrice. Vega, Eida de la, tr. 2009. 25.70 *(978-1-58415-843-1(3))*; What It's Like to Be Ryan Howard: Como Es Ser Ryan Howard. Sherman, Patrice & Murica, Rebecca Thatcher. de la Vega, Eida, tr. Rasemas, Joe, illus. 2009. 25.70 *(978-1-58415-845-5(X))*; What It's Like to Be Shakira. Thatcher Murcia, Rebecca. de la Vega, Eida, tr. 2010. lib. bdg. 25.70 *(978-1-58415-851-6(4))*; What Its Like to Be Sonia Sotomayor. Gagne, Tammy. de la Vega, Eida, tr. 2010. lib. bdg. 25.70 *(978-1-58415-853-0(0))*; What It's Like to Be the Jonas Brothers: Que Se Siente Al Ser Los Hermanos Jonas. Leavitt, Amie Jane. Vega, Eida de la, tr. 2009. 25.70 *(978-1-58415-842-4(5))*; (Illus.). 32p. (J). (gr. -1-2). 2010. Set lib. bdg. 205.60 *(978-1-58415-855-4(7))* Mitchell Lane Pubs., Inc.

What's So Great About...?, 10 vols., Set. 2006. (J). (gr. 1-4). lib. bdg. 169.50 *(978-1-58415-297-2(4))* Mitchell Lane Pubs., Inc.

Wheeler, Jill C. Ezra Jack Keats, 1 vol. 2005. (Children's Illustrators Set 1 Ser.). (ENG., Illus.). 24p. (gr. k-6). 25.65 *(978-1-59197-718-6(5)*, Checkerboard Library) ABDO Publishing Co.

White, Joseph C. Forged in a Country Crucible. 2003. (Illus.). 278p. per. 19.95 *(978-0-9726095-1-7(2)*, FCC2003) Crossing Trails Pubns.

Whitehurst, Susan. William Bradford & Plymouth: A Colony Grows. 2009. (Library of the Pilgrims Ser.). 24p. (gr. 3-4). 42.50 *(978-1-60853-916-1(4)*, PowerKids Pr.) Rosen Publishing Group, Inc., The.

Whiting, Jim. Jim Beckwourth: The Man Who Opened the West. 2007. (Illus.). 144p. (YA). (gr. 6-18). lib. bdg. 25.95 *(978-1-59556-027-8(0))* OTTN Publishing.

—The Maryland Colony: Lord Baltimore. 2007. (Building America Ser.). (Illus.). 48p. (J). (gr. 4-8). lib. bdg. 29.95 *(978-1-58415-547-8(7))* Mitchell Lane Pubs., Inc.

Whiting, Jim. Russell Westbrook. 2017. (J). lib. bdg. 25.70 ***(978-1-68020-133-8(6))*** Mitchell Lane Pubs., Inc.

Wilcoxson, Billy. The CB Cowboys: The Saga of the Legendary Christensen Family. 2003. (Illus.). 217p. pap. 26.95 *(978-1-57168-823-1(4))* Eakin Pr.

Willett, Edward. Jimi Hendrix: Kiss the Sky. 2006. (American Rebels Ser.). (Illus.). 160p. (YA). (gr. 6-9). lib. bdg. 35.94 *(978-0-7660-2449-6(0))* Enslow Pubs., Inc.

William Dawes. 2006. (J). lib. bdg. *(978-1-58415-444-0(6))* Mitchell Lane Pubs., Inc.

Williams, Mary E. Mark Zuckerberg. Greenhaven Press Staff, ed. 2012. (People in the News Ser.). (ENG., Illus.). 128p. (gr. 7-10). lib. bdg. 39.40 *(978-1-4205-0758-4(3)*, Lucent Bks.) Cengage Gale.

Williams, Mel. Taylor Lautner: Overnight Sizzlin' Sensation. 2009. (ENG.). 48p. (YA). pap. 9.99 *(978-1-4424-0368-0(3)*, Simon Pulse) Simon Pulse.

Williams, Zella. America Ferrera: Award-Winning Actress. 2010. (Hispanic Headliners Ser.). (ENG.). 24p. (J). pap. 8.25 *(978-1-4488-1478-7(2))*; lib. bdg. 22.60 *(978-1-4488-1473-2(1))* Rosen Publishing Group, Inc., The. (PowerKids Pr.).

—America Ferrera: Award-Winning Actress = Estrella de la Pantalla. 2010. (Hispanic Headliners / Hispanos en Las Noticias Ser.). (ENG & SPA.). 24p. (J). (gr. 2-5). lib. bdg. 22.60 *(978-1-4488-0713-0(1))* Rosen Publishing Group, Inc., The.

—Mark Sanchez: Quarterback on the Rise - Mariscal de Campo en Ascenso. 2010. (Hispanic Headliners / Hispanos en Las Noticias Ser.). (ENG & SPA.). 24p. (J). (gr. 2-5). 22.60 *(978-1-4488-1171-7(6))* Rosen Publishing Group, Inc., The.

Wilner, Barry. Football's Top 10 Quarterbacks. 2010. (Top 10 Sports Stars Ser.). (Illus.). 48p. (J). (gr. 5-9). 25.27 *(978-0-7660-3469-3(0))* Enslow Pubs., Inc.

—Football's Top 10 Running Backs. 2010. (Top 10 Sports Stars Ser.). (Illus.). 48p. (J). (gr. 5-9). 25.27 *(978-0-7660-3468-6(2))* Enslow Pubs., Inc.

—Peyton Manning: A Football Star Who Cares. 2011. (Sports Stars Who Care Ser.). (Illus.). 48p. (J). (gr. 2-5). lib. bdg. 25.27 *(978-0-7660-3774-8(6))* Enslow Pubs., Inc.

Wilson, Rene. Kenny Chesney. 2010. (Country Music Stars Ser.). (Illus.). 32p. (J). (gr. 3-8). pap. 10.50 *(978-1-4339-3608-1(9))*; lib. bdg. 25.25 *(978-1-4339-3607-4(0))* Stevens, Gareth Publishing LLLP.

Winter, Jonah. Dizzy. Qualls, Sean, illus. 2006. (J). 16.99 *(978-0-439-50736-3(7)*, Levine, Arthur A. Bks.) Scholastic, Inc.

—Sonia Sotomayor: A Judge Grows in the Bronx. Ziegler, Argentina Palacios, tr. from SPA. Rodriguez, Edel, illus. 2009. (ENG & SPA.). 40p. (J). (gr. -1-3). 17.99 *(978-1-4424-0303-1(9)*, Atheneum Bks. for Young Readers) Simon & Schuster Children's Publishing.

Winters, Kay. John Appleseed: A Trail of Trees. Pullen, Zachary, illus. 2007. (J). *(978-1-4263-0101-8(4))* National Geographic Society.

Wise, Bill. Louis Sockalexis: Native American Baseball Pioneer, 1 vol. Farnsworth, Bill, illus. 2007. (ENG.). 32p. (J). (gr. 1-7). 16.95 *(978-1-58430-269-8(0))* Lee & Low Bks., Inc.

Wittekind, Erika. Gloria Steinem: Women's Liberation Leader, 1 vol. 2011. (Essential Lives Set 7 Ser.). (ENG., Illus.). 112p. (J). (gr. 6-12). lib. bdg. 35.64 *(978-1-61783-007-5(0))* ABDO Publishing Co.

Wong, Angi Ma. Barack Obama: Historymaker. 2009. (Illus.). 104p. (J). *(978-1-928753-86-5(8))* Pacific Heritage Bks.

Wong, Angi Ma, illus. Meet President Obama: America's 44th President. 2009. 32p. (J). *(978-1-928753-28-5(0))* Pacific Heritage Bks.

Wong, Li Keng. Good Fortune: My Journey to Gold Mountain, 1 vol. 2006. (ENG., Illus.). 144p. (J). (gr. 3-7). 14.95 *(978-1-56145-367-2(6))* Peachtree Pubs.

Woodside, Martin. Thomas Edison: The Man Who Lit up the World. 2007. (Sterling Biographies(r) Ser.). (ENG., Illus.). 128p. (J). (gr. 5-9). pap. 5.95 *(978-1-4027-3229-4(5))* Sterling Publishing Co., Inc.

Woog, Adam. Joe Montana. 2008. (Football Superstars Ser.). (Illus.). 120p. (YA). (gr. 7-12). 30.00 *(978-0-7910-9568-3(1))* Facts On File, Inc.

—Pierre M. Omidyar: Creator of Ebay. 2007. (Innovators Ser.). (ENG., Illus.). 64p. (J). (gr. 4-8). lib. bdg. 29.95 *(978-0-7377-3864-3(2)*, LML02109-234925, Kidhaven) Cengage Gale.

Wooldridge, Connie N. & Wooldridge, Connie Nordhielm. Thank You Very Much, Captain Ericsson! Glass, Andrew, photos by. 2004. (ENG., Illus.). 32p. (J). (gr. k-3). tchr. ed. 16.95 *(978-0-8234-1626-4(7))* Holiday Hse., Inc.

Wooten, Sara McIntosh. Tim McGraw: Celebrity with Heart. 2010. (Celebrities with Heart Ser.). (Illus.). 128p. (J). pap. 10.95 *(978-1-59845-207-5(X))* Enslow Pubs., Inc.

Wright, David K. The Life of Paul Robeson: Actor, Singer, Political Activist. 2014. (Legendary African Americans Ser.). 96p. (J). (gr. 6-12). 27.94 *(978-0-7660-6157-6(4))* Enslow Pubs., Inc.

Wyborny, Sheila. Frederick W. Smith: Founder of FedEx. 2007. (Innovators Ser.). (ENG., Illus.). 64p. (J). (gr. 4-8). lib. bdg. 28.75 *(978-0-7377-3861-2(8)*, LML02109-234922, Kidhaven) Cengage Gale.

Wyckoff, Edwin Brit. The African-American Heart Surgery Pioneer: The Genius of Vivien Thomas. 2013. (Genius Inventors & Their Great Ideas Ser.). (Illus.). 48p. (J). (gr. 3-18). 25.27 *(978-0-7660-4140-0(9)*, Enslow Elementary) Enslow Pubs., Inc.

—The Man Who Invented Television: The Genius of Philo T. Farnsworth. 2013. (Genius Inventors & Their Great Ideas Ser.). (Illus.). 48p. (J). (gr. 3-18). 25.27 *(978-0-7660-4139-4(5)*, Enslow Elementary) Enslow Pubs., Inc.

—The Man Who Invented the Electric Guitar: The Genius of les Paul. 2013. (Genius Inventors & Their Great Ideas Ser.). (Illus.). 48p. (J). (gr. 3-18). 25.27 *(978-0-7660-4137-0(9))* Enslow Pubs., Inc.

—The Man Who Invented the Laser: The Genius of Theodore H. Maiman. 2013. (Genius Inventors & Their Great Ideas Ser.). (Illus.). 48p. (J). (gr. 3-18). 25.27 *(978-0-7660-4138-7(7)*, Enslow Elementary) Enslow Pubs., Inc.

—The Woman Who Invented the Thread That Stops Bullets: The Genius of Stephanie Kwolek. 2013. (Genius Inventors & Their Great Ideas Ser.). (Illus.). 48p. (J). (gr. 3-18). 25.27 *(978-0-7660-4141-7(7))* Enslow Pubs., Inc.

Wyckoff, Edwin Brit & Library. Sign Language Man: Thomas H. Gallaudet & His Incredible Work. 2010. (Genius at Work! Great Inventor Biographies Ser.). (Illus.). 32p. (J). (gr. 2-5). lib. bdg. 23.94 *(978-0-7660-3447-1(X))* Enslow Pubs., Inc.

Yancey, Diane. The Case of the Green River Killer. 2007. (Crime Scene Investigations Ser.). (ENG., Illus.). 104p. (YA). (gr. 7-12). lib. bdg. 35.45 *(978-1-59018-955-9(8))* Cengage Gale.

Yasuda, Anita. Kristen Stewart. 2010. (Remarkable People Ser.). (Illus.). 24p. (J). (gr. 4-6). pap. 11.95 *(978-1-61690-164-6(0))*; lib. bdg. 25.70 *(978-1-61690-163-9(2))* Weigl Pubs., Inc.

—Miranda Cosgrove. 2011. (J). (gr. 4-6). pap. 12.95 *(978-1-61690-673-3(1)*, AV2 by Weigl); (Illus.). 24p. (YA). (gr. 3-6). 27.13 *(978-1-61690-668-9(5))* Weigl Pubs., Inc.

—Taylor Lautner. 2010. (Remarkable People Ser.). (Illus.). 24p. (J). (gr. 4-6). pap. 11.95 *(978-1-61690-161-5(6))*; lib. bdg. 25.70 *(978-1-61690-160-8(8))* Weigl Pubs., Inc.

Yomtov, Nel & Biskup, Agnieszka. American Graphic Fall 2011. 2011. (American Graphic Ser.). (ENG.). 32p. (gr. 3-4). lib. bdg. 61.30 *(978-1-4296-6584-1(X)*, Graphic Library) Capstone Press of Coughlan Cos.

Young, Jeff C. Albert Pujols: A Baseball Star Who Cares. 2013. (Sports Stars Who Care Ser.). 48p. (J). lib. bdg. 25.27 *(978-0-7660-4228-5(6))* Enslow Pubs., Inc.

—Dwyane Wade. 2012. (Role Model Athletes Ser.). 64p. (J). (gr. 7). 22.95 *(978-1-4222-2709-1(X))* Mason Crest.

Yount, Lisa. Craig Venter. 2011. (Trailblazers in Science & Technology Ser.). 160p. (gr. 6-12). 35.00 *(978-1-60413-662-3(6)*, Chelsea Hse.) Facts On File, Inc.

Zaunders, Bo. The Great Bridge-Building Contest. Munro, Roxie, illus. 2006. 30p. (J). (gr. 4-8). reprint ed. 17.00 *(978-1-4223-5239-7(0))* DIANE Publishing Co.

Zepke, Terrance. Pirates of the Carolinas for Kids. 2009. (Carolinas for Kids Ser.). (ENG.). 71p. (J). (gr. 4-18). pap. 9.95 *(978-1-56164-459-9(5))* Pineapple Pr., Inc.

Zimmer, Kyle, frwd. Who Wrote That? Incl. Avi. Speaker-Yuan, Margaret. 112p. lib. bdg. 35.00 *(978-0-7910-8230-0(X))*; Beatrix Potter. Yuan, Margaret Speaker. 120p. lib. bdg. 35.00 *(978-0-7910-8655-1(0))*; Beverly Cleary. Peltak, Jennifer. 112p. lib. bdg. 35.00 *(978-0-7910-8231-7(8))*; Bruce Coville. Marcovitz, Hal. 128p. 35.00 *(978-0-7910-8656-8(9))*; Charles Dickens. Dailey, Donna. 112p. lib. bdg. 35.00 *(978-0-7910-8233-1(4))*; E. B. White. LaBrie, Aimie. 112p. (YA). 35.00 *(978-0-7910-8235-5(0))*; Jane Yolen. 128p. lib. bdg. 35.00 *(978-0-7910-8660-5(7))*; L. M. Montgomery. Kjelle, Marylou Morano. 112p. lib. bdg. 35.00 *(978-0-7910-8234-8(2))*; Phillip Pullman. Speaker-Yuan, Margaret & Yuan, Margaret Speaker. 120p. lib. bdg. 35.00 *(978-0-7910-8658-2(5))*; R. L. Stine. Marcovitz, Hal. 136p. lib. bdg. 35.00 *(978-0-7910-8659-9(3))*; Robert Cormier. Hyde, Margaret O. 112p. lib. bdg. 35.00 *(978-0-7910-8232-4(6))*; Will Hobbs. Marcovitz, Hal. 128p. lib. bdg. 35.00 *(978-0-7910-8657-5(7))*; (Illus.). (gr. 6-12). (Who Wrote That? Ser.). 2005. 660.00 o.p. *(978-0-7910-9155-5(4)*, Chelsea Hse.) Facts On File, Inc.

Zuehlke, Jeffrey. Ben Roethlisberger. 2007. (Amazing Athletes Ser.). (ENG., Illus.). 32p. (gr. 2-5). lib. bdg. 25.26 *(978-0-8225-7660-0(0))* Lerner Publishing Group.

—Joe Mauer. 2011. 32p. 25.26 *(978-0-7613-7204-2(0))*; (ENG.). (gr. 2-5). pap. 7.95 *(978-0-7613-7068-0(4))* Lerner Publishing Group.

—Joe Mauer (Revised Edition) 2011. (Amazing Athletes Ser.). 32p. (J). pap. 45.32 *(978-0-7613-7653-8(4))* Lerner Publishing Group.

—Kevin Garnett. rev. ed. 2010. (Amazing Athletes Ser.). (ENG.). 32p. (gr. 2-5). pap. 7.95 *(978-0-7613-5595-3(2))* Lerner Publishing Group.

—Kevin Garnett (Revised Edition) 2010. pap. 39.62 *(978-0-7613-6969-1(4))* Lerner Publishing Group.

Zumbusch, Amelie von. Michelle Obama: Our First Lady. 2010. (Making History: the Obamas Ser.). (Illus.). 24p. (J). pap. 8.25 *(978-1-4358-9868-4(0))*; (gr. 2-3). lib. bdg. 22.60 *(978-1-4358-9388-7(3))* Rosen Publishing Group, Inc., The. (PowerKids Pr.).

UNITED STATES—BIOGRAPHY—DICTIONARIES

Eggleston, Edward. Stories of Great Americans for Little Americans. 2008. 124p. 24.99 *(978-0-554-30270-6(5))* Creative Media Partners, LLC.

Founding Fathers. (J). tchr. ed. 41.95 *(978-0-382-40882-3(9))* Cobblestone Publishing Co.

Rudin, Ronald. Founding Fathers: The Celebration of Champlain & Laval in the Streets of Quebec, 1878-1908. 2003. (ENG., Illus.). 304p. *(978-0-8020-3645-2(7))*; pap. *(978-0-8020-8479-8(6))* Univ. of Toronto Pr.

Wilson, Hoyt R. They Never Gave Up. 2006. (Illus.). 112p. (J). (gr. 4-7). pap. 7.95 *(978-0-9706429-0-5(3))* Resource Publishing.

UNITED STATES—BIOGRAPHY—POETRY

Grady, Cynthia. I Lay My Stitches Down. Wood, Michele, illus. 2012. (ENG.). 34p. (YA). 17.00 *(978-0-8028-5386-8(2)*, Eerdmans Bks For Young Readers) Eerdmans, William B. Publishing Co.

UNITED STATES—BUREAU OF CUSTOMS

Kerrigan, Michael. Customs & Border Protection. 2017. (J). ***(978-1-4222-3761-8(3))*** Mason Crest.

UNITED STATES—CENSUS

Wilson, Natashya. The Census & America's People: Analyzing Data Using Line Graphs & Tables. (PowerMath Ser.). (ENG., 32p. (gr. 4-5). 2009. Illus.). pap. 10.00 *(978-0-8239-8903-4(8)*, PowerKids Pr.) 2004. 47.50 *(978-0-8239-7647-8(5))* Rosen Publishing Group, Inc., The.

UNITED STATES—CENTRAL INTELLIGENCE AGENCY

Besel, Jennifer M., et al. American Special Ops. 2012. (American Special Ops Ser.). (ENG.). 48p. (gr. 3-4). lib. bdg. 127.96 *(978-1-4296-9184-0(0))* Capstone Press of Coughlan Cos.

Cobb, Allan B. How the US Security Agencies Work, 1 vol. 2014. (How the US Government Works). (ENG., Illus.). 48p. (gr. 3-6). lib. bdg. 32.79 *(978-1-62403-636-5(4))* ABDO Publishing Co.

Goodman, Michael E. The CIA & Other American Spies. 2012. (Spies Around the World Ser.). (Illus.). 48p. (J). (gr. 5-12). 23.95 *(978-1-60818-226-8(6))* Creative Co., The.

—Modern Spies. 2015. (Illus.). 48p. (J). *(978-1-60818-600-6(8)*, Creative Education) Creative Co., The.

—Modern Spies: Wartime Spies. 2016. (Wartime Spies Ser.). (ENG., Illus.). 48p. (J). (gr. 5-9). pap. 12.00 *(978-1-62832-205-7(5)*, Creative Paperbacks) Creative Co., The.

—Spies Around the World: the CIA & Other American Spies. 2014. (Spies Around the World Ser.). (ENG., Illus.). 48p. (J). (gr. 4-7). pap. 12.00 *(978-0-89812-969-4(9)*, Creative Paperbacks) Creative Co., The.

Hamilton, John. The CIA, 1 vol. 2007. (Defending the Nation Ser.). (ENG., Illus.). 32p. (gr. -1-3). 27.07 *(978-1-59679-756-7(8)*, Checkerboard Library) ABDO Publishing Co.

Hines, Janet. Inside America's CIA: The Central Intelligence Agency. (Inside the World's Most Famous Intelligence Agencies Ser.). 64p. 2009. (gr. 5-5). 58.50 *(978-1-61513-567-7(7))* 2005. (Illus.). (YA). (gr. 7-12). lib. bdg. 31.95 *(978-0-8239-3811-7(5))* Rosen Publishing Group, Inc., The.

McCollum, Sean. The CIA: The Missions. 2012. (American Special Ops Ser.). (ENG., Illus.). 48p. (gr. 3-4). lib. bdg. 31.99 *(978-1-4296-8660-0(X))* Capstone Press of Coughlan Cos.

TUV

Murray, Laura K. Spies in the CIA. 2016. 24p. (J). *(978-1-60818-616-7(4)*, Creative Education) Creative Co., The.

Streissguth, Tom. America's Security Agencies: The Department of Homeland Security, FBI, NSA, & CIA. 2008. (Federal Government Ser.). (Illus.). 128p. (J). (gr. 3-7). lib. bdg. 34.60 *(978-1-59845-058-3(1)*, MyReportLinks.com Bks.) Enslow Pubs., Inc.

—The Security Agencies of the United States: How the CIA, FBI, NSA, & Homeland Security Keep Us Safe. 2012. (Constitution & the United States Government Ser.). (Illus.). 104p. (J). (gr. 5-18). 33.27 *(978-0-7660-4064-9(X))* Enslow Pubs., Inc.

Wagner, Heather Lehr. The Central Intelligence Agency. 2007. (U. S. Government Ser.). (Illus.). 104p. (YA). (gr. 5-9). lib. bdg. 30.00 *(978-0-7910-9282-8(8))* Facts On File, Inc.

Wright, John D. Counterterrorist Forces with the CIA. 2004. (Rescue & Prevention Ser.). (Illus.). 96p. (YA). (gr. 7-18). lib. bdg. 22.95 *(978-1-59084-407-6(6))* Mason Crest.

UNITED STATES—CHURCH HISTORY

Manuel, David, et al. From Sea to Shining Sea for Young Readers: 1787-1837. 2011. (Discovering God's Plan for America Ser.: 2). (ENG.). 208p. (J). pap. 16.00 *(978-0-8007-3374-2(6))* Revell.

UNITED STATES—CIVIL AIR PATROL

Feinstein, Stephen. The 1980s. 2015. (Decades of the 20th & 21st Centuries Ser.). (ENG., Illus.). 96p. (J). (gr. 7-7). 34.60 *(978-0-7660-6935-0(4))* Enslow Pubs., Inc.

UNITED STATES—CIVILIZATION

Benchmark Education Co., LLC. The Middle Colonies. 2014. (PRIME Ser.). (J). (gr. 6-8). pap. *(978-1-4509-9487-3(3))* Benchmark Education Co.

Bingham, Jane. Popular Culture: 1920-1939, 1 vol. 2012. (History of Popular Culture Ser.). (ENG.). 64p. (gr. 6-9). pap. 10.95 *(978-1-4109-4629-4(0))*; lib. bdg. 35.99 *(978-1-4109-4622-5(3))* Heinemann-Raintree.

Bix, Cynthia Overbeck. Fad Mania! A History of American Crazes. 2014. 64p. (J). (gr. 6-12). lib. bdg. 34.60 *(978-1-4677-1034-3(2)*, Twenty-First Century Bks.) Lerner Publishing Group.

Brill, Marlene Targ. America in the 1990s. 2009. (Decades of Twentieth-Century America Ser.). (ENG.). 144p. (gr. 5-12). lib. bdg. 38.60 *(978-0-8225-7603-7(1))* Lerner Publishing Group.

Burgan, Michael. Popular Culture: 1960-1979, 1 vol. 2012. (History of Popular Culture Ser.). (ENG.). 64p. (gr. 6-9). pap. 10.95 *(978-1-4109-4631-7(2))*; lib. bdg. 35.99 *(978-1-4109-4624-9(X))* Heinemann-Raintree.

Carlisle, Rodney P. Contemporary America, 1970 to Present, 9 vols. 2009. (Handbook to Life in America Ser.). (Illus.). 291p. (C). (gr. 9-18). 50.00 *(978-0-8160-7182-1(9))* Facts On File, Inc.

—The Gilded Age, 1870-1900, 9 vols. 2009. (Handbook to Life in America Ser.). (Illus.). 272p. (C). (gr. 9-18). 50.00 *(978-0-8160-7177-7(2))* Facts On File, Inc.

Ciment, James. Postwar America: An Encyclopedia of Social, Political, Cultural, & Economic History, 4 vols., Set. 2006. (ENG., Illus.). 2008p. (C). (gr. 7-18). 158.00 *(978-0-7656-8067-9(X)*, Y183409) Routledge.

Combs, Maggie. Postwar United States. 2011. (Explorer Library: Language Arts Explorer Ser.). (ENG.). 32p. (gr. 4-8). pap. 14.21 *(978-1-61080-284-0(5)*, 201207); lib. bdg. 28.50 *(978-1-61080-196-6(2)*, 201168) Cherry Lake Publishing.

Craats, Rennay. Trends. 2008. (USA Past Present Future Ser.). (Illus.). 48p. (J). (gr. 4-6). pap. 10.95 *(978-1-59036-977-7(7))*; lib. bdg. 29.05 *(978-1-59036-976-0(9))* Weigl Pubs., Inc.

Dustman, Jeanne. American Culture. rev. ed. 2014. (Primary Source Readers Content & Literacy Ser.). (ENG., Illus.). 32p. (gr. 3-3). pap. 8.99 *(978-1-4333-7360-2(2))* Teacher Created Materials, Inc.

Feinstein, Stephen. The 1900s. 2015. (Decades of the 20th & 21st Centuries Ser.). (ENG., Illus.). 96p. (J). (gr. 7-7). 34.60 *(978-0-7660-6920-6(6))* Enslow Pubs., Inc.

—The 1900s from Teddy Roosevelt to Flying Machines. rev. ed. 2006. (Decades of the 20th Century in Color Ser.). (Illus.). 64p. (J). (gr. 5-9). lib. bdg. 29.27 *(978-0-7660-2630-8(2))* Enslow Pubs., Inc.

—The 1910s. 2015. (Decades of the 20th & 21st Centuries Ser.). (ENG., Illus.). 96p. (J). (gr. 7-7). 34.60 *(978-0-7660-6922-0(2))* Enslow Pubs., Inc.

—The 1910s from World War I to Ragtime Music. rev. ed. 2006. (Decades of the 20th Century in Color Ser.). (Illus.). 64p. (J). (gr. 5-9). lib. bdg. 29.27 *(978-0-7660-2631-5(0))* Enslow Pubs., Inc.

—The 1920s. 2015. (Decades of the 20th & 21st Centuries Ser.). (ENG., Illus.). 96p. (J). (gr. 7-7). 34.60 *(978-0-7660-6924-4(9))* Enslow Pubs., Inc.

—The 1930s. 2015. (Decades of the 20th & 21st Centuries Ser.). (ENG., Illus.). 96p. (J). (gr. 7-7). 34.60 *(978-0-7660-6926-8(5))* Enslow Pubs., Inc.

—The 1930s from the Great Depression to the Wizard of Oz. rev. ed. 2006. (Decades of the 20th Century in Color Ser.). (Illus.). 64p. (J). (gr. 4-7). lib. bdg. 29.27 *(978-0-7660-2633-9(7))* Enslow Pubs., Inc.

—The 1940s. 2015. (Decades of the 20th & 21st Centuries Ser.). (ENG., Illus.). 96p. (J). (gr. 7-7). 34.60 *(978-0-7660-6928-2(1))* Enslow Pubs., Inc.

—The 1940s from World War II to Jackie Robinson. rev. ed. 2006. (Decades of the 20th Century in Color Ser.). (Illus.). 64p. (J). (gr. 4-7). lib. bdg. 29.27 *(978-0-7660-2634-6(5))* Enslow Pubs., Inc.

—The 1950s. 2015. (Decades of the 20th & 21st Centuries Ser.). (ENG., Illus.). 96p. (J). (gr. 7-7). 34.60 *(978-0-7660-6930-5(3))* Enslow Pubs., Inc.

—The 1950s from the Korean War to Elvis. rev. ed. 2006. (Decades of the 20th Century in Color Ser.). (Illus.). 64p. (J). (gr. 5). lib. bdg. 29.27 *(978-0-7660-2635-3(3))* Enslow Pubs., Inc.

—The 1960s. 2015. (Decades of the 20th & 21st Centuries Ser.). (ENG., Illus.). 96p. (J). (gr. 7-7). 34.60 *(978-0-7660-6932-9(X))* Enslow Pubs., Inc.

—The 1960s from the Vietnam War to Flower Power. rev. ed. 2006. (Decades of the 20th Century in Color Ser.). (Illus.). 64p. (J). (gr. 5). lib. bdg. 29.27 *(978-0-7660-2636-0(1))* Enslow Pubs., Inc.

—The 1970s. 2015. (Decades of the 20th & 21st Centuries Ser.). (ENG., Illus.). 96p. (J). (gr. 7-7). 34.60 *(978-0-7660-6934-3(6))* Enslow Pubs., Inc.

—The 1990s. 2015. (Decades of the 20th & 21st Centuries Ser.). (ENG., Illus.). 96p. (J). (gr. 7-7). 34.60 *(978-0-7660-6937-4(0))* Enslow Pubs., Inc.

—The 1990s from the Persian Gulf War to Y2K. rev. ed. 2006. (Decades of the 20th Century in Color Ser.). (Illus.). 64p. (J). (gr. 5-9). lib. bdg. 29.27 *(978-0-7660-2639-1(6))* Enslow Pubs., Inc.

—The 2000s. 2015. (Decades of the 20th & 21st Centuries Ser.). (ENG., Illus.). 96p. (J). (gr. 7-7). 34.60 *(978-0-7660-6939-8(7))* Enslow Pubs., Inc.

Fredriksen, John C. Chronology of American History, 4 vols., Set. 2008. 2592p. (C). (gr. 9-18). 350.00 *(978-0-8160-6800-5(3))* Facts On File, Inc.

Gale. Bwlng Btnks Bell Btms 2, 6 vols. 2nd ed. 2012. (Bowling, Beatniks, & Bell-Bottoms Ser.). (ENG., Illus.). 1650p. lib. bdg. 522.00 *(978-1-4144-1165-1(0)*, UXL) Cengage Gale.

George, Enzo. America in the Fifties. 2015. (Primary Sources in U. S. History Ser.). (ENG., Illus.). 48p. (J). (gr. 4-4). 31.36 *(978-1-5026-0494-1(9))* Cavendish Square Publishing.

Grolier Educational Staff, contrib. by. USA 1950s, 6 vols., Set. 2005. (Illus.). (J). (gr. 9-12). lib. bdg. 479.00 *(978-0-7172-6082-9(8)*, Grolier) Scholastic Library Publishing.

Hardyman, Robyn. Celebrate: United States. 2009. (Celebrate Country Ser.). 32p. (gr. 4-6). 28.00 *(978-1-60413-264-9(7)*, Chelsea Clubhouse) Facts On File, Inc.

Hidden History. 2016. (Hidden History Ser.). 00032p. (J). pap. 63.00 ***(978-1-4824-5838-1(1))*** Stevens, Gareth Publishing LLLP.

Hunt, Jilly. Popular Culture: 1900-1919, 1 vol. 2012. (History of Popular Culture Ser.). (ENG.). 64p. (gr. 6-9). pap. 10.95 *(978-1-4109-4628-7(2))*; lib. bdg. 35.99 *(978-1-4109-4621-8(5))* Heinemann-Raintree.

—Popular Culture: 1980-1999, 1 vol. 2012. (History of Popular Culture Ser.). (ENG.). 64p. (gr. 6-9). pap. 10.95 *(978-1-4109-4632-4(0))*; lib. bdg. 35.99 *(978-1-4109-4625-6(8))* Heinemann-Raintree.

Hunter, Nick. Popular Culture: 1940-1959, 1 vol. 2012. (History of Popular Culture Ser.). (ENG.). 64p. (gr. 6-9). pap. 10.95 *(978-1-4109-4630-0(4))*; lib. bdg. 35.99 *(978-1-4109-4623-2(1))* Heinemann-Raintree.

Johnson, Cynthia & Baker, Lawrence W. Bowling, Beatniks, & Bell-Bottoms: Pop Culture of 20th- & 21st-Century America, 6 vols. 2nd ed. 2012. (Illus.). (J). *(978-1-4144-1166-8(9))*; *(978-1-4144-1171-2(5))*; *(978-1-4144-1170-5(7))*; *(978-1-4144-1168-2(5))*; *(978-1-4144-1169-9(3))*; *(978-1-4144-1167-5(7))* Cengage Gale. (UXL).

Kingston, Anna. Respecting the Contributions of African Americans. 2012. (Stop Bullying Now! Ser.). (ENG., Illus.). 24p. (J). (gr. 3-6). 22.60 *(978-1-4488-7448-4(3))*; pap. 8.25 *(978-1-4488-7521-4(8))* Rosen Publishing Group, Inc., The. (PowerKids Pr.).

Kuskowski, Alex. Super Simple American Art: Fun & Easy Art from Around the World, 1 vol. 2012. (ENG.). 32p. 27.07 *(978-1-61783-211-6(1)*, Super SandCastle) ABDO Publishing Co.

Lindop, Edmund & DeCapua, Sarah. America in the 1950s. 2009. (Decades of Twentieth-Century America Ser.). (ENG.). 144p. (gr. 5-12). lib. bdg. 38.60 *(978-0-8225-7642-6(2))* Lerner Publishing Group.

Mellors, Julie. U-X-L American Decades 2000-09 Cumulative Index. 2012. (U-X-L American Decades Ser.). (ENG.). pap. 5.00 *(978-1-4144-9723-5(7)*, UXL) Cengage Gale.

Nelson, Kadir. Heart & Soul: The Story of America & African Americans. Nelson, Kadir, illus. (Illus.). (J). (gr. 1-5). 2013. (ENG.). 112p. pap. 8.99 *(978-0-06-173079-5(3))* 2011. (ENG., 108p. 19.99 *(978-0-06-173074-0(2))* 2011. 108p. lib. bdg. 20.89 *(978-0-06-173076-4(9))* HarperCollins Pubs.

—Heart & Soul: The Story of America & African Americans. 2013. (J). lib. bdg. 19.65 *(978-0-606-35050-1(0)*, Turtleback) Turtleback Bks.

Ollhoff, Jim. Freedom & the Future, 1 vol. 2011. (Hispanic American History Ser.). (ENG., Illus.). 32p. (YA). (gr. 5-9). 27.07 *(978-1-61783-056-3(9))* ABDO Publishing Co.

Schwartz, Eric. What Makes America America? 2006. (How America Became America Ser.). (Illus.). 96p. (YA). lib. bdg. 22.95 *(978-1-59084-913-2(2))* Mason Crest.

Stone, Amy. Jewish Americans. 2006. (World Almanac Library of American Immigration). (Illus.). 48p. (gr. 5-12). pap. 14.05 *(978-0-8368-7327-6(0))*; lib. bdg. 31.00 *(978-0-8368-7314-6(9))* Stevens, Gareth Publishing LLLP. (Gareth Stevens Secondary Library).

Wirkner, Linda. Learning about Life in the New American Nation with Graphic Organizers. (Graphic Organizers in Social Studies). 24p. 2009. (gr. 3-4). 42.50 *(978-1-61513-082-5(9)*, PowerKids Pr.) 2006. (ENG.). (gr. 4-6). pap. 8.25 *(978-1-4042-5050-5(6)*, Rosen Classroom) 2005. (Illus.). (J). (gr. 3-5). lib. bdg. 22.60 *(978-1-4042-2810-8(1)*, PowerKids Pr.) Rosen Publishing Group, Inc., The.

UNITED STATES—COAST GUARD

Benson, Michael. The U. S. Coast Guard. 2004. (U. S. Armed Forces Ser.). (ENG., Illus.). 64p. (gr. 4-8). lib. bdg. 26.60 *(978-0-8225-1647-7(0))* Lerner Publishing Group.

Bergaust, Erik & Foss, William O. Coast Guard in Action. 2012. 96p. 38.95 *(978-1-258-25246-5(5))*; pap. 23.95 *(978-1-258-25728-6(9))* Literary Licensing, LLC.

Best, B. J. Coast Guard Boats. 2017. (J). ***(978-1-5026-2556-4(3))*** Cavendish Square Publishing.

David, Jack. United States Coast Guard. 2008. (Armed Forces Ser.). (ENG., Illus.). 24p. (J). (gr. 3-7). lib. bdg. 25.95 *(978-1-60014-163-8(3))* Bellwether Media.

Demarest, Chris L. Mayday! Mayday! A Coast Guard Rescue. Demarest, Chris L., illus. 2004. (ENG., Illus.). 40p. (J). (gr. -1-5). 17.99 *(978-0-689-85161-2(8)*, McElderry, Margaret K. Bks.) McElderry, Margaret K. Bks.

Dolan, Edward F. Military Service, 5 vols., Set. Incl. Careers in the U. S. Air Force. (YA). (gr. 7-9). 35.64 *(978-0-7614-4205-9(7))*; Careers in the U. S. Army. (YA). (gr. 7-9). 35.64 *(978-0-7614-4206-6(5))*; Careers in the U. S. Coast Guard. (gr. 7-9). 35.64 *(978-0-7614-4207-3(3))*; Careers in the U. S. Marine Corps. (YA). (gr. 8-18). 35.64 *(978-0-7614-4209-7(X))*; Careers in the U. S. Navy. (gr. 7-18). 35.64 *(978-0-7614-4210-3(3))*; 80p. 2009. 2010. Set lib. bdg. 178.21 o.p. *(978-0-7614-4203-5(0))* Marshall Cavendish Corp.

Goldish, Meish. Coast Guard: Civilian to Guardian. 2010. (Becoming a Soldier Ser.). 24p. (YA). (gr. 3-6). lib. bdg. 22.61 *(978-1-936088-12-6(6))* Bearport Publishing Co., Inc.

Gordon, Nick. Coast Guard Rescue Swimmer. 2012. (Dangerous Jobs Ser.). (ENG., Illus.). 24p. (J). (gr. 3-7). lib. bdg. 25.95 *(978-1-60014-778-4(X)*, Torque Bks.) Bellwether Media.

—U. S. Coast Guard. 2012. (U. S. Military Ser.). (ENG., Illus.). 24p. (J). (gr. 3-7). lib. bdg. 25.95 *(978-1-60014-828-6(X)*, Epic Bks.) Bellwether Media.

Gray, Judy Silverstein. The U. S. Coast Guard & Military Careers. 2007. (U.S. Armed Forces & Military Careers Ser.). (Illus.). 128p. (J). (gr. 5). lib. bdg. 33.27 *(978-0-7660-2493-9(8))* Enslow Pubs., Inc.

Gray, Judy Silverstein & Kiland, Taylor Baldwin. Careers in the US Coast Guard. 2015. (Careers in the US Armed Forces Ser.). (ENG., Illus.). 128p. (J). (gr. 6-7). 37.27 *(978-0-7660-6945-9(1))* Enslow Pubs., Inc.

Hamilton, John. The Coast Guard, 1 vol. 2007. (Defending the Nation Ser.). (ENG., Illus.). 32p. (gr. -1-3). 27.07 *(978-1-59679-755-0(X)*, Checkerboard Library) ABDO Publishing Co.

Lyons, Lewis. Rescue at Sea with the U. S. & Canadian Coast Guards. 2004. (Rescue & Prevention Ser.). (Illus.). 96p. (YA). (gr. 7-18). lib. bdg. 22.95 *(978-1-59084-405-2(X))* Mason Crest.

Marciniak, Kristin. US Coast Guard, 1 vol. 2014. (Essential Library of the US Military Ser.). (ENG.). 112p. (J). (gr. 6-12). lib. bdg. 35.64 *(978-1-62403-434-3(9)*, Essential Library) ABDO Publishing Co.

Markovics, Joyce L. Today's Coast Guard Heroes. 2012. (Acts of Courage: Inside America's Military Ser.). 32p. (J). (gr. 2-7). lib. bdg. 25.27 *(978-1-61772-448-0(3))* Bearport Publishing Co., Inc.

Mitchell, P. P. Join the Coast Guard. 2017. (U. S. Armed Forces Ser.). 32p. (gr. 1-2). pap. 10.50 ***(978-1-5382-0538-9(6))*** Stevens, Gareth Publishing LLLP.

Murray, Julie. United States Coast Guard, 1 vol. 2014. (U. S. Armed Forces Ser.). (ENG.). 24p. (J). (gr. 4-8). lib. bdg. 28.50 *(978-1-62970-095-3(9))* ABDO Publishing Co.

Noble, Dennis L. The U. S. Coast Guard. 2004. (America's Armed Forces Ser.). (Illus.). 48p. (J). (gr. 5-12). lib. bdg. 31.00 *(978-0-8368-5681-1(3)*, Gareth Stevens Secondary Library) Stevens, Gareth Publishing LLLP.

Orr, Tamra. Your Career in the Coast Guard. 2011. (Call of Duty: Careers in the Armed Forces Ser.). (ENG.). 128p. (YA). (gr. 9-12). lib. bdg. 34.60 *(978-1-4488-5514-8(4))* Rosen Publishing Group, Inc., The.

Randolph, Joanne. Coast Guard Boats. (To the Rescue! Ser.). 24p. 2009. (gr. 1-1). 42.50 *(978-1-60854-395-3(1))* 2008. (Illus.). (J). (gr. 3-7). lib. bdg. 22.60 *(978-1-4042-4152-7(3))* Rosen Publishing Group, Inc., The. (PowerKids Pr.).

—Coastguard Boats/Lanchas Guardacostas. 2009. (To the Rescue! / ¡Al rescate! Ser.). (ENG & SPA.). 24p. (gr. 1-1). 42.50 *(978-1-60854-401-1(X)*, Editorial Buenas Letras) Rosen Publishing Group, Inc., The.

Rose, Simon. Coast Guard. 2012. (J). *(978-1-61913-630-4(9))*; pap. *(978-1-61913-631-1(7))* Weigl Pubs., Inc.

Roza, Greg. Careers in the Coast Guard's Search & Rescue Units. 2009. (Careers in Search & Rescue Operations Ser.). 64p. (gr. 5-8). 58.50 *(978-1-61511-808-3(X)*, Rosen Reference) Rosen Publishing Group, Inc., The.

Shea, John M. Heroes of the US Coast Guard. 2012. (Heroes of the US Military Ser.). 32p. (J). (gr. 3-6). pap. 10.50 *(978-1-4339-7241-6(7))*; lib. bdg. 26.60 *(978-1-4339-7240-9(9))* Stevens, Gareth Publishing LLLP.

Toth, Vince. My Sister Is in the Coast Guard, 01 vols., 1. 2016. (Military Families Ser.). (ENG., Illus.). 24p. (J). pap. 8.25 *(978-1-5081-4442-7(7)*, PowerKids Pr.) Rosen Publishing Group, Inc., The.

Wood, Alix. Serving in the Coast Guard. 2013. (Protecting Our Country Ser.). 32p. (J). (gr. 3-6). pap. 60.00 *(978-1-4777-1403-4(0))*; (ENG., Illus.). pap. 10.00 *(978-1-4777-1402-7(2))*; (ENG., Illus.). lib. bdg. 25.25 *(978-1-4777-1298-6(4))* Rosen Publishing Group, Inc., The. (PowerKids Pr.).

UNITED STATES—COLONIES

see United States—Territories and Possessions

UNITED STATES—COMMERCE

Burgan, Michael. American Capitalism. 2012. (ENG.). 64p. (J). lib. bdg. 30.00 *(978-0-531-23054-1(6))*; (gr. 4-6). pap. 8.95 *(978-0-531-28154-3(X))* Scholastic Library Publishing.

Currie, Stephen. Outsourcing America. 2007. (Ripped from the Headlines Ser.). 64p. (J). (gr. 7-12). 23.95 *(978-1-60217-008-7(8))* Erickson Pr.

Egendorf, Laura K. Should the U. S. Do Business with China? 2008. (At Issue Ser.). (ENG., Illus.). 128p. (gr. 10-12). 39.40 *(978-0-7377-4112-4(0))*; pap. 27.80 *(978-0-7377-4113-1(9))* Cengage Gale. (Greenhaven Pr., Inc.).

Francis, Amy. The U. S. Policy on Cuba. 2008. (At Issue Ser.). (ENG., Illus.). 128p. (gr. 10-12). 39.40 *(978-0-7377-4108-7(2))*; pap. 27.80 *(978-0-7377-4109-4(0))* Cengage Gale. (Greenhaven Pr., Inc.).

Frohnapfel-Krueger, Lisa. Does Outsourcing Harm America? 2010. (At Issue Ser.). (Illus.). 128p. pap. 24.45 *(978-0-7377-4674-7(2))*; (YA). (gr. 7-18). 34.45 *(978-0-7377-4673-0(4))* Cengage Gale. (Greenhaven Pr., Inc.).

Goldberg, Jan. The Department of Commerce. 2005. (This Is Your Government Ser.). (Illus.). 64p. (J). (gr. k-3). lib. bdg. 31.95 *(978-1-4042-0207-8(2))* Rosen Publishing Group, Inc., The.

UNITED STATES—COMMERCIAL POLICY

Goldberg, Jan. The Department of Commerce. (This Is Your Government Ser.). 64p. 2009. (gr. 5-6). 58.50 *(978-1-60854-365-6(X)*, Rosen Reference) 2006. (ENG., Illus.). (gr. 4-8). per. 12.95 *(978-1-4042-0660-1(4))* Rosen Publishing Group, Inc., The.

UNITED STATES—CONGRESS

Alexander, Heather & dePaola, Tomie. Who Is Hillary Clinton? Harrison, Nancy & Putra, Dede, illus. 2016. (Who Was? Ser.). (ENG.). 112p. (J). (gr. 3-7). lib. bdg. 15.99 *(978-0-399-54234-3(5)*, Grosset & Dunlap) Penguin Young Readers Group.

Allen, Charles F. David Crockett: Scout, Small Boy, Pilgrim, Mountaineer, Soldier, Bear-Hunter, & Congressman, Defender of the Alamo. (Illus.). 308p. reprint ed. lib. bdg. 98.00 *(978-0-7222-4856-0(3))* Library Reprints, Inc.

Benson, Kathleen & Haskins, Jim. John Lewis in the Lead: A Story of the Civil Rights Movement, 1 vol. Andrews, Benny, illus. 2006. (ENG.). 40p. (gr. 2-7). 17.95 *(978-1-58430-250-6(X))* Lee & Low Bks., Inc.

Bow, James. What Is the Legislative Branch? 2013. (ENG.). 32p. (J). *(978-0-7787-0879-7(9))*; pap. *(978-0-7787-0905-3(1))* Crabtree Publishing Co.

Brexel, Bernadette. Congress. 2009. (Primary Source Library of American Citizenship Ser.). 32p. (gr. 5-5). 47.90 *(978-1-61511-218-0(9)*, Rosen Reference) Rosen Publishing Group, Inc., The.

Cane, Ella. The U. S. House of Representatives, 1 vol. 2014. (Our Government Ser.). (ENG.). 24p. (gr. 1-2). lib. bdg. 25.32 *(978-1-4765-4201-0(5)*, First Facts) Capstone Press of Coughlan Cos.

—The U. S. Senate, 1 vol. 2014. (Our Government Ser.). (ENG.). 24p. (gr. 1-2). lib. bdg. 25.32 *(978-1-4765-4202-7(3)*, First Facts) Capstone Press of Coughlan Cos.

Collins, David R. Huey P. Long: Talker & Doer, 1 vol. Smith, Jack K., illus. 2003. (ENG.). 32p. (J). (gr. k-3). 16.99 *(978-1-56554-913-5(9))* Pelican Publishing Co., Inc.

Connors, Kathleen. What Does Congress Do? 2017. (Look at Your Government Ser.). 32p. (gr. 2-2). pap. 10.50 ***(978-1-4824-6047-6(5))*** Stevens, Gareth Publishing LLLP.

Cooper, Ilene. A Woman in the House (and Senate) How Women Came to the United States Congress, Broke down Barriers, & Changed the Country. Baddeley, Elizabeth, illus. 2014. (ENG.). 144p. (J). (gr. 3-7). 24.95 *(978-1-4197-1036-0(2)*, Abrams Bks. for Young Readers) Abrams, Inc.

Crawford, Ann Fears. Barbara Jordan: Breaking the Barriers. 2003. (Illus.). 90p. (J). (gr. 7-9). lib. bdg. 19.95 *(978-1-931823-11-1(1))* Halcyon Pr., Ltd.

Cummings, Matthew. What Is the Legislative Branch? 2015. (Let's Find Out! Government Ser.). (ENG., Illus.). 32p. (J). (gr. 2-3). 23.45 *(978-1-62275-956-9(7)*, Britannica Educational Publishing) Rosen Publishing Group, Inc., The.

Davy Crockett. 2010. (Legends of the Wild West Ser.). (Illus.). 120p. (gr. 6-12). 35.00 *(978-1-60413-592-3(1)*, Chelsea Hse.) Facts On File, Inc.

Dodge, Andrew. Exploring Capitol Hill: A Kid's Guide to the U. S. Capitol & Congress. Wasniewski, Matthew, ed. Gibson, Barbara, illus. 12p. (J). pap. 1.95 *(978-0-916200-25-1(6))* U. S. Capitol Historical Society.

Doeden, Matt. Michele Bachmann: Tea Party Champion. 2011. (Gateway Biographies Ser.). (YA). (gr. 4-7). lib. bdg. 26.60 *(978-0-7613-9074-9(X))* Lerner Publishing Group.

Egan, Tracie. How a Bill Becomes a Law. 2009. (Primary Source Library of American Citizenship Ser.). 32p. (gr. 5-5). 47.90 *(978-1-61511-219-7(7)*, Rosen Reference) Rosen Publishing Group, Inc., The.

Feldman, Ruth Tenzer. How Congress Works: A Look at the Legislative Branch. 2003. (How Government Works). (ENG., Illus.). 56p. (gr. 4-8). lib. bdg. 25.26 *(978-0-8225-1347-6(1))* Lerner Publishing Group.

Finley, Toiya Kristen. Russell Simmons. 2007. (Sharing the American Dream Ser.). 64p. (YA). (gr. 7-18). pap. 9.95 *(978-1-4222-0762-8(5))* Mason Crest.

Fitzgerald, Stephanie. Hillary Clinton. rev. ed. 2017. (Rookie Biographies(tm) Ser.). (ENG., Illus.). 32p. (J). lib. bdg. 25.00 ***(978-0-531-22931-6(9))*** Scholastic Library Publishing.

Furgang, Kathy. The Declaration of Independence & Roger Sherman of Connecticut. 2009. (Framers of the Declaration of Independence Ser.). 24p. (gr. 3-3). 42.50 *(978-1-61512-632-3(5)*, PowerKids Pr.) Rosen Publishing Group, Inc., The.

Goldsworthy, Kaite. Gabrielle Giffords. 2012. (J). *(978-1-61913-535-2(3))*; pap. *(978-1-61913-590-1(6))* Weigl Pubs., Inc.

Gorman, Jacqueline Laks. Miembro del Congreso (Member of Congress) 2009. (Conoce tu gobierno (Know Your Government) Ser.). (SPA.). 24p. (J). (gr. 2-4). lib. bdg. 22.00 *(978-1-4339-0101-0(3)*, Weekly Reader Leveled Readers) Stevens, Gareth Publishing LLLP.

Gorman, Jacqueline Laks & Nations, Susan. Member of Congress. 2009. (Know Your Government Ser.). 24p. (J). (gr. 2-4). pap. 8.15 *(978-1-4339-0122-5(6))*; lib. bdg. 22.00 *(978-1-4339-0094-5(7))* Stevens, Gareth Publishing LLLP. (Weekly Reader Leveled Readers).

Gutner, Howard. The Speaker of the House. 2003. (America's Leaders Ser.). (Illus.). 32p. (J). 23.70 *(978-1-56711-964-0(6)*, Blackbirch Pr., Inc.) Cengage Gale.

Haldy, Emma E. Davy Crockett. Bane, Jeff, illus. 2017. (My Early Library: My Itty-Bitty Bio Ser.). (ENG.). 24p. (J). (gr. k-1). lib. bdg. 28.50 *(978-1-63472-151-6(9)*, 209176) Cherry Lake Publishing.

Haskins, Jim, et al. John Lewis in the Lead: A Story of the Civil Rights Movement, 1 vol. 2006. (ENG., Illus.). 40p. (J). pap. 11.95 *(978-1-60060-849-0(3))* Lee & Low Bks., Inc.

Hillard, Stephanie. The U. S. Capitol: The History of U. S. Congress. 2017. (Landmarks of Democracy: American Institutions Ser.). 24p. (J). (gr. 7-8). pap. 8.25 ***(978-1-5081-6097-7(X)*** PowerKids Pr.) Rosen Publishing Group, Inc., The.

Horn, Geoffrey M. Nancy Pelosi. 2009. (People We Should Know Ser.). 32p. (J). (gr. 3-5). pap. 10.50 *(978-1-4339-0162-1(5))*; lib. bdg. 31.00 *(978-1-4339-0021-1(1))* Stevens, Gareth Publishing LLLP. (Gareth Stevens Learning Library).

Jakubiak, David J. What Does a Congressional Representative Do? 2010. (How Our Government Works Ser.). 24p. (J). (gr. 3-6). lib. bdg., E-Book 42.50 *(978-1-4488-0033-9(1))* Rosen Publishing Group, Inc., The.

Jarnow, Jesse. Davy Crockett: Defensor de la frontera (Davy Crockett: Frontier Hero) 2009. (Grandes personajes en la historia de los Estados Unidos (Famous People in American History) Ser.). (SPA.). 32p. (gr. 2-3). 47.90 *(978-1-61512-797-9(6)*, Editorial Buenas Letras) Rosen Publishing Group, Inc., The.

—Davy Crockett: Frontier Hero / Defensor de la Frontera. 2009. (Famous People in American History/Grandes personajes en la historia de los Estados Unidos Ser.). (ENG

& SPA.). 32p. (gr. 2-3). 47.90 (978-1-61512-543-2(4), Editorial Buenas Letras) Rosen Publishing Group, Inc., The.

Johnston, Marianne. Davy Crockett. 2009. (American Legends Ser.). 24p. (gr. 3-3). 42.50 (978-1-61511-381-1(9), PowerKids Pr.) Rosen Publishing Group, Inc., The.

Kennedy, Edward M. My Senator & Me: A Dog's-Eye View of Washington, D. C. Small, David, illus. 2011. (J). (gr. 2-5). 29.95 (978-0-545-04379-3(4)) Weston Woods Studios, Inc.

Koestler-Grack, Rachel A. The House of Representatives. 2nd rev. ed. 2007. (U. S. Government Ser.). 112p. (YA). (gr. 5-9). 30.00 (978-0-7910-9285-9(2)) Facts On File, Inc.

Krieg, Katherine. Congress. 2014. (ENG.). 24p. (gr. 3-5). 28.50 (978-1-62717-679-8(9)) Rourke Educational Media.

Kunstler, James Howard. Davy Crockett, 1 vol. Brodner, Steve, illus. 2004. (Rabbit Ears-A Classic Tale Ser.). (ENG.). 36p. (gr. k-5). 25.65 (978-1-59197-762-9(2)) Spotlight.

Laks Gorman, Jacqueline. Miembro del Congreso (Member of Congress) 2009. (Conoce tu gobierno (Know Your Government) Ser.). (SPA.). 24p. (gr. 2-4). pap. 8.15 (978-1-4339-0129-4(3), Weekly Reader Leveled Readers) Stevens, Gareth Publishing LLLP.

Leavitt, Amie Jane. Nancy Pelosi. 2007. (Blue Banner Biography Ser.). (Illus.). 32p. (YA). (gr. 4-7). lib. bdg. 25.70 (978-1-58415-613-0(9)) Mitchell Lane Pubs., Inc.

Lee, Georgia. Tour the U. S. Capitol. 2013. (InfoMax Readers Ser.). (ENG.). 24p. (J). (gr. 3-4). pap. 49.50 (978-1-4777-2574-0(1)); pap. 8.25 (978-1-4777-2769-0(8)) Rosen Publishing Group, Inc., The. (Rosen Classroom).

Marcovitz, Hal. Nancy Pelosi: Politician. 2009. (Women of Achievement Ser.). (Illus.). 160p. (gr. 6-12). 35.00 (978-1-60413-075-1(X), Chelsea Hse.) Facts On File, Inc.

Marx, Trish. Jeannette Rankin: First Lady of Congress. Andreasen, Dan, illus. 2013. (ENG.). 48p. (J). (gr. 2-5). 19.99 (978-1-4424-9618-7(5), McElderry, Margaret K. Bks.) McElderry, Margaret K. Bks.

McAuliffe, Bill. The U. S. House of Representatives. 2017. (By the People Ser.). (ENG., Illus.). 48p. (J). (gr. 7-11). pap. 12.00 (978-1-62832-271-2(3), Creative Paperbacks) Creative Co., The.

—The U.S. House of Representatives. 2016. (Illus.). 48p. (J). 39.95 (978-1-60818-675-4(X), Creative Education) Creative Co., The.

McElroy, Lisa Tucker. Nancy Pelosi. 2008. pap. 52.95 (978-0-8225-9477-2(3)) Lerner Publishing Group.

—Nancy Pelosi: First Woman Speaker of the House. 2007. (Gateway Biographies Ser.). (ENG., Illus.). 48p. (gr. 4-8). lib. bdg. 26.60 (978-0-8225-8685-2(1), Lerner Pubns.) Lerner Publishing Group.

Modifica, Lisa. A Timeline of Congress. 2009. (Timelines of American History Ser.). 32p. (gr. 4-4). 47.90 (978-1-60854-380-9(3), Rosen Reference) Rosen Publishing Group, Inc., The.

Moriarty, J. T. Davy Crockett: Defensor de la Frontera. 2004. (Grandes personajes en la historia de los Estados Unidos Ser.). (SPA.). 32p. (gr. 3-6). pap. 10.00 (978-0-8239-4226-8(0), Rosen Classroom) Rosen Publishing Group, Inc., The.

—Davy Crockett: Frontier Hero. 2009. (Primary Sources of Famous People in American History Ser.). 32p. (gr. 2-3). 47.90 (978-1-60851-670-4(9)) Rosen Publishing Group, Inc., The.

Murcia, Rebecca Thatcher. The Legislative Branch. 2011. (My Guide to the Constitution Ser.). (Illus.). 48p. (J). (gr. 3-6). lib. bdg. 29.95 (978-1-58415-942-1(1)) Mitchell Lane Pubs., Inc.

Nelson, Maria. Becoming a House Representative. 2016. (Who's Your Candidate? Choosing Government Leaders Ser.). (ENG., Illus.). 32p. (J). (gr. 3-4). pap. 10.50 (978-1-4824-4035-5(0)) Stevens, Gareth Publishing LLLP.

Nelson, Robin & Donovan, Sandra. The Congress: A Look at the Legislative Branch. 2012. (Searchlight Books How Does Government Work Ser.). (ENG., Illus.). 40p. (gr. 3-5). lib. bdg. 27.93 (978-0-7613-6518-1(4)) Lerner Publishing Group.

Nelson, Robin & Donovan, Sandy. The Congress: A Look at the Legislative Branch. 2012. (Searchlight Books How Does Government Work Ser.). (ENG., Illus.). 40p. (gr. 3-5). pap. 51.01 (978-0-7613-9230-9(0)); pap. 8.95 (978-0-7613-8559-2(2)) Lerner Publishing Group.

Nichols, Kaitlyn. Davey Crockett. 2009. pap. 13.25 (978-1-60559-057-8(6)) Hameray Publishing Group, Inc.

Pulditor, Seth H. The House of Representatives Today. 2016. (Illus.). 64p. (J). (978-1-61900-089-6(X)) Eldorado Ink.

Raatma, Lucia. Barbara Jordan. 2013. 96p. (YA). (gr. 7-12). 39.93 (978-0-7614-4956-0(6)); pap. 19.99 (978-1-62712-114-9(5)) Cavendish Square Publishing.

—Shirley Chisholm. 2010. (Leading Women Ser.). 96p. (YA). (gr. 7-12). 39.93 (978-0-7614-4953-9(1)) Marshall Cavendish Corp.

Reis, Ronald A. The US Congress for Kids: Over 200 Years of Lawmaking, Deal-Breaking, & Compromising, with 21 Activities. 2014. (For Kids Ser.). (ENG., Illus.). 144p. (J). (gr. 5). pap. 16.95 (978-1-61374-977-7(5)) Chicago Review Pr., Inc.

Rice, Liz. Bill Richardson. 2007. (Sharing the American Dream Ser.). 64p. (YA). (gr. 7-18). pap. 9.95 (978-1-4222-0761-1(7)) Mason Crest.

Rose, Simon. The House of Representatives. 2014. (J). (978-1-4896-1938-9(0)) Weigl Pubs., Inc.

Rose, Simon. House of Representatives. 2016. (J). **(978-1-5105-2245-9(X))** SmartBook Media, Inc.

Sanford, William R. & Green, Carl R. Davy Crockett: Courageous Hero of the Alamo. 2012. (Courageous Heroes of the American West Ser.). (Illus.). 48p. (J). pap. 8.95 (978-1-4644-0086-5(5)) Enslow Pubs., Inc.

Sapet, Kerrily. John Lewis. 2009. (Political Profiles Ser.). 100p. (YA). (gr. 5-9). 28.95 (978-1-59935-130-8(7)) Reynolds, Morgan Inc.

Schuh, Mari C. The U. S. House of Representatives, 1 vol. 2012. (U. S. Government Ser.). (ENG.). 24p. (gr. k-1). lib. bdg. 26.65 (978-1-4296-7565-9(9), Pebble Plus) Capstone Press of Coughlan Cos.

Shea, Therese. Meet the House of Representatives. 2012. (Guide to Your Government Ser.). (Illus.). 32p. (J). (gr. 4-6). 26.60 (978-1-4339-7252-2(2)); pap. 10.50 (978-1-4339-7253-9(0)) Stevens, Gareth Publishing LLLP. (Gareth Stevens Learning Library).

Shichtman, Sandra H. Nancy Pelosi. 2008. (Political Profiles Ser.). (Illus.). 112p. (YA). (gr. 5-9). lib. bdg. 27.95 (978-1-59935-049-3(1)) Reynolds, Morgan Inc.

Smith, Andrea P. Davy Crockett. 2012. (Illus.). 24p. (J). 63.60 (978-1-4488-5223-9(4)); pap. 10.60 (978-1-4488-5222-2(6)); lib. bdg. 25.25 (978-1-4488-5192-8(0)) Rosen Publishing Group, Inc., The. (PowerKids Pr.).

Spalding, Maddie. How the Legislative Branch Works. 2016. (How America Works). (ENG.). 24p. (J). (gr. 3-6). 28.50 (978-1-5038-0906-2(4), 210663) Child's World, Inc., The.

Steinkraus, Kyla. How a Bill Becomes a Law. 2014. (ENG.). 24p. (gr. 3-5). 28.50 (978-1-62717-682-8(9)) Rourke Educational Media.

Taylor-Butler, Christine. The Congress of the United States. (True Bks.). (ENG., Illus.). 48p. (J). (gr. 3-5). 2008. pap. 6.95 (978-0-531-14778-8(9)) 2007. lib. bdg. 29.00 (978-0-531-12628-8(5)) Scholastic Library Publishing. (Children's Pr.).

White, Carolyn. Standing in the Shoes of a Member of the House of Representatives. 2015. (My Government Ser.). (ENG., Illus.). 32p. (J). (gr. 4-4). lib. bdg. 28.50 (978-1-5026-0470-5(1)) Cavendish Square Publishing.

Winders, Richard Bruce. Davy Crockett: The Legend of the Wild Frontier. 2009. (Library of American Lives & Times Ser.). 112p. (gr. 5-5). 69.20 (978-1-60853-476-0(6)) Rosen Publishing Group, Inc., The.

Zurlo, Tony. The Legislative Branch: Creating America's Laws. 2008. (Federal Government Ser.). (Illus.). 128p. (J). (gr. 3-7). lib. bdg. 34.60 (978-1-59845-056-9(5), MyReportLinks.com Bks.) Enslow Pubs., Inc.

—The United States Congress & the Legislative Branch: How the Senate & House of Representatives Create Our Laws. 2012. (Constitution & the United States Government Ser.). 104p. (J). (gr. 5-18). 33.27 (978-0-7660-4066-3(6)) Enslow Pubs., Inc.

UNITED STATES—CONGRESS—FICTION

Law, Janice. Capitol Cat & Watch Dog Unite Lady Freedoms. Eckhardt, Jason C., illus. 2008. 64p. (J). (978-1-934645-71-0(0), Eakin Pr.) Eakin Pr.

Santrey, Laurence & Macken, JoAnn Early. Davy Crockett: Young Pioneer. Livingston, Francis, illus. 2008. 55p. (J). pap. (978-0-439-02048-0(4)) Scholastic, Inc.

Van Dyne, Edith. Aunt Jane's Nieces at Work. 2005. 204p. pap. 12.95 (978-1-4218-1523-7(0), 1st World Library - Literary Society) 1st World Publishing, Inc.

UNITED STATES—CONGRESS—SENATE

Anderson, Janet. The Senate. 2007. (U. S. Government Ser.). 112p. (YA). (gr. 5-9). 30.00 (978-0-7910-9291-0(7)) Facts On File, Inc.

Brill, Marlene Targ. Barack Obama: Working to Make a Difference. 2006. (Gateway Biography Ser.). (Illus.). 48p. (J). 23.93 (978-0-8225-3417-4(7)) Lerner Publishing Group.

Burgan, Michael. Hillary Clinton, 1 vol. 2014. (Extraordinary Women Ser.). (ENG.). 48p. (gr. 6-6). lib. bdg. 32.65 (978-1-4109-5941-6(4)) Heinemann-Raintree.

Cohen, Sheila & Terman Cohen, Sheila. Gaylord Nelson: Champion for Our Earth. 2010. (Badger Biographies Ser.). (ENG., Illus.). 120p. (J). pap. 12.95 (978-0-87020-443-2(2)) Wisconsin Historical Society.

Corey, Shana. Hillary Clinton: the Life of a Leader. Gustavson, Adam, illus. 2016. (Step into Reading Ser.). (ENG.). 48p. (J). (gr. k-3). 3.99 (978-1-101-93235-3(X), Random Hse. Bks. for Young Readers) Random Hse. Children's Bks.

Glaser, Jason. Meet the Senate. 2012. (Guide to Your Government Ser.). (Illus.). 32p. (J). (gr. 4-6). 26.60 (978-1-4339-7267-6(0)); pap. 10.50 (978-1-4339-7264-5(6)) Stevens, Gareth Publishing LLLP. (Gareth Stevens Learning Library).

Grimes, Nikki. Barack Obama: Son of Promise, Child of Hope. Collier, Bryan, illus. 2012. (ENG.). 48p. (J). (gr. k-3). pap. 9.99 (978-1-4424-5077-6(0), Little Simon) Little Simon.

—Barack Obama: Son of Promise, Child of Hope. Collier, Bryan, illus. 2012. (ENG.). 48p. (J). (gr. k-3). 9.99 (978-1-4424-4092-0(9), Simon & Schuster Bks. For Young Readers) Simon & Schuster Bks. For Young Readers.

Jakubiak, David J. What Does a Senator Do? 2010. (How Our Government Works Ser.). 24p. (J). (gr. 3-6). lib. bdg., E-Book 42.50 (978-1-4488-0029-2(3)); (Illus.). pap. 8.25 (978-1-4358-9816-5(8), PowerKids Pr.); (Illus.). (gr. 3-6). lib. bdg. 22.60 (978-1-4358-9360-3(3), PowerKids Pr.) Rosen Publishing Group, Inc., The.

Mapua, Jeff. Hillary Clinton, 1 vol. 2015. (ENG., Illus.). 32p. (J). 23.45 (978-1-62275-689-6(4), Britannica Educational Publishing) Rosen Publishing Group, Inc., The.

McAuliffe, Bill. The U. S. Senate. 2017. (By the People Ser.). (ENG., Illus.). 48p. (J). (gr. 7-11). pap. 12.00 (978-1-62832-273-6(X), Creative Paperbacks) Creative Co., The.

—The U.S. Senate. 2016. (Illus.). 48p. (J). 39.95 (978-1-60818-677-8(6), Creative Education) Creative Co., The.

Nagelhout, Ryan. Standing in a Senator's Shoes. 2015. (My Government Ser.). (ENG.). 32p. (J). (gr. 4-4). pap. 10.58 (978-1-5026-0472-9(8)) Cavendish Square Publishing.

Nelson, Maria. Becoming a Senator. 2016. (Who's Your Candidate? Choosing Government Leaders Ser.). (ENG., Illus.). 32p. (J). (gr. 3-4). pap. 10.50 (978-1-4824-4043-0(1)) Stevens, Gareth Publishing LLLP.

Rose, Simon. Senate. 2016. (J). **(978-1-5105-2249-7(2))** SmartBook Media, Inc.

Schuh, Mari C. The U. S. Senate, 1 vol. 2012. (U. S. Government Ser.). (ENG., Illus.). 24p. (gr. k-1). lib. bdg. 26.65 (978-1-4296-7567-3(5), Pebble Plus) Capstone Press of Coughlan Cos.

Shepherd, Jodie. Hillary Clinton. 2015. (Rookie Biographies(r) Ser.). (ENG., Illus.). 32p. (J). lib. bdg. 23.00 (978-0-531-20592-1(4)) Scholastic Library Publishing.

Sherman, Jill. Donald Trump: Outspoken Personality & President. 2017. (Gateway Biographies Ser.). (ENG., Illus.). 48p. (J). (gr. 4-8). lib. bdg. 26.65 (978-1-5124-2596-3(6)) Lerner Publishing Group.

Ziff, John. The United States Senate. 2016. 64p. (J). (978-1-61900-096-4(2)) Eldorado Ink.

UNITED STATES—CONGRESS—SENATE—BIOGRAPHY

Abrams, Dennis. Hillary Rodham Clinton: Politician. 2009. (Women of Achievement Ser.). (Illus.). 144p. (gr. 6-12). 35.00 (978-1-60413-077-5(6), Chelsea Hse.) Facts On File, Inc.

Anderson, Dale. Al Gore: A Wake-Up Call to Global Warming. 2009. (Voices for Green Choices Ser.). (ENG., Illus.). 48p. (J). (gr. 5-9). pap. (978-0-7787-4679-9(8)); lib. bdg. (978-0-7787-4666-9(6)) Crabtree Publishing Co.

Baptiste, Tracey. Al Gore. 2011. (Conservation Heroes Ser.). (Illus.). 120p. (YA). (gr. 6-12). 35.00 (978-1-60413-949-5(8), Chelsea Hse.) Facts On File, Inc.

Barack Obama. 2007. (Political Profiles Ser.). (Illus.). 128p. (YA). (gr. 5-9). lib. bdg. 27.95 (978-1-59935-045-5(9)) Reynolds, Morgan Inc.

Barton, Chris. The Amazing Age of John Roy Lynch. Tate, Don, illus. 2015. (ENG.). 50p. (J). 17.00 (978-0-8028-5379-0(X), Eerdmans Bks For Young Readers) Eerdmans, William B. Publishing Co.

Blashfield, Jean F. Hillary Clinton. 2010. (Leading Women Ser.). 96p. (YA). (gr. 7-12). 39.93 (978-0-7614-4954-6(X)) Marshall Cavendish Corp.

Blohm, Craig E. Hillary Clinton. 2016. (ENG.). 80p. (J). 38.60 (978-1-60152-950-3(3)) ReferencePoint Pr., Inc.

Blumenthal, Karen. Hillary Rodham Clinton: A Woman Living History. 2016. (ENG., Illus.). 448p. (J). 18.99 (978-1-250-06014-3(1), 9781250060143) Feiwel & Friends.

Bodden, Valerie. Hillary Clinton: Historic Leader, 1 vol. 2009. (Essential Lives Set 4 Ser.). (ENG., Illus.). 112p. (J). (gr. 6-12). lib. bdg. 35.64 (978-1-60453-699-7(3)) ABDO Publishing Co.

—Samuel Houston: Army Leader & Historic Politician, 1 vol. 2010. (Military Heroes Ser.). (ENG.). 112p. (J). (gr. 6-12). lib. bdg. 35.64 (978-1-60453-962-2(3)) ABDO Publishing Co.

Bourcier, Cammy S. Barack Obama. 2009. (Sharing the American Dream Ser.). (Illus.). 64p. (YA). (gr. 7-12). 22.95 (978-1-4222-0574-7(6)) Mason Crest.

Brager, Bruce L. John Kerry: Senator from Massachusetts. 2005. (Twentieth Century Leaders Ser.). (Illus.). 128p. (J). (gr. 6-12). lib. bdg. 23.95 (978-1-931798-64-8(8)) Reynolds, Morgan Inc.

Brill, Marlene Targ. Barack Obama: Working to Make a Difference. 2006. (J). pap. 6.95 (978-0-8225-6056-2(9), First Avenue Editions) Lerner Publishing Group.

—Barack Obama (Revised Edition) 2009. pap. 52.95 (978-0-7613-5031-6(4)) Lerner Publishing Group.

Burlingame, Jeff. Hillary Clinton: A Life in Politics. 2008. (People to Know Today Ser.). (Illus.). 112p. (J). (gr. 3-7). lib. bdg. 33.27 (978-0-7660-2892-0(5)) Enslow Pubs., Inc.

Caravantes, Peggy. American in Texas: The Story of Sam Houston. 2004. (Notable Americans Ser.). (Illus.). 144p. (YA). (gr. 6-12). 23.95 (978-1-931798-19-8(2)) Reynolds, Morgan Inc.

Coddington, Andrew. Davy Crockett. Lapegüe, Matias, illus. 2016. (American Legends & Folktales Ser.). 32p. (J). 28.50 (978-1-5026-2193-1(2)) Cavendish Square Publishing.

Cohen, Sheila & Terman Cohen, Sheila. Gaylord Nelson: Champion for Our Earth. 2010. (Badger Biographies Ser.). (ENG., Illus.). 120p. (J). pap. 12.95 (978-0-87020-443-2(2)) Wisconsin Historical Society.

Collard, Sneed B., III. John Glenn: Hooked on Flying. 2008. (American Heroes Ser.). (Illus.). 48p. (J). (gr. 3-18). lib. bdg. 29.93 (978-0-7614-3066-7(0), Benchmark Bks.) Marshall Cavendish Corp.

Davis, William Michael. Barack Obama: The Politics of Hope. 2007. (Illus.). 168p. (J). (gr. 10-18). lib. bdg. 25.95 (978-1-59556-024-7(6)); (YA). (gr. 8-18). pap. 16.99 (978-1-59556-032-2(7)) OTTN Publishing.

De Medeiros, James. Al Gore. 2008. (Remarkable People Ser.). (Illus.). 24p. (J). (gr. 4-6). pap. 8.95 (978-1-59036-993-7(9)); lib. bdg. 24.45 (978-1-59036-992-0(0)) Weigl Pubs., Inc.

De Medeiros, Michael. Barack Obama. (J). 2013. (978-1-62127-388-2(1)) 2008. (Illus.). 24p. (gr. 4-6). pap. 8.95 (978-1-59036-989-0(0)) 2008. (Illus.). 24p. (gr. 4-6). lib. bdg. 24.45 (978-1-59036-988-3(2)) Weigl Pubs., Inc.

Devaney, Sherri, et al. Barack Obama. 2009. (People in the News Ser.). (ENG.). 104p. (YA). (gr. 7-12). lib. bdg. 33.45 (978-1-4205-0206-0(9), LML02109-248525) Cengage Gale.

Doak, Robin S. Hillary Clinton. 2013. (True Book™—Biographies Ser.). (ENG., Illus.). 48p. (J). pap. 6.95 (978-0-531-23877-6(6)); lib. bdg. 29.00 (978-0-531-21906-5(2)) Scholastic Library Publishing.

Edwards, Roberta. Barack Obama: United States President. Call, Ken, illus. rev. exp. ed. 2009. (ENG.). 64p. (J). (gr. 1-3). mass mkt. 5.99 (978-0-448-45234-0(0), Grosset & Dunlap) Penguin Young Readers Group.

Egan, Jill. Hillary Rodham Clinton. 2009. (People We Should Know Ser.). (ENG., Illus.). 48p. (J). (gr. 3-5). pap. 10.50 (978-1-4339-2193-3(6)); lib. bdg. 31.00 (978-1-4339-2188-9(X)) Stevens, Gareth Publishing LLLP. (Gareth Stevens Learning Library).

Epstein, Brad M. Barack Obama 101. l.t. ed. 2009. (My First Presidential Board Book Ser.). (Illus.). 28p. (J). (gr. -1-1). bds. (978-1-60730-044-1(3), 101 Bk.) Michaelson Entertainment.

Epstein, Dwayne. Hillary Clinton. 2010. (People in the News Ser.). (Illus.). 128p. (J). 33.95 (978-1-4205-0268-8(9), Lucent Bks.) Cengage Gale.

Falk, Laine. Meet President Barack Obama. 2009. (Scholastic News Nonfiction Readers Ser.). (ENG.). 24p. (J). (gr. 1-2). 20.00 (978-0-531-23403-7(7), Children's Pr.) Scholastic Library Publishing.

—Meet President John McCain. 2009. (J). (978-0-531-23650-5(1)) Children's Pr., Ltd.

Feinstein, Stephen. Barack Obama. 2008. (African-American Heroes Ser.). (Illus.). 24p. (J). (gr. 1-3). lib. bdg. 22.60 (978-0-7660-2893-7(3), Enslow Elementary) Enslow Pubs., Inc.

Freedman, Jeri. Elizabeth Warren: Democratic Senator from Massachusetts. 2017. (J). **(978-1-5026-2699-8(3))** Cavendish Square Publishing.

Freedman, Jeri. Hillary Rodham Clinton: Profile of a Leading Democrat. (Career Profiles Ser.). 112p. 2009. (gr. 9-10). 63.90 (978-1-61511-794-9(6)) 2007. (YA). (gr. 7-12). lib. bdg. 34.60 (978-1-4042-1910-6(2)) Rosen Publishing Group, Inc., The.

Giblin, James Cross. The Rise & Fall of Senator Joe McCarthy. 2009. (ENG., Illus.). 304p. (YA). (gr. 7-18). 22.00 (978-0-618-61058-7(8)) Houghton Mifflin Harcourt Publishing Co.

Gibson, Karen Bush. The Historic Fight for the 2008 Democratic Presidential Nomination: The Obama View. 2009. (Monumental Milestones Ser.). (Illus.). 48p. (YA). (gr. 4-7). lib. bdg. 29.95 (978-1-58415-732-8(1)) Mitchell Lane Pubs., Inc.

Goldsworthy, Steve. Edward Kennedy. 2010. (Remarkable People Ser.). (Illus.). 24p. (J). (gr. 4-6). pap. 11.95 (978-1-61690-170-7(5)); lib. bdg. 25.70 (978-1-61690-169-1(1)) Weigl Pubs., Inc.

Grimes, Nikki. Barack Obama: Son of Promise, Child of Hope. Collier, Bryan, illus. 2008. (ENG.). 48p. (J). (gr. k-3). 16.99 (978-1-4169-7144-3(0), Simon & Schuster Bks. For Young Readers) Simon & Schuster Bks. For Young Readers.

Guernsey, JoAnn B. Hillary Rodham Clinton. 2005. (Biography Ser.). (Illus.). 112p. (J). (gr. 6-18). pap. 7.95 (978-0-8225-9613-4(X)) Lerner Publishing Group.

Guernsey, Joann Bren. Hillary Rodham Clinton. 2005. (Biography Ser.). (Illus.). 112p. (J). (gr. 3-7). lib. bdg. 29.27 (978-0-8225-2372-7(8), Lerner Pubns.) Lerner Publishing Group.

—Hillary Rodham Clinton: Secretary of State. 2009. (USA TODAY Lifeline Biographies Ser.). (ENG.). 112p. (gr. 6-12). lib. bdg. 34.60 (978-0-7613-5122-1(1)) Lerner Publishing Group.

Harmon, Daniel E. Al Gore & Global Warming. 2009. (Celebrity Activists Ser.). 112p. (gr. 8-8). 66.50 (978-1-61511-826-7(8)) Rosen Publishing Group, Inc., The.

Hillstrom, Kevin. McCarthyism & the Communist Threat. 2011. (Defining Moments Ser.). 266p. 55.00 (978-0-7808-1184-3(4)) Omnigraphics, Inc.

Hillstrom, Kevin & Hillstrom, Laurie Collier. Al Gore. 2008. (People in the News Ser.). (ENG., Illus.). 128p. (gr. 7-10). lib. bdg. 39.40 (978-1-4205-0086-8(4), LML02109-242090, Lucent Bks.) Cengage Gale.

Hiram Bingham & the Dream of Gold. 2014. (ENG.). 192p. (J). (gr. 3-7). pap. 13.95 (978-1-59077-350-5(0)) Evans, M. & Co., Inc.

Hoe, Susan. Rosa Parks. 2007. (Sharing the American Dream Ser.). 64p. (YA). (gr. 7-18). pap. 9.95 (978-1-4222-0760-4(9)) Mason Crest.

Horn, Geoffrey M. John Mccain. 2009. (People We Should Know Ser.). 32p. (J). (gr. 3-5). pap. 10.50 (978-1-4339-0160-7(9), Gareth Stevens Learning Library) Stevens, Gareth Publishing LLLP.

—John McCain. 2009. (People We Should Know Ser.). 32p. (J). (gr. 3-5). lib. bdg. 31.00 (978-1-4339-0020-4(3), Gareth Stevens Learning Library) Stevens, Gareth Publishing LLLP.

Immell, Myra. The McCarthy Era. Gale Editors, ed. 2011. (Perspectives on Modern World History Ser.). (ENG.). 224p. (gr. 12-12). lib. bdg. 47.80 (978-0-7377-5260-1(2), Greenhaven Pr., Inc.) Cengage Gale.

Iorio, Nicole. Joe Biden. 2009. (People We Should Know Ser.). 48p. (J). (gr. 3-5). pap. 10.50 (978-1-4339-2148-3(0)); lib. bdg. 31.00 (978-1-4339-1949-7(4)) Stevens, Gareth Publishing LLLP. (Gareth Stevens Learning Library).

Kann, Bob. Belle & Bob la Follette: Partners in Politics. 2008. (Badger Biographies Ser.). (ENG., Illus.). 144p. (J). (gr. 3-7). pap. 12.95 (978-0-87020-407-4(6)) Wisconsin Historical Society.

Klein, Adria F. Barack Obama. 2009. pap. 13.25 (978-1-60559-055-4(X)) Hameray Publishing Group, Inc.

Krull, Kathleen. The Brothers Kennedy: John, Robert, Edward. Bates, Amy June, illus. 2010. (ENG.). 40p. (J). (gr. -1-3). 16.99 (978-1-4169-9158-8(1), Simon & Schuster Bks. For Young Readers) Simon & Schuster Bks. For Young Readers.

Lee, Sally. Hillary Clinton, 1 vol. 2010. (First Ladies Ser.). (ENG.). 24p. (gr. k-1). lib. bdg. 26.65 (978-1-4296-5327-5(2), Pebble Plus) Capstone Press of Coughlan Cos.

Marcovitz, Hal. Barack. 2007. (Obamas Ser.). (Illus.). 64p. (YA). (gr. 3-6). pap. 9.95 (978-1-4222-1484-8(2)); (gr. 4-7). lib. bdg. 19.95 (978-1-4222-1477-0(X)) Mason Crest.

Markel, Michelle. Hillary Rodham Clinton: Some Girls Are Born to Lead. Pham, LeUyen, illus. 2016. 40p. (J). (gr. -1-3). 17.99 (978-0-06-238122-4(9)) HarperCollins Pubs.

Marsh, Carole. John Kerry: Successful Senator & 2004 Presidential Candidate. 2004. (J). 24p. pap. 5.95 (978-0-635-02537-1(X)); 24.95 (978-0-635-02542-5(6)) Gallopade International.

Mattern, Joanne. Hillary Rodham Clinton, 1 vol. 2008. (First Ladies Set 1 Ser.). (ENG., Illus.). 32p. (YA). (gr. 1-4). 27.07 (978-1-59928-792-8(7)) ABDO Publishing Co.

McGowan, Joe. Al Gore. 2009. (People We Should Know Ser.). (ENG.). 48p. (J). (gr. 3-5). pap. 10.50 (978-1-4339-2146-9(4), Gareth Stevens Learning Library) Stevens, Gareth Publishing LLLP.

McGowan, Joseph. Al Gore. 2009. (People We Should Know Ser.). (ENG.). 48p. (J). (gr. 3-5). lib. bdg. 31.00 (978-1-4339-1947-3(8), Gareth Stevens Learning Library) Stevens, Gareth Publishing LLLP.

Mendell, David & Thomson, Sarah L. Obama: A Promise of Change. 2008. (ENG., Illus.). 192p. (J). (gr. 3-7). pap. 6.99 (978-0-06-169700-5(1), Amistad) HarperCollins Pubs.

Miller, Barbara Kiely. Sam Houston. 2007. (Grandes Personajes (Great Americans) Ser.). 24p. (gr. 1-4). (SPA.). pap. 8.15 (978-0-8368-8336-7(5)); pap. 8.15 (978-0-8368-8323-7(3)); lib. bdg. 22.00 (978-0-8368-8316-9(0)); (SPA., Illus.). lib. bdg. 22.00 (978-0-8368-8329-9(2)) Stevens, Gareth Publishing LLLP. (Weekly Reader Leveled Readers).

Peppas, Lynn. Why Sam Houston Matters to Texas. 2014. (Illus.). 32p. (J). lib. bdg. 26.25 (978-1-4777-0912-2(6)) Rosen Publishing Group, Inc., The.

Riddolls, Tom & Wearing, Judy. Hillary Clinton. 2009. (Remarkable People Ser.). (Illus.). 24p. (J). (gr. 4-6). pap. 8.95 (978-1-60596-621-2(5)); lib. bdg. 24.45 (978-1-60596-620-5(7)) Weigl Pubs., Inc.

Robinson, Tom. Barack Obama: 44th U. S. President. 2009. (J). lib. bdg. 32.79 (978-1-60453-528-0(8), Essential Library) ABDO Publishing Co.

—John McCain: POW & Statesman, 1 vol. 2010. (Military Heroes Ser.). (ENG.). 112p. (J). (gr. 6-12). lib. bdg. 35.64 (978-1-60453-963-9(1)) ABDO Publishing Co.

Ryan, Bernard. Hillary Rodham Clinton: First Lady & Senator. 2004. (Ferguson Career Biographies Ser.). (Illus.). 160p. (gr. 6-12). 25.00 (978-0-8160-5544-9(0), Ferguson Publishing Co.) Facts On File, Inc.

Saddleback Educational Publishing Staff, ed. Davy Crockett, 1 vol. unabr. ed. 2008. (Graphic Biographies Ser.). (ENG., Illus.). 25p. (YA). (gr. 9-12). pap. 7.95 (978-1-59905-220-5(2)) Saddleback Educational Publishing, Inc.

Sanford, William R. & Green, Carl R. Sam Houston: Courageous Texas Hero. 2012. (Courageous Heroes of the American West Ser.). (Illus.). 48p. (J). pap. 8.95 (978-1-4644-0092-6(X)); (gr. 5-18). lib. bdg. 22.60 (978-0-7660-4009-0(7)) Enslow Pubs., Inc.

Sapet, Kerrily. Al Gore. 2007. (Political Profiles Ser.). (Illus.). 112p. (YA). (gr. 5-9). lib. bdg. 27.95 (978-1-59935-070-7(X)) Reynolds, Morgan Inc.

Schuman, Michael A. Barack Obama: We Are One People. 2008. (African-American Biography Library). (Illus.). 128p. (J). (gr. 3-7). lib. bdg. 33.27 (978-0-7660-2891-3(7)) Enslow Pubs., Inc.

—Barack Obama: We Are One People, Revised & Expanded. rev. ed. 2009. (African-American Biography Library). (Illus.). 160p. (J). (gr. 6). lib. bdg. 33.27 (978-0-7660-3649-9(9)) Enslow Pubs., Inc.

Slavicek, Louise Chipley. Daniel Inouye. 2nd ed. 2007. (Asian Americans of Achievement Ser.). (Illus.). 128p. (YA). (gr. 7-12). lib. bdg. 35.00 (978-0-7910-9271-2(2)) Facts On File, Inc.

Stefoff, Rebecca. Al Gore: Fighting for a Greener Planet. rev. ed. 2008. (Gateway Biographies Ser.). (ENG.). 48p. (gr. 4-8). 26.60 (978-1-57505-948-8(7)) Lerner Publishing Group.

Streissguth, Tom. John Glenn. 2004. (Just the Facts Biographies Ser.). (ENG., Illus.). 112p. (J). (gr. 5-12). lib. bdg. 27.93 (978-0-8225-2274-4(8)) Lerner Publishing Group.

Ted Kennedy. 2009. (Political Profiles Ser.). 144p. (YA). (gr. 5-9). 28.95 (978-1-59935-089-9(0)) Reynolds, Morgan Inc.

Tibbitts, Alison Davis. Henry Clay: From War Hawk to the Great Compromiser. 2003. (Historical American Biographies Ser.). (Illus.). 128p. (J). lib. bdg. 27.94 (978-0-7660-1980-5(2)) Enslow Pubs., Inc.

Tieck, Sarah. Hillary Rodham Clinton, 1 vol. 2010. (First Biographies Set 6 Ser.). (ENG.). 32p. (J). (gr. 1-4). 27.07 (978-1-60453-983-7(6)) ABDO Publishing Co.

Tracy, Kathleen. The Historic Fight for the 2008 Democratic Presidential Nomination: The Clinton View. 2009. (Monumental Milestones Ser.). (Illus.). 48p. (YA). (gr. 4-7). lib. bdg. 29.95 (978-1-58415-731-1(3)) Mitchell Lane Pubs., Inc.

—The McCarthy Era. 2008. (Monumental Milestones Ser.). (Illus.). 48p. (YA). (gr. 4-7). lib. bdg. 29.95 (978-1-58415-694-9(5)) Mitchell Lane Pubs., Inc.

Turner, Carolyn. Sam Houston. 2010. pap. 9.95 (978-1-61690-066-3(0)); 24p. (J). (gr. 2-4). lib. bdg. 25.70 (978-1-61690-065-6(2)) Weigl Pubs., Inc.

Uschan, Michael V. Joe Biden. 2010. (People in the News Ser.). (Illus.). 128p. (J). 33.95 (978-1-4205-0260-2(3), Lucent Bks.) Cengage Gale.

Wade, Mary Dodson. David Crockett: Creating a Legend. Hein, Joy Fisher, illus. 2009. (ENG.). 24p. (J). (gr. k-2). 16.95 (978-1-933979-12-0(7), 9781933979120) Bright Sky Pr.

Wagner, Heather Lehr. Barack Obama. 2008. (Black Americans of Achievement: Legacy Edition Ser.). 104p. (gr. 6-12). pap. 11.95 (978-1-60413-324-0(4), Checkmark Bks.) Facts On File, Inc.

—Barack Obama: Politician. 2008. (Black Americans of Achievement Ser.). (Illus.). 104p. (YA). (gr. 7-12). lib. bdg. 35.00 (978-0-7910-9716-8(1)) Facts On File, Inc.

Watson, Marilyn Myrick. Barry Goldwater: State Greats Arizona. 2007. (Acacia Biographies Ser.). (Illus.). 28p. (J). (gr. 4-7). per. 6.95 (978-0-9790826-0-3(9)) Acacia Publishing, Inc.

—Bary Goldwater: State Greats Arizona. 2007. (Acacia Biographies Ser.). (Illus.). 28p. (J). (gr. 3-7). lib. bdg. 16.95 (978-0-9788283-4-9(8)) Acacia Publishing, Inc.

Wells, Catherine. Hillary Clinton. 2007. (Political Profiles Ser.). (Illus.). 112p. (YA). (gr. 5-9). lib. bdg. 27.95 (978-1-59935-047-9(5)) Reynolds, Morgan Inc.

—John McCain. 2008. (Political Profiles Ser.). (Illus.). 112p. (YA). (gr. 5-9). lib. bdg. 27.95 (978-1-59935-046-2(7)) Reynolds, Morgan Inc.

Winget, Mary Mueller. Gerald R. Ford. 2007. (Presidential Leaders Ser.). (Illus.). 112p. (J). (gr. 3-7). lib. bdg. 29.27 (978-0-8225-1509-8(1), Twenty-First Century Bks.) Lerner Publishing Group.

Winter, Jonah. Barack. Ford, A. G., illus. 32p. (J). (gr. -1-2). 2010. (ENG.). pap. 7.99 (978-0-06-170396-6(6), Tegen, Katherine Bks) 2008. lib. bdg. 18.89 (978-0-06-170393-5(1)) 2008. (ENG.). 17.99 (978-0-06-170392-8(3), Tegen, Katherine Bks) HarperCollins Pubs.

—Barack, 2 vols, 2009. (J). 38.75 (978-1-4407-3624-7(3)); 40.75 (978-1-4407-3618-6(9)); 38.75 (978-1-4407-3620-9(0)); 40.75 (978-1-4407-3622-3(7)); 1.25 (978-1-4407-3625-4(1)); 222.75 (978-1-4407-3619-3(7)) Recorded Bks., Inc.

—Hillary. Colón, Raúl, illus. 2016. (ENG.). 40p. (J). (gr. -1-3). lib. bdg. 20.99 (978-0-553-53389-7(4), Schwartz & Wade Bks.) Random Hse. Children's Bks.

Winter, Jonah & Colón, Raúl. Hillary. 2016. (ENG., Illus.). 40p. (J). (gr. -1-3). 17.99 (978-0-553-53388-0(6), Schwartz & Wade Bks.) Random Hse. Children's Bks.

Woodward, Mac. Sam Houston: For Texas & the Union. 2009. (Library of American Lives & Times Ser.). 112p. (gr. 5-5). 69.20 (978-1-60853-504-0(5)) Rosen Publishing Group, Inc., The.

Young, Jeff C. Joe Biden. 2009. (Political Profiles Ser.). 100p. (YA). (gr. 5-9). 28.95 (978-1-59935-131-5(5)) Reynolds, Morgan Inc.

UNITED STATES—CONSTITUTION

Allen, Kathy. The U. S. Constitution. 2016. (Pebble Plus Ser.). (ENG.). 24p. (gr. k-1). pap. 7.29 (978-1-5157-5967-6(9), Pebble Plus) Capstone Press of Coughlan Cos.

Aloian, Molly. Constitution Day. 2008. (Celebrations in My World Ser.). (ENG., Illus.). 32p. (J). (gr. k-3). pap. (978-0-7787-4304-0(7)) Crabtree Publishing Co.

Barden, Cindy & Mark Twain Media Staff. Jumpstarters for the U. S. Constitution: Short Daily Warm-Ups for the Classroom. 2005. (Jumpstarters Ser.). (ENG., Illus.). 48p. (gr. 4-8). pap. 8.99 (978-1-58037-304-3(6)) Twain, Mark Media, Inc. Pubs.

Baxter, Roberta. The Creation of the U. S. Constitution: A History Perspectives Book. 2014. (Perspectives Library). (ENG., Illus.). 32p. (J). (gr. 4-8). 28.50 (978-1-63137-616-0(0), 205247) Cherry Lake Publishing.

Beckett, Leslie & Dunn, John M. The Story of the Constitution: Creating the U. S. Government. 2017. (American History Ser.). 104p. (J). (gr. 7-7). lib. bdg. 39.40 **(978-1-5345-6044-4(0)**, Lucent Pr.) Greenhaven Publishing LLC.

Benchmark Education Company, LLC Staff, compiled by. Freedom's Trail & U. S. Constitution. 2005. spiral bd. 75.00 (978-1-4108-5826-9(X)) Benchmark Education Co.

Bradley, B. J. We the People- the 27 Amendments of the United States Constitution. 2012. 34p. pap. 15.95 (978-0-578-10413-3(X)) Winding Road Pubs.

Brezina, Corona. Fifth Amendment: Double Jeopardy, Self-Incrimination, & Due Process of Law. 2011. (Amendments to the United States Constitution: the Bill of Rights Ser.). (ENG., Illus.). 64p. (J). pap. 12.95 (978-1-4488-2306-2(4), Rosen Reference) Rosen Publishing Group, Inc., The.

—The Fifth Amendment: Double Jeopardy, Self-Incrimination, & Due Process of Law. 2011. (Amendments to the United States Constitution: the Bill of Rights Ser.). (Illus.). 64p. (YA). (gr. 5-9). lib. bdg. 31.95 (978-1-4488-1260-8(7)) Rosen Publishing Group, Inc., The.

Brinkman, Patricia. Discover Writing the Constitution. 2006. (J). pap. (978-1-4108-6453-6(7)) Benchmark Education Co.

Buchanan, Shelly. The U. S. Constitution & You. rev. ed. 2014. (Primary Source Readers Content & Literacy Ser.). (ENG., Illus.). 32p. (gr. 3-3). pap. 8.99 (978-1-4333-7364-0(5)) Teacher Created Materials, Inc.

Burgan, Michael. The Creation of the U. S. Constitution. Purcell, Gordon & Beatty, Terry, illus. 2006. (Graphic History Ser.). (ENG.). 32p. (gr. 3-4). pap. 8.10 (978-0-7368-9653-5(8), Graphic Library) Capstone Press of Coughlan Cos.

—The U. S. Constitution. 2011. (Cornerstones of Freedom, Third Ser.). (ENG., Illus.). 64p. (J). pap. 8.95 (978-0-531-26567-3(6), Children's Pr.) Scholastic Library Publishing.

—The U.S. Constitution/By Michael Burgan. 2011. (Cornerstones of Freedom, Third Ser.). (Illus.). 64p. (J). lib. bdg. 30.00 (978-0-531-25042-6(3), Children's Pr.) Scholastic Library Publishing.

Carson, Brian & Ramen, Catherine. Understanding Your Right to Freedom from Searches. 2011. (Personal Freedom & Civic Duty Ser.). (Illus.). 160p. (YA). (gr. 7-12). lib. bdg. 35.95 (978-1-4488-4670-2(6)) Rosen Publishing Group, Inc., The.

Catrow, David. We the Kids: The Preamble of the Constitution of the United States. Catrow, David, illus. 2004. (Illus.). (J). (gr. k-5). 27.90 incl. audio (978-0-8045-6914-9(2)) Spoken Arts, Inc.

Cefrey, Holly. The United States Constitution & Early State Constitutions: Law & Order in the New Nation & States. 2009. (Life in the New American Nation Ser.). 32p. (gr. 4-4). 47.90 (978-1-61514-287-3(8)) Rosen Publishing Group, Inc., The.

Cheney, Lynne. We the People: The Story of Our Constitution. Harlin, Greg, illus. (ENG.). 40p. (J). (gr. k-4). 2012. 7.99 (978-1-4424-4422-5(3)) 2008. 17.99 (978-1-4169-5418-7(X)) Simon & Schuster/Paula Wiseman Bks. (Simon & Schuster/Paula Wiseman Bks.).

Clay, Kathryn. The U. S. Constitution: Introducing Primary Sources. 2016. (Introducing Primary Sources Ser.). (ENG., Illus.). 32p. (gr. 1-2). lib. bdg. 27.99 (978-1-4914-8225-4(7)) Capstone Press of Coughlan Cos.

Coleman, Wim. The Constitution & the Bill of Rights. Perrin, Pat, ed. 2nd ed. 2006. (Researching American History Ser.). (ENG., Illus.). 56p. (J). pap. 8.95 (978-1-932663-11-2(8)) History Compass, LLC.

DeRubertis, Barbara. Let's Celebrate Constitution Day. 2015. (ENG., Illus.). 32p. (J). (gr. 1-4). pap. 7.95 (978-1-57565-749-3(X)) Kane Press, Inc.

Donnelly, Karen. The Bill of Rights. 2009. (Primary Source Library of American Citizenship Ser.). 32p. (gr. 5-5). 47.90 (978-1-61511-221-0(9), Rosen Reference) Rosen Publishing Group, Inc., The.

Eck, Kristin. Drafting the Constitution: Weighing Evidence to Draw Sound Conclusions. 2006. (Critical Thinking in American History Ser.). (ENG., Illus.). 48p. (YA). (gr. 5-8). lib. bdg. 29.25 (978-1-4042-0412-6(1)) Rosen Publishing Group, Inc., The.

The Evolution of the Bill of Rights (NCHS) (YA). (gr. 8-12). spiral bd., tchr.'s planning gde. ed. 13.50 (978-0-382-40938-7(8)) Cobblestone Publishing Co.

Fradin, Dennis Brindell. The U. S. Constitution. 2007. (Turning Points in U. S. History Ser.). (Illus.). 47p. (J). (gr. 4-7). lib. bdg. 31.36 (978-0-7614-2036-1(3), Benchmark Bks.) Marshall Cavendish Corp.

Furgang, Kathy. The Ninth Amendment: Rights Retained by the People. 2011. (Amendments to the United States Constitution: the Bill of Rights Ser.). (Illus.). 64p. (YA). (gr. 5-9). lib. bdg. 31.95 (978-1-4488-1264-6(X)) Rosen Publishing Group, Inc., The.

Ganchy, Sally & Isler, Claudia. Understanding Your Right to Free Speech. 2011. (Personal Freedom & Civic Duty Ser.). (Illus.). 152p. (YA). (gr. 7-12). lib. bdg. 35.95 (978-1-4488-4667-2(6)) Rosen Publishing Group, Inc., The.

Gonzales, Doreen. A Look at the Second Amendment: To Keep & Bear Arms. 2007. (Constitution of the United States Ser.). (Illus.). 128p. (J). (gr. 5). lib. bdg. 34.60 (978-1-59845-061-3(1), MyReportLinks.com Bks.) Enslow Pubs., Inc.

Graham, Amy. A Look at the Bill of Rights: Protecting the Rights of Americans. 2007. (Constitution of the United States Ser.). (Illus.). 128p. (J). (gr. 3-7). lib. bdg. 34.60 (978-1-59845-064-4(6), MyReportLinks.com Bks.) Enslow Pubs., Inc.

Griffin, Maave. Constitution Day. 2009. (Explore Citizenship Ser.). 24p. (gr. 3-3). 42.50 (978-1-61512-340-7(7), PowerKids Pr.) Rosen Publishing Group, Inc., The.

Griffin, Maeve. Constitution Day. 2009. (Real Life Readers Ser.). 24p. (gr. 3-4). pap. 8.25 (978-1-4358-0139-4(3), Rosen Classroom); (J). 22.60 (978-1-4358-2978-7(6), PowerKids Pr.) Rosen Publishing Group, Inc., The.

Harris, Nancy. What's the U. S. Constitution? 2016. (First Guide to Government Ser.). (ENG.). 32p. (gr. 1-3). pap. 8.29 (978-1-4846-3690-9(2), Heinemann First Library) Heinemann-Raintree.

Isaacs, Sally & Bedeksy, Baron. Understanding the US Constitution. 2008. (Documenting Early America Ser.). (ENG.). 32p. (J). (gr. 3-6). pap. (978-0-7787-4378-1(0)) Crabtree Publishing Co.

Jacobson, Bray. The US Constitution. 2017. (Look at U. S. History Ser.). 32p. (gr. 2-2). pap. 10.50 **(978-1-4824-6043-8(2))** Stevens, Gareth Publishing LLLP.

Jones, Molly. First Amendment: Freedom of Speech, the Press, & Religion. 2011. (Amendments to the United States Constitution: the Bill of Rights Ser.). (ENG., Illus.). 64p. (YA). pap. 12.95 (978-1-4488-2302-4(1), Rosen Reference) Rosen Publishing Group, Inc., The.

—The First Amendment: Freedom of Speech, the Press, & Religion. 2011. (Amendments to the United States Constitution: the Bill of Rights Ser.). (Illus.). 64p. (YA). (gr. 5-9). lib. bdg. 31.95 (978-1-4488-1252-3(6)) Rosen Publishing Group, Inc., The.

Kawa, Katie. Bill of Rights. 2016. (Documents of American Democracy Ser.). (Illus.). 32p. (J). (gr. 5-5). pap. 10.00 (978-1-4994-2073-9(0), PowerKids Pr.) Rosen Publishing Group, Inc., The.

Keegan, Anna. The United States Constitution & the Bill of Rights: The Law of the Land. 2015. (Spotlight on American History Ser.). (ENG., Illus.). 24p. (J). (gr. 4-6). pap. 10.00 (978-1-4994-1773-9(X), PowerKids Pr.) Rosen Publishing Group, Inc., The.

Krensky, Stephen. The Constitution. 2011. (Documents of Democracy Ser.). 96p. (gr. 8). 34.21 (978-0-7614-4917-1(5)) Marshall Cavendish Corp.

Krull, Kathleen. A Kids' Guide to America's Bill of Rights. DiVito, Anna, illus. 2015. (ENG.). 240p. (J). (gr. 3-7). pap. 6.99 (978-0-06-235230-9(X)) HarperCollins Pubs.

LearningExpress Staff. U. S. Constitution in 15 Minutes a Day. 2011. (15 Minutes a Day Ser.). (ENG.). 256p. pap. 14.95 (978-1-57685-767-0(0)) LearningExpress, LLC.

Leavitt, Amie Jane. The Bill of Rights in Translation: What It Really Means. (Kids' Translations Ser.). (ENG.). 32p. (gr. 3-4). 2017. lib. bdg. 27.32 **(978-1-5157-9138-6(6))** 2016. pap. 8.10 (978-1-5157-4218-0(0)) Capstone Press of Coughlan Cos. (Fact Finders).

Lusted, Marcia Amidon. The U. S. Constitution. 2016. (How America Works). (ENG.). 24p. (J). (gr. 3-6). 28.50 (978-1-5038-0907-9(2), 210664) Child's World, Inc., The.

Maestro, Betsy. A More Perfect Union: The Story of Our Constitution. Maestro, Giulio, illus. 2008. (American Story Ser.). (ENG.). 48p. (J). (gr. 2-7). pap. 7.99 (978-0-688-10192-3(5)) HarperCollins Pubs.

Manger, Katherine. The U.S. Constitution. 2016. (J). (978-1-5081-0455-1(7)) Rosen Publishing Group, Inc., The.

Marsh, Carole. The Counterfeit Constitution Mystery. 2009. (Real Kids, Real Places Ser.). (Illus.). 144p. (J). lib. bdg. 18.99 (978-0-635-07043-2(X), Marsh, Carole Mysteries) Gallopade International.

—I'm Reading about the U. S. Constitution. 2016. (I'm Reading About Ser.). (ENG., Illus.). (J). lib. bdg. 24.99 **(978-0-635-12219-3(7))**; pap. 7.99 **(978-0-635-12220-9(0))** Gallopade International.

Marsh, Carole. The U. S. Constitution. Beard, Chad, ed. 2004. (American Milestones Ser.). (Illus.). 28p. (J). (gr. 4-12). pap. 5.95 (978-0-635-02696-5(1)) Gallopade International.

Metz, Lorijo. La Constitucin de los Estados Unidos y la Carta de Derechos / the United States Constitution & the Bill of Rights. Beullens-Maoui, Nathalie, ed. 2014. (¡Celebremos la Libertad! / Let's Celebrate Freedom! Ser.). (SPA & BYN.). 24p. (J). (gr. 3-6). 23.60 (978-1-4777-3247-2(0), PowerKids Pr.) Rosen Publishing Group, Inc., The.

—The United States Constitution & the Bill of Rights, 1 vol., 1. 2014. (Let's Celebrate Freedom! Ser.). (ENG.). 24p. (J). (gr. 3-6). 23.60 (978-1-4777-2895-6(3), PowerKids Pr.) Rosen Publishing Group, Inc., The.

Micklos, John. The Making of the United States from Thirteen Colonies — Through Primary Sources. 2013. (American Revolution Through Primary Sources Ser.). 48p. (J). (gr. 4-18). 25.27 (978-0-7660-4133-2(6)) Enslow Pubs., Inc.

—The Making of the United States from Thirteen Colonies—Through Primary Sources. 2013. (American Revolution Through Primary Sources Ser.). 48p. (J). (gr. 4-10). pap. 8.95 (978-1-4644-0191-6(8)) Enslow Pubs., Inc.

Micklos, John & Micklos, John, Jr. From Thirteen Colonies to One Nation. 2008. (Revolutionary War Library). (Illus.). 48p. (J). (gr. 3-7). lib. bdg. 25.27 (978-0-7660-3015-2(6), Enslow Elementary) Enslow Pubs., Inc.

Mooney, Carla. U. S. Constitution: Discover How Democracy Works. Casteel, Tom, illus. 2016. (Build It Yourself Ser.). (ENG.). 128p. (J). (gr. 3-7). pap. 17.95 (978-1-61930-445-1(7)) Open City Bks.

—The U. S. Constitution: Discover How Democracy Works. Casteel, Tom, illus. 2016. (Build It Yourself Ser.). (ENG.). 128p. (J). (gr. 3-7). 22.95 (978-1-61930-441-3(4)) Open City Bks.

Murray, Hallie. The Right to Bear Arms: The Second Amendment. 2017. (Bill of Rights Ser.). 48p. (J). (gr. 5-6). lib. bdg. 27.93 **(978-0-7660-8551-0(1))** Enslow Pubs., Inc.

—Unreasonable Search & Seizure: The Fourth Amendment. 2017. (Bill of Rights Ser.). 48p. (J). (gr. 5-6). lib. bdg. 27.93 **(978-0-7660-8555-8(4))** Enslow Pubs., Inc.

Nelson, Robin. Constitution Day. 2009. (First Step Nonfiction - American Holidays Ser.). (ENG.). 24p. (gr. k-2). 23.93 (978-0-7613-4930-3(8)) Lerner Publishing Group.

Orr, Tamra. The Story of the Constitution. 2011. (My Guide to the Constitution Ser.). 48p. (J). (gr. 3-6). pap. 16.50 (978-1-61228-188-9(5)); (Illus.). lib. bdg. 29.95 (978-1-58415-946-9(4)) Mitchell Lane Pubs., Inc.

Otfinoski, Steven. The U. S. Constitution, Bill of Rights, & a New Nation. 2012. (Story of the American Revolution Ser.). (ENG.). 32p. (gr. 3-4). pap. 47.70 (978-1-4296-9293-9(6), Fact Finders); (Illus.). lib. bdg. 27.32 (978-1-4296-8589-4(1)) Capstone Press of Coughlan Cos.

Otfinoski, Steven Anthony. The U. S. Constitution, Bill of Rights, & a New Nation, 1 vol. 2012. (Story of the American Revolution Ser.). (ENG.). 32p. (gr. 3-4). pap. 8.10 (978-1-4296-9292-2(8), Fact Finders) Capstone Press of Coughlan Cos.

Pearl, Norman. The U. S. Constitution, 1 vol. Skeens, Matthew, illus. 2006. (American Symbols Ser.). (ENG.). 24p. (gr. 1-2). 9.95 (978-1-4048-2646-5(7)) Picture Window Bks.

Pederson, Charles E. The U. S. Constitution & Bill of Rights, 1 vol. 2010. (Essential Events Set 4 Ser.). (ENG.). 112p. (J). (gr. 6-12). lib. bdg. 35.64 (978-1-60453-948-6(8)) ABDO Publishing Co.

Porterfield, Jason. The Third Amendment: The Right to Privacy in the Home. 2011. (Amendments to the United States Constitution: the Bill of Rights Ser.). (Illus.). 64p. (YA). (gr. 5-9). lib. bdg. 31.95 (978-1-4488-1256-1(9)) Rosen Publishing Group, Inc., The.

—Third Amendment: Upholding the Right to Privacy. 2011. (Amendments to the United States Constitution: the Bill of Rights Ser.). (ENG.). 64p. (YA). pap. 12.95 (978-1-4488-2304-8(8), Rosen Reference) Rosen Publishing Group, Inc., The.

Rajczak Nelson, Kristen. U.S. Constitution. 2016. (Documents of American Democracy Ser.). (Illus.). 32p. (J). (gr. 5-5). pap. 10.00 (978-1-4994-2089-0(7), PowerKids Pr.) Rosen Publishing Group, Inc., The.

Ransom, Candice. George Washington & the Story of the U. S. Constitution. Reeves, Jeni, illus. 2011. (History Speaks: Picture Books Plus Reader's Theater Ser.). 48p. pap. 56.72 (978-0-7613-7632-3(1)); (ENG.). (gr. 2-4). 27.93 (978-0-7613-5877-0(3), Millbrook Pr.); (ENG.). (gr. 2-4). pap. 9.95 (978-0-7613-7116-8(8)) Lerner Publishing Group.

—Who Wrote the U. S. Constitution? And Other Questions about the Constitutional Convention of 1787. 2010. (Six Questions of American History Ser.). (ENG.). (gr. 4-6). pap. 56.72 (978-0-7613-6949-3(X)); 48p. pap. 9.95 (978-0-7613-6126-8(X)); 48p. lib. bdg. 30.60 (978-1-58013-669-3(9)) Lerner Publishing Group.

Richmond, Benjamin. What Are the Three Branches of the Government? And Other Questions about the U. S. Constitution. 2015. (Good Question! Ser.). (ENG., Illus.). 32p. (J). (gr. 2). pap. 5.95 (978-1-4549-1244-6(8)) Sterling Publishing Co., Inc.

Rokutani, John. Freedom of Speech, the Press, & Religion: The First Amendment. 2017. (Bill of Rights Ser.). 48p. (J). (gr. 5-6). 27.93 **(978-0-7660-8549-7(X))** Enslow Pubs., Inc.

Schmidt, Maegan. Us Constitution & Bill of Rights, 1 vol. 2013. (Foundations of Our Nation Ser.). (ENG.). 48p. (J). (gr. 3-6). lib. bdg. 32.79 (978-1-61783-713-5(X)) ABDO Publishing Co.

—US Constitution & Bill of Rights. 2013. (Foundations of Our Nation EBook Ser.). (ENG., Illus.). 48p. (J). pap. 15.64 (978-1-61783-763-0(6), Core Library) ABDO Publishing Co.

Shamir, Ruby. What's the Big Deal about Freedom. Faulkner, Matt, illus. 2017. (What's the Big Deal About Ser.). (ENG.). 32p. (J). (gr. -1-3). 17.99 (978-0-399-54728-7(2), Philomel Bks.) Penguin Young Readers Group.

Shea, Therese. The United States Constitution. 2013. (Documents That Shaped America Ser.). (ENG., Illus.). 32p. (J). (gr. 4-6). lib. bdg. 26.60 (978-1-4339-9009-0(1)) Stevens, Gareth Publishing LLLP.

—20 Fun Facts about the US Constitution. 2013. 32p. (J). (gr. 3-6). 25.25 (978-1-4339-9198-1(5)); pap. 63.00 (978-1-4339-9200-1(0)); pap. 10.50 (978-1-4339-9199-8(3)) Stevens, Gareth Publishing LLLP.

Sonneborn, Liz. The United States Constitution, 1 vol. 2012. (Documenting U. S. History Ser.). (ENG.). 48p. (gr. 3-6). pap. 9.95 (978-1-4329-6761-1(4), NA-h) Heinemann-Raintree.

Steinkraus, Kyla. Constitution. 2014. (ENG.). 24p. (gr. 3-5). 28.50 (978-1-62717-681-1(0)) Rourke Educational Media.

Swain, Gwenyth. Documents of Freedom: A Look at the Declaration of Independence, the Bill of Rights, & the U. S. Constitution. 2012. (Searchlight Books How Does Government Work Ser.). (ENG., Illus.). 40p. (gr. 3-5). pap. 51.01 (978-0-7613-9231-6(9)); pap. 8.95 (978-0-7613-8560-8(6)) Lerner Publishing Group.

—Documents of Freedom: A Look at the Declaration of Independence, the Bill of Rights, & the U.S. Constitution. 2012. (Searchlight Books How Does Government Work Ser.). (ENG., Illus.). 40p. (gr. 3-5). lib. bdg. 27.93 (978-0-7613-6514-3(1)) Lerner Publishing Group.

Taylor-Butler, Christine. The Constitution of the United States. 2008. (True Bks.). (ENG., Illus.). 48p. (J). (gr. 3-5). pap. 6.95 (978-0-531-14779-5(7), Children's Pr.) Scholastic Library Publishing.

Thomas, William David. ¿Qué Es una Constitución? 2008. (Mi gobierno de Estados Unidos (My American Government) Ser.). (SPA., Illus.). 32p. (gr. 3-7). pap. 10.50 (978-0-8368-8878-2(2), Gareth Stevens Learning Library) Stevens, Gareth Publishing LLLP.

—¿Qué Es Una Constitucion? 2008. (Mi gobierno de Estados Unidos (My American Government) Ser.). (SPA.). 32p. (gr. 3-7). lib. bdg. 26.00 (978-0-8368-8873-7(1), Gareth Stevens Learning Library) Stevens, Gareth Publishing LLLP.

—What Is a Constitution? 2008. (My American Government Ser.). 32p. (gr. 3-7). pap. 10.50 (978-0-8368-8868-3(5)); (Illus.). lib. bdg. 26.00 (978-0-8368-8863-8(4)) Stevens, Gareth Publishing LLLP. (Gareth Stevens Learning Library).

Thompson, Gare. Shaping the Constitution: Text Pairs. 2008. (Bridges/Navigators Ser.). (J). (gr. 5). 89.00 (978-1-4108-8422-0(8)) Benchmark Education Co.

Travis, Cathy. Constitution Translated for Kids. 3rd ed. 2008. (ENG.). 112p. (J). (gr. 5-17). pap. 11.95 (978-0-9814534-1-5(4)) Ovation Bks.

—Constitution Translated for Kids / la Constitución traducida para Niños. 2008. (SPA & ENG., Illus.). 176p. (J). (gr. 3-7). pap. 12.95 (978-0-9814534-2-2(2)) Ovation Bks.

Understanding the United States Constitution. 2014. (Understanding the United States Constitution Ser.). 112p. (YA). (gr. 7-12). 249.20 (978-1-4777-7503-5(X)) Rosen Publishing Group, Inc., The.

The United States Constitution Student Workbook. 2nd ed. 2003. pap. (978-0-9635364-8-8(6)) Academic Solutions, Inc.

Webster, Christine. The Pledge of Allegiance. 2003. (Cornerstones of Freedom Ser.). (ENG., Illus.). 48p. (J). (gr. 4-6). 26.00 (978-0-516-22674-3(6), Children's Pr.) Scholastic Library Publishing.

Wolfe, James & Stair, Nancy L. Understanding the Bill of Rights. 2015. (Primary Sources of American Political

Documents Ser.). (ENG., Illus.). 112p. (J). (gr. 7-7). 37.27 *(978-0-7660-6882-7(X))* Enslow Pubs., Inc.

Yero, Judith Lloyd & National Geographic Learning Staff. The Bill of Rights. 2007. (Reading Expeditions Ser.). (ENG., Illus.). 32p. (J). pap. 17.95 *(978-0-7922-4552-0(0))* CENGAGE Learning.

UNITED STATES—CONSTITUTION—AMENDMENTS

see Constitutional Amendments—United States

UNITED STATES—CONSTITUTIONAL CONVENTION (1787)

Conklin, Wendy. Early Congresses, 1 vol. 2004. (Primary Source Readers Ser.). (ENG.). 24p. (J). (gr. 5-5). pap. 8.99 *(978-0-7439-8750-9(0))* Shell Educational Publishing.

Giddens, Sandra. A Timeline of the Constitutional Convention. 2009. (Timelines of American History Ser.). 32p. (gr. 4-4). 47.90 *(978-1-60854-382-3(X)*, Rosen Reference) Rosen Publishing Group, Inc., The.

Hughes, Chris. The Constitutional Convention. 2005. (People at the Center of Ser.). (Illus.). 48p. (J). (gr. -1-7). lib. bdg. 24.95 *(978-1-56711-918-3(2)*, Blackbirch Pr., Inc.) Cengage Gale.

Maestro, Betsy & Maestro, Giulio. A More Perfect Union: The Story of Our Constitution. 2008. (Illus.). 48p. (J). (gr. -1-3). 18.40 *(978-0-8335-6055-1(7)*, Turtleback) Turtleback Bks.

Ransom, Candice. George Washington & the Story of the U. S. Constitution. Reeves, Jeni, illus. 2011. (History Speaks: Picture Books Plus Reader's Theater Ser.). 48p. pap. 56.72 *(978-0-7613-7632-3(1))*; (ENG.). (gr. 2-4). 27.93 *(978-0-7613-5877-0(3)*, Millbrook Pr.); (ENG.). (gr. 2-4). pap. 9.95 *(978-0-7613-7116-8(8))* Lerner Publishing Group.

—Who Wrote the U. S. Constitution? And Other Questions about the Constitutional Convention of 1787. 2010. (Six Questions of American History Ser.). (ENG.). (gr. 4-6). pap. 56.72 *(978-0-7613-6949-3(X))*; 48p. pap. 9.95 *(978-0-7613-6126-8(X))*; 48p. lib. bdg. 30.60 *(978-1-58013-669-3(9))* Lerner Publishing Group.

Weston Woods Staff, creator. Shh! We're Writing the Constitution. 2011. 38.75 *(978-0-439-72886-7(X))* 2004. 18.95 *(978-1-55592-681-6(9))* 2004. 29.95 *(978-1-55592-682-3(7))* Weston Woods Studios, Inc.

UNITED STATES—CONSTITUTIONAL HISTORY

see Constitutional History—United States

UNITED STATES—CONSTITUTIONAL LAW

see Constitutional Law—United States

UNITED STATES—CONSULAR SERVICE

see United States—Diplomatic and Consular Service

UNITED STATES—CONTINENTAL CONGRESS

Adler, David A. A Picture Book of Patrick Henry. Wallner, John et al, illus. 2005. (ENG.). 32p. (J). (gr. k-3). pap. 6.95 *(978-0-8234-1678-3(X))* Holiday Hse., Inc.

Betti, Matthew. The Declaration of Independence & the Continental Congress. 2015. (Spotlight on American History Ser.). (ENG., Illus.). 24p. (J). (gr. 4-6). pap. 10.00 *(978-1-4994-1728-9(4)*, PowerKids Pr.) Rosen Publishing Group, Inc., The.

Conklin, Wendy. Early Congresses, 1 vol. 2004. (Primary Source Readers Ser.). (ENG.). 24p. (J). (gr. 5-5). pap. 8.99 *(978-0-7439-8750-9(0))* Shell Educational Publishing.

Espinosa, Rod. Patrick Henry, 1 vol. Espinosa, Rod, illus. 2007. (Bio-Graphics Ser.). (ENG., Illus.). 32p. (gr. 3-6). 28.50 *(978-1-60270-070-3(2)*, Graphic Planet- Nonfiction) ABDO Publishing Co.

Jarnow, Jesse. Patrick Henry's Liberty or Death Speech: A Primary Source Investigation. (Great Historic Debates & Speeches Ser.). 64p. 2009. (gr. 5-8). 58.50 *(978-1-61513-120-4(5))* 2004. (Illus.). (J). lib. bdg. 31.95 *(978-1-4042-0152-1(1))* Rosen Publishing Group, Inc., The.

Ransom, Candice. John Hancock. 2005. (History Maker Bios Ser.). (Illus.). 48p. (J). (gr. 3-4). 26.60 *(978-0-8225-1547-0(4)*, Lerner Pubns.) Lerner Publishing Group.

—What Was the Continental Congress? And Other Questions about the Declaration of Independence. 2011. (Six Questions of American History Ser.). (ENG.). 48p. (gr. 4-6). 30.60 *(978-0-7613-5227-3(9))*; pap. 9.95 *(978-0-7613-7135-9(4))*; pap. 56.72 *(978-0-7613-7642-2(9))* Lerner Publishing Group.

Rosaler, Maxine. A Timeline of the First Continental Congress. 2009. (Timelines of American History Ser.). 32p. (gr. 4-4). 47.90 *(978-1-60854-384-7(6)*, Rosen Reference) Rosen Publishing Group, Inc., The.

Welch, Catherine A. Patrick Henry. 2006. (History Maker Bios Ser.). (Illus.). 48p. (J). (gr. 3-6). lib. bdg. 26.60 *(978-0-8225-5941-2(2)*, Lerner Pubns.) Lerner Publishing Group.

UNITED STATES—DEBTS, PUBLIC

see Debts, Public

UNITED STATES—DECLARATION OF INDEPENDENCE

Adler, David A. & Adler, Michael S. A Picture Book of Sam Houston. Collins, Matt, illus. 2012. (ENG.). 32p. (J). (gr. -1-3). 17.95 *(978-0-8234-2369-9(7))* Holiday Hse., Inc.

—A Picture Book of Samuel Adams. Himler, Ronald, illus. 2005. (ENG.). 32p. (J). 16.95 *(978-0-8234-1846-6(4))* Holiday Hse., Inc.

Armentrout, David & Armentrout, Patricia. La Declaración de Independencia. 2005. (Documentos Que Formaron la Nacion Ser.). (Illus.). 48p. (J). (gr. 3-7). lib. bdg. 31.36 *(978-1-59515-644-0(5))* Rourke Educational Media.

Betti, Matthew. The Declaration of Independence & the Continental Congress. 2015. (Spotlight on American History Ser.). (ENG., Illus.). 24p. (J). (gr. 4-6). pap. 10.00 *(978-1-4994-1728-9(4)*, PowerKids Pr.) Rosen Publishing Group, Inc., The.

Bodden, Valerie. The Declaration of American Independence. 2009. (Days of Change Ser.). (Illus.). 48p. (YA). (gr. 4-7). 22.95 *(978-1-58341-733-1(8))* Creative Co., The.

Boyer, Marilyn. For you they Signed. 2010. (YA). lib. bdg. 34.99 *(978-0-89051-598-3(0))* Master Bks.

Castellano, Peter. The Declaration of Independence. 2017. (Look at U. S. History Ser.). 32p. (gr. 2-2). pap. 10.50 ***(978-1-4824-6031-5(9))*** Stevens, Gareth Publishing LLLP.

Clark, Willow. The True Story of the Declaration of Independence. 2013. (What Really Happened? Ser.). (ENG., Illus.). 24p. (J). (gr. 3-6). pap. 8.25 *(978-1-4488-9840-4(4))*; lib. bdg. 22.60 *(978-1-4488-9691-2(6))* Rosen Publishing Group, Inc., The. (PowerKids Pr.).

Clay, Kathryn. The Declaration of Independence: Introducing Primary Sources. 2017. (Introducing Primary Sources Ser.). (ENG.). 32p. (gr. 1-2). lib. bdg. 27.99 ***(978-1-5157-6355-0(2))*** Capstone Press of Coughlan Cos.

Coddington, Andrew. Thomas Jefferson: Architect of the Declaration of Independence. 2016. (Great American Thinkers Ser.). (Illus.). 128p. (J). (gr. 9-9). 45.64 *(978-1-5026-1924-2(5))* Cavendish Square Publishing.

Fingeroth, Danny. Democracy's Signature: Benjamin Franklin & the Declaration of Independence. 2009. (Great Moments in American History Ser.). 32p. (gr. 3-3). 47.90 *(978-1-61513-141-9(8))* Rosen Publishing Group, Inc., The.

Fink, Sam. The Declaration of Independence: The Words That Made America. Fink, Sam, illus. 2007. (Illus.). 160p. (YA). (gr. 7). 19.65 *(978-0-7569-8187-7(5))* Perfection Learning Corp.

Fradin, Dennis Brindell. The Declaration of Independence. 2006. (Turning Points in U. S. History Ser.). (Illus.). 46p. (J). (gr. 3-7). lib. bdg. 31.36 *(978-0-7614-2129-0(7)*, Benchmark Bks.) Marshall Cavendish Corp.

—The Signers: The 56 Stories Behind the Declaration of Independence. McCurdy, Michael, illus. 2003. (ENG.). 176p. (J). (gr. 5-18). 24.95 *(978-0-8027-8849-8(1)*, 9780802788498, Bloomsbury USA Childrens) Bloomsbury Publishing USA.

Furgang, Kathy. The Declaration of Independence & Benjamin Franklin of Pennsylvania. 2009. (Framers of the Declaration of Independence Ser.). 24p. (gr. 3-3). 42.50 *(978-1-61512-629-3(5)*, PowerKids Pr.) Rosen Publishing Group, Inc., The.

—The Declaration of Independence & Richard Henry Lee of Virginia. 2009. (Framers of the Declaration of Independence Ser.). 24p. (gr. 3-3). 42.50 *(978-1-61512-630-9(9)*, PowerKids Pr.) Rosen Publishing Group, Inc., The.

—The Declaration of Independence & Robert Livingston of New York. 2009. (Framers of the Declaration of Independence Ser.). 24p. (gr. 3-3). 42.50 *(978-1-61512-631-6(7)*, PowerKids Pr.) Rosen Publishing Group, Inc., The.

—The Declaration of Independence & Roger Sherman of Connecticut. 2009. (Framers of the Declaration of Independence Ser.). 24p. (gr. 3-3). 42.50 *(978-1-61512-632-3(5)*, PowerKids Pr.) Rosen Publishing Group, Inc., The.

—The Declaration of Independence & Thomas Jefferson of Virginia. 2009. (Framers of the Declaration of Independence Ser.). 24p. (gr. 3-3). 42.50 *(978-1-61512-633-0(3)*, PowerKids Pr.) Rosen Publishing Group, Inc., The.

Gagne, Tammy. Who Were the Signers of the Declaration of Independence? 2017. (Young America Ser.). (gr. 3-6). 29.95 *(978-1-61228-983-0(5))* Mitchell Lane Pubs., Inc.

Graves, Kerry A. The Declaration of Independence: The Story Behind America's Founding Document. 2003. (America in Words & Song Ser.). (Illus.). 32p. (gr. 4-6). 23.00 *(978-0-7910-7334-6(3)*, Chelsea Hse.) Facts On File, Inc.

Harris, Michael C. What Is the Declaration of Independence? Hoare, Jerry & McVeigh, Kevin, illus. 2016. (What Was? Ser.). (ENG.). 112p. (J). (gr. 3-7). lib. bdg. 15.99 *(978-0-399-54230-5(2)*, Grosset & Dunlap) Penguin Young Readers Group.

Hicks, Terry Allan. The Declaration of Independence. 2006. (Symbols of America Ser.). (Illus.). 40p. (gr. 3-7). lib. bdg. 20.95 *(978-0-7614-2135-1(1)*, Benchmark Bks.) Marshall Cavendish Corp.

Isaacs, Sally. Understanding the Declaration of Independence. 2008. (Documenting Early America Ser.). (ENG.). 32p. (J). (gr. 3-6). lib. bdg. *(978-0-7787-4371-2(3))* Crabtree Publishing Co.

Isaacs, Sally & Bedeksy, Baron. Understanding the Declaration of Independence. 2008. (Documenting Early America Ser.). (ENG.). 32p. (J). (gr. 3-6). pap. *(978-0-7787-4376-7(4))* Crabtree Publishing Co.

Jeffrey, Gary. Thomas Jefferson & the Declaration of Independence. 2011. (Graphic Heroes of the American Revolution Ser.). (Illus.). 24p. (J). (gr. 3-6). 23.95 *(978-1-4339-6025-3(7))*; pap. 8.15 *(978-1-4339-6026-0(5)*, Gareth Stevens Learning Library) Stevens, Gareth Publishing LLLP.

Kawa, Katie. The Declaration of Independence Wasn't Signed on July 4th: Exposing Myths about Independence Day. 2016. (Exposed! Myths about Early American History Ser.). 00032p. (J). pap. 10.50 ***(978-1-4824-5720-9(2))*** Stevens, Gareth Publishing LLLP.

Kerley, Barbara. Those Rebels, John & Tom. Fotheringham, Edwin, illus. 2012. (ENG.). 48p. (J). (gr. 2-5). 17.99 *(978-0-545-22268-6(0)*, Scholastic Pr.) Scholastic, Inc.

Krensky, Stephen. The Declaration of Independence. 2011. (Documents of Democracy Ser.). (Illus.). 96p. (J). (gr. 8). 34.21 *(978-0-7614-4913-3(2))* Marshall Cavendish Corp.

Landau, Elaine. The Declaration of Independence. 2008. (True Bks.). (ENG., Illus.). 48p. (J). (gr. 3-5). pap. 6.95 *(978-0-531-14780-1(0)*, Children's Pr.) Scholastic Library Publishing.

—The Declaration of Independence: American History. 2007. (True Bks.). (ENG., Illus.). 48p. (J). (gr. 3-5). lib. bdg. 29.00 *(978-0-531-12630-1(7)*, Children's Pr.) Scholastic Library Publishing.

Leavitt, Amie Jane. Declaration of Independence in Translation: What It Really Means. 2016. (Kids' Translations Ser.). (ENG.). 32p. (gr. 3-4). pap. 8.10 *(978-1-5157-6250-8(5)*, Fact Finders) Capstone Press of Coughlan Cos.

Leavitt, Amie Jane, et al. Kids' Translations. 2017. (Kids' Translations Ser.). (ENG.). 32p. (gr. 3-4). pap. 40.50 ***(978-1-5157-9765-4(1)***, Fact Finders) Capstone Press of Coughlan Cos.

Machajewski, Sarah. Declaration of Independence. 2016. (Documents of American Democracy Ser.). (Illus.). 32p. (J). (gr. 5-6). pap. 10.00 *(978-1-4994-2077-7(3)*, PowerKids Pr.) Rosen Publishing Group, Inc., The.

Manger, Katherine. The Declaration of Independence. 2016. (Let's Find Out! Primary Sources Ser.). 00032p. (J). (gr. 2-3). lib. bdg. 24.45 *(978-1-5081-0395-0(X))* Rosen Publishing Group, Inc., The.

Marcovitz, Hal. The Declaration of Independence. 2014. (Understanding American History). (ENG., Illus.). 96p. (J). lib. bdg. *(978-1-60152-736-3(5))* ReferencePoint Pr., Inc.

—The Declaration of Independence: Forming a New Nation. Moreno, Barry, ed. 2014. (Patriotic Symbols of America Ser.: 20). 48p. (J). (gr. 4-18). lib. bdg. 20.95 *(978-1-4222-3122-7(4))* Mason Crest.

McDaniel, Melissa. The Declaration of Independence. 2011. (Cornerstones of Freedom, Third Ser.). (Illus.). 64p. (J). (ENG.). pap. 8.95 *(978-0-531-26555-0(2))*; lib. bdg. 30.00 *(978-0-531-25030-3(X))* Scholastic Library Publishing. (Children's Pr.).

Meinking, Mary. The Declaration of Independence. 2016. (How America Works). (ENG.). 24p. (J). (gr. 3-6). 28.50 *(978-1-5038-0901-7(3)*, 210666) Child's World, Inc., The.

Metz, Lorijo. La Declaracin de Independencia / the Declaration of Independence, 1 vol., 1. Beullens-Maoui, Nathalie, ed. 2014. (¡Celebremos la Libertad! / Let's Celebrate Freedom! Ser.). (SPA, BYN & ENG., Illus.). 24p. (J). (gr. 3-6). 23.60 *(978-1-4777-3246-5(2)*, PowerKids Pr.) Rosen Publishing Group, Inc., The.

—The Declaration of Independence, 1 vol., 1. 2014. (Let's Celebrate Freedom! Ser.). (ENG.). 24p. (J). (gr. 3-6). 23.60 *(978-1-4777-2894-9(5)*, PowerKids Pr.) Rosen Publishing Group, Inc., The.

Micklos, John. The Making of the United States from Thirteen Colonies — Through Primary Sources. 2013. (American Revolution Through Primary Sources Ser.). 48p. (J). (gr. 4-18). 25.27 *(978-0-7660-4133-2(6))* Enslow Pubs., Inc.

—The Making of the United States from Thirteen Colonies—Through Primary Sources. 2013. (American Revolution Through Primary Sources Ser.). 48p. (J). (gr. 4-10). pap. 8.95 *(978-1-4644-0191-6(8))* Enslow Pubs., Inc.

Micklos, John & Micklos, John, Jr. From Thirteen Colonies to One Nation. 2008. (Revolutionary War Library). (Illus.). 48p. (J). (gr. 3-7). lib. bdg. 25.27 *(978-0-7660-3015-2(6)*, Enslow Elementary) Enslow Pubs., Inc.

Miller, Mirella S. 12 Questions about the Declaration of Independence. 2017. (Examining Primary Sources Ser.). (ENG., Illus.). 32p. (J). (gr. 3-6). 21.95 *(978-1-63235-283-5(4))* Pr. Room Editions LLC.

Morey, Allan. A Timeline History of the Declaration of Independence. 2014. (Timeline Trackers: America's Beginnings Ser.). (Illus.). 48p. (gr. 5-8). (J). lib. bdg. 30.60 *(978-1-4677-3640-4(6)*, Lerner Pubns.); pap. 9.95 *(978-1-4677-4571-0(5))* Lerner Publishing Group.

Mortensen, Lori. The Declaration of Independence, 1 vol. Skeens, Matthew, illus. 2009. (American Symbols Ser.). (ENG.). 24p. (gr. 1-2). lib. bdg. 26.65 *(978-1-4048-5165-8(8))* Picture Window Bks.

—Thomas Jefferson: A Founding Father of the United States of America, 1 vol. Ebert, Len, illus. 2008. (Biographies Ser.). (ENG.). 24p. (gr. k-3). lib. bdg. 26.65 *(978-1-4048-3729-4(9))* Picture Window Bks.

Mulhall, Jill K. Declaration of Independence, 1 vol. 2004. (Primary Source Readers Ser.). (SPA & ENG.). 24p. (J). (gr. 5-5). pap. 8.99 *(978-0-7439-8746-2(2))* Shell Educational Publishing.

Nardo, Don. The Declaration of Independence. 2003. (World History Ser.). (ENG., Illus.). 112p. (J). 34.95 *(978-1-59018-293-2(6)*, Lucent Bks.) Cengage Gale.

—The Declaration of Independence. 2006. (Illus.). 48p. (J). (gr. 4-8). reprint ed. 17.80 *(978-1-4223-5323-3(0))* DIANE Publishing Co.

Niver, Heather Moore. 20 Fun Facts about the Declaration of Independence. 2013. (Fun Fact File: US History! Ser.). 32p. (J). (gr. 3-6). pap. 10.50 *(978-1-4339-9184-4(5))*; pap. 63.00 *(978-1-4339-9185-1(3))* Stevens, Gareth Publishing LLLP.

Niver, Heather Moore & Moore Niver, Heather. 20 Fun Facts about the Declaration of Independence. 2013. 32p. (J). (gr. 3-6). 25.25 *(978-1-4339-9183-7(7))* Stevens, Gareth Publishing LLLP.

Osornio, Catherine L. The Declaration of Independence from A to Z, 1 vol. Johnson, Layne, illus. 2010. (ENG.). 32p. (J). (gr. 1-7). 16.99 *(978-1-58980-676-4(X))* Pelican Publishing Co., Inc.

Ransom, Candice. What Was the Continental Congress? And Other Questions about the Declaration of Independence. 2011. (Six Questions of American History Ser.). (ENG.). 48p. (gr. 4-6). 30.60 *(978-0-7613-5227-3(9))*; pap. 9.95 *(978-0-7613-7135-9(4))*; pap. 56.72 *(978-0-7613-7642-2(9))* Lerner Publishing Group.

Raum, Elizabeth. The Declaration of Independence, 1 vol. 2012. (Documenting U. S. History Ser.). (ENG.). 48p. (gr. 3-6). pap. 9.95 *(978-1-4329-6762-8(2))*; lib. bdg. 32.65 *(978-1-4329-6753-6(3))* Heinemann-Raintree. (NA-h).

Rissman, Rebecca. Declaration of Independence, 1 vol. 2013. (Foundations of Our Nation Ser.). 48p. (J). (ENG.). (gr. 3-6). lib. bdg. 32.79 *(978-1-61783-708-1(3))*; (Illus.). pap. 15.64 *(978-1-61783-758-6(X)*, Core Library) ABDO Publishing Co.

Sargent, Dave & Sargent, Pat. Duke: (Dappled Palomino) Good Behavior, 30 vols., Vol. 23. Lenoir, Jane, illus. 2003. (Saddle up Ser.: Vol. 23). 42p. (J). pap. 10.95 *(978-1-56763-682-6(9))*; lib. bdg. 23.60 *(978-1-56763-681-9(0))* Ozark Publishing.

St. George, Judith. The Journey of the One & Only Declaration of Independence. Hillenbrand, Will, illus. (ENG.). 48p. (J). (gr. 2-5). 2014. 8.99 *(978-0-14-751164-5(X)*, Puffin Books) 2005. 17.99 *(978-0-399-23738-6(0)*, Philomel Bks.) Penguin Young Readers Group.

—The Journey of the One & Only Declaration of Independence. Hillenbrand, Will, illus. 2011. (J). (gr. 1-7). 29.95 *(978-0-439-02760-1(8)*, WHCD806) Weston Woods Studios, Inc.

Stanton, Terence M. The Declaration of Independence. 2009. (Real Life Readers Ser.). 32p. (gr. 4-5). pap. 10.00 *(978-1-4358-0163-9(6)*, Rosen Classroom); 32p. (gr. 4-4). 47.90 *(978-1-61511-371-2(1)*, PowerKids Pr.); (J). pap. 60.00 *(978-1-4358-0164-6(4)*, PowerKids Pr.); (J). lib. bdg. 25.25 *(978-1-4358-2990-9(5)*, PowerKids Pr.) Rosen Publishing Group, Inc., The.

Steiner, Howard. The Declaration of Independence. 2012. 54p. pap. 14.95 *(978-1-105-24573-2(X))* Lulu Pr., Inc.

Swain, Gwenyth. Declaring Freedom: A Look at the Declaration of Independence, the Bill of Rights, & the Constitution. 2003. (How Government Works). (ENG., Illus.). 56p. (gr. 4-8). lib. bdg. 25.26 *(978-0-8225-1348-3(X))* Lerner Publishing Group.

—Documents of Freedom: A Look at the Declaration of Independence, the Bill of Rights, & the U. S. Constitution. 2012. (Searchlight Books How Does Government Work Ser.). (ENG., Illus.). 40p. (gr. 3-5). pap. 51.01 *(978-0-7613-9231-6(9))*; pap. 8.95 *(978-0-7613-8560-8(6))* Lerner Publishing Group.

—Documents of Freedom: A Look at the Declaration of Independence, the Bill of Rights, & the U.S. Constitution. 2012. (Searchlight Books How Does Government Work Ser.). (ENG., Illus.). 40p. (gr. 3-5). lib. bdg. 27.93 *(978-0-7613-6514-3(1))* Lerner Publishing Group.

Wolfe, James & Viegas, Jennifer. Understanding the Declaration of Independence. 2015. (Primary Sources of American Political Documents Ser.). (ENG., Illus.). 112p. (J). (gr. 7-7). 37.27 *(978-0-7660-6874-2(9))* Enslow Pubs., Inc.

Yero, Judith Lloyd. The Declaration of Independence. 2007. (Reading Expeditions Ser.). (ENG., Illus.). 32p. (J). pap. 17.95 *(978-0-7922-4554-4(7))* CENGAGE Learning.

UNITED STATES—DEFENSES

Beyer, Mark. Homeland Security & Weapons of Mass Destruction: How Prepared Are We? 2004. (Library of Weapons of Mass Destruction Ser.). (Illus.). 64p. (J). lib. bdg. 31.95 *(978-1-4042-0289-4(7))* Rosen Publishing Group, Inc., The.

—Nuclear Weapons & the Cold War. 2009. (Library of Weapons of Mass Destruction Ser.). 64p. (gr. 5-5). 58.50 *(978-1-60853-953-6(9))* Rosen Publishing Group, Inc., The.

Campbell, Geoffrey A. A Vulnerable America: An Overview of National Security. 2007. (Lucent Library of Homeland Security). (ENG., Illus.). 112p. (J). 30.85 *(978-1-59018-383-0(5)*, Lucent Bks.) Cengage Gale.

Keeter, Hunter. The U. S. Homeland Security Forces. 2004. (America's Armed Forces Ser.). (Illus.). 48p. (gr. 5-12). lib. bdg. 31.00 *(978-0-8368-5682-8(1)*, Gareth Stevens Secondary Library) Stevens, Gareth Publishing LLLP.

Meyer, Jared. Working in a War Zone: Military Contractors. 2006. (Extreme Careers Ser.). (Illus.). 64p. (J). (gr. 5-8). lib. bdg. 31.95 *(978-1-4042-0959-6(X))* Rosen Publishing Group, Inc., The.

Schuler, Harold H. Fort Sisseton. 2012. (Prairie Plains Ser.: No. 5). (Illus.). 283p. (Orig.). reprint ed. pap. 22.95 *(978-0-931170-62-1(1))* Ctr. for Western Studies.

UNITED STATES—DEPARTMENT OF AGRICULTURE

Rosaler, Maxine. The Department of Agriculture. (This Is Your Government Ser.). 64p. 2009. (gr. 5-6). 58.50 *(978-1-60854-362-5(5)*, Rosen Reference) 2006. (ENG., Illus.). (gr. 4-8). per. 12.95 *(978-1-4042-0659-5(0))* 2005. (Illus.). (J). (gr. k-3). lib. bdg. 31.95 *(978-1-4042-0206-1(4))* Rosen Publishing Group, Inc., The.

UNITED STATES—DEPARTMENT OF COMMERCE

Goldberg, Jan. The Department of Commerce. (This Is Your Government Ser.). 64p. 2009. (gr. 5-6). 58.50 *(978-1-60854-365-6(X)*, Rosen Reference) 2006. (ENG., Illus.). (gr. 4-8). per. 12.95 *(978-1-4042-0660-1(4))* 2005. (Illus.). (J). (gr. k-3). lib. bdg. 31.95 *(978-1-4042-0207-8(2))* Rosen Publishing Group, Inc., The.

UNITED STATES—DEPARTMENT OF DEFENSE

Ruffin, David C. The Duties & Responsibilities of the Secretary of Defense. (Your Government in Action Ser.). 32p. (gr. 3-3). 2009. 43.90 *(978-1-60854-915-3(1))* 2005. (Illus.). (J). lib. bdg. 23.95 *(978-1-4042-2689-0(3))* Rosen Publishing Group, Inc., The. (PowerKids Pr.).

—The Duties & Responsibilities of the Secretary of Education. 2005. (Your Government in Action Ser.). (Illus.). 32p. (J). lib. bdg. 23.95 *(978-1-4042-2692-0(3)*, PowerKids Pr.) Rosen Publishing Group, Inc., The.

UNITED STATES—DEPARTMENT OF HEALTH, EDUCATION, AND WELFARE

Ruffin, David C. The Duties & Responsibilities of the Secretary of Education. 2009. (Your Government in Action Ser.). 32p. (gr. 3-3). 43.90 *(978-1-60854-916-0(X)*, PowerKids Pr.) Rosen Publishing Group, Inc., The.

UNITED STATES—DEPARTMENT OF JUSTICE

Mattern, Joanne. Attorney General. 2003. (America's Leaders Ser.). (Illus.). 32p. (J). 24.94 *(978-1-56711-278-8(1)*, Blackbirch Pr., Inc.) Cengage Gale.

McElroy, Lisa Tucker. Alberto Gonzales: Attorney General. 2006. (Gateway Biographies Ser.). (Illus.). 48p. (J). (gr. 4-8). lib. bdg. 23.93 *(978-0-8225-3418-1(5))* Lerner Publishing Group.

UNITED STATES—DEPARTMENT OF LABOR

Casil, Amy Sterling. The Department of Labor. (This Is Your Government Ser.). 64p. 2009. (gr. 5-6). 58.50 *(978-1-60854-374-8(9)*, Rosen Reference) 2005. (Illus.). (J). (gr. k-3). lib. bdg. 31.95 *(978-1-4042-0210-8(2))* Rosen Publishing Group, Inc., The.

UNITED STATES—DEPARTMENT OF STATE

Alexander, Heather & dePaola, Tomie. Who Is Hillary Clinton? Harrison, Nancy & Putra, Dede, illus. 2016. (Who Was? Ser.). (ENG.). 112p. (J). (gr. 3-7). lib. bdg. 15.99 *(978-0-399-54234-3(5)*, Grosset & Dunlap) Penguin Young Readers Group.

Burgan, Michael. Hillary Clinton, 1 vol. 2014. (Extraordinary Women Ser.). (ENG.). 48p. (gr. 6-6). lib. bdg. 32.65 *(978-1-4109-5941-6(4))* Heinemann-Raintree.

Corey, Shana. Hillary Clinton: the Life of a Leader. Gustavson, Adam, illus. 2016. (Step into Reading Ser.). (ENG.). 48p. (J). (gr. k-3). 3.99 *(978-1-101-93235-3(X)*, Random Hse. Bks. for Young Readers) Random Hse. Children's Bks.

Fitzgerald, Stephanie. Hillary Clinton. rev. ed. 2017. (Rookie Biographies(tm) Ser.). (ENG., Illus.). 32p. (J). lib. bdg. 25.00 ***(978-0-531-22931-6(9))*** Scholastic Library Publishing.

Markel, Michelle. Hillary Rodham Clinton: Some Girls Are Born to Lead. Pham, LeUyen, illus. 2016. 40p. (J). (gr. -1-3). 17.99 *(978-0-06-238122-4(9))* HarperCollins Pubs.

Ruffin, David C. The Duties & Responsibilities of the Secretary of State. (Your Government in Action Ser.). 32p. (gr. 3-3). 2009. 43.90 *(978-1-60854-919-1(4))* 2005. (Illus.). (J). lib. bdg. 23.95 *(978-1-4042-2688-3(5))* Rosen Publishing Group, Inc., The. (PowerKids Pr.).

Sherman, Jill. Donald Trump: Outspoken Personality & President. 2017. (Gateway Biographies Ser.). (ENG., Illus.).

T U V

48p. (J). (gr. 4-8). lib. bdg. 26.65 *(978-1-5124-2596-3(6))* Lerner Publishing Group.

Winter, Jonah & Colón, Raúl. Hillary. 2016. (ENG., Illus.). 40p. (J). (gr. -1-3). 17.99 *(978-0-553-53388-0(6)*, Schwartz & Wade Bks.) Random Hse. Children's Bks.

UNITED STATES—DEPARTMENT OF THE TREASURY

Ruffin, David C. The Duties & Responsibilities of the Secretary of the Treasury. (Your Government in Action Ser.). 32p. (gr. 3-3). 2009. 43.90 *(978-1-60854-920-7(8))* 2005. (Illus.). (J). lib. bdg. 23.95 *(978-1-4042-2690-6(7))* Rosen Publishing Group, Inc., The. (PowerKids Pr.).

UNITED STATES—DESCRIPTION AND TRAVEL

ABC Travel Guides for Kids-Philadelphia. 2004. (J). per. 12.95 *(978-0-9760047-0-7(4))* Rosenberger, Matthew.

Acampora, Courtney. Sticker Road Trip: 50 States. Cramb, Sara Lynn, illus. 2017. (ENG.). 96p. (J). (gr. k). pap. 12.99 *(978-1-62686-706-2(2)*, Silver Dolphin Bks.) Readerlink Distribution Services, LLC.

Allen, Nancy. Northeast & Metropolitan Regions. 2014. (ENG.). 32p. (gr. 3-5). 32.79 *(978-1-62717-673-6(X))* Rourke Educational Media.

America the Beautiful, Third Series (Revised Edition) (Fall 2014 Set Of 26) 2014. (America the Beautiful, Third Ser. (Revised Edition) Ser.). (J). lib. bdg. 1040.00 *(978-0-531-27324-1(5))* Scholastic Library Publishing.

Andrews, Barbara. The Southeast Region. 2006. (J). pap. *(978-1-4108-6432-1(4))* Benchmark Education Co.

Barter, James. San Francisco in the 1960s. 2003. (Travel Guide To Ser.). (ENG., Illus.). 96p. (J). 30.85 *(978-1-59018-359-5(2)*, Lucent Bks.) Cengage Gale.

Beken, Robert A. Tijuana River Estuary & Border Field State Park: Land of diversity, land of Hope. l.t. ed. 2004. (Illus.). 260p. spiral bd. 34.95 *(978-0-9761726-0-4(7))* Tritium Pr.

Benchmark Education Company. The Northeast Region (Teacher Guide) 2005. *(978-1-4108-4660-0(1))* Benchmark Education Co.

Boyer, Crispin. National Geographic Kids Ultimate U. S. Road Trip Atlas: Maps, Games, Activities, & More for Hours of Backseat Fun. 2012. (ENG., Illus.). 128p. (J). (gr. 3-7). pap. 5.99 *(978-1-4263-0933-5(3))*; lib. bdg. 14.90 *(978-1-4263-0934-2(1))* National Geographic Society. (National Geographic Children's Bks.).

Cain, Marie Mowery. America the Beautiful. 2013. (Big Books, Red Ser.). (ENG & SPA., Illus.). 16p. pap. 33.00 *(978-1-59246-225-4(1))* Big Books, by George!

Carole Marsh. Atlanta Coloring. 2004. (City Bks.). 24p. (gr. k-5). pap., act. bk. ed. 3.95 *(978-0-635-02230-1(3))* Gallopade International.

Clawson, Calvin C. A Ride to the Infernal Regions: Yellowstone's First Tourists. Silliman, Lee, ed. 2003. per. 19.95 *(978-1-931832-18-2(8)*, 8667872363) Riverbend Publishing.

Cohen, Stephanie. The Northeast: Set Of 6. 2011. (Navigators Ser.). (J). pap. 48.00 net. *(978-1-4108-5102-4(8))* Benchmark Education Co.

Colorado Coloring Book. 2003. (J). *(978-0-9726022-0-4(8))* Mountain States Specialties.

Colorado Pocket Guide. 2003. (Illus.). 32p. (YA). 1.75 net. *(978-0-9726022-5-9(9))* Mountain States Specialties.

Columbia in Pictures. 2004. (Illus.). lib. bdg. 27.93 *(978-0-8225-1996-6(8))* Lerner Publishing Group.

Coming to America. (Illus.). (J). (gr. 3-6). 103.50 *(978-0-8239-7282-1(8)*, Reading Power) Rosen Publishing Group, Inc., The.

Corrigan, Jim. The 1930s Decade in Photos: Depression & Hope. 2010. (Amazing Decades in Photos Ser.). (Illus.). 64p. (J). (gr. 5-9). lib. bdg. 29.27 *(978-0-7660-3132-6(2))* Enslow Pubs., Inc.

—The 1940s Decade in Photos: A World at War. 2010. (Amazing Decades in Photos Ser.). (Illus.). 64p. (J). (gr. 5-9). lib. bdg. 29.27 *(978-0-7660-3133-3(0))* Enslow Pubs., Inc.

—The 1950s Decade in Photos: The American Decade. 2010. (Amazing Decades in Photos Ser.). (Illus.). 64p. (J). (gr. 5-9). lib. bdg. 29.27 *(978-0-7660-3134-0(9))* Enslow Pubs., Inc.

—The 1970s Decade in Photos: Protest & Change. 2010. (Amazing Decades in Photos Ser.). (Illus.). 64p. (J). (gr. 5-9). lib. bdg. 29.27 *(978-0-7660-3136-4(5))* Enslow Pubs., Inc.

—The 1980s Decade in Photos: The Triumph of Democracy. 2010. (Amazing Decades in Photos Ser.). (Illus.). 64p. (J). (gr. 5-9). lib. bdg. 29.27 *(978-0-7660-3137-1(3))* Enslow Pubs., Inc.

—The 1990s Decade in Photos: The Rise of Technology. 2010. (Amazing Decades in Photos Ser.). (Illus.). 64p. (J). (gr. 5-9). lib. bdg. 29.27 *(978-0-7660-3138-8(1))* Enslow Pubs., Inc.

—The 2000s Decade in Photos: A New Millennium. 2010. (Amazing Decades in Photos Ser.). (Illus.). 64p. (J). (gr. 5-9). lib. bdg. 29.27 *(978-0-7660-3139-5(X))* Enslow Pubs., Inc.

Crabtree Publishing Company Staff & Greil, Marlene. United States: The Land. 2012. (ENG.). 32p. (J). *(978-0-7787-9835-4(6))*; pap. *(978-0-7787-9838-5(0))* Crabtree Publishing Co.

DaSilva, Barbara, ed. Roosters. 2011. (Applewood's Pictorial America Ser.). (ENG., Illus.). 56p. pap. 9.95 *(978-1-60889-011-8(2))* Applewood Bks.

Ditchfield, Christin. The Lewis & Clark Expedition. 2006. (True Bks.). (ENG., Illus.). 48p. (J). (gr. 3-7). pap. 6.95 *(978-0-516-25222-3(4)*, Children's Pr.) Scholastic Library Publishing.

Egginton, Jane. Pick Your Brains about the USA. Williams, Caspar, illus. 2005. (Pick Your Brains - Cadogan Ser.). (ENG.). 128p. pap. 9.95 *(978-1-86011-222-5(6))* Cadogan Guides GBR. Dist: Globe Pequot Pr., The.

Espinosa, Rod. Lewis & Clark, 1 vol. Espinosa, Rod, illus. 2007. (Bio-Graphics Ser.). (ENG., Illus.). 32p. (gr. 3-6). 28.50 *(978-1-60270-069-7(9)*, Graphic Planet- Nonfiction) ABDO Publishing Co.

Gallardo, Yuri, ed. Houses & Apartments under 1000 Square Feet. 2013. (ENG., Illus.). 256p. pap. 24.95 *(978-1-77085-214-3(X)*, 9781770852143) Firefly Bks., Ltd.

Gamble, Adam. Good Night America. Chan, Suwin, illus. 2006. (Good Night Our World Ser.). (ENG.). 28p. (J). (gr. k — 1). bds. 9.95 *(978-0-9777979-0-5(2))* Good Night Bks.

Gamble, Adam & Jasper, Mark. Count to Sleep America. Veno, Joe, illus. 2015. (Count to Sleep Ser.). (ENG.). 20p. (J). (— 1). bds. 7.95 *(978-1-60219-231-7(6))* Good Night Bks.

—Good Night Illinois. 2013. (Good Night Our World Ser.). (ENG., Illus.). 20p. (J). (— 1). bds. 9.95 *(978-1-60219-086-3(0))* Good Night Bks.

Gondosch, Linda. Where Did Sacagawea Join the Corps of Discovery? And Other Questions about the Lewis & Clark Expedition. 2011. (Six Questions of American History Ser.). (ENG.). 48p. (gr. 4-6). lib. bdg. 30.60 *(978-0-7613-5226-6(0))* Lerner Publishing Group.

Group/McGraw-Hill, Wright. The United States Coast to Coast, 6 vols. (Book2WebTM Ser.). (gr. 4-8). 36.50 *(978-0-322-04443-2(X))* Wright Group/McGraw-Hill.

Hall, Hannah. God Bless Our Country, 1 vol. Whitlow, Steve, illus. 2016. (God Bless Book Ser.). (ENG.). 20p. (J). bds. 9.99 *(978-0-7180-4017-8(1))* Nelson, Thomas Inc.

Horowitz, Joseph. Dvoerak in America. 2003. (Illus.). x, 158p. (J). pap. 8.95 *(978-0-8126-2692-6(3))* Cricket Bks.

—Dvorak in America: In Search of the New World. 2003. (ENG., Illus.). 160p. (YA). 17.95 *(978-0-8126-2681-0(8))* Cricket Bks.

Houghton, Raymond C. A Revolutionary War Road Trip on US Route 202: Spend a Revolutionary Day along One of America's Most Historic Routes. 2004. (Illus.). 154p. per. 12.99 *(978-1-931373-13-5(2))* Cyber Haus.

—A Revolutionary War Road Trip on US Route 7: Spend a Revolutionary Day along One of America's Most Historic Routes. 2004. (Illus.). 150p. per. 12.99 *(978-1-931373-10-4(8))* Cyber Haus.

—A Revolutionary War Road Trip on US Route 9W: Spend a Revolutionary Day along One of America's Most Historic Routes. 2004. (Illus.). 174p. per. 12.99 *(978-1-931373-11-1(6))* Cyber Haus.

It's My State: Group 2, 6 vols. 2003. (YA). (gr. 3). lib. bdg. 162.43 *(978-0-7614-1521-3(1))* Marshall Cavendish Corp.

It's My State 5. 2nd rev. ed. 2013. (J). (gr. 4-8). 188.16 *(978-0-7614-7997-0(X))* Cavendish Square Publishing.

Jackson, Elaine. America. 2004. (QEB Travel Through Ser.). (Illus.). 32p. (J). lib. bdg. 18.95 *(978-1-59566-057-2(7))* QEB Publishing Inc.

Jackson, Robert B. The Remarkable Ride of the Abernathy Boys. 2003. (Land We Belong to Is Grand Ser.). (Illus.). 69p. (J). pap. *(978-1-57168-798-2(X)*, Eakin Pr.) Eakin Pr.

Keller, Susanna. The True Story of Lewis & Clark. 2013. (What Really Happened? Ser.). (ENG., Illus.). 24p. (J). (gr. 3-6). pap. 8.25 *(978-1-4488-9846-6(3))*; lib. bdg. 22.60 *(978-1-4488-9694-3(0))* Rosen Publishing Group, Inc., The. (PowerKids Pr.).

Lantos, James, ed. & compiled by. Benjamin Franklin. Lantos, James, compiled by. 2010. (Applewood's Pictorial America Ser.). (ENG., Illus.). 56p. pap. 9.95 *(978-1-60889-016-3(3))* Applewood Bks.

—Love: Vintage Images of America's Living Past. Lantos, James, compiled by. 2010. (Applewood's Pictorial America Ser.). (ENG.). 56p. pap. 9.95 *(978-1-60889-008-8(2))* Applewood Bks.

Leonardo, Victoria. The Northeast Region. 2005. (J). pap. *(978-1-4108-4612-9(1))* Benchmark Education Co.

Levy, Janey. Spanish Explorers of North America. 2009. (Real Life Readers Ser.). 32p. (gr. 4-5). pap. 10.00 *(978-1-4358-0171-4(7)*, Rosen Classroom) Rosen Publishing Group, Inc., The.

Linde, Barbara M. Traveling Around the United States: Learning to Add 2 Three-Digit Numbers Without Regrouping. 2009. (Math for the REAL World Ser.). 16p. (gr. 2-3). pap. 7.05 *(978-0-8239-8899-0(6)*, Rosen Classroom) Rosen Publishing Group, Inc., The.

Lonely Planet Publications Staff. U. S. A. Everything You Ever Wanted to Know, 1 vol. 2012. (Lonely Planet Kids Ser.). (ENG., Illus.). 96p. (J). pap. 14.99 *(978-1-74321-423-7(5)*, 4354) Lonely Planet Pubns.

Matrishon, Maible. Island Experiences - Adventures in Bocas Del Toro, on the Caribbean Coast of Panama. 2013. 40p. pap. *(978-0-9808653-9-4(5)*, Matrishon Media) Wider Vision Publishing.

Meachen Rau, Dana. Travel in American History. 2006. (How People Lived in America Ser.). (Illus.). 24p. (gr. 1-4). pap. 8.15 *(978-0-8368-7217-0(7)*, Weekly Reader Leveled Readers) Stevens, Gareth Publishing LLLP.

Morley, Jacqueline. You Wouldn't Want to... Be an American Pioneer! Antram, David, illus. rev. ed. 2012. (ENG.). (J). 40p. pap. 9.95 *(978-0-531-28025-6(X))*; 32p. lib. bdg. 29.00 *(978-0-531-27500-9(0))* Scholastic Library Publishing.

Murphy, Jim. Across America on an Emigrant Train. 2003. (ENG., Illus.). 168p. (J). (gr. 5-7). pap. 10.95 *(978-0-395-76483-1(1))* Houghton Mifflin Harcourt Publishing Co.

National Geographic Kids Staff. National Parks Guide U. S. A. The Most Amazing Sights, Scenes, & Cool Activities from Coast to Coast! 2012. (ENG., Illus.). 160p. (J). (gr. 2-4). pap. 14.95 *(978-1-4263-0931-1(7)*, National Geographic Children's Bks.) National Geographic Society.

National Geographic Society (U.S.) Staff, contrib. by. National Parks Guide U. S. A: The Most Amazing Sights, Scenes, & Cool Activities from Coast to Coast! 2012. (ENG., Illus.). 160p. (J). (gr. 2-4). lib. bdg. 21.90 *(978-1-4263-0932-8(5)*, National Geographic Children's Bks.) National Geographic Society.

Nelson, Ray & Nelson, Douglas. Greetings from America: Postcards from Donovan Willoughby. Tronslin, Andrea, ed. Nelson, Ray & Nelson, Douglas, illus. 2nd ed. (Illus.). 48p. (J). (gr. k-5). 14.95 *(978-1-56977-409-0(9))* Flying Rhinoceros, Inc.

Nikola-Lisa, W. America: A Book of Opposites/Un Libro de Contrarios. 14 Outstanding American Artists Staff, illus. 2013. (ENG & SPA.). 32p. (J). (gr. -1). bds. 8.95 *(978-1-58430-028-1(0))* Lee & Low Bks., Inc.

Otfinoski, Steven, et al. Exploring the 13 Colonies. 2016. (Exploring the 13 Colonies Ser.). (ENG.). 48p. (gr. 3-4). 415.87 *(978-1-5157-2398-1(4))* Capstone Press of Coughlan Cos.

Owens, Lisa. Southern Region. 2014. (ENG.). 32p. (gr. 3-5). 32.79 *(978-1-62717-675-0(6))* Rourke Educational Media.

—Southwestern Region. 2014. (ENG.). 32p. (gr. 3-5). 32.79 *(978-1-62717-668-2(3))* Rourke Educational Media.

Ray, Liz. Famous U. S. Landmarks, 6 vols., Set. 2004. (Phonics Readers Books 37-72 Ser.). (ENG.). 8p. (gr. k-1). pap. 35.70 *(978-0-7368-4067-5(2)*, Phonics Readers) Capstone Press of Coughlan Cos.

Redmond, Shirley Raye. Lewis & Clark: A Prairie Dog for the President. Manders, John, illus. 2003. (Step into Reading Ser.). 48p. 14.00 *(978-0-7569-1697-8(6))* Perfection Learning Corp.

—Lewis & Clark: A Prairie Dog for the President. Manders, John, illus. 2003. (Step into Reading Ser.: No. 3). (ENG.). 48p. (J). (gr. k-3). pap. 3.99 *(978-0-375-81120-3(6)*, Random Hse. Bks. for Young Readers) Random Hse. Children's Bks.

Road Trip: Exploring America's Regions. 2013. (Road Trip: Exploring America's Regions Ser.). 24p. (J). (gr. 2-5). 135.60 *(978-1-4339-9675-7(8))*; pap. 293.40 *(978-1-4339-9744-0(4))*; pap. 48.90 *(978-1-4339-9743-3(6))* Stevens, Gareth Publishing LLLP.

Rossi, Ann. The Southeast: Set Of 6. 2011. (Navigators Ser.). (J). pap. 48.00 net. *(978-1-4108-5103-1(6))* Benchmark Education Co.

Rowland, Wickie. Good Morning Piscataqua. 2014. (Illus.). 48p. (J). pap. 12.95 *(978-0-9603896-3-5(6))* Strawbery Banke Museum.

Sabuda, Robert. America the Beautiful. Sabuda, Robert, illus. 2004. (ENG., Illus.). 16p. (J). (gr. -1-3). 35.00 *(978-0-689-84744-8(0)*, Little Simon) Little Simon.

Saddleback Educational Publishing Staff, ed. Daniel Boone, 1 vol. unabr. ed. 2008. (Graphic Biographies Ser.). (ENG., Illus.). 25p. (YA). (gr. 9-12). pap. 7.95 *(978-1-59905-219-9(9))* Saddleback Educational Publishing, Inc.

Sasek, Miroslav. This Is America: A National Treasury. 2016. (ENG., Illus.). 80p. (J). (gr. 5). 19.95 *(978-0-7893-3258-5(2))* Universe Publishing.

Stout, Mary Gallagher & Gascot, John. Usa to Z. 2012. 60p. pap. 14.95 *(978-1-62006-161-9(9))* Sunbury Press, Inc.

Streissguth, Thomas. United States in Pictures. 2007. (Visual Geography (Lerner) Ser.). (Illus.). 80p. (YA). (gr. 7-12). lib. bdg. 31.93 *(978-0-8225-8567-1(7))* Twenty First Century Bks.

Suen, Anastasia. Great Plains Region. 2014. (ENG.). 32p. (gr. 3-5). 32.79 *(978-1-62717-670-5(5))* Rourke Educational Media.

—Gulf Coast Region. 2014. (ENG.). 32p. (gr. 3-5). 32.79 *(978-1-62717-672-9(1))* Rourke Educational Media.

—Mountain Region. 2014. (ENG., Illus.). 32p. (gr. 3-5). 32.79 *(978-1-62717-669-9(1))* Rourke Educational Media.

Sylvester, Alden W. Five Minutes in America a Voyage in Life. 2012. (ENG.). (J). pap. 13.95 *(978-1-4675-2936-5(2))* Independent Pub.

Tallarico, Tony. Across America. 2003. (Ultimate Hidden Pictures Ser.). (ENG., Illus.). 48p. (J). (gr. -1-3). 5.99 *(978-0-8431-0265-9(9)*, Price Stern Sloan) Penguin Young Readers Group.

Teacher Created Resources Staff. America: Come on a Journey of Discovery. 2008. (Qeb Travel Through Ser.). (ENG., Illus.). 32p. (gr. 4-7). pap. 7.99 *(978-1-4206-8277-9(6))* Teacher Created Resources, Inc.

Toufexis, George. U. S. A. Facts & Fun Activity Book. 2017. (Dover Children's Activity Bks.). (ENG.). 48p. (J). (gr. 3-6). pap. 4.99 *(978-0-486-81379-0(7))* Dover Pubns., Inc.

Vander Hook, Sue. West Coast Region. 2014. (ENG.). 32p. (gr. 3-5). 32.79 *(978-1-62717-667-5(5))* Rourke Educational Media.

Wilder, Laura Ingalls. A Little House Traveler: Writings from Laura Ingalls Wilder's Journeys Across America. 2011. (Little House Nonfiction Ser.). (ENG., Illus.). 368p. (J). (gr. 5). pap. 7.99 *(978-0-06-072492-4(7)*, Collins) HarperCollins Pubs.

Woodcock, John, illus. Color & Doodle Your Way Across the USA. 2013. 108p. *(978-1-78157-023-4(X)*, Ilex Pr.) Octopus Publishing Group.

Zschock, Martha Day. Hello, America! 2012. (ENG., Illus.). 16p. (J). (gr. -1-k). bds. 7.95 *(978-1-933212-88-3(8)*, Commonwealth Editions) Applewood Bks.

UNITED STATES—DESCRIPTION AND TRAVEL—MAPS

see United States—Maps

UNITED STATES—DIPLOMATIC AND CONSULAR SERVICE

Broderick, Kevin Joyce. The JipiJapa Hat. 2007. 124p. per. 12.95 *(978-0-595-45071-8(7))* iUniverse, Inc.

UNITED STATES—DISCOVERY AND EXPLORATION

see America—Discovery and Exploration; United States—Exploring Expeditions

UNITED STATES—ECONOMIC CONDITIONS

Amidon Lusted, Marcia. The Great Depression: Experience the 1930s from the Dust Bowl to the New Deal. Casteel, Tom, illus. 2016. (Inquire & Investigate Ser.). (ENG.). 128p. (J). (gr. 6-10). 22.95 *(978-1-61930-336-2(1)*, 1401073) Open City Bks.

—The Great Depression: Experience the 1930's from the Dust Bowl to the New Deal. Casteel, Tom, illus. 2016. (Inquire & Investigate Ser.). (ENG.). 128p. (J). (gr. 6-10). pap. 17.95 *(978-1-61930-340-9(X)*, 1401073) Octavio Publishing.

Bailey Association Staff, et al. Women of Today. 2011. (Cultural History of Women in America Ser.). (Illus.). 64p. (gr. 6-12). 35.00 *(978-1-60413-936-5(6)*, Chelsea Hse.) Facts On File, Inc.

Bair, Sheila. The Bullies of Wall Street: How Greedy Adults Messed up Our Economy. 2016. (ENG.). 288p. (YA). (gr. 7). pap. 11.99 *(978-1-4814-0086-2(X)*, Simon & Schuster Bks. For Young Readers) Simon & Schuster Bks. For Young Readers.

—The Bullies of Wall Street: This Is How Greedy Adults Messed up Our Economy. 2015. (ENG., Illus.). 272p. (YA). (gr. 7). 17.99 *(978-1-4814-0085-5(1)*, Simon & Schuster Bks. For Young Readers) Simon & Schuster Bks. For Young Readers.

Bezdecheck, Bethany. Bailout! Government Intervention in Business. 2010. (In the News Ser.). (ENG.). 64p. (YA). pap. 12.95 *(978-1-4488-1681-1(5))*; (gr. 7-12). lib. bdg. 31.95 *(978-1-4358-9449-5(9))* Rosen Publishing Group, Inc., The.

Bolden, Tonya. FDR's Alphabet Soup: New Deal America, 1932-1939. 2010. (ENG.). 144p. (YA). (gr. 7). 19.99 *(978-0-375-85214-5(X)*, Knopf Bks. for Young Readers) Random Hse. Children's Bks.

Brezina, Corona. America's Recession: The Effects of the Economic Downturn. 2011. (Headlines! Ser.). (ENG.). 64p. (YA). lib. bdg. 31.95 *(978-1-4488-1296-7(8))* Rosen Publishing Group, Inc., The.

—The Industrial Revolution in America: A Primary Source History of America's Transformation into an Industrial Society. (Primary Sources in American History Ser.). 64p. (gr. 5-8). 2009. 58.50 *(978-1-60851-497-7(8))* 2005. (Illus.). (YA). lib. bdg. 31.95 *(978-1-4042-0179-8(3))* Rosen Publishing Group, Inc., The.

Buckley, Susan Washburn & National Geographic Learning Staff. The Industrial Revolution. 2006. (Nonfiction Reading & Writing Workshops Ser.). (ENG., Illus.). 40p. (J). pap. 19.95 *(978-0-7922-8685-1(5))* CENGAGE Learning.

Burgan, Michael. American Capitalism. 2012. (ENG.). 64p. (J). lib. bdg. 30.00 *(978-0-531-23054-1(6))*; (gr. 4-6). pap. 8.95 *(978-0-531-28154-3(X))* Scholastic Library Publishing.

—The Great Depression: An Interactive History Adventure, 1 vol. (You Choose: Historical Eras Ser.). (ENG.). 112p. (gr. 3-4). 2011. pap. 6.95 *(978-1-4296-6276-5(X))* 2011. pap. 41.70 *(978-1-4296-6740-1(0))* 2010. 31.99 *(978-1-4296-5480-7(5))* Capstone Press of Coughlan Cos. (You Choose Bks.).

Coleman, Wim & Perrin, Pat. The Amazing Erie Canal & How a Big Ditch Opened up the West. 2006. (Wild History of the American West Ser.). (Illus.). 128p. (J). (gr. 5-9). lib. bdg. 34.60 *(978-1-59845-017-0(4)*, MyReportLinks.com Bks.) Enslow Pubs., Inc.

Cornerstones of Freedom & Trade 2013, Set. 2013. (Cornerstones of Freedom™, Third Ser.). (J). 300.00 *(978-0-531-23848-6(2)*, Children's Pr.) Scholastic Library Publishing.

Craats, Rennay. Economy. 2008. (USA Past Present Future Ser.). (Illus.). 48p. (J). (gr. 4-6). pap. 10.95 *(978-1-59036-981-4(5))*; lib. bdg. 29.05 *(978-1-59036-980-7(7))* Weigl Pubs., Inc.

Crayton, Lisa A. & Nagle, Jeanne. Recession: What It Is & How It Works. 2016. (Economics in the 21st Century Ser.). (ENG., Illus.). 96p. (J). (gr. 8-8). lib. bdg. 34.60 *(978-0-7660-7356-2(4)*, 1399425) Enslow Pubs., Inc.

Desenfants, Millie. Long Ago Sally. 2011. 28p. pap. 15.99 *(978-1-4628-7305-0(7))* Xlibris Corp.

Fankford, Ronald, Jr. What Is the Future of the U. S. Economy? Lankford, Ronnie D., ed. 2012. (At Issue Ser.). (ENG.). 128p. (gr. 10-12). lib. bdg. 39.40 *(978-0-7377-6213-6(6)*, Greenhaven Pr., Inc.) Cengage Gale.

Freedman, Jeri. The U.S. Auto Industry: American Carmakers & the Economic Crisis. 2010. (In the News Ser.). (ENG.). 64p. (YA). pap. 12.95 *(978-1-4488-1680-4(7))*; (gr. 7-12). lib. bdg. 31.95 *(978-1-4358-9448-8(0))* Rosen Publishing Group, Inc., The.

Fremon, David K. The Great Depression in United States History. 2014. (In United States History Ser.). 96p. (J). (gr. 5-12). 27.94 *(978-0-7660-6087-6(X))*; (Illus.). pap. 10.95 *(978-0-7660-6088-3(8))* Enslow Pubs., Inc.

Frohnapfel-Krueger, Lisa. Does Outsourcing Harm America? 2010. (At Issue Ser.). (Illus.). 128p. pap. 24.45 *(978-0-7377-4674-7(2))*; (YA). (gr. 7-18). 34.45 *(978-0-7377-4673-0(4))* Cengage Gale. (Greenhaven Pr., Inc.).

Garstecki, Julia. Life During the Industrial Revolution, 1 vol. 2014. (Daily Life in US History Ser.). (ENG.). 48p. (gr. 3-6). lib. bdg. 32.79 *(978-1-62403-627-9(9))* ABDO Publishing Co.

Gedney, Mona K. The Story of the Great Depression. 2005. (Monumental Milestones Ser.). (Illus.). 48p. (YA). (gr. 4-7). lib. bdg. 29.95 *(978-1-58415-403-7(9))* Mitchell Lane Pubs., Inc.

George, Linda & George, Charles. The Great Depression. 2013. (Illus.). 96p. (J). lib. bdg. *(978-1-60152-492-8(7))* ReferencePoint Pr., Inc.

Gow, Mary. The Stock Market Crash Of 1929: Dawn of the Great Depression. 2003. (American Disasters Ser.). (Illus.). 48p. (J). lib. bdg. 23.93 *(978-0-7660-2111-2(4))* Enslow Pubs., Inc.

Grant, R. G. The Great Depression. 2005. (How Did It Happen? Ser.). (ENG., Illus.). 48p. (YA). (gr. 7-10). lib. bdg. 32.10 *(978-1-59018-606-0(0)*, Lucent Bks.) Cengage Gale.

—Why Did the Great Depression Happen? 2010. (Moments in History Ser.). (Illus.). 48p. (YA). (gr. 6-8). lib. bdg. 31.95 *(978-1-4339-4169-6(4))*; (gr. 6-8). pap. 14.05 *(978-1-4339-4170-2(8)*, Gareth Stevens Secondary Library) Stevens, Gareth Publishing LLLP.

Grayson, Robert. The U. S. Industrial Revolution, 1 vol. 2010. (Essential Events Set 5 Ser.). (ENG.). 112p. (J). (gr. 6-12). lib. bdg. 35.64 *(978-1-61613-687-1(1))* ABDO Publishing Co.

The Great Depression 1929-1938. 2010. (Discovering U. S. History Ser.). (Illus.). 136p. (gr. 5-8). 35.00 *(978-1-60413-357-8(0)*, Chelsea Hse.) Facts On File, Inc.

Gregory, Joy. The Great Depression. 2016. (Illus.). 48p. (J). *(978-1-5105-1286-3(1))* SmartBook Media, Inc.

Gunderson, Cory. Great Depression, 1 vol. 2004. (American Moments Ser.). (ENG.). 48p. (gr. 4-8). 27.07 *(978-1-59197-286-0(8)*, Abdo & Daughters) ABDO Publishing Co.

Hakim, Joy. An Age of Extremes, 1880-1917. 2nd rev. ed. 2007. (History of US Ser.: Vol. 8). (ENG., Illus.). 224p. (gr. 4-7). per. 15.95 *(978-0-19-532722-9(5))* Oxford Univ. Pr., Inc.

Hamilton, Jill. The U. S. Economy. 2010. (Introducing Issues with Opposing Viewpoints Ser.). (ENG.). 144p. (gr. 7-10). 42.00 *(978-0-7377-4945-8(8)*, Greenhaven Pr., Inc.) Cengage Gale.

Haugen, David M. Should the U. S. Reduce Its Consumption? 2010. (At Issue Ser.). (ENG.). 128p. (gr. 10-12). 39.40 *(978-0-7377-4894-9(X))*; pap. 27.80 *(978-0-7377-4895-6(8)*, Greenhaven Pr., Inc.) Cengage Gale.

Haugen, David M., et al. The Great Depression. 2010. (Perspectives on Modern World History Ser.). (Illus.). 224p. (YA). (gr. 10-12). 42.45 *(978-0-7377-4795-9(1)*, Greenhaven Pr., Inc.) Cengage Gale.

Hill, Jeff. The WPA— Putting America to Work. 2013. (Defining Moments Ser.). (ENG.). 264p. lib. bdg. 55.00 *(978-0-7808-1331-1(6))* Omnigraphics, Inc.

Hurt, Avery. The Great Depression. 2017. (J). *(978-1-5026-2713-1(2))* Cavendish Square Publishing.

Industrialism. 2010. (Key Concepts in American History Ser.). (Illus.). 128p. (gr. 6-12). 45.00 *(978-1-60413-222-9(1)*, Chelsea Hse.) Facts On File, Inc.

Ingram, Scott. The Stock Market Crash of 1929. 2004. (Landmark Events in American History Ser.). (Illus.). 48p. (gr. 5-12). pap. 14.05 *(978-0-8368-5425-1(X)*, Gareth Stevens Secondary Library) Stevens, Gareth Publishing LLLP.

Kleinmartin, Hex. The Erie Canal. 2016. (Expanding America Ser.). (ENG., Illus.). 96p. (J). (gr. 8-8). lib. bdg. 42.79 *(978-1-5026-0966-3(5))* Cavendish Square Publishing.

Lange, Brenda. The Stock Market Crash Of 1929: The End of Prosperity. 2007. (Milestones in American History Ser.). (Illus.). 114p. (YA). (gr. 7-12). lib. bdg. 35.00 *(978-0-7910-9354-2(9))* Facts On File, Inc.

Lanier, Wendy H. Life During the Great Depression, 1 vol. 2014. (Daily Life in US History Ser.). (ENG., Illus.). 48p. (J). (gr. 3-6). lib. bdg. 32.79 *(978-1-62403-626-2(0))* ABDO Publishing Co.

Lankford, Ronnie D., ed. What Is the Future of the U. S. Economy? 2012. (At Issue Ser.). (ENG.). 128p. (gr. 10-12). pap. 27.80 *(978-0-7377-6214-3(4),* Greenhaven Pr., Inc.) Cengage Gale.

Lawrence, Katherine. Labor Legislation: The Struggle to Gain Rights for America's Workforce. (Progressive Movement 1900-1920: Efforts to Reform America's New Industrial Society Ser.). 32p. 2009. (gr. 3-4). 47.90 *(978-1-60854-166-9(5))* 2004. (Illus.). (YA). (gr. 5-9). lib. bdg. 22.50 *(978-1-4042-0191-0(2))* Rosen Publishing Group, Inc., The.

Marsh, Carole. Industrial Revolution from Muscles to Machines! 2004. (American Milestones Ser.). (Illus.). 28p. (J). (gr. 4-12). pap. 5.95 *(978-0-635-02694-1(5))* Gallopade International.

—Industrial Revolution Reproducible Activity Book (HC) 2004. 28p. (gr. 4-12). 29.95 *(978-0-635-02695-8(3))* Gallopade International.

Mattern, Joanne. Florida's Economy: From the Mouse to the Moon. 2016. (Primary Source Readers Ser.). (Illus.). 32p. (J). (gr. 4-4). pap. 8.99 *(978-1-4938-3548-5(3))* Teacher Created Materials, Inc.

McCormick, Anita Louise. The Industrial Revolution in United States History. 2014. (In United States History Ser.). (Illus.). 96p. (J). (gr. 5-12). 27.94 *(978-0-7660-6102-6(7));* pap. 10.95 *(978-0-7660-6103-3(5))* Enslow Pubs., Inc.

McNeilly, Linden K. Perspectives on the Great Depression. 2018. (ENG.). 32p. (gr. 3-6). ***(978-1-63235-401-3(2),*** 12-Story Library) Pr. Room Editions LLC.

Miller, Debra A. The U. S. Economy. 2010. (Current Controversies Ser.). (Illus.). 240p. (J). 40.95 *(978-0-7377-4711-9(0),* Greenhaven Pr., Inc.) Cengage Gale.

Mooney, Carla. Perspectives on the Industrial Revolution. 2018. (ENG.). 32p. (gr. 3-6). ***(978-1-63235-402-0(0),*** 12-Story Library) Pr. Room Editions LLC.

Peterson, Sheryl. The Great Depression & World War II. 2011. (Explorer Library: Language Arts Explorer Ser.). (ENG.). 32p. (gr. 4-8). pap. 14.21 *(978-1-61080-287-1(X),* 201210); lib. bdg. 28.50 *(978-1-61080-199-7(7),* 201174) Cherry Lake Publishing.

Quinby, Michelle. Connecting the 21st Century to the Past: What Makes America America, 2000-The Present. 2013. (Illus.). 48p. (J). pap. *(978-1-4222-2423-6(6))* Mason Crest.

—Connecting the 21st Century to the Past: What Makes America America, 2000-The Present. Rakove, Jack N., ed. 2012. (How America Became America Ser.). (Illus.). 48p. (J). (gr. 3-4). 19.95 *(978-1-4222-2409-0(0))* Mason Crest.

Reis, Ronald A. The Great Depression & the New Deal: America's Economy in Crisis. 2011. (Milestones in American History Ser.). (Illus.). 150p. (gr. 6-12). 35.00 *(978-1-60413-766-8(5),* Chelsea Hse.) Facts On File, Inc.

Riggs, Kate. The Great Recession. 2016. 48p. (J). *(978-1-60818-749-2(7),* Creative Education) Creative Co., The.

Ripped from the Headlines, 10 bks., Set. Incl. Downloading Music. Allman, Toney. (J). 23.95 *(978-1-60217-006-3(1));* Fat in America. Stewart, Gail. (J). 23.95 *(978-1-60217-002-5(9));* Gas Crisis. Kallan, Stuart A. (YA). 23.95 *(978-1-60217-001-8(0));* Illegal Immigration. Stewart, Gail. (J). 23.95 *(978-1-60217-003-2(7));* Internet Predators. Allman, Toney. (J). 23.95 *(978-1-60217-000-1(2));* Nuclear Weapons. Sheen, Barbara. (YA). 23.95 *(978-1-60217-004-9(5));* Outsourcing America. Currie, Stephen. (J). 23.95 *(978-1-60217-008-7(8));* Reality TV. Woog, Adam. (YA). 23.95 *(978-1-60217-005-6(3));* Street Crime. Parks, Peggy. (Illus.). (YA). 23.95 *(978-1-60217-007-0(X));* Your Sexuality. Hirschmann, Kris. (YA). 23.95 *(978-1-60217-009-4(6));* 64p. (gr. 7-12). 2007. 214.95 *(978-1-60217-010-0(X))* Erickson Pr.

Robinson, Tom. The Development of the Industrial United States: 1870-1900. 2007. (Presidents of the United States Ser.). (Illus.). 48p. (J). (gr. 4-7). lib. bdg. 29.05 *(978-1-59036-745-2(6))* Weigl Pubs., Inc.

—Development of the Industrial United States: 1870-1900. 2007. (Presidents of the United States Ser.). (Illus.). 48p. (J). (gr. 4-7). per. 10.95 *(978-1-59036-746-9(4))* Weigl Pubs., Inc.

Roza, Greg. America's Transition from Agriculture to Industry: Drawing Inferences & Conclusions. (Critical Thinking in American History Ser.). 48p. 2009. (gr. 5-8). 53.00 *(978-1-61512-087-1(4),* Rosen Reference) 2005. (Illus.). (J). (gr. k-3). lib. bdg. 29.25 *(978-1-4042-0410-2(5))* Rosen Publishing Group, Inc., The.

Smith, Robert W. Spotlight on America: Industrial Revolution. 2006. (ENG., Illus.). 48p. pap. 9.99 *(978-1-4206-3220-0(5))* Teacher Created Resources, Inc.

South, Victor. America in the 20th Century (1913-1999) 2013. (Illus.). 48p. (J). *(978-1-4222-2410-6(4));* *(978-1-4222-2396-3(5))* Mason Crest.

Stein, R. Conrad. The Industrial Revolution: Manufacturing a Better America. 2006. (American Saga Ser.). (Illus.). 128p. (J). (gr. 5-12). lib. bdg. 31.93 *(978-0-7660-2571-4(3))* Enslow Pubs., Inc.

Wolfe, James. The Industrial Revolution: Steam & Steel. 2015. (Age of Revolution Ser.). (ENG., Illus.). 128p. (J). (gr. 9-10). 35.25 *(978-1-68048-026-9(X),* Britannica Educational Publishing) Rosen Publishing Group, Inc., The.

World Book, Inc Staff, contrib. by. The Great Depression. 2010. (J). *(978-0-7166-1505-7(3))* World Bk., Inc.

UNITED STATES—ECONOMIC POLICY

Bolden, Tonya. FDR's Alphabet Soup: New Deal America, 1932-1939. 2010. (ENG.). 144p. (YA). (gr. 7). 19.99 *(978-0-375-85214-5(X),* Knopf Bks. for Young Readers) Random Hse. Children's Bks.

Brezina, Corona. America's Recession: The Effects of the Economic Downturn. 2011. (Headlines! Ser.). (ENG.). 64p. (YA). lib. bdg. 31.95 *(978-1-4488-1296-7(8))* Rosen Publishing Group, Inc., The.

—How Stimulus Plans Work. 2010. (Real World Economics Ser.). (Illus.). 80p. (YA). (gr. 7-18). lib. bdg. 33.25 *(978-1-4358-9464-8(2))* Rosen Publishing Group, Inc., The.

Crayton, Lisa A. & Nagle, Jeanne. Recession: What It Is & How It Works. 2016. (Economics in the 21st Century Ser.). (ENG., Illus.). 96p. (J). (gr. 8-8). lib. bdg. 34.60 *(978-0-7660-7356-2(4),* 1399425) Enslow Pubs., Inc.

Gitlin, Martin. U. S. Sanctions on Cuba, 1 vol. 2010. (Essential Viewpoints Set 5 Ser.). (ENG., Illus.). 112p. (J). (gr. 6-12). lib. bdg. 35.64 *(978-1-61613-525-6(5),* 1315619, Essential Library) ABDO Publishing Co.

Hamilton, Jill. The U. S. Economy. 2010. (Introducing Issues with Opposing Viewpoints Ser.). (ENG.). 144p. (gr. 7-10). 42.00 *(978-0-7377-4945-8(8),* Greenhaven Pr., Inc.) Cengage Gale.

Haugen, David M. Should the Federal Government Bail Out Private Industry? 2010. (At Issue Ser.). (Illus.). 128p. (J). 34.45 *(978-0-7377-4656-3(4));* pap. 24.45 *(978-0-7377-4657-0(2))* Cengage Gale. (Greenhaven Pr., Inc.).

Heinrichs, Ann. The Great Recession. 2011. (Cornerstones of Freedom, Third Ser.). (ENG., Illus.). 64p. (J). pap. 8.95 *(978-0-531-26560-4(9),* Children's Pr.) Scholastic Library Publishing.

Hunnicutt, Susan C. The Federal Budget Deficit. 2010. (At Issue Ser.). (Illus.). 128p. pap. 24.45 *(978-0-7377-4686-0(6),* Greenhaven Pr., Inc.) Cengage Gale.

Miller, Debra A. The U. S. Economy. 2010. (Current Controversies Ser.). (Illus.). 240p. (J). pap. 28.45 *(978-0-7377-4712-6(9),* Greenhaven Pr., Inc.) Cengage Gale.

Moriarty, J. T. The Rise of American Capitalism: The Growth of American Banks. 2009. (America's Industrial Society in the 19th Century Ser.). 32p. (gr. 4-4). 47.90 *(978-1-61511-346-0(0))* Rosen Publishing Group, Inc., The.

Randolph, Ryan. Alexander Hamilton's Economic Plan: Solving Problems in America's New Economy. 2009. (Life in the New American Nation Ser.). 32p. (gr. 4-4). 47.90 *(978-1-61514-276-7(2))* Rosen Publishing Group, Inc., The.

UNITED STATES—EMIGRATION AND IMMIGRATION

Alvarez, Pilar. New Jobs, New Opportunities: British Immigrants Arrive in America (1830s-1890s), 01 vols., 1. 2016. (Spotlight on Immigration & Migration Ser.). (ENG., Illus.). 24p. (J). pap. 10.00 *(978-1-5081-4090-0(1),* PowerKids Pr.) Rosen Publishing Group, Inc., The.

Ambrosek, Renee. America Debates United States Policy on Immigration. (America Debates Ser.). 64p. (gr. 5-6). 2009. 58.50 *(978-1-61511-335-4(5),* Rosen Reference) 2007. (Illus.). (YA). lib. bdg. 31.95 *(978-1-4042-1924-3(2))* Rosen Publishing Group, Inc., The.

The American Mosaic: Immigration Today. 2014. (American Mosaic: Immigration Today Ser.). 24p. (J). (gr. 3-6). 141.60 *(978-1-4777-6653-8(7));* pap. 49.50 *(978-1-4777-7248-5(0))* Rosen Publishing Group, Inc., The. (PowerKids Pr.).

American Voices - Group 2, 6 bks., Set. 205.29 *(978-0-7614-1200-7(X),* Benchmark Bks.) Marshall Cavendish Corp.

Anderson, Dale. Chinese Americans. 2006. (World Almanac Library of American Immigration). (Illus.). 48p. (gr. 5-12). pap. 14.05 *(978-0-8368-7321-4(1));* lib. bdg. 31.00 *(978-0-8368-7308-5(4))* Stevens, Gareth Publishing LLLP. (Gareth Stevens Secondary Library).

—Cuban Americans. 2006. (World Almanac Library of American Immigration). (Illus.). 48p. (gr. 5-12). pap. 14.05 *(978-0-8368-7322-1(X));* lib. bdg. 31.00 *(978-0-8368-7309-2(2))* Stevens, Gareth Publishing LLLP. (Gareth Stevens Secondary Library).

—Italian Americans. 2006. (World Almanac Library of American Immigration). 48p. (gr. 5-12). pap. 14.05 *(978-0-8368-7325-2(4));* (Illus.). lib. bdg. 31.00 *(978-0-8368-7312-2(2))* Stevens, Gareth Publishing LLLP. (Gareth Stevens Secondary Library).

—Japanese Americans. 2006. (World Almanac Library of American Immigration). (Illus.). 48p. (gr. 5-12). pap. 14.05 *(978-0-8368-7326-9(2));* lib. bdg. 31.00 *(978-0-8368-7313-9(0))* Stevens, Gareth Publishing LLLP. (Gareth Stevens Secondary Library).

—Polish Americans. 2006. (World Almanac Library of American Immigration). (Illus.). 48p. (gr. 5-12). pap. 14.05 *(978-0-8368-7330-6(0));* lib. bdg. 31.00 *(978-0-8368-7317-7(3))* Stevens, Gareth Publishing LLLP. (Gareth Stevens Secondary Library).

Anderson, Marilyn D. Arab Americans. 2006. (World Almanac Library of American Immigration). (Illus.). 48p. (gr. 5-12). lib. bdg. 31.00 *(978-0-8368-7307-8(6),* Gareth Stevens Secondary Library) Stevens, Gareth Publishing LLLP.

Anderson, Stuart, ed. The Changing Face of America: Immigration Since 1965, 16 vols., Set. 2003. (Illus.). 112p. (YA). lib. bdg. *(978-1-59084-679-7(6))* Mason Crest.

Arnéz, Lynda. My Journey Through Ellis Island. 2016. (My Place in History Ser.). (ENG., Illus.). 24p. (J). (gr. 2-3). 22.60 *(978-1-4824-4000-3(8))* Stevens, Gareth Publishing LLLP.

Aykroyd, Clarissa. Refugees. 2005. (Changing Face of North America Ser.). (Illus.). 112p. (YA). lib. bdg. 24.95 *(978-1-59084-692-6(3))* Mason Crest.

Baker, Brynn. Life in America: Comparing Immigrant Experiences. 2015. (U. S. Immigration in The 1900s Ser.). (ENG., Illus.). 48p. (gr. 3-4). pap. 8.95 *(978-1-4914-4174-9(7))* Capstone Press of Coughlan Cos.

Baker, Brynn & Kravitz, Danny. U. S. Immigration in The 1900s. 2015. (U. S. Immigration in The 1900s Ser.). (ENG.). (gr. 3-4). 114.61 *(978-1-4914-6658-2(8),* Connect) Stone Arch Bks.

Barnett, Tracy. Immigration from South America. 2005. (Changing Face of North America Ser.). (Illus.). 112p. (YA). lib. bdg. 24.95 *(978-1-59084-687-2(7))* Mason Crest.

Bausum, Ann. Denied, Detained, Deported: Stories from the Dark Side of American Immigration. 2009. (ENG., Illus.). 112p. (J). (gr. 5). lib. bdg. 32.90 *(978-1-4263-0333-3(5));* 21.95 *(978-1-4263-0332-6(7))* National Geographic Society. (National Geographic Children's Bks.).

Benoit, Peter. Immigration. 2012. (Cornerstones of Freedom, Third Ser.). (ENG., Illus.). 64p. (J). pap. 8.95 *(978-0-531-28157-4(4));* (gr. 4-6). lib. bdg. 30.00 *(978-0-531-23057-2(0))* Scholastic Library Publishing. (Children's Pr.).

Benson, Sonia. U. S. Immigration & Migration: Almanac, 2.0. 2004. (US Immigration & Migration Reference Library). (ENG., Illus.). 685p. (J). 191.00 *(978-0-7876-7732-9(9),* UXL) Cengage Gale.

—U.S. Immigration & Migration Almanac, 2 vols. 2004. (U. S. Immigration & Migration Reference Library). (Illus.). (J). *(978-0-7876-7566-0(0)); (978-0-7876-7567-7(9))* Cengage Gale. (UXL).

Berger, Melvin. Where Did Your Family Come From? (Discovery Readers Ser.). (ENG.). 48p. (J). pap. 3.95 *(978-0-8249-5320-1(7),* Ideal Pubns.) Worthy Publishing.

Bjorklund, Ruth. Immigration. 2011. (Debating the Issues Ser.). 64p. (gr. 6). 32.79 *(978-0-7614-4973-7(6))* Marshall Cavendish Corp.

Bliss, John. Nineteenth Century Migration to America, 1 vol. 2011. (Children's True Stories: Migration Ser.). (ENG.). 32p. (gr. 3-3). pap. 8.29 *(978-1-4109-4080-3(2),* Raintree Perspectives) Heinemann-Raintree.

Broida, Marian. Projects about Nineteenth-Century European Immigrants. 2005. (Hands-On History Ser.). (Illus.). 48p. (J). (gr. 3-7). lib. bdg. *(978-0-7614-1980-8(2),* Benchmark Bks.) Marshall Cavendish Corp.

Bryan, Nichol. Greek Americans, 1 vol. 2004. (One Nation Set 2 Ser.). (ENG.). 32p. (gr. k-6). 27.07 *(978-1-59197-527-4(1),* Checkerboard Library) ABDO Publishing Co.

—Japanese Americans, 1 vol. 2004. (One Nation Set 2 Ser.). (ENG.). 32p. (gr. k-6). 27.07 *(978-1-59197-529-8(8),* Checkerboard Library) ABDO Publishing Co.

Budhos, Marina. Remix: Conversations with Immigrant Teenagers. 2007. (Illus.). 158p. (gr. 9-12). pap. 20.00 *(978-1-55635-610-0(2))* Wipf & Stock Pubs.

Burgan, Michael. Ellis Island: An Interactive History Adventure, 1 vol. 2013. (You Choose: History Ser.). (ENG.). 112p. (gr. 3-4). pap. 6.95 *(978-1-4765-3606-4(6));* 31.99 *(978-1-4765-0253-3(6))* Capstone Press of Coughlan Cos. (You Choose Bks.).

Byers, Ann. The History of U. S. Immigration: Coming to America. 2006. (American Saga Ser.). (Illus.). 128p. (J). (gr. 5). lib. bdg. 33.27 *(978-0-7660-2574-5(8))* Enslow Pubs., Inc.

—Immigration: Interpreting the Constitution. 2014. (Understanding the United States Constitution Ser.). 112p. (YA). (gr. 7-12). 35.60 *(978-1-4777-7512-7(9))* Rosen Publishing Group, Inc., The.

Campbell, Wallis. Angel Island. 2006. (Illus.). 48p. (J). pap. *(978-1-59034-808-6(7))* Mondo Publishing.

Choi, Anne Soon. Korean Americans. 2007. (New Immigrants Ser.). (Illus.). 132p. (gr. 6-12). lib. bdg. 30.00 *(978-0-7910-8788-6(3),* Chelsea Hse.) Facts On File, Inc.

Ciongoli, A. Kenneth & Parini, Jay. Passage to Liberty: The Story of Italian Immigration & the Rebirth of America. 2003. (Illus.). 32p. (YA). (gr. 9-12). 30.00 *(978-0-7567-6841-6(1))* DIANE Publishing Co.

Conley, Kate A. The Puerto Rican Americans. 2003. (Immigrants in America Ser.). (ENG., Illus.). 112p. (J). (gr. 4-7). lib. bdg. 30.85 *(978-1-59018-432-5(7),* Lucent Bks.) Cengage Gale.

Coy, John. Their Great Gift: Courage, Sacrifice, & Hope in a New Land. Huie, Wing Young, photos by. 2016. (ENG., Illus.). 32p. (J). (gr. k-3). 19.99 *(978-1-4677-8054-4(5));* 38.65 *(978-1-4677-9756-6(1))* Lerner Publishing Group. (Carolrhoda Bks.).

Cunningham, Kevin. Migration from Africa, 1 vol. 2011. (Children's True Stories: Migration Ser.). (ENG.). 32p. (gr. 3-3). pap. 8.29 *(978-1-4109-4078-0(0));* 30.65 *(978-1-4109-4072-8(1))* Heinemann-Raintree. (Raintree Perspectives).

Currie, Stephen. Undocumented Immigrant Youth. 2016. (ENG.). 80p. (J). (gr. 5-12). lib. bdg. *(978-1-60152-980-0(5))* ReferencePoint Pr., Inc.

Demuth, Patricia Brennan. What Was Ellis Island? 2014. (What Was... ? Ser.). lib. bdg. 16.00 *(978-0-606-34156-1(0),* Turtleback) Turtleback Bks.

DePietro, Frank. Latino Americans & Immigration Laws. 2013. (Illus.). 64p. pap. *(978-1-4222-2338-3(8))* Mason Crest.

—Latino Americans & Immigration Laws. Limón, José E., ed. 2012. (Hispanic Americans: Major Minority Ser.). (Illus.). 64p. (J). (gr. 4). 22.95 *(978-1-4222-2321-5(3))* Mason Crest.

—South American Immigrants. 2013. (Illus.). 64p. (J). pap. *(978-1-4222-2346-8(9))* Mason Crest.

—South American Immigrants. Limón, José E., ed. 2012. (Hispanic Americans: Major Minority Ser.). (Illus.). 64p. (J). (gr. 4). 22.95 *(978-1-4222-2329-1(9))* Mason Crest.

DiConsiglio, John. Young Americans: Tales of Teenage Immigrants. 2005. (Illus.). 43p. *(978-0-439-12405-8(0))* Scholastic, Inc.

Doak, Robin Santos. Fighting for American Values: 1941-1985. Overmyer-Velazquez, Mark, ed. 2007. (Latino-American History Ser.). (Illus.). 106p. (YA). (gr. 5-9). lib. bdg. 35.00 *(978-0-8160-6444-1(X))* Facts On File, Inc.

—Indian Americans. 2007. (American Immigrants Ser.). (Illus.). 48p. (J). (gr. 4-6). lib. bdg. *(978-1-60044-612-2(4))* Rourke Educational Media.

Egendorf, Laura K. Immigration. (History of Issues Ser.). 192-240p. (gr. 10-12). pap. 23.70 *(978-0-7377-2872-9(8),* Greenhaven Pr., Inc.) Cengage Gale.

Faria, Joseph D. The Statue of Liberty & Ellis Island: A MyReportLinks.com Book. 2005. (Virtual Field Trips Ser.). (Illus.). 48p. (J). (gr. 4-10). lib. bdg. 26.60 *(978-0-7660-5226-0(5),* MyReportLinks.com Bks.) Enslow Pubs., Inc.

Ferguson, John E. & Allport, Alan. Immigration Policy. 2nd rev. ed. 2009. (Point/Counterpoint Ser.). (Illus.). 152p. (C). (gr. 9-18). 35.00 *(978-1-60413-126-0(8),* Chelsea Hse.) Facts On File, Inc.

Ferry, Joseph. Vietnamese Immigration. 2005. (Changing Face of North America Ser.). (Illus.). 112p. (YA). lib. bdg. 24.95 *(978-1-59084-682-7(6))* Mason Crest.

Fields, Julianna. First-Generation Immigrant Families. 2010. (Changing Face of Modern Families Ser.). (Illus.). 64p. (YA). (gr. 6-18). lib. bdg. 22.95 *(978-1-4222-1499-2(0))* Mason Crest.

Figorito, Marcus. Ellis Island: Welcome to America. (Reading Room Collection 1 Ser.). 16p. 2009. (gr. 2-3). 37.50 *(978-1-60851-943-9(0),* PowerKids Pr.) 2006. (Illus.). (J). (gr. 3-7). lib. bdg. 17.25 *(978-1-4042-3347-8(4))* Rosen Publishing Group, Inc., The.

Flor Ada, Alma & Campoy, F. Isabel. Yes! We Are Latinos. Diaz, David, illus. 2016. (ENG & SPA.). 96p. (J). (gr. 5). pap. 9.95 *(978-1-58089-549-1(2))* Charlesbridge Publishing, Inc.

Freedman, Russell. Angel Island: Gateway to Gold Mountain. 2014. (ENG., Illus.). 96p. (J). (gr. 5-7). 17.99 *(978-0-547-90378-1(2))* Houghton Mifflin Harcourt Publishing Co.

—Angel Island: Gateway to Gold Mountain. 2016. lib. bdg. 22.10 ***(978-0-606-39677-6(2))*** Turtleback Bks.

Gaines, Jena. Haitian Immigration. 2003. (Changing Face of North America Ser.). (Illus.). 112p. (J). lib. bdg. *(978-1-59084-691-9(5))* Mason Crest.

Gale Editors & Miller, Debra A. Immigration. 2014. (Current Controversies Ser.). (ENG., Illus.). 224p. (gr. 7-12). lib. bdg. 46.40 *(978-0-7377-6874-9(6),* Greenhaven Pr., Inc.) Cengage Gale.

Gallegos, Yuliana. Mi Sueno de America/My American Dream. Baeza, Georgina, tr. 2009. (ENG & SPA., Illus.). 55p. (J). (gr. 4-7). pap. 9.95 *(978-1-55885-534-2(3),* Piñata Books) Arte Publico Pr.

Gelletly, LeeAnne. Mexican Immigration. 2005. (Changing Face of North America Ser.). (Illus.). 112p. (YA). lib. bdg. 24.95 *(978-1-59084-680-3(X))* Mason Crest.

Green, Robert. Immigration. 2008. (21st Century Skills Library: Global Perspectives Ser.). (ENG.). 32p. (gr. 4-8). lib. bdg. 28.50 *(978-1-60279-128-2(7),* 200101) Cherry Lake Publishing.

Greve, Tom. Angel Island. 2015. (ENG.). 32p. (gr. 3-6). 32.79 *(978-1-63430-044-5(0))* Rourke Educational Media.

Haerens, Margaret. Illegal Immigration. 2006. (Opposing Viewpoints Ser.). (ENG.). 212p. (J). (gr. 7-18). pap. 39.70 *(978-0-7377-3356-3(X));* (Illus.). 27.50 *(978-0-7377-3357-0(8))* Cengage Gale. (Greenhaven Pr., Inc.).

Heaney, Shane. The Scotch-Irish Immigration to America: Economic Hardship in Ireland (1603-1775), 01 vols., 1. 2016. (Spotlight on Immigration & Migration Ser.). (ENG., Illus.). 24p. (J). pap. 10.00 *(978-1-5081-4095-5(2),* PowerKids Pr.) Rosen Publishing Group, Inc., The.

Heckt, Jackie. Immigration to Colonial America, 01 vols., 1. 2016. (Spotlight on Immigration & Migration Ser.). (ENG., Illus.). 24p. (J). pap. 10.00 *(978-1-5081-4081-8(2),* PowerKids Pr.) Rosen Publishing Group, Inc., The.

Hernandez, Roger E. Immigration. 2008. (Gallup Major Trends & Events Ser.). (Illus.). 120p. (YA). (gr. 7-18). lib. bdg. 22.95 *(978-1-59084-965-1(5))* Mason Crest.

Hernandez, Romel. Immigration from Central America. 2005. (Changing Face of North America Ser.). (Illus.). 112p. (YA). lib. bdg. 24.95 *(978-1-59084-688-9(5))* Mason Crest.

Hicks, Terry Allan. Ellis Island. (Symbols of America Ser.). (Illus.). 40p. 2007. (J). pap. 6.99 *(978-0-7614-3377-4(5))* 2006. (gr. 3-7). lib. bdg. 20.95 *(978-0-7614-2134-4(3))* Marshall Cavendish Corp. (Benchmark Bks.).

Honovich, Nancy. Immigration from the Former Yugoslavia. 2005. (Changing Face of North America Ser.). (Illus.). 112p. (YA). lib. bdg. 24.95 *(978-1-59084-690-2(7))* Mason Crest.

Horst, Heather A. & Garner, Andrew. Jamaican Americans. 2007. (New Immigrants Ser.). (Illus.). 144p. (gr. 6-12). lib. bdg. 30.00 *(978-0-7910-8790-9(5),* Chelsea Hse.) Facts On File, Inc.

Hossell, Karen Price. The Irish Americans. 2003. (Immigrants in America Ser.). (ENG., Illus.). 112p. (J). 30.85 *(978-1-56006-752-8(7),* Lucent Bks.) Cengage Gale.

Houghton, Gillian. Ellis Island: A Primary Source History of an Immigrant's Arrival in America. (Primary Sources in American History Ser.). 64p. (gr. 5-8). 2009. 58.50 *(978-1-60851-489-2(7))* 2004. (Illus.). (YA). lib. bdg. 31.95 *(978-0-8239-4003-5(9),* Rosen Reference) Rosen Publishing Group, Inc., The.

Howell, Sara. Famous Immigrants & Their Stories. 2014. (American Mosaic: Immigration Today Ser.). 24p. (J). (gr. 3-6). pap. 49.50 *(978-1-4777-6652-1(9))* Rosen Publishing Group, Inc., The.

—First-Generation Americans. 2014. (American Mosaic: Immigration Today Ser.). (Illus.). 24p. (J). (gr. 3-6). pap. 49.50 *(978-1-4777-6651-4(0),* PowerKids Pr.) Rosen Publishing Group, Inc., The.

—Immigrants' Rights, Citizens' Rights. 2014. (American Mosaic: Immigration Today Ser.). 24p. (J). (gr. 3-6). pap. 49.50 *(978-1-4777-6647-7(2),* PowerKids Pr.) Rosen Publishing Group, Inc., The.

—Inmigrantes Famosos y Sus Historias. 2014. (Mosaico Americano: la Inmigración Hoy en día (the American Mosaic: Immigration Today) Ser.). (SPA., Illus.). 24p. (J). (gr. 3-6). lib. bdg. 23.60 *(978-1-4777-6803-7(3),* PowerKids Pr.) Rosen Publishing Group, Inc., The.

—Los Derechos de los Inmigrantes, Los Derechos de Los Ciudadanos. 2014. (Mosaico Americano: la Inmigración Hoy en día (the American Mosaic: Immigration Today) Ser.). (SPA., Illus.). 24p. (J). (gr. 3-6). lib. bdg. 23.60 *(978-1-4777-6819-8(X),* PowerKids Pr.) Rosen Publishing Group, Inc., The.

—Los Inmigrantes Indocumentados. 2014. (Mosaico Americano: la Inmigración Hoy en día (the American Mosaic: Immigration Today) Ser.). (SPA., Illus.). 24p. (J). (gr. 3-6). pap. 49.50 *(978-1-4777-6811-2(4),* PowerKids Pr.) Rosen Publishing Group, Inc., The.

—Los Refugiados. 2014. (Mosaico Americano: la Inmigración Hoy en día (the American Mosaic: Immigration Today) Ser.). (SPA & ENG., Illus.). 24p. (J). (gr. 3-6). pap. 8.25 *(978-1-4777-6817-4(3),* PowerKids Pr.) Rosen Publishing Group, Inc., The.

—Primera Generación de Estadounidenses. 2014. (Mosaico Americano: la Inmigración Hoy en día (the American Mosaic: Immigration Today) Ser.). (SPA., Illus.). 24p. (J). (gr. 3-6). lib. bdg. 23.60 *(978-1-4777-6807-5(6),* PowerKids Pr.) Rosen Publishing Group, Inc., The.

—Refugees. 2014. (American Mosaic: Immigration Today Ser.). (Illus.). 24p. (J). (gr. 3-6). pap. 49.50 *(978-1-4777-6649-1(9),* PowerKids Pr.) Rosen Publishing Group, Inc., The.

—Undocumented Immigrants. 2014. (American Mosaic: Immigration Today Ser.). (Illus.). 24p. (J). (gr. 3-6). pap. 8.25 *(978-1-4777-6745-0(2));* pap. 49.50 *(978-1-4777-6650-7(2));*

lib. bdg. 23.60 *(978-1-4777-6744-3(4))* Rosen Publishing Group, Inc., The. (PowerKids Pr.).

Ingram, Scott. Korean Americans. 2006. (World Almanac Library of American Immigration). (Illus.). 48p. (gr. 5-12). pap. 14.05 *(978-0-8368-7328-3(9))*; lib. bdg. 31.00 *(978-0-8368-7315-3(7))* Stevens, Gareth Publishing LLLP. (Gareth Stevens Secondary Library).

—Mexican Americans. 2006. (World Almanac Library of American Immigration). (Illus.). 48p. (gr. 5-12). pap. 14.05 *(978-0-8368-7329-0(7))*; lib. bdg. 31.00 *(978-0-8368-7316-0(5))* Stevens, Gareth Publishing LLLP. (Gareth Stevens Secondary Library).

—South Asian Americans. 2006. (World Almanac Library of American Immigration). (Illus.). 48p. (gr. 5-12). pap. 14.05 *(978-0-8368-7331-3(9))*; lib. bdg. 31.00 *(978-0-8368-7318-4(1))* Stevens, Gareth Publishing LLLP. (Gareth Stevens Secondary Library).

Kallen, Stuart A. Twentieth-Century Immigration to the United States. (American History Ser.). 2009. pap. 24.10 *(978-1-4205-0299-2(9))* 2007. (ENG., Illus.). 104p. (gr. 3-7). lib. bdg. 39.40 *(978-1-59018-186-7(7))* Cengage Gale. (Lucent Bks.).

Kallio, Jamie. Angel Island Immigration: A History Perspectives Book. 2014. (Perspectives Library). (ENG.). 32p. (J). (gr. 4-8). 28.50 *(978-1-63137-614-6(4)*, 205239) Cherry Lake Publishing.

Keedle, Jayne. West African Americans. 2009. (New Americans Ser.). (Illus.). 80p. (J). (gr. 5-8). 35.64 *(978-0-7614-4313-1(4))* Marshall Cavendish Corp.

Kenney, Karen. Illegal Immigration, 1 vol. 2007. (Essential Viewpoints Set 1 Ser.). (ENG., Illus.). 112p. (J). (gr. 6-12). lib. bdg. 35.64 *(978-1-59928-861-1(3))* ABDO Publishing Co.

Kenney, Karen Latchana. Ellis Island, 1 vol. Hunt, Judith A., illus. 2011. (Our Nation's Pride Set 2 Ser.). (ENG.). 32p. (J). (gr. 1-4). 28.50 *(978-1-61641-150-3(3))* Magic Wagon.

Kim, Patti. Here I Am. Sánchez, Sonia, illus. 2013. (ENG.). 40p. (gr. k-5). 14.95 *(978-1-62370-036-2(1))* Capstone Young Readers of Coughlan Cos.

—Here I Am, 1 vol. Sánchez, Sonia, illus. (ENG.). 40p. (gr. k-5). 2015. pap. 7.95 *(978-1-4795-1931-6(6))* 2013. 28.65 *(978-1-4048-8299-7(5))* Picture Window Bks.

Knight, Margy Burns. Who Belongs Here? An American Story. O'Brien, Anne Sibley, illus. 2004. 32p. 19.45 *(978-0-7569-2426-3(X))* Perfection Learning Corp.

—Who Belongs Here? An American Story, 1 vol. O'Brien, Anne Sibley, illus. 2nd ed. 2003. (SPA & ENG.). 40p. (gr. 2-6). 8.95 *(978-0-88448-169-0(7)*, 884169) Tilbury Hse. Pubs.

Knight, Margy Burns, et al. Who Belongs Here? An American Story. 2nd ed. 2004. (Illus.). 40p. (gr. 3-8). 16.95 *(978-0-88448-110-2(7))* Tilbury Hse. Pubs.

Kravitz, Danny. In the Shadow of Lady Liberty: Immigrant Stories from Ellis Island. 2015. (U. S. Immigration in The 1900s Ser.). (ENG.). 48p. (gr. 3-4). pap. 8.95 *(978-1-4914-4173-2(9))* Capstone Press of Coughlan Cos.

—Journey to America: A Chronology of Immigration in the 1900s. 2015. (U. S. Immigration in The 1900s Ser.). (ENG., Illus.). 48p. (gr. 3-4). pap. 8.95 *(978-1-4914-4172-5(0))* Capstone Press of Coughlan Cos.

Kroll, Steven. Ellis Island: Doorway to Freedom. 2009. (ENG.). 31p. (J). 18.00 *(978-1-4379-6699-2(3))* DIANE Publishing Co.

Kule, Elaine A. Beginning Again: Immigrating to America. Thermes, Jennifer, illus. 2006. 40p. *(978-1-59137-473-2(1))* Options Publishing.

Landau, Elaine & National Geographic Learning Staff. Ellis Island. 2012. (ENG., Illus.). 48p. (C). (gr. 3-5). pap. 10.95 *(978-0-531-14781-8(9))* National Geographic School Publishing, Inc.

Larson, Kirsten W. U.S. Border Patrol. 2016. (Protecting Our People Ser.). (ENG., Illus.). 32p. (J). (gr. 1-4). 20.95 *(978-1-60753-986-5(1))* Amicus Publishing.

Lemke, Donald B. The Schoolchildren's Blizzard. 2007. (Disasters in History Ser.). (ENG., Illus.). 32p. (gr. 3-4). 30.65 *(978-1-4296-0157-3(4)*, Graphic Library) Capstone Press of Coughlan Cos.

Levy, Janey. Illegal Immigration & Amnesty: Open Borders & National Security. 2010. (In the News Ser.). (Illus.). 64p. (YA). (gr. 7-12). lib. bdg. 31.95 *(978-1-4358-3583-2(2))* Rosen Publishing Group, Inc., The.

Lingen, Marissa. Chinese Immigration. 2005. (Changing Face of North America Ser.). (Illus.). 112p. (YA). lib. bdg. 24.95 *(978-1-59084-694-0(X))* Mason Crest.

Maestro, Betsy. Coming to America. Ryan, Susannah, illus. 2015. 40p. pap. 9.00 *(978-1-61003-543-9(7))* Center for the Collaborative Classroom.

Marcovitz, Hal. Ellis Island: The Story of a Gateway to America. Moreno, Barry, ed. 2014. (Patriotic Symbols of America Ser.: 20). 48p. (J). (gr. 4-18). lib. bdg. 20.95 *(978-1-4222-3123-4(2))* Mason Crest.

Marroquin, Feliciano. The American Dream Journey. 2008. 96p. pap. 28.95 *(978-1-59754-342-2(X))* Editorial Libros en Red.

Martin, Jennifer C. The Korean Americans. 2003. (Immigrants in America Ser.). (ENG., Illus.). 112p. (J). (gr. 4-7). lib. bdg. 30.85 *(978-1-59018-079-2(8)*, Lucent Bks.) Cengage Gale.

Maury, Rob. Citizenship: Rights & Responsibilities. (Major American Immigration Ser.). (YA). 2010. (Illus.). 64p. (gr. 9-12). lib. bdg. 22.95 *(978-1-4222-0618-8(1))* 2007. pap. 9.95 *(978-1-4222-0685-0(8))* Mason Crest.

—Immigration from the Middle East. 2005. (Changing Face of North America Ser.). (Illus.). 112p. (YA). lib. bdg. 24.95 *(978-1-59084-695-7(8))* Mason Crest.

McDaniel, Jan. Indian Immigration. 2005. (Changing Face of North America Ser.). (Illus.). 112p. (YA). lib. bdg. 24.95 *(978-1-59084-683-4(4))* Mason Crest.

McDaniel, Melissa & National Geographic Learning Staff. Ellis Island. 3rd ed. 2011. (ENG., Illus.). 64p. (J). pap. 14.95 *(978-0-531-26556-7(0))* National Geographic School Publishing, Inc.

Merino, Noël. Illegal Immigration. Greenhaven Press Staff, ed. 2015. (Opposing Viewpoints Ser.). (ENG., Illus.). 224p. (gr. 10-12). pap. 33.80 *(978-0-7377-7273-9(5))*; lib. bdg. 48.80 *(978-0-7377-7272-2(7))* Cengage Gale. (Greenhaven Pr., Inc.).

Merrick, Caitlin & Houghton, Gillian. A Primary Source Investigation of Ellis Island. 2015. (Uncovering American History Ser.). (ENG., Illus.). 64p. (J). (gr. 5-6). 32.95 *(978-1-4994-3505-4(3)*, Rosen Central) Rosen Publishing Group, Inc., The.

Metz, Lorijo. Una Nacin de Inmigrantes / a Nation of Immigrants, 1 vol., 1. Beullens-Maoui, Nathalie, ed. 2014. (¡Celebremos la Libertad! / Let's Celebrate Freedom! Ser.). (SPA & BYN.). 24p. (J). (gr. 3-6). 23.60 *(978-1-4777-3251-9(9)*, PowerKids Pr.) Rosen Publishing Group, Inc., The.

—A Nation of Immigrants, 1 vol., 1. 2014. (Let's Celebrate Freedom! Ser.). (ENG.). 24p. (J). (gr. 3-6). 23.60 *(978-1-4777-2899-4(6)*, PowerKids Pr.) Rosen Publishing Group, Inc., The.

Meyer, Jared. Frequently Asked Questions about Being an Immigrant Teen. (FAQ: Teen Life Ser.). 64p. 2009. (gr. 5-6). 58.50 *(978-1-61512-565-4(5))* 2007. (Illus.). (YA). (gr. 7-12). lib. bdg. 31.95 *(978-1-4042-1079-0(2))* Rosen Publishing Group, Inc., The.

Miller, Debra A. Illegal Immigration. 2007. (Compact Research Ser.). (Illus.). 110p. (YA). (gr. 7-12). lib. bdg. 25.95 *(978-1-60152-009-8(3))* ReferencePoint Pr., Inc.

Miller, Debra A., ed. Illegal Immigration. 2007. (Current Controversies Ser.). (ENG., Illus.). (YA). 222p. (gr. 8-12). 27.50 *(978-0-7377-3724-0(7)*, Greenhaven Pr., Inc.); 240p. (gr. 9-12). pap. 39.70 *(978-0-7377-3723-3(9))* Cengage Gale.

Moreno, Barry. The Chinese Americans. 2007. (Major American Immigration Ser.). (YA). pap. 9.95 *(978-1-4222-0672-0(6))* Mason Crest.

—The Cuban Americans. (Major American Immigration Ser.). (YA). 2010. (Illus.). 64p. (gr. 9-12). 22.95 *(978-1-4222-0606-5(8))* 2007. pap. 9.95 *(978-1-4222-0673-7(4))* Mason Crest.

—The German Americans. 2007. (Major American Immigration Ser.). (YA). pap. 9.95 *(978-1-4222-0674-4(2))* Mason Crest.

—History of American Immigration. (Major American Immigration Ser.). (YA). 2010. (Illus.). 64p. (gr. 9-12). lib. bdg. 22.95 *(978-1-4222-0613-3(0))* 2007. pap. 9.95 *(978-1-4222-0680-5(7))* Mason Crest.

—The Irish Americans. 2007. (Major American Immigration Ser.). (YA). pap. 9.95 *(978-1-4222-0675-1(0))* Mason Crest.

—The Italian Americans. 2007. (Major American Immigration Ser.). (YA). pap. 9.95 *(978-1-4222-0676-8(9))* Mason Crest.

—The Japanese Americans. (Major American Immigration Ser.). (YA). 2010. (Illus.). 64p. (gr. 9-12). 22.95 *(978-1-4222-0610-2(6))* 2007. pap. 9.95 *(978-1-4222-0677-5(7))* Mason Crest.

—The Jewish Americans. (Major American Immigration Ser.). (YA). 2010. (Illus.). 64p. (gr. 9-12). 22.95 *(978-1-4222-0611-9(4))* 2007. pap. 9.95 *(978-1-4222-0678-2(5))* Mason Crest.

—The Korean Americans. (Major American Immigration Ser.). (YA). 2010. (Illus.). 64p. (gr. 9-12). 22.95 *(978-1-4222-0612-6(2))* 2007. pap. 9.95 *(978-1-4222-0679-9(3))* Mason Crest.

—The Mexican Americans. (Major American Immigration Ser.). (YA). 2010. (Illus.). 64p. (gr. 9-12). 22.95 *(978-1-4222-0614-0(9))* 2007. pap. 9.95 *(978-1-4222-0681-2(5))* Mason Crest.

—The Polish Americans. (Major American Immigration Ser.). (YA). 2010. (Illus.). 64p. (gr. 9-12). 22.95 *(978-1-4222-0616-4(5))* 2007. pap. 9.95 *(978-1-4222-0683-6(1))* Mason Crest.

—The Russian Americans. 2007. (Major American Immigration Ser.). (YA). pap. 9.95 *(978-1-4222-0684-3(X))* Mason Crest.

Moreno, Barry & Ashbrock, Peg. The German Americans. 2010. (Major American Immigration Ser.). (Illus.). 64p. (YA). (gr. 9-12). 22.95 *(978-1-4222-0607-2(6))* Mason Crest.

Moreno, Barry & Bowen, Richard A. The Italian Americans. 2010. (Major American Immigration Ser.). (Illus.). 64p. (YA). (gr. 9-12). 22.95 *(978-1-4222-0609-6(2))* Mason Crest.

Moreno, Barry & Haugen, Brenda. The Irish Americans. 2010. (Major American Immigration Ser.). (Illus.). 64p. (YA). (gr. 9-12). 22.95 *(978-1-4222-0608-9(4))* Mason Crest.

Moreno, Barry & Lingen, Marissa. The Chinese Americans. 2010. (Major American Immigration Ser.). (Illus.). 64p. (YA). (gr. 9-12). 22.95 *(978-1-4222-0605-8(X))* Mason Crest.

Mortensen, Lori. Ellis Island, 1 vol. Skeens, Matthew, illus. 2008. (American Symbols Ser.). (ENG.). 24p. (gr. 1-2). 26.65 *(978-1-4048-4705-7(7))* Picture Window Bks.

Moynihan, Daniel Patrick, intro. Immigrants in America. 2005. (Immigrants in America Ser.). (Illus.). 112p. (gr. 6-12). 180.00 *(978-0-7910-7125-0(1)*, Chelsea Hse.) Facts On File, Inc.

Nazario, Sonia. La Travesía de Enrique. 2015. (ENG & SPA.). 304p. (YA). (gr. 7). pap. 9.99 *(978-0-553-53554-9(4)*, Ember) Random Hse. Children's Bks.

Newman, Lori M. What Rights Should Illegal Immigrants Have? 2006. (At Issue Ser.). (ENG., Illus.). 90p. (YA). (gr. 8-12). 22.50 *(978-0-7377-3481-2(7))*; lib. bdg. 31.80 *(978-0-7377-3480-5(9))* Cengage Gale. (Greenhaven Pr., Inc.).

Nichol, Bryan. Irish Americans, 1 vol. 2004. (One Nation Set 2 Ser.). (ENG.). 32p. (gr. k-6). 27.07 *(978-1-59197-528-1(X)*, Checkerboard Library) ABDO Publishing Co.

Noonan, Sheila Smith. Korean Immigration. 2005. (Changing Face of North America Ser.). (Illus.). 112p. (YA). lib. bdg. 24.95 *(978-1-59084-693-3(1))* Mason Crest.

O'Donnell, Liam. U. S. Immigration. Barnett, Charles, illus. 2008. (Cartoon Nation Ser.). (ENG.). 32p. (gr. 3-4). 30.65 *(978-1-4296-1983-7(X)*, Graphic Library) Capstone Press of Coughlan Cos.

O'Donoghue, Sean. The Disaster of the Irish Potato Famine: Irish Immigrants Arrive in America (1845-1850), 01 vols., 1. 2016. (Spotlight on Immigration & Migration Ser.). (ENG., Illus.). 24p. (J). pap. 10.00 *(978-1-5081-4066-5(9)*, PowerKids Pr.) Rosen Publishing Group, Inc., The.

Ollhoff, Jim. Exploring Immigration, 1 vol. 2010. (Your Family Tree Ser.). (ENG.). 32p. (gr. 4-7). 27.07 *(978-1-61613-463-1(1)*, Abdo & Daughters) ABDO Publishing Co.

Osborne, Linda Barrett. This Land Is Our Land: The History of American Immigration. 2016. (ENG., Illus.). 128p. (J). (gr. 8-17). 24.95 *(978-1-4197-1660-7(3)*, Abrams Bks. for Young Readers) Abrams, Inc.

Otfinoski, Steven. 1990-2010. 2009. (Hispanic America 2 Ser.). 80p. (gr. 5). 34.21 *(978-0-7614-4180-9(8))* Marshall Cavendish Corp.

Outman, James L. & Baker, Lawrence W. U. S. Immigration & Migration: Primary Sources. 2004. (US Immigration & Migration Reference Library). (ENG., Illus.). 272p. (J). 106.00 *(978-0-7876-7669-8(1)*, UXL) Cengage Gale.

Outman, James L., et al. U. S. Immigration & Migration: Biographies, 2.0. 2004. (US Immigration & Migration Reference Library). (ENG., Illus.). 410p. (J). 191.00 *(978-0-7876-7733-6(7)*, UXL) Cengage Gale.

—U.S. Immigration & Migration, 2 vols. 2004. ([U.S. Immigration & Migration Reference Library]). (Illus.). (J). *(978-0-7876-7668-1(3))*; 110.00 *(978-0-7876-7568-4(7))* Cengage Gale. (UXL).

Parker, Lewis K. Why German Immigrants Came to America. 2009. (Coming to America Ser.). 24p. (gr. 2-3). 42.50 *(978-1-61511-883-0(7)*, PowerKids Pr.) Rosen Publishing Group, Inc., The.

—Why Irish Immigrants Came to America. 2009. (Coming to America Ser.). 24p. (gr. 2-3). 42.50 *(978-1-61511-884-7(5)*, PowerKids Pr.) Rosen Publishing Group, Inc., The.

—Why Italian Immigrants Came to America. 2009. (Coming to America Ser.). 24p. (gr. 2-3). 42.50 *(978-1-61511-885-4(3)*, PowerKids Pr.) Rosen Publishing Group, Inc., The.

—Why Japanese Immigrants Came to America. 2009. (Coming to America Ser.). 24p. (gr. 2-3). 42.50 *(978-1-61511-886-1(1)*, PowerKids Pr.) Rosen Publishing Group, Inc., The.

—Why Mexican Immigrants Came to America. (Coming to America Ser.). 24p. 2009. (gr. 2-3). 42.50 *(978-1-61511-887-8(X))* 2003. (Illus.). (J). lib. bdg. 22.60 *(978-0-8239-6459-8(0))* Rosen Publishing Group, Inc., The. (PowerKids Pr.).

—Why Vietnamese Immigrants Came to America. 2009. (Coming to America Ser.). 24p. (gr. 2-3). 42.50 *(978-1-61511-888-5(8)*, PowerKids Pr.) Rosen Publishing Group, Inc., The.

Perl, Lila. Immigration: This Land Is Whose Land? 2009. (Controversy! Ser.). 112p. (gr. 7-9). lib. bdg. 37.07 *(978-0-7614-4232-5(4))* Marshall Cavendish Corp.

Pobst, Sandy. The Newest Americans, 5 vols. 2003. (Middle School Reference Ser.). (Illus.). 144p. (C). (gr. 6-8). 242.00 *(978-0-313-32553-3(7)*, MS2553, Greenwood) ABC-CLIO, LLC.

Powell, John. Immigration. 2006. (Library in a Book). (Illus.). 320p. (C). (gr. 9). 45.00 *(978-0-8160-6234-8(X))* Facts On File, Inc.

Primary Sources of Immigration & Migration. 2004. (Primary Source Big Bookstm Ser.). (ENG.). 24p. (gr. 4-8). 43.95 *(978-0-8239-4594-8(4))* Rosen Publishing Group, Inc., The.

Rinker, Kimberly. Immigration from the Dominican Republic. 2005. (Changing Face of North America Ser.). (Illus.). 112p. (YA). lib. bdg. 24.95 *(978-1-59084-689-6(3))* Mason Crest.

RJF Publishing Staff & Staton, Hilarie. Ellis Island. 2009. (Symbols of American Freedom Ser.). 48p. (gr. 4-6). 30.00 *(978-1-60413-519-0(0)*, Chelsea Clubhouse) Facts On File, Inc.

Rosen Classroom, creator. Map Activities for Primary Sources of Immigration & Migration in America: Reproducible Blackline Masters. 2011. (Illus.). 15p. (J). pap. 15.99 *(978-0-8239-4597-9(9)*, Rosen Classroom) Rosen Publishing Group, Inc., The.

Roza, Greg. Immigration & Migration. 2011. (Story of America Ser.). (Illus.). 32p. (J). (gr. 4-6). lib. bdg. 26.60 *(978-1-4339-4768-1(4)*, Gareth Stevens Learning Library) Stevens, Gareth Publishing LLLP.

Ruffin, Frances E. Ellis Island. 2006. (Places in American History Ser.). (Illus.). 24p. (gr. 1-4). pap. 8.15 *(978-0-8368-6415-1(8))*; lib. bdg. 22.00 *(978-0-8368-6408-3(5))* Stevens, Gareth Publishing LLLP. (Weekly Reader Leveled Readers).

Russell, Freedman. Immigrant Kids. 2014. (ENG.). 80p. (J). (gr. k-3). 13.24 *(978-1-63245-247-4(2))* Lectorum Pubns., Inc.

Sánchez, Sonia, illus. Here I Am. 2014. (J). ***(978-1-4795-1932-3(4))*** Picture Window Bks.

Santos, Edward J. Everything You Need to Know If You & Your Parents Are New Americans. 2005. (Need to Know Library). (Illus.). 64p. (YA). (gr. 4-6). lib. bdg. 31.95 *(978-0-8239-3547-5(7))* Rosen Publishing Group, Inc., The.

—Everything You Need to Know If You & Your Parents are New Americans. 2009. (Need to Know Library). 64p. (gr. 5-5). 58.50 *(978-1-60854-099-0(5))* Rosen Publishing Group, Inc., The.

Saxon-Ford, Stephanie. The Czech Americans: The Immigrant Experience. 2006. (Illus.). 111p. (J). (gr. 4-8). reprint ed. 20.00 *(978-1-4223-5547-3(0))* DIANE Publishing Co.

Schmermund, Elizabeth. Immigration Bans. 2017. (J). pap. ***(978-1-5345-0057-0(X))*** Greenhaven Publishing LLC.

Seymour, Isobel. I am Mexican American. 2009. (Our American Family Ser.). 24p. (gr. 2-3). 42.50 *(978-1-60851-149-5(9)*, PowerKids Pr.) Rosen Publishing Group, Inc., The.

Shea, Therese. Immigration to America: Identifying Different Points of View about an Issue. 2009. (Critical Thinking in American History Ser.). 48p. (gr. 5-8). 53.00 *(978-1-61512-093-2(9)*, Rosen Reference) Rosen Publishing Group, Inc., The.

—Immigration to America: Identifying Different Points of View About an Issue. 2005. (Critical Thinking in American History Ser.). (Illus.). 48p. (J). (gr. k-3). lib. bdg. 29.25 *(978-1-4042-0414-0(8))* Rosen Publishing Group, Inc., The.

Sioux, Tracee. Immigrants & the Westward Expansion. 2009. (Primary Sources of Immigration & Migration in America Ser.). 24p. (gr. 3-4). 42.50 *(978-1-60851-776-3(4)*, PowerKids Pr.) Rosen Publishing Group, Inc., The.

—Immigrants, Migration, & the Growth of the American City. 2009. (Primary Sources of Immigration & Migration in America Ser.). 24p. (gr. 3-4). 42.50 *(978-1-60851-778-7(0)*, PowerKids Pr.) Rosen Publishing Group, Inc., The.

—Immigrants, Migration, & the Industrial Revolution. 2009. (Primary Sources of Immigration & Migration in America Ser.). 24p. (gr. 3-4). 42.50 *(978-1-60851-779-4(9)*, PowerKids Pr.) Rosen Publishing Group, Inc., The.

—Immigration, Migration, & the Industrial Revolution. 2004. (Primary Sources of Immigration & Migration in America Ser.). (ENG., Illus.). 24p. (gr. 4-8). pap. 9.40 *(978-0-8239-8998-0(4)*, PowerKids Pr.) Rosen Publishing Group, Inc., The.

Snyder, Elaine. Anna & Solomon. Bliss, Harry, illus. 2014. (ENG.). 32p. (J). (gr. -1-3). 17.99 *(978-0-374-30362-4(2)*, 9780374303624, Farrar, Straus & Giroux (BYR)) Farrar, Straus & Giroux.

Staley, Erin. I'm an Undocumented Immigrant, Now What? 2016. (Teen Life 411 Ser.). 00112p. (J). (gr. 7-7). 37.10 *(978-1-5081-7193-5(9))* Rosen Publishing Group, Inc., The.

Stefoff, Rebecca. A Century of Immigration: 1820-1924. 2006. (American Voices Ser.). (Illus.). 115p. (J). (gr. 3-7). lib. bdg. 38.50 *(978-0-7614-2172-6(6)*, Benchmark Bks.) Marshall Cavendish Corp.

Stewart, Gail. Illegal Immigration. 2007. (Ripped from the Headlines Ser.). 64p. (J). (gr. 7-12). 23.95 *(978-1-60217-003-2(7))* Erickson Pr.

Swain, Gwenyth. Hope & Tears: Ellis Island Voices. 2012. (ENG., Illus.). 128p. (J). (gr. 3). 17.95 *(978-1-59078-765-6(X))* Boyds Mills Pr.

Thomas, William David. Korean Americans. 2009. (New Americans Ser.). 80p. (gr. 5). 35.64 *(978-0-7614-4306-3(1))* Marshall Cavendish Corp.

Thornton, Jeremy. Hard Times in Ireland: The Scotch-Irish Come to America (1603-1775) (Primary Sources of Immigration & Migration in America Ser.). 24p. 2009. (gr. 3-4). 42.50 *(978-1-60851-775-6(6))* 2004. (Illus.). (J). lib. bdg. 22.60 *(978-0-8239-6830-5(8))* Rosen Publishing Group, Inc., The. (PowerKids Pr.).

—Hard Times in Ireland: The Scotch-Irish Come to America, 1603-1775. 2004. (Primary Sources of Immigration & Migration in America Ser.). (ENG., Illus.). 24p. (gr. 4-8). pap. 9.40 *(978-0-8239-8956-0(9)*, PowerKids Pr.) Rosen Publishing Group, Inc., The.

—New Industries, New Jobs: British Immigrants Come to America (1830s-1890s) 2004. (Primary Sources of Immigration & Migration Ser.). (Illus.). 24p. (ENG.). (gr. 4-8). pap. 9.40 *(978-0-8239-8958-4(5)*, Rosen Classroom); (J). lib. bdg. 22.60 *(978-0-8239-6832-9(4)*, PowerKids Pr.) Rosen Publishing Group, Inc., The.

—New Industries, New Jobs: British Immigrants Come to America(1830s-1890s) 2009. (Primary Sources of Immigration & Migration in America Ser.). 24p. (gr. 3-4). 42.50 *(978-1-60851-782-4(9)*, PowerKids Pr.) Rosen Publishing Group, Inc., The.

—Religious Intolerance: Jewish Immigrants Come to America (1881-1914) 2009. (Primary Sources of Immigration & Migration in America Ser.). 24p. (gr. 3-4). 42.50 *(978-1-60851-783-1(7)*, PowerKids Pr.) Rosen Publishing Group, Inc., The.

Townsend, Dana E. Ellis Island. (Illus.). 32p. (J). *(978-0-7367-2944-4(5))* Zaner-Bloser, Inc.

U. S. Immigration & Migration, 5.0. Incl. U. S. Immigration & Migration: Almanac. Benson, Sonia. 685p. 191.00 *(978-0-7876-7732-9(9))*; U. S. Immigration & Migration: Biographies. Outman, James L., et al. 410p. 191.00 *(978-0-7876-7733-6(7))*; U. S. Immigration & Migration: Primary Sources. Outman, James L. & Baker, Lawrence W. 272p. 106.00 *(978-0-7876-7669-8(1))*; (Illus.). (J). (US Immigration & Migration Reference Library). (ENG.). 1,327p. 2004. 458.00 *(978-0-7876-7565-3(2)*, UXL) Cengage Gale.

Uschan, Michael V. German Americans. 2006. (World Almanac Library of American Immigration). (Illus.). 48p. (gr. 5-12). pap. 14.05 *(978-0-8368-7323-8(8))*; lib. bdg. 31.00 *(978-0-8368-7310-8(6))* Stevens, Gareth Publishing LLLP. (Gareth Stevens Secondary Library).

—Irish Americans. 2006. (World Almanac Library of American Immigration). (Illus.). 48p. (gr. 5-12). pap. 14.05 *(978-0-8368-7324-5(6))*; lib. bdg. 31.00 *(978-0-8368-7311-5(4))* Stevens, Gareth Publishing LLLP. (Gareth Stevens Secondary Library).

Weber, Valerie J. I Come from Afghanistan. 2006. (This Is My Story Ser.). (Illus.). 24p. (gr. 1-4). pap. 8.15 *(978-0-8368-7240-8(1))*; lib. bdg. 22.00 *(978-0-8368-7233-0(9))* Stevens, Gareth Publishing LLLP. (Weekly Reader Leveled Readers).

—I Come from Chile. 2006. (This Is My Story Ser.). (Illus.). 24p. (gr. 1-4). lib. bdg. 22.00 *(978-0-8368-7234-7(7)*, Weekly Reader Leveled Readers) Stevens, Gareth Publishing LLLP.

—I Come from Chile. 2006. (This Is My Story Ser.). (Illus.). 24p. (gr. 1-4). pap. 8.15 *(978-0-8368-7241-5(X)*, Weekly Reader Leveled Readers) Stevens, Gareth Publishing LLLP.

—I Come from India. 2006. (This Is My Story Ser.). (Illus.). 24p. (gr. 1-4). pap. 8.15 *(978-0-8368-7242-2(8))*; lib. bdg. 22.00 *(978-0-8368-7235-4(5))* Stevens, Gareth Publishing LLLP. (Weekly Reader Leveled Readers).

—I Come from Ivory Coast. 2006. (This Is My Story Ser.). (Illus.). 24p. (gr. 1-4). pap. 8.15 *(978-0-8368-7243-9(6))*; lib. bdg. 22.00 *(978-0-8368-7236-1(3))* Stevens, Gareth Publishing LLLP. (Weekly Reader Leveled Readers).

—I Come from South Korea. 2006. (This Is My Story Ser.). (Illus.). 24p. (gr. 1-4). lib. bdg. 22.00 *(978-0-8368-7237-8(1)*, Weekly Reader Leveled Readers) Stevens, Gareth Publishing LLLP.

—I Come from Ukraine. 2006. (This Is My Story Ser.). (Illus.). 24p. (gr. 1-4). pap. 8.15 *(978-0-8368-7245-3(2)*, Weekly Reader Leveled Readers) Stevens, Gareth Publishing LLLP.

—I Come from Ukraine. 2006. (This Is My Story Ser.). (Illus.). 24p. (gr. 1-4). lib. bdg. 22.00 *(978-0-8368-7238-5(X)*, Weekly Reader Leveled Readers) Stevens, Gareth Publishing LLLP.

Weber, Valerie J. & Weber, Valerie J. I Come from South Korea. 2006. (This Is My Story Ser.). (Illus.). 24p. (gr. 1-4). pap. 8.15 *(978-0-8368-7244-6(4)*, Weekly Reader Leveled Readers) Stevens, Gareth Publishing LLLP.

Whitman, Sylvia. Immigrant Children. 2005. (Picture the American Past Ser.). (Illus.). 48p. (gr. 2-5). lib. bdg. 22.60 *(978-1-57505-395-0(0))* Lerner Publishing Group.

Wong, Li Keng. Good Fortune: My Journey to Gold Mountain, 1 vol. 2006. (ENG., Illus.). 144p. (J). (gr. 3-7). 14.95 *(978-1-56145-367-2(6))* Peachtree Pubs.

World Book, Inc. Staff, contrib. by. The World Book of America's Multicultural Heritage, 2 vols. 2003. (Illus.). 384p. (gr. 4-12). 86.99 *(978-0-7166-7303-3(7))* World Bk., Inc.

Young, Robert. A Personal Tour of Ellis Island. 64p. (J). (gr. 3-6). 6.95 *(978-1-58013-154-4(9))*; 2003. (Illus.). 18.95 *(978-1-58013-079-0(8))* Lerner Publishing Group. (Kar-Ben Publishing).

UNITED STATES—EMPLOYEES

see United States—Officials and Employees

UNITED STATES—EXECUTIVE POWER

see Executive Power

UNITED STATES—EXPLORING EXPEDITIONS

Here are entered works on exploration within the United States and for explorations in other countries which are sponsored by the United States. Works on early exploration in territory which became a part of the United States are entered under America—Discovery and Exploration.

see also names of expeditions, e.g. Lewis and Clark expedition

Benge, Janet & Benge, Geoff. Heroes of History - Daniel Boone: Frontiersman. 2004. (ENG.). 224p. (YA). pap. 9.99 *(978-1-932096-09-5(4))* Emerald Bks.

Levy, Janey. Mapping America's Westward Expansion: Applying Geographic Tools & Interpreting Maps. 2005. (Critical Thinking in American History Ser.). (Illus.). 48p. (J). (gr. k-3). lib. bdg. 29.25 *(978-1-4042-0416-4(4))* Rosen Publishing Group, Inc., The.

Lyne, William Rayford. Galisteo: Thothmes III's Colony in America, C. 1626 B. C.: the Tanoan-Egyptian Djed Festival Stone. Lyne, William Rayford, illus. 2011. (ENG., Illus.). 250p. pap. 25.00 *(978-0-9637467-3-3(1))* Creatopia Productions - Lamy, New Mexico.

Redmond, Shirley Raye. Lewis & Clark: A Prairie Dog for the President. Manders, John, illus. 2003. (Step into Reading Ser.: No. 3). (ENG.). 48p. (J). (gr. k-3). pap. 3.99 *(978-0-375-81120-3(6)*, Random Hse. Bks. for Young Readers) Random Hse. Children's Bks.

UNITED STATES—FEDERAL BUREAU OF INVESTIGATION

Anderson, Dale. The FBI & Civil Rights. 2009. (FBI Story Ser.). 64p. (J). (gr. 4-7). lib. bdg. 22.95 *(978-1-4222-0569-3(X))* Mason Crest.

—The FBI & Organized Crime. 2009. (FBI Story Ser.). 64p. (J). (gr. 4-7). lib. bdg. 22.95 *(978-1-4222-0565-5(7))* Mason Crest.

—The FBI & White-Collar Crime. 2009. (FBI Story Ser.). 64p. (J). (gr. 4-7). lib. bdg. 22.95 *(978-1-4222-0566-2(5))* Mason Crest.

—The FBI Files: Successful Investigations. 2009. (FBI Story Ser.). 64p. (J). (gr. 4-7). lib. bdg. 22.95 *(978-1-4222-0561-7(4))* Mason Crest.

Aronson, Marc. Master of Deceit: J. Edgar Hoover & America in the Age of Lies. 2012. (ENG., Illus.). 230p. (J). (gr. 9). 25.99 *(978-0-7636-5025-4(0))* Candlewick Pr.

Collins, Terry. The FBI. Brown, Kelly, illus. 2008. (Cartoon Nation Ser.). (ENG.). 32p. (gr. 3-4). 30.65 *(978-1-4296-1982-0(1)*, Graphic Library) Capstone Press of Coughlan Cos.

Crewe, Sabrina. The FBI & Crimes Against Children. 2009. (FBI Story Ser.). 64p. (J). (gr. 4-7). lib. bdg. 22.95 *(978-1-4222-0570-9(3))* Mason Crest.

—A History of the FBI. 2009. (FBI Story Ser.). 64p. (J). (gr. 4-7). lib. bdg. 22.95 *(978-1-4222-0563-1(0))* Mason Crest.

Faust, Daniel R. A Career As an FBI Special Agent. 2015. (Federal Forces: Careers As Federal Agents Ser.). (ENG., Illus.). 32p. (J). (gr. 4-5). pap. 10.00 *(978-1-4994-1060-0(3)*, PowerKids Pr.) Rosen Publishing Group, Inc., The.

FBI Agent. 2009. (Virtual Apprentice Ser.). 64p. (gr. 4-9). 29.95 *(978-0-8160-6758-9(9)*, Ferguson Publishing Co.) Facts On File, Inc.

The FBI Story, 12 vols., Set. Incl. FBI & Civil Rights. Anderson, Dale. lib. bdg. 22.95 *(978-1-4222-0569-3(X))*; FBI & Crimes Against Children. Crewe, Sabrina. lib. bdg. 22.95 *(978-1-4222-0570-9(3))*; FBI & Cyber Crimes. Grayson, Robert. lib. bdg. 22.95 *(978-1-4222-0568-6(1))*; FBI & National Security. Grayson, Robert. lib. bdg. 22.95 *(978-1-4222-0564-8(9))*; FBI & Organized Crime. Anderson, Dale. lib. bdg. 22.95 *(978-1-4222-0565-5(7))*; FBI & Public Corruption. Grayson, Robert. lib. bdg. 22.95 *(978-1-4222-0567-9(3))*; FBI & White-Collar Crime. Anderson, Dale. lib. bdg. 22.95 *(978-1-4222-0566-2(5))*; FBI Files: Successful Investigations. Anderson, Dale. lib. bdg. 22.95 *(978-1-4222-0561-7(4))*; FBI's Most Wanted. Wachtel, Alan. lib. bdg. 22.95 *(978-1-4222-0562-4(2))*; History of the FBI. Crewe, Sabrina. lib. bdg. 22.95 *(978-1-4222-0563-1(0))*; How to Become an FBI Agent. Thomas, William David. lib. bdg. 22.95 *(978-1-4222-0571-6(1))*; Investigative Techniques of the FBI. Wachtel, Alan. lib. bdg. 22.95 *(978-1-4222-0572-3(X))*; 64p. (J). (gr. 4-7). 2009. 2010. Set lib. bdg. 275.40 *(978-1-4222-0560-0(6))* Mason Crest.

Federal Forces: Careers As Federal Agents. 2015. (Federal Forces: Careers As Federal Agents Ser.). (ENG.). 32p. (J). (gr. 4-5). pap., pap., pap. 360.00 *(978-1-4994-1291-8(6)*, PowerKids Pr.) Rosen Publishing Group, Inc., The.

Gaines, Ann Graham. Special Agent & Careers in the FBI. 2006. (Homeland Security & Counterterrorism Careers Ser.). (Illus.). 128p. (J). (gr. 5-9). lib. bdg. 33.27 *(978-0-7660-2648-3(5))* Enslow Pubs., Inc.

Grayson, Robert. The FBI & Cyber Crimes. 2009. (FBI Story Ser.). 64p. (J). (gr. 4-7). lib. bdg. 22.95 *(978-1-4222-0568-6(1))* Mason Crest.

—The FBI & National Security. 2009. (FBI Story Ser.). 64p. (J). (gr. 4-7). lib. bdg. 22.95 *(978-1-4222-0564-8(9))* Mason Crest.

—The FBI & Public Corruption. 2009. (FBI Story Ser.). 64p. (J). (gr. 4-7). lib. bdg. 22.95 *(978-1-4222-0567-9(3))* Mason Crest.

Hamilton, John. The FBI, 1 vol. 2007. (Defending the Nation Ser.). (ENG., Illus.). 32p. (gr. 4-7). 27.07 *(978-1-59679-757-4(6)*, Checkerboard Library) ABDO Publishing Co.

Horn, Geoffrey M. FBI Agent. 2008. (Cool Careers Ser.). 32p. (gr. 5-8). pap. 10.50 *(978-0-8368-9326-7(3))*; lib. bdg. 26.00 *(978-0-8368-9193-5(7))* Stevens, Gareth Publishing LLLP.

Karlitz, Gail. Virtual Apprentice: FBI Agent. 2009. (Virtual Apprentice Ser.). 64p. (gr. 4-9). pap. 9.95 *(978-0-8160-7894-3(7)*, Checkmark Bks.) Facts On File, Inc.

Lewis, Brenda Ralph. Hostage Rescue with the FBI. 2004. (Rescue & Prevention Ser.). (Illus.). 96p. (YA). (gr. 7-18). lib. bdg. 22.95 *(978-1-59084-403-8(3))* Mason Crest.

Lewis, Brenda Ralph. Rescuing Hostages: The FBI. 2017. (J). ***(978-1-4222-3770-0(2))*** Mason Crest.

Mara, Wil. FBI Special Agent. 2015. (21st Century Skills Library: Cool STEAM Careers Ser.). (ENG., Illus.). 32p. (J). (gr. 4-7). pap. 14.21 *(978-1-63362-648-5(2)*, 1391909) Cherry Lake Publishing.

Newcomb, Tim. FBI Agent, Vol. 12. 2015. (On a Mission Ser.). 48p. (J). (gr. 5). 20.95 *(978-1-4222-3394-8(4))* Mason Crest.

Poolos, Jamie. Hostage Rescuers. (Extreme Careers Ser.). 64p. (gr. 5-5). 2009. 58.50 *(978-1-61512-399-5(7)*, Rosen Reference) 2007. (Illus.). lib. bdg. 31.95 *(978-1-4042-0941-1(7))* Rosen Publishing Group, Inc., The.

Prentzas, Scott. FBI Special Agent. 2008. (21st Century Skills Library: Cool Careers Ser.). (ENG., Illus.). 32p. (gr. 4-8). lib. bdg. 28.50 *(978-1-60279-304-0(2)*, 200143) Cherry Lake Publishing.

Rapine, Dawn. Federal Forces: Careers As Federal Agents Set. 2015. (Federal Forces: Careers As Federal Agents Ser.). (ENG.). 32p. (J). (gr. 4-5). 157.50 *(978-1-4994-0772-3(6)*, PowerKids Pr.) Rosen Publishing Group, Inc., The.

Ricciuti, Edward R. Federal Bureau of Investigation. 2010. (Law Enforcement Agencies Ser.). (Illus.). 144p. (gr. 6-12). 35.00 *(978-1-60413-636-4(7)*, Chelsea Hse.) Facts On File, Inc.

Streissguth, Tom. America's Security Agencies: The Department of Homeland Security, FBI, NSA, & CIA. 2008. (Federal Government Ser.). (Illus.). 128p. (J). (gr. 3-7). lib. bdg. 34.60 *(978-1-59845-058-3(1)*, MyReportLinks.com Bks.) Enslow Pubs., Inc.

—The Security Agencies of the United States: How the CIA, FBI, NSA, & Homeland Security Keep Us Safe. 2012. (Constitution & the United States Government Ser.). (Illus.). 104p. (J). (gr. 5-18). 33.27 *(978-0-7660-4064-9(X))* Enslow Pubs., Inc.

Thomas, William David. How to Become an FBI Agent. 2009. (FBI Story Ser.). 64p. (J). (gr. 4-7). lib. bdg. 22.95 *(978-1-4222-0571-6(1))* Mason Crest.

Wachtel, Alan. The FBI's Most Wanted. 2009. (FBI Story Ser.). 64p. (J). (gr. 4-7). lib. bdg. 22.95 *(978-1-4222-0562-4(2))* Mason Crest.

—Investigative Techniques of the FBI. 2009. (FBI Story Ser.). 64p. (J). (gr. 4-7). lib. bdg. 22.95 *(978-1-4222-0572-3(X))* Mason Crest.

Wagner, Heather Lehr. The Federal Bureau of Investigation. 2007. (U. S. Government Ser.). (Illus.). 104p. (YA). (gr. 5-9). lib. bdg. 30.00 *(978-0-7910-9281-1(X))* Facts On File, Inc.

Whiting, Jim. FBI Hostage Rescue & Swat Teams. 2014. (U. S. Special Forces Ser.). (ENG., Illus.). 48p. (J). (gr. 5-8). lib. bdg. 35.65 *(978-1-60818-462-0(5)*, Creative Education) Creative Co., The.

—U. S. Special Forces: FBI Hostage Rescue & SWAT Teams. 2015. (U. S. Special Forces Ser.). (ENG.). 48p. (J). (gr. 5-8). pap. 12.00 *(978-1-62832-048-0(6)*, Creative Paperbacks) Creative Co., The.

Wimmer, Teresa. Federal Bureau of Investigation: Agents of Government. 2016. (Agents of Government Ser.). (ENG.). 48p. (J). (gr. 5-9). pap. 12.00 *(978-1-62832-146-3(6)*, Creative Paperbacks) Creative Co., The.

Woog, Adam. Careers in the FBI. 2014. 96p. 39.92 *(978-1-62712-431-7(4))* Cavendish Square Publishing.

—Careers in the FBI. 2013. (J). *(978-1-60870-957-1(4))* Marshall Cavendish.

UNITED STATES—FICTION

Aaron, Chester. Alex, Who Won His War. 2014. 225p. (YA). *(978-1-936144-26-6(3))* Zumaya Pubns. LLC.

Adams, Nick K. The Uncivil War: Battle in the Classroom. 2010. 84p. pap. 9.99 *(978-1-60911-711-5(5)*, Eloquent Bks.) Strategic Book Publishing & Rights Agency (SBPRA).

Alcott, Louisa May. Little Women. 2015. (ENG.). 408p. (J). (gr. 2-4). 14.99 *(978-1-4052-7179-0(5))* Egmont Bks., Ltd. GBR. Dist: Independent Pubs. Group.

Alexander, Lyndi. Windmills. 2013. 248p. (J). pap. 14.99 *(978-1-61271-226-0(6))* Zumaya Pubns. LLC.

Ali, S. K. Saints, Misfits, Monsters, & Mayhem. 2017. (ENG., Illus.). 336p. (YA). (gr. 9). 18.99 ***(978-1-4814-9924-8(6)***, Salaam Reads) Simon & Schuster Bks. For Young Readers.

Allen, Justin. The American. 2008. (ENG.). 320p. (gr. 12). 21.95 *(978-1-59020-100-8(0))* Overlook Pr., The.

Alsaid, Adi. North of Happy. 2017. (ENG.). 304p. 18.99 *(978-0-373-21228-6(3)*, Harlequin Teen) Harlequin Enterprises, Ltd. CAN. Dist: HarperCollins Pubs.

Alvarez, Julia. How the Garcia Girls Lost Their Accent. 2011. 13.46 *(978-0-7848-3532-6(2)*, Everbind) Marco Bk. Co.

—Return to Sender. 2010. (ENG.). 352p. (J). (gr. 3-7). 6.99 *(978-0-375-85123-0(2)*, Yearling) Random Hse. Children's Bks.

American Girl Magazine: Jan/Feb 2004. (J). 19.75 *(978-1-58485-925-3(3))* American Girl Publishing, Inc.

American Girl Magazine: July/Aug 2004 Jumbo Issue. (J). 24.75 *(978-1-58485-928-4(8))* American Girl Publishing, Inc.

American Girl Magazine: March/April 2004. (J). 19.75 *(978-1-58485-926-0(1))* American Girl Publishing, Inc.

American Girl Magazine: May/June 2004. (J). 19.75 *(978-1-58485-927-7(X))* American Girl Publishing, Inc.

American Girl Magazine: Sept/Oct 2004. (J). 19.75 *(978-1-58485-929-1(6))* American Girl Publishing, Inc.

Anderson, Laurie Halse. Seeds of America: Chains; Forge; Ashes. 2016. (Seeds of America Trilogy Ser.: 4). (ENG., Illus.). 928p. (J). (gr. 5-9). 52.99 *(978-1-4814-8678-1(0)*, Atheneum/Caitlyn Dlouhy Books) Simon & Schuster Children's Publishing.

Anderson, Matt & Hutchins, Eric. White Picket Fences: Double Feature One-shot. 2008. (Illus.). 52p. (YA). pap. 6.95 *(978-0-9801314-9-9(9))* Ape Entertainment.

Andre Alice Norton, Alice Norton & Andre Alice Norton. The Time Traders. 2009. 148p. pap. 5.95 *(978-1-60386-204-2(8)*, Merchant Bks.) Rough Draft Printing.

Avi. Don't You Know There's a War On? 2nd ed. 2003. 208p. (J). pap. *(978-0-439-53096-5(2)*, HarperCollins) HarperCollins Pubs.

—Don't You Know There's a War On? 2003. 193p. (gr. 3-7). 18.00 *(978-0-7569-1383-0(7))* Perfection Learning Corp.

—Who Was That Masked Man, Anyway? 2014. (ENG.). 176p. (J). (gr. 3-7). pap. 6.99 *(978-0-439-52355-4(9)*, Scholastic Paperbacks) Scholastic, Inc.

Bacho, Peter. Leaving Yesler. 2010. 285p. (YA). pap. 16.00 *(978-1-929355-57-0(2))* Pleasure Boat Studio: A Literary Pr.

Ballard, John. The Shining Thing, 1 vol. Hume, Jeff, illus. 2009. 35p. pap. 19.95 *(978-1-61546-655-9(X))* PublishAmerica, Inc.

Bandy, Michael S. & Stein, Eric. White Water. Stickland, Shadra, illus. 2015. (ENG.). 40p. (J). (gr. k-3). 7.99 *(978-0-7636-7945-3(3))* Candlewick Pr.

Barnaby, Hannah. Wonder Show. (ENG., 288p. (YA). (gr. 7). 2013. Illus.). pap. 8.99 *(978-0-544-10483-9(8))* 2012. 16.99 *(978-0-547-59980-9(3))* Houghton Mifflin Harcourt Publishing Co.

Barnes, Jennifer Lynn. Bad Blood (the Naturals #4) ((the Naturals #4)) 2016. (Naturals Ser.). (ENG.). 384p. (YA). (gr. 7-12). 17.99 *(978-1-4847-5732-1(7))* Hyperion Bks. for Children.

—Killer Instinct. 2014. (Naturals Ser.: Bk. 2). (ENG.). 384p. (YA). (gr. 9-17). 17.99 *(978-1-4231-6832-4(1))* Hyperion Pr.

Barnes, Peter W. Little Miss Patriot. Barnes, Cheryl Shaw, illus. 2007. 32p. (J). lib. bdg. 17.95 *(978-1-893622-20-3(7)*, VSP Bks.) Vacation Spot Publishing.

—Marshall, the Courthouse Mouse: A Tail of the U. S. Supreme Court. Barnes, Cheryl S., illus. 2012. (ENG.). 40p. (J). (gr. k). 16.95 *(978-1-59698-789-0(8)*, Little Patriot Pr.) Regnery Publishing, Inc., An Eagle Publishing Co.

Bart, Kathleen. Town Teddy & Country Bear Tour the USA. Bart, Kathleen, illus. 2008. (Illus.). 32p. (J). (gr. -1-3). pap. 16.95 *(978-1-932485-50-9(3))* Reverie Publishing Co.

Bates, Katherine. America the Beautiful. 2015. (ENG., Illus.). 100p. pap. 7.95 *(978-1-894997-10-2(7)*, Fox Music Bks.) Quarry Pr. CAN. Dist: SCB Distributors.

Baucom, Ian. Through the Skylight. Gerard, Justin, illus. 2013. (ENG.). 400p. (J). (gr. 4-8). 17.99 *(978-1-4169-1777-9(2)*, Atheneum Bks. for Young Readers) Simon & Schuster Children's Publishing.

Bauld, Jane Scoggins. Hector Saves the Moon, Vol. 2. Laronde, Gary, illus. 2003. (Hector's Escapades Ser.). 34p. (J). (gr. -1-3). per. 7.95 *(978-1-57168-312-0(7))* Eakin Pr.

Baum, L. Frank. Mary Louise & the Liberty Girls. 2007. (ENG.). 144p. pap. 18.99 *(978-1-4346-4333-9(6))*; 160p. pap. 21.99 *(978-1-4346-4334-6(4))* Creative Media Partners, LLC.

Bennett, Virginia. The Pigeon Tale. Hardy, E. Stuart, illus. 2007. 48p. per. *(978-1-4065-4810-5(3))* Dodo Pr.

Bilbrey, Heather. The Cookie Man. Green, Megan, illus. 2008. 20p. pap. 24.95 *(978-1-60703-328-8(3))* America Star Bks.

Billingsley, ReShonda Tate. Drama Queens. 2010. (Good Girlz Ser.: 8). (ENG., Illus.). 256p. pap. 12.99 *(978-1-4391-5687-2(5)*, Gallery Bks.) Gallery Bks.

Binder, John. The Girl Who Applied Everywhere. 2011. 160p. (YA). 17.99 *(978-1-936679-02-7(7))* Wicker Park Pr., Ltd.

Bishop, Barbara L. Children Today Around the U S A. Bishop, Barbara L., illus. 2008. (Illus.). 40p. pap. 13.95 *(978-1-934246-25-2(5))* Peppertree Pr., The.

Blaine, John. The Boy Scouts on a Submarine. 2007. 112p. pap. 18.99 *(978-1-4346-3960-8(6))*; 124p. pap. 19.99 *(978-1-4346-3961-5(4))* Creative Media Partners, LLC.

Blessing, Charlotte. New Old Shoes. Phillips, Gary R., illus. 2009. (ENG.). 32p. (J). (gr. k-3). 16.95 *(978-0-9792035-6-5(2))* Pleasant St. Pr.

Boeve, Eunice. The Summer of the Crow. 2013. 306p. pap. 14.95 *(978-1-939054-06-7(0))* Rowe Publishing and Design.

Bourgeois, Paulette. Postal Workers. LaFave, Kim, illus. 2005. 32p. (J). lib. bdg. 15.38 *(978-1-4242-1192-0(1))* Fitzgerald Bks.

Bowen, Carl. Firestormers: Elite Firefighting Crew. Lee, Marc, illus. 2016. (ENG.). 224p. (gr. 4-8). pap. 8.95 *(978-1-62370-756-9(0))* Capstone Young Readers of Coughlan Cos.

Bowen, Carl & Fuentes, Benny. Critical Strike. Tortosa, Wilson, illus. 2014. (Shadow Squadron Ser.). (ENG.). 224p. (gr. 4-8). pap. 8.95 *(978-1-62370-109-3(0))* Capstone Young Readers of Coughlan Cos.

—Dragon Teeth. Tortosa, Wilson, illus. 2015. (Shadow Squadron Ser.). (ENG.). 112p. (gr. 4-8). lib. bdg. 26.65 *(978-1-4965-0383-1(X))* Stone Arch Bks.

—Rogue Agent. Tortosa, Wilson, illus. 2015. (Shadow Squadron Ser.). (ENG.). 224p. (gr. 4-8). pap. 8.95 *(978-1-62370-296-0(8))* Capstone Young Readers of Coughlan Cos.

—Steel Hammer. Tortosa, Wilson, illus. 2015. (Shadow Squadron Ser.). (ENG.). 112p. (gr. 4-8). lib. bdg. 26.65 *(978-1-4965-0385-5(6))* Stone Arch Bks.

Bowlby, Linda S. Nasaria's Family/la Familia de Nasaria. Helms, Dana, illus. 2008. 45p. (J). (gr. -1-3). pap. 10.95 *(978-0-9779993-9-2(4))* Red Earth Publishing.

Boyd, Bentley. Moving & Grooving. 2009. (Chester Comix Ser.). (Illus.). 24p. pap. 6.95 *(978-1-933122-36-6(6))* Chester Comix, LLC.

—Reconstruction Junction. 2010. (Chester Comix Ser.). (Illus.). 24p. pap. *(978-1-933122-43-4(9))* Chester Comix, LLC.

Bray, Diane E. B. First Generation: The Story of Annie. 2008. 53p. pap. 16.95 *(978-1-60563-516-3(2))* America Star Bks.

Bridwell, Norman. Clifford Sees America. 2012. (Scholastic Reader Level 1 Ser.). (ENG.). 32p. (J). (gr. -1-3). pap. 3.99 *(978-0-545-23144-2(2)*, Cartwheel Bks.) Scholastic, Inc.

—Clifford Sees America. 2012. (Clifford: Scholastic Readers Level 1 Ser.). lib. bdg. 13.55 *(978-0-606-23908-0(1)*, Turtleback) Turtleback Bks.

Bruchac, Joseph. Brothers of the Buffalo: A Novel of the Red River War. 2016. (ENG.). 392p. (YA). (gr. 7). pap. 16.95 *(978-1-938486-92-0(7))* Fulcrum Publishing.

—Crazy Horse's Vision. Nelson, S. D., illus. 2006. (gr. 1-4). 20.45 *(978-0-7569-6691-1(4))* Perfection Learning Corp.

Buckey, Sarah Masters. The Light in the Cellar: A Molly Mystery. 2003. (American Girl Mysteries Ser.). (ENG., Illus.). 176p. (gr. 4-7). 10.95 *(978-1-59369-159-2(9))* American Girl Publishing, Inc.

Bunting, Eve. My Red Balloon. Life, Kay, illus. 2005. (ENG.). 32p. (J). (gr. -1-2). 15.95 *(978-1-59078-263-7(1))* Boyds Mills Pr.

Burg, Ann. Rebekkah's Journey: A World War II Refugee Story. Iskowitz, Joel, illus. 2006. (Tales of Young Americans Ser.). (ENG.). 32p. (J). (gr. 3-7). 17.95 *(978-1-58536-275-2(1))* Sleeping Bear Pr.

Burgan, Michael, et al. U. S. Special Ops. 2016. (U. S. Special Ops Ser.). (ENG.). 48p. (gr. 3-4). 114.61 *(978-1-5157-1865-9(4)*, Connect) Stone Arch Bks.

Butler, Ethel And Steven, creator. Callie the Kangie Traveling America. 2012. 32p. pap. 15.99 *(978-1-4685-6197-5(9))* AuthorHouse.

Carbone, Elisa & Wells, Rosemary. Diana's White House Garden. Hill, Jen, illus. 2016. (ENG.). 44p. (J). (gr. k-3). bds. 17.99 *(978-0-670-01649-5(7)*, Viking Books for Young Readers) Penguin Young Readers Group.

Carol Muller-Funk. Proxmire & the Exodus of Prairieville. 2009. 400p. pap. 17.99 *(978-1-4389-4013-7(0))* AuthorHouse.

Carter, Rachel. So Close to You. 2013. (ENG.). 336p. (YA). (gr. 9). pap. 9.99 *(978-0-06-208106-3(3)*, HarperTeen) HarperCollins Pubs.

Choat, Beth. Soccerland, 0 vols. Beck, Robert, illus. 2012. (International Sports Academy Ser.: 0). (ENG.). 242p. (YA). (gr. 7-9). pap. 8.99 *(978-0-7614-6249-1(X)*, 9780761462491, Amazon Children's Publishing) Amazon Publishing.

Clack, Cynthia. Doodles the American Hero. 2007. (ENG., Illus.). 60p. (J). lib. bdg. 20.95 *(978-0-9787533-0-6(5))* Tiger Tale Publishing Co.

Clenott, Peter. Devolution. 2013. 280p. pap. *(978-1-927792-14-8(2))* Imajin Bks.

Cole, Lisa. Chessie of the Chesapeake Bay. Cole, Lisa, illus. 2011. (Illus.). 110p. pap. 9.95 *(978-1-936343-94-2(0))* Peppertree Pr., The.

Collier, Kevin Scott. Journeys of Hope, Pearl of Wisdom. Collier, Kevin Scott, illus. 2006. (Illus.). 28p. (J). E-Book 9.95 incl. cd-rom *(978-1-933090-31-3(6))* Guardian Angel Publishing, Inc.

Cooper, Afua. My Name Is Henry Bibb: A Story of Slavery & Freedom. 2009. (ENG., Illus.). 160p. (J). (gr. 5-9). 16.95 *(978-1-55337-813-6(X))* Kids Can Pr., Ltd. CAN. Dist: Hachette Bk. Group.

Cox, Stephen Angus. The Dare Boys of 1776. 2004. reprint ed. pap. 15.95 *(978-1-4191-5856-8(2))*; pap. 1.99 *(978-1-4192-5856-5(7))* Kessinger Publishing, LLC.

Crabtree, Zona Mae. The Travelers. 2004. (Corn Cave Ser.: 2). (Illus.). 155p. (YA). per. 8.00 *(978-0-9726826-1-9(9))* Owl Hollow Publishing.

Crocker, Nancy. Billie Standish Was Here. 2007. (ENG.). 288p. (YA). (gr. 9-12). 16.99 *(978-1-4169-2423-4(X)*, Simon & Schuster Bks. For Young Readers) Simon & Schuster Bks. For Young Readers.

Crossan, Sarah. Resist. 2013. (Breathe Ser.: 2). (ENG.). 368p. (YA). (gr. 8). 17.99 *(978-0-06-211872-1(2)*, Greenwillow Bks.) HarperCollins Pubs.

Crowley, Kieran Mark. Colm & the Lazarus Key. 2009. (ENG., Illus.). 224p. (J). pap. 14.95 *(978-1-85635-646-6(9))* Mercier Pr., Ltd., The IRL. Dist: Dufour Editions, Inc.

Cusick, John M. Cherry Money Baby. 2013. (ENG.). 400p. (YA). (gr. 9). 16.99 *(978-0-7636-5557-0(0))* Candlewick Pr.

Czekaj, Jef. Austin, Lost in America: A Geography Adventure. Czekaj, Jef, illus. 2015. (ENG., Illus.). 40p. (J). (gr. -1-3). 17.99 *(978-0-06-228017-6(1))* HarperCollins Pubs.

Daffern, Brian. Prince Albert in a Can, Bk. 1. 2004. 256p. (YA). per. 13.95 *(978-0-9709104-5-5(2))* Hickory Tales Publishing.

Dagg, Carole Estby. The Year We Were Famous. 2011. (ENG.). 256p. (YA). (gr. 7-18). 17.99 *(978-0-618-99983-5(3))* Houghton Mifflin Harcourt Publishing Co.

Dalhaimer Bartkowski, Anna. Maggie Visits Grandpa: A Coloring Adventure. Dalhaimer Bartkowski, Anna, illus. 2007. (Illus.). 32p. pap. 8.99 *(978-0-9790720-1-7(8))* Infinite Adventure.

Dallas, Sandra. Red Berries, White Clouds, Blue Sky. 2015. (ENG.). 216p. (J). (gr. 3-6). pap. 9.99 *(978-1-58536-907-2(1)*, 203820) Sleeping Bear Pr.

David Iii, Paul. Brave Americans. 2013. 28p. pap. 15.95 *(978-0-7414-9638-6(0))* Infinity Publishing.

Davies, Jacqueline. Where the Ground Meets the Sky, 0 vols. unabr. ed. 2004. (ENG.). 224p. (gr. 4-6). pap. 9.99 *(978-0-7614-5187-7(0)*, 9780761451877, Amazon Children's Publishing) Amazon Publishing.

Daviess, Maria Thompson. The Golden Bird. 2007. 92p. per. *(978-1-4068-1853-6(4))* Echo Library.

Day, Williamson. The Pretorius Stories. 2011. 96p. pap. 9.99 *(978-1-4634-7430-0(X))* AuthorHouse.

de Brunhoff, Laurent. Babar's USA. 2008. (ENG., Illus.). 64p. (J). (gr. -1-k). 17.95 *(978-0-8109-7096-0(1)*, Abrams Bks. for Young Readers) Abrams, Inc.

de Brunhoff, Laurent & Rose, Phyllis. Babar Comes to America. 2008. (ENG., Illus.). 72p. (J). (gr. -1-k). 18.95 *(978-0-8109-7244-5(1)*, Abrams Bks. for Young Readers) Abrams, Inc.

Deering, Leta. Patriotic Samáand the Mendez Twins at the Alamo. 2008. 112p. pap. 19.95 *(978-1-60610-689-1(9))* America Star Bks.

Dennett, Kathleen. The 4 Corners Mystery. 2008. 32p. pap. 24.95 *(978-1-4137-2603-9(8))* America Star Bks.

Deutsch, Stacia & Cohon, Rhody. Bell's Breakthrough. Wenzel, David, illus. 2013. (Blast to the Past Ser.: 3). (ENG.). 128p. (J). (gr. 2-5). pap. 5.99 *(978-1-4424-9536-4(7)*, Simon & Schuster/Paula Wiseman Bks.) Simon & Schuster/Paula Wiseman Bks.

—Betsy Ross's Star. Francis, Guy, illus. 2015. (Blast to the Past Ser.: 8). (ENG.). 128p. (J). (gr. 2-5). pap. 6.99 *(978-1-4424-9541-8(3)*, Simon & Schuster/Paula Wiseman Bks.) Simon & Schuster/Paula Wiseman Bks.

Diggs, Dylan. The Palladium. 2006. 112p. (YA). mass mkt. 3.80 *(978-1-886366-12-1(8)*, 10,000) Sights Productions.

Doherty, Ellen. William's Journal. 2011. (Early Connections Ser.). (J). *(978-1-61672-680-5(6))* Benchmark Education Co.

Don, Lari. The Hungry Wolf: A Story from North America. Williamson, Melanie, illus. 2013. (Animal Stories Ser.). (ENG.). 48p. (J). (gr. 1-4). pap. 8.99 *(978-1-84686-872-6(6))* Barefoot Bks., Inc.

Douglas, Alan. Afloat: Or Adventures on Watery Trails. 2007. 120p. pap. 18.99 *(978-1-4346-6016-9(8))*; (ENG.). 134p. pap. 19.99 *(978-1-4346-6017-6(6))* Creative Media Partners, LLC.

Down, Heather. A Deadly Distance. 2005. (Illus.). 128p. (YA). pap. *(978-0-88878-455-1(4)*, Sandcastle Bks.) Dundurn.

Dunn, Matthew. Spy Trade: A Spycatcher Novella. 2015. 208p. mass mkt. 4.99 *(978-0-06-244142-3(6)*, Witness Impulse) HarperCollins Pubs.

Durbin, William. Until the Last Spike: The Journal of Sean Sullivan, a Transcontinental Railroad Worker, Nebraska & Points West 1867. 2013. (My Name Is America Ser.). lib.

bdg. 17.20 *(978-0-606-32342-0(2)*, Turtleback) Turtleback Bks.

Dyan, Penelope. Even More of My Life As I Know It. 2011. 100p. pap. 8.95 *(978-1-935630-50-0(4))* Bellissima Publishing, LLC.

Elkeles, Simone. How to Ruin My Teenage Life. 2007. (How to Ruin a Summer Vacation Novel Ser.: 2). (ENG.). 288p. (YA). (gr. 7-12). per. 11.99 *(978-0-7387-1019-8(9)*, Flux) North Star Editions.

Elliott, L. M. Suspect Red. 2017. (ENG.). 304p. (J). (gr. 5-9). 16.99 ***(978-1-4231-5754-0(0))*** Hyperion Bks. for Children.

English, Karen. Nadia's Hands. Weiner, Jonathan, illus. 2009. (ENG.). 32p. (J). pap. 9.95 *(978-1-59078-784-7(6))* Boyds Mills Pr.

Epstein, Estelle Pottern. I Heard My Father's Voice. 2007. 124p. pap. 11.95 *(978-0-7414-4053-2(9))* Infinity Publishing.

Erdrich, Louise. Chickadee. Erdrich, Louise, illus. 2012. (Birchbark House Ser.: 4). (Illus.). 208p. (J). (gr. 3-7). (ENG.). 16.99 *(978-0-06-057790-2(8))*; lib. bdg. 17.89 *(978-0-06-057791-9(6))* HarperCollins Pubs.

Eyre, David. Sacred Awa Piercing Spears. Kalahele, Imaikalani, illus. 2009. 31p. 14.95 *(978-0-87336-217-7(9))* Kamehameha Publishing.

Farnsworth, Frances. Cubby in Wonderland. 2005. pap. 20.95 *(978-1-4179-8778-8(2))* Kessinger Publishing, LLC.

Fidler, Mark. Blaze of the Great Cliff. 2003. 196p. 24.95 *(978-0-595-65847-3(4))* iUniverse, Inc.

Fleury, Mike Stevenson. Natural Disaster 2222. 2003. (ENG.). 112p. 19.95 *(978-0-595-65436-9(3))*; 108p. (YA). pap. 9.95 *(978-0-595-25921-2(9))* iUniverse, Inc. (Writers Club Pr.).

Flint, Ann. Charlotte's Curtain Call. 2011. 190p. pap. *(978-1-908105-51-6(8))* Grosvenor Hse. Publishing Ltd.

Flood, Nancy Bo. Warriors in the Crossfire. 2013. (ENG.). 144p. (J). (gr. 6-9). pap. 7.95 *(978-1-62091-026-9(8))* Boyds Mills Pr.

Flower, Graham Jessie. Grace Harlowe's Overland Riders on the Great American Desert. 2007. (ENG.). 132p. pap. 18.99 *(978-1-4264-1676-7(8))* Creative Media Partners, LLC.

—Grace Harlowe's Overland Riders on the Great American Desert. 2004. reprint ed. pap. 20.95 *(978-1-4191-2221-7(5))*; pap. 1.99 *(978-1-4192-2221-4(X))* Kessinger Publishing, LLC.

Floyd, Belinda D. Going to America. 2005. 28p. per. 25.49 *(978-1-4208-8693-1(2))* AuthorHouse.

Forest, Heather. The Baker's Dozen. Gaber, Susan, illus. 2013. (ENG.). 32p. (J). (gr. -1-3). 8.95 *(978-1-939160-70-6(7))* August Hse. Pubs., Inc.

Francis, Peter, illus. God Bless America, 1 vol. 2016. (Land That I Love Book Ser.). (ENG.). 18p. (J). bds. 9.99 *(978-0-310-75347-6(3))* Zonderkidz.

Furman, A. L., ed. Pioneer Stories: Young Readers. Geer, Charles, illus. 2011. 190p. 42.95 *(978-1-258-09907-7(1))* Literary Licensing, LLC.

Gardner, Sheldon. Converso Legacy. 2005. 264p. (J). pap. 12.95 *(978-1-932687-19-4(X)*, Devora Publishing) Simcha Media Group.

Gerber, Linda. Lights, Camera, Cassidy - Hacked. 2012. (Lights, Camera, Cassidy Ser.: 3). (ENG.). 224p. (J). (gr. 3-7). pap. 7.99 *(978-0-14-241816-1(1)*, Puffin Books) Penguin Young Readers Group.

Gildea, Kathy. The Adventures of Baylee Beagle — Greenville. 2005. (Illus.). 20p. (J). 7.95 *(978-0-9767096-0-2(0))* Maxim Pr.

Gingrich, Callista. Christmas in America. Arciero, Susan, illus. 2015. (Ellis the Elephant Ser.). (ENG.). 40p. (J). (gr. -1-3). 16.99 *(978-1-62157-345-6(1)*, Regnery Kids) Regnery Publishing, Inc., An Eagle Publishing Co.

Glick, Susan. Jemma's Got the Travel Bug, 1 vol. Nash, Kelli, illus. 2010. (ENG.). 32p. (J). 14.99 *(978-0-7643-3632-4(0)*, 9780764336324) Schiffer Publishing, Ltd.

Goelman, Ari. The Path of Names. 2013. (Illus.). 339p. (J). pap. *(978-0-545-47431-3(0)*, Levine, Arthur A. Bks.) Scholastic, Inc.

Gordon, Meryl G. The Flower Girl Wore Celery. Clifton-Brown, Holly, illus. 2016. (ENG.). 32p. (J). (gr. -1-5). 17.99 *(978-1-4677-7844-2(3)*, Kar-Ben Publishing) Lerner Publishing Group.

Goring, Ruth. Adriana's Angels. Meza, Erika, illus. 2017. (J). 16.99 ***(978-1-5064-1832-2(5)***, Sparkhouse Family) Augsburg Fortress, Pubs.

Green, Tim. Deep Zone. 2012. (Football Genius Ser.: 5). (ENG.). 304p. (J). (gr. 3-7). pap. 6.99 *(978-0-06-201245-6(2))* HarperCollins Pubs.

—Perfect Season. 2013. (Football Genius Ser.: 6). (ENG.). 400p. (J). (gr. 3-7). 16.99 *(978-0-06-220869-9(1))* HarperCollins Pubs.

Greenwell, Ivo. The Ancestor. 2003. 264p. (YA). pap. 16.95 *(978-0-595-29494-7(4))* iUniverse, Inc.

Griesmer, Russell. My Hometown. Wong, Priscilla, illus. 2015. (ENG.). 40p. (gr. 1-4). 15.95 *(978-1-62370-174-1(0))* Capstone Young Readers of Coughlan Cos.

Hale, Edward Everett. Margaret Percival in America; a Tale Ed by a New England Minister, a B Being a Sequel to Margaret Percival a Tale Ed by Rev William Sewell, B. 2006. 288p. per. 23.99 *(978-1-4255-2654-2(3))* Michigan Publishing.

Hall, Annalisa. Tak & Lolly: Santa Clause at Church. 2009. 51p. pap. 6.99 *(978-0-557-04923-3(7))* Lulu Pr., Inc.

Hall, Donald. Lucy's Christmas. McCurdy, Michael, illus. 2007. (ENG.). 32p. (J). (gr. 1). pap. 10.95 *(978-1-56792-342-1(9))* Godine, David R. Pub.

Hampstead, Tom. The Kingdom of the Two Great Houses. 2011. 86p. pap. 10.95 *(978-1-60911-895-2(2)*, Strategic Bk. Publishing) Strategic Book Publishing & Rights Agency (SBPRA).

Hancock, H. Irving. Dave Darrin at Vera Cruz. 2007. 180p. per. *(978-1-4065-1973-0(1))* Dodo Pr.

Harper, Chris. The Dogges of Barkshire - the Grand Kennel. Harper, Chris, illus. 2013. (Illus.). 26p. (J). pap. *(978-1-78222-086-2(0))* Paragon Publishing, Rothersthorpe.

Harper, Ken. Mystery in Mansfield. 2008. 60p. pap. 19.95 *(978-1-60441-055-6(8))* America Star Bks.

Harris, Joel Chandler. Told by Uncle Remus: New Stories of the. 2006. (Illus.). pap. 31.95 *(978-1-4254-9964-8(3))* Kessinger Publishing, LLC.

Harstad, Johan. 172 Hours on the Moon. 2013. (ENG.). 384p. (J). (gr. 8-17). pap. 10.99 *(978-0-316-18289-8(3))* Little, Brown Bks. for Young Readers.

Harstad, Johan & Chace, Tara. 172 Hours on the Moon. 2012. (ENG.). 368p. (gr. 7-17). 17.99 *(978-0-316-18288-1(5))* Little Brown & Co.

Havran, Melissa. George Washington. 2013. 32p. pap. 19.99 *(978-1-4817-0157-0(6))* AuthorHouse.

Hearne, Betsy. Seven Brave Women. Andersen, Bethanne, illus. 2006. (gr. -1-3). 17.00 *(978-0-7569-6669-0(8))* Perfection Learning Corp.

Hergé. America. Orig. Title: Tintin en Amerique. (Illus.). 62p. (J). 24.95 *(978-0-8288-5000-1(3))* French & European Pubns., Inc.

—Tintin en Amerique. Orig. Title: Tintin in America. (Illus.). 62p. (J). (FRE.). 24.95 *(978-0-8288-5093-3(3))*; (SPA., 24.95 *(978-0-8288-5094-0(1))* French & European Pubns., Inc.

Hergé & I, Herge-tintin Rustica. Tintin en Amerique. (Tintin Ser.). Orig. Title: Tintin in America. (SPA.). 64p. (J). 14.95 *(978-84-261-1400-6(8))* Juventud, Editorial ESP. Dist: Distribooks, Inc.

Herman, Debbie. Rosie Saves the World. Lyon, Tammie, illus. 2017. (ENG.). 32p. (gr. -1-2). 17.99 ***(978-1-5124-2085-2(9)***, Kar-Ben Publishing) Lerner Publishing Group.

Hesse, Karen. Safekeeping. 2016. (YA). lib. bdg. 20.85 *(978-0-606-38437-7(5))* Turtleback Bks.

Hinton, S. E. Rumble Fish. 2013. (ENG.). 144p. (YA). (gr. 7). pap. 7.99 *(978-0-385-37568-9(9)*, Delacorte Pr.) Random Hse. Children's Bks.

Hobbs, Will. Beardance. 2004. (ENG., Illus.). 208p. (J). (gr. 5-9). pap. 7.99 *(978-0-689-87072-9(8)*, Simon & Schuster/Paula Wiseman Bks.) Simon & Schuster Children's Publishing.

—Crossing the Wire. 2007. (Illus.). 216p. (gr. 5-9). 17.00 *(978-0-7569-8053-5(4))* Perfection Learning Corp.

Hoberman, Mary Ann. Very Short Tall Tales to Read Together. Emberley, Michael, illus. 2014. (ENG.). 32p. (J). (gr. -1-3). 17.00 *(978-0-316-18329-1(6))* Little Brown & Co.

Holt, Kimberly Willis. Navy Brat. Davenier, Christine, illus. 2011. (Piper Reed Ser.: 1). (ENG.). 176p. (J). (gr. 3-6). pap. 6.99 *(978-0-312-62548-1(0)*, 9780312625481) Square Fish.

—Piper Reed, Campfire Girl. Davenier, Christine, illus. 2011. (Piper Reed Ser.: 4). (ENG.). 176p. (J). (gr. 3-6). pap. 6.99 *(978-0-312-67482-3(1)*, 9780312674823) Square Fish.

—Piper Reed, Clubhouse Queen. Davenier, Christine, illus. 2011. (Piper Reed Ser.: 2). (ENG.). 176p. (J). (gr. 3-6). pap. 6.99 *(978-0-312-61676-2(7)*, 9780312616762) Square Fish.

—Piper Reed, Forever Friend. Davenier, Christine, illus. 2012. (Piper Reed Ser.: 6). (ENG.). 160p. (J). (gr. 3-6). 15.99 *(978-0-8050-9008-6(8)*, 9780805090086, Holt, Henry & Co. Bks. For Young Readers) Holt, Henry & Co.

—Piper Reed, Forever Friend. Davenier, Christine, illus. 2013. (Piper Reed Ser.: 6). (ENG.). 176p. (J). (gr. 3-6). pap. 6.99 *(978-1-250-02725-2(X)*, 9781250027252) Square Fish.

—Piper Reed Gets a Job. Davenier, Christine, illus. 2009. (Piper Reed Ser.: 3). (ENG.). 160p. (J). (gr. 3-6). 14.99 *(978-0-8050-8199-2(2)*, 9780805081992, Holt, Henry & Co. Bks. For Young Readers) Holt, Henry & Co.

—Piper Reed, Party Planner. Davenier, Christine, illus. 2011. (Piper Reed Ser.: 3). (ENG.). 176p. (J). (gr. 3-6). pap. 7.99 *(978-0-312-61677-9(5)*, 9780312616779) Square Fish.

Hossfeld, Harald. Rapacious Kings Sagacious Kids. 2010. 186p. pap. *(978-3-8391-4994-2(0))* Books on Demand GmbH.

Howe, Kim, illus. American Life Series: Family, Teacher, Friend, 3 books. 2006. 80p. 19.95 *(978-1-59971-554-4(6))* Aardvark Global Publishing.

Hu, Jennifer. Dodo's Story: Journey in America. 2010. 40p. 16.99 *(978-1-4520-6095-8(9))* AuthorHouse.

Hubbard, Crystal. Catching the Moon: The Story of a Young Girl's Baseball Dream. DuBurke, Randy, illus. 2005. (ENG.). 32p. (J). pap. 9.95 *(978-1-60060-572-7(9))* Lee & Low Bks., Inc.

Hubbard, Jenny. Paper Covers Rock. 2012. (ENG.). 192p. (YA). (gr. 9). pap. 7.99 *(978-0-385-74056-2(5)*, Ember) Random Hse. Children's Bks.

Huber, Morgan. Nanite. 2013. 140p. pap. 19.95 *(978-1-63004-633-0(7))* America Star Bks.

Huber, Randolph. Monsters from the ID. 2007. 48p. per. 16.95 *(978-1-4241-4682-6(8))* PublishAmerica, Inc.

Hughes, Dean. Four-Four-Two. 2016. (ENG., Illus.). 272p. (YA). (gr. 7). 17.99 *(978-1-4814-6252-5(0)*, Atheneum Bks. for Young Readers) Simon & Schuster Children's Publishing.

Hughes, Virginia. Peggy Finds the Theater. Leone, Sergio, illus. 2011. 186p. 42.95 *(978-1-258-10513-6(6))* Literary Licensing, LLC.

Husain, Aliya. Neither This nor That. 2010. 260p. pap. 19.99 *(978-0-557-22302-2(4))* Lulu Pr., Inc.

John, Antony. Elemental. (ENG., (YA). (gr. 7). 2013. Illus.). 352p. pap. 8.99 *(978-0-14-242516-9(8)*, Speak) 2012. 336p. 17.99 *(978-0-8037-3682-5(7)*, Dial Bks) Penguin Young Readers Group.

—Renegade. 2014. (ENG.). 304p. (YA). (gr. 7). 17.99 *(978-0-8037-3685-6(1)*, Dial Bks) Penguin Young Readers Group.

Johnston, Annie Fellows. The Little Colonel. 2004. reprint ed. pap. 1.99 *(978-1-4192-7020-8(6))* Kessinger Publishing, LLC.

Jones, Marcia Thornton. Woodford Brave. Whipple, Kevin, illus. 2015. (ENG.). 200p. (J). (gr. 3-7). 16.95 *(978-1-62979-305-4(1)*, Calkins Creek) Boyds Mills Pr.

Jordan-Tegtmeier. Jennifer. The Small Shady Tree. 2008. 16p. pap. 8.49 *(978-1-4343-7382-3(7))* AuthorHouse.

Judybee. Danny Strikes Out in Americ: A R. E. A. d Book. Kecskés, Anna, illus. 2013. 32p. pap. *(978-1-78092-335-2(X))* MX Publishing, Ltd.

Jules, Jacqueline. Sofia Martinez. 2015. (Sofia Martinez Ser.). (ENG.). 32p. (gr. k-2). lib. bdg. 85.28 *(978-1-4795-6168-1(1)*, Sofia Martinez) Picture Window Bks.

Kay, Susan. Abby & Gabby Tales. 2009. 16p. pap. 9.99 *(978-1-4389-6467-6(6))* AuthorHouse.

Keller, Laurie. The Scrambled States of America. 2011. (J). (gr. k-4). 29.95 *(978-0-545-19702-1(3))* Weston Woods Studios, Inc.

—Scrambled States of America. 2009. (ENG., Illus.). 32p. (J). (gr. -1-4). 9.99 *(978-1-4272-0730-2(5)*, 9781427207302) Macmillan Audio.

—The Scrambled States of America Talent Show. Keller, Laurie, illus. 2010. (ENG., Illus.). 40p. (J). (gr. 2-5). pap. 7.99 *(978-0-312-62824-6(2)*, 9780312628246) Square Fish.

Kelly, Cheryl. Adam the Adventurous Ant. 2011. 24p. pap. 15.99 *(978-1-4568-6366-1(5))* Xlibris Corp.

Kennedy, Katie. Learning to Swear in America. 2017. (ENG.). 368p. (YA). pap. 9.99 *(978-1-61963-911-9(4)*, 9781619639119, Bloomsbury USA Childrens) Bloomsbury Publishing USA.

Kent, Elizabeth. The Enchanted Adventures of the Caroline Kemps. 2007. 148p. pap. 24.95 *(978-1-4241-9915-0(8))* America Star Bks.

Ketchum, Liza. The Life Fantastic. 2017. (ENG.). 256p. (YA). 17.99 *(978-1-4405-9876-0(2)*, Simon Pulse) Simon Pulse.

Kiem, Elizabeth. Dancer, Daughter, Traitor, Spy. 2014. (Bolshoi Saga Ser.: 1). (ENG., Illus.). 292p. (YA). (gr. 9). pap. 10.99 *(978-1-61695-422-2(1)*, Soho Teen) Soho Pr., Inc.

Kimpton, Paul & Kimpton, Ann Kaczkowski. Starting Early: A Boy & His Bugle in America During WWII. 2011. (Adventures with Music Ser.: 1). (ENG., Illus.). 204p. (J). (gr. 4-7). pap. 8.95 *(978-1-57999-805-9(4))* G I A Pubns., Inc.

Kirby, Matthew J. The Lost Kingdom. 2013. (ENG.). 352p. (J). (gr. 3-7). 18.99 *(978-0-545-27426-5(5)*, Scholastic Pr.) Scholastic, Inc.

Knapp, Jodi. The Adventures of Kelly & Lucky: The Beginning. 2010. 76p. pap. 20.99 *(978-1-60976-090-8(5)*, Eloquent Bks.) Strategic Book Publishing & Rights Agency (SBPRA).

Konigsburg, E. L. The Outcasts of 19 Schuyler Place. 2005. 296p. (J). (gr. 5). 13.65 *(978-0-7569-6307-1(9))* Perfection Learning Corp.

Kravitz, Danny. Tommy Mcknight & the Great Election. 2016. (Presidential Politics Ser.). (ENG.). 96p. (gr. 3-4). lib. bdg. 26.65 *(978-1-4965-2585-7(X)*, Connect) Stone Arch Bks.

Krensky, Stephen. John Henry. Oldroyd, Mark, illus. 2007. (On My Own Folklore Ser.). (ENG.). 48p. (gr. 2-4). per. 6.95 *(978-0-8225-6477-5(7)*, First Avenue Editions) Lerner Publishing Group.

Kurchinski, Alessandra. Disney Story. 2010. 36p. pap. 17.30 *(978-0-557-25447-7(7))* Lulu Pr., Inc.

Lachtman, Ofelia Dumas. The Truth about las Mariposas. 2007. 144p. (J). (gr. 6-18). pap. 9.95 *(978-1-55885-494-9(0)*, Piñata Books) Arte Publico Pr.

Landon, Lucinda. Meg Mackintosh Solves Seven American History Mysteries: A Solve-It-Yourself Mystery. 2008. (Meg Mackintosh Mystery Ser.: 9). (ENG.). 96p. (J). (gr. 2-4). pap. 8.95 *(978-1-888695-12-0(9))* Secret Passage Pr.

Langridge, Roger. The Muppet Show Comic Book: The Treasure of Peg-Leg Wilson. Langridge, Roger, illus. 2010. (Muppet Show Ser.). (ENG., Illus.). 112p. (J). 24.99 *(978-1-60886-530-7(4))*; (gr. 4-7). pap. 9.99 *(978-1-60886-504-8(5))* Boom! Studios.

Larson, Kirby. Duke. 2015. (Dogs of World War II Ser.). (ENG.). 240p. (J). (gr. 3-7). pap. 7.99 *(978-0-545-41638-2(8)*, Scholastic Paperbacks) Scholastic, Inc.

Lawlor, Laurie. He Will Go Fearless. 2012. (ENG.). 224p. (J). (gr. 5-9). pap. 10.99 *(978-0-689-86580-0(5)*, Simon & Schuster Bks. For Young Readers) Simon & Schuster Bks. For Young Readers.

Lazo Gilmore, Dorina K. Cora Cooks Pancit. Valiant, Kristi, illus. 2014. (ENG.). 32p. (J). (gr. -1-3). 17.95 *(978-1-885008-35-0(X)*, Shen's Bks.) Lee & Low Bks., Inc.

Leipold, Judith. Destiny's Wild Ride, a Tall Tale of the Legendary Hub Hubbell. White, David, illus. 2013. 32p. 24.95 *(978-1-61493-168-3(2))*; pap. 14.95 *(978-1-61493-167-6(4))* Peppertree Pr., The.

Lester, Julius. Day of Tears. 2007. (ENG., Illus.). 192p. (J). (gr. 5-9). pap. 7.99 *(978-1-4231-0409-4(9)*, Jump at the Sun) Hyperion Bks. for Children.

Levitin, Sonia. Junk Man's Daughter. Porfirio, Guy, illus. rev. ed. 2007. (Tales of Young Americans Ser.). (ENG.). 32p. (J). (gr. 3-7). 17.95 *(978-1-58536-315-5(4))* Sleeping Bear Pr.

Lewis, Fiona. Dreaming in Color. 2011. (ENG.). 304p. (J). (gr. 7). pap. 16.95 *(978-0-9845318-5-1(8))* Tiny Stachel Pr.

Lieurance, Suzanne. The Lucky Baseball: My Story in a Japanese-American Internment Camp. 2009. (Historical Fiction Adventures (HFA) Ser.). (Illus.). 160p. (J). (gr. 3-6). lib. bdg. 29.27 *(978-0-7660-3311-5(2))* Enslow Pubs., Inc.

Lockard, Donna Lee. Sasha the Tortoise's Summer Vacation. 2013. (ENG.). 36p. (J). pap. 19.95 *(978-1-4787-0938-1(3))* Outskirts Pr., Inc.

Loeper, John J. Galloping Gertrude: By Motorcar In 1908. Chironna, Ronald, illus. 2011. 80p. (J). lib. bdg. 19.95 *(978-0-9727940-1-5(8))* Hieropub LLC.

Lois, Lowry. Crow Call. Ibatoulline, Bagram, illus. 2009. (ENG.). 32p. (J). (gr. 3-7). 19.99 *(978-0-545-03035-9(8)*, Scholastic Pr.) Scholastic, Inc.

—Gooney Bird on the Map. Thomas, Middy, illus. (Gooney Bird Greene Ser.). (ENG.). 128p. (J). (gr. 1-4). 2013. pap. 5.99 *(978-0-547-85088-7(3))* 2011. 16.99 *(978-0-547-55622-2(5))* Houghton Mifflin Harcourt Publishing Co.

Loiske, Jennifer. Black Diamond. 2013. 246p. (J). pap. 13.61 *(978-1-291-30145-8(3))* Lulu Pr., Inc.

Lombardo, Constance. Mr. Puffball: Stunt Cat Across America. Lombardo, Constance, illus. 2016. (Mr. Puffball Ser.: 2). (Illus.). 240p. (J). (gr. 3-7). 12.99 *(978-0-06-232068-1(8)*, Tegen, Katherine Bks) HarperCollins Pubs.

London, C. Alexander. Blood in the Water. 2014. (Tides of War Ser.: 1). (ENG.). 224p. (J). (gr. 5-9). pap. 5.99 *(978-0-545-66298-7(2)*, Scholastic Paperbacks) Scholastic, Inc.

—Honor Bound. 2014. (Tides of War Ser.: 2). (ENG.). 224p. (J). (gr. 5-9). pap. 5.99 *(978-0-545-66301-4(6)*, Scholastic Paperbacks) Scholastic, Inc.

Long, Loren & Bildner, Phil. Horsin' Around. Long, Loren, illus. 2009. (Sluggers Ser.: 2). (ENG., Illus.). 224p. (J). (gr. 3-7). pap. 8.99 *(978-1-4169-1888-2(4)*, Simon & Schuster Bks. For Young Readers) Simon & Schuster Bks. For Young Readers.

Lucan, Dawn. My Challenge Memories. 2011. 108p. pap. 8.95 *(978-1-4583-4714-5(1))* Lulu Pr., Inc.

Lucas, Lexie. The Adventures of Little Boy Brown. 2011. (Illus.). 40p. pap. 16.59 *(978-1-4567-4035-1(0))* AuthorHouse.

Lyford, Cabot. Arthur the Moose. Lyford, Cabot, illus. l.t. ed. 2004. (Illus.). 32p. (J). lib. bdg. *(978-0-9748145-0-6(4))* Castlebay, Inc.

Lynch, Chris. Casualties of War. 2013. (Vietnam Ser.: 4). lib. bdg. 18.40 *(978-0-606-31964-5(6)*, Turtleback) Turtleback Bks.

—Free-Fire Zone. 2012. (Vietnam Ser.). (J). (ENG.). 192p. (gr. 5-9). 16.99 *(978-0-545-27025-0(1))*; 183p. *(978-0-545-49427-4(3))* Scholastic, Inc. (Scholastic Pr.).

—Free-Fire Zone. 2013. (Vietnam Ser.: 3). lib. bdg. 18.40 *(978-0-606-31963-8(8)*, Turtleback) Turtleback Bks.

—I Pledge Allegiance. 2011. 183p. (YA). *(978-0-545-38415-5(X))* Scholastic, Inc.

—I Pledge Allegiance. 2013. (Vietnam Ser.: 1). lib. bdg. 17.20 *(978-0-606-31961-4(1)*, Turtleback) Turtleback Bks.

—The Liberators. 2015. (World War II Ser.: 4). (ENG.). 192p. (J). (gr. 5-9). 18.99 *(978-0-545-52304-2(4)*, Scholastic Pr.) Scholastic, Inc.

—Walking Wounded, Bk. 5. 2014. (Vietnam Ser.: 5). (ENG.). 208p. (J). (gr. 5-9). 17.99 *(978-0-545-64013-8(X)*, Scholastic Pr.) Scholastic, Inc.

MacDonald, Jerry. Red Eyes & Crazy Jake. 2009. 24p. pap. 15.95 *(978-1-4389-2706-0(1))* AuthorHouse.

MacKenzie-Krysko, Claudia & Krysko, Kenneth L. The Adventures of Granville, Coming to America. Cotton, Sue Lynn, illus. 2013. 24p. pap. 12.95 *(978-1-61493-227-7(1))* Peppertree Pr., The.

MacLachlan, Patricia. More Perfect Than the Moon. 2005. 16.00 *(978-0-7569-5437-6(1))* Perfection Learning Corp.

—Nora's Chicks. Brown, Kathryn, illus. 2013. (ENG.). 40p. (J). (gr. -1-2). 15.99 *(978-0-7636-4753-7(5))* Candlewick Pr.

Madison, Ron. Ned & the General: A Lesson about Deployment. Covolo, David, illus. 2004. 26p. (J). (gr. -1-3). *(978-1-887206-25-9(6))* Ned's Head Productions.

Magenta, Emma. Orlando on a Thursday. Magenta, Emma, illus. 2010. (ENG., Illus.). 32p. (J). (gr. -1-2). 15.99 *(978-0-7636-4560-1(5))* Candlewick Pr.

Marsh, Carole. The Counterfeit Constitution Mystery. 2008. (Real Kids, Real Places Ser.). (Illus.). 144p. (J). (gr. 3-5). 14.95 *(978-0-635-06517-9(7))*; per. 5.95 *(978-0-635-06512-4(6))* Gallopade International.

Martinez, Manuel. Ana Is a Citizen! Digital Citizenship. 2017. (Computer Science for the Real World Ser.). 16p. (gr. 7-8). pap. 7.95 ***(978-1-5383-5216-8(8)***, Rosen Classroom) Rosen Publishing Group, Inc., The.

Marvel. Marvel's the Avengers Storybook Collection. 2015. (ENG., Illus.). 192p. (J). (gr. -1-3). 11.99 *(978-0-316-25631-5(5))* Little, Brown Bks. for Young Readers.

Matagrano, Joseph F. Forever Brothers. 2007. 396p. 26.95 *(978-1-4327-0963-1(1))*; per. 16.95 *(978-1-4327-1524-3(0))* Outskirts Pr., Inc.

Mayhar, Ardath. Medicine Walk. 2007. (ENG.). 96p. (YA). (gr. 9). pap. 7.95 *(978-1-4169-6846-7(6)*, Simon Pulse) Simon Pulse.

McCaffrey, Debra. Fly...Ball: Illustrated by 2nd Grade Students of Mrs. Young's 2KY at Mohansic Elementary School. 2007. pap. 20.00 *(978-0-8059-8781-2(9))* Dorrance Publishing Co., Inc.

McCully, Emily Arnold. My Heart Glow: Alice Cogswell, Thomas Gallaudet, & the Birth of American Sign Language. McCully, Emily Arnold, illus. 2008. (ENG., Illus.). 40p. (gr. 1-4). 15.99 *(978-1-4231-0028-7(X))* Hyperion Pr.

McDavid-Jones, Elizabeth. Ghost Light on Graveyard Shoal. 2009. (Mysteries Through Time Ser.). 144 - 176p. (YA). (gr. 4-8). 31.95 *(978-1-60754-443-2(1))*; pap. 15.25 *(978-1-60754-444-9(X))* Windmill Bks.

McGovern, DeeDee Jean. The Heartland of Home: Tight Quarters in the City. 2008. 58p. pap. 16.95 *(978-1-60610-058-5(0))* America Star Bks.

McMann, Lisa. The Trap Door. 2015. (Infinity Ring Ser.: 3). lib. bdg. 17.20 *(978-0-606-37788-1(3))* Turtleback Bks.

McSpadden, Judy. Heart for Thunder. 2010. 148p. 22.95 *(978-1-4401-9487-0(4))*; pap. 12.95 *(978-1-4401-9489-4(0))* iUniverse, Inc.

Meehan, Thomas. Annie. 2013. (Annie Book Ser.). (ENG.). 272p. (J). (gr. 5). pap. 7.99 *(978-0-14-751114-0(3)*, Puffin Books) Penguin Young Readers Group.

Merry Christmas USA. 2007. (J). bds. 21.95 *(978-0-9745191-3-5(8))* Lynn Tyner Mitchum & James Rogers.

Messner, Kate. Capture the Flag. 2012. (ENG.). 240p. (J). (gr. 3-7). 16.99 *(978-0-545-39539-7(9)*, Scholastic Pr.) Scholastic, Inc.

Miller, Bobbi. One Fine Trade. Hillenbrand, Will, illus. 2009. (ENG.). 32p. (J). (gr. -1-3). 16.95 *(978-0-8234-1836-7(7))* Holiday Hse., Inc.

Mochizuki, Ken. Baseball Saved Us. 97th rev. ed. 2014. (ENG.). 30p. (J). (gr. k-12). 15.65 *(978-1-63245-249-8(9))* Lectorum Pubns., Inc.

Montgomery, R. A. Blood on the Handle. 2010. (Illus.). 144p. (J). pap. 6.99 *(978-1-933390-33-8(6))* Chooseco LLC.

—Smoke Jumpers. Peguy, Laurence, illus. 2009. (Choose Your Own Adventure Ser.: No. 29). 144p. (J). (gr. 2-7). pap. 6.99 *(978-1-933390-29-1(8))* Chooseco LLC.

Moreland, Janet & Webb, Shirley G. Dance in the Rain. 2005. (Howell Women Saga: Bk. II). 209p. (YA). pap. 14.95 *(978-0-595-34022-4(9))* iUniverse, Inc.

Musilli Whitesell, Marjorie. I Have Four Parents. 2009. (Illus.). 20p. pap. 10.95 *(978-1-60860-448-7(9)*, Eloquent Bks.) Strategic Book Publishing & Rights Agency (SBPRA).

The Mystery of the Tiny Key. 2008. 32p. pap. 4.99 *(978-0-8341-2351-9(7)*, 083-412-3517) Beacon Hill Pr. of Kansas City.

Naberhaus, Sarvinder. Blue Sky White Stars. Nelson, Kadir, illus. 2017. (ENG.). 40p. (J). (gr. -1-3). 17.99 *(978-0-8037-3700-6(9)*, Dial Bks) Penguin Young Readers Group.

Naifeh, Ted. The League of Ordinary Gentleman. 2011. (Courtney Crumrin Tales Ser.). (Illus.). 56p. (J). (gr. 2). pap. 5.99 *(978-1-934964-68-2(9))* Oni Pr., Inc.

Nextext, creator. Tales of O. Henry. 2006. (Classic Retelling Ser.). (Illus.). 144p. (YA). (gr. 8-12). lib. bdg. *(978-0-618-08596-5(3)*, 2-00189) Holt McDougal.

Olivas, John D. Endeavour's Long Journey/la Larga Travesía de Endeavour. Roski, Gayle G., illus. 2016. (SPA.). 40p. (J). 19.95 ***(978-0-9973947-2-6(2))*** East West Discovery Pr.

Orback, Craig, illus. Paul Bunyan. 2006. (On My Own Folklore Ser.). 48p. (J). (gr. -1-3). lib. bdg. 25.26 *(978-1-57505-888-7(X)*, Millbrook Pr.) Lerner Publishing Group.

Osa, Nancy. Cuba 15. 2005. (ENG.). 304p. (YA). (gr. 7). reprint ed. pap. 9.99 (978-0-385-73233-8(3), Ember) Random Hse. Children's Bks.

Osborne, Mary Pope. Magic Tree House Volumes 21-24 Boxed Set: American History Quartet, 4 vols. Murdocca, Sal, illus. 2014. (ENG.). 96p. (J). (gr. 1-4). 23.96 (978-0-385-38957-0(4), Random Hse. Bks. for Young Readers) Random Hse. Children's Bks.

Pacileo, Janis. A Shrimp Called Pee Wee. 2012. 24p. pap. 12.45 (978-1-4624-0135-2(X), Inspiring Voices) Author Solutions, Inc.

Parkinson, Curtis. Death in Kingsport. 2007. (ENG.). 224p. (YA). (gr. 5-9). per. 11.95 (978-0-88776-827-9(X), Tundra Bks.) Tundra Bks. CAN. Dist: Penguin Random Hse. LLC.

Parry, Rosanne. Heart of a Shepherd. 2010. (ENG.). 176p. (J). (gr. 3-7). pap. 7.99 (978-0-375-84803-2(7), Yearling) Random Hse. Children's Bks.

Paulsen, Gary. The Quilt. 2005. 83p. (gr. 3-7). 16.00 (978-0-7569-4781-1(2)) Perfection Learning Corp.

Payne, Sandy. Find Your Magic. Goodpaster, Nancy, illus. 2013. 50p. pap. 12.95 (978-1-937508-16-6(1)) Bearhead Publishing, LLC.

Payson, Howard. The Boy Scouts under Sealed Orders. 2005. (Illus.). pap. 30.95 (978-1-885529-57-2(0)) Stevens Publishing.

Pearsall, Shelley. Jump into the Sky. 2012. (ENG.). 352p. (J). (gr. 5). 16.99 (978-0-375-83699-2(3), Knopf Bks. for Young Readers) Random Hse. Children's Bks.

Pedersen, Elsa. Alaska Harvest. Werth, Kurt, illus. 2012. 194p. 42.95 (978-1-258-23211-5(1)); pap. 27.95 (978-1-258-23973-2(6)) Literary Licensing, LLC.

Peirce, Lincoln. I Can't Take It! 2013. (Big Nate Graphic Novels Ser.). lib. bdg. 20.85 (978-0-606-32313-0(9), Turtleback) Turtleback Bks.

Penner, Stephen. Professor Barrister's Dinosaur Mysteries #2: The Case of the Armored Allosaurus. 2010. 54p. pap. 19.60 (978-1-60888-018-8(4)) Nimble Bks. LLC.

Perkins, Mitali. The Not-So-Star-Spangled Life of Sunita Sen. 2nd rev. ed. 2005. (ENG.). 192p. (J). (gr. 3-7). reprint ed. pap. 17.99 (978-0-316-73453-0(5)) Little, Brown Bks. for Young Readers.

Petersen, Jean. Moose Shoes. Morrow, E., illus. 2007. 52p. per. 24.95 (978-1-4241-8399-9(5)) America Star Bks.

Peterson, Esther Allen. The House That Cared. 2010. (J). pap. (978-0-88092-505-1(1)) Royal Fireworks Publishing Co.

Phanton, Rick. Boston & the Bean. 2012. 112p. pap. 19.95 (978-1-4626-4809-2(6)) America Star Bks.

Phillips, Dee. A Dream of America, 1 vol., Bk. 12. 2015. (Yesterday's Voices Ser.). (ENG.). 48p. (YA). (gr. 9-12). pap. 8.95 (978-1-62250-914-0(5)) Saddleback Educational Publishing, Inc.

—A Dream of America: The Story of an Immigrant. 2015. (Yesterday's Voices Ser.). (YA). lib. bdg. 19.60 (978-0-606-36672-4(5)) Turtleback Bks.

Pickett, Anola. Callahan Crossroads. 2015. (ENG.). 192p. (J). pap. 12.99 (978-1-4621-1715-4(5), Sweetwater Bks.) Cedar Fort, Inc./CFI Distribution.

Pinkney, Andrea Davis. Bird in a Box. Qualls, Sean, illus. 2012. (ENG.). 288p. (J). (gr. 3-7). pap. 8.99 (978-0-316-07402-5(0)) Little, Brown Bks. for Young Readers.

Pintozzi, Nick. Bentley & the Cactus Rustlers. Pintozzi, Nick & Pintozzi, Connie, illus. 2006. per. 11.00 (978-0-9749465-4-2(0)) BentDaiSha, LLC.

Polacco, Patricia. Someone for Mr. Sussman. Polacco, Patricia, illus. 2008. (ENG., Illus.). 40p. (J). (gr. 1-3). 17.99 (978-0-399-25075-0(1), Philomel Bks.) Penguin Young Readers Group.

Ponti, James. Framed! 2017. (Framed! Ser.: 1). (ENG., Illus.). 320p. (J). (gr. 3-7). pap. 7.99 **(978-1-4814-3631-1(7)**, Aladdin) Simon & Schuster Children's Publishing.

Priceman, Marjorie. How to Make a Cherry Pie & See the U. S. A. 2013. lib. bdg. 18.40 (978-0-606-32190-7(X), Turtleback) Turtleback Bks.

Prinz, Yvonne. All You Get Is Me. 2010. (ENG.). 288p. (YA). (gr. 9-18). 16.99 (978-0-06-171580-8(8)) HarperCollins Pubs.

Pynn, Susan. Jelly Bean Row, 1 vol. Pratt, Liz, illus. 2011. (ENG.). 32p. (J). (gr. k-5). pap. 9.95 (978-1-897174-80-7(2), Tuckamore Bks) Creative Bk. Publishing CAN. Dist: Orca Bk. Pubs. USA.

Ralphson, G. Harvey. Boy Scouts in a Submarine. 2007. 104p. per. (978-1-4068-3726-1(1)) Echo Library.

—Boy Scouts in an Airship. 2007. 104p. per. (978-1-4068-3727-8(X)) Echo Library.

—Boy Scouts in Southern Waters. 2007. 128p. (gr. -1-7). per. (978-1-4068-3730-8(X)) Echo Library.

Rexroth, Sharon. America from the Sky. 2006. (J). 9.95 (978-1-57166-429-7(7)); per. 22.95 (978-1-57166-430-3(0)) Quixote Pr.

RIGBY. Now We Live in the USA! Third Grade Big Books. 2009. (Rigby on Our Way to English Ser.). (ENG.). 24p. (gr. 3-3). pap. 50.70 (978-0-7578-4207-8(0)) Rigby Education.

Robbins, Dean. Two Friends: Susan B. Anthony & Frederick Douglass: Susan B. Anthony & Frederick Douglass. Qualls, Sean & Alko, Selina, illus. 2016. (ENG.). 32p. (J). (gr. -1-3). 17.99 (978-0-545-39996-8(3), Orchard Bks.) Scholastic, Inc.

Robles, Tony. Joey Gonzalez, Great American. Pryor, Jim, illus. 2008. (ENG.). (J). (gr. 2-3). 15.95 (978-0-9767269-3-7(9)) WND Bks, Inc.

Rocklin, Joanne. Fleabrain Loves Franny. 2015. (ENG.). 288p. (J). (gr. 3-7). pap. 8.95 (978-1-4197-1676-8(X), Amulet Bks.) Abrams, Inc.

Rockwood, Roy. Dave Dashaway & His Hydroplane. 2009. 128p. 23.95 (978-1-60664-625-0(7)); pap. 10.95 (978-1-60664-364-8(9)) Rodgers, Alan Bks.

Rolt-Wheeler, Francis. The Boy with the U. S. Census. 2006. (ENG.). 220p. pap. 20.99 (978-1-4264-6792-9(3)); 242p. pap. 22.99 (978-1-4264-6855-1(5)) Creative Media Partners, LLC.

Rossi, Veronica. Riders. 2017. (Riders Ser.: 1). (ENG.). 384p. (YA). pap. 9.99 (978-0-7653-8255-9(5), 9780765382559, Tor Teen) Doherty, Tom Assocs., LLC.

Roy, Ron. A Thief at the National Zoo. Bush, Timothy, illus. 2007. (Capital Mysteries Ser.: No. 9). (ENG.). 96p. (J). (gr. 1-4). per. 4.99 (978-0-375-84804-9(5), Random Hse. Bks. for Young Readers) Random Hse. Children's Bks.

Rylant, Cynthia & National Geographic Learning Staff. Tulip Sees America. Desimini, Lisa, illus. 2010. (Rise & Shine Ser.). (ENG.). 32p. (C). (gr. -1-18). pap. 21.95 (978-0-439-39978-4(5)) National Geographic School Publishing, Inc.

Santacroce, John P. Running Across the Moon. 2013. 146p. pap. 14.98 (978-0-615-76887-8(3)) Santacroce, John.

Saunders, Jami Lynn. Rabid: Book II of the Werecat Saga. 2012. 94p. (YA). pap. 4.99 (978-1-936307-16-6(2), 711Press) Vendera Publishing.

Say, Allen. Grandfather's Journey. Say, Allen, illus. 2008. (ENG., Illus.). 32p. (J). (gr. -1-3). 7.99 (978-0-547-07680-5(0)) Houghton Mifflin Harcourt Publishing Co.

—Grandfather's Journey. 2008. (ENG.). 32p. (J). (gr. -1-3). pap. 7.99 (978-0-547-14178-7(5), Sandpiper) Houghton Mifflin Harcourt Trade & Reference Pubs.

—Grandfather's Journey. 2011. (J). (gr. k-5). 29.95 (978-0-545-10696-2(6)); 18.95 (978-0-545-12708-0(4)) Weston Woods Studios, Inc.

Schorr, Titus. The Stars & Stripes, 01 vols., 1. 2016. (Rosen REAL Readers: Social Studies Nonfiction / Fiction: Family, Community, & the World Ser.). (ENG.). 12p. (J). pap. 6.33 (978-1-5081-1958-6(9), Rosen Classroom) Rosen Publishing Group, Inc., The.

Schraff, Anne. Urban Underground Class Set. 2010. (J). pap. 119.50 (978-1-61651-012-1(9)) Saddleback Educational Publishing, Inc.

—Urban Underground Complete Set. 2010. (J). pap. 190.20 (978-1-61651-011-4(0)) Saddleback Educational Publishing, Inc.

—Wildflower, 1 vol. unabr. ed. 2011. (Urban Underground Ser.). (ENG.). 183p. (YA). (gr. 9-12). pap. 9.95 (978-1-61651-009-1(9)) Saddleback Educational Publishing, Inc.

Schuette, Leslie Elaine. Little Autumn's Adventure in the Smoky Mountains. 2013. 30p. 24.95 (978-1-63004-952-2(2)) America Star Bks.

Sedgwick, Marcus. Saint Death. 2017. (ENG.). 240p. (YA). 17.99 (978-1-62672-549-2(7), 9781626725492) Roaring Brook Pr.

Seeger, K R. Asa-Birdie Corn. 2007. 244p. 26.95 (978-0-595-69522-5(1)); per. 16.95 (978-0-595-45553-9(0)) iUniverse, Inc.

Seerattan, Tanya. Uncle Noel's Journey to Americ. 2011. 28p. pap. 15.99 (978-1-4568-3065-6(1)) Xlibris Corp.

Shea, Therese. A Trip to the White House. 2006. (Neighborhood Readers Ser.). (ENG.). 16p. (gr. 1-3). pap. 6.50 (978-1-4042-7204-0(6), Rosen Classroom) Rosen Publishing Group, Inc., The.

Shepherd, David & Plummer, William K. We Were There at the Driving of the Golden Spike. 2013. (ENG., Illus.). 192p. (J). (gr. 3-8). pap. 6.99 (978-0-486-49259-9(1)) Dover Pubns., Inc.

Sherman, M. Zachary. Control under Fire, 1 vol. Casas, Fritz, illus. 2011. (Bloodlines Ser.). (ENG.). 88p. (gr. 4-8). pap. 6.95 (978-1-4342-3100-0(3)); lib. bdg. 26.65 (978-1-4342-2561-0(5)) Stone Arch Bks.

Sherman, M. Zachary & Iligan, Marlon. Damage Control, 1 vol. Cage, Josef, illus. 2012. (Bloodlines Ser.). (ENG.). 88p. (gr. 4-8). pap. 6.95 (978-1-4342-3875-7(X)); lib. bdg. 26.65 (978-1-4342-3765-1(6)) Stone Arch Bks.

Sherman, M. Zachary & Lee, Raymund. Depth Charge, 1 vol. Bermudez, Raymund, illus. 2012. (Bloodlines Ser.). (ENG.). 88p. (gr. 4-8). pap. 6.95 (978-1-4342-3876-4(8)); lib. bdg. 26.65 (978-1-4342-3764-4(8)) Stone Arch Bks.

Shore, Diane Z. This Is the Feast. Lloyd, Megan, illus. 2011. (ENG.). 32p. (J). (gr. -1-3). pap. 6.99 (978-0-06-443850-6(3)) HarperCollins Pubs.

Shulman, Dee. On Stage in America. 2012. (My Totally Secret Diary Ser.). (ENG., Illus.). 144p. (J). (gr. 2-4). pap. 12.99 (978-1-86230-423-9(8), Red Fox) Random House Children's Books GBR. Dist: Independent Pubs. Group.

Signore, Marco. The Hunting Pack: Allosaurus. Bacchin, Matteo, illus. 2009. (Dinosaurs: Ser.). (ENG.). 64p. (J). (gr. 4-9). 15.95 (978-0-7892-1011-1(8), Abbeville Kids) Abbeville Pr., Inc.

Simmons, John M. Katya's Prayer. 2006. 15p. 4.95 (978-0-9725916-2-1(1), 21206) White Knight Printing and Publishing.

Sisco, K. B. Jackpot's Tail. 2008. (ENG.). 32p. pap. 15.99 (978-1-4196-4475-7(0)) CreateSpace Independent Publishing Platform.

Smallman, Steve. Santa Is Coming to the Quad Cities. Dunn, Robert, illus. 2013. (ENG.). 32p. (J). (-3). 9.99 (978-1-4022-9060-2(8), Sourcebooks Jabberwocky) Sourcebooks, Inc.

Smith, Sherri L. Flygirl. 2010. (ENG.). 304p. (YA). (gr. 7-18). 9.99 (978-0-14-241725-6(4), Speak) Penguin Young Readers Group.

Stanley, George E. Teddy Kennedy: Lion of the Senate. Faricy, Patrick, illus. 2010. (Childhood of Famous Americans Ser.). (ENG.). 224p. (J). (gr. 3-7). pap. 5.99 (978-1-4169-9041-3(0), Simon & Schuster/Paula Wiseman Bks.) Simon & Schuster/Paula Wiseman Bks.

Stewart, Jane L. The Camp Fire Girls at Long Lake: Bessie King in Summer Camp. 2007. 112p. pap. 18.99 (978-1-4346-2295-2(9)); (ENG.). 126p. pap. 19.99 (978-1-4346-2353-9(X)) Creative Media Partners, LLC.

Stiles, Martha Bennett. Sailing to Freedom. 2012. (ENG.). 256p. (J). (gr. 3-7). 16.99 (978-0-8050-9238-7(2), 9780805092387, Holt, Henry & Co. Bks. For Young Readers) Holt, Henry & Co.

Stilton, Geronimo. The Race Across America. 2009. (Geronimo Stilton Ser.: 37). (ENG.). 128p. (J). (gr. 2-5). pap. 7.99 (978-0-545-02137-1(5), Scholastic Paperbacks) Scholastic, Inc.

—The Race Across America. 2009. (Geronimo Stilton Ser.: 37). lib. bdg. 18.40 (978-0-606-00228-8(6), Turtleback) Turtleback Bks.

Stockton, Frank Richard. John Gayther's Garden & the Stories Told Therein. 2008. 220p. 26.95 (978-1-60664-746-2(6)) Rodgers, Alan Bks.

Stone, Judith. Billie the Buffalo Goes to Great Sand Dunes National Park. 2009. 24p. pap. 15.95 (978-1-4490-1495-7(X)) AuthorHouse.

Stowe, Harriet Beecher. Uncle Toms Cabin Young Folks Edition Ill. 2006. pap. (978-1-4065-1077-5(7)) Dodo Pr.

Stratton, Allan. Borderline. 2012. (ENG.). 320p. (YA). (gr. 8). pap. 9.99 (978-0-06-145113-3(4), HarperTeen) HarperCollins Pubs.

Straub-Martin, Susan M. Legends, Loves & Great Lakes. 2013. 28p. pap. 15.00 (978-0-9830321-6-8(5)) Strauberry Studios.

Tal, Eve. Double Crossing. 2007. (ENG.). 262p. (J). (gr. 7-9). pap. 9.95 (978-1-933693-15-6(0)) Cinco Puntos Pr.

Taylor, Richard B. Chispita Service Dog Extraordinaire: Volume 5. Indian Country. 2010. 60p. pap. 21.99 (978-1-4490-5617-9(2)) AuthorHouse.

Taylor, Theodore & Taylor, Theodore. The Bomb. 2007. (ENG., Illus.). 208p. (YA). (gr. 7-12). pap. 6.95 (978-0-15-206165-4(7)) Houghton Mifflin Harcourt Publishing Co.

Thompson, Lisa. The Wreck of the Atocha. 2007. (Illus.). 52p. (J). pap. (978-1-4207-0719-9(1)) Sundance/Newbridge Educational Publishing.

To Keep Me SAFE! A Story for Children Affected by Military Deployments. 2003. (J). 12.00 (978-0-9740289-0-3(8)) State of Growth Publishing Co.

Tocher, Timothy. Chief Sunrise, John McGraw, & Me. 2004. (ENG.). 168p. (J). (gr. 4-8). 16.95 (978-0-8126-2711-4(3)) Cricket Bks.

Tong, Paul, illus. Pecos Bill. 2006. (On My Own Folklore Ser.). 48p. (J). (gr. -1-3). lib. bdg. 25.26 (978-1-57505-889-4(8), Millbrook Pr.) Lerner Publishing Group.

Trout, Richard. Eclipse of the Jaguar, 1 vol. 2011. (ENG., Illus.). 224p. (YA). (gr. 8-12). 16.99 (978-1-58980-872-0(X)) Pelican Publishing Co., Inc.

Tucker, Zekita. Don't Call Me N!gga. 2007. per. 0.01 net. (978-1-60402-249-0(3)) Independent Pub.

Van Hamme, Jean. The Strange Encounter, Vol. 5. 2009. (Blake & Mortimer Ser.: 5). (ENG., Illus.). 66p. pap. 15.95 (978-1-905460-75-5(9)) CineBook GBR. Dist: National Bk. Network.

Van Riper, Guernsey, Jr. Will Rogers, Young Cowboy. 2011. 196p. 42.95 (978-1-258-06291-0(7)) Literary Licensing, LLC.

Vawter, Vince. Paperboy. 2013. (ENG.). 240p. (J). (gr. 5). 16.99 (978-0-385-74244-3(4)); lib. bdg. 19.99 (978-0-375-99058-8(5)) Random Hse. Children's Bks. (Delacorte Bks. for Young Readers).

Waldman, Alan/A. Erica from America & the Start of the Gang of Four. Scobie, Andrea, illus. 2013. 44p. pap. (978-0-9840514-2-7(2)) Roxby Media Ltd.

Walsh, Alice. A Long Way from Home, 1 vol. 2012. (ENG.). 232p. (J). (gr. 6-8). 11.95 (978-1-926920-79-5(1)) Second Story Pr. CAN. Dist: Orca Bk. Pubs. USA.

Walsh, Patrick M., Jr. Who Says Timmy Can't Play: The Derby: A Timmy Wallings Story. McGriff, Aaron, ed. WFM Services, illus. 2011. 135p. (J). (978-0-9842929-3-6(4)) Daddy Bean Bks.

Walters, Eric. We All Fall Down. 2006. (ENG.). 192p. (J). (gr. 5). pap. 9.99 (978-0-385-66192-8(4), Doubleday Canada) Penguin Random House Canada Young Readers CAN. Dist: Penguin Random Hse. LLC.

Warner, Charles Dudley. Being A Boy. 2005. 26.95 (978-1-4218-0314-2(3)); 124p. pap. 10.95 (978-1-4218-0414-9(X)) 1st World Publishing, Inc. (1st World Library - Literary Society).

—Being A Boy. 2004. reprint ed. pap. 15.95 (978-1-4191-0953-9(7)); pap. 1.99 (978-1-4192-0953-6(1)) Kessinger Publishing, LLC.

Warner, Susan & Wetherell, Elizabeth. Queechy. 2008. 328p. per. 16.95 (978-1-60312-446-1(2)) Aegypan.

Watson, Michael. Search, Secrets, & Spies. 2011. 32p. pap. 13.00 (978-1-61204-357-9(7), Strategic Bk. Publishing) Strategic Book Publishing & Rights Agency (SBPRA).

Webster, Frank V. The Boy Scouts of Lenox: Or the Hike over Big Bear Mountain. 2007. 146p. pap. 18.99 (978-1-4346-4443-5(X)) Creative Media Partners, LLC.

Weeks, Sarah & Varadarajan, Gita. Save Me a Seat. 2016. (ENG.). 240p. (J). (gr. 3-7). 16.99 (978-0-545-84660-8(9), Scholastic Pr.) Scholastic, Inc.

Weston, Elise. The Coastwatcher, 1 vol. 2005. (ENG.). 144p. (J). (gr. 3-7). 14.95 (978-1-56145-350-4(1)) Peachtree Pubs.

Weston Woods Staff, creator. Grandfather's Journey. 2011. 38.75 (978-0-545-12710-3(6)) Weston Woods Studios, Inc.

—Scrambled States of America Talent Show. 2011. 18.95 (978-0-545-34618-4(5)); 38.75 (978-0-545-34954-3(0)) Weston Woods Studios, Inc.

Whitby, Adele. Kate's Story 1914. 2014. (Secrets of the Manor Ser.: 2). (ENG., Illus.). 160p. (J). (gr. 3-7). 16.99 (978-1-4814-0635-2(3), Simon Spotlight) Simon Spotlight.

Whyman, Matt. Goldstrike: A Thriller. 2010. (ENG.). 272p. (YA). (gr. 7-18). 16.99 (978-1-4169-9510-4(2), Atheneum Bks. for Young Readers) Simon & Schuster Children's Publishing.

Wiederblank. Save Our School. 2006. 144p. (J). 14.99 (978-1-56871-392-2(4)) Targum Pr., Inc.

Wiesner, Leona Shew. Lundy: Adventures of A Little Boy in Early America. 2007. 72p. per. 8.95 (978-0-595-47200-0(1)) iUniverse, Inc.

Wiggin, Kate Douglas. New Chronicles of Rebecc. 2008. 152p. (gr. 4-7). pap. 12.95 (978-1-60664-257-3(X)) Rodgers, Alan Bks.

Wilbur, Helen. Lily's Victory Garden. Steele, Robert, illus. 2010. (Tales of Young Americans Ser.). (ENG.). 32p. (J). (gr. 2-4). 16.95 (978-1-58536-450-3(9)) Sleeping Bear Pr.

Wilder, Laura Ingalls. Little House on the Prairie. 2007. (Little House Ser.). 336p. (J). (gr. 3-7). pap. 6.99 (978-0-06-088539-7(4), Harper Trophy) HarperCollins Pubs.

Wyatt, Ellen. Sheriff Buzzy Bullet & the Bank Robbers. 2009. 28p. pap. 12.25 (978-1-60860-391-6(1), Eloquent Bks.) Strategic Book Publishing & Rights Agency (SBPRA).

Yates, Donnalyn. Let's Memorize States & Capitals Using Pictures & Stories. 2011. 128p. pap. 14.95 (978-1-257-07566-9(7)) Lulu Pr., Inc.

Yunisa. Schoolaholic Princess 3: Simfoni Cinta. 2008. 220p. pap. 14.88 (978-1-4357-6045-5(X)) Lulu Pr., Inc.

Yusuf. Butterfly & Bumble Bee: Adventure in Yellow Stone National Park. 2010. 16p. 8.49 (978-1-4520-4022-6(2)) AuthorHouse.

Zamor, Nehemie Djose. The Adventures of Naoomi. 2011. 34p. pap. 14.99 (978-1-61379-327-5(8)) Salem Author Services.

Zamora, Peter. A Story about Kandie Cole. 2010. 28p. pap. 13.99 (978-1-4520-5632-6(3)) AuthorHouse.

UNITED STATES—FINANCE

see Finance—United States

UNITED STATES—FOOD AND DRUG ADMINISTRATION

Esherick, Joan. The FDA & Psychiatric Drugs: How a Drug Is Approved. McDonnell, Mary Ann & Esherick, Donald, eds. 2013. (State of Mental Illness & Its Therapy Ser.: 19). 128p. (J). (gr. 7-18). 24.95 (978-1-4222-2826-5(6)) Mason Crest.

—The FDA & Psychiatric Drugs: How a Drug Is Approved. 2004. (Encyclopedia of Psychiatric Drugs & Their Disorders Ser.). (Illus.). 128p. (YA). lib. bdg. 24.95 (978-1-59084-578-3(1)) Mason Crest.

—How a Drug Is Approved: The FDA & Psychiatric Drugs. 2003. (Psychiatric Disorders: Drugs & Psychology for the Mind & Bod Ser.). (Illus.). 124p. (YA). (gr. 7). pap. 14.95 (978-1-4222-0402-3(2)) Mason Crest.

UNITED STATES—FOREIGN POLICY

see United States—Foreign Relations

UNITED STATES—FOREIGN POPULATION

see Immigrants; Minorities

also Italians—United States; and similar headings

UNITED STATES—FOREIGN PUBLIC OPINION

Berlatsky, Noah. Does the World Hate the U. S. ? 2012. (At Issue Ser.). (ENG.). 128p. (gr. 10-12). lib. bdg. 39.40 (978-0-7377-6171-9(7), Greenhaven Pr., Inc.) Cengage Gale.

Berlatsky, Noah, ed. Does the World Hate the U. S. ? 2012. (At Issue Ser.). (ENG.). 128p. (gr. 10-12). pap. 24.45 (978-0-7377-6172-6(5), Greenhaven Pr., Inc.) Cengage Gale.

UNITED STATES—FOREIGN RELATIONS

see also Monroe Doctrine

Alagna, Magdalena. The Monroe Doctrine: An End to European Colonies in America. (Life in the New American Nation Ser.). 32p. 2009. (gr. 4-4). 47.90 (978-1-61514-285-9(1)) 2004. (Illus.). (gr. 5-8). pap. 10.00 (978-0-8239-4258-9(9)) Rosen Publishing Group, Inc., The.

America Debates, 6 vols., Set. Incl. America Debates Civil Liberties & Terrorism. Freedman, Jeri. lib. bdg. 31.95 (978-1-4042-1927-4(7)); America Debates Global Warming: Crisis or Myth? Robinson, Matthew. lib. bdg. 31.95 (978-1-4042-1925-0(0)); America Debates Privacy Versus Security. Freedman, Jeri. lib. bdg. 31.95 (978-1-4042-1929-8(3)); America Debates Stem Cell Research. Freedman, Jeri. lib. bdg. 31.95 (978-1-4042-1928-1(5)); America Debates United States Policy on Immigration. Ambrosek, Renee. lib. bdg. 31.95 (978-1-4042-1924-3(2)); (Illus.). 64p. (YA). (gr. 5-9). 2007. 2007. Set lib. bdg. 175.50 (978-1-4042-1100-1(4)) Rosen Publishing Group, Inc., The.

America's Role in a Changing World. 2010. (Global Connections Ser.). (Illus.). 120p. (gr. 5-8). 35.00 (978-1-60413-287-8(6), Chelsea Hse.) Facts On File, Inc.

Baker, Lawrence W. Cold War Reference Library Cumulative Index. 2003. (Cold War Reference Library). (ENG.). 85p. (J). 5.00 (978-0-7876-7667-4(5), UXL) Cengage Gale.

—Immigration & Migration Reference. 2004. (US Immigration & Migration Reference Library). (ENG.). (J). 5.00 (978-0-7876-7734-3(5), UXL) Cengage Gale.

Berlatsky, Noah. Syria. Greenhaven Press Staff, ed. 2014. (Opposing Viewpoints Ser.). (ENG., Illus.). 224p. (gr. 10-12). lib. bdg. 48.80 (978-0-7377-7006-3(6), Greenhaven Pr., Inc.) Cengage Gale.

Blumberg, Rhoda. Commodore Perry in the Land of the Shogun. 2003. (ENG., Illus.). 144p. (J). (gr. 3-18). pap. 9.99 (978-0-06-008625-1(4)) HarperCollins Pubs.

—Commodore Perry in the Land of the Shogun. 2003. (Illus.). 144p. (gr. 3-7). 20.00 (978-0-7569-1440-0(X)) Perfection Learning Corp.

Burgan, Michael. The Vietnam War. 2006. (Wars That Changed American History Ser.). (Illus.). 48p. (gr. 5-12). pap. 14.05 (978-0-8368-7304-7(1)); lib. bdg. 31.00 (978-0-8368-7295-8(9)) Stevens, Gareth Publishing LLLP. (Gareth Stevens Secondary Library).

Burnett, Betty. The Attack on the USS Cole in Yemen on October 12 2000. 2009. (Terrorist Attacks Ser.). 64p. (gr. 5-5). 58.50 (978-1-60853-311-4(5)) Rosen Publishing Group, Inc., The.

Cefrey, Holly. The Pinckney Treaty: America Wins the Right to Travel the Mississippi River. 2009. (Life in the New American Nation Ser.). 32p. (gr. 4-4). 47.90 (978-1-61514-286-6(X)) Rosen Publishing Group, Inc., The.

Cloud Tapper, Suzanne. America as a World Power: From the Spanish-American War to Today. 2006. (American Saga Ser.). (Illus.). 128p. (J). (gr. 5-9). lib. bdg. 33.27 (978-0-7660-2606-3(X)) Enslow Pubs., Inc.

The Cold War & Postwar America 1946-1963. 2010. (Discovering U. S. History Ser.). (Illus.). 136p. (gr. 5-8). 35.00 (978-1-60413-360-8(0), Chelsea Hse.) Facts On File, Inc.

Corona, Laurel. War Within a War: Vietnam & the Cold War. 2004. (Lucent Library of Historical Eras). (ENG., Illus.). 112p. (J). 33.45 (978-1-59018-389-2(4), Lucent Bks.) Cengage Gale.

Craats, Rennay. Foreign Affairs. 2008. (USA Past Present Future Ser.). (Illus.). 48p. (J). (gr. 4-6). pap. 10.95 (978-1-59036-979-1(3)); lib. bdg. 29.05 (978-1-59036-978-4(5)) Weigl Pubs., Inc.

Creative Media Applications Staff, contrib. by. American Presidents in World History, 5 vols., Vol. 1. 2003. (Middle School Reference Ser.). (Illus.). 144p. (C). (gr. 6-8). 242.00 (978-0-313-32564-9(2), MS2564, Greenwood) ABC-CLIO, LLC.

Deedy, Carmen Agra. 14 Cows for America, 1 vol. González, Thomas, illus. 2009. (ENG.). 36p. (J). (gr. 1-5). 17.95 (978-1-56145-490-7(7)) Peachtree Pubs.

—14 Cows for America. Gonzalez, Thomas, illus. 2016. (ENG.). 36p. (J). (gr. -1-3). lib. bdg. 19.60 (978-0-606-39065-1(0)) Turtleback Bks.

Deedy, Carmen Agra & Naiyomah, Wilson Kimeli. 14 Cows for America, 1 vol. González, Thomas, illus. 2016. (ENG.). 36p. (J). (gr. 1-5). pap. 8.95 (978-1-56145-961-2(5)) Peachtree Pubs.

Dougherty, Steve. Attack on Pearl Harbor: World War II Strikes Home in the USA. 2011. (J). pap. (978-0-545-32930-9(2)) Scholastic, Inc.

Dudley, William. How Should the U. S. Proceed in Iraq? 2008. (At Issue Ser.). (ENG., Illus.). 128p. (gr. 10-12). 39.40 *(978-0-7377-4056-1(6))*; pap. 27.80 *(978-0-7377-4057-8(4))*, Greenhaven Pr., Inc.) Cengage Gale.

Egendorf, Laura K. Should the U. S. Do Business with China? 2008. (At Issue Ser.). (ENG., Illus.). 128p. (gr. 10-12). 39.40 *(978-0-7377-4112-4(0))*; pap. 27.80 *(978-0-7377-4113-1(9))* Cengage Gale. (Greenhaven Pr., Inc.).

Espejo, Roman. Does the World Hate the U. S. ? 2008. (At Issue Ser.). (ENG., Illus.). 80-128p. (gr. 10-12). 24.45 *(978-0-7377-4097-4(3))*; pap. 34.45 *(978-0-7377-4096-7(5))* Cengage Gale. (Greenhaven Pr., Inc.).

Feldman, Ruth Tenzer. World War I. 2004. (Chronicle of America's Wars Ser.). (Illus.). 88p. (gr. 5-12). lib. bdg. 27.93 *(978-0-8225-0148-0(1))* Lerner Publishing Group.

Gitlin, Martin. U. S. Sanctions on Cuba, 1 vol. 2010. (Essential Viewpoints Set 5 Ser.). (ENG., Illus.). 112p. (J). (gr. 6-12). lib. bdg. 35.64 *(978-1-61613-525-6(5)*, 1315619, Essential Library) ABDO Publishing Co.

Greene, Meg. The Transcontinental Treaty 1819: A Primary Source Examination of the Treaty Between the United States & Spain over the American West. 2006. (Primary Sources of American Treaties Ser.). (Illus.). 64p. (J). (gr. k-3). lib. bdg. 31.95 *(978-1-4042-0439-3(3))* Rosen Publishing Group, Inc., The.

Hanes, Sharon M., et al. Cold War: Almanac, 2 vols. 2003. (Cold War Reference Library). (Illus.). (J). 200p. 55.00 *(978-0-7876-7662-9(4))*; *(978-0-7876-9087-8(2))*; (ENG., 376p. lib. bdg. 191.00 *(978-0-7876-9089-2(9))* Cengage Gale. (UXL).

Harness, Cheryl. The Remarkable Rough-Riding Life of Theodore Roosevelt & the Rise of Empire America. 2007. (Cheryl Harness Histories Ser.). (ENG., Illus.). 144p. (J). (gr. 4-7). lib. bdg. 25.90 *(978-1-4263-0009-7(3)*, National Geographic Children's Bks.) National Geographic Society.

Haugen, David M., et al. Iraq. 2009. (Opposing Viewpoints Ser.). (ENG., Illus.). 240p. (YA). (gr. 10-12). 29.45 *(978-0-7377-4525-2(8)*, LML02109-246006);No. 9. pap. 42.95 *(978-0-7377-4524-5(X)*, LML02109-245978) Cengage Gale. (Greenhaven Pr., Inc.).

Isolationism. 2010. (Key Concepts in American History Ser.). (Illus.). 128p. (gr. 6-12). 45.00 *(978-1-60413-224-3(8)*, Chelsea Hse.) Facts On File, Inc.

Johnson, Robin. Pearl Harbor. 2014. (ENG., Illus.). 48p. (J). *(978-0-7787-1367-8(9))* Crabtree Publishing Co.

Kallen, Stuart A. Primary Sources. 2003. (American War Library). (ENG., Illus.). 112p. (J). 30.85 *(978-1-59018-243-7(X)*, Lucent Bks.) Cengage Gale.

Katchur, Matthew & Sterngass, Jon. Spanish Settlement in North America: 1822-1898. Overmyer-Velazquez, Mark, ed. 2006. (Latino-American History Ser.). (Illus.). 106p. (YA). (gr. 5-9). lib. bdg. 35.00 *(978-0-8160-6442-7(3))* Facts On File, Inc.

Keeley, Jennifer. Containing the Communists: America's Foreign Entanglements. 2003. (American War Library). (ENG., Illus.). 112p. (J). 30.85 *(978-1-59018-225-3(1)*, Lucent Bks.) Cengage Gale.

Kiesbye, Stefan. How Should the U. S. Proceed in Afghanistan? 2009. (At Issue Ser.). (ENG., Illus.). 128p. (gr. 10-12). 24.45 *(978-0-7377-4425-5(1))*; 39.40 *(978-0-7377-4424-8(3))* Cengage Gale. (Greenhaven Pr., Inc.).

Laxer, James. Empire, 1 vol. 2007. (Groundwork Guides). (ENG., Illus.). 144p. (gr. 8-12). pap. 9.95 *(978-0-88899-707-4(8))* Groundwood Bks. CAN. Dist: Publishers Group West (PGW).

Marshall Cavendish. The Attack on Pearl Harbor. 2011. (Perspectives on 3 Ser.). (Illus.). 112p. (J). (gr. 7). 39.93 *(978-1-60870-448-4(3))* Marshall Cavendish Corp.

McAneney, Caitie. Standing in the Secretary of State's Shoes. 2015. (My Government Ser.). (ENG., Illus.). 32p. (J). (gr. 4-4). pap. 10.58 *(978-1-5026-0466-8(3))* Cavendish Square Publishing.

McNeese, Tim. The Perry Expedition & the Opening of Japan. 2012. (J). 35.00 *(978-1-60413-924-2(2)*, Chelsea Hse.) Facts On File, Inc.

Meyer, Edith Patterson. The Friendly Frontier: The Story of the Canadian-American Border. Mars, W. T., illus. 2011. 304p. 48.95 *(978-1-258-09384-6(7))* Literary Licensing, LLC.

Miller, Debra A. Iran. Gale Editors, ed. 2010. (Current Controversies Ser.). (ENG.). 240p. 40.95 *(978-0-7377-5181-9(9))*; pap. 28.45 *(978-0-7377-5182-6(7))* Cengage Gale. (Greenhaven Pr., Inc.).

Murdico, Suzanne J. Osama bin Laden. 2009. (Middle East Leaders Ser.). 112p. (gr. 5-8). 66.50 *(978-1-61514-647-5(4)*, Rosen Reference) Rosen Publishing Group, Inc., The.

Piddock, Charles. The Cold War. 2016. (Illus.). 48p. (J). *(978-1-5105-1282-5(9))* SmartBook Media, Inc.

Porterfield, Jason. How Lyndon B. Johnson Fought the Vietnam War. 2017. (Presidents at War Ser.). 128p. (J). (gr. 8-8). lib. bdg. 37.27 ***(978-0-7660-8531-2(7))*** Enslow Pubs., Inc.

Rauf, Don. How George W. Bush Fought the Wars in Iraq & Afghanistan. 2017. (Presidents at War Ser.). 128p. (J). (gr. 8-8). lib. bdg. 37.27 ***(978-0-7660-8533-6(3))*** Enslow Pubs., Inc.

Ross, Stewart & Woodward, Joe. Pearl Harbor. 2011. (Place in History Ser.). (Illus.). 48p. (YA). (gr. 5-9). lib. bdg. 34.25 *(978-1-84837-676-2(6))* Arcturus Publishing GBR. Dist: Black Rabbit Bks.

Roxburgh, Ellis. John F. Kennedy vs. Nikita Khrushchev. 2015. (History's Greatest Rivals Ser.). (ENG., Illus.). 48p. (J). (gr. 6-8). lib. bdg. 31.95 *(978-1-4824-2221-4(2))* Stevens, Gareth Publishing LLLP.

Ruffin, David C. The Duties & Responsibilities of the Secretary of State. (Your Government in Action Ser.). 32p. (gr. 3-3). 2009. 43.90 *(978-1-60854-919-1(4))* 2005. (Illus.). (J). lib. bdg. 23.95 *(978-1-4042-2688-3(5))* Rosen Publishing Group, Inc., The. (PowerKids Pr.).

Samuels, Charlie. The Attack on Pearl Harbor, Vol. 1. 2014. (Turning Points in US Military History Ser.). (ENG.). 48p. (J). (gr. 5-6). 31.95 *(978-1-4824-0409-8(5))* Stevens, Gareth Publishing LLLP.

Schwartz, Eric. A World Contender. 2006. (How America Became America Ser.). (Illus.). 96p. (YA). lib. bdg. 22.95 *(978-1-59084-911-8(6))* Mason Crest.

Sharp, Constance. Beyond Our Shores: America Extends Its Reach,1890-1899. 2013. (Illus.). 48p. (J). pap. *(978-1-4222-2420-5(1))* Mason Crest.

—Beyond Our Shores: America Extends Its Reach,1890-1899. Rakove, Jack N., ed. 2012. (How America Became America Ser.). (Illus.). 48p. (J). (gr. 3-4). 19.95 *(978-1-4222-2406-9(6))* Mason Crest.

Sonneborn, Liz. The Acquisition of Florida: America's Twenty-Seventh State. 2009. (Milestones in American History Ser.). (Illus.). 120p. (gr. 6-12). 35.00 *(978-1-60413-054-6(7)*, Chelsea Hse.) Facts On File, Inc.

South, Victor. America in the 20th Century (1913-1999) 2013. (Illus.). 48p. (J). pap. *(978-1-4222-2422-9(8))* Mason Crest.

—America in the 20th Century (1913-1999) Rakove, Jack N., ed. 2012. (How America Became America Ser.). (Illus.). 48p. (J). (gr. 3-4). 19.95 *(978-1-4222-2408-3(2))* Mason Crest.

—A Shifting Role: America & the World, 1900-1912. 2013. 48p. (J). pap. *(978-1-4222-2421-2(X))* Mason Crest.

—A Shifting Role: America & the World, 1900-1912. Rakove, Jack N., ed. 2012. (How America Became America Ser.). 48p. (J). (gr. 3-4). 19.95 *(978-1-4222-2407-6(4))* Mason Crest.

Stanley, George Edward. America in Today's World (1969-2004) 2005. (Primary Source History of the United States Ser.). (Illus.). 48p. (gr. 5-12). pap. 14.05 *(978-0-8368-5840-2(9))*; lib. bdg. 31.00 *(978-0-8368-5831-0(X))* Stevens, Gareth Publishing LLLP. (Gareth Stevens Secondary Library).

—An Emerging World Power, 1900-1929. 2005. (Primary Source History of the United States Ser.). (Illus.). 48p. (gr. 5-12). pap. 14.05 *(978-0-8368-5837-2(9))*; lib. bdg. 31.00 *(978-0-8368-5828-0(X))* Stevens, Gareth Publishing LLLP. (Gareth Stevens Secondary Library).

Wallenfeldt, Jeff, ed. A New World Power: America from 1920 To 1945. 2012. (Documenting America: the Primary Source Documents of a Nation Ser.). (ENG., Illus.). 192p. (YA). (gr. 10-12). 82.20 *(978-1-61530-784-5(2))* Rosen Publishing Group, Inc., The.

Wood, Douglas. Franklin & Winston: A Christmas That Changed the World. Moser, Barry, illus. 2011. (ENG.). 40p. (J). (gr. 1-4). 16.99 *(978-0-7636-3383-7(6))* Candlewick Pr.

Yomtov, Nel. The Attack on Pearl Harbor: December 7 1941, 1 vol. 2014. (24-Hour History Ser.). (ENG.). 48p. (gr. 3-5). pap. 8.95 *(978-1-4329-9299-6(6))*; (Illus.). lib. bdg. 33.32 *(978-1-4329-9293-4(7))* Heinemann-Raintree. (NA-h).

Yomtov, Nelson. The United States & Mexico. 2013. (Cornerstones of Freedom™, Third Ser.). (ENG., Illus.). 64p. (J). pap. 8.95 *(978-0-531-21963-8(1))*; lib. bdg. 30.00 *(978-0-531-23605-5(6))* Scholastic Library Publishing.

Zimmerman, Andrea. Eliza's Cherry Trees: Japan's Gift to America, 1 vol. Chen, Ju-Hong, illus. 2011. (ENG.). 32p. (J). (gr. k-3). 16.99 *(978-1-58980-954-3(8))* Pelican Publishing Co., Inc.

UNITED STATES—FOREIGN RELATIONS—TREATIES

Greene, Meg. The Transcontinental Treaty 1819: A Primary Source Examination of the Treaty Between the United States & Spain over the American West. 2009. (Primary Sources of American Treaties Ser.). 64p. (gr. 5-8). 58.50 *(978-1-60851-514-1(1))* Rosen Publishing Group, Inc., The.

Primary Sources of American Treaties. (Illus.). (YA). (gr. 5-8). 175.50 *(978-1-4042-0626-7(4))* Rosen Publishing Group, Inc., The.

UNITED STATES—FOREST SERVICE—FICTION

Rolt-Wheeler, Francis. The Boy with the U S Foresters. 2007. 128p. per. *(978-1-4068-4018-6(1))* Echo Library.

UNITED STATES—GOVERNMENT

see United States—Politics and Government

UNITED STATES—GOVERNMENT EMPLOYEES

see United States—Officials and Employees

UNITED STATES—HISTORY

Aaseng, Nathan. Michael Jordan: Hall of Fame Basketball Superstar. 2013. (Hall of Fame Sports Greats Ser.). 64p. (J). (gr. 4-18). 15.95 *(978-1-62285-035-8(1))* Enslow Pubs., Inc.

ABDO. Daily Life in US History, 1 vol. 2014. (Daily Life in US History Ser.: 8). (ENG.). 48p. (gr. 3-6). lib. bdg. 262.32 *(978-1-62403-623-1(6))* ABDO Publishing Co.

Abdo Publishing. Foundations of Our Nation, 1 vol. 2013. (Foundations of Our Nation Ser.: 8). (ENG.). 48p. (J). (gr. 3-6). lib. bdg. 262.32 *(978-1-61783-705-0(9))* ABDO Publishing Co.

ABDO Publishing Company Staff. American Moments Set 1. 2004. (American Moments Set 1 Ser.). (gr. 4-8). 324.84 *(978-1-59197-276-1(0)*, Abdo & Daughters) ABDO Publishing Co.

—Story of the United States. 2014. (Story of the United States Ser.: 10). (ENG.). 48p. (gr. 3-6). lib. bdg. 327.90 *(978-1-62403-170-0(6))* ABDO Publishing Co.

Abitz, Diana, et al. Know-the-Facts Review Game: 100 Must-Know Facts in a Q & A Game Format to Help Kids Really Remember Standards-Based Social Studies Information. 2005. (Ancient Civilizations Ser.). (ENG.). 144p. pap. 14.99 *(978-0-439-37432-3(4)*, Teaching Resources) Scholastic, Inc.

Abramovitz, Melissa. Old Cars, 1 vol. 2013. (Cars, Cars, Cars Ser.). (ENG.). 24p. (gr. k-1). lib. bdg. 26.65 *(978-1-62065-090-5(8)*, Pebble Plus) Capstone Press of Coughlan Cos.

Akyroyd, Clarissa. Native American Horsemanship. Johnson, Troy, ed. 2013. (Native American Life Ser.: 15). 64p. (J). (gr. 5-18). 19.95 *(978-1-4222-2971-2(8))* Mason Crest.

All the People: A History of the Us Book 10. 2011. 14.78 *(978-0-7848-3647-7(7)*, Everbind) Marco Bk. Co.

Allman, Toney. The Enlightenment. 2014. (Understanding World History Ser.). (Illus.). 96p. (J). lib. bdg. *(978-1-60152-740-0(3))* ReferencePoint Pr., Inc.

Aloian, Molly. The Mojave Desert. 2012. (ENG.). 32p. (J). *(978-0-7787-0713-4(X))*; (Illus.). pap. *(978-0-7787-0721-9(0))* Crabtree Publishing Co.

Altman, Linda Jacobs. The Politics of Slavery: Fiery National Debates Fueled by the Slave Economy. 2004. (Slavery in American History Ser.). (Illus.). 128p. (J). lib. bdg. 27.94 *(978-0-7660-2150-1(5))* Enslow Pubs., Inc.

American Graphic. (American Graphic Ser.). (ENG.). 32p. (gr. 3-4). 2011. pap. 286.20 *(978-1-4296-6439-4(8))* 2010. pap. 40.50 *(978-1-4296-6271-0(9))* Capstone Press of Coughlan Cos. (Graphic Library).

American History. (YA). 20.00 *(978-1-931555-47-0(8))* Our Lady of Victory Schl.

American History Playing Card Deck. 2004. (History Channel Ser.). (Illus.). 120p. pap. 12.00 *(978-1-57281-440-0(3)*, AMH55) U.S. Games Systems, Inc.

American Voices Group 3, 5 bks., Set. Incl. American Voices from the Women's Movement. Schomp, Virginia. 128p. (gr. 6-7). lib. bdg. 26.95 *(978-0-7614-2171-9(8))*; Century of Immigration: 1820-1924. Steloff, Rebecca. 115p. (J). (gr. 3-7). lib. bdg. 38.50 *(978-0-7614-2172-6(6))*; Time of Slavery. Sirimarco, Elizabeth. 114p. (J). (gr. 3-7). lib. bdg. 38.50 *(978-0-7614-2169-6(6))*; Wild West. Steloff, Rebecca. 128p. (gr. 6-7). lib. bdg. 26.95 *(978-0-7614-2170-2(X))*; (Illus.). 2006. 2007. Set lib. bdg. 185.36 *(978-0-7614-2167-2(X)*, Benchmark Bks.) Marshall Cavendish Corp.

The Americans. 2005. (gr. 6-12). *(978-0-618-17618-2(7)*, 2-37951); *(978-0-618-17568-0(7)*, 2-37933); tchr. ed. *(978-0-618-16260-4(7)*, 2-37912) Holt McDougal.

America's Role in a Changing World. 2010. (Global Connections Ser.). (Illus.). 120p. (gr. 5-8). 35.00 *(978-1-60413-287-8(6)*, Chelsea Hse.) Facts On File, Inc.

Ancient Americas DBA. 2003. spiral bd. 16.95 *(978-1-56004-156-6(0))* Social Studies Schl. Service.

Anderson, Dale. The Aftermath of the Civil War. 2004. (World Almanac Library of the Civil War). (Illus.). 48p. (gr. 5-12). pap. 14.05 *(978-0-8368-5597-5(3))*; lib. bdg. 31.00 *(978-0-8368-5588-3(4))* Stevens, Gareth Publishing LLLP. (Gareth Stevens Secondary Library).

—The Atom Bomb Project. 2004. (Landmark Events in American History Ser.). (Illus.). 48p. (gr. 5-12). lib. bdg. 31.00 *(978-0-8368-5385-8(7)*, Gareth Stevens Secondary Library) Stevens, Gareth Publishing LLLP.

Anderson, Jameson. Lebron James, 1 vol. 2014. (Awesome Athletes Ser.). (ENG.). 32p. (gr. 8-12). 27.07 *(978-1-62403-330-8(X))* ABDO Publishing Co.

Anderson, Jennifer Joline. Women's Rights Movement, 1 vol. 2013. (Essential Library of Social Change Ser.). (ENG.). 112p. (J). (gr. 6-12). lib. bdg. 35.64 *(978-1-61783-889-7(6)*, Essential Library) ABDO Publishing Co.

Anderson, Michael. Biographies of the New World Power: Rutherford B. Hayes, Thomas Alva Edison, Margaret Sanger, & More. 2012. (Impact on America: Collective Biographies Ser.). (ENG., Illus.). 112p. (J). (gr. 7-12). 32.90 *(978-1-61530-691-6(9))* Rosen Publishing Group, Inc., The.

Anderson, Michael, ed. Biographies of the New World: Leif Eriksson, Henry Hudson, Charles Darwin, & More. 2012. (Impact on America: Collective Biographies Ser.). (ENG., Illus.). 112p. (YA). (gr. 7-12). 65.80 *(978-1-61530-803-3(2))* Rosen Publishing Group, Inc., The.

Andrews, Barbara. Discover the Southwest Region. 2006. (J). pap. *(978-1-4108-6436-9(7))* Benchmark Education Co.

Appleby, Joyce, et al. The American Journey: Early Years. 2008. (American Journey Ser.). (Illus.). 660p. (J). 93.32 *(978-0-07-877715-8(1)*, 9780078777158) Glencoe/McGraw-Hill.

—The American Republic since 1877. 2nd ed. 2004. (U. S. History - the Modern Era Ser.). (ENG., Illus.). 1096p. (gr. 8-10). stu. ed. 124.84 *(978-0-07-860712-7(4)*, 0078607124) McGraw-Hill Education.

—The American Republic to 1877. 3rd ed. 2006. (American Journey (survey) Ser.). (ENG., Illus.). 720p. (gr. 6-9). stu. ed. 121.64 *(978-0-07-874675-8(2)*, 0078746752) McGraw-Hill Higher Education.

—The American Vision. 2nd ed. 2004. (United States History (hs) Ser.). (ENG., Illus.). 1138p. (gr. 9-12). stu. ed. 119.32 *(978-0-07-860719-6(1)*, 0078607191) McGraw-Hill Higher Education.

—La Republica Estadounidense Hasta 1877. 2nd ed. 2005.Tr. of American Republic to 1877. (SPA., Illus.). 670p. (C). (gr. 4-7). 101.28 *(978-0-07-867372-6(0)*, 0078673720) McGraw-Hill Higher Education.

—El Viaje Estadounidense. 2005. (American Journey (survey) Ser.).Tr. of American Journey. (SPA., Illus.). 1112p. (gr. 6-9). stu. ed. 127.92 *(978-0-07-867380-1(1)*, 0078673801) McGraw-Hill Higher Education.

—El Viaje Estadounidense: Reconstruccion Hasta el Presente. 2005. (Amer Journey Recon/present Ser.).Tr. of American Journey, Reconstruction to the Present. Spanish Student Edition. (SPA., Illus.). 1044p. (gr. 6-9). 126.24 *(978-0-07-868134-9(0)*, 0078681340) McGraw-Hill Higher Education.

Applesauce Press, Applesauce, et al. The Patriot Papers: Bursting with Fascinating Tidbits about the Declaration of Independence & the Bill of Rights. 2016. (ENG., Illus.). 96p. (J). (gr. 3). pap. 14.95 *(978-1-60433-605-4(6)*, Applesauce Pr.) Cider Mill Pr. Bk. Pubs., LLC.

Aretha, David. Sabotage, Sedition, & Sundry Acts of Rebellion. 2014. (J). *(978-1-59935-406-4(3))* Reynolds, Morgan Inc.

Army JROTC: Leadership Education & Training, Cadet Reference. 2nd ed. 2003. (Illus.). vi, 56p. (J). *(978-0-536-74189-9(1)*, Dept. of the Army) United States Government Printing Office.

Ashabranner, Brent. Great American Memorials, 5 vols. Incl. No Better Hope: What the Lincoln Memorial Means to America. Ashabranner, Jennifer. (J). 2001. lib. bdg. 25.90 *(978-0-7613-1523-0(3))*; Remembering Korea: Korean War. Ashabranner, Jennifer, photos by. 2001. lib. bdg. 25.90 *(978-0-7613-2156-9(X))*; Their Names to Live: What the Vietnam Veterans Memorial Means to America. Ashabranner, Jennifer, photos by. 1998. lib. bdg. 24.90 *(978-0-7613-3235-0(9))*; Washington Monument: A Beacon for America. Ashabranner, Jennifer, photos by. 2002. lib. bdg. 25.90 *(978-0-7613-1524-7(1))*; 64p. (gr. 4-8). (Illus.). 2004. 155.40 o.p. *(978-0-7613-3142-1(5)*, Twenty-First Century Bks.) Lerner Publishing Group.

Bailey, Martha. New Mexico: Uno de muchos, de muchos Uno, 1. Bailey, Martha, illus. l.t. ed. 2006. (SPA., Illus.). 96p. (J). per. *(978-0-9786448-0-2(8))* Bailey, Martha.

Baker, et al. Nueva Historia de los Estados Unidos. (SPA.). 350p. (J). 32.95 *(978-0-8056-0124-4(4)*, MI010) Minerva Bks., Ltd.

Balkan, Gabrielle. The 50 States: Explore the U.S.A. with 50 Fact-Filled Maps! Linero, Sol, illus. 2015. (50 States Ser.). (ENG.). 112p. (J). (gr. 2-5). 30.00 *(978-1-84780-711-3(9)*, Wide Eyed Editions) Quarto Publishing Group UK GBR. Dist: Hachette Bk. Group.

Ball, Lea. The Federalist — Anti-Federalist Debate over States' Rights: A Primary Source Investigation. 2004. (Great Historic Debates & Speeches Ser.). (Illus.). 64p. (J). lib. bdg. 31.95 *(978-1-4042-0149-1(1))* Rosen Publishing Group, Inc., The.

Bartley, Niccole. Land That I Love: Regions of the United States. 2014. (Land That I Love: Regions of the United States Ser.). 32p. (J). (gr. 3-6). 157.50 *(978-1-4777-6639-2(1)*, PowerKids Pr.) Rosen Publishing Group, Inc., The.

—The Southwest. 2014. (Land That I Love: Regions of the United States Ser.). (Illus.). 32p. (J). (gr. 3-6). pap. 60.00 *(978-1-4777-6638-5(3)*, PowerKids Pr.) Rosen Publishing Group, Inc., The.

Bausum, Ann. Our Country's Presidents: A Complete Encyclopedia of the U.S. Presidency. 2017. (Illus.). 224p. (J). ***(978-1-4263-2944-9(X))*** National Geographic Society.

Beall, Pamela Conn & Nipp, Susan Hagen. Wee Sing America, 1 vol. 2005. (Wee Sing Ser.). (ENG., Illus.). 64p. (J). (gr. -1-2). 10.99 *(978-0-8431-1279-5(4)*, Price Stern Sloan) Penguin Young Readers Group.

Beard, Daniel C. American Boy's Handy Book. 2014. (ENG., Illus.). 320p. (J). (gr. -1-3). pap. 12.95 *(978-0-8048-4403-1(8))* Tuttle Publishing.

Benchmark Education Company, LLC Staff. Coming to America: Immigration from 1840 to 1930 Teacher's Guide. 2004. *(978-1-4108-2580-3(9))* Benchmark Education Co.

Benchmark Education Company, LLC Staff, compiled by. U. S. History. 2006. (J). 173.00 *(978-1-4108-7113-8(4))* Benchmark Education Co.

—United States History: Theme Set. 2006. (J). 173.00 *(978-1-4108-7128-2(2))* Benchmark Education Co.

Benoit, Peter. Cornerstones of Freedom, Third Series: the Trail of Tears. 2012. (ENG.). 64p. (J). lib. bdg. 30.00 *(978-0-531-23067-1(8)*, Children's Pr.) Scholastic Library Publishing.

—Immigration. 2012. (Cornerstones of Freedom, Third Ser.). (ENG., Illus.). 64p. (J). pap. 8.95 *(978-0-531-28157-4(4))*; (gr. 4-6). lib. bdg. 30.00 *(978-0-531-23057-2(0))* Scholastic Library Publishing. (Children's Pr.).

—The Trail of Tears. 2012. (Cornerstones of Freedom, Third Ser.). (ENG.). 64p. (J). pap. 8.95 *(978-0-531-28167-3(1))* Scholastic Library Publishing.

Benson, Sonia, et al. UXL Encyclopedia of U.S. History. 2008. (J). *(978-1-4144-3044-7(2))*; *(978-1-4144-3045-4(0))*; *(978-1-4144-3047-8(7))*; *(978-1-4144-3048-5(5))*; *(978-1-4144-3049-2(3))*; *(978-1-4144-3050-8(7))*; *(978-1-4144-3051-5(5))*; *(978-1-4144-3046-1(9))* Cengage Gale. (UXL).

Bernstein, Vivian. America's Story. 2005. (America's Story Ser.). (ENG., Illus.). 400p. (gr. 5-10). 51.00 *(978-0-7398-9716-4(0))* Houghton Mifflin Harcourt Publishing Co.

Berry, Carrie, et al. First-Person Histories, 1 vol. 2014. (First-Person Histories Ser.). (ENG.). 32p. (gr. 3-4). 163.92 *(978-1-4765-7686-2(6)*, Fact Finders) Capstone Press of Coughlan Cos.

Boardworks Learning Centers: Across the U. S. A. 2006. (J). bds. *(978-0-9755252-5-8(5))* Evergreen Pr. of Brainerd, LLC.

Bockenhauer, Mark H. & Cunha, Stephen F. National Geographic Our Fifty States. 2004. (ENG., Illus.). 240p. (J). (gr. 5). 24.95 *(978-0-7922-6402-6(9)*, National Geographic Children's Bks.) National Geographic Society.

Boerst, William J. Marching in Birmingham. 2007. (Civil Rights Movement Ser.). (Illus.). 112p. (J). (gr. 3-7). lib. bdg. 27.95 *(978-1-59935-055-4(6))* Reynolds, Morgan Inc.

Bonner, John. A Child's History of the United States, 2 vol., set. reprint ed. 250.00 *(978-0-7222-7249-7(9))* Library Reprints, Inc.

Books, Golson. Multicultural America, 7 vols., Set. 2011. (Multicultural America Ser.). (Illus.). (gr. 6-12). 385.00 *(978-0-8160-7810-3(6))* Facts On File, Inc.

Boorstin, Daniel J., et al. A History of the United States. 6th ed. 2005. (Illus.). (YA). (gr. 9-12). 85.20 *(978-0-13-181542-1(3))* Prentice Hall Pr.

Borden, Louise. America Is... Schuett, Stacey, illus. 2005. (ENG.). 40p. (J). (gr. 1-4). 7.99 *(978-1-4169-0286-7(4)*, McElderry, Margaret K. Bks.) McElderry, Margaret K. Bks.

Boyd, Bentley. George Washington Leads the Way. 2011. (Mount Vernon Comix Ser.). (Illus.). 24p. (J). (gr. 3-9). pap. 6.95 *(978-1-933122-44-1(7))* Chester Comix, LLC.

Boyer, Paul S. Holt American Nation: Online Edition Plus. 3rd ed. 2003. 17.26 *(978-0-03-074332-6(4))* Holt McDougal.

Boyer, Rick & Boyer, Marilyn. America's Struggle to Become a Nation: Understanding the Foundations of Freedom. 2015. (ENG.). 384p. pap. 34.99 *(978-0-89051-910-3(2))* Master Bks.

Boyer's Staff. The American Nation: Modern Era: Online Edition. 5th ed. 2004. (gr. 1). 17.26 *(978-0-03-038831-6(7))*; (gr. 6). 77.26 *(978-0-03-038832-3(5))* Holt McDougal.

Brain Quest Editors. Brain Quest America: 850 Questions 850 Answers Celebrating Our Nation's History People & Culture. rev. ed. 2013. (ENG.). 152p. (J). (gr. 3-6). 11.95 *(978-0-7611-7239-0(4)*, 17239) Workman Publishing Co., Inc.

Brannon, Barbara. Discover the Northeast Region. 2005. (J). pap. *(978-1-4108-5152-9(4))* Benchmark Education Co.

Brezina, Corona. The Industrial Revolution in America: A Primary Source History of America's Transformation into an Industrial Society. 2009. (Primary Sources in American History Ser.). 64p. (gr. 5-8). 58.50 *(978-1-60851-497-7(8))* Rosen Publishing Group, Inc., The.

Brinkley, Alan. The Unfinished Nation with PowerWeb. 4th rev. ed. 2003. (Unfinished Nation Ser.). (J). (gr. 6-12). (Illus.). pap., pap. 70.31 *(978-0-07-293522-6(7)*, 9780072935226); Vol. 2. pap., pap. 67.19 *(978-0-07-293525-7(1)*, 9780072935257) Glencoe/McGraw-Hill.

Brook, Henry. True Stories of D-Day. 2006. (Illus.). 160p. (J). per. 4.99 *(978-0-7945-1161-6(9)*, Usborne) EDC Publishing.

Brown, Fannie T. Where Are the Children? 2011. 114p. pap. 11.95 *(978-1-4269-6661-3(X))* Trafford Publishing.

Bruccoli, Matthew J., et al. Conflicts in American History: A Documentary Encyclopedia, 8 vols., Set. 2010. 3200p. (C). (gr. 9-18). 720.00 *(978-0-8160-7093-0(8))* Facts On File, Inc.

Bruchac, Margaret M. & Grace, Catherine O'Neill. 1621: A New Look at Thanksgiving. Coulson, Cotton & Brimberg, Sisse, photos by. 2004. (I Am American Ser.). (ENG., Illus.).

48p. (J). (gr. 3-7). pap. 7.95 *(978-0-7922-6139-1(9)*, National Geographic Children's Bks.) National Geographic Society.
Buell, Tonya. Slavery in America: A Primary Source History of the Intolerable Practice of Slavery. 2009. (Primary Sources in American History Ser.). 64p. (gr. 5-8). 58.50 *(978-1-60851-491-5(9))* Rosen Publishing Group, Inc., The.
Building America, 11 vols., Set. Incl. Colonial Virginia. Harkins, Susan Sales & Harkins, William H. (gr. 4-8). 2007. lib. bdg. 29.95 *(978-1-58415-548-5(5))*; Georgia: The Debtors Colony. Harkins, Susan Sales & Harkins, William H. (gr. 3-7). 2006. lib. bdg. 29.95 *(978-1-58415-465-5(9))*; Holidays & Celebrations in Colonial America. Roberts, Russell. (gr. 3-7). 2006. lib. bdg. 29.95 *(978-1-58415-467-9(5))*; Jamestown: The First Colony. Harkins, William H. & Harkins, Susan Sales. (gr. 3-7). 2006. lib. bdg. 29.95 *(978-1-58415-458-7(6))*; Life in Colonial America. Roberts, Russell. (gr. 4-8). 2007. lib. bdg. 29.95 *(978-1-58415-549-2(3))*; Maryland Colony: Lord Baltimore. Whiting, Jim. (gr. 4-8). 2007. lib. bdg. 29.95 *(978-1-58415-547-8(7))*; Massachusetts Bay Colony: The Puritans Arrive from England. Hinman, Bonnie. (gr. 3-7). 2006. lib. bdg. 29.95 *(978-1-58415-460-0(8))*; New Netherland: The Dutch Settle the Hudson Valley. Gibson, Karen Bush. (gr. 3-7). 2006. lib. bdg. 29.95 *(978-1-58415-461-7(6))*; Pennsylvania: William Penn & the City of Brotherly Love. Hinman, Bonnie. (gr. 3-7). 2006. lib. bdg. 29.95 *(978-1-58415-463-1(2))*; Plymouth Colony: The Pilgrims Settle in New England. Tracy, Kathleen. (gr. 3-7). 2006. lib. bdg. 29.95 *(978-1-58415-459-4(4))*; Texas Joins the United States. Roberts, Russell. (gr. 4-8). 2007. lib. bdg. 29.95 *(978-1-58415-550-8(7))*; (Illus.). 48p. (J). (Building America Ser.). 2007. Set lib. bdg. 329.45 *(978-1-58415-551-5(5))* Mitchell Lane Pubs., Inc.
Buller, Jon, et al. Smart about the Fifty States. Buller, Jon et al, illus. 2003. (Smart about History Ser.). (ENG.). 64p. (J). (gr. k-4). mass mkt. 6.99 *(978-0-448-43131-4(9))*, Grosset & Dunlap) Penguin Young Readers Group.
Burgan, Michael. The Great Depression: An Interactive History Adventure, 1 vol. (You Choose: Historical Eras Ser.). (ENG.). 112p. (gr. 3-4). 2011. pap. 6.95 *(978-1-4296-6276-5(X))* 2010. 31.99 *(978-1-4296-5480-7(5))* Capstone Press of Coughlan Cos. (You Choose Bks.).
—United States of America. 2013. (ENG.). 144p. (J). 40.00 *(978-0-531-23680-2(3))* Scholastic Library Publishing.
Burleigh, Robert. The Adventures of Mark Twain by Huckleberry Finn. Blitt, Barry, illus. 2011. (ENG.). 48p. (J). (gr. 2-5). 17.99 *(978-0-689-83041-9(6)*, Atheneum Bks. for Young Readers) Simon & Schuster Children's Publishing.
Burlingame, Jeff. Demi! Latina Star Demi Lovato. 2013. (Sizzling Celebrities Ser.). 48p. (J). (gr. 4-9). pap. 8.95 *(978-1-4644-0277-7(9))* Enslow Pubs., Inc.
C. Q. Press Staff. Landmark Events in U. S. History, 05 vols., Set. rev. ed. 2005. (Landmark Events in U. S. History Ser.). (ENG.). 400p. (gr. 9-18). 590.00 *(978-1-933116-27-3(7))* CQ Pr.
Cain, Marie Mowery. American Symbols. 2013. (Big Books, Blue Ser.). (ENG & SPA., Illus.). 16p. pap. 33.00 *(978-1-59246-014-4(3))* Big Books, by George!
Callan, Jim. America in the 1900s And 1910s. 2005. (Decades of American History Ser.). (Illus.). 128p. (gr. 5-8). 35.00 *(978-0-8160-5636-1(6))* Facts On File, Inc.
Campbell, Ballard C. Disasters, Accidents, & Crises in American History: A Reference Guide to the Nation's Most Catastrophic Events. 2008. (Facts on File Library of American History Ser.). (Illus.). 461p. (C). (gr. 9-18). 95.00 *(978-0-8160-6603-2(5))* Facts On File, Inc.
Campbell, Wallis. Angel Island. 2006. (Illus.). 48p. (J). pap. *(978-1-59034-808-6(7))* Mondo Publishing.
Cane, Ella. States in My World, 1 vol. 2013. (My World Ser.). (ENG.). 24p. (gr. k-1). 21.99 *(978-1-4765-3121-2(8))*; pap. 6.95 *(978-1-4765-3463-3(2))* Capstone Press of Coughlan Cos. (Pebble Bks.).
Capriola, Arlene & Swensen, Rigmor. US History 8: Reconstruction to the Present. 2005. (Taking the High Road to Social Studies Ser.). 5.95 *(978-0-7915-1672-0(5))*; 24.95 *(978-0-7915-1666-9(0))* Phoenix Learning Resources, LLC.
Carlisle, Rodney P. The Age of Reform, 1890-1920, 9 vols. 2009. (Handbook to Life in America Ser.). (Illus.). 291p. (C). (gr. 9-18). 50.00 *(978-0-8160-7178-4(0))* Facts On File, Inc.
—The Civil War & Reconstruction, 1860 - 1876, 9 vols. 2009. (Handbook to Life in America Ser.). (Illus.). 272p. (C). (gr. 9-18). 50.00 *(978-0-8160-7176-0(4))* Facts On File, Inc.
—The Colonial Revolutionary Era: Beginnings To 1783, 9 vols. 2009. (Handbook to Life in America Ser.). (Illus.). 288p. (C). (gr. 9-18). 50.00 *(978-0-8160-7174-6(8))* Facts On File, Inc.
—Contemporary America, 1970 to Present, 9 vols. 2009. (Handbook to Life in America Ser.). (Illus.). 291p. (C). (gr. 9-18). 50.00 *(978-0-8160-7182-1(9))* Facts On File, Inc.
—The Early National Period & Expansion, 1783 - 1859, 9 vols. 2009. (Handbook to Life in America Ser.). (Illus.). 275p. (C). (gr. 9-18). 50.00 *(978-0-8160-7175-3(6))* Facts On File, Inc.
—The Gilded Age, 1870-1900, 9 vols. 2009. (Handbook to Life in America Ser.). (Illus.). 272p. (C). (gr. 9-18). 50.00 *(978-0-8160-7177-7(2))* Facts On File, Inc.
—The Great Depression & World War II, 1929-1949, 9 vols. 2009. (Handbook to Life in America Ser.). (Illus.). 287p. (C). (gr. 9-18). 50.00 *(978-0-8160-7180-7(2))* Facts On File, Inc.
—Postwar America, 1950-1969, 9 vols. 2009. (Handbook to Life in America Ser.). (Illus.). 292p. (C). (gr. 9-18). 50.00 *(978-0-8160-7181-4(0))* Facts On File, Inc.
—The Roaring Twenties, 1920 - 1929, 9 vols. 2009. (Handbook to Life in America Ser.). (Illus.). 282p. (C). (gr. 9-18). 50.00 *(978-0-8160-7179-1(9))* Facts On File, Inc.
Cassells, E. Steve. Tracing the Past: Archaeology along the Rocky Mountain Expansion Loop Pipeline, 1. 2003. (Illus.). 40p. 6.95 *(978-0-9743137-0-2(X))* Alpine Archaeological Consultants, Inc.
Cayton, Andrew & Prentice Hall Staff. America: Pathways to the Present. 2004. (ENG.). (YA). (gr. 11-12). 88.00 *(978-0-13-181545-2(8)*, Prentice Hall) Pearson Schl.
—America: Pathways to the Present, Modern American History. 2004. (ENG.). (YA). (gr. 11-12). 85.90 *(978-0-13-181547-6(4)*, Prentice Hall) Pearson Schl.
Celebrate the States - Group 7, 5 bks., Set. 2nd rev. ed. Incl. Arkansas. Altman, Linda Jacobs. lib. bdg. 42.79 *(978-0-7614-3001-8(6))*; Idaho. Stefoff, Rebecca. lib. bdg. 42.79 *(978-0-7614-3003-2(2))*; Maryland. Pietrzyk, Leslie & Kneib, Martha. lib. bdg. 42.79 *(978-0-7614-3004-9(0))*; Massachusetts. LeVert, Suzanne & Orr, Tamra. lib. bdg. 42.79 *(978-0-7614-3005-6(9))*; New Jersey. Moragne, Wendy & Orr, Tamra. lib. bdg. 42.79 *(978-0-7614-3006-3(7))*; (gr. 6-18). (Celebrate the States 7 Ser.). 144p. 2008. Set lib. bdg. 213.93 *(978-0-7614-3000-1(8)*, Benchmark Bks.) Marshall Cavendish Corp.
Center for Learning Network Staff. U. S. History & Geography 2 Bk. 2: Curriculum Unit, 2 vols. 2003. (Social Studies Ser.). 210p. tchr. ed., spiral bd. 29.95 *(978-1-56077-655-0(2))* Center for Learning, The.
Center for Learning Staff. The Age of Imperialism: 1895-1930 — - Elementary U. S. History Series, 11 vols. 2003. (Social Studies Ser.). (Illus.). 143p. (J). tchr. ed., spiral bd. 29.95 *(978-1-56077-748-9(6))* Center for Learning, The.
—Using Literature to Teach U. S. History: Elementary U. S. History Series, 12 vols. 2003. (Social Studies Ser.). (Illus.). 227p. (J). tchr. ed., spiral bd. 37.95 *(978-1-56077-736-6(2))* Center for Learning, The.
Chalberg, John C., ed. Opposing Viewpoints in American History, Volume 1: From Colonial Times to Reconstruction. 2006. (Opposing Viewpoints in American History Ser.: Vol. 1). (ENG.). 187p. (J). (gr. 3-7). 44.95 *(978-0-7377-3185-9(0)*, Greenhaven Pr., Inc.); (YA). (gr. 9-12). pap. 67.45 *(978-0-7377-3184-2(2))* Cengage Gale.
—Opposing Viewpoints in American History, Volume 2: From Reconstruction to the Present. 2006. (Opposing Viewpoints in American History Ser.: Vol. 2). (ENG.). 226p. (J). (gr. 3-7). 44.95 *(978-0-7377-3187-3(7)*, Greenhaven Pr., Inc.); (YA). (gr. 9-12). pap. 63.60 *(978-0-7377-3186-6(9))* Cengage Gale.
Chandler, Matt & Garbe, Suzanne. Haunted America, 1 vol. 2014. (Haunted America Ser.). (ENG.). 32p. (gr. 3-4). lib. bdg. 111.96 *(978-1-4765-7925-2(3)*, Edge Bks.) Capstone Press of Coughlan Cos.
Cheney, Lynne. A Is for Abigail: An Almanac of Amazing American Women. Glasser, Robin Preiss, illus. 2003. (ENG.). 48p. (J). (gr. 1-7). 19.99 *(978-0-689-85819-2(1)*, Simon & Schuster Bks. For Young Readers) Simon & Schuster Bks. For Young Readers.
—Our 50 States: A Family Adventure Across America. Glasser, Robin Preiss, illus. 2006. (ENG.). 74p. (J). (gr. 2-5). 19.99 *(978-0-689-86717-0(4)*, Simon & Schuster/Paula Wiseman Bks.) Simon & Schuster/Paula Wiseman Bks.
—A Time for Freedom: What Happened When in America. 2005. (ENG., Illus.). 304p. (J). (gr. 5-9). 19.99 *(978-1-4169-0925-5(7)*, Simon & Schuster/Paula Wiseman Bks.) Simon & Schuster/Paula Wiseman Bks.
Child, Hamilton. Gazetteer & Business Directory of Sullivan County For 1872-73: Republished on CD-ROM by Between the Lakes Group 2003. (Illus.). 380p. cd-rom 20.00 *(978-0-9727403-4-0(1)*, EJ03-03C) Between the Lakes Group, LLC.
Chudacoff, Howard, et al. Major Problems in American Urban & Suburban History: Documents & Essays. 2nd ed. 2004. (Major Problems in American History Ser.). (ENG., Illus.). 528p. (C). per. 119.95 *(978-0-618-43276-9(0)*, 309820) CENGAGE Learning.
Clark, Katie. The Lincoln Memorial: Myths, Legends, & Facts, 1 vol. 2014. (Monumental History Ser.). (ENG.). 32p. (gr. 3-4). 27.32 *(978-1-4914-0205-4(9)*, Fact Finders) Capstone Press of Coughlan Cos.
Clickard, Carrie. Thomas Jefferson & the Mammoth Hunt. Carpenter, Nancy, illus. 2017. (J). *(978-1-4814-4268-8(6)*, Beach Lane Bks.) Beach Lane Bks.
Coletti, Sharon. Everything You Need to Supplement U. S. & State Studies. 2005. (YA). Pt. 1. ring bd. 249.95 *(978-1-933558-08-0(3))*Pt. 2. ring bd. 249.95 *(978-1-933558-09-7(1))* InspirEd Educators.
Collins, Terry. Liberty, 1 vol. Bascle, Brian, illus. 2009. (Cartoon Nation Ser.). (ENG.). 32p. (gr. 3-4). lib. bdg. 30.65 *(978-1-4296-2340-7(3)*, Graphic Library) Capstone Press of Coughlan Cos.
Color All About: America: A Giant Coloring Book about the Birth of a Nation. 2004. (Illus.). (J). *(978-0-9763307-3-8(3))* Food Marketing Consultants, Inc.
Connors, Kathleen. Let's Explore the Northeast. 2013. 24p. (J). (gr. 2-5). 22.60 *(978-1-4339-9134-9(9))*; pap. 8.15 *(978-1-4339-9135-6(7))* Stevens, Gareth Publishing LLLP.
Cornerstones of Freedom, Second Series, 4 bks., Set. Incl. Building the New York Subway. Santella, Andrew. 26.00 *(978-0-516-23638-4(5))*; Gilded Age. Morrow, Ann. 26.00 *(978-0-516-23641-4(5))*; Manhattan Project. Elish, Dan. 26.00 *(978-0-516-23299-7(1))*; U. S. Supreme Court. Elish, Dan. 26.00 *(978-0-516-23637-7(7))*; (Illus.). 48p. (J). (gr. 4-6). 2007. 104.00 o.p. *(978-0-531-17731-0(9)*, Children's Pr.) Scholastic Library Publishing.
Cornerstones of Freedom, Third Series Spring 2012 Set Of 10. 2012. (Cornerstones of Freedom, Third Ser.). 300.00 *(978-0-531-25834-7(3)*, Children's Pr.) Scholastic Library Publishing.
Cosson, M. J. Three Worlds Meet. 2011. (Explorer Library: Language Arts Explorer Ser.). (ENG.). 32p. (gr. 4-8). lib. bdg. 28.50 *(978-1-61080-193-5(8)*, 201162) Cherry Lake Publishing.
Crabtree Publishing Company Staff & Morss, Martha. United States: The People. 2012. (ENG.). 32p. (J). pap. *(978-0-7787-9839-2(9))* Crabtree Publishing Co.
Creating America: A History of the United States: Creating America Workbook Answer Key. 2005. (gr. 6-12). *(978-0-618-15629-0(1)*, 2-01341) Holt McDougal.
Creating America: A History of the United States: EEdition Plus Online. 2005. (gr. 6-12). *(978-0-618-42734-5(1)*, 2-00718) Holt McDougal.
Creating America: A History of the United States: EEdition Plus Online with purchase of print Pupil'sYear. 2005. (gr. 6-12). *(978-0-618-42727-7(9)*, 2-00711) Holt McDougal.
Creating America: A History of the United States: ETest Plus Online-1 year (per Student) 2005. (gr. 6-12). *(978-0-618-28361-3(7)*, 2-90117) Holt McDougal.
Creating America: A History of the United States: ETest Plus Online-6 year (per Student) 2005. (gr. 6-12). *(978-0-618-28382-8(X)*, 2-90122) Holt McDougal.
Creating America: A History of the United States: GeoQuest. 2005. (gr. 6-12). cd-rom *(978-0-618-03712-4(8)*, 2-81168) Holt McDougal.
Creating America: A History of the United States: Primary Source Explorer. 2005. (gr. 6-12). cd-rom *(978-0-618-03708-7(X)*, 2-81164) Holt McDougal.
Creating America: Beginnings through Reconstruction: Creating America: Beginnings through Reconstruction Workbook. 2005. (gr. 6-12). *(978-0-618-19420-9(7)*, 2-70061) Holt McDougal.
Creating America: Beginnings Through Reconstruction: EEdition Plus Online. 2005. (gr. 6-12). *(978-0-618-19411-7(8)*, 2-70053) Holt McDougal.
Creating America: Beginnings Through Reconstruction: EEdition Plus Online with purchase of print Pupil's Year. 2005. (gr. 6-12). *(978-0-618-18720-1(0)*, 2-70030) Holt McDougal.
Creating America: Beginnings Through World War I. 2005. (gr. 6-12). *(978-0-618-16522-3(3)*, 2-81245) Holt McDougal.
Creating America: Beginnings Through World War I: EEdition Plus Online. 2005. (gr. 6-12). *(978-0-618-42758-1(9)*, 2-00742) Holt McDougal.
Creating America: Beginnings Through World War I: EEdition Plus Online with purchase of print Pupil's Year. 2005. (gr. 6-12). *(978-0-618-42751-2(1)*, 2-00735) Holt McDougal.
Creative Media Applications Staff, contrib. by. Debatable Issues in U. S. History: A World Power 1934 to the Present, 5 vols. 2004. (Middle School Reference Ser.). (Illus.). 144p. (C). (gr. 6-8). 242.00 *(978-0-313-32910-4(9)*, MS2910, Greenwood) ABC-CLIO, LLC.
Crewe, Sabrina & Anderson, Dale. The Atom Bomb Project. 2004. (Events That Shaped America Ser.). (Illus.). 32p. (gr. 3-6). lib. bdg. 26.00 *(978-0-8368-3404-8(6)*, Gareth Stevens Learning Library) Stevens, Gareth Publishing LLLP.
—The Seneca Falls Women's Rights Convention. 2004. (Events That Shaped America Ser.). (Illus.). 32p. (J). (gr. 3-6). lib. bdg. 26.00 *(978-0-8368-3408-6(9)*, Gareth Stevens Learning Library) Stevens, Gareth Publishing LLLP.
Critical Anthologies of Nonfiction Writing. 2005. (gr. 7-12). lib. bdg. 183.60 *(978-1-4042-0354-9(0))* Rosen Publishing Group, Inc., The.
Croy, Elden. United States. 2010. (Countries of the World Ser.). (ENG., Illus.). 64p. (J). (gr. 5-18). 27.90 *(978-1-4263-0632-7(6)*, National Geographic Children's Bks.) National Geographic Society.
Cudeyro, Erica M. American History for Young Minds - Volume 1, Looking Towards the Sky, Book 1, the First Airplane. Butler, Lindsay L., illus. 2008. 20p. pap. 11.95 *(978-1-934925-34-8(9)*, Eloquent Bks.) Strategic Book Publishing & Rights Agency (SBPRA).
Cunningham, Kevin. Contemporary United States. 2011. (Explorer Library: Language Arts Explorer Ser.). (ENG.). 32p. (gr. 4-8). pap. 14.21 *(978-1-61080-283-3(7)*, 201206); (Illus.). lib. bdg. 28.50 *(978-1-61080-195-9(4)*, 201166) Cherry Lake Publishing.
Currie, Stephen. Environmentalism in America. 2010. (American History Ser.). (Illus.). 128p. (J). 34.80 *(978-1-4205-0210-7(7)*, Lucent Bks.) Cengage Gale.
—The Quest for Freedom: The Abolitionist Movement. 2005. (Lucent Library of Black History). (ENG., Illus.). 112p. (YA). (gr. 7-10). lib. bdg. 33.45 *(978-1-59018-703-6(2)*, Lucent Bks.) Cengage Gale.
Currie, Stephen & National Geographic Learning Staff. Expeditions in the Americas, 1492-1700. 2007. (Nonfiction Reading & Writing Workshops Ser.). (ENG., Illus.). 32p. (J). pap. 17.95 *(978-0-7922-4544-5(X))* CENGAGE Learning.
D'Amico, Joan & Drummond, Karen Eich. The U. S. History Cookbook: Delicious Recipes & Exciting Events from the Past. Cline, Jeff & Cash-Walsh, Tina, illus. 2003. (ENG.). 192p. (J). (gr. 3-7). pap. 16.00 *(978-0-471-13602-6(6)*, Jossey-Bass) Wiley, John & Sons, Inc.
D'Amico, Joan & Drumond, Karen Eich. The US History Cook Book: Delicious Recipes & Exciting Events from the Past. 2006. (Illus.). 180p. (J). (gr. 4-8). reprint ed. pap. 15.00 *(978-1-4223-5809-2(7))* DIANE Publishing Co.
David Haugen. Colonists. 2004. (Voices from the Revolution Ser.). lib. bdg. 22.45 *(978-1-4103-0413-1(2))* Cengage Gale.
—Leaders. 2004. lib. bdg. 22.45 *(978-1-56711-958-9(1)*, Blackbirch Pr., Inc.) Cengage Gale.
Davies, Gill. The Thirteen Colonies 1584 - 1776. 2005. (National Geographic Timelines Ser.). (Illus.). 64p. (J). 27.90 *(978-0-7922-4171-3(1))* CENGAGE Learning.
Davis, Kenneth C. Don't Know Much About American History. Faulkner, Matt, illus. 2003. (Don't Know Much About Ser.). (ENG.). 224p. (J). (gr. 3-7). pap. 6.99 *(978-0-06-440836-3(1))* HarperCollins Pubs.
—Don't Know Much About American History. 2004. (Don't Know Much about Ser.). 224p. (J). (gr. 4-7). pap. 40.00 incl. audio *(978-0-8072-2092-4(2)*, Listening Library) Random Hse. Audio Publishing Group.
Day, Reed B. Two Families: A History of the Lives & Times of the Families of Isaac Newton Day & Lucilla Caroline Blachly 1640-1940. 2004. (Illus.). 296p. per. 29.95 *(978-0-9760563-1-7(3)*, 7796) Mechling Bookbindery.
DBQ Practice U. S. History. 2003. spiral bd. 19.95 *(978-1-56004-144-3(7))* Social Studies Schl. Service.
Discover America State by State, 51 vols., Set. 2005. (Discover America State by State Ser.). (ENG., Illus.). (J). (gr. 1-3). 915.45 *(978-1-58536-294-3(8)*, 202286) Sleeping Bear Pr.
Discovering U. S. History, 12 vols., Set. 2010. (Discovering U. S. History Ser.). (gr. 5-8). 420.00 *(978-1-60413-864-1(5)*, Chelsea Hse.) Facts On File, Inc.
Disgusting History. (Disgusting History Ser.). 32p. 2010. lib. bdg. 103.96 *(978-1-4296-5851-5(7))* 2009. (ENG.). (gr. 3-4). lib. bdg. 81.96 *(978-1-4296-4443-3(5))* Capstone Press of Coughlan Cos. (Fact Finders).
Documents That Shaped America. 2013. (Documents That Shaped America Ser.). 32p. (J). (gr. 4-6). 159.60 *(978-1-4339-9678-8(2))*; pap. 378.00 *(978-1-4339-9746-4(0))*; pap. 63.00 *(978-1-4339-9745-7(2))* Stevens, Gareth Publishing LLLP.
Donner, Candie. American Girl: Assembled: Meet Kaya Lapbook. Kinney, Cyndi, ed. 2013. (J). pap. 35.99 *(978-1-61625-515-2(3))* Knowledge Box Central.
—American Girl: Meet Kaya Lapbook. Kinney, Cyndi, ed. 2013. (J). pap. 25.99 *(978-1-61625-513-8(7))*; cd-rom 19.99 *(978-1-61625-512-1(9))* Knowledge Box Central.
Doucet, Bob, illus. Fact & Fable: State Stories, 6 vols., Set 2. Incl. Buster's Trip to Cape Cod: A Story about Massachusetts. Gaarder-Juntti, Oona. 25.65 *(978-1-60453-921-9(6))*; Frenchy's Float: A Story about Louisiana. Scheunemann, Pam. 25.65 *(978-1-60453-922-6(4))*; Great Lei Race: A Story about Hawaii. Salzmann, Mary Elizabeth. 25.65 *(978-1-60453-923-3(2))*; Leaping Lily: A Story about Georgia. Dolphin, Colleen. 25.65 *(978-1-60453-924-0(0))*; Monty's Ice Pick: A Story about Alaska. Hengel, Katherine. 25.65 *(978-1-60453-925-7(9))*; Rupert & the Liberty Bell: A Story about Pennsylvania. Hengel, Katherine. 25.65 *(978-1-60453-926-4(7))*; (J). (gr. -1-3). (Fact & Fable: State Stories Set 2 Ser.). (Illus.). 24p. 2010. 153.90 *(978-1-60453-920-2(8))*; 153.90 *(978-1-61714-678-7(1))* ABDO Publishing Co. (Super SandCastle).
Downing, Brian M. The Paths of Glory: Social Change in America from the Great War to Vietnam. 2003. 324p. (YA). per. 22.95 *(978-1-877275-58-6(1)*, Cybereditions (TM)) Lisa Loucks Christenson Publishing, LLC.
Draper, Allison Stark. Clothing, Costumes & Uniforms Throughout American History, 6 bks. Incl. What People Wore During the American Revolution. lib. bdg. 22.60 *(978-0-8239-5666-1(0)*, PKCLRE); What People Wore During the Civil War. lib. bdg. 22.60 *(978-0-8239-5669-2(5)*, PKCLCI); What People Wore in Early America. lib. bdg. 22.60 *(978-0-8239-5664-7(4)*, PKCLEA); What People Wore on Southern Plantations. lib. bdg. 22.60 *(978-0-8239-5668-5(7)*, PKCLPL); 24p. (J). (gr. 3). 2001. (Illus.). Set lib. bdg. 117.00 *(978-0-8239-7060-5(4)*, PKCLAM, PowerKids Pr.) Rosen Publishing Group, Inc., The.
Duby, Marjorie. From Caravels to the Constitution: Puzzles Trageting Historical Themes That Reinforce Logic & Problem-Solving Skills. Armstrong, Bev, illus. 2006. (Learning Works). 112p. (J). (gr. 5-8). per. 13.99 *(978-0-88160-385-9(6)*, LW405, Learning Works, The) Creative Teaching Pr., Inc.
Due Process DBA. 2003. spiral bd. 16.95 *(978-1-56004-148-1(X))* Social Studies Schl. Service.
Dunn, Joeming W. The Pony Express, 1 vol. Martin, Cynthia, illus. 2008. (Graphic History Ser.). (ENG.). 32p. 28.50 *(978-1-60270-184-7(9)*, Graphic Planet- Nonfiction) ABDO Publishing Co.
Elissa Grodin. Everyone Counts: A Citizens' Number Book. Juhasz, Victor, illus. rev. ed. 2006. (Count Your Way Across the U. S. A. Ser.). (ENG.). 40p. (J). (gr. -1-3). 17.95 *(978-1-58536-295-0(6))* Sleeping Bear Pr.
Encyclopaedia Britannica, Inc. Staff, compiled by. Views of the Americas. 2003. (Illus.). 64p. 14.95 *(978-1-59339-043-3(2))* Encyclopaedia Britannica, Inc.
Encyclopedia Britannica's Annals of America 2003, 22 vols. 2003. 13000p. (YA). (gr. 5-18). 529.00 *(978-0-85229-960-9(5))* Encyclopaedia Britannica, Inc.
Ervin, Robert Edgar. The John Hunt Morgan Raid of 1863. 2003. (Illus.). 306p. lib. bdg. 29.95 net. *(978-0-9746189-0-6(X))* Ervin, Robert E.
Esty, Amos. The Liberator: The Story of William Lloyd Garrison. 2011. (Civil Rights Leaders Ser.). 144p. 28.95 *(978-1-59935-137-7(4))* Reynolds, Morgan Inc.
European Colonies in the Americas. (Illus.). (J). (gr. 3-6). 103.50 *(978-0-8239-7283-8(6)*, Reading Power) Rosen Publishing Group, Inc., The.
Evan-Moor. US Facts & Fun, Grades 1-3. 2005. (ENG.). 192p. (J). (gr. 1-3). pap. 14.99 *(978-1-59673-002-1(1)*, EMC 6305) Evan-Moor Educational Pubs.
—US Facts & Fun, Grades 4-6. 2005. (ENG.). 192p. (J). (gr. 4-6). pap. 14.99 *(978-1-59673-003-8(X)*, EMC 6306) Evan-Moor Educational Pubs.
Exposed! Myths about Early American History. 2016. (Exposed! Myths about Early American History Ser.). 00032p. (J). pap. 63.00 ***(978-1-4824-5845-9(4))*** Stevens, Gareth Publishing LLLP.
Eyewitness to History: Set 2. 2014. (Eyewitness to History Ser.). 32p. (J). (gr. 4-6). 159.60 *(978-1-4824-1172-0(5))* Stevens, Gareth Publishing LLLP.
Eyewitness to History: Sets 1-2. 2014. (Eyewitness to History Ser.). 32p. (J). (gr. 4-6). 319.20 *(978-1-4824-1450-9(3))* Stevens, Gareth Publishing LLLP.
Facts on File, Inc. Staff, creator. Eyewitness History Set, 16-Volumes. 2007. (Eyewitness History Ser.). 688p. (C). (gr. 9). 1280.00 *(978-0-8160-7438-9(0))* Facts On File, Inc.
First Americans, 6 bks., Set. Incl. Apache. Casey, Carolyn. lib. bdg. *(978-0-7614-1894-8(6))*; Cherokee. De Capua, Sarah. lib. bdg. *(978-0-7614-1895-5(4))*; Iroquois. De Capua, Sarah. lib. bdg. *(978-0-7614-1896-2(2))*; Navajo. King, David C. lib. bdg. *(978-0-7614-1897-9(0))*; Pueblo. Broida, Marian. lib. bdg. *(978-0-7614-1898-6(9))*; Sioux. King, David C. lib. bdg. *(978-0-7614-1899-3(7))*; (Illus.). 48p. (J). (gr. 3-7). 2005. *(978-0-7614-1893-1(8)*, Benchmark Bks.) Marshall Cavendish Corp.
Fisher, Douglas & McGraw-Hill Book Company Staff. The American Vision, Modern Times, Active Reading & Note-Taking Guide. 2005. (American Vision: Mod Times Ser.). (ENG., Illus.). 360p. (gr. 9-12). stu. ed., per., wbk. ed. 12.80 *(978-0-07-872764-1(2)*, 0078727642) McGraw-Hill Higher Education.
Fisher, Douglas & McGraw-Hill-Glencoe Staff. The American Republic to 1877. 2nd ed. 2004. (U. S. History - the Early Years Ser.). (ENG., Illus.). 314p. (gr. 6-9). stu. ed., per. 12.80 *(978-0-07-866250-8(8)*, 0078662508) McGraw-Hill Higher Education.
Fisher, Douglas & McGraw-Hill Staff. The American Journey: Reconstruction to the Present. 2004. (Amer Journey Recon/present Ser.). (ENG., Illus.). 310p. (gr. 6-9). stu. ed. 12.80 *(978-0-07-868547-7(8)*, 0078685478) McGraw-Hill Higher Education.
—The American Republic since 1877: Active Reading Note-Taking Guide. 2nd ed. 2004. (U. S. History - the Modern Era Ser.). (ENG., Illus.). 530p. (gr. 8-10). stu. ed., per. 12.80 *(978-0-07-867995-7(8)*, 0078679958) McGraw-Hill Higher Education.
—The American Vision Active Reading Note-Taking Guide: Student Workbook. 2nd ed. 2004. (United States History (hs) Ser.). (ENG., Illus.). 574p. (gr. 9-12). stu. ed., per. 12.80 *(978-0-07-868002-1(6)*, 0078680026) McGraw-Hill Higher Education.

TUV

Fishman, Jon M. Miguel Cabrera. 2013. (Amazing Athletes Ser.). (ENG., Illus.). 32p. (gr. 2-5). pap. 7.95 (978-1-4677-1559-1(X)) Lerner Publishing Group.

Forest, Christopher. This Book Is History: A Collection of Cool U. S. History Trivia, 1 vol. 2012. (Super Trivia Collection). (ENG.). 32p. (gr. 3-4). lib. bdg. 27.99 (978-1-4296-8419-4(4)) Capstone Press of Coughlan Cos.

Foster James, Helen. Little America. 2011. (My Little State Ser.). (ENG., Illus.). 22p. (J). 7.95 (978-1-58536-179-3(8)) Sleeping Bear Pr.

Fradin, Dennis Brindell. Turning Points in History, 6 vols., Group 4. Incl. First Lunar Landing. 31.36 (978-0-7614-4256-1(1)); Hurricane Katrina. Fradin, Judith Bloom. 31.36 (978-0-7614-4261-5(8)); Louisiana Purchase. 31.36 (978-0-7614-4257-8(X)); Montgomery Bus Boycott. 31.36 (978-0-7614-4258-5(8)); September 11, 2001. 31.36 (978-0-7614-4259-2(6)); Stamp Act of 1765. (Illus.). (J). 31.36 (978-0-7614-4260-8(X)); 48p. (gr. 3-18). (Turning Points in U. S. History 4 Ser.). 2009. Set lib. bdg. 188.16 o.p. (978-0-7614-4255-4(3)) Marshall Cavendish Corp.

—Turning Points in U. S. History - Group 3, 6 bks., Set. Incl. Battle of Yorktown. lib. bdg. 31.36 (978-0-7614-3008-7(3)); Bill of Rights. lib. bdg. 31.36 (978-0-7614-3009-4(1)); Boston Massacre. lib. bdg. 31.36 (978-0-7614-3010-0(5)); California Gold Rush. lib. bdg. 31.36 (978-0-7614-3012-4(1)); Salem Witch Trials. Fradin, Judith Bloom. lib. bdg. 31.36 (978-0-7614-3013-1(X)); Underground Railroad. lib. bdg. 31.36 (978-0-7614-3014-8(8)); 48p. (gr. 3-18). (Turning Points in U. S. History 3 Ser.). 2008. Set lib. bdg. 188.16 (978-0-7614-3007-0(5), Benchmark Bks.) Marshall Cavendish Corp.

Franchino, Vicky. Northeast. 2011. (Explorer Library: Social Studies Explorer Ser.). (ENG.). 48p. (gr. 4-8). lib. bdg. 31.36 (978-1-61080-180-5(6), 201154) Cherry Lake Publishing.

Franck, Irene M. & Brownstone, David M. Frontier America, 10 vols. 2004. (Illus.). (J). 369.00 (978-0-7172-5990-8(0), Grolier) Scholastic Library Publishing.

Frank, Nicole & Berg, Elizabeth. The United States. 2010. (Welcome to My Country Ser.). 48p. (gr. 3). 28.50 (978-1-60870-160-5(3)) Marshall Cavendish Corp.

Frank, Sarah. Filipinos in America. 2005. (In America Ser.). (ENG., Illus.). 72p. (gr. 5-8). lib. bdg. 27.93 (978-0-8225-4873-7(9), Lerner Pubns.) Lerner Publishing Group.

Frederick, Shane. The Ultimate Collection of Pro Football Records. 2012. (For the Record Ser.). (ENG.). 64p. (gr. 4-6). pap. 53.70 (978-1-4296-9433-9(5)) Capstone Press of Coughlan Cos.

Freedman, Jeri. Careers in Child Care, 1 vol. 2015. (ENG.). 80p. (J). 34.25 (978-1-4777-7884-5(5), Rosen Young Adult) Rosen Publishing Group, Inc., The.

Fridell, Ron. Prisoners of War. 2007. (Open for Debate Ser.). (Illus.). 128p. (gr. 7-7). lib. bdg. 42.79 (978-0-7614-2577-9(2), Benchmark Bks.) Marshall Cavendish Corp.

Friedman-Brunt, Elyse. Conflict Resolution in American History, Gr. 8: Lessons from the Past, Lessons for Today. Chandler, Terrence, illus. 2003. 48p. (YA). pap., wbk. ed. 19.95 (978-1-878227-89-8(0)) Peace Education Foundation.

—Conflict Resolution in American History, Grade 8: Lessons from the Past, Lessons for Today. Chandler, Terrence, illus. 2003. 200p. pap., instr.'s training gde. ed. 29.95 (978-1-878227-88-1(2)) Peace Education Foundation.

Friedman, Ian C. Freedom of Speech & the Press. 2005. (American Rights Ser.). (Illus.). 144p. (gr. 5-8). 35.00 (978-0-8160-5662-0(5)) Facts On File, Inc.

Friedman, Michael & Friedman, Brett. Settlement Houses: Improving the Social Welfare of America's Immigrants. 2004. (Progressive Movement, 1900-1920 Ser.). (Illus.). 32p. (YA). (gr. 5-9). lib. bdg. 22.50 (978-1-4042-0194-1(7)) Rosen Publishing Group, Inc., The.

Frisch, Aaron. Aaron Rodgers. 2013. (Illus.). 24 p.p. (J). 25.65 (978-1-60818-334-0(3), Creative Education) Creative Co., The.

—Adrian Peterson. 2013. (Illus.). 24 p.p. (J). 25.65 (978-1-60818-335-7(1), Creative Education) Creative Co., The.

—Katy Perry. 2013. (Illus.). 24p. (J). 25.65 (978-1-60818-331-9(9), Creative Education) Creative Co., The.

—Lady Gaga. 2013. (Illus.). 24p. (J). 25.65 (978-1-60818-332-6(7), Creative Education) Creative Co., The.

Fun Fact File. 2013. (Fun Fact File Ser.). 32p. (J). (gr. 3-6). 606.00 (978-1-4339-9734-1(7)); pap. 252.00 (978-1-4339-9826-3(2)); pap. 1512.00 (978-1-4339-9827-0(0)) Stevens, Gareth Publishing LLLP.

Fun Fact File: Complete Set. 2017. (Fun Fact File Ser.). 32p. (gr. 2-3). lib. bdg. 1515.00 **(978-1-5382-0470-2(3))** Stevens, Gareth Publishing LLLP.

Fun Fact File: Founding Fathers. 2017. (Fun Fact File: Founding Fathers Ser.). 32p. (gr. 2-3). pap. 63.00 **(978-1-5382-0484-9(3))** Stevens, Gareth Publishing LLLP.

Fun Fact File: US History! 2013. (Fun Fact File: US History! Ser.). 32p. (J). (gr. 3-6). 151.50 (978-1-4339-9698-6(7)); pap. 63.00 (978-1-4339-9804-1(1)); pap. 378.00 (978-1-4339-9805-8(X)) Stevens, Gareth Publishing LLLP.

Gale Editor, ed. Junior Worldmark Encyclopedia of the States: 4 Volume Set, 4 vols. 6th ed. 2013. (Junior Worldmark Encyclopedia of the States Ser.). (ENG., Illus.). 372.00 (978-1-4144-9859-1(4), UXL) Cengage Gale.

Ganeri, Anita. United States of America. Isik, Semur, illus. 2015. (Country Guides, with Benjamin Blog & His Inquisitive Dog Ser.). (ENG.). 32p. (gr. 1-3). 29.99 (978-1-4109-6851-7(0), Read Me!) Heinemann-Raintree.

Garbe, Suzanne. Ghosts of Gettysburg & Other Hauntings of the East, 1 vol. 2014. (Haunted America Ser.). (ENG.). 32p. (gr. 3-4). lib. bdg. 27.99 (978-1-4765-3916-4(2), Edge Bks.) Capstone Press of Coughlan Cos.

Garcia, Jesus, et al. *Creating America: A History of the United* States. 2006. (Illus.). 890p. (gr. 6-12). stu. ed. (978-0-395-92899-8(0), 2-88557) Holt McDougal.

—Creating America: A History of the United States: Beginnings Through Reconstruction, 2 vols. l.t. ed. 2003. (McDougal Littell Creating America Ser.). (ENG., Illus.). 816p. (gr. 8-8). stu. ed. 111.95 (978-0-618-37698-8(4), 2-00479) Great Source Education Group, Inc.

—Creating America: A History of the United States: with Atlas by Rand Mcnally. l.t. ed. 2006. (Illus.). 917p. (gr. 7-9). stu. ed. 78.64 (978-0-618-37690-2(9), 2-00471) Holt McDougal.

—Creating America: Beginnings Through World War I. 2006. (Illus.). 751p. (gr. 6-12). stu. ed. (978-0-618-16252-9(6), 2-81241) Holt McDougal.

—Creating America: Beginnings Through World War I: A History of the United States. l.t. ed. 2005. (Illus.). 757p. (gr. 7-9). (978-0-618-37708-4(5), 2-00489) Holt McDougal.

—McDougal Littell Creating America: A History of the United States, 2 vols. l.t. ed. 2003. (McDougal Littell Creating America Ser.). (ENG., Illus.). 704p. (gr. 8-8). stu. ed. 111.95 (978-0-618-37684-1(4), 2-00465) Great Source Education Group, Inc.

Gave, Marc. La historia de los Estados Unidos en Suma. 2011. (SPA.). 32p. (J). pap. 49.00 net. (978-1-4108-2342-7(3), A23423) Benchmark Education Co.

Gilbert, Sara. Built for Success: the Story of CNN. 2013. (Built for Success Ser.). (ENG.). 48p. (J). (gr. 4-7). pap. 12.00 (978-0-89812-760-7(2), Creative Paperbacks) Creative Co., The.

—The Story of Amazon. Com. 2013. (Built for Success Ser.). (ENG.). 48p. (J). (gr. 4-7). pap. 12.00 (978-0-89812-759-1(9), Creative Paperbacks) Creative Co., The.

The Gilded Age & Progressivism, 1891-1913. 2010. (Discovering U. S. History Ser.). (Illus.). 136p. (gr. 5-8). 35.00 (978-1-60413-355-4(4), Chelsea Hse.) Facts On File, Inc.

Gingrich, Callista. Sweet Land of Liberty. Arciero, Susan, illus. 2011. (Ellis the Elephant Ser.). (ENG.). 28p. (J). (gr. -1-3). 14.95 (978-1-59698-292-5(6)) Regnery Publishing, Inc., An Eagle Publishing Co.

Glencoe McGraw-Hill Staff. The American Journey. 7th ed. 2008. (American Journey (survey) Ser.). (ENG., Illus.). 62p. (gr. 6-8). pap., wbk. ed. 6.96 (978-0-07-880612-4(7), 0078806127) McGraw-Hill Education.

—The American Journey: Modern Times. 2nd ed. 2008. (American Journey (survey) Ser.). (ENG.). 784p. (gr. 6-8). 130.28 (978-0-07-877718-9(6), 0078777186) McGraw-Hill Education.

—The American Vision. 2007. (United States History (hs) Ser.). (ENG., Illus.). 72p. (gr. 9-12). pap. 8.08 (978-0-07-878431-6(X), 007878431X) McGraw-Hill Higher Education.

—The American Vision. 2007. (United States History (hs) Ser.). (ENG., Illus.). 58p. (gr. 9-12). pap. 8.08 (978-0-07-878510-8(3), 0078785103) McGraw-Hill Higher Education.

—The American Vision: Modern Times. 2007. (United States History (hs) Ser.). (ENG., (gr. 9-12). Illus.). 280p. per. 12.08 (978-0-07-878518-4(9), 0078785189); 1024p. stu. ed. 130.24 (978-0-07-874523-2(3), 0078745233) McGraw-Hill Higher Education.

—The American Vision: Modern Times, Spanish Reading Essentials & Note-Taking Guide. 2007. (United States History (hs) Ser.). (ENG & SPA.). (gr. 9-12). pap. 12.08 (978-0-07-878520-7(0), 0078785200) McGraw-Hill Higher Education.

Glencoe McGraw-Hill Staff, creator. The American Journey - Modern Times: Reading Essentials & Note-Taking Guide. 2nd ed. 2008. (American Journey (survey) Ser.). (ENG., Illus.). 216p. (gr. 6-8). per. 11.68 (978-0-07-880638-4(0), 0078806380) McGraw-Hill Education.

—The American Journey: Modern Times, Spanish Reading Essentials & Note-Taking Guide. 2nd ed. 2008. (American Journey (survey) Ser.). (ENG & SPA., Illus.). 210p. (gr. 6-8). per. 11.68 (978-0-07-880648-3(8), 0078806488) McGraw-Hill Education.

—The American Republic since 1877 Spanish Reading Essentials & Study Guide. 2nd ed. 2004. (U. S. History - the Modern Era Ser.). (SPA., Illus.). 479p. (gr. 8-10). stu. ed., per. 15.12 (978-0-07-865407-7(6), 0078654076) McGraw-Hill Higher Education.

—The American Vision Reading Essentials & Study Guide Student Workbook. 2nd ed. 2004. (United States History (hs) Ser.). (ENG., Illus.). 534p. (gr. 9-12). per. 16.00 (978-0-07-865439-8(4), 0078654394) McGraw-Hill Higher Education.

GLOBE. Globe Fearon American History Vol. 2: Civil War to the Present. 2003. (ENG.). 524p. (YA). (gr. 6-12). 50.95 (978-0-13-024411-6(2), GLOBE) Pearson Schl.

Globe Fearon American History Vol. 1: Prehistory Through Reconstruction. 2003. (American History Ser.). 542p. (YA). (gr. 6-12). 50.95 (978-0-13-024400-0(7)) Globe Fearon Educational Publishing.

Goldish, Meish. Animal Control Officers to the Rescue. 2013. (Work of Heroes: First Responders in Action Ser.). 32p. (J). (gr. 1-6). lib. bdg. 25.27 (978-1-61772-747-4(4)) Bearport Publishing Co., Inc.

Goldsmith, Marcia. Important Years: The 1980s. 2005. (Illus.). 16p. (J). (978-0-618-56043-1(2)) Houghton Mifflin Harcourt Publishing Co.

Goldsworthy, Kaite. Bald Eagle with Code. 2012. (AV2 American Icons Ser.). (ENG., Illus.). 24p. (J). pap. 12.95 (978-1-61913-300-6(8)); lib. bdg. 27.13 (978-1-61913-077-7(7)) Weigl Pubs., Inc. (AV2 by Weigl).

Gonzales, Doreen. The Secret of the Manhattan Project. 2012. (Stories in American History Ser.). (Illus.). 128p. (J). (gr. 5-18). 33.27 (978-0-7660-3954-4(4)) Enslow Pubs., Inc.

Gonzalez, Libia. Geografia e Historia de los Estados Unidos. (SPA.). 376p. (J). pap. 52.50 (978-958-04-3011-7(X), NOR011) Norma S.A. COL. Dist: AIMS International Bks., Inc.

Goodall, Barry, Jr. Glory Gone Forgotten: The Untold Story of the 12th Kentucky Cavalry. Embry, Eugene, ed. Brown, Stevi, illus. 2nd rev. ed. 2005. 182p. (978-0-9763932-1-4(2), 500) Goodall, Barry.

Goodrich, Charles Augustus. A Child's History of the United States. 2013. (Notable American Authors Ser.). 425p. reprint ed. lthr. 79.00 (978-0-7812-2935-7(9)) Reprint Services Corp.

Goodrich, Samuel G. A Child's History of the United States. reprint ed. 150.00 (978-0-7222-7251-0(0)) Library Reprints, Inc.

Goodrich, Samuel Griswol. Peter Parleys Tales about America & Au. 2006. pap. (978-1-4068-3320-1(7)) Echo Library.

Gordon, Minette, et al. Understanding Women's Rights. 2011. (Personal Freedom & Civic Duty Ser.). (J). lib. bdg. 35.95 (978-1-4488-4671-9(4)) Rosen Publishing Group, Inc., The.

Gordon, Sharon. United States. 2015. (Illus.). 32p. (J). 10.58 (978-1-5026-0576-4(7)) Musa Publishing.

Gosman, Gillian. Franklin D. Roosevelt. 2011. (Life Stories Ser.). (Illus.). 24p. (J). pap. 8.25 (978-1-4488-3182-1(2), PowerKids Pr.); (ENG & SPA., (gr. 1-4). lib. bdg. 22.60 (978-1-4488-3222-4(5)); (gr. 1-4). lib. bdg. 22.60 (978-1-4488-3179-1(2), PowerKids Pr.) Rosen Publishing Group, Inc., The.

—Life Stories, 8 vols., Set. Incl. Abraham Lincoln. lib. bdg. 22.60 (978-1-4488-2582-0(2)); Benjamin Franklin. lib. bdg. 22.60 (978-1-4488-2585-1(7)); Franklin D. Roosevelt. lib. bdg. 22.60 (978-1-4488-3179-1(2)); George Washington. lib. bdg. 22.60 (978-1-4488-2581-3(4)); Harriet Tubman. lib. bdg. 22.60 (978-1-4488-2586-8(5)); Martin Luther King, Jr. lib. bdg. 22.60 (978-1-4488-2583-7(0)); Rosa Parks. lib. bdg. 22.60 (978-1-4488-2584-4(9)); Thomas Jefferson. lib. bdg. 22.60 (978-1-4488-3178-4(4)); (J). (gr. 1-4). (Life Stories Ser.). (Illus.). 24p. 2011. Set lib. bdg. 170.00 (978-1-4488-2793-0(0), PowerKids Pr.) Rosen Publishing Group, Inc., The.

Grant, R. G. The Great Depression. 2005. (How Did It Happen? Ser.). (ENG., Illus.). 48p. (YA). (gr. 7-10). lib. bdg. 32.10 (978-1-59018-606-0(0), Lucent Bks.) Cengage Gale.

Graphic Organizers in Social Studies. (Illus.). (J). (gr. 3-5). 119.70 (978-1-4042-2956-3(6)) Rosen Publishing Group, Inc., The.

Graves, Karen M., et al. It's Back to School ... Way Back! 2016. (It's Back to School ... Way Back! Ser.). (ENG.). 32p. (gr. 3-4). 109.28 (978-1-5157-2116-1(7), Fact Finders) Capstone Press of Coughlan Cos.

The Great Depression 1929-1938. 2010. (Discovering U. S. History Ser.). (Illus.). 136p. (gr. 5-8). 35.00 (978-1-60413-357-8(0), Chelsea Hse.) Facts On File, Inc.

Green, Carl R. The Gemini 4 Spacewalk Mission: A MyReportLinks. com Book. 2004. (Space Flight Adventures & Disasters Ser.). (Illus.). 48p. (J). lib. bdg. 26.60 (978-0-7660-5163-8(3), MyReportLinks.com Bks.) Enslow Pubs., Inc.

Gregory, Josh. Bill & Melinda Gates. 2013. (True Book(tm), A — Biographies Ser.). (ENG., Illus.). 48p. (J). lib. bdg. 31.00 (978-0-531-21905-8(4)); pap. 6.95 (978-0-531-23876-9(8)) Scholastic Library Publishing.

Gritzner, Charles F. The United States. 2007. (Modern World Nations Ser.). (Illus.). 142p. (YA). (gr. 7-12). lib. bdg. 35.00 (978-0-7910-9511-9(8)) Facts On File, Inc.

Gutman, Dan. My Weird School Fast Facts: Explorers, Presidents, & Toilets. Paillot, Jim, illus. 2017. (My Weird School Fast Facts Ser.). 192p. (J). (gr. 1-5). pap. 5.99 (978-0-06-230623-4(5)) HarperCollins Pubs.

Hakim, Joy. An Age of Extremes, 1880-1917. 2nd rev. ed. 2007. (History of US Ser.: Vol. 8). (ENG., Illus.). 224p. (gr. 4-7). per. 15.95 (978-0-19-532722-9(5)) Oxford Univ. Pr., Inc.

—A History of Us, 10 vols. 3rd ed. 2003. (Illus.). 186p. (J). 199.50 (978-0-19-515259-3(X)) Oxford Univ. Pr., Inc.

—A History of US: Sourcebook & Index. 3rd rev. ed. 2006. (History of US Ser.: 11). (ENG., Illus.). 160p. (gr. 4-7). 24.95 (978-0-19-518903-2(5)) Oxford Univ. Pr., Inc.

—A History of US: Ten-volume Set, 10 vols. 3rd rev. ed. 2006. (History of US Ser.). (ENG., Illus.). 249.50 (978-0-19-531491-5(3)) Oxford Univ. Pr., Inc.

Hall, Brianna & Levine, Becky. Cause & Effect, 1 vol. 2014. (Cause & Effect Ser.). (ENG.). 32p. (gr. 3-4). lib. bdg. 54.64 (978-1-4765-7824-8(9), Fact Finders) Capstone Press of Coughlan Cos.

Hallett, R. B. The 10 Most Decisive Battles on American Soil. 2008. 14.99 (978-1-55448-538-3(X)) Scholastic Library Publishing.

Hammond World Atlas Corporation Staff. American History Through Maps. 2004. (Atlas Ser.). (Illus.). 48p. (gr. 5). 8.95 (978-0-8437-7435-1(5), 774355) Hammond World Atlas Corp.

Harasymiw, Mark. Extreme Jobs in Extreme Places: Life on a Submarine. 2013. (Extreme Jobs in Extreme Places Ser.). (Illus.). 32p. (gr. 3-6). pap. 10.50 (978-1-4339-8503-4(9)); lib. bdg. 26.60 (978-1-4339-8502-7(0)) Stevens, Gareth Publishing LLLP.

Harcourt School Publishers Staff. Harcourt School Publishers Horizons Vol. 1: Us History 2003. 3rd ed. 2003. (Harcourt School Publishers Horizons Ser.). (ENG.). 780p. (gr. 5-5). tchr. ed. 202.15 (978-0-15-320189-9(4)) Harcourt Schl. Pubs.

—Horizons. 3rd ed. 2003. (Harcourt Horizons Ser.). (ENG.). 336p. (gr. 1-1). stu. ed. 58.00 (978-0-15-339615-1(6)); (ENG.). 390p. (gr. 2-2). stu. ed. 58.00 (978-0-15-339616-8(4)); (ENG.). 520p. (gr. 3-3). 79.75 (978-0-15-339617-5(2)); Vol. 1. tchr. ed. 104.40 (978-0-15-339626-7(1)); Vol. 2. tchr. ed. 104.40 (978-0-15-339627-4(X)) Harcourt Schl. Pubs.

—Horizons: Time for Kids Readers: US History. 3rd ed. 2003. (Harcourt Horizons Ser.). (gr. k-7). tchr. ed. 57.40 (978-0-15-334654-5(X)) Harcourt Schl. Pubs.

—Horizons Big Book. 3rd ed. 2003. (Harcourt Horizons Ser.). (ENG.). 100p. (gr. k-k). spiral bd. 312.10 (978-0-15-339673-1(3)) Harcourt Schl. Pubs.

—Horizons, Grade 1. 3rd ed. 2003. Vol. 1. tchr. ed. 98.30 (978-0-15-339624-3(5)) Vol. 2. tchr. ed. 98.30 (978-0-15-339625-0(3)) Harcourt Schl. Pubs.

—Horizons, Grade 3. 3rd ed. 2003. (Harcourt Horizons Ser.). (ENG.). (gr. 3-3). Vol. 1. 492p. tchr. ed., spiral bd. 153.45 (978-0-15-339628-1(8)) Vol. 2. 540p. tchr. ed., spiral bd. 153.45 (978-0-15-339629-8(6)) Harcourt Schl. Pubs.

—Horizons, Grade K. 3rd ed. 2003. tchr. ed. 113.40 (978-0-15-339623-6(7)) Harcourt Schl. Pubs.

—Horizontes: US History. 3rd ed. 2003. (Harcourt Horizontes Ser.). (SPA., (gr. k-6). Illus.). act. bk. ed. 11.80 (978-0-15-324555-8(7)); Vol. 1. tchr. ed. 133.80 (978-0-15-321981-8(5)); Vol. 2. tchr. ed. 133.80 (978-0-15-321982-5(3)) Harcourt Schl. Pubs.

—Social Studies: Stories in Time: Library Book Collection. 2003. (Harcourt Brace Social Studies). (Illus.). (gr. k-7). 130.90 (978-0-15-308394-5(8)) Harcourt Schl. Pubs.

—U. S. History. 3rd ed. 2003. (Harcourt Horizons Ser.). (ENG.). 808p. (gr. 4-5). stu. ed. 89.15 (978-0-15-339619-9(9)) Harcourt Schl. Pubs.

—United States History 2003, Vol. 1. 3rd ed. 2003. (Harcourt School Publishers Horizons Ser.). (ENG., Illus.). 464p. (gr. 4-6). 86.80 (978-0-15-339681-6(4)) Harcourt Schl. Pubs.

—US History. 3rd ed. 2003. (Horizontes (Social Studies) Ser.). (SPA., Illus.). (gr. k-6). pupil's gde. ed. 71.90 (978-0-15-324536-7(0)) Harcourt Schl. Pubs.

—US History - Beginning to the Civil War. 3rd ed. 2003. (Harcourt Electronic Test Ser.). pap., tchr. ed. 10.70 (978-0-15-340792-5(1)) Harcourt Schl. Pubs.

—US History - Civil War to the Present. 3rd ed. 2003. (Harcourt Electronic Test Ser.). pap., tchr. ed. 10.70 (978-0-15-340790-1(5)) Harcourt Schl. Pubs.

Hardyman, Robyn. Celebrate: United States. 2009. (Celebrate Country Ser.). 32p. (gr. 4-6). 28.00 (978-1-60413-264-9(7), Chelsea Clubhouse) Facts On File, Inc.

Harker, John B. Betsy Ross's Five Pointed Star: Elizabeth Claypoole, Quaker Flag Maker: A Historical Perspective. 2004. (Illus.). 166p. per. 20.00 (978-1-887774-15-4(7)) Canmore Pr.

Hazen, Walter A. Everyday Life: Reform in America. 2004. (Illus.). iv, 100p. pap. 12.95 (978-0-673-58898-2(X)) Good Year Bks.

Heeg, Berg Heeg. Voyage to Victory: The Voice of a Sailor in the Pacific 1943-1945. 2004. (YA). per. 9.95 (978-0-938682-79-0(2), 682-79-2) River Road Pubns., Inc.

Hein, Connie L. Toliver in Time: For a Fourth of July Celebration. Theobald, Denise, illus. 2003. 40p. (J). lib. bdg. 19.95 (978-0-9740855-8-6(8)); per. 12.95 (978-0-9740855-9-3(6)) Still Water Publishing.

Henretta, James A. America's History: High School Edition. 5th ed. 2004. 74.50 (978-0-312-44303-0(X)) Bedford/Saint Martin's.

Hernandez, Roger E. Teens & Relationships. Developed in Association with the Gallup Organization Staff, ed. 2013. (Gallup Youth Survey: Major Issues & Trends Ser.: 14). 112p. (J). (gr. 7-18). 24.95 (978-1-4222-2956-9(4)) Mason Crest.

Herweck, Dona. Susan B. Anthony, 1 vol. 2nd rev. ed. 2014. (TIME for KIDS(r) Nonfiction Readers Ser.). (ENG., Illus.). 28p. (J). (gr. 2-2). pap. 23.96 (978-1-4807-1063-4(6)) Shell Educational Publishing.

Herwick Rice, Dona & Bradley, Kathleen. Reconstruction: After the Civil War, 1 vol. 2009. (Building Fluency Through Reader's Theater Ser.). (ENG.). 32p. (J). (gr. 3-5). pap. 7.99 (978-1-4333-0547-4(X)) Teacher Created Materials, Inc.

Hewitt, David. Uncle Sam's America. Hewitt, Kathryn, illus. 2011. (ENG.). 40p. (J). (gr. 2-5). pap. 19.99 (978-1-4424-3092-1(3)) Simon & Schuster Children's Publishing.

Hicks, Terry Allan. The Bald Eagle. 2006. (Symbols of America Ser.). (Illus.). 40p. (J). (gr. 3-7). lib. bdg. 28.50 (978-0-7614-2133-7(5), Benchmark Bks.) Marshall Cavendish Corp.

Higgins, Melissa. We All Come from Different Cultures, 1 vol. 2012. (Celebrating Differences Ser.). (ENG.). 24p. (gr. k-1). 26.65 (978-1-4296-7577-2(2)); pap. 7.29 (978-1-4296-7887-2(9)) Capstone Press of Coughlan Cos. (Pebble Plus).

Higgins, Nadia. Perspective Flip Books. 2014. (Perspectives Flip Bks.). (ENG.). 64p. (gr. 5-6). pap. 17.90 (978-0-7565-4801-8(2), CPB Grades 4-8) Compass Point Bks.

Higginson, Thomas W. Young Folks' History of the United States. 2013. (Notable American Authors Ser.). (Illus.). 425p. reprint ed. lthr. 79.00 (978-0-7812-3113-8(2)) Reprint Services Corp.

Hill, Jeff. The WPA — Putting America to Work. 2013. (Defining Moments Ser.). (ENG.). 264p. lib. bdg. 55.00 (978-0-7808-1331-1(6)) Omnigraphics, Inc.

Hinman, Bonnie. Fascinating History. 2018. (ENG.). 32p. (gr. 3-6). 31.35 **(978-1-63235-420-4(9)**, 12-Story Library) Pr. Room Editions LLC.

Hirsch, E. D., Jr., ed. The Age of Exploration, Level 5. 2003. tchr. ed. 9.95 (978-0-7690-5077-5(8)); stu. ed. 49.95 (978-0-7690-2852-1(7)) Pearson Learning.

—Americans Move West. 2003. tchr. ed. 9.95 (978-0-7690-5050-8(6)); stu. ed. 49.95 (978-0-7690-2955-9(8)) Pearson Learning.

—From Colonies to Independence. 2003. tchr. ed. 9.95 (978-0-7690-5042-3(5)); stu. ed. 49.95 (978-0-7690-2947-4(7)) Pearson Learning.

—Geography of the United States, Level 5. tchr. ed. 9.95 (978-0-7690-5084-3(0)); stu. ed. 49.95 (978-0-7690-2849-1(7)) Pearson Learning.

—Industrialization & Urbanization in America, Level 6. tchr. ed. 9.95 (978-0-7690-5092-8(1)); stu. ed. 49.95 (978-0-7690-2857-6(8)) Pearson Learning.

—Westward Expansion after the Civil War, Level 5. tchr. ed. 9.95 (978-0-7690-5082-9(4)); stu. ed. 49.95 (978-0-7690-2851-4(9)) Pearson Learning.

—Westward Expansion Before the Civil War, Level 5. tchr. ed. 9.95 (978-0-7690-5080-5(8)); 2003. stu. ed. 49.95 (978-0-7690-2850-7(0)) Pearson Learning.

Hirschmann, Kris & Herndon, Ryan. Test Your Smarts! 2009. (Illus.). 80p. (J). (978-0-545-12042-5(X)) Scholastic, Inc.

Hispanic America, 6 bks., Set. Incl. Civil War, 1840s-1890s. Hernández, Roger E. lib. bdg. 34.21 (978-0-7614-2939-5(5)); Early Explorations: The 1500s. Hernández, Roger E. lib. bdg. 34.21 (978-0-7614-2937-1(9)); New Republic. Otfinoski, Steven. lib. bdg. 34.21 (978-0-7614-2938-8(7)); New Spain: 1600-1760s. Hernández, Roger E. lib. bdg. 34.21 (978-0-7614-2936-4(0)); Texas War of Independence. Worth, Richard. lib. bdg. 34.21 (978-0-7614-2934-0(4)); 80p. (gr. 5-18). (Hispanic America Ser.). 2008. Set lib. bdg. 171.07 (978-0-7614-2933-3(6), Benchmark Bks.) Marshall Cavendish Corp.

Historia y Geografia de America. (SPA.). (J). 45.00 (978-958-04-5985-9(1)); (Illus.). wbk. ed. 15.00 (978-958-04-5986-6(X)) Norma S.A. COL. Dist: Distribuidora Norma, Inc.

History Through Sources, 5 bks., Set. (YA). (gr. 6-8). lib. bdg. 128.20 (978-1-57572-222-1(4)) Heinemann-Raintree.

Hoena, Blake A., et al. You Choose: Modern History, 1 vol. 2014. (You Choose: Modern History Ser.). (ENG.). 112p. (gr. 3-4). 127.96 (978-1-4765-6174-5(5), You Choose Bks.) Capstone Press of Coughlan Cos.

Holmes, Parker. Amazing Snakes of the Southwest & West Coast. 2014. (Amazing Snakes Ser.). (Illus.). 24p. (J). (gr. 3-6). pap. 8.25 *(978-1-4777-6503-6(4),* PowerKids Pr.) Rosen Publishing Group, Inc., The.
—Texas vs. Oklahoma. 2013. (J). *(978-1-4777-1162-0(7));* pap. *(978-1-4777-1161-3(9));* lib. bdg. *(978-1-4777-1157-6(0))* Rosen Publishing Group, Inc., The. (PowerKids Pr.).
How Our Nation Began. (YA). 15.00 *(978-1-931555-45-6(1))* Our Lady of Victory Schl.
Howell, Brian. U. S. Growth & Change in the 19th Century, 1801 to 1861. 2011. (Explorer Library: Language Arts Explorer Ser.). (ENG.). 32p. (gr. 4-8). lib. bdg. 28.50 *(978-1-61080-202-4(0),* 201180) Cherry Lake Publishing.
Huey, Lois Miner. American Archaeology Uncovers the Westward Movement. 2009. (American Archaeology Ser.). (Illus.). 64p. (J). (gr. 5-6). 31.36 *(978-0-7614-4265-3(0))* Marshall Cavendish Corp.
—Ick! Yuck! Eew! Our Gross American History. 48p. 2015. (ENG., Illus.). (gr. 4-6). 34.65 *(978-1-4677-5989-2(9),* Lerner Digital) 2013. 29.27 *(978-1-4677-1710-6(X))* 2013. (ENG., Illus.). (gr. 4-6). 29.27 *(978-0-7613-9091-6(X),* Millbrook Pr.) Lerner Publishing Group.
Hults, Alaska, ed. American History Reader's Theater Vol. 2244: Develop Reading Fluency & Text Comprehension Skills. Hillam, Corbin & Vangsgard, Amy, illus. 2004. 96p. (J). pap. 14.99 *(978-1-59198-039-1(9),* 2244) Creative Teaching Pr., Inc.
Hunter, Nick. Talking about the Past, 1 vol. 2014. (History at Home Ser.). (ENG., Illus.). 32p. (gr. 1-3). 27.32 *(978-1-4846-0232-4(3));* pap. 7.99 *(978-1-4846-0236-2(6))* Heinemann-Raintree. (Heinemann First Library).
Hurley, Michael. United States of America, 1 vol. 2012. (Countries Around the World Ser.). (ENG.). 48p. (gr. 3-6). pap. 9.95 *(978-1-4329-6141-1(1),* NA-h) Heinemann-Raintree.
Ichord, Loretta Frances & Millbrook Press. Skillet Bread, Sourdough, & Vinegar Days: Cooking in Pioneer Days. Ellis, Jan Davey, illus. 2005. 64p. (J). (gr. 4-8). per. 8.95 *(978-0-7613-9521-8(0),* First Avenue Editions) Lerner Publishing Group.
In American History, 56 bks., Set. (Illus.). (YA). (gr. 5-12). lib. bdg. 1215.10 *(978-0-89490-972-6(X))* Enslow Pubs., Inc.
In the Early Days: Southern Humboldt History 1853-1920, 1. 5th ed. 2006. (Illus.). 141p. per. 20.95 *(978-0-9672162-3-2(0))* Hawk Mountaintop Publishing.
It's My State: Group 5, 6 Bks, Set. 2004. (J). 162.43 *(978-0-7614-1821-4(0))* Marshall Cavendish Corp.
Jeffrey, Laura S. Amazing American Inventors of the 20th Century. 2013. (Inspiring Collective Biographies Ser.). 112p. (J). (gr. 5-12). pap. 10.95 *(978-1-4644-0245-6(0))* Enslow Pubs., Inc.
Johnson, Drew, et al. Junior Worldmark Encyclopedia of the States, 4 vols. 6th ed. 2013. (Illus.). (J). *(978-1-4144-9860-7(8))* Cengage Gale.
Johnston, Robert D. The Making of America: The History of the United States from 1492 to the Present. 2010. (ENG., Illus.). 240p. (J). (gr. 5-18). 29.95 *(978-1-4263-0663-1(6));* 38.90 *(978-1-4263-0665-5(2))* National Geographic Society. (National Geographic Children's Bks.).
Jones, Charlotte Foltz. Westward Ho! Eleven Explorers of the American West. 2005. (ENG., Illus.). 240p. (J). (gr. 4-6). tchr. ed. 22.95 *(978-0-8234-1586-1(4))* Holiday Hse., Inc.
Jones, Stephen A. So What Did the People Find? 2009. 24p. pap. 11.50 *(978-1-4389-2736-7(3))* AuthorHouse.
Jones, Stephen Anderton. America Is Good. 2008. 60p. (gr. -1). pap. 22.50 *(978-1-4343-6321-3(X))* AuthorHouse.
Joseph, Frank. Ancient America's Lost History. 2017. (Discovering Ancient America Ser.). 200p. (gr. 12-14). 39.75 ***(978-1-4994-6677-5(3),*** Rosen Young Adult) Rosen Publishing Group, Inc., The.
Jr. Graphic African American History. 2013. (Jr. Graphic African American History Ser.). 24p. (J). (gr. 3-6). 151.50 *(978-1-4777-1547-5(9));* pap. 63.60 *(978-1-4777-2671-6(3));* pap. 381.60 *(978-1-4777-2672-3(1))* Rosen Publishing Group, Inc., The. (PowerKids Pr.).
Juarez, Christine. United States of America. 2013. (Countries Ser.). (ENG.). 24p. (gr. k-1). pap. 6.95 *(978-1-4765-3514-2(0),* Pebble Bks.) Capstone Press of Coughlan Cos.
Kaleidoscope - American History Series - Group 2, 4 bks., Set. 102.57 *(978-0-7614-1459-9(2),* Benchmark Bks.) Marshall Cavendish Corp.
Kalman, Bobbie & Walker, Niki. Conoce los Estados Unidos de América. 2009. (SPA.). 32p. (J). *(978-0-7787-8196-7(8));* (gr. 2-5). pap. *(978-0-7787-8216-2(6))* Crabtree Publishing Co.
—Spotlight on the United States of America. 2007. (Spotlight on My Country Ser.). (ENG., Illus.). 32p. (J). (gr. 2-5). pap. *(978-0-7787-3478-9(1))* Crabtree Publishing Co.
Kamma, Anne. If You Lived When There Was Slavery in America. Johnson, Pamela, illus. 2004. (If You... Ser.). (ENG.). 64p. (J). (gr. 2-5). pap. 6.99 *(978-0-439-56706-0(8))* Scholastic, Inc.
Karapetian, Marjam. Bilingual Content Dictionary: English to Spanish: Social Studies - American History Through 1776. 2004. (SPA & ENG.). 14.95 *(978-0-9764829-3-2(2))* Wizdomlnc.
Kaserman & Haberkern, E. The United States of America, 50 vols. 2nd ed. 2003. (Illus.). 46p. (J). cd-rom *(978-0-9714299-1-8(X))* I Save A Tree.
Kelley, K. C. Hottest NASCAR Machines. 2007. (Wild Wheels! Ser.). (Illus.). 48p. (J). (gr. 3-7). lib. bdg. 25.27 *(978-0-7660-2869-2(0))* Enslow Pubs., Inc.
Kennelly, Sean. All Around America. Paiva, Johannah Gilman, ed. 2014. (ENG., Illus.). 48p. (J). (gr. 4). 8.99 *(978-1-4867-0256-5(2))* Flowerpot Children's Pr. Inc. CAN. Dist: Cardinal Pubs. Group.
Kennelly, Sean & Carpenter, Dan. Amazing America. Flowerpot Press, ed. 2012. (Illus.). 48p. (J). *(978-1-926988-94-8(9))* Flowerpot Children's Pr. Inc.
—Amazing America: An Adventure into American History. Gilman, Thomas W. & Paiva, Johannah Gilman, eds. 2014. (ENG., Illus.). 48p. (J). (gr. 4). 8.99 *(978-1-4867-0255-8(4))* Flowerpot Children's Pr. Inc. CAN. Dist: Cardinal Pubs. Group.
—Great Americans. Flowerpot Press, ed. 2012. (Illus.). 48p. (J). *(978-1-926988-93-1(0))* Flowerpot Children's Pr. Inc.
Kenney, Karen. US History Through Infographics. Westlund, Laura, illus. 2014. (Super Social Studies Infographics Ser.). 32p. (gr. 3-5). pap. 8.95 *(978-1-4677-4568-0(5))* Lerner Publishing Group.
Kenney, Karen Latchana. Our Nation's Pride, 6 vols., Set 2. Hunt, Judith A., illus. Incl. Bald Eagle. 28.50 *(978-1-61641-149-7(X));* Ellis Island. 28.50 *(978-1-61641-150-3(3));* Lincoln Memorial. 28.50 *(978-1-61641-151-0(1));* Memorial Day. 28.50 *(978-1-61641-152-7(X));* Mount Rushmore. 28.50 *(978-1-61641-153-4(8));* White House. 28.50 *(978-1-61641-154-1(6));* (J). (gr. 1-4). (Our Nation's Pride Set 2 Ser.). (Illus.). 32p. 2011. 171.00 *(978-1-61641-148-0(1),* Looking Glass Library- Nonfiction) Magic Wagon.
—US History Through Infographics. Westlund, Laura, illus. 2014. (Super Social Studies Infographics Ser.). (ENG.). 32p. (gr. 3-5). lib. bdg. 26.60 *(978-1-4677-3459-2(4),* Lerner Pubns.) Lerner Publishing Group.
Keppeler, Jill. Betsy Ross Didn't Create the American Flag: Exposing Myths about US Symbols. 2016. (Exposed! Myths about Early American History Ser.). 00032p. (J). pap. 10.50 *(978-1-4824-5717-9(2))* Stevens, Gareth Publishing LLLP.
Kinney, Cyndi & Trout, Judy. State History for ALL 50 States - 100 Lapbooks & Lapbook Journals & Study Guides. 2013. (YA). cd-rom 99.00 *(978-1-61625-540-4(4))* Knowledge Box Central.
Kirkman, Marissa. Life & Times. 2016. (Life & Times Ser.). (ENG.). 24p. (gr. 1-2). 101.28 *(978-1-5157-2498-8(0),* First Facts) Capstone Press of Coughlan Cos.
Klobuchar, Lisa. USA in Our World. 2011. (Countries in Our World Ser.). 32p. (YA). (gr. 4-7). lib. bdg. 28.50 *(978-1-59920-436-9(3))* Black Rabbit Bks.
Knox, Barbara J. Hearst Castle: An American Palace. 2005. (Castles, Palaces, & Tombs Ser.). (Illus.). 32p. (J). lib. bdg. 25.27 *(978-1-59716-069-8(5))* Bearport Publishing Co., Inc.
Kopp, Megan. United States. 2013. (J). *(978-1-62127-255-7(9));* pap. *(978-1-62127-261-8(3))* Weigl Pubs., Inc.
Kowalski, Kathiann M. Salvadorans in America. 2005. (In America Ser.). (Illus.). 80p. (J). (gr. 4-7). lib. bdg. 27.93 *(978-0-8225-2424-3(4),* Lerner Pubns.) Lerner Publishing Group.
LaClair, Teresa. The Northern Colonies: Freedom to Worship (1600-1770) 2012. (J). pap. *(978-1-4222-2411-3(2))* Mason Crest.
Lader, Curt. Painless American History. 2nd rev. ed. 2009. (Painless Ser.). (ENG., Illus.). 320p. pap. 9.99 *(978-0-7641-4231-4(3))* Barron's Educational Series, Inc.
Landau, Elaine. The Bald Eagle. 2007. (True Book(tm), a — American History Ser.). (ENG., Illus.). 48p. (J). (gr. 3-5). lib. bdg. 31.00 *(978-0-531-12626-4(9),* Children's Pr.) Scholastic Library Publishing.
—The Wounded Knee Massacre. 2004. (Cornerstones of Freedom Ser.). (ENG., Illus.). 48p. (YA). (gr. 4-7). 26.00 *(978-0-516-24244-6(X))* Scholastic Library Publishing.
Lanser, Amanda. America at War by the Numbers. 2015. (America at War by the Numbers Ser.). (ENG.). 32p. (gr. 3-4). 111.96 *(978-1-4914-6661-2(8),* Edge Bks.) Capstone Press of Coughlan Cos.
Larkin, Tanya. Cooking Throughout American History Set 2, 6 bks. Incl. What Was Cooking in Abigail Adam's White House? lib. bdg. 22.60 *(978-0-8239-5607-4(5));* What Was Cooking in Dolly Madison's White House? lib. bdg. 21.25 *(978-0-8239-5608-1(3));* What Was Cooking in Edith Roosevelt's White House? lib. bdg. 22.60 *(978-0-8239-5610-4(5));* What Was Cooking in Julia Grant's White House? lib. bdg. 22.60 *(978-0-8239-5611-1(3));* What Was Cooking in Martha Washington's Presidential Mansion? lib. bdg. 21.25 *(978-0-8239-5606-7(7));* What Was Cooking in Mary Todd Lincoln's White House? lib. bdg. 21.25 *(978-0-8239-5609-8(1));* 24p. (J). (gr. 3). 2001. (Illus.). Set lib. bdg. 117.00 *(978-0-8239-7062-9(0),* PowerKids Pr.) Rosen Publishing Group, Inc., The.
Lassieur, Allison. The Dust Bowl: An Interactive History Adventure. 2016. (You Choose: History Ser.). (ENG.). 112p. (gr. 3-4). pap. 6.95 *(978-1-5157-4262-3(8),* You Choose Bks.) Capstone Press of Coughlan Cos.
—The Navajo: A Proud People. 2005. (American Indians Ser.). (Illus.). 48p. (J). (gr. 4-7). lib. bdg. 25.27 *(978-0-7660-2453-3(9),* Enslow Elementary) Enslow Pubs., Inc.
Lassieur, Allison & Otfinoski, Steven. You Choose: History, 1 vol. (You Choose: History Ser.). (ENG.). 112p. (gr. 3-4). 2014. 63.98 *(978-1-4765-6183-7(4))* 2013. pap. 166.80 *(978-1-4914-1515-3(0))* Capstone Press of Coughlan Cos. (You Choose Bks.).
Latham, Donna. Hurricane! The 1900 Galveston Night of Terror. 2005. (X-Treme Disasters That Changed America Ser.). (Illus.). 32p. (J). (gr. 3-7). lib. bdg. 25.27 *(978-1-59716-071-1(7))* Bearport Publishing Co., Inc.
Leacock, Elspeth & Buckley, Susan. Places in Time: A New Atlas of American History. Jones, Randy, illus. 2006. 48p. (J). (gr. 4-8). reprint ed. 15.00 *(978-1-4223-5555-8(1))* DIANE Publishing Co.
Leacock, Elspeth & Buckley, Susan Washburn. Places in Time: A New Atlas of American History. Jones, Randy, illus. 2003. (ENG.). 48p. (J). (gr. 5-7). pap. 6.99 *(978-0-618-31113-2(0))* Houghton Mifflin Harcourt Publishing Co.
Lerner Publishing Group Staff. History Speaks: Picture Books Plus Reader's Theater, 6 vols., Set. 2011. (J). (gr. 2-4). lib. bdg. 167.58 *(978-0-7613-7483-1(3))* Lerner Publishing Group.
LernerClassroom Editors. On My Own History Teaching Guide. 2009. pap. 7.95 *(978-0-8225-5321-2(X))* Lerner Publishing Group.
LernerClassroom Editors, ed. Teaching Guide for Six Questions of American History. 2010. pap. 5.95 *(978-0-7613-6685-0(7))* Lerner Publishing Group.
Let's Explore the Northeast. 2013. (Road Trip: Exploring America's Regions Ser.). 24p. (J). (gr. 2-5). pap. 48.90 *(978-1-4339-9136-3(5))* Stevens, Gareth Publishing LLLP.
Liberman, Sherri. A Historical Atlas of the Industrial Age & the Growth of America's Cities. 2005. (United States: Historical Atlases of the Growth of a New Nation Ser.). (Illus.). 64p. (J). (gr. 7-12). lib. bdg. 31.95 *(978-1-4042-0205-4(6))* Rosen Publishing Group, Inc., The.
The Library of American Lives & Times, 12 vols., Set 3. 2005. (Illus.). (gr. 4-8). lib. bdg. 383.40 *(978-0-8239-6657-8(7))* Rosen Publishing Group, Inc., The.
The Library of the Thirteen Colonies & the Lost Colony, 14 bks. Incl. Colony of Connecticut. Whitehurst, Susan. (J). (gr. 3). lib. bdg. 19.95 *(978-0-8239-5479-7(X),* PowerKids Pr.); Colony of Delaware. Whitehurst, Susan. (YA). (gr. 1-4). lib. bdg. 19.95 *(978-0-8239-5482-7(X));* Colony of Georgia. Coleman, Brooke. (YA). (gr. 1-4). lib. bdg. 22.60 *(978-0-8239-5474-2(9));* Colony of Maryland. Coleman, Brooke. (YA). (gr. 1-4). lib. bdg. 22.60 *(978-0-8239-5483-4(8));* Colony of Massachusetts. Whitehurst, Susan. (J). (gr. 3). lib. bdg. 19.95 *(978-0-8239-5475-9(7),* PowerKids Pr.); Colony of New Hampshire. Whitehurst, Susan. (YA). (gr. 1-4). lib. bdg. 22.60 *(978-0-8239-5477-3(3));* Colony of New Jersey. Whitehurst, Susan. (J). (gr. 3). lib. bdg. 19.95 *(978-0-8239-5480-3(3),* PowerKids Pr.); Colony of Pennsylvania. Whitehurst, Susan. (J). (gr. 3). lib. bdg. 22.60 *(978-0-8239-5481-0(1),* PowerKids Pr.); Colony of Rhode Island. Whitehurst, Susan. (J). (gr. 3). lib. bdg. 22.60 *(978-0-8239-5476-6(5),* PowerKids Pr.); Colony of Virginia. Coleman, Brooke. (YA). (gr. 1-4). lib. bdg. 19.95 *(978-0-8239-5484-1(6));* Roanoke: The Lost Colony. Coleman, Brooke. (J). (gr. 3). lib. bdg. 19.95 *(978-0-8239-5473-5(0),* PowerKids Pr.); 24p. 2000. (Illus.). Set lib. bdg. 273.00 *(978-0-8239-7005-6(1),* PowerKids Pr.) Rosen Publishing Group, Inc., The.
Lindeen, Mary. Welcome to North America. 2011. (Wonder Readers Fluent Level Ser.). (ENG.). 16p. (gr. -1-2). pap. 35.94 *(978-1-4296-8204-6(3),* Wonder Readers) Capstone Press of Coughlan Cos.
Lloyd, Jon. A View of America's Future by America's. 2005. 51p. pap. 16.95 *(978-1-4137-9110-5(7))* PublishAmerica, Inc.
Logiudice, Carolyn. US History Reading Comrehension Book. 2003. (Illus.). 167p. (J). per. 37.95 *(978-0-7606-0449-6(5))* LinguiSystems, Inc.
A Look at U. S. History. 2017. (Look at U. S. History Ser.). 32p. (gr. 2-2). pap. 63.00 ***(978-1-4824-6286-9(9));*** lib. bdg. 159.60 ***(978-1-4824-6284-5(2))*** Stevens, Gareth Publishing LLLP.
Machajewski, Sarah. Our Country's Symbols. 2012. (InfoMax Readers Ser.). (ENG., Illus.). 24p. (J). (gr. 1-2). pap. 8.25 *(978-1-4488-8980-8(4),* Rosen Classroom) Rosen Publishing Group, Inc., The.
MacRae, Sloan. Rajon Rondo. 2012. (Sports Heroes Ser.). (ENG.). 24p. (J). (gr. 3-6). pap. 8.25 *(978-1-4488-6288-7(4),* PowerKids Pr.) Rosen Publishing Group, Inc., The.
Maga, Timothy P. The 1960s. 2003. (Eyewitness History Ser.). (Illus.). 416p. (C). (gr. 9). 80.00 *(978-0-8160-4809-0(6))* Facts On File, Inc.
Magsamen, Sandra. I Love America - An ABC Adventure. 2016. (ENG.). 40p. (J). (-5). 12.99 *(978-1-4926-2854-5(9),* Sourcebooks Jabberwocky) Sourcebooks, Inc.
Mara, Wil. The Gunsmith. 2013. 48p. (J). (gr. 4-8). 29.93 *(978-1-60870-414-9(9))* Cavendish Square Publishing.
Marcovitz, Hal. Teens & Career Choices. Developed in Association with the Gallup Organization Staff, ed. 2013. (Gallup Youth Survey: Major Issues & Trends Ser.: 14). 112p. (J). (gr. 7-18). 24.95 *(978-1-4222-2950-7(5))* Mason Crest.
—Teens & Family Issues. Developed in Association with the Gallup Organization Staff, ed. 2013. (Gallup Youth Survey: Major Issues & Trends Ser.: 14). 112p. (J). (gr. 7-18). 24.95 *(978-1-4222-2952-1(1))* Mason Crest.
—Teens & LGBT Issues. Developed in Association with the Gallup Organization Staff, ed. 2013. (Gallup Youth Survey: Major Issues & Trends Ser.: 14). 112p. (J). (gr. 7-18). 24.95 *(978-1-4222-2953-8(X))* Mason Crest.
—Teens & Suicide. Developed in Association with the Gallup Organization Staff, ed. 2013. (Gallup Youth Survey: Major Issues & Trends Ser.: 14). 112p. (J). (gr. 7-18). 24.95 *(978-1-4222-2958-3(0))* Mason Crest.
Marsh, Carole. Quit Bossing Us Around! The Declaration of Independence. 2004. (American Milestones Ser.). (Illus.). 28p. (J). (gr. 4-12). pap. 5.95 *(978-0-635-02680-4(5))* Gallopade International.
—The Young Patriot's Book of Puzzles, Games, Riddles, Stories, Poems, & Activities. 2004. (Patriotic Favorites Ser.). 48p. (gr. 1-4). pap. 5.95 *(978-0-635-01032-2(1))* Gallopade International.
Marshall, H. E. This Country of Ours. 2007. 500p. per. 17.95 *(978-1-60206-874-2(7))* Cosimo, Inc.
—This Country of Ours (Yesterday's Classics) 2006. (Illus.). 636p. (J). per. 19.95 *(978-1-59915-010-9(7))* Yesterday's Classics.
Marx, Trish. Jeannette Rankin: First Lady of Congress. Andreasen, Dan, illus. 2006. (ENG.). 48p. (J). (gr. 3-7). 18.95 *(978-0-689-86290-8(3),* McElderry, Margaret K. Bks.) McElderry, Margaret K. Bks.
McDougal-Littell Publishing Staff, creator. Creating America Workbook: A History of the United States. 2006. (Illus.). 120p. (gr. 6-12). pap. *(978-0-618-16521-6(5),* 2-81244) Holt McDougal.
McGraw-Hill - Jamestown Education Staff. American History Ink: Taming Horses on the Great Plains. 2007. (Jt Am Hist Graph Novel Ser.). (ENG.). 24p. (gr. 6-12). spiral bd. 12.72 *(978-0-07-878023-3(3),* 0078780233) McGraw-Hill Cos., The.
McGraw-Hill Education Editors. The American Journey, Active Reading Note-Taking Guide, Student Edition. 2nd ed. 2004. (American Journey (survey) Ser.). (ENG.). (gr. 6-9). pap. 12.80 *(978-0-07-867397-9(6),* 0078673976) McGraw-Hill Higher Education.
—The American Vision: Modern Times, StudentWorks Plus. 2005. (American Vision: Mod Times Ser.). (ENG.). (gr. 9-12). cd-rom 161.96 *(978-0-07-872733-7(2),* 0078727332) McGraw-Hill Higher Education.
—American Vision, Spanish Reading Essentials & Study Guide, Student Edition. 2nd ed. 2004. (United States History (hs) Ser.). (SPA.). (gr. 9-12). pap. 16.00 *(978-0-07-865441-1(6),* 0078654416) McGraw-Hill Higher Education.
—The American Vision, StudentWorks Plus CD-ROM. 2nd ed. 2005. (United States History (hs) Ser.). (ENG.). (gr. 9-12). 152.24 *(978-0-07-865456-5(4),* 0078654564) McGraw-Hill Higher Education.
—Our World Today Reading Essentials & Study Guide Student Workbook: People, Places, & Issues. 2003. (GEOGRAPHY: WORLD & ITS PEOPLE Ser.). (ENG., Illus.). 305p. (gr. 6-9). stu. ed., per. 13.40 *(978-0-07-860531-4(8),* 0078605318) McGraw-Hill Higher Education.
McGraw-Hill Education Staff. The American Journey. 5th ed. 2005. (American Journey (survey) Ser.). (ENG.). (gr. 6-9). 147.48 *(978-0-07-866280-5(X),* 007866280X) McGraw-Hill Higher Education.
—The American Journey, Interactive Tutor Self Assessment CD-ROM. 5th ed. 2005. (American Journey (survey) Ser.). (ENG.). (gr. 6-9). 107.12 *(978-0-07-867794-6(7),* 0078677947) McGraw-Hill Higher Education.
—The American Journey Modern Times. 2nd ed. 2008. (American Journey (survey) Ser.). (ENG.). (gr. 6-8). cd-rom 156.12 *(978-0-07-880651-3(8),* 0078806518) McGraw-Hill Education.
—The American Journey Spanish Reading Essentials & Note-Taking Guide. 7th ed. 2008. (American Journey (survey) Ser.). (ENG & SPA., Illus.). 360p. (gr. 6-8). per., wbk. ed. 12.04 *(978-0-07-880618-6(6),* 0078806186) McGraw-Hill Education.
—The American Republic to 1877 StudentWorks Plus. 2nd ed. 2005. (U. S. History - the Early Years Ser.). (ENG.). (gr. 6-9). stu. ed. 152.64 *(978-0-07-866248-5(6),* 0078662486) McGraw-Hill Higher Education.
—The American Vision: Modern Times, Interactive Tutor Self-Assessment. 2007. (United States History (hs) Ser.). (ENG.). (gr. 9-12). cd-rom 107.12 *(978-0-07-878527-6(8),* 0078785278) McGraw-Hill Higher Education.
—The American Vision, Interactive Tutor. 2007. (United States History (hs) Ser.). (ENG.). (gr. 9-12). cd-rom 107.12 *(978-0-07-878450-7(6),* 0078784506) McGraw-Hill Higher Education.
McGraw-Hill-Glencoe Staff, creator. The American Journey, Early Years: Reading Essentials & Note-Taking Guide. 2008. (American Journey (survey) Ser.). (ENG., Illus.). 200p. (gr. 6-8). pap., wbk. ed. 12.08 *(978-0-07-880671-1(2),* 0078806712) McGraw-Hill Education.
McGraw-Hill Staff. American Journey. 2nd ed. 2004. (American Journey (survey) Ser.). (ENG., Illus.). 445p. (gr. 6-9). stu. ed., per., wbk. ed. 12.80 *(978-0-07-865550-0(1),* 0078655501) McGraw-Hill Higher Education.
—The American Journey. 4th ed. 2004. (American Journey (survey) Ser.). (ENG.). (gr. 6-9). stu. ed. 115.60 *(978-0-07-860980-0(1),* 0078609801) McGraw-Hill Higher Education.
—The American Journey, Student Edition. 6th ed. 2008. (American Journey Ser.). (Illus.). 1116p. (J). 95.32 *(978-0-07-877712-7(7),* 9780078777127) Glencoe/McGraw-Hill.
—The American Republic since 1877: StudentWorks. 2nd ed. 2005. (U. S. History - the Modern Era Ser.). (ENG.). (gr. 8-10). stu. ed. 156.64 *(978-0-07-865416-9(5),* 0078654165) McGraw-Hill Higher Education.
—The American Republic since 1877, Reading Essentials & Study Guide, Student Edition. 2nd ed. 2004. (U. S. History - the Modern Era Ser.). (ENG.). (gr. 8-10). pap. 15.12 *(978-0-07-865405-3(X),* 007865405X) McGraw-Hill Higher Education.
McGraw-Hill Staff, creator. The American Vision: Modern Times, Reading Essentials & Study Guide: Student Workbook. 2005. (American Vision: Mod Times Ser.). (ENG., Illus.). 360p. (gr. 9-12). stu. ed., per., wbk. ed. 12.80 *(978-0-07-872768-9(5),* 0078727685) McGraw-Hill Higher Education.
McHugh, Erin. 50 States: A State-by-State Tour of the USA. Schrier, Albert, illus. 2010. (ENG.). 240p. (J). (gr. -1-17). 24.95 *(978-1-57912-851-7(3),* 81851, Black Dog & Leventhal Pubs. Inc.) Hachette Bks.
McKissack, Patricia C. & McKissack, Fredrick L. Booker T. Washington: African-American Leader. 2013. (Famous African Americans Ser.). 24p. (J). (gr. k-3). pap. 7.95 *(978-1-4644-0194-7(2));* (Illus.). lib. bdg. 22.60 *(978-0-7660-4100-4(X))* Enslow Pubs., Inc. (Enslow Elementary).
—Carter G. Woodson: Black History Pioneer. 2013. (Famous African Americans Ser.). 24p. (J). (gr. k-3). pap. 7.95 *(978-1-4644-0195-4(0),* Enslow Elementary) Enslow Pubs., Inc.
—Jesse Owens: Legendary Track Star. 2013. (Famous African Americans Ser.). (Illus.). 24p. (J). (gr. k-18). 22.60 *(978-0-7660-4104-2(2))* Enslow Pubs., Inc.
—Madam C. J. Walker: Inventor & Millionaire. 2013. (Famous African Americans Ser.). 24p. (J). (gr. k-3). pap. 7.95 *(978-1-4644-0201-2(9),* Enslow Elementary) Enslow Pubs., Inc.
McLeese, Don. Robert Fulton. 2005. (Rourke Discovery Library). (Illus.). 24p. (J). (gr. 2-5). lib. bdg. *(978-1-59515-434-7(5),* 1244323) Rourke Educational Media.
McNeese, Tim. Plessy V. Ferguson: Separate but Equal. 2006. (Great Supreme Court Decisions Ser.). (Illus.). 136p. (YA). (gr. 5-9). lib. bdg. 32.95 *(978-0-7910-9237-8(2))* Facts On File, Inc.
—Reform Movements in American History Set, 8-Volumes. 2007. (Reform Movements in American History Ser.). (gr. 6-12). 260.00 *(978-0-7910-9821-9(4),* Chelsea Hse.) Facts On File, Inc.
—The Rise & Fall of American Slavery: Freedom Denied, Freedom Gained. 2004. (Slavery in American History Ser.). (Illus.). 128p. (J). lib. bdg. 27.94 *(978-0-7660-2156-3(4))* Enslow Pubs., Inc.
McNeese, Tim, ed. Rivers in American Life & Times. (Illus.). (gr. 9-13). pap. *(978-0-7910-8059-7(5));* 2005. 120p. (C). 195.00 *(978-0-7910-7722-1(5))* Facts On File, Inc. (Chelsea Hse.).
McPherson, Stephanie Sammartino. Biography Coretta Scott King. 2007. (Biography Ser.). (Illus.). 112p. (YA). (gr. 7-12). lib. bdg. 29.27 *(978-0-8225-7156-8(0))* Twenty First Century Bks.
Meinking, Mary. Cash Crop to Cash Cow: The History of Tobacco & Smoking in America. 2007. (Tobacco: the Deadly Drug Ser.). (Illus.). 112p. (YA). pap. 12.95 *(978-1-4222-0811-3(7))* Mason Crest.

Melbo, Irving Robert. Our Americ: A Textbook for Elementary School History & Social Studies. 2011. 414p. 54.95 (978-1-258-07894-2(5)) Literary Licensing, LLC.

Miller, Barbara Kiely. Grandes Personajes (Great Americans), 6 vols., Set. Incl. Anne Hutchinson. (Illus.). lib. bdg. 22.00 (978-0-8368-8330-5(6)); Frederick Douglass. (Illus.). lib. bdg. 22.00 (978-0-8368-8328-2(4)); George Washington Carver. (Illus.). lib. bdg. 22.00 (978-0-8368-8327-5(6)); Jefe Joseph. lib. bdg. 22.00 (978-0-8368-8331-2(4)); John Muir. lib. bdg. 22.00 (978-0-8368-8332-9(2)); Sam Houston. (Illus.). lib. bdg. 22.00 (978-0-8368-8329-9(2)); 24p. (gr. 1-4). 2007., Weekly Reader Leveled Readers (SPA.). 2007. Set lib. bdg. 119.58 o.p. (978-0-8368-8326-8(8)); Set pap. 35.70 o.p. (978-0-8368-8333-6(0)) Stevens, Gareth Publishing LLLP.

—Great Americans, 6 vols., Set. Incl. Anne Hutchinson. Nations, Susan. (Illus.). lib. bdg. 22.00 (978-0-8368-8317-6(9)); Chief Joseph. lib. bdg. 22.00 (978-0-8368-8314-5(4)); Frederick Douglass. lib. bdg. 22.00 (978-0-8368-8315-2(2)); George Washington Carver. lib. bdg. 22.00 (978-0-8368-8313-8(6)); John Muir. lib. bdg. 22.00 (978-0-8368-8318-3(7)); Sam Houston. lib. bdg. 22.00 (978-0-8368-8316-9(0)); 24p. (gr. 1-4). 2007., Weekly Reader Leveled Readers 2007. Set lib. bdg. 119.58 o.p. (978-0-8368-8312-1(8)) Stevens, Gareth Publishing LLLP.

Mitchell Lane Publishers Inc. Staff. Profiles in American History. 2007. (YA). lib. bdg. 460.90 (978-1-58415-532-4(9)) Mitchell Lane Pubs., Inc.

Mitcheltree, Frani B. Liberty Blue. 2013. 30p. pap. 16.95 (978-1-4497-8113-2(6), WestBow Pr.) Author Solutions, Inc.

Mitten, Ellen. Appalachian Region. 2014. (ENG.). 32p. (gr. 3-5). 32.79 (978-1-62717-674-3(8)) Rourke Educational Media.

Monteverde, Matthew. Giants vs. Cowboys. 2014. (Sports Greatest Rivalries Ser.). 24p. (J). (gr. 2-5). lib. bdg. 22.60 (978-1-4777-2781-2(7), PowerKids Pr.) Rosen Publishing Group, Inc., The.

—Michigan vs. Ohio State. 2013. (J). (978-1-4777-1166-8(X)); pap. (978-1-4777-1165-1(1)); lib. bdg. (978-1-4777-1159-0(7)) Rosen Publishing Group, Inc., The. (PowerKids Pr.).

Monumental Milestones: Great Events of Modern Times, 16 vols., Set. 2006. (J). (gr. 4-8). lib. bdg. 319.20 (978-1-58415-292-7(3)) Mitchell Lane Pubs., Inc.

Moran, Margaret. Coming to America Immigration from 1840 To 1930: Set Of 6. 2011. (Navigators Ser.). (J). pap. 50.00 net. (978-1-4108-2565-0(5)) Benchmark Education Co.

Moreno, Barry. The Arab Americans. 2007. (Major American Immigration Ser.). (YA). pap. 9.95 (978-1-4222-0671-3(8)) Mason Crest.

—History of American Immigration. (Major American Immigration Ser.). (YA). 2010. (Illus.). 64p. (gr. 9-12). lib. bdg. 22.95 (978-1-4222-0613-3(0)) 2007. pap. 9.95 (978-1-4222-0680-5(7)) Mason Crest.

Moreno, Barry & Temple, Bob. The Arab Americans. 2010. (Major American Immigration Ser.). (Illus.). 64p. (YA). (gr. 9-12). 22.95 (978-1-4222-0604-1(1)) Mason Crest.

Morrow, Ann. The Gilded Age. 2007. (Cornerstones of Freedom Ser.). (Illus.). 48p. (J). (gr. 4-6). 26.00 (978-0-516-23641-4(5), Children's Pr.) Scholastic Library Publishing.

Mulhall, Jill K. Lewis & Clark, 1 vol. 2005. (Primary Source Readers Ser.). (ENG.). 24p. (J). (gr. 4-4). pap. 8.99 (978-0-7439-8906-0(6)) Shell Educational Publishing.

Murray, Julie. United States, 1 vol. 2016. (Explore the Countries Set 3 Ser.). (ENG., Illus.). 40p. (J). (gr. 2-5). 29.93 (978-1-68078-072-7(7)) ABDO Publishing Co.

My Place in History: Set 2. 2017. (My Place in History Ser.). 24p. (gr. 2-3). pap. 48.90 **(978-1-5382-0486-3(X))**; lib. bdg. 135.60 **(978-1-5382-0472-6(X))** Stevens, Gareth Publishing LLLP.

Nagara, Innosanto. A Is for Activist. 2013. (ENG., Illus.). 28p. (J). (gr. -1-2). 9.99 (978-1-60980-539-5(9), Triangle Square) Seven Stories Pr.

Nagelhout, Ryan. CM Punk. 2013. (Superstars of Wrestling Ser.). (Illus.). 32p. (J). (gr. 3-6). pap. 10.50 (978-1-4339-8523-2(3)); lib. bdg. 25.25 (978-1-4339-8522-5(5)) Stevens, Gareth Publishing LLLP.

Nardo, Don. Early Native North Americans. 2008. (American History Ser.). (ENG., Illus.). 104p. (YA). (gr. 7-10). 34.80 (978-1-4205-0034-9(1), Lucent Bks.) Cengage Gale.

—The Rise of Industrial America. 2016. (Illus.). 48p. (J). (978-1-5105-1290-0(X)) SmartBook Media, Inc.

Nathan, Amy. Round & Round Together: Taking a Merry-Go-Round Ride into the Civil Rights Movement. 2011. (Nautilus Ser.). (ENG., Illus.). 200p. (gr. 4-10). pap. 14.95 (978-1-58988-071-9(4)) Dry, Paul Bks., Inc.

Nelson, Sheila. Thomas Jefferson's America: The Louisiana Purchase (1800-1811) 2006. (How America Became America Ser.). (Illus.). 96p. (YA). lib. bdg. 22.95 (978-1-59084-904-0(3)) Mason Crest.

Obama, Barack. Of Thee I Sing: A Letter to My Daughters. Long, Loren, illus. 2010. (ENG.). 40p. (J). (gr. k-12). 17.99 (978-0-375-83527-8(X), Knopf Bks. for Young Readers) Random Hse. Children's Bks.

Omoth, Tyler. The Ultimate Collection of Pro Basketball Records. 2012. (For the Record Ser.). (ENG.). 64p. (gr. 4-6). pap. 53.70 (978-1-4296-9431-5(9)) Capstone Press of Coughlan Cos.

Omoth, Tyler Dean. The Ultimate Collection of Pro Basketball Records, 1 vol. 2012. (For the Record Ser.). (ENG.). 64p. (gr. 4-6). pap. 8.95 (978-1-4296-9430-8(0)) Capstone Press of Coughlan Cos.

O'Neal, Michael J. America in The 1920s. 2005. (Decades of American History Ser.). (Illus.). 128p. (gr. 5-8). 35.00 (978-0-8160-5637-8(4)) Facts On File, Inc.

Open for Debate Group 3, 5 bks., Set. Incl. Affirmative Action. Kowalski, Kathiann M. lib. bdg. 42.79 (978-0-7614-2300-3(1)); Arab-Israeli Conflict. Worth, Richard. lib. bdg. 42.79 (978-0-7614-2295-2(3)); Marriage. Steffoff, Rebecca. lib. bdg. 42.79 (978-0-7614-2299-0(4)); Media Bias. Streissguth, Thomas. lib. bdg. 42.79 (978-0-7614-2296-9(X)); Racial Profiling. Kops, Deborah. lib. bdg. 42.79 (978-0-7614-2298-3(6)); (Illus.). 128p. (gr. 7-7). (Open for Debate 3 Ser.). 2006. Set lib. bdg. 213.93 (978-0-7614-2294-5(3), Benchmark Bks.) Marshall Cavendish Corp.

Orr, Tamra. Southwest. 2011. (Explorer Library: Social Studies Explorer Ser.). (ENG.). 48p. (gr. 4-8). lib. bdg. 31.36 (978-1-61080-183-6(0), 201160) Cherry Lake Publishing.

Orr, Tamra B. & Clay, Kathryn. Introducing Primary Sources. 2016. (Introducing Primary Sources Ser.). (ENG.). 32p. (gr. 1-2). 167.94 (978-1-4914-8688-7(0)) Capstone Press of Coughlan Cos.

Otfinoski, Steven. Gun Control. 2014. (Cornerstones of Freedom Ser.: 3). (ENG.). 64p. (J). lib. bdg. 30.00 (978-0-531-21331-5(5)) Scholastic Library Publishing.

—Major Disasters in U.S. History. 2005. (Illus.). 48p. (J). (978-0-669-51416-2(0)) Great Source Education Group, Inc.

Pack, Linda Hager. Appalachian Toys & Games from a to Z. Banks, Pat, illus. 2013. (ENG.). 56p. 17.95 (978-0-8131-4104-6(4)) Univ. Pr. of Kentucky.

Paises del Mundo.Tr. of Lands & People. (SPA., Illus.). (YA). (gr. 5-8). 38.95 (978-84-241-9401-7(2)) Everest Editora ESP. Dist: Lectorum Pubns., Inc.

Penton, ed. United States Flipper. 2003. (Smart Kids Flippers Ser.). (ENG.). (J). pap. 14.95 (978-1-59125-250-4(4)) Penton Overseas, Inc.

Perrin, Pat. Getting Started-America's Melting Pot. 2004. (Illus.). (J). (978-1-932663-04-4(5)) History Compass, LLC.

—Getting Started-Our 50 United States. 2004. (Illus.). (J). (978-1-932663-03-7(7)) History Compass, LLC.

—Getting Started-Our Government. 2004. (Illus.). (J). (978-1-932663-02-0(9)) History Compass, LLC.

Perrin, Pat, ed. America's Founders. 2003. (Researching American History Ser.). (ENG.). 52p. (J). pap. 8.95 (978-1-57960-097-6(2)) History Compass, LLC.

—Communications. 2003. (Researching American History Ser.). (ENG., Illus.). 52p. (J). pap. 8.95 (978-1-57960-099-0(9)) History Compass, LLC.

—Spanish Explorers. 2003. (Researching American History Ser.). (ENG., Illus.). 56p. pap. 8.95 (978-1-57960-088-4(3)) History Compass, LLC.

—Transportation Stories. 2003. (Researching American History Ser.). (ENG., Illus.). 52p. (J). pap. 8.95 (978-1-57960-098-3(0)) History Compass, LLC.

Petersen, Christine. The Surveyor. 2010. (Colonial People Ser.). 48p. (gr. 3-18). 29.93 (978-0-7614-4805-1(5)) Marshall Cavendish Corp.

Pinborough, Jan. Miss Moore Thought Otherwise: How Anne Carroll Moore Created Libraries for Children. Atwell, Debby, illus. 2013. (ENG.). 40p. (J). (gr. 1-4). 17.99 (978-0-547-47105-1(X)) Houghton Mifflin Harcourt Publishing Co.

Pinkney, Andrea Davis. Martin & Mahalia: His Words, Her Song. 2013. (ENG., Illus.). 40p. (J). (gr. 1-17). 18.99 (978-0-316-07013-3(0)) Little Brown & Co.

Platt, D. D. & Conkling, Philip, eds. Island Journal: An Annual Publication of the Island Institute, 20. Ralston, Peter, photos by. 20th ed. 2003. (Island Journals: 20). (Illus.). 96p. pap. 9.95 (978-0-942719-33-8(6)) Island Institute.

Plummer, Barbara. Kids in the Backyard. 2007. 60p. per. 16.95 (978-1-4241-9064-5(9)) America Star Bks.

Pofahl, Jane. Westward Movement: United States History. (Time Traveler Ser.). (Illus.). 32p. (gr. 3-6). 6.99 (978-0-513-02222-5(8), TSD22228) Denison, T. S. & Co., Inc.

Pohl, Kathleen. Descubramos Estados Unidos. 2008. (Descubramos países del mundo (Looking at Countries) Ser.). (SPA., Illus.). 32p. (gr. 1-5). (J). lib. bdg. 26.00 (978-0-8368-9072-3(8)); pap. 10.50 (978-0-8368-9073-0(6)) Stevens, Gareth Publishing LLLP. (Gareth Stevens Learning Library).

—Looking at the United States. 2008. (Looking at Countries Ser.). (Illus.). 32p. (gr. 1-5). (J). lib. bdg. 26.00 (978-0-8368-9070-9(1)); pap. 10.50 (978-0-8368-9071-6(X)) Stevens, Gareth Publishing LLLP. (Gareth Stevens Learning Library).

Powerkids Readers: American Symbols. 2013. (PowerKids Readers: American Symbols Ser.). 24p. (J). (gr. k-2). 135.60 (978-1-4777-1138-5(4)); pap. 49.50 (978-1-4777-2673-0(X)); pap. 297.00 (978-1-4777-2674-7(8)) Rosen Publishing Group, Inc., The. (PowerKids Pr.).

Powerkids Readers: American Symbols / SMbolos de Amrica. 2013. (PowerKids Readers: American Symbols / Smbolos de Amrica Ser.). (ENG & SPA.). 24p. (J). (gr. k-2). 135.60 (978-1-4777-1237-5(2), PowerKids Pr.) Rosen Publishing Group, Inc., The.

Pratt, Mara L. American History Stories, Volume I - with Original Illustrations. 2011. (Illus.). 212p. (978-1-84902-412-9(X)) Benediction Classics.

—American History Stories, Volume II - with Original Illustrations. 2011. 218p. (978-1-84902-410-5(3)) Benediction Classics.

—American History Stories, Volume III - with Original Illustrations. 2011. 208p. (978-1-84902-409-9(X)) Benediction Classics.

—American History Stories, Volume Iv - with Original Illustrations. 2011. 246p. (978-1-84902-407-5(3)) Benediction Classics.

Primary Sources in U. S. History. 2015. (Primary Sources in U. S. History Ser.). (ENG.). 48p. (J). (gr. 4-4). 156.80 (978-1-5026-0312-8(8)) Cavendish Square Publishing.

Primary Sources of American Wars. (J). (gr. 3-5). 119.70 (978-1-4042-3304-1(0)) Rosen Publishing Group, Inc., The.

Publications International Ltd. Staff, ed. Electronic Time for Learning: States. 2010. 120p. 18.98 (978-1-4127-9853-2(1), PIL Kids) Publications International, Ltd.

Publishers, Chelsea House, creator. Building America: Then & Now Set, 8-Volumes. 2009. (Building America: Then & Now Ser.). (gr. 5-8). 280.00 (978-1-60413-601-2(4), Chelsea Hse.) Facts On File, Inc.

Radomski, Kassandra, et al. What Went Wrong?, 1 vol. 2014. (What Went Wrong? Ser.). (ENG.). 32p. (gr. 3-4). lib. bdg. 109.28 (978-1-4765-7815-6(X), Fact Finders) Capstone Press of Coughlan Cos.

Rajczak, Michael. How Did the Liberty Bell Get Its Crack? — & Other FAQs about American History. 2016. (Q & a: Life's Mysteries Solved! Ser.). (Illus.). 32p. (J). (gr. 4-3). pap. 10.50 (978-1-4824-4737-8(1)) Stevens, Gareth Publishing LLLP.

Rakes, Celeste W. All American History Student Reader Vol. 1: The Explorers to the Jacksonians. 2005. (All American History Ser.). (Illus.). 442p. 44.95 (978-1-892427-12-0(5)) Bright Ideas! Educational Resources.

Randolph, Ryan. Alexander Hamilton's Economic Plan: Solving Problems in America's New Economy. 2009. (Life in the New American Nation Ser.). 32p. (gr. 4-4). 47.90 (978-1-61514-276-7(2)) Rosen Publishing Group, Inc., The.

Rau, Dana Meachen. The Northeast. 2012. (True Book Ser.). (ENG., Illus.). 48p. (J). pap. 6.95 (978-0-531-28326-4(7)); (gr. 3-5). 29.00 (978-0-531-24851-5(8)) Scholastic Library Publishing. (Children's Pr.).

—The Southwest. 2012. (True Book Ser.). (ENG., Illus.). 48p. (J). pap. 6.95 (978-0-531-28328-8(3)); (gr. 3-5). lib. bdg. 29.00 (978-0-531-24853-9(4)) Scholastic Library Publishing. (Children's Pr.).

—U. S. Landforms. 2012. (True Book Ser.). (ENG., Illus.). 48p. (J). pap. 6.95 (978-0-531-28329-5(1)); lib. bdg. 29.00 (978-0-531-24854-6(2)) Scholastic Library Publishing. (Children's Pr.).

Reader's Digest Editors. The 50 States. 2011. (Panorama Sticker Storybook Ser.). (ENG., Illus.). 48p. (J). (gr. 1-3). pap. 9.99 (978-0-7944-2265-3(9)) Reader's Digest Assn., Inc., The.

Rebellions, Revolts, & Uprisings. 2017. (Rebellions, Revolts, & Uprisings Ser.). 48p. (gr. 5-5). pap. 84.30 **(978-1-5382-0838-0(5))**; lib. bdg. 191.70 **(978-1-5382-0837-3(7))** Stevens, Gareth Publishing LLLP.

Remembering Medicine Creek: The Story of the First Treaty Signed in Washington. 2005. (YA). pap. 10.00 (978-0-9772528-0-0(9)) Fireweed Pr.

Research American History Series: Series Set. 2004. (Researching American History Ser.). (Illus.). (J). (978-1-932663-05-1(3)) History Compass, LLC.

Rice, Dona. Grand Old Flag (Foundations) 2015. (TIME for KIDS(r) Nonfiction Readers Ser.). (ENG., Illus.). 12p. (gr. k-k). 4.99 (978-1-4938-2055-9(9)) Teacher Created Materials, Inc.

Road Trip: Exploring America's Regions. 2013. (Road Trip: Exploring America's Regions Ser.). 24p. (J). (gr. 2-5). 135.60 (978-1-4339-9675-7(8)); pap. 293.40 (978-1-4339-9744-0(4)); pap. 48.90 (978-1-4339-9743-3(6)) Stevens, Gareth Publishing LLLP.

Robertson, Jean. Pictures of America. 2014. (ENG.). 32p. (gr. 3-6). 32.79 (978-1-62717-736-8(1)) Rourke Educational Media.

Robinson, Tom. The Development of the Industrial United States: 1870-1900. 2007. (Presidents of the United States Ser.). (Illus.). 48p. (J). (gr. 4-7). lib. bdg. 29.05 (978-1-59036-745-2(6)) Weigl Pubs., Inc.

—Development of the Industrial United States: 1870-1900. 2007. (Presidents of the United States Ser.). (Illus.). 48p. (J). (gr. 4-7). per. 10.95 (978-1-59036-746-9(4)) Weigl Pubs., Inc.

Rodhe, Paul. Kids Meet the Presidents 3rd Edition. 2017. (Kids Meet Ser.: 9). (ENG.). 96p. (J). (gr. 3). spiral bd. 14.95 (978-1-60433-657-3(9), Applesauce Pr.) Cider Mill Pr. Bk. Pubs., LLC.

Roop, Peter & Roop, Connie. Louisiana Purchase. Comport, Sally Wern, illus. 2004. (Ready-For-Chapters Ser.). (ENG.). 80p. (J). (gr. 2-5). pap. 6.99 (978-0-689-86443-8(4), Simon & Schuster/Paula Wiseman Bks.) Simon & Schuster/Paula Wiseman Bks.

—Manten Las Luces Encendidas, Abbie. Hanson, Peter E., illus. 2005. (Yo Solo Biografias Ser.). (SPA.). 40p. (J). (gr. 2-5). per. 6.95 (978-0-8225-3099-2(6)) Lerner Publishing Group.

Rosen, Daniel. New Beginnings: Jamestown & the Virginia Colony 1607-1699. 2005. (Crossroads America Ser.). (ENG.). 40p. (J). (gr. 5-9). 12.95 (978-0-7922-8277-8(9)); (Illus.). 21.90 (978-0-7922-8357-7(0)) National Geographic Society. (National Geographic Children's Bks.).

Rossi, Ann. Bright Ideas: The Age of Invention in America 1870-1910. 2005. (Crossroads America Ser.). (ENG., Illus.). 40p. (J). (gr. 5-9). 21.90 (978-0-7922-8356-0(2), National Geographic Children's Bks.) National Geographic Society.

—Created Equal: Women Campaign for the Right to Vote 1840 - 1920. 2005. (Crossroads America Ser.). (ENG., Illus.). 40p. (J). (gr. 5-9). 12.95 (978-0-7922-8275-4(2)); 21.90 (978-0-7922-8285-3(X)) National Geographic Society. (National Geographic Children's Bks.).

—Cultures Collide: Native American & Europeans 1492-1700. 2004. (Crossroads America Ser.). (ENG., Illus.). 40p. (J). (gr. 5-9). 12.95 (978-0-7922-7189-5(0), National Geographic Children's Bks.) National Geographic Society.

Rous, Sheri, ed. United States History. 2004. (Illus.). 32p. (J). pap. 10.99 (978-1-59198-053-7(4), CTP 2797) Creative Teaching Pr., Inc.

Rubel, David. Scholastic Encyclopedia of the Presidents & Their Times. 2013. (ENG.). 256p. (J). (gr. 5-9). 24.99 (978-0-545-49985-9(2), Scholastic Reference) Scholastic, Inc.

Rulers & Their Times - Group 3, 4 bks. 119.71 (978-0-7614-1486-5(X), Benchmark Bks.) Marshall Cavendish Corp.

Sakolsky, Josh. Critical Perspectives on the Industrial Revolution. 2005. (Critical Anthologies of Nonfiction Writing Ser.). (Illus.). 176p. (YA). (gr. 7-12). lib. bdg. 37.95 (978-1-4042-0062-3(2)) Rosen Publishing Group, Inc., The.

Sanders, Doug. Superstorm Sandy. 2013. (Code Red Ser.). 32p. (J). (gr. 2-7). lib. bdg. 25.27 (978-1-61772-898-3(5)) Bearport Publishing Co., Inc.

Sandler, Martin W. America's Great Disasters. Sandler, Martin W., illus. 2003. (Illus.). 96p. (J). (gr. 3-18). 17.99 (978-0-06-029107-5(9)) HarperCollins Pubs.

Sanna, Ellyn. Politician. Riggs, Ernestine G. & Gholar, Cheryl, eds. 2013. (Careers with Character Ser.: 18). 96p. (J). (gr. 7-18). 22.95 (978-1-4222-2762-6(6)) Mason Crest.

Savitz, Harriet May. Dear Daughters & Sons: Three Essays on the American Spirit... a Tribute. 2003. 40p. per. 4.95 (978-0-9639838-9-3(X)) Little Treasure Bks.

Saxena, Shalini. Paul Revere Didn't Say "The British Are Coming!" Exposing Myths about the American Revolution. 2016. (Exposed! Myths about Early American History Ser.). 00032p. (J). pap. 10.50 (978-1-4824-5727-8(X)) Stevens, Gareth Publishing LLLP.

Scholastic Library Publishing. Cornerstones of Freedom. 2012. (Third Ser.). (J). 300.00 (978-0-531-22774-9(X), Children's Pr.) Scholastic Library Publishing.

—Cornerstones of Freedom, Third Series. 2011. (Third Ser.). (J). 1200.00 (978-0-531-27644-0(9), Children's Pr.) Scholastic Library Publishing.

—A True Book-the U. S. Regions. 2012. (True Book Ser.). (J). 174.00 (978-0-531-26024-1(0), Children's Pr.) Scholastic Library Publishing.

Schraff, Anne. Daredevil American Heroes of Exploration & Flight. 2013. (Inspiring Collective Biographies Ser.). 112p. (J). (gr. 5-12). pap. 10.95 (978-1-4644-0247-0(7)) Enslow Pubs., Inc.

Schraff, Anne E. Daredevil American Heroes of Exploration & Flight. 2013. (Inspiring Collective Biographies Ser.). (Illus.). 112p. (J). (gr. 5-18). 33.27 (978-0-7660-4163-9(8)) Enslow Pubs., Inc.

Scillian, Devin. One Nation: America by the Numbers. Carroll, Pam, illus. 2004. (ENG.). 40p. (J). (gr. k-6). pap. 7.95 (978-1-58536-249-3(2)) Sleeping Bear Pr.

Selzer, Adam. The Smart Aleck's Guide to American History. 2009. (ENG., Illus.). 336p. (J). (gr. 4-7). pap. 13.99 (978-0-385-73650-3(9), Delacorte Bks. for Young Readers) Random Hse. Children's Bks.

Seneca Falls, Grades 4-9: Achieving Women's Rights. (Teaching with Primary Sources Ser.). (J). tchr. ed. 32.95 (978-0-382-40975-2(2)) Cobblestone Publishing Co.

Serber, Michael & Peiser, Andrew. U. S. History & Government. rev. ed. 2005. 688p. (gr. 10-12). (978-0-87720-882-2(4), R036H) AMSCO Schl. Pubns., Inc.

Sets 1, 2, 3 & 4. 2005. (Primary Sources in American History Ser.). (Illus.). 64p. (gr. 5-8). lib. bdg. (978-1-4042-0352-5(4)) Rosen Publishing Group, Inc., The.

Sharp, Constance. Thomas Jefferson & the Growing United States (1800-1811) 2012. (J). pap. (978-1-4222-2414-4(7)) Mason Crest.

Shelton, Karen. Famous Americans: Ready-to-Go Units That Include Mini-Books, Read-Aloud Plays, Graphic Organizers, & Writing Activities That Teach about 12 Important Americans. 2011. (Person of the Month Ser.). (ENG.). 96p. (gr. k-2). pap. 14.99 (978-0-545-28076-1(1), Teaching Resources) Scholastic, Inc.

Show Me America, 5 vols., Set. Incl. Dorothea Lange: Photographer of the People. King, David C. 88p. (C). 2009. lib. bdg. 158.00 (978-0-7656-8154-6(4), Y181941); George Catlin: Painter of Indian Life. Worth, Richard. 80p. (C). 2009. lib. bdg. 158.00 (978-0-7656-8152-2(8), Y182314); John Trumbull: Painter of the Revolutionary War. Murray, Stuart A. P. 83p. (C). 2008. lib. bdg. 158.00 (978-0-7656-8150-8(1), Y182501); Lewis Hine: Photographer of Americans at Work. Worth, Richard. 83p. (C). 2009. lib. bdg. 158.00 (978-0-7656-8153-9(6), Y182862); Mathew Brady: Photographer of Our Nation. Murray, Stuart A. P. 83p. 2009. lib. bdg. 158.00 (978-0-7656-8151-5(X), Y182957); (Illus.). (gr. 6-18). (ENG.). 2009. Set lib. bdg. 140.00 (978-0-7656-8149-2(8), Y183560) Routledge.

Shuh, Mari. Adrian Peterson. 2013. (Football Stars up Close Ser.). 24p. (J). (gr. k-5). lib. bdg. 23.93 (978-1-61772-718-4(0)) Bearport Publishing Co., Inc.

Shukin, Barbara. Renaissance History Portfolio: A History of Europe & the Americas from the 14th -18th Centuries. 2004. (J). ring bd. 29.95 (978-0-9762918-2-4(7)) Homeschool Journey.

Siebert, Anne & Clark, Raymond C. All Around America: The Time Traveler's Talk Show. 2004. (gr. 6-12). pap., wbk. ed. 39.00 incl. cd-rom (978-0-86647-186-2(3)) Pro Lingua Assocs., Inc.

—All Around America Activities: The Time Traveler's Talk Show. 2004. 76p. (gr. 6-12). pap., stu. ed., wbk. ed. 16.50 (978-0-86647-184-8(7)) Pro Lingua Assocs., Inc.

Sikora, Frank & Batcheler, Michelle. Frank M. Johnson, Jr: Courageous Judge. 2009. (Illus.). 104p. (978-1-59421-045-7(4)) Seacoast Publishing, Inc.

Silbert, Jack. Honest Abe's Funny Money Book. 2012. (Illus.). 32p. (978-0-545-36740-0(9)) Scholastic, Inc.

Six Questions of American History. 2012. (Six Questions of American History Ser.). (ENG.). 48p. (gr. 4-6). Set III. pap. 56.72 (978-0-7613-9243-9(2))Set III, Pack. pap. 340.29 (978-0-7613-9244-6(0)) Lerner Publishing Group.

Six Questions of American History: Spring 2012 New Releases. 2012. (Six Questions of American History Ser.). 48p. (gr. 4-6). lib. bdg. 183.60 (978-0-7613-8909-5(1), Lerner Pubns.) Lerner Publishing Group.

Smith, A. G. Historic American Landmarks. 2005. (Dover History Coloring Book Ser.). (ENG., Illus.). 32p. (J). (gr. 3-5). 3.99 (978-0-486-44489-5(9)) Dover Pubns., Inc.

Smith, Ruth J. Divine Providence: A Child's History of the United States. Mikler, Lisa M., illus. 2005. 224p. (J). per. 19.95 net. (978-0-9705618-5-5(7)) Bradford Pr., Inc.

—Liberty & Justice for All: A Child's History of the United States of America. Mikler, Lisa M., illus. 2003. 208p. (J). per. 19.95 (978-0-9705618-3-1(0)) Bradford Pr., Inc.

—Liberty & Justice for All Teacher's Guide: Liberty & Justice for All. 2003. (J). tchr. ed., per. 34.95 (978-0-9705618-4-8(9)) Bradford Pr., Inc.

Smith, Shuford. ABC All-American Riddles. 2003. (Illus.). (J). 13.95 (978-0-939217-56-4(2)) Peel Productions, Inc.

Smith, Tamara. The Story of Ulysses S. Grant. Britt, Stephanie, illus. 2005. 26p. (J). bds. 7.69 (978-0-8249-6565-5(5), Ideal Pubns.) Worthy Publishing.

Social Studies Explorer: It's Cool to Learn about the United States, 5 vols., Set. Incl. Midwest. Orr, Tamra B. lib. bdg. 31.36 (978-1-61080-179-9(2), 201152); Northeast. Franchino, Vicky. lib. bdg. 31.36 (978-1-61080-180-5(6), 201154); Southeast. Marsico, Katie. lib. bdg. 31.36 (978-1-61080-181-2(4), 201156); Southwest. Orr, Tamra. lib. bdg. 31.36 (978-1-61080-183-6(0), 201160); West. Somervill, Barbara A. lib. bdg. 31.36 (978-1-61080-182-9(2), 201158); 48p. (gr. 4-8). (Social Studies Explorer Ser.). 2011. Set lib. bdg. 156.80 (978-1-61080-191-1(1)) Cherry Lake Publishing.

Spotlight on American History. 2015. (Spotlight on American History Ser.). (ENG.). 24p. (J). (gr. 4-6). pap., pap., pap. 720.00 (978-1-4994-1836-1(1), PowerKids Pr.) Rosen Publishing Group, Inc., The.

Spotlight on American History: Set 2. 2016. (Spotlight on American History Ser.). 24p. (gr. 6-4). 315.00 (978-1-4994-1894-1(9)); pap. 120.00 (978-1-4994-2480-5(9)) Rosen Publishing Group, Inc., The. (PowerKids Pr.).

Stanley, George Edward. The Great Depression & World War II (1929-1949) 2005. (Primary Source History of the United States Ser.). (Illus.). 48p. (gr. 5-12). pap. 14.05

(978-0-8368-5838-9(7)); lib. bdg. 31.00 *(978-0-8368-5829-7(8))* Stevens, Gareth Publishing LLLP. (Gareth Stevens Secondary Library).

The Star-Spangled State Book: Have Fun Learning about All 50 States. 2006. (YA). per. *(978-0-9787820-0-9(3))* King, Joel.

States. 2005. (Illus.). 96p. 12.98 *(978-0-7853-9600-0(4)*, 7127301) Phoenix International Publications, Inc.

Stckvagn. Americas Story Complete Book S. 2005. pap. *(978-0-7398-9717-1(9))* Harcourt Schl. Pubs.

Steck-Vaughn Staff. Social Studies Level E: History of Our Country. 2005. (Steck-Vaughn Social Studies). (ENG., Illus.). 208p. (gr. 5-5). pap. 37.65 *(978-0-7398-9222-0(3))* Houghton Mifflin Harcourt Publishing Co.

Steele, Philip. Iran & the West. 2012. (Our World Divided Ser.). (ENG., Illus.). 48p. (J). (gr. 5-8). 27.95 *(978-1-4488-6031-9(8)*, Rosen Reference) Rosen Publishing Group, Inc., The.

Stephens, Edna Cucksey. Rock U. S. A. & the American Way! A Freedom Handbook. Herrick, Mark J., illus. 2004. (Connect-It Ser.). 124p. (J). (gr. -1-3). pap. 29.95 *(978-0-9749412-1-9(2))* EDCO Publishing, Inc.

Stewart, Mark. The United States & Canada. 2016. (Regions of the World Ser.). (ENG.). 64p. (gr. 6-9). pap. 9.99 *(978-1-4846-3814-9(X)*, NA-h) Heinemann-Raintree.

Stille, Darlene R. The Emergence of Modern America: 1890-1930. 2007. (Presidents of the United States Ser.). (Illus.). 48p. (J). (gr. 4-7). lib. bdg. 29.05 *(978-1-59036-747-6(2))*; per. 10.95 *(978-1-59036-748-3(0))* Weigl Pubs., Inc.

Stone, Oliver & Kuznick, Peter. The Untold History of the United States Vol. 1: Young Readers Edition, 1898-1963. 2015. lib. bdg. 24.50 *(978-0-606-37853-6(7))* Turtleback Bks.

—The Untold History of the United States, 1898-1945, Vol. 1. 2015. (ENG., Illus.). 400p. (J). (gr. 5). pap. 12.99 *(978-1-4814-2174-4(3)*, Atheneum Bks. for Young Readers) Simon & Schuster Children's Publishing.

Stone, Tanya Lee. A Is for America: A Patriotic Alphabet Book. Kelley, Gerald, illus. 2011. (ENG.). 24p. (J). (gr. -1-k). mass mkt. 4.99 *(978-0-8431-9877-5(X)*, Price Stern Sloan) Penguin Young Readers Group.

Stout, Glenn & Williams, Ike. From Hardships to Championships. 2013. (Good Sports Ser.). (ENG., Illus.). 144p. (J). (gr. 5-7). pap. 5.99 *(978-0-547-88735-7(3))* Houghton Mifflin Harcourt Publishing Co.

Streissguth, Thomas. United States in Pictures. 2007. (Visual Geography (Lerner) Ser.). (Illus.). 80p. (YA). (gr. 7-12). lib. bdg. 31.93 *(978-0-8225-8567-1(7))* Twenty First Century Bks.

Sundance/Newbridge LLC Staff. It's on the Map. 2004. (Reading PowerWorks Ser.). (gr. 1-3). 37.50 *(978-0-7608-7823-1(4))*; pap. 6.10 *(978-0-7608-7824-8(2))* Sundance/Newbridge Educational Publishing.

Swanson Sateren, Shelley, et al. It's Back to School ... Way Back! 2016. (It's Back to School ... Way Back! Ser.). (ENG.). 32p. (gr. 3-4). pap. 31.80 *(978-1-5157-2117-8(5)*, Fact Finders) Capstone Press of Coughlan Cos.

Tate, Suzanne. Color with the Wright Brothers: See How They Made History. Melvin, James, illus. 2003. (Suzanne Tate's History Ser.). 32p. (J). pap. 2.95 *(978-1-878405-41-8(1))* Nags Head Art, Inc.

Teacher Created Materials. Early America, Set. rev. ed. 2009. (Teacher Created Materials Library). (ENG., Illus.). (J). (gr. 4-6). spiral bd. 55.92 *(978-1-4333-1895-5(4))* Shell Educational Publishing.

Teaching Hello U.S.A. 2004. (Illus.). lib. bdg., tchr. ed. 7.95 *(978-0-8225-3748-9(6))* Lerner Publishing Group.

Theresine, Mary. Challenge to Freedom. O'Leary, Timothy F. & Veronica, M., eds. 2011. 322p. 50.95 *(978-1-258-07535-4(0))* Literary Licensing, LLC.

Thompson, Carol & Thompson, Carol. America the Good: Stories of Goodwill by Good Americans. 2003. (Illus.). 95p. bds. 15.95 *(978-0-9744111-0-1(8))* Wren's Nest Publishing, Inc.

Thompson, Jerry D., contrib. by. Symbols of American Freedom Set, 10-Volumes. 2009. (Symbols of American Freedom Ser.). (gr. 4-6). 300.00 *(978-1-60413-830-6(0)*, Chelsea Clubhouse) Facts On File, Inc.

Tiner, John. The Story of the Pledge of Allegiance: Discovering Our Nations Heritage. 2003. (Discovering Our Nation's Heritage Ser.). (Illus.). 48p. (J). 9.99 *(978-0-89051-393-4(7))* Master Bks.

Todd, Francine E. The Todds in America: 1741-2005: An American History/Genealogy Curriculum for Grades 3-5. 2006. (ENG., Illus.). 68p. per. 17.75 *(978-1-4120-7834-4(2))* Trafford Publishing.

Townsend, Dana E. Ellis Island. (Illus.). 32p. (J). *(978-0-7367-2944-4(5))* Zaner-Bloser, Inc.

Tracy, Kathleen. Top Secret: The Story of the Manhattan Project. 2005. (Monumental Milestones Ser.). (Illus.). 48p. (YA). (gr. 4-7). lib. bdg. 29.95 *(978-1-58415-399-3(7))* Mitchell Lane Pubs., Inc.

Troupe, Thomas Kingsley. Fly on the Wall History. Tejido, Jomike, illus. 2017. (Fly on the Wall History Ser.). (ENG.). 32p. (gr. 1-3). 109.28 *(978-1-4795-9801-4(1))* Picture Window Bks.

Turning Points in U. S. History, 6 bks., Set. Incl. Alamo. Fradin, Dennis Brindell. 46p. (J). 2006. lib. bdg. 29.93 *(978-0-7614-2127-6(0))*; Assassination of Abraham Lincoln. Brindell, Dennis Fradin. 48p. 2006. lib. bdg. 31.36 *(978-0-7614-2123-8(8))*; Custer's Last Stand. Fradin, Dennis Brindell. 48p. 2006. lib. bdg. 31.36 *(978-0-7614-2124-5(6))*; Declaration of Independence. Fradin, Dennis Brindell. 46p. (J). 2006. lib. bdg. 31.36 *(978-0-7614-2129-0(7))*; Jamestown, Virginia. Fradin, Dennis Brindell. 48p. 2007. lib. bdg. 31.36 *(978-0-7614-2122-1(X))*; Mayflower Compact. Fradin, Dennis Brindell. 47p. (J). 2006. lib. bdg. 31.36 *(978-0-7614-2125-2(4))*; (Illus.). (gr. 3-7). 2007. Set lib. bdg. 179.57 *(978-0-7614-2121-4(1)*, Benchmark Bks.) Marshall Cavendish Corp.

U. S. National Geographic Society Staff, contrib. by. The Northeast Today. 2007. (Reading Expeditions Ser.). (ENG., Illus.). 32p. (J). pap. 17.95 *(978-0-7922-4532-2(6))* National Geographic School Publishing, Inc.

Uhlig, Elizabeth. I See America! Uhlig, Elizabeth, illus. 2009. (Illus.). (J). pap. 12.95 *(978-0-9815345-7-2(0))* Marble Hse. Editions.

The United States: Historical Atlases of the Growth of a New Nation. 2005. (Illus.). (gr. 7-12). lib. bdg. 183.60 *(978-1-4042-0357-0(5))* Rosen Publishing Group, Inc., The.

United States History, 3 vols. 2004. (Pacemaker United States History Ser.). 738p. (YA). (gr. 6-12). 43.95 *(978-0-13-024410-9(4))* Globe Fearon Educational Publishing.

The United States Past & Present. (J). (gr. 5). *(978-0-669-11398-3(0))*; suppl. ed. *(978-0-669-11382-2(4))* Houghton Mifflin Harcourt School Pubs.

The United States Past to Present: Heath Social Studies. Incl. United States Past & Present. suppl. ed. *(978-0-669-11382-2(4))*; United States Past & Present. *(978-0-669-11398-3(0))*; The United States Past to Present. suppl. ed. *(978-0-669-11424-9(3))*; The United States Past to Present. pap., wbk. ed. *(978-0-669-11404-1(9))*; The United States Past to Present. tchr. ed., wbk. ed. *(978-0-669-11409-6(X))*; The United States Past to Present. suppl. ed. *(978-0-669-11430-0(8))*; The United States Past to Present. suppl. ed. *(978-0-669-11725-7(0))*; The United States Past to Present. suppl. ed. (J). (gr. 5-6). *(978-0-669-11390-7(5))* Houghton Mifflin Harcourt School Pubs.

Uschan, Michael V. Reconstruction. 2007. (Lucent Library of Black History Ser.). (ENG., Illus.). 128p. (gr. 3-7). lib. bdg. 39.40 *(978-1-4205-0009-7(0)*, Lucent Bks.) Cengage Gale.

Vescia, Monique. Battle Reenactments, 01 vols., 1. 2016. (Role-Playing for Fun & Profit Ser.). (ENG.). 48p. (J). pap. 11.75 *(978-1-4994-3728-7(5)*, Rosen Central) Rosen Publishing Group, Inc., The.

Victor, Rae Anna. George Washington's Revolutionary Marshals. 2004. (Illus.). 62p. (J). pap. 9.95 *(978-0-7414-2302-3(2))* Infinity Publishing.

Wacholtz, Anthony. Joe Mauer: Baseball Superstar, 1 vol. 2012. (Superstar Athletes Ser.). (ENG.). 24p. (gr. 1-2). pap. 7.29 *(978-1-4296-8003-5(2))*; lib. bdg. 25.32 *(978-1-4296-7683-0(3))* Capstone Press of Coughlan Cos.

—The Ultimate Collection of Pro Baseball Records. 2012. (For the Record Ser.). (ENG.). 64p. (gr. 4-6). pap. 53.70 *(978-1-4296-9429-2(7))* Capstone Press of Coughlan Cos.

Waldman, Neil. A Land of Big Dreamers: Voices of Courage in America. Waldman, Neil, illus. 2011. (Single Titles Ser.). (ENG., Illus.). 32p. (gr. 3-5). lib. bdg. 16.95 *(978-0-8225-6810-0(1))* Lerner Publishing Group.

Walter Foster Creative Team. My Learning Adventures: USA. 2013. (My Learning Adventures Ser.). (ENG., Illus.). 80p. (J). (gr. -1). spiral bd. 12.95 *(978-1-60710-629-6(9)*, Silver Dolphin Bks.) Readerlink Distribution Services, LLC.

Warner, Roxie & Warner, Christian. Land of the Free, A to Z. Schartup, Adam, illus. 2014. (J). *(978-1-62086-801-0(6))* Mascot Bks., Inc.

Waryncia, Lou. Antietam: Day of Courage & Sacrifice. Hale, Sarah Elder, ed. 2005. (ENG., Illus.). 48p. (J). (gr. 3-9). 17.95 *(978-0-8126-7904-5(0))* Cobblestone Publishing Co.

Waxman, Laura Hamilton. Why Did the Pilgrims Come to the New World? & Other Questions about the Plymouth Colony. 2010. (Six Questions of American History Ser.). 48p. (J). pap. 9.95 *(978-0-7613-6123-7(5))* Lerner Publishing Group.

Weber, Jennifer L. Key Concepts in American History, 10 vols., Set. 2010. (Key Concepts in American History Ser.). (gr. 6-12). 450.00 *(978-1-60413-961-7(7)*, Chelsea Hse.) Facts On File, Inc.

Weintraub, Aileen. The Library of Pirates, 6 bks. Incl. Barbarossa Brothers: 16th-Century Pirates of the Barbary Coast. (YA). (gr. 2-5). lib. bdg. 22.60 *(978-0-8239-5799-6(3))*; Captain Kidd: 17th-Century Pirate of the Indian Ocean & African Coast. (YA). (gr. 2-5). lib. bdg. 22.60 *(978-0-8239-5797-2(7))*; Henry Morgan: 17th-Century Buccaneer. (J). (gr. 3). lib. bdg. 22.60 *(978-0-8239-5798-9(5)*, PowerKids Pr.); Jean Lafitte: Pirate Hero of the War of 1812. (J). (gr. 3). lib. bdg. 22.60 *(978-0-8239-5796-5(9)*, PowerKids Pr.); 24p. 2002. (Illus.). 112.50 *(978-0-8239-7133-6(3)*, PowerKids Pr.) Rosen Publishing Group, Inc., The.

What Really Happened?, 6 vols., Set. Incl. True Story of Pocahontas. Adams, Colleen. (J). lib. bdg. 22.60 *(978-1-4042-4475-7(1))*; True Story of the American Flag. Zumbusch, Amelie von. (YA). lib. bdg. 22.60 *(978-1-4042-4478-8(6))*; True Story of the Battle of Lexington & Concord. Von Zumbusch, Amelie. (YA). lib. bdg. 22.60 *(978-1-4042-4480-1(8))*; True Story of the Battle of the Alamo. Adams, Colleen. (YA). lib. bdg. 22.60 *(978-1-4042-4477-1(8))*; True Story of the First Thanksgiving. Adams, Colleen. (YA). lib. bdg. 22.60 *(978-1-4042-4476-4(X))*; True Story of the Salem Witch Hunts. Von Zumbusch, Amelie. (YA). lib. bdg. 22.60 *(978-1-4042-4479-5(4))*; (Illus.). 24p. (gr. 3-6). 2009. 2008. Set lib. bdg. 127.50 *(978-1-4358-2540-6(3)*, PowerKids Pr.) Rosen Publishing Group, Inc., The.

Williams, Colleen. Native American Family Life. Johnson, Troy, ed. 2013. (Native American Life Ser.: 15). 64p. (J). (gr. 5-18). 19.95 *(978-1-4222-2969-9(6))* Mason Crest.

Williams, Dinah. Terrible but True: Awful Events in American History. 2016. (ENG., Illus.). 192p. (J). (gr. 4-7). pap. 9.99 *(978-0-545-90972-3(4)*, Scholastic Nonfiction) Scholastic, Inc.

Willis, Carrie (Hunter) & Saunders, Lucy S. Those Who Dared: Stories of Early Days in Our Country. 2011. 322p. 50.95 *(978-1-258-05701-5(8))* Literary Licensing, LLC.

Wingate, Katherine. Political Reforms: American Citizens Gain More Control over Their Government. 2004. (Progressive Movement, 1900-1920 Ser.). (Illus.). 32p. (YA). (gr. 5-9). lib. bdg. 22.50 *(978-1-4042-0192-7(0))* Rosen Publishing Group, Inc., The.

Winter, Jonah. The Founding Fathers! Those Horse-Ridin', Fiddle-Playin', Book-Readin', Gun-Totin' Gentlemen Who Started America. Blitt, Barry, illus. 2015. (ENG.). 48p. (J). (gr. k-3). 17.99 *(978-1-4424-4274-0(3))* Simon & Schuster Children's Publishing.

Wiseman, Blaine. Baseball. 2010. (Record Breakers Ser.). (Illus.). 24p. (YA). (gr. 3-6). lib. bdg. 27.13 *(978-1-61690-109-7(8))*; (J). (gr. 4-6). pap. 12.95 *(978-1-61690-110-3(1))* Weigl Pubs., Inc.

Wolfson, Evelyn. Wayland A-Z: A Dictionary of Then & Now. Wolfson, Evelyn, ed. 2004. per. 15.00 *(978-0-9762756-0-2(0))* Wayland Historical Society.

Woods, Bob. Smokin' Muscle Cars. 2013. (Fast Wheels! Ser.). 48p. (J). (gr. 4-18). 14.95 *(978-1-62285-090-7(4))* Enslow Pubs., Inc.

Wooster, Patricia. Show Me the United States: My First Picture Encyclopedia, 1 vol. 2013. (My First Picture Encyclopedias Ser.). (ENG.). 32p. (gr. 1-2). 7.95 *(978-1-4765-3347-6(4))*; 27.32 *(978-1-4765-0117-8(3))*; pap. 8.10 *(978-1-4765-3351-3(2))* Capstone Press of Coughlan Cos. (Aplus Bks.).

Working Americans 1880-1999, 5 vols., 5. 2003. 675.00 *(978-1-59237-034-4(9))* Grey Hse. Publishing.

Workman Publishing Company Staff. Everything You Need to Ace American History in One Big Fat Notebook: A Middle School Study Guide. 2016. (Big Fat Notebooks Ser.). (ENG., Illus.). 512p. (J). (gr. 6-8). pap. 14.95 *(978-0-7611-6083-0(3))* Workman Publishing Co., Inc.

World Almanac Puzzler Deck for Kids: U. S. History (BoMC) World Almanac U. S. History, 9-11. 2007. 9.95 *(978-0-8118-6241-7(0))* Chronicle Bks. LLC.

Young, Jeff C. Albert Pujols: A Baseball Star Who Cares. 2013. (Sports Stars Who Care Ser.). 48p. (J). (gr. 3-4). pap. 8.95 *(978-1-4644-0399-6(6)*, Enslow Elementary) Enslow Pubs., Inc.

Zehnder, Christopher. History: Sea to Shining Sea. 2003. (Illus.). ix, 462p. (J). (gr. 5). 55.00 *(978-0-89870-961-2(X))* Ignatius Pr.

Zeman, Anne & Kelly, Kate. Everything You Need to Know about American History Homework. 2011. (Illus.). 152p. (J). pap. *(978-0-545-37471-2(5))* Scholastic, Inc.

Ziefert, Harriet. Use Isbn 1593541627. 2006. (J). 15.95 *(978-1-59354-094-4(9))* Blue Apple Bks.

Zinn, Howard. Class Struggle to the War on Terror. 2007. (For Young People Ser.). (ENG., Illus.). 192p. (J). (gr. 5-10). 17.95 *(978-1-58322-760-2(1)*, Triangle Square) Seven Stories Pr.

—A Young People's History of the United States Vol. 1: Columbus to the Spanish-American War. 2007. (For Young People Ser.). (ENG., Illus.). 192p. (J). (gr. 5-10). 16.95 *(978-1-58322-759-6(8)*, Triangle Square) Seven Stories Pr.

Zocchi, Judy. In the United States. Brodie, Neale, illus. 2005. (Global Adventures II Ser.). 32p. (J). pap. 10.95 *(978-1-59646-172-7(1))*; lib. bdg. 21.65 *(978-1-59646-085-0(7))* Dingles & Co.

—In the United States/en los Estados Unidos. Brodie, Neale, illus. 2005. (Global Adventures II Ser.).Tr. of En los Estados Unidos. (ENG & SPA.). 32p. (J). pap. 10.95 *(978-1-59646-174-1(8))*; lib. bdg. 21.65 *(978-1-59646-086-7(5))* Dingles & Co.

Zschock, Martha Day. Hello, America! 2012. (ENG., Illus.). 16p. (J). (gr. -1-k). bds. 7.95 *(978-1-933212-88-3(8)*, Commonwealth Editions) Applewood Bks.

The 50 States. Date not set. (Illus.). 32p. (J). 3.98 *(978-0-7525-9870-3(8))* Parragon, Inc.

UNITED STATES—HISTORY—CHRONOLOGY

Bowman, John S. Chronology of Wars. 2nd rev. ed. 2010. (America at War Ser.). 304p. (gr. 6-12). 45.00 *(978-0-8160-8193-6(X)*, Chelsea Hse.) Facts On File, Inc.

Corey, Melinda. Chronology of 20th-Century America. 2005. (Decades of American History Ser.). (Illus.). 128p. (gr. 5-8). 35.00 *(978-0-8160-5646-0(3))* Facts On File, Inc.

Englar, Mary. An Illustrated Timeline of U. S. Presidents, 1 vol. Epstein, Len, illus. 2012. (Visual Timelines in History Ser.). (ENG.). 32p. (gr. 3-4). pap. 7.49 *(978-1-4048-7254-7(X))*; lib. bdg. 28.65 *(978-1-4048-7161-8(6))* Picture Window Bks.

Fredriksen, John C. Chronology of American History, 4 vols., Set. 2008. 2592p. (C). (gr. 9-18). 350.00 *(978-0-8160-6800-5(3))* Facts On File, Inc.

Time Chart of American History: A Chronological History of the United States. 2014. (Illus.). (J). *(978-1-4351-5393-6(6))* Metro Bks.

Wooster, Patricia. An Illustrated Timeline of U. S. States, 1 vol. Morgan, Rick, illus. 2011. (Visual Timelines in History Ser.). (ENG.). 32p. (gr. 3-4). pap. 7.49 *(978-1-4048-7020-8(2))* Picture Window Bks.

UNITED STATES—HISTORY—DICTIONARIES

Abolitionism. 2010. (Key Concepts in American History Ser.). (Illus.). 128p. (gr. 6-12). 45.00 *(978-1-60413-220-5(5)*, Chelsea Hse.) Facts On File, Inc.

Conflicts in American History: A Documentary Encyclopedia. 2010. (J). *(978-0-8160-7101-2(2))*; *(978-0-8160-7094-7(6))*; *(978-0-8160-7096-1(2))*; *(978-0-8160-7097-8(0))*; *(978-0-8160-7098-5(9))*; *(978-0-8160-7099-2(7))*; *(978-0-8160-7100-5(4))* Facts On File, Inc.

Dorling Kindersley Publishing Staff. Children's Encyclopedia of American History. 2014. (ENG.). 320p. (J). (gr. 3-7). 29.99 *(978-1-4654-2843-1(7)*, DK Children) Dorling Kindersley Publishing, Inc.

Gale Cengage Learning, ed. Junior Worldmark Encyclopedia of the States: 4 Volume Set. 2013. 1260p. pap. 307.00 *(978-1-4144-9864-5(0))* Cengage Gale.

Gale Encyclopedia US Hist: Bus, 2 Vol. 2007. 220.00 *(978-1-4144-3126-0(0))* Cengage Gale.

Gale Encyclopedia US Hist: Fam, 2 Vol. 2007. 220.00 *(978-1-4144-3122-2(8))* Cengage Gale.

Gale Encyclopedia US Hist: Sci Tech, 2 Vol. 2007. 220.00 *(978-1-4144-3110-9(4))* Cengage Gale.

National Geographic Kids Staff. United States Encyclopedia: America's People, Places, & Events. 2015. (ENG., Illus.). 272p. (J). (gr. 3-7). 24.99 *(978-1-4263-2092-7(2)*, National Geographic Children's Bks.) National Geographic Society.

U-X-L Encyclopedia of U. S. History, 8 vols., Vol. 10. rev. ed. 2008. (ENG.). (YA). (gr. 6-8). 664.00 *(978-1-4144-3043-0(4)*, UXL) Cengage Gale.

UNITED STATES—HISTORY—DRAMA

Fredericks, Anthony D. American Folklore, Legends, & Tall Tales for Readers Theatre, 1 vol. 2008. (Readers Theatre Ser.). 156p. (C). pap. 40.00 *(978-1-59158-734-7(4)*, TIP8734, Libraries Unlimited) ABC-CLIO, LLC.

GLOBE. Eight Plays of U.S. History. 2012. (ENG., Illus.). vi, 201p. (J). (gr. 6-12). pap. 15.50 *(978-0-8359-1374-4(0)*, GLOBE) Pearson Schl.

Twain, Mark, pseud. Huckleberry Finn. 2009. (Foundation Classics Ser.). (Illus.). 56p. (J). (gr. 5-9). lib. bdg. 27.95 *(978-1-60754-541-5(1))* Windmill Bks.

UNITED STATES—HISTORY, ECONOMIC

see United States—Economic Conditions

UNITED STATES—HISTORY—FICTION

Alter, Judy. Sam Houston Is My Hero. 2003. (Chaparral Bks.). (ENG.). 130p. (J). pap. 11.95 *(978-0-87565-277-1(8))* Texas Christian Univ. Pr.

Atamer, Billie. Banjo Billy & the River Rat Kids. 2009. 130p. pap. 7.99 *(978-1-61667-004-7(5))* Raider Publishing International.

Babson, Jane F. A Story of Us: The Dolls' History of People of the United States. Babson, Jane F., illus. 2003. (Illus.). 56p. (J). (gr. 4-5). 10.95 *(978-0-940787-03-2(2))* Winstead Pr., Ltd.

Bain, Michelle. The Adventures of Thumbs up Johnnie Thumbs up to Red, White & Blue! Thumbs up to Red, White & Blue! Lizana, Lorenzo, illus. 2007. 48p. (J). 14.95 *(978-0-9795832-2-3(5))* Pixie Stuff LLC.

Barone, Michelle. Out of the Ordinary. 2004. (Adventures in History Ser.). (Illus.). 120p. (J). pap. *(978-1-932663-08-2(8))* History Compass, LLC.

Bartelme, Elizabeth. Simon Brute & the Western Adventure. 2012. 132p. pap. 12.95 *(978-0-9831800-8-1(3))* Hillside Education.

Birtha, Becky. Lucky Beans. Tadgell, Nicole, illus. 2012. (J). 34.28 *(978-1-61913-129-3(3))* Weigl Pubs., Inc.

Blos, Joan W. Letters from the Corrugated Castle: A Novel of Gold Rush California, 1850-1852. 2007. (ENG., Illus.). 320p. (J). (gr. 5-9). 17.99 *(978-0-689-87077-4(9)*, Atheneum Bks. for Young Readers) Simon & Schuster Children's Publishing.

Brannon, Tom, illus. Who Cares, Charlie Brown? 2014. (Peanuts Great American Adventure Ser.). (ENG.). 40p. (J). (gr. -1). 16.99 *(978-1-62157-259-6(5)*, Little Patriot Pr.) Regnery Publishing, Inc., An Eagle Publishing Co.

Call me. 2003. (J). pap. 2.25 *(978-0-590-33766-3(1))* Scholastic, Inc.

Clark, Betsy Huhn. Lizzie's Extraordinary Adventure. 2006. (Illus.). 24p. (J). 9.99 *(978-1-4276-0116-2(X))* Aardvark Global Publishing.

Columbia River Stories. 2007. (J). per. 15.00 *(978-0-9792207-0-8(X))* Earth Arts NW.

Connors, Faith Raymond. Love, Midgie. Connors, Tracy D., ed. 2008. (ENG., Illus.). 308p. pap. 12.95 *(978-0-9640138-1-0(9)*, 9780964013810) BelleAire Pr.

Cooney, Caroline B. The Ransom of Mercy Carter. 2011. (ENG.). 256p. (YA). (gr. 7). pap. 8.99 *(978-0-385-74046-3(8)*, Ember) Random Hse. Children's Bks.

Cox, Stephen Angus. The Dare Boys of 1776. 2007. (ENG.). 106p. pap. 18.99 *(978-1-4264-3400-6(6))* Creative Media Partners, LLC.

Davies, Jacqueline. Tricking the Tallyman. Schindler, S. D., illus. 2014. (ENG.). 40p. (J). (gr. k-3). 7.99 *(978-0-385-75519-1(8)*, Dragonfly Bks.) Random Hse. Children's Bks.

Deutsch, Stacia & Cohon, Rhody. Sacagawea's Strength. Wenzel, David T. & Wenzel, David, illus. 2006. (Blast to the Past Ser.: 5). (ENG.). 128p. (J). (gr. 2-5). pap. 9.99 *(978-1-4169-1270-5(3)*, Simon & Schuster/Paula Wiseman Bks.) Simon & Schuster/Paula Wiseman Bks.

Doyle, Bill. Trapped! The 2031 Journal of Otis Fitzmorgan. 6th ed. 2006. (ENG., Illus.). 144p. (J). (gr. 3-7). per. 16.99 *(978-0-316-05754-7(1))* Little, Brown Bks. for Young Readers.

Doyle, Bill H. Betrayed! The 1977 Journal of Zeke Moorie. 4th ed. 2006. (ENG., Illus.). 144p. (J). (gr. 3-7). per. 16.99 *(978-0-316-05741-7(X))* Little, Brown Bks. for Young Readers.

Flaherty, Mildred. The Great Saint Patrick's Day Flood. 2004. (Illus.). 104p. (J). pap. *(978-0-9711835-8-2(9))* Local History Co., The.

Fleming, Candace. Imogene's Last Stand. Carpenter, Nancy, illus. 2014. (ENG.). 40p. (J). (gr. -1-3). 7.99 *(978-0-385-38654-8(0)*, Dragonfly Bks.) Random Hse. Children's Bks.

Forbes, Esther Hoskins. Johnny Tremain. 2011. (ENG., Illus.). 320p. (J). (gr. 5-7). pap. 7.99 *(978-0-547-61432-8(2))* Houghton Mifflin Harcourt Publishing Co.

Furtney, Charles S. Tryconnel: An Antebellum Adventure along the C & O Canal. 2004. (Illus.). iii, 156p. (J). pap. *(978-0-9711835-3-7(8))* Local History Co., The.

Gaillard, Frye. Go South to Freedom. 2016. (ENG., Illus.). 72p. (J). 17.95 *(978-1-58838-316-7(4)*, NewSouth Bks.) NewSouth, Inc.

Gratz, Alan. The Brooklyn Nine. 2010. (ENG.). 320p. (J). (gr. 3-7). 8.99 *(978-0-14-241544-3(8)*, Puffin Books) Penguin Young Readers Group.

Gunderson, Jessica & Collins, Terry. American Graphic. Kinsella, Pat & Byers, Michael, illus. 2012. (American Graphic Ser.). (ENG.). 32p. (gr. 3-4). pap. 15.90 *(978-1-4296-9505-3(6))*; pap. 477.00 *(978-1-4296-8478-1(X))*; pap. 72.90 *(978-1-4296-8477-4(1))*; lib. bdg. 61.30 *(978-1-4296-8178-0(0))*; lib. bdg. 275.85 *(978-1-4296-8179-7(9))* Capstone Press of Coughlan Cos. (Graphic Library).

Haislip, Phyllis Hall. Divided Loyalties: A Revolutionary War Fifer's Story. 2005. (Illus.). 212p. (J). (gr. 4-7). per. 7.95 *(978-1-57249-369-8(0)*, White Mane Kids) White Mane Publishing Co., Inc.

Hancock, H. Irving. Uncle Sam's Boys with Pershing's Troops. 2006. 27.95 *(978-1-4218-2944-9(4))*; pap. 12.95 *(978-1-4218-3044-5(2))* 1st World Publishing, Inc.

Hayhurst, James L. The Adventures of Mercury Lane: Bad Commandments, Book No. 1. 2008. (Illus.). 212p. (YA). pap. 13.95 *(978-0-9729380-1-3(X)*, Parascension Pr.) Parascension, Inc.

Hayhurst/Parascension Press, James/Lyle. The Adventures of Mercury Lane: Bad Commandments, Book No.1. 2008. (Illus.). 212p. (YA). lib. bdg. 21.95 *(978-0-615-18212-4(7)*, Parascension Pr.) Parascension, Inc.

Hedstrom-Page, Deborah. From Settlement to City with Benjamin Franklin. Martinez, Sergio, illus. 2007. (My American Journey Ser.). 84p. (J). (gr. 3-9). 9.99 *(978-0-8054-3267-1(1))* B&H Publishing Group.

Heibel, Dorothy. Message for a Spy. 2004. (Illus.). 94p. (J). pap. *(978-1-932663-07-5(X))* History Compass, LLC.

Hemphill, Helen. The Adventurous Deeds of Deadwood Jones. 2008. (ENG.). 232p. (J). (gr. 5-18). 16.95 *(978-1-59078-637-6(8)*, Front Street) Boyds Mills Pr.

Hernandez, Natalie Nelson. Mapmakers of the Western Trails: Adventures with John Chrles Fremont, 3 bks. 2003. (Illus.).

130p. (J). per. 10.95 (978-1-885852-31-1(2)) James Stevenson Pub.

Hill, Joyce. A Penny in My Pocket. 2007. 220p. 27.95 (978-0-9795818-0-9(X)); pap. 14.95 (978-0-9795818-1-6(8)) Mushgush Pr.

History Speaks: Picture Books Plus Reader's Theater, 12 vols., Set. Incl. Alice Ray & the Salem Witch Trials. Knudsen, Shannon. Palmer, Ruth, illus. 2011. 27.93 (978-0-7613-5879-4(X)); Annie Shapiro & the Clothing Workers' Strike. Brill, Marlene Targ. Akib, Jamel, illus. 2010. lib. bdg. 27.93 (978-1-58013-672-3(9)); Benjamin Brown & the Great Steamboat Race. Jordan, Shirley. Chayka, Doug & Kemly, Kathleen, illus. 2011. lib. bdg. 27.93 (978-1-58013-674-7(5)); Clara Morgan & the Oregon Trail Journey. Figley, Marthy Rhodes. Orback, Craig, illus. 2011. 27.93 (978-0-7613-5878-7(1)); Ellen Craft's Escape from Slavery. Moore, Cathy. Braught, Mark, illus. 2010. lib. bdg. 27.93 (978-0-7613-5875-6(7)); Enrique Esparza & the Battle of the Alamo. Brown, Susan Taylor. Reeves, Jeni, illus. 2010. lib. bdg. 27.93 (978-0-8225-8566-4(9)); George Washington & the Story of the U. S. Constitution. Ransom, Candice. Reeves, Jeni, illus. 2011. 27.93 (978-0-7613-5877-0(3)); John Greenwood's Journey to Bunker Hill. Figley, Marty Rhodes. Orback, Craig, illus. 2010. lib. bdg. 27.93 (978-1-58013-673-0(7)); Johnny Moore & the Wright Brothers' Flying Machine. Schulz, Walter A. Bowles, Doug, illus. 2011. lib. bdg. 27.93 (978-0-7613-5876-3(5)); Little Rock Nine Stand up for Their Rights. Lucas, Eileen. Gustavson, Adam, illus. 2011. lib. bdg. 27.93 (978-0-7613-5874-9(9)); Lizzie Newton & the San Francisco Earthquake. Krensky, Stephen. Tugeau, Jeremy, illus. 2010. lib. bdg. 27.93 (978-0-8225-9031-6(X)); 48p. (gr. 2-4)., Millbrook Pr. 2011. Set lib. bdg. 335.16 (978-0-7613-5100-9(0)) Lerner Publishing Group.

Hoobler, Dorothy & Hoobler, Thomas. The Century Kids, 10 vols. Hoffman, Robin, illus. Incl. 1940s: Secrets. (J). 2001. lib. bdg. 22.90 (978-0-7613-1604-6(3)); 1950's: Music. (J). 2001. lib. bdg. 22.90 (978-0-7613-1605-3(1)); 1960's: Rebels. (J). 2001. lib. bdg. 22.90 (978-0-7613-1606-0(X)); 1970's: Arguments. 2002. lib. bdg. 22.90 (978-0-7613-1607-7(8)); 1980s: Earthsong. 2002. lib. bdg. 22.90 (978-0-7613-1608-4(6)); 1990s: Families. 2002. lib. bdg. 22.90 (978-0-7613-1609-1(4)); 160p. (gr. 5-8). (Illus.). 2004. 229.00 (978-0-7613-2985-5(4), Twenty-First Century Bks.) Lerner Publishing Group.

Hughes, Barbara. Then & Now. (Livewire Ser.). 192p. (YA). (gr. 6-9). pap. 8.95 (978-0-7043-4930-8(2)) Women's Pr., Ltd., The GBR. Dist: Trafalgar Square Publishing.

Hunt, Wayne. Zack & the Validators: Good As Gold. 2011. 138p. pap. 19.99 (978-1-4653-5816-5(1)) Xlibris Corp.

Igneri, David S. The Boy & Girl Who Hated History. Wigley, Audrey Watson, illus. 2009. 44p. pap. 24.95 (978-1-61546-828-7(5)) America Star Bks.

Ingold, Jeanette. Hitch. 2006. (ENG., Illus.). 288p. (YA). (gr. 7-12). pap. 7.99 (978-0-15-205619-3(X)) Houghton Mifflin Harcourt Publishing Co.

Kennedy Center Staff. Chasing George Washington. Hoyt, Ard, illus. 2011. (ENG.). 80p. (J). (gr. 2-5). pap. 5.99 (978-1-4169-4861-2(9), Simon & Schuster Bks. For Young Readers) Simon & Schuster Bks. For Young Readers.

Kinsey-Warnock, Natalie. Gifts from the Sea. Pederson, Judy, illus. 2005. (ENG.). 128p. (J). (gr. 3-7). 5.99 (978-0-440-41970-9(0), Yearling) Random Hse. Children's Bks.

Krull, Kathleen. Hillary Rodham Clinton: Dreams Taking Flight. Bates, Amy June, illus. 2015. (ENG.). 48p. (J). (gr. k-5). 17.99 (978-1-4814-5113-0(8), Simon & Schuster Bks. For Young Readers) Simon & Schuster Bks. For Young Readers.

Larson, Kirby. Duke. 2013. (Dogs of World War II Ser.). (ENG.). 240p. (J). (gr. 3-7). 16.99 (978-0-545-41637-5(X), Scholastic Pr.) Scholastic, Inc.

Lefevre-Garros. The Wright Brothers. 2009. (ENG., Illus.). 48p. pap. 11.95 (978-1-905460-73-1(2)) CineBook GBR. Dist: National Bk. Network.

MacColl, Michaela. Lost Ones. 2016. (Hidden Histories Ser.). (ENG.). 256p. (J). (gr. 3-7). 17.95 (978-1-62091-625-4(8), Calkins Creek) Boyds Mills Pr.

Marlow, Susan K. Andi under the Big Top, 1 vol. 2017. (Circle C Stepping Stones Ser.: 2). (J). pap. 7.99 **(978-0-8254-4431-9(4))** Kregel Pubns.

Maxson, H. A. & Young, Claudia H. Tea Party at Chestertown. Kosits, Andrew, illus. 2003. (Magical History Tours Ser.). 55p. (J). per. 8.95 (978-0-9741713-0-2(1)) Bay Oak Pubs., Ltd.

Michelson, Richard. Across the Alley. Lewis, E. B., illus. 2006. (ENG.). 32p. (J). (gr. -1-3). 16.99 (978-0-399-23970-0(7), G.P. Putnam's Sons Books for Young Readers) Penguin Young Readers Group.

Minor, Wendell. How Big Could Your Pumpkin Grow? Minor, Wendell, illus. 2013. (ENG., Illus.). 32p. (J). (gr. -1-k). 16.99 (978-0-399-24684-5(3), Nancy Paulsen Books) Penguin Young Readers Group.

Morse, William A. and & Morse, William A. And Dana Jo. Kurkle Kids: Spirit of America. 2009. 44p. pap. 16.99 (978-1-4490-1009-6(1)) AuthorHouse.

National Children's Book and Literacy Alliance Staff. Our White House: Looking in, Looking Out. 2008. (ENG., Illus.). 256p. (J). (gr. 5). 29.99 (978-0-7636-2067-7(X)) Candlewick Pr.

Nicodemus, Laura Konger. Growing up on the Farm in The 1930s' 2011. 60p. pap. 24.20 (978-1-4269-3201-4(4)) Trafford Publishing.

Parton, Paula. Room 17 Where History Comes Alive Book I—Indians. Parton, Paula, illus. 2007. (Illus.). 128p. per. 8.95 (978-0-9794815-0-5(3)) Bellissima Publishing, LLC.

—Room 17 Where History Comes Alive! Book I-Indians. Parton, Paua, illus. 2007. 128p. 19.95 (978-0-9794815-2-9(X)) Bellissima Publishing, LLC.

Pearsall, Shelley. Jump into the Sky. 2013. (ENG.). 352p. (J). (gr. 4-7). pap. 7.99 (978-0-440-42140-5(3), Yearling) Random Hse. Children's Bks.

Pinkney, Andrea Davis. Sojourner Truth's Step-Stomp Stride. Pinkney, Brian, illus. 2009. (ENG.). 32p. (J). (gr. k-4). 16.99 (978-0-7868-0767-3(9), Jump at the Sun) Hyperion Bks. for Children.

Polisar, Barry Louis. Stolen Man: The Story of the Amistad Rebellion. 2007. (ENG.). 32p. (J). (gr. 4-7). per. 7.95 (978-0-938663-50-8(X)) Rainbow Morning Music Alternatives.

Rack, Charlene. The Adventures of Delaware Bear & Young George Washington. 2011. 24p. (gr. 1-2). pap. 12.79 (978-1-4567-5681-9(8)) AuthorHouse.

Richards, J. Stuart. Hard Coal Times, Volume Two: Mules, Drivers & Spraggers, 2. 2003. (Illus.). 44p. (YA). 5.95 (978-0-9709630-3-1(3)) Coal Hole Productions.

Riley, D. H. The Mysterians, 1 vol. 2009. 54p. pap. 16.95 (978-1-60836-374-2(0)) America Star Bks.

Rubay, Donnell. Emma & the Oyster Pirate. 2011. 172p. pap. 13.95 (978-1-885852-52-6(5)) James Stevenson Pub.

Sargent, Dave & Sargent, Pat. Freckles: (Flea-bitten Grey) Be Proud of Old Glory, 30 vols., Vol. 26. Lenoir, Jane, illus. 2003. (Saddle up Ser.: Vol. 26). 42p. (J). pap. 10.95 (978-1-56763-810-3(4)); lib. bdg. 23.60 (978-1-56763-809-7(0)) Ozark Publishing.

Sipperley, Keli. Doughnuts with Francis Scott Key. 2016. (Time Hop Sweets Shop Ser.). (ENG.). 32p. (gr. k-3). 25.65 (978-1-68191-377-3(1)) Rourke Educational Media.

Slanina, Anne Maro. Annie Mouse's Route 66 Adventure: A Photo Journal, vols. 6, vol. 5. Collins, Kelsey, illus. 2011. (ENG.). 48p. (J). pap. 14.99 (978-0-9793379-6-3(8)) Annie Mouse Bks.

Steinkraus, Kyla. Apple Pie with Amelia Earhart. 2016. (Time Hop Sweets Shop Ser.). (ENG.). 32p. (gr. k-3). 25.65 (978-1-68191-369-8(0)) Rourke Educational Media.

—Cookies with Clara Barton. 2016. (Time Hop Sweets Shop Ser.). (ENG.). 32p. (gr. k-3). 25.65 (978-1-68191-370-4(4)) Rourke Educational Media.

Stiles, Martha Bennett. Sailing to Freedom. 2014. (ENG.). 256p. (J). (gr. 3-7). pap. 6.99 (978-1-250-03991-0(6), 9781250039910) Square Fish.

Stockton, Frank Richard. John Gayther's Garden & the Stories Told Therein. 2008. 220p. pap. 15.95 (978-1-60664-247-4(2)) Rodgers, Alan Bks.

Stone, Phoebe. The Romeo & Juliet Code. 2012. (ENG.). 320p. (J). (gr. 3-7). pap. 7.99 (978-0-545-21827-6(6), Levine, Arthur A. Bks.) Scholastic, Inc.

Sun Edit and Book Design, ed. Abraham Lincoln & the Forest of Little Pigeon Creek. 2007. (Illus.). 56p. (J). 19.95 (978-0-9798739-0-4(8)) AmeriTales Entertainment, LLC.

Uchilla, Canchi. 1532: A Test of Courage. 2008. 108p. pap. 10.00 (978-0-9769989-5-2(5)) Edit et Cetera Ltd.

Vail, Emily Blake. The Search for Ole Ben's Treasure. 2011. 82p. 24.99 (978-1-4568-9874-8(4)); pap. 15.99 (978-1-4568-9873-1(6)) Xlibris Corp.

Varonka, Steve. Hard Coal Times: Pennsylvania Anthracite Stories, Vol. 1. 2003. (Illus.). 40p. (J). 4.72 (978-0-9709630-2-4(5)) Coal Hole Productions.

Walters, Scott. Woman Too Young of Panther Cave. 2007. 20.95 (978-1-934248-14-0(2)) Salem Author Services.

Weigman, Matthew. Liberty's Journey: The Story of Our Freedom. Eve, Lealand, illus. 2004. 31p. (J). 16.95 (978-0-9747981-0-3(X)) Fahnestock Pr.

Whitby, Adele. Kay's Story 1934. 2015. (Secrets of the Manor Ser.: 6). lib. bdg. 17.20 (978-0-606-36305-1(X)) Turtleback Bks.

Wiggin, Kate Douglas. New Chronicles of Rebecc. 2008. 152p. (gr. 4-7). 24.95 (978-1-60664-756-1(3)) Rodgers, Alan Bks.

Winfield, Arthur M. Rover Boys at School. 2006. pap. (978-1-4068-3129-0(8)) Echo Library.

Yolen, Jane. Naming Liberty. Burke, Jim, illus. 2008. (ENG.). 32p. (J). (gr. 1-4). 16.99 (978-0-399-24250-2(3), Philomel Bks.) Penguin Young Readers Group.

UNITED STATES—HISTORY, LOCAL

Benchmark Education Company, LLC Staff, compiled by. This State Is Mine & State HIST. 2005. spiral bd. 110.00 (978-1-4108-5817-7(0)) Benchmark Education Co.

Gillis, Jennifer Blizin. Restored Villages. 2007. (Field Trips Ser.). (Illus.). 24p. (J). (gr. 2-5). lib. bdg. 27.07 (978-1-60044-563-7(2)) Rourke Educational Media.

Herman, Debbie. From Pie Town to Yum Yum: Weird & Wacky Place Names Across the United States. Goldman, Linda Sarah, illus. 2011. (ENG.). 120p. (J). pap. 10.99 (978-1-935279-79-2(3)) Kane Miller.

Hurtig, Jennifer. Capitals. 2008. (U. S. Sites & Symbols Ser.). (Illus.). 48p. (J). (gr. 3-5). lib. bdg. 29.05 (978-1-59036-896-1(7)); (gr. 4-6). pap. 10.95 (978-1-59036-897-8(5)) Weigl Pubs., Inc.

Prior, Jennifer. America's Man-Made Landmarks. rev. ed. 2014. (Primary Source Readers Content & Literacy Ser.). (ENG., Illus.). 32p. (gr. 3-3). pap. 8.99 (978-1-4333-7370-1(X)) Teacher Created Materials, Inc.

Putnam, Jeff. National Monuments: Events & Times. 2004. (ZB Reads Trio Books). (Illus.). iii, 75p. (gr. 4-6). pap. 5.00 (978-0-7367-1787-8(0)) Zaner-Bloser, Inc.

Stuckey, Rachel. Women in the West. 2015. (True History of the Wild West Ser.). (ENG., Illus.). 32p. (J). (gr. 5-5). pap. 10.00 (978-1-4994-1181-2(2), 1391528, PowerKids Pr.) Rosen Publishing Group, Inc., The.

UNITED STATES—HISTORY, MILITARY

ABDO Publishing Company Staff. Essential Library of the US Military. 2014. (Essential Library of the US Military Ser.: 6). (ENG.). 112p. (J). (gr. 6-12). lib. bdg. 213.84 (978-1-62403-431-2(4), Essential Library) ABDO Publishing Co.

America at War, 5 vols., Set. Incl. American Civil War & Reconstruction: People, Politics, & Power. Wallenfeldt, Jeffrey H., ed. 264p. lib. bdg. 49.00 (978-1-61530-007-5(4)); American Revolutionary War & the War of 1812: People, Politics, & Power. Wallenfeldt, Jeffrey H. 240p. lib. bdg. 49.00 (978-1-61530-022-8(8)); Korean War & the Vietnam War: People, Politics, & Power. Hosch, William L. 232p. lib. bdg. 49.00 (978-1-61530-011-2(2)); World War I: People, Politics, & Power. Hosch, William L., ed. 240p. lib. bdg. 49.00 (978-1-61530-013-6(9)); World War II: People, Politics, & Power. Hosch, William L. 264p. lib. bdg. 49.00 (978-1-61530-008-2(2)); (YA). (gr. 9-12). (America at War Ser.). (Illus.). 264p. 2009. Set lib. bdg. 245.00 (978-1-61530-030-3(9)) Rosen Publishing Group, Inc., The.

Ammon, Richard. Valley Forge. Farnsworth, Bill, illus. 2006. (ENG.). 32p. (J). (gr. 1-5). 6.95 (978-0-8234-2016-2(7)) Holiday Hse., Inc.

Anderson, Dale. The Civil War in the East (1861-July 1863) 2004. (World Almanac Library of the Civil War). (Illus.). 48p. (gr. 5-12). pap. 14.05 (978-0-8368-5591-3(4)); lib. bdg. 31.00 (978-0-8368-5582-1(5)) Stevens, Gareth Publishing LLLP. (Gareth Stevens Secondary Library).

Asselin, Kristine Carlson. The Real Story on the Weapons & Battles of Colonial America, 1 vol. 2012. (Life in the American Colonies Ser.). (ENG.). 32p. (gr. 3-4). 27.32 (978-1-4296-6491-2(6)); pap. 8.10 (978-1-4296-7985-5(9)); pap. 47.70 (978-1-4296-8462-0(3)) Capstone Press of Coughlan Cos. (Fact Finders).

Benge, Janet & Benge, Geoff. Heroes of History - Douglas MacArthur: What Greater Honor. 2005. (ENG., Illus.). 205p. (YA). pap. 9.99 (978-1-932096-15-6(9)) Emerald Bks.

Bowman, John S. Chronology of Wars. 2nd rev. ed. 2010. (America at War Ser.). 304p. (gr. 6-12). 45.00 (978-0-8160-8193-6(X), Chelsea Hse.) Facts On File, Inc.

Burgan, Michael. The Battle of Bunker Hill: An Interactive History Adventure. 2016. (You Choose: History Ser.). (ENG.). 112p. (gr. 3-4). pap. 6.95 (978-1-5157-3387-4(4), You Choose Bks.) Capstone Press of Coughlan Cos.

Cheatham, Mark. The Life of a Colonial Soldier. 2013. (Jr. Graphic Colonial America Ser.). (ENG., Illus.). 24p. (J). (gr. 3-6). pap. 10.60 (978-1-4777-1439-3(1)); lib. bdg. 25.25 (978-1-4777-1310-5(7)) Rosen Publishing Group, Inc., The. (PowerKids Pr.).

Daniel Fernandez Memorial Center Projec. Man of Honor: The Story of Daniel Fernandez. 2009. 32p. pap. 15.49 (978-1-4389-8338-7(7)) AuthorHouse.

Donelly, Karen. American Women Pilots of World War II. 2009. 112p. (YA). (gr. 7-12). pap. 12.95 (978-1-4358-3274-9(4)) Rosen Publishing Group, Inc., The.

The G. I. Series: The Illustrated History of the American Soldier, His Uniform, & His Equipment, 21. 2005. (G. I. Ser.). 84p. (gr. 6-12). 495.00 (978-0-7910-8077-1(3), Chelsea Hse.) Facts On File, Inc.

Gallagher, Jim. US-Led Wars in Iraq, 1991-Present, Vol. 11. Musteen, Jason R., ed. 2015. (Major U. S. Historical Wars Ser.). (Illus.). 64p. (J). (gr. 7). lib. bdg. 23.95 (978-1-4222-3358-0(8)) Mason Crest.

Gitlin, Martin. George S. Patton: World War II General & Military Innovator, 1 vol. 2010. (Military Heroes Ser.). (ENG.). 112p. (J). (gr. 6-12). lib. bdg. 35.64 (978-1-60453-964-6(X)) ABDO Publishing Co.

Gonzales, Doreen. The Secret of the Manhattan Project: Stories in American History. 2012. (Stories in American History Ser.). (Illus.). 128p. (J). (gr. 5-18). pap. 10.95 (978-1-4644-0024-7(5)) Enslow Pubs., Inc.

Hamilton, John. Humvees. 2011. (Military Vehicles Ser.). (Illus.). 32p. (YA). (gr. 4-7). 27.07 (978-1-61783-076-1(3)) ABDO Publishing Co.

Hogue, Richard, Sr. We Were the Third Herd. 2003. per. 17.95 (978-0-9722264-0-0(0)) Richlyn Publishing.

Honders, Christine. Buffalo Soldiers. 2015. (Heroes of Black History Ser.). (ENG., Illus.). 32p. (J). (gr. 3-4). pap. 10.50 (978-1-4824-2900-8(4)) Stevens, Gareth Publishing LLLP.

Janeczko, Paul B. The Dark Game: True Spy Stories from Invisible Ink to CIA Moles. 2012. (ENG.). 256p. (YA). (gr. 5-9). pap. 9.99 (978-0-7636-6066-6(3)) Candlewick Pr.

Keeter, Hunter. American Ground Forces in the Vietnam War. 2005. (American Experience in Vietnam Ser.). (Illus.). 48p. (gr. 5-12). lib. bdg. 31.00 (978-0-8368-5774-0(7), Gareth Stevens Secondary Library) Stevens, Gareth Publishing LLLP.

Krick, Robert K. The Civil War: Gettysburg & Other Eastern Battles, 1863-1865. 2010. (Civil War: Essential Histories Ser.). (ENG.). 96p. (YA). lib. bdg. 33.25 (978-1-4488-0388-0(8)) Rosen Publishing Group, Inc., The.

The Life of a Colonial Soldier. 2013. (Jr. Graphic Colonial America Ser.). 24p. (J). (gr. 3-6). pap. 63.60 (978-1-4777-1440-9(5), PowerKids Pr.) Rosen Publishing Group, Inc., The.

Looney, Michael. Battle of the Bulge Vol. III: The Untold Story of Hofen. 2005. 179p. 29.95 (978-0-9700567-4-0(5)) Victory WW 2 Publishing Ltd.

Lusted, Marcia Amidon. African Americans in the Military. 2012. (J). pap. (978-1-4222-2392-5(2)) Mason Crest.

—African Americans in the Military. Hill, Marc Lamont, ed. 2012. (Major Black Contributions from Emancipation to Civil Rights Ser.). 64p. (J). (gr. 5). 22.95 (978-1-4222-2379-6(5)) Mason Crest.

McPherson, Stephanie Sammartino. Douglas MacArthur. 2005. (History Maker Bios Ser.). (Illus.). 48p. (J). 26.60 (978-0-8225-2434-2(1)) Lerner Publishing Group.

Micklos, John. Washington's Crossing the Delaware & the Winter at Valley Forge: Through Primary Sources. 2013. (American Revolution Through Primary Sources Ser.). 48p. (J). (gr. 4-18). 25.27 (978-0-7660-4132-5(8)) Enslow Pubs., Inc.

O'Maley, Elizabeth. Bones on the Ground. 2014. (J). (978-0-87195-362-9(5)) Indiana Historical Society.

O'Neill, Robert John & Gallagher, Gary W. The Civil War: Bull Run & Other Eastern Battles, 1861-May 1863. 2010. (Civil War: Essential Histories Ser.). (ENG.). 96p. (YA). lib. bdg. 33.25 (978-1-4488-0387-3(X)) Rosen Publishing Group, Inc., The.

Orozco, Mike. The War-Time Paragons. 2011. 74p. pap. 15.99 (978-1-4535-8533-7(8)) Xlibris Corp.

Pugh, Harry F. & PERKOWSKI, Gary. U. S. Special Forces Group Insignia (Post 1975) 2004. (Elite Insignia Guides Ser.). (YA). pap. (978-0-9633231-8-7(0)) C&D Enterprises.

Raum, Elizabeth, et al. True War Stories: Personal Accounts of History's Greatest Conflicts. Kinsella, Pat et al, illus. 2017. (J). (978-1-4914-1965-6(2)) Capstone Press of Coughlan Cos.

Ross, Thomas A. Privileges of War: A Good Story of American Service in South Vietnam. 2004. (Illus.). 356p. 24.95 (978-0-9754859-0-3(3), 9005710) American Heritage Publishing.

Sabin, Edwin L. Boys' Book of Border Battles. 2013. (ENG., Illus.). 352p. pap. 14.95 (978-1-62087-158-4(0), 620158) Skyhorse Publishing Co., Inc.

Saddleback Educational Publishing Staff, ed. American History 1, 1 vol. 2013. (American History Ser.). (ENG.). 110p. (gr. 6-12). pap. 44.95 (978-1-62250-032-1(6)) Saddleback Educational Publishing, Inc.

—American History 2, 1 vol. 2013. (American History Ser.). (ENG.). 110p. (gr. 6-12). pap. 44.95 (978-1-62250-033-8(4)) Saddleback Educational Publishing, Inc.

Snyder, Sally. Hold the Fort. Snyder, Sally, illus. 2003. (Illus.). 45p. (J). 20.00 (978-1-882203-99-4(2)) Orange Frazer Pr.

Sorrels, Roy. The Legend of the Alamo: Stories in American History. 2012. (Stories in American History Ser.). (Illus.). 128p. (J). (gr. 5-18). pap. 10.95 (978-1-4644-0022-3(9)) Enslow Pubs., Inc.

Stanley, George E. George S. Patton: War Hero. Henderson, Meryl, illus. 2007. (Childhood of Famous Americans Ser.). (ENG.). 192p. (J). (gr. 3-7). pap. 6.99 (978-1-4169-1547-8(8), Simon & Schuster/Paula Wiseman Bks.) Simon & Schuster/Paula Wiseman Bks.

Stewart, Gail B. Fighting for Freedom: Blacks in the American Military. 2006. (Lucent Library of Black History Ser.). (ENG., Illus.). 104p. (J). (gr. 3-7). lib. bdg. 34.80 (978-1-59018-952-8(3), Lucent Bks.) Cengage Gale.

Strange, Matthew. America at War: Military Conflicts, Home & Abroad in the 1800s. 2009. (Daily Life in America in the 1800s Ser.). 64p. (YA). (gr. 7-18). lib. bdg. 22.95 (978-1-4222-1778-8(7)) Mason Crest.

Sutcliffe, Jane. George S. Patton JR. 2006. (History Maker Bios Ser.). (Illus.). 48p. (J). (gr. 3-7). lib. bdg. 26.60 (978-0-8225-2436-6(8), Lerner Pubns.) Lerner Publishing Group.

Taylor, Kathleen. Eddie & Bingo: A Friendship Tale. Taylor, Kathleen, illus. 2011. (Illus.). 42p. (J). pap. 21.95 (978-1-59299-558-5(6)) Inkwater Pr.

U. S. Military [Scholastic]. 2010. (Military Branches Ser.). pap. 2.08 (978-1-4296-5073-1(7), Pebble Plus) Capstone Press of Coughlan Cos.

The United States at War. 2016. (United States at War Ser.). 128p. (gr. 6-6). lib. bdg. 223.62 (978-0-7660-7501-6(X)) Enslow Pubs., Inc.

Welch, Catherine A. George C. Marshall. (History Maker Bios Ser.). 48p. (J). 2006. (Illus.). (gr. 3-7). lib. bdg. 26.60 (978-0-8225-2435-9(X), Lerner Pubns.) 2005. pap. 8.95 (978-0-8225-5460-8(7)) Lerner Publishing Group.

Wilson, Patrick. Survival First Aid. Carney, John, ed. 2014. (Extreme Survival in the Military Ser.: 12). (Illus.). 64p. (J). (gr. 7-18). lib. bdg. 23.95 (978-1-4222-3086-2(4)) Mason Crest.

Yasuda, Anita. The 12 Most Amazing American Battles. 2014. (ENG., Illus.). 32p. (J). (978-1-63235-006-0(8)) Pr. Room Editions LLC.

UNITED STATES—HISTORY, NAVAL

Baum, L. Frank. Navy Alphabet Book. 2004. (ENG., Illus.). 60p. (J). (gr. -1-3). per. 14.95 (978-1-55709-570-1(1)) Applewood Bks.

Blumberg, Rhoda. Commodore Perry in the Land of the Shogun. 2003. (ENG., Illus.). 144p. (J). (gr. 3-18). pap. 9.99 (978-0-06-008625-1(4)) HarperCollins Pubs.

—Commodore Perry in the Land of the Shogun. 2003. (Illus.). 144p. (gr. 3-7). 20.00 (978-0-7569-1440-0(X)) Perfection Learning Corp.

Hobbs, Richard R. Naval Science 2 2: Maritime History, Leadership, & Nautical Sciences for the NJROTC Student. 2nd ed. 2006. (ENG., Illus.). 360p. 34.95 (978-1-59114-366-6(7)) Naval Institute Pr.

Kevin, McDonald. Tin Can Sailors Save the Day. 2015. (J). pap. 10.95 (978-1-55571-786-5(1), Paloma Bks.) L & R Publishing, LLC.

Myers, Walter Dean. USS Constellation: Pride of the American Navy. 2004. (ENG., Illus.). 96p. (J). (gr. 4-6). tchr. ed. 16.95 (978-0-8234-1816-9(2)) Holiday Hse., Inc.

Thornton, Jeremy. The Birth of the American Navy. 2009. (Building America's Democracy Ser.). 24p. (gr. 3-3). 42.50 (978-1-61511-765-9(2), PowerKids Pr.) Rosen Publishing Group, Inc., The.

Wittner, David G. Commodore Matthew Perry & the Perry Expedition to Japan. 2009. (Library of American Lives & Times Ser.). 112p. (gr. 5-5). 69.20 (978-1-60853-474-6(X)) Rosen Publishing Group, Inc., The.

UNITED STATES—HISTORY—POETRY

Dyan, Penelope. Gold Rush! a Kid's Guide to Techatticup Gold Mine, Eldorado Canyon, Nevad. Weigand, John D., photos by. 2010. (Illus.). 48p. pap. 11.95 (978-1-935630-11-1(3)) Bellissima Publishing, LLC.

—Happy Birthday Usa! Dyan, Penelope, illus. 2010. (Illus.). 32p. pap. 11.95 (978-1-935630-15-9(6)) Bellissima Publishing, LLC.

Grady, Cynthia. I Lay My Stitches Down. Wood, Michele, illus. 2012. (ENG.). 34p. (YA). 17.00 (978-0-8028-5386-8(2), Eerdmans Bks For Young Readers) Eerdmans, William B. Publishing Co.

Hopkins, Lee Bennett, ed. America at War. Alcorn, Stephen, illus. 2008. (ENG.). 96p. (J). (gr. 3-7). 24.99 (978-1-4169-1832-5(9), McElderry, Margaret K. Bks.) McElderry, Margaret K. Bks.

Longfellow, Henry Wadsworth. Paul Revere's Ride: The Landlord's Tale. Santore, Charles, illus. 2003. 40p. (J). lib. bdg. 17.89 (978-0-06-623747-3(5)) HarperCollins Pubs.

Voorhees, Sue. I'm Your Very Own Flag. 2006. (J). per. 12.50 (978-0-9764167-4-6(3)) Old Soldier Publishing.

UNITED STATES—HISTORY, POLITICAL

see United States—Politics and Government

UNITED STATES—HISTORY—SOURCES

Colonial Life: Exploration & Settlement - Cities & Town - Daily Living - Government - Trade & Commerce, 5 bks., Set. Incl. Cities & Towns. Stefoff, Rebecca. 96p. lib. bdg. 140.00 (978-0-7656-8109-6(9), Y181735); Daily Living. Hinds, Kathryn. 96p. lib. bdg. 158.00 (978-0-7656-8110-2(2), Y181908); Exploration & Settlement. Stefoff, Rebecca. 96p. lib. bdg. 158.00 (978-0-7656-8108-9(0), Y182272); Government. Kelly, Martin & Kelly, Melissa. 96p. lib. bdg. 158.00 (978-0-7656-8112-6(9), Y182476); Trade & Commerce. Altman, Linda Jacobs. 98p. lib. bdg. 175.00 (978-0-7656-8111-9(0), Y184849); (C). (gr. 6-18). (ENG., Illus.). 96p. 2007. Set lib. bdg. 140.00 (978-0-7656-8107-2(2), Y181691) Routledge.

Flanagan, Timothy. Reconstruction: A Primary Source History of the Struggle to Unite the North & South after the Civil War. 2005. (Primary Sources in American History Ser.). (Illus.). 64p. (J). (gr. 5-8). lib. bdg. 31.95 (978-1-4042-0177-4(7)) Rosen Publishing Group, Inc., The.

Hakim, Joy. All the People. 2nd rev. ed. 2007. (History of US Ser.: 11). (ENG., Illus.). 352p. (gr. 4-7). per. 15.95 (978-0-19-532725-0(X)) Oxford Univ. Pr., Inc.

Primary Sources in American History Set 4. 2005. (Illus.). 64p. (gr. 5-8). lib. bdg. 175.50 *(978-1-4042-0351-8(6))* Rosen Publishing Group, Inc., The.

Primary Sources of Life in the New American Nation. 2004. (Primary Source Big Bookstm Ser.). (ENG.). 24p. (gr. 4-8). 43.95 *(978-0-8239-4602-0(9))* Rosen Publishing Group, Inc., The.

Scholastic, Inc. Staff & Keenan, Sheila. O, Say Can You See? America's Symbols, Landmarks, & Important Words. Boyajian, Ann, illus. 2007. (ENG.). 64p. (J). (gr. -1-3). pap. 6.99 *(978-0-439-59360-1(3)*, Scholastic Nonfiction) Scholastic, Inc.

Stites, Bill. Democracy: A Primary Source Analysis. 2003. (Primary Sources of Political Systems Ser.). (Illus.). 64p. (YA). (gr. 5-9). lib. bdg. 31.95 *(978-0-8239-4518-4(9))* Rosen Publishing Group, Inc., The.

Tait, Leia. Primary Sources. 2007. (Social Studies Essential Skills Ser.). (Illus.). 24p. (J). lib. bdg. 24.45 *(978-1-59036-763-6(4))*; (gr. 4-7). per. 8.95 *(978-1-59036-764-3(2))* Weigl Pubs., Inc.

UNITED STATES—HISTORY—COLONIAL PERIOD, CA. 1600-1775

see also Pilgrims (New Plymouth Colony); United States—History—French and Indian War, 1755-1763

Alexander, Richard. The Colony of Connecticut. 2015. (Spotlight on the 13 Colonies Ser.). (ENG., Illus.). 24p. (J). (gr. 4-5). pap. 8.25 *(978-1-4994-0314-5(3)*, PowerKids Pr.) Rosen Publishing Group, Inc., The.

Altman, Linda Jacobs. Trade & Commerce. 2007. (ENG., Illus.). 98p. (C). (gr. 6-18). lib. bdg. 175.00 *(978-0-7656-8111-9(0)*, Y184849) Routledge.

Appleby, Joyce, et al. The American Republic to 1877. 2003. (Illus.). 670p. stu. ed. 122.75 *(978-0-07-826474-0(X))* McGraw-Hill Cos., The.

Archaeology of Early Colonial Life: Grades 4-9. (Teaching with Primary Sources Ser.). (J). tchr. ed., ring bd. 28.95 *(978-0-382-44366-4(7))* Cobblestone Publishing Co.

Arnéz, Lynda. My Life in the American Colonies. 2016. (My Place in History Ser.). (ENG., Illus.). 24p. (J). (gr. 2-3). pap. 8.15 *(978-1-4824-3992-2(1))* Stevens, Gareth Publishing LLLP.

Aronson, Marc. Witch-Hunt: Mysteries of the Salem Witch Trials. Anderson, Stephanie, illus. 2005. (ENG.). 288p. (YA). (gr. 7). reprint ed. pap. 11.99 *(978-1-4169-0315-4(1)*, Atheneum Bks. for Young Readers) Simon & Schuster Children's Publishing.

Asselin, Kristine Carlson. The Real Story on the Weapons & Battles of Colonial America, 1 vol. 2012. (Life in the American Colonies Ser.). (ENG.). 32p. (gr. 3-4). 27.32 *(978-1-4296-6491-2(6))*; pap. 47.70 *(978-1-4296-8462-0(3))*; pap. 8.10 *(978-1-4296-7985-5(9))* Capstone Press of Coughlan Cos. (Fact Finders).

Athan, Polly, et al. Felicity's Cooking Studio. Mahal, Susan, illus. 2007. (American Girl Ser.). 55p. (J). (gr. 3-7). 15.95 *(978-1-59369-266-7(8))* American Girl Publishing, Inc.

Axelrod-Contrada, Joan. A Historical Atlas of Colonial America. (United States: Historical Atlases of the Growth of a New Nation Ser.). 64p. 2009. (gr. 5-5). 61.20 *(978-1-60854-251-2(3))* 2005. (Illus.). (J). (gr. 7-12). lib. bdg. 31.95 *(978-1-4042-0200-9(5))* Rosen Publishing Group, Inc., The.

—A Primary Source History of the Colony of Rhode Island. 2006. (Primary Sources of the Thirteen Colonies & the Lost Colony Ser.). (Illus.). 64p. (YA). (gr. 4-7). lib. bdg. 31.95 *(978-1-4042-0434-8(2))* Rosen Publishing Group, Inc., The.

Beck, Glenn. Book of American Heroes. Ajhar, Brian, illus. 2011. (ENG.). 276p. (J). 19.99 *(978-1-4424-2332-9(3)*, Simon & Schuster/Paula Wiseman Bks.) Simon & Schuster/Paula Wiseman Bks.

Benchmark Education Company. The Thirteen Colonies (Teacher Guide) 2005. *(978-1-4108-4667-9(9))* Benchmark Education Co.

Benoit, Peter. The British Colonies in North America. 2013. (Cornerstones of Freedom™, Third Ser.). (ENG., Illus.). 64p. (J). pap. 8.95 *(978-0-531-21960-7(7))*; lib. bdg. 30.00 *(978-0-531-23602-4(1))* Scholastic Library Publishing.

Bjornlund, Lydia D. Women in Colonial America. 2003. (Women in History Ser.). (ENG., Illus.). 112p. (J). 33.45 *(978-1-59018-470-7(X)*, Lucent Bks.) Cengage Gale.

Bodden, Valerie. The Declaration of American Independence. 2009. (Days of Change Ser.). (Illus.). 48p. (YA). (gr. 4-7). 22.95 *(978-1-58341-733-1(8))* Creative Co., The.

Bordessa, Kris. Great Colonial America Projects: You Can Build Yourself! 2006. (Build It Yourself Ser.). (ENG., Illus.). 128p. (J). (gr. 3-7). pap. 15.95 *(978-0-9771294-0-9(3))* Northern Trails Pr.

Brannon, Barbara. Discover the Thirteen Colonies. 2005. (J). pap. *(978-1-4108-5156-7(7))* Benchmark Education Co.

Branse, J. L. A Day in the Life of a Colonial Sea Captain. 2009. (Library of Living & Working in Colonial Times Ser.). 24p. (gr. 3-3). 42.50 *(978-1-60853-737-2(4)*, PowerKids Pr.) Rosen Publishing Group, Inc., The.

Buckley, James. Who Was Blackbeard? 2015. (Who Was... ? Ser.). lib. bdg. 16.00 *(978-0-606-37556-6(2))* Turtleback Bks.

Buckley, James & dePaola, Tomie. Who Was Blackbeard? Harrison, Nancy & Qiu, Joseph J. M. , illus. 2015. (Who Was? Ser.). (ENG.). 112p. (J). (gr. 3-7). 5.99 *(978-0-448-48308-5(4)*, Grosset & Dunlap) Penguin Young Readers Group.

Burgan, Michael. The Carpenter. 2013. 48p. (J). (gr. 4-8). 29.93 *(978-1-60870-411-8(4))* Cavendish Square Publishing.

Burt, Barbara & Schifini, Alfredo. Colonial Life. 2007. (Avenues Ser.). (ENG., Illus.). 40p. (J). pap. 19.95 *(978-0-7922-8678-3(2))* CENGAGE Learning.

Capaccio, George. The Countryside. 2014. (Life in Colonial America Ser.). (Illus.). 80p. (J). (gr. 6-8). lib. bdg. 35.64 *(978-1-62712-885-8(9))* Cavendish Square Publishing.

Carlisle, Rodney P. & Golson, J. Geoffrey, eds. Turning Points-Actual & Alternate Histories: Colonial America from Settlement to the Revolution, 1 vol. 2006. (Turning Points-Actual & Alternate Histories Ser.). (Illus.). 266p. (C). 94.00 *(978-1-85109-827-9(5)*, TPHCAM1C) ABC-CLIO, LLC.

Clark, Willow. The True Story of the Declaration of Independence. 2013. (What Really Happened? Ser.). (ENG., Illus.). 24p. (J). (gr. 3-6). pap. 8.25 *(978-1-4488-9840-4(4))*; lib. bdg. 22.60 *(978-1-4488-9691-2(6))* Rosen Publishing Group, Inc., The. (PowerKids Pr.).

Colligan, L. H. The City. 2014. (J). pap. *(978-1-62712-883-4(2))*; 80p. (YA). (gr. 6-8). lib. bdg. 35.64 *(978-1-62712-882-7(4))* Cavendish Square Publishing.

Colonial America, 1543-1763. 2010. (Discovering U. S. History Ser.). (Illus.). 136p. (gr. 5-8). 35.00 *(978-1-60413-349-3(X)*, Chelsea Hse.) Facts On File, Inc.

Colonial Leaders. 2005. (Colonial Leaders Ser.). 80p. (gr. 5-8). 275.00 *(978-0-7910-6279-1(1)*, Chelsea Hse.) Facts On File, Inc.

Colonial Life: Exploration & Settlement - Cities & Town - Daily Living - Government - Trade & Commerce, 5 bks., Set. Incl. Cities & Towns. Stefoff, Rebecca. 96p. lib. bdg. 140.00 *(978-0-7656-8109-6(9)*, Y181735); Daily Living. Hinds, Kathryn. 96p. lib. bdg. 158.00 *(978-0-7656-8110-2(2)*, Y181908); Exploration & Settlement. Stefoff, Rebecca. 96p. lib. bdg. 158.00 *(978-0-7656-8108-9(0)*, Y182272); Government. Kelly, Martin & Kelly, Melissa. 96p. lib. bdg. 158.00 *(978-0-7656-8112-6(9)*, Y182476); Trade & Commerce. Altman, Linda Jacobs. 98p. lib. bdg. 175.00 *(978-0-7656-8111-9(0)*, Y184849); (C). (gr. 6-18). (ENG., Illus.). 96p. 2007. Set lib. bdg. 140.00 *(978-0-7656-8107-2(2)*, Y181691) Routledge.

Connell, Kate. The Thirteen Colonies. 2006. (Language, Literacy, & Vocabulary - Reading Expeditions Ser.). (ENG., Illus.). 36p. (J). pap. 18.95 *(978-0-7922-5453-9(8))* CENGAGE Learning.

Cook, Peter. You Wouldn't Want to Be at the Boston Tea Party! Wharf Water You'd Rather Not Drink. Antram, David, illus. 2013. (ENG.). (J). 32p. 29.00 *(978-0-531-27105-6(6))*; 40p. pap. 9.95 *(978-0-531-23856-1(3))* Scholastic Library Publishing. (Watts, Franklin).

Cooke, Tim. Blackbeard: A Notorious Pirate in the Caribbean. 2016. (Wanted! Famous Outlaws Ser.). (ENG., Illus.). 48p. (J). (gr. 6-8). pap. 14.05 *(978-1-4824-4247-2(7))* Stevens, Gareth Publishing LLLP.

Cunningham, Kevin. The Delaware Colony. 2011. (True Bk Ser.). (ENG., Illus.). 48p. (J). pap. 6.95 *(978-0-531-26601-4(X))*; lib. bdg. 29.00 *(978-0-531-25388-5(0))* Scholastic Library Publishing. (Children's Pr.).

—The Georgia Colony. 2011. (True Bk Ser.). (ENG., Illus.). 48p. (J). pap. 6.95 *(978-0-531-26602-1(8))*; lib. bdg. 29.00 *(978-0-531-25389-2(9))* Scholastic Library Publishing. (Children's Pr.).

Dimartino, Catherine. Early American Alliances. 2005. (ENG., Illus.). 16p. (J). (gr. 5-5). pap. 7.47 net. *(978-0-328-14893-6(8)*, Scott Foresman) Pearson Schl.

Doherty, Craig A. & Doherty, Katherine M. New Hampshire. 2005. (Thirteen Colonies Ser.). (Illus.). 144p. (gr. 5-8). 35.00 *(978-0-8160-5411-4(8))* Facts On File, Inc.

—New Jersey, 13 vols. 2005. (Thirteen Colonies Ser.). (Illus.). 144p. (gr. 5-8). 35.00 *(978-0-8160-5408-4(8))* Facts On File, Inc.

Dosier, Susan. Colonial Cooking. 2016. (Exploring History Through Food Ser.). (ENG., Illus.). 32p. (gr. 3-4). lib. bdg. 27.32 *(978-1-5157-2356-1(9))* Capstone Press of Coughlan Cos.

Evan-Moor. History Pockets: Colonial America, Grades 4-6. 2003. (History Pockets Ser.). (ENG., Illus.). 96p. (J). (gr. 4-6). pap., suppl. ed. 14.99 *(978-1-55799-906-1(6)*, EMC 3709) Evan-Moor Educational Pubs.

Explore Colonial America. 2016. (Explore Colonial America Ser.). 48p. (gr. 5-4). pap. 70.20 *(978-0-7660-7986-1(4))*; lib. bdg. 167.58 *(978-0-7660-7498-9(6))* Enslow Pubs., Inc.

Fajardo, Anika. The Dish on Food & Farming in Colonial America. (Life in the American Colonies Ser.). (ENG.). 32p. (gr. 3-4). 2017. pap. 8.10 ***(978-1-5157-9748-7(1))*** 2011. pap. 8.10 *(978-1-4296-7217-7(X))* 2011. pap. 47.70 *(978-1-4296-7218-4(8))* Capstone Press of Coughlan Cos. (Fact Finders).

Fisher, Verna & Stone, Bryan. Explore Colonial America! 25 Great Projects, Activities, Experiments. 2009. (Explore Your World Ser.). (ENG., Illus.). 96p. (J). (gr. k-4). pap. 12.95 *(978-1-934670-37-8(5))* Octavio Publishing.

Forest, Christopher. The Rebellious Colonists & the Causes of the American Revolution. 2012. (Story of the American Revolution Ser.). (ENG.). 32p. (gr. 3-4). pap. 47.70 *(978-1-4296-9291-5(X)*, Fact Finders) Capstone Press of Coughlan Cos.

Fremon, David K. The Salem Witchcraft Trials in United States History. 2015. (In United States History Ser.). 96p. (J). (gr. 5-12). 27.94 *(978-0-7660-6340-2(2))* Enslow Pubs., Inc.

Fritz, Jean. The Lost Colony of Roanoke. Talbott, Hudson, illus. 2004. (ENG.). 64p. (J). (gr. 2-5). 18.99 *(978-0-399-24027-0(6)*, G.P. Putnam's Sons Books for Young Readers) Penguin Young Readers Group.

Garstecki, Julia. Life in Colonial America, 1 vol. 2014. (Daily Life in US History Ser.). (ENG., Illus.). 48p. (J). (gr. 3-6). lib. bdg. 32.79 *(978-1-62403-630-9(9))* ABDO Publishing Co.

George, Enzo. Colonial America. 2015. (J). lib. bdg. *(978-1-62713-485-9(9))*; (ENG.). 48p. (gr. 4-4). lib. bdg. 31.36 *(978-1-5026-0256-5(3))* Cavendish Square Publishing.

George, Lynn. What Do You Know about Colonial America? (20 Questions: History Ser.). 24p. 2009. (gr. 2-3). 42.50 *(978-1-60854-955-9(0)*, PowerKids Pr.) 2008. (Illus.). (J). (gr. 3-7). lib. bdg. 21.25 *(978-1-4042-4185-5(X))* Rosen Publishing Group, Inc., The.

Glencoe McGraw-Hill Staff, creator. The American Republic to 1877 Reading Essentials & Study Guide Student Workbook. 2nd ed. 2004. (U. S. History - the Early Years Ser.). (ENG., Illus.). 264p. (gr. 6-9). stu. ed., per. 12.80 *(978-0-07-865487-9(4)*, 0078654874) McGraw-Hill Higher Education.

Goddu, Krystyna Poray. A Primary Source History of U. S. Independence. 2015. (Primary Source History Ser.). (ENG.). 32p. (gr. 3-4). pap. 7.95 *(978-1-4914-1846-8(X))* Capstone Press of Coughlan Cos.

Hakim, Joy. From Colonies to Country, 1735-1791. 3rd rev. ed. 2006. (History of US Ser.: 3). (ENG., Illus.). 224p. (gr. 4-7). 24.95 *(978-0-19-518896-7(9))* Oxford Univ. Pr., Inc.

—Making Thirteen Colonies, 1600-1740. (History of US Ser.: 2). (ENG., Illus.). 192p. (gr. 4-7). 2nd rev. ed. 2007. per. 15.95 *(978-0-19-532716-8(0))* 3rd rev. ed. 2006. 24.95 *(978-0-19-518895-0(0))* Oxford Univ. Pr., Inc.

Hamen, Susan E. Thirteen Colonies, 1 vol. 2013. (Foundations of Our Nation Ser.). (ENG.). 48p. (J). (gr. 3-6). lib. bdg. 32.79 *(978-1-61783-712-8(1))* ABDO Publishing Co.

Harasymiw, M. Alexander. The British Colonies. 2011. (Story of America Ser.). (Illus.). 32p. (J). (gr. 4-6). pap. 10.50 *(978-1-4339-4765-0(X))*; lib. bdg. 26.60 *(978-1-4339-4764-3(1))* Stevens, Gareth Publishing LLLP. (Gareth Stevens Learning Library).

Harris, Laurie Lanzen. Colonial America & the Revolutionary War: The Story of the People of the Colonies, from Early Settlers to Revolutionary Leaders. 2009. 399p. (J). (gr. 5-7). lib. bdg. 49.00 *(978-1-931360-34-0(0))* Favorable Impressions.

Hartwiger, Heidi. Tricorn Trivia: Colonial Facts & Fun for Kids. 2007. 5.00 *(978-1-59712-065-4(0))* Catawba Publishing Co.

Heckt, Jackie. The Colony of Virginia. 2015. (Spotlight on the 13 Colonies Ser.). (ENG., Illus.). 24p. (J). (gr. 4-5). pap. 8.25 *(978-1-4994-0587-3(1)*, PowerKids Pr.) Rosen Publishing Group, Inc., The.

—Immigration to Colonial America, 01 vols., 1. 2016. (Spotlight on Immigration & Migration Ser.). (ENG., Illus.). 24p. (J). pap. 10.00 *(978-1-5081-4081-8(2)*, PowerKids Pr.) Rosen Publishing Group, Inc., The.

Heinrichs, Ann. The Barber. 2010. (Colonial People Ser.). 48p. (gr. 3-18). 29.93 *(978-0-7614-4800-6(4))* Marshall Cavendish Corp.

—The Shipbuilder. 2013. 48p. (J). (gr. 4-8). 29.93 *(978-0-7614-0005-9(2))* Cavendish Square Publishing.

—The Shoemaker. 2010. (Colonial People Ser.). 48p. (gr. 3-18). 29.93 *(978-0-7614-4798-6(9))* Marshall Cavendish Corp.

Hollar, Sherman. Biographies of Colonial America: From Sir Walter Raleigh to Phillis Wheatley. 2012. (Impact on America: Collective Biographies Ser.). (ENG., Illus.). 112p. (J). (gr. 7-12). lib. bdg. 32.90 *(978-1-61530-683-1(8))* Rosen Publishing Group, Inc., The.

—Biographies of Colonial America: Sir Walter Raleigh, Powhatan, Phillis Wheatley, & More. 2012. (Impact on America: Collective Biographies Ser.). (ENG., Illus.). 112p. (YA). (gr. 7-12). 65.80 *(978-1-61530-763-0(X))* Rosen Publishing Group, Inc., The.

Holt, Rinehart and Winston Staff. Call to Freedom: Beginning 1877 - Texas Online Edition. 2003. cd-rom 77.60 *(978-0-03-073346-8(4))* Holt McDougal.

Isaacs, Sally. Understanding the Declaration of Independence. 2008. (Documenting Early America Ser.). (ENG.). 32p. (J). (gr. 3-6). lib. bdg. *(978-0-7787-4371-2(3))* Crabtree Publishing Co.

Jacobson, Bray. The Thirteen Colonies. 2017. (Look at U. S. History Ser.). 32p. (gr. 2-2). pap. 10.50 *(978-1-4824-6039-1(4))* Stevens, Gareth Publishing LLLP.

Jedson, Lee. The Treaty of Paris 1783: A Primary Source Examination of the Treaty That Recognized American Independence. (Primary Sources of American Treaties Ser.). 64p. 2009. (gr. 5-8). 58.50 *(978-1-60851-517-2(6))* 2006. (Illus.). (J). (gr. k-3). lib. bdg. 31.95 *(978-1-4042-0441-6(5))* Rosen Publishing Group, Inc., The.

Jeffries, Joyce. The Colony of North Carolina. 2015. (Spotlight on the 13 Colonies Ser.). (ENG., Illus.). 24p. (J). (gr. 4-5). pap. 8.25 *(978-1-4994-0554-5(5)*, PowerKids Pr.) Rosen Publishing Group, Inc., The.

—The Colony of South Carolina. 2015. (Spotlight on the 13 Colonies Ser.). (ENG., Illus.). 24p. (J). (gr. 4-5). pap. 8.25 *(978-1-4994-0582-8(0)*, PowerKids Pr.) Rosen Publishing Group, Inc., The.

Jeffries, Joyce. Recipes of the Thirteen Colonies. 2017. (Cooking Your Way Through American History Ser.). (J). (gr. 3-3). pap. 63.60 ***(978-1-5345-2109-4(7))***; 24p. pap. 10.60 ***(978-1-5345-2108-7(9))***; 24p. lib. bdg. 27.25 ***(978-1-5345-2110-0(0))*** Greenhaven Publishing LLC. (KidHaven Publishing).

Jobes, Cecily. The Colony of Maryland. 2015. (Spotlight on the 13 Colonies Ser.). (ENG., Illus.). 24p. (J). (gr. 4-5). pap. 8.25 *(978-1-4994-0504-0(9)*, PowerKids Pr.) Rosen Publishing Group, Inc., The.

Jr. Graphic Colonial America: Set 2. 2013. (Jr. Graphic Colonial America Ser.). 24p. (J). (gr. 3-6). 151.50 *(978-1-4777-1546-8(0)*, PowerKids Pr.) Rosen Publishing Group, Inc., The.

Jr. Graphic Colonial America: Sets 1 - 2. 2013. (Jr. Graphic Colonial America Ser.). 24p. (J). (gr. 3-6). 303.00 *(978-1-4777-1553-6(3))*; pap. 127.20 *(978-1-4777-2730-0(2))*; pap. 763.20 *(978-1-4777-2731-7(0))* Rosen Publishing Group, Inc., The. (PowerKids Pr.).

Kalman, Bobbie. A Visual Dictionary of a Colonial Community. 2007. (Visual Dictionaries Ser.). (ENG., Illus.). 32p. (J). (gr. 4-7). pap. *(978-0-7787-3522-9(2))* Crabtree Publishing Co.

Kalman, Maira. Thomas Jefferson: Life, Liberty & the Pursuit of Everything. Kalman, Maira, illus. 2014. (ENG., Illus.). 40p. (J). (gr. k-3). 17.99 *(978-0-399-24040-9(3)*, Nancy Paulsen Books) Penguin Young Readers Group.

Katz, Vladimir. A Timeline of the Life of George Washington. 2009. (Timelines of American History Ser.). 32p. (gr. 4-4). 47.90 *(978-1-60854-388-5(9)*, Rosen Reference) Rosen Publishing Group, Inc., The.

Kenison, Misti. Cheer up, Ben Franklin! 2017. (ENG.). 28p. (J). bds. 9.99 ***(978-1-4926-5247-2(4)***, Sourcebooks Jabberwocky) Sourcebooks, Inc.

King, David C. & American Heritage, American. Colonies & Revolution. 2003. (American Heritage, American Voices Ser.). (ENG.). 144p. (J). (gr. 5-9). pap. 22.95 *(978-1-119-10345-5(2))* Wiley, John & Sons, Inc.

Kit, Oscar. A Timeline of the Life of Thomas Jefferson. 2009. (Timelines of American History Ser.). 32p. (gr. 4-4). 47.90 *(978-1-60854-389-2(7)*, Rosen Reference) Rosen Publishing Group, Inc., The.

Konstam, Angus. America Speaks, 10 vols. 2005. (Illus.). (J). *(978-0-7172-6024-9(0))*; *(978-0-7172-6029-4(1))*; *(978-0-7172-6028-7(3))*; *(978-0-7172-6027-0(5))*; *(978-0-7172-6026-3(7))*; *(978-0-7172-6020-1(8))*; *(978-0-7172-6021-8(6))*; *(978-0-7172-6022-5(4))*; *(978-0-7172-6023-2(2))*; *(978-0-7172-6025-6(9))* Grolier, Ltd.

—America Speaks, 10 vols., Set. 2005. (Illus.). (J). (gr. 5-10). lib. bdg. 269.00 *(978-0-7172-6030-0(5)*, Grolier) Scholastic Library Publishing.

Krebs, Laurie. A Day in the Life of a Colonial Miller. 2004. (Library of Living & Working in Colonial Times). (Illus.). 24p. (J). lib. bdg. 19.95 *(978-0-8239-6230-3(X)*, PowerKids Pr.) Rosen Publishing Group, Inc., The.

—A Day in the Life of a Colonial Shipwright. (Library of Living & Working in Colonial Times Ser.). 24p. 2009. (gr. 3-3). 42.50 *(978-1-60853-738-9(2)*, PowerKids Pr.) 2004. (Illus.). (J). lib. bdg. 22.60 *(978-0-8239-6227-3(X))* Rosen Publishing Group, Inc., The.

Krizner, L. J. & Sita, Lisa. Peter Stuyvesant: New Amsterdam & the Origins of New York. 2005. (Library of American Lives & Times). (Illus.). 112p. (J). (gr. 4-8). lib. bdg. 34.60 *(978-0-8239-5732-3(2))* Rosen Publishing Group, Inc., The.

LaClair, Teresa. The Northern Colonies: Freedom to Worship (1600-1770) Rakove, Jack N., ed. 2012. (How America Became America Ser.). 48p. (J). (gr. 3-4). 19.95 *(978-1-4222-2397-0(3))* Mason Crest.

Landau, Elaine. The Declaration of Independence. 2008. (True Bks.). (ENG., Illus.). 48p. (J). (gr. 3-5). pap. 6.95 *(978-0-531-14780-1(0)*, Children's Pr.) Scholastic Library Publishing.

—The Declaration of Independence: American History. 2007. (True Bks.). (ENG., Illus.). 48p. (J). (gr. 3-5). lib. bdg. 29.00 *(978-0-531-12630-1(7)*, Children's Pr.) Scholastic Library Publishing.

Lassieur, Allison. Colonial America: An Interactive History Adventure, 1 vol. (You Choose: Historical Eras Ser.). (ENG.). 112p. (gr. 3-4). 2011. pap. 6.95 *(978-1-4296-6277-2(8))* 2011. pap. 41.70 *(978-1-4296-6739-5(7))* 2010. 31.99 *(978-1-4296-5481-4(3))* Capstone Press of Coughlan Cos. (You Choose Bks.).

Lee, David. The Colony of Delaware. 2015. (Spotlight on the 13 Colonies Ser.). (ENG., Illus.). 24p. (J). (gr. 4-5). pap. 8.25 *(978-1-4994-0351-0(8)*, PowerKids Pr.) Rosen Publishing Group, Inc., The.

Levy, Janey. William Penn: Shaping a Nation. 2009. (Illus.). 32p. (J). 60.00 *(978-1-4358-0196-7(2)*, 1291824, PowerKids Pr.) Rosen Publishing Group, Inc., The.

Life in Colonial America. 2014. (Life in Colonial America Ser.). 80p. (YA). (gr. 6-8). 213.84 *(978-1-62713-128-5(0))* Cavendish Square Publishing.

Life in the American Colonies. 2011. (Life in the American Colonies Ser.). (ENG.). 32p. (gr. 3-4). pap. 31.80 *(978-1-4296-7221-4(8)*, Fact Finders) Capstone Press of Coughlan Cos.

The Life of a Colonial Innkeeper. 2013. (Jr. Graphic Colonial America Ser.). 24p. (J). (gr. 3-6). pap. 63.60 *(978-1-4777-1436-2(7)*, PowerKids Pr.) Rosen Publishing Group, Inc., The.

Linde, Barbara M. Slavery in Early America. 2011. (Story of America Ser.). (Illus.). 32p. (J). (gr. 4-6). lib. bdg. 26.60 *(978-1-4339-4776-6(5)*, Gareth Stevens Learning Library) Stevens, Gareth Publishing LLLP.

Lusted, Marcia Amidon. America's Colonization & Settlement. 2011. (Explorer Library: Language Arts Explorer Ser.). (ENG.). 32p. (gr. 4-8). pap. 14.21 *(978-1-61080-282-6(9)*, 201205); lib. bdg. 28.50 *(978-1-61080-194-2(6)*, 201164) Cherry Lake Publishing.

Machajewski, Sarah. The Colony of Georgia. 2015. (Spotlight on the 13 Colonies Ser.). (ENG., Illus.). 24p. (J). (gr. 4-5). pap. 8.25 *(978-1-4994-0493-7(X)*, PowerKids Pr.) Rosen Publishing Group, Inc., The.

—A Kid's Life in Colonial America, 1 vol. 2015. (ENG., Illus.). 24p. (J). lib. bdg. 23.60 *(978-1-4994-0006-9(3)*, PowerKids Pr.) Rosen Publishing Group, Inc., The.

Malaspina, Ann. A Primary Source History of the Colony of Connecticut. 2005. (Primary Sources of the Thirteen Colonies & the Lost Colony Ser.). (Illus.). 64p. (YA). (gr. 4-7). lib. bdg. 31.95 *(978-1-4042-0424-9(5))* Rosen Publishing Group, Inc., The.

Maloof, Torrey. James Oglethorpe: Not for Self, but for Others. 2016. (Primary Source Readers Ser.). (Illus.). 32p. (gr. 2-2). 8.99 *(978-1-4938-2555-4(0))* Teacher Created Materials, Inc.

Mara, Wil. If You Were a Kid in the Thirteen Colonies. Farré, Lluís, illus. 2016. (If You Were a Kid Ser.). (ENG.). 32p. (J). lib. bdg. 26.00 *(978-0-531-21972-0(0)*, Children's Pr.) Scholastic Library Publishing.

—The Innkeeper. 2010. (Colonial People Ser.). 48p. (gr. 3-18). 29.93 *(978-0-7614-4796-2(2))* Marshall Cavendish Corp.

—The Schoolmaster. 2010. (Colonial People Ser.). 48p. (gr. 3-18). 29.93 *(978-0-7614-4801-3(2))* Marshall Cavendish Corp.

—The Silversmith. 2010. (Colonial People Ser.). 48p. (gr. 3-18). 29.93 *(978-0-7614-4804-4(7))* Marshall Cavendish Corp.

Marciniak, Kristin. 12 Incredible Facts about the Boston Tea Party. 2015. (Turning Points in US History Ser.). (ENG., Illus.). 32p. (J). (gr. 3-5). *(978-1-63235-126-5(9)*, 12-Story Library) Pr. Room Editions LLC.

Marsh, Carole. Colonial America - Common Core Lessons & Activities. 2015. (Common Core Ser.). (ENG.). (J). pap. 4.99 *(978-0-635-11984-1(6))* Gallopade International.

—Roger Williams. 2003. 12p. (gr. k-4). 2.95 *(978-0-635-02361-2(X))* Gallopade International.

Marshall Cavendish. The Miller. 2011. (Colonial People 2 Ser.). 48p. (gr. 3). 29.93 *(978-1-60870-416-3(5))* Marshall Cavendish Corp.

Marsico, Katie. The Doctor. 2011. (Colonial People 2 Ser.). 48p. (gr. 3). 29.93 *(978-1-60870-412-5(2))* Marshall Cavendish Corp.

Martin, David. The Colony of Pennsylvania. 2015. (Spotlight on the 13 Colonies Ser.). (ENG., Illus.). 24p. (J). (gr. 4-5). pap. 8.25 *(978-1-4994-0572-9(3)*, PowerKids Pr.) Rosen Publishing Group, Inc., The.

Masters, Nancy Robinson. Extraordinary Patriots of the United States of America: Colonial Times to Pre-Civil War. 2005. (Extraordinary People Ser.). (ENG., Illus.). 288p. (J). (gr. 4-7). 40.00 *(978-0-516-24404-4(3)*, Children's Pr.) Scholastic Library Publishing.

Mattern, Joanne. Pocahontas. 2015. (Rookie Biographies(tm) Ser.). (ENG., Illus.). 32p. (J). lib. bdg. 25.00 *(978-0-531-20596-9(7))* Scholastic Library Publishing.

McAneney, Caitie. Hidden History: Uncovering the Jamestown Colony. 2016. (Hidden History Ser.). 00032p. (J). pap. 10.50 *(978-1-4824-5806-0(3))* Stevens, Gareth Publishing LLLP.

McCallum, Ann. Eat Your U. S. History Homework: Recipes for Revolutionary Minds. Hernandez, Leeza, illus. 2015. (Eat

Your Homework Ser.). (ENG.). 48p. (J). (gr. 2-5). lib. bdg. 15.95 *(978-1-57091-923-7(2))* Charlesbridge Publishing, Inc.

McCarthy, Pat. The Thirteen Colonies from Founding to Revolution in American History. 2004. (In American History Ser.). (Illus.). 128p. (J). lib. bdg. 27.94 *(978-0-7660-1990-4(X))* Enslow Pubs., Inc.

McDonnell, Julia. The Pilgrims Didn't Celebrate the First Thanksgiving: Exposing Myths about Colonial History. 2016. (Exposed! Myths about Early American History Ser.). 00032p. (J). pap. 10.50 *(978-1-4824-5731-5(8))* Stevens, Gareth Publishing LLLP.

McKissack, Fredrick, Jr. & McKissack, Patricia C. Hard Labor: The First African-Americans 1619. Fiedler, Joseph Daniel, illus. 2004. (Milestone Ser.). (ENG.). 64p. (J). (gr. 2-5). pap. 6.99 *(978-0-689-86149-9(4)*, Simon & Schuster/Paula Wiseman Bks.) Simon & Schuster/Paula Wiseman Bks.

McLeese, Don. Phillis Wheatley. 2004. (Heroes of the American Revolution Ser.). (Illus.). 32p. (J). (gr. -1 — 1). pap. 5.95 *(978-1-59515-320-3(9))* Rourke Educational Media.

Merrill, Amy French. A Day in the Life of a Colonial Cabinetmaker. 2009. (Library of Living & Working in Colonial Times Ser.). 24p. (gr. 3-3). 42.50 *(978-1-60853-729-7(3)*, PowerKids Pr.) Rosen Publishing Group, Inc., The.

—A Day in the Life of a Colonial Dressmaker. 2009. (Library of Living & Working in Colonial Times Ser.). 24p. (gr. 3-3). 42.50 *(978-1-60853-730-3(7)*, PowerKids Pr.) Rosen Publishing Group, Inc., The.

—A Day in the Life of a Colonial Surveyor. 2009. (Library of Living & Working in Colonial Times Ser.). 24p. (gr. 3-3). 42.50 *(978-1-60853-740-2(4)*, PowerKids Pr.) Rosen Publishing Group, Inc., The.

Miller, Brandon Marie. Growing up in Revolution & the New Nation, 1775 to 1800. 2003. (Our America Ser.). (Illus.). 64p. (J). (gr. 4-7). lib. bdg. 26.60 *(978-0-8225-0078-0(7))* Lerner Publishing Group.

—Women of Colonial America: 13 Stories of Courage & Survival in the New World. 2016. (Women of Action Ser.). (ENG., Illus.). 256p. (YA). (gr. 7). 19.95 *(978-1-55652-487-5(0))* Chicago Review Pr., Inc.

Misztal, Maggie. The Colony of New Jersey. 2015. (Spotlight on the 13 Colonies Ser.). (ENG., Illus.). 24p. (J). (gr. 4-5). pap. 8.25 *(978-1-4994-0531-6(6)*, PowerKids Pr.) Rosen Publishing Group, Inc., The.

Morley, Jacqueline. You Wouldn't Want to Be an American Colonist! A Settlement You'd Rather Not Start. Antram, David, illus. 2013. (You Wouldn't Want to... Ser.). (ENG.). (J). 32p. 29.00 *(978-0-531-25946-7(3))*; 40p. pap. 9.95 *(978-0-531-24502-6(0))* Scholastic Library Publishing. (Watts, Franklin).

Muhall, Jill K. & Alarcon, Jill. Causes of the Revolution, 1 vol. 2004. (Primary Source Readers Ser.). (ENG., Illus.). 24p. (J). (gr. 5-5). pap. 8.99 *(978-0-7439-8785-1(3))* Shell Educational Publishing.

Nardo, Don. Daily Life in Colonial America. 2010. (Lucent Library of Historical Eras Ser.). 144p. (YA). (gr. 7-12). 34.80 *(978-1-4205-0264-0(6))* Cengage Gale.

—The Establishment of the Thirteen Colonies. 2010. (Lucent Library of Historical Eras Ser.). (ENG., Illus.). 128p. (gr. 7-12). 39.40 *(978-1-4205-0267-1(0))* Cengage Gale.

Nelson, Sheila. The Original United States of America. 2006. (How America Became America Ser.). (Illus.). 96p. (YA). lib. bdg. 22.95 *(978-1-59084-903-3(5))* Mason Crest.

Oney, Yannick. First American Colonies. 2004. (World Discovery History Readers Ser.). (Illus.). 32p. (J). pap. *(978-0-439-66555-1(8))* Scholastic, Inc.

Osborne, Mary Pope & Boyce, Natalie Pope. American Revolution: A Nonfiction Companion to Revolutionary War on Wednesday. Murdocca, Sal, illus. 2004. (Magic Tree House - Fact Tracker Ser.: 11). (ENG.). 128p. (J). (gr. 2-5). pap. 6.99 *(978-0-375-82379-4(4)*, Random Hse. Bks. for Young Readers) Random Hse. Children's Bks.

Parker, Lewis K. Dutch Colonies in the Americas. (European Colonies in the Americas Ser.). 24p. 2009. (gr. 2-2). 42.50 *(978-1-61512-316-2(4))* 2003. (Illus.). (J). lib. bdg. 22.60 *(978-0-8239-6472-7(8))* Rosen Publishing Group, Inc., The. (PowerKids Pr.).

—English Colonies in the Americas. (European Colonies in the Americas Ser.). 24p. 2009. (gr. 2-2). 42.50 *(978-1-61512-317-9(2))* 2003. (Illus.). (J). lib. bdg. 22.60 *(978-0-8239-6475-8(2))* Rosen Publishing Group, Inc., The. (PowerKids Pr.).

—French Colonies in the Americas. 2009. (European Colonies in the Americas Ser.). 24p. (gr. 2-2). 42.50 *(978-1-61512-318-6(0)*, PowerKids Pr.) Rosen Publishing Group, Inc., The.

—Russian Colonies in the Americas. 2009. (European Colonies in the Americas Ser.). 24p. (gr. 2-2). 42.50 *(978-1-61512-319-3(9)*, PowerKids Pr.) Rosen Publishing Group, Inc., The.

—Spanish Colonies in the Americas. 2009. (European Colonies in the Americas Ser.). 24p. (gr. 2-2). 42.50 *(978-1-61512-320-9(2)*, PowerKids Pr.) Rosen Publishing Group, Inc., The.

Pelleschi, Andrea. The Life of a Colonial Innkeeper. 2013. (Jr. Graphic Colonial America Ser.). 24p. (J). (gr. 3-6). 25.25 *(978-1-4777-1309-9(3))*; pap. 10.60 *(978-1-4777-1435-5(9))* Rosen Publishing Group, Inc., The. (PowerKids Pr.).

Perritano, John. Colonization & Settlement. 2016. (Illus.). 48p. (J). *(978-1-5105-1284-9(5))* SmartBook Media, Inc.

Petersen, Christine. The Apothecary. 2010. (Colonial People Ser.). 48p. (gr. 3-18). 29.93 *(978-0-7614-4795-5(4))* Marshall Cavendish Corp.

—The Blacksmith. 2010. (Colonial People Ser.). 48p. (gr. 3-18). 29.93 *(978-0-7614-4799-3(7))* Marshall Cavendish Corp.

—The Printer. 2010. (Colonial People Ser.). 48p. (gr. 3-18). 29.93 *(978-0-7614-4802-0(0))* Marshall Cavendish Corp.

—The Tailor. 2011. (Colonial People 2 Ser.). 48p. (gr. 3). 29.93 *(978-1-60870-417-0(3))* Marshall Cavendish Corp.

—The Tanner. 2011. (Colonial People 2 Ser.). (Illus.). 48p. (J). (gr. 3). 29.93 *(978-1-60870-418-7(1))* Marshall Cavendish Corp.

Pratt, Mary. A Timeline History of the Thirteen Colonies. 2014. (Timeline Trackers: America's Beginnings Ser.). (Illus.). 48p. (gr. 5-8). (J). lib. bdg. 30.60 *(978-1-4677-3639-8(2)*, Lerner Pubns.); pap. 9.95 *(978-1-4677-4573-4(1))* Lerner Publishing Group.

Publishers, Chelsea House, creator. Colonial Settlements in America Set, 8-Volumes. 2007. (Colonial Settlements in America Ser.). 112p. (gr. 5-8). 240.00 *(978-0-7910-9589-8(4)*, Chelsea Hse.) Facts On File, Inc.

The Puritans, Algonkians & Roger Williams (NCHS) (J). (gr. 5-8). spiral bd., tchr.'s planning gde. ed. 13.50 *(978-0-382-44447-0(7))* Cobblestone Publishing Co.

The Puritans, Algonkians & Roger Williams (NCHS) Grades 5-8. (J). tchr. ed. 18.00 *(978-0-382-44537-8(6))* Cobblestone Publishing Co.

Raum, Elizabeth. The Cold, Hard Facts about Science & Medicine in Colonial America, 1 vol. 2011. (Life in the American Colonies Ser.). (ENG.). 32p. (gr. 3-4). pap. 8.10 *(978-1-4296-7215-3(3))*; pap. 47.70 *(978-1-4296-7216-0(1))* Capstone Press of Coughlan Cos. (Fact Finders).

Raum, Elizabeth, et al. Life in the American Colonies. 2011. (Life in the American Colonies Ser.). (ENG.). 32p. (gr. 3-4). pap. 190.80 *(978-1-4296-7222-1(6))*; lib. bdg. 54.64 *(978-1-4296-6493-6(2))* Capstone Press of Coughlan Cos. (Fact Finders).

Rausch, Monica. Crispus Attucks. 2007. (Great Americans Ser.). (Illus.). 24p. (gr. 1-4). lib. bdg. 22.00 *(978-0-8368-7681-9(4)*, Weekly Reader Leveled Readers) Stevens, Gareth Publishing LLLP.

Raymond, Aaron. A Primary Source History of the Colony of Delaware. 2006. (Primary Sources of the Thirteen Colonies & the Lost Colony Ser.). (Illus.). 64p. (YA). (gr. 4-7). lib. bdg. 31.95 *(978-1-4042-0425-6(3))* Rosen Publishing Group, Inc., The.

Roberts, Russell. Holidays & Celebrations in Colonial America. 2006. (Building America Ser.). (Illus.). 48p. (J). (gr. 3-7). lib. bdg. 29.95 *(978-1-58415-467-9(5))* Mitchell Lane Pubs., Inc.

—Life in Colonial America. 2007. (Building America Ser.). (Illus.). 48p. (J). (gr. 4-8). lib. bdg. 29.95 *(978-1-58415-549-2(3))* Mitchell Lane Pubs., Inc.

Robson, David. Colonial America. 2012. (Illus.). 96p. (YA). lib. bdg. *(978-1-60152-246-7(0))* ReferencePoint Pr., Inc.

Rodgers, Kelly. The Middle Colonies: Breadbasket of the New World. 2016. (Primary Source Readers Ser.). (Illus.). 32p. (J). (gr. 4-5). pap. 8.99 *(978-1-4938-3076-3(7))* Teacher Created Materials, Inc.

—The New England Colonies: A Place for Puritans. 2016. (Primary Source Readers Ser.). (Illus.). 32p. (J). (gr. 4-5). pap. 8.99 *(978-1-4938-3075-6(9))* Teacher Created Materials, Inc.

—The Southern Colonies: First & Last of 13. 2016. (Primary Source Readers Ser.). (Illus.). 32p. (J). (gr. 4-5). pap. 8.99 *(978-1-4938-3077-0(5))* Teacher Created Materials, Inc.

Rosen, Daniel. Independence Now: The American Revolution, 1763-1783. 2004. (Crossroads America Ser.). (ENG., Illus.). 40p. (J). (gr. 5-9). 21.90 *(978-0-7922-6990-8(X)*, National Geographic Children's Bks.) National Geographic Society.

Roza, Greg. Analyzing the Boston Tea Party: Establishing Cause-and-Effect Relationships. 2005. (Critical Thinking in American History Ser.). (Illus.). 48p. (J). (gr. k-3). lib. bdg. 29.25 *(978-1-4042-0411-9(3))* Rosen Publishing Group, Inc., The.

—The Colony of New York. 2015. (Spotlight on the 13 Colonies Ser.). (ENG., Illus.). 24p. (J). (gr. 4-5). pap. 8.25 *(978-1-4994-0537-8(5)*, PowerKids Pr.) Rosen Publishing Group, Inc., The.

—The Colony of Rhode Island. 2015. (Spotlight on the 13 Colonies Ser.). (ENG.). 24p. (J). (gr. 4-5). pap. 8.25 *(978-1-4994-0577-4(4)*, PowerKids Pr.) Rosen Publishing Group, Inc., The.

Ruffin, Frances E. Molly Pitcher. 2009. (American Legends Ser.). 24p. (gr. 3-3). 42.50 *(978-1-61511-384-2(3)*, PowerKids Pr.) Rosen Publishing Group, Inc., The.

Saddleback Educational Publishing Staff, ed. American History 1, 1 vol. 2013. (American History Ser.). (ENG.). 110p. (gr. 6-12). pap. 44.95 *(978-1-62250-032-1(6))* Saddleback Educational Publishing, Inc.

Schanzer, Rosalyn. George vs. George: The American Revolution as Seen from Both Sides. 2007. (ENG., Illus.). 64p. (J). (gr. 4-7). per. 6.95 *(978-1-4263-0042-4(5)*, National Geographic Children's Bks.) National Geographic Society.

—George vs. George: The Revolutionary War as Seen by Both Sides. 2004. (ENG., Illus.). 64p. (J). (gr. 4-7). 25.90 *(978-0-7922-6999-1(3))*; 16.95 *(978-0-7922-7349-3(4))* National Geographic Society. (National Geographic Children's Bks.).

Sioux, Tracee. Immigrants in Colonial America. (Primary Sources of Immigration & Migration in America Ser.). 24p. 2009. (gr. 3-4). 42.50 *(978-1-60851-777-0(2))* 2004. (ENG., Illus.). (gr. 4-8). pap. 9.40 *(978-0-8239-8949-2(6))* 2004. (Illus.). (J). lib. bdg. 22.60 *(978-0-8239-6823-7(5))* Rosen Publishing Group, Inc., The. (PowerKids Pr.).

Smith, Emily R. Life in the Colonies, 1 vol. 2004. (Primary Source Readers Ser.). (ENG.). 24p. (J). (gr. 5-5). pap. 8.99 *(978-0-7439-8742-4(X))* Shell Educational Publishing.

—Phillis Wheatley, 1 vol. 2004. (Primary Source Readers Ser.). (ENG.). 24p. (J). (gr. 4-4). pap. 8.99 *(978-0-7439-8743-1(8))* Shell Educational Publishing.

Spotlight on the 13 Colonies. 2015. (Spotlight on the 13 Colonies Ser.). (ENG.). 24p. (J). (gr. 4-5). pap., pap., pap. 693.00 *(978-1-4994-1313-7(0)*, PowerKids Pr.) Rosen Publishing Group, Inc., The.

Stanley, George Edward. The New Republic (1763-1815) 2005. (Primary Source History of the United States Ser.). (Illus.). 48p. (gr. 5-12). pap. 14.05 *(978-0-8368-5834-1(4))*; lib. bdg. 31.00 *(978-0-8368-5825-9(5))* Stevens, Gareth Publishing LLLP. (Gareth Stevens Secondary Library).

Stefoff, Rebecca. Cities & Towns. 2007. (ENG., Illus.). 96p. (C). (gr. 6-18). lib. bdg. 140.00 *(978-0-7656-8109-6(9)*, Y181735) Routledge.

—Exploration & Settlement. 2007. (ENG., Illus.). 96p. (C). (gr. 6-18). lib. bdg. 158.00 *(978-0-7656-8108-9(0)*, Y182272) Routledge.

Sullivan, Laura L. Blackbeard. 2015. (J). lib. bdg. *(978-1-62713-525-2(1))* Cavendish Square Publishing.

—The Colonial Slave Family. 2015. (Colonial People Ser.). (ENG., Illus.). 48p. (J). (gr. 4-4). 31.36 *(978-1-5026-0486-6(8))* Cavendish Square Publishing.

—The Colonial Woodworker. 2015. (Colonial People Ser.). (ENG.). 48p. (J). (gr. 4-4). 31.36 *(978-1-5026-0484-2(1))* Cavendish Square Publishing.

Swanson Sateren, Shelley. School in Colonial America. 2016. (It's Back to School ... Way Back! Ser.). (ENG., Illus.). 32p. (gr. 3-4). lib. bdg. 27.32 *(978-1-5157-2097-3(7)*, Fact Finders) Capstone Press of Coughlan Cos.

Thomas, Mark & National Geographic Learning Staff. Clothes in Colonial America. 2012. (ENG., Illus.). 24p. (C). (gr. -1-2). pap. 7.95 *(978-0-516-23490-8(0))* National Geographic School Publishing, Inc.

Uschan, Michael V. The Salem Witch Trials. 2004. (Landmark Events in American History Ser.). (Illus.). 48p. (gr. 5-12). pap. 14.05 *(978-0-8368-5415-2(2))*; lib. bdg. 31.00 *(978-0-8368-5387-2(3))* Stevens, Gareth Publishing LLLP. (Gareth Stevens Secondary Library).

Wachter, Joanne. The Thirteen Colonies. 2005. (J). pap. *(978-1-4108-4619-8(9))* Benchmark Education Co.

Wagner, Heather Lehr. Benjamin Banneker. 2010. (Leaders of the Colonial Era Ser.). 104p. (gr. 5-8). 35.00 *(978-1-60413-744-6(4)*, Chelsea Hse.) Facts On File, Inc.

Walker, Sally. Ghost Walls: The Story of a 17th-Century Colonial Homestead. 2014. (Illus.). 136p. (J). (gr. 6-12). lib. bdg. 20.95 *(978-0-7613-5408-6(5)*, Carolrhoda Bks.) Lerner Publishing Group.

Wells-Cole, Catherine. Slavery & the Forging of Early America. 2014. (J). *(978-1-59935-410-1(1))* Reynolds, Morgan Inc.

Whitman Publishing, creator. Discover the American Revolution: History Project Toolkit. 2011. pap. 19.95 *(978-0-7948-3590-3(2))* Whitman Publishing LLC.

Wiener. The 13 Colonies, 13 vols. 2004. (Illus.). *(978-0-7398-6890-4(X))* Harcourt Schl. Pubs.

Wirkner, Linda. Learning about America's Colonial Period with Graphic Organizers. (Graphic Organizers in Social Studies). 24p. 2009. (gr. 3-4). 42.50 *(978-1-61513-078-8(0)*, PowerKids Pr.) 2006. (ENG.). (gr. 4-6). pap. 8.25 *(978-1-4042-5052-9(2)*, Rosen Classroom) 2005. (Illus.). (J). (gr. 3-5). lib. bdg. 22.60 *(978-1-4042-2811-5(X)*, PowerKids Pr.) Rosen Publishing Group, Inc., The.

—Learning about America's Industrial Growth & Expansion with Graphic Organizers. 2009. (Graphic Organizers in Social Studies). 24p. (gr. 3-4). 42.50 *(978-1-61513-081-8(0)*, PowerKids Pr.) Rosen Publishing Group, Inc., The.

Wolfe, James. The Colonial Period, 01 vols., 1. 2016. (Early American History Ser.). (ENG., Illus.). 80p. (J). 32.90 *(978-1-68048-268-3(8)*, Britannica Educational Publishing) Rosen Publishing Group, Inc., The.

Worth, Richard. Colonial America: Building Toward Independence. 2006. (American Saga Ser.). (Illus.). 128p. (J). (gr. 5-12). lib. bdg. 33.27 *(978-0-7660-2569-1(1))* Enslow Pubs., Inc.

Yale, Dallas. The Colony of New Hampshire. 2015. (Spotlight on the 13 Colonies Ser.). (ENG., Illus.). 24p. (J). (gr. 4-5). pap. 8.25 *(978-1-4994-0526-2(X)*, PowerKids Pr.) Rosen Publishing Group, Inc., The.

Yero, Judith Lloyd. The Bill of Rights. 2006. (American Documents Ser.). (ENG., Illus.). 40p. (J). (gr. 5-9). 15.95 *(978-0-7922-5395-2(7))*; lib. bdg. 23.90 *(978-0-7922-5396-9(5))* National Geographic Society. (National Geographic Children's Bks.).

—The Declaration of Independence. 2006. (American Documents Ser.). (ENG., Illus.). 40p. (J). (gr. 5-9). 15.95 *(978-0-7922-5397-6(3))*; lib. bdg. 23.90 *(978-0-7922-5398-3(1))* National Geographic Society. (National Geographic Children's Bks.).

—The Mayflower Compact. 2006. (American Documents Ser.). (ENG., Illus.). 40p. (J). (gr. 5-9). 15.95 *(978-0-7922-5891-9(6))*; lib. bdg. 23.90 *(978-0-7922-5892-6(4))* National Geographic Society. (National Geographic Children's Bks.).

Yomtov, Nel. Night of Rebellion! Nickolas Flux & the Boston Tea Party, 1 vol. Ginevra, Dante, illus. 2014. (Nickolas Flux History Chronicles Ser.). (ENG.). 32p. (gr. 3-4). lib. bdg. 30.65 *(978-1-4765-3946-1(4)*, Graphic Library) Capstone Press of Coughlan Cos.

Yorinks, Adrienne. Quilt of States: Piecing Together America. Larson, Jeanette, ed. 2005. (ENG., Illus.). 128p. (J). (gr. 5-8). 19.95 *(978-0-7922-7285-4(4))*; 29.90 *(978-0-7922-7286-1(2))* National Geographic Society. (National Geographic Children's Bks.).

UNITED STATES—HISTORY—COLONIAL PERIOD, CA. 1600-1775—FICTION

Alsheimer, Jeanette E. & Friedle, Patricia J. Path to Punishment. 2008. 220p. (J). (gr. 8-12). per. 18.95 *(978-1-57197-482-2(2)*, Ivy House Publishing Group) Pentland Pr., Inc.

Ayers, Linda. The Time Bridge Travelers & the Time Travel Station, 3 bks., Bk. 3. Ayers, Ryan, illus. l.t. ed. 2007. (Time Bridge Travelers Ser.: 3). 140p. (J). lib. bdg. 16.95 *(978-0-9786302-8-7(9))*; per. 7.95 *(978-0-9786302-7-0(0))* Blue Thistle Pr.

Bailey, Carolyn Sherwin. Boys & Girls of Colonial Days. 2008. (Illus.). 152p. pap. 8.95 *(978-1-59915-246-2(0))* Yesterday's Classics.

Butters, Dorothy Gilman, pseud. The Bells of Freedom. Wilde, Carol, illus. 2008. (J). (gr. 4-6). 21.00 *(978-0-8446-6162-9(7))* Smith, Peter Pub., Inc.

Cocca-Leffler, Maryann, illus. Spotlight on Stacey. 2007. (Social Studies Connects). 32p. (J). (gr. -1-3). pap. 5.95 *(978-1-57565-236-8(6))* Kane Press, Inc.

Colonial People, 10 vols., Set. Incl. Apothecary. Petersen, Christine. 29.93 *(978-0-7614-4795-5(4))*; Barber. Heinrichs, Ann. 29.93 *(978-0-7614-4800-6(4))*; Blacksmith. Petersen, Christine. 29.93 *(978-0-7614-4799-3(7))*; Farmer. Mara, Wil. 29.93 *(978-0-7614-4797-9(0))*; Innkeeper. Mara, Wil. 29.93 *(978-0-7614-4796-2(2))*; Printer. Petersen, Christine. 29.93 *(978-0-7614-4802-0(0))*; Schoolmaster. Mara, Wil. 29.93 *(978-0-7614-4801-3(2))*; Shoemaker. Heinrichs, Ann. 29.93 *(978-0-7614-4798-6(9))*; Silversmith. Mara, Wil. 29.93 *(978-0-7614-4804-4(7))*; Surveyor. Petersen, Christine. 29.93 *(978-0-7614-4805-1(5))*; 48p. (gr. 3-18). (Colonial People Ser.). 2010. Set lib. bdg. 299.30 o.p. *(978-0-7614-4794-8(6))* Marshall Cavendish Corp.

Cornelia Meigs. Master Simon's Garden. 2010. (Illus.). 244p. pap. 6.95 *(978-1-60386-299-8(4)*, Watchmaker Publishing) Wexford College Pr.

Curtis, Alice. A Little Maid of Newport. Price, Hattie Longstreet, illus. 2006. (Little Maid Ser.). (ENG.). 212p. (J). (gr. 4-7). pap. 12.95 *(978-1-55709-339-4(3))* Applewood Bks.

de Angeli, Marguerite. Elin's Amerika. 3rd ed. 2007. (Illus.). 98p. (J). pap. 15.99 *(978-0-9800761-0-3(2))* American Swedish Historical Museum.

Draper, Sharon M. Copper Sun. 2006. (ENG.). 320p. (YA). (gr. 8-18). 19.99 *(978-0-689-82181-3(6)*, Atheneum Bks. for Young Readers) Simon & Schuster Children's Publishing.

Frazier, Jan. Catch the Watercolored Wind: Jamestown 1617. 2015. (YA). pap. 14.95 *(978-1-55571-788-9(8)*, Paloma Bks.) L & R Publishing, LLC.

Gibbs, Gretchen. The Book of Maggie Bradstreet. 2012. (Bradstreet Chronicles). (ENG.). 183p. (YA). pap. 9.99 *(978-0-9852948-0-9(9))* Glenmere Pr.

Gilberstadt, Debra Pack. Unmarked Grave: Remembering an American Patriot. 2005. (YA). lib. bdg. 29.95 *(978-0-9763033-0-5(2))* Eslinger Hse. Publishing.

Gingrich, Callista. Land of the Pilgrims Pride. Arciero, Susan, illus. 2012. (Ellis the Elephant Ser.). (ENG.). 28p. (J). (gr. k-3). 14.95 *(978-1-59698-829-3(0)*, Little Patriot Pr.) Regnery Publishing, Inc., An Eagle Publishing Co.

Hopkins, K. C. The Night the Spirits Danced. 2008. 115p. pap. 15.00 *(978-0-615-23929-3(3))* Hopkins, KC.

Horender, Philip M. Patriotic Mouse: Boston Tea Party Participant, 1 vol. Wolek, Guy, illus. 2013. (Maximilian P. Mouse, Time Traveler Ser.). (ENG.). 112p. (J). (gr. 3-6). lib. bdg. 27.07 *(978-1-61641-957-8(1)*, Calico Chapter Bks) Magic Wagon.

Kastner, Janet. The Snake Fence: A Novel. 2012. (J). pap. 14.95 *(978-1-937768-13-3(9))* QuakerPress.

Leatherman, Diane. Abigail Before the Revolution. 2005. (Illus.). 64p. (J). *(978-0-9665861-2-1(3))* Bounty Project, The.

Limbaugh, Rush H., III. Rush Revere & the First Patriots: Time-Travel Adventures with Exceptional Americans. 2014. (Rush Revere Ser.: 2). (ENG., Illus.). 256p. 19.99 *(978-1-4767-5588-5(4)*, Threshold Editions) Threshold Editions.

McCall, Edith S. Adventures of the American Colonies. Rogers, Carol, illus. 2011. 126p. 40.95 *(978-1-258-06470-9(7))* Literary Licensing, LLC.

Nixon, Joan Lowery. Ann's Story, 1747. 2004. (J). *(978-0-87935-198-4(5))* Colonial Williamsburg Foundation.

—Caesar's Story, 1759. 2004. (J). *(978-0-87935-199-1(3))* Colonial Williamsburg Foundation.

—Maria's Story, 1773. 2004. (J). *(978-0-87935-227-1(2))* Colonial Williamsburg Foundation.

—Nancy's Story, 1765. 2004. (J). *(978-0-87935-225-7(6))* Colonial Williamsburg Foundation.

—Will's Story, 1771. 2004. (J). *(978-0-87935-226-4(4))* Colonial Williamsburg Foundation.

Otis, James. Neal, the Miller: A Son of Liberty. 2007. 48p. per. *(978-1-4068-4368-2(7))* Echo Library.

Prescott, Della. A Day in a Colonial Home. Dana, John Cotton, ed. 2006. (ENG.). 96p. (J). (gr. 4-7). per. 12.95 *(978-1-55709-374-5(1))* Applewood Bks.

Richter, Conrad. The Light in the Forest. (YA). (gr. 7-18). 21.95 *(978-0-89190-333-8(X))* Amereon Ltd.

Rinaldi, Ann. The Fifth of March: A Story of the Boston Massacre. 2004. (Great Episodes Ser.). (ENG.). 352p. (J). (gr. 5-7). pap. 8.99 *(978-0-15-205078-8(7))* Houghton Mifflin Harcourt Publishing Co.

Smith, Mary P. Wells. The Young Puritans in King Philip's War. Bridgman, L. J., illus. 2011. 396p. 54.95 *(978-1-258-05550-9(3))* Literary Licensing, LLC.

Soup, Cuthbert. Another Whole Nother Story. Timmins, Jeffrey Stewart, illus. 2010. (Whole Nother Story Ser.). (ENG.). 304p. (YA). (gr. 3-6). 16.99 *(978-1-59990-436-8(5)*, 9781599904368, Bloomsbury USA Childrens) Bloomsbury Publishing USA.

Stowe, Harriet Beecher. The First Christmas of New England & O. 2006. 108p. per. 9.95 *(978-1-59818-758-8(9))* Aegypan.

Tripp, Valerie. Very Funny, Elizabeth! England, Tamara, ed. Andreasen, Dan, illus. 2005. (ENG.). 96p. (gr. 3). pap. 6.95 *(978-1-59369-061-8(4)*, American Girl) American Girl Publishing, Inc.

UNITED STATES—HISTORY—FRENCH AND INDIAN WAR, 1755-1763

Bruchac, Marge. Malian's Song. Maughan, William L., illus. 2006. (Vermont Folklife Center Children's Book Ser.). (ENG.). 32p. (J). (gr. -1-3). 16.95 *(978-0-916718-26-8(3))* Vermont Folklife Ctr.

Caravantes, Peggy. French & Indian War. 2013. (Foundations of Our Nation Ser.). (ENG.). 48p. (J). pap. 15.64 *(978-1-61783-759-3(8)*, Core Library); (gr. 3-6). lib. bdg. 32.79 *(978-1-61783-709-8(1))* ABDO Publishing Co.

Cheatham, Mark. The Life of a Colonial Soldier. 2013. (Jr. Graphic Colonial America Ser.). (ENG., Illus.). 24p. (J). (gr. 3-6). pap. 10.60 *(978-1-4777-1439-3(1))*; lib. bdg. 25.25 *(978-1-4777-1310-5(7))* Rosen Publishing Group, Inc., The. (PowerKids Pr.).

Dipiazza, Francesca. When Did George Washington Fight His First Military Battle? And Other Questions about the French & Indian War. 2011. (Six Questions of American History Ser.). (ENG.). 48p. (gr. 4-6). pap. 56.72 *(978-0-7613-7643-9(7))* Lerner Publishing Group.

DiPiazza, Francesca Davis. When Did George Washington Fight His First Military Battle? And Other Questions about the French & Indian War. 2011. (Six Questions of American History Ser.). (ENG.). 48p. (gr. 4-6). 30.60 *(978-0-7613-5329-4(1))*; pap. 9.95 *(978-0-7613-7492-3(2))* Lerner Publishing Group.

French & Indian War. 2003. (ENG., Illus.). 240p. (J). lib. bdg. 106.00 *(978-0-7876-6560-9(6)*, UXL) Cengage Gale.

Gard, Carolyn. The French & Indian War: A Primary Source History of the Fight for Territory in North America. 2009. (Primary Sources in American History Ser.). 64p. (gr. 5-8). 58.50 *(978-1-60851-495-3(1))* Rosen Publishing Group, Inc., The.

—The French Indian War. 2004. (Primary Sources in American History Ser.). (Illus.). 64p. (J). (gr. 5-8). lib. bdg. 31.95 *(978-0-8239-4511-5(1)*, Rosen Reference) Rosen Publishing Group, Inc., The.

The Life of a Colonial Soldier. 2013. (Jr. Graphic Colonial America Ser.). 24p. (J). (gr. 3-6). pap. 63.60 *(978-1-4777-1440-9(5)*, PowerKids Pr.) Rosen Publishing Group, Inc., The.

Maynard, Charles W. Fort Ticonderoga. 2009. (Famous Forts Throughout American History Ser.). 24p. (gr. 3-4). 42.50

(978-1-61512-521-0(3), PowerKids Pr.) Rosen Publishing Group, Inc., The.
Pederson, Charles E. The French & Indian War, 1 vol. 2010. (Essential Events Set 4 Ser.). (ENG.). 112p. (J). (gr. 6-12). lib. bdg. 35.64 *(978-1-60453-943-1(7))* ABDO Publishing Co.
Quasha, Jennifer. Robert Rogers: Rogers' Rangers & the French & Indian War. 2005. (Library of American Lives & Times). (Illus.). 112p. (J). (gr. 4-8). lib. bdg. 34.60 *(978-0-8239-5731-6(4))* Rosen Publishing Group, Inc., The.
—Robert Rogers: Rogers' Rangers, & the French & Indian War. 2009. (Library of American Lives & Times Ser.). 112p. (gr. 5-5). 69.20 *(978-1-60853-503-3(7))* Rosen Publishing Group, Inc., The.
Santella, Andrew. The French & Indian War. 2011. (Cornerstones of Freedom, Third Ser.). 64p. (J). lib. bdg. 30.00 *(978-0-531-25033-4(4),* Children's Pr.); (ENG.). (gr. 4-6). pap. 8.95 *(978-0-531-26558-1(7))* Scholastic Library Publishing.
Thornton, Jeremy. The French & Indian War. (Building America's Democracy Ser.). 24p. 2009. (gr. 3-3). 42.50 *(978-1-61511-766-6(0))* 2003. (J). lib. bdg. 22.60 *(978-0-8239-6275-4(X))* Rosen Publishing Group, Inc., The. (PowerKids Pr.).

UNITED STATES—HISTORY—FRENCH AND INDIAN WAR, 1755-1763—FICTION

Altsheler, Joseph A. The French & Indian War Novels: The Hunters of the Hills & The Shadow of the North, Vol. 1. 2008. 464p. (J). *(978-1-84677-586-4(8));* pap. *(978-1-84677-585-7(X))* Leonaur Ltd.
—The French & Indian War Novels: The Lords of the Wild & The Sun of Quebec, Vol. 3. 2008. (J). reprint ed. 428p. *(978-1-84677-590-1(6));* 424p. pap. *(978-1-84677-589-5(2))* Leonaur Ltd.
—The French & Indian War Novels: The Rulers of the Lakes & The Masters of the Peaks, Vol. 2. 2008. 416p. (J). reprint ed. *(978-1-84677-588-8(4));* pap. *(978-1-84677-587-1(6))* Leonaur Ltd.
—The Hunters of the Hills: A Story of the Great French & Indian War. rev. ed. 2006. (French & Indian War Ser.). 316p. (J). 29.95 *(978-1-4218-2334-8(9));* pap. 14.95 *(978-1-4218-2434-5(5))* 1st World Publishing, Inc. (1st World Library - Literary Society).
—The Hunters of the Hills: A Story of the Great French & Indian War. (French & Indian War Ser.: Vol. 1). (J). reprint ed. 26.95 *(978-0-8488-0904-1(1))* Amereon Ltd.
—The Hunters of the Hills: A Story of the Great French & Indian War. 2009. (French & Indian War Ser.: Vol. 1). 200p. (J). reprint ed. pap. *(978-0-217-62835-8(4))* Books LLC.
—The Hunters of the Hills: A Story of the Great French & Indian War. l.t. ed. 2007. (French & Indian War Ser.). (ENG.). 282p. (J). pap. 23.99 *(978-1-4264-8308-0(2))* 2012. 392p. reprint ed. pap. 33.75 *(978-1-277-16849-5(0))* 2008. (French & Indian War Ser.: Vol. 2). 284p. (J). reprint ed. 28.99 *(978-0-554-25147-9(7))* 2008. (French & Indian War Ser.: Vol. 2). 284p. (J). reprint ed. 25.99 *(978-0-554-34450-8(5))* 2007. (French & Indian War Ser.). (ENG.). 256p. (J). pap. 21.99 *(978-1-4264-8271-7(X))* Creative Media Partners, LLC.
—The Hunters of the Hills: A Story of the Great French & Indian War. 2006. (French & Indian War Ser.). (J). pap. *(978-1-4065-0815-4(2))* Dodo Pr.
—The Hunters of the Hills: A Story of the Great French & Indian War. 2007. (French & Indian War Ser.). 188p. (J). per. *(978-1-4068-1680-8(9))* Echo Library.
—The Hunters of the Hills: A Story of the Great French & Indian War. 2010. (French & Indian War Ser.: Vol. 1). (Illus.). 168p. (J). (gr. 4-7). reprint ed. pap. 19.99 *(978-1-153-70670-4(9))* General Bks. LLC.
—The Hunters of the Hills: A Story of the Great French & Indian War. (French & Indian War Ser.: Vol. 1). (J). reprint ed. 2011. 372p. (gr. 4-7). 48.95 *(978-1-169-83864-2(2))* 2010. 372p. (gr. 4-7). 39.16 *(978-1-163-20015-5(8))* 2010. 372p. (gr. 4-7). pap. 27.16 *(978-1-162-64218-5(1))* 2004. pap. 33.95 *(978-1-4179-1500-2(5))* Kessinger Publishing, LLC.
—The Hunters of the Hills: A Story of the Great French & Indian War. 2011. (French & Indian War Ser.: Vol. 1). 284p. (J). (gr. 4-7). reprint ed. pap. *(978-3-8424-7700-1(7))* Tredition GmbH.
—The Lords of the Wild: A Story of the Old New York Border. rev. ed. 2006. (French & Indian War Ser.). 264p. (J). 28.95 *(978-1-4218-2335-5(7));* pap. 13.95 *(978-1-4218-2435-2(3))* 1st World Publishing, Inc. (1st World Library - Literary Society).
—The Lords of the Wild: A Story of the Old New York Border. (French & Indian War Ser.: Vol. 1). (J). reprint ed. 24.95 *(978-0-8488-0905-8(X))* Amereon Ltd.
—The Lords of the Wild: A Story of the Old New York Border. (French & Indian War Ser.). (J). 2007. (ENG.). 212p. pap. 20.99 *(978-1-4264-5696-1(4))* 2007. (ENG.). 234p. pap. 22.99 *(978-1-4264-5741-8(3))* 2008. 236p. reprint ed. 27.99 *(978-0-554-24080-0(7))* 2008. 236p. reprint ed. 24.99 *(978-0-554-33383-0(X))* Creative Media Partners, LLC.
—The Lords of the Wild: A Story of the Old New York Border. 2006. (French & Indian War Ser.). (J). pap. *(978-1-4065-0816-1(0))* Dodo Pr.
—The Lords of the Wild: A Story of the Old New York Border. 2007. (French & Indian War Ser.). 156p. (J). per. *(978-1-4068-1681-5(7))* Echo Library.
—The Lords of the Wild: A Story of the Old New York Border. 2010. (French & Indian War Ser.: Vol. 5). (Illus.). 138p. (J). (gr. 4-7). reprint ed. pap. 19.99 *(978-1-153-71020-6(X))* General Bks. LLC.
—The Lords of the Wild: A Story of the Old New York Border. (French & Indian War Ser.: Vol. 5). (J). reprint ed. 2010. 208p. (gr. 4-7). 31.96 *(978-1-169-28834-8(0))* 2010. 208p. (gr. 4-7). pap. 19.96 *(978-1-162-70072-4(6))* 2010. 39.95 *(978-1-161-46937-0(0))* 2004. pap. 1.99 *(978-1-4192-7070-3(2))* 2004. pap. 24.95 *(978-1-4191-7070-6(8))* Kessinger Publishing, LLC.
—The Lords of the Wild: A Story of the Old New York Border. 2011. (French & Indian War Ser.: Vol. 5). 236p. (J). reprint ed. pap. *(978-3-8424-4395-2(1))* Tredition GmbH.
—The Rulers of the Lakes: A Story of George & Champlain. 2006. (French & Indian War Ser.: Vol. 3). 300p. (J). reprint ed. 29.95 *(978-1-4218-1778-1(0));* pap. 14.95 *(978-1-4218-1878-8(7))* 1st World Publishing, Inc. (1st World Library - Literary Society).
—The Rulers of the Lakes: A Story of George & Champlain. (French & Indian War Ser.: Vol. 3). (J). reprint ed. 25.95 *(978-0-8488-0906-5(8))* Amereon Ltd.
—The Rulers of the Lakes: A Story of George & Champlain. 2008. (French & Indian War Ser.: Vol. 3). 272p. (J). 25.99 *(978-0-554-34451-5(3))* 2008. (French & Indian War Ser.: Vol. 3). 272p. (J). 28.99 *(978-0-554-25148-6(5))* 2007. (ENG.). 268p. reprint ed. pap. 23.99 *(978-1-4264-8309-7(0))* 2010. (French & Indian War Ser.: Vol. 3). (ENG.). 370p. (J). (gr. 4-7). reprint ed. pap. 32.75 *(978-1-177-56810-4(1))* Creative Media Partners, LLC.
—The Rulers of the Lakes: A Story of George & Champlain. Henry, J., illus. 2007. (French & Indian War Ser.: Vol. 3). 214p. (J). reprint ed. pap. 20.99 *(978-1-4264-8272-4(8))* Creative Media Partners, LLC.
—The Rulers of the Lakes: A Story of George & Champlain. 2006. (French & Indian War Ser.: Vol. 3). (J). reprint ed. pap. *(978-1-4065-0819-2(5))* Dodo Pr.
—The Rulers of the Lakes: A Story of George & Champlain. 2010. 166p. pap. 24.67 *(978-1-152-80290-2(9));* (French & Indian War Ser.: Vol. 3). (Illus.). 160p. (J). (gr. 4-7). reprint ed. pap. 19.99 *(978-1-153-71979-7(7))* General Bks. LLC.
—The Rulers of the Lakes: A Story of George & Champlain. reprint ed. 2010. 366p. 39.16 *(978-1-163-74095-8(0))* 2010. 366p. pap. 27.16 *(978-1-163-71977-0(3))* 2007. (French & Indian War Ser.: Vol. 3). 368p. (J). 48.95 *(978-0-548-43205-1(8))* 2007. (French & Indian War Ser.: Vol. 3). 368p. (J). pap. 33.95 *(978-0-548-40955-8(2))* Kessinger Publishing, LLC.
—The Rulers of the Lakes: A Story of George & Champlain. 2011. (French & Indian War Ser.: Vol. 3). 272p. (J). (gr. 4-7). reprint ed. pap. *(978-3-8424-7701-8(5))* Tredition GmbH.
—The Shadow of the North: A Story of Old New York & a Lost Campaign. l.t. ed. (French & Indian War Ser.: Vol. 2). (J). reprint ed. 2007. (ENG.). 290p. pap. 23.99 *(978-1-4264-5705-0(7))* 2010. (ENG.). 378p. (gr. 4-7). pap. 33.75 *(978-1-176-98060-0(2))* 2008. 292p. 28.99 *(978-0-554-24046-6(7))* 2008. 292p. 25.99 *(978-0-554-33349-6(X))* 2007. (ENG.). 260p. pap. 21.99 *(978-1-4264-5660-2(3))* Creative Media Partners, LLC.
—The Shadow of the North: A Story of Old New York & a Lost Campaign. 2006. (French & Indian War Ser.: Vol. 2). (J). reprint ed. pap. *(978-1-4065-0823-9(3))* Dodo Pr.
—The Shadow of the North: A Story of Old New York & a Lost Campaign. 2007. (French & Indian War Ser.: Vol. 2). 188p. (J). reprint ed. per. *(978-1-4068-1687-7(6))* Echo Library.
—The Shadow of the North: A Story of Old New York & a Lost Campaign. 2010. (French & Indian War Ser.: Vol. 2). (Illus.). 170p. (J). (gr. 4-7). reprint ed. pap. 19.99 *(978-1-153-72063-2(9))* General Bks. LLC.
—The Shadow of the North: A Story of Old New York & a Lost Campaign. (French & Indian War Ser.: Vol. 2). (J). reprint ed. 2010. 256p. (gr. 4-7). 34.36 *(978-1-169-30396-6(X))* 2010. 256p. (gr. 4-7). pap. 22.36 *(978-1-162-70813-3(1))* 2010. 42.95 *(978-1-161-47677-4(6))* 2004. pap. 27.95 *(978-1-4191-8225-9(0))* 2004. pap. 1.99 *(978-1-4192-8225-6(5))* Kessinger Publishing, LLC.
—The Shadow of the North: A Story of Old New York & a Lost Campaign. 2011. (French & Indian War Ser.: Vol. 2). 286p. (J). reprint ed. pap. *(978-3-8424-4397-6(8))* Tredition GmbH.
—The Sun of Quebec: A Story of a Great Crisis. 2006. (French & Indian War Ser.: Vol. 6). 324p. (J). reprint ed. 29.95 *(978-1-4218-2337-9(3));* pap. 14.95 *(978-1-4218-2437-6(X))* 1st World Publishing, Inc. (1st World Library - Literary Society).
—The Sun of Quebec: A Story of a Great Crisis. (French & Indian War Ser.: Vol. 6). (J). reprint ed. 25.95 *(978-0-8488-0907-2(6))* Amereon Ltd.
—The Sun of Quebec: A Story of a Great Crisis. l.t. ed. (French & Indian War Ser.: Vol. 6). (J). reprint ed. 2007. 296p. pap. 23.99 *(978-1-4264-9822-0(5))* 2008. 300p. 28.99 *(978-0-554-25710-5(6))* 2008. 300p. 25.99 *(978-0-554-35013-4(0))* 2007. (ENG.). 264p. pap. 21.99 *(978-1-4264-9441-3(6))* Creative Media Partners, LLC.
—The Sun of Quebec: A Story of a Great Crisis. 2007. (French & Indian War Ser.: Vol. 6). 280p. (J). reprint ed. per. *(978-1-4065-6552-2(0))* Dodo Pr.
—The Sun of Quebec: A Story of a Great Crisis. 2007. (French & Indian War Ser.: Vol. 6). 196p. (J). reprint ed. per. *(978-1-4068-1689-1(2))* Echo Library.
—The Sun of Quebec: A Story of a Great Crisis. 2010. (French & Indian War Ser.: Vol. 6). (Illus.). 176p. (J). (gr. 4-7). reprint ed. pap. 19.99 *(978-1-153-72258-2(5))* General Bks. LLC.
—The Sun of Quebec: A Story of a Great Crisis. 2011. (French & Indian War Ser.: Vol. 6). (J). (gr. 4-7). reprint ed. *(978-1-164-50609-6(9))* Kessinger Publishing, LLC.
—The Sun of Quebec: A Story of a Great Crisis. Wrenn, Charles L., illus. (French & Indian War Ser.: Vol. 6). 356p. (J). reprint ed. 2010. (gr. 4-7). pap. 25.56 *(978-1-163-19471-3(9))* 2008. 46.95 *(978-1-4366-7287-0(2))* 2007. per. 31.95 *(978-1-4325-9779-5(5))* Kessinger Publishing, LLC.
—The Sun of Quebec: A Story of a Great Crisis. 2012. (French & Indian War Ser.: Vol. 6). 276p. (J). (gr. 4-7). reprint ed. pap. *(978-3-8472-3211-7(8))* Tredition GmbH.
Altsheler, Joseph A., ed. The Masters of the Peaks: A Story of the Great North Woods. (French & Indian War Ser.: Vol. 4). 311p. (J). reprint ed. lib. bdg. 24.95 *(978-0-88411-938-8(6))* Amereon Ltd.
—The Masters of the Peaks: A Story of the Great North Woods. 2010. (French & Indian War Ser.: Vol. 4). (Illus.). 144p. (J). (gr. 4-7). reprint ed. pap. *(978-1-4432-2285-3(2))* Books LLC.
—The Masters of the Peaks: A Story of the Great North Woods. l.t. ed. reprint ed. 2007. (French & Indian War Ser.: Vol. 4). (ENG.). 248p. (J). pap. 22.99 *(978-1-4264-4882-9(1))* 2012. 182p. pap. 22.75 *(978-1-276-49474-8(2))* 2010. (French & Indian War Ser.: Vol. 4). 320p. (J). pap. 30.75 *(978-1-142-51783-0(7))* 2008. (French & Indian War Ser.: Vol. 4). 252p. (J). 27.99 *(978-0-554-23650-6(8))* 2008. (French & Indian War Ser.: Vol. 4). 252p. (J). 24.99 *(978-0-554-32953-6(0))* 2007. (French & Indian War Ser.: Vol. 4). (ENG.). 222p. (J). pap. 20.99 *(978-1-4264-4839-3(2))* Creative Media Partners, LLC.
—The Masters of the Peaks: A Story of the Great North Woods. 2006. (French & Indian War Ser.: Vol. 4). (J). reprint ed. pap. *(978-1-4065-0817-8(9))* Dodo Pr.
—The Masters of the Peaks: A Story of the Great North Woods. 2006. (French & Indian War Ser.: Vol. 4). (J). reprint ed. pap. *(978-1-4068-0762-2(1))* Echo Library.
—The Masters of the Peaks: A Story of the Great North Woods. 2009. (French & Indian War Ser.: Vol. 4). 162p. (J). reprint ed. pap. 8.85 *(978-1-150-40712-3(3))* General Bks. LLC.
—The Masters of the Peaks: A Story of the Great North Woods. (French & Indian War Ser.: Vol. 4). (J). reprint ed. 2010. 220p. (gr. 4-7). 31.96 *(978-1-169-29283-3(6))* 2010. 220p. (gr. 4-7). pap. 19.96 *(978-1-162-70171-4(4))* 2010. 39.95 *(978-1-161-47035-2(2))* 2004. pap. 1.99 *(978-1-4192-7205-9(5))* 2004. pap. 24.95 *(978-1-4191-7205-2(0))* Kessinger Publishing, LLC.
—The Masters of the Peaks: A Story of the Great North Woods. 2011. (French & Indian War Ser.: Vol. 4). 228p. (J). reprint ed. pap. *(978-3-8424-4394-5(3))* Tredition GmbH.
Cooper, James Fenimore. The Last of the Mohicans. Wyeth, N. C., illus. 2013. (Scribner Classics Ser.). (ENG.). 368p. (J). (gr. 5). 24.99 *(978-1-4424-8130-5(7),* Atheneum Bks. for Young Readers) Simon & Schuster Children's Publishing.
—The Last of the Mohicans. Howell, Troy, illus. 2008. (Classic Starts(tm) Ser.). (ENG.). 160p. (J). (gr. 2-4). 6.95 *(978-1-4027-4577-5(X))* Sterling Publishing Co., Inc.
—Last of the Mohicans, 1 vol. Fields, Jan, illus. 2010. (Calico Illustrated Classics Ser.: No. 1). (ENG.). 112p. (J). (gr. 3-6). 27.07 *(978-1-60270-708-5(1))* Magic Wagon.
Hemphill, Kris. Ambush in the Wilderness. 2003. (Adventures in America Ser.). (Illus.). 90p. (gr. 4). 14.95 *(978-1-893110-34-2(6))* Silver Moon Pr.
Henty, George Alfred. With Wolfe in Canad: The Winning of a Continent. 2011. 378p. pap. 19.95 *(978-1-61179-149-5(9))* Fireship Pr.
—With Wolfe in Canada: The Winning of a Continent. 2006. per. 8.95 *(978-1-57646-980-4(8))* Quiet Vision Publishing.
Kastner, Janet. The Snake Fence: A Novel. 2012. (J). pap. 14.95 *(978-1-937768-13-3(9))* QuakerPress.

UNITED STATES—HISTORY—REVOLUTION, 1775-1783

Abnett, Dan. George Washington & the American Revolution. (Jr. Graphic Biographies Ser.). (ENG.). 24p. 2009. (J). (gr. 2-3). 47.90 *(978-1-61513-813-5(7),* PowerKids Pr.) 2007. (Illus.). (J). (gr. 2-5). lib. bdg. 25.25 *(978-1-4042-3395-9(4))* 2007. (Illus.). (gr. 3-8). pap. 10.60 *(978-1-4042-2148-2(4),* PowerKids Pr.) Rosen Publishing Group, Inc., The.
—George Washington y la Guerra de Independencia. 2009. (Historietas Juveniles: Biografías (Jr. Graphic Biographies) Ser.). (SPA & ENG., Illus.). 24p. (YA). (gr. 2-5). 25.25 *(978-1-4358-8564-6(3))* Rosen Publishing Group, Inc., The.
Adams, Colleen. Results of the American Revolution: Summarizing Information. (Critical Thinking in American History Ser.). 48p. 2009. (gr. 5-8). 53.00 *(978-1-61512-096-3(3),* Rosen Reference) 2005. (Illus.). (J). (gr. k-3). lib. bdg. 29.25 *(978-1-4042-0417-1(2))* Rosen Publishing Group, Inc., The.
Adamson, Thomas K. The American Revolution. 2015. (Wars in U. S. History Ser.). (ENG.). 32p. (J). (gr. 2-5). 28.50 *(978-1-63143-707-6(0),* 208539) Child's World, Inc., The.
Adler, David A. Heroes of the Revolution. Smith, Donald A., illus. 2006. (ENG.). 32p. (J). (gr. 1-4). 7.99 *(978-0-8234-2017-9(5))* Holiday Hse., Inc.
Adler, David A. & Adler, Michael S. A Picture Book of Sam Houston. Collins, Matt, illus. 2012. (ENG.). 32p. (J). (gr. -1-3). 17.95 *(978-0-8234-2369-9(7))* Holiday Hse., Inc.
—A Picture Book of Samuel Adams. Himler, Ronald, illus. 2005. (ENG.). 32p. (J). 16.95 *(978-0-8234-1846-6(4))* Holiday Hse., Inc.
Allen, Thomas B. George Washington, Spymaster: How the Americans Outspied the British & Won the Revolutionary War. Harness, Cheryl, illus. 2007. (ENG.). 192p. (J). (gr. 5-7). per. 7.95 *(978-1-4263-0041-7(7),* National Geographic Children's Bks.) National Geographic Society.
American Revolution. 2013. (American Revolution Ser.: 6). 32p. (J). (gr. 5-9). lib. bdg. 162.42 *(978-1-61783-677-0(X),* Abdo & Daughters) ABDO Publishing Co.
The American Revolution Complete Program. (gr. 2-5). 430.95 *(978-0-7368-4502-1(X))* Red Brick Learning.
Amler, Jane Frances. Haym Salomon: Patriot Banker of the American Revolution. 2009. (Library of American Lives & Times Ser.). 112p. (gr. 5-5). 69.20 *(978-1-60853-487-6(1))* Rosen Publishing Group, Inc., The.
Anderson, Dale. The American Colonies Declare Independence. 2005. (World Almanac Library of the American Revolution Ser.). (Illus.). 48p. (gr. 5-12). lib. bdg. 31.00 *(978-0-8368-5926-3(X),* Gareth Stevens Secondary Library) Stevens, Gareth Publishing LLLP.
—The American Revolution: Events & Outcomes. 2006. (Illus.). 78p. (YA). (gr. 5-9). reprint ed. 17.00 *(978-1-4223-5441-4(5))* DIANE Publishing Co.
—The Causes of the American Revolution. 2005. (World Almanac Library of the American Revolution Ser.). 48p. (gr. 5-12). pap. 14.05 *(978-0-8368-5934-8(0));* (Illus.). lib. bdg. 31.00 *(978-0-8368-5925-6(1))* Stevens, Gareth Publishing LLLP. (Gareth Stevens Secondary Library).
—Daily Life During the American Revolution. 2005. (World Almanac Library of the American Revolution Ser.). 48p. (gr. 5-12). pap. 14.05 *(978-0-8368-5939-3(1));* lib. bdg. 31.00 *(978-0-8368-5930-0(8))* Stevens, Gareth Publishing LLLP. (Gareth Stevens Secondary Library).
—Leaders of the American Revolution. 2005. (World Almanac Library of the American Revolution Ser.). 48p. (gr. 5-12). pap. 14.05 *(978-0-8368-5940-9(5));* lib. bdg. 31.00 *(978-0-8368-5931-7(6))* Stevens, Gareth Publishing LLLP. (Gareth Stevens Secondary Library).
—Soldiers & Sailors in the American Revolution. 2005. (World Almanac Library of the American Revolution Ser.). 48p. (gr. 5-12). pap. 14.05 *(978-0-8368-5938-6(3));* lib. bdg. 31.00 *(978-0-8368-5929-4(4))* Stevens, Gareth Publishing LLLP. (Gareth Stevens Secondary Library).
Anderson, Floyd. Father of the American Navy: John Barry. Orban, Paul, illus. 2011. 188p. 42.95 *(978-1-258-07454-8(0))* Literary Licensing, LLC.
Appleby, Joyce, et al. The American Republic to 1877. 2003. (Illus.). 670p. stu. ed. 122.75 *(978-0-07-826474-0(X))* McGraw-Hill Cos., The.
Aronson, Marc. The Real Revolution: The Global Story of American Independence. 2005. (ENG., Illus.). 256p. (YA). (gr. 7-12). 22.00 *(978-0-618-18179-7(2))* Houghton Mifflin Harcourt Publishing Co.
The Atlas of Famous Battles of the American Revolution. (Illus.). (J). (gr. k-5). 127.50 *(978-0-8239-7269-2(0))* Rosen Publishing Group, Inc., The.
Axelrod, Alan. The Revolutionary War. Künstler, Mort, illus. 2016. (See American History Ser.). (ENG.). 48p. (J). (gr. 2-7). 13.95 *(978-0-7892-1253-5(6),* Abbeville Kids) Abbeville Pr., Inc.
Bearce, Stephanie. The American Revolution: Spies, Secret Missions, & Hidden Facts from the American Revolution. 2014. (Top Secret Files of History Ser.: 0). (ENG.). 125p. (J). (gr. 4-7). pap. 8.95 *(978-1-61821-247-4(8))* Prufrock Pr.
Beller, Susan Provost. Yankee Doodle & the Redcoats: Soldiering in the Revolutionary War. rev. ed. 2007. (Soldiers on the Battlefront Ser.). (ENG., Illus.). 112p. (gr. 6-8). lib. bdg. 33.26 *(978-0-8225-6655-7(9))* Lerner Publishing Group.
Benchmark Education Co., LLC. The Causes of the American Revolution. 2014. (PRIME Ser.). (J). (gr. 6-8). pap. *(978-1-4509-9489-7(X))* Benchmark Education Co.
—The Faces of the American Revolution. 2014. (PRIME Ser.). (J). (gr. 6-8). pap. *(978-1-4509-9491-0(1))* Benchmark Education Co.
Benchmark Education Company. George Washington & the American Revolution (Teacher Guide) 2005. *(978-1-4108-4681-5(4))* Benchmark Education Co.
Benchmark Education Company, LLC Staff, compiled by. The AMER Revolution. 2006. spiral bd. 330.00 *(978-1-4108-7010-0(3))* Benchmark Education Co.
—The American Revolution. 2005. (English Explorers Ser.). (J). spiral bd. 265.00 *(978-1-4108-5771-2(9))* Benchmark Education Co.
—The American Revolution: Theme Set. 2006. (J). 131.00 *(978-1-4108-7125-1(8))* Benchmark Education Co.
—Freedom's Trail & AMER Revolution. 2005. spiral bd. 225.00 *(978-1-4108-5825-2(1))* Benchmark Education Co.
—Social Studies Theme: The AMER Revolution. 2005. spiral bd. 115.00 *(978-1-4108-5326-4(8))* Benchmark Education Co.
Blair, Margaret Whitman. Liberty or Death: The Surprising Story of Runaway Slaves Who Sided with the British During the American Revolution. 2010. (ENG., Illus.). 64p. (J). (gr. 5-8). 27.90 *(978-1-4263-0591-7(5));* 18.95 *(978-1-4263-0590-0(7))* National Geographic Society. (National Geographic Children's Bks.).
Bober, Natalie S. Countdown to Independence. 2007. (ENG.). 368p. (YA). (gr. 7). pap. 19.95 *(978-1-4169-6392-9(8),* Atheneum Bks. for Young Readers) Simon & Schuster Children's Publishing.
Bobrick, Benson. Fight for Freedom: The American Revolutionary War. 2004. (ENG., Illus.). 96p. (J). 24.99 *(978-0-689-86422-3(1),* Atheneum Bks. for Young Readers) Simon & Schuster Children's Publishing.
Bodden, Valerie. The Declaration of American Independence. 2009. (Days of Change Ser.). (Illus.). 48p. (YA). (gr. 4-7). 22.95 *(978-1-58341-733-1(8))* Creative Co., The.
Botones para el General Washington (Buttons for General Washington) 2006. (J). pap. 6.95 *(978-0-8225-6617-5(6),* Ediciones Lerner) Lerner Publishing Group.
Boyer, Marilyn. For you they Signed. 2010. (YA). lib. bdg. 34.99 *(978-0-89051-598-3(0))* Master Bks.
Brennan, Linda. The Black Regiment of the American Revolution. Noll, Cheryl Kirk, illus. 2005. 32p. (J). (gr. 4-7). per. 8.95 *(978-1-931659-18-5(4))* Moon Mountain Publishing, Inc.
Brennan, Linda Crotta. The Birth of the United States. 2011. (Explorer Library: Language Arts Explorer Ser.). (ENG.). 32p. (gr. 4-8). pap. 14.21 *(978-1-61080-285-7(3),* 201208); lib. bdg. 28.50 *(978-1-61080-197-3(0),* 201170) Cherry Lake Publishing.
Broida, Marian. Projects about the American Revolution. 2005. (Hands-On History Ser.). (Illus.). 48p. (J). (gr. 3-7). lib. bdg. *(978-0-7614-1981-5(0),* Benchmark Bks.) Marshall Cavendish Corp.
Brooks, Philip. King George III: America's Enemy. 2009. (Wicked History Ser.). (ENG.). 128p. (J). (gr. 6-12). pap. 5.95 *(978-0-531-20739-0(0));* (Illus.). 31.00 *(978-0-531-21803-7(1))* Scholastic Library Publishing. (Watts, Franklin).
Burgan, Michael. The Battle of Bunker Hill: An Interactive History Adventure. 2016. (You Choose: History Ser.). (ENG.). 112p. (gr. 3-4). lib. bdg. 31.99 *(978-1-5157-3384-3(X),* You Choose Bks.) Capstone Press of Coughlan Cos.
—Benedict Arnold: American Hero & Traitor, 1 vol. Beatty, Terry, illus. 2007. (Graphic Biographies Ser.). (ENG.). 32p. (gr. 3-4). per. 8.10 *(978-0-7368-7906-4(4),* Graphic Library) Capstone Press of Coughlan Cos.
—The Split History of the American Revolution: A Perspectives Flip Book, 1 vol. 2012. (Perspectives Flip Bks.). (ENG.). 64p. (gr. 5-6). pap. 8.95 *(978-0-7565-4592-5(7));* lib. bdg. 33.99 *(978-0-7565-4570-3(6))* Compass Point Bks.
—The Untold Story of the Black Regiment: Fighting in the Revolutionary War. 2015. (What You Didn't Know about the American Revolution Ser.). (ENG.). 64p. (gr. 4-8). 34.65 *(978-0-7565-4975-6(2))* Compass Point Bks.
—Weapons, Gear, & Uniforms of the American Revolution, 1 vol. 2012. (Equipped for Battle Ser.). (ENG.). 32p. (gr. 3-4). lib. bdg. 27.99 *(978-1-4296-7647-2(7),* Edge Bks.) Capstone Press of Coughlan Cos.
Burt, Barbara & Schifini, Alfredo. Colonial Life. 2007. (Avenues Ser.). (ENG., Illus.). 40p. (J). pap. 19.95 *(978-0-7922-8678-3(2))* CENGAGE Learning.
Butcher, Andrew & Toohey, Vincent. Analysing the American Revolution Pack (Textbook & Interactive Textbook) 2nd ed. 2015. (ENG.). pap. *(978-1-107-50647-3(6))* Cambridge Univ. Pr.
Caravantes, Peggy. The American Revolution: 12 Things to Know. 2017. (America at War Ser.). (ENG., Illus.). 32p. (J). (gr. 3-6). 21.95 *(978-1-63235-264-4(8))* Pr. Room Editions LLC.
Carole Marsh. How Our Nation Was Born: the American Revolution. 2004. (American Milestones Ser.). 32p. (gr. 3-8). pap. 5.95 *(978-0-635-02348-3(2));* (gr. 4-12). 29.95 *(978-0-635-02349-0(0))* Gallopade International.

TUV

Carr, Joaquin. The American Revolution: Set Of 6. 2011. (Navigators Ser.). (J). pap. 48.00 net. (978-1-4108-5108-6(7)) Benchmark Education Co.

—The American Revolution: Text Pairs. 2008. (BridgesNavigators Ser.). (J). (gr. 5). 89.00 (978-1-4108-8403-9(1)) Benchmark Education Co.

Carson, Mary Kay. Did It All Start with a Snowball Fight? And Other Questions about... the American Revolution. Elliott, Mark & Hunt, Robert, illus. 2012. (Good Question! Ser.). (ENG.). 40p. (J). 12.95 (978-1-4027-9626-5(9)) Sterling Publishing Co., Inc.

—Did It All Start with a Snowball Fight? And Other Questions about... The American Revolution. Elliott, Mark & Hunt, Robert, illus. 2012. (Good Question! Ser.). (ENG.). 32p. (J). pap. 5.95 (978-1-4027-8734-8(0)) Sterling Publishing Co., Inc.

Casey, Susan. Women Heroes of the American Revolution: 20 Stories of Espionage, Sabotage, Defiance, & Rescue. 2017. (Women of Action Ser.). (ENG.). 240p. (YA). (gr. 7). pap. 12.99 **(978-1-61373-831-3(5))** Chicago Review Pr., Inc.

Castellano, Peter. The American Revolution. 2017. (Look at U. S. History Ser.). 32p. (J). (gr. 2-2). pap. 10.50 (978-1-4824-6023-0(8)) Stevens, Gareth Publishing LLLP.

Castrovilla, Selene. Revolutionary Friends: General George Washington & the Marquis de Lafayette. Kozjan, Drazen, illus. 2013. (ENG.). 40p. (J). (gr. 3). 16.95 (978-1-59078-880-6(X), Calkins Creek) Boyds Mills Pr.

Catel, Patrick. The Home Front of the Revolutionary War, 1 vol. (Why We Fought: the Revolutionary War Ser.). (ENG.). 48p. (gr. 3-6). 2011. pap. 9.95 (978-1-4329-3900-7(9)) 2010. 33.32 (978-1-4329-3895-6(9)) Heinemann-Raintree. (Heinemann InfoSearch).

—Soldiers of the Revolutionary War, 1 vol. (Why We Fought: the Revolutionary War Ser.). (ENG.). 48p. (gr. 3-6). 2011. pap. 9.95 (978-1-4329-3903-8(3)) 2010. 33.32 (978-1-4329-3898-7(3)) Heinemann-Raintree. (Heinemann InfoSearch).

—Why We Fought Set: The Revolutionary War, 4 vols. Incl. Battles of the Revolutionary War. pap. 9.95 (978-1-4329-3901-4(7)); Home Front of the Revolutionary War. pap. 9.95 (978-1-4329-3900-7(9)); Soldiers of the Revolutionary War. pap. 9.95 (978-1-4329-3903-8(3)); (gr. 3-6). (Why We Fought: the Revolutionary War Ser.). (ENG.). 48p. 2011. Set pap. 29.85 (978-1-4329-3904-5(1), Heinemann InfoSearch) Heinemann-Raintree.

Causes of the American Revolution (NCHS) Grades 7-9. (J). tchr. ed., spiral bd. 13.50 (978-0-382-44448-7(5)) Cobblestone Publishing Co.

Cefrey, Holly. One Life to Lose for My Country: The Arrest & Execution of Nathan Hale. (Great Moments in American History Ser.). 32p. 2009. (gr. 3-3). 47.90 (978-1-61513-135-8(3)) 2004. (Illus.). (gr. 4-8). lib. bdg. 22.50 (978-0-8239-4371-5(2), Rosen Reference) Rosen Publishing Group, Inc., The.

Cheatham, Mark. The Life of a Colonial Soldier. 2013. (Jr. Graphic Colonial America Ser.). (ENG., Illus.). 24p. (J). (gr. 3-6). pap. 10.60 (978-1-4777-1439-3(1)); lib. bdg. 25.25 (978-1-4777-1310-5(7)) Rosen Publishing Group, Inc., The. (PowerKids Pr.).

Clark, Willow. The True Story of the Declaration of Independence. 2013. (What Really Happened? Ser.). (ENG., Illus.). 24p. (J). (gr. 3-6). pap. 8.25 (978-1-4488-9840-4(4)); lib. bdg. 22.60 (978-1-4488-9691-2(6)) Rosen Publishing Group, Inc., The. (PowerKids Pr.).

Collins, Kathleen. El Marques de Lafayette: Heroe Frances de la Guerra de Independencia. 2004. (Grandes personajes en la historia de los Estados Unidos Ser.). (SPA.). 32p. (gr. 3-6). pap. 10.00 (978-0-8239-4233-6(3), Rosen Classroom) Rosen Publishing Group, Inc., The.

—Marquis de Lafayette: French Hero of the American Revolution. 2009. (Primary Sources of Famous People in American History Ser.). 32p. (gr. 2-3). 47.90 (978-1-60851-703-9(9)) Rosen Publishing Group, Inc., The.

—Marquis de Lafayette / el Marques de Lafayette: French Hero of the American Revolution / Héroe francés de la Revolución Estadounidense. 2009. (Famous People in American History/Grandes personajes en la historia de los Estados Unidos Ser.). (ENG & SPA.). 32p. (gr. 2-3). 47.90 (978-1-61512-550-0(7), Editorial Buenas Letras) Rosen Publishing Group, Inc., The.

Colonial America, 1543-1763. 2010. (Discovering U. S. History Ser.). (Illus.). 136p. (gr. 5-8). 35.00 (978-1-60413-349-3(X), Chelsea Hse.) Facts On File, Inc.

Conklin, Wendy. Benjamin Franklin, 1 vol. 2004. (Primary Source Readers Ser.). (ENG.). 24p. (J). (gr. 4-4). pap. 8.99 (978-0-7439-8755-4(1)) Shell Educational Publishing.

Corporate Contibutor & Perritano, John. The Causes of the American Revolution. 2012. (ENG.). 48p. (J). (978-0-7787-0804-9(7)) Crabtree Publishing Co.

—The Outcome of the American Revolution. 2012. (ENG.). 48p. (J). (978-0-7787-0805-6(5)) Crabtree Publishing Co.

Corporate Contibutor Staff & Clarke, Gordon. Significant Battles of the American Revolution. 2012. (ENG.). 48p. (J). (978-0-7787-0806-3(3)) Crabtree Publishing Co.

Corporate Contibutor Staff & Mason, Helen. Life on the Homefront During the American Revolution. 2012. (ENG.). 48p. (J). (978-0-7787-0801-8(2)); pap. (978-0-7787-0812-4(8)) Crabtree Publishing Co.

Cox, Vicki. Betsy Ross: Flag for a New Nation. 2005. (Leaders of the American Revolution Ser.). (Illus.). 100p. (gr. 5-8). lib. bdg. 30.00 (978-0-7910-8618-6(6)) Facts On File, Inc.

Crabtree Staff & Perritano, John. The Outcome of the American Revolution. 2012. (ENG., Illus.). 48p. (J). pap. (978-0-7787-0816-2(0)) Crabtree Publishing Co.

Crawford, Laura. The American Revolution from A to Z, 1 vol. Hierstein, Judith, illus. 2009. (ENG.). 32p. (J). (gr. k-3). 16.99 (978-1-58980-515-6(1)) Pelican Publishing Co., Inc.

Crompton, Samuel Willard. Thomas Paine: Fighting for American Independence. 2017. (Rebels with a Cause Ser.). 128p. (gr. 8-8). lib. bdg. 37.27 **(978-0-7660-8515-2(5))** Enslow Pubs., Inc.

Crompton, Samuel Willard. Thomas Paine & the Fight for Liberty. 2005. (Leaders of the American Revolution Ser.). (Illus.). 100p. (J). (gr. 5-8). lib. bdg. 30.00 (978-0-7910-8625-4(9)) Facts On File, Inc.

Davenport, John. The American Revolution. (American History Ser.). 2009. pap. 24.10 (978-1-4205-0300-5(6)) 2007. (ENG., Illus.). 104p. (J). (gr. 3-7). lib. bdg. 33.45 (978-1-59018-939-9(6)) Cengage Gale. (Lucent Bks.).

Davies, Monika. True Life: Alexander Hamilton. 2016. (TIME for KIDS(r) Nonfiction Readers Ser.). (Illus.). 48p. (J). (gr. 8-8). pap. 9.99 **(978-1-4938-3633-8(1))** Teacher Created Materials, Inc.

Davis, Graeme. The Weapons & Gear of the Revolutionary War. 2012. (Story of the American Revolution Ser.). (ENG.). 32p. (gr. 3-4). pap. 47.70 (978-1-4296-9289-2(8), Fact Finders); (Illus.). lib. bdg. 27.32 (978-1-4296-8588-7(3)) Capstone Press of Coughlan Cos.

Deem, James M. Primary Source Accounts of the Revolutionary War. 2006. (America's Wars Through Primary Sources Ser.). (Illus.). 128p. (J). (gr. 4-7). lib. bdg. 34.60 (978-1-59845-004-0(2), MyReportLinks.com Bks.) Enslow Pubs., Inc.

DeFord, Deborah H. The American Revolution. 2006. (Wars That Changed American History Ser.). (Illus.). 48p. (gr. 5-12). pap. 14.05 (978-0-8368-7298-9(3)); lib. bdg. 31.00 (978-0-8368-7289-7(4)) Stevens, Gareth Publishing LLLP. (Gareth Stevens Secondary Library).

Dodge Cummings, Judy. The American Revolution: Experience the Battle for Independence. Casteel, Tom, illus. 2015. (Build It Yourself Ser.). (ENG.). 128p. (J). (gr. 3-7). 22.95 (978-1-61930-255-6(1)); pap. 17.95 (978-1-61930-246-4(2)) Open City Bks.

Doeden, Matt. Weapons of the Revolutionary War. 2017. (Weapons of War Ser.). (ENG.). 32p. (gr. 2-3). lib. bdg. 26.65 **(978-1-5157-7908-7(4))** Capstone Press of Coughlan Cos.

Dorais, Katherine M. The Revolutionary War & a Few Things More. 2011. 32p. (gr. -1). pap. 15.50 (978-1-4567-1193-1(8)) AuthorHouse.

Draper, Allison Stark. The Boston Tea Party: Angry Colonists Dump British Tea. 2009. (Headlines from History Ser.). 24p. (gr. 3-3). 42.50 (978-1-61513-244-7(9), PowerKids Pr.) Rosen Publishing Group, Inc., The.

—What People Wore During the American Revolution. 2009. (Clothing, Costumes, & Uniforms Throughout American History Ser.). 24p. (gr. 3-3). 42.50 (978-1-61511-875-5(6), PowerKids Pr.) Rosen Publishing Group, Inc., The.

Early American Wars, 4 vols., Set. Incl. American Revolutionary War. Marston, Daniel & O'Neill, Robert John. lib. bdg. 33.25 (978-1-4488-1331-5(X)); Texas War of Independence. Huffines, Alan C. lib. bdg. 33.25 (978-1-4488-1332-2(8)); War of 1812: The Fight for American Trade Rights. Benn, Carl. lib. bdg. 33.25 (978-1-4488-1333-9(6)); (YA). (gr. 9-18). 2011. (Early American Wars Ser.). (Illus.). 96p. 2011. Set lib. bdg. 127.80 (978-1-4488-1387-2(5)) Rosen Publishing Group, Inc., The.

Espinosa, Rod. American Revolution, 1 vol. 2008. (Graphic History Ser.). (ENG., Illus.). 32p. 28.50 (978-1-60270-179-3(2), Graphic Planet- Nonfiction) ABDO Publishing Co.

Farshtey, Greg. The American Revolution. 2003. (Daily Life Ser.). (Illus.). 48p. (J). (gr. 3-5). 26.20 (978-0-7377-1402-9(6), Kidhaven) Cengage Gale.

Figley, Marty Rhodes. John Greenwood's Journey to Bunker Hill. 2010. pap. 56.72 (978-0-7613-6927-1(9)) Lerner Publishing Group.

—Prisoner for Liberty. Orback, Craig, illus. (On My Own History Ser.). (ENG.). 48p. (gr. 2-4). 2009. pap. 6.95 (978-0-8225-9022-4(0), First Avenue Editions) 2008. lib. bdg. 25.26 (978-0-8225-7280-0(X), Millbrook Pr.) Lerner Publishing Group.

—Salvar a la Campana de la Libertad. Lepp, Kevin, illus. 2005. (Yo Solo Biografías Ser.). (SPA.). 48p. (J). (gr. 2-5). per. 6.95 (978-0-8225-3095-4(3)) Lerner Publishing Group.

—Salvar a la Campana de la Libertad; Saving the Liberty Bell. 2008. pap. 40.95 (978-0-7613-3933-5(7)) Lerner Publishing Group.

—Saving the Liberty Bell. Lepp, Kevin, illus. 2005. (On My Own History Ser.). (ENG.). 48p. (gr. 2-4). pap. 6.95 (978-1-57505-696-8(8)) Lerner Publishing Group.

Figley, Mary Rhodes. Prisoner for Liberty. 2009. pap. 40.95 (978-0-7613-4796-5(8)) Lerner Publishing Group.

Fitzgerald, Stephanie & Burgan, Michael. Perspective Flip Books. 2013. (Perspectives Flip Bks.). (ENG.). 64p. (gr. 5-6). pap. 17.90 (978-0-7565-4727-1(X), CPB Grades 4-8) Compass Point Bks.

Fitzgerald, Stephanie, et al. Perspective Flip Books. 2013. (Perspectives Flip Bks.). (ENG.). 64p. (gr. 5-6). pap. 53.70 (978-0-7565-4728-8(8), CPB Grades 4-8) Compass Point Bks.

Ford, Barbara. Paul Revere: American Patriot. 2015. (Legendary American Biographies Ser.). 96p. (J). (gr. 6-12). 27.94 (978-0-7660-6485-0(9)) Enslow Pubs., Inc.

Forest, Christopher. The Biggest Battles of the Revolutionary War, 1 vol. 2012. (Story of the American Revolution Ser.). (ENG.). 32p. (gr. 3-4). lib. bdg. 27.32 (978-1-4296-8429-3(1)) Capstone Press of Coughlan Cos.

—The Rebellious Colonists & the Causes of the American Revolution. 2012. (Story of the American Revolution Ser.). (ENG.). 32p. (gr. 3-4). pap. 47.70 (978-1-4296-9291-5(X), Fact Finders); (Illus.). pap. 8.10 (978-1-4296-9290-8(1)); (Illus.). lib. bdg. 27.32 (978-1-4296-8428-6(3)) Capstone Press of Coughlan Cos.

Forest, Christopher, et al. The Story of the American Revolution. 2012. (Story of the American Revolution Ser.). (ENG.). 32p. (gr. 3-4). 163.92 (978-1-4296-9152-9(2), Fact Finders) Capstone Press of Coughlan Cos.

Founding Fathers. (J). tchr. ed. 41.95 (978-0-382-40882-3(9)) Cobblestone Publishing Co.

Fradin, Dennis Brindell. The Stamp Act of 1765. 2009. (Turning Points in U. S. History Ser.). (Illus.). 48p. (J). (gr. 3-18). 31.36 (978-0-7614-4260-8(X)) Marshall Cavendish Corp.

Fremont-Barnes, Gregory & Ryerson, Richard A., eds. American Revolutionary War Set, Vol. 5: A Student Encyclopedia, 5 vols. 2006. (Illus.). 2548p. (C). (gr. 9-18). 439.00 (978-1-85109-839-2(9), RYFRES1C) ABC-CLIO, LLC.

Friddell, Claudia. George Washington's Spies. Lowe, Wesley, illus. 2016. (Totally True Adventures Ser.). (ENG.). 112p. (J). (gr. 2-5). pap. 4.99 (978-0-399-55077-5(1), Random Hse. Bks. for Young Readers) Random Hse. Children's Bks.

Fritz, Jean. Alexander Hamilton: The Outsider. 2012. (ENG.). 144p. (J). (gr. 3-7). 8.99 (978-0-14-241986-1(9), Puffin Books) Penguin Young Readers Group.

Garstecki, Julia. The Complete Guide to the Revolutionary War. 2016. (Illus.). 144p. (J). **(978-1-4351-6359-1(1))** Barnes & Noble, Inc.

George, Enzo. The American Revolution. 2015. (J). lib. bdg. (978-1-62713-487-3(5)) Cavendish Square Publishing.

George, Lynn. What Do You Know about the American Revolution? (20 Questions: History Ser.). 24p. (gr. 2-3). 2009. 42.50 (978-1-60854-957-3(7), PowerKids Pr.) 2008. (Illus.). (J). lib. bdg. 22.60 (978-1-4042-4186-2(8)) Rosen Publishing Group, Inc., The.

Glencoe McGraw-Hill Staff, creator. The American Republic to 1877 Reading Essentials & Study Guide Student Workbook. 2nd ed. 2004. (U. S. History - the Early Years Ser.). (ENG., Illus.). 264p. (gr. 6-9). stu. ed., per. 12.80 (978-0-07-865487-9(4), 0078654874) McGraw-Hill Higher Education.

Goodman, Michael E. Revolutionary War Spies. 2015. (Illus.). 48p. (J). (978-1-60818-601-3(6), Creative Education) Creative Co., The.

—Revolutionary War Spies: Wartime Spies. 2016. (Wartime Spies Ser.). (ENG.). 48p. (J). (gr. 5-9). pap. 12.00 (978-1-62832-206-4(3), Creative Paperbacks) Creative Co., The.

Grayson, Robert. Revolutionary War, 1 vol. 2013. (Essential Library of American Wars Ser.). (ENG.). 112p. (J). (gr. 6-12). lib. bdg. 35.64 (978-1-61783-879-8(9), Essential Library) ABDO Publishing Co.

Gregory, Josh. The Revolutionary War. 2011. (Cornerstones of Freedom, Third Ser.). 64p. (J). (ENG.). pap. 8.95 (978-0-531-26564-2(1)); lib. bdg. 30.00 (978-0-531-25039-6(3)) Scholastic Library Publishing. (Children's Pr.).

Group/McGraw-Hill, Wright. History: Revolutionary War, 6 vols. (Book2WebTM Ser.). (gr. 4-8). 36.50 (978-0-322-04450-0(2)) Wright Group/McGraw-Hill.

Gunderson, Cory. Boston Tea Party, 1 vol. 2004. (American Moments Ser.). (ENG., Illus.). 48p. (gr. 4-8). 27.07 (978-1-59197-280-8(9), Abdo & Daughters) ABDO Publishing Co.

Gunderson, Jessica. Benedict Arnold: Battlefield Hero or Selfish Traitor?, 1 vol. 2013. (Perspectives on History Ser.). (ENG.). 32p. (gr. 3-4). 27.32 (978-1-4765-0243-4(9)); pap. 7.95 (978-1-4765-3407-7(1)) Capstone Press of Coughlan Cos. (Fact Finders).

Hakim, Joy. From Colonies to Country, 1735-1791. 3rd rev. ed. 2006. (History of US Ser.: 3). (ENG., Illus.). 224p. (gr. 4-7). 24.95 (978-0-19-518896-7(9)) Oxford Univ. Pr., Inc.

Hall, Brianna. Great Women of the American Revolution. 2012. (Story of the American Revolution Ser.). (ENG.). 32p. (gr. 3-4). pap. 47.70 (978-1-4296-9285-4(5), Fact Finders) Capstone Press of Coughlan Cos.

Hall, Brianna, et al. The Story of the American Revolution. 2012. (Story of the American Revolution Ser.). (ENG.). 32p. (gr. 3-4). pap. 40.50 (978-1-4296-9294-6(4)); pap. 286.20 (978-1-4296-9295-3(2)) Capstone Press of Coughlan Cos. (Fact Finders).

Hamilton, John. American Revolution: Road to War. 2013. (American Revolution Ser.). 32p. (J). (gr. 5-9). lib. bdg. 27.07 (978-1-61783-678-7(8), Abdo & Daughters) ABDO Publishing Co.

—Turning Points of the American Revolution. 2013. (American Revolution Ser.). 32p. (J). (gr. 5-9). lib. bdg. 27.07 (978-1-61783-682-4(6), Abdo & Daughters) ABDO Publishing Co.

—Weapons of the American Revolution. 2013. (American Revolution Ser.). 32p. (J). (gr. 5-9). lib. bdg. 27.07 (978-1-61783-683-1(4), Abdo & Daughters) ABDO Publishing Co.

Hamilton, Robert M. Recipes of the American Revolution. 2017. (Cooking Your Way Through American History Ser.). 24p. (J). (gr. 3-3). 27.25 **(978-1-5345-2106-3(2))**; pap. 63.60 **(978-1-5345-2105-6(4))**; pap. 10.60 **(978-1-5345-2104-9(6))** Greenhaven Publishing LLC. (KidHaven Publishing).

Hargrove, Julia. Bostons Trail to Freedom. 2003. (Historic Monuments Ser.). (Illus.). 48p. (J). (gr. 4-8). pap. 6.95 (978-1-57310-403-6(5)) Teaching & Learning Co.

Hazen, Walter A. Everyday Life: Revolutionary War. 2004. (Illus.). 104p. (J). pap. 13.50 (978-0-673-58899-9(8)) Good Year Bks.

Heims, Neil. Reading Johnny Tremain. 2005. (Engaged Reader Ser.). (Illus.). 96p. (gr. 5-8). lib. bdg. 25.00 (978-0-7910-8831-9(6), Chelsea Hse.) Facts On File, Inc.

Henrickson, Beth. The Marquis de Lafayette & Other International Champions of the American Revolution. 2015. (Spotlight on American History Ser.). (ENG., Illus.). 24p. (J). (gr. 4-6). pap. 10.00 (978-1-4994-1745-6(4), PowerKids Pr.) Rosen Publishing Group, Inc., The.

Hinman, Bonnie. Life During the Revolutionary War, 1 vol. 2014. (Daily Life in US History Ser.). (ENG., Illus.). 48p. (J). (gr. 3-6). lib. bdg. 32.79 (978-1-62403-628-6(7)) ABDO Publishing Co.

—The Second Continental Congress. 2017. (Young America Ser.). 29.95 (978-1-61228-979-3(7)) Mitchell Lane Pubs., Inc.

Hirsch, E. D., Jr., ed. The American Revolution, Level 4. 2003. stu. ed. 9.95 (978-0-7690-5101-7(4)); stu. ed. 49.95 (978-0-7690-2845-3(4)); tchr. ed. 9.95 (978-0-7690-5068-3(9)) Pearson Learning.

Houghton, Raymond C. A Revolutionary War Road Trip on US Route 4: Spend a Revolutionary Day along One of America's Most Historic Routes 2004. (Illus.). 162p. per. 12.99 (978-1-931373-09-8(4)) Cyber Haus.

—A Revolutionary War Road Trip on US Route 9: Spend a Revolutionary Day along One of America's Most Historic Routes. 2004. (Illus.). 166p. per. 12.99 (978-1-931373-12-8(4)) Cyber Haus.

Howell, Sara. The American Revolution: Frontline Soldiers & Their Families. 2015. (Frontline Families Ser.). (ENG., Illus.). 48p. (J). (gr. 5-6). pap. 14.05 (978-1-4824-3053-0(3)) Stevens, Gareth Publishing LLLP.

Huey, Lois Miner. Voices of the American Revolution: Stories from the Battlefields, 1 vol. 2010. (Voices of War Ser.). (ENG., Illus.). 32p. (gr. 3-4). pap. 8.29 (978-1-4296-5628-3(X), Edge Bks.) Capstone Press of Coughlan Cos.

Ingram, Scott. The Battle of Valcour Bay. 2003. (Triangle Histories of the American Revolution Ser.). (Illus.). 32p. (J). 22.45 (978-1-56711-778-3(3), Blackbirch Pr., Inc.) Cengage Gale.

Isaacs, Sally. Understanding the Declaration of Independence. 2008. (Documenting Early America Ser.). (ENG.). 32p. (J). (gr. 3-6). lib. bdg. (978-0-7787-4371-2(3)) Crabtree Publishing Co.

Isaacs, Sally & Bedeksy, Baron. Understanding the Declaration of Independence. 2008. (Documenting Early America Ser.). (ENG.). 32p. (J). (gr. 3-6). pap. (978-0-7787-4376-7(4)) Crabtree Publishing Co.

Jedson, Lee. The Treaty of Paris 1783: A Primary Source Examination of the Treaty That Recognized American Independence. (Primary Sources of American Treaties Ser.). 64p. 2009. (gr. 5-8). 58.50 (978-1-60851-517-2(6)) 2006. (Illus.). (J). (gr. k-3). lib. bdg. 31.95 (978-1-4042-0441-6(5)) Rosen Publishing Group, Inc., The.

Jeffrey, Gary. George Washington & the Winter at Valley Forge. 2011. (Graphic Heroes of the American Revolution Ser.). 24p. (J). (gr. 3-8). pap. 8.15 (978-1-4339-6014-7(1), Gareth Stevens Learning Library); (Illus.). lib. bdg. 23.95 (978-1-4339-6174-8(1)) Stevens, Gareth Publishing LLLP.

Jeffries, Joyce. The Colony of North Carolina. 2015. (Spotlight on the 13 Colonies Ser.). (ENG., Illus.). 24p. (J). (gr. 4-5). pap. 8.25 (978-1-4994-0554-5(5), PowerKids Pr.) Rosen Publishing Group, Inc., The.

—The Colony of South Carolina. 2015. (Spotlight on the 13 Colonies Ser.). (ENG., Illus.). 24p. (J). (gr. 4-5). pap. 8.25 (978-1-4994-0582-8(0), PowerKids Pr.) Rosen Publishing Group, Inc., The.

Jensen, Ann. The World Turned Upside Down: Children of 1776, 1 vol. Ramsey, Marcy Dunn, illus. 2009. (ENG.). 80p. (J). pap. 9.95 (978-0-87033-534-1(0), 9780870335341, Cornell Maritime Pr./Tidewater Pubs.) Schiffer Publishing, Ltd.

Kajencki, AnnMarie Francis. Count Casimir Pulaski: From Poland to America, a Hero's Fight for Liberty. 2009. (Library of American Lives & Times Ser.). 112p. (gr. 5-5). 69.20 (978-1-60853-475-3(8)) Rosen Publishing Group, Inc., The.

Kalman, Maira. Thomas Jefferson: Life, Liberty & the Pursuit of Everything. Kalman, Maira, illus. 2014. (ENG., Illus.). 40p. (J). (gr. k-3). 17.99 (978-0-399-24040-9(3), Nancy Paulsen Books) Penguin Young Readers Group.

Katz, Vladimir. A Timeline of the Life of George Washington. 2009. (Timelines of American History Ser.). 32p. (gr. 4-4). 47.90 (978-1-60854-388-5(9), Rosen Reference) Rosen Publishing Group, Inc., The.

Kelley, True. Who Was Abigail Adams? O'brien, John, illus. 2014. (Who Was? Ser.). (ENG.). 112p. (J). (gr. 3-7). 5.99 (978-0-448-47890-6(0), Grosset & Dunlap) Penguin Young Readers Group.

—Who Was Abigail Adams? 2014. (Who Was... ? Ser.). lib. bdg. 16.00 (978-0-606-34166-0(8), Turtleback) Turtleback Bks.

Kent, Deborah. The American Revolution: From Bunker Hill to Yorktown. 2011. (United States at War Ser.). (Illus.). 128p. (J). (gr. 5-18). lib. bdg. 33.27 (978-0-7660-3642-0(1)) Enslow Pubs., Inc.

Kent, Jacqueline C. Molly Pitcher. 2003. (Women of the Revolution Ser.). (J). pap. (978-1-58417-088-4(3)); lib. bdg. (978-1-58417-025-9(5)) Lake Street Pubs.

Kent, Zachary. Alexander Hamilton: Creating a Nation. 2004. (America's Founding Fathers Ser.). (Illus.). 128p. (J). lib. bdg. 26.60 (978-0-7660-2181-5(5)) Enslow Pubs., Inc.

Kit, Oscar. A Timeline of the Life of Thomas Jefferson. 2009. (Timelines of American History Ser.). 32p. (gr. 4-4). 47.90 (978-1-60854-389-2(7), Rosen Reference) Rosen Publishing Group, Inc., The.

Kjelle, Marylou. The First Continental Congress. 2017. (Young America Ser.). (gr. 3-6). 29.95 (978-1-61228-977-9(0)) Mitchell Lane Pubs., Inc.

Klepeis, Alicia. Stamp Act Congress. 2017. (Young America Ser.). (gr. 3-6). 29.95 (978-1-61228-991-5(6)) Mitchell Lane Pubs., Inc.

Kneib, Martha. A Historical Atlas of the American Revolution. (United States: Historical Atlases of the Growth of a New Nation Ser.). 64p. 2009. (gr. 5-5). 61.20 (978-1-60854-253-6(X)) 2005. (Illus.). (J). (gr. 7-12). lib. bdg. 31.95 (978-1-4042-0204-7(8)) Rosen Publishing Group, Inc., The.

Konstam, Angus. America Speaks, 10 vols. 2005. (Illus.). (J). (978-0-7172-6025-6(9)); (978-0-7172-6024-9(0)); (978-0-7172-6023-2(2)); (978-0-7172-6022-5(4)); (978-0-7172-6021-8(6)); (978-0-7172-6020-1(8)); (978-0-7172-6027-0(5)); (978-0-7172-6028-7(3)); (978-0-7172-6026-3(7)); (978-0-7172-6029-4(1)) Grolier, Ltd.

—America Speaks, 10 vols., Set. 2005. (Illus.). (J). (gr. 5-10). lib. bdg. 269.00 (978-0-7172-6030-0(5), Grolier) Scholastic Library Publishing.

Kravitz, Danny. The Untold Story of Henry Knox: The Man Who Saved Boston. 2015. (What You Didn't Know about the American Revolution Ser.). (ENG., Illus.). 64p. (gr. 4-8). 34.65 (978-0-7565-4972-5(8)) Compass Point Bks.

Kravitz, Danny & Burgan, Michael. What You Didn't Know about the American Revolution. 2015. (What You Didn't Know about the American Revolution Ser.). (ENG.). 64p. (gr. 4-8). lib. bdg. 138.60 (978-0-7565-4988-6(4), CPB Grades 4-8) Compass Point Bks.

Krull, Kathleen. What Was the Boston Tea Party? Mortimer, Lauren & Bennett, James, illus. 2013. (What Was? Ser.). (ENG.). 112p. (J). (gr. 3-7). pap. 5.99 (978-0-448-46288-2(5), Penguin Workshop) Penguin Young Readers Group.

—What Was the Boston Tea Party? 2013. (What Was... ? Ser.). lib. bdg. 16.00 (978-0-606-29971-8(8), Turtleback) Turtleback Bks.

Lakin, Patricia. Abigail Adams: First Lady of the American Revolution. Bandelin, Debra & Dacey, Bob, illus. 2006. 48p. (J). lib. bdg. 15.00 (978-1-4242-1560-7(9)) Fitzgerald Bks.

—Abigail Adams: First Lady of the American Revolution. Dacey, Bob & Bandelin, Debra, illus. 2006. (Ready-To-read SOFA Ser.). (ENG.). 48p. (J). (gr. 1-3). pap. 3.99 (978-0-689-87032-3(9), Simon Spotlight) Simon Spotlight.

Landau, Elaine. Celebrate the Founding of America with Elaine Landau. 2006. (Explore Colonial America with Elaine

Landau Ser.). (Illus.). 48p. (J). (gr. 3-7). lib. bdg. 25.27 *(978-0-7660-2557-8(8)*, Enslow Elementary) Enslow Pubs., Inc.

—The Declaration of Independence. 2008. (True Bks.). (ENG., Illus.). 48p. (J). (gr. 3-5). pap. 6.95 *(978-0-531-14780-1(0)*, Children's Pr.) Scholastic Library Publishing.

—The Declaration of Independence: American History. 2007. (True Bks.). (ENG., Illus.). 48p. (J). (gr. 3-5). lib. bdg. 29.00 *(978-0-531-12630-1(7)*, Children's Pr.) Scholastic Library Publishing.

—General Washington Crosses the Delaware: Would You Join the American Revolution? 2015. (What Would You Do? Ser.). 48p. (J). (gr. 3-4). pap. 8.95 *(978-0-7660-6316-7(X)*, Enslow Elementary) Enslow Pubs., Inc.

—The Revolutionary War Begins: Would You Join the Fight? (What Would You Do? Ser.). (Illus.). 48p. (J). 2010. pap. 8.95 *(978-1-59845-197-9(9))* 2008. (gr. 3-4). lib. bdg. 25.27 *(978-0-7660-2900-2(X))* Enslow Pubs., Inc. (Enslow Elementary).

—The Start of the Revolutionary War: Would You Fight for Independence? 2015. (What Would You Do? Ser.). 48p. (J). (gr. 3-4). 25.27 *(978-0-7660-6310-5(0))*; pap. 8.95 *(978-0-7660-6311-2(9)*, Enslow Elementary) Enslow Pubs., Inc.

Lanser, Amanda. The American Revolution by the Numbers. 2015. (America at War by the Numbers Ser.). (ENG., Illus.). 32p. (gr. 3-4). lib. bdg. 27.99 *(978-1-4914-4294-4(8))* Capstone Press of Coughlan Cos.

Lee, David. The Colony of Delaware. 2015. (Spotlight on the 13 Colonies Ser.). (ENG., Illus.). 24p. (J). (gr. 4-5). pap. 8.25 *(978-1-4994-0351-0(8)*, PowerKids Pr.) Rosen Publishing Group, Inc., The.

Levine, Becky. For Life & Liberty: Causes & Effects of the Declaration of Independence, 1 vol. 2014. (Cause & Effect Ser.). (ENG.). 32p. (gr. 3-4). lib. bdg. 27.32 *(978-1-4765-3931-7(6)*, Fact Finders) Capstone Press of Coughlan Cos.

Liberston, Jody. Nathan Hale: Heroe de la guerra de Independencia. 2004. (Grandes personajes en la historia de los Estados Unidos Ser.). (SPA.). 32p. (gr. 3-6). pap. 10.00 *(978-0-8239-4235-0(X)*, Rosen Classroom) Rosen Publishing Group, Inc., The.

Libertson, Jody. Nathan Hale: Hero of the American Revolution. 2009. (Primary Sources of Famous People in American History Ser.). 32p. (gr. 2-3). 47.90 *(978-1-60851-709-1(8))* Rosen Publishing Group, Inc., The.

—Nathan Hale: Héroe revolucionario / Hero of the American Revolution. 2009. (Famous People in American History/Grandes personajes en la historia de los Estados Unidos Ser.). (ENG & SPA.). 32p. (gr. 2-3). 47.90 *(978-1-61512-552-4(3)*, Editorial Buenas Letras) Rosen Publishing Group, Inc., The.

—Nathan Hale: Héroe revolucionario (Nathan Hale: Hero of the American Revolution) 2009. (Grandes personajes en la historia de los Estados Unidos (Famous People in American History) Ser.). (SPA.). 32p. (gr. 2-3). 47.90 *(978-1-61512-805-1(0)*, Editorial Buenas Letras) Rosen Publishing Group, Inc., The.

The Life of a Colonial Soldier. 2013. (Jr. Graphic Colonial America Ser.). 24p. (J). (gr. 3-6). pap. 63.60 *(978-1-4777-1440-9(5)*, PowerKids Pr.) Rosen Publishing Group, Inc., The.

Linde, Barbara M. Slavery in Early America. 2011. (Story of America Ser.). (Illus.). 32p. (J). (gr. 4-6). lib. bdg. 26.60 *(978-1-4339-4776-6(5)*, Gareth Stevens Learning Library) Stevens, Gareth Publishing LLLP.

Lowery, Zoe. The American Revolution, 01 vols., 1. 2016. (Early American History Ser.). (ENG., Illus.). 80p. (J). 32.90 *(978-1-68048-269-0(6)*, Britannica Educational Publishing) Rosen Publishing Group, Inc., The.

—The American Revolution: Life, Liberty, & the Pursuit of Happiness. 2015. (Age of Revolution Ser.). (ENG., Illus.). 128p. (J). (gr. 9-10). 35.25 *(978-1-68048-020-7(0)*, Britannica Educational Publishing) Rosen Publishing Group, Inc., The.

Lowery, Zoe, ed. The American Revolution. 2015. (Age of Revolution Ser.). (ENG.). 128p. (YA). (gr. 9-10). 70.50 *(978-1-68048-021-4(9)*, Britannica Educational Publishing) Rosen Publishing Group, Inc., The.

Lusted, Marcia Amidon. Revolution & the New Nation: 1750-Early 1800s. 2007. (Presidents of the United States Ser.). (Illus.). 48p. (J). (gr. 4-7). lib. bdg. 29.05 *(978-1-59036-739-1(1))*; per. 10.95 *(978-1-59036-740-7(5))* Weigl Pubs., Inc.

Maestro, Betsy. Liberty or Death: The American Revolution: 1763-1783. Maestro, Giulio, illus. 2005. 64p. (J). lib. bdg. 17.89 *(978-0-688-08803-3(1))*; (ENG.). (gr. 2-7). 18.99 *(978-0-688-08802-6(3))* HarperCollins Pubs.

Maloof, Torrey. Abigail Adams & the Women Who Shaped America. 2016. (Primary Source Readers Ser.). (Illus.). 32p. (J). (gr. 4-5). 8.99 *(978-1-4938-3080-0(5))* Teacher Created Materials, Inc.

—The American Revolution: Fighting for Freedom. 2016. (Primary Source Readers Ser.). (Illus.). 32p. (J). (gr. 4-5). pap. 8.99 *(978-1-4938-3079-4(1))* Teacher Created Materials, Inc.

Mara, Wil. If You Were a Kid During the American Revolution. 2016. (If You Were a Kid Ser.). (ENG., Illus.). 32p. (J). lib. bdg. 26.00 *(978-0-531-21971-3(2)*, Children's Pr.) Scholastic Library Publishing.

Marciniak, Kristin. The Revolutionary War: Why They Fought. 2015. (What Were They Fighting For? Ser.). (ENG., Illus.). 64p. (gr. 5-9). lib. bdg. 34.65 *(978-0-7565-5169-8(2))* Compass Point Bks.

Marcovitz, Hal. Cause & Effect the American Revolution: The American Revolution. 2015. (ENG., Illus.). 80p. (J). lib. bdg. *(978-1-60152-790-5(X))* ReferencePoint Pr., Inc.

Margulies, Phillip. A Timeline of the Continental Army. 2009. (Timelines of American History Ser.). 32p. (gr. 4-4). 47.90 *(978-1-60854-383-0(8)*, Rosen Reference) Rosen Publishing Group, Inc., The.

Marrin, Albert. Thomas Paine: Crusader for Liberty: an Adventure in the History of Ideas. 2014. (ENG., Illus.). 176p. (YA). (gr. 7). lib. bdg. 20.99 *(978-0-375-96674-3(9)*, Knopf Bks. for Young Readers) Random Hse. Children's Bks.

—Thomas Paine: Crusader for Liberty: How One Man's Ideas Helped Form a New Nation. (ENG.). (YA). (gr. 7). 2016. 144p. pap. 15.99 *(978-0-375-85969-4(1)*, Ember) 2014. (Illus.). 176p. 17.99 *(978-0-375-86674-6(4)*, Knopf Bks. for Young Readers) Random Hse. Children's Bks.

Marsh, Carole. Samuel Adams. 2003. 12p. (gr. k-4). 2.95 *(978-0-635-02367-4(9))* Gallopade International.

Marston, Daniel & O'Neill, Robert John. The American Revolutionary War. 2011. (Early American Wars Ser.). (Illus.). 96p. (YA). (gr. 9-18). lib. bdg. 33.25 *(978-1-4488-1331-5(X))* Rosen Publishing Group, Inc., The.

Martin, David. The Colony of Pennsylvania. 2015. (Spotlight on the 13 Colonies Ser.). (ENG., Illus.). 24p. (J). (gr. 4-5). pap. 8.25 *(978-1-4994-0572-9(3)*, PowerKids Pr.) Rosen Publishing Group, Inc., The.

Mayr, Diane & Sisters, Write. Women of the Constitution State: 25 Connecticut Women You Should Know. Greenleaf, Lisa, illus. 2012. 136p. (J). pap. 16.00 *(978-0-9842549-1-0(9))* Apprentice Shop Bks., LLC.

McCallum, Ann. Eat Your U. S. History Homework: Recipes for Revolutionary Minds. Hernandez, Leeza, illus. 2015. (Eat Your Homework Ser.). (ENG.). 48p. (J). (gr. 2-5). lib. bdg. 15.95 *(978-1-57091-923-7(2))* Charlesbridge Publishing, Inc.

McCarthy, Pat. The Thirteen Colonies from Founding to Revolution in American History. 2004. (In American History Ser.). (Illus.). 128p. (J). lib. bdg. 27.94 *(978-0-7660-1990-4(X))* Enslow Pubs., Inc.

McDonnell, Peter. A Soldier in Disguise. Tormey, Carlotta, illus. 2005. 16p. (J). pap. *(978-0-7367-2909-3(7))* Zaner-Bloser, Inc.

McKissack, Fredrick, Jr. & McKissack, Patricia C. Hard Labor: The First African-Americans 1619. Fiedler, Joseph Daniel, illus. 2004. (Milestone Ser.). (ENG.). 64p. (J). (gr. 2-5). pap. 6.99 *(978-0-689-86149-9(4)*, Simon & Schuster/Paula Wiseman Bks.) Simon & Schuster/Paula Wiseman Bks.

McLeese, Don. Alexander Hamilton. 2004. (Heroes of the American Revolution Ser.). (Illus.). 32p. (gr. 2-5). lib. bdg. *(978-1-59515-219-0(9))* Rourke Educational Media.

McNeese, Tim. Alexander Hamilton: Framer of the Constitution. 2005. (Leaders of the American Revolution Ser.). (Illus.). 100p. (gr. 5-8). lib. bdg. 30.00 *(978-0-7910-8616-2(X))* Facts On File, Inc.

McNeil, Niki, et al. HOCPP 1061 American Revolution. 2006. spiral bd. 24.00 *(978-1-60308-061-3(9))* In the Hands of a Child.

McPherson, Stephanie. My Dear Husband: Important Letters of Abigail Adams. 2009. (Great Moments in American History Ser.). 32p. (gr. 3-3). 47.90 *(978-1-61513-134-1(5))* Rosen Publishing Group, Inc., The.

Metz, Lorijo. The American Revolution, 1 vol., 1. 2014. (Let's Celebrate Freedom! Ser.). (ENG.). 24p. (J). (gr. 3-6). 23.60 *(978-1-4777-2896-3(1)*, PowerKids Pr.) Rosen Publishing Group, Inc., The.

—La Revolucin Americana / the American Revolution, 1 vol., 1. Beullens-Maoui, Nathalie, ed. 2014. (¡Celebremos la Libertad! / Let's Celebrate Freedom! Ser.). (SPA & BYN.). 24p. (J). (gr. 3-6). 23.60 *(978-1-4777-3248-9(9)*, PowerKids Pr.) Rosen Publishing Group, Inc., The.

Micklos, John. African Americans & American Indians Fighting in the Revolutionary War. 2008. (Revolutionary War Library). (Illus.). 48p. (J). (gr. 3-4). lib. bdg. 25.27 *(978-0-7660-3018-3(0)*, Enslow Elementary) Enslow Pubs., Inc.

—American Indians & African Americans of the American Revolution — Through Primary Sources. 2013. (American Revolution Through Primary Sources Ser.). 48p. (J). (gr. 4-18). lib. bdg. 25.27 *(978-0-7660-4130-1(1))* Enslow Pubs., Inc.

—American Indians & African Americans of the American Revolution—Through Primary Sources. 2013. (American Revolution Through Primary Sources Ser.). 48p. (J). (gr. 4-10). pap. 8.95 *(978-1-4644-0188-6(8))* Enslow Pubs., Inc.

—The Brave Women & Children of the American Revolution. 2008. (Revolutionary War Library). (Illus.). 48p. (J). (gr. 3-4). lib. bdg. 25.27 *(978-0-7660-3019-0(9)*, Enslow Elementary) Enslow Pubs., Inc.

—Courageous Children & Women of the American Revolution: Through Primary Sources. 2013. (American Revolution Through Primary Sources Ser.). 48p. (J). (gr. 4-18). 25.27 *(978-0-7660-4131-8(X))* Enslow Pubs., Inc.

—Courageous Children & Women of the American Revolution—Through Primary Sources. 2013. (American Revolution Through Primary Sources Ser.). 48p. (J). (gr. 4-10). pap. 8.95 *(978-1-4644-0189-3(6))* Enslow Pubs., Inc.

—The Making of the United States from Thirteen Colonies — Through Primary Sources. 2013. (American Revolution Through Primary Sources Ser.). 48p. (J). (gr. 4-18). 25.27 *(978-0-7660-4133-2(6))* Enslow Pubs., Inc.

—The Making of the United States from Thirteen Colonies—Through Primary Sources. 2013. (American Revolution Through Primary Sources Ser.). 48p. (J). (gr. 4-10). pap. 8.95 *(978-1-4644-0191-6(8))* Enslow Pubs., Inc.

—An Overview of the American Revolution-Through Primary Sources. 2013. (American Revolution Through Primary Sources Ser.). 48p. (J). (gr. 4-18). lib. bdg. 25.27 *(978-0-7660-4135-6(2))* Enslow Pubs., Inc.

—An Overview of the American Revolution—Through Primary Sources. 2013. (American Revolution Through Primary Sources Ser.). 48p. (J). (gr. 4-10). pap. 8.95 *(978-1-4644-0193-0(4))* Enslow Pubs., Inc.

Micklos, John & Micklos, John, Jr. What Was the Revolutionary War All About? 2008. (Revolutionary War Library). (Illus.). 48p. (J). (gr. 3-7). lib. bdg. 25.27 *(978-0-7660-3014-5(8)*, Enslow Elementary) Enslow Pubs., Inc.

Mierka, Gregg A. Nathanael Greene: The General Who Saved the Revolution. 2006. (J). pap. *(978-1-59556-017-9(3))*; (Illus.). 88p. (gr. 5-11). lib. bdg. 23.95 *(978-1-59556-012-4(2))* OTTN Publishing.

Miller, Brandon Marie. Declaring Independence: Life During the American Revolution. 2005. (People's History Ser.). (ENG., Illus.). 96p. (gr. 5-12). 33.26 *(978-0-8225-1275-2(0))* Lerner Publishing Group.

Minor, Wendell. Yankee Doodle Alphabet: The Spirit of 1776 from a to Z. 2016. (J). *(978-1-56792-566-1(9))* Godine, David R. Pub.

Misztal, Maggie. The Colony of New Jersey. 2015. (Spotlight on the 13 Colonies Ser.). (ENG., Illus.). 24p. (J). (gr. 4-5). pap. 8.25 *(978-1-4994-0531-6(6)*, PowerKids Pr.) Rosen Publishing Group, Inc., The.

Morey, Allan. A Timeline History of the Early American Republic. 2014. (Timeline Trackers: America's Beginnings Ser.). (Illus.). 48p. (gr. 5-8). (J). lib. bdg. 30.60 *(978-1-4677-3641-1(4)*, Lerner Pubns.); pap. 9.95 *(978-1-4677-4572-7(3))* Lerner Publishing Group.

Moss, Marissa. America's Tea Parties: Not One but Four!: Boston, Charleston, New York, Philadelphia. 2016. (ENG., Illus.). 56p. (J). (gr. 3-7). 19.95 *(978-1-4197-1874-8(6)*, Abrams Bks. for Young Readers) Abrams, Inc.

Muhall, Jill K. & Alarcon, Jill. Causes of the Revolution, 1 vol. 2004. (Primary Source Readers Ser.). (ENG., Illus.). 24p. (J). (gr. 5-5). pap. 8.99 *(978-0-7439-8785-1(3))* Shell Educational Publishing.

Mulhall, Jill K. Abigail Adams, 1 vol. 2004. (Primary Source Readers Ser.). (ENG.). 24p. (J). (gr. 4-4). pap. 8.99 *(978-0-7439-8786-8(1))* Shell Educational Publishing.

Murray, Stuart. American Revolution. 2015. (DK Eyewitness Bks.). (ENG., Illus.). 72p. (J). (gr. 3-7). lib. bdg. 19.99 *(978-1-4654-3859-1(9)*, DK Children) Dorling Kindersley Publishing, Inc.

—DK Eyewitness Books: American Revolution. 2015. (DK Eyewitness Bks.). (ENG., Illus.). 72p. (J). (gr. 3-7). pap. 9.99 *(978-1-4654-3858-4(0)*, DK Children) Dorling Kindersley Publishing, Inc.

Nagle, Jeanne. How George Washington Fought the Revolutionary War. 2017. (Presidents at War Ser.). 128p. (J). (gr. 8-8). lib. bdg. 37.27 ***(978-0-7660-8523-7(6))*** Enslow Pubs., Inc.

Nardo, Don. The American Revolution. 2003. (History of Weapons & Warfare Ser.). (ENG., Illus.). 112p. (J). 32.10 *(978-1-59018-326-7(6))* Cengage Gale.

Nell, William C. Black Patriots of the American Revolution, with Sketches of Several Distinguished Black Persons to Which Is Added a Brief Survey of the Condition & Prospects of Black Americans. 2017. (ENG., Illus.). 396p. (J). (gr. 4-12). act. bk. ed. incl. cd-rom *(978-1-892824-87-5(6))* AFCHRON.

Nelson, Sheila. The Original United States of America. 2006. (How America Became America Ser.). (Illus.). 96p. (YA). lib. bdg. 22.95 *(978-1-59084-903-3(5))* Mason Crest.

Ohlin, Nancy. The American Revolution. Larkum, Adam, illus. 2016. (Blast Back! Ser.). (ENG.). 112p. (J). (gr. 2-5). pap. 5.99 *(978-1-4998-0122-4(X))* Little Bee Books Inc.

Olson, Kay Melchisedech. Betsy Ross & the American Flag, 1 vol. Cool, Anna Maria et al, illus. 2005. (Graphic History Ser.). (ENG.). 32p. (gr. 3-4). 30.65 *(978-0-7368-4962-3(9)*, Graphic Library) Capstone Press of Coughlan Cos.

Olson, Nathan. Nathan Hale: Revolutionary Spy. Martin, Cynthia & Schoonover, Brent, illus. 2005. (Graphic Biographies Ser.). (ENG.). 32p. (gr. 3-4). 30.65 *(978-0-7368-4968-5(8)*, Graphic Library) Capstone Press of Coughlan Cos.

Olson, Nathan & Glaser, Jason. Nathan Hale: Revolutionary Spy, 1 vol. Martin, Cynthia & Schoonover, Brent, illus. 2006. (Graphic Biographies Ser.). (ENG.). 32p. (gr. 3-4). per. 8.10 *(978-0-7368-6199-1(8)*, Graphic Library) Capstone Press of Coughlan Cos.

Omoth, Tyler. Secrets of the American Revolution. 2017. (Top Secret Files Ser.). (ENG.). 32p. (gr. 3-4). pap. 7.95 *(978-1-5157-4141-1(9))*; (Illus.). lib. bdg. 27.99 *(978-1-5157-4137-4(0))* Capstone Press of Coughlan Cos. (Edge Bks.).

Osborne, Mary Pope & Boyce, Natalie Pope. American Revolution: A Nonfiction Companion to Revolutionary War on Wednesday. Murdocca, Sal, illus. 2004. (Magic Tree House - Fact Tracker Ser.: 11). (ENG.). 128p. (J). (gr. 2-5). pap. 6.99 *(978-0-375-82379-4(4)*, Random Hse. Bks. for Young Readers) Random Hse. Children's Bks.

Otfinoski, Steven. People of the American Revolution: Text Pairs. 2008. (Bridges/Navigators Ser.). (J). (gr. 5). 89.00 *(978-1-4108-8421-3(X))* Benchmark Education Co.

Palazzo-Craig, Janet. The Making of the American Flag: Betsy Ross & George Washington. 2009. (Great Moments in American History Ser.). 32p. (gr. 3-3). 47.90 *(978-1-61513-155-6(8))* Rosen Publishing Group, Inc., The.

Paley, Caitlyn. Strategic Inventions of the Revolutionary War. 2016. (Tech in the Trenches Ser.). (ENG., Illus.). 112p. (J). (gr. 9-9). lib. bdg. 42.79 *(978-1-5026-1028-7(0))* Cavendish Square Publishing.

Palmer, Kate Salley. Almost Invisible Blk Patriots. Palmer, Kate Salley, illus. 2008. (ENG., Illus.). 56p. (J). pap. 11.95 *(978-0-9667114-6-2(7))* Warbranch Pr., Inc.

Paris, Stephanie. Forming a New Government (America's Early Years) 2016. (Primary Source Readers Ser.). (ENG., Illus.). 32p. (J). (gr. 4-5). pap. 8.99 *(978-1-4938-3083-1(X))* Teacher Created Materials, Inc.

Parker, Christi E. American Revolution, 1 vol. 2004. (Primary Source Readers Ser.). (ENG.). 24p. (J). (gr. 5-5). pap. 8.99 *(978-0-7439-8748-6(9))* Shell Educational Publishing.

Peal, Robert. Modern Britain - The Americas. 2017. (Knowing History Ser.). (ENG.). 16p. (J). (gr. 6-9). 3.99 *(978-0-00-819539-7(0))* HarperCollins Pubs. Ltd. GBR. Dist: Independent Pubs. Group.

Pfeffer, Wendy. Many Ways to Be a Soldier. Verstraete, Elaine, illus. 2008. (On My Own History Ser.). (ENG.). 48p. (gr. 2-4). lib. bdg. 25.26 *(978-0-8225-7279-4(6)*, Millbrook Pr.) Lerner Publishing Group.

Powell, Walter L. Benedict Arnold: Revolutionary War Hero & Traitor. (Library of American Lives & Timestm Ser.). 112p. (Illus.). (J). (gr. 4-8). lib. bdg. 31.95 *(978-1-4042-6627-8(5))*; 2009. (gr. 5-5). 69.20 *(978-1-60853-471-5(5))* Rosen Publishing Group, Inc., The.

Prior, Jennifer Overend. Reasons for a Revolution. 2016. (Primary Source Readers Ser.). (Illus.). 32p. (J). (gr. 4-5). pap. 8.99 *(978-1-4938-3078-7(3))* Teacher Created Materials, Inc.

Purcell, Martha Sias. Spies of the American Revolution. 2003. (Reading Essentials in Social Studies). (Illus.). 48p. pap. 9.00 *(978-0-7891-5854-3(X))* Perfection Learning Corp.

Quirk, Anne. The Good Fight: The Feuds of the Founding Fathers (and How They Shaped the Nation) Baddeley, Elizabeth, illus. 2017. (ENG.). 128p. (J). (gr. 2-5). 16.99 *(978-1-5247-0035-5(5)*, Knopf Bks. for Young Readers) Random Hse. Children's Bks.

Radomski, Kassandra. Battle for a New Nation: Causes & Effects of the Revolutionary War. 2015. (Revolutionary War Ser.). (ENG., Illus.). 48p. (gr. 3-4). pap. 8.95 *(978-1-4914-2159-8(2))* Capstone Press of Coughlan Cos.

Randolph, Ryan. Betsy Ross: The American Flag, & Life in a Young America. 2009. (Library of American Lives & Times Ser.). 112p. (gr. 5-5). 69.20 *(978-1-60853-473-9(1))* Rosen Publishing Group, Inc., The.

Ransom, Candice. John Hancock. 2005. (History Maker Bios Ser.). (Illus.). 48p. (J). (gr. 3-4). 26.60 *(978-0-8225-1547-0(4)*, Lerner Pubns.) Lerner Publishing Group.

Ratliff, Thamas. Do You Want to Be a Revolutionary War Soldier? 2015. (Do You Want to Be... Ser.). (Illus.). 32p. (gr. 3-6). 28.50 *(978-1-909645-37-0(0))* Book Hse. GBR. Dist: Black Rabbit Bks.

Ratliff, Thomas. How to Be a Revolutionary War Soldier. 2008. (How to Be Ser.). (ENG., Illus.). 32p. (J). (gr. 4-7). pap. 5.95 *(978-1-4263-0247-3(9)*, National Geographic Children's Bks.) National Geographic Society.

—How to Be a Revolutionary War Soldier. James, John, illus. 2006. (How to Be Ser.). (ENG.). 32p. (J). (gr. 4-7). 14.95 *(978-0-7922-7489-6(X))*; lib. bdg. 21.90 *(978-0-7922-7546-6(2))* National Geographic Society. (National Geographic Children's Bks.).

Rauf, Don. Thomas Paine: Author of Common Sense. 2017. (J). ***(978-1-5383-8100-7(1))***; pap. ***(978-1-5383-8097-0(8))*** Rosen Publishing Group, Inc., The.

Raum, Elizabeth. At Battle in the Revolutionary War: An Interactive Battlefield Adventure. 2015. (You Choose: Battlefields Ser.). (ENG., Illus.). 112p. (gr. 3-4). pap. 6.95 *(978-1-4914-2392-9(7)*, You Choose Bks.) Capstone Press of Coughlan Cos.

—The Revolutionary War: An Interactive History Adventure. 2016. (You Choose: History Ser.). (ENG.). 112p. (gr. 3-4). pap. 6.95 *(978-1-5157-4264-7(4)*, You Choose Bks.) Capstone Press of Coughlan Cos.

—A Revolutionary War Timeline, 1 vol. 2014. (War Timelines Ser.). (ENG.). 48p. (gr. 4-6). lib. bdg. 34.65 *(978-1-4765-4157-0(4))* Capstone Press of Coughlan Cos.

—Spies of the American Revolution: An Interactive Espionage Adventure. 2015. (You Choose: Spies Ser.). (ENG., Illus.). 112p. (gr. 3-4). lib. bdg. 31.99 *(978-1-4914-5858-7(5)*, You Choose Bks.) Capstone Press of Coughlan Cos.

Raum, Elizabeth & Burgan, Michael. The Revolutionary War Experience: An Interactive History Adventure. 2014. (Illus.). 327p. (J). *(978-1-4914-1712-6(9))* Capstone Press of Coughlan Cos.

Raum, Elizabeth, et al. Stories of War. 2012. (Stories of War Ser.). (ENG.). 32p. (gr. 3-4). lib. bdg. 122.60 *(978-1-4296-9164-2(6)*, Graphic Library) Capstone Press of Coughlan Cos.

Reeder, Eric. Minority Soldiers Fighting in the American Revolution. 2017. (J). ***(978-1-5026-2661-5(6))*** Cavendish Square Publishing.

Renehan, Edward J., Jr. The Treaty of Paris: The Precursor to a New Nation. 2007. (Milestones in American History Ser.). (Illus.). 121p. (YA). (gr. 7-12). lib. bdg. 35.00 *(978-0-7910-9352-8(2))* Facts On File, Inc.

Revolutionary America, 1783-1799. 2010. (Discovering U. S. History Ser.). (Illus.). 128p. (gr. 5-8). 35.00 *(978-1-60413-350-9(3)*, Chelsea Hse.) Facts On File, Inc.

Rife, Douglas M. & Capaldi, Gina. The American Revolution. Lyall, Dennis, illus. 2009. (ENG.). 44p. (J). (gr. 3-17). 19.99 *(978-1-58476-612-4(3))* Innovative Kids.

Rissman, Rebecca. Declaration of Independence, 1 vol. 2013. (Foundations of Our Nation Ser.). 48p. (J). (ENG.). (gr. 3-6). lib. bdg. 32.79 *(978-1-61783-708-1(3))*; (Illus.). pap. 15.64 *(978-1-61783-758-6(X)*, Core Library) ABDO Publishing Co.

Roberts, Cokie. Founding Mothers: Remembering the Ladies. Goode, Diane, illus. 2014. 40p. (J). (gr. 2-7). (ENG.). 17.99 *(978-0-06-078002-9(9))*; lib. bdg. 18.89 *(978-0-06-078003-6(7))* HarperCollins Pubs.

Rogers, Amy B. & Davenport, John. The American Revolution: Fighting for Independence. 2017. (American History Ser.). 104p. (J). (gr. 7-7). 39.40 *(978-1-5345-6041-3(6)*, Lucent Pr.) Greenhaven Publishing LLC.

Roop, Peter & Roop, Connie. Botones Para el General Washington. Hanson, Peter E., illus. 2006. (Yo Solo - Historia (on My Own - History) Ser.).Tr. of Buttons for General Washington. (SPA.). 48p. (gr. 2-4). lib. bdg. 25.26 *(978-0-8225-6261-0(8))* Lerner Publishing Group.

—Let's Ride, Paul Revere! 2004. (Before I Made History Ser.). (Illus.). 60p. (J). pap. *(978-0-439-67623-6(1))* Scholastic, Inc.

—Who Cracked the Liberty Bell? And Other Questions about the American Revolution. 2007. (Chapters in History Ser.). (Illus.). 44p. (J). *(978-0-439-02523-2(0))* Scholastic, Inc.

Rose, Simon. American Revolutionary War. 2014. 49p. (J). *(978-1-4896-0512-2(6))* Weigl Pubs., Inc.

Rosen, Daniel. Independence Now: The American Revolution 1763-1783. 2004. (Crossroads America Ser.). (ENG., Illus.). 40p. (J). (gr. 5-9). 12.95 *(978-0-7922-6766-9(4)*, National Geographic Children's Bks.) National Geographic Society.

—Independence Now: The American Revolution, 1763-1783. 2004. (Crossroads America Ser.). (ENG., Illus.). 40p. (J). (gr. 5-9). 21.90 *(978-0-7922-6990-8(X)*, National Geographic Children's Bks.) National Geographic Society.

Roxburgh, Ellis. The Founding Fathers vs. King George III: The Fight for a New Nation. 2015. (History's Greatest Rivals Ser.). (ENG., Illus.). 48p. (J). (gr. 6-8). lib. bdg. 31.95 *(978-1-4824-2217-7(4))* Stevens, Gareth Publishing LLLP.

Roza, Greg. The Colony of New York. 2015. (Spotlight on the 13 Colonies Ser.). (ENG., Illus.). 24p. (J). (gr. 4-5). pap. 8.25 *(978-1-4994-0537-8(5)*, PowerKids Pr.) Rosen Publishing Group, Inc., The.

Rudin, Ronald. Founding Fathers: The Celebration of Champlain & Laval in the Streets of Quebec, 1878-1908. 2003. (ENG., Illus.). 304p. *(978-0-8020-3645-2(7))*; pap. *(978-0-8020-8479-8(6))* Univ. of Toronto Pr.

Rushworth, Victoria. Battles of the American Revolution: Saratoga: Text Pairs. 2008. (Bridges/Navigators Ser.). (J). (gr. 5). 81.00 *(978-1-4108-8404-6(X))* Benchmark Education Co.

Samuels, Charlie. Timeline of the Revolutionary War. 2011. (Americans at War: a Gareth Stevens Timeline Ser.). (Illus.). 48p. (J). (gr. 6-8). 31.95 *(978-1-4339-5914-1(3))*; pap. 14.05 *(978-1-4339-5916-5(X))* Stevens, Gareth Publishing LLLP. (Gareth Stevens Secondary Library).

Schanzer, Rosalyn. George vs. George: The American Revolution as Seen from Both Sides. 2007. (ENG., Illus.).

64p. (J). (gr. 4-7). per. 6.95 (978-1-4263-0042-4(5), National Geographic Children's Bks.) National Geographic Society.

—George vs. George: The Revolutionary War as Seen by Both Sides. 2004. (ENG., Illus.). 64p. (J). (gr. 4-7). 25.90 (978-0-7922-6999-1(3)); 16.95 (978-0-7922-7349-3(4)) National Geographic Society. (National Geographic Children's Bks.).

Schiffman, Jessica, illus. Sybil Ludington: Freedom's Brave Rider. 2005. 32p. (J). pap. (978-0-7367-2931-4(3)) Zaner-Bloser, Inc.

Shea, Nicole. The American Revolution. 2011. (Story of America Ser.). (Illus.). 32p. (J). (gr. 4-6). pap. 10.50 (978-1-4339-4761-2(7)); lib. bdg. 26.60 (978-1-4339-4760-5(9)) Stevens, Gareth Publishing LLLP. (Gareth Stevens Learning Library).

Shea, Therese. The Boston Massacre, Vol. 1. 2014. (What You Didn't Know about History Ser.). 24p. (J). (gr. 2-3). (ENG.). 22.60 (978-1-4824-0580-4(6)); pap. 8.15 (978-1-4824-3328-9(1)) Stevens, Gareth Publishing LLLP.

Sheinkin, Steve. King George: What Was His Problem? 2015. (YA). lib. bdg. 20.85 (978-0-606-37587-0(2)) Turtleback Bks.

—The Notorious Benedict Arnold: A True Story of Adventure, Heroism & Treachery. 2013. (ENG., Illus.). 368p. (YA). (gr. 6-9). pap. 9.99 (978-1-250-02460-2(9), 9781250024602) Square Fish.

—The Notorious Benedict Arnold: A True Story of Adventure, Heroism & Treachery. 2013. (YA). lib. bdg. 20.85 (978-0-606-28487-5(7), Turtleback) Turtleback Bks.

—Storyteller's History: The American Revolution. 2005. (Storyteller's History Ser.). (Illus.). 144p. (J). (gr. 4-8). per. 10.95 (978-0-9766367-0-0(0)) Summer Street Pr.

Siddons, Brian. Crispus Attucks & African American Patriots of the American Revolution. 2015. (Spotlight on American History Ser.). (ENG., Illus.). 24p. (J). (gr. 4-6). pap. 10.00 (978-1-4994-1739-5(X), PowerKids Pr.) Rosen Publishing Group, Inc., The.

Silate, Jennifer. Betsy Ross: Creadora de la bandera Estadounidense. 2004. (Grandes personajes en la historia de los Estados Unidos Ser.). (SPA.). 32p. (gr. 3-6). pap. 10.00 (978-0-8239-4222-0(8), Rosen Classroom) Rosen Publishing Group, Inc., The.

—Betsy Ross: Creadora de la bandera estadounidense (Betsy Ross: Creator of the American Flag) 2009. (Grandes personajes en la historia de los Estados Unidos (Famous People in American History) Ser.). (SPA.). 32p. (gr. 2-3). 47.90 (978-1-61512-791-7(7), Editorial Buenas Letras) Rosen Publishing Group, Inc., The.

—Betsy Ross: Creator of the American Flag. 2009. (Primary Sources of Famous People in American History Ser.). 32p. (gr. 2-3). 47.90 (978-1-60851-657-5(1)) Rosen Publishing Group, Inc., The.

—Betsy Ross: Creator of the American Flag / Creadora de la bandera Estadounidense. 2009. (Famous People in American History/Grandes personajes en la historia de los Estados Unidos Ser.). (ENG & SPA.). 32p. (gr. 2-3). 47.90 (978-1-61512-539-5(6), Editorial Buenas Letras) Rosen Publishing Group, Inc., The.

Smith, Emily R. Phillis Wheatley, 1 vol. 2004. (Primary Source Readers Ser.). (ENG.). 24p. (J). (gr. 4-4). pap. 8.99 (978-0-7439-8743-1(8)) Shell Educational Publishing.

Smith-Llera, Danielle. The Revoutionary War: A Chronology of America's Fight for Independence. 2015. (Revolutionary War Ser.). (ENG.). 48p. (gr. 3-4). pap. 8.95 (978-1-4914-2160-4(6)) Capstone Press of Coughlan Cos.

Smith, Robert. American Revolution. 2004. (Spotlight on America Ser.). (ENG., Illus.). 80p. (gr. 4-8). pap. 12.99 (978-0-7439-3212-7(9)) Teacher Created Resources, Inc.

Somervill, Barbara A. The Life & Times of James Madison. 2008. (Profiles in American History Ser.). (Illus.). 48p. (J). (gr. 4-7). lib. bdg. 29.95 (978-1-58415-530-0(2)) Mitchell Lane Pubs., Inc.

Sonneborn, Liz. John Paul Jones: American Naval Hero. 2005. (Leaders of the American Revolution Ser.). (Illus.). 100p. (gr. 5-8). lib. bdg. 30.00 (978-0-7910-8621-6(6)) Facts On File, Inc.

South, Victor. Remember the Alamo: Americans Fight for Texas, 1820-1845. 2012. (J). pap. (978-1-4222-2416-8(3)) Mason Crest.

—Remember the Alamo: Americans Fight for Texas, 1820-1845. Rakove, Jack N., ed. 2012. (How America Became America Ser.). 48p. (J). (gr. 3-4). 19.95 (978-1-4222-2402-1(3)) Mason Crest.

Stanley, George Edward. The New Republic (1763-1815) 2005. (Primary Source History of the United States Ser.). (Illus.). 48p. (gr. 5-12). pap. 14.05 (978-0-8368-5834-1(4)); lib. bdg. 31.00 (978-0-8368-5825-9(5)) Stevens, Gareth Publishing LLLP. (Gareth Stevens Secondary Library).

Stewart, Gail B. Life of a Soldier in Washington's Army. 2003. (American War Library). (ENG., Illus.). 112p. (J). 30.85 (978-1-59018-215-4(4), Lucent Bks.) Cengage Gale.

Stokes, Betty Southard. Postcards from George, 1763-1781: George Rogers Clark Writes Home to Virginia from the Kentucky Wilderness. Cable, Annette, illus. 2010. (J). (978-1-935497-12-7(X)) Butler Bk. Publishing.

Strum, Richard M. Causes of the American Revolution. 2005. (Road to War Ser.). (Illus.). 64p. (J). pap. 12.95 (978-1-59556-005-6(X)); (gr. 4-18). lib. bdg. 22.95 (978-1-59556-001-8(7)) OTTN Publishing.

Sullivan, Laura L. Life As a Spy in the American Revolution. 2016. (Life As... Ser.). (ENG., Illus.). 32p. (J). (gr. 3-3). 28.50 (978-1-5026-1081-2(7)) Cavendish Square Publishing.

Thompson, Ben. The American Revolution. Butzer, C. M., illus. 2017. (Guts & Glory Ser.: 4). (ENG.). 336p. (J). (gr. 3-7). 17.99 (978-0-316-31209-7(6)) Little Brown & Co.

Thompson, Gare. Main Idea & Details/Determine Importance - Forward, March! 2010. (Connect to Literacy Ser.). 8p. pap. (978-1-4334-0543-3(1)) Millmark Education.

Thompson, Gare & Peratt, Karen. Seeking the American Revolution - History Comes Alive! 2010. (Connect to Literacy Ser.). 8p. pap. (978-1-4334-0544-0(X)) Millmark Education.

Thompson, Gare & West, Elizabeth. Main Idea & Details/Determine Importance: Symbols of Freedom. 2010. (Connect to Literacy Ser.). 8p. pap. (978-1-4334-0515-0(6)) Millmark Education.

Thornton, Jeremy. Foreign-Born Champions of the American Revolution. 2003. (Building America's Democracy Ser.). (Illus.). 24p. (J). lib. bdg. 22.60 (978-0-8239-6277-8(6), PowerKids Pr.) Rosen Publishing Group, Inc., The.

Tracy, Kathleen. Nathan Hale. 2006. (Profiles in American History Ser.). (Illus.). 48p. (J). (gr. 3-7). lib. bdg. 29.95 (978-1-58415-447-1(0)) Mitchell Lane Pubs., Inc.

Urwin, Kirsten. Betsy Ross & the Creation of the American Flag. 2015. (Spotlight on American History Ser.). (ENG., Illus.). 24p. (J). (gr. 4-6). pap. 10.00 (978-1-4994-1789-0(6), PowerKids Pr.) Rosen Publishing Group, Inc., The.

Wachter, Joanne. George Washington & the American Revolution. 2005. (J). pap. (978-1-4108-4633-4(4)) Benchmark Education Co.

Walker, Robert. Flag Day. 2012. (ENG.). 32p. (J). (978-0-7787-4087-2(0)); pap. (978-0-7787-4092-6(7)) Crabtree Publishing Co.

Warrick, Karen Clemens. Independence National Historical Park: A MyReportLinks.com Book. 2005. (Virtual Field Trips Ser.). (Illus.). 48p. (J). (gr. 4-10). lib. bdg. 26.60 (978-0-7660-5224-6(9), MyReportLinks.com Bks.) Enslow Pubs., Inc.

Webb, Sarah Powers. The American Revolution. 2016. (Primary Source History Ser.). (ENG., Illus.). 32p. (gr. 3-4). lib. bdg. 27.32 (978-1-4914-8487-6(X), Fact Finders) Capstone Press of Coughlan Cos.

Wells-Cole, Catherine. Slavery & the Forging of Early America. 2014. (J). (978-1-59935-410-1(1)) Reynolds, Morgan Inc.

Whig Against Tory or the Military Advent. 2004. reprint ed. pap. 15.95 (978-1-4191-9382-8(1)) Kessinger Publishing, LLC.

Whiting, Jim. The Life & Times of Abigail Adams. 2007. (Profiles in American History Ser.). (Illus.). 48p. (J). (gr. 4-7). lib. bdg. 29.95 (978-1-58415-527-0(2)) Mitchell Lane Pubs., Inc.

Whitman Blair, Margaret. Liberty or Death: The Surprising Story of Runaway Slaves Who Sided with the British During the American Revolution (Large Print 16pt) l.t. ed. 2013. 122p. pap. (978-1-4596-6716-7(6)) ReadHowYouWant.com, Ltd.

Winter, Jonah. Paul Revere & the Bell Ringers. Dodson, Bert, illus. 2003. (Ready-To-read COFA Ser.). (ENG.). 32p. (J). (gr. k-2). pap. 3.99 (978-0-689-85635-8(0), Simon Spotlight) Simon Spotlight.

Winters, Kay. Colonial Voices: Hear Them Speak. Day, Larry, illus. 2008. (ENG.). 32p. (J). (gr. 4-7). 17.99 (978-0-525-47872-0(8), Dutton Books for Young Readers) Penguin Young Readers Group.

—Colonial Voices - Hear Them Speak: The Outbreak of the Boston Tea Party Told from Multiple Points-of-View! Day, Larry, illus. 2015. (ENG.). 48p. (J). (gr. 4-7). pap. 8.99 (978-0-14-751162-1(3), Puffin Books) Penguin Young Readers Group.

Wirkner, Linda. Learning about the American Revolution with Graphic Organizers. (Graphic Organizers in Social Studies). 24p. 2009. (gr. 3-4). 42.50 (978-1-61513-083-2(7), PowerKids Pr.) 2006. (ENG.). (gr. 4-6). pap. 8.25 (978-1-4042-5055-0(7), Rosen Classroom) Rosen Publishing Group, Inc., The.

—Learning about the American Revolutionary War with Graphic Organizers. 2005. (Graphic Organizers in Social Studies). (Illus.). 24p. (J). (gr. 3-5). lib. bdg. 22.60 (978-1-4042-2813-9(6), PowerKids Pr.) Rosen Publishing Group, Inc., The.

Wister, Sally. Diary of Sally Wister: A Colonial Quaker Girl, 1 vol. 2014. (First-Person Histories Ser.). (ENG.). 32p. (gr. 3-4). lib. bdg. 27.32 (978-1-4765-4191-4(4), Fact Finders) Capstone Press of Coughlan Cos.

Woelfle, Gretchen. Answering the Cry for Freedom: Stories of African Americans & the American Revolution. Christie, R. Gregory, illus. 2016. (ENG.). 240p. (J). (gr. 3-7). 18.95 (978-1-62979-306-1(X), Calkins Creek) Boyds Mills Pr.

—Write on, Mercy! The Secret Life of Mercy Otis Warren. Wallner, Alexandra, illus. 2012. (ENG.). 40p. (J). (gr. 3). 16.95 (978-1-59078-822-6(2), Calkins Creek) Boyds Mills Pr.

Yasuda, Anita. The American Revolutionary War. 2016. (Illus.). 48p. (J). (978-1-5105-1278-8(0)) SmartBook Media, Inc.

Yero, Judith Lloyd. The Mayflower Compact. 2006. (American Documents Ser.). (ENG., Illus.). 40p. (J). (gr. 5-9). 15.95 (978-0-7922-5891-9(6)); lib. bdg. 23.90 (978-0-7922-5892-6(4)) National Geographic Society. (National Geographic Children's Bks.).

Yomtov, Nel. Revolutionary War Spies, 1 vol. 2013. (Classified Ser.). (ENG.). 48p. (gr. 3-4). 31.99 (978-1-4296-9977-8(9)) Capstone Press of Coughlan Cos.

Ziff, John. The American Revolution, Vol. 11. Musteen, Jason R., ed. 2015. (Major U. S. Historical Wars Ser.). (Illus.). 64p. (J). (gr. 7). lib. bdg. 23.95 (978-1-4222-3353-5(7)) Mason Crest.

UNITED STATES—HISTORY—REVOLUTION, 1775-1783—BIOGRAPHY

Ades, Audrey. Ethan Allen & the Green Mountain Boys. 2017. 25.70 (978-1-61228-952-6(5)) Mitchell Lane Pubs., Inc.

Adler, David A. & Adler, Peter S. Heroes of the Revolution. 2003. (ENG., Illus.). 32p. (J). (gr. 1-5). tchr. ed. 17.95 (978-0-8234-1471-0(X)) Holiday Hse., Inc.

Aluri, Rao. Backcountry Fury: A Sixteen-Year-Old Patriot in the Revolutionary War. 2010. (J). pap. 19.95 (978-1-59712-409-6(5)) Catawba Publishing Co.

Amler, Jane Frances. Haym Salomon: Patriot Banker of the American Revolution. 2009. (Library of American Lives & Times Ser.). 112p. (gr. 5-5). 69.20 (978-1-60853-487-6(1)) Rosen Publishing Group, Inc., The.

Anderson, Dale. The Patriots Win the American Revolution. 2005. (World Almanac Library of the American Revolution Ser.). 48p. (gr. 5-12). pap. 14.05 (978-0-8368-5937-9(5)); lib. bdg. 31.00 (978-0-8368-5928-7(6)) Stevens, Gareth Publishing LLLP. (Gareth Stevens Secondary Library).

Anderson, Laurie Halse. Independent Dames: What You Never Knew about the Women & Girls of the American Revolution. Faulkner, Matt, illus. 2008. (ENG.). 40p. (J). (gr. 1-5). 17.99 (978-0-689-85808-6(6), Simon & Schuster Bks. For Young Readers) Simon & Schuster Bks. For Young Readers.

Anderson, Michael. Biographies of the American Revolution: Benjamin Franklin to John Paul Jones. 2012. (Impact on America: Collective Biographies Ser.). (ENG., Illus.). 112p. (J). (gr. 7-12). lib. bdg. 32.90 (978-1-61530-685-5(4)) Rosen Publishing Group, Inc., The.

Anderson, Michael, ed. Biographies of the American Revolution: Benjamin Franklin, John Adams, John Paul Jones, & More. 2012. (Impact on America: Collective Biographies Ser.). (ENG., Illus.). 112p. (YA). (gr. 7-12). 65.80 (978-1-61530-764-7(8)) Rosen Publishing Group, Inc., The.

Archer, Jules. They Made a Revolution: The Sons & Daughters of the American Revolution. 2016. (Jules Archer History for Young Readers Ser.). (ENG.). 170p. (J). (gr. 6). 16.99 (978-1-63450-195-8(0), Sky Pony Pr.) Skyhorse Publishing Co., Inc.

Beller, Susan Provost. Yankee Doodle & the Redcoats: Soldiering in the Revolutionary War. Day, Larry, illus. 2003. (Single Titles Ser.). (ENG.). 96p. (gr. 5-8). lib. bdg. 26.60 (978-0-7613-2612-0(X), Twenty-First Century Bks.) Lerner Publishing Group.

Bodie, Idella. Heroes & Heroines of the American Revolution. 2004. (Illus.). 48p. (J). pap., instr.'s gde. ed. (978-0-87844-173-0(5)) Sandlapper Publishing Co., Inc.

—Heroines of the American Revolution. 2003. (Illus.). 99p. (J). pap. 6.95 (978-0-87844-170-9(0)) Sandlapper Publishing Co., Inc.

Boyer, Marilyn & Tumas, Grace. Profiles of Valor: Character Studies from the War of Independence. 2013. (Illus.). 352p. (J). (978-0-9777685-9-2(7)) Learning Parent, The.

Castrovilla, Selene. By the Sword. Farnsworth, Bill, illus. 2007. (ENG.). 40p. (J). (gr. 5-7). 17.95 (978-1-59078-427-3(8)) Boyds Mills Pr.

Crannell, Karl. John Stark: Live Free or Die. 2006. (Forgotten Heroes of the American Revolution Ser.). (Illus.). 80p. (J). (gr. 5-11). lib. bdg. 23.95 (978-1-59556-016-2(5)) OTTN Publishing.

—John Stark: Live Free or Die! 2006. (J). pap. (978-1-59556-021-6(1)) OTTN Publishing.

Cunningham, Mark. Molly Pitcher. 2014. (Illus.). 31p. (J). pap. (978-1-62712-290-0(7)) Cavendish Square Publishing.

DeVillier, Christy. Nathan Hale, 1 vol. 2004. (First Biographies Set Iv Ser.). (ENG., Illus.). 32p. (gr. k-4). 27.07 (978-1-59197-513-7(1), Buddy Bks.) ABDO Publishing Co.

Draper, Allison Stark. The Start of the American Revolutionary War: Paul Revere Rides at Midnight. 2009. (Headlines from History Ser.). 24p. (gr. 3-3). 42.50 (978-1-61513-247-8(3), PowerKids Pr.) Rosen Publishing Group, Inc., The.

Fedyszyn, Kirra. Molly Pitcher. 2014. (Jr. Graphic American Legends Ser.). 24p. (J). (gr. 3-6). lib. bdg. 26.25 (978-1-4777-7205-8(7), PowerKids Pr.) Rosen Publishing Group, Inc., The.

Gagne, Tammy. Who Were the Signers of the Declaration of Independence? 2017. (Young America Ser.). (gr. 3-6). 29.95 (978-1-61228-983-0(5)) Mitchell Lane Pubs., Inc.

Glaser, Jason. Molly Pitcher: Young American Patriot, 1 vol. Smith, Tod G. et al, illus. 2006. (Graphic Biographies Ser.). (ENG.). 32p. (gr. 3-4). 30.65 (978-0-7368-5486-3(X), Graphic Library) Capstone Press of Coughlan Cos.

Green, Joanne. An American Hero. 2008. 56p. per. (978-1-897512-04-3(X)) Saga Bks.

Hale, Nathan. One Dead Spy. 2012. (Nathan Hale's Hazardous Tales Ser.). (ENG., Illus.). 128p. (J). (gr. 3-7). 12.95 (978-1-4197-0396-6(X), Amulet Bks.) Abrams, Inc.

Hall, Brianna. Great Women of the American Revolution, 1 vol. 2012. (Story of the American Revolution Ser.). (ENG., Illus.). 32p. (gr. 3-4). pap. 8.10 (978-1-4296-9284-7(7)); lib. bdg. 27.32 (978-1-4296-8451-4(8), Fact Finders) Capstone Press of Coughlan Cos.

Hamilton, John. Leaders & Generals of the American Revolution. 2013. (American Revolution Ser.). 32p. (J). (gr. 5-9). lib. bdg. 27.07 (978-1-61783-681-7(8), Abdo & Daughters) ABDO Publishing Co.

Harness, Cheryl. The Revolutionary John Adams. 2003. (ENG., Illus.). 48p. (J). (gr. 3-7). 17.95 (978-0-7922-6970-0(5), National Geographic Children's Bks.) National Geographic Society.

Harris, Laurie Lanzen. Colonial America & the Revolutionary War: The Story of the People of the Colonies, from Early Settlers to Revolutionary Leaders. 2009. 399p. (J). (gr. 5-7). lib. bdg. 49.00 (978-1-931360-34-0(0)) Favorable Impressions.

Hollar, Sherman. Biographies of Colonial America: From Sir Walter Raleigh to Phillis Wheatley. 2012. (Impact on America: Collective Biographies Ser.). (ENG., Illus.). 112p. (J). (gr. 7-12). lib. bdg. 32.90 (978-1-61530-683-1(8)) Rosen Publishing Group, Inc., The.

—Biographies of Colonial America: Sir Walter Raleigh, Powhatan, Phillis Wheatley, & More. 2012. (Impact on America: Collective Biographies Ser.). (ENG., Illus.). 112p. (YA). (gr. 7-12). 65.80 (978-1-61530-763-0(X)) Rosen Publishing Group, Inc., The.

Huey, Lois Miner. Voices of the American Revolution. 2010. (Voices of War Ser.). (ENG.). 32p. (gr. 3-4). pap. 47.70 (978-1-4296-5699-3(9), Edge Bks.) Capstone Press of Coughlan Cos.

—Voices of the American Revolution: Stories from the Battlefields, 1 vol. 2010. (Voices of War Ser.). (ENG.). 32p. (gr. 3-4). lib. bdg. 27.99 (978-1-4296-4739-7(6), Edge Bks.) Capstone Press of Coughlan Cos.

Jeffrey, Gary. Paul Revere & His Midnight Ride. 2011. (Graphic Heroes of the American Revolution Ser.). 24p. (J). (gr. 3-6). lib. bdg. 23.95 (978-1-4339-6019-2(2)); pap. 8.15 (978-1-4339-6020-8(6), Gareth Stevens Learning Library) Stevens, Gareth Publishing LLLP.

—Thomas Jefferson & the Declaration of Independence. 2011. (Graphic Heroes of the American Revolution Ser.). (Illus.). 24p. (J). (gr. 3-6). 23.95 (978-1-4339-6025-3(7)); pap. 8.15 (978-1-4339-6026-0(5), Gareth Stevens Learning Library) Stevens, Gareth Publishing LLLP.

Kauffman, Scott. Francis Marion: Swamp Fox of South Carolina. 2006. (Forgotten Heroes of the American Revolution Ser.). (Illus.). 88p. (YA). (gr. 5-11). lib. bdg. 23.95 (978-1-59556-014-8(9)) OTTN Publishing.

Koestler-Grack, Rachel A. Nathan Hale: Courageous Spy. 2005. (Leaders of the American Revolution Ser.). (Illus.). 100p. (gr. 5-8). lib. bdg. 30.00 (978-0-7910-8623-0(2)) Facts On File, Inc.

Kudlinski, Kathleen V. Rebel with a Cause: The Daring Adventure of Dicey Langston, Girl Spy of the American Revolution. Faber, Rudy, illus. 2015. (Encounter: Narrative Nonfiction Picture Bks.). (ENG.). 40p. (gr. 3-4). lib. bdg. 28.65 (978-1-4914-6073-3(3)) Encounter Bks.

The Legend of Jocko: Hero of the American Revolution. 2003. (YA). pap. 9.95 (978-0-9761778-0-7(3)) Lefall & Co., Inc.

Libertson, Jody. Nathan Hale: Hero of the American Revolution. 2004. (Famous People in American History Ser.). (ENG., Illus.). 32p. (gr. 4-8). pap. 10.00 (978-0-8239-4189-6(2)) Rosen Publishing Group, Inc., The.

Madison, Richard & Cunningham, Mark. Molly Pitcher: The Woman Who Fought the War. 2014. (Illus.). 31p. (J). 28.50 (978-1-62712-289-4(3)) Cavendish Square Publishing.

Maloof, Torrey. George Washington & the Men Who Shaped America. 2016. (Primary Source Readers Ser.). (Illus.). 32p. (J). (gr. 4-5). pap. 8.99 (978-1-4938-3081-7(3)) Teacher Created Materials, Inc.

Masters, Nancy Robinson. Extraordinary Patriots of the United States of America: Colonial Times to Pre-Civil War. 2005. (Extraordinary People Ser.). (ENG., Illus.). 288p. (J). (gr. 4-7). 40.00 (978-0-516-24404-4(3), Children's Pr.) Scholastic Library Publishing.

Murray, Stuart A. P. John Trumbull: Painter of the Revolutionary War. 2008. (ENG., Illus.). 83p. (C). (gr. 6-18). lib. bdg. 158.00 (978-0-7656-8150-8(1), Y182501) Routledge.

Newton, Michael E. Alexander Hamilton: The Formative Years. 2015. (ENG., Illus.). 774p. 40.00 (978-0-9826040-3-8(3)) Eleftheria Publishing.

Otfinoski, Steven. Patriots & Redcoats: Stories of American Revolutionary War Leaders. 2015. (Revolutionary War Ser.). (ENG.). 48p. (gr. 3-4). pap. 8.95 (978-1-4914-2158-1(4)) Capstone Press of Coughlan Cos.

—People of the American Revolution: Set Of 6. 2011. (Navigators Ser.). (J). pap. 48.00 net. (978-1-4108-5110-9(9)) Benchmark Education Co.

Parker, Christi E. George Washington, 1 vol. 2004. (Primary Source Readers Ser.). (ENG.). 24p. (J). (gr. 4-4). pap. 8.99 (978-0-7439-8749-3(7)) Shell Educational Publishing.

Pfeffer, Wendy. Many Ways to Be A Soldier. 2009. pap. 40.95 (978-0-7613-4795-8(X)) Lerner Publishing Group.

Publishers, Chelsea House, creator. Leaders of the American Revolution Set, 11-Volumes. 2006. (Leaders of the American Revolution Ser.). 100p. (gr. 5-8). 270.00 (978-0-7910-9320-7(4), Chelsea Hse.) Facts On File, Inc.

Raum, Elizabeth. True Stories of the Revolutionary War, 1 vol. Kinsella, Pat, illus. 2012. (Stories of War Ser.). (ENG.). 32p. (gr. 3-4). 30.65 (978-1-4296-8674-7(X)); pap. 8.10 (978-1-4296-9342-4(8)); pap. 47.70 (978-1-4296-9343-1(6)) Capstone Press of Coughlan Cos. (Graphic Library).

Revolutionary War Leaders. 2005. (Revolutionary War Leaders Ser.). (gr. 5-8). 440.00 (978-0-7910-9157-9(0), Chelsea Hse.) Facts On File, Inc.

Riley, John B. John Paul Jones: A Photo Biography. l.t. ed. 2004. (First Biographies Ser.). (Illus.). 24p. (YA). (gr. 5-18). 16.95 (978-1-883846-63-3(3), First Biographies) Reynolds, Morgan Inc.

Rockliff, Mara. Gingerbread for Liberty! How a German Baker Helped Win the American Revolution. Kirsch, Vincent X., illus. 2015. (ENG.). 32p. (J). (gr. 1-4). 17.99 (978-0-544-13001-2(4), HMH Books For Young Readers) Houghton Mifflin Harcourt Publishing Co.

Rockwell, Anne. A Spy Called James: The True Story of James Lafayette, Revolutionary War Double Agent. Cooper, Floyd, illus. 2016. (ENG.). 32p. (gr. 2-5). lib. bdg. 17.99 (978-1-4677-4933-6(8)); 35.99 (978-1-4677-6178-9(8)) Lerner Publishing Group. (Carolrhoda Bks.).

Rosen, Daniel & National Geographic Learning Staff. Fight for Freedom. 2007. (Reading Expeditions Social Studies). (ENG., Illus.). 40p. (J). pap. 19.95 (978-0-7922-8620-2(0)) CENGAGE Learning.

Ruffin, Frances E. Molly Pitcher. 2009. (American Legends Ser.). 24p. (gr. 3-3). 42.50 (978-1-61511-384-2(3), PowerKids Pr.) Rosen Publishing Group, Inc., The.

Scarbrough, Mary Hertz. Heroes of the American Revolution. 2012. (Story of the American Revolution Ser.). (ENG.). 32p. (gr. 3-4). pap. 47.70 (978-1-4296-9287-8(1), Fact Finders); (Illus.). pap. 8.10 (978-1-4296-9286-1(3)); (Illus.). lib. bdg. 27.32 (978-1-4296-8590-0(5)) Capstone Press of Coughlan Cos.

Silate, Jennifer. Betsy Ross. 2004. (Famous People in American History Ser.). (ENG., Illus.). 32p. (gr. 4-8). pap. 10.00 (978-0-8239-4176-6(0)) Rosen Publishing Group, Inc., The.

Stewart, Gail B. The Revolutionary War. 2003. (People at the Center of Ser.). (Illus.). 48p. (J). 26.20 (978-1-56711-769-1(4), Blackbirch Pr., Inc.) Cengage Gale.

Thornton, Jeremy. Famous Women of the American Revolution. 2009. (Building America's Democracy Ser.). 24p. (gr. 3-3). 42.50 (978-1-61511-763-5(6), PowerKids Pr.) Rosen Publishing Group, Inc., The.

—Foreign-Born Champions of the American Revolution. 2003. (Building America's Democracy Ser.). (Illus.). 24p. (J). lib. bdg. 22.60 (978-0-8239-6277-8(6), PowerKids Pr.) Rosen Publishing Group, Inc., The.

—Tories & Patriots: Neighbors at War. (Building America's Democracy Ser.). 24p. 2009. (gr. 3-3). 42.50 (978-1-61511-768-0(7)) 2003. (Illus.). (J). lib. bdg. 22.60 (978-0-8239-6279-2(2)) Rosen Publishing Group, Inc., The. (PowerKids Pr.).

Wales, Dirk. Twice a Hero: Polish American Heroes of the American Revolutuion. Peterson, Lynn Ihsen, illus. 2007. 31p. (J). (gr. 4-9). 18.95 incl. audio compact disk (978-0-9632459-4-6(5)) Great Plains Pr.

Walsh, Francis. Daring Women of the American Revolution. 2009. (Real Life Readers Ser.). 32p. (gr. 4-5). pap. 10.00 (978-1-4358-0177-6(6), Rosen Classroom); (gr. 4-4). 47.90 (978-1-61511-367-5(3), PowerKids Pr.); (J). (gr. 3-4). lib. bdg. 25.25 (978-1-4358-2994-7(8), PowerKids Pr.) Rosen Publishing Group, Inc., The.

Weston Woods Staff, creator. And Then What Happened, Paul Revere? 2011. 18.95 (978-0-439-72661-0(1)); 29.95 (978-0-439-73467-7(3)); 38.75 (978-0-439-72663-4(8)) Weston Woods Studios, Inc.

Women of the American Revolution (NCHS) (YA). (gr. 5-8). spiral bd., tchr.'s planning gde. ed. 11.50 (978-0-382-40933-2(7)) Cobblestone Publishing Co.

Women of the American Revolution (NCHS) Grades 5-8. 58p. (J). tchr. ed. 29.45 (978-0-382-40934-9(5)) Cobblestone Publishing Co.

Yomtov, Nel, et al. Stories of War. 2012. (Stories of War Ser.). (ENG.). 32p. (gr. 3-4). pap. 190.80 *(978-1-4296-9349-3(5))*; pap. 31.80 *(978-1-4296-9348-6(7))* Capstone Press of Coughlan Cos. (Graphic Library).

UNITED STATES—HISTORY—REVOLUTION, 1775-1783—CAMPAIGNS

see also Yorktown (Va.)—History—Siege, 1781

Abnett, Dan. George Washington y la Guerra de Independencia. 2009. (Historietas Juveniles: Biografías (Jr. Graphic Biographies) Ser.). (SPA & ENG., Illus.). 24p. (gr. 3-8). pap. 10.60 *(978-1-4358-3322-7(8))* Rosen Publishing Group, Inc., The.

Aluri, Rao. Backcountry Fury: A Sixteen-Year-Old Patriot in the Revolutionary War. 2010. (J). pap. 19.95 *(978-1-59712-409-6(5))* Catawba Publishing Co.

Ammon, Richard. Valley Forge. Farnsworth, Bill, illus. 2004. (ENG.). 32p. (J). (gr. 4-6). tchr. ed. 17.95 *(978-0-8234-1746-9(8))* Holiday Hse., Inc.

Anderson, Dale. Key Battles of the American Revolution, 1776-1778. 2005. (World Almanac Library of the American Revolution Ser.). 48p. (gr. 5-12). pap. 14.05 *(978-0-8368-5936-2(7))*; lib. bdg. 31.00 *(978-0-8368-5927-0(8))* Stevens, Gareth Publishing LLLP. (Gareth Stevens Secondary Library).

—The Patriots Win the American Revolution. 2005. (World Almanac Library of the American Revolution Ser.). 48p. (gr. 5-12). pap. 14.05 *(978-0-8368-5937-9(5))*; lib. bdg. 31.00 *(978-0-8368-5928-7(6))* Stevens, Gareth Publishing LLLP. (Gareth Stevens Secondary Library).

Benchmark Education Co., LLC. The Battles of the American Revolution. 2014. (PRIME Ser.). (J). (gr. 6-8). pap. *(978-1-4509-9490-3(3))* Benchmark Education Co.

Bodie, Idella. Light-Horse Harry. 2004. (Illus.). 86p. (J). pap. 6.95 *(978-0-87844-172-3(7))* Sandlapper Publishing Co., Inc.

Brown Reference Group Staff. Revolutionary War. 2009. (Battle Box Ser.). (ENG.). 64p. (J). (gr. 5-9). 21.99 *(978-1-4169-7126-9(2)*, Simon & Schuster Bks. For Young Readers) Simon & Schuster Bks. For Young Readers.

Catel, Patrick. Battles of the Revolutionary War, 1 vol. (Why We Fought: the Revolutionary War Ser.). (ENG.). 48p. (gr. 3-6). 2011. pap. 9.95 *(978-1-4329-3901-4(7))* 2010. 33.32 *(978-1-4329-3896-3(7))* Heinemann-Raintree. (Heinemann InfoSearch).

Cheney, Lynne. When Washington Crossed the Delaware: A Wintertime Story for Young Patriots. Fiore, Peter M., illus. 2012. (ENG.). 40p. (J). (gr. k-4). 7.99 *(978-1-4424-4423-2(1)*, Simon & Schuster/Paula Wiseman Bks.) Simon & Schuster/Paula Wiseman Bks.

Cheney, Lynne & Fiore, Peter. When Washington Crossed the Delaware: A Wintertime Story for Young Patriots. 2004. (ENG., Illus.). 32p. (J). (gr. k-4). 19.99 *(978-0-689-87043-9(4)*, Simon & Schuster/Paula Wiseman Bks.) Simon & Schuster/Paula Wiseman Bks.

Corporate Contributor Staff & Roberts, Steve. King George Iii: England's Struggle to Keep America. 2012. (ENG.). 48p. (J). *(978-0-7787-0800-1(4))* Crabtree Publishing Co.

Crabtree Staff & Clarke, Gordon. Significant Battles of the American Revolution. 2012. (ENG., Illus.). 48p. (J). pap. *(978-0-7787-0817-9(9))* Crabtree Publishing Co.

Crabtree Staff & Perritano, John. The Causes of the American Revolution. 2012. (ENG., Illus.). 48p. (J). pap. *(978-0-7787-0815-5(2))* Crabtree Publishing Co.

Crannell, Karl. John Stark: Live Free or Die. 2006. (Forgotten Heroes of the American Revolution Ser.). (Illus.). 80p. (J). (gr. 5-11). lib. bdg. 23.95 *(978-1-59556-016-2(5))* OTTN Publishing.

—John Stark: Live Free or Die! 2006. (J). pap. *(978-1-59556-021-6(1))* OTTN Publishing.

Crewe, Sabrina & Uschan, Michael V. Lexington & Concord. 2004. (Events That Shaped America Ser.). (Illus.). 32p. (gr. 3-6). lib. bdg. 26.00 *(978-0-8368-3398-0(8)*, Gareth Stevens Learning Library) Stevens, Gareth Publishing LLLP.

Dean, Arlan. Crossing the Delaware: George Washington & the Battle of Trenton. 2009. (Great Moments in American History Ser.). 32p. (gr. 3-3). 47.90 *(978-1-61513-140-2(X))* Rosen Publishing Group, Inc., The.

Forest, Christopher. The Biggest Battles of the Revolutionary War, 1 vol. 2012. (Story of the American Revolution Ser.). (ENG.). 32p. (gr. 3-4). pap. 8.10 *(978-1-4296-9282-3(0))*; pap. 47.70 *(978-1-4296-9283-0(9)*, Fact Finders) Capstone Press of Coughlan Cos.

Gallagher, Jim. Daniel Morgan: Fighting Frontiersman. 2006. (J). pap. *(978-1-59556-020-9(3))*; (Illus.). 88p. (gr. 5-11). lib. bdg. 23.95 *(978-1-59556-015-5(7))* OTTN Publishing.

Hamilton, John. Early Battles of the American Revolution. 2013. (American Revolution Ser.). 32p. (J). (gr. 5-9). lib. bdg. 27.07 *(978-1-61783-679-4(6)*, Abdo & Daughters) ABDO Publishing Co.

—Final Years of the American Revolution. 2013. (American Revolution Ser.). 32p. (J). (gr. 5-9). lib. bdg. 27.07 *(978-1-61783-680-0(X)*, Abdo & Daughters) ABDO Publishing Co.

Kravitz, Danny. The Untold Story of Washington's Surprise Attack: The Daring Crossing of the Delaware River. 2015. (What You Didn't Know about the American Revolution Ser.). (ENG.). 64p. (gr. 4-8). 34.65 *(978-0-7565-4973-2(6))* Compass Point Bks.

Landau, Elaine. George Washington Crosses the Delaware: Would You Risk the Revolution? 2010. (What Would You Do? Ser.). (Illus.). 48p. (J). pap. 8.95 *(978-1-59845-195-5(2)*, Enslow Elementary) Enslow Pubs., Inc.

Levin, Jack E. & Levin, Mark R. George Washington: The Crossing. 2013. (ENG., Illus.). 64p. 18.00 *(978-1-4767-3193-3(4)*, Threshold Editions) Threshold Editions.

McGowen, Tom. The Revolutionary War & George Washington's Army in American History. 2004. (In American History Ser.). (Illus.). 128p. (J). lib. bdg. 26.60 *(978-0-7660-2143-3(2))* Enslow Pubs., Inc.

Micklos, John. Washington's Crossing the Delaware & the Winter at Valley Forge: Through Primary Sources. 2013. (American Revolution Through Primary Sources Ser.). 48p. (J). (gr. 4-18). 25.27 *(978-0-7660-4132-5(8))* Enslow Pubs., Inc.

—Washington's Crossing the Delaware & the Winter at Valley Forge—Through Primary Sources. 2013. (American Revolution Through Primary Sources Ser.). 48p. (J). (gr. 4-10). pap. 8.95 *(978-1-4644-0190-9(X))* Enslow Pubs., Inc.

—Why We Won the American Revolution — Through Primary Sources. 2013. (American Revolution Through Primary Sources Ser.). 48p. (J). (gr. 4-18). 25.27 *(978-0-7660-4134-9(4))* Enslow Pubs., Inc.

—Why We Won the American Revolution—Through Primary Sources. 2013. (American Revolution Through Primary Sources Ser.). 48p. (J). (gr. 4-10). pap. 8.95 *(978-1-4644-0192-3(6))* Enslow Pubs., Inc.

Peacock, Louise. Crossing the Delaware: A History in Many Voices. Krudop, Walter Lyon, illus. 2007. (ENG.). 48p. (J). (gr. 3-7). 12.99 *(978-1-4169-5890-1(8)*, Simon & Schuster/Paula Wiseman Bks.) Simon & Schuster/Paula Wiseman Bks.

Randolph, Joanne. The Call of Liberty: Marquis de Lafayette & the American Revolution. 2009. (Great Moments in American History Ser.). 32p. (gr. 3-3). 47.90 *(978-1-61513-152-5(3))* Rosen Publishing Group, Inc., The.

Rushworth, Victoria. Battles of the American Revolution: Set of 6: Saratoga. 2011. (Navigators Ser.). (J). pap. 48.00 net. *(978-1-4108-5109-3(5))* Benchmark Education Co.

Strum, Richard. Henry Knox: Washington's Artilleryman. 2006. (Forgotten Heroes of the American Revolution Ser.). (Illus.). 88p. (J). (gr. 5-11). lib. bdg. 23.95 *(978-1-59556-013-1(0))* OTTN Publishing.

Strum, Richard M. Henry Knox: Washington's Artilleryman. 2006. (J). pap. *(978-1-59556-018-6(1))* OTTN Publishing.

Thornton, Jeremy. Foreign-Born Champions of the American Revolution. 2009. (Building America's Democracy Ser.). 24p. (gr. 3-3). 42.50 *(978-1-61511-764-2(4)*, PowerKids Pr.) Rosen Publishing Group, Inc., The.

Uschan, Michael V. Lexington & Concord. 2003. (Landmark Events in American History Ser.). (Illus.). 48p. (gr. 5-12). pap. 14.05 *(978-0-8368-5407-7(1)*, Gareth Stevens Secondary Library) Stevens, Gareth Publishing LLLP.

Vierow, Wendy. The Battle of Saratoga. 2009. (Atlas of Famous Battles of the American Revolution Ser.). 24p. (gr. 3-3). 42.50 *(978-1-60853-330-5(1)*, PowerKids Pr.) Rosen Publishing Group, Inc., The.

—The Battle of Trenton. 2009. (Atlas of Famous Battles of the American Revolution Ser.). 24p. (gr. 3-3). 42.50 *(978-1-60853-331-2(X)*, PowerKids Pr.) Rosen Publishing Group, Inc., The.

—The Battle of Yorktown. 2009. (Atlas of Famous Battles of the American Revolution Ser.). 24p. (gr. 3-3). 42.50 *(978-1-60853-332-9(8)*, PowerKids Pr.) Rosen Publishing Group, Inc., The.

Waldman, Scott P. The Battle of Bunker Hill. 2003. (Atlas of Famous Battles of the American Revolution Ser.). (Illus.). 24p. (J). lib. bdg. 22.60 *(978-0-8239-6329-4(2)*, PowerKids Pr.) Rosen Publishing Group, Inc., The.

—The Battle of Lexington & Concord. (Atlas of Famous Battles of the American Revolution Ser.). 24p. 2009. (gr. 3-3). 42.50 *(978-1-60853-328-2(X))* 2003. (Illus.). (J). lib. bdg. 22.60 *(978-0-8239-6328-7(4))* Rosen Publishing Group, Inc., The. (PowerKids Pr.).

—The Battle of Monmouth. (Atlas of Famous Battles of the American Revolution Ser.). 24p. 2009. (gr. 3-3). 42.50 *(978-1-60853-329-9(8))* 2003. (Illus.). (J). lib. bdg. 22.60 *(978-0-8239-6330-0(6))* Rosen Publishing Group, Inc., The. (PowerKids Pr.).

—The Battle of Trenton. 2003. (Atlas of Famous Battles of the American Revolution Ser.). (Illus.). 24p. (J). lib. bdg. 22.60 *(978-0-8239-6333-1(0)*, PowerKids Pr.) Rosen Publishing Group, Inc., The.

—The Battle of Yorktown. 2003. (Atlas of Famous Battles of the American Revolution Ser.). (Illus.). 24p. (J). lib. bdg. 22.60 *(978-0-8239-6331-7(4))* Rosen Publishing Group, Inc., The.

Whitelaw, Nancy. The Shot Heard Round the World: The Battles of Lexington & Concord. 2004. (First Battles Ser.). (Illus.). 112p. (J). (gr. 6-12). 23.95 *(978-1-883846-75-6(7)*, First Biographies) Reynolds, Morgan Inc.

UNITED STATES—HISTORY—REVOLUTION, 1775-1783—DRAMA

McCaslin, Nellie. Brave New Banner. 2003. (Players Press Nellie McCaslin Ser.). (Illus.). 20p. (YA). (gr. 6-12). pap. 5.00 *(978-0-88734-436-7(4))* Players Pr., Inc.

UNITED STATES—HISTORY—REVOLUTION, 1775-1783—FICTION

Abbott, E. F. Sybil Ludington: Revolutionary War Rider. 2016. (Based on a True Story Ser.). (ENG., Illus.). 192p. (J). 15.99 *(978-1-250-06836-1(3)*, 9781250068361) Feiwel & Friends.

Amstel, Marsha. The Horse-Riding Adventure of Sybil Ludington, Revolutionary War Messenger. Hammond, Ted & Carbajal, Richard Pimentel, illus. 2011. (History's Kid Heroes Set III Ser.). pap. 51.02 *(978-0-7613-7636-1(4)*, Graphic Universe™) Lerner Publishing Group.

—The Horse-Riding Adventure of Sybil Ludington, Revolutionary War Messenger. Hammond, Ted & Carbajal, Richard, illus. 2011. (History's Kid Heroes Ser.). (ENG.). 32p. (gr. 3-5). 26.60 *(978-0-7613-6181-7(2))*; pap. 8.95 *(978-0-7613-7073-4(0)*, Graphic Universe™) Lerner Publishing Group.

Anderson, Laurie Halse. Ashes. l.t. ed. 2017. (Seeds of America Ser.: 3). (ENG.). 430p. 23.99 ***(978-1-4104-9607-2(4))*** Cengage Gale.

—Ashes. (Seeds of America Trilogy Ser.: Bk. 3). (ENG., Illus.). (J). (gr. 5). 2017. 320p. pap. 8.99 *(978-1-4169-6147-5(X))* 2016. 304p. 16.99 *(978-1-4169-6146-8(1)*, Atheneum/Caitlyn Dlouhy Books) Simon & Schuster Children's Publishing.

—Chains. l.t. ed. 2017. (Seeds of America Ser.). (ENG.). 442p. 22.99 ***(978-1-4104-9917-2(0))*** Cengage Gale.

—Chains. 2014. (Seeds of America Trilogy). (ENG.). 336p. (J). 12.24 *(978-1-63245-094-4(1))* Lectorum Pubns., Inc.

—Chains. 2009. 9.00 *(978-0-7848-3678-1(7)*, Everbind) Marco Bk. Co.

—Chains. (Seeds of America Trilogy Ser.). (ENG., Illus.). (J). (gr. 5-9). 2010. 336p. pap. 8.99 *(978-1-4169-0586-8(3))* 2008. 320p. 18.99 *(978-1-4169-0585-1(5))* Simon & Schuster Children's Publishing. (Atheneum Bks. for Young Readers).

—Chains. l.t. ed. 2009. (ENG.). 390p. (YA). 23.95 *(978-1-4104-1425-0(6))* Thorndike Pr.

—Chains. 2010. (Seeds of America Trilogy Ser.: 1). lib. bdg. 19.65 *(978-0-606-14520-6(6)*, Turtleback) Turtleback Bks.

—Forge. 2012. 18.00 *(978-1-61383-316-2(4))* Perfection Learning Corp.

—Forge. (Seeds of America Trilogy Ser.). (ENG., Illus.). (J). (gr. 5-9). 2012. 320p. pap. 8.99 *(978-1-4169-6145-1(3))* 2010. 304p. 18.99 *(978-1-4169-6144-4(5))* Simon & Schuster Children's Publishing. (Atheneum Bks. for Young Readers).

—Forge. 2012. (Seeds of America Trilogy Ser.: 2). lib. bdg. 18.40 *(978-0-606-23680-5(5)*, Turtleback) Turtleback Bks.

Anderson, M. T. The Kingdom on the Waves. (Astonishing Life of Octavian Nothing, Traitor to the Nation Ser.: Vol. 2). (ENG., Illus.). 592p. 2011. pap. 14.00 *(978-0-7636-5377-4(2))* 2009. (YA). (gr. 9). pap. 12.99 *(978-0-7636-4626-4(1))* Candlewick Pr.

—The Pox Party. (Astonishing Life of Octavian Nothing, Traitor to the Nation Ser.: Vol. 1). (ENG., Illus.). 2006. 368p. (YA). (gr. 9-12). 17.99 *(978-0-7636-2402-6(0))* Vol. I. 2011. 384p. pap. 14.00 *(978-0-7636-5376-7(4))* Candlewick Pr.

Avery, Ben G. Turtle Trouble, 1 vol. Gaudiamo, Adi Darda, illus. 2007. (Z Graphic Novels / TimeFlyz Ser.). (ENG.). 160p. (J). (gr. 3-7). pap. 6.99 *(978-0-310-71362-3(5))* Zondervan.

Avi. The Fighting Ground. 25th anniv. ed. 2009. (Trophy Bk.). (ENG.). 160p. (J). (gr. 3-7). reprint ed. pap. 6.99 *(978-0-06-440185-2(5))* HarperCollins Pubs.

—The Fighting Ground. 2009. 157p. (J). (gr. 4-7). 17.20 *(978-0-8085-9452-9(4)*, Turtleback) Turtleback Bks.

—Fighting Ground. 25th rev. ed. 2014. (Trophy Bk Ser.). (ENG.). 160p. (J). (gr. 3-7). 10.24 *(978-1-63245-315-0(0))* Lectorum Pubns., Inc.

—Sophia's War: A Tale of the Revolution. 2012. (ENG., Illus.). 320p. (J). (gr. 3-7). 17.99 *(978-1-4424-1441-9(3)*, Beach Lane Bks.) Beach Lane Bks.

—Sophia's War: A Tale of the Revolution. 2013. (ENG., Illus.). 336p. (J). (gr. 3-7). pap. 7.99 *(978-1-4424-1442-6(1))* Simon & Schuster Children's Publishing.

Barnes, Cheryl Shaw & Barnes, Peter W., illus. Liberty Lee's Tail of Independence. 2012. (ENG.). 36p. (J). (gr. k-3). 16.95 *(978-1-59698-792-0(8)*, Little Patriot Pr.) Regnery Publishing, Inc., An Eagle Publishing Co.

Baxter, Jean Rae. Freedom Bound. 2012. (ENG., Illus.). 246p. pap. 11.95 *(978-1-55380-143-6(1))* Ronsdale Pr. CAN. Dist: SPD-Small Pr. Distribution.

Beaty, Mary, et al. George Johnson's War, 1 vol. 2003. (ENG., Illus.). 224p. (J). (gr. 7-18). pap. 8.95 *(978-0-88899-468-4(0))* Groundwood Bks. CAN. Dist: Publishers Group West (PGW).

Berleth, Richard. Samuel's Choice. Watling, James, illus. 2012. (ENG.). 40p. (J). (gr. 2-3). pap. 6.99 *(978-0-8075-7219-1(5))* Whitman, Albert & Co.

Blackwood, Gary. The Year of the Hangman. 2004. 261p. (YA). (gr. 8-12). 14.65 *(978-0-7569-4274-8(8))* Perfection Learning Corp.

Blackwood, Gary L. & Blackwood, Gary. Year of the Hangman. 2004. (ENG.). 272p. (YA). (gr. 9-18). 6.99 *(978-0-14-240078-4(5)*, Speak) Penguin Young Readers Group.

Bond, Douglas. Guns of Providence. 2010. (J). pap. *(978-1-59638-156-8(6))* P & R Publishing.

Carlson, Drew. Attack of the Turtle. Johnson, David A., illus. 2008. (ENG.). 157p. (YA). (gr. 4-9). per. 8.00 *(978-0-8028-5338-7(2))* Eerdmans, William B. Publishing Co.

Clark, Eleanor. Victoria Grace: Courageous Patriot. 2007. (Eleanor Ser.: Bk. 2). 209p. (J). (gr. 4-7). 14.99 *(978-0-9753036-8-9(6))* HonorNet.

Collier, James Lincoln & Collier, Christopher. My Brother Sam Is Dead. 2005. (Apple Signature Ser.). (ENG.). 240p. (J). (gr. 7-12). per. 6.99 *(978-0-439-78360-6(7)*, Scholastic Paperbacks) Scholastic, Inc.

De la Cruz, Melissa. Alex & Eliza: A Love Story. 9 vols. 2017. (ENG.). (YA). 161.91 ***(978-0-525-48665-7(8))***; 368p. (gr. 7). 17.99 ***(978-1-5247-3962-1(6))*** Penguin Young Readers Group. (G.P. Putnam's Sons Books for Young Readers).

DeMitchell, Terri A. The Portsmouth Alarm. 2013. 161p. pap. 16.95 *(978-1-932278-92-7(3))* Mayhaven Publishing, Inc.

Elliott, L. M. Give Me Liberty. 2008. (ENG., Illus.). 384p. (J). (gr. 4-7). per. 7.99 *(978-0-06-074423-6(5)*, Tegen, Katherine Bks) HarperCollins Pubs.

Ellis, Edward S. The Boy Patriot. 2007. (Illus.). 88p. per. *(978-1-4065-3449-8(8))* Dodo Pr.

Evan, Frances Y. The Forgotten Flag: Revolutionary Struggle in Connecticut. 2003. (Illus.). 92p. (J). 5.95 *(978-1-57249-338-4(0)*, White Mane Kids) White Mane Publishing Co., Inc.

Falk, Elizabeth Sullivan. Freedom's Fire. Wang, Qi Z., illus. 2004. (J). *(978-1-59336-321-5(4))*; pap. *(978-1-59336-322-2(2))* Mondo Publishing.

Figley, Marthy Rhodes & Figley, Marty Rhodes. The Prison-Ship Adventure of James Forten, Revolutionary War Captive. Hammond, Ted & Carbajal, Richard, illus. 2011. (History's Kid Heroes Ser.). (ENG.). 32p. (gr. 3-5). 26.60 *(978-0-7613-6183-1(9))*; pap. 8.95 *(978-0-7613-7075-8(7)*, Graphic Universe™) Lerner Publishing Group.

Figley, Marty Rhodes. The Prison-Ship Adventure of James Forten, Revolutionary War Captive. Hammond, Ted & Carbajal, Richard, illus. 2011. (History's Kid Heroes Ser.). 32p. pap. 51.02 *(978-0-7613-7637-8(2)*, Graphic Universe™) Lerner Publishing Group.

Fleming, Candace, et al. The Hatmaker's Sign: A Story Benjamin Franklin. Parker, Robert Andrew, illus. 2003. (Avenues Ser.). (ENG.). 40p. (C). (gr. k-4). pap. 10.95 *(978-0-531-07174-8(X))* National Geographic School Publishing, Inc.

Forbes, Esther. Johnny Tremain. 2003. (EMC Masterpiece Series Access Editions). (Illus.). xvi, 308p. (J). 13.99 *(978-0-8219-2408-2(7))* EMC/Paradigm Publishing.

—Johnny Tremain. McCurdy, Michael, illus. l.t. ed. 2005. (ENG.). 440p. (YA). pap. 10.95 *(978-0-7862-7178-8(7))* Thorndike Pr.

Forbes, Esther Hoskins. Johnny Tremain: Illustrated American Classics. Date not set. (J). lib. bdg. 22.95 *(978-0-8488-1318-5(9))* Amereon Ltd.

—Johnny Tremain: Illustrated American Classics. Random House Publishing Group.

—Johnny Tremain Set: Illustrated American Classics, 2 vols., l.t. ed. (J). reprint ed. *(978-0-89064-029-6(7))* National Assn. for Visually Handicapped.

Forman, Sam A. Twenty-One Heroes, 1 vol. 2015. (ENG., Illus.). 224p. (YA). (gr. 7-12). 17.95 *(978-1-4556-2087-6(4))* Pelican Publishing Co., Inc.

Giff, Patricia Reilly. Storyteller. 2011. (ENG.). 176p. (J). (gr. 3-7). pap. 6.99 *(978-0-440-42175-7(6)*, Yearling) Random Hse. Children's Bks.

Gingrich, Callista & Arciero, Susan. Yankee Doodle Dandy. 2013. (Ellis the Elephant Ser.). (ENG., Illus.). 40p. (J). (gr. -1-3). 14.95 *(978-1-62157-087-5(8)*, Regnery Kids) Regnery Publishing, Inc., An Eagle Publishing Co.

Gregory, Kristiana. Cannons at Dawn: The Second Diary of Abigail Jane Stewart, Valley Forge, Pennsylvania, 1779. 2011. (Dear America Ser.). (ENG.). 256p. (J). (gr. 5-9). 12.99 *(978-0-545-21319-6(3))* Scholastic, Inc.

—The Winter of Red Snow. 2010. (Dear America Ser.). (ENG.). 192p. (J). (gr. 3-7). 12.99 *(978-0-545-23802-1(1)*, Scholastic Pr.) Scholastic, Inc.

Griffin, Kitty. The Ride: The Legend of Betsy Dowdy. Priceman, Marjorie, illus. 2010. (ENG.). 40p. (J). (gr. -1-3). 16.99 *(978-1-4169-2816-4(2)*, Atheneum Bks. for Young Readers) Simon & Schuster Children's Publishing.

Gunderson, Jessica. A Rebel among Redcoats: A Revolutionary War Novel. 2015. (Revolutionary War Ser.). (ENG., Illus.). 96p. (gr. 4-4). lib. bdg. 26.65 *(978-1-4342-9701-3(2))* Stone Arch Bks.

—Secret Weapons: A Tale of the Revolutionary War, 1 vol. Aburto, Jesus, illus. 2008. (Historical Fiction Ser.). (ENG.). 56p. (gr. 2-3). pap. 6.25 *(978-1-4342-0848-4(6)*, Graphic Flash) Stone Arch Bks.

Guzman, Lila & Guzman, Rick. Lorenzo & the Turncoat. 2006. 183p. (J). (gr. 5). per. 9.95 *(978-1-55885-471-0(1)*, Piñata Books) Arte Publico Pr.

—Lorenzo's Revolutionary Quest. 2003. 176p. (J). pap. 9.95 *(978-1-55885-392-8(8)*, Piñata Books) Arte Publico Pr.

—Lorenzo's Secret Mission. 2005. 153p. (gr. 4-7). 19.95 *(978-0-7569-5599-1(8))* Perfection Learning Corp.

Haislip, Phyllis Hall. Between the Lines: A Revolutionary War Slave's Journey to Freedom. 2012. (ENG., Illus.). 190p. (J). pap. 8.95 *(978-1-57249-409-1(3)*, White Mane Kids) White Mane Publishing Co., Inc.

Hardman, Ron & Hardman, Jessica. Shadow Fox: Sons of Liberty. Barnecut, Suzanne, ed. Harrigan, Mike, illus. 2010. (Shadow Fox Ser.). 186p. (J). (gr. 4-8). 22.99 *(978-0-9819607-1-5(5))* Fox Run Pr., LLC.

—Shadow Fox: Sons of Liberty. Barnecut, Suzanne, ed. Harrigan, Mike, illus. 2010. (Shadow Fox Ser.). 186p. (J). (gr. 4-8). pap. 11.99 *(978-0-9819607-0-8(7))* Fox Run Pr., LLC.

—Shadow Fox: Sons of Liberty Teacher's Edition. Barnecut, Suzanne, ed. Harrigan, Mike, illus. 2010. (Shadow Fox Ser.: 1). 186p. (J). 34.99 *(978-0-9819607-2-2(3))* Fox Run Pr., LLC.

Harlow, Joan Hiatt. Midnight Rider. 2006. (ENG.). 384p. (J). (gr. 4-9). pap. 8.99 *(978-0-689-87010-1(8)*, McElderry, Margaret K. Bks.) McElderry, Margaret K. Bks.

Hedstrom-Page, Deborah. From Colonies to Country with George Washington. Martinez, Sergio, illus. 2007. (My American Journey Ser.). 82p. (J). (gr. 3-9). 9.99 *(978-0-8054-3265-7(5))* B&H Publishing Group.

Henty, George Alfred. True to the Old Flag: A Novel of the Loyalists in the American War of Independence. 2011. 344p. pap. 19.95 *(978-1-61179-114-3(6))* Fireship Pr.

Hering, Marianne & Sanders, Nancy I. Captured on the High Seas. 2014. (AIO Imagination Station Bks.: 14). (ENG.). 144p. (J). pap. 4.99 *(978-1-58997-775-4(0))* Tyndale Hse. Pubs.

Hogan, Stephen. Johnny Lynch: Patriot Drummerboy. rev. ed. 2007. (J). *(978-0-9795474-0-9(7))* KAM Publishing.

—Johnny Lynch: Road to Camden. 2007. (J). *(978-0-9795474-1-6(5))* KAM Publishing.

Hunter, John P. Red Thunder: Secrets, Spies, & Scoundrels at Yorktown. 2006. 234p. (YA). (gr. 6-8). 7.95 *(978-0-87935-231-8(0))* Colonial Williamsburg Foundation.

Ingle, Sheila. Courageous Kate: A Daughter of the American Revolution. 2006. (ENG.). 130p. pap. 11.95 *(978-1-891885-52-5(9))* Hub City Pr.

Klimo, Kate. Sweetie, No. 6. Jessell, Tim, illus. 2015. (Dog Diaries: 6). (ENG.). 160p. (J). (gr. 2-5). pap. 7.99 *(978-0-385-39240-2(0)*, Random Hse. Bks. for Young Readers) Random Hse. Children's Bks.

Lane, Marion T. Patriots of African Descent in the Revolutionary War: Part 1. 2011. 56p. 30.00 *(978-1-60976-517-0(6)*, Eloquent Bks.) Strategic Book Publishing & Rights Agency (SBPRA).

Lavender, William. Just Jane: A Daughter of England Caught in the Struggle of the American Revolution. 2005. (Great Episodes Ser.). (ENG.). 336p. (YA). (gr. 7-12). pap. 15.95 *(978-0-15-205472-4(3))* Houghton Mifflin Harcourt Publishing Co.

Limbaugh, Rush H., III & Limbaugh, Kathryn Adams. Rush Revere & the American Revolution. 2014. (ENG.). 256p. 19.99 *(978-1-4767-8987-3(8)*, Threshold Editions) Threshold Editions.

—Rush Revere & the American Revolution. Hiers, Christopher, illus. 2014. 244p. (J). pap. *(978-1-4767-8989-7(4)*, Threshold Editions) Threshold Editions.

Mansbach, Adam & Zweibel, Alan. Benjamin Franklin: Huge Pain in My... 2015. (Benjamin Franklin Ser.). (ENG., Illus.). 208p. (J). (gr. 5-9). 12.99 *(978-1-4847-1304-4(4))* Hyperion Bks. for Children.

Marshall, Peter, et al. Nate Donovan: Revolutionary Spy. 2007. 208p. (J). pap. 9.99 *(978-0-8054-4394-3(0)*, B&H Bks.) B&H Publishing Group.

McIntyre, John T. Fighting King George. 2006. (Illus.). pap. 33.95 *(978-1-4286-1853-4(8))* Kessinger Publishing, LLC.

Messner, Kate. Spitfire. 2007. (J). *(978-1-59531-018-7(5))* North Country Bks., Inc.

Moore, Ruth Nulton. The Christmas Surprise. Eitzen, Allan, illus. 2007. 160p. (gr. 4-7). pap. 20.00 *(978-1-55635-418-2(5)*, Resource Pubns.(OR)) Wipf & Stock Pubs.

Morgan, Helen L. Liberty Maid: The Story of Abigail Adams. 2011. 252p. 46.95 *(978-1-258-03202-9(3))* Literary Licensing, LLC.

Moss, Marissa. Emma's Journal. 2004. (Young American Voice Bks.). (Illus.). (gr. 3-7). 17.00 *(978-0-7569-4110-9(5))* Perfection Learning Corp.

Nixon, Joan Lowery. John's Story, 1775. 2004. (J). *(978-0-87935-228-8(0))* Colonial Williamsburg Foundation.

Noble, Trinka Hakes. The Scarlet Stockings Spy. Papp, Robert, illus. 2004. (Tales of Young Americans Ser.). (ENG.). 48p. (J). (gr. 1-7). 16.95 *(978-1-58536-230-1(1))* Sleeping Bear Pr.

Olasky, Susan. Annie Henry: Adventures in the American Revolution. 2005. (Illus.). 528p. (J). pap. 16.99 *(978-1-58134-521-6(6)*, Crossway Bibles) Crossway.

—Annie Henry & the Birth of Liberty. 2011. (J). pap. *(978-1-59638-375-3(5))* P & R Publishing.

—Annie Henry & the Redcoats. 2011. (J). pap. *(978-1-59638-377-7(1))* P & R Publishing.

Osborne, Mary Pope. Revolutionary War on Wednesday. unabr. ed. 2004. (Magic Tree House Ser.: No. 22). 69p. (J). (gr. k-3). pap. 17.00 incl. audio *(978-0-8072-0931-8(7)*, S FTR 254 SP, Listening Library) Random Hse. Audio Publishing Group.

Otis, James. The Minute Boys of Mohawk Valley. 2005. 29.95 *(978-1-4218-0059-2(4)*, 1st World Library - Literary Society) 1st World Publishing, Inc.

—Under the Liberty Tree, a Story of the Boston Massacre. 2011. 84p. pap. 9.99 *(978-1-61203-273-3(7))* Bottom of the Hill Publishing.

Papp, Lisa & Noble, Trinka Hakes. The Battles. Papp, Robert, illus. 2013. (American Adventures Ser.). (ENG.). 88p. (J). (gr. 3-6). pap. 9.99 *(978-1-58536-861-7(X)*, 202368) Sleeping Bear Pr.

Paulsen, Gary. The Rifle. 2006. (ENG.). 112p. (YA). (gr. 7-12). pap. 6.99 *(978-0-15-205839-5(7))* Houghton Mifflin Harcourt Publishing Co.

—Woods Runner. 2011. (ENG.). 176p. (YA). (gr. 7). pap. 7.99 *(978-0-375-85908-3(X)*, Lamb, Wendy Bks.) Random Hse. Children's Bks.

Perkins, Lucy. The American Twins of the Revolution. Perkins, Lucy, illus. 2007. (Illus.). 232p. per. 12.95 *(978-0-9776786-7-9(9))* Salem Ridge Press LLC.

Perkins, Lucy Fitch. The American Twins of the Revolution. Perkins, Lucy Fitch, illus. 2008. (Illus.). 240p. 22.95 *(978-1-934671-19-1(3))* Salem Ridge Press LLC.

Pettinato, Laura. Thirteen Americas: American Revolution & Constitution. Tiwari, Saral, illus. 2004. (J). 18.95 *(978-0-9742502-7-4(9))* Gossamer Bks., LLC.

—Thirteen Americas: The Declaration of Independence. Tiwari, Saral, illus. 2nd ed. 2004. (J). lib. bdg. *(978-0-9742502-6-7(0))* Gossamer Bks., LLC.

Pfaff, Eugene E. Guns at Guilford Court House. 2008. 132p. (YA). (gr. 6-9). pap. 14.95 *(978-0-936389-97-4(4))* Tudor Pubs., Inc.

Philbrick, Nathaniel. Ben's Revolution: Benjamin Russell & the Battle of Bunker Hill. Minor, Wendell, illus. 2017. (ENG.). 64p. (J). (gr. 2-4). 17.99 *(978-0-399-16674-7(2)*, Nancy Paulsen Books) Penguin Young Readers Group.

Pierpoint, Eric. The Secret Mission of William Tuck. 2015. (ENG.). 320p. (J). (gr. 4-7). pap. 7.99 *(978-1-4022-8174-7(9)*, 9781402281747, Sourcebooks Jabberwocky) Sourcebooks, Inc.

Poe, Marshall. Sons of Liberty. Purvis, Leland, illus. 2008. (Turning Points Ser.). (ENG.). 128p. (J). (gr. 3-7). pap. 8.99 *(978-1-4169-5067-7(2)*, Aladdin) Simon & Schuster Children's Publishing.

Prentice-Hall Staff. J. Tremain. 2nd ed. (J). stu. ed. *(978-0-13-717174-3(9))* Prentice Hall (Schl. Div.).

Pryor, Bonnie. Captain Hannah Pritchard: The Hunt for Pirate Gold. 2011. (Historical Fiction Adventures (HFA) Ser.). (Illus.). 160p. (J). (gr. 3-18). pap. 10.95 *(978-1-59845-283-9(5))*; (gr. 4-7). lib. bdg. 29.27 *(978-0-7660-3817-2(3))* Enslow Pubs., Inc.

—Hannah Pritchard: Pirate of the Revolution. 2008. (Historical Fiction Adventures (HFA) Ser.). (Illus.). 160p. (J). (gr. 3-7). lib. bdg. 29.27 *(978-0-7660-2851-7(8))* Enslow Pubs., Inc.

—Pirate Hannah Pritchard: Captured! 2009. (Historical Fiction Adventures (HFA) Ser.). (Illus.). 160p. (J). (gr. 3-6). lib. bdg. 29.27 *(978-0-7660-3310-8(4))* Enslow Pubs., Inc.

Rice, Dona Herwick & Bradley, Kathleen. Molly Pitcher, 1 vol. 2009. (Building Fluency Through Reader's Theater Ser.). (ENG., Illus.). 24p. (J). (gr. 2-4). pap. 6.99 *(978-1-4333-0993-9(9))* Teacher Created Materials, Inc.

Rinaldi, Ann. The Family Greene. 2011. (ENG.). 256p. (YA). (gr. 7). pap. 14.95 *(978-0-547-57723-4(0))* Houghton Mifflin Harcourt Publishing Co.

—Finishing Becca: A Story about Peggy Shippen & Benedict Arnold. 2004. (Great Episodes Ser.). (ENG.). 384p. (YA). (gr. 7-8). pap. 17.95 *(978-0-15-205079-5(5))* Houghton Mifflin Harcourt Publishing Co.

—Or Give Me Death. 2004. (Great Episodes Ser.). 226p. (gr. 5-9). 17.00 *(978-0-7569-3462-0(1))* Perfection Learning Corp.

—Or Give Me Death: A Novel of Patrick Henry's Family. 2004. (Great Episodes Ser.). (ENG.). 240p. (YA). (gr. 7-8). pap. 6.99 *(978-0-15-205076-4(0))* Houghton Mifflin Harcourt Publishing Co.

—The Secret of Sarah Revere. 2003. (Great Episodes Ser.). (ENG.). 336p. (J). (gr. 5-7). pap. 8.99 *(978-0-15-204684-2(4))* Houghton Mifflin Harcourt Publishing Co.

Roop, Peter & Roop, Connie. An Eye for an Eye. 2004. 168p. (J). lib. bdg. 16.92 *(978-1-4242-0772-5(X))* Fitzgerald Bks.

—The Top-Secret Adventure of John Darragh, Revolutionary War Spy. 2010. pap. 51.02 *(978-0-7613-6923-3(6))* Lerner Publishing Group.

—The Top-Secret Adventure of John Darragh, Revolutionary War Spy. Trover, Zachary, illus. 2010. (History's Kid Heroes Ser.). (ENG.). 32p. (gr. 3-5). pap. 8.95 *(978-0-7613-6193-0(6)*, Graphic Universe™); lib. bdg. 26.60 *(978-0-7613-6174-9(X))* Lerner Publishing Group.

Scieszka, Jon. Oh Say, I Can't See, No. 15. McCauley, Adam, illus. 2007. (Time Warp Trio Ser.: 15). (ENG.). 80p. (J). (gr. 2-4). 5.99 *(978-0-14-240808-7(5)*, Puffin Books) Penguin Young Readers Group.

Singmaster, Elsie. Rifles for Washington. 2005. pap. 30.95 *(978-1-4191-0108-3(0))* Kessinger Publishing, LLC.

Skead, Robert A. & Skead, Robert J. Patriots, Redcoats & Spies, 1 vol. 2015. (American Revolutionary War Adventures Ser.). (ENG.). 192p. (J). 14.99 *(978-0-310-74841-0(0))* Zonderkidz.

Skead, Robert J. Submarines, Secrets & a Daring Rescue, 1 vol. 2015. (American Revolutionary War Adventures Ser.). (ENG., Illus.). 208p. (J). 14.99 *(978-0-310-74747-5(3))* Zonderkidz.

Skinner, Constance Lindsay. Becky Landers: Frontier Warrior. 2006. (Living History Library). 198p. (YA). (gr. 10). per. 12.95 *(978-1-932350-06-7(3))* Bethlehem Bks.

Smith, Donna Campbell. An Independent Spirit: The Tale of Betsy Dowdy & Black Bess. 2006. (Illus.). 182p. (J). per. 11.95 *(978-0-9779889-0-7(2))* Faithful Publishing.

Smith, Lane. John, Paul, George & Ben. Smith, Lane, illus. 2006. (ENG., Illus.). 40p. (J). (gr. -1 — 1). 17.99 *(978-0-7868-4893-5(6))* Hyperion Pr.

—John, Paul, George & Ben. 2011. (J). (gr. 2-5). 29.95 *(978-0-439-02754-0(3)*, WHCD807) Weston Woods Studios, Inc.

Stevenson, Chris. The Drum of Destiny. 2016. (Middle-Grade Novels Ser.). (ENG., Illus.). 224p. (gr. 4-7). lib. bdg. 26.65 *(978-1-4965-2673-1(2))* Stone Arch Bks.

Stratemeyer, Edward. Marching on Niagara: The Soldier Boys of the Old Frontier. 2011. 191p. (YA). pap. *(978-0-9843717-2-3(9))* Gask Castle Pr.

—With Washington in the West: A Soldier Boy's Battles in the Wilderness. 2011. 198p. (J). pap. *(978-0-9843717-1-6(0))* Gask Castle Pr.

Tripp, Valerie. Felicity Story Collection. Andreasen, Dan, illus. 2008. (ENG.). 404p. (J). 29.95 *(978-1-59369-452-4(0))* American Girl Publishing, Inc.

Turner, Ann Warren. When Mr. Jefferson Came to Philadelphia: What I Learned of Freedom 1776. Hess, Mark, illus. 2004. 32p. (J). (gr. -1-3). 15.99 *(978-0-06-027579-2(0))* HarperCollins Pubs.

VanRiper, Justin & VanRiper, Gary. The Fall of Fort Ticonderoga. 2011. (Adirondack Kids Ser.: Vol. 11). 96p. (J). (gr. 2-7). pap. 9.95 *(978-0-9826250-1-9(4))* Adirondack Kids Pr.

Washington, Ida H. Brave Enough: The Story of Rob Sanford, Vermont Pioneer Boy. Smoak, I. W. & Washington, C. E., illus. 2003. vii, 128p. (J). (gr. 4-6). pap. 12.95 *(978-0-9666832-7-1(7))* Cherry Tree Bks.

Weston Woods Staff, creator. Will You Sign Here, John Hancock? 2011. 38.75 *(978-0-439-76748-4(2))*; 18.95 *(978-0-439-76741-5(5))* Weston Woods Studios, Inc.

Wibberley, Leonard. John Treegate's Musket. 2007. (Living History Library). 173p. (YA). (gr. 8-12). pap. 12.95 *(978-1-932350-16-6(0))* Bethlehem Bks.

—Peter Treegate's War. 2009. 134p. (YA). pap. 12.95 *(978-1-932350-21-0(7))* Bethlehem Bks.

—Treegate's Raiders. 2011. (ENG.). 186p. (YA). pap. 12.95 *(978-1-932350-48-7(9))* Bethlehem Bks.

Winnick, Karen B. Sybil's Night Ride. 2009. (ENG., Illus.). 32p. (J). pap. 10.95 *(978-1-59078-771-7(4))* Boyds Mills Pr.

UNITED STATES—HISTORY—REVOLUTION, 1775-1783—NAVAL OPERATIONS

Abbot, Willis J. Blue Jackets of 1876: A History of the Naval Battles of the American Revolution Together with a Narrative of the War with Tripoli. 2006. (Illus.). pap. 30.95 *(978-1-4286-1609-7(8))* Kessinger Publishing, LLC.

Alphin, Elaine Marie & Alphin, Arthur B. I Have Not Yet Begun to Fight: A Story about John Paul Jones. Casale, Paul, tr. Casale, Paul, illus. 2004. (Creative Minds Biography Ser.). 64p. (J). 22.60 *(978-1-57505-601-2(1)*, Carolrhoda Bks.); (ENG.). (gr. 4-8). pap. 8.95 *(978-1-57505-635-7(6))* Lerner Publishing Group.

Brager, Bruce L. John Paul Jones: America's Sailor. 2006. (Founders of the Republic Ser.). (Illus.). 160p. (J). (gr. 6-12). lib. bdg. 26.95 *(978-1-931798-84-6(2))* Reynolds, Morgan Inc.

Cooper, Michael L. Hero of the High Seas: John Paul Jones & the American Revolution. 2006. (ENG., Illus.). 128p. (gr. 5-7). 21.95 *(978-0-7922-5547-5(X))*; lib. bdg. 32.90 *(978-0-7922-5548-2(8))* National Geographic Society. (National Geographic Children's Bks.).

Crickard, Sarah. John Paul Jones & the Birth of the American Navy. 2015. (Spotlight on American History Ser.). (ENG., Illus.). 24p. (J). (gr. 4-6). pap. 10.00 *(978-1-4994-1759-3(4)*, PowerKids Pr.) Rosen Publishing Group, Inc., The.

Harkins, Susan Sales & Harkins, William H. The Life & Times of John Paul Jones. 2007. (Profiles in American History Ser.). (Illus.). 48p. (J). (gr. 4-8). lib. bdg. 29.95 *(978-1-58415-529-4(9))* Mitchell Lane Pubs., Inc.

Micklos, John. Why We Won the American Revolution—Through Primary Sources. 2013. (American Revolution Through Primary Sources Ser.). 48p. (J). (gr. 4-10). pap. 8.95 *(978-1-4644-0192-3(6))* Enslow Pubs., Inc.

Riley, John B. John Paul Jones: A Photo Biography. l.t. ed. 2004. (First Biographies Ser.). (Illus.). 24p. (YA). (gr. 5-18). 16.95 *(978-1-883846-63-3(3)*, First Biographies) Reynolds, Morgan Inc.

Sperry, Armstrong. John Paul Jones: The Pirate Patriot. (Great Leaders & Events Ser.). (ENG.). (J). (gr. 4-8). 2017. lib. bdg. 35.99 ***(978-1-942875-42-0(8))*** 2016. (Illus.). 168p. pap. 12.99 *(978-0-7603-5230-4(5)*, Voyageur Pr.) Quarto Publishing Group USA.

UNITED STATES—HISTORY—1783-1815

see also Constitutional History—United States; Lewis and Clark Expedition (1804-1806); Louisiana Purchase

Beyer, Mark. The Election of 1800: Congress Helps Settle a Three-Way Vote. 2004. (Life in the New American Nation Ser.). (ENG., Illus.). 32p. (gr. 5-8). pap. 10.00 *(978-0-8239-4255-8(4))* Rosen Publishing Group, Inc., The.

—The Election Of 1800: Congress Helps Settle a Three-Way Vote. 2009. (Life in the New American Nation Ser.). 32p. (gr. 4-4). 47.90 *(978-1-61514-282-8(7))* Rosen Publishing Group, Inc., The.

Brown, Don. Aaron & Alexander: The Most Famous Duel in American History. 2015. (ENG., Illus.). 32p. (J). (gr. k-4). 17.99 *(978-1-59643-998-6(X)*, 9781596439986) Roaring Brook Pr.

Clifton, Chuck & Clifton, Joyce. A Daily Walk with Lewis & Clark - 1805. 2003. 390p. (J). spiral bd. 14.95 *(978-0-9669760-4-5(5))* Maple Canyon Co.

—A Daily Walk with Lewis & Clark - 1806. 2003. 292p. (J). spiral bd. 14.95 *(978-0-9669760-5-2(3))* Maple Canyon Co.

Connell, Kate, et al. The Spirit of a New Nation. 2007. (Avenues Ser.). (ENG., Illus.). 40p. (J). pap. 19.95 *(978-0-7922-8684-4(7))* CENGAGE Learning.

Kalman, Maira. Thomas Jefferson: Life, Liberty & the Pursuit of Everything. Kalman, Maira, illus. 2014. (ENG., Illus.). 40p. (J). (gr. k-3). 17.99 *(978-0-399-24040-9(3)*, Nancy Paulsen Books) Penguin Young Readers Group.

Konstam, Angus. America Speaks, 10 vols. 2005. (Illus.). (J). *(978-0-7172-6028-7(3))*; *(978-0-7172-6029-4(1))*; *(978-0-7172-6020-1(8))*; *(978-0-7172-6027-0(5))*; *(978-0-7172-6026-3(7))*; *(978-0-7172-6021-8(6))*; *(978-0-7172-6022-5(4))*; *(978-0-7172-6023-2(2))*; *(978-0-7172-6024-9(0))*; *(978-0-7172-6025-6(9))* Grolier, Ltd.

—America Speaks, 10 vols., Set. 2005. (Illus.). (J). (gr. 5-10). lib. bdg. 269.00 *(978-0-7172-6030-0(5)*, Grolier) Scholastic Library Publishing.

Lynette, Rachel. The Louisiana Purchase. 2013. (Pioneer Spirit: the Westward Expansion Ser.). (Illus.). 24p. (J). (gr. 3-6). pap. 49.50 *(978-1-4777-0896-5(0))*; pap. 8.25 *(978-1-4777-0895-8(2))*; lib. bdg. 22.60 *(978-1-4777-0781-4(6))* Rosen Publishing Group, Inc., The. (PowerKids Pr.).

Marsh, Carole. Louisiana Purchase. 2003. 12p. (gr. k-4). 2.95 *(978-0-635-02132-8(3))* Gallopade International.

Micklos, John. The Making of the United States from Thirteen Colonies — Through Primary Sources. 2013. (American Revolution Through Primary Sources Ser.). 48p. (J). (gr. 4-18). 25.27 *(978-0-7660-4133-2(6))* Enslow Pubs., Inc.

Mooney, Carla. Perspectives on the Industrial Revolution. 2018. (ENG.). 32p. (gr. 3-6). ***(978-1-63235-402-0(0)***, 12-Story Library) Pr. Room Editions LLC.

Yasuda, Anita. 12 Incredible Facts about the Louisiana Purchase. 2015. (Turning Points in US History Ser.). (ENG., Illus.). 32p. (J). (gr. 3-5). *(978-1-63235-131-9(5)*, 12-Story Library) Pr. Room Editions LLC.

UNITED STATES—HISTORY—1783-1815—FICTION

Jensen, Dorothea. A Buss from Lafayette. 2016. (ENG.). 266p. (J). (gr. 5-9). pap. 16.95 *(978-1-939371-90-4(2))* Boutique of Quality Books Publishing Co., Inc.

Limbaugh, Rush H., III & Limbaugh, Kathryn Adams. Rush Revere & the Presidency. 2016. (Rush Revere Ser.: 5). (ENG., Illus.). 272p. (gr. 4-7). 19.99 *(978-1-5011-5689-2(6)*, Threshold Editions) Threshold Editions.

McCully, Emily Arnold. The Escape of Oney Judge: Martha Washington's Slave Finds Freedom. McCully, Emily Arnold, illus. 2007. (ENG., Illus.). 32p. (J). (gr. 1-4). 17.99 *(978-0-374-32225-0(2)*, 9780374322250, Farrar, Straus & Giroux (BYR)) Farrar, Straus & Giroux.

UNITED STATES—HISTORY—1783-1865

Appleby, Joyce, et al. The American Republic to 1877. 2003. (Illus.). 670p. stu. ed. 122.75 *(978-0-07-826474-0(X))* McGraw-Hill Cos., The.

Cloud Tapper, Suzanne. The Abolition of Slavery: Fighting for a Free America. 2006. (American Saga Ser.). (Illus.). 128p. (J). (gr. 5-18). lib. bdg. 33.27 *(978-0-7660-2605-6(1))* Enslow Pubs., Inc.

Early National America ,1790-1850. 2010. (Discovering U. S. History Ser.). (Illus.). 136p. (gr. 5-8). 35.00 *(978-1-60413-351-6(1)*, Chelsea Hse.) Facts On File, Inc.

Hakim, Joy. The New Nation, 1789-1850, Bk. 4. 2nd rev. ed. 2007. (History of US Ser.: 4). (ENG., Illus.). 208p. (gr. 4-7). per. 15.95 *(978-0-19-532718-2(7))* Oxford Univ. Pr., Inc.

Hanes, Richard Clay, et al. Shaping of America, 1783-1815, Reference Library, 5 vols. 2005. (Illus.). (J). *(978-1-4144-0185-0(X))*; *(978-1-4144-0184-3(1))* Cengage Gale. (UXL).

Hollar, Sherman. Biographies of Colonial America: From Sir Walter Raleigh to Phillis Wheatley. 2012. (Impact on America: Collective Biographies Ser.). (ENG., Illus.). 112p. (J). (gr. 7-12). lib. bdg. 32.90 *(978-1-61530-683-1(8))* Rosen Publishing Group, Inc., The.

Lusted, Marcia Amidon. Revolution & the New Nation: 1750-Early 1800s. 2007. (Presidents of the United States Ser.). (Illus.). 48p. (J). (gr. 4-7). lib. bdg. 29.05 *(978-1-59036-739-1(1))*; per. 10.95 *(978-1-59036-740-7(5))* Weigl Pubs., Inc.

Manuel, David, et al. From Sea to Shining Sea for Young Readers: 1787-1837. 2011. (Discovering God's Plan for America Ser.: 2). (ENG.). 208p. (J). pap. 16.00 *(978-0-8007-3374-2(6))* Revell.

Marsh, Carole. The U. S. Constitution. Beard, Chad, ed. 2004. (American Milestones Ser.). (Illus.). 28p. (J). (gr. 4-12). pap. 5.95 *(978-0-635-02696-5(1))* Gallopade International.

Morey, Allan. A Timeline History of the Early American Republic. 2014. (Timeline Trackers: America's Beginnings Ser.). (Illus.). 48p. (gr. 5-8). (J). lib. bdg. 30.60 *(978-1-4677-3641-1(4)*, Lerner Pubns.); pap. 9.95 *(978-1-4677-4572-7(3))* Lerner Publishing Group.

Porterfield, Jason. The Lincoln-Douglas Senatorial Debates of 1858: A Primary Source Investigation. 2004. (Great Historic Debates & Speeches Ser.). (ENG., Illus.). 64p. (YA). (gr. 5-8). lib. bdg. 31.95 *(978-1-4042-0153-8(X))* Rosen Publishing Group, Inc., The.

Roberts, Cokie. Founding Mothers: Remembering the Ladies. Goode, Diane, illus. 2014. 40p. (J). (gr. 2-7). (ENG.). 17.99 *(978-0-06-078002-9(9))*; lib. bdg. 18.89 *(978-0-06-078003-6(7))* HarperCollins Pubs.

Stanley, George Edward. The New Republic (1763-1815) 2005. (Primary Source History of the United States Ser.). (Illus.). 48p. (gr. 5-12). pap. 14.05 *(978-0-8368-5834-1(4))*; lib. bdg. 31.00 *(978-0-8368-5825-9(5))* Stevens, Gareth Publishing LLLP. (Gareth Stevens Secondary Library).

Wolny, Philip, ed. The New Nation, 01 vols., 1. 2016. (Early American History Ser.). (ENG., Illus.). 80p. (J). 32.90 *(978-1-68048-270-6(X)*, Britannica Educational Publishing) Rosen Publishing Group, Inc., The.

UNITED STATES—HISTORY—1783-1865—BIOGRAPHY

Hollar, Sherman. Biographies of Colonial America: Sir Walter Raleigh, Powhatan, Phillis Wheatley, & More. 2012. (Impact on America: Collective Biographies Ser.). (ENG., Illus.). 112p. (YA). (gr. 7-12). 65.80 *(978-1-61530-763-0(X))* Rosen Publishing Group, Inc., The.

—Biographies of the New American Nation: From George Washington to Frederick Douglass. 2012. (Impact on America: Collective Biographies Ser.). (ENG., Illus.). 112p. (J). (gr. 7-12). lib. bdg. 32.90 *(978-1-61530-686-2(2))* Rosen Publishing Group, Inc., The.

—Biographies of the New American Nation: George Washington, Thomas Jefferson, Frederick Douglass, & More. 2012. (Impact on America: Collective Biographies Ser.). (ENG., Illus.). 112p. (YA). (gr. 7-12). 65.80 *(978-1-61530-802-6(4))* Rosen Publishing Group, Inc., The.

Masters, Nancy Robinson. Extraordinary Patriots of the United States of America: Colonial Times to Pre-Civil War. 2005. (Extraordinary People Ser.). (ENG., Illus.). 288p. (J). (gr. 4-7). 40.00 *(978-0-516-24404-4(3)*, Children's Pr.) Scholastic Library Publishing.

UNITED STATES—HISTORY—1783-1865—FICTION

Hopkinson, Deborah. Independence Cake: A Revolutionary Confection Inspired by Amelia Simmons, Whose True History Is Unfortunately Unknown. Potter, Giselle, illus. 2017. (ENG.). 44p. (J). (gr. -1-3). 17.99 *(978-0-385-39017-0(3)*, Schwartz & Wade Bks.) Random Hse. Children's Bks.

—Under the Quilt of Night. Ransome, James E., illus. 2005. (ENG.). 40p. (J). (gr. k-5). reprint ed. 7.99 *(978-0-689-87700-1(5)*, Aladdin) Simon & Schuster Children's Publishing.

Lyons, Mary E. The Poison Place. 2007. (ENG.). 160p. (YA). (gr. 7). pap. 9.95 *(978-1-4169-6842-9(3)*, Simon & Schuster/Paula Wiseman Bks.) Simon & Schuster/Paula Wiseman Bks.

Mosley, Walter. 47. 2006. (ENG., Illus.). 240p. (J). (gr. 7-17). reprint ed. per. 10.99 *(978-0-316-01635-3(7))* Little, Brown Bks. for Young Readers.

Turner, Diane D. My Name Is Oney Judge. Massey, Cal, illus. 2010. (J). pap. *(978-0-88378-321-4(5))* Third World Press.

—My Name Is Oney Judge. Massey, Call, illus. 2010. (ENG.). 40p. (J). 19.95 *(978-0-88378-304-7(5))* Third World Press.

UNITED STATES—HISTORY—19TH CENTURY

Abolitionism. 2010. (Key Concepts in American History Ser.). (Illus.). 128p. (gr. 6-12). 45.00 *(978-1-60413-220-5(5)*, Chelsea Hse.) Facts On File, Inc.

Alarcon, Roben. American Indians in the 1800s, 1 vol. 2005. (Primary Source Readers Ser.). (ENG., Illus.). 24p. (J). (gr. 5-5). pap. 8.99 *(978-0-7439-8913-8(9))* Shell Educational Publishing.

Anderson, Dale. A Soldier's Life in the Civil War. 2004. (World Almanac Library of the Civil War). (Illus.). 48p. (gr. 5-12). pap. 14.05 *(978-0-8368-5595-1(7))*; lib. bdg. 31.00 *(978-0-8368-5586-9(8))* Stevens, Gareth Publishing LLLP. (Gareth Stevens Secondary Library).

Brannon, Cecelia H. Zoom in on the National Anthem. 2016. (Zoom in on American Symbols Ser.). (Illus.). 24p. (J). pap. 9.35 *(978-0-7660-8446-9(9))* Enslow Pubs., Inc.

Burgan, Michael. The Underground Railroad. Schwarz, Philip, ed. 2006. (Slavery in the Americas Ser.). (Illus.). 112p. (gr. 5-8). 35.00 *(978-0-8160-6137-2(8))* Facts On File, Inc.

Bussey, Jennifer. 1820-1840 (Events That Changed the World) 2004. (gr. 10-12). 22.45 *(978-0-7377-2032-7(8)*, Greenhaven Pr., Inc.) Cengage Gale.

Carson, Mary Kay. The Underground Railroad for Kids: From Slavery to Freedom with 21 Activities. 2005. (For Kids Ser.). (ENG., Illus.). 176p. (J). (gr. 4). pap. 18.95 *(978-1-55652-554-4(0))* Chicago Review Pr., Inc.

Chastain, Zachary. Scandals & Glory: Politics in the 1800s. 2009. (Daily Life in America in the 1800s Ser.). 64p. (YA). (gr. 7-18). lib. bdg. 22.95 *(978-1-4222-1787-0(6))* Mason Crest.

—Scandals & Glory: Politics in The 1800s. 2009. (Daily Life in America in the 1800s Ser.). 64p. (YA). (gr. 7-18). pap. 9.95 *(978-1-4222-1860-0(0))* Mason Crest.

Connell, Kate & Feresten, Nancy. Servant to Abigail Adams: The Early Colonial Adventures of Hannah Cooper. 2003. (I Am American Ser.). (ENG., Illus.). 40p. (J). (gr. 3-7). pap. 6.99 *(978-0-7922-5828-5(2)*, National Geographic Children's Bks.) National Geographic Society.

Depew, Lanette. A Bridge Spanning Time. 2003. (ENG.). 128p. (J). pap. 9.95 *(978-1-57072-236-3(6))* Overmountain Pr.

Down, Susan. Theodore Weld: Architect of Abolitionism. 2013. (ENG., Illus.). 64p. (J). *(978-0-7787-1062-2(9))*; pap. *(978-0-7787-1065-3(3))* Crabtree Publishing Co.

Doyle, Kelly. 1880-1900 (Events That Changed the World) 2004. (Illus.). (gr. 10-12). 22.45 *(978-0-7377-2036-5(0)*, Greenhaven Pr., Inc.) Cengage Gale.

Fisanick, Christina. 1800-1820 (Events That Changed the World) 2004. (gr. 10-12). 22.45 *(978-0-7377-2030-3(1)*, Greenhaven Pr., Inc.) Cengage Gale.

Howell, Brian. U.S. Growth & Change in the 19th Century. 2011. (Explorer Library: Language Arts Explorer Ser.). (ENG.). 32p. (gr. 4-8). pap. 14.21 *(978-1-61080-290-1(X)*, 201213) Cherry Lake Publishing.

Kawa, Katie. Recipes of the Westward Expansion. 2017. (Cooking Your Way Through American History Ser.). (J). (gr. 3-3). 24p. pap. 10.60 ***(978-1-5345-2100-1(3))***; pap. 63.60 ***(978-1-5345-2101-8(1))***; 24p. lib. bdg. 27.25 ***(978-1-5345-2102-5(X))*** Greenhaven Publishing LLC. (KidHaven Publishing).

Kerns, Ann. Was There Really a Gunfight at the O. K. Corral? And Other Questions about the Wild West. Thompson, Colin W., illus. 2011. (Is That a Fact? Ser.). (ENG.). 40p. (gr. 4-6). lib. bdg. 26.60 *(978-0-7613-6100-8(6))* Lerner Publishing Group.

Krull, Kathleen & Brewer, Paul. Lincoln Tells a Joke: How Laughter Saved the President (and the Country) Innerst, Stacy, illus. 2010. (ENG.). 40p. (J). (gr. 1-4). 17.99 *(978-0-15-206639-0(X))* Houghton Mifflin Harcourt Publishing Co.

Malaspina, Ann. Heart on Fire: Susan B. Anthony Votes for President. James, Steven, illus. 2012. (ENG.). 32p. (J). (gr. 1-3). 16.99 *(978-0-8075-3188-4(X))* Whitman, Albert & Co.

McKissack, Patricia C. & McKissack, Fredrick L. Frederick Douglass: Fighter Against Slavery. 2013. (Famous African Americans Ser.). (Illus.). 24p. (J). (gr. k-18). 22.60 *(978-0-7660-4098-4(4)*, Enslow Elementary) Enslow Pubs., Inc.

McNeese, Tim. The Pony Express: Bringing Mail to the American West. 2009. (Milestones in American History Ser.). (Illus.). 128p. (gr. 6-12). 35.00 *(978-1-60413-028-7(8)*, Chelsea Hse.) Facts On File, Inc.

Miller, Reagan & Claus, J. Matteson. Life on a Civil War Battlefield. 2011. (ENG.). 48p. (J). pap. *(978-0-7787-5357-5(3))*; lib. bdg. *(978-0-7787-5340-7(9))* Crabtree Publishing Co.

Ochiltree, Dianne. Molly, by Golly! The Legend of Molly Williams, America's First Female Firefighter. Kemly, Kathleen, illus. 2012. (ENG.). 32p. (J). (gr. 2-4). 16.95 *(978-1-59078-721-2(8)*, Calkins Creek) Boyds Mills Pr.
Olhoff, Jim. Identity & Civil Rights, 1 vol. 2011. (Hispanic American History Ser.). (ENG., Illus.). 32p. (YA). (gr. 5-9). 27.07 *(978-1-61783-057-0(7))* ABDO Publishing Co.
Pierce, Alan. Lincoln-Douglas Debates, 1 vol. 2005. (American Moments Set Ii Ser.). (ENG., Illus.). 48p. (gr. 4-8). 27.07 *(978-1-59197-734-6(7)*, Abdo & Daughters) ABDO Publishing Co.
Primary Sources of America's Industrial Society in the 19th Century. 2004. (Primary Source Big Bookstm Ser.). (ENG.). 24p. (gr. 4-8). 43.95 *(978-0-8239-4598-6(7))* Rosen Publishing Group, Inc., The.
Raum, Elizabeth. Expanding a Nation: Causes & Effects of the Louisiana Purchase, 1 vol. 2013. (Cause & Effect Ser.). (ENG.). 32p. (gr. 3-4). 27.32 *(978-1-4765-0236-6(6))*; pap. 8.95 *(978-1-4765-3402-2(0))* Capstone Press of Coughlan Cos. (Fact Finders).
Raum, Elizabeth, et al. Cause & Effect, 1 vol. (Cause & Effect Ser.). (ENG.). 32p. (gr. 3-4). 2014. lib. bdg. 163.92 *(978-1-4765-7825-5(7))* 2013. pap. 31.80 *(978-1-4765-3634-7(1))* 2013. lib. bdg. 109.28 *(978-1-4765-0371-4(0))* Capstone Press of Coughlan Cos. (Fact Finders).
Schaffer, David. The Louisiana Purchase: The Deal of the Century That Doubled the Nation. 2006. (Wild History of the American West Ser.). (Illus.). 128p. (J). (gr. 5-9). lib. bdg. 34.60 *(978-1-59845-018-7(2)*, MyReportLinks.com Bks.) Enslow Pubs., Inc.
Seguin, Marilyn. Young & Courageous: American Girls Who Made History. 2012. (J). pap. *(978-0-8283-2463-2(8))* Branden Bks.
Sharp, Constance. Thomas Jefferson & the Growing United States (1800-1811) Rakove, Jack N., ed. 2012. (How America Became America Ser.). 48p. (J). (gr. 3-4). 19.95 *(978-1-4222-2400-7(7))* Mason Crest.
Zdrok, Jodie L. 1840-1860 (Events That Changed the World) 2004. (Events That Changed the World Ser.). (Illus.). 175p. (gr. 10-12). 22.45 *(978-0-7377-2034-1(4)*, Greenhaven Pr., Inc.) Cengage Gale.

UNITED STATES—HISTORY—19TH CENTURY—FICTION

Alger, Horatio. The Young Musician. reprint ed. pap. 79.00 *(978-1-4047-3629-0(8))* Classic Textbooks.
—The Young Musician. 2006. pap. *(978-1-4068-0673-1(0))* Echo Library.
Edinger, Monica. Africa Is My Home: A Child of the Amistad. Byrd, Robert, illus. 2015. (ENG.). 64p. (J). (gr. 5). pap. 8.99 *(978-0-7636-7647-6(0))* Candlewick Pr.
Fletcher, Susan. Walk Across the Sea. Jakesevic, Nenad, illus. 2003. (ENG.). 224p. (J). (gr. 4-8). pap. 11.95 *(978-0-689-85707-2(1)*, Atheneum Bks. for Young Readers) Simon & Schuster Children's Publishing.
Hart, Alison. Fires of Jubilee. 2003. (ENG., Illus.). 192p. (J). (gr. 3-7). pap. 9.99 *(978-0-689-85528-3(1)*, Simon & Schuster/Paula Wiseman Bks.) Simon & Schuster/Paula Wiseman Bks.
Hedstrom-Page, Deborah. From Log Cabin to White House with Abraham Lincoln. Martinez, Sergio, illus. 2007. (My American Journey Ser.). 82p. (J). (gr. 3-9). 9.99 *(978-0-8054-3269-5(8))* B&H Publishing Group.
Howard, Elizabeth Fitzgerald. Virgie Goes to School with Us Boys. Lewis, E. B., illus. 2005. (gr. k-3). 18.00 *(978-0-7569-5088-0(0))* Perfection Learning Corp.
Hughes, Lynn Gordon. To Live a Truer Life: A Story of the Hopedale Community. Lindro, illus. 2003. 32p. (J). 10.00 *(978-0-9725017-2-9(X))* Blackstone Editions.
Kirkle, Diane Luise. Rachel Serves a Stew. Batson, Susann, illus. 2009. 28p. pap. 10.95 *(978-1-935137-59-7(X))* Guardian Angel Publishing, Inc.
Morpurgo, Michael. Twist of Gold. 2nd ed. 2009. (ENG.). 304p. (J). (gr. 4-7). pap. 10.99 *(978-1-4052-2928-9(4))* Egmont Bks., Ltd. GBR. Dist: Independent Pubs. Group.
Ralphson, G. Harvey. Boy Scouts in the Philippines: Or the Key to the Treaty Box. 2007. (ENG.). 146p. pap. 18.99 *(978-1-4346-3798-7(0))*; 164p. pap. 21.99 *(978-1-4346-3799-4(9))* Creative Media Partners, LLC.
Reed, Wilfred. Andy & Mark & the Time Machine: Custer's Last Stand. 2003. 240p. (YA). pap. 15.95 *(978-0-595-26496-4(4)*, Writers Club Pr.) iUniverse, Inc.
Rinaldi, Ann. An Unlikely Friendship: A Novel of Mary Todd Lincoln & Elizabeth Keckley. 2008. (ENG., Illus.). 256p. (J). (gr. 5-7). pap. 7.99 *(978-0-15-206398-6(6))* Houghton Mifflin Harcourt Publishing Co.
Stratemeyer, Edward. The Rover Boys at College: The Right Road & the Wrong. l.t. ed. 2007. (ENG.). 464p. pap. 30.99 *(978-1-4264-4101-1(0))*; 180p. pap. 19.99 *(978-1-4264-4042-7(1))* Creative Media Partners, LLC.
Sutherland, Robert. The Schooner's Revenge. 2008. (ENG.). 176p. (J). pap. 11.99 *(978-0-00-200853-2(X)*, Harper Trophy) HarperCollins Pubs.
Winfield, Arthur M. Rover Boys at College or the Right Road. 2006. pap. 30.95 *(978-1-4286-4106-8(8))* Kessinger Publishing, LLC.

UNITED STATES—HISTORY—TRIPOLITAN WAR, 1801-1805

Abbot, Willis J. Blue Jackets of 1876: A History of the Naval Battles of the American Revolution Together with a Narrative of the War with Tripoli. 2006. (Illus.). pap. 30.95 *(978-1-4286-1609-7(8))* Kessinger Publishing, LLC.
January, Brendan. The Aftermath of the Wars Against the Barbary Pirates. 2009. (Aftermath of History Ser.). (ENG.). 160p. (gr. 9-12). 38.60 *(978-0-8225-9094-1(8))* Lerner Publishing Group.

UNITED STATES—HISTORY—WAR OF 1812

Alvarez, Pilar F. The War of 1812: New Challenges for a New Nation. 2016. (Spotlight on American History Ser.). (Illus.). 24p. (J). (gr. 6-4). 26.25 *(978-1-5081-4947-7(X)*, PowerKids Pr.) Rosen Publishing Group, Inc., The.
Barile, Mary. Alphonso Wetmore: Soldier, Adventurer, & Writer. 2015. (ENG., Illus.). 48p. (J). 24.00 *(978-1-61248-147-0(7))* Truman State Univ. Pr.
Bartoletti, Susan Campbell. The Flag Maker: A Story of the Star-Spangled Banner. Nivola, Claire A., illus. 2007. (ENG.). 32p. (J). (gr. 2-5). 7.99 *(978-0-618-80911-0(2))* Houghton Mifflin Harcourt Publishing Co.
Benn, Carl. The War of 1812: The Fight for American Trade Rights. 2011. (Early American Wars Ser.). (Illus.). 96p. (YA). (gr. 9-18). lib. bdg. 33.25 *(978-1-4488-1333-9(6))* Rosen Publishing Group, Inc., The.
Beyer, Mark. The War of 1812: The New American Nation Goes to War with England. (Life in the New American Nation Ser.). 32p. 2009. (gr. 4-4). 47.90 *(978-1-61514-288-0(6))* 2004. (ENG., Illus.). (gr. 5-8). pap. 10.00 *(978-0-8239-4261-9(9))* Rosen Publishing Group, Inc., The.
Bozonelis, Helen Koutras. Primary Source Accounts of the War of 1812. 2006. (America's Wars Through Primary Sources Ser.). (Illus.). 128p. (J). (gr. 4-7). lib. bdg. 34.60 *(978-1-59845-006-4(9)*, MyReportLinks.com Bks.) Enslow Pubs., Inc.
Childress, Diana. The War of 1812. 2004. (Chronicle of America's Wars Ser.). (ENG., Illus.). 96p. (gr. 5-12). 27.93 *(978-0-8225-0800-7(1))* Lerner Publishing Group.
Crewe, Sabrina & Ingram, Scott. The Writing of "The Star-Spangled Banner" 2004. (Events That Shaped America Ser.). (Illus.). 32p. (gr. 3-6). lib. bdg. 26.00 *(978-0-8368-3409-3(7)*, Gareth Stevens Learning Library) Stevens, Gareth Publishing LLLP.
Crump, Jennifer. Canada on Fire: The War of 1812. 2011. (Canadians at War Ser.: 4). (ENG., Illus.). 208p. (YA). (gr. 6). pap. 19.99 *(978-1-55488-753-8(4))* Dundurn CAN. Dist: Ingram Publisher Services.
Cunningham, Alvin Robert. Washington Is Burning! The War of 1812. 2003. (Reading Essentials in Social Studies). (Illus.). 48p. (J). 9.00 *(978-0-7891-5896-3(5))* Perfection Learning Corp.
Figley, Marty Rhodes. Washington Is Burning. Orback, Craig, illus. (On My Own History Ser.). 48p. (gr. 2-4). 2007. (ENG.). per. 6.95 *(978-0-8225-6050-0(X)*, First Avenue Editions) 2006. (J). lib. bdg. 25.26 *(978-1-57505-875-7(8))* Lerner Publishing Group.
Flatt, Lizann. The Legacy of the War of 1812. 2011. (ENG.). 48p. (J). pap. *(978-0-7787-7966-7(1))*; (gr. 5-9). lib. bdg. *(978-0-7787-7961-2(0))* Crabtree Publishing Co.
Fulton, Kristen. Long May She Wave. Berry, Holly, illus. 2017. (ENG.). 40p. (J). (gr. -1-3). 17.99 *(978-1-4814-6096-5(X)*, McElderry, Margaret K. Bks.) McElderry, Margaret K. Bks.
Gaspar, Joe. The National Anthem. 2013. (PowerKids Readers: American Symbols Ser.). 24p. (J). (gr. k-2). 22.60 *(978-1-4777-0740-1(9))*; (ENG., Illus.). pap. 8.25 *(978-1-4777-0821-7(9))* Rosen Publishing Group, Inc., The. (PowerKids Pr.).
—The National Anthem / el Himno Nacional. Alamn, Eduardo, ed. 2013. (PowerKids Readers: American Symbols / Smbolos de Amrica Ser.). (ENG & SPA.). 24p. (J). (gr. k-2). 22.60 *(978-1-4777-1208-5(9)*, PowerKids Pr.) Rosen Publishing Group, Inc., The.
Giddens, Sandra. A Timeline of the War of 1812. 2009. (Timelines of American History Ser.). 32p. (gr. 4-4). 47.90 *(978-1-60854-392-2(7)*, Rosen Reference) Rosen Publishing Group, Inc., The.
Greenblatt, Miriam. War of 1812. 3rd rev. ed. 2010. (America at War Ser.). (Illus.). 192p. (gr. 6-12). 45.00 *(978-0-8160-8194-3(8))* Facts On File, Inc.
Hall, M. C. The National Anthem, 1 vol. Ouren, Todd, illus. 2008. (Our Nation's Pride Ser.). (ENG.). 32p. (gr. -1-3). 28.50 *(978-1-60270-113-7(X)*, Looking Glass Library- Nonfiction) Magic Wagon.
Hess, Deborah. The Star-Spangled Banner. 2007. (J). pap. 6.99 *(978-0-7614-3392-7(9))* Marshall Cavendish Corp.
Hinman, Bonnie. The War of 1812: 12 Things to Know. 2017. (America at War Ser.). (ENG., Illus.). 32p. (J). (gr. 3-6). 21.95 *(978-1-63235-269-9(9))* Pr. Room Editions LLC.
Ingram, Scott. The Writing of The Star-Spangled Banner. 2004. (Landmark Events in American History Ser.). (Illus.). 48p. (gr. 5-12). pap. 14.05 *(978-0-8368-5418-3(7)*, Gareth Stevens Secondary Library) Stevens, Gareth Publishing LLLP.
Isaacs, Sally Senzell. What Caused the War of 1812? 2011. (ENG.). 48p. (J). pap. *(978-0-7787-7967-4(X))* Crabtree Publishing Co.
Jacobson, Ryan. The Story of the Star-Spangled Banner, 1 vol. Martin, Cynthia & Beatty, Terry, illus. 2006. (Graphic History Ser.). (ENG.). 32p. (gr. 3-4). 30.65 *(978-0-7368-5493-1(2)*, Graphic Library) Capstone Press of Coughlan Cos.
Johnson, Robin. Famous People of the War of 1812. 2011. (ENG.). 48p. (J). pap. *(978-0-7787-7964-3(5))*; (gr. 5-9). lib. bdg. *(978-0-7787-7959-9(9))* Crabtree Publishing Co.
Kjelle, Marylou Morano. Francis Scott Key. 2006. (What's So Great About...? Ser.). (Illus.). 32p. (YA). (gr. 2-4). lib. bdg. 25.70 *(978-1-58415-474-7(8))* Mitchell Lane Pubs., Inc.
Kulling, Monica. Francis Scott Key's Star-Spangled Banner. 2012. (Step into Reading Level 3 Ser.). lib. bdg. 13.55 *(978-0-606-23857-1(3)*, Turtleback) Turtleback Bks.
Lowitz, Sadyebeth & Lowitz, Anson. Mr Key's Song: The Star Spangled Banner. 2011. 58p. 36.95 *(978-1-258-10511-2(X))* Literary Licensing, LLC.
Marsico, Katie. The War of 1812, 1 vol. 2010. (Essential Events Set 5 Ser.). (ENG.). 112p. (J). (gr. 6-12). lib. bdg. 35.64 *(978-1-61613-688-8(X))* ABDO Publishing Co.
Maynard, Charles W. Fort McHenry. 2009. (Famous Forts Throughout American History Ser.). 24p. (gr. 3-4). 42.50 *(978-1-61512-519-7(1)*, PowerKids Pr.) Rosen Publishing Group, Inc., The.
Micklos, John, Jr. Primary Source History of the War of 1812. 2016. (Primary Source History Ser.). (ENG., Illus.). 32p. (gr. 3-4). lib. bdg. 27.32 *(978-1-4914-8488-3(8)*, Fact Finders) Capstone Press of Coughlan Cos.
Mulhall, Jill K. The War of 1812, 1 vol. 2005. (Primary Source Readers Ser.). (ENG.). 24p. (J). (gr. 5-5). pap. 8.99 *(978-0-7439-8907-7(4))* Shell Educational Publishing.
The National Anthem. 2013. (PowerKids Readers: American Symbols Ser.). 24p. (J). (gr. k-2). pap. 49.50 *(978-1-4777-0822-4(7)*, PowerKids Pr.) Rosen Publishing Group, Inc., The.
Nelson, Maria. The National Anthem. 2015. (Symbols of America Ser.). (ENG.). 24p. (J). (gr. 1-2). 22.60 *(978-1-4824-1874-3(6))* Stevens, Gareth Publishing LLLP.
Orr, Tamra B. The Star-Spangled Banner: Introducing Primary Sources. 2016. (Introducing Primary Sources Ser.). (ENG., Illus.). 32p. (gr. 1-2). lib. bdg. 27.99 *(978-1-4914-8226-1(5))* Capstone Press of Coughlan Cos.
Owens, Tom. The Star-Spangled Banner: The Flag & Its Anthem. 2003. (Illus.). 48p. (J). pap. *(978-0-7891-5890-1(6))* Perfection Learning Corp.
Pearl, Norman. Our National Anthem, 1 vol. Skeens, Matthew, illus. 2006. (American Symbols Ser.). (ENG.). 24p. (gr. 1-2). 9.95 *(978-1-4048-2221-4(6))* Picture Window Bks.
Poulakidas, Georgene. The War of 1812. (Primary Sources of American Wars Ser.). 24p. 2009. (gr. 3-4). 42.50 *(978-1-60851-529-5(X)*, PowerKids Pr.) 2006. (Illus.). (YA). (gr. 4-7). lib. bdg. 22.60 *(978-1-4042-2681-4(8))* Rosen Publishing Group, Inc., The.
Quinby, Michelle. Wars at Home: America Forms an Identity (1812-1820) 2012. (J). pap. *(978-1-4222-2415-1(5))* Mason Crest.
—Wars at Home: America Forms an Identity (1812-1820) Rakove, Jack N., ed. 2012. (How America Became America Ser.). 48p. (J). (gr. 3-4). 19.95 *(978-1-4222-2401-4(5))* Mason Crest.
Radomski, Kassandra. Mr. Madison's War: Causes & Effects of the War of 1812. 2013. (Cause & Effect Ser.). (ENG.). 32p. (gr. 3-4). pap. 8.95 *(978-1-4765-3405-3(5))*; lib. bdg. 27.32 *(978-1-4765-0239-7(0))* Capstone Press of Coughlan Cos.
RJF Publishing Staff & Burgan, Michael. Fort McHenry. 2009. (Symbols of American Freedom Ser.). 48p. (gr. 4-6). 30.00 *(978-1-60413-520-6(4)*, Chelsea Clubhouse) Facts On File, Inc.
Schwaeber, Barbie. The Star-Spangled Banner. 2006. (American Favorites Ser.). (ENG., Illus.). 32p. (J). (gr. 3-7). 9.85 *(978-1-59249-652-5(0))* Soundprints.
Schwartz, Heather E. The War of 1812: By the Dawn's Early Light. 2017. (Primary Source Readers Ser.). (Illus.). 32p. (J). (gr. 4-5). pap. 8.99 *(978-1-4938-3794-6(X))* Teacher Created Materials, Inc.
Silate, Jennifer. The Calhoun-Randolph Debate on the Eve of the War of 1812: A Primary Source Investigation. 2004. (Great Historic Debates & Speeches Ser.). (Illus.). 64p. (YA). (gr. 5-9). lib. bdg. 31.95 *(978-1-4042-0150-7(5))* Rosen Publishing Group, Inc., The.
—The Calhoun-Randolph Debate on the Eve of the War Of 1812: A Primary Source Investigation. 2009. (Great Historic Debates & Speeches Ser.). 64p. (gr. 5-8). 58.50 *(978-1-61513-124-2(8))* Rosen Publishing Group, Inc., The.
Sonneborn, Liz. The War of 1812. 2004. (Primary Sources in American History Ser.). (Illus.). 64p. (gr. 5-8). lib. bdg. 31.95 *(978-0-8239-4515-3(4)*, Rosen Reference) Rosen Publishing Group, Inc., The.
—The War of 1812: A Primary Source History of America's Second War with Britain. 2009. (Primary Sources in American History Ser.). 64p. (gr. 5-8). 58.50 *(978-1-60851-506-6(0))* Rosen Publishing Group, Inc., The.
Spier, Peter. The Star-Spangled Banner. 2014. (ENG., Illus.). 56p. (J). (gr. k-4). 17.99 *(978-0-385-37618-1(9)*, Doubleday Bks. for Young Readers) Random Hse. Children's Bks.
Toler, Pamela. The War Of 1812, Vol. 11. Musteen, Jason R., ed. 2015. (Major U. S. Historical Wars Ser.). (Illus.). 64p. (J). (gr. 7). lib. bdg. 23.95 *(978-1-4222-3361-0(8))* Mason Crest.
Toler, Pamela D. Causes of the War of 1812. 2009. (J). lib. bdg. *(978-1-59556-036-0(X))* OTTN Publishing.
Warrick, Karen & Clemens Warrick, Karen. The War Of 1812. 2016. (United States at War Ser.). (ENG., Illus.). 128p. (J). (gr. 6-6). 37.27 *(978-0-7660-7671-6(7))* Enslow Pubs., Inc.
Welch, Catherine A. La Bandera de Estrellas Centelleantes; the Star-Spangled Banner. 2008. pap. 40.95 *(978-0-7613-3867-3(5))* Lerner Publishing Group.
—The Star-Spangled Banner. Warwick, Carrie, illus. 2004. (On My Own History Ser.). 48p. (J). (gr. 1-3). pap. 6.95 *(978-1-57505-697-5(6))*; (ENG.). (gr. 2-4). 25.26 *(978-1-57505-590-9(2))* Lerner Publishing Group.
Zee, Amy Van. The War Of 1812: A History Perspectives Book. 2013. (Perspectives Library). (ENG., Illus.). 32p. (J). (gr. 4-8). 28.50 *(978-1-62431-424-7(4)*, 202816); pap. 14.21 *(978-1-62431-500-8(3)*, 202818) Cherry Lake Publishing.

UNITED STATES—HISTORY—WAR OF 1812—CAMPAIGNS

see also New Orleans, Battle of, New Orleans, La., 1815

Clarke, Gordon. Major Battles of the War of 1812. 2011. (ENG.). 48p. (J). pap. *(978-0-7787-7965-0(3))*; (gr. 5-9). lib. bdg. *(978-0-7787-7960-5(2))* Crabtree Publishing Co.
Crump, Jennifer. The War of 1812: Heroes of a Great Canadian Victory. 2007. (Amazing Stories Ser.). (ENG.). 96p. (J). pap. 9.95 *(978-1-55439-711-2(1)*, 9781554397112) Lorimer, James & Co., Ltd., Pubs. CAN. Dist: Casemate Pubs. & Bk. Distributors, LLC.
Gordon, Irene Ternier. Tecumseh: Diplomat & Warrior in the War of 1812. 2009. (Amazing Stories Ser.). (ENG., Illus.). 128p. (J). (gr. 6-12). pap. 9.95 *(978-1-55277-430-4(9)*, 9781552774304) Lorimer, James & Co., Ltd., Pubs. CAN. Dist: Casemate Pubs. & Bk. Distributors, LLC.
Monroe, Tyler. Star-Spangled Banner. 2013. (U. S. Symbols Ser.). (ENG.). 24p. (gr. k-1). 26.65 *(978-1-4765-3087-1(4))*; pap. 7.95 *(978-1-4765-3536-4(1))* Capstone Press of Coughlan Cos. (Pebble Plus).

UNITED STATES—HISTORY—WAR OF 1812—FICTION

Cook, Kajsa C. The Untold Story: About the War of 1812. 2011. 84p. pap. 12.99 *(978-1-4520-6557-1(8))* AuthorHouse.
Crook, Connie Brummel. Acts of Courage: Laura Secord & the War of 1812. 2012. (ENG., Illus.). 272p. (J). (gr. 5-9). pap. 11.95 *(978-0-9869495-7-9(4))* Pajama Pr. CAN. Dist: Ingram Publisher Services.
Frost, Helen. Salt: A Story of Friendship in a Time of War. 2013. (ENG.). 160p. (J). (gr. 5-9). 17.99 *(978-0-374-36387-1(0)*, 9780374363871, Farrar, Straus & Giroux (BYR)) Farrar, Straus & Giroux.
George Cary Eggleston. Captain Sam: The Boy Scouts of 1814. 2007. (ENG.). 124p. per. 18.99 *(978-1-4346-3940-0(1))*; 132p. per. 19.99 *(978-1-4346-3941-7(X))* Creative Media Partners, LLC.
Guyatt, Ben. Billy Green Saves the Day. 2009. (ENG.). 160p. (J). (gr. 7-18). pap. 10.99 *(978-1-55488-041-6(6)*, Dundurn Pr.) Dundurn CAN. Dist: Ingram Publisher Services.
Hall, Marjory. The Gold-Lined Box. 2003. 224p. 11.95 *(978-0-9714612-6-0(0))* Green Mansion Pr. LLC.
Kramer, Alan & Kramer, Candice. The Star-Spangled Banner Story. 2005. (J). pap. *(978-1-4108-4203-9(7))* Benchmark Education Co.
Milford, Kate. The Left-Handed Fate. Wheeler, Eliza, illus. 2016. (ENG.). 384p. (J). 16.99 *(978-0-8050-9800-6(3)*, 9780805098006, Holt, Henry & Co. Bks. For Young Readers) Holt, Henry & Co.
—The Left-Handed Fate. Wheeler, Eliza, illus. 2017. (ENG.). 384p. (J). pap. 7.99 *(978-1-250-12183-7(3)*, 9781250121837) Square Fish.
Papp, Lisa & Noble, Trinka Hakes. The Battles. Papp, Robert, illus. 2013. (American Adventures Ser.). (ENG.). 88p. (J). (gr. 3-6). pap. 9.99 *(978-1-58536-861-7(X)*, 202368) Sleeping Bear Pr.
Papp, Lisa & Papp, Robert. The Town That Fooled the British: A War of 1812 Story. Papp, Lisa & Papp, Robert, illus. 2011. (Tales of Young Americans Ser.). (ENG., Illus.). 32p. (J). (gr. 1-5). 16.95 *(978-1-58536-484-8(3))* Sleeping Bear Pr.
Perkins, Lucy Fitch. American Twins of 1812. (J). (gr. 2-5). 20.95 *(978-0-89190-473-1(5))* Amereon Ltd.
—The American Twins of 1812. 2009. (Illus.). 112p. (J). pap. 13.95 *(978-1-934610-17-6(8))* Bluewater Pubns.
Peterson, Mike. Freehand: A Young Boy's Adventures in the War Of 1812. Baldwin, Christopher, illus. 2012. (ENG.). 44p. (J). pap. 6.95 *(978-1-938384-03-5(2))* Baldwin, Christopher John.
Riley, Clifford. Spymasters. 2013. (39 Clues: the Cahill Files Ser.). (ENG., Illus.). 256p. (J). (gr. 3-7). 12.99 *(978-0-545-56468-7(9))* Scholastic, Inc.
Sanchez, Anita. The Invasion of Sandy Bay. 2008. (ENG.). 148p. (J). (gr. 5-7). 16.95 *(978-1-59078-560-7(6)*, Calkins Creek) Boyds Mills Pr.
Scheffler, Stephanie. Elizabeth & the War of 1812. 2010. 292p. (YA). 28.95 *(978-1-4502-3539-6(5))*; (ENG.). pap. 18.95 *(978-1-4502-3540-2(9))* iUniverse, Inc.
Tomlinson, Everett T. The War of 1812. 2010. 204p. reprint ed. pap. 24.75 *(978-1-146-39267-9(2))* Creative Media Partners, LLC.
—The War of 1812. 2009. 112p. reprint ed. pap. 14.14 *(978-0-217-61361-3(6))* General Bks. LLC.
Wiley, Melissa. Little House by Boston Bay. 2007. (Little House Prequel Ser.). (ENG.). 160p. (J). (gr. 3-7). pap. 5.99 *(978-0-06-114828-6(8))* HarperCollins Pubs.
Winstead, Amy. The Star-Spangled Banner. Dacey, Bob & Bandelin, Debra, illus. 2003. (ENG.). 32p. (J). 18.65 *(978-0-8249-5462-8(9)*, Ideal Pubns.) Worthy Publishing.

UNITED STATES—HISTORY—1815-1861

The Antebellum Women's Movement, 1820-1860. (YA). (gr. 6-9). spiral bd., tchr.'s planning gde. ed. 12.00 *(978-0-382-44465-4(5))* Cobblestone Publishing Co.
Blumberg, Rhoda. Commodore Perry in the Land of the Shogun. 2003. (ENG., Illus.). 144p. (J). (gr. 3-18). pap. 9.99 *(978-0-06-008625-1(4))* HarperCollins Pubs.
—Commodore Perry in the Land of the Shogun. 2003. (Illus.). 144p. (gr. 3-7). 20.00 *(978-0-7569-1440-0(X))* Perfection Learning Corp.
Casciato, Daniel. Expansion & Reform: (Early 1800s-1861) 2007. (Presidents of the United States Ser.). (Illus.). 48p. (J). (gr. 4-7). lib. bdg. 29.05 *(978-1-59036-741-4(3))* Weigl Pubs., Inc.
—Expansion & Reform: Early 1800s-1861. 2007. (Presidents of the United States Ser.). (Illus.). 48p. (J). (gr. 4-7). per. 11.95 *(978-1-59036-742-1(1))* Weigl Pubs., Inc.
Hakim, Joy. Liberty for All, 1789-1850, Bk. 5. 2nd rev. ed. 2007. (History of US Ser.: 5). (ENG., Illus.). 224p. (gr. 4-7). per. 15.95 *(978-0-19-532719-9(5))* Oxford Univ. Pr., Inc.
Helfand, Lewis. Abraham Lincoln: From the Log Cabin to the White House - Campfire Heroes Line. Jones, K. L. & Manikandan, illus. 2013. (Campfire Graphic Novels Ser.). (ENG.). 108p. (YA). (gr. 5-12). pap. 12.99 *(978-93-80741-21-5(9)*, Campfire) Steerforth Pr.
Lanier, Wendy. What Was the Missouri Compromise? And Other Questions about the Struggle over Slavery. 2012. (Six Questions of American History Ser.). (ENG.). 48p. (gr. 4-6). pap. 9.95 *(978-0-7613-8565-3(7))* Lerner Publishing Group.
Lanier, Wendy & Nelson, Robin. What Was the Missouri Compromise? And Other Questions about the Struggle over Slavery. 2012. (Start to Finish, Second Series: Nature's Cycles Ser.). (ENG.). 48p. (gr. k-3). pap. 39.62 *(978-0-7613-9293-4(9))* Lerner Publishing Group.
Larkin, Tanya. What Was Cooking in Julia Grant's White House? 2009. (Cooking Throughout American History Ser.). 24p. (gr. 3-3). 42.50 *(978-1-61511-952-3(3)*, PowerKids Pr.) Rosen Publishing Group, Inc., The.
McDougal-Littell Publishing Staff, contrib. by. A Nation Dividing 1800-1860. 2004. (Stories in History Ser.). (Illus.). 176p. (gr. 6-12). 13.32 *(978-0-618-14222-4(3)*, 2-00242) Holt McDougal.
Quinby, Michelle. Wars at Home: America Forms an Identity (1812-1820) 2012. (J). pap. *(978-1-4222-2415-1(5))* Mason Crest.
—Wars at Home: America Forms an Identity (1812-1820) Rakove, Jack N., ed. 2012. (How America Became America Ser.). 48p. (J). (gr. 3-4). 19.95 *(978-1-4222-2401-4(5))* Mason Crest.

UNITED STATES—HISTORY—1815-1861—FICTION

Brill, Marlene Targ. Allen Jay & the Undergound Railroad, 4 bks., Set. Porter, Janice Lee, illus. 2007. (Readalongs for Beginning Readers Ser.). (J). (gr. 1-3). pap. 37.95 incl. audio *(978-1-59519-947-8(0))* Live Oak Media.
Broyles, Anne. Priscilla & the Hollyhocks. Alter, Anna, illus. 2008. (ENG.). 32p. (J). (gr. 1-4). 15.95 *(978-1-57091-675-5(6))* Charlesbridge Publishing, Inc.
Crawford, Neil. The Journeyers. 2006. (ENG.). 248p. (J). per. *(978-0-9778205-4-2(8))* Helm Publishing.
Edinger, Monica. Africa Is My Home: A Child of the Amistad. Byrd, Robert, illus. 2013. (ENG.). 64p. (J). (gr. 5). 17.99 *(978-0-7636-5038-4(2))* Candlewick Pr.
Porter, Janice Lee, illus. Allen Jay & the Underground Railroad, 4 bks., Set. 2006. (Readalongs for Beginning Readers Ser.). (J). (gr. 2-5). pap. 39.95 incl. audio compact disk *(978-1-59519-951-5(9))* Live Oak Media.
Wilson, Diane Lee. Black Storm Comin' 2006. (ENG.). 240p. (J). (gr. 5-9). pap. 7.99 *(978-0-689-87138-2(4)*, McElderry, Margaret K. Bks.) McElderry, Margaret K. Bks.
—Black Storm Comin' 2006. (Illus.). 291p. (gr. 5-9). 17.00 *(978-0-7569-6908-0(5))* Perfection Learning Corp.

TUV

UNITED STATES—HISTORY—WAR WITH MEXICO, 1845-1848

see Mexican War, 1846-1848

UNITED STATES—HISTORY—CIVIL WAR, 1861-1865

see also Slavery—United States

Ablard, Michelle. The Civil War: Brother Against Brother. 2017. (Primary Source Readers Ser.). (Illus.). 32p. (J). (gr. 4-5). pap. 8.99 ***(978-1-4938-3804-2(0))*** Teacher Created Materials, Inc.

Abnett, Dan. Abraham Lincoln & the Civil War. (Jr. Graphic Biographies Ser.). (ENG.). 24p. 2009. (J). (gr. 2-3). 47.90 *(978-1-61513-807-4(2),* PowerKids Pr.) 2007. (Illus.). (J). (gr. 2-5). lib. bdg. 25.25 *(978-1-4042-3392-8(X))* 2007. (Illus.). (gr. 3-8). pap. 10.60 *(978-1-4042-2145-1(X),* PowerKids Pr.) Rosen Publishing Group, Inc., The.

—Abraham Lincoln y la Guerra Civil. 2009. (Historietas Juveniles: Biografías (Jr. Graphic Biographies) Ser.). (SPA., Illus.). 24p. (J). (gr. 2-5). 25.25 *(978-1-4358-8561-5(9));* (gr. 3-8). pap. 10.60 *(978-1-4358-3316-6(3))* Rosen Publishing Group, Inc., The.

—The Monitor versus the Merrimac: Ironclads at War. 2009. (Graphic Civil War Battles Ser.). (ENG.). 48p. (YA). (gr. 4-5). 58.50 *(978-1-61512-902-7(2),* Rosen Reference) Rosen Publishing Group, Inc., The.

—The Monitor vs. the Merrimack: Ironclads at War! 2007. (Graphic Battles: Civil War Ser.). (ENG., Illus.). 48p. (gr. 5-8). pap. 14.05 *(978-1-4042-6480-9(9),* Rosen Classroom) Rosen Publishing Group, Inc., The.

Adamson, Deanna. The Other Side of the Lines: Southern Heroes of the US Civil War. 2011. 88p. pap. 10.95 *(978-1-4327-7194-2(9))* Outskirts Pr., Inc.

Adamson, Thomas K. The Civil War. 2015. (Wars in U. S. History Ser.). (ENG.). 32p. (J). (gr. 2-5). 28.50 *(978-1-63143-706-9(2),* 208536) Child's World, Inc., The.

Adler, David A. A Picture Book of Harriet Beecher Stowe. Bootman, Colin, illus. 2003. (ENG.). 32p. (J). (gr. k-3). tchr. ed. 17.95 *(978-0-8234-1646-2(1))* Holiday Hse., Inc.

Allen, Thomas B. & Allen, Roger MacBride. Mr. Lincoln's High-Tech War: How the North Used the Telegraph, Railroads, Surveillance Balloons, Ironclads, High-Powered Weapons, & More to Win the Civil War. 2009. (ENG., Illus.). 144p. (J). (gr. 5-18). 18.95 *(978-1-4263-0379-1(3));* lib. bdg. 25.90 *(978-1-4263-0380-7(7))* National Geographic Society. (National Geographic Children's Bks.).

Aloian, Molly. Emancipation. 2013. (ENG.). 48p. (J). *(978-0-7787-1100-1(5));* pap. *(978-0-7787-1120-9(X))* Crabtree Publishing Co.

Anderson, Dale. The Aftermath of the Civil War. 2004. (World Almanac Library of the Civil War). (Illus.). 48p. (gr. 5-12). pap. 14.05 *(978-0-8368-5597-5(3));* lib. bdg. 31.00 *(978-0-8368-5588-3(4))* Stevens, Gareth Publishing LLLP. (Gareth Stevens Secondary Library).

—The Causes of the Civil War. 2004. (World Almanac Library of the Civil War). (Illus.). 48p. (gr. 5-12). pap. 14.05 *(978-0-8368-5590-6(6));* lib. bdg. 31.00 *(978-0-8368-5581-4(7))* Stevens, Gareth Publishing LLLP. (Gareth Stevens Secondary Library).

—The Civil War in the West (1861-July 1863) 2004. (World Almanac Library of the Civil War). (Illus.). 48p. (gr. 5-12). pap. 14.05 *(978-0-8368-5592-0(2));* lib. bdg. 31.00 *(978-0-8368-5583-8(3))* Stevens, Gareth Publishing LLLP. (Gareth Stevens Secondary Library).

—The Home Fronts in the Civil War. 2004. (World Almanac Library of the Civil War). (Illus.). 48p. (gr. 5-12). lib. bdg. 31.00 *(978-0-8368-5587-6(6),* Gareth Stevens Secondary Library) Stevens, Gareth Publishing LLLP.

—A Soldier's Life in the Civil War. 2004. (World Almanac Library of the Civil War). (Illus.). 48p. (gr. 5-12). pap. 14.05 *(978-0-8368-5595-1(7));* lib. bdg. 31.00 *(978-0-8368-5586-9(8))* Stevens, Gareth Publishing LLLP. (Gareth Stevens Secondary Library).

—World Almanac Library of the Civil War, 8 bks. Incl. Aftermath of the Civil War. pap. 14.05 *(978-0-8368-5597-5(3));* Causes of the Civil War. pap. 14.05 *(978-0-8368-5590-6(6));* Civil War at Sea. pap. 14.05 *(978-0-8368-5594-4(9));* Civil War in the East (1861-July 1863) pap. 14.05 *(978-0-8368-5591-3(4));* Civil War in the West (1861-July 1863) pap. 14.05 *(978-0-8368-5592-0(2));* Soldier's Life in the Civil War. pap. 14.05 *(978-0-8368-5595-1(7));* Union Victory (July 1863-1865) pap. 14.05 *(978-0-8368-5593-7(0));* (gr. 5-12)., Gareth Stevens Secondary Library (World Almanac Library of the Civil War). (Illus.). 48p. 2004. Set pap. 95.60 o.p. *(978-0-8368-5589-0(2),* World Almanac Library) Stevens, Gareth Publishing LLLP.

Anderson, Maxine. Great Civil War Projects: You Can Build Yourself. 2nd ed. 2012. (Build It Yourself Ser.). (ENG.). 128p. (J). (gr. 3-7). 21.95 *(978-1-936749-46-1(7));* pap. 15.95 *(978-1-936749-45-4(9))* Open City Bks.

—Proyectos Impresionantes de la Guerra Civil: Que Puedes Construir Tú Mismo. 2012. (Construyelo Tu Mismo Ser.). (SPA & ENG.). 128p. (J). (gr. 3-7). pap. 15.95 *(978-1-936749-47-8(5))* Open City Bks.

Anderson, Michael, contrib. by. Abraham Lincoln. 2012. (Pivotal Presidents: Profiles in Leadership Ser.). (ENG., Illus.). 80p. (gr. 7-12). (J). lib. bdg. 32.90 *(978-1-61530-942-9(X));* (YA). 65.80 *(978-1-61530-953-5(5))* Rosen Publishing Group, Inc., The.

Archer, Jules. A House Divided: The Lives of Ulysses S. Grant & Robert E. Lee. rev. ed. 2015. (Jules Archer History for Young Readers Ser.). (ENG., Illus.). 176p. (J). (gr. 6). 16.99 *(978-1-63220-604-6(8),* Sky Pony Pr.) Skyhorse Publishing Co., Inc.

Armentrout, David, et al. The Gettysburg Address. 2005. (Documents that Shaped the Nation Ser.). (Illus.). 48p. (gr. 4-6). 20.95 *(978-1-59515-232-9(6))* Rourke Educational Media.

Armstrong, Jennifer. Photo by Brady: A Picture of the Civil War. 2013. (ENG., Illus.). 128p. (J). pap. 11.95 *(978-0-689-85786-7(1),* Simon & Schuster/Paula Wiseman Bks.) Simon & Schuster/Paula Wiseman Bks.

Arnold, James R. The Civil War. 2005. (Chronicle of America's Wars Ser.). (Illus.). 96p. (J). (gr. 5-12). 27.93 *(978-0-8225-0140-4(6))* Lerner Publishing Group.

Arnold, James R. & Wiener, Roberta. Life Goes On: The Civil War at Home, 1861-1865. 2005. (Civil War Ser.). (Illus.). 72p. (gr. 5-12). lib. bdg. 25.26 *(978-0-8225-2315-4(9))* Lerner Publishing Group.

Aronson, Billy. Abraham Lincoln. 2008. (Presidents & Their Times Ser.). 96p. (gr. 6-18). lib. bdg. 34.21 *(978-0-7614-2839-8(9),* Benchmark Bks.) Marshall Cavendish Corp.

Bader, Bonnie. Who Was Robert E. Lee? Harrison, Nancy & O'brien, John, illus. 2014. (Who Was? Ser.). (ENG.). 112p. (J). (gr. 3-7). 5.99 *(978-0-448-47909-5(5),* Grosset & Dunlap) Penguin Young Readers Group.

Baptiste, Tracey. The Civil War & Reconstruction Eras. 2015. (African American Experience: from Slavery to the Presidency Ser.). (ENG., Illus.). 80p. (J). (gr. 7-8). 32.90 *(978-1-68048-039-9(1),* Britannica Educational Publishing) Rosen Publishing Group, Inc., The.

Baptiste, Tracey, ed. The Civil War & Reconstruction Eras. 2015. (African American Experience: from Slavery to the Presidency Ser.). (ENG.). 80p. (YA). (gr. 7-8). 65.80 *(978-1-68048-040-5(5),* Britannica Educational Publishing) Rosen Publishing Group, Inc., The.

Bauer, Patricia. B Is for Battle Cry: A Civil War Alphabet. Geister, David, illus. 2009. (History Ser.). (ENG.). 40p. (J). (gr. 2-5). 17.95 *(978-1-58536-356-8(1))* Sleeping Bear Pr.

Baumann, Susan K. Black Civil War Soldiers: The 54th Massachusetts Regiment. 2013. (Jr. Graphic African American History Ser.). (ENG., Illus.). 24p. (J). (gr. 3-6). pap. 10.60 *(978-1-4777-1457-7(X));* lib. bdg. 25.25 *(978-1-4777-1316-7(6))* Rosen Publishing Group, Inc., The. (PowerKids Pr.).

Baxter, Kathleen & McConnell, Robert L., contrib. by. Civil War Witness: Mathew Brady's Photos Reveal the Horrors of War, 1 vol. 2013. (Captured History Ser.). (ENG.). 64p. (gr. 5-7). 34.65 *(978-0-7565-4693-9(1),* CPB Grades 4-8) Compass Point Bks.

Baxter, Roberta. The Northern Home Front of the Civil War, 1 vol. (Why We Fought: the Civil War Ser.). (ENG.). 48p. (gr. 3-6). 2011. pap. 9.95 *(978-1-4329-3917-5(3))* 2010. 33.32 *(978-1-4329-3911-3(4))* Heinemann-Raintree. (Heinemann InfoSearch).

—The Southern Home Front of the Civil War, 1 vol. (Why We Fought: the Civil War Ser.). (ENG.). 48p. (gr. 3-6). 2011. pap. 9.95 *(978-1-4329-3918-2(1))* 2010. 33.32 *(978-1-4329-3912-0(2))* Heinemann-Raintree. (Heinemann InfoSearch).

Bearce, Stephanie. The Civil War: Spies, Secret Missions, & Hidden Facts from the Civil War. 2014. (Top Secret Files of History Ser.: 0). (ENG., Illus.). 125p. (J). (gr. 4-7). pap. 8.95 *(978-1-61821-250-4(8))* Prufrock Pr.

Bednarz, Robert, et al. Horizons: Us History - Civil War-Present. 3rd ed. 2003. (Harcourt School Publishers Horizons Ser.). (ENG., Illus.). 680p. (gr. 5-6). pupil's gde. ed. 93.85 *(978-0-15-321350-2(7))* Harcourt Schl. Pubs.

Beller, Susan Provost. Billy Yank & Johnny Reb: Soldiering in the Civil War. rev. ed. 2007. (Soldiers on the Battlefront Ser.). (ENG., Illus.). 112p. (gr. 6-8). lib. bdg. 33.26 *(978-0-8225-6803-2(9))* Lerner Publishing Group.

Benchmark Education Company, LLC Staff, compiled by. The Civil War: Theme Set. 2006. (J). 173.00 *(978-1-4108-7127-5(4))* Benchmark Education Co.

Benoit, Peter. The Confederate States of America. 2011. (True Book(tm), a — Civil War Ser.). (ENG.). 48p. (J). lib. bdg. 31.00 *(978-0-531-26310-5(X));* pap. 6.95 *(978-0-531-26623-6(0))* Scholastic Library Publishing. (Children's Pr.).

—The Surrender at Appomattox. 2011. (Cornerstones of Freedom, Third Ser.). 64p. (J). (ENG.). pap. 8.95 *(978-0-531-26566-6(8));* lib. bdg. 30.00 *(978-0-531-25041-9(5))* Scholastic Library Publishing. (Children's Pr.).

Berry, Carrie. Diary of Carrie Berry: A Confederate Girl, 1 vol. 2014. (First-Person Histories Ser.). (ENG.). 32p. (gr. 3-4). lib. bdg. 27.32 *(978-1-4765-4192-1(2),* Fact Finders) Capstone Press of Coughlan Cos.

Bickerstaff, Linda. The Red Badge of Courage & the Civil War. 2009. (Looking at Literature Through Primary Sources Ser.). 64p. (gr. 5-8). 58.50 *(978-1-61514-307-8(6))* Rosen Publishing Group, Inc., The.

Bircher, William. Diary of William Bircher: A Civil War Drummer, 1 vol. 2014. (First-Person Histories Ser.). (ENG.). 32p. (gr. 3-4). lib. bdg. 27.32 *(978-1-4765-4195-2(7),* Fact Finders) Capstone Press of Coughlan Cos.

Black Civil War Soldiers: The 54th Massachusetts Regiment. 2013. (Jr. Graphic African American History Ser.). 24p. (J). (gr. 3-6). pap. 63.60 *(978-1-4777-1458-4(8),* PowerKids Pr.) Rosen Publishing Group, Inc., The.

Borges, Antonion. Cocoa & Company: A Civil War Classic. 2007. (ENG.). 124p. per. 19.95 *(978-1-4241-4829-5(4))* America Star Bks.

Brocker, Susan. Voices from the Civil War & Voces de la Guerra Civil: 6 English, 6 Spanish Adaptations. 2011. (ENG & SPA.). (J). 97.00 net. *(978-1-4108-5714-9(X))* Benchmark Education Co.

Brown, Susan Taylor. Robert Smalls Sails to Freedom. Marshall, Felicia, illus. 2006. (On My Own History Ser.). 48p. (J). (gr. 3-7). pap. 6.95 *(978-0-8225-6051-7(8),* First Avenue Editions); (ENG.). (gr. 2-4). lib. bdg. 25.26 *(978-1-57505-872-6(3))* Lerner Publishing Group.

Brownell, Richard. The Civil War: The Fall of the Confederacy & the End of Slavery. 2005. (History's Great Defeats Ser.). (ENG., Illus.). 109p. (YA). (gr. 7-10). lib. bdg. 30.85 *(978-1-59018-429-5(7),* Lucent Bks.) Cengage Gale.

Burgan, Michael. Spies of the Civil War: An Interactive History Adventure. 2015. (You Choose: Spies Ser.). (ENG., Illus.). 112p. (gr. 3-4). pap. 6.95 *(978-1-4914-5932-4(8),* You Choose Bks.) Capstone Press of Coughlan Cos.

Burton, Melissa. Divided They Stood. 2014. 42p. pap. 14.95 *(978-1-934898-46-8(5))* McClanahan Publishing Hse., Inc.

Byers, Ann. Strategic Inventions of the Civil War. 2016. (Tech in the Trenches Ser.). (ENG., Illus.). 112p. (J). (gr. 9-9). lib. bdg. 42.79 *(978-1-5026-1030-0(2))* Cavendish Square Publishing.

Calkins, Chris. Auto Tour of Civil War Petersburg: 1861-1865, 1 vol. 2003. (Illus.). 80p. per. 7.66 *(978-0-9744824-0-8(4))* Petersburg Museums, The.

Capek, Michael. The Battle over Slavery: Causes & Effects of the U.S. Civil War. 2015. (Civil War Ser.). (ENG.). 48p. (gr. 3-4). lib. bdg. 29.32 *(978-1-4914-2009-6(X))* Capstone Press of Coughlan Cos.

Caravantes, Peggy. Petticoat Spies: Six Women Spies of the US Civil War. 2004. (Notable Americans Ser.). (Illus.). 112p. (YA). (gr. 6-12). 23.95 *(978-1-883846-88-6(9),* First Biographies) Reynolds, Morgan Inc.

Carole Marsh. When Brother Fought Brother: the American Civil War. 2004. (American Milestones Ser.). 32p. (gr. 3-8). pap. 5.95 *(978-0-635-02346-9(6));* (gr. 4-12). 29.95 *(978-0-635-02347-6(4))* Gallopade International.

Castellano, Peter. The Civil War. 2017. (Look at U. S. History Ser.). 32p. (J). (gr. 2-2). pap. 10.50 *(978-1-4824-6027-8(0))* Stevens, Gareth Publishing LLLP.

Chorlian, Meg & Hale, Sarah Elder, eds. Ulysses S. Grant: Confident Leader & Hero. 2005. (ENG., Illus.). 48p. (J). (gr. 3-9). 17.95 *(978-0-8126-7906-9(7))* Cobblestone Publishing Co.

Civil War. (Color & Learn Ser.). 36p. (J). (gr. 1-5). pap. *(978-1-882210-07-7(7))* Action Publishing, Inc.

The Civil War: The American Civil War 1861-1865. 2007. (Illus.). 33p. (J). (gr. 4-7). per. 6.95 *(978-0-9795887-1-6(5))* EZ Comics.

The Civil War Era, 1851-1865. 2010. (Discovering U. S. History Ser.). (Illus.). 144p. (gr. 5-8). 35.00 *(978-1-60413-352-3(X),* Chelsea Hse.) Facts On File, Inc.

The Civil War Instructional Guide. 2009. (Grade 8: Social Studies Exit Project Kits Ser.). spiral bd. *(978-1-4042-4027-8(6),* Rosen Classroom) Rosen Publishing Group, Inc., The.

Civil War Tales of the Tennessee Valley 2003. (Illus.). 241p. per. 17.95 *(978-0-9719946-7-6(6))* Bluewater Pubns.

Clark, Willow. The True Story of the Civil War. 2013. (What Really Happened? Ser.). (ENG., Illus.). 24p. (J). (gr. 3-6). pap. 8.25 *(978-1-4488-9844-2(7));* lib. bdg. 22.60 *(978-1-4488-9693-6(2))* Rosen Publishing Group, Inc., The. (PowerKids Pr.).

—The True Story of the Emancipation Proclamation. 2013. (What Really Happened? Ser.). (ENG., Illus.). 24p. (J). (gr. 3-6). 22.60 *(978-1-4488-9695-0(9));* pap. 8.25 *(978-1-4488-9848-0(X))* Rosen Publishing Group, Inc., The. (PowerKids Pr.).

Colbert, Nancy A. The Firing on Fort Sumter: A Splintered Nation Goes to War. 2004. (First Battles Ser.). (Illus.). 112p. (J). (gr. 6-12). 23.95 *(978-1-883846-51-0(X),* First Biographies) Reynolds, Morgan Inc.

Colorado Historical Society Staff, ed. A Civil War Scrapbook: I Was There Too! 2012. (ENG., Illus.). 64p. (J). (gr. 4-7). pap. 14.95 *(978-1-55591-668-8(6))* Fulcrum Publishing.

Conklin, Wendy. Battles of the Civil War, 1 vol. 2005. (Primary Source Readers Ser.). (ENG., Illus.). 24p. (J). (gr. 5-5). pap. 8.99 *(978-0-7439-8919-0(8))* Shell Educational Publishing.

—Civil War Leaders. 2017. (Primary Source Readers Ser.). 32p. (J). (gr. 4-5). pap. 8.99 *(978-1-4938-3887-5(3))* Teacher Created Materials, Inc.

—Robert E. Lee, 1 vol. 2005. (Primary Source Readers Ser.). (ENG.). 24p. (J). (gr. 4-4). pap. 8.99 *(978-0-7439-8918-3(X))* Shell Educational Publishing.

Cooke, Tim. After the War. 2012. (American Civil War: the Right Answer Ser.). (Illus.). 48p. (J). (gr. 6-8). 31.95 *(978-1-4339-7531-8(9));* pap. 14.05 *(978-1-4339-7532-5(7))* Stevens, Gareth Publishing LLLP. (Gareth Stevens Secondary Library).

—Causes of the War. 2012. (American Civil War: the Right Answer Ser.). (Illus.). 48p. (J). (gr. 6-8). pap. 14.05 *(978-1-4339-7536-3(X));* lib. bdg. 31.95 *(978-1-4339-7535-6(1))* Stevens, Gareth Publishing LLLP.

—Causes of the War: 1860-1861. 2012. (Civil War Highlights Ser.). (Illus.). 48p. (gr. 5-12). lib. bdg. 37.10 *(978-1-59920-813-8(X))* Black Rabbit Bks.

—The Home Front. 2012. (American Civil War: the Right Answer Ser.). (Illus.). 48p. (J). (gr. 6-8). 31.95 *(978-1-4339-7543-1(2));* pap. 14.05 *(978-1-4339-7544-8(0))* Stevens, Gareth Publishing LLLP. (Gareth Stevens Secondary Library).

—Home Front, 1861-1865. 2012. (Civil War Highlights Ser.). (Illus.). 48p. (gr. 5-12). 37.10 *(978-1-59920-817-6(2))* Black Rabbit Bks.

—Politics of the War: 1861-1865. 2012. (Civil War Highlights Ser.). (Illus.). 48p. (gr. 5-12). lib. bdg. 37.10 *(978-1-59920-818-3(0))* Black Rabbit Bks.

—The U. S. Civil War on the Front Lines, 1 vol. 2014. (Life on the Front Lines Ser.). (ENG., Illus.). 32p. (gr. 3-4). 27.99 *(978-1-4914-0842-1(1),* Edge Bks.) Capstone Press of Coughlan Cos.

—Weapons & Tactics. 2012. (American Civil War: the Right Answer Ser.). (Illus.). 48p. (J). (gr. 6-8). 31.95 *(978-1-4339-7551-6(3));* pap. 14.05 *(978-1-4339-7552-3(1))* Stevens, Gareth Publishing LLLP. (Gareth Stevens Secondary Library).

Cooke, Tim, ed. Politics. 2011. (CC: Civil War Ser.). 112p. (gr. 6-12). 42.80 *(978-1-936333-48-6(1))* Brown Bear Bks.

—Weapons, Tactics, & Strategy. 2011. (CC: Civil War Ser.). 112p. (gr. 6-12). 42.80 *(978-1-936333-46-2(5))* Brown Bear Bks.

Cordell, M. R. Courageous Women of the Civil War: Soldiers, Spies, Medics, & More. 2016. (Women of Action Ser.). (ENG., Illus.). 256p. (YA). (gr. 7). 19.99 *(978-1-61373-200-7(7))* Chicago Review Pr., Inc.

Corrick, James A. The Civil War & Emancipation. 2007. (Lucent Library of Black History Ser.). (ENG., Illus.). 128p. (gr. 3-7). lib. bdg. 39.40 *(978-1-4205-0008-0(2),* Lucent Bks.) Cengage Gale.

Cosson, Jody. Civil War & Reconstruction: 1850-1877. 2007. (Presidents of the United States Ser.). (Illus.). (J). (gr. 4-7). 47p. lib. bdg. 29.05 *(978-1-59036-743-8(X));* 48p. per. 10.95 *(978-1-59036-744-5(8))* Weigl Pubs., Inc.

Cotugno, Megan. Why We Fought - The Civil War Set, 5 vols. Incl. Battles of the Civil War. Fay, Gail. pap. 9.95 *(978-1-4329-3916-8(5));* Key People of the Civil War. McManus, Lori. pap. 9.95 *(978-1-4329-3919-9(X));* Northern Home Front of the Civil War. Baxter, Roberta. pap. 9.95 *(978-1-4329-3917-5(3));* Soldiers of the Civil War. Roche, Tim. pap. 9.95 *(978-1-4329-3920-5(3));* Southern Home Front of the Civil War. Baxter, Roberta. pap. 9.95 *(978-1-4329-3918-2(1));* (gr. 3-6). (Why We Fought: the Civil War Ser.). (ENG.). 48p. 2011. Set pap. 44.95 *(978-1-4329-3921-2(1),* Heinemann InfoSearch) Heinemann-Raintree.

Crewe, Sabrina & Uschan, Michael V. Fort Sumter: The Civil War Begins. 2005. (Events That Shaped America Ser.). (Illus.). 32p. (gr. 3-6). lib. bdg. 26.00 *(978-0-8368-3414-7(3),* Gareth Stevens Learning Library) Stevens, Gareth Publishing LLLP.

Crompton, Samuel W. The Civil War, Vol. 11. Musteen, Jason R., ed. 2015. (Major U. S. Historical Wars Ser.). (Illus.). 64p. (J). (gr. 7). lib. bdg. 23.95 *(978-1-4222-3354-2(5))* Mason Crest.

Crozier, A. J. Technology & the Civil War: Set Of 6. 2011. (Navigators Ser.). (J). pap. 48.00 net. *(978-1-4108-6260-0(7))* Benchmark Education Co.

—Technology & the Civil War: Text Pairs. 2008. (Bridges/Navigators Ser.). (J). (gr. 5). 89.00 *(978-1-4108-8423-7(6))* Benchmark Education Co.

Cummings, Judy Dodge. Civil War, 1 vol. 2013. (Essential Library of American Wars Ser.). (ENG.). 112p. (J). (gr. 6-12). lib. bdg. 35.64 *(978-1-61783-877-4(2),* Essential Library) ABDO Publishing Co.

Cunningham, Anne C., ed. Reparations. 2017. (Opposing Viewpoints Ser.). 224p. (YA). (gr. 10-12). pap. 33.80 ***(978-1-5345-0031-0(6));*** lib. bdg. 48.80 ***(978-1-5345-0025-9(1))*** Greenhaven Publishing LLC. (Greenhaven Publishing).

Day, Nancy. Your Travel Guide to Civil War America. 2005. (Passport to History Ser.). (Illus.). 96p. (gr. 5-8). lib. bdg. 26.50 *(978-0-8225-3078-7(3))* Lerner Publishing Group.

DeFord, Deborah H. The Civil War. 2006. (Wars That Changed American History Ser.). 48p. (gr. 5-12). pap. 14.05 *(978-0-8368-7300-9(9));* (Illus.). lib. bdg. 31.00 *(978-0-8368-7291-0(6))* Stevens, Gareth Publishing LLLP. (Gareth Stevens Secondary Library).

Del Adelman, Garry. The Civil War Kids 150: Fifty Fun Things to Do, See, Make, & Find. 150th anniv. ed. 2012. (ENG., Illus.). 96p. pap. 12.95 *(978-0-7627-8205-5(6),* Lyons Pr.) Globe Pequot Pr., The.

Delmar, Pete. Vehicles of the Civil War, 1 vol. 2013. (War Vehicles Ser.). (ENG.). 32p. (gr. 3-4). 27.99 *(978-1-4296-9912-9(4),* Edge Bks.) Capstone Press of Coughlan Cos.

Doeden, Matt. The Civil War: An Interactive History Adventure. 2016. (You Choose: History Ser.). (ENG.). 112p. (gr. 3-4). pap. 6.95 *(978-1-5157-3389-8(0));* lib. bdg. 31.99 *(978-1-5157-3386-7(6))* Capstone Press of Coughlan Cos. (You Choose Bks.).

—The Civil War [Scholastic]: An Interactive History Adventure. 2010. (You Choose: History Ser.). 112p. pap. 0.90 *(978-1-4296-5977-2(7),* You Choose Bks.) Capstone Press of Coughlan Cos.

Doeden, Matt. Weapons of the Civil War. 2017. (Weapons of War Ser.). (ENG.). 32p. (gr. 2-3). lib. bdg. 26.65 ***(978-1-5157-7909-4(2))*** Capstone Press of Coughlan Cos.

Dorling Kindersley Publishing Staff. Civil War. 2015. (DK Eyewitness Bks.). (ENG., Illus.). 72p. (J). (gr. 3-7). pap. 9.99 *(978-1-4654-3186-8(1),* DK Children) Dorling Kindersley Publishing, Inc.

—DK Eyewitness Books: Civil War: Civil War. 2015. (DK Eyewitness Bks.). (ENG., Illus.). 72p. (J). (gr. 3-7). 19.99 *(978-1-4654-3360-2(0),* DK Children) Dorling Kindersley Publishing, Inc.

Dosier, Susan. Civil War Cooking: The Confederacy. 2016. (Exploring History Through Food Ser.). (ENG., Illus.). 32p. (gr. 3-4). lib. bdg. 27.32 *(978-1-5157-2354-7(2))* Capstone Press of Coughlan Cos.

—Civil War Cooking: The Union. 2016. (Exploring History Through Food Ser.). (ENG., Illus.). 32p. (gr. 3-4). lib. bdg. 27.32 *(978-1-5157-2353-0(4))* Capstone Press of Coughlan Cos.

Downey, Fairfax. Famous Horses of the Civil War. Chapman, Frederick T., illus. 2011. 128p. 40.95 *(978-1-258-00351-7(1))* Literary Licensing, LLC.

Drama of African-American History, 5 bks., Set. Incl. Africa: A Look Back. Haskins, James & Benson, Kathleen. 80p. (J). (gr. 6-7). lib. bdg. 35.64 *(978-0-7614-2148-1(3));* Civil War. Jordan, Anne Devereaux. 72p. (J). (gr. 3-7). lib. bdg. 35.64 *(978-0-7614-2179-5(3));* Reconstruction Era. Stroud, Bettye. 80p. (gr. 6-7). lib. bdg. 35.64 *(978-0-7614-2181-8(5));* Slave Trade & the Middle Passage. Sharp, S. Pearl. 80p. (gr. 6-7). lib. bdg. 35.64 *(978-0-7614-2176-4(9));* Slavery & Resistance. Jordan, Anne Devereaux. 80p. (gr. 6-7). lib. bdg. 35.64 *(978-0-7614-2178-8(5));* (Illus.). 2006. 2007. Set lib. bdg. 178.21 *(978-0-7614-2174-0(2),* Benchmark Bks.) Marshall Cavendish Corp.

Draper, Allison Stark. What People Wore During the Civil War. 2009. (Clothing, Costumes, & Uniforms Throughout American History Ser.). 24p. (gr. 3-3). 42.50 *(978-1-61511-876-2(4),* PowerKids Pr.) Rosen Publishing Group, Inc., The.

Dreyer, Ellen. A Band of Brave Men: The Story of the 54th Massachusetts Regiment. 2004. (ENG., Illus.). 31p. (J). (gr. 5-5). pap. 11.47 net. *(978-0-7652-5247-0(3),* Celebration Pr.) Pearson Schl.

Edwards, Judith. Abolitionists & Slave Resistance: Breaking the Chains of Slavery. 2004. (Slavery in American History Ser.). (Illus.). 128p. (J). lib. bdg. 27.94 *(978-0-7660-2155-6(6))* Enslow Pubs., Inc.

Elliot, Henry. Harriet Beecher Stowe: The Voice of Humanity in White America. 2009. (Voices for Freedom Ser.). (ENG., Illus.). 64p. (J). (gr. 5-8). pap. *(978-0-7787-4837-3(5));* lib. bdg. *(978-0-7787-4821-2(9))* Crabtree Publishing Co.

Epperson, James F. Causes of the Civil War. 2005. (Road to War Ser.). (Illus.). 64p. (J). pap. 12.95 *(978-1-59556-006-3(8));* (gr. 4-18). lib. bdg. 22.95 *(978-1-59556-002-5(5))* OTTN Publishing.

Fein, Eric. Weapons, Gear, & Uniforms of the Civil War, 1 vol. 2012. (Equipped for Battle Ser.). (ENG.). 32p. (gr. 3-4). lib. bdg. 27.99 *(978-1-4296-7648-9(5),* Edge Bks.) Capstone Press of Coughlan Cos.

Ferry, Joseph. The Star-Spangled Banner: Story of Our National Anthem. Moreno, Barry, ed. 2014. (Patriotic Symbols of America Ser.: 20). 48p. (J). (gr. 4-18). 20.95 *(978-1-4222-3132-6(1))* Mason Crest.

Figley, Marty Rhodes. President Lincoln, Willie Kettles, & the Telegraph Machine. 2010. pap. 56.72 *(978-0-7613-6929-5(5))* Lerner Publishing Group.

Fiore, C. A. Young Heros of the Civil War. (J). pap. 9.99 (978-0-88092-486-3(1)) Royal Fireworks Publishing Co.

Fiore, Carmen Anthony. Young Heroes of the Civil War. 2006. (J). pap. (978-0-88092-639-3(2)); lib. bdg. (978-0-88092-638-6(4)) Royal Fireworks Publishing Co.

Fitzgerald, Stephanie. A Civil War Timeline, 1 vol. 2014. (War Timelines Ser.). (ENG.). 48p. (gr. 4-6). lib. bdg. 34.65 (978-1-4765-4156-3(6)) Capstone Press of Coughlan Cos.

Fitzgerald, Stephanie & Burgan, Michael. Perspectives Flip Books. 2013. (Perspectives Flip Bks.). (ENG.). 64p. (gr. 5-6). 67.98 (978-0-7565-4725-7(3), CPB Grades 4-8) Compass Point Bks.

Fitzgerald, Stephanie, et al. Perspectives Flip Books. 2013. (Perspectives Flip Bks.). (ENG.). 64p. (gr. 5-6). 203.94 (978-0-7565-4726-4(1), CPB Grades 4-8) Compass Point Bks.

—War Timelines, 1 vol. 2014. (War Timelines Ser.). (ENG.). 48p. (gr. 4-6). lib. bdg. 138.60 (978-1-4765-6962-8(2)) Capstone Press of Coughlan Cos.

Fluharty, Linda Cunningham. Civil War - West Virginia: Union Lives Lost. 2004. (Illus.). 175p. lib. bdg. 35.00 (978-0-9759097-1-3(1)) Fluharty, Linda Cunningham.

Ford, Carin T. African-American Soldiers in the Civil War: Fighting for Freedom. 2004. (Civil War Library). (Illus.). 48p. (J). (gr. 3-4). lib. bdg. 25.27 (978-0-7660-2254-6(4)) Enslow Pubs., Inc.

—The American Civil War: An Overview. 2004. (Civil War Library). (Illus.). 48p. (J). lib. bdg. 25.27 (978-0-7660-2255-3(2)) Enslow Pubs., Inc.

—The Civil War's African-American Soldiers Through Primary Sources. 2013. (Civil War Through Primary Sources Ser.). 48p. (J). (gr. 4-10). pap. 8.95 (978-1-4644-0183-1(7)); 25.27 (978-0-7660-4125-7(5)) Enslow Pubs., Inc.

—An Overview of the American Civil War Through Primary Sources. 2013. (Civil War Through Primary Sources Ser.). 48p. (J). (gr. 4-10). pap. 8.95 (978-1-4644-0182-4(9)); lib. bdg. 25.27 (978-0-7660-4124-0(7)) Enslow Pubs., Inc.

—Women of the Civil War Through Primary Sources. 2013. (Civil War Through Primary Sources Ser.). 48p. (J). (gr. 4-10). pap. 8.95 (978-1-4644-0186-2(1)); lib. bdg. 25.27 (978-0-7660-4128-8(X)) Enslow Pubs., Inc.

Fox, Arthur B. Pittsburgh During the American Civil War 1860-1865. 2004. (Illus.). 236p. pap. 29.95 (978-0-9760563-0-0(5), 7526S) Mechling Bookbindery.

Fredriksen, John C. Civil War Almanac. 2007. (Almanacs of American Wars Ser.). (Illus.). 672p. (C). (gr. 9). 95.00 (978-0-8160-6459-5(8)) Facts On File, Inc.

Furbee, Mary Rodd. Outrageous Women of Civil War Times. 2003. (Outrageous Women Ser.: 7). (ENG., Illus.). 132p. (J). (gr. 5-9). pap. 14.95 (978-0-471-22926-1(1), Jossey-Bass) Wiley, John & Sons, Inc.

George, Enzo. The Civil War. 2015. (J). lib. bdg. (978-1-62713-491-0(3)); (ENG.). 48p. (gr. 4-4). 31.36 (978-1-5026-0251-0(2)) Cavendish Square Publishing.

George, Lynn. What Do You Know about the Civil War? (20 Questions: History Ser.). 24p. (gr. 2-3). 2009. 42.50 (978-1-60854-958-0(5), PowerKids Pr.) 2008. (Illus.). (J). lib. bdg. 22.60 (978-1-4042-4187-9(6)) Rosen Publishing Group, Inc., The.

Golay, Michael. Civil War. 3rd rev. ed. 2010. (America at War Ser.). 288p. (gr. 6-12). 45.00 (978-0-8160-8190-5(5), Chelsea Hse.) Facts On File, Inc.

Goldsmith, Bonnie Zucker. Dr. Mary Edwards Walker: Civil War Surgeon & Medal of Honor Recipient, 1 vol. 2010. (Military Heroes Ser.). (ENG.). 112p. (J). (gr. 6-12). lib. bdg. 35.64 (978-1-60453-966-0(6)) ABDO Publishing Co.

Goodman, Michael E. Civil War Spies. 2015. (Illus.). 48p. (J). (978-1-60818-598-6(2), Creative Education) Creative Co., The.

—Civil War Spies: Wartime Spies. 2016. (Wartime Spies Ser.). (ENG.). 48p. (J). (gr. 5-9). pap. 12.00 (978-1-62832-203-3(9), Creative Paperbacks) Creative Co., The.

Goodman, Susan E. Robert Henry Hendershot. Ettlinger, Doris, illus. 2003. (Brave Kids Ser.). (ENG.). 64p. (J). (gr. 1-4). pap. 6.99 (978-0-689-84980-0(X), Simon & Schuster/Paula Wiseman Bks.) Simon & Schuster/Paula Wiseman Bks.

Gourley, Catherine. The Horrors of Andersonville: Life & Death Inside a Civil War Prison. 2010. (ENG.). 192p. (gr. 9-12). lib. bdg. 38.60 (978-0-7613-4212-0(5)) Lerner Publishing Group.

Grayson, Robert. The U. S. Civil War: Why They Fought. 2015. (What Were They Fighting For? Ser.). (ENG., Illus.). 64p. (gr. 5-9). lib. bdg. 34.65 (978-0-7565-5168-1(4)) Compass Point Bks.

—12 Incredible Facts about the US Civil War. 2015. (Turning Points in US History Ser.). (ENG., Illus.). 32p. (J). (gr. 3-5). (978-1-63235-133-3(1), 12-Story Library) Pr. Room Editions LLC.

Gregory, Josh. The Gettysburg Address. 2013. (ENG.). 64p. (J). 30.00 (978-0-531-28204-5(X)); pap. 8.95 (978-0-531-27669-3(4)) Scholastic Library Publishing.

Griskey, Michele. Harriet Beecher Stowe. 2005. (Classic Storytellers Ser.). (Illus.). 48p. (J). (gr. 4-8). lib. bdg. 29.95 (978-1-58415-375-7(X)) Mitchell Lane Pubs., Inc.

Grolier Educational Staff, contrib. by. The Civil War, 10 Vols. 2004. (Illus.). (J). 339.00 (978-0-7172-5883-3(1), Grolier) Scholastic Library Publishing.

Hakim, Joy. War, Terrible War, 1855-1865. (History of US Ser.: 6). (ENG., Illus.). 176p. (gr. 4-7). 3rd rev. ed. 2006. 24.95 (978-0-19-518899-8(3))Bk. 6. 2nd rev. ed. 2007. per. 15.95 (978-0-19-532720-5(9)) Oxford Univ. Pr., Inc.

Hale, Nathan. Big Bad Ironclad! 2012. (Nathan Hale's Hazardous Tales Ser.). (ENG., Illus.). 128p. (J). (gr. 3-7). 12.95 (978-1-4197-0395-9(1), Amulet Bks.) Abrams, Inc.

—The Underground Abductor. 2015. (Nathan Hale's Hazardous Tales Ser.). (ENG., Illus.). 128p. (J). (gr. 3-9). 12.95 (978-1-4197-1536-5(4), Amulet Bks.) Abrams, Inc.

—The Underground Abductor. 2017. (Nathan Hale's Hazardous Tales Ser.). (J). lib. bdg. 24.45 **(978-0-606-40708-3(1))** Turtleback Bks.

Hale, Sarah Elder, ed. Robert E. Lee: Duty & Honor. 2005. (ENG., Illus.). 48p. (J). (gr. 3-9). 17.95 (978-0-8126-7905-2(9)) Cobblestone Publishing Co.

Halfmann, Janet. Seven Miles to Freedom: The Robert Smalls Story. Smith, Duane, illus. 2008. 40p. (J). (gr. 1-6). 17.95 (978-1-60060-232-0(0)) Lee & Low Bks., Inc.

Halfmann, Janet & Smith, Duane. Seven Miles to Freedom: The Robert Smalls Story, 1 vol. 2008. (ENG., Illus.). 40p. (J). pap. 10.95 (978-1-60060-986-2(4)) Lee & Low Bks., Inc.

Halls, Kelly Milner. Life During the Civil War, 1 vol. 2014. (Daily Life in US History Ser.). (ENG., Illus.). 48p. (J). (gr. 3-6). lib. bdg. 32.79 (978-1-62403-625-5(2)) ABDO Publishing Co.

Harkrader, Lisa. Reconstruction & Aftermath of the Civil War: A MyReportLinks. com Book. 2004. (American Civil War Ser.). (Illus.). 48p. (J). lib. bdg. 25.26 (978-0-7660-5265-9(6), MyReportLinks.com Bks.) Enslow Pubs., Inc.

Harness, Cheryl. Mary Walker Wears the Pants: The True Story of the Doctor, Reformer, & Civil War Hero. Molinari, Carlo, illus. 2013. (ENG.). 32p. (J). (gr. 1-3). 16.99 (978-0-8075-4990-2(8)) Whitman, Albert & Co.

Havelin, Kate. Hoopskirts, Union Blues, & Confederate Grays: Civil War Fashions from 1861 to 1865. 2011. (Dressing a Nation: the History of U. S. Fashion Ser.). (ENG., Illus.). 64p. (gr. 5-12). lib. bdg. 31.93 (978-0-7613-5889-3(7), Twenty-First Century Bks.) Lerner Publishing Group.

Hazen, Walter A. The Civil War. 2007. (Everyday Life (Good Year Books) Ser.). (Illus.). 92p. (J). (gr. 5-12). per. 12.95 (978-1-59647-199-3(9)) Good Year Bks.

Helfand, Lewis. Abraham Lincoln: From the Log Cabin to the White House - Campfire Heroes Line. Jones, K. L. & Manikandan, illus. 2013. (Campfire Graphic Novels Ser.). (ENG.). 108p. (YA). (gr. 5-12). pap. 12.99 (978-93-80741-21-5(9), Campfire) Steerforth Pr.

Helwig, Laura. How Abraham Lincoln Fought the Civil War. 2017. (Presidents at War Ser.). 128p. (J). (gr. 8-8). lib. bdg. 37.27 **(978-0-7660-8525-1(2))** Enslow Pubs., Inc.

Hernández, Roger E. The Civil War, 1840s-1890s. 2008. (Hispanic America Ser.). 80p. (gr. 5-18). lib. bdg. 34.21 (978-0-7614-2939-5(5), Benchmark Bks.) Marshall Cavendish Corp.

Herwick Rice, Dona & Conklin, Wendy. Causes of the Civil War, 1 vol. 2009. (Building Fluency Through Reader's Theater Ser.). (ENG.). 32p. (J). (gr. 3-5). pap. 7.99 (978-1-4333-0545-0(3)) Teacher Created Materials, Inc.

Hirsch, E. D., Jr., ed. The Civil War, Level 5. tchr. ed. 9.95 (978-0-7690-5081-2(6)); stu. ed. 49.95 (978-0-7690-2848-4(9)) Pearson Learning.

Hoogenboom, Lynn. William Tecumseh Sherman: The Fight to Preserve the Union. 2009. (Library of American Lives & Times Ser.). 112p. (gr. 5-5). 69.20 (978-1-60853-511-8(8)) Rosen Publishing Group, Inc., The.

Howell, Brian. The US Civil War & Reconstruction. 2011. (Explorer Library: Language Arts Explorer Ser.). (ENG.). 32p. (gr. 4-8). lib. bdg. 28.50 (978-1-61080-201-7(2), 201178) Cherry Lake Publishing.

—The U.S. Civil War & Reconstruction. 2011. (Explorer Library: Language Arts Explorer Ser.). (ENG.). 32p. (gr. 4-8). pap. 14.21 (978-1-61080-289-5(6), 201212) Cherry Lake Publishing.

Howell, Sara. The Civil War: Frontline Soldiers & Their Families. 2015. (Frontline Families Ser.). (ENG., Illus.). 48p. (J). (gr. 5-6). pap. 14.05 (978-1-4824-3057-8(6)) Stevens, Gareth Publishing LLLP.

Howse, Jennifer. The Civil War. 2008. (African American History Ser.). (Illus.). 48p. (YA). (gr. 5-8). pap. 10.95 (978-1-59036-877-0(0)); lib. bdg. 29.05 (978-1-59036-876-3(2)) Weigl Pubs., Inc.

—Civil War. 2013. (J). (978-1-62127-191-8(9)); pap. (978-1-62127-197-0(8)) Weigl Pubs., Inc.

Hutchison, Patricia. The Civil War: 12 Things to Know. 2017. (America at War Ser.). (ENG., Illus.). 32p. (J). (gr. 3-6). 21.95 (978-1-63235-265-1(6)) Pr. Room Editions LLC.

Imbriaco, Alison. Causes of the Civil War: A MyReportLinks. com Book. 2004. (American Civil War Ser.). (Illus.). 48p. (J). lib. bdg. 25.26 (978-0-7660-5186-7(2), MyReportLinks.com Bks.) Enslow Pubs., Inc.

Jarrow, Gail. Lincoln's Flying Spies: Thaddeus Lowe & the Civil War Balloon Corps. 2010. (ENG., Illus.). 112p. (J). (gr. 4-12). 18.95 (978-1-59078-719-9(6), Calkins Creek) Boyds Mills Pr.

Jones, Carrie. Sarah Emma Edmonds Was a Great Pretender: The True Story of a Civil War Spy. Oldroyd, Mark, illus. 2011. (Carolrhoda Picture Bks.). (ENG.). 32p. (J). (gr. 2-5). 17.95 (978-0-7613-5399-7(2)) Lerner Publishing Group.

Jordan, Anne Devereaux. The Civil War. 2006. (Drama of African-American History Ser.). (Illus.). 72p. (J). (gr. 3-7). lib. bdg. 35.64 (978-0-7614-2179-5(3), Benchmark Bks.) Marshall Cavendish Corp.

Junyk, Myra. The 10 Most Defining Moments of the Civil War. 2008. (J). 14.99 (978-1-55448-518-5(5)) Scholastic Library Publishing.

Kantor, MacKinlay. Lee & Grant at Appomattox. 2015. (ENG.). 144p. pap. 9.95 (978-0-9904604-0-4(1)) Flying Point Pr.

—Lee & Grant at Appomattox. (Great Leaders & Events Ser.). (ENG.). 208p. (J). (gr. 4-8). 2017. lib. bdg. 35.99 **(978-1-942875-25-3(8))** 2016. (Illus.). pap. 12.99 (978-0-7603-5226-7(7)) Quarto Publishing Group USA. (Voyageur Pr.).

Kay, Betty Carlson. The Civil War from A to Z: Two Points of View. 2010. 144p. pap. 11.70 (978-1-4520-9451-9(9)) AuthorHouse.

Kelman, Ari & Fetter-Vorm, Jonathan. Battle Lines: A Graphic History of the Civil War. Fetter-Vorm, Jonathan, illus. 2015. (ENG., Illus.). 224p. 26.00 (978-0-8090-9474-5(6), 9780809094745, Hill & Wang) Farrar, Straus & Giroux.

Kent, Deborah. The Great Civil War Draft Riots. 2005. (Cornerstones of Freedom Ser.). (ENG., Illus.). 48p. (YA). (gr. 4-7). lib. bdg. 26.00 (978-0-516-23632-2(6)) Scholastic Library Publishing.

Kent, Zachary. The Civil War: From Fort Sumter to Appomattox. 2011. (United States at War Ser.). (Illus.). 128p. (J). (gr. 5-18). lib. bdg. 33.27 (978-0-7660-3638-3(3)) Enslow Pubs., Inc.

Kerley, Barbara. Walt Whitman: Words for America. Selznick, Brian, illus. 2004. (ENG.). 56p. (J). (gr. 2-5). 17.99 (978-0-439-35791-3(8), Scholastic Pr.) Scholastic, Inc.

Kirkman, Marissa. The Life & Times of Abraham Lincoln & the US Civil War. 2016. (Life & Times Ser.). (ENG., Illus.). 24p. (gr. 1-2). lib. bdg. 25.32 (978-1-5157-2474-2(3), First Facts) Capstone Press of Coughlan Cos.

Kissock, Heather. Civil War & Reconstruction. 2016. (Illus.). 48p. (J). (978-1-5105-1280-1(2)) SmartBook Media, Inc.

Kolpin, Amanda & Kolpin, Molly. The Story of the Civil War, 1 vol. 2014. (Story of the Civil War Ser.). (ENG.). 32p. (gr. 3-4). pap. 31.80 (978-1-4914-0738-7(7), Fact Finders) Capstone Press of Coughlan Cos.

Kolpin, Molly & Kolpin, Amanda. The Story of the Civil War, 1 vol. 2014. (Story of the Civil War Ser.). (ENG.). 32p. (gr. 3-4). 109.28 (978-1-4914-0737-0(9), Fact Finders) Capstone Press of Coughlan Cos.

Kostyal, Karen. 1862 - Fredericksburg: A New Look at a Bitter Civil War Battle. Epstein, Lori, photos by. 2011. (ENG., Illus.). 48p. (J). (gr. 3-7). 17.95 (978-1-4263-0835-2(3)); lib. bdg. 27.90 (978-1-4263-0836-9(1)) National Geographic Society. (National Geographic Children's Bks.).

Krull, Kathleen & Brewer, Paul. Lincoln Tells a Joke: How Laughter Saved the President (and the Country) Innerst, Stacy, illus. 2010. (ENG.). 40p. (J). (gr. 1-4). 17.99 (978-0-15-206639-0(X)) Houghton Mifflin Harcourt Publishing Co.

Lanser, Amanda. The Civil War by the Numbers. 2015. (America at War by the Numbers Ser.). (ENG., Illus.). 32p. (gr. 3-4). lib. bdg. 27.99 (978-1-4914-4295-1(6)) Capstone Press of Coughlan Cos.

Lassieur, Allison. At Battle in the Civil War: An Interactive Battlefield Adventure. 2015. (You Choose: Battlefields Ser.). (ENG.). 112p. (gr. 3-4). lib. bdg. 31.99 (978-1-4914-2149-9(5), You Choose Bks.) Capstone Press of Coughlan Cos.

Lassieur, Allison & Doeden, Matt. The Civil War Experience: An Interactive History Adventure, 1 vol. 2014. (You Choose: History Ser.). (ENG.). 328p. (gr. 3-4). pap. 14.95 (978-1-4765-0839-9(9), You Choose Bks.) Capstone Press of Coughlan Cos.

LeBoutillier, Linda. Secrets of the U. S. Civil War. 2017. (Top Secret Files Ser.). (ENG.). 32p. (gr. 3-4). pap. 7.95 (978-1-5157-4142-8(7)); (Illus.). lib. bdg. 27.99 (978-1-5157-4138-1(9)) Capstone Press of Coughlan Cos. (Edge Bks.).

Levy, Debbie. Soldier Song: A True Story of the Civil War. Ford, Gilbert, illus. 2017. (ENG.). 80p. (J). (gr. 3-5). 18.99 (978-1-4847-2598-6(0)) Disney Pr.

Lieurance, Suzanne. Weapons & Strategies of the Civil War: A MyReportLinks. com Book. 2004. (American Civil War Ser.). (Illus.). 48p. (J). lib. bdg. 25.26 (978-0-7660-5185-0(4), MyReportLinks.com Bks.) Enslow Pubs., Inc.

Machajewski, Sarah. A Kid's Life During the American Civil War, 1 vol. 2015. (ENG., Illus.). 24p. (J). lib. bdg. 23.60 (978-1-4994-0004-5(7), PowerKids Pr.) Rosen Publishing Group, Inc., The.

Mara, Wil. If You Were a Kid During the Civil War. 2016. (If You Were a Kid Ser.). (ENG., Illus.). 32p. (J). lib. bdg. 26.00 (978-0-531-21969-0(0), Children's Pr.) Scholastic Library Publishing.

Marcovitz, Hal. Confederate Flag: Controversial Symbol of the South. Moreno, Barry, ed. 2014. (Patriotic Symbols of America Ser.: 20). 48p. (J). (gr. 4-18). 20.95 (978-1-4222-3121-0(6)) Mason Crest.

Marinelli, Deborah A. The Assassination of Abraham Lincoln. 2003. (Library of Political Assassinations Ser.). (Illus.). 64p. (YA). (gr. 7-12). lib. bdg. 31.95 (978-0-8239-3539-0(6)) Rosen Publishing Group, Inc., The.

Marsh, Carole. What Was the Civil War All about Anyway? 2010. (Student's Civil War, 150th Anniversary: 1861-1865 Ser.). (Illus.). 36p. (J). pap. 9.99 (978-0-635-07640-3(3)) Gallopade International.

—When Did It Happen in the Civil War? 2010. (Civil War Ser.). (Illus.). 36p. (J). pap. 9.99 (978-0-635-07641-0(1)) Gallopade International.

—Where Did the Civil War Happen? 2010. (Student's Civil War, 150th Anniversary: 1861-1865 Ser.). (Illus.). 36p. (J). pap. 9.99 (978-0-635-07642-7(X)) Gallopade International.

—Who Were the Key Players in the Civil War? 2010. (Student's Civil War, 150th Anniversary: 1861-1865 Ser.). (Illus.). 36p. (J). pap. 9.99 (978-0-635-07639-7(X)) Gallopade International.

Martin, Iain C. Gettysburg: The True Account of Two Young Heroes in the Greatest Battle of the Civil War. (ENG., Illus.). 208p. (gr. 6). 2015. (J). pap. 16.99 (978-1-63220-438-7(X)) 2013. (YA). 16.95 (978-1-62087-532-2(2), 620532) Skyhorse Publishing Co., Inc. (Sky Pony Pr.).

Mattern, Joanne. Fort Sumter. 2015. (ENG.). 32p. (gr. 3-6). 32.79 (978-1-63430-046-9(7)) Rourke Educational Media.

McCarthy, Pat. Famous Confederate Generals & Leaders of the South: A Myreportlinks. com Book. 2004. (American Civil War Ser.). (Illus.). 48p. (J). lib. bdg. 26.60 (978-0-7660-5189-8(7), MyReportLinks.com Bks.) Enslow Pubs., Inc.

—Famous Union Generals & Leaders of the North: A MyReportLinks. com Book. 2004. (American Civil War Ser.). (Illus.). 48p. (J). lib. bdg. 26.60 (978-0-7660-5188-1(9), MyReportLinks.com Bks.) Enslow Pubs., Inc.

McConnell, Robert L., contrib. by. Civil War Witness: Mathew Brady's Photos Reveal the Horrors of War, 1 vol. 2013. (Captured History Ser.). (ENG.). 64p. (gr. 5-7). pap. 9.10 (978-0-7565-4699-1(0), CPB Grades 4-8) Compass Point Bks.

McDonald, Archie P. Primary Source Accounts of the Civil War. 2006. (America's Wars Through Primary Sources Ser.). (Illus.). 128p. (J). (gr. 5-12). lib. bdg. 33.27 (978-1-59845-000-2(X), MyReportLinks.com Bks.) Enslow Pubs., Inc.

McNamara, Margaret. Discover the North & the South. 2006. (J). pap. (978-1-4108-6447-5(2)) Benchmark Education Co.

—The North & the South. 2006. (J). pap. (978-1-4108-6444-4(8)) Benchmark Education Co.

McNeese, Tim. The Civil War: A Nation Divided Set, 8-Volumes. 2009. (Civil War: A Nation Divided Ser.). (gr. 6-12). 280.00 (978-1-60413-653-1(7), Chelsea Hse.) Facts On File, Inc.

—Civil War Leaders. 2009. (Civil War: A Nation Divided Ser.). (Illus.). 144p. (gr. 6-12). 35.00 (978-1-60413-033-1(4), Chelsea Hse.) Facts On File, Inc.

—Robert E. Lee. 2009. (Leaders of the Civil War Era Ser.). (Illus.). 152p. (gr. 6-12). lib. bdg. 35.00 (978-1-60413-304-2(X), Chelsea Hse.) Facts On File, Inc.

Meacham, Margaret. Oyster Moon, 1 vol. Ramsey, Marcy Dunn, illus. 2009. (ENG.). 112p. (J). (gr. 8-18). pap. 9.95 (978-0-87033-459-7(X), 9780870334597, Cornell Maritime Pr./Tidewater Pubs.) Schiffer Publishing, Ltd.

Meltzer, Brad. I Am Abraham Lincoln. Eliopoulos, Christopher, illus. 2014. (Ordinary People Change World Ser.). (ENG.). 40p. (J). (gr. k-3). 14.99 (978-0-8037-4083-9(2), Dial Bks) Penguin Publishing Group.

Micklos, John, Jr. The United States Civil War. 2016. (Primary Source History Ser.). (ENG., Illus.). 32p. (gr. 3-4). lib. bdg. 27.32 (978-1-4914-8489-0(6), Fact Finders) Capstone Press of Coughlan Cos.

Miller, Mirella S. 12 Questions about the Gettysburg Address. 2017. (Examining Primary Sources Ser.). (ENG., Illus.). 32p. (J). (gr. 3-6). 21.95 (978-1-63235-284-2(2)) Pr. Room Editions LLC.

Miller, Reagan & Claus, J. Matteson. Life on a Civil War Battlefield. 2011. (ENG.). 48p. (J). pap. (978-0-7787-5357-5(3)); lib. bdg. (978-0-7787-5340-7(9)) Crabtree Publishing Co.

Miller, Reagan & Cocca, Lisa Colozza. Reconstruction & the Aftermath of the Civil War. 2011. (ENG.). 48p. (J). pap. (978-0-7787-5358-2(1)); lib. bdg. (978-0-7787-5341-4(7)) Crabtree Publishing Co.

Miller, Reagan & Doak, Melissa J. Life on the Homefront During the Civil War. 2011. (ENG.). 48p. (J). pap. (978-0-7787-5361-2(1)); lib. bdg. (978-0-7787-5344-5(1)) Crabtree Publishing Co.

Miller, Reagan & Gould, Jane H. The Civil War Begins. 2011. (ENG.). 48p. (J). pap. (978-0-7787-5355-1(7)); lib. bdg. (978-0-7787-5338-4(7)) Crabtree Publishing Co.

Miller, Reagan & Putnam, Jeff. A Nation Divided: Causes of the Civil War. 2011. (ENG.). 48p. (J). pap. (978-0-7787-5354-4(9)); lib. bdg. (978-0-7787-5337-7(9)) Crabtree Publishing Co.

Morris, Rob & Marcello, Paul. The Civil War Close Up. 2015. (War Chronicles Ser.). (ENG., Illus.). 72p. (YA). (gr. 9-9). 32.95 (978-1-4994-6160-2(7), Rosen Young Adult) Rosen Publishing Group, Inc., The.

Moss, Marissa. Nurse, Soldier, Spy: The Story of Sarah Edmonds, a Civil War Hero. Hendrix, John, illus. (ENG.). 48p. (J). 2016. (gr. 1-4). pap. 9.95 (978-1-4197-2065-9(1)) 2011. (gr. 3-7). 19.95 (978-0-8109-9735-6(5)) Abrams, Inc. (Abrams Bks. for Young Readers).

Mountjoy, Shane. Causes of the Civil War: The Differences Between the North & South. McNeese, Tim, ed. 2009. (Civil War: A Nation Divided Ser.). (Illus.). 144p. (gr. 6-12). 35.00 (978-1-60413-036-2(9), Chelsea Hse.) Facts On File, Inc.

—Technology & the Civil War. McNeese, Tim, ed. 2009. (Civil War: A Nation Divided Ser.). 136p. (gr. 6-12). 35.00 (978-1-60413-037-9(7), Chelsea Hse.) Facts On File, Inc.

Murray, Stuart A. P. Mathew Brady: Photographer of Our Nation. 2009. (ENG., Illus.). 83p. (gr. 6-18). lib. bdg. 158.00 (978-0-7656-8151-5(X), Y182957) Routledge.

Nardo, Don. Bull Run to Gettysburg: Early Battles of the Civil War, 1 vol. 2010. (Civil War Ser.). (ENG.). 64p. (gr. 6-7). lib. bdg. 33.99 (978-0-7565-4368-6(1), CPB Grades 4-8) Compass Point Bks.

—The Civil War. (American History Ser.). 2009. pap. 24.10 (978-1-4205-0302-9(2)) 2008. (ENG., Illus.). 96-128p. (J). (gr. 7-10). 34.80 (978-1-4205-0065-3(1)) Cengage Gale. (Lucent Bks.).

Nelson, Sheila. Americans Divided: The Civil War. 2006. (How America Became America Ser.). (Illus.). 96p. (YA). lib. bdg. 22.95 (978-1-59084-908-8(6)) Mason Crest.

Nemeth, Jason D. Voices of the Civil War: Stories from the Battlefields, 1 vol. 2010. (Voices of War Ser.). (ENG., Illus.). 32p. (gr. 3-4). pap. 8.29 (978-1-4296-5625-2(5), Edge Bks.) Capstone Press of Coughlan Cos.

Newsome, Joel. Minority Soldiers Fighting in the Civil War. 2017. (J). **(978-1-5026-2662-2(4))** Cavendish Square Publishing.

Nextext, creator. The Civil War: 1860-1865. 2004. (Stories in History Ser.). (Illus.). 205p. (J). (gr. 3-7). 13.32 (978-0-618-14214-9(2), 2-00234) Holt McDougal.

O'Connell, Kim A. The Civil War: A MyReportLinks. Com Book. 2003. (U.S. Wars Ser.). (Illus.). 48p. (J). lib. bdg. 26.60 (978-0-7660-5130-0(7)) Enslow Pubs., Inc.

—Slavery, Emancipation, & the Civil War: A MyReportLinks. com Book. 2004. (American Civil War Ser.). (Illus.). 48p. (J). lib. bdg. 26.60 (978-0-7660-5190-4(0), MyReportLinks.com Bks.) Enslow Pubs., Inc.

Ohlin, Nancy. The Civil War. Larkum, Adam, illus. 2016. (Blast Back! Ser.). (ENG.). 112p. (J). (gr. 2-5). pap. 5.99 (978-1-4998-0120-0(3)) Little Bee Books Inc.

Ollhoff, Jim. The Civil War, 1 vol. 2011. (African American History Ser.). (ENG., Illus.). 32p. (YA). (gr. 5-9). lib. bdg. 27.07 (978-1-61714-710-4(9)) ABDO Publishing Co.

—The Civil War: Slavery, 1 vol. 2012. (Civil War Ser.). (ENG.). 32p. (YA). (gr. 5-9). 27.07 (978-1-61783-276-5(6)) ABDO Publishing Co.

—The Civil War: Weapons, 1 vol. 2012. (Civil War Ser.). (ENG.). 32p. (J). (gr. 5-9). 27.07 (978-1-61783-278-9(2)) ABDO Publishing Co.

Olson, Kay Melchisedech. The Terrible, Awful Civil War: The Disgusting Details about Life During America's. 2011. (Disgusting History Ser.). (ENG.). 32p. (gr. 3-4). pap. 47.70 (978-1-4296-6480-6(0), Fact Finders) Capstone Press of Coughlan Cos.

—The Terrible, Awful Civil War: The Disgusting Details about Life During America's Bloodiest War. (Disgusting History Ser.). (ENG.). 32p. (gr. 3-4). 2011. pap. 8.10 (978-1-4296-6349-6(9)) 2010. lib. bdg. 27.32 (978-1-4296-3960-6(1)) Capstone Press of Coughlan Cos. (Fact Finders).

Olson, Steve. Lincoln's Gettysburg Address: A Primary Source Investigation. 2009. 64p. (YA). (gr. 5-8). pap. 12.95 (978-1-4358-3275-6(2)) Rosen Publishing Group, Inc., The.

Olson, Steven P. Lincoln's Gettysburg Address: A Primary Source Investigation. 2009. (Great Historic Debates & Speeches Ser.). 64p. (gr. 5-8). 58.50 (978-1-61513-115-0(9)) Rosen Publishing Group, Inc., The.

O'Muhr, G. Causes & Effects of the American Civil War. 2009. (Real Life Readers Ser.). (ENG., Illus.). 32p. (J). (gr. 5-6). pap. 10.00 (978-1-4358-0203-2(9)); 32p. (gr. 5-5). 47.90 (978-1-61511-373-6(8)); (J). lib. bdg. 25.25 (978-1-4358-3013-4(X)) Rosen Publishing Group, Inc., The. (PowerKids Pr.).

Orr, Tamra. The Railroad & the Civil War (1860s) 2012. (J). lib. bdg. 29.95 (978-1-61228-289-3(X)) Mitchell Lane Pubs., Inc.

Otfinoski, Steven. The Civil War. 2017. (Step into History(tm) Ser.). (ENG., Illus.). 144p. (J). lib. bdg. 36.00 (978-0-531-22569-1(0), Children's Pr.) Scholastic Library Publishing.

Otfinoski, Steven, et al. The Civil War. 2015. (Civil War Ser.). (ENG.). 48p. (gr. 3-4). lib. bdg. 114.61 (978-1-4914-2434-6(6), Connect) Stone Arch Bks.

Page, Thomas Nelson. A Captured Santa Claus. reprint ed. pap. 28.00 (978-1-4047-4699-2(4)) Classic Textbooks.

—A Captured Santa Claus. 2013. (Notable American Authors Ser.). reprint ed. lthr. 79.00 (978-0-7812-4699-6(7)) Reprint Services Corp.

Parker, Christi E. Abraham Lincoln, 1 vol. 2005. (Primary Source Readers Ser.). (ENG.). 24p. (J). (gr. 4-4). pap. 8.99 (978-0-7439-8916-9(3)) Shell Educational Publishing.

—Civil War Is Coming, 1 vol. 2005. (Primary Source Readers Ser.). (ENG.). 24p. (J). (gr. 5-5). pap. 8.99 (978-0-7439-8915-2(5)) Shell Educational Publishing.

Perritano, John. The Ghosts of Civil War Soldiers. 2014. (Jr. Graphic Ghost Stories Ser.). 24p. (J). (gr. 3-6). lib. bdg. 26.25 (978-1-4777-7133-4(6), PowerKids Pr.) Rosen Publishing Group, Inc., The.

Peterson, Amanda. The U. S. Civil War: A Chronology of a Divided Nation. 2015. (Civil War Ser.). (ENG.). 48p. (gr. 3-4). lib. bdg. 29.32 (978-1-4914-2010-2(3)) Capstone Press of Coughlan Cos.

Phillips, Larissa. Women Civil War Spies of the Confederacy. 2004. (American Women at War Ser.). (Illus.). 112p. (gr. 7-12). lib. bdg. 34.60 (978-0-8239-4451-4(4)) Rosen Publishing Group, Inc., The.

Pingry, Patricia A. Meet Robert E. Lee. Johnson, Meredith, illus. 2004. (J). 9.95 (978-0-8249-5465-9(3), Ideal Pubns.) Worthy Publishing.

—The Story of Robert E. Lee. Johnson, Meredith, illus. 2004. (ENG.). 26p. (J). (gr. -1-k). bds. 6.95 (978-0-8249-6501-3(9), Ideal Pubns.) Worthy Publishing.

—The Story of the Star-Spangled Banner. Munger, Nancy, illus. 2014. (Story of Ser.). 24p. (J). bds. 6.99 (978-0-8249-1930-6(0), Ideal Pubns.) Worthy Publishing.

Pittman, Rickey E. Confederate Alphabet, 1 vol. Ford, Stephanie A., illus. 2011. (ENG.). 32p. (J). (gr. k-3). 16.99 (978-1-58980-760-0(X)) Pelican Publishing Co., Inc.

Poulakidas, Georgene. The Civil War. 2009. (Illus.). 24p. (J). (gr. 3-6). pap. 8.25 (978-1-4358-3276-3(0), PowerKids Pr.) Rosen Publishing Group, Inc., The.

Publishers, Chelsea House, creator. Leaders of the Civil War Era Set, 10-Volumes. 2009. (Leaders of the Civil War Era Ser.). (gr. 6-12). 350.00 (978-1-60413-643-2(X), Chelsea Hse.) Facts On File, Inc.

Randolph, Jennifer & Benchmark Education Co. Staff. Women of the Civil War. 2014. (Text Connections Ser.). (J). (gr. 5). (978-1-4900-1377-0(6)) Benchmark Education Co.

Ransom, Candice. Willie McLean & the Civil War Surrender. Reeves, Jeni, illus. 2004. (On My Own History Ser.). (ENG.). 48p. (gr. 2-4). 25.26 (978-1-57505-588-6(0)); pap. 6.95 (978-1-57505-698-2(4)) Lerner Publishing Group.

Rappaport, Doreen & Verniero, Joan C. United No More! Stories of the Civil War. Reeves, Rick, illus. 2006. 144p. (J). (gr. 3-7). lib. bdg. 17.89 (978-0-06-050600-1(8)) HarperCollins Pubs.

Ratliff, Thomas. You Wouldn't Want to Be a Civil War Soldier! A War You'd Rather Not Fight. Antram, David, illus. 2013. (You Wouldn't Want to... Ser.). (ENG.). (J). 32p. 29.00 (978-0-531-25947-4(1)); 40p. pap. 9.95 (978-0-531-24503-3(9)) Scholastic Library Publishing. (Watts, Franklin).

Rees, Bob. The Civil War, 1 vol. 2012. (Living Through... Ser.). (ENG.). 80p. (gr. 7-8). lib. bdg. 37.32 (978-1-4329-5996-8(4)) Heinemann-Raintree.

Rice, Earle. The Life & Times of the Brothers Custer: Galloping to Glory. 2008. (Profiles in American History Ser.). (Illus.). 48p. (J). (gr. 4-8). lib. bdg. 29.95 (978-1-58415-665-9(1)) Mitchell Lane Pubs., Inc.

Rife, Douglas M. & Capaldi, Gina. Letters for Freedom: the Civil War. Lyall, Dennis, illus. 2011. (ENG.). 44p. (J). (gr. 3-17). 19.99 (978-1-60169-018-0(5)) Innovative Kids.

Rivera, Sheila. Gettysburg Address, 1 vol. 2004. (American Moments Ser.). (ENG., Illus.). 48p. (gr. 4-8). 27.07 (978-1-59197-285-3(X), Abdo & Daughters) ABDO Publishing Co.

Roche, Tim. Soldiers of the Civil War, 1 vol. (Why We Fought: the Civil War Ser.). (ENG.). 48p. (gr. 3-6). 2011. pap. 9.95 (978-1-4329-3920-5(3)) 2010. 33.32 (978-1-4329-3914-4(9)) Heinemann-Raintree. (Heinemann InfoSearch).

Rodgers, Kelly. Civil War & Reconstruction in Florida. 2016. (Primary Source Readers Ser.). 32p. (J). (gr. 4-4). pap. 8.99 (978-1-4938-3539-3(4)) Teacher Created Materials, Inc.

Rogers, Amy B. Recipes of the Civil War. 2017. (Cooking Your Way Through American History Ser.). 24p. (J). (gr. 3-3). pap. 10.60 (978-1-5345-2088-2(0), KidHaven Publishing) Greenhaven Publishing LLC.

Rose, Simon. Civil War. 2014. (Illus.). 48p. (J). (978-1-4896-1554-1(7)) Weigl Pubs., Inc.

—The War of 1812. 2014. (Illus.). 48p. (J). (978-1-4896-0516-0(9)) Weigl Pubs., Inc.

Roxburgh, Ellis. Abraham Lincoln vs. Jefferson Davis: Presidents of a Divided Nation. 2016. (History's Greatest Rivals Ser.). (ENG., Illus.). 48p. (J). (gr. 6-8). pap. 14.05 (978-1-4824-4219-9(1)) Stevens, Gareth Publishing LLLP.

—Ulysses S. Grant vs. Robert E. Lee: Civil War Rivals. 2015. (History's Greatest Rivals Ser.). (ENG.). 48p. (J). (gr. 6-8). lib. bdg. 31.95 (978-1-4824-2225-2(5)) Stevens, Gareth Publishing LLLP.

Ruffin, Frances E. Clara Barton. 2009. (American Legends Ser.). 24p. (gr. 3-3). 42.50 (978-1-61511-379-8(7), PowerKids Pr.) Rosen Publishing Group, Inc., The.

Sakany, Lois. Women Civil War Spies of the Union. 2004. (American Women at War Ser.). (Illus.). 112p. (gr. 7-12). lib. bdg. 34.60 (978-0-8239-4450-7(6)) Rosen Publishing Group, Inc., The.

Samuels, Charlie. The Attack on Fort Sumter, Vol. 1. 2014. (Turning Points in US Military History Ser.). (ENG.). 48p. (J). (gr. 5-6). 31.95 (978-1-4824-0401-2(X)) Stevens, Gareth Publishing LLLP.

Samuels, Charlie & George, Enzo. The Civil War: The War Between Brothers. 2014. (Voices of War Ser.). 48p. (J). (gr. 4-6). lib. bdg. 31.36 (978-1-62712-858-2(1)) Cavendish Square Publishing.

Sandler, Martin W. Civil War. 2014. (Library of Congress Classics). (ENG., Illus.). 96p. (J). (gr. 3-18). pap. 12.99 (978-0-06-446264-8(1)) HarperCollins Pubs.

—What Was America's Deadliest War? And Other Questions about the Civil War. Hunt, Robert, illus. 2014. (Good Question! Ser.). (ENG.). 32p. (J). pap. 5.95 (978-1-4027-9046-1(5)) Sterling Publishing Co., Inc.

Scholastic Library Publishing. A True Book-the Civil War. 2011. (True Book-the Civil War Ser.). (J). 116.00 (978-0-531-24922-2(0), Children's Pr.) Scholastic Library Publishing.

Schroeder-Lein, Glenna R. The Encyclopedia of Civil War Medicine. 2008. (ENG., Illus.). 457p. (C). 158.00 (978-0-7656-1171-0(6), Y184328) Routledge.

Schwartz, Heather E. Causes of the Civil War: A House Divided. 2017. (Primary Source Readers Ser.). (Illus.). 32p. (J). (gr. 4-5). pap. 8.99 (978-1-4938-3803-5(2)) Teacher Created Materials, Inc.

Seabrook, Lochlainn. Honest Jeff & Dishonest Abe: A Southern Children's Guide to the Civil War. 2012. 318p. pap. 24.95 (978-0-9838185-9-5(2)) Sea Raven Pr.

—The Quotable Nathan Bedford Forrest: Selections from the Writings & Speeches of the Confederacy's Most Brilliant Cavalryman. 2012. (Illus.). 130p. pap. 12.95 (978-0-9838185-5-7(X)) Sea Raven Pr.

Senior, Kathryn. You Wouldn't Want to Be a Nurse During the American Civil War! A Job That's Not for the Squeamish. 2010. (You Wouldn't Want to... Ser.). 32p. (J). 29.00 (978-0-531-20506-8(1)); (ENG., Illus.). (gr. 3-18). pap. 9.95 (978-0-531-13786-4(4)) Scholastic Library Publishing. (Watts, Franklin).

Shattuck, Jason. The Civil War, 01 vols., 1. 2016. (Early American History Ser.). (ENG., Illus.). 80p. (J). 32.90 (978-1-68048-272-0(6), Britannica Educational Publishing) Rosen Publishing Group, Inc., The.

Shea, Therese. Interpreting America's Civil War: Organizing & Interpreting Information in Outlines, Graphs, Timelines, Maps, & Charts. (Critical Thinking in American History Ser.). 48p. 2009. (gr. 5-8). 53.00 (978-1-61512-094-9(7), Rosen Reference) 2005. (Illus.). (J). (gr. k-3). lib. bdg. 26.50 (978-1-4042-0415-7(6)) Rosen Publishing Group, Inc., The.

Sheffield, Sarah. Life During the American Civil War. 2009. (Reading Room Collection 2 Ser.). 24p. (gr. 3-4). 42.50 (978-1-60851-978-1(3), PowerKids Pr.) Rosen Publishing Group, Inc., The.

Shoup, Kate. Life As a Soldier in the Civil War. 2016. (Life As... Ser.). (ENG., Illus.). 32p. (J). (gr. 3-3). pap. 10.58 (978-1-5026-1083-6(3)) Cavendish Square Publishing.

Silvey, Anita. I'll Pass for Your Comrade: Women Soldiers in the Civil War. 2008. (ENG., Illus.). 128p. (J). (gr. 5-7). 19.99 (978-0-618-57491-9(3)) Houghton Mifflin Harcourt Publishing Co.

Smith, Debra. Young Heroes of the Confederacy, 1 vol. 2012. (ENG., Illus.). 128p. (J). (gr. 3-7). pap. 12.95 (978-1-4556-1684-8(2)) Pelican Publishing Co., Inc.

Sodaro, Craig. Civil War Spies, 1 vol. 2013. (Classified Ser.). 48p. (ENG.). (gr. 3-4). 31.99 (978-1-4296-9976-1(0)); pap. 9.95 (978-1-4765-3590-6(6)) Capstone Press of Coughlan Cos.

Stanley, George Edward. The Crisis of the Union (1815-1865) 2005. (Primary Source History of the United States Ser.). (Illus.). 48p. (gr. 5-12). pap. 14.05 (978-0-8368-5835-8(2)); lib. bdg. 31.00 (978-0-8368-5826-6(3)) Stevens, Gareth Publishing LLLP. (Gareth Stevens Secondary Library).

Steele, Philip. Did Anything Good Come Out of the Civil War?, 01 vols., 1. 2016. (Innovation Through Adversity Ser.). (ENG.). 48p. (J). 30.25 (978-1-5081-7074-7(6), Rosen Young Adult) Rosen Publishing Group, Inc., The.

Stewart, Whitney. Mr. Lincoln's Gift: A Civil War Story. Dunham Akiyama, Laine, illus. 2008. 32p. (J). 19.95 (978-0-9754917-4-4(1)) Friends of Hildene, Inc.

Stille, Darlene R. The Civil War Through Photography, 1 vol. 2012. (Documenting U. S. History Ser.). (ENG.). 48p. (gr. 3-6). pap. 9.95 (978-1-4329-6764-2(9)); lib. bdg. 32.65 (978-1-4329-6755-0(X)) Heinemann-Raintree. (NA-h).

Stotts, Stuart. Lucius Fairchild: Civil War Hero. 2011. (Badger Biographies Ser.). (ENG., Illus.). 112p. (J). pap. 12.95 (978-0-87020-460-9(2)) Wisconsin Historical Society.

Suen, Anastasia. From Accident to Hospital. 2015. (ENG.). 24p. (gr. k-2). 28.50 (978-1-63430-058-2(0)) Rourke Educational Media.

Sutherland, Jonathan. Civil War Victory & the Costly Aftermath. 2017. (Civil War Ser.: Vol. 5). (ENG.). (YA). (gr. 7-12). 24.95 **(978-1-4222-3886-8(5))** Mason Crest.

—The Origins of the Civil War. 2017. (Civil War Ser.: Vol. 5). (ENG.). (YA). (gr. 7-12). 24.95 **(978-1-4222-3882-0(2))** Mason Crest.

—The Politics of the Civil War. 2017. (Civil War Ser.: Vol. 5). (ENG.). (YA). (gr. 7-12). 24.95 **(978-1-4222-3885-1(7))** Mason Crest.

—Slavery & the Abolition Movement. 2017. (Civil War Ser.: Vol. 5). (ENG.). (YA). (gr. 7-12). 24.95 **(978-1-4222-3883-7(0))** Mason Crest.

Thompson, Ben. The American Civil War. Butzer, C. M., illus. 2015. (Guts & Glory Ser.: 1). (ENG.). 352p. (J). (gr. 3-7). pap. 7.99 (978-0-316-32051-1(X)) Little, Brown Bks. for Young Readers.

Trumbauer, Lisa. Abraham Lincoln & the Civil War. 2016. (Life in the Time Of Ser.). (ENG.). 32p. pap. 8.29 (978-1-4846-3822-4(0), Heinemann First Library) Heinemann-Raintree.

Uschan, Michael V. Fort Sumter: The Civil War Begins. 2004. (Landmark Events in American History Ser.). (Illus.). 48p. (gr. 5-12). pap. 14.05 (978-0-8368-5423-7(3), Gareth Stevens Secondary Library) Stevens, Gareth Publishing LLLP.

Van Steenwyk, Elizabeth. How Kate Warne Saved President Lincoln. Belloni, Valentina, illus. 2016. (ENG.). 32p. (J). (gr. -1-3). 16.99 (978-0-8075-4117-3(6)) Whitman, Albert & Co.

Vierow, Wendy. The Assault on Fort Wagner: Black Union Soldiers Make a Stand in South Carolina Battle. (Headlines from History Ser.). 24p. 2009. (gr. 3-3). 42.50 (978-1-61513-240-9(6), PowerKids Pr.) 2004. (Illus.). (YA). (gr. 2-5). lib. bdg. 22.60 (978-0-8239-6223-5(7)) Rosen Publishing Group, Inc., The.

—Shots Fired at Fort Sumter. 2004. (Headlines from History Ser.). (Illus.). 24p. (J). lib. bdg. 22.60 (978-0-8239-6220-4(2)) Rosen Publishing Group, Inc., The.

—Shots Fired at Fort Sumter: Civil War Breaks Out! 2009. (Headlines from History Ser.). 24p. (gr. 3-3). 42.50 (978-1-61513-238-6(4), PowerKids Pr.) Rosen Publishing Group, Inc., The.

Vonne, Mira. Gross Facts about the American Civil War. 2017. (Gross History Ser.). (ENG., Illus.). 32p. (gr. 1-2). lib. bdg. 26.65 (978-1-5157-4155-8(9)) Capstone Press of Coughlan Cos.

Wagner, Heather Lehr. The Outbreak of the Civil War. 2008. (Milestones in American History Ser.). (Illus.). 112p. (YA). (gr. 7-12). 35.00 (978-1-60413-053-9(9)) Facts On File, Inc.

Walker, Sally M. Shipwreck Search: Discovery of the H. L. Hunley. Verstraete, Elaine, illus. 2007. (On My Own Science Ser.). (ENG.). 48p. (gr. 2-4). per. 6.95 (978-0-8225-6449-2(1), First Avenue Editions) Lerner Publishing Group.

Warren, Andrea. Under Siege! Three Children at the Civil War Battle for Vicksburg. 2009. (ENG., Illus.). 176p. (YA). (gr. 4-8). 21.95 (978-0-374-31255-8(9), 9780374312558, Farrar, Straus & Giroux (BYR)) Farrar, Straus & Giroux.

Waryncia, Lou. Abraham Lincoln: Defender of the Union. Hale, Sarah Elder, ed. 2005. (ENG., Illus.). 48p. (J). (gr. 3-9). 17.95 (978-0-8126-7902-1(4)) Cobblestone Publishing Co.

—Nation at War: Soldiers, Saints, & Spies. Hale, Sarah Elder, ed. 2005. (ENG., Illus.). 48p. (J). (gr. 3-9). 17.95 (978-0-8126-7900-7(8)) Cobblestone Publishing Co.

—Young Heroes of the North & South. Hale, Sarah Elder, ed. 2005. (ENG., Illus.). 48p. (J). (gr. 3-9). 17.95 (978-0-8126-7901-4(6)) Cobblestone Publishing Co.

We the People: Civil War Era. 2011. (We the People: Civil War Era Ser.). (ENG.). 48p. (gr. 5-6). pap. 477.00 (978-0-7565-4539-0(0)); pap. 79.50 (978-0-7565-4538-3(2)) Compass Point Bks. (We the People).

Westwell, Ian. The Civil War. 2008. (Wars Day by Day Ser.). 48p. (gr. 5-9). 37.10 (978-1-933834-38-2(2)) Brown Bear Bks.

Whitman Publishing, creator. Discover the Civil War: History Project Toolkit. 2011. pap. 19.95 (978-0-7948-3587-3(2)) Whitman Publishing LLC.

Wilson, Camilla. Civil War Spies: Behind Enemy Lines. 2010. vii, 104p. (J). pap. (978-0-545-13002-8(6)) Scholastic, Inc.

Windsor, Wesley. The Civil War: America Torn Apart, 1860-1865. 2012. (J). pap. (978-1-4222-2418-2(X)) Mason Crest.

—The Civil War: America Torn Apart, 1860-1865. Rakove, Jack N., ed. 2012. (How America Became America Ser.). 48p. (J). (gr. 3-4). 19.95 (978-1-4222-2404-5(X)) Mason Crest.

Wood, Ira. Fort Sumter: Where the Civil War Began. (Reading Room Collection 1 Ser.). 16p. 2009. (gr. 2-3). 37.50 (978-1-60851-944-6(9)) 2006. (Illus.). (J). (gr. 3-7). lib. bdg. 17.25 (978-1-4042-3349-2(0)) Rosen Publishing Group, Inc., The. (PowerKids Pr.).

Woog, Adam. The Emancipation Proclamation: Ending Slavery in America. 2009. (Milestones in American History Ser.). (Illus.). 128p. (gr. 6-12). 35.00 (978-1-60413-307-3(4), Chelsea Hse.) Facts On File, Inc.

World Book, Inc. Staff. Documenting History, 12 vols., Set. 2010. 768p. (YA). 329.00 (978-0-7166-1498-2(7)) World Bk., Inc.

UNITED STATES—HISTORY—CIVIL WAR, 1861-1865—BIOGRAPHY

Anderson, Paul C. George Armstrong Custer: The Indian Wars & the Battle of the Little Bighorn. 2009. (Library of American Lives & Times Ser.). 112p. (gr. 5-5). 69.20 (978-1-60853-483-8(9)) Rosen Publishing Group, Inc., The.

Bailey, Diane. General George Thomas: The Rock of Chickamauga. 2011. (J). (978-1-59556-045-2(9)); pap. (978-1-59556-051-3(3)) OTTN Publishing.

Capstone Press. Voices of War. 2010. (Voices of War Ser.). (ENG.). 32p. lib. bdg. 106.60 (978-1-4296-5905-5(X), Edge Bks.) Capstone Press of Coughlan Cos.

Conklin, Wendy. Civil War Leaders, 1 vol. 2005. (Primary Source Readers Ser.). (ENG.). 24p. (J). (gr. 5-5). pap. 8.99 (978-0-7439-8917-6(1)) Shell Educational Publishing.

—Civil War Leaders. 2017. (Primary Source Readers Ser.). 32p. (J). (gr. 4-5). pap. 8.99 (978-1-4938-3887-5(3)) Teacher Created Materials, Inc.

Cooke, Tim. Key Figures. 2012. (American Civil War: the Right Answer Ser.). (Illus.). 48p. (J). (gr. 6-8). 31.95 (978-1-4339-7547-9(5)); pap. 14.05 (978-1-4339-7548-6(3)) Stevens, Gareth Publishing LLLP. (Gareth Stevens Secondary Library).

Cooke, Tim, ed. People. 2011. (CC: Civil War Ser.). 112p. (gr. 6-12). 42.80 (978-1-936333-47-9(3)) Brown Bear Bks.

Corrigan, Jim. General George G. Meade: Victor at Gettysburg. 2011. (J). (978-1-59556-044-5(0)); pap. (978-1-59556-050-6(5)) OTTN Publishing.

—General James Longstreet: Lee's "Old War Horse" 2012. (J). (978-1-59556-043-8(2)); pap. (978-1-59556-049-0(1)) OTTN Publishing.

Dell, Pamela. Memoir of Susie King Taylor: A Civil War Nurse. 2017. (First-Person Histories Ser.). (ENG.). 32p. (gr. 3-4). pap. 8.95 (978-1-5157-3356-0(4)); (Illus.). lib. bdg. 27.32 (978-1-5157-3354-6(8)) Capstone Press of Coughlan Cos. (Fact Finders).

Dougherty, Terri. Admiral David Farragut: "Full Speed Ahead!" 2011. (J). (978-1-59556-041-4(6)); pap. (978-1-59556-047-6(5)) OTTN Publishing.

Favor, Lesli J. Women Doctors & Nurses of the Civil War. 2009. (American Women at War Ser.). 112p. (gr. 8-8). 63.90 (978-1-61511-404-7(1)) Rosen Publishing Group, Inc., The.

Favor, Leslie. Women Doctors & Nurses of the Civil War. 2009. 112p. (YA). (gr. 7-12). pap. 12.95 (978-1-4358-3273-2(6)) Rosen Publishing Group, Inc., The.

Fiore, Carmen Anthony. Young Heroes of the Civil War. 2006. (J). pap. (978-0-88092-639-3(2)); lib. bdg. (978-0-88092-638-6(4)) Royal Fireworks Publishing Co.

Friedman, Robin. The Silent Witness: A True Story of the Civil War. Nivola, Claire A., illus. 2008. (ENG.). 32p. (J). (gr. -1-3). pap. 7.99 (978-0-547-01436-4(8)) Houghton Mifflin Harcourt Publishing Co.

Giovanni, Nikki. Rosa Storytime Set, 1 vol. Collier, Bryan, illus. unabr. ed. 2014. (ENG.). 40p. (J). (gr. -1-3). 12.99 (978-1-4272-4397-3(2), 9781427243973) Macmillan Audio.

Haines, J. D. Put the Boys In: The Story of the Virginia Military Institute Cadets at the Battle of New Market. 2003. (Illus.). 69p. per. (978-1-57168-816-3(1)) Eakin Pr.

Haskins, James, et al. Black Stars of Civil War Times. 2003. (Black Stars Ser.: 2). (ENG., Illus.). 132p. (J). (gr. 5-9). pap. 12.95 (978-0-471-22069-5(8), Wiley) Wiley, John & Sons, Inc.

Hughes, Christopher. The Civil War. 2003. (People at the Center of Ser.). (Illus.). 48p. (J). 24.95 (978-1-56711-764-6(3), Blackbirch Pr., Inc.) Cengage Gale.

Kolpin, Molly. Great Women of the Civil War, 1 vol. 2014. (Story of the Civil War Ser.). (ENG.). 32p. (gr. 3-4). lib. bdg. 27.32 (978-1-4914-0719-6(0)) Capstone Press of Coughlan Cos.

Lakin, Patricia. Clara Barton: Spirit of the American Red Cross. Sullivan, Simon, illus. 2004. (Ready-To-read SOFA Ser.). (ENG.). 48p. (J). (gr. 1-3). pap. 3.99 (978-0-689-86513-8(9), Simon Spotlight) Simon Spotlight.

Link, Theodore. George Armstrong Custer: General de la caballeria Estadounidense. 2004. (Grandes personajes en la historia de los Estados Unidos Ser.). (SPA.). 32p. (gr. 3-6). pap. 10.00 (978-0-8239-4228-2(7), Rosen Classroom) Rosen Publishing Group, Inc., The.

—George Armstrong Custer: General of the U. S. Cavalry. 2009. (Primary Sources of Famous People in American History Ser.).Tr. of George Armstrong Custer: General de la Caballeria Estadounidense. 32p. (gr. 2-3). 47.90 (978-1-60851-680-3(6)) Rosen Publishing Group, Inc., The.

McManus, Lori. Key People of the Civil War, 1 vol. (Why We Fought: the Civil War Ser.). (ENG.). 48p. (gr. 3-6). 2011. pap. 9.95 (978-1-4329-3919-9(X)) 2010. 33.32 (978-1-4329-3913-7(0)) Heinemann-Raintree. (Heinemann InfoSearch).

Miller, Reagan & Arthur, Martin. Great Leaders of the Civil War. 2011. (ENG.). 48p. (J). pap. (978-0-7787-5359-9(X)); lib. bdg. (978-0-7787-5342-1(5)) Crabtree Publishing Co.

Nemeth, Jason D. Voices of the Civil War. 2010. (Voices of War Ser.). (ENG.). 32p. (gr. 3-4). pap. 47.70 (978-1-4296-5700-6(6), Edge Bks.) Capstone Press of Coughlan Cos.

—Voices of the Civil War: Stories from the Battlefields, 1 vol. 2010. (Voices of War Ser.). (ENG.). 32p. (gr. 3-4). lib. bdg. 27.99 (978-1-4296-4736-6(1), Edge Bks.) Capstone Press of Coughlan Cos.

Nichols, Joan Kane. Civil War Heroines. 2005. (ENG., Illus.). 16p. (J). (gr. 5-5). pap. 7.47 net. (978-0-328-14901-8(2), Scott Foresman) Pearson Schl.

—The Civil War Sisterhood: Women Who Made a Difference. 2005. (ENG., Illus.). 16p. (J). (gr. 5-5). pap. 7.47 net. (978-0-328-14902-5(0), Scott Foresman) Pearson Schl.

—Women of the Civil War. 2005. (ENG., Illus.). 16p. (J). (gr. 5-5). pap. 7.47 net. (978-0-328-14900-1(4), Scott Foresman) Pearson Schl.

Otfinoski, Steven. Yankees & Rebels: Stories of U.S. Civil War Leaders. 2015. (Civil War Ser.). (ENG.). 48p. (gr. 3-4). lib. bdg. 29.32 (978-1-4914-2008-9(1)) Capstone Press of Coughlan Cos.

Phillips, Larissa. Women Civil War Spies of the Confederacy. (American Women at War Ser.). 112p. 2009. (gr. 8-8). 63.90 (978-1-61511-402-3(5)) 2004. (Illus.). (gr. 7-12). lib. bdg. 34.60 (978-0-8239-4451-4(4)) Rosen Publishing Group, Inc., The.

Raum, Elizabeth, et al. Stories of War. 2012. (Stories of War Ser.). (ENG.). 32p. (gr. 3-4). lib. bdg. 122.60 (978-1-4296-9164-2(6), Graphic Library) Capstone Press of Coughlan Cos.

Rice, Dona Herwick & Housel, Debra. Civil War Hero of Marye's Heights, 1 vol. 2009. (Building Fluency Through Reader's Theater Ser.). (ENG., Illus.). 32p. (J). (gr. 3-5). pap. 7.99 (978-1-4333-0546-7(1)) Teacher Created Materials, Inc.

Roppelt, Donna J. & DeAngelis, Therese. General A.P. Hill: Light Division Leader. 2011. (J). (978-1-59556-042-1(4)); pap. (978-1-59556-048-3(3)) OTTN Publishing.

Sakany, Lois. Women Civil War Spies of the Union. (American Women at War Ser.). 112p. 2009. (gr. 8-8). 63.90 (978-1-61511-403-0(3)) 2004. (Illus.). (gr. 7-12). lib. bdg. 34.60 (978-0-8239-4450-7(6)) Rosen Publishing Group, Inc., The.

Sterngass, Jon. Frederick Douglass. 2009. (Leaders of the Civil War Era Ser.). (Illus.). 160p. (gr. 6-12). 35.00 (978-1-60413-306-6(6), Chelsea Hse.) Facts On File, Inc.

Voices of War, 1 vol. 2010. (Voices of War Ser.). (ENG.). 32p. (gr. 3-4). lib. bdg. 83.97 (978-1-4296-4740-3(X), Edge Bks.) Capstone Press of Coughlan Cos.

Waryncia, Lou. Nation at War: Soldiers, Saints, & Spies. Hale, Sarah Elder, ed. 2005. (ENG., Illus.). 48p. (J). (gr. 3-9). 17.95 (978-0-8126-7900-7(8)) Cobblestone Publishing Co.

—Young Heroes of the North & South. Hale, Sarah Elder, ed. 2005. (ENG., Illus.). 48p. (J). (gr. 3-9). 17.95 (978-0-8126-7901-4(6)) Cobblestone Publishing Co.

Wittman, Susan S. Heroes of the Civil War, 1 vol. 2014. (Story of the Civil War Ser.). (ENG.). 32p. (gr. 3-4). lib. bdg. 27.32 (978-1-4914-0720-2(4)) Capstone Press of Coughlan Cos.

A Woman Officer in the Confederate Army. (J). pap. 9.95 (978-0-88388-211-5(6)) Bellerophon Bks.

Yomtov, Nel. True Stories of the Civil War. Molinari, Carlo, illus. 2012. (Stories of War Ser.). (ENG.). 32p. (gr. 3-4). pap. 47.70 (978-1-4296-9341-7(X), Graphic Library) Capstone Press of Coughlan Cos.

Yomtov, Nel, et al. Stories of War. 2012. (Stories of War Ser.). (ENG.). 32p. (gr. 3-4). pap. 31.80 (978-1-4296-9348-6(7)); pap. 190.80 (978-1-4296-9349-3(5)) Capstone Press of Coughlan Cos. (Graphic Library).

Yomtov, Nelson. True Stories of the Civil War, 1 vol. Molinari, Carlo, illus. 2012. (Stories of War Ser.). (ENG.). 32p. (gr. 3-4). pap. 8.10 (978-1-4296-9340-0(1)); lib. bdg. 30.65 (978-1-4296-8624-2(3)) Capstone Press of Coughlan Cos. (Graphic Library).

UNITED STATES—HISTORY—CIVIL WAR, 1861-1865—CAMPAIGNS

see also Bull Run, 1st Battle of, Va., 1861; Gettysburg, Battle of, Gettysburg, Pa., 1863; Sherman's March to the Sea; Vicksburg (Miss.)—History—Siege, 1863

Abnett, Dan. The Battle of the Wilderness: Deadly Inferno. (Graphic Civil War Battles Ser.). (ENG.). 48p. 2009. (YA). (gr.

4-5). 58.50 *(978-1-61512-901-0(4)*, Rosen Reference) 2007. (Illus.). (gr. 5-8). pap. 14.05 *(978-1-4042-6479-3(5)*, Rosen Classroom) Rosen Publishing Group, Inc., The.

—The Battle of the Wilderness: Deadly Inferno. Verma, Dheeraj, illus. 2007. (Graphic Battles of the Civil War Ser.). (ENG.). 48p. (YA). (gr. 4-7). lib. bdg. 31.95 *(978-1-4042-0780-6(5))* Rosen Publishing Group, Inc., The.

Anderson, Dale. The Civil War in the East (1861-July 1863) 2004. (World Almanac Library of the Civil War). (Illus.). 48p. (gr. 5-12). pap. 14.05 *(978-0-8368-5591-3(4))*; lib. bdg. 31.00 *(978-0-8368-5582-1(5))* Stevens, Gareth Publishing LLLP. (Gareth Stevens Secondary Library).

—The Union Victory (July 1863-1865) 2004. (World Almanac Library of the Civil War). (Illus.). 48p. (gr. 5-12). pap. 14.05 *(978-0-8368-5593-7(0))*; lib. bdg. 31.00 *(978-0-8368-5584-5(1))* Stevens, Gareth Publishing LLLP. (Gareth Stevens Secondary Library).

Anderson, Paul Christopher. Robert E. Lee: Legendary Commander of the Confederacy. (Library of American Lives & Times Ser.). 112p. 2009. (gr. 5-5). 69.20 *(978-1-60853-501-9(0))* 2005. (Illus.). (YA). (gr. 4-8). lib. bdg. 34.60 *(978-0-8239-5748-4(9))* Rosen Publishing Group, Inc., The.

Bailey, Diane. General George Thomas: The Rock of Chickamauga. 2011. (J). *(978-1-59556-045-2(9))*; pap. *(978-1-59556-051-3(3))* OTTN Publishing.

Brager, Bruce L. There He Stands: The Story of Stonewall Jackson. 2005. (Civil War Leaders Ser.). (Illus.). 176p. (J). (gr. 6-12). 26.95 *(978-1-931798-44-0(3))* Reynolds, Morgan Inc.

Collins, Terry. Robert E. Lee: The Story of the Great Confederate General. Mallea, Cristian, illus. (American Graphic Ser.). (ENG.). 32p. (gr. 3-4). 2011. pap. 47.70 *(978-1-4296-6436-3(3))* 2010. lib. bdg. 30.65 *(978-1-4296-5475-3(9))* Capstone Press of Coughlan Cos. (Graphic Library).

Cooke, Tim. The Confederacy on the Advance: 1861-1862. 2012. (Civil War Highlights Ser.). (Illus.). 48p. (gr. 5-12). lib. bdg. 37.10 *(978-1-59920-814-5(8))* Black Rabbit Bks.

—Triumph of the Union: 1864-1865. 2012. (Civil War Highlights Ser.). (Illus.). 48p. (gr. 5-12). 37.10 *(978-1-59920-816-9(4))* Black Rabbit Bks.

—The Turning Point, 1863. 2012. (Civil War Highlights Ser.). (Illus.). 48p. (gr. 5-12). 37.10 *(978-1-59920-815-2(6))* Black Rabbit Bks.

Cooke, Tim, ed. Battles & Campaigns. 2011. (CC: Civil War Ser.). 112p. (gr. 6-12). lib. bdg. 42.80 *(978-1-936333-43-1(0))* Brown Bear Bks.

Corrigan, Jim. Civil War in the West. 2004. (History of the Old West Ser.). (Illus.). 64p. (YA). (gr. 5-18). lib. bdg. 19.95 *(978-1-59084-067-2(4))* Mason Crest.

—General George G. Meade: Victor at Gettysburg. 2011. (J). *(978-1-59556-044-5(0))*; pap. *(978-1-59556-050-6(5))* OTTN Publishing.

Dupuy, Trevor Nevitt. The Military History of Civil War Land Battles. Fisher, Leonard Everett, illus. 2011. 98p. 38.95 *(978-1-258-07607-8(1))*; 38.95 *(978-1-258-01405-6(X))* Literary Licensing, LLC.

Engle, Stephen Douglas. The Civil War: The Siege of Vicksburg & Other Western Battles, 1861-July 1863. O'Neill, Robert, ed. 2010. (Civil War: Essential Histories Ser.). (ENG.). 96p. (YA). lib. bdg. 33.25 *(978-1-4488-0390-3(X))* Rosen Publishing Group, Inc., The.

Fay, Gail. Battles of the Civil War, 1 vol. (Why We Fought: the Civil War Ser.). (ENG.). 48p. (gr. 3-6). 2011. pap. 9.95 *(978-1-4329-3916-8(5))* 2010. 33.32 *(978-1-4329-3910-6(6))* Heinemann-Raintree. (Heinemann InfoSearch).

Ford, Carin T. The Battle of Gettysburg & Lincoln's Gettysburg Address. 2004. (Civil War Library). (Illus.). 48p. (J). lib. bdg. 25.27 *(978-0-7660-2253-9(6))* Enslow Pubs., Inc.

Hale, Sarah Elder, ed. Stonewall Jackson: Spirit of the South. 2005. (ENG., Illus.). 48p. (J). (gr. 3-9). 17.95 *(978-0-8126-7907-6(5))* Cobblestone Publishing Co.

Hama, Larry. The Battle of First Bull Run: The Civil War Begins. 2009. (Graphic Civil War Battles Ser.). (ENG.). 48p. (YA). (gr. 4-5). 58.50 *(978-1-61512-898-3(0)*, Rosen Reference) Rosen Publishing Group, Inc., The.

Koestler-Grack, Rachel A. Stonewall Jackson. 2009. (Leaders of the Civil War Era Ser.). (Illus.). 136p. (gr. 6-12). 35.00 *(978-1-60413-299-1(X)*, Chelsea Hse.) Facts On File, Inc.

—William Tecumseh Sherman. 2009. (Leaders of the Civil War Era Ser.). (Illus.). 149p. (gr. 6-12). 35.00 *(978-1-60413-300-4(7)*, Chelsea Hse.) Facts On File, Inc.

Kolpin, Molly. The Biggest Battles of the Civil War, 1 vol. 2014. (Story of the Civil War Ser.). (ENG.). 32p. (gr. 3-4). lib. bdg. 27.32 *(978-1-4914-0718-9(2))* Capstone Press of Coughlan Cos.

Krick, Robert K. The Civil War: Gettysburg & Other Eastern Battles, 1863-1865. 2010. (Civil War: Essential Histories Ser.). (ENG.). 96p. (YA). lib. bdg. 33.25 *(978-1-4488-0388-0(8))* Rosen Publishing Group, Inc., The.

Landau, Elaine. The Battle of Gettysburg: Would You Lead the Fight? 2010. (What Would You Do? Ser.). (Illus.). 48p. (J). pap. 8.95 *(978-1-59845-192-4(8)*, Enslow Elementary) Enslow Pubs., Inc.

—The Great Battle of Gettysburg: Would You Stand & Fight? 2015. (What Would You Do? Ser.). 48p. (J). (gr. 3-4). 25.27 *(978-0-7660-6295-5(3))*; pap. 8.95 *(978-0-7660-6296-2(1)*, Enslow Elementary) Enslow Pubs., Inc.

Lieurance, Suzanne. Weapons & Strategies of the Civil War: A MyReportLinks. com Book. 2004. (American Civil War Ser.). (Illus.). 48p. (J). lib. bdg. 25.26 *(978-0-7660-5185-0(4)*, MyReportLinks.com Bks.) Enslow Pubs., Inc.

Marrin, Albert. Virginia's General: Robert E. Lee & the Civil War. 2003. (Illus.). 201p. (YA). pap. 14.95 *(978-1-893103-14-6(5))* Beautiful Feet Bks.

McLeese, Don. Stonewall Jackson. 2005. (Civil War Military Leaders Ser.). (Illus.). 32p. (J). (gr. 3-6). lib. bdg. 19.95 *(978-1-59515-477-4(9))* Rourke Educational Media.

McNeese, Tim. Civil War Battles. 2009. (Civil War: A Nation Divided Ser.). (Illus.). 144p. (gr. 6-12). 35.00 *(978-1-60413-034-8(2)*, Chelsea Hse.) Facts On File, Inc.

Miller, Reagan & Hiller, Sandi J. Turning Point Battles of the Civil War. 2011. (ENG.). 48p. (J). pap. *(978-0-7787-5360-5(3))*; lib. bdg. *(978-0-7787-5343-8(3))* Crabtree Publishing Co.

Miller, Reagan & Stowell, Cinci. Final Campaigns of the Civil War. 2011. (ENG.). 48p. (J). pap. *(978-0-7787-5356-8(5))*; lib. bdg. *(978-0-7787-5339-1(5))* Crabtree Publishing Co.

O'Connell, Kim A. Major Battles of the Civil War: A MyReportLinks. com Book. 2004. (American Civil War Ser.). (Illus.). 48p. (J). lib. bdg. 25.26 *(978-0-7660-5187-4(0)*, MyReportLinks.com Bks.) Enslow Pubs., Inc.

Ollhoff, Jim. The Civil War: Early Battles, 1 vol. 2012. (Civil War Ser.). (ENG.). 32p. (YA). (gr. 5-9). 27.07 *(978-1-61783-273-4(1))* ABDO Publishing Co.

—The Civil War: Leaders & Generals, 1 vol. 2012. (Civil War Ser.). (ENG.). 32p. (YA). (gr. 5-9). 27.07 *(978-1-61783-275-8(8))* ABDO Publishing Co.

—The Civil War: The Final Years, 1 vol. 2012. (Civil War Ser.). (ENG.). 32p. (YA). (gr. 5-9). 27.07 *(978-1-61783-274-1(X))* ABDO Publishing Co.

—The Civil War: Turning Points, 1 vol. 2012. (Civil War Ser.). (ENG.). 32p. (YA). (gr. 5-9). 27.07 *(978-1-61783-277-2(4))* ABDO Publishing Co.

Olson, Steven P. Lincoln's Gettysburg Address: A Primary Source Investigation. 2004. (Great Historic Debates & Speeches Ser.). (Illus.). 64p. (J). lib. bdg. 31.95 *(978-1-4042-0151-4(3))* Rosen Publishing Group, Inc., The.

O'Neill, Robert John & Gallagher, Gary W. The Civil War: Bull Run & Other Eastern Battles, 1861-May 1863. 2010. (Civil War: Essential Histories Ser.). (ENG.). 96p. (YA). lib. bdg. 33.25 *(978-1-4488-0387-3(X))* Rosen Publishing Group, Inc., The.

O'Neill, Robert John & Glatthaar, Joseph T. The Civil War: Sherman's Capture of Atlanta & Other Western Battles, 1863-1865. 2010. (Civil War: Essential Histories Ser.). (ENG.). 96p. (YA). lib. bdg. 33.25 *(978-1-4488-0389-7(6))* Rosen Publishing Group, Inc., The.

Pingry, Patricia A. The Story of Gettysburg. Britt, Stephanie, illus. 2003. (ENG.). 26p. (J). (gr. -1-k). bds. 7.69 *(978-0-8249-6503-7(5)*, Ideal Pubns.) Worthy Publishing.

Power, J. Tracey. Stonewall Jackson: Hero of the Confederacy. 2009. (Library of American Lives & Times Ser.). 112p. (gr. 5-5). 69.20 *(978-1-60853-507-1(X))* Rosen Publishing Group, Inc., The.

Rice, Earle, Jr. Robert E. Lee: First Soldier of the Confederacy. 2005. (Civil War Leaders Ser.). (Illus.). 176p. (gr. 6-12). 28.95 *(978-1-931798-47-1(8))* Reynolds, Morgan Inc.

Robertson, James I., Jr. Robert E. Lee: Virginian Soldier, American Citizen. 2005. (ENG., Illus.). 176p. (YA). (gr. 7-12). 29.99 *(978-0-689-85731-7(4)*, Atheneum Bks. for Young Readers) Simon & Schuster Children's Publishing.

Roppelt, Donna J. & DeAngelis, Therese. General A.P. Hill: Light Division Leader. 2011. (J). *(978-1-59556-042-1(4))*; pap. *(978-1-59556-048-3(3))* OTTN Publishing.

Rosen, Daniel. Battles of the Civil War: Set of 6: Antietam. 2011. (Navigators Ser.). (J). pap. 48.00 net. *(978-1-4108-6259-4(3))* Benchmark Education Co.

—Battles of the Civil War: Antietam: Text Pairs. 2008. (Bridges/Navigators Ser.). (J). (gr. 5). 89.00 *(978-1-4108-8405-3(8))* Benchmark Education Co.

Samuels, Charlie. The Civil War. 2011. (Americans at War: a Gareth Stevens Timeline Ser.). 48p. (J). (gr. 6-8). pap. 14.05 *(978-1-4339-5912-7(7))*; lib. bdg. 31.95 *(978-1-4339-5910-3(0))* Stevens, Gareth Publishing LLLP. (Gareth Stevens Secondary Library).

Tanaka, Shelley. Gettysburg: The Legendary Battle & the Address That Inspired a Nation. Craig, David, illus. 2003. (Day That Changed America Ser.). (ENG.). 48p. 16.99 *(978-0-7868-1922-5(7))* Hyperion Pr.

Vansant, Wayne. Grant vs. Lee: The Graphic History of the Civil War's Greatest Rivals During the Last Year of the War. Vansant, Wayne, illus. 2015. (Graphic Histories Ser.). (ENG., Illus.). 104p. (J). (gr. 8-12). 34.65 *(978-1-939581-78-5(8))* Quarto Publishing Group USA.

—Grant vs. Lee: The Graphic History of the Civil War's Greatest Rivals During the Last Year of the War. 2013. (Zenith Graphic Histories Ser.). (ENG., Illus.). 104p. pap. 19.99 *(978-0-7603-4531-3(7)*, 0760345317, Zenith Pr.) Quarto Publishing Group USA.

Vierow, Wendy. The Battle of Bull Run. 2004. (Headlines from History Ser.). (Illus.). 24p. (YA). (gr. 2-5). lib. bdg. 22.60 *(978-0-8239-6221-1(0))* Rosen Publishing Group, Inc., The.

—The Battle of Bull Run: Confederate Forces Overwhelm Union Troops. 2009. (Headlines from History Ser.). 24p. (gr. 3-3). 42.50 *(978-1-61513-241-6(4)*, PowerKids Pr.) Rosen Publishing Group, Inc., The.

—The Battle of Gettysburg: The Civil War's Biggest Battle. 2009. (Headlines from History Ser.). 24p. (gr. 3-3). 42.50 *(978-1-61513-242-3(2)*, PowerKids Pr.) Rosen Publishing Group, Inc., The.

—The Battle of Saratoga. 2003. (Atlas of Famous Battles of the American Revolution Ser.). (Illus.). 24p. (J). lib. bdg. 22.60 *(978-0-8239-6332-4(2)*, PowerKids Pr.) Rosen Publishing Group, Inc., The.

—The Capture of New Orleans: Union Fleet Takes Control of the Lower Mississippi. 2009. (Headlines from History Ser.). 24p. (gr. 3-3). 42.50 *(978-1-61513-245-4(7)*, PowerKids Pr.) Rosen Publishing Group, Inc., The.

—The Capture of New Orleans: Union Fleet Takes Control of the Lower Mississippi River. 2004. (Headlines from History Ser.). (Illus.). 24p. (YA). (gr. 2-5). lib. bdg. 22.60 *(978-0-8239-6222-8(9))* Rosen Publishing Group, Inc., The.

Waldman, Scott P. The Battle of Bunker Hill. 2009. (Atlas of Famous Battles of the American Revolution Ser.). 24p. (gr. 3-3). 42.50 *(978-1-60853-327-5(1)*, PowerKids Pr.) Rosen Publishing Group, Inc., The.

UNITED STATES—HISTORY—CIVIL WAR, 1861-1865—FICTION

Abbott, E. F. John Lincoln Clem: Civil War Drummer Boy. 2016. (Based on a True Story Ser.). (ENG., Illus.). 192p. (J). 15.99 *(978-1-250-06837-8(1)*, 9781250068378) Feiwel & Friends.

Alcorn, Anita C. Caught in the Crossfire: A Boy's View of the Battle of Mill Springs, KY. 2006. 48p. pap. 8.95 *(978-0-7414-3581-1(0))* Infinity Publishing.

Alger, Horatio. Frank's Campaign: Or, The Farm & the Camp. 2006. (ENG.). 196p. pap. 19.99 *(978-1-4264-0484-9(0))*; 188p. pap. 21.99 *(978-1-4264-0527-3(8))* Creative Media Partners, LLC.

—Frank's Campaign: Or, The Farm & the Camp. 2006. pap. *(978-1-4065-0705-8(9))* Dodo Pr.

Alger Jr. Horatio Staff. Frank's Campaign. rev. ed. 2006. 300p. 29.95 *(978-1-4218-1761-3(6))*; pap. 14.95 *(978-1-4218-1861-0(2))* 1st World Publishing, Inc. (1st World Library - Literary Society).

Altsheler, Joseph A. The Guns of Bull Run: A Story of the Civil War's Eve. 2006. (Civil War Ser.: Vol. 1). 300p. (J). reprint ed. 29.95 *(978-1-4218-1777-4(2))*; pap. 14.95 *(978-1-4218-1877-1(9))* 1st World Publishing, Inc. (1st World Library - Literary Society).

—The Guns of Bull Run: A Story of the Civil War's Eve. 2009. 278p. reprint ed. pap. 14.99 *(978-1-60512-409-4(5))*; (Civil War Ser.: Vol. 1). (J). 27.99 *(978-1-60512-309-7(9))* Akasha Publishing, LLC. (Akasha Classics).

—The Guns of Bull Run: A Story of the Civil War's Eve. l.t. ed. (Civil War Ser.: Vol. 1). (J). 2007. 272p. per. 23.99 *(978-1-4346-7679-5(X))* 2008. 272p. reprint ed. 28.99 *(978-0-554-29458-2(3))* 2008. 272p. reprint ed. 25.99 *(978-0-554-38761-1(1))* 2007. (ENG.). 238p. reprint ed. per. 20.99 *(978-1-4346-7678-8(1))* Creative Media Partners, LLC.

—The Guns of Bull Run: A Story of the Civil War's Eve. 2006. (Civil War Ser.: Vol. 1). (J). reprint ed. pap. *(978-1-4065-0812-3(8))* Dodo Pr.

—The Guns of Bull Run: A Story of the Civil War's Eve. 2007. (Civil War Ser.: Vol. 1). 176p. (J). reprint ed. per. *(978-1-4068-1678-5(7))* Echo Library.

—The Guns of Bull Run: A Story of the Civil War's Eve. 2010. (Civil War Ser.: Vol. 1). (Illus.). 162p. (J). (gr. 4-7). reprint ed. pap. 19.99 *(978-1-153-70504-2(4))* General Bks. LLC.

—The Guns of Bull Run: A Story of the Civil War's Eve. (Civil War Ser.: Vol. 1). (J). reprint ed. 2010. 238p. (gr. 4-7). 33.56 *(978-1-169-29842-2(7))* 2010. 238p. (gr. 4-7). pap. 21.56 *(978-1-162-69670-6(2))* 2010. 41.95 *(978-1-161-46535-8(9))* 2004. pap. 1.99 *(978-1-4192-6519-8(9))* 2004. pap. 26.95 *(978-1-4191-6519-1(4))* Kessinger Publishing, LLC.

—The Guns of Bull Run: A Story of the Civil War's Eve. 2011. (Civil War Ser.: Vol. 1). 256p. (J). (gr. 4-7). reprint ed. pap. *(978-3-8424-5271-8(3))* Tredition GmbH.

—The Guns of Bull Run: A Story of the Civil War's Eve. 2009. (Civil War Ser.: Vol. 1). (YA). (gr. 4-7). reprint ed. pap. 16.95 *(978-1-933573-82-3(1))* Zeezok Publishing, LLC.

—The Guns of Bull Run (Webster's French Thesaurus Edition) 2008. (Civil War Ser.: Vol. 1). (ENG & FRE.). 306p. reprint ed. pap. 28.95 *(978-0-497-97879-2(2))* Icon Group International, Inc.

—The Guns of Bull Run (Webster's Spanish Thesaurus Edition) 2008. (Civil War Ser.: Vol. 1). (ENG & SPA.). 313p. pap. 28.95 *(978-0-497-99968-1(4))* Icon Group International, Inc.

—The Guns of Shiloh. 2006. (Civil War Ser.: Vol. 2). 292p. (J). reprint ed. 28.95 *(978-1-4218-1774-3(8))*; pap. 13.95 *(978-1-4218-1874-0(4))* 1st World Publishing, Inc. (1st World Library - Literary Society).

—The Guns of Shiloh. l.t. ed. (Civil War Ser.: Vol. 2). (J). 2007. (ENG.). 260p. per. 23.99 *(978-1-4346-7681-8(1))* 2010. (ENG.). 356p. (gr. 4-7). reprint ed. pap. 32.75 *(978-1-177-56053-5(4))* 2008. 264p. reprint ed. 28.99 *(978-0-554-29459-9(1))* 2008. 264p. reprint ed. 25.99 *(978-0-554-38762-8(X))* 2007. 240p. reprint ed. per. 20.99 *(978-1-4346-7680-1(3))* Creative Media Partners, LLC.

—The Guns of Shiloh. 2006. (Civil War Ser.: Vol. 2). (J). reprint ed. pap. *(978-1-4065-0813-0(6))* Dodo Pr.

—The Guns of Shiloh. 2006. (Civil War Ser.: Vol. 2). (J). reprint ed. pap. *(978-1-4068-0745-5(1))* Echo Library.

—The Guns of Shiloh. 2010. 156p. pap. 24.39 *(978-1-152-46676-0(3))*; (Civil War Ser.: Vol. 2). (Illus.). (J). (gr. 4-7). reprint ed. pap. 19.99 *(978-1-153-70505-9(2))* General Bks. LLC.

—The Guns of Shiloh. (Civil War Ser.: Vol. 2). (J). 2010. 216p. pap. *(978-1-4076-3068-7(7))* 2012. 362p. reprint ed. pap. *(978-1-290-02433-4(2))* HardPr.

—The Guns of Shiloh. 2003. (Civil War Ser.: Vol. 2). 232p. (J). reprint ed. pap. 36.99 *(978-1-4043-5087-8(X))* IndyPublish.com.

—The Guns of Shiloh. (Civil War Ser.: Vol. 2). (J). reprint ed. 2010. 226p. (gr. 4-7). 31.96 *(978-1-169-29437-0(5))* 2010. 226p. (gr. 4-7). pap. 19.96 *(978-1-162-69671-3(0))* 2010. 39.95 *(978-1-161-46536-5(7))* 2004. pap. 1.99 *(978-1-4192-6520-4(2))* 2004. pap. 24.95 *(978-1-4191-6520-7(8))* Kessinger Publishing, LLC.

—The Guns of Shiloh. (Civil War Ser.: Vol. 2). reprint ed. 2008. 228p. (J). pap. 14.45 *(978-1-60597-269-5(X))* 2007. 232p. per. 12.45 *(978-1-60424-259-1(0))* Standard Pubns., Inc. (Book Jungle).

—The Guns of Shiloh. 2011. (Civil War Ser.: Vol. 2). 260p. (J). (gr. 4-7). reprint ed. pap. *(978-3-8424-2812-6(X))* Tredition GmbH.

—The Guns of Shiloh. 2009. (Civil War Ser.: Vol. 2). 278p. (J). (gr. 4-7). reprint ed. pap. 16.95 *(978-1-933573-83-0(X))* Zeezok Publishing, LLC.

—The Rock of Chickamauga: A Story of the Western Crisis. 2006. (Civil War Ser.: Vol. 6). 292p. (J). reprint ed. 28.95 *(978-1-4218-1775-0(6))*; pap. 13.95 *(978-1-4218-1875-7(2))* 1st World Publishing, Inc. (1st World Library - Literary Society).

—The Rock of Chickamauga: A Story of the Western Crisis. (Civil War Ser.: Vol. 6). (J). reprint ed. 25.95 *(978-0-8488-0071-0(0))* Amereon Ltd.

—The Rock of Chickamauga: A Story of the Western Crisis. l.t. ed. (Civil War Ser.: Vol. 6). (J). reprint ed. 2007. (ENG.). 258p. pap. 23.99 *(978-1-4346-2064-4(6))* 2010. 360p. (gr. 4-7). pap. 32.75 *(978-1-177-86302-5(2))* 2010. 356p. pap. 32.75 *(978-1-142-78423-2(1))* 2008. 260p. 28.99 *(978-0-554-26869-9(8))* 2008. 260p. 25.99 *(978-0-554-36172-7(8))* 2007. (ENG.). 234p. pap. 20.99 *(978-1-4346-2035-4(2))* Creative Media Partners, LLC.

—The Rock of Chickamauga: A Story of the Western Crisis. 2006. (Civil War Ser.: Vol. 6). (J). reprint ed. pap. *(978-1-4065-0818-5(7))* Dodo Pr.

—The Rock of Chickamauga: A Story of the Western Crisis. 2007. (Civil War Ser.: Vol. 6). 176p. (J). reprint ed. per. *(978-1-4068-1682-2(5))* Echo Library.

—The Rock of Chickamauga: A Story of the Western Crisis. 2010. (Civil War Ser.: Vol. 6). (Illus.). 154p. (J). (gr. 4-7). reprint ed. pap. 19.99 *(978-1-153-71942-1(8))* General Bks. LLC.

—The Rock of Chickamauga: A Story of the Western Crisis. 2010. (Civil War Ser.: Vol. 6). 220p. (J). pap. *(978-1-4076-5409-6(8))* HardPr.

—The Rock of Chickamauga: A Story of the Western Crisis. (Civil War Ser.: Vol. 6). (J). 2010. 236p. (gr. 4-7). pap. 21.56 *(978-1-162-70708-2(9))* 2010. 236p. (gr. 4-7). reprint ed. 33.56 *(978-1-169-29814-9(1))* 2010. reprint ed. 41.95 *(978-1-161-47572-2(9))* 2004. reprint ed. pap. 26.95 *(978-1-4191-8082-8(7))* 2004. reprint ed. pap. 1.99 *(978-1-4192-8082-5(1))* Kessinger Publishing, LLC.

—The Rock of Chickamauga: A Story of the Western Crisis. 2011. (Civil War Ser.: Vol. 6). 260p. (J). (gr. 4-7). reprint ed. pap. *(978-3-8424-7218-1(8))* Tredition GmbH.

—The Scouts of Stonewall: The Story of the Great Valley Campaign. 2006. (Civil War Ser.: Vol. 3). 312p. (J). reprint ed. 29.95 *(978-1-4218-1779-8(9))*; pap. 14.95 *(978-1-4218-1879-5(5))* 1st World Publishing, Inc. (1st World Library - Literary Society).

—The Scouts of Stonewall: The Story of the Great Valley Campaign. l.t. ed. (Civil War Ser.: Vol. 3). (J). reprint ed. 2007. (ENG.). 240p. pap. 22.99 *(978-1-4264-1531-9(1))* 2011. 370p. (gr. 4-7). pap. 32.75 *(978-1-245-65787-7(9))* 2008. 244p. 24.99 *(978-0-554-31333-7(2))* 2008. 244p. 27.99 *(978-0-554-22030-7(X))* 2006. 250p. pap. 20.99 *(978-1-4264-1498-5(6))* Creative Media Partners, LLC.

—The Scouts of Stonewall: The Story of the Great Valley Campaign. 2006. (Civil War Ser.: Vol. 3). (J). reprint ed. pap. *(978-1-4065-0820-8(9))* Dodo Pr.

—The Scouts of Stonewall: The Story of the Great Valley Campaign. 2007. (Civil War Ser.: Vol. 3). 184p. (J). reprint ed. per. *(978-1-4068-1684-6(1))* Echo Library.

—The Scouts of Stonewall: The Story of the Great Valley Campaign. 2010. (Civil War Ser.: Vol. 3). (Illus.). 166p. (J). (gr. 4-7). reprint ed. pap. 19.99 *(978-1-153-72009-0(4))* General Bks. LLC.

—The Scouts of Stonewall: The Story of the Great Valley Campaign. reprint ed. 2010. (Civil War Ser.: Vol. 3). 252p. (J). (gr. 4-7). 33.56 *(978-1-169-30265-5(3))* 2010. (Civil War Ser.: Vol. 3). 252p. (J). (gr. 4-7). pap. 21.56 *(978-1-162-70768-6(2))* 2010. (Civil War Ser.: Vol. 3). 252p. (J). 41.95 *(978-1-161-47632-3(6))* 2004. pap. 26.95 *(978-1-4191-8162-7(9))* 2004. (Civil War Ser.: Vol. 3). (J). pap. 1.99 *(978-1-4192-8162-4(3))* Kessinger Publishing, LLC.

—The Scouts of Stonewall: The Story of the Great Valley Campaign. 2011. (Civil War Ser.: Vol. 3). 278p. (J). (gr. 4-7). reprint ed. pap. *(978-3-8424-6100-0(3))* Tredition GmbH.

—The Shades of the Wilderness: A Story of Lee's Great Stand. 2006. (Civil War Ser.: Vol. 7). 308p. (J). reprint ed. 29.95 *(978-1-4218-2336-2(5))*; pap. 14.95 *(978-1-4218-2436-9(1))* 1st World Publishing, Inc. (1st World Library - Literary Society).

—The Shades of the Wilderness: A Story of Lee's Great Stand. (Civil War Ser.: Vol. 7). 312p. (J). reprint ed. lib. bdg. 25.95 *(978-0-88411-940-1(8))* Amereon Ltd.

—The Shades of the Wilderness: A Story of Lee's Great Stand. l.t. ed. (Civil War Ser.: Vol. 7). (J). reprint ed. 2006. (ENG.). 278p. pap. 23.99 *(978-1-4264-6220-7(4))* 2008. 280p. 28.99 *(978-0-554-24300-9(8))* 2008. 280p. 25.99 *(978-0-554-33603-9(0))* 2006. (ENG.). 250p. pap. 20.99 *(978-1-4264-6165-1(8))* Creative Media Partners, LLC.

—The Shades of the Wilderness: A Story of Lee's Great Stand. 2006. (Civil War Ser.: Vol. 7). (J). reprint ed. pap. *(978-1-4065-0822-2(5))* Dodo Pr.

—The Shades of the Wilderness: A Story of Lee's Great Stand. 2007. (Civil War Ser.: Vol. 7). 180p. (J). reprint ed. per. *(978-1-4068-1686-0(8))* Echo Library.

—The Shades of the Wilderness: A Story of Lee's Great Stand. 2010. (Civil War Ser.: Vol. 7). (Illus.). 162p. (J). (gr. 4-7). reprint ed. pap. 19.99 *(978-1-153-72059-5(0))* General Bks. LLC.

—The Shades of the Wilderness: A Story of Lee's Great Stand. (Civil War Ser.: Vol. 7). (J). reprint ed. 2011. (gr. 4-7). *(978-1-164-50265-4(4))* 2010. 324p. (gr. 4-7). pap. 24.76 *(978-1-163-19558-1(8))* 2008. 324p. 45.95 *(978-1-4366-8424-8(2))* 2007. 324p. per. 30.95 *(978-1-4325-9861-7(9))* Kessinger Publishing, LLC.

—The Shades of the Wilderness: A Story of Lee's Great Stand. 2007. (Civil War Ser.: Vol. 7). 308p. reprint ed. per. 16.45 *(978-1-60424-029-0(6)*, Book Jungle) Standard Pubns., Inc.

—The Shades of the Wilderness: A Story of Lee's Great Stand. 2011. (Civil War Ser.: Vol. 7). 280p. (J). reprint ed. pap. *(978-3-8424-4396-9(X))* Tredition GmbH.

—The Star of Gettysburg: A Story of Southern High Tide. 2006. (Civil War Ser.: Vol. 5). 324p. (J). reprint ed. 29.95 *(978-1-4218-1780-4(2))*; pap. 14.95 *(978-1-4218-1880-1(9))* 1st World Publishing, Inc. (1st World Library - Literary Society).

—The Star of Gettysburg: A Story of Southern High Tide. l.t. ed. (Civil War Ser.: Vol. 5). (J). reprint ed. 2007. (ENG.). 290p. per. 23.99 *(978-1-4346-7685-6(4))* 2008. 292p. 25.99 *(978-0-554-38764-2(6))* 2008. 292p. 28.99 *(978-0-554-29461-2(3))* 2007. (ENG.). 258p. per. 21.99 *(978-1-4346-7684-9(6))* Creative Media Partners, LLC.

—The Star of Gettysburg: A Story of Southern High Tide. 2006. (Civil War Ser.: Vol. 5). (J). reprint ed. pap. *(978-1-4065-0824-6(1))* Dodo Pr.

—The Star of Gettysburg: A Story of Southern High Tide. 2007. (Civil War Ser.: Vol. 5). 192p. (J). reprint ed. per. *(978-1-4068-1688-4(4))* Echo Library.

—The Star of Gettysburg: A Story of Southern High Tide. 2010. (Civil War Ser.: Vol. 5). 174p. (J). (gr. 4-7). reprint ed. pap. 19.99 *(978-1-153-72161-5(9))* General Bks. LLC.

—The Star of Gettysburg: A Story of Southern High Tide. (Civil War Ser.: Vol. 5). (J). reprint ed. 2010. 262p. (gr. 4-7). 34.36 *(978-1-169-30586-1(5))* 2010. 262p. (gr. 4-7). pap. 22.36 *(978-1-162-70899-7(9))* 2010. 42.95 *(978-1-161-47763-4(2))* 2004. pap. 1.99 *(978-1-4192-8344-4(8))* 2004. pap. 27.95 *(978-1-4191-8344-7(3))* Kessinger Publishing, LLC.

—The Star of Gettysburg: A Story of Southern High Tide. 2011. (Civil War Ser.: Vol. 5). 280p. (J). (gr. 4-7). reprint ed. pap. *(978-3-8424-5317-3(5))* Tredition GmbH.

—The Star of Gettysburg (Webster's Korean Thesaurus Edition) 2008. (Civil War Ser.: Vol. 5). (Illus.). 340p. (C). pap. 28.95 *(978-0-546-50036-3(6))* Icon Group International, Inc.

—The Sword of Antietam: A Story of the Nation's Crisis. 2006. (Civil War Ser.: Vol. 4). 296p. (J). reprint ed. 28.95 (978-1-4218-1776-7(4)); pap. 13.95 (978-1-4218-1876-4(0)) 1st World Publishing, Inc. (1st World Library - Literary Society).

—The Sword of Antietam: A Story of the Nation's Crisis. l.t. ed. (Civil War Ser.: Vol. 4). (J). reprint ed. 2006. 262p. pap. 23.99 (978-1-4264-2714-5(X)) 2011. 358p. (gr. 4-7). pap. 32.75 (978-1-245-13385-2(3)) 2008. 264p. 28.99 (978-0-554-22582-1(4)) 2008. 264p. 25.99 (978-0-554-31885-1(7)) 2007. (ENG.). 242p. pap. 20.99 (978-1-4264-2657-5(7)) Creative Media Partners, LLC.

—The Sword of Antietam: A Story of the Nation's Crisis. 2006. (Civil War Ser.: Vol. 4). (J). reprint ed. pap. (978-1-4065-0825-3(X)) Dodo Pr.

—The Sword of Antietam: A Story of the Nation's Crisis. 2007. (Civil War Ser.: Vol. 4). 176p. (J). reprint ed. per. (978-1-4068-1690-7(6)) Echo Library.

—The Sword of Antietam: A Story of the Nation's Crisis. 2010. (Civil War Ser.: Vol. 4). (Illus.). 160p. (J). (gr. 4-7). reprint ed. pap. 19.99 (978-1-153-72276-6(3)) General Bks. LLC.

—The Sword of Antietam: A Story of the Nation's Crisis. 2010. (Civil War Ser.: Vol. 4). 224p. (J). reprint ed. pap. (978-1-4076-4642-8(7)) HardPr.

—The Sword of Antietam: A Story of the Nation's Crisis. (Civil War Ser.: Vol. 4). (J). reprint ed. 2011. 352p. (gr. 4-7). 46.95 (978-1-169-87969-0(1)) 2010. 352p. (gr. 4-7). 37.56 (978-1-163-20537-2(0)) 2010. 352p. (gr. 4-7). pap. 25.56 (978-1-162-77564-7(5)) 2005. 352p. 46.95 (978-1-4326-1485-0(1)) 2005. pap. 31.95 (978-0-7661-9405-2(1)) 2004. pap. 1.99 (978-1-4192-8469-4(X)) Kessinger Publishing, LLC.

—The Sword of Antietam: A Story of the Nation's Crisis. 2011. (Civil War Ser.: Vol. 4). 264p. (J). (gr. 4-7). reprint ed. pap. (978-3-8424-3211-6(9)) Tredition GmbH.

—The Sword of Antietam: A Story of the Nation's Crisis. 2009. (Civil War Ser.: Vol. 4). (J). reprint ed. pap. 16.95 (978-1-933573-85-4(6)) Zeezok Publishing, LLC.

—The Sword of Antietam (Webster's French Thesaurus Edition) 2008. (ENG & FRE.). 299p. (C). reprint ed. pap. 28.95 (978-0-497-97890-7(3)) Icon Group International, Inc.

—The Tree of Appomattox: A Story of the Civil War's Close. 2006. (Civil War Ser.: Vol. 8). 324p. (J). reprint ed. 29.95 (978-1-4218-2338-6(1)); pap. 14.95 (978-1-4218-2438-3(8)) 1st World Publishing, Inc. (1st World Library - Literary Society).

—The Tree of Appomattox: A Story of the Civil War's Close. l.t. ed. (Civil War Ser.: Vol. 8). (J). reprint ed. 2007. (ENG.). 298p. pap. 23.99 (978-1-4346-1261-8(9)) 2008. 300p. 28.99 (978-0-554-26479-0(X)) 2008. 300p. 25.99 (978-0-554-35782-9(8)) 2007. (ENG.). 266p. pap. 21.99 (978-1-4346-1190-1(6)) Creative Media Partners, LLC.

—The Tree of Appomattox: A Story of the Civil War's Close. 2006. (Civil War Ser.: Vol. 8). (J). reprint ed. pap. (978-1-4065-0828-4(4)) Dodo Pr.

—The Tree of Appomattox: A Story of the Civil War's Close. 2007. (Civil War Ser.: Vol. 8). 192p. (J). reprint ed. per. (978-1-4068-1693-8(0)) Echo Library.

—The Tree of Appomattox: A Story of the Civil War's Close. 2010. (Civil War Ser.: Vol. 8). (Illus.). 174p. (J). (gr. 4-7). reprint ed. pap. 19.99 (978-1-153-72402-9(2)) General Bks. LLC.

—The Tree of Appomattox: A Story of the Civil War's Close. Wrenn, Charles L., illus. (Civil War Ser.: Vol. 8). 332p. (J). (gr. 4-7). reprint ed. 2011. 45.95 (978-1-169-88135-8(1)) 2010. 36.76 (978-1-163-21361-2(6)) 2010. pap. 24.76 (978-1-162-78752-7(X)) Kessinger Publishing, LLC.

—The Tree of Appomattox: A Story of the Civil War's Close. 2005. (Civil War Ser.: Vol. 8). (J). reprint ed. pap. 30.95 (978-1-4179-2071-6(8)) Kessinger Publishing, LLC.

—The Tree of Appomattox: A Story of the Civil War's Close. Wrenn, Charles L., illus. 2005. (Civil War Ser.: Vol. 8). 332p. (J). reprint ed. 45.95 (978-1-4326-1333-4(2)) Kessinger Publishing, LLC.

—The Tree of Appomattox: A Story of the Civil War's Close. 2011. (Civil War Ser.: Vol. 8). 294p. (J). (gr. 4-7). reprint ed. pap. (978-3-8424-8485-6(2)) Tredition GmbH.

Aviation Staff. Iron Thunder: The Battle Between the Monitor & the Merrimac. 2009. (ENG.). 208p. (J). (gr. 3-7). pap. 7.99 (978-1-4231-0518-3(4)) Hyperion Pr.

Ballard, Allen. Where Im Bound. 2006. pap. 18.95 (978-0-595-39856-0(1), Backinprint.com) iUniverse, Inc.

Barnhart, Aaron. Firebrand. 2015. (ENG., Illus.). 168p. (J). 19.95 (978-0-9669258-6-9(6)) Quindaro Pr.

Barrows, Annie. Magic in the Mix. 2014. (ENG.). 288p. (YA). (gr. 3-6). 16.99 (978-1-61963-482-4(1), 9781619634824, Bloomsbury USA Childrens) Bloomsbury Publishing USA.

Bearden, Romare. Li'l Dan the Drummer Boy: A Civil War Story. Bearden, Romare, illus. 2003. (ENG., Illus.). 40p. (J). (gr. -1-3). 24.99 (978-0-689-86237-3(7), Simon & Schuster Bks. For Young Readers) Simon & Schuster Bks. For Young Readers.

Beddor, Frank & Cavalier, Liz. Mad with Wonder. Wrobel, C. J., ed. 2009. (ENG., Illus.). 208p. (gr. 7). 24.99 (978-0-9818737-1-8(5)); Vol. 2. pap. 14.95 (978-0-9818737-2-5(3)) Automatic Pictures Publishing.

Bierce, Ambrose. An Occurrence at Owl Creek Bridge. 2010. (J). 19.95 (978-1-58341-922-9(5), Creative Education) Creative Co., The.

Blackwood, Gary L. Second Sight. 2007. (Illus.). 279p. (J). (gr. 5-9). 14.65 (978-0-7569-8132-7(8)) Perfection Learning Corp.

Blackwood, Gary L. & Blackwood, Gary. Second Sight. 2007. (ENG.). 288p. (J). (gr. 5-18). 8.99 (978-0-14-240747-9(X), Speak) Penguin Young Readers Group.

Blaine, John. The Blue Ghost Mystery: A Rick Brant Science Adventure Story. 2011. 188p. 42.95 (978-1-258-09526-0(2)) Literary Licensing, LLC.

Blair, Margaret Whitman. The Sand Castle: Blockade Running & the Battle of Fort Fisher. 2005. (White Mane Kids Ser.: 17). (Illus.). 187p. (J). (gr. 4-7). per. 8.95 (978-1-57249-346-9(1), White Mane Kids) White Mane Publishing Co., Inc.

Bruchac, Joseph. March Toward the Thunder. 2009. (ENG.). 320p. (YA). (gr. 7-18). 9.99 (978-0-14-241446-0(8), Speak) Penguin Young Readers Group.

Burgan, Michael. Hot Iron: The Adventures of a Civil War Powder Boy. Rodriquez, Pedro, illus. 2007. (Historical Fiction Ser.). (ENG.). 56p. (gr. 2-3). pap. 6.25 (978-1-59889-406-6(4), Graphic Flash) Stone Arch Bks.

Calkhoven, Laurie. Will at the Battle of Gettysburg. 2012. (Boys of Wartime Ser.: 2). (ENG.). 256p. (J). (gr. 4-7). 7.99 (978-0-14-241987-8(7), Puffin Books) Penguin Young Readers Group.

Carolyn, Reeder. Shades of Gray. 2014. (ENG.). 160p. (J). (gr. 5-12). 11.24 (978-1-63245-242-9(1)) Lectorum Pubns., Inc.

Cauvin, Raoul. Bluecoats - Greenhorn, Vol. 4. Lambil, Willy, illus. 4th ed. 2011. (Bluecoats Ser.: 4). (ENG.). 48p. (gr. 3-17). pap. 11.95 (978-1-84918-066-5(0)) CineBook GBR. Dist: National Bk. Network.

—The Blues in the Mud. Lambil, Willy, illus. 2014. (Bluecoats Ser.: 7). (ENG.). 48p. pap. 11.95 (978-1-84918-183-9(7)) CineBook GBR. Dist: National Bk. Network.

—Bronco Benny. Lambil, Willy, illus. 2013. (Bluecoats Ser.: 6). (ENG.). 48p. pap. 11.95 (978-1-84918-146-4(2)) CineBook GBR. Dist: National Bk. Network.

—The Navy Blues. Lambil, Willy, illus. 2009. (Bluecoats Ser.: 2). (ENG.). 46p. (J). (gr. 4-7). pap. 11.95 (978-1-905460-82-3(1)) CineBook GBR. Dist: National Bk. Network.

—Robertsonville Prison, Volume 1. Lambil, Willy, illus. 2009. (Bluecoats Ser.: 1). (ENG.). 46p. (J). (gr. -1-17). pap. 11.95 (978-1-905460-71-7(6)) CineBook GBR. Dist: National Bk. Network.

—Rumberley. Lambil, Willy, illus. 2012. (Bluecoats Ser.: 5). (ENG.). 48p. (J). (gr. 3-8). pap. 11.95 (978-1-84918-108-2(X)) CineBook GBR. Dist: National Bk. Network.

Chickasaw Adventures: The Civil War. 2005. (J). (978-1-4265-0000-8(9)) Layne Morgan Media, Inc.

Connell, Kate. Yankee Blue or Rebel Grey? The Civil War Adventures of Sam Shaw. 2003. (I Am American Ser.). (ENG., Illus.). 40p. (J). (gr. 3-7). pap. 6.99 (978-0-7922-5179-8(2), National Geographic Children's Bks.) National Geographic Society.

Cook, Kajsa. Discoveries in the Shriver Family Attic: How a Woman & Her Children Dealt with the Battle of Gettysburg. 2009. (Illus.). 122p. (J). (gr. 4-8). pap. 8.95 (978-1-57249-398-8(4), White Mane Kids) White Mane Publishing Co., Inc.

Crane, Stephen. The Red Badge of Courage. 2004. (Dover Children's Evergreen Classics Ser.). (ENG.). 160p. (YA). (gr. 3-8). pap. 4.99 (978-0-486-43422-3(2)) Dover Pubns., Inc.

—The Red Badge of Courage. 2008. (Bring the Classics to Life Ser.). (ENG., Illus.). 72p. (gr. 3-12). pap., act. bk. ed. 10.95 (978-0-931334-42-9(X), EDCTR-302B) EDCON Publishing Group.

—The Red Badge of Courage. (EMC Masterpiece Series Access Editions). (J). 11.99 (978-0-8219-1981-1(4)) EMC/Paradigm Publishing.

—The Red Badge of Courage. 2005. (Illus.). 175p. (gr. 3-7). 21.00 (978-0-7569-5810-7(5)) Perfection Learning Corp.

—The Red Badge of Courage. 2005. (Aladdin Classics Ser.). (ENG.). 256p. (J). (gr. 5-9). pap. 5.99 (978-0-689-87835-0(4), Aladdin) Simon & Schuster Children's Publishing.

—The Red Badge of Courage. 2008. (ENG.). 160p. pap. 11.45 (978-1-60597-411-8(0), Book Jungle) Standard Pubns., Inc.

—The Red Badge of Courage. Akib, Jamel, illus. 2006. (Classic Starts(tm) Ser.). (ENG.). 160p. (J). (gr. 2-4). 6.95 (978-1-4027-2663-7(5)) Sterling Publishing Co., Inc.

—The Red Badge of Courage: With a Discussion of Self-Esteem. Clift, Eva, illus. 2003. (Values in Action Illustrated Classics Ser.). 190p. (J). (978-1-59203-034-7(3)) Learning Challenge, Inc.

Cregar, Elyse M. Hanna's Courage: A Story of Love & Betrayal at the Battle of Gettysburg. 2012. 212p. pap. 8.99 (978-0-9621292-2-3(4)) Tamerac Publishing.

Crist-Evans, Craig. Moon over Tennessee: A Boy's Civil War Journal. Christensen, Bonnie, illus. 2003. (ENG.). 64p. (J). (gr. 5-7). pap. 8.95 (978-0-618-31107-1(6)) Houghton Mifflin Harcourt Publishing Co.

Curtis, Alice Turner. A Yankee Girl at Fort Sumter. 2005. 26.95 (978-1-4218-0301-2(1), 1st World Library - Literary Society) 1st World Publishing, Inc.

—Yankee Girl at Fort Sumter. 2004. reprint ed. pap. 1.99 (978-1-4192-9516-4(0)); pap. 19.95 (978-1-4191-9516-7(6)) Kessinger Publishing, LLC.

Denenberg, Barry. When Will This Cruel War Be Over? The Diary of Emma Simpson, Gordonsville, Virginia 1864. 2011. (Dear America Ser.). (ENG.). 176p. (J). (gr. 3-7). 12.99 (978-0-545-27598-9(9)) Scholastic, Inc.

Dixon, Chuck & Kwapisz, Gary. Civil War Adventure: Book One. 2015. (Dover Graphic Novels Ser.). (ENG., Illus.). 144p. pap. 9.95 (978-0-486-79509-6(8)) Dover Pubns., Inc.

Ekberg, Nancy. What Kind of War Was It, Anyhow? Reynolds, Rhonda, tr. Reynolds, Rhonda, illus. 2003. 45p. (J). pap. 8.95 (978-1-58838-085-2(8), Junebug Bks.) NewSouth, Inc.

Elliott, L. M. Annie, Between the States. 2006. (ENG.). 544p. (YA). (gr. 8-12). per. 9.99 (978-0-06-001213-7(7), Tegen, Katherine Bks) 2004. (Illus.). 496p. (J). (gr. 7-18). 16.99 (978-0-06-001211-3(0)) HarperCollins Pubs.

Ernst, Kathleen. Ghosts of Vicksburg. 2003. (White Main Kids Ser.: 13). (Illus.). 180p. (J). pap. 8.95 (978-1-57249-322-3(4), White Mane Kids) White Mane Publishing Co., Inc.

—Retreat from Gettysburg. 2010. (White Mane Kids Ser.). (Illus.). 145p. (YA). pap. (978-1-57249-403-9(4), White Mane Kids) White Mane Publishing Co., Inc.

Fireside, Bryna J. Private Joel & the Sewell Mountain Seder. Costello, Shawn, illus. 2008. (Passover Ser.). (J). (gr. 3-6). 47p. lib. bdg. 16.95 (978-0-8225-7240-4(0)); (ENG.). 48p. per. 6.95 (978-0-8225-9050-7(6)) Lerner Publishing Group. (Kar-Ben Publishing).

Fletcher, Susan. Dadblamed Union Army Cow. Root, Kimberly Bulcken, illus. 2016. (ENG.). 32p. (J). (gr. k-3). 7.99 (978-0-7636-8770-0(7)) Candlewick Pr.

Frazier, Jan. Prairie Points:: a Civil War Sanctuary. 2017. (ENG., Illus.). (J). pap. 12.95 **(978-1-55571-864-0(7)**, Hellgate Pr.) L & R Publishing, LLC.

Garcia, Kami & Stohl, Margaret. Beautiful Creatures. 2009. (Beautiful Creatures Ser.: 1). (ENG.). 576p. (YA). (gr. 7-17). 17.99 (978-0-316-04267-3(6)) Little Brown & Co.

—Beautiful Creatures. (Beautiful Creatures Ser.: 1). (ENG.). 592p. (YA). (gr. 7-17). 2010. pap. 12.99 (978-0-316-07703-3(8)) 2012. mass mkt. 7.99 (978-0-316-23165-7(7)) 2012. pap. 10.99 (978-0-316-23167-1(3)) Little, Brown Bks. for Young Readers.

—Beautiful Creatures. 2013. (ENG., Illus.). 240p. (gr. 8-17). 20.00 (978-0-316-18271-3(0), Yen Pr.) Orbit.

—Beautiful Creatures. 2010. (Beautiful Creatures Ser.: 1). (YA). lib. bdg. 23.30 (978-0-606-26699-4(2), Turtleback) Turtleback Bks.

Garland, Sherry. Voices of Gettysburg, 1 vol. Hierstein, Judith, illus. 2010. (Voices of History Ser.). (ENG.). 40p. (J). (gr. 3-3). 17.99 (978-1-58980-653-5(0)) Pelican Publishing Co., Inc.

Gunderson, Jessica. The Songs of Stones River: A Civil War Novel. 2015. (Civil War Ser.). (ENG., Illus.). 96p. (gr. 4-4). lib. bdg. 26.65 (978-1-4342-9703-7(9)) Stone Arch Bks.

Gutman, Dan. Abner & Me. 2007. (Baseball Card Adventures Ser.). (ENG., Illus.). 176p. (J). (gr. 5-9). pap. 5.99 (978-0-06-053445-5(1)) HarperCollins Pubs.

—Abner & Me. 2007. (Baseball Card Adventures Ser.). (Illus.). 166p. (gr. 5-9). 16.00 (978-0-7569-7920-1(X)) Perfection Learning Corp.

Hahn, Mary Downing. Hear the Wind Blow. (ENG.). (J). (gr. 5-7). 2017. 288p. pap. 7.99 **(978-1-328-74092-2(7)**, HMH Books For Young Readers) 2003. (Illus.). 224p. tchr. ed. 17.99 (978-0-618-18190-2(3)) Houghton Mifflin Harcourt Publishing Co.

Hahn, Mary Downing. Promises to the Dead. 2009. (ENG.). 208p. (J). (gr. 5-7). pap. 7.99 (978-0-547-25838-6(0)) Houghton Mifflin Harcourt Publishing Co.

Haislip, Phyllis Hall. Anybody's Hero: The Battle of Old Men & Young Boys. 2004. (Illus.). 220p. (J). pap. 8.95 (978-1-57249-343-8(7), White Mane Kids) White Mane Publishing Co., Inc.

—Lili's Gift: A Civil War Healer's Story. 2008. (ENG., Illus.). 204p. (J). pap. 8.95 (978-1-57249-392-6(5), White Mane Kids) White Mane Publishing Co., Inc.

—Lottie's Courage: A Contraband Slave's Story. 2003. (Illus.). 120p. (J). pap. 7.95 (978-1-57249-311-7(9), White Mane Kids) White Mane Publishing Co., Inc.

Harness, Cheryl. Ghosts of the Civil War. Harness, Cheryl, illus. 2004. (ENG., Illus.). 48p. (J). (gr. 2-5). 8.99 (978-0-689-86992-1(4), Simon & Schuster Bks. For Young Readers) Simon & Schuster Bks. For Young Readers.

Harris, Dorthy. Taylor's Dream Ends Summer School Nightm. 2006. 95p. pap. 16.95 (978-1-4241-3574-5(5)) PublishAmerica, Inc.

Hart, Alison. Gabriel's Horses, 1 vol. 2007. (Racing to Freedom Trilogy). (ENG.). 160p. (J). (gr. 3-7). 14.95 (978-1-56145-398-6(6)) Peachtree Pubs.

—Gabriel's Journey, 1 vol. (Racing to Freedom Ser.). (ENG.). 160p. (J). 2011. pap. 4.99 (978-1-56145-530-0(X)) 2008. (Illus.). (gr. 3-7). 14.95 (978-1-56145-442-6(7)) Peachtree Pubs.

—Gabriel's Triumph, 1 vol. 2007. (Racing to Freedom Trilogy). (ENG.). 160p. (J). (gr. 3-7). 14.95 (978-1-56145-410-5(9)) Peachtree Pubs.

Haynes, Betsy. Cowslip. 2008. (J). (gr. 4-7). 22.50 (978-0-8446-6244-2(5)) Smith, Peter Pub., Inc.

Hemphill, Michael & Angleberger, Tom. Stonewall Hinkleman & the Battle of Bull Run. 2014. (ENG.). 192p. (J). (gr. 3-7). pap. 7.99 (978-0-14-751182-9(8), Puffin Books) Penguin Young Readers Group.

Henty, George Alfred. With Lee in Virgini. 2007. 392p. 39.95 (978-1-4344-8351-5(7)); per. 24.95 (978-1-4344-8350-8(9)) Wildside Pr., LLC.

—With Lee in Virgini: A Story of the American Civil War. 2011. 404p. pap. 19.95 (978-1-61179-178-5(2)) Fireship Pr.

Hopkinson, Deborah. Billy & the Rebel: Based on a True Civil War Story. Floca, Brian, illus. 2005. 44p. (J). lib. bdg. 15.00 (978-1-4242-1148-7(4)) Fitzgerald Bks.

—Billy & the Rebel: Based on a True Civil War Story. Floca, Brian, illus. 2006. (Ready-to-Read Ser.). 44p. (gr. 1-3). 14.00 (978-0-7569-6390-3(7)) Perfection Learning Corp.

—Billy & the Rebel: Based on a True Civil War Story. Floca, Brian, illus. 2006. (Ready-To-Reads Ser.). (ENG.). 48p. (J). (gr. 1-3). pap. 3.99 (978-0-689-83396-0(2), Simon Spotlight) Simon Spotlight.

—Billy & the Rebel: Based on a True Civil War Story. Anderson, Bethanne & Floca, Brian, illus. 2005. (Ready-To-Reads Ser.). (ENG.). 48p. (J). (gr. 1-3). 16.99 (978-0-689-83964-1(2), Simon Spotlight) Simon Spotlight.

—From Slave to Soldier: Based on a True Civil War Story. Floca, Brian, illus. 2007. (Ready-To-Reads Ser.). (ENG.). 48p. (J). (gr. 1-3). pap. 3.99 (978-0-689-83966-5(9), Simon Spotlight) Simon Spotlight.

Horender, Philip M. Yankee Mouse: Gettysburg Address Observer, 1 vol. Wolek, Guy, illus. 2013. (Maximilian P. Mouse, Time Traveler Ser.). (ENG.). 112p. (J). (gr. 3-6). lib. bdg. 27.07 (978-1-61641-958-5(X), Calico Chapter Bks) Magic Wagon.

Hubbs, M. E. The Secret of Wattensaw Bayou. Lyndon, Tracy S., illus. 2013. 170p. pap. 12.95 (978-1-934610-76-3(3)) Bluewater Pubns.

Immel, Mary Blair. Captured! A Boy Trapped in the Civil War. 2005. (Illus.). xi, 153p. (J). (978-0-87195-184-7(3)); pap. 6.95 (978-0-87195-188-5(6)) Indiana Historical Society.

Johnson, Nancy. A Sweet-Sounding Place: A Civil War Story. 2008. (ENG.). 128p. (J). (gr. 3-7). pap. 10.95 (978-0-89272-770-4(5)) Down East Bks.

Johnston, Annie Fell. The Little Colonel. 2006. (Illus.). pap. (978-1-4065-1132-1(3)) Dodo Pr.

—The Little Colonel. 2005. reprint ed. pap. 21.95 (978-0-7661-9402-1(7)) Kessinger Publishing, LLC.

—The Little Colonel's Chum: Mary Ware (il. 2006. (Illus.). pap. (978-1-4065-1125-3(0)) Dodo Pr.

Johnston, K. E. M. The Witness Tree & the Shadow of the Noose: Mystery, Lies, & Spies in Manassas. 2009. 111p. (J). (gr. 5-7). pap. 8.95 (978-1-57249-397-1(6), White Mane Kids) White Mane Publishing Co., Inc.

Joyce, Alexandria. Trail of the Caribou: A Tale of Dire Wolves in the Time of the Ice Age. 2011. 216p. (gr. 4-6). pap. 15.95 (978-1-4620-5066-6(2)) iUniverse, Inc.

Kantorek, Keith A. A Soldier's Choice. 2009. 108p. 24.50 (978-0-557-10928-9(0)); pap. 9.50 (978-0-557-10764-3(4)) Lulu Pr., Inc.

Kay, Alan. Breaking the Rules. 2007. (Young Heroes of History Ser.: 7). 149p. (J). pap. 7.95 (978-1-57249-389-6(5), White Mane Kids) White Mane Publishing Co., Inc.

Kay, Alan N. Crossroads at Gettysburg. 2005. (Young Heroes of History Ser.: 6). (Illus.). 166p. (J). (gr. 3-7). per. 7.95 (978-1-57249-359-9(3), White Mane Kids) White Mane Publishing Co., Inc.

—No Girls Allowed. 2003. (Young Heroes of History Ser.: Vol. 5). (Illus.). 140p. (J). pap. 6.95 (978-1-57249-324-7(0), White Mane Kids) White Mane Publishing Co., Inc.

Kay, Verla. Civil War Drummer Boy. Day, Larry, illus. 2012. (ENG.). 32p. (J). (gr. 1-3). 16.99 (978-0-399-23992-2(8), G.P. Putnam's Sons Books for Young Readers) Penguin Young Readers Group.

Kendall, Jane F. Tennessee Rose. Sheckels, Astrid, illus. 2012. (Horse Diaries). (ENG.). 160p. (J). (gr. 3-7). pap. 7.99 (978-0-375-87006-4(7), Random Hse. Bks. for Young Readers) Random Hse. Children's Bks.

Kilgore, James. The Passage, 1 vol. 2006. (ENG., Illus.). 256p. (YA). (gr. 7-18). 15.95 (978-1-56145-384-9(6)) Peachtree Pubs.

Kirkland, Joseph. The Captain of Company K. (Americans in Fiction Ser.). (Illus.). (J). reprint ed. lib. bdg. 27.00 (978-0-8398-1057-5(1)) Irvington Pubs.

—The Captain of Company K. 2013. (Collected Works of Joseph Kirkland). 351p. reprint ed. lthr. 79.00 (978-0-7812-1319-6(3)) Reprint Services Corp.

Klingel, Deanna K. Avery's Battlefield. 2011. (J). (978-1-60682-171-8(7)) BJU Pr.

—Avery's Crossroad. 2011. (J). (978-1-60682-193-0(8)) BJU Pr.

LaFaye, A. Stella Stands Alone. 2008. (ENG., Illus.). 256p. (YA). (gr. 7-9). 16.99 (978-1-4169-1164-7(2), Simon & Schuster Bks. For Young Readers) Simon & Schuster Bks. For Young Readers.

Lambil, Willy & Raoul, Cauvin. The Blues in Black & White. 2004. (Blue Tunics Ser.: Vol. 1). (Illus.). (J). 12.45 (978-0-9752688-0-3(5)) Reney Editions, Inc.

Law, Preston E. Drummer Boy for the Bonnie Blue: Marching Through Maryland, Virginia, & Pennsylvania with Robert E. Lee's Army. 2012. (J). pap. (978-1-57249-410-7(7), White Mane Kids) White Mane Publishing Co., Inc.

Lawlor, Laurie. Wind on the River. 2004. 156p. (J). lib. bdg. 16.92 (978-1-4242-0771-8(1)) Fitzgerald Bks.

Lyons, Kelly Starling. Hope's Gift. Tate, Don, illus. 2012. (ENG.). 32p. (J). (gr. 1-3). 16.99 (978-0-399-16001-1(9), G.P. Putnam's Sons Books for Young Readers) Penguin Young Readers Group.

Malkus, Alida Sims. We Were There at the Battle of Gettysburg. Vosburgh, Leonard, illus. 2013. (ENG.). 192p. (J). (gr. 3-8). pap. 6.99 (978-0-486-49261-2(3)) Dover Pubns., Inc.

Marsh, Carole. The Mystery at Fort Sumter. Friedlander, Randolyn, illus. 2010. (Real Kids, Real Places Ser.). 32p. (J). pap. 7.99 (978-0-635-07432-4(X), Marsh, Carole Mysteries) Gallopade International.

—The Mystery at Fort Sumter: First Shot Fired in the Civil War! 2010. (Real Kids, Real Places Ser.). (Illus.). 158p. (J). 18.99 (978-0-635-07430-0(3), Marsh, Carole Mysteries) Gallopade International.

Marvel Editors. Genuine Sweet. 2016. (J). lib. bdg. 14.75 (978-0-606-38314-1(X)) Turtleback Bks.

—Marvel's Captain America Civil War Junior Novel. 2016. (J). lib. bdg. 17.20 (978-0-606-38313-4(1)) Turtleback Bks.

Masters, Susan Rowan. Night Journey to Vicksburg. Killcoyne, Hope L., ed. Smith, Duane A., illus. 2003. (Adventures in America Ser.). 74p. (gr. 4). 14.95 (978-1-893110-30-4(3)) Silver Moon Pr.

McDavid-Jones, Elizabeth. Watcher in the Piney Woods. 2009. (Mysteries Through Time Ser.). 160p. (YA). (gr. 4-8). 31.95 (978-1-60754-304-6(4)); pap. 15.25 (978-1-60754-305-3(2)) Windmill Bks.

McDivitt, Barry. The Youngest Spy. 2007. (ENG.). 176p. (YA). (gr. 3-9). per. 12.95 (978-1-897235-17-1(8)) Thistledown Pr., Ltd. CAN. Dist: Univ. of Toronto Pr.

McGee, Anne Loader. Anni's Attic. 2012. 326p. (-18). pap. 12.99 (978-1-936307-24-1(3)) Vendera Publishing.

McGowen, Tom. Jesse Bowman: A Union Boy's War Story. 2008. (Historical Fiction Adventures (HFA) Ser.). (Illus.). 160p. (J). (gr. 3-7). lib. bdg. 29.27 (978-0-7660-2929-3(8)) Enslow Pubs., Inc.

McMann, Lisa. The Trap Door. 2013. (Infinity Ring Ser.: Bk. 3). (ENG.). 192p. (J). (gr. 3-7). 16.99 (978-0-545-48456-5(1)); (Illus.). 12.99 (978-0-545-38698-2(5)) Scholastic, Inc.

McMullan, Margaret. How I Found the Strong: A Civil War Story. 2006. (ENG.). 144p. (YA). (gr. 7-12). reprint ed. mass mkt. 5.99 (978-0-553-49492-1(9), Laurel Leaf) Random Hse. Children's Bks.

Meehan, William. Fife. 2006. (ENG.). 180p. (YA). (gr. 4-6). per. 12.95 (978-0-595-39223-0(7)) iUniverse, Inc.

Meloy, Alice McFeely. As the Crow Flies: Preface to Gettysburg: the Enemy Is Here! 2012. 106p. (J). pap. 8.95 (978-1-57249-411-4(5), White Mane Kids) White Mane Publishing Co., Inc.

Michael R. Zomber. Sweet Betsy That's Me: A child of the Civil War. 2009. 116p. pap. 10.95 (978-1-4401-6323-4(5)) iUniverse, Inc.

Mickles Sr., Robert T. S. Blood Kin, a Savannah Story. 2007. 108p. per. 9.95 (978-0-595-45129-6(2)) iUniverse, Inc.

Miller, Bobbi. The Girls of Gettysburg. 2014. (ENG.). 160p. (J). (gr. 2-7). 16.95 (978-0-8234-3163-2(0)) Holiday Hse., Inc.

Montgomery, R. A. House of Danger. 2005. (Choose Your Own Adventure Ser.). (Illus.). 108p. (gr. 4-8). pap. 5.50 (978-0-7608-9694-5(1)) Sundance/Newbridge Educational Publishing.

—House of Danger. Sundaravej, Sittisan, illus. 2006. (Choose Your Own Adventure Ser.: No. 6). 144p. (J). (gr. 4-8). per. 6.99 (978-1-933390-06-2(9), CHCL06) Chooseco LLC.

Morris, Gilbert. Drummer Boy at Bull Run. 2011. (Bonnets & Bugles Ser.: 1). (ENG.). 192p. (J). (gr. 4-9). pap. 6.99 (978-0-8024-0911-9(3), 566) Moody Pubs.

Murphy, Jim. On Enemy Soil: The Journal of James Edmond Pease, a Civil War Union Soldier. 2012. (ENG.). 176p. (J). (gr. 3-7). pap. 6.99 (978-0-545-39887-9(8)) Scholastic, Inc.

Myers, Anna. Assassin. 2005. (J). (978-978-080-278-3(9)) Walker & Co.

Myers, Laurie. Escape by Night: A Civil War Adventure. Bates, Amy June, illus. 2011. (ENG.). 128p. (J). (gr. 3-7). 14.99 (978-0-8050-8825-0(3), 9780805088250, Holt, Henry & Co. Bks. For Young Readers) Holt, Henry & Co.

Nickerson, Jane. The Mirk & Midnight Hour. 2014. (ENG.). 384p. (YA). (gr. 9). 16.99 *(978-0-385-75286-2(5)*, Knopf Bks. for Young Readers) Random Hse. Children's Bks.

Nix, Josef. My Mama's War. 2009. 104p. pap. 9.99 *(978-1-60860-666-5(X)*, Strategic Bk. Publishing) Strategic Book Publishing & Rights Agency (SBPRA).

Noble, Trinka Hakes. The Last Brother: A Civil War Tale. Papp, Robert, illus. 2006. (Tales of Young Americans Ser.). (ENG.). 32p. (J). (gr. 3-7). 17.95 *(978-1-58536-253-0(0))* Sleeping Bear Pr.

Nolen, Jerdine. Calico Girl. 2017. (ENG., Illus.). 192p. (J). (gr. 3-7). 16.99 *(978-1-4814-5981-5(3)*, Simon & Schuster/Paula Wiseman Bks.) Simon & Schuster/Paula Wiseman Bks.

O'Dell, Scott. 290. 2008. (ENG.). 128p. (J). (gr. 4-7). pap. 8.99 *(978-1-4022-1326-7(3)*, Sourcebooks Jabberwocky) Sourcebooks, Inc.

Optic, Oliver, pseud. Fighting for the Right. 2007. 136p. per. *(978-1-4068-3635-6(4))* Echo Library.

—The Soldier Boy; or, Tom Somers in the Army. 2007. 156p. per. *(978-1-4068-4347-7(4))* Echo Library.

—Stand by the Union. 2007. 140p. (gr. 4-7). per. *(978-1-4068-4345-3(8))* Echo Library.

—Taken by the Enemy. 2007. 132p. (gr. 4-7). per. *(978-1-4068-4346-0(6))* Echo Library.

—Within the Enemy's Lines. 2007. 132p. (gr. 4-7). per. *(978-1-4068-4348-4(2))* Echo Library.

—Within the Enemy's Lines: SERIES: the Blue & the Gray — Afloat. 2007. (ENG.). 196p. per. 19.99 *(978-1-4346-2937-1(6))*; 208p. per. 22.99 *(978-1-4346-2961-6(9))* Creative Media Partners, LLC.

Orzechowski, Shawneen. Sarah's Secret: Civil War Deserter at Fredericksburg. 2011. 104p. (J). pap. 8.95 *(978-1-57249-400-8(X)*, White Mane Kids) White Mane Publishing Co., Inc.

Osborne, Mary Pope. Civil War on Sunday. unabr. ed. 2004. (Magic Tree House Ser.: No. 21). 76p. (J). (gr. k-3). pap. 17.00 incl. audio *(978-0-8072-0930-1(9)*, S FTR 253 SP, Listening Library) Random Hse. Audio Publishing Group.

Papp, Lisa & Noble, Trinka Hakes. The Battles. Papp, Robert, illus. 2013. (American Adventures Ser.). (ENG.). 88p. (J). (gr. 3-6). pap. 9.99 *(978-1-58536-861-7(X)*, 202368) Sleeping Bear Pr.

Parsons, Bruce. Siah Carter & the Ship Monitor. 2009. 36p. pap. 16.99 *(978-1-4490-3435-1(7))* AuthorHouse.

Peck, Richard. The River Between Us. 2005. (ENG.). 176p. (J). (gr. 3-7). reprint ed. pap. 7.99 *(978-0-14-240310-5(5)*, Puffin Books) Penguin Young Readers Group.

Perez, Norah A. The Slopes of War. 2008. (ENG., Illus.). 224p. (YA). (gr. 7-12). pap. 7.99 *(978-0-547-01614-6(X))* Houghton Mifflin Harcourt Publishing Co.

Philbrick, Rodman. The Mostly True Adventures of Homer P. Figg. (ENG.). (J). (gr. 3-7). 2011. 240p. pap. 7.99 *(978-0-439-66821-7(2)*, Scholastic Paperbacks) 2009. 224p. 16.99 *(978-0-439-66818-7(2)*, Blue Sky Pr., The) Scholastic, Inc.

Poe, Marshall. A House Divided. Lindner, Ellen & Purvis, Leland, illus. 2009. (Turning Points Ser.). (ENG.). 128p. (J). (gr. 3-7). pap. 8.99 *(978-1-4169-5057-8(5)*, Simon & Schuster/Paula Wiseman Bks.) Simon & Schuster/Paula Wiseman Bks.

Polacco, Patricia. Just in Time, Abraham Lincoln. Polacco, Patricia, illus. 2011. (ENG., Illus.). 48p. (J). (gr. 2-4). 17.99 *(978-0-399-25471-0(4)*, G.P. Putnam's Sons Books for Young Readers) Penguin Young Readers Group.

—Just in Time Abraham Lincoln. 2012. 29.95 *(978-0-8045-4240-1(6))* Spoken Arts, Inc.

—Pink & Say. (Illus.). (J). (gr. 3-4). pap. 7.99 net. *(978-1-930332-54-6(8))* Lectorum Pubns., Inc.

Potter, David. The Left Behinds: Abe Lincoln & the Selfie That Saved the Union. 2016. (Left Behinds Ser.). (ENG.). 304p. (J). (gr. 3-7). 16.99 *(978-0-385-39060-6(2)*, Crown Books For Young Readers) Random Hse. Children's Bks.

Riddleburger, Sam & Michael Hemphill. Stonewall Hinkleman & the Battle of Bull Run. 2014. lib. bdg. 18.40 *(978-0-606-35709-8(2))* Turtleback Bks.

Rimer, David & Robertson, William P. The Bucktails' Antietam Trials. 2005. (White Mane Kids Ser.: No.14). (Illus.). 175p. (J). (gr. 4-7). per. 7.95 *(978-1-57249-337-7(2)*, White Mane Kids) White Mane Publishing Co., Inc.

Rinaldi, Ann. An Acquaintance with Darkness. 2005. (Great Episodes Ser.). (ENG.). 384p. (YA). (gr. 7-8). pap. 9.99 *(978-0-15-205387-1(5))* Houghton Mifflin Harcourt Publishing Co.

—Juliet's Moon. 2010. (ENG., Illus.). 256p. (YA). (gr. 7). pap. 14.99 *(978-0-547-25874-4(7))* Houghton Mifflin Harcourt Publishing Co.

—Leigh Ann's Civil War. 2011. (ENG.). 320p. (YA). (gr. 7). pap. 17.99 *(978-0-547-54999-6(7))* Houghton Mifflin Harcourt Publishing Co.

—My Vicksburg. 2011. (ENG.). 160p. (YA). (gr. 7). pap. 11.95 *(978-0-547-55000-8(6))* Houghton Mifflin Harcourt Publishing Co.

—Sarah's Ground. (ENG.). 192p. (YA). 2012. (gr. 7). pap. 9.99 *(978-1-4424-8107-7(2))* 2004. (Illus.). 15.95 *(978-0-689-85924-3(4))* Simon & Schuster Bks. For Young Readers. (Simon & Schuster Bks. For Young Readers).

Robertson, William P. & Rimer, David. The Battling Bucktails at Fredericksburg. 2005. (WM Kids Ser.: Vol. 16). (Illus.). 154p. (J). (gr. 4-7). per. 7.95 *(978-1-57249-345-2(3)*, White Mane Kids) White Mane Publishing Co., Inc.

Savage, Bridgette Z. Fly Like the Wind. Savage, Charles J., ed. Savage, Bridgette Z., illus. Savage, Charles J., photos by. 2005. (ENG., Illus.). 112p. (YA). (gr. 5). per. 16.99 *(978-0-9771494-0-7(4))* Buckbeech Studios.

Schraff, Anne. The Burning of the Valley. 2008. (Passages to History Ser.). 115p. (J). (gr. 4-6). lib. bdg. 13.95 *(978-0-7569-8400-7(9))* Perfection Learning Corp.

Schwabach, Karen. The Storm Before Atlanta. 2011. (ENG.). 320p. (J). (gr. 3-7). pap. 6.99 *(978-0-375-85867-3(9)*, Yearling) Random Hse. Children's Bks.

Scott, Kathy. Beacon Hill. 2005. 85p. pap. 16.95 *(978-1-4137-8423-7(2))* PublishAmerica, Inc.

Secrets at Pine Haven: Civil War Comes to Florida. 2006. (Illus.). 180p. (J). per. 12.95 *(978-1-878398-75-8(X)*, Blue Note Bks.) Blue Note Pubns.

Shoulders, Michael. Crossing the Dead Line: Stephen's Journey Through the Civil War. 2016. (ENG.). 384p. (YA). (gr. 4-7). 16.99 *(978-1-58536-951-5(9)*, 204098) Sleeping Bear Pr.

Spain, Susan. The Deep Cut, 0 vols. 2014. (ENG.). 228p. pap. 9.99 *(978-1-4778-4768-8(5)*, 9781477847688, Amazon Children's Publishing) Amazon Publishing.

Spain, Susan Rosson. The Deep Cut, 1 vol. 2006. (ENG., Illus.). 224p. (J). (gr. 5-9). 16.99 *(978-0-7614-5316-1(4))* Marshall Cavendish Corp.

Spier, Peter. The Star-Spangled Banner. 2004. (J). (gr. -1-6). 18.95 *(978-1-55592-143-9(4))* Weston Woods Studios, Inc.

Steele, William O. The Perilous Road. 2004. (ENG., Illus.). 176p. (J). (gr. 2-5). pap. 6.99 *(978-0-15-205204-1(6))* Houghton Mifflin Harcourt Publishing Co.

Sykes, Shelley & Szymanski, Lois. A Whisper of War. 2003. (J). 5.95 *(978-1-57249-327-8(5)*, White Mane Kids) White Mane Publishing Co., Inc.

Trout, Robert J. Drumbeat: The Story of a Civil War Drummer Boy. 2007. 190p. (J). (gr. 4-9). pap. 12.95 *(978-1-57249-390-2(9)*, White Mane Kids) White Mane Publishing Co., Inc.

Verne, Jules. The Secret of the Island. Kingston, W. H. G., tr. 2008. 160p. 24.95 *(978-1-60664-753-0(9))* Rodgers, Alan Bks.

Vigenère, Sator & Alberti, Enigma. Mary Bowser & the Civil War Spy Ring. Cliff, Tony, illus. 2016. (Spy on History Ser.). (ENG.). 96p. (J). (gr. 4). 12.95 *(978-0-7611-8739-4(1))* Workman Publishing Co., Inc.

Walter, Jon. My Name Is Not Friday. 2017. (ENG.). 400p. (J). (gr. 7). pap. 9.99 ***(978-1-338-16064-2(8))*** Scholastic, Inc.

Walter, Jon. My Name's Not Friday. 2016. (ENG.). 384p. (YA). (gr. 7). 18.99 *(978-0-545-85522-8(5))* Scholastic, Inc.

Wargin, Kathy-jo. The Legend of Old Abe: A Civil War Eagle. Caple, Laurie, illus. 2006. (Legend (Sleeping Bear) Ser.). (ENG.). 40p. (J). (gr. 3-7). 17.95 *(978-1-58536-232-5(8))* Sleeping Bear Pr.

Warner, Susan & Wetherell, Elizabeth. Daisy in the Field. 2011. 272p. 29.95 *(978-1-4638-9964-6(5))*; pap. 16.95 *(978-1-4638-0163-2(7))* Rodgers, Alan Bks.

Watkins, Steve. Fallen in Fredericksburg. 2016. (Ghosts of War Ser.: 4). (ENG.). 208p. (J). (gr. 3-7). pap. 5.99 *(978-0-545-83707-1(3)*, Scholastic Paperbacks) Scholastic, Inc.

Wells, Rosemary. Red Moon at Sharpsburg. 2008. (ENG.). 256p. (YA). (gr. 7-18). 7.99 *(978-0-14-241205-3(8)*, Speak) Penguin Young Readers Group.

Wiechman, Kathy Cannon. Like a River. 2015. (ENG.). 336p. (J). (gr. 3). 17.95 *(978-1-62979-209-5(8)*, Calkins Creek) Boyds Mills Pr.

William Murray Hogben. Johnny & Mr Reb: A Civil War Tale. 2009. 40p. pap. 18.99 *(978-1-4389-4326-8(1))* AuthorHouse.

Wilson, John. Battle Scars. 2005. (ENG., Illus.). 168p. (J). (gr. 5-9). 6.95 *(978-1-55337-703-0(6))* Kids Can Pr., Ltd. CAN. Dist: Hachette Bk. Group.

—Death on the River, 1 vol. 2009. (ENG., Illus.). (YA). (gr. 7-12). 212p. 18.95 *(978-1-55469-257-6(1))*; 208p. pap. 12.95 *(978-1-55469-111-1(7))* Orca Bk. Pubs. USA.

—The Flags of War. 2004. (ENG.). 168p. (J). (gr. 5-9). 6.95 *(978-1-55337-568-5(8))* Kids Can Pr., Ltd. CAN. Dist: Hachette Bk. Group.

—The Flags of War: Fields of Conflict-The American Civil War, Part One. 2015. (ENG.). 192p. pap. 12.95 *(978-1-77203-070-9(8))* Heritage Hse. CAN. Dist: Orca Bk. Pubs. USA.

Wincik, Stephanie. The Journey: A Northern Lights Adventure. 2007. 111p. (J). per. 9.99 *(978-0-9725650-4-2(3))* One Horse Pr.

Winnick, Karen B. Cassie's Sweet Berry Pie: A Civil War Story. 2005. (ENG., Illus.). 32p. (J). (gr. 1-4). 16.95 *(978-1-56397-984-2(5))* Boyds Mills Pr.

—Lucy's Cave: A Story of Vicksburg 1863. 2008. (ENG.). 32p. (J). (gr. 4-6). 16.95 *(978-1-59078-194-4(5))* Boyds Mills Pr.

UNITED STATES—HISTORY—CIVIL WAR, 1861-1865—NAVAL OPERATIONS

Abnett, Dan. The Monitor Versus the Merrimac: Ironclads at War. Verma, Dheeraj, illus. 2007. (Graphic Battles of the Civil War Ser.). (ENG.). 48p. (YA). (gr. 4-7). lib. bdg. 31.95 *(978-1-4042-0778-3(3))* Rosen Publishing Group, Inc., The.

Anderson, Dale. The Civil War at Sea. 2004. (World Almanac Library of the Civil War). (Illus.). 48p. (gr. 5-12). pap. 14.05 *(978-0-8368-5594-4(9))*; lib. bdg. 31.00 *(978-0-8368-5585-2(X))* Stevens, Gareth Publishing LLLP. (Gareth Stevens Secondary Library).

Bailey, Tom. Raphael Semmes: Commander of the Alabama. 2011. (Illus.). 120p. (J). *(978-1-59421-062-4(4))* Seacoast Publishing, Inc.

Brager, Bruce L. The Monitor vs. the Merrimack. 2003. (Great Battles Through the Ages Ser.). (Illus.). 112p. (gr. 6-12). 30.00 *(978-0-7910-7439-8(0)*, Chelsea Hse.) Facts On File, Inc.

Dougherty, Terri. Admiral David Farragut: "Full Speed Ahead!" 2011. (J). *(978-1-59556-041-4(6))*; pap. *(978-1-59556-047-6(5))* OTTN Publishing.

Hawk, Frank. The Story of the H. L. Hunley & Queenie's Coin. Nance, Dan, illus. 2004. (ENG.). 40p. (J). (gr. k-6). 16.95 *(978-1-58536-218-9(2))* Sleeping Bear Pr.

O'Brien, Patrick. Duel of the Ironclads: The Monitor vs. the Virginia. 2003. (Illus.). 40p. (J). (gr. 1-5). 18.85 *(978-0-8027-8863-6(2))* Walker & Co.

Thompson, Gare. Civil War Battleship: The Monitor. Day, Larry, illus. 2003. (Penguin Young Readers, Level 4 Ser.). (ENG.). 48p. (J). (gr. 3-4). mass mkt. 3.99 *(978-0-448-43245-8(5)*, Penguin Young Readers) Penguin Young Readers Group.

Walker, Sally M. Secrets of a Civil War Submarine: Solving the Mysteries of the H. L. Hunley. 2005. (ENG., Illus.). 112p. (gr. 4-12). 18.95 *(978-1-57505-830-6(8)*, Carolrhoda Bks.) Lerner Publishing Group.

—Shipwreck Search: Discovery of the H. L. Hunley. Verstraete, Elaine, illus. 2006. (On My Own Science Ser.). (ENG.). 48p. (gr. 2-4). lib. bdg. 25.26 *(978-1-57505-878-8(2)*, Millbrook Pr.) Lerner Publishing Group.

UNITED STATES—HISTORY—CIVIL WAR, 1861-1865—POETRY

Lewis, J. Patrick. The Brothers' War: Civil War Voices in Verse. Civil War Photographers Staff, photos by. 2007. (ENG., Illus.). 48p. (J). (gr. 5-9). 25.90 *(978-1-4263-0037-0(9)*, National Geographic Children's Bks.) National Geographic Society.

UNITED STATES—HISTORY—1865-1898

see also Reconstruction (U.S. History, 1865-1877)

Anderson, Michael, ed. Biographies of the New World Power: Rutherford B. Hayes, Thomas Alva Edison, Margaret Sanger, & More. 2012. (Impact on America: Collective Biographies Ser.). (ENG., Illus.). 112p. (YA). (gr. 7-12). 65.80 *(978-1-61530-765-4(6))* Rosen Publishing Group, Inc., The.

Cooke, Tim. After the War. 2012. (American Civil War: the Right Answer Ser.). (Illus.). 48p. (J). (gr. 6-8). 31.95 *(978-1-4339-7531-8(9))*; pap. 14.05 *(978-1-4339-7532-5(7))* Stevens, Gareth Publishing LLLP. (Gareth Stevens Secondary Library).

Flanagan, Timothy. Reconstruction: A Primary Source History of the Struggle to Unite the North & South after the Civil War. 2005. (Primary Sources in American History Ser.). (Illus.). 64p. (J). (gr. 5-8). lib. bdg. 31.95 *(978-1-4042-0177-4(7))* Rosen Publishing Group, Inc., The.

Hakim, Joy. Reconstructing America, 1865-1890. (History of US Ser.: 7). (ENG., Illus.). 208p. (gr. 4-7). 3rd rev. ed. 2006. 24.95 *(978-0-19-518900-1(0))*Bk. 7. 2nd rev. ed. 2007. per. 15.95 *(978-0-19-532721-2(7))* Oxford Univ. Pr., Inc.

Hale, Sarah Elder, ed. Rebuilding a Nation: Picking up the Pieces. 2005. (ENG., Illus.). 48p. (J). (gr. 3-9). 17.95 *(978-0-8126-7909-0(1))* Cobblestone Publishing Co.

Harkrader, Lisa. Reconstruction & Aftermath of the Civil War: A MyReportLinks. com Book. 2004. (American Civil War Ser.). (Illus.). 48p. (J). lib. bdg. 25.26 *(978-0-7660-5265-9(6)*, MyReportLinks.com Bks.) Enslow Pubs., Inc.

Herringshaw, DeAnn. The United States Enters the 20th Century. 2011. (Explorer Library: Language Arts Explorer Ser.). (ENG.). 32p. (gr. 4-8). pap. 14.21 *(978-1-61080-288-8(8)*, 201211); lib. bdg. 28.50 *(978-1-61080-200-0(4)*, 201176) Cherry Lake Publishing.

Kenison, Misti. Where's Your Hat, Abe Lincoln? 2017. (ENG.). 28p. (J). bds. 9.99 ***(978-1-4926-5250-2(4)***, Sourcebooks Jabberwocky) Sourcebooks, Inc.

Miller, Reagan & Cocca, Lisa Colozza. Reconstruction & the Aftermath of the Civil War. 2011. (ENG.). 48p. (J). lib. bdg. *(978-0-7787-5341-4(7))* Crabtree Publishing Co.

Mooney, Carla. Perspectives on the Industrial Revolution. 2018. (ENG.). 32p. (gr. 3-6). ***(978-1-63235-402-0(0)***, 12-Story Library) Pr. Room Editions LLC.

The New South & the Old West, 1866-1890. 2010. (Discovering U. S. History Ser.). (Illus.). 136p. (gr. 5-8). 35.00 *(978-1-60413-354-7(6)*, Chelsea Hse.) Facts On File, Inc.

Pierce, Alan. Reconstruction, 1 vol. 2005. (American Moments Ser.). (ENG., Illus.). 48p. (gr. 4-8). 27.07 *(978-1-59197-939-5(0)*, Abdo & Daughters) ABDO Publishing Co.

Stanley, George Edward. The Era of Reconstruction & Expansion (1865-1900) 2005. (Primary Source History of the United States Ser.). (Illus.). 48p. (gr. 5-12). pap. 14.05 *(978-0-8368-5836-5(0))*; lib. bdg. 31.00 *(978-0-8368-5827-3(1))* Stevens, Gareth Publishing LLLP. (Gareth Stevens Secondary Library).

Stuckey. Call to Freedom: 1877-Present: Online Edition Plus. 3rd ed. 2003. 17.26 *(978-0-03-037431-9(6))*; 17.26 *(978-0-03-037427-2(8))* Holt McDougal.

—Call to Freedom: Beginning-1877: Online Edition Plus. 3rd ed. 2003. 17.26 *(978-0-03-037428-9(6))*; 17.26 *(978-0-03-037429-6(4))* Holt McDougal.

UNITED STATES—HISTORY—1865-1898—FICTION

Abnett, Dan. Dragon Frontier. 2015. (Dragon Frontier Ser.). (ENG., Illus.). 330p. (J). (gr. 4). pap. 9.99 *(978-0-14-134296-2(X))* Penguin Bks., Ltd. GBR. Dist: Independent Pubs. Group.

Bradbury, Bianca. Flight into Spring. 2005. (Sally (Bethlehem Books) Ser.). 184p. (YA). (gr. 7). per. 11.95 *(978-1-932350-01-2(2))* Bethlehem Bks.

Cast, P. C. & Cast, Kristin. Neferet's Curse. 2013. (House of Night Novellas Ser.: 3). (ENG., Illus.). 160p. (YA). (gr. 7). 12.99 *(978-1-250-00025-5(4)*, 9781250000255, St. Martin's Griffin) St. Martin's Pr.

Hannigan, Kate. The Detective's Assistant. 2016. (ENG.). 368p. (J). (gr. 3-7). pap. 6.99 *(978-0-316-40349-8(0))* Little, Brown Bks. for Young Readers.

LaFaye, A. Walking Home to Rosie Lee. Shepherd, Keith D., illus. 2011. (ENG.). 32p. (J). (gr. 1-6). 16.95 *(978-1-933693-97-2(5))* Cinco Puntos Pr.

Lawlor, Laurie. He Will Go Fearless. 2006. (ENG.). 224p. (J). (gr. 5). 15.95 *(978-0-689-86579-4(1)*, Simon & Schuster Bks. For Young Readers) Simon & Schuster Bks. For Young Readers.

Walsh, Alice. Pomiuk, Prince of the North. Whitehead, Jerry, illus. 2006. (ENG.). 64p. (J). (gr. 3). pap., tchr. ed. 6.95 *(978-0-88878-447-6(3))* Dundum CAN. Dist: Ingram Publisher Services.

UNITED STATES—HISTORY—1898-

Boyer, Paul. Holt American Nation: Modern Era: Online Edition Plus. 3rd ed. 2003. 17.26 *(978-0-03-037433-3(2))* Holt McDougal.

Stuckey. Call to Freedom: 1877-Present: Online Edition Plus. 3rd ed. 2003. 17.26 *(978-0-03-037427-2(8))*; 17.26 *(978-0-03-037431-9(6))* Holt McDougal.

—Call to Freedom: Beginning-1877: Online Edition Plus. 3rd ed. 2003. 17.26 *(978-0-03-037429-6(4))*; 17.26 *(978-0-03-037428-9(6))* Holt McDougal.

UNITED STATES—HISTORY—1898-1919

Brill, Marlene Targ. America in the 1900s. 2009. (Decades of Twentieth-Century America Ser.). (ENG.). 144p. (gr. 5-12). lib. bdg. 38.60 *(978-0-8225-3436-5(3))* Lerner Publishing Group.

Brill, Marlene Targ & Richards, Marlee. America in the 1910s. 2009. (Decades of Twentieth-Century America Ser.). (ENG.). 144p. (gr. 5-12). lib. bdg. 38.60 *(978-0-8225-3437-2(1))* Lerner Publishing Group.

Corrigan, Jim. The 1900s Decade in Photos: A Decade of Discovery. 2010. (Amazing Decades in Photos Ser.). (Illus.). 64p. (J). (gr. 5-9). lib. bdg. 29.27 *(978-0-7660-3129-6(2))* Enslow Pubs., Inc.

UNITED STATES—HISTORY—WAR OF 1898

see Spanish-American War, 1898

UNITED STATES—HISTORY—20TH CENTURY

Amidon Lusted, Marcia. The Roaring Twenties: Discover the Era of Prohibition, Flappers, & Jazz. Keller, Jennifer, illus. 2014. (Inquire & Investigate Ser.). (ENG.). 128p. (J). (gr. 6-10). 22.95 *(978-1-61930-260-0(8))* Open City Bks.

Anderson, Michael, ed. Biographies of the New World Power: Rutherford B. Hayes, Thomas Alva Edison, Margaret Sanger, & More. 2012. (Impact on America: Collective Biographies Ser.). (ENG., Illus.). 112p. (YA). (gr. 7-12). 65.80 *(978-1-61530-765-4(6))* Rosen Publishing Group, Inc., The.

Archer, Jules. The Incredible '60s: The Stormy Years That Changed America. rev. ed. 2015. (Jules Archer History for Young Readers Ser.). (ENG., Illus.). 288p. (J). (gr. 6). 16.99 *(978-1-63220-605-3(6)*, Sky Pony Pr.) Skyhorse Publishing Co., Inc.

Aronson, Marc. Master of Deceit: J. Edgar Hoover & America in the Age of Lies. 2012. (ENG., Illus.). 230p. (J). (gr. 9). 25.99 *(978-0-7636-5025-4(0))* Candlewick Pr.

Barber, Nicola. Who Broke the Wartime Codes?, 1 vol. 2014. (Primary Source Detectives Ser.). (ENG., Illus.). 64p. (gr. 7-8). lib. bdg. 35.99 *(978-1-4329-9606-2(1))* Heinemann-Raintree.

Bartoletti, Susan Campbell, adapted by. The Untold History of the United States, 1898-1945, Vol. 1. 2014. (ENG., Illus.). 400p. (J). (gr. 5-9). 19.99 *(978-1-4814-2173-7(5)*, Atheneum Bks. for Young Readers) Simon & Schuster Children's Publishing.

Boyer, Paul S. Promises to Keep: The United States since World War II. 3rd ed. 2004. (ENG., Illus.). 560p. (C). per. 152.95 *(978-0-618-43383-4(X)*, 305248) CENGAGE Learning.

Brill, Marlene Targ. America in the 1980s. 2009. (Decades of Twentieth-Century America Ser.). (ENG.). 144p. (gr. 5-12). lib. bdg. 38.60 *(978-0-8225-7602-0(3))* Lerner Publishing Group.

—America in the 1990s. 2009. (Decades of Twentieth-Century America Ser.). (ENG.). 144p. (gr. 5-12). lib. bdg. 38.60 *(978-0-8225-7603-7(1))* Lerner Publishing Group.

—Annie Shapiro & the Clothing Workers' Strike. Akib, Jamel, illus. 2010. (History Speaks: Picture Books Plus Reader's Theater Ser.). (ENG.). 48p. (gr. 2-4). pap. 9.95 *(978-0-7613-6132-9(4))* Lerner Publishing Group.

Brown, Jonatha A., et al. César Chávez. McHargue, D., illus. 2007. (Biografías Gráficas (Graphic Biographies) Ser.). (SPA.). 32p. (gr. 5-8). lib. bdg. 27.00 *(978-0-8368-7879-0(5))* Stevens, Gareth Publishing LLLP.

Burns, Bree. America in The 1970s. 2005. (Decades of American History Ser.). (Illus.). 128p. (gr. 5-8). 35.00 *(978-0-8160-5643-9(9))* Facts On File, Inc.

Coates, Tim. The Shooting of John F. Kennedy 1963: The Warren Commission. 2003. (Moments of History Ser.). (Illus.). 320p. *(978-1-84381-025-4(5))* Coates, Tim.

The Cold War & Postwar America 1946-1963. 2010. (Discovering U. S. History Ser.). (Illus.). 136p. (gr. 5-8). 35.00 *(978-1-60413-360-8(0)*, Chelsea Hse.) Facts On File, Inc.

Combs, Maggie. Postwar United States. 2011. (Explorer Library: Language Arts Explorer Ser.). (ENG.). 32p. (gr. 4-8). pap. 14.21 *(978-1-61080-284-0(5)*, 201207); lib. bdg. 28.50 *(978-1-61080-196-6(2)*, 201168) Cherry Lake Publishing.

Corey, Melinda. Chronology of 20th-Century America. 2005. (Decades of American History Ser.). (Illus.). 128p. (gr. 5-8). 35.00 *(978-0-8160-5646-0(3))* Facts On File, Inc.

The Decades of Twentieth-Century America, 10 vols., Set. Incl. America in the 1900s. Brill, Marlene Targ. lib. bdg. 38.60 *(978-0-8225-3436-5(3))*; America in the 1910s. Brill, Marlene Targ & Richards, Marlee. lib. bdg. 38.60 *(978-0-8225-3437-2(1))*; America in the 1920s. Lindop, Edmund & Goldstein, Margaret. (Illus.). lib. bdg. 38.60 *(978-0-7613-2831-5(9))*; America in the 1930s. Lindop, Edmund & Goldstein, Margaret. lib. bdg. 38.60 *(978-0-7613-2832-2(7))*; America in the 1940s. Lindop, Edmund & Goldstein, Margaret. lib. bdg. 38.60 *(978-0-7613-2945-9(5))*; America in the 1950s. Lindop, Edmund & DeCapua, Sarah. lib. bdg. 38.60 *(978-0-8225-7642-6(2))*; America in the 1960s. Lindop, Edmund & Goldstein, Margaret. lib. bdg. 38.60 *(978-0-7613-3453-8(X))*; America in the 1970s. Brill, Marlene Targ & Richards, Marlee. lib. bdg. 38.60 *(978-0-8225-3438-9(X))*; America in the 1980s. Brill, Marlene Targ. lib. bdg. 38.60 *(978-0-8225-7602-0(3))*; America in the 1990s. Brill, Marlene Targ. lib. bdg. 38.60 *(978-0-8225-7603-7(1))*; 144p. (gr. 5-12). 2009. (Decades of Twentieth-Century America Ser.). (ENG.). 2010. Set lib. bdg. 386.00 *(978-0-8225-8172-7(8)*, Twenty-First Century Bks.) Lerner Publishing Group.

Deutsch, Stacia & Cohon, Rhody. Hot Pursuit: Murder in Mississippi. Orback, Craig, illus. 2010. (ENG.). 40p. (J). (gr. 3-5). pap. 7.95 *(978-0-7613-3956-4(6)*, Kar-Ben Publishing) Lerner Publishing Group.

Fandel, Jennifer. Martin Luther King, Jr. 2005. (Genius Ser.). (Illus.). 48p. (J). (gr. 5-9). lib. bdg. 21.95 *(978-1-58341-329-6(4)*, Creative Education) Creative Co., The.

Feinstein, Stephen. Decades of the 20th Century, 10 bks., Set. Incl. 1900s from Teddy Roosevelt to Flying Machines. (J). 2001. lib. bdg. 23.94 *(978-0-7660-1612-5(9))*; 1910s from World War I to Ragtime Music. (J). 2001. lib. bdg. 22.60 *(978-0-7660-1611-8(0))*; 1920s from Prohibition to Charles Lindbergh. (J). 2001. lib. bdg. 22.60 *(978-0-7660-1610-1(2))*; 1930s from the Great Depression to the Wizard of Oz. (J). 2001. lib. bdg. 23.94 *(978-0-7660-1609-5(9))*; 1940s from World War II to Jackie Robinson. (J). 2000. lib. bdg. 23.94 *(978-0-7660-1428-2(2))*; 1950s from the Korean War to Elvis. (J). 2000. lib. bdg. 23.94 *(978-0-7660-1427-5(4))*; 1960s from the Vietnam War to Flower Power. (J). 2000. lib. bdg. 23.94 *(978-0-7660-1426-8(6))*; 1970s from Watergate to Disco. (J). 2000. lib. bdg. 23.94 *(978-0-7660-1425-1(8))*; 1980s from Ronald Reagan to MTV. (YA). 2000. lib. bdg. 22.60 *(978-0-7660-1424-4(X))*; 1990s from the Persian Gulf War to Y2K. (J). 2001. lib. bdg. 22.60 *(978-0-7660-1613-2(7))*; 64p. (gr. 5-12). (Illus.). Set lib. bdg. 179.50 *(978-0-7660-1605-7(6))* Enslow Pubs., Inc.

—The 1970s from Watergate to Disco. rev. ed. 2006. (Decades of the 20th Century in Color Ser.). (Illus.). 64p. (J). (gr. 5). lib. bdg. 29.27 *(978-0-7660-2637-7(X))* Enslow Pubs., Inc.

TUV

—The 1980s from Ronald Reagan to MTV. rev. ed. 2006. (Decades of the 20th Century in Color Ser.). (Illus.). 64p. (J). (gr. 5). lib. bdg. 29.27 *(978-0-7660-2638-4(8))* Enslow Pubs., Inc.

Fiorelli, June Estep. Fannie Lou Hamer: A Voice for Freedom. 2004. (Avisson Young Adult Ser.). (Illus.). 117p. (J). pap. 19.95 *(978-1-888105-62-9(3))* Avisson Pr., Inc.

Gaines, Jena. Haitian Immigration. 2003. (Changing Face of North America Ser.). (Illus.). 112p. (J). lib. bdg. *(978-1-59084-691-9(5))* Mason Crest.

Ganeri, Anita. I Have a Dream: Martin Luther King, Jr. & the Fight for Equal Rights. 2013. (Turning Points in History Ser.). (Illus.). 48p. (gr. 5-12). 37.10 *(978-1-59920-972-2(1))* Black Rabbit Bks.

Gershenson, Harold P. America the Musical 1900-2000: A Nation's History Through Music. Chesworth, Michael, illus. 2006. (J). *(978-1-58987-201-1(0))* Kindermusik International.

Goodman, Susan E. Hazelle Boxberg. Ettlinger, Doris, illus. 2004. (Brave Kids Ser.). (ENG.). 64p. (J). (gr. 1-4). pap. 5.99 *(978-0-689-84982-4(6),* Simon & Schuster/Paula Wiseman Bks.) Simon & Schuster/Paula Wiseman Bks.

Hakim, Joy. All the People since 1945. 4th ed. 2010. (History of US Ser.: 10). (ENG., Illus.). 304p. (YA). (gr. 5-18). pap. 15.95 *(978-0-19-973553-2(0))* Oxford Univ. Pr., Inc.

—A History of US Bk. 10: All the People since 1945. 4th ed. 2010. (History of US Ser.: 10). (ENG., Illus.). 304p. (YA). (gr. 5-18). 24.95 *(978-0-19-973502-0(6))* Oxford Univ. Pr., Inc.

—War, Peace, & All That Jazz, 1918-1945. 3rd rev. ed. 2006. (History of US Ser.: 9). (ENG., Illus.). 224p. (gr. 4-7). 24.95 *(978-0-19-530738-2(0))* Oxford Univ. Pr., Inc.

Hamilton, Neil A. The 1970s. 2006. (Eyewitness History Ser.). (Illus.). 480p. (C). (gr. 9). 80.00 *(978-0-8160-5778-8(8))* Facts On File, Inc.

Hardy, P. Stephen & Hardy, Sheila. Extraordinary People of the Civil Rights Movement. 2006. (Extraordinary People Ser.). (ENG., Illus.). 288p. (J). (gr. 6-18). lib. bdg. 40.00 *(978-0-516-25461-6(8),* Children's Pr.) Scholastic Library Publishing.

Hillstrom, Kevin. The Progressive Era. 2008. (American History Ser.). (ENG., Illus.). 104p. (gr. 7-10). 39.40 *(978-1-4205-0067-7(8),* Lucent Bks.) Cengage Gale.

Hinton, Kerry. The Black Power Movement & Civil Unrest. 2017. (J). pap. ***(978-1-5383-8016-1(1))*** Rosen Publishing Group, Inc., The.

Honovich, Nancy. Immigration from the Former Yugoslavia. 2005. (Changing Face of North America Ser.). (Illus.). 112p. (YA). lib. bdg. 24.95 *(978-1-59084-690-2(7))* Mason Crest.

Hudak, Heather C. McCarthyism & the Red Scare. 2017. 48p. (J). ***(978-0-7787-3939-5(2))*** Crabtree Publishing Co.

Hudson Goff, Elizabeth, et al. César Chávez. 2007. (Biografias Graficas (Graphic Biographies) Ser.). (SPA.). 32p. (gr. 5-8). pap. 10.50 *(978-0-8368-7886-8(8))* Stevens, Gareth Publishing LLLP.

Jackson, Robert B. The Remarkable Ride of the Abernathy Boys. 2003. (Land We Belong to Is Grand Ser.). (Illus.). 69p. (J). pap. *(978-1-57168-798-2(X),* Eakin Pr.) Eakin Pr.

Jarrow, Gail. Red Madness: How a Medical Mystery Changed What We Eat. 2014. (ENG., Illus.). 192p. (J). (gr. 5). 17.95 *(978-1-59078-732-8(3),* Calkins Creek) Boyds Mills Pr.

Kops, Deborah. Racial Profiling. 2006. (Open for Debate Ser.). (Illus.). 128p. (gr. 7-7). lib. bdg. 42.79 *(978-0-7614-2298-3(6),* Benchmark Bks.) Marshall Cavendish Corp.

Lüsted, Marcia Amidon. Lyndon B. Johnson & the Civil Rights ACT. 2017. (J). ***(978-1-5383-8048-2(X))*** Rosen Publishing Group, Inc., The.

Lynne, Douglas. Contemporary United States: 1968 to the Present. 2007. (Presidents of the United States Ser.). (Illus.). 48p. (J). (gr. 4-7). lib. bdg. 29.05 *(978-1-59036-753-7(7));* per. 10.95 *(978-1-59036-754-4(5))* Weigl Pubs., Inc.

Mellors, Julie. U-X-L American Decades 2000-09 Cumulative Index. 2012. (U-X-L American Decades Ser.). (ENG.). pap. 5.00 *(978-1-4144-9723-5(7),* UXL) Cengage Gale.

Miklowitz, Gloria D. Bill Gates. 2004. (ENG., Illus.). 37p. (J). (gr. 2-5). pap. 7.33 *(978-0-7685-1214-4(X),* Dominie Elementary) Pearson Schl.

Noonan, Sheila Smith. Korean Immigration. 2005. (Changing Face of North America Ser.). (Illus.). 112p. (YA). lib. bdg. 24.95 *(978-1-59084-693-3(1))* Mason Crest.

Ochoa, George. America in The 1990s. 2005. (Decades of American History Ser.). (Illus.). 128p. (gr. 5-8). 35.00 *(978-0-8160-5645-3(5))* Facts On File, Inc.

Ollhoff, Jim. Identity & Civil Rights, 1 vol. 2011. (Hispanic American History Ser.). (ENG., Illus.). 32p. (YA). (gr. 5-9). 27.07 *(978-1-61783-057-0(7))* ABDO Publishing Co.

Potter, Tony, prod. Plantation Home Model. 2005. 3p. (J). pap. 19.95 *(978-1-58980-274-2(8))* Pelican Publishing Co., Inc.

Rice, Dona Herwick & Isecke, Harriet. Civil Rights: Freedom Riders, 1 vol. 2009. (Building Fluency Through Reader's Theater Ser.). (ENG., Illus.). 32p. (J). (gr. 3-5). pap. 7.99 *(978-1-4333-0554-2(2))* Teacher Created Materials, Inc.

The Sixties in America, 3 vols. 2004. (ENG.). 600p. 286.00 *(978-0-7876-9249-0(2),* UXL) Cengage Gale.

Smith, Robert W. 20th Century Wars. Hoffman, Nancy, ed. McCarthy, Kevin, illus. 2006. (Spotlight on America Ser.). (ENG.). 96p. (gr. 5-9). pap. 13.99 *(978-1-4206-3219-4(1))* Teacher Created Resources, Inc.

South, Victor. America in the 20th Century (1913-1999) 2013. (Illus.). 48p. (J). pap. *(978-1-4222-2422-9(8))* Mason Crest.

—America in the 20th Century (1913-1999) Rakove, Jack N., ed. 2012. (How America Became America Ser.). (Illus.). 48p. (J). (gr. 3-4). 19.95 *(978-1-4222-2408-3(2))* Mason Crest.

Southwell, David. Unsolved Political Mysteries. 2009. (Mysteries & Conspiracies Ser.). 80p. (gr. 10-10). 61.20 *(978-1-61514-747-2(0))* Rosen Publishing Group, Inc., The.

Southwell, David & Twist, Sean. Unsolved Political Mysteries. 2007. (Mysteries & Conspiracies Ser.). (Illus.). 80p. (YA). (gr. 9-12). lib. bdg. 33.25 *(978-1-4042-1083-7(0))* Rosen Publishing Group, Inc., The.

Stone, Oliver & Kuznick, Peter J. The Untold History of the *United States: Young Readers Edition.* 2014. (Illus.). 383p. (J). pap. *(978-1-4814-2177-5(8))* Simon & Schuster Children's Publishing.

Streissguth, Tom. Clay V. United States & How Muhammad Ali Fought the Draft: Debating Supreme Court Decisions. 2006. (Debating Supreme Court Decisions Ser.). (Illus.). 112p. (J). (gr. 6-12). lib. bdg. 27.94 *(978-0-7660-2393-2(1))* Enslow Pubs., Inc.

Supples, Kevin, et al. The Civil Rights Movement. 2006. (Nonfiction Reading & Writing Workshops Ser.). (ENG., Illus.). 40p. (J). pap. 19.95 *(978-0-7922-8628-8(6))* CENGAGE Learning.

Telgen, Diane. The Gilded Age. 2012. (Defining Moments Ser.). 249p. lib. bdg. 55.00 *(978-0-7808-1238-3(7))* Omnigraphics, Inc.

Vietze, Andrew. The Life & Death of Martin Luther King Jr. 2017. (J). pap. ***(978-1-5383-8039-0(0))*** Rosen Publishing Group, Inc., The.

Woog, Adam. The Fight Renewed: The Civil Rights Movement. 2005. (Lucent Library of Black History). (ENG., Illus.). 112p. (YA). (gr. 7-10). lib. bdg. 33.45 *(978-1-59018-701-2(6),* Lucent Bks.) Cengage Gale.

Wright, John & Waugh, Steven. The USA, 1929-1980. 2005. (Illus.). 144p. pap. 38.50 *(978-0-340-88903-9(9),* Hodder Education) Hodder Education Group GBR. Dist: Trans-Atlantic Pubns., Inc.

UNITED STATES—HISTORY—20TH CENTURY—FICTION

Birtha, Becky. Grandmama's Pride. Bootman, Colin, illus. 2005. (ENG.). 32p. (J). (gr. 2-3). 16.99 *(978-0-8075-3028-3(X))* Whitman, Albert & Co.

—Lucky Beans. Tadgell, Nicole, illus. 2010. (ENG.). 32p. (J). (gr. 2-3). 16.99 *(978-0-8075-4782-3(4))* Whitman, Albert & Co.

Blakemore, Megan Frazer. The Spy Catchers of Maple Hill. 2014. (ENG.). 320p. (YA). (gr. 3-6). 16.99 *(978-1-61963-348-3(5),* 9781619633483, Bloomsbury USA Childrens) Bloomsbury Publishing USA.

Chaconas, Dori. Pennies in a Jar, 1 vol. Lewin, Ted, illus. 2007. (ENG.). 32p. (J). (gr. 1-5). 16.95 *(978-1-56145-422-8(2))* Peachtree Pubs.

Crenshaw, Mills. The Christmas of 45. 2010. 176p. pap. 11.99 *(978-1-59955-455-6(0))* Cedar Fort, Inc./CFI Distribution.

Easton, Kelly. Walking on Air. 2010. (ENG.). 240p. (YA). (gr. 7). pap. 11.99 *(978-1-4424-1437-2(5),* McElderry, Margaret K. Bks.) McElderry, Margaret K. Bks.

Gibson, Julia Mary. Copper Magic. 2014. (ENG., Illus.). 336p. (J). (gr. 5-9). 16.99 *(978-0-7653-3211-0(6),* 9780765332110, Starscape) Doherty, Tom Assocs., LLC.

Greenwood, Diana. Insight, 1 vol. 2012. (ENG.). 224p. (YA). pap. 7.99 *(978-0-310-72315-8(9))* Zondervan.

Hartry, Nancy. Watching Jimmy. 2012. (ENG., Illus.). 152p. (J). (gr. 4-7). pap. 9.95 *(978-1-77049-360-5(3),* Tundra Bks.) Tundra Bks. CAN. Dist: Penguin Random Hse. LLC.

Holm, Jennifer L. Full of Beans. 2016. (ENG.). 208p. (J). (gr. 3-7). 16.99 *(978-0-553-51036-2(3));* lib. bdg. 19.99 *(978-0-553-51037-9(1))* Random Hse. Children's Bks. (Random Hse. Bks. for Young Readers).

Holubitsky, Katherine. Hippie House, 1 vol. 2004. (ENG.). 244p. (YA). (gr. 8-12). lib. bdg. 16.95 *(978-1-55143-316-5(8))* Orca Bk. Pubs. USA.

Johnson, Angela. A Sweet Smell of Roses. Velasquez, Eric, illus. 2007. (ENG.). 32p. (J). (gr. k-3). 7.99 *(978-1-4169-5361-6(2),* Simon & Schuster Bks. For Young Readers) Simon & Schuster Bks. For Young Readers.

Kidd, Ronald. The Year of the Bomb. 2009. (ENG.). 208p. (YA). (gr. 7). pap. 5.99 *(978-1-4169-9625-5(7));* 16.99 *(978-1-4169-5892-5(4))* Simon & Schuster Bks. For Young Readers. (Simon & Schuster Bks. For Young Readers).

Larson, Kirby. The Friendship Doll. 2012. (ENG.). 208p. (J). (gr. 4-7). 6.99 *(978-0-375-85089-9(9),* Yearling) Random Hse. Children's Bks.

Magoon, Kekla. The Rock & the River. (ENG.). 304p. (J). (gr. 5-9). 2010. pap. 7.99 *(978-1-4169-7803-9(8))* 2009. 17.99 *(978-1-4169-7582-3(9))* Simon & Schuster Children's Publishing. (Aladdin).

Matti, Truus. Mister Orange. 2013. (ENG., Illus.). 156p. (J). (gr. 3). 16.95 *(978-1-59270-123-0(X))* Enchanted Lion Bks., LLC.

Mitchell, Margaree King. When Grandmama Sings. Ransome, James E., illus. 2012. (ENG.). 40p. (J). (gr. k-4). 16.99 *(978-0-688-17563-4(5),* Amistad) HarperCollins Pubs.

Myers, Edward. Duck & Cover. 2004. 200p. (J). per. 11.95 *(978-0-9674477-8-0(X))* Montemayor Pr.

Myers, Walter Dean. Patrol: An American Soldier in Vietnam. Grifalconi, Ann, illus. 2005. (ENG.). 40p. (J). (gr. 3-7). pap. 6.99 *(978-0-06-073159-5(1))* HarperCollins Pubs.

Schlitz, Laura Amy. The Hired Girl. 2015. (ENG., Illus.). 400p. (J). (gr. 7-10). 17.99 *(978-0-7636-7818-0(X))* Candlewick Pr.

—The Hired Girl. 2018. lib. bdg. 22.10 ***(978-0-606-40389-4(2))*** Turtleback Bks.

Schwabach, Karen. The Hope Chest. 2010. (ENG.). 288p. (J). (gr. 3-7). 7.99 *(978-0-375-84096-8(6),* Yearling) Random Hse. Children's Bks.

Sepahban, Lois. Paper Wishes. 2016. (ENG.). 192p. (J). 16.99 *(978-0-374-30216-0(2),* 9780374302160, Farrar, Straus & Giroux (BYR)) Farrar, Straus & Giroux.

Shaw, Deirdre. Fair Play. 2005. (American Dreams Ser.: 5). (ENG.). 176p. (YA). mass mkt. 5.99 *(978-0-689-87850-3(8))* Pocket Books.

Smith, Montez Roller. Growing Pains. 2007. (Illus.). 226p. (J). (gr. 4-7). pap. 14.95 *(978-0-9795826-2-2(8))* House Upon A Hill Bks.

—Growing Tall. 2007. (Illus.). 199p. (J). (gr. 4-7). pap. 14.95 *(978-0-9795826-0-8(1))* House Upon A Hill Bks.

Stentiford, Tyler Michael. A Darker Secret. 2009. (ENG.). 128p. (YA). pap. 9.99 *(978-1-60138-315-0(0))* Atlantic Publishing Group, Inc.

Stevenson, Robin. Record Breaker, 1 vol. 2013. (ENG.). 152p. (J). (gr. 4-7). pap. 9.95 *(978-1-55469-959-9(2))* Orca Bk. Pubs. USA.

Strasser, Todd. Fallout. 2013. (ENG.). 272p. (J). (gr. 5). 16.99 *(978-0-7636-5534-1(1))* Candlewick Pr.

Trimble, Tonya. Curiosity, with a Capital S. Enik, Ted, illus. 2011. 144p. (J). pap. 9.95 *(978-0-9816453-9-1(9));* 16.95 *(978-0-9829421-5-4(X))* Tell Me Pr., LLC.

Watts, Jeri. Kizzy Ann Stamps. 2013. (ENG., Illus.). 192p. (J). (gr. 4-7). pap. 5.99 *(978-0-7636-6976-8(8))* Candlewick Pr.

Williams-Garcia, Rita. One Crazy Summer. 2009. (KOR.). 272p. (J). pap. *(978-89-7199-494-8(0))* Dolbegae Publishing Co.

—One Crazy Summer. (J). (gr. 4-7). 2011. (ENG.). 240p. pap. 7.99 *(978-0-06-076090-8(7))* 2010. (ENG.). 224p. 16.99 *(978-0-06-076088-5(5))* 2010. 224p. lib. bdg. 16.89 *(978-0-06-076089-2(3))* HarperCollins Pubs. (Amistad).

—One Crazy Summer. (J). 2011. 1.25 *(978-1-4498-2201-9(0))* 2010. 69.75 *(978-1-4498-2197-5(9))* 2010. 67.75 *(978-1-4498-2199-9(5))* Recorded Bks., Inc.

—One Crazy Summer. 2011. (J). lib. bdg. 17.20 *(978-0-606-23555-6(8),* Turtleback) Turtleback Bks.

UNITED STATES—HISTORY—1919-1933

Baxter, Roberta. The Great Depression: A History Perspectives Book. 2014. (Perspectives Library). (ENG., Illus.). 32p. (J). (gr. 4-8). 28.50 *(978-1-63137-618-4(7),* 205255) Cherry Lake Publishing.

Bearce, Stephanie. Top Secret Files: Gangsters & Bootleggers: Secrets, Strange Tales, & Hidden Facts about the Roaring 20s. rev. ed. 2015. (Top Secret Files Ser.: 0). (ENG., Illus.). 125p. (J). (gr. 4-7). 8.95 *(978-1-61821-461-4(6))* Prufrock Pr.

Beyer, Mark. Temperance & Prohibition: The Movement to Pass Anti-Liquor Laws in America. 2006. (Progressive Movement, 1900-1920 — Efforts to Reform America's New Industrial Society Ser.). (Illus.). 32p. (ENG.). (gr. 4-8). pap. 10.00 *(978-1-4042-0861-2(5));* (YA). (gr. 5-9). lib. bdg. 22.50 *(978-1-4042-0195-8(5))* Rosen Publishing Group, Inc., The.

—Temperance & Prohibition: The Movement to Pass Anti-liquor Laws in America. 2009. (Progressive Movement 1900-1920: Efforts to Reform America's New Industrial Society Ser.). 32p. (gr. 3-4). 47.90 *(978-1-60854-171-3(1))* Rosen Publishing Group, Inc., The.

Blumenthal, Karen. Bootleg: Murder, Moonshine, & the Lawless Years of Prohibition. 2013. (ENG., Illus.). 176p. (YA). (gr. 7-12). pap. 13.99 *(978-1-250-03427-4(2),* 9781250034274) Square Fish.

Burg, David F. The Great Depression. 2nd rev. ed. 2005. (Eyewitness History Ser.). (Illus.). 464p. (C). (gr. 9). 80.00 *(978-0-8160-5709-2(5))* Facts On File, Inc.

Burgan, Michael. The Great Depression: An Interactive History Adventure. 2011. (You Choose: Historical Eras Ser.). (ENG.). 112p. (gr. 3-4). pap. 41.70 *(978-1-4296-6740-1(0),* You Choose Bks.) Capstone Press of Coughlan Cos.

Callan, Jim. America in The 1930s. 2005. (Decades of American History Ser.). (Illus.). 128p. (gr. 5-8). 35.00 *(978-0-8160-5638-5(2))* Facts On File, Inc.

Corrigan, Jim. The 1920s Decade in Photos: The Roaring Twenties. 2010. (Amazing Decades in Photos Ser.). (Illus.). 64p. (J). (gr. 5-9). lib. bdg. 29.27 *(978-0-7660-3131-9(4))* Enslow Pubs., Inc.

—The 1930s Decade in Photos: Depression & Hope. 2010. (Amazing Decades in Photos Ser.). (Illus.). 64p. (J). (gr. 5-9). lib. bdg. 29.27 *(978-0-7660-3132-6(2))* Enslow Pubs., Inc.

Feinstein, Stephen. The 1920s from Prohibition to Charles Lindbergh. rev. ed. 2006. (Decades of the 20th Century in Color Ser.). (Illus.). 64p. (J). (gr. 5). lib. bdg. 29.27 *(978-0-7660-2632-2(9))* Enslow Pubs., Inc.

Gedney, Mona K. The Story of the Great Depression. 2005. (Monumental Milestones Ser.). (Illus.). 48p. (YA). (gr. 4-7). lib. bdg. 29.95 *(978-1-58415-403-7(9))* Mitchell Lane Pubs., Inc.

George, Enzo. The Jazz Age & the Great Depression. 2015. (Primary Sources in U. S. History Ser.). (ENG., Illus.). 48p. (J). (gr. 4-4). 31.36 *(978-1-5026-0490-3(6))* Cavendish Square Publishing.

Gregory, Joy. The Great Depression. 2016. (Illus.). 48p. (J). *(978-1-5105-1286-3(1))* SmartBook Media, Inc.

Hamen, Susan E. The New Deal, 1 vol. 2010. (Essential Events Set 5 Ser.). (ENG.). 112p. (J). (gr. 6-12). lib. bdg. 35.64 *(978-1-61613-684-0(7))* ABDO Publishing Co.

Haugen, David M., et al. The Great Depression. 2010. (Perspectives on Modern World History Ser.). (Illus.). 224p. (YA). (gr. 10-12). 42.45 *(978-0-7377-4795-9(1),* Greenhaven Pr., Inc.) Cengage Gale.

Herringshaw, DeAnn. The United States Enters the 20th Century. 2011. (Explorer Library: Language Arts Explorer Ser.). (ENG.). 32p. (gr. 4-8). pap. 14.21 *(978-1-61080-288-8(8),* 201211); lib. bdg. 28.50 *(978-1-61080-200-0(4),* 201176) Cherry Lake Publishing.

Howes, Kelly King & Carnagie, Julie L. The Roaring Twenties Almanac & Primary Sources. 2005. (Roaring 20's Reference Library). (ENG., Illus.). 352p. (J). (gr. 3-7). 106.00 *(978-1-4144-0212-3(0),* UXL) Cengage Gale.

—The Roaring Twenties Biographies. 2005. (Roaring 20's Reference Library). (ENG., Illus.). 304p. (J). (gr. 3-7). 106.00 *(978-1-4144-0211-6(2),* UXL) Cengage Gale.

Hurt, Avery. The Great Depression. 2017. (J). ***(978-1-5026-2713-1(2))*** Cavendish Square Publishing.

Kupperberg, Paul. Critical Perspectives on the Great Depression. 2005. (Critical Anthologies of Nonfiction Writing Ser.). 176p. (YA). (gr. 7-12). lib. bdg. 37.95 *(978-1-4042-0061-6(4))* Rosen Publishing Group, Inc., The.

Kupperberg, Paul, ed. Critical Perspectives on the Great Depression. 2009. (Critical Anthologies of Nonfiction Writing Ser.). 176p. (gr. 8-8). 63.90 *(978-1-61512-081-9(5))* Rosen Publishing Group, Inc., The.

Lieurance, Suzanne. The Prohibition Era in American History. 2003. (In American History Ser.). (Illus.). 112p. (J). (gr. 5-12). lib. bdg. 27.94 *(978-0-7660-1840-2(7))* Enslow Pubs., Inc.

Lindop, Edmund & Goldstein, Margaret. America in the 1920s. 2009. (Decades of Twentieth-Century America Ser.). (ENG., Illus.). 144p. (gr. 5-12). lib. bdg. 38.60 *(978-0-7613-2831-5(9))* Lerner Publishing Group.

McDaniel, Melissa. The Great Depression. 2012. (Cornerstones of Freedom, Third Ser.). (ENG., Illus.). 64p. (J). pap. 8.95 *(978-0-531-28156-7(6));* (gr. 4-6). lib. bdg. 30.00 *(978-0-531-23056-5(2))* Scholastic Library Publishing.

Mullenbach, Cheryl. The Great Depression for Kids: Hardship & Hope in 1930s America, with 21 Activities. 2015. (For Kids Ser.). (ENG., Illus.). 144p. (J). (gr. 4). pap. 16.95 *(978-1-61373-051-5(9))* Chicago Review Pr., Inc.

Nardo, Don. Migrant Mother: How a Photograph Defined the Great Depression, 1 vol. 2011. (Captured History Ser.). (ENG.). 64p. (gr. 5-7). pap. 9.10 *(978-0-7565-4448-5(3));* lib. bdg. 34.65 *(978-0-7565-4397-6(5))* Compass Point Bks. (CPB Grades 4-8).

Pascal, Janet. What Was the Great Depression? 2015. (What Was... ? Ser.). lib. bdg. 16.00 *(978-0-606-37550-4(3))* Turtleback Bks.

Pascal, Janet & dePaola, Tomie. What Was the Great Depression? Putra, Dede, illus. 2015. (What Was? Ser.). (ENG.). 112p. (J). (gr. 3-7). 5.99 *(978-0-448-48427-3(7),* Penguin Workshop) Penguin Young Readers Group.

Peterson, Sheryl. The Great Depression & World War II. 2011. (Explorer Library: Language Arts Explorer Ser.). (ENG.). 32p. (gr. 4-8). pap. 14.21 *(978-1-61080-287-1(X),* 201210); lib. bdg. 28.50 *(978-1-61080-199-7(7),* 201174) Cherry Lake Publishing.

Ruth, Amy. Growing up in the Great Depression, 1929 to 1941. 2003. (Our America Ser.). (Illus.). 64p. (J). (gr. 4-7). lib. bdg. 26.60 *(978-0-8225-0655-3(6))* Lerner Publishing Group.

Stein, R. Conrad. The New Deal: Pulling America Out of the Great Depression. 2006. (American Saga Ser.). (Illus.). 128p. (J). (gr. 5-9). lib. bdg. 33.27 *(978-0-7660-2570-7(5))* Enslow Pubs., Inc.

Thompson, Gare. The Roaring 20s: Voices from America's Past. 2007. (Reading Expeditions Ser.). (ENG., Illus.). 40p. (J). pap. 19.95 *(978-0-7922-4551-3(2))* National Geographic School Publishing, Inc.

Wallenfeldt, Jeff, ed. A New World Power: America from 1920 To 1945. 2012. (Documenting America: the Primary Source Documents of a Nation Ser.). (ENG., Illus.). 192p. (YA). (gr. 10-12). 82.20 *(978-1-61530-784-5(2))* Rosen Publishing Group, Inc., The.

Wallenfeldt, Jeffrey H. A New World Power: America from 1920 to 1945. 2012. (Documenting America: the Primary Source Documents of a Nation Ser.). (ENG., Illus.). 192p. (J). (gr. 10-12). lib. bdg. 41.10 *(978-1-61530-694-7(3))* Rosen Publishing Group, Inc., The.

World Book, Inc Staff, contrib. by. The Great Depression. 2010. (J). *(978-0-7166-1505-7(3))* World Bk., Inc.

UNITED STATES—HISTORY—1933-1945

Amidon Lusted, Marcia. The Great Depression: Experience the 1930s from the Dust Bowl to the New Deal. Casteel, Tom, illus. 2016. (Inquire & Investigate Ser.). (ENG.). 128p. (J). (gr. 6-10). 22.95 *(978-1-61930-336-2(1),* 1401073) Open City Bks.

—The Great Depression: Experience the 1930's from the Dust Bowl to the New Deal. Casteel, Tom, illus. 2016. (Inquire & Investigate Ser.). (ENG.). 128p. (J). (gr. 6-10). pap. 17.95 *(978-1-61930-340-9(X),* 1401073) Octavio Publishing.

Baxter, Roberta. The Great Depression. 2014. (Perspectives Library). (ENG., Illus.). 32p. (J). (gr. 4-8). pap. 14.21 *(978-1-63137-663-4(2),* 205256) Cherry Lake Publishing.

—The Great Depression: A History Perspectives Book. 2014. (Perspectives Library). (ENG., Illus.). 32p. (J). (gr. 4-8). 28.50 *(978-1-63137-618-4(7),* 205255) Cherry Lake Publishing.

Bolden, Tonya. FDR's Alphabet Soup: New Deal America, 1932-1939. 2010. (ENG.). 144p. (YA). (gr. 7). 19.99 *(978-0-375-85214-5(X),* Knopf Bks. for Young Readers) Random Hse. Children's Bks.

Brown, Don. The Great American Dust Bowl. 2017. (ENG., Illus.). 80p. (YA). (gr. 7). pap. 9.99 ***(978-1-328-74087-8(0),*** HMH Books For Young Readers) Houghton Mifflin Harcourt Publishing Co.

—The Great American Dust Bowl. Brown, Don, illus. 2013. (ENG., Illus.). 80p. (YA). (gr. 7). 18.99 *(978-0-547-81550-3(6))* Houghton Mifflin Harcourt Publishing Co.

Burg, David F. The Great Depression. 2nd rev. ed. 2005. (Eyewitness History Ser.). (Illus.). 464p. (C). (gr. 9). 80.00 *(978-0-8160-5709-2(5))* Facts On File, Inc.

Burgan, Michael. The Great Depression: An Interactive History Adventure. 2011. (You Choose: Historical Eras Ser.). (ENG.). 112p. (gr. 3-4). pap. 41.70 *(978-1-4296-6740-1(0),* You Choose Bks.) Capstone Press of Coughlan Cos.

Callan, Jim. America in The 1930s. 2005. (Decades of American History Ser.). (Illus.). 128p. (gr. 5-8). 35.00 *(978-0-8160-5638-5(2))* Facts On File, Inc.

Corrigan, Jim. The 1940s Decade in Photos: A World at War. 2010. (Amazing Decades in Photos Ser.). (Illus.). 64p. (J). (gr. 5-9). lib. bdg. 29.27 *(978-0-7660-3133-3(0))* Enslow Pubs., Inc.

George, Linda & George, Charles. The Great Depression. 2013. (Illus.). 96p. (J). lib. bdg. *(978-1-60152-492-8(7))* ReferencePoint Pr., Inc.

Gitlin, Martin. The Great Depression & World War II: 1929-1945. 2007. (Presidents of the United States Ser.). (Illus.). 48p. (J). (gr. 4-7). lib. bdg. 29.05 *(978-1-59036-749-0(9));* per. 10.95 *(978-1-59036-750-6(2))* Weigl Pubs., Inc.

—World War II on the Home Front: An Interactive History Adventure, 1 vol. 2012. (You Choose: History Ser.). (ENG.). 112p. (gr. 3-4). pap. 6.95 *(978-1-4296-7998-5(0));* lib. bdg. 31.99 *(978-1-4296-6019-8(8))* Capstone Press of Coughlan Cos. (You Choose Bks.).

Graves, Kerry A. School in the Great Depression. 2016. (It's Back to School ... Way Back! Ser.). (ENG., Illus.). 32p. (gr. 3-4). lib. bdg. 27.32 *(978-1-5157-2098-0(5),* Fact Finders) Capstone Press of Coughlan Cos.

Gregory, Joy. The Great Depression. 2016. (Illus.). 48p. (J). *(978-1-5105-1286-3(1))* SmartBook Media, Inc.

Halpern, Monica & National Geographic Learning Staff. The Home Front During World War II. 2007. (Nonfiction Reading & Writing Workshops Ser.). (ENG., Illus.). 40p. pap. 19.95 *(978-0-7922-4558-2(X))* CENGAGE Learning.

Hamen, Susan E. The New Deal, 1 vol. 2010. (Essential Events Set 5 Ser.). (ENG.). 112p. (J). (gr. 6-12). lib. bdg. 35.64 *(978-1-61613-684-0(7))* ABDO Publishing Co.

Haugen, David M., et al. The Great Depression. 2010. (Perspectives on Modern World History Ser.). (Illus.). 224p. (YA). (gr. 10-12). 42.45 *(978-0-7377-4795-9(1),* Greenhaven Pr., Inc.) Cengage Gale.

Hurt, Avery. The Great Depression. 2017. (J). ***(978-1-5026-2713-1(2))*** Cavendish Square Publishing.

Immell, Myra. The McCarthy Era. Gale Editors, ed. 2011. (Perspectives on Modern World History Ser.). (ENG.). 224p. (gr. 12-12). lib. bdg. 47.80 *(978-0-7377-5260-1(2),* Greenhaven Pr., Inc.) Cengage Gale.

Isserman, Maurice. World War II. 2nd rev. ed. 2010. (America at War Ser.). 272p. (gr. 6-12). 45.00 *(978-0-8160-8185-1(9),* Chelsea Hse.) Facts On File, Inc.

Kimmelman, Leslie & Juhasz, Victor. Hot Dog! Eleanor Roosevelt Throws a Picnic. 2014. (ENG., Illus.). 40p. (J). (gr. 3-6). 16.99 *(978-1-58536-830-3(X),* 203013) Sleeping Bear Pr.

Kupperberg, Paul. Critical Perspectives on the Great Depression. 2005. (Critical Anthologies of Nonfiction Writing Ser.). 176p. (YA). (gr. 7-12). lib. bdg. 37.95 *(978-1-4042-0061-6(4))* Rosen Publishing Group, Inc., The.

Kupperberg, Paul, ed. Critical Perspectives on the Great Depression. 2009. (Critical Anthologies of Nonfiction Writing Ser.). 176p. (gr. 8-8). 63.90 *(978-1-61512-081-9(5))* Rosen Publishing Group, Inc., The.
Lassieur, Allison, et al. The World War II Experience: An Interactive History Adventure, 1 vol. 2014. (You Choose: History Ser.). (ENG.). 328p. (gr. 3-4). pap. 14.95 *(978-1-4765-2169-5(7),* You Choose Bks.) Capstone Press of Coughlan Cos.
Lindop, Edmund & Goldstein, Margaret. America in the 1940s. 2009. (Decades of Twentieth-Century America Ser.). (ENG.). 144p. (gr. 5-12). lib. bdg. 38.60 *(978-0-7613-2945-9(5))* Lerner Publishing Group.
Marriott, Emma. Did Anything Good Come Out of the Great Depression?, 01 vols., 1. 2016. (Innovation Through Adversity Ser.). (ENG.). 48p. (J). 30.25 *(978-1-5081-7072-3(X),* Rosen Young Adult) Rosen Publishing Group, Inc., The.
McCarthy, Meghan. Aliens Are Coming! The True Account of the 1938 War of the Worlds Radio Broadcast. 2009. (ENG.). 40p. (J). (gr. -1-2). pap. 7.99 *(978-0-385-73678-7(9),* Dragonfly Bks.) Random Hse. Children's Bks.
McDaniel, Melissa. The Great Depression. 2012. (Cornerstones of Freedom, Third Ser.). (ENG., Illus.). 64p. (J). pap. 8.95 *(978-0-531-28156-7(6));* (gr. 4-6). lib. bdg. 30.00 *(978-0-531-23056-5(2))* Scholastic Library Publishing.
McNeill, Allison & Hanes, Richard Clay. American Home Front in World War II Reference Library Cumulative Index. 2004. (American Homefront in World War II Reference Library). (ENG.). 32p. 5.00 *(978-0-7876-9125-7(9),* UXL) Cengage Gale.
McNeilly, Linden K. Perspectives on the Great Depression. 2018. (ENG.). 32p. (gr. 3-6). ***(978-1-63235-401-3(2),*** 12-Story Library) Pr. Room Editions LLC.
Mullenbach, Cheryl. The Great Depression for Kids: Hardship & Hope in 1930s America, with 21 Activities. 2015. (For Kids Ser.). (ENG., Illus.). 144p. (J). (gr. 4). pap. 16.95 *(978-1-61373-051-5(9))* Chicago Review Pr., Inc.
Nardo, Don. Migrant Mother: How a Photograph Defined the Great Depression, 1 vol. 2011. (Captured History Ser.). (ENG.). 64p. (gr. 5-7). pap. 9.10 *(978-0-7565-4448-5(3));* lib. bdg. 34.65 *(978-0-7565-4397-6(5))* Compass Point Bks. (CPB Grades 4-8).
Pascal, Janet. What Was the Great Depression? 2015. (What Was... ? Ser.). lib. bdg. 16.00 *(978-0-606-37550-4(3))* Turtleback Bks.
Pascal, Janet & dePaola, Tomie. What Was the Great Depression? Putra, Dede, illus. 2015. (What Was? Ser.). (ENG.). 112p. (J). (gr. 3-7). 5.99 *(978-0-448-48427-3(7),* Penguin Workshop) Penguin Young Readers Group.
Peterson, Sheryl. The Great Depression & World War II. 2011. (Explorer Library: Language Arts Explorer Ser.). (ENG.). 32p. (gr. 4-8). pap. 14.21 *(978-1-61080-287-1(X),* 201210); lib. bdg. 28.50 *(978-1-61080-199-7(7),* 201174) Cherry Lake Publishing.
Reis, Ronald A. The Great Depression & the New Deal: America's Economy in Crisis. 2011. (Milestones in American History Ser.). (Illus.). 150p. (gr. 6-12). 35.00 *(978-1-60413-766-8(5),* Chelsea Hse.) Facts On File, Inc.
Ruth, Amy. Growing up in the Great Depression, 1929 to 1941. 2003. (Our America Ser.). (Illus.). 64p. (J). (gr. 4-7). lib. bdg. 26.60 *(978-0-8225-0655-3(6))* Lerner Publishing Group.
Stein, R. Conrad. The New Deal: Pulling America Out of the Great Depression. 2006. (American Saga Ser.). (Illus.). 128p. (J). (gr. 5-9). lib. bdg. 33.27 *(978-0-7660-2570-7(5))* Enslow Pubs., Inc.
Wallenfeldt, Jeff, ed. A New World Power: America from 1920 To 1945. 2012. (Documenting America: the Primary Source Documents of a Nation Ser.). (ENG., Illus.). 192p. (YA). (gr. 10-12). 82.20 *(978-1-61530-784-5(2))* Rosen Publishing Group, Inc., The.
Wills, Charles. America in The 1940s. 2005. (Decades of American History Ser.). (Illus.). 128p. (gr. 5-8). 35.00 *(978-0-8160-5639-2(0))* Facts On File, Inc.
World Book, Inc Staff, contrib. by. The Great Depression. 2010. (J). *(978-0-7166-1505-7(3))* World Bk., Inc.

UNITED STATES—HISTORY—WORLD WAR, 1939-1945
see World War, 1939-1945—United States

UNITED STATES—HISTORY—1945-1953
Corrigan, Jim. The 1950s Decade in Photos: The American Decade. 2010. (Amazing Decades in Photos Ser.). (Illus.). 64p. (J). (gr. 5-9). lib. bdg. 29.27 *(978-0-7660-3134-0(9))* Enslow Pubs., Inc.
Cunningham, Jesse G., ed. The McCarthy Hearings. 2003. (At Issue in History Ser.). (Illus.). 144p. (YA). (gr. 7-10). pap. 18.70 *(978-0-7377-1347-3(X),* Greenhaven Pr., Inc.) Cengage Gale.
Gitlin, Martin. Post-War United States: 1945-Early 1970s. 2007. (Presidents of the United States Ser.). (Illus.). 48p. (J). (gr. 4-7). lib. bdg. 29.05 *(978-1-59036-751-3(0));* per. 10.95 *(978-1-59036-752-0(9))* Weigl Pubs., Inc.
Immell, Myra. The McCarthy Era. Gale Editors, ed. 2011. (Perspectives on Modern World History Ser.). (ENG.). 224p. (gr. 12-12). lib. bdg. 47.80 *(978-0-7377-5260-1(2),* Greenhaven Pr., Inc.) Cengage Gale.
Lindop, Edmund & DeCapua, Sarah. America in the 1950s. 2009. (Decades of Twentieth-Century America Ser.). (ENG.). 144p. (gr. 5-12). lib. bdg. 38.60 *(978-0-8225-7642-6(2))* Lerner Publishing Group.
Lindop, Edmund & Goldstein, Margaret. America in the 1940s. 2009. (Decades of Twentieth-Century America Ser.). (ENG.). 144p. (gr. 5-12). lib. bdg. 38.60 *(978-0-7613-2945-9(5))* Lerner Publishing Group.
Stanley, George Edward. America & the Cold War (1949-1969) 2005. (Primary Source History of the United States Ser.). (Illus.). 48p. (gr. 5-12). lib. bdg. 31.00 *(978-0-8368-5830-3(1),* Gareth Stevens Secondary Library) Stevens, Gareth Publishing LLLP.
Tracy, Kathleen. The McCarthy Era. 2008. (Monumental Milestones Ser.). (Illus.). 48p. (YA). (gr. 4-7). lib. bdg. 29.95 *(978-1-58415-694-9(5))* Mitchell Lane Pubs., Inc.
Wills, Charles. America in The 1940s. 2005. (Decades of American History Ser.). (Illus.). 128p. (gr. 5-8). 35.00 *(978-0-8160-5639-2(0))* Facts On File, Inc.
Wills, Charles A. America in The 1950s. 2005. (Decades of American History Ser.). (Illus.). 128p. (gr. 5-8). 35.00 *(978-0-8160-5640-8(4))* Facts On File, Inc.
World War I & the Roaring Twenties, 1914-1928. 2010. (Discovering U. S. History Ser.). (Illus.). 136p. (J). (gr. 5-8). 35.00 *(978-1-60413-356-1(2),* Chelsea Hse.) Facts On File, Inc.

UNITED STATES—HISTORY—1961-
ABDO Publishing Company Staff & Scheunemann, Pam. United We Stand, Set. 2003. (United We Stand Ser.: 4). (ENG.). (J). (gr. k-3). lib. bdg. 96.84 *(978-1-57765-876-4(0),* SandCastle) ABDO Publishing Co.
Brill, Marlene Targ & Richards, Marlee. America in the 1970s. 2009. (Decades of Twentieth-Century America Ser.). (ENG.). 144p. (gr. 5-12). lib. bdg. 38.60 *(978-0-8225-3438-9(X))* Lerner Publishing Group.
Callan, Jim. America in The 1960s. 2005. (Decades of American History Ser.). (Illus.). 128p. (gr. 5-8). 35.00 *(978-0-8160-5642-2(0))* Facts On File, Inc.
Corrigan, Jim. The 1960s Decade in Photos: Love, Freedom, & Flower Power. 2010. (Amazing Decades in Photos Ser.). (Illus.). 64p. (J). (gr. 5-9). lib. bdg. 29.27 *(978-0-7660-3135-7(7))* Enslow Pubs., Inc.
—The 1970s Decade in Photos: Protest & Change. 2010. (Amazing Decades in Photos Ser.). (Illus.). 64p. (J). (gr. 5-9). lib. bdg. 29.27 *(978-0-7660-3136-4(5))* Enslow Pubs., Inc.
—The 1980s Decade in Photos: The Triumph of Democracy. 2010. (Amazing Decades in Photos Ser.). (Illus.). 64p. (J). (gr. 5-9). lib. bdg. 29.27 *(978-0-7660-3137-1(3))* Enslow Pubs., Inc.
—The 1990s Decade in Photos: The Rise of Technology. 2010. (Amazing Decades in Photos Ser.). (Illus.). 64p. (J). (gr. 5-9). lib. bdg. 29.27 *(978-0-7660-3138-8(1))* Enslow Pubs., Inc.
Fleming, Candace. The Lincolns: A Scrapbook Look at Abraham & Mary. 2008. (ENG., Illus.). 200p. (J). (gr. 5-9). 24.99 *(978-0-375-83618-3(7),* Schwartz & Wade Bks.) Random Hse. Children's Bks.
Gitlin, Martin. U. S. Involvement in Vietnam, 1 vol. 2010. (Essential Events Set 4 Ser.). (ENG.). 112p. (J). (gr. 6-12). lib. bdg. 35.64 *(978-1-60453-949-3(6))* ABDO Publishing Co.
Hibbert, Clare. A Day That Changed History: The Assassination of John F Kennedy. 2013. (Turning Points in History Ser.). 48p. (gr. 5-12). 37.10 *(978-1-59920-971-5(3))* Black Rabbit Bks.
Kelley, Tracey. Assassination of John F. Kennedy. 2013. (Turning Points in History Ser.). 48p. (gr. 5-9). 24.95 *(978-1-59920-771-1(0))* Black Rabbit Bks.
Levy, Debbie. The Vietnam War. 2004. (Chronicle of America's Wars Ser.). (Illus.). 96p. (J). (gr. 5-12). 27.93 *(978-0-8225-0421-4(9))* Lerner Publishing Group.
Lindop, Edmund & Goldstein, Margaret. America in the 1960s. 2009. (Decades of Twentieth-Century America Ser.). (ENG.). 144p. (gr. 5-12). lib. bdg. 38.60 *(978-0-7613-3453-8(X))* Lerner Publishing Group.
Marcovitz, Hal & marcovitz, hal. The 1960s: Part of the Understanding American History Series. 2013. (Illus.). 96p. (YA). lib. bdg. *(978-1-60152-494-2(3))* ReferencePoint Pr., Inc.
Primary Sources, Sixties in America. 2004. (Sixties in America Reference Library). (ENG., Illus.). 304p. (J). lib. bdg. 106.00 *(978-0-7876-9248-3(4),* UXL) Cengage Gale.
Schwartz, Richard Alan. The 1990s. 2006. (Eyewitness History Ser.). (Illus.). 512p. (C). (gr. 9). 80.00 *(978-0-8160-5696-5(X))* Facts On File, Inc.

UNITED STATES—HISTORY—21ST CENTURY
Bartoletti, Susan Campbell, adapted by. The Untold History of the United States, 1898-1945, Vol. 1. 2014. (ENG., Illus.). 400p. (J). (gr. 5-9). 19.99 *(978-1-4814-2173-7(5),* Atheneum Bks. for Young Readers) Simon & Schuster Children's Publishing.
Corrigan, Jim. The 2000s Decade in Photos: A New Millennium. 2010. (Amazing Decades in Photos Ser.). (Illus.). 64p. (J). (gr. 5-9). lib. bdg. 29.27 *(978-0-7660-3139-5(X))* Enslow Pubs., Inc.
Stone, Oliver & Kuznick, Peter J. The Untold History of the United States: Young Readers Edition. 2014. (Illus.). 383p. (J). pap. *(978-1-4814-2177-5(8))* Simon & Schuster Children's Publishing.
TIME Annual 2009. 2009. (Time Inc. Home Entertainment Library-Bound Titles Ser.). (gr. 5-12). 39.93 *(978-0-7613-4232-8(X),* Twenty-First Century Bks.) Lerner Publishing Group.
Time Inc. Home Entertainment Library-Bound Titles, 9 vols., Set. Incl. GOLF Magazine: The Best Instruction Guide Ever. 144p. (YA). (gr. 5-12). 2008. lib. bdg. 39.93 *(978-0-8225-7278-7(8),* Twenty-First Century Bks.); Life Nature's Fury. 144p. (gr. 5-12). 2008. lib. bdg. 39.93 *(978-0-7613-4051-5(3),* Twenty-First Century Bks.); Life Remembering Martin Luther King, Jr. His Life & Crusade in Pictures. Johnson, Charles & Adelman, Bob. 144p. (gr. 5-12). 2008. lib. bdg. 39.93 *(978-0-7613-4178-9(1),* Twenty-First Century Bks.); Life Strange but True. 128p. (gr. 5-12). 2009. 39.93 *(978-0-7613-4231-1(1),* Twenty-First Century Bks.); Time: The Year in Review. Twenty-First Century Books, creator. (Illus.). 122p. (YA). (gr. 7-12). 2008. lib. bdg. 33.27 *(978-1-57505-972-3(X));* TIME for Kids Almanac 2009. 256p. (YA). (gr. 5-12). 2008. lib. bdg. 39.93 *(978-0-7613-4052-2(1),* Twenty-First Century Bks.); Time Living Wonders: The Marvels & Mysteries of Life on Earth. 128p. (gr. 5-12). 2009. 39.93 *(978-0-7613-4229-8(X),* Twenty-First Century Bks.); Time Nature's Wonders: The Science & Splendor of Earth's Most Fascinating Places. Lerner Publishing Group Staff, ed. 128p. (gr. 5-12). 2008. lib. bdg. 39.93 *(978-0-7613-4228-1(1),* Twenty-First Century Bks.); 2008. Set lib. bdg. 389.97 *(978-0-8225-7275-6(3),* Twenty-First Century Bks.) Lerner Publishing Group.
Twenty-First Century Books, creator. Time: The Year in Review. 2008. (Time Inc. Home Entertainment Library-Bound Titles Ser.). (Illus.). 122p. (YA). (gr. 7-12). lib. bdg. 33.27 *(978-1-57505-972-3(X))* Lerner Publishing Group.

UNITED STATES—HISTORY—21ST CENTURY—FICTION
Obama, Barack. Yes We Can! A Salute to Children from President Obama's Victory Speech. 2010. (Rise & Shine Ser.). (ENG.). 32p. (C). (gr. -1-3). pap. 8.95 *(978-0-545-16366-8(8))* National Geographic School Publishing, Inc.

UNITED STATES—INSULAR POSSESSIONS
see United States—Territories and Possessions

UNITED STATES—LABOR AND LABORING CLASSES
see Labor—United States

UNITED STATES—LAW
see Law—United States

UNITED STATES—MAIL
see Postal Service

UNITED STATES—MANNERS AND CUSTOMS
see United States—Social Life and Customs

UNITED STATES—MANUFACTURES
see Industries—United States

UNITED STATES—MAPS
The Atlas of Famous Battles of the American Revolution. (Illus.). (J). (gr. k-5). 127.50 *(978-0-8239-7269-2(0))* Rosen Publishing Group, Inc., The.
Attainment Company, prod. Geography Reader: 96 Lessons Focus on USA Destinations. 2005. 203p. (YA). (gr. 7-12). spiral bd. 39.00 incl. audio compact disk *(978-1-57861-547-6(X),* IEP Resources) Attainment Co., Inc.
Balkan, Gabrielle. The 50 States. Linero, Sol, illus. 2016. (50 States Ser.). (ENG.). 32p. (J). (gr. 3-6). pap., act. bk. ed. 9.99 *(978-1-84780-862-2(X),* Wide Eyed Editions) Quarto Publishing Group UK GBR. Dist: Hachette Bk. Group.
Balkan, Gabrielle. The 50 States - B&N: Explore the U. S. a with 50 Fact-Filled Maps! Linero, Sol, illus. 2016. (ENG.). (J). (gr. 2-5). 19.99 ***(978-1-84780-934-6(0),*** Wide Eyed Editions) Quarto Publishing Group UK GBR. Dist: Hachette Bk. Group.
Boyer, Crispin. National Geographic Kids Ultimate U. S. Road Trip Atlas: Maps, Games, Activities, & More for Hours of Backseat Fun. 2012. (ENG., Illus.). 128p. (J). (gr. 3-7). lib. bdg. 14.90 *(978-1-4263-0934-2(1),* National Geographic Children's Bks.) National Geographic Society.
Chadow, Alysa. US States. 2003. pap. 14.00 *(978-0-8059-6054-9(6))* Dorrance Publishing Co., Inc.
Emerald Books, creator. Heroes of History - Maps of the United States Workbook: A Reproducible Workbook & Curriculum Guide. 2005. (Heroes of History Ser.). (ENG., Illus.). 127p. (gr. 5-9). per. 17.99 *(978-1-932096-26-2(4))* Emerald Bks.
Equipo Staff. Atlas Enciclopedico Paises de America. (SPA., Illus.). 224p. (YA). (gr. 5-8). *(978-84-241-2522-6(3),* EV5866) Everest Editora ESP. Dist: Lectorum Pubns., Inc.
Evan-Moor. Maps of the USA, Grades 1-6. 2004. (ENG.). 128p. (J). pap. 16.99 *(978-1-55799-955-9(4),* EMC 3721) Evan-Moor Educational Pubs.
In the United States. (J). (gr. 4). 3.80 *(978-0-8374-1453-9(9),* 404) Weekly Reader Corp.
Map - United States. 2004. (Wall Charts Ser.). (J). 4.99 *(978-1-85997-987-7(4))* Byeway Bks.
Martonyi, E. Andrew. The Little Man in the Map: With Clues to Remember All 50 States. Olson, Ed, illus. 2007. (ENG.). 64p. (gr. -1-3). lib. bdg. 19.95 *(978-0-9785100-4-6(6))* Schoolside Pr.
Miller, Millie & Nelson, Cyndi. United States of America: A State-by-State Guide. 2006. (United States of America Ser.). (ENG., Illus.). 64p. (J). (gr. 3-7). pap. 7.99 *(978-0-439-82765-2(5),* Scholastic Reference) Scholastic, Inc.
National Geographic Kids. National Geographic Kids United States Atlas. 2017. (ENG.). 176p. (J). (gr. 3-7). lib. bdg. 22.90 ***(978-1-4263-2832-9(X),*** National Geographic Children's Bks.) National Geographic Society.
National Geographic Kids Staff. National Geographic Kids Beginner's United States Atlas. 2016. (ENG.). 128p. (J). (gr. k-4). 18.99 *(978-1-4263-2434-5(0),* National Geographic Children's Bks.) National Geographic Society.
National Geographic Kids Staff. National Geographic Kids United States Atlas. 2017. (ENG., Illus.). 176p. (J). (gr. 3-7). pap. 12.99 ***(978-1-4263-2831-2(1),*** National Geographic Children's Bks.) National Geographic Society.
National Geographic Staff. National Geographic Kids United States Atlas. 2012. (ENG., Illus.). 176p. (J). (gr. 3-7). pap. 12.95 *(978-1-4263-1052-2(8),* National Geographic Children's Bks.) National Geographic Society.
Rand McNally Staff. Atlas Schoolhouse Illustrated United States Atlas. 2005. 112p. (J). 9.95 *(978-0-528-93459-9(7))* Rand McNally.
—Kids' Road Atlas. (Backseat Bks.). 80p. (J). pap. 3.95 *(978-0-528-96544-9(1))* Rand McNally.
State by State Sticker Book. 2012. (J). 5.95 *(978-0-8437-0985-8(5))* Hammond World Atlas Corp.
Treasure Maps of Clarion County. 2004. per. 19.95 *(978-0-9743881-1-3(4))* Hufnagel Software.
U. S. A. History Map. 2004. (J). *(978-0-9759433-3-5(2))* Maps For Kids Inc.
U. S. A. History Notebook Map. 2004. (J). *(978-0-9759433-5-9(9))* Maps For Kids Inc.
U. S. A. History Poster Map. 2004. (J). *(978-0-9759433-4-2(0))* Maps For Kids Inc.
U. S. National Geographic Society Staff. Beginner's United States Atlas. 2009. (ENG., Illus.). 128p. (J). (gr. 1-4). 27.90 *(978-1-4263-0558-0(3),* National Geographic Children's Bks.) National Geographic Society.
U. S. National Geographic Society Staff & National Geographic Learning Staff. Beginner's United States: It's Your Country. Be a Part of It! 3rd ed. 2009. (ENG., Illus.). 128p. (J). (gr. 1-4). 18.95 *(978-1-4263-0512-2(5),* National Geographic Children's Bks.) National Geographic Society.

UNITED STATES—MARINE CORPS
Alvarez, Carlos. Marine Expeditionary Units. 2009. (Armed Forces Ser.). (ENG., Illus.). 24p. (J). (gr. 3-7). lib. bdg. 25.95 *(978-1-60014-278-9(8))* Bellwether Media.
Baker, Brynn. Navajo Code Talkers: Secret American Indian Heroes of World War II. 2015. (Military Heroes Ser.). (ENG., Illus.). 32p. (gr. 3-4). lib. bdg. 27.32 *(978-1-4914-4837-3(7))* Capstone Press of Coughlan Cos.
Benson, Michael. The U. S. Marine Corps. 2004. (U. S. Armed Forces Ser.). (ENG., Illus.). 64p. (gr. 4-8). lib. bdg. 26.60 *(978-0-8225-1648-4(9))* Lerner Publishing Group.
Berne, Emma Carlson. Today's U. S. Marines, 1 vol. 2013. (U. S. Armed Forces Ser.). (ENG.). 48p. (gr. 5-6). pap. 9.10 *(978-0-7565-4637-3(0));* lib. bdg. 29.32 *(978-0-7565-4621-2(4))* Compass Point Bks.
Boothroyd, Jennifer. Inside the US Marine Corps. 2017. (Lightning Bolt Books (tm) — US Armed Forces Ser.). (ENG.). (J). (gr. 1-3). 24p. 25.32 *(978-1-5124-3393-7(4));* pap. 6.99 ***(978-1-5124-5601-1(2))*** Lerner Publishing Group.
Bozzo, Linda. Marine Expeditionary Units. 2015. (Serving in the Military Ser.). (Illus.). 32p. (J). 28.50 *(978-1-60753-493-8(2))* Amicus Publishing.
Broyles, Janell. Chemical Biological Incident Response Force. (Inside Special Operations Ser.). 2009. (Illus.). 64p. (gr. 5-8). pap. 12.95 *(978-1-4358-5129-0(3),* Rosen Classroom) 2009. 64p. (gr. 6-6). 58.50 *(978-1-61513-551-6(0),* Rosen Reference) 2008. (Illus.). 54p. (J). lib. bdg. 31.95 *(978-1-4042-1751-5(7))* Rosen Publishing Group, Inc., The.
Cook, Colleen Ryckert. Your Career in the Marines. 2011. (Call of Duty: Careers in the Armed Forces Ser.). (ENG.). 128p. (YA). (gr. 9-12). lib. bdg. 34.60 *(978-1-4488-5512-4(8))* Rosen Publishing Group, Inc., The.
Cooke, Tim. US Marine Corps. 2012. (Ultimate Special Forces Ser.). (ENG., Illus.). 48p. (J). (gr. 4-8). 27.95 *(978-1-4488-7880-2(2));* pap. 11.75 *(978-1-4488-7957-1(4))* Rosen Publishing Group, Inc., The. (PowerKids Pr.).
David, Jack. United States Marine Corps. 2008. (Armed Forces Ser.). (ENG., Illus.). 24p. (YA). (gr. 3-7). lib. bdg. 25.95 *(978-1-60014-164-5(1))* Bellwether Media.
Goldish, Meish. Marine Corps: Civilian to Marine. 2010. (Becoming a Soldier Ser.). 24p. (YA). (gr. 3-6). lib. bdg. 22.61 *(978-1-936088-13-3(4))* Bearport Publishing Co., Inc.
Goldish, Meish & Parkhurst, Anthony. Horses, Donkeys, & Mules in the Marines. 2012. (America's Animal Soldiers Ser.). 24p. (J). (gr. 1-6). lib. bdg. 23.93 *(978-1-61772-453-4(X))* Bearport Publishing Co., Inc.
Gordon, Nick. Marine Corps Force Recon. 2013. (U. S. Military Ser.). (ENG., Illus.). 24p. (J). (gr. 3-7). lib. bdg. 25.95 *(978-1-60014-875-0(1),* Epic Bks.) Bellwether Media.
—Marine Expeditionary Units. 2013. (U. S. Military Ser.). (ENG., Illus.). 24p. (J). (gr. 3-7). lib. bdg. 25.95 *(978-1-60014-876-7(X),* Epic Bks.) Bellwether Media.
—U. S. Marine Corps. 2012. (U. S. Military Ser.). (ENG., Illus.). 24p. (J). (gr. 3-7). lib. bdg. 25.95 *(978-1-60014-829-3(8),* Epic Bks.) Bellwether Media.
Green, Michael. The United States Marines, 1 vol. 2013. (U. S. Military Forces Ser.). (ENG.). 24p. (gr. 1-2). lib. bdg. 25.32 *(978-1-4765-0072-0(X))* Capstone Press of Coughlan Cos.
Gutner, Howard. America's Secret Weapon: The Navajo Code Talkers of World War II. 2003. (ENG., Illus.). 32p. (J). (gr. 6-8). pap. 7.97 net. *(978-0-7652-3266-3(9),* Celebration Pr.) Pearson Schl.
Hamilton, John. The Marine Corps, 1 vol. 2007. (Defending the Nation Ser.). (ENG., Illus.). 32p. (gr. 4-7). 27.07 *(978-1-59679-758-1(4),* Checkerboard Library) ABDO Publishing Co.
—United States Marine Corps. 2011. (Armed Forces Ser.). (Illus.). 32p. (YA). (gr. 3-6). 27.07 *(978-1-61783-070-9(4))* ABDO Publishing Co.
Higgins, Melissa. Sgt. Reckless - The War Horse: Korean War Hero. Iglesias, Álvaro, illus. 2014. (Animal Heroes Ser.). (ENG.). 32p. (gr. k-2). 28.65 *(978-1-4795-5462-1(6))* Picture Window Bks.
Jones, Keisha. My Brother Is in the Marine Corps, 01 vols., 1. 2016. (Military Families Ser.). (ENG., Illus.). 24p. (J). pap. 8.25 *(978-1-5081-4430-4(3),* PowerKids Pr.) Rosen Publishing Group, Inc., The.
Keeter, Hunter. American Ground Forces in the Vietnam War. 2005. (American Experience in Vietnam Ser.). (Illus.). 48p. (gr. 5-12). lib. bdg. 31.00 *(978-0-8368-5774-0(7),* Gareth Stevens Secondary Library) Stevens, Gareth Publishing LLLP.
—The U. S. Marine Corps. 2004. (America's Armed Forces Ser.). (Illus.). 48p. (J). (gr. 5-12). lib. bdg. 31.00 *(978-0-8368-5683-5(X),* Gareth Stevens Secondary Library) Stevens, Gareth Publishing LLLP.
Lewis, J. Patrick. The Navajo Code Talkers. Kelley, Gary, illus. 2016. (ENG.). 32p. (J). (gr. 2-4). 18.99 *(978-1-56846-295-0(6),* Creative Editions) Creative Co., The.
Loria, Laura. Marine Force Recon. 2012. (US Special Forces Ser.). (ENG.). 32p. (J). (gr. 3-6). pap. 10.50 *(978-1-4339-6563-0(1));* lib. bdg. 26.60 *(978-1-4339-6561-6(5))* Stevens, Gareth Publishing LLLP. (Gareth Stevens Learning Library).
Lusted, Marcia Amidon. Marine Force Recon: Elite Operations. 2013. (Military Special Ops Ser.). (ENG., Illus.). 32p. (gr. 3-8). lib. bdg. 26.60 *(978-0-7613-9079-4(0),* Lerner Pubns.) Lerner Publishing Group.
Marinaro, Stacy. If I Became a U. S. Marine. 2009. 46p. 24.95 *(978-0-615-21988-2(8))* Marinaro, Stacy.
Marx, Mandy R. Amazing U. S. Marine Facts. 2016. (Amazing Military Facts Ser.). (ENG., Illus.). 24p. (gr. k-1). lib. bdg. 26.65 *(978-1-5157-0954-1(X),* Pebble Plus) Capstone Press of Coughlan Cos.
Miller, Adam. U. S. Marines True Stories: Tales of Bravery. 2014. (Courage under Fire Ser.). (ENG.). 32p. (gr. 3-4). lib. bdg. 27.99 *(978-1-4765-9935-9(1))* Capstone Press of Coughlan Cos.
Mitchell, P. P. Join the Marines. 2017. (U. S. Armed Forces Ser.). 32p. (gr. 1-2). pap. 10.50 ***(978-1-5382-0544-0(0))*** Stevens, Gareth Publishing LLLP.
Montana, Jack. Marines. 2010. (Special Forces Ser.). 64p. (YA). (gr. 7-18). lib. bdg. 22.95 *(978-1-4222-1842-6(2))* Mason Crest.
Murray, Julie. United States Marine Corps, 1 vol. 2014. (U. S. Armed Forces Ser.). (ENG.). 24p. (J). (gr. 4-8). lib. bdg. 28.50 *(978-1-62970-096-0(7))* ABDO Publishing Co.
Nelson, Maria. Heroes of the US Marines. 2012. (Heroes of the US Military Ser.). (Illus.). 32p. (J). (gr. 3-6). pap. 10.50 *(978-1-4339-7245-4(X));* lib. bdg. 26.60 *(978-1-4339-7244-7(1))* Stevens, Gareth Publishing LLLP.
Orr, Tamra B. USMC Special Reaction Teams. 2009. (Inside Special Operations Ser.). (Illus.). 64p. (gr. 5-8). pap. 12.95 *(978-1-4358-5130-6(7),* Rosen Classroom) Rosen Publishing Group, Inc., The.
Portman, Michael. Marine Corps. 2011. (Us Military Forces Ser.). (Illus.). 32p. (gr. 3-6). (J). pap. 10.50 *(978-1-4339-5856-4(2),* Gareth Stevens Learning Library); (YA). lib. bdg. 26.60 *(978-1-4339-5854-0(6))* Stevens, Gareth Publishing LLLP.
Raum, Elizabeth. U. S. Marines by the Numbers, 1 vol. 2014. (Military by the Numbers Ser.). (ENG.). 32p. (gr. 3-4). lib.

TUV

bdg. 27.99 *(978-1-4765-3919-5(7),* Edge Bks.) Capstone Press of Coughlan Cos.

Reed, Jennifer. Marines de la Infantería de Marina de EE. UU. 2010. (Gente de Las Fuerzas Armadas de EE. UU. /People of the Armed Forces Ser.) Tr. of Marines of the U. S. Marine Corps. (ENG, SPA & MUL.). 24p. (gr. k-1). lib. bdg. 26.65 *(978-1-4296-6116-4(X))* Capstone Press of Coughlan Cos.

—Marines of the U. S. Marine Corps [Scholastic]. 2010. (People of the U. S. Armed Forces Ser.). (ENG.). 24p. pap. 0.49 *(978-1-4296-5805-8(3),* Pebble Plus) Capstone Press of Coughlan Cos.

—The U. S. Marine Corps [Scholastic]. 2010. (Military Branches Ser.). (ENG.). 24p. pap. 0.52 *(978-1-4296-5072-4(9),* Pebble Plus) Capstone Press of Coughlan Cos.

Reed, Jennifer. The U.S. Marine Corps. 2017. (U. S. Military Branches Ser.). (ENG.). 24p. (gr. k-1). lib. bdg. 26.65 ***(978-1-5157-6772-5(8))*** Capstone Press of Coughlan Cos.

Rose, Simon. Marine Corps. 2012. (J). *(978-1-61913-294-8(X));* pap. *(978-1-61913-298-6(2))* Weigl Pubs., Inc.

—Marine Corps Special Operations. 2013. (J). 27.13 *(978-1-62127-452-0(7));* pap. *(978-1-62127-458-2(6))* Weigl Pubs., Inc.

Rowell, Rebecca. US Marine Corps, 1 vol. 2014. (Essential Library of the US Military Ser.). (ENG.). 112p. (J). (gr. 6-12). lib. bdg. 35.64 *(978-1-62403-435-0(7),* Essential Library) ABDO Publishing Co.

Rudolph, Jessica & Pushies, Fred J. Marine Scout Snipers in Action. 2013. (Special Ops II Ser.). 32p. (J). (gr. 2-7). lib. bdg. 26.60 *(978-1-61772-891-4(8))* Bearport Publishing Co., Inc.

Russo, Kristen J. Surprising Facts about Being a Marine. 2017. (What You Didn't Know about the U. S. Military Life Ser.). (ENG.). 32p. (gr. 3-4). lib. bdg. 27.99 ***(978-1-5157-7427-3(9),*** Edge Bks.) Capstone Press of Coughlan Cos.

Sandler, Michael. Marine Force Recon in Action. 2008. (Special Ops Ser.). (Illus.). 32p. (J). (gr. 3-6). lib. bdg. 25.27 *(978-1-59716-634-8(0))* Bearport Publishing Co., Inc.

Santella, Andrew. Navajo Code Talkers. 2005. (Reader's Workshop Ser.). (ENG., Illus.). 45p. (C). pap. 21.95 *(978-0-7362-2794-0(6))* National Geographic School Publishing, Inc.

Saxena, Shalini, ed. The History of Marines Around the World, 1 vol., 1. 2014. (World's Armed Forces Ser.). (ENG.). 120p. (YA). (gr. 7-12). 35.25 *(978-1-62275-148-8(5))* Rosen Publishing Group, Inc., The.

Schwartz, Heather E. Women of the U. S. Marine Corps: Breaking Barriers. 2010. (Women in the U. S. Armed Forces Ser.). (ENG.). 32p. (gr. 3-4). lib. bdg. 27.99 *(978-1-4296-5450-0(3),* Snap Bks.) Capstone Press of Coughlan Cos.

Simons, Lisa M. Bolt. U. S. Marine Raider Missions: A Timeline. 2016. (Special Ops Mission Timelines Ser.). (ENG., Illus.). 32p. (gr. 1-2). lib. bdg. 26.65 *(978-1-4914-8704-4(6),* Blazers) Capstone Press of Coughlan Cos.

Slater, Lee. Marine Force Recon, 1 vol. 2016. (Special Ops Ser.). (ENG., Illus.). 32p. (J). (gr. 3-6). 27.07 *(978-1-62403-970-6(7))* ABDO Publishing Co.

Sodaro, Craig. The U. S. Marines Special Operations Regiment: The Missions. 2012. (American Special Ops Ser.). (ENG., Illus.). 48p. (gr. 3-4). 31.99 *(978-1-4296-8658-7(8))* Capstone Press of Coughlan Cos.

Stein, R. Conrad. The U. S. Marine Corps & Military Careers. 2006. (U.S. Armed Forces & Military Careers Ser.). (Illus.). 128p. (J). (gr. 5-8). lib. bdg. 31.93 *(978-0-7660-2521-9(7))* Enslow Pubs., Inc.

Whiting, Jim. Marine Corps Forces Special Operations Command. 2014. (J). *(978-1-60818-464-4(1),* Creative Education) Creative Co., The.

—U. S. Special Forces: Marine Corps Forces Special Operations Command. 2015. (U. S. Special Forces Ser.). (ENG.). 48p. (J). (gr. 5-8). pap. 12.00 *(978-1-62832-050-3(8),* Creative Paperbacks) Creative Co., The.

Witcher, Monte L. Cleared Hot: A Story of the Battle of Observation Post 4. 2011. 94p. 24.99 *(978-1-4653-4952-1(9));* pap. 15.99 *(978-1-4653-4951-4(0))* Xlibris Corp.

Wood, Alix. Serving in the Marine Corps. 2013. (Protecting Our Country Ser.). 32p. (J). (gr. 3-6). pap. 60.00 *(978-1-4777-1399-0(9));* pap. 10.00 *(978-1-4777-1398-3(0));* lib. bdg. 25.25 *(978-1-4777-1296-2(8))* Rosen Publishing Group, Inc., The. (PowerKids Pr.).

Yomtov, Nel. Recon. 2016. (Military Missions Ser.). (ENG., Illus.). 24p. (J). (gr. 3-7). 25.95 *(978-1-62617-437-5(7),* Epic Bks.) Bellwether Media.

UNITED STATES—MARINE CORPS—BIOGRAPHY

Bradley, James & Powers, Ron. Flags of Our Fathers: A Young People's Edition. 2005. (ENG., Illus.). 224p. (YA). (gr. 4-7). mass mkt. 7.99 *(978-0-440-22920-9(0),* Laurel Leaf) Random Hse. Children's Bks.

—Flags of Our Fathers: Heroes of Iwo Jima. 2003. (ENG., Illus.). 232p. (YA). (gr. 4-7). reprint ed. pap. 8.99 *(978-0-385-73064-8(0),* Delacorte Bks. for Young Readers) Random Hse. Children's Bks.

Sandler, Michael & Pushies, Fred J. Today's Marine Heroes. 2012. (Acts of Courage: Inside America's Military Ser.). 32p. (J). (gr. 2-7). lib. bdg. 25.27 *(978-1-61772-444-2(0))* Bearport Publishing Co., Inc.

UNITED STATES—MARINE CORPS—VOCATIONAL GUIDANCE

Dolan, Edward F. Military Service, 5 vols., Set. Incl. Careers in the U. S. Air Force. (YA). (gr. 7-9). 35.64 *(978-0-7614-4205-9(7));* Careers in the U. S. Army. (YA). (gr. 7-9). 35.64 *(978-0-7614-4206-6(5));* Careers in the U. S. Coast Guard. (gr. 7-9). 35.64 *(978-0-7614-4207-3(3));* Careers in the U. S. Marine Corps. (YA). (gr. 8-18). 35.64 *(978-0-7614-4209-7(X));* Careers in the U. S. Navy. (gr. 7-18). 35.64 *(978-0-7614-4210-3(3));* 80p. 2009. 2010. Set lib. bdg. 178.21 o.p. *(978-0-7614-4203-5(0))* Marshall Cavendish Corp.

Kiland, Taylor Baldwin & Stein, R. Conrad. Careers in the US Marine Corps. 2015. (Careers in the US Armed Forces Ser.). (ENG., Illus.). 128p. (J). (gr. 6-7). 37.27 *(978-0-7660-6947-3(8))* Enslow Pubs., Inc.

McNab, Chris. Learning Mental Endurance for Survival. Carney, John, ed. 2014. (Extreme Survival in the Military Ser.: 12). 64p. (J). (gr. 7-18). lib. bdg. 23.95 *(978-1-4222-3082-4(1))* Mason Crest.

UNITED STATES MARSHALS

Alagna, Magdalena. Wyatt Earp: Lawman of the American West. 2009. (Primary Sources of Famous People in American History Ser.). 32p. (gr. 2-3). 47.90 *(978-1-60851-747-3(0))* Rosen Publishing Group, Inc., The.

—Wyatt Earp: Lawman of the American West / Sheriff del oeste Americano. 2009. (Famous People in American History/Grandes personajes en la historia de los Estados Unidos Ser.). (ENG & SPA.). 32p. (gr. 2-3). 47.90 *(978-1-61512-558-6(2),* Editorial Buenas Letras) Rosen Publishing Group, Inc., The.

—Wyatt Earp: Sheriff del lejano Oeste. 2004. (Grandes personajes en la historia de los Estados Unidos Ser.). (SPA.). 32p. (gr. 3-6). pap. 10.00 *(978-0-8239-4241-1(4),* Rosen Classroom) Rosen Publishing Group, Inc., The.

—Wyatt Earp: Sheriff del oeste americano (Wyatt Earp: Lawman of the American West) 2009. (Grandes personajes en la historia de los Estados Unidos (Famous People in American History) Ser.). (SPA.). 32p. (gr. 2-3). 47.90 *(978-1-61512-811-2(5),* Editorial Buenas Letras) Rosen Publishing Group, Inc., The.

Goodman, Michael E. Wyatt Earp. 2005. (Legends of the West Ser.). (Illus.). 48p. (J). (gr. 5-9). lib. bdg. 21.95 *(978-1-58341-339-5(1),* Creative Education) Creative Co., The.

Green, Carl R. & Sanford, William R. Wyatt Earp. rev. ed. 2008. (Outlaws & Lawmen of the Wild West, Revised Edition Ser.). (Illus.). 48p. (J). (gr. 5-18). lib. bdg. 25.27 *(978-0-7660-3174-6(8))* Enslow Pubs., Inc.

Nelson, Vaunda Micheaux. Bad News for Outlaws: The Remarkable Life of Bass Reeves, Deputy U. S. Marshall. Christie, R. Gregory, illus. 2009. (Exceptional Social Studies Titles for Intermediate Grades). (ENG.). 40p. (J). (gr. 3-6). lib. bdg. 17.95 *(978-0-8225-6764-6(4))* Lerner Publishing Group.

Rogers, Kate. Air Marshals, 01 vols., 1. 2016. (Careers for Heroes Ser.). (ENG., Illus.). 24p. (J). pap. 8.25 *(978-1-5081-4387-1(0),* PowerKids Pr.) Rosen Publishing Group, Inc., The.

Urban, William. Wyatt Earp: The O. K. Corral & the Law of the American West. 2009. (Library of American Lives & Times Ser.). 112p. (gr. 5-5). 69.20 *(978-1-60853-512-5(6))* Rosen Publishing Group, Inc., The.

—Wyatt Earp: The OK Corral & the Law of the American West. 2005. (Library of American Lives & Times). (Illus.). 112p. (YA). (gr. 4-8). lib. bdg. 34.60 *(978-0-8239-5740-8(3))* Rosen Publishing Group, Inc., The.

UNITED STATES MILITARY ACADEMY

Epstein, Brad M. Army 101: My First Text-Board-Book. l.t. ed. 2007. (101 — My First Text-Board Books). (Illus.). 20p. (J). bds. *(978-1-932530-42-1(8),* 101 Bk.) Michaelson Entertainment.

Kimmel, Heidi. West Point. 2008. (Cornerstones of Freedom Ser.). (ENG.). 48p. (J). pap. 5.95 *(978-0-531-21109-0(6),* Children's Pr.) Scholastic Library Publishing.

UNITED STATES MILITARY ACADEMY—FICTION

Efaw, Amy. Battle Dress. 2003. 400p. (J). (gr. 7-18). pap. 6.99 *(978-0-06-053520-9(2))* HarperCollins Pubs.

—Battle Dress. 2010. (ENG.). 304p. (YA). (gr. 7-18). 8.99 *(978-0-14-241397-5(6),* Speak) Penguin Young Readers Group.

Hancock, H. Irving. Dick Prescott's First Year at West Point. 2007. 144p. per. *(978-1-4065-1978-5(2))* Dodo Pr.

—Dick Prescott's Fourth Year at West Point. rev. ed. 2006. 208p. 27.95 *(978-1-4218-1735-4(7));* pap. 12.95 *(978-1-4218-1835-1(3))* 1st World Publishing, Inc. (1st World Library - Literary Society).

—Dick Prescott's Fourth Year at West Point. 2007. 176p. per. *(978-1-4065-1981-5(2))* Dodo Pr.

—Dick Prescott's Second Year at West Point. rev. ed. 2006. 208p. 27.95 *(978-1-4218-1736-1(5));* pap. 12.95 *(978-1-4218-1836-8(1))* 1st World Publishing, Inc. (1st World Library - Literary Society).

—Dick Prescott's Second Year at West Point. 2006. (ENG.). 156p. pap. 19.99 *(978-1-4264-6424-9(X));* 174p. pap. 21.99 *(978-1-4264-6498-0(3))* Creative Media Partners, LLC.

—Dick Prescott's Second Year at West Point. 2007. 176p. per. *(978-1-4065-1979-2(0))* Dodo Pr.

—Dick Prescott's Third Year at West Point. rev. ed. 2006. 208p. 27.95 *(978-1-4218-1737-8(3));* pap. 12.95 *(978-1-4218-1837-5(X))* 1st World Publishing, Inc. (1st World Library - Literary Society).

—Dick Prescott's Third Year at West Point. 2007. 176p. per. *(978-1-4065-1980-8(4))* Dodo Pr.

UNITED STATES—MILITARY HISTORY

see United States—History, Military

UNITED STATES—MILITARY POLICY

Allport, Alan. American Military Policy. 2003. (Point/Counterpoint Ser.). (Illus.). 112p. (C). (gr. 9-13). 35.00 *(978-0-7910-7488-6(9),* Chelsea Hse.) Facts On File, Inc.

Cunningham, Anne C., ed. Drones, Surveillance, & Targeted Killings. 2017. (Current Controversies Ser.). 224p. (J). (gr. 10-12). pap. 32.00 ***(978-1-5345-0036-5(7));*** lib. bdg. 46.40 ***(978-1-5345-0020-4(0))*** Greenhaven Publishing LLC. (Greenhaven Publishing).

Egan, Tracie. Weapons of Mass Destruction & North Korea. (Library of Weapons of Mass Destruction Ser.). 64p. 2009. (gr. 5-5). 58.50 *(978-1-60853-961-1(X))* 2004. (Illus.). (J). lib. bdg. 31.95 *(978-1-4042-0296-2(X))* Rosen Publishing Group, Inc., The.

Laxer, James. Empire, 1 vol. 2007. (Groundwork Guides). (ENG., Illus.). 144p. (gr. 8-12). pap. 9.95 *(978-0-88899-707-4(8))* Groundwood Bks. CAN. Dist: Publishers Group West (PGW).

UNITED STATES—MORAL CONDITIONS

Crompton, Samuel Willard. The Family Values Movement: Promoting Faith Through Action. 2007. (Reform Movements in American History Ser.). (Illus.). 120p. (J). (gr. 7-12). lib. bdg. 32.50 *(978-0-7910-9608-6(4))* Facts On File, Inc.

Haugen, David M., et al. American Values. 2014. (Opposing Viewpoints Ser.). (ENG., Illus.). 224p. (gr. 7-12). lib. bdg. 48.80 *(978-0-7377-6945-6(9),* Greenhaven Pr., Inc.) Cengage Gale.

UNITED STATES—NATIONAL AERONAUTICS AND SPACE ADMINISTRATION

Anderson, Rane. Stem: Mission to Mars: Problem Solving (Grade 3) 2017. (Mathematics Readers Ser.). (Illus.). 32p. (gr. 3-3). 8.99 ***(978-1-4807-5801-8(9))*** Teacher Created Materials, Inc.

Avera, Randy. The Truth about Challenger. 2003. (Illus.). 344p. 34.00 *(978-1-932258-00-4(0),* SAN # 254-9522) Randolph Publishing.

Elish, Dan. NASA. 2006. (Kaleidoscope Space Ser.). (Illus.). 48p. (gr. 3-7). lib. bdg. 20.95 *(978-0-7614-2046-0(0),* Benchmark Bks.) Marshall Cavendish Corp.

Greve, Tom. Thanks, Nasa! 2012. (ENG.). 48p. (gr. 4-6). pap. 10.95 *(978-1-61810-253-9(2))* Rourke Educational Media.

Krumm, Brian. Shuttle in the Sky: The Story of the Space Shuttle Columbia. 2015. (Exploring Space & Beyond Ser.). (ENG., Illus.). 48p. (gr. 3-4). lib. bdg. 29.32 *(978-1-4914-4161-9(5))* Capstone Press of Coughlan Cos.

Laser-Sailing Starships: Meet NASA Inventor Philip Lubin & His Team's. 2017. (J). ***(978-0-7166-6159-7(4))*** World Bk., Inc.

Meet NASA Inventor Kendra Short & Her Printable Probes & Cosmic Confetti. 2017. (J). ***(978-0-7166-6158-0(6))*** World Bk., Inc.

Meet NASA Inventor Masahiro Ono & His Team's Asteroid-Harpooning Hitcher. 2017. (J). ***(978-0-7166-6161-0(6))*** World Bk., Inc.

Meet NASA Inventor Robert Hoyt & His Team's Web-Spinning Space Spiders. 2017. (J). ***(978-0-7166-6157-3(8))*** World Bk., Inc.

Rauf, Don & Vescia, Monique. Choose Your Own Career Adventure at NASA. 2016. (Bright Futures Press: Choose Your Own Career Adventure Ser.). (ENG., Illus.). 32p. (J). (gr. 4-6). 29.93 *(978-1-63471-913-1(1),* 208973) Cherry Lake Publishing.

Redfern, Nick. True Stories of Space Exploration Conspiracies. 2014. (Off the Record! Ser.). 248p. (YA). (gr. 7-12). 38.25 *(978-1-4777-7833-3(0))* Rosen Publishing Group, Inc., The.

Riddolls, Tom. Sally Ride: The First American Woman in Space. 2010. (Crabtree Groundbreaker Biographies Ser.). (ENG., Illus.). 112p. (J). pap. *(978-0-7787-2550-3(2));* (gr. 5-8). lib. bdg. *(978-0-7787-2541-1(3))* Crabtree Publishing Co.

Rustad, Martha E. H. NASA, 1 vol. 2012. (Exploring Space Ser.). (ENG.). 24p. (gr. k-1). pap. 7.29 *(978-1-4296-7894-0(1));* pap. 41.70 *(978-1-4296-8329-6(5));* lib. bdg. 26.65 *(978-1-4296-7581-9(0))* Capstone Press of Coughlan Cos. (Pebble Plus).

Wimmer, Teresa. National Aeronautics & Space Administration. (Agents of Government Ser.). 48p. 2016. (ENG.). (J). (gr. 5-9). pap. 12.00 *(978-1-62832-148-7(2),* Creative Paperbacks) 2015. (Illus.). (YA). *(978-1-60818-547-4(8),* Creative Education) Creative Co., The.

Zappa, Marcia. NASA, 1 vol. 2011. (Universe Set 2 Ser.). (ENG., Illus.). 32p. (gr. 3-5). 27.07 *(978-1-61714-690-9(0),* Buddy Bks.) ABDO Publishing Co.

Zobel, Derek. NASA. 2010. (Exploring Space Ser.). (ENG., Illus.). 24p. (J). (gr. k-3). lib. bdg. 25.95 *(978-1-60014-293-2(1),* Blastoff! Readers) Bellwether Media.

UNITED STATES—NATIONAL GUARD

Bryan, Nichol. The National Guard, 1 vol. 2003. (Everyday Heroes Ser.). (ENG., Illus.). 32p. (gr. k-6). 27.07 *(978-1-57765-858-0(2),* Checkerboard Library) ABDO Publishing Co.

Greene, Meg. Careers in the National Guards' Search & Rescue Units. (Careers in Search & Rescue Operations Ser.). 64p. (gr. 5-8). 2009. 58.50 *(978-1-61511-812-0(8),* Rosen Reference) 2005. (Illus.). (YA). lib. bdg. 31.95 *(978-0-8239-3836-0(0))* Rosen Publishing Group, Inc., The.

Kerrigan, Michael. The National Guard. 2004. (Rescue & Prevention Ser.). (Illus.). 96p. (J). (gr. 7-18). lib. bdg. 22.95 *(978-1-59084-410-6(6))* Mason Crest.

Lusted, Marcia Amidon. US National Guard, 1 vol. 2014. (Essential Library of the US Military Ser.). (ENG.). 112p. (J). (gr. 6-12). lib. bdg. 35.64 *(978-1-62403-436-7(5),* Essential Library) ABDO Publishing Co.

Mitchell, P. P. Join the National Guard. 2017. (U. S. Armed Forces Ser.). 32p. (gr. 1-2). pap. 63.00 ***(978-1-5382-0552-5(1))*** Stevens, Gareth Publishing LLLP.

Thompson, Jim. My Cousin Is in the National Guard, 01 vols., 1. 2016. (Military Families Ser.). (ENG., Illus.). 24p. (J). 23.60 *(978-1-5081-4448-9(6),* PowerKids Pr.) Rosen Publishing Group, Inc., The.

UNITED STATES—NATIONAL PARK SERVICE

Pimentel, Annette Bay & Lo, Rich. Mountain Chef: How One Man Lost His Groceries, Changed His Plans, & Helped Cook up the National Park Service. 2016. (ENG., Illus.). 40p. (J). (gr. 1-4). 16.95 *(978-1-58089-711-2(8))* Charlesbridge Publishing, Inc.

Tomio, Stacy & Keffer, Ken. The National Parks! 2016. (Ranger Rick's Travels Ser.). (ENG., Illus.). 144p. (J). (gr. 2-6). pap. 14.95 *(978-1-63076-230-8(X))* Muddy Boots Pr.

UNITED STATES—NATIONAL PARKS AND RESERVES

see National Parks and Reserves—United States

UNITED STATES—NATURAL HISTORY

see Natural History—United States

UNITED STATES—NATURAL MONUMENTS

see Natural Monuments

UNITED STATES—NATURAL RESOURCES

see Natural Resources—United States; United States—Economic Conditions

UNITED STATES NAVAL ACADEMY—FICTION

Hancock, H. Irving. Dave Darrin's First Year at Annapolis. rev. ed. 2006. 212p. 27.95 *(978-1-4218-1739-2(X));* pap. 12.95 *(978-1-4218-1839-9(6))* 1st World Publishing, Inc. (1st World Library - Literary Society).

—Dave Darrin's First Year at Annapolis. 2007. 160p. pap. 19.99 *(978-1-4264-6408-9(8))* 2006. (ENG.). 172p. pap. 21.99 *(978-1-4264-6482-9(7))* Creative Media Partners, LLC.

—Dave Darrin's First Year at Annapolis. 2007. 180p. per. *(978-1-4065-1974-7(X))* Dodo Pr.

—Dave Darrin's Fourth Year at Annapolis. rev. ed. 2006. 216p. 27.95 *(978-1-4218-1746-0(2));* pap. 12.95 *(978-1-4218-1846-7(9))* 1st World Publishing, Inc. (1st World Library - Literary Society).

—Dave Darrin's Second Year at Annapolis. rev. ed. 2006. 184p. 26.95 *(978-1-4218-1734-7(9));* pap. 11.95 *(978-1-4218-1834-4(5))* 1st World Publishing, Inc. (1st World Library - Literary Society).

—Dave Darrin's Second Year at Annapolis. 2007. 152p. per. *(978-1-4065-1976-1(6))* Dodo Pr.

—Dave Darrin's Second Year at Annapolis, or Two Midshipmen As Naval Academy Youngsters. l.t. ed. 2007. (ENG.). 132p. pap. 18.99 *(978-1-4264-3913-1(X));* 166p. pap. 21.99 *(978-1-4264-3971-1(7))* Creative Media Partners, LLC.

—Dave Darrin's Third Year at Annapolis. rev. ed. 2006. 216p. 27.95 *(978-1-4218-1747-7(0));* pap. 12.95 *(978-1-4218-1847-4(7))* 1st World Publishing, Inc. (1st World Library - Literary Society).

—Dave Darrin's Third Year at Annapolis. l.t. ed. 2007. (ENG.). 160p. pap. 19.99 *(978-1-4264-4039-7(1));* 464p. pap. 30.99 *(978-1-4264-4098-4(7))* Creative Media Partners, LLC.

—Dave Darrin's Third Year at Annapolis. 2007. 184p. per. *(978-1-4065-1977-8(4))* Dodo Pr.

Sherman, M. Zachary & Iligan, Marlon. Heart of the Enemy, 1 vol. Cage, Josef, illus. 2012. (Bloodlines Ser.). (ENG.). 88p. (gr. 4-8). lib. bdg. 26.65 *(978-1-4342-3767-5(2))* Stone Arch Bks.

UNITED STATES—NAVY

Albright, Rosie. Military Dolphins. 2012. (Animal Detectives Ser.). (ENG., Illus.). 24p. (J). (gr. k-3). pap. 8.25 *(978-1-4488-6258-0(2));* lib. bdg. 22.60 *(978-1-4488-6153-8(5))* Rosen Publishing Group, Inc., The. (PowerKids Pr.).

—Military Dolphins: Delfines Del Ejército. Alamán, Eduardo, tr. 2012. (Animal Detectives / Detectives Del Reino Animal Ser.). (SPA & ENG., Illus.). 24p. (J). (gr. k-3). lib. bdg. 22.60 *(978-1-4488-6716-5(9),* PowerKids Pr.) Rosen Publishing Group, Inc., The.

Alvarez, Carlos. MH-53E Sea Dragons. 2010. (Military Machines Ser.). (ENG., Illus.). 24p. (J). (gr. 3-7). lib. bdg. 25.95 *(978-1-60014-495-0(0),* Torque Bks.) Bellwether Media.

Anderson, Dale. Soldiers & Sailors in the American Revolution. 2005. (World Almanac Library of the American Revolution Ser.). 48p. (gr. 5-12). pap. 14.05 *(978-0-8368-5938-6(3));* lib. bdg. 31.00 *(978-0-8368-5929-4(4))* Stevens, Gareth Publishing LLLP. (Gareth Stevens Secondary Library).

Besel, Jennifer M. The Navy SEALs, 1 vol. 2010. (Elite Military Forces Ser.). (ENG.). 24p. (gr. 1-2). lib. bdg. 25.32 *(978-1-4296-5380-0(9),* First Facts) Capstone Press of Coughlan Cos.

—The U. S. Navy SEALs: The Missions, 1 vol. 2012. (American Special Ops Ser.). (ENG.). 48p. (gr. 3-4). lib. bdg. 31.99 *(978-1-4296-8715-7(0))* Capstone Press of Coughlan Cos.

Boothroyd, Jennifer. Inside the US Navy. 2017. (Lightning Bolt Books (tm) — US Armed Forces Ser.). (ENG.). (J). (gr. 1-3). 24p. lib. bdg. 25.32 *(978-1-5124-3394-4(2));* pap. 6.99 ***(978-1-5124-5602-8(0))*** Lerner Publishing Group.

Bow, James. Navy Seals. 2012. (ENG.). 48p. (J). *(978-0-7787-7926-1(2));* pap. *(978-0-7787-7935-3(1))* Crabtree Publishing Co.

Bozzo, Linda. Navy SEALs. 2015. (Serving in the Military Ser.). (Illus.). 32p. (J). 28.50 *(978-1-60753-494-5(0))* Amicus Publishing.

Cooke, Tim. US Navy SEALs. 2012. (Ultimate Special Forces Ser.). (ENG., Illus.). 48p. (J). (gr. 4-8). 27.95 *(978-1-4488-7881-9(0));* pap. 11.75 *(978-1-4488-7958-8(2))* Rosen Publishing Group, Inc., The. (PowerKids Pr.).

David, Jack. Navy SEALs. 2009. (Armed Forces Ser.). (ENG., Illus.). 24p. (YA). (gr. 3-7). lib. bdg. 25.95 *(978-1-60014-265-9(6))* Bellwether Media.

—United States Navy. 2008. (Armed Forces Ser.). (ENG., Illus.). 24p. (J). (gr. 3-7). lib. bdg. 25.95 *(978-1-60014-165-2(X))* Bellwether Media.

Dolan, Edward F. Careers in the U. S. Navy. 2009. (Military Service Ser.). 80p. (gr. 7-18). 35.64 *(978-0-7614-4210-3(3))* Marshall Cavendish Corp.

—Military Service, 5 vols., Set. Incl. Careers in the U. S. Air Force. (YA). (gr. 7-9). 35.64 *(978-0-7614-4205-9(7));* Careers in the U. S. Army. (YA). (gr. 7-9). 35.64 *(978-0-7614-4206-6(5));* Careers in the U. S. Coast Guard. (gr. 7-9). 35.64 *(978-0-7614-4207-3(3));* Careers in the U. S. Marine Corps. (YA). (gr. 8-18). 35.64 *(978-0-7614-4209-7(X));* Careers in the U. S. Navy. (gr. 7-18). 35.64 *(978-0-7614-4210-3(3));* 80p. 2009. 2010. Set lib. bdg. 178.21 o.p. *(978-0-7614-4203-5(0))* Marshall Cavendish Corp.

Donovan, Sandy. U. S. Naval Special Warfare Forces. 2004. (U. S. Armed Forces Ser.). (ENG., Illus.). 64p. (gr. 4-8). lib. bdg. 26.60 *(978-0-8225-1650-7(0))* Lerner Publishing Group.

Foster, Linda. United States Naval Academy: Annapolis. Miller, Roger, photos by. 2006. (Illus.). 168p. 39.95 *(978-0-911897-49-4(6))* Image Publishing, Ltd.

Goldish, Meish. Navy: Civilian to Sailor. 2010. (Becoming a Soldier Ser.). 24p. (YA). (gr. 3-6). lib. bdg. 22.61 *(978-1-936088-14-0(2))* Bearport Publishing Co., Inc.

Gordon, Nick. Navy SEALs. 2012. (U. S. Military Ser.). (ENG., Illus.). 24p. (J). (gr. 3-7). lib. bdg. 25.95 *(978-1-60014-825-5(5),* Epic Bks.) Bellwether Media.

—U. S. Navy. 2012. (U. S. Military Ser.). (ENG., Illus.). 24p. (J). (gr. 3-7). lib. bdg. 25.95 *(978-1-60014-830-9(1),* Epic Bks.) Bellwether Media.

Gregory, Josh. Avionics Technician. 2012. (21st Century Skills Library: Cool Military Careers Ser.). (ENG.). 32p. (gr. 4-8). 28.50 *(978-1-61080-445-5(7),* 202055); pap. 14.21 *(978-1-61080-619-0(0),* 202229) Cherry Lake Publishing.

—The Hunt for Bin Laden: Operation Neptune Spear. 2013. (ENG.). 64p. (J). 30.00 *(978-0-531-28209-0(0));* pap. 8.95 *(978-0-531-27674-7(0))* Scholastic Library Publishing.

Gunderson, Jessica. U. S. Navy True Stories: Tales of Bravery. 2014. (Courage under Fire Ser.). (ENG.). 32p. (gr. 3-4). lib. bdg. 27.99 *(978-1-4765-9937-3(8))* Capstone Press of Coughlan Cos.

Hamilton, John. The Navy, 1 vol. 2007. (Defending the Nation Ser.). (ENG., Illus.). 32p. (gr. 3-7). 27.07 *(978-1-59679-760-4(6),* Checkerboard Library) ABDO Publishing Co.

—Navy SEALs. 2011. (Armed Forces Ser.). (Illus.). 32p. (YA). (gr. 3-6). 27.07 *(978-1-61783-067-9(4))* ABDO Publishing Co.

—United States Navy. 2011. (Armed Forces Ser.). (Illus.). 32p. (YA). (gr. 3-6). 27.07 *(978-1-61783-071-6(2))* ABDO Publishing Co.

Hodges, Tammy. Breakfast with the Blues. l.t. ed. 2006. (Illus.). 32p. (J). *(978-1-934035-00-9(9))* Trent's Prints.

Jackson, Kay. Navy Ships in Action. 2009. (Amazing Military Vehicles Ser.). 24p. (gr. 3-5). (Illus.). (J). pap. 8.25 *(978-1-4358-3160-5(8),* PowerKids Pr.); 42.50 *(978-1-61511-321-7(5),* PowerKids Pr.); (YA). lib. bdg. 22.60 *(978-1-4358-2750-9(3))* Rosen Publishing Group, Inc., The.

—Navy Submarines in Action. 2009. (Amazing Military Vehicles Ser.). 24p. (gr. 3-5). (J). pap. 8.25 *(978-1-4358-3161-2(6),* PowerKids Pr.); 42.50 *(978-1-61511-324-8(X),* PowerKids Pr.); (YA). lib. bdg. 22.60 *(978-1-4358-2751-6(1))* Rosen Publishing Group, Inc., The.

Jordan, David. The U. S. Navy. 2004. (America's Armed Forces Ser.). (Illus.). 48p. (gr. 5-12). lib. bdg. 31.00 *(978-0-8368-5684-2(8),* Gareth Stevens Secondary Library) Stevens, Gareth Publishing LLLP.

Kiland, Taylor Baldwin. Careers in the US Navy. 2015. (Careers in the US Armed Forces Ser.). (ENG., Illus.). 128p. (J). (gr. 6-7). 37.27 *(978-0-7660-6949-7(4))* Enslow Pubs., Inc.

—The U. S. Navy & Military Careers. 2006. (U.S. Armed Forces & Military Careers Ser.). (Illus.). 128p. (J). (gr. 5-8). lib. bdg. 33.27 *(978-0-7660-2523-3(3))* Enslow Pubs., Inc.

Kiland, Taylor Baldwin & Teitelbaum, Michael. Military Submarines: Sea Power. 2015. (Military Engineering in Action Ser.). (ENG., Illus.). 48p. (J). (gr. 6-6). 27.93 *(978-0-7660-6918-3(4));* pap. 11.70 *(978-0-7660-7069-1(7))* Enslow Pubs., Inc.

Leavitt, Amie Jane. U. S. Navy by the Numbers, 1 vol. 2014. (Military by the Numbers Ser.). (ENG.). 32p. (J). lib. bdg. 27.99 *(978-1-4765-3918-8(9),* Edge Bks.) Capstone Press of Coughlan Cos.

Llanas, Sheila Griffin. Women of the U. S. Navy: Making Waves, 1 vol. 2010. (Women in the U. S. Armed Forces Ser.). (ENG.). 32p. (gr. 3-4). lib. bdg. 27.99 *(978-1-4296-5448-7(1),* Snap Bks.) Capstone Press of Coughlan Cos.

Lunis, Natalie & Pushies, Fred J. The Takedown of Osama Bin Laden. 2012. (Special Ops Ser.). 32p. (J). (gr. 2-7). lib. bdg. 25.27 *(978-1-61772-459-6(9))* Bearport Publishing Co., Inc.

Marciniak, Kristin. Navy Seals, 1 vol. 2013. (Great Warriors Ser.). (ENG.). 48p. (J). (gr. 3-6). lib. bdg. 32.79 *(978-1-61783-725-8(3))* ABDO Publishing Co.

—Navy SEALs. 2013. (Great Warriors EBook Ser.). (ENG., Illus.). 48p. (J). pap. 15.64 *(978-1-61783-775-3(X),* Core Library) ABDO Publishing Co.

Marini, Matthew. Special Forces, Vol. 12. 2015. (On a Mission Ser.). (Illus.). 48p. (J). (gr. 5). 20.95 *(978-1-4222-3401-3(0))* Mason Crest.

Marx, Mandy R. Amazing U. S. Navy Facts. 2016. (Amazing Military Facts Ser.). (ENG., Illus.). 24p. (gr. k-1). lib. bdg. 26.65 *(978-1-5157-0952-7(3),* Pebble Plus) Capstone Press of Coughlan Cos.

McNab, Chris. Survival at Sea. Carney, John, ed. 2014. (Extreme Survival in the Military Ser.: 12). 64p. (J). (gr. 7-18). lib. bdg. 23.95 *(978-1-4222-3084-8(8))* Mason Crest.

McNeil, Niki, et al. HOCPP 1106 the United States Navy. 2006. spiral bd. 23.50 *(978-1-60308-106-1(2))* In the Hands of a Child.

Miller, Nancy. My Mom Is in the Navy, 01 vols., 1. 2016. (Military Families Ser.). (ENG., Illus.). 24p. (J). pap. 8.25 *(978-1-5081-4438-0(9),* PowerKids Pr.) Rosen Publishing Group, Inc., The.

Mitchell, P. P. Join the Navy. 2017. (U. S. Armed Forces Ser.). 32p. (gr. 1-2). pap. 10.50 ***(978-1-5382-0548-8(3))*** Stevens, Gareth Publishing LLLP.

Montana, Jack. Navy SEALs. 2010. (Special Forces Ser.). 64p. (YA). (gr. 7-18). lib. bdg. 22.95 *(978-1-4222-1843-3(0))* Mason Crest.

Murphy, Patricia J. Grace Hopper: Computer Pioneer. 2004. (Famous Inventors Ser.). (Illus.). 32p. (J). lib. bdg. 22.60 *(978-0-7660-2273-7(0))* Enslow Pubs., Inc.

Murray, Julie. Navy SEALs, 1 vol. 2014. (U. S. Armed Forces Ser.). (ENG.). 24p. (J). (gr. 4-8). lib. bdg. 28.50 *(978-1-62970-092-2(4))* ABDO Publishing Co.

Nardo, Don. In the Water: Frogmen & Commandos. 2015. (J). *(978-1-59935-462-0(4))* Reynolds, Morgan Inc.

—Today's U. S. Navy, 1 vol. 2013. (U. S. Armed Forces Ser.). (ENG.). 48p. (gr. 5-6). pap. 9.10 *(978-0-7565-4641-0(9));* lib. bdg. 29.32 *(978-0-7565-4617-5(6))* Compass Point Bks.

Nelson, Drew. Navy SEALs. 2012. (US Special Forces Ser.). (ENG., Illus.). 32p. (J). (gr. 3-6). pap. 10.50 *(978-1-4339-6567-8(4));* lib. bdg. 26.60 *(978-1-4339-6565-4(8))* Stevens, Gareth Publishing LLLP. (Gareth Stevens Learning Library).

Newman, Patricia. Navy Seals: Elite Operations. 2013. (Military Special Ops Ser.). (ENG., Illus.). 32p. (gr. 3-8). lib. bdg. 26.60 *(978-0-7613-9080-0(4),* Lerner Pubns.) Lerner Publishing Group.

Orr, Tamra. Your Career in the Navy. 2011. (Call of Duty: Careers in the Armed Forces Ser.). (ENG.). 128p. (YA). (gr. 9-12). lib. bdg. 34.60 *(978-1-4488-5511-7(X))* Rosen Publishing Group, Inc., The.

Payment, Simone. Black Ops & Other Special Missions of the U. S. Navy Seals. 2012. (Inside Special Forces Ser.). (ENG., Illus.). 64p. (YA). (gr. 5-8). pap. 12.95 *(978-1-4488-8385-1(7));* lib. bdg. 31.95 *(978-1-4488-8380-6(6))* Rosen Publishing Group, Inc., The.

—Navy SEALs: Special Operations for the U. S. Navy. 2003. (Inside Special Operations Ser.). (Illus.). 64p. (YA). (gr. 5-8). lib. bdg. 26.50 *(978-0-8239-3809-4(3),* Rosen Reference) Rosen Publishing Group, Inc., The.

—Navy Seals: Special Operations for the U. S. Navy. (Inside Special Operations Ser.). 64p. 2009. (gr. 6-6). 58.50 *(978-1-61513-556-1(1))* 2006. (Illus.). (J). (gr. 5-8). lib. bdg. 31.95 *(978-1-4042-0874-2(7))* Rosen Publishing Group, Inc., The. (Rosen Reference).

Person, Stephen. Navy SEAL Team Six in Action. 2013. (Special Ops II Ser.). (Illus.). 32p. (J). (gr. 2-7). lib. bdg. 26.60 *(978-1-61772-890-7(X))* Bearport Publishing Co., Inc.

Peters, Gregory N. Trailblazers, 1 vol. 2014. (Trailblazers Ser.). (ENG.). 48p. (gr. 2-3). 255.92 *(978-1-4765-8598-7(9))* Capstone Press of Coughlan Cos.

—U. S. Navy SEALs Elite Force, 1 vol. 2014. (Real World Adventures Ser.). (ENG.). 48p. (gr. 4-12). 31.99 *(978-1-4765-8470-6(2))* Capstone Press of Coughlan Cos.

Reed, Jennifer. Marineros de la Armada de EE. UU. 2010. (Gente de Las Fuerzas Armadas de EE. UU. /People of the Armed Forces Ser.),Tr. of Sailors of the U. S. Navy. (MUL & SPA.). 24p. (gr. k-1). lib. bdg. 26.65 *(978-1-4296-6117-1(8))* Capstone Press of Coughlan Cos.

—Sailors of the U. S. Navy [Scholastic]. 2010. (People of the U. S. Armed Forces Ser.). (ENG.). 24p. pap. 0.49 *(978-1-4296-5806-5(1),* Pebble Plus) Capstone Press of Coughlan Cos.

—The U. S. Navy [Scholastic]. 2010. (Military Branches Ser.). (ENG.). 24p. pap. 0.52 *(978-1-4296-5071-7(0),* Pebble Plus) Capstone Press of Coughlan Cos.

Reed, Jennifer. The U.S. Navy. 2017. (U. S. Military Branches Ser.). (ENG.). 24p. (gr. k-1). lib. bdg. 26.65 ***(978-1-5157-6755-8(8))*** Capstone Press of Coughlan Cos.

Richards, Tracy. My Navy Dad. 2010. 20p. pap. 14.95 *(978-1-4490-3217-3(6))* AuthorHouse.

Rose, Simon. Navy SEALs. 2013. (J). *(978-1-62127-453-7(5));* pap. *(978-1-62127-459-9(4))* Weigl Pubs., Inc.

Simons, Lisa M. Bolt. U. S. Navy SEAL Missions: A Timeline. 2016. (Special Ops Mission Timelines Ser.). (ENG., Illus.). 32p. (gr. 1-2). lib. bdg. 26.65 *(978-1-4914-8703-7(8),* Blazers) Capstone Press of Coughlan Cos.

Slater, Lee. Navy SEALs, 1 vol. 2016. (Special Ops Ser.). (ENG., Illus.). 32p. (J). (gr. 3-6). 27.07 *(978-1-62403-971-3(5))* ABDO Publishing Co.

Snedden, Robert. The Navy. 2016. (Defend & Protect Ser.). (ENG.). 48p. (J). (gr. 4-5). pap. 14.05 *(978-1-4824-4123-9(3))* Stevens, Gareth Publishing LLLP.

Stillwell, Alexander. Military Jobs: Navy SEALs. 2015. (J). lib. bdg. *(978-1-62713-465-1(4))* Cavendish Square Publishing.

Stilwell, Alexander. Navy SEALs: What It Takes to Join the Elite. 2015. (Military Jobs Ser.). (ENG.). 48p. (YA). (gr. 8-8). 31.36 *(978-1-5026-0226-8(1))* Cavendish Square Publishing.

Streissguth, Tom. The U. S. Navy. 2004. (U. S. Armed Forces Ser.). (ENG., Illus.). 64p. (gr. 4-8). lib. bdg. 26.60 *(978-0-8225-1649-1(7))* Lerner Publishing Group.

Thornton, Jeremy. The Birth of the American Navy. 2003. (Building America's Democracy Ser.). (Illus.). 24p. (J). lib. bdg. 22.60 *(978-0-8239-6274-7(1),* PowerKids Pr.) Rosen Publishing Group, Inc., The.

Townsend, John. Navy. 2016. (Action Force: World War II Ser.). 32p. (gr. 3-7). 31.35 *(978-1-59920-984-5(5),* Smart Apple Media) Black Rabbit Bks.

White, Steve. Naval Warship: FSF-1 Sea Fighter. 2007. (High-Tech Military Weapons Ser.). (ENG., Illus.). 48p. (J). (gr. 4-7). pap. 6.95 *(978-0-531-18707-4(1))* Scholastic Library Publishing.

Whiting, Jim. Navy SEALs. 2014. (J). *(978-1-60818-465-1(X),* Creative Education) Creative Co., The.

—U. S. Special Forces: Navy SEALs. 2015. (U. S. Special Forces Ser.). (ENG.). 48p. (J). (gr. 5-8). pap. 12.00 *(978-1-62832-051-0(6),* Creative Paperbacks) Creative Co., The.

Wood, Alix. Serving in the Navy. 2013. 32p. (J). (gr. 3-6). 25.25 *(978-1-4777-1295-5(X));* pap. 60.00 *(978-1-4777-1397-6(2))* Rosen Publishing Group, Inc., The. (PowerKids Pr.).

Yomtov, Nel. Navy Seals in Action. 2008. (Special Ops Ser.). (Illus.). 32p. (YA). (gr. 3-6). lib. bdg. 25.27 *(978-1-59716-630-0(8))* Bearport Publishing Co., Inc.

UNITED STATES—NAVY—BIOGRAPHY

Alphin, Elaine Marie & Alphin, Arthur B. I Have Not Yet Begun to Fight: A Story about John Paul Jones. Casale, Paul, tr. Casale, Paul, illus. 2004. (Creative Minds Biography Ser.). 64p. (J). 22.60 *(978-1-57505-601-2(1),* Carolrhoda Bks.); (ENG.). (gr. 4-8). pap. 8.95 *(978-1-57505-635-7(6))* Lerner Publishing Group.

Bradford, James C. John Paul Jones: And the American Navy. 2005. (Library of American Lives & Times). (Illus.). 112p. (J). (gr. 4-8). lib. bdg. 34.60 *(978-0-8239-5726-2(8))* Rosen Publishing Group, Inc., The.

—John Paul Jones & the American Navy. 2009. (Library of American Lives & Times Ser.). 112p. (gr. 5-6). 69.20 *(978-1-60853-490-6(1))* Rosen Publishing Group, Inc., The.

Brager, Bruce L. John Paul Jones: America's Sailor. 2006. (Founders of the Republic Ser.). (Illus.). 160p. (J). (gr. 6-12). lib. bdg. 26.95 *(978-1-931798-84-6(2))* Reynolds, Morgan Inc.

Cooper, Michael L. Hero of the High Seas: John Paul Jones & the American Revolution. 2006. (ENG., Illus.). 128p. (gr. 5-7). 21.95 *(978-0-7922-5547-5(X));* lib. bdg. 32.90 *(978-0-7922-5548-2(8))* National Geographic Society. (National Geographic Children's Bks.).

Crickard, Sarah. John Paul Jones & the Birth of the American Navy. 2015. (Spotlight on American History Ser.). (ENG., Illus.). 24p. (J). (gr. 4-6). pap. 10.00 *(978-1-4994-1759-3(4),* PowerKids Pr.) Rosen Publishing Group, Inc., The.

Dougherty, Terri. Admiral David Farragut: "Full Speed Ahead!" 2011. (J). *(978-1-59556-041-4(6));* pap. *(978-1-59556-047-6(5))* OTTN Publishing.

Egan, Tracie. John Paul Jones: Héroe de la marina estadounidense (John Paul Jones: American Naval Hero) 2009. (Grandes personajes en la historia de los Estados Unidos (Famous People in American History) Ser.). (SPA.). 32p. (gr. 2-3). 47.90 *(978-1-61512-802-0(6),* Editorial Buenas Letras) Rosen Publishing Group, Inc., The.

Greitens, Eric. The Warrior's Heart: Becoming a Man of Compassion & Courage. (ENG., Illus.). (YA). (gr. 7). 2015. 288p. pap. 9.99 *(978-0-544-10481-5(1),* HMH Books For Young Readers) 2012. 272p. 16.99 *(978-0-547-86852-3(9))* Houghton Mifflin Harcourt Publishing Co.

Harasymiw, Mark. Heroes of the US Navy. 2012. (Heroes of the US Military Ser.). (Illus.). 32p. (J). (gr. 3-6). 26.60 *(978-1-4339-7248-5(4));* pap. 10.50 *(978-1-4339-7249-2(2))* Stevens, Gareth Publishing LLLP.

Harkins, Susan Sales & Harkins, William H. The Life & Times of John Paul Jones. 2007. (Profiles in American History Ser.). (Illus.). 48p. (J). (gr. 4-8). lib. bdg. 29.95 *(978-1-58415-529-4(9))* Mitchell Lane Pubs., Inc.

McDoniel, Estelle. Registered Nurse to Rear Admiral: A First for Navy Women. 2003. (Illus.). viii, 81p. (J). 16.95 *(978-1-57168-766-1(1),* Eakin Pr.) Eakin Pr.

Micklos, John, Jr. SEAL Team Six: Battling Terrorism Worldwide. 2017. (Military Heroes Ser.). (ENG., Illus.). 32p. (gr. 3-4). lib. bdg. 27.32 *(978-1-5157-3347-8(5))* Capstone Press of Coughlan Cos.

A Navy Medical Corpsman's Journey. 2003. 37p. (YA). lib. bdg. 20.00 net. *(978-0-9747035-1-0(6))* Strickland, Wilton.

Ritland, Mike, et al. Navy SEAL Dogs: My Tale of Training Canines for Combat. 2013. (ENG., Illus.). 208p. (YA). (gr. 7). 17.99 *(978-1-250-04182-1(1),* 9781250041821, St. Martin's Griffin) St. Martin's Pr.

Rudolph, Jessica & Pushies, Fred J. Today's Navy Heroes. 2012. (Acts of Courage: Inside America's Military Ser.). 32p. (J). (gr. 2-7). lib. bdg. 25.27 *(978-1-61772-446-6(7))* Bearport Publishing Co., Inc.

Russo, Kristen J. Surprising Facts about Being a Navy Sailor. 2017. (What You Didn't Know about the U. S. Military Life Ser.). (ENG.). 32p. (gr. 3-4). lib. bdg. 27.99 ***(978-1-5157-7430-3(9),*** Edge Bks.) Capstone Press of Coughlan Cos.

Sonneborn, Liz. John Paul Jones: American Naval Hero. 2005. (Leaders of the American Revolution Ser.). (Illus.). 100p. (gr. 5-8). lib. bdg. 30.00 *(978-0-7910-8621-6(6))* Facts On File, Inc.

Sperry, Armstrong. John Paul Jones: The Pirate Patriot. (Great Leaders & Events Ser.). (ENG.). (J). (gr. 4-8). 2017. lib. bdg. 35.99 ***(978-1-942875-42-0(8))*** 2016. (Illus.). 168p. pap. 12.99 *(978-0-7603-5230-4(5),* Voyageur Pr.) Quarto Publishing Group USA.

Sutcliffe, Jane & Kodera, Craig. Chester Nimitz & the Sea, 1 vol. 2013. (ENG., Illus.). 32p. (J). (gr. k-3). 16.99 *(978-1-4556-1796-8(2))* Pelican Publishing Co., Inc.

Taylor, Kathleen. Eddie & Bingo: A Friendship Tale. Taylor, Kathleen, illus. 2011. (Illus.). 42p. (J). pap. 21.95 *(978-1-59299-558-5(6))* Inkwater Pr.

Wasdin, Howard E. & Templin, Stephen. I Am a Seal Team Six Warrior. 2012. (YA). lib. bdg. 19.65 *(978-0-606-26244-6(X),* Turtleback) Turtleback Bks.

—I Am a Seal Team Six Warrior: Memoirs of an American Soldier. 2012. (ENG., Illus.). 192p. (YA). (gr. 6). pap. 9.99 *(978-1-250-01643-0(6),* 9781250016430, St. Martin's Griffin) St. Martin's Pr.

Wittner, David G. Commodore Matthew Perry & the Perry Expedition to Japan. 2009. (Library of American Lives & Times Ser.). 112p. (gr. 5-5). 69.20 *(978-1-60853-474-6(X))* Rosen Publishing Group, Inc., The.

UNITED STATES—NAVY—HISTORY

Abbot, Willis J. Blue Jackets of 1876: A History of the Naval Battles of the American Revolution Together with a Narrative of the War with Tripoli. 2006. (Illus.). pap. 30.95 *(978-1-4286-1609-7(8))* Kessinger Publishing, LLC.

Goldish, Meish. Sea Lions in the Navy. 2012. (America's Animal Soldiers Ser.). 24p. (J). (gr. 1-6). lib. bdg. 23.93 *(978-1-61772-450-3(5))* Bearport Publishing Co., Inc.

Goldish, Meish & Ridgway, Sam H. Bottlenose Dolphins in the Navy. 2012. (America's Animal Soldiers Ser.). 24p. (J). (gr. 1-6). lib. bdg. 23.93 *(978-1-61772-451-0(3))* Bearport Publishing Co., Inc.

Gomez-Centurion, Carlos. Armada Invencible. (SPA.). 96p. (J). *(978-84-207-3813-0(1))* Grupo Anaya, S.A.

Green, Michael. The United States Navy, 1 vol. 2013. (U. S. Military Forces Ser.). (ENG., Illus.). 24p. (gr. 1-2). lib. bdg. 25.32 *(978-1-4765-0070-6(3))* Capstone Press of Coughlan Cos.

Hamen, Susan E. US Navy, 1 vol. 2014. (Essential Library of the US Military Ser.). (ENG.). 112p. (J). (gr. 6-12). lib. bdg. 35.64 *(978-1-62403-437-4(3),* Essential Library) ABDO Publishing Co.

Hemingway, Albert. American Naval Forces in the Vietnam War. 2005. (American Experience in Vietnam Ser.). (Illus.). 48p. (gr. 5-12). lib. bdg. 31.00 *(978-0-8368-5776-4(3),* Gareth Stevens Secondary Library) Stevens, Gareth Publishing LLLP.

Micklos, John. How the Revolutionary War Was Won. 2008. (Revolutionary War Library). (Illus.). 48p. (J). (gr. 3-4). lib. bdg. 25.27 *(978-0-7660-3016-9(4),* Enslow Elementary) Enslow Pubs., Inc.

—Why We Won the American Revolution — Through Primary Sources. 2013. (American Revolution Through Primary Sources Ser.). 48p. (J). (gr. 4-18). 25.27 *(978-0-7660-4134-9(4))* Enslow Pubs., Inc.

—Why We Won the American Revolution—Through Primary Sources. 2013. (American Revolution Through Primary Sources Ser.). 48p. (J). (gr. 4-10). pap. 8.95 *(978-1-4644-0192-3(6))* Enslow Pubs., Inc.

Murray, Julie. United States Navy, 1 vol. 2014. (U. S. Armed Forces Ser.). (ENG.). 24p. (J). (gr. 4-8). lib. bdg. 28.50 *(978-1-62970-097-7(5))* ABDO Publishing Co.

Nagle, Jeanne. Navy. 2011. (Us Military Forces Ser.). (Illus.). 32p. (gr. 3-6). (J). pap. 10.50 *(978-1-4339-5860-1(0),* Gareth Stevens Learning Library); (YA). 26.60 *(978-1-4339-5858-8(9))* Stevens, Gareth Publishing LLLP.

Rose, Simon. Navy. 2012. (J). *(978-1-61913-293-1(1));* pap. *(978-1-61913-297-9(4))* Weigl Pubs., Inc.

Rutherford, David B. A Navy SEAL's Guide for Helping Kids Get Squared Away: Field Manuals for Kids, Vol. 1. 2007. (ENG.). 118p. (J). per. 15.00 *(978-0-9801464-0-0(2))* Leadline Publishing.

Sheinkin, Steve. The Port Chicago 50: Disaster, Mutiny, & the Fight for Civil Rights. 2014. (ENG., Illus.). 208p. (J). (gr. 5-9). 19.99 *(978-1-59643-796-8(0),* 9781596437968) Roaring Brook Pr.

Stein, R. Conrad. Annapolis. 2009. (Cornerstones of Freedom Ser.). (ENG.). 48p. (J). (gr. 4-6). pap. 5.95 *(978-0-531-21100-7(2),* Children's Pr.) Scholastic Library Publishing.

Thornton, Jeremy. The Birth of the American Navy. 2009. (Building America's Democracy Ser.). 24p. (gr. 3-3). 42.50 *(978-1-61511-765-9(2),* PowerKids Pr.) Rosen Publishing Group, Inc., The.

The U.S. Navy in World War II. 2014. (True Book(tm), a — World at War Ser.). (ENG.). 48p. (J). lib. bdg. 31.00 *(978-0-531-20497-9(9))* Scholastic Library Publishing.

USS Wisconsin: Hampton Roads Naval Historical Foundation Photo Museum Guide. 2003. per. 12.95 *(978-1-930127-05-0(7))* Oxford Museum Pr.

Waldman, Scott. Victory at Sea: John Paul Jones & the Continental Navy. 2009. (Great Moments in American History Ser.). 32p. (gr. 3-3). 47.90 *(978-1-61513-156-3(6))* Rosen Publishing Group, Inc., The.

UNITED STATES—OFFICIALS AND EMPLOYEES

Brown, Monica. Lado a Lado: La Historia de Dolores Huerta y Cesar Chavez. Cepeda, Joe, illus. 2010.Tr. of Side by Side - The Story of Dolores Huerta & Cesar Chavez. (SPA & ENG.). 32p. (J). (gr. -1-3). 16.99 *(978-0-06-122781-3(1),* Rayo) HarperCollins Pubs.

Cuesta, Vivian. It Can Be Done: The Life & Legacy of César Chávez. 2003. (ENG., Illus.). 32p. (J). (gr. 6-8). pap. 8.47 net. *(978-0-7652-3271-7(5),* Celebration Pr.) Pearson Schl.

Faust, Daniel R. A Career As an FBI Special Agent. 2015. (Federal Forces: Careers As Federal Agents Ser.). (ENG., Illus.). 32p. (J). (gr. 4-5). pap. 10.00 *(978-1-4994-1060-0(3),* PowerKids Pr.) Rosen Publishing Group, Inc., The.

Ferguson. Careers in Focus: Government. 2nd rev. ed. 2007. (Careers in Focus Ser.). 208p. (gr. 6-12). 32.95 *(978-0-8160-6568-4(3),* Ferguson Publishing Co.) Facts On File, Inc.

Jakubiak, David J. What Does a Supreme Court Justice Do? 2010. (How Our Government Works Ser.). 24p. (J). (gr. 3-6). lib. bdg., E-Book 42.50 *(978-1-4488-0031-5(5))* Rosen Publishing Group, Inc., The.

Stevens, Stewart, Sr. The White House Chandeliers: My Experiences While Working for Seven U. S. Presidents. 2016. (ENG., Illus.). xi, 127p. (gr. 6-17). pap. 25.00 *(978-0-9974925-0-7(3))* Lightning Fast Bk. Publishing.

Storrs, Landon & Storrs, Landon R. Y. The Second Red Scare & the Unmaking of the New Deal Left. 2012. (Politics & Society in Modern America Ser.). (ENG., Illus.). 424p. (C). 47.95 *(978-0-691-15396-4(5))* Princeton Univ. Pr.

Topinka, Joseph Baar. Just Judy: A Citizen & Leader for Illinois. 2017. (ENG.). (J). pap. 16.95 ***(978-0-9983282-2-5(7))*** Hilton Publishing Co.

Woog, Adam. Careers in Homeland Security. 2014. 112p. (J). *(978-1-62712-422-5(5))* Cavendish Square Publishing.

—Careers in Homeland Security. 2013. (J). 34.21 *(978-1-60870-959-5(0))* Marshall Cavendish Corp.

UNITED STATES—PAINTERS

see Painters—United States

UNITED STATES—POETRY

Adams, Michelle Medlock. Ha! Ha! Ha! Halloween. Johnson, Meredith, illus. 2005. 30p. (J). (gr. 3-7). 12.95 *(978-0-8249-5508-3(0),* Ideal Pubns.) Worthy Publishing.

Blanco, Richard. One Today: The Inaugural Poems for President Barack Obama. Pilkey, Dav, illus. 2015. (ENG.). 40p. (J). (gr. -1-3). 18.00 *(978-0-316-37144-5(0))* Little, Brown Bks. for Young Readers.

Dyan, Penelope. An Apple a Day! a Kid's Guide to Julian, Californi. Weigand, John D., photos by. 2010. (Illus.). 48p. pap. 11.95 *(978-1-935630-12-8(1))* Bellissima Publishing, LLC.

—One Big Hole in the Ground, a Kid's Guide to Grand Canyon, Us. Weigand, John D., photos by. 2010. (Illus.). 50p. pap. 11.95 *(978-1-935630-02-9(4))* Bellissima Publishing, LLC.

—Take a Dam Tour! a Kid's Guide to Hoover Dam, Nevad. Weigand, John D., photos by. 2010. (Illus.). 50p. pap. 11.95 *(978-1-935630-05-0(9))* Bellissima Publishing, LLC.

—What Happens in Vegas a Kid's Guide to Las Vegas, Nevad. Weigand, John D., photos by. 2010. (Illus.). 48p. pap. 11.95 *(978-1-935630-06-7(7))* Bellissima Publishing, LLC.

Landry, Cornell P. Goodnight Nola: An Endearing Bedtime Book for All Ages. Schmitt, Louis J., illus. 2009. (ENG.). 36p. (J). 16.95 *(978-0-9818126-4-9(3))* Ampersand, Inc.

Lee Bates, Katharine & Gamwell, Calvert. America the Beautiful: A Pop-up Book about the Famous Song by Katharine Lee Bates. Jordan, Carrie, illus. 2006. 16p. (J). (gr. 4-8). reprint ed. 17.00 *(978-1-4223-5447-6(4))* DIANE Publishing Co.

Myers, Walter Dean. We Are America. 2015. (J). lib. bdg. 17.20 *(978-0-606-36963-3(5))* Turtleback Bks.

—We Are America: A Tribute from the Heart. Myers, Christopher, illus. (ENG.). 40p. (J). (gr. 1-5). 2015. pap. 6.99 *(978-0-06-052310-7(7))* 2011. 16.99 *(978-0-06-052308-4(5))* HarperCollins Pubs. (Collins).

Myers, Walter Dean & Myers, Christopher. We Are America: A Tribute from the Heart. 2012. (ENG.). (J). (gr. 3-6). 29.95 incl. audio compact disk *(978-1-4301-1112-2(7))* Live Oak Media.

Perdomo, Willie. Visiting Langston. Collier, Bryan, illus. 2005. (ENG.). 32p. (J). (gr. -1-3). reprint ed. pap. 9.99 *(978-0-8050-7681-7(9),* 9780805078817) Square Fish.

Salas, Laura Purdie. Tiny Dreams, Sprouting Tall: Poems about the United States, 1 vol. 2008. (Poetry Ser.). (ENG., Illus.). 32p. (gr. 1-2). per. 8.10 *(978-1-4296-1748-2(9),* Aplus Bks.) Capstone Press of Coughlan Cos.

Sardelli, Darren. Galaxy Pizza & Meteor Pie. 2009. 12.95 *(978-0-615-28469-9(8))* Laugh-A-Lot Bks.

Soto, Gary. A Fire in My Hands. exp. rev. ed. 2013. (ENG.). 96p. (YA). (gr. 7-12). pap. 6.99 *(978-0-544-10482-2(X))* Houghton Mifflin Harcourt Publishing Co.

Testa, Maria. Something about America. 2007. (ENG., Illus.). 96p. (YA). (gr. 7-18). pap. 6.99 *(978-0-7636-3415-5(8))* Candlewick Pr.

Van Wassenhove, Sue. The Seldom-Ever-Shady Glades. 2008. (ENG., Illus.). 32p. (J). (gr. 3-7). 17.95 *(978-1-59078-352-8(2),* Wordsong) Boyds Mills Pr.

Yanique, Tiphanie & Djeli, Moses. I Am the Virgin Islands. 2012. *(978-1-934370-30-8(4))* Editorial Campana.

UNITED STATES—POLITICS AND GOVERNMENT

ABDO. How the US Government Works, 1 vol. 2014. (How the US Government Works: 6). (ENG.). 48p. (gr. 3-6). lib. bdg. 196.74 *(978-1-62403-632-3(5))* ABDO Publishing Co.

ABDO Publishing Company. American Moments Set 2. 2005. (American Moments Set Ii Ser.). (gr. 4-8). 324.84 *(978-1-59197-724-7(X),* Abdo & Daughters) ABDO Publishing Co.

Adler, David A. A Picture Book of Patrick Henry. Wallner, John et al, illus. 2005. (ENG.). 32p. (J). (gr. k-3). pap. 6.95 *(978-0-8234-1678-3(X))* Holiday Hse., Inc.

T U V

Alarcon, Robert. John Jay, 1 vol. 2004. (Primary Source Readers Ser.). (ENG.). 24p. (J). (gr. 4-4). pap. 8.99 (978-0-7439-8784-4(5)) Shell Educational Publishing.

Aldritt, Jeremy. Thomas Paine & the Power of Common Sense. 2015. (Spotlight on American History Ser.). (ENG., Illus.). 24p. (J). (gr. 4-6). pap. 10.00 (978-1-4994-1765-4(9), PowerKids Pr.) Rosen Publishing Group, Inc., The.

Aloian, Molly. Constitution Day. 2008. (Celebrations in My World Ser.). (ENG., Illus.). 32p. (J). (gr. k-3). pap. (978-0-7787-4304-0(7)) Crabtree Publishing Co.

Altman, Linda Jacobs. The Politics of Slavery: Fiery National Debates Fueled by the Slave Economy. 2004. (Slavery in American History Ser.). (Illus.). 128p. (J). lib. bdg. 27.94 (978-0-7660-2150-1(5)) Enslow Pubs., Inc.

American Political Biographies, 3 vols., Set. 2010. (Political Biographies Ser.). (C). (gr. 9). 255.00 (978-0-8160-8310-7(X)) Facts On File, Inc.

Anderson, Dale. The Aftermath of the Civil War. 2004. (World Almanac Library of the Civil War). (Illus.). 48p. (gr. 5-12). pap. 14.05 (978-0-8368-5597-5(3)); lib. bdg. 31.00 (978-0-8368-5588-3(4)) Stevens, Gareth Publishing LLLP. (Gareth Stevens Secondary Library).

—The American Colonies Declare Independence. 2005. (World Almanac Library of the American Revolution Ser.). (Illus.). 48p. (gr. 5-12). lib. bdg. 31.00 (978-0-8368-5926-3(X), Gareth Stevens Secondary Library) Stevens, Gareth Publishing LLLP.

—The Causes of the Civil War. 2004. (World Almanac Library of the Civil War). (Illus.). 48p. (gr. 5-12). pap. 14.05 (978-0-8368-5590-6(6)); lib. bdg. 31.00 (978-0-8368-5581-4(7)) Stevens, Gareth Publishing LLLP. (Gareth Stevens Secondary Library).

—Forming a New American Government. 2005. (World Almanac Library of the American Revolution Ser.). 48p. (gr. 5-12). pap. 14.05 (978-0-8368-5941-6(3)); (Illus.). lib. bdg. 31.00 (978-0-8368-5932-4(4)) Stevens, Gareth Publishing LLLP. (Gareth Stevens Secondary Library).

—The Home Fronts in the Civil War. 2004. (World Almanac Library of the Civil War). (Illus.). 48p. (gr. 5-12). lib. bdg. 31.00 (978-0-8368-5587-6(6), Gareth Stevens Secondary Library) Stevens, Gareth Publishing LLLP.

—Leaders of the American Revolution. 2005. (World Almanac Library of the American Revolution Ser.). 48p. (gr. 5-12). pap. 14.05 (978-0-8368-5940-9(5)); lib. bdg. 31.00 (978-0-8368-5931-7(6)) Stevens, Gareth Publishing LLLP. (Gareth Stevens Secondary Library).

Anderson, Michael, contrib. by. Abraham Lincoln. 2012. (Pivotal Presidents: Profiles in Leadership Ser.). (ENG., Illus.). 80p. (gr. 7-12). (J). lib. bdg. 32.90 (978-1-61530-942-9(X)); (YA). 65.80 (978-1-61530-953-5(5)) Rosen Publishing Group, Inc., The.

—Ronald Reagan. 2012. (Pivotal Presidents: Profiles in Leadership Ser.). (ENG., Illus.). 80p. (YA). (gr. 7-12). 65.80 (978-1-61530-958-0(6)) Rosen Publishing Group, Inc., The.

Anderson, Nancy. I Am a Citizen of the United States. 2016. (Rosen REAL Readers: Social Studies Nonfiction / Fiction: Family, Community, & the World Ser.). 12p. (gr. 1-k). pap. 6.33 (978-1-5081-2323-1(3), Rosen Classroom) Rosen Publishing Group, Inc., The.

Anderson, Wayne. Fighting Racial Discrimination: Treating All Americans Fairly under the Law. (Progressive Movement 1900-1920: Efforts to Reform America's New Industrial Society Ser.). 32p. 2009. (gr. 3-4). 47.90 (978-1-60854-164-5(9)) 2004. (Illus.). (YA). (gr. 5-9). lib. bdg. 22.50 (978-1-4042-0189-7(0)) Rosen Publishing Group, Inc., The.

Andronik, Catherine M. & Kenney, Karen Latchana. Abraham Lincoln's Presidency. 2016. (Presidential Powerhouses Ser.). (ENG., Illus.). 104p. (J). (gr. 6-12). 35.99 (978-1-4677-7925-8(3), Lerner Pubns.) Lerner Publishing Group.

Apel, Melani. The Federal Reserve Act: Making the American Banking System Stronger. 2009. (Progressive Movement 1900-1920: Efforts to Reform America's New Industrial Society Ser.). 32p. (gr. 3-4). 47.90 (978-1-60854-172-0(X)) Rosen Publishing Group, Inc., The.

Apel, Melanie Ann. The Federal Reserve Act: Making the American Banking System Stronger. 2004. (Progressive Movement, 1900-1920 Ser.). (Illus.). 32p. (YA). (gr. 5-9). lib. bdg. 22.50 (978-1-4042-0196-5(3)) Rosen Publishing Group, Inc., The.

Armentrout, David & Armentrout, Patricia. The Emancipation Proclamation. 2005. (Documents that Shaped the Nation Ser.). (Illus.). 48p. (gr. 4-6). 20.95 (978-1-59515-233-6(4)) Rourke Educational Media.

Aronin, Miriam. Dwight D. Eisenhower. 2016. (First Look at America's Presidents Ser.). (ENG., Illus.). 24p. (J). (gr. -1-3). 17.95 (978-1-943553-31-0(9)) Bearport Publishing Co., Inc.

—Woodrow Wilson. 2016. (First Look at America's Presidents Ser.). (ENG., Illus.). 24p. (J). (gr. -1-3). 17.95 (978-1-943553-30-3(0)) Bearport Publishing Co., Inc.

Aronson, Billy. Richard M. Nixon. 2007. (Presidents & Their Times Ser.). (Illus.). 96p. (J). (gr. 4-7). lib. bdg. 34.21 (978-0-7614-2428-4(8), Benchmark Bks.) Marshall Cavendish Corp.

Aronson, Marc. The Real Revolution: The Global Story of American Independence. 2005. (ENG., Illus.). 256p. (YA). (gr. 7-12). 22.00 (978-0-618-18179-7(2)) Houghton Mifflin Harcourt Publishing Co.

Asselin, Kristine Carlson. The Real Story about Government & Politics in Colonial America. (Life in the American Colonies Ser.). (ENG.). 32p. (gr. 3-4). 2017. pap. 8.10 **(978-1-5157-9747-0(3))** 2011. pap. 8.10 (978-1-4296-7219-1(6)) 2011. pap. 47.70 (978-1-4296-7220-7(X)) Capstone Press of Coughlan Cos. (Fact Finders).

Ball, Lea. The Federalist — Anti-Federalist Debate over States' Rights: A Primary Source Investigation. 2004. (Great Historic Debates & Speeches Ser.). (Illus.). 64p. (J). lib. bdg. 31.95 (978-1-4042-0149-1(1)) Rosen Publishing Group, Inc., The.

—The Federalist-Anti-Federalist Debate over States' Rights: A Primary Source Investigation. 2009. (Great Historic Debates & Speeches Ser.). 64p. (gr. 5-8). 58.50 (978-1-61513-125-9(6)) Rosen Publishing Group, Inc., The.

Bamaton, Paul. Elections: Choosing Our Leaders. 2009. (Explore Citizenship Ser.). 24p. (J). (gr. 3-5). 22.60 (978-1-4358-2979-4(4), PowerKids Pr.) Rosen Publishing Group, Inc., The.

Bari, Ellen. Our Government: Text Pairs. 2008. (Bridges/Navigators Ser.). (J). (gr. 3). 89.00 (978-1-4108-8368-1(X)) Benchmark Education Co.

Bartoletti, Susan Campbell, adapted by. The Untold History of the United States, 1898-1945, Vol. 1. 2014. (ENG., Illus.). 400p. (J). (gr. 5-9). 19.99 (978-1-4814-2173-7(5), Atheneum Bks. for Young Readers) Simon & Schuster Children's Publishing.

Barton, Chris. The Amazing Age of John Roy Lynch. Tate, Don, illus. 2015. (ENG.). 50p. (J). 17.00 (978-0-8028-5379-0(X), Eerdmans Bks For Young Readers) Eerdmans, William B. Publishing Co.

Bausum, Ann. Our Country's Presidents: A Complete Encyclopedia of the U.S. Presidency. 2017. (Illus.). 224p. (J). **(978-1-4263-2944-9(X))** National Geographic Society.

Bausum, Ann. Unraveling Freedom: The Battle for Democracy on the Homefront During World War I. 2010. (ENG., Illus.). 96p. (J). (gr. 5-18). 19.95 (978-1-4263-0702-7(0)); 28.90 (978-1-4263-0703-4(9)) National Geographic Society. (National Geographic Children's Bks.).

Belton, Blair. The Articles of Confederation. 2013. 32p. (J). (gr. 4-6). 26.60 (978-1-4339-8993-3(X)); pap. 63.00 (978-1-4339-8995-7(6)); pap. 10.50 (978-1-4339-8994-0(8)) Stevens, Gareth Publishing LLLP.

Benchmark Education Company. The United States Government (Teacher Guide) 2005. (978-1-4108-4640-2(7)) Benchmark Education Co.

Benchmark Education Company, LLC Staff, compiled by. Government & Citizenship. 2005. (English Explorers Ser.). (J). spiral bd. 265.00 (978-1-4108-5767-5(0)) Benchmark Education Co.

—Government & Citizenship: Theme Set. 2006. (J). 121.00 (978-1-4108-7096-4(0)) Benchmark Education Co.

—GOVT & Citizenship. 2006. spiral bd. 330.00 (978-1-4108-7007-0(3)) Benchmark Education Co.

Benoit, Peter. Forms of Government. 2014. (Cornerstones of Freedom Ser.: 3). (ENG.). 64p. (J). lib. bdg. 30.00 (978-0-531-21330-8(7)) Scholastic Library Publishing.

—Immigration. 2012. (Cornerstones of Freedom, Third Ser.). (ENG., Illus.). 64p. (J). pap. 8.95 (978-0-531-28157-4(4)); (gr. 4-6). lib. bdg. 30.00 (978-0-531-23057-2(0)) Scholastic Library Publishing. (Children's Pr.).

Berlatsky, Noah. The Republican Party. Greenhaven Press Staff, ed. 2015. (Opposing Viewpoints Ser.). (ENG.). 224p. (gr. 10-12). pap. 33.80 (978-0-7377-7285-2(9), Greenhaven Pr., Inc.) Cengage Gale.

—Voting Rights. Greenhaven Press Staff, ed. 2015. (Opposing Viewpoints Ser.). (ENG.). 224p. (gr. 10-12). pap. 33.80 (978-0-7377-7301-9(4), Greenhaven Pr., Inc.) Cengage Gale.

Berne, Emma Carlson. The Presidency of Theodore Roosevelt: Leading from the Bully Pulpit, 1 vol. 2014. (Greatest U. S. Presidents Ser.). (ENG.). 64p. (gr. 5-7). lib. bdg. 33.99 (978-0-7565-4925-1(6)) Compass Point Bks.

Best, B. J. Abraham Lincoln, the Emancipation Proclamation, & the 13th Amendment. 2015. (Primary Sources of the Abolitionist Movement Ser.). (ENG., Illus.). 64p. (J). (gr. 6-6). lib. bdg. 34.21 (978-1-5026-0530-6(9)) Cavendish Square Publishing.

Betti, Matthew. The Declaration of Independence & the Continental Congress. 2015. (Spotlight on American History Ser.). (ENG., Illus.). 24p. (J). (gr. 4-6). pap. 10.00 (978-1-4994-1728-9(4), PowerKids Pr.) Rosen Publishing Group, Inc., The.

Beyer, Mark. The Election of 1800: Congress Helps Settle a Three-Way Vote. 2004. (Life in the New American Nation Ser.). (ENG., Illus.). 32p. (gr. 5-8). pap. 10.00 (978-0-8239-4255-8(4)) Rosen Publishing Group, Inc., The.

—The Election Of 1800: Congress Helps Settle a Three-Way Vote. 2009. (Life in the New American Nation Ser.). 32p. (gr. 4-4). 47.90 (978-1-61514-282-8(7)) Rosen Publishing Group, Inc., The.

Bishirjian, Richard J. The American Political Tradition & the Nature of Public Philosophy. 2004. (C). per. 12.50 (978-1-58152-339-3(4), Copley Publishing Group) Copley Custom Textbooks.

Blake, Kevin. Harry S. Truman: The 33rd President. 2016. (First Look at America's Presidents Ser.). (ENG., Illus.). 24p. (J). (gr. -1-3). lib. bdg. 17.95 (978-1-943553-29-7(7)) Bearport Publishing Co., Inc.

—Lyndon B. Johnson. 2016. (First Look at America's Presidents Ser.). (ENG., Illus.). 24p. (J). (gr. -1-3). lib. bdg. 17.95 (978-1-943553-32-7(7)) Bearport Publishing Co., Inc.

Bober, Natalie S. Countdown to Independence. 2007. (ENG.). 368p. (YA). (gr. 7). pap. 19.95 (978-1-4169-6392-9(8), Atheneum Bks. for Young Readers) Simon & Schuster Children's Publishing.

—Thomas Jefferson: Draftsman of a Nation. 2008. (ENG., Illus.). 376p. per. 16.95 (978-0-8139-2732-9(3)) University of Virginia Pr.

Bodden, Valerie. The Declaration of American Independence. 2009. (Days of Change Ser.). (Illus.). 48p. (YA). (gr. 4-7). 22.95 (978-1-58341-733-1(8)) Creative Co., The.

Boehme, Gerry. Edward Snowden: Heroic Whistleblower or Traitorous Spy? 2017. (J). **(978-1-5026-2673-8(X))** Cavendish Square Publishing.

Bolden, Tonya. The Emancipation Proclamation: Lincoln & the Dawn of Liberty. 2013. (ENG., Illus.). 128p. (J). (gr. 3-7). 24.95 (978-1-4197-0390-4(0), Abrams Bks. for Young Readers) Abrams, Inc.

—FDR's Alphabet Soup: New Deal America, 1932-1939. 2010. (ENG.). 144p. (YA). (gr. 7). 19.99 (978-0-375-85214-5(X), Knopf Bks. for Young Readers) Random Hse. Children's Bks.

Boothroyd, Jennifer. What Are the Branches of Government? 2015. (ENG., Illus.). 24p. (J). (gr. k-2). 23.99 (978-1-4677-8573-0(3), Lerner Pubns.) Lerner Publishing Group.

Boshier, Rosa. Ronald Reagan: 40th US President, 1 vol. 2013. (Essential Lives Set 8 Ser.). (ENG.). 112p. (J). (gr. 6-12). lib. bdg. 35.64 (978-1-61783-895-8(0), Essential Library) ABDO Publishing Co.

Bouchard, David. The Elders Are Watching. Vickers, Roy Henry, illus. 5th rev. deluxe ed. 2003. (ENG.). 56p. (J). 18.95 (978-1-55192-641-4(5)) Raincoast Bk. Distribution CAN. Dist: Publishers Group West (PGW).

Boyd, Bentley. Government. 2nd ed. 2010. (Chester the Crab's Comix with Content Ser.). (Illus.). 24p. pap. 6.95 (978-1-933122-38-0(2)) Chester Comix, LLC.

Brannon, Barbara. Discover the United States Government. 2005. (J). pap. (978-1-4108-5146-8(X)) Benchmark Education Co.

Brennan, Linda Crotta. Franklin D. Roosevelt's Presidency. 2016. (Presidential Powerhouses Ser.). (ENG., Illus.). 104p. (J). (gr. 6-12). 35.99 (978-1-4677-7928-9(8)); 53.32 (978-1-4677-8549-5(0)) Lerner Publishing Group. (Lerner Pubns.).

Brexel, Bernadette. The Populist Party: A Voice for the Farmers in an Industrial Society. 2009. (America's Industrial Society in the 19th Century Ser.). 32p. (gr. 4-4). 47.90 (978-1-61511-344-6(4)) Rosen Publishing Group, Inc., The.

—The Populist Party: A Voice for the Farmers in the Industrialized Society. 2004. (America's Industrial Society in the 19th Century Ser.). (ENG., Illus.). 32p. (gr. 5-8). pap. 10.00 (978-0-8239-4284-8(8)) Rosen Publishing Group, Inc., The.

—Prosecuting Trusts: The Courts Break up Monopolies in America. (Progressive Movement 1900-1920: Efforts to Reform America's New Industrial Society Ser.). 32p. 2009. (gr. 3-4). 47.90 (978-1-60854-169-0(X)) 2004. (Illus.). (YA). (gr. 5-9). lib. bdg. 22.50 (978-1-4042-0188-0(2)) Rosen Publishing Group, Inc., The.

Bright-Moore, Susan & Bedesky, Baron. How Is a Government Elected? 2008. (Your Guide to Government Ser.). (ENG.). 32p. (J). (gr. k-5). lib. bdg. (978-0-7787-4325-5(X)); (Illus.). pap. (978-0-7787-4330-9(6)) Crabtree Publishing Co.

Brockenbrough, Martha. Alexander Hamilton, Revolutionary. 2017. (ENG.). 384p. (YA). 19.99 **(978-1-250-12319-0(4),** 9781250123190) Feiwel & Friends.

Brown, Liz. Civics. 2007. (Social Studies Essential Skills Ser.). (Illus.). 24p. (J). (gr. 4-7). lib. bdg. 24.45 (978-1-59036-765-0(0)); per. 8.95 (978-1-59036-766-7(9)) Weigl Pubs., Inc.

Brownell, Richard. The Civil War: The Fall of the Confederacy & the End of Slavery. 2005. (History's Great Defeats Ser.). (ENG., Illus.). 109p. (YA). (gr. 7-10). lib. bdg. 30.85 (978-1-59018-429-5(7), Lucent Bks.) Cengage Gale.

Bryfonski, Dedria. Deregulation. 2010. (Opposing Viewpoints Ser.). (ENG., Illus.). 240p. 42.95 (978-0-7377-5108-6(8)); 224p. (gr. 10-12). pap. 33.80 (978-0-7377-5109-3(6)) Cengage Gale. (Greenhaven Pr., Inc.).

Buchanan, Shelly. Our Government: The Three Branches, 1 vol. rev. ed. 2014. (Primary Source Readers Content & Literacy Ser.). (ENG., Illus.). 32p. (gr. 3-3). pap. 8.99 (978-1-4333-7365-7(3)) Teacher Created Materials, Inc.

Buckwalter, Stephanie. Independent Government Agencies: Working for America. 2008. (Federal Government Ser.). (Illus.). 128p. (J). (gr. 6-18). lib. bdg. 34.60 (978-1-59845-057-6(3), MyReportLinks.com Bks.) Enslow Pubs., Inc.

Burgan, Michael. The Branches of U. S. Government. 2011. (Cornerstones of Freedom, Third Ser.). (Illus.). 64p. (J). (ENG.). pap. 8.95 (978-0-531-26553-6(6)); lib. bdg. 30.00 (978-0-531-25028-0(8)) Scholastic Library Publishing. (Children's Pr.).

—The Creation of the U. S. Constitution. Purcell, Gordon & Beatty, Terry, illus. 2006. (Graphic History Ser.). (ENG.). 32p. (gr. 3-4). pap. 8.10 (978-0-7368-9653-5(8), Graphic Library) Capstone Press of Coughlan Cos.

—The U. S. Constitution. 2011. (Cornerstones of Freedom, Third Ser.). (ENG., Illus.). 64p. (J). pap. 8.95 (978-0-531-26567-3(6), Children's Pr.) Scholastic Library Publishing.

—The U.S. Constitution/By Michael Burgan. 2011. (Cornerstones of Freedom, Third Ser.). (Illus.). 64p. (J). lib. bdg. 30.00 (978-0-531-25042-6(3), Children's Pr.) Scholastic Library Publishing.

—The Voting Rights Act of 1965: An Interactive History Adventure. 2015. (You Choose: History Ser.). (ENG.). 112p. (gr. 3-4). pap. 6.95 (978-1-4914-1805-5(2), You Choose Bks.) Capstone Press of Coughlan Cos.

Burgan, Michael & Hoena, Blake A. The Creation of the U. S. Constitution, 1 vol. Purcell, Gordon & Beatty, Terry, illus. 2006. (Graphic History Ser.). (ENG.). 32p. (gr. 3-4). 30.65 (978-0-7368-6491-6(1), Graphic Library) Capstone Press of Coughlan Cos.

Burnett, Iris & Greager, Clay. So You Think You Can Be President? 200 Questions to Determine If You Are Right (Or Left) Enough to Be the Next Commander-in-Chief. 2008. (ENG.). 240p. pap. 12.95 (978-1-60239-202-1(1)) Skyhorse Publishing Co., Inc.

Camardella, Michele L. America in The 1980s. 2005. (Decades of American History Ser.). (Illus.). 128p. (gr. 5-8). per. 35.00 (978-0-8160-5644-6(7)) Facts On File, Inc.

Carey, Charles W., Jr. The Emancipation Proclamation. 2009. (Journey to Freedom Ser.). (ENG., Illus.). 32p. (J). (gr. 4-7). 29.93 (978-1-60253-137-6(4), 200403) Child's World, Inc., The.

Casciato, Daniel. Expansion & Reform: (Early 1800s-1861) 2007. (Presidents of the United States Ser.). (Illus.). 48p. (J). (gr. 4-7). lib. bdg. 29.05 (978-1-59036-741-4(3)) Weigl Pubs., Inc.

—Expansion & Reform: Early 1800s-1861. 2007. (Presidents of the United States Ser.). (Illus.). 48p. (J). (gr. 4-7). per. 11.95 (978-1-59036-742-1(1)) Weigl Pubs., Inc.

Cefrey, Holly. The Interstate Commerce Act: The Government Takes Control of Trade Between States. 2009. (America's Industrial Society in the 19th Century Ser.). 32p. (gr. 4-4). 47.90 (978-1-61511-342-2(8)) Rosen Publishing Group, Inc., The.

—The United States Constitution & Early State Constitutions: Law & Order in the New Nation & States. 2009. (Life in the New American Nation Ser.). 32p. (gr. 4-4). 47.90 (978-1-61514-287-3(8)) Rosen Publishing Group, Inc., The.

Chastain, Zachary. Scandals & Glory: Politics in the 1800s. 2009. (Daily Life in America in the 1800s Ser.). 64p. (YA). (gr. 7-18). lib. bdg. 22.95 (978-1-4222-1787-0(6)) Mason Crest.

—Scandals & Glory: Politics in The 1800s. 2009. (Daily Life in America in the 1800s Ser.). 64p. (YA). (gr. 7-18). pap. 9.95 (978-1-4222-1860-0(0)) Mason Crest.

Cheney, Lynne. We the People: The Story of Our Constitution. Harlin, Greg, illus. (ENG.). 40p. (J). (gr. k-4). 2012. 7.99 (978-1-4424-4422-5(3)) 2008. 17.99 (978-1-4169-5418-7(X)) Simon & Schuster/Paula Wiseman Bks. (Simon & Schuster/Paula Wiseman Bks.).

Clark, Willow. The True Story of the Declaration of Independence. 2013. (What Really Happened? Ser.). (ENG., Illus.). 24p. (J). (gr. 3-6). pap. 8.25 (978-1-4488-9840-4(4)); lib. bdg. 22.60 (978-1-4488-9691-2(6)) Rosen Publishing Group, Inc., The. (PowerKids Pr.).

—The True Story of the Emancipation Proclamation. 2013. (What Really Happened? Ser.). (ENG., Illus.). 24p. (J). (gr. 3-6). 22.60 (978-1-4488-9695-0(9)); pap. 8.25 (978-1-4488-9848-0(X)) Rosen Publishing Group, Inc., The. (PowerKids Pr.).

Clay, Kathryn. The Declaration of Independence: Introducing Primary Sources. 2017. (Introducing Primary Sources Ser.). (ENG.). 32p. (gr. 1-2). lib. bdg. 27.99 **(978-1-5157-6355-0(2))** Capstone Press of Coughlan Cos.

Colbert, David. Benjamin Franklin. 2008. (10 Days Ser.). (ENG.). 160p. (J). (gr. 3-8). pap. 8.99 (978-1-4169-6446-9(0), Simon & Schuster/Paula Wiseman Bks.) Simon & Schuster/Paula Wiseman Bks.

Colligan, Louise H. Government. 2014. (Life in Colonial America Ser.). 80p. (YA). (gr. 6-8). lib. bdg. 35.64 (978-1-62712-891-9(3)) Cavendish Square Publishing.

Connell, Kate. Servant to Abigail Adams: The Early American Adventures of Hannah Cooper. 2004. (Illus.). 40p. (J). (gr. 4-8). pap. 7.00 (978-0-7567-8216-0(3)) DIANE Publishing Co.

Connell, Kate, et al. The Spirit of a New Nation. 2007. (Avenues Ser.). (ENG., Illus.). 40p. (J). pap. 19.95 (978-0-7922-8684-4(7)) CENGAGE Learning.

Cooke, Tim. Causes of the War. 2012. (American Civil War: the Right Answer Ser.). (Illus.). 48p. (J). (gr. 6-8). pap. 14.05 (978-1-4339-7536-3(X)); lib. bdg. 31.95 (978-1-4339-7535-6(1)) Stevens, Gareth Publishing LLLP.

—Politics of the War: 1861-1865. 2012. (Civil War Highlights Ser.). (Illus.). 48p. (gr. 5-12). lib. bdg. 37.10 (978-1-59920-818-3(0)) Black Rabbit Bks.

Cooke, Tim, ed. Politics. 2011. (CC: Civil War Ser.). 112p. (gr. 6-12). 42.80 (978-1-936333-48-6(1)) Brown Bear Bks.

Corey, Shana. A Time to Act: John F. Kennedy's Big Speech. Christie, R. Gregory, illus. 2017. (ENG.). 56p. (J). (gr. 3). 18.95 (978-0-7358-4275-5(2)) North-South Bks., Inc.

Cosson, Jody. Civil War & Reconstruction: 1850-1877. 2007. (Presidents of the United States Ser.). (Illus.). (J). (gr. 4-7). 47p. lib. bdg. 29.05 (978-1-59036-743-8(X)); 48p. per. 10.95 (978-1-59036-744-5(8)) Weigl Pubs., Inc.

Cox, Vicki. The History of Third Parties. 2007. (U. S. Government Ser.). (Illus.). 125p. (YA). (gr. 5-9). lib. bdg. 30.00 (978-0-7910-9421-1(9)) Facts On File, Inc.

CQ Press Editors. Guide to Current American Government 2004. 2004. (ENG.). 153p. pap. 26.95 (978-1-56802-901-6(2)) CQ Pr.

Creative Media Applications Staff, contrib. by. American Presidents in World History, 5 vols., Vol. 1. 2003. (Middle School Reference Ser.). (Illus.). 144p. (C). (gr. 6-8). 242.00 (978-0-313-32564-9(2), MS2564, Greenwood) ABC-CLIO, LLC.

—Debatable Issues in U. S. History: A World Power 1934 to the Present, 5 vols. 2004. (Middle School Reference Ser.). (Illus.). 144p. (C). (gr. 6-8). 242.00 (978-0-313-32910-4(9), MS2910, Greenwood) ABC-CLIO, LLC.

Crompton, Samuel Willard. Gouverneur Morris: Creating a Nation. 2004. (America's Founding Fathers Ser.). (Illus.). 128p. (J). lib. bdg. 26.60 (978-0-7660-2213-3(7)) Enslow Pubs., Inc.

Crompton, Samuel Willard. How Woodrow Wilson Fought World War I. 2017. (Presidents at War Ser.). 128p. (J). (gr. 8-8). lib. bdg. 37.27 **(978-0-7660-8529-9(5))** Enslow Pubs., Inc.

Darby, Jean. Dwight D. Eisenhower. 2004. (Presidential Leaders Ser.). (Illus.). 112p. (J). (gr. 6-12). lib. bdg. 29.27 (978-0-8225-0813-7(3)) Lerner Publishing Group.

Davies, Monika. True Life: Alexander Hamilton. 2016. (TIME for KIDS(r) Nonfiction Readers Ser.). (Illus.). 48p. (J). (gr. 8-8). pap. 9.99 **(978-1-4938-3633-8(1))** Teacher Created Materials, Inc.

Day, Meredith, ed. Lyndon B. Johnson. 2016. (Pivotal Presidents: Profiles in Leadership Ser.). 80p. (gr. 8-8). lib. bdg. 33.90 (978-1-68048-527-1(X)) Rosen Publishing Group, Inc., The.

DeCarolis, Lisa. Alexander Hamilton: Federalist & Founding Father. 2009. (Library of American Lives & Times Ser.). 112p. (gr. 5-5). 69.20 (978-1-60853-470-8(7)) Rosen Publishing Group, Inc., The.

DeGraw, Aleine. Alexander Hamilton: American Statesman. 2009. (Primary Sources of Famous People in American History Ser.). 32p. (gr. 2-3). 47.90 (978-1-60851-646-9(6)) Rosen Publishing Group, Inc., The.

—Alexander Hamilton: American Statesman / Estadista Estadounidense. 2009. (Famous People in American History/Grandes personajes en la historia de los Estados Unidos Ser.). (SPA.). 32p. (gr. 2-3). 47.90 (978-1-61512-536-4(1), Editorial Buenas Letras) Rosen Publishing Group, Inc., The.

—Alexander Hamilton: Estadista Estadounidense. 2004. (Grandes Personajes en la Historia de Los Estados Unidos Ser.). (SPA., Illus.). 32p. (gr. 5-8). pap. 10.00 (978-0-8239-4219-0(8)) Rosen Publishing Group, Inc., The.

—Alexander Hamilton: Estadista estadounidense (Alexander Hamilton: American Statesman) 2009. (Grandes personajes en la historia de los Estados Unidos (Famous People in American History) Ser.). 32p. (gr. 2-3). 47.90 (978-1-61512-788-7(7), Editorial Buenas Letras) Rosen Publishing Group, Inc., The.

DeRubertis, Barbara. Let's Celebrate Constitution Day. 2015. (ENG., Illus.). 32p. (J). (gr. 1-4). pap. 7.95 (978-1-57565-749-3(X)) Kane Press, Inc.

Doak, Robin. Conflicts in Iraq & Afghanistan. 2006. (Wars That Changed American History Ser.). (Illus.). 48p. (gr. 5-12). pap. 14.05 (978-0-8368-7305-4(X), Gareth Stevens Secondary Library) Stevens, Gareth Publishing LLLP.

Doak, Robin S. Eleanor Roosevelt, 1 vol. 2012. (American Biographies Ser.). (ENG.). 48p. (gr. 4-6). pap. 9.95 *(978-1-4329-6461-0(5)*, NA-h) Heinemann-Raintree.
Doak, Robin Santos. Conflicts in Iraq & Afghanistan. 2006. (Wars That Changed American History Ser.). (Illus.). 48p. (gr. 5-12). lib. bdg. 31.00 *(978-0-8368-7296-5(7)*, Gareth Stevens Secondary Library) Stevens, Gareth Publishing LLLP.
Doeden, Matt & Hoena, Blake. War in Afghanistan: An Interactive Modern History Adventure, 1 vol. 2014. (You Choose: Modern History Ser.). (ENG.). 112p. (gr. 3-4). 31.99 *(978-1-4765-4190-7(6)*, You Choose Bks.) Capstone Press of Coughlan Cos.
[DS529] Our Government [Lakeshore]. 2010. (Our Government Ser.). 24p. pap. 27.80 *(978-1-4296-4806-6(6)*, First Facts) Capstone Press of Coughlan Cos.
Eck, Kristin. Drafting the Constitution: Weighing Evidence to Draw Sound Conclusions. 2006. (Critical Thinking in American History Ser.). (ENG., Illus.). 48p. (YA). (gr. 5-8). lib. bdg. 29.25 *(978-1-4042-0412-6(1))* Rosen Publishing Group, Inc., The.
Egan, Tracie. The President & the Executive Branch. 2009. (Primary Source Library of American Citizenship Ser.). 32p. (gr. 5-5). 47.90 *(978-1-61511-229-6(4)*, Rosen Reference) Rosen Publishing Group, Inc., The.
Elish, Dan. The Watergate Scandal. 2004. (Cornerstones of Freedom Ser.). (ENG., Illus.). 48p. (J). 26.00 *(978-0-516-24239-2(3)*, Children's Pr.) Scholastic Library Publishing.
Elston, Heidi. George H. W. Bush, 1 vol. 2009. (United States Presidents Ser.). (ENG.). (YA). 40p. (YA). (gr. 3-6). 27.07 *(978-1-60453-443-6(5))* ABDO Publishing Co.
—Harry S. Truman, 1 vol. 2016. (ENG., Illus.). 40p. (J). *(978-1-68078-119-9(7))* ABDO Publishing Co.
The Emancipation Proclamation & the End of Slavery in America. 2014. (Celebration of the Civil Rights Movement Ser.). (Illus.). 80p. (J). (gr. 7-12). 34.25 *(978-1-4777-7749-7(0))* Rosen Publishing Group, Inc., The.
Encyclopaedia Britannica, ed. The American Presidency. 2009. (Illus.). 144p. (YA). (gr. 7-12). 29.95 *(978-1-59339-843-9(3))* Encyclopaedia Britannica, Inc.
Englar, Mary. An Illustrated Timeline of U. S. Presidents, 1 vol. Epstein, Len, illus. 2012. (Visual Timelines in History Ser.). (ENG.). 32p. (gr. 3-4). pap. 7.49 *(978-1-4048-7254-7(X))*; lib. bdg. 28.65 *(978-1-4048-7161-8(6))* Picture Window Bks.
Epperson, James F. Causes of the Civil War. 2005. (Road to War Ser.). (Illus.). 64p. (J). pap. 12.95 *(978-1-59556-006-3(8))*; (gr. 4-18). lib. bdg. 22.95 *(978-1-59556-002-5(5))* OTTN Publishing.
Epstein, Brad M. Barack Obama 101. l.t. ed. 2009. (My First Presidential Board Book Ser.). (Illus.). 28p. (J). (gr. -1-1). bds. *(978-1-60730-044-1(3)*, 101 Bk.) Michaelson Entertainment.
Espinosa, Rod. Patrick Henry, 1 vol. Espinosa, Rod, illus. 2007. (Bio-Graphics Ser.). (ENG., Illus.). 32p. (gr. 3-6). 28.50 *(978-1-60270-070-3(2)*, Graphic Planet- Nonfiction) ABDO Publishing Co.
Etingoff, Kim. Harry Truman: From Farmer to President. 2012. (J). pap. *(978-1-4222-2485-4(6))*; 64p. (gr. 7-8). 22.95 *(978-1-4222-2482-3(1))* Mason Crest.
EZ Comics, ed. James A. Baker, III: The Authorised Comic Book Biography. 2009. (ENG., Illus.). 44p. (YA). *(978-0-9795887-3-0(1))* EZ Comics.
Federalism. 2010. (Key Concepts in American History Ser.). (Illus.). 128p. (gr. 6-12). 45.00 *(978-1-60413-218-2(3)*, Chelsea Hse.) Facts On File, Inc.
Feinstein, Stephen. The 1900s. 2015. (Decades of the 20th & 21st Centuries Ser.). (ENG., Illus.). 96p. (J). (gr. 7-7). 34.60 *(978-0-7660-6920-6(6))* Enslow Pubs., Inc.
—The 1910s. 2015. (Decades of the 20th & 21st Centuries Ser.). (ENG., Illus.). 96p. (J). (gr. 7-7). 34.60 *(978-0-7660-6922-0(2))* Enslow Pubs., Inc.
—The 1920s. 2015. (Decades of the 20th & 21st Centuries Ser.). (ENG., Illus.). 96p. (J). (gr. 7-7). 34.60 *(978-0-7660-6924-4(9))* Enslow Pubs., Inc.
—The 1930s. 2015. (Decades of the 20th & 21st Centuries Ser.). (ENG., Illus.). 96p. (J). (gr. 7-7). 34.60 *(978-0-7660-6926-8(5))* Enslow Pubs., Inc.
—The 1940s. 2015. (Decades of the 20th & 21st Centuries Ser.). (ENG., Illus.). 96p. (J). (gr. 7-7). 34.60 *(978-0-7660-6928-2(1))* Enslow Pubs., Inc.
—The 1950s. 2015. (Decades of the 20th & 21st Centuries Ser.). (ENG., Illus.). 96p. (J). (gr. 7-7). 34.60 *(978-0-7660-6930-5(3))* Enslow Pubs., Inc.
—The 1960s. 2015. (Decades of the 20th & 21st Centuries Ser.). (ENG., Illus.). 96p. (J). (gr. 7-7). 34.60 *(978-0-7660-6932-9(X))* Enslow Pubs., Inc.
—The 1970s. 2015. (Decades of the 20th & 21st Centuries Ser.). (ENG., Illus.). 96p. (J). (gr. 7-7). 34.60 *(978-0-7660-6934-3(6))* Enslow Pubs., Inc.
—The 1980s. 2015. (Decades of the 20th & 21st Centuries Ser.). (ENG., Illus.). 96p. (J). (gr. 7-7). 34.60 *(978-0-7660-6935-0(4))* Enslow Pubs., Inc.
—The 1990s. 2015. (Decades of the 20th & 21st Centuries Ser.). (ENG., Illus.). 96p. (J). (gr. 7-7). 34.60 *(978-0-7660-6937-4(0))* Enslow Pubs., Inc.
—The 2000s. 2015. (Decades of the 20th & 21st Centuries Ser.). (ENG., Illus.). 96p. (J). (gr. 7-7). 34.60 *(978-0-7660-6939-8(7))* Enslow Pubs., Inc.
Ferguson, Melissa. U. S. Government: What You Need to Know. 2017. (Fact Files Ser.). (ENG.). 24p. (gr. 1-2). lib. bdg. 25.32 ***(978-1-5157-8118-9(6)***, First Facts) Capstone Press of Coughlan Cos.
Fingeroth, Danny. Democracy's Signature: Benjamin Franklin & the Declaration of Independence. 2009. (Great Moments in American History Ser.). 32p. (gr. 3-3). 47.90 *(978-1-61513-141-9(8))* Rosen Publishing Group, Inc., The.
Fink, Sam. The Declaration of Independence: The Words That Made America. Fink, Sam, illus. 2007. (Illus.). 160p. (YA). (gr. 7). 19.65 *(978-0-7569-8187-7(5))* Perfection Learning Corp.
Finley, Toiya Kristen. Russell Simmons. 2007. (Sharing the American Dream Ser.). 64p. (YA). (gr. 7-18). pap. 9.95 *(978-1-4222-0762-8(5))* Mason Crest.
Ford, Carin T. The Emancipation Proclamation, Lincoln, & Slavery Through Primary Sources. 2013. (Civil War Through Primary Sources Ser.). 48p. (J). (gr. 4-10). pap. 8.95 *(978-1-4644-0187-9(X))*; lib. bdg. 25.27 *(978-0-7660-4129-5(8))* Enslow Pubs., Inc.
—Lincoln, Slavery, & the Emancipation Proclamation. 2004. (Civil War Library). (Illus.). 48p. (J). lib. bdg. 25.27 *(978-0-7660-2252-2(8))* Enslow Pubs., Inc.
Ford, Jeanne Marie. How the Government Works. 2016. (How America Works). (ENG.). 24p. (J). (gr. 3-6). 28.50 *(978-1-5038-0904-8(8)*, 210661) Child's World, Inc., The.
Fradin, Dennis Brindell. The Declaration of Independence. 2006. (Turning Points in U. S. History Ser.). (Illus.). 46p. (J). (gr. 3-7). lib. bdg. 31.36 *(978-0-7614-2129-0(7)*, Benchmark Bks.) Marshall Cavendish Corp.
—The Emancipation Proclamation. 2007. (Turning Points in U. S. History Ser.). (J). lib. bdg. 31.36 *(978-0-7614-2038-5(X)*, Benchmark Bks.) Marshall Cavendish Corp.
—September 11, 2001. 2009. (Turning Points in U. S. History Ser.). 48p. (gr. 3-6). 31.36 *(978-0-7614-4259-2(6))* Marshall Cavendish Corp.
—The U. S. Constitution. 2007. (Turning Points in U. S. History Ser.). (Illus.). 47p. (J). (gr. 4-7). lib. bdg. 31.36 *(978-0-7614-2036-1(3)*, Benchmark Bks.) Marshall Cavendish Corp.
Francis, Amy. The U. S. Policy on Cuba. 2008. (At Issue Ser.). (ENG., Illus.). 128p. (gr. 10-12). 39.40 *(978-0-7377-4108-7(2))*; pap. 27.80 *(978-0-7377-4109-4(0))* Cengage Gale. (Greenhaven Pr., Inc.).
Frank, Michael. Government in Action. 2006. (Language, Literacy, & Vocabulary - Reading Expeditions Ser.). (ENG., Illus.). 36p. (J). pap. 18.95 *(978-0-7922-5447-8(3))* CENGAGE Learning.
Freedman, Jeri. Elizabeth Warren: Democratic Senator from Massachusetts. 2017. (J). ***(978-1-5026-2699-8(3))*** Cavendish Square Publishing.
Fremon, David K. The Watergate Scandal in United States History. 2014. (In United States History Ser.). (Illus.). 96p. (J). (gr. 5-12). 27.94 *(978-0-7660-6107-1(8))*; pap. 10.95 *(978-0-7660-6108-8(6))* Enslow Pubs., Inc.
Friedman, Mark. The Democratic Process. 2012. (Cornerstones of Freedom, Third Ser.). (ENG., Illus.). 64p. (J). pap. 8.95 *(978-0-531-28155-0(8))*; (gr. 4-6). lib. bdg. 30.00 *(978-0-531-23055-8(4))* Scholastic Library Publishing. (Children's Pr.).
Friesen, Helen Lepp. El Tío Sam. 2014. (SPA., Illus.). 24p. (J). *(978-1-62127-625-8(2))* Weigl Pubs., Inc.
Fritz, Jean. Alexander Hamilton: The Outsider. 2012. (ENG.). 144p. (J). (gr. 3-7). 8.99 *(978-0-14-241986-1(9)*, Puffin Books) Penguin Young Readers Group.
Furgang, Kathy. The Declaration of Independence & Benjamin Franklin of Pennsylvania. 2009. (Framers of the Declaration of Independence Ser.). 24p. (gr. 3-3). 42.50 *(978-1-61512-629-3(5)*, PowerKids Pr.) Rosen Publishing Group, Inc., The.
—The Declaration of Independence & Richard Henry Lee of Virginia. 2009. (Framers of the Declaration of Independence Ser.). 24p. (gr. 3-3). 42.50 *(978-1-61512-630-9(9)*, PowerKids Pr.) Rosen Publishing Group, Inc., The.
—The Declaration of Independence & Robert Livingston of New York. 2009. (Framers of the Declaration of Independence Ser.). 24p. (gr. 3-3). 42.50 *(978-1-61512-631-6(7)*, PowerKids Pr.) Rosen Publishing Group, Inc., The.
—The Declaration of Independence & Roger Sherman of Connecticut. 2009. (Framers of the Declaration of Independence Ser.). 24p. (gr. 3-3). 42.50 *(978-1-61512-632-3(5)*, PowerKids Pr.) Rosen Publishing Group, Inc., The.
—The Declaration of Independence & Thomas Jefferson of Virginia. 2009. (Framers of the Declaration of Independence Ser.). 24p. (gr. 3-3). 42.50 *(978-1-61512-633-0(3)*, PowerKids Pr.) Rosen Publishing Group, Inc., The.
Gagne, Tammy. The Power of the States. 2011. (My Guide to the Constitution Ser.). (Illus.). 48p. (J). (gr. 3-6). lib. bdg. 29.95 *(978-1-58415-945-2(6))* Mitchell Lane Pubs., Inc.
Gale Encyclopedia of U. S. History: Government & Politics, 2 vols. rev. ed. 2008. (Gale Encyclopedia of U. S. History Ser.). (ENG., Illus.). 900p. 339.00 *(978-1-4144-3118-5(X))* Cengage Gale.
Gamble, Amy. U. S. Government & Presidents, Grades 3 - 5. Fox, Carrie, ed. 2008. (Skills for Success Ser.). (ENG.). 128p. (gr. 3-5). pap. 16.99 *(978-1-60418-602-4(X))* Carson-Dellosa Publishing, LLC.
Geller, Kevin. Harry S. Truman. 2017. (Pivotal Presidents: Profiles in Leadership Ser.). 80p. (gr. 12-13). lib. bdg. 33.90 ***(978-1-68048-633-9(0)***, Britannica Educational Publishing) Rosen Publishing Group, Inc., The.
Gelletly, LeeAnne. A Woman's Place in Early America. 2012. (J). pap. *(978-1-4222-2365-9(5))* Mason Crest.
—A Woman's Place in Early America. Harrington, A. Page, ed. 2012. (Finding a Voice: Women's Fight for Equality in U. S. Society Ser.). 64p. (J). (gr. 5). 22.95 *(978-1-4222-2355-0(8))* Mason Crest.
Gerdes, Louise. National Service. 2011. (Opposing Viewpoints Ser.). (ENG.). 224p. (gr. 12-12). lib. bdg. 48.80 *(978-0-7377-5233-5(5)*, Greenhaven Pr., Inc.) Cengage Gale.
Gerdes, Louise I. National Service. 2011. (Opposing Viewpoints Ser.). (ENG.). 224p. (gr. 12-12). pap. 33.80 *(978-0-7377-5234-2(3)*, Greenhaven Pr., Inc.) Cengage Gale.
Giddens, Sandra. A Timeline of the Constitutional Convention. 2009. (Timelines of American History Ser.). 32p. (gr. 4-4). 47.90 *(978-1-60854-382-3(X)*, Rosen Reference) Rosen Publishing Group, Inc., The.
Giesecke, Ernestine. National Government. 2016. (Kids' Guide to Government Ser.). (ENG.). 32p. (gr. 3-5). pap. 7.99 *(978-1-4846-3812-5(3)*, NA-h) Heinemann-Raintree.
Gigliotti, Jim. Ronald Reagan, the 40th President. 2016. (First Look at America's Presidents Ser.). (ENG.). 24p. (J). (gr. -1-3). lib. bdg. 17.95 *(978-1-944102-69-2(8))* Bearport Publishing Co., Inc.
The Gilded Age & Progressivism, 1891-1913. 2010. (Discovering U. S. History Ser.). (Illus.). 136p. (gr. 5-8). 35.00 *(978-1-60413-355-4(4)*, Chelsea Hse.) Facts On File, Inc.
Gitlin, Martin. The Great Depression & World War II: 1929-1945. 2007. (Presidents of the United States Ser.). (Illus.). 48p. (J). (gr. 4-7). lib. bdg. 29.05 *(978-1-59036-749-0(9))*; per. 10.95 *(978-1-59036-750-6(2))* Weigl Pubs., Inc.
—Post-War United States: 1945-Early 1970s. 2007. (Presidents of the United States Ser.). (Illus.). 48p. (J). (gr. 4-7). lib. bdg. 29.05 *(978-1-59036-751-3(0))*; per. 10.95 *(978-1-59036-752-0(9))* Weigl Pubs., Inc.
Glaser, Jason. Patrick Henry: Liberty or Death. McDonnell, Peter, illus. 2005. (Graphic Biographies Ser.). (ENG.). 32p. (gr. 3-4). 30.65 *(978-0-7368-4970-8(X)*, Graphic Library) Capstone Press of Coughlan Cos.
Glencoe McGraw-Hill Staff. United States Government: Democracy in Action, StudentWorks with Audio Summaries. 2007. (Government in the U. S. Ser.). (ENG.). (gr. 9-12). cd-rom 135.60 *(978-0-07-878365-4(8)*, 0078783658) McGraw-Hill Higher Education.
Glencoe McGraw-Hill Staff, creator. United States Government: Democracy in Action. 2007. (Government in the U. S. Ser.). (ENG., Illus.). 309p. (gr. 9-12). per. 11.20 *(978-0-07-878125-4(6)*, 007878125 6) McGraw-Hill Higher Education.
Gold, Susan Dudley. The Civil Rights ACT of 1964. 2010. (Landmark Legislation Ser.). 128p. (YA). (gr. 7-12). 39.93 *(978-1-60870-040-0(2))* Marshall Cavendish GBR. Dist: Marshall Cavendish Corp.
—The Missouri Compromise. 2010. (Landmark Legislation Ser.). 128p. (YA). (gr. 7-12). 39.93 *(978-1-60870-041-7(0))* Marshall Cavendish Corp.
Goldsmith, Marcia. Important Years: The 1980s. 2005. (Illus.). 16p. (J). *(978-0-618-56043-1(2))* Houghton Mifflin Harcourt Publishing Co.
Gonzales, Doreen. A Look at the Second Amendment: To Keep & Bear Arms. 2007. (Constitution of the United States Ser.). (Illus.). 128p. (J). (gr. 5). lib. bdg. 34.60 *(978-1-59845-061-3(1)*, MyReportLinks.com Bks.) Enslow Pubs., Inc.
Gorman, Jacqueline Laks. Gobernador (Governor) 2009. (Conoce tu gobierno (Know Your Government) Ser.). (SPA., Illus.). 24p. (J). (gr. 2-4). lib. bdg. 22.00 *(978-1-4339-0098-3(X)*, Weekly Reader Leveled Readers) Stevens, Gareth Publishing LLLP.
—Quiénes Gobiernan Nuestro País? 2008. (Conoce tu gobierno (Know Your Government) Ser.). (SPA.). 24p. (gr. 1-4). pap. 8.15 *(978-0-8368-8856-0(1)*, Weekly Reader Leveled Readers) Stevens, Gareth Publishing LLLP.
—Quienes Gobiernan Nuestro País? 2008. (Conoce tu gobierno (Know Your Government) Ser.). (SPA., Illus.). 24p. (gr. 1-4). lib. bdg. 22.00 *(978-0-8368-8851-5(0)*, Weekly Reader Leveled Readers) Stevens, Gareth Publishing LLLP.
—Who Leads Our Country? 2008. (Know Your Government Ser.). 24p. (gr. 1-4). pap. 8.15 *(978-0-8368-8846-1(4))*; (Illus.). lib. bdg. 22.00 *(978-0-8368-8841-6(3))* Stevens, Gareth Publishing LLLP. (Weekly Reader Leveled Readers).
Gorman, Jacqueline Laks & Nations, Susan. Member of Congress. 2009. (Know Your Government Ser.). 24p. (J). (gr. 2-4). pap. 8.15 *(978-1-4339-0122-5(6))*; lib. bdg. 22.00 *(978-1-4339-0094-5(7))* Stevens, Gareth Publishing LLLP. (Weekly Reader Leveled Readers).
Gormley, Beatrice. George W. Bush: Our 43rd President. 2015. (Real-Life Story Ser.). (ENG., Illus.). 256p. (J). (gr. 3-7). 17.99 *(978-1-4814-4645-7(2)*, Aladdin) Simon & Schuster Children's Publishing.
Gosman, Gillian. Thomas Jefferson. 2011. (Life Stories Ser.). (Illus.). 24p. (J). pap. 8.25 *(978-1-4488-3180-7(6)*, PowerKids Pr.); (SPA & ENG., (gr. 1-4). lib. bdg. 22.60 *(978-1-4488-3221-7(7))*; (gr. 1-4). lib. bdg. 22.60 *(978-1-4488-3178-4(4)*, PowerKids Pr.) Rosen Publishing Group, Inc., The.
Gottfried, Ted. Millard Fillmore. 2007. (Presidents & Their Times Ser.). (Illus.). 96p. (gr. 6-7). lib. bdg. 34.21 *(978-0-7614-2431-4(8)*, Benchmark Bks.) Marshall Cavendish Corp.
Gould, Jane H. Alexander Hamilton. 2012. (Jr. Graphic Founding Fathers Ser.). (ENG., Illus.). 24p. (J). (gr. 3-6). pap. 10.60 *(978-1-4488-7989-2(2))*; lib. bdg. 25.25 *(978-1-4488-7895-6(0))* Rosen Publishing Group, Inc., The. (PowerKids Pr.).
Graves, Kerry A. The Constitution: The Story Behind America's Governing Document. 2004. (America in Words & Song Ser.). (Illus.). 32p. (gr. 4-6). 23.00 *(978-0-7910-7333-9(5)*, Chelsea Hse.) Facts On File, Inc.
Grayson, Robert. The U. S. Civil War: Why They Fought. 2015. (What Were They Fighting For? Ser.). (ENG., Illus.). 64p. (gr. 5-9). lib. bdg. 34.65 *(978-0-7565-5168-1(4))* Compass Point Bks.
Griffin, Maave. Constitution Day. 2009. (Explore Citizenship Ser.). 24p. (gr. 3-3). 42.50 *(978-1-61512-340-7(7)*, PowerKids Pr.) Rosen Publishing Group, Inc., The.
Griffin, Maeve. Constitution Day. 2009. (Real Life Readers Ser.). 24p. (gr. 3-4). pap. 8.25 *(978-1-4358-0139-4(3)*, Rosen Classroom); (J). 22.60 *(978-1-4358-2978-7(6)*, PowerKids Pr.) Rosen Publishing Group, Inc., The.
Grodin, Elissa. D Is for Democracy: A Citizen's Alphabet. Juhasz, Victor, illus. 2004. (ENG.). 40p. (J). (gr. 1-4). 16.95 *(978-1-58536-234-9(4)*, 202059) Sleeping Bear Pr.
Grolier Educational Staff, contrib. by. Flash Focus, 4 vols. 2004. (Illus.). (J). Vol. 1. *(978-0-7172-5934-2(X))* Vol. 2. *(978-0-7172-5938-0(2))* Vol. 3. *(978-0-7172-5937-3(4))* Vol. 4. *(978-0-7172-5940-3(4))* Grolier, Ltd.
Gunderson, Jessica. The Election Of 1860: A Nation Divides on the Eve of War. 2016. (Presidential Politics Ser.). (ENG., Illus.). 48p. (gr. 3-4). lib. bdg. 29.32 *(978-1-4914-8240-7(0)*, Connect) Stone Arch Bks.
—Election of 1860: A Nation Divides on the Eve of War. 2016. (J). pap. *(978-1-4914-8737-2(2))* Capstone Press of Coughlan Cos.
Haerens, Margaret. Government Gridlock. 2015. (Opposing Viewpoints Ser.). (ENG., Illus.). 224p. (J). (gr. 10-12). 48.80 *(978-0-7377-7266-1(2)*, Greenhaven Pr., Inc.) Cengage Gale.
Haldy, Emma E. Abraham Lincoln. Bane, Jeff, illus. 2016. (My Early Library: My Itty-Bitty Bio Ser.). (ENG.). 24p. (J). (gr. k-1). 28.50 *(978-1-63470-476-2(2)*, 207635) Cherry Lake Publishing.
Halpern, Monica & National Geographic Learning Staff. The Progressives. 2006. (Nonfiction Reading & Writing Workshops Ser.). (ENG., Illus.). 40p. (J). pap. 19.95 *(978-0-7922-8624-0(3))* CENGAGE Learning.
Han, Tomislav & Han, Lori Cox. Handbook to American Democracy, 4 vols. 2012. (Illus.). 224p. (C). (gr. 9). 220.00 *(978-0-8160-7854-7(8))* Facts On File, Inc.
Harness, Cheryl. The Remarkable Rough-Riding Life of Theodore Roosevelt & the Rise of Empire America. 2007. (Cheryl Harness Histories Ser.). (ENG., Illus.). 144p. (J). (gr. 4-7). lib. bdg. 25.90 *(978-1-4263-0009-7(3)*, National Geographic Children's Bks.) National Geographic Society.
Harper, Leslie. How Do Laws Get Passed? 2012. (Civics Q & A Ser.). (ENG., Illus.). 24p. (J). (gr. 3-6). pap. 8.25 *(978-1-4488-7509-2(9))*; lib. bdg. 22.60 *(978-1-4488-7436-1(X))* Rosen Publishing Group, Inc., The. (PowerKids Pr.).
—What Are Checks & Balances? 2012. (Civics Q & A Ser.). (ENG., Illus.). 24p. (J). (gr. 3-6). 22.60 *(978-1-4488-7433-0(5))*; pap. 8.25 *(978-1-4488-7506-1(4))* Rosen Publishing Group, Inc., The. (PowerKids Pr.).
Harris, Michael C. What Is the Declaration of Independence? Hoare, Jerry & McVeigh, Kevin, illus. 2016. (What Was? Ser.). (ENG.). 112p. (J). (gr. 3-7). lib. bdg. 15.99 *(978-0-399-54230-5(2)*, Grosset & Dunlap) Penguin Young Readers Group.
Harris, Nancy. Mount Rushmore. 2016. (Patriotic Symbols Ser.). (ENG.). 24p. (gr. -1-1). pap. 6.29 *(978-1-4846-3588-9(4)*, Acorn) Heinemann-Raintree.
Hartley, John. Holt American Civics. 5th ed. 2005. (Holt American Civics Ser.). (ENG., Illus.). 784p. (gr. 9-9). 98.35 *(978-0-03-037778-5(1))* Houghton Mifflin Harcourt Publishing Co.
Haugen, David M. & Bauder, Julia. Is the Political Divide Harming America? 2006. (At Issue Ser.). (ENG., Illus.). 128p. (gr. 10-12). 39.40 *(978-0-7377-3521-5(X))* Cengage Gale.
Haulley, Fletcher. The Deparment of Homeland Security. 2005. (This Is Your Government Ser.). (Illus.). 64p. (J). (gr. k-3). lib. bdg. 31.95 *(978-1-4042-0209-2(9))* Rosen Publishing Group, Inc., The.
—The Department of Homeland Security. 2009. (This Is Your Government Ser.). 64p. (gr. 5-6). 58.50 *(978-1-60854-371-7(4)*, Rosen Reference) Rosen Publishing Group, Inc., The.
Herringshaw, DeAnn. The United States Enters the 20th Century. 2011. (Explorer Library: Language Arts Explorer Ser.). (ENG.). 32p. (gr. 4-8). pap. 14.21 *(978-1-61080-288-8(8)*, 201211); lib. bdg. 28.50 *(978-1-61080-200-0(4)*, 201176) Cherry Lake Publishing.
Herwick Rice, Dona & Conklin, Wendy. Causes of the Civil War, 1 vol. 2009. (Building Fluency Through Reader's Theater Ser.). (ENG.). 32p. (J). (gr. 3-5). pap. 7.99 *(978-1-4333-0545-0(3))* Teacher Created Materials, Inc.
Hiber, Amanda. Is the U. S. Ready for a Minority President? 2007. (At Issue Ser.). (ENG., Illus.). 128p. (gr. 10-12). pap. 27.80 *(978-0-7377-3879-7(0)*, Greenhaven Pr., Inc.) Cengage Gale.
—Is the United States Ready for a Minority President? 2007. (At Issue Ser.). (ENG., Illus.). 128p. (gr. 10-12). 39.40 *(978-0-7377-3878-0(2)*, Greenhaven Pr., Inc.) Cengage Gale.
Hicks, Terry Allan. The Declaration of Independence. 2006. (Symbols of America Ser.). (Illus.). 40p. (gr. 3-7). lib. bdg. 20.95 *(978-0-7614-2135-1(1)*, Benchmark Bks.) Marshall Cavendish Corp.
Higgins, Nadia. US Government Through Infographics. Sciuto, Alex, illus. 2014. (Super Social Studies Infographics Ser.). 32p. (J). (gr. 3-5). lib. bdg. 26.60 *(978-1-4677-3463-9(2)*, Lerner Pubns.) Lerner Publishing Group.
Hillstrom, Kevin. The Progressive Era. 2008. (American History Ser.). (ENG., Illus.). 104p. (gr. 7-10). 39.40 *(978-1-4205-0067-7(8)*, Lucent Bks.) Cengage Gale.
—Watergate. 2004. (Defining Moments Ser.). (Illus.). 195p. lib. bdg. 55.00 *(978-0-7808-0769-3(3))* Omnigraphics, Inc.
Hinman, Bonnie. The Second Continental Congress. 2017. (Young America Ser.). 29.95 *(978-1-61228-979-3(7))* Mitchell Lane Pubs., Inc.
Hinton, KaaVonia. To Preserve the Union: Causes & Effects of the Missouri Compromise, 1 vol. 2013. (Cause & Effect Ser.). (ENG.). 32p. (gr. 3-4). 27.32 *(978-1-4765-0238-0(2))*; pap. 8.95 *(978-1-4765-3404-6(7))* Capstone Press of Coughlan Cos. (Fact Finders).
Hobbes, Emma. Thomas More & Utopia. 2016. (J). lib. bdg. *(978-1-68048-551-6(2))* Rosen Publishing Group, Inc., The.
Hoffman, Mary Ann. I Am a Good Citizen. 2011. (Kids of Character Ser.). (Illus.). 24p. (J). (gr. 1-3). pap. 8.15 *(978-1-4339-4851-0(6))*; lib. bdg. 22.60 *(978-1-4339-4850-3(8))* Stevens, Gareth Publishing LLLP.
Holt, Rinehart and Winston Staff. American Civics: Online Edition Plus. 3rd ed. 2003. 17.26 *(978-0-03-037434-0(0))* Holt McDougal.
Horn, Geoffrey M. The Cabinet & Federal Agencies. 2003. (World Almanac Library of American Government). (Illus.). 48p. (gr. 5-12). pap. 14.05 *(978-0-8368-5481-7(0))*; lib. bdg. 31.00 *(978-0-8368-5476-3(4))* Stevens, Gareth Publishing LLLP. (Gareth Stevens Secondary Library).
—The Presidency. 2003. (World Almanac Library of American Government). (Illus.). 48p. (gr. 5-12). lib. bdg. 31.00 *(978-0-8368-5458-9(6)*, Gareth Stevens Secondary Library) Stevens, Gareth Publishing LLLP.
How to Contact an Elected Official. 2014. (Be a Community Leader Ser.). 32p. (J). (gr. 4-6). lib. bdg. 26.25 *(978-1-4777-6689-7(8)*, PowerKids Pr.) Rosen Publishing Group, Inc., The.
Hubbard-Brown, Janet. How the Constitution Was Created. 2007. (U. S. Government Ser.). (Illus.). 104p. (YA). (gr. 5-9). lib. bdg. 30.00 *(978-0-7910-9420-4(0))* Facts On File, Inc.
Hudak, Heather C. McCarthyism & the Red Scare. 2017. 48p. (J). ***(978-0-7787-3939-5(2))*** Crabtree Publishing Co.
Huddle, Lorena. Woodrow Wilson. 2017. (Pivotal Presidents: Profiles in Leadership Ser.). 80p. (gr. 12-13). lib. bdg. 33.90 ***(978-1-68048-635-3(7)***, Britannica Educational Publishing) Rosen Publishing Group, Inc., The.
Hughes, Chris. The Constitutional Convention. 2005. (People at the Center of Ser.). (Illus.). 48p. (J). (gr. -1-7). lib. bdg. 24.95 *(978-1-56711-918-3(2)*, Blackbirch Pr., Inc.) Cengage Gale.
Isaacs, Sally. Understanding the Articles of Confederation. 2008. (Documenting Early America Ser.). (ENG., Illus.). 32p. (J). (gr. 3-6). lib. bdg. *(978-0-7787-4372-9(1))* Crabtree Publishing Co.

—Understanding the Declaration of Independence. 2008. (Documenting Early America Ser.). (ENG.). 32p. (J). (gr. 3-6). lib. bdg. *(978-0-7787-4371-2(3))* Crabtree Publishing Co.

Isaacs, Sally & Bedeksy, Baron. Understanding the Declaration of Independence. 2008. (Documenting Early America Ser.). (ENG.). 32p. (J). (gr. 3-6). pap. *(978-0-7787-4376-7(4))* Crabtree Publishing Co.

—Understanding the US Constitution. 2008. (Documenting Early America Ser.). (ENG.). 32p. (J). (gr. 3-6). pap. *(978-0-7787-4378-1(0))* Crabtree Publishing Co.

Isecke, Harriet. Lyndon B. Johnson: Un Texano en la Casa Blanca / Lyndon B. Johnson - A Texan in the White House. 2013. (Primary Source Readers Ser.). (SPA.). lib. bdg. 19.65 *(978-0-606-31873-0(9)*, Turtleback) Turtleback Bks.

It's My State! - Group 6. Incl. Georgia. Haywood, Karen Diane. 79p. lib. bdg. 27.07 *(978-0-7614-1862-7(8))*; Louisiana. Bjorklund, Ruth. 80p. lib. bdg. 27.07 *(978-0-7614-1863-4(6))*; Michigan. Haney, Johannah. 79p. lib. bdg. 27.07 *(978-0-7614-1861-0(X))*; Nevada. Hicks, Terry Allan. 80p. lib. bdg. 27.07 *(978-0-7614-1860-3(1))*; Rhode Island. Petreycik, Rick. 80p. lib. bdg. 27.07 *(978-0-7614-1859-7(8))*; Vermont. Dornfeld, Margaret. 80p. lib. bdg. 27.07 *(978-0-7614-1864-1(4))*; (Illus.). (J). (gr. 4-7). 2005. 2005. 162.43 *(978-0-7614-1858-0(X)*, Benchmark Bks.) Marshall Cavendish Corp.

Jain, Varun. Understanding American Politics: A Book for Teenangers. 2014. 54p. pap. 15.99 *(978-1-4931-6161-4(X))* Xlibris Corp.

Jakubiak, David J. How Our Government Works, 6 vols., Set. Incl. What Does a Congressional Representative Do? lib. bdg. 22.60 *(978-1-4358-9362-7(X))*; What Does a Governor Do? lib. bdg. 22.60 *(978-1-4358-9358-0(1))*; What Does a Mayor Do? lib. bdg. 22.60 *(978-1-4358-9359-7(X))*; What Does a Senator Do? lib. bdg. 22.60 *(978-1-4358-9360-3(3))*; What Does a Supreme Court Justice Do? lib. bdg. 22.60 *(978-1-4358-9361-0(1))*; What Does the President Do? lib. bdg. 22.60 *(978-1-4358-9357-3(3))*; (J). (gr. 3-6). (Illus.). 24p. 2010. Set lib. bdg. 127.50 *(978-1-4358-9405-1(7)*, PowerKids Pr.) Rosen Publishing Group, Inc., The.

—What Does a Congressional Representative Do? 2010. (How Our Government Works Ser.). (Illus.). 24p. (J). pap. 8.25 *(978-1-4358-9820-2(6))*; (gr. 3-6). lib. bdg. 22.60 *(978-1-4358-9362-7(X))* Rosen Publishing Group, Inc., The. (PowerKids Pr.).

—What Does a Governor Do? 2010. (How Our Government Works Ser.). 24p. (J). (gr. 3-6). lib. bdg., E-Book 42.50 *(978-1-4488-0022-3(6))*; (Illus.). pap. 8.25 *(978-1-4358-9812-7(5)*, PowerKids Pr.); (Illus.). (gr. 3-6). lib. bdg. 22.60 *(978-1-4358-9358-0(1)*, PowerKids Pr.) Rosen Publishing Group, Inc., The.

—What Does a Senator Do? 2010. (How Our Government Works Ser.). 24p. (J). (gr. 3-6). lib. bdg., E-Book 42.50 *(978-1-4488-0029-2(3))*; (Illus.). pap. 8.25 *(978-1-4358-9816-5(8)*, PowerKids Pr.); (Illus.). (gr. 3-6). lib. bdg. 22.60 *(978-1-4358-9360-3(3)*, PowerKids Pr.) Rosen Publishing Group, Inc., The.

—What Does the President Do? 2010. (How Our Government Works Ser.). 24p. (J). (ENG.). pap. 8.25 *(978-1-4358-9810-3(9)*, PowerKids Pr.); (gr. 3-6). lib. bdg., E-Book 42.50 *(978-1-4488-0020-9(X))*; (Illus.). (gr. 3-6). lib. bdg. 22.60 *(978-1-4358-9357-3(3)*, PowerKids Pr.) Rosen Publishing Group, Inc., The.

Jarnow, Jesse. Patrick Henry's Liberty or Death Speech: A Primary Source Investigation. (Great Historic Debates & Speeches Ser.). 64p. 2009. (gr. 5-8). 58.50 *(978-1-61513-120-4(5))* 2004. (Illus.). (J). lib. bdg. 31.95 *(978-1-4042-0152-1(1))* Rosen Publishing Group, Inc., The.

Jeffrey, Gary. Thomas Paine Writes Common Sense. 2011. (Graphic Heroes of the American Revolution Ser.). 24p. (gr. 3-6). (YA). lib. bdg. 23.95 *(978-1-4339-6028-4(1))*; (J). pap. 8.15 *(978-1-4339-6029-1(X)*, Gareth Stevens Learning Library) Stevens, Gareth Publishing LLLP.

Jianmei, Wang. America: My Hom, Your Country. 2009. pap. 29.00 *(978-1-61584-424-1(4))* Independent Pub.

Johnson, Etta. The United States Government. 2005. (J). pap. *(978-1-4108-4592-4(3))* Benchmark Education Co.

Kaleidoscope - Government Series, 4 bks., Set. 102.57 *(978-0-7614-1450-6(9)*, Benchmark Bks.) Marshall Cavendish Corp.

Kallen, Stuart A. Does Equality Exist in America? 2006. (At Issue Ser.). (ENG., Illus.). 106p. (YA). (gr. 9-12). pap. 34.45 *(978-0-7377-3433-1(7))* Cengage Gale.

Keegan, Anna. The United States Constitution & the Bill of Rights: The Law of the Land. 2015. (Spotlight on American History Ser.). (ENG., Illus.). 24p. (J). (gr. 4-6). pap. 10.00 *(978-1-4994-1773-9(X)*, PowerKids Pr.) Rosen Publishing Group, Inc., The.

Keller, Susanna. Alexander Hamilton: America's First Treasury Secretary. 2017. (J). pap. ***(978-1-68048-808-1(2))***; lib. bdg. ***(978-1-68048-809-8(0))*** Rosen Publishing Group, Inc., The. (Britannica Educational Publishing).

Kelley, K. C. Alexander Hamilton: American Hero. 2017. (Rookie Biographies(tm) Ser.). (ENG., Illus.). 32p. (J). lib. bdg. 25.00 *(978-0-531-22290-4(X))* Scholastic Library Publishing.

Kelly, Martin & Kelly, Melissa. Government. 2007. (ENG., Illus.). 96p. (C). (gr. 6-18). lib. bdg. 158.00 *(978-0-7656-8112-6(9)*, Y182476) Routledge.

Kenison, Misti. Where's Your Hat, Abe Lincoln? 2017. (ENG.). 28p. (J). bds. 9.99 ***(978-1-4926-5250-2(4)***, Sourcebooks Jabberwocky) Sourcebooks, Inc.

Kenney, Karen Latchana & Andronik, Catherine M. Abraham Lincoln's Presidency. 2016. (Presidential Powerhouses Ser.). (ENG., Illus.). 104p. (J). (gr. 6-12). 53.32 *(978-1-4677-8547-1(4)*, Lerner Pubns.) Lerner Publishing Group.

Kent, Zachary. Alexander Hamilton: Creating a Nation. 2004. (America's Founding Fathers Ser.). (Illus.). 128p. (J). lib. bdg. 26.60 *(978-0-7660-2181-5(5))* Enslow Pubs., Inc.

Kerrigan, Michael. Homeland Security. 2017. (J). ***(978-1-4222-3767-0(2))*** Mason Crest.

King, David C. Herbert Hoover. 2009. (Presidents & Their Times 3 Ser.). 96p. (gr. 6). 34.21 *(978-0-7614-3626-3(X))* Marshall Cavendish Corp.

King, Margaret. Just Right Words: Revising the Constitution (Level 5) 2017. (Exploring Reading Ser.). (Illus.). 48p. (J). (gr. 5-5). pap. 10.99 ***(978-1-4258-4992-4(X))*** Teacher Created Materials, Inc.

Kishel, Ann-Marie. Government Services. 2007. (First Step Nonfiction - Government Ser.). (ENG., Illus.). 24p. (gr. k-2). lib. bdg. 23.93 *(978-0-8225-6397-6(5)*, Lerner Pubns.) Lerner Publishing Group.

Kjelle, Marylou. The First Continental Congress. 2017. (Young America Ser.). (gr. 3-6). 29.95 *(978-1-61228-977-9(0))* Mitchell Lane Pubs., Inc.

Klein, Adria F. Barack Obama. 2009. pap. 13.25 *(978-1-60559-055-4(X))* Hameray Publishing Group, Inc.

Klepeis, Alicia. Stamp Act Congress. 2017. (Young America Ser.). (gr. 3-6). 29.95 *(978-1-61228-991-5(6))* Mitchell Lane Pubs., Inc.

Knudsen, Shannon. When Were the First Slaves Set Free During the Civil War? And Other Questions about the Emancipation Proclamation. 2010. (Six Questions of American History Ser.). (ENG.). (gr. 4-6). pap. 56.72 *(978-0-7613-6948-6(1))*; (Illus.). 48p. lib. bdg. 30.60 *(978-1-58013-670-9(2))* Lerner Publishing Group.

—When Were the First Slaves Set Free During the Civil War? And Other Questions about the Emancipation Proclamation. 2010. (Six Questions of American History Ser.). (ENG.). 48p. (gr. 4-6). pap. 9.95 *(978-0-7613-6121-3(9))* Lerner Publishing Group.

Kovach, John. Bob Ehrlich: His Historical Campaign for Governor & How a Young Girl Made a Difference. 2003. (Illus.). 52p. (J). pap. 9.95 *(978-0-7414-1497-7(X))* Infinity Publishing.

Kowalski, Kathiann M. A Balancing Act: A Look at Checks & Balances. 2003. (How Government Works). (ENG., Illus.). 56p. (gr. 4-8). lib. bdg. 25.26 *(978-0-8225-1350-6(1))* Lerner Publishing Group.

—Checks & Balances: A Look at the Powers of Government. 2012. (Searchlight Books How Does Government Work Ser.). (ENG., Illus.). 40p. (gr. 3-5). pap. 51.01 *(978-0-7613-9229-3(7))*; pap. 8.95 *(978-0-7613-8558-5(4))*; lib. bdg. 27.93 *(978-0-7613-6515-0(X))* Lerner Publishing Group.

Krensky, Stephen. The Constitution. 2011. (Documents of Democracy Ser.). 96p. (gr. 8). 34.21 *(978-0-7614-4917-1(5))* Marshall Cavendish Corp.

—The Declaration of Independence. 2011. (Documents of Democracy Ser.). (Illus.). 96p. (J). (gr. 8). 34.21 *(978-0-7614-4913-3(2))* Marshall Cavendish Corp.

—The Emancipaton Proclamation. 2011. (Documents of Democracy Ser.). 96p. (gr. 8). 34.21 *(978-0-7614-4915-7(9))* Marshall Cavendish Corp.

Krick, Robert K. The Civil War: Gettysburg & Other Eastern Battles, 1863-1865. 2010. (Civil War: Essential Histories Ser.). (ENG.). 96p. (YA). lib. bdg. 33.25 *(978-1-4488-0388-0(8))* Rosen Publishing Group, Inc., The.

Kulling, Monica. Alexander Hamilton: From Orphan to Founding Father. 2017. (Step into Reading Ser.). (ENG., Illus.). 48p. (J). (gr. k-3). pap. 3.99 *(978-1-5247-1698-1(7)*, Random Hse. Bks. for Young Readers) Random Hse. Children's Bks.

Laks Gorman, Jacqueline. Gobernador (Governor) 2009. (Conoce tu gobierno (Know Your Government) Ser.). (SPA., Illus.). 24p. (J). (gr. 2-4). pap. 8.15 *(978-1-4339-0126-3(9)*, Weekly Reader Leveled Readers) Stevens, Gareth Publishing LLLP.

Landau, Elaine. The Declaration of Independence. 2008. (True Bks.). (ENG., Illus.). 48p. (J). (gr. 3-5). pap. 6.95 *(978-0-531-14780-1(0)*, Children's Pr.) Scholastic Library Publishing.

—The Declaration of Independence: American History. 2007. (True Bks.). (ENG., Illus.). 48p. (J). (gr. 3-5). lib. bdg. 29.00 *(978-0-531-12630-1(7)*, Children's Pr.) Scholastic Library Publishing.

—The Emancipation Proclamation: Would You Do What Lincoln Did? 2008. (What Would You Do? Ser.). (Illus.). 48p. (J). (gr. 3-7). lib. bdg. 25.27 *(978-0-7660-2899-9(2)*, Enslow Elementary) Enslow Pubs., Inc.

—Lincoln's Emancipation Proclamation: Would You Sign the Great Document? 2015. (What Would You Do? Ser.). 48p. (J). (gr. 3-4). 25.27 *(978-0-7660-6290-0(2))*; pap. 8.95 *(978-0-7660-6291-7(0)*, Enslow Elementary) Enslow Pubs., Inc.

Landmarks of Democracy: American Institutions. 2017. (Landmarks of Democracy: American Institutions Ser.). 24p. (gr. 7-8). 118.00 ***(978-1-5081-6109-7(7))***; pap. 41.25 ***(978-1-5081-6110-3(0))*** Rosen Publishing Group, Inc., The. (PowerKids Pr.).

Lanier, Wendy. What Was the Missouri Compromise? And Other Questions about the Struggle over Slavery. 2012. (Six Questions of American History Ser.). (ENG.). 48p. (gr. 4-6). pap. 9.95 *(978-0-7613-8565-3(7))*; (Illus.). lib. bdg. 30.60 *(978-0-7613-5331-7(3))* Lerner Publishing Group.

Lanier, Wendy & Nelson, Robin. What Was the Missouri Compromise? And Other Questions about the Struggle over Slavery. 2012. (Start to Finish, Second Series: Nature's Cycles Ser.). (ENG.). 48p. (gr. k-3). pap. 39.62 *(978-0-7613-9293-4(9))* Lerner Publishing Group.

Lansford, Tom & Watson, Robert P. George W. Bush. 2004. (gr. 10-12). 22.45 *(978-0-7377-2598-8(2)*, Greenhaven Pr., Inc.) Cengage Gale.

Larson, Kirsten W. The CIA. 2016. (Protecting Our People Ser.). (ENG., Illus.). 32p. (J). (gr. 1-4). 20.95 *(978-1-60753-982-7(9))* Amicus Publishing.

LearningExpress Staff. U. S. Constitution in 15 Minutes a Day. 2011. (15 Minutes a Day Ser.). (ENG.). 256p. pap. 14.95 *(978-1-57685-767-0(0))* LearningExpress, LLC.

Leavitt, Amie Jane. Declaration of Independence in Translation: What It Really Means. 2016. (Kids' Translations Ser.). (ENG.). 32p. (gr. 3-4). pap. 8.10 *(978-1-5157-6250-8(5)*, Fact Finders) Capstone Press of Coughlan Cos.

—A History of the Republican Party. 2012. (J). lib. bdg. 29.95 *(978-1-61228-261-9(X))* Mitchell Lane Pubs., Inc.

Lee, Sally. Arnold Schwarzenegger: From Superstar to Governor. 2006. (People to Know Today Ser.). (Illus.). 128p. (J). (gr. 6-12). lib. bdg. 33.27 *(978-0-7660-2625-4(6))* Enslow Pubs., Inc.

Leonard, Barry, ed. Symbols of the US Government: Ben's Activity Book. 2005. (Illus.). 46p. (J). (gr. k-4). pap. 15.00 *(978-0-7567-4540-0(3))* DIANE Publishing Co.

Let's Find Out! Government. 2015. (Let's Find Out! Government Ser.). (ENG.). 32p. (J). (gr. 2-3). pap., pap., pap. 619.20 *(978-1-68048-148-8(7)*, Britannica Educational Publishing) Rosen Publishing Group, Inc., The.

LeVert, Suzanne. State Government. 2003. (Kaleidoscope Ser.). (Illus.). 48p. (gr. 3-18). lib. bdg. 20.95 *(978-0-7614-1596-1(3)*, Benchmark Bks.) Marshall Cavendish Corp.

Levinson, Cynthia & Levinson, Sanford. Fault Lines in the Constitution: The Framers, Their Fights, & the Flaws That Affect Us Today. 2017. (ENG.). 192p. (J). (gr. 5-9). 19.95 ***(978-1-56145-945-2(3))*** Peachtree Pubs.

Liljeblad, Fredrik. Democracy at Work. 2007. (21st Century Skills Library: Citizens & Their Governments Ser.). (ENG., Illus.). 32p. (gr. 4-8). lib. bdg. 28.50 *(978-1-60279-058-2(2)*, 200003) Cherry Lake Publishing.

Linde, Barbara M. Becoming a Supreme Court Justice. 2016. (Who's Your Candidate? Choosing Government Leaders Ser.). (ENG., Illus.). 32p. (J). (gr. 3-4). pap. 10.50 *(978-1-4824-4051-5(2))* Stevens, Gareth Publishing LLLP.

Lloyd, Jon. A View of America's Future by America's. 2005. 51p. pap. 16.95 *(978-1-4137-9110-5(7))* PublishAmerica, Inc.

Loria, Laura. What Is Citizenship? 2015. (Let's Find Out! Government Ser.). (ENG., Illus.). 32p. (J). (gr. 2-3). 23.45 *(978-1-62275-976-7(1)*, Britannica Educational Publishing) Rosen Publishing Group, Inc., The.

Lukes, Bonnie L. Woodrow Wilson & the Progressive Era. 2006. (World Leaders Ser.). (Illus.). 192p. (J). (gr. 6-10). lib. bdg. 26.95 *(978-1-931798-79-2(6))* Reynolds, Morgan Inc.

Lusted, Marcia Amidon. Revolution & the New Nation: 1750-Early 1800s. 2007. (Presidents of the United States Ser.). (Illus.). 48p. (J). (gr. 4-7). lib. bdg. 29.05 *(978-1-59036-739-1(1))*; per. 10.95 *(978-1-59036-740-7(5))* Weigl Pubs., Inc.

Lynne, Douglas. Contemporary United States: 1968 to the Present. 2007. (Presidents of the United States Ser.). (Illus.). 48p. (J). (gr. 4-7). lib. bdg. 29.05 *(978-1-59036-753-7(7))*; per. 10.95 *(978-1-59036-754-4(5))* Weigl Pubs., Inc.

Machajewski, Sarah. Declaration of Independence. 2016. (Documents of American Democracy Ser.). (Illus.). 32p. (J). (gr. 5-5). pap. 10.00 *(978-1-4994-2077-7(3)*, PowerKids Pr.) Rosen Publishing Group, Inc., The.

Magoon, Kekla. Gun Control, 1 vol. 2007. (Essential Viewpoints Set 1 Ser.). (ENG., Illus.). 112p. (J). (gr. 6-12). lib. bdg. 35.64 *(978-1-59928-860-4(5))* ABDO Publishing Co.

Maloof, Torrey. We the People: Founding Documents (America's Early Years) 2016. (Primary Source Readers Ser.). (ENG., Illus.). 32p. (J). (gr. 4-5). pap. 8.99 *(978-1-4938-3084-8(8))* Teacher Created Materials, Inc.

Manger, Katherine. The Declaration of Independence. 2016. (Let's Find Out! Primary Sources Ser.). 00032p. (J). (gr. 2-3). lib. bdg. 24.45 *(978-1-5081-0395-0(X))* Rosen Publishing Group, Inc., The.

—The U.S. Constitution. 2016. (J). *(978-1-5081-0455-1(7))* Rosen Publishing Group, Inc., The.

Manning, Jack. Our Government, 1 vol. 2014. (Our Government Ser.). (ENG.). 24p. (gr. 1-2). 101.28 *(978-1-4914-0345-7(4)*, First Facts) Capstone Press of Coughlan Cos.

—Voting in Elections, 1 vol. 2014. (Our Government Ser.). (ENG.). 24p. (gr. 1-2). lib. bdg. 25.32 *(978-1-4914-0334-1(9))* Capstone Press of Coughlan Cos.

Mapua, Jeff. Bill & Hillary Clinton. 2014. (Making a Difference: Leaders Who Are Changing the World Ser.). 48p. (YA). (gr. 5-8). 25.85 *(978-1-62275-425-0(5))*; pap. 14.05 *(978-1-62275-427-4(1))*; pap. 84.30 *(978-1-62275-428-1(X))* Rosen Publishing Group, Inc., The.

Mara, Wil. Democracy at Work. 2016. (21st Century Skills Library: a Citizen's Guide Ser.). (ENG., Illus.). 32p. (J). (gr. 4-7). 29.93 *(978-1-63471-065-7(7)*, 208339) Cherry Lake Publishing.

—FBI Special Agent. 2015. (21st Century Skills Library: Cool STEAM Careers Ser.). (ENG., Illus.). 32p. (J). (gr. 4-7). pap. 14.21 *(978-1-63362-648-5(2)*, 1391909) Cherry Lake Publishing.

—Gerald Ford. 2009. (Presidents & Their Times 3 Ser.). 96p. (gr. 6). 34.21 *(978-0-7614-3629-4(4))* Marshall Cavendish GBR. Dist: Marshall Cavendish Corp.

—Harry Truman. 2011. (Presidents & Their Times 5 Ser.). (Illus.). 96p. (J). (gr. 6). 34.21 *(978-1-60870-185-8(9))* Marshall Cavendish Corp.

—John F. Kennedy. 2009. (Presidents & Their Times 3 Ser.). 96p. (gr. 6). 34.21 *(978-0-7614-3628-7(6))* Marshall Cavendish Corp.

Marciniak, Kristin. The Revolutionary War: Why They Fought. 2015. (What Were They Fighting For? Ser.). (ENG., Illus.). 64p. (gr. 5-9). lib. bdg. 34.65 *(978-0-7565-5169-8(2))* Compass Point Bks.

Marcovitz, Hal. The Declaration of Independence. 2014. (Understanding American History). (ENG., Illus.). 96p. (J). lib. bdg. *(978-1-60152-736-3(5))* ReferencePoint Pr., Inc.

—The Declaration of Independence: Forming a New Nation. Moreno, Barry, ed. 2014. (Patriotic Symbols of America Ser.: 20). 48p. (J). (gr. 4-18). lib. bdg. 20.95 *(978-1-4222-3122-7(4))* Mason Crest.

—Independence Hall: Birthplace of Freedom. Moreno, Barry, ed. 2014. (Patriotic Symbols of America Ser.: 20). 48p. (J). (gr. 4-18). lib. bdg. 20.95 *(978-1-4222-3124-1(0))* Mason Crest.

Margulies, Philip. The Deparatment of Energy. 2005. (This Is Your Government Ser.). (Illus.). 64p. (J). (gr. k-3). lib. bdg. 31.95 *(978-1-4042-0208-5(0))* Rosen Publishing Group, Inc., The.

Margulies, Phillip. The Department of Energy. 2009. (This Is Your Government Ser.). 64p. (gr. 5-6). 58.50 *(978-1-60854-368-7(4)*, Rosen Reference) Rosen Publishing Group, Inc., The.

Marrin, Albert. FDR & the American Crisis. (ENG.). 336p. (YA). (gr. 7). 2016. pap. 15.99 *(978-0-385-75362-3(4)*, Ember) 2015. (Illus.). 24.99 *(978-0-385-75359-3(4)*, Knopf Bks. for Young Readers) 2015. (Illus.). lib. bdg. 27.99 *(978-0-385-75360-9(8)*, Knopf Bks. for Young Readers) Random Hse. Children's Bks.

Marsh, Carole. Barack Obama - America's 44th President. 2009. (Here & Now Ser.). 40p. (J). (gr. 2-9). 29.99 *(978-0-635-06983-2(0))* Gallopade International.

—Georgia Government: the Cornerstone of Everyday Life in Our State! The Cornerstone of Everyday Life in Our State! 2004. 28p. pap. 5.95 *(978-0-635-02682-8(1))* Gallopade International.

—The Obama Family - Life in the White House: President Barack Obama, First Lady Michelle Obama, First Children Malia & Sasha. 2008. (Here & Now Ser.). 32p. (J). (gr. 2-9). pap. 8.99 *(978-0-635-07051-7(0))* Gallopade International.

Martin, Bill, Jr. & Sampson, Michael. I Pledge Allegiance. Raschka, Chris, illus. 2004. (ENG.). 40p. (J). (gr. 1-4). reprint ed. pap. 8.99 *(978-0-7636-2527-6(2))* Candlewick Pr.

Martin, David. The Colony of Pennsylvania. 2015. (Spotlight on the 13 Colonies Ser.). (ENG., Illus.). 24p. (J). (gr. 4-5). pap. 8.25 *(978-1-4994-0572-9(3)*, PowerKids Pr.) Rosen Publishing Group, Inc., The.

Matzke, Ann H. What Are the Branches of Democracy? 2012. (ENG., Illus.). 24p. (J). (gr. k-2). pap. 8.95 *(978-1-61810-279-9(6))* Rourke Educational Media.

McCarthy, Pat. Famous Union Generals & Leaders of the North: A MyReportLinks. com Book. 2004. (American Civil War Ser.). (Illus.). 48p. (J). lib. bdg. 26.60 *(978-0-7660-5188-1(9)*, MyReportLinks.com Bks.) Enslow Pubs., Inc.

McDaniel, Melissa. The Declaration of Independence. 2011. (Cornerstones of Freedom, Third Ser.). (Illus.). 64p. (J). (ENG.). pap. 8.95 *(978-0-531-26555-0(2))*; lib. bdg. 30.00 *(978-0-531-25030-3(X))* Scholastic Library Publishing. (Children's Pr.).

McElroy, Lisa Tucker. Alberto Gonzalez. 2006. (J). pap. 8.95 *(978-0-8225-6058-6(5)*, First Avenue Editions) Lerner Publishing Group.

McGraw-Hill Education Staff. United States Government: Democracy in Action. 2nd ed. 2005. (Government in the U. S. Ser.). (ENG., Illus.). 320p. (gr. 9-12). per., wbk. ed., pupil's gde. ed. 17.96 *(978-0-07-865918-8(3)*, 0078659183) McGraw-Hill Higher Education.

—United States Government: Democracy in Action: Spanish Reading Essentials & Study Guide. 2007. (Government in the U. S. Ser.). (ENG & SPA., Illus.). 309p. (gr. 9-12). per. 11.20 *(978-0-07-878362-3(3)*, 0078783623) McGraw-Hill Higher Education.

—United States Government: Democracy in Action, Spanish Reading Essentials & Study Guide: Student Workbook. 2nd ed. 2005. (Government in the U. S. Ser.). (SPA., Illus.). 309p. (gr. 9-12). stu. ed., per., wbk. ed. 17.96 *(978-0-07-865920-1(5)*, 0078659205) McGraw-Hill Higher Education.

McGraw-Hill Staff. United States Government, Democracy in Action, StudentWorks CD-ROM. 2nd ed. 2005. (Government in the U. S. Ser.). (ENG.). (gr. 9-12). 136.96 *(978-0-07-865936-2(1)*, 0078659361) McGraw-Hill Higher Education.

McLeese, Don. Alexander Hamilton. 2004. (Heroes of the American Revolution Ser.). (Illus.). 32p. (gr. 2-5). lib. bdg. *(978-1-59515-219-0(9))* Rourke Educational Media.

McNeese, Tim. Alexander Hamilton: Framer of the Constitution. 2005. (Leaders of the American Revolution Ser.). (Illus.). 100p. (gr. 5-8). lib. bdg. 30.00 *(978-0-7910-8616-2(X))* Facts On File, Inc.

—The Progressive Movement: Advocating Social Change. 2007. (Reform Movements in American History Ser.). (Illus.). 144p. (YA). (gr. 7-12). lib. bdg. 32.50 *(978-0-7910-9501-0(0))* Facts On File, Inc.

McNeil, Niki, et al. HOCPP1032 American Government. 2004. spiral bd. 20.00 *(978-1-60308-032-3(5))* In the Hands of a Child.

McPherson, Stephanie Sammartino. Liberty or Death: A Story about Patrick Henry. Debon, Nicolas, illus. 2003. (Creative Minds Biographies Ser.). (ENG.). 64p. (gr. 4-8). 22.60 *(978-1-57505-178-9(8)*, Carolrhoda Bks.) Lerner Publishing Group.

—Martha Washington: Legendary First Lady of the United States. 2015. (Legendary American Biographies Ser.). 96p. (J). (gr. 6-12). 27.94 *(978-0-7660-6475-1(1))* Enslow Pubs., Inc.

Meacham, Jon. Thomas Jefferson: President & Philosopher. (ENG., Illus.). 336p. (J). (gr. 5). 2016. pap. 12.99 *(978-0-385-38752-1(0)*, Yearling) 2014. 19.99 *(978-0-385-38749-1(0)*, Crown Books For Young Readers) 2014. lib. bdg. 22.99 *(978-0-385-38750-7(4)*, Crown Books For Young Readers) Random Hse. Children's Bks.

Melton, Buckner F. Aaron Burr: The Rise & Fall of an American Politician. 2009. (Library of American Lives & Times Ser.). 112p. (gr. 5-5). 69.20 *(978-1-60853-468-5(5))* Rosen Publishing Group, Inc., The.

Metz, Lorijo. La Declaracin de Independencia / the Declaration of Independence, 1 vol., 1. Beullens-Maoui, Nathalie, ed. 2014. (¡Celebremos la Libertad! / Let's Celebrate Freedom! Ser.). (SPA, BYN & ENG., Illus.). 24p. (J). (gr. 3-6). 23.60 *(978-1-4777-3246-5(2)*, PowerKids Pr.) Rosen Publishing Group, Inc., The.

—The Declaration of Independence, 1 vol., 1. 2014. (Let's Celebrate Freedom! Ser.). (ENG.). 24p. (J). (gr. 3-6). 23.60 *(978-1-4777-2894-9(5)*, PowerKids Pr.) Rosen Publishing Group, Inc., The.

Meyer, Jared. Working in a War Zone: Military Contractors. 2009. (Extreme Careers Ser.). 64p. (gr. 5-5). 58.50 *(978-1-61512-422-0(5)*, Rosen Reference) Rosen Publishing Group, Inc., The.

Miller, Amanda. What Does the President Do? 2009. (Scholastic News Nonfiction Readers Ser.). 24p. (J). (gr. 1-2). (ENG.). pap. 6.95 *(978-0-531-22425-0(2))*; (Illus.). 22.00 *(978-0-531-21088-8(X))* Scholastic Library Publishing.

Miller, Mirella S. 12 Questions about the Declaration of Independence. 2017. (Examining Primary Sources Ser.). (ENG., Illus.). 32p. (J). (gr. 3-6). 21.95 *(978-1-63235-283-5(4))* Pr. Room Editions LLC.

Mis, Melody S. Meet Jesse Jackson. 2008. (Civil Rights Leaders Ser.). (Illus.). 24p. (YA). (gr. 2-5). lib. bdg. 22.60 *(978-1-4042-4212-8(0))* Rosen Publishing Group, Inc., The.

Modern America 1964-present. 2010. (Discovering U. S. History Ser.). (Illus.). 144p. (gr. 5-8). 35.00 *(978-1-60413-361-5(9)*, Chelsea Hse.) Facts On File, Inc.

Morey, Allan. A Timeline History of the Declaration of Independence. 2014. (Timeline Trackers: America's Beginnings Ser.). (Illus.). 48p. (gr. 5-8). (J). lib. bdg. 30.60

(978-1-4677-3640-4(6), Lerner Pubns.); pap. 9.95 *(978-1-4677-4571-0(5))* Lerner Publishing Group.

Morris-Lipsman, Arlene. Presidential Races: Campaigning for the White House. rev. ed. 2011. (People's History Ser.). (ENG., Illus.). 112p. (gr. 5-12). lib. bdg. 33.26 *(978-0-7613-7395-7(0)*, Twenty-First Century Bks.) Lerner Publishing Group.

—Presidential Races: The Battle for Power in the United States. 2007. (People's History Ser.). (ENG., Illus.). 112p. (gr. 5-12). lib. bdg. 33.26 *(978-0-8225-6783-7(0))* Lerner Publishing Group.

Mortensen, Lori. The Declaration of Independence, 1 vol. Skeens, Matthew, illus. 2009. (American Symbols Ser.). (ENG.). 24p. (gr. 1-2). lib. bdg. 26.65 *(978-1-4048-5165-8(8))* Picture Window Bks.

—Thomas Jefferson: A Founding Father of the United States of America, 1 vol. Ebert, Len, illus. 2008. (Biographies Ser.). (ENG.). 24p. (gr. k-3). lib. bdg. 26.65 *(978-1-4048-3729-4(9))* Picture Window Bks.

Mountjoy, Shane. Causes of the Civil War: The Differences Between the North & South. McNeese, Tim, ed. 2009. (Civil War: A Nation Divided Ser.). (Illus.). 144p. (gr. 6-12). 35.00 *(978-1-60413-036-2(9)*, Chelsea Hse.) Facts On File, Inc.

Moxon, Kay & Magee, Eric. A2 US Government & Politics: Representation in the USA. 2009. 64p. pap., wbk. ed. 15.95 *(978-0-340-99002-5(3))* Hodder Education Group GBR. Dist: Trans-Atlantic Pubns., Inc.

Mulhall, Jill K. James Madison, 1 vol. 2005. (Primary Source Readers Ser.). (ENG.). 24p. (J). (gr. 4-4). pap. 8.99 *(978-0-7439-8908-4(2))* Shell Educational Publishing.

—Thomas Jefferson, 1 vol. 2004. (Primary Source Readers Ser.). (ENG.). 24p. (J). (gr. 4-4). pap. 8.99 *(978-0-7439-8747-9(0))* Shell Educational Publishing.

Murcia, Rebecca Thatcher. The Legislative Branch. 2011. (My Guide to the Constitution Ser.). 48p. (J). (gr. 3-6). pap. 16.50 *(978-1-61228-184-1(2))*; (Illus.). lib. bdg. 29.95 *(978-1-58415-942-1(1))* Mitchell Lane Pubs., Inc.

Murphy, John A. The Impeachment Process. 2007. (U. S. Government Ser.). (Illus.). 102p. (YA). (gr. 5-9). lib. bdg. 30.00 *(978-0-7910-9465-5(0))* Facts On File, Inc.

Murray, Glen L. The Dumbing down of Americ. 2009. 68p. pap. 15.99 *(978-1-4415-1642-8(5))* Xlibris Corp.

Musser, Susan, ed. America's Global Influence. 2007. (Opposing Viewpoints Ser.). (ENG., Illus.). 223p. (J). (gr. 10-12). 27.50 *(978-0-7377-3424-9(8))*; (YA). (gr. 8-12). pap. 39.70 *(978-0-7377-3423-2(X))* Cengage Gale. (Greenhaven Pr., Inc.).

Nagelhout, Ryan. Emancipation Proclamation. 2016. (Documents of American Democracy Ser.). (Illus.). 32p. (J). (gr. 5-5). pap. 10.00 *(978-1-4994-2081-4(1)*, PowerKids Pr.) Rosen Publishing Group, Inc., The.

—Thomas Paine's Common Sense. 2013. 32p. (J). (gr. 4-6). 26.60 *(978-1-4339-9013-7(X))*; pap. 10.50 *(978-1-4339-9014-4(8))* Stevens, Gareth Publishing LLLP.

Nardo, Don. The Declaration of Independence. 2003. (World History Ser.). (ENG., Illus.). 112p. (J). 34.95 *(978-1-59018-293-2(6)*, Lucent Bks.) Cengage Gale.

—The Declaration of Independence. 2006. (Illus.). 48p. (J). (gr. 4-8). reprint ed. 17.80 *(978-1-4223-5323-3(0))* DIANE Publishing Co.

—The Presidency of Abraham Lincoln: The Triumph of Freedom & Unity, 1 vol. 2014. (Greatest U. S. Presidents Ser.). (ENG.). 64p. (gr. 5-7). lib. bdg. 33.99 *(978-0-7565-4926-8(4))* Compass Point Bks.

—The Presidency of Franklin D. Roosevelt: Confronting the Great Depression & World War II. 2014. (Greatest U. S. Presidents Ser.). (ENG.). 64p. (gr. 5-7). lib. bdg. 33.99 *(978-0-7565-4927-5(2))* Compass Point Bks.

Nationalism. 2010. (Key Concepts in American History Ser.). (Illus.). 128p. (gr. 6-12). 45.00 *(978-1-60413-219-9(1)*, Chelsea Hse.) Facts On File, Inc.

Nelson, Maria. Becoming a House Representative. 2016. (Who's Your Candidate? Choosing Government Leaders Ser.). (ENG., Illus.). 32p. (J). (gr. 3-4). pap. 10.50 *(978-1-4824-4035-5(0))* Stevens, Gareth Publishing LLLP.

—Becoming a Senator. 2016. (Who's Your Candidate? Choosing Government Leaders Ser.). (ENG., Illus.). 32p. (J). (gr. 3-4). pap. 10.50 *(978-1-4824-4043-0(1))* Stevens, Gareth Publishing LLLP.

Nelson, Sheila. The Original United States of America. 2006. (How America Became America Ser.). (Illus.). 96p. (YA). lib. bdg. 22.95 *(978-1-59084-903-3(5))* Mason Crest.

Niver, Heather Moore. Articles of Confederation. 2016. (Documents of American Democracy Ser.). (Illus.). 32p. (J). (gr. 5-5). pap. 10.00 *(978-1-4994-2069-2(2)*, PowerKids Pr.) Rosen Publishing Group, Inc., The.

—20 Fun Facts about the Declaration of Independence. 2013. (Fun Fact File: US History! Ser.). 32p. (J). (gr. 3-6). pap. 10.50 *(978-1-4339-9184-4(5))*; pap. 63.00 *(978-1-4339-9185-1(3))* Stevens, Gareth Publishing LLLP.

Niver, Heather Moore & Moore Niver, Heather. 20 Fun Facts about the Declaration of Independence. 2013. 32p. (J). (gr. 3-6). 25.25 *(978-1-4339-9183-7(7))* Stevens, Gareth Publishing LLLP.

Oachs, Emily Rose. Thomas Jefferson's Presidency. 2016. (Presidential Powerhouses Ser.). (ENG., Illus.). 104p. (J). (gr. 6-12). 35.99 *(978-1-4677-7923-4(7))*; 53.32 *(978-1-4677-8602-7(0))* Lerner Publishing Group. (Lerner Pubns.).

Obama, Barack. Our Enduring Spirit: President Barack Obama's First Words to America. Ruth, Greg, illus. 2009. 48p. lib. bdg. 18.89 *(978-0-06-183456-1(4))* HarperCollins Pubs.

Obama, Barack & Nelson, Kadir. Change Has Come: An Artist Celebrates Our American Spirit. Nelson, Kadir, illus. 2009. (ENG., Illus.). 64p. (J). (gr. 1). 12.99 *(978-1-4169-8955-4(2)*, Simon & Schuster Bks. For Young Readers) Simon & Schuster Bks. For Young Readers.

O'Neill, Robert John & Gallagher, Gary W. The Civil War: Bull Run & Other Eastern Battles, 1861-May 1863. 2010. (Civil War: Essential Histories Ser.). (ENG.). 96p. (YA). lib. bdg. 33.25 *(978-1-4488-0387-3(X))* Rosen Publishing Group, Inc., The.

Orr, Tamra. Government at Work. 2007. (21st Century Skills Library: Citizens & Their Governments Ser.). (ENG., Illus.). 32p. (gr. 4-8). lib. bdg. 28.50 *(978-1-60279-059-9(0)*, 200005) Cherry Lake Publishing.

—The Story of the Constitution. 2011. (My Guide to the Constitution Ser.). 48p. (J). (gr. 3-6). pap. 16.50 *(978-1-61228-188-9(5))*; (Illus.). lib. bdg. 29.95 *(978-1-58415-946-9(4))* Mitchell Lane Pubs., Inc.

—Tenth Amendment: Limiting Federal Powers. 2011. (Amendments to the United States Constitution: the Bill of Rights Ser.). (ENG., Illus.). 64p. (YA). pap. 12.95 *(978-1-4488-2311-6(0))* Rosen Publishing Group, Inc., The.

—The Tenth Amendment: Limiting Federal Powers. 2011. (Amendments to the United States Constitution: the Bill of Rights Ser.). (Illus.). 64p. (YA). (gr. 5-9). lib. bdg. 31.95 *(978-1-4488-1265-3(8))* Rosen Publishing Group, Inc., The.

Osborne, Linda Barrett. Traveling the Freedom Road: From Slavery & the Civil War Through Reconstructon. 2009. (ENG., Illus.). 128p. (J). (gr. 3-7). 25.95 *(978-0-8109-8338-0(9)*, Abrams Bks. for Young Readers) Abrams, Inc.

Osornio, Catherine L. The Declaration of Independence from A to Z, 1 vol. Johnson, Layne, illus. 2010. (ENG.). 32p. (J). (gr. 1-7). 16.99 *(978-1-58980-676-4(X))* Pelican Publishing Co., Inc.

Otfinoski, Steven. Patriots & Redcoats: Stories of American Revolutionary War Leaders. 2015. (Revolutionary War Ser.). (ENG.). 48p. (gr. 3-4). pap. 8.95 *(978-1-4914-2158-1(4))* Capstone Press of Coughlan Cos.

—The U. S. Constitution, Bill of Rights, & a New Nation. 2012. (Story of the American Revolution Ser.). (ENG.). 32p. (gr. 3-4). pap. 47.70 *(978-1-4296-9293-9(6)*, Fact Finders); (Illus.). lib. bdg. 27.32 *(978-1-4296-8589-4(1))* Capstone Press of Coughlan Cos.

Otfinoski, Steven Anthony. The U. S. Constitution, Bill of Rights, & a New Nation, 1 vol. 2012. (Story of the American Revolution Ser.). (ENG.). 32p. (gr. 3-4). pap. 8.10 *(978-1-4296-9292-2(8)*, Fact Finders) Capstone Press of Coughlan Cos.

Panchyk, Richard. Franklin Delano Roosevelt for Kids: His Life & Times with 21 Activities. 2007. (For Kids Ser.). (ENG., Illus.). 160p. (J). (gr. 4-8). pap. 14.95 *(978-1-55652-657-2(1))* Chicago Review Pr., Inc.

Paris, Stephanie. Forming a New Government (America's Early Years) 2016. (Primary Source Readers Ser.). (ENG., Illus.). 32p. (J). (gr. 4-5). pap. 8.99 *(978-1-4938-3083-1(X))* Teacher Created Materials, Inc.

Parker, Christi E. Abraham Lincoln, 1 vol. 2005. (Primary Source Readers Ser.). (ENG.). 24p. (J). (gr. 4-4). pap. 8.99 *(978-0-7439-8916-9(3))* Shell Educational Publishing.

—George Washington, 1 vol. 2004. (Primary Source Readers Ser.). (ENG.). 24p. (J). (gr. 4-4). pap. 8.99 *(978-0-7439-8749-3(7))* Shell Educational Publishing.

Paul, Michael. Pan Am 103 & State-Sponsored Terrorism. 2006. (Terrorism in Today's World Ser.). (Illus.). 48p. (gr. 5-12). pap. 14.05 *(978-0-8368-6566-0(9))*; lib. bdg. 31.00 *(978-0-8368-6559-2(6))* Stevens, Gareth Publishing LLLP. (Gareth Stevens Secondary Library).

Payan, Gregory. The Federalists & Anti-Federalists: How & Why Political Parties Were Formed in Young America. 2009. (Life in the New American Nation Ser.). 32p. (gr. 4-4). 47.90 *(978-1-61514-283-5(5))* Rosen Publishing Group, Inc., The.

Pederson, Charles E. The U. S. Constitution & Bill of Rights, 1 vol. 2010. (Essential Events Set 4 Ser.). (ENG.). 112p. (J). (gr. 6-12). lib. bdg. 35.64 *(978-1-60453-948-6(8))* ABDO Publishing Co.

Peppas, Lynn. The Battle of the Alamo. 2017. 48p. (J). ***(978-0-7787-3940-1(6))*** Crabtree Publishing Co.

Perrin, Pat. Getting Started-America's Melting Pot. 2004. (Illus.). (J). *(978-1-932663-04-4(5))* History Compass, LLC.

—Getting Started-Our 50 United States. 2004. (Illus.). (J). *(978-1-932663-03-7(7))* History Compass, LLC.

—Getting Started-Our Government. 2004. (Illus.). (J). *(978-1-932663-02-0(9))* History Compass, LLC.

Perritano, John. Radical Republicans: The Struggle for Equality. 2008. (Graphic America Ser.). (ENG., Illus.). 32p. (J). (gr. 3-6). lib. bdg. *(978-0-7787-4187-9(7))* Crabtree Publishing Co.

Petechuk, David. PACs, Super PACs, & Fundraising. 2016. (Illus.). 64p. (J). *(978-1-61900-093-3(8))* Eldorado Ink.

Petersen, Christine. How the Legislative Branch Works, 1 vol. 2014. (How the US Government Works). (ENG.). 48p. (gr. 3-6). lib. bdg. 32.79 *(978-1-62403-637-8(6))* ABDO Publishing Co.

Pettiford, Rebecca. El Capitolio. 2016. (Los Primeros Viajes Escolares (First Field Trips)).Tr. of State Capitol. (SPA.). 24p. (J). (gr. k-2). lib. bdg. 25.65 *(978-1-62031-328-2(6)*, Bullfrog Bks.) Jump! Inc.

—State Capitol. Fretland VanVoorst, Jenny, ed. 2016. (First Field Trips). 24p. (J). (gr. k-2). lib. bdg. 25.65 *(978-1-62031-297-1(2)*, Bullfrog Bks.) Jump! Inc.

Piddock, Charles. The Cold War. 2016. (Illus.). 48p. (J). *(978-1-5105-1282-5(9))* SmartBook Media, Inc.

Pierce, Alan. Constitution, 1 vol. 2005. (American Moments Set Ii Ser.). (ENG., Illus.). 48p. (gr. 4-8). 27.07 *(978-1-59197-731-5(2)*, Abdo & Daughters) ABDO Publishing Co.

—Declaration of Independence, 1 vol. 2005. (American Moments Set Ii Ser.). (ENG., Illus.). 48p. (gr. 4-8). 27.07 *(978-1-59197-732-2(0)*, Abdo & Daughters) ABDO Publishing Co.

Pingry, Patricia A. The Story of Ronald Reagan. Mahan, Ben, illus. 2006. (ENG.). 26p. (J). (gr. -1-k). bds. 7.69 *(978-0-8249-6621-8(X)*, Ideal Pubns.) Worthy Publishing.

Political Profiles Set, vols. 13, vol. 13. Incl. Al Gore. Sapet, Kerrily. (Illus.). 112p. 2007. lib. bdg. 27.95 *(978-1-59935-070-7(X))*; Arnold Schwarzenegger. Young, Jeff C. (Illus.). 112p. 2007. 27.95 *(978-1-59935-050-9(5))*; Barack Obama. (Illus.). 128p. 2007. lib. bdg. 27.95 *(978-1-59935-045-5(9))*; Hillary Clinton. Wells, Catherine. (Illus.). 112p. 2007. lib. bdg. 27.95 *(978-1-59935-047-9(5))*; Joe Biden. Young, Jeff C. 100p. 2009. 28.95 *(978-1-59935-131-5(5))*; John Lewis. Sapet, Kerrily. 100p. 2009. 28.95 *(978-1-59935-130-8(7))*; John McCain. Wells, Catherine. (Illus.). 112p. 2008. lib. bdg. 27.95 *(978-1-59935-046-2(7))*; Michelle Obama. 112p. 2009. lib. bdg. 28.95 *(978-1-59935-090-5(4))*; Nancy Pelosi. Shichtman, Sandra H. (Illus.). 112p. 2008. lib. bdg. 27.95 *(978-1-59935-049-3(1))*; Rudy Giuliani. Sharp, Anna Layton. (Illus.). 128p. 2008. lib. bdg. 27.95 *(978-1-59935-048-6(3))*; Ted Kennedy. 144p. 2009. 28.95 *(978-1-59935-089-9(0))*; (YA). (gr. 5-9). 2007. Set lib. bdg. 376.35 *(978-1-59935-072-1(6))* Reynolds, Morgan Inc.

Pollack, Pam & Belviso, Meg. Who Was Alexander Hamilton? Putra, Dede, illus. 2017. (Who Was? Ser.). (ENG.). 112p. (J). (gr. 3-7). 5.99 ***(978-0-399-54427-9(5))***; lib. bdg. 15.99 ***(978-0-399-54429-3(1))*** Penguin Young Readers Group. (Penguin Workshop).

Porterfield, Jason. How Lyndon B. Johnson Fought the Vietnam War. 2017. (Presidents at War Ser.). 128p. (J). (gr. 8-8). lib. bdg. 37.27 ***(978-0-7660-8531-2(7))*** Enslow Pubs., Inc.

Porterfield, Jason. Problems & Progress in American Politics: The Growth of the Democratic Party in the Late 1800s. 2009. (America's Industrial Society in the 19th Century Ser.). 32p. (gr. 4-4). 47.90 *(978-1-61511-339-2(8))* Rosen Publishing Group, Inc., The.

Prentzas, G. S. The Emancipation Proclamation. 2011. (Cornerstones of Freedom, Third Ser.). (Illus.). 64p. (J). (ENG.). pap. 8.95 *(978-0-531-26557-4(9))*; lib. bdg. 30.00 *(978-0-531-25032-7(6))* Scholastic Library Publishing. (Children's Pr.).

Price, Sean Stewart. U. S. Presidents: Truth & Rumors. Doty, Eldon, illus. 2010. (Truth & Rumors Ser.). (ENG.). 32p. (gr. 3-4). lib. bdg. 27.99 *(978-1-4296-3952-1(0)*, Edge Bks.) Capstone Press of Coughlan Cos.

Primary Sources of American Political Documents. 2015. (Primary Sources of American Political Documents Ser.). (ENG.). 112p. (J). (gr. 7-7). 223.62 *(978-0-7660-6686-1(X))* Enslow Pubs., Inc.

Progressivism. 2010. (Key Concepts in American History Ser.). (Illus.). 128p. (gr. 6-12). 45.00 *(978-1-60413-223-6(X)*, Chelsea Hse.) Facts On File, Inc.

Publishers, Chelsea House, creator. The U. S. Government: How It Works Set, 14-Volumes. 2007. (U. S. Government Ser.). (gr. 5-8). 420.00 *(978-0-7910-9819-6(2)*, Chelsea Hse.) Facts On File, Inc.

Quinby, Michelle. Connecting the 21st Century to the Past: What Makes America America, 2000-The Present. 2013. (Illus.). 48p. (J). pap. *(978-1-4222-2423-6(6))* Mason Crest.

—Connecting the 21st Century to the Past: What Makes America America, 2000-The Present. Rakove, Jack N., ed. 2012. (How America Became America Ser.). (Illus.). 48p. (J). (gr. 3-4). 19.95 *(978-1-4222-2409-0(0))* Mason Crest.

Quirk, Anne. The Good Fight: The Feuds of the Founding Fathers (and How They Shaped the Nation) Baddeley, Elizabeth, illus. 2017. (ENG.). 128p. (J). (gr. 2-5). 16.99 *(978-1-5247-0035-5(5)*, Knopf Bks. for Young Readers) Random Hse. Children's Bks.

Raatma, Lucia. Barbara Jordan. 2013. 96p. (YA). (gr. 7-12). 39.93 *(978-0-7614-4956-0(6))* Cavendish Square Publishing.

Rajczak, Michael. Becoming President. 2016. (Who's Your Candidate? Choosing Government Leaders Ser.). (ENG., Illus.). 32p. (J). (gr. 3-4). pap. 10.50 *(978-1-4824-4039-3(3))* Stevens, Gareth Publishing LLLP.

Randolph, Joanne. The Iroquois League. (Reading Room Collection 2 Ser.). 24p. 2009. (gr. 3-4). 42.50 *(978-1-60851-995-8(3)*, PowerKids Pr.) 2003. (Illus.). (J). lib. bdg. 22.60 *(978-0-8239-3703-5(8))* Rosen Publishing Group, Inc., The.

Ransom, Candice. George Washington & the Story of the U. S. Constitution. Reeves, Jeni, illus. 2011. (History Speaks: Picture Books Plus Reader's Theater Ser.). 48p. pap. 56.72 *(978-0-7613-7632-3(1))*; (ENG.). (gr. 2-4). 27.93 *(978-0-7613-5877-0(3)*, Millbrook Pr.); (ENG.). (gr. 2-4). pap. 9.95 *(978-0-7613-7116-8(8))* Lerner Publishing Group.

—What Was the Continental Congress? And Other Questions about the Declaration of Independence. 2011. (Six Questions of American History Ser.). (ENG.). 48p. (gr. 4-6). 30.60 *(978-0-7613-5227-3(9))*; pap. 9.95 *(978-0-7613-7135-9(4))*; pap. 56.72 *(978-0-7613-7642-2(9))* Lerner Publishing Group.

—Who Wrote the U. S. Constitution? And Other Questions about the Constitutional Convention of 1787. 2010. (Six Questions of American History Ser.). (ENG.). (gr. 4-6). pap. 56.72 *(978-0-7613-6949-3(X))*; 48p. pap. 9.95 *(978-0-7613-6126-8(X))*; 48p. lib. bdg. 30.60 *(978-1-58013-669-3(9))* Lerner Publishing Group.

Rauf, Don. How George W. Bush Fought the Wars in Iraq & Afghanistan. 2017. (Presidents at War Ser.). 128p. (J). (gr. 8-8). lib. bdg. 37.27 ***(978-0-7660-8533-6(3))*** Enslow Pubs., Inc.

Rauf, Don. Washington's Farewell Address. 2016. (Let's Find Out! Primary Sources Ser.). 00032p. (J). (gr. 2-3). lib. bdg. 24.45 *(978-1-5081-0407-0(7))* Rosen Publishing Group, Inc., The.

Raum, Elizabeth. The Declaration of Independence, 1 vol. 2012. (Documenting U. S. History Ser.). (ENG.). 48p. (gr. 3-6). pap. 9.95 *(978-1-4329-6762-8(2))*; lib. bdg. 32.65 *(978-1-4329-6753-6(3))* Heinemann-Raintree. (NA-h).

Remy, Richard C. United States Government: Democracy in Action. 2007. (Illus.). 898p. (J). 94.64 *(978-0-07-874762-5(7)*, 9780078747625) Glencoe/McGraw-Hill.

Rice, Earle. FDR & the New Deal. 2009. (Monumental Milestones Ser.). 48p. (YA). (gr. 4-7). lib. bdg. 29.95 *(978-1-58415-828-8(X))* Mitchell Lane Pubs., Inc.

Rice, Earle, Jr. How Franklin D. Roosevelt Fought World War II. 2017. (Presidents at War Ser.). 128p. (J). (gr. 8-8). lib. bdg. 37.27 ***(978-0-7660-8527-5(9))*** Enslow Pubs., Inc.

Rice, Liz. Bill Richardson. (Sharing the American Dream Ser.). 64p. (YA). (gr. 7-12). 2009. 22.95 *(978-1-4222-0589-1(4))* 2007. pap. 9.95 *(978-1-4222-0761-1(7))* Mason Crest.

Rissman, Rebecca. Declaration of Independence, 1 vol. 2013. (Foundations of Our Nation Ser.). 48p. (J). (ENG.). (gr. 3-6). lib. bdg. 32.79 *(978-1-61783-708-1(3))*; (Illus.). pap. 15.64 *(978-1-61783-758-6(X)*, Core Library) ABDO Publishing Co.

RJF Publishing Staff & Staton, Hilarie. Independence Hall. 2009. (Symbols of American Freedom Ser.). 48p. (gr. 4-6). 30.00 *(978-1-60413-521-3(2)*, Chelsea Clubhouse) Facts On File, Inc.

Roberts, Russell. A History of the Democratic Party. 2012. 48p. (J). (gr. 3-6). lib. bdg. 29.95 *(978-1-61228-259-6(8))* Mitchell Lane Pubs., Inc.

Robinson, Tom. The Development of the Industrial United States: 1870-1900. 2007. (Presidents of the United States Ser.). (Illus.). 48p. (J). (gr. 4-7). lib. bdg. 29.05 *(978-1-59036-745-2(6))* Weigl Pubs., Inc.

—Development of the Industrial United States: 1870-1900. 2007. (Presidents of the United States Ser.). (Illus.). 48p. (J). (gr. 4-7). per. 10.95 *(978-1-59036-746-9(4))* Weigl Pubs., Inc.

—Media Ownership, 1 vol. 2009. (Essential Viewpoints Set 4 Ser.). (ENG., Illus.). 112p. (J). (gr. 6-12). lib. bdg. 35.64 *(978-1-60453-534-1(2))* ABDO Publishing Co.

Roome, Hugh. Franklin D. Roosevelt. 2017. (Rookie Biographies Ser.). (ENG.). 32p. (J). pap. 5.95 ***(978-0-531-23863-9(6)***, Children's Pr.) Scholastic Library Publishing.

—Franklin D. Roosevelt: American Hero. 2017. (Rookie Biographies Ser.). (ENG.). 32p. (J). lib. bdg. 25.00 ***(978-0-531-23229-3(8)***, Children's Pr.) Scholastic Library Publishing.

Rosaler, Maxine. A Timeline of the First Continental Congress. 2009. (Timelines of American History Ser.). 32p. (gr. 4-4). 47.90 *(978-1-60854-384-7(6)*, Rosen Reference) Rosen Publishing Group, Inc., The.

Rowell, Rebecca. John F. Kennedy's Presidency. 2016. (Presidential Powerhouses Ser.). (ENG.). 104p. (J). (gr. 6-12). 53.32 *(978-1-4677-8600-3(4)*, Lerner Pubns.) Lerner Publishing Group.

Roxburgh, Ellis. Thomas Jefferson vs. John Adams: Founding Fathers & Political Rivals. 2016. (History's Greatest Rivals Ser.). (ENG., Illus.). 48p. (J). (gr. 6-8). pap. 14.05 *(978-1-4824-4239-7(6))* Stevens, Gareth Publishing LLLP.

Roza, Greg. Evaluating the Articles of Confederation: Determining the Validity of Information & Arguments. 2009. (Critical Thinking in American History Ser.). 48p. (gr. 5-8). 53.00 *(978-1-61512-092-5(0)*, Rosen Reference) Rosen Publishing Group, Inc., The.

Rubel, David. Scholastic Encyclopedia of the Presidents & Their Times. 2013. (ENG.). 256p. (J). (gr. 5-9). 24.99 *(978-0-545-49985-9(2)*, Scholastic Reference) Scholastic, Inc.

Ruffin, David C. The Duties & Responsibilities of the Secretary of Defense. 2009. (Your Government in Action Ser.). 32p. (gr. 3-3). 43.90 *(978-1-60854-915-3(1)*, PowerKids Pr.) Rosen Publishing Group, Inc., The.

—The Duties & Responsibilities of the Secretary of Education. 2009. (Your Government in Action Ser.). 32p. (gr. 3-3). 43.90 *(978-1-60854-916-0(X)*, PowerKids Pr.) Rosen Publishing Group, Inc., The.

—The Duties & Responsibilities of the Secretary of Homeland Security. 2009. (Your Government in Action Ser.). 32p. (gr. 3-3). 43.90 *(978-1-60854-918-4(6)*, PowerKids Pr.) Rosen Publishing Group, Inc., The.

Ruschmann, Paul. Energy Policy. 2009. (Point/Counterpoint Ser.). 144p. (C). (gr. 9-18). 35.00 *(978-1-60413-333-2(3)*, Chelsea Hse.) Facts On File, Inc.

Ryckman, Tatiana. Alexander Hamilton: The First Secretary of Treasury & an Author of the Federalist Papers. 2016. (Great American Thinkers Ser.). (Illus.). 128p. (J). (gr. 9-9). 45.64 *(978-1-5026-1934-1(2))* Cavendish Square Publishing.

Sakany, Lois. Progressive Leaders: The Platforms & Policies of America's Reform Politicians. (Progressive Movement 1900-1920: Efforts to Reform America's New Industrial Society Ser.). 32p. 2009. (gr. 3-4). 47.90 *(978-1-60854-168-3(1))* 2004. (Illus.). (YA). (gr. 5-9). lib. bdg. 22.50 *(978-1-4042-0193-4(9))* Rosen Publishing Group, Inc., The.

Samuel, Charlie. Government & Politics in Colonial America. (Primary Sources of Everyday Life in Colonial America Ser.). 24p. 2009. (gr. 3-4). 42.50 *(978-1-60851-625-4(3))* 2003. (Illus.). (J). lib. bdg. 21.25 *(978-0-8239-6597-7(X))* Rosen Publishing Group, Inc., The. (PowerKids Pr.).

Sanders, Bernie. Bernie Sanders's Guide to Political Revolution. 2017. (ENG., Illus.). 240p. (YA). 16.99 ***(978-1-250-13890-3(6)***, 9781250138903, Holt, Henry & Co. Bks. For Young Readers) Holt, Henry & Co.

Sapet, Kerrily. Al Gore. 2007. (Political Profiles Ser.). (Illus.). 112p. (YA). (gr. 5-9). lib. bdg. 27.95 *(978-1-59935-070-7(X))* Reynolds, Morgan Inc.

Scherer, Lauri S. Social Protest. Gale, ed. 2014. (Issues That Concern You Ser.). (ENG., Illus.). 144p. (gr. 7-10). lib. bdg. 42.00 *(978-0-7377-6934-0(3)*, Greenhaven Pr., Inc.) Cengage Gale.

Scherer, Randy. Political Scandals. 2007. (At Issue Ser.). (ENG., Illus.). 128p. (gr. 10-12). pap. 27.80 *(978-0-7377-3764-6(6)*, Greenhaven Pr., Inc.) Cengage Gale.

Schlesinger, Arthur M., Jr., et al. History of American Presidential Elections, 1789-2008, 3 vols. 4th rev. ed. 2011. (Illus.). 1742p. (C). (gr. 9). 225.00 *(978-0-8160-8220-9(0))* Facts On File, Inc.

Schmidt, Maegan. Us Constitution & Bill of Rights, 1 vol. 2013. (Foundations of Our Nation Ser.). (ENG.). 48p. (J). (gr. 3-6). lib. bdg. 32.79 *(978-1-61783-713-5(X))* ABDO Publishing Co.

—US Constitution & Bill of Rights. 2013. (Foundations of Our Nation EBook Ser.). (ENG., Illus.). 48p. (J). pap. 15.64 *(978-1-61783-763-0(6)*, Core Library) ABDO Publishing Co.

Schuh, Mari. The U. S. Government. 2012. (U. S. Government Ser.). (ENG.). 24p. (gr. k-1). lib. bdg. 79.95 *(978-1-4296-8111-7(X)*, Pebble Plus) Capstone Press of Coughlan Cos.

Schuman, Michael A. Bill Clinton. rev. ed. 2003. (United States Presidents Ser.). (Illus.). 128p. (J). (gr. 5-12). lib. bdg. 27.94 *(978-0-7660-2032-0(0))* Enslow Pubs., Inc.

Schwartz, Eric. What Makes America America? 2006. (How America Became America Ser.). (Illus.). 96p. (YA). lib. bdg. 22.95 *(978-1-59084-913-2(2))* Mason Crest.

Schwartz, Heather E. Causes of the Civil War: A House Divided. 2017. (Primary Source Readers Ser.). (Illus.). 32p. (J). (gr. 4-5). pap. 8.99 *(978-1-4938-3803-5(2))* Teacher Created Materials, Inc.

—Our Leaders in Government. 2016. (Primary Source Readers Ser.). (Illus.). 32p. (gr. 2-2). 8.99 *(978-1-4938-2552-3(6))* Teacher Created Materials, Inc.

—Theodore Roosevelt's Presidency. 2016. (Presidential Powerhouses Ser.). (ENG., Illus.). 104p. (J). (gr. 6-12). 35.99 *(978-1-4677-7930-2(X))*; 53.32 *(978-1-4677-8601-0(2))* Lerner Publishing Group. (Lerner Pubns.).

Schwartz, Richard Alan. The 1990s. 2006. (Eyewitness History Ser.). (Illus.). 512p. (C). (gr. 9). 80.00 *(978-0-8160-5696-5(X))* Facts On File, Inc.

T
U
V

Searchlight Books - How Does Government Work? 2012. (Searchlight Books How Does Government Work Ser.). (ENG., Illus.). 40p. (gr. 3-5). lib. bdg. 167.58 *(978-0-7613-6513-6(3)*, Lerner Pubns.);Set. pap. 51.02 *(978-0-7613-9235-4(1))*;Set, Pack. pap. 306.09 *(978-0-7613-9236-1(X))* Lerner Publishing Group.

Seeley, M. H. 20 Fun Facts about Alexander Hamilton. 2017. (Fun Fact File: Founding Fathers Ser.). 32p. (gr. 2-3). pap. 10.50 ***(978-1-5382-0288-3(3))*** Stevens, Gareth Publishing LLLP.

Serber, Michael & Peiser, Andrew. U. S. History & Government. rev. ed. 2005. 688p. (gr. 10-12). *(978-0-87720-882-2(4)*, R036H) AMSCO Schl. Pubns., Inc.

Sexton, Colleen A. Arnold Schwarzenegger. 2005. (A&E Biography Ser.). (Illus.). 112p. (J). (gr. 6-12). 29.27 *(978-0-8225-1634-7(9))*; (ENG & SPA., pap. 7.95 *(978-0-8225-5328-1(7))* Lerner Publishing Group.

Sharp, Constance. America Is Born, 1770-1800. 2012. (J). pap. *(978-1-4222-2413-7(9))* Mason Crest.

—America Is Born, 1770-1800. Rakove, Jack N., ed. 2012. (How America Became America Ser.). 48p. (J). (gr. 3-4). 19.95 *(978-1-4222-2399-4(X))* Mason Crest.

Shattuck, Randy. Theodore Roosevelt. 2016. lib. bdg. *(978-1-68048-529-5(6))* Rosen Publishing Group, Inc., The.

Shea, John. The Declaration of Independence. 2013. (Documents That Shaped America Ser.). 32p. (J). (gr. 4-6). pap. 63.00 *(978-1-4339-8999-5(9))*; pap. 10.50 *(978-1-4339-8998-8(0))* Stevens, Gareth Publishing LLLP.

Shea, John & Shea, John M. The Declaration of Independence. 2013. 32p. (J). (gr. 4-6). 26.60 *(978-1-4339-8997-1(2))* Stevens, Gareth Publishing LLLP.

Shea, Therese M. Alexander Hamilton: Founding Father & Treasury Secretary. 2017. (J). pap. ***(978-0-7660-9045-3(0))*** Enslow Pubs., Inc.

Silate, Jennifer. The Calhoun-Randolph Debate on the Eve of the War of 1812: A Primary Source Investigation. 2004. (Great Historic Debates & Speeches Ser.). (Illus.). 64p. (YA). (gr. 5-9). lib. bdg. 31.95 *(978-1-4042-0150-7(5))* Rosen Publishing Group, Inc., The.

—The Calhoun-Randolph Debate on the Eve of the War Of 1812: A Primary Source Investigation. 2009. (Great Historic Debates & Speeches Ser.). 64p. (gr. 5-8). 58.50 *(978-1-61513-124-2(8))* Rosen Publishing Group, Inc., The.

Skahill, Carolyn M. The Socialist Party: Eugene V. Debs & the Radical Politics of the American Working Class. 2006. (Progressive Movement, 1900-1920 Ser.). (Illus.). 32p. (YA). (gr. 5-9). lib. bdg. 22.50 *(978-1-4042-0198-9(X))* Rosen Publishing Group, Inc., The.

Slater, Lee. Marine Force Recon, 1 vol. 2016. (Special Ops Ser.). (ENG., Illus.). 32p. (J). (gr. 3-6). 27.07 *(978-1-62403-970-6(7))* ABDO Publishing Co.

Slepian, Curtis. Hamilton vs. Jefferson (Alexander Hamilton) 2017. (Primary Source Readers Focus On Ser.). (Illus.). 32p. (J). (gr. 4-8). pap. 8.99 ***(978-1-4258-6354-8(X))*** Teacher Created Materials, Inc.

Smith, Adam I. P. Abraham Lincoln. 2016. (History Makers Ser.). 144p. (J). (gr. 9-9). 45.64 *(978-1-5026-1912-9(1))* Cavendish Square Publishing.

Smith-Llera, Danielle. The Presidency of George Washington: Inspiring a Young Nation, 1 vol. 2014. (Greatest U. S. Presidents Ser.). (ENG.). 64p. (gr. 5-7). lib. bdg. 33.99 *(978-0-7565-4928-2(0))* Compass Point Bks.

Sobel, Syl. How the U. S. Government Works. 2nd rev. ed. 2012. (ENG.). 48p. (J). (gr. 2-6). pap. 6.99 *(978-0-7641-4792-0(7))* Barron's Educational Series, Inc.

Somervill, Barbara A. The Life & Times of James Madison. 2008. (Profiles in American History Ser.). (Illus.). 48p. (J). (gr. 4-7). lib. bdg. 29.95 *(978-1-58415-530-0(2))* Mitchell Lane Pubs., Inc.

Somerville, Clive. The Drug Enforcement Administration. 2017. (J). ***(978-1-4222-3765-6(6))*** Mason Crest.

Sonneborn, Liz. The Articles of Confederation, 1 vol. 2012. (Documenting U. S. History Ser.). (ENG.). 48p. (gr. 3-6). pap. 9.95 *(978-1-4329-6758-1(4))*; lib. bdg. 32.65 *(978-1-4329-6749-9(5))* Heinemann-Raintree. (NA-h).

South, Victor. America in the 20th Century (1913-1999) 2013. (Illus.). 48p. (J). *(978-1-4222-2410-6(4))*; *(978-1-4222-2396-3(5))* Mason Crest.

Southwell, David. Unsolved Political Mysteries. 2009. (Mysteries & Conspiracies Ser.). 80p. (gr. 10-10). 61.20 *(978-1-61514-747-2(0))* Rosen Publishing Group, Inc., The.

Southwell, David & Twist, Sean. Unsolved Political Mysteries. 2007. (Mysteries & Conspiracies Ser.). (Illus.). 80p. (YA). (gr. 9-12). lib. bdg. 33.25 *(978-1-4042-1083-7(0))* Rosen Publishing Group, Inc., The.

St. George, Judith. The Journey of the One & Only Declaration of Independence. Hillenbrand, Will, illus. 2005. (ENG.). 48p. (J). (gr. 2-5). 17.99 *(978-0-399-23738-6(0)*, Philomel Bks.) Penguin Young Readers Group.

—The Journey of the One & Only Declaration of Independence. Hillenbrand, Will, illus. 2011. (J). (gr. 1-7). 29.95 *(978-0-439-02760-1(8)*, WHCD806) Weston Woods Studios, Inc.

Stabler, David. Kid Presidents: True Tales of Childhood from America's Presidents. Horner, Doogie, illus. 2014. (Kid Legends Ser.: 1). (ENG.). 224p. (J). (gr. 4-7). 13.95 *(978-1-59474-731-1(8))* Quirk Bks.

Stanley, George Edward. America & the Cold War (1949-1969) 2005. (Primary Source History of the United States Ser.). (Illus.). 48p. (gr. 5-12). lib. bdg. 31.00 *(978-0-8368-5830-3(1)*, Gareth Stevens Secondary Library) Stevens, Gareth Publishing LLLP.

—America in Today's World (1969-2004) 2005. (Primary Source History of the United States Ser.). (Illus.). 48p. (gr. 5-12). pap. 14.05 *(978-0-8368-5840-2(9))*; lib. bdg. 31.00 *(978-0-8368-5831-0(X))* Stevens, Gareth Publishing LLLP. (Gareth Stevens Secondary Library).

—The Crisis of the Union (1815-1865) 2005. (Primary Source History of the United States Ser.). (Illus.). 48p. (gr. 5-12). pap. 14.05 *(978-0-8368-5835-8(2))*; lib. bdg. 31.00 *(978-0-8368-5826-6(3))* Stevens, Gareth Publishing LLLP. (Gareth Stevens Secondary Library).

—An Emerging World Power, 1900-1929. 2005. (Primary Source History of the United States Ser.). (Illus.). 48p. (gr. 5-12). pap. 14.05 *(978-0-8368-5837-2(9))*; lib. bdg. 31.00 *(978-0-8368-5828-0(X))* Stevens, Gareth Publishing LLLP. (Gareth Stevens Secondary Library).

Stanton, Terence M. The Branches of the U. S. Government. 2009. (Real Life Readers Ser.). 32p. (gr. 4-5). pap. 10.00 *(978-1-4358-0173-8(3)*, Rosen Classroom) Rosen Publishing Group, Inc., The.

—The Declaration of Independence. 2009. (Real Life Readers Ser.). 32p. (gr. 4-5). pap. 10.00 *(978-1-4358-0163-9(6)*, Rosen Classroom); 32p. (gr. 4-4). 47.90 *(978-1-61511-371-2(1)*, PowerKids Pr.); (J). pap. 60.00 *(978-1-4358-0164-6(4)*, PowerKids Pr.); (J). lib. bdg. 25.25 *(978-1-4358-2990-9(5)*, PowerKids Pr.) Rosen Publishing Group, Inc., The.

Steck-Vaughn, creator. Cast Your Vote!: High School: National, State, & Local Government. 2007. (Illus.). 72p. (J). (gr. 4-7). pap. 12.99 *(978-1-4190-3637-8(8))* Steck-Vaughn.

Steck-Vaughn Staff, creator. Cast Your Vote! Grades 3-5: National, State, & Local Government. 2007. (Illus.). 72p. (J). (gr. 4-7). pap. 12.99 *(978-1-4190-3635-4(1))* Steck-Vaughn.

Steinberg, Arnold. Whiplash! From JFK to Donald Trump, a Political Odyssey. 2017. (J). ***(978-0-89803-180-5(X))*** Jameson Bks., Inc.

Stille, Darlene R. The Emergence of Modern America: 1890-1930. 2007. (Presidents of the United States Ser.). (Illus.). 48p. (J). (gr. 4-7). lib. bdg. 29.05 *(978-1-59036-747-6(2))*; per. 10.95 *(978-1-59036-748-3(0))* Weigl Pubs., Inc.

Stone, Oliver & Kuznick, Peter J. The Untold History of the United States: Young Readers Edition. 2014. (Illus.). 383p. (J). pap. *(978-1-4814-2177-5(8))* Simon & Schuster Children's Publishing.

Storrs, Landon & Storrs, Landon R. Y. The Second Red Scare & the Unmaking of the New Deal Left. 2012. (Politics & Society in Modern America Ser.). (ENG., Illus.). 424p. (C). 47.95 *(978-0-691-15396-4(5))* Princeton Univ. Pr.

Strum, Richard. Henry Knox: Washington's Artilleryman. 2006. (Forgotten Heroes of the American Revolution Ser.). (Illus.). 88p. (J). (gr. 5-11). lib. bdg. 23.95 *(978-1-59556-013-1(0))* OTTN Publishing.

Strum, Richard M. Causes of the American Revolution. 2005. (Road to War Ser.). (Illus.). 64p. (J). pap. 12.95 *(978-1-59556-005-6(X))*; (gr. 4-18). lib. bdg. 22.95 *(978-1-59556-001-8(7))* OTTN Publishing.

—Henry Knox: Washington's Artilleryman. 2006. (J). pap. *(978-1-59556-018-6(1))* OTTN Publishing.

Stumpff, April D. & Messersmith, Patrick. Ann Richards: A Woman's Place Is in the Dome. 2006. (Stars of Texas Ser.: 6). (ENG., Illus.). 80p. (gr. 4-7). 14.95 *(978-1-933337-12-8(5))* State Hse. Pr.

Sundance/Newbridge LLC Staff. America Is Voting. 2004. (Reading PowerWorks Ser.). (gr. 1-3). 37.50 *(978-0-7608-9723-2(9))* Sundance/Newbridge Educational Publishing.

Swain, Gwenyth. Documents of Freedom: A Look at the Declaration of Independence, the Bill of Rights, & the U. S. Constitution. 2012. (Searchlight Books How Does Government Work Ser.). (ENG., Illus.). 40p. (gr. 3-5). pap. 51.01 *(978-0-7613-9231-6(9))*; pap. 8.95 *(978-0-7613-8560-8(6))* Lerner Publishing Group.

—Documents of Freedom: A Look at the Declaration of Independence, the Bill of Rights, & the U.S. Constitution. 2012. (Searchlight Books How Does Government Work Ser.). (ENG., Illus.). 40p. (gr. 3-5). lib. bdg. 27.93 *(978-0-7613-6514-3(1))* Lerner Publishing Group.

Taylor-Butler, Christine. The Congress of the United States. (True Bks.). (ENG., Illus.). 48p. (J). (gr. 3-5). 2008. pap. 6.95 *(978-0-531-14778-8(9))* 2007. lib. bdg. 29.00 *(978-0-531-12628-8(5))* Scholastic Library Publishing. (Children's Pr.).

—The Constitution. 2007. (True Book(tm), a — American History Ser.). (ENG., Illus.). 48p. (J). (gr. 3-5). lib. bdg. 31.00 *(978-0-531-12629-5(3)*, Children's Pr.) Scholastic Library Publishing.

—The Constitution of the United States. 2008. (True Bks.). (ENG., Illus.). 48p. (J). (gr. 3-5). pap. 6.95 *(978-0-531-14779-5(7)*, Children's Pr.) Scholastic Library Publishing.

Teigen, Diane. The Gilded Age. 2012. (Defining Moments Ser.). 249p. lib. bdg. 55.00 *(978-0-7808-1238-3(7))* Omnigraphics, Inc.

The Choices Program - Brown University Staff. A More Perfect Union: Shaping American Government, 2 vols. 5th ed. 2005. (Illus.). 168p. (YA). pap. 34.00 *(978-1-891306-88-4(X))* Choices Program, Watson Institute, Brown Univ.

This Is Your Governement. (Illus.). (YA). (gr. 5-8). 159.00 *(978-1-4042-0371-6(0)*, Rosen Reference) Rosen Publishing Group, Inc., The.

Thomas, Garen. Yes We Can: A Biography of President Barack Obama. 2nd rev. ed. 2008. (ENG., Illus.). 256p. (J). (gr. 3-7). pap. 12.99 *(978-0-312-58639-3(6)*, 9780312586393) Feiwel & Friends.

Thomas Paine's Common Sense. 2013. (Documents That Shaped America Ser.). 32p. (J). (gr. 4-6). pap. 63.00 *(978-1-4339-9015-1(6))* Stevens, Gareth Publishing LLLP.

Thomas, Ray aka The Bull Cutter. What's Wrong in America. 2008. 216p. pap. 14.95 *(978-1-4327-2531-0(9))* Outskirts Pr., Inc.

Thomas, William David. Como Elegimos a Nuestros Lideres? 2008. (Mi gobierno de Estados Unidos (My American Government) Ser.). (SPA & ENG., Illus.). 32p. (gr. 3-7). lib. bdg. 26.00 *(978-0-8368-8870-6(7)*, Gareth Stevens Learning Library) Stevens, Gareth Publishing LLLP.

—¿Cómo Elegimos a Nuestros Líderes? 2008. (Mi gobierno de Estados Unidos (My American Government) Ser.). (SPA & ENG.). 32p. (gr. 3-7). pap. 10.50 *(978-0-8368-8875-1(8)*, Gareth Stevens Learning Library) Stevens, Gareth Publishing LLLP.

—¿Cuáles son las partes del gobierno? (What Are the Parts of Government?) 2008. (Mi gobierno de Estados Unidos (My American Government) Ser.). (SPA.). 32p. (gr. 3-7). pap. 10.50 *(978-0-8368-8877-5(4)*, Gareth Stevens Learning Library) Stevens, Gareth Publishing LLLP.

—The Home Front in the Vietnam War. 2005. (American Experience in Vietnam Ser.). (Illus.). 48p. (gr. 5-12). lib. bdg. 31.00 *(978-0-8368-5775-7(5)*, Gareth Stevens Secondary Library) Stevens, Gareth Publishing LLLP.

—How Do We Elect Our Leaders? 2008. (My American Government Ser.). (Illus.). 32p. (gr. 3-7). pap. 10.50 *(978-0-8368-8865-2(0))*; lib. bdg. 26.00 *(978-0-8368-8860-7(X))* Stevens, Gareth Publishing LLLP. (Gareth Stevens Learning Library).

—What Are the Parts of Government? 2008. (My American Government Ser.). 32p. (gr. 3-7). pap. 10.50 *(978-0-8368-8867-6(7)*, Gareth Stevens Learning Library) Stevens, Gareth Publishing LLLP.

—What Are the Parts of Government? 2008. (My American Government Ser.). (Illus.). 32p. (gr. 3-7). lib. bdg. 26.00 *(978-0-8368-8862-1(6)*, Gareth Stevens Learning Library) Stevens, Gareth Publishing LLLP.

Thompson, Jerry D., contrib. by. Symbols of American Freedom Set, 10-Volumes. 2009. (Symbols of American Freedom Ser.). (gr. 4-6). 300.00 *(978-1-60413-830-6(0)*, Chelsea Clubhouse) Facts On File, Inc.

Thornton, Jeremy. Tories & Patriots: Neighbors at War. 2009. (Building America's Democracy Ser.). 24p. (gr. 3-3). 42.50 *(978-1-61511-768-0(7)*, PowerKids Pr.) Rosen Publishing Group, Inc., The.

Torres, John. How Barack Obama Fought the War on Terrorism. 2017. (Presidents at War Ser.). 128p. (J). (gr. 8-8). lib. bdg. 37.27 ***(978-0-7660-8535-0(X))*** Enslow Pubs., Inc.

Tracy, Kathleen. The McCarthy Era. 2008. (Monumental Milestones Ser.). (Illus.). 48p. (YA). (gr. 4-7). lib. bdg. 29.95 *(978-1-58415-694-9(5))* Mitchell Lane Pubs., Inc.

—The Watergate Scandal. 2006. (Monumental Milestones Ser.). (Illus.). 48p. (YA). (gr. 4-7). lib. bdg. 29.95 *(978-1-58415-470-9(5))* Mitchell Lane Pubs., Inc.

Trumbauer, Lisa. Abraham Lincoln & the Civil War. 2016. (Life in the Time Of Ser.). (ENG.). 32p. pap. 8.29 *(978-1-4846-3822-4(0)*, Heinemann First Library) Heinemann-Raintree.

Tukan, Jaytoe Anthony, Sr. John Reid Edwards: The People's Senator. 2003. per. 19.95 *(978-0-9665909-4-4(5))* Kalawantis Publishing Services, Inc.

U. S. Government. (J). tchr. ed. 41.95 *(978-0-382-40684-3(2))* Cobblestone Publishing Co.

The U. S. Government Set: How It Works, 7 vols. Incl. Central Intelligence Agency. Wagner, Heather Lehr. (Illus.). 104p. (YA). lib. bdg. 30.00 *(978-0-7910-9282-8(8))*; Department of Homeland Security. Koestler-Grack, Rachel A. (Illus.). 104p. (J). lib. bdg. 30.00 *(978-0-7910-9286-6(0))*; Federal Bureau of Investigation. Wagner, Heather Lehr. (Illus.). 104p. (YA). lib. bdg. 30.00 *(978-0-7910-9281-1(X))*; House of Representatives. 2nd rev. ed. Koestler-Grack, Rachel A. 112p. (YA). 30.00 *(978-0-7910-9285-9(2))*; Presidency. 2nd rev. ed. Wagner, Heather Lehr. (Illus.). 112p. (YA). lib. bdg. 30.00 *(978-0-7910-9284-2(4))*; Senate. Anderson, Janet. 112p. (YA). 30.00 *(978-0-7910-9291-0(7))*; Supreme Court. 2nd rev. ed. Wagner, Heather Lehr. (Illus.). 104p. (YA). lib. bdg. 30.00 *(978-0-7910-9283-5(6))*; (gr. 5-9). 2007. (U. S. Government Ser.). 2007. 210.00 o.p. *(978-0-7910-9678-9(5)*, Chelsea Hse.) Facts On File, Inc.

Uschan, Michael V. Watergate. 2009. (American History Ser.). (ENG., Illus.). 104p. 39.40 *(978-1-4205-0135-3(6)*, Lucent Bks.) Cengage Gale.

Valelly, Richard M. The Voting Rights Act: Securing the Ballot, 00 vols. CQ Press Staff, ed. rev. ed. 2005. (Landmark Events in U. S. History Ser.). (ENG., Illus.). 400p. (gr. 9-18). 145.00 *(978-1-56802-989-4(6))* CQ Pr.

Vaughn, Wally G. & Davis, Mattie Campbell, eds. The Selma Campaign, 1963-1965: The Decisive Battle of the Civil Rights Movement. 2006. (ENG., Illus.). 244p. pap. 19.95 *(978-0-912469-44-7(7))* Majority Pr., The.

Vescia, Monique. The Emancipation Proclamation. 2016. (Let's Find Out! Primary Sources Ser.). 00032p. (J). (gr. 2-3). lib. bdg. 24.45 *(978-1-5081-0405-6(0))* Rosen Publishing Group, Inc., The.

Vierow, Wendy. The 1864 Presidential Election: A War-Weary Nation Reelects President Abraham Lincoln. 2009. (Headlines from History Ser.). 24p. (gr. 3-3). 42.50 *(978-1-61513-239-3(2)*, PowerKids Pr.) Rosen Publishing Group, Inc., The.

Wagner, Heather Lehr. Barack Obama. 2008. (Black Americans of Achievement: Legacy Edition Ser.). 104p. (gr. 6-12). pap. 11.95 *(978-1-60413-324-0(4)*, Checkmark Bks.) Facts On File, Inc.

Wallenfeldt, Jeff, ed. A New World Power: America from 1920 To 1945. 2012. (Documenting America: the Primary Source Documents of a Nation Ser.). (ENG., Illus.). 192p. (YA). (gr. 10-12). 82.20 *(978-1-61530-784-5(2))* Rosen Publishing Group, Inc., The.

Wallenfeldt, Jeffrey H. A New World Power: America from 1920 to 1945. 2012. (Documenting America: the Primary Source Documents of a Nation Ser.). (ENG., Illus.). 192p. (J). (gr. 10-12). lib. bdg. 41.10 *(978-1-61530-694-7(3))* Rosen Publishing Group, Inc., The.

Waryncia, Lou. Abraham Lincoln: Defender of the Union. Hale, Sarah Elder, ed. 2005. (ENG., Illus.). 48p. (J). (gr. 3-9). 17.95 *(978-0-8126-7902-1(4))* Cobblestone Publishing Co.

Watts, Duncan. US/UK Government & Politics, Vol. 2003. (Understandings MUP Ser.). (ENG.). 352p. pap., instr.'s gde. ed. 23.95 *(978-0-7190-6721-1(9))* Manchester Univ. Pr. GBR. Dist: Oxford Univ. Pr., Inc.

Waxman, Laura Hamilton. What Are the Articles of Confederation? And Other Questions about the Birth of the United States. 2012. (Six Questions of American History Ser.). (ENG.). 48p. (gr. 4-6). pap. 56.72 *(978-0-7613-9238-5(6))*; pap. 9.95 *(978-0-7613-8564-6(9))*; lib. bdg. 30.60 *(978-0-7613-5330-0(5))* Lerner Publishing Group.

Welch, Catherine A. Patrick Henry. 2006. (History Maker Bios Ser.). (Illus.). 48p. (J). (gr. 3-6). lib. bdg. 26.60 *(978-0-8225-5941-2(2)*, Lerner Pubns.) Lerner Publishing Group.

Westcott, Jim. Tea Party, Libertarian, & Other Political Parties. 2016. (Illus.). 64p. (J). *(978-1-61900-095-7(4))* Eldorado Ink.

Wheeler, Jill C. Abigail Adams, 1 vol. 2010. (First Ladies Set 2 Ser.). (ENG., Illus.). 32p. (YA). (gr. 1-4). 27.07 *(978-1-60453-629-4(2))* ABDO Publishing Co.

White, Casey. John Jay: Diplomat of the American Experiment. (Library of American Thinkers Ser.). 112p. 2009. (gr. 6-6). 66.50 *(978-1-60853-515-6(0)*, Rosen Reference) 2005. (Illus.). (YA). (gr. 5-9). lib. bdg. 34.60 *(978-1-4042-0507-9(1))* Rosen Publishing Group, Inc., The.

Williams, Robert F. & Williams, Mabel, as told by. Robert & Mabel Williams Resource Guide. 2005. (ENG., Illus.). 86p. pap. 10.00 *(978-0-9727422-7-6(1))* Freedom Archives, The.

Wilson, Steve. Andrew Jackson's Presidency: Democracy in Action. 2016. (Spotlight on American History Ser.). (Illus.). 24p. (J). (gr. 6-4). 26.25 *(978-1-5081-4938-5(0)*, PowerKids Pr.) Rosen Publishing Group, Inc., The.

Wingate, Kate. Political Reforms: American Citizens Gain More Control over Their Government. 2009. (Progressive Movement 1900-1920: Efforts to Reform America's New Industrial Society Ser.). 32p. (gr. 3-4). 47.90 *(978-1-60854-167-6(3))* Rosen Publishing Group, Inc., The.

Wingate, Katherine. Political Reforms: American Citizens Gain More Control over Their Government. (Progressive Movement, 1900-1920 — Efforts to Reform America's New Industrial Society Ser.). (Illus.). 32p. 2006. (ENG.). (gr. 4-8). pap. 10.00 *(978-1-4042-0853-7(4))* 2004. (YA). (gr. 5-9). lib. bdg. 22.50 *(978-1-4042-0192-7(0))* Rosen Publishing Group, Inc., The.

Wirkner, Linda. Learning about Life in the New American Nation with Graphic Organizers. (Graphic Organizers in Social Studies). 24p. 2009. (gr. 3-4). 42.50 *(978-1-61513-082-5(9)*, PowerKids Pr.) 2006. (ENG.). (gr. 4-6). pap. 8.25 *(978-1-4042-5050-5(6)*, Rosen Classroom) 2005. (Illus.). (J). (gr. 3-5). lib. bdg. 22.60 *(978-1-4042-2810-8(1)*, PowerKids Pr.) Rosen Publishing Group, Inc., The.

Wittekind, Erika. James Madison's Presidency. 2016. (Presidential Powerhouses Ser.). (ENG., Illus.). 104p. (J). (gr. 6-12). 35.99 *(978-1-4677-7929-6(6))*; 53.32 *(978-1-4677-8599-0(7)*, Lerner Pubns.) Lerner Publishing Group.

Wolfe, James & Callahan, Kerry P. Understanding the Articles of Confederation. 2015. (Primary Sources of American Political Documents Ser.). (ENG.). 128p. (J). (gr. 7-7). 37.27 *(978-0-7660-6866-7(8))* Enslow Pubs., Inc.

Wolfe, James & Viegas, Jennifer. Understanding the Declaration of Independence. 2015. (Primary Sources of American Political Documents Ser.). (ENG., Illus.). 112p. (J). (gr. 7-7). 37.27 *(978-0-7660-6874-2(9))* Enslow Pubs., Inc.

Wood, Alexander. Visit Independence Hall. 2012. (Landmarks of Liberty Ser.). (ENG.). 24p. (gr. 2-5). pap. 8.15 *(978-1-4339-6386-5(8)*, Gareth Stevens Learning Library); (J). lib. bdg. 22.60 *(978-1-4339-6384-1(1))* Stevens, Gareth Publishing LLLP.

Wood, Ethel, compiled by. The Presidency. 2004. (Historical Reader Ser.). (Illus.). 240p. (gr. 6-12). 13.32 *(978-0-618-04821-2(9)*, 2-00153) Holt McDougal.

Woog, Adam. The Emancipation Proclamation: Ending Slavery in America. 2009. (Milestones in American History Ser.). (Illus.). 128p. (gr. 6-12). 35.00 *(978-1-60413-307-3(4)*, Chelsea Hse.) Facts On File, Inc.

World Book, Inc. Staff, contrib. by. The World Book of America's Presidents, 2 vols. 2005. (Illus.). (gr. 5-12). 99.00 *(978-0-7166-3698-4(0))* World Bk., Inc.

Yero, Judith Lloyd. The Declaration of Independence. 2007. (Reading Expeditions Ser.). (ENG., Illus.). 32p. (J). pap. 17.95 *(978-0-7922-4554-4(7))* CENGAGE Learning.

Your Government in Action. (Illus.). (J). (gr. 3-6). 127.50 *(978-1-4042-2966-2(3))* Rosen Publishing Group, Inc., The.

Zahensky, Kenneth. George W. Bush. 2016. (J). lib. bdg. *(978-1-68048-526-4(1))* Rosen Publishing Group, Inc., The.

Zahensky, Kenneth, ed. George W. Bush. 2017. (Pivotal Presidents: Profiles in Leadership Ser.). 80p. (J). (gr. 12-13). 33.90 ***(978-1-68048-629-2(2)***, Britannica Educational Publishing) Rosen Publishing Group, Inc., The.

Ziff, John. The Modern Democratic Party. 2016. 64p. (J). *(978-1-61900-091-9(1))* Eldorado Ink.

—The Modern Republican Party. 2016. 64p. (J). *(978-1-61900-092-6(X))* Eldorado Ink.

—The United States Senate. 2016. 64p. (J). *(978-1-61900-096-4(2))* Eldorado Ink.

Zimmerman, Bob. The American Challenge: Twenty-One Winning Strategies for the 21st Century. 2003. (Illus.). 303p. (gr. 8-18). bds. 25.00 *(978-0-932555-04-5(7))* Uxor Pr., Inc.

Zuchora-Walske, Christine. Andrew Jackson's Presidency. 2016. (Presidential Powerhouses Ser.). (ENG., Illus.). 104p. (J). (gr. 6-12). 35.99 *(978-1-4677-7926-5(1))*; 53.32 *(978-1-4677-8548-8(2))* Lerner Publishing Group. (Lerner Pubns.).

UNITED STATES—POLITICS AND GOVERNMENT—FICTION

Barnes, Peter W. House Mouse, Senate Mouse. Barnes, Cheryl S., illus. 2012. (ENG.). 40p. (J). (gr. k-3). 16.99 *(978-1-59698-790-6(1)*, Little Patriot Pr.) Regnery Publishing, Inc., An Eagle Publishing Co.

Higgins, Helen Boyd. Alexander Hamilton: Young Statesman. Underdown, Harold D., ed. Morrison, Cathy, illus. 2nd rev. ed. 2008. (Young Patriots Ser.: 14). (ENG.). 120p. (J). (gr. 4-7). 15.95 *(978-1-882859-61-0(8)*, Young Patriots Series); per. 9.95 *(978-1-882859-62-7(6))* Patria Pr., Inc.

Levine, Ellen. In Trouble. 2011. (Carolrhoda YA Ser.). (ENG.). 208p. (YA). (gr. 9-12). 17.95 *(978-0-7613-6558-7(3)*, Carolrhoda Lab™) Lerner Publishing Group.

Limbaugh, Rush H., III & Limbaugh, Kathryn Adams. Rush Revere & the Presidency. 2016. (Rush Revere Ser.: 5). (ENG., Illus.). 272p. (gr. 4-7). 19.99 *(978-1-5011-5689-2(6)*, Threshold Editions) Threshold Editions.

Sargent, Dave & Sargent, Pat. Duke: (Dappled Palomino) Good Behavior, 30 vols., Vol. 23. Lenoir, Jane, illus. 2003. (Saddle up Ser.: Vol. 23). 42p. (J). pap. 10.95 *(978-1-56763-682-6(9))*; lib. bdg. 23.60 *(978-1-56763-681-9(0))* Ozark Publishing.

UNITED STATES—POST OFFICE DEPARTMENT

Wales, Dirk. A Lucky Dog: Owney, U.S. Rail Mail Mascot. Kenna, Diane, illus. 2003. 32p. (J). 15.95 *(978-0-9632459-0-8(2))* Great Plains Pr.

UNITED STATES—POSTAL SERVICE

see Postal Service

UNITED STATES—PRESIDENTS

see Presidents—United States

UNITED STATES—PUBLIC DEBTS

see Debts, Public

UNITED STATES—RACE RELATIONS

Adamson, Heather. The Civil Rights Movement [Scholastic]: An Interactive History Adventure. (You Choose: History Ser.). 112p. 2010. pap. 0.86 *(978-1-4296-5179-0(2))* 2009. (gr. 3-4). pap. 0.86 *(978-1-4296-4047-3(2))* Capstone Press of Coughlan Cos. (You Choose Bks.).

Adler, David A. A Picture Book of Rosa Parks. Casilla, Robert, illus. 2015. 32p. pap. 8.00 *(978-1-61003-405-0(8))* Center for the Collaborative Classroom.

African American Eras. 2010. *(978-1-4144-3600-5(9)); (978-1-4144-3598-5(3)); (978-1-4144-3597-8(5)); (978-1-4144-3599-2(1))* Cengage Gale. (UXL).

Altman, Linda Jacobs. The Politics of Slavery: Fiery National Debates Fueled by the Slave Economy. 2004. (Slavery in American History Ser.). (Illus.). 128p. (J). lib. bdg. 27.94 *(978-0-7660-2150-1(5))* Enslow Pubs., Inc.

Anderson, Wayne. Fighting Racial Discrimination: Treating All Americans Fairly under the Law. (Progressive Movement 1900-1920: Efforts to Reform America's New Industrial Society Ser.). 32p. 2009. (gr. 3-4). 47.90 *(978-1-60854-164-5(9))* 2004. (Illus.). (YA). (gr. 5-9). lib. bdg. 22.50 *(978-1-4042-0189-7(0))* Rosen Publishing Group, Inc., The.

Banting, Erinn. The Civil Rights Movement. 2008. (African American History Ser.). (Illus.). 48p. (YA). (gr. 5-8). lib. bdg. 29.05 *(978-1-59036-882-4(7))*; pap. 10.95 *(978-1-59036-883-1(5))* Weigl Pubs., Inc.

Bartoletti, Susan Campbell. They Called Themselves the K. K. K. The Birth of an American Terrorist Group. (ENG., Illus.). 176p. (YA). (gr. 7). 2014. pap. 12.99 *(978-0-544-22582-4(1)*, HMH Books For Young Readers) 2010. 19.00 *(978-0-618-44033-7(X))* Houghton Mifflin Harcourt Publishing Co.

Bauchner, Elizabeth. Teen Minorities in Rural North America: Growing up Different. 2009. (Youth in Rural North America Ser.). (Illus.). 96p. (YA). (gr. 3-7). lib. bdg. 22.95 *(978-1-4222-0014-8(0))* Mason Crest.

Bausum, Ann. Marching to the Mountaintop: How Poverty, Labor Fights, & Civil Rights Set the Stage for Martin Luther King Jr.'s Final Hours. 2012. (ENG., Illus.). 112p. (J). (gr. 5-9). lib. bdg. 28.90 *(978-1-4263-0940-3(6)*, National Geographic Children's Bks.) National Geographic Society.

Bausum, Ann & National Geographic Kids Staff. The March Against Fear: The Last Great Walk of the Civil Rights Movement & the Emergence of Black Power. 2017. (ENG., Illus.). 144p. (J). (gr. 7-9). 18.99 *(978-1-4263-2665-3(3)*, National Geographic Children's Bks.) National Geographic Society.

—Marching to the Mountaintop: How Poverty, Labor Fights, & Civil Rights Set the Stage for Martin Luther King Jr.'s Final Hours. 2012. (ENG., Illus.). 112p. (J). (gr. 5-9). 19.95 *(978-1-4263-0939-7(2)*, National Geographic Children's Bks.) National Geographic Society.

Berlatsky, Noah, ed. Interracial America. 2011. (Opposing Viewpoints Ser.). (Illus.). 240p. pap. 29.45 *(978-0-7377-5728-6(0)*, Greenhaven Pr., Inc.) Cengage Gale.

Berne, Emma. Face of Freedom: How the Photos of Frederick Douglass Celebrated Racial Equality. 2017. (Captured History Ser.). (ENG.). 64p. (gr. 5-7). pap. 9.10 ***(978-0-7565-5619-8(8)***, CPB Grades 4-8) Compass Point Bks.

Berne, Emma Carlson. Face of Freedom: How the Photos of Frederick Douglass Celebrated Racial Equality. 2017. (Captured History Ser.). (ENG.). 64p. (gr. 5-7). lib. bdg. 34.65 ***(978-0-7565-5617-4(1)***, CPB Grades 4-8) Compass Point Bks.

bjornlund, lydia. The Civil Rights Movement. 2012. (Illus.). 96p. (J). lib. bdg. *(978-1-60152-476-2(1))* ReferencePoint Pr., Inc.

Bolden, Tonya. Capital Days: Michael Shiner's Journal & the Growth of Our Nation's Capital. 2015. (ENG., Illus.). 96p. (J). (gr. 3-7). 21.95 *(978-1-4197-0733-9(7)*, Abrams Bks. for Young Readers) Abrams, Inc.

Bridges, Ruby. Ruby Bridges Goes to School: My True Story. 2009. (Scholastic Reader Level 2 Ser.). lib. bdg. 13.55 *(978-0-606-06808-6(2)*, Turtleback) Turtleback Bks.

Brimner, Larry Dane. Birmingham Sunday. 2010. (ENG., Illus.). 48p. (J). (gr. 5-18). 17.95 *(978-1-59078-613-0(0)*, Calkins Creek) Boyds Mills Pr.

Byers, Ann. African-American History from Emancipation to Today: Rising above the Ashes of Slavery. 2004. (Slavery in American History Ser.). (Illus.). 128p. (J). lib. bdg. 27.94 *(978-0-7660-2153-2(X))* Enslow Pubs., Inc.

Capek, Michael. Civil Rights Movement, 1 vol. 2013. (Essential Library of Social Change Ser.). (ENG.). 112p. (J). (gr. 6-12). lib. bdg. 35.64 *(978-1-61783-885-9(3)*, Essential Library) ABDO Publishing Co.

Coleman, Wim & Perrin, Pat. Racism on Trial: From the Medgar Evers Murder Case to Ghosts of Mississippi. 2009. (Famous Court Cases That Became Movies Ser.). (Illus.). 112p. (J). (gr. 7-12). lib. bdg. 33.27 *(978-0-7660-3059-6(8))* Enslow Pubs., Inc.

Conklin, Wendy. Civil Rights Movement, 1 vol. 2007. (Primary Source Readers Ser.). (ENG.). 32p. (J). (gr. 5-5). pap. 8.99 *(978-0-7439-0670-8(5))* Shell Educational Publishing.

Connolly, Sean. Racial & Ethnic Equality. 2005. (Campaigns for Change Ser.). (Illus.). 48p. (J). (gr. 6-9). lib. bdg. 29.95 *(978-1-58340-516-1(X))* Black Rabbit Bks.

Daly, Ruth. Rosa Parks. 2014. (J). *(978-1-4896-2452-9(X))* Weigl Pubs., Inc.

Davis, Kenneth C. In the Shadow of Liberty: The Hidden History of Slavery, Four Presidents, & Five Black Lives. 2016. (ENG., Illus.). 304p. (J). 17.99 *(978-1-62779-311-7(9)*, 9781627793117, Holt, Henry & Co. Bks. For Young Readers) Holt, Henry & Co.

De Medeiros, James. The Migration North. 2013. (J). 29.99 *(978-1-62127-193-2(5))* 2013. (J). pap. 14.95 *(978-1-62127-199-4(4))* 2008. (Illus.). 48p. (YA). (gr. 5-8). pap. 10.95 *(978-1-59036-881-7(9))* 2008. (Illus.). 48p. (YA). (gr. 5-8). lib. bdg. 29.05 *(978-1-59036-880-0(0))* Weigl Pubs., Inc.

Deal, Heidi. Perspectives on the Civil Rights Movement. 2018. (ENG.). 32p. (gr. 3-6). ***(978-1-63235-398-6(9)***, 12-Story Library) Pr. Room Editions LLC.

Deutsch, Stacia & Cohon, Rhody. Hot Pursuit: Murder in Mississippi. Orback, Craig, illus. 2010. (ENG.). 40p. (J). (gr. 3-5). pap. 7.95 *(978-0-7613-3956-4(6))*; lib. bdg. 17.95 *(978-0-7613-3955-7(8))* Lerner Publishing Group. (Kar-Ben Publishing).

Donaldson, Madeline. Ruby Bridges. 2009. (History Maker Biographies Ser.). (ENG., Illus.). 48p. (gr. 3-6). 27.93 *(978-0-7613-4220-5(6)*, Lerner Pubns.) Lerner Publishing Group.

Dray, Philip. Yours for Justice, Ida B. Wells: The Daring Life of a Crusading Journalist, 1 vol. Alcorn, Stephen, illus. 2008. (ENG.). 48p. (J). (gr. 5-9). 18.95 *(978-1-56145-417-4(6))* Peachtree Pubs.

Edwards, Judith. The History of the American Indians & the Reservation. 2008. (From Many Cultures, One History Ser.). (Illus.). 128p. (J). (gr. 3-7). lib. bdg. 33.27 *(978-0-7660-2798-5(8))* Enslow Pubs., Inc.

Ellis, Carol. African American Activists. 2012. (J). pap. *(978-1-4222-2384-0(1))* Mason Crest.

—African American Activists. Hill, Marc Lamont, ed. 2012. (Major Black Contributions from Emancipation to Civil Rights Ser.). 64p. (J). (gr. 5). 22.95 *(978-1-4222-2371-0(X))* Mason Crest.

Esty, Amos. Plessy V. Ferguson. 2012. (Civil Rights Movement Ser.). (Illus.). 112p. (YA). (gr. 7-12). 28.95 *(978-1-59935-182-7(X))* Reynolds, Morgan Inc.

Finegan, Jeffrey E., Sr. Colonel Washington & Me: George Washington, His Slave William Lee & Their Incredible Journey Together. Nikolopoulos, Stephanie, ed. 2012. (ENG., Illus.). 32p. (J). 16.95 *(978-0-9852819-0-8(1))* Seigle Bks.

Finlayson, Reggie. We Shall Overcome: The History of the American Civil Rights Movement. 2005. (People's History Ser.). (Illus.). 96p. (gr. 6-12). lib. bdg. 26.60 *(978-0-8225-0647-8(5))* Lerner Publishing Group.

Fireside, Harvey & Rauf, Don. Separate but Equal: Plessy V. Ferguson. 2016. (US Supreme Court Landmark Cases Ser.). (Illus.). 128p. (J). 37.27 *(978-0-7660-8434-6(5))* Enslow Pubs., Inc.

George, Charles. Black Nationalism. 2009. (Lucent Library of Black History Ser.). (ENG., Illus.). 128p. (gr. 7-10). 39.40 *(978-1-4205-0083-7(X)*, Lucent Bks.) Cengage Gale.

—Racism. Haugen, Hayley Mitchell, ed. 2007. (Social Issues Firsthand Ser.). (ENG.). 192p. (gr. 10-12). lib. bdg. 38.30 *(978-0-7377-2901-6(5)*, Greenhaven Pr., Inc.) Cengage Gale.

George, Enzo. The Civil Rights Movement. 2015. (Primary Sources in U. S. History Ser.). (ENG., Illus.). 48p. (J). (gr. 4-4). 31.36 *(978-1-5026-0496-5(5))* Cavendish Square Publishing.

Hardy, P. Stephen & Hardy, Sheila. Extraordinary People of the Civil Rights Movement. 2006. (Extraordinary People Ser.). (ENG., Illus.). 288p. (J). (gr. 6-18). lib. bdg. 40.00 *(978-0-516-25461-6(8)*, Children's Pr.) Scholastic Library Publishing.

Haskins, Jim. Delivering Justice: W. W. Law & the Fight for Civil Rights. Andrews, Benny, illus. 2008. (ENG.). 32p. (J). (gr. k-3). pap. 7.99 *(978-0-7636-3880-1(3))* Candlewick Pr.

Haugen, David M. Interracial Relationships. 2006. (At Issue Ser.). (ENG.). 128p. (gr. 10-12). 39.40 *(978-0-7377-2390-8(4))*; 98p. (YA). (gr. 8-12). 24.45 *(978-0-7377-2391-5(2)*, Greenhaven Pr., Inc.) Cengage Gale.

Haugen, Hayley Mitchell, ed. Race in Ralph Ellison's Invisible Man. 2011. (Social Issues in Literature Ser.). (Illus.). 224p. pap. 28.45 *(978-0-7377-5812-2(0)*, Greenhaven Pr., Inc.); (YA). (gr. 9-12). 40.95 *(978-0-7377-5811-5(2))* Cengage Gale.

Henneberg, Susan, ed. Race in America. 2017. (Opposing Viewpoints Ser.). 224p. (YA). (gr. 10-12). pap. 33.80 ***(978-1-5345-0028-0(6))***; lib. bdg. 48.80 ***(978-1-5345-0022-8(7))*** Greenhaven Publishing LLC. (Greenhaven Publishing).

Herda, D. J. Slavery & Citizenship: The Dred Scott Case. 2016. (US Supreme Court Landmark Cases Ser.). 128p. (J). 37.27 *(978-0-7660-8426-1(4))* Enslow Pubs., Inc.

Hermann, Spring. The Struggle for Equality: Women & Minorities in America. 2006. (American Saga Ser.). (Illus.). 128p. (J). (gr. 5-9). lib. bdg. 33.27 *(978-0-7660-2573-8(X))* Enslow Pubs., Inc.

Hiber, Amanda. Is the United States Ready for a Minority President? 2007. (At Issue Ser.). (ENG., Illus.). 128p. (gr. 10-12). 39.40 *(978-0-7377-3878-0(2)*, Greenhaven Pr., Inc.) Cengage Gale.

Hinman, Bonnie. Eternal Vigilance: The Story of Ida B. Wells-Barnett. 2011. (Civil Rights Leaders Ser.). 128p. (gr. 6-10). lib. bdg. 28.95 *(978-1-59935-111-7(0))* Reynolds, Morgan Inc.

Hinton, Kerry. The Black Power Movement & Civil Unrest. 2017. (J). pap. ***(978-1-5383-8016-1(1))*** Rosen Publishing Group, Inc., The.

Hoe, Susan C. Rosa Parks. 2009. (Sharing the American Dream Ser.). 64p. (YA). (gr. 7-12). 22.95 *(978-1-4222-0597-6(5))* Mason Crest.

Holliday, Laurel. Dreaming in Color Living in Black & White: Our Own Stories of Growing up Black in America. 2012. (ENG.). 208p. (YA). (gr. 7). pap. 10.99 *(978-1-4424-7177-1(8)*, Simon Pulse) Simon Pulse.

Honders, Christine. Mexican American Rights Movement. 2016. (Civic Participation: Working for Civil Rights Ser.). 00032p. (J). (gr. 5-5). pap. 10.00 *(978-1-4994-2684-7(4)*, PowerKids Pr.) Rosen Publishing Group, Inc., The.

Hooks, Gwendolyn. If You Were a Kid During the Civil Rights Movement. 2017. (If You Were a Kid Ser.). (ENG., Illus.). 32p. (J). lib. bdg. 26.00 *(978-0-531-22384-0(1)*, Children's Pr.) Scholastic Library Publishing.

Hopkinson, Deborah. Sweet Land of Liberty, 1 vol. Jenkins, Leonard, illus. 2007. (ENG.). 32p. (J). (gr. 1-5). 16.95 *(978-1-56145-395-5(1))* Peachtree Pubs.

Houtman, Jacqueline, et al. Bayard Rustin: The Invisible Activist. 2014. (J). pap. *(978-1-937768-58-4(9))* QuakerPress.

Howard, Melanie A. Civil Rights Marches, 1 vol. 2004. (American Moments Ser.). (ENG.). 48p. (gr. 4-8). 27.07 *(978-1-59197-282-2(5)*, Abdo & Daughters) ABDO Publishing Co.

Jakoubek, Robert. Martin Luther King Jr. 2008. (Black Americans of Achievement: Legacy Edition Ser.). 112p. (gr. 6-12). pap. 11.95 *(978-1-60413-328-8(7)*, Checkmark Bks.) Facts On File, Inc.

Jakoubek, Robert E. Martin Luther King, Jr. Civil Rights Leader. 2004. (Black Americans of Achievement Ser.). (Illus.). 112p. (gr. 6-12). 35.00 *(978-0-7910-8161-7(3)*, Chelsea Hse.) Facts On File, Inc.

Jeffrey, Gary. The Little Rock Nine & the Fight for Equal Education. 2012. (Graphic History of the Civil Rights Movement Ser.). (Illus.). 24p. (J). (gr. 3-8). lib. bdg. 23.95 *(978-1-4339-7483-0(5))* Stevens, Gareth Publishing LLLP.

—Medgar Evers & the NAACP. 2012. (Graphic History of the Civil Rights Movement Ser.). 24p. (J). (gr. 3-8). pap. 8.15 *(978-1-4339-7496-0(7))*; lib. bdg. 23.95 *(978-1-4339-7495-3(9))* Stevens, Gareth Publishing LLLP.

—Rosa Parks & the Montgomery Bus Boycott. 2012. (Graphic History of the Civil Rights Movement Ser.). (Illus.). 24p. (J). (gr. 3-8). pap. 8.15 *(978-1-4339-7500-4(9))*; lib. bdg. 23.95 *(978-1-4339-7499-1(1))* Stevens, Gareth Publishing LLLP.

Kallen, Stuart A. A History of Free Blacks in America. 2006. (Lucent Library of Black History). (ENG., Illus.). 112p. (YA). (gr. 7-10). lib. bdg. 33.45 *(978-1-59018-776-0(8)*, Lucent Bks.) Cengage Gale.

Kanefield, Teri. The Girl from the Tar Paper School: Barbara Rose Johns & the Advent of the Civil Rights Movement. 2014. (ENG., Illus.). 56p. (J). (gr. 3-7). 19.95 *(978-1-4197-0796-4(5)*, Abrams Bks. for Young Readers) Abrams, Inc.

Kemp, Kristin. Amazing Americans: Rosa Parks, 1 vol. rev. ed. 2014. (Primary Source Readers Content & Literacy Ser.). (ENG., Illus.). 32p. (gr. 3-3). pap. 8.99 *(978-1-4333-7375-6(0))* Teacher Created Materials, Inc.

—Amazing Americans: Thurgood Marshall, 1 vol. rev. ed. 2014. (Primary Source Readers Content & Literacy Ser.). (ENG., Illus.). 32p. (gr. 3-3). pap. 8.99 *(978-1-4333-7374-9(2))* Teacher Created Materials, Inc.

King, Martin Luther, Jr. I Have a Dream. 2007. (Illus.). 40p. (J). (gr. -1-3). 14.65 *(978-0-7569-8119-8(0))* Perfection Learning Corp.

Klein, Carol Swartout. Painting for Peace in Ferguson. 2nd ed. 2015. (ENG.). 54p. (J). (gr. 2-3). 25.95 *(978-0-9963901-0-1(3))*; pap. 15.95 *(978-0-9892079-9-7(4))* TreeHse. Publishing Group.

Krumm, Brian. The Little Rock Nine: A Primary Source Exploration of the Battle for School Integration, 1 vol. 2014. (We Shall Overcome Ser.). (ENG.). 32p. (gr. 3-4). lib. bdg. 27.32 *(978-1-4914-0225-2(3))* Capstone Press of Coughlan Cos.

Levinson, Cynthia. The Youngest Marcher: The Story of a Young Civil Rights Activist. Brantley-Newton, Vanessa, illus. 2017. (ENG.). 40p. (J). (gr. k-5). 17.99 *(978-1-4814-0070-1(3))* Simon & Schuster, Inc.

Linde, Barbara M. Rosa Parks. 2011. (Civil Rights Crusaders Ser.). (Illus.). 24p. (gr. 2-5). (J). pap. 8.15 *(978-1-4339-5696-6(9)*, Gareth Stevens Learning Library); (YA). lib. bdg. 22.60 *(978-1-4339-5694-2(2))* Stevens, Gareth Publishing LLLP.

Lo Bosco, Maryellen. Confronting Racism. 2017. pap. ***(978-1-5383-8176-2(1))*** Rosen Publishing Group, Inc., The.

Loughran, P. J., illus. Turning 15 on the Road to Freedom: My Story of the Selma Voting Rights March. 2015. (ENG.). 128p. (YA). (gr. 7). 19.99 *(978-0-8037-4123-2(5)*, Dial Bks) Penguin Young Readers Group.

Lowery, Zoe. Barack Obama & a "Post-Racial Society" 2015. (African American Experience: from Slavery to the Presidency Ser.). (ENG., Illus.). 80p. (J). (gr. 7-8). 32.90 *(978-1-68048-051-1(0)*, Britannica Educational Publishing) Rosen Publishing Group, Inc., The.

Lowery, Zoe, ed. Barack Obama & the Idea of a Postracial Society. 2015. (African American Experience: from Slavery to the Presidency Ser.). (ENG.). 80p. (YA). (gr. 7-8). 65.80 *(978-1-68048-052-8(9)*, Britannica Educational Publishing) Rosen Publishing Group, Inc., The.

Lucas, Eileen. Cracking the Wall: The Struggles of the Little Rock Nine. Anthony, Mark, illus. 2007. pap. 37.95 incl. audio *(978-1-59519-939-3(X))*; pap. 39.95 incl. audio compact disk *(978-1-59519-943-0(8))* Live Oak Media.

Mahoney, Emily Jankowski. American Civil Rights Movement. 2016. (Civic Participation: Working for Civil Rights Ser.). 00032p. (J). (gr. 5-5). pap. 10.00 *(978-1-4994-2791-2(3)*, PowerKids Pr.) Rosen Publishing Group, Inc., The.

Main, Mary & Thomason, Cathy. African-Americans in Law & Politics. 2012. (J). pap. *(978-1-4222-2391-8(4))* Mason Crest.

—African-Americans in Law & Politics. Hill, Marc Lamont, ed. 2012. (Major Black Contributions from Emancipation to Civil Rights Ser.). 64p. (J). (gr. 5). 22.95 *(978-1-4222-2378-9(7))* Mason Crest.

Mara, Wil. Rosa Parks: Mother of the Civil Rights Movement. 2014. (Rookie Biographies(tm) Ser.). (ENG.). 32p. (J). lib. bdg. 25.00 *(978-0-531-20561-7(4))* Scholastic Library Publishing.

Marcovitz, Hal. Race Relations. 2008. (Gallup Major Trends & Events Ser.). (Illus.). 127p. (YA). (gr. 7-18). lib. bdg. 22.95 *(978-1-59084-968-2(X))* Mason Crest.

—Teens & Race. Developed in Association with the Gallup Organization Staff, ed. 2013. (Gallup Youth Survey: Major Issues & Trends Ser.: 14). 112p. (J). (gr. 7-18). 24.95 *(978-1-4222-2955-2(6))* Mason Crest.

McClaurin, Irma & Schomp, Virginia. Facing the Future. 2007. (Drama of African-American History Ser.). 80p. (gr. 6). lib. bdg. 35.64 *(978-0-7614-2644-8(2)*, Benchmark Bks.) Marshall Cavendish Corp.

McKissack, Patricia C. & McKissack, Fredrick L. Ida B. Wells-Barnett: Fighter for Justice. 2013. (Famous African Americans Ser.). 24p. (J). (gr. k-3). pap. 7.95 *(978-1-4644-0198-5(5)*, Enslow Elementary); (Illus.). 22.60 *(978-0-7660-4108-0(5))* Enslow Pubs., Inc.

McNeese, Tim. Plessy V. Ferguson: Separate but Equal. 2006. (Great Supreme Court Decisions Ser.). (Illus.). 136p. (YA). (gr. 5-9). lib. bdg. 32.95 *(978-0-7910-9237-8(2))* Facts On File, Inc.

Michelson, Richard. As Good As Anybody. Colón, Raúl, illus. 2013. (ENG.). 40p. (J). (gr. 1-4). 7.99 *(978-0-385-75387-6(X)*, Dragonfly Bks.) Random Hse. Children's Bks.

Miller, Jake. The March from Selma to Montgomery: African Americans Demand the Vote. 2004. (Library of the Civil Rights Movement Ser.). (Illus.). 24p. (J). lib. bdg. 22.60 *(978-0-8239-6254-9(7)*, PowerKids Pr.) Rosen Publishing Group, Inc., The.

Mooney, Carla. Confronting Discrimination Against Immigrants. 2017. (J). pap. ***(978-1-5383-8164-9(8)***, Rosen Young Adult) Rosen Publishing Group, Inc., The.

Morretta, Alison. Ida B. Wells-Barnett & the Crusade Against Lynching. 2016. (Primary Sources of the Civil Rights Movement Ser.). (Illus.). 64p. (J). (gr. 6-6). 34.21 *(978-1-5026-1874-0(5))* Cavendish Square Publishing.

Myers, Walter Dean. Ida B. Wells: Let the Truth Be Told. Christensen, Bonnie, illus. 2008. (ENG.). 40p. (J). (gr. -1-3). 16.99 *(978-0-06-027705-5(X)*, Amistad) HarperCollins Pubs.

Nathan, Amy. Round & Round Together: Taking a Merry-Go-Round Ride into the Civil Rights Movement. 2011. (Nautilus Ser.). (ENG., Illus.). 200p. (gr. 4-10). pap. 14.95 *(978-1-58988-071-9(4))* Dry, Paul Bks., Inc.

Ollhoff, Jim. The Civil Rights Movement, 1 vol. 2011. (African American History Ser.). (ENG., Illus.). 32p. (YA). (gr. 5-9). 27.07 *(978-1-61714-709-8(5))* ABDO Publishing Co.

—Courage & Growth, 1 vol. 2011. (African American History Ser.). (ENG., Illus.). 32p. (YA). (gr. 5-9). lib. bdg. 27.07 *(978-1-61714-711-1(7))* ABDO Publishing Co.

O'Maley, Elizabeth. Bones on the Ground. 2014. (J). *(978-0-87195-362-9(5))* Indiana Historical Society.

Orr, Tamra. Coping with Racial Inequality. 2017. (Coping Ser.). 112p. (gr. 12-12). 37.10 ***(978-1-5081-7396-0(6)***, Rosen Young Adult) Rosen Publishing Group, Inc., The.

Osborne, Linda Barrett. Miles to Go for Freedom: Segregation & Civil Rights in the Jim Crow Years. 2012. (ENG., Illus.). 128p. (J). (gr. 3-7). 25.99 *(978-1-4197-0020-0(0)*, Abrams Bks. for Young Readers) Abrams, Inc.

Otfinoski, Steven. 1990-2010. 2009. (Hispanic America 2 Ser.). 80p. (gr. 5). 34.21 *(978-0-7614-4180-9(8))* Marshall Cavendish Corp.

Parks, Peggy J. How Prevalent Is Racism in Society? 2014. (In Controversy Ser.). (ENG., Illus.). 96p. (J). lib. bdg. *(978-1-60152-716-5(0))* ReferencePoint Pr., Inc.

Partridge, Elizabeth. Marching for Freedom: Walk Together, Children, & Don't You Grow Weary. 2009. (ENG.). 80p. (J). (gr. 5-18). 19.99 *(978-0-670-01189-6(4)*, Viking Books for Young Readers) Penguin Young Readers Group.

Peacock, Thomas Love & Wisuri, Marlene. To Be Free: Understanding & eliminating Racism. 2010. (ENG., Illus.). 104p. (J). 24.00 *(978-1-890434-80-9(9))* Afton Historical Society Pr.

Perritano, John. Free at Last! How the Freeing of the Slaves Changed American History. 2008. (Graphic America Ser.). (ENG., Illus.). 32p. (J). (gr. 3-6). pap. *(978-0-7787-4212-8(1))*; lib. bdg. *(978-0-7787-4185-5(0))* Crabtree Publishing Co.

Perry, M. LaVora. A History of the Civil Rights Movement. 2012. (J). pap. *(978-1-4222-2395-6(7))* Mason Crest.

—A History of the Civil Rights Movement. Hill, Marc Lamont, ed. 2012. (Major Black Contributions from Emancipation to Civil Rights Ser.). 64p. (J). (gr. 5). 22.95 *(978-1-4222-2382-6(5))* Mason Crest.

Pferdehirt, Julia. Blue Jenkins: Working for Workers. 2011. (Badger Biographies Ser.). (ENG., Illus.). 160p. (J). pap. 12.95 *(978-0-87020-427-2(0))* Wisconsin Historical Society.

Pingry, Patricia A. The Story of Rosa Parks. Walker, Steven, illus. 2016. (J). *(978-0-8249-1987-0(4)*, Ideal Pubns.) Worthy Publishing.

Rappaport, Doreen. Nobody Gonna Turn Me 'Round: Stories & Songs of the Civil Rights Movement. Evans, Shane W., illus. 2006. (ENG.). 64p. (J). (gr. 4-7). 19.99 *(978-0-7636-1927-5(2))* Candlewick Pr.

—Nobody Gonna Turn Me 'Round: Stories & Songs of the Civil Rights Movement. Evans, Shane W., illus. 2008. (ENG.). 64p. (J). (gr. 4-7). pap. 9.99 *(978-0-7636-3892-4(7))* Candlewick Pr.

Regis, Frankye. A Voice from the Civil Rights Era, 1 vol. 2004. (Voices of Twentieth-Century Conflict Ser.). (Illus.). 184p. (C). 43.00 *(978-0-313-32998-2(2)*, GR2998, Greenwood) ABC-CLIO, LLC.

Robinson, Sharon. Promises to Keep: How Jackie Robinson Changed America. 2004. (ENG., Illus.). 64p. (J). (gr. 3-7). 17.99 *(978-0-439-42592-6(1))* Scholastic, Inc.

Robinson, Tom. Malcolm X: Rights Activist & Nation of Islam Leader, 1 vol. 2013. (Essential Lives Set 8 Ser.). (ENG.). 112p. (J). (gr. 6-12). lib. bdg. 35.64 *(978-1-61783-893-4(4)*, Essential Library) ABDO Publishing Co.

Sanna, Ellyn. Native North American Indians. 2012. (Gallup Guides for Youth Facing Persistent Prejudice Ser.). 64p. (J). (gr. 7-8). 22.95 *(978-1-4222-2469-4(4))*; pap. 9.95 *(978-1-4222-2478-6(3))* Mason Crest.

Schraff, Anne E. Ida B. Wells-Barnett: Strike a Blow Against Glaring Evil. 2008. (African-American Biography Library). (Illus.). 128p. (J). (gr. 6-18). lib. bdg. 33.27 *(978-0-7660-2704-6(X))* Enslow Pubs., Inc.

Schuetz, Rachael Law. The Long Road to Change: An American Story of Civil Rights & Barack Obama's Journey to the White House. 2009. 36p. (J). 16.00 *(978-0-615-27983-1(X))* NRS Enterprises.

Schwartz, Heather E. Freedom Riders: A Primary Source Exploration of the Struggle for Racial Justice. 2014. (We Shall Overcome Ser.). (ENG.). 32p. (gr. 3-4). lib. bdg. 27.32 *(978-1-4914-0222-1(9))* Capstone Press of Coughlan Cos.

Shea, Therese. Rosa Parks, 1 vol. 2015. (ENG., Illus.). 32p. (J). 23.45 *(978-1-62275-697-1(5)*, Britannica Educational Publishing) Rosen Publishing Group, Inc., The.

Shelton, Paula Young. Child of the Civil Rights Movement. Colón, Raúl, illus. 2013. (ENG.). 48p. (J). (gr. -1-3). 7.99 *(978-0-385-37606-8(5)*, Dragonfly Bks.) Random Hse. Children's Bks.

Spilsbury, Richard. Who Marched for Civil Rights?, 1 vol. HL Studios Staff, illus. 2014. (Primary Source Detectives Ser.). (ENG.). 64p. (gr. 7-8). lib. bdg. 35.99 *(978-1-4329-9604-8(5))* Heinemann-Raintree.

Staley, Erin. Martin Luther King Jr. & the Speech That Inspired the World. 2014. (Celebration of the Civil Rights Movement Ser.). 80p. (YA). (gr. 7-12). 34.25 *(978-1-4777-7745-9(8))* Rosen Publishing Group, Inc., The.

Staton, Hilarie N. Civil Rights. 2015. (ENG.). 48p. (J). *(978-0-7787-1549-8(3))* Crabtree Publishing Co.

Supples, Kevin, et al. The Civil Rights Movement. 2006. (Nonfiction Reading & Writing Workshops Ser.). (ENG., Illus.). 40p. (J). pap. 19.95 *(978-0-7922-8628-8(6))* CENGAGE Learning.

Takaki, Ronald. A Different Mirror for Young People: A History of Multicultural America. 2012. (For Young People Ser.). (ENG., Illus.). 378p. (J). (gr. 5). pap. 18.95 *(978-1-60980-416-9(3)*, Triangle Square) Seven Stories Pr.

Taylor-Butler, Christine. Rosa Parks. 2015. (ENG., Illus.). 48p. (J). pap. 6.95 (978-0-531-21209-7(2), Orchard Bks.) Scholastic Library Publishing.

Tisdale, Rachel. The Little Rock Nine, 1 vol., 1. 2014. (We Shall Overcome Ser.). (ENG.). 32p. (J). (gr. 3-6). 26.25 (978-1-4777-6057-4(1), PowerKids Pr.) Rosen Publishing Group, Inc., The.

—The Montgomery Bus Boycott, 1 vol., 1. 2014. (We Shall Overcome Ser.). (ENG., Illus.). 32p. (J). (gr. 3-6). 26.25 (978-1-4777-6053-6(9), PowerKids Pr.) Rosen Publishing Group, Inc., The.

Toth, Henrietta. The Murder of Emmett Till. 2017. pap. **(978-1-5383-8054-3(4))** Rosen Publishing Group, Inc., The.

Tougas, Shelley. Birmingham 1963: How a Photograph Rallied Civil Rights Support, 1 vol. 2011. (Captured History Ser.). (ENG.). 64p. (gr. 5-7). pap. 9.10 (978-0-7565-4446-1(7), CPB Grades 4-8) Compass Point Bks.

—Little Rock Girl 1957: How a Photograph Changed the Fight for Integration, 1 vol. 2011. (Captured History Ser.). (ENG.). 64p. (gr. 5-7). pap. 9.10 (978-0-7565-4512-3(9)); lib. bdg. 34.65 (978-0-7565-4440-9(8)) Compass Point Bks. (CPB Grades 4-8).

Tracy, Kathleen. The Life & Times of Rosa Parks. 2008. (Illus.). 48p. (J). (gr. 4-8). lib. bdg. 29.95 (978-1-58415-666-6(X)) Mitchell Lane Pubs., Inc.

Uschan, Michael V. The Civil Rights Movement. 2010. (American History Ser.). (ENG.). 128p. 34.80 (978-1-4205-0261-9(1), Lucent Bks.) Cengage Gale.

Walsh, Frank & O'Hern, Kerri. The Montgomery Bus Boycott. McHargue, D., illus. 2006. (Graphic Histories Ser.). 32p. (gr. 5-8). lib. bdg. 27.00 (978-0-8368-6205-8(8)) Stevens, Gareth Publishing LLLP.

Weatherford, Carole Boston. The Beatitudes: From Slavery to Civil Rights. Ladwig, Tim, illus. 2009. (ENG.). 36p. (J). (gr. 3-7). 17.00 (978-0-8028-5352-3(8), Eerdmans Bks For Young Readers) Eerdmans, William B. Publishing Co.

Weil, Ann. Medgar Evers, 1 vol. 2012. (American Biographies Ser.). (ENG.). 48p. (gr. 4-6). pap. 9.95 (978-1-4329-6465-8(8), NA-h) Heinemann-Raintree.

—Medgar Evers, 1 vol. Oxford Bible Staff, illus. 2012. (American Biographies Ser.). (ENG.). 48p. (gr. 4-6). lib. bdg. 32.65 (978-1-4329-6454-2(2), NA-h) Heinemann-Raintree.

Welch, Catherine A. Ida B. Wells-Barnett: Powerhouse with a Pen. 2005. (Trailblazers Biographies Ser.). (Illus.). 112p. (gr. 5-9). 27.93 (978-1-57505-352-3(7)) Lerner Publishing Group.

Winter, Max. Civil Rights Movement, 1 vol. 2014. (African-American History Ser.). (ENG.). 48p. (gr. 8-12). lib. bdg. 32.79 (978-1-62403-145-8(5)) ABDO Publishing Co.

Woog, Adam. The Fight Renewed: The Civil Rights Movement. 2005. (Lucent Library of Black History). (ENG., Illus.). 112p. (YA). (gr. 7-10). lib. bdg. 33.45 (978-1-59018-701-2(6), Lucent Bks.) Cengage Gale.

World Book, Inc Staff, contrib. by. African American Civil Rights Movement. 2010. (J). (978-0-7166-1500-2(2)) World Bk., Inc.

Worth, Richard. 1950s to 1960s. 2009. (Hispanic America 2 Ser.). 80p. (gr. 5). 34.21 (978-0-7614-4177-9(8)) Marshall Cavendish GBR. Dist: Marshall Cavendish Corp.

Zeiger, Jennifer. The Civil Rights Movement. 2011. (Cornerstones of Freedom, Third Ser.). (Illus.). 64p. (J). (ENG.). pap. 8.95 (978-0-531-26554-3(4)); (ABK., lib. bdg. 30.00 (978-0-531-25029-7(6)) Scholastic Library Publishing. (Children's Pr.).

UNITED STATES—RELIGION

Capaccio, George. Religion. 2014. (Illus.). 80p. (J). pap. (978-1-62712-889-6(1)) Cavendish Square Publishing.

—Religion in Colonial America. 2014. (Life in Colonial America Ser.). (Illus.). 80p. (J). (gr. 6-8). lib. bdg. 35.64 (978-1-62712-888-9(3)) Cavendish Square Publishing.

Haugen, David M. & Musser, Susan. Religion in America. 2010. (Opposing Viewpoints Ser.). (ENG.). 224p. (gr. 10-12). pap. 33.80 (978-0-7377-4989-2(X), Greenhaven Pr., Inc.) Cengage Gale.

Head, Tom. Freedom of Religion. 2005. (American Rights Ser.). (Illus.). 144p. (gr. 5-8). 35.00 (978-0-8160-5664-4(1)) Facts On File, Inc.

Melman, Anna. Muslims in America. 2010. (World of Islam Ser.). (Illus.). 64p. (YA). (gr. 4-7). lib. bdg. 22.95 (978-1-4222-0535-8(5)) Mason Crest.

Musser, Susan. Religion in America. Haugen, David M., ed. 2010. (Opposing Viewpoints Ser.). (ENG.). 240p. 42.95 (978-0-7377-4988-5(1), Greenhaven Pr., Inc.) Cengage Gale.

Nardo, Don. Religious Beliefs in Colonial America. 2010. (Lucent Library of Historical Eras Ser.). (ENG., Illus.). 128p. (gr. 7-10). 39.40 (978-1-4205-0266-4(2)) Cengage Gale.

Radomski, Kassandra, et al. United States by Region. 2016. (United States by Region Ser.). (ENG.). 32p. (gr. 3-4). 136.60 (978-1-5157-2465-0(4), Fact Finders) Capstone Press of Coughlan Cos.

Smith-Llera, Danielle, et al. United States by Region. 2016. (United States by Region Ser.). (ENG.). 32p. (gr. 3-4). pap. 39.75 (978-1-5157-2466-7(2), Fact Finders) Capstone Press of Coughlan Cos.

Tiner, John. The Story of the Pledge of Allegiance: Discovering Our Nations Heritage. 2003. (Discovering Our Nation's Heritage Ser.). (Illus.). 48p. (J). 9.99 (978-0-89051-393-4(7)) Master Bks.

UNITED STATES—SOCIAL CONDITIONS

America Debates, 6 vols., Set. Incl. America Debates Civil Liberties & Terrorism. Freedman, Jeri. lib. bdg. 31.95 (978-1-4042-1927-4(7)); America Debates Global Warming: Crisis or Myth? Robinson, Matthew. lib. bdg. 31.95 (978-1-4042-1925-0(0)); America Debates Privacy Versus Security. Freedman, Jeri. lib. bdg. 31.95 (978-1-4042-1929-8(3)); America Debates Stem Cell Research. Freedman, Jeri. lib. bdg. 31.95 (978-1-4042-1928-1(5)); America Debates United States Policy on Immigration. Ambrosek, Renee. lib. bdg. 31.95 (978-1-4042-1924-3(2)); (Illus.). 64p. (YA). (gr. 5-9). 2007. 2007. Set lib. bdg. 175.50 (978-1-4042-1100-1(4)) Rosen Publishing Group, Inc., The.

Amidon Lusted, Marcia. The Great Depression: Experience the 1930s from the Dust Bowl to the New Deal. Casteel, Tom, illus. 2016. (Inquire & Investigate Ser.). (ENG.). 128p. (J). (gr. 6-10). 22.95 (978-1-61930-336-2(1), 1401073) Open City Bks.

—The Great Depression: Experience the 1930's from the Dust Bowl to the New Deal. Casteel, Tom, illus. 2016. (Inquire & Investigate Ser.). (ENG.). 128p. (J). (gr. 6-10). pap. 17.95 (978-1-61930-340-9(X), 1401073) Octavio Publishing.

—The Roaring Twenties: Discover the Era of Prohibition, Flappers, & Jazz. Keller, Jennifer, illus. 2014. (Inquire & Investigate Ser.). (ENG.). 128p. (J). (gr. 6-10). 22.95 (978-1-61930-260-0(8)) Open City Bks.

Anderson, Dale. The Home Fronts in the Civil War. 2004. (World Almanac Library of the Civil War). (Illus.). 48p. (gr. 5-12). lib. bdg. 31.00 (978-0-8368-5587-6(6), Gareth Stevens Secondary Library) Stevens, Gareth Publishing LLLP.

Bailey Association Staff & Gorman, Jacqueline Laks. The Modern Feminist Movement. 2011. (Cultural History of Women in America Ser.). (Illus.). 64p. (gr. 6-12). 35.00 (978-1-60413-935-8(8), Chelsea Hse.) Facts On File, Inc.

Bailey Association Staff & Senker, Cath. Strength in Numbers. 2011. (Cultural History of Women in America Ser.). (Illus.). 64p. (gr. 6-12). 35.00 (978-1-60413-931-0(5), Chelsea Hse.) Facts On File, Inc.

—Women Claim the Vote. 2011. (Cultural History of Women in America Ser.). (Illus.). 64p. (gr. 6-12). 35.00 (978-1-60413-930-3(7), Chelsea Hse.) Facts On File, Inc.

Bailey Association Staff, et al. Women of Today. 2011. (Cultural History of Women in America Ser.). (Illus.). 64p. (gr. 6-12). 35.00 (978-1-60413-936-5(6), Chelsea Hse.) Facts On File, Inc.

Bauchner, Elizabeth. Teen Minorities in Rural North America: Growing up Different. 2009. (Youth in Rural North America Ser.). (Illus.). 96p. (YA). (gr. 3-7). lib. bdg. 22.95 (978-1-4222-0014-8(0)) Mason Crest.

Bausum, Ann. Muckrakers: How Ida Tarbell, Upton Sinclair, & Lincoln Steffens Helped Expose Scandal, Inspire Reform, & Invent Investigative Journalism. 2007. (ENG., Illus.). 112p. (J). (gr. 5-9). 21.95 (978-1-4263-0137-7(5), National Geographic Children's Bks.) National Geographic Society.

—Unraveling Freedom: The Battle for Democracy on the Homefront During World War I. 2010. (ENG., Illus.). 96p. (J). (gr. 5-18). 19.95 (978-1-4263-0702-7(0)); 28.90 (978-1-4263-0703-4(9)) National Geographic Society. (National Geographic Children's Bks.).

Baxter, Roberta. The Northern Home Front of the Civil War, 1 vol. (Why We Fought: the Civil War Ser.). (ENG.). 48p. (gr. 3-6). 2011. pap. 9.95 (978-1-4329-3917-5(3)) 2010. 33.32 (978-1-4329-3911-3(4)) Heinemann-Raintree. (Heinemann InfoSearch).

Boehm, Richard G., et al. Game Time! United States. 2003. (Harcourt Brace Social Studies). (gr. k-7). 7.80 (978-0-15-312367-2(2)) Harcourt Schl. Pubs.

Bolden, Tonya. FDR's Alphabet Soup: New Deal America, 1932-1939. 2010. (ENG.). 144p. (YA). (gr. 7). 19.99 (978-0-375-85214-5(X), Knopf Bks. for Young Readers) Random Hse. Children's Bks.

Brill, Marlene Targ. America in the 1900s. 2009. (Decades of Twentieth-Century America Ser.). (ENG.). 144p. (gr. 5-12). lib. bdg. 38.60 (978-0-8225-3436-5(3)) Lerner Publishing Group.

Bringle, Jennifer. Homelessness in America Today. 2010. (In the News Ser.). (ENG.). 64p. (YA). pap. 12.95 (978-1-4488-1683-5(1)); (gr. 7-12). lib. bdg. 31.95 (978-1-4358-9451-8(0)) Rosen Publishing Group, Inc., The.

Brown, Harriet & Witowski, Teri. Kit's World: A Girl's-Eye View of the Great Depression. Rane, Walter & Hood, Philip, illus. 2008. 30p. (YA). (gr. 3-18). 24.95 (978-1-59369-459-3(8)) American Girl Publishing, Inc.

Cartlidge, Cherese. Homeless Youth. 2016. (ENG., Illus.). 80p. (J). (gr. 5-12). (978-1-60152-978-7(3)) ReferencePoint Pr., Inc.

Catalano, Angela. Community Plans: Making Choices about Money in Communities. 2005. (Communities at Work Ser.). (ENG., Illus.). 24p. (gr. 2-3). pap. 8.25 (978-1-4042-5014-7(X), PowerKids Pr.) Rosen Publishing Group, Inc., The.

—Community Resources: The Land & the People in Communities. 2005. (Communities at Work Ser.). (ENG., Illus.). 24p. (gr. 2-3). pap. 8.25 (978-1-4042-5016-1(6), PowerKids Pr.) Rosen Publishing Group, Inc., The.

Catel, Patrick. The Home Front of the Revolutionary War, 1 vol. (Why We Fought: the Revolutionary War Ser.). (ENG.). 48p. (gr. 3-6). 2011. pap. 9.95 (978-1-4329-3900-7(9)) 2010. 33.32 (978-1-4329-3895-6(9)) Heinemann-Raintree. (Heinemann InfoSearch).

Center for Learning Network Staff. Violence in America. 2005. (Social Studies Ser.). 83p. (YA). tchr. ed., spiral bd. 20.95 (978-1-56077-793-9(1)) Center for Learning, The.

Chastain, Zachary. Rooting for the Home Team: Sports in The 1800s. 2009. (Daily Life in America in the 1800s Ser.). 64p. (YA). (gr. 7-18). pap. 9.95 (978-1-4222-1859-4(7)); lib. bdg. 22.95 (978-1-4222-1786-3(8)) Mason Crest.

Coletti, Sharon. Everything You Need to Supplement U. S. & State Studies. 2005. (YA). Pt. 1. ring bd. 249.95 (978-1-933558-08-0(3))Pt. 2. ring bd. 249.95 (978-1-933558-09-7(1)) InspirEd Educators.

Combs, Maggie. Postwar United States. 2011. (Explorer Library: Language Arts Explorer Ser.). (ENG.). 32p. (gr. 4-8). pap. 14.21 (978-1-61080-284-0(5), 201207); lib. bdg. 28.50 (978-1-61080-196-6(2), 201168) Cherry Lake Publishing.

Cooke, Tim, ed. The War & U. S. Society. 2013. (NAM: the Vietnam War Ser.). 48p. (gr. 5-9). 37.10 (978-1-78121-045-1(4), Brown Bear Bks.) Windmill Bks. Ltd. GBR. Dist: Black Rabbit Bks.

Corrigan, Jim. The 1990s Decade in Photos: The Rise of Technology. 2010. (Amazing Decades in Photos Ser.). (Illus.). 64p. (J). (gr. 5-9). lib. bdg. 29.27 (978-0-7660-3138-8(1)) Enslow Pubs., Inc.

—The 2000s Decade in Photos: A New Millennium. 2010. (Amazing Decades in Photos Ser.). (Illus.). 64p. (J). (gr. 5-9). lib. bdg. 29.27 (978-0-7660-3139-5(X)) Enslow Pubs., Inc.

Coster, Patience & Walker, Pamela. A New Deal for Women. 2011. (Cultural History of Women in America Ser.). (Illus.). 64p. (gr. 6-12). 35.00 (978-1-60413-934-1(X), Chelsea Hse.) Facts On File, Inc.

Crompton, Samuel Willard. The Family Values Movement: Promoting Faith Through Action. 2007. (Reform Movements in American History Ser.). (Illus.). 120p. (J). (gr. 7-12). lib. bdg. 32.50 (978-0-7910-9608-6(4)) Facts On File, Inc.

Daily Life in America in the 1800s, 15 vols., Set. Incl. America at War: Military Conflicts, Home & Abroad in the 1800s. Strange, Matthew. pap. 9.95 (978-1-4222-1851-8(1)); Bleeding, Blistering, & Purging: Health & Medicine in The 1800s. Strange, Matthew. pap. 9.95 (978-1-4222-1848-8(1)); Buggies, Bicycles & Iron Horses: Transportation in the 1800s. McIntosh, Kenneth. pap. 9.95 (978-1-4222-1849-5(X)); Cornmeal & Cider: Food & Drink in the 1800s. Chastain, Zachary. pap. 9.95 (978-1-4222-1850-1(3)); From the Parlor to the Altar: Romance & Marriage in The 1800s. Chastain, Zachary. pap. 9.95 (978-1-4222-1852-5(X)); Guardians of the Home: Women's Lives in The 1800s. Strange, Matthew. pap. 9.95 (978-1-4222-1853-2(8)); Home Sweet Home: Around the House in the 1800s. Chastain, Zachary. pap. 9.95 (978-1-4222-1854-9(6)); Jump Ropes, Jacks, & Endless Chores: Children's Lives in The 1800s. Strange, Matthew. pap. 9.95 (978-1-4222-1855-6(4)); Outlaws & Lawmen: Crime & Punishment in the 1800s. McIntosh, Kenneth. pap. 9.95 (978-1-4222-1857-0(0)); Passing the Time: Entertainment in The 1800s. Chastain, Zachary. pap. 9.95 (978-1-4222-1858-7(9)); Reviving the Spirit, Reforming Society: Religion in The 1800s. McIntosh, Kenneth. pap. 9.95 (978-1-4222-1856-3(2)); Rooting for the Home Team: Sports in The 1800s. Chastain, Zachary. pap. 9.95 (978-1-4222-1859-4(7)); Saloons, Shootouts, & Spurs: The Wild West in The 1800's. McIntosh, Kenneth. pap. 9.95 (978-1-4222-1862-4(7)); Scandals & Glory: Politics in The 1800s. Chastain, Zachary. pap. 9.95 (978-1-4222-1860-0(0)); Sweat of Their Brow: Occupations in the 1800s. Chastain, Zachary. pap. 9.95 (978-1-4222-1861-7(9)); (YA). (gr. 7-18). 2009. (Illus.). 64p. 2011. Set pap. 149.25 (978-1-4222-1847-1(3), 1317825); Set lib. bdg. 344.25 (978-1-4222-1774-0(4), 1317825) Mason Crest.

DePietro, Frank. Central American Immigrants. 2012. (J). pap. (978-1-4222-2334-5(5)) Mason Crest.

—Central American Immigrants. Limón, José E., ed. 2012. (Hispanic Americans: Major Minority Ser.). 64p. (J). (gr. 4). 22.95 (978-1-4222-2317-8(5)) Mason Crest.

Duse Sr, Phillip M. Phil Duse Exposes Government Quack Silliness to Us Law-Abiding Citizens. 2013. 76p. pap. 9.95 (978-1-60414-724-7(5)) Fideli Publishing, Inc.

Ferguson, Amanda. The Attack Against the U. S. Embassies in Kenya & Tanzania. 2009. (Terrorist Attacks Ser.). 64p. (gr. 5-5). 58.50 (978-1-60853-309-1(3)) Rosen Publishing Group, Inc., The.

Fighting the Monster. 2004. (YA). ring bd. 59.95 (978-0-9661256-2-7(2)) Youth Communication - New York Center.

Fradin, Dennis Brindell. September 11, 2001. 2009. (Turning Points in U. S. History Ser.). 48p. (gr. 3-6). 31.36 (978-0-7614-4259-2(6)) Marshall Cavendish Corp.

Freedman, Russell. Children of the Great Depression. 2010. (ENG., Illus.). 128p. (J). (gr. 5-7). pap. 10.99 (978-0-547-48035-0(0)) Houghton Mifflin Harcourt Publishing Co.

Friedman, Lauri S. Abortion. 2008. (Compact Research Ser.). (YA). (gr. 7-12). lib. bdg. 25.95 (978-1-60152-047-0(6)) ReferencePoint Pr., Inc.

Gallagher, Aileen. The Muckrakers: American Journalism During the Age of Reform. 2009. (Progressive Movement 1900-1920: Efforts to Reform America's New Industrial Society Ser.). 32p. (gr. 3-4). 47.90 (978-1-60854-173-7(8)) Rosen Publishing Group, Inc., The.

The Gilded Age & Progressivism, 1891-1913. 2010. (Discovering U. S. History Ser.). (Illus.). 136p. (gr. 5-8). 35.00 (978-1-60413-355-4(4), Chelsea Hse.) Facts On File, Inc.

Gitlin, Martin. World War II on the Home Front: An Interactive History Adventure, 1 vol. 2012. (You Choose: History Ser.). (ENG.). 112p. (gr. 3-4). pap. 6.95 (978-1-4296-7998-5(0)); lib. bdg. 31.99 (978-1-4296-6019-8(8)) Capstone Press of Coughlan Cos. (You Choose Bks.).

—World War II U. S. Homefront: A History Perspectives Book. 2014. (Perspectives Library). (ENG., Illus.). 32p. (J). (gr. 4-8). 28.50 (978-1-63137-621-4(7), 205267) Cherry Lake Publishing.

Hakim, Joy. An Age of Extremes, 1880-1917. 2nd rev. ed. 2007. (History of US Ser.: Vol. 8). (ENG., Illus.). 224p. (gr. 4-7). per. 15.95 (978-0-19-532722-9(5)) Oxford Univ. Pr., Inc.

—Reconstructing America, 1865-1890. (History of US Ser.: 7). (ENG., Illus.). 208p. (gr. 4-7). 3rd rev. ed. 2006. 24.95 (978-0-19-518900-1(0))Bk. 7. 2nd rev. ed. 2007. per. 15.95 (978-0-19-532721-2(7)) Oxford Univ. Pr., Inc.

Halpern, Monica & National Geographic Learning Staff. The Home Front During World War II. 2007. (Nonfiction Reading & Writing Workshops Ser.). (ENG., Illus.). 40p. pap. 19.95 (978-0-7922-4558-2(X)) CENGAGE Learning.

Harrison, Geoffrey C. & Scott, Thomas F. The Fight for Freedom. Stewart, Mark & Kennedy, Mike, eds. 2014. (Great Debates Ser.). (ENG.). 48p. (J). (gr. 5-8). lib. bdg. 29.27 (978-1-59953-588-3(2)) Norwood Hse. Pr.

Haugen, David M., et al. The Great Depression. 2010. (Perspectives on Modern World History Ser.). (Illus.). 224p. (YA). (gr. 10-12). 42.45 (978-0-7377-4795-9(1), Greenhaven Pr., Inc.) Cengage Gale.

Hazen, Walter. Reform Movement. 2005. (Illus.). 112p. pap. 12.95 (978-1-59647-085-9(2)) Good Year Bks.

Heitkamp, Kristina Lyn. Confronting Anti-Semitism. 2017. (J). **(978-1-5081-7742-5(2)**, Rosen Young Adult) Rosen Publishing Group, Inc., The.

Hermann, Spring. The Struggle for Equality: Women & Minorities in America. 2006. (American Saga Ser.). (Illus.). 128p. (J). (gr. 5-9). lib. bdg. 33.27 (978-0-7660-2573-8(X)) Enslow Pubs., Inc.

Howard, Melanie A. Civil Rights Marches, 1 vol. 2004. (American Moments Ser.). (ENG.). 48p. (gr. 4-8). 27.07 (978-1-59197-282-2(5), Abdo & Daughters) ABDO Publishing Co.

Hyde, Natalie. Life in a Mining Community. 2009. (Learn about Rural Life Ser.). (ENG., Illus.). 32p. (J). (gr. 3-6). pap. (978-0-7787-5087-1(6)); lib. bdg. (978-0-7787-5074-1(4)) Crabtree Publishing Co.

Josephson, Judith Pinkerton. Growing up in World War II, 1941-1945. 2003. (Our America Ser.). (Illus.). 64p. (J). (gr. 4-7). lib. bdg. 26.60 (978-0-8225-0660-7(2)) Lerner Publishing Group.

Kamma, Anne. If You Lived When Women Won Their Rights. Johnson, Pamela, illus. 2008. (If You... Ser.). (ENG.). 64p. (J). (gr. 2-5). pap. 7.99 (978-0-439-74869-8(0), Scholastic Reference) Scholastic, Inc.

Kiesbye, Stefan. Can Busy Teens Succeed Academically? 2009. (At Issue Ser.). (ENG.). 128p. (J). (gr. 10-12). 34.45 (978-0-7377-4286-2(0), Greenhaven Pr., Inc.) Cengage Gale.

King, David C. & American Heritage, American. Colonies & Revolution. 2003. (American Heritage, American Voices Ser.). (ENG.). 144p. (J). (gr. 5-9). pap. 22.95 (978-1-119-10345-5(2)) Wiley, John & Sons, Inc.

Konstam, Angus. America Speaks, 10 vols. 2005. (Illus.). (J). (978-0-7172-6023-2(2)); (978-0-7172-6024-9(0)); (978-0-7172-6026-3(7)); (978-0-7172-6027-0(5)); (978-0-7172-6028-7(3)); (978-0-7172-6029-4(1)); (978-0-7172-6022-5(4)); (978-0-7172-6021-8(6)); (978-0-7172-6020-1(8)); (978-0-7172-6025-6(9)) Grolier, Ltd.

—America Speaks, 10 vols., Set. 2005. (Illus.). (J). (gr. 5-10). lib. bdg. 269.00 (978-0-7172-6030-0(5), Grolier) Scholastic Library Publishing.

Levy, Debbie. Slaves on a Southern Plantation. 2004. (Daily Life Ser.). (ENG., Illus.). 48p. (J). 27.50 (978-0-7377-1827-0(7), Greenhaven Pr., Inc.) Cengage Gale.

Libal, Joyce. Migrant Youth: Falling Between the Cracks. 2009. (Youth in Rural North America Ser.). (Illus.). 96p. (YA). (gr. 3-7). lib. bdg. 22.95 (978-1-4222-0020-9(5)) Mason Crest.

Lynette, Rachel. What to Do When Your Parent Is Out of Work. 2010. (Let's Work It Out Ser.). 24p. (J). (ENG.). pap. 8.25 (978-1-4358-9764-9(1), PowerKids Pr.); (Illus.). (gr. 2-5). lib. bdg. 22.60 (978-1-4358-9338-2(7)) Rosen Publishing Group, Inc., The.

Manuel, David, et al. From Sea to Shining Sea for Young Readers: 1787-1837. 2011. (Discovering God's Plan for America Ser.: 2). (ENG.). 208p. (J). pap. 16.00 (978-0-8007-3374-2(6)) Revell.

Marcovitz, Hal. Race Relations. 2008. (Gallup Major Trends & Events Ser.). (Illus.). 127p. (YA). (gr. 7-18). lib. bdg. 22.95 (978-1-59084-968-2(X)) Mason Crest.

—Teens & Volunteerism. Developed in Association with the Gallup Organization Staff, ed. 2013. (Gallup Youth Survey: Major Issues & Trends Ser.: 14). 112p. (J). (gr. 7-18). 24.95 (978-1-4222-2960-6(2)) Mason Crest.

Marcovitz, Hal & marcovitz, hal. The 1960s: Part of the Understanding American History Series. 2013. (Illus.). 96p. (YA). lib. bdg. (978-1-60152-494-2(3)) ReferencePoint Pr., Inc.

Martin, Iain C. Gettysburg: The True Account of Two Young Heroes in the Greatest Battle of the Civil War. 2013. (ENG., Illus.). 208p. (YA). (gr. 6-12). 16.95 (978-1-62087-532-2(2), 620532, Sky Pony Pr.) Skyhorse Publishing Co., Inc.

McIntosh, Kenneth & Livingston, Phyllis. Youth with Alcohol & Drug Addiction: Escape from Bondage. 2009. (Helping Youth with Mental, Physical, & Social Challenges Ser.). (Illus.). 128p. (YA). (gr. 7-18). lib. bdg. 24.95 (978-1-4222-0143-5(0)) Mason Crest.

McNeill, Allison & Hanes, Richard Clay. American Home Front in World War II Reference Library Cumulative Index. 2004. (American Homefront in World War II Reference Library). (ENG.). 32p. 5.00 (978-0-7876-9125-7(9), UXL) Cengage Gale.

Meade, Marion. Free Woman: The Life & Times of Victoria Woodhull. 2011. 176p. pap. 15.95 (978-1-61756-052-1(9)) Open Road Integrated Media, Inc.

Miller, Brandon Marie. Declaring Independence: Life During the American Revolution. 2005. (People's History Ser.). (ENG., Illus.). 96p. (gr. 5-12). 33.26 (978-0-8225-1275-2(0)) Lerner Publishing Group.

Miller, Debra A. The Patriot Act. 2007. (Hot Topics Ser.). (ENG., Illus.). 112p. (YA). (gr. 7-12). lib. bdg. 33.95 (978-1-59018-981-8(7), LML02109-229790) Cengage Gale.

Miller, Reagan & Doak, Melissa J. Life on the Homefront During the Civil War. 2011. (ENG.). 48p. (J). lib. bdg. (978-0-7787-5344-5(1)) Crabtree Publishing Co.

Monk, Linda R. The Words We Live By: Your Annotated Guide to the Constitution. annot. rev. ed. 2004. (ENG., Illus.). 304p. (gr. -1-17). pap. 18.99 (978-0-7868-8620-3(X)) Hyperion Pr.

Murray, Glen L. The Dumbing down of Americ. 2009. 68p. pap. 15.99 (978-1-4415-1642-8(5)) Xlibris Corp.

Nardo, Don. The Atlantic Slave Trade. 2007. (Lucent Library of Black History Ser.). (ENG., Illus.). 128p. (gr. 8-12). lib. bdg. 39.40 (978-1-4205-0007-3(4), Lucent Bks.) Cengage Gale.

Nazario, Sonia. La Travesía de Enrique. 2015. (ENG & SPA.). 304p. (YA). (gr. 7). pap. 9.99 (978-0-553-53554-9(4), Ember) Random Hse. Children's Bks.

Piehl, Norah. Underage Drinking. 2010. (Social Issues Firsthand Ser.). (Illus.). 192p. (J). 33.75 (978-0-7377-4799-7(4), Greenhaven Pr., Inc.) Cengage Gale.

Progressivism. 2010. (Key Concepts in American History Ser.). (Illus.). 128p. (gr. 6-12). 45.00 (978-1-60413-223-6(X), Chelsea Hse.) Facts On File, Inc.

Rodger, Ellen. A Refugee's Journey from Myanmar. 2017. 32p. (J). **(978-0-7787-3674-5(1))** Crabtree Publishing Co.

Rossi, Ann & National Geographic Learning Staff. Immigrants Today. 2007. (Reading Expeditions Ser.). (ENG., Illus.). 40p. (J). pap. 19.95 (978-0-7922-4560-5(1)) CENGAGE Learning.

Ruffner, Peter & Hillstrom, Kevin. Worker's Unite! The American Labor Movement. 2010. (Defining Moments Ser.). (Illus.). 248p. (gr. 9-18). lib. bdg. 55.00 (978-0-7808-1130-0(5)) Omnigraphics, Inc.

Sakany, Lois. Progressive Leaders: The Platforms & Policies of America's Reform Politicians. (Progressive Movement 1900-1920: Efforts to Reform America's New Industrial Society Ser.). 32p. 2009. (gr. 3-4). 47.90 (978-1-60854-168-3(1)) 2004. (Illus.). (YA). (gr. 5-9). lib. bdg. 22.50 (978-1-4042-0193-4(9)) Rosen Publishing Group, Inc., The.

Seeley, M. H. America's Oddest Fads. 2016. (Weird America Ser.). 00032p. (J). pap. 10.50 **(978-1-4824-5747-6(4))** Stevens, Gareth Publishing LLLP.

Senker, Cath. Who Traveled the Underground Railroad?, 1 vol. 2014. (Primary Source Detectives Ser.). (ENG., Illus.). 64p. (gr. 7-8). lib. bdg. 35.99 (978-1-4329-9603-1(7)) Heinemann-Raintree.

Snyder, Gail. Teens & Alcohol. Developed in Association with the Gallup Organization Staff, ed. 2013. (Gallup Youth Survey: Major Issues & Trends Ser.: 14). 112p. (J). (gr. 7-18). 24.95 (978-1-4222-2949-1(1)) Mason Crest.

Steck-Vaughn Staff. Social Studies Level H-J: America Is... 2003. (Steck-Vaughn Shutterbug Bks.). (ENG., Illus.). 16p. (gr. 1-2). pap. 41.55 (978-0-7398-7652-7(X)) Harcourt Schl. Pubs.

Stein, R. Conrad. The Home Front During World War II in American History. 2003. (In American History Ser.). (Illus.). 112p. (J). (gr. 5-12). lib. bdg. 26.60 (978-0-7660-1984-3(5)) Enslow Pubs., Inc.

Stone, Tanya Lee. The House That Jane Built: A Story about Jane Addams. Brown, Kathryn, illus. 2015. (ENG.). 32p. (J). (gr. 1-4). 17.99 (978-0-8050-9049-9(5), 9780805090499, Holt, Henry & Co. Bks. For Young Readers) Holt, Henry & Co.

Strange, Matthew. Guardians of the Home: Women's Lives in The 1800s. 2009. (Daily Life in America in the 1800s Ser.). 64p. (YA). (gr. 7-18). pap. 9.95 (978-1-4222-1853-2(8)); lib. bdg. 22.95 (978-1-4222-1780-1(9)) Mason Crest.

Thomas, William David. Korean Americans. 2009. (New Americans Ser.). 80p. (gr. 5). 35.64 (978-0-7614-4306-3(1)) Marshall Cavendish Corp.

Vonne, Mira. Gross Facts about the American Colonies. 2017. (Gross History Ser.). (ENG., Illus.). 32p. (gr. 1-2). lib. bdg. 26.65 (978-1-5157-4154-1(0)) Capstone Press of Coughlan Cos.

World War I & the Roaring Twenties, 1914-1928. 2010. (Discovering U. S. History Ser.). (Illus.). 136p. (J). (gr. 5-8). 35.00 (978-1-60413-356-1(2), Chelsea Hse.) Facts On File, Inc.

Worth, Richard. Lewis Hine: Photographer of Americans at Work. 2009. (ENG., Illus.). 83p. (C). (gr. 6-18). lib. bdg. 158.00 (978-0-7656-8153-9(6), Y182862) Routledge.

Zoldak, Joyce. When Danger Hits Home: Survivors of Domestic Violence. 2009. (J). pap. 24.95 (978-1-4222-1473-2(7)) Mason Crest.

UNITED STATES—SOCIAL LIFE AND CUSTOMS

Acker, Kerry. Everything You Need to Know about the Goth Scene. 2005. (Need to Know Library). (Illus.). 64p. (YA). (gr. 7-12). lib. bdg. 31.95 (978-0-8239-3223-8(0), NTGOSC) Rosen Publishing Group, Inc., The.

Allen, Nancy Kelly. My Life As an Early Settler. 2012. (ENG.). 24p. (gr. k-2). pap. 8.95 (978-1-61810-273-7(7)) Rourke Educational Media.

Aloian, Molly. Cultural Traditions in the United States. 2014. (ENG., Illus.). 32p. (J). (978-0-7787-0305-1(3)) Crabtree Publishing Co.

Ancona, George. Mi Casa: My House. 2005. (Somos Latinos (We Are Latinos) Ser.). (SPA & ENG., Illus.). 32p. (J). (gr. 1-3). pap. 8.95 (978-0-516-25065-6(5), Children's Pr.) Scholastic Library Publishing.

Anderson, Dale. Daily Life During the American Revolution. 2005. (World Almanac Library of the American Revolution Ser.). 48p. (gr. 5-12). pap. 14.05 (978-0-8368-5939-3(1)); lib. bdg. 31.00 (978-0-8368-5930-0(8)) Stevens, Gareth Publishing LLLP. (Gareth Stevens Secondary Library).

Anderson, Laurie Halse. Thank You, Sarah: The Woman Who Saved Thanksgiving. Faulkner, Matt, illus. 2005. (ENG.). 40p. (J). (gr. k-3). 7.99 (978-0-689-85143-8(X), Simon & Schuster Bks. For Young Readers) Simon & Schuster Bks. For Young Readers.

Bailey Publishing Staff & McEvoy, Anne. The 20s & 30s. 2009. (Costume Source Bks). (Illus.). 32p. (gr. 6-12). 35.00 (978-1-60413-383-7(X), Chelsea Hse.) Facts On File, Inc.

Bailey Publishing Staff & Steer, Deirdre Clancy. The 1980s & 1990s. 2009. (Costume Source Bks). (Illus.). 32p. (gr. 6-12). 35.00 (978-1-60413-386-8(4), Chelsea Hse.) Facts On File, Inc.

Barter, James. San Francisco in the 1960s. 2003. (Travel Guide To Ser.). (ENG., Illus.). 96p. (J). 30.85 (978-1-59018-359-5(2), Lucent Bks.) Cengage Gale.

Bearce, Stephanie. Top Secret Files: Gangsters & Bootleggers: Secrets, Strange Tales, & Hidden Facts about the Roaring 20s. rev. ed. 2015. (Top Secret Files Ser.: 0). (ENG., Illus.). 125p. (J). (gr. 4-7). 8.95 (978-1-61821-461-4(6)) Prufrock Pr.

Behnke, Alison. The Little Black Dress & Zoot Suits: Depression & Wartime Fashions from the 1930s to the 1950s. 2011. (Dressing a Nation: the History of U. S. Fashion Ser.). (ENG., Illus.). 64p. (gr. 5-12). lib. bdg. 31.93 (978-0-7613-5892-3(7), Twenty-First Century Bks.) Lerner Publishing Group.

Berg, Elizabeth. The United States. 2010. (Festivals of the World Ser.). 32p. (gr. 3). 28.50 (978-1-60870-106-3(9)) Marshall Cavendish GBR. Dist: Marshall Cavendish Corp.

Bingham, Jane. Popular Culture: 1920-1939, 1 vol. 2012. (History of Popular Culture Ser.). (ENG.). 64p. (gr. 6-9). pap. 10.95 (978-1-4109-4629-4(0)); lib. bdg. 35.99 (978-1-4109-4622-5(3)) Heinemann-Raintree.

Books, Golson. The African Americans, 7 vols. 2011. (Multicultural America Ser.). (Illus.). 256p. (gr. 6-12). 55.00 (978-0-8160-7813-4(0)) Facts On File, Inc.

—The Arab Americans, 7 vols. 2011. (Multicultural America Ser.). (Illus.). 208p. (gr. 6-12). 55.00 (978-0-8160-7812-7(2)) Facts On File, Inc.

—The Asian Americans, 7 vols. 2011. (Multicultural America Ser.). (Illus.). 272p. (gr. 6-12). 55.00 (978-0-8160-7814-1(9)) Facts On File, Inc.

—The European Americans, 7 vols. 2011. (Multicultural America Ser.). (Illus.). 256p. (gr. 6-12). 55.00 (978-0-8160-7816-5(5)) Facts On File, Inc.

—The Hispanic Americans, 7 vols. 2011. (Multicultural America Ser.). (Illus.). 256p. (gr. 6-12). 55.00 (978-0-8160-7811-0(4)) Facts On File, Inc.

—The Jewish Americans, 7 vols. 2011. (Multicultural America Ser.). (Illus.). 256p. (gr. 6-12). 55.00 (978-0-8160-7815-8(7)) Facts On File, Inc.

—The Native Americans, 7 vols. 2011. (Multicultural America Ser.). (Illus.). 256p. (gr. 6-12). 55.00 (978-0-8160-7817-2(3)) Facts On File, Inc.

Books, Golson & Purdy, Elizabeth. Celebrating Women in American History, 5 vols., Set. 2011. (Celebrating Women in American History Ser.). 1280p. (gr. 6-12). 315.00 (978-0-8160-7878-3(5)) Facts On File, Inc.

Braun, Eric. If I Were a Cowboy, 1 vol. Reid, Mick, illus. 2010. (Dream Big! Ser.). (ENG.). 24p. (gr. k-3). lib. bdg. 26.65 (978-1-4048-5531-1(9)) Picture Window Bks.

Brill, Marlene Targ. America in the 1980s. 2009. (Decades of Twentieth-Century America Ser.). (ENG.). 144p. (gr. 5-12). lib. bdg. 38.60 (978-0-8225-7602-0(3)) Lerner Publishing Group.

Broida, Marian. Projects about the American Revolution. 2005. (Hands-On History Ser.). (Illus.). 48p. (J). (gr. 3-7). lib. bdg. (978-0-7614-1981-5(0), Benchmark Bks.) Marshall Cavendish Corp.

Brown, Harriet & Witowski, Teri. Kit's World: A Girl's-Eye View of the Great Depression. Rane, Walter & Hood, Philip, illus. 2008. 30p. (YA). (gr. 3-18). 24.95 (978-1-59369-459-3(8)) American Girl Publishing, Inc.

Bryfonski, Dedria. Deregulation. 2010. (Opposing Viewpoints Ser.). (ENG., Illus.). 240p. 42.95 (978-0-7377-5108-6(8)); 224p. (gr. 10-12). pap. 33.80 (978-0-7377-5109-3(6)) Cengage Gale. (Greenhaven Pr., Inc.).

Bullard, Lisa. Chelsea's Chinese New Year. Saunders, Katie, illus. 2012. (Holidays & Special Days Ser.). 24p. (gr. k-2). (J). pap. 39.62 (978-0-7613-9247-7(5), Millbrook Pr.); (ENG.). pap. 6.95 (978-0-7613-8579-0(7), Millbrook Pr.); (ENG.). lib. bdg. 23.93 (978-0-7613-5078-1(0)) Lerner Publishing Group.

Burgan, Michael. Popular Culture: 1960-1979, 1 vol. 2012. (History of Popular Culture Ser.). (ENG.). 64p. (gr. 6-9). pap. 10.95 (978-1-4109-4631-7(2)); lib. bdg. 35.99 (978-1-4109-4624-9(X)) Heinemann-Raintree.

Catel, Patrick. The Home Front of the Revolutionary War, 1 vol. (Why We Fought: the Revolutionary War Ser.). (ENG.). 48p. (gr. 3-6). 2011. pap. 9.95 (978-1-4329-3900-7(9)) 2010. 33.32 (978-1-4329-3895-6(9)) Heinemann-Raintree. (Heinemann InfoSearch).

Center for Learning Network Staff. Catch-22: Curriculum Unit. 2005. (Novel Ser.). 76p. (YA). tchr. ed., spiral bd. 19.95 (978-1-56077-792-2(3)) Center for Learning, The.

Chastain, Zachary. From the Parlor to the Altar: Romance & Marriage in The 1800s. 2009. (Daily Life in America in the 1800s Ser.). 64p. (YA). (gr. 7-18). pap. 9.95 (978-1-4222-1852-5(X)); lib. bdg. 22.95 (978-1-4222-1779-5(5)) Mason Crest.

—Home Sweet Home: Around the House in the 1800s. 2009. (Daily Life in America in the 1800s Ser.). 64p. (YA). (gr. 7-18). pap. 9.95 (978-1-4222-1854-9(6)); lib. bdg. 22.95 (978-1-4222-1781-8(7)) Mason Crest.

—Passing the Time: Entertainment in The 1800s. 2009. (Daily Life in America in the 1800s Ser.). 64p. (YA). (gr. 7-18). pap. 9.95 (978-1-4222-1858-7(9)); lib. bdg. 22.95 (978-1-4222-1785-6(X)) Mason Crest.

Colligan, L. H. The City. 2014. (J). pap. (978-1-62712-883-4(2)); 80p. (YA). (gr. 6-8). lib. bdg. 35.64 (978-1-62712-882-7(4)) Cavendish Square Publishing.

Colman, Penny. Thanksgiving: The True Story. 2008. (ENG., Illus.). 160p. (YA). (gr. 5-11). 29.99 (978-0-8050-8229-6(8), Holt, Henry & Co. Bks. For Young Readers) Holt, Henry & Co.

Colonial Life: Exploration & Settlement - Cities & Town - Daily Living - Government - Trade & Commerce, 5 bks., Set. Incl. Cities & Towns. Stefoff, Rebecca. 96p. lib. bdg. 140.00 (978-0-7656-8109-6(9), Y181735); Daily Living. Hinds, Kathryn. 96p. lib. bdg. 158.00 (978-0-7656-8110-2(2), Y181908); Exploration & Settlement. Stefoff, Rebecca. 96p. lib. bdg. 158.00 (978-0-7656-8108-9(0), Y182272); Government. Kelly, Martin & Kelly, Melissa. 96p. lib. bdg. 158.00 (978-0-7656-8112-6(9), Y182476); Trade & Commerce. Altman, Linda Jacobs. 98p. lib. bdg. 175.00 (978-0-7656-8111-9(0), Y184849); (C). (gr. 6-18). (ENG., Illus.). 96p. 2007. Set lib. bdg. 140.00 (978-0-7656-8107-2(2), Y181691) Routledge.

Combs, Maggie. Postwar United States. 2011. (Explorer Library: Language Arts Explorer Ser.). (ENG.). 32p. (gr. 4-8). pap. 14.21 (978-1-61080-284-0(5), 201207); lib. bdg. 28.50 (978-1-61080-196-6(2), 201168) Cherry Lake Publishing.

Connell, Kate. Servant to Abigail Adams: The Early American Adventures of Hannah Cooper. 2004. (Illus.). 40p. (J). (gr. 4-8). pap. 7.00 (978-0-7567-8216-0(3)) DIANE Publishing Co.

Crabtree Publishing Company Staff & Morss, Martha. United States: The People. 2012. (ENG.). 32p. (J). (978-0-7787-9836-1(4)) Crabtree Publishing Co.

Crabtree Publishing Company Staff & Weiss, Lynne. United States: The Culture. 2012. (ENG.). 32p. (J). pap. (978-0-7787-9837-8(2)) Crabtree Publishing Co.

Dawson, Emily C. Holidays & Celebrations. 2010. (Special Days Ser.). 24p. 25.65 (978-1-60753-030-5(9)) Amicus Publishing.

Day, Nancy. Your Travel Guide to Civil War America. 2005. (Passport to History Ser.). (Illus.). 96p. (gr. 5-8). lib. bdg. 26.50 (978-0-8225-3078-7(3)) Lerner Publishing Group.

—Your Travel Guide to Colonial America. 2005. (Passport to History Ser.). (Illus.). 96p. (gr. 5-8). lib. bdg. 26.50 (978-0-8225-3079-4(1)) Lerner Publishing Group.

dePaola, Tomie. Things Will Never Be the Same. dePaola, Tomie, illus. 2004. (26 Fairmount Avenue Bks.). (Illus.). 69p. (J). (gr. 3-7). 13.65 (978-0-7569-2951-0(2)) Perfection Learning Corp.

Doak, Robin Santos. Struggling to Become American: 1899-1940. Overmyer-Velazquez, Mark, ed. 2006. (Latino-American History Ser.). (Illus.). 106p. (YA). (gr. 5-9). lib. bdg. 35.00 (978-0-8160-6443-4(1)) Facts On File, Inc.

Domnauer, Teresa. Life in the West. 2010. (True Book Ser.). (ENG., Illus.). 48p. (J). pap. 6.95 (978-0-531-21246-2(7)) Scholastic Library Publishing.

Donovan, Sandra. The Middle Eastern American Experience. 2010. (USA TODAY Cultural Mosaic Ser.). (ENG., Illus.). 80p. (gr. 6-8). lib. bdg. 33.26 (978-0-7613-4087-4(4)) Lerner Publishing Group.

Draper, Allison Stark. What People Wore During the American Revolution. 2009. (Clothing, Costumes, & Uniforms Throughout American History Ser.). 24p. (gr. 3-3). 42.50 (978-1-61511-875-5(6), PowerKids Pr.) Rosen Publishing Group, Inc., The.

—What People Wore During the Civil War. 2009. (Clothing, Costumes, & Uniforms Throughout American History Ser.). 24p. (gr. 3-3). 42.50 (978-1-61511-876-2(4), PowerKids Pr.) Rosen Publishing Group, Inc., The.

—What People Wore in Early America. 2009. (Clothing, Costumes, & Uniforms Throughout American History Ser.). 24p. (gr. 3-3). 42.50 (978-1-61511-881-6(0), PowerKids Pr.) Rosen Publishing Group, Inc., The.

—What People Wore on Southern Plantations. 2009. (Clothing, Costumes, & Uniforms Throughout American History Ser.). 24p. (gr. 3-3). 42.50 (978-1-61511-882-3(9), PowerKids Pr.) Rosen Publishing Group, Inc., The.

Dustman, Jeanne. American Culture. rev. ed. 2014. (Primary Source Readers Content & Literacy Ser.). (ENG., Illus.). 32p. (gr. 3-3). pap. 8.99 (978-1-4333-7360-2(2)) Teacher Created Materials, Inc.

Ehrlich, Amy, ed. When I Was Your Age Vol. 2: Original Stories about Growing Up. 2006. (Illus.). 187p. (YA). (gr. 8-11). reprint ed. 17.00 (978-1-4223-5199-4(8)) DIANE Publishing Co.

—When I Was Your Age Vols. I & II: Original Stories about Growing Up. 2012. lib. bdg. 26.95 (978-0-606-23806-9(9), Turtleback) Turtleback Bks.

Engdahl, Sylvia. Free Press. 2011. (Teen Rights & Freedoms Ser.). (ENG., Illus.). 176p. (gr. 10-12). 42.00 (978-0-7377-5827-6(9)) Cengage Gale.

Fajardo, Anika. The Dish on Food & Farming in Colonial America, 1 vol. 2011. (Life in the American Colonies Ser.). (ENG.). 32p. (gr. 3-4). pap. 8.10 (978-1-4296-7217-7(X)); pap. 47.70 (978-1-4296-7218-4(8)) Capstone Press of Coughlan Cos. (Fact Finders).

Feinstein, Stephen. The 1920s from Prohibition to Charles Lindbergh. rev. ed. 2006. (Decades of the 20th Century in Color Ser.). (Illus.). 64p. (J). (gr. 5). lib. bdg. 29.27 (978-0-7660-2632-2(9)) Enslow Pubs., Inc.

—The 1970s from Watergate to Disco. rev. ed. 2006. (Decades of the 20th Century in Color Ser.). (Illus.). 64p. (J). (gr. 5). lib. bdg. 29.27 (978-0-7660-2637-7(X)) Enslow Pubs., Inc.

—The 1980s from Ronald Reagan to MTV. rev. ed. 2006. (Decades of the 20th Century in Color Ser.). (Illus.). 64p. (J). (gr. 5). lib. bdg. 29.27 (978-0-7660-2638-4(8)) Enslow Pubs., Inc.

Friedman, Hannah. Everything Sucks: Losing My Mind & Finding Myself in a High School Quest for Cool. 2009. (ENG.). 264p. (YA). (gr. 8-12). pap. 12.95 (978-0-7573-0775-1(2), HCI Teens) Health Communications, Inc.

Gelletly, LeeAnne. A Woman's Place in Early America. 2012. (J). pap. (978-1-4222-2365-9(5)) Mason Crest.

—A Woman's Place in Early America. Harrington, A. Page, ed. 2012. (Finding a Voice: Women's Fight for Equality in U. S. Society Ser.). 64p. (J). (gr. 5). 22.95 (978-1-4222-2355-0(8)) Mason Crest.

George, Enzo. America in the Fifties. 2015. (Primary Sources in U. S. History Ser.). (ENG., Illus.). 48p. (J). (gr. 4-4). 31.36 (978-1-5026-0494-1(9)) Cavendish Square Publishing.

Gerber, Larry. Torture. 2011. (Headlines! Ser.). (ENG.). 64p. (YA). lib. bdg. 31.95 (978-1-4488-1291-2(7)) Rosen Publishing Group, Inc., The.

Gillis, Jennifer Blizin. Restored Villages. 2007. (Field Trips Ser.). (Illus.). 24p. (J). (gr. 2-5). lib. bdg. 27.07 (978-1-60044-563-7(2)) Rourke Educational Media.

Glasser, Debbie & Schenck, Emily. New Kid, New Scene: A Guide to Moving & Switching Schools. 2011. (Illus.). 112p. (J). 14.95 (978-1-4338-1039-8(5), Magination Pr.) American Psychological Assn.

Gogerly, Liz. United States. 2008. (Costume Around the World Ser.). (Illus.). 32p. (gr. 4-6). 28.00 (978-0-7910-9774-8(9), Chelsea Clubhouse) Facts On File, Inc.

Golson Books, Ltd. Staff. Handbooks to Life in America, 9 vols., Set. 2009. (Handbook to Life in America Ser.). (Illus.). 304p. (C). (gr. 9-18). 450.00 (978-0-8160-7785-4(1)) Facts On File, Inc.

Hanauer, Jodi. A Child of the 80's Looks Back. 2004. 60p. pap. 19.95 (978-1-4137-2461-5(2)) America Star Bks.

Harasymiw, Teppo. Customs & Celebrations Across America. 2009. (Real Life Readers Ser.). 12p. (gr. 2-3). pap. 5.90 (978-1-4042-7954-4(7), Rosen Classroom) Rosen Publishing Group, Inc., The.

Hardyman, Robyn. Celebrate: United States. 2009. (Celebrate Country Ser.). 32p. (gr. 4-6). 28.00 (978-1-60413-264-9(7), Chelsea Clubhouse) Facts On File, Inc.

Harness, Cheryl. Our Colonial Year. Harness, Cheryl, illus. 2005. (ENG., Illus.). 40p. (J). (gr. -1-3). 16.95 (978-0-689-83479-0(9), Simon & Schuster Bks. For Young Readers) Simon & Schuster Bks. For Young Readers.

Havelin, Kate. Hoopskirts, Union Blues, & Confederate Grays: Civil War Fashions from 1861 to 1865. 2011. (Dressing a Nation: the History of U. S. Fashion Ser.). (ENG., Illus.). 64p. (gr. 5-12). lib. bdg. 31.93 (978-0-7613-5889-3(7), Twenty-First Century Bks.) Lerner Publishing Group.

Hazen, Walter A. Colonial Times: With Cross-Curricular Activities in Each Chapter: Colonial Times. 2008. (ENG., Illus.). 96p. (J). pap. 12.95 (978-1-59647-266-2(9)) Good Year Bks.

—The Frontier: With Cross-Curricular Activities in Each Chapter: the Frontier. 2008. (Illus.). 96p. (J). pap. 12.95 (978-1-59647-268-6(5)) Good Year Bks.

Heinz, Brian J. Nathan of Yesteryear & Michael of Today. Friar, Joanne, illus. 2006. (Exceptional Social Studies Titles for Intermediate Grades). (ENG.). 32p. (J). (gr. 3-6). lib. bdg. 22.60 (978-0-7613-2893-3(9), Millbrook Pr.) Lerner Publishing Group.

Hernández, Roger E. The Civil War, 1840s-1890s. 2008. (Hispanic America Ser.). 80p. (gr. 5-18). lib. bdg. 34.21 (978-0-7614-2939-5(5), Benchmark Bks.) Marshall Cavendish Corp.

Herrera, Juan Felipe. El Canto de las Palomas/Calling the Doves. 2004. (Illus.). (J). (gr. 3-6). spiral bd. (978-0-616-14607-1(8)) Canadian National Institute for the Blind/Institut National Canadien pour les Aveugles.

Higgins, Nadia. US Culture Through Infographics. Kulihin, Vic, illus. 2014. (Super Social Studies Infographics Ser.). 32p. (gr. 3-5). pap. 8.95 (978-1-4677-4565-9(0)) Lerner Publishing Group.

—US Culture Through Infographics. Thompson, Bryon & Kulihin, Vic, illus. 2014. (Super Social Studies Infographics Ser.). (ENG.). 32p. (gr. 3-5). lib. bdg. 26.60 (978-1-4677-3464-6(0), Lerner Pubns.) Lerner Publishing Group.

—US Government Through Infographics. Sciuto, Alex, illus. 2014. (Super Social Studies Infographics Ser.). 32p. (gr. 3-5). pap. 8.95 (978-1-4677-4567-3(7)) Lerner Publishing Group.

Hinds, Kathryn. Daily Living. 2007. (ENG., Illus.). 96p. (C). (gr. 6-18). lib. bdg. 158.00 (978-0-7656-8110-2(2), Y181908) Routledge.

Hooks, Earnest. Let's go see Mother Wilkerson's Farm. 2011. 72p. pap. 27.08 (978-1-4389-5072-3(1)) AuthorHouse.

Hunt, Jilly. Popular Culture: 1900-1919, 1 vol. 2012. (History of Popular Culture Ser.). (ENG.). 64p. (gr. 6-9). pap. 10.95 (978-1-4109-4628-7(2)); lib. bdg. 35.99 (978-1-4109-4621-8(5)) Heinemann-Raintree.

—Popular Culture: 1980-1999, 1 vol. 2012. (History of Popular Culture Ser.). (ENG.). 64p. (gr. 6-9). pap. 10.95 (978-1-4109-4632-4(0)); lib. bdg. 35.99 (978-1-4109-4625-6(8)) Heinemann-Raintree.

Hunter, Nick. Popular Culture: 1940-1959, 1 vol. 2012. (History of Popular Culture Ser.). (ENG.). 64p. (gr. 6-9). pap. 10.95 (978-1-4109-4630-0(4)); lib. bdg. 35.99 (978-1-4109-4623-2(1)) Heinemann-Raintree.

Jessup, Dylan. We're All Americans. 2012. (InfoMax Readers Ser.). (ENG., Illus.). 24p. (J). (gr. 1-2). pap. 8.25 (978-1-4488-9079-8(9), Rosen Classroom) Rosen Publishing Group, Inc., The.

Kalman, Bobbie. A Visual Dictionary of Victorian Life. 2010. (Crabtree Visual Dictionaries Ser.). (ENG.). 32p. (J). (gr. 1-7). lib. bdg. (978-0-7787-3507-6(9)) Crabtree Publishing Co.

Kocienda, Genevieve. Only in America Low Intermediate Book with Online Access. 2014. (ENG.). 28p. (J). pap. 9.50 (978-1-107-63700-9(7)) Cambridge Univ. Pr.

Krebs, Laurie. A Day in the Life of a Colonial Shipwright. 2004. (Library of Living & Working in Colonial Times Ser.). (Illus.). 24p. (J). lib. bdg. 22.60 (978-0-8239-6227-3(X)) Rosen Publishing Group, Inc., The.

Landau, Elaine. El Dia de San Valentin: Caramelos, Amor y Corazones. 2005. (Días Festivos Ser.). (SPA., Illus.). 48p. (J). (gr. 3-4). lib. bdg. 25.27 (978-0-7660-2613-1(2), Enslow Elementary) Enslow Pubs., Inc.

Lanier, Wendy H. Life During the Great Depression, 1 vol. 2014. (Daily Life in US History Ser.). (ENG., Illus.). 48p. (J). (gr. 3-6). lib. bdg. 32.79 (978-1-62403-626-2(0)) ABDO Publishing Co.

Lassieur, Allison. Colonial America: An Interactive History Adventure, 1 vol. (You Choose: Historical Eras Ser.). (ENG.). 112p. (gr. 3-4). 2011. pap. 6.95 (978-1-4296-6277-2(8)) 2011. pap. 41.70 (978-1-4296-6739-5(7)) 2010. 31.99 (978-1-4296-5481-4(3)) Capstone Press of Coughlan Cos. (You Choose Bks.).

Lieurance, Suzanne. The Prohibition Era in American History. 2003. (In American History Ser.). (Illus.). 112p. (J). (gr. 5-12). lib. bdg. 27.94 (978-0-7660-1840-2(7)) Enslow Pubs., Inc.

The Life of a Colonial Innkeeper. 2013. (Jr. Graphic Colonial America Ser.). 24p. (J). (gr. 3-6). pap. 63.60 (978-1-4777-1436-2(7), PowerKids Pr.) Rosen Publishing Group, Inc., The.

The Life of a Colonial Schoolteacher. 2013. (Jr. Graphic Colonial America Ser.). 24p. (J). (gr. 3-6). pap. 63.60 (978-1-4777-1428-7(6), PowerKids Pr.) Rosen Publishing Group, Inc., The.

Lindop, Edmund & Goldstein, Margaret. America in the 1930s. 2009. (Decades of Twentieth-Century America Ser.). (ENG.). 144p. (gr. 5-12). lib. bdg. 38.60 (978-0-7613-2832-2(7)) Lerner Publishing Group.

Loh-Hagan, Virginia. PoPo's Lucky Chinese New Year. Benoit, Renné, illus. 2016. (ENG.). 32p. (J). (gr. 1-4). 16.99 (978-1-58536-978-2(0), 204113) Sleeping Bear Pr.

Lowery, Linda. El Dia de los Muertos. Knutson, Barbara, illus. 2005. (Yo Solo Festividades Ser.).Tr. of Day of the Dead. (SPA.). 48p. (J). (gr. 2-4). per. 5.95 (978-0-8225-3123-4(2)) Lerner Publishing Group.

—El Dia de los Muertos. Translations.com Staff, tr. Knutson, Barbara, illus. 2005. (Yo Solo - Festividades (on My Own - Holidays) Ser.).Tr. of Day of the Dead. (SPA & ENG.). 48p. (gr. 2-4). lib. bdg. 25.26 (978-0-8225-3122-7(4)) Lerner Publishing Group.

Lusted, Marcia Amidon. America's Colonization & Settlement. 2011. (Explorer Library: Language Arts Explorer Ser.). (ENG.). 32p. (gr. 4-8). pap. 14.21 (978-1-61080-282-6(9), 201205); lib. bdg. 28.50 (978-1-61080-194-2(6), 201164) Cherry Lake Publishing.

MacElroy, Mary H. Work & Play in Colonial Days. reprint ed. 150.00 (978-0-7222-6600-7(6)) Library Reprints, Inc.

Machajewski, Sarah. A Kid's Life in Colonial America, 1 vol. 2015. (ENG., Illus.). 24p. (J). lib. bdg. 23.60 (978-1-4994-0006-9(3), PowerKids Pr.) Rosen Publishing Group, Inc., The.

Mara, Wil. The Farmer. 2010. (Colonial People Ser.). 48p. (gr. 3-18). 29.93 (978-0-7614-4797-9(0)) Marshall Cavendish Corp.

—If You Were a Kid in the Thirteen Colonies. Farré, Lluís, illus. 2016. (If You Were a Kid Ser.). (ENG.). 32p. (J). lib. bdg. 26.00 (978-0-531-21972-0(0), Children's Pr.) Scholastic Library Publishing.

Marcovitz, Hal. Teens, Religion & Values. Developed in Association with the Gallup Organization Staff, ed. 2013. (Gallup Youth Survey: Major Issues & Trends Ser.: 14). 112p. (J). (gr. 7-18). 24.95 (978-1-4222-2962-0(9)) Mason Crest.

Marcovitz, Hal & marcovitz, hal. The 1960s: Part of the Understanding American History Series. 2013. (Illus.). 96p. (YA). lib. bdg. (978-1-60152-494-2(3)) ReferencePoint Pr., Inc.

Matzke, Ann H. My Life As a Pioneer. 2012. (ENG.). 24p. (gr. k-2). pap. 8.95 (978-1-61810-280-5(X)) Rourke Educational Media.

Meachen Rau, Dana. Clothing in American History. 2006. (How People Lived in America Ser.). (Illus.). 24p. (gr. 1-4). pap. 8.15 (978-0-8368-7212-5(6), Weekly Reader Leveled Readers) Stevens, Gareth Publishing LLLP.

Meachen Rau, Dana & Meachen Rau, Dana. Clothing in American History. 2006. (How People Lived in America Ser.). (Illus.). 24p. (gr. 1-4). lib. bdg. 22.00 (978-0-8368-7205-7(3), Weekly Reader Leveled Readers) Stevens, Gareth Publishing LLLP.

Michaels, Vanessa Lynn & Harrow, Jeremy. Frequently Asked Questions about Family Violence. 2011. (FAQ: Teen Life

Ser.). lib. bdg. 31.95 *(978-1-4488-4628-3(5))* Rosen Publishing Group, Inc., The.
Miller, Brandon Marie. Good Women of a Well-Blessed Land: Women's Lives in Colonial America. 2003. (People's History Ser.). (Illus.). 96p. (J). 29.27 *(978-0-8225-0032-2(9))* Lerner Publishing Group.
—Women of Colonial America: 13 Stories of Courage & Survival in the New World. 2016. (Women of Action Ser.). (ENG., Illus.). 256p. (YA). (gr. 7). 19.95 *(978-1-55652-487-5(0))* Chicago Review Pr., Inc.
Moriarty, J. T. Manifest Destiny: A Primary Source History of America's Territorial Expansion in the 19th Century. 2009. (Primary Sources in American History Ser.). 64p. (gr. 5-8). 58.50 *(978-1-60851-490-8(0))* Rosen Publishing Group, Inc., The.
Murray, Julie. Chinese New Year, 1 vol. 2005. (Buddy Book Ser.). (ENG., Illus.). 24p. (gr. k-4). 25.65 *(978-1-59197-585-4(9),* Buddy Bks.) ABDO Publishing Co.
Nardo, Don. Daily Life in Colonial America. 2010. (Lucent Library of Historical Eras Ser.). 144p. (YA). (gr. 7-12). 34.80 *(978-1-4205-0264-0(6))* Cengage Gale.
Olson, Kay Melchisedech. The Terrible, Awful Civil War: The Disgusting Details about Life During America's. 2011. (Disgusting History Ser.). (ENG.). 32p. (gr. 3-4). pap. 47.70 *(978-1-4296-6480-6(0),* Fact Finders) Capstone Press of Coughlan Cos.
—The Terrible, Awful Civil War: The Disgusting Details about Life During America's Bloodiest War. (Disgusting History Ser.). (ENG.). 32p. (gr. 3-4). 2011. pap. 8.10 *(978-1-4296-6349-6(9))* 2010. lib. bdg. 27.32 *(978-1-4296-3960-6(1))* Capstone Press of Coughlan Cos. (Fact Finders).
Otto, Carolyn B. Celebrate Kwanzaa: With Candles, Community, & the Fruits of the Harvest. 2008. (Holidays Around the World Ser.). (ENG., Illus.). 32p. (J). (gr. 1-4). 15.95 *(978-1-4263-0319-7(X))*; lib. bdg. 23.90 *(978-1-4263-0320-3(3))* National Geographic Society. (National Geographic Children's Bks.).
—Holidays Around the World: Celebrate Kwanzaa: With Candles, Community, & the Fruits of the Harvest. 2010. (Holidays Around the World Ser.). (ENG., Illus.). 32p. (J). (gr. 1-4). pap. 6.95 *(978-1-4263-0705-8(5),* National Geographic Children's Bks.) National Geographic Society.
Parks, Peggy J. Teenage Suicide. 2011. (Compact Research Ser.). 96p. (YA). (gr. 7-12). lib. bdg. 27.95 *(978-1-60152-156-9(1))* ReferencePoint Pr., Inc.
Pelleschi, Andrea. The Life of a Colonial Innkeeper. 2013. (Jr. Graphic Colonial America Ser.). 24p. (J). (gr. 3-6). 25.25 *(978-1-4777-1309-9(3))*; pap. 10.60 *(978-1-4777-1435-5(9))* Rosen Publishing Group, Inc., The. (PowerKids Pr.).
—The Life of a Colonial Schoolteacher. 2013. (Jr. Graphic Colonial America Ser.). 24p. (J). (gr. 3-6). 25.25 *(978-1-4777-1305-1(0))*; pap. 10.60 *(978-1-4777-1427-0(8))* Rosen Publishing Group, Inc., The. (PowerKids Pr.).
Pelletier, Fran. Little Pine to King Spruce: A Franco-American Childhood, 1 vol. 2003. (ENG., Illus.). 192p. pap. 15.00 *(978-0-88448-254-3(5),* 884254) Tilbury Hse. Pubs.
Penne, Barbra & Renehan, Patrick. Your Rights As an LGBTQ+ Teen. 2017. (LGBTQ+ Guide to Beating Bullying Ser.). 64p. (J). (gr. 12-11). 34.45 ***(978-1-5081-7439-4(3),*** Rosen Young Adult) Rosen Publishing Group, Inc., The.
Ponto, Joanna. Mardi Gras. 2016. (Illus.). 32p. (J). pap. *(978-0-7660-7472-5(0))*; (ENG.). (gr. 3-3). 25.27 *(978-0-7660-7460-6(9))* Enslow Pubs., Inc.
Purdy, Elizabeth Rholetter. Celebrating Women in American History. 2011. (J). *(978-0-8160-7879-0(3))*; *(978-0-8160-7883-7(1))*; *(978-0-8160-7882-0(3))*; *(978-0-8160-7881-3(5))*; *(978-0-8160-7880-6(7))* Facts On File, Inc.
Rajczak, Kristen. Life in the American Colonies. 2013. (What You Didn't Know about History Ser.). (Illus.). 24p. (J). (gr. 2-5). pap. 8.15 *(978-1-4339-8435-8(0))*; lib. bdg. 22.60 *(978-1-4339-8434-1(2))* Stevens, Gareth Publishing LLLP.
—Life on a Wagon Train. 2013. (What You Didn't Know about History Ser.). (Illus.). 24p. (J). (gr. 2-5). pap. 8.15 *(978-1-4339-8445-7(8))*; lib. bdg. 22.60 *(978-1-4339-8444-0(X))* Stevens, Gareth Publishing LLLP.
Raum, Elizabeth. The Dreadful, Smelly Colonies: The Disgusting Details about Life in Colonial Amer. 2011. (Disgusting History Ser.). (ENG.). 32p. (gr. 3-4). pap. 47.70 *(978-1-4296-6477-6(0),* Fact Finders) Capstone Press of Coughlan Cos.
—The Dreadful, Smelly Colonies: The Disgusting Details about Life in Colonial America, 1 vol. (Disgusting History Ser.). (ENG.). 32p. (gr. 3-4). 2011. pap. 8.10 *(978-1-4296-6351-9(0))* 2010. lib. bdg. 27.32 *(978-1-4296-3959-0(8))* Capstone Press of Coughlan Cos. (Fact Finders).
—The Scoop on Clothes, Homes, & Daily Life in Colonial America, 1 vol. 2011. (Life in the American Colonies Ser.). (ENG.). 32p. (gr. 3-4). 27.32 *(978-1-4296-6138-6(0))*; pap. 47.70 *(978-1-4296-7214-6(5))* Capstone Press of Coughlan Cos. (Fact Finders).
Roberts, Russell. Holidays & Celebrations in Colonial America. 2006. (Building America Ser.). (Illus.). 48p. (J). (gr. 3-7). lib. bdg. 29.95 *(978-1-58415-467-9(5))* Mitchell Lane Pubs., Inc.
—Life in Colonial America. 2007. (Building America Ser.). (Illus.). 48p. (J). (gr. 4-8). lib. bdg. 29.95 *(978-1-58415-549-2(3))* Mitchell Lane Pubs., Inc.
Robins, Maureen Picard. One Land, Many Cultures. 2012. (ENG.). 24p. (gr. k-2). pap. 8.95 *(978-1-61810-276-8(1))* Rourke Educational Media.
Robinson, Fay. Celebrating Chinese New Year. 2012. (Celebrating Holidays Ser.). (Illus.). 48p. (J). (gr. 3-4). pap. 8.95 *(978-1-59845-398-0(X))*; lib. bdg. 25.27 *(978-0-7660-4031-1(3))* Enslow Pubs., Inc. (Enslow Elementary).
—Chinese New Year. 2016. (Story of Our Holidays Ser.). (Illus.). 32p. (J). pap. 10.52 *(978-0-7660-8324-0(1))* Enslow Pubs., Inc.
Rooney, Anne. The 50s & 60s. 2009. (Costume Source Bks). (Illus.). 32p. (gr. 6-12). 35.00 *(978-1-60413-385-1(6),* Chelsea Hse.) Facts On File, Inc.
Samuel, Charlie. Entertainment in Colonial America. 2003. (Primary Sources of Everyday Life in Colonial America Ser.). (Illus.). 24p. (J). lib. bdg. 22.60 *(978-0-8239-6600-4(3),* PowerKids Pr.) Rosen Publishing Group, Inc., The.
Sheffield, Sarah. Life During the American Civil War. 2009. (Reading Room Collection 2 Ser.). 24p. (gr. 3-4). 42.50 *(978-1-60851-978-1(3),* PowerKids Pr.) Rosen Publishing Group, Inc., The.
Sirvaitis, Karen. The European American Experience. 2010. (USA TODAY Cultural Mosaic Ser.). (ENG.). 80p. (gr. 6-8). lib. bdg. 33.26 *(978-0-7613-4088-1(2))* Lerner Publishing Group.
Small, Cathleen. American Life & Communication from the Telephone to Twitter. 2016. (Pop Culture Ser.). 112p. (J). (gr. 7-7). 39.93 *(978-1-5026-1977-8(6))* Cavendish Square Publishing.
Spangenburg, Ray & Moser, Kit. Teen Fads: Fun, Foolish, or Fatal? 2003. (Teen Issues Ser.). (Illus.). 64p. (J). (gr. 6-12). lib. bdg. 22.60 *(978-0-7660-1665-1(X))* Enslow Pubs., Inc.
Spilsbury, Louise. Horrible Jobs in Colonial Times, Vol. 1. 2014. (History's Most Horrible Jobs Ser.). (ENG.). 48p. (J). (gr. 5-6). 31.95 *(978-1-4824-0330-5(7))* Stevens, Gareth Publishing LLLP.
Sterngass, Jon. Same Sex Marriage. 2011. (Controversy! 3 Ser.). 112p. (gr. 7). 37.07 *(978-1-60870-490-3(4))* Marshall Cavendish Corp.
Stewart, Gail B. Missing Persons. 2011. (Crime Scene Investigations Ser.). (ENG.). 128p. (gr. 10-10). lib. bdg. 40.40 *(978-1-4205-0534-4(3),* Lucent Bks.) Cengage Gale.
Sullivan, Laura L. The Colonial Wigmaker. 2015. (Colonial People Ser.). (ENG.). 48p. (J). (gr. 4-4). 31.36 *(978-1-5026-0480-4(9))* Cavendish Square Publishing.
—The Colonial Woodworker. 2015. (Colonial People Ser.). (ENG.). 48p. (J). (gr. 4-4). 31.36 *(978-1-5026-0484-2(1))* Cavendish Square Publishing.
Tabor, Nancy Maria Grande. Celebraciones: Dias Feriados de los Estados Unidos y Mexico. Tabor, Nancy Maria Grande, illus. 2004.Tr. of Celebrations - Holidays of the United States of America & Mexico. (SPA & ENG., Illus.). 32p. (J). (gr. -1-2). pap. 7.95 *(978-1-57091-550-5(4))* Charlesbridge Publishing, Inc.
Teacher Created Resources Staff. America: Come on a Journey of Discovery. 2008. (Qeb Travel Through Ser.). (ENG., Illus.). 32p. (gr. 4-7). pap. 7.99 *(978-1-4206-8277-9(6))* Teacher Created Resources, Inc.
Thompson, Gare. The Roaring 20s: Voices from America's Past. 2007. (Reading Expeditions Ser.). (ENG., Illus.). 40p. (J). pap. 19.95 *(978-0-7922-4551-3(2))* National Geographic School Publishing, Inc.
—When the Mission Padre Came to the Rancho: The Early California Adventures of Rosalinda & Simon Delgado. 2004. (I Am American Ser.). (ENG., Illus.). 40p. (J). (gr. 3-7). pap. 6.99 *(978-0-7922-6945-8(4),* National Geographic Children's Bks.) National Geographic Society.
Troupe, Thomas Kingsley. Your Life as a Settler in Colonial America. Canga, C. B., illus. 2012. (Way It Was Ser.). (ENG.). 32p. (gr. 2-3). pap. 8.95 *(978-1-4048-7251-6(5))*; lib. bdg. 26.65 *(978-1-4048-7156-4(X))* Picture Window Bks.
Uhlig, Elizabeth. I See America! Uhlig, Elizabeth, illus. 2009. (Illus.). (J). pap. 12.95 *(978-0-9815345-7-2(0))* Marble Hse. Editions.
Weber, Valerie J. I Come from Afghanistan. 2006. (This Is My Story Ser.). (Illus.). 24p. (gr. 1-4). pap. 8.15 *(978-0-8368-7240-8(1))*; lib. bdg. 22.00 *(978-0-8368-7233-0(9))* Stevens, Gareth Publishing LLLP. (Weekly Reader Leveled Readers).
—I Come from Chile. 2006. (This Is My Story Ser.). (Illus.). 24p. (gr. 1-4). lib. bdg. 22.00 *(978-0-8368-7234-7(7),* Weekly Reader Leveled Readers) Stevens, Gareth Publishing LLLP.
—I Come from Chile. 2006. (This Is My Story Ser.). (Illus.). 24p. (gr. 1-4). pap. 8.15 *(978-0-8368-7241-5(X),* Weekly Reader Leveled Readers) Stevens, Gareth Publishing LLLP.
—I Come from India. 2006. (This Is My Story Ser.). (Illus.). 24p. (gr. 1-4). pap. 8.15 *(978-0-8368-7242-2(8))*; lib. bdg. 22.00 *(978-0-8368-7235-4(5))* Stevens, Gareth Publishing LLLP. (Weekly Reader Leveled Readers).
—I Come from Ivory Coast. 2006. (This Is My Story Ser.). (Illus.). 24p. (gr. 1-4). pap. 8.15 *(978-0-8368-7243-9(6))*; lib. bdg. 22.00 *(978-0-8368-7236-1(3))* Stevens, Gareth Publishing LLLP. (Weekly Reader Leveled Readers).
—I Come from South Korea. 2006. (This Is My Story Ser.). (Illus.). 24p. (gr. 1-4). lib. bdg. 22.00 *(978-0-8368-7237-8(1),* Weekly Reader Leveled Readers) Stevens, Gareth Publishing LLLP.
—I Come from Ukraine. 2006. (This Is My Story Ser.). (Illus.). 24p. (gr. 1-4). pap. 8.15 *(978-0-8368-7245-3(2),* Weekly Reader Leveled Readers) Stevens, Gareth Publishing LLLP.
—I Come from Ukraine. 2006. (This Is My Story Ser.). (Illus.). 24p. (gr. 1-4). lib. bdg. 22.00 *(978-0-8368-7238-5(X),* Weekly Reader Leveled Readers) Stevens, Gareth Publishing LLLP.
Weber, Valerie J. & Weber, Valerie J. I Come from South Korea. 2006. (This Is My Story Ser.). (Illus.). 24p. (gr. 1-4). pap. 8.15 *(978-0-8368-7244-6(4),* Weekly Reader Leveled Readers) Stevens, Gareth Publishing LLLP.
Whitman, Sylvia. Children of the World War II Home Front. 2005. (Picture the American Past Ser.). (Illus.). 48p. (J). (gr. 2-5). lib. bdg. 22.60 *(978-1-57505-484-1(1))* Lerner Publishing Group.
Whitney, Gleaves & Whitney, Louise Doak. B Is for Buckaroo: A Cowboy Alphabet. Guy, Sue & Guy, Susan, illus. rev. ed. 2003. (Sports Ser.). (ENG.). 40p. (J). (gr. 1-4). 17.95 *(978-1-58536-139-7(9),* 202000) Sleeping Bear Pr.
Wilder, Laura Ingalls. A Little House Traveler: Writings from Laura Ingalls Wilder's Journeys Across America. 2011. (Little House Nonfiction Ser.). (ENG., Illus.). 368p. (J). (gr. 5). pap. 7.99 *(978-0-06-072492-4(7),* Collins) HarperCollins Pubs.
World War I & the Roaring Twenties, 1914-1928. 2010. (Discovering U. S. History Ser.). (Illus.). 136p. (J). (gr. 5-8). 35.00 *(978-1-60413-356-1(2),* Chelsea Hse.) Facts On File, Inc.
Worth, Richard. The 1970s to the 1980s. 2009. (Hispanic America 2 Ser.). 80p. (gr. 5). 34.21 *(978-0-7614-4178-6(6))* Marshall Cavendish Corp.
Zocchi, Judy. In the United States. Brodie, Neale, illus. 2005. (Global Adventures II Ser.). 32p. (J). pap. 10.95 *(978-1-59646-172-7(1))*; lib. bdg. 21.65 *(978-1-59646-085-0(7))* Dingles & Co.
—In the United States/en los Estados Unidos. Brodie, Neale, illus. 2005. (Global Adventures II Ser.).Tr. of En los Estados Unidos. (ENG & SPA.). 32p. (J). pap. 10.95 *(978-1-59646-174-1(8))*; lib. bdg. 21.65 *(978-1-59646-086-7(5))* Dingles & Co.

UNITED STATES—SOCIAL LIFE AND CUSTOMS—COLONIAL PERIOD, CA. 1600-1775

Bailey Publishing Staff, et al. Colonial America. 2009. (Costume Source Bks). (Illus.). 32p. (gr. 6-12). 35.00 *(978-1-60413-380-6(5),* Chelsea Hse.) Facts On File, Inc.
Barter, James. Colonial New York. 2003. (Travel Guide To Ser.). (ENG., Illus.). 112p. (J). 30.85 *(978-1-59018-250-5(2),* Lucent Bks.) Cengage Gale.
Broida, Marian. Projects about Colonial Life. 2003. (Hands-On History Ser.). (Illus.). 48p. (gr. 3-8). lib. bdg. 21.95 *(978-0-7614-1603-6(X),* Benchmark Bks.) Marshall Cavendish Corp.
Burgan, Michael. The Carpenter. 2013. (Colonial People 3 Ser.). 48p. (J). (gr. 4-8). pap. 12.93 *(978-1-62712-045-6(9))* Cavendish Square Publishing.
—The Carpenter. 2013. 48p. (J). (gr. 4-8). 29.93 *(978-1-60870-411-8(4))* Cavendish Square Publishing.
Colonial Life. (J). tchr. ed. 41.95 *(978-0-382-40663-8(X))* Cobblestone Publishing Co.
Colonial Life: Exploration & Settlement - Cities & Town - Daily Living - Government - Trade & Commerce, 5 bks., Set. Incl. Cities & Towns. Stefoff, Rebecca. 96p. lib. bdg. 140.00 *(978-0-7656-8109-6(9),* Y181735); Daily Living. Hinds, Kathryn. 96p. lib. bdg. 158.00 *(978-0-7656-8110-2(2),* Y181908); Exploration & Settlement. Stefoff, Rebecca. 96p. lib. bdg. 158.00 *(978-0-7656-8108-9(0),* Y182272); Government. Kelly, Martin & Kelly, Melissa. 96p. lib. bdg. 158.00 *(978-0-7656-8112-6(9),* Y182476); Trade & Commerce. Altman, Linda Jacobs. 98p. lib. bdg. 175.00 *(978-0-7656-8111-9(0),* Y184849); (C). (gr. 6-18). (ENG., Illus.). 96p. 2007. Set lib. bdg. 140.00 *(978-0-7656-8107-2(2),* Y181691) Routledge.
Gravois, Michael. Hands-On History: Colonial America. 2003. 48p. pap., tchr. ed. 10.99 *(978-0-590-66115-7(9),* Teaching Resources) Scholastic, Inc.
Heinrichs, Ann. The Shipbuilder. 2013. (Colonial People 3 Ser.). 48p. (J). (gr. 4-8). pap. 12.93 *(978-1-62712-048-7(3))* Cavendish Square Publishing.
Hinman, Bonnie. The Scoop on School & Work in Colonial America, 1 vol. 2012. (Life in the American Colonies Ser.). (ENG.). 32p. (gr. 3-4). pap. 8.10 *(978-1-4296-7986-2(7))*; pap. 47.70 *(978-1-4296-8461-3(5))* Capstone Press of Coughlan Cos. (Fact Finders).
Krebs, Laurie. A Day in the Life of a Colonial Shipwright. 2009. (Library of Living & Working in Colonial Times Ser.). 24p. (gr. 3-3). 42.50 *(978-1-60853-738-9(2),* PowerKids Pr.) Rosen Publishing Group, Inc., The.
Maestro, Betsy. The New Americans: Colonial Times: 1620-1689. Maestro, Giulio, illus. 2004. (American Story Ser.). (ENG.). 48p. (J). (gr. 2-7). pap. 7.99 *(978-0-06-057572-4(7))* HarperCollins Pubs.
Mara, Wil. The Gunsmith. 2013. 48p. (J). (gr. 4-8). 29.93 *(978-1-60870-414-9(9))*; pap. 12.93 *(978-1-62712-046-3(7))* Cavendish Square Publishing.
Mead, Wendy. The Merchant. 2013. 48p. (J). (gr. 4-8). 29.93 *(978-1-60870-415-6(7))*; pap. 12.93 *(978-1-62712-047-0(5))* Cavendish Square Publishing.
Petersen, Christine. The Wheelwright. 2013. 48p. (J). (gr. 4-8). 29.93 *(978-1-60870-419-4(X))*; pap. 12.93 *(978-1-62712-049-4(1))* Cavendish Square Publishing.
Sherman, Patrice. Colonial America. 2009. (How'd They Do That? Ser.). (Illus.). 64p. (J). (gr. 4-8). lib. bdg. 33.95 *(978-1-58415-817-2(4))* Mitchell Lane Pubs., Inc.
Vonne, Mira. Gross Facts about the American Colonies. 2017. (Gross History Ser.). (ENG., Illus.). 32p. (gr. 1-2). lib. bdg. 26.65 *(978-1-5157-4154-1(0))* Capstone Press of Coughlan Cos.

UNITED STATES—SOCIAL POLICY

Burlingame, Jeff. Government Entitlement. 2011. (Controversy! 3 Ser.). 112p. (gr. 7). 37.07 *(978-1-60870-491-0(2))* Marshall Cavendish Corp.
Forman, Lillian E. Health Care Reform, 1 vol. 2009. (Essential Viewpoints Set 4 Ser.). (ENG., Illus.). 112p. (J). (gr. 6-12). lib. bdg. 35.64 *(978-1-60453-532-7(6))* ABDO Publishing Co.
Hiber, Amanda. Are Adoption Policies Fair? 2008. (At Issue Ser.). (ENG., Illus.). 80-128p. (YA). (gr. 9-12). pap. 34.45 *(978-0-7377-3910-7(X))*; (J). (gr. 10-12). 24.45 *(978-0-7377-3911-4(8),* Greenhaven Pr., Inc.) Cengage Gale.

UNITED STATES—SOLDIERS

see Soldiers—United States

UNITED STATES—STATE GOVERNMENTS

see State Governments

UNITED STATES—STATISTICS

TIME for Kids Almanac 2009. 2008. (Time Inc. Home Entertainment Library-Bound Titles Ser.). 256p. (YA). (gr. 5-12). lib. bdg. 39.93 *(978-0-7613-4052-2(1),* Twenty-First Century Bks.) Lerner Publishing Group.

UNITED STATES—SUPREME COURT

Abrams, Dennis. Sandra Day O'Connor: U. S. Supreme Court Justice. 2009. (Women of Achievement Ser.). (Illus.). 136p. (gr. 6-12). 35.00 *(978-1-60413-337-0(6),* Chelsea Hse.) Facts On File, Inc.
Barrington, Richard. Sonia Sotomayor. 2014. (Making a Difference: Leaders Who Are Changing the World Ser.). 48p. (YA). (gr. 5-8). 25.85 *(978-1-62275-435-9(2))* Rosen Publishing Group, Inc., The.
Beier, Anne. The Supreme Court & the Judicial Branch. 2009. (Primary Source Library of American Citizenship Ser.). 32p. (gr. 5-5). 47.90 *(978-1-61511-230-2(8),* Rosen Reference) Rosen Publishing Group, Inc., The.
Benoit, Peter. The Supreme Court. 2014. (Cornerstones of Freedom Ser.: 3). (ENG., Illus.). 64p. (J). lib. bdg. 30.00 *(978-0-531-21332-2(3))* Scholastic Library Publishing.
Benson, Michael. William H. Taft. 2004. (Presidential Leaders Ser.). (ENG., Illus.). 112p. (gr. 6-12). 29.27 *(978-0-8225-0849-6(4),* Lerner Pubns.) Lerner Publishing Group.
Boerst, William J. Galileo Galilei & the Science of Motion. 2004. (Profiles in Science Ser.). (Illus.). 144p. (YA). (gr. 6-12). lib. bdg. 26.95 *(978-1-931798-00-6(1))* Reynolds, Morgan Inc.
Brannen, Daniel E., et al. Supreme Court Drama: Cases That Changed America. 2nd ed. 2011. *(978-1-4144-8658-1(8))*; *(978-1-4144-8657-4(X))*; *(978-1-4144-8660-4(X))*; *(978-1-4144-8668-0(5))*; *(978-1-4144-8659-8(6))*;Set. (ENG.). 1119p. 458.00 *(978-1-4144-8656-7(1))* Cengage Gale. (UXL).
Branscomb, Leslie Wolf. Earl Warren. 2011. (Supreme Court Justices Ser.). (Illus.). 112p. 28.95 *(978-1-59935-158-2(7))* Reynolds, Morgan Inc.
Cane, Ella. The U. S. Supreme Court, 1 vol. 2014. (Our Government Ser.). (ENG., Illus.). 24p. (gr. 1-2). lib. bdg. 25.32 *(978-1-4765-4203-4(1),* First Facts) Capstone Press of Coughlan Cos.
Colins, Luke. Thurgood Marshall, 1 vol. 2014. (Great African-Americans Ser.). (ENG.). 24p. (gr. k-1). lib. bdg. 21.99 *(978-1-4765-3956-0(1),* Pebble Bks.) Capstone Press of Coughlan Cos.
Corrigan, Jim. John Marshall: The Story of John Marshall. 2011. (Supreme Court Justices Ser.). (Illus.). 112p. (J). 28.95 *(978-1-59935-159-9(5))* Reynolds, Morgan Inc.
Cox, Vicki. Clarence Thomas. 2008. (Black Americans of Achievement Ser.). (Illus.). 120p. (YA). (gr. 7-12). 35.00 *(978-0-7910-9683-5(2))* Facts On File, Inc.
Davis, Jenny B. The U. S. Supreme Court Coloring & Activity Book. 2007. (ENG., Illus.). 32p. (J). (gr. 1-17). pap. 5.95 *(978-1-59031-924-6(9))* American Bar Assn.
De Capua, Sarah. Sandra Day O'Connor. 2013. 96p. (YA). (gr. 7-12). 39.93 *(978-0-7614-4961-4(2))* Cavendish Square Publishing.
DeCapua, Sarah. Sandra Day O'Connor. 2013. (Leading Women 2 Ser.). 96p. (YA). (gr. 7-12). pap. 19.99 *(978-1-62712-117-0(X))* Cavendish Square Publishing.
DiPrimio, Pete. The Judicial Branch. 2011. (My Guide to the Constitution Ser.). (Illus.). 48p. (J). (gr. 3-6). lib. bdg. 29.95 *(978-1-58415-944-5(8))* Mitchell Lane Pubs., Inc.
Elish, Dan. The U. S. Supreme Court. 2007. (Cornerstones of Freedom Ser.). (Illus.). 48p. (J). (gr. 4-6). 26.00 *(978-0-516-23637-7(7),* Children's Pr.) Scholastic Library Publishing.
Fridell, Ron. Gideon V. Wainwright: The Right to Free Counsel. 2006. (Supreme Court Milestones Ser.). (Illus.). 128p. (gr. 7). lib. bdg. 42.79 *(978-0-7614-2146-7(7),* Benchmark Bks.) Marshall Cavendish Corp.
Gallagher, Brigid. Sonia Sotomayor, 1 vol. 2014. (Extraordinary Women Ser.). (ENG., Illus.). 48p. (gr. 6-6). pap. 9.95 *(978-1-4109-5954-6(6))*; lib. bdg. 32.65 *(978-1-4109-5946-1(5))* Heinemann-Raintree.
Heppermann, Christine & Friedman, Richard D. Bush v. Gore: The Florida Recounts of the 2000 Presidential Election, 1 vol. 2012. (Landmark Supreme Court Cases Ser.). (ENG., Illus.). 160p. (J). (gr. 6-12). 37.07 *(978-1-61783-471-4(8))* ABDO Publishing Co.
Horn, Geoffrey M. The Supreme Court. 2003. (World Almanac Library of American Government). (Illus.). 48p. (gr. 5-12). lib. bdg. 31.00 *(978-0-8368-5459-6(4),* Gareth Stevens Secondary Library) Stevens, Gareth Publishing LLLP.
—Thurgood Marshall. 2004. (Trailblazers of the Modern World Ser.). (Illus.). 48p. (gr. 5-12). pap. 14.05 *(978-0-8368-5258-5(3))*; lib. bdg. 31.00 *(978-0-8368-5098-7(X))* Stevens, Gareth Publishing LLLP. (Gareth Stevens Secondary Library).
Howse, Jennifer. Sandra Day O'Connor. 2007. (Remarkable People Ser.). (Illus.). 24p. (J). (gr. 3-7). pap. 8.95 *(978-1-59036-648-6(4))*; lib. bdg. 24.45 *(978-1-59036-647-9(6))* Weigl Pubs., Inc.
Hunt, Santana. What Does the U.S. Supreme Court Do? 2017. (Look at Your Government Ser.). 32p. (gr. 2-2). pap. 10.50 *(978-1-4824-6059-9(9))* Stevens, Gareth Publishing LLLP.
Isle, Mick. A Timeline of the Supreme Court. 2009. (Timelines of American History Ser.). 32p. (gr. 4-4). 47.90 *(978-1-60854-391-5(9),* Rosen Reference) Rosen Publishing Group, Inc., The.
Jakubiak, David J. What Does a Supreme Court Justice Do? 2010. (How Our Government Works Ser.). 24p. (J). (gr. 3-6). lib. bdg., E-Book 42.50 *(978-1-4488-0031-5(5))*; (Illus.). pap. 8.25 *(978-1-4358-9818-9(4),* PowerKids Pr.); (Illus.). (gr. 3-6). lib. bdg. 22.60 *(978-1-4358-9361-0(1),* PowerKids Pr.) Rosen Publishing Group, Inc., The.
Jarrow, Gail. Robert H. Jackson: New Deal Lawyer, Supreme Court Justice, Nuremberg Prosecutor. 2008. (ENG., Illus.). 104p. (J). (gr. 4-6). 18.95 *(978-1-59078-511-9(8),* Calkins Creek) Boyds Mills Pr.
Jones, Brenn. Learning about Equal Rights from the Life of Ruth Bader Ginsburg. 2009. (Character Building Book Ser.). 24p. (gr. 2-3). 42.50 *(978-1-61511-000-1(3),* PowerKids Pr.) Rosen Publishing Group, Inc., The.
Kemp, Kristin. Amazing Americans: Thurgood Marshall, 1 vol. rev. ed. 2014. (Primary Source Readers Content & Literacy Ser.). (ENG., Illus.). 32p. (gr. 3-3). pap. 8.99 *(978-1-4333-7374-9(2))* Teacher Created Materials, Inc.
Kramer, Barbara. National Geographic Kids Readers: Sonia Sotomayor. 2016. (J). pap. *(978-1-4263-2291-4(7))* National Geographic Society.
Krieg, Katherine. Supreme Court. 2014. (ENG.). 24p. (gr. 3-5). 28.50 *(978-1-62717-680-4(2))* Rourke Educational Media.
Levy, Debbie. I Dissent: Ruth Bader Ginsburg Makes Her Mark. Baddeley, Elizabeth, illus. 2016. (ENG.). 40p. (J). (gr. -1-3). 17.99 *(978-1-4814-6559-5(7),* Simon & Schuster Bks. For Young Readers) Simon & Schuster Bks. For Young Readers.
Linde, Barbara. Thurgood Marshall. 2011. (Civil Rights Crusaders Ser.). (Illus.). 24p. (gr. 2-5). (J). pap. 8.15 *(978-1-4339-5700-0(0),* Gareth Stevens Learning Library); (YA). 22.60 *(978-1-4339-5698-0(5))* Stevens, Gareth Publishing LLLP.
Linde, Barbara M. Becoming a Supreme Court Justice. 2016. (Who's Your Candidate? Choosing Government Leaders Ser.). (ENG., Illus.). 32p. (J). (gr. 3-4). pap. 10.50 *(978-1-4824-4051-5(2))* Stevens, Gareth Publishing LLLP.
Littlefield, Sophie. Oliver Wendell Holmes Jr: The Supreme Court & American Legal Thought. 2009. (Library of American Lives & Times Ser.). 112p. (gr. 5-5). 69.20 *(978-1-60853-496-8(0))* Rosen Publishing Group, Inc., The.
Madani, Hamed. The Judicial Branch: Interpreting America's Laws. 2008. (Federal Government Ser.). (Illus.). 128p. (J). (gr. 6-18). lib. bdg. 34.60 *(978-1-59845-059-0(X),* MyReportLinks.com Bks.) Enslow Pubs., Inc.

—The Supreme Court & the Judicial Branch: How the Federal Courts Interpret Our Laws. 2012. (Constitution & the United States Government Ser.). (Illus.). 104p. (J). (gr. 5-18). 33.27 *(978-0-7660-4065-6(8))* Enslow Pubs., Inc.

Marshall, Thurgood. Thurgood Marshall. 2004. (Black Americans of Achievement Ser.). (Illus.). 112p. (gr. 6-12). 35.00 *(978-0-7910-8163-1(X)*, Chelsea Hse.) Facts On File, Inc.

McElroy, Lisa Tucker. John G. Roberts, Jr: Chief Justice. 2006. (Gateway Biographies Ser.). (ENG., Illus.). 48p. (gr. 4-8). lib. bdg. 26.60 *(978-0-8225-6389-1(4)*, Lerner Pubns.) Lerner Publishing Group.

McNeese, Tim, ed. Great Supreme Court Decisions Set, 12-Volumes. 2007. (Great Supreme Court Decisions Ser.). (gr. 5-8). 395.40 *(978-0-7910-9679-6(3)*, Chelsea Hse.) Facts On File, Inc.

Mead, Wendy. William H. Taft. 2011. (Presidents & Their Times 5 Ser.). 96p. (gr. 6). 34.21 *(978-1-60870-186-5(7))* Marshall Cavendish Corp.

Mountjoy, Shane & McNeese, Tim. Marbury V. Madison. 2006. (Great Supreme Court Decisions Ser.). (Illus.). 144p. (YA). (gr. 5-9). 32.95 *(978-0-7910-9240-8(2))* Facts On File, Inc.

National Geographic Kids Staff & Kramer, Barbara. Sonia Sotomayor. 2016. (Readers Bios Ser.). (ENG., Illus.). 48p. (J). (gr. 1-4). pap. 3.99 *(978-1-4263-2289-1(5)*, National Geographic Children's Bks.) National Geographic Society.

Nelson, Drew. Meet the Supreme Court. 2012. (Guide to Your Government Ser.). (Illus.). 32p. (J). (gr. 4-6). 26.60 *(978-1-4339-7268-3(9))*; pap. 10.50 *(978-1-4339-7269-0(7))* Stevens, Gareth Publishing LLLP. (Gareth Stevens Learning Library).

Panchyk, Richard. Our Supreme Court: A History with 14 Activities. 2006. (For Kids Ser.). (ENG., Illus.). 208p. (J). (gr. 5-7). pap. 18.95 *(978-1-55652-607-7(5))* Chicago Review Pr., Inc.

Patrick, John J. The Supreme Court of the United States: A Student Companion. 3rd rev. ed. 2006. (ENG., Illus.). 416p. (YA). (gr. 6-18). 65.00 *(978-0-19-530925-6(1))* Oxford Univ. Pr., Inc.

Prentzas, G. S. Gideon V. Wainwright: The Right to Free Legal Counsel. 2007. (Great Supreme Court Decisions Ser.). (Illus.). 120p. (YA). (gr. 5-9). lib. bdg. 32.95 *(978-0-7910-9383-2(2))* Facts On File, Inc.

Randolph, Ryan P. How to Draw the Life & Times of William Howard Taft. 2007. (Kid's Guide to Drawing the Presidents of the United States of America Ser.). (Illus.). 32p. (YA). (gr. 2-5). 26.50 *(978-1-4042-3003-3(3))* Rosen Publishing Group, Inc., The.

Rohan, Rebecca Carey. Thurgood Marshall: The First African-American Supreme Court Justice. 2016. (Great American Thinkers Ser.). 128p. (J). (gr. 9-9). 45.64 *(978-1-5026-1932-7(6))* Cavendish Square Publishing.

Roland, James. Ruth Bader Ginsburg: Iconic Supreme Court Justice. 2016. (Gateway Biographies Ser.). (ENG., Illus.). 48p. (J). (gr. 4-8). 26.65 *(978-1-5124-0596-5(5))*; 39.99 *(978-1-5124-0597-2(3))* Lerner Publishing Group. (Lerner Pubns.).

Rose, Simon. Supreme Court. 2016. (J). ***(978-1-5105-2251-0(4))*** SmartBook Media, Inc.

Rosen, Daniel. Dred Scott & the Supreme Court: Text Pairs. 2008. (Bridges/Navigators Ser.). (J). (gr. 5). 94.00 *(978-1-4108-8413-8(9))* Benchmark Education Co.

Rumsch, BreAnn. William Taft, 1 vol. 2009. (United States Presidents Ser.). (ENG., Illus.). 40p. (YA). (gr. 3-6). 27.07 *(978-1-60453-474-0(5))* ABDO Publishing Co.

Sandra Day O'Connor. 2005. 12p. (gr. k-4). 2.95 *(978-0-635-02621-7(X))* Gallopade International.

Shichtman, Sandra H. Sonia Sotomayor. 2011. (Supreme Court Justices Ser.). (Illus.). 111p. 28.95 *(978-1-59935-156-8(0))* Reynolds, Morgan Inc.

Suen, Anastasia. The U. S. Supreme Court, 1 vol. Skeens, Matthew, illus. 2008. (American Symbols Ser.). (ENG.). 24p. (gr. 1-2). 26.65 *(978-1-4048-4707-1(3))* Picture Window Bks.

Supreme Court DBQs: Exploring the Cases that Changed History. 2007. (YA). spiral bd. 29.95 *(978-1-932785-28-9(0))* Bill of Rights Institute, The.

Supreme Court Milestones - Group 5, 5 bks., Set. Incl. Plessy v. Ferguson: Separate but Unequal. Axelrod-Contrada, Joan. lib. bdg. 42.79 *(978-0-7614-2951-7(4))*; Roberts v. Jaycees: Women's Rights. Gold, Susan Dudley. lib. bdg. 42.79 *(978-0-7614-2952-4(2))*; U. S. v. Eichman: Flag-Burning & Free Speech. Fridell, Ron. lib. bdg. 42.79 *(978-0-7614-2953-1(0))*; U. S. v. Nixon: The Limits of Presidential Privilege. Stefoff, Rebecca. lib. bdg. 42.79 *(978-0-7614-2955-5(7))*; Worcester v. Georgia: Native American Rights. Gold, Susan Dudley. lib. bdg. 42.79 *(978-0-7614-2956-2(5))*; 128p. (gr. 7-18). (Supreme Court Milestones 5 Ser.). 2008. Set lib. bdg. 213.95 *(978-0-7614-2949-4(2)*, Benchmark Bks.) Marshall Cavendish Corp.

Supreme Court Milestones Group 3, 5 bks., Set. Incl. Gideon V. Wainwright: The Right to Free Counsel. Fridell, Ron. lib. bdg. 42.79 *(978-0-7614-2146-7(7))*; New York Times Co. V. Sullivan: Freedom of the Press or Libel? Gold, Susan Dudley. lib. bdg. 42.79 *(978-0-7614-2145-0(9))*; Reno V. ACLU Internet Censorship. Axelrod-Contrada, Joan. lib. bdg. 42.79 *(978-0-7614-2144-3(0))*; Tinker V. des Moines: Free Speech for Students. Gold, Susan Dudley. lib. bdg. 42.79 *(978-0-7614-2142-9(4))*; United States V. Amistad: Slave Ship Mutiny. Gold, Susan Dudley. lib. bdg. 42.79 *(978-0-7614-2143-6(2))*; (Illus.). 128p. (gr. 7-7). (Supreme Court Milestones 3 Ser.). 2006. Set lib. bdg. 213.95 *(978-0-7614-2140-5(8)*, Benchmark Bks.) Marshall Cavendish Corp.

Taylor-Butler, Christine. The Supreme Court. (True Bks.). (ENG., Illus.). 48p. (J). (gr. 3-5). 2008. pap. 6.95 *(978-0-531-14786-3(X))* 2007. 29.00 *(978-0-531-12636-3(6))* Scholastic Library Publishing. (Children's Pr.).

—Thurgood Marshall. 2006. (Rookie Biographies Ser.). (ENG., Illus.). 32p. (J). (gr. 1-2). pap. 4.95 *(978-0-516-27099-9(0)*, Children's Pr.) Scholastic Library Publishing.

Torres, John. Sonia Sotomayor: First Latina Supreme Court Justice. 2015. (Influential Latinos Ser.). (ENG., Illus.). 128p. (J). (gr. 7-7). 37.27 *(978-0-7660-7001-1(8))* Enslow Pubs., Inc.

US Supreme Court Landmark Cases. 2016. (US Supreme Court Landmark Cases Ser.). 128p. (J). lib. bdg. 298.16 *(978-0-7660-8418-6(3))* Enslow Pubs., Inc.

Wagner, Heather Lehr. The Supreme Court. 2nd rev. ed. 2007. (U. S. Government Ser.). (Illus.). 104p. (YA). (gr. 5-9). lib. bdg. 30.00 *(978-0-7910-9283-5(6))* Facts On File, Inc.

Wetterer, Charles M. & Wetterer, Margaret K. Chief Justice. Walters, Kurt K. C., illus. 2005. 32p. (J). *(978-1-59336-306-2(0))*; pap. *(978-1-59336-307-9(9))* Mondo Publishing.

Wheeler, Jill C. Thurgood Marshall. 2003. (Breaking Barriers Ser.). 64p. (gr. 3-8). 27.07 *(978-1-57765-907-5(4)*, Abdo & Daughters) ABDO Publishing Co.

Whitelaw, Nancy. Mr. Civil Rights: The Story of Thurgood Marshall. 2nd rev. exp. ed. 2004. (Notable Americans Ser.). (Illus.). 144p. (YA). (gr. 6-12). 23.95 *(978-1-931798-02-0(8))* Reynolds, Morgan Inc.

—Thurgood Marshall. 2011. (Supreme Court Justices Ser.). (Illus.). 128p. 28.95 *(978-1-59935-157-5(9))* Reynolds, Morgan Inc.

Wilson, Natashya. How to Draw the Life & Times of William Howard Taft. 2009. (Kid's Guide to Drawing the Presidents of the United States of America Ser.). 32p. (gr. 4-4). 50.50 *(978-1-61511-165-7(4)*, PowerKids Pr.) Rosen Publishing Group, Inc., The.

Winter, Jonah. Ruth Bader Ginsburg: The Case of R. B. G. vs. Inequality. Innerst, Stacy, illus. 2017. (ENG.). 48p. (J). (gr. 1-4). 18.95 ***(978-1-4197-2559-3(9)***, Abrams Bks. for Young Readers) Abrams, Inc.

—Sonia Sotomayor. Rodriguez, Edel, illus. 2015. 40p. pap. 8.00 *(978-1-61003-616-0(6))* Center for the Collaborative Classroom.

—Sonia Sotomayor: A Judge Grows in the Bronx. Ziegler, Argentina Palacios, tr. from SPA. Rodriguez, Edel, illus. 2009. (ENG & SPA.). 40p. (J). (gr. -1-3). 17.99 *(978-1-4424-0303-1(9)*, Atheneum Bks. for Young Readers) Simon & Schuster Children's Publishing.

Wroble, Lisa A. The Right to Counsel: From Gideon V. Wainwright to Gideon's Trumpet. 2009. (Famous Court Cases That Became Movies Ser.). (Illus.). 104p. (J). (gr. 7-12). lib. bdg. 33.27 *(978-0-7660-3057-2(1))* Enslow Pubs., Inc.

Zimmerman, W. Frederick. The Nine Current Supreme Court Justices: Colorful Info for Curious Minds #3. 2007. 36p. per. 17.81 *(978-1-934840-01-6(7))* Nimble Bks. LLC.

UNITED STATES—TAXATION

see Taxation—United States

UNITED STATES—TERRITORIAL EXPANSION

Alagna, Magdalena. The Louisiana Purchase: Expanding America's Boundaries. 2009. (Life in the New American Nation Ser.). 32p. (gr. 4-4). 47.90 *(978-1-61514-284-2(3))* Rosen Publishing Group, Inc., The.

Behnke, Alison. A Timeline History of the Transcontinental Railroad. 2015. (ENG., Illus.). 48p. (J). (gr. 5-8). 30.65 *(978-1-4677-8581-5(4))* Lerner Publishing Group.

Burgan, Michael. The Louisiana Purchase. 2016. (Making a New Nation Ser.). (ENG.). 48p. (gr. 4-4). pap. 8.99 *(978-1-4846-3596-4(5)*, NA-h) Heinemann-Raintree.

Casciato, Daniel. Expansion & Reform: (Early 1800s-1861) 2007. (Presidents of the United States Ser.). (Illus.). 48p. (J). (gr. 4-7). lib. bdg. 29.05 *(978-1-59036-741-4(3))* Weigl Pubs., Inc.

—Expansion & Reform: Early 1800s-1861. 2007. (Presidents of the United States Ser.). (Illus.). 48p. (J). (gr. 4-7). per. 11.95 *(978-1-59036-742-1(1))* Weigl Pubs., Inc.

Chastain, Zachary. Scandals & Glory: Politics in the 1800s. 2009. (Daily Life in America in the 1800s Ser.). 64p. (YA). (gr. 7-18). lib. bdg. 22.95 *(978-1-4222-1787-0(6))* Mason Crest.

—Scandals & Glory: Politics in The 1800s. 2009. (Daily Life in America in the 1800s Ser.). 64p. (YA). (gr. 7-18). pap. 9.95 *(978-1-4222-1860-0(0))* Mason Crest.

Christopher, Nick. The Dream of Manifest Destiny: Immigrants & the Westward Expansion, 01 vols., 1. 2016. (Spotlight on Immigration & Migration Ser.). (ENG., Illus.). 24p. (J). pap. 10.00 *(978-1-5081-4071-9(5)*, PowerKids Pr.) Rosen Publishing Group, Inc., The.

Clinton, Greg. The Louisiana Purchase. 2016. (Expanding America Ser.). (ENG., Illus.). 96p. (J). (gr. 8-8). lib. bdg. 42.79 *(978-1-5026-0962-5(2))* Cavendish Square Publishing.

Collins, Terry. Into the West: Causes & Effects of U. S. Westward Expansion, 1 vol. 2013. (Cause & Effect Ser.). (ENG.). 32p. (gr. 3-4). 27.32 *(978-1-4765-0237-3(4))*; pap. 8.95 *(978-1-4765-3403-9(9))* Capstone Press of Coughlan Cos. (Fact Finders).

Deibel, Zachary. Native American Resistance. 2017. ***(978-1-5026-2644-8(6))*** Cavendish Square Publishing.

Domnauer, Teresa. Westward Expansion. 2010. (True Book Ser.). (ENG., Illus.). 48p. (J). pap. 6.95 *(978-0-531-21249-3(1))*; (gr. 2-5). 29.00 *(978-0-531-20586-0(X))* Scholastic Library Publishing.

Expansionism. 2010. (Key Concepts in American History Ser.). (Illus.). 128p. (gr. 6-12). 45.00 *(978-1-60413-221-2(3)*, Chelsea Hse.) Facts On File, Inc.

Favor, Lesli J. A Historical Atlas of America's Manifest Destiny. (United States: Historical Atlases of the Growth of a New Nation Ser.). 64p. 2009. (gr. 5-5). 61.20 *(978-1-60854-250-5(5))* 2005. (Illus.). (J). (gr. 7-12). lib. bdg. 31.95 *(978-1-4042-0201-6(3))* Rosen Publishing Group, Inc., The.

George, Enzo. The Expanding Frontier. 2015. (J). lib. bdg. *(978-1-62713-489-7(1))*; (ENG.). 48p. (gr. 4-4). lib. bdg. 31.36 *(978-1-5026-0248-0(2))* Cavendish Square Publishing.

George, Lynn. What Do You Know about Westward Expansion? (20 Questions: History Ser.). 24p. (gr. 2-3). 2009. 42.50 *(978-1-60854-960-3(7)*, PowerKids Pr.) 2008. (Illus.). (J). lib. bdg. 22.60 *(978-1-4042-4189-3(2))* Rosen Publishing Group, Inc., The.

Harness, Cheryl. The Remarkable Rough-Riding Life of Theodore Roosevelt & the Rise of Empire America. 2007. (Cheryl Harness Histories Ser.). (ENG., Illus.). 144p. (J). (gr. 4-7). lib. bdg. 25.90 *(978-1-4263-0009-7(3)*, National Geographic Children's Bks.) National Geographic Society.

Howell, Brian. U. S. Growth & Change in the 19th Century, 1801 to 1861. 2011. (Explorer Library: Language Arts Explorer Ser.). (ENG.). 32p. (gr. 4-8). lib. bdg. 28.50 *(978-1-61080-202-4(0)*, 201180) Cherry Lake Publishing.

—U.S. Growth & Change in the 19th Century. 2011. (Explorer Library: Language Arts Explorer Ser.). (ENG.). 32p. (gr. 4-8). pap. 14.21 *(978-1-61080-290-1(X)*, 201213) Cherry Lake Publishing.

Huey, Lois Miner. American Archaeology Uncovers the Westward Movement. 2009. (American Archaeology Ser.). (Illus.). 64p. (J). (gr. 5-6). 31.36 *(978-0-7614-4265-3(0))* Marshall Cavendish Corp.

Jarnow, Jesse. Manifest Destiny: A Primary Source History of the Settlement of the American Heartland in the Late 19th Century. 2005. (Primary Sources in American History Ser.). (Illus.). 64p. (J). (gr. 5-8). lib. bdg. 31.95 *(978-1-4042-0176-7(9))* Rosen Publishing Group, Inc., The.

Klar, Jeremy. The Louisiana Purchase & Westward Expansion, 01 vols., 1. 2016. (Early American History Ser.). (ENG., Illus.). 80p. (J). lib. bdg. 32.90 *(978-1-68048-271-3(8)*, Britannica Educational Publishing) Rosen Publishing Group, Inc., The.

Kleinmartin, Hex. The Erie Canal. 2016. (Expanding America Ser.). (ENG., Illus.). 96p. (J). (gr. 8-8). lib. bdg. 42.79 *(978-1-5026-0966-3(5))* Cavendish Square Publishing.

Landau, Elaine. Jefferson's Louisiana Purchase: Would You Make the Deal of the Century? 2015. (What Would You Do? Ser.). 48p. (J). (gr. 3-4). 25.27 *(978-0-7660-6305-1(4))*; pap. 8.95 *(978-0-7660-6306-8(2)*, Enslow Elementary) Enslow Pubs., Inc.

—The Louisiana Purchase: Would You Close the Deal? (What Would You Do? Ser.). (Illus.). 48p. (J). 2010. pap. 8.95 *(978-1-59845-196-2(0))* 2008. (gr. 3-7). lib. bdg. 25.27 *(978-0-7660-2902-6(6))* Enslow Pubs., Inc. (Enslow Elementary).

Lassieur, Allison. Westward Expansion: An Interactive History Adventure. 2016. (You Choose: History Ser.). (ENG.). 112p. (gr. 3-4). pap. 6.95 *(978-1-5157-4259-3(8)*, You Choose Bks.) Capstone Press of Coughlan Cos.

Levy, Janey. Mapping America's Westward Expansion: Applying Geographic Tools & Interpreting Maps. 2009. (Critical Thinking in American History Ser.). 48p. (gr. 5-8). 53.00 *(978-1-61512-095-6(5)*, Rosen Reference) Rosen Publishing Group, Inc., The.

Lynette, Rachel. The Louisiana Purchase. 2013. (Pioneer Spirit: the Westward Expansion Ser.). (Illus.). 24p. (J). (gr. 3-6). pap. 8.25 *(978-1-4777-0895-8(2))*; pap. 49.50 *(978-1-4777-0896-5(0))*; lib. bdg. 22.60 *(978-1-4777-0781-4(6))* Rosen Publishing Group, Inc., The. (PowerKids Pr.).

—The Oregon Trail. 2013. (Pioneer Spirit: the Westward Expansion Ser.). 24p. (J). (gr. 3-6). 22.60 *(978-1-4777-0786-9(7))*; (ENG., Illus.). pap. 8.25 *(978-1-4777-0905-4(3))* Rosen Publishing Group, Inc., The. (PowerKids Pr.).

Marsh, Carole. John C. Fremont. 2004. 12p. (gr. k-4). 2.95 *(978-0-635-02380-3(6))* Gallopade International.

—What a Deal! The Louisiana Purchase. 2003. 32p. (J). (gr. 3-8). pap. 5.95 *(978-0-635-02123-6(4))* Gallopade International.

Maynard, Charles W. John Charles Fremont: The Pathfinder. (Famous Explorers of the American West Ser.). 24p. 2009. (gr. 3-4). 42.50 *(978-1-61512-503-6(5))* 2003. (Illus.). (J). lib. bdg. 22.60 *(978-0-8239-6289-1(X))* Rosen Publishing Group, Inc., The. (PowerKids Pr.).

Moriarty, J. T. Manifest Destiny: A Primary Source History of America's Territorial Expansion in the 19th Century. 2009. (Primary Sources in American History Ser.). 64p. (gr. 5-8). 58.50 *(978-1-60851-490-8(0))* Rosen Publishing Group, Inc., The.

Mountjoy, Shane. Manifest Destiny: Westward Expansion. 2009. (Milestones in American History Ser.). (Illus.). 128p. (gr. 6-12). 35.00 *(978-1-60413-055-3(5)*, Chelsea Hse.) Facts On File, Inc.

Mulhall, Jill K. Expanding the Nation, 1 vol. 2005. (Primary Source Readers Ser.). (ENG.). 24p. (J). (gr. 5-5). pap. 8.99 *(978-0-7439-8905-3(8))* Shell Educational Publishing.

Musolf, Nell. The Split History of Westward Expansion in the United States: A Perspectives Flip Book, 1 vol. 2012. (Perspectives Flip Bks.). (ENG.). 64p. (gr. 5-6). pap. 8.95 *(978-0-7565-4596-3(X))*; lib. bdg. 33.99 *(978-0-7565-4571-0(4))* Compass Point Bks.

Nelson, Sheila. From Sea to Shining Sea: Americans Move West, 13 vols. 2005. (How America Became America Ser.). (Illus.). 96p. (J). lib. bdg. *(978-1-59084-900-2(0))* Mason Crest.

—Thomas Jefferson's America: The Louisiana Purchase (1800-1811) 2006. (How America Became America Ser.). (Illus.). 96p. (YA). lib. bdg. 22.95 *(978-1-59084-904-0(3))* Mason Crest.

O'Donoghue, Sean. Thomas Jefferson & the Louisiana Purchase. 2016. (Spotlight on American History Ser.). (Illus.). 24p. (J). (gr. 6-4). 26.25 *(978-1-5081-4948-4(8)*, PowerKids Pr.) Rosen Publishing Group, Inc., The.

Olson, Steven. The Oregon Trail: A Primary Source History of the Route to the American West. 2009. (Primary Sources in American History Ser.). 64p. (gr. 5-8). 58.50 *(978-1-60851-501-1(X))* Rosen Publishing Group, Inc., The.

The Oregon Trail. 2013. (Pioneer Spirit: the Westward Expansion Ser.). 24p. (J). (gr. 3-6). pap. 49.50 *(978-1-4777-0906-1(1)*, PowerKids Pr.) Rosen Publishing Group, Inc., The.

Otfinoski, Steven. A Primary Source History of Westward Expansion. 2015. (Primary Source History Ser.). (ENG., Illus.). 32p. (gr. 3-4). lib. bdg. 27.32 *(978-1-4914-1841-3(9))* Capstone Press of Coughlan Cos.

Raabe, Emily. Thomas Jefferson & the Louisiana Purchase. 2009. (Westward Ho! Ser.). 24p. (gr. 2-3). 42.50 *(978-1-60854-763-0(9)*, PowerKids Pr.) Rosen Publishing Group, Inc., The.

Rajczak, Kristen. Life As a Pioneer. 2013. (What You Didn't Know about History Ser.). (Illus.). 24p. (J). (gr. 2-5). pap. 8.15 *(978-1-4339-8420-4(2))*; lib. bdg. 22.60 *(978-1-4339-8419-8(9))* Stevens, Gareth Publishing LLLP.

Randolph, Ryan P. Following the Great Herds: The Plains Indians & the American Buffalo. 2009. (Library of the Westward Expansion Ser.). 24p. (gr. 3-4). 42.50 *(978-1-60853-934-5(2)*, PowerKids Pr.) Rosen Publishing Group, Inc., The.

Raum, Elizabeth. Cutting a Path: Daniel Boone & the Cumberland Gap. 2015. (Adventures on the American Frontier Ser.). (ENG., Illus.). 32p. (gr. 3-4). pap. 7.95 *(978-1-4914-4909-7(8))* Capstone Press of Coughlan Cos.

—Expanding a Nation: Causes & Effects of the Louisiana Purchase, 1 vol. 2013. (Cause & Effect Ser.). (ENG.). 32p. (gr. 3-4). 27.32 *(978-1-4765-0236-6(6))*; pap. 8.95 *(978-1-4765-3402-2(0))* Capstone Press of Coughlan Cos. (Fact Finders).

Raum, Elizabeth, et al. Cause & Effect. 2013. (Cause & Effect Ser.). (ENG.). 32p. (gr. 3-4). pap. 31.80 *(978-1-4765-3634-7(1))*; lib. bdg. 109.28 *(978-1-4765-0371-4(0))* Capstone Press of Coughlan Cos. (Fact Finders).

Rice, Katelyn. The Great Leap Westward. 2017. (J). pap. *(978-1-4938-3791-5(5))* Teacher Created Materials, Inc.

RJF Publishing Staff & Hankins, Chelsey. The Gateway Arch. 2009. (Symbols of American Freedom Ser.). 48p. (gr. 4-6). 30.00 *(978-1-60413-513-8(1)*, Chelsea Clubhouse) Facts On File, Inc.

Roberts, Russell. The Railroad Fuels Westward Expansion (1870s) 2012. (Illus.). 47p. (J). lib. bdg. 29.95 *(978-1-61228-290-9(3))* Mitchell Lane Pubs., Inc.

Romano, Amy. A Historical Atlas of the United States & Its Territories. 2009. (United States: Historical Atlases of the Growth of a New Nation Ser.). 64p. (gr. 5-5). 61.20 *(978-1-60854-255-0(6))* Rosen Publishing Group, Inc., The.

Roza, Greg. Westward Expansion. 2011. (Story of America Ser.). (Illus.). 32p. (J). (gr. 4-6). pap. 10.50 *(978-1-4339-4781-0(1))*; lib. bdg. 26.60 *(978-1-4339-4780-3(3))* Stevens, Gareth Publishing LLLP. (Gareth Stevens Learning Library).

Schaffer, David. The Louisiana Purchase: The Deal of the Century That Doubled the Nation. 2006. (Wild History of the American West Ser.). (Illus.). 128p. (J). (gr. 5-9). lib. bdg. 34.60 *(978-1-59845-018-7(2)*, MyReportLinks.com Bks.) Enslow Pubs., Inc.

Sechrist, Darren. Westward, Ho! 2008. (ENG.). 32p. (J). pap. *(978-0-7787-4217-3(2))* Crabtree Publishing Co.

Sharp, Constance. Beyond Our Shores: America Extends Its Reach,1890-1899. 2013. (Illus.). 48p. (J). pap. *(978-1-4222-2420-5(1))* Mason Crest.

—Beyond Our Shores: America Extends Its Reach,1890-1899. Rakove, Jack N., ed. 2012. (How America Became America Ser.). (Illus.). 48p. (J). (gr. 3-4). 19.95 *(978-1-4222-2406-9(6))* Mason Crest.

Smith, Robert W. & Smith, Robert. Westward Movement. 2006. (Spotlight on America Ser.). (ENG., Illus.). 96p. (gr. 5-9). pap. 13.99 *(978-1-4206-3216-3(7))* Teacher Created Resources, Inc.

Steele, Christy. California & the Southwest Join the United States. 2005. (America's Westward Expansion Ser.). (Illus.). 48p. (gr. 5-12). lib. bdg. 31.00 *(978-0-8368-5786-3(0)*, Gareth Stevens Secondary Library) Stevens, Gareth Publishing LLLP.

—Pioneer Life in the American West. 2005. (America's Westward Expansion Ser.). (Illus.). 48p. (gr. 5-12). pap. 14.05 *(978-0-8368-5797-9(6))*; lib. bdg. 31.00 *(978-0-8368-5790-0(9))* Stevens, Gareth Publishing LLLP. (Gareth Stevens Secondary Library).

—Texas Joins the United States. 2005. (America's Westward Expansion Ser.). (Illus.). 48p. (gr. 5-12). lib. bdg. 31.00 *(978-0-8368-5791-7(7)*, Gareth Stevens Secondary Library) Stevens, Gareth Publishing LLLP.

Streissguth, Thomas. Perspectives on Westward Expansion. 2018. (ENG.). 32p. (gr. 3-6). ***(978-1-63235-404-4(7)***, 12-Story Library) Pr. Room Editions LLC.

Torr, James D., ed. Westward Expansion. 2003. (Interpreting American History Through Primary Documents Ser.x). (Illus.). 208p. (J). 32.45 *(978-0-7377-1134-9(5)*, Greenhaven Pr., Inc.) Cengage Gale.

Whitman Publishing, creator. Discover Westward Expansion History Project Toolkit. 2011. (Illus.). 19.95 *(978-0-7948-3589-7(9))* Whitman Publishing LLC.

Zurn, Jon. The Louisiana Purchase, 1 vol. 2007. (Essential Events Set 1 Ser.). (ENG., Illus.). 112p. (J). (gr. 6-12). lib. bdg. 35.64 *(978-1-59928-853-6(2))* ABDO Publishing Co.

UNITED STATES—TERRITORIES AND POSSESSIONS

Benchmark Education Co., LLC. The New England Colonies. 2014. (PRIME Ser.). (J). (gr. 6-8). pap. *(978-1-4509-9486-6(5))* Benchmark Education Co.

—The Southern Colonies. 2014. (PRIME Ser.). (J). (gr. 6-8). pap. *(978-1-4509-9488-0(1))* Benchmark Education Co.

Bradley, Jada. U. S. Territories & Possessions, Vol. 19. 2015. (Let's Explore the States Ser.). (Illus.). 64p. (J). (gr. 5). 23.95 *(978-1-4222-3335-1(9))* Mason Crest.

Brown, Jonatha A. Puerto Rico & Other Outlying Areas. 2006. (Portraits of the States Ser.). (Illus.). 32p. (gr. 2-6). pap. 10.50 *(978-0-8368-4693-5(1))*; lib. bdg. 26.00 *(978-0-8368-4674-4(5))* Stevens, Gareth Publishing LLLP. (Gareth Stevens Learning Library).

Doherty, Craig A. & Doherty, Katherine M. The Thirteen Colonies Set. 2005. (Thirteen Colonies Ser.). 160p. (gr. 5-8). 455.00 *(978-0-8160-5406-0(1))* Facts On File, Inc.

Romano, Amy. A Historical Atlas of the United States & Its Territories. 2009. (United States: Historical Atlases of the Growth of a New Nation Ser.). 64p. (gr. 5-5). 61.20 *(978-1-60854-255-0(6))* Rosen Publishing Group, Inc., The.

Scholastic Library Publishing. A True Book-the Thirteen Colonies. 2011. (True Book-the Thirteen Colonies Ser.). (J). (gr. 3-5). 377.00 *(978-0-531-22149-5(0)*, Children's Pr.) Scholastic Library Publishing.

UNITED STATES—TREATIES

see United States—Foreign Relations—Treaties

UNITED STATES—VICE-PRESIDENTS

see Vice-presidents—United States

UNITED STATES—WOMEN

see Women—United States

UNITED STATES—WORLD WAR, 1939-1945

see World War, 1939-1945—United States

UNITED STATES CAPITOL (WASHINGTON, D.C.)

Campodonica, Carol A. How Congress Works. Miller, Bondell, ed. Anderson, Bill, illus. Uni Photo Picture Agency Staff, photos by. Date not set. (J). (gr. 4-5). pap. *(978-0-9648488-9-4(9))* Buzzard Pr. International.

Carr, Aaron. Capitol Building. 2014. (J). *(978-1-4896-2890-9(8))* Weigl Pubs., Inc.

Clay, Kathryn. The U. S. Capitol: Introducing Primary Sources. 2017. (Introducing Primary Sources Ser.). (ENG.). 32p. (gr. 1-2). lib. bdg. 27.99 **(978-1-5157-6354-3(4))** Capstone Press of Coughlan Cos.

Curlee, Lynn. Capital. Curlee, Lynn, illus. 2006. (ENG., Illus.). 48p. (J). (gr. 4-7). 22.99 (978-1-4169-1801-1(9), Atheneum Bks. for Young Readers) Simon & Schuster Children's Publishing.

Hicks, Terry Allan. The Capitol. (Symbols of America Ser.). (Illus.). 40p. 2007. (J). (gr. 4-7). pap. 6.99 (978-0-7614-3374-3(0)) 2006. (gr. 3-7). lib. bdg. 20.95 (978-0-7614-2132-0(7)) Marshall Cavendish Corp. (Benchmark Bks.).

Hillard, Stephane. The U. S. Capitol: The History of U. S. Congress. 2017. (Landmarks of Democracy: American Institutions Ser.). 24p. (J). (gr. 7-8). pap. 8.25 **(978-1-5081-6097-7(X)**, PowerKids Pr.) Rosen Publishing Group, Inc., The.

Lee, Georgia. Tour the U. S. Capitol. 2013. (InfoMax Readers Ser.). (ENG.). 24p. (J). (gr. 3-4). pap. 49.50 (978-1-4777-2574-0(1)); pap. 8.25 (978-1-4777-2769-0(8)) Rosen Publishing Group, Inc., The. (Rosen Classroom).

Piehl, Janet. The Capitol Building. 2009. (Lightning Bolt Books (tm) — Famous Places Ser.). (ENG.). 32p. (gr. k-2). 26.60 (978-1-57505-966-2(5), Lerner Pubns.) Lerner Publishing Group.

Silate, Jennifer. The United States Capitol. (Primary Sources of American Symbols Ser.). 24p. 2009. (gr. 3-3). 42.50 (978-1-60851-511-0(7), PowerKids Pr.) 2006. (Illus.). (J). (gr. 4-7). lib. bdg. 22.60 (978-1-4042-2694-4(X)) Rosen Publishing Group, Inc., The.

Sirota, Lyn & Sirota, Lyn A. Capitol. 2013. (Illus.). 24p. (J). (978-1-62127-460-5(8)) Weigl Pubs., Inc.

Sirota, Lyn A. Capitol. 2013. (Illus.). 24p. (J). pap. (978-1-62127-466-7(7)) Weigl Pubs., Inc.

Stille, Darlene R. The Capitol Building, 1 vol. Ouren, Todd, illus. 2008. (Our Nation's Pride Ser.). (ENG.). 32p. (gr. -1-3). 28.50 (978-1-60270-112-0(1), Looking Glass Library- Nonfiction) Magic Wagon.

UNITED STATES PEACE CORPS

see Peace Corps (U.S.)

UNIVERSAL HISTORY

see World History

UNIVERSE

Alex, Joanne DeFilipp. I Wonder What's Out There: A Vision of the Universe for Primary Classes. 2003. (Illus.). 64p. (J). spiral bd. (978-0-939195-32-9(1)) Parent Child Pr., Inc.

American Museum of Natural History. ABC Universe. 2015. (AMNH ABC Board Bks.). (ENG., Illus.). 18p. (J). (gr. -1-k). bds. 7.95 (978-1-4549-1409-9(2)) Sterling Publishing Co., Inc.

Asimov, Isaac & Hantula, Richard. The Birth of Our Universe. 2005. (Isaac Asimov's 21st Century Library of the Universe). (Illus.). 32p. (gr. 2-6). lib. bdg. 26.00 (978-0-8368-3964-7(1), Gareth Stevens Learning Library) Stevens, Gareth Publishing LLLP.

—Black Holes, Pulsars, & Quasars. 2005. (Isaac Asimov's 21st Century Library of the Universe). (Illus.). 32p. (gr. 2-6). lib. bdg. 26.00 (978-0-8368-3965-4(X), Gareth Stevens Learning Library) Stevens, Gareth Publishing LLLP.

—Is There Life in Outer Space? 2005. (Isaac Asimov's 21st Century Library of the Universe). (Illus.). 32p. (gr. 2-6). lib. bdg. 26.00 (978-0-8368-3950-0(1), Gareth Stevens Learning Library) Stevens, Gareth Publishing LLLP.

Bankston, John. Stephen Hawking: Breaking the Boundaries of Time & Space. 2005. (Great Minds of Science Ser.). (Illus.). 128p. (J). lib. bdg. 27.94 (978-0-7660-2281-2(1)) Enslow Pubs., Inc.

Benchmark Education Company, LLC Staff, compiled by. The Universe: Theme Set. 2006. (J). 135.00 (978-1-4108-7149-7(5)) Benchmark Education Co.

Bennett, Jeffrey. I, Humanity. 2016. (ENG., Illus.). 32p. (J). (gr. 2-4). 15.00 (978-1-937548-52-0(X)) Big Kid Science.

Bortz, Fred. Beyond Jupiter: The Story of Planetary Astronomer Heidi Hammel. 2006. (ENG., Illus.). 128p. (gr. 7-9). per. 19.95 (978-0-309-09552-5(2), Joseph Henry Pr.) National Academies Pr.

—The Big Bang Theory: Edwin Hubble & the Origins of the Universe. 2013. (Revolutionary Discoveries of Scientific Pioneers Ser.). (Illus.). 80p. (J). (gr. 7-12). 33.25 (978-1-4777-1803-2(6)) Rosen Publishing Group, Inc., The.

Burbank, Shirley Ann. Where Did I Come From? 2010. 40p. pap. 21.32 (978-1-4535-3304-8(4)) Xlibris Corp.

Butt, Kyle. God Made the World. 2006. (ENG., Illus.). (J). (gr. -1-3). 3.00 (978-0-932859-69-3(0)) Apologetics Pr., Inc.

Carson, Mary Kay. The Universe: From the Big Bang to Deep Space. 2014. (ENG.). 24p. (gr. k-3). 28.50 (978-1-62717-731-3(0)) Rourke Educational Media.

Clark, Stuart. Discovering the Universe. 2012. (ENG., Illus.). 48p. (J). 15.00 (978-1-899762-77-4(9)) Award Pubns. Ltd. GBR. Dist: Parkwest Pubns., Inc.

Cornell, Kari. Theoretical Physicist Stephen Hawking. 2016. (STEM Trailblazer Bios Ser.). (ENG., Illus.). 32p. (J). (gr. 2-5). 26.65 (978-1-4677-9528-9(3), Lerner Pubns.) Lerner Publishing Group.

El Cosmos. (SPA.). (YA). (gr. 5-8). pap. (978-84-7131-925-8(X)) Editex, Editorial S.A. ESP. Dist: Lectorum Pubns., Inc.

Culp, Jennifer. Neil DeGrasse Tyson. 2014. (Great Science Writers Ser.). (Illus.). 112p. (J). (gr. 7-12). 35.60 (978-1-4777-7691-9(5)) Rosen Publishing Group, Inc., The.

DeCristofano, Carolyn Cinami. Big Bang! The Tongue-Tickling Tale of a Speck That Became Spectacular. Carroll, Michael, illus. 2005. (ENG.). 32p. (J). (gr. k-3). pap. 7.95 (978-1-57091-619-9(5)) Charlesbridge Publishing, Inc.

Dorling Kindersley Publishing Staff. It Can't Be True. 2016. (DK Braille Ser.). (ENG.). 72p. (J). (gr. 4-7). 29.99 (978-1-4654-4406-6(8), DK Children) Dorling Kindersley Publishing, Inc.

Doudna, Kelly. The Universe, 1 vol. 2015. (ENG., Illus.). 24p. (J). (978-1-62403-747-4(X)) ABDO Publishing Co.

Earth Cosmology: The Destroyer Comet. 2004. (YA). cd-rom 15.00 (978-0-934269-61-2(0)) UFO Photo Archives.

Earth Cosmology: The Effects of the Giant Destroyer Comet. 2004. (UFO Fact Bks.). (YA). cd-rom 15.00 (978-0-934269-41-4(6)) UFO Photo Archives.

Editors of Kingfisher. Amazing Universe: Come Face to Face with Faraway Stars. 2016. (Fast Facts Ser.). (ENG., Illus.). 32p. (J). pap. 6.99 (978-0-7534-7277-4(5), 9780753472774, Kingfisher) Roaring Brook Pr.

—Amazing Universe: Come Face to Face with Life Faraway Stars. 2016. (Fast Facts Ser.). (ENG., Illus.). 32p. 11.99 (978-0-7534-7276-7(7), 9780753472767, Kingfisher) Roaring Brook Pr.

Encyclopaedia Britannica, Inc. Staff. Britannica Illustrated Science Library Series (18 Title Series), 18 vols. 2010. 599.00 (978-1-61535-423-8(9)) Encyclopaedia Britannica, Inc.

Encyclopaedia Britannica, Inc. Staff, compiled by. Britannica Illustrated Science Library: Universe, 16 vols. 2008. (Illus.). (J). 29.95 (978-1-59339-399-1(7)) Encyclopaedia Britannica, Inc.

Encyclopedia Britannica Staff, creator. Universe. 2011. (Britannica Illustrated Science Library Ser.). 104p. (J). 37.44 (978-1-61535-457-3(3)) Encyclopaedia Britannica, Inc.

Fleisher, Paul. The Big Bang. 2005. (Great Ideas of Science Ser.). (Illus.). 80p. (YA). (gr. 9-12). lib. bdg. 27.93 (978-0-8225-2133-4(4)) Lerner Publishing Group.

Ford, Harry & Barnham, Kay. Outer Space. 2003. (Knowledge Masters Ser.). (Illus.). 32p. (YA). pap. incl. cd-rom (978-1-903954-09-6(6), Pavilion Children's Books) Pavilion Bks.

Garcia, Gloria. El Universo. (SPA.). 8p. 9.95 (978-84-272-7277-4(4)) Molino, Editorial ESP. Dist: Distribooks, Inc.

Garlick, Mark A. Atlas of the Universe. 2008. (Insiders Ser.). (ENG., Illus.). 128p. (J). (gr. 4-9). 24.99 (978-1-4169-5558-0(5), Simon & Schuster Bks. For Young Readers) Simon & Schuster Bks. For Young Readers.

Germadnik, Mary. How Do We Know the Age of the Universe? 2009. (Great Scientific Questions & the Scientists Who Answered Them Ser.). 112p. (gr. 7-12). 63.90 (978-1-61513-197-6(3)) Rosen Publishing Group, Inc., The.

Gifford, Clive. The Universe, Black Holes, & the Big Bang. 2015. (Watch This Space! Ser.). (ENG., Illus.). 32p. (J). (gr. 3-7). lib. bdg. (978-0-7787-2024-9(1)) Crabtree Publishing Co.

Graham, Ian. Earth & the Universe. 2008. (World of Wonder Ser.). (ENG.). 32p. (J). 29.00 (978-0-531-24025-0(8), Children's Pr.) Scholastic Library Publishing.

Hasan, Heather, ed. How Mathematical Models, Computer Simulations, & Exploration Can Be Used to Study the Universe: An Anthology of Current Thought. 2009. (Contemporary Discourse in the Field of Astronomy Ser.). 240p. (gr. 10-10). 63.90 (978-1-61511-904-2(3)) Rosen Publishing Group, Inc., The.

Hixson, Bryce. Galactic Cookie Dough. Hixson, Bryce, illus. 2003. (Illus.). (J). per. 14.95 (978-1-931801-06-5(1)) Loose In The Lab.

Holden, Barry. The Milky Way BIG BOOK Edition. 2014. (ENG.). 16p. (gr. 2-2). Beta (978-1-77654-100-3(6), Red Rocket Readers) Flying Start Bks.

Holt, Rinehart and Winston Staff. Holt Science & Technology Chapter 18: Earth Science: Studying Space. 5th ed. 2004. (Illus.). pap. 12.86 (978-0-03-030331-9(1)) Holt McDougal.

Howard, Fran. The Universe, 8 vols., Set. Incl. Asteroids, Comets, & Meteoroids. 27.07 (978-1-59928-925-0(3)); Dwarf Planets. 27.07 (978-1-59928-926-7(1)); Kuiper Belt. 27.07 (978-1-59928-927-4(X)); Milky Way. 27.07 (978-1-59928-928-1(8)); Moon. 27.07 (978-1-59928-929-8(6)); Solar System. 27.07 (978-1-59928-930-4(X)); Stars. 27.07 (978-1-59928-931-1(8)); Sun. 27.07 (978-1-59928-932-8(6)); 32p. (gr. k-4). (On the Map Ser.). 2008. 216.56 (978-1-59928-924-3(5), Buddy Bks.) ABDO Publishing Co.

Jackson, Tom. The Universe: An Illustrated History of Astronomy. 2012. (Illus.). 144p. (J). (978-0-9853230-2-8(7)) Shelter Harbor Pr.

James, Muirden. El Universo.Tr. of Universe. (SPA.). 96p. (YA). (gr. 5-8). 18.36 (978-84-241-1993-5(2)) Everest Editora ESP. Dist: Lectorum Pubns., Inc.

Jedicke, Peter. Cosmology: Exploring the Universe. 2003. (Hot Science Ser.). (J). lib. bdg. 28.50 (978-1-58340-366-2(3)) Black Rabbit Bks.

Keranen, Rachel. The Big Bang Theory. 2017. (J). **(978-1-5026-2770-4(1))** Cavendish Square Publishing.

—The Big Bang Theory & Light Spectra. 2016. (Space Systems Ser.). 112p. (J). lib. bdg. 42.79 (978-1-5026-2295-2(5)) Cavendish Square Publishing.

—The Composition of the Universe: The Evolution of Stars & Galaxies. 2016. (Space Systems Ser.). 112p. (J). 42.79 (978-1-5026-2285-3(8)) Cavendish Square Publishing.

Kook, Ima. Big Bang Theory: The Bang That Created Our Universe. 2008. (As Dreamed by Itsy Ser.). (Illus.). 24p. (J). pap. 12.00 (978-1-892298-21-8(X)) Abique Pub.

May, Brian, et al. Exploring the Mysteries of the Universe. 2016. (STEM Guide to the Universe Ser.). (ENG.). 200p. (J). (gr. 9-9). lib. bdg. 46.10 (978-1-4994-6407-8(X)) Rosen Publishing Group, Inc., The.

McMahon, Michael. Why Do the Stars Shine? Level 4 Factbook. 2010. (Cambridge Young Readers Ser.). (ENG., Illus.). 16p. pap. 6.00 (978-0-521-13723-2(3)) Cambridge Univ. Pr.

Media, Cont. The Cosmos. 2008. 96p. (YA). 17.99 (978-1-931703-01-7(9)) Creative Publishing Consultants.

Miotto, Enrico. El Universo.Tr. of Universe. (SPA.). 40p. (YA). (gr. 5-8). 10.36 (978-84-207-5192-4(8)) Grupo Anaya, S.A. ESP. Dist: Lectorum Pubns., Inc.

Morgan, Jennifer. Born with a Bang: The Universe Tells Our Cosmic Story. Andersen, Dana Lynne, illus. 2004. (Sharing Nature with Children Book Ser.). 48p. (YA). (gr. 2-18). 19.95 (978-1-58469-033-7(X)); pap. 9.95 (978-1-58469-032-0(1)) Dawn Pubns.

Murphy, Pat & Klutz Editors. Guide to the Galaxy. 2011. (ENG.). 50p. (J). (gr. 3-3). 19.99 (978-1-59174-920-2(4)) Klutz.

Our Universe. 2004. (Illus.). lib. bdg. 7.95 (978-0-8225-4790-7(2)) Lerner Publishing Group.

Paiva, Johannah Gilman, ed. The Awesome Book of the Universe. Various, illus. 2013. (ENG.). 32p. (J). (gr. 3-7). 7.99 (978-1-77093-779-6(X)) Flowerpot Pr.

Pamplona, Alberto Hernández. A Visual Guide to the Universe. 2017. (Visual Exploration of Science Ser.). 96p. (J). (gr. 12-13). 37.10 **(978-1-5081-7585-8(3)**, Rosen Young Adult) Rosen Publishing Group, Inc., The.

Parragon Publishing Staff, contrib. by. The Universe: The Ultimate Guided Tour of the Cosmos from the Formation of Stars to the Farthest Reaches of the Universe. 2014. (Illus.). 224p. (J). (978-1-4723-4675-9(0)) Parragon Bk. Service Ltd.

Pissanos, Paul. From Aristotle to Hawking. 2012. (Illus.). 272p. pap. 73.23 (978-1-4678-8506-5(1)) AuthorHouse.

Priddy, Roger. Space: For Kids Who Really Love Space! 2012. (ENG., Illus.). 30p. (J). (gr. -1-2). 9.99 (978-0-312-51459-4(X), 9780312514594, Priddy Bks.) St. Martin's Pr.

—The Sun. 2011. (ENG., Illus.). 30p. (J). (978-1-84915-726-1(X), Priddy Bks.) St. Martin's Pr.

Pulliam, Christine & Daniels, Patricia. Space Encyclopedia: A Tour of Our Solar System & Beyond. Aguilar, David A., illus. 2013. 191p. (J). (978-1-4263-1629-6(1)) National Geographic Society.

Rice, Dona. We Are Here. 2015. (Science Readers: Content & Literacy Ser.). (ENG., Illus.). 32p. (J). (gr. 4-4). pap. 8.99 (978-1-4807-4687-9(8)) Teacher Created Materials, Inc.

Rockett, Paul. 70 Thousand Million, Million, Million Stars in Space. Ruffle, Mark, illus. 2015. (Big Countdown Ser.). (ENG.). 32p. (gr. 3-5). 29.99 (978-1-4109-6875-3(8), Raintree Perspectives) Heinemann-Raintree.

Rubino, Michael. Bang! How We Came to Be. 2011. (ENG.). 69p. (J). (gr. 4-7). pap. 17.00 (978-1-61614-472-2(6)) Prometheus Bks., Pubs.

Saddleback Educational Publishing Staff, creator. Universe. 2008. (Factoscope Ser.). (Illus.). 64p. (YA). per. 10.95 (978-1-59905-237-3(7)) Saddleback Educational Publishing, Inc.

Schmermund, Elizabeth. New Frontiers in Astronomy. 2016. (Great Discoveries in Science Ser.). (Illus.). 128p. (J). (gr. 9-9). 45.64 (978-1-5026-1959-4(8)) Cavendish Square Publishing.

Schomp, Virginia. The Ancient Maya. 2009. (Myths of the World 3 Ser.). 96p. (gr. 6). 34.21 (978-0-7614-4217-2(0)) Marshall Cavendish Corp.

Science, Punk & Punk Science Staff. Punk Science - Intergalactic, Supermassive Space Book, Vol. 1. unabr. ed. 2015. (ENG., Illus.). 96p. (J). (gr. 2). pap. 7.99 (978-1-4472-5384-6(1)) Pan Macmillan GBR. Dist: Independent Pubs. Group.

Scientific American Staff. Extreme Physics. 2009. (Scientific American Cutting-Edge Science Ser.). 176p. (gr. 9-9). 63.90 (978-1-60853-076-2(0)) Rosen Publishing Group, Inc., The.

Senker, Cath. Stephen Hawking. 2015. (Against the Odds Biographies Ser.). (ENG., Illus.). 48p. (gr. 3-6). 33.32 (978-1-4846-2466-1(1)) Heinemann-Raintree.

Senker, Cath & Throp, Claire. Against the Odds Biographies. 2015. (Against the Odds Biographies Ser.). (ENG.). 48p. (gr. 3-6). lib. bdg. 133.28 (978-1-4846-2468-5(8), Heinemann InfoSearch) Heinemann-Raintree.

Silverstein, Alvin, et al. The Universe. 2003. (Science Concepts Ser.). (ENG., Illus.). 64p. (gr. 5-9). lib. bdg. 26.60 (978-0-7613-2255-9(8), Twenty-First Century Bks.) Lerner Publishing Group.

Simon, Seymour. The Universe. 2006. (ENG., Illus.). 32p. (J). (gr. k-4). pap. 6.99 (978-0-06-087725-5(1), Collins) HarperCollins Pubs.

Solway, Andrew. The Universe. 2010. (CC: 21st Century Science Ser.). 112p. (gr. 6-12). 42.80 (978-1-933834-76-4(5)) Brown Bear Bks.

Sparrow, Giles. Our Universe. 2017. (J). **(978-0-7660-9263-1(1))** Enslow Pubs., Inc.

Sparrow, Giles. Probing Deep Space. 2006. (Secrets of the Universe Ser.). (Illus.). 48p. (gr. 6-12). lib. bdg. 31.00 (978-0-8368-7279-8(7), Gareth Stevens Secondary Library) Stevens, Gareth Publishing LLLP.

Sparrow, Giles & John, Judith. How the Universe Works. 2016. (Discoveries in Space Science Ser.). (ENG., Illus.). 80p. (YA). (gr. 9-9). lib. bdg. 35.64 (978-1-5026-1014-0(0)) Cavendish Square Publishing.

Teacher Created Resources Staff. Space Guides - Discovering the Universe: A Galaxy of Mind-Expanding Information! 2008. (ENG., Illus.). 32p. (gr. 4-13). pap. 7.99 (978-1-4206-8268-7(7)) Teacher Created Resources, Inc.

The Universe. (Jump Ser.). 36p. (J). (gr. 2-7). pap. (978-1-882210-21-3(2)) Action Publishing, Inc.

Venezia, Mike. Stephen Hawking: Cosmologist Who Gets a Big Bang Out of the Universe. Venezia, Mike, illus. 2009. (Getting to Know the World's Greatest Inventors & Scientists Ser.). (ENG., Illus.). 32p. (J). (gr. 3-4). pap. 6.95 (978-0-531-21337-7(4), Children's Pr.); (gr. 2-5). 28.00 (978-0-531-23728-1(1)) Scholastic Library Publishing.

Ventura, Marne. Astrophysicist & Space Advocate Neil Degrasse Tyson. 2014. (STEM Trailblazer Bios Ser.). (ENG., Illus.). 32p. (gr. 2-5). lib. bdg. 26.60 (978-1-4677-2461-6(0), Lerner Pubns.) Lerner Publishing Group.

Walsh, Kenneth. Outer Space, 1 vol. 2nd rev. ed. 2013. (Nonfiction Readers Ser.). (ENG., Illus.). 28p. (J). (gr. 2-2). pap. 23.96 (978-1-4807-1053-5(9)) Shell Educational Publishing.

Whitt, Stephen. The Turtle & the Universe. Hernandez, Stephanie, illus. 2008. (ENG.). 86p. (J). (gr. 3-7). pap. 14.99 (978-1-59102-626-6(1)) Prometheus Bks., Pubs.

Williams, Brian. The Universe. 2010. (What About... Ser.). (Illus.). 40p. (J). (gr. 6-8). lib. bdg. 19.95 (978-1-4222-1566-1(0)) Mason Crest.

—Universe: Biggest & Best. 2004. (Biggest & Best Ser.). (Illus.). 40p. (J). pap. 7.95 (978-1-84236-025-5(6)) Miles Kelly Publishing, Ltd. GBR. Dist: Independent Pubs. Group.

—What about the Universe. 2008. 40p. pap. (978-1-84810-075-6(2)) Miles Kelly Publishing, Ltd.

World Book, Inc Staff, contrib. by. The Universe — Mysteries & Marvels. 2010. (J). (978-0-7166-9546-2(4)) World Bk., Inc.

—The Universe — A Cosmic Tour. 2010. (J). (978-0-7166-9545-5(6)) World Bk., Inc.

Zappa, Marcia. The Universe, 8 vols., Set 2. Incl. Black Holes. 27.07 (978-1-61714-686-2(2)); Constellations. 27.07 (978-1-61714-687-9(0)); Eclipses. 27.07 (978-1-61714-688-6(9)); Galaxies. 27.07 (978-1-61714-689-3(7)); NASA. 27.07 (978-1-61714-690-9(0)); Rockets & Satellites. 27.07 (978-1-61714-691-6(9)); Space Exploration. 27.07 (978-1-61714-692-3(7)); Space Stations. 27.07 (978-1-61714-693-0(5)); (gr. 3-5). (Universe Set 2 Ser.). (Illus.). 32p. 2011. 216.56 (978-1-61714-685-5(4), Buddy Bks.) ABDO Publishing Co.

Zuchora-Walske, Christine. We're the Center of the Universe! Science's Biggest Mistakes about Astronomy & Physics. 2014. (Science Gets It Wrong Ser.). (Illus.). 32p. (gr. 4-6). pap. 7.95 (978-1-4677-4552-9(9)); (ENG., lib. bdg. 26.60 (978-1-4677-3663-3(5), Lerner Pubns.) Lerner Publishing Group.

UNIVERSITIES AND COLLEGES

see also Education, Higher; Scholarships; Students also headings beginning with the word College and names of individual institutions

Allshouse, Sara & Burns, Adam. University of San Francisco College Prowler off the Record. 2005. (College Prowler off the Record Guides: Vol. 181). 160p. (YA). (gr. 12-18). pap., stu. ed. 14.95 (978-1-59658-180-7(8)) College Prowler, Inc.

Alter, Austin & Lyon, Abby. Rhode Island School of Design College Prowler off the Record. 2005. (College Prowler off the Record Guides: Vol. 106). 160p. (YA). (gr. 12-18). pap., stu. ed. 14.95 (978-1-59658-105-0(0)) College Prowler, Inc.

Amboba, Ethan & Lyon, Abby. Occidental College College Prowler off the Record. 2nd ed. 2005. (College Prowler off the Record Guides: Vol. 94). 160p. (YA). (gr. 12-18). pap., stu. ed. 14.95 (978-1-59658-093-0(3)) College Prowler, Inc.

Amodeo, Jessica & Pecsenye, Jessica. University of Colorado College Prowler off the Record. 2nd ed. 2005. (College Prowler off the Record Guides: Vol. 151). 160p. (YA). (gr. 12-18). pap., stu. ed. 14.95 (978-1-59658-150-0(6)) College Prowler, Inc.

Andrew, Stacy & Davis, Cristine. Morehouse College College Prowler off the Record. 2005. (College Prowler off the Record Guides: Vol. 86). 160p. (YA). (gr. 12-18). pap., stu. ed. 14.95 (978-1-59658-085-5(2), Off The Record) College Prowler, Inc.

Ayala, Anikka & Nash, Kevin. University of Notre Dame College Prowler off the Record. 2nd ed. 2005. (College Prowler off the Record Guides: Vol. 171). 160p. (YA). (gr. 12-18). pap., stu. ed. 14.95 (978-1-59658-170-8(0)) College Prowler, Inc.

Baier, Ellen & Skindzier, Jon. Franklin & Marshall College College Prowler off the Record. 2005. (College Prowler off the Record Guides: Vol. 52). 160p. (YA). (gr. 12-18). pap., stu. ed. 14.95 (978-1-59658-051-0(8)) College Prowler, Inc.

Bailey, Diane. Kansas Basketball. 2013. (America's Most Winning Teams Ser.). 48p. (J). (gr. 5-8). 29.25 (978-1-4488-9405-5(0)); pap. 11.75 (978-1-4488-9429-1(8)) Rosen Publishing Group, Inc., The.

Ballow, Jonah & Gray, Kevan. University of Kansas College Prowler off the Record. 2nd ed. 2005. (College Prowler off the Record Guides: Vol. 159). 160p. (YA). (gr. 12-18). pap., stu. ed. 14.95 (978-1-59658-158-6(1)) College Prowler, Inc.

Barrish, Lily & Pecsenye, Jessice. University of Central Florida College Prowler off the Record. 2005. (College Prowler off the Record Guides: Vol. 149). 160p. (YA). (gr. 12-18). pap., stu. ed. 14.95 (978-1-59658-148-7(4)) College Prowler, Inc.

Beane, Abbie, et al. Middlebury College College Prowler off the Record. 2005. (College Prowler off the Record Guides: Vol. 85). 160p. (YA). (gr. 12-18). pap., stu. ed. 14.95 (978-1-59658-084-8(4)) College Prowler, Inc.

Bender, Abby & Weisgerber, Amy. Purdue University College Prowler off the Record. 2005. (College Prowler off the Record Guides: Vol. 103). 160p. (YA). (gr. 12-18). pap., stu. ed. 14.95 (978-1-59658-102-9(6)) College Prowler, Inc.

Benson, Elisa & Gohari, Omid. Colgate University College Prowler off the Record. 2005. (College Prowler off the Record Guides: Vol. 29). 160p. (YA). (gr. 12-18). pap., stu. ed. 14.95 (978-1-59658-028-2(3)) College Prowler, Inc.

Biggers, Nikki & Mason, Chris. Cal Poly College Prowler off the Record: Inside California Polytechnic State University. 2005. (College Prowler off the Record Guides: Vol. 21). 160p. (YA). (gr. 12-18). pap., stu. ed. 14.95 (978-1-59658-020-6(8)) College Prowler, Inc.

Bist, Richard & Skindzier, Jon. Florida State University College Prowler off the Record. 2005. (College Prowler off the Record Guides: Vol. 50). 160p. (YA). (gr. 12-18). pap., stu. ed. 14.95 (978-1-59658-049-7(6)) College Prowler, Inc.

Bohler, Victoria & Gray, Kevan. Loyola College in Maryland College Prowler off the Record. 2005. (College Prowler off the Record Guides: Vol. 76). 160p. (YA). (gr. 12-18). pap., stu. ed. 14.95 (978-1-59658-075-6(5)) College Prowler, Inc.

Brennan, Genevieve. Wellesley College College Prowler off the Record. 2005. (College Prowler off the Record Guides: Vol. 200). 160p. (YA). (gr. 12-18). pap., stu. ed. 14.95 (978-1-59658-199-9(9)) College Prowler, Inc.

Bretzius Matthew. West Virginia University College Prowler off the Record. 2005. (College Prowler off the Record Guides: Vol. 203). 160p. (YA). (gr. 12-18). pap., stu. ed. 14.95 (978-1-59658-202-6(2)) College Prowler, Inc.

Brown, Antoinette & Skindzier, Jon. St John's University NY College Prowler off the Record: Inside Saint Johns New York. 2nd ed. 2005. (College Prowler off the Record Guides: Vol. 122). 160p. (YA). (gr. 12-18). pap., stu. ed. 14.95 (978-1-59658-121-0(2)) College Prowler, Inc.

Burgan, Michael. Death at Kent State: How a Photograph Brought the Vietnam War Home to America. 2016. (Captured History Ser.). (ENG., Illus.). 64p. (gr. 5-7). lib. bdg. 34.65 (978-0-7565-5424-8(1), CPB Grades 4-8) Compass Point Bks.

Byers, Ann. Ohio State Football. 2013. (America's Most Winning Teams Ser.). 48p. (J). (gr. 5-8). 29.25 (978-1-4488-9401-7(8)); pap. 11.75 (978-1-4488-9438-3(7)); pap. 70.50 (978-1-4488-9439-0(5)) Rosen Publishing Group, Inc., The.

C. Ridley, Joi & Gray, Kevan. Howard University College Prowler off the Record. 2nd ed. 2005. (College Prowler off the Record Guides: Vol. 66). 160p. (YA). (gr. 12-18). pap., stu. ed. 14.95 (978-1-59658-065-7(8), Off The Record) College Prowler, Inc.

Campbell, Margaret & Gohari, Omid. Duke University College Prowler off the Record. 2nd ed. 2005. (College Prowler off the Record Guides: Vol. 45). 160p. (YA). (gr. 12-18). pap., stu. ed. 14.95 (978-1-59658-044-2(5)) College Prowler, Inc.

Carlin, Daniel. Washington University in St Louis College Prowler off the Record. 2nd ed. 2005. (College Prowler off the Record Guides: Vol. 199). 160p. (YA). (gr. 12-18). pap., stu. ed. 14.95 (978-1-59658-198-2(0)) College Prowler, Inc.

Chadderdon, Andrea & Nash, Kevin. University of Oklahoma College Prowler off the Record. 2nd ed. 2005. (College Prowler off the Record Guides: Vol. 172). 160p. (YA). (gr. 12-18). pap., stu. ed. 14.95 *(978-1-59658-171-5(9))* College Prowler, Inc.

Chang, Tristen & Pecsenye, Jessica. UC Davis College Prowler off the Record: Inside University of California Davis. 2nd ed. 2005. (College Prowler off the Record Guides: Vol. 142). 160p. (YA). (gr. 12-18). pap., stu. ed. 14.95 *(978-1-59658-141-8(7))* College Prowler, Inc.

Chasan, Emily & Gray, Kevan. Tufts University College Prowler off the Record. 2nd ed. 2005. (College Prowler off the Record Guides: Vol. 136). 160p. (YA). (gr. 12-18). pap., stu. ed. 14.95 *(978-1-59658-135-7(2))* College Prowler, Inc.

C.Laird, Elizabeth & Skindzier, Jon. Guilford College College Prowler off the Record. 2005. (College Prowler off the Record Guides: Vol. 59). 160p. (YA). (gr. 12-18). pap., stu. ed. 14.95 *(978-1-59658-058-9(5))* College Prowler, Inc.

Clapp, Sarah & Varacalli, Lauren. Denison University College Prowler off the Record. 2005. (College Prowler off the Record Guides: Vol. 41). 160p. (YA). (gr. 12-18). pap., stu. ed. 14.95 *(978-1-59658-040-4(2))* College Prowler, Inc.

Cloud, Megan & Nash, Kevin. Barnard College College Prowler off the Record. 2005. (College Prowler off the Record Guides: Vol. 8). 160p. (YA). (gr. 12-18). pap., stu. ed. 14.95 *(978-1-59658-007-7(0))* College Prowler, Inc.

Cole, Kristin & Burns, Adam. Loyola Marymount University College Prowler off the Record. 2005. (College Prowler off the Record Guides: Vol. 77). 160p. (YA). (gr. 12-18). pap., stu. ed. 14.95 *(978-1-59658-076-3(3))* College Prowler, Inc.

Coleman, Andrew & Mason, Chris. Clemson University College Prowler off the Record. 2nd ed. 2005. (College Prowler off the Record Guides: Vol. 27). 160p. (YA). (gr. 12-18). pap., stu. ed. 14.95 *(978-1-59658-026-8(7))* College Prowler, Inc.

Coleman, Miriam. Plan It: Conducting Short-Term & Long-Term Research. 2012. (Core Skills Ser.). (ENG., Illus.). 32p. (J). (gr. 3-6). pap. 10.00 *(978-1-4488-7523-8(4))*; lib. bdg. 25.25 *(978-1-4488-7450-7(5))* Rosen Publishing Group, Inc., The. (PowerKids Pr.).

Collins, Elizabeth & Lyon, Abby. Swarthmore College College Prowler off the Record. 2nd ed. 2005. (College Prowler off the Record Guides: Vol. 129). 160p. (YA). (gr. 12-18). pap., stu. ed. 14.95 *(978-1-59658-128-9(X))* College Prowler, Inc.

Connell, Sarah & Nash, Kevin. Bates College College Prowler off the Record. 2005. (College Prowler off the Record Guides: Vol. 9). 160p. (YA). (gr. 12-18). pap., stu. ed. 14.95 *(978-1-59658-008-4(9))* College Prowler, Inc.

Cook, Jane Hampton. B Is for Baylor. Dobbins, Erin & Connally, Erin, illus. 2010. (Big Bear Bks.). (ENG.). 64p. (gr. 17). 29.95 *(978-1-60258-270-5(X))* Baylor Univ. Pr.

Cook, Peter & Nash, Kevin. Pomona College College Prowler off the Record. 2nd ed. 2005. (College Prowler off the Record Guides: Vol. 100). 160p. (YA). (gr. 12-18). pap., stu. ed. 14.95 *(978-1-59658-099-2(2))* College Prowler, Inc.

Cooper, Amy & Keller, Carolyn. Rochester Institute of Technology College Prowler off the Record: Inside RIT. 2005. (College Prowler off the Record Guides: Vol. 109). 160p. (YA). (gr. 12-18). pap., stu. ed. 14.95 *(978-1-59658-108-1(5))* College Prowler, Inc.

Core, Sarah & Varacalli, Lauren. College of Wooster College Prowler off the Record. 2005. (College Prowler off the Record Guides: Vol. 33). 160p. (YA). (gr. 12-18). pap., stu. ed. 14.95 *(978-1-59658-032-9(1))* College Prowler, Inc.

Cruttenden, Jamie & Pecsenye, Jessica. University of Pittsburgh College Prowler off the Record. 2nd ed. 2005. (College Prowler off the Record Guides: Vol. 175). 160p. (YA). (gr. 12-18). pap., stu. ed. 14.95 *(978-1-59658-174-6(3))* College Prowler, Inc.

Cusick, John. Wesleyan University College Prowler off the Record. 2005. (College Prowler off the Record Guides: Vol. 201). 160p. (YA). (gr. 12-18). pap., stu. ed. 14.95 *(978-1-59658-200-2(6))* College Prowler, Inc.

Cyr, Jessica & Keller, Carolyn. Ohio University College Prowler off the Record. 2nd ed. 2005. (College Prowler off the Record Guides: Vol. 96). 160p. (YA). (gr. 12-18). pap., stu. ed. 14.95 *(978-1-59658-095-4(X))* College Prowler, Inc.

Davis, Amy & Mandelbaum, Jolie. Michigan State University College Prowler off the Record. 2nd ed. 2005. (College Prowler off the Record Guides: Vol. 84). 160p. (YA). (gr. 12-18). pap., stu. ed. 14.95 *(978-1-59658-083-1(6))* College Prowler, Inc.

Davis, Jenny & Skindzier, Jon. Indiana University College Prowler off the Record. 2nd ed. 2005. (College Prowler off the Record Guides: Vol. 67). 160p. (YA). (gr. 12-18). pap., stu. ed. 14.95 *(978-1-59658-066-4(6))* College Prowler, Inc.

Davis, Lauren & Varacalli, Lauren. Bucknell University College Prowler off the Record. 2005. (College Prowler off the Record Guides: Vol. 20). 160p. (YA). (gr. 12-18). pap., stu. ed. 14.95 *(978-1-59658-019-0(4))* College Prowler, Inc.

Dearing, Kate & Lyon, Abby. Tulane University College Prowler off the Record. 2nd ed. 2005. (College Prowler off the Record Guides: Vol. 137). 160p. (YA). (gr. 12-18). pap., stu. ed. 14.95 *(978-1-59658-136-4(0))* College Prowler, Inc.

Dickson, Kristin & Pecsenye, Jessica. Trinity University Texas College Prowler off the Record. 2005. (College Prowler off the Record Guides: Vol. 135). 160p. (YA). (gr. 12-18). pap., stu. ed. 14.95 *(978-1-59658-134-0(4))* College Prowler, Inc.

Doctorick, Jonathan & Gohari, Omid. Duquesne University College Prowler off the Record. 2005. (College Prowler off the Record Guides: Vol. 46). 160p. (YA). (gr. 12-18). pap., stu. ed. 14.95 *(978-1-59658-045-9(3))* College Prowler, Inc.

Doscher, Melissa. Yale University College Prowler off the Record. 2nd ed. 2005. (College Prowler off the Record Guides: Vol. 208). 160p. (YA). (gr. 12-18). pap., stu. ed. 14.95 *(978-1-59658-207-1(3))* College Prowler, Inc.

DuPree, Ben & Skindzier, Jon. Reed College College Prowler off the Record. 2nd ed. 2005. (College Prowler off the Record Guides: Vol. 104). 160p. (YA). (gr. 12-18). pap., stu. ed. 14.95 *(978-1-59658-103-6(4))* College Prowler, Inc.

Dutt, Arjun & Varacalli, Lauren. Claremont Mckenna College College Prowler off the Record. 2005. (College Prowler off the Record Guides: Vol. 26). 160p. (YA). (gr. 12-18). pap., stu. ed. 14.95 *(978-1-59658-025-1(9)*, Off The Record) College Prowler, Inc.

Eagan, Colin & Varacalli, Lauren. Davidson College College Prowler off the Record. 2005. (College Prowler off the Record Guides: Vol. 40). 160p. (YA). (gr. 12-18). pap., stu. ed. 14.95 *(978-1-59658-039-8(9))* College Prowler, Inc.

Earl, Archie William, Sr. The Inside Scoop on American Colleges & Universities. 2004. (YA). pap. 6.99 *(978-1-884169-32-8(5))* International Educational Improvement Ctr. Pr.

Easley, Michael F. Look Out, College, Here I Come! 2007. (J). *(978-0-8106-2037-7(5))*; pap. *(978-0-8106-2038-4(3))* National Education Assn.

Epstein, Brad M. Arizona State University 101: My First Text-Board-Book. I.t. ed. 2003. (101 — My First Text-Board Books). (Illus.). 20p. (J). bds. *(978-0-9727702-3-1(2)*, 101 Bk.) Michaelson Entertainment.

—Clemson University 101: My First Text-Board-Book. I.t. ed. 2004. (101 — My First Text-Board Books). (ENG., Illus.). 20p. (J). bds. *(978-1-932530-06-3(1)*, 101 Bk.) Michaelson Entertainment.

—Kansas State Univ 101: My First Text-Board-Book. I.t. ed. 2007. (101 — My First Text-Board Books). (Illus.). 20p. (J). bds. *(978-1-932530-57-5(6)*, 101 Bk.) Michaelson Entertainment.

—Louisiana State University 101: My First Text-Board-Book. I.t. ed. 2004. (My First Text Board Bks.). (Illus.). 20p. (J). bds. *(978-1-932530-09-4(6))* Michaelson Entertainment.

—Ohio State 101. 2013. (My First Text-Board-Book Ser.). (ENG., Illus.). 24p. (J). bds. *(978-1-60730-064-9(8)*, 101 Bk.) Michaelson Entertainment.

—Purdue University 101: My First Text-Board-Book. I.t. ed. 2004. (101 — My First Text-Board Books). (ENG., Illus.). 20p. (J). bds. *(978-1-932530-11-7(8)*, 101 Bk.) Michaelson Entertainment.

—Stanford 101. 2013. (My First Text-Board-Book Ser.). (ENG., Illus.). 20p. (J). (gr. -1). bds. *(978-1-60730-066-3(4)*, 101 Bk.) Michaelson Entertainment.

—UCLA 101: My First Text-Board-Book. I.t. ed. 2004. (My First Text Board Bks.). (Illus.). 20p. (J). bds. *(978-1-932530-15-5(0)*, 101 Bk.) Michaelson Entertainment.

—University of Florida 101: My First Text-Board-Book. I.t. ed. 2004. (101 — My First Text-Board Books). (Illus.). 20p. (J). bds. *(978-1-932530-21-6(5)*, 101 Bk.) Michaelson Entertainment.

—University of Georgia 101: My First Text-Board-Book. I.t. ed. 2004. (101 — My First Text-Board Books). (ENG., Illus.). 20p. (J). bds. *(978-1-932530-08-7(8)*, 101 Bk.) Michaelson Entertainment.

—University of Illinois 101: My First Text-Board-Book. I.t. ed. 2004. (101 — My First Text-Board Books). (ENG., Illus.). 20p. (J). bds. *(978-1-932530-17-9(7)*, 101 Bk.) Michaelson Entertainment.

—University of Kansas 101: My First Text-Board-Book. 2006. (101 — My First Text-Board Books). (ENG., Illus.). 20p. (J). bds. *(978-1-932530-40-7(1)*, 101 Bk.) Michaelson Entertainment.

—University of Nebraska 101: My First Text-Board-book. 2013. (My First Text-Board-Book Ser.). (ENG., Illus.). 20p. (J). bds. *(978-1-60730-063-2(X))* Michaelson Entertainment.

—University of Washington 101. 2013. (My First Text-Board-Book Ser.). (ENG., Illus.). 20p. (J). (gr. -1). bds. *(978-1-60730-068-7(0)*, 101 Bk.) Michaelson Entertainment.

—Usc 101: My First Text-Board-Book. I.t. ed. 2004. (101 — My First Text-Board Books). (ENG., Illus.). 20p. (J). bds. *(978-0-9727702-0-0(8)*, 101 Bk.) Michaelson Entertainment.

Eske, Aaron & Nash, Kevin. University of Nebraska College Prowler off the Record. 2nd ed. 2005. (College Prowler off the Record Guides: Vol. 168). 160p. (YA). (gr. 12-18). pap., stu. ed. 14.95 *(978-1-59658-167-8(0))* College Prowler, Inc.

Evans, Moana & Pecsenye, Jessica. Harvey Mudd College College Prowler off the Record. 2005. (College Prowler off the Record Guides: Vol. 63). 160p. (YA). (gr. 12-18). pap., stu. ed. 14.95 *(978-1-59658-062-6(3))* College Prowler, Inc.

Ewing, Drew & Burns, Adam. St Louis University College Prowler off the Record: Inside Saint Louis. 2nd ed. 2005. (College Prowler off the Record Guides: Vol. 123). 160p. (YA). (gr. 12-18). pap., stu. ed. 14.95 *(978-1-59658-122-7(0))* College Prowler, Inc.

Fackrell, Caitlin & Lyon, Abby. Lewis & Clark College College Prowler off the Record. 2005. (College Prowler off the Record Guides: Vol. 75). 160p. (YA). (gr. 12-18). pap., stu. ed. 14.95 *(978-1-59658-074-9(7))* College Prowler, Inc.

Fassio, Dan & Burns, Adam. Washington & Lee University College Prowler off the Record. 2005. (College Prowler off the Record Guides: Vol. 198). 160p. (YA). (gr. 12-18). pap., stu. ed. 14.95 *(978-1-59658-197-5(2))* College Prowler, Inc.

Fitzgerald, Brendan & Burns, Adam. Hofstra University College Prowler off the Record. 2005. (College Prowler off the Record Guides: Vol. 65). 160p. (YA). (gr. 12-18). pap., stu. ed. 14.95 *(978-1-59658-064-0(X))* College Prowler, Inc.

Flegal, Eric & Pecsenye, Jessica. UCLA College Prowler off the Record: Inside University of California Los Angeles. 2nd ed. 2005. (College Prowler off the Record Guides: Vol. 144). 160p. (YA). (gr. 12-18). pap., stu. ed. 14.95 *(978-1-59658-143-2(3))* College Prowler, Inc.

Fleming, Jessica & Burns, Adam. Texas Christian University College Prowler off the Record. 2005. (College Prowler off the Record Guides: Vol. 133). 160p. (YA). (gr. 12-18). pap., stu. ed. 14.95 *(978-1-59658-132-6(8))* College Prowler, Inc.

Florence, Sylvia & Keller, Carolyn. James Madison University College Prowler off the Record. 2nd ed. 2005. (College Prowler off the Record Guides: Vol. 70). 160p. (YA). (gr. 12-18). pap., stu. ed. 14.95 *(978-1-59658-069-5(0))* College Prowler, Inc.

Foster, Jessica & Pecsenye, Jessice. University of South Carolina College Prowler off the Record. 2nd ed. 2005. (College Prowler off the Record Guides: Vol. 182). 160p. (YA). (gr. 12-18). pap., stu. ed. 14.95 *(978-1-59658-181-4(6))* College Prowler, Inc.

Fosyth, Rebekah & Burns, Adam. Rose-Hulman Institute of Technology College Prowler off the Record. 2005. (College Prowler off the Record Guides: Vol. 111). 160p. (YA). (gr. 12-18). pap., stu. ed. 14.95 *(978-1-59658-110-4(7)*, Off The Record) College Prowler, Inc.

Fraser, Alison & Lyon, Abby. Princeton University College Prowler off the Record. 2005. (College Prowler off the Record Guides: Vol. 101). 160p. (YA). (gr. 12-18). pap., stu. ed. 14.95 *(978-1-59658-100-5(X))* College Prowler, Inc.

Fried, Alyssa & Seaman, Jim. Penn State College Prowler off the Record: Inside Pennsylvania State University. 2nd ed. 2005. (College Prowler off the Record Guides: Vol. 97). 160p. (YA). (gr. 12-18). pap., stu. ed. 14.95 *(978-1-59658-096-1(8))* College Prowler, Inc.

Friedman, Sarah & Gohari, Omid. Bryn Mawr College College Prowler off the Record. 2005. (College Prowler off the Record Guides: Vol. 19). 160p. (YA). (gr. 12-18). pap., stu. ed. 14.95 *(978-1-59658-018-3(6))* College Prowler, Inc.

G. de la Parra, John & Rahimi, Joey. The Cooper Union College Prowler off the Record. 2nd ed. 2005. (College Prowler off the Record Guides: Vol. 37). 160p. (YA). (gr. 12-18). pap., stu. ed. 14.95 *(978-1-59658-036-7(4)*, Off The Record) College Prowler, Inc.

Garrett, Tiffany & Seaman, Jim. Miami University of Ohio College Prowler off the Record. 2005. (College Prowler off the Record Guides: Vol. 83). 160p. (YA). (gr. 12-18). pap., stu. ed. 14.95 *(978-1-59658-082-4(8))* College Prowler, Inc.

Gatker, Anna & Varacalli, Lauren. Babson College College Prowler off the Record. 2005. (College Prowler off the Record Guides: Vol. 6). 160p. (YA). (gr. 12-18). pap., stu. ed. 14.95 *(978-1-59658-005-3(4))* College Prowler, Inc.

Gilbert, Heather & Nash, Kevin. Virginia Tech College Prowler off the Record: Inside Virginia Polytechnic Institute. 2nd ed. 2005. (College Prowler off the Record Guides: Vol. 196). 160p. (YA). (gr. 12-18). pap., stu. ed. 14.95 *(978-1-59658-195-1(6))* College Prowler, Inc.

Gilmore, David. Xavier University College Prowler off the Record. 2005. (College Prowler off the Record Guides: Vol. 207). 160p. (YA). (gr. 12-18). pap., stu. ed. 14.95 *(978-1-59658-206-4(5))* College Prowler, Inc.

Gitlin, Martin. Wisconsin Badgers, 1 vol. 2013. (Inside College Football Set 2 Ser.). (ENG.). 48p. (J). (gr. 3-6). lib. bdg. 32.79 *(978-1-61783-658-9(3)*, SportsZone) ABDO Publishing Co.

Glabe, Scott & Rahimi, Joey. Dartmouth College College Prowler off the Record. 2nd ed. 2005. (College Prowler off the Record Guides: Vol. 39). 160p. (YA). (gr. 12-18). pap., stu. ed. 14.95 *(978-1-59658-038-1(0))* College Prowler, Inc.

Goldsmith, Emily & Nash, Kevin. Vassar College College Prowler off the Record. 2005. (College Prowler off the Record Guides: Vol. 194). 160p. (YA). (gr. 12-18). pap., stu. ed. 14.95 *(978-1-59658-193-7(X))* College Prowler, Inc.

Gordon, Josh & Pecsenye, Jessica. Pitzer College College Prowler off the Record. 2005. (College Prowler off the Record Guides: Vol. 99). 160p. (YA). (gr. 12-18). pap., stu. ed. 14.95 *(978-1-59658-098-5(4))* College Prowler, Inc.

Gordon, Julie & Skindzier, Jon. George Washington University College Prowler off the Record. 2nd ed. 2005. (College Prowler off the Record Guides: Vol. 54). 160p. (YA). (gr. 12-18). pap., stu. ed. 14.95 *(978-1-59658-053-4(4))* College Prowler, Inc.

Gordon, Lily & Nash, Kevin. Union College College Prowler off the Record. 2nd ed. 2005. (College Prowler off the Record Guides: Vol. 138). 160p. (YA). (gr. 12-18). pap., stu. ed. 14.95 *(978-1-59658-137-1(9))* College Prowler, Inc.

Goss, Nicole, et al. University of Georgia College Prowler off the Record. 2nd ed. 2005. (College Prowler off the Record Guides: Vol. 156). 160p. (YA). (gr. 12-18). pap., stu. ed. 14.95 *(978-1-59658-155-5(7))* College Prowler, Inc.

Gossett, Kelley & Nash, Kevin. Boston College College Prowler off the Record. 2nd ed. 2005. (College Prowler off the Record Guides: Vol. 13). 160p. (YA). (gr. 12-18). pap., stu. ed. 14.95 *(978-1-59658-012-1(7))* College Prowler, Inc.

Granberry, Debra & Skindzier, Jon. Furman University College Prowler off the Record. 2nd ed. 2005. (College Prowler off the Record Guides: Vol. 53). 160p. (YA). (gr. 12-18). pap., stu. ed. 14.95 *(978-1-59658-052-7(6))* College Prowler, Inc.

Grashkina, Alexandra. Williams College College Prowler off the Record. 2005. (College Prowler off the Record Guides: Vol. 206). 160p. (YA). (gr. 12-18). pap., stu. ed. 14.95 *(978-1-59658-205-7(7))* College Prowler, Inc.

Gray, Kevan. Spelman College College Prowler off the Record. 2005. (College Prowler off the Record Guides: Vol. 121). 160p. (YA). (gr. 12-18). pap., stu. ed. 14.95 *(978-1-59658-120-3(4)*, Off The Record) College Prowler, Inc.

Greenfeld, Barbara & Weinstein, Robert A. The Kids' College Almanac Fourth Edition: A First Look at College. 4th ed. 2010. (ENG., Illus.). 352p. pap. 16.95 *(978-1-59357-736-0(2)*, JIST Works) JIST Publishing.

Gunderman, Shelby & Burns, Adam. UC San Diego College Prowler off the Record: Inside University of California San Diego. 2005. (College Prowler off the Record Guides: Vol. 146). 160p. (YA). (gr. 12-18). pap., stu. ed. 14.95 *(978-1-59658-145-6(X))* College Prowler, Inc.

Hall, Erin & Skindzier, Jon. University of Texas College Prowler off the Record. 2nd ed. 2005. (College Prowler off the Record Guides: Vol. 186). 160p. (YA). (gr. 12-18). pap., stu. ed. 14.95 *(978-1-59658-185-2(9))* College Prowler, Inc.

Hansen, Peter & Skindzier, Jon. University of Richmond College Prowler off the Record. 2005. (College Prowler off the Record Guides: Vol. 178). 160p. (YA). (gr. 12-18). pap., stu. ed. 14.95 *(978-1-59658-177-7(8))* College Prowler, Inc.

Harmon, Daniel E. Notre Dame Football. 2013. (America's Most Winning Teams Ser.). 48p. (J). (gr. 5-8). 29.25 *(978-1-4488-9399-7(2))*; pap. 70.50 *(978-1-4488-9437-6(9))*; pap. 11.75 *(978-1-4488-9436-9(0))* Rosen Publishing Group, Inc., The.

Hasslebeck, Kellie & Gohari, Omid. Depauw University College Prowler off the Record. 2005. (College Prowler off the Record Guides: Vol. 42). 160p. (YA). (gr. 12-18). pap., stu. ed. 14.95 *(978-1-59658-041-1(0))* College Prowler, Inc.

Hein, Michelle & Skindzier, Jon. Muhlenberg College College Prowler off the Record. 2005. (College Prowler off the Record Guides: Vol. 88). 160p. (YA). (gr. 12-18). pap., stu. ed. 14.95 *(978-1-59658-087-9(9))* College Prowler, Inc.

Heing, Bridget & Baldino, Greg. Critical Perspectives on the College Admissions Process. 2017. (Analyzing the Issues Ser.). 208p. (J). (gr. 8-8). lib. bdg. 47.93 ***(978-0-7660-8479-7(5))*** Enslow Pubs., Inc.

Helmer, Jay & Skindzier, Jon. Kenyon College College Prowler off the Record. 2005. (College Prowler off the Record Guides: Vol. 72). 160p. (YA). (gr. 12-18). pap., stu. ed. 14.95 *(978-1-59658-071-8(2))* College Prowler, Inc.

Hofius, Sarah & Skindzier, Jon. Ithaca College College Prowler off the Record. 2005. (College Prowler off the Record Guides: Vol. 69). 160p. (YA). (gr. 12-18). pap., stu. ed. 14.95 *(978-1-59658-068-8(2))* College Prowler, Inc.

Hondorp, Michael & Nash, Kevin. University of Michigan College Prowler off the Record. 2nd ed. 2005. (College Prowler off the Record Guides: Vol. 164). 160p. (YA). (gr. 12-18). pap., stu. ed. 14.95 *(978-1-59658-163-0(8))* College Prowler, Inc.

Hood, Dominic & Skindzier, Jon. Harvard University College Prowler off the Record. 2005. (College Prowler off the Record Guides: Vol. 62). 160p. (YA). (gr. 12-18). pap., stu. ed. 14.95 *(978-1-59658-061-9(5))* College Prowler, Inc.

Hopkins, Adrianna & Lyon, Abby. University of North Carolina College Prowler off the Record. 2nd ed. 2005. (College Prowler off the Record Guides: Vol. 170). 160p. (YA). (gr. 12-18). pap., stu. ed. 14.95 *(978-1-59658-169-2(7))* College Prowler, Inc.

Huang, Christine & Nash, Kevin. UC Berkeley College Prowler off the Record: Inside University of California Berkeley. 2nd ed. 2005. (College Prowler off the Record Guides: Vol. 141). 160p. (YA). (gr. 12-18). pap., stu. ed. 14.95 *(978-1-59658-140-1(9))* College Prowler, Inc.

Intravia, Emily & Swope, Gretchen. Fordham University College Prowler off the Record. 2005. (College Prowler off the Record Guides: Vol. 51). 160p. (YA). (gr. 12-18). pap., stu. ed. 14.95 *(978-1-59658-050-3(X))* College Prowler, Inc.

Jade, Torea, et al. Northwestern University College Prowler off the Record. 2005. (College Prowler off the Record Guides: Vol. 92). 160p. (YA). (gr. 12-18). pap., stu. ed. 14.95 *(978-1-59658-091-6(7))* College Prowler, Inc.

Jardy, Adam & Pecsenye, Jessica. Ohio State University College Prowler off the Record. 2005. (College Prowler off the Record Guides: Vol. 95). 160p. (YA). (gr. 12-18). pap., stu. ed. 14.95 *(978-1-59658-094-7(1))* College Prowler, Inc.

Jendrey, Julie. San Diego State University College Prowler off the Record. 2005. (College Prowler off the Record Guides: Vol. 113). 160p. (YA). (gr. 12-18). pap., stu. ed. 14.95 *(978-1-59658-112-8(3))* College Prowler, Inc.

Johnston, Cathy & Pecsenye, Jessica. Hamilton College College Prowler off the Record. 2005. (College Prowler off the Record Guides: Vol. 60). 160p. (YA). (gr. 12-18). pap., stu. ed. 14.95 *(978-1-59658-059-6(3))* College Prowler, Inc.

Jordan, Keith. Don't Stress the Process: The College Plan. 2005. (J). lib. bdg. 18.95 *(978-0-9761218-0-0(8))* Knowledge College Planning.

Joseph, Jessica, et al. Suny Albany College Prowler off the Record: Inside State University of New York. 2005. (College Prowler off the Record Guides: Vol. 126). 160p. (YA). (gr. 12-18). pap., stu. ed. 14.95 *(978-1-59658-125-8(5))* College Prowler, Inc.

Joseph, Tiffani & Keller, Carolyn. Temple University College Prowler off the Record. 2nd ed. 2005. (College Prowler off the Record Guides: Vol. 131). 160p. (YA). (gr. 12-18). pap., stu. ed. 14.95 *(978-1-59658-130-2(1))* College Prowler, Inc.

J.S., Monroe-Daley. A Is for Arizona. 2009. (J). 14.95 *(978-1-934878-65-1(0))* Mascot Bks., Inc.

Kamberg, Mary-Lane. North Carolina Basketball. 2013. (America's Most Winning Teams Ser.). 48p. (J). (gr. 5-8). 29.25 *(978-1-4488-9404-8(2))*; pap. 11.75 *(978-1-4488-9435-2(2))*; pap. 70.50 *(978-1-4488-9444-4(1))* Rosen Publishing Group, Inc., The.

Katz, Andrew & Gohari, Omid. Brandeis University College Prowler off the Record. 2nd ed. 2005. (College Prowler off the Record Guides: Vol. 16). 160p. (YA). (gr. 12-18). pap., stu. ed. 14.95 *(978-1-59658-015-2(1))* College Prowler, Inc.

Keller, Carolyn & Seaman, Jim. Allegheny College College Prowler off the Record. 2005. (College Prowler off the Record Guides: Vol. 1). 160p. (YA). (gr. 12-18). pap., stu. ed. 14.95 *(978-1-59658-000-8(3))* College Prowler, Inc.

Kennedy, Lauren, et al. Arizona State University College Prowler off the Record. 2005. (College Prowler off the Record Guides: Vol. 4). 160p. (YA). (gr. 12-18). pap., stu. ed. 14.95 *(978-1-59658-003-9(8))* College Prowler, Inc.

Killeen, Jared & Nash, Kevin. Bard College College Prowler off the Record. 2005. (College Prowler off the Record Guides: Vol. 7). 160p. (YA). (gr. 12-18). pap., stu. ed. 14.95 *(978-1-59658-006-0(2))* College Prowler, Inc.

Kittay, Matthew & Mason, Chris. Brown University College Prowler off the Record. 2nd ed. 2005. (College Prowler off the Record Guides: Vol. 18). 160p. (YA). (gr. 12-18). pap., stu. ed. 14.95 *(978-1-59658-017-6(8))* College Prowler, Inc.

Klein, Jennifer & Gray, Kevan. University of Pennsylvania College Prowler off the Record. 2nd ed. 2005. (College Prowler off the Record Guides: Vol. 174). 160p. (YA). (gr. 12-18). pap., stu. ed. 14.95 *(978-1-59658-173-9(5))* College Prowler, Inc.

Klein, Nadav & Varacalli, Lauren. Amherst College College Prowler off the Record. 2005. (College Prowler off the Record Guides: Vol. 3). 160p. (YA). (gr. 12-18). pap., stu. ed. 14.95 *(978-1-59658-002-2(X))* College Prowler, Inc.

Knight, Russell & Williams, Tim. University of Puget Sound College Prowler off the Record. 2005. (College Prowler off the Record Guides: Vol. 176). 160p. (YA). (gr. 12-18). pap., stu. ed. 14.95 *(978-1-59658-175-3(1))* College Prowler, Inc.

Koestler-Grack, Rachel A. Kent State Tragedy, 1 vol. 2005. (American Moments Ser.). (ENG., Illus.). 48p. (gr. 4-8). 27.07 *(978-1-59197-934-0(X)*, Abdo & Daughters) ABDO Publishing Co.

Koestler, Larry & Scheff, William. Lehigh University College Prowler off the Record. 2005. (College Prowler off the Record Guides: Vol. 74). 160p. (YA). (gr. 12-18). pap., stu. ed. 14.95 *(978-1-59658-073-2(9))* College Prowler, Inc.

Krakauer, Steve & Skindzier, Jon. Syracuse University College Prowler off the Record. 2005. (College Prowler off the Record Guides: Vol. 130). 160p. (YA). (gr. 12-18). pap., stu. ed. 14.95 *(978-1-59658-129-6(8))* College Prowler, Inc.

Kutscher, Scott & Lyon, Abby. Suny Binghamton College Prowler off the Record: Inside State University of New York. 2005. (College Prowler off the Record Guides: Vol. 125). 160p. (YA). (gr. 12-18). pap., stu. ed. 14.95 *(978-1-59658-124-1(7))* College Prowler, Inc.

L, Jessica & Skindzier, Jon. Grove City College College Prowler off the Record. 2005. (College Prowler off the Record Guides: Vol. 58). 160p. (YA). (gr. 12-18). pap., stu. ed. 14.95 *(978-1-59658-057-2(7))* College Prowler, Inc.

L. Wright, Sean & Nash, Kevin. Villanova University College Prowler off the Record. 2005. (College Prowler off the Record Guides: Vol. 195). 160p. (YA). (gr. 12-18). pap., stu. ed. 14.95 *(978-1-59658-194-4(8))* College Prowler, Inc.

Lang, Alex & Burns, Adam. University of Iowa College Prowler off the Record. 2nd ed. 2005. (College Prowler off the Record Guides: Vol. 158). 160p. (YA). (gr. 12-18). pap., stu. ed. 14.95 *(978-1-59658-157-9(3))* College Prowler, Inc.

Langlieb, David & Burns, Adam. Haverford College College Prowler off the Record. 2005. (College Prowler off the Record Guides: Vol. 64). 160p. (YA). (gr. 12-18). pap., stu. ed. 14.95 *(978-1-59658-063-3(1))* College Prowler, Inc.

Langston, Mandy & Nash, Kevin. University of Kentucky College Prowler off the Record. 2nd ed. 2005. (College Prowler off the Record Guides: Vol. 160). 160p. (YA). (gr. 12-18). pap., stu. ed. 14.95 *(978-1-59658-159-3(X))* College Prowler, Inc.

Langwith, Jacqueline. College. 2009. (Introducing Issues with Opposing Viewpoints Ser.). (ENG.). 144p. (gr. 10-12). 42.00 *(978-0-7377-4336-4(0),* Greenhaven Pr., Inc.) Cengage Gale.

Latina, Paul A. The Places You'll Go: While at the University of Florida. 2012. 20p. pap. 16.50 *(978-1-61204-831-4(5),* Strategic Bk. Publishing) Strategic Book Publishing & Rights Agency (SBPRA).

Leanoard, James & Nash, Kevin. University of San Diego College Prowler off the Record. 2nd ed. 2005. (College Prowler off the Record Guides: Vol. 180). 160p. (YA). (gr. 12-18). pap., stu. ed. 14.95 *(978-1-59658-179-1(4))* College Prowler, Inc.

LeBaron, Sarah & Dawson, Kai. Oberlin College College Prowler off the Record. 2005. (College Prowler off the Record Guides: Vol. 93). 160p. (YA). (gr. 12-18). pap., stu. ed. 14.95 *(978-1-59658-092-3(5))* College Prowler, Inc.

Lee, Brittany. Rollins College. Moore, Kim & Burns, Adam, eds. 2005. (College Prowler off the Record Guides: Vol. 110). (Illus.). 150p. (gr. 12-18). pap., stu. ed. 14.95 *(978-1-59658-109-8(3))* College Prowler, Inc.

Lee, Danielle. JumpStart Your Future: A Guide for the College-Bound Christian. 2006. (Illus.). iii, 123p. (YA). per. 12.99 *(978-0-9769298-9-5(9))* Olive Pr., The.

Lee, Susie & Skindzier, Jon. MIT College Prowler off the Record: Inside Massachusetts Institute of Technology. 2nd ed. 2005. (College Prowler off the Record Guides: Vol. 82). 160p. (YA). (gr. 12-18). pap., stu. ed. 14.95 *(978-1-59658-081-7(X))* College Prowler, Inc.

Leitikow, Greg & Varacalli, Lauren. Colorado College College Prowler off the Record. 2005. (College Prowler off the Record Guides: Vol. 34). 160p. (YA). (gr. 12-18). pap., stu. ed. 14.95 *(978-1-59658-033-6(X))* College Prowler, Inc.

Lenfest, Kevyn & Mandelbaum, Jolie. University of Vermont College Prowler off the Record. 2nd ed. 2005. (College Prowler off the Record Guides: Vol. 188). 160p. (YA). (gr. 12-18). pap., stu. ed. 14.95 *(978-1-59658-187-6(5))* College Prowler, Inc.

Lewis, Brooke & Varacalli, Lauren. Dickinson College College Prowler off the Record. 2005. (College Prowler off the Record Guides: Vol. 43). 160p. (YA). (gr. 12-18). pap., stu. ed. 14.95 *(978-1-59658-042-8(9))* College Prowler, Inc.

Lewis, Jeff & Burns, Adam. University of New Hampshire College Prowler off the Record. 2nd ed. 2005. (College Prowler off the Record Guides: Vol. 169). 160p. (YA). (gr. 12-18). pap., stu. ed. 14.95 *(978-1-59658-168-5(9))* College Prowler, Inc.

Lewis, Jennifer & Williams, Tim. Mount Holyoke College College Prowler off the Record. 2005. (College Prowler off the Record Guides: Vol. 87). 160p. (YA). (gr. 12-18). pap., stu. ed. 14.95 *(978-1-59658-086-2(0))* College Prowler, Inc.

Lexa, Katrina & Skindzier, Jon. Hampton University College Prowler off the Record. 2nd ed. 2005. (College Prowler off the Record Guides: Vol. 61). 160p. (YA). (gr. 12-18). pap., stu. ed. 14.95 *(978-1-59658-060-2(7))* College Prowler, Inc.

Lieberman, Dan & Rahimi, Joey. Carnegie Mellon University College Prowler off the Record. 2nd ed. 2005. (College Prowler off the Record Guides: Vol. 24). 160p. (YA). (gr. 12-18). pap., stu. ed. 14.95 *(978-1-59658-023-7(2))* College Prowler, Inc.

Lindin, Kerri & Pecsenye, Jessica. University of Rochester College Prowler off the Record. 2nd ed. 2005. (College Prowler off the Record Guides: Vol. 179). 160p. (YA). (gr. 12-18). pap., stu. ed. 14.95 *(978-1-59658-178-4(6))* College Prowler, Inc.

Low, Jessica & Nash, Kevin. Bentley College College Prowler off the Record. 2005. (College Prowler off the Record Guides: Vol. 12). 160p. (YA). (gr. 12-18). pap., stu. ed. 14.95 *(978-1-59658-011-4(9))* College Prowler, Inc.

Lunis, Natalie. Spooky Schools. 2013. (Scary Places Ser.). 32p. (J). (gr. 4-8). lib. bdg. 25.27 *(978-1-61772-750-4(4))* Bearport Publishing Co., Inc.

Lynn Sauthoff, Taryn & Williams, Tim. Rutgers New Brunswick College Prowler off the Record. 2005. (College Prowler off the Record Guides: Vol. 112). 160p. (YA). (gr. 12-18). pap., stu. ed. 14.95 *(978-1-59658-111-1(5))* College Prowler, Inc.

Maehl, Sarah & Nash, Kevin. Beloit College College Prowler off the Record. 2005. (College Prowler off the Record Guides: Vol. 11). 160p. (YA). (gr. 12-18). pap., stu. ed. 14.95 *(978-1-59658-010-7(0))* College Prowler, Inc.

Mahon, Amy & Gohari, Omid. Elon University College Prowler off the Record. 2005. (College Prowler off the Record Guides: Vol. 47). 160p. (YA). (gr. 12-18). pap., stu. ed. 14.95 *(978-1-59658-046-6(1))* College Prowler, Inc.

Marshall, Ashley & Keller, Carolyn. Texas a & M University College Prowler off the Record. 2nd ed. 2005. (College Prowler off the Record Guides: Vol. 132). 160p. (YA). (gr. 12-18). pap., stu. ed. 14.95 *(978-1-59658-131-9(X))* College Prowler, Inc.

Mass, Aaron & Burns, Adam. Wake Forest University College Prowler off the Record. 2nd ed. 2005. (College Prowler off the Record Guides: Vol. 197). 160p. (YA). (gr. 12-18). pap., stu. ed. 14.95 *(978-1-59658-196-8(4))* College Prowler, Inc.

McNeese, Tim. Regents of the University of California V. Bakke: American Education & Affirmative Action. 2007. (Great Supreme Court Decisions Ser.). (Illus.). 152p. (YA). (gr. 5-9). lib. bdg. 32.95 *(978-0-7910-9260-6(7))* Facts On File, Inc.

McRobert, Megan & Skindzier, Jon. Smith College College Prowler off the Record. 2005. (College Prowler off the Record Guides: Vol. 119). 160p. (YA). (gr. 12-18). pap., stu. ed. 14.95 *(978-1-59658-118-0(2))* College Prowler, Inc.

Meers, Whitney & Nash, Kevin. University of South Florida College Prowler off the Record. 2005. (College Prowler off the Record Guides: Vol. 183). 160p. (YA). (gr. 12-18). pap., stu. ed. 14.95 *(978-1-59658-182-1(4))* College Prowler, Inc.

Megill, Colin & Davis, Cristine. University of Connecticut College Prowler off the Record. 2nd ed. 2005. (College Prowler off the Record Guides: Vol. 152). 160p. (YA). (gr. 12-18). pap., stu. ed. 14.95 *(978-1-59658-151-7(4))* College Prowler, Inc.

Meyer, Jared & Jolis, Annie. University of Maryland College Prowler off the Record. 2nd ed. 2005. (College Prowler off the Record Guides: Vol. 161). 160p. (YA). (gr. 12-18). pap., stu. ed. 14.95 *(978-1-59658-160-9(3))* College Prowler, Inc.

Miller, Kirystan & Burns, Adam. Iowa State University College Prowler off the Record. 2005. (College Prowler off the Record Guides: Vol. 68). 160p. (YA). (gr. 12-18). pap., stu. ed. 14.95 *(978-1-59658-067-1(4))* College Prowler, Inc.

Mitchell, Kyra & Varacalli, Lauren. Baylor University College Prowler off the Record. 2005. (College Prowler off the Record Guides: Vol. 10). 160p. (YA). (gr. 12-18). pap., stu. ed. 14.95 *(978-1-59658-009-1(7))* College Prowler, Inc.

Mooney, Carla. Duke Basketball. 2013. (America's Most Winning Teams Ser.). 48p. (J). (gr. 5-8). 29.25 *(978-1-4488-9406-2(9))*; pap. 11.75 *(978-1-4488-9427-7(1))*; pap. 70.50 *(978-1-4488-9428-4(X))* Rosen Publishing Group, Inc., The.

—Nebraska Football. 2013. (America's Most Winning Teams Ser.). 48p. (J). (gr. 5-8). 29.25 *(978-1-4488-9400-0(X))*; pap. 70.50 *(978-1-4488-9434-5(4))*; pap. 11.75 *(978-1-4488-9433-8(6))* Rosen Publishing Group, Inc., The.

—Teen Guide to Paying for College. 2016. (ENG.). 64p. (J). (gr. 5-12). lib. bdg. *(978-1-68282-084-1(X))* ReferencePoint Pr., Inc.

Murphy, Ryan & Varacalli, Lauren. Drexel University College Prowler off the Record. 2nd ed. 2005. (College Prowler off the Record Guides: Vol. 44). 160p. (YA). (gr. 12-18). pap., stu. ed. 14.95 *(978-1-59658-043-5(7))* College Prowler, Inc.

Murray, Melanie & Varacalli, Lauren. College of Charleston College Prowler off the Record. 2005. (College Prowler off the Record Guides: Vol. 30). 160p. (YA). (gr. 12-18). pap., stu. ed. 14.95 *(978-1-59658-029-9(1))* College Prowler, Inc.

Nash, Kevin. Suny Stony Brook College Prowler off the Record: Inside State University of New York. 2005. (College Prowler off the Record Guides: Vol. 128). 160p. (YA). (gr. 12-18). pap., stu. ed. 14.95 *(978-1-59658-127-2(1))* College Prowler, Inc.

—Valparaiso University College Prowler off the Record. 2005. (College Prowler off the Record Guides: Vol. 192). 160p. (YA). (gr. 12-18). pap., stu. ed. 14.95 *(978-1-59658-191-3(3))* College Prowler, Inc.

Nicklin, Miriam & Pecsenye, Jessica. University of Virginia College Prowler off the Record. 2nd ed. 2005. (College Prowler off the Record Guides: Vol. 189). 160p. (YA). (gr. 12-18). pap., stu. ed. 14.95 *(978-1-59658-188-3(3))* College Prowler, Inc.

Nicole, Bridget & Gray, Kevan. University of Illinois College Prowler off the Record. 2nd ed. 2005. (College Prowler off the Record Guides: Vol. 157). 160p. (YA). (gr. 12-18). pap., stu. ed. 14.95 *(978-1-59658-156-2(5))* College Prowler, Inc.

Niekerk, Katie & Seaman, Jim. University of Denver College Prowler off the Record. 2nd ed. 2005. (College Prowler off the Record Guides: Vol. 154). 160p. (YA). (gr. 12-18). pap., stu. ed. 14.95 *(978-1-59658-153-1(0))* College Prowler, Inc.

Nolan, Lindsey & Varacalli, Lauren. Auburn University College Prowler off the Record. 2nd ed. 2005. (College Prowler off the Record Guides: Vol. 5). 160p. (YA). (gr. 12-18). pap., stu. ed. 14.95 *(978-1-59658-004-6(6))* College Prowler, Inc.

Olson, Remy & Mason, Chris. Case Western Reserve University College Prowler off the Record. 2nd ed. 2005. (College Prowler off the Record Guides: Vol. 25). 160p. (YA). (gr. 12-18). pap., stu. ed. 14.95 *(978-1-59658-024-4(0))* College Prowler, Inc.

Paley, Briyah. Northeastern University. Belinsky, Robin et al, eds. 2nd ed. 2005. (College Prowler off the Record Guides: Vol. 91). (Illus.). 154p. (gr. 12-18). pap., stu. ed. 14.95 *(978-1-59658-090-9(9))* College Prowler, Inc.

Palmer, Amy & Keller, Carolyn. University of Minnesota College Prowler off the Record. 2nd ed. 2005. (College Prowler off the Record Guides: Vol. 165). 160p. (YA). (gr. 12-18). pap., stu. ed. 14.95 *(978-1-59658-164-7(6))* College Prowler, Inc.

Pattinson, Darcy. Kentucky Basketball. 2013. (America's Most Winning Teams Ser.). 48p. (J). (gr. 5-8). pap. 70.50 *(978-1-4488-9432-1(8))* Rosen Publishing Group, Inc., The.

Pattison, Darcy. Kentucky Basketball. 2013. (America's Most Winning Teams Ser.). 48p. (J). (gr. 5-8). 29.25 *(978-1-4488-9403-1(4))*; pap. 11.75 *(978-1-4488-9431-4(X))* Rosen Publishing Group, Inc., The.

Peckyno, Ryan. West Point Military Academy College Prowler off the Record. 2005. (College Prowler off the Record Guides: Vol. 202). 160p. (YA). (gr. 12-18). pap., stu. ed. 14.95 *(978-1-59658-201-9(4))* College Prowler, Inc.

Piehl, Norah, ed. Choosing a College. 2012. (Issues That Concern You Ser.). (ENG., Illus.). 144p. (gr. 7-10). lib. bdg. 42.00 *(978-0-7377-5691-3(8))* Cengage Gale.

Pinkerton, Steve & Pecsenye, Jessica. Pepperdine University College Prowler off the Record. 2005. (College Prowler off the Record Guides: Vol. 98). 160p. (YA). (gr. 12-18). pap., stu. ed. 14.95 *(978-1-59658-097-8(6))* College Prowler, Inc.

Pommer, Christina & Skindzier, Jon. Johns Hopkins University College Prowler off the Record. 2005. (College Prowler off the Record Guides: Vol. 71). 160p. (YA). (gr. 12-18). pap., stu. ed. 14.95 *(978-1-59658-070-1(4))* College Prowler, Inc.

Pope-Roush, Jordan & Skindzier, Jon. Emory University College Prowler off the Record. 2nd ed. 2005. (College Prowler off the Record Guides: Vol. 49). 160p. (YA). (gr. 12-18). pap., stu. ed. 14.95 *(978-1-59658-048-0(8))* College Prowler, Inc.

Pouliot, Seth & Nash, Kevin. University of Massachusetts College Prowler off the Record. 2nd ed. 2005. (College Prowler off the Record Guides: Vol. 162). 160p. (YA). (gr. 12-18). pap., stu. ed. 14.95 *(978-1-59658-161-6(1))* College Prowler, Inc.

R., Ben & Nash, Kevin. Suny Buffalo College Prowler off the Record: Inside State University of New York. 2005. (College Prowler off the Record Guides: Vol. 127). 160p. (YA). (gr. 12-18). pap., stu. ed. 14.95 *(978-1-59658-126-5(3))* College Prowler, Inc.

R, Sarah & Seaman, Jim. Rhodes College College Prowler off the Record. 2nd ed. 2005. (College Prowler off the Record Guides: Vol. 107). 160p. (YA). (gr. 12-18). pap., stu. ed. 14.95 *(978-1-59658-106-7(9))* College Prowler, Inc.

Rakovic, Robert & Pecsenye, Jessica. Seton Hall University College Prowler off the Record. 2005. (College Prowler off the Record Guides: Vol. 117). 160p. (YA). (gr. 12-18). pap., stu. ed. 14.95 *(978-1-59658-116-6(6))* College Prowler, Inc.

Renick, Ricki & Swope, Gretchen. University of Mississippi College Prowler off the Record. 2005. (College Prowler off the Record Guides: Vol. 166). 160p. (YA). (gr. 12-18). pap., stu. ed. 14.95 *(978-1-59658-165-4(4))* College Prowler, Inc.

Richmond, Derek & Skindzier, Jon. Georgetown University College Prowler off the Record. 2nd ed. 2005. (College Prowler off the Record Guides: Vol. 55). 160p. (YA). (gr. 12-18). pap., stu. ed. 14.95 *(978-1-59658-054-1(2))* College Prowler, Inc.

Robinson, Hadley & Seaman, Jim. UC Santa Cruz College Prowler off the Record: Inside University of California Santa Cruz. 2nd ed. 2005. (College Prowler off the Record Guides: Vol. 148). 160p. (YA). (gr. 12-18). pap., stu. ed. 14.95 *(978-1-59658-147-0(6))* College Prowler, Inc.

Rosario, Nicole & Williams, Tim. University of Wisconsin College Prowler off the Record. 2nd ed. 2005. (College Prowler off the Record Guides: Vol. 191). 160p. (YA). (gr. 12-18). pap., stu. ed. 14.95 *(978-1-59658-190-6(5))* College Prowler, Inc.

Rosenbaum, Jason & Weisgerber, Amy. University of Missouri College Prowler off the Record. 2nd ed. 2005. (College Prowler off the Record Guides: Vol. 167). 160p. (YA). (gr. 12-18). pap., stu. ed. 14.95 *(978-1-59658-166-1(2))* College Prowler, Inc.

Ross, Jordan & Gohari, Omid. Emerson College College Prowler off the Record. 2nd ed. 2005. (College Prowler off the Record Guides: Vol. 48). 160p. (YA). (gr. 12-18). pap., stu. ed. 14.95 *(978-1-59658-047-3(X))* College Prowler, Inc.

Rossi, Regine & Dawson, Kai. Rensselaer Polytechnic Institute College Prowler off the Record: Inside RPI. 2005. (College Prowler off the Record Guides: Vol. 105). 160p. (YA). (gr. 12-18). pap., stu. ed. 14.95 *(978-1-59658-104-3(2))* College Prowler, Inc.

Rossi, Regine & Nash, Kevin. University of Florida College Prowler off the Record. 2nd ed. 2005. (College Prowler off the Record Guides: Vol. 155). 160p. (YA). (gr. 12-18). pap., stu. ed. 14.95 *(978-1-59658-154-8(9))* College Prowler, Inc.

Roth, Pam & Williams, Tim. Lafayette College College Prowler off the Record. 2nd ed. 2005. (College Prowler off the Record Guides: Vol. 73). 160p. (YA). (gr. 12-18). pap., stu. ed. 14.95 *(978-1-59658-072-5(0))* College Prowler, Inc.

Rudolph, Allyson & Gohari, Omid. Colby College College Prowler off the Record. 2005. (College Prowler off the Record Guides: Vol. 28). 160p. (YA). (gr. 12-18). pap., stu. ed. 14.95 *(978-1-59658-027-5(5))* College Prowler, Inc.

Rugg, Frederick E. Rugg's Recommendations on the Colleges. 20th rev. ed. 2003. 220p. (YA). (gr. 10-12). pap. 22.95 *(978-1-883062-48-4(9))* Rugg's Recommendations.

—Twenty More Tips on the Colleges. 6p. (YA). 9th rev. ed. 2003. (gr. 10-12). pap. 8.95 *(978-1-883062-49-1(7))* 10th rev. ed. 2004. pap. 8.95 *(978-1-883062-54-5(3))* 11th rev. ed. 2005. pap. 8.95 *(978-1-883062-59-0(4))* Rugg's Recommendations.

S. Wong, Derrick & Varacalli, Lauren. Bowdoin College College Prowler off the Record. 2005. (College Prowler off the Record Guides: Vol. 15). 160p. (YA). (gr. 12-18). pap., stu. ed. 14.95 *(978-1-59658-014-5(3))* College Prowler, Inc.

Salaver, Jillianne & Williams, Tim. UC Irvine College Prowler off the Record: Inside University of California Irvine. 2nd ed. 2005. (College Prowler off the Record Guides: Vol. 143). 160p. (YA). (gr. 12-18). pap., stu. ed. 14.95 *(978-1-59658-142-5(5))* College Prowler, Inc.

Sanders, Carly. Whitman College College Prowler off the Record. 2005. (College Prowler off the Record Guides: Vol. 205). 160p. (YA). (gr. 12-18). pap., stu. ed. 14.95 *(978-1-59658-204-0(9))* College Prowler, Inc.

Sandoval, Kate & Keller, Carolyn. UC Santa Barbara College Prowler off the Record: Inside University of California Santa Barbara. 2nd ed. 2005. (College Prowler off the Record Guides: Vol. 147). 160p. (YA). (gr. 12-18). pap., stu. ed. 14.95 *(978-1-59658-146-3(8))* College Prowler, Inc.

Schubach, Alanna & Pecsenye, Jessica. American University College Prowler off the Record. 2nd ed. 2005. (College Prowler off the Record Guides: Vol. 2). 160p. (YA). (gr. 12-18). pap., stu. ed. 14.95 *(978-1-59658-001-5(1))* College Prowler, Inc.

Schuvent, Julia & Skindzier, Jon. Rice University College Prowler off the Record. 2005. (College Prowler off the Record Guides: Vol. 108). 160p. (YA). (gr. 12-18). pap., stu. ed. 14.95 *(978-1-59658-107-4(7))* College Prowler, Inc.

Sendrowski, Brian, Jr. & Gohari, Omid. Connecticut College College Prowler off the Record. 2005. (College Prowler off the Record Guides: Vol. 36). 160p. (YA). (gr. 12-18). pap., stu. ed. 14.95 *(978-1-59658-035-0(6))* College Prowler, Inc.

Shaw, Katie & Nash, Kevin. University of Washington College Prowler off the Record. 2nd ed. 2005. (College Prowler off the Record Guides: Vol. 190). 160p. (YA). (gr. 12-18). pap., stu. ed. 14.95 *(978-1-59658-189-0(1))* College Prowler, Inc.

Sheik, Mayra & Varacalli, Lauren. Caltech College Prowler off the Record: Inside California Institute of Technology. 2nd ed. 2005. (College Prowler off the Record Guides: Vol. 22). 160p. (YA). (gr. 12-18). pap., stu. ed. 14.95 *(978-1-59658-021-3(6))* College Prowler, Inc.

Singer, Jenny & Scheff, William. Marquette University College Prowler off the Record. 2nd ed. 2005. (College Prowler off the Record Guides: Vol. 81). 160p. (YA). (gr. 12-18). pap., stu. ed. 14.95 *(978-1-59658-080-0(1))* College Prowler, Inc.

Skindzier, Jon. Southern Methodist University College Prowler off the Record. 2005. (College Prowler off the Record Guides: Vol. 120). 160p. (YA). (gr. 12-18). pap., stu. ed. 14.95 *(978-1-59658-119-7(0))* College Prowler, Inc.

Smith, Stacy & Davis, Cristine. University of Rhode Island College Prowler off the Record. 2005. (College Prowler off the Record Guides: Vol. 177). 160p. (YA). (gr. 12-18). pap., stu. ed. 14.95 *(978-1-59658-176-0(X))* College Prowler, Inc.

Spiro, Ian & Jendrey, Julie. Stanford University College Prowler off the Record. 2nd ed. 2005. (College Prowler off the Record Guides: Vol. 124). 160p. (YA). (gr. 12-18). pap., stu. ed. 14.95 *(978-1-59658-123-4(9))* College Prowler, Inc.

Standifer, Lauren, et al. Grinnell College College Prowler off the Record. 2005. (College Prowler off the Record Guides: Vol. 57). 160p. (YA). (gr. 12-18). pap., stu. ed. 14.95 *(978-1-59658-056-5(9))* College Prowler, Inc.

Steinman, Joshua & Nash, Kevin. University of Chicago College Prowler off the Record. 2nd ed. 2005. (College Prowler off the Record Guides: Vol. 150). 160p. (YA). (gr. 12-18). pap., stu. ed. 14.95 *(978-1-59658-149-4(2))* College Prowler, Inc.

Stephens, Kate. College, Quicker: 24 Practical Ways to Save Money & Get Your Degree Faster. 2015. (ENG., Illus.). 288p. (J). (gr. 9-13). pap. 14.99 *(978-1-4926-1338-1(X))* Sourcebooks, Inc.

Stewart, Mark. The Florida Gators. 2010. (Team Spirit Ser.). 48p. (J). (gr. 3-6). 26.60 *(978-1-59953-333-9(2))* Norwood Hse. Pr.

—The Georgia Bulldogs. 2010. (Team Spirit Ser.). 48p. (J). (gr. 3-6). lib. bdg. 26.60 *(978-1-59953-334-6(0))* Norwood Hse. Pr.

—The Illinois Fighting Illini. 2010. (Team Spirit Ser.). (ENG.). 48p. (J). (gr. 3-6). lib. bdg. 26.60 *(978-1-59953-365-0(0))* Norwood Hse. Pr.

—The Michigan Wolverines. 2009. (Team Spirit College Ser.). 48p. (J). (gr. 3-6). lib. bdg. 26.60 *(978-1-59953-278-3(6))* Norwood Hse. Pr.

—The Ohio State Buckeyes. 2009. (Team Spirit College Ser.). 48p. (J). (gr. 3-6). lib. bdg. 26.60 *(978-1-59953-277-6(8))* Norwood Hse. Pr.

Stewart, Nicolette & Nash, Kevin. Skidmore College College Prowler off the Record. 2005. (College Prowler off the Record Guides: Vol. 118). 160p. (YA). (gr. 12-18). pap., stu. ed. 14.95 *(978-1-59658-117-3(4))* College Prowler, Inc.

Striker, Oliver & Varacalli, Lauren. Cornell University College Prowler off the Record. 2005. (College Prowler off the Record Guides: Vol. 38). 160p. (YA). (gr. 12-18). pap., stu. ed. 14.95 *(978-1-59658-037-4(2))* College Prowler, Inc.

Tafoya, Nathan & Nash, Kevin. University of Arizona College Prowler off the Record. 2nd ed. 2005. (College Prowler off the Record Guides: Vol. 140). 160p. (YA). (gr. 12-18). pap., stu. ed. 14.95 *(978-1-59658-139-5(5))* College Prowler, Inc.

Thomas, Jesse & Keller, Carolyn. University of Oregon College Prowler off the Record. 2nd ed. 2005. (College Prowler off the Record Guides: Vol. 173). 160p. (YA). (gr. 12-18). pap., stu. ed. 14.95 *(978-1-59658-172-2(7))* College Prowler, Inc.

Todd, Danielle & Keller, Carolyn. University of Delaware College Prowler off the Record. 2nd ed. 2005. (College Prowler off the Record Guides: Vol. 153). 160p. (YA). (gr. 12-18). pap., stu. ed. 14.95 *(978-1-59658-152-4(2))* College Prowler, Inc.

Tompkins, Michelle & Rahimi, Joey. Columbia University College Prowler off the Record. 2nd ed. 2005. (College Prowler off the Record Guides: Vol. 35). 160p. (YA). (gr. 12-18). pap., stu. ed. 14.95 *(978-1-59658-034-3(8))* College Prowler, Inc.

Tran, Christine & Nash, Kevin. Scripps College College Prowler off the Record. 2005. (College Prowler off the Record Guides: Vol. 115). 160p. (YA). (gr. 12-18). pap., stu. ed. 14.95 *(978-1-59658-114-2(X))* College Prowler, Inc.

Treadway, Kathryn & Seaman, Jim. Providence College College Prowler off the Record. 2nd ed. 2005. (College Prowler off the Record Guides: Vol. 102). 160p. (YA). (gr. 12-18). pap., stu. ed. 14.95 *(978-1-59658-101-2(8))* College Prowler, Inc.

Trousdale, Jonathan & Skindzier, Jon. Georgia Tech College Prowler off the Record: Inside Georgia Institute of Technology. 2005. (College Prowler off the Record Guides: Vol. 56). 160p. (YA). (gr. 12-18). pap., stu. ed. 14.95 *(978-1-59658-055-8(0))* College Prowler, Inc.

Turley, Meredith & Burns, Adam. New York University College Prowler off the Record: Inside NYU. 2005. (College Prowler off the Record Guides: Vol. 90). 160p. (YA). (gr. 12-18). pap., stu. ed. 14.95 *(978-1-59658-089-3(5))* College Prowler, Inc.

Tylevich, Katherine & Skindzier, Jon. Macalester College College Prowler off the Record. 2nd ed. 2005. (College Prowler off the Record Guides: Vol. 80). 160p. (YA). (gr. 12-18). pap., stu. ed. 14.95 *(978-1-59658-079-4(8))* College Prowler, Inc.

Ucla Basketball. 2013. (America's Most Winning Teams Ser.). 48p. (J). (gr. 5-8). pap. 70.50 *(978-1-4488-9446-8(8))* Rosen Publishing Group, Inc., The.

Ugarte, Julia & Jendrey, Julie. Seattle University College Prowler off the Record. 2nd ed. 2005. (College Prowler off the Record Guides: Vol. 116). 160p. (YA). (gr. 12-18). pap., stu. ed. 14.95 *(978-1-59658-115-9(8))* College Prowler, Inc.

Unkovic, Rachel & Burns, Adam. Trinity College Connecticut College Prowler off the Record. 2005. (College Prowler off the Record Guides: Vol. 134). 160p. (YA). (gr. 12-18). pap., stu. ed. 14.95 *(978-1-59658-133-3(6))* College Prowler, Inc.

Valhouli, Alex & Skindzier, Jon. University of Southern California College Prowler off the Record. 2nd ed. 2005. (College Prowler off the Record Guides: Vol. 184). 160p. (YA). (gr. 12-18). pap., stu. ed. 14.95 *(978-1-59658-183-8(2))* College Prowler, Inc.

Vance, Ashley & Gohari, Omid. Brigham Young University College Prowler off the Record: Inside BYU. 2nd ed. 2005. (College Prowler off the Record Guides: Vol. 17). 160p. (YA). (gr. 12-18). pap., stu. ed. 14.95 *(978-1-59658-016-9(X))* College Prowler, Inc.

Wade McCormick, Lisa. Ucla Basketball. 2013. (America's Most Winning Teams Ser.). 48p. (J). (gr. 5-8). 29.25 *(978-1-4488-9408-6(5))*; pap. 11.75 *(978-1-4488-9443-7(3))* Rosen Publishing Group, Inc., The.

Walker, Caren & Varacalli, Lauren. Boston University College Prowler off the Record. 2nd ed. 2005. (College Prowler off the Record Guides: Vol. 14). 160p. (YA). (gr. 12-18). pap., stu. ed. 14.95 *(978-1-59658-013-8(5))* College Prowler, Inc.

Watkins, Boyce. Everything You Ever Wanted to Know about College: A Guide for Minority Students. 2004. xiii, 330p. (YA). per. 25.00 *(978-0-9742632-0-5(6))* Blue Boy Publishing Co.

Webb, Anne Aldridge. Appalachian State, A to Z. Bostian, Laurie, illus. 2010. (J). 18.95 *(978-1-933251-69-1(7))* Parkway Pubs., Inc.

Whitley, Jared & Mandelbaum, Jolie. University of Utah College Prowler off the Record. 2nd ed. 2005. (College Prowler off the Record Guides: Vol. 187). 160p. (YA). (gr. 12-18). pap., stu. ed. 14.95 *(978-1-59658-186-9(7))* College Prowler, Inc.

Wiedrich, Merrick & Scheff, William. University of Alabama College Prowler off the Record. 2nd ed. 2005. (College Prowler off the Record Guides: Vol. 139). 160p. (YA). (gr. 12-18). pap., stu. ed. 14.95 *(978-1-59658-138-8(7))* College Prowler, Inc.
Wild, Cynthia & Nash, Kevin. UC Riverside College Prowler off the Record: Inside University of California Riverside. 2nd ed. 2005. (College Prowler off the Record Guides: Vol. 145). 160p. (YA). (gr. 12-18). pap., stu. ed. 14.95 *(978-1-59658-144-9(1))* College Prowler, Inc.
Williams, Jacob & Burns, Adam. University of Tennessee College Prowler off the Record. 2nd ed. 2005. (College Prowler off the Record Guides: Vol. 185). 160p. (YA). (gr. 12-18). pap., stu. ed. 14.95 *(978-1-59658-184-5(0))* College Prowler, Inc.
Williams, Rozalia. College FAQ Book: Over 5,000 Not Frequently Asked Questions about College! 2005. (Illus.). 494p. (YA). per. 24.95 *(978-0-9755103-0-8(4))* Hidden Curriculum Education.
Williams, Tim. New School University College Prowler off the Record. 2nd ed. 2005. (College Prowler off the Record Guides: Vol. 89). 160p. (YA). (gr. 12-18). pap., stu. ed. 14.95 *(978-1-59658-088-6(7)*, Off The Record) College Prowler, Inc.
Wines, Shawn & Pecsenye, Jessica. University of Miami College Prowler off the Record. 2nd ed. 2005. (College Prowler off the Record Guides: Vol. 163). 160p. (YA). (gr. 12-18). pap., stu. ed. 14.95 *(978-1-59658-162-3(X))* College Prowler, Inc.
Woolsey, Matthew & Keller, Carolyn. Vanderbilt University College Prowler off the Record. 2nd ed. 2005. (College Prowler off the Record Guides: Vol. 193). 160p. (YA). (gr. 12-18). pap., stu. ed. 14.95 *(978-1-59658-192-0(1))* College Prowler, Inc.
Zang, Adam & Varacalli, Lauren. Carleton College College Prowler off the Record. 2005. (College Prowler off the Record Guides: Vol. 23). 160p. (YA). (gr. 12-18). pap., stu. ed. 14.95 *(978-1-59658-022-0(4))* College Prowler, Inc.

UNIVERSITIES AND COLLEGES—DIRECTORIES

Kwapong, Ohene. 12 Steps to Getting Admitted into Colleges & Universities in the United States. 2003. 79p. (YA). pap. 10.95 *(978-0-595-29647-7(5))* iUniverse, Inc.
Rugg, Frederick E. Thirty Questions & Answers on the Colleges. (YA). 9th rev. ed. 2003. 20p. pap. 9.95 *(978-1-883062-52-1(7))* 10th rev. ed. 2004. 20p. pap. 9.95 *(978-1-883062-56-9(X))* 11th rev. ed. 2005. 21p. pap. 9.95 *(978-1-883062-61-3(6))* Rugg's Recommendations.

UNIVERSITIES AND COLLEGES—ENTRANCE REQUIREMENTS

Learning Express Editors. Catholic High School Entrance Exams. 5th ed. 2013. (ENG.). 256p. pap. 18.95 *(978-1-57685-933-9(9))* LearningExpress, LLC.

UNIVERSITIES AND COLLEGES—FICTION

see also Schools—Fiction

Ahmad, M. I. Aldebaram. 2009. 95p. pap. 13.00 *(978-0-557-08323-7(0))* Lulu Pr., Inc.
Beck, Lynn G. & Sesa. Powercat, the Pacific Tiger. 2012. (J). 14.95 *(978-1-937406-00-4(8))* Mascot Bks., Inc.
Bee, Clair. Buzzer Basket: A Chip Hilton Sports Story. 2011. 184p. (gr. 4-7). 42.95 *(978-1-258-06936-0(9))* Literary Licensing, LLC.
—Freshman Quarterback: Chip Hilton Sports Story No. 9. 2011. 222p. (gr. 8-12). 44.95 *(978-1-258-07328-2(5))* Literary Licensing, LLC.
—Hardcourt Upset: A Chip Hilton Sports Story. 2011. 190p. (gr. 3-8). 42.95 *(978-1-258-08011-2(7))* Literary Licensing, LLC.
—Pay-off Pitch: A Chip Hilton Sports Story. 2011. 192p. (gr. 3-8). 42.95 *(978-1-258-09970-1(5))* Literary Licensing, LLC.
Binder, John. The Girl Who Applied Everywhere. 2011. 160p. (YA). 17.99 *(978-1-936679-02-7(7))* Wicker Park Pr., Ltd.
Blumenthal, Bliss & Alarcon, Claudia. Wiley's Way: El Camino de Wiley. Gonzalez, Ricky & Gonzalez, Crysol, illus. 2004. (ENG & SPA.). 96p. mass mkt. 9.95 *(978-0-292-70615-6(4))* Univ. of Texas Pr.
Butler, Dori H. Campus Attack, Sabotage! 2011. (Readers' & Writers' Genre Workshop Ser.). (YA). pap. *(978-1-4509-3018-5(2))* Benchmark Education Co.
Caine, Rachel, pseud. Bite Club. 10 vols. 2011. (Morganville Vampires Ser.: 10). (ENG.). 368p. (YA). (gr. 9). pap. 9.99 *(978-0-451-23468-1(5)*, Berkley) Penguin Publishing Group.
—Black Dawn. 2012. (Morganville Vampires Ser.: 12). (ENG.). 400p. (YA). (gr. 9). pap. 9.99 *(978-0-451-23793-4(5)*, Berkley) Penguin Publishing Group.
—Ghost Town. 9 vols. 2011. (Morganville Vampires Ser.: 9). (ENG.). 368p. (YA). (gr. 9-18). 9.99 *(978-0-451-23291-5(7)*, Berkley) Penguin Publishing Group.
—Last Breath. 11 vols. 2012. (Morganville Vampires Ser.: 11). (ENG.). 368p. (YA). (gr. 9). 9.99 *(978-0-451-23580-0(0)*, Berkley) Penguin Publishing Group.
—Lord of Misrule. 2009. (Morganville Vampires Ser.: Bk. 5). 352p. (YA). lib. bdg. 20.00 *(978-1-4242-4704-2(7))* Fitzgerald Bks.
—Lord of Misrule. 2009. (Morganville Vampires Ser.: 5). (ENG.). 256p. (YA). (gr. 9-18). mass mkt. 7.99 *(978-0-451-22572-6(4)*, Berkley) Penguin Publishing Group.
—Midnight Alley. 2007. (Morganville Vampires Ser.: Bk. 3). 256p. (YA). lib. bdg. 20.00 *(978-1-4242-4705-9(5))* Fitzgerald Bks.
—Midnight Alley. 2007. (Morganville Vampires Ser.: 3). (ENG.). 256p. (YA). (gr. 9-18). mass mkt. 7.99 *(978-0-451-22238-1(5)*, Berkley) Penguin Publishing Group.
—The Morganville Vampires, Vol. 4. 2011. (Morganville Vampires Ser.: Bks. 7-8). (ENG.). 464p. (YA). (gr. 9-18). 9.99 *(978-0-451-23426-1(X)*, Berkley) Penguin Publishing Group.
Charbonneau, Joelle. Independent Study. (ENG.). (YA). (gr. 7). 2015. (Testing Ser.: 2). 336p. pap. 9.99 *(978-0-544-43945-0(7)*, HMH Books For Young Readers) 2014. (Testing Trilogy: Bk. 2). 320p. 17.99 *(978-0-547-95920-7(6))* Houghton Mifflin Harcourt Publishing Co.
—Independent Study. 2015. (Testing Ser.: 2). lib. bdg. 20.85 *(978-0-606-36832-2(9))* Turtleback Bks.
—The Testing. (Testing Ser.: 1). (ENG.). 352p. (YA). (gr. 7). 2015. pap. 9.99 *(978-0-544-33623-0(2)*, HMH Books For Young Readers) 2013. 17.99 *(978-0-547-95910-8(9))* Houghton Mifflin Harcourt Publishing Co.
Choi, Sook Nyul. Gathering of Pearls. 2007. (ENG.). 176p. (YA). (gr. 7). pap. 11.95 *(978-0-618-80918-9(X))* Houghton Mifflin Harcourt Publishing Co.
Clement-Moore, Rosemary. Hell Week. 2009. (Maggie Quinn: Girl vs Evil Ser.). (ENG.). 336p. (YA). (gr. 9). pap. 9.99 *(978-0-385-73415-8(8)*, Delacorte Bks. for Young Readers) Random Hse. Children's Bks.
Colasanti, Susane. All I Need. 2014. (ENG.). 240p. (YA). (gr. 7). pap. 9.99 *(978-0-14-242676-0(8)*, Speak) Penguin Young Readers Group.
Condie, Ally. First Day. 2007. 304p. (YA). pap. 15.95 *(978-1-59038-775-7(9))* Deseret Bk. Co.
—Reunion. 2008. 288p. (YA). pap. 15.95 *(978-1-59038-989-8(1))* Deseret Bk. Co.
Cooney, Caroline B. Janie Face to Face. 2013. (ENG.). 352p. (YA). (gr. 7). 17.99 *(978-0-385-74206-1(1)*, Delacorte Bks. for Young Readers) Random Hse. Children's Bks.
Davis, Catherine Jennings & Thompson, Traci Shirley. Goodnight Cavaliers. 2013. (J). 17.95 *(978-1-62086-038-0(4))* Mascot Bks., Inc.
Durst, Sarah Beth. Enchanted Ivy. (ENG.). (YA). (gr. 7). 2011. 336p. pap. 9.99 *(978-1-4169-8646-1(4))* 2010. 320p. 16.99 *(978-1-4169-8645-4(6))* McElderry, Margaret K. Bks. (McElderry, Margaret K. Bks.).
Flower, Graham Jessie. Grace Harlowe's Second Year at Overton College. 2004. reprint ed. pap. 20.95 *(978-1-4191-2223-1(1))* Kessinger Publishing, LLC.
Hazuka, Tom. Last Chance for First. 2008. 296p. (YA). (gr. 9-18). pap. 8.95 *(978-0-9798824-0-1(0))* Brown Barn Bks.
Hoffman, Nina Kiriki. Spirits That Walk in Shadow. 2008. (ENG.). 320p. (YA). (gr. 7-18). 9.99 *(978-0-14-241158-2(2)*, Firebird) Penguin Young Readers Group.
Johnson-Choong, Shelly. A Light to Come Home By. 2nd unabr. ed. 2004. 212p. (C). reprint ed. pap. 12.95 *(978-1-932280-52-4(9)*, 80529) Granite Publishing & Distribution.
Karras, Kim. Accidentally Me. 2016. (ENG.). (YA). pap. 15.99 *(978-1-4621-1867-0(4)*, Sweetwater Bks.) Cedar Fort, Inc./CFI Distribution.
Kearney, Meg. When You Never Said Goodbye: An Adoptee's Search for Her Birth Mother. 2017. (ENG.). 224p. (YA). (gr. 9-17). 17.95 *(978-0-89255-479-9(7)*, 255479) Persea Bks., Inc.
Korman, Gordon. Son of the Mob (repackage) 2017. (ENG.). 240p. (J). (gr. 5-9). pap. 8.99 ***(978-1-4847-9845-4(7))*** Hyperion Bks. for Children.
Kropp, Paul. Home Run. 2006. (ENG.). 208p. (J). (gr. 7). pap. 11.95 *(978-0-385-66148-5(7)*, Doubleday Canada) Penguin Random House Canada Young Readers CAN. Dist: Penguin Random Hse. LLC.
Kunze, Lauren & Onur, Rina. The Ivy. (Ivy Ser.: 1). (ENG.). (YA). (gr. 9). 2011. 336p. pap. 8.99 *(978-0-06-196046-8(2))* 2010. 320p. 16.99 *(978-0-06-196045-1(4))* HarperCollins Pubs. (Greenwillow Bks.).
—Rivals. 2012. (Ivy Ser.: 3). (ENG.). 384p. (YA). (gr. 9). 16.99 *(978-0-06-196049-9(7)*, Greenwillow Bks.) HarperCollins Pubs.
—Scandal. 2013. (Ivy Ser.: 4). (ENG.). 336p. (YA). (gr. 9). 17.99 *(978-0-06-196051-2(9)*, Greenwillow Bks.) HarperCollins Pubs.
—Secrets. 2011. (Ivy Ser.: 2). (ENG.). 320p. (YA). (gr. 9-18). 16.99 *(978-0-06-196047-5(0)*, Greenwillow Bks.) HarperCollins Pubs.
Lazebnik, Claire. The Trouble with Flirting. 2013. (ENG.). 336p. (YA). (gr. 8). pap. 9.99 *(978-0-06-192127-8(0)*, HarperTeen) HarperCollins Pubs.
Lithgow, John. Mahalia Mouse Goes to College. Oleynikov, Igor, illus. 2007. (ENG.). 40p. (J). (gr. -1-3). 17.99 *(978-1-4169-2715-0(8)*, Simon & Schuster Bks. For Young Readers) Simon & Schuster Bks. For Young Readers.
Malloy, Brian. Twelve Long Months. 2010. (ENG.). 320p. (J). (gr. 7). 9.99 *(978-0-439-87763-3(6)*, Scholastic Paperbacks) Scholastic, Inc.
Mc Daniel, Jessica & Morgan, Amanda. Goodnight Tigers. 2010. 32p. (J). 17.95 *(978-1-4507-0621-6(5))* Independent Pub.
McDonald, Megan. Judy Moody Goes to College. (Judy Moody Ser.: 8). 2010. lib. bdg. 16.00 *(978-0-606-12352-5(0))* 2009. lib. bdg. 16.00 *(978-0-606-01313-0(X))* Turtleback Bks. (Turtleback).
—Judy Moody Goes to College, Bk. 8. Reynolds, Peter H., illus. 2010. (Judy Moody Ser.: 8). (ENG.). (J). (gr. 1-4). 144p. 15.99 *(978-0-7636-4856-5(6))*; 160p. pap. 5.99 *(978-0-7636-4855-8(8))* Candlewick Pr.
Miller, Lauren. Parallel. 2013. (ENG.). 432p. (YA). (gr. 8). 17.99 *(978-0-06-219977-5(3)*, HarperTeen) HarperCollins Pubs.
Montgomery, L. M. Anne of the Island. 2012. (World Classics Ser.). (ENG.). 212p. pap. 19.99 *(978-1-909438-92-7(8)*, Sovereign) Bollinger, Max GBR. Dist: Lightning Source UK, Ltd.
—Anne of the Island. 2008. (Anne of Green Gables Ser.). (ENG.). 272p. (J). (gr. 4-7). pap. 9.95 *(978-0-9782552-8-2(3))* Davenport Pr. CAN. Dist: Independent Pubs. Group.
—Anne of the Island. 2006. (ENG.). pap. *(978-1-4068-2171-0(3))*; pap. *(978-1-4068-3175-7(1))* Echo Library.
—Anne of the Island. 2004. reprint ed. pap. 1.99 *(978-1-4192-0718-1(0))*; pap. 30.95 *(978-1-4179-0885-1(8))* Kessinger Publishing, LLC.
—Anne of the Island. l.t. ed. 2004. 396p. 26.00 *(978-1-58287-640-5(1))* North Bks.
—Anne of the Island. 2010. (Puffin Classics Ser.). (ENG.). 368p. (J). (gr. 5-7). pap. 5.99 *(978-0-14-132736-5(7)*, Puffin Books) Penguin Young Readers Group.
Moore, Stephanie Perry. Finally Sure, Vol. 5. 2004. (Laurel Shadrach Ser.: 5). (ENG.). 176p. (YA). (gr. 8). pap. 7.99 *(978-0-8024-4039-6(8))* Moody Pubs.
Myracle, Lauren. Yolo. 2014. (Internet Girls Ser.). (ENG., Illus.). 208p. (YA). (gr. 8-17). 16.95 *(978-1-4197-0871-8(6)*, Amulet Bks.) Abrams, Inc.
Naylor, Phyllis Reynolds. Now I'll Tell You Everything. 2013. (Alice Ser.: 25). (ENG., Illus.). 528p. (YA). (gr. 9). 17.99 *(978-1-4424-4590-1(4))* Simon & Schuster Children's Publishing.
Oliver, Jasmine. Prada Princesses. 2007. (Project Fashion Ser.: 3). (ENG.). 192p. (YA). (gr. 9-12). pap. 9.99 *(978-1-4169-3812-5(5)*, Simon Pulse) Simon Pulse.
Olsen, Kaki. Swan & Shadow: A Swan Lake Story. 2016. (ENG.). 299p. (YA). pap. 18.99 *(978-1-4621-1814-4(3)*, Sweetwater Bks.) Cedar Fort, Inc./CFI Distribution.
Padian, Maria. Wrecked. 2016. (ENG.). 368p. (YA). (gr. 9-12). 17.95 *(978-1-61620-624-6(1))* Algonquin Bks. of Chapel Hill.
Pascal, Francine. Libertad Incondicional.Tr. of Love, Lies & Jessica Wakefield. (SPA.). 224p. (J). 8.95 *(978-84-272-3162-7(8))* Molino, Editorial ESP. Dist: AIMS International Bks., Inc.
—Otra Oportunidad.Tr. of Love of Her Life. (SPA.). 200p. (J). 8.95 *(978-84-272-3166-5(0))* Molino, Editorial ESP. Dist: AIMS International Bks., Inc.
Perry, Jolene. The Next Door Boys. 2011. (YA). *(978-1-59955-910-0(2)*, Bonneville Bks.) Cedar Fort, Inc./CFI Distribution.
Roux, Madeleine. Asylum. (ENG.). (gr. 9). 2014. 336p. (J). pap. 9.99 *(978-0-06-222097-4(7))* 2013. (Illus.). 320p. (YA). 17.99 *(978-0-06-222096-7(9))* HarperCollins Pubs.
—Asylum. 2015. (SPA.). 320p. (YA). (gr. 9-12). pap. 20.99 *(978-987-612-778-3(0))* V&R Editoras.
—Sanctum. 2014. (Illus.). 343p. (YA). *(978-0-06-235182-1(6))* Harper & Row Ltd.
—Sanctum. 2014. (Asylum Ser.: 2). (ENG., Illus.). 352p. (YA). (gr. 9). 17.99 *(978-0-06-222099-8(3))* HarperCollins Pubs.
Shine, Joe. I Become Shadow. 2015. (ENG.). 304p. (YA). (gr. 9). pap. 10.99 *(978-1-61695-537-3(6)*, Soho Teen) Soho Pr., Inc.
Soto, Gary. Jesse. 2006. (ENG., Illus.). 192p. (YA). (gr. 7-12). pap. 7.99 *(978-0-15-205425-0(1))* Houghton Mifflin Harcourt Publishing Co.
—Jesse. 2006. 166p. (gr. 7-12). 16.95 *(978-0-7569-6688-1(4))* Perfection Learning Corp.
Stolarz, Laurie Faria. Red Is for Remembrance. l.t. ed. 2008. (Blue Is for Nightmares Ser.: Bk. 4). 385p. (YA). (gr. 7). 22.95 *(978-1-4104-0339-1(4))* Thorndike Pr.
Thompson, Alicia. Psych Major Syndrome. 2010. (ENG.). 336p. pap. 8.99 *(978-1-4231-1549-6(X))* Disney Pr.
Tillworth, Mary. Big Monster, Little Monster. Random House Disney Staff, illus. 2014. (Step into Reading Ser.). (ENG.). 24p. (J). (gr. -1-1). 3.99 *(978-0-7364-3094-4(6)*, RH/Disney) Random Hse. Children's Bks.
Warner, Gertrude Chandler. The Mystery of the Grinning Gargoyle. VanArsdale, Anthony, illus. 2014. (Boxcar Children Mysteries Ser.: 137). (ENG.). 128p. (J). (gr. 1-5). pap. 5.99 *(978-0-8075-0893-0(4))* Whitman, Albert & Co.

UNIVERSITY OF NOTRE DAME

Howell, Brian. Notre Dame Fighting Irish, 1 vol. 2012. (Inside College Football Ser.). (ENG., Illus.). 48p. (J). (gr. 3-6). 32.79 *(978-1-61783-500-1(5))* ABDO Publishing Co.
Monteverde, Matthew. Notre Dame vs. USC. 2013. (J). *(978-1-4777-1164-4(3))*; pap. *(978-1-4777-1163-7(5))*; lib. bdg. *(978-1-4777-1158-3(9))* Rosen Publishing Group, Inc., The. (PowerKids Pr.).
Stewart, Mark. The Notre Dame Fighting Irish. 2010. (Team Spirit Ser.). (ENG.). 48p. (J). (gr. 3-6). lib. bdg. 26.60 *(978-1-59953-279-0(4))* Norwood Hse. Pr.

UNMARRIED MOTHERS—FICTION

Chambers, Aidan. Postcards from No Man's Land. 2007. (ENG.). 320p. (YA). (gr. 9-18). 10.00 *(978-0-14-240788-2(7)*, Speak) Penguin Young Readers Group.
Dessen, Sarah. Someone Like You. 2011. 10.36 *(978-0-7848-3539-5(X)*, Everbind) Marco Bk. Co.
—Someone Like You. 2004. (ENG.). 304p. (YA). (gr. 7-7). 10.99 *(978-0-14-240177-4(3)*, Speak) Penguin Young Readers Group.
—Someone Like You. 2004. 281p. (YA). (gr. 7). 16.65 *(978-0-7569-4967-9(X))* Perfection Learning Corp.
—Someone Like You. 2004. 281p. (gr. 7). lib. bdg. 22.10 *(978-1-4176-2674-8(7)*, Turtleback) Turtleback Bks.
Millward, Carol. Star in the Middle. 2009. 304p. (YA). (gr. 9-12). 16.95 *(978-1-934813-13-3(3))* Westside Bks.
Woodson, Jacqueline. The Dear One. 2010. (ENG.). 176p. (YA). (gr. 7-18). 7.99 *(978-0-14-241705-8(X)*, Puffin Books) Penguin Young Readers Group.
Wright, Julie. My Not-So-Fairytale Life. 2005. 256p. (YA). pap. 15.95 *(978-1-59038-476-3(8))* Deseret Bk. Co.

UPPER ATMOSPHERE

see Atmosphere, Upper

UPPER CLASS—FICTION

MacLean, Sarah. The Season. (ENG.). 352p. (J). (gr. 7). 2010. 8.99 *(978-0-545-04887-3(7))* 2009. 17.99 *(978-0-545-04886-6(9))* Scholastic, Inc. (Orchard Bks.).
Smedley, Frank E. Frank Fairlegh. 2008. 224p. pap. 15.95 *(978-1-60664-179-8(4))*; 244p. pap. 15.95 *(978-1-60664-178-1(6))* Aegypan.
—Frank Fairlegh: Scenes from the Life of a Private Pupil. 2007. (ENG.). 570p. per. 30.99 *(978-1-4346-4557-9(6))*; 640p. per. 45.75 *(978-1-4346-4558-6(4))* Creative Media Partners, LLC.
Van Dyne, Edith. Aunt Jane's Nieces in Society. 2005. 28.95 *(978-1-4218-1424-7(2))*; 276p. pap. 13.95 *(978-1-4218-1524-4(9))* 1st World Publishing, Inc. (1st World Library - Literary Society).
—Aunt Jane's Nieces in Society. 2007. (ENG.). 144p. pap. 18.99 *(978-1-4264-4161-5(4))*; 156p. pap. 21.99 *(978-1-4264-4202-5(5))* Creative Media Partners, LLC.
—Aunt Jane's Nieces in Society. 2004. reprint ed. pap. 20.95 *(978-1-4191-0824-2(7))*; pap. 1.99 *(978-1-4192-0824-9(1))* Kessinger Publishing, LLC.

URANIUM

Gardner, Jane P. Uranium. 2017. (Chemistry of Everyday Elements Ser.: Vol. 10). (ENG.). (YA). (gr. 7-12). 23.95 ***(978-1-4222-3847-9(4))*** Mason Crest.
Mineo, Tyrone. Uranium, Vol. 1. 2014. (Rare & Precious Metals Ser.). (ENG.). 24p. (J). (gr. 2-3). 22.60 *(978-1-4824-0531-6(8))* Stevens, Gareth Publishing LLLP.
Perritano, John. Uranium, Vol. 12. 2015. (North American Natural Resources Ser.). (Illus.). 64p. (J). (gr. 7). 23.95 *(978-1-4222-3390-0(1))* Mason Crest.
Tiner, John Hudson. Uranium & Plutonium Make Nuclear Power. 2003. (From Resource to Energy Source Ser.). (J). *(978-1-58417-288-8(6))*; pap. *(978-1-58417-289-5(4))* Lake Street Pubs.

URANIUM—FICTION

Friend, Gaythel & Miller, Dalton. The Mystery of the Green Box. 2006. 88p. per. 8.95 *(978-1-59824-147-1(8))* E-BookTime LLC.
Gilligan, Shannon. Struggle down Under. Burphon, S. et al, illus. 2007. (Choose Your Own Adventure Ser.: No. 21). 123p. (J). (gr. 4-7). pap. 6.99 *(978-1-933390-21-5(2))* Chooseco LLC.

URANUS (PLANET)

Adamson, Thomas K. The Secrets of Uranus. 2015. (Planets Ser.). (ENG., Illus.). 32p. (gr. 2-4). lib. bdg. 31.99 *(978-1-4914-5869-3(0))* Capstone Press of Coughlan Cos.
—Uranus [Scholastic]: Revised Edition. 2010. (Exploring the Galaxy Ser.). (ENG.). 24p. pap. 0.49 *(978-1-4296-5815-7(0)*, Pebble Plus) Capstone Press of Coughlan Cos.
Asimov, Isaac & Hantula, Richard. Urano: El Planeta Inclinado. Porras, Carlos & D'Andrea, Patricia, trs. from ENG. 2003. (Isaac Asimov's Biblioteca del Universo del Siglo XXI).Tr. of Uranus: The Sideways Planet. (SPA., Illus.). 32p. (gr. 2-6). lib. bdg. 26.00 *(978-0-8368-3863-3(7)*, Gareth Stevens Learning Library) Stevens, Gareth Publishing LLLP.
Bloom, J. P. Uranus, 1 vol. 2014. (Planets Ser.). (ENG.). 24p. (J). (gr. 2-4). lib. bdg. 28.50 *(978-1-62970-721-1(X))* ABDO Publishing Co.
Carson, Mary Kay. Far-Out Guide to Uranus. 2010. (Far-Out Guide to the Solar System Ser.). (Illus.). 48p. (J). pap. 8.95 *(978-1-59845-188-7(X)*, Enslow Elementary); (gr. 2-5). 25.27 *(978-0-7660-3185-2(3))* Enslow Pubs., Inc.
Elkins-Tanton, Linda T. Uranus, Neptune, Pluto, & the Outer Solar System. 2nd rev. ed. 2010. (Solar System Ser.). (Illus.). 272p. (C). (gr. 9). 39.50 *(978-0-8160-7701-4(0))* Facts On File, Inc.
Glaser, Chaya. Urano: Frío y Azul. 2015. (Fuera de Este Mundo Ser.). (SPA., Illus.). 24p. (J). (gr. -1-3). lib. bdg. 23.93 *(978-1-62724-598-2(7))* Bearport Publishing Co., Inc.
—Uranus: Cold & Blue. 2015. (Out of This World Ser.). (ENG.). 24p. (J). (gr. -1-3). lib. bdg. 23.93 *(978-1-62724-567-8(7))* Bearport Publishing Co., Inc.
Goldstein, Margaret J. Uranus. 2005. (Pull Ahead Bks.). (Illus.). 32p. (gr. 2-4). lib. bdg. 22.60 *(978-0-8225-4654-2(X))* Lerner Publishing Group.
Howard, Fran. Uranus, 1 vol. 2007. (Planets Ser.). (ENG.). 32p. (gr. 3-7). 27.07 *(978-1-59928-829-1(X)*, Buddy Bks.) ABDO Publishing Co.
Hunter, Valerie. Journey to Uranus, 1 vol. 2014. (Spotlight on Space Science Ser.). (ENG.). 32p. (J). (gr. 5-5). pap. 11.75 *(978-1-4994-0379-4(8)*, PowerKids Pr.) Rosen Publishing Group, Inc., The.
Jefferis, David. Gas Giants: Huge Far off Worlds. 2008. (ENG., Illus.). 32p. (J). (gr. 3-7). pap. *(978-0-7787-3750-6(0))* Crabtree Publishing Co.
Kazunas, Ariel. Uranus. 2011. (21st Century Junior Library: Solar System Ser.). (ENG.). 24p. (gr. 2-5). lib. bdg. 25.64 *(978-1-61080-084-6(2)*, 201078) Cherry Lake Publishing.
Keiser, Cody. Exploring Uranus. 2017. (J). ***(978-1-5345-2253-4(0)***, KidHaven Publishing) Greenhaven Publishing LLC.
Lawrence, Ellen. Uranus: The Sideways-Spinning Planet. 2013. (Zoom into Space Ser.). 24p. (J). (gr. -1-3). lib. bdg. 23.93 *(978-1-909673-16-8(1))* Ruby Tuesday Books Limited GBR. Dist: Bearport Publishing Co., Inc.
Orme, Helen & Orme, David. Let's Explore Uranus. 2007. (Space Launch! Ser.). (Illus.). 24p. (J). (gr. 1-4). pap. 8.15 *(978-0-8368-8134-9(6))*; lib. bdg. 23.00 *(978-0-8368-7949-0(X))* Stevens, Gareth Publishing LLLP. (Gareth Stevens Learning Library).
Owen, Ruth. Uranus. 2013. (Explore Outer Space Ser.). 32p. (J). (gr. 3-6). 25.25 *(978-1-61533-728-6(8)*, PowerKids Pr.) Rosen Publishing Group, Inc., The.
—Uranus. 2013. (Explore Outer Space Ser.). 32p. (J). (gr. 3-6). pap. 60.00 *(978-1-61533-774-3(1))*; pap. 10.00 *(978-1-61533-773-6(3))* Windmill Bks.
Owens, L. L. Uranus. McGeehan, Dan, illus. 2011. (Space Neighbors Ser.). (ENG.). 32p. (J). (gr. 1-4). lib. bdg. 27.07 *(978-1-60954-389-1(0)*, 200889) Child's World, Inc., The.
Ring, Susan. Uranus. (J). 2013. 27.13 *(978-1-62127-269-4(9))* 2013. pap. 12.95 *(978-1-62127-278-6(8))* 2004. (Illus.). pap. 8.95 *(978-1-59036-224-2(1))* 2004. (Illus.). 24p. (gr. 4-7). lib. bdg. 24.45 *(978-1-59036-097-2(4))* Weigl Pubs., Inc.
Ring, Susan & Roumanis, Alexis. Uranus. 2016. (Illus.). 24p. (J). *(978-1-5105-0992-4(5))* SmartBook Media, Inc.
Roumanis, Alexis. Uranus. 2016. (J). ***(978-1-5105-2057-8(0))*** SmartBook Media, Inc.
—Uranus. 2015. (J). *(978-1-4896-3304-0(9))* Weigl Pubs., Inc.
Scherer, Glenn & Fletcher, Marty. Uranus: A MyReportLinks.com Book. 2005. (Solar System Ser.). (Illus.). 48p. (J). lib. bdg. 26.60 *(978-0-7660-5307-6(5)*, MyReportLinks.com Bks.) Enslow Pubs., Inc.
Sexton, Colleen. Uranus. 2010. (Exploring Space Ser.). (ENG., Illus.). 24p. (J). (gr. k-3). lib. bdg. 25.95 *(978-1-60014-408-0(X)*, Blastoff! Readers) Bellwether Media.
Sherman, Josepha. Uranus. 2009. (Space!). 64p. (gr. 5-18). lib. bdg. 32.79 *(978-0-7614-4248-6(0))* Marshall Cavendish Corp.
Slade, Suzanne. A Look at Uranus. (Astronomy Now! Ser.). 24p. (gr. 2-3). 2009. 42.50 *(978-1-61511-474-0(2)*, PowerKids Pr.) 2007. (Illus.). (J). lib. bdg. 22.60 *(978-1-4042-3831-2(X))* Rosen Publishing Group, Inc., The.
Sparrow, Giles. Destination Uranus, Neptune, & Pluto. 2009. (Destination Solar System Ser.). (Illus.). 32p. (J). 25.25 *(978-1-4358-3446-0(1))*; pap. 10.00 *(978-1-4358-3463-7(1))* Rosen Publishing Group, Inc., The. (PowerKids Pr.).
Steinkraus, Kyla. Giant Gas Planets: Jupiter, Saturn, Uranus, & Neptune. 2014. (ENG.). 24p. (gr. k-3). 28.50 *(978-1-62717-728-3(0))* Rourke Educational Media.
Taylor-Butler, Christine. Planet Uranus. 2014. (True Book(tm), A — Space Ser.). (ENG.). 48p. (J). lib. bdg. 31.00 *(978-0-531-21158-8(4))* Scholastic Library Publishing.
—Uranus. 2007. (Scholastic News Nonfiction Readers Ser.). (ENG., Illus.). 24p. (J). (gr. 1-2). 22.00 *(978-0-531-14754-2(1))* Scholastic Library Publishing.
Uranus. 2nd rev. ed. 2008. (New Solar System Ser.). 32p. (YA). (gr. 3-6). 23.00 *(978-1-60413-214-4(0))* Facts On File, Inc.
Viegas, Jennifer. Uranus. (Library of Planets Ser.). 48p. (gr. 5-8). 2009. 55.90 *(978-1-60853-822-5(2)*, Rosen Reference)

T U V

2008. (Illus.). (YA). lib. bdg. 29.25 *(978-1-4042-1428-6(3))* Rosen Publishing Group, Inc., The.

Vogt, Gregory. Uranus. 2009. (Early Bird Astronomy Ser.). (ENG.). 48p. (gr. 2-5). lib. bdg. 26.60 *(978-0-7613-4156-7(0))* Lerner Publishing Group.

Wimmer, Teresa. Uranus. 2007. (My First Look at: Planets Ser.). (Illus.). 24p. (J). (gr. -1-3). lib. bdg. 24.25 *(978-1-58341-523-8(8)*, Creative Education) Creative Co., The.

World Book, contrib. by. Saturn & Uranus. 2nd ed. 2006. (World Book's Solar System & Space Exploration Library). (Illus.). 64p. (J). *(978-0-7166-9519-6(7))* World Bk., Inc.

World Book, Inc. Staff, contrib. by. Saturn & Uranus. 2006. (World Book's Solar System & Space Exploration Library). (Illus.). 63p. (J). *(978-0-7166-9506-6(5))* World Bk., Inc.

World Book, Inc Staff, contrib. by. Saturn & Uranus. 2010. (J). *(978-0-7166-9535-6(9))* World Bk., Inc.

Zuchora-Walske, Christine. Your Mission to Uranus, 1 vol. 2011. (Planets Ser.). (ENG., Illus.). 32p. (J). (gr. k-3). 28.50 *(978-1-61641-683-6(1))* Magic Wagon.

URBAN RENEWAL

see also City Planning; Sociology, Urban

WalkerTheo. THE CITY EXPERIMENT: REBUILDING GREENSBURG, KANSAS LOW INTERMEDIATE BOOK WITH ONLINE ACCESS. 2014. (ENG., Illus.). 24p. (J). pap. 9.50 *(978-1-107-62256-2(5))* Cambridge Univ. Pr.

URBAN RENEWAL—FICTION

Simonet, Evan, illus. Jake & the Sailing Tree. 2009. (J). *(978-1-60108-019-6(0))* Red Cygnet Pr.

Thornton, D. S. Scrap City. Bowater, Charlie, illus. 2015. (Middle-Grade Novels Ser.). (ENG.). 352p. (gr. 4-7). lib. bdg. 27.99 *(978-1-4965-0475-3(5))* Stone Arch Bks.

URBAN SOCIOLOGY

see Sociology, Urban

URUGUAY

Behnke, Alison. Uruguay in Pictures. 2009. (Visual Geography Series, Second Ser.). (ENG.). 80p. (gr. 5-12). 31.93 *(978-1-57505-961-7(4)*, Twenty-First Century Bks.) Lerner Publishing Group.

Jermyn, Leslie & Wong, Winnie. Uruguay. 2nd rev. ed. 2009. (Cultures of the World 17 Ser.). 144p. (gr. 6). 42.79 *(978-0-7614-4482-4(3))* Marshall Cavendish Corp.

Oachs, Emily Rose. Uruguay. 2016. (Exploring Countries Ser.). (ENG., Illus.). 32p. (J). (gr. 3-7). 26.95 *(978-1-62617-406-1(7)*, Blastoff! Readers) Bellwether Media.

Oldfield, Matt & Oldfield, Tom. Luis Suarez: el Pistolero. 2016. (ENG., Illus.). 160p. (J). (gr. 4-7). pap. 8.99 *(978-1-78606-012-9(4))* Blake, John Publishing, Ltd. GBR. Dist: Independent Pubs. Group.

Shields, Charles J. Uruguay. (South America Today Ser.). 2009. (Illus.). 63p. (J). (gr. 4-7). 21.95 *(978-1-4222-0642-3(4))* 2007. 64p. (YA). (gr. 7-18). pap. 9.95 *(978-1-4222-0709-3(9))* Mason Crest.

—Uruguay, Vol. 13. Henderson, James D., ed. 2015. (Discovering South America: History, Politics, & Culture Ser.). (Illus.). 64p. (J). (gr. 7). lib. bdg. 22.95 *(978-1-4222-3305-4(7))* Mason Crest.

USEFUL ARTS

see Technology

UTAH

Brown, Jonatha A. Utah. 2006. (Portraits of the States Ser.). 32p. (gr. 2-6). pap. 10.50 *(978-0-8368-4726-0(1))*; (Illus.). lib. bdg. 26.00 *(978-0-8368-4709-3(1))* Stevens, Gareth Publishing LLLP. (Gareth Stevens Learning Library).

Fein, E. How to Draw Utah's Sights & Symbols. 2009. (Kid's Guide to Drawing America Ser.). 32p. (gr. k-k). 50.50 *(978-1-61511-100-8(X)*, PowerKids Pr.) Rosen Publishing Group, Inc., The.

Feinstein, Stephen. Utah: A MyReportLinks. Com Book. 2003. (States Ser.). (Illus.). 48p. (J). (gr. 4-10). lib. bdg. 25.26 *(978-0-7660-5097-6(1)*, MyReportLinks.com Bks.) Enslow Pubs., Inc.

Hall, Rebecca. A Is for Arches: A Utah Alphabet. Larson, Katherine & Langton, Bruce, illus. 2003. (Discover America State by State Ser.). (ENG.). 40p. (J). (gr. 1-3). 17.95 *(978-1-58536-096-3(1)*, 201976) Sleeping Bear Pr.

Hansen Moench, Megan. Know Your State Activity Book Utah, 1 vol. Padavick, Nate, illus. 2015. (ENG.). 272p. (J). pap. 14.99 *(978-1-4236-4056-1(X))* Gibbs Smith, Publisher.

Hirschmann, Kris. Utah. 2003. (World Almanac Library of the States). (Illus.). 48p. (gr. 4-9). pap. 14.05 *(978-0-8368-5332-2(6))*; lib. bdg. 31.00 *(978-0-8368-5161-8(7))* Stevens, Gareth Publishing LLLP. (Gareth Stevens Learning Library).

Marsh, Carole. Utah Current Events Projects: 30 Cool, Activities, Crafts, Experiments & More for Kids to Do to Learn about Your State! 2003. (Utah Experience Ser.). 32p. (gr. k-5). pap. 5.95 *(978-0-635-02063-5(7)*, Marsh, Carole Bks.) Gallopade International.

—Utah Geography Projects: 30 Cool, Activities, Crafts, Experiments & More for Kids to Do to Learn about Your State! 2003. (Utah Experience Ser.). 32p. (gr. k-5). pap. 5.95 *(978-0-635-01862-5(4)*, Marsh, Carole Bks.) Gallopade International.

—Utah Government Projects: 30 Cool, Activities, Crafts, Experiments & More for Kids to Do to Learn about Your State! 2003. (Utah Experience Ser.). 32p. (gr. k-5). pap. 5.95 *(978-0-635-01963-9(9)*, Marsh, Carole Bks.) Gallopade International.

—Utah Symbols & Facts Projects: 30 Cool, Activities, Crafts, Experiments & More for Kids to Do to Learn about Your State! 2003. (Utah Experience Ser.). 32p. (gr. k-5). pap. 5.95 *(978-0-635-01913-4(2)*, Marsh, Carole Bks.) Gallopade International.

Murray, Julie. Utah, 1 vol. 2006. (United States Ser.). (ENG., Illus.). 32p. (gr. 2-4). 27.07 *(978-1-59197-703-2(7)*, Buddy Bks.) ABDO Publishing Co.

Obregon, Jose Maria. Utah. Brusca, Maria Cristina, tr. from ENG. 2006. (Bilingual Library of the United States of America Ser.: Set 2). (ENG & SPA., Illus.). 32p. (J). (gr. 3-6). lib. bdg. 25.25 *(978-1-4042-3110-8(2))* Rosen Publishing Group, Inc., The.

Obregón, José María. Utah. 2009. (Bilingual Library of the United States of America Ser.). (ENG & SPA.). 32p. (gr. 2-2). 47.90 *(978-1-60853-388-6(3)*, Editorial Buenas Letras) Rosen Publishing Group, Inc., The.

Orr, Tamra B. Zion. 2017. (True Book — National Parks Ser.). (ENG.). 48p. (J). pap. 7.95 ***(978-0-531-24024-3(X))***; lib. bdg. 31.00 ***(978-0-531-23397-9(9))*** Scholastic Library Publishing. (Children's Pr.).

Stefoff, Rebecca & Mead, Wendy. Utah. 2nd rev. ed. 2009. (Celebrate the States 9 Ser.). 144p. (gr. 6). 42.79 *(978-0-7614-4035-2(6))* Marshall Cavendish Corp.

Trueit, Trudi Strain. Utah. 2007. (Rookie Read-About Geography Ser.). (Illus.). 31p. (J). (gr. 1-2). 20.50 *(978-0-531-12574-8(2)*, Children's Pr.) Scholastic Library Publishing.

UTAH—FICTION

Amato, Carol J. The Lost Treasure of the Golden Sun. 2005. 172p. (J). *(978-0-9713756-3-5(1))* Stargazer Publishing Co.

Beaty, Janice J. & Beaty, Lillian C., illus. Jarod & the Mystery of the Utah Arches: A National Park Adventure Series Book. 2016. 118p. (J). pap. *(978-1-63293-122-1(2))* Sunstone Pr.

Crane, Cheri J. Moment of Truth: A Novel. 2005. 238p. (YA). *(978-1-59156-727-1(0))* Covenant Communications.

Evans, Richard. If Only. 2015. (ENG., Illus.). 288p. (YA). (gr. 9). pap. 11.99 *(978-1-4814-4853-6(6)*, Simon Pulse) Simon Pulse.

Fitzgerald, John. Great Brain. 2006. 20.75 *(978-0-8446-7293-9(9))* Smith, Peter Pub., Inc.

Fitzgerald, John D. More Adventures of the Great Brain. Mayer, Mercer, illus. 2004. (Great Brain Ser.). (ENG.). 176p. (J). (gr. 3-7). pap. 6.99 *(978-0-14-240065-4(3)*, Puffin Books) Penguin Young Readers Group.

—More Adventures of the Great Brain. 2004. (Great Brain Ser.). 142p. (J). (gr. 3-7). pap., tchr.'s training gde. ed. 36.00 incl. audio *(978-0-8072-0860-1(4)*, Listening Library) Random Hse. Audio Publishing Group.

Fogg, K. L. Diamondback Cave: A Novel. 2008. 377p. (J). *(978-1-59811-512-3(X))* Covenant Communications.

Gamble, Adam & Jasper, Mark. Good Night Utah. Rosen, Anne & Hart, Jason, illus. 2012. (Good Night Our World Ser.). (ENG.). 20p. (J). (gr. k — 1). bds. 9.95 *(978-1-60219-059-7(3))* Good Night Bks.

Greene, Michele Dominguez. Keep Sweet. 2011. (ENG.). 224p. (YA). (gr. 9). pap. 9.99 *(978-1-4424-0977-4(0)*, Simon Pulse) Simon Pulse.

Hall, Susan Liberty. Scented Adventures of the Bouquet Sisters in Fairyland. Josephine, Wall, illus. 2011. 85p. (YA). pap. 21.50 *(978-0-9833247-6-8(X))* Inkwell Books LLC.

Horender, Philip M. Head West, Young Mouse: Transcontinental Railroad Traveler, 1 vol. Wolek, Guy, illus. 2013. (Maximilian P. Mouse, Time Traveler Ser.). (ENG.). 112p. (J). (gr. 3-6). lib. bdg. 27.07 *(978-1-61641-959-2(8)*, Calico Chapter Bks) Magic Wagon.

Hughes, Dean. Missing in Action. 2010. (ENG.). 240p. (J). (gr. 5-9). 16.99 *(978-1-4169-1502-7(8)*, Atheneum Bks. for Young Readers) Simon & Schuster Children's Publishing.

Hulet, Debra. Independence Rock. 2011. 208p. pap. 13.99 *(978-1-59955-441-9(0)*, Bonneville Bks.) Cedar Fort, Inc./CFI Distribution.

Hurley, Jeanette Clinger. The Crystal Prince: Love Is the Only Way. 2010. (Illus.). 77p. pap. 32.95 *(978-0-578-03963-3(X))* Outskirts Pr., Inc.

Jacobs, Lily. The Littlest Bunny in Utah: An Easter Adventure. Dunn, Robert, illus. 2015. (ENG.). 32p. (J). (-3). 9.99 *(978-1-4926-1219-3(7)*, Sourcebooks Jabberwocky) Sourcebooks, Inc.

James, Eric. A Halloween Scare in Utah. La Ray, Marina, illus. 2015. (ENG.). 32p. (J). (-5). 9.99 *(978-1-4926-2405-9(5)*, 9781492624059, Sourcebooks Jabberwocky) Sourcebooks, Inc.

—Santa's Sleigh Is on Its Way to Utah: A Christmas Adventure. Dunn, Robert, illus. 2016. (ENG.). 32p. (J). (-2). 12.99 *(978-1-4926-4360-9(2)*, 9781492643609, Sourcebooks Jabberwocky) Sourcebooks, Inc.

Jenkins, Jerry B. & Fabry, Chris. Canyon Echoes. 2005. (Red Rock Mysteries Ser.: 8). (ENG.). 234p. (YA). pap. 6.99 *(978-1-4143-0147-1(2)*, Tyndale Kids) Tyndale Hse. Pubs.

Johnson, Annabel & Johnson, Edgar. Wilderness Bride. 2003. 232p. 12.95 *(978-0-9714612-7-7(9))* Green Mansion Pr. LLC.

Kearns, Ann. Dell's Discovery. 2006. 108p. (YA). per. 9.95 *(978-0-9710696-6-4(2))* Jordan Publishing, Inc.

London, Jonathan. Desolation Canyon. London, Sean, illus. 2015. (Aaron's Wilderness Ser.: 1). (ENG.). 168p. (YA). pap. 12.99 *(978-1-941821-29-9(4)*, West Winds Pr.) Graphic Arts Ctr. Publishing Co.

Mangum, Kay Lynn. A Love Like Lilly. 2006. 336p. (YA). pap. 15.95 *(978-1-59038-580-7(2))* Deseret Bk. Co.

Nichols, Walter H. The Measure of a Boy. 2005. (Illus.). pap. 28.95 *(978-1-885529-73-2(2))* Stevens Publishing.

Nielsen, Gwyn English. Torey the Turkey Goes Skiing. 2003. (Illus.). 24p. (Orig.). (gr. -1-4). pap. 5.99 *(978-0-9660726-0-0(X))* C.G.S. Pr.

Norton, Charles. The Perfect Plan & the Four Brother's Pact. 2012. 24p. pap. 15.99 *(978-1-4691-6503-5(1))* Xlibris Corp.

O'Neill, Elizabeth. Alfred Visits Utah. 2009. 24p. (J). pap. 12.00 *(978-0-9822288-3-8(X))* Global Business Information Strategies, Inc.

Pearson, Carol Lynn. Summer of Truth. 2007. 104p. per. 9.99 *(978-1-59955-046-6(6))* Cedar Fort, Inc./CFI Distribution.

Perry, Jolene. The Next Door Boys. 2011. (YA). *(978-1-59955-910-0(2)*, Bonneville Bks.) Cedar Fort, Inc./CFI Distribution.

Raleigh, Michael H. Ted & Jimmy, 1 vol. 2010. 99p. pap. 19.95 *(978-1-4489-6225-9(0))* America Star Bks.

Randall, Alison L. The Wheat Doll, 1 vol. Farnsworth, Bill, illus. 2008. (ENG.). 32p. (J). (gr. k-3). 16.95 *(978-1-56145-456-3(7))* Peachtree Pubs.

Sargent, Dave & Sargent, Pat. Bashful: (Dusty Dun) Be Brave. Lenoir, Jane, illus. 2003. (Saddle up Ser.: Vol. 1). 42p. (J). pap. 10.95 *(978-1-56763-684-0(5))*; lib. bdg. 23.60 *(978-1-56763-683-3(7))* Ozark Publishing.

Silvano, Wendi. Love Is All Around Utah. Czernichowska, Joanna, illus. 2016. (ENG.). 32p. (J). (-6). 12.99 *(978-1-4926-2968-9(5)*, Sourcebooks Jabberwocky) Sourcebooks, Inc.

Smallman, Steve. Santa Is Coming to Salt Lake City. Dunn, Robert, illus. 2015. (ENG.). 32p. (J). (-3). 9.99 *(978-1-4926-2645-9(7)*, Sourcebooks Jabberwocky) Sourcebooks, Inc.

—Santa Is Coming to Utah. Dunn, Robert, illus. 2013. (ENG.). 32p. (J). (-3). 9.99 *(978-1-4022-8827-2(1)*, Sourcebooks Jabberwocky) Sourcebooks, Inc.

Smith, Emily Wing. The Way He Lived. 2016. (ENG.). 224p. (YA). (gr. 9). 17.99 *(978-0-399-18722-3(7)*, Dutton Books for Young Readers) Penguin Young Readers Group.

Stanley, Brenda. I Am Nuchu. 2010. 334p. (YA). (gr. 9-18). 16.95 *(978-1-934813-47-8(8))* Westside Bks.

Stilton, Geronimo. The Fastest Train in the West. Cooper-McGuinness, Nanette, tr. 2013. (Geronimo Stilton Graphic Novels Ser.). (ENG., Illus.). 56p. (J). (gr. 2-6). 9.99 *(978-1-59707-448-3(9)*, 9781597074483) Papercutz.

Sumner Johnson, Janet. The Last Great Adventure of the PB & J Society. 2016. (Middle-Grade Novels Ser.). (ENG.). 256p. (gr. 4-7). lib. bdg. 26.65 *(978-1-4965-2695-3(3))* Stone Arch Bks.

Tipton, R. Kent. Kid Posse & the Phantom Robber. 2003. (ENG., Illus.). (J). pap. 14.95 *(978-1-878044-89-1(3))* Mayhaven Publishing, Inc.

Williams, Sarah DeFord. Palace Beautiful. 2011. (ENG.). 240p. (J). (gr. 5-18). 6.99 *(978-0-14-241745-4(9)*, Puffin Books) Penguin Young Readers Group.

UTAH—HISTORY

Alvarez, Carlos & Finn, Denny Von. Salt Flat Racers. 2010. (World's Fastest Ser.). (ENG., Illus.). 24p. (J). (gr. 3-7). lib. bdg. 25.95 *(978-1-60014-334-2(2))* Bellwether Media.

Ching, Jacqueline. Utah: Past & Present. 2010. (United States: Past & Present Ser.). (ENG.). 48p. (YA). pap. 11.75 *(978-1-4358-9524-9(X))*; lib. bdg. 29.25 *(978-1-4358-9497-6(9))* Rosen Publishing Group, Inc., The. (Rosen Reference).

Felix, Rebecca. What's Great about Utah? 2015. (Our Great States Ser.). (ENG., Illus.). 32p. (J). (gr. 2-5). pap. 7.95 *(978-1-4677-6088-1(9)*, Lerner Pubns.) Lerner Publishing Group.

Gish, Melissa. Utah. 2009. (This Land Called America Ser.). (Illus.). 32p. (YA). (gr. 3-6). 19.95 *(978-1-58341-797-3(4))* Creative Co., The.

Hall, Carol S. & Hansen, T. J. This Is Utah. 257p. (J). (gr. 1-6). pap. 39.95 *(978-1-56861-048-1(3))* Swift Learning Resources.

Hamilton, John. Zion National Park. 2008. (National Parks Set II Ser.). 32p. (gr. 4-9). 27.07 *(978-1-60453-096-4(0)*, Abdo & Daughters) ABDO Publishing Co.

Harvey, Dan. Rocky Mountain: Colorado, Utah, Wyoming, Vol. 19. 2015. (Let's Explore the States Ser.). (Illus.). 64p. (J). (gr. 5). 23.95 *(978-1-4222-3332-0(4))* Mason Crest.

Jerome, Kate B. Lucky to Live in Utah. 2017. (Arcadia Kids Ser.). (ENG., Illus.). 32p. (J). 16.99 ***(978-0-7385-2793-2(9))*** Arcadia Publishing.

—The Wise Animal Handbook Utah. 2017. (Arcadia Kids Ser.). (ENG., Illus.). 32p. (J). 16.99 ***(978-0-7385-2846-5(3))*** Arcadia Publishing.

Kent, Deborah. Utah (Revised Edition) 2014. (America the Beautiful, Third Ser. (Revised Edition) Ser.). (ENG.). 144p. (J). lib. bdg. 40.00 *(978-0-531-28295-3(3))* Scholastic Library Publishing.

LeBoutillier, Nate. The Story of the Utah Jazz. 2010. (NBA — A History of Hoops Ser.). 48p. (YA). (gr. 5-18). 23.95 *(978-1-58341-964-9(0)*, Creative Education) Creative Co., The.

Lusted, Marcia Amidon. Utah: The Beehive State. 2010. (Our Amazing States Ser.). (ENG.). 24p. (J). pap. 8.25 *(978-1-4488-0752-9(2)*, PowerKids Pr.) Rosen Publishing Group, Inc., The.

Marsh, Carole. Exploring Utah Through Project-Based Learning: Geography, History, Government, Economics & More. 2016. (Utah Experience Ser.). (ENG.). (J). pap. 9.99 *(978-0-635-12368-8(1))* Gallopade International.

—I'm Reading about Utah. 2014. (Utah Experience Ser.). (ENG., Illus.). (J). pap., pap. 8.99 *(978-0-635-11319-1(8))* Gallopade International.

—Utah History Projects: 30 Cool, Activities, Crafts, Experiments & More for Kids to Do to Learn about Your State! 2003. (Utah Experience Ser.). 32p. (gr. k-5). pap. 5.95 *(978-0-635-01813-7(6)*, Marsh, Carole Bks.) Gallopade International.

Olhoff, Jim. Utah, 1 vol. 2009. (United States Ser.). (ENG., Illus.). 48p. (YA). (gr. 2-5). 27.07 *(978-1-60453-680-5(2))* ABDO Publishing Co.

Parker, Janice. Utah. 2011. (Illus.). 48p. (J). *(978-1-61690-493-7(3))* Weigl Pubs., Inc.

—Utah: The Beehive State. 2016. (J). *(978-1-4896-4950-8(6))* Weigl Pubs., Inc.

Rodriguez, Cindy. Utah: The Beehive State. 2012. (J). 27.13 *(978-1-61913-409-6(8))* Weigl Pubs., Inc.

Sanders, Doug, et al. Utah. 2016. (ENG., Illus.). 80p. (J). 34.21 *(978-1-62713-178-0(7))* Cavendish Square Publishing.

Skogen, J. M. Utah Jazz. 2013. (On the Hardwood Ser.). (ENG., Illus.). 48p. (gr. 3-8). pap. 8.95 *(978-1-61570-833-8(2))* Scobre Pr. Corp.

Tieck, Sarah. Utah, 1 vol. 2012. (Explore the United States Ser.). (ENG.). 32p. (J). (gr. k-5). lib. bdg. 28.50 *(978-1-61783-383-0(5)*, Big Buddy Bks.) ABDO Publishing Co.

The Utah Journey Program Kit: All program components for the Utah Journey, 1 vol. 2009. 129.95 *(978-1-4236-0733-5(3))* Gibbs Smith, Publisher.

UTENSILS, KITCHEN

see Household Equipment and Supplies

UTILITIES, PUBLIC

see Public Utilities

UTOPIAS—FICTION

Blakemore, Megan Frazer. The Daybreak Bond. 2017. (ENG.). 336p. (J). 16.99 ***(978-1-68119-479-0(1)***, 9781681194790, Bloomsbury USA Childrens) Bloomsbury Publishing USA.

Booraem, Ellen. The Unnameables. 2011. (ENG., Illus.). 336p. (J). (gr. 5-7). pap. 18.99 *(978-0-547-55213-2(0))* Houghton Mifflin Harcourt Publishing Co.

DeStefano, Lauren. Perfect Ruin. White, Teagan, illus. 2013. (Internment Chronicles Ser.: 1). (ENG.). 368p. (YA). (gr. 7). 18.99 *(978-1-4424-8061-2(0)*, Simon & Schuster Bks. For Young Readers) Simon & Schuster Bks. For Young Readers.

—Perfect Ruin. White, Teagan, illus. 2013. (Internment Chronicles Ser.: 1). (ENG.). 368p. (YA). (gr. 7). pap. 10.99 *(978-1-4814-1538-5(7))* Simon & Schuster Children's Publishing.

Fiedler, Lisa. Hopper's Destiny. To, Vivienne, illus. 2016. (Mouseheart Ser.: 2). (ENG.). 368p. (J). (gr. 3-7). pap. 7.99 *(978-1-4814-2090-7(9)*, McElderry, Margaret K. Bks.) McElderry, Margaret K. Bks.

—Mouseheart. To, Vivienne, illus. 2015. (Mouseheart Ser.: 1). (ENG.). 336p. (J). (gr. 3-7). pap. 7.99 *(978-1-4424-8783-3(6)*, McElderry, Margaret K. Bks.) McElderry, Margaret K. Bks.

Grant, Michael. BZRK. (ENG.). 400p. (gr. 9). 2013. (J). pap. 9.99 *(978-1-60684-418-2(0))* 2012. 17.99 *(978-1-60684-312-3(5))* Lerner Publishing Group. (Carolrhoda Lab™).

—BZRK Apocalypse. 2014. (ENG.). 400p. (J). (gr. 9). 18.99 *(978-1-60684-408-3(3)*, Carolrhoda Lab™) Lerner Publishing Group.

—BZRK Reloaded. (ENG.). 432p. (J). (gr. 9). 2014. pap. 9.99 *(978-1-60684-504-2(7))* 2013. 18.99 *(978-1-60684-394-9(X))* Lerner Publishing Group. (Carolrhoda Lab™).

Hawk, Delores. The Edge of Finali. 2012. 350p. pap. 14.25 *(978-0-9859522-0-4(2))* Asimow, Dyanne.

Hinchliffe, Stuart Jarod. Princess Tiffany Arabella & the Time of Dreams. 2009. 196p. 24.50 *(978-1-60860-627-6(9)*, Strategic Bk. Publishing) Strategic Book Publishing & Rights Agency (SBPRA).

Hirsch, Jeff. The Darkest Path. 2013. (YA). pap. *(978-0-545-51224-4(7)*, Scholastic Pr.) Scholastic, Inc.

Hourlier, Sylvaine. Blacky & the Enchanted Mountain, 1 vol. 2010. 48p. pap. 16.95 *(978-1-4512-1140-5(6))* America Star Bks.

Jolley, Dan & Nelson, O. T. The Girl Who Owned a City: The Graphic Novel. Jones, Joëlle, illus. 2012. (Single Titles Ser.). (ENG.). 128p. (YA). (gr. 5-12). pap. *(978-0-7613-5634-9(7)*, Graphic Universe™) Lerner Publishing Group.

Layne, Steven L. Paradise Lost, 1 vol. (ENG.). 312p. (YA). (gr. 7-12). 2013. pap. 8.95 *(978-1-4556-1775-3(X))* 2011. 15.99 *(978-1-58980-590-3(9))* Pelican Publishing Co., Inc.

Lois, Lowry. Messenger. 2012. (Giver Quartet Ser.: 3). (ENG.). 192p. (YA). (gr. 7). 17.99 *(978-0-547-99567-0(9))* Houghton Mifflin Harcourt Publishing Co.

—Messenger. (ENG.). (J). 2009. 176p. (gr. 3-7). mass mkt. 7.99 *(978-0-385-73716-6(5)*, Bantam Bks. for Young Readers) 2006. 192p. (gr. 4-7). pap. 9.99 *(978-0-385-73253-6(8)*, Ember) Random Hse. Children's Bks.

—Son. 2014. (Giver Quartet Ser.: 4). lib. bdg. 20.85 *(978-0-606-35979-5(6))* Turtleback Bks.

Metzger, Joanna. The Space Program. Elizalde, Marcelo, illus. 2006. 142p. (J). *(978-1-59336-695-7(7))* Mondo Publishing.

Parker, Amy Christine. Astray (Gated Sequel) 2014. (ENG.). 352p. (YA). (gr. 9). 17.99 *(978-0-449-81602-8(8)*, Random Hse. Bks. for Young Readers) Random Hse. Children's Bks.

—Gated. 2013. (ENG.). 352p. (YA). (gr. 9). 17.99 *(978-0-449-81597-7(8)*, Random Hse. Bks. for Young Readers) Random Hse. Children's Bks.

Simmons, Kristen. Article 5. 2013. (Article 5 Ser.: 1). (ENG.). 384p. (YA). (gr. 8-12). pap. 10.99 *(978-0-7653-2961-5(1)*, 9780765329615, Tor Teen) Doherty, Tom Assocs., LLC.

Thomas, John Ira. Zoo Force: Dear Eniko. Smith, Jeremy, illus. 2003. 68p. per. 6.95 *(978-0-9743147-1-6(4))* Candle Light Pr.

White, Ruth. You'll Like It Here (Everybody Does) 2012. (ENG.). 272p. (J). (gr. 4-7). 7.99 *(978-0-375-86596-1(9)*, Yearling) Random Hse. Children's Bks.

V

VACATIONS

Adamson, Heather. Family Vacations. 2010. (Special Days Ser.). 24p. (J). 25.65 *(978-1-60753-029-9(5))* Amicus Publishing.

Allen, Francesca, illus. Vacation. 2006. (Usborne Look & Say Ser.). 10p. (J). (gr. -1-k). bds. 7.99 *(978-0-7945-1315-3(8)*, Usborne) EDC Publishing.

Auld, Mary. Going on Vacation. 2011. (My Family & Me Ser.). (Illus.). 24p. (J). lib. bdg. 24.25 *(978-1-59771-230-9(2))* Sea-To-Sea Pubns.

Bernardo, Kat. Stem: The Science of Travel: Multiplication (Grade 3) 2017. (Mathematics Readers Ser.). (Illus.). 32p. (J). (gr. 3-3). pap. 8.99 ***(978-1-4807-5797-4(7))*** Teacher Created Materials, Inc.

Brode, Robyn. August/agosto. 2009. (Months of the Year/Meses del año Ser.). (ENG & SPA.). 24p. (J). (gr. -1-3). pap. 8.15 *(978-1-4339-2113-1(8)*, Weekly Reader Leveled Readers) Stevens, Gareth Publishing LLLP.

—August/Agosto. 2009. (Months of the Year/Meses del año Ser.). (ENG & SPA.). 24p. (J). (gr. -1-3). lib. bdg. 22.00 *(978-1-4339-1936-7(2)*, Weekly Reader Leveled Readers) Stevens, Gareth Publishing LLLP.

—July/julio. 2009. (Months of the Year/Meses del año Ser.). (ENG & SPA.). 24p. (J). (gr. -1-3). pap. 8.15 *(978-1-4339-2112-4(X)*, Weekly Reader Leveled Readers) Stevens, Gareth Publishing LLLP.

—July/Julio. 2009. (Months of the Year/Meses del año Ser.). (ENG & SPA.). 24p. (J). (gr. -1-3). lib. bdg. 22.00 *(978-1-4339-1935-0(4)*, Weekly Reader Leveled Readers) Stevens, Gareth Publishing LLLP.

—June/junio. 2009. (Months of the Year/Meses del año Ser.). (ENG & SPA.). 24p. (J). (gr. -1-3). pap. 8.15 *(978-1-4339-2111-7(1)*, Weekly Reader Leveled Readers) Stevens, Gareth Publishing LLLP.

—June/Junio. 2009. (Months of the Year/Meses del año Ser.). (ENG & SPA.). 24p. (J). (gr. -1-3). lib. bdg. 22.00 *(978-1-4339-1934-3(6)*, Weekly Reader Leveled Readers) Stevens, Gareth Publishing LLLP.

Brode, Robyn & Nations, Susan. August. 2nd rev. ed. 2009. (Months of the Year Ser.). (ENG.). 24p. (J). (gr. -1-3). pap. 8.15 *(978-1-4339-2101-8(4))*; lib. bdg. 22.00 *(978-1-4339-1924-4(9))* Stevens, Gareth Publishing LLLP. (Weekly Reader Leveled Readers).

—July. 2nd rev. ed. 2009. (Months of the Year Ser.). (ENG.). 24p. (J). (gr. -1-3). pap. 8.15 *(978-1-4339-2100-1(6))*; lib. bdg. 22.00 *(978-1-4339-1923-7(0))* Stevens, Gareth Publishing LLLP. (Weekly Reader Leveled Readers).
—June. 2nd rev. ed. 2009. (Months of the Year Ser.). (ENG.). 24p. (J). (gr. -1-3). pap. 8.15 *(978-1-4339-2099-8(9))*; lib. bdg. 22.00 *(978-1-4339-1922-0(2))* Stevens, Gareth Publishing LLLP. (Weekly Reader Leveled Readers).
Carlton Books, ed. Vacation Doodles: Doodle Your Way to Vacation Heaven! 2010. (ENG., Illus.). 96p. (J). (gr. 2). pap. 7.95 *(978-1-84732-652-2(8))* Carlton Bks., Ltd. GBR. Dist: Sterling Publishing Co., Inc.
Color All About: A Giant Coloring Book about Summer Vacation: Summer Vacation. 2004. (Illus.). 36p. (J). *(978-1-59949-006-9(4))* Food Marketing Consultants, Inc.
Day, Amelia. Olivia's Ocean Adventure. 2013. (Core Math Skills: Numbers & Operations in Base 10 Ser.). 24p. (J). (gr. 1-2). 22.60 *(978-1-4777-2222-0(X)*, Rosen Classroom) Rosen Publishing Group, Inc., The.
—Olivia's Ocean Adventure: Understand Place Value. 2013. (Rosen Math Readers Ser.). (ENG.). 24p. (J). (gr. 1-2). pap. 49.50 *(978-1-4777-2038-7(3))*; pap. 8.25 *(978-1-4777-2037-0(5))* Rosen Publishing Group, Inc., The. (Rosen Classroom).
EventoSusan. YOUR DREAM VACATION HIGH BEGINNING BOOK WITH ONLINE ACCESS. 2014. (ENG.). 24p. (J). pap. 9.50 *(978-1-107-69043-1(9))* Cambridge Univ. Pr.
Eystad, Janet Lynn. What I Got into Last Summer. 2012. 28p. 24.95 *(978-1-4626-5316-4(2))* America Star Bks.
George, Lucy M. Holidays: Then & Now. 2015. (Collins Big Cat Ser.). (ENG.). 24p. (J). (gr. 2-2). pap. 6.95 *(978-0-00-759108-4(X))* HarperCollins Pubs. Ltd. GBR. Dist: Independent Pubs. Group.
Gibson, Ray. Little book of vacation Activities. 2005. (ENG.). 96p. (J). 7.95 *(978-0-7945-1171-5(6)*, Usborne) EDC Publishing.
Gilpin, Rebecca. Travel Activity Book. 2013. (Doodle Bks). 96p. (J). pap. 12.99 *(978-0-7945-3287-1(X)*, Usborne) EDC Publishing.
Hanson, Anders. Let's Go by RV, 1 vol. 2008. (Let's Go Ser.). (ENG., Illus.). 24p. (J). (gr. k-3). lib. bdg. 24.21 *(978-1-59928-902-1(4)*, SandCastle) ABDO Publishing Co.
Harper, Suzanne & Sheppard, Bonnie. The 10 Most Extreme Vacations. 2008. (J). 14.99 *(978-1-55448-534-5(7))* Scholastic Library Publishing.
Heos, Bridget. Manners on Vacation. Longhi, Katya, illus. 2015. (Monstrous Manners Ser.). (ENG.). 24p. (J). (gr. 1-3). 19.95 *(978-1-60753-747-2(8))* Amicus Publishing.
Highlights for Children, compiled by. Highlights Hidden Picture Playground: on Vacation. 2009. (Highlights Hidden Pictures Ser.). (ENG., Illus.). 32p. (J). (gr. -1-1). pap. 5.49 *(978-0-87534-321-1(X))* Highlights for Children.
The Land & the People. 2016. (Land & the People Ser.). 48p. (gr. 5-5). pap. 84.30 *(978-1-4824-5327-0(4))*; lib. bdg. 191.70 *(978-1-4824-4975-4(7))* Stevens, Gareth Publishing LLLP.
Laval, Thierry. Look & Find on Vacation. 2017. (Mini Look & Find Ser.). (ENG.). 14p. (J). 9.95 ***(978-0-531-23083-1(X)***, Children's Pr.) Scholastic Library Publishing.
Lennon, Liz. What I Like: Holidays. 2017. (Little Stars Ser.). (ENG., Illus.). 24p. (J). (gr. -1-k). pap. 6.99 *(978-1-4451-4766-6(1)*, Franklin Watts) Hachette Children's Group GBR. Dist: Hachette Bk. Group.
Maskel, Hazel. 1001 Things to Spot on Vacation. 2011. (1001 Things to Spot Ser.). 32p. (J). ring bd. 9.99 *(978-0-7945-3087-7(7)*, Usborne) EDC Publishing.
Mercado, Nancy E. Boredom Busters! Activities to Do for Kids Like You! 2003. (Illus.). 38p. (J). *(978-0-439-52312-7(5))* Scholastic, Inc.
Nez, John, illus. My Vacation Diary. 2008. (ENG.). 24p. (J). (gr. -1-3). pap. 14.99 *(978-0-8249-5581-6(1)*, Ideal Pubns.) Worthy Publishing.
Phillips, Clifton. Waterworld Wonderways. 2007. 36p. 9.99 *(978-0-9797106-2-9(6))* Avid Readers Publishing Group.
Richards, Jon. Vacations & Holidays. 2005. (How Things Have Changed Ser.). (Illus.). 32p. (J). (gr. 3-7). lib. bdg. 27.10 *(978-1-59389-197-8(0))* Chrysalis Education.
Robson, Kirsteen. Wipe-Clean Vacation Activities. 2015. (Wipe-Clean Bks.). (ENG.). 22p. (J). (gr. k-5). pap. 7.99 *(978-0-7945-3480-6(5)*, Usborne) EDC Publishing.
Ross, Stewart. Seaside Holidays. 2013. (Start-Up Connections Ser.). (ENG., Illus.). 32p. (J). pap. 12.99 *(978-0-237-54421-8(0))* Evans Brothers, Ltd. GBR. Dist: Independent Pubs. Group.
Rowe, Brooke. What's Your Perfect Vacation? 2015. 32p. (J). *(978-1-63470-037-5(6))* Cherry Lake Publishing.
Ticktock Media, Ltd. Staff. Summer Vacation. 2009. (Busy Tots Ser.). (ENG.). 10p. (J). (gr. -1-k). bds. 6.95 *(978-1-84696-800-6(3)*, TickTock Books) Octopus Publishing Group GBR. Dist: Independent Pubs. Group.
Tocquigny, Rick. Life Lessons from Family Vacations. 2015. (ENG., Illus.). 224p. 14.95 *(978-1-63076-081-6(1))* Taylor Trade Publishing.
Woolf, Alex. A Photographic View of Holidays. 2016. (Past in Pictures Ser.). (ENG., Illus.). 32p. (J). (gr. 4-6). pap. 11.99 *(978-0-7502-8353-3(X)*, Wayland) Hachette Children's Group GBR. Dist: Hachette Bk. Group.

VACATIONS—FICTION

Adams, Sherred Willcox. Five Little Friends. 2006. pap. 15.95 *(978-1-4304-4149-6(6))* Kessinger Publishing, LLC.
Agee, Jon. Terrific. 2017. (ENG., Illus.). 40p. (J). (gr. k-3). 17.99 ***(978-0-7352-2988-4(0)***, Dial Bks) Penguin Young Readers Group.
Altreche, Jeanine. Talula Goes to New York. 2007. 32p. per. 12.95 *(978-1-4327-0538-1(5))* Outskirts Pr., Inc.
Ameen, Judith. Harold & the Magic Books. 2005. 40p. pap. 8.95 *(978-1-933265-42-1(6))* Wasteland Pr.
Andersen, C. B. The Forgotten Treasure. 2004. 215p. (J). pap. *(978-1-59038-314-8(1))* Deseret Bk. Co.
Applegate, Katherine. Spring Break. 2010. (Summer Ser.). (ENG., Illus.). 240p. (YA). (gr. 9-18). pap. 8.99 *(978-1-4169-9094-9(1)*, Simon Pulse) Simon Pulse.
Arena, Jen. Lady Liberty's Holiday. Hunt, Matt, illus. 2016. (ENG.). 40p. (J). (gr. k-3). 17.99 *(978-0-553-52067-5(9)*, Knopf Bks. for Young Readers) Random Hse. Children's Bks.
Azurmendi, Mattie. Sock Vacation. 2011. 20p. pap. 14.95 *(978-1-257-64550-3(1))* Lulu Pr., Inc.
Bader, Arlys Elaine. The Adventures of Garth & Cloey. 2008. 40p. pap. 16.99 *(978-1-4389-2472-4(0))* AuthorHouse.
Bailey, Ethel M. T. Lily Pond Village, 1 vol. 2009. 57p. pap. 16.95 *(978-1-60703-379-0(8))* America Star Bks.
Banks, Kate. Dillon Dillon. 2005. 149p. (gr. 3-7). 18.00 *(978-0-7569-5767-4(2))* Perfection Learning Corp.
Baratz-Logsted, Lauren. Zinnia's Zaniness. 2011. (Sisters Eight Ser.: 8). (ENG., Illus.). 128p. (J). (gr. 1-4). pap. 5.99 *(978-0-547-55439-6(7))* Houghton Mifflin Harcourt Publishing Co.
Barks, Carl, et al. Walt Disney's Vacation Parade Volume 5. Clark, John, ed. 2008. (ENG., Illus.). 80p. pap. 9.95 *(978-1-60360-031-6(0)*, 9781603600316) Gemstone Publishing, Inc.
—Walt Disney's Vacation Parade Volume 6. 2009. 80p. pap. 9.99 *(978-1-60360-096-5(5))* Gemstone Publishing, Inc.
Barnett, Angela. Mystic Grove. 2006. pap. 10.00 *(978-1-4257-1912-8(0))* Xlibris Corp.
Barrow, David. Fergus Barnaby. 2017. (ENG.). 32p. (J). (gr. -1-k). 12.99 ***(978-1-4380-5009-6(7))*** Barron's Educational Series, Inc.
Battiste, Alyse. Super Sally's Fantastic Fun Day. 2007. (Illus.). 68p. (J). pap. 15.97 *(978-0-9798217-1-4(1))* Candalyse Publishing.
Beachy, Elaine. Biff & Becka's Stupendous Vacation. 2013. 156p. (J). 30.95 *(978-1-4497-9069-1(0))*; pap. 13.95 *(978-1-4497-9070-7(4))* Author Solutions, Inc. (WestBow Pr.).
Behrens, Rebecca. Summer of Lost & Found. 2016. (ENG., Illus.). 288p. (J). (gr. 3-7). 16.99 *(978-1-4814-5896-2(5)*, Aladdin) Simon & Schuster Children's Publishing.
Bentley, Sue. A Forest Charm, 6 vols. Farley, Andrew & Swan, Angela, illus. 2010. (Magic Puppy Ser.: 6). (ENG.). 128p. (J). (gr. 1-3). pap. 5.99 *(978-0-448-45065-0(8)*, Grosset & Dunlap) Penguin Young Readers Group.
—Sunshine Shimmers. 2014. (Magic Puppy Ser.: 12). lib. bdg. 14.75 *(978-0-606-34141-7(2)*, Turtleback) Turtleback Bks.
—Sunshine Shimmers #12. Swan, Angela & Farley, Andrew, illus. 2014. (Magic Puppy Ser.: 12). (ENG.). 128p. (J). (gr. 1-3). 5.99 *(978-0-448-46791-7(7)*, Grosset & Dunlap) Penguin Young Readers Group.
—Vacation Dreams. 2013. (Magic Bunny Ser.: 2). lib. bdg. 16.00 *(978-0-606-31676-7(0)*, Turtleback) Turtleback Bks.
—Vacation Dreams #2. Swan, Angela, illus. 2013. (Magic Bunny Ser.: 2). (ENG.). 128p. (J). (gr. 1-3). pap. 5.99 *(978-0-448-46728-3(3)*, Grosset & Dunlap) Penguin Young Readers Group.
—Winter Wonderland #5. Swan, Angela, illus. 2013. (Magic Ponies Ser.: 5). (ENG.). 128p. (J). (gr. 1-3). 5.99 *(978-0-448-46786-3(0)*, Grosset & Dunlap) Penguin Young Readers Group.
Benton, Jim. The Super-Nice Are Super-Annoying. Benton, Jim, illus. 2012. (Dear Dumb Diary Year Two Ser.). (ENG., Illus.). 144p. (J). (gr. 3-7). pap. 5.99 *(978-0-545-37763-8(3)*, Scholastic Paperbacks) Scholastic, Inc.
Berenstain, Jan, et al. The Berenstain Bears Go on Vacation. Berenstain, Jan & Berenstain, Mike, illus. 2010. (Berenstain Bears Ser.). (ENG.). 32p. (J). (gr. -1-3). pap. 6.99 *(978-0-06-057433-8(X))* HarperCollins Pubs.
Berenstain, Stan & Berenstain, Jan. The Berenstain Bears Out West. Berenstain, Stan & Berenstain, Jan, illus. 2006. (I Can Read Level 1 Ser.). (ENG., Illus.). 32p. (J). (gr. k-3). pap. 3.99 *(978-0-06-058354-5(1))* HarperCollins Pubs.
Bevin, Teresa. Tina Springs into Summer/Tina Se Lanza Al Verano. Rodriguez, Perfecto, illus. 2005. (ENG & SPA.). 114p. (J). pap. 21.00 *(978-1-928589-28-0(6))* Gival Pr., LLC.
Beyers, Kathryn. Babe's Vacation. 2012. 32p. pap. 17.49 *(978-1-4771-5671-1(2))* Xlibris Corp.
Bickford, Janette. Vern's Vacation. 2012. 16p. pap. 12.68 *(978-1-4669-2311-9(3))* Trafford Publishing.
Birdsall, Jeanne. The Penderwicks: A Summer Tale of Four Sisters, Two Rabbits, & a Very Interesting Boy. (Penderwicks Ser.). (ENG.). (J). (gr. 3-7). 2007. 288p. 7.99 *(978-0-440-42047-7(4)*, Yearling) 2005. 272p. 16.99 *(978-0-375-83143-0(6)*, Knopf Bks. for Young Readers) Random Hse. Children's Bks.
—The Penderwicks: A Summer Tale of Four Sisters, Two Rabbits & a Very Interesting Boy. 2007. (Penderwicks (Hardback) Ser.). 262p. (gr. 3-7). 18.00 *(978-0-7569-7798-6(3))* Perfection Learning Corp.
—The Penderwicks: A Summer Tale of Four Sisters, Two Rabbits, & a Very Interesting Boy. 2007. (Penderwicks Ser.: 1). (Illus.). 262p. (gr. 4-7). lib. bdg. 18.40 *(978-1-4177-7275-9(1))* Turtleback Bks.
—The Penderwicks: A Summer Tale of Four Sisters, Two Rabbits & a Very Interesting Boy. 2009. 8.80 *(978-0-7848-2826-7(1)*, Everbind) Marco Bk. Co.
—The Penderwicks: A Summer Tale of Four Sisters, Two Rabbits & a Very Interesting Boy. l.t. ed. 2006. (Penderwick Ser.). 304p. (J). (gr. 3-7). 23.95 *(978-0-7862-8897-7(3))* Thorndike Pr.
—The Penderwicks at Point Mouette. 2011. (Playaway Children Ser.). (J). (gr. k). 44.99 *(978-1-61707-434-9(9))* Findaway World, LLC.
—The Penderwicks at Point Mouette. (Penderwicks Ser.). (ENG.). (J). (gr. 3-7). 2012. 320p. 7.99 *(978-0-375-85135-3(6)*, Yearling) 2011. 304p. 16.99 *(978-0-375-85851-2(2)*, Knopf Bks. for Young Readers) Random Hse. Children's Bks.
—The Penderwicks Paperback 4-Book Boxed Set, 4 vols. 2016. (ENG.). 270p. (J). (gr. 3-7). 31.96 *(978-1-101-93760-0(2)*, Yearling) Random Hse. Children's Bks.
Blackstone, Stella & Harter, Debbie. Bear Takes a Trip. 2012. (ENG., Illus.). 24p. (J). (gr. -1-1). pap. 6.99 *(978-1-84686-756-9(8))* Barefoot Bks., Inc.
Blackstone, Stella & Parker, Elizabeth. L'Ours Fait un Voyage. Harter, Debbie, illus. 2013.Tr. of Bear Takes a Trip. (FRE & ENG.). 24p. (J). (gr. k-1). pap. 6.99 *(978-1-84686-946-4(3))* Barefoot Bks., Inc.
Blume, Judy. Fudge-a-Mania. 2007. (ENG.). 176p. (J). (gr. 3-7). 7.99 *(978-0-14-240877-3(8)*, Puffin Books) Penguin Young Readers Group.
—Otherwise Known as Sheila the Great. 2004. (ENG.). 160p. (J). (gr. 3-7). 7.99 *(978-0-425-19380-8(2)*, Berkley) Penguin Publishing Group.
—Otherwise Known as Sheila the Great. 2007. (ENG.). 176p. (J). (gr. 3-7). 7.99 *(978-0-14-240879-7(4)*, Puffin Books) Penguin Young Readers Group.
—Otherwise Known as Sheila the Great. 2007. 154p. (gr. 4-7). 16.00 *(978-0-7569-7915-7(3))* Perfection Learning Corp.
—Otherwise Known as Sheila the Great. 2007. (Fudge Bks.: 2). 138p. (gr. 4-7). lib. bdg. 18.40 *(978-1-4177-8370-0(2)*, Turtleback) Turtleback Bks.
Bodeen, S. A. Shipwreck Island. 2014. (Shipwreck Island Ser.: 1). (ENG.). 192p. (J). (gr. 5-8). 16.99 *(978-1-250-02777-1(2)*, 9781250027771) Feiwel & Friends.
Bond, Michael. Paddington Abroad. Fortnum, Peggy, illus. 2015. (Paddington Ser.). 176p. (J). (gr. 3-7). 9.99 *(978-0-06-231222-8(7))* HarperCollins Pubs.
Bowman, Lucy. Sticker Dolly Dressing on Vacation (Revised Cover) 2015. (Sticker Dolly Dressing Ser.). (ENG.). 24+p. (J). (gr. k-5). pap. 8.99 *(978-0-7945-3555-1(0)*, Usborne) EDC Publishing.
Bracken- Murphy, Julie. Sammy's Summer Vacation. 2007. 52p. per. 13.95 *(978-1-4327-0615-9(2))* Outskirts Pr., Inc.
Brauner, Susan. The Adventures of Sohi: Mystery of Moon Island. 2011. 207p. 28.95 *(978-1-4327-6752-5(6))*; pap. 15.95 *(978-1-4327-6536-1(1))* Outskirts Pr., Inc.
Brege, K. B. Champ... A Wave of Terror! Five Ways to Finish. 2006. (Mick Morris Myth Solver Ser.: No. 3). (J). mass mkt. 6.99 *(978-0-9774119-2-4(3))* Team B Creative LLC.
Bridgman, C. A. Santa's Hawaiian Vacation. (J). 14.95 *(978-0-681-32827-3(4))* Booklines Hawaii, Ltd.
Bridwell, Norman. Clifford Sees America. 2012. (Scholastic Reader Level 1 Ser.). (ENG.). 32p. (J). (gr. -1-3). pap. 3.99 *(978-0-545-23144-2(2)*, Cartwheel Bks.) Scholastic, Inc.
—Clifford Sees America. 2012. (Clifford: Scholastic Readers Level 1 Ser.). lib. bdg. 13.55 *(978-0-606-23908-0(1)*, Turtleback) Turtleback Bks.
Brown, Jeff. Flat Stanley's Worldwide Adventures #10: Showdown at the Alamo. Pamintuan, Macky, illus. 2013. (Flat Stanley's Worldwide Adventures Ser.: 10). (ENG.). 112p. (J). (gr. 1-5). 15.99 *(978-0-06-218988-2(3))* HarperCollins Pubs.
—The Mount Rushmore Calamity. Pamintuan, Macky, illus. 2009. (Flat Stanley's Worldwide Adventures Ser.: 1). (ENG.). 96p. (J). (gr. 2-5). 15.99 *(978-0-06-142991-0(0))*; pap. 4.99 *(978-0-06-142990-3(2))* HarperCollins Pubs.
—Showdown at the Alamo. Pamintuan, Macky, illus. 2013. (Flat Stanley's Worldwide Adventures Ser.: 10). (ENG.). 112p. (J). (gr. 1-5). pap. 4.99 *(978-0-06-218987-5(5))* HarperCollins Pubs.
—Showdown at the Alamo. 2013. (Flat Stanley's Worldwide Adventures Ser.: 10). (J). lib. bdg. 14.75 *(978-0-606-35046-4(2)*, Turtleback) Turtleback Bks.
Brown, Marc. Arthur & the School Pet. 2005. (Step into Reading Sticker Bks.). (Illus.). 24p. 14.00 *(978-0-7569-5571-7(8))* Perfection Learning Corp.
—Arthur & the School Pet. 2003. (Step into Reading Ser.). (ENG., Illus.). 24p. (J). (gr. k-3). pap. 3.99 *(978-0-375-81001-5(3)*, Random Hse. Bks. for Young Readers) Random Hse. Children's Bks.
—Arthur & the School Pet. 2003. (Arthur Step into Reading Ser.). (gr. -1-2). lib. bdg. 13.55 *(978-0-613-57492-1(3)*, Turtleback) Turtleback Bks.
—Arthur in New York. 2008. (Step into Reading Ser.). (ENG., Illus.). 24p. (J). (gr. k-3). pap. 3.99 *(978-0-375-82976-5(8)*, Random Hse. Bks. for Young Readers) Random Hse. Children's Bks.
—Arthur's Classroom Fib. 2007. (Arthur Step into Reading Ser.). lib. bdg. 13.55 *(978-1-4177-7281-0(6)*, Turtleback) Turtleback Bks.
Brown, Monica. Lola Levine & the Vacation Dream. 2017. (Lola Levine Ser.: 5). (J). lib. bdg. 16.00 ***(978-0-606-40222-4(5))*** Turtleback Bks.
Brown, Ruth Alberta. Tabitha's Vacation. 2005. reprint ed. pap. 27.95 *(978-1-4191-1538-7(3))* Kessinger Publishing, LLC.
Buffie, Margaret. Who Is Frances Rain? 20th ed. 2007. (ENG.). 184p. (J). (gr. 7-9). 7.95 *(978-1-55453-209-4(4))* Kids Can Pr., Ltd. CAN. Dist: Hachette Bk. Group.
Burn, Michael. Childhood at Oriol. 2005. (ENG., Illus.). 360p. pap. 16.95 *(978-1-885586-32-2(9))* Turtle Point Pr.
Burshek, Edward & Burshek, Tonja. Explorers of the Word: Episode 1: the Creation. Peterson, Melanie, illus. 2007. (ENG.). 76p. per. 19.95 *(978-1-4241-6691-6(8))* America Star Bks.
Bush, Laura & Hager, Jenna Bush. Our Great Big Backyard. Rogers, Jacqueline, illus. 40p. (J). (gr. -1-3). 2018. pap. 7.99 ***(978-0-06-246841-3(3))*** 2016. (ENG.). 18.99 *(978-0-06-246835-2(9))* 2016. lib. bdg. 19.89 *(978-0-06-246836-9(7))* HarperCollins Pubs.
Buske, Jody. Wilderness Awakening. 2006. 108p. pap. 19.95 *(978-1-4241-2685-9(1))* PublishAmerica, Inc.
Candlewick Press Editors. Peppa Pig & the Great Vacation. 2015. (Peppa Pig Ser.). lib. bdg. 16.00 *(978-0-606-36857-5(4))* Turtleback Bks.
Candlewick Press Staff. Peppa Pig & the Great Vacation. 2014. (Peppa Pig Ser.). (ENG.). 32p. (J). (-k). 12.99 *(978-0-7636-6986-7(5)*, Candlewick Entertainment) Candlewick Pr.
Capucilli, Alyssa Satin. Biscuit's First Trip. 2010. (Biscuit 8x8 Ser.). (J). lib. bdg. 13.55 *(978-0-606-10115-8(2)*, Turtleback) Turtleback Bks.
Carey, Rosa Nouchette. Uncle Max. 2007. pap. *(978-1-4065-1269-4(9))* Dodo Pr.
Carr, Annie Roe. Nan Sherwoods Winter Holidays or Rescuin. 2007. pap. *(978-1-4065-1296-0(6))* Dodo Pr.
Carroll, D. L. Sir Licksalot & the Island Fools. 2012. 120p. pap. 19.95 *(978-1-4626-8092-4(5))* America Star Bks.
Carson, John E. & Carson, Marlene R. The Wire Forest of Peru. 2007. (Ramblin' Rose Ser.). 205p. (YA). (gr. 8-12). per. 8.99 *(978-0-9776043-9-5(X))* Aspirations Media, Inc.
Champman, Joan. Val's Vacation. 2006. (Neighborhood Readers Ser.). (ENG.). 16p. (gr. 1-3). pap. 6.50 *(978-1-4042-6990-3(8)*, Rosen Classroom) Rosen Publishing Group, Inc., The.
Chandler, Ann. Siena Summer, 1 vol. 2009. (ENG., Illus.). 142p. (YA). (gr. 6-9). pap. 12.95 *(978-1-896580-17-3(3))* Tradewind Bks. CAN. Dist: Orca Bk. Pubs. USA.
Chase, L. P. Elliot Stone & the Mystery of the Summer Vacation Sea Monster. DiRocco, Carl, illus. 2011. (ENG.). 165p. (J). pap. 8.99 *(978-0-9792918-7-6(9))* Blue Marlin Pubns.
Chaud, Benjamin & Cali, Davide. The Truth about My Unbelievable Summer ... 2016. (ENG., Illus.). 44p. (J). (gr. 1-4). 12.99 *(978-1-4521-4483-2(4))* Chronicle Bks. LLC.
Chittenden, Charlotte E. What Two Children Did. 2007. (ENG., Illus.). 132p. per. *(978-1-4065-1360-8(1))* Dodo Pr.
Christie, Ed. The Sweet Smell of Rotten Eggs: Volume Two, the Dude Ranch Rangers. 2009. 108p. pap. 10.95 *(978-1-4401-3764-8(1))* iUniverse, Inc.
Christopherson, Keven. Adventures of the Sky Kids: Lost Treasure of Kolob Canyon. 2005. 58p. pap. 16.95 *(978-1-4137-6514-4(9))* America Star Bks.
Citra, Becky. After the Fire, 1 vol. 2010. (ENG.). 192p. (J). (gr. 4-7). pap. 10.95 *(978-1-55469-246-0(6))* Orca Bk. Pubs. USA.
Clover, Peter. Rescue Riders: Race Against Time. l.t. ed. 2007. 88p. per. *(978-1-905665-29-7(6))* Pollinger In Print.
Cocca-Leffler, Maryann. A Vacation for Pooch. Cocca-Leffler, Maryann, illus. 2013. (ENG., Illus.). 32p. (J). (gr. -1-2). 16.99 *(978-0-8050-9106-9(8)*, 9780805091069, Holt, Henry & Co. Bks. For Young Readers) Holt, Henry & Co.
Coman, Carolyn. Sneaking Suspicions. Shepperson, Rob, illus. 2007. (ENG.). 204p. (J). (gr. 4-6). 16.95 *(978-1-59078-491-4(X)*, Front Street) Boyds Mills Pr.
Conforto, Lisa. The Very Compromising Adventures of Thumby Blackstone, 1 vol. 2010. 34p. 24.95 *(978-1-4512-0270-0(9))* PublishAmerica, Inc.
Cook, Jessica & Stephens, Michael. What If Mommy Took a Vacation? 2011. 28p. pap. 13.99 *(978-1-4634-3601-8(7))* AuthorHouse.
Corwin, Jeff. The Great Alaska Adventure!, 2 vols., Bk. 2. 2010. (Jeff Corwin Ser.: 2). (ENG.). 112p. (J). (gr. 1-3). 4.99 *(978-0-14-241409-5(3)*, Puffin Books) Penguin Young Readers Group.
—Your Backyard Is Wild. 2009. (Jeff Corwin Ser.: 1). (ENG.). 96p. (J). (gr. 1-3). 4.99 *(978-0-14-241404-0(2)*, Puffin Books) Penguin Young Readers Group.
Cottrell-Bentley, Lisa M. Wright on Time: Collection 1. Bauerle, Tanja, illus. 2012. 376p. pap. 19.99 *(978-1-937848-00-2(0))* Do Life Right, Inc.
—Wright on Time: Minnesota. Bauerle, Tanja, illus. 2012. 126p. pap. 12.99 *(978-1-937848-02-6(7))* Do Life Right, Inc.
Couloumbis, Audrey. Lexie. Denos, Julia, illus. 2012. (ENG.). 208p. (J). (gr. 3-7). pap. 6.99 *(978-0-375-85633-4(1)*, Yearling) Random Hse. Children's Bks.
Cousins, Lucy. Maisy Goes on Vacation. Cousins, Lucy, illus. 2012. (Maisy Ser.). (ENG., Illus.). 32p. (J). (gr. -1-2). pap. 6.99 *(978-0-7636-6039-0(6))* Candlewick Pr.
Cowan, Charlotte. Moose with Loose Poops. Neal, Penelope, illus. 2008. (Dr. Hippo Ser.). (ENG.). 32p. (J). (gr. -1-2). 17.95 *(978-0-9753516-5-9(6))* Hippocratic Pr., The.
Cowdell, Nikki. The Bradshaw Vacation. 2008. 77p. pap. 12.33 *(978-1-4092-3667-2(6))* Lulu Pr., Inc.
Crane, C. H. A Christmas Quest: A Young Boy's Unexpected Christmas Vacation. 2013. 122p. (gr. 4-6). 22.33 *(978-1-4907-0807-2(3))*; pap. 12.33 *(978-1-4907-0808-9(1))* Trafford Publishing.
Cross, P. C. Summer Job: A Virgil & Cy Mystery. 2008. 260p. pap. 16.95 *(978-0-595-50921-8(5))* iUniverse, Inc.
Cuillain, Adam & Cuillain, Charlotte. The Pirates on Holiday. Van Wyk, Rupert, illus. 2014. (ENG.). 32p. (J). *(978-0-7787-1311-1(3))* Crabtree Publishing Co.
Culbertson, Jan E. The Legend of Dunsmoor Manor. 2006. 88p. pap. 13.95 *(978-1-58909-348-5(8))* Bookstand Publishing.
—The Legend of the Lost Tiki. 2006. 95p. (YA). pap. 13.95 *(978-1-58909-315-7(1))* Bookstand Publishing.
Cummings, Quasheba Giri. The World's First Submarine. 2008. 20p. pap. 15.49 *(978-1-4389-1273-8(0))* AuthorHouse.
Daniels, Darla. Carrie Goes Camping. 2011. 24p. pap. 16.95 *(978-1-4626-0642-9(3))* America Star Bks.
—The Magic Ring: Summer Vacation in London. 2012. 30p. 16.95 *(978-1-4626-6252-4(8))* America Star Bks.
Daniels, J. M. The Secret of the Little Dutch Doll. 2009. 68p. pap. 25.49 *(978-1-4343-9356-2(9))* AuthorHouse.
Danziger, Paula. What a Trip, Amber Brown. 2003. (Amber Brown Ser.). (Illus.). (J). (gr. -1-2). audio compact disk 28.95 *(978-1-59112-569-3(3))* Live Oak Media.
Davie, Jan. Arthur's Amulet. 2004. 86p. pap. *(978-1-84401-228-2(X))* Athena Pr.
Davies, Jacqueline. The House Takes a Vacation, 0 vols. 2013. (ENG.). 34p. (J). (gr. -1-3). pap. 9.99 *(978-1-4778-1619-6(4)*, 9781477816196, Amazon Children's Publishing) Amazon Publishing.
Delhohne, Jean-Philippe. Visit to Another Planet. 2004. (Illus.). 31p. (J). (gr. k-4). reprint ed. *(978-0-7567-7768-5(2))* DIANE Publishing Co.
dePaola, Tomie. Strega Nona Takes a Vacation. dePaola, Tomie, illus. 2003. (ENG., Illus.). 32p. (J). (gr. -1-3). pap. 5.99 *(978-0-14-250076-7(3)*, Puffin Books) Penguin Young Readers Group.
—Strega Nona Takes a Vacation. dePaola, Tomie, illus. 2003. (Illus.). (J). (gr. -1-3). 13.65 *(978-0-7569-1469-1(8))* Perfection Learning Corp.
DeSio, Delores . Up a Tree with Mary Mcphee: A Mystery for Children. 2006. 86p. pap. 16.95 *(978-1-4241-4309-2(8))* PublishAmerica, Inc.
Destiny, A. & Helms, Rhonda. Sparks in Scotland. 2015. (Flirt Ser.). (ENG.). 224p. (YA). (gr. 7). pap. 9.99 *(978-1-4814-2121-8(2)*, Simon Pulse) Simon Pulse.
Deutsch, Neil. Rose & the Pelican. 2013. 32p. pap. 19.99 *(978-1-4817-0947-7(X))* AuthorHouse.
Diesen, Deborah. The Pout-Pout Fish, Far, Far from Home. Hanna, Dan, illus. 2017. (Pout-Pout Fish Adventure Ser.). (ENG.). 32p. (J). 16.99 *(978-0-374-30194-1(8)*, 9780374301941, Farrar, Straus & Giroux (BYR)) Farrar, Straus & Giroux.
Disney Book Group. World of Reading: Miles from Tomorrowland How I Saved My Summer Vacation: Level 1. Disney Storybook Art Team, illus. 2016. (World of Reading Ser.). (ENG.). 32p. (J). (gr. -1-k). pap. 3.99 *(978-1-4847-2962-5(5))* Disney Pr.
Disney Press Staff & Disney Book Group Staff. Road Trip. Disney Storybook Art Team, illus. 2011. (ENG.). 10p. (J). (gr. -1-k). bds. 8.99 *(978-1-4231-4416-8(3))* Disney Pr.

TUV

Douglas, Ryke Leigh. The Big Wheel. 2010. (Illus.). 21p. (J). pap. 15.95 *(978-1-4327-4495-3(X))* Outskirts Pr., Inc.

Dower, Laura. Give Me a Break. 2004. 166p. (J). lib. bdg. 16.92 *(978-1-4242-0649-0(9))* Fitzgerald Bks.

Dudek, V. A. Soldiers of Fate. 2009. 94p. pap. 15.99 *(978-1-4415-2702-8(8))* Xlibris Corp.

Dyne, Edith Van. Aunt Jane's Nieces on Vacation. 2007. (ENG.). 154p. pap. 19.99 *(978-1-4346-2111-5(1))*; 172p. pap. 21.99 *(978-1-4346-2139-9(1))* Creative Media Partners, LLC.

Earls, Nick. After Summer. 2005. (ENG.). 240p. (YA). (gr. 7). pap. 13.99 *(978-0-618-45781-6(X))* Houghton Mifflin Harcourt Publishing Co.

Ellen, Connie. Marvel Mansion Gang. 2012. 114p. 22.19 *(978-1-4269-6666-8(0))* Trafford Publishing.

Emzer, Counselor. The Day Before Summer Vacation. 2004. 31p. pap. 24.95 *(978-1-4137-2680-0(1))* PublishAmerica, Inc.

Enright, Elizabeth. Gone-Away Lake. Krush, Beth & Krush, Joe, illus. 2006. 256p. (J). (gr. 4-8). reprint ed. pap. 6.00 *(978-1-4223-5436-0(9))* DIANE Publishing Co.

Falconer, Ian. Olivia Goes to Venice. Falconer, Ian, illus. 2010. (ENG., Illus.). 48p. (J). (gr. -1-2). 17.99 *(978-1-4169-9674-3(5),* Atheneum Bks. for Young Readers) Simon & Schuster Children's Publishing.

Feldkamp, Jim And Cate. The Adventures of Tommy & Clara on Mount Catherine. 2008. 32p. pap. 14.49 *(978-1-4389-1366-7(4))* AuthorHouse.

Fenton, Geleta. Joel's Adventure at Sea. Siniard, Ricky, illus. 2013. 50p. (J). mass mkt. 9.95 *(978-0-9824433-2-3(3))* Octopus Publishing Co.

Finley, Martha. Elsie's Vacation & after Events. 2006. 27.95 *(978-1-4218-2997-5(5))*; pap. 12.95 *(978-1-4218-3097-1(3))* 1st World Publishing, Inc.

Flaggert, Candy. Ok, Said Carrie Katherine, 1 vol. Chipka, Sandy, illus. 2008. (ENG.). 25p. 24.95 *(978-1-60563-502-6(2))* America Star Bks.

Fogelin, Adrian. My Brother's Hero, 1 vol. 2005. (ENG.). 224p. (J). (gr. 3-7). reprint ed. pap. 7.95 *(978-1-56145-352-8(8))* Peachtree Pubs.

Frazee, Marla. A Couple of Boys Have the Best Week Ever. 2008. (ENG., Illus.). 40p. (J). (gr. 1-4). 17.99 *(978-0-15-206020-6(0))* Houghton Mifflin Harcourt Publishing Co.

Fromental, Jean-Luc. Oops! Connors, Thomas, tr. from FRE. Jolivet, Joëlle, illus. 2010. (ENG.). 42p. (J). (gr. -1-k). 17.95 *(978-0-8109-8749-4(X))* Abrams, Inc.

Gallagher, Diana G. Beach Blues: The Complicated Life of Claudia Cristina Cortez, 1 vol. Garvey, Brann, illus. 2008. (Claudia Cristina Cortez Ser.). (ENG.). 88p. (gr. 2-3). pap. 6.10 *(978-1-4342-0869-9(9),* Claudia Cristina Cortez) Stone Arch Bks.

Garsee, Linmarie. Annabelle's Vacation with Grandma Hayley: A Mountain Quiltfest Adventure. 2012. 50p. pap. 21.99 *(978-1-4772-7737-9(4))* AuthorHouse.

Gateley, Edwina. God Goes on Vacation. Gateley, Edwina, illus. 2009. (Illus.). 32p. (Orig.). (J). pap. 9.95 *(978-0-8091-6747-0(6))* Paulist Pr.

Gay, Marie-Louise. Summer in the City. 2013. 148p. pap. *(978-1-4596-6493-7(0))* ReadHowYouWant.com, Ltd.

Gehrke, William & Gehrke, Dolores. Sonia's Choice. 2011. 28p. pap. 15.99 *(978-1-4634-0825-1(0))* AuthorHouse.

Geraldi, Michele J. Pennies at Piper Park. 2009. 24p. pap. 12.99 *(978-1-4389-2829-6(7))* AuthorHouse.

Germain, Kerry. Kimo's Summer Vacation. Montes, Keoni, illus. 2003. 52p. (J). 12.95 *(978-0-9705889-4-4(1))* Island Paradise Publishing.

Gilliam, David. Gingertown. Gilliam, David, illus. 2012. 216p. (J). 29.99 *(978-1-60131-122-1(2))* Big Tent Bks.

Gingras, Marie Claude. Let's Spend Summer with Fred. 2012. 198p. 24.95 *(978-1-4626-4413-1(9))* America Star Bks.

Ginoschio De Osceola, Ibrahim. Enter the Corn Bunny, Vol. 1. 2007. 56p. per. 8.95 *(978-0-595-45273-6(6))* iUniverse, Inc.

Glass, June. Poker Fat: Takes a Vacation. 2005. (J). pap. 9.00 *(978-0-8059-6150-8(X))* Dorrance Publishing Co., Inc.

Golden Books. Thomas Takes a Vacation (Thomas & Friends) Durk, Jim, illus. 2015. (Hologramatic Sticker Book Ser.). (ENG.). 64p. (J). (gr. -1-2). pap. 4.99 *(978-0-553-50846-8(6),* Golden Bks.) Random Hse. Children's Bks.

Gonzalez, Genaro. A So-Called Vacation. 2009. 192p. (YA). (gr. 9-18). pap. 10.95 *(978-1-55885-545-8(9),* Piñata Books) Arte Publico Pr.

Goode, Suzi. The Lost Wizard Series Bk 1. 2007. pap. 11.95 *(978-1-59374-817-3(5))* Whiskey Creek Pr., LLC.

Goscinny, René. Nicholas on Vacation. Bell, Anthea, tr. Sempé, Jean-Jacques, illus. 2013. (ENG.). 136p. (J). (gr. 1-4). pap. 9.95 *(978-0-7148-6224-8(X))* Phaidon Pr., Inc.

—Nicholas on Vacation. Bell, Anthea, tr. from FRE. Sempé, Jean-Jacques, illus. rev. ed. 2006. (ENG.). 132p. (gr. 8-17). 19.95 *(978-0-7148-4678-1(3))* Phaidon Pr., Inc.

Gowar, Mick. Dad's Van. 2009. (ENG., Illus.). 24p. (J). pap. *(978-0-7787-3897-8(3))*; lib. bdg. *(978-0-7787-3866-4(3))* Crabtree Publishing Co.

Gram, Golden. Gail the Snail: Goes on Vacation. 2008. 20p. pap. 11.95 *(978-1-59858-860-6(5))* Dog Ear Publishing, LLC.

Grandpa Casey. Another Mush-Mice Adventure: Florida Vacation, 1 vol. Brennan, Lisa, illus. 2009. 45p. pap. 24.95 *(978-1-60813-329-1(X))* America Star Bks.

Gray, Kes. Daisy & the Trouble with Kittens. Sharratt, Nick & Parsons, Garry, illus. 2010. (Daisy Ser.). (ENG.). 256p. (J). (gr. 2-4). pap. 11.99 *(978-1-86230-834-3(9),* Red Fox) Random House Children's Books GBR. Dist: Independent Pubs. Group.

Greene, Stephanie. Princess Posey & the Crazy, Lazy Vacation. Sisson, Stéphanie Roth, illus. 2016. (Princess Posey, First Grader Ser.: 10). (ENG.). 96p. (J). (gr. k-3). 5.99 *(978-0-14-751293-2(X),* Puffin Books) Penguin Young Readers Group.

Greenwald, Lisa. Dog Beach Unleashed. (Seagate Summers Ser.). (ENG.). (YA). 2016. 256p. (gr. 3-7). pap. 7.95 *(978-1-4197-2056-7(2))* 2015. (Illus.). 240p. (gr. 5-9). 15.95 *(978-1-4197-1481-8(3))* Abrams, Inc. (Amulet Bks.).

—Welcome to Dog Beach. (Seagate Summers Ser.). (ENG.). (YA). (gr. 3-7). 2015. 288p. pap. 6.95 *(978-1-4197-1497-9(X))* 2014. 272p. 15.95 *(978-1-4197-1018-6(4))* Abrams, Inc. (Amulet Bks.).

Greer, Hannah. The Lighthouse Summer Greer, Tica, illus. 2009. 156p. pap. 24.95 *(978-1-60813-493-9(8))* America Star Bks.

Grey, C. R. Animas, Book Two Flight of the King. 2016. (Animas Ser.). (ENG.). 320p. (J). (gr. 3-7). pap. 7.99 *(978-1-4231-8467-6(X))* Hyperion Bks. for Children.

Gutman, Dan. Back to School, Weird Kids Rule! 2014. (My Weird School Ser.). (J). lib. bdg. 16.00 *(978-0-606-35502-5(2))* Turtleback Bks.

—The Get Rich Quick Club. (ENG.). 128p. (J). 2006. (gr. 3-7). pap. 5.99 *(978-0-06-053442-4(7))* 2004. 15.99 *(978-0-06-053440-0(0))* HarperCollins Pubs.

Haber, Shel & dePaola, Tomie. The Animals' Vacation. Haber, Jan, illus. 2015. (G&d Vintage Ser.). (ENG.). 24p. (J). (gr. -1-k). bds. 7.99 *(978-0-448-48399-3(8),* Grosset & Dunlap) Penguin Young Readers Group.

Haesche, Richard Paul, Sr. The Treasure of Pirates Cave. 2007. (ENG.). 378p. (YA). 11.99 *(978-0-9798536-7-8(2))* Kreative X-Pressions Pubns.

Hale, Shannon & Hale, Dean. The Princess in Black Takes a Vacation. Pham, LeUyen, illus. 2016. (Princess in Black Ser.). (ENG.). 96p. (J). (gr. k-3). 14.99 *(978-0-7636-6512-8(6))* Candlewick Pr.

Hall, Angela Marie. Priscilla Pennybrook: Hello World, I Have Arrived!, 1 vol. 2009. 55p. pap. 16.95 *(978-1-61582-899-9(0))* America Star Bks.

Han, Jenny. It's Not Summer Without You, 6 vols. 2010. (Summer I Turned Pretty Ser.: 2). (YA). 90.75 *(978-1-4498-2018-3(2))*; 1.25 *(978-1-4498-2022-0(0))*; 230.75 *(978-1-4498-2015-2(8))*; 88.75 *(978-1-4498-2020-6(4))*; 73.75 *(978-1-4498-2016-9(6))* Recorded Bks., Inc.

—It's Not Summer Without You. (Summer I Turned Pretty Ser.). (ENG.). (YA). (gr. 7). 2011. 320p. pap. 10.99 *(978-1-4169-9556-2(0))* 2010. 288p. 18.99 *(978-1-4169-9555-5(2))* Simon & Schuster Bks. For Young Readers. (Simon & Schuster Bks. For Young Readers).

—The Summer I Turned Pretty. (Summer I Turned Pretty Ser.). (ENG.). (YA). (gr. 7). 2010. 304p. pap. 10.99 *(978-1-4169-6829-0(6))* 2009. 288p. 19.99 *(978-1-4169-6823-8(7))* Simon & Schuster Bks. For Young Readers. (Simon & Schuster Bks. For Young Readers).

—The Summer I Turned Pretty. 2010. lib. bdg. 22.10 *(978-0-606-14529-9(X),* Turtleback) Turtleback Bks.

—We'll Always Have Summer. 2011. (YA). 1.25 *(978-1-4640-1977-7(0))* Recorded Bks., Inc.

—We'll Always Have Summer. (Summer I Turned Pretty Ser.). (ENG.). (YA). (gr. 7). 2012. 320p. pap. 10.99 *(978-1-4169-9559-3(5))* 2011. 304p. 17.99 *(978-1-4169-9558-6(7))* Simon & Schuster Bks. For Young Readers. (Simon & Schuster Bks. For Young Readers).

Hanson, Ed. Desert Ordeal. 2003. (Barclay Family Adventure Ser.: Bk. 3). (Illus.). 64p. (J). (gr. k-6). per. 3.95 *(978-1-56254-552-9(3),* SP 5523) Saddleback Educational Publishing, Inc.

Hapka, Catherine, pseud. Vacation in the Wild. 2014. (I Can Read! Level 2 Ser.). (J). lib. bdg. 13.55 *(978-0-606-35064-8(0),* Turtleback) Turtleback Bks.

Harvey, Jacqueline. Alice-Miranda in the Alps. 2016. (Alice-Miranda Ser.: 12). (ENG.). 336p. (J). (gr. 3-7). pap. 9.99 *(978-0-85798-274-2(5))* Random Hse. Australia AUS. Dist: Independent Pubs. Group.

—Alice-Miranda on Vacation. 2013. (ENG.). 288p. (J). (gr. 2-5). 7.99 *(978-0-385-73996-2(6),* Yearling) Random Hse. Children's Bks.

Harvey, Roland. At the Beach: Postcards from Crabby Spit. Harvey, Roland, illus. 2007. (ENG., Illus.). 32p. (J). (gr. -1-k). pap. 11.99 *(978-1-74114-704-9(2))* Allen & Unwin AUS. Dist: Independent Pubs. Group.

Hawthorne, Rachel. Island Girls & Boys. 2005. (ENG.). 336p. (YA). (gr. 9). pap. 8.99 *(978-0-06-075546-1(6),* HarperTeen) HarperCollins Pubs.

Hay, Angela. Grace S Incredible! Unforgettable! Summer! 2012. 38p. pap. 19.99 *(978-1-62419-562-4(8))* Salem Author Services.

Hayes, Celeste. Cacao & the Jaded Orb: A Sphinx & Trevi Adventure. 2011. (Illus.). 62p. (J). pap. 22.95 *(978-0-9785695-2-5(0))* Adam's Creations Publishing, LLC.

Henighan, Tom. Doom Lake Holiday. 2009. (ENG.). 240p. (YA). (gr. 6). pap. 12.99 *(978-1-55002-847-8(2))* Dundurn CAN. Dist: Ingram Publisher Services.

Henning, Ann. Cow Patty Patti. 2004. 47p. pap. 24.95 *(978-1-4137-3456-0(1))* PublishAmerica, Inc.

Herman, Alison & Grossman, Lynne. Dolly Goes on Vacation. Eve, Lealand, illus. 2007. 22p. (J). 24.95 *(978-0-9746153-2-5(3))* DMH Pr., Inc.

Herring, Bruce D. The Wizard of Wonderland, 1 vol. 2010. 192p. pap. 24.95 *(978-1-4489-5844-3(X))* America Star Bks.

Hibbs, Gillian. Tilly's at Home Holiday. Hibbs, Gillian, illus. 2014. (Child's Play Library). (ENG., Illus.). 32p. (J). *(978-1-84643-601-7(X))* Child's Play International Ltd.

Hinkelman, Carole & Rebik, Nan. The Herman Chronicles: *Herman the Horrible Trailer Mouse *Herman & the Donkeys * Herman's Midnight Trek * Herman's Vacation. 2012. 84p. (gr. 2-4). pap. 11.50 *(978-1-4669-5202-7(4))* Trafford Publishing.

Hitchcock, Fleur. Sunk! A Shrunk! Adventure. 2016. (Shrunk! Adventure Ser.: 4). (ENG., Illus.). 240p. (J). (gr. 3-7). pap. 9.99 *(978-1-84812-448-6(1))* Bonnier Publishing GBR. Dist: Independent Pubs. Group.

Hobbs, Leigh. Old Tom's Holiday. Hobbs, Leigh, illus. 2004. (ENG., Illus.). 32p. (J). 16.95 *(978-1-56145-316-0(1))* Peachtree Pubs.

Homel, David & Gay, Marie-Louise. Travels with My Family, 1 vol. 2007. (ENG., Illus.). 120p. (J). (gr. 1-5). pap. 8.95 *(978-0-88899-833-0(3))* Groundwood Bks. CAN. Dist: Publishers Group West (PGW).

Hopkins, Cathy. Mates, Dates, & Great Escapes. 2011. (Mates, Dates Ser.). (ENG.). 224p. (YA). (gr. 7). pap. 10.99 *(978-1-4424-3080-8(X),* Simon Pulse) Simon Pulse.

Hordos, Sandra. Marissa Plans a Princess Tea Party. Allen, Joshua, illus. 2010. 28p. pap. 12.49 *(978-1-4520-2557-5(6))* AuthorHouse.

Horsfall, S. J. Jodie & Lilly... & the Fake Mansion. 2009. 58p. pap. 7.50 *(978-0-557-12474-9(3))* Lulu Pr., Inc.

Horvath, Polly. The Vacation, 1 vol. (ENG.). 208p. pap. 12.95 *(978-0-88899-693-0(4))* Groundwood Bks. CAN. Dist: Publishers Group West (PGW).

Huelin, Jodi. Alvin & the Chipmunks: Alvin's Easter Break. Artful Doodlers Limited Staff & Carzon, Walter, illus. 2014. (ENG.). 24p. (J). (gr. -1-3). pap. 3.99 *(978-0-06-225222-7(4),* HarperFestival) HarperCollins Pubs.

Hueller, Andy. Dizzy Fantastic & Her Flying Bicycle. 2010. (Illus.). 155p. (J). pap. 8.99 *(978-1-59955-395-5(3))* Cedar Fort, Inc./CFI Distribution.

Ibeh, Chinwe. Tishan Worst Moment. 2010. 28p. pap. 21.99 *(978-1-4500-9385-9(X))* Xlibris Corp.

Ireland, Mary E. & Brandstaedter, German H. Vacaciones de Éric,Las. Clingan, Darrell, tr. 2011.Tr. of Eric's Vacation. (Illus.). 237p. (YA). (gr. 11). pap. 7.25 *(978-0-7399-7766-8(0))* Rod & Staff Pubs., Inc.

Irwin, Chris. Nightmare of Shadows. 2007. 140p. pap. 18.95 *(978-0-615-15008-6(X))* Irwin, Christine.

Irwin, Inez Haynes. Maida's Little House. 2004. reprint ed. pap. 27.95 *(978-1-4179-4236-7(3))* Kessinger Publishing, LLC.

Joan, Marler. Secrets of the Wind. 2006. pap. *(978-1-888251-37-1(9))* Voice & Vision Pubns.

Jones, Jen. Willow's Spring Break Adventure. Franco, Paula, illus. 2015. (Sleepover Girls Ser.). (ENG.). 128p. (gr. 3-5). pap. 6.95 *(978-1-62370-305-9(0))* Stone Arch Bks.

Joseph, Curtis M. Order of Godalming: Max Baxter, 1 vol. 2009. 64p. pap. 19.95 *(978-1-60836-525-8(5))* America Star Bks.

Jules, Jacqueline. The Beach Trip. Smith, Kim, illus. 2016. (Sofia Martinez Ser.). (ENG.). 32p. (gr. k-2). lib. bdg. 21.32 *(978-1-4795-8719-3(2),* Sofia Martinez) Picture Window Bks.

Jungle Crossing. 2011. (ENG.). 228p. (J). (gr. 5-7). pap. 13.99 *(978-0-547-55009-1(X))* Houghton Mifflin Harcourt Publishing Co.

Kane, Bob. Tropical Getaway & Bird Watching. Nguyen, Dustin, illus. 2015. (Batman: Li'l Gotham Ser.). (ENG.). 32p. (gr. 2-3). lib. bdg. 22.60 *(978-1-4342-9735-8(7))* Stone Arch Bks.

Keast, Ellen Frances. A Rainy Week. 2011. 16p. pap. 10.00 *(978-1-60976-777-8(2),* Eloquent Bks.) Strategic Book Publishing & Rights Agency (SBPRA).

Kessler, Liz. Poppy the Pirate Dog. Phillips, Mike, illus. 2015. (Candlewick Sparks Ser.). (ENG.). 64p. (J). (gr. k-4). pap. 3.99 *(978-0-7636-7661-2(6))* Candlewick Pr.

—A Year Without Autumn. (ENG.). 304p. (J). (gr. 4-7). 2012. pap. 7.99 *(978-0-7636-6060-4(4))* 2011. (Illus.). 15.99 *(978-0-7636-5595-2(3))* Candlewick Pr.

Khalsa, Dayal Kaur. My Family Vacation. 2003. (ENG., Illus.). 24p. (J). (gr. 1-4). pap. 6.95 *(978-0-88776-629-9(3),* Tundra Bks.) Tundra Bks. CAN. Dist: Penguin Random Hse. LLC.

Kimmelman, Leslie. In the Doghouse: An Emma & Bo Story. Kelley, True, illus. 2006. (Holiday House Reader Ser.: Level 2). (ENG.). 32p. (J). (gr. 5-8). 14.95 *(978-0-8234-1882-4(0))* Holiday Hse., Inc.

Kinney, Jeff. The Long Haul. Kinney, Jeff, illus. 2014. (Diary of a Wimpy Kid Ser.: Bk. 9). (ENG., Illus.). 224p. (J). (gr. 3-7). 13.95 *(978-1-4197-1189-3(X),* Amulet Bks.) Abrams, Inc.

—The Long Haul. (CHI.). (J). 2015. 368p. (gr. 4-8). pap. *(978-986-6104-59-6(1))* 2014. *(978-986-6104-52-7(4))* DaskoviK, Izdatel'sko-torgovaja korporacija.

—The Long Haul. 2014. (JPN.). 221p. (J). *(978-4-591-14196-0(9))* Poplar Publishing.

—The Long Haul. 2013. (Diary of a Wimpy Kid Ser.: 9). (J). 40.75 *(978-1-4906-4383-0(4))*; 43.75 *(978-1-4906-4058-7(4))* Recorded Bks., Inc.

—The Long Haul. 2014. (Diary of a Wimpy Kid Ser.: 9). (J). lib. bdg. 25.70 *(978-0-606-36074-6(3))* Turtleback Bks.

Kirkpatrick, Teresa. The Adventures of Four Friends on Vacation, 1 vol. 2009. 119p. pap. 19.95 *(978-1-60836-927-0(7))* America Star Bks.

Knowles, Kent. Lucius & the Storm. Knowles, Kent, illus. 2007. (Illus.). 32p. (J). (gr. -1-3). 15.95 *(978-1-60108-005-9(0))* Red Cygnet Pr.

Kondrchek, Jamie & Rasemas, Joe. What Day Is It? (Que Dia Es Hoy?) Vega, Eida de la, tr. Rasemas, Joe, illus. 2009. (Day in the Life Ser.). (SPA & ENG., Illus.). 32p. (J). (gr. -1-1). 25.70 *(978-1-58415-838-7(7))* Mitchell Lane Pubs., Inc.

Kraft, Erik P. Lenny & Mel's Summer Vacation. Kraft, Erik P., illus. 2012. (Ready-For-Chapters Ser.). (ENG., Illus.). 64p. (J). (gr. 2-5). pap. 6.99 *(978-0-689-86874-0(X),* Simon & Schuster/Paula Wiseman Bks.) Simon & Schuster/Paula Wiseman Bks.

Krulik, Nancy. Going Overboard! John and Wendy Staff, illus. 2012. (Katie Kazoo, Switcheroo Ser.: No. 9). (ENG.). 144p. (J). (gr. 2-4). pap. 5.99 *(978-0-448-45681-2(8),* Grosset & Dunlap) Penguin Young Readers Group.

LaBree Stute, Lela. Summer Pugs. 2010. 44p. pap. 19.99 *(978-0-557-41763-6(5))* Lulu Pr., Inc.

Lagercrantz, Rose. Life According to Dani. Eriksson, Eva, illus. 2016. (My Happy Life Ser.: 4). (ENG.). 108p. (gr. k-3). 16.99 *(978-1-77657-070-6(7))* Gecko Pr. NZL. Dist: Lerner Publishing Group.

Langlois, Annie. L' Evasion d'Alfred le Dindon. Beaulieu, Jimmÿ, illus. 2004. (Roman Jeunesse Ser.). (FRE.). 96p. (J). (gr. 4-7). pap. *(978-2-89021-687-7(X))* Diffusion du livre Mirabel (DLM).

Latimer, Àlex. Stay! a Top Dog Story, 1 vol. Latimer, Àlex, illus. 2015. (ENG., Illus.). 32p. (J). (gr. -1-3). 16.95 *(978-1-56145-884-4(8))* Peachtree Pubs.

Leray, Merrill. The Kidnapping. 2009. 58p. pap. 15.99 *(978-1-4415-4380-6(5))* Xlibris Corp.

Lewis, Steven & Parker, Shelley. Return to Allapatria. 2006. 395p. (J). pap. *(978-0-9547092-9-7(2))* Accent Pr. Ltd.

Lim, Rebecca. The Sweet Life. 2012. (ENG.). 196p. (YA). (gr. 7). pap. 11.99 *(978-1-74237-770-4(X))* Allen & Unwin AUS. Dist: Independent Pubs. Group.

Logan, Dottie Colegrove. Picnic on the Beach: Nana & Me Series, Book Three. 2010. 16p. 12.99 *(978-1-4490-3689-8(9))* AuthorHouse.

London, Jonathan. Froggy Goes to Hawaii. Remkiewicz, Frank, illus. 2012. (Froggy Ser.). (ENG.). 32p. (J). (gr. -1-k). pap. 6.99 *(978-0-14-242219-2(7),* Puffin Books) Penguin Young Readers Group.

—Froggy Goes to Hawaii. 2012. (Froggy Ser.). lib. bdg. 17.20 *(978-0-606-26083-1(8),* Turtleback) Turtleback Bks.

Lopez, Christopher P. The Absolute Truth about Lying. Racine, Victoria, illus. 2011. 36p. pap. 24.95 *(978-1-4626-3245-9(9))* America Star Bks.

Loving, Winifred "Oyoko". My Grandma Loves to Play. 2013. 28p. pap. 16.99 *(978-1-4669-7405-0(2))* Trafford Publishing.

Mackler, Carolyn. Tangled. 2011. (ENG.). 336p. (YA). (gr. 9). pap. 9.99 *(978-0-06-173106-8(4),* HarperTeen) HarperCollins Pubs.

Marsh, Carole. The Secret of Skullcracker Swamp. 2006. (Pretty Darn Scary Mysteries Ser.). (Illus.). 113p. (YA). (gr. 7-14). 14.95 *(978-0-635-06238-3(0))*; (J). (gr. 3-5). per. 7.99 *(978-0-635-06234-5(8))* Gallopade International.

Matas, Carol. Far. 2008. (Freak Ser.). (ENG.). 152p. (J). (gr. 5-18). pap. *(978-1-55470-094-3(9))* Me to We.

Mattel. Monster High Diaries: Lagoona Blue & the Big Sea Scarecation. 2016. (Monster High Diaries: 3). (ENG.). 160p. (J). (gr. 3-7). 9.99 *(978-0-316-30080-3(2))* Little, Brown Bks. for Young Readers.

McGirr, Randel W. Bible Camp. 2007. 176p. per. 13.95 *(978-0-595-44663-6(9))* iUniverse, Inc.

McKay, Hilary. Lulu & the Dog from the Sea. Lamont, Priscilla, illus. (Lulu Ser.: Book 2). (ENG.). 112p. (J). (gr. 1-5). 2014. pap. 4.99 *(978-0-8075-4821-9(9))* 2013. 13.99 *(978-0-8075-4820-2(0))* Whitman, Albert & Co.

McLean, Matthew. A Bewitching Summer, 1 vol. 2009. 100p. pap. 19.95 *(978-1-60836-686-6(3))* America Star Bks.

McPhail, David. Pig Pig Returns. McPhail, David, illus. 2011. (ENG., Illus.). 32p. (J). (gr. -1-3). 15.95 *(978-1-58089-356-5(2))* Charlesbridge Publishing, Inc.

Meadows, Daisy. Joy the Summer Vacation Fairy. Ripper, Georgie, illus. 2007. (Rainbow Magic Ser.). (ENG.). 192p. (J). (gr. -1-3). 6.99 *(978-0-439-93442-8(7),* Scholastic Paperbacks) Scholastic, Inc.

—Joy the Summer Vacation Fairy. Ripper, Georgie, illus. 2007. (Rainbow Magic — Special Edition Ser.). 177p. (gr. -1-3). lib. bdg. 17.20 *(978-1-4177-7081-6(3),* Turtleback) Turtleback Bks.

Menefee, Angelo K. Billy's First Summer Vacation. 2007. (Illus.). (J). per. 16.95 *(978-1-60002-249-4(9))* Mountain Valley Publishing, LLC.

Menge, Dawn. Queen Vernita Visits the Blue Ice Mountains. 2009. 32p. (J). pap. 19.95 *(978-1-4327-1169-6(5))* Outskirts Pr., Inc.

Miller, Ed, illus. Minions Paradise: Phil Saves the Day! 2016. (ENG.). 24p. (J). (gr. -1-3). pap. 5.99 *(978-0-316-39296-9(0))* Little, Brown Bks. for Young Readers.

Millner, Robert W. The Chicken Coop Gang. 2011. 130p. 29.99 *(978-1-4568-5517-8(4))*; pap. 19.99 *(978-1-4568-5516-1(6))* Xlibris Corp.

Mincin, Sabrina. Catching a Shooting Star. 2012. 28p. pap. 12.95 *(978-1-4575-0862-2(1))* Dog Ear Publishing, LLC.

Mitchell, Charlie. The Great M & M Caper. 2009. 82p. pap. 15.99 *(978-1-4415-2242-9(5))* Xlibris Corp.

Montague, Chester. Timmy's Vacation. 2008. 40p. pap. 24.95 *(978-1-60441-225-3(9))* America Star Bks.

Montgomery, E. j. Hailey Walker & the Mystery of the Absent Professor. 2013. 180p. pap. 13.95 *(978-1-4575-2068-6(0))* Dog Ear Publishing, LLC.

Morgan, Retta & Morgan, Kris. Love Hates. 2011. 152p. pap. 11.99 *(978-1-4567-1448-2(1))* AuthorHouse.

Moundlic, Charlotte. The Bathing Costume. Tallec, Olivier & Sorman, Joy, illus. 2013. (ENG.). 40p. (J). (gr. k-3). 15.95 *(978-1-59270-141-4(8))* Enchanted Lion Bks., LLC.

Mullin, Michael & Skewes, John. Larry Gets Lost in the Twin Cities. Skewes, John, illus. 2012. (Larry Gets Lost Ser.). (ENG., Illus.). 32p. (J). (gr. -1-2). 17.99 *(978-1-57061-754-6(6),* Little Bigfoot) Sasquatch Bks.

Mumford, Carole. Christmas Vacation in Colorado: A Magnificent Six Adventure, 1 vol. 2009. 75p. pap. 19.95 *(978-1-60749-231-3(8))* America Star Bks.

Mun-Ensor, Michelle. Aloh. 2011. 32p. pap. 24.95 *(978-1-4560-9848-3(9))* America Star Bks.

Napoli, Donna Jo & Johnston, Shelagh. Hotel Jungle. Spengler, Kenneth, tr. Spengler, Kenneth, illus. 2004. 33p. (J). 15.95 *(978-1-59336-002-3(9))*; pap. *(978-1-59336-003-0(7))* Mondo Publishing.

Nash, Tim. The Club. 2009. 112p. pap. 12.49 *(978-1-4490-2087-3(9))* AuthorHouse.

Neel, Julien. The Perfect Summer. Neel, Julien, illus. 2012. (Lou! Ser.: 4). (ENG., Illus.). 48p. (J). (gr. 6-9). pap. 8.95 *(978-0-8225-9169-6(3),* Graphic Universe™) Lerner Publishing Group.

Neel, Julien & Burrell, Carol klio. The Perfect Summer. Neel, Julien, illus. 2012. (Lou! Ser.: 4). (ENG., Illus.). 48p. (J). (gr. 6-9). lib. bdg. 27.93 *(978-0-7613-8780-0(3),* Graphic Universe™) Lerner Publishing Group.

Norman, Donna Marie. Just a Swim? Widowati, Marini, illus. 2008. 29p. pap. 24.95 *(978-1-60672-182-7(8))* America Star Bks.

North, Merry. My Vacation: Picture, Play, & Tote. 2003. (Picture, Play & Tote-Book Ser.). (Illus.). 10p. (J). (gr. -1-18). bds. 5.99 *(978-1-57151-720-3(0))* Playhouse Publishing.

Oakley, Graham. Church Mice Take a Break. (Illus.). 25p. (J). 17.99 *(978-0-340-73254-0(7))* Hodder & Stoughton GBR. Dist: Trafalgar Square Publishing.

Oceanak, Karla. Bogus: An Aldo Zelnick Comic Novel. Spanjer, Kendra, illus. 2016. (Aldo Zelnick Comic Novel Ser.: 2). (ENG.). 160p. (J). (gr. 3-7). pap. 8.95 *(978-1-934649-66-4(X))* Bailiwick Pr.

—Cahoots. Spanjer, Kendra, illus. 2011. (Aldo Zelnick Comic Novel Ser.: 3). (ENG.). 151p. (J). (gr. 3-7). 12.95 *(978-1-934649-08-4(2))* Bailiwick Pr.

—Cahoots: An Aldo Zelnick Comic Novel. Spanjer, Kendra, illus. 2016. (Aldo Zelnick Comic Novel Ser.: 3). (ENG.). 160p. (J). (gr. 1-8). pap. 8.95 *(978-1-934649-67-1(8))* Bailiwick Pr.

—Dumbstruck: An Aldo Zelnick Comic Novel. Spanjer, Kendra, illus. 2016. (Aldo Zelnick Comic Novel Ser.: 4). (ENG.). 160p. (J). (gr. 1-8). pap. 8.95 *(978-1-934649-68-8(6))* Bailiwick Pr.

—Egghead: An Aldo Zelnick Comic Novel. Spanjer, Kendra, illus. 2016. (Aldo Zelnick Comic Novel Ser.: 5). (ENG.). 160p. (J). (gr. 1-8). pap. 8.95 *(978-1-934649-69-5(4))* Bailiwick Pr.

—Finicky: An Aldo Zelnick Comic Novel. Spanjer, Kendra, illus. 2016. (Aldo Zelnick Comic Novel Ser.: 6). (ENG.). 160p. (J). (gr. 1-8). pap. 8.95 *(978-1-934649-70-1(8))* Bailiwick Pr.

—Hotdogger: An Aldo Zelnick Comic Novel. Spanjer, Kendra, illus. 2016. (Aldo Zelnick Comic Novel Ser.: 8). (ENG.). 160p. (J). (gr. 1-8). pap. 8.95 *(978-1-934649-72-5(4))* Bailiwick Pr.

—Ignoramus: An Aldo Zelnick Comic Novel. Spanjer, Kendra, illus. 2016. (Aldo Zelnick Comic Novel Ser.: 9). (ENG.). 160p. (J). (gr. 1-8). pap. 8.95 *(978-1-934649-73-2(2))* Bailiwick Pr.
—Logjam. Spanjer, Kendra, illus. 2016. (Aldo Zelnick Comic Novel Ser.: 12). (ENG.). 160p. (gr. 1-8). 12.95 *(978-1-934649-64-0(3))* Bailiwick Pr.
Ockler, Sarah. Twenty Boy Summer. 2010. (ENG.). 320p. (YA). (gr. 7-17). pap. 10.99 *(978-0-316-05158-3(6))* Little, Brown Bks. for Young Readers.
Odhiambo, Tori. Close to Home: The African Savannah. 2012. 32p. pap. 21.99 *(978-1-4691-9510-0(0))* Xlibris Corp.
Olds, Laurie. Cars on Vacation. 2009. 24p. pap. 12.25 *(978-1-4490-1633-3(2))* AuthorHouse.
Oso Se Va de Viaje. 2014. (ENG & SPA., Illus.). (J). *(978-1-78285-088-5(0))* Barefoot Bks., Inc.
Palmer, Robin. Little Miss Red. 2010. (ENG.). 320p. (YA). (gr. 7-18). 9.99 *(978-0-14-241123-0(X),* Speak) Penguin Young Readers Group.
Papademetriou, Lisa & Minsky, Terri. A Very Lizzie Summer. 2005. (Lizzie Mcguire Super Special Ser.). (Illus.). 265p. (J). *(978-1-4155-9625-8(5))* Disney Pr.
Papell, David. Harlem Awakenings Color Edition. 2007. 50p. pap. 26.95 *(978-0-615-17931-5(2))* Papell, David.
Parish, Herman. Amelia Bedelia Chapter Book #3: Amelia Bedelia Road Trip! (Special Edition) 2013. (ENG., Illus.). 160p. (J). *(978-0-06-227057-3(5),* Collins Design) HarperCollins Pubs.
—Amelia Bedelia Road Trip! 2013. (Amelia Bedelia Chapter Book Ser.: 3). (J). lib. bdg. 14.75 *(978-0-606-32453-3(4),* Turtleback) Turtleback Bks.
Parisi, Bettie. The Quiet. 2009. 36p. pap. 15.00 *(978-1-4269-1015-9(0))* Trafford Publishing.
Park, Barbara. Aloha-Ha-Ha! Brunkus, Denise, illus. (Junie B. Jones Ser.: 26). (ENG.). 128p. (J). (gr. 1-4). 2007. per. 4.99 *(978-0-375-83404-2(4))* 2006. lib. bdg. 13.95 *(978-0-375-93403-2(0))* Random Hse. Children's Bks. (Random Hse. Bks. for Young Readers).
—Junie B., First Grader - Aloha-Ha-Ha! Brunkus, Denise, illus. 2007. (Junie B. Jones Ser.). 119p. (gr. 1-4). 15.00 *(978-0-7569-8085-6(2))* Perfection Learning Corp.
—Junie B. First Grader - Aloha-Ha-Ha! 2007. (Junie B. Jones Ser.: 26). lib. bdg. 14.75 *(978-1-4177-8157-7(2),* Turtleback) Turtleback Bks.
Payne, Helen. Vacation Paws. Youngblood, Carol, illus. 2006. 50p. per. 10.00 *(978-0-9786276-6-9(0))* Mentzer Printing Ink.
Payot Karpathakis, Emmanuelle. Pixie en Vacaciones. 2013. 40p. pap. *(978-1-909193-28-4(3))* Summertime Publishing.
—Pixie's Holidays. 2013. 40p. pap. *(978-1-909193-25-3(9))* Summertime Publishing.
Peeler, Gail. Jackson's Magic Wishing Well. 2008. 25p. 35.50 *(978-1-4357-2950-6(1))* Lulu Pr., Inc.
Perez, Angela J. Zack Attack! Hazard, Andrea, illus. 2007. 36p. (J). 17.95 *(978-0-9778328-9-7(9))* His Work Christian Publishing.
Perisic, Zoran. An Alien Called Freddy. 2012. 152p. pap. 9.95 *(978-1-60594-907-9(8),* Llumina Pr.) Aeon Publishing Inc.
Perkins, Lynne Rae. Pictures from Our Vacation. Perkins, Lynne Rae, illus. 2007. (Illus.). 32p. (J). (gr. k-3). 17.89 *(978-0-06-085098-2(1),* Greenwillow Bks.) HarperCollins Pubs.
Perkins, Lynne Rae & Perkins, Lynne R. Pictures from Our Vacation. Perkins, Lynne Rae, illus. 2007. (ENG., Illus.). 32p. (J). (gr. k-3). 17.99 *(978-0-06-085097-5(3),* Greenwillow Bks.) HarperCollins Pubs.
Perry, Tristan. Cinnamon Takes a Vacation: Furry Tails #2, 1 vol. 2009. 122p. pap. 19.95 *(978-1-60836-451-0(8))* America Star Bks.
Peschke, M. Vacation Queen. Mourning, Tuesday, illus. 2016. (Kylie Jean Ser.). (ENG.). 112p. (gr. 2-3). 8.95 *(978-1-5158-0059-0(8))* Picture Window Bks.
Peschke, Marci. Vacation Queen. Mourning, Tuesday, illus. 2016. (Kylie Jean Ser.). (ENG.). 112p. (gr. 2-3). lib. bdg. 22.65 *(978-1-5158-0058-3(X))* Picture Window Bks.
Peterson, Doug. LarryBoy Versus the Volcano, 1 vol., No. 9. 2004. (Big Idea Books / LarryBoy Ser.). (ENG., Illus.). 96p. (J). pap. 4.99 *(978-0-310-70728-8(5))* Zonderkidz.
Peterson, Jim. The Summer House Kitten. 2007. 48p. pap. 16.95 *(978-1-60441-914-6(8))* America Star Bks.
Potter, Barbara L. The Fly That Went on Vacation. 2010. 16p. 8.49 *(978-1-4490-9353-2(1))* AuthorHouse.
Prime, D. De Nuevo en Vacaciones. (Serie Sara y Pablo - Sarah & Paul Ser.: No. 6).Tr. of Go on Vacation. (SPA.). (J). 2.99 *(978-0-7899-0495-9(0),* 498900) Editorial Unilit.
Princess Protection Program Staff. The Palace of Mystery, No. 4. 2010. (Princess Protection Program Ser.). 144p. pap. 4.99 *(978-1-4231-2727-7(7))* Disney Pr.
Ramirez, Terry. Growing up with Olivi. The Beguiling Blue-Haired Beauty of Boysenberry Lane. 2009. 96p. pap. 9.95 *(978-0-595-47668-8(6))* iUniverse, Inc.
Rand, Johnathan. American Chillers #22 Nuclear Jelly Fish of New Jersey. 2007. 208p. (J). pap. 5.99 *(978-1-893699-93-9(5))* AudioCraft Publishing, Inc.
Ransom, Candice. Iva Honeysuckle Meets Her Match. Ross, Heather, illus. 2014. (Iva Honeysuckle Book Ser.). (ENG.). 192p. (J). (gr. 1-3). pap. 4.99 *(978-1-4231-3516-6(4))* Hyperion Bks. for Children.
—Iva Honeysuckle Meets Her Match. Ross, Heather, illus. 2013. (Iva Honeysuckle Book Ser.). (ENG.). 192p. (J). (gr. 2-5). 14.99 *(978-1-4231-3514-2(8))* Hyperion Pr.
Reberg, Evelyne. Vacances infernales Tom Tom. pap. 21.95 *(978-2-227-73108-0(7))* Bayard Editions FRA. Dist: Distribooks, Inc.
Reed, Lynn Rowe. Roscoe & the Pelican Rescue. Reed, Lynn Rowe, illus. 2011. (ENG., Illus.). 32p. (J). (gr. -1-3). 14.95 *(978-0-8234-2352-1(2))* Holiday Hse., Inc.
Reiff, Lauren & Geiser, Christina. Meows-Key Motel: A Great Vacation Spot for Hip Cats. 2009. 12p. pap. 8.95 *(978-1-4389-8801-6(X))* AuthorHouse.
Reimiller, Diane. Brayden & Ryan's Summer Vacation. Jastrzebski, Brandy, illus. 2012. 24p. pap. 24.95 *(978-1-4626-7792-4(4))* America Star Bks.
Rey, H. A. & Rey, Margret. Takes a Trip. 2007. (Curious George Ser.). (ENG., Illus.). 24p. (J). (gr. -1-3). pap. 3.99 *(978-0-618-88403-2(3))* Houghton Mifflin Harcourt Publishing Co.
Reynolds, Evan. My Vacation. 2004. (J). 12.95 *(978-0-9759790-0-6(0))* Plant the Seed Publishing.
Richardson, Tracy. Indian Summer. 2010. (ENG.). 198p. (YA). (gr. 7). pap. 11.95 *(978-1-935462-25-5(3))* Luminis Bks., Inc.
Richens, Carol & Smith, Lori. Lori's Summer Fun with Tamara! 2009. 33p. 16.40 *(978-1-4357-1113-6(0))* Lulu Pr., Inc.
Rigby Education Staff. Mr. Merton's Vacation. (Sails Literacy Ser.). (Illus.). 16p. (gr. 2-3). 27.00 *(978-0-7635-9948-5(4))* Rigby Education.
Rippin, Sally. The Spotty Vacation. Fukuoka, Aki, illus. 2013. 43p. (J). *(978-1-61067-233-7(X))* Kane Miller.
—The Spotty Vacation: Billie B. Brown. Fukuoka, Aki, illus. 2014. (ENG.). 48p. (J). pap. 4.99 *(978-1-61067-183-5(X))* Kane Miller.
Roberts, Johanna Lonsdorf. Summer at the Cabin. Shaggy Dog Press, ed. Challoner, Audrey, illus. 2007. 32p. (J). per. *(978-0-9722007-2-1(X))* Shaggy Dog Pr.
Rohan, Margaret de. Celia & Granny Meg go to Paris: A survival Guide. 2011. (ENG., Illus.). 184p. pap. *(978-1-84876-650-1(5))* Troubador Publishing Ltd.
—Celia & Granny Meg Return to Paris: The man with no Face. 2012. (ENG., Illus.). 176p. pap. *(978-1-78088-243-7(2))* Troubador Publishing Ltd.
Rooks, Elizabeth. Where Does Santa Go on Vacation after Christmas? 2012. 24p. pap. 17.99 *(978-1-4772-6535-2(X))* AuthorHouse.
Rose, Valerie. The Family Reunion Is Not A Real Vacation. 2003. 28p. (J). 9.95 *(978-0-9703489-2-0(4),* Little Petals) Roses Are READ Productions.
Ross, Jill. The Blake Family Vacation. Pruitt, Gwendolyn, illus. 2010. (ENG.). 130p. (J). (gr. 3-7). pap. 9.95 *(978-1-59825-950-6(4))* Shenanigans Series.
Rouse, Betty Munn. The Adventures of the Phillyfab Family. 2011. 68p. pap. 12.95 *(978-1-4567-3005-5(3))* AuthorHouse.
Rutledge, Eddie. Amani's World: Amani & Friends Go to New York City. 2012. 24p. pap. 17.99 *(978-1-4772-9554-0(2))* AuthorHouse.
—Amani's World: Amani Goes to Washington D. C. Anderson, Susan, illus. 2009. 16p. pap. 8.75 *(978-1-4490-2095-8(X))* AuthorHouse.
Rylant, Cynthia. Henry & Mudge & the Tumbling Trip. Bracken, Carolyn, illus. 2006. (Henry & Mudge Ser.). 40p. (gr. k-3). 14.00 *(978-0-7569-6904-2(2))* Perfection Learning Corp.
—Henry & Mudge & the Tumbling Trip. Bracken, Carolyn, illus. 2006. (Henry & Mudge Ser.: 27). (ENG.). 40p. (J). (gr. k-2). pap. 3.99 *(978-0-689-83452-3(7),* Simon Spotlight) Simon Spotlight.
Sanchez, Alex. Rainbow Road. 2007. (ENG., Illus.). 266p. (YA). (gr. 7-12). pap. 11.99 *(978-1-4169-1191-3(X),* Simon & Schuster Bks. For Young Readers) Simon & Schuster Bks. For Young Readers.
Sanchez, Alex & Louth, Jack. Rainbow Road. 2005. (ENG., Illus.). 256p. (J). (gr. 7). 16.95 *(978-0-689-86565-7(1),* Simon & Schuster Bks. For Young Readers) Simon & Schuster Bks. For Young Readers.
Santa Takes A Vacation. 2005. (J). 5.95 *(978-0-9769321-4-7(8))* Steingart, Nathan Publishing.
Santillo, LuAnn. At the Beach, 6 vols. Santillo, LuAnn, ed. 2003. (Half-Pint Kids Readers Ser.). (Illus.). 42p. (J). (gr. -1-1). pap. 6.95 *(978-1-59256-084-4(9))* Half-Pint Kids, Inc.
—A Fun Trip. Santillo, LuAnn, ed. 2003. (Half-Pint Kids Readers Ser.). (Illus.). 7p. (J). (gr. -1-1). pap. 1.00 *(978-1-59256-085-1(7))* Half-Pint Kids, Inc.
—The Picnic. Santillo, LuAnn, ed. 2003. (Half-Pint Kids Readers Ser.). (Illus.). 7p. (J). (gr. -1-1). pap. 1.00 *(978-1-59256-090-5(3))* Half-Pint Kids, Inc.
Sclafani, Terry. The Thompson Twins Cruise Adventure. 2007. 84p. per. 10.95 *(978-1-4327-1542-7(9))* Outskirts Pr., Inc.
Sconyers, Jennifer. John Bunny Goes on Vacation. 2010. 20p. pap. 12.99 *(978-1-4490-7774-7(9))* AuthorHouse.
Sempe, Goscinny. Las Vacaciones del Pequeno Nicolas. 2003. (SPA., Illus.). 150p. (J). (gr. 5-8). pap. 9.95 *(978-84-204-4813-8(3))* Santillana USA Publishing Co., Inc.
Sheldon, Dyan. Sophie Pitt-Turnbull Discovers America. 2007. (ENG.). 192p. (YA). (gr. 7-12). per. 7.99 *(978-0-7636-3295-3(3))* Candlewick Pr.
Shortle, Stacy & Mooney, Dean J. M. A Train Ride to Grandma's (with NO Chocolate Donut!) Wulfing, Amy J., illus. 2009. 48p. (J). 18.95 *(978-0-9759850-5-2(1))* Maple Leaf Ctr.
Simmons, J. A. Hannah's First Airplane Ride. 2013. 32p. pap. 24.95 *(978-1-63004-197-7(1))* America Star Bks.
Simon, Leslie & Kelley, Trevor. Wish You Were Here: An Essential Guide to Your Favorite Music Scenes - From Punk to Indie & Everything in Between. Dobi, Rob, illus. 2009. (ENG.). 256p. pap. 14.99 *(978-0-06-157371-2(X))* HarperCollins Pubs.
Sinha, Rhea. Latte's Vacation. Sinha, Rhea, illus. 2011. (Illus.). 20p. pap. 7.50 *(978-1-61170-045-9(0))* Robertson Publishing.
Smith, Clete Barrett. Aliens on Vacation. Slade, Christian, illus. 2012. (Intergalactic Bed & Breakfast Ser.). (ENG.). 272p. (J). (gr. 3-7). pap. 6.99 *(978-1-4231-5723-6(0))* Hyperion Pr.
Smith, William. Frankie & Earnie Meet, 1 vol. 2009. pap. 24.95 *(978-1-60749-333-4(0))* America Star Bks.
Snider, Jesse Blaze. Toy Story: Toy Overboard. Watson, Nathan, illus. 2011. 128p. (J). pap. 9.99 *(978-1-60886-605-2(X))* Boom! Studios.
Soffer, Gilad. Duck's Vacation. 2015. (ENG., Illus.). 48p. (J). (gr. -1-k). 17.99 *(978-1-250-05647-4(0),* 9781250056474) Feiwel & Friends.
Sprague, Howard Lee. Snowflake's Vacation. Borrajero, Judy, illus. 2011. 40p. pap. 9.95 *(978-1-881276-16-6(3))* Serey/Jones Pubs.
Sproule, Acquanetta M. Scamp. 2010. 40p. pap. 18.00 *(978-0-557-37187-7(2))* Lulu Pr., Inc.
Spykman, E. C. Terrible, Horrible Edie. 2010. (ENG.). 232p. (J). (gr. 4-7). 16.95 *(978-1-59017-353-4(8),* NYR Children's Collection) New York Review of Bks., Inc., The.
St. Anthony, Jane. Grace above All. 2015. (Fesler-Lampert Minnesota Heritage Ser.). (ENG.). 176p. pap. 9.95 *(978-0-8166-9814-1(7))* Univ. of Minnesota Pr.
St. Antoine, Sarah. Three Bird Summer. 2014. (ENG.). 256p. (J). (gr. 5). 16.99 *(978-0-7636-6564-7(9))* Candlewick Pr.
St John, Patricia. Other Kitten. 2007. (Illus.). 96p. pap. *(978-1-84427-290-7(7))* Scripture Union.
Standish, Burt L. Frank Merriwell's Vacation. Rudman, Jack, ed. 2003. (Frank Merriwell Ser.). (YA). (gr. 9-18). 29.95 *(978-0-8373-9325-4(6));* pap. 9.95 *(978-0-8373-9025-3(7),* FM-025) Merriwell, Frank Inc.
Stanek, Robert, pseud. The Bugville Critters Go on Vacation. 2008. (ENG., Illus.). (J). 32p. per. 9.95 *(978-1-57545-148-0(4));* 52p. per. 19.95 *(978-1-57545-125-1(5))* RP Media.
—Bugville Critters Start Summer Vacation. 2011. (Illus.). 32p. pap. 4.99 *(978-1-57545-257-9(X),* Reagent Pr. Bks. for Young Readers) RP Media.
—The Bugville Critters Vacation Surprise: Buster Bee's School Days #3. 2008. (ENG., Illus.). 68p. (J). per. 18.95 *(978-1-57545-172-5(7))* RP Media.
—Go on Vacation. 2008. (ENG., Illus.). 32p. (J). pap. 5.59 *(978-1-57545-191-6(3))* RP Media.
—Start Summer Vacation. 2010. (Illus.). 32p. pap. 8.99 *(978-1-57545-174-9(3),* Reagent Pr. Bks. for Young Readers) RP Media.
Staniszewski, Anna. Once upon a Cruise: a Wish Novel. 2016. (ENG.). 256p. (J). (gr. 3-7). pap. 6.99 *(978-0-545-87986-6(8),* Scholastic Paperbacks) Scholastic, Inc.
Stanton, Angie. Royally Lost. 2014. (ENG.). 336p. (YA). (gr. 8). pap. 9.99 *(978-0-06-227258-4(6),* HarperTeen) HarperCollins Pubs.
Stein, Tammar. High Dive. 2011. (ENG.). 208p. (YA). (gr. 7). pap. 7.99 *(978-0-440-23903-1(6),* Knopf Bks. for Young Readers) Random Hse. Children's Bks.
Steiner, Barbara. The Cry of the Loon: A Samantha Mystery. Tibbles, Jean-Paul, illus. (ENG.). 192p. (gr. 4-18). 2009. (YA). pap. 6.95 *(978-1-59369-480-7(6))* 2006. 10.95 *(978-1-59369-479-1(2))* American Girl Publishing, Inc.
Steinkraus, Kyla. The Trouble with Trading. Reese, Bob, illus. 2011. (ENG.). 24p. (gr. 2-3). pap. 8.95 *(978-1-61236-034-8(3))* Rourke Educational Media.
Stern, Jacqueline. Mystery of the Whispering Walls. 2004. (J). 148p. pap. *(978-1-57168-844-6(7));* (Hollow Tree Mystery Ser.: Bk. 6). (Illus.). v, 142p. *(978-1-57168-850-7(1),* Eakin Pr.) Eakin Pr.
Stephens, Sarah Hines. Spring Break-Up. 2006. (Zoey 101 Ser.). 103p. (J). *(978-1-4156-8963-9(6))* Scholastic, Inc.
Stewart, Bob. Baily Bumble Bee. 2009. 32p. pap. 14.49 *(978-1-4389-7254-1(7))* AuthorHouse.
Sticker Dolly Dressing on Vacation (Revised) 2017. (Sticker Dolly Dressing Ser.). (ENG.). (J). pap. 9.99 ***(978-0-7945-3791-3(X),*** Usborne) EDC Publishing.
Stilton, Geronimo. A Fabumouse Vacation for Geronimo. Keys, Larry, illus. 2004. (Geronimo Stilton Ser.: 9). (ENG.). 128p. (J). (gr. 2-5). pap. 7.99 *(978-0-439-55971-3(5),* Scholastic Paperbacks) Scholastic, Inc.
—Run for the Hills, Geronimo! 2011. (Geronimo Stilton Ser.: Bk. 47). (ENG.). 128p. (J). (gr. 2-5). pap. 7.99 *(978-0-545-33132-6(3),* Scholastic Paperbacks) Scholastic, Inc.
—Save the White Whale! 2011. (ENG.). 128p. (J). (gr. 2-5). pap. 7.99 *(978-0-545-10377-0(0),* Scholastic Paperbacks) Scholastic, Inc.
—The Stinky Cheese Vacation. 2014. (Geronimo Stilton Ser.: 57). lib. bdg. 18.40 *(978-0-606-35843-9(9))* Turtleback Bks.
Stinson, Kathy. Seven Clues, 1 vol. 2005. (Lorimer Streetlights Ser.). (ENG.). 104p. (J). (gr. 2-5). 7.95 *(978-1-55028-889-6(X),* 9781550288896) Lorimer, James & Co., Ltd., Pubs. CAN. Dist: Casemate Pubs. & Bk. Distributors, LLC.
Stock, Catherine. A Porc in New York. 2007. (ENG., Illus.). 32p. (J). (gr. -1-3). 16.95 *(978-0-8234-1994-4(0))* Holiday Hse., Inc.
Swallow, Pamela Curtis. Melvil & Dewey Gone Fishin', 1 vol. Eliasen, Lorena, ed. 2004. (Illus.). 56p. (C). pap. 14.00 *(978-1-59158-153-6(2),* LU1532) Pearson Education GBR. Dist: ABC-CLIO, LLC.
Tackett, Wendy. The Jefferson Wish. 2011. 124p. (gr. 4-6). 20.95 *(978-1-4620-3771-1(2));* pap. 10.95 *(978-1-4620-3768-1(2))* iUniverse, Inc.
Tamaki, Mariko. This One Summer. Tamaki, Jillian, illus. 2014. (ENG.). 320p. (YA). (gr. 7). 21.99 *(978-1-62672-094-7(0),* 9781626720947); pap. 18.99 *(978-1-59643-774-6(X),* 9781596437746) Roaring Brook Pr. (First Second Bks.).
Thrasher, Grady. Tim & Sally's Beach Adventure. Rabon, Elaine Hearn, illus. 2008. 48p. (J). (gr. -1-3). 18.95 *(978-1-58818-161-9(8))* Hill Street Pr., LLC.
Tremblay, Amanda. The Tornado Trial. 2010. 65p. pap. 12.00 *(978-0-557-14051-0(X))* Lulu Pr., Inc.
Trinidad Joe. Santa's Key West Vacation. 2007. (Illus.). 80p. per. 12.95 *(978-0-9799474-0-7(5))* Seastory Pr.
Tucker, Valerie Nell. The Hermit's Box. 2009. 36p. pap. 15.49 *(978-1-4490-2285-3(5))* AuthorHouse.
Tuthill, Louisa C. Hurrah for New England! or the Virginia Boy's Vacation. 2004. reprint ed. pap. 1.99 *(978-1-4192-2504-8(9));* pap. 15.95 *(978-1-4191-2504-1(4))* Kessinger Publishing, LLC.
Udvari, Joseph G. Courage. 2012. 132p. pap. *(978-1-84961-169-5(6))* RealTime Publishing.
Vacations: Set B Individual Title Six-Packs. (Smart Start Ser.). (gr. k-1). 23.00 *(978-0-7635-0418-2(1))* Rigby Education.
Van Dyne, Edith. Aunt Jane's Nieces on Vacation. 2005. 27.95 *(978-1-4218-1027-0(1));* 200p. pap. 12.95 *(978-1-4218-1127-7(8))* 1st World Publishing, Inc. (1st World Library - Literary Society).
—Aunt Jane's Nieces on Vacation. 2004. reprint ed. pap. 21.95 *(978-1-4191-0825-9(5));* pap. 1.99 *(978-1-4192-0825-6(X))* Kessinger Publishing, LLC.
Viguié, Debbie. The Summer of Cotton Candy, 1 vol. 2008. (Sweet Seasons Novel Ser.). (ENG., Illus.). 224p. (YA). (gr. 8-11). pap. 9.99 *(978-0-310-71558-0(X))* Zondervan.
Voake, Steve. Daisy Dawson at the Beach. Meserve, Jessica, illus. (Daisy Dawson Ser.: 4). (ENG.). (J). (gr. 1-4). 2012. 96p. pap. 5.99 *(978-0-7636-5946-2(0))* 2011. 87p. 14.99 *(978-0-7636-5306-4(3))* Candlewick Pr.
—Daisy Dawson on the Farm. Meserve, Jessica, illus. 2012. (Daisy Dawson Ser.: 5). (ENG.). 96p. (J). (gr. 1-4). 14.99 *(978-0-7636-5882-3(0))* Candlewick Pr.
Voelkel, Jon & Voelkel, Pamela. Middleworld. 2007. (Jaguar Stones Ser.: Bk. 1). (Illus.). 397p. (gr. 6-9). *(978-1-57525-561-3(8))* Smith & Kraus Pubs., Inc.
Waldman, Maya, illus. To-Do List. 2007. (ENG.). 48p. (J). (gr. k). 12.95 *(978-0-9741319-5-5(4))* 4N Publishing LLC.
Waldron, Kathleen Cook. Five Stars for Emily, 1 vol. 2004. (Orca Young Readers Ser.). (ENG., Illus.). 144p. (J). (gr. 3-6). pap., tchr. ed. 4.99 *(978-1-55143-296-0(X),* 1234541) Orca Bk. Pubs. USA.
Walker, Anna. I Love Vacations. Walker, Anna, illus. 2011. (ENG., Illus.). 32p. (J). (gr. -1-1). 9.99 *(978-1-4169-8321-7(X),* Simon & Schuster Bks. For Young Readers) Simon & Schuster Bks. For Young Readers.
Wallace, Sheila Ryan. Diving for the Gold. 2004. 142p. (YA). pap. 15.95 *(978-0-7414-2269-9(7))* Infinity Publishing.
Walters, Eric. Skye Above, 1 vol. Parkins, David, illus. 2014. (Orca Echoes Ser.). (ENG.). 64p. (J). (gr. 2-3). pap. 6.95 *(978-1-4598-0701-3(4))* Orca Bk. Pubs. USA.
Webb, Holly. The Secret Puppy. Williams, Sophy, illus. 2016. (Pet Rescue Adventures Ser.). (ENG.). 128p. (J). (gr. 2-6). 4.99 *(978-1-58925-483-1(X))* Tiger Tales.
Weetman, Nova. A Hot Cold Summer: Choose Your Own Ever After. 2016. (ENG.). 256p. (J). pap. 5.99 *(978-1-61067-354-9(9))* Kane Miller.
Wetherby, Mark. The Tales of Mossy Dell. 2009. (Illus.). 88p. pap. 10.49 *(978-1-4389-7726-3(3))* AuthorHouse.
Williams, Alan. Archy the Flying Dolphin & the Vampire's Curse. 2007. pap. 15.38 *(978-1-4251-3151-7(4))* Trafford Publishing.
Winter, Christopher. Henrietta the Farmer & the Long, Long, Long, Long Vacation! O'Shea, Bonnie, illus. 2012. 32p. pap. 13.95 *(978-1-60594-856-0(X))* Aeon Publishing Inc.
Wisdom, Gail Ann. Trouble with Bullies. 2013. 48p. pap. 20.45 *(978-1-4908-0026-4(3),* WestBow Pr.) Author Solutions, Inc.
Wittlinger, Ellen. Zigzag. (ENG., Illus.). (YA). (gr. 7). 2003. 272p. 16.95 *(978-0-689-84996-1(6))* 2005. 288p. reprint ed. pap. 9.99 *(978-0-689-84998-5(2))* Simon & Schuster Bks. For Young Readers. (Simon & Schuster Bks. For Young Readers).
Wojciechowski, Susan. Beany Goes to Camp. Natti, Susanna, illus. 2005. (Beany Adventures Ser.). 104p. (J). (gr. 4-7). 13.65 *(978-0-7569-6499-3(7))* Perfection Learning Corp.
Wright, Kiyah. Vacation Fun. 2011. 24p. pap. 14.95 *(978-1-4634-4055-8(3))* AuthorHouse.
Wright, Mary. Justice for All. 2004. 177p. pap. 24.95 *(978-1-4137-4083-7(9))* America Star Bks.
Yeager, Graham. Diablo: The Third Millersburg Novel. 2006. 145p. (YA). per. 7.99 *(978-0-9765478-4-6(8))* Stone Acres Publishing Co.
Yoon, Salina. Penguin on Vacation. Yoon, Salina, illus. (Penguin Ser.). (ENG., Illus.). (J). (gr. -1-1). 2015. 34p. bds. 7.99 *(978-0-8027-3837-0(0),* 9780802738370) 2013. 40p. 14.99 *(978-0-8027-3397-9(2),* 9780802733979) Bloomsbury Publishing USA. (Bloomsbury USA Childrens).
Zadunajsky, Donna M. Tayla Takes a Trip. Bicking, Judith, illus. 2013. (ENG.). 40p. pap. 9.99 *(978-1-938037-36-8(7))* Zadunajsky, Donna M.

VACCINATION

see also Immunity

Abramovitz, Melissa. 12 Ways to Prevent Disease. 2017. (J). *(978-1-62143-512-9(1))* Pr. Room Editions LLC.
Abramovitz, Melissa & Smibert, Angie. 12 Ways to Prevent Disease. 2016. (Healthy Living Ser.). (ENG., Illus.). 32p. (J). pap. 9.95 *(978-1-63235-388-7(1))* Pr. Room Editions LLC.
Alter, Judy. Vaccines. 2008. (21st Century Skills Innovation Library: Innovation in Medicine Ser.). (ENG., Illus.). 32p. (gr. 4-8). lib. bdg. 28.50 *(978-1-60279-223-4(2),* 200154) Cherry Lake Publishing.
De la Bédoyère, Guy. The First Polio Vaccine. 2005. (Milestones in Modern Science Ser.). (Illus.). 48p. (gr. 6-12). pap. 14.05 *(978-0-8368-5862-4(X),* Gareth Stevens Secondary Library) Stevens, Gareth Publishing LLLP.
De la Bédoyère, Guy & De la Bédoyère, Camilla. The First Polio Vaccine. 2005. (Milestones in Modern Science Ser.). (Illus.). 48p. (gr. 6-12). lib. bdg. 31.00 *(978-0-8368-5855-6(7),* Gareth Stevens Secondary Library) Stevens, Gareth Publishing LLLP.
Ellis, Carol. Vaccines. 2013. (Advances in Medicine Ser.). 64p. (J). (gr. 6-9). pap. 15.28 *(978-1-62712-012-8(2));* (Illus.). 34.21 *(978-1-60870-470-5(X))* Cavendish Square Publishing.
Espejo, Roman. Should Vaccinations Be Mandatory? Gale, G., ed. 2014. (At Issue Ser.). (ENG.). 128p. (gr. 10-12). lib. bdg. 39.40 *(978-0-7377-6862-6(2),* Greenhaven Pr., Inc.) Cengage Gale.
Hand, Carol. Vaccines, 1 vol. 2013. (Medical Marvels Ser.). (ENG., Illus.). 112p. (YA). (gr. 6-12). lib. bdg. 35.64 *(978-1-61783-905-4(1),* Essential Library) ABDO Publishing Co.
Hantula, Richard. Jonas Salk. 2004. (Trailblazers of the Modern World Ser.). (Illus.). 48p. (gr. 5-12). lib. bdg. 31.00 *(978-0-8368-5100-7(5),* Gareth Stevens Secondary Library) Stevens, Gareth Publishing LLLP.
Hillstrom, Laurie, ed. Vaccinations. 2012. (Nutrition & Health Ser.). (ENG., Illus.). 80p. (gr. 7-10). lib. bdg. 30.95 *(978-1-4205-0724-9(9),* Lucent Bks.) Cengage Gale.
Hunter, Nick. Louis Pasteur, 1 vol. 2014. (Science Biographies Ser.). (ENG.). 32p. (gr. 2-4). lib. bdg. 30.65 *(978-1-4109-6236-2(9),* Raintree Perspectives) Heinemann-Raintree.
Llanas, Sheila. Jonas Salk: Medical Innovator & Polio Vaccine Developer, 1 vol. 2013. (Essential Lives Set 8 Ser.). (ENG., Illus.). 112p. (J). (gr. 6-12). lib. bdg. 35.64 *(978-1-61783-896-5(9),* Essential Library) ABDO Publishing Co.
Merino, Noël. Vaccines. 2015. (J). *(978-0-7377-7193-0(3),* Greenhaven Pr., Inc.) Cengage Gale.
Merino, Noel. Vaccines. Greenhaven Press Staff, ed. 2015. (At Issue Ser.). (ENG.). 128p. (gr. 10-12). pap. 27.80 *(978-0-7377-7194-7(1),* Greenhaven Pr., Inc.) Cengage Gale.
Petersen, Christine. Frequently Asked Questions about Vaccines & Vaccinations. 2011. (FAQ: Teen Life Ser.). (ENG., Illus.). 64p. (YA). lib. bdg. 31.95 *(978-1-4488-1328-5(X))* Rosen Publishing Group, Inc., The.
Phelan, Glen. Killing Germs, Saving Lives: The Quest for the First Vaccines. 2006. (Science Quest Ser.). (ENG., Illus.). 64p. (J). (gr. 5-9). 17.95 *(978-0-7922-5537-6(2));* lib. bdg. 25.90 *(978-0-7922-5538-3(0))* National Geographic Society. (National Geographic Children's Bks.).
Rooney, Anne. You Wouldn't Want to Live Without Vaccinations! Antram, David, illus. 2015. (You Wouldn't Want

TUV

to Live Without... Ser.). (ENG.). 40p. (J). pap. 9.95 *(978-0-531-21409-1(5),* Watts, Franklin) Scholastic Library Publishing.

Sherman, Jill. The Vaccination Debate, 1 vol. 2010. (Essential Viewpoints Set 5 Ser.). (ENG.). 112p. (J). (gr. 6-12). lib. bdg. 35.64 *(978-1-61613-526-3(3),* Essential Library) ABDO Publishing Co.

Shulman, Neil, et al. The Germ Patrol: All about Shots for Tots... & Big Kids, Too! 2004. (Illus.). 36p. (gr. -1-3). pap. 14.95 *(978-0-9639002-8-9(5))* Rx Humor.

Vaccines. 2010. (Science Foundations Ser.). (Illus.). 120p. (gr. 6-12). 35.00 *(978-1-60413-339-4(2),* Chelsea Hse.) Facts On File, Inc.

VADER, DARTH (FICTITIOUS CHARACTER)—FICTION

Angleberger, Tom. Star Wars - Return of the Jedi: Beware the Power of the Dark Side! McCaig, Iain, illus. 2015. (ENG.). 432p. (J). (gr. 3-7). 17.99 *(978-1-4847-0913-9(6),* Disney Lucasfilm Press) Disney Publishing Worldwide.

Beecroft, Simon. DK Readers L3: Star Wars: Death Star Battles. 2016. (DK Readers Ser.). (ENG.). 48p. (J). (gr. 2-4). pap. 3.99 *(978-1-4654-6004-2(7),* DK Children) Dorling Kindersley Publishing, Inc.

Blackman, Haden. Darth Vader & the Lost Command: Vol 1, 1 vol. 2012. (Star Wars: Darth Vader & the Lost Command Ser.). (ENG., Illus.). 24p. (J). 24.21 *(978-1-59961-980-4(6),* Graphic Novels) Spotlight.

—Darth Vader & the Lost Command: Vol 2, 1 vol. Leonardi, Rick, illus. 2012. (Star Wars: Darth Vader & the Lost Command Ser.). (ENG.). 24p. (J). 24.21 *(978-1-59961-981-1(4),* Graphic Novels) Spotlight.

—Darth Vader & the Lost Command: Vol 3, 1 vol. Leonardi, Rick, illus. 2012. (Star Wars: Darth Vader & the Lost Command Ser.). (ENG.). 24p. (J). 24.21 *(978-1-59961-982-8(2),* Graphic Novels) Spotlight.

—Darth Vader & the Lost Command: Vol 4, 1 vol. Leonardi, Rick, illus. 2012. (Star Wars: Darth Vader & the Lost Command Ser.). (ENG.). 24p. (J). 24.21 *(978-1-59961-983-5(0),* Graphic Novels) Spotlight.

—Darth Vader & the Lost Command: Vol 5, 1 vol. Leonardi, Rick, illus. 2012. (Star Wars: Darth Vader & the Lost Command Ser.). (ENG.). 24p. (J). 24.21 *(978-1-59961-984-2(9),* Graphic Novels) Spotlight.

Bracken, Alexandra. Star Wars - A New Hope: The Princess, the Scoundrel, & the Farm Boy. McCaig, Iain, illus. 2015. (ENG.). 336p. (J). (gr. 3-7). 17.99 *(978-1-4847-0912-2(8),* 1384321, Disney Lucasfilm Press) Disney Publishing Worldwide.

Disney Press Editors. Star Wars: Escape from Darth Vader. 2014. (Star Wars: World of Reading Ser.). (J). lib. bdg. 13.55 *(978-0-606-35924-5(9))* Turtleback Bks.

Dorling Kindersley Publishing Staff & Beecroft, Simon. Anakin in Action! 2008. (DK Readers Ser.). (ENG.). 32p. (J). (gr. 1-3). pap. 3.99 *(978-0-7566-4031-6(8),* DK Children) Dorling Kindersley Publishing, Inc.

—Watch Out for Jabba the Hutt!, Level 1. 2008. (DK Readers Ser.). (ENG.). 32p. (J). (gr. k-2). pap. 3.99 *(978-0-7566-4083-5(0),* DK Children) Dorling Kindersley Publishing, Inc.

Dorling Kindersley Publishing Staff & Hibbert, Clare. Tatooine Adventures, Level 1. 2011. (DK Readers Ser.). (ENG.). 48p. (J). (gr. k-4). 3.99 *(978-0-7566-7128-0(0),* DK Children) Dorling Kindersley Publishing, Inc.

Dorling Kindersley Publishing Staff & Nesworthy, Lauren. Rebels: Darth Vader, Jedi Hunter! 2016. (DK Readers Ser.). (ENG., Illus.). 48p. (J). (gr. 1-3). pap. 3.99 *(978-1-4654-5212-2(5),* DK Children) Dorling Kindersley Publishing, Inc.

Harper, Benjamin. Star Wars: the Power of the Dark Side. 2015. (ENG.). 32p. (J). (gr. 1-4). 17.99 *(978-0-7944-3532-5(7))* Reader's Digest Assn., Inc., The.

Landers, Ace. A New Hope. 2015. (Lego Star Wars Ser.). (ENG.). 24p. (J). (gr. -1-3). pap. 3.99 *(978-0-545-80135-5(4))* Scholastic, Inc.

—Revenge of the Sith. 2015. (LEGO Star Wars 8X8 Ser.). lib. bdg. 13.55 *(978-0-606-37767-6(0))* Turtleback Bks.

Landers, Ace. Vader's Secret Missions. Ameet Studio Staff, illus. 2015. (Lego Star Wars Ser.: 2). (ENG.). 64p. (J). (gr. 2-5). pap. 4.99 *(978-0-545-83557-2(7))* Scholastic, Inc.

—Vader's Secret Missions. 2015. (Illus.). 63p. (J). ***(978-1-4806-8324-2(8))*** Scholastic, Inc.

Nesworthy, Lauren. Darth Vader, Rebel Hunter! 2016. (Illus.). 48p. (J). ***(978-1-5182-1849-1(0))*** Dorling Kindersley Publishing, Inc.

Scholastic Editors & Fry, Jason. Darth Vader. 2017. (Backstories Ser.: Vol. 6). (ENG., Illus.). 128p. (J). (gr. 3-7). 16.00 *(978-0-606-39145-0(2))* Turtleback Bks.

Wallace, Daniel. Darth Vader: A 3-D Reconstruction Log. Reiff, Chris & Trevas, Chris, illus. 2011. (Star Wars Ser.). (ENG.). 24p. (J). bds. 19.99 *(978-0-545-31215-8(9))* Scholastic, Inc.

VALENTINE'S DAY

Appleby, Alex. Happy Valentine's Day!, Vol. 1. 2014. (Happy Holidays! Ser.). (Illus.). 24p. (J). (gr. k-k). (ENG.). 22.60 *(978-1-4339-9951-2(X));* pap. 8.15 *(978-1-4339-9953-6(6))* Stevens, Gareth Publishing LLLP.

Bloomsbury USA. I Love You. 2015. (ENG., Illus.). 10p. (J). (gr. -1-1). bds. 6.99 *(978-1-61963-802-0(9),* 9781619638020, Bloomsbury USA Childrens) Bloomsbury Publishing USA.

Bodden, Valerie. Valentine's Day. 2005. (My First Look at Holidays Ser.). (Illus.). 24p. (J). (gr. k-3). lib. bdg. 15.95 *(978-1-58341-371-5(5),* Creative Education) Creative Co., The.

Erlbach, Arlene & Erlbach, Herbert. Valentine's Day Crafts. 2004. (Fun Holiday Crafts Kids Can Do! Ser.). (Illus.). 32p. (J). lib. bdg. 23.94 *(978-0-7660-2237-9(4))* Enslow Pubs., Inc.

Farmer, Jacqueline. Valentine Be Mine. Halsey, Megan & Addy, Sean, illus. 2013. (ENG.). 32p. (J). (gr. k-3). pap. 7.95 *(978-1-58089-390-9(2))* Charlesbridge Publishing, Inc.

Gibbons, Gail. Valentine's Day Is... Gibbons, Gail, illus. 2005. (ENG., Illus.). 32p. (J). (gr. -1-3). 17.95 *(978-0-8234-1852-7(9))* Holiday Hse., Inc.

—Valentine's Day Is. Gibbons, Gail, illus. 2006. (ENG., Illus.). 32p. (J). (gr. k-3). 6.95 *(978-0-8234-2036-0(1))* Holiday Hse., Inc.

Gilpin, Rebecca. Valentine Things to Make & Do. 2006. (Usborne Activities Ser.). (Illus.). 31p. (J). *(978-0-439-78705-5(X))* Scholastic, Inc.

Goeller, Dorothy. Valentine's Day. 2010. (All about Holidays Ser.). (Illus.). 24p. (J). 22.60 *(978-0-7660-3810-3(6));* pap. 7.95 *(978-1-59845-179-5(0))* Enslow Pubs., Inc. (Enslow Elementary).

Golden Books Staff. Vintage Valentines. 2005. (Press Out Book Ser.). (ENG., Illus.). 12p. (J). (gr. -1-2). pap. 4.99 *(978-0-375-87514-4(X),* Golden Bks.) Random Hse. Children's Bks.

Hayes, Amy. Celebrate Valentine's Day. 2015. (Our Holidays Ser.). (ENG.). 24p. (J). (gr. 1-1). 24.21 *(978-1-5026-0236-7(9))* Cavendish Square Publishing.

—Valentine's Day. 2015. (J). *(978-1-62713-481-1(6))* Cavendish Square Publishing.

Keogh, Josie. Valentine's Day. 2013. (PowerKids Readers: Happy Holidays! Ser.). (ENG., Illus.). 24p. (J). (gr. k-2). pap. 8.25 *(978-1-4488-9710-0(6));* lib. bdg. 22.60 *(978-1-4488-9627-1(4))* Rosen Publishing Group, Inc., The. (PowerKids Pr.).

—Valentine's Day: Día de San Valentín. Alamán, Eduardo, tr. from SPA. 2013. (PowerKids Readers: Happy Holidays! / ¡Felices Fiestas! Ser.). (ENG., Illus.). 24p. (gr. k-2). lib. bdg. 22.60 *(978-1-4488-9970-8(2),* PowerKids Pr.) Rosen Publishing Group, Inc., The.

Landau, Elaine. El Día de San Valentín: Caramelos, Amor y Corazones. 2005. (Días Festivos Ser.). (SPA., Illus.). 48p. (J). (gr. 3-4). lib. bdg. 25.27 *(978-0-7660-2613-1(2),* Enslow Elementary) Enslow Pubs., Inc.

—What Is Valentine's Day? 2011. (I Like Holidays! Ser.). (Illus.). 24p. (J). (gr. k-18). pap. 7.95 *(978-1-59845-296-9(7),* Enslow Elementary); (gr. 1-4). lib. bdg. 22.60 *(978-0-7660-3699-4(5))* Enslow Pubs., Inc.

Lee, Sally. A Short History of Valentine's Day. 2015. (Holiday Histories Ser.). (ENG., Illus.). 24p. (gr. k-1). lib. bdg. 26.65 *(978-1-4914-6098-6(9))* Capstone Press of Coughlan Cos.

Lynette, Rachel. Let's Throw a Valentine's Day Party! 2011. (J). 49.50 *(978-1-4488-2730-5(2));* pap. 8.25 *(978-1-4488-2729-9(9));* lib. bdg. 22.60 *(978-1-4488-2570-7(9))* Rosen Publishing Group, Inc., The. (PowerKids Pr.).

McGee, Randel. Paper Crafts for Valentine's Day. 2012. (Paper Craft Fun for Holidays Ser.). (Illus.). 48p. (J). (gr. 3-4). pap. 8.95 *(978-1-4644-0329-3(5),* Enslow Elementary) Enslow Pubs., Inc.

McGrath, Barbara Barbieri. The M & M's(r) Brand Valentine Book. Tagel, Peggy, illus. 2004. 12p. (J). (gr. -1-k). bds. 6.95 *(978-1-57091-422-5(2))* Charlesbridge Publishing, Inc.

McNeil, Niki, et al. HOCPP 1033 Valentine's Day. 2005. spiral bd. 20.00 *(978-1-60308-033-0(3))* In the Hands of a Child.

—HOCPP 1145 Be My Valentine. 2007. spiral bd. 15.50 *(978-1-60308-145-0(3))* In the Hands of a Child.

Mercer, Abbie. Happy Valentine's Day. (Holiday Fun Ser.). 24p. 2009. (gr. 2-3). 42.50 *(978-1-61513-379-6(8),* PowerKids Pr.) 2007. (Illus.). (J). (gr. 3-7). lib. bdg. 22.60 *(978-1-4042-3809-1(3))* Rosen Publishing Group, Inc., The.

Miller, Reagan. Valentine's Day. 2009. (Celebrations in My World Ser.). (ENG., Illus.). 32p. (J). (gr. k-2). pap. *(978-0-7787-4777-2(8));* (gr. 1-3). *(978-0-7787-4759-8(X))* Crabtree Publishing Co.

Murray, Julie. Valentine's Day, 1 vol. 2003. (Holidays Ser.). (ENG.). 24p. (gr. k-4). 25.65 *(978-1-57765-954-9(6),* Buddy Bks.) ABDO Publishing Co.

Otto, Carolyn. Valentine's Day: With Love, Cards, & Candy. 2016. (Holidays Around the World Ser.). (ENG.). 32p. (J). (gr. 2-5). pap. 7.99 *(978-1-4263-2747-6(1),* National Geographic Children's Bks.) National Geographic Society.

Owen, Ruth. More Valentine's Day Origami, 1 vol. 2015. (Holiday Origami Ser.). (ENG.). 32p. (J). 27.50 *(978-1-4777-5698-0(1),* PowerKids Pr.) Rosen Publishing Group, Inc., The.

—Valentine's Day Origami. 2012. (Holiday Origami Ser.). (ENG., Illus.). 32p. (J). (gr. 3-6). 26.50 *(978-1-4488-7865-9(9));* pap. 11.75 *(978-1-4488-7924-3(8))* Rosen Publishing Group, Inc., The. (PowerKids Pr.).

—Valentine's Day Sweets & Treats. 2012. (Holiday Cooking for Kids! Ser.). (ENG., Illus.). 32p. (J). (gr. 3-6). 26.50 *(978-1-4488-8080-5(7));* pap. 11.75 *(978-1-4488-8127-7(7))* Windmill Bks.

Pettiford, Rebecca. Día de San Valentín. 2015.Tr. of Valentine's Day. (SPA., Illus.). 24p. (J). lib. bdg. *(978-1-62031-244-5(1),* Bullfrog Bks.) Jump! Inc.

—Valentine's Day. 2015. (Illus.). 24p. (J). lib. bdg. *(978-1-62031-187-5(9),* Bullfrog Bks.) Jump! Inc.

Ponto, Joanna. Valentine's Day. 2016. (Story of Our Holidays Ser.). (ENG., Illus.). 32p. (J). (gr. 3-3). 25.27 *(978-0-7660-7462-0(5));* pap. 10.52 *(978-0-7660-7474-3(9))* Enslow Pubs., Inc.

Price, Roger, et al. Dear Valentine Letters Mad Libs. 2006. (Mad Libs Junior Ser.). (ENG., Illus.). 48p. (J). (gr. 3-7). 6.99 *(978-0-8431-2088-2(6),* Mad Libs) Penguin Young Readers Group.

Priddy, Roger. My Fold Out Books I Love You. 2011. (ENG., Illus.). 12p. (J). (gr. -1 — 1). bds. 6.99 *(978-0-312-51334-4(8),* 9780312513344, Priddy Bks.) St. Martin's Pr.

Ritter, Elizabeth A. Happy Valentine's Day! 2016. (Celebrations Ser.). 00024p. (J). (gr. 1-1). pap. 8.25 *(978-1-4994-2673-1(9),* PowerKids Pr.) Rosen Publishing Group, Inc., The.

Sebra, Richard. It's Valentine's Day! 2017. (Bumba Books (tm) — It's a Holiday! Ser.). (ENG.). 24p. (J). (gr. -1-1). 12.99 ***(978-1-5124-3708-9(5),*** Lerner Pubns.); 38.65 ***(978-1-5124-3707-2(7),*** Lerner Pubns.); (Illus.). 25.32 *(978-1-5124-2562-8(1));* (Illus.). 38.65 ***(978-1-5124-2741-7(1),*** Lerner Pubns.) Lerner Publishing Group.

Sévigny, Eric, illus. Caillou: Mystery Valentine. 2016. (Clubhouse Ser.). (ENG.). 24p. (J). (gr. -1-1). pap. 4.99 *(978-2-89718-181-9(8))* Caillouet, Gerry.

Siewert, Pauline, illus. It's Valentine's Day! A Valentine Book & Activity Kit. 2005. 10p. (J). bds. 9.95 *(978-1-58117-377-2(6),* Intervisual/Piggy Toes) Bendon, Inc.

Strain-Trueit, Trudi. Valentine's Day. 2013. (ENG.). 32p. (J). 23.00 *(978-0-531-27207-7(9));* pap. 5.95 *(978-0-531-27357-9(1))* Scholastic Library Publishing.

Trueit, Trudi Strain. Valentine's Day. 2010. (Benchmark Rebus: Holiday Fun Ser.). 24p. (gr. k-1). 15.95 *(978-0-7614-4889-1(6))* Marshall Cavendish Corp.

Williams, Colleen Madonna Flood. My Adventure on Valentine's Day. 2009. (ENG.). 44p. (J). 8.99 *(978-1-59092-558-4(0))* Blue Forge Pr.

Yasuda, Anita. Valentine's Day. 2011. (J). (gr. 3-5). pap. 12.95 *(978-1-61690-684-9(7),* AV2 by Weigl); (Illus.). 24p. (gr. 2-5). 27.13 *(978-1-61690-678-8(2))* Weigl Pubs., Inc.

Zocchi, Judy. On Valentine's Day. Wallis, Rebecca, illus. 2005. (Holiday Happenings Ser.). 32p. (J). lib. bdg. 21.65 *(978-1-891997-79-2(3));* per. 10.95 *(978-1-59646-229-8(9))* Dingles & Co.

—On Valentine's Day/el día de San Valentín. Wallis, Rebecca, illus. 2005. (Holiday Happenings Ser.).Tr. of Día de San Valentín. (ENG & SPA.). 32p. (J). pap. 10.95 *(978-1-59646-230-4(2));* lib. bdg. 21.65 *(978-1-891997-78-5(5));* per. 10.95 *(978-1-59646-231-1(0))* Dingles & Co.

VALENTINE'S DAY—FICTION

Ackelsberg, Amy. Valentine's Day Mix-Up. MJ Illustrations Staff, illus. 2011. (Strawberry Shortcake Ser.). (ENG.). 24p. (J). (gr. -1-k). mass mkt. 4.99 *(978-0-448-45696-6(6),* Grosset & Dunlap) Penguin Young Readers Group.

Andrews, Julie & Hamilton, Emma Walton. Valentines from the Heart. 2015. (Very Fairy Princess Ser.). (J). lib. bdg. 16.00 *(978-0-606-37466-8(3))* Turtleback Bks.

—The Very Fairy Princess Follows Her Heart. Davenier, Christine, illus. 2013. (Very Fairy Princess Ser.). (ENG.). 32p. (J). (gr. -1-3). 16.99 *(978-0-316-18559-2(0))* Little Brown & Co.

Awdry, W. A Valentine for Percy. 2015. (Thomas & Friends Step into Reading Ser.). lib. bdg. 14.75 *(978-0-606-38471-1(5))* Turtleback Bks.

Awdry, Wilbert V. Thomas' Valentine Party. Durk, Jim, illus. 2011. (Full-Color Activity Book with Stickers Ser.). (ENG.). 32p. (J). (gr. -1-2). pap. 3.99 *(978-0-375-86815-3(1),* Golden Bks.) Random Hse. Children's Bks.

—Valentine's Day in Vicarstown. 2008. (Thomas in Town Ser.). (ENG., Illus.). 32p. (J). (gr. -1-2). 5.99 *(978-0-375-84755-4(3),* Random Hse. Bks. for Young Readers) Random Hse. Children's Bks.

Baglio, Ben M. Corgi in the Cupcakes. Baum, Ann, illus. 2008. 142p. (J). pap. *(978-0-439-02533-1(8))* Scholastic, Inc.

—Kitty in the Candy Hearts. 2007. (Illus.). 147p. (J). pap. *(978-0-439-87119-8(0))* Scholastic, Inc.

Balian, Lorna. A Sweetheart for Valentine, 1 vol. Balian, Lorna, illus. 2005. (ENG., Illus.). 32p. (J). 15.95 *(978-1-932065-14-5(8))* Star Bright Bks., Inc.

Barkley, Callie. Ellie's Lovely Idea. Riti, Marsha, illus. 2013. (Critter Club Ser.: 6). (ENG.). 128p. (J). (gr. k-4). 16.99 *(978-1-4424-8219-7(2));* pap. 5.99 *(978-1-4424-8218-0(4))* Little Simon. (Little Simon).

—Ellie's Lovely Idea. 2013. (Critter Club Ser.: 6). (J). lib. bdg. 16.00 *(978-0-606-32321-5(X),* Turtleback) Turtleback Bks.

Beardshaw, Rosalind, illus. Kiss the Frog. 2013. (J). *(978-1-4351-4925-0(4))* Barnes & Noble, Inc.

Benton, Jim. Attack of the 50-Ft. Cupid. Benton, Jim, illus. 2004. (Franny K. Stein, Mad Scientist Ser.: 2). (ENG., Illus.). 112p. (J). (gr. 2-5). 16.99 *(978-0-689-86292-2(X),* Simon & Schuster Bks. For Young Readers) Simon & Schuster Bks. For Young Readers.

—Attack of the 50-Ft. Cupid, 1 vol. Benton, Jim, illus. 2011. (Franny K. Stein, Mad Scientist Ser.). (ENG., Illus.). 112p. (gr. 3-6). 24.21 *(978-1-59961-818-0(4))* Spotlight.

Berenstain, Mike. Valentine Love Bug. Berenstain, Mike, illus. 2014. (Berenstain Bears Ser.). (ENG., Illus.). 24p. (J). (gr. -1-3). pap. 6.99 *(978-0-06-207562-8(4))* HarperCollins Pubs.

Berger, Samantha. A Crankenstein Valentine. Santat, Dan, illus. 2014. (ENG.). 40p. (J). (gr. -1-3). 17.99 *(978-0-316-37638-9(8))* Little, Brown Bks. for Young Readers.

Bickel, Karla. Fishnet Valentine. Bickel, Karla, illus. l.t. ed. 2004. (Illus.). 16p. (J). (gr. -1-5). pap. 5.00 *(978-1-891452-13-0(4),* 4) Heart Arbor Bks.

Bond, Felicia. Day It Rained Hearts. Bond, Felicia, illus. 2006. (ENG., Illus.). 36p. (J). (gr. -1-3). pap. 6.99 *(978-0-06-073123-6(0))* HarperCollins Pubs.

Bunting, Eve. Mr. Goat's Valentine. Zimmer, Kevin, illus. 2016. (ENG.). 32p. (J). (gr. k-2). 16.99 *(978-1-58536-944-7(6),* 204024) Sleeping Bear Pr.

Cabot, Meg. Valentine Princess. 2006. (Princess Diaries: 7.75). (ENG.). 96p. (YA). (gr. 8-12). 12.99 *(978-0-06-084718-0(2),* HarperTeen) HarperCollins Pubs.

Carlson, Melody. Secret Admirer, 1 vol. 2016. (Faithgirlz / Girls of Harbor View Ser.). (ENG.). 272p. (J). pap. 9.99 *(978-0-310-75371-1(6))* Zonderkidz.

Carlson, Nancy. Henry & the Valentine Surprise. 2008. (ENG.). 32p. (J). (gr. -1-1). 15.99 *(978-0-670-06267-6(7),* Viking Books for Young Readers) Penguin Young Readers Group.

—Louanne Pig in the Mysterious Valentine. rev. ed. 2004. (Carolrhoda Picture Books Ser.). (Illus.). 32p. (J). (gr. k-2). 15.95 *(978-1-57505-671-5(2));* (ENG., per. 6.95 *(978-1-57505-722-4(0))* Lerner Publishing Group.

Carr, Jan. Sweet Hearts. Donohue, Dorothy, illus. 2004. (ENG.). 32p. (gr. -1-1). reprint ed. 6.95 *(978-0-8234-1879-4(0))* Holiday Hse., Inc.

Carter, David A. Love Bugs. Carter, David A., illus. 2003. (ENG., Illus.). 12p. (J). (gr. 2-5). 6.99 *(978-0-689-85815-4(9),* Little Simon) Little Simon.

Cazet, Denys, reader. Minnie & Moo: Will You Be My Valentine? 2004. (Read-Alongs for Beginning Readers Ser.). (Illus.). (J). (gr. -1-3). 25.95 incl. audio *(978-1-59112-892-2(7));* pap. 31.95 incl. audio compact disk *(978-1-59112-897-7(8));* pap. 29.95 incl. audio *(978-1-59112-893-9(5))* Live Oak Media.

Chand, Emlyn. Vicky Finds a Valentine: Bird Brain Books. Giffin, Noelle, illus. ed. 2013. (ENG.). 50p. (gr. k-1). pap. 10.95 *(978-1-62253-116-5(7));* 21.95 *(978-1-62253-117-2(5))* Evolved Publishing.

Clough, Lisa & Briant, Ed. Petal & Poppy & the Mystery Valentine. 2015. (Green Light Readers — Level 2 Ser.). lib. bdg. 13.55 *(978-0-606-37452-1(3))* Turtleback Bks.

Cohen, Miriam. Bee My Valentine, 1 vol. Himmler, Ronald, illus. 2009. (ENG.). 32p. (J). (gr. k-3). pap. 5.95 *(978-1-59572-086-3(3))* Star Bright Bks., Inc.

—Bee My Valentine!, 1 vol. Himler, Ronald, illus. 2008. (ENG.). 32p. (J). (gr. k-3). 15.95 *(978-1-59572-085-6(5))* Star Bright Bks., Inc.

Cooke, Brandy. My Valentine. Wilkinson, Annie, illus. 2010. (ENG.). 12p. (J). (gr. -1 — 1). bds. 4.99 *(978-1-4424-0779-4(4),* Little Simon) Little Simon.

Cooper, Mimi. Me Versus Cooties. 2006. 17p. 9.99 *(978-1-4116-8256-6(4))* Lulu Pr., Inc.

D'Andrea, Deborah, concept. Picture Me Bee My Honey. 2003. 10p. (J). (gr. -1-18). bds. 2.99 *(978-1-57151-520-9(8))* Playhouse Publishing.

Darling, Angela. Rachel's Valentine Crush. 2013. (Crush Ser.: 5). (ENG., Illus.). 160p. (J). (gr. 3-7). 15.99 *(978-1-4424-8641-6(4));* pap. 5.99 *(978-1-4424-8640-9(6))* Simon Spotlight. (Simon Spotlight).

Davenport, Kathy. Holly's Chocolate Heart. 2011. 40p. 17.49 *(978-1-4567-1520-5(8))* AuthorHouse.

Dean, James, illus. Valentine's Day Is Cool. 2013. (Pete the Cat Ser.). (ENG.). 24p. (J). (gr. -1-3). 9.99 *(978-0-06-219865-5(3),* HarperFestival) HarperCollins Pubs.

Disney Book Group Staff. I Love You! Disney Storybook Artists Staff, illus. 2012. (ENG.). 10p. (J). (gr. -1-k). pap. 7.99 *(978-1-4231-6571-2(3))* Disney Pr.

Disney Book Group Staff & Higginson, Sheila Sweeny. Minnie: Minnie's Valentine. Disney Storybook Artists Staff, illus. 2013. 10p. 5.99 *(978-1-4231-8811-7(X))* Disney Pr.

—My Huggy Valentine. Disney Storybook Art Team, illus. 2013. (ENG.). 24p. (J). (gr. -1-k). pap. 5.99 *(978-1-4847-0425-7(8))* Disney Pr.

Dougherty, Brandi. The Valentine's Day Disaster. 2008. 204p. (J). pap. *(978-0-545-03168-4(0))* Scholastic, Inc.

Dunrea, Olivier. Ollie's Valentine. 2015. (Gossie & Friends Ser.). (ENG., Illus.). 14p. (J). (— 1). bds. 6.99 *(978-0-544-50269-7(8),* HMH Books For Young Readers) Houghton Mifflin Harcourt Publishing Co.

Dyan, Penelope. Mikey & Me & the Valentines — -the Continuing Story of a Girl & Her Dog. Dyan, Penelope, illus. 2010. (Illus.). 50p. pap. 14.95 *(978-1-935118-96-1(X))* Bellissima Publishing, LLC.

—My Valentines. 2011. 34p. pap. 11.95 *(978-1-935630-52-4(0))* Bellissima Publishing, LLC.

Elliott, Laura Malone. String of Hearts. Munsinger, Lynn, illus. 2010. (ENG.). 32p. (J). (gr. -1-2). 16.99 *(978-0-06-000085-1(6),* Tegen, Katherine Bks) HarperCollins Pubs.

Emerson, Carl. Monster Boy's Valentine, 1 vol. Levin, Lon, illus. 2010. (Monster Boy Set 2 Ser.). (ENG.). 32p. (J). (gr. k-3). 28.50 *(978-1-60270-782-5(0))* ABDO Publishing Co.

Engelbreit, Mary. Queen of Hearts. Engelbreit, Mary, illus. 2008. (Ann Estelle Stories Ser.). (ENG., Illus.). 32p. (J). (gr. -1-3). pap. 6.99 *(978-0-06-008183-6(X))* HarperCollins Pubs.

Eubank, Patricia Reeder. Valentine ABCs. Eubank, Patricia Reeder, illus. 2009. (Illus.). 32p. (J). (gr. -1-3). 9.99 *(978-0-8249-5597-7(8),* Ideal Pubns.) Worthy Publishing.

Farley, Robin. The Sweetest Valentine. Ivanov, Aleksey & Ivanov, Olga, illus. 2012. (Mia Ser.). (ENG.). 24p. (J). (gr. -1-3). pap. 4.99 *(978-0-06-210012-2(2),* HarperFestival) HarperCollins Pubs.

Ferber, Brenda. The Yuckiest, Stinkiest, Best Valentine Ever. Arnold, Tedd, illus. 2015. (ENG.). 32p. (J). (gr. -1-2). 8.99 *(978-0-14-751709-8(5),* Puffin Books) Penguin Young Readers Group.

Friedman, Laurie. Heart to Heart with Mallory. 2008. pap. 34.95 *(978-0-8225-9439-0(0))* Lerner Publishing Group.

—Heart to Heart with Mallory. Pollak, Barbara, illus. (Mallory Ser.: 6). (ENG.). 160p. (J). (gr. 2-5). 2007. per. 5.95 *(978-0-8225-7133-9(1),* First Avenue Editions) 2006. lib. bdg. 15.95 *(978-1-57505-932-7(0),* Twenty-First Century Bks.) Lerner Publishing Group.

—Love, Ruby Valentine. Cravath, Lynne Avril, illus. 2006. (ENG.). 32p. (J). (gr. k-3). lib. bdg. 16.95 *(978-1-57505-899-3(5),* Carolrhoda Bks.) Lerner Publishing Group.

—Ruby Valentine & the Sweet Surprise. Avril, Lynne, illus. 2014. (ENG.). 32p. (J). (gr. k-3). 16.95 *(978-0-7613-8873-9(7),* Carolrhoda Bks.) Lerner Publishing Group.

—Ruby Valentine Saves the Day. Avril, Lynne, illus. 2010. (Carolrhoda Picture Bks.). (ENG.). 32p. (J). (gr. k-3). lib. bdg. 16.95 *(978-0-7613-4213-7(3))* Lerner Publishing Group.

Froeb, Lori & Mitter, Matt. Fisher-Price Little People Valentine's Day Is Here! 2015. (Fisher Price Lift the Flap Ser.). (ENG.). 10p. (J). (gr. -1-k). bds. 9.99 *(978-0-7944-3535-6(1))* Reader's Digest Assn., Inc., The.

Fruchter, Jason, illus. Happy Love Day, Daniel Tiger! 2015. (Daniel Tiger's Neighborhood Ser.). (ENG.). 14p. (J). (gr. -1-2). bds. 6.99 *(978-1-4814-4855-0(2),* Simon Spotlight) Simon Spotlight.

Gallo, Tina. Where's My Valentine? (Yo Gabba Gabba! Ser.). (ENG., 12p. (J). (gr. -1-1). 2013. Illus.). bds. 5.99 *(978-1-4424-8647-8(3))* 2009. 7.99 *(978-1-4169-9063-5(1))* Simon Spotlight. (Simon Spotlight).

Garcia, Mary. Play with Me: Togetherness Time for Your Preschooler & You: St. Valentine's Day. 2007. (J). *(978-0-9790931-1-1(2))* SMARTseeds Co., LLC, The.

Golden Books. Puppy Love! (Bubble Guppies) Golden Books, illus. 2012. (Full-Color Activity Book with Stickers Ser.). (ENG., Illus.). 32p. (J). (gr. -1-2). pap. 3.99 *(978-0-307-98197-4(5),* Golden Bks.) Random Hse. Children's Bks.

Golden Books Staff. Dora's Big Valentine! Golden Books Staff, illus. 2010. (Full-Color Activity Book with Stickers Ser.). (ENG., Illus.). 32p. (J). (gr. -1-2). pap. 3.99 *(978-0-375-87321-8(X),* Golden Bks.) Random Hse. Children's Bks.

—Puppy Hugs & Kisses! Golden Books Staff & Lovett, Nate, illus. 2016. (Hologramatic Sticker Book Ser.). (ENG.). 64p. (J). (gr. -1-2). pap. 4.99 *(978-0-399-55878-8(0),* Golden Bks.) Random Hse. Children's Bks.

Greene, Stephanie. Princess Posey & the First Grade Ballet. Sisson, Stephanie Roth, illus. 2014. (Princess Posey, First Grader Ser.: 9). (ENG.). 96p. (J). (gr. k-3). pap. 5.99 *(978-0-14-751292-5(1),* Puffin Books) Penguin Young Readers Group.

Greenwald, Lisa. Sweet Treats & Secret Crushes. (ENG.). (YA). (gr. 3-7). 2011. 320p. pap. 7.95 *(978-1-4197-0029-3(4))* 2010. 304p. 16.95 *(978-0-8109-8990-0(5))* Abrams, Inc. (Amulet Bks.).

Gutman, Dan. Mr. Louie Is Screwy! Paillot, Jim, illus. 2007. (My Weird School Ser.: 20). (ENG.). 112p. (J). (gr. 1-5). pap. 4.99 *(978-0-06-123479-8(6))* HarperCollins Pubs.
—Oh, Valentine, We've Lost Our Minds! Paillot, Jim, illus. 2014. (My Weird School Special Ser.). (ENG.). 144p. (J). (gr. 1-5). pap. 5.99 *(978-0-06-228403-7(7))* HarperCollins Pubs.
—Oh, Valentine, We've Lost Our Minds! 2014. (My Weird School Ser.). (J). lib. bdg. 16.00 *(978-0-606-36460-7(9))* Turtleback Bks.
Harrod-Eagles, Cynthia & Bennett, Elizabeth. Happy Valentine's Day. Hino, Sachiho, illus. 2016. (Hello Kitty Ser.). (ENG.). 32p. (J). (gr. k-2). pap. 3.99 *(978-1-338-11366-2(6))* Scholastic, Inc.
Hasbro. My Little Pony: Ponyville Reading Adventures. 2015. (Passport to Reading Level 2 Ser.). (ENG., Illus.). 192p. (J). (gr. -1-3). 9.99 *(978-0-316-33740-3(4))* Little, Brown Bks. for Young Readers.
Higginson, Sheila Sweeny & Disney Book Group Staff. Minnie's Valentine. Loter Inc. Staff & Disney Storybook Art Team, illus. rev. ed. 2007. (ENG.). 24p. (J). (gr. -1-k). pap. 4.99 *(978-1-4231-0746-0(2))* Disney Pr.
Hillert, Margaret. I Love You, Dear Dragon. Pullan, Jack, illus. 2016. (BeginningtoRead Ser.). (ENG.). 32p. (J). (-2). lib. bdg. 22.60 *(978-1-59953-770-2(2))* Norwood Hse. Pr.
Hillert, Margaret. Te Quiero, Querido Dragón. Pullan, Jack, illus. 2017. (BeginningtoRead Ser.).Tr. of I Love You, Dear Dragon. (ENG & SPA.). 32p. (J). (-2). 22.60 ***(978-1-59953-833-4(4))*** Norwood Hse. Pr.
Hills, Tad. Duck & Goose, Goose Needs a Hug. Hills, Tad, illus. 2012. (Duck & Goose Ser.). (ENG., Illus.). 22p. (J). (-k). bds. 6.99 *(978-0-307-98293-3(9))*, Schwartz & Wade Bks.) Random Hse. Children's Bks.
Hoff, Syd. Danny & the Dinosaur: First Valentine's Day. Hoff, Syd, illus. 2016. (Illus.). 24p. (J). (gr. -1-3). pap. 6.99 *(978-0-06-241044-3(X)*, HarperFestival) HarperCollins Pubs.
Hoien, Ruth S. Ruthie's Four Hearts. (J). pap. 3.99 *(978-0-88019-105-0(8))* Schmul Publishing Co., Inc.
Holub, Joan. Big Heart! A Valentine's Day Tale. Terry, Will, illus. 2007. (Ant Hill Ser.). (ENG.). 24p. (J). (gr. -1-k). lib. bdg. 13.89 *(978-1-4169-2562-0(7)*, Simon & Schuster/Paula Wiseman Bks.) Simon & Schuster/Paula Wiseman Bks.
—Big Heart! A Valentine's Day Tale. Terry, Will, illus. 2007. (Ant Hill Ser.). (ENG.). 24p. (J). (gr. -1-k). pap. 3.99 *(978-1-4169-0957-6(5)*, Simon Spotlight) Simon Spotlight.
Humphrey, Anna. Rhymes with Cupid. 2010. (ENG.). 240p. (YA). (gr. 8). pap. 7.99 *(978-0-06-193501-5(8)*, HarperTeen) HarperCollins Pubs.
Inches, Alison. Dora Quiere Mucho a Boots. Saunders, Zina, illus. 2005. (Dora the Explorer Ser.). (SPA.). 24p. (J). (gr. -1-2). pap. 3.99 *(978-1-4169-0620-9(7)*, Libros Para Ninos) Libros Para Ninos.
Jackson, Everett E. Kimme Gets a Valentine. 2008. 28p. pap. 16.99 *(978-1-4389-0982-0(9))* AuthorHouse.
Jahn-Clough, Lisa, et al. Petal & Poppy & the Mystery Valentine. Briant, Ed, illus. 2015. (Green Light Readers Level 2 Ser.). (ENG.). 32p. (J). (gr. 1-4). pap. 3.99 *(978-0-544-55549-5(X)*, HMH Books For Young Readers) Houghton Mifflin Harcourt Publishing Co.
Jennings, Sharon. Batnapped. *(978-1-897039-30-4(1))* High Interest Publishing (HIP).
Kann, Victoria. Pink of Hearts. Kann, Victoria, illus. 2011. (Pinkalicious Ser.). (ENG., Illus.). 24p. (J). (gr. -1-2). pap. 6.99 *(978-0-06-198923-0(1)*, HarperFestival) HarperCollins Pubs.
Kaye, Marilyn. Valentine's Day Surprise: The after School Club. 2014. (ENG., Illus.). 80p. (J). (gr. 3-7). pap. 13.99 *(978-1-4814-2886-6(1)*, Simon & Schuster/Paula Wiseman Bks.) Simon & Schuster/Paula Wiseman Bks.
Kent, Renee Holmes. Adventures in Misty Falls, Vol. 8. 2004. (Adventures in Misty Falls Ser.: Vol. 8). (Illus.). 100p. (gr. 4-7). pap. 4.99 *(978-1-56309-456-9(8)*, N017104) Woman's Missionary Union.
Killian, Beth. Everything She Wants. 2006. (310 Ser.). (ENG.). 240p. (gr. 8-12). pap. 15.99 *(978-1-4165-2168-6(2)*, MTV Bks.) MTV Books.
King, Trey. Wrecking Valentine's Day! Wang, Sean, illus. 2015. (Lego City Ser.). (ENG.). 24p. (J). (gr. -1-3). pap. 3.99 *(978-0-545-85984-4(0))* Scholastic, Inc.
Kirby, Stan. Captain Awesome Gets Crushed. O'Connor, George, illus. 2013. (Captain Awesome Ser.: 9). (ENG.). 128p. (J). (gr. k-2). pap. 5.99 *(978-1-4424-8212-8(5))*; 16.99 *(978-1-4424-8213-5(3))* Little Simon. (Little Simon).
—Captain Awesome Gets Crushed. 2013. (Captain Awesome Ser.: 9). lib. bdg. 16.00 *(978-0-606-32331-4(7)*, Turtleback) Turtleback Bks.
Kleinberg, Naomi. My Fuzzy Valentine. Womble, Louis, illus. 2005. (Board Books). (ENG.). 12p. (J). (gr. k — 1). bds. 4.99 *(978-0-375-83392-2(7)*, Random Hse. Bks. for Young Readers) Random Hse. Children's Bks.
Kline, Suzy. Horrible Harry on the Ropes. Remkiewicz, Frank & Wummer, Amy, illus. 2011. (Horrible Harry Ser.). (ENG.). 80p. (J). (gr. 2-4). 4.99 *(978-0-14-241695-2(9)*, Puffin Books) Penguin Young Readers Group.
—Horrible Harry on the Ropes, 24 vols. Wummer, Amy, illus. 2009. (Horrible Harry Ser.: 24). (ENG.). 80p. (J). (gr. 2-4). 14.99 *(978-0-670-01097-4(9)*, Viking Books for Young Readers) Penguin Young Readers Group.
Knowlton, Laurie Lazzaro. My Valentine for Jesus, 1 vol. Erdogan, Buket, illus. 2009. (ENG.). 10p. (J). bds. 4.99 *(978-0-310-71333-3(1))* Zonderkidz.
Knudson, Mike & Wilkinson, Steve. Dancing Dudes. Curtis, Stacy, illus. 2010. (Raymond & Graham Ser.). (ENG.). 144p. (J). (gr. 3-7). 6.99 *(978-0-14-241508-5(1)*, Puffin Books) Penguin Young Readers Group.
Kroll, Steven. The Biggest Valentine Ever. Bassett, Jeni, illus. 2006. (ENG.). 32p. (J). (gr. -1-1). pap. 3.99 *(978-0-439-76419-3(X))* Scholastic, Inc.
LaFleur, John & Dubin, Shawn. Dreary & Naughty: Friday the 13th of February, 1 vol. 2013. (ENG., Illus.). 64p. (J). 14.99 *(978-0-7643-4495-4(1)*, 9780764344954) Schiffer Publishing, Ltd.
Lee, Quinlan B. Valentine Surprise. Haefele, Steve, illus. 2008. (Clifford the Big Red Dog Ser.). (J). *(978-0-545-02845-5(0))* Scholastic, Inc.
Levithan, David. Marly's Ghost. Selznick, Brian, illus. 2007. (ENG.). 208p. (YA). (gr. 7-18). 7.99 *(978-0-14-240912-1(X)*, Speak) Penguin Young Readers Group.
Lunsford, Susie. The Magical Wishing Well Forest Series. 2006. pap. 25.32 *(978-1-4134-9491-4(9))* Xlibris Corp.
Mayer, Mercer. Happy Valentine's Day, Little Critter! Mayer, Mercer, illus. 2005. (Little Critter Ser.). (ENG., Illus.). 20p. (J). (gr. -1-3). pap. 6.99 *(978-0-06-053973-3(9)*, HarperFestival) HarperCollins Pubs.
—Just a Little Love. 2013. (Little Critter: I Can Read! Ser.). (J). lib. bdg. 13.55 *(978-0-606-32176-1(4)*, Turtleback) Turtleback Bks.
McGrath, Barbara Barbieri & Tagel, Peggy. Valentine's Shapes. 2016. (First Celebrations Ser.). (ENG., Illus.). 12p. (J). (— 1). bds. 6.95 *(978-1-58089-532-3(8))* Charlesbridge Publishing, Inc.
McGuirk, Leslie. Tucker's Valentine. McGuirk, Leslie, illus. 2010. (ENG., Illus.). 28p. (J). (gr. -1-k). bds. 6.99 *(978-0-7636-4357-7(2))* Candlewick Pr.
McNamara, Margaret. Clara & the Magical Charms. Denos, Julia, illus. 2013. (Fairy Bell Sisters Ser.: 4). (ENG.). 128p. (J). (gr. 1-5). 15.99 *(978-0-06-222811-6(0))*; pap. 4.99 *(978-0-06-222810-9(2))* HarperCollins Pubs.
—Too Many Valentines. Gordon, Mike, illus. 2003. (Robin Hill School Ser.). (ENG.). 32p. (J). (gr. -1-1). pap. 3.99 *(978-0-689-85537-5(0)*, Simon Spotlight) Simon Spotlight.
Meadows, Daisy. Juliet the Valentine Fairy. 2009. (Rainbow Magic Ser.). (ENG., Illus.). 192p. (J). (gr. 2-5). pap. 6.99 *(978-0-545-14886-3(3)*, Scholastic Paperbacks) Scholastic, Inc.
Moffitt, Debra. Girls in Charge. 2011. (Pink Locker Society Novels Ser.: 4). (ENG.). 208p. (J). (gr. 3-7). pap. 18.99 *(978-0-312-64506-9(6)*, 9780312645069, St. Martin's Griffin) St. Martin's Pr.
Mongredien, Sue. Be My Valentine. 2010. (Sleepover Club Ser.). (ENG.). 128p. (J). (gr. 2-6). pap. 6.99 *(978-0-00-727705-6(9))* Lion Hudson PLC GBR. Dist: Independent Pubs. Group.
My Little Love. 2003. (Illus.). 256p. (J). (gr. -1-1). pap. 14.99 *(978-0-06-051764-9(6))* HarperCollins Pubs.
Nagda, Ann Whitehead. The Valentine Cat. Roth, Stephanie, illus. 2008. (ENG.). 32p. (J). (gr. 2-5). 16.95 *(978-0-8234-2123-7(6))* Holiday Hse., Inc.
Numeroff, Laura Joffe. Happy Valentine's Day, Mouse! Lap Edition. Bond, Felicia, illus. 2015. (If You Give... Ser.). (ENG.). 24p. (J). (gr. -1-3). bds. 12.99 *(978-0-06-242740-3(7))* HarperCollins Pubs.
Oceanak, Karla. Ignoramus. Spanjer, Kendra, illus. 2013. (Aldo Zelnick Comic Novel Ser.: 9). (ENG.). 160p. (J). (gr. 3-7). 12.95 *(978-1-934649-41-1(4))* Bailiwick Pr.
O'Connor, Jane. Fancy Nancy: Nancy Clancy Seeks a Fortune. Glasser, Robin Preiss & Bracken, Carolyn, illus. 2016. (Nancy Clancy Ser.: 7). 144p. (J). (gr. 1-5). 9.99 *(978-0-06-226969-0(0))* HarperCollins Pubs.
—Heart to Heart. Glasser, Robin Preiss & Bracken, Carolyn, illus. 2009. (Fancy Nancy Ser.). (ENG.). 24p. (J). (gr. -1-3). pap. 4.99 *(978-0-06-123596-2(2)*, HarperFestival) HarperCollins Pubs.
—Nancy Clancy, Secret Admirer. Glasser, Robin Preiss, illus. 2013. (Nancy Clancy Ser.: 2). (ENG.). 144p. (J). (gr. 1-5). pap. 4.99 *(978-0-06-208420-0(8))* HarperCollins Pubs.
—Nancy Clancy, Secret Admirer. 2013. (Nancy Clancy Ser.: 2). (J). lib. bdg. 14.75 *(978-0-606-35045-7(4)*, Turtleback) Turtleback Bks.
—Nancy Clancy's Tres Charming, 3 vols., Set. Glasser, Robin Preiss, illus. 2013. (Fancy Nancy Ser.). (ENG.). 384p. (J). (gr. 1-5). 24.99 *(978-0-06-227793-0(6))* HarperCollins Pubs.
—Secret Admirer, 3 vols. Glasser, Robin Preiss, illus. 2013. (Fancy Nancy Ser.: Bk. 2). (ENG.). 128p. (J). (gr. 1-5). 9.99 *(978-0-06-208295-4(7))* HarperCollins Pubs.
Parish, Herman. Amelia Bedelia's First Valentine. Avril, Lynne, illus. (Amelia Bedelia Ser.). (ENG.). 32p. (J). (gr. -1-3). 2014. pap. 6.99 *(978-0-06-154460-6(4))* 2011. 9.99 *(978-0-06-203275-1(5))* 2009. 16.99 *(978-0-06-154458-3(2))* HarperCollins Pubs. (Greenwillow Bks.).
—Amelia Bedelia's First Valentine. 2014. (Amelia Bedelia Picture Bks.). (J). lib. bdg. 17.20 *(978-0-606-35971-9(0))* Turtleback Bks.
Park, Barbara. Junie B. Jones & the Mushy Gushy Valentine. unabr. ed. 2004. (Junie B. Jones Ser.: No. 14). 69p. (J). (gr. k-3). pap. 17.00 incl. audio *(978-0-8072-0335-4(1)*, Listening Library) Random Hse. Audio Publishing Group.
—Junie B. My Valentime. Brunkus, Denise, illus. 2013. (Junie B. Jones Ser.). (ENG.). 12p. (gr. -1-2). pap. 5.99 *(978-0-385-37302-9(3)*, Random Hse. Bks. for Young Readers) Random Hse. Children's Bks.
Perelman, Helen. Heart to Heart. 2007. (High School Musical Stories from East High Ser.). 125p. (J). (gr. 3-7). 12.65 *(978-0-7569-8340-6(1))* Perfection Learning Corp.
Perry, Naresha. Zora's Valentine. 2005. per. 17.00 *(978-0-8059-9751-4(2))* Dorrance Publishing Co., Inc.
Peschke, Marci. Valentine Queen, 1 vol. Mourning, Tuesday, illus. 2014. (Kylie Jean Ser.). (ENG.). 112p. (gr. 2-3). 22.65 *(978-1-4795-2352-8(6)*, Kylie Jean) Picture Window Bks.
Petersen, David. Snowy Valentine. Petersen, David, illus. 2011. (ENG., Illus.). 32p. (J). (gr. -1-3). 14.99 *(978-0-06-146378-5(7))* HarperCollins Pubs.
Peterson, John & Slater, Teddy. The Littles Have a Happy Valentine's Day. Rogers, Jacqueline, illus. 2003. (Littles First Readers Ser.: No. 11). (ENG.). 32p. (J). (gr. k-2). pap. 3.99 *(978-0-439-42499-8(2)*, Scholastic Paperbacks) Scholastic, Inc.
Priddy, Roger. Love You Always. 2016. (Shiny Shapes Ser.). (ENG.). 10p. (J). bds. 7.99 *(978-0-312-52053-3(0)*, 9780312520533, Priddy Bks.) St. Martin's Pr.
Publications International Ltd. Staff, ed. Sesame Street(r) Elmo's Valentine. 2013. 12p. (J). bds. 7.98 *(978-1-4508-7410-6(X)*, 95d0f5ac-f093-4d77-bf25-5caf2a717091) Phoenix International Publications, Inc.
Quin-Harkin, Janet. Secret Valentine. 2014. (Tgif Ser.: 6). (ENG., Illus.). 128p. (J). (gr. 3-7). pap. 13.99 *(978-1-4814-2884-2(5)*, Simon & Schuster/Paula Wiseman Bks.) Simon & Schuster/Paula Wiseman Bks.
Random House Disney Staff. A Valentine for Percy (Thomas & Friends) Courtney, Richard, illus. 2015. (Step into Reading Ser.). (ENG.). 24p. (J). (gr. -1-1). 4.99 *(978-1-101-93287-2(2)*, Random Hse. Bks. for Young Readers) Random Hse. Children's Bks.
Rey, H. A. Happy Valentine's Day. Young, Mary O'Keefe, illus. 2011. (Curious George Ser.). (ENG.). 14p. (J). (gr. -1-3). 8.99 *(978-0-547-13107-8(0))* Houghton Mifflin Harcourt Publishing Co.
Ricci, Christine. Dora's Valentine Adventure. A and J Studios Staff, illus. 2006. (Dora the Explorer Ser.). (ENG.). 14p. (J). (gr. -1-k). bds. 6.99 *(978-1-4169-1754-0(3)*, Simon Spotlight/Nickelodeon) Simon Spotlight/Nickelodeon.
Ritchie, Joseph. Peek-A-Boo! Valentine. Halverson, Lydia, illus. 2006. (ENG.). 14p. (J). (gr. -1-k). bds. 7.95 *(978-0-8249-6674-4(0)*, Ideal Pubns.) Worthy Publishing.
Roberts, Bethany. Valentine Mice! Cushman, Doug, illus. 2016. (Green Light Readers Level 1 Ser.). (ENG.). 32p. (J). (gr. -1-3). 12.99 *(978-0-544-80897-3(5)*, HMH Books For Young Readers) Houghton Mifflin Harcourt Publishing Co.
—Valentine Mice! Board Book. Cushman, Doug, illus. 2011. (ENG.). 28p. (J). (gr. k — 1). bds. 5.99 *(978-0-547-37144-3(6))* Houghton Mifflin Harcourt Publishing Co.
Rose, Nancy. The Secret Life of Squirrels: A Love Story. 2016. (ENG., Illus.). 32p. (J). (gr. -1-3). 16.99 *(978-0-316-27263-6(9))* Little, Brown Bks. for Young Readers.
Roy, Ron. February Friend. Gurney, John Steven, illus. 2009. (Calendar Mysteries Ser.: 2). (ENG.). 80p. (J). (gr. 1-4). 4.99 *(978-0-375-85662-4(5)*, Random Hse. Bks. for Young Readers) Random Hse. Children's Bks.
—Secret Admirer. Gurney, John Steven, illus. 2015. (to Z Mysteries Ser.: No. 8). (ENG.). 144p. (J). (gr. 1-4). 5.99 *(978-0-553-52399-7(6)*, Random Hse. Bks. for Young Readers) Random Hse. Children's Bks.
Roza, Greg. El Día de San Valentín (Valentines for Vinnie) 2007. (Lecturas del barrio (Neighborhood Readers) Ser.). (SPA.). 12p. 33.50 *(978-1-4042-7301-6(8)*, Rosen Classroom) Rosen Publishing Group, Inc., The.
—Valentines for Vinnie. (Neighborhood Readers Ser.). (ENG.). 12p. 2007. 33.50 *(978-1-4042-7300-9(X))* 2006. (gr. 1-3). pap. 5.90 *(978-1-4042-6799-2(9))* Rosen Publishing Group, Inc., The. (Rosen Classroom).
Rylant, Cynthia. Henry & Mudge & Mrs. Hopper's House. Bracken, Carolyn, illus. 2004. (Ready-to-Read Ser.). 40p. (gr. k-2). 14.00 *(978-0-7569-2200-9(3))* Perfection Learning Corp.
—Henry & Mudge & Mrs. Hopper's House. Bracken, Carolyn, illus. (Henry & Mudge Ser.: 22). (ENG.). 40p. (J). (gr. k-2). 2004. pap. 3.99 *(978-0-689-83446-2(2))* 2003. 15.99 *(978-0-689-81153-1(5))* Simon Spotlight. (Simon Spotlight).
—Henry & Mudge & Mrs. Hopper's House. Bracken, Carolyn, illus. 2004. (Henry & Mudge Ready-To-Read Ser.: 22). 40p. (gr. k-2). lib. bdg. 13.55 *(978-0-613-90376-9(5)*, Turtleback) Turtleback Bks.
—If You'll Be My Valentine. Kosaka, Fumi, illus. 2005. (ENG.). 32p. (J). (gr. -1-3). pap. 6.99 *(978-0-06-009271-9(8))* HarperCollins Pubs.
Schigiel, Gregg. Feel the Love. 2013. (SpongeBob Squarepants 8X8 Ser.). lib. bdg. 14.75 *(978-0-606-35559-9(6))* Turtleback Bks.
Schulman, Janet. 10 Valentine Friends. Davick, Linda, illus. 2012. (ENG.). 26p. (J). (gr. -1 — 1). bds. 6.99 *(978-0-375-87130-6(6)*, Knopf Bks. for Young Readers) Random Hse. Children's Bks.
Schulz. Buon San Valentino Dolce. pap. 19.95 *(978-88-451-2996-4(9))* Fabbri Editori - RCS Libri ITA. Dist: Distribooks, Inc.
Schulz, Charles. Be My Valentine, Charlie Brown. (J). pap. 46.80 *(978-0-590-06610-5(2))* Scholastic, Inc.
Schulz, Charles M. Be My Valentine, Charlie Brown. 2007. (Miniature Editions Ser.). (ENG., Illus.). 128p. (gr. 1-17). 5.95 *(978-0-7624-2754-3(X))* Running Pr. Bk. Pubs.
Scieszka, Jon. Melvin's Valentine. Shannon, David et al, illus. 2009. (Jon Scieszka's Trucktown Ser.). (ENG.). 24p. (J). (gr. -1-1). lib. bdg. 15.99 *(978-1-4169-4155-2(X)*, Simon Spotlight) Simon Spotlight.
Scollon, William. Minnie: Be My Sparkly Valentine. 2014. (Mickey Mouse 8x8 Ser.). (J). lib. bdg. 16.00 *(978-0-606-35903-0(5))* Turtleback Bks.
Scollon, William, et al. Minnie Be My Sparkly Valentine. Disney Storybook Art Team Staff, illus. 2014. (ENG.). 24p. (J). (gr. -1-k). pap. 5.99 *(978-1-4231-6414-2(8))* Disney Pr.
Scotton, Rob. Love, Splat. Scotton, Rob, illus. (Splat the Cat Ser.). (ENG., Illus.). 40p. (J). (gr. -1-2). 2011. 9.99 *(978-0-06-207776-9(7))* 2008. 16.99 *(978-0-06-083157-8(X))* HarperCollins Pubs.
Setzer, Lee Ann. Sariah Mcduff: Book Three of the Sariah Mcduff Series: Valentine's Day Scrooge. Bonham, Bob, illus. 2005. (J). per. 5.95 *(978-1-55517-841-3(3))* Cedar Fort, Inc./CFI Distribution.
Shaw, Natalie. OLIVIA & the Perfect Valentine. Johnson, Shane L., illus. 2013. (Olivia TV Tie-In Ser.). (ENG.). 24p. (J). (gr. -1-2). pap. 4.99 *(978-1-4424-8484-9(5)*, Simon Spotlight) Simon Spotlight.
—Olivia & the Perfect Valentine. 2013. (Olivia 8x8 Ser.). lib. bdg. 14.75 *(978-0-606-35200-0(7))* Turtleback Bks.
Silvano, Wendi. Love Is All Around Alabama. Czernichowska, Joanna, illus. 2016. (ENG.). 32p. (J). (-6). 12.99 *(978-1-4926-2900-9(6)*, Sourcebooks Jabberwocky) Sourcebooks, Inc.
—Love Is All Around Alaska. Czernichowska, Joanna, illus. 2016. (ENG.). 32p. (J). (-6). 12.99 *(978-1-4926-2901-6(4)*, Sourcebooks Jabberwocky) Sourcebooks, Inc.
—Love Is All Around Albuquerque. Czernichowska, Joanna, illus. 2016. (ENG.). 32p. (J). (-6). 12.99 *(978-1-4926-2902-3(2)*, Sourcebooks Jabberwocky) Sourcebooks, Inc.
—Love Is All Around Arizona. Czernichowska, Joanna, illus. 2016. (ENG.). 32p. (J). (-6). 12.99 *(978-1-4926-2903-0(0)*, Sourcebooks Jabberwocky) Sourcebooks, Inc.
—Love Is All Around Arkansas. Czernichowska, Joanna, illus. 2016. (ENG.). 32p. (J). (-6). 12.99 *(978-1-4926-2904-7(9)*, Sourcebooks Jabberwocky) Sourcebooks, Inc.
—Love Is All Around Boise. Czernichowska, Joanna, illus. 2016. (ENG.). 32p. (J). (-6). 12.99 *(978-1-4926-2906-1(5)*, Sourcebooks Jabberwocky) Sourcebooks, Inc.
—Love Is All Around Boston. Czernichowska, Joanna, illus. 2016. (ENG.). 32p. (J). (-6). 12.99 *(978-1-4926-2907-8(3)*, Sourcebooks Jabberwocky) Sourcebooks, Inc.
—Love Is All Around Calgary. Czernichowska, Joanna, illus. 2016. (ENG.). 32p. (J). (-6). 12.99 *(978-1-4926-2908-5(1)*, Sourcebooks Jabberwocky) Sourcebooks, Inc.
—Love Is All Around California. Czernichowska, Joanna, illus. 2016. (ENG.). 32p. (J). (-10). 12.99 *(978-1-4926-2909-2(X)*, Sourcebooks Jabberwocky) Sourcebooks, Inc.
—Love Is All Around Canada. Czernichowska, Joanna, illus. 2016. (ENG.). 32p. (J). (-10). 12.99 *(978-1-4926-2910-8(3)*, Sourcebooks Jabberwocky) Sourcebooks, Inc.
—Love Is All Around Charleston. Czernichowska, Joanna, illus. 2016. (ENG.). 32p. (J). (-6). 12.99 *(978-1-4926-2911-5(1)*, Sourcebooks Jabberwocky) Sourcebooks, Inc.
—Love Is All Around Chicago. Czernichowska, Joanna, illus. 2016. (ENG.). 32p. (J). (-6). 12.99 *(978-1-4926-2912-2(X)*, Sourcebooks Jabberwocky) Sourcebooks, Inc.
—Love Is All Around Cincinnati. Czernichowska, Joanna, illus. 2016. (ENG.). 32p. (J). (-6). 12.99 *(978-1-4926-2913-9(8)*, Sourcebooks Jabberwocky) Sourcebooks, Inc.
—Love Is All Around Colorado. Czernichowska, Joanna, illus. 2016. (ENG.). 32p. (J). (-6). 12.99 *(978-1-4926-2914-6(6)*, Sourcebooks Jabberwocky) Sourcebooks, Inc.
—Love Is All Around Connecticut. Czernichowska, Joanna, illus. 2016. (ENG.). 32p. (J). (-6). 12.99 *(978-1-4926-2915-3(4)*, Sourcebooks Jabberwocky) Sourcebooks, Inc.
—Love Is All Around Delaware. Czernichowska, Joanna, illus. 2016. (ENG.). 32p. (J). (-6). 12.99 *(978-1-4926-2916-0(2)*, Sourcebooks Jabberwocky) Sourcebooks, Inc.
—Love Is All Around Edmonton. Czernichowska, Joanna, illus. 2016. (ENG.). 32p. (J). (-6). 12.99 *(978-1-4926-2917-7(0)*, Sourcebooks Jabberwocky) Sourcebooks, Inc.
—Love Is All Around Florida. Czernichowska, Joanna, illus. 2016. (ENG.). 32p. (J). (-6). 12.99 *(978-1-4926-2918-4(9)*, Sourcebooks Jabberwocky) Sourcebooks, Inc.
—Love Is All Around Georgia. Czernichowska, Joanna, illus. 2016. (ENG.). 32p. (J). (-6). 12.99 *(978-1-4926-2919-1(7)*, Sourcebooks Jabberwocky) Sourcebooks, Inc.
—Love Is All Around Hawaii. Czernichowska, Joanna, illus. 2016. (ENG.). 32p. (J). (-6). 12.99 *(978-1-4926-2920-7(0)*, Sourcebooks Jabberwocky) Sourcebooks, Inc.
—Love Is All Around Idaho. Czernichowska, Joanna, illus. 2016. (ENG.). 32p. (J). (-6). 12.99 *(978-1-4926-2921-4(9)*, Sourcebooks Jabberwocky) Sourcebooks, Inc.
—Love Is All Around Illinois. Czernichowska, Joanna, illus. 2016. (ENG.). 32p. (J). (-6). 12.99 *(978-1-4926-2922-1(7)*, Sourcebooks Jabberwocky) Sourcebooks, Inc.
—Love Is All Around Indiana. Czernichowska, Joanna, illus. 2016. (ENG.). 32p. (J). (-6). 12.99 *(978-1-4926-2923-8(5)*, Sourcebooks Jabberwocky) Sourcebooks, Inc.
—Love Is All Around Iowa. Czernichowska, Joanna, illus. 2016. (ENG.). 32p. (J). (-6). 12.99 *(978-1-4926-2924-5(3)*, Sourcebooks Jabberwocky) Sourcebooks, Inc.
—Love Is All Around Kansas. Czernichowska, Joanna, illus. 2016. (ENG.). 32p. (J). (-6). 12.99 *(978-1-4926-2925-2(1)*, Sourcebooks Jabberwocky) Sourcebooks, Inc.
—Love Is All Around Kansas City. Czernichowska, Joanna, illus. 2016. (ENG.). 32p. (J). (-6). 12.99 *(978-1-4926-2926-9(X)*, Sourcebooks Jabberwocky) Sourcebooks, Inc.
—Love Is All Around Kentucky. Czernichowska, Joanna, illus. 2016. (ENG.). 32p. (J). (-6). 12.99 *(978-1-4926-2927-6(8)*, 9781492629276, Sourcebooks Jabberwocky) Sourcebooks, Inc.
—Love Is All Around Las Vegas. Czernichowska, Joanna, illus. 2016. (ENG.). 32p. (J). (-6). 12.99 *(978-1-4926-2928-3(6)*, Sourcebooks Jabberwocky) Sourcebooks, Inc.
—Love Is All Around Los Angeles. Czernichowska, Joanna, illus. 2016. (ENG.). 32p. (J). (-6). 12.99 *(978-1-4926-2929-0(4)*, Sourcebooks Jabberwocky) Sourcebooks, Inc.
—Love Is All Around Louisiana. Czernichowska, Joanna, illus. 2016. (ENG.). 32p. (J). (-6). 12.99 *(978-1-4926-2930-6(8)*, Sourcebooks Jabberwocky) Sourcebooks, Inc.
—Love Is All Around Maine. Czernichowska, Joanna, illus. 2016. (ENG.). 32p. (J). (-6). 12.99 *(978-1-4926-2931-3(6)*, Sourcebooks Jabberwocky) Sourcebooks, Inc.
—Love Is All Around Maryland. Czernichowska, Joanna, illus. 2016. (ENG.). 32p. (J). (-6). 12.99 *(978-1-4926-2932-0(4)*, Sourcebooks Jabberwocky) Sourcebooks, Inc.
—Love Is All Around Massachusetts. Czernichowska, Joanna, illus. 2016. (ENG.). 32p. (J). (-6). 12.99 *(978-1-4926-2933-7(2)*, Sourcebooks Jabberwocky) Sourcebooks, Inc.
—Love Is All Around Michigan. Czernichowska, Joanna, illus. 2016. (ENG.). 32p. (J). (-6). 12.99 *(978-1-4926-2934-4(0)*, 9781492629344, Sourcebooks Jabberwocky) Sourcebooks, Inc.
—Love Is All Around Minnesota. Czernichowska, Joanna, illus. 2016. (ENG.). 32p. (J). (-6). 12.99 *(978-1-4926-2935-1(9)*, Sourcebooks Jabberwocky) Sourcebooks, Inc.
—Love Is All Around Mississippi. Czernichowska, Joanna, illus. 2016. (ENG.). 32p. (J). (-6). 12.99 *(978-1-4926-2936-8(7)*, Sourcebooks Jabberwocky) Sourcebooks, Inc.
—Love Is All Around Missouri. Czernichowska, Joanna, illus. 2016. (ENG.). 32p. (J). (-6). 12.99 *(978-1-4926-2937-5(5)*, Sourcebooks Jabberwocky) Sourcebooks, Inc.
—Love Is All Around Montana. Czernichowska, Joanna, illus. 2016. (ENG.). 32p. (J). (-6). 12.99 *(978-1-4926-2938-2(3)*, Sourcebooks Jabberwocky) Sourcebooks, Inc.
—Love Is All Around Nebraska. Czernichowska, Joanna, illus. 2016. (ENG.). 32p. (J). (-6). 12.99 *(978-1-4926-2939-9(1)*, Sourcebooks Jabberwocky) Sourcebooks, Inc.
—Love Is All Around Nevada. Czernichowska, Joanna, illus. 2016. (ENG.). 32p. (J). (-6). 12.99 *(978-1-4926-2940-5(5)*, Sourcebooks Jabberwocky) Sourcebooks, Inc.
—Love Is All Around New England. Czernichowska, Joanna, illus. 2016. (ENG.). 32p. (J). (-6). 12.99 *(978-1-4926-2941-2(3)*, Sourcebooks Jabberwocky) Sourcebooks, Inc.
—Love Is All Around New Hampshire. Czernichowska, Joanna, illus. 2016. (ENG.). 32p. (J). (-6). 12.99 *(978-1-4926-2942-9(1)*, Sourcebooks Jabberwocky) Sourcebooks, Inc.
—Love Is All Around New Jersey. Czernichowska, Joanna, illus. 2016. (ENG.). 32p. (J). (-6). 12.99

(978-1-4926-2943-6(X), Sourcebooks Jabberwocky) Sourcebooks, Inc.

—Love Is All Around New Mexico. Czernichowska, Joanna, illus. 2016. (ENG.). 32p. (J). (-6). 12.99 (978-1-4926-2944-3(8), Sourcebooks Jabberwocky) Sourcebooks, Inc.

—Love Is All Around New York. Czernichowska, Joanna, illus. 2016. (ENG.). 32p. (J). (-6). 12.99 (978-1-4926-2945-0(6), Sourcebooks Jabberwocky) Sourcebooks, Inc.

—Love Is All Around New York City. Czernichowska, Joanna, illus. 2016. (ENG.). 32p. (J). (-6). 12.99 (978-1-4926-2946-7(4), Sourcebooks Jabberwocky) Sourcebooks, Inc.

—Love Is All Around North Carolina. Czernichowska, Joanna, illus. 2016. (ENG.). 32p. (J). (-6). 12.99 (978-1-4926-2947-4(2), Sourcebooks Jabberwocky) Sourcebooks, Inc.

—Love Is All Around North Dakota. Czernichowska, Joanna, illus. 2016. (ENG.). 32p. (J). (-6). 12.99 (978-1-4926-2948-1(0), Sourcebooks Jabberwocky) Sourcebooks, Inc.

—Love Is All Around Ohio. Czernichowska, Joanna, illus. 2016. (ENG.). 32p. (J). (-6). 12.99 (978-1-4926-2949-8(9), Sourcebooks Jabberwocky) Sourcebooks, Inc.

—Love Is All Around Oklahoma. Czernichowska, Joanna, illus. 2016. (ENG.). 32p. (J). (-6). 12.99 (978-1-4926-2950-4(2), Sourcebooks Jabberwocky) Sourcebooks, Inc.

—Love Is All Around Omaha. Czernichowska, Joanna, illus. 2016. (ENG.). 32p. (J). (-6). 12.99 (978-1-4926-2951-1(0), Sourcebooks Jabberwocky) Sourcebooks, Inc.

—Love Is All Around Oregon. Czernichowska, Joanna, illus. 2016. (ENG.). 32p. (J). (-6). 12.99 (978-1-4926-2952-8(9), Sourcebooks Jabberwocky) Sourcebooks, Inc.

—Love Is All Around Ottawa. Czernichowska, Joanna, illus. 2016. (ENG.). 32p. (J). (-6). 12.99 (978-1-4926-2953-5(7), Sourcebooks Jabberwocky) Sourcebooks, Inc.

—Love Is All Around Pennsylvania. Czernichowska, Joanna, illus. 2016. (ENG.). 32p. (J). (-6). 12.99 (978-1-4926-2954-2(5), Sourcebooks Jabberwocky) Sourcebooks, Inc.

—Love Is All Around Philadelphia. Czernichowska, Joanna, illus. 2016. (ENG.). 32p. (J). (-6). 12.99 (978-1-4926-2955-9(3), Sourcebooks Jabberwocky) Sourcebooks, Inc.

—Love Is All Around Pittsburgh. Czernichowska, Joanna, illus. 2016. (ENG.). 32p. (J). (-6). 12.99 (978-1-4926-2956-6(1), Sourcebooks Jabberwocky) Sourcebooks, Inc.

—Love Is All Around Portland. Czernichowska, Joanna, illus. 2016. (ENG.). 32p. (J). (-6). 12.99 (978-1-4926-2957-3(X), Sourcebooks Jabberwocky) Sourcebooks, Inc.

—Love Is All Around Rhode Island. Czernichowska, Joanna, illus. 2016. (ENG.). 32p. (J). (-6). 12.99 (978-1-4926-2958-0(8), Sourcebooks Jabberwocky) Sourcebooks, Inc.

—Love Is All Around San Francisco. Czernichowska, Joanna, illus. 2016. (ENG.). 32p. (J). (-6). 12.99 (978-1-4926-2959-7(6), Sourcebooks Jabberwocky) Sourcebooks, Inc.

—Love Is All Around South Carolina. Czernichowska, Joanna, illus. 2016. (ENG.). 32p. (J). (-6). 12.99 (978-1-4926-2960-3(X), Sourcebooks Jabberwocky) Sourcebooks, Inc.

—Love Is All Around South Dakota. Czernichowska, Joanna, illus. 2016. (ENG.). 32p. (J). (-6). 12.99 (978-1-4926-2961-0(8), Sourcebooks Jabberwocky) Sourcebooks, Inc.

—Love Is All Around St. Louis. Czernichowska, Joanna, illus. 2016. (ENG.). 32p. (J). (-6). 12.99 (978-1-4926-2962-7(6), Sourcebooks Jabberwocky) Sourcebooks, Inc.

—Love Is All Around Tennessee. Czernichowska, Joanna, illus. 2016. (ENG.). 32p. (J). (-6). 12.99 (978-1-4926-2964-1(2), Sourcebooks Jabberwocky) Sourcebooks, Inc.

—Love Is All Around Texas. Czernichowska, Joanna, illus. 2016. (ENG.). 32p. (J). (-6). 12.99 (978-1-4926-2965-8(0), Sourcebooks Jabberwocky) Sourcebooks, Inc.

—Love Is All Around the World. Czernichowska, Joanna, illus. 2016. (ENG.). 32p. (J). (-6). 12.99 (978-1-4926-3163-7(9), Sourcebooks Jabberwocky) Sourcebooks, Inc.

—Love Is All Around Toronto. Czernichowska, Joanna, illus. 2016. (ENG.). 32p. (J). (-6). 12.99 (978-1-4926-2966-5(9), Sourcebooks Jabberwocky) Sourcebooks, Inc.

—Love Is All Around Tulsa. Czernichowska, Joanna, illus. 2016. (ENG.). 32p. (J). (-6). 12.99 (978-1-4926-2967-2(7), Sourcebooks Jabberwocky) Sourcebooks, Inc.

—Love Is All Around Utah. Czernichowska, Joanna, illus. 2016. (ENG.). 32p. (J). (-6). 12.99 (978-1-4926-2968-9(5), Sourcebooks Jabberwocky) Sourcebooks, Inc.

—Love Is All Around Vermont. Czernichowska, Joanna, illus. 2016. (ENG.). 32p. (J). (-6). 12.99 (978-1-4926-2970-2(7), Sourcebooks Jabberwocky) Sourcebooks, Inc.

—Love Is All Around Virginia. Czernichowska, Joanna, illus. 2016. (ENG.). 32p. (J). (-6). 12.99 (978-1-4926-2971-9(5), Sourcebooks Jabberwocky) Sourcebooks, Inc.

—Love Is All Around Washington. Czernichowska, Joanna, illus. 2016. (ENG.). 32p. (J). (-6). 12.99 (978-1-4926-2972-6(3), Sourcebooks Jabberwocky) Sourcebooks, Inc.

—Love Is All Around Washington, DC. Czernichowska, Joanna, illus. 2016. (ENG.). 32p. (J). (-6). 12.99 (978-1-4926-2973-3(1), Sourcebooks Jabberwocky) Sourcebooks, Inc.

—Love Is All Around West Virginia. Czernichowska, Joanna, illus. 2016. (ENG.). 32p. (J). (-6). 12.99 (978-1-4926-2974-0(X), Sourcebooks Jabberwocky) Sourcebooks, Inc.

—Love Is All Around Wisconsin. Czernichowska, Joanna, illus. 2016. (ENG.). 32p. (J). (-6). 12.99 (978-1-4926-2975-7(8), Sourcebooks Jabberwocky) Sourcebooks, Inc.

—Love Is All Around Wyoming. Czernichowska, Joanna, illus. 2016. (ENG.). 32p. (J). (-6). 12.99 (978-1-4926-2976-4(6), Sourcebooks Jabberwocky) Sourcebooks, Inc.

Smith, Jane. It's Valentine's Day, Chloe Zoe! Smith, Jane, illus. 2016. (Chloe Zoe Ser.). (ENG., Illus.). 32p. (J). (gr. -1-3). 12.99 (978-0-8075-2462-6(X)) Whitman, Albert & Co.

Sourcebooks, Inc. My Little Valentine: Coupons & Stickers for the Sweetest Girl I Know. 2013. (ENG.). 48p. (J). (-4). 7.99 (978-1-4022-7959-1(0)) Sourcebooks, Inc.

Star, Nancy. Case of the Kidnapped Cupid. Bernardin, James, illus. 2005. (Calendar Club Mysteries Ser.). 79p. (J). (978-0-439-67263-4(5)) Scholastic, Inc.

Stilton, Geronimo. Geronimo's Valentine, No. 36. 2009. (Geronimo Stilton Ser.: 36). (ENG.). 128p. (J). (gr. 2-5). pap. 7.99 (978-0-545-02136-4(7), Scholastic Paperbacks) Scholastic, Inc.

—Geronimo's Valentine. 2009. (Geronimo Stilton Ser.: 36). (Illus.). 103p. (J). 18.40 (978-1-4364-5051-5(9), Turtleback) Turtleback Bks.

—Valentine's Day Disaster. Keys, Larry et al, illus. 2006. (Geronimo Stilton Ser.: No. 23). 122p. (J). lib. bdg. 18.46 (978-1-4242-0292-8(2)) Fitzgerald Bks.

—Valentine's Day Disaster. 2006. (Geronimo Stilton Ser.: No. 23). (ENG., Illus.). 128p. (J). (gr. 2-5). pap. 7.99 (978-0-439-69147-5(8), Scholastic Paperbacks) Scholastic, Inc.

Stone Arch Books. Valentine's Day & the Lunar New Year, 1 vol. Nguyen, Dustin, illus. 2014. (Batman: Li'l Gotham Ser.). (ENG.). 32p. (gr. 2-3). 22.60 (978-1-4342-9218-6(5)) Stone Arch Bks.

Sutherland, Margaret. Valentines Are for Saying I Love You. Wummer, Amy, illus. 2007. (Reading Railroad Ser.). (ENG.). 24p. (J). (gr. -1-k). mass mkt. 4.99 (978-0-448-44702-5(9), Grosset & Dunlap) Penguin Young Readers Group.

Testa, Maggie. Sealed with a Kick. 2015. (Kung Fu Panda Ready-To-Read Ser.). lib. bdg. 13.55 (978-0-606-37871-0(5)) Turtleback Bks.

Thaler, Mike. Valentine's Day from the Black Lagoon, 1 vol. 2014. (Black Lagoon Adventures Set 3 Ser.). (ENG.). 64p. (J). (gr. 3-6). lib. bdg. 24.21 (978-1-61479-209-3(7)) Spotlight.

Thompson, Lauren. Mouse's First Valentine. Erdogan, Buket, illus. 2004. (Classic Board Bks.). (ENG.). 34p. (J). (gr. -1 — 1). bds. 7.99 (978-0-689-85585-6(0), Little Simon) Little Simon.

Torres, J., et al. My Crummy Valentine, 1 vol. 2014. (Teen Titans GO! Ser.). (ENG., Illus.). 32p. (gr. 2-3). 22.60 (978-1-4342-6468-8(8)) Stone Arch Bks.

Underwood, Deborah. Here Comes Valentine Cat. Rueda, Claudia, illus. 2015. (ENG.). 88p. (J). (-k). 16.99 (978-0-525-42915-9(8), Dial Bks) Penguin Young Readers Group.

Wallace, Nancy Elizabeth. Valentine Express, 0 vols. 2008. (ENG., Illus.). 32p. (J). (gr. -1-2). pap. 9.99 (978-0-7614-5447-2(0), 9780761454472, Amazon Children's Publishing) Amazon Publishing.

Weeks, Sarah. Be Mine, Be Mine, Sweet Valentine. Kosaka, Fumi, illus. 2005. (ENG.). 20p. (J). (gr. -1-k). 9.99 (978-0-694-01514-6(8), HarperFestival) HarperCollins Pubs.

Weinberg, Jennifer Liberts. Princess Hearts. 2012. (Disney Princess Step into Reading Ser.). lib. bdg. 13.55 (978-0-606-26975-9(4), Turtleback) Turtleback Bks.

Wells, Rosemary. Max's Valentine. 2003. (Max & Ruby Ser.). (ENG., Illus.). 32p. (J). (gr. -1 — 1). bds. 5.99 (978-0-670-03668-4(4), Viking Books for Young Readers) Penguin Young Readers Group.

Wilhelm, Hans. I Love Valentine's Day! 2010. (Illus.). (J). pap. (978-0-545-13475-0(7), Cartwheel Bks.) Scholastic, Inc.

Yee, Wong Herbert. Secret Valentine. Yee, Wong Herbert, illus. 2013. (Mouse & Mole Story Ser.). (ENG., Illus.). 48p. (J). (gr. 1-4). 15.99 (978-0-547-88719-7(1)) Houghton Mifflin Harcourt Publishing Co.

VALLEY FORGE (PA.)

Allen, Thomas B. Remember Valley Forge: Patriots, Tories, & Redcoats Tell Their Stories. (ENG., Illus.). 64p. (J). (gr. 5). 2015. pap. 7.99 (978-1-4263-2250-1(X)) 2007. 17.95 (978-1-4263-0149-0(9)) 2007. lib. bdg. 27.90 (978-1-4263-0150-6(2)) National Geographic Society. (National Geographic Children's Bks.).

Jeffrey, Gary. George Washington & the Winter at Valley Forge. 2011. (Graphic Heroes of the American Revolution Ser.). 24p. (J). (gr. 3-8). pap. 8.15 (978-1-4339-6014-7(1), Gareth Stevens Learning Library) Stevens, Gareth Publishing LLLP.

Micklos, John. Washington's Crossing the Delaware & the Winter at Valley Forge: Through Primary Sources. 2013. (American Revolution Through Primary Sources Ser.). 48p. (J). (gr. 4-18). 25.27 (978-0-7660-4132-5(8)) Enslow Pubs., Inc.

VALUES

see also Ethics

ABDO Publishing Company Staff. What We Stand For. 2014. (What We Stand For Ser.: 6). (ENG.). 24p. (gr. 5-10). lib. bdg. 153.90 (978-1-62403-291-2(5), Super SandCastle) ABDO Publishing Co.

ABDO Publishing Company Staff & Doudna, Kelly. Character Concepts, 1 vol. 2007. (Character Concepts Ser.: 8). (ENG.). 24p. (J). (gr. k-3). lib. bdg. 193.68 (978-1-59928-734-8(X), SandCastle) ABDO Publishing Co.

Aguilera, Dana, et al. Character in Motion! Real Life Stories Series 5th Grade Student Workbook. 2006. 68p. (J). per. 5.95 (978-0-9765722-8-2(1)) Positively for Kids, Inc.

Allan, Delores. Magical Moments with Roy & Toni: Have You Ever. 2011. 24p. pap. 12.79 (978-1-4634-2687-3(9)) AuthorHouse.

Aloian, Molly. Live It: Respect. 2009. (Crabtree Character Sketches Ser.). (ENG., Illus.). 32p. (J). (gr. 3-6). pap. (978-0-7787-4912-7(6)); lib. bdg. (978-0-7787-4879-3(0)) Crabtree Publishing Co.

—Live It: Responsibility. 2009. (Crabtree Character Sketches Ser.). (ENG., Illus.). 32p. (J). (gr. 3-6). pap. (978-0-7787-4913-4(4)); lib. bdg. (978-0-7787-4880-9(4)) Crabtree Publishing Co.

Amoroso, Cynthia. Courage. 2013. (Values to Live By Ser.). (ENG.). 24p. (J). (gr. -1-2). 25.64 (978-1-62323-516-1(2), 206287) Child's World, Inc., The.

—Forgiveness. 2013. (Values to Live By Ser.). (ENG.). 24p. (J). (gr. -1-2). 25.64 (978-1-62323-517-8(0), 206288) Child's World, Inc., The.

—Friendliness. 2013. (Values to Live By Ser.). (ENG.). 24p. (J). (gr. -1-2). 25.64 (978-1-62323-518-5(9), 206289) Child's World, Inc., The.

—Loyalty. 2013. (Values to Live By Ser.). (ENG.). 24p. (J). (gr. -1-2). 25.64 (978-1-62323-521-5(9), 206292) Child's World, Inc., The.

—Patience. 2013. (Values to Live By Ser.). (ENG.). 24p. (J). (gr. -1-2). 25.64 (978-1-62323-522-2(7), 206293) Child's World, Inc., The.

—Tolerance. 2013. (Values to Live By Ser.). (ENG.). 24p. (J). (gr. -1-2). 25.64 (978-1-62323-527-7(8), 206298) Child's World, Inc., The.

Barron, T. A. The Hero's Trail: A Guide for a Heroic Life. 2007. (ENG., Illus.). 192p. (J). (gr. 3-7). 8.99 (978-0-14-240760-8(7), Puffin Books) Penguin Young Readers Group.

Bell, Rob. Love Wins: For Teens. 2013. (ENG., Illus.). 160p. (YA). (gr. 8). 17.99 (978-0-06-222187-2(6), Collins) HarperCollins Pubs.

Bergeron, Pastor Susan "Suzy". A Preteens Mothers Best Friend. 2012. 16p. pap. 12.68 (978-1-4669-5618-6(6)) Trafford Publishing.

Bireda, Martha. Trabue Woods Book of Values. 2006. 108p. per. (978-4-902837-20-9(X)) Aoishima Kenkyusha.

Boykin, Timothy. Timster's World: So What Makes You So Special? 2010. 36p. pap. 16.99 (978-1-4389-8506-0(1)) AuthorHouse.

Burch, Regina G. & Donovan Guntly, Jenette. I Can Show I Care. Jarrett, Michael, photos by. 2004. (Doing the Right Thing Ser.). (Illus.). 16p. (gr. -1-2). lib. bdg. 20.00 (978-0-8368-4247-0(2), Gareth Stevens Learning Library) Stevens, Gareth Publishing LLLP.

—I Can Show Respect. Ember, Kathi, illus. 2004. (Doing the Right Thing Ser.). 16p. (gr. -1-2). lib. bdg. 20.00 (978-0-8368-4248-7(0), Gareth Stevens Learning Library) Stevens, Gareth Publishing LLLP.

Character Values [Really Good Stuff]. 2011. (Character Values Ser.). 24p. pap. 35.70 (978-1-4296-6086-0(4), Pebble Bks.) Capstone Press of Coughlan Cos.

Clayton, Dallas. An Awesome Book of Thanks!, 0 vols. unabr. ed. 2010. (ENG.). 86p. (gr. 4-6). 17.95 (978-1-935597-37-7(X), 9781935597377, Two Lions) Amazon Publishing.

Cohen, Marina. Live It: Cooperation. 2009. (Crabtree Character Sketches Ser.). (ENG., Illus.). 32p. (J). (gr. 3-6). lib. bdg. (978-0-7787-4889-2(X)) Crabtree Publishing Co.

—Live It: Inclusiveness. 2009. (ENG., Illus.). 32p. (J). (gr. 3-6). lib. bdg. (978-0-7787-4890-8(1)) Crabtree Publishing Co.

Dalmatian Press Staff. A Lesson In... Thankfulness: Book to Color with Stickers. 2003. (Big Idea's Veggie Tales Ser.). (ENG., Illus.). 32p. (J). pap. 2.99 (978-1-4037-0293-7(4), Spirit Pr.) Bendon, Inc.

Deroche, Ed, et al. Character: A Guide for Middle Grade Students. 2004. (ENG.). 176p. pap., wbk. ed. 9.95 (978-1-55864-152-5(1), JIST Life) JIST Publishing.

Dyan, Penelope. Life Is a Dream! Dyan, Penelope, illus. 2013. (Illus.). 34p. pap. 11.95 (978-1-61477-091-6(3)) Bellissima Publishing, LLC.

—What Is Truth? Dyan, Penelope, illus. 2011. (Illus.). 34p. pap. 11.95 (978-1-935630-96-8(2)) Bellissima Publishing, LLC.

Edgar, Kathleen J., et al. Compassion. 2003. (J). (978-1-59203-055-2(6)) Learning Challenge, Inc.

—Courage. 2003. (J). (978-1-59203-056-9(4)) Learning Challenge, Inc.

—Determination. 2003. (J). (978-1-59203-057-6(2)) Learning Challenge, Inc.

—Imagination. 2003. (J). (978-1-59203-058-3(0)) Learning Challenge, Inc.

—Responsibility. 2003. (J). (978-1-59203-059-0(9)) Learning Challenge, Inc.

—Vision. 2003. (J). (978-1-59203-060-6(2)) Learning Challenge, Inc.

Engelhardt, Lisa O. Making Good Choices: Just for Me Book. Fitzgerald, Anne, illus. 2012. 32p. (J). pap. 7.95 (978-0-87029-514-0(4)) Abbey Pr.

Erroll, Mark. I Am Honest / Soy Honesto. 2011. (Kids of Character / Chicos con carácter Ser.). (ENG & SPA., Illus.). 24p. (J). (gr. -1-2). 22.60 (978-1-4339-4866-4(4)) Stevens, Gareth Publishing LLLP.

Espeland, Pamela & Verdick, Elizabeth. Knowing & Doing What's Right: The Positive Values Assets. 2005. (Adding Assets Series for Kids Ser.). (ENG., Illus.). 80p. (J). (gr. 3-7). pap. 7.99 (978-1-57542-184-1(4)) Free Spirit Publishing, Inc.

Geisen, Cynthia. We Are Different & Alike: A Book about Diversity. Fitzgerald, Anne, illus. 2013. 32p. (J). 7.95 (978-0-87029-557-7(8)) Abbey Pr.

Goodman, Errol. I Am Helpful / Soy Acomedida. 2011. (Kids of Character / Chicos con carácter Ser.). (ENG & SPA., Illus.). 24p. (J). (gr. -1-2). 22.60 (978-1-4339-4860-2(5)) Stevens, Gareth Publishing LLLP.

Greve, Meg. Integrity. 2012. (ENG.). 24p. (gr. k-2). pap. 8.95 (978-1-61810-270-6(2)) Rourke Educational Media.

Guzman, Maria Del C. Sheep of Many Colors: Coloring Book. Lovell, Edith, illus. 2013. 26p. pap. 5.99 (978-0-9855639-4-3(X)) Guzman, Maria del C.

Havergal, Frances Ridley. Little Pillows & Morning Bells: Good-Night Thoughts & Waking Thoughts for the Little Ones. 2004. 200p. (J). per. 14.95 (978-1-932474-25-1(0)) Solid Ground Christian Bks.

Hood, Karen Jean Matsko. Kids' Kindness: Adventures in Learning, Vol. 9. Whispering Pine Press International, ed. Artistic Design Services Staff, illus. 2015. 160p. (J). 29.95 (978-1-59808-759-8(2)); per. 19.95 (978-1-59808-757-4(6)) Whispering Pine Pr. International, Inc.

It's Good 2b Good Staff & Zemer, Sandra. It's Good 2B Good: Why It's Not Bad to Be Good. 2011. (ENG., Illus.). 106p. (J). pap. 12.95 (978-0-615-51275-4(5)) It's Good 2B Good LLC.

Jackson, Sharinese. Choices: Upper Elementary. Nyamor, Eric, illus. 2010. 112p. pap. 12.95 (978-0-9840660-3-2(9)) Second Time Media & Communications.

James, Emily. How to Be Respectful: A Question & Answer Book about Respect. 2017. (Character Matters Ser.). (ENG.). 32p. (gr. 1-2). lib. bdg. 27.32 **(978-1-5157-7200-2(4)**, Aplus Bks.) Capstone Press of Coughlan Cos.

—How to Be Responsible: A Question & Answer Book about Responsibility. 2017. (Character Matters Ser.). (ENG.). 32p. (gr. 1-2). lib. bdg. 27.32 **(978-1-5157-7201-9(2)**, Aplus Bks.) Capstone Press of Coughlan Cos.

James, Wayan. We Honor Our Elders. 2016. (Rosen REAL Readers: Social Studies Nonfiction / Fiction: Family, Community, & the World Ser.). 8p. (gr. 1-k). pap. 5.46 (978-1-5081-2275-3(X), Rosen Classroom) Rosen Publishing Group, Inc., The.

Joseph, Kurt. I Am Respectful / Soy Respetuoso. 2011. (Kids of Character / Chicos con carácter Ser.). (ENG & SPA., Illus.). 24p. (J). (gr. -1-2). 22.60 (978-1-4339-4878-7(8)) Stevens, Gareth Publishing LLLP.

Kent, Susan. Learning How to Say You Are Sorry. 2009. (Violence Prevention Library). 24p. (gr. 2-3). 42.50 (978-1-60854-267-3(X), PowerKids Pr.) Rosen Publishing Group, Inc., The.

Keuss, Jeff & Sloth, Lia. Character in Motion! Athlete Series. 2006. (Illus.). 136p. (YA). per. 5.95 (978-0-9765722-0-6(6)) Positively for Kids, Inc.

Kunjufu, Jawanza. A Culture of Respect. 2007. (ENG., Illus.). 24p. (J). (gr. k-2). pap. 9.95 (978-1-934155-06-6(3)) African American Images.

Lang, Carol, et al. Character in Motion! Real Life Stories Series 3rd Grade Student Workbook. 2006. 63p. (J). per. 5.95 (978-0-9765722-9-9(X)) Positively for Kids, Inc.

Lasi, Cindy. A B C d Is for Down. 2013. 32p. pap. 13.95 (978-1-4525-8235-1(1), Balboa Pr.) Author Solutions, Inc.

Lewis, Barbara A. What Do You Stand for? a Kid's Guide ToBuilding Character. 2014. 30.00 (978-1-63419-753-3(4)) Perfection Learning Corp.

Lewis, Barbara A. & Free Spirit Publishing Staff. What Do You Stand For? Character Building. 2006. (ENG., Illus.). 60p. (gr. 1-6). 13.99 (978-1-57542-217-6(4)) Free Spirit Publishing, Inc.

MacKenzie, Carine. My First Book of Christian Values. 2008. (My First Bks.). (ENG., Illus.). 64p. (J). (gr. -1-2). pap. 3.99 (978-1-84550-262-1(0), 7f7e41fe-7f77-4552-9163-a10f885274fd) Christian Focus Pubns. GBR. Dist: Bookmasters Distribution.

Marcovitz, Hal. Teens, Religion, & Values. 2008. (Gallup Youth Survey, Major Issues & Trends Ser.). (Illus.). 112,128p. (YA). (gr. 7-9). lib. bdg. 22.95 (978-1-59084-726-8(1)) Mason Crest.

Marshall, Shelley. Molly the Great Misses the Bus: A Book about Being on Time. Mahan, Ben, illus. 2010. (Character Education with Super Ben & Molly the Great Ser.). 24p. (J). 22.60 (978-0-7660-3518-8(2), Enslow Elementary) Enslow Pubs., Inc.

—Molly the Great's Messy Bed: A Book about Responsibility. Mahan, Ben, illus. 2010. (Character Education with Super Ben & Molly the Great Ser.). 24p. (J). 22.60 (978-0-7660-3517-1(4)) Enslow Pubs., Inc.

Mead, David. Little Ben Franklin Learns a Lesson in Generosity: Generosity. Sharp, Chris, illus. 2003. (American Virtues for Kids Ser.). (J). bds. 6.95 (978-0-9746440-2-8(1), Ideal Pubns.) Worthy Publishing.

Merino, Noël. Ethics. Greenhaven Press Staff, ed. 2015. (Opposing Viewpoints Ser.). (ENG.). 224p. (gr. 10-12). pap. 33.80 (978-0-7377-7261-6(1), Greenhaven Pr., Inc.) Cengage Gale.

Mundy, Michaelene. It's Great to Be Grateful! A Kid's Guide to Being Thankful. Alley, R. W., illus. 2012. 32p. (J). pap. 7.95 (978-0-87029-512-6(8)) Abbey Pr.

Munroe, Terri, et al. Rachel's Challenge: A Columbine Legacy Student Workbook. 2006. (YA). per. 5.95 (978-0-9765722-4-4(9)) Positively for Kids, Inc.

Mutyala, Sita. What Is Vemana Saying? 2009. (ENG., Illus.). 32p. (J). 14.95 (978-0-9818113-0-7(2)) WeShine Pr. Co.

Nettleton, Pamela Hill. Pitch In! Kids Talk about Cooperation. Muehlenhardt, Amy Bailey, illus. 2004. (Kids Talk Ser.). (ENG.). 32p. (gr. 2-5). 27.99 (978-1-4048-0621-4(0)) Picture Window Bks.

Obama, Barack. Of Thee I Sing: A Letter to My Daughters. Long, Loren, illus. 2010. (ENG.). 40p. (J). (gr. k-12). 17.99 (978-0-375-83527-8(X), Knopf Bks. for Young Readers) Random Hse. Children's Bks.

Parker, Natasha. You - Are Special Like the World: (English/French/Spanish/German/Italian/Portugese/Chinese) 2012. 50p. pap. 20.95 (978-1-4633-3940-1(2)) Palibrio.

Pittau, Francesco & Gervais, Bernadette. That's Disgusting! 2004. (ENG., Illus.). 80p. (J). (gr. -1-17). bds. 9.99 (978-1-57912-351-2(1), 81351, Black Dog & Leventhal Pubs. Inc.) Hachette Bks.

—That's Mean! 2004. (ENG., Illus.). 80p. bds. 9.95 (978-1-57912-352-9(X), 81352, Black Dog & Leventhal Pubs. Inc.) Hachette Bks.

Pryor, Kimberley Jane. Doing Your Best. 2010. (Values 2 Ser.). 32p. (gr. 1). 18.56 (978-1-60870-142-1(5)) Marshall Cavendish Corp.

—Values, 6 bks., Set. Incl. Cooperation. (J). lib. bdg. 18.56 (978-0-7614-3124-4(1)); Courage. lib. bdg. 18.56 (978-0-7614-3131-2(4), Benchmark Bks.); Honesty. lib. bdg. 18.56 (978-0-7614-3125-1(X), Benchmark Bks.); Kindness. lib. bdg. 18.56 (978-0-7614-3126-8(8), Benchmark Bks.); Respect. (J). lib. bdg. 18.56 (978-0-7614-3128-2(4)); Tolerance. (J). lib. bdg. 18.56 (978-0-7614-3129-9(2)); 32p. (gr. 1-3). (Values Ser.). 2008. Set lib. bdg. 111.36 (978-0-7614-3123-7(3), Benchmark Bks.) Marshall Cavendish Corp.

Puppet Rescue, creator. Rosie & Yellowtail Share. 2007. (Illus.). 10p. (J). 4.95 (978-0-9799958-0-4(9)) Puppet Rescue.

Raatma, Lucia. Caring. 2016. (Character Education Ser.). (ENG.). 24p. (gr. 2-3). pap. 8.10 (978-1-5157-5629-3(7), Bridgestone Bks.) Capstone Press of Coughlan Cos.

Rich, Winifred. Wake Up! To All You Are. 2011. 44p. pap. 16.95 (978-1-4525-3460-2(8)) Get Published.

Richmond, Marianne. Bedtime Blessings. 2017. (ENG.). 24p. (J). bds. 8.99 (978-1-4926-4183-4(9), 9781492641834, Sourcebooks Jabberwocky) Sourcebooks, Inc.

Rogers, Jennifer. While the Stars Are at Play. 2013. 30p. pap. 13.99 (978-1-4525-6681-8(X)) Balboa Pr.

Rorick, William. Society. 2008. 60p. pap. 17.95 (978-1-4327-2481-8(9)) Outskirts Pr., Inc.

Scheunemann, Pam. Acting with Kindness, 1 vol. 2004. (Keeping the Peace Ser.). (ENG., Illus.). 24p. (J). (gr. k-3). lib. bdg. 24.21 (978-1-59197-557-1(3), SandCastle) ABDO Publishing Co.

Schuette, Sarah L. Character Values Bilingual. Saunders-Smith, Gail, ed. (Pebble Ser.). (Illus.). (J). (gr. k-1). lib. bdg. 95.58 (978-0-7368-2353-1(0)) Capstone Press of Coughlan Cos.

Singh, Rajinder. Journey of the Phoenix. Bergen, Brenda, illus. 2011. 24p. (J). (gr. -1-3). 10.00 *(978-0-918224-83-5(7))* Radiance Pubs.
—The King's Mascot. Williams-El, Belinda Irene, illus. 2011. (ENG & ACE.). 28p. (J). (gr. -1-3). 10.00 *(978-0-918224-85-9(3))* Radiance Pubs.
Stern, Robin. We Follow the Rules. 2012. (InfoMax Readers Ser.). (ENG., Illus.). 16 pp.p. (J). (gr. k-1). pap. 7.00 *(978-1-4488-8911-2(1),* Rosen Classroom) Rosen Publishing Group, Inc., The.
Swainston, Jeani. Grandma Stuff: ... it's what love Is made Of. 2006. (J). *(978-0-9791384-0-9(X))* Rock Cliff Media.
Thomas, Pat. Everyone Matters: A First Look at Respect for Others. Harker, Lesley, illus. 2010. (First Look At... Ser.). (ENG.). 32p. (J). (gr. -1-3). pap. 7.99 *(978-0-7641-4517-9(7))* Barron's Educational Series, Inc.
Thompson, Freida. Believe. 2010. 16p. pap. 8.49 *(978-1-4490-5128-0(6))* AuthorHouse.
Walker, Robert. Live It: Initiative. 2009. (ENG., Illus.). 32p. (J). (gr. 3-6). lib. bdg. *(978-0-7787-4888-5(X))* Crabtree Publishing Co.
Weinstein, Bruce D. Is It Still Cheating If I Don't Get Caught? Russell, Harriet, illus. 2009. (ENG.). 160p. (YA). (gr. 5-9). pap. 14.99 *(978-1-59643-306-9(X),* 9781596433069) Roaring Brook Pr.
What Really Matters. 2007. (J). per. 10.00 *(978-1-930052-35-2(9))* Cherokee Bks.
Whiteside, Doug. Thank You... No, Thank You! 2009. 80p. pap. 10.49 *(978-1-4389-8173-4(2))* AuthorHouse.

VALUES—FICTION

Adame, Marie. Lemonade & Piglet in the Curse of the Rock of Musim. 2012. pap. 8.95 *(978-0-7414-7251-9(1))* Infinity Publishing.
Alam, Sarah H. Enchanting Fables. 2008. 48p. pap. 16.95 *(978-1-60441-768-5(4))* America Star Bks.
Alimonti, Frederick & Tedesco, Ann. Tommy & the T-Tops: Helping Children Overcome Prejudice. Hazard, John, illus. 2009. (Let's Talk Ser.). (ENG.). 48p. (J). (gr. -1-4). pap. 8.95 *(978-0-88282-305-8(1))* New Horizon Pr. Pubs., Inc.
Allen-Wilson, Regina. Bobo & the Pooch. 2013. 26p. pap. 12.00 *(978-1-4575-2084-6(2))* Dog Ear Publishing, LLC.
Andreae, Giles. My Little World of Happy, 9 vols. Cronin, Janet, illus. 2013. (World of Happy Ser.). (ENG.). 90p. (J). (— 1). bds. 15.99 *(978-1-4052-6082-4(3))* Egmont Bks., Ltd. GBR. Dist: Independent Pubs. Group.
Angelo, Tony. Go-bez Nibe: Very Clever Firefly, 1 vol. Lubitsky, Maribeth Jenkins, illus. 2010. 48p. 24.95 *(978-1-4489-5184-0(4))* PublishAmerica, Inc.
Baker, Lavayne L. The Return of the Black Dinosaur. 2009. 28p. pap. 12.49 *(978-1-4490-1723-1(1))* AuthorHouse.
Bakker, Merel. Maks & Mila on a Special Journey. Mini Pois Etc, illus. 2013. 54p. *(978-2-9700865-0-5(6))* Mila Publishing, Merel Bakker.
Barth, Kathleen E. The Amazing Adventures of Quigley D Pigley & His Friends. 2009. 16p. pap. 8.49 *(978-1-4389-8322-6(0))* AuthorHouse.
—The Amazing Adventures of Quigley D Pigley & His Friends: How to Become an Astronaut. 2009. 16p. pap. 8.49 *(978-1-4389-8606-7(6))* AuthorHouse.
Batten, Scott A. Johnny the Phoenix. 2008. 64p. pap. 23.95 *(978-1-4343-7297-0(9))* AuthorHouse.
Benchimol, Brigitte. Jadyn & the Magic Bubble: I Met Gandhi. Adams, Mark Wayne, illus. 2008. (J). 24.95 *(978-0-9799339-7-4(8))* East West Discovery Pr.
Berry, Ron. Let Your Light Shine. 2007. (ENG., Illus.). 16p. (J). (gr. -1-k). bds. 12.99 *(978-0-8249-6723-9(2),* Ideal Pubns.) Worthy Publishing.
Biachi, Kelvin K. Tortoise the King. 2010. 74p. pap. 21.50 *(978-1-60911-875-4(8),* Eloquent Bks.) Strategic Book Publishing & Rights Agency (SBPRA).
Binkow, Howard. Howard B. Wigglebottom on Yes or No: A Fable about Trust. Long, Taillefer, illus. 2013. (Howard B. Wigglebottom Ser.). 32p. (J). (gr. -1-3). 15.00 *(978-0-9826165-8-1(9),* We Do Listen) We Do Listen Foundation.
Blitz, Shmuel & Zakon, Miriam Stark. The Search for the Stones. Lumer, Marc, illus. 2009. 96p. (J). *(978-1-4226-0934-7(0),* Shaar Pr.) Mesorah Pubns., Ltd.
Blosser, Connie S. A Bear Named Blue. 2013. 20p. pap. 24.95 *(978-1-4626-9340-5(7))* America Star Bks.
Bohlken, Robert L. Listening to the Mukies: And Their Character Building Adventures. Veasey, Michele, illus. 2003. (J). pap. 14.95 *(978-0-930643-15-7(1))* Images Unlimited Publishing.
—Listening to the Mukies & Their Character Building Adventures. Veasey, Michele, illus. 2003. (J). 24.95 *(978-0-930643-17-1(8))* Images Unlimited Publishing.
Bombaci, James J. The Million Dollar Dog. 2010. 32p. pap. 14.99 *(978-1-4490-4936-2(2))* AuthorHouse.
Brière, Paule. The Undesirables. Beha, Philippe, illus. 2009. (ENG.). 32p. (J). (gr. -1-3). 16.95 *(978-1-894965-88-0(4))* Simply Read Bks. CAN. Dist: Ingram Publisher Services.
Broach, Elise. Gumption! Egielski, Richard, illus. 2010. (ENG.). 40p. (J). (gr. k-3). 18.99 *(978-1-4169-1628-4(8),* Atheneum Bks. for Young Readers) Simon & Schuster Children's Publishing.
Brookover, Brian D. Neddy & Little Roy Go to Town. 2013. 40p. pap. 20.99 *(978-1-4817-1185-2(7))* AuthorHouse.
Bunny, Hull. The Hidden Treasure. Fleming, Kye, illus. 2007. (Young Masters Ser.). (J). (gr. -1). 13.95 incl. audio compact disk *(978-0-9721478-8-0(8))* BrassHeart Music.
Bush, Leanne. A Very Special Christmas with Grandm. 2008. 18p. pap. 24.95 *(978-1-4241-9777-4(5))* America Star Bks.
Calvert, Ellen Hasenecz. Nine Goldfish in David's Pond. Fleming, Diana Trucks, illus. 2013. 36p. pap. 14.99 *(978-1-936745-18-0(6))* Nuevo Bks.
Camara-Macauley, Marcella. The Candy Girl. 2008. 32p. pap. 21.99 *(978-1-4415-2957-2(8))* Xlibris Corp.
Campbell, Yma Orne. Manners & Morals in Minutes for Children. 2010. 44p. pap. 16.99 *(978-1-4520-8251-6(0))* AuthorHouse.
Centineo Durrett, Marjorie. Stick People Stories. 2009. 20p. pap. 10.49 *(978-1-4490-2856-5(X))* AuthorHouse.
Chachas, George & Wojtak, James. Doolittle's Very, Very Bad Day. De Soto, Ben, illus. 2011. 26p. (J). pap. 9.95 *(978-0-9793144-2-1(9))* Dragonetti.
—The Story of Doolittle: An Exceptional Young Gorilla. De Soto, Ben, illus. 2011. 32p. (J). pap. 9.95 *(978-0-9793144-0-7(2))* Dragonetti.
Chambers, Aidan. The Kissing Game: Short Stories. 2013. (ENG.). 224p. (YA). (gr. 9-17). pap. 7.95 *(978-1-4197-0531-1(8),* Amulet Bks.) Abrams, Inc.
Ching, Brent & Santos, Jordan. Little Lima Bean. 2009. 16p. pap. 9.95 *(978-0-9821698-5-8(X))* Watermark Publishing, LLC.
Choi, JeongIm. Who's Coming Tonight? Gang, MinJeong, illus. rev. ed. 2014. (MySELF Bookshelf Ser.). (ENG.). 32p. (J). (gr. k-2). lib. bdg. 25.27 *(978-1-59953-653-8(6))* Norwood Hse. Pr.
Christenson, Jonathan. Maximilian's Mistake. Gerecke, Bretta, illus. 2012. (ENG.). 42p. (J). pap. 9.95 *(978-1-897411-35-3(9))* Bayeux Arts, Inc. CAN. Dist: Chicago Distribution Ctr.
Cline, Renee. Kawndra the Tiger. 2009. 28p. pap. 15.49 *(978-1-4389-6484-3(6))* AuthorHouse.
Compestine, Ying Chang. Revolution Is Not a Dinner Party. 2009. (ENG.). 272p. (J). (gr. 5-9). pap. 9.99 *(978-0-312-58149-7(1),* 9780312581497) Square Fish.
Cook, Julia. Cheaters Never Prosper. DuFalla, Anita, illus. 2016. (ENG.). 32p. (J). pap. 10.95 ***(978-1-944882-08-2(1))*** Boys Town Pr.
Cook, Julia. The Judgmental Flower. DuFalla, Anita, illus. 2016. (ENG.). 32p. (J). pap. 10.95 *(978-1-944882-05-1(7))* Boys Town Pr.
Cooper, Dolores Thorne. Hands Are Not for Hitting. 2005. (Illus.). 32p. (J). 7.95 *(978-1-881539-39-1(3))* Tabby Hse. Bks.
Cox, Phil Roxbee. Give That Back, Jack. 2004. (Cautionary Tales Ser.). 24p. (J). pap. 7.95 *(978-0-7945-0466-3(3),* Usborne) EDC Publishing.
Curtis, Morgan. Second-hand Alligata: A Cajun Tale. 2010. 20p. 13.99 *(978-1-4520-1673-3(9))* AuthorHouse.
Dalrymple, Marilyn. Bartholomew's Buttons. 2006. 18p. (J). 9.73 *(978-1-4116-9200-8(4))* Lulu Pr., Inc.
Davis, Holly. Thankful Together. Sokolova, Valerie, illus. 2006. 36p. (J). 5.99 *(978-0-7847-1436-2(3),* 04077) Standard Publishing.
Day, Alexandra. Frank & Ernest. 2010. (ENG., Illus.). 40p. (J). 15.95 *(978-1-59583-424-9(9),* 9781595834249, Green Tiger Pr.) Laughing Elephant.
Defosse, Rosana Curiel. Santiago y el talisman de la Luz. Barradas, Leticia, illus. (Santiago Y Los Valores Ser.). (SPA.). 32p. (J). (gr. 3-5). pap. 7.95 *(978-970-29-0131-0(6))* Santillana USA Publishing Co., Inc.
—Santiago y los Dobraks. Barradas, Leticia, illus. (SPA.). 32p. (J). (gr. 3-5). pap. 7.95 *(978-970-29-0111-2(1))* Santillana USA Publishing Co., Inc.
DeLaCroix, Alice. The Best Horse Ever. Himler, Ronald, illus. 2010. (ENG.). 80p. (J). (gr. 1-5). 15.95 *(978-0-8234-2254-8(2))* Holiday Hse., Inc.
dePaola, Tomie, illus. Look & Be Grateful. 2015. (ENG.). 32p. (J). (gr. -1). 16.95 *(978-0-8234-3443-5(5))* Holiday Hse., Inc.
Dharma Publishing Staff. The Monkey King: A Story about Compassion & Leadership. 2nd ed. 2013. (ENG.). 36p. (gr. -1-7). pap. 8.95 *(978-0-89800-495-3(0))* Dharma Publishing.
—The Spade Sage: The Story about Finding Happiness. 2nd ed. 2013. (ENG.). 36p. (gr. -1-7). pap. 8.95 *(978-0-89800-522-6(1))* Dharma Publishing.
—Three Wise Birds: A Story about Wisdom & Leadership. 3rd ed. 2013. (ENG.). 36p. (gr. -1-7). pap. 8.95 *(978-0-89800-521-9(3))* Dharma Publishing.
Dimplechin, Lord Reginald. McKenzie Was Here. 2012. 24p. pap. 24.95 *(978-1-4626-8674-2(5))* America Star Bks.
Dober, Jim. Hickory Woods Adventures: Waiting for A Bubble. 2010. pap. 14.99 *(978-1-61579-688-5(6))* Salem Author Services.
Doll, Nancy L. Buddee the Bugger & Me: Told by Mac, 1 vol. 2009. 48p. pap. 24.95 *(978-1-60749-979-4(7))* America Star Bks.
Duncan-Pauley, Chadney. A Bull's Paradise. 2009. 32p. pap. 15.60 *(978-0-557-17660-1(3))* Lulu Pr., Inc.
Dunston, Marc. The Magic of Giving, 1 vol. Cantrell, Katie, illus. 2010. (ENG.). 32p. (J). (gr. k-3). 16.99 *(978-1-58980-805-8(3))* Pelican Publishing Co., Inc.
Dureke, Jottn O. Z - the Goodluck Bird. Dureke, Jottn O., tr. 2004. (Illus.). 44p. (YA). pap. 6.95 *(978-0-9701144-1-9(9))* Jahs Publishing Group.
Dyan, Penelope. I Did It, & I Hid It! a Book about Taking Responsibility. Dyan, Penelope, illus. 2009. (Illus.). 44p. pap. 11.95 *(978-1-935118-68-8(4))* Bellissima Publishing, LLC.
Ebanks, Timali. A Caymanian Heritage Series: Christmas Time. 2013. 24p. pap. 12.50 *(978-1-4575-1726-6(4))* Dog Ear Publishing, LLC.
Edgeworth, Maria. The Bracelets or Amiability & Industry Rewarded. 2004. reprint ed. pap. 15.95 *(978-1-4191-5513-0(X));* pap. 1.99 *(978-1-4192-5513-7(4))* Kessinger Publishing, LLC.
Elkins, Christy. The Seedling Heart. 2010. (ENG.). 33p. pap. 12.00 *(978-0-557-23498-1(0))* Lulu Pr., Inc.
Emory, Kb. Tyler Tales: What Is My Color/ Different Families. 2012. 36p. pap. 21.99 *(978-1-4797-2504-5(8))* Xlibris Corp.
Escalante, Travis. The Story of Rocks & Balloons. 2013. 28p. 16.99 *(978-0-9897168-5-7(6))* Mindstir Media.
Espopo. El Leon y la Zorra. 2003. (SPA.). 24p. *(978-84-246-1564-2(6),* GL0475) La Galera, S.A. Editorial ESP. Dist: Lectorum Pubns., Inc.
Ferreira, Ann Devine & Bailey. Hi I'm Bailey & I'm Getting A New Special Family. 2011. 32p. 17.95 *(978-1-4269-5303-3(8))* Trafford Publishing.
Finch, Susan M. Dino Manners: Some Prehistoric Lessons Featuring Our Friends from the Cretaceous Period. Seda, Alison, illus. 2009. 32p. pap. 16.50 *(978-1-4490-5102-0(2))* AuthorHouse.
Finkelstein, Ruth. Guess-the-Ending Mitzvah Book. Lazewnik, Sara, illus. 2004. 26p. (J). (gr. k-3). 9.95 *(978-0-9628157-4-4(8))* Finkelstein, Ruth.
Finnan, Gary. Hector: At Ground Level a Very Simple Love Story. 2013. 112p. (gr. 10-12). 28.99 *(978-1-4525-7345-8(X));* pap. 11.99 *(978-1-4525-7343-4(3))* Author Solutions, Inc. (Balboa Pr.).
Fontaine, La. EL LEÓN Y EL RATÓN. 2003. (SPA.). 24p. *(978-84-246-1925-1(0),* GL0474) La Galera, S.A. Editorial ESP. Dist: Lectorum Pubns., Inc.
Fox, Jeannine. Feeding Penny Pig. 2009. 32p. (J). 14.95 *(978-0-9841589-1-1(X))* Mincing Mockingbird, The.
Frias, Miriam Rocio. Cuentos para Ninos Buenos - Relatos Reafirman Valores Humanos. (SPA.). (J). 7.98 *(978-970-643-238-4(8))* Selector, S.A. de C.V. MEX. Dist: AIMS International Bks., Inc.
Friedman, Laurie. Mallory & Mary Ann Take New York. Kalis, Jennifer, illus. 2013. (Mallory Ser.: 19). (ENG.). 160p. (J). (gr. 2-5). 15.95 *(978-0-7613-6074-2(3))* Lerner Publishing Group.
Fun Short Stories on Values & Morals of Life. 2003. (Illus.). 90p. (YA). per. *(978-0-9742122-0-3(2))* Aunty Ems Boutique.
Gales, Rick. Granny Puckerlips: Keepin' It Real with Kindness & Respect. 2013. 108p. (gr. 9-12). 28.95 *(978-1-4908-0438-5(2));* pap. 11.95 *(978-1-4908-0437-8(4))* Author Solutions, Inc. (WestBow Pr.).
Garcia, Katherine. Jojo & the Tule Tree. 2013. 20p. pap. 9.95 *(978-1-935752-39-4(1))* Bryce Cullen Publishing.
Gayle, Sherri. Bubbles of Faith. 2013. 48p. pap. 11.95 *(978-1-61244-076-7(2))* Halo Publishing International.
Gentilin, Isabella. Whispers of an Angel. 2010. 32p. pap. 13.00 *(978-1-60911-778-8(6),* Eloquent Bks.) Strategic Book Publishing & Rights Agency (SBPRA).
Goetz, Bracha. My Own Thank You Story in Rainbow Colored Land. 2012. (ENG.). (J). pap. *(978-1-4675-2407-0(7))* Independent Pub.
Goobie, Beth & Fernández, Queta. Ni un Día Más, 1 vol. 2009. (Spanish Soundings Ser.). (SPA.). 112p. (YA). (gr. 8-12). pap. 9.95 *(978-1-55469-137-1(0))* Orca Bk. Pubs. USA.
Gordon, Jon. Thank You & Good Night. Wallace, Donald, illus. 2016. (ENG.). 36p. (J). (gr. -1-4). 18.00 *(978-1-118-98691-2(1))* Wiley, John & Sons, Inc.
Gragg, Karla. Memphis Learns the Hard Way. Unger, Erin, illus. 2013. 28p. pap. 6.95 *(978-0-9818396-7-7(3))* True Horizon Publishing.
Grateful Steps Publishing & Tipton, Angela. Butterflies Don't Crawl. Irvine, Wil, illus. 2009. 32p. (J). 16.95 *(978-1-935130-14-7(5))* Grateful Steps.
Green, John. Terdellaline: A Free-Spirited, Energeti. 2005. 48p. pap. 16.95 *(978-1-4137-9528-8(5))* PublishAmerica, Inc.
Greene, Janice. I Spy E-Spy (Spy), 1 vol. 2017. (Pageturners Ser.). (ENG.). 76p. (YA). (gr. 9-12). 8.95 ***(978-1-68021-400-0(4))*** Saddleback Educational Publishing, Inc.
Griffin, Dorothy J. What Goes Around Comes Around. 2013. 20p. pap. 12.45 *(978-1-4908-1053-9(6),* WestBow Pr.) Author Solutions, Inc.
Grooms, Molly. We Are Puppies. 2005. 40p. bds. *(978-90-5843-815-7(5))* YoYo Bks.
Harris, Brian. Joe's Bedtime Stories for Boys & Girls. 2009. (Illus.). 240p. pap. 16.99 *(978-1-4389-7600-6(3))* AuthorHouse.
Harris, Rita & Long, Paul. The 19 Cats of Alabama. 2004. (ENG.). 35p. 24.95 *(978-1-4137-3006-7(X))* America Star Bks.
Hautman, Pete. Eden West. 2015. (ENG.). 320p. (YA). (gr. 9). 17.99 *(978-0-7636-7418-2(4))* Candlewick Pr.
Hawkins, Phycillia Maria. What's up Chuck? The Little Boy with ADHD. 2011. 16p. (gr. -1). pap. 9.36 *(978-1-4567-6200-1(1))* AuthorHouse.
Herman, Alison & Grossman, Lynne. Dolly Goes on Vacation. Eve, Lealand, illus. 2007. 22p. (J). 24.95 *(978-0-9746153-2-5(3))* DMH Pr., Inc.
—Dolly Goes to the Beach. Eve, Lealand, illus. 2007. 24p. (J). 24.95 *(978-0-9746153-1-8(5))* DMH Pr., Inc.
—Dolly Goes to the Supermarket. Eve, Lealand, illus. 2007. 22p. (J). 24.96 *(978-0-9746153-0-1(7))* DMH Pr., Inc.
Hermes, Patricia. Emma Dilemma & the New Nanny, 0 vols. Carter, Abby, illus. 2010. (Emma Dilemma Ser.: 1). (ENG.). 114p. (J). (gr. 3-6). pap. 6.99 *(978-0-7614-5619-3(8),* 9780761456193, Amazon Children's Publishing) Amazon Publishing.
—Emma Dilemma, the Nanny, & the Secret Ferret, 0 vols. Carter, Abby, illus. 2010. (Emma Dilemma Ser.: 5). (ENG.). 112p. (J). (gr. 3-6). 15.99 *(978-0-7614-5650-6(3),* 9780761456506, Amazon Children's Publishing) Amazon Publishing.
Herndon, S. N. Uncle Deek's Boating Adventure. 2012. 46p. 24.95 *(978-1-4512-7187-4(5))* America Star Bks.
Hibbs, Lisa. Allie Doogledorf & the Mighty Mess. 2009. 36p. pap. 21.99 *(978-1-4500-0777-1(5))* Xlibris Corp.
Higgs, Carolyn. The Little Knight, 1 vol. 2009. 20p. pap. 24.95 *(978-1-61546-095-3(0))* America Star Bks.
Hile, Doretta. A Place for All of Us. Barnes, William, illus. 2007. 36p. per. 14.94 *(978-1-59858-421-9(9))* Dog Ear Publishing, LLC.
Hinton, Maureen. William's Troublesome Tongue. 2010. 36p. pap. 13.95 *(978-1-60911-396-4(9),* Eloquent Bks.) Strategic Book Publishing & Rights Agency (SBPRA).
Hoban, Russell. The Sorely Trying Day. Hoban, Lillian, illus. 2010. (ENG.). 48p. (J). (gr. -1-3). 14.95 *(978-1-59017-343-5(0),* NYR Children's Collection) New York Review of Bks., Inc., The.
Hoena, Blake. Trouble with Cheating. Regan, Dana, illus. 2014. (Jess & Jaylen Ser.). (ENG.). 48p. (J). (gr. 1-4). 27.07 *(978-1-63143-442-6(X),* 208266) Child's World, Inc., The.
Holiday, Michael. Clam Land: Lessons in Life. 2013. 48p. pap. *(978-1-4602-2094-8(3))* FriesenPress.
Hoose, Phillip & Hoose, Hannah. Oye, Hormiguita. Tilley, Debbie, illus. 2004.Tr. of Hey Little Ant! (SPA.). 32p. (J). (gr. -1-2). pap. 7.99 *(978-1-58246-089-5(2),* Tricycle Pr.) Random Hse. Children's Bks.
Hopkins, Ellen. Burned. 2006. (ENG., Illus.). 544p. (YA). (gr. 9-12). 21.99 *(978-1-4169-0354-3(2),* McElderry, Margaret K. Bks.) McElderry, Margaret K. Bks.
Hotton, Rick. Holy Mole: Life Is What You Make It: Subtle Wisdom from an Unconventional Comic Strip. 2013. (ENG.). 96p. pap. *(978-1-62343-164-8(6))* Willow Creek Pr., Inc.
House, Brandy. Scorch the Dragon, 1 vol. 2009. 32p. pap. 24.95 *(978-1-60749-209-2(1))* America Star Bks.
Hull, Bunny. Young Masters: The Magic Eye. Fleming, Kye, illus. 2007. (Young Masters Ser.). (J). (gr. -1). 13.95 incl. audio compact disk *(978-0-9721478-7-3(X))* BrassHeart Music.
Ikegwuonu, Patricia Ryan. I Love My Hair, Too! 2013. 20p. pap. 24.95 *(978-1-4626-7556-2(5))* PublishAmerica, Inc.
Ivan, Benson. The Snow That Just Wouldn't Stop. Scott, Rosseau, illus. 2008. 24p. (J). pap. 8.95 *(978-0-9774754-4-5(1))* Spiritbuilding.
Jackson, Amani D. I'm a Big Boy Now. 2009. 16p. pap. 9.99 *(978-1-4389-2195-2(0))* AuthorHouse.
Jaysree. Drama. 2004. 134p. (YA). pap. 11.95 *(978-0-595-29662-0(9))* iUniverse, Inc.
Jean-Baptiste, Marie V. Goodnight & Seeyoutomorrow. 2013. 28p. pap. 24.95 *(978-1-4626-9551-5(5))* America Star Bks.
Johnston, Camille. A Gifted Book. Donahue, Linda, illus. 2008. 19p. pap. 24.95 *(978-1-60563-329-9(1))* America Star Bks.
Johnston, Carrie Lynn. Sir Bear Knight. 2008. 20p. per. 24.95 *(978-1-4241-9224-3(2))* America Star Bks.
Kallander, Susan & Boomgaarden, Larry. Up in Smoke. 2010. (Illus.). 24p. pap. 11.50 *(978-1-60860-934-5(0),* Eloquent Bks.) Strategic Book Publishing & Rights Agency (SBPRA).
Katz, Karen. No Hitting! Katz, Karen, illus. 2004. (ENG., Illus.). 14p. (J). (gr. -1-k). 5.99 *(978-0-448-43612-8(4),* Grosset & Dunlap) Penguin Young Readers Group.
Kenney, Cindy. Project Precious Paws, Bk. 3. 2009. 86p. (J). 9.95 *(978-0-9817159-5-7(8));* pap. 5.99 *(978-0-9817159-4-0(X))* Precious Moments, Inc.
Kline, Lpc. Flutter Flies Away: A Book about Rules. 2009. 32p. pap. 14.99 *(978-1-4389-9747-6(7))* AuthorHouse.
Korman, Gordon. Slacker. 2017. (ENG.). 240p. (J). (gr. 3-7). pap. 6.99 ***(978-0-545-82316-6(1),*** Scholastic Pr.) Scholastic, Inc.
Lammertink, Ilona. Don't Be Afraid to Say No! Georger, Lucie, illus. 2013. (ENG.). 32p. (J). (gr. k-2). 15.95 *(978-1-60537-148-1(3))* Cobblestone Publishing Co.
Lamphere-Slaughter, Sharyn. Droopy Drawers & the Peg Leg Pirate. 2009. 24p. pap. 12.99 *(978-1-4490-6055-8(2))* AuthorHouse.
Law, Felicia. Cairo the Camel: A Tale of Responsibility. Danson, Lesley, illus. 2010. (Animal Fair Values Ser.). (ENG.). 32p. (J). (gr. -1-3). pap. 10.55 *(978-1-60754-911-6(5));* lib. bdg. 22.60 *(978-1-60754-903-1(4))* Windmill Bks.
Lee, R. Lacey Learns: Love & Beauty. 2012. 44p. pap. 21.99 *(978-1-4797-1535-0(2))* Xlibris Corp.
Lee, Spike & Lee, Tonya Lewis. Giant Steps to Change the World. Qualls, Sean, illus. 2011. (ENG.). 40p. (J). (gr. -1). 18.99 *(978-0-689-86815-3(4),* Simon & Schuster Bks. For Young Readers) Simon & Schuster Bks. For Young Readers.
Lescuyer, Moira. Little Life Reminders. 2010. 16p. 7.95 *(978-1-4525-0037-9(1))* Get Published.
Liette, Chad. The Downy Duck. 2013. 16p. pap. 12.70 *(978-1-4669-8469-1(4))* Trafford Publishing.
Lilly, T. S. The Upgrade. 2008. 60p. pap. 16.95 *(978-1-60441-536-0(3))* America Star Bks.
Lima, Rick. Redd: The Beta Fish. 2009. 28p. pap. 12.49 *(978-1-4389-4320-6(2))* AuthorHouse.
Linseman, Daniel. Shroobear's First Swim: Book I of the Shroobear Short Stories. 2008. 36p. pap. 15.49 *(978-1-4343-8252-8(4))* AuthorHouse.
Litzenberg, Corinne M. Grandpa's Basement, 1 vol. 2007. (ENG., Illus.). 32p. (J). 14.95 *(978-0-7643-2720-9(8),* 9780764327209) Schiffer Publishing, Ltd.
Logsted, Greg. Something Happened. 2008. (ENG.). 208p. (YA). (gr. 7-9). pap. 8.99 *(978-1-4169-5078-3(8),* Simon Pulse) Simon Pulse.
Longus. The ADVENTURES of SILVANA & the MAGIC UNICORN. 2008. 48p. 18.95 *(978-1-4357-1877-7(1))* Lulu Pr., Inc.
Lorenzo, Alejandro. Mateo's Progress/Jornadas de Mateo: Tales for Children of All Ages/Cuentos para Niños de Todas las Edades. 2004. (SPA & ENG., Illus.). 96p. (J). 20.00 *(978-0-9714366-3-3(0))* Pureplay Pr.
Lowery, Marie Hayes. Beau & Friends. 2012. 20p. pap. 17.99 *(978-1-4817-0106-8(1))* AuthorHouse.
Luscier, Kim. Steven Learns about Temper Tantrums, 1 vol. 2009. 48p. pap. 16.95 *(978-1-60749-692-2(5))* America Star Bks.
Maddox, Jake. The Hunter's Code. Tiffany, Sean, illus. 2008. (Jake Maddox Sports Stories Ser.). (ENG.). 72p. (gr. 2-3). 25.32 *(978-1-4342-0782-1(X));* pap. 5.95 *(978-1-4342-0878-1(8))* Stone Arch Bks.
—Off the Bench, 1 vol. Tiffany, Sean, illus. 2010. (Team Jake Maddox Sports Stories Ser.). (ENG.). 72p. (gr. 2-3). pap. 5.95 *(978-1-4342-2278-7(0));* lib. bdg. 25.32 *(978-1-4342-1922-0(4))* Stone Arch Bks.
—Win or Lose. Tiffany, Sean, illus. 2010. (Team Jake Maddox Sports Stories Ser.). (ENG.). 72p. (gr. 2-3). pap. 5.95 *(978-1-4342-2281-7(0))* Stone Arch Bks.
Magsamen, Sandra. I Love You Beary Much. 2014. (Earisistables Ser.). (ENG., Illus.). 14p. (J). (gr. -1 — 1). bds. 7.99 *(978-0-316-25516-5(5))* Little, Brown Bks. for Young Readers.
Maidment, Stella & Wilde, Oscar. The Star Child. Whelan, Olwyn, tr. Whelan, Olwyn, illus. gif. ed. 2003. 40p. (YA). *(978-1-84365-012-6(6),* Pavilion Children's Books) Pavilion Bks.
Mallory, Barbara. Shantelle: Angels, Stars & Faith. 2008. pap. 16.95 *(978-1-60563-038-0(1))* America Star Bks.
Marie, Tina. Isabella Learns the Value of Money. 2011. 24p. pap. 12.95 *(978-1-4567-4537-0(9))* AuthorHouse.
Marr, Kendra Lynn. I Was Rufus. 2013. 20p. pap. 24.95 *(978-1-4626-9917-9(0))* America Star Bks.
Marro, Barbara. Smitty's Cave Adventures. 2010. 147p. pap. 12.95 *(978-1-4327-4340-6(6))* Outskirts Pr., Inc.
Marrs, J. Pierce & Marrs, S. Nick. Andy Goes to the Aquarium. 2013. 48p. pap. 14.99 *(978-0-9896681-0-1(X))* 4mPr.
Matyas, Diane. The Terrible Captain Jack Visits the Museum: Or A Guide of Museum Manners for Incorrigible Pirates & the Like. 2008. (Illus.). 24p. (J). *(978-0-9623017-2-8(8))* Noble Maritime Collection, The.
Mayer, Mercer. You Go First, 1 vol. 2013. (ENG., Illus.). 24p. (J). pap. 3.99 *(978-1-4003-2245-9(6));* bds. 9.99 *(978-1-4003-2244-2(8))* Nelson, Thomas Inc.
McCann, Thomas P. "Tom". The Tree Nobody Wanted: A Christmas Story. 2007. 14.95 *(978-0-9797407-0-1(3))* Exeter Pr.
McClain M.Ed. Ncc, Ashley. Not So Perfect Polly. 2011. 40p. pap. *(978-1-4269-7126-6(5))* Trafford Publishing (UK) Ltd.

TUV

McClure, Brian D. The Ants. Plumlee, Buddy, illus. 2009. (Brian D. Mcclure Childrens Book Collection). 57p. (J). (gr. -1-3). 16.95 *(978-1-933426-10-5(1))* Universal Flag Publishing.

—The Birds & the Frogs. Plumlee, Buddy, illus. 2009. (Brian D. Mcclure Childrens Book Collection). 37p. (J). (gr. -1-3). 16.95 *(978-1-933426-13-6(6))* Universal Flag Publishing.

—The Meal. Plumlee, Buddy, illus. 2009. (Brian D. Mcclure Childrens Book Collection). 59p. (J). (gr. -1-3). 16.95 *(978-1-933426-04-4(7))* Universal Flag Publishing.

—The Up down Day. Plumlee, Buddy, illus. 2009. (Brian D. Mcclure Childrens Book Collection). 47p. (J). (gr. -1-3). 14.95 *(978-1-933426-07-5(1))* Universal Flag Publishing.

McDine, Donna M. Hockey Agony. Hammond, Julie, illus. 2013. 20p. pap. 9.95 *(978-1-61633-360-7(X))* Guardian Angel Publishing, Inc.

McDonald, Megan. Judy Moody Declares Independence. 2010. (Judy Moody Ser.: 6). lib. bdg. 16.00 *(978-0-606-12345-7(8),* Turtleback) Turtleback Bks.

Meadows, Thomas. The Tales of Tommy Tucker: My Private Parts Are Private! 2013. 20p. pap. 13.77 *(978-1-4669-8895-8(9))* Trafford Publishing.

—The Tales of Tommy Tucker: Pizza Pie Patty! 2013. 36p. pap. 17.25 *(978-1-4669-8894-1(0))* Trafford Publishing.

Mendoza, S. J. How about Me. 2012. 156p. pap. 19.99 *(978-1-4797-0704-1(X))* Xlibris Corp.

Mescall, Ron. The Adventures of Goo Goo Malou: A Parent's Guide for Teaching Values. 2009. 24p. pap. 10.96 *(978-1-4269-0836-1(9))* Trafford Publishing.

Miller, Dennis. ABCs of Character. Wallace, Sam Amber, illus. 2003. 52p. (J). lib. bdg. 15.95 *(978-0-9722259-1-5(9))* Twin Peaks Publishing, Inc.

Miller, Gary R. Taming Chaos Workbook: Leaders Discussion Guide. 2017. (ENG., Illus.). 70p. (J). (gr. 7-9). pap. 14.95 *(978-1-68350-155-8(1))* Morgan James Publishing.

Miller, Jennifer. Christmas Tails. Knight, Vanessa, illus. 2009. 56p. pap. 17.26 *(978-1-4251-8987-7(3))* Trafford Publishing.

Miller, Linda K. Ronald the Church Mouse. 2008. 96p. pap. 12.00 *(978-1-60693-063-2(X),* Eloquent Bks.) Strategic Book Publishing & Rights Agency (SBPRA).

Miner, Deb. I get Around. Miner, Deb, illus. 2007. (ENG., Illus.). 32p. (J). bds. 11.00 *(978-0-9794262-0-9(0))* do be you.

Murphy, Stuart J. Good Job, Ajay! 2010. (I See I Learn Ser.). (ENG., Illus.). 32p. (J). (gr. -1-k). pap. 6.95 *(978-1-58089-455-5(0))* Charlesbridge Publishing, Inc.

Nambiar, Vinesh. Adventures in Human Values - Series 4: Strength, Bravery, Gratitude, Acceptance, Discipline, Happiness, Cooperation, Hope, Self-Control. Ralte, Albert Lalmuanpuia, illus. 2012. (J). pap. 9.99 *(978-0-9798986-3-1(3))* Human Values 4 Kids Foundation, The.

Neylon, Robbie. The Real Me. 2013. 24p. pap. 15.99 *(978-1-4797-5718-3(7))* Xlibris Corp.

Nighthawk, Tori. Don't Judge a Bird by Its Feathers. Nighthawk, Tori, illus. 2013. (ENG., Illus.). 60p. (J). (gr. -1-3). 17.99 *(978-0-9858811-9-1(4))* Stone, Anne Publishing.

Oliver, Lauren. Before I Fall Movie Tie-In Edition. 2017. 496p. (YA). (gr. 9). pap. 10.99 *(978-0-06-265632-2(5))* HarperCollins Pubs.

Orr, Fran E. When Mommy Was a Soldier, 1 vol. 2008. (ENG.). 26p. 24.95 *(978-1-4241-9576-3(4))* America Star Bks.

Otoshi, Kathryn. Zero. 2010. (ENG., Illus.). 32p. (J). (gr. -1-3). 17.95 *(978-0-9723946-3-5(X))* KO Kids Bks.

Page, Shari. Little Master of Tall Tales. 2004. 17p. pap. 11.07 *(978-1-4116-1568-7(9))* Lulu Pr., Inc.

Pallone, Robert. The Adventures of Main Man: A Child's View of the World. 2010. 28p. pap. 12.95 *(978-1-4490-5598-1(2))* AuthorHouse.

Paratore, Coleen Murtagh. Big. O'Malley, Judy, ed. Fennell, Clare, illus. 2012. (ENG.). 32p. (J). (gr. -1-2). 18.95 *(978-0-9829938-5-9(4))* March 4th, Inc.

Parrish, Terry. Wiffenpoof. 2012. 28p. pap. 24.95 *(978-1-4626-7942-3(0))* America Star Bks.

Pearce, Jackson. Purity. 2013. (ENG.). 224p. (YA). (gr. 10-17). pap. 9.00 *(978-0-316-18247-8(8))* Little, Brown Bks. for Young Readers.

Pearson, Mary E. The Adoration of Jenna Fox. 2009. (Jenna Fox Chronicles Ser.: 1). (ENG.). 288p. (YA). (gr. 7-12). pap. 10.99 *(978-0-312-59441-1(0),* 9780312594411) Square Fish.

Peeler, Casey. Losing Charley. 2015. (ENG.). (C). pap. 12.99 *(978-0-9961521-2-9(1))* Peeler, Casey.

Peirce, Lincoln. Big Nate — Great Minds Think Alike. 2014. (Big Nate Graphic Novels Ser.). lib. bdg. 20.85 *(978-0-606-35229-1(5))* Turtleback Bks.

Perez, Angela J. Zack Attack! Hazard, Andrea, illus. 2007. 36p. (J). 17.95 *(978-0-9778328-9-7(9))* His Work Christian Publishing.

Pham, LeUyen. There's No Such Thing As Little. 2015. (ENG., Illus.). 48p. (J). (gr. -1-2). 17.99 *(978-0-385-39150-4(1),* Knopf Bks. for Young Readers) Random Hse. Children's Bks.

Pittau, Francesco & Gervais, Bernadette. That's Dangerous! 2004. (ENG., Illus.). 80p. 9.99 *(978-1-57912-350-5(3),* 81350, Black Dog & Leventhal Pubs. Inc.) Hachette Bks.

Price, Diane J. Tiny Story, Vol. 1. Csavas, Sally, illus. 2008. 28p. (J). 9.00 *(978-0-9789637-0-5(9))* Price, Diane Joan.

Puzzanghera, Marcia. Holly the Multi-Colored Girl. 2012. 24p. pap. 19.99 *(978-1-4685-6249-1(5))* AuthorHouse.

Quinn, Gloria W. Lemon Water. 2012. 24p. pap. 24.95 *(978-1-4626-8877-7(2))* America Star Bks.

Raghbeer, Anjali. Rescue by Design: Madhubani Art. Modak, Tejas, illus. 2012. (Art Tales from India Ser.). (ENG.). 24p. 14.95 *(978-81-8328-194-2(X))* Wisdom Tree IND. Dist: SCB Distributors.

Raichert, Lance, illus. Treasury of Values for Children. 2012. 159p. (J). *(978-1-4508-3729-3(8))* Phoenix International Publications, Inc.

Raines, Jennifer. Laughs for Porcupine, 1 vol. 2009. 18p. pap. 24.95 *(978-1-60836-784-9(3))* America Star Bks.

Ramrattan Smith, Sherry & Smith, Benjamin Eric. Brothers: Best Friends Growing Up. 2010. 28p. pap. 14.95 *(978-1-4490-6339-9(X))* AuthorHouse.

Rawlings, John S. Sometimes Boxes Make the Best Forts. Espina, Vito, illus. 2006. (J). pap. 15.00 *(978-0-8059-7181-1(5))* Dorrance Publishing Co., Inc.

Rice, Clay. The Stick. Rice, Clay, illus. 2014. (ENG., Illus.). 32p. (J). 16.95 *(978-1-939629-28-9(4),* 9781939629289) Familius LLC.

Richards, Arlene. That's Bingzy! Busy Building Self-Esteem. 2007. (J). per. 15.95 *(978-0-9794323-2-3(4))* Bing Note, Inc.

Romero, Vivian. On the Lam with Lambert. 2009. 24p. pap. 12.99 *(978-1-4490-2773-5(3))* AuthorHouse.

Rosales, Irene González. Esmeralda Does Very Good Things. 2012. 46p. pap. 14.95 *(978-0-9824348-2-6(0))* Rosales, Irene.

Rosenthal, Amy Krouse. It's Not Fair! Lichtenheld, Tom, illus. 2008. (ENG.). 40p. (J). (gr. -1-3). 16.99 *(978-0-06-115257-3(9))* HarperCollins Pubs.

Rushford, Betty. Best Buddies: And the Fruit of the Spirit. 2003. 41p. pap. 24.95 *(978-1-59286-746-2(4))* America Star Bks.

Russell, Allyson. The Lizard Who Wanted to Be a Mouse. Bubp, Jennifer, illus. 2009. 28p. pap. 12.95 *(978-1-59858-938-2(5))* Dog Ear Publishing, LLC.

Sangha Mitra, Ms Janice. Golden Bear: The Story of a Flowering Heart. Sangha Mitra, Ms Janice, illus. 4th ed. 2013. (ENG., Illus.). 38p. pap. *(978-0-9805945-2-2(9))* Little Bear Values.

Sankey, Erica. Magic Dust. 2010. 32p. pap. 16.49 *(978-1-4490-0893-2(3))* AuthorHouse.

Santana, Sr. Stella. We Are the People of This World: Book One. Bear, Andrea, illus. 2011. 40p. pap. 14.95 *(978-1-61204-643-3(6),* Eloquent Bks.) Strategic Book Publishing & Rights Agency (SBPRA).

Sapp, Brent. Teknon & the Champion Warriors. Cariello, Sergio, illus. 2003. 7.99 *(978-1-57229-219-2(9))* FamilyLife.

Schraff, Anne. The Quality of Mercy, 1 vol. unabr. ed. 2011. (Urban Underground Ser.). (ENG.). 183p. (YA). (gr. 9-12). pap. 9.95 *(978-1-61651-006-0(4))* Saddleback Educational Publishing, Inc.

—The Terrible Orchid Sky (Adventure), 1 vol. 2017. (Pageturners Ser.). (ENG.). 76p. (YA). (gr. 9-12). 8.95 ***(978-1-68021-380-5(6))*** Saddleback Educational Publishing, Inc.

—To Be a Man, 1 vol. unabr. ed. 2011. (Urban Underground Ser.). (ENG.). 181p. (YA). (gr. 9-12). pap. 9.95 *(978-1-61651-008-4(0))* Saddleback Educational Publishing, Inc.

—Urban Underground Class Set. 2010. (J). pap. 119.50 *(978-1-61651-012-1(9))* Saddleback Educational Publishing, Inc.

—Urban Underground Complete Set. 2010. (J). pap. 190.20 *(978-1-61651-011-4(0))* Saddleback Educational Publishing, Inc.

Seuss, Dr. Dr. Seuss's Ultimate Horton Collection, 3 vols., Set. 2015. (ENG., Illus.). 192p. (J). (gr. -1-3). 44.95 *(978-0-553-50908-3(X),* Random Hse. Bks. for Young Readers) Random Hse. Children's Bks.

Shang, Anthony. When Jack Meets Jill: A Backstory to the Nursery Rhyme. 2014. 80p. (gr. 2-2). pap. 12.17 *(978-1-4828-9675-6(3))* Partridge Pub.

Shelton, Donna. Breaking Dawn, 1 vol. unabr. ed. 2012. (Cutting Edge Ser.). (ENG.). 170p. (YA). (gr. 9-12). pap. 9.95 *(978-1-61651-758-8(1))* Saddleback Educational Publishing, Inc.

Short M.S., Jeff. A Kid's World, 1 vol. 2009. (Illus.). 48p. pap. 24.95 *(978-1-60836-760-3(6))* America Star Bks.

Silberman, Dani. The Three Monkey Brothers. 2009. 28p. pap. 14.50 *(978-1-60860-366-4(0),* Eloquent Bks.) Strategic Book Publishing & Rights Agency (SBPRA).

Simon, Mary Manz. Tiger Forgives. Clearwater, Linda & Couri, Kathy, illus. 2006. (First Virtues for Toddlers Ser.). 20p. (J). 5.99 *(978-0-7847-1413-3(4),* 04065) Standard Publishing.

Singletary, Gladys Renae. A Snowman with a Heart. 2012. 24p. pap. 17.99 *(978-1-4685-9642-7(X))* AuthorHouse.

Sinke, Grandma Janet Mary. I Wanna Go to Grandma's House. Pennington, Craig, illus. 2003. (Grandma Janet Mary Ser.). 50p. (J). *(978-0-9742732-0-4(1))* My Grandma & Me Pubs.

Skocz, Anita Joyce. Kite Tale. 2011. 40p. pap. 16.95 *(978-1-4525-3889-1(1))* Get Published.

Smith, Jennifer & Morgan, Andre. Zelza Zero. 2010. 20p. pap. 12.99 *(978-1-4490-4546-3(4))* AuthorHouse.

Smith, Sindy. Little Lucy Lou. Smith, Sindy, illus. 2012. (Illus.). 38p. 29.95 *(978-1-4489-3350-1(1))* America Star Bks.

Sommer, Carl. If Only I Were... 2003. (Another Sommer-Time Story Ser.). (Illus.). 48p. (J). (gr. k-4). lib. bdg. 23.95 incl. audio *(978-1-57537-752-0(7))* Advance Publishing, Inc.

—If Only I Were... James, Kennon, illus. 2003. (Another Sommer-Time Story Ser.). (ENG.). 48p. (J). (gr. k-4). lib. bdg. 23.95 incl. audio compact disk *(978-1-57537-702-5(0))* Advance Publishing, Inc.

—Mayor for A Day Read-along 2003. (Another Sommer-Time Story Ser.). (Illus.). 48p. (J). lib. bdg. 23.95 incl. audio *(978-1-57537-763-6(2))* Advance Publishing, Inc.

—No One Will Ever Know Read-Along. 2003. (Another Sommer-Time Story Ser.). (Illus.). 48p. (J). lib. bdg. 23.95 incl. audio *(978-1-57537-756-8(X))* Advance Publishing, Inc.

—No One Will Ever Know Read-Along, 1 bk. Westbrook, Dick, illus. 2003. (Another Sommer-Time Story Ser.). (ENG.). 48p. (J). lib. bdg. 23.95 incl. audio compact disk *(978-1-57537-706-3(3))* Advance Publishing, Inc.

—Noise! Noise! Noise! James, Kennon, illus. 2003. (Another Sommer-Time Story Ser.). (ENG.). 48p. (J). lib. bdg. 23.95 incl. audio compact disk *(978-1-57537-719-3(5))* Advance Publishing, Inc.

—Proud Rooster & Little Hen 2003. (Another Sommer-Time Story Ser.). (Illus.). 48p. (J). lib. bdg. 23.95 incl. audio *(978-1-57537-760-5(8))* Advance Publishing, Inc.

—Proud Rooster & Little Hen. Budwine, Greg, illus. 2003. (Another Great Achiever Ser.). (ENG.). 48p. (J). lib. bdg. 23.95 incl. audio compact disk *(978-1-57537-710-0(1))* Advance Publishing, Inc.

Spinelli, Eileen. Thankful, 1 vol. Preston, Archie, illus. 2015. (ENG.). 32p. (J). 16.99 *(978-0-310-00088-4(2))* Zonderkidz.

Springstubb, Tricia. Cody & the Rules of Life. Wheeler, Eliza, illus. 2017. (ENG.). 176p. (J). (gr. 2-5). 14.99 *(978-0-7636-7920-0(8))* Candlewick Pr.

St. John, Patricia. Friska My Friend & the Other Kitten. 2003. (Illus.). 192p. 6.49 *(978-1-85999-312-5(5))* Scripture Union GBR. Dist: Gabriel Resources.

Standish, Burt L. Frank Merriwell's Generosity. Rudman, Jack, ed. 2003. (Frank Merriwell Ser.). 29.95 *(978-0-8373-9352-0(3))*; pap. 9.95 *(978-0-8373-9052-9(4))* Merriwell, Frank Inc.

Stein, Catherine. Madley Doesn't Want To. 2011. 24p. pap. 11.32 *(978-1-4634-2259-2(8))* AuthorHouse.

Stewart, Bob. Baily Bumble Bee. 2009. 32p. pap. 14.49 *(978-1-4389-7254-1(7))* AuthorHouse.

Stripland, Rubye Weldon. Lucy Bell, Queen of the Pasture Book Four. 2009. 94p. pap. 10.96 *(978-1-4357-4742-5(9))* Lulu Pr., Inc.

Sydor, Colleen. Timmerman Was Here. Debon, Nicolas, illus. 2009. (ENG.). 32p. (J). (gr. -1-1). 19.95 *(978-0-88776-890-3(3),* Tundra Bks.) Tundra Bks. CAN. Dist: Penguin Random Hse. LLC.

Tewkesbury, Alexa. Danny's Daring Days, 1 vol. 2009. (Topz Secret Diaries). (ENG., Illus.). 128p. pap. *(978-1-85345-502-5(4))* Crusade for World Revival.

Thomas, Jason. The Adventures of Bird & Gator: Best Friends. 2012. 24p. pap. 12.56 *(978-1-4669-4973-7(2))* Trafford Publishing.

Thomas, Nayomi. The Thankables: Three Little Creatures with Very Large Features. 2013. 20p. pap. 10.99 *(978-1-4908-0562-7(1),* WestBow Pr.) Author Solutions, Inc.

Thomas The Toad. Willie the Frog Learns to Fly. 2009. 68p. pap. 27.49 *(978-1-4389-6997-8(X))* AuthorHouse.

Thrasher, Amanda M. Mischief in the Mushroom Patch. 2009. 174p. 23.75 *(978-1-60860-722-8(4),* Strategic Bk. Publishing) Strategic Book Publishing & Rights Agency (SBPRA).

Tidwell, Deborah Swayne. Magic Eraser: And the Substitute Teacher. 2008. 24p. pap. 12.99 *(978-1-4343-8107-1(2))* AuthorHouse.

Todd, Chelva E. Up from the Barber's Chair. 2012. 44p. pap. 17.49 *(978-1-4691-4476-4(X))* Xlibris Corp.

Tommy. Bubba & Cecil. 2009. 52p. pap. 16.95 *(978-1-60836-860-0(2))* America Star Bks.

Torrance-Matthews, Armer, et al. Miss Bertha, the Talking Tree: A Delightful Story of a Talking Tree. 2010. 36p. pap. 18.95 *(978-1-4269-2051-6(2))* Trafford Publishing.

Valentine, Billy. Trust Love: A Tale of Angels. 2008. 176p. (J). 23.95 *(978-0-595-48801-8(3))* iUniverse, Inc.

VanCil, Marybelle. Sadie Fourpaws & the Magic Rocking Chair. 2009. (Illus.). 57p. pap. 26.95 *(978-1-4327-3642-2(6))* Outskirts Pr., Inc.

Vertley, Barbara. Back in the Day. 2007. 52p. per. 16.95 *(978-1-4241-9549-7(7))* PublishAmerica, Inc.

Vishpriya. Tales from Indi: Character Counts! RESPECT. Ruble, Eugene, illus. 2009. 24p. pap. 10.95 *(978-1-933090-57-3(X))* Guardian Angel Publishing, Inc.

Walder, Lysa. Katie the Paramedic. 2009. (Illus.). 28p. pap. 12.49 *(978-1-4389-7134-6(6))* AuthorHouse.

Walters, Eric. House Party, 1 vol. 2007. (Orca Soundings Ser.). (ENG.). (YA). (gr. 8-12). 112p. 14.95 *(978-1-55143-743-9(0))*; 128p. pap. 9.95 *(978-1-55143-741-5(4))* Orca Bk. Pubs. USA.

Waterton, Betty. A Salmon for Simon, 1 vol. Blades, Ann, illus. 35th ed. 2013. (ENG.). 32p. (J). (gr. -1-k). 14.95 *(978-1-55498-392-6(4))* Groundwood Bks. CAN. Dist: Publishers Group West (PGW).

Weiss, Fred G. Mag-Nan-I-Mous Monkey & Gerald Giraffe. 2013. 28p. 18.99 *(978-0-9898820-5-7(5))* Mindstir Media.

Westling, Vicki Diane. Cats Keep Out: Sam & Friends. 2009. 40p. pap. 16.99 *(978-1-4490-3623-2(6))* AuthorHouse.

White, Andrea. Radiant Girl. 2008. (ENG.). 256p. (J). (gr. 4-7). 19.95 *(978-1-933979-23-6(2),* 9781933979236) Bright Sky Pr.

White, Becky. PawPrints on Your Heart. Cranford, Darren, illus. 2013. 64p. (J). 18.95 *(978-0-9860169-0-5(X))* Vision Chapters Publishing Co.

White, Jamie Nicole. How I Wish I Could Share My Nice Words. 2013. 28p. pap. 24.95 *(978-1-4626-6953-0(0))* America Star Bks.

White, Pauline. Jewel Baxter & Friends, 1 vol. 2009. 48p. pap. 16.95 *(978-1-60813-541-7(1))* America Star Bks.

Wilhelm, Kj. Grandma Coocoonutts Goes to Boston. 2009. 28p. pap. 15.99 *(978-1-4363-9933-3(5))* Xlibris Corp.

Willard, Gerald. Amy Firefly. 2009. 40p. pap. 18.50 *(978-1-60693-448-7(1),* Eloquent Bks.) Strategic Book Publishing & Rights Agency (SBPRA).

Williams, Shannon. School Rules! Nelson, Anndria, illus. 2010. 36p. pap. 16.99 *(978-1-4520-3924-4(0))* AuthorHouse.

Wilson, Rosalee. A Mushy Mouse Tale. 2009. 69p. pap. 24.58 *(978-0-557-10084-2(4))* Lulu Pr., Inc.

Womack, Vernesia. What If... 2004. (J). pap. 7.00 *(978-0-8059-6383-0(9))* Dorrance Publishing Co., Inc.

Wyatt, Cherokee. The Adventures of Margaret Mouse: Harvest Carnival. l.t. ed. 2006. (Illus.). 32p. (J). 6.95 *(978-0-9761326-5-3(6))* www.margaretmouse.com publishing co.

Yang, John, Sr. You Can Eat Cheese but Don't Be Cheesy. 2003. (Illus.). 58p. (J). per. *(978-0-9743080-0-5(5))* Painting With Words.

Yasuda, Anita. I've Got the No-Skateboard Blues, 1 vol. Santillan, Jorge H., illus. 2012. (Sports Illustrated Kids Victory School Superstars Ser.). (ENG.). 56p. (gr. 1-3). pap. 5.95 *(978-1-4342-3866-5(0))*; lib. bdg. 26.65 *(978-1-4342-2244-2(6))* Stone Arch Bks.

Zambak Çucok Publishing Staff, ed. Lost: Niloya 3. 2016. (J). pap. 4.99 *(978-1-4621-1864-9(X),* Horizon Pubs.) Cedar Fort, Inc./CFI Distribution.

—The Onion: Niloya 2. 2016. (J). pap. 4.99 *(978-1-4621-1863-2(1),* Horizon Pubs.) Cedar Fort, Inc./CFI Distribution.

—The Rainbow: Niloya 1. 2016. (J). pap. 4.99 *(978-1-4621-1862-5(3),* Horizon Pubs.) Cedar Fort, Inc./CFI Distribution.

VAMPIRES

ABDO Publishing Company Staff. Creatures of Legend. 2014. (Creatures of Legend Ser.: 6). (ENG.). 48p. (gr. 3-6). lib. bdg. 196.74 *(978-1-62403-149-6(8))* ABDO Publishing Co.

Altmann, Scott. Vampire Mazes. 2011. (Dover Children's Activity Bks.). (ENG., Illus.). 48p. (J). (gr. 3-4). pap. 4.99 *(978-0-486-47922-4(6))* Dover Pubns., Inc.

Bennett, Adelaide. Ancient Werewolves & Vampires: The Roots of the Teeth. 2010. (Making of a Monster Ser.). (Illus.). 64p. (YA). (gr. 7-18). pap. 9.95 *(978-1-4222-1955-3(0))*; lib. bdg. 22.95 *(978-1-4222-1802-0(3))* Mason Crest.

—Global Legends & Lore: Vampires & Werewolves Around the World. 2010. (Making of a Monster Ser.). 64p. (YA). (gr. 7-18). pap. 9.95 *(978-1-4222-1963-8(1))* Mason Crest.

Bingham, Jane. Vampires & Werewolves, 1 vol. King, Chris, illus. 2013. (Solving Mysteries with Science Ser.). (ENG.). 48p. (gr. 3-6). pap. 9.95 *(978-1-4109-5507-4(9))* Heinemann-Raintree.

—Vampires & Werewolves, 1 vol. 2013. (Solving Mysteries with Science Ser.). (ENG.). 48p. (gr. 3-6). 29.99 *(978-1-4109-5501-2(X))* Heinemann-Raintree.

Biskup, Agnieszka. Vampires & Cells, 1 vol. Jok, Diego, illus. 2011. (Monster Science Ser.). (ENG.). 32p. (gr. 3-4). pap. 8.10 *(978-1-4296-7331-0(1),* Graphic Library) Capstone Press of Coughlan Cos.

—Vampires & Cells. Jok, illus. 2011. (Monster Science Ser.). (ENG.). 32p. (gr. 3-4). pap. 47.70 *(978-1-4296-7332-7(X),* Graphic Library) Capstone Press of Coughlan Cos.

—Vampires & Cells, 1 vol. Jok, Diego, illus. 2011. (Monster Science Ser.). (ENG.). 32p. (gr. 3-4). lib. bdg. 30.65 *(978-1-4296-6582-7(3),* Graphic Library) Capstone Press of Coughlan Cos.

Bringle, Jennifer. Vampires in Film & Television. 2011. 77.70 *(978-1-4488-2236-2(X),* Rosen Reference); pap. 12.95 *(978-1-4488-2229-4(7),* Rosen Reference); (YA). (gr. 5-9). lib. bdg. 31.95 *(978-1-4488-1226-4(7))* Rosen Publishing Group, Inc., The.

Brinker, Spencer. More or Less & a Vampire's Guess. 2015. (Illus.). 32p. (J). lib. bdg. *(978-1-62724-330-8(5))* Bearport Publishing Co., Inc.

Bullard, Lisa. I'M a Midnight Snacker! - Meet a Vampire. Buccheri, Chiara, illus. 2014. (Monster Buddies Ser.). (ENG.). 24p. (gr. k-2). lib. bdg. 23.93 *(978-0-7613-9191-3(6),* Millbrook Pr.) Lerner Publishing Group.

Cast, P. C. & Doner, Kim. The Fledgling Handbook 101. 2010. (House of Night Novels Ser.). (ENG., Illus.). 176p. (YA). (gr. 7-12). pap. 14.99 *(978-0-312-59512-8(3),* 9780312595128, St. Martin's Griffin) St. Martin's Pr.

Castellano, Peter. Vampires. 2016. (Monsters! Ser.). (ENG.). 32p. (J). (gr. 1-2). pap. 10.50 *(978-1-4824-4095-9(4))* Stevens, Gareth Publishing LLLP.

Cohen, Robert Z. Transylvania: Birthplace of Vampires. 2011. (J). 77.70 *(978-1-4488-2234-8(3),* Rosen Reference); (J). pap. 12.95 *(978-1-4488-2231-7(9),* Rosen Reference); (YA). (gr. 5-9). lib. bdg. 31.95 *(978-1-4488-1228-8(3))* Rosen Publishing Group, Inc., The.

Collins, Sophie. How to Love a Werewolf. 2010. (ENG., Illus.). 128p. (gr. -1-17). 12.50 *(978-1-84601-368-3(2),* Spruce) Octopus Publishing Group GBR. Dist: Hachette Bk. Group.

Dutton, Michael & Roytman, Arkady. 3-D Coloring Book — Vampires & Zombies. 2011. (Dover 3-D Coloring Book Ser.). (ENG., Illus.). 32p. (J). (gr. 2-6). pap. 5.99 *(978-0-486-48415-0(7))* Dover Pubns., Inc.

Etingoff, Kim. Howling at the Moon: Vampires & Werewolves in the New World. 2010. (Making of a Monster Ser.). (Illus.). 64p. (YA). (gr. 7-18). pap. 9.95 *(978-1-4222-1958-4(5))*; lib. bdg. 22.95 *(978-1-4222-1805-1(8))* Mason Crest.

—The Science of the Beast: The Facts Behind the Fangs. 2010. (Making of a Monster Ser.). (Illus.). 64p. (YA). (gr. 7-18). pap. 9.95 *(978-1-4222-1961-4(5))*; lib. bdg. 22.95 *(978-1-4222-1808-2(2))* Mason Crest.

Frisch, Aaron. That's Spooky: Vampires. 2013. (That's Spooky Ser.). (ENG., Illus.). 24p. (J). (gr. 1-3). pap. 7.99 *(978-0-89812-805-5(6),* Creative Paperbacks) Creative Co., The.

—Vampires. 2013. (That's Spooky! Ser.). (ENG., Illus.). 24p. (J). (gr. 3-7). 25.65 *(978-1-60818-248-0(7),* Creative Education) Creative Co., The.

Griffiths, Katie. Vampires. 2016. (Creatures of Fantasy Ser.). (ENG.). 64p. (J). (gr. 6-6). 34.21 *(978-1-5026-0928-1(2))* Cavendish Square Publishing.

Guiley, Rosemary Ellen. Vampires. 2009. (Mysteries, Legends, & Unexplained Phenomena Ser.). 128p. (gr. 6-12). pap. 10.95 *(978-0-7910-9895-0(8),* Checkmark Bks.) Facts On File, Inc.

Guillain, Charlotte. Vampires, 1 vol. 2010. (Mythical Creatures Ser.). (ENG., Illus.). 32p. (gr. 1-2). 29.99 *(978-1-4109-3801-5(8),* Read Me!) Heinemann-Raintree.

Hamilton, John. Vampires, 1 vol. 2007. (World of Horror Ser.). (ENG., Illus.). 32p. (gr. 4-8). 27.07 *(978-1-59928-774-4(9),* Abdo & Daughters) ABDO Publishing Co.

Hamilton, S. L. Vampires. 2010. (Xtreme Monsters Ser.). 32p. (gr. 3-9). 27.07 *(978-1-61613-470-9(4),* A&D Xtreme) ABDO Publishing Co.

Jeffrey, Gary. Vampires. Verma, Dheeraj, illus. 2012. (Graphic Mythical Creatures Ser.). (ENG.). 24p. (J). (gr. 3-5). pap. 8.15 *(978-1-4339-6773-3(1))*; lib. bdg. 23.95 *(978-1-4339-6771-9(5))* Stevens, Gareth Publishing LLLP. (Gareth Stevens Learning Library).

Jensen Shaffer, Jody. Vampires & Light, 1 vol. Gervasio, illus. 2013. (Monster Science Ser.). (ENG.). 32p. (gr. 3-4). pap. 8.10 *(978-1-62065-820-8(8),* Graphic Library) Capstone Press of Coughlan Cos.

Jones, Jen. The Girls' Guide to Vampires: Everything Enchanting about These Immortal Creatures. 2010. (Girls' Guides to Everything Unexplained Ser.). (ENG.). 32p. (gr. 3-4). lib. bdg. 27.99 *(978-1-4296-5452-4(X),* Snap Bks.) Capstone Press of Coughlan Cos.

Kespert, Deborah. 3-D Chillers: Vampires, Zombies, & Werewolves. 2012. (3-D Chillers Ser.). (ENG.). 48p. (J). (gr. 3-7). pap. 7.99 *(978-0-545-38779-8(5),* Scholastic Paperbacks) Scholastic, Inc.

Klepeis, Alicia. Vampires: The Truth Behind History's Creepiest Bloodsuckers. 2015. (Monster Handbooks Ser.). (ENG., Illus.). 32p. (gr. 3-4). lib. bdg. 27.99 *(978-1-4914-4250-0(6))* Capstone Press of Coughlan Cos.

Knudsen, Shannon. Giants, Trolls, & Ogres. 2009. (Fantasy Chronicles Ser.). (ENG., Illus.). 48p. (gr. 4-7). lib. bdg. 27.93 *(978-0-8225-9985-2(6))* Lerner Publishing Group.

Loh-Hagan, Virginia. Vampires: Magic, Myth, & Mystery. 2016. (Magic, Myth, & Mystery Ser.). (ENG., Illus.). 32p. (J). (gr. 4-8). 29.93 *(978-1-63471-109-8(2),* 208547, 45th Parallel Press) Cherry Lake Publishing.

Martin, Nicholas. Fighting the Fangs: A Guide to Vampires & Werewolves. 2010. (Making of a Monster Ser.). (Illus.). 64p. (YA). (gr. 7-18). pap. 9.95 *(978-1-4222-1957-7(7))*; lib. bdg. 22.95 *(978-1-4222-1804-4(X))* Mason Crest.

Marx, Mandy R. Great Vampire Legends, 1 vol. 2010. (Vampires Ser.). (ENG.). 32p. (gr. 3-4). lib. bdg. 27.99 *(978-1-4296-4576-8(8),* Edge Bks.) Capstone Press of Coughlan Cos.

Mason, Paul & Hachette Children's Group. The Vampire Hunter's Guide. 2012. (Monster Tracker Ser.). (Illus.). 32p. (gr. 4-6). lib. bdg. 28.50 *(978-1-59771-317-7(1))* Sea-To-Sea Pubns.

McMeans, Bonnie. Vampires. 2006. (Mysterious Encounters Ser.). (ENG., Illus.). 48p. (gr. 3-7). lib. bdg. 33.60 *(978-0-7377-3476-8(0),* Greenhaven Pr., Inc.) Cengage Gale.

Mead, Richelle. Vampire Academy. movie tie-in ed. 2013. (Vampire Academy Ser.: 1). (ENG.). 352p. (YA). (gr. 7). pap. 10.99 *(978-1-59514-360-0(2),* Razorbill) Penguin Publishing Group.

Navarre, Sam. Vampires in America. 2011. (America's Supernatural Secrets Ser.). (ENG.). 48p. (YA). (gr. 5-8). pap. 11.75 *(978-1-4488-5574-2(8));* lib. bdg. 29.25 *(978-1-4488-5528-5(4))* Rosen Publishing Group, Inc., The. (Rosen Reference).

Netzley, Patricia D. Do Vampires Exist? 2015. (ENG., Illus.). 80p. (J). lib. bdg. *(978-1-60152-860-5(4))* ReferencePoint Pr., Inc.

O'Hearn, Michael. Vampires vs. Werewolves: Battle of the Bloodthirsty Beasts. Kendree, McLean, illus. 2011. (Monster Wars Ser.). (ENG.). 32p. (gr. 3-4). pap. 47.70 *(978-1-4296-7266-5(8));* lib. bdg. 27.99 *(978-1-4296-6521-6(1))* Capstone Press of Coughlan Cos. (Edge Bks.).

Orme, David. Vampires. 2010. (Fact to Fiction Grafx Ser.). (Illus.). 36p. (J). lib. bdg. 16.95 *(978-1-60686-474-6(2))* Perfection Learning Corp.

Owen, Ruth. Vampires & Other Bloodsuckers. 2013. (Not near Normal: the Paranormal Ser.). 32p. (J). (gr. 3-8). lib. bdg. 26.60 *(978-1-61772-722-1(9))* Bearport Publishing Co., Inc.

Petechuk, David. The Undead: Vampires, Zombies, & Other Strange Monsters. 2015. (J). *(978-1-61900-070-4(9))* Eldorado Ink.

Peter Pauper Press Staff, et al. Vampires, Werewolves, Zombies: from the papers of Herr Doktor Max Sturm & Baron Ludwig Von Drang. Waldman, Bruce, illus. 2010. 168p. 9.95 *(978-1-59359-647-7(2))* Peter Pauper Pr. Inc.

Pipe, Jim. The Undead. 2013. (Twilight Realm Ser.). (Illus.). 32p. (J). (gr. 4-6). 26.60 *(978-1-4339-8759-5(7));* pap. 10.50 *(978-1-4339-8760-1(0))* Stevens, Gareth Publishing LLLP. (Gareth Stevens Learning Library).

Rainey, Rich. Vampire Life, 1 vol. 2010. (Vampires Ser.). (ENG.). 32p. (gr. 3-4). lib. bdg. 27.99 *(978-1-4296-4577-5(6),* Edge Bks.) Capstone Press of Coughlan Cos.

Roberts, Steven. The Undead!, 1 vol., 1. 2014. (Jr. Graphic Monster Stories Ser.). (ENG.). 24p. (J). (gr. 3-6). 26.25 *(978-1-4777-6207-3(8),* PowerKids Pr.) Rosen Publishing Group, Inc., The.

—Vampires! 2012. (Jr. Graphic Monster Stories Ser.). (ENG., Illus.). 24p. (J). (gr. 3-6). pap. 10.60 *(978-1-4488-8006-5(8));* lib. bdg. 25.25 *(978-1-4488-7906-9(X))* Rosen Publishing Group, Inc., The. (PowerKids Pr.).

Rooney, Anne. Vampire Castle. 2008. (Crabtree Contact Ser.). (ENG.). 32p. (J). (gr. 3-7). pap. *(978-0-7787-3788-9(8));* (Illus.). lib. bdg. *(978-0-7787-3766-7(7))* Crabtree Publishing Co.

Roytman, Arkady. Vampire Nights. 2010. (Dover Stained Glass Coloring Book Ser.). (ENG., Illus.). 32p. (J). (gr. 3-5). pap. 6.99 *(978-0-486-47638-4(3))* Dover Pubns., Inc.

Sabatino, Michael. The Legend of Dracula. 2015. (Famous Legends Ser.). (ENG., Illus.). 32p. (J). (gr. 2-3). 25.25 *(978-1-4824-2734-9(6))* Stevens, Gareth Publishing LLLP.

Sanna, Emily. Pop Monsters: The Modern-Day Craze for Vampires & Werewolves. 2010. (Making of a Monster Ser.). 64p. (YA). (gr. 7-18). pap. 9.95 *(978-1-4222-1959-1(3))* Mason Crest.

Spencer, Liv. Love Bites: The Unofficial Saga of Twilight. 2010. (ENG., Illus.). 203p. (YA). (gr. 7). pap. *(978-1-55022-930-1(3))* Filmer Ltd.

Stefoff, Rebecca. Vampires, Zombies, & Shape-Shifters. 2007. (Secrets of the Supernatural Ser.). (Illus.). 79p. (J). (gr. 4-7). lib. bdg. 32.79 *(978-0-7614-2635-6(3),* Benchmark Bks.) Marshall Cavendish Corp.

Stewart, Sheila. The Psychology of Our Dark Side: Humans' Love Affair with Vampires & Werewolves. 2010. (Making of a Monster Ser.). (Illus.). 64p. (YA). (gr. 7-18). pap. 9.95 *(978-1-4222-1960-7(7));* lib. bdg. 22.95 *(978-1-4222-1807-5(4))* Mason Crest.

Streissguth, Thomas & Streissguth, Tom. Legends of Dracula. 2003. (Biography Ser.). (Illus.). 112p. (YA). (gr. 6-18). pap. 7.95 *(978-0-8225-9682-0(2),* Carolrhoda Bks.) Lerner Publishing Group.

Ticktock Media, Ltd. Staff. Undead: Zombies, Vampires, Werewolves. 2008. (ENG.). 96p. (J). (gr. 4-7). pap. 9.95 *(978-1-84696-797-9(X),* TickTock Books) Octopus Publishing Group GBR. Dist: Independent Pubs. Group.

Tieck, Sarah. Vampires, 1 vol. 2016. (ENG., Illus.). 32p. (J). *(978-1-62403-767-2(4))* ABDO Publishing Co.

Troupe, Thomas Kingsley. The Legend of the Vampire, 1 vol. Kemarskaya, Oksana, illus. 2010. (Legend Has It Ser.). (ENG.). 32p. (gr. 2-4). lib. bdg. 27.32 *(978-1-4048-6031-5(2))* Picture Window Bks.

Vampire Sticker Book. 2003. (Illus.). 16p. (J). 2.98 *(978-1-84273-119-2(X),* Exclusive Editions) Parragon, Inc.

Vampires. 2009. (FACT ATLAS Ser.). 72p. (J). (gr. 3-7). pap. 13.99 *(978-0-8416-1100-9(9))* Hammond World Atlas Corp.

Vampires: The Myths, Legends, & Lore. 2014. (ENG., Illus.). 224p. 16.99 *(978-1-4405-8076-5(6))* Adams Media Corp.

Weakland, Mark Andrew & Collins, Terry Lee. Scooby Doo Unmasks the Truth Behind Vampires. 2016. (Illus.). 24p. (J). *(978-1-4062-8895-7(0))* Capstone Press of Coughlan Cos.

Weingarten, Ethan. Transylvania. 2013. (Scariest Places on Earth Ser.). 24p. (J). (gr. 2-5). 22.60 *(978-1-4824-1161-4(X))* Stevens, Gareth Publishing LLLP.

West, David & Ganeri, Anita. Vampires & the Undead. West, David & Ganeri, Anita, illus. 2010. (Dark Side Ser.). (Illus.). 32p. (J). (ENG.). pap. 10.50 *(978-1-4488-1570-8(3));* lib. bdg. 26.50 *(978-1-61531-899-5(2))* Rosen Publishing Group, Inc., The.

—Witches & Warlocks. West, David & Ganeri, Anita, illus. 2010. (Dark Side Ser.). (Illus.). 32p. (J). pap. 10.50 *(978-1-4488-1574-6(6),* PowerKids Pr.) Rosen Publishing Group, Inc., The.

White, Steve & McKenzie-Ray, Mark. Hunting Vampires. 2016. (Monster Hunting Ser.). 00088p. (YA). (gr. 8-8). 37.10 *(978-1-4994-6530-3(0),* Rosen Young Adult) Rosen Publishing Group, Inc., The.

World Book, Inc Staff, contrib. by. Searching for the Real Dracula. 2015. (Illus.). 48p. (J). *(978-0-7166-2674-9(8))* World Bk., Inc.

VAMPIRES—FICTION

Adams, James D. Creepy Campfire Tales: Halloween Campout, Vol. 1. 2008. 132p. (J). per. 12.95 *(978-1-60404-103-3(X))* Owl Creek Media Ltd.

—Creepy Campfire Tales Vol. 1: Halloween Campout. 2008. 132p. (YA). 26.95 *(978-1-60404-104-0(8))* Owl Creek Media Ltd.

Adamson, Ged & Rylance, Ulrike. Elsie Clarke & the Vampire Hairdresser. Adamson, Ged, illus. 2013. (ENG., Illus.). 28p. (J). (gr. -1-1). 16.95 *(978-1-62087-983-2(2),* 620983, Sky Pony Pr.) Skyhorse Publishing Co., Inc.

Anderson, M. T. Thirsty. 2008. (ENG., Illus.). 256p. (YA). (gr. 7). pap. 8.99 *(978-0-7636-3895-5(1))* Candlewick Pr.

Atwater-Rhodes, Amelia. The Den of Shadows Quartet. 2009. (ENG.). 608p. (YA). (gr. 7). pap. 11.99 *(978-0-385-73894-1(3),* Ember) Random Hse. Children's Bks.

—Persistence of Memory. 2010. (Den of Shadows Ser.: Bk. 4). (ENG.). 224p. (YA). (gr. 7). pap. 8.99 *(978-0-440-24004-4(2),* Delacorte Pr.) Random Hse. Children's Bks.

—Poison Tree. 2013. (ENG.). 240p. (YA). (gr. 7). pap. 8.99 *(978-0-385-73755-5(6),* Ember) Random Hse. Children's Bks.

AZ Books Staff & Evans, Olivia. Haunted Castle. Shumovich, Nadezhda, ed. 2012. (Terribly Funny Monsters Ser.). (ENG., Illus.). 10p. (J). bds. 15.95 *(978-1-61889-134-1(0))* AZ Bks. LLC.

Bardhan-Quallen, Sudipta. Hampire! Fine, Howard, illus. 2011. (ENG.). 32p. (J). (gr. -1-3). 16.99 *(978-0-06-114239-0(5))* HarperCollins Pubs.

The Beautiful & the Damned. 2014. (ENG., Illus.). 288p. (YA). (gr. 7). pap. 11.99 *(978-1-4424-8836-6(0),* Simon Pulse) Simon Pulse.

Becket. Key the Steampunk Vampire Girl - Book One: And the Dungeon of Despair. 2013. 242p. (J). pap. 9.99 *(978-0-9898785-2-4(X))* Becket.

Bell, Amber Dawn. Cave of Terror. 2008. 280p. pap. 12.95 *(978-0-9818550-3-5(2))* Highland Pr. Publishing.

Bickle, Laura. The Outside. (ENG.). 320p. (YA). (gr. 7). 2014. pap. 8.99 *(978-0-544-33635-3(6),* HMH Books For Young Readers) 2013. 16.99 *(978-0-544-00013-1(7))* Houghton Mifflin Harcourt Publishing Co.

Black, Bekka. IDrakula. 2010. (ENG., Illus.). 160p. (YA). (gr. 7-12). pap. 9.99 *(978-1-4022-4465-0(7))* Sourcebooks, Inc.

Black, Holly. The Coldest Girl in Coldtown. 2013. 419p. (YA). *(978-0-316-27755-6(X))* Little Brown & Co.

—The Coldest Girl in Coldtown. (ENG.). (gr. 10-17). 2014. 448p. pap. 10.99 *(978-0-316-21309-7(8))* 2013. 432p. 19.00 *(978-0-316-21310-3(1))* Little, Brown Bks. for Young Readers.

Blackhurst, Rebecca. Count Grumpula & the Wood Witch. Errington, Rachael, illus. 2013. 18p. *(978-0-473-24899-4(9))* Cobble Creep Productions.

Blevins, Wiley. Cinderella & the Vampire Prince. Cox, Steve, illus. 2016. (Scary Tales Retold Ser.). (ENG.). 24p. (gr. k-3). lib. bdg. 23.99 *(978-1-63440-090-9(9))* Red Chair Pr.

Block, Francesca Lia. Pretty Dead. (ENG.). (YA). (gr. 9). 2010. 224p. pap. 8.99 *(978-0-06-154787-4(5))* 2009. 208p. 16.99 *(978-0-06-154785-0(9))* HarperCollins Pubs. (HarperTeen).

Bloom, Ira. Hearts & Other Body Parts. 2017. (ENG.). 352p. (J). (gr. 9). 17.99 *(978-1-338-03073-0(6),* Scholastic Pr.) Scholastic, Inc.

Bloom, M. Beth. Drain You. 2012. (ENG.). 400p. (YA). (gr. 8). pap. 8.99 *(978-0-06-203686-5(6),* HarperTeen) HarperCollins Pubs.

Blue, Parker. Catch Me. 2015. (ENG., Illus.). 222p. (J). pap. 14.95 *(978-1-61194-623-9(9))* BelleBks., Inc.

—Try Me. 2010. 218p. pap. 14.95 *(978-0-9843256-6-5(2),* Bell Bridge Bks.) BelleBks., Inc.

Brambles, Lindsay. Becoming Darkness. 2015. (ENG.). 496p. 17.95 *(978-1-63079-017-2(6))* Switch Pr.

Brereton, Dan, et al. Buffy the Vampire Slayer Omnibus, 7 vols., Vol. 1. Golden, Christopher, illus. 2007. (Buffy the Vampire Slayer Ser.). (ENG.). 408p. pap. 24.99 *(978-1-59307-784-6(X))* Dark Horse Comics.

Brewer, Heather. Chronicles of Vladimir Tod, 2 vols. 2009. (Chronicles of Vladimir Tod Ser.: 2). (ENG.). 288p. (YA). (gr. 7-18). 8.99 *(978-0-14-241342-5(9),* Speak) Penguin Young Readers Group.

—Eighth Grade Bites. Laud, Julia, illus. 2013. (Chronicles of Vladimir Tod Ser.: 1). (ENG.). 144p. (YA). (gr. 7). pap. 12.99 *(978-0-8037-3811-9(0),* Dial Bks) Penguin Young Readers Group.

—Eighth Grade Bites. 2008. (Chronicles of Vladimir Tod Ser.: 1). (ENG.). 192p. (YA). (gr. 7). 8.99 *(978-0-14-241187-2(6),* Speak) Penguin Young Readers Group.

—Eleventh Grade Burns, 4 vols. 2010. (Chronicles of Vladimir Tod Ser.: 4). (ENG.). 320p. (YA). (gr. 7-18). 8.99 *(978-0-14-241647-1(9),* Speak); 4th ed. 16.99 *(978-0-525-42243-3(9),* Dutton Books for Young Readers) Penguin Young Readers Group.

—First Kill. 2012. (Slayer Chronicles Ser.: 1). (ENG.). 336p. (YA). (gr. 7). pap. 8.99 *(978-0-14-242196-3(0),* Speak) Penguin Young Readers Group.

—First Kill. 2012. (Slayer Chronicles Ser.: 1). lib. bdg. 19.65 *(978-0-606-26670-3(4),* Turtleback) Turtleback Bks.

—Tenth Grade Bleeds. Preseault, N., ed. 2010. (Chronicles of Vladimir Tod Ser.: 3). (ENG.). 304p. (YA). (gr. 7-18). pap. 8.99 *(978-0-14-241560-3(X),* Speak) Penguin Young Readers Group.

—Tenth Grade Bleeds. 2009. (Chronicles of Vladimir Tod Ser.: 3). (ENG., Illus.). 304p. (YA). (gr. 7-18). 16.99 *(978-0-525-42135-1(1),* Dutton Books for Young Readers) Penguin Young Readers Group.

—Tenth Grade Bleeds. 2010. (Chronicles of Vladimir Tod Ser.: 03). lib. bdg. 19.65 *(978-0-606-10594-1(8),* Turtleback) Turtleback Bks.

—The Chronicles of Vladimir Tod. 2011. (Chronicles of Vladimir Tod Ser.: 5). (ENG.). 336p. (YA). (gr. 7-18). 8.99 *(978-0-14-241752-2(1),* Speak) Penguin Young Readers Group.

—Twelfth Grade Kills. 5th ed. 2010. (Chronicles of Vladimir Tod Ser.: 5). (ENG.). 340p. (YA). (gr. 7-18). 16.99 *(978-0-525-42224-2(2),* Dutton Books for Young Readers) Penguin Young Readers Group.

Brezenoff, Steve. Bites, 1 vol. Pinelli, Amerigo, illus. 2013. (Ravens Pass Ser.). (ENG.). 96p. (gr. 2-3). pap. 6.15 *(978-1-4342-6217-2(0))* Stone Arch Bks.

—Bites. 2013. (Ravens Pass Ser.). (ENG.). 96p. (gr. 2-3). pap. 35.70 *(978-1-4342-6289-9(8))* Stone Arch Bks.

—Bites, 1 vol. Pinelli, Amerigo, illus. 2013. (Ravens Pass Ser.). (ENG.). 96p. (gr. 2-3). lib. bdg. 25.32 *(978-1-4342-4617-2(5))* Stone Arch Bks.

Brookes, Archer. Vampireology: The True History of the Fallen. Holt, Nick, ed. 2010. (Ologies Ser.: 9). (ENG., Illus.). 30p. (YA). (gr. 7-9). 21.99 *(978-0-7636-4914-2(7))* Candlewick Pr.

Brown, Lisa. Vampire Boy's Good Night. Brown, Lisa, illus. 2010. (ENG., Illus.). 32p. (J). (gr. -1-2). 16.99 *(978-0-06-114011-2(2))* HarperCollins Pubs.

Brown, Mick. From Round about Midnight until about Five! 2012. 60p. pap. 27.45 *(978-1-4772-2701-5(6))* AuthorHouse.

Brush Creations & Holmes, A. M. X. Robbie Virtual vs. Vlad the Vampire: Book 1. 2007. 56p. pap. 9.95 *(978-0-7414-3621-4(3))* Infinity Publishing.

Bundy, E. A. Phillip Marrow, Jr. 2013. (ENG.). 206p. (YA). pap. 10.99 *(978-1-61955-008-7(3))* Singing Winds Pr.

Burghall, Johan. The Vale of the Faeries. 2012. 274p. (-18). pap. *(978-0-9571863-3-0(9))* Burghall, Johan.

Burke, Anjalena Anita. Ghost: The Dead End Series Book 1, 1 vol. 2009. 73p. pap. 16.95 *(978-1-61582-686-5(6))* PublishAmerica, Inc.

Burns, Laura J. & Metz, Melinda. Sacrifice. 2011. (ENG.). 272p. (YA). (gr. 9). 17.99 *(978-1-4424-3900-9(9));* pap. 9.99 *(978-1-4424-0818-0(9))* Simon & Schuster Bks. For Young Readers. (Simon & Schuster Bks. For Young Readers).

Caine, Rachel, pseud. Bite Club, 10 vols. 2011. (Morganville Vampires Ser.: 10). (ENG.). 368p. (YA). (gr. 9). pap. 9.99 *(978-0-451-23468-1(5),* Berkley) Penguin Publishing Group.

—Bitter Blood. 2013. (Morganville Vampires Ser.: 13). (ENG.). 432p. (YA). (gr. 9). pap. 9.99 *(978-0-451-41424-3(1),* Berkley) Penguin Publishing Group.

—Black Dawn. 2012. (Morganville Vampires Ser.: 12). (ENG.). 400p. (YA). (gr. 9). pap. 9.99 *(978-0-451-23793-4(5),* Berkley) Penguin Publishing Group.

—Carpe Corpus. 2009. (Morganville Vampires Ser.: 6). (ENG.). 256p. (YA). (gr. 9-18). mass mkt. 7.99 *(978-0-451-22719-5(0),* Berkley) Penguin Publishing Group.

—Fade Out. 2009. (Morganville Vampires Ser.: Bk. 7). 256p. (YA). lib. bdg. 20.00 *(978-1-4242-4701-1(2))* Fitzgerald Bks.

—Fade Out. 2009. (Morganville Vampires Ser.: 7). (ENG.). 256p. (YA). (gr. 9-18). mass mkt. 7.99 *(978-0-451-22866-6(9),* Berkley) Penguin Publishing Group.

—Fall of Night. 2013. (Morganville Vampires Ser.: 14). (ENG.). 368p. (YA). (gr. 9). pap. 9.99 *(978-0-451-41426-7(8),* Berkley) Penguin Publishing Group.

—Feast of Fools. 2008. (Morganville Vampires Ser.: Bk. 4). 256p. (YA). lib. bdg. 20.00 *(978-1-4242-4702-8(0))* Fitzgerald Bks.

—Feast of Fools. 2008. (Morganville Vampires Ser.: 4). (ENG.). 256p. (YA). (gr. 9-18). mass mkt. 7.99 *(978-0-451-22463-7(9),* Berkley) Penguin Publishing Group.

—Ghost Town, 9 vols. 2011. (Morganville Vampires Ser.: 9). (ENG.). 368p. (YA). (gr. 9-18). 9.99 *(978-0-451-23291-5(7),* Berkley) Penguin Publishing Group.

—Kiss of Death, 8 vols. 2010. (Morganville Vampires Ser.: 8). (ENG.). 256p. (YA). (gr. 9-18). 6.99 *(978-0-451-22973-1(8),* Berkley) Penguin Publishing Group.

—Last Breath, 11 vols. 2012. (Morganville Vampires Ser.: 11). (ENG.). 368p. (YA). (gr. 9). 9.99 *(978-0-451-23580-0(0),* Berkley) Penguin Publishing Group.

—Lord of Misrule. 2009. (Morganville Vampires Ser.: Bk. 5). 352p. (YA). lib. bdg. 20.00 *(978-1-4242-4704-2(7))* Fitzgerald Bks.

—Lord of Misrule. 2009. (Morganville Vampires Ser.: 5). (ENG.). 256p. (YA). (gr. 9-18). mass mkt. 7.99 *(978-0-451-22572-6(4),* Berkley) Penguin Publishing Group.

—Midnight Alley. 2007. (Morganville Vampires Ser.: Bk. 3). 256p. (YA). lib. bdg. 20.00 *(978-1-4242-4705-9(5))* Fitzgerald Bks.

—Midnight Alley. 2007. (Morganville Vampires Ser.: 3). (ENG.). 256p. (YA). (gr. 9-18). mass mkt. 7.99 *(978-0-451-22238-1(5),* Berkley) Penguin Publishing Group.

—Midnight Bites: Stories of the Morganville Vampires. 2016. (Morganville Vampires Ser.). (ENG.). 512p. (YA). (gr. 9). pap. 9.99 *(978-1-101-98978-4(5),* Berkley) Penguin Publishing Group.

—The Morganville Vampires. (Morganville Vampires Ser.: Bks. 1-2). (ENG.). (YA). (gr. 9-18). 2009. 480p. 9.99 *(978-0-451-23054-6(X))* Vol. 2. 2010. 464p. 9.99 *(978-0-451-23289-2(5))* Vol. 3. 2011. 464p. 9.99 *(978-0-451-23355-4(7))* Vol. 4. 2011. 464p. 9.99 *(978-0-451-23426-1(X))* Penguin Publishing Group. (Berkley).

Caine, Rachel, pseud, et al. Immortal: Love Stories with Bite. Cast, P. C., ed. 2009. (ENG., Illus.). 280p. (J). (gr. 9-12). pap. 8.95 *(978-1-933771-92-2(5))* BenBella Bks.

Capstone Press. Vampires. 2010. (Vampires Ser.). (ENG.). 32p. lib. bdg. 79.95 *(978-1-4296-5906-2(8),* Edge Bks.) Capstone Press of Coughlan Cos.

Carter, Rebecca. Moonlit Daydreams. 2010. 71p. pap. 11.99 *(978-0-557-35588-4(5))* Lulu Pr., Inc.

Cary, Kate. Bloodline. 2006. (ENG.). 352p. (YA). (gr. 7-12). 9.99 *(978-1-59514-078-4(6),* Razorbill) Penguin Young Readers Group.

—Reckoning. 2008. (ENG.). 320p. (YA). (gr. 7-18). pap. 9.99 *(978-1-59514-179-8(0),* Razorbill) Penguin Young Readers Group.

Cast, P. C. & Cast, Kristin. Awakened. (House of Night Novels Ser.: 8). (ENG.). 304p. (YA). (gr. 7-12). 2013. mass mkt. 9.99 *(978-1-250-04692-5(0),* 9781250046925, St. Martin's Paperbacks) 2012. pap. 10.99 *(978-0-312-38797-6(0),* 9780312387976, St. Martin's Griffin) 2011. 17.99 *(978-0-312-65024-7(8),* 9780312650247, St. Martin's Griffin) St. Martin's Pr.

—Awakened. l.t. ed. 2011. (House of Night Ser.). (ENG.). 436p. 23.99 *(978-1-4104-3776-1(0))* Thorndike Pr.

—Betrayed. (House of Night Novels Ser.: 2). (ENG.). 320p. (YA). (gr. 7-12). 2009. 19.99 *(978-0-312-59629-3(4),* 9780312596293) 2007. pap. 10.99 *(978-0-312-36028-3(2),* 9780312360283, St. Martin's Griffin) St. Martin's Pr.

—Betrayed. l.t. ed. 2008. (House of Night Ser.: No. 2). (ENG.). 472p. (YA). 23.95 *(978-1-4104-1025-2(0))* Thorndike Pr.

—Burned. (House of Night Novels Ser.: 7). (ENG.). 336p. (YA). (gr. 7-12). 2011. pap. 10.99 *(978-0-312-38796-9(2),* 9780312387969) 2010. 17.99 *(978-0-312-60616-9(8),* 9780312606169) St. Martin's Pr. (St. Martin's Griffin).

—Burned. l.t. ed. 2011. (House of Night Ser.). (ENG.). 552p. 23.99 *(978-1-4104-3440-1(0))* Thorndike Pr.

—Chosen. 2010. (House of Night Novels (Quality) Ser.). (CHI.). 367p. pap. *(978-957-0316-42-1(X))* Locus Publishing Co.

—Chosen. 2008. (House of Night Novels Ser.: 3). (ENG.). 320p. (YA). (gr. 8-12). pap. 10.99 *(978-0-312-36030-6(4),* 9780312360306, St. Martin's Griffin) St. Martin's Pr.

—Chosen. l.t. ed. 2009. (House of Night Ser.: Bk. 3). (ENG.). 406p. (YA). 23.95 *(978-1-4104-1608-7(9))* Thorndike Pr.

—Destined. 2013. (House of Night Novels Ser.: 9). (ENG.). 336p. (YA). (gr. 7-12). pap. 10.99 *(978-0-312-38798-3(9),* 9780312387983, St. Martin's Griffin) St. Martin's Pr.

—Hidden. 2012. (House of Night Novels Ser.: 10). (ENG.). 320p. (YA). (gr. 7-12). 18.99 *(978-0-312-59442-8(9),* 9780312594428, St. Martin's Griffin) St. Martin's Pr.

—House of Night: the Beginning: Marked & Betrayed. 2013. (House of Night Novels Ser.). (ENG.). 640p. (YA). (gr. 7-12). pap. 11.99 *(978-1-250-03723-7(9),* 9781250037237, St. Martin's Griffin) St. Martin's Pr.

—Hunted. 2010. (House of Night Novels Ser.: 5). (ENG.). 336p. (YA). (gr. 7-12). pap. 10.99 *(978-0-312-57799-5(0),* 9780312577995, St. Martin's Griffin) St. Martin's Pr.

—Hunted. l.t. ed. 2010. (House of Night Ser.: Bk. 5). (ENG.). 548p. 23.95 *(978-1-4104-1951-4(7))* Thorndike Pr.

—Marcada: Una Casa de la Noche Novela. 2009. (House of Night Novels Ser.: 1). (SPA & ENG.). 320p. (YA). (gr. 7-12). pap. 16.99 *(978-0-312-63830-6(2),* 9780312638306, St. Martin's Griffin) St. Martin's Pr.

—Marked. (House of Night Novels Ser.: 1). (ENG.). 320p. (YA). (gr. 8-12). 2009. 19.99 *(978-0-312-36025-2(8),* 9780312360252) 2007. pap. 10.99 *(978-0-312-36026-9(6),* 9780312360269, St. Martin's Griffin) St. Martin's Pr.

—Marked. l.t. ed. 2008. (House of Night Ser.: No. 1). (ENG.). 442p. (YA). 23.95 *(978-1-4104-1021-4(8))* Thorndike Pr.

—Marked. 2007. (House of Night Ser.: 1). 306p. (YA). lib. bdg. 22.10 *(978-1-4178-0853-3(5),* Turtleback) Turtleback Bks.

—Neferet's Curse. 2013. (House of Night Novellas Ser.: 3). (ENG., Illus.). 160p. (YA). (gr. 7). 12.99 *(978-1-250-00025-5(4),* 9781250000255, St. Martin's Griffin) St. Martin's Pr.

—Redeemed: A House of Night Novel. 2014. (YA). *(978-1-250-05952-9(6));* (House of Night Ser.: Vol. 12). (ENG.). 320p. (gr. 7-12). 18.99 *(978-0-312-59444-2(5),* 9780312594442, St. Martin's Griffin) St. Martin's Pr.

—Tempted. (House of Night Novels Ser.: 6). (ENG.). (YA). (gr. 7-12). 2013. 352p. mass mkt. 9.99 *(978-1-250-04698-7(X),* 9781250046987, St. Martin's Paperbacks) 2011. 336p. pap. 10.99 *(978-0-312-60938-2(8),* 9780312609382, St. Martin's Griffin) 2009. 336p. 17.99 *(978-0-312-56748-4(0),* 9780312567484, St. Martin's Griffin) St. Martin's Pr.

—Tempted. l.t. ed. 2010. (House of Night Novel Ser.). (ENG.). 552p. 23.99 *(978-1-4104-3141-7(X))* Thorndike Pr.

—Untamed. 2008. (House of Night Novels Ser.: 4). (ENG.). 352p. (YA). (gr. 8-12). pap. 10.99 *(978-0-312-37983-4(8),* 9780312379834, St. Martin's Griffin) St. Martin's Pr.

—Untamed. l.t. ed. 2009. (House of Night Ser.: Bk. 4). (ENG.). 510p. (YA). 23.95 *(978-1-4104-1965-1(7))* Thorndike Pr.

Cast, P. C. & Doner, Kim. The Fledgling Handbook 101. 2010. (House of Night Novels Ser.). (ENG., Illus.). 176p. (YA). (gr. 7-12). pap. 14.99 *(978-0-312-59512-8(3),* 9780312595128, St. Martin's Griffin) St. Martin's Pr.

Church, Oliver. Living Dead - the Reaper's Reward. 2009. 258p. pap. 12.99 *(978-0-578-00160-9(8))* Folk Prophet Bks.

Clare, Cassandra. City of Fallen Angels. 2011. (Mortal Instruments Ser.: 4). (ENG.). 432p. (YA). (gr. 9-18). 24.99 *(978-1-4424-0354-3(3),* McElderry, Margaret K. Bks.) McElderry, Margaret K. Bks.

—City of Fallen Angels, 11 vols. (Mortal Instruments Ser.: 4). (YA). 2012. 133.75 *(978-1-4618-0638-7(0))* 2011. 135.75 *(978-1-4618-0637-0(2))* 2011. 317.75 *(978-1-4618-0642-4(9))* 2011. 133.75 *(978-1-4618-0641-7(0))* 2011. 1.25 *(978-1-4640-2483-2(9))* Recorded Bks., Inc.

—City of Glass. (Mortal Instruments Ser.: Bk. 3). (ENG., (YA). (gr. 9). 2015. Illus.). 592p. pap. 13.99 *(978-1-4814-5598-5(2))* 2009. 560p. 24.99 *(978-1-4169-1430-3(7))* McElderry, Margaret K. Bks. (McElderry, Margaret K. Bks.).

—City of Glass. 2010. 23.00 *(978-1-60686-827-0(6))* Perfection Learning Corp.

—City of Glass. 2009. pap. *(978-1-4424-9308-7(9))* Simon & Schuster.

—City of Glass. 2015. (Mortal Instruments Ser.: Bk. 3). 592p. (YA). lib. bdg. 25.75 *(978-0-606-37733-1(6))* Turtleback Bks.

—City of Heavenly Fire. 2014. (Mortal Instruments Ser.: No. 6). (ENG., Illus.). 752p. (YA). (gr. 9). 24.99 *(978-1-4424-1689-5(0),* McElderry, Margaret K. Bks.) McElderry, Margaret K. Bks.

—City of Lost Souls. (Mortal Instruments Ser.: Bk. 5). (ENG., (YA). (gr. 9). 2015. Illus.). 592p. pap. 13.99 *(978-1-4814-5600-5(8))* 2012. 544p. 21.99 *(978-1-4424-1686-4(6))* McElderry, Margaret K. Bks. (McElderry, Margaret K. Bks.).

—City of Lost Souls, 16 vols. 2012. (Mortal Instruments Ser.: Bk. 5). (YA). 135.75 *(978-1-4640-3948-5(8));* 133.75 *(978-1-4640-3952-2(6));* 133.75 *(978-1-4640-3951-5(8));* 317.75 *(978-1-4640-3949-2(6))* Recorded Bks., Inc.

—City of Lost Souls. 2015. (Mortal Instruments Ser.: Bk. 5). 592p. (YA). lib. bdg. 25.75 *(978-0-606-37736-2(0))* Turtleback Bks.

—City of Lost Souls. 2012. 512p. pap. *(978-1-4063-3760-0(9))* Walker Bks., Ltd.

TUV

Clare, Cassandra, et al. The Bane Chronicles. Clare, Cassandra, ed. 2014. (Bane Chronicles Ser.). (ENG., Illus.). 528p. (YA). (gr. 9). 22.99 (978-1-4424-9599-9(5), McElderry, Margaret K. Bks.) McElderry, Margaret K. Bks.

—Tales from the Shadowhunter Academy. (Tales from the Shadowhunter Academy Ser.). (ENG.). (YA). (gr. 9). 2017. 704p. pap. 14.99 **(978-1-4814-4326-5(7))** 2016. (Illus.). 672p. 23.99 (978-1-4814-4325-8(9)) McElderry, Margaret K. Bks. (McElderry, Margaret K. Bks.).

Cold Moon. 2nd ed. 2014. 180p. pap. 14.99 (978-1-62798-459-1(3), Harmony Ink Pr.) Dreamspinner Pr.

Collins, Nancy A. After Dark. 3rd ed. 2009. (Vamps Ser.: 3). (ENG.). 192p. (YA). (gr. 9-18). pap. 8.99 (978-0-06-134919-5(4), HarperTeen) HarperCollins Pubs.

—Night Life. 2009. (Vamps Ser.: 2). (ENG.). 256p. (YA). (gr. 9-18). pap. 8.99 (978-0-06-134918-8(6), HarperTeen) HarperCollins Pubs.

—Vamps. 2008. (Vamps Ser.: 1). (ENG.). 256p. (YA). (gr. 9-18). pap. 8.99 (978-0-06-134917-1(8), HarperTeen) HarperCollins Pubs.

Collins, Tim. Fang-Tastic Collection! Notes from a Totally Lame Vampire; Prince of Dorkness; Notes from a Hairy-Not-Scary Werewolf; Fangs a Lot. Pindar, Andrew, illus. 2016. (ENG.). 1280p. (J). (gr. 3-7). 52.99 (978-1-4814-6980-7(0), Aladdin) Simon & Schuster Children's Publishing.

—Fangs a Lot: Final Notes from a Totally Lame Vampire. Pinder, Andrew, illus. 2014. (ENG.). 320p. (J). (gr. 5-9). 13.99 (978-1-4814-2134-8(4), Aladdin) Simon & Schuster Children's Publishing.

—Notes from a Hairy-Not-Scary Werewolf. Pinder, Andrew, illus. 2013. (ENG.). 288p. (J). (gr. 5-9). 12.99 (978-1-4424-8207-4(9), Aladdin) Simon & Schuster Children's Publishing.

—Notes from a Totally Lame Vampire: Because the Undead Have Feelings Too! Pinder, Andrew, illus. 2010. (ENG.). 336p. (J). (gr. 5-9). 12.99 (978-1-4424-1183-8(X), Aladdin) Simon & Schuster Children's Publishing.

—Prince of Dorkness: More Notes from a Totally Lame Vampire. Pinder, Andrew, illus. 2011. (ENG.). 336p. (J). (gr. 5-9). 12.99 (978-1-4424-3388-5(4), Aladdin) Simon & Schuster Children's Publishing.

Cook, Kristi. Eternal. (ENG., Illus.). (YA). (gr. 9). 2014. 432p. pap. 9.99 (978-1-4424-8531-0(0)) 2013. 416p. 16.99 (978-1-4424-8532-7(9)) Simon Pulse. (Simon Pulse).

Cooney, Caroline B. The Vampire's Promise. 2011. (ENG.). 496p. (J). (gr. 7-7). pap. 9.99 (978-0-545-28976-4(9)) Scholastic, Inc.

Cooper, Helen Wendy. The Vegetarian Vampire. 2012. (Illus.). 53p. pap. 8.50 (978-1-78035-365-4(0), Fastprint Publishing) Upfront Publishing Ltd. GBR. Dist: Printondemand-worldwide.com.

—The Vegetarian Vampire: The Lost Fangs. 2013. (Illus.). 50p. pap. 8.50 (978-1-78035-651-8(X), Fastprint Publishing) Upfront Publishing Ltd. GBR. Dist: Printondemand-worldwide.com.

Cosby, Sam & Metzger, Clancy. Ceruladons: Blue dreams rain to Tears. 2008. 304p. 28.95 (978-0-595-51125-9(2)) iUniverse, Inc.

Cox, Michael & Smedley. Invasion of the Sausage Snatchers. 2003. (Illus.). 128p. pap. (978-0-340-79592-7(1), Hodder Children's Books) Hachette Children's Group.

Crowson, Andrew. Flip Flap Spooky. Crowson, Andrew, illus. 2003. (Illus.). 12p. (J). bds. (978-1-85602-475-4(X), Pavilion Children's Books) Pavilion Bks.

Cunningham, P. E. Slayer for Hire. 2013. 204p. pap. (978-1-77130-285-2(2)) Evernight Publishing.

Dahl, Michael. The Vampire Chapter, 1 vol. Kendall, Bradford, illus. 2010. (Return to the Library of Doom Ser.). (ENG.). 72p. (gr. 1-3). 23.99 (978-1-4342-2143-8(1), Zone Bks.) Stone Arch Bks.

Darrows, Eva. The Awesome. 2015. (ENG.). 352p. (YA). (gr. 10). pap. 9.99 (978-1-78108-324-6(X), Ravenstone) Rebellion GBR. Dist: Simon & Schuster, Inc.

Datlow, Ellen & Windling, Terri. Teeth: Vampire Tales. 2011. (ENG.). 480p. (YA). (gr. 8-18). 17.99 (978-0-06-193515-2(8)); pap. 9.99 (978-0-06-193514-5(X)) HarperCollins Pubs.

De la Cruz, Melissa. Blue Bloods. (Blue Bloods Ser.). (ENG.). (J). (gr. 5-9). 2007. 336p. pap. 9.99 (978-1-4231-0126-0(X))Set. 2009. 944p. pap. 24.99 (978-1-4231-2595-2(9)) Hyperion Pr.

—Blue Bloods. 2007. (Blue Bloods Ser.: 1). (J). lib. bdg. 20.85 (978-1-4178-2375-8(5), Turtleback) Turtleback Bks.

—Gates of Paradise. 2013. (ENG.). 368p. (Blue Bloods Ser.: Bk. 7). (J). (gr. 5-9). pap. 9.99 (978-1-4231-6110-3(6)); (YA). (gr. 7-17). 16.99 (978-1-4231-5741-0(9)) Hyperion Pr.

—Lost in Time. 2012. (Blue Bloods Ser.). (ENG.). 368p. (J). (gr. 5-9). pap. 8.99 (978-1-4231-3413-8(3)) Hyperion Pr.

—Masquerade. 2008. (Blue Bloods Ser.). (ENG.). 336p. (J). (gr. 5-9). pap. 9.99 (978-1-4231-0127-7(8)) Hyperion Pr.

—Revelations. 2009. (ENG.). 288p. (J). (gr. 7-17). pap. 8.99 (978-1-4231-0229-8(0)) Hyperion Pr.

DEKELB-RITTENHOUSE, Diane. Immortal Longings. 2012. (ENG.). 340p. (J). (gr. 7). pap. 14.95 (978-0-9845318-4-4(X)) Tiny Stachel Pr.

Dent, Sue. Never Ceese: Can Two Who Were Wronged Make It Right? 2006. 336p. (YA). lib. bdg. 17.99 (978-1-59958-017-3(9)) Journey Stone Creations, LLC.

Despeyroux, Denise. The Big Book of Vampires. Falcone, Fernando, illus. 2012. (ENG.). 112p. (J). (gr. 4-7). 17.95 (978-1-77049-371-1(9), Tundra Bks.) Tundra Bks. CAN. Dist: Penguin Random Hse. LLC.

Deutsch, Stacia, adapted by. Hotel Transylvania 2: Movie Novelization. 2015. (Illus.). 141p. (J). (978-1-4806-9404-0(5), Simon Spotlight) Simon Spotlight.

Donbavand, Tommy. Attack of the Trolls. 2012. (Scream Street Ser.: 8). (ENG., Illus.). 128p. (J). (gr. 3-7). pap. 5.99 (978-0-7636-5760-4(3)) Candlewick Pr.

—Attack of the Trolls. 2012. (Scream Street Ser.: 8). lib. bdg. 16.00 (978-0-606-31471-8(7), Turtleback) Turtleback Bks.

—Blood of the Witch. 2009. (Scream Street Ser.: 2). (ENG., Illus.). 128p. (J). (gr. 3-7). pap. 5.99 (978-0-7636-4607-3(5)) Candlewick Pr.

—Blood of the Witch: Book 2, 1 vol. Cartoon Saloon, illus. 2012. (ENG.). 120p. (J). 24.21 (978-1-59961-993-4(8), Chapter Bks.) Spotlight.

—Claw of the Werewolf, Bk. 6. Cartoon Saloon Staff, illus. 2010. (Scream Street Ser.: 6). (ENG.). 128p. (J). (gr. 3-7). pap. 5.99 (978-0-7636-4638-7(5)) Candlewick Pr.

—Claw of the Werewolf: Book 6, 1 vol. Cartoon Saloon, illus. 2012. (ENG.). 120p. (J). 24.21 (978-1-59961-997-2(0), Chapter Bks.) Spotlight.

—Fang of the Vampire. Cartoon Saloon Staff, illus. 2009. (Scream Street Ser.: 1). (ENG.). 160p. (J). (gr. 3-7). pap. 5.99 (978-0-7636-4608-0(3)) Candlewick Pr.

—Fang of the Vampire: Book 1, 1 vol. Cartoon Saloon, illus. 2012. (ENG.). 129p. (J). 24.21 (978-1-59961-992-7(X), Chapter Bks.) Spotlight.

—Invasion of the Normals. 2012. (Scream Street Ser.: 7). (ENG., Illus.). 128p. (J). (gr. 3-7). pap. 5.99 (978-0-7636-5759-8(X)) Candlewick Pr.

—Secret of the Changeling. Donbavand, Tommy, illus. 2015. (Scream Street Ser.: 12). (ENG., Illus.). 128p. (J). (gr. 3-7). pap. 5.99 (978-0-7636-5764-2(6)) Candlewick Pr.

—Skull of the Skeleton, Bk. 5. Cartoon Saloon Staff, illus. 2010. (Scream Street Ser.: 5). (ENG.). 128p. (J). (gr. 3-7). pap. 5.99 (978-0-7636-4635-6(0)) Candlewick Pr.

—Skull of the Skeleton: Book 5, 1 vol. Cartoon Saloon, illus. 2012. (ENG.). 120p. (J). 24.21 (978-1-59961-996-5(2), Chapter Bks.) Spotlight.

—Terror of the Nightwatchman. 2014. (Scream Street Ser.: 9). lib. bdg. 16.00 (978-0-606-35872-9(2)) Turtleback Bks.

Dufaux, Jean. Rapaces. Marini, Enrico, illus. 2004. (SPA.). Vol. 1. 56p. pap. 17.95 (978-1-59497-003-0(3)) Vol. 2. 56p. pap. 17.95 (978-1-59497-004-7(1)) Vol. 3. 64p. pap. 17.95 (978-1-59497-005-4(X)) Public Square Bks.

Durst, Sarah Beth. Drink, Slay, Love. (ENG., Illus.). 400p. (YA). (gr. 9). 2012. pap. 10.99 (978-1-4424-2374-9(9)) 2011. 17.99 (978-1-4424-2373-2(0)) McElderry, Margaret K. Bks. (McElderry, Margaret K. Bks.).

Duval, Alex. Bloodlust. 2006. (Vampire Beach Ser.: 1). (ENG.). 208p. (YA). (gr. 7-12). mass mkt. 6.99 (978-1-4169-1166-1(9), Simon Pulse) Simon Pulse.

—Bloodlust - Initiation. 2010. (Vampire Beach Ser.: 1). (ENG.). 416p. (YA). (gr. 9). pap. 9.99 (978-1-4424-0693-3(3), Simon Pulse) Simon Pulse.

—Ritual. 2007. (Vampire Beach Ser.). (ENG.). 208p. (YA). (gr. 9-12). mass mkt. 5.99 (978-1-4169-1168-5(5), Simon Pulse) Simon Pulse.

—Vampire Beach 2 - Ritual - Legacy. 2011. (Vampire Beach Ser.: 2). (ENG.). 448p. (YA). (gr. 9). pap. 9.99 (978-1-4424-0694-0(1), Simon Pulse) Simon Pulse.

Egielski, Richard. The Sleepless Little Vampire. 2011. (J). pap. (978-0-545-14598-5(8), Levine, Arthur A. Bks.) Scholastic, Inc.

Fangs for the Memories. 2008. (Looney Tunes 8*8 Ser.). 24p. pap. (978-1-4075-2630-0(8)); pap. (978-1-4075-2640-9(5)) Parragon, Inc.

Fantaskey, Beth. Jessica Rules the Dark Side. 2012. (ENG.). 320p. (YA). (gr. 9). 16.99 (978-0-547-39309-4(1)) Houghton Mifflin Harcourt Publishing Co.

—Jessica's Guide to Dating on the Dark Side. 2010. (ENG., Illus.). 384p. (YA). (gr. 9-18). pap. 8.99 (978-0-547-25940-6(9)) Houghton Mifflin Harcourt Publishing Co.

Feasey, Steve. Dark Moon. 2011. (Wereling Ser.: 2). (ENG.). 336p. (YA). (gr. 7-18). pap. 18.99 (978-0-312-64643-1(7), 9780312646431) Feiwel & Friends.

—Wereling. 2010. (Wereling Ser.: 1). (ENG.). 288p. (YA). (gr. 7-18). pap. 9.99 (978-0-312-59612-5(X), 9780312596125) Feiwel & Friends.

Feder, Jane. Spooky Friends. Downing, Julie, illus. 2013. (ENG.). 40p. (J). (gr. k-2). 16.99 (978-0-545-47815-1(4), Scholastic Pr.) Scholastic, Inc.

—Spooky Friends, Level 2. Downing, Julie, illus. 2013. (Scholastic Reader Level 2 Ser.). (ENG.). 40p. (J). (gr. 1-2). pap. 3.99 (978-0-545-47816-8(2), Scholastic Pr.) Scholastic, Inc.

Fischer, Rusty. Vamplayers. 2011. (Living Dead Love Story Ser.). (ENG.). 384p. (YA). (gr. 6). pap. 9.95 (978-1-60542-449-1(8), Gold Medallion) Medallion Pr., Inc.

Fisher, Rusty. Littlest Vampire's Story, 1 vol. 2014. (Story Time for Little Monsters Ser.). (ENG., Illus.). 24p. (J). (gr. -1-4). lib. bdg. 27.07 (978-1-62402-020-9(8), Looking Glass Library) Magic Wagon.

Fontes, Justine & Fontes, Ron. Casebook: Vampires. 2009. (Top Secret Graphica Mysteries Ser.). (Illus.). 48p. (YA). (gr. 2-6). 29.25 (978-1-60754-606-1(X)); pap. 11.75 (978-1-60754-607-8(8)) Windmill Bks.

Frade, B. A. Vampire Vacation. 2017. (Tales from the Scaremaster Ser.: 5). (ENG.). 160p. (J). (gr. 3-7). pap. 5.99 **(978-0-316-46409-3(0))** Little, Brown Bks. for Young Readers.

—Vampire Vacation. 2017. (Tales of the Scaremaster Ser.). (J). lib. bdg. 16.00 **(978-0-606-40225-5(X))** Turtleback Bks.

Francis, Melissa. Bite Me! 2009. (ENG.). 304p. (YA). (gr. 9-18). pap. 8.99 (978-0-06-143098-5(6), HarperTeen) HarperCollins Pubs.

Francis, Melissa Mckenzie. Love Sucks! 2010. (ENG.). 288p. (YA). (gr. 9-18). pap. 8.99 (978-0-06-143099-2(4), HarperTeen) HarperCollins Pubs.

Fry, Sonali. I'm a Little Vampire. Rescek, Sanja, illus. 2014. (ENG.). 16p. (J). (gr. -1 — 1). bds. 5.99 (978-1-4814-0504-1(7), Little Simon) Little Simon.

Fukuda, Andrew. The Hunt. 2012. (Hunt Trilogy Ser.: 1). (ENG.). 304p. (YA). (gr. 7). pap. 11.99 (978-1-250-00529-8(9), 9781250005298); 17.99 (978-1-250-00514-4(0), 9781250005144) St. Martin's Pr. (St. Martin's Griffin).

—The Trap. 2013. (Hunt Trilogy Ser.: 3). (ENG.). 320p. (YA). (gr. 7). 18.99 (978-1-250-00512-0(4), 9781250005120, St. Martin's Griffin) St. Martin's Pr.

Gelsey, James & Duendes Del Sur Staff. Scooby-Doo & the Vampire's Revenge, 1 vol. 2011. (Scooby-Doo Mysteries Ser.). (ENG., Illus.). 64p. (J). (gr. 3-6). 24.21 (978-1-59961-894-4(X)) Spotlight.

Gilson. Melusine Vol. 3: The Vampires' Ball. 2008. (Melusine Ser.: 3). (ENG., Illus.). 48p. (J). (gr. 4-7). pap. 11.95 (978-1-905460-69-4(4)) CineBook GBR. Dist: National Bk. Network.

Gleason, Colleen. The Chess Queen Enigma: A Stoker & Holmes Novel. (ENG.). 360p. (YA). (gr. 7-12). 2016. pap. 9.99 (978-1-4521-5649-1(2)) 2015. (Stoker & Holmes Ser.: 3). 17.99 (978-1-4521-4317-0(X)) Chronicle Bks. LLC.

—The Clockwork Scarab. 2014. (Stoker & Holmes Ser.: 1). (ENG.). 384p. (YA). (gr. 7-12). pap. 11.99 (978-1-4521-2873-3(1)) Chronicle Bks. LLC.

Goddard, Drew, et al. No Future for You, 8 vols., Vol. 2. Jeanty, Georges et al, illus. 2008. (Buffy the Vampire Slayer Ser.). (ENG.). 320p. pap. 15.99 (978-1-59307-963-5(X)) Dark Horse Comics.

Golightly, Holly, creator. School Bites. 2004. 64p. (YA). per. (978-0-9745367-2-9(5), SB1A) BroadSword Comics/ Jim Balent Studios.

Gow, Kailin. The Stoker Sisters. 2010. 266p. (YA). pap. (978-1-59748-947-8(6)) Sparklesoup LLC.

Gran, Meredith. Marceline & the Scream Queens. Gran, Meredith, illus. 2013. (Adventure Time Ser.). (ENG., Illus.). 128p. (J). (gr. 4). pap. 19.99 (978-1-60886-313-6(1)) Boom! Studios.

Grandma. There Is a Vampire in Our Cellar: Adventures of Butterfly Nectar Meadows. 2008. 20p. pap. 24.95 (978-1-60813-128-0(9)) America Star Bks.

Graves, Judith. Second Skin. 2011. 280p. (J). pap. 16.99 (978-1-61603-006-3(2)) Leap Bks.

—Under My Skin. Cox, Val, illus. 2010. 328p. (YA). (gr. 8-18). pap. 16.99 (978-1-61603-000-1(3)) Leap Bks.

Gray, Amy. How to Be a Vampire: A Fangs-On Guide for the Newly Undead. Erwert, Scott, illus. 2009. (ENG.). 144p. (YA). (gr. 7-18). 14.99 (978-0-7636-4915-9(5)) Candlewick Pr.

Gray, Claudia. Afterlife. 2012. (Evernight Ser.: 4). (ENG.). 384p. (YA). (gr. 8). pap. 9.99 (978-0-06-128451-9(3), HarperTeen) HarperCollins Pubs.

—Balthazar. (Evernight Ser.: 5). (ENG.). (YA). (gr. 8). 2013. 400p. pap. 9.99 (978-0-06-196119-9(1)) 2012. 384p. 17.99 (978-0-06-196118-2(3)) HarperCollins Pubs. (HarperTeen).

—Evernight. 2009. (Evernight Ser.: 1). (ENG.). 352p. (YA). (gr. 8). pap. 8.99 (978-0-06-128444-1(0), HarperTeen) HarperCollins Pubs.

—Hourglass. 2011. (Evernight Ser.: 3). (ENG.). 368p. (YA). (gr. 8). pap. 8.99 (978-0-06-128448-9(3), HarperTeen) HarperCollins Pubs.

—Stargazer. (Evernight Ser.: 2). (ENG.). (YA). (gr. 8). 2010. 352p. pap. 8.99 (978-0-06-128446-5(7)) 2009. 336p. 17.99 (978-0-06-128440-3(8)) HarperCollins Pubs. (HarperTeen).

Greenburg, Dan. Don't Count on Dracula. Davis, Jack E., illus. 2004. (Zack Files Ser.). 58p. lib. bdg. 15.00 (978-0-7569-2236-8(4)) Perfection Learning Corp.

—Secrets of Dripping Fang: Attack of the Giant Octopus. Fischer, Scott M., illus. 2009. (Secrets of Dripping Fang Ser.). (ENG.). 160p. 25.65 (978-1-59961-537-0(1)) Spotlight.

—Secrets of Dripping Fang: Fall of the House of Mandible. Fischer, Scott M., illus. 2009. (Secrets of Dripping Fang Ser.). (ENG.). 160p. 25.65 (978-1-59961-535-6(5)) Spotlight.

—Secrets of Dripping Fang: Please Don't Eat the Children: Book 7: Book 7. Fischer, Scott M., illus. 2009. (Secrets of Dripping Fang Ser.). (ENG.). 160p. 25.65 (978-1-59961-538-7(X)) Spotlight.

—Secrets of Dripping Fang: The Onts. Fischer, Scott M., illus. 2009. (Secrets of Dripping Fang Ser.). (ENG.). 144p. 25.65 (978-1-59961-532-5(0)) Spotlight.

—Secrets of Dripping Fang: The Shluffmuffin Boy Is History. Fischer, Scott M., illus. 2009. (Secrets of Dripping Fang Ser.). (ENG.). 176p. 25.65 (978-1-59961-536-3(3)) Spotlight.

—Secrets of Dripping Fang: The Vampire's Curse: Book 3: Book 3. Fischer, Scott M., illus. 2009. (Secrets of Dripping Fang Ser.). (ENG.). 144p. 25.65 (978-1-59961-534-9(7)) Spotlight.

—Secrets of Dripping Fang: Treachery & Betrayal at Jolly Days. Fischer, Scott M., illus. 2009. (Secrets of Dripping Fang Ser.). (ENG.). 144p. 25.65 (978-1-59961-533-2(9)) Spotlight.

—Secrets of Dripping Fang: When Bad Snakes Attack Good Children. Fischer, Scott M., illus. 2009. (Secrets of Dripping Fang Ser.). (ENG.). 144p. 25.65 (978-1-59961-539-4(8)) Spotlight.

—Secrets of Dripping Fang, Book Seven: Please Don't Eat the Children. Fischer, Scott M., illus. 2007. (Secrets of Dripping Fang Ser.: Bk. 7). (ENG.). 160p. (J). (gr. 2-5). 11.95 (978-0-15-206047-3(2)) Houghton Mifflin Harcourt Publishing Co.

Greenwald, Tom. My Dog Is Better Than Your Dog. Stower, Adam, illus. 2015. 198p. (J). pap. (978-0-545-91669-1(0), Scholastic Pr.) Scholastic, Inc.

Greenwald, Tommy. It's a Doggy Dog World. Stower, Adam, illus. 2016. (Crimebiters Ser.: 2). (ENG.). 240p. (J). (gr. 3-7). 12.99 (978-0-545-78397-2(6), Scholastic Pr.) Scholastic, Inc.

—My Dog Is Better Than Your Dog (Crimebiters! #1) Stower, Adam, illus. 2015. (Crimebiters Ser.: 1). (ENG.). 208p. (J). (gr. 3-7). 12.99 (978-0-545-77332-4(6), Scholastic Pr.) Scholastic, Inc.

Griffin, Adele. The Knaveheart's Curse. 2009. (Vampire Island Ser.). (ENG.). 160p. (J). (gr. 3-7). 6.99 (978-0-14-241407-1(7), Puffin Books) Penguin Young Readers Group.

Griffo, Michael. Unwelcome. 2011. (ENG.). 352p. (YA). (gr. 9). pap. 9.95 (978-0-7582-5339-2(7), K-Teen) Kensington Publishing Corp.

Gunter, Miles & Shannon, Kelsey. Yeti vs. Vampire. 2012. (Illus.). 96p. (YA). pap. 12.95 (978-0-9822253-5-6(0)) Antarctic Pr., Inc.

Hahn, Mary Downing. Look for Me by Moonlight. 2008. (ENG.). 208p. (YA). (gr. 7). pap. 7.99 (978-0-547-07616-4(9)) Houghton Mifflin Harcourt Publishing Co.

HarperCollins Publishers Ltd. Staff, et al. Origins No. 5. 2010. (Vampire Diaries: Stefan's Diaries: 1). (ENG.). 256p. (YA). (gr. 9-18). pap. 9.99 (978-0-06-200393-5(3), HarperTeen) HarperCollins Pubs.

Harris, Lewis. A Taste for Red. 2010. (ENG.). 180p. (J). (gr. 5-7). pap. 12.95 (978-0-547-39851-8(4)) Houghton Mifflin Harcourt Publishing Co.

Hautman, Pete. Sweetblood. 2010. (ENG.). 208p. (YA). (gr. 7). pap. 8.99 (978-1-4424-0755-8(7), Simon & Schuster Bks. For Young Readers) Simon & Schuster Bks. For Young Readers.

Havard, Amanda. The Survivors. 2011. (ENG.). (YA). 294p. 21.99 (978-0-9833190-0-9(6)); 300p. pap. 11.99 (978-0-9833190-2-3(2)) Chafie Pr., LLC.

Hawkins, Rachel. Hex Hall, Bk. 1. 2010. (ENG.). 336p. (J). (gr. 7-17). 16.99 (978-1-4231-2130-5(9)) Hyperion Pr.

Henderson, Jason. The Triumph of Death. 2012. (Alex Van Helsing Ser.: 3). (ENG.). 320p. (YA). (gr. 8). 17.99 (978-0-06-195103-9(X), HarperTeen) HarperCollins Pubs.

—Vampire Rising. (Alex Van Helsing Ser.: 1). (ENG.). (YA). (gr. 8). 2011. 272p. pap. 8.99 (978-0-06-195100-8(5)) 2010. 256p. 16.99 (978-0-06-195099-5(8)) HarperCollins Pubs. (HarperTeen).

—Voice of the Undead. 2011. (Alex Van Helsing Ser.: 2). (ENG.). 304p. (YA). (gr. 8). 16.99 (978-0-06-195101-5(3), HarperTeen) HarperCollins Pubs.

Henson, Heather, et al. The Vampire Bunny. Mack, Jeff, tr. Mack, Jeff, illus. 2004. (Bunnicula & Friends Ser.: 1). (ENG.). 48p. (J). (gr. 1-3). 16.99 (978-0-689-85724-9(1), Simon Spotlight) Simon Spotlight.

Hicks, Rebecca. Little Vampires. Hicks, Rebecca, illus. 2007. (Illus.). 56p. per. 8.95 (978-0-9799290-0-7(8)) Lunasea Studios.

Higginson, Sheila Sweeny & Deutsch, Stacia, adapted by. Hotel Transylvania 2 Movie Novelization. 2015. (Hotel Transylvania 2 Ser.). (ENG., Illus.). 144p. (J). (gr. 3-7). pap. 6.99 (978-1-4814-4819-2(6), Simon Spotlight) Simon Spotlight.

Hill, Will. Darkest Night (Department 19, Book 5) 2016. (Department 19 Ser.: 5). (ENG.). 736p. (J). pap. 9.99 (978-0-00-815427-1(9), HarperCollins Children's Bks.) HarperCollins Pubs. Ltd. GBR. Dist: HarperCollins Pubs.

—The Rising: A Department 19 Novel. 2013. (Department Nineteen Ser.: 2). (ENG.). 592p. (YA). (gr. 9). pap. 9.99 (978-1-59514-629-8(6), Razorbill) Penguin Young Readers Group.

Hill, William. Department Nineteen. 2012. (Department Nineteen Ser.: 1). (ENG.). 544p. (YA). (gr. 9). 9.99 (978-1-59514-485-0(4), Razorbill) Penguin Young Readers Group.

Hoena, Blake & Hoena, Blake A. Vampires & Veggies. Bardin, Dave, illus. 2016. (Monster Heroes Ser.). (ENG.). 32p. (gr. 1-2). lib. bdg. 21.32 (978-1-4965-3755-3(6)) Stone Arch Bks.

Holder, Nancy & Viguié, Debbie. Crusade. (Crusade Ser.). (ENG.). (YA). (gr. 9). 2011. 496p. pap. 9.99 (978-1-4169-9803-7(9)) 2010. 480p. 16.99 (978-1-4169-9802-0(0)) Simon Pulse. (Simon Pulse).

—Damned. 2011. (Crusade Ser.). (ENG.). 544p. (YA). (gr. 9). pap. 9.99 (978-1-4169-9805-1(5), Simon Pulse) Simon Pulse.

—Vanquished. 2012. (Crusade Ser.). (ENG.). 496p. (YA). (gr. 9). 16.99 (978-1-4169-9806-8(3)); pap. 9.99 (978-1-4169-9807-5(1)) Simon Pulse. (Simon Pulse).

Holloway, Christopher. Glourmain Chronicles Book 1. the Aznadac Heir. 2013. 262p. (J). pap. (978-1-78299-219-6(7)) FeedARead.com.

Holub, Joan. Vampoodle. Bowers, Tim, illus. 2017. (Step into Reading Ser.). (ENG.). 32p. (J). (gr. -1-1). pap. 3.99 (978-1-101-93666-5(5), Random Hse. Bks. for Young Readers) Random Hse. Children's Bks.

Hopkins, Audrey. Vinny Drake Is One. Flook, Helen, illus. 2007. (Tiger Ser.). (ENG.). 64p. (J). (gr. 2-4). pap. 9.95 (978-1-84270-437-0(0)) Andersen Pr. GBR. Dist: Independent Pubs. Group.

Hopkins, Ellen, ed. A New Dawn: Your Favorite Authors on Stephenie Meyer's Twilight Series. 2009. (ENG., Illus.). 200p. (J). (gr. 9-12). pap. 12.95 (978-1-933771-93-9(3)) BenBella Bks.

Howard, Kate. Hotel of Horrors. 2012. (Scooby Doo 8X8 Ser.). lib. bdg. 14.75 (978-0-606-31559-3(4), Turtleback) Turtleback Bks.

Howe, Deborah & Howe, James. Bunnicula. Daniel, Alan, illus. 2006. (Bunnicula & Friends Ser.). (ENG.). 128p. (J). (gr. 3-7). pap. 7.99 (978-1-4169-2817-1(0), Atheneum Bks. for Young Readers) Simon & Schuster Children's Publishing.

Howe, James. Bunnicula Strikes Again! 2004. (Bunnicula Ser.). 116p. (J). (gr. 3-7). pap. 29.00 incl. audio (978-0-8072-8213-7(8), Listening Library) Random Hse. Audio Publishing Group.

—Bunnicula Strikes Again! Daniel, Alan, illus. 2007. (Bunnicula & Friends Ser.). (ENG.). 144p. (J). (gr. 3-7). pap. 6.99 (978-1-4169-3968-9(7), Atheneum Bks. for Young Readers) Simon & Schuster Children's Publishing.

—The Celery Stalks at Midnight. unabr. ed. 2004. (Bunnicula Ser.). 111p. (J). (gr. 3-7). pap. 29.00 incl. audio (978-0-8072-8357-8(6), YA173SP, Listening Library) Random Hse. Audio Publishing Group.

—The Celery Stalks at Midnight. Morrill, Leslie H., illus. 2006. (Bunnicula & Friends Ser.). (ENG.). 144p. (J). (gr. 3-7). pap. 6.99 (978-1-4169-2814-0(6), Atheneum Bks. for Young Readers) Simon & Schuster Children's Publishing.

—Hot Fudge. Mack, Jeff, illus. 2006. (Bunnicula & Friends Ser.). 42p. (gr. k-4). 14.00 (978-0-7569-7224-0(8)) Perfection Learning Corp.

—Hot Fudge. Mack, Jeff, tr. Mack, Jeff, illus. 2004. (Bunnicula & Friends Ser.: 2). (ENG.). 48p. (J). (gr. 1-3). 16.99 (978-0-689-85725-6(X), Atheneum Bks. for Young Readers) Simon & Schuster Children's Publishing.

—The Vampire Bunny. Mack, Jeff, illus. 2005. (Bunnicula & Friends Ser.). 41p. (J). (gr. 1-3). 11.65 (978-0-7569-6832-8(1)) Perfection Learning Corp.

Hulme-Cross, Benjamin. The Red Thirst. Evergreen, Nelson, illus. 2015. (Dark Hunter Ser.). (ENG.). 64p. (J). (gr. 4-8). pap. 4.99 (978-1-4677-8088-9(X)) Lerner Publishing Group.

Hunter, C. C. Awake at Dawn. 2013. (Shadow Falls Novel Ser.: 2). (ENG.). 400p. (YA). (gr. 7-12). mass mkt. 9.99 (978-1-250-04679-6(3), 9781250046796, St. Martin's Paperbacks) St. Martin's Pr.

—Eternal. 2014. (Shadow Falls: after Dark Ser.: 2). (ENG.). 400p. (YA). mass mkt. 9.99 (978-1-250-07016-6(3), 9781250070166, St. Martin's Paperbacks); (gr. 7-12). 19.99 (978-1-250-05630-6(6), St. Martin's Griffin) St. Martin's Pr.

—Eternal: Shadow Falls: After Dark. 2014. (Shadow Falls: after Dark Ser.: 2). (ENG.). 400p. (YA). (gr. 7-12). pap. 9.99 (978-1-250-04461-7(8), 9781250044617, St. Martin's Griffin) St. Martin's Pr.

—Reborn. 2014. (Shadow Falls: after Dark Ser.: 1). (ENG.). 400p. (YA). (gr. 7). pap. 10.99 (978-1-250-03591-2(0), 9781250035912, St. Martin's Griffin) St. Martin's Pr.

Jeanty, Georges, et al. The Core, Vol. 5. Allie, Scott & Hahn, Sierra, eds. 2014. (ENG., Illus.). 168p. pap. 17.99 *(978-1-61655-254-1(9))* Dark Horse Comics.
Jefford, Nikki. Aurora Sky: Vampire Hunter, Vol. 1. 2013. 260p. pap. 10.99 *(978-1-939997-48-7(8))* Boyce, S. M.
Jenkins, A. M. Night Road. (ENG.). 368p. (YA). (gr. 8). 2010. pap. 8.99 *(978-0-06-054606-9(9))*No. 1. 2008. 16.99 *(978-0-06-054604-5(2))* HarperCollins Pubs. (HarperTeen).
Jinks, Catherine. The Reformed Vampire Support Group. 2010. (ENG.). 384p. (YA). (gr. 7). pap. 8.99 *(978-0-547-41166-8(9))* Houghton Mifflin Harcourt Publishing Co.
Johnson, Pete. The Vampire Fighters. 2012. (ENG., Illus.). 272p. (J). (gr. 4-7). pap. 10.99 *(978-0-440-86940-5(4))* Transworld Publishers Ltd. GBR. Dist: Independent Pubs. Group.
Jolley, Dan. My Boyfriend Bites, 3 vols., No. 3. Martinez, Alitha E., illus. 2011. (My Boyfriend Is a Monster Ser.: 3). (ENG.). 128p. (YA). (gr. 7-12). 29.27 *(978-0-7613-5599-1(5))* Lerner Publishing Group.
—My Boyfriend Is a Monster - My Boyfriend Bites. Martinez, Alitha E., illus. 2011. (My Boyfriend Is a Monster Ser.: 3). (ENG.). 128p. (YA). (gr. 7-12). pap. 9.95 *(978-0-7613-7078-9(1),* Graphic Universe™) Lerner Publishing Group.
—Vampire Hunt. Titus, Gregory, illus. 2008. (Twisted Journeys (r) Ser.: 7). (ENG.). 112p. (J). (gr. 4-7). 27.93 *(978-0-8225-8877-1(3),* Graphic Universe™); pap. 7.95 *(978-0-8225-8879-5(X))* Lerner Publishing Group.
Jozev. Claws of Darkness. 2006. (Journal of the Vampire Hunter; Claws of Darkness Ser.). (ENG., Illus.). 64p. (YA). pap. 5.95 *(978-1-59796-090-8(X))* DrMaster Pubns. Inc.
—Journal of the Vampire Hunter Vol. 3: Claws of Darkness. Zhao, Yun, tr. 2006. (Journal of the Vampire Hunter; Claws of Darkness Ser.). (ENG., Illus.). 64p. (YA). pap. 5.95 *(978-1-59796-088-5(8))* DrMaster Pubns. Inc.
—Journal of the Vampire Hunter Vol. 4: Claws of Darkness. 2006. (Journal of the Vampire Hunter; Claws of Darkness Ser.). (ENG., Illus.). 64p. (YA). pap. 5.95 *(978-1-59796-089-2(6))* DrMaster Pubns. Inc.
Julie Shelton. World of Vampires Part 1: The Huntress. 2006. 49p. pap. 10.00 *(978-1-59926-998-6(8))* Xlibris Corp.
Jungman, Ann. Vlad the Drac. Thompson, George, illus. 2006. (Vlad the Drac Ser.). 124p. (J). (gr. 2-4). per. 6.95 *(978-1-903015-22-3(7))* Barn Owl Bks, London GBR. Dist: Independent Pubs. Group.
—Vlad the Drac Superstar. Thompson, George, illus. 2006. (Vlad the Drac Ser.). 122p. (J). (gr. 2-4). pap. 6.95 *(978-1-903015-45-2(6))* Barn Owl Bks, London GBR. Dist: Independent Pubs. Group.
Jungman, Ann & Quarto Generic Staff. Vlad the Drac: The Adventures of a Vegetarian Vampire. rev. ed. 2014. (ENG., Illus.). 120p. (J). (gr. 2-5). pap. 7.99 *(978-1-84780-487-7(X),* Frances Lincoln) Quarto Publishing Group UK GBR. Dist: Hachette Bk. Group.
Kadence, Sam. Evolution. 2013. 230p. pap. 14.99 *(978-1-62380-410-7(8),* Harmony Ink Pr.) Dreamspinner Pr.
—Evolution [Library Edition]. 2013. 230p. pap. 14.99 *(978-1-62380-924-9(X),* Harmony Ink Pr.) Dreamspinner Pr.
Kagawa, Julie. The Immortal Rules. 2013. (Blood of Eden Ser.: 1). lib. bdg. 20.85 *(978-0-606-26947-6(9),* Turtleback) Turtleback Bks.
Katcher, Brian. The Improbable Theory of Ana & Zak. 2016. (ENG.). 336p. (YA). (gr. 8). 20.85 *(978-0-606-39261-7(0))* Turtleback Bks.
Kayla Taylor. Fatal Elements: Book 1. 2009. 368p. pap. 20.95 *(978-1-4401-8495-6(X))* iUniverse, Inc.
Keating, T. P. Bleeding Hearts: the Diary of a Country Vampire. 2005. 272p. (YA). pap. 12.48 *(978-1-4116-4815-9(3))* Lulu Pr., Inc.
Keeble, Helen. Fang Girl. 2012. (ENG.). 352p. (YA). (gr. 8). pap. 9.99 *(978-0-06-208225-1(6),* HarperTeen) HarperCollins Pubs.
Kelly, Nikki. Gabriel. 2015. (Styclar Saga Ser.: 2). (ENG.). 384p. (YA). (gr. 7). 17.99 *(978-1-250-05153-0(3),* 9781250051530) Feiwel & Friends.
—Jonah. 2017. (Styclar Saga Ser.: 3). (ENG.). 352p. (YA). 17.99 *(978-1-250-05154-7(1),* 9781250051547) Feiwel & Friends.
—Lailah. 2014. (Styclar Saga Ser.: 1). (ENG.). 416p. (YA). (gr. 7). 17.99 *(978-1-250-05151-6(7),* 9781250051516) Feiwel & Friends.
Klause, Annette Curtis. The Silver Kiss. 2007. (ENG.). 224p. (YA). (gr. 7). pap. 8.99 *(978-0-385-73422-6(0),* Delacorte Bks. for Young Readers) Random Hse. Children's Bks.
Kokoro, Natsume & Natsume, Kokoro. Lovephobia Volume 2. 2012. (ENG., Illus.). 200p. (YA). pap. 12.95 *(978-1-56970-283-3(7),* 9781569702833) Digital Manga Publishing.
Lake, Nick. The Betrayal of the Living. (ENG., Illus.). 368p. (YA). (gr. 9). 2013. (Blood Ninja Ser.: Bk. 3). pap. 9.99 *(978-1-4424-2680-1(2))* 2012. 17.99 *(978-1-4424-2679-5(9))* Simon & Schuster Bks. For Young Readers. (Simon & Schuster Bks. For Young Readers).
—Blood Ninja. (ENG., Illus.). (YA). (gr. 7). 2010. (Blood Ninja Ser.: Bk. 1). 400p. pap. 9.99 *(978-1-4169-8628-7(6))* 2009. 384p. 16.99 *(978-1-4169-8627-0(8))* Simon & Schuster Bks. For Young Readers. (Simon & Schuster Bks. For Young Readers).
—The Revenge of Lord Oda. (ENG., Illus.). (YA). (gr. 7). 2011. (Blood Ninja Ser.: Bk. 2). 416p. pap. 9.99 *(978-1-4169-8630-0(8))* 2010. 400p. 16.99 *(978-1-4169-8629-4(4))* Simon & Schuster Bks. For Young Readers. (Simon & Schuster Bks. For Young Readers).
Lane, Travis. Redhaze: Trilogy. 2004. 192p. pap. 24.95 *(978-1-4137-6094-1(5))* PublishAmerica, Inc.
Larbalestier, Justine & Brennan, Sarah Rees. Team Human. (ENG.). 352p. (YA). (gr. 8). 2013. pap. 9.99 *(978-0-06-208965-6(X))* 2012. 17.99 *(978-0-06-208964-9(1))* HarperCollins Pubs. (HarperTeen).
Lawrence, Michael. Jiggy the Vampire Slayer: A Bloodcurdling Caper! 2011. (ENG.). 224p. (J). (gr. 4-6). pap. 7.99 *(978-1-4083-0804-2(5))* Hodder & Stoughton GBR. Dist: Hachette Bk. Group.
Leamon, Kevin. Oh No. Not Again! 2010. 27p. 14.95 *(978-0-557-63078-3(9))* Lulu Pr., Inc.
Leblanc, Louise. Leo's Midnight Rescue. Prud'homme, Jules, illus. 2004. 62p. (J). lib. bdg. 12.00 *(978-1-4242-1217-0(0))* Fitzgerald Bks.
—Leo's Midnight Rescue, 1 vol. Cummins, Sarah, tr. from FRE. Prud'homme, Jules & Jules, Prud'homme, illus. 2004. (Formac First Novels Ser.: 53). (ENG.). 64p. (J). (gr. 2-5). 4.95 *(978-0-88780-640-7(6),* 9780887806407); 14.95 *(978-0-88780-641-4(4),* 9780887806414) Formac Publishing Co., Ltd. CAN. Dist: Casemate Pubs. & Bk. Distributors, LLC.
—Leo's Skiing Surprise. Prud'homme, Jules, illus. 2007. (Formac First Novels Ser.). (ENG.). 64p. (J). (gr. 2-5). 14.95 *(978-0-88780-738-1(0),* 9780887807381) Formac Publishing Co., Ltd. CAN. Dist: Casemate Pubs. & Bk. Distributors, LLC.
—Leo's Skiing Surprise, 1 vol. Cummins, Sarah, tr. from FRE. Prud'homme, Jules, illus. 2007. (Formac First Novels Ser.). (ENG.). 64p. (J). (gr. 2-5). 4.95 *(978-0-88780-736-7(4),* 9780887807367) Formac Publishing Co., Ltd. CAN. Dist: Casemate Pubs. & Bk. Distributors, LLC.
Leblanc, Louise & Prud'homme, Jules. Les Vampires Sortent de L'ombre. 2003. (Premier Roman Ser.). (FRE., Illus.). 64p. (J). (gr. 1-4). pap. *(978-2-89021-609-9(8))* Diffusion du livre Mirabel (DLM).
Lockard, Lynn. Gone Batty!!! 2009. 40p. pap. 16.99 *(978-1-4389-8516-9(9))* AuthorHouse.
London, J. A. After Daybreak. 2013. (Darkness Before Dawn Ser.: 3). (ENG., Illus.). 336p. (YA). (gr. 9). pap. 9.99 *(978-0-06-202067-3(6),* HarperTeen) HarperCollins Pubs.
—Darkness Before Dawn. 2012. (Darkness Before Dawn Ser.: 1). (ENG., Illus.). 368p. (YA). (gr. 9). pap. 9.99 *(978-0-06-202065-9(X),* HarperTeen) HarperCollins Pubs.
Lowe, E. Van. Never Slow Dance with a Zombie. 2009. (ENG.). 256p. (J). (gr. 8-12). pap. 18.99 *(978-0-7653-2040-7(1),* 9780765320407, Tor Teen) Doherty, Tom Assocs., LLC.
Lubar, David. Attack of the Vampire Weenies: And Other Warped & Creepy Tales. 2011. (Weenies Stories Ser.). (ENG.). 224p. (J). (gr. 4-7). 15.99 *(978-0-7653-2345-3(1),* 9780765323453, Starscape) Doherty, Tom Assocs., LLC.
—Strikeout of the Bleacher Weenies: And Other Warped & Creepy Tales. 2016. (Weenies Stories Ser.: 8). (ENG.). 208p. (J). 15.99 *(978-0-7653-7726-5(8),* 9780765377265, Starscape) Doherty, Tom Assocs., LLC.
—The Vanishing Vampire: A Monsterrific Tale. 2013. (Monsterrific Tales Ser.). (ENG., Illus.). 144p. (J). (gr. 3-7). 15.99 *(978-0-7653-3077-2(6),* 9780765330772, Starscape) Doherty, Tom Assocs., LLC.
Maizel, Rebecca. Infinite Days. 2010. (Vampire Queen Ser.: 1). (ENG.). 336p. (YA). (gr. 7-18). pap. 9.99 *(978-0-312-64991-3(6),* 9780312649913, St. Martin's Griffin) St. Martin's Pr.
—Stolen Nights. 2013. (Vampire Queen Ser.: 2). (ENG.). 320p. (YA). (gr. 7-18). pap. 9.99 *(978-0-312-64992-0(4),* 9780312649920, St. Martin's Griffin) St. Martin's Pr.
Maniscalco, Kerri. Hunting Prince Dracula. 2017. (Stalking Jack the Ripper Ser.: 2). (ENG., Illus.). (YA). (gr. 10-17). 448p. 18.99 ***(978-0-316-55166-3(X))***; 608p. 20.99 ***(978-0-316-43986-2(X))*** Little Brown & Co. (Jimmy Patterson).
Marini, Enrico & Dufaux, Jean. Rapaces, Vol. 4. 2005. (SPA., Illus.). 56p. pap. 17.95 *(978-1-59497-107-5(2))* Public Square Bks.
Marrone, Amanda. Devoured. 2009. (ENG.). 304p. (YA). (gr. 9-18). pap. 9.99 *(978-1-4169-7890-9(9),* Simon Pulse) Simon Pulse.
—Slayed. 2010. (ENG., Illus.). 272p. (YA). (gr. 9-18). pap. 9.99 *(978-1-4169-9487-9(4),* Simon Pulse) Simon Pulse.
Marsh, Carole. The Mystery at Dracula's Castle: Transylvania, Romania. (Around the World in 80 Mysteries Ser.). 133p. (J). 2009. 18.99 *(978-0-635-07039-5(1),* Marsh, Carole Mysteries) 2008. (Illus.). (gr. 3-5). 14.95 *(978-0-635-06471-4(5))* 2008. (Illus.). (gr. 3-5). per. 5.95 *(978-0-635-06469-1(3),* Marsh, Carole Mysteries) Gallopade International.
Marshall, Carol. A Vampire's Story: Bella's Diary. 2009. 194p. pap. 9.99 *(978-1-61667-011-5(8))* Raider Publishing International.
McGowan, Maureen. Sleeping Beauty: Vampire Slayer. 2010. 320p. pap. 8.95 *(978-1-60747-779-2(3),* Pickwick Pr.) Phoenix Bks., Inc.
McHeffey, Adam. Asiago, 0 vols. McHeffey, Adam, illus. 2012. (ENG., Illus.). 32p. (J). (gr. k-3). 16.99 *(978-0-7614-6138-8(8),* 9780761461388, Amazon Children's Publishing) Amazon Publishing.
McIntyre, Sarah & O'Connell, David. Jampires. 2015. (ENG., Illus.). 32p. (J). (gr. -1-k). 16.99 *(978-0-545-81663-2(7))* Scholastic, Inc.
McKenzie, J. Lee. Vampires Don't Believe in Mermaids. 2011. 54p. pap. 16.95 *(978-1-4560-1157-4(X))* America Star Bks.
McNaughton, Colin. Dracula's Tomb. McNaughton, Colin, illus. 2009. (ENG., Illus.). 24p. (J). (gr. k-4). 14.99 *(978-0-7636-4488-8(9))* Candlewick Pr.
Mead, Richelle. Blood Promise. 2010. (Vampire Academy Ser.: 4). (ENG.). 528p. (YA). (gr. 7-18). 9.99 *(978-1-59514-310-5(6),* Razorbill) Penguin Young Readers Group.
—Blood Promise. 2010. (Vampire Academy Ser.: 4). lib. bdg. 20.85 *(978-0-606-14565-7(6),* Turtleback) Turtleback Bks.
—Bloodlines. 2012. (Bloodlines Ser.: 1). (ENG.). 448p. (YA). (gr. 7-18). pap. 10.99 *(978-1-59514-473-7(0),* Razorbill) Penguin Young Readers Group.
—The Fiery Heart. 2014. (Bloodlines Ser.: 4). (ENG.). 448p. (YA). (gr. 7). pap. 9.99 *(978-1-59514-631-1(8),* Razorbill) Penguin Young Readers Group.
—Frostbite. 2008. (Vampire Academy Ser.: Bk. 2). (ENG.). 335p. (YA). (gr. 7-18). pap. 10.99 *(978-1-59514-175-0(8),* Razorbill) Penguin Publishing Group.
—Frostbite. Vieceli, Emma, illus. 2012. (Vampire Academy Ser.: 2). (ENG.). 144p. (YA). (gr. 7-18). pap. 12.99 *(978-1-59514-430-0(7),* Razorbill) Penguin Young Readers Group.
—Frostbite. 2012. (Vampire Academy (Graphic Novels) Ser.: 2). lib. bdg. 24.50 *(978-0-606-23631-7(7),* Turtleback) Turtleback Bks.
—The Golden Lily. (Bloodlines Ser.: 2). (ENG.). (YA). (gr. 7). 2013. 448p. pap. 10.99 *(978-1-59514-602-1(4))* 2012. 432p. 18.99 *(978-1-59514-318-1(1))* Penguin Young Readers Group. (Razorbill).
—The Indigo Spell. 2013. (Bloodlines Ser.: Bk. 3). (ENG.). 416p. (YA). (gr. 7). 18.99 *(978-1-59514-319-8(X),* Razorbill) Penguin Publishing Group.
—The Indigo Spell. 2013. (Bloodlines Ser.: 3). (ENG.). 448p. (YA). (gr. 7). pap. 10.99 *(978-1-59514-613-7(X),* Razorbill) Penguin Young Readers Group.
—Last Sacrifice. 2011. (Vampire Academy Ser.: 6). (ENG.). 608p. (YA). (gr. 7-18). 10.99 *(978-1-59514-440-9(4),* Razorbill) Penguin Young Readers Group.
—The Ruby Circle. 2015. (Bloodlines Ser.: 6). (ENG.). (YA). (gr. 7). 384p. pap. 10.99 *(978-1-59514-633-5(4))*; 368p. 18.99 *(978-1-59514-322-8(X))* Penguin Young Readers Group. (Razorbill).
—Shadow Kiss. 2008. (Vampire Academy Ser.: 3). (ENG.). 448p. (YA). (gr. 7-18). pap. 10.99 *(978-1-59514-197-2(9),* Razorbill) Penguin Publishing Group.
—Shadow Kiss. Vieceli, Emma, illus. 2013. (Vampire Academy Ser.: 3). (ENG.). 160p. (YA). (gr. 7). pap. 12.99 *(978-1-59514-431-7(5),* Razorbill) Penguin Young Readers Group.
—Shadow Kiss. 2013. (Vampire Academy (Graphic Novels) Ser.: 3). lib. bdg. 24.50 *(978-0-606-34129-5(3),* Turtleback) Turtleback Bks.
—Silver Shadows. 2014. (Bloodlines Ser.: Bk. 5). (ENG.). 416p. (YA). (gr. 7). 18.99 *(978-1-59514-321-1(1),* Razorbill) Penguin Publishing Group.
—Silver Shadows. 2015. (Bloodlines Ser.: 5). (ENG.). 416p. (YA). (gr. 7). pap. 9.99 *(978-1-59514-632-8(6),* Razorbill) Penguin Young Readers Group.
—Spirit Bound. 2011. (Vampire Academy Ser.: 5). (ENG.). 512p. (YA). (gr. 7-18). 9.99 *(978-1-59514-366-2(1),* Razorbill) Penguin Young Readers Group.
—Vampire Academy. 2007. (Vampire Academy Ser.: Bk. 1). (ENG.). 336p. (J). (gr. 7-18). pap. 10.99 *(978-1-59514-174-3(X),* Razorbill) Penguin Publishing Group.
—Vampire Academy. 2010. (SPA.). 256p. (gr. 8-12). pap. 16.99 *(978-607-11-0456-4(4),* Alfaguara) Santillana USA Publishing Co., Inc.
—Vampire Academy. Vieceli, Emma, illus. 2011. (Vampire Academy Ser.: 1). (ENG.). 144p. (J). (gr. 7-18). pap. 12.99 *(978-1-59514-429-4(3),* Razorbill) Penguin Young Readers Group.
—Vampire Academy 10th Anniversary Edition. 2016. (ENG.). 512p. (YA). (gr. 7). pap. 11.99 *(978-0-448-49429-6(9),* Razorbill) Penguin Young Readers Group.
—Vampire Academy Box Set 1-3, 3 vols. 2013. (Vampire Academy Ser.). (ENG.). 1152p. (YA). (gr. 7). pap., pap., pap. 30.97 *(978-1-59514-775-2(6),* Razorbill) Penguin Young Readers Group.
—Vampire Academy Box Set 1-6, 6 vols. 2013. (Vampire Academy Ser.). (ENG.). 2784p. (YA). (gr. 7). pap., pap., pap. 60.94 *(978-1-59514-758-5(6),* Razorbill) Penguin Young Readers Group.
—Vampire Academy Box Set 4-6, 3 vols. 2013. (Vampire Academy Ser.). (ENG.). 1648p. (YA). (gr. 7). pap., pap., pap. 29.97 *(978-1-59514-787-5(X),* Razorbill) Penguin Young Readers Group.
Meehl, Brian. Suck It Up. 2009. (ENG.). 336p. (YA). (gr. 7). pap. 8.99 *(978-0-440-42091-0(1),* Delacorte Bks. for Young Readers) Random Hse. Children's Bks.
Meistle, Jarrod. Victor the Vampire. 2011. 28p. pap. 12.99 *(978-1-4628-4514-9(2))* Xlibris Corp.
—Victor the Vampire & the Bully. 2012. 28p. pap. 14.99 *(978-1-4691-3879-4(4))* Xlibris Corp.
Merasty, Maria Paul. Chuck the Different Vampire. 2012. 32p. pap. *(978-1-77067-501-8(9))* FriesenPress.
Mercer, Sienna. Date with Destiny. 2014. (My Sister the Vampire Ser.: 10). (ENG.). 224p. (J). (gr. 4-6). 6.99 *(978-1-4052-5985-9(X))* Egmont Bks., Ltd. GBR. Dist: Independent Pubs. Group.
—Fangs for the Memories. 2017. (My Sister the Vampire Ser.: 18). (ENG.). 208p. (J). (gr. 4-6). pap. 8.99 *(978-1-4052-7844-7(7))* Egmont Bks., Ltd. GBR. Dist: Independent Pubs. Group.
—Fangtastic! 2007. (My Sister the Vampire Ser.: 2). (ENG.). 208p. (J). (gr. 3-7). per. 6.99 *(978-0-06-087115-4(6))* HarperCollins Pubs.
—Fashion Frightmare! 2014. (My Sister the Vampire Ser.: 16). (ENG.). 240p. (J). (gr. 4-6). pap. 6.99 *(978-1-4052-6573-7(6))* Egmont Bks., Ltd. GBR. Dist: Independent Pubs. Group.
—Flipping Out ! 2014. (My Sister the Vampire Ser.: 14). (ENG.). 256p. (J). (gr. 4-6). pap. 6.99 *(978-1-4052-6571-3(X))* Egmont Bks., Ltd. GBR. Dist: Independent Pubs. Group.
—Love Bites. 2014. (My Sister the Vampire Ser.: 6). (ENG.). 256p. (J). (gr. 4-6). pap. 6.99 *(978-1-4052-5698-8(2))* Egmont Bks., Ltd. GBR. Dist: Independent Pubs. Group.
—Lucky Break. 2014. (My Sister the Vampire Ser.: 7). (ENG.). 256p. (J). (gr. 4-6). 6.99 *(978-1-4052-5699-5(0))* Egmont Bks., Ltd. GBR. Dist: Independent Pubs. Group.
—My Sister the Vampire - Twin Spins! 2014. (My Sister the Vampire Ser.: 9). (ENG.). 224p. (J). (gr. 4-6). pap. 6.99 *(978-1-4052-5984-2(1))* Egmont Bks., Ltd. GBR. Dist: Independent Pubs. Group.
—Re-Vamped! 2007. (My Sister the Vampire Ser.: 3). (ENG.). 208p. (J). (gr. 3-7). pap. 6.99 *(978-0-06-087118-5(0))* HarperCollins Pubs.
—Secrets & Spies. 2014. (My Sister the Vampire Ser.: 15). (ENG.). 224p. (J). (gr. 4-6). pap. 8.99 *(978-1-4052-6572-0(8))* Egmont Bks., Ltd. GBR. Dist: Independent Pubs. Group.
—Star Style. 2014. (My Sister the Vampire Ser.: 8). (ENG.). 256p. (J). (gr. 4-6). pap. 6.99 *(978-1-4052-5700-8(8))* Egmont Bks., Ltd. GBR. Dist: Independent Pubs. Group.
—Switched. 2007. (My Sister the Vampire Ser.: 1). (ENG.). 208p. (J). (gr. 3-7). pap. 6.99 *(978-0-06-087113-0(X))* HarperCollins Pubs.
—Vampalicious! 2008. (My Sister the Vampire Ser.: 4). (ENG.). 208p. (J). (gr. 3-7). per. 6.99 *(978-0-06-087121-5(0))* HarperCollins Pubs.
Mercer, Sienna & Miller, Sienna. Double Disaster! 2014. (My Sister the Vampire Ser.: 13). (ENG.). 256p. (J). (gr. 4-6). pap. 6.99 *(978-1-4052-6570-6(1))* Egmont Bks., Ltd. GBR. Dist: Independent Pubs. Group.
—Flying Solo. 2014. (My Sister the Vampire Ser.: 11). (ENG.). 224p. (J). (gr. 4-6). pap. 6.99 *(978-1-4052-5987-3(6))* Egmont Bks., Ltd. GBR. Dist: Independent Pubs. Group.
—Stake Out! 2014. (My Sister the Vampire Ser.: 12). (ENG.). 240p. (J). (gr. 4-6). pap. 6.99 *(978-1-4052-5988-0(4))* Egmont Bks., Ltd. GBR. Dist: Independent Pubs. Group.
Meyer, Stephenie. Amanecer. Pallarés, José Miguel & Sánchez, María Jesús, trs. 2008.Tr. of Breaking Dawn. (SPA.). 832p. (gr. 8-12). pap. 19.99 *(978-607-11-0033-7(X),* Alfaguara Juvenil) Santillana USA Publishing Co., Inc.
—Breaking Dawn. (Twilight Saga Ser.: 4). (ENG.). 768p. (YA). (gr. 7-17). 2012. mass mkt. 7.99 *(978-0-316-22613-4(0))* 2010. pap. 16.99 *(978-0-316-06793-5(8))* 2008. 22.99 *(978-0-316-06792-8(X),* Tingley, Megan Bks.)Pt. II. 2012. pap. 14.99 *(978-0-316-22642-4(4))* Little, Brown Bks. for Young Readers.
—Breaking Dawn. 2010. (Twilight Saga Ser.: 4). (YA). lib. bdg. 29.40 *(978-0-606-23108-4(0),* Turtleback) Turtleback Bks.
—Crepusculo. 2015.Tr. of Twilight. (ENG & SPA.). 736p. (gr. 7). pap. 14.99 *(978-607-11-0163-1(8),* Punto de Lectura) Santillana USA Publishing Co., Inc.
—Crepúsculo, Vol. 1. Kim, Young, illus. 2010.Tr. of Twilight. (SPA.). 216p. (gr. 8-12). pap. 19.99 *(978-607-11-0482-3(3),* Alfaguara Juvenil) Santillana USA Publishing Co., Inc.
—Eclipse. 2009. (Twilight Saga Ser.: 3). (ENG.). 640p. (YA). (gr. 7-17). pap. 15.99 *(978-0-316-02765-6(0))* Little Brown & Co.
—Eclipse. 2007. (Twilight Saga Ser.: 3). (ENG.). 640p. (YA). (gr. 7-17). 19.99 *(978-0-316-16020-9(2))* Little, Brown Bks. for Young Readers.
—Eclipse. 2008. 576p. *(978-1-904233-91-6(0),* Atom Books) Little, Brown Book Group Ltd.
—Eclipse. 2011. (Twilight Saga: Bk. 3). 13.08 *(978-0-7848-3531-9(4),* Everbind) Marco Bk. Co.
—Eclipse. 2010. (Twilight Saga: Bk. 3). 629p. (YA). (gr. 9-12). 22.10 *(978-1-60686-303-9(7))* Perfection Learning Corp.
—Eclipse. Pallarés, José Miguel & Sánchez, María Jesús, trs. 2007. (SPA.). 870p. (YA). (gr. 8-12). pap. 15.99 *(978-1-60396-022-9(8),* Punto de Lectura) Santillana USA Publishing Co., Inc.
—Eclipse. 2007. (Twilight Saga Spanish Ser.: 3). (SPA.). 637p. (gr. 7-12). lib. bdg. 28.15 *(978-1-4177-9862-9(9),* Turtleback) Turtleback Bks.
—Luna Nueva. Pallares, Jose Miguel, tr. from ENG. 2009.Tr. of New Moon. (SPA.). 280p. (YA). (gr. 8-12). pap. 11.99 *(978-1-60396-698-6(6),* Punto de Lectura) Santillana USA Publishing Co., Inc.
—Luna Nueva. Pallarés, José Miguel & Sánchez, María Jesús, trs. from ENG. 2007.Tr. of New Moon. (SPA.). 696p. (YA). (gr. 8-12). per. 15.99 *(978-970-58-0023-8(5),* Alfaguara) Santillana USA Publishing Co., Inc.
—New Moon. (Twilight Saga Ser.: 2). (ENG.). 608p. (gr. 7-17). 2008. (YA). pap. 15.99 *(978-0-316-02496-9(1))* 2006. (J). 19.99 *(978-0-316-16019-3(9),* Tingley, Megan Bks.) Little, Brown Bks. for Young Readers.
—New Moon. 2011. (Twilight Saga: Bk. 2). 11.72 *(978-0-7848-3535-7(7),* Everbind) Marco Bk. Co.
—New Moon. 2008. (Twilight Saga: Bk. 2). 563p. (gr. 9-12). 21.00 *(978-1-60686-336-7(3))* Perfection Learning Corp.
—La Segunda Vida de Bree Tanner. Oliveras, Julio Hermoso, tr. 2010. (SPA.). 240p. (YA). (gr. 8-12). mass mkt. 14.99 *(978-1-61605-142-6(6),* Alfaguara) Santillana USA Publishing Co., Inc.
—The Short Second Life of Bree Tanner. (Twilight Saga Ser.). (ENG.). (YA). (gr. 7-17). 2012. 224p. pap. 8.99 *(978-0-316-22852-7(4))* 2010. 192p. 16.00 *(978-0-316-12558-1(X))* Little, Brown Bks. for Young Readers.
—Twilight. 2008. (Twilight Saga: Bk. 1). (CHI.). 375p. (YA). pap. *(978-7-5448-0333-5(3))* Jieli Publishing Hse.
—Twilight. (Twilight Saga Ser.: 1). (ENG.). 544p. (YA). (gr. 7-17). 2005. 19.99 *(978-0-316-16017-9(2))* 2006. reprint ed. pap. 15.99 *(978-0-316-01584-4(9))* Little, Brown Bks. for Young Readers. (Tingley, Megan Bks.).
—Twilight. 2008. 480p. pap. *(978-1-905654-34-5(0),* Atom Books) Little, Brown Book Group Ltd.
—Twilight. 2009. (Twilight Saga: Bk. 1). 11.72 *(978-0-7848-1934-0(3),* Everbind) Marco Bk. Co.
—Twilight. (Twilight Saga Ser.: 1). (ENG.). 2012. 224p. (gr. 7-17). pap. 14.99 *(978-0-316-20488-0(9))* 2011. (Illus.). 240p. (gr. 7-17). 19.99 *(978-0-316-13319-7(1))* 2010. (Illus.). 224p. 19.99 *(978-0-7595-2943-4(4))* Orbit. (Yen Pr.).
—Twilight. Kim, Young, illus. collector's ed. 2012. (Twilight Saga Ser.: 0). (ENG.). 464p. (gr. 7-17). 24.99 *(978-0-316-21717-0(4),* Yen Pr.) Orbit.
—Twilight. (Twilight Saga: Bk. 1). 2010. 498p. (YA). (gr. 9-12). 20.10 *(978-1-60686-352-7(5))* 2006. 21.00 *(978-0-7569-6825-0(9))* Perfection Learning Corp.
—Twilight. (Twilight Ser.: 1). (YA). 2007. 1.25 *(978-1-4193-9974-9(8))* 2006. 87.75 *(978-1-4193-9975-6(6))* Recorded Bks., Inc.
—Twilight. 2006. (Twilight Saga Ser.: 1). (Illus.). 498p. (YA). (gr. 9-12). lib. bdg. 28.15 *(978-1-4177-5591-2(1),* Turtleback) Turtleback Bks.
Mikumo, Gakuto. Strike the Blood. Manyako, illus. 2017. (Strike the Blood Ser.: 6). (ENG.). 224p. (YA). (gr. 8-17). pap. 14.00 *(978-0-316-34558-3(X),* Yen Pr.) Orbit.
Millard, Adam. Peter Crombie, Teenage Zombie. 2012. 238p. pap. *(978-0-9573999-7-6(9))* Crowded Quarantine Pubns.
Mongredien, Sue. Oliver Moon's Fangtastic Sleepover. 2011. (Oliver Moon Ser.). 92p. (J). pap. 4.99 *(978-0-7945-3094-5(X),* Usborne) EDC Publishing.
Monstrata, Nessi. Monster High Diaries: Draculaura & the New Stepmomster. 2015. (Monster High Diaries: 1). (ENG.). 160p. (J). (gr. 3-7). 9.99 *(978-0-316-30084-1(5))* Little, Brown Bks. for Young Readers.
Moore, Peter. Red Moon Rising. 2012. (ENG.). 352p. (J). (gr. 5-9). pap. 9.99 *(978-1-4231-1939-5(8))* Hyperion Pr.
Morris, Dave. Crypt of the Vampire. Hartas, Leo, illus. 2013. 122p. pap. *(978-1-909905-05-4(4))* Fabled Lands Publishing.
Mosley, Walter. When the Thrill Is Gone, 3 vols. 2012. (Leonid McGill Mystery Ser.: Bk. 3). (ENG.). 384p. (gr. 12). 16.00 *(978-0-451-23565-7(7),* Berkley) Penguin Publishing Group.

T U V

Moss, Marissa. Blood Diaries: Tales of a 6th-Grade Vampire. Moss, Marissa, illus. 2014. (ENG., Illus.). 136p. (J). (gr. 2-7). 13.00 (978-1-939547-05-7(9)) Creston Bks.
Muncaster, Harriet. Isadora Moon Goes Camping. 2017. (Isadora Moon Ser.: 2). (ENG.). 128p. (J). (gr. 1-4). 5.99 (978-0-399-55827-6(6)); 14.99 (978-0-399-55825-2(X)); lib. bdg. 17.99 (978-0-399-55826-9(8)) Random Hse. Children's Bks. (Random Hse. Bks. for Young Readers).
—Isadora Moon Goes to School. 2017. (Isadora Moon Ser.: 1). (ENG.). 128p. (J). (gr. 1-4). 5.99 (978-0-399-55823-8(3)); 14.99 (978-0-399-55821-4(7)); lib. bdg. 17.99 (978-0-399-55822-1(5)) Random Hse. Children's Bks. (Random Hse. Bks. for Young Readers).
Mungin, Shanyece. Entwined, 1 vol. 2010. 117p. pap. 19.95 (978-1-4489-9685-8(6)) America Star Bks.
Murphy, Lisa. Little Vampire. 2009. 262p. pap. 16.95 (978-1-4092-9494-8(3)) Lulu Pr., Inc.
Nash, Susan Smith. The Good Deeds Society: Family Plot. 2008. (Illus.). 220p. (YA). pap. 18.00 (978-0-9797573-2-7(0)) Texture Pr.
Natsume, Kokoro. Lovephobia, Vol. 3. 2016. (Illus.). 200p. (YA). pap. 12.95 (978-1-56970-300-7(0)) Digital Manga Publishing.
Neill, Chloe. Charmfall. 2012. (Dark Elite Ser.: 3). (ENG.). 288p. (YA). (gr. 9). 9.99 (978-0-451-23080-5(9), Berkley) Penguin Publishing Group.
Nickel, Scott. Buzz Beaker vs Dracula: A Buzz Beaker Brainstorm, 1 vol. Smith, Andy J., illus. 2009. (Buzz Beaker Brainstorm Ser.). (ENG.). 40p. (gr. 1-3). lib. bdg. 23.99 (978-1-4342-1191-0(6), Graphic Sparks) Stone Arch Bks.
Night, P. J. You Can't Come in Here!, 1 vol. 2013. (You're Invited to a Creepover Ser.). (ENG.). 160p. (J). (gr. 3-6). lib. bdg. 24.21 (978-1-61479-066-2(3), Essential Library) ABDO Publishing Co.
—You Can't Come in Here! 2011. (You're Invited to a Creepover Ser.: 2). (ENG.). 160p. (J). (gr. 3-7). pap. 6.99 (978-1-4424-2095-3(2), Simon Spotlight) Simon Spotlight.
Noble, Marty. Vampires Coloring Book. 2010. (Dover Coloring Bks.). (ENG., Illus.). 32p. (gr. 6-8). pap. 3.99 (978-0-486-47848-7(3)) Dover Pubns., Inc.
O'Callaghan, G. The Eternals. 2007. 376p. per. (978-1-84693-055-3(3)) Best Global Publishing Ltd.
O'Hara, Mo. Any Fin Is Possible. Jagucki, Marek, illus. 2016. (My Big Fat Zombie Goldfish Ser.: 4). (ENG.). 224p. (J). (gr. 3-5). 12.99 (978-1-250-06353-3(1), 9781250063533) Feiwel & Friends.
O'Reilly, Sean. The Gremlin's Curse, 1 vol. 2012. (Mighty Mighty Monsters Ser.). (ENG.). 48p. (gr. 2-3). lib. bdg. 23.99 (978-1-4342-3894-8(6)) Stone Arch Bks.
—Gremlin's Curse. 2013. (Mighty Mighty Monsters Ser.). (ENG., Illus.). 48p. (gr. 2-3). pap. 6.10 (978-1-4342-4228-0(5)) Stone Arch Bks.
Orme, David & Orme, David. Vampires. 2008. (ENG., Illus.). 36p. pap. (978-1-84167-692-0(6)) Ransom Publishing Ltd.
O'Shea, M.J. Blood Moon. 2016. (ENG., Illus.). (J). 24.99 (978-1-63477-941-8(X), Harmony Ink Pr.) Dreamspinner Pr.
—Cold Moon. 2nd ed. 2016. (ENG., Illus.). (J). 24.99 (978-1-63477-954-8(1), Harmony Ink Pr.) Dreamspinner Pr.
O'Shea, M.J. Cold Moon [Library Edition]. 2nd ed. 2014. 180p. pap. 14.99 (978-1-62798-460-7(7), Harmony Ink Pr.) Dreamspinner Pr.
Pace, Anne Marie. Vampirina at the Beach. Pham, LeUyen, illus. 2017. (Vampirina Ser.). (ENG.). 40p. (J). (gr. -1-k). 16.99 (978-1-4847-7342-0(X)) Disney Pr.
—Vampirina Ballerina. Pham, LeUyen, illus. 2012. (Vampirina Ser.). (ENG.). 40p. (J). (gr. -1-k). 16.99 (978-1-4231-5753-3(2)) Hyperion Pr.
Papineau, Lucie. Bebe-Vampire, Gloups! 2004. (FRE., Illus.). (J). (gr. k-3). spiral bd. (978-0-616-07259-2(7)) Canadian National Institute for the Blind/Institut National Canadien pour les Aveugles.
Papp, Robert L., illus. The Vampire Mystery. 2009. (Boxcar Children Mysteries Ser.: 120). (ENG.). 128p. (J). (gr. 1-5). pap. 5.99 (978-0-8075-8461-3(4)); lib. bdg. 14.99 (978-0-8075-8460-6(6)) Whitman, Albert & Co.
Patrick, David. Nero Demare & the Legend of the Vampires. 2007. 284p. (YA). per. 17.95 (978-0-595-42014-8(1)) iUniverse, Inc.
Paulk, William. The Creatures of Vision City: Pokie's Party, Book One. 2009. 48p. pap. 10.99 (978-1-4389-5659-6(2)) AuthorHouse.
Pavanello, Roberto. The Dancing Vampire. Zeni, Marco, tr. from ITA. Pisapia, Blasco & Brughera, Pamela, illus. 2012. (Echo & the Bat Pack Ser.). (ENG.). 128p. (gr. 2-3). 25.32 (978-1-4342-3837-5(7), Echo & the Bat Pack) Stone Arch Bks.
Perry, Pete. The Secret of Bedside Manor. 2009. (Illus.). 140p. pap. 36.49 (978-1-4389-6668-7(7)) AuthorHouse.
Petrucha, Stefan. Breaking Down, No. 2. Parker, Rick, illus. 2011. (Papercutz Slices Ser.: 2). (ENG.). 64p. (J). (gr. 5-12). 10.99 (978-1-59707-245-8(1), 9781597072458) Papercutz.
Petrucha, Stefan & Kinney, Sarah. Vampire Slayer. Murase, Sho, illus. 2010. (Nancy Drew the New Case Files Ser.: 2). (ENG.). 64p. (J). (gr. 3-7). 10.99 (978-1-59707-234-2(6), 9781597072342) Papercutz.
Phillips, Dee. The Vampire's Lair. 2016. (Cold Whispers II Ser.). (ENG.). 32p. (J). (gr. 2-6). 19.95 (978-1-944102-30-2(2)) Bearport Publishing Co., Inc.
Pike, Christopher, pseud. Deepest Desires, Instant Remorse No. 2, Bk. 2. 2010. (Thirst Ser.: 2). (ENG.). 608p. (YA). (gr. 9). pap. 11.99 (978-1-4169-8309-5(0), Simon Pulse) Simon Pulse.
—The Eternal Dawn. 2010. (Thirst Ser.: 3). (ENG.). 512p. (YA). (gr. 9-18). pap. 11.99 (978-1-4424-1317-7(4), Simon Pulse) Simon Pulse.
—Human Urges, Fatal Consequences. 2009. (Thirst Ser.: 1). (ENG., Illus.). 624p. (YA). (gr. 9). pap. 12.99 (978-1-4169-8308-8(2), Simon Pulse) Simon Pulse.
—The Sacred Veil. 2013. (Thirst Ser.: 5). (ENG., Illus.). 512p. (YA). (gr. 7). pap. 12.99 (978-1-4424-6731-6(2), Simon Pulse) Simon Pulse.
—The Shadow of Death. 2011. (Thirst Ser.: 4). (ENG., Illus.). 528p. (YA). (gr. 9). pap. 10.99 (978-1-4424-1319-1(0), Simon Pulse) Simon Pulse.
—Thirst, 3 vols. 2013. (Thirst Ser.). (ENG.). 1744p. (YA). (gr. 9). pap. 30.99 (978-1-4424-8375-0(X), Simon Pulse) Simon Pulse.
Pixie, B. R. Just a Little Human. 2011. 98p. pap. 19.95 (978-1-4512-3551-7(8)) America Star Bks.
Poulsen, David A. The Book of Vampire. 4th rev. ed. 2007. (Salt & Pepper Chronicles). (ENG., Illus.). 160p. (J). (gr. 4-7). 6.95 (978-1-55263-805-7(7)) Leaf Storm Pr.
—The Vampire's Visit. 2007. (Salt & Pepper Chronicles). (ENG.). 160p. (J). (gr. 4-7). 6.95 (978-1-55263-721-0(2)) Leaf Storm Pr.
Publications International Ltd. Staff, ed. Vampires & Other Scary Creatures(Look & Find) 2010. 24p. (J). 7.98 (978-1-60553-839-6(6)) Publications International, Ltd.
Rand, Johnathan. Amer Ch Double Thrillers. 2010. 256p. pap. 6.99 (978-1-893699-26-7(9)) AudioCraft Publishing, Inc.
Ratnett, Michael. Dracula Steps Out. Goulding, June & Smyth, Iain, illus. 2005. 12p. (J). (gr. k-4). reprint ed. 16.00 (978-0-7567-8585-7(5)) DIANE Publishing Co.
Rees, Douglas. Vampire High. 2010. (ENG.). 240p. (YA). (gr. 7-18). pap. 9.99 (978-0-385-73920-7(6), Delacorte Bks. for Young Readers) Random Hse. Children's Bks.
Reid, Katie. Blood Driven. 2011. 370p. pap. 29.95 (978-1-4560-5417-5(1)) PublishAmerica, Inc.
Rex, Adam. Fat Vampire: A Never Coming of Age Story. 2011. (ENG.). 336p. (YA). (gr. 9). pap. 8.99 (978-0-06-192092-9(4)) HarperCollins Pubs.
Rice, Morgan. Before Dawn (Vampire, Fallen-Book 1) 2016. (ENG., Illus.). 118p. (J). pap. 6.99 (978-1-63291-611-2(8)) Morgan Rice Bks.
Richardson, E. E. The Curse Box. 2013. (ENG.). 64p. (YA). (gr. 6-12). pap. 6.95 (978-1-78112-176-4(1)); lib. bdg. 22.60 (978-1-78112-175-7(3)) Lerner Publishing Group.
Riviello, Linda. Werewolves, Vampires & Ghosts... Oh My! 2009. (J). pap. 12.95 (978-1-61623-088-3(6)) Independent Pub.
Robinson, A. M. Vampire Crush. 2010. (ENG.). 416p. (YA). (gr. 8-18). pap. 8.99 (978-0-06-198971-1(1), HarperTeen) HarperCollins Pubs.
Rowen, Michelle & Mead, Richelle. Vampire Academy: The Ultimate Guide. 2011. (ENG.). 320p. (YA). (gr. 7-18). 9.99 (978-1-59514-451-5(X), Razorbill) Penguin Young Readers Group.
Roy, Ron. The Vampire's Vacation. Gurney, John Steven, illus. 2004. (to Z Mysteries Ser.: 22). (ENG.). 96p. (J). (gr. 1-4). pap. 4.99 (978-0-375-82479-1(0), Random Hse. Bks. for Young Readers) Random Hse. Children's Bks.
Rykken, John. Bloodwood: The Chronicles of Max Mayhem. 2011. 264p. (gr. 10-12). 26.95 (978-1-4620-0656-4(6)); pap. 16.95 (978-1-4620-0657-1(4)) iUniverse, Inc.
Sage, Angie. Frognapped. Pickering, Jimmy, illus. 2008. (Araminta Spookie Ser.: 3). (ENG.). 224p. (J). (gr. 2-5). pap. 6.99 (978-0-06-077489-9(4), Tegen, Katherine Bks) HarperCollins Pubs.
—Vampire Brat. Pickering, Jimmy, illus. 2009. (Araminta Spookie Ser.: 4). (ENG.). 224p. (J). (gr. 2-5). pap. 6.99 (978-0-06-077492-9(4), Tegen, Katherine Bks) HarperCollins Pubs.
Saveley, Barb. Dusky II: Journey of Tears. 2010. 40p. 18.95 (978-1-4389-8243-4(7)) AuthorHouse.
Schaefer, Peggy. A Haunted Halloween Activity Book. Arif, Tasneem & Reed, Lisa, illus. 2014. 16p. (J). 4.99 (978-0-8249-5666-0(4), Ideal Pubns.) Worthy Publishing.
Schreiber, Ellen. The Beginning. 2009. (Vampire Kisses Ser.: Nos. 1-3). (ENG.). 576p. (YA). (gr. 8). pap. 9.99 (978-0-06-177894-0(X), Tegen, Katherine Bks) HarperCollins Pubs.
—Blood Relatives, Vol. II. Rem, illus. 2008. (Vampire Kisses: Blood Relatives Ser.: Vol. 2). (ENG.). 192p. (YA). (gr. 8-18). pap. 9.99 (978-0-06-134082-6(0), Tegen, Katherine Bks) HarperCollins Pubs.
—Blood Relatives, Vol. 3. Kwon, Elisa, illus. 2009. (Vampire Kisses: Blood Relatives Ser.: Vol. 3). (ENG.). 192p. (YA). (gr. 8-18). pap. 9.99 (978-0-06-134083-3(9), Tegen, Katherine Bks) HarperCollins Pubs.
—The Coffin Club. 2009. (Vampire Kisses Ser.: 5). (ENG.). 208p. (YA). (gr. 8). pap. 8.99 (978-0-06-128886-9(1), Tegen, Katherine Bks) HarperCollins Pubs.
—Cryptic Cravings. 2012. (Vampire Kisses Ser.: 8). (ENG.). 240p. (YA). (gr. 8). pap. 9.99 (978-0-06-168947-5(5), Tegen, Katherine Bks) HarperCollins Pubs.
—Dance with a Vampire. 2009. (Vampire Kisses Ser.: 4). (ENG.). 208p. (YA). (gr. 8). pap. 8.99 (978-0-06-177898-8(2), Tegen, Katherine Bks) HarperCollins Pubs.
—Graveyard Games, No. 1. Xian Nu Studio Staff, illus. 2011. (Vampire Kisses: Blood Relatives Ser.). (ENG.). 192p. (YA). (gr. 8). pap. 9.99 (978-0-06-202672-9(0), Tegen, Katherine Bks) HarperCollins Pubs.
—Immortal Hearts. (Vampire Kisses Ser.: 9). (ENG.). 272p. (YA). (gr. 8). 2013. pap. 9.99 (978-0-06-207009-8(6)) 2012. 17.99 (978-0-06-207008-1(8)) HarperCollins Pubs. (Tegen, Katherine Bks).
—Kissing Coffins. (Vampire Kisses Ser.: No. 2). (ENG.). 2007. 240p. (J). pap., pap. 5.99 (978-0-06-077624-4(2), HarperTeen) 2005. 176p. (YA). (gr. 8-18). 17.99 (978-0-06-077622-0(6), Tegen, Katherine Bks) HarperCollins Pubs.
—Love Bites. 2011. (Vampire Kisses Ser.: 7). (ENG.). 208p. (YA). (gr. 8). pap. 8.99 (978-0-06-168944-4(0), Tegen, Katherine Bks) HarperCollins Pubs.
—Royal Blood No. 6. 2009. (Vampire Kisses Ser.: 6). (ENG.). 208p. (YA). (gr. 8-18). 17.99 (978-0-06-128887-6(X), Tegen, Katherine Bks) HarperCollins Pubs.
—Vampire Kisses. 2003. (Vampire Kisses Ser.: 1). (ENG.). 208p. (YA). (gr. 8-18). 17.99 (978-0-06-009334-1(X), Tegen, Katherine Bks) HarperCollins Pubs.
—Vampire Kisses: Finstere Sehnsucht / Dunkle Ahnung / Düsteres Versprechen. 2005. (Vampire Kisses Ser.: No. 1). 272p. (YA). (gr. 7-18). reprint ed. pap. 5.99 (978-0-06-009336-5(6), Harper Trophy) HarperCollins Pubs.
—Vampire Kisses: Finstere Sehnsucht / Dunkle Ahnung / Düsteres Versprechen. l.t. ed. 2008. (Vampire Kisses Ser.: No. 1). 294p. (YA). 22.95 (978-1-4104-0727-6(5)) Thorndike Pr.
—Vampire Kisses Boxed Set: Vampire Kisses; Kissing Coffins; Vampireville. 2008. (Vampire Kisses Ser.: Nos. 1-3). (J). pap. 15.99 (978-0-06-169160-7(7), HarperTeen) HarperCollins Pubs.
—Vampireville. (Vampire Kisses Ser.: No. 3). (ENG.). (YA). 2007. 208p. (gr. 7-12). pap., pap. 5.99 (978-0-06-077627-5(7), HarperTeen) 2006. 192p. (gr. 8-12). 17.99 (978-0-06-077625-1(0), Tegen, Katherine Bks) HarperCollins Pubs.
Schwartz, Alvin. More Scary Stories to Tell in the Dark. Helquist, Brett, illus. 2010. (Scary Stories Ser.). (ENG.). 128p. (J). (gr. 4-18). 16.99 (978-0-06-083521-7(4)); pap. 5.99 (978-0-06-083522-4(2)) HarperCollins Pubs.
Seibold, J. Otto. Count, Dagmar! 2011. (ENG.). 20p. (J). (gr. -1 — 1). 8.99 (978-0-8118-7773-2(6)) Chronicle Bks. LLC.
Selzer, Adam. I Kissed a Zombie, & I Liked It. 2010. (ENG.). 192p. (YA). (gr. 7-18). pap. 7.99 (978-0-385-73503-2(0), Delacorte Bks. for Young Readers) Random Hse. Children's Bks.
Serra, Louis. The Reluctant Vampire. 2006. (YA). per. 12.00 (978-0-9769132-5-2(9)) Capri Publishing.
Shakespeare, William & Gabel, Claudia. Romeo & Juliet & Vampires. 2010. (ENG.). 256p. (YA). (gr. 9-18). pap. 8.99 (978-0-06-197624-7(5), HarperTeen) HarperCollins Pubs.
Shan, Darren, pseud. Allies of the Night. 2005. (Cirque du Freak Ser.: 8). (ENG., Illus.). 256p. (J). (gr. 7-17). pap. 10.99 (978-0-316-11437-0(5)) Little, Brown Bks. for Young Readers.
—Birth of a Killer. 2011. (Saga of Larten Crepsley Ser.: 1). (ENG.). 288p. (YA). (gr. 10-17). pap. 10.99 (978-0-316-07862-7(X)) Little, Brown Bks. for Young Readers.
—Brothers to the Death. 2013. (Saga of Larten Crepsley Ser.: 4). (ENG.). 272p. (YA). (gr. 10-17). pap. 10.00 (978-0-316-07871-9(9)) Little, Brown Bks. for Young Readers.
—Hunters of the Dusk. 2005. (Cirque du Freak Ser.: 7). (ENG., Illus.). 224p. (J). (gr. 7-17). pap. 10.99 (978-0-316-60211-2(6)) Little, Brown Bks. for Young Readers.
—Hunters of the Dusk. 2005. (Cirque du Freak Ser.: 7). (J). lib. bdg. 22.10 (978-1-4177-3731-4(X), Turtleback) Turtleback Bks.
—Killers of the Dawn, 9. 2004. (ENG.). 192p. (978-0-00-713781-7(8)) HarperCollins Pubs. Australia.
—Killers of the Dawn. 2006. (Cirque du Freak Ser.: 9). (ENG., Illus.). 224p. (J). (gr. 7-17). per. 10.99 (978-0-316-10654-2(2)) Little, Brown Bks. for Young Readers.
—The Lake of Souls, 10. 2004. (Darren Shan Saga: Bk. 10). (ENG.). 224p. (978-0-00-715919-2(6)) HarperCollins Pubs. Australia.
—The Lake of Souls. 2006. (Cirque du Freak Ser.: 10). (ENG., Illus.). 272p. (J). (gr. 7-17). per. 10.99 (978-0-316-01665-0(9)) Little, Brown Bks. for Young Readers.
—Lord of the Shadows, 11. 2005. (Darren Shan Saga: Bk. 11). (ENG.). 192p. (978-0-00-715920-8(X)) HarperCollins Pubs. Australia.
—Lord of the Shadows. 2007. (Cirque du Freak Ser.: 11). (ENG., Illus.). 256p. (J). (gr. 7-17). per. 10.99 (978-0-316-01661-2(6)) Little, Brown Bks. for Young Readers.
—Lord of the Shadows. 2007. (Cirque du Freak Ser.: 11). (J). lib. bdg. 22.10 (978-1-4177-7441-8(X), Turtleback) Turtleback Bks.
—Ocean of Blood. 2012. (Saga of Larten Crepsley Ser.: 2). (ENG.). 272p. (YA). (gr. 10-17). pap. 10.99 (978-0-316-07867-2(0)) Little, Brown Bks. for Young Readers.
—Palace of the Damned. (Saga of Larten Crepsley Ser.: 3). (ENG.). (YA). (gr. 10-17). 2012. 272p. pap. 10.00 (978-0-316-07869-6(7)) 2011. 256p. 17.99 (978-0-316-07870-2(0)) Little, Brown Bks. for Young Readers.
—Sons of Destiny, 12. 2005. (Darren Shan Saga: Bk. 12). (ENG.). 208p. (978-0-00-715921-5(8)) HarperCollins Pubs. Australia.
—Sons of Destiny. 2007. (Cirque du Freak Ser.: 12). (ENG., Illus.). 272p. (J). (gr. 7-17). per. 9.99 (978-0-316-01663-6(2)) Little, Brown Bks. for Young Readers.
—Sons of Destiny. 2012. (Cirque du Freak, the Manga Ser.: 12). lib. bdg. 24.55 (978-0-606-26471-6(X), Turtleback) Turtleback Bks.
—Trials of Death. 2004. (Cirque du Freak Ser.: 5). (ENG., Illus.). 224p. (J). (gr. 7-17). pap. 10.99 (978-0-316-60395-9(3)) Little, Brown Bks. for Young Readers.
—Tunnels of Blood. 2003. (Cirque du Freak Ser.: 3). (ENG., Illus.). 240p. (J). (gr. 7-17). pap. 10.99 (978-0-316-60608-0(1)) Little, Brown Bks. for Young Readers.
—Tunnels of Blood. 2003. (Cirque du Freak Ser.: 3). (J). (gr. 3-6). lib. bdg. 20.85 (978-0-613-71782-3(1), Turtleback) Turtleback Bks.
—Vampire Destiny Trilogy: The Lake of Souls; Lord of the Shadows; Sons of Destiny. 2005. (ENG.). 592p. pap., pap., pap. (978-0-00-717959-6(6)) HarperCollins Pubs. Australia.
—Vampire Mountain. 2003. (Cirque du Freak Ser.: 4). (ENG., Illus.). 208p. (J). (gr. 7-17). pap. 10.99 (978-0-316-60542-7(5)) Little, Brown Bks. for Young Readers.
—Vampire Mountain. (Cirque du Freak Ser.: 4). 2003. (J). (gr. 5-8). lib. bdg. 22.10 (978-0-613-71781-6(3)) Vol. 4. 2010. lib. bdg. 24.55 (978-0-606-14433-9(1)) Turtleback Bks. (Turtleback).
—The Vampire Prince. 2004. (Cirque du Freak Ser.: 6). (ENG., Illus.). 208p. (J). (gr. 7-17). pap. 10.99 (978-0-316-60274-7(4)) Little, Brown Bks. for Young Readers.
—The Vampire Prince. 2004. (Cirque du Freak Ser.: 6). (J). lib. bdg. 19.65 (978-1-4177-3732-1(8), Turtleback) Turtleback Bks.
—Vampire War Trilogy. 2005. (ENG.). 496p. (978-0-00-717958-9(8)) HarperCollins Pubs. Australia.
—Wolf Island. 2010. (ENG.). 216p. (YA). (gr. 10-17). pap. 10.00 (978-0-316-04881-1(X)) Little, Brown Bks. for Young Readers.
Shaw, Stephanie. Schnitzel: A Cautionary Tale for Lazy Louts. Barry, Kevin, illus. 2016. (ENG.). 32p. (J). (gr. k-3). 16.99 (978-1-58536-957-7(8), 204104) Sleeping Bear Pr.
Shouoto, Aya. He's My Only Vampire, Vol. 10. 2017. (He's My Only Vampire Ser.: 10). (ENG., Illus.). 176p. (gr. 11-17). pap. 13.00 (978-0-316-39912-8(4), Yen Pr.) Orbit.
—He's My Only Vampire, Vol. 4. 2015. (He's My Only Vampire Ser.: 4). (ENG., Illus.). 160p. (gr. 11-17). pap. 13.00 (978-0-316-26168-5(8), Yen Pr.) Orbit.
—He's My Only Vampire, Vol. 9. 2016. (He's My Only Vampire Ser.: 9). (ENG., Illus.). 160p. (gr. 11-17). pap. 13.00 (978-0-316-34584-2(9), Yen Pr.) Orbit.
Simon, Francesca. Horrid Henry & the Zombie Vampire. Ross, Tony, illus. 2012. (Horrid Henry Ser.: 0). (ENG.). 112p. (J). (gr. 2-5). pap. 7.99 (978-1-4022-6785-7(1), Sourcebooks Jabberwocky) Sourcebooks, Inc.
Sinden, David, et al. The Jungle Vampire. Duddle, Jonny, illus. 2009. (Awfully Beastly Business Ser.: 4). (ENG.). 208p. (J). (gr. 3-7). 9.99 (978-1-4169-8652-2(9), Aladdin) Simon & Schuster Children's Publishing.
Smith, Cynthia Leitich. Blessed. (Tantalize Ser.). (ENG., Illus.). (YA). (gr. 9). 2012. 464p. pap. 8.99 (978-0-7636-5479-5(5)) 2011. 480p. 17.99 (978-0-7636-4326-3(2)) Candlewick Pr.
—Eternal. (Tantalize Ser.). (ENG., Illus.). 320p. (YA). (gr. 9). 2010. pap. 8.99 (978-0-7636-4773-5(X)) 2009. 17.99 (978-0-7636-3573-2(1)) Candlewick Pr.
—Tantalize. 2007. (Tantalize Ser.). (ENG., Illus.). 336p. (YA). (gr. 9-12). 16.99 (978-0-7636-2791-1(7)) Candlewick Pr.
Smith, L. J. The Awakening & the Struggle, 2 vols. 2007. (Vampire Diaries: Nos. 1-2). (ENG.). 512p. (YA). (gr. 8). pap. 9.99 (978-0-06-114097-6(X), HarperTeen) HarperCollins Pubs.
—The Awakening & the Struggle, 2 vols. 2007. (Vampire Diaries: 1). 492p. (YA). (gr. 7). lib. bdg. 20.85 (978-1-4178-2599-8(5), Turtleback) Turtleback Bks.
—Dark Angel - The Chosen - Soulmate, 3 vols. 2008. (Night World Ser.: 2). (ENG.). 688p. (YA). (gr. 9). pap. 9.99 (978-1-4169-7451-2(2), Simon Pulse) Simon Pulse.
—Destiny Rising. (Vampire Diaries: the Hunters Ser.: 3). (ENG.). (YA). (gr. 9). 2013. 416p. pap. 9.99 (978-0-06-201774-1(8)) 2012. 400p. 17.99 (978-0-06-201773-4(X)) HarperCollins Pubs. (HarperTeen).
—The Fury & Dark Reunion, 2 vols. 2007. (Vampire Diaries: Nos. 3-4). (ENG.). 528p. (YA). (gr. 8-12). pap. 9.99 (978-0-06-114098-3(8), HarperTeen) HarperCollins Pubs.
—The Fury & Dark Reunion. 2007. (Vampire Diaries: 3). (YA). lib. bdg. 20.85 (978-0-606-07135-2(0), Turtleback) Turtleback Bks.
—Huntress, Black Dawn, Witchlight, 3 vols. 2009. (Night World Ser.: 3). (ENG., Illus.). 752p. (YA). (gr. 9). pap. 9.99 (978-1-4169-7452-9(0), Simon Pulse) Simon Pulse.
—Midnight. (Vampire Diaries: the Return Ser.: 3). (ENG.). (YA). (gr. 8). 2012. 592p. pap. 9.99 (978-0-06-172086-4(0)) 2011. 576p. 17.99 (978-0-06-172085-7(2)) HarperCollins Pubs. (HarperTeen).
—Moonsong. 2012. (Vampire Diaries: the Hunters Ser.: 2). (ENG.). 400p. (YA). (gr. 9). 17.99 (978-0-06-201770-3(5), HarperTeen) HarperCollins Pubs.
—Moonsong Vol. 9. 2013. (Vampire Diaries: the Hunters Ser.: 2). (ENG.). 416p. (YA). (gr. 9). pap. 10.99 (978-0-06-201771-0(3), HarperTeen) HarperCollins Pubs.
—Night World: Secret Vampire; Daughters of Darkness; Spellbinder. 2008. (Night World Ser.: 1). (ENG.). 752p. (YA). (gr. 9). pap. 9.99 (978-1-4169-7450-5(4), Simon Pulse) Simon Pulse.
—Nightfall. (Vampire Diaries: the Return Ser.: 1). (ENG.). (YA). (gr. 8). 2010. 608p. pap. 9.99 (978-0-06-172080-2(1)) 2009. 592p. 17.99 (978-0-06-172077-2(1)) HarperCollins Pubs. (HarperTeen).
—Phantom. (Vampire Diaries: the Hunters Ser.: 1). (ENG.). (YA). (gr. 9). 2012. 432p. pap. 9.99 (978-0-06-201769-7(1)) 2011. 416p. 17.99 (978-0-06-201768-0(3)) HarperCollins Pubs. (HarperTeen).
—Shadow Souls. (Vampire Diaries: the Return Ser.: 2). (ENG.). (YA). (gr. 8). 2011. 624p. pap. 9.99 (978-0-06-172083-3(6)) 2010. (Illus.). 608p. 17.99 (978-0-06-172081-9(X)) HarperCollins Pubs. (HarperTeen).
—The Struggle. 2010. (Vampire Diaries: 2). (ENG.). 304p. (YA). (gr. 8). mass mkt. 7.99 (978-0-06-199076-2(0)) HarperCollins Pubs.
Smith, L. J. & Clark, Aubrey. Unmasked, 0 vols. 2014. (Vampire Diaries: the Salvation Ser.). (ENG.). 310p. (gr. 7-12). pap. 9.99 (978-1-4778-2335-4(2), 9781477823354, 47North) Amazon Publishing.
—Unseen, 0 vols. 2013. (Vampire Diaries: the Salvation Ser.: 1). (ENG.). 306p. (YA). (gr. 7-9). pap. 9.99 (978-1-4778-0967-9(8), 9781477809679, 47North) Amazon Publishing.
—Unspoken, 0 vols. 2013. (Vampire Diaries: the Salvation Ser.: 2). (ENG.). 308p. (YA). (gr. 7-12). pap. 9.99 (978-1-61218-462-3(6), 9781612184623, 47North) Amazon Publishing.
Smith, L. J. & Williamson, Kevin. The Asylum. 2012. (Vampire Diaries: Stefan's Diaries: 5). (ENG.). 256p. (YA). (gr. 9). pap. 9.99 (978-0-06-211395-5(X), HarperTeen) HarperCollins Pubs.
—The Compelled. 2012. (Vampire Diaries: Stefan's Diaries: 6). (ENG.). 256p. (YA). (gr. 9). pap. 10.99 (978-0-06-211398-6(4), HarperTeen) HarperCollins Pubs.
Smith, L. J., et al. Bloodlust. 2011. (Vampire Diaries: Stefan's Diaries: 2). (ENG.). 256p. (YA). (gr. 9-18). pap. 9.99 (978-0-06-200394-2(1), HarperTeen) HarperCollins Pubs.
—The Ripper. 2011. (Vampire Diaries: Stefan's Diaries: 4). (ENG.). 256p. (YA). (gr. 9). pap. 10.99 (978-0-06-211393-1(3), HarperTeen) HarperCollins Pubs.
Sommer-Bodenburg, Angela. El Pequeno Vampiro. Glienke, Amelie, illus. 2003. (SPA.). 192p. (J). (gr. 3-5). pap. 11.95 (978-968-19-0673-3(X)) Santillana USA Publishing Co., Inc.
Somper, Justin. Black Heart. 2010. (Vampirates Ser.: 4). (ENG.). 512p. (J). (gr. 3-7). pap. 8.99 (978-0-316-02088-6(5)) Little, Brown Bks. for Young Readers.
—Blood Captain. 2009. (Vampirates Ser.: 3). (ENG.). 592p. (J). (gr. 3-7). pap. 10.99 (978-0-316-02086-2(9)) Little Brown & Co.
—Dead Deep. 2009. pap. 1.00 (978-1-4074-4559-5(6)) Recorded Bks., Inc.
—Demons of the Ocean. 2007. (Vampirates Ser.: 1). (ENG.). 352p. (J). (gr. 3-7). per. 8.99 (978-0-316-01444-1(3)) Little, Brown Bks. for Young Readers.

—Demons of the Ocean. 2006. 1.00 *(978-1-4294-1974-1(1))* Recorded Bks., Inc.
—Demons of the Ocean. 2007. (Vampirates Ser.: 1). (Illus.). 330p. (J). 19.65 *(978-1-4177-8287-1(0)*, Turtleback) Turtleback Bks.
—Empire of Night. (Vampirates Ser.: 5). (ENG.). (J). (gr. 3-7). 2011. 512p. pap. 10.99 *(978-0-316-03323-7(5))* 2010. 496p. 15.99 *(978-0-316-03322-0(7))* Little, Brown Bks. for Young Readers.
—Immortal War. 2013. (Vampirates Ser.: 6). (ENG.). 512p. (J). (gr. 3-7). pap. 10.99 *(978-0-316-03325-1(1))* Little, Brown Bks. for Young Readers.
—Immortal War. 2013. (Vampirates Ser.: 6). (J). lib. bdg. 22.10 *(978-0-606-26696-3(8)*, Turtleback) Turtleback Bks.
—Tide of Terror. 2008. (Vampirates Ser.: 2). (ENG.). 480p. (J). (gr. 3-7). pap. 10.99 *(978-0-316-01445-8(1))* Little, Brown Bks. for Young Readers.
Sonneborn, Scott. No Guts, No Gloria. Banks, Timothy, illus. 2015. (Frankenstein Journals). (ENG.). 80p. (gr. 2-3). 22.65 *(978-1-4965-0221-6(3))* Stone Arch Bks.
Sowles, Joann I. Martin. Darkness (the Brookehaven Vampires Series #2) The Brookehaven Vampires. 2011. (YA). *(978-0-9844867-3-1(9))* Brookehaven Publishing.
Specter, Baron. Vampires Are Not Your Friends, 1 vol. Kneupper, Setch, illus. 2012. (Graveyard Diaries Ser.). (ENG.). 128p. (J). (gr. 3-8). 27.07 *(978-1-61641-902-8(4))* Magic Wagon.
Speer, Cindy Lynn. Unbalanced. 2010. pap. *(978-1-934841-90-7(0))* Zumaya Pubns. LLC.
St. Crow, Lili. Betrayals. 2009. (Strange Angels Ser.: 2). (ENG., Illus.). 304p. (YA). (gr. 7-18). 9.99 *(978-1-59514-252-8(5)*, Razorbill) Penguin Young Readers Group.
—Betrayals. 10 vols. 2010. (Strange Angels Ser.: 2). (YA). 95.75 *(978-1-4407-7156-9(1))* Recorded Bks., Inc.
—Betrayals. 2009. (Strange Angels Ser.: 2). lib. bdg. 20.85 *(978-0-606-09020-9(7)*, Turtleback) Turtleback Bks.
—Jealousy. 2010. (Strange Angels Ser.: 3). (ENG.). 320p. (YA). (gr. 7-18). 9.99 *(978-1-59514-290-0(8)*, Razorbill) Penguin Young Readers Group.
—Jealousy, 10 vols. 2010. (Strange Angels Ser.: 3). (J). 86.75 *(978-1-4498-2774-8(8))*; 83.75 *(978-1-4498-2776-2(4))*; 68.75 *(978-1-4498-2773-1(X))*; 1.25 *(978-1-4498-2777-9(2))*; 209.75 *(978-1-4498-2772-4(1))* Recorded Bks., Inc.
—Jealousy. 2010. (Strange Angels Ser.: 3). lib. bdg. 20.85 *(978-0-606-14566-4(4)*, Turtleback) Turtleback Bks.
—Reckoning. 2011. (Strange Angels Ser.: 5). (ENG.). 320p. (YA). (gr. 7-18). 9.99 *(978-1-59514-395-2(5)*, Razorbill) Penguin Young Readers Group.
—Strange Angels. 2009. (Strange Angels Ser.: 1). (ENG., Illus.). 304p. (YA). (gr. 7-18). pap. 9.99 *(978-1-59514-251-1(7)*, Razorbill) Penguin Young Readers Group.
—Strange Angels, 9 vols. 2009. (Strange Angels Ser.: 1). (J). 84.75 *(978-1-4407-6195-9(7))*; 114.75 *(978-1-4407-6199-7(X))*; 181.75 *(978-1-4407-6194-2(9))*; 117.75 *(978-1-4407-6197-3(3))*; 87.75 *(978-1-4407-6193-5(0))* Recorded Bks., Inc.
—Strange Angels. 2009. (Strange Angels Ser.: 1). lib. bdg. 20.85 *(978-0-606-08957-9(8)*, Turtleback) Turtleback Bks.
Steele, Michael Anthony. Vampire Zoo Hullabaloo. Jeralds, Scott, illus. 2017. (Scooby-Doo! Beginner Mysteries Ser.). (ENG.). 112p. (gr. 2-3). lib. bdg. 22.65 ***(978-1-4965-4770-5(5))*** Capstone Press of Coughlan Cos.
Stilton, Geronimo. Un granizado de moscas para el Conde. Wolf, Matt, illus. (SPA.). 128p. (J). (gr. 3-5). pap. 7.95 *(978-1-59437-452-4(X))* Santillana USA Publishing Co., Inc.
—My Name Is Stilton, Geronimo Stilton. 2005. (Geronimo Stilton Ser.: 19). (ENG., Illus.). 128p. (J). (gr. 2-5). pap. 7.99 *(978-0-439-69142-0(7)*, Scholastic Paperbacks) Scholastic, Inc.
—Red Pizzas for a Blue Count. Wolf, Matt & Keys, Larry, illus. 2004. (Geronimo Stilton Ser.: 7). (ENG.). 128p. (J). (gr. 2-5). pap. 7.99 *(978-0-439-55969-0(3))* Scholastic, Inc.
—Return of the Vampire. 2012. (Creepella Von Cacklefur Ser.: 4). (ENG.). 128p. (J). (gr. 2-5). pap. 7.99 *(978-0-545-39348-5(5)*, Scholastic Paperbacks) Scholastic, Inc.
—Return of the Vampire. 2012. (Geronimo Stilton — Creepella Von Cacklefur Ser.: 4). lib. bdg. 18.40 *(978-0-606-26180-7(X)*, Turtleback) Turtleback Bks.
Stine, R. L. Bitten: Dangerous Girls & the Taste of Night. 2010. (ENG.). 496p. (YA). (gr. 9). pap. 9.99 *(978-0-06-200739-1(4)*, HarperTeen) HarperCollins Pubs.
—Dangerous Girls. 2003. 256p. (J). 111.92 *(978-0-06-056910-5(7))*; 111.92 *(978-0-06-056909-9(3))*; (ENG., Illus.). (gr. 7-18). 13.99 *(978-0-06-053080-8(4))* HarperCollins Pubs.
—How to Be a Vampire. 2011. (R. L. Stine's Ghosts of Fear Street Ser.). (ENG.). 128p. (J). (gr. 3-7). pap. 6.99 *(978-1-4424-2760-0(4)*, Aladdin) Simon & Schuster Children's Publishing.
—Please Don't Feed the Vampire a Give Yourself Goosebumps Book. 2015. (Goosebumps Ser.: 32). lib. bdg. 17.20 *(978-0-606-37070-7(6))* Turtleback Bks.
—Temptation. 2012. (ENG.). 416p. (YA). (gr. 7). pap. 10.99 *(978-1-4424-5068-4(1)*, Simon Pulse) Simon Pulse.
—Vampire Breath. 2011. (Classic Goosebumps Ser.: 21). (ENG.). 160p. (J). (gr. 3-7). pap. 6.99 *(978-0-545-29837-7(7)*, Scholastic Paperbacks) Scholastic, Inc.
Stoker, Bram. Count Dracula. 2004. (Fast Track Classics Ser.). (Illus.). 48p. (J). pap. *(978-0-237-52401-2(5))* Evans Brothers, Ltd.
—Dracula. 2009. (Foundation Classics Ser.). (Illus.). 56p. (J). (gr. 5-9). lib. bdg. 27.95 *(978-1-60754-847-8(X))* Windmill Bks.
—Dracula. Gilbert, Anne Yvonne, illus. 2010. (ENG.). 96p. (J). (gr. 7-18). 19.99 *(978-0-7636-4793-3(4)*, Templar) Candlewick Pr.
—Dracula, 1 vol. Simon, Ute, illus. 2011. (Calico Illustrated Classics Ser.: No. 3). (ENG.). 112p. (J). (gr. 3-6). 27.07 *(978-1-61641-101-5(5))* Magic Wagon.
—Dracula. Bryant, Clive, ed. Johnson, Staz et al, illus. 2012. (ENG.). 144p. (gr. 6). pap. 16.95 *(978-1-906332-67-9(3)*, Classical Comics, Ltd.); pap. 16.95 *(978-1-906332-68-6(1))* Classical Comics GBR. Dist: Publishers Group West (PGW).
—Dracula. Williams, Anthony, illus. 2014. (ENG.). 32p. 8.95 *(978-1-78404-355-1(9))* Arcturus Publishing GBR. Dist: Bookmasters Distribution.
—Dracula. Kliros, Thea, illus. abr. ed. 2011. (Dover Children's Thrift Classics Ser.). (ENG.). 96p. (J). (gr. 3-8). reprint ed. pap. 4.00 *(978-0-486-29567-1(2))* Dover Pubns., Inc.
—Dracula. 2006. (Clasicos Para La Juventud). (SPA.). 126p. (YA). *(978-987-1129-52-2(1))* Grupo Visor E.A.S.A.
—Dracula. DiTerlizzi, Tony, illus. 2009. (Puffin Classics Ser.). (ENG.). 640p. (J). (gr. 5-7). 6.99 *(978-0-14-132566-8(6)*, Puffin Books) Penguin Young Readers Group.
—Dracula. McKowen, Scott, illus. 2010. (Sterling Unabridged Classics Ser.). (ENG.). 416p. (J). (gr. 5-18). 14.95 *(978-1-4027-7324-2(2))* Sterling Publishing Co., Inc.
Summers, Tamara. Never Bite a Boy on the First Date. 2009. (ENG.). 288p. (YA). (gr. 9-18). pap. 5.99 *(978-0-06-172154-0(9)*, HarperTeen) HarperCollins Pubs.
Surrisi, C. M. Vampires on the Run: A Quinnie Boyd Mystery. 2017. (Quinnie Boyd Mysteries Ser.: 2). (ENG.). 296p. (gr. 4-8). 33.32 ***(978-1-5124-2692-2(X)***, Carolrhoda Bks.) Lerner Publishing Group.
Surrisi, Cynthia & Surrisi, C. M. Vampires on the Run: A Quinnie Boyd Mystery. 2017. (Quinnie Boyd Mysteries Ser.: 2). (ENG.). 296p. (J). (gr. 4-8). 16.99 *(978-1-5124-1150-8(7)*, Carolrhoda Bks.) Lerner Publishing Group.
Sutton, Laurie S. Goldilocks & the Three Vampires: A Graphic Novel. Jennings, C. S., illus. 2016. (Far Out Fairy Tales Ser.). (ENG.). 40p. (gr. 3-4). lib. bdg. 25.32 *(978-1-4965-3783-6(1)*, Far Out Fairy Tales) Stone Arch Bks.
Swift, John. Tea with a Vampire. 2007. pap. 9.00 *(978-0-8059-8963-2(3))* Dorrance Publishing Co., Inc.
Taylor, Dereen. The Mystery of the Vampire Boy: Dare You Peek Through the Pop-Up Windows? Spoor, Mike, illus. 2014. (ENG.). 12p. (J). (gr. k-5). 16.99 *(978-1-86147-410-0(5)*, Armadillo) Anness Publishing GBR. Dist: National Bk. Network.
Taylor, Drew Hayden. The Night Wanderer: A Native Gothic Novel. Wyatt, Michael, illus. 2007. (ENG.). 228p. (YA). (gr. 7-12). 21.95 *(978-1-55451-100-6(3)*, 9781554511006); 5th ed. pap. 12.95 *(978-1-55451-099-3(6)*, 9781554510993) Annick Pr., Ltd. CAN. Dist: Publishers Group West (PGW).
Thaler, Mike. Hubie Cool: Vampire Hunter. Lee, Jared D., illus. 2015. 64p. (J). pap. ***(978-0-545-85075-9(4))*** Scholastic, Inc.
Thompson, Kate. Midnight's Choice. unabr. ed. 2004. (Switchers Ser.: Vol. 2). 240p. (J). (gr. 5-9). pap. 38.00 incl. audio *(978-0-8072-8769-9(5)*, Listening Library) Random Hse. Audio Publishing Group.
Thomson, Sarah L. Mercy: The Last New England Vampire, 1 vol. 2011. (ENG.). 178p. (J). pap. 16.95 *(978-1-934031-36-0(4)*, 9caae975-eeb4-4b56-8673-b3abbf16fc2f) Islandport Pr., Inc.
Toft, Di. The Twilight Circus. 2011. (Wolven Ser.: 2). (ENG.). 384p. (J). (gr. 3-7). 17.99 *(978-0-545-29492-8(4)*, Chicken Hse., The) Scholastic, Inc.
Troupe, Thomas Kingsley. The Voiceless Vampire. Gilpin, Stephen, illus. 2015. (Furry & Flo Ser.). (ENG.). 128p. (gr. 2-3). lib. bdg. 25.32 *(978-1-4342-9645-0(8))* Stone Arch Bks.
Turner, Max. End of Days. 2010. (Night Runner Novels Ser.: 2). (ENG.). 304p. (YA). (gr. 8-12). pap. 20.99 *(978-0-312-59252-3(3)*, 9780312592523, St. Martin's Griffin) St. Martin's Pr.
Vampires, 1 vol. 2010. (Vampires Ser.). (ENG.). 32p. (gr. 3-4). lib. bdg. 83.97 *(978-1-4296-4579-9(2)*, Edge Bks.) Capstone Press of Coughlan Cos.
van Diepen, Allison. The Vampire Stalker. 2011. (ENG.). 272p. (J). (gr. 7-7). 17.99 *(978-0-545-28375-5(2))* Scholastic, Inc.
Vanholme, Virginie. The Vampire from the Marshes. Mauricet, illus. 2008. (Scared to Death Ser.: 1). (ENG.). 46p. pap. 11.95 *(978-1-905460-47-2(3))* CineBook GBR. Dist: National Bk. Network.
Verday, Jessica. The Beautiful & the Damned. 2013. (ENG., Illus.). 272p. (YA). (gr. 7). 17.99 *(978-1-4424-8835-9(2)*, Simon Pulse) Simon Pulse.
Verstraete, Majanka. Valentina & the Haunted Mansion (Valentina's Spooky Adventures - 1) Giffin, Noelle, illus. I.t. ed. 2013. (ENG.). 48p. 21.95 *(978-1-62253-057-1(8))*; pap. 10.95 *(978-1-62253-056-4(X))* Evolved Publishing.
—Valentina & the Whackadoodle Witch: Valentina's Spooky Adventures. Giffin, Noelle, illus. I.t. ed. 2013. 2. (ENG.). 46p. (gr. k-4). pap. 10.95 *(978-1-62253-059-5(4))* Evolved Publishing.
Viehl, Lynn. Dead of Night. 2012. (Youngbloods Ser.: 2). (ENG.). 312p. (YA). pap. 9.95 *(978-0-7387-2646-5(X)*, Flux) North Star Editions.
Wells, Craig. Fangs for God: A Vampire Satire. 2011. 252p. pap. 16.95 *(978-1-4620-2136-9(0))* iUniverse, Inc.
West, Temple. Velvet. 2015. (ENG.). 416p. (YA). (gr. 8). pap. 9.99 *(978-1-250-05708-2(6)*, 9781250057082) Feiwel & Friends.
Westerfeld, Scott. Peeps: So süss, dass ich ihn fressen musste. 2006. (ENG.). 288p. (YA). (gr. 9-12). 8.99 *(978-1-59514-083-8(2)*, Razorbill) Penguin Young Readers Group.
Whiteside, S. K. Inheritance. 2013. 320p. (YA). pap. 12.99 *(978-1-939769-27-5(2))* Crushing Hearts and Black Butterfly Publishing.
Wignall, K. J. Alchemy. Book Two of the Mercian Trilogy: Alchemy. 2012. (ENG.). 336p. (J). (gr. 7). 17.99 *(978-1-60684-265-2(X)*, Carolrhoda Lab™) Lerner Publishing Group.
—Blood: Book One of the Mercian Trilogy. 2012. (ENG.). 272p. (J). (gr. 7). pap. 9.99 *(978-1-60684-387-1(7)*, Carolrhoda Lab™) Lerner Publishing Group.
Wilde, Terry Lee. The Vampire... in My Dreams. 2008. (ENG.). 244p. (YA). (gr. 7-12). pap. 13.00 *(978-1-59998-837-5(2))* Samhain Publishing, LTD.
Winters, Ben H. Literally Disturbed No. 1: Tales to Keep You up at Night. Watkins, Adam F., illus. 2013. (ENG.). 64p. (J). (gr. 3-7). 9.99 *(978-0-8431-7194-5(4)*, Price Stern Sloan) Penguin Young Readers Group.
Yancey, Rick. The Curse of the Wendigo. 2010. (Monstrumologist Ser.: 2). (ENG., Illus.). 448p. (YA). (gr. 9-18). 17.99 *(978-1-4169-8450-4(X)*, Simon & Schuster Bks. For Young Readers) Simon & Schuster Bks. For Young Readers.
Zornow, Jeff. Werewolf, 1 vol. Zornow, Jeff, illus. 2007. (Graphic Horror Ser.). (ENG., Illus.). 32p. (gr. 3-7). 28.50 *(978-1-60270-062-8(1)*, Graphic Planet- Fiction) ABDO Publishing Co.

VAN BUREN, MARTIN, 1782-1862

Ferry, Steven. Martin Van Buren. 2008. (Presidents of the U. S. A. Ser.). (ENG., Illus.). 48p. (J). (gr. 3-6). 32.79 *(978-1-60253-037-9(8)*, 200676) Child's World, Inc., The.
Lazo, Caroline Evensen. Martin Van Buren. 2005. (Presidential Leaders Ser.). (Illus.). 112p. (J). (gr. 3-7). lib. bdg. 29.27 *(978-0-8225-1394-0(3))* Lerner Publishing Group.
Rumsch, BreAnn. Martin Van Buren, 1 vol. 2009. (United States Presidents Ser.). (ENG., Illus.). 40p. (YA). (gr. 3-6). 27.07 *(978-1-60453-478-8(8))* ABDO Publishing Co.
Schmidt, Roderic. How to Draw the Life & Times of Martin Van Buren. (Kid's Guide to Drawing the Presidents of the United States of America Ser.). 2009. 32p. (gr. 4-4). 50.50 *(978-1-61511-155-8(7)*, PowerKids Pr.) 2006. (YA). (gr. 2-5). 26.50 *(978-1-4042-2985-3(X))* Rosen Publishing Group, Inc., The.
Venezia, Mike. Martin Van Buren. Venezia, Mike, illus. 2005. (Getting to Know the U. S. Presidents Ser.). (ENG., Illus.). 32p. (J). (gr. 3-4). 28.00 *(978-0-516-22613-2(4)*, Children's Pr.) Scholastic Library Publishing.

VAN DIEMAN'S LAND

see Tasmania

VAN GOGH, VINCENT, 1853-1890

see Gogh, Vincent Van, 1853-1890

VANILLA

Karner, Julie. The Biography of Vanilla. 2006. (How Did That Get Here? Ser.). (ENG., Illus.). 32p. (J). (gr. 4-7). pap. *(978-0-7787-2526-8(X))*; lib. bdg. *(978-0-7787-2490-2(5))* Crabtree Publishing Co.

VAN WINKLE, RIP (FICTITIOUS CHARACTER)—FICTION

Irving, Washington & Busch, Jeffrey. Rip Van Winkle. (Classics Illustrated Ser.). (Illus.). 52p. (YA). pap. 4.95 *(978-1-57209-009-5(X))* Classics International Entertainment, Inc.

VASQUEZ DE CORONADO, FRANCISCO, 1510-1549

see Coronado, Francisco Vasquez de, 1510-1554

VASSALS

see Feudalism

VATICAN CITY

Fox, Martha Capwell. Vatican City. 2005. (Modern Nations Ser.). (ENG., Illus.). 112p. (YA). (gr. 7-10). lib. bdg. 30.85 *(978-1-59018-733-3(4)*, 1244593, Lucent Bks.) Cengage Gale.
Nanji, Shenaaz. Vatican City. 2014. (J). *(978-1-4896-1158-1(4))* Weigl Pubs., Inc.

VEGETABLE ANATOMY

see Plant Anatomy

VEGETABLE GARDENING

see also Vegetables

Amstutz, Lisa J. Edible Gardening: Growing Your Own Vegetables, Fruits, & More. 2016. (Gardening Guides). (ENG., Illus.). 32p. (gr. 3-4). lib. bdg. 27.99 *(978-1-4914-8235-3(4)*, Snap Bks.) Capstone Press of Coughlan Cos.
Bath, Louella. Growing Vegetables. 2015. (Garden Squad! Ser.). (ENG.). 24p. (J). (gr. 3-4). 23.60 *(978-1-4994-1014-3(X)*, PowerKids Pr.) Rosen Publishing Group, Inc., The.
Berkes, Marianne. What's in the Garden?, 1 vol. Arbo, Cris, illus. 2013. (ENG.). 32p. (J). (gr. -1-4). 16.95 *(978-1-58469-189-1(1))*; pap. 8.95 *(978-1-58469-190-7(5))* Dawn Pubns.
Brown, Robert L. Daddy Grows Colors, 1 vol. 2009. 28p. pap. 24.95 *(978-1-60836-124-3(1))* America Star Bks.
Burns Chong, Susan. Community Gardens. 2013. (Urban Gardening & Farming for Teens Ser.). 64p. (YA). (gr. 7-12). 33.25 *(978-1-4777-1777-6(3))* Rosen Publishing Group, Inc., The.
Collins, Chris & Lia, Leendertz. Grow Your Own: For Kids! 2012. (ENG., Illus.). 112p. (gr. -1-17). 14.99 *(978-1-84533-606-6(2)*, Mitchell Beazley) Octopus Publishing Group GBR. Dist: Hachette Bk. Group.
Gourley, Robbin. First Garden: The White House Garden & How It Grew. 2011. (ENG., Illus.). 48p. (J). (gr. 1-4). 16.99 *(978-0-547-48224-8(8))* Houghton Mifflin Harcourt Publishing Co.
Grant, Amanda. Grow It, Cook It with Kids. 2010. (ENG., Illus.). 128p. (J). *(978-1-84597-969-0(9))* Ryland Peters & Small.
Hengel, Katherine. Garden to Table: A Kid's Guide to Planting, Growing, & Preparing Food. 2014. (ENG., Illus.). 144p. (J). (gr. 2-7). pap. 15.95 *(978-1-938063-42-8(2)*, Mighty Media Junior Readers) Mighty Media Pr.
Heos, Bridget. So You Want to Grow a Salad? Fabbri, Daniele, illus. 2015. (Grow Your Food Ser.). (ENG.). 24p. (gr. 1-3). 19.95 *(978-1-60753-741-0(9))* Amicus Publishing.
Hirsch, Rebecca. Save the Planet: Growing Your Own Garden. 2010. (Explorer Library: Language Arts Explorer Ser.). (ENG.). 32p. (gr. 4-8). pap. 14.21 *(978-1-60279-666-9(1)*, 200913) Cherry Lake Publishing.
How Fruits & Vegetables Grow, 5 vols. 2010. (How Fruits & Vegetables Grow Ser.). (ENG.). 24p. (gr. k-1). pap. 29.75 *(978-1-4296-6189-8(5)*, Pebble Bks.) Capstone Press of Coughlan Cos.
Kesselring, Susan. Grow a Garden: Sustainable Foods, 1 vol. Avakyan, Tatevik, illus. 2012. (Move & Get Healthy Ser.). (ENG.). 32p. (J). (gr. k-3). 28.50 *(978-1-61641-861-8(3))* Magic Wagon.
Kuskowski, Alex. Super Simple Kitchen Gardens: A Kid's Guide to Gardening, 1 vol. 2014. (Super Simple Gardening Ser.). (ENG.). 32p. (gr. k-4). 27.07 *(978-1-62403-525-8(6))* ABDO Publishing Co.
—Super Simple Salad Gardens: A Kid's Guide to Gardening, 1 vol. 2014. (Super Simple Gardening Ser.). (ENG.). 32p. (gr. k-4). 27.07 *(978-1-62403-526-5(4))* ABDO Publishing Co.
Lanz, Helen. Grow Your Own Lettuce. 2012. (Grow Your Own Ser.). (Illus.). 32p. (gr. 3-6). lib. bdg. 28.50 *(978-1-59771-311-5(2))* Sea-To-Sea Pubns.
—Grow Your Own Potatoes. 2012. (Grow Your Own Ser.). (Illus.). 32p. (gr. 3-6). lib. bdg. 28.50 *(978-1-59771-312-2(0))* Sea-To-Sea Pubns.
—Grow Your Own Tomatoes. 2012. (Grow Your Own Ser.). (Illus.). 32p. (gr. 3-6). lib. bdg. 28.50 *(978-1-59771-314-6(7))* Sea-To-Sea Pubns.
Leavitt, Amie. A Backyard Vegetable Garden for Kids. 2008. (Gardening for Kids Ser.). 48p. (YA). (gr. 1-4). lib. bdg. 29.95 *(978-1-58415-634-5(1))* Mitchell Lane Pubs., Inc.
Liversidge, Cassie. Pasta Sauce! Grow Your Own Ingredients. 2013. (ENG., Illus.). 40p. (J). (gr. k-3). 14.95 *(978-1-62087-533-9(0)*, 620533, Sky Pony Pr.) Skyhorse Publishing Co., Inc.
Martin, Jacqueline Briggs. Farmer Will Allen & the Growing Table. Larkin, Eric, illus. 2013. (ENG.). 32p. (J). (gr. k). 17.95 *(978-0-9836615-3-5(7))* READERS to EATERS.
McDougall, Nancy & Hendy, Jenny. 300 Step-By-Step Cooking & Gardening Projects for Kids: The Ultimate Book for Budding Gardeners & Super Chefs with Amazing Things to Grow & Cook Yourself, Shown in over 2300 Photographs. 2012. (ENG., Illus.). 512p. 25.00 *(978-0-7548-2383-4(0))* Anness Publishing GBR. Dist: National Bk. Network.
—300 Step-By-Step Cooking & Gardening Projects for Kids: The Ultimate Book for Budding Gardeners & Super Chefs, with Amazing Things to Grow & Cook Yourself, Shown in over 2300 Photographs. 2015. (ENG., Illus.). 512p. pap. 14.99 *(978-1-86147-707-1(4)*, Armadillo) Anness Publishing GBR. Dist: National Bk. Network.
Minden, Cecilia. Gardening by the Numbers. 2007. (21st Century Skills Library: Real World Math Ser.). (ENG., Illus.). 32p. (gr. 4-8). lib. bdg. 28.50 *(978-1-60279-008-7(6)*, 200064) Cherry Lake Publishing.
Pettiford, Rebecca. Vegetables. Fretland VanVoorst, Jenny, ed. 2015. (J). lib. bdg. 25.65 *(978-1-62031-233-9(6))* Jump! Inc.
Rand, Casey. Producing Vegetables, 1 vol. 2012. (Technology of Farming Ser.). (ENG.). 48p. (gr. 4-6). lib. bdg. 33.32 *(978-1-4329-6407-8(0)*, Heinemann InfoSearch) Heinemann-Raintree.
Rigby Education Staff. The Vegetable Garden. (Chiquilibros Ser.). (Illus.). (gr. -1-1). 12.00 *(978-0-7635-8538-9(6))* Rigby Education.
Schuh, Mari C. How Fruits & Vegetables Grow, 5 vols., Set. Incl. Blueberries Grow on a Bush. Saunders-Smith, Gail, contrib. by. lib. bdg. 21.99 *(978-1-4296-5282-7(9))*; Lettuce Grows on the Ground. Saunders-Smith, Gail. lib. bdg. 21.99 *(978-1-4296-5281-0(0))*; Tomatoes Grow on a Vine. Saunders-Smith, Gail. lib. bdg. 21.99 *(978-1-4296-5278-0(0))*; (gr. k-1). (How Fruits & Vegetables Grow Ser.). (ENG.). 24p. 2010. Set lib. bdg. 65.97 *(978-1-4296-5283-4(7)*, Pebble Bks.) Capstone Press of Coughlan Cos.
Sévigny, Eric, illus. In the Garden. 2005. (Playtime Ser.). (ENG.). 24p. (J). (gr. -1-1). pap. 4.99 *(978-2-89450-383-6(0))* Caillouet, Gerry.
Stagliano, Katie. Katie's Cabbage. Heid, Karen, illus. 2014. (Young Palmetto Bks.). (ENG.). 40p. 19.95 *(978-1-61117-504-2(6))* Univ. of South Carolina Pr.
Sundance/Newbridge LLC Staff. The Vegetable Garden. 2007. (Early Science Ser.). (gr. k-3). 18.95 *(978-1-4007-6287-3(1))*; pap. 6.10 *(978-1-4007-6283-5(9))* Sundance/Newbridge Educational Publishing.

VEGETABLE GARDENING—FICTION

Brown, Robert L. Daddy Grows Colors, 1 vol. 2010. 26p. 24.95 *(978-1-4512-1746-9(3))* PublishAmerica, Inc.
Candlewick Press Staff. Peppa Pig & the Vegetable Garden. 2014. (Peppa Pig Ser.). (ENG.). 32p. (J). (-k). 12.99 *(978-0-7636-6987-4(3)*, Candlewick Entertainment) Candlewick Pr.
Coy, John. Two Old Potatoes & Me. Fisher, Carolyn, illus. 2013. (ENG.). (J). (gr. k-3). pap. 7.99 *(978-1-935666-46-2(0))* Nodin Pr.
dePaola, Tomie. Strega Nona's Harvest. dePaola, Tomie, illus. (ENG., Illus.). 32p. (J). (gr. -1-3). 2012. mass mkt. 7.99 *(978-0-14-242338-7(6)*, Puffin Books) 2009. 16.99 *(978-0-399-25291-4(6)*, G.P. Putnam's Sons Books for Young Readers) Penguin Young Readers Group.
Dillard, Sarah. Mouse Scouts. 2016. (Mouse Scouts Ser.). (ENG., Illus.). 128p. (J). (gr. 2-5). 12.99 *(978-0-385-75599-3(6)*, Knopf Bks. for Young Readers) Random Hse. Children's Bks.
Ehlert, Lois. A Sembrar Sopa de Verduras. 2012.Tr. of Growing Vegetable Soup. (ENG & SPA., Illus.). 32p. (J). (gr. -1 — 1). bds. 4.99 *(978-0-547-73497-2(2))* Houghton Mifflin Harcourt Publishing Co.
Gibson, James E. Rico, the Mysterious Worm, 1 vol. 2009. 17p. pap. 24.95 *(978-1-60749-148-4(6))* America Star Bks.
Hillert, Margaret. Dear Dragon Grows a Garden. Schimmell, David, illus. rev. ed. 2014. (BeginningtoRead Ser.). (ENG.). 32p. (J). (gr. k-2). pap. 11.94 *(978-1-60357-414-3(X))*; lib. bdg. 22.60 *(978-1-59953-578-4(5))* Norwood Hse. Pr.
January, Rick. Come Out to the Garden. January, Stella, illus. 2012. (ENG.). 30p. (J). (gr. k-3). pap. 12.95 *(978-1-937084-66-0(3))* Boutique of Quality Books Publishing Co., Inc.
January, Rick & January, Stella. Come Out to the Garden. 2012. (ENG., Illus.). 30p. (J). 24.95 *(978-1-937084-40-0(X)*, BQB Publishing) Boutique of Quality Books Publishing Co., Inc.
Koehn, Wendel. Wendel Plants Potatoes. 2012. 24p. pap. 14.93 *(978-1-4669-5956-9(8))* Trafford Publishing.
Peterson, Mary. Snail Has Lunch. Peterson, Mary, illus. 2016. (Pix Ser.). (ENG., Illus.). 64p. (J). (gr. 1-4). 12.99 *(978-1-4814-5302-8(5)*, Aladdin) Simon & Schuster Children's Publishing.
Picou, Lin & Moreta, Gladys. Too Much Tv! Reese, Bob, illus. 2011. (ENG.). 24p. (gr. 1-2). pap. 8.95 *(978-1-61236-019-5(X))* Rourke Educational Media.
Rey, H. A. The Perfect Carrot. 2010. (Curious George Ser.). (ENG., Illus.). 24p. (J). (gr. -1-3). pap. 3.99 *(978-0-547-24299-6(9))* Houghton Mifflin Harcourt Publishing Co.
Roberts, Margiad & Owen, Carys Eurwen. Tecwyn Yn Plannu Tatws. 2005. (WEL., Illus.). 36p. pap. *(978-0-86381-408-2(5))* Gwasg Carreg Gwalch.
Square Cat ABC. 2014. (ENG., Illus.). 32p. (J). (gr. -1-3). 15.99 *(978-1-4424-9895-2(1)*, Aladdin) Simon & Schuster Children's Publishing.
Tolstoy, Alexei. Enormous Turnip. 2003. (Green Light Readers — Level 2 Ser.). (gr. k-3). lib. bdg. 13.50 *(978-0-613-64495-2(6)*, Turtleback) Turtleback Bks.
Waddell, Barbara. Hooray, Hooray, Today's the Day. 2010. 36p. 15.49 *(978-1-4269-4477-2(2))* Trafford Publishing.

T U V

White, Gene. Billy's Big Tomato. Davis, Shelley & Davis, Betsy, illus. 2013. 24p. pap. 11.00 (978-0-9886360-9-5(3)) Kids At Heart Publishing, LLC.

Worcester, Sue. Ernesto Nia Lakeru. 2011. 28p. pap. 28.03 (978-1-4568-8257-0(0)) Xlibris Corp.

Young, Jessica. Room to Bloom. Secheret, Jessica, illus. 2017. (Finley Flowers Ser.). (ENG.). 128p. (gr. 2-3). lib. bdg. 25.32 (978-1-4795-9806-9(2), Finley Flowers) Picture Window Bks.

Zoehfeld, Kathleen Weidner. Secrets of the Garden: Food Chains & the Food Web in Our Backyard. Lamont, Priscilla, illus. 2014. (ENG.). 40p. (J). (gr. k-3). 7.99 (978-0-385-75364-7(0), Dragonfly Bks.) Random Hse. Children's Bks.

VEGETABLE KINGDOM

see Botany; Plants

VEGETABLES

see also Vegetable Gardening; Vegetarianism

Aboff, Marcie. The Incredible Vegetable Group, 1 vol. Poling, Kyle, illus. 2011. (First Graphics: Myplate & Healthy Eating Ser.). (ENG.). 24p. (gr. 1-2). pap. 6.29 (978-1-4296-7163-7(7)); lib. bdg. 23.99 (978-1-4296-6089-1(9)); pap. 35.70 (978-1-4296-7169-9(6)) Capstone Press of Coughlan Cos.

Adams, Julia. Vegetables. 2011. (Good Food Ser.). (ENG.). 24p. (J). lib. bdg. 22.60 (978-1-4488-3274-3(8), PowerKids Pr.) Rosen Publishing Group, Inc., The.

AZ Books Staff. Fruits & Vegetables. Slusar, Julia, ed. 2012. (Pull It Out Ser.). (ENG.). 10p. (J). (— 1). 7.95 (978-1-61889-192-1(8)) AZ Bks. LLC.

Bass, Jennifer Vogel. Edible Colors. Bass, Jennifer Vogel, photos by. (ENG., Illus.). (J). 2016. 30p. bds. 7.99 (978-1-62672-284-2(6), 9781626722842) 2014. 32p. (gr. -1-k). 12.99 (978-1-62672-002-2(9), 9781626720022) Roaring Brook Pr.

—Edible Numbers. (ENG., Illus.). (J). 2016. 30p. bds. 8.99 (978-1-62672-285-9(4), 9781626722859) 2015. 32p. (gr. -1-k). 12.99 (978-1-62672-003-9(7), 9781626720039) Roaring Brook Pr.

Bath, Louella. Growing Vegetables. 2015. (Garden Squad! Ser.). (ENG.). 24p. (J). (gr. 3-4). 23.60 (978-1-4994-1014-3(X), PowerKids Pr.) Rosen Publishing Group, Inc., The.

Benduhn, Tea. Vegetables. 2007. (Find Out about Food Ser.). 24p. (gr. k-3). pap. 8.15 (978-0-8368-8262-9(8)); (Illus.). lib. bdg. 22.00 (978-0-8368-8255-1(5)) Stevens, Gareth Publishing LLLP. (Weekly Reader Leveled Readers).

—Vegetables (Vegetales) 2007. (Find Out about Food/ Conoce la comida Ser.). (SPA & ENG.). 24p. (gr. k-3). pap. 8.15 (978-0-8368-8466-1(3), Weekly Reader Leveled Readers) Stevens, Gareth Publishing LLLP.

—Vegetables/Vegetales. 2007. (Find Out about Food/Conoce la Comida Ser.). (SPA., Illus.). 24p. (gr. k-3). lib. bdg. 22.00 (978-0-8368-8459-3(0), Weekly Reader Leveled Readers) Stevens, Gareth Publishing LLLP.

Blanch, Xavier. Hortalizas. 2003. (SPA & CAT.). (J). (978-84-246-0693-0(0), GL30335) La Galera, S.A. Editorial ESP. Dist: Lectorum Pubns., Inc.

Blane, Francisco. Vegetables Are Good! Lap Book. 2009. (My First Reader's Theater Set B Ser.). (J). 28.00 (978-1-60634-990-8(2)) Benchmark Education Co.

Bodden, Valerie. Healthy Plates: Vegetables. 2015. (Healthy Plates Ser.). (ENG.). 24p. (J). (gr. 1-3). pap. 9.99 (978-1-62832-112-8(1), Creative Paperbacks) Creative Co., The.

—Vegetables. 2015. (J). (978-1-60818-512-2(5), Creative Education) Creative Co., The.

Borgert-Spaniol, Megan. Vegetable Group. 2012. (Eating Right with Myplate Ser.). (ENG., Illus.). 24p. (J). (gr. k-3). lib. bdg. 25.95 (978-1-60014-760-9(7), Blastoff! Readers) Bellwether Media.

Byers, Ann. Fruits & Vegetables: From the Garden to Your Table. 2012. (Truth about the Food Supply Ser.). (ENG., Illus.). 48p. (J). (gr. 5-8). lib. bdg. 27.95 (978-1-4488-6799-8(1), Rosen Reference) Rosen Publishing Group, Inc., The.

Byrd, Tracy. Fruits & Vegetables & How They Grow: A to Z. 2012. 60p. pap. 24.99 (978-1-4772-4897-3(8)) AuthorHouse.

Cardenas, Ernesto A. Vegetables for Me! 2009. 19.95 (978-1-60698-017-0(3)); pap. 3.95 (978-1-60698-015-6(7)) Milo Educational Bks. & Resources.

Charney, Steve & Goldbeck, David. The ABC's of Fruits & Vegetables & Beyond: Delicious Alphabet Poems Plus Food, Facts & Fun for Everyone. Larson, Maria Burgaleta, illus. 2007. 112p. (J). (gr. -1-4). per. 16.95 (978-1-886101-07-4(8)) Ceres Pr.

Christian, Cheryl. What's in My Garden? A Book of Colors. Ericsson, Annie Beth, illus. 2009. 16p. (J). (gr. -1). bds. 6.25 (978-1-59572-166-2(5)) Star Bright Bks., Inc.

Cleary, Brian P. Green Beans, Potatoes, & Even Tomatoes: What Is in the Vegetables Group? Goneau, Martin, illus. 2011. (Food Is CATegorical Ser.). (ENG.). 32p. (gr. k-3). pap. 7.95 (978-0-7613-6391-0(2)) Lerner Publishing Group.

Cleary, Brian P. & Goneau, Martin. Green Beans, Potatoes, & Even Tomatoes: What Is in the Vegetables Group? 2011. (Food Is CATegorical Ser.). pap. 45.32 (978-0-7613-8350-5(6), Millbrook Pr.) Lerner Publishing Group.

Cleary, Brian P. & Nelson, Jennifer K. Green Beans, Potatoes, & Even Tomatoes: What Is in the Vegetables Group? Goneau, Martin, illus. 2010. (Food Is CATegorical Ser.). (ENG.). 32p. (gr. k-3). 25.26 (978-1-58013-588-7(9)) Lerner Publishing Group.

Deal, Darlene. Play with Your Food & Learn How to Eat Right: Nutritional Book about Fruits & Vegetables. 2004. (ENG & SPA., Illus.). 22p. (J). (gr. 1-4). pap. 9.95 (978-0-9747299-0-9(6)) Deal, Darlene.

Derkazarian, Susan. Fruits & Vegetables. (Rookie Read-About Health Ser.). (ENG., Illus.). 32p. (J). (gr. k-2). 2006. pap. 5.95 (978-0-516-25926-0(1)) 2005. lib. bdg. 20.50 (978-0-516-23673-5(3)) Scholastic Library Publishing. (Children's Pr.).

Dickmann, Nancy. A Bean's Life, 1 vol. 2010. (Watch It Grow Ser.). (ENG., Illus.). 24p. (gr. -1-1). pap. 6.29 (978-1-4329-4151-2(8), Acorn) Heinemann-Raintree.

Dilkes, D. H. Vegetables. 2011. (All about Good Foods We Eat Ser.). (Illus.). 24p. (J). (gr. -1-18). pap. 7.95 (978-1-59845-255-6(X), Enslow Elementary); (gr. k-3). lib. bdg. 22.60 (978-0-7660-3926-1(9)) Enslow Pubs., Inc.

Dolbear, Emily. How Did That Get to My Table? Salad. 2009. (Community Connections: How Did That Get to My Table? Ser.). (ENG.). 24p. (gr. 2-5). lib. bdg. 25.64 (978-1-60279-473-3(1), 200262) Cherry Lake Publishing.

Dorling Kindersley Publishing Staff. Eat Your Greens, Reds, Yellows, & Purples. 2016. (ENG., Illus.). 80p. (J). (gr. 3-7). 12.99 (978-1-4654-5152-1(8), DK Children) Dorling Kindersley Publishing, Inc.

Edwards, Nicola. Vegetables. 2007. (See How Plants Grow Ser.). (Illus.). 24p. (J). (gr. 3-7). lib. bdg. 22.60 (978-1-4042-3700-1(3), PowerKids Pr.) Rosen Publishing Group, Inc., The.

Ehlert, Lois. Eating the Alphabet: Fruits & Vegetables from A to Z. alt. ed. 2006. (ENG., Illus.). 28p. (J). (gr. -1 — 1). bds. 11.99 (978-0-15-205688-9(2)) Houghton Mifflin Harcourt Publishing Co.

Ericsson, Annie Beth & Christian, Cheryl. ¿Que hay en mi Jardin? (Spanish/English) Un libro de colores/A Book of Colors. del Risco, Eida, tr. 2009. (ENG & SPA., Illus.). 16p. (J). bds. 6.25 (978-1-59572-181-5(9)) Star Bright Bks., Inc.

Esperanzate-Buenafe, Norma. You Don't Have to Like It. 2011. (ENG.). 25p. (J). pap. 16.95 (978-1-4327-7771-5(8)) Outskirts Pr., Inc.

Franklin, Jean. Get the Carrot. 2016. (Spring Forward Ser.). (J). (gr. 1). (978-1-4900-6014-9(6)) Benchmark Education Co.

Fruits & Vegetables I Like to Eat - English Take Home Book. 2007. (Journeys Ser.). (J). pap. 15.00 (978-1-4042-5462-6(5), Rosen Classroom) Rosen Publishing Group, Inc., The.

Fruits & Vegetables I Like to Eat - Spanish Take Home Book. 2007. (Journeys Ser.). (J). pap. 49.95 (978-1-4042-5513-5(3), Rosen Classroom) Rosen Publishing Group, Inc., The.

Gibbons, Gail. The Vegetables We Eat. (ENG., Illus.). 32p. (J). 2008. (gr. 4-7). pap. 7.99 (978-0-8234-2153-4(8)) 2007. (gr. 3-7). 17.95 (978-0-8234-2001-8(9)) Holiday Hse., Inc.

Graham, Pamela. Big Red Tomato. 2007. (Rise & Shine Ser.). (ENG.). 24p. (C). (gr. k-2). pap. 13.95 (978-0-7922-9221-0(9)) CENGAGE Learning.

Green, Emily K. Vegetables. 2006. (Blastoff! Readers Ser.). (ENG., Illus.). 24p. (J). (gr. k-3). lib. bdg. 24.95 (978-1-60014-002-0(5), Blastoff! Readers) Bellwether Media.

—Vegetables. 2011. (Blastoff! Readers Ser.). (Illus.). 24p. (J). pap. 5.95 (978-0-531-25857-6(2), Children's Pr.) Scholastic Library Publishing.

Gul, Hasibe, et al. Nutritious Vegetables. 2011. (ENG.). 16p. (J). (gr. -1 — 1). pap. 3.95 (978-1-59784-239-6(7)) Tughra Bks.

Hartley, Jill, photos by. Vegetables of India. 2010. (ENG., Illus.). 24p. (J). (gr. k — 1). bds. 7.95 (978-81-907546-9-9(6)) Tara Books Agency IND. Dist: Publishers Group West (PGW).

Head, Honor. Salad. 2010. (J). 24.25 (978-1-59920-259-4(X)) Black Rabbit Bks.

Hengel, Katherine. Cool Leaf Lettuce from Garden to Table: How to Plant, Grow, & Prepare Leaf Lettuce, 1 vol. 2012. (Cool Garden to Table Ser.). (ENG.). 32p. 28.50 (978-1-61783-185-0(9), Checkerboard Library) ABDO Publishing Co.

Heos, Bridget. So You Want to Grow a Salad? Fabbri, Daniele, illus. 2015. (Grow Your Food Ser.). (ENG.). 24p. (gr. 1-3). 19.95 (978-1-60753-741-0(9)) Amicus Publishing.

Herrington, Lisa M. Tomatoes to Ketchup. 2013. (Rookie Read-About(r) Science Ser.). (ENG.). 32p. (J). pap. 5.95 (978-0-531-24709-9(0), Children's Pr.); lib. bdg. 23.00 (978-0-531-24743-3(0)) Scholastic Library Publishing.

Hoffmann, Sara. Kinds of Vegetables. 2012. (First Step Nonfiction - Kinds of Plants Ser.). (ENG., Illus.). 8p. (gr. -1-1). pap. 4.95 (978-1-4677-0499-1(7), Lerner Pubns.) Lerner Publishing Group.

Houbre, Gilbert. Vegetables. Houbre, Gilbert, illus. 2012. (ENG., Illus.). 36p. (J). (gr. -1-k). 12.99 (978-1-85103-402-4(1)) Moonlight Publishing, Ltd. GBR. Dist: Independent Pubs. Group.

How Fruits & Vegetables Grow. 2011. (How Fruits & Vegetables Grow Ser.). (ENG.). 24p. (gr. k-1). pap. 178.50 (978-1-4296-6358-8(8), Pebble Bks.) Capstone Press of Coughlan Cos.

Hughes, Meredith Sayles. Green Power: Leaf & Flower Vegetables. 2005. (Plants We Eat Ser.). (Illus.). 104p. (gr. 6-9). 26.60 (978-0-8225-2839-5(8)) Lerner Publishing Group.

Jones, Bryony. Very Tasty Vegetables. 2011. (ENG., Illus.). 14p. (J). (gr. -1-k). bds. (978-1-84089-615-2(9)) Zero to Ten, Ltd.

Kalz, Jill. Vegetables. 2003. 24p. (J). lib. bdg. 21.35 (978-1-58340-300-6(0)) Black Rabbit Bks.

Kesselring, Susan. Eat a Rainbow: Healthy Foods, 1 vol. Avakyan, Tatevik, illus. 2012. (Move & Get Healthy Ser.). (ENG.). 32p. (J). (gr. k-3). 28.50 (978-1-61641-858-8(3)) Magic Wagon.

Klepeis, Alicia. Fruits & Vegetables Explained. 2016. (Distinctions in Nature Ser.). 32p. (J). (gr. 3-3). 28.50 (978-1-5026-1744-6(7)) Cavendish Square Publishing.

Kuskowski, Alex. Super Simple Salad Gardens: A Kid's Guide to Gardening, 1 vol. 2014. (Super Simple Gardening Ser.). (ENG.). 32p. (gr. k-4). 27.07 (978-1-62403-526-5(4)) ABDO Publishing Co.

Lanz, Helen. Grow Your Own Potatoes. 2012. (Grow Your Own Ser.). (Illus.). 32p. (gr. 3-6). lib. bdg. 28.50 (978-1-59771-312-2(0)) Sea-To-Sea Pubns.

—Grow Your Own Tomatoes. 2012. (Grow Your Own Ser.). (Illus.). 32p. (gr. 3-6). lib. bdg. 28.50 (978-1-59771-314-6(7)) Sea-To-Sea Pubns.

Lassieur, Allison. Vegetables. 2015. (Illus.). 32p. (J). lib. bdg. 28.50 (978-1-60753-496-9(7)) Amicus Publishing.

Malam, John. Grow Your Own Sandwich, 1 vol. 2011. (Grow It Yourself! Ser.). (ENG.). 32p. (gr. k-2). pap. 8.29 (978-1-4329-5115-3(7)); 27.32 (978-1-4329-5108-5(4)) Heinemann-Raintree. (Heinemann First Library).

Marsico, Katie. Your Healthy Plate - Vegetables. 2012. (21st Century Basic Skills Library: Your Healthy Plate Ser.). (ENG.). 24p. (gr. k-3). lib. bdg. 22.79 (978-1-61080-347-2(7), 201290) Cherry Lake Publishing.

—Your Healthy Plate: Vegetables. 2012. (21st Century Basic Skills Library: Your Healthy Plate Ser.). (ENG.). 24p. (gr. k-3). pap. 12.79 (978-1-61080-399-1(X), 201334) Cherry Lake Publishing.

Martineau, Susan & James, Hel. Fruits & Vegetables. 2012. (Healthy Eating Ser.). (Illus.). 32p. (gr. 2-6). pap. 8.95 (978-1-59920-243-3(3)) Black Rabbit Bks.

Matthews, Colin. I Know Fruits & Vegetables. 2017. (What I Know Ser.). 24p. (J). (gr. k-k). pap. 8.15 (978-1-4824-6293-7(1)) Stevens, Gareth Publishing LLLP.

Milet Publishing Staff. My First Bilingual Book - Vegetables. 2011. (My First Bilingual Book Ser.). (Illus.). 24p. (J). (gr. k — 1). (FRE & ENG.). bds. 8.99 (978-1-84059-660-1(0)); (ENG., bds. 7.99 (978-1-84059-658-8(9)); (ENG., bds. 8.99 (978-1-84059-666-3(X)); (ENG., bds. 7.99 (978-1-84059-669-4(4)) Milet Publishing.

—My First Bilingual Book-Vegetables. 2011. (My First Bilingual Book Ser.). (ENG., Illus.). 24p. (J). (gr. k — 1). bds. 7.99 (978-1-84059-663-2(5)) Milet Publishing.

—My First Bilingual Book-Vegetables (English-Arabic) 2011. (My First Bilingual Book Ser.). (ENG., Illus.). 24p. (J). (gr. k — 1). bds. 8.99 (978-1-84059-656-4(2)) Milet Publishing.

—My First Bilingual Book-Vegetables (English-Farsi) 2011. (My First Bilingual Book Ser.). (ENG., Illus.). 24p. (J). (gr. k — 1). bds. 7.99 (978-1-84059-659-5(7)) Milet Publishing.

—My First Bilingual Book-Vegetables (English-Spanish) 2011. (My First Bilingual Book Ser.). (SPA & ENG., Illus.). 24p. (J). (gr. k — 1). bds. 8.99 (978-1-84059-668-7(6)) Milet Publishing.

—My First Bilingual Book-Vegetables (English-Urdu) 2011. (My First Bilingual Book Ser.). (ENG., Illus.). 24p. (J). (gr. k — 1). bds. 7.99 (978-1-84059-670-0(8)) Milet Publishing.

—My First Bilingual Book-Vegetables (English-Vietnamese) 2011. (My First Bilingual Book Ser.). (ENG., Illus.). 24p. (J). (gr. k — 1). bds. 8.99 (978-1-84059-671-7(6)) Milet Publishing.

—Vegetables. 2011. (My First Bilingual Book Ser.). (ENG., Illus.). 24p. (J). (gr. k — 1). bds. 7.99 (978-1-84059-667-0(8)); bds. 7.99 (978-1-84059-664-9(3)); bds. 7.99 (978-1-84059-657-1(0)) Milet Publishing.

—Vegetables - My First Bilingual Book. 2011. (My First Bilingual Book Ser.). (ENG., Illus.). 24p. (J). (gr. k — 1). bds. 7.99 (978-1-84059-665-6(1)); bds. 7.99 (978-1-84059-661-8(9)) Milet Publishing.

—Vegetables (Le Verdure) 2011. (My First Bilingual Book Ser.). (ENG & ITA., Illus.). 24p. (J). (gr. k — 1). bds. 7.99 (978-1-84059-662-5(7)) Milet Publishing.

Mitchell, Melanie S. Potatoes. (First Step Nonfiction Ser.). (Illus.). (gr. k-2). 2005. 24p. lib. bdg. 17.27 (978-0-8225-4612-2(4)) 2003. 23p. (J). pap. 5.95 (978-0-8225-4613-9(2), Lerner Pubns.) Lerner Publishing Group.

Morganelli, Adrianna. The Biography of Tomatoes. 2007. (How Did That Get Here? Ser.). (ENG., Illus.). 32p. (J). (gr. 2-9). lib. bdg. (978-0-7787-2494-0(8)); pap. (978-0-7787-2530-5(8)) Crabtree Publishing Co.

Murray, Laura K. Bean. 2015. (Illus.). 32p. (J). (978-1-60818-560-3(5), Creative Education) Creative Co., The.

National Geographic Learning Staff. Frozen Vegetables. 2012. (ENG., Illus.). 24p. (C). (gr. 1-4). pap. 12.95 (978-0-8368-4073-5(9)) National Geographic School Publishing, Inc.

Nelson, Robin. Las Verduras. Castañer, Mercedes & Fitzpatrick, Julia, trs. 2003. (Mi Primer Paso Al Mundo Real - Los Grupos de Alimentos (First Step Nonfiction - Food Groups) Ser.).Tr. of Vegetables. (SPA., Illus.). 24p. (gr. k-2). lib. bdg. 23.93 (978-0-8225-5059-4(8)) Lerner Publishing Group.

—Tomatoes. 2009. pap. 34.95 (978-0-7613-4124-6(2)) Lerner Publishing Group.

—Vegetables. 2003. (First Step Nonfiction - Food Groups Ser.). (ENG., Illus.). 24p. (gr. k-2). lib. bdg. 23.93 (978-0-8225-4626-9(4)) Lerner Publishing Group.

Nugent, Samantha. Vegetables. 2015. (Let's Learn about Food Ser.). (ENG.). (J). lib. bdg. 27.13 (978-1-4896-4003-1(7), AV2 by Weigl) Weigl Pubs., Inc.

Owen, Ruth. Vegetables! Life on a Produce Farm. 2012. (Food from Farmers Ser.). (Illus.). 32p. (J). (gr. k-3). pap. 11.75 (978-1-61533-540-4(4)); lib. bdg. 26.50 (978-1-61533-531-2(5)) Windmill Bks.

Pankova, Yuliya, ed. Veggies - Guess What? 2013. (Guess What? Ser.). (ENG.). 10p. (J). (— 1). bds. 5.95 (978-1-61889-319-2(X)) AZ Bks. LLC.

Peanuckle. Mrs. Peanuckle's Vegetable Alphabet. Ford, Jessie, illus. 2017. (Mrs. Peanuckle's Alphabet Library: 1). (ENG.). 28p. (J). bds. 7.99 (978-1-62336-870-8(7), 9781623368708, Rodale Kids) Rodale Pr., Inc.

Pettiford, Rebecca. Vegetables. Fretland VanVoorst, Jenny, ed. 2015. (J). lib. bdg. 25.65 (978-1-62031-233-9(6)) Jump! Inc.

Potato. 2003. 38.95 (978-0-8136-4132-4(2)); 36.95 (978-0-8136-9263-0(6)) Modern Curriculum Pr.

Potatoes, Potatoes: Level J, 6 vols. (Wonder Worldtm Ser.). 16p. 29.95 (978-0-7802-2904-4(5)) Wright Group/McGraw-Hill.

Puppet Rescue, creator. Caterpillar says Eat Your Greens. 2007. (Illus.). 10p. (J). 4.95 (978-0-9799958-1-1(7)) Puppet Rescue.

Rajczak, Kristen. Very Tasty Vegetable Recipes. 2014. (Ingredients for a Healthy Life Ser.). (Illus.). 24p. (J). (gr. 2-5). 22.60 (978-1-4824-0575-0(X)) Stevens, Gareth Publishing LLLP.

Rand, Casey. Producing Vegetables, 1 vol. 2012. (Technology of Farming Ser.). (ENG.). 48p. (gr. 4-6). lib. bdg. 33.32 (978-1-4329-6407-8(0), Heinemann InfoSearch) Heinemann-Raintree.

Riggs, Kate. Grow with Me: Tomato. 2013. (Grow with Me Ser.). (ENG.). 32p. (J). (gr. 1-3). pap. 9.99 (978-0-89812-772-0(6), Creative Paperbacks) Creative Co., The.

—Tomato. 2012. (Grow with Me Ser.). (Illus.). 32p. (J). (gr. 3-8). 19.95 (978-1-60818-219-0(3), Creative Education) Creative Co., The.

Robbins, Eliza. Vegetables & How They Grow. 2008. (Rosen Real Readers: Upper Emergent Ser.). (ENG., Illus.). 12p. (gr. 1-2). pap. 5.90 (978-0-8239-8128-1(2)) Rosen Publishing Group, Inc., The.

Rodger, Ellen. The Biography of Potatoes. 2007. (How Did That Get Here? Ser.). (ENG., Illus.). 32p. (J). (gr. 2-9). lib. bdg. (978-0-7787-2492-6(1)); pap. (978-0-7787-2528-2(6)) Crabtree Publishing Co.

Rondeau, Amanda. Vegetables Are Vital, 1 vol. 2003. (What Should I Eat? Ser.). (ENG., Illus.). 24p. (J). (gr. k-3). lib. bdg. 24.21 (978-1-57765-835-1(3), SandCastle) ABDO Publishing Co.

Rosa-Mendoza, Gladys, creator. Fruits & Vegetables. 2004. (English-Spanish Foundations Ser.: Vol. 10).Tr. of Frutas y Vegetales. (SPA & ENG., Illus.). 22p. (J). bds. 6.95 (978-1-931398-10-7(0)) Me+Mi Publishing.

Samson, Tess. We Like Vegetables. 2010. (Sight Word Readers Ser.). (J). 3.49 (978-1-60719-615-0(8)) Newmark Learning LLC.

Sayre, April Pulley. Rah, Rah, Radishes! A Vegetable Chant. Sayre, April Pulley, photos by. 2014. (Classic Board Bks.). (ENG., Illus.). 34p. (J). (gr. -1 — 1). bds. 7.99 (978-1-4424-9927-0(3), Little Simon) Little Simon.

Schuette, Sarah L. Eating Pairs (Comer Pares) Counting Fruits & Vegetables by Two (Contar Frutas y Vegetales de DOS en DOS) 2012. (Vamos a Contar / Counting Bks.). (ENG, SPA & MUL.). 32p. (gr. 1-2). lib. bdg. 27.32 (978-1-4296-8251-0(5), A+ Bilingue/Bilingual) Capstone Press of Coughlan Cos.

Schuh, Mari. Carrots Grow Underground. 2011. (How Fruits & Vegetables Grow Ser.). (ENG.). 24p. (gr. k-1). pap. 35.70 (978-1-4296-6186-7(0), Pebble Bks.) Capstone Press of Coughlan Cos.

—Tomatoes Grow on a Vine, 1 vol. 2011. (How Fruits & Vegetables Grow Ser.). (ENG., 24p. (gr. k-1). Illus.). pap. 6.29 (978-1-4296-6187-4(9)); pap. 35.70 (978-1-4296-6357-1(X)) Capstone Press of Coughlan Cos. (Pebble Bks.).

—Vegetables on Myplate. 2012. (What's on Myplate? Ser.). (ENG.). 24p. (gr. k-1). pap. 41.70 (978-1-4296-9425-4(4), Pebble Plus) Capstone Press of Coughlan Cos.

Schuh, Mari C. Lettuce Grows on the Ground, 1 vol. 2010. (How Fruits & Vegetables Grow Ser.). (ENG.). 24p. (gr. k-1). lib. bdg. 21.99 (978-1-4296-5281-0(0), Pebble Bks.) Capstone Press of Coughlan Cos.

—Tomatoes Grow on a Vine, 1 vol. 2010. (How Fruits & Vegetables Grow Ser.). (ENG.). 24p. (gr. k-1). lib. bdg. 21.99 (978-1-4296-5278-0(0), Pebble Bks.) Capstone Press of Coughlan Cos.

Scott, Celicia. My Daily Diet: Vegetables. Prock, Lisa Albers, ed. 2014. (On My Plate Ser.: 6). 48p. (J). (gr. 5-18). 20.95 (978-1-4222-3100-5(3)) Mason Crest.

Staniford, Linda. Where Do Vegetables Come From? 2016. (From Farm to Fork: Where Does My Food Come From? Ser.). (ENG.). 24p. (gr. k-2). lib. bdg. 23.99 (978-1-4846-3351-9(2)) Heinemann-Raintree.

Tofts, Hannah. One Cool Watermelon. Tofts, Hannah, illus. 2008. (Things I Eat Ser.). (ENG., Illus.). 24p. (J). (gr. -1-k). (978-1-84089-555-1(1)) Zero to Ten, Ltd.

Tometich, Annabelle. The Vegetables Group. 2013. (Healthy Eating with Myplate Ser.). (ENG.). 24p. (J). (gr. 1-4). 28.50 (978-1-62323-606-9(1), 206408) Child's World, Inc., The.

Turning Tomatoes into Ketchup. 2014. (Step-By-Step Transformations Ser.). 24p. (J). (gr. k-2). lib. bdg. 24.21 (978-1-62713-010-3(1)) Cavendish Square Publishing.

Vaughn, Inés. Potatoes/Papas. 2009. (Native Foods of Latin America / Alimentos indígenas de Latino América Ser.). (ENG & SPA.). 24p. (gr. 2-3). 42.50 (978-1-61514-798-4(5), Editorial Buenas Letras) Rosen Publishing Group, Inc., The.

—Squash/Calabazas. 2009. (Native Foods of Latin America / Alimentos indígenas de Latino América Ser.). (ENG & SPA.). 24p. (gr. 2-3). 42.50 (978-1-61514-799-1(3), Editorial Buenas Letras) Rosen Publishing Group, Inc., The.

—Tomatoes/Tomates. 2009. (Native Foods of Latin America / Alimentos indígenas de Latino América Ser.). (ENG & SPA.). 24p. (gr. 2-3). 42.50 (978-1-61514-800-4(0), Editorial Buenas Letras) Rosen Publishing Group, Inc., The.

Vaughn, Inés & Sanz, Ma Pilar. Squash: Calabazas. 2009. (Native Foods of Latin America / Alimentos Indígenas de Latinoamérica Ser.). (SPA, ENG & MUL., Illus.). 24p. (J). lib. bdg. 22.60 (978-1-4358-2727-1(9), Everett Pr.) Rosen Publishing Group, Inc., The.

—Tomatoes: Tomates. 2009. (Native Foods of Latin America / Alimentos Indígenas de Latinoamérica Ser.). (SPA & ENG.). (J). lib. bdg. 22.60 (978-1-4358-2724-0(4), Editorial Buenas Letras) Rosen Publishing Group, Inc., The.

Waters, Rosa. My Daily Diet: Dairy. 2014. (J). (978-1-4222-3094-7(5)) Mason Crest.

Weiss, Ellen. From Eye to Potato. 2007. (Scholastic News Nonfiction Readers Ser.). (ENG., Illus.). 24p. (J). (gr. 1-2). 22.00 (978-0-531-18535-3(4)); pap. 6.95 (978-0-531-18788-3(8)) Scholastic Library Publishing.

Wellington, Monica. Color & Garden VEGETABLES. 2011. (Dover Children's Activity Bks.). (ENG., Illus.). 32p. (J). (gr. -1-3). pap. 4.99 (978-0-486-47959-0(5)) Dover Pubns., Inc.

Woolf, Alex. You Wouldn't Want to Live Without Vegetables! Antram, David, illus. 2016. (You Wouldn't Want to Live Without... Ser.). (ENG.). 32p. (J). lib. bdg. 29.00 (978-0-531-21490-9(7), Watts, Franklin) Scholastic Library Publishing.

Yasuda, Anita. Eating Green. 2016. (J). (978-1-5105-2213-8(1)) SmartBook Media, Inc.

Yummy Yummy Vegetables. 2004. (J). per. 15.99 (978-0-9744205-4-7(9)) Golden Eagle Publishing Hse., Inc.

VEGETABLES—CANNING

see Canning and Preserving

VEGETABLES—FICTION

Andrews, Jackie. Great Big Enormous Turnip. Taylor, Lawrie, illus. 2012. (ENG.). 32p. (J). pap. 6.50 (978-1-84135-192-6(X)) Award Pubns. Ltd. GBR. Dist: Parkwest Pubns., Inc.

Aspinall, Sheila. Cep & the Forest. 2015. (ENG., Illus.). 64p. (J). (gr. 3-4). pap. 18.95 (978-1-78455-263-3(1), 87a70ad0-da83-446b-854b-eedce1296e3a) Austin, Stan AUS. Dist: Bookmasters Distribution.

Bailey, Lori Gayle. The Dog Who Loved Cucumbers. 2009. 24p. pap. 11.95 (978-1-4490-2457-4(2)) AuthorHouse.

Baker, Keith. LMNO Peas. Baker, Keith, illus. 2010. (Peas Ser.). (ENG., Illus.). 40p. (J). (gr. -1-3). 17.99 (978-1-4169-9141-0(7), Beach Lane Bks.) Beach Lane Bks.

—LMNO Peas. Baker, Keith, illus. 2014. (Peas Ser.). (ENG., Illus.). 36p. (J). (gr. -1-k). bds. 7.99 *(978-1-4424-8978-3(2),* Little Simon) Little Simon.
—1-2-3 Peas. Baker, Keith, illus. 2012. (Peas Ser.). (ENG., Illus.). 40p. (J). (gr. -1-3). 17.99 *(978-1-4424-4551-2(3),* Beach Lane Bks.) Beach Lane Bks.
Barkow, Henriette. Giant Turnip - Big Book. Johnson, Richard, illus. 2004. (ENG & MAY.). 23p. (J). *(978-1-85269-896-6(9))* Mantra Lingua.
Barkow, Henriette & Johnson, Richard, illus. The Giant Turnip: Rrepa Gjigante. 2004. 24p. (J). *(978-1-85269-732-7(6))* Mantra Lingua.
Barnes, Ben. Don't Eat My Garden. Barnes, Page, illus. 2007. 28p. per. 24.95 *(978-1-4241-8964-9(0))* America Star Bks.
Bass, Jules. Herb, the Vegetarian Dragon. Harter, Debbie, illus. 2005. 32p. (J). (gr. 1-5). reprint ed. pap. 6.99 *(978-1-84148-127-2(0))* Barefoot Bks., Inc.
Benson, Sherry. Introducing Jelly Bean. 2008. 27p. pap. 24.95 *(978-1-60672-427-9(4))* America Star Bks.
Bertrand, Diane Gonzales, et al. Adelita & the Veggie Cousins / Adelita y las primas Verduritas. Rodriguez, Tina, illus. 2011. (SPA.). (J). 16.95 *(978-1-55885-699-8(4),* Piñata Books) Arte Publico Pr.
Big Idea Entertainment, LLC. The Ballad of Little Joe. Jones, Cory, illus. 2016. (VeggieTales Ser.). (ENG.). 32p. (J). (gr. -1-3). pap. 3.99 *(978-1-4336-4349-1(9),* B&H Kids) B&H Publishing Group.
—King George & the Ducky. Jones, Cory, illus. 2016. (VeggieTales Ser.). (ENG.). 32p. (J). (gr. -1-3). pap. 3.99 *(978-1-4336-4339-2(1),* B&H Kids) B&H Publishing Group.
—LarryBoy & the Merciless Mango. Jones, Cory, illus. 2016. (VeggieTales Ser.). (ENG.). 32p. (J). (gr. -1-3). pap. 3.99 *(978-1-4336-4338-5(3),* B&H Kids) B&H Publishing Group.
—LarryBoy & the Prideosaurus. Jones, Cory, illus. 2016. (VeggieTales Ser.). (ENG.). 32p. (J). (gr. -1-3). pap. 3.99 *(978-1-4336-4341-5(3),* B&H Kids) B&H Publishing Group.
—LarryBoy & the Quitter Critter Quad Squad. Jones, Cory, illus. 2016. (VeggieTales Ser.). (ENG.). 32p. (J). (gr. -1-3). pap. 3.99 *(978-1-4336-4342-2(1),* B&H Kids) B&H Publishing Group.
—LarryBoy & the Reckless Ruckus. Jones, Cory, illus. 2016. (VeggieTales Ser.). (ENG.). 32p. (J). (gr. -1-3). pap. 3.99 *(978-1-4336-4343-9(X),* B&H Kids) B&H Publishing Group.
—LarryBoy & the Rude Beet. Jones, Cory, illus. 2016. (VeggieTales Ser.). (ENG.). 32p. (J). (gr. -1-3). pap. 3.99 *(978-1-4336-4344-6(8),* B&H Kids) B&H Publishing Group.
—The League of Incredible Vegetables. Jones, Cory, illus. 2016. (VeggieTales Ser.). (ENG.). 32p. (J). (gr. -1-3). pap. 3.99 *(978-1-4336-4350-7(2),* B&H Kids) B&H Publishing Group.
—Lyle the Kindly Viking. Jones, Cory, illus. 2016. (VeggieTales Ser.). (ENG.). 32p. (J). (gr. -1-3). pap. 3.99 *(978-1-4336-4345-3(6),* B&H Kids) B&H Publishing Group.
—MacLarry & the Stinky Cheese Battle. Jones, Cory, illus. 2016. (VeggieTales Ser.). (ENG.). 32p. (J). (gr. -1-3). pap. 3.99 *(978-1-4336-4346-0(4),* B&H Kids) B&H Publishing Group.
—Minnesota Cuke & the Search for Samson's Hairbrush. Jones, Cory, illus. 2016. (VeggieTales Ser.). (ENG.). 32p. (J). (gr. -1-3). pap. 3.99 *(978-1-4336-4347-7(2),* B&H Kids) B&H Publishing Group.
—VeggieTales SuperComics: Vol 3. Jones, Cory, illus. 2015. (VeggieTales Super Comics Ser.: 1). (ENG.). 104p. (J). (gr. -1-3). pap. 12.99 *(978-1-4336-8536-1(1),* B&H Kids) B&H Publishing Group.
—VeggieTales SuperComics: Vol 4. Jones, Cory, illus. 2015. (VeggieTales Super Comics Ser.: 1). (ENG.). 104p. (J). (gr. -1-3). pap. 12.99 *(978-1-4336-8537-8(X),* B&H Kids) B&H Publishing Group.
Black, Michael Ian. I'm Bored. Ohi, Debbie Ridpath, illus. 2012. (ENG.). 40p. (J). (gr. -1-3). 17.99 *(978-1-4424-1403-7(0),* Simon & Schuster Bks. For Young Readers) Simon & Schuster Bks. For Young Readers.
—Qué Aburrido! 2014. (SPA.). 36p. (J). (gr. k-1). pap. 16.95 *(978-1-933032-90-0(1))* Lectorum Pubns., Inc.
Bloom, Amy. Little Sweet Potato. Jones, Noah Z., illus. 2012. (ENG.). 32p. (J). (gr. -1-2). 16.99 *(978-0-06-180439-7(8),* Tegen, Katherine Bks) HarperCollins Pubs.
Blu De Golyer. The Adventures of Captain Greenspud. 2009. 28p. pap. 13.99 *(978-1-4389-6582-6(6))* AuthorHouse.
Bookins, Daddy. Outside with Lil Boo. Piotti, Dania, illus. 2012. 38p. pap. 13.50 *(978-0-9848019-3-0(6))* Inkwell Books LLC.
Brett, Jan & McPike, Elizabeth. The Turnip. Brett, Jan, illus. 2015. (ENG., Illus.). 32p. (J). (-k). bds. 17.99 *(978-0-399-17070-6(7),* G.P. Putnam's Sons Books for Young Readers) Penguin Young Readers Group.
Brewer, Jo Ann. Miss Q-Cee & the Sweet Potatoes. 2011. 28p. pap. 15.99 *(978-1-4568-6245-9(6))* Xlibris Corp.
Brown, Jr. Jimmy's Alphabet Garden. 2013. 32p. pap. 13.50 *(978-1-4575-1797-6(3))* Dog Ear Publishing, LLC.
Bruel, Nick. Bad Kitty's Tasty Treats. 2014. (Slide & Find Ser.). (ENG., Illus.). 16p. (J). (gr. -1 — 1). bds. 12.99 *(978-0-312-51723-6(8),* 9780312517236) Roaring Brook Pr.
Bryant, Janine. Yucky Green Beans. Lt. ed. 2005. 12p. (J). per. 5.00 *(978-0-9703474-8-0(0))* Pinniti Pubs.
Carter, Denzel T. Pedro's Carrot. 2015. (Rosen REAL Readers: STEM & STEAM Collection). (ENG.). 8p. pap. 5.46 *(978-1-4994-9548-5(X),* Rosen Classroom) Rosen Publishing Group, Inc., The.
Chapman, Jared. Fruits in Suits. 2017. (ENG., Illus.). 40p. (J). (gr. -1-k). 14.95 *(978-1-4197-2298-1(0),* Abrams Appleseed) Abrams, Inc.
—Vegetables in Underwear. 2015. (ENG., Illus.). 40p. (J). (gr. -1-k). 14.95 *(978-1-4197-1464-1(3))* Abrams, Inc.
Chen, Sam. A Real Meal Table Fable. Peschel, Georgia, illus. 2007. 60p. (J). *(978-0-9800764-0-0(4))* Uncle Jim's Publishing.
Christie, Jackie. Wacky WaterSlide Wipeout. 2011. 28p. (gr. -1). pap. 16.09 *(978-1-4269-5821-2(8))* Trafford Publishing.
Cowley, Joy. Freddy Bear & the Green Peas. Webb, Philip, illus. 2016. (Freddy Bear Ser.). (ENG.). 20p. (J). (gr. -1-k). bds. 12.99 *(978-1-927262-57-3(7))* Upstart Pr. NZL. Dist: Independent Pubs. Group.
Crabb, James Anthony. The Dinosaur & Dragon Juice Café. 2008. (Illus.). 32p. pap. 17.95 *(978-0-9556105-8-5(3))* Picnic Publishing Ltd. GBR. Dist: Trans-Atlantic Pubns., Inc.
Daynes, Katie. Enormous Turnip. Overwater, Georgien, illus. 2006. (First Reading Level 3 Ser.). 48p. (J). (gr. 1-4). 8.99 *(978-0-7945-1376-4(X),* Usborne) EDC Publishing.
De Anda, Diane. The Patchwork Garden. Ventura, Gabriela Baeza, tr. Kemarskaya, Oksana, illus. 2013.Tr. of Pedacitos de Huerto. (ENG & SPA.). 32p. (J). 16.95 *(978-1-55885-763-6(X),* Piñata Books) Arte Publico Pr.
De Golyer, Blu. The Adventures of Captain Greenspud. 2009. 28p. pap. 14.50 *(978-1-60860-425-8(X),* Eloquent Bks.) Strategic Book Publishing & Rights Agency (SBPRA).
de Las Casas, Dianne. The Gigantic Sweet Potato, 1 vol. Gentry, Marita, illus. 2010. (ENG.). 32p. (J). (gr. k-3). 16.99 *(978-1-58980-755-6(3))* Pelican Publishing Co., Inc.
DeFelice, Cynthia C. One Potato, Two Potato. U'Ren, Andrea, illus. 2006. (ENG.). 32p. (J). (gr. -1-3). 18.99 *(978-0-374-35640-8(8),* 9780374356408, Farrar, Straus & Giroux (BYR)) Farrar, Straus & Giroux.
dePaola, Tomie. Strega Nona & Her Tomatoes. 2017. (Simon & Schuster Ready-To-Read Level 1 Ser.). lib. bdg. 13.55 ***(978-0-606-40214-9(4))*** Turtleback Bks.
Dickson, Vivian. To Be a Bean. 2nd ed. 2013. 24p. pap. *(978-0-9873438-1-9(5))* Link Spots.
Dippy Doodle's Beary Big Tomato. 2003. (J). 7.95 *(978-0-9713174-9-9(6))* Boyds Collection Ltd., The.
Doodler, Todd H. One Potato, Two Potato. Doodler, Todd H., illus. 2013. (ENG., Illus.). 32p. (J). (gr. -1-k). 14.99 *(978-1-4424-8517-4(5),* Little Simon) Little Simon.
—Veggies with Wedgies. Doodler, Todd H., illus. 2014. (ENG., Illus.). 32p. (J). (gr. -1-k). 14.99 *(978-1-4424-9340-7(2),* Little Simon) Little Simon.
Dowell, Frances O'Roark. Sam the Man & the Rutabaga Plan. Bates, Amy June, illus. 2017. (Sam the Man Ser.: 2). (ENG.). 128p. (J). (gr. 1-4). 16.99 *(978-1-4814-4069-1(1),* Atheneum/Caitlyn Dlouhy Books) Simon & Schuster Children's Publishing.
Elkins, J. Theron. You Are the Pea, & I Am the Carrot. Lemaitre, Pascal, illus. 2013. (ENG.). 32p. (J). (gr. k-2). 16.95 *(978-1-4197-0850-3(3),* Abrams Bks. for Young Readers) Abrams, Inc.
The Enormous Turnip, Level 1. 2016. (Ladybird Readers Ser.). (ENG., Illus.). 48p. (J). pap., act. bk. ed. 9.99 *(978-0-241-25408-0(6))* Penguin Bks., Ltd. GBR. Dist: Independent Pubs. Group.
Evans, Cordelia, adapted by. Doozers Have Green Thumbs. 2015. (Doozers Ser.). (ENG., Illus.). 32p. (J). (gr. -1-1). pap. 3.99 *(978-1-4814-3220-7(6),* Simon Spotlight) Simon Spotlight.
Falwell, Cathryn. Mystery Vine. Falwell, Cathryn, illus. 2009. (Illus.). 32p. (J). lib. bdg. 17.89 *(978-0-06-177197-2(X),* Greenwillow Bks.) HarperCollins Pubs.
Fashion Parade: Individual Title, 6 pack. (Bookweb Ser.). 32p. (gr. 6-18). 34.00 *(978-0-7578-0890-6(5))* Rigby Education.
Fine, Karen. Veggiesaurus Lex. 2009. 24p. pap. 12.99 *(978-1-4490-0290-9(0))* AuthorHouse.
Foster, Lisa. 5 Little Tomatoes. 2008. 44p. pap. 17.95 *(978-1-4327-2306-4(5))* Outskirts Pr., Inc.
Ganzer, Diane & St. Croix, Sammy. Adventures of a Kitten Named Raspberry & Other Tales. 2009. 176p. pap. 9.95 *(978-1-935105-30-5(2))* Avid Readers Publishing Group.
Goodrow, Carol. The Treasure of Health & Happiness. Goodrow, Carol, illus. 2006. (ENG., Illus.). 96p. (J). (gr. 4-7). 14.00 *(978-1-891369-60-5(1))* Breakaway Bks.
Grimly, Gris. Little Jordan Ray's Muddy Spud. Grimly, Gris, illus. 2015. (ENG., Illus.). 100p. (J). pap. 19.95 *(978-0-9729388-6-0(9))* Baby Tattoo Bks.
Hansen, Chance. Green Pea Makes a Flourless Cookie. 2012. 28p. pap. 13.50 *(978-1-4669-2637-0(6))* Trafford Publishing.
Harriton, Maxine. A School Trip to the Fruit Planet, 1. 1.t. ed. 2006. 34p. (J). (gr. -1-1). lib. bdg. 18.95 *(978-0-9787248-0-1(1),* 00-01-851-447X) UpTree Publishing.
Hawkins, Linda J. Alexander & the Great Vegetable Feud. Bowles, Jennifer, illus. 2004. 40p. (J). (gr. k-5). 19.99 *(978-0-9742806-1-5(5))* Heart to Heart Publishing, Inc.
Haydon, David J. The Spuds - the Windy Day. Ferns, Kevin, illus. 2010. 20p. pap. *(978-1-907611-11-7(8))* Paragon Publishing, Rothersthorpe.
HB Staff. Four Very Big Beans. 97th ed. 2003. (First-Place Reading Ser.). (gr. 1-18). pap. 16.50 *(978-0-15-308144-6(9))* Harcourt Schl. Pubs.
Hebert, J. J. Weepy the Dragon. 2012. 36p. pap. 9.99 *(978-0-9853650-7-3(2))* Mindstir Media.
Helmore Wall Staff & Helmore, Jim. Oh No, Monster Tomato! Wall, Karen, illus. 2009. (ENG.). 32p. (J). (gr. -1). 16.99 *(978-1-4052-4740-5(1))* Egmont Bks., Ltd. GBR. Dist: Independent Pubs. Group.
Hensdill, Norma Mae. I'm Granny's Little Mess, Just Look at the Rest. 2009. 36p. pap. 17.99 *(978-1-4389-5054-9(3))* AuthorHouse.
Holt, Kimberly Willis. Piggy's Sweet Potato Pie Lesson. 2007. (Illus.). 22p. (J). per. 18.99 *(978-0-9759691-4-4(5))* Catch 22 Publishing Inc.
Hood, Morag. Carrot & Pea. 2017. (ENG., Illus.). 32p. (J). (gr. -1-3). 16.99 *(978-0-544-86842-7(0),* HMH Books For Young Readers) Houghton Mifflin Harcourt Publishing Co.
Houdek, Andi. Stop That Pudding! Collier, Kevin, illus. 2010. 16p. pap. 9.95 *(978-1-61633-079-8(1))* Guardian Angel Publishing, Inc.
Howell, Trisha Adelena. The Adventures of Melon & Turnip. Lopez, Paul, illus. 2004. 32p. 15.95 *(978-1-931210-04-1(7))* Howell Canyon Pr.
Jacqueline Juin Snow. A Potato Tale. 2009. 16p. pap. 8.49 *(978-1-4389-6360-0(2))* AuthorHouse.
Jasnoch, Dorothy. Frankie the Bunny the Fall Scramble Begins. Korzeniowski, Samson, ed. Jasnoch, Dorothy, illus. 2012. (Illus.). 28p. pap. 12.99 *(978-1-937752-04-0(6))* Owl About Bks. Pub., Inc.
Jeffers, Dawn. Vegetable Dreams/Huerto Sonado. de La Vega, Eida, tr. Schneider, Claude, illus. 2006. (SPA & ENG.). 32p. (J). (gr. -1-3). 16.95 *(978-0-9741992-9-0(X),* 626999, Raven Tree Pr.,Csi) Continental Sales, Inc.
Jin, Susie Lee. Mine! Jin, Susie Lee, illus. 2016. (ENG., Illus.). 40p. (J). (gr. -1-3). 16.99 *(978-1-4814-2772-2(5),* Simon & Schuster Bks. For Young Readers) Simon & Schuster Bks. For Young Readers.
Joelson. Oliver Mccoy - the Vegetable Boy. 2011. (ENG., Illus.). 60p. (J). 19.95 *(978-0-9830039-1-5(2))* SLM Bk. Publishing.
Johnson, Marion. Caillou: The Carrot Patch. Sevigny, Eric, illus. 2017. (Read with Caillou Ser.). (ENG.). 32p. (J). (gr. -1-k). 3.99 *(978-2-89718-367-7(5))* Caillouet, Gerry.
Jones, Christianne C. Pruebalo, 1 vol. Ruiz, Carlos, tr. Yi, Hye Won, illus. 2006. (Read-It! Readers en Español: Story Collection).Tr. of Just Try it. (SPA.). 24p. (gr. -1-3). 21.32 *(978-1-4048-1692-3(5),* Easy Readers) Picture Window Bks.
Jones, Dennis. The Adventures of the Fruitiebears: Book 2 Fruitiecars. 2011. (Illus.). 48p. pap. 19.48 *(978-1-4567-9001-1(3))* AuthorHouse.
Kann, Victoria & Kann, Elizabeth. Pinkalicious, 1 vol. Kann, Victoria, illus. 2011. (Pinkalicious Ser.). (SPA., Illus.). 40p. (J). (gr. k-3). 17.99 *(978-0-06-179959-4(9))* HarperCollins Pubs.
Kaus, Cathy. The Bean Bandit, 1 vol. 2010. 24p. 24.95 *(978-1-4489-2202-4(X))* PublishAmerica, Inc.
Kenney, Cindy. Cool Hand Cuke Vol. 5: A Lesson in Giving, 1 vol. Moore, Michael, illus. 2006. (Big Idea Books / VeggieTown Values Ser.: Bk. 5). (ENG.). 32p. (J). (gr. -1-3). pap. 3.99 *(978-0-310-70738-7(2))* Zonderkidz.
—Junior Asparagus. 2004. (ENG., Illus.). 100p. (J). pap. 3.99 *(978-0-310-70722-6(6))* Zonderkidz.
—Laura Carrot. 2004. (ENG., Illus.). 100p. (J). pap. 3.99 *(978-0-310-70723-3(4))* Zonderkidz.
—Veggietales Bible Storybook, 1 vol. 2006. (Big Idea Bks.). (ENG., Illus.). 256p. (J). (gr. -1-3). 16.99 *(978-0-310-71008-0(1))* Zonderkidz.
Kenney, Cindy, et al. Frog Wars, 1 vol. 2005. (Big Idea Books / VeggieTown Values Ser.: Bk. 2). (ENG., Illus.). 32p. (J). pap. 3.99 *(978-0-310-70627-4(0))* Zonderkidz.
—Veggietown Voyage, 1 vol. Moore, Michael, illus. 2013. (Big Idea Books / VeggieTales Ser.). (ENG.). 96p. (J). 7.99 *(978-0-310-72352-3(3))* Zonderkidz.
Kramer, Alan. The Jack & the Beanstalk Trial. 2006. (J). pap. *(978-1-4108-6181-8(3))* Benchmark Education Co.
Lasky, Kathryn. My Uncle Eats Carrots on the Roof. 2008. (J). 16.99 *(978-0-374-35119-9(8),* Farrar, Straus & Giroux (BYR)) Farrar, Straus & Giroux.
Lassiter, Erin & Garcia, Jolanda. EarTwiggle's Adventure 1: The Treasure Hunt. 2004. (Illus.). (J). 12.99 *(978-0-9762573-0-1(0))* Ear Twiggles Productions, Inc.
Lavoie, Rejean. Des Legumes Pour Frank Einstein. Begin, Jean-Guy, illus. 2004. (Des 9 Ans. Ser.: Vol. 44). (FRE.). 120p. (J). 8.95 *(978-2-89599-006-2(9))* Editions de la Paix CAN. Dist: World of Reading, Ltd.
Lea, Larry, et al. Larry Learns to Listen, 1 vol. 2003. (Big Idea Books / VeggieTales Ser.). (ENG., Illus.). 12p. (J). (gr. -1-1). bds. 4.99 *(978-0-310-70539-0(8))* Zonderkidz.
Lima Bean Dream. (J). (gr. 3-5). pap. 9.90 *(978-0-669-15612-6(4));* pap. 9.90 *(978-0-669-15895-3(X))* Houghton Mifflin Harcourt School Pubs.
Lin, Grace. Ugly Vegetables. 2014. 16.95 *(978-1-63419-748-9(8))* Perfection Learning Corp.
Manning, Dennis & Crisalli, Joseph. The Turnip War. 2011. 120p. pap. 7.76 *(978-1-4357-1566-0(7))* Lulu Pr., Inc.
Marie, Cherry. The President Eats Vegetables & So Do I! 2012. 44p. pap. 12.00 *(978-0-9853259-0-9(9))* Professional Publishing Hse. LLC.
Marshall, Linda Elovitz. Talia & the Rude Vegetables. Assirelli, Francesca, illus. 2011. (High Holidays Ser.). (ENG.). 24p. (J). (gr. k-3). pap. 6.95 *(978-0-7613-5218-1(X),* Kar-Ben Publishing) Lerner Publishing Group.
Masson, Lynne. The Vegetable Patch. 2012. (Illus.). 64p. pap. 28.99 *(978-1-4772-3859-2(X))* AuthorHouse.
Matsumoto, Reiko Odate. The Sweet Potato. 2012. 24p. pap. 17.99 *(978-1-4685-7456-2(6))* AuthorHouse.
Mattern, Joanne. The Food Pyramid Disaster. 2005. (J). pap. *(978-1-4108-4195-7(2))* Benchmark Education Co.
McCall, Val. Twelve Rabbits & a Turtle: Bilingual English French. 2012. 46p. pap. 9.95 *(978-1-938367-00-7(6))* Destinee Media.
McClements, George. Night of the Veggie Monster. McClements, George, illus. (ENG., Illus.). 32p. (J). (gr. -1-1). 2014. 7.99 *(978-1-61963-180-9(6),* 9781619631809) 2008. 16.99 *(978-1-59990-061-2(0),* 9781599900612) Bloomsbury Publishing USA. (Bloomsbury USA Childrens).
McCreadie, Sandi. Thistle Fables. 2013. 64p. pap. 23.99 *(978-1-4808-0313-8(8))* Archway Publishing.
McDonald, Susan. Only Just One Mushroom. 2012. 32p. pap. 32.70 *(978-1-4771-3617-1(7))* Xlibris Corp.
Mckenzie, Precious. Who Stole the Veggies from the Veggie Patch? Snape, Jenny, illus. 2012. (ENG.). 24p. (gr. k-1). pap. 8.95 *(978-1-61810-298-0(2))* Rourke Educational Media.
McTrustry, Chris. Red Goes Green, 1 vol. rev. ed. 2013. (Fiction Readers Ser.). (ENG., Illus.). 32p. (J). (gr. 3-3). pap. 8.99 *(978-1-4333-5641-4(4))* Shell Educational Publishing.
Meyers, Dolores. Herbie's New Home. 2011. 20p. pap. 24.95 *(978-1-60749-665-6(8))* America Star Bks.
Miller, Pat Zietlow. Sophie's Squash. Wilsdorf, Anne, illus. 2013. (ENG.). 40p. (J). (gr. -1-2). 16.99 *(978-0-307-97896-7(6),* Schwartz & Wade Bks.) Random Hse. Children's Bks.
Morrow. Lima Bean Dream. (J). (gr. 3-5). 75.00 *(978-0-669-13451-3(1))* Houghton Mifflin Harcourt School Pubs.
My Vegetable Garden. 2003. (J). per. *(978-1-57657-896-4(8))* Paradise Pr., Inc.
North, Laura. Jack & the Bean Pie. 2014. (ENG., Illus.). 32p. (J). *(978-0-7787-0441-6(6));* pap. *(978-0-7787-0449-2(1))* Crabtree Publishing Co.
Padua, Grace. The Travels of Chikippo. Baker, David, illus. 2012. 26p. 24.95 *(978-1-4626-9782-3(8))* America Star Bks.
Parks, Carmen. Farmers Market/Dia de Mercado. Flor Ada, Alma & Campoy, F. Isabel, trs. from ENG. Martinez, Edward, illus. 2010. (Green Light Readers Level 2 Ser.). (SPA & ENG.). 28p. (J). (gr. -1-3). pap. 3.99 *(978-0-547-36900-6(X))* Houghton Mifflin Harcourt Publishing Co.
Peachey, Ted. The Adventures of Ryan & His Magic Carrot. 2010. 90p. pap. 9.99 *(978-1-60911-222-6(9),* Eloquent Bks.) Strategic Book Publishing & Rights Agency (SBPRA).
Peterson, Doug. Ben Hurry: A Lesson in Patience, 1 vol. Moore, Michael, illus. 2006. (Big Idea Books / VeggieTown Values Ser.: Bk. 8). (ENG.). 32p. (J). (gr. -1-3). pap. 3.99 *(978-0-310-70743-1(9))* Zonderkidz.
—Field of Beans: A Lesson in Faith, 1 vol. 2005. (Big Idea Books / VeggieTown Values Ser.: Bk. 3). (ENG., Illus.). 32p. (J). pap. 3.99 *(978-0-310-70628-1(9))* Zonderkidz.
Peterson, Doug & Kenney, Cindy. Lost in Place: A Lesson in Overcoming Fear, 1 vol. Big Idea Productions Staff, illus. 2005. (Big Idea Books / VeggieTown Values Ser.: Bk. 4). (ENG.). 32p. (J). pap. 3.99 *(978-0-310-70629-8(7))* Zonderkidz.
Piernas-Davenport, Gail. Shante Keys & the New Year's Peas. Eldridge, Marion, illus. 2007. (ENG.). 32p. (J). (gr. k-3). lib. bdg. 16.99 *(978-0-8075-7330-3(2))* Whitman, Albert & Co.
Pierro, Rita. No Veggies for Me. Iukel, Onur, illus. 2011. 32p. pap. 24.95 *(978-1-4626-4554-1(2))* America Star Bks.
Pisella, Donna. The Blue Goblin. 2013. (ENG.). 30p. (J). 22.95 *(978-1-4787-1269-5(4))* Outskirts Pr., Inc.
Prignano, Barbara. The Tiny Tomato & His Terrific Manners. Kalpart, illus. 2013. 32p. pap. 12.95 *(978-1-62857-080-9(6),* Strategic Bk. Publishing) Strategic Book Publishing & Rights Agency (SBPRA).
Pryor, Katherine. Zora's Zucchini. Raff, Anna, illus. 2015. (ENG.). 32p. (J). (gr. -1-5). 16.95 *(978-0-9836615-7-3(X))* READERS to EATERS.
—Zora's Zucchini (1 Hardcover/1 CD) 2016. (ENG.). (J). (gr. -1-2). audio compact disk 29.95 *(978-1-4301-2183-1(1))* Live Oak Media.
Ras, J. J. The Ketchup Story. 2007. 48p. pap. 19.94 *(978-1-84728-470-9(1))* Lulu Pr., Inc.
Reeder, Kim Cooley. Runaway Tomato. Agnew, Lincoln, illus. 2014. (ENG.). 34p. (J). (gr. -1-k). 16.99 *(978-0-8037-3694-8(0),* Dial Bks) Penguin Young Readers Group.
Reynolds, Aaron. Creepy Carrots! Brown, Peter, illus. 2012. (ENG.). 40p. (J). (gr. -1-3). 17.99 *(978-1-4424-0297-3(0),* Simon & Schuster Bks. For Young Readers) Simon & Schuster Bks. For Young Readers.
—Las Zanahorias Maléficas. 2015.Tr. of Creepy Carrots. (SPA.). 40p. (J). (gr. k-3). 24.95 *(978-84-16117-13-0(6))* Ediciones Obelisco ESP. Dist: Spanish Pubs., LLC.
Rinaldi, Francis. Brock Lee & the Salad Kids. 2005. 20p. 7.53 *(978-1-4116-5552-2(4))* Lulu Pr., Inc.
Rivoal, Marine, creator. Three Little Peas. 2014. (ENG., Illus.). 48p. (J). (gr. -1-3). 16.95 *(978-1-59270-155-1(8))* Enchanted Lion Bks., LLC.
Robb, Jackie & Stringle, Berny. The Story of Pea Brain. Duncan, Karen & Stringle, Sam, illus. 2004. (Bang on the Door Ser.). 32p. (YA). pap. *(978-1-85602-383-2(4),* Pavilion Children's Books) Pavilion Bks.
Robinson, Hilary. Snow White & the Enormous Turnip. Sanfilippo, Simona, illus. 2012. (ENG.). 32p. (J). pap. *(978-0-7787-8035-9(X))* Crabtree Publishing Co.
Rumbaugh, Melinda. The Great Easter Egg Hunt. Reed, Lisa, illus. 2014. (VeggieTales Bk Ser.). 16p. (J). 12.99 *(978-0-8249-1928-3(9),* Ideal Pubns.) Worthy Publishing.
Sayre, April Pulley. Rah, Rah, Radishes! A Vegetable Chant. Sayre, April Pulley, photos by. 2011. (ENG., Illus.). 32p. (J). (gr. -1-3). 17.99 *(978-1-4424-2141-7(X),* Beach Lane Bks.) Beach Lane Bks.
Scelsa, Greg. I Like Potatoes. Faulkner, Stacey, ed. Ostrom, Bob, illus. 2006. (J). pap. 2.99 *(978-1-59198-316-3(9))* Creative Teaching Pr., Inc.
Scholastic, Inc. Staff, contrib. by. Red Pepper, Yellow Squash: A Book of Colors. 2014. (Rookie Toddler(r) Ser.). (ENG.). 12p. (J). bds. 6.95 *(978-0-531-20917-2(2))* Scholastic Library Publishing.
Scroggs, Kirk. Snoop Troop: Attack of the Ninja Potato Clones. 2015. (Snoop Troop Ser.: 2). (ENG., Illus.). 192p. (J). (gr. 1-4). 13.99 *(978-0-316-24277-6(2))* Little, Brown Bks. for Young Readers.
Segal, John. Carrot Soup. Segal, John, illus. 2006. (ENG., Illus.). 32p. (J). (gr. -1-3). 17.99 *(978-0-689-87702-5(1),* McElderry, Margaret K. Bks.) McElderry, Margaret K. Bks.
—Sopa de Zanahoria. Mlawer, Teresa, tr. from ENG. 2006. (Illus.). (J). (gr. -1-k). 12.99 *(978-1-933032-13-9(8))* Lectorum Pubns., Inc.
Selig, Josh. Ride the Potato Train. Gibbons, Cassandra, illus. 2013. 30p. (J). *(978-1-4844-0420-1(3),* Planet Dexter) Penguin Publishing Group.
Seplowitz, P'Nina. Once upon a Vegetable. 2012. 32p. pap. 14.51 *(978-1-4669-1414-8(9))* Trafford Publishing.
Sims, Janice. Grandma's Basket. Storr, Nicola, illus. 2010. 28p. pap. *(978-1-904408-68-0(0))* Bank House Bks.
Smith, Carrie. The Enormous Turnip: Classic Tales Edition. Rogers, Jacqueline, illus. 2011. (Classic Tales Ser.). (J). *(978-1-936258-70-3(6))* Benchmark Education Co.
Stanek, Robert, pseud. Visit Garden Box Farms. 2008. (ENG., Illus.). 28p. (J). pap. 5.29 *(978-1-57545-190-9(5))* RP Media.
Stango, Diane. Too Many Tomatoes. 2006. (Neighborhood Readers Ser.). (ENG.). 12p. (gr. -1-3). pap. 5.90 *(978-1-4042-6718-3(2),* Rosen Classroom) Rosen Publishing Group, Inc., The.
—Vicky's Vegetables. 2006. (Neighborhood Readers Ser.). (ENG.). 16p. (gr. 1-3). pap. 6.50 *(978-1-4042-7156-2(2),* Rosen Classroom) Rosen Publishing Group, Inc., The.
Stremanos, A. M., illus. Rosemary's Taken over My Potatoes. 2008. 20p. (J). 5.00 *(978-0-9801372-0-0(9))* Benedetti, Jef.
Stroud, David Wayne. Funny, Dust & Honey & the Giant Carrot. Nardandrea, Swannee, illus. I.t. ed. 2005. 32p. (J). 17.95 *(978-0-9762835-2-2(2))* Shooting Star Publishing.
Sunday Potatoes, Monday Potatoes. (Early Intervention Levels Ser.). 63.00 *(978-0-7362-2139-9(5));* 10.50 *(978-0-7362-0509-2(8))* CENGAGE Learning.
Sylvander, Matthieu. The Battle of the Vegetables. Barrier, Perceval, illus. 2016. (ENG.). 48p. (J). (gr. 1-4). 15.99 *(978-0-544-35942-0(9),* Clarion Bks.) Houghton Mifflin Harcourt Trade & Reference Pubs.
Talbot Healy, John Adrian. The Flea & the Cauliflower. 2009. (Illus.). 92p. pap. 30.49 *(978-1-4490-1360-8(0))* AuthorHouse.
Tel-Or, Nava. Tristan & the Magical Vegetable Stew. 2011. (Illus.). 36p. (gr. -1). pap. 22.24 *(978-1-4567-7024-2(1))* AuthorHouse.
Tolstoy, Aleksei & Sharkey, Niamh. The Gigantic Turnip. 2006. (ENG., Illus.). 40p. (J). (gr. -1-2). 10.99 *(978-1-905236-72-5(7))* Barefoot Bks., Inc.
Tolstoy, Aleksei, et al. The Gigantic Turnip. 2009. (ENG., Illus.). (J). 16.99 *(978-1-84686-298-4(1))* Barefoot Bks., Inc.
Tone, Satoe. The Very Big Carrot. 2013. (ENG., Illus.). 26p. (J). 12.00 *(978-0-8028-5426-1(5),* Eerdmans Bks For Young Readers) Eerdmans, William B. Publishing Co.

Toscano, Leesa. Eat Your Vegetables. Bodoff, Janet, illus. 2012. 24p. pap. 24.95 *(978-1-4626-5278-5(6))* America Star Bks.

Triplett, Annette. From the Farm to You Coloring Book. Vale, Joe, ed. Murphy, Dennis, illus. 2012. 28p. (J). *(978-0-933842-34-2(1))* Univ. of Missouri, Extension.

Van Lemon, M. Champions of the Garden Games: Winter Fun for Everyone. 2009. 48p. pap. 20.95 *(978-1-4490-3580-8(9))* AuthorHouse.

Warner, Gertrude Chandler, creator. The Mystery of the Traveling Tomatoes. 2008. (Boxcar Children Mysteries Ser.: 117). (ENG.). 128p. (J). (gr. 1-5). 14.99 *(978-0-8075-5579-8(7))*; pap. 6.99 *(978-0-8075-5580-4(0))* Whitman, Albert & Co.

Warren, Donna E. Colors of the Rainbow. 2011. 26p. pap. 12.00 *(978-1-61204-318-0(6))*, Eloquent Bks.) Strategic Book Publishing & Rights Agency (SBPRA).

Waszak, Madonna. Mason's Mashed Potato Tree. Johnston, Lisa Harp, illus. 2011. 34p. pap. 14.95 *(978-1-4575-0159-3(7))* Dog Ear Publishing, LLC.

Watson, M. Veg Patch Gang. 2005. (Illus.). 40p. pap. *(978-1-84401-005-9(8))* Athena Pr.

Waxman, Melanie Brown. The Little Carrot, 1 vol. Friend, Bonnie, illus. 2009. 39p. pap. 24.95 *(978-1-61546-046-5(2))* America Star Bks.

Wenger, Shaunda. The Farm Stand Mystery. 2006. (Early Explorers Ser.). (J). pap. *(978-1-4108-6121-4(X))* Benchmark Education Co.

Wilson, CeCe. Lily's Tomato. 2015. (Rosen REAL Readers: STEM & STEAM Collection). (ENG.). 12p. (gr. 1-2). pap. 6.33 *(978-1-4994-9620-8(6)*, Rosen Classroom) Rosen Publishing Group, Inc., The.

Winningham, Barbara. The Turtle Pit. 2013. 36p. 24.95 *(978-1-62709-875-5(5))*; pap. 24.95 *(978-1-62709-493-1(8))* America Star Bks.

Yaldezian, Lisa M. 500 Presents for Penelope Potts. Seltzer, Jerry, illus. 2006. (J). 16.95 *(978-1-60131-005-7(6))* Big Tent Bks.

Yumel, Demain. Little Yellow Pear Tomatoes. Tamarin, Nicole, illus. 2005. 32p. (J). 15.95 *(978-0-9740190-2-4(X))* Illumination Arts Publishing Co., Inc.

VEGETABLES—MARKETING

see Farm Produce—Marketing

VEGETARIANISM

Askew, Claire. Generation V: The Complete Guide to Going, Being, & Staying Vegan as a Teenager. 2011. (Tofu Hound Press Ser.). (ENG., Illus.). 160p. pap. 14.95 *(978-1-60486-338-3(2))* PM Pr.

Boothroyd, Jennifer. Why Doesn't Everyone Eat Meat? Vegetarianism & Special Diets. 2016. (Lightning Bolt Books — Healthy Eating Ser.). (ENG., Illus.). 32p. (J). (gr. 1-3). 26.65 *(978-1-4677-9471-8(6)*, Lerner Pubns.) Lerner Publishing Group.

Cornell, Kari. Terrific Veggies on the Side. Cohen, Brie, photos by. 2013. (You're the Chef Ser.). (ENG., Illus.). 32p. (gr. 3-5). lib. bdg. 26.60 *(978-0-7613-6640-9(7)*, Millbrook Pr.) Lerner Publishing Group.

DeMaris, Sheri-Lynn. Macro Magic for Kids & Parents: Taking the Mystery Out of Macrobiotic Cooking. (J). 2010. *(978-89-21-42450-1(4))* 2009. *(978-1-892142-45-0(7))* Cedar Tree Bks.

Elton, Sarah. Meatless? A Fresh Look at What You Eat. McLaughlin, Julie, illus. 2017. (ENG.). 48p. (J). (gr. 4-8). 16.95 *(978-1-926818-43-6(1))* Owlkids Bks. Inc. CAN. Dist: Publishers Group West (PGW).

Francis, Amy. Vegetarianism. 2015. (Current Controversies Ser.). (ENG.). 224p. (J). (gr. 10-12). 46.40 *(978-0-7377-7227-2(1)*, Greenhaven Pr., Inc.) Cengage Gale.

Gillard, Arthur. Vegetarianism. Gale Editors, ed. 2014. (Issues That Concern You Ser.). (ENG., Illus.). 144p. (gr. 7-10). lib. bdg. 42.00 *(978-0-7377-6936-4(X)*, Greenhaven Pr., Inc.) Cengage Gale.

Langely, Andrew. Should We Eat Animals? 2007. (What Do You Think? Ser.). (Illus.). 56p. (J). pap. 9.49 *(978-1-4329-0369-5(1))* Heinemann.

Larson, Jennifer S. Delicious Vegetarian Main Dishes. Cohen, Brie, photos by. 2013. (You're the Chef Ser.). (ENG., Illus.). 32p. (gr. 3-5). lib. bdg. 26.60 *(978-0-7613-6635-5(0)*, Millbrook Pr.) Lerner Publishing Group.

Miller, Debra A. Vegetarianism. Gale Editors, ed. 2010. (Current Controversies Ser.). (ENG.). 208p. (gr. 10-12). 44.10 *(978-0-7377-4925-0(3))*; pap. 30.45 *(978-0-7377-4926-7(1))* Cengage Gale. (Greenhaven Pr., Inc.).

Rau, Dana Meachen. Going Vegan: A Healthy Guide to Making the Switch, 1 vol. 2012. (Food Revolution Ser.). (ENG.). 64p. (gr. 6-7). lib. bdg. 34.65 *(978-0-7565-4521-5(8)*, CPB Grades 4-8) Compass Point Bks.

—Going Vegetarian: A Healthy Guide to Making the Switch, 1 vol. 2012. (Food Revolution Ser.). (ENG., Illus.). 64p. (gr. 6-7). 34.65 *(978-0-7565-4522-2(6))*; pap. 9.10 *(978-0-7565-4530-7(7))* Compass Point Bks. (CPB Grades 4-8).

El Reino Vegetal, 6 vols., Vol. 2. (Explorers. Exploradores Nonfiction Sets Ser.). (SPA.). 32p. (gr. 3-6). 44.95 *(978-0-7699-0641-6(9))* Shortland Pubns. (U. S. A.) Inc.

Roth, Ruby. That's Why We Don't Eat Animals: A Book about Vegans, Vegetarians, & All Living Things. Roth, Ruby, illus. 2009. (ENG., Illus.). 48p. (J). (gr. 1-4). 16.95 *(978-1-55643-785-4(4))* North Atlantic Bks.

—V Is for Vegan: The ABCs of Being Kind. Roth, Ruby, illus. 2013. (ENG., Illus.). 32p. (J). (gr. -1-2). 12.95 *(978-1-58394-649-7(7))* North Atlantic Bks.

—Vegan Is Love: Having Heart & Taking Action. Roth, Ruby, illus. 2012. (ENG., Illus.). 44p. (J). (gr. 2-5). 16.95 *(978-1-58394-354-0(4))* North Atlantic Bks.

VEHICLES

Abbot, Henry. I Want to Drive a Police Car. 2016. (At the Wheel Ser.). 00024p. (J). (gr. 1-1). 23.60 *(978-1-4994-2943-5(6))*; pap. 8.25 *(978-1-4994-2664-9(X))* Rosen Publishing Group, Inc., The. (PowerKids Pr.).

Abbott, John A. Press-Out & Play Autoshop Fun. 2013. (ENG.). 18p. (J). pap. 4.99 *(978-1-78235-569-4(3))* Make Believe Ideas GBR. Dist: Nelson, Thomas Inc.

Abramovitz, Melissa. Emergency Vehicles. 2015. (Wild about Wheels Ser.). (ENG.). 24p. (gr. k-1). lib. bdg. 26.65 *(978-1-4914-2115-4(0)*, Pebble Plus) Capstone Press of Coughlan Cos.

Acampora, Courtney & DiPerna, Kaitlyn. Read with Me! Pre, Level 1. 2016. (Smithsonian Readers Ser.). (ENG., Illus.). 200p. (J). (gr. -1). 14.95 *(978-1-62686-571-6(X)*, Silver Dolphin Bks.) Readerlink Distribution Services, LLC.

Ackland, Nick. Zoom! Bradley, Jennie, illus. 2016. (Baby Sparkler Ser.). (ENG.). 10p. (J). (gr. -1 — 1). bds. 5.99 *(978-0-7641-6849-9(5))* Barron's Educational Series, Inc.

Adamson, Thomas K. Garbage Trucks. 2017. (Mighty Machines in Action Ser.). (ENG., Illus.). 24p. (J). (gr. k-3). lib. bdg. 25.95 *(978-1-62617-605-8(1)*, Blastoff! Readers) Bellwether Media.

Ambramson, Andra Serlin. Emergency & Rescue Vehicles. 2014. (Kids Meet Ser.: 1). (ENG., Illus.). 96p. (J). 14.95 *(978-1-60433-468-5(1)*, Applesauce Pr.) Cider Mill Pr. Bk. Pubs., LLC.

Anderson, Jill, ed. Let's Go!/Vamos a Viajar! Evrard, Gaetan, illus. 2005. (Word Play/Juegos con Pala Ser.). (ENG & SPA.). 20p. (J). (gr. -1-17). bds. 6.95 *(978-1-58728-513-4(4))* Cooper Square Publishing Llc.

Anness Publishing Ltd. Let's Look & See: Vehicles. 2014. (ENG., Illus.). 24p. (J). (gr. -1-k). bds. 6.99 *(978-1-86147-375-2(3)*, Armadillo) Anness Publishing GBR. Dist: National Bk. Network.

Appleby, Alex. Dinosaurs on the Go. 2013. (Dinosaur School Ser.). 24p. (J). (gr. k-1). pap. 8.15 *(978-1-4339-9062-5(8))*; pap. 48.90 *(978-1-4339-9063-2(6))*; (ENG., Illus.). lib. bdg. 22.60 *(978-1-4339-9061-8(X))* Stevens, Gareth Publishing LLLP.

Armadillo. Things That Go! Tractors Trucks Trains Planes Helicopters Balloons Ships Ferries Boats Bicycles Motorcycles Cars. 2016. (ENG., Illus.). 48p. (J). (gr. -1-12). bds. 9.99 *(978-1-86147-693-7(0)*, Armadillo) Anness Publishing GBR. Dist: National Bk. Network.

Awa, Solomon. Igluvigaliumiq Qamusiumirlu: How to Build an Iglu & a Qamutik, 1 vol. Breithaupt, Andrew, illus. 2013. (ENG.). 32p. (J). (gr. 3-6). 9.95 *(978-1-927095-31-7(X))* Inhabit Media Inc. CAN. Dist: Independent Pubs. Group.

Baer, Edith. This Is the Way We Go to School. 2014. 17.00 *(978-1-63419-734-2(8))* Perfection Learning Corp.

Barlow, Amanda. Things That Go. 2004. (Baby Board Bks.). (ENG., Illus.). 1p. (J). (gr. -1-18). bds. 4.99 *(978-0-7460-4101-7(2))* EDC Publishing.

Basic Vehicles. 2005. (Transportation Ser.). (YA). (gr. k-3). 118.80 *(978-0-7368-4191-7(1)*, Pebble Bks.) Capstone Press of Coughlan Cos.

Beck, Isabel L., et al. Trophies Kindergarten: A Big, Big Van. 2003. (Trophies Ser.). (gr. k-6). 13.80 *(978-0-15-329546-1(5))* Harcourt Schl. Pubs.

Bell, Samantha. Farm Quad. 2016. (21st Century Basic Skills Library: Welcome to the Farm Ser.). (ENG.). 24p. (J). (gr. k-3). 24.21 *(978-1-63471-040-4(1)*, 208240) Cherry Lake Publishing.

—Four-Wheel Drive Utility Tractor. 2016. (21st Century Basic Skills Library: Welcome to the Farm Ser.). (ENG.). 24p. (J). (gr. k-3). 24.21 *(978-1-63471-038-1(X)*, 208232) Cherry Lake Publishing.

Best, B. J. Ambulances. 2017. (J). ***(978-1-5026-2553-3(9))*** Cavendish Square Publishing.

—Police Cars. 2017. (J). ***(978-1-5026-2555-7(5))*** Cavendish Square Publishing.

Bidder, Jane. Inventions We Use to Go Places. 2006. (Everyday Inventions Ser.). (Illus.). 32p. (gr. 1-4). lib. bdg. 26.00 *(978-0-8368-6901-9(X)*, Gareth Stevens Learning Library) Stevens, Gareth Publishing LLLP.

Biggs, Brian. Blue Bus, Red Balloon: A Book of Colors. Biggs, Brian, illus. 2013. (ENG., Illus.). 24p. (J). (gr. -1 — 1). bds. 7.99 *(978-0-06-195814-4(X))* HarperCollins Pubs.

Blaine, Victor. My Scooter, 1 vol. 2015. (ENG.). 24p. (J). lib. bdg. 23.60 *(978-1-4994-0253-7(8)*, PowerKids Pr.) Rosen Publishing Group, Inc., The.

—My Sled, 1 vol. 2015. (ENG., Illus.). 24p. (J). lib. bdg. 23.60 *(978-1-4994-0249-0(X)*, PowerKids Pr.) Rosen Publishing Group, Inc., The.

—Watch Me Go!, 1 vol. 2015. (Watch Me Go! Ser.). (ENG.). 24p. (J). 141.60 *(978-1-4777-5729-1(5)*, PowerKids Pr.) Rosen Publishing Group, Inc., The.

Bloomsbury USA. Baby's First Words: Things That Go. 2016. (ENG., Illus.). 10p. (J). bds. 5.99 *(978-1-61963-995-9(5)*, 9781619639959, Bloomsbury Activity Bks.) Bloomsbury Publishing USA.

Boothroyd, Jennifer. From the Model T to Hybrid Cars: How Transportation Has Changed. 2011. (Comparing Past & Present Ser.). pap. 7.95 *(978-0-7613-7837-2(5))*; pap. 45.32 *(978-0-7613-8392-5(1))*; (ENG., Illus.). 32p. lib. bdg. 26.60 *(978-0-7613-6743-7(8))* Lerner Publishing Group.

Braithwaite, Jill. Police Cars. 2004. (Pull Ahead Books-Mighty Movers Ser.). (ENG., Illus.). 32p. (gr. k-3). pap. 7.95 *(978-0-8225-9919-7(8))*; lib. bdg. 22.60 *(978-0-8225-0770-3(6))* Lerner Publishing Group.

Bridges, Sarah. I Drive a Snowplow, 1 vol. Alderman, Derrick & Shea, Denise, illus. 2004. (Working Wheels Ser.). (ENG.). 24p. (gr. -1-2). 26.65 *(978-1-4048-0617-7(2))* Picture Window Bks.

Brooks, Felicity. Usborne Lift & Look Emergency Vehicles. Van Wyk, Hanri, illus. 2007. (Lift & Look Board Bks.). 10p. (J). (gr. -1-k). bds. 9.99 *(978-0-7945-1596-6(7)*, Usborne) EDC Publishing.

Bulleman, Curtis David & Coloring Books Staff. Car Crazy! 2011. (Dover 3-D Coloring Book Ser.). (ENG., Illus.). 32p. (J). (gr. 2-6). 5.99 *(978-0-486-48418-1(1))* Dover Pubns., Inc.

Burch, Lynda S. Wicky Wacky Things that Go! Emergency Vehicles. Burch, Lynda S., photos by. 2004. (Illus.). 30p. (J). E-Book 9.95 incl. cd-rom *(978-1-933090-13-9(8))* Guardian Angel Publishing, Inc.

Chancellor, Deborah. Fire Rescue. 2013. (Emergency Vehicles Ser.). 24p. (gr. k-3). 28.50 *(978-1-59920-889-3(X))* Black Rabbit Bks.

—Police Rescue. 2013. (Emergency Vehicles Ser.). (Illus.). 24p. (gr. k-3). lib. bdg. 28.50 *(978-1-59920-890-9(3))* Black Rabbit Bks.

Channing, Margot. On the Go. Claude, Jean, illus. 2017. (First Words & Pictures Ser.). (ENG.). 14p. (J). (gr. -1 — 1). bds. 9.99 *(978-1-68152-201-2(2))* Amicus.

Colson, Rob. SUVs & Off-Roaders. 2016. (Top Marques Ser.). (ENG., Illus.). 32p. (J). (gr. 2-4). 17.99 *(978-0-7502-8588-9(5)*, Wayland) Hachette Children's Group GBR. Dist: Hachette Bk. Group.

Community Vehicles. 2005. (Transportation Ser.). (YA). (gr. k-3). 118.80 *(978-0-7368-4192-4(X)*, Pebble Bks.) Capstone Press of Coughlan Cos.

Coppendale, Jean. Fire Trucks & Rescue Vehicles. 2010. (Mighty Machines Ser.). (ENG., Illus.). 24p. (J). (gr. -1-2). pap. 5.95 *(978-1-55407-621-5(8)*, 9781554076215) Firefly Bks., Ltd.

Dale, Jay. Ways We Go to School, 1 vol. 2012. (Engage Literacy Green Ser.). (ENG.). 32p. (gr. k-2). pap. 5.99 *(978-1-4296-9020-1(8)*, Engage Literacy) Capstone Press of Coughlan Cos.

David, Jack. ATVs. 2008. (Cool Rides Ser.). (ENG., Illus.). 24p. (J). (gr. 3-7). lib. bdg. 25.95 *(978-1-60014-146-1(3))* Bellwether Media.

de Seve, Karen. National Geographic Little Kids First Big Book of Things That Go. 2017. (National Geographic Little Kids First Big Bks.). (ENG.). 128p. (J). (gr. -1-3). lib. bdg. 24.90 ***(978-1-4263-2805-3(2)***, National Geographic Children's Bks.) National Geographic Society.

de Seve, Karen & National Geographic Kids Staff. Little Kids First Big Book of Things That Go. 2017. (National Geographic Little Kids First Big Bks.). (ENG.). 128p. (J). (gr. -1-3). 14.99 ***(978-1-4263-2804-6(4)***, National Geographic Children's Bks.) National Geographic Society.

Deneux, Xavier. TouchThinkLearn: Vehicles. 2015. (ENG., Illus.). 22p. (J). (gr. -1 — 1). bds. 14.99 *(978-1-4521-4516-7(4))* Chronicle Bks. LLC.

Dinmont, Kerry. Ambulances on the Go. 2016. (Bumba Books (tm) — Machines That Go Ser.). (ENG.). 24p. (J). (gr. -1-1). lib. bdg. 25.32 *(978-1-5124-1448-6(4))* Lerner Publishing Group.

Dinmont, Kerry & Granat, Annette. ¡Ambulancias en Acción! 2017. (Bumba Books (tm) en Español — Máquinas en Acción (Machines That Go) Ser.). (SPA., Illus.). 24p. (J). (gr. -1-1). 25.32 *(978-1-5124-2876-6(0))* Lerner Publishing Group.

Dittmer, Lori. The Future of Transportation. 2012. (What's Next? Ser.). (Illus.). 48p. (J). (gr. 5-12). 23.95 *(978-1-60818-224-4(X)*, Creative Education) Creative Co., The.

Doman, Mary Kate. Rescue Vehicles. 2011. (All about Big Machines Ser.). (Illus.). 24p. (J). (gr. -1-18). pap. 7.95 *(978-1-59845-244-0(4)*, Enslow Elementary); (gr. k-3). lib. bdg. 22.60 *(978-0-7660-3934-6(X))* Enslow Pubs., Inc.

Dorling Kindersley Publishing Staff. The Big Book of Things That Go. 2016. (DK Adventures Ser.). (ENG., Illus.). 32p. (J). (gr. k-4). 14.99 *(978-1-4654-4509-4(9)*, DK Children) Dorling Kindersley Publishing, Inc.

—Cars, Trains, Ships, & Planes. 2015. (ENG., Illus.). 256p. (J). (gr. 3-7). 24.99 *(978-1-4654-3805-8(X)*, DK Children) Dorling Kindersley Publishing, Inc.

—Hide & Seek: Things That Go. 2013. (ENG., Illus.). 48p. (J). (gr. -1 — 1). 12.99 *(978-1-4654-0931-7(9)*, DK Children) Dorling Kindersley Publishing, Inc.

—My First Things That Go. 2016. (ENG., Illus.). 36p. (J). (— 1). bds. 5.99 *(978-1-4654-4490-5(4)*, DK Children) Dorling Kindersley Publishing, Inc.

—Things That Go. 2009. (Baby Touch & Feel Ser.). (ENG., Illus.). 14p. (J). (gr. -1 — 1). bds. 5.99 *(978-0-7566-5841-0(1)*, DK Children) Dorling Kindersley Publishing, Inc.

—Things That Go! 2013. (ENG.). 14p. (J). (gr. -1 — 1). bds. 7.99 *(978-1-4654-1428-1(2)*, DK Children) Dorling Kindersley Publishing, Inc.

Ebel, Julia Taylor, Jr. Hansi & the Ice Man. Canter, Idalia, illus. 2014. 32p. (YA). lib. bdg. 19.95 *(978-1-933251-81-3(6))* Parkway Pubs., Inc.

Enz, Tammy. The Science Behind Batman's Ground Vehicles. Vecchio, Luciano, illus. 2016. (Science Behind Batman Ser.). (ENG.). 24p. (gr. 1-2). lib. bdg. 25.32 *(978-1-5157-2034-8(9)*, DC Super Heroes) Stone Arch Bks.

Felix, Rebecca. Heavy, Heavier, Heaviest. 2015. (Size It Up Ser.). (Illus.). 16p. (J). 25.65 *(978-1-60753-576-8(9))* Amicus Publishing.

Fortuna, Lois. Ambulances. 2016. (To the Rescue! Ser.). 24p. (J). (gr. k-k). 22.60 *(978-1-4824-4659-3(6))* Stevens, Gareth Publishing LLLP.

—Police Cars. 2016. (To the Rescue! Ser.). (ENG., Illus.). 24p. (J). (gr. k-k). lib. bdg. 22.60 *(978-1-4824-4661-6(8))* Stevens, Gareth Publishing LLLP.

—Rescue Helicopters. 2016. (To the Rescue! Ser.). 24p. (J). (gr. k-k). pap. 8.15 *(978-1-4824-4663-0(4))* Stevens, Gareth Publishing LLLP.

—Snowmobiles. 2016. (To the Rescue! Ser.). 24p. (J). (gr. k-k). pap. 8.15 *(978-1-4824-4665-4(0))* Stevens, Gareth Publishing LLLP.

Freeman, Marcia S. Police Cars [Scholastic]. 2009. (Community Vehicles Ser.). 24p. (gr. k-1). pap. 0.36 *(978-1-4296-4244-6(0)*, Pebble Bks.) Capstone Press of Coughlan Cos.

Gabrielson, Curt. Kinetic Contraptions: Build a Hovercraft, Airboat, & More with a Hobby Motor. 2010. (ENG., Illus.). 192p. (J). (gr. 7-18). pap. 16.95 *(978-1-55652-957-3(0))* Chicago Review Pr., Inc.

Galloway, Fhiona. Look Through: Things That Go. 2016. (Look Through Ser.). (ENG., Illus.). 10p. (J). bds. 8.99 *(978-1-62686-579-2(5)*, Silver Dolphin Bks.) Readerlink Distribution Services, LLC.

Galvin, Laura Gates. First Look at Rescue Vehicles. Eaddy, Susan, illus. 2009. (ENG.). 16p. (J). (gr. -1-k). 6.95 *(978-1-60727-106-2(0))*; bds. 6.95 *(978-1-60727-093-5(5))* Soundprints.

Ganeri, Anita. Flip the Flaps: Things That Go! Humphries, Tudor, illus. 2014. (Flip the Flaps Ser.). (ENG.). 32p. (J). (gr. -1-1). pap. 6.99 *(978-0-7534-7133-3(7)*, 9780753471333, Kingfisher) Roaring Brook Pr.

George, Joshua. Vehicles. Crisp, Dan, illus. 2017. (Search & Find Ser.). (ENG.). 48p. (J). (gr. k-2). pap. 6.99 ***(978-1-78700-030-8(3))*** Top That! Publishing PLC GBR. Dist: Independent Pubs. Group.

Gordon, Sharon. Fast/Slow. 2007. (J). pap. 6.99 *(978-0-7614-3281-4(7))* Marshall Cavendish Corp.

—Fast/Slow/Rapido/Lento. 2006. (Bookworms Ser.). (ENG & SPA., Illus.). 24p. (gr. k-1). lib. bdg. 15.95 *(978-0-7614-2447-5(4))* Marshall Cavendish Corp.

—Que Hay Dentro de un Carro de Policia? 2006. (Bookworms Ser.). (SPA & ENG., Illus.). 32p. (gr. 1-2). lib. bdg. 15.95 *(978-0-7614-2396-6(6))* Marshall Cavendish Corp.

—Rapido Lento. 2006. (Bookworms Ser.). (SPA & ENG., Illus.). 24p. (gr. k-1). lib. bdg. 15.95 *(978-0-7614-2367-6(2))* Marshall Cavendish Corp.

—What's Inside a Police Car? 2007. (Bookworms Ser.). (Illus.). 31p. (J). (gr. -1-3). pap. 6.99 *(978-0-7614-3348-4(1)*, Benchmark Bks.) Marshall Cavendish Corp.

—What's Inside a Police Car/Que Hay Dentro de un Carro de Policia? 2006. (Bookworms Ser.). (ENG & SPA., Illus.). 32p. (gr. 1-2). lib. bdg. 15.95 *(978-0-7614-2475-8(X))* Marshall Cavendish Corp.

Gould, Robert. Rescue Vehicles. Gould, Robert, photos by. 2005. (Big Stuff Ser.). (ENG., Illus.). 16p. (J). bds. 7.95 *(978-1-929945-51-1(5))* Big Guy Bks., Inc.

Graham, Buck. My First Big Book of Questions & Answers: Things That Go. 2005. (Illus.). 10p. bds. 9.98 *(978-0-7853-7227-1(X)*, 7171500) Publications International, Ltd.

Graham, Ian. Emergency! 2006. (QEB Machines at Work Ser.). (Illus.). 36p. (J). lib. bdg. 16.95 *(978-1-59566-188-3(3))* QEB Publishing Inc.

—Machines & Inventions. Antram, David et al, illus. 2008. (World of Wonder Ser.). (ENG.). 32p. (J). (gr. 1-4). pap. 9.95 *(978-0-531-23823-3(7)*, Children's Pr.) Scholastic Library Publishing.

Graubart, Norman D. Ambulances, 1 vol. 2015. (ENG.). 24p. (J). lib. bdg. 23.60 *(978-1-4994-0029-8(2)*, PowerKids Pr.) Rosen Publishing Group, Inc., The.

Green, Rod. Emergency Vehicles. Biesty, Stephen, illus. 2015. (ENG.). 16p. (J). (gr. k-4). 15.99 *(978-0-7636-7959-0(3)*, Templar) Candlewick Pr.

—Giant Vehicles. Biesty, Stephen, illus. 2014. (ENG.). 16p. (J). (gr. k-4). 15.99 *(978-0-7636-7404-5(4)*, Templar) Candlewick Pr.

Hammelef, Danielle S. & Omoth, Tyler. See How It's Made, 1 vol. 2014. (See How It's Made Ser.). (ENG.). 32p. (gr. 1-2). lib. bdg. 106.60 *(978-1-4765-7851-4(6)*, Blazers) Capstone Press of Coughlan Cos.

Harrison, Paul. Speed Machines. 2009. (Up Close Ser.). 24p. (gr. 3-3). 47.90 *(978-1-60854-705-0(1)*, PowerKids Pr.) Rosen Publishing Group, Inc., The.

Haughom, Lisa, illus. Things That Go! 2010. 16p. (J). *(978-1-58865-542-4(3))* Kidsbooks, LLC.

Hinkler Books, creator. 101 First Words: Things That Go. 2011. (101 First Words Ser.). (Illus.). 16p. (J). (gr. -1). bds. 7.99 *(978-1-74184-818-2(0))* Hinkler Bks. Pty, Ltd. AUS. Dist: Ideals Pubns.

Home, Jane. Rough & Tough: Tractors & Trucks/Cars/Diggers & Dumpers/Emergency. 2007. (Illus.). 12p. (gr. -1-k). *(978-1-84610-559-3(5))* Make Believe Ideas.

—Rough & Tough Emergency. 2008. 12p. *(978-1-84610-414-5(9))* Make Believe Ideas.

—101 First Things That Go. 2013. (ENG.). 16p. (J). bds. 8.99 *(978-1-78235-607-3(X))* Make Believe Ideas GBR. Dist: Nelson, Thomas Inc.

Horsepower [Really Good Stuff]. 2010. (Horsepower Ser.). 32p. pap. 79.50 *(978-1-4296-5361-9(2)*, Blazers) Capstone Press of Coughlan Cos.

Imperato, Teresa. Speed Machines: A Pop-up Book with Moving Gears. Robinson, Keith, illus. 2005. 8p. (J). 14.95 *(978-1-58117-323-9(7)*, Intervisual/Piggy Toes) Bendon, Inc.

Innovative Kids Staff, creator. Vehicles. 2012. (ENG., Illus.). 1p. (J). (gr. -1 — 1). 10.99 *(978-1-60169-224-5(2))* Innovative Kids.

Ipcizade, Catherine. H Is for Honk! A Transportation Alphabet, 1 vol. 2010. (Alphabet Fun Ser.). (ENG.). 32p. (gr. 1-2). lib. bdg. 27.32 *(978-1-4296-4464-8(8)*, Aplus Bks.) Capstone Press of Coughlan Cos.

Jonath, Leslie & Nash, Josh. On the Go. 2010. (ENG., Illus.). 12p. (J). (gr. -1). 9.99 *(978-0-7407-9800-9(6))* Andrews McMeel Publishing.

Joyce, Bridget & Furman, Eric. Tonka Rescue Trucks! Dean Kleven Studios & Finley, Shawn, illus. 2007. (Fold & Go Vehicles Ser.). 15.98 *(978-1-4127-2981-9(5))* Publications International, Ltd.

Jugran, Jan. Hugs. Larranaga, Ana Martin, illus. 2007. (ENG.). 12p. (J). (gr. -1 — 1). 9.99 *(978-1-58476-620-9(4)*, IKIDS) Innovative Kids.

Kenney, Karen Latchana. What Makes Vehicles Safer? 2015. (ENG., Illus.). 32p. (gr. 4-8). (J). 26.65 *(978-1-4677-7913-5(X))*; 26.65 *(978-1-4677-8652-2(7))* Lerner Publishing Group. (Lerner Pubns.).

Kilby, Don. In the Country. Kilby, Don, illus. 2006. (Wheels at Work Ser.). (ENG., Illus.). 24p. (J). (gr. -1-2). 5.95 *(978-1-55337-985-0(3))* Kids Can Pr., Ltd. CAN. Dist: Hachette Bk. Group.

Knight, M. J. Why Should I Walk More Often? 2009. (One Small Step Ser.). (YA). (gr. 2-5). 28.50 *(978-1-59920-268-6(9))* Black Rabbit Bks.

Knight M. J. Why Should I Walk More Often? 2009. (One Small Step Ser.). (Illus.). 32p. (J). (gr. -1-3). pap. *(978-1-897563-50-2(7))* Saunders Bk. Co.

Kramer, Nash. What Goes Fastest? 2014. (Little Books of Answers: Level B Ser.). (Illus.). 16p. (gr. k-2). pap. 7.95 *(978-1-927136-19-5(9))* Three Crows Media NZL. Dist: RiverStream Publishing.

Krych, Elizabeth. Magnetic Learning: Vehicles. 2015. (Magnetic Learning Ser.). (ENG., Illus.). 56p. (J). (gr. -1). 19.95 *(978-1-62686-334-7(2)*, Silver Dolphin Bks.) Readerlink Distribution Services, LLC.

La Coccinella. Look & See: Wheels on the Go! 2008. (Look & See! Ser.). (ENG., Illus.). 24p. (J). (gr. -1-1). bds. 6.95 *(978-1-4027-5826-3(X))* Sterling Publishing Co., Inc.

Learning Fun, Early & Priddy, Roger. Things That Go. 2010. (ENG., Illus.). 20p. (J). bds. *(978-1-84915-141-2(5)*, Priddy Bks.) St. Martin's Pr.

Levine, Michelle & Waxman, Laura Hamilton. Ambulances on the Move. 2011. (Lightning Bolt Books Vroom-Vroom Ser.). (ENG., Illus.). 32p. (J). (gr. k-2). lib. bdg. 26.60 *(978-0-7613-3922-9(1))* Lerner Publishing Group.

Life in the Fast Lane. 2014. (Life in the Fast Lane Ser.). 48p. (J). (gr. 4-6). 219.52 *(978-1-62713-146-9(9))* Cavendish Square Publishing.

Lindeen, Mary. Snowplows. 2007. (Mighty Machines Ser.). (ENG., Illus.). 24p. (J). (gr. k-3). lib. bdg. 25.95 *(978-1-60014-120-1(X))* Bellwether Media.

Litchfield, J. & Brooks, F. Rescue Vehicles. 2004. (ENG., Illus.). 10p. (J). bds. 4.99 *(978-0-7945-0589-9(9))* EDC Publishing.

Loh-Hagan, Virginia. Parade Float Designer: Odd Jobs. 2015. 32p. (J). *(978-1-63470-027-6(9))* Cherry Lake Publishing.

Machines in Motion. 2013. (Machines in Motion Ser.). 48p. (J). (gr. 3-5). 191.70 *(978-1-4339-9685-6(5))*; pap. 84.30 *(978-1-4339-9817-1(3))*; pap. 505.80 *(978-1-4339-9818-8(1))* Stevens, Gareth Publishing LLLP.

MacNeill, Scott. How Things Work Vehicles - Motorcycle. 2013. (ENG.). 48p. (J). (gr. 3-8). pap. 4.99 *(978-0-486-49221-6(4))* Dover Pubns., Inc.

Mahaney, Ian F. Extreme off-Road Vehicles. 2015. (Extreme Machines Ser.). (ENG.). 32p. (J). (gr. 3-4). pap. 10.00 *(978-1-4994-1185-0(5)*, PowerKids Pr.) Rosen Publishing Group, Inc., The.

—Extreme Snow Vehicles. 2015. (Extreme Machines Ser.). (ENG.). 32p. (J). (gr. 3-4). pap. 10.00 *(978-1-4994-1187-4(1)*, PowerKids Pr.) Rosen Publishing Group, Inc., The.

—Extreme Unmanned Vehicles. 2015. (Extreme Machines Ser.). (ENG.). 32p. (J). (gr. 3-4). pap. 10.00 *(978-1-4994-1189-8(8)*, PowerKids Pr.) Rosen Publishing Group, Inc., The.

Manolis, Kay. Police Cars. 2008. (Mighty Machines Ser.). (ENG., Illus.). 24p. (J). (gr. k-3). lib. bdg. 25.95 *(978-1-60014-179-9(X))* Bellwether Media.

Marshall, Jane. Rescue Vehicles. 2013. (Wild Rides Ser.). 32p. (gr. 2-4). *(978-1-84898-620-6(3)*, TickTock Books) Octopus Publishing Group.

Masters, Neil. Working Vehicles Coloring Book. 2013. (ENG.). 32p. 11.98 *(978-1-62884-655-3(0)*, Baby Professor (Education Kids)) Speedy Publishing LLC.

Max & Sid, Max &, illus. My First Vehicles. 2016. (My First Ser.). (ENG.). 12p. (J). (gr. -1 — 1). bds. 5.99 *(978-1-4998-0188-0(2))* Little Bee Books Inc.

Maynard, Christopher. I Wonder Why Planes Have Wings: And Other Questions about Transportation. 2012. (I Wonder Why Ser.). (ENG., Illus.). 32p. (J). (gr. k-3). pap. 6.99 *(978-0-7534-6703-9(8)*, 9780753467039, Kingfisher) Roaring Brook Pr.

McDonnell, Rory. Matemáticas con Ruedas / Math with Wheels. de la Vega, Eida, tr. 2016. (¡Matemáticas en Todas Partes! / Math Is Everywhere! Ser.). (ENG & SPA.). 24p. (gr. k-k). lib. bdg. 22.60 *(978-1-4824-5218-1(9))* Stevens, Gareth Publishing LLLP.

McMahon, Peter. Ultimate Trains. Mora, Andy, illus. 2010. (Machines of the Future Ser.). (ENG.). 40p. (J). (gr. 4-7). 16.95 *(978-1-55453-366-4(X))* Kids Can Pr., Ltd. CAN. Dist: Hachette Bk. Group.

Meachen Rau, Dana, ed. A Conducir! 2006. (En Movimiento Ser.). (SPA & ENG., Illus.). 24p. (gr. k-1). lib. bdg. 15.95 *(978-0-7614-2422-2(9)*, Benchmark Bks.) Marshall Cavendish Corp.

Meister, Cari. Tow Trucks. 2013. (ENG., Illus.). 24p. (J). lib. bdg. 25.65 *(978-1-62031-048-9(1))* Jump! Inc.

Metsola, Aino-Maija. Traffic Jam: Puzzle Book. 2016. (Learning Garden Ser.). (ENG., Illus.). 14p. (J). bds. 14.99 *(978-1-84780-746-5(1)*, Wide Eyed Editions) Quarto Publishing Group UK GBR. Dist: Littlehampton Bk Services, Ltd.

Mighty Machines. Date not set. (Illus.). (J). 48p. 5.98 *(978-1-4054-0207-1(5))*; 256p. *(978-1-4054-1538-5(X))* Parragon, Inc.

Milet Publishing Staff. My First Bilingual Book - Vehicles. 2014. (My First Bilingual Book Ser.). (ENG & KOR., Illus.). 20p. (J). (— 1). bds. 7.99 *(978-1-84059-929-9(4))*; bds. 7.99 *(978-1-84059-925-1(1))*; bds. 7.99 *(978-1-84059-937-4(5))*; bds. 7.99 *(978-1-84059-935-0(9))*; bds. 7.99 *(978-1-84059-924-4(3))*; bds. 7.99 *(978-1-84059-933-6(2))* Milet Publishing.

—My First Bilingual Book - Vehicles (English-Russian) 2014. (My First Bilingual Book Ser.). (ENG & RUS., Illus.). 20p. (J). (— 1). bds. 7.99 *(978-1-84059-932-9(4))* Milet Publishing.

—Vehicles. 2014. (My First Bilingual Book Ser.). (Illus.). 20p. (J). (— 1). (ENG & ITA.). bds. 7.99 *(978-1-84059-928-2(6))*; (SPA & ENG., bds. 7.99 *(978-1-84059-934-3(0))*; (ENG & ARA., bds. 7.99 *(978-1-84059-922-0(7))* Milet Publishing.

—Vehicles - My First Bilingual Book. 2014. (My First Bilingual Book Ser.). (Illus.). 20p. (J). (— 1). (FRE & ENG.). bds. 7.99 *(978-1-84059-926-8(X))*; (ENG & URD., bds. 7.99 *(978-1-84059-936-7(7))*; (POR & ENG., bds. 7.99 *(978-1-84059-931-2(6))*; (ENG & BEN., bds. 7.99 *(978-1-84059-923-7(5))*; (ENG, POL & POR., bds. 7.99 *(978-1-84059-930-5(8))* Milet Publishing.

—Vehicles (English-German) 2014. (My First Bilingual Book Ser.). (ENG & GER., Illus.). 20p. (J). (— 1). bds. 7.99 *(978-1-84059-927-5(8))* Milet Publishing.

Mitton, Tony & Parker, Ant. Amazing Machines. 2003. (Illus.). 93p. (J). *(978-0-7534-5938-6(8)*, Kingfisher) Roaring Brook Pr.

—Cool Cars. 2014. (Amazing Machines Ser.). (ENG., Illus.). 24p. (J). (gr. -1-k). 4.99 *(978-0-7534-7207-1(4)*, 9780753472071, Kingfisher) Roaring Brook Pr.

—Cool Cars. 2014. (Amazing Machines Ser.). (J). lib. bdg. 14.75 *(978-0-606-36132-3(4))* Turtleback Bks.

Morey, Allan. Police Cars. 2014. (Illus.). 24p. (J). lib. bdg. 25.65 *(978-1-62031-104-2(6)*, Bullfrog Bks.) Jump! Inc.

Morris, Neil. Transportation, 1 vol. 2010. (From Fail to Win! Learning from Bad Ideas Ser.). (ENG., Illus.). 56p. (gr. 5-8). 34.65 *(978-1-4109-3911-1(1)*, Raintree Freestyle) Heinemann-Raintree.

Murray, Julie. My Community: Vehicles. 2016. (My Community: Vehicles Ser.: 6). (ENG.). 24p. (J). (gr. k-2). lib. bdg. 162.42 *(978-1-68080-127-9(9))* ABDO Publishing Co.

My Big Book of Vehicles. 2004. 12p. (J). bds. 7.99 *(978-1-85854-660-5(5))* Brimax Books Ltd. GBR. Dist: Byeway Bks.

National Geographic Kids Staff. Things That Go. 2014. (Look & Learn Ser.). (ENG.). 24p. (J). (-k). bds. 6.99 *(978-1-4263-1706-4(9)*, National Geographic Children's Bks.) National Geographic Society.

Nishida, Masaki. Drawing Manga Vehicles. (How to Draw Manga Ser.). 24p. 2009. (gr. 3-3). 47.90 *(978-1-61513-442-7(5)*, PowerKids Pr.) 2007. (Illus.). (J). (gr. 5-8). lib. bdg. 25.25 *(978-1-4042-3848-0(4))* Rosen Publishing Group, Inc., The.

Off Road Vehicles. 2004. (Mega MacHines Ser.). (Illus.). 16p. (J). *(978-2-7643-0200-2(2))* Phidal Publishing, Inc./Editions Phidal, Inc.

Olivera, Ramon. ABCs on Wheels. Olivera, Ramon, illus. 2016. (ENG., Illus.). 40p. (J). (gr. -1-k). 17.99 *(978-1-4814-3244-3(3)*, Little Simon) Little Simon.

O'Toole, Janet & Anness Publishing Staff. Vehicles: Lift the Flaps to Find Out about Vehicles! Adams, Ben, illus. 2013. (ENG.). 16p. bds. 6.99 *(978-1-84322-728-1(2)*, Armadillo) Anness Publishing GBR. Dist: National Bk. Network.

Oxlade, Chris. The History of Transportation. 2017. (History of Technology Ser.). (ENG.). 32p. (gr. 2-5). lib. bdg. 27.32 ***(978-1-4846-4038-8(1)***, Heinemann First Library) Heinemann-Raintree.

Page, Claire. Hide & Seek Vehicles. 2008. (Hide & Seek Ser.). (Illus.). 20p. (gr. -1). bds. *(978-1-84610-586-9(2))* Make Believe Ideas.

Parker, Steve. Emergency Vehicles. 2010. (How It Works Ser.). (Illus.). 40p. (J). (gr. 3-18). lib. bdg. 19.95 *(978-1-4222-1793-1(0)*, 1317906) Mason Crest.

—On the Road. 2010. (J). 28.50 *(978-1-59920-283-9(2))* Black Rabbit Bks.

—Speed Machines. Pang, Alex, illus. 2010. (How It Works Ser.). 40p. (J). (gr. 3-18). lib. bdg. 19.95 *(978-1-4222-1800-6(7)*, 1317938) Mason Crest.

Parker, Steven. On Land. 2011. (Future Transport Ser.). (Illus.). 32p. (J). (gr. 4). 28.50 *(978-1-60870-779-9(2))* Marshall Cavendish Corp.

Pearson, Debora. Alphabeep! A Zipping, Zooming ABC. Miller, Edward, illus. 2007. (ENG.). 36p. (J). (gr. -1-3). 6.95 *(978-0-8234-2076-6(0))* Holiday Hse., Inc.

Pearson, Deborah. Animachines. Hilb, Nora, illus. 2016. (ENG.). 16p. (J). (— 1). bds. 7.99 *(978-1-55451-831-9(8))* Annick Pr., Ltd. CAN. Dist: Publishers Group West (PGW).

Penguin Books Staff. Vehicles. (Learners Ser.). (Illus.). 48p. (J). 3.50 *(978-0-7214-1704-2(3)*, Dutton Juvenile) Penguin Publishing Group.

Peppas, Lynn. Atvs & Off-Roaders. 2012. (ENG.). 32p. (J). *(978-0-7787-3017-0(4))*; pap. *(978-0-7787-3022-4(0))* Crabtree Publishing Co.

—Green Machines: Eco-Friendly Rides. 2011. (ENG., Illus.). 32p. (J). lib. bdg. *(978-0-7787-2729-3(7))*; (Vehicles on the Move Ser.: No. 15). pap. *(978-0-7787-2736-1(X))* Crabtree Publishing Co.

Poolos, J. ATVs/Vehículos Todo Terreno. Alaman, Eduardo, tr. from ENG. 2007. (Wild Rides / Autos de Locura Ser.). (SPA., Illus.). 24p. (J). (gr. 2-5). lib. bdg. 22.60 *(978-1-4042-7641-3(6))* Rosen Publishing Group, Inc., The.

—Wild about ATVs. (Wild Rides Ser.). 24p. (gr. 2-3). 2009. 42.50 *(978-1-60854-797-5(3)*, PowerKids Pr.) 2007. (Illus.). (J). lib. bdg. 22.60 *(978-1-4042-3793-3(3))* Rosen Publishing Group, Inc., The.

—Wild about ATVs/Vehículos todo Terreno. 2009. (Wild Rides/Autos de locura Ser.). 24p. (gr. 2-3). 42.50 *(978-1-60854-802-6(3)*, Editorial Buenas Letras) Rosen Publishing Group, Inc., The.

—Wild about Lowriders. 2009. (Wild Rides/Autos de locura Ser.). 24p. (gr. 2-3). (SPA.). 42.50 *(978-1-60854-807-1(4)*, Editorial Buenas Letras); 42.50 *(978-1-60854-800-2(7)*, PowerKids Pr.) Rosen Publishing Group, Inc., The.

Potts, Nikki. My First Guide to Fire Vehicles. 2017. (My First Guides). (ENG., Illus.). 24p. (gr. 1-2). lib. bdg. 25.32 *(978-1-5157-3594-6(X)*, First Facts) Capstone Press of Coughlan Cos.

Priddy, Roger. My Big Rescue Book. 2004. (Illus.). 10p. (J). *(978-1-84332-215-3(3))* St. Martin's Pr.

—Playtown: Emergency. 2016. (ENG.). 14p. (J). bds. 9.99 *(978-0-312-52009-0(3)*, 9780312520090, Priddy Bks.) St. Martin's Pr.

Publications International Ltd. Staff, ed. Things That Go Board Book. 2014. (Illus.). 22p. (J). bds. 4.98 *(978-1-4508-8581-2(0)*, 1450885810) Phoenix International Publications, Inc.

Randolph, Joanne. Ambulances. 2008. (To the Rescue! Ser.). (Illus.). 24p. (J). (gr. 3-7). lib. bdg. 22.60 *(978-1-4042-4150-3(7)*, PowerKids Pr.) Rosen Publishing Group, Inc., The.

—Ambulances/Ambulancias. Alaman, Eduardo, tr. from ENG. 2008. (To the Rescue! / ¡Al Rescate! Ser.). (Illus.). 24p. (J). (gr. 3-7). lib. bdg. 22.60 *(978-1-4042-7670-3(X)*, Editorial Buenas Letras) Rosen Publishing Group, Inc., The.

—Police Cars. 2008. (To the Rescue! Ser.). (Illus.). 24p. (J). (gr. -1-3). lib. bdg. 22.60 *(978-1-4042-4153-4(1)*, PowerKids Pr.) Rosen Publishing Group, Inc., The.

—Police Cars/Patrullas. Alaman, Eduardo, tr. 2008. (To the Rescue! / ¡Al Rescate! Ser.). (Illus.). 24p. (J). (gr. -1-3). lib. bdg. 22.60 *(978-1-4042-7674-1(2)*, Editorial Buenas Letras) Rosen Publishing Group, Inc., The.

Rice, Dona Herweck. En Movimiento, 1 vol. 2nd rev. ed. 2011. (Nonfiction Readers Ser.). (SPA.). 12p. (J). (gr. 1-1). pap. 4.99 *(978-1-4333-4410-7(6))* Teacher Created Materials, Inc.

—On the Go, 1 vol. 2nd rev. ed. 2011. (Nonfiction Readers Ser.). (ENG.). 12p. (J). (gr. 1-1). pap. 4.99 *(978-1-4333-3571-6(9))* Teacher Created Materials, Inc.

Riggs, Kate. To the Rescue! Williams, Nate, illus. 2016. (ENG.). 14p. (J). (gr. -1 — 1). bds. 7.99 *(978-1-56846-288-2(3)*, Creative Editions) Creative Co., The.

Ripley Entertainment. Life in the Fast Lane. 2010. (Ripley's Believe It or Not Ser.). 36p. (YA). (gr. 3-18). lib. bdg. 19.95 *(978-1-4222-1538-8(5))* Mason Crest.

Ripley's Believe It Or Not! Staff & Ripley's Believe It Or Not! Editors. Ripley Twists: Mighty Machines PORTRAIT EDN. 2014. (Twist Ser.). (ENG.). 48p. (J). 12.95 *(978-1-893951-85-3(5))* Ripley Entertainment, Inc.

Rosen, Michael J. & Kassoy, Ben. Bizarre Vehicles. Sandy, J. P., illus. 2013. (No Way! Ser.). (ENG.). 32p. (gr. 3-5). lib. bdg. 26.60 *(978-0-7613-8985-9(7)*, Millbrook Pr.) Lerner Publishing Group.

Royston, Angela. Race That Bike! Forces in Vehicles. 2015. (Feel the Force Ser.). (ENG., Illus.). 48p. (gr. 3-6). 33.32 *(978-1-4846-2599-6(4))* Heinemann-Raintree.

Rutherford, Peter. Let's Look on the Move. Spong, Clive, illus. 2015. (ENG.). 24p. (J). (gr. -1-2). bds. 6.99 *(978-1-86147-414-8(8)*, Armadillo) Anness Publishing GBR. Dist: National Bk. Network.

Scarry, Richard. Richard Scarry's Hop Aboard! Here We Go! 2012. (ENG., Illus.). 48p. (J). (gr. -1-2). 12.95 *(978-1-4027-7222-1(X))* Sterling Publishing Co., Inc.

Schaefer, Lola M. Tow Trucks in Action, 1 vol. 2012. (Transportation Zone Ser.). (ENG., Illus.). 24p. (gr. 1-2). lib. bdg. 25.32 *(978-1-4296-7691-5(4)*, First Facts) Capstone Press of Coughlan Cos.

Scheff, Matt. ATVs, 1 vol. 2014. (Speed Machines Ser.). (ENG.). 32p. (gr. 3-6). lib. bdg. 27.07 *(978-1-62403-608-8(2)*, SportsZone) ABDO Publishing Co.

Scholastic, Inc. Staff, contrib. by. Shapes That Go. 2014. (Rookie Toddler(r) Ser.). (ENG.). 12p. (J). bds. 6.95 *(978-0-531-20915-8(6))* Scholastic Library Publishing.

—The Wheels on the Truck Go 'Round & 'Round. 2012. (Rookie Toddler Ser.). (ENG.). 12p. (J). bds. 6.95 *(978-0-531-20855-7(9)*, Children's Pr.) Scholastic Library Publishing.

Schuh, Mari C. Show Me Transportation: My First Picture Encyclopedia, 1 vol. 2012. (My First Picture Encyclopedias Ser.). (ENG., Illus.). 32p. (gr. 1-2). lib. bdg. 27.32 *(978-1-4296-8570-2(0))* Capstone Press of Coughlan Cos.

Sheen, Barbara. Cutting Edge Transportation Technology. 2016. (ENG.). 80p. (J). (gr. 5-12). lib. bdg. *(978-1-68282-046-9(7))* ReferencePoint Pr., Inc.

Spaight, Anne J. & Granat, Annette. Carros de Policía en Acción. 2017. (Bumba Books (tm) en Español — Máquinas en Acción (Machines That Go) Ser.). (SPA., Illus.). 24p. (J). (gr. -1-1). 25.32 *(978-1-5124-2880-3(9))* Lerner Publishing Group.

Speed Machines: Set 2. 2013. (Speed Machines Ser.). 32p. (J). (gr. 3-6). 151.50 *(978-1-4777-1149-1(X)*, PowerKids Pr.) Rosen Publishing Group, Inc., The.

Spengler, Kremena T. An Illustrated Timeline of Transportation, 1 vol. Doty, Eldon, illus. 2011. (Visual Timelines in History Ser.). (ENG.). 32p. (gr. 3-4). pap. 7.49 *(978-1-4048-7019-2(9))*; lib. bdg. 28.65 *(978-1-4048-6661-4(2))* Picture Window Bks.

Sterling Children's, Sterling. Things That Go Vroom: A Book of Vehicles. 2016. (ENG., Illus.). 28p. (J). (— 1). bds. 6.95 *(978-1-4114-7589-2(5)*, Spark Publishing Group) Sterling Publishing Co., Inc.

Sweeney, Bernadette. Monster Machines. 2007. (Steck-Vaughn BOLDPRINT Anthologies Ser.). (ENG., Illus.). 48p. (gr. 5-8). pap. 16.90 *(978-1-4190-4024-5(3))* Houghton Mifflin Harcourt Publishing Co.

Tagel, Peggy, illus. On the Go. 2003. (Squishy Shapes Ser.). 10p. (J). 12.95 *(978-1-57145-739-4(9)*, Silver Dolphin Bks.) Readerlink Distribution Services, LLC.

Thomas Nelson. First 100 Things That Go. 2016. (ENG.). 15p. (gr. -1). bds. *(978-1-78598-468-6(3))* Make Believe Ideas.

Tieck, Sarah. ATVs, 1 vol. 2009. (Amazing Vehicles Ser.). (ENG., Illus.). 32p. (J). (gr. 2-5). 28.50 *(978-1-60453-539-6(3))* ABDO Publishing Co.

—Dune Buggies, 1 vol. 2009. (Amazing Vehicles Ser.). (ENG., Illus.). 32p. (gr. 2-5). 28.50 *(978-1-60453-541-9(5)*, Big Buddy Bks.) ABDO Publishing Co.

—The LEGO Build-It Book: Amazing Vehicles, 1 vol., Set 2. Incl. Choppers. 28.50 *(978-1-61714-695-4(1))*; Dragsters. 28.50 *(978-1-61714-696-1(X))*; Helicopters. 28.50 *(978-1-61714-697-8(8))*; Hovercraft. 28.50 *(978-1-61714-698-5(6))*; Jets. 28.50 *(978-1-61714-699-2(4))*; Superbikes. 28.50 *(978-1-61714-700-5(1))*; (J). (gr. 2-5). (Amazing Vehicles Set 2 Ser.). (ENG., Illus.). 32p. 2011. 171.00 *(978-1-61714-694-7(3)*, Big Buddy Bks.) ABDO Publishing Co.

To the Rescue! 2016. (To the Rescue! Ser.). 24p. (gr. k-k). pap. 48.90 *(978-1-4824-5346-1(0))*; lib. bdg. 135.60 *(978-1-4824-4522-0(0))* Stevens, Gareth Publishing LLLP.

Tuxworth, Nicola. Things That Go. 2016. (ENG., Illus.). 20p. bds. 6.99 *(978-1-84322-752-6(5)*, Armadillo) Anness Publishing GBR. Dist: National Bk. Network.

Vehicles. 2003. (First Concepts Book Ser.). 32p. (J). 3.98 *(978-0-7525-8894-0(X))* Parragon, Inc.

Vehicles. (Cute & Cushy Ser.). 10p. (J). bds. *(978-2-7643-0207-1(X))* Phidal Publishing, Inc./Editions Phidal, Inc.

Veitch, Catherine. Big Machines Rescue!, 1 vol. 2014. (Big Machines Ser.). (ENG.). 24p. (gr. k-1). 23.32 *(978-1-4846-0588-2(8)*, Heinemann Read & Learn) Heinemann-Raintree.

Wheeler, Jill C. Alternative Cars, 1 vol. 2008. (Eye on Energy Ser.). (ENG., Illus.). 32p. (gr. k-6). 27.07 *(978-1-59928-803-1(6)*, Checkerboard Library) ABDO Publishing Co.

Will, Sandra. Transportation Inventions: From Subways to Submarines. 2006. (Which Came First? Ser.). (Illus.). 32p. (YA). (gr. 3-6). lib. bdg. 25.27 *(978-1-59716-133-6(0))* Bearport Publishing Co., Inc.

Wolfe, Jane. Pull the Lever: Who's in Here? Benham, Tors, illus. 2014. (ENG.). 8p. (J). (gr. -1-2). bds. 6.99 *(978-1-86147-394-3(X)*, Armadillo) Anness Publishing GBR. Dist: National Bk. Network.

Worms, Penny. Off-Road Vehicles. 2016. (Motormania Ser.). 32p. (gr. 2-7). 31.35 *(978-1-59920-995-1(0)*, Smart Apple Media) Black Rabbit Bks.

VEHICLES, MILITARY

ABDO Publishing Company Staff. Military Vehicles. 2011. (Military Vehicles Ser.). (Illus.). 32p. 162.42 *(978-1-61783-072-3(0)*, A&D Xtreme) ABDO Publishing Co.

Abramovitz, Melissa. Military Helicopters. 2012. (Military Machines Ser.). (ENG.). 24p. (gr. k-1). pap. 41.70 *(978-1-4296-8314-2(7)*, Pebble Plus) Capstone Press of Coughlan Cos.

—Military Trucks. 2012. (Military Machines Ser.). (ENG.). 24p. (gr. k-1). pap. 41.70 *(978-1-4296-8317-3(1)*, Pebble Plus) Capstone Press of Coughlan Cos.

—Military Vehicles. 2015. (Wild about Wheels Ser.). (ENG.). 24p. (gr. k-1). lib. bdg. 26.65 *(978-1-4914-2116-1(9)*, Pebble Plus) Capstone Press of Coughlan Cos.

Alpert, Barbara. Military Amphibious Vehicles. 2012. (Military Machines Ser.). (ENG.). 24p. (gr. k-1). pap. 41.70 *(978-1-4296-8313-5(9))*; (Illus.). lib. bdg. 26.65 *(978-1-4296-7569-7(1))* Capstone Press of Coughlan Cos. (Pebble Plus).

—Military Ships. 2012. (Military Machines Ser.). (ENG.). 24p. (gr. k-1). pap. 41.70 *(978-1-4296-8316-6(3)*, Pebble Plus) Capstone Press of Coughlan Cos.

Alvarez, Carlos. MH-53J Pave Lows. 2009. (Military Machines Ser.). (ENG., Illus.). 24p. (J). (gr. 3-7). lib. bdg. 25.95 *(978-1-60014-281-9(8))* Bellwether Media.

—Strykers. 2010. (Military Machines Ser.). (ENG., Illus.). 24p. (YA). (gr. 3-7). lib. bdg. 25.95 *(978-1-60014-496-7(9)*, Torque Bks.) Bellwether Media.

Barnhart, Norm, et al. My First Guides. 2015. (My First Guides). (ENG.). 24p. (gr. 1-2). lib. bdg. 101.28 *(978-1-4914-2554-1(7)*, First Facts) Capstone Press of Coughlan Cos.

Bell, Samantha S. Powerful Military Vehicles, 1 vol. 2014. (Ready for Military Action Ser.). (ENG.). 48p. (gr. 3-6). lib. bdg. 32.79 *(978-1-62403-654-5(6))* ABDO Publishing Co.

Bodden, Valerie. Armored Vehicles. 2012. (Illus.). 22p. (J). 25.65 *(978-1-60818-123-0(5)*, Creative Education) Creative Co., The.

Burrows, Terry. Hovercraft & Humvees: Engineering Goes to War. 2017. (STEM on the Battlefield Ser.). (ENG.). 48p. (J). (gr. 4-6). 31.99 ***(978-1-5124-3929-8(0))*** Lerner Publishing Group.

Cain, Bill & Hama, Larry. Tank of Tomorrow. 2007. (High-Tech Military Weapons Ser.). (ENG., Illus.). 48p. (J). (gr. 4-7). pap. 6.95 *(978-0-531-18710-4(1))* Scholastic Library Publishing.

Chambers, Catherine. Mighty Fighting Machines. Bustamante, Martin, illus. 2016. (Warriors! Ser.). (ENG.). 32p. (J). (gr. 3-6). lib. bdg. 26.65 *(978-1-4677-9358-2(2))* Lerner Publishing Group.

Clay, Kathryn & Vonne, Mira. My First Guide to Military Vehicles. 2015. (My First Guides). (ENG.). 24p. (gr. 1-2). lib. bdg. 25.32 *(978-1-4914-2050-8(2))* Capstone Press of Coughlan Cos.

Cohn, Jessica. Military Machines. 2013. (Machines in Motion Ser.). 48p. (J). (gr. 3-5). pap. 84.30 *(978-1-4339-9606-1(5))*; pap. 14.05 *(978-1-4339-9605-4(7))*; (ENG., Illus.). lib. bdg. 31.95 *(978-1-4339-9604-7(9))* Stevens, Gareth Publishing LLLP.

Colson, Rob Scott. Tanks & Military Vehicles. 2013. (Ultimate Machines Ser.). (ENG., Illus.). 24p. (J). (gr. 3-6). pap. 8.25 *(978-1-4777-0119-5(2))*; lib. bdg. 22.60 *(978-1-4777-0067-9(6))* Rosen Publishing Group, Inc., The. (PowerKids Pr.).

Cornish, Geoff. Battleground Support. 2004. (Military Hardware in Action Ser.). (Illus.). 48p. (J). (gr. 4-9). lib. bdg. 25.26 *(978-0-8225-4708-2(2))* Lerner Publishing Group.

—Tanks. 2003. (Military Hardware in Action Ser.). (ENG., Illus.). 48p. (gr. 5-9). lib. bdg. 25.26 *(978-0-8225-4701-3(5))* Lerner Publishing Group.

David, Jack. M2A2 Bradleys. 2009. (Military Machines Ser.). (ENG., Illus.). 24p. (J). (gr. 3-7). lib. bdg. 25.95 *(978-1-60014-261-1(3))* Bellwether Media.

—Torque: M2A2 Bradleys. 2009. (Torque Ser.). 24p. (J). (gr. 3-7). 20.00 *(978-0-531-21737-5(X)*, Children's Pr.) Scholastic Library Publishing.

—Torque - Military Machines, 4 vols., Set. Incl. Torque: B-1B Lancers. 20.00 *(978-0-531-21736-8(1))*; Torque: B-52 Stratofortresses. 20.00 *(978-0-531-21735-1(3))*; Torque: Humvees. 20.00 *(978-0-531-21734-4(5))*; Torque: M2A2 Bradleys. 20.00 *(978-0-531-21737-5(X))*; 24p. (J). (gr. 3-7). 2009. 2009. Set lib. bdg. 80.00 *(978-0-531-26137-8(9)*, Children's Pr.) Scholastic Library Publishing.

Dell, Pamela & Delmar, Peter. The Science of Military Vehicles, 1 vol. 2012. (Science of War Ser.). (ENG.). 48p. (gr. 5-6). pap. 9.10 *(978-0-7565-4525-3(0)*, CPB Grades 4-8) Compass Point Bks.

Delmar, Pete. Vehicles of the Civil War, 1 vol. 2013. (War Vehicles Ser.). (ENG.). 32p. (gr. 3-4). 27.99 *(978-1-4296-9912-9(4)*, Edge Bks.) Capstone Press of Coughlan Cos.

Doman, Mary Kate. Big Military Machines. 2011. (All about Big Machines Ser.). (Illus.). 24p. (J). (gr. -1-18). pap. 7.95 *(978-1-59845-243-3(6)*, Enslow Elementary) Enslow Pubs., Inc.

Ellis, Catherine. Cars & Trucks. 2009. (Mega Military Machines Ser.). 24p. (gr. 1-1). 42.50 *(978-1-61514-634-5(2)*, PowerKids Pr.) Rosen Publishing Group, Inc., The.

—Cars & Trucks/Autos y Camiones. 2009. (Mega Military Machines/Megamaquinas militares Ser.). (ENG & SPA.). 24p. (gr. 1-1). 42.50 *(978-1-61514-639-0(3)*, Editorial Buenas Letras) Rosen Publishing Group, Inc., The.

—Cars & Trucks/Autos y Camiones. Brusca, Maria Cristina, tr. from ENG. 2007. (Mega Military Machines / Megamaquinas Militares Ser.). (Illus.). 24p. (J). lib. bdg. 22.60 *(978-1-4042-7624-6(6)*, Editorial Buenas Letras) Rosen Publishing Group, Inc., The.

—Mega Military Machines, 6 bks., Set. Incl. Cars & Trucks. lib. bdg. 22.60 *(978-1-4042-3669-1(4))*; Helicopters. lib. bdg. 22.60 *(978-1-4042-3666-0(X))*; Planes. lib. bdg. 22.60 *(978-1-4042-3667-7(8))*; Ships. lib. bdg. 22.60 *(978-1-4042-3668-4(6))*; Submarines. lib. bdg. 22.60 *(978-1-4042-3665-3(1))*; Tanks. lib. bdg. 21.25 *(978-1-4042-3664-6(3))*; (Illus.). 24p. (J). (gr. 3-7). 2007. 2007. Set lib. bdg. 127.50 *(978-1-4042-3606-6(6))* Rosen Publishing Group, Inc., The.

Fein, Eric. Vehicles of World War II, 1 vol. 2013. (War Vehicles Ser.). (ENG.). 32p. (gr. 3-4). 27.99 *(978-1-4296-9915-0(9)*, Edge Bks.) Capstone Press of Coughlan Cos.

Fein, Eric, et al. War Vehicles. 2013. (War Vehicles Ser.). (ENG.). 32p. (gr. 3-4). lib. bdg. 139.95 *(978-1-4296-9916-7(7)*, Edge Bks.) Capstone Press of Coughlan Cos.

Finn, Denny Von. M-ATVs. 2013. (Military Vehicles Ser.). (ENG., Illus.). 24p. (J). (gr. 3-7). lib. bdg. 25.95 *(978-1-60014-943-6(X)*, Epic Bks.) Bellwether Media.

—Strykers. 2014. (Military Vehicles Ser.). (ENG., Illus.). 24p. (J). (gr. 3-7). lib. bdg. 25.95 *(978-1-62617-082-7(7)*, Epic Bks.) Bellwether Media.

Fishkin, Rebecca Love. Vehicles of the Iraq War, 1 vol. 2013. (War Vehicles Ser.). (ENG.). 32p. (gr. 3-4). 27.99 *(978-1-4296-9914-3(0)*, Edge Bks.) Capstone Press of Coughlan Cos.

T U V

Gilpin, Daniel & Pang, Alex. Military Fighting Machines. 2010. (Machines Close-Up Ser.). 32p. (J). (gr. 4-7). 28.50 (978-1-60870-109-4(3)) Marshall Cavendish Corp.

Gosman, Gillian. Simple Machines in the Military. 2014. (Simple Machines Everywhere Ser.). (Illus.). 24p. (J). (gr. k-3). pap. 8.25 (978-1-4777-6834-1(3), PowerKids Pr.) Rosen Publishing Group, Inc., The.

Hamilton, John. Cougars. 2011. (Military Vehicles Ser.). (Illus.). 32p. (YA). (gr. 4-7). 27.07 (978-1-61783-075-4(5)) ABDO Publishing Co.

—Strykers. 2011. (Military Vehicles Ser.). (Illus.). 32p. (YA). (gr. 4-7). 27.07 (978-1-61783-078-5(X)) ABDO Publishing Co.

Jackson, Kay. Armored Vehicles in Action. 2009. (Amazing Military Vehicles Ser.). 24p. (gr. 3-3). 42.50 (978-1-61511-309-5(6), PowerKids Pr.) Rosen Publishing Group, Inc., The.

Jackson, Robert. 101 Great Tanks. 2010. (101 Greatest Weapons of All Times Ser.). (Illus.). 112p. (YA). (gr. 9-12). lib. bdg. 34.60 (978-1-4358-3595-5(6)) Rosen Publishing Group, Inc., The.

Kiland, Taylor Baldwin & Souter, Gerry. Armored Tanks: Battlefield Dominance. 2015. (Military Engineering in Action Ser.). (ENG., Illus.). 48p. (J). (gr. 6-6). 27.93 (978-0-7660-6908-4(7)) Enslow Pubs., Inc.

Kiland, Taylor Baldwin & Teitelbaum, Michael. Military Humvees: Armored Mobility. 2015. (Military Engineering in Action Ser.). (ENG.). 48p. (J). (gr. 6-6). pap. 11.70 (978-0-7660-7065-3(4)) Enslow Pubs., Inc.

LaPadula, Tom & Shelly, Jeff. All about Drawing Cool Cars, Fast Planes & Military Machines: Learn How to Draw More Than 40 High-Powered Vehicles Step by Step. 2011. (All about Drawing Ser.). (ENG., Illus.). 80p. (J). (gr. 1-3). pap. 9.95 (978-1-60058-235-6(4), 1600582354) Quarto Publishing Group USA.

Levine, Michelle. Vehicles of the Vietnam War, 1 vol. 2013. (War Vehicles Ser.). (ENG.). 32p. (gr. 3-4). 27.99 (978-1-4296-9913-6(2), Edge Bks.) Capstone Press of Coughlan Cos.

Mattern, Joanne. Remote Control Planes. 2015. (Rookie Read-About(tm) Science: How Things Work Ser.). (ENG.). 32p. (J). lib. bdg. 25.00 (978-0-531-21369-8(2), Children's Pr.) Scholastic Library Publishing.

Meister, Cari. Totally Amazing Facts about Military Land Vehicles. 2017. (Mind Benders Ser.). (ENG., Illus.). 112p. (gr. 1-3). lib. bdg. 23.32 (978-1-5157-4527-3(9)) Capstone Press of Coughlan Cos.

—Totally Amazing Facts about Military Vehicles. 2017. (Mind Benders Ser.). (ENG., Illus.). 240p. (gr. 1-3). pap. 7.95 (978-1-5157-4542-6(2)) Capstone Press of Coughlan Cos.

Mighty Military Machines. 2015. (Mighty Military Machines Ser.). (ENG.). 32p. (J). (gr. 1-1). 159.60 (978-1-4824-1649-7(2)) Stevens, Gareth Publishing LLLP.

Nelson, Drew. Armored Vehicles. 2013. (Military Machines Ser.). (Illus.). 32p. (J). (gr. 3-6). pap. 10.50 (978-1-4339-8453-2(9)); lib. bdg. 26.60 (978-1-4339-8452-5(0)) Stevens, Gareth Publishing LLLP.

Parker, Steve. Military Machines. 2010. (How It Works Ser.). 40p. (J). (gr. 3-18). lib. bdg. 19.95 (978-1-4222-1797-9(3)) Mason Crest.

Peppas, Lynn. Powerful Armored Vehicles. 2011. (ENG.). 32p. (J). pap. (978-0-7787-2755-2(6)) Crabtree Publishing Co.

Riggs, Kate. Armored Vehicles. 2016. (Seedlings Ser.). (Illus.). 24p. (J). 28.50 (978-1-60818-659-4(8), Creative Education) Creative Co., The.

Schaub, Michelle. Vehicles of World War I, 1 vol. 2013. (War Vehicles Ser.). (ENG.). 32p. (gr. 3-4). 27.99 (978-1-4296-9911-2(6), Edge Bks.) Capstone Press of Coughlan Cos.

Stark, William N. Mighty Military Land Vehicles. 2016. (Military Machines on Duty Ser.). (ENG., Illus.). 24p. (gr. 1-2). lib. bdg. 25.32 (978-1-4914-8848-5(4), First Facts) Capstone Press of Coughlan Cos.

Summers, Elizabeth. Weapons & Vehicles of the Iraq War. 2015. (Tools of War Ser.). (ENG., Illus.). 32p. (gr. 1-2). lib. bdg. 26.65 (978-1-4914-4081-0(3)) Capstone Press of Coughlan Cos.

—Weapons & Vehicles of the Vietnam War. 2015. (Tools of War Ser.). (ENG., Illus.). 32p. (gr. 1-2). lib. bdg. 26.65 (978-1-4914-4082-7(1)) Capstone Press of Coughlan Cos.

—Weapons & Vehicles of World War I. 2015. (Tools of War Ser.). (ENG., Illus.). 32p. (gr. 1-2). lib. bdg. 26.65 (978-1-4914-4095-7(3)) Capstone Press of Coughlan Cos.

—Weapons & Vehicles of World War II. 2015. (Tools of War Ser.). (ENG., Illus.). 32p. (gr. 1-2). lib. bdg. 26.65 (978-1-4914-4080-3(5)) Capstone Press of Coughlan Cos.

Turner, Tracy. Weapons of War. 2015. (Head-To-Head Ser.). (ENG., Illus.). 24p. (gr. 3-8). 28.50 (978-1-62588-151-9(7)) Black Rabbit Bks.

Walter Foster Creative Team. Learn to Draw Cars, Planes & Moving Machines: Step-By-Step Instructions for More Than 25 High-Powered Vehicles. LaPadula, Tom & Shelly, Jeff, illus. 2015. (Learn to Draw: Expanded Edition Ser.). (ENG.). 64p. (J). (gr. 3-5). 33.32 (978-1-939581-69-3(9)) Quarto Publishing Group USA.

VELAZQUEZ, DIEGO, 1599-1660

Venezia, Mike. Diego Velázquez. Venezia, Mike, illus. 2004. (Getting to Know the World's Greatest Artists Ser.). (ENG., Illus.). 32p. (J). (gr. 3-4). pap. 6.95 (978-0-516-26980-1(1), Children's Pr.) Scholastic Library Publishing.

VELAZQUEZ, DIEGO, 1599-1660—FICTION

de Trevino, Elizabeth Borton. I, Juan de Pareja. 3rd ed. pap. 3.95 (978-0-13-800129-2(4)) Prentice Hall (Schl. Div.).

—I, Juan de Pareja. 2008. (ENG.). 192p. (YA). (gr. 7-12). pap. 7.99 (978-0-312-38005-2(4), 9780312380052) Square Fish.

—I, Juan de Pareja. l.t. ed. 2005. 244p. 20.95 (978-0-7862-7666-0(5)) Thorndike Pr.

I, Juan de Pareja. 3rd ed. (J). pap., stu. ed. (978-0-13-667452-8(6)) Prentice Hall (Schl. Div.).

Mayhew, James. Katie & the Spanish Princess. 2015. (Katie Ser.). (ENG., Illus.). 32p. (J). (gr. -1-k). pap. 11.99 (978-1-4083-3242-9(6)) Hodder & Stoughton GBR. Dist: Hachette Bk. Group.

VELOCITY

see Speed

VENEREAL DISEASES

see Sexually Transmitted Diseases

VENEZUELA

Baguley, Kitt. Venezuela, 1 vol. 2009. (ENG., Illus.). 288p. pap. 17.99 (978-0-7614-5569-1(8), Cavendish Children's Bks.) Marshall Cavendish Corp.

Crooker, Richard A. Venezuela. Gritzner, Charles F., ed. 2006. (Modern World Nations Ser.). (Illus.). 114p. (gr. 6-12). lib. bdg. 35.00 (978-0-7910-8834-0(0)) Facts On File, Inc.

Dawson, Mike. Growing up Yanomamö: Missionary Adventures in the Amazon Rainforest. Pintor, Ruben, illus. 2009. (ENG.). 336p. (J). pap. 19.95 (978-1-60265-009-1(8)) Grace Acres Pr.

Dillon, Doug. We Visit Venezuela. 2010. (Your Land & My Land Ser.). (Illus.). 64p. (J). (gr. 3-6). lib. bdg. 33.95 (978-1-58415-884-4(0)) Mitchell Lane Pubs., Inc.

Doeden, Matt. Miguel Cabrera: Baseball Superstar, 1 vol. 2014. (Superstar Athletes Ser.). (ENG.). 24p. (gr. 1-2). lib. bdg. 25.32 (978-1-4765-8602-1(0)) Capstone Press of Coughlan Cos.

Flynn, Brendan. Miguel Cabrera: MVP & Triple Crown Winner. 2015. (Today's MVPs & Champions Ser.). (ENG.). 24p. (J). (gr. 2-5). 27.07 (978-1-63143-736-6(4), 208572) Child's World, Inc., The.

Gagne, Tammy. The Evolution of Government & Politics in Venezuela. 2014. (gr. 4-8). 29.95 (978-1-61228-582-5(1)) Mitchell Lane Pubs., Inc.

Jones, Helga. Venezuela. (Country Explorers Ser.). (Illus.). 48p. (gr. 2-4). 2008. (ENG.). lib. bdg. 29.27 (978-0-8225-8663-0(0)) 2005. lib. bdg. 22.60 (978-1-57505-146-8(X)) Lerner Publishing Group.

Mattern, Joanne. Cataratas Ángel. 2004. (Maravillas Naturales (Natures Greatest Hits) Ser.). (SPA.). 24p. (J). (gr. 2-4). lib. bdg. 22.60 (978-0-8239-6878-7(2)) Rosen Publishing Group, Inc., The.

Ng, Yumi. Welcome to Venezuela. 2004. (Welcome to My Country Ser.). (Illus.). 48p. (gr. 2-5). lib. bdg. 27.00 (978-0-8368-3123-8(3)) Stevens, Gareth Publishing LLLP.

Patterson, Irania & McElvane, Catherine. Wings & Dreams (Alas y Suenos) The Legend of Angel Falls (La Leyenda del Salto Angel) 2010. (ENG & SPA.). 40p. (J). (gr. 1-3). 19.95 (978-0-9815192-4-1(5)) Novello Festival Pr.

Pohl, Kathleen. Looking at Venezuela. 2008. (Looking at Countries Ser.). (Illus.). 32p. (gr. 1-5). (J). lib. bdg. 26.00 (978-0-8368-9074-7(4)); pap. 10.50 (978-0-8368-9075-4(2)) Stevens, Gareth Publishing LLLP. (Gareth Stevens Learning Library).

Rauf, Don. Miguel Cabrera: Triple Crown Winner. 2015. (Living Legends of Sports Ser.). (ENG., Illus.). 48p. (J). (gr. 5-6). 25.85 (978-1-68048-094-8(4), Britannica Educational Publishing) Rosen Publishing Group, Inc., The.

Shields, Charles J. Venezuela. (South America Today Ser.). 2009. (Illus.). 63p. (J). (gr. 4-7). 21.95 (978-1-4222-0643-0(2)) 2007. 64p. (YA). (gr. 7-18). pap. 9.95 (978-1-4222-0710-9(2)) Mason Crest.

Wardrope, William. Venezuela. 2003. (Countries of the World Ser.). (Illus.). 96p. (gr. 5-12). lib. bdg. 31.00 (978-0-8368-2369-1(9)) Stevens, Gareth Publishing LLLP.

Watson, Galadriel. Angel Falls. 2005. (Natural Wonders of the U. S. A. Ser.). (Illus.). 32p. (J). (gr. 4-7). per. 9.95 (978-1-59036-273-0(X)) Weigl Pubs., Inc.

Watson, Galadriel Findlay. Angel Falls. 2013. (J). 28.55 (978-1-62127-472-8(1)) Weigl Pubs., Inc.

—Angel Falls: The Largest Waterfall in the World. 2004. (Illus.). 32p. (J). lib. bdg. 26.00 (978-1-59036-267-9(5)) Weigl Pubs., Inc.

Willis, Terri. Venezuela. 2003. (Enchantment of the World Ser.). (ENG., Illus.). 144p. (YA). (gr. 5-9). 37.00 (978-0-516-24214-9(8), Children's Pr.) Scholastic Library Publishing.

VENEZUELA—FICTION

Carney, Lacy & Robey, Samantha. The Last Name Banks. 2012. 148p. (J). pap. 11.99 (978-0-9856863-1-4(6)) FireFly Lights.

Cowcher, Helen. Jaguar. (J). (gr. 1-2). (978-0-590-36037-1(X)); (SPA., Illus.). pap. 3.96 net. (978-0-590-87599-8(X), SO30738, Scholastic Pr.) Scholastic, Inc.

Ficklin, Jonene H. Orinoco Intrigue. 2005. (YA). 14.95 (978-0-9761188-1-7(5)) Victor's Crown Publishing.

L'Engle, Madeleine. Dragons in the Waters. 2011. (ENG.). 320p. (YA). (gr. 6-10). pap. 11.99 (978-0-312-67442-7(2), 9780312674427) Square Fish.

Paterson Jr., John B. & Paterson Sr, John B. Roberto's Trip to the Top. Alarcao, Renato, illus. 2010. (ENG.). 40p. (J). (gr. -1-3). pap. 6.99 (978-0-7636-4755-1(1)) Candlewick Pr.

VENEZUELA—HISTORY

Cunill, Pedro. Venezuela II. (Biblioteca Iberoamericana Ser.). (SPA., Illus.). 128p. (978-84-207-3096-7(3), BI-2036) Grupo Anaya, S.A.

Doeden, Matt. Miguel Cabrera: Baseball Superstar, 1 vol. 2014. (Superstar Athletes Ser.). (ENG.). 24p. (gr. 1-2). pap. 7.29 (978-1-4765-9431-6(7)) Capstone Press of Coughlan Cos.

Fishman, Jon M. Miguel Cabrera. 2013. (Amazing Athletes Ser.). (ENG., Illus.). 32p. (gr. 2-5). pap. 7.95 (978-1-4677-1559-1(X)) Lerner Publishing Group.

Gibson, Karen Bush. Venezuela. 2009. (J). (978-1-58415-791-5(7)) Mitchell Lane Pubs., Inc.

Houser, Aimee. Venezuela, 1 vol. 2011. (Countries of the World Set 1 Ser.). (ENG., Illus.). 144p. (J). (gr. 6-12). lib. bdg. 37.07 (978-1-61783-120-1(4)) ABDO Publishing Co.

Jones, Helga. Venezuela. 2008. pap. 40.95 (978-0-8225-9308-9(4)) Lerner Publishing Group.

Mattern, Joanne. Angel Falls: World's Highest Waterfall. 2009. (Nature's Greatest Hits Ser.). 24p. (gr. 2-2). 42.50 (978-1-61514-837-0(X), PowerKids Pr.) Rosen Publishing Group, Inc., The.

—Cataratas Ángel: Las cataratas más altas del mundo (Angel Falls: World's Highest Waterfall) 2009. (Maravillas naturales (Natures Greatest Hits) Ser.). (SPA.). 24p. (gr. 2-2). 42.50 (978-1-61514-362-7(9), Editorial Buenas Letras) Rosen Publishing Group, Inc., The.

Pohl, Kathleen & Nations, Susan. Descubramos Venezuela. 2008. (Descubramos países del mundo (Looking at Countries) Ser.). (SPA.). 32p. (gr. 1-5). (J). lib. bdg. 26.00 (978-0-8368-9076-1(0)); pap. 10.50 (978-0-8368-9077-8(9)) Stevens, Gareth Publishing LLLP. (Gareth Stevens Learning Library).

Schuetz, Kari. Venezuela. 2012. (Exploring Countries Ser.). (ENG., Illus.). 32p. (J). (gr. 3-7). lib. bdg. 26.95 (978-1-60014-735-7(6), Blastoff! Readers) Bellwether Media.

Shields, Charles J. Venezuela, Vol. 13. Henderson, James D., ed. 2015. (Discovering South America: History, Politics, & Culture Ser.). (Illus.). 64p. (J). (gr. 7). lib. bdg. 22.95 (978-1-4222-3306-1(5)) Mason Crest.

Watson, Galadriel Findlay. Angel Falls. 2013. (J). pap. 13.95 (978-1-62127-478-0(0)) Weigl Pubs., Inc.

Willis, Terri. Venezuela. 2013. (Enchantment of the World™, Second Ser.). (ENG.). 144p. (J). 40.00 (978-0-531-25604-6(9), Children's Pr.) Scholastic Library Publishing.

VENICE (ITALY)

Kids Go Europe: Treasure Hunt Venice. 2006. (J). spiral bd. 9.95 (978-0-9772699-0-7(6)) Kids Go Europe, Inc.

Rossi, Renzo. Venice. 2004. (Great Cities Through the Ages Ser.). (Illus.). 44p. (J). (gr. 5). 18.95 (978-1-59270-014-1(4)) Enchanted Lion Bks., LLC.

Sasek, M. This Is Venice. 2005. (ENG., Illus.). 64p. (J). (gr. 2-12). 17.95 (978-0-7893-1223-5(9)) Universe Publishing.

VENICE (ITALY)—FICTION

Baucom, Ian. Through the Skylight. Gerard, Justin, illus. (ENG.). 400p. (J). (gr. 4-8). 2014. pap. 6.99 (978-1-4424-8167-1(6)) 2013. 17.99 (978-1-4169-1777-9(2)) Simon & Schuster Children's Publishing. (Atheneum Bks. for Young Readers).

Christopher, Nicholas. The True Adventures of Nicolo Zen. 2014. (ENG.). 304p. (YA). (gr. 7). 17.99 (978-0-375-86738-5(4), Knopf Bks. for Young Readers) Random Hse. Children's Bks.

Collins, Pat Lowery. Hidden Voices: The Orphan Musicians of Venice. 2009. (ENG., Illus.). 352p. (YA). (gr. 7). 17.99 (978-0-7636-3917-4(6)) Candlewick Pr.

Cowling, Douglas. Vivaldi's Ring of Mystery. Fernandez, Laura & Jacobson, Rick, illus. 2004. (ENG.). 44p. (J). (978-0-439-96904-8(2), North Winds Pr) Scholastic Canada, Ltd.

Demi. Marco Polo, 0 vols. 2008. (ENG., Illus.). 56p. (J). (gr. 4-7). 19.99 (978-0-7614-5433-5(0), 9780761454335, Amazon Children's Publishing) Amazon Publishing.

Funke, Cornelia. The Thief Lord. 2004.Tr. of Herr der Diebe. 376p. (J). (gr. 5-18). pap. 44.00 incl. audio (978-0-8072-2278-2(X), Listening Library) Random Hse. Audio Publishing Group.

—The Thief Lord. 2003.Tr. of Herr der Diebe. (gr. 3-6). 18.40 (978-0-613-84572-4(2), Turtleback) Turtleback Bks.

Gregory, Philippa. Fools' Gold. van Deelen, Fred, illus. 2014. (Order of Darkness Ser.: 3). (ENG.). 384p. (YA). (gr. 9). pap. 9.99 (978-1-4424-7691-2(5)); 19.99 (978-1-4424-7690-5(7)) Simon Pulse. (Simon Pulse).

Hemphill, Stephanie. Sisters of Glass. 2013. (ENG.). 160p. (YA). (gr. 7). pap. 7.99 (978-0-307-98141-7(X), Ember) Random Hse. Children's Bks.

Henty, George Alfred. The Lion of Saint Mark: A Story of Venice in the Fourteenth Century. 2007. (ENG.). 310p. pap. 23.99 (978-1-4346-1158-1(2)); 346p. pap. 24.99 (978-1-4346-1229-8(5)) Creative Media Partners, LLC.

Higgins, Jack & Richards, Justin. Death Run. 2009. (Rich & Jade Ser.: Bk. 2). (ENG.). 288p. (YA). (gr. 7-18). 8.99 (978-0-14-241475-0(1), Speak) Penguin Young Readers Group.

Lovric, Michelle. The Undrowned Child. 2012. (ENG.). 464p. (J). (gr. 5). 7.99 (978-0-375-86597-8(7), Yearling) Random Hse. Children's Bks.

Monks, Julie. Let's Read! Marcello Mouse & the Masked Ball, 7. 2014. (Let's Read! Ser.). (ENG., Illus.). 32p. (J). (gr. k-2). pap. 7.99 (978-1-4472-3695-5(5)) Pan Macmillan GBR. Dist: Independent Pubs. Group.

Napoli, Donna Jo. Daughter of Venice. 2003. (ENG.). 288p. (YA). (gr. 7). mass mkt. 7.99 (978-0-440-22928-5(6), Laurel Leaf) Random Hse. Children's Bks.

Osborne, Mary Pope. Carnival at Candlelight. Murdocca, Sal, illus. 2006. (Magic Tree House Merlin Mission Ser.: 5). (ENG.). 144p. (J). (gr. 2-5). 5.99 (978-0-375-83034-1(0), Random Hse. Bks. for Young Readers) Random Hse. Children's Bks.

Osborne, Mary Pope & PLC Editors Staff. Carnival at Candlelight. Murdocca, Sal, illus. 2006. (Magic Tree House Merlin Missions Ser.: No. 5). 105p. (gr. 2-6). 15.00 (978-0-7569-6690-4(6)) Perfection Learning Corp.

Papa Piccolo: Evaluation Guide. 2006. (J). 17.95 (978-1-55942-419-6(2)) Witcher Productions.

Paris, Harper. The Mystery of the Mosaic. Calo, Marcos, illus. 2014. (Greetings from Somewhere Ser.: 2). (ENG.). 128p. (J). (gr. k-2). pap. 5.99 (978-1-4424-9721-4(1), Little Simon) Little Simon.

Rabley, Stephen. Marcel & the Mona Lisa. 2nd ed. 2009. (ENG., Illus.). 20p. pap. 11.99 (978-1-4058-6955-3(0)) Pearson Education.

Renek, Nava. Venice Is for Cats. 2013. (Illus.). pap. 20.00 (978-0-923389-53-6(9)) Spuyten Duyvil Publishing.

Shefelman, Janice Jordan. Anna Maria's Gift. Papp, Robert, illus. 2011. (Stepping Stone Book Ser.). (ENG.). 112p. (J). (gr. 2-5). pap. 4.99 (978-0-375-85882-6(2), Random Hse. Bks. for Young Readers) Random Hse. Children's Bks.

Stevenson, Steve. The Crown of Venice, No. 7. Turconi, Stefano, illus. 2014. (Agatha: Girl of Mystery Ser.: 7). (ENG.). 144p. (J). (gr. 2-5). 5.99 (978-0-448-46225-7(7), Grosset & Dunlap) Penguin Young Readers Group.

Stilton, Geronimo. The Mystery in Venice. 2012. (Geronimo Stilton Ser.: Bk. 48). (ENG.). 128p. (J). (gr. 2-5). pap. 7.99 (978-0-545-34097-7(7), Scholastic Paperbacks) Scholastic, Inc.

—The Mystery in Venice. 2012. (Geronimo Stilton Ser.: 48). lib. bdg. 18.40 (978-0-606-23729-1(1), Turtleback) Turtleback Bks.

—Who Stole the Mona Lisa? Cooper-McGuinness, Nanette, tr. 2010. (Geronimo Stilton Graphic Novels Ser.). (ENG., Illus.). 56p. (J). (gr. 2-6). 9.99 (978-1-59707-221-2(4), 9781597072212) Papercutz.

Warner, Emilia & Garland, Peter. Micia. 2007. (ENG.). 56p. 20.25 (978-1-905299-39-3(7), Stacey International) Stacey Publishing GBR. Dist: Casemate Pubs. & Bk. Distributors, LLC.

Woodford, Pamela. Lilly & Harry. 2013. (Brighter Little Minds Ser.). (ENG., Illus.). 24p. (J). pap. 10.95 (978-1-871305-79-1(9)) Orpen Pr. IRL. Dist: Dufour Editions, Inc.

VENICE (ITALY)—HISTORY

Candlewick Press, Candlewick. Venice: a 3D Keepsake Cityscape. McMenemy, Sarah, illus. 2014. (Panorama Pops Ser.). (ENG.). 20p. (J). (gr. k-4). 8.99 (978-0-7636-7186-0(X)) Candlewick Pr.

Dyan, Penelope. Marco Polo Was Here! a Kid's Guide to Venice, Italy. Weigand, John D., photos by. 2009. (Illus.). 42p. pap. 11.95 (978-1-935118-69-5(2)) Bellissima Publishing, LLC.

Naughton, Diane. Venice: The Floating City. 2014. (ENG., Illus.). 28p. (J). pap. 9.50 (978-1-107-62163-3(1)) Cambridge Univ. Pr.

Verzov, Ella & Oirechman, Chana. Tamar of Venice. 2013. (Illus.). 54p. (J). (978-1-61465-170-3(1)) Menucha Pubs. Inc.

VENOM

see Poisons

VENUS (PLANET)

Adamson, Thomas K. Do You Really Want to Visit Venus? Fabbri, Daniele, illus. 2013. (Do You Really Want to Visit... ? Ser.). (ENG.). 24p. (gr. 1-4). 27.10 (978-1-60753-196-8(8)) Amicus Publishing.

—Venus [Scholastic]: Revised Edition. 2010. (Exploring the Galaxy Ser.). (ENG.). 24p. pap. 0.49 (978-1-4296-5816-4(9), Pebble Plus) Capstone Press of Coughlan Cos.

Asimov, Isaac & Hantula, Richard. Venus. Porras, Carlos & D'Andrea, Patricia, trs. from ENG. 2003. (Isaac Asimov's Biblioteca del Universo del Siglo XXI). (SPA., Illus.). 32p. (gr. 2-6). lib. bdg. 26.00 (978-0-8368-3864-0(5), Gareth Stevens Learning Library) Stevens, Gareth Publishing LLLP.

Berne, Emma Carlson. The Secrets of Venus. 2015. (Planets Ser.). (ENG., Illus.). 32p. (gr. 2-4). lib. bdg. 31.99 (978-1-4914-5870-9(4)) Capstone Press of Coughlan Cos.

Bjorklund, Ruth. Venus. 2009. (Space!). 64p. (gr. 5-18). lib. bdg. 32.79 (978-0-7614-4251-6(0)) Marshall Cavendish Corp.

Bloom, J. P. Venus, 1 vol. 2014. (Planets Ser.). (ENG.). 24p. (J). (gr. 2-4). lib. bdg. 28.50 (978-1-62970-722-8(8)) ABDO Publishing Co.

Carson, Mary Kay. Far-Out Guide to Venus. 2010. (Far-Out Guide to the Solar System Ser.). 48p. (J). (gr. 2-5). 25.27 (978-0-7660-3181-4(0)); (Illus.). pap. 8.95 (978-1-59845-182-5(0), Enslow Elementary) Enslow Pubs., Inc.

Chrismer, Melanie. Venus. 2007. (Scholastic News Nonfiction Readers Ser.). (ENG., Illus.). 24p. (J). (gr. 1-2). 22.00 (978-0-531-14755-9(X)) Scholastic Library Publishing.

Dickmann, Nancy. Exploring the Inner Planets. 2015. (Spectacular Space Science Ser.). (ENG., Illus.). 48p. (J). (gr. 5-6). 30.25 (978-1-4994-3629-7(7), Rosen Central) Rosen Publishing Group, Inc., The.

Dunn, Mary R. A Look at Venus. (Astronomy Now! Ser.). 24p. (gr. 2-3). 2009. 42.50 (978-1-61511-475-7(0), PowerKids Pr.) 2007. (Illus.). (YA). lib. bdg. 22.60 (978-1-4042-3826-8(3)) Rosen Publishing Group, Inc., The.

Feinstein, Stephen. Venus: A MyReportLinks. com Book. 2005. (Solar System Ser.). (Illus.). 48p. (J). lib. bdg. 26.60 (978-0-7660-5300-7(8), MyReportLinks.com Bks.) Enslow Pubs., Inc.

Fleisher, Paul. Venus. 2009. (Early Bird Astronomy Ser.). (ENG.). 48p. (gr. 2-5). lib. bdg. 26.60 (978-0-7613-4151-2(X)) Lerner Publishing Group.

Goldstein, Margaret J. Venus. 2003. (Our Universe Ser.). (ENG., Illus.). 32p. (gr. 2-4). lib. bdg. 22.60 (978-0-8225-4649-8(3)) Lerner Publishing Group.

Hollar, Sherman. The Inner Planets: Mercury, Venus, & Mars. 2011. (Illus.). 96p. (J). 31.70 (978-1-61530-512-4(2)) Rosen Publishing Group, Inc., The.

Howard, Fran. Venus, 1 vol. 2007. (Planets Ser.). (ENG.). 32p. (gr. 3-7). 27.07 (978-1-59928-824-6(9), Buddy Bks.) ABDO Publishing Co.

James, Lincoln. Venus: The Masked Planet. 2010. (Our Solar System Ser.). 24p. (J). (gr. k-3). (ENG.). pap. 8.15 (978-1-4339-3846-7(4)); (Illus.). lib. bdg. 22.60 (978-1-4339-3845-0(6)) Stevens, Gareth Publishing LLLP.

Jefferis, David. Hot Planets: Mercury & Venus. 2008. (ENG., Illus.). 32p. (J). (gr. 3-7). pap. (978-0-7787-3751-3(9)) Crabtree Publishing Co.

Kazunas, Ariel. Venus. 2011. (21st Century Junior Library: Solar System Ser.). (ENG.). 24p. (gr. 2-5). lib. bdg. 25.64 (978-1-61080-085-3(0), 201080) Cherry Lake Publishing.

Land-Sailing Venus Rover: Meet NASA Inventor Geoffrey Landis & His Team's. 2017. (J). **(978-0-7166-6160-3(8))** World Bk., Inc.

Lawrence, Ellen. Venus: The Hot & Toxic Planet. 2013. (Zoom into Space Ser.). 24p. (J). (gr. -1-3). lib. bdg. 23.93 (978-1-909673-04-5(8)) Ruby Tuesday Books Limited GBR. Dist: Bearport Publishing Co., Inc.

Margaret, Amy. Venus. 2009. (Library of the Planets Ser.). 24p. (gr. 3-3). 42.50 (978-1-60853-920-8(2), PowerKids Pr.) Rosen Publishing Group, Inc., The.

Oldfield, Dawn Bluemel. Venus: Super Hot. 2015. (Out of This World Ser.). (ENG.). 24p. (J). (gr. -1-3). lib. bdg. 23.93 (978-1-62724-562-3(6)) Bearport Publishing Co., Inc.

—Venus: Supercaliente. 2015. (Fuera de Este Mundo Ser.). (SPA., Illus.). 24p. (J). (gr. -1-3). lib. bdg. 23.93 (978-1-62724-599-9(5)) Bearport Publishing Co., Inc.

Orme, Helen & Orme, David. Let's Explore Venus. 2007. (Space Launch! Ser.). 24p. (gr. 1-4). pap. 8.15 (978-0-8368-8135-6(4)); (Illus.). lib. bdg. 23.00 (978-0-8368-7950-6(3)) Stevens, Gareth Publishing LLLP. (Gareth Stevens Learning Library).

Owen, Ruth. Venus. 2013. (Explore Outer Space Ser.). 32p. (J). (gr. 3-6). pap. 10.00 (978-1-61533-763-7(6)); pap. 60.00 (978-1-61533-764-4(4)); lib. bdg. 25.25 (978-1-61533-723-1(7)) Windmill Bks.

Owens, L. L. Venus. McGeehan, Dan, illus. 2011. (Space Neighbors Ser.). (ENG.). 32p. (J). (gr. 1-4). lib. bdg. 27.07 (978-1-60954-390-7(4), 200884) Child's World, Inc., The.

Renfield, R. K. Venus. (Library of Planets Ser.). 2009. 48p. (gr. 5-8). 55.90 (978-1-60853-823-2(0), Rosen Reference) 2006. (J). 29.25 (978-1-4042-1968-7(4)) Rosen Publishing Group, Inc., The.

Ring, Susan. Venus. (J). 2013. (978-1-62127-270-0(2)) 2013. pap. (978-1-62127-279-3(6)) 2004. (Illus.). pap. 8.95

(978-1-59036-223-5(3)) 2004. (Illus.). 24p. (gr. 4-7). lib. bdg. 24.45 (978-1-59036-096-5(6)) Weigl Pubs., Inc.
Ring, Susan & Roumanis, Alexis. Venus. 2016. (Illus.). 24p. (J). (978-1-5105-0995-5(X)) SmartBook Media, Inc.
Romero, Libby. Discover Mars & Venus. 2006. (J). pap. (978-1-4108-6507-6(X)) Benchmark Education Co.
—Mars & Venus. 2006. (J). pap. (978-1-4108-6504-5(5)) Benchmark Education Co.
Roumanis, Alexis. Venus. 2016. (J). **(978-1-5105-2059-2(7))** SmartBook Media, Inc.
—Venus. 2015. (J). (978-1-4896-3308-8(1)) Weigl Pubs., Inc.
Sexton, Colleen. Venus. 2010. (Exploring Space Ser.). (ENG., Illus.). 24p. (J). (gr. k-3). lib. bdg. 25.95 (978-1-60014-403-5(9), Blastoff! Readers) Bellwether Media.
Snyder, J. M. Journey to Venus, 1 vol. 2014. (Spotlight on Space Science Ser.). (ENG.). 32p. (J). (gr. 5-5). pap. 11.75 (978-1-4994-0380-0(1), PowerKids Pr.) Rosen Publishing Group, Inc., The.
Sparrow, Giles. Destination Venus. 32p. (J). 2010. (Illus.). pap. 10.00 (978-1-4358-3457-6(7)) 2009. (ENG.). lib. bdg. 25.25 (978-1-4358-3442-2(9)) Rosen Publishing Group, Inc., The. (PowerKids Pr.).
Steinkraus, Kyla. Rocky Planets: Mercury, Venus, Earth, & Mars. 2014. (ENG.). 24p. (gr. k-3). 28.50 (978-1-62717-727-6(2)) Rourke Educational Media.
Taylor-Butler, Christine. Planet Venus. 2014. (True Book(tm), A — Space Ser.). (ENG.). 48p. (J). lib. bdg. 31.00 (978-0-531-21159-5(2)) Scholastic Library Publishing.
Teitelbaum, Michael. Mars & Venus Space Exploration: Set Of 6. 2011. (Navigators Ser.). (J). pap. 50.00 net. (978-1-4108-6243-3(7)) Benchmark Education Co.
Thomas, Isabel. Mercury & Venus, 1 vol. 2012. (Astronaut Travel Guides). (ENG.). 48p. (gr. 3-6). lib. bdg. 32.65 (978-1-4109-4571-6(5), NA-r) Heinemann-Raintree.
Venus. 2nd rev. ed. 2008. (New Solar System Ser.). 32p. (YA). (gr. 3-6). 23.00 (978-1-60413-209-0(4)) Facts On File, Inc.
Wimmer, Teresa. Venus. 2007. (My First Look at: Planets Ser.). (Illus.). 24p. (J). (gr. -1-3). lib. bdg. 24.25 (978-1-58341-524-5(6), Creative Education) Creative Co., The.
World Book, contrib. by. Mercury & Venus. 2nd ed. 2006. (World Book's Solar System & Space Exploration Library). (Illus.). 64p. (J). (978-0-7166-9517-2(0)) World Bk., Inc.
World Book, Inc. Staff, contrib. by. Mercury & Venus. 2006. (World Book's Solar System & Space Exploration Library). (Illus.). 63p. (J). (978-0-7166-9502-8(2)) World Bk., Inc.
World Book, Inc Staff, contrib. by. Mercury & Venus. 2010. (J). (978-0-7166-9534-9(0)) World Bk., Inc.
Zuchora-Walske, Christine. Your Mission to Venus, 1 vol. 2011. (Planets Ser.). (ENG., Illus.). 32p. (J). (gr. k-3). 28.50 (978-1-61641-684-3(X)) Magic Wagon.

VERDI, GIUSEPPE, 1813-1901

Bauer, Helen. Verdi for Kids: His Life & Music with 21 Activities. 2013. (For Kids Ser.). (ENG., Illus.). 144p. (J). (gr. 4). pap. 16.95 (978-1-61374-500-7(1)) Chicago Review Pr., Inc.
Schoell, William. Giuseppe Verdi & Italian Opera. 2007. (Classical Composers Ser.). (Illus.). 128p. (J). (gr. 3-7). lib. bdg. 27.95 (978-1-59935-041-7(6)) Reynolds, Morgan Inc.
Snowman, Daniel. Giuseppe Verdi: Composer. 2016. (History Makers Ser.). 144p. (J). 45.64 (978-1-5026-2449-9(4)) Cavendish Square Publishing.
Whiting, Jim. The Life & Times of Guiseppe Verdi. 2004. (Masters of Music Ser.). (Illus.). 48p. (gr. 4-8). lib. bdg. 20.95 (978-1-58415-281-1(8)) Mitchell Lane Pubs., Inc.

VERMEER, JOHANNES, 1632-1675

Mis, Melody S. Vermeer. 2009. (Meet the Artist Ser.). 24p. (gr. 2-3). 42.50 (978-1-61514-633-8(4), PowerKids Pr.) Rosen Publishing Group, Inc., The.
Raczka, Bob. The Vermeer Interviews: Conversations with Seven Works of Art. 2010. (Bob Raczka's Art Adventures Ser.). (ENG.). 32p. (gr. 3-12). pap. 9.95 (978-1-58013-882-6(9), First Avenue Editions) Lerner Publishing Group.
Wood, Alix. Johannes Vermeer. 2013. (Artists Through the Ages Ser.). (ENG., Illus.). 32p. (J). (gr. 3-6). pap. 10.00 (978-1-61533-633-3(8)); lib. bdg. 25.25 (978-1-61533-623-4(0)) Windmill Bks.

VERMONT

Adam, Sarah E., illus. Abby in Vermont Coloring & Activity Book. 2008. 32p. (J). 4.95 (978-0-9793790-1-7(6)) Howard Printing, Inc.
Brown, Jonatha A. Vermont. 2006. (Portraits of the States Ser.). 32p. (gr. 2-6). pap. 10.50 (978-0-8368-4727-7(X)); (Illus.). lib. bdg. 26.00 (978-0-8368-4710-9(5)) Stevens, Gareth Publishing LLLP. (Gareth Stevens Learning Library).
Czech, Jan M. Vermont. 2008. (ENG.). 80p. (J). pap. 7.95 (978-0-531-20816-8(8), Children's Pr.) Scholastic Library Publishing.
Dornfeld, Margaret. Vermont. 2005. (It's My State! Ser.). (Illus.). 80p. (J). (gr. 4-7). lib. bdg. 27.07 (978-0-7614-1864-1(4), Benchmark Bks.) Marshall Cavendish Corp.
Dupeyron, Sarah, illus. The ABC's of Vermont Coloring Book. 2007. 32p. (J). 4.95 (978-0-9793790-0-0(8)) Howard Printing, Inc.
Elish, Dan. Vermont. 2nd rev. ed. 2005. (Celebrate the States Ser.). (Illus.). 144p. (gr. 6-7). lib. bdg. 42.79 (978-0-7614-2018-7(5), Benchmark Bks.) Marshall Cavendish Corp.
Hassig, Susan M. & Quek, Lynette. Panama. 2nd rev. ed. 2006. (Cultures of the World Ser.). (Illus.). 144p. (gr. 6-7). lib. bdg. 42.79 (978-0-7614-2028-6(2), Benchmark Bks.) Marshall Cavendish Corp.
Keizer, Garret, et al, contrib. by. The Twelve Seasons of Vermont: A Vermont Life Book. 2005. (Illus.). 112p. 34.95 (978-1-931389-07-5(1)) Vermont Life Magazine.
Marsh, Carole. Vermont Current Events Projects: 30 Cool, Activities, Crafts, Experiments & More for Kids to Do to Learn about Your State! 2003. (Vermont Experience Ser.). 32p. (gr. k-5). pap. 5.95 (978-0-635-02065-9(3), Marsh, Carole Bks.) Gallopade International.
—Vermont Geography Projects: 30 Cool, Activities, Crafts, Experiments & More for Kids to Do to Learn about Your State! 2003. (Vermont Experience Ser.). 32p. (gr. k-5). pap. 5.95 (978-0-635-01863-2(2), Marsh, Carole Bks.) Gallopade International.
—Vermont Government Projects: 30 Cool, Activities, Crafts, Experiments & More for Kids to Do to Learn about Your State! 2003. (Vermont Experience Ser.). 32p. (gr. k-5). pap. 5.95 (978-0-635-01964-6(7), Marsh, Carole Bks.) Gallopade International.
—Vermont People Projects: 30 Cool, Activities, Crafts, Experiments & More for Kids to Do to Learn about Your State! 2003. (Vermont Experience Ser.). 32p. (gr. k-5). pap. 5.95 (978-0-635-02014-7(9), Marsh, Carole Bks.) Gallopade International.
—Vermont Symbols & Facts Projects: 30 Cool, Activities, Crafts, Experiments & More for Kids to Do to Learn about Your State! 2003. (Vermont Experience Ser.). 32p. (gr. k-5). pap. 5.95 (978-0-635-01914-1(0), Marsh, Carole Bks.) Gallopade International.
Murray, Julie. Vermont, 1 vol. 2006. (Buddy Book Ser.). (ENG., Illus.). 32p. (gr. 2-4). 27.07 (978-1-59197-704-9(5), Buddy Bks.) ABDO Publishing Co.
Parker, Bridget. Vermont. 2016. (States Ser.). (ENG., Illus.). 32p. (gr. 3-4). lib. bdg. 27.32 (978-1-5157-0433-1(5)) Next Page Pr., The.
Peters, S. True. How to Draw Vermont's Sights & Symbols. 2009. (Kid's Guide to Drawing America Ser.). 32p. (gr. k-k). 50.50 (978-1-61511-101-5(8), PowerKids Pr.) Rosen Publishing Group, Inc., The.
Schaffer, David. Vermont: A MyReportLinks.com Book. 2003. (States Ser.). (Illus.). 48p. (J). (gr. 4-10). lib. bdg. 25.26 (978-0-7660-5110-2(2), MyReportLinks.com Bks.) Enslow Pubs., Inc.
Taylor-Butler, Christine. Vermont. 2007. (Rookie Read-About Geography Ser.). (Illus.). 31p. (J). (gr. 1-2). 20.50 (978-0-531-12593-9(9), Children's Pr.) Scholastic Library Publishing.
Way, Jennifer. Vermont. 2009. (Bilingual Library of the United States of America Ser.). (ENG & SPA.). 32p. (gr. 2-2). 47.90 (978-1-60853-389-3(1), Editorial Buenas Letras) Rosen Publishing Group, Inc., The.
—Vermont. Brusca, Maria Cristina, tr. from ENG. 2006. (Bilingual Library of the United States of America Ser.: Set 2). (ENG & SPA., Illus.). 32p. (J). (gr. 3-6). lib. bdg. 25.25 (978-1-4042-3111-5(0)) Rosen Publishing Group, Inc., The.

VERMONT—FICTION

Alvarez, Julia. De Como la Tia Lola Aprendio a Ensenar. 2011. (Tia Lola Stories Ser.). (SPA & ENG.). 160p. (J). (gr. 3-7). 7.99 (978-0-375-85793-5(1), Yearling) Random Hse. Children's Bks.
—De Como Tia Lola Salvo el Verano. 2012. (Tia Lola Stories Ser.). (ENG & SPA.). 192p. (J). (gr. 3-7). 6.99 (978-0-307-93023-1(8), Yearling) Random Hse. Children's Bks.
—Devolver Al Remitente. 2010.Tr. of Return to Sender. (SPA & ENG.). 368p. (J). (gr. 3-7). 7.99 (978-0-375-85124-7(0), Yearling) Random Hse. Children's Bks.
—How Tia Lola Came to Visit Stay. 2004. 147p. (gr. 3-7). 17.00 (978-0-7569-3641-9(1)) Perfection Learning Corp.
—How Tía Lola Ended up Starting Over. 2012. (Tia Lola Stories Ser.). (ENG.). 160p. (J). (gr. 3-7). pap. 6.99 (978-0-375-87320-1(1), Yearling) Random Hse. Children's Bks.
—How Tia Lola Learned to Teach. 2011. (Tia Lola Stories Ser.). (ENG., Illus.). 144p. (J). (gr. 3-7). pap. 7.99 (978-0-375-85792-8(3), Yearling) Random Hse. Children's Bks.
—How Tia Lola Saved the Summer. (Tia Lola Stories Ser.). (ENG.). (J). (gr. 3-7). 2012. 176p. 6.99 (978-0-375-86687-6(6), Yearling) 2011. 160p. 15.99 (978-0-375-86727-9(9), Knopf Bks. for Young Readers) Random Hse. Children's Bks.
Anderson, M. T. The Chamber in the Sky. 2012. (Norumbegan Quartet Ser.: 4). (ENG.). 288p. (J). (gr. 3-7). 17.99 (978-0-545-33493-8(4), Scholastic Pr.) Scholastic, Inc.
—The Game of Sunken Places. 2005. (Norumbegan Quartet: No. 1). 260p. (J). (gr. 4-7). 13.65 (978-0-7569-5253-2(0)) Perfection Learning Corp.
Arenstam, Peter. Nicholas: A Vermont Tale. Holman, Karen Busch, illus. 2010. (Nicholas Northeastern Ser.: 4). (ENG.). 144p. (J). (gr. k-7). 14.95 (978-1-58726-522-8(2), Mitten Pr.) Ann Arbor Editions LLC.
Beres, E. Jean. The Sugaring Season. 2008. 92p. pap. 19.95 (978-1-60610-633-4(3)) America Star Bks.
Blakemore, Megan Frazer. The Spy Catchers of Maple Hill. 2014. (ENG.). 320p. (YA). (gr. 3-6). 16.99 (978-1-61963-348-3(5), 9781619633483, Bloomsbury USA Childrens) Bloomsbury Publishing USA.
Blaushild, A. M. Angel Radio. 2016. (ENG., Illus.). (YA). 27.99 **(978-1-63477-935-7(5)**, Harmony Ink Pr.) Dreamspinner Pr.
Carlson, Melody. Viva Vermont!, 1 vol. 2014. (Carter House Girls Ser.). (ENG.). 224p. (YA). pap. 9.99 (978-0-310-74714-7(7)) Zondervan.
Chase, L. P. Elliot Stone & the Mystery of the Summer Vacation Sea Monster. DiRocco, Carl, illus. 2011. (ENG.). 165p. (J). pap. 8.99 (978-0-9792918-7-6(9)) Blue Marlin Pubns.
Clark, Seneca & Giardi, Sandy. Frankie Goes to Fenway: The Tale of the Faithful, Red Sox-Loving Mouse. Decedue, Julie, illus. 2008. 56p. (J). 18.95 (978-0-9767276-3-7(3)) Three Bean Pr.
Conforto, Lisa. The Very Compromising Adventures of Thumby Blackstone, 1 vol. 2010. 34p. 24.95 (978-1-4512-0270-0(9)) PublishAmerica, Inc.
Cook, Eileen. The Education of Hailey Kendrick. 2011. (ENG.). 288p. (YA). (gr. 9). pap. 9.99 (978-1-4424-1326-9(3), Simon Pulse) Simon Pulse.
Dugger, Elizabeth L. & Kanell, Beth. The Darkness under the Water. 2008. (ENG., Illus.). 320p. (YA). (gr. 7). 16.99 (978-0-7636-3719-4(X)) Candlewick Pr.
Edwards, Judith. At the Top of the Mountain: The Adventures of Will Ryan & the Civilian Conservation Corps, 1936-38, Book III. 2013. (ENG., Illus.). 144p. (J). (gr. 3-7). pap. 12.95 (978-1-884592-63-8(5)) Images from the Past, Inc.
—Invasion on the Mountain: The Adventures of Will Ryan & the Civilian Conservation Corps 1933. 2011. (ENG., Illus.). 90p. (J). (gr. 3-7). pap. 12.50 (978-1-884592-55-3(4)) Images from the Past, Inc.
—Trouble on the Mountain: The Adventures of Will Ryan & the Civilian Conservation Corps, 1934-35. 2012. (ENG., Illus.). 118p. (J). (gr. 3-7). pap. 12.50 (978-1-884592-60-7(0)) Images from the Past, Inc.
Fisher, Dorothy Canfield. Understood Betsy. 2004. reprint ed. pap. 1.99 (978-1-4192-9201-9(3)); pap. 24.95 (978-1-4179-0955-1(2)) Kessinger Publishing, LLC.
Galante, Cecilia. The Sweetness of Salt. 2012. (ENG.). 320p. (YA). (gr. 7). pap. 9.99 (978-1-59990-853-3(0), 9781599908533, Bloomsbury USA Childrens) Bloomsbury Publishing USA.
Gilligan, Shannon. The Lake Monster Mystery. Newton, Keith, illus. 2009. (Dragonlarks Ser.). 80p. (J). (gr. k-3). pap. 7.99 (978-1-933390-60-4(3)) Chooseco LLC.
Hahn, Mary Downing. All the Lovely Bad Ones. 2009. (ENG.). 192p. (J). (gr. 2-5). pap. 7.99 (978-0-547-24878-3(4)) Houghton Mifflin Harcourt Publishing Co.
Hart, Alison. Bell's Star. Sanderson, Ruth, illus. 2009. (Horse Diaries: No. 2). (ENG.). 144p. (J). (gr. 3-7). pap. 7.99 (978-0-375-85204-6(2), Random Hse. Bks. for Young Readers) Random Hse. Children's Bks.
Henry, Marguerite. Justin Morgan Had a Horse. 2011. 8.32 (978-0-7848-3468-8(7), Everbind) Marco Bk. Co.
—Justin Morgan Had a Horse. Dennis, Wesley, illus. (ENG.). 176p. (J). (gr. 3-7). 2015. 19.99 (978-1-4814-2562-9(5)) 2006. pap. 7.99 (978-1-4169-2785-3(9)) Simon & Schuster Children's Publishing. (Aladdin).
Hesse, Karen. Witness. 2004. 168p. (J). (gr. 5-9). pap. 29.00 incl. audio (978-0-8072-2094-8(9), Listening Library) Random Hse. Audio Publishing Group.
—Witness. 2003. (ENG., Illus.). 176p. (J). (gr. 3-7). pap. 7.99 (978-0-439-27200-1(9), Scholastic Paperbacks) Scholastic, Inc.
Higginson, Hadley. Keeker & the Crazy, Upside-Down Birthday. Perrett, Lisa, illus. 2008. (ENG.). 56p. (J). (gr. k-3). pap. 4.99 (978-0-8118-6256-1(9)) Chronicle Bks. LLC.
—Keeker & the Springtime Surprise. Perrett, Lisa, illus. 2007. (Keeker & the Sneaky Pony Ser.: KEEK). (ENG.). 58p. (J). (gr. k-3). per. 4.99 (978-0-8118-5599-0(6)) Chronicle Bks. LLC.
Hilton, Marilyn. Full Cicada Moon. 2017. lib. bdg. 19.65 **(978-0-606-39789-6(2))** Turtleback Bks.
Jacobs, Caroline E. The S. W. F. Club. 2007. (ENG.). 120p. pap. 18.99 (978-1-4346-2899-2(X)); 134p. pap. 19.99 (978-1-4346-2900-5(7)) Creative Media Partners, LLC.
Jacobs, Lily. The Littlest Bunny in Vermont: An Easter Adventure. Dunn, Robert, illus. 2015. (ENG.). 32p. (J). (-3). 9.99 (978-1-4926-1225-4(1), Sourcebooks Jabberwocky) Sourcebooks, Inc.
Jaimet, Kate. Edge of Flight, 1 vol. 2012. (Orca Sports Ser.). (ENG.). 160p. (YA). (gr. 6-10). pap. 9.95 (978-1-4598-0160-8(1)) Orca Bk. Pubs. USA.
James, Brian. Zombie Blondes. 2009. (ENG.). 256p. (YA). (gr. 7-12). pap. 8.99 (978-0-312-57375-1(8), 9780312573751) Square Fish.
James, Eric. A Halloween Scare in Vermont. Le Ray, Marina, illus. 2015. (ENG.). 32p. (J). (-5). 9.99 (978-1-4926-2407-3(1), 9781492624073, Sourcebooks Jabberwocky) Sourcebooks, Inc.
—Santa's Sleigh Is on Its Way to Vermont: A Christmas Adventure. Dunn, Robert, illus. 2016. (ENG.). 32p. (J). (-2). 12.99 (978-1-4926-4362-3(9), 9781492643623, Sourcebooks Jabberwocky) Sourcebooks, Inc.
Julia, Alvarez. How Tia Lola Came to Visit Stay. 2014. (Tia Lola Stories Ser.). (ENG.). 160p. (J). (gr. 3-7). 11.24 (978-1-63245-289-4(8)) Lectorum Pubns., Inc.
Kelley, Jane. Nature Girl. 2011. (ENG., Illus.). 256p. (J). (gr. 3-7). pap. 6.99 (978-0-375-85635-8(8), Yearling) Random Hse. Children's Bks.
LaFleur, Suzanne. Love, Aubrey. 2011. (ENG.). 272p. (J). (gr. 3-7). pap. 7.99 (978-0-375-85159-9(3), Yearling) Random Hse. Children's Bks.
Lasky, Kathryn. Sugaring Time. 2003. (Illus.). 21.25 (978-0-8446-7248-9(3)) Smith, Peter Pub., Inc.
Logan, Kenneth. True Letters from a Fictional Life. 2016. 336p. (J). (gr. 8). 17.99 (978-0-06-238025-8(7), HarperTeen) HarperCollins Pubs.
Mademann Vaughan, Kathryn. My Day at the Zoo. Martin, Don, illus. 2004. (J). per. 19.95 (978-0-9747447-1-1(9)) Chaser Media LLC.
Messner, Kate. The Brilliant Fall of Gianna Z. (ENG.). 224p. 2017. (J). pap. 8.99 **(978-1-68119-547-6(X)**, 9781681195476) 2010. (YA). (gr. 3-6). pap. 8.99 (978-0-8027-2173-0(7), 9780802721730) Bloomsbury Publishing USA. (Bloomsbury USA Childrens).
—The Brilliant Fall of Gianna Z. 2017. (J). lib. bdg. 19.65 **(978-0-606-40595-9(X))** Turtleback Bks.
Moulton, Erin E. Flutter: The Story of Four Sisters & an Incredible Journey. 2012. (ENG.). 224p. (J). (gr. 3-7). pap. 6.99 (978-0-14-242133-8(2), Puffin Books) Penguin Young Readers Group.
Oneill, Elizabeth. Alfred Visits Vermont. 2008. 24p. pap. 12.00 (978-0-9799121-9-1(9)) Global Business Information Strategies, Inc.
Parent, David D. Drummers Forward! Marching with Angels: The Exciting Tale of a Drummer Boy Serving with the First Vermont Brigade & His Adventures During the Americ. 2013. 188p. pap. 13.50 (978-1-62516-582-4(X), Strategic Bk. Publishing) Strategic Book Publishing & Rights Agency (SBPRA).
Parkhurst, Johanna. Here's to You, Zeb Pike [Library Edition]. 2014. 180p. pap. 14.99 (978-1-62798-526-0(3), Harmony Ink Pr.) Dreamspinner Pr.
Paterson, Katherine. Preacher's Boy. 2013. (ENG.). 176p. (J). (gr. 5-7). pap. 7.99 (978-0-544-10490-7(0)) Houghton Mifflin Harcourt Publishing Co.
Peck, Robert Newton. A Day No Pigs Would Die. 139p. (YA). (gr. 7-18). pap. 4.99 (978-0-8072-1384-1(5)); pap. 4.99 (978-0-8072-1357-5(8)) Random Hse. Audio Publishing Group. (Listening Library).
Perl, Erica S. Aces Wild. 2013. (ENG.). 224p. (J). (gr. 3-7). 15.99 (978-0-307-93172-6(2), Knopf Bks. for Young Readers) Random Hse. Children's Bks.
—When Life Gives You O. J. (ENG.). 224p. (J). (gr. 3-7). 2013. 6.99 (978-0-375-85902-1(0), Yearling) 2011. 15.99 (978-0-375-85924-3(1), Knopf Bks. for Young Readers) Random Hse. Children's Bks.
Porter, Eleanor H. Pollyanna. 2007. (ENG.). 184p. pap. 19.99 (978-1-4346-0972-4(3)) Creative Media Partners, LLC.
—Pollyanna. 2016. (J). pap. (978-1-5124-2614-4(8)) Lerner Publishing Group.
—Pollyanna. McKowen, Scott, illus. 2013. (Sterling Unabridged Classics Ser.). (ENG.). 208p. (J). (gr. 5). 9.95 (978-1-4027-9718-7(4)) Sterling Publishing Co., Inc.
—Pollyanna. Akib, Jamel, illus. 2007. (Classic Starts(tm) Ser.). (ENG.). 160p. (J). (gr. 2-4). 6.95 (978-1-4027-3692-6(4)) Sterling Publishing Co., Inc.
—Pollyanna. l.t. ed. 2007. (ENG.). 206p. pap. 22.99 (978-1-4346-1071-3(3)) Creative Media Partners, LLC.
Rupp, Rebecca. Octavia Boone's Big Questions about Life, the Universe & Everything. 2010. (ENG., Illus.). 192p. (J). (gr. 4-7). 15.99 (978-0-7636-4491-8(9)) Candlewick Pr.
—Sarah Simpson's Rules for Living. 2008. (ENG., Illus.). 96p. (J). (gr. 3-7). 14.99 (978-0-7636-3220-5(1)) Candlewick Pr.
Shankman, Ed. Champ & Me by the Maple Tree. O'Neill, Dave, illus. 2010. (Shankman & O'Neill Ser.). (ENG.). 32p. (gr. -1-3). 14.95 (978-0-9819430-5-3(5), Commonwealth Editions) Applewood Bks.
Silvano, Wendi. Love Is All Around Vermont. Czernichowska, Joanna, illus. 2016. (ENG.). 32p. (J). (-6). 12.99 (978-1-4926-2970-2(7), Sourcebooks Jabberwocky) Sourcebooks, Inc.
Smallman, Steve. Santa Is Coming to Vermont. Dunn, Robert, illus. 2013. (ENG.). 32p. (J). (-3). 9.99 (978-1-4022-9127-2(2), Sourcebooks Jabberwocky) Sourcebooks, Inc.
Stahler, David, Jr. Gathering of Shades. 2006. (ENG.). 256p. pap. (978-0-06-052296-4(8)) HarperCollins Canada, Ltd.
—A Gathering of Shades. 2005. (ENG.). 304p. (J). 15.99 (978-0-06-052294-0(1), HarperTeen) HarperCollins Pubs.
—Spinning Out. 2011. (ENG.). 288p. (YA). (gr. 7-17). 16.99 (978-0-8118-7780-0(9)) Chronicle Bks. LLC.
Strohm, Stephanie Kate. The Taming of the Drew. 2016. (ENG.). 304p. (J). (gr. 6). 17.99 (978-1-5107-0215-8(6), Sky Pony Pr.) Skyhorse Publishing Co., Inc.
Tougias, Michael, et al. Good Night Vermont. Kelly, Cooper, illus. 2007. (Good Night Our World Ser.). (ENG.). 20p. (J). (gr. k — 1). bds. 9.95 (978-1-60219-017-7(8)) Good Night Bks.
Tracy, Kristen. Hung Up. 2014. (ENG., Illus.). 288p. (YA). (gr. 9). 17.99 (978-1-4424-6075-1(X), Simon Pulse) Simon Pulse.
Villanueva, Pedro. Chronicle of a New Kid. 2017. (Text Connections Guided Close Reading Ser.). (J). (gr. 1). (978-1-4900-1825-6(5)) Benchmark Education Co.
Wallace, Kali. The Memory Trees. 2017. 432p. (YA). (gr. 9). 17.99 **(978-0-06-236623-8(8)**, Tegen, Katherine Bks) HarperCollins Pubs.
Washington, Ida H. Brave Enough: The Story of Rob Sanford, Vermont Pioneer Boy. Smoak, I. W. & Washington, C. E., illus. 2003. vii, 128p. (J). (gr. 4-6). pap. 12.95 (978-0-9666832-7-1(7)) Cherry Tree Bks.
Winthrop, Elizabeth. Counting on Grace. 2007. (ENG., Illus.). 240p. (J). (gr. 3-7). 6.99 (978-0-553-48783-1(3), Yearling) Random Hse. Children's Bks.
Wise, Anna. The Vala of Trinity: Book One Norse Series, 1 vol. 2009. 195p. pap. 24.95 (978-1-61582-763-3(3)) America Star Bks.
Wojciechowska, Maia & Manna, Sal. A Kingdom in a Horse. 2012. (ENG.). 160p. (J). (gr. 2-7). pap. 9.95 (978-1-61608-481-3(2), 608481, Sky Pony Pr.) Skyhorse Publishing Co., Inc.
Wolitzer, Meg. Belzhar. 2015. lib. bdg. 22.10 (978-0-606-37573-3(2)) Turtleback Bks.
Wolper, Joanna. The Man Who Could Be Santa. 2008. (Illus.). 78p. (J). pap. (978-0-88092-765-9(8)); lib. bdg. (978-0-88092-764-2(X)) Royal Fireworks Publishing Co.

VERMONT—HISTORY

Ades, Audrey. Ethan Allen & the Green Mountain Boys. 2017. 25.70 (978-1-61228-952-6(5)) Mitchell Lane Pubs., Inc.
Bailer, Darice. What's Great about Vermont? 2015. (ENG., Illus.). 32p. (J). (gr. 2-5). 26.65 (978-1-4677-3876-7(X)) Lerner Publishing Group.
Carole Marsh. Vermont Indians. 2004. (Vermont Experience Ser.). 36p. (gr. 3-8). pap. 7.95 (978-0-635-02334-6(2)); lib. bdg. 29.95 (978-0-635-02335-3(0)) Gallopade International.
Davies, Jean S. Neighborly Notes: From Turn of the Century Small Town Vermont 2004. (Illus.). 256p. per. 24.95 (978-0-9749151-9-7(X)) CoZi Publishing LLC.
Foran, Jill. Vermont. 2011. (Guide to American States Ser.). (Illus.). 48p. (YA). (gr. 3-6). 29.99 (978-1-61690-818-8(1)); (J). 29.99 (978-1-61690-494-4(1)) Weigl Pubs., Inc.
—Vermont: The Green Mountain State. 2016. (J). (978-1-4896-4953-9(0)) Weigl Pubs., Inc.
Friesen, Helen Lepp. Vermont: The Green Mountain State. 2012. (J). (978-1-61913-411-9(X)); pap. (978-1-61913-412-6(8)) Weigl Pubs., Inc.
Gilbert, Sara. Vermont. 2009. (This Land Called America Ser.). (Illus.). 32p. (YA). (gr. 3-6). 19.95 (978-1-58341-798-0(2)) Creative Co., The.
Heinrichs, Ann. Vermont (Revised Edition) 2014. (America the Beautiful, Third Ser. (Revised Edition) Ser.). (ENG.). 144p. (J). lib. bdg. 40.00 (978-0-531-28296-0(1)) Scholastic Library Publishing.
Jensen, Niels R. Vermont, 1 vol. 2009. (United States Ser.). (ENG., Illus.). 48p. (YA). (gr. 2-5). 27.07 (978-1-60453-681-2(0)) ABDO Publishing Co.
Koontz, Robin Michal. Vermont: The Green Mountain State. 2010. (Our Amazing States Ser.). (ENG.). 24p. (J). pap. 8.25 (978-1-4488-0730-7(1), PowerKids Pr.) Rosen Publishing Group, Inc., The.
Marsh, Carole. Exploring Vermont Through Project-Based Learning: Geography, History, Government, Economics & More. 2016. (Vermont Experience Ser.). (ENG.). (J). pap. 9.99 (978-0-635-12369-5(X)) Gallopade International.
—I'm Reading about Vermont. 2014. (Vermont Experience Ser.). (ENG., Illus.). (J). pap., pap. 8.99 (978-0-635-11320-7(1)) Gallopade International.
—Vermont History Projects: 30 Cool, Activities, Crafts, Experiments & More for Kids to Do to Learn about Your State! 2003. (Vermont Experience Ser.). 32p. (gr. k-5). pap. 5.95 (978-0-635-01814-4(4), Marsh, Carole Bks.) Gallopade International.
Otfinoski, Steven, et al. Vermont. 2015. (It's My State! (r) Ser.). (ENG., Illus.). 80p. (J). (gr. 4-4). 34.21 (978-1-62713-181-0(7)) Cavendish Square Publishing.

Sommers, Michael. Vermont: Past & Present. 2010. (United States: Past & Present Ser.). (ENG.). 48p. (YA). pap. 11.75 *(978-1-4358-9525-6(8))*; lib. bdg. 29.25 *(978-1-4358-9498-3(7))* Rosen Publishing Group, Inc., The. (Rosen Reference).

Tieck, Sarah. Vermont, 1 vol. 2012. (Explore the United States Ser.). (ENG., Illus.). 32p. (J). (gr. 2-5). lib. bdg. 28.50 *(978-1-61783-384-7(3)*, Big Buddy Bks.) ABDO Publishing Co.

Ziff, John. Northern New England: Maine, New Hampshire, Vermont, Vol. 19. 2015. (Let's Explore the States Ser.). (Illus.). 64p. (J). (gr. 5). 23.95 *(978-1-4222-3330-6(8))* Mason Crest.

VERNE, JULES, 1828-1905

Buckley, James. Who Was Jules Verne? 2016. (Who Was... ? Ser.). lib. bdg. 16.00 *(978-0-606-38861-0(3))* Turtleback Bks.

Saddleback Educational Publishing Staff, ed. Around the World in 80 Days. 2011. (Timeless Classics Ser.). (ENG.). 48p. (YA). (gr. 9-12). pupil's gde. ed. 19.95 incl. cd-rom *(978-1-61651-127-2(3))* Saddleback Educational Publishing, Inc.

—20,000 Leagues under the Sea. 2011. (Timeless Classics Ser.). (ENG.). 48p. (YA). (gr. 9-12). pupil's gde. ed. 19.95 incl. cd-rom *(978-1-61651-156-2(7))* Saddleback Educational Publishing, Inc.

Schoell, William. Remarkable Journeys: The Story of Jules Verne. 2004. (World Writers Ser.). (Illus.). 112p. (YA). (gr. 6-12). 23.95 *(978-1-883846-92-3(7)*, First Biographies) Reynolds, Morgan Inc.

Streissguth, Tom. Science Fiction Pioneer: A Story about Jules Verne. Ramstad, Ralph L., illus. 2003. (Creative Minds Biographies Ser.). (ENG.). 64p. (gr. 4-8). pap. 8.95 *(978-1-57505-623-4(2))* Lerner Publishing Group.

VERRAZANO, GIOVANNI DA, 1485-1527

Healy, Nick. Giovanni Da Verrazano. 2003. (Explorers of the Unknown Ser.). (J). *(978-1-58417-037-2(9))*; pap. *(978-1-58417-100-3(6))* Lake Street Pubs.

VERS LIBRE

see Free Verse

VERSIFICATION

see also Poetry

Fandel, Jennifer. Rhyme, Meter, & Other Word Music. 2005. (Understanding Poetry Ser.). (Illus.). 48p. (YA). (gr. 4-7). lib. bdg. 21.95 *(978-1-58341-342-5(1))* Creative Co., The.

Roza, Greg. Patterns in Poetry: Recognizing & Analyzing Poetic Form & Meter. (PowerMath Ser.). 32p. 2009. (ENG.). (gr. 5-6). pap. 10.00 *(978-1-4042-5146-5(4))* 2009. (gr. 4-5). 47.90 *(978-1-60851-415-1(3))* 2005. (Illus.). (J). (gr. 3-6). lib. bdg. 25.25 *(978-1-4042-2941-9(8))* Rosen Publishing Group, Inc., The. (PowerKids Pr.).

Zschock, Martha Day. Journey Around Nantucket from A to Z. Zschock, Martha Day, illus. 2008. (Journeys Ser.). (Illus.). 32p. (J). (gr. 1-6). 17.95 *(978-1-933212-82-1(9)*, Commonwealth Editions) Applewood Bks.

VERTEBRATES

see also Amphibians; Birds; Fishes; Mammals; Reptiles

Boothroyd, Jennifer. On the Ground. 2006. (First Step Nonfiction - Animal Homes Ser.). (ENG., Illus.). 8p. (gr. -1-1). pap. 4.95 *(978-0-8225-5665-7(0)*, Lerner Pubns.) Lerner Publishing Group.

Collard, Sneed B., III. Catching Air: Making the Leap with Gliding Animals, 1 vol. 2017. (How Nature Works: 0). (ENG., Illus.). 48p. (gr. 3-7). 17.95 *(978-0-88448-496-7(3)*, 884496) Tilbury Hse. Pubs.

Duke, Shirley Smith. Vertebrates & Invertebrates Explained. 2016. (Distinctions in Nature Ser.). (Illus.). 32p. (J). (gr. 3-3). pap. 10.58 *(978-1-5026-1779-8(X))* Cavendish Square Publishing.

Johnston, Ginny & Cutchins, Judy. Ice Age Giants of the South. 2015. (Southern Fossil Discoveries Ser.). (ENG., Illus.). 48p. (J). pap. 14.95 *(978-1-56164-793-4(4))* Pineapple Pr., Inc.

Kalman, Bobbie. What Is a Vertebrate? (ENG.). 32p. (J). 2008. *(978-0-7787-7673-4(5))* 2007. (Illus.). (gr. 1-4). lib. bdg. *(978-0-7787-3277-8(0))* 2007. (Illus.). (gr. 1-5). pap. *(978-0-7787-3297-6(5))* Crabtree Publishing Co.

—What Is a Vertibrate? 2008. (ENG.). 32p. (J). *(978-0-7787-7672-7(7))* Crabtree Publishing Co.

Lord, Michelle. Animal School: What Class Are You? Garland, Michael, illus. 2014. (ENG.). 32p. (J). (gr. -1-3). 16.95 *(978-0-8234-3045-1(6))* Holiday Hse., Inc.

McNeil, Niki, et al. HOCPP 1133 Vertebrates. 2006. spiral bd. 24.00 *(978-1-60308-133-7(X))* In the Hands of a Child.

O'Hare, Ted. Vertebrates. 2005. (What Is an Animal Ser.). (Illus.). 24p. (J). (gr. 1-4). lib. bdg. 22.97 *(978-1-59515-422-4(1))* Rourke Educational Media.

Pascoe, Elaine. Animals with Backbones. 2009. (Kid's Guide to the Classification of Living Things Ser.). 32p. (gr. 3-4). 47.90 *(978-1-61511-198-5(0)*, PowerKids Pr.) Rosen Publishing Group, Inc., The.

Rissman, Rebecca. Animals: Real Size Science, 1 vol. 2013. (Real Size Science Ser.). (ENG.). 24p. (gr. -1-1). 22.65 *(978-1-4329-7879-2(9))*; pap. 6.95 *(978-1-4329-7886-0(1))* Heinemann-Raintree. (Acorn).

Selsam, Millicent E. & Hunt, Joyce. First Look at Animals with Backbones & a First Look at Animals Without Backbones. 2003. 68p. pap. 14.95 *(978-0-595-29122-9(8)*, Backinprint.com) iUniverse, Inc.

Williams, Judith. The Discovery & Mystery of a Dinosaur Named Jane. 2007. (Prime (Elementary) Ser.). (Illus.). 48p. (J). (gr. 4-7). per. 8.95 *(978-0-7660-2709-1(0))* Enslow Pubs., Inc.

Zondervan Staff. Spiders, Snakes, Bees, & Bats, 1 vol. 2010. (I Can Read! / Made by God Ser.). (ENG., Illus.). 32p. (J). (gr. -1-2). pap. 3.99 *(978-0-310-72007-2(9))* Zonderkidz.

VESPUCCI, AMERIGO, 1451-1512

Hoogenboom, Lynn. Amerigo Vespucci. 2009. (Primary Source Library of Famous Explorers Ser.). 24p. (gr. 4-4). 42.50 *(978-1-60854-118-8(5)*, PowerKids Pr.) Rosen Publishing Group, Inc., The.

—Amerigo Vespucci: A Primary Source Biography. 2005. (Primary Source Library of Famous Explorers Ser.). (Illus.). 24p. (J). (gr. 3-7). lib. bdg. 21.25 *(978-1-4042-3037-8(8)*, PowerKids Pr.) Rosen Publishing Group, Inc., The.

Lambert, Lorene & Mickle, Jed. The Forgotten Explorer? The Story of Amerigo Vespucci. 2005. (Who in the World Ser.: 0). (ENG., Illus.). 48p. (gr. 2-4). per. 9.50 *(978-0-9728603-8-3(X)*, 86038) Well-Trained Mind Pr.

VESSELS (SHIPS)

see Ships

VETERINARIANS

Acevedo, Gianira Candelario. Becoming a Veterinarian. 2017. (Text Connections Guided Close Reading Ser.). (J). (gr. 1). *(978-1-4900-1813-3(1))* Benchmark Education Co.

Adamson, Heather. A Day in the Life of a Veterinarian, 1 vol. 2003. (Community Helpers at Work Ser.). (ENG., Illus.). 24p. (gr. 1-2). 25.32 *(978-0-7368-2287-9(9)*, First Facts) Capstone Press of Coughlan Cos.

Ames, Michelle. Veterinarians in Our Community. 2009. (On the Job Ser.). (Illus.). 24p. (J). (ENG.). pap. 8.25 *(978-1-4358-2457-7(1))*; lib. bdg. 22.60 *(978-1-4042-8071-7(5))* Rosen Publishing Group, Inc., The. (PowerKids Pr.).

Andrus, Aubre. A Visit to the Vet (Scholastic Reader, Level 2) Kuo, Linda, illus. 2017. (Scholastic Reader, Level 2 Ser.). (ENG.). 32p. (J). (gr. 1-3). pap. 3.99 *(978-1-338-08761-1(4))* Scholastic, Inc.

Arnold, Quinn M. Veterinarians. 2017. (J). ***(978-1-60818-876-5(0)***, Creative Education) Creative Co., The.

Ask the Veterinarians: Fourth Grade Guided Comprehension Level O. (On Our Way to English Ser.). (gr. 4-18). 34.50 *(978-0-7578-7169-6(0))* Rigby Education.

Askew, Amanda & Crowson, Andrew. Vet. 2012. (Illus.). 24p. (gr. 1-3). pap. 7.95 *(978-1-926853-51-2(2))* Saunders Bk. Co. CAN. Dist: RiverStream Publishing.

Bellisario, Gina. Let's Meet a Veterinarian. Atkinson, Cale, illus. 2013. (Cloverleaf Books — Community Helpers Ser.). (ENG.). 24p. (gr. k-2). pap. 6.95 *(978-1-4677-0806-7(2))*; lib. bdg. 23.93 *(978-0-7613-9030-5(8))* Lerner Publishing Group. (Millbrook Pr.).

Brooks, Felicity. Vicky the Vet. Litchfield, Jo, illus. 2004. (Jobs People Do Ser.). 24p. (J). (gr. -1). lib. bdg. 14.95 *(978-1-58086-699-6(9)*, Usborne) EDC Publishing.

—Vicky the Vet Kid Kit. Litchfield, Jo, illus. 2007. (Kid Kits Ser.). 23p. (J). pap. 15.99 *(978-1-60130-008-9(5)*, Usborne) EDC Publishing.

Buckley, James, Jr. Classic Cars. 2008. (Reading Rocks! Ser.). (ENG., Illus.). 32p. (J). (gr. 2-5). 28.50 *(978-1-60253-095-9(5)*, 200758) Child's World, Inc., The.

—A Day with a Zoo Veterinarian. 2008. (Reading Rocks! Ser.). (ENG., Illus.). 32p. (J). (gr. 2-5). 28.50 *(978-1-60253-098-0(X)*, 200756) Child's World, Inc., The.

Carson, J. Visiting the Vet: Learning the V Sound. 2009. (PowerPhonics Ser.). 24p. (gr. 1-1). 39.90 *(978-1-60851-476-2(5)*, PowerKids Pr.) Rosen Publishing Group, Inc., The.

Clendening, John. Veterinary Hospitals. 2014. (Animal Rescue Ser.). 32p. (J). (gr. 3-6). lib. bdg. 26.25 *(978-1-4777-7023-8(2)*, PowerKids Pr.) Rosen Publishing Group, Inc., The.

Edgar, Sherra G. Large Animal Veterinarian. 2015. (Gross Jobs Ser.). (ENG.). 24p. (J). (gr. 2-5). 27.07 *(978-1-63143-687-1(2)*, 208522) Child's World, Inc., The.

Facts on File, Inc. Staff. Animals. 2010. (New Discovering Careers for Your Future Ser.). (Illus.). 128p. (gr. 4-9). 24.95 *(978-0-8160-8044-1(5)*, Ferguson Publishing Co.) Facts On File, Inc.

Forest, Anne. Veterinarians on the Job. 2017. (Jobs in Our Community Ser.). (J). (gr. 1-1). 24p. 24.60 ***(978-1-5345-2151-3(8))***; pap. 49.50 ***(978-1-5345-2150-6(X))***; 24p. pap. 8.25 ***(978-1-5345-2149-0(6))*** Greenhaven Publishing LLC. (KidHaven Publishing).

Gibbons, Gail. Say Woof! 2014. (ENG.). 32p. (J). (gr. -1-3). pap. 13.99 *(978-1-4814-3622-9(8)*, Atheneum Bks. for Young Readers) Simon & Schuster Children's Publishing.

Gregory, Josh. What Do They Do? Veterinarians. 2010. (Community Connections: What Do They Do? Ser.). (ENG.). 24p. (gr. 2-5). lib. bdg. 25.64 *(978-1-60279-810-6(9)*, 200510) Cherry Lake Publishing.

Hutchings, Amy. What Happens at a Vet's Office? 2009. (Where People Work Ser.). 24p. (gr. -1-3). (J). lib. bdg. 22.00 *(978-1-4339-0071-6(8))*; pap. 8.15 *(978-1-4339-0135-5(8))* Stevens, Gareth Publishing LLLP. (Weekly Reader Leveled Readers).

—What Happens at a Vet's Office?/Que Pasa En Una Clinica Veterinaria? 2009. (Where People Work/Dónde Trabaja la Gente? Ser.). (SPA & ENG., Illus.). 24p. (J). (gr. -1-3). pap. 8.15 *(978-1-4339-0143-0(9)*, Weekly Reader Leveled Readers) Stevens, Gareth Publishing LLLP.

—What Happens at a Vet's Office?/¿Qué Pasa en Una Clínica Veterinaria? 2009. (Where People Work/Dónde Trabaja la Gente? Ser.). (SPA & ENG., Illus.). 24p. (J). (gr. -1-3). lib. bdg. 22.00 *(978-1-4339-0079-2(3)*, Weekly Reader Leveled Readers) Stevens, Gareth Publishing LLLP.

Jackson, Donna M. ER Vets: Life in an Animal Emergency Room. 2009. (ENG., Illus.). 96p. (J). (gr. 2-5). pap. 8.99 *(978-0-547-23758-9(8))* Houghton Mifflin Harcourt Publishing Co.

Jeffries, Joyce. Meet the Vet. 2013. (People Around Town Ser.). 24p. (J). (gr. k-2). pap. 8.15 *(978-1-4339-9388-6(0))*; pap. 48.90 *(978-1-4339-9389-3(9))*; (ENG., Illus.). lib. bdg. 22.60 *(978-1-4339-9387-9(2))* Stevens, Gareth Publishing LLLP.

—Meet the Vet/Conoce a Los Veterinarios. 2013. (People Around Town / Gente de Mi Ciudad Ser.). (ENG & SPA., Illus.). 24p. (J). (gr. k-2). lib. bdg. 22.60 *(978-1-4339-9474-6(7))* Stevens, Gareth Publishing LLLP.

Kalman, Bobbie. Veterinarians Help Keep Animals Healthy. 2004. (My Community & Its Helpers Ser.). (ENG., Illus.). 32p. (J). pap. *(978-0-7787-2125-3(6))* Crabtree Publishing Co.

—Los Veterinarios Cuidan la Salud de los Animales. 2006. (Mi Communidad y Quienes Contribuyen a Ella Ser.). (SPA., Illus.). 32p. (J). (gr. 3-7). pap. *(978-0-7787-8443-2(6))*; lib. bdg. *(978-0-7787-8429-6(0))* Crabtree Publishing Co.

Liebman, Dan. Veterinaire. Lior, Tsipora, tr. from ENG. 2006. (Je Veux Etre Ser.). (FRE., Illus.). 24p. (J). (gr. -1-2). pap. 5.95 *(978-1-55407-105-0(4)*, 9781554071050) Firefly Bks., Ltd.

Lowenstein, Felicia. What Does a Veterinarian Do? 2006. (What Does a Community Helper Do? Ser.). (Illus.). 24p. (J). (gr. 1-3). lib. bdg. 22.60 *(978-0-7660-2322-2(2)*, Enslow Elementary) Enslow Pubs., Inc.

Macken, JoAnn Early. Veterinarians. 2010. (People in My Community Ser.). (ENG.). 24p. (J). (gr. k-3). pap. 8.15 *(978-1-4339-3813-9(8))*; lib. bdg. 22.60 *(978-1-4339-3812-2(X))* Stevens, Gareth Publishing LLLP.

McKenzie, Precious. People Who Care for Animals. 2015. (ENG.). 24p. (gr. 1-4). 28.50 *(978-1-63430-069-8(6))* Rourke Educational Media.

McKinnon, Elaine. Pets at the Vet. 2016. (Community Helpers Ser.). 00024p. (J). (gr. 1-1). pap. 8.25 *(978-1-4994-2706-6(9)*, PowerKids Pr.) Rosen Publishing Group, Inc., The.

Meachen Rau, Dana. Una Veterinaria. 2007. (En el Trabajo Ser.). (SPA., Illus.). 24p. (gr. k-1). lib. bdg. 15.95 *(978-0-7614-2787-2(2)*, Benchmark Bks.) Marshall Cavendish Corp.

—Veterinarian. 2007. (Jobs in Town Ser.). (SPA., Illus.). 24p. (gr. k-1). lib. bdg. 15.95 *(978-0-7614-2622-6(1)*, Benchmark Bks.) Marshall Cavendish Corp.

Miller, Connie Colwell. I'll Be a Veterinarian. Baroncelli, Silvia, illus. 2016. (When I Grow Up Ser.). (ENG.). 24p. (J). (gr. k-3). 20.95 *(978-1-60753-764-9(8))* Amicus Publishing.

Minden, Cecilia. Veterinarians. 2014. (People in Our Community Ser.). (ENG.). 24p. (J). (gr. k-3). 27.07 *(978-1-62687-020-8(9)*, 206810) Child's World, Inc., The.

Murray, Aaron R. Veterinarians Help Us. 2012. (All about Community Helpers Ser.). (Illus.). 24p. (J). (gr. -1-1). 22.60 *(978-0-7660-4046-5(1)*, Enslow Elementary) Enslow Pubs., Inc.

Nixon, James. Vet. 2016. (Here to Help Ser.). (ENG., Illus.). 24p. (J). (gr. k-2). 16.99 *(978-1-4451-4017-9(9)*, Franklin Watts) Hachette Children's Group GBR. Dist: Hachette Bk. Group.

Parks, Peggy J. Veterinarian. 2004. (EXPLORING CAREERS Ser.). (ENG.). (J). 27.50 *(978-0-7377-2068-6(9)*, Greenhaven Pr., Inc.) Cengage Gale.

Ready, Dee. Veterinarians Help, 1 vol. 2013. (Our Community Helpers Ser.). (ENG.). 24p. (gr. k-1). pap. 6.29 *(978-1-62065-851-2(8))*; pap. 35.70 *(978-1-62065-852-9(6))*; lib. bdg. 21.99 *(978-1-62065-083-7(5))* Capstone Press of Coughlan Cos. (Pebble Bks.).

Rich, Mari. Big-Animal Vets!, Vol. 10. 2015. (Scientists in Action Ser.). (Illus.). 48p. (J). (gr. 5). 20.95 *(978-1-4222-3419-8(3))* Mason Crest.

Riddle, John & Simons, Rae. Veterinarian. Gholar, Cheryl & Riggs, Ernestine G., eds. 2013. (Careers with Character Ser.: 18). 96p. (J). (gr. 7-18). 22.95 *(978-1-4222-2768-8(5))* Mason Crest.

Riggs, Kate. Seedlings: Veterinarians. 2017. (Seedlings Ser.). (ENG.). 24p. (J). (gr. -1-1). pap. 7.99 ***(978-1-62832-491-4(0)***, Creative Paperbacks) Creative Co., The.

Salzmann, Mary Elizabeth. Veterinarian's Tools, 1 vol. 2011. (Professional Tools Ser.). (ENG., Illus.). 24p. (J). (gr. 3-5). lib. bdg. 25.65 *(978-1-61613-582-9(4)*, Super SandCastle) ABDO Publishing Co.

Shaw, Gina & dePaola, Tomie. Curious about Zoo Vets. 2015. (Smithsonian Ser.). (ENG., Illus.). 32p. (J). (gr. 1-3). bds. 3.99 *(978-0-448-48687-1(3)*, Grosset & Dunlap) Penguin Young Readers Group.

Siemens, Jared. Veterinarians. 2016. (J). ***(978-1-5105-2113-1(5))*** SmartBook Media, Inc.

—Veterinarians. 2015. (Illus.). 24p. (J). pap. *(978-1-4896-3662-1(5))* Weigl Pubs., Inc.

Somervill, Barbara A. Veterinarian. (21st Century Skills Library: Cool STEAM Careers Ser.). (ENG., Illus.). 32p. (gr. 4-7). 2015. (J). 29.93 *(978-1-63362-566-2(4)*, 206448) 2008. lib. bdg. 28.50 *(978-1-60279-301-9(8)*, 200140) Cherry Lake Publishing.

Steffora, Tracey. Math at the Vet, 1 vol. 2013. (Math on the Job Ser.). (ENG., Illus.). 24p. (gr. k-2). pap. 6.29 *(978-1-4329-7162-5(X))*; lib. bdg. 22.65 *(978-1-4329-7155-7(7))* Heinemann-Raintree. (Acorn).

Thomas, William David. Veterinarian. 2008. (Cool Careers Ser.). 32p. (gr. 5-8). pap. 10.50 *(978-0-8368-9330-4(1))*; lib. bdg. 26.00 *(978-0-8368-9197-3(X))* Stevens, Gareth Publishing LLLP.

Truett, Trudi Strain. Animal Physical Therapist. 2014. (J). *(978-0-7614-8074-7(9))* Marshall Cavendish Corp.

—Veterinarian. 2014. (J). *(978-0-7614-8076-1(5))* Marshall Cavendish Corp.

Waldendorf, Kurt. Hooray for Veterinarians! 2016. (Bumba Books (tm) — Hooray for Community Helpers! Ser.). (ENG., Illus.). 24p. (J). (gr. -1-1). 25.32 *(978-1-5124-1438-7(7))* Lerner Publishing Group.

Waldendorf, Kurt. Que Vivan los Veterinarios! 2017. (Bumba Books (tm) en Español — ¡Que Vivan Los Ayudantes Comunitarios! (Hooray for Community Helpers!) Ser.). (SPA.). 24p. (J). (gr. -1-1). 25.32 ***(978-1-5124-4133-8(3))*** Lerner Publishing Group.

VETERINARIANS—FICTION

Abbott, Simon, illus. Happy Street: Vet. 2016. (Happy Street Ser.). (ENG.). 10p. (J). (gr. -1-k). 9.99 *(978-1-4052-7518-7(9))* Egmont Bks., Ltd. GBR. Dist: Independent Pubs. Group.

Anderson, Laurie Halse. Acting Out, 14 vols. 2012. (Vet Volunteers Ser.: 14). (ENG.). 144p. (J). (gr. 3-7). pap. 6.99 *(978-0-14-241676-1(2)*, Puffin Books) Penguin Young Readers Group.

—End of the Race, 12 vols. 2012. (Vet Volunteers Ser.: 12). (ENG.). 160p. (J). (gr. 3-7). 6.99 *(978-0-14-241228-2(7)*, Puffin Books) Penguin Young Readers Group.

—Fight for Life. 2007. (Vet Volunteers Ser.: 1). (ENG.). 160p. (J). (gr. 3-7). 6.99 *(978-0-14-240862-9(X)*, Puffin Books) Penguin Young Readers Group.

—Helping Hands. 2013. (Vet Volunteers Ser.: 15). (ENG.). 144p. (J). (gr. 3-7). pap. 6.99 *(978-0-14-241677-8(0)*, Puffin Books) Penguin Young Readers Group.

—Homeless. 2007. (Vet Volunteers Ser.: 2). (ENG.). 160p. (J). (gr. 3-7). 6.99 *(978-0-14-240863-6(8)*, Puffin Books) Penguin Young Readers Group.

—Left Behind. 2016. (Vet Volunteers Ser.: 17). (ENG.). 128p. (J). (gr. 3-7). 7.99 *(978-0-14-241679-2(7)*, Puffin Books) Penguin Young Readers Group.

—Masks, 11 vols. 2012. (Vet Volunteers Ser.: 11). (ENG.). 128p. (J). (gr. 3-7). 6.99 *(978-0-14-241257-2(0)*, Puffin Books) Penguin Young Readers Group.

—New Beginnings #13, 13 vols. 2012. (Vet Volunteers Ser.: 13). (ENG.). 192p. (J). (gr. 3-7). 6.99 *(978-0-14-241675-4(4)*, Puffin Books) Penguin Young Readers Group.

—Say Good-Bye, No. 5. 2008. (Vet Volunteers Ser.: 5). (ENG.). 160p. (J). (gr. 3-7). 7.99 *(978-0-14-241100-1(0)*, Puffin Books) Penguin Young Readers Group.

—Storm Rescue. 2008. (Vet Volunteers Ser.: 6). (ENG.). 144p. (J). (gr. 3-7). 6.99 *(978-0-14-241101-8(9)*, Puffin Books) Penguin Young Readers Group.

—Teacher's Pet. 2009. (Vet Volunteers Ser.: 7). (ENG.). 160p. (J). (gr. 3-7). 6.99 *(978-0-14-241252-7(X)*, Puffin Books) Penguin Young Readers Group.

—Trapped. 2009. (Vet Volunteers Ser.: 8). (ENG.). 144p. (J). (gr. 3-7). 6.99 *(978-0-14-241223-7(6)*, Puffin Books) Penguin Young Readers Group.

—Trickster. 2008. (Vet Volunteers Ser.: 3). (ENG.). 144p. (J). (gr. 3-7). 6.99 *(978-0-14-241083-7(7)*, Puffin Books) Penguin Young Readers Group.

Banerjee, Anjali. Seaglass Summer. 2011. (ENG., Illus.). 176p. (J). (gr. 3-7). pap. 7.99 *(978-0-375-84399-0(X)*, Yearling) Random Hse. Children's Bks.

Bier, Erich & Bier, Donna. Lester the Bear. 2013. (ENG., Illus.). 22p. (J). (gr. -1-3). 14.95 *(978-1-62086-297-1(2))* Mascot Bks., Inc.

Biggs, Brian. I'm a Veterinarian. 2016. (Tinyville Town Ser.). (ENG., Illus.). 22p. (J). (gr. -1 — 1). bds. 7.95 *(978-1-4197-2135-9(6)*, Abrams Appleseed) Abrams, Inc.

Bruel, Nick. Bad Kitty Goes to the Vet. 2016. (Bad Kitty Ser.). (ENG., Illus.). 144p. (J). 13.99 *(978-1-59643-977-1(7)*, 9781596439771) Roaring Brook Pr.

Carris, Joan. Magic at the Bed & Biscuit. Jones, Noah Z., illus. 2012. (ENG.). 112p. (J). (gr. 1-4). pap. 5.99 *(978-0-7636-5849-6(9))* Candlewick Pr.

—Welcome to the Bed & Biscuit. Jones, Noah Z., illus. 2009. (ENG.). 128p. (J). (gr. 1-4). 5.99 *(978-0-7636-4621-9(0))* Candlewick Pr.

—Wild Times at the Bed & Biscuit. Jones, Noah Z., illus. 2011. (ENG.). 128p. (J). (gr. 1-4). pap. 5.99 *(978-0-7636-5294-4(6))* Candlewick Pr.

Carris, Joan Davenport. Magic at the Bed & Biscuit. Meserve, Jessica & Jones, Noah Z., illus. 2011. (Daisy Dawson Ser.). (ENG.). 128p. (J). (gr. 1-4). 15.99 *(978-0-7636-4306-5(8))* Candlewick Pr.

Chukovsky, Kornei. Doctor Ouch. Seabaugh, Jan, tr. from RUS. Seabaugh, Jan, illus. 2004. (Children's International Ser.: 1). Orig. Title: Aibolit. 43p. (J). pap. 6.99 *(978-0-9740551-0-7(7))* Smith, Viveca Publishing.

Chwast, Seymour & Lofting, Hugh. Dr. Dolittle. Chwast, Seymour, illus. 2015. (ENG., Illus.). 40p. (J). (gr. 4-7). 18.99 *(978-1-56846-258-5(1)*, Creative Editions) Creative Co., The.

Clarke, Jane. Clover the Bunny. 2016. (Dr. KittyCat Ser.: 2). (ENG.). 96p. (J). (gr. 2-5). pap. 4.99 *(978-0-545-87336-9(3)*, Scholastic Paperbacks) Scholastic, Inc.

—Posy the Puppy. 2016. (Dr. KittyCat Ser.: 1). (ENG.). 96p. (J). (gr. 2-5). pap. 4.99 *(978-0-545-87333-8(9)*, Scholastic Paperbacks) Scholastic, Inc.

Crow, Melinda Melton. Rocky & Daisy Go to the Vet. Sassin, Eva, illus. 2013. (My Two Dogs Ser.). (ENG.). 32p. (gr. 1-3). pap. 29.70 *(978-1-4342-6297-4(9))*; (gr. 2-3). pap. 5.95 *(978-1-4342-6203-5(0))*; (gr. 2-3). lib. bdg. 22.65 *(978-1-4342-6009-3(7))* Stone Arch Bks.

Davis, David Denton. Polly's Promise: A Story about Thriving Rather Than Simply Surviving... Turning Apparent Disability into Gifted Ability. 2013. 80p. pap. 21.95 *(978-1-4787-0275-7(3))* Outskirts Pr., Inc.

Davis, Kauline, et al. Fat Dogs & Coughing Horses. 2012. (ENG.). 61p. (J). pap. 12.95 *(978-1-932739-22-0(X)*, affc1c85-635d-4f6b-8285-dcef4a125771) Purdue Univ. Pr.

Dempsey, Tami. We Are a Champion! 2010. 36p. pap. 15.49 *(978-1-4490-8102-7(9))* AuthorHouse.

Disney Book Group. Doc Mcstuffins Smitten with a Kitten. Disney Storybook Art Team, illus. 2016. (ENG.). 24p. (J). (gr. -1-k). pap. 4.99 *(978-1-4847-6203-5(7))* Disney Pr.

—World of Reading: Doc Mcstuffins Take Your Pet to the Vet: Level 1. Disney Storybook Art Team, illus. 2015. (World of Reading Ser.). (ENG.). 32p. (J). (gr. -1-k). pap. 3.99 *(978-1-4847-1966-4(2))* Disney Pr.

Disney Book Group Staff & Miller, Sara. Doc Mcstuffins: Take Your Pet to the Vet. 2015. (World of Reading Ser.). (J). lib. bdg. 13.55 *(978-0-606-37535-1(X))* Turtleback Bks.

Dyan, Penelope. Blake the Cat & His Very Loose Tooth! Dyan, Penelope, illus. 2011. (Illus.). 34p. pap. 10.95 *(978-1-935630-77-7(6))* Bellissima Publishing, LLC.

Garcia, Randolph. The Steamer Trunk Adventures #2: The Ghosts of Machu Picchu. 2006. (ENG.). 88p. per. 16.95 *(978-1-4241-1843-4(3))* PublishAmerica, Inc.

Henry, Heather French. Pepper's Purple Heart: A Veteran's Day Story. Henry, Heather French, illus. 2004. (Claire's Holiday Adventures Ser.: Vol. 1). (Illus.). 32p. (J). (gr. k-4). pap. 8.95 *(978-0-9706341-1-5(0))* Cubbie Blue Publishing.

Hensley, Terri Anne. Henry visits the Veterinarian. 2007. (J). per. 6.95 *(978-0-9789057-2-9(5))* Huntington Ludlow Media Group.

Hillert, Margaret. Ayuda para Querido Dragón. Pullan, Jack, illus. 2017. (BeginningtoRead Ser.). Orig. Title: Help for Dear Dragon. (ENG & SPA.). 32p. (J). (-2). 22.60 ***(978-1-59953-832-7(6))*** Norwood Hse. Pr.

Hillert, Margaret. Help for Dear Dragon. Pullan, Jack, illus. 2016. (BeginningtoRead Ser.). (ENG.). 32p. (J). (-2). lib. bdg. 22.60 *(978-1-59953-769-6(9))* Norwood Hse. Pr.

Huneck, Stephen. Sally Goes to the Vet. Huneck, Stephen, illus. 2004. (ENG., Illus.). 32p. (J). (gr. -1-3). 19.95 *(978-0-8109-4813-6(3))* Abrams, Inc.

Jordan, Apple. I Can Be a Farm Vet (Barbie) Riley, Kellee, illus. 2016. (Step into Reading Ser.). (ENG.). 24p. (J). (gr. -1-1). 4.99 *(978-1-101-93245-2(7)*, Random Hse. Bks. for Young Readers) Random Hse. Children's Bks.

Kelly, Jacqueline. Counting Sheep: Calpurnia Tate, Girl Vet. White, Teagan & Meyer, Jennifer L., illus. 2017. (Calpurnia Tate, Girl Vet Ser.). (ENG.). 112p. (J). 15.99 *(978-1-62779-870-9(6)*, 9781627798709, Holt, Henry & Co. Bks. For Young Readers) Holt, Henry & Co.

—The Curious World of Calpurnia Tate. 2015. (Calpurnia Tate Ser.: 2). (ENG.). 320p. (J). (gr. 4-7). 16.99 *(978-0-8050-9744-3(9)*, 9780805097443, Holt, Henry & Co. Bks. For Young Readers) Holt, Henry & Co.

—The Curious World of Calpurnia Tate. 2017. (Calpurnia Tate Ser.: 2). (J). lib. bdg. 18.40 ***(978-0-606-39939-5(9))*** Turtleback Bks.
—Skunked! White, Teagan & Meyer, Jennifer L., illus. 2016. (Calpurnia Tate, Girl Vet Ser.). (ENG.). 112p. (J). 15.99 *(978-1-62779-868-6(4)*, 9781627798686, Holt, Henry & Co. Bks. For Young Readers) Holt, Henry & Co.
Kelly, Jacqueline. Who Gives a Hoot?: Calpurnia Tate, Girl Vet. Meyer, Jennifer L., illus. 2017. (Calpurnia Tate, Girl Vet Ser.). (ENG.). 112p. (J). 15.99 ***(978-1-62779-873-0(0)***, 9781627798730, Holt, Henry & Co. Bks. For Young Readers) Holt, Henry & Co.
Leonard, Marcia & Handelman, Dorothy. The Pet Vet. Handelman, Dorothy, illus. Leonard, Marcia, photos by. 2005. (ENG & SPA., Illus.). 32p. (J). (gr. -1-1). pap. 4.99 *(978-0-8225-3299-6(9))* Lerner Publishing Group.
Lively, Deborah Dreher. Vanishing Treasure of the Virungas. 2008. 88p. pap. 11.50 *(978-1-934925-54-6(3)*, Strategic Bk. Publishing) Strategic Book Publishing & Rights Agency (SBPRA).
Lofting, Hugh. The Voyages of Doctor Dolittle. McKowen, Scott, illus. 2012. (Sterling Unabridged Classics Ser.). (ENG.). 256p. (J). (gr. 5). 9.95 *(978-1-4027-9721-7(4))* Sterling Publishing Co., Inc.
Lynch, Chris. Cyberia. 2008. (Cyberia Ser.: 1). (ENG.). 160p. (J). (gr. 3-7). 16.99 *(978-0-545-02793-9(4)*, Scholastic Pr.) Scholastic, Inc.
—Monkey See, Monkey Don't. (Cyberia Ser.: 2). (ENG.). 144p. (J). (gr. 3-7). 2011. pap. 5.99 *(978-0-545-02797-7(7)*, Scholastic Paperbacks) 2009. 16.99 *(978-0-545-02794-6(2)*, Scholastic Pr.) Scholastic, Inc.
Mackall, Dandi Daley. Double Trouble, 1 vol. Wolf, Claudia, illus. 2011. (I Can Read! / a Horse Named Bob Ser.). (ENG.). 32p. (J). pap. 3.99 *(978-0-310-71785-0(X))* Zonderkidz.
Mitchell, Sherry. Fernando the Veterinarian. 2012. 20p. pap. 17.99 *(978-1-4685-8098-3(1))* AuthorHouse.
Moncomble, Gerard & Van den Dries, Sidonie. Half & Half-A Doctor for the Animals. Fortier, Natali & Brenier, Claire, illus. 32p. (J). 2009. 9.95 *(978-1-60115-203-9(5))* 2008. pap. 4.99 *(978-1-60115-204-6(3))* Treasure Bay, Inc.
Odgers, Darrel & Odgers, Sally. Cranky Paws. Dawson, Janine, illus. 2009. (Pet Vet Ser.: 1). 96p. (J). (gr. 2-6). pap. 4.99 *(978-1-935279-01-3(7))* Kane Miller.
—The Mare's Tale. Dawson, Janine, illus. 2009. (Pet Vet Ser.: 2). 96p. (J). (gr. 2-6). pap. 4.99 *(978-1-935279-02-0(5))* Kane Miller.
Odgers, Darrel & Sally. The Pup's Tale: Pet Vet Book 6. Dawson, Janine, illus. 2015. 96p. (J). pap. 4.99 *(978-1-61067-351-8(4))* Kane Miller.
Phillips, Matthew. Ingo Flamingo, 1 vol. 2009. 19p. pap. 24.95 *(978-1-60836-340-7(6))* America Star Bks.
Popper, Garry. The Beast of Didley Dale. Forshaw, John, illus. 2004. (Bret the Vet Ser.). 40p. 7.00 *(978-1-84161-024-5(0))* Ravette Publishing, Ltd. GBR. Dist: Parkwest Pubns., Inc.
Riley, Ford & Nee, Chris. Take Your Pet to the Vet. 2015. (Illus.). 32p. (J). *(978-1-4844-6746-6(9))* Disney Publishing Worldwide.
Santillo, LuAnn. The Vet. Santillo, LuAnn, ed. 2003. (Half-Pint Kids Readers Ser.). (Illus.). 7p. (J). (gr. -1-1). pap. 1.00 *(978-1-59256-123-0(3))* Half-Pint Kids, Inc.
Schoon, Christian. Under Nameless Stars. 2014. (ENG.). 368p. (J). (gr. 9). pap. 9.99 *(978-1-908844-87-3(6)*, Strange Chemistry) Watkins Media Limited GBR. Dist: Penguin Random Hse. LLC.
Schwartz, Jean. The Snake with a Bellyache. Fisher, Todd, illus. 2007. 20p. per. 10.95 *(978-1-934246-41-2(7))* Peppertree Pr., The.
Selfors, Suzanne. The Fairy Swarm. Santat, Dan, illus. 2016. (Imaginary Veterinary Ser.: 6). (ENG.). 240p. (J). (gr. 2-7). pap. 7.99 *(978-0-316-28692-3(3))* Little, Brown Bks. for Young Readers.
—The Lonely Lake Monster. Santat, Dan, illus. 2014. (Imaginary Veterinary Ser.: 2). (ENG.). 240p. (J). (gr. 2-7). pap. 7.99 *(978-0-316-22561-8(4))* Little, Brown Bks. for Young Readers.
—The Order of the Unicorn. Santat, Dan, illus. 2014. 197p. (J). *(978-0-316-32339-0(X))* Little Brown & Co.
—The Order of the Unicorn: The Imaginary Veterinary. Santat, Dan, illus. 2014. (Imaginary Veterinary Ser.: 4). (ENG.). 208p. (J). (gr. 2-7). 16.00 *(978-0-316-36406-5(1))* Little, Brown Bks. for Young Readers.
—The Sasquatch Escape. Santat, Dan, illus. 2014. (Imaginary Veterinary Ser.: 1). (ENG.). 240p. (J). (gr. 2-7). pap. 7.99 *(978-0-316-22569-4(X))* Little, Brown Bks. for Young Readers.
Skafish, Brad. Red Letter Day: The Bad Cats Learn about Letters! 2012. 20p. pap. 11.95 *(978-1-62141-260-1(1))* Booklocker.com, Inc.
Smith, Maggie Caldwell. Tommy Wilson, Junior Veterinarian: The Case of the Orphaned Bobcat. Heyer, Carol & White, Charlotte L., illus. 2006. (J). per. 7.95 *(978-0-9788391-1-6(0))* Magpie Pr., Pine Mountain Club, CA.
Smith, Margaret Ann. A New Kind of Life for Eddie Eagle. 2008. 36p. pap. 24.95 *(978-1-60441-168-3(6))* America Star Bks.
Stern, A. J. Doggy Day Care, 2 vols. Marts, Doreen Mulryan, illus. 2010. (Frankly, Frannie Ser.: 2). (ENG.). 128p. (J). (gr. 1-3). pap. 4.99 *(978-0-448-45350-7(9)*, Grosset & Dunlap) Penguin Young Readers Group.
Stockham, Jessica, illus. Visiting the Vet. 2011. (First Time Ser.). (ENG.). 24p. (J). (gr. 2-2). pap. *(978-1-84643-337-5(1))* Child's Play International Ltd.
Travitzky, Paul Joseph & Travitzky, Brianna Marie. Brianna Marie Wants to Be... A Veterinarian. 2010. 20p. 11.00 *(978-1-4490-7701-3(3))* AuthorHouse.
Viselman, Kenn. Li'l Pet Hospital: The Great Race. 2003. 32p. pap. 3.99 *(978-0-06-054840-7(1)*, Harper Entertainment) HarperCollins Pubs.

VETERINARY MEDICINE

Ames, Michelle. Veterinarians in Our Community. 2009. (On the Job Ser.). (Illus.). 24p. (J). (ENG.). pap. 8.25 *(978-1-4358-2457-7(1))*; lib. bdg. 22.60 *(978-1-4042-8071-7(5))* Rosen Publishing Group, Inc., The. (PowerKids Pr.)
Andrus, Aubre. A Visit to the Vet (Scholastic Reader, Level 2) Kuo, Linda, illus. 2017. (Scholastic Reader, Level 2 Ser.). (ENG.). 32p. (J). (gr. 1-3). pap. 3.99 *(978-1-338-08761-1(4))* Scholastic, Inc.
Arnold, Quinn M. Veterinarians. 2017. (J). ***(978-1-60818-876-5(0)***, Creative Education) Creative Co., The.
Bedell, J. M. So, You Want to Work with Animals? Discover Fantastic Ways to Work with Animals, from Veterinary Science to Aquatic Biology. 2017. (Be What You Want Ser.). (ENG., Illus.). 256p. (J). (gr. 3-7). 19.99 *(978-1-58270-596-5(8))* Aladdin/Beyond Words.
Bellisario, Gina. Let's Meet a Veterinarian. Atkinson, Cale, illus. 2013. (Cloverleaf Books — Community Helpers Ser.). (ENG.). 24p. (J). (gr. k-2). pap. 6.95 *(978-1-4677-0806-7(2))*; lib. bdg. 23.93 *(978-0-7613-9030-5(8))* Lerner Publishing Group. (Millbrook Pr.).
Brooks, Felicity. Vicky the Vet. Litchfield, Jo, illus. 2004. (Jobs People Do Ser.). 24p. (J). (gr. -1). lib. bdg. 14.95 *(978-1-58086-699-6(9)*, Usborne) EDC Publishing.
—Vicky the Vet Kid Kit. Litchfield, Jo, illus. 2007. (Kid Kits Ser.). 23p. (J). pap. 15.99 *(978-1-60130-008-9(5)*, Usborne) EDC Publishing.
Buckley, James, Jr. Classic Cars. 2008. (Reading Rocks! Ser.). (ENG., Illus.). 32p. (J). (gr. 2-5). 28.50 *(978-1-60253-095-9(5)*, 200758) Child's World, Inc., The.
—A Day with a Zoo Veterinarian. 2008. (Reading Rocks! Ser.). (ENG., Illus.). 32p. (J). (gr. 2-5). 28.50 *(978-1-60253-098-0(X)*, 200756) Child's World, Inc., The.
Chilman-Blair, Kim. Medikidz Explain Swine Flu. 2010. (Superheroes on a Medical Mission Ser.). (Illus.). 40p. (YA). pap. 11.75 *(978-1-4488-1843-3(5))*; (gr. 5-8). lib. bdg. 29.25 *(978-1-4358-9457-0(X))* Rosen Publishing Group, Inc., The. (Rosen Reference).
Clendening, John. Veterinary Hospitals. 2014. (Animal Rescue Ser.). 32p. (J). (gr. 3-6). lib. bdg. 26.25 *(978-1-4777-7023-8(2)*, PowerKids Pr.) Rosen Publishing Group, Inc., The.
Diconsiglio, John. When Birds Get Flu & Cows Go Mad! How Safe Are We? 2007. (24/7: Science Behind the Scenes Ser.). (ENG., Illus.). 64p. (J). (gr. 8-12). 29.00 *(978-0-531-12069-9(4)*, Watts, Franklin) Scholastic Library Publishing.
Evento, Susan & Meredith Books Staff. Vet Emergencies 24/7. 2008. (Illus.). 48p. (J). (gr. 4-7). per. 6.99 *(978-0-696-23979-3(5))* Meredith Bks.
Ewing, Susan M. Working with Animals. 2018. (ENG.). 32p. (gr. 3-6). ***(978-1-63235-452-5(7)***, 12-Story Library) Pr. Room Editions LLC.
Extraordinary Jobs with Animals. 2006. (Extraordinary Jobs Ser.). 160p. (gr. 6-12). 40.00 *(978-0-8160-5862-4(8)*, Ferguson Publishing Co.) Facts On File, Inc.
Facts on File, Inc. Staff. Animals. 2010. (New Discovering Careers for Your Future Ser.). (Illus.). 128p. (gr. 4-9). 24.95 *(978-0-8160-8044-1(5)*, Ferguson Publishing Co.) Facts On File, Inc.
Forest, Anne. Veterinarians on the Job. 2017. (Jobs in Our Community Ser.). (J). (gr. 1-1). 24p. 24.60 ***(978-1-5345-2151-3(8))***; pap. 49.50 ***(978-1-5345-2150-6(X))***; 24p. pap. 8.25 ***(978-1-5345-2149-0(6))*** Greenhaven Publishing LLC. (KidHaven Publishing).
Gregory, Josh. What Do They Do? Veterinarians. 2010. (Community Connections: What Do They Do? Ser.). (ENG.). 24p. (gr. 2-5). lib. bdg. 25.64 *(978-1-60279-810-6(9)*, 200510) Cherry Lake Publishing.
Halls, Kelly Milner. Albino Animals. 2004. (Illus.). 72p. (J). pap. 8.95 *(978-1-58196-016-7(6))* Lerner Publishing Group.
Jackson, Donna M. ER Vets: Life in an Animal Emergency Room. 2009. (ENG., Illus.). 96p. (J). (gr. 2-5). pap. 8.99 *(978-0-547-23758-9(8))* Houghton Mifflin Harcourt Publishing Co.
Kalman, Bobbie. Veterinarians Help Keep Animals Healthy. 2004. (My Community & Its Helpers Ser.). (ENG., Illus.). 32p. (J). pap. *(978-0-7787-2125-3(6))* Crabtree Publishing Co.
Macken, JoAnn Early. Veterinarians. 2010. (People in My Community Ser.). (ENG.). 24p. (J). (gr. k-3). pap. 8.15 *(978-1-4339-3813-9(8))*; lib. bdg. 22.60 *(978-1-4339-3812-2(X))* Stevens, Gareth Publishing LLLP.
Markle, Sandra. The Case of the Vanishing Little Brown Bats: A Scientific Mystery. 2014. (ENG., Illus.). 48p. (gr. 4-6). lib. bdg. 29.27 *(978-1-4677-1463-1(1)*, Millbrook Pr.) Lerner Publishing Group.
McKinnon, Elaine. Pets at the Vet. 2016. (Community Helpers Ser.). 00024p. (J). (gr. 1-1). pap. 8.25 *(978-1-4994-2706-6(9)*, PowerKids Pr.) Rosen Publishing Group, Inc., The.
Miller, Connie Colwell. I'll Be a Veterinarian. Baroncelli, Silvia, illus. 2016. (When I Grow Up Ser.). (ENG.). 24p. (J). (gr. k-3). 20.95 *(978-1-60753-764-9(8))* Amicus Publishing.
Minden, Cecilia. Veterinarians. 2014. (People in Our Community Ser.). (ENG.). 24p. (J). (gr. k-3). 27.07 *(978-1-62687-020-8(9)*, 206810) Child's World, Inc., The.
Murray, Aaron R. Veterinarians Help Us. 2012. (All about Community Helpers Ser.). (Illus.). 24p. (J). (gr. -1-1). 22.60 *(978-0-7660-4046-5(1)*, Enslow Elementary) Enslow Pubs., Inc.
Nixon, James. Vet. 2016. (Here to Help Ser.). (ENG., Illus.). 24p. (J). (gr. k-2). 16.99 *(978-1-4451-4017-9(9)*, Franklin Watts) Hachette Children's Group GBR. Dist: Hachette Bk. Group.
Orr, Tamra. Avian Flu. 2009. (Coping in a Changing World Ser.). 112p. (gr. 7-7). 63.90 *(978-1-61512-018-5(1))* Rosen Publishing Group, Inc., The.
Ready, Dee. Veterinarians Help. 2013. (Our Community Helpers Ser.). (ENG.). 24p. (gr. k-1). pap. 35.70 *(978-1-62065-852-9(6))*; pap. 6.29 *(978-1-62065-851-2(8))*; lib. bdg. 21.99 *(978-1-62065-083-7(5))* Capstone Press of Coughlan Cos. (Pebble Bks.).
Rich, Mari. Big-Animal Vets!, Vol. 10. 2015. (Scientists in Action Ser.). (Illus.). 48p. (J). (gr. 5). 20.95 *(978-1-4222-3419-8(3))* Mason Crest.
Salzmann, Mary Elizabeth. Veterinarian's Tools, 1 vol. 2011. (Professional Tools Ser.). (ENG., Illus.). 24p. (J). (gr. 3-5). lib. bdg. 25.65 *(978-1-61613-582-9(4)*, Super SandCastle) ABDO Publishing Co.
Somervill, Barbara A. Veterinarian. 2008. (21st Century Skills Library: Cool Careers Ser.). (ENG., Illus.). 32p. (gr. 4-8). lib. bdg. 28.50 *(978-1-60279-301-9(8)*, 200140) Cherry Lake Publishing.
Thomas, William David. Veterinarian. 2008. (Cool Careers Ser.). 32p. (gr. 5-8). lib. bdg. 26.00 *(978-0-8368-9197-3(X))* Stevens, Gareth Publishing LLLP.
Truett, Trudi Strain. Animal Physical Therapist. 2014. (Illus.). 64p. (J). *(978-1-62712-458-4(6))* Musa Publishing.
Worthington, Niles. A Vet's Job. 2015. (Community Workers Ser.). (ENG., Illus.). 24p. (J). (gr. 1-1). pap. 8.22 *(978-1-5026-0436-1(1))* Cavendish Square Publishing.
Zombie Animals: Parasites Take Control! 2015. (Zombie Animals: Parasites Take Control! Ser.). (ENG.). 24p. (J). (gr. 2-3). pap., pap., pap. 293.40 *(978-1-4824-3500-9(4))* Stevens, Gareth Publishing LLLP.

VETERINARY MEDICINE—FICTION

Ahlberg, Allan. Mrs. Vole the Vet. Chichester Clark, Emma, illus. (ENG.). 24p. (J). pap. 6.95 *(978-0-14-037880-1(4))* Penguin Bks., Ltd. GBR. Dist: Trafalgar Square Publishing.
Anderson, Laurie Halse. End of the Race, 12 vols. 2012. (Vet Volunteers Ser.: 12). (ENG.). 160p. (J). (gr. 3-7). 6.99 *(978-0-14-241228-2(7)*, Puffin Books) Penguin Young Readers Group.
—Helping Hands. 2013. (Vet Volunteers Ser.: 15). (ENG.). 144p. (J). (gr. 3-7). pap. 6.99 *(978-0-14-241677-8(0)*, Puffin Books) Penguin Young Readers Group.
—Left Behind. 2016. (Vet Volunteers Ser.: 17). (ENG.). 128p. (J). (gr. 3-7). 7.99 *(978-0-14-241679-2(7)*, Puffin Books) Penguin Young Readers Group.
Baglio, Ben M. Collie with a Card. Baum, Ann, illus. 2004. 136p. (J). pap. *(978-0-439-68760-7(8))* Scholastic, Inc.
Carpenter, Christopher, illus. Lilly's Heart: The Veterinary Clinic Cases Series. 2006. 32p. (J). per. 9.95 *(978-0-9766641-0-9(0))* Ichabod Ink.
Goldman, Marcia, photos by. Lola Goes to the Doctor. 2014. (Lola Ser.). (ENG., Illus.). 32p. (J). (gr. -1-3). 16.95 *(978-1-939547-11-8(3))* Creston Bks.
Henson, Heather. The Whole Sky. 2017. (ENG., Illus.). 256p. (J). (gr. 5-7). 16.99 ***(978-1-4424-1405-1(7)***, Atheneum/Caitlyn Dlouhy Books) Simon & Schuster Children's Publishing.
Kerr, Judith. Mog & the Vet. (ENG., Illus.). 32p. (J). pap. 9.99 *(978-0-00-664620-4(4))* HarperCollins Pubs. Ltd. GBR. Dist: Trafalgar Square Publishing.
Lynn, Elizabeth B. Forget the Vet. Meyer, Ashley M., illus. 2012. 32p. 24.95 *(978-1-936688-21-0(2))* AKA:yoLa.
Morpurgo, Michael. Out of the Ashes. 1. unabr. ed. 2012. (ENG., Illus.). 128p. (J). (gr. 4-7). pap. 9.95 *(978-1-4472-0733-7(5))* Pan Macmillan GBR. Dist: Independent Pubs. Group.
North, Sherry. Champ's Story: Dogs Get Cancer Too!, 1 vol. Rietz, Kathleen, illus. 2010. (ENG.). 32p. (J). (gr. -1-4). 16.95 *(978-1-60718-077-7(4))*; pap. 8.95 *(978-1-60718-088-3(X))* Arbordale Publishing.
—La Historia de Campeona: ¡a Los Perros También les Da Cáncer!, 1 vol. Rietz, Kathleen, illus. 2010. (SPA & ENG.). 32p. (J). (gr. -1-4). 17.95 *(978-1-60718-681-6(0))* Arbordale Publishing.
Ries, Lori. Aggie the Brave. Dormer, Frank W., illus. (ENG.). 48p. (J). (gr. -1-3). 2012. pap. 5.95 *(978-1-57091-636-6(5))* 2010. 12.95 *(978-1-57091-635-9(7))* Charlesbridge Publishing, Inc.
Wilson, Diane Lee. Firehorse. (ENG.). 336p. (YA). (gr. 7). 2010. pap. 8.99 *(978-1-4424-0331-4(4))* 2006. (Illus.). 17.99 *(978-1-4169-1551-5(6))* McElderry, Margaret K. Bks. (McElderry, Margaret K. Bks.).

VETERINARY MEDICINE—VOCATIONAL GUIDANCE

Adamson, Heather. A Day in the Life of a Veterinarian, 1 vol. 2003. (Community Helpers at Work Ser.). (ENG., Illus.). 24p. (gr. 1-2). 25.32 *(978-0-7368-2287-9(9)*, First Facts) Capstone Press of Coughlan Cos.
Allman, Toney. Careers If You Like Animals. 2017. (Career Discovery Ser.). (ENG.). 80p. (YA). (gr. 5-12). ***(978-1-68282-134-3(X))*** ReferencePoint Pr., Inc.
Byers, Ann. Internship & Volunteer Opportunities for People Who Love Animals. 2012. (Foot in the Door Ser.). (ENG., Illus.). 80p. (YA). (gr. 7-12). lib. bdg. 33.25 *(978-1-4488-8293-9(1))* Rosen Publishing Group, Inc., The.
Gibbons, Gail. Say Woof! 2014. (ENG.). 32p. (J). (gr. -1-3). pap. 13.99 *(978-1-4814-3622-9(8)*, Atheneum Bks. for Young Readers) Simon & Schuster Children's Publishing.
Hutchings, Amy. What Happens at a Vet's Office? 2009. (Where People Work Ser.). 24p. (gr. -1-3). (J). lib. bdg. 22.00 *(978-1-4339-0071-6(8))*; pap. 8.15 *(978-1-4339-0135-5(8))* Stevens, Gareth Publishing LLLP. (Weekly Reader Leveled Readers).
—What Happens at a Vet's Office?/Que Pasa En Una Clinica Veterinaria? 2009. (Where People Work/Dónde Trabaja la Gente? Ser.). (SPA & ENG., Illus.). 24p. (J). (gr. -1-3). pap. 8.15 *(978-1-4339-0143-0(9)*, Weekly Reader Leveled Readers) Stevens, Gareth Publishing LLLP.
—What Happens at a Vet's Office?/¿Qué Pasa en Una Clínica Veterinaria? 2009. (Where People Work/Dónde Trabaja la Gente? Ser.). (SPA & ENG., Illus.). 24p. (J). (gr. -1-3). lib. bdg. 22.00 *(978-1-4339-0079-2(3)*, Weekly Reader Leveled Readers) Stevens, Gareth Publishing LLLP.
Kalman, Bobbie. Veterinarians Help Keep Animals Healthy. 2004. (My Community & Its Helpers Ser.). (ENG., Illus.). 32p. (J). pap. *(978-0-7787-2125-3(6))* Crabtree Publishing Co.
Lowenstein, Felicia. What Does a Veterinarian Do? 2006. (What Does a Community Helper Do? Ser.). (Illus.). 24p. (J). (gr. 1-3). lib. bdg. 22.60 *(978-0-7660-2322-2(2)*, Enslow Elementary) Enslow Pubs., Inc.
Parks, Peggy J. Veterinarian. 2004. (EXPLORING CAREERS Ser.). (ENG.). (J). 27.50 *(978-0-7377-2068-6(9)*, Greenhaven Pr., Inc.) Cengage Gale.
Riddle, John & Simons, Rae. Veterinarian. Gholar, Cheryl & Riggs, Ernestine G., eds. 2013. (Careers with Character Ser.: 18). 96p. (J). (gr. 7-18). 22.95 *(978-1-4222-2768-8(5))* Mason Crest.
Somervill, Barbara A. Veterinarian. 2015. (21st Century Skills Library: Cool STEAM Careers Ser.). (ENG., Illus.). 32p. (J). (gr. 4-7). 29.93 *(978-1-63362-566-2(4)*, 206448) Cherry Lake Publishing.
Thomas, William David. Veterinarian. 2008. (Cool Careers Ser.). 32p. (gr. 5-8). pap. 10.50 *(978-0-8368-9330-4(1))* Stevens, Gareth Publishing LLLP.
Truett, Trudi Strain. Animal Physical Therapist. 2014. (J). *(978-0-7614-8074-7(9))* Marshall Cavendish Corp.
—Veterinarian. 2014. (J). *(978-0-7614-8076-1(5))* Marshall Cavendish Corp.
—Veterinarian. 2014. (Illus.). 64p. (J). *(978-1-62712-464-5(0))* Musa Publishing.

VIADUCTS

see Bridges

VIANNEY, JEAN BAPTISTE, MARIE, SAINT, 1786-1859

DeDomenico, Elizabeth Marie. Saint John Vianney: A Priest for All People. Hatke, Ben, illus. 2008. (Encounter the Saints Ser.). 122p. (J). (gr. 4-7). pap. 7.95 *(978-0-8198-7115-2(X))* Pauline Bks. & Media.

VIBRATION

see also Light; Waves

Boothroyd, Jennifer. Sensing Light & Sound. 2014. (First Step Nonfiction - Light & Sound Ser.). (ENG., Illus.). 24p. (gr. k-2). lib. bdg. 23.93 *(978-1-4677-3915-3(4)*, Lerner Pubns.) Lerner Publishing Group.
—Vibrations Make Sound. 2014. (First Step Nonfiction - Light & Sound Ser.). (ENG., Illus.). 24p. (gr. k-2). lib. bdg. 23.93 *(978-1-4677-3910-8(3)*, Lerner Pubns.) Lerner Publishing Group.
McAneney, Caitlin. How Elephants & Other Animals Hear the Earth. 2015. (Superior Animal Senses Ser.). (ENG., Illus.). 24p. (J). (gr. 3-4). pap. 8.25 *(978-1-4994-0991-8(5)*, PowerKids Pr.) Rosen Publishing Group, Inc., The.
Solway, Andrew. Exploring Sound, Light, & Radiation. 2007. (Exploring Physical Science Ser.). (Illus.). 48p. (YA). (gr. 5-9). lib. bdg. 29.25 *(978-1-4042-3746-9(1))* Rosen Publishing Group, Inc., The.
Spilsbury, Louise & Spilsbury, Richard. Why Can't I Hear That?: Pitch & Frequency, 1 vol. HL Studios Staff, illus. 2014. (Exploring Sound Ser.). (ENG.). 32p. (gr. 2-4). lib. bdg. 30.65 *(978-1-4109-6000-9(5)*, Raintree Perspectives) Heinemann-Raintree.

VICE-PRESIDENTS—UNITED STATES

Anderson, Dale. Al Gore: A Wake-Up Call to Global Warming. 2009. (Voices for Green Choices Ser.). (ENG., Illus.). 48p. (J). (gr. 5-9). pap. *(978-0-7787-4679-9(8))*; lib. bdg. *(978-0-7787-4666-9(6))* Crabtree Publishing Co.
Baptiste, Tracey. Al Gore. 2011. (Conservation Heroes Ser.). (Illus.). 120p. (YA). (gr. 6-12). 35.00 *(978-1-60413-949-5(8)*, Chelsea Hse.) Facts On File, Inc.
De Medeiros, James. Al Gore. 2008. (Remarkable People Ser.). (Illus.). 24p. (J). (gr. 4-6). pap. 8.95 *(978-1-59036-993-7(9))*; lib. bdg. 24.45 *(978-1-59036-992-0(0))* Weigl Pubs., Inc.
Gorman, Jacqueline Laks. Vice President. 2009. (Know Your Government Ser.). 24p. (J). (gr. 2-4). pap. 8.15 *(978-1-4339-0124-9(2))*; lib. bdg. 22.00 *(978-1-4339-0096-9(3))* Stevens, Gareth Publishing LLLP. (Weekly Reader Leveled Readers).
Harmon, Daniel E. Al Gore & Global Warming. (Celebrity Activists Ser.). 112p. 2009. (gr. 8-8). 66.50 *(978-1-61511-826-7(8))* 2008. (Illus.). (YA). (gr. 7-12). lib. bdg. 34.60 *(978-1-4042-1761-4(4))* Rosen Publishing Group, Inc., The.
Hillstrom, Kevin & Hillstrom, Laurie Collier. Al Gore. 2008. (People in the News Ser.). (ENG., Illus.). 128p. (gr. 7-10). lib. bdg. 39.40 *(978-1-4205-0086-8(4)*, LML02109-242090, Lucent Bks.) Cengage Gale.
Laks Gorman, Jacqueline. Vicepresidente (Vice President) 2009. (Conoce tu gobierno (Know Your Government) Ser.). (SPA.). 24p. (J). (gr. 2-4). pap. 8.15 *(978-1-4339-0131-7(5))*; lib. bdg. 22.00 *(978-1-4339-0103-4(X))* Stevens, Gareth Publishing LLLP. (Weekly Reader Leveled Readers).
Lucas, Eileen. The Aaron Burr Treason Trial. 2003. (Headline Court Cases Ser.). (Illus.). 112p. (J). (gr. 6-12). lib. bdg. 27.94 *(978-0-7660-1765-8(6))* Enslow Pubs., Inc.
Marsh, Carole. Dick Cheney: U. S. Vice President. 2004. (1000 Readers Ser.). (Illus.). 14p. (J). (gr. k-4). pap. 2.95 *(978-0-635-02670-5(8))* Gallopade International.
—John Edwards: Vice Presidential Hopeful. 2004. (Did You Know... ? Ser.). (Illus.). 12p. (J). (gr. k-4). pap. 2.95 *(978-0-635-02671-2(6))* Gallopade International.
McGowan, Joe. Al Gore. 2009. (People We Should Know Ser.). (ENG.). 48p. (J). (gr. 3-5). pap. 10.50 *(978-1-4339-2146-9(4)*, Gareth Stevens Learning Library) Stevens, Gareth Publishing LLLP.
McGowan, Joseph. Al Gore. 2009. (People We Should Know Ser.). (ENG.). 48p. (J). (gr. 3-5). lib. bdg. 31.00 *(978-1-4339-1947-3(8)*, Gareth Stevens Learning Library) Stevens, Gareth Publishing LLLP.
McGrath, Brian. Aaron Burr: More Than a Villain (Alexander Hamilton) 2017. (Primary Source Readers Focus On Ser.). (Illus.). 32p. (J). (gr. 4-8). pap. 8.99 ***(978-1-4258-6355-5(8))*** Teacher Created Materials, Inc.
Melton, Buckner F. Aaron Burr: The Rise & Fall of an American Politician. 2009. (Library of American Lives & Times Ser.). 112p. (gr. 5-5). 69.20 *(978-1-60853-468-5(5))* Rosen Publishing Group, Inc., The.
Nelson, Maria. Becoming Vice President. 2016. (Who's Your Candidate? Choosing Government Leaders Ser.). (ENG., Illus.). 32p. (J). (gr. 3-4). pap. 10.50 *(978-1-4824-4055-3(5))* Stevens, Gareth Publishing LLLP.
Sapet, Kerrily. Al Gore. 2007. (Political Profiles Ser.). (Illus.). 112p. (YA). (gr. 5-9). lib. bdg. 27.95 *(978-1-59935-070-7(X))* Reynolds, Morgan Inc.
Stefoff, Rebecca. Al Gore. rev. ed. 2009. pap. 52.95 *(978-0-7613-9899-8(6))* Lerner Publishing Group.
—Al Gore: Fighting for a Greener Planet. rev. ed. 2008. (Gateway Biographies Ser.). (ENG.). 48p. (gr. 4-8). 26.60 *(978-1-57505-948-8(7))* Lerner Publishing Group.
Uschan, Michael V. Joe Biden. 2010. (People in the News Ser.). (Illus.). 128p. (J). 33.95 *(978-1-4205-0260-2(3)*, Lucent Bks.) Cengage Gale.
Winget, Mary Mueller. Gerald R. Ford. 2007. (Presidential Leaders Ser.). (Illus.). 112p. (J). (gr. 3-7). lib. bdg. 29.27 *(978-0-8225-1509-8(1)*, Twenty-First Century Bks.) Lerner Publishing Group.
Young, Jeff C. Joe Biden. 2009. (Political Profiles Ser.). 100p. (YA). (gr. 5-9). 28.95 *(978-1-59935-131-5(5))* Reynolds, Morgan Inc.

VICKSBURG (MISS.)—HISTORY—SIEGE, 1863

Warren, Andrea. Under Siege! Three Children at the Civil War Battle for Vicksburg. 2009. (ENG., Illus.). 176p. (YA). (gr.

T
U
V

4-8). 21.95 *(978-0-374-31255-8(9)*, 9780374312558, Farrar, Straus & Giroux (BYR)) Farrar, Straus & Giroux.

VICTORIA, QUEEN OF GREAT BRITAIN, 1819-1901

Bailey, Gerry & Foster, Karen. Queen Victoria's Diamond. Noyes, Leighton & Radford, Karen, illus. 2008. (Stories of Great People Ser.). (ENG.). 40p. (J). (gr. 3-6). lib. bdg. *(978-0-7787-3697-4(0))*; pap. *(978-0-7787-3719-3(5))* Crabtree Publishing Co.

Bernard, Catherine J. The British Empire & Queen Victoria in World History. 2003. (In World History Ser.). (Illus.). 128p. (J). (gr. 5-12). lib. bdg. 26.60 *(978-0-7660-1824-2(5))* Enslow Pubs., Inc.

Gigliotti, Jim. Who Was Queen Victoria? Harrison, Nancy & Hergenrother, Max, illus. 2014. (Who Was? Ser.). (ENG.). 112p. (J). (gr. 3-7). 5.99 *(978-0-448-48182-1(0)*, Grosset & Dunlap) Penguin Young Readers Group.

—Who Was Queen Victoria? 2014. (Who Was... ? Ser.). lib. bdg. 16.00 *(978-0-606-35697-8(5))* Turtleback Bks.

Guy, John. Victoria. 2004. (Illus.). 32p. (J). (gr. 4-7). pap. 5.95 *(978-1-86007-033-4(7)*, TickTock Books) Octopus Publishing Group GBR. Dist: Independent Pubs. Group.

Hicks, Kyra E. Martha Ann's Quilt for Queen Victoria. Födi, Lee Edward, illus. 2012. 32p. (J). pap. 12.95 *(978-0-9824796-8-1(9))* Black Threads Pr.

—Martha Ann's Quilt for Queen Victoria. Fodi, Lee Edward, illus. 2006. 28p. (J). (gr. -1-3). 16.95 *(978-1-933285-59-7(1))* Brown Books Publishing Group.

Lacey, Saskia. The History of Victorian Innovations: Equivalent Fractions (Grade 3) 2017. (Mathematics Readers Ser.). (Illus.). 32p. (gr. 3-3). 8.99 ***(978-1-4807-5803-2(5))*** Teacher Created Materials, Inc.

Schomp, Virginia. Victoria & Her Court. 2010. (Life in Victorian England Ser.). 80p. (gr. 6). 34.21 *(978-1-60870-028-8(3))* Marshall Cavendish Corp.

Whitelaw, Nancy. Queen Victoria & the British Empire. 2004. (World Leaders Ser.). (Illus.). 160p. (YA). (gr. 6-12). lib. bdg. 26.95 *(978-1-931798-29-7(X))* Reynolds, Morgan Inc.

VIDEO GAMES

Austic, Greg. Game Design. 2013. (21st Century Skills Innovation Library: Makers As Innovators Ser.). (ENG., Illus.). 32p. (J). (gr. 4-8). 28.50 *(978-1-62431-142-0(3)*, 202888); pap. 14.21 *(978-1-62431-274-8(8)*, 202890) Cherry Lake Publishing.

Barba, Rick. Assassin's Creed: A Walk Through History 1189-1868. 2016. (ENG., Illus.). 128p. (J). (gr. 7). pap. 12.99 *(978-1-338-09914-0(0))* Scholastic, Inc.

Barton, Chris. Attack! Boss! Cheat Code! A Gamer's Alphabet. Spiotto, Joey, illus. 2014. (ENG.). 32p. (J). (gr. 1-4). 14.95 *(978-1-57687-701-2(9)*, powerHouse Bks.) powerHouse Cultural Entertainment, Inc.

Bjornlund, Lydia. The History of Video Games. 2014. (Video Games & Society Ser.). (ENG., Illus.). 96p. (J). lib. bdg. *(978-1-60152-746-2(2))* ReferencePoint Pr., Inc.

BradyGames. Pokémon Visual Companion: Second Edition. 2016. (ENG., Illus.). 272p. (J). (gr. 1-4). 16.99 *(978-0-7440-1760-1(2)*, DK) DK Games.

BradyGames Staff & Birlew, Dan. Monster Hunter Official Strategy Guide. 2004. (ENG., Illus.). 144p. pap. 14.99 *(978-0-7440-0362-8(8))* Pearson Education.

Burns, Jan. Shigeru Miyamoto: Nintendo Game Designer. 2006. (Inventors & Creators Ser.). (ENG., Illus.). 48p. (J). (gr. 3-7). lib. bdg. 29.95 *(978-0-7377-3534-5(1)*, Greenhaven Pr., Inc.) Cengage Gale.

Camille, Hayley. The Ultimate Player's Guide to Skylanders Superchargers. 2016. (ENG., Illus.). 336p. pap. 19.99 *(978-0-7897-5715-9(X))* Pearson Education.

Carmichael, L. E. How Do Video Games Work? 2015. (ENG., Illus.). 32p. (J). (gr. k-2). 26.65 *(978-1-4677-8079-7(0))* Lerner Publishing Group.

Carson, Mary Kay. Who Invented Home Video Games? Ralph Baer. 2012. (I Like Inventors! Ser.). (Illus.). 24p. (J). (gr. k-3). pap. 7.95 *(978-1-4644-0135-0(7)*, Enslow Elementary) Enslow Pubs., Inc.

Ceceri, Kathy. Video Games: Design & Code Your Own Adventure. Crosier, Mike, illus. 2015. (Build It Yourself Ser.). (ENG.). 128p. (J). (gr. 3-7). 22.95 *(978-1-61930-291-4(8))* Open City Bks.

Cefrey, Holly. Career Building Through Machinima: Using Video Games to Make Movies. 2009. (Digital Career Building Ser.). 64p. (gr. 6-6). 58.50 *(978-1-61512-168-7(4))* Rosen Publishing Group, Inc., The.

Cohen, Judith Love. You Can Be A Woman Video Game Producer. l.t. ed. 2005. (Illus.). 72p. (J). 17.95 *(978-1-880599-74-7(0))*; pap. 12.95 *(978-1-880599-73-0(2))* Cascade Pass, Inc.

ConCrafter. Minecraft by Concrafter: An Unofficial Guide with New Facts & Commands. 2016. (ENG., Illus.). 240p. (J). pap. 12.99 *(978-1-250-10566-0(8)*, 9781250105660) Feiwel & Friends.

Cornell, Kari. Nintendo Video Game Designer Shigeru Miyamoto. 2016. (STEM Trailblazer Bios Ser.). (ENG., Illus.). 32p. (J). (gr. 2-5). 26.65 *(978-1-4677-9531-9(3))* Lerner Publishing Group.

Corporate Contributor Staff. The Economics of a Video Game. 2013. (ENG.). 48p. (J). *(978-0-7787-7970-4(X))*; pap. *(978-0-7787-7975-9(0))* Crabtree Publishing Co.

Creative Team at Walter Foster Publishing Staff. Learn to Draw Angry Birds: Learn to Draw All of Your Favorite Angry Birds & Those Bad Piggies! 2012. (Licensed Learn to Draw Ser.). (ENG., Illus.). 64p. (J). (gr. 1-3). pap. 9.95 *(978-1-60058-306-3(7)*, 1600583067) Quarto Publishing Group USA.

Croce, Nicholas. Cool Careers Without College for People Who Love Video Games. 2006. (Cool Careers Without College Ser.). (Illus.). 144p. (YA). (gr. 7-12). lib. bdg. 35.95 *(978-1-4042-0747-9(3))* Rosen Publishing Group, Inc., The.

—Cool Careers Without College for people who love Video Games. 2009. (Cool Careers Without College Ser.). 144p. (gr. 6-6). 66.50 *(978-1-61511-982-0(5))* Rosen Publishing Group, Inc., The.

Culp, Jennifer. Call of Duty: Vince Zampella, Grant Collier, & Jason West, 1 vol. 2015. (ENG., Illus.). 128p. (J). 35.60 *(978-1-4777-7923-1(X)*, Rosen Young Adult) Rosen Publishing Group, Inc., The.

Cunningham, Kevin. Video Game Designer. 2015. (21st Century Skills Library: Cool STEAM Careers Ser.). (ENG., Illus.). 32p. (J). (gr. 4-7). 29.93 *(978-1-63362-567-9(2)*, 206452) Cherry Lake Publishing.

—Video Games: From Concept to Consumer. 2013. (Calling All Innovators). (ENG.). 64p. (J). pap. 8.95 *(978-0-531-22011-5(7)*, Children's Pr.); lib. bdg. 30.00 *(978-0-531-26523-9(4))* Scholastic Library Publishing.

Donovan, Sandy. Technology Top Tens. 2014. (Entertainment's Top 10 Ser.). (Illus.). 32p. (J). (gr. 5-8). lib. bdg. 26.60 *(978-1-4677-3841-5(7)*, Lerner Pubns.) Lerner Publishing Group.

Dorling Kindersley Publishing Staff. The Clone Wars. 2008. (Ultimate Sticker Bks.). (ENG.). 16p. (J). (gr. k-3). 6.99 *(978-0-7566-4029-3(6)*, DK Children) Dorling Kindersley Publishing, Inc.

—Disney Infinity Character Encyclopedia. 2015. (ENG., Illus.). 192p. (J). (gr. 1-4). 16.99 *(978-1-4654-2895-0(X)*, DK Children) Dorling Kindersley Publishing, Inc.

—Skylanders Universe Chronicles. 2014. (ENG.). 96p. (J). (gr. 2-4). 12.99 *(978-1-4654-2129-6(7)*, DK Children) Dorling Kindersley Publishing, Inc.

Egan, Jill & Stewart, Rhea A. How Video Game Designers Use Math. 2009. (Math in the Real World Ser.). 32p. (gr. 4-6). 28.00 *(978-1-60413-603-6(0)*, Chelsea Clubhouse) Facts On File, Inc.

Farkas, Bart G. Way of the Samurai 2 Official Strategy Guide. 2004. (ENG., Illus.). 128p. pap. 14.99 *(978-0-7440-0371-0(7))* Pearson Education.

Farshtey, Greg. Lego Ninjago Official Guide. 2011. (Illus.). 128p. (J). pap. *(978-0-545-38285-4(8))* Scholastic, Inc.

Farwell, Nick. Minecraft. Burlinson, James & Cordner, Theo, illus. 2014. 79p. (J). *(978-0-545-68575-7(3))* Scholastic, Inc.

—Minecraft: Redstone Handbook (Updated Edition) An Official Mojang Book. 2015. (Minecraft Ser.). (ENG., Illus.). 96p. (J). (gr. 3-7). 8.99 *(978-0-545-82324-1(2))* Scholastic, Inc.

Farwell, Nick & Steer, Don. Minecraft Redstone Handbook. Burlinson, James et al, illus. 2015. 93p. (J). *(978-0-545-82320-3(X))* Scholastic, Inc.

Furgang, Adam. For People Who Love Gaming. 2016. (Cool Careers Without College Ser.). 00104p. (J). (gr. 7-7). 38.45 *(978-1-5081-7282-6(X))* Rosen Publishing Group, Inc., The.

Gimpel, Diane Marczely. Violence in Video Games. 2013. (Hot Topics in Media EBook Ser.). (ENG.). 48p. (J). pap. 15.64 *(978-1-61783-786-9(5))*; (Illus.). (gr. 3-6). lib. bdg. 32.79 *(978-1-61783-736-4(9))* ABDO Publishing Co.

Green, Sara. Nintendo. 2016. (Brands We Know Ser.). (ENG., Illus.). 24p. (J). (gr. 3-8). lib. bdg. 25.95 *(978-1-62617-350-7(8)*, Pilot Bks.) Bellwether Media.

Gregory, Josh. Minecraft: Guide to Building. 2017. (21st Century Skills Innovation Library: Unofficial Guides). (ENG., Illus.). 32p. (J). (gr. 4-8). lib. bdg. 29.93 *(978-1-63472-195-0(0)*, 209352) Cherry Lake Publishing.

—Minecraft: Guide to Combat. 2017. (21st Century Skills Innovation Library: Unofficial Guides). (ENG., Illus.). 32p. (J). (gr. 4-8). lib. bdg. 29.93 *(978-1-63472-196-7(9)*, 209356) Cherry Lake Publishing.

Hackett, Jennifer. Game Design. 2017. (True Book — Behind the Scenes Ser.). (ENG.). 48p. (J). pap. 7.95 ***(978-0-531-24146-2(7))***; lib. bdg. 31.00 ***(978-0-531-23503-4(3))*** Scholastic Library Publishing. (Children's Pr.).

Hamilton, Jill. Video Games. 2010. (Introducing Issues with Opposing Viewpoints Ser.). (ENG.). 144p. 36.95 *(978-0-7377-4946-5(6)*, Greenhaven Pr., Inc.) Cengage Gale.

Hile, Kevin. Video Games. 2009. (Technology 360 Ser.). (ENG., Illus.). 128p. (YA). (gr. 7-10). lib. bdg. 34.95 *(978-1-4205-0170-4(4)*, LML02109-246082, Lucent Bks.) Cengage Gale.

Hollinger, Elizabeth M. Star Ocean(r) Till the End of Time: Official Strategy Guide. 2004. (ENG., Illus.). 272p. (YA). pap. 15.99 *(978-0-7440-0390-1(3))* Pearson Education.

Hulick, Kathryn. American Life & Video Games from Pong to Minecraft. 2016. (Pop Culture Ser.). (Illus.). 112p. (J). (gr. 7-7). 39.93 *(978-1-5026-1975-4(X))* Cavendish Square Publishing.

Jakubiak, David J. A Smart Kid's Guide to Playing Online Games. 2009. (Kids Online Ser.). 24p. (J). (ENG.). pap. 8.25 *(978-1-4358-3350-0(3))*; (Illus.). (gr. 2-6). lib. bdg. 22.60 *(978-1-4042-8115-8(0))* Rosen Publishing Group, Inc., The. (PowerKids Pr.).

Jozefowicz, Chris. Video Game Developer. 2009. (Cool Careers: Cutting Edge Ser.). (ENG., Illus.). 32p. (J). (gr. 5-8). pap. 10.50 *(978-1-4339-2157-5(X))* Stevens, Gareth Publishing LLLP.

—Video Games. 2009. (Ultimate 10: Entertainment Ser.). (ENG.). 48p. (J). (gr. 4-8). pap. 10.50 *(978-1-4339-2215-2(0))*; (YA). (gr. 5-9). lib. bdg. 31.00 *(978-0-8368-9167-6(8))* Stevens, Gareth Publishing LLLP.

Kaplan, Arie. The Awesome Inner Workings of Video Games. (ShockZone (tm) — Games & Gamers Ser.). (ENG., Illus.). 32p. (gr. 5-8). 2015. 21.32 *(978-1-4677-5994-6(5)*, Lerner Digital) 2013. pap. 8.95 *(978-1-4677-1584-3(0))* 2013. lib. bdg. 26.60 *(978-1-4677-1250-7(7)*, Lerner Pubns.) Lerner Publishing Group.

—The Biggest Names of Video Games. (ShockZone (tm) — Games & Gamers Ser.). (ENG., Illus.). 32p. (gr. 5-8). 2015. 21.32 *(978-1-4677-5995-3(3)*, Lerner Digital) 2013. pap. 8.95 *(978-1-4677-1589-8(1))* 2013. lib. bdg. 26.60 *(978-1-4677-1253-8(1)*, Lerner Pubns.) Lerner Publishing Group.

—The Brain-Boosting Benefits of Gaming. (ShockZone (tm) — Games & Gamers Ser.). (ENG., 32p. (gr. 5-8). 2015. Illus.). 21.32 *(978-1-4677-5996-0(1)*, Lerner Digital) 2013. lib. bdg. 26.60 *(978-1-4677-1251-4(5)*, Lerner Pubns.) 2013. (Illus.). pap. 8.95 *(978-1-4677-1588-1(3))* Lerner Publishing Group.

—The Epic Evolution of Video Games. (ShockZone (tm) — Games & Gamers Ser.). (ENG., Illus.). 32p. (gr. 5-8). 2015. 21.32 *(978-1-4677-5998-4(8)*, Lerner Digital) 2013. pap. 8.95 *(978-1-4677-1585-0(9))* 2013. lib. bdg. 26.60 *(978-1-4677-1248-4(5)*, Lerner Pubns.) Lerner Publishing Group.

Keppeler, Jill. The Inventors of Minecraft: Markus Notch Persson & His Coding Team. 2017. (Breakout Biographies Ser.). 32p. (J). (gr. 9-10). pap. 10.00 ***(978-1-5081-6062-5(7)***, PowerKids Pr.) Rosen Publishing Group, Inc., The.

Krensky, Stephen. The High Score & Lowdown on Video Games! Burroughs, Scott, illus. 2015. (History of Fun Stuff Ser.). (ENG.). 48p. (J). (gr. 1-3). 16.99 *(978-1-4814-2916-0(7))*; pap. 3.99 *(978-1-4814-2915-3(9))* Simon Spotlight. (Simon Spotlight).

La Bella, Laura. Careers for Tech Girls in Video Game Development. 2015. (Tech Girls Ser.). (ENG., Illus.). 80p. (J). (gr. 7-8). 34.25 *(978-1-4994-6107-7(0)*, Rosen Young Adult) Rosen Publishing Group, Inc., The.

Loh-Hagan, Virginia. Sound Effects Artist. 2015. (Illus.). 32p. (J). pap. *(978-1-63470-056-6(2))* Cherry Lake Publishing.

McCarthy, Cecilia Pinto. E-Sports Game Design. 2017. (ESports: Game On! Ser.). (ENG.). 48p. (J). (gr. 5-8). 29.27 ***(978-1-59953-892-1(X))*** Norwood Hse. Pr.

Miko, Christopher & Romines, Garrett. Unofficial Holy Bible for Minecrafters: A Children's Guide to the New Testament. 2016. (ENG.). 316p. (J). (gr. k). pap. 19.99 *(978-1-5107-0182-3(6))* Skyhorse Publishing Co., Inc.

Miller, Megan. Hacks for Minecrafters - Master Builder: The Unofficial Guide to Tips & Tricks That Other Guides Won't Teach You. 2014. (ENG., Illus.). 128p. (J). (gr. 1). 12.99 *(978-1-63450-043-2(1)*, Sky Pony Pr.) Skyhorse Publishing Co., Inc.

—Hacks for Minecrafters: Command Blocks: The Unofficial Guide to Tips & Tricks That Other Guides Won't Teach You. 2015. (ENG., Illus.). 128p. (J). (gr. 1-7). 12.99 *(978-1-63450-663-2(4)*, Sky Pony Pr.) Skyhorse Publishing Co., Inc.

—Hacks for Minecrafters: Redstone: The Unofficial Guide to Tips & Tricks That Other Guides Won't Teach You. 2015. (ENG., Illus.). 128p. (J). (gr. 1-7). 12.99 *(978-1-63450-665-6(0)*, Sky Pony Pr.) Skyhorse Publishing Co., Inc.

Milton, Stephanie. Minecraft: Combat Handbook (Updated Edition) An Official Mojang Book. 2015. (Minecraft Ser.). (ENG., Illus.). 96p. (J). (gr. 3-7). 8.99 *(978-0-545-82323-4(4))* Scholastic, Inc.

Milton, Stephanie & Soares, Paul. Minecraft Combat Handbook. Cordner, Theo & Bolder, Joe, illus. 2015. 95p. (J). *(978-0-545-82319-7(6))* Scholastic, Inc.

Milton, Stephanie, et al. Minecraft: Essential Handbook (Updated Edition) An Official Mojang Book. 2015. (Minecraft Ser.). (ENG., Illus.). 96p. (J). (gr. 3-7). 8.99 *(978-0-545-82326-5(9))* Scholastic, Inc.

Mooney, Carla. Inside the e-Sports Industry. 2017. (ESports: Game On! Ser.). (ENG.). 48p. (J). (gr. 5-8). 29.27 ***(978-1-59953-891-4(1))*** Norwood Hse. Pr.

Morgan, Winter. Discoveries in the Overworld: Lost Minecraft Journals, Book One. 2015. (Lost Minecraft Journals Ser.). (ENG.). 112p. (J). (gr. 1-7). pap. 7.99 *(978-1-5107-0350-6(0)*, Sky Pony Pr.) Skyhorse Publishing Co., Inc.

Nakaya, Andrea C. Are Video Games Harmful? 2016. (ENG.). 80p. (J). (gr. 5-12). *(978-1-68282-070-4(X))* ReferencePoint Pr., Inc.

—Video Games & Youth. 2014. (Video Games & Society Ser.). (ENG., Illus.). 80p. (J). lib. bdg. *(978-1-60152-750-9(0))* ReferencePoint Pr., Inc.

National Geographic Kids Staff. Angry Birds Explore the World. 2014. (ENG., Illus.). 104p. (J). (gr. 3-7). lib. bdg. 18.90 *(978-1-4263-1987-7(8)*, National Geographic Children's Bks.) National Geographic Society.

Needler, Matthew & Southam, Phil. Minecraft Construction Handbook. Barker, James et al, illus. 2015. 87p. (J). *(978-0-545-82321-0(8))* Scholastic, Inc.

—Minecraft: Construction Handbook (Updated Edition) An Official Mojang Book. 2015. (Minecraft Ser.). (ENG., Illus.). 96p. (J). (gr. 3-7). 8.99 *(978-0-545-82325-8(0))* Scholastic, Inc.

Netzley, Patricia. How Do Video Games Affect Society? 2014. (Video Games & Society Ser.). (ENG., Illus.). 80p. (J). lib. bdg. *(978-1-60152-748-6(9))* ReferencePoint Pr., Inc.

Netzley, Patricia D. How Does Video Game Violence Affect Society? 2013. (Illus.). 96p. (YA). lib. bdg. *(978-1-60152-490-4(0))* ReferencePoint Pr., Inc.

—Video Games, Violence & Crime. 2014. (Video Games & Society Ser.). (ENG., Illus.). 80p. (J). lib. bdg. *(978-1-60152-752-3(7))* ReferencePoint Pr., Inc.

Owen, Ruth. The Wonderful Worlds of a Video Game Designer. 2015. (Get to Work with Science & Technology Ser.). (ENG.). 32p. (J). (gr. 2-7). lib. bdg. 26.60 *(978-1-910549-32-2(0))* Bearport Publishing Co., Inc.

Oxlade, Chris. Gaming Technology. 2011. (New Technology Ser.). 48p. (YA). (gr. 7-12). lib. bdg. 34.25 *(978-1-59920-531-1(9))* Black Rabbit Bks.

Palmer, Erin. Video Games, Yes or No. 2015. (ENG.). 24p. (gr. k-3). 28.50 *(978-1-63430-349-1(0))* Rourke Educational Media.

Paris, David. History of Video Games (Grade 6) 2016. (TIME for KIDS(r) Nonfiction Readers Ser.). (Illus.). 48p. (J). (gr. 6-6). pap. 9.99 *(978-1-4938-3594-2(7))* Teacher Created Materials, Inc.

Parker, K. J. Guardian Universe Core Fuzion. 2004. (Illus.). 228p. (YA). per. 25.00 *(978-0-9744698-0-5(7))* Dilly Green Bean Games.

parks, peggy j. Video Games. 2008. (Compact Research Ser.). (Illus.). 104p. (YA). (gr. 7-12). lib. bdg. 25.95 *(978-1-60152-053-1(0))* ReferencePoint Pr., Inc.

Peters, Diane. Gaming: Before It Outplays You, 1 vol. Shannon, Ben, illus. 2010. (Lorimer Deal with It Ser.). (ENG.). 32p. (YA). (gr. 4-6). 24.95 *(978-1-55277-490-8(2)*, 9781552774908) Lorimer, James & Co., Ltd., Pubs. CAN. Dist: Casemate Pubs. & Bk. Distributors, LLC.

—Gaming: Deal with It Before It Outplays You, 1 vol. Shannon, Ben, illus. 2010. (Lorimer Deal with It Ser.). (ENG.). 32p. (J). (gr. 4-9). pap. 12.95 *(978-1-55277-434-2(1)*, 9781552774342) Lorimer, James & Co., Ltd., Pubs. CAN. Dist: Orca Bk. Pubs. USA.

Peterson, Tara & Hogan, Joyce W. Should We Play Video Games? A Persuasive Text. 2006. (Illus.). 30p. (J). pap. *(978-1-59336-338-3(9))* Mondo Publishing.

Polette, Nancy. Improvisation & Theatre Games with Children's Literature. 2004. (J). pap. 10.95 *(978-1-931334-41-9(2))* Pieces of Learning.

Polydoros, Lori. Awesome Video Game Competitions. 2017. (Cool Competitions Ser.). (ENG.). 32p. (gr. 1-2). lib. bdg. 26.65 ***(978-1-5157-7353-5(1)***, Blazers) Capstone Press of Coughlan Cos.

Powell, Marie. Asking Questions about Video Games. 2015. (21st Century Skills Library: Asking Questions about Media Ser.). (ENG., Illus.). 32p. (J). (gr. 4-8). 29.93 *(978-1-63362-491-7(9)*, 206872); pap. 14.21 *(978-1-63362-507-5(9)*, 206873) Cherry Lake Publishing.

Pratchett, Rhianna & Robson, Eddie. Video Games. 2008. (ENG., Illus.). 32p. (J). (gr. 6-10). lib. bdg. *(978-0-7787-3817-6(5))* Crabtree Publishing Co.

Ross, Michael & Ross, Christopher. Finding Faith in a Minecrafty World: 80 a-To-Z (Kid Only) Survival Secrets [an Unofficial Guide]. 2017. (ENG., Illus.). 256p. (J). pap. 14.99 *(978-0-7369-7085-3(1))* Harvest Hse. Pubs.

Roy, Daniel. Crafting & Construction Handbook. 2016. (Terraria Ser.). (ENG., Illus.). 80p. (J). (gr. 3-7). pap. 8.99 *(978-0-399-54134-6(9)*, Grosset & Dunlap) Penguin Young Readers Group.

—The Ultimate Survival Handbook. 2016. (Terraria Ser.). (ENG., Illus.). 80p. (J). (gr. 3-7). pap. 8.99 *(978-0-399-54133-9(0)*, Grosset & Dunlap) Penguin Young Readers Group.

Rubenstein, Glenn. Sports Gamer: The Best in Sports Video Games. (J). (gr. 3-9). pap. 3.99 *(978-1-930623-22-4(4))* Sports Illustrated For Kids.

Scholastic & Imagine Publishing Staff. Game on! 2017: All the Best Games: Awesome Facts & Coolest Secrets. 2016. (ENG., Illus.). 224p. (J). (gr. 3-7). pap. 14.99 *(978-1-338-03272-7(0))* Scholastic, Inc.

Scholastic Editors & Wiltshire, Alex. Minecraft: Blockopedia. 2015. (ENG., Illus.). 312p. (J). (gr. 4-5). 49.99 *(978-0-545-82011-0(1))* Scholastic, Inc.

Scholastic Inc, contrib. by. Game On! 2016. 2015. (ENG., Illus.). 224p. (J). (gr. 3-7). pap. 14.99 *(978-0-545-85031-5(2)*, Scholastic Paperbacks) Scholastic, Inc.

—The League of Superhero Games. 2017. (Game On! Ser.). (ENG., Illus.). 128p. (J). (gr. 3-7). pap. 8.99 *(978-1-338-11813-1(7))* Scholastic, Inc.

Scott, Cavan & Snider, Brandon T. Skylanders Universe: The Complete Collection. 2015. (Illus.). 224p. (J). ***(978-0-448-48904-9(X)***, Grosset & Dunlap) Penguin Publishing Group.

Simon, Philip, ed. The Art of Plants vs. Zombies: A Visual Book. 2014. (Plants vs. Zombies Ser.). (ENG., Illus.). 88p. (gr. 3-7). 9.99 *(978-1-61655-331-9(6))* Dark Horse Comics.

Stolze, Greg. Rites of the Dragon. 2004. (Vampire, the Requiem Ser.). (Illus.). 120p. (YA). 24.99 *(978-1-58846-254-1(4))* White Wolf Publishing, Inc.

Suen, Anastasia. Alternate Reality Game Designer Jane Mcgonigal. 2014. (STEM Trailblazer Bios Ser.). (ENG., Illus.). 32p. (gr. 2-5). lib. bdg. 26.60 *(978-1-4677-2458-6(0)*, Lerner Pubns.) Lerner Publishing Group.

Swatman, Simon. Plants vs. Zombies: Official Guide to Protecting Your Brains. Howling, Adam, illus. 2013. (Plants vs. Zombies Ser.). (ENG.). 176p. (J). (gr. 1-5). pap. 7.99 *(978-0-06-222855-0(2)*, HarperFestival) HarperCollins Pubs.

Terry, Paul. Top 10 for Kids Gaming. 2015. (ENG., Illus.). 96p. (J). (gr. 3-6). pap. 9.95 *(978-1-77085-564-9(5)*, 9781770855649) Firefly Bks., Ltd.

Thomas Nelson Publishing Staff. Adventures in Odyssey & the Great Escape: The Ultimate Test of Time Awaits You Inside! 2008. cd-rom 19.95 *(978-0-9754280-2-3(0))* Nelson, Thomas Inc.

—Adventures in Odyssey & the Treasure of the Incas: The Chase Is on. Discover the Treasure. Reveal the Truth. 2008. cd-rom 19.95 *(978-0-9754280-0-9(4))* Nelson, Thomas Inc.

Trueit, Trudi Strain. Video Gaming. 2008. (21st Century Skills Innovation Library: Innovation in Entertainment Ser.). (ENG., Illus.). 32p. (gr. 4-8). lib. bdg. 28.50 *(978-1-60279-218-0(6)*, 200149) Cherry Lake Publishing.

Video Games. 2010. (Career Launcher Ser.). 160p. (C). (gr. 9-18). 34.95 *(978-0-8160-7960-5(9)*, Ferguson Publishing Co.); pap. 14.95 *(978-0-8160-7982-7(X)*, Checkmark Bks.) Facts On File, Inc.

Watson, Stephanie. Video Game Designer. 2017. (ENG.). 64p. (YA). (gr. 5-12). ***(978-1-68282-184-8(6))*** ReferencePoint Pr., Inc.

West, Tracey. Normal Pokédex. 2005. (Pokemon Ser.). 47p. *(978-0-439-72200-1(4))* Scholastic, Inc.

—Temple Run: Race Through Time to Unlock Secrets of Ancient Worlds. 2014. (ENG., Illus.). 128p. (J). (gr. 3-7). pap. 12.99 *(978-1-4263-1780-4(8)*, National Geographic Children's Bks.) National Geographic Society.

West, Tracey & Noll, Katherine. Psychic Pokédex. 2005. (Illus.). 47p. (J). pap. *(978-0-439-81051-7(5))* Scholastic, Inc.

West, Tracey & Nolls, Katherine. Ice & Fighting Pokédex. 2005. 47p. *(978-0-439-72194-3(6))* Scholastic, Inc.

—Official Pokémon Pokédex. 2006. (Illus.). 111p. (J). *(978-0-439-85586-0(1))* Scholastic, Inc.

Wilkinson, Colin. Gaming: Playing Safe & Playing Smart. 2011. (Digital & Information Literacy Ser.). (ENG.). 48p. (YA). (gr. 5-8). pap. 11.75 *(978-1-4488-5611-4(6))*; lib. bdg. 29.25 *(978-1-4488-5552-0(7))* Rosen Publishing Group, Inc., The. (Rosen Reference).

Wood, Alix. Video Game Designer, 1 vol., 1. 2014. (World's Coolest Jobs Ser.). (ENG.). 32p. (J). (gr. 3-6). 26.25 *(978-1-4777-6015-4(6)*, PowerKids Pr.) Rosen Publishing Group, Inc., The.

Wyckoff, Edwin Brit. The Guy Who Invented Home Video Games: Ralph Baer & His Awesome Invention. 2010. (Genius at Work! Great Inventor Biographies Ser.). (Illus.). 32p. (J). (gr. 2-5). 23.94 *(978-0-7660-3450-1(X))* Enslow Pubs., Inc.

Yogscast Staff. Yogscast: the Diggy Diggy Book. 2016. (ENG., Illus.). 112p. (J). (gr. 3-7). pap. 8.99 *(978-0-545-95663-5(3))* Scholastic, Inc.

Zalme, Ron, illus. How to Draw Nintendo Greatest Heroes & Villains. 2007. *(978-0-439-91324-9(1))* Scholastic, Inc.

Zeiger, James. Minecraft: Redstone & Transportation. 2016. (21st Century Skills Innovation Library: Unofficial Guides). (ENG., Illus.). 32p. (J). (gr. 4-8). 29.93 *(978-1-63470-522-6(X)*, 207819) Cherry Lake Publishing.

VIENNA (AUSTRIA)—FICTION

Clifford, Ross. The Shiddakovich Adventure. 2009. 122p. pap. 12.88 *(978-1-4092-3520-0(3))* Lulu Pr., Inc.

Dunlap, Susanne. The Musician's Daughter. (ENG.). (YA). (gr. 7). 2010. 352p. pap. 8.99 *(978-1-59990-452-8(7)*, 9781599904528) 2009. 336p. 16.99 *(978-1-59990-332-3(6)*, 9781599903323) Bloomsbury Publishing USA. (Bloomsbury USA Childrens).

Glatshteyn, Yankev. Emil & Karl. Shandler, Jeffrey, tr. 2008. (ENG.). 208p. (J). (gr. 4-9). per. 9.99 *(978-0-312-37387-0(2),* 9780312373870) Square Fish.

Henry, Marguerite. White Stallion of Lipizza. Dennis, Wesley, illus. 2014. (ENG.). 192p. (J). (gr. 3-7). pap. 7.99 *(978-1-4814-0391-7(5),* Aladdin) Simon & Schuster Children's Publishing.

Ibbotson, Eva. The Star of Kazan. Hawkes, Kevin, illus. 2006. (ENG.). 416p. (J). (gr. 3-7). reprint ed. 8.99 *(978-0-14-240582-6(5),* Puffin Books) Penguin Young Readers Group.

Lodding, Linda Ravin. A Gift for Mama. Jay, Alison, illus. 2014. (ENG.). 32p. (J). (gr. -1-3). 17.99 *(978-0-385-75331-9(4),* Knopf Bks. for Young Readers) Random Hse. Children's Bks.

Osborne, Mary Pope. Moonlight on the Magic Flute. Murdocca, Sal, illus. 2010. (Magic Tree House Merlin Mission Ser.: No. 13). (ENG.). 144p. (J). (gr. 2-5). pap. 5.99 *(978-0-375-85647-1(1),* Random Hse. Bks. for Young Readers) Random Hse. Children's Bks.

Salten, Felix. The Hound of Florence. Paterson, Huntley, tr. from GER. 2014. (Bambi's Classic Animal Tales Ser.). (ENG., Illus.). 288p. (J). (gr. 3-7). pap. 6.99 *(978-1-4424-8748-2(8),* Aladdin) Simon & Schuster Children's Publishing.

Watts, Irene N. A Telling Time, 1 vol. Shoemaker, Kathryn E., illus. 2004. (ENG.). 32p. (J). (gr. 2-5). 17.95 *(978-1-896580-39-5(4))* Tradewind Bks. CAN. Dist: Orca Bk. Pubs. USA.

VIENNA (AUSTRIA)—HISTORY

Allport, Alan. The Congress of Vienna. 2011. (Milestones in Modern World History Ser.). (Illus.). 126p. (J). (gr. 9). 35.00 *(978-1-60413-497-1(6),* Chelsea Hse.) Facts On File, Inc.

Dyan, Penelope. Oh Vienna! a Kid's Guide to Vienna, Austri. Weigand, John D., photos by. 2013. (Illus.). 34p. pap. 11.95 *(978-1-61477-073-2(5))* Bellissima Publishing, LLC.

Rauch, Georg. Unlikely Warrior: A Jewish Soldier in Hitler's Army. 2015. (ENG., Illus.). 352p. (YA). (gr. 7). 17.99 *(978-0-374-30142-2(5),* Farrar, Straus & Giroux (BYR)) Farrar, Straus & Giroux.

VIETNAM

Alberti, Theresa. Vietnam ABCs: A Book about the People & Places of Vietnam, 1 vol. Blanks, Natascha Alex, illus. 2007. (Country ABCs Ser.). (ENG.). 32p. (gr. k-5). lib. bdg. 27.99 *(978-1-4048-2251-1(8))* Picture Window Bks.

Gray, Shirley W. & Gray, Shirley Wimbish. Vietnam. 2003. (True Bks.). (ENG., Illus.). 48p. (J). 25.00 *(978-0-516-24211-8(3),* Children's Pr.) Scholastic Library Publishing.

Green, Jen. National Geographic Countries of the World - Vietnam. 2008. (National Geographic Countries of the World Ser.). (ENG., Illus.). 64p. (J). (gr. 5-9). lib. bdg. 27.90 *(978-1-4263-0202-2(9),* National Geographic Children's Bks.) National Geographic Society.

Guillain, Charlotte. Vietnam, 1 vol. 2012. (Countries Around the World Ser.). (ENG.). 48p. (gr. 3-6). pap. 9.95 *(978-1-4329-6142-8(X),* NA-h) Heinemann-Raintree.

Imbriaco, Alison. Vietnam: A MyReportLinks. com Book. 2004. (Top Ten Countries of Recent Immigrants Ser.). (Illus.). 48p. (J). lib. bdg. 26.60 *(978-0-7660-5182-9(X),* MyReportLinks.com Bks.) Enslow Pubs., Inc.

Phillips, Douglas A. Vietnam. Gritzner, Charles F., ed. 2006. (Modern World Nations Ser.). (Illus.). 108p. (gr. 6-12). lib. bdg. 35.00 *(978-0-7910-8835-7(9))* Facts On File, Inc.

Rau, Dana Meachen. Vietnam. 2011. (Explorer Library: Social Studies Explorer Ser.). (ENG.). 48p. (gr. 4-8). lib. bdg. 31.36 *(978-1-61080-097-6(4),* 201088) Cherry Lake Publishing.

Robinson, Tom. John McCain: POW & Statesman, 1 vol. 2010. (Military Heroes Ser.). (ENG.). 112p. (J). (gr. 6-12). lib. bdg. 35.64 *(978-1-60453-963-9(1))* ABDO Publishing Co.

Rose, Elizabeth. A Primary Source Guide to Vietnam. 2009. (Countries of the World). 24p. (gr. 2-3). 42.50 *(978-1-61512-049-9(1),* PowerKids Pr.) Rosen Publishing Group, Inc., The.

Seah, Audrey & Nair, Charissa M. Vietnam. 2nd rev. ed. 2004. (Cultures of the World Ser.). (Illus.). 144p. (gr. 6-7). lib. bdg. 42.79 *(978-0-7614-1789-7(3))* Marshall Cavendish Corp.

Simmons, Pat. Vietnam. (World Focus Ser.). (Illus.). 31p. (J). (gr. 3-7). pap. 3.99 *(978-0-431-07264-7(7))* Oxfam Publishing GBR. Dist: Stylus Publishing, LLC.

Taus-Bolstad, Stacy. Vietnam in Pictures. 2003. (Visual Geography Ser.). (Illus.). 80p. (J). (gr. 5-12). 27.93 *(978-0-8225-4678-8(7))* Lerner Publishing Group.

Zocchi, Judy. In Vietnam. Brodie, Neale, illus. 2005. (Global Adventures II Ser.). 32p. (J). per. 10.95 *(978-1-59646-165-9(9))* Dingles & Co.

VIETNAM—FICTION

Choi, Na-mi. Song of the Mekong River: Vietnam. Cowley, Joy, ed. Jo, Sinae, illus. 2015. (Global Kids Storybooks Ser.). (ENG.). 32p. (gr. 1-4). 7.99 *(978-1-925246-53-7(1));* 26.65 *(978-1-925246-27-8(2));* 26.65 *(978-1-925246-01-8(9))* ChoiceMaker Pty. Ltd., The AUS. (Big and SMALL). Dist: Lerner Publishing Group.

—Song of the Mekong River: Vietnam. Cowley, Joy, ed. Jo, Sinae, illus. 2015. (Global Kids Storybooks Ser.). (ENG.). 32p. (J). (gr. 1-4). pap. 7.99 *(978-1-925233-44-5(8))* Lerner Publishing Group.

Dowell, Frances O'Roark. Shooting the Moon. 2009. (ENG.). 192p. (J). (gr. 5-9). pap. 7.99 *(978-1-4169-7986-9(7),* Atheneum Bks. for Young Readers) Simon & Schuster Children's Publishing.

Dunivan, Dennis W. Escape from Communist Heaven. 2013. (ENG., Illus.). 392p. 17.99 *(978-1-59181-229-6(1))* Sentient Pubns.

Garland, Sherry. Children of the Dragon: Selected Tales from Vietnam, 1 vol. Hyman, Trina Schart, illus. 2012. (ENG.). 32p. (J). (gr. 3-7). 16.99 *(978-1-4556-1709-8(1))* Pelican Publishing Co., Inc.

—The Lotus Seed. Kiuchi, Tatsuro, illus. 2014. 32p. pap. 7.00 *(978-1-61003-219-3(5))* Center for the Collaborative Classroom.

Hoffmire, Baird, illus. How Tiger Got His Stripes: A Folktale from Vietnam. 2006. (Story Cove Ser.). (ENG.). 32p. (J). (gr. -1-3). pap. 4.95 *(978-0-87483-799-5(5))* August Hse. Pubs., Inc.

Hoppey, Tim. Jungle Scout: A Vietnam War Story, 1 vol. Espinoza, Ramon, illus. 2008. (Historical Fiction Ser.). (ENG.). 56p. (gr. 2-3). pap. 6.25 *(978-1-4342-0846-0(X),* Graphic Flash) Stone Arch Bks.

Kadohata, Cynthia. A Million Shades of Gray. 2011. (ENG., Illus.). 240p. (J). (gr. 5-9). pap. 7.99 *(978-1-4424-2919-2(4),* Atheneum Bks. for Young Readers) Simon & Schuster Children's Publishing.

Lai, Thanhhà. Inside Out & Back Again. (ENG.). (J). (gr. 3-7). 2013. 288p. pap. 8.99 *(978-0-06-196279-0(1))* 2011. 272p. 16.99 *(978-0-06-196278-3(3))* HarperCollins Pubs.

—Inside Out & Back Again. 2014. (ENG.). 288p. (J). (gr. 3-7). 12.24 *(978-1-63245-350-1(9))* Lectorum Pubns., Inc.

—Inside Out & Back Again. 2009. 9.68 *(978-0-7848-3887-7(9),* Everbind) Marco Bk. Co.

—Inside Out & Back Again. 2013. 18.00 *(978-1-61383-970-6(7))* Perfection Learning Corp.

—Inside Out & Back Again. 2013. (J). lib. bdg. 18.40 *(978-0-606-27126-4(0),* Turtleback) Turtleback Bks.

—Listen, Slowly. 2015. (ENG.). (J). (gr. 3-7). 272p. 16.99 *(978-0-06-222918-2(4));* 288p. E-Book *(978-0-06-222920-5(6))* HarperCollins Pubs.

Literature Connections English: Fallen Angels. 2004. (gr. 6-12). *(978-0-395-83360-5(4),* 2-70783) Holt McDougal.

Lynch, Chris. Free-Fire Zone. 2012. (Vietnam Ser.). (J). (ENG.). 192p. (gr. 5-9). 16.99 *(978-0-545-27025-0(1));* 183p. *(978-0-545-49427-4(3))* Scholastic, Inc. (Scholastic Pr.).

—I Pledge Allegiance. 2011. 183p. (YA). *(978-0-545-38415-5(X))* Scholastic, Inc.

—I Pledge Allegiance. 2013. (Vietnam Ser.: 1). lib. bdg. 17.20 *(978-0-606-31961-4(1),* Turtleback) Turtleback Bks.

—Vietnam #1: I Pledge Allegiance. 2013. (Vietnam Ser.: 1). (ENG.). 192p. (J). (gr. 5-9). pap. 7.99 *(978-0-545-27030-4(8),* Scholastic Paperbacks) Scholastic, Inc.

Marsden, Carolyn. When Heaven Fell. 2007. (ENG., Illus.). 192p. (J). (gr. 3-7). 15.99 *(978-0-7636-3175-8(2))* Candlewick Pr.

Marsden, Carolyn & Niem, Thay. The Buddha's Diamonds. 2010. (ENG., Illus.). 112p. (J). (gr. 3-7). pap. 5.99 *(978-0-7636-4828-2(0))* Candlewick Pr.

McAfee, Joan K. The Road to el Dorado. 2003. (Illus.). 186p. (YA). pap. 12.95 *(978-0-89745-273-1(9))* Sunflower Univ. Pr.

McKay, Lawrence, Jr., et al. Journey Home. Lee, Keunhee et al, illus. 2003. (Avenues Ser.). (ENG.). 32p. (C). (gr. -1-5). pap. 13.95 *(978-1-58430-005-2(1))* National Geographic School Publishing, Inc.

Meloy, Maile. The Apprentices. Schoenherr, Ian, illus. 2014. (Apothecary Ser.: 2). (ENG.). 432p. (J). (gr. 5). pap. 8.99 *(978-0-14-242598-5(2),* Puffin Books) Penguin Young Readers Group.

Nuo, Johnny. Dinh Van Binh: Vietnamese Village Boy. 2006. (Illus.). 176p. per. 15.12 *(978-1-4120-9966-0(8))* Trafford Publishing.

Phillips, Dee. Vietnam, 1 vol., Bk. 9. 2015. (Yesterday's Voices Ser.). (ENG.). 48p. (YA). (gr. 9-12). pap. 8.95 *(978-1-62250-911-9(0))* Saddleback Educational Publishing, Inc.

Poulsen, David A. Old Man. 2013. 276p. pap. *(978-1-4596-6325-1(X))* ReadHowYouWant.com, Ltd.

Sherman, M. Zachary. Fighting Phantoms, 1 vol. Casas, Fritz, illus. 2011. (Bloodlines Ser.). (ENG.). 88p. (gr. 4-8). lib. bdg. 26.65 *(978-1-4342-2560-3(7))* Stone Arch Bks.

Thong, Roseanne Greenfield. Fly Free! Neilan, Eujin Kim, illus. 2010. (ENG.). 32p. (J). (gr. 2-4). 17.95 *(978-1-59078-550-8(9))* Boyds Mills Pr.

Tran, Truong. Going Home, Coming Home. Phong, Ann, illus. 2003.Tr. of Ve Nha Tham Que Hu'o'Ng. (ENG & VIE.). 32p. (J). 16.95 *(978-0-89239-179-0(0))* Lee & Low Bks., Inc.

Vander Zee, Ruth. Always with You. Himler, Ronald, illus. 2008. (ENG.). 32p. (J). (gr. -1-3). 17.00 *(978-0-8028-5295-3(5),* Eerdmans Bks For Young Readers) Eerdmans, William B. Publishing Co.

VIETNAM—FOREIGN RELATIONS—UNITED STATES

Burgan, Michael. The Vietnam War. 2006. (Wars That Changed American History Ser.). (Illus.). 48p. (gr. 5-12). pap. 14.05 *(978-0-8368-7304-7(1),* Gareth Stevens Secondary Library) Stevens, Gareth Publishing LLLP.

VIETNAM—HISTORY

Bui, Nam. Fish over Diamond. 2012. 138p. 30.99 *(978-1-4691-9624-4(7))* Xlibris Corp.

Clare, John D. Vietnam, 1939-75. 2nd rev. ed. 2004. (Hodder 20th Century History Ser.). (Illus.). 48p. (YA). pap. 26.50 *(978-0-340-81476-5(4),* Hodder Education) Hodder Education Group GBR. Dist: Trans-Atlantic Pubns., Inc.

Cottrell, Robert C. Vietnam: The 17th Parallel. 2004. (Arbitrary Borders Ser.). (Illus.). 112p. (J). (gr. 9-13). 35.00 *(978-0-7910-7834-1(5),* Chelsea Hse.) Facts On File, Inc.

DeMarco, Neil. Vietnam, 1939-75. 2nd rev. ed. 2004. (Illus.). 48p. pap. 26.50 *(978-0-340-81475-8(6),* Hodder Education) Hodder Education Group GBR. Dist: Trans-Atlantic Pubns., Inc.

DiConsiglio, John. Vietnam: The Bloodbath at Hamburger Hill. 2009. (24/7 Goes to War Ser.). (ENG.). 64p. (J). (gr. 6-12). lib. bdg. 29.00 *(978-0-531-25526-1(3),* Children's Pr.) Scholastic Library Publishing.

Johnson, Kristin F. Ho Chi Minh: North Vietnamese President, 1 vol. 2011. (Essential Lives Set 7 Ser.). (ENG., Illus.). 112p. (J). (gr. 6-12). lib. bdg. 35.64 *(978-1-61783-006-8(2))* ABDO Publishing Co.

Kjelle, Marylou Morano. Saigon. 2009. (J). *(978-1-58415-793-9(3))* Mitchell Lane Pubs., Inc.

Labrie, Julia. Cultural Traditions in Vietnam. 2017. 32p. (J). ***(978-0-7787-8101-1(1))*** Crabtree Publishing Co.

LeBoutillier, Kris, photos by & rev. National Geographic Traveler: Vietnam, 3rd Edition. LeBoutillier, Kris, rev. 3rd rev. ed. 2015. (National Geographic Traveler Ser.). (ENG., Illus.). 272p. pap. 22.95 *(978-1-4262-1363-2(8))* National Geographic Society.

Markovics, Joyce L. Vietnam. 2015. (Countries We Come From Ser.). (ENG., Illus.). 32p. (J). (gr. k-3). lib. bdg. 26.60 *(978-1-62724-860-0(9))* Bearport Publishing Co., Inc.

O'Connor, Karen. Vietnam. 2009. pap. 52.95 *(978-0-7613-4736-1(4))* 2008. (Illus.). 48p. (J). (gr. 2-5). 27.93 *(978-0-8225-9415-4(3))* Lerner Publishing Group.

Parker, Lewis K. Why Vietnamese Immigrants Came to America. 2009. (Coming to America Ser.). 24p. (gr. 2-3). 42.50 *(978-1-61511-888-5(8),* PowerKids Pr.) Rosen Publishing Group, Inc., The.

Rush, Elizabeth. H Is for Hanoi. Nguyen, Nghia Cuong, illus. 2013. (Alphabetical World Ser.). (ENG & VIE.). 48p. (gr. k-4). 12.95 *(978-1-934159-42-2(5))* ThingsAsian Pr.

Seah, Audrey, et al. Vietnam. 2015. (Cultures of the World Ser.). (ENG., Illus.). 144p. (J). (gr. 6-6). lib. bdg. 47.07 *(978-1-5026-0080-6(3))* Cavendish Square Publishing.

Sexton, Colleen & Simmons, Walter. Vietnam. 2010. (Exploring Countries Ser.). (ENG., Illus.). 32p. (J). (gr. 3-7). lib. bdg. 26.95 *(978-1-60014-492-9(6),* Blastoff! Readers) Bellwether Media.

Simmons, Walter. Vietnam. 2011. (ENG., Illus.). 32p. (J). *(978-0-531-26473-7(4))* Bellwether Media.

Stibbens, Steve. Knights over the Delta: An Oral History of the 114th Aviation Company in Vietnam, 1963-72. Stibbens, Steve, ed. 2003. 60.00 *(978-0-9742465-0-5(6))* 114th Aviation Co. Assn.

Taylor, Trace. Vietnam. 2010. pap. 39.62 *(978-1-61541-093-4(7))* American Reading Co.

Taylor, Trace & SáNchez, LucíA M. Viet Nam. 2010. pap. 39.62 *(978-1-61541-123-8(2))* American Reading Co.

Taylor, Trace & Sánchez, Lucía M. Vietnam. 2010. (1Y Nuestro Mundo Ser.). (SPA.). 16p. (J). (gr. k-1). pap. 6.99 *(978-1-61541-122-1(4))* American Reading Co.

Willis, Terri. Vietnam. 2013. (Enchantment of the World™, Second Ser.). (ENG.). 144p. (J). 40.00 *(978-0-531-25605-3(7),* Children's Pr.) Scholastic Library Publishing.

Winter, Max. Vietnam. 2015. (One World, Many Countries Ser.). (ENG.). 32p. (J). (gr. 1-4). 28.50 *(978-1-63407-060-7(7),* 208879) Child's World, Inc., The.

Yasuda, Anita. Vietnam. 2016. (Illus.). 32p. (J). *(978-1-4896-4615-6(9))* Weigl Pubs., Inc.

Zocchi, Judy. In Vietnam. Brodie, Neale, illus. 2005. (Global Adventures II Ser.). 32p. (J). pap. 10.95 *(978-1-59646-164-2(0));* lib. bdg. 21.65 *(978-1-59646-081-2(4))* Dingles & Co.

—In Vietnam/en Vietnam. Brodie, N. eale, illus. 2005. (Global Adventures II Ser.).Tr. of En Vietnam. (ENG & SPA.). 32p. (J). pap. 10.95 *(978-1-59646-166-6(7))* Dingles & Co.

—In Vietnam/en Vietnam. Brodie, Neale, illus. 2005. (Global Adventures II Ser.).Tr. of En Vietnam. (ENG & SPA.). 32p. (J). lib. bdg. 21.65 *(978-1-59646-082-9(2));* per. 10.95 *(978-1-59646-167-3(5))* Dingles & Co.

VIETNAM WAR, 1961-1975

Barr, Linda. Long Road to Freedom: Journey of the Hmong. 2004. (High Five Reading - Purple Ser.). (ENG., Illus.). 64p. (gr. 3-4). per. 9.00 *(978-0-7368-3852-8(X),* High Five Reading (RBL)) Capstone Press of Coughlan Cos.

Benoit, Peter. The Vietnam War. 2013. (Cornerstones of Freedom™, Third Ser.). (ENG., Illus.). 64p. (J). pap. 8.95 *(978-0-531-21966-9(6));* lib. bdg. 30.00 *(978-0-531-23608-6(0))* Scholastic Library Publishing.

Burgan, Michael. Death at Kent State: How a Photograph Brought the Vietnam War Home to America. 2016. (Captured History Ser.). (ENG., Illus.). 64p. (gr. 5-7). lib. bdg. 34.65 *(978-0-7565-5424-8(1),* CPB Grades 4-8) Compass Point Bks.

—The Vietnam War. 2006. (Wars That Changed American History Ser.). (Illus.). 48p. (gr. 5-12). pap. 14.05 *(978-0-8368-7304-7(1));* lib. bdg. 31.00 *(978-0-8368-7295-8(9))* Stevens, Gareth Publishing LLLP. (Gareth Stevens Secondary Library).

—The Vietnam War: An Interactive Modern History Adventure, 1 vol. 2014. (You Choose: Modern History Ser.). (ENG.). 112p. (gr. 3-4). 31.99 *(978-1-4765-4187-7(6),* You Choose Bks.) Capstone Press of Coughlan Cos.

Chant, Christopher. The Escalation of American Involvement in the Vietnam War. 2017. (Vietnam War Ser.: Vol. 5). (ENG.). (YA). (gr. 7-12). 24.95 ***(978-1-4222-3889-9(X))*** Mason Crest.

—The Fall of Saigon & the End of the Vietnam War. 2017. (Vietnam War Ser.: Vol. 5). (ENG.). (YA). (gr. 7-12). 24.95 ***(978-1-4222-3892-9(X))*** Mason Crest.

—The Origins of Conflict in the Vietnam War. 2017. (Vietnam War Ser.: Vol. 5). (ENG.). (YA). (gr. 7-12). 24.95 ***(978-1-4222-3888-2(1))*** Mason Crest.

—Stalemate: U. S. Public Opinion of the War in Vietnam. 2017. (Vietnam War Ser.: Vol. 5). (ENG.). (YA). (gr. 7-12). 24.95 ***(978-1-4222-3891-2(1))*** Mason Crest.

—The U. S. Ground War in Vietnam 1965 1973. 2017. (Vietnam War Ser.: Vol. 5). (ENG.). (YA). (gr. 7-12). 24.95 ***(978-1-4222-3890-5(3))*** Mason Crest.

Clare, John D. Vietnam, 1939-75. 2nd rev. ed. 2004. (Hodder 20th Century History Ser.). (Illus.). 48p. (YA). pap. 26.50 *(978-0-340-81476-5(4),* Hodder Education) Hodder Education Group GBR. Dist: Trans-Atlantic Pubns., Inc.

Cooke, Tim. The Vietnam War on the Front Lines, 1 vol. 2014. (Life on the Front Lines Ser.). (ENG.). 32p. (gr. 3-4). 27.99 *(978-1-4914-0846-9(4),* Edge Bks.) Capstone Press of Coughlan Cos.

Cooke, Tim, ed. The Experience of the War. 2013. (NAM: the Vietnam War Ser.). 48p. (gr. 5-9). 37.10 *(978-1-78121-047-5(0),* Brown Bear Bks.) Windmill Bks. Ltd. GBR. Dist: Black Rabbit Bks.

—The International War. 2013. (NAM: the Vietnam War Ser.). 48p. (gr. 5-9). 37.10 *(978-1-78121-046-8(2),* Brown Bear Bks.) Windmill Bks. Ltd. GBR. Dist: Black Rabbit Bks.

—The Johnson Years 1965-68. 2013. (NAM: the Vietnam War Ser.). 48p. (gr. 5-9). 37.10 *(978-1-78121-043-7(8),* Brown Bear Bks.) Windmill Bks. Ltd. GBR. Dist: Black Rabbit Bks.

—NAM - The Vietnam War: Causes & Outbreak. 2013. (NAM: the Vietnam War Ser.). (Illus.). 48p. (gr. 5-9). 37.10 *(978-1-78121-042-0(X),* Brown Bear Bks.) Windmill Bks. Ltd. GBR. Dist: Black Rabbit Bks.

—The War & U. S. Society. 2013. (NAM: the Vietnam War Ser.). 48p. (gr. 5-9). 37.10 *(978-1-78121-045-1(4),* Brown Bear Bks.) Windmill Bks. Ltd. GBR. Dist: Black Rabbit Bks.

Cooke, Tim, ed. NAM - The Vietnam War: Disengagement & Defeat 1969-75. Cooke, Tim, . 2013. (NAM: the Vietnam War Ser.). (Illus.). 48p. (gr. 5-9). 37.10 *(978-1-78121-044-4(6),* Brown Bear Bks.) Windmill Bks. Ltd. GBR. Dist: Black Rabbit Bks.

Cooper, Candy J. P.O.W. 2011. (J). *(978-0-531-22553-0(4))* Scholastic, Inc.

Corona, Laurel. War Within a War: Vietnam & the Cold War. 2004. (Lucent Library of Historical Eras). (ENG., Illus.). 112p. (J). 33.45 *(978-1-59018-389-2(4),* Lucent Bks.) Cengage Gale.

Cottrell, Robert C. Vietnam: The 17th Parallel. 2004. (Arbitrary Borders Ser.). (Illus.). 112p. (J). (gr. 9-13). 35.00 *(978-0-7910-7834-1(5),* Chelsea Hse.) Facts On File, Inc.

Cunningham, Mark E. & Zwier, Lawrence. The Aftermath of the French Defeat in Vietnam. 2009. (Aftermath of History Ser.). (ENG.). 160p. (gr. 9-12). 38.60 *(978-0-8225-9093-4(X))* Lerner Publishing Group.

Daugherty, Leo J. Vietnam War. 2010. (FAYFT: Modern Military History Ser.). 64p. (gr. 4-10). 39.95 *(978-1-933834-51-1(X))* Brown Bear Bks.

Daynes, Katie. The Vietnam War. 2008. (Young Reading Series 3 Gift Books Ser.). (Illus.). 64p. (J). 8.99 *(978-0-7945-1991-9(1),* Usborne) EDC Publishing.

Dorling Kindersley Publishing Staff. Vietnam War. 2017. (DK Eyewitness Bks.). (ENG., Illus.). 72p. (J). (gr. 3-7). lib. bdg. 19.99 *(978-1-4654-5985-5(5),* DK Children) Dorling Kindersley Publishing, Inc.

Duffield, Katy. The TET Offensive: Crucial Battles of the Vietnam War. 2017. (Major Battles in US History (paperback) Ser.). (ENG., Illus.). 32p. (J). (gr. 4-7). pap. 9.95 ***(978-1-63517-081-8(8),*** Focus Readers) North Star Editions.

Feinstein, Stephen. The 1960s from the Vietnam War to Flower Power. rev. ed. 2006. (Decades of the 20th Century in Color Ser.). (Illus.). 64p. (J). (gr. 5). lib. bdg. 29.27 *(978-0-7660-2636-0(1))* Enslow Pubs., Inc.

Ferguson, Amanda. American Women of the Vietnam War. (American Women at War Ser.). 112p. 2009. (gr. 8-8). 63.90 *(978-1-61511-395-8(9))* 2004. (Illus.). (YA). (gr. 7-12). lib. bdg. 34.60 *(978-0-8239-4448-4(4))* Rosen Publishing Group, Inc., The.

Ferry, Joseph. The Vietnam Veterans Memorial. 2004. (American Symbols & Their Meanings Ser.). (Illus.). 48p. (J). (gr. 4-18). lib. bdg. 19.95 *(978-1-59084-039-9(9))* Mason Crest.

Freedman, Russell. Vietnam: A History of the War. 2016. (ENG., Illus.). 160p. (J). 20.00 *(978-0-8234-3658-3(6))* Holiday Hse., Inc.

Gagne, Tammy. The Vietnam War. 2016. (Illus.). 48p. (J). *(978-1-5105-1292-4(6))* SmartBook Media, Inc.

Galt, Margot Fortunato. Stop This War! American Protest of the Conflict in Vietnam. 2005. (People's History Ser.). (Illus.). 96p. (gr. 6-12). lib. bdg. 26.60 *(978-0-8225-1740-5(X))* Lerner Publishing Group.

Gibson, Karen Bush. The Vietnam War. (Monumental Milestones Ser.). (J). 2007. (Illus.). 48p. (gr. 4-8). lib. bdg. 29.95 *(978-1-58415-541-6(8))* 2006. lib. bdg. *(978-1-58415-469-3(1))* Mitchell Lane Pubs., Inc.

Gifford, Clive. The Vietnam War. 2005. (How Did It Happen? Ser.). (ENG., Illus.). 48p. (YA). (gr. 7-10). lib. bdg. 32.10 *(978-1-59018-609-1(5),* Lucent Bks.) Cengage Gale.

—Why Did the Vietnam War Happen? 2010. (Moments in History Ser.). 48p. (ENG.). (J). (gr. 6-8). pap. 14.05 *(978-1-4339-4179-5(1),* Gareth Stevens Secondary Library); (Illus.). (YA). (gr. 5-9). lib. bdg. 31.95 *(978-1-4339-4178-8(3))* Stevens, Gareth Publishing LLLP.

Gitlin, Martin. U. S. Involvement in Vietnam, 1 vol. 2010. (Essential Events Set 4 Ser.). (ENG.). 112p. (J). (gr. 6-12). lib. bdg. 35.64 *(978-1-60453-949-3(6))* ABDO Publishing Co.

—Vietnam War, 1 vol. 2013. (Essential Library of American Wars Ser.). (ENG., Illus.). 112p. (J). (gr. 6-12). lib. bdg. 35.64 *(978-1-61783-880-4(2),* Essential Library) ABDO Publishing Co.

Grant, R. G. The Vietnam War. 2004. (Atlas of Conflicts Ser.). (Illus.). 64p. (gr. 6-12). pap. 14.05 *(978-0-8368-5674-3(0));* lib. bdg. 34.00 *(978-0-8368-5667-5(8))* Stevens, Gareth Publishing LLLP. (Gareth Stevens Secondary Library).

Green, Carl R. The Vietnam War: A MyReportLinks. Com Book. 2003. (U.S. Wars Ser.). (Illus.). 48p. (J). lib. bdg. 26.60 *(978-0-7660-5147-8(1))* Enslow Pubs., Inc.

Haugen, David M. The Vietnam War. Gale Editors, ed. 2011. (Perspectives on Modern World History Ser.). 224p. (YA). (gr. 10-12). 42.45 *(978-0-7377-5008-9(1),* Greenhaven Pr., Inc.) Cengage Gale.

Hemingway, Albert. American Naval Forces in the Vietnam War. 2005. (American Experience in Vietnam Ser.). (Illus.). 48p. (gr. 5-12). lib. bdg. 31.00 *(978-0-8368-5776-4(3),* Gareth Stevens Secondary Library) Stevens, Gareth Publishing LLLP.

Hogue, Richard, Sr. We Were the Third Herd. 2003. per. 17.95 *(978-0-9722264-0-0(0))* Richlyn Publishing.

Horn, Geoffrey M. John Mccain. 2009. (People We Should Know Ser.). 32p. (J). (gr. 3-5). pap. 10.50 *(978-1-4339-0160-7(9),* Gareth Stevens Learning Library) Stevens, Gareth Publishing LLLP.

—John McCain. 2009. (People We Should Know Ser.). 32p. (J). (gr. 3-5). lib. bdg. 31.00 *(978-1-4339-0020-4(3),* Gareth Stevens Learning Library) Stevens, Gareth Publishing LLLP.

Hosch, William L. Korean War & the Vietnam War: People, Politics, & Power. 2009. (America at War Ser.). (Illus.). 232p. (YA). (gr. 9-12). lib. bdg. 49.00 *(978-1-61530-011-2(2))* Rosen Publishing Group, Inc., The.

—The Korean War & the Vietnam War: People, Politics, & Power. 2009. (America at War Ser.). (ENG.). 232p. (YA). 98.00 *(978-1-61530-088-4(0))* Rosen Publishing Group, Inc., The.

Isserman, Maurice. Vietnam War. 3rd rev. ed. 2010. (America at War Ser.). (Illus.). 224p. (gr. 6-12). 45.00 *(978-0-8160-8187-5(5),* Chelsea Hse.) Facts On File, Inc.

Jeffrey, Gary & Spender, Nik, illus. The Vietnam War. 2013. (ENG.). 48p. (J). *(978-0-7787-1236-7(2));* pap. *(978-0-7787-1240-4(0))* Crabtree Publishing Co.

Keeter, Hunter. American Air Forces in the Vietnam War. 2005. (American Experience in Vietnam Ser.). (Illus.). 48p. (gr. 5-12). lib. bdg. 31.00 *(978-0-8368-5773-3(9),* Gareth Stevens Secondary Library) Stevens, Gareth Publishing LLLP.

—American Ground Forces in the Vietnam War. 2005. (American Experience in Vietnam Ser.). (Illus.). 48p. (gr. 5-12). lib. bdg. 31.00 *(978-0-8368-5774-0(7),* Gareth Stevens Secondary Library) Stevens, Gareth Publishing LLLP.

Kent, Deborah. The Vietnam War: From Da Nang to Saigon. 2011. (United States at War Ser.). (Illus.). 128p. (J). (gr. 5-18). lib. bdg. 33.27 *(978-0-7660-3637-6(5))* Enslow Pubs., Inc.

TUV

Killcoyne, Hope Lourie. Key Figures of the Vietnam War. 2015. (Biographies of War Ser.). (ENG., Illus.). 112p. (J). (gr. 7-8). 32.90 (978-1-68048-063-4(4), Britannica Educational Publishing) Rosen Publishing Group, Inc., The.

Kjelle, Marylou Morano. Saigon. 2009. (J). (978-1-58415-793-9(3)) Mitchell Lane Pubs., Inc.

Kohler, Dean Ellis & VanHecke, Susan. Rock 'n' Roll Soldier: A Memoir. 2009. (ENG.). 288p. (YA). (gr. 9-18). 17.99 (978-0-06-124255-7(1), HarperTeen) HarperCollins Pubs.

Levete, Sarah. The Vietnam War: Frontline Soldiers & Their Families. 2015. (Frontline Families Ser.). (ENG., Illus.). 48p. (J). (gr. 5-6). pap. 14.05 (978-1-4824-3061-5(4)) Stevens, Gareth Publishing LLLP.

Levine, Michelle. Vehicles of the Vietnam War, 1 vol. 2013. (War Vehicles Ser.). (ENG.). 32p. (gr. 3-4). 27.99 (978-1-4296-9913-6(2), Edge Bks.) Capstone Press of Coughlan Cos.

Levy, Debbie. The Vietnam War. 2004. (Chronicle of America's Wars Ser.). (Illus.). 96p. (J). (gr. 5-12). 27.93 (978-0-8225-0421-4(9)) Lerner Publishing Group.

Lusted, Marcia Amidon & Thain, Gerald J. Tinker v. Des Moines: The Right to Protest in Schools, 1 vol. 2012. (Landmark Supreme Court Cases Ser.). (ENG., Illus.). 160p. (J). (gr. 6-12). 37.07 (978-1-61783-477-6(7)) ABDO Publishing Co.

Marcovitz, Hal. The Vietnam War. 2007. (World History Ser.). (ENG., Illus.). 128p. (gr. 7-10). lib. bdg. 39.90 (978-1-4205-0024-0(4), Lucent Bks.) Cengage Gale.

McCune, Susan. Lihn Is from Vietnam, 01 vols., 1. 2016. (Rosen REAL Readers: Social Studies Nonfiction / Fiction: Family, Community, & the World Ser.). (ENG.). 12p. (J). pap. 6.33 (978-1-5081-1827-5(2), Rosen Classroom) Rosen Publishing Group, Inc., The.

Morales, Gilbert, ed. Critical Perspectives on the Vietnam War. 2009. (Critical Anthologies of Nonfiction Writing Ser.). 176p. (gr. 8-8). 63.90 (978-1-61512-082-6(3)) Rosen Publishing Group, Inc., The.

Murray, Stuart & Dorling Kindersley Publishing Staff. DK Eyewitness Books - Vietnam War. 2005. (DK Eyewitness Bks.). (ENG., Illus.). 72p. (J). (gr. 3-7). 16.99 (978-0-7566-1166-8(0)); lib. bdg. 19.99 (978-0-7566-1165-1(2)) Dorling Kindersley Publishing, Inc. (DK Children).

O'Connell, Kim A. Primary Source Accounts of the Vietnam War. 2006. (America's Wars Through Primary Sources Ser.). (Illus.). 128p. (J). (gr. 4-7). lib. bdg. 34.60 (978-1-59845-001-9(8), MyReportLinks.com Bks.) Enslow Pubs., Inc.

Otfinoski, Steven. The Vietnam War. 2017. (Step into History(tm) Ser.). (ENG., Illus.). 144p. (J). lib. bdg. 36.00 (978-0-531-22570-7(4), Children's Pr.) Scholastic Library Publishing.

Polansky, Daniel. Profiles #5: the Vietnam War. 2013. (Profiles Ser.). (ENG.). 144p. (J). (gr. 5-9). pap. 6.99 (978-0-545-48855-6(9), Scholastic Paperbacks) Scholastic, Inc.

Porterfield, Jason. How Lyndon B. Johnson Fought the Vietnam War. 2017. (Presidents at War Ser.). 128p. (J). (gr. 8-8). lib. bdg. 37.27 **(978-0-7660-8531-2(7))** Enslow Pubs., Inc.

Rice, Earle. Causes of the Vietnam War. 2009. (J). lib. bdg. (978-1-59556-034-6(3)) OTTN Publishing.

Rice, Earle, Jr. Point of No Return: Tonkin Gulf & the Vietnam War. 2004. (First Battles Ser.). (Illus.). 144p. (YA). (gr. 6-12). 23.95 (978-1-931798-16-7(8)) Reynolds, Morgan Inc.

Rice, Earle. The Vietnam War, Vol. 11. Musteen, Jason R., ed. 2015. (Major U. S. Historical Wars Ser.). (Illus.). 64p. (J). (gr. 7). lib. bdg. 23.95 (978-1-4222-3359-7(6)) Mason Crest.

Rose, Simon. The Vietnam War: 1954-1975. 2014. (Illus.). 48p. (J). pap. (978-1-62127-656-2(2)) Weigl Pubs., Inc.

Samuels, Charlie. Machines & Weaponry of the Vietnam War. 2013. (Machines That Won the War Ser.). (Illus.). 48p. (J). (gr. 5-8). pap. 14.05 (978-1-4339-8600-0(0)); lib. bdg. 31.95 (978-1-4339-8599-7(3)) Stevens, Gareth Publishing LLLP.

—Timeline of the Vietnam War. 2011. (Americans at War: a Gareth Stevens Timeline Ser.). (Illus.). 48p. (J). (gr. 6-8). pap. 14.05 (978-1-4339-5920-2(8)); lib. bdg. 31.95 (978-1-4339-5918-9(6)) Stevens, Gareth Publishing LLLP. (Gareth Stevens Secondary Library).

Samuels, Charlie & George, Enzo. The Vietnam Conflict: War with Communism. 2014. (Voices of War Ser.). 48p. (J). (gr. 4-6). lib. bdg. 31.36 (978-1-62712-873-5(5)) Cavendish Square Publishing.

Schynert, Mark. Women of the Vietnam War. 2004. (Women in History Ser.). (ENG., Illus.). 112p. (J). (gr. 7-10). 34.80 (978-1-59018-474-5(2), Lucent Bks.) Cengage Gale.

Senker, Cath. The Vietnam War, 1 vol. 2012. (Living Through... Ser.). (ENG.). 80p. (gr. 7-8). pap. 11.95 (978-1-4329-6009-4(1)); lib. bdg. 37.32 (978-1-4329-6000-1(8)) Heinemann-Raintree.

Sheinkin, Steve. Most Dangerous: Daniel Ellsberg & the Secret History of the Vietnam War. 2015. (ENG., Illus.). 384p. (J). (gr. 5-9). 19.99 (978-1-59643-952-8(1), 9781596439528) Roaring Brook Pr.

Sherman, Jill. The Vietnam War: 12 Things to Know. 2017. (America at War Ser.). (ENG., Illus.). 32p. (J). (gr. 3-6). 21.95 (978-1-63235-267-5(2)) Pr. Room Editions LLC.

Skrypuch, Marsha Forchuk. Adrift at Sea: A Vietnamese Boy's Story of Survival. Deines, Brian, illus. 2016. (ENG.). 40p. (J). (gr. 1-4). 18.95 (978-1-77278-005-5(7)) Pajama Pr. CAN. Dist: Ingram Publisher Services.

—Last Airlift: A Vietnamese Orphan's Rescue from War. 2013. (ENG., Illus.). 120p. (J). (gr. 3-7). pap. 9.95 (978-0-9869495-1-7(5)) Pajama Pr. CAN. Dist: Ingram Publisher Services.

—One Step at a Time: A Vietnamese Child Finds Her Way. (ENG., Illus.). 128p. (J). (gr. 3-7). 2014. pap. 12.95 (978-1-927485-02-6(9)) 2013. 13.95 (978-1-927485-01-9(0)) Pajama Pr. CAN. Dist: Ingram Publisher Services.

Small, Cathleen. Strategic Inventions of the Vietnam War. 2016. (Tech in the Trenches Ser.). (ENG., Illus.). 112p. (J). (gr. 9-9). lib. bdg. 42.79 (978-1-5026-1032-4(9)) Cavendish Square Publishing.

Spilsbury, Richard. Who Protested Against the Vietnam War?, 1 vol. 2014. (Primary Source Detectives Ser.). (ENG.). 64p. (gr. 7-8). lib. bdg. 35.99 (978-1-4329-9607-9(X)) Heinemann-Raintree.

Steele, Philip. Did Anything Good Come Out of the Vietnam War?, 01 vols., 1. 2016. (Innovation Through Adversity Ser.). (ENG.). 48p. (J). 30.25 (978-1-5081-7076-1(2), Rosen Young Adult) Rosen Publishing Group, Inc., The.

Streissguth, Tom. The Vietnam War. 2015. (Wars in U. S. History Ser.). (ENG.). 32p. (J). (gr. 2-5). 28.50 (978-1-63143-711-3(9), 208540) Child's World, Inc., The.

Summers, Elizabeth. Weapons & Vehicles of the Vietnam War. 2015. (Tools of War Ser.). (ENG., Illus.). 32p. (gr. 1-2). lib. bdg. 26.65 (978-1-4914-4082-7(1)) Capstone Press of Coughlan Cos.

Sutherland, Jonathan & Canwell, Diane. American Women in the Vietnam War. 2005. (American Experience in Vietnam Ser.). (Illus.). 48p. (gr. 5-12). lib. bdg. 31.00 (978-0-8368-5777-1(1), Gareth Stevens Secondary Library) Stevens, Gareth Publishing LLLP.

Thomas, William David. The Home Front in the Vietnam War. 2005. (American Experience in Vietnam Ser.). (Illus.). 48p. (gr. 5-12). lib. bdg. 31.00 (978-0-8368-5775-7(5), Gareth Stevens Secondary Library) Stevens, Gareth Publishing LLLP.

Tougas, Shelley. Weapons, Gear, & Uniforms of the Vietnam War, 1 vol. 2012. (Equipped for Battle Ser.). (ENG.). 32p. (gr. 3-4). lib. bdg. 27.99 (978-1-4296-7651-9(5), Edge Bks.) Capstone Press of Coughlan Cos.

Warren, Andrea & National Geographic Learning Staff. Escape from Saigon: How a Vietnam War Orphan Became an American Boy. 2008. (ENG., Illus.). 128p. (J). (gr. 5-9). pap. 12.99 (978-0-374-40023-1(7), 9780374400231) Square Fish.

Westwell, Ian. The Vietnam War. 2008. (Wars Day by Day Ser.). 48p. (gr. 5-9). 37.10 (978-1-933834-39-9(0)) Brown Bear Bks.

Wiest, Andrew & McNab, Chris. The Vietnam War. 2016. (Primary Sources in World Warfare Ser.). 256p. (YA). lib. bdg. 55.00 (978-1-5026-2468-0(0)) Cavendish Square Publishing.

Zullo, Allan. Vietnam War Heroes. 2015. (Ten True Tales Ser.). (ENG.). 192p. (J). (gr. 3-7). pap. 5.99 (978-0-545-83750-7(2)) Scholastic, Inc.

VIETNAM WAR, 1961-1975—AFRICAN AMERICANS

Schmermund, Elizabeth. Minority Soldiers Fighting in the Vietnam War. 2017. (J). **(978-1-5026-2666-0(7))** Cavendish Square Publishing.

Sutherland, Jonathan & Canwell, Diane. African Americans in the Vietnam War. 2005. (American Experience in Vietnam Ser.). (Illus.). 48p. (gr. 5-12). lib. bdg. 31.00 (978-0-8368-5772-6(0), Gareth Stevens Secondary Library) Stevens, Gareth Publishing LLLP.

VIETNAM WAR, 1961-1975—FICTION

Arnold, Tedd. Rat Life. 2009. (ENG.). 208p. (YA). (gr. 7-18). pap. 7.99 (978-0-14-241431-6(X), Puffin Books) Penguin Young Readers Group.

Bauer, Michael Gerard. The Running Man. 2008. 304p. (YA). (gr. 9-18). lib. bdg. 17.89 (978-0-06-145509-4(1), HarperTeen) HarperCollins Pubs.

—The Running Man. 2004. 280p. (YA). pap. (978-1-86291-575-6(X), Omnibus Bks.) Scholastic Australia.

Boyd, Candy Dawson. Charlie Pippin. 2011. (ENG.). 190p. (J). (gr. 4-7). pap. 9.99 (978-1-4424-5232-9(3), Simon & Schuster Bks. For Young Readers) Simon & Schuster Bks. For Young Readers.

Bryant, Jen. Kaleidoscope Eyes. 2010. (ENG.). 272p. (J). (gr. 3-7). 7.99 (978-0-440-42190-0(X), Yearling) Random Hse. Children's Bks.

Burg, Ann E. All the Broken Pieces. (ENG.). 240p. (J). 2012. (gr. 7). pap. 6.99 (978-0-545-08093-4(2), Scholastic Paperbacks) 2009. (gr. 5-9). 16.99 (978-0-545-08092-7(4), Scholastic Pr.) Scholastic, Inc.

Cataneo, D. M. Eggplant Alley. 2013. (ENG.). 352p. (YA). (gr. 7-9). 17.95 (978-1-59373-146-5(9)) Bunker Hill Publishing, Inc.

Choyce, Lesley. Reckless, 1 vol. 2010. (Orca Currents Ser.). (ENG.). (gr. 5-9). 128p. (J). pap. 9.95 (978-1-55469-223-1(7)); 112p. (YA). lib. bdg. 16.95 (978-1-55469-224-8(5)) Orca Bk. Pubs. USA.

Collins, Suzanne. Year of the Jungle. Proimos, James, illus. 2013. (ENG.). 40p. (J). (gr. -1-7). 17.99 (978-0-545-42516-2(6), Scholastic Pr.) Scholastic, Inc.

Dowell, Frances O'Roark. Shooting the Moon. 2008. (ENG., Illus.). 176p. (J). (gr. 5-9). 16.99 (978-1-4169-2690-0(9), Atheneum Bks. for Young Readers) Simon & Schuster Children's Publishing.

Franklin, Kristine L. Dove Song. 2006. (ENG.). 192p. (J). (gr. 5-9). per. 5.99 (978-0-7636-3219-9(8)) Candlewick Pr.

Golden, Mike & Vansant, Wayne, illus. The 'Nam, Vol. 1. 2009. (ENG.). 248p. (YA). (gr. 8-17). pap. 29.99 (978-0-7851-3750-4(5)) Marvel Worldwide, Inc.

Hoppey, Tim. Jungle Scout: A Vietnam War Story, 1 vol. Espinoza, Ramon, illus. 2008. (Historical Fiction Ser.). (ENG.). 56p. (gr. 2-3). pap. 6.25 (978-1-4342-0846-0(X), Graphic Flash) Stone Arch Bks.

Hughes, Dean. Search & Destroy. 2005. (ENG., Illus.). 224p. (YA). 16.95 (978-0-689-87023-1(X), Atheneum Bks. for Young Readers) Simon & Schuster Children's Publishing.

—Search & Destroy. 2015. (ENG., Illus.). 256p. (YA). (gr. 7). pap. 9.99 (978-1-4814-2703-6(2), Atheneum Bks. for Young Readers) Simon & Schuster Children's Publishing.

Kadohata, Cynthia. Cracker! The Best Dog in Vietnam. (ENG.). 320p. (J). (gr. 5-9). 2008. pap. 8.99 (978-1-4169-0638-4(X)) 2007. (Illus.). 18.99 (978-1-4169-0637-7(1)) Simon & Schuster Children's Publishing. (Atheneum Bks. for Young Readers).

Keenan, Sheila. Dogs of War. Fox, Nathan, illus. 2013. (ENG.). 176p. (J). (gr. 3-7). pap. 12.99 (978-0-545-12888-9(9), Graphix) Scholastic, Inc.

Kimball, Richard. Shadows of the Men with Green Faces. 2011. 162p. 29.99 (978-1-4653-5070-1(5)); pap. 19.99 (978-1-4653-5069-5(1)) Xlibris Corp.

King, A. S. Everybody Sees the Ants. 2011. (ENG.). 288p. (YA). (gr. 10-17). 18.00 (978-0-316-12928-2(3)) Little Brown & Co.

—Everybody Sees the Ants. 2012. (ENG.). 320p. (YA). (gr. 10-17). pap. 10.00 (978-0-316-12927-5(5)) Little, Brown Bks. for Young Readers.

Lai, Thanhhà. Listen, Slowly. (J). (gr. 3-7). 2016. 288p. pap. 6.99 (978-0-06-222919-9(2)) 2015. (ENG.). 272p. 16.99 (978-0-06-222918-2(4)) 2015. (ENG.). 288p. E-Book (978-0-06-222920-5(6)) HarperCollins Pubs.

Lai, Thanhha. Listen, Slowly. 2016. (J). lib. bdg. 17.20 (978-0-606-38747-7(1)) Turtleback Bks.

Lynch, Chris. Casualties of War. 2013. (Vietnam Ser.: 4). (ENG.). 192p. (J). (gr. 5-9). pap. 7.99 (978-0-545-27024-3(3), Scholastic Pr.) Scholastic, Inc.

—Casualties of War. 2013. (Vietnam Ser.: 4). lib. bdg. 18.40 (978-0-606-31964-5(6), Turtleback) Turtleback Bks.

—Free-Fire Zone. 2012. (Vietnam Ser.). (J). (ENG.). 192p. (gr. 5-9). 16.99 (978-0-545-27025-0(1)); 183p. (978-0-545-49427-4(3)) Scholastic, Inc. (Scholastic Pr.).

—Free-Fire Zone. 2013. (Vietnam Ser.: 3). lib. bdg. 18.40 (978-0-606-31963-8(8), Turtleback) Turtleback Bks.

—I Pledge Allegiance. 2011. (Vietnam Ser.: 1). (ENG.). 192p. (J). (gr. 3-7). 16.99 (978-0-545-27029-8(4), Scholastic Pr.); 183p. (YA). (978-0-545-38415-5(X)) Scholastic, Inc.

—I Pledge Allegiance. 2013. (Vietnam Ser.: 1). lib. bdg. 17.20 (978-0-606-31961-4(1), Turtleback) Turtleback Bks.

—Sharpshooter. (J). 2013. (Vietnam Ser.: 2). (ENG.). 192p. (gr. 5-9). pap. 7.99 (978-0-545-27027-4(8)) 2012. (978-0-545-43650-2(8)) Scholastic, Inc. (Scholastic Pr.).

—Sharpshooter. 2013. (Vietnam Ser.: 2). lib. bdg. 18.40 (978-0-606-31962-1(X), Turtleback) Turtleback Bks.

—Vietnam #1: I Pledge Allegiance. 2013. (Vietnam Ser.: 1). (ENG.). 192p. (J). (gr. 5-9). pap. 7.99 (978-0-545-27030-4(8), Scholastic Paperbacks) Scholastic, Inc.

—Walking Wounded, Bk. 5. (Vietnam Ser.: 5). (ENG.). 208p. (J). (gr. 5-9). 2016. pap. 7.99 (978-0-545-64016-9(4)) 2014. 17.99 (978-0-545-64013-8(X)) Scholastic, Inc. (Scholastic Pr.).

Metivier, Gary. Cody & Grandpa's Christmas Tradition, 1 vol. Van Wagoner, Traci, illus. 2016. (ENG.). 32p. (J). (gr. k-3). 16.99 (978-1-4556-2170-5(6)) Pelican Publishing Co., Inc.

Myers, Walter Dean. Fallen Angels. 2008. (ENG.). 336p. (J). (gr. 7). pap. 9.99 (978-0-545-05576-5(8), Scholastic Paperbacks) Scholastic, Inc.

—Patrol: An American Soldier in Vietnam. Grifalconi, Ann, illus. 2005. (ENG.). 40p. (J). (gr. 3-7). pap. 6.99 (978-0-06-073159-5(1)) HarperCollins Pubs.

—Patrol: An American Soldier in Vietnam. 2005. 17.00 (978-0-7569-5428-4(2)) Perfection Learning Corp.

Partridge, Elizabeth. Dogtag Summer. (ENG.). 240p. (YA). (gr. 3-12). 2012. pap. 7.99 (978-1-59990-829-8(8), 9781599908298) 2011. 16.99 (978-1-59990-183-1(8), 9781599901831) Bloomsbury Publishing USA. (Bloomsbury USA Childrens).

Paulsen, Gary. The Car. 2006. (ENG., Illus.). 192p. (YA). (gr. 7-12). pap. 7.99 (978-0-15-205827-2(3)) Houghton Mifflin Harcourt Publishing Co.

—The Car. 2006. 182p. (gr. 7-12). 17.00 (978-0-7569-6685-0(X)) Perfection Learning Corp.

Phillips, Dee. Vietnam: The Story of a Marine. 2015. (Yesterday's Voices Ser.). (YA). lib. bdg. 19.60 (978-0-606-36677-9(6)) Turtleback Bks.

Poulsen, David A. Old Man. 2013. (ENG.). 224p. (YA). pap. 12.99 (978-1-4597-0547-0(5)) Dundurn CAN. Dist: Ingram Publisher Services.

—Old Man. 2013. 276p. pap. (978-1-4596-6325-1(X)) ReadHowYouWant.com, Ltd.

Qualey, Marsha. Come in from the Cold. 2008. (ENG.). 224p. (YA). (gr. 7). pap. 14.95 (978-0-547-01439-5(2)) Houghton Mifflin Harcourt Publishing Co.

Santacroce, John P. Running Across the Moon. 2013. 146p. pap. 14.98 (978-0-615-76887-8(3)) Santacroce, John.

Sherlock, Patti. Letters from Wolfie. 2007. (ENG.). 240p. (J). (gr. 5-18). 7.99 (978-0-14-240358-7(X), Puffin Books) Penguin Young Readers Group.

Sherman, M. Zachary. Fighting Phantoms, 1 vol. Casas, Fritz, illus. 2011. (Bloodlines Ser.). (ENG.). 88p. (gr. 4-8). lib. bdg. 26.65 (978-1-4342-2560-3(7)) Stone Arch Bks.

Sherman, M. Zachary & Lee, Raymund. Emergency Ops, 1 vol. Bermudez, Raymund, illus. 2012. (Bloodlines Ser.). (ENG.). 88p. (gr. 4-8). pap. 6.95 (978-1-4342-3877-1(6)); lib. bdg. 26.65 (978-1-4342-3766-8(4)) Stone Arch Bks.

Smith, Andrew. In the Path of Falling Objects. 2010. (ENG.). 352p. (YA). (gr. 8-12). pap. 12.99 (978-0-312-65929-5(6), 9780312659295) Square Fish.

Stentiford, Tyler Michael. A Darker Secret. 2009. (ENG.). 128p. (YA). pap. 9.99 (978-1-60138-315-0(0)) Atlantic Publishing Group, Inc.

Tashjian, Janet. For What It's Worth. 2012. (ENG.). 288p. (YA). (gr. 7-12). 16.99 (978-0-8050-9365-0(6), 9780805093650, Holt, Henry & Co. Bks. For Young Readers) Holt, Henry & Co.

Trip to Freedom: Six-Pack. (Greetings Ser.: Vol. 3). (gr. 3-5). 31.00 (978-0-7635-1777-9(1)) Rigby Education.

Wallace, Rich. War & Watermelon. 2012. (ENG.). 192p. (J). (gr. 5-18). pap. 6.99 (978-0-14-242138-3(3), Puffin Books) Penguin Young Readers Group.

VIETNAMESE AMERICANS

Bryan, Nichol. Vietnamese Americans, 1 vol. 2004. (One Nation Set 2 Ser.). (ENG.). 32p. (gr. k-6). 27.07 (978-1-59197-534-2(4), Checkerboard Library) ABDO Publishing Co.

Coleman, Lori. Vietnamese in America. 2005. (In America Ser.). (Illus.). 80p. (J). (gr. 5-8). lib. bdg. 27.93 (978-0-8225-3951-3(9)) Lerner Publishing Group.

Ferry, Joseph. Vietnamese Immigration. 2005. (Changing Face of North America Ser.). (Illus.). 112p. (YA). lib. bdg. 24.95 (978-1-59084-682-7(6)) Mason Crest.

Grabowski, John F. Vietnamese Americans. (Successful Americans Ser.). 64p. (YA). 2009. (gr. 9-12). 22.95 (978-1-4222-0522-8(3)) 2007. (gr. 7-18). pap. 9.95 (978-1-4222-0869-4(9)) Mason Crest.

Hall, Margaret C. Vietnamese Americans. 2003. (We Are America Ser.). (Illus.). 32p. (J). (gr. 2-4). lib. bdg. 24.22 (978-1-4034-0738-2(X)) Heinemann-Raintree.

Imbriaco, Alison. Vietnam: A MyReportLinks. com Book. 2004. (Top Ten Countries of Recent Immigrants Ser.). (Illus.). 48p. (J). lib. bdg. 26.60 (978-0-7660-5182-9(X), MyReportLinks.com Bks.) Enslow Pubs., Inc.

National Geographic Learning. Huong's Journey. 2009. (Inside the USA Ser.). (ENG., Illus.). 16p. (C). pap. 13.95 (978-0-7362-7059-5(0)) CENGAGE Learning.

Parker, Lewis K. Why Vietnamese Immigrants Came to America. (Coming to America Ser.). 24p. 2009. (gr. 2-3). 42.50 (978-1-61511-888-5(8)) 2003. (Illus.). (J). lib. bdg. 22.60 (978-0-8239-6461-1(2)) Rosen Publishing Group, Inc., The. (PowerKids Pr.).

Warren, Andrea & National Geographic Learning Staff. Escape from Saigon: How a Vietnam War Orphan Became an American Boy. 2008. (ENG., Illus.). 128p. (J). (gr. 5-9). pap. 12.99 (978-0-374-40023-1(7), 9780374400231) Square Fish.

VIETNAMESE AMERICANS—FICTION

Burg, Ann E. All the Broken Pieces. (ENG.). 240p. (J). 2012. (gr. 7). pap. 6.99 (978-0-545-08093-4(2), Scholastic Paperbacks) 2009. (gr. 5-9). 16.99 (978-0-545-08092-7(4), Scholastic Pr.) Scholastic, Inc.

Cobb, Amy. Shredding with the Geeks, 1 vol. Cattish, Anna, illus. 2015. (ENG.). 112p. (J). (978-1-62402-076-6(3)) Magic Wagon.

Jules, Jacqueline. Duck for Turkey Day. Mitter, Kathryn, illus. (ENG.). 32p. (J). 2017. (gr. k-2). pap. 7.99 **(978-0-8075-1735-2(6))** 2009. (gr. 1-3). 16.99 (978-0-8075-1734-5(8)) Whitman, Albert & Co.

Lai, Thanhhà. Inside Out & Back Again. (ENG.). (J). (gr. 3-7). 2013. 288p. pap. 8.99 (978-0-06-196279-0(1)) 2011. 272p. 16.99 (978-0-06-196278-3(3)) HarperCollins Pubs.

—Inside Out & Back Again. 2014. (ENG.). 288p. (J). (gr. 3-7). 12.24 (978-1-63245-350-1(9)) Lectorum Pubns., Inc.

—Inside Out & Back Again. 2009. 9.68 (978-0-7848-3887-7(9), Everbind) Marco Bk. Co.

—Inside Out & Back Again. 2013. 18.00 (978-1-61383-970-6(7)) Perfection Learning Corp.

—Inside Out & Back Again. 2013. (J). lib. bdg. 18.40 (978-0-606-27126-4(0), Turtleback) Turtleback Bks.

Lai, Thanhha. Inside Out & Back Again: a Harper Classic. 2017. (Harper Classic Ser.). 288p. (J). (gr. 3-7). 16.99 **(978-0-06-257402-2(7))** HarperCollins Pubs.

McKay, Lawrence, Jr., et al. Journey Home. Lee, Keunhee et al, illus. 2003. (Avenues Ser.). (ENG.). 32p. (C). (gr. -1-5). pap. 13.95 (978-1-58430-005-2(1)) National Geographic School Publishing, Inc.

Mosher, Richard. Zazoo. 2004. (ENG.). 272p. (YA). (gr. 7-18). reprint ed. pap. 15.95 (978-0-618-43904-1(8)) Houghton Mifflin Harcourt Publishing Co.

Partridge, Elizabeth. Dogtag Summer. (ENG.). 240p. (YA). (gr. 3-12). 2012. pap. 7.99 (978-1-59990-829-8(8), 9781599908298) 2011. 16.99 (978-1-59990-183-1(8), 9781599901831) Bloomsbury Publishing USA. (Bloomsbury USA Childrens).

Perera, Hilda. MAI. (SPA.). 120p. (J). 7.95 (978-84-348-1149-2(9), SM1210) SM Ediciones ESP. Dist: AIMS International Bks., Inc., Lectorum Pubns., Inc.

Pung, Alice & Masciullo, Lucia. Marly Walks on the Moon. 2016. (Our Australian Girl Ser.: 4). (ENG.). 144p. (J). (gr. 3-7). 12.99 (978-0-14-330852-2(1)) Penguin Books Australia AUS. Dist: Independent Pubs. Group.

Schraff, Anne. Memories Are Forever. 2008. (Passages Ser.). 135p. lib. bdg. 13.95 (978-0-7569-8405-2(X)) Perfection Learning Corp.

Silver, Gail. Steps & Stones: An Anh's Anger Story. Krömer, Christiane, illus. 2007. (ENG.). 40p. (J). (gr. -1-3). 16.95 (978-1-935209-87-4(6), Plum Blossom Bks.) Parallax Pr.

Sugarman, Brynn Olenberg. Rebecca's Journey Home. Shapiro, Michelle, illus. (Life Cycle Ser.). 32p. (J). 2014. (ENG.). (gr. k-4). 8.95 (978-1-4677-4937-4(0)) 2006. (gr. -1-3). lib. bdg. 17.95 (978-1-58013-157-5(3)) Lerner Publishing Group. (Kar-Ben Publishing).

Tran, Truong. Going Home, Coming Home. Phong, Ann, illus. 2003.Tr. of Ve Nha Tham Que Hu'o'Ng. (ENG & VIE.). 32p. (J). 16.95 (978-0-89239-179-0(0)) Lee & Low Bks., Inc.

VIETNAMESE CONFLICT, 1961-1975

see Vietnam War, 1961-1975

VIETNAMESE LANGUAGE

Beullens-Maoui, Nathalie, ed. Animals Habitats: Vietnamese, 01 vols., 1. 2016. (Our Wonderful World Ser.). (ENG & SPA.). 8p. (J). pap. 9.35 (978-1-5081-1257-0(6), Rosen Classroom) Rosen Publishing Group, Inc., The.

Doan, Linh. Let's Learn Vietnamese Kit: 64 Basic Vietnamese Words & Their Uses. 2017. (ENG., Illus.). (J). (gr. k-8). 14.95 (978-0-8048-4696-7(0)) Tuttle Publishing.

Kudela, Katy R. My First Book of Vietnamese Words, 1 vol. Translations.com Staff, tr. 2011. (Bilingual Picture Dictionaries Ser.). 32p. (gr. 1-2). (ENG, VIE & MUL., Illus.). pap. 8.10 (978-1-4296-6163-8(1)); (MUL.). pap. 47.70 (978-1-4296-6164-5(X)) Capstone Press of Coughlan Cos. (Aplus Bks.).

Lanchais, Aurelie, et al. Kto A? 2005. (Who Am I? What Am I? Ser.).Tr. of Who Am I? (RUS, ENG, TUR, VIE & CHI., Illus.). 16p. (J). (gr. -1-1). 9.95 (978-1-84059-232-0(X)) Milet Publishing.

—Who Am I? 2005. (Who Am I? What Am I? Ser.). (CHI, ENG, VIE, GUJ & RUS., Illus.). 16p. (J). (gr. -1-1). 9.95 (978-1-84059-229-0(X)) Milet Publishing.

Martin, Robert, Jr. Vietnamese Children's Picture Dictionary: English-Vietnamese/Vietnamese-English. Voltaggio, Nicholas, illus. 2006. (ENG & VIE.). 112p. (J). (gr. 3-7). pap. 14.95 (978-0-7818-1133-0(3)) Hippocrene Bks., Inc.

Milet Publishing Staff. Animals - My First Bilingual Book. 2011. (My First Bilingual Book Ser.). (ENG., Illus.). 24p. (J). (gr. k — 1). bds. 8.99 (978-1-84059-623-6(6)) Milet Publishing.

—Bilingual Visual Dictionary. 2011. (Milet Multimedia Ser.). (ENG & VIE., Illus.). 1p. (J). (gr. k-2). cd-rom 19.95 (978-1-84059-595-6(7)) Milet Publishing.

—Colors. 2011. (My First Bilingual Book Ser.). (ENG.). 24p. (J). (gr. k — 1). bds. 7.99 (978-1-84059-606-9(6)) Milet Publishing.

—My Bilingual Book-Hearing (English-Vietnamese) 2014. (My Bilingual Book Ser.). (ENG & VIE., Illus.). 28p. (J). (gr. -1-k). 9.95 (978-1-84059-787-5(9)) Milet Publishing.

—My Bilingual Book-Sight (English-Vietnamese) 2014. (My Bilingual Book Ser.). (ENG & VIE., Illus.). 28p. (J). (gr. -1-k). 9.95 (978-1-84059-803-2(4)) Milet Publishing.

—My Bilingual Book-Smell (English-Vietnamese) 2014. (My Bilingual Book Ser.). (ENG & VIE., Illus.). 28p. (J). (gr. -1-k). 9.95 (978-1-84059-819-3(0)) Milet Publishing.

—My Bilingual Book-Touch (English-Vietnamese) 2014. (My Bilingual Book Ser.). (ENG & VIE., Illus.). 28p. (J). (gr. -1-k). 9.95 (978-1-84059-851-3(4)) Milet Publishing.
—My First Bilingual Book-Home (English-Vietnamese) 2011. (My First Bilingual Book Ser.). (ENG., Illus.). 24p. (J). (gr. k — 1). bds. 8.99 (978-1-84059-655-7(4)) Milet Publishing.
—My First Bilingual Book-Jobs (English-Vietnamese) 2012. (My First Bilingual Book Ser.). (ENG & VIE., Illus.). 24p. (J). (gr. k — 1). bds. 7.99 (978-1-84059-715-8(1)) Milet Publishing.
—My First Bilingual Book-Music (English-Vietnamese) 2012. (My First Bilingual Book Ser.). (ENG & VIE., Illus.). 24p. (J). (gr. k — 1). bds. 7.99 (978-1-84059-731-8(3)) Milet Publishing.
—My First Bilingual Book-Opposites (English-Vietnamese) 2012. (My First Bilingual Book Ser.). (ENG & VIE., Illus.). 24p. (J). (gr. k — 1). bds. 7.99 (978-1-84059-747-9(X)) Milet Publishing.
—My First Bilingual Book-Sports (English-Vietnamese) 2012. (My First Bilingual Book Ser.). (ENG & VIE., Illus.). 24p. (J). (gr. k — 1). bds. 7.99 (978-1-84059-763-9(1)) Milet Publishing.
—My First Bilingual Book-Vegetables (English-Vietnamese) 2011. (My First Bilingual Book Ser.). (ENG., Illus.). 24p. (J). (gr. k — 1). bds. 8.99 (978-1-84059-671-7(6)) Milet Publishing.
Nguyen, An Mai. Let's Learn Animals in Vietnamese. 2006. (VIE & ENG., Illus.). (J). bds. 6.95 (978-0-9776482-3-8(0)) Viet Baby, LLC.
—Let's Learn Colors in Vietnamese. 2006. (VIE & ENG., Illus.). (J). bds. 6.95 (978-0-9776482-1-4(4)) Viet Baby, LLC.
—Let's Learn How to Count in Vietnamese. 2006. (VIE & ENG., Illus.). (J). bds. 6.95 (978-0-9776482-2-1(2)) Viet Baby, LLC.
—Let's Learn the Vietnamese Alphabet. 2006. (VIE & ENG., Illus.). (J). bds. 6.95 (978-0-9776482-0-7(6)) Viet Baby, LLC.
Turhan, Sedat. New Bilingual Visual Dictionary (English-Vietnamese) 2nd ed. 2017. (New Bilingual Visual Dictionary Ser.). (ENG & VIE., Illus.). 144p. (J). (gr. k-2). 19.95 **(978-1-78508-896-4(3))** Milet Publishing.

VIEWS

Barlowe, Dot. Tropical Paradise Scenes to Paint or Color. 2009. (Dover Art Coloring Book Ser.). (ENG., Illus.). 48p. (gr. 6-8). pap. 5.99 (978-0-486-46562-3(4)) Dover Pubns., Inc.
Baxter, Nicola. Learn about Our World. Elliott, Rebecca, illus. 2013. (ENG.). 16p. (J). (gr. k-2). bds. 17.99 (978-1-84322-985-8(4), Armadillo) Anness Publishing GBR. Dist: National Bk. Network.
Hawkins, Emily. Atlas of Miniature Adventures: A Pocket-Sized Collection of Small-scale Wonders - Because Bigger Isn't Always Better. Letherland, Lucy, illus. 2016. (Atlas Of Ser.). (ENG.). 64p. (J). 9.99 (978-1-84780-909-4(X), Wide Eyed Editions) Quarto Publishing Group UK GBR. Dist: Littlehampton Bk Services, Ltd.
It's My State: Group 2, 6 vols. 2003. (YA). (gr. 3). lib. bdg. 162.43 (978-0-7614-1521-3(1)) Marshall Cavendish Corp.
Tullet, Hervé. The Finger Travel Game. 2015. (ENG., Illus.). 14p. (gr. -1 — 1). 12.95 (978-0-7148-6977-3(5)) Phaidon Pr., Inc.

VIKINGS

Here are entered works on the Scandinavian sea-warriors who plundered the northern and western coasts of Europe from the 8th to the 10th centuries. Works on the inhabitants of Scandinavia since the 10th century are entered under Scandinavians. Works on the inhabitants of Scandinavia prior to the 10th century are entered under Northmen.
see also Northmen

Allan, Tony. Exploring the Life, Myth, & Art of Ancient Vikings. 2011. 39.95 (978-1-4488-4837-9(7)) Rosen Publishing Group, Inc., The.
—Exploring the Life, Myth, & Art of the Vikings. 2011. (Civilizations of the World Ser.). (YA). (gr. 7-12). lib. bdg. 42.60 (978-1-4488-4833-1(4)) Rosen Publishing Group, Inc., The.
Anderson, Peter. Vikings. 2011. (History's Greatest Warriors Ser.). (ENG., Illus.). 24p. (J). (gr. 3-7). lib. bdg. 25.95 (978-1-60014-632-9(5), Torque Bks.) Bellwether Media.
Anderson, Scoular. How to Be a Viking in 13 Easy Stages. Anderson, Scoular, illus. 2007. (Collins Big Cat Ser.). (ENG., Illus.). 192p. (J). (gr. 2-4). pap. 7.99 (978-0-00-723079-2(6)) HarperCollins Pubs. Ltd. GBR. Dist: Independent Pubs. Group.
Bedford, Kate. The Vikings. 2011. (Children in History Ser.). (Illus.). 32p. (YA). (gr. 4-7). lib. bdg. 28.50 (978-1-59771-272-9(8)) Sea-To-Sea Pubns.
Bingham, Jane. Vikings. 2017. (Explore! Ser.). (ENG., Illus.). 32p. (J). (gr. 4-6). pap. 12.99 **(978-0-7502-9737-0(9),** Wayland) Hachette Children's Group GBR. Dist: Hachette Bk. Group.
Bodden, Valerie. Great Warriors: Vikings. 2014. (Great Warriors Ser.). (ENG.). 24p. (J). (gr. 1-3). pap. 9.99 (978-1-62832-069-5(9), Creative Paperbacks) Creative Co., The.
—Vikings. 2017. (J). **(978-1-60818-816-1(7),** Creative Education) Creative Co., The.
Bodden, Valerie. Vikings (Great Warriors) 2013. 24p. pap. (978-1-60818-469-9(2)) Creative Co., The.
Butterfield, Moira. Vikings. 2017. (Britain in the Past Ser.). (ENG., Illus.). 32p. (J). (gr. 2-5). pap. 12.99 **(978-1-4451-4068-1(3),** Franklin Watts) Hachette Children's Group GBR. Dist: Hachette Bk. Group.
Clements, J. M. Vikings. 2012. (Illus.). 205p. (J). (978-1-4351-4591-7(7)) Metro Bks.
Cooke, Tim. The Vikings. 2015. (At Home With... Ser.). (Illus.). 32p. (gr. 5-9). lib. bdg. 31.35 (978-1-78121-085-7(3), Brown Bear Bks.) Windmill Bks. Ltd. GBR. Dist: Black Rabbit Bks.
Corrick, James A. The Rough, Stormy Age of Vikings: The Disgusting Details about Viking Life, 1 vol. 2010. (Disgusting History Ser.). (ENG.). 32p. (gr. 3-4). lib. bdg. 27.32 (978-1-4296-5405-0(8), Fact Finders) Capstone Press of Coughlan Cos.
Cox, P. Roxbee. Who Were the Vikings? rev. ed. (Starting Point History Ser.). (ENG.). 1p. (J). (gr. 1-18). pap. 4.99 (978-0-7945-0177-8(X)) EDC Publishing.
D'Aulaire, Ingri & D'Aulaire, Edgar Parin. Leif the Lucky. 2014. (ENG., Illus.). 60p. 16.95 (978-0-8166-9545-4(8)) Univ. of Minnesota Pr.
Deem, James M. The Vikings: A MyReportLinks. com Book. 2004. (Civilizations of the Ancient World Ser.). (Illus.). 48p. (J). lib. bdg. 25.26 (978-0-7660-5198-0(6), MyReportLinks.com Bks.) Enslow Pubs., Inc.
DeFries, Cheryl L. Leif Eriksson: Viking Explorer of the New World. 2010. (Great Explorers of the World Ser.). (Illus.). 112p. (J). (gr. 7-12). lib. bdg. 33.27 (978-1-59845-126-9(X)) Enslow Pubs., Inc.
Dillard, Sheri. Viking Warriors. 2015. (Ancient Warriors Ser.). (ENG.). 32p. (J). (gr. 2-5). 28.50 (978-1-63143-761-8(5), 208593) Child's World, Inc., The.
Dorling Kindersley Publishing Staff. Eye Wonder: Vikings. 2016. (Eye Wonder Ser.). (ENG., Illus.). 56p. (J). (gr. k-4). 10.99 (978-1-4654-1855-5(5), DK Children) Dorling Kindersley Publishing, Inc.
Dougherty, Martin J. The Untold History of the Vikings. 2016. (History Exposed Ser.). (ENG.). 224p. (YA). (gr. 9-9). 55.00 (978-1-5026-1902-0(4)) Cavendish Square Publishing.
Dowling, Lucy. Why Why Why... Were Vikings So Fierce? 2010. (Why Why Why Ser.). 32p. (YA). (gr. 1-3). lib. bdg. 18.95 (978-1-4222-1591-3(1)) Mason Crest.
Fowke, Robert. Vikings. (Illus.). 128p. (J). pap. (978-0-340-68611-9(1)) Hodder & Stoughton.
Gandolfi, Claudine. Scratch & Sketch Vikings: An Art Activity Book for Legendary Artists & Explorers of All Ages. Zschock, Martha Day, illus. 2015. (ENG.). 64p. (J). 12.99 (978-1-4413-1813-8(5), 9781441318138) Peter Pauper Pr. Inc.
Ganeri, Anita. How to Live Like a Viking Warrior. Epelbaum, Mariano, illus. 2015. (How to Live Like... Ser.). (ENG.). 32p. (J). (gr. 3-6). lib. bdg. 26.65 (978-1-4677-6354-7(3)) Lerner Publishing Group.
Gitlin, Martin. Vikings, 1 vol. 2013. (Great Warriors Ser.). (ENG.). 48p. (J). (gr. 3-6). lib. bdg. 32.79 (978-1-61783-729-6(6)); (Illus.). pap. 15.64 (978-1-61783-779-1(2), Core Library) ABDO Publishing Co.
Goldsmith, Rose. How Did the Vikings Come to Canada? 2014. (Little Books of Answers: Level F Ser.). (Illus.). 16p. (gr. k-2). pap. 7.95 (978-1-927136-51-5(2)) Three Crows Media NZL. Dist: RiverStream Publishing.
Grant, Neil. Everyday Life of the Vikings. 2005. (Uncovering History Ser.). (Illus.). 46p. (J). (gr. 6-9). lib. bdg. 29.95 (978-1-58340-706-6(5)) Black Rabbit Bks.
Greenling, Jason. The Technology of the Vikings. 2016. (Ancient Innovations Ser.). 64p. (J). 34.21 (978-1-5026-2241-9(6)) Cavendish Square Publishing.
Gunderson, Jessica. Vikings. 2012. (Fearsome Fighters Ser.). (Illus.). 48p. (J). (gr. 5-12). 23.95 (978-1-60818-185-8(5), Creative Education) Creative Co., The.
Higgins, Nadia. National Geographic Kids Everything Vikings: All the Incredible Facts & Fierce Fun You Can Plunder. 2015. (National Geographic Kids Everything Ser.). (ENG., Illus.). 64p. (J). (gr. 3-7). pap. 12.99 (978-1-4263-2076-7(0), National Geographic Children's Bks.) National Geographic Society.
Hinds, Kathryn. Vikings: Masters of the Sea. 2009. (Barbarians! Ser.). 80p. (gr. 6-8). 35.64 (978-0-7614-4074-1(7)) Marshall Cavendish Corp.
Hopkins, Andrea. Viking Explorers & Settlers. 2009. (Viking Library). 24p. (gr. 3-3). 42.50 (978-1-60854-256-7(4), PowerKids Pr.) Rosen Publishing Group, Inc., The.
—Viking Families & Farms. 2009. (Viking Library). 24p. (gr. 3-3). 42.50 (978-1-60854-257-4(2), PowerKids Pr.) Rosen Publishing Group, Inc., The.
—Viking Longships. 2009. (Viking Library). 24p. (gr. 3-3). 42.50 (978-1-60854-259-8(9), PowerKids Pr.) Rosen Publishing Group, Inc., The.
—Viking Raiders & Traders. 2009. (Viking Library). 24p. (gr. 3-3). 42.50 (978-1-60854-260-4(2), PowerKids Pr.) Rosen Publishing Group, Inc., The.
—Vikings: The Norse Discovery of America. 2009. (Viking Library). 24p. (gr. 3-3). 42.50 (978-1-60854-261-1(0), PowerKids Pr.) Rosen Publishing Group, Inc., The.
Howell, Izzi. Vikings. (Fact Cat: History: Early Britons Ser.). (ENG., Illus.). 24p. (J). (gr. k-2). 2017. 16.99 (978-0-7502-9581-9(3)) 2016. pap. 9.99 (978-0-7502-9935-0(5)) Hachette Children's Group GBR. (Wayland). Dist: Hachette Bk. Group.
Hubbard, Ben. Viking Warriors. 2016. (Conquerors & Combatants Ser.). 224p. (YA). lib. bdg. 55.00 (978-1-5026-2455-0(9)) Cavendish Square Publishing.
Huey, Lois Miner. American Archaeology Uncovers the Vikings. 2009. (American Archaeology Ser.). 64p. (gr. 5-6). 31.36 (978-0-7614-4270-7(7)) Marshall Cavendish Corp.
Hyde, Natalie. Explore with Leif Eriksson. 2014. (ENG., Illus.). 32p. (J). (978-0-7787-1427-9(2)) Crabtree Publishing Co.
Hynson, Colin. How People Lived in Viking Times. (How People Lived Ser.). (Illus.). 2009. 32p. (gr. 4-8). pap. 10.60 (978-1-4358-2624-3(8), Rosen Classroom) 2008. 30p. (J). lib. bdg. 26.50 (978-1-4042-4434-4(4), PowerKids Pr.) Rosen Publishing Group, Inc., The.
Jeffrey, Gary. The Dark Ages & the Vikings. 2014. (ENG., Illus.). 48p. (J). (978-0-7787-0401-0(7)) Crabtree Publishing Co.
Knudsen, Shannon. Leif Eriksson. Oldroyd, Mark, illus. 2005. (On My Own Biography Ser.). (ENG.). 48p. (gr. 2-4). pap. 6.95 (978-1-57505-828-3(6)); lib. bdg. 25.26 (978-1-57505-649-4(6), Carolrhoda Bks.) Lerner Publishing Group.
Landau, Elaine. Exploring the World of the Vikings. 2005. (Exploring Ancient Civilizations with Elaine Landau Ser.). (Illus.). 48p. (J). (gr. 4-7). lib. bdg. 25.27 (978-0-7660-2340-6(0), Enslow Elementary) Enslow Pubs., Inc.
Langley, Andrew. You Wouldn't Want to Be a Viking Explorer! Voyages You'd Rather Not Make. Antram, David, illus. rev. ed. 2013. (ENG.). (J). 32p. 29.00 (978-0-531-27103-2(X)); 40p. pap. 9.95 (978-0-531-23854-7(7)) Scholastic Library Publishing. (Watts, Franklin).
Lassieur, Allison. Life as a Viking. 2010. (You Choose: Warriors Ser.). (ENG.). 112p. (gr. 3-4). pap. 41.70 (978-1-4296-5727-3(8), You Choose Bks.) Capstone Press of Coughlan Cos.
—Life as a Viking: An Interactive History Adventure. 2010. (You Choose: Warriors Ser.). (ENG., Illus.). 112p. (gr. 3-4). pap. 6.95 (978-1-4296-5639-9(5), You Choose Bks.) Capstone Press of Coughlan Cos.
Lee, Adrienne. Vikings, 1 vol. Martin, Cynthia, illus. 2013. (Legendary Warriors Ser.). (ENG.). 32p. (gr. 1-2). 26.65 (978-1-4765-3116-8(1), Blazers) Capstone Press of Coughlan Cos.
Leonard, Kiri Ostergaard. Vikings of Legend & Lore Paper Dolls. 2013. (ENG.). 32p. (gr. 3-8). pap. 9.99 (978-0-486-49334-3(2)) Dover Pubns., Inc.
Levy, Janey. At Sea on a Viking Ship: Solving Problems of Length & Weight Using the Four Math Operations. 2004. (Math Big Bookstm Ser.). (ENG.). 24p. (gr. 3-4). 43.95 (978-0-8239-7642-3(4)) Rosen Publishing Group, Inc., The.
Macdonald, Fiona. The Medieval Chronicles: Vikings, Knights, & Castles. Antram, David, illus. 2013. 92p. (J). (978-1-4351-5067-6(8)) Barnes & Noble, Inc.
MacDonald, Fiona. Viking Raiders. 2009. (History Explorers Ser.). (ENG.). 24p. (J). (gr. k-2). pap. 5.95 (978-1-84696-216-5(1), TickTock Books) Octopus Publishing Group GBR. Dist: Independent Pubs. Group.
Macdonald, Fiona. Vikings. 2010. (Remarkable Man & Beast Ser.). (Illus.). 48p. (J). (gr. 3-18). lib. bdg. 19.95 (978-1-4222-1977-5(1)) Mason Crest.
MacDonald, Fiona. Vikings: Dress, Eat, Write & Play Just Like the Vikings. 2008. (Hands-on History Ser.). (ENG., Illus.). 32p. (J). (gr. 3-7). pap. (978-0-7787-4072-8(2)) Crabtree Publishing Co.
Macleod, Robert. Vikingworld: The Age of Seafarers & Sagas. 2014. (ENG., Illus.). 80p. (J). (gr. 3). 19.95 (978-1-78312-046-8(0)) Carlton Bks., Ltd. GBR. Dist: Sterling Publishing Co., Inc.
MacPhail, David. Vikings in Britain. 2017. (ENG., Illus.). 48p. (J). pap. 8.99 **(978-0-00-820883-7(2))** HarperCollins Pubs. Ltd. GBR. Dist: Independent Pubs. Group.
Malam, John. The Vikings. 2011. (Dig It: History from Objects Ser.). (Illus.). 32p. (YA). (gr. 2-5). lib. bdg. 26.50 (978-1-4488-3286-6(1)) Rosen Publishing Group, Inc., The.
Margeson, Susan M. & Dorling Kindersley Publishing Staff. Viking. 2009. (DK Eyewitness Bks.). (ENG.). 72p. (J). (gr. 3-7). 16.99 (978-0-7566-5829-8(2), DK Children) Dorling Kindersley Publishing, Inc.
Mattern, Joanne. Leif Eriksson: Viking Explorer. 2004. (Explorers! Ser.). (Illus.). 48p. (J). lib. bdg. 25.27 (978-0-7660-2146-4(7)) Enslow Pubs., Inc.
McCollum, Sean. Vikings: A Guide to the Terrifying Conquerors, 1 vol. 2011. (History's Greatest Warriors Ser.). (ENG.). 48p. (gr. 3-4). lib. bdg. 31.99 (978-1-4296-6603-9(X)) Capstone Press of Coughlan Cos.
McKinley, Herald. Vikings: Raiders & Explorers. 2015. (J). lib. bdg. (978-1-62713-409-5(3)) Cavendish Square Publishing.
McLeese, Don. Vikings. 2009. 32p. pap. 7.99 (978-0-8249-1445-5(7), Ideal Pubns.) Worthy Publishing.
McNeil, Niki, et al. HOCPP 1082 Vikings. 2006. spiral bd. 24.00 (978-1-60308-082-8(1)) In the Hands of a Child.
McRae, Anne & Agosta, Loredana. The Vikings. Cecchi, Lorenzo et al, illus. 2008. (Back to Basics Ser.). 32p. (J). (gr. 2-5). lib. bdg. (978-88-6098-051-9(8)) McRae Bks. Srl.
Miles, John C. Everyday Life, Art & Culture. 2016. (Discover the Vikings Ser.). (ENG., Illus.). 32p. (J). (gr. 2-4). 17.99 (978-1-4451-4887-8(0), Franklin Watts) Hachette Children's Group GBR. Dist: Hachette Bk. Group.
—Warriors, Exploration & Trade. 2016. (Discover the Vikings Ser.). (ENG., Illus.). 32p. (J). (gr. 3-6). 17.99 (978-1-4451-4886-1(2), Franklin Watts) Hachette Children's Group GBR. Dist: Hachette Bk. Group.
Nardo, Don. The Vikings. 2010. (World History Ser.). (ENG.). 96-128p. 34.95 (978-1-4205-0316-6(2), Lucent Bks.) Cengage Gale.
Ohlin, Nancy. Vikings. Larkum, Adam, illus. 2017. (Blast Back! Ser.). (ENG.). 112p. (J). (gr. 2-5). 16.99 (978-1-4998-0386-0(9)) Little Bee Books Inc.
Osborne, Mary Pope & Boyce, Natalie Pope. Magic Tree House Fact Tracker: A Nonfiction Companion to Magic Tree House. Molinari, Carlo, illus. 2015. (Magic Tree House - Fact Tracker Ser.). (ENG.). 128p. (J). (gr. 2-5). 6.99 (978-0-385-38638-8(9), Random Hse. Bks. for Young Readers) Random Hse. Children's Bks.
—Vikings: A Nonfiction Companion to Magic Tree House 15 Viking Ships at Sunrise. 2015. (Magic Tree House Fact Tracker Ser.: 33). lib. bdg. 16.00 (978-0-606-37707-2(7)) Turtleback Bks.
Owen, Ruth. The World of a Viking Warrior. 2015. (It's a Fact Ser.). (ENG.). 32p. (J). (gr. 3-6). lib. bdg. 26.60 (978-1-909673-90-8(0)) Bearport Publishing Co., Inc.
Park, Louise & Love, Timothy. The Scandinavian Vikings. 2009. (Ancient & Medieval People Ser.). 32p. (gr. 5). 28.50 (978-0-7614-4445-9(9)) Marshall Cavendish GBR. Dist: Marshall Cavendish Corp.
Phipps, Liza & Thompson, Avril. Vikings. 2017. (History Showtime Ser.). (ENG., Illus.). 32p. (J). (gr. 2-4). pap. 11.99 (978-1-4451-1487-3(9), Franklin Watts) Hachette Children's Group GBR. Dist: Hachette Bk. Group.
Powell, Jillian. The Vikings. 2010. (Gruesome Truth about Ser.). (ENG.). 32p. (J). (gr. 4-6). lib. bdg. 22.60 (978-1-61533-221-2(9)) Windmill Bks.
Raum, Elizabeth. What Did the Vikings Do for Me?, 1 vol. 2010. (Linking the Past & Present Ser.). (ENG., Illus.). 32p. (gr. 3-6). 33.32 (978-1-4329-3745-4(6)); pap. 8.29 (978-1-4329-3752-2(9)) Heinemann-Raintree. (Heinemann InfoSearch).
Rice, Earle. The Life & Times of Erik the Red. 2008. (Biography from Ancient Civilizations Ser.). (Illus.). 48p. (J). (gr. 4-8). lib. bdg. 29.95 (978-1-58415-701-4(1)) Mitchell Lane Pubs., Inc.
—The Life & Times of Leif Eriksson. 2008. (Biography from Ancient Civilizations Ser.). (Illus.). 48p. (J). (gr. 4-8). lib. bdg. 29.95 (978-1-58415-702-1(X)) Mitchell Lane Pubs., Inc.
Richardson, Hazel. Life of the Ancient Vikings. 2005. (Peoples of the Ancient World Ser.). (ENG., Illus.). 32p. (J). (gr. -1-9). pap. (978-0-7787-2074-4(8)); lib. bdg. (978-0-7787-2044-7(6)) Crabtree Publishing Co.
Ridley, Sarah. Life in Viking Times. 2015. (Everyday History Ser.). (Illus.). 32p. (J). 31.35 (978-1-59920-952-4(7)) Black Rabbit Bks.
Smith, A. G. BOOST Story of the Vikings Coloring Book. 2013. (BOOST Educational Ser.). (ENG.). 48p. (J). (gr. 3-5). pap. 5.99 (978-0-486-49439-5(X)) Dover Pubns., Inc.
Steele, Philip. Hands-On History! Viking World: Learn about the Legendary Norse Raiders, with 15 Step-By-step Projects & More Than 350 Exciting Pictures. 2013. (ENG., Illus.). 64p. (J). (gr. 3-7). 12.99 (978-1-84322-694-9(4)) Anness Publishing GBR. Dist: National Bk. Network.
—Kingfisher Readers L3: Vikings. 2014. (Kingfisher Readers Ser.). (ENG., Illus.). 32p. (J). (gr. k-3). 12.99 (978-0-7534-7148-7(5), 9780753471487, Kingfisher) Roaring Brook Pr.
Steele, Philip & MacDonald, Fiona. The Vikings & the Celts: Ancient Warriors & Raiders. 2010. (ENG., Illus.). 128p. (J). (gr. -1-12). pap. 17.99 (978-1-84476-878-3(3)) Anness Publishing GBR. Dist: National Bk. Network.
Taylor, Dereen. Vikings. 2009. (Flashback History Ser.). (Illus.). 48p. (J). pap. 11.75 (978-1-4358-5502-1(7), PowerKids Pr.); (YA). (gr. 3-6). 29.25 (978-1-4358-5501-4(9)) Rosen Publishing Group, Inc., The.
Thompson, Ben. The Vikings. (Guts & Glory Ser.: 2). (ENG., Illus.). 320p. (J). (gr. 3-7). 2016. pap. 6.99 (978-0-316-32057-3(9)) 2015. 17.00 (978-0-316-32056-6(0)) Little, Brown Bks. for Young Readers.
Toth, Henrietta. Viking Explorers. 2016. (Spotlight on Explorers & Colonization Ser.). 48p. (J). (gr. 6-6). pap. 11.75 (978-1-4777-8832-5(8)) Rosen Publishing Group, Inc., The.
Troupe, Thomas Kingsley. Your Life As an Explorer on a Viking Ship. Ebbeler, Jeffrey, illus. 2012. (Way It Was Ser.). (ENG.). 32p. (gr. 2-3). pap. 8.95 (978-1-4048-7252-3(3)); lib. bdg. 26.65 (978-1-4048-7160-1(8)) Picture Window Bks.
Truett, Trudi Strain. The Vikings. 2011. (Technology of the Ancients Ser.). 64p. (gr. 5). 32.79 (978-1-60870-769-0(5)) Marshall Cavendish Corp.
The Vikings. 2014. (Ladybird Histories Ser.). (ENG., Illus.). 64p. (J). (gr. 2-4). 13.99 **(978-0-7232-8841-1(0))** Penguin Bks., Ltd. GBR. Dist: Independent Pubs. Group.
Vonne, Mira. Gross Facts about Vikings. 2017. (Gross History Ser.). (ENG., Illus.). 32p. (gr. 1-2). lib. bdg. 26.65 (978-1-5157-4158-9(3)) Capstone Press of Coughlan Cos.
Wayland Publishers & Bingham, Jane. Vikings. 2017. (Explore! Ser.). (ENG., Illus.). 32p. (J). (gr. 4-6). 17.99 (978-0-7502-9548-2(1), Wayland) Hachette Children's Group GBR. Dist: Hachette Bk. Group.
West, David. The Vikings. 2016. (Discovering Ancient Civilizations Ser.). 32p. (gr. 3-3). pap. 10.50 (978-1-4824-5047-7(X)) Stevens, Gareth Publishing LLLP.
Williams, Colleen Madonna Flood. My Adventure with Vikings. 2009. (ENG.). 44p. (J). 8.99 (978-1-59092-474-7(6)) Blue Forge Pr.
Wingate, Philippa & Millard, Anne. Viking World. Wood, Gerald, illus. 2004. (Illustrated World History Ser.). 64p. (J). (gr. 6). lib. bdg. 19.95 (978-1-58086-628-6(X), Usborne) EDC Publishing.
Woolf, Alex. Meet the Vikings. 2014. (Encounters with the Past Ser.). 32p. (J). (gr. 3-6). pap. 63.00 (978-1-4824-0900-0(3)) Stevens, Gareth Publishing LLLP.
Yasuda, Anita. Explore Norse Myths! With 25 Great Projects. Stone, Bryan, illus. 2015. (Explore Your World Ser.). (ENG.). 96p. (J). (gr. 1-5). 19.95 (978-1-61930-316-4(7), 1398135) Open City Bks.

VIKINGS—FICTION

Aptekar, Devan. How to Train Your Dragon - Befriending a Foe. 2010. (How to Train Your Dragon Ser.). 24p. (J). (gr. -1-2). pap. 3.99 (978-0-06-156735-3(3), HarperFestival) HarperCollins Pubs.
Batson, Wayne Thomas. Isle of Fire, 1 vol. 2009. (ENG.). 352p. pap. 9.99 (978-1-4003-1512-3(3)) Nelson, Thomas Inc.
Bowen, Carl. Loki & Thor. Smith, Tod & Lokus, Rex, illus. 2016. (Norse Myths: a Viking Graphic Novel Ser.). (ENG.). 56p. (gr. 3-4). lib. bdg. 27.99 (978-1-4965-3490-3(5)) Stone Arch Bks.
Bowen, Carl, et al. Norse Myths, 4 vols. Smith, Tod & Garcia, Eduardo, illus. 2016. (Norse Myths: a Viking Graphic Novel Ser.). (ENG.). 56p. (gr. 3-4). 111.96 (978-1-4965-3519-1(7)) Stone Arch Bks.
Boyd, David. Beware the Vikings. Rooth, Mike, illus. 2007. 48p. (J). lib. bdg. 23.08 (978-1-4242-1624-6(9)) Fitzgerald Bks.
Chabert, Jack. Mystery of the Map. Merritt, Kory, illus. 2016. (Poptropica Ser.: bk.1). (ENG.). 112p. (J). (gr. 1-4). 9.95 (978-1-4197-2067-3(8), Amulet Bks.) Abrams, Inc.
Ciddor, Anna. Runestone: The First Book about the Adventures of Oddo & Thora. 2007. (Viking Magic Ser.). (ENG., Illus.). 192p. (Orig.). (J). (gr. 4-7). pap. 11.99 (978-1-86508-689-7(4)) Allen & Unwin AUS. Dist: Independent Pubs. Group.
—Wolfspell. 2007. (Viking Magic Ser.). (ENG., Illus.). 192p. (J). (gr. 4-7). pap. 12.99 (978-1-74114-013-2(7)) Allen & Unwin AUS. Dist: Independent Pubs. Group.
Cowell, Cressida. A Hero's Guide to Deadly Dragons. 2010. (ENG., Illus.). 272p. (J). (978-0-340-99913-4(6), Hodder Children's Books) Hachette Children's Group GBR. Dist: Hachette Bk. Group.
—A Hero's Guide to Deadly Dragons. (How to Train Your Dragon Ser.: 6). (ENG.). (J). (gr. 3-7). 2010. 272p. pap. 8.00 (978-0-316-08532-8(4)) 2009. 256p. 12.99 (978-0-316-11779-1(X)) Little, Brown Bks. for Young Readers.
—How to Be a Pirate. 2010. (ENG., Illus.). 240p. (J). (978-0-340-99908-0(X), Hodder Children's Books) Hachette Children's Group GBR. Dist: Hachette Bk. Group.
—How to Be a Pirate. (How to Train Your Dragon Ser.: 2). (ENG.). (J). (gr. 3-7). 2010. 240p. pap. 8.99 (978-0-316-08528-1(6)) 2005. (Illus.). 224p. 13.99 (978-0-316-15598-4(5)) Little, Brown Bks. for Young Readers.
—How to Be a Viking. 2014. (ENG.). 32p. (J). (gr. -1-3). 15.00 (978-0-316-28635-0(4)) Little, Brown Bks. for Young Readers.
—How to Betray a Dragon's Hero. 2014. (How to Train Your Dragon Ser.: 11). (J). lib. bdg. 18.45 (978-0-606-35943-6(5)) Turtleback Bks.
—How to Break a Dragon's Heart. 2010. (ENG., Illus.). 320p. (J). (978-0-340-99692-8(7), Hodder Children's Books) Hachette Children's Group GBR. Dist: Hachette Bk. Group.

T U V

—How to Break a Dragon's Heart. 2012. (How to Train Your Dragon Ser.: 8). (J). lib. bdg. 18.45 *(978-0-606-26163-0(X),* Turtleback) Turtleback Bks.

—How to Cheat a Dragon's Curse. 2010. (ENG., Illus.). 256p. (J). *(978-0-340-99910-3(1),* Hodder Children's Books) Hachette Children's Group GBR. Dist: Hachette Bk. Group.

—How to Cheat a Dragon's Curse. 2010. (How to Train Your Dragon Ser.: 4). (ENG.). 272p. (J). (gr. 3-7). pap. 8.99 *(978-0-316-08530-4(8))* Little, Brown Bks. for Young Readers.

—How to Cheat a Dragon's Curse. Cowell, Cressida, illus. 2007. (How to Train Your Dragon Ser.: 4). (ENG., Illus.). 256p. (J). (gr. 3-7). 14.99 *(978-0-316-11425-7(1))* Little, Brown Bks. for Young Readers.

—How to Fight a Dragon's Fury. 2015. (How to Train Your Dragon Ser.: 12). (ENG., Illus.). 496p. (J). (gr. 3-7). 13.99 *(978-0-316-36515-4(7))* Little, Brown Bks. for Young Readers.

—How to Fight a Dragon's Fury. 2016. (How to Train Your Dragon Ser.: 12). (J). lib. bdg. 18.40 *(978-0-606-39195-5(9))* Turtleback Bks.

—How to Ride a Dragon's Storm. 2010. (ENG., Illus.). 288p. (J). *(978-0-340-99912-7(8),* Hodder Children's Books) Hachette Children's Group GBR. Dist: Hachette Bk. Group.

—How to Ride a Dragon's Storm. (How to Train Your Dragon Ser.: 7). (ENG.). (J). (gr. 3-7). 2011. 288p. pap. 8.99 *(978-0-316-07909-9(X))* 2010. 272p. 12.99 *(978-0-316-07916-7(2))* Little, Brown Bks. for Young Readers.

—How to Seize a Dragon's Jewel. (How to Train Your Dragon Ser.: 10). (ENG., Illus.). 416p. (J). (gr. 3-7). 2014. pap. 8.00 *(978-0-316-24408-4(2))* 2013. 12.99 *(978-0-316-24409-1(0))* Little, Brown Bks. for Young Readers.

—How to Seize a Dragon's Jewel. 2014. (How to Train Your Dragon Ser.: 10). (J). lib. bdg. 18.45 *(978-0-606-35307-6(0))* Turtleback Bks.

—How to Speak Dragonese. 2010. (ENG., Illus.). 256p. (J). *(978-0-340-99909-7(8),* Hodder Children's Books) Hachette Children's Group GBR. Dist: Hachette Bk. Group.

—How to Speak Dragonese. (How to Train Your Dragon Ser.: 3). (ENG.). (J). (gr. 3-7). 2010. 256p. pap. 8.99 *(978-0-316-08529-8(4))* 2006. (Illus.). 240p. 12.99 *(978-0-316-15600-4(0))* Little, Brown Bks. for Young Readers.

—How to Steal a Dragon's Sword. 2013. (How to Train Your Dragon Ser.: 9). (ENG.). 384p. (J). (gr. 3-7). pap. 8.00 *(978-0-316-20570-2(2))* Little, Brown Bks. for Young Readers.

—How to Steal a Dragon's Sword. 2013. (How to Train Your Dragon Ser.: 9). (J). lib. bdg. 18.45 *(978-0-606-31742-9(2),* Turtleback) Turtleback Bks.

—How to Train Your Dragon. 2010. (ENG., Illus.). (J). 240p. *(978-0-340-99907-3(1))*; 240p. pap. *(978-0-340-99716-1(8))*;No. 1. 304p. *(978-0-340-99717-8(6))* Hachette Children's Group GBR. (Hodder Children's Books). Dist: Hachette Bk. Group.

—How to Train Your Dragon. (How to Train Your Dragon Ser.: 1). (ENG., (J). (gr. 3-7). 2004. Illus.). 224p. 13.99 *(978-0-316-73737-1(2))*Bk. 1. 2010. 240p. pap. 8.99 *(978-0-316-08527-4(8))* Little, Brown Bks. for Young Readers.

—How to Train Your Dragon: How to Betray a Dragon's Hero. (How to Train Your Dragon Ser.: 11). (ENG., Illus.). 416p. (J). (gr. 3-7). 2014. pap. 8.99 *(978-0-316-24411-4(2))* 2013. 13.99 *(978-0-316-24412-1(0))* Little, Brown Bks. for Young Readers.

—How to Train Your Dragon: How to Fight a Dragon's Fury. 2016. (How to Train Your Dragon Ser.: 12). (ENG., Illus.). 496p. (J). (gr. 3-7). pap. 7.99 *(978-0-316-36516-1(5))* Little, Brown Bks. for Young Readers.

—How to Train Your Dragon Special Edition: With Brand New Short Stories! 2014. (ENG., Illus.). 432p. (J). (gr. 3-7). pap. 10.00 *(978-0-316-40747-2(X))* Little, Brown Bks. for Young Readers.

—How to Twist a Dragon's Tale. 2010. (ENG., Illus.). 272p. (J). *(978-0-340-99911-0(X),* Hodder Children's Books) Hachette Children's Group GBR. Dist: Hachette Bk. Group.

—How to Twist a Dragon's Tale. (How to Train Your Dragon Ser.: 5). (ENG., (J). (gr. 3-7). 2008. Illus.). 256p. 10.99 *(978-0-316-11774-6(9))*Bk. 5. 2010. 272p. pap. 8.99 *(978-0-316-08531-1(6))* Little, Brown Bks. for Young Readers.

—A Journal for Heroes. 2015. (How to Train Your Dragon Ser.). (ENG.). 176p. (J). (gr. 3-7). 10.99 *(978-0-316-30743-7(2))* Little, Brown Bks. for Young Readers.

Cross, Gillian. Brother Aelred's Feet. Stevens, Tim, illus. 2007. (Collins Big Cat Ser.). (ENG.). 544p. (J). (gr. 3-4). pap. 8.99 *(978-0-00-723093-8(1))* HarperCollins Pubs. Ltd. GBR. Dist: Independent Pubs. Group.

Dahl, Lisa. Gorm the Viking: The Lost Voyage. 2013. 282p. (gr. 4-6). 26.95 *(978-1-4759-5809-6(9))*; pap. 16.95 *(978-1-4759-5807-2(2))* iUniverse, Inc.

Dahl, Michael. The Viking Claw. 2011. (Finnegan Zwake Ser.: 4). (ENG.). 192p. (YA). (gr. 7). pap. 9.99 *(978-1-4424-3101-0(6),* Simon Pulse) Simon Pulse.

David, Erica. How to Track a Dragon. 2016. (Simon & Schuster Ready-To-Read Level 2 Ser.). lib. bdg. 13.55 *(978-0-606-38992-1(X))* Turtleback Bks.

Davis, Mike. Land of the Lost Mammoths: A Science Adventure. 2003. (Illus.). 174p. (J). 15.95 *(978-0-9747078-0-8(5))* Perceval Pr.

DeBlois, Dean, et al. The Serpent's Heir. Wheatley, Doug, illus. 2017. (ENG.). 80p. (gr. 4-7). pap. 10.99 *(978-1-61655-931-1(4))* Dark Horse Comics.

Dinsdale, Christopher. Stolen Away. 2006. (ENG., Illus.). 240p. (J). per. 10.95 *(978-1-894917-20-9(0),* Napoleon & Co.) Dundurn CAN. Dist: Ingram Publisher Services.

Dixon, Sean. The Winter Drey. 2009. (Trilogy of the Tree Ser.: Pt. 2). (ENG., Illus.). 200p. (J). (gr. 4-9). pap. *(978-1-55470-190-2(2))* Me to We.

Don, Lari. The Dragon's Hoard. James, Cate, illus. 2016. (ENG.). 64p. (J). (gr. 3-6). 22.99 *(978-1-84780-681-9(3),* Frances Lincoln Children's Bks.) Quarto Publishing Group UK GBR. Dist: Hachette Bk. Group.

Dreamworks How to Train Your Dragon, Dreamworks How. Dreamworks How to Train Your Dragon 2: Time to Race! 2014. (Build It Ser.: 4). (ENG.). 24p. (J). (gr. -1-1). 14.99 *(978-0-7944-3111-2(9),* Reader's Digest Children's Bks.) Studio Fun International.

Erich, James. Seidman [Library Edition]. 2012. 210p. pap. 14.99 *(978-1-62380-904-1(5),* Harmony Ink Pr.) Dreamspinner Pr.

Evans, Cordelia, adapted by. The Dragon That Rides on Lightning. 2015. (How to Train Your Dragon TV Ser.). (ENG., Illus.). 24p. (J). (gr. -1-3). 12.99 *(978-1-4814-3613-7(9),* Simon Spotlight) Simon Spotlight.

Farmer, Nancy. The Islands of the Blessed. 2012. (ENG., Illus.). 496p. (YA). (gr. 7). pap. 11.99 *(978-1-4169-0738-1(6),* Atheneum Bks. for Young Readers) Simon & Schuster Children's Publishing.

—The Islands of the Blessed. Foster, Jon, illus. 2009. (ENG.). 496p. (YA). (gr. 7-9). 18.99 *(978-1-4169-0737-4(8),* Atheneum/Richard Jackson Bks.) Simon & Schuster Children's Publishing.

—The Islands of the Blessed. l.t. ed. 2010. (Sequel to the Land of the Silver Apples Ser.). (ENG.). 520p. (J). 23.95 *(978-1-4104-2253-8(4))* Thorndike Pr.

—The Sea of Trolls. (ENG., Illus.). 480p. 2004. (J). (gr. 5-8). 19.99 *(978-0-689-86744-6(1),* Atheneum/Richard Jackson Bks.) 2006. (YA). (gr. 9-8). reprint ed. pap. 11.99 *(978-0-689-86746-0(8),* Atheneum Bks. for Young Readers) Simon & Schuster Children's Publishing.

French, Allen. The Story of Rolf: A Viking Adventure. 2005. (Dover Children's Classics Ser.). (ENG.). 154p. (J). (gr. 3-6). per. 9.95 *(978-0-486-44133-7(4))* Dover Pubns., Inc.

—The Story of Rolf & the Viking Bow. 2008. 148p. (gr. 7-12). pap. 8.15 *(978-1-60459-522-2(1))* Wilder Pubns., Corp.

Furman, Simon. Dragons Vol.4: The Stowaway. 2015. (Riders of Berk Ser.). (ENG., Illus.). 64p. (J). (gr. 3-7). pap. 6.99 *(978-1-78276-079-5(2))* Titan Bks. Ltd. GBR. Dist: Penguin Random Hse. LLC.

—Dragons - Defenders of Berk Vol. 1: The Endless Night. Florean, Arianna, illus. 2016. (ENG.). 64p. (J). (gr. 3-7). pap. 6.99 *(978-1-78276-214-0(0))* Titan Bks. Ltd. GBR. Dist: Penguin Random Hse. LLC.

—Dragons: Riders of Berk Collection Volume 3. Nasif, Iwan, illus. 2016. (ENG.). 112p. (J). (gr. 1-4). pap. 12.99 *(978-1-78585-177-3(2))* Titan Bks. Ltd. GBR. Dist: Penguin Random Hse. LLC.

—Riders of Berk - Tales from Berk, Vol. 1. 2016. (ENG., Illus.). 64p. (J). (gr. 3-7). pap. 12.99 *(978-1-78276-696-4(0))* Titan Bks. Ltd. GBR. Dist: Penguin Random Hse. LLC.

Furman, Simon & Nazif, Iwan. Dragons - Riders of Berk, Vol. 2. Lawrence, Jack, illus. 2016. (ENG.). 112p. (J). (gr. 3-7). pap. 12.99 *(978-1-78585-176-6(4))* Titan Bks. Ltd. GBR. Dist: Penguin Random Hse. LLC.

Furman, Simon & Titan Comics Staff. The Legend of Ragnarok, Vol. 5. 2015. (Riders of Berk Ser.). (ENG., Illus.). 64p. (J). (gr. 3-7). pap. 6.99 *(978-1-78276-080-1(6))* Titan Bks. Ltd. GBR. Dist: Penguin Random Hse. LLC.

Golding, Julia. The Silver Sea, 0 vols. 2013. (ENG.). 352p. (YA). (gr. 7-11). pap. 9.99 *(978-1-4778-1598-4(8),* 9781477815984, Amazon Children's Publishing) Amazon Publishing.

Goscinny, René. Asterix & the Vikings: The Book of the Film. Uderzo, Albert, illus. 2007. (ENG.). 72p. pap. 12.99 *(978-0-7528-8876-7(5),* Orion) Orion Publishing Group, Ltd. GBR. Dist: Hachette Bk. Group.

—Asterix & the Vikings: The Book of the Film. Bell, Anthea, tr. Uderzo, Albert, illus. 2006. (ENG.). 72p. (gr. 4-7). 17.99 *(978-0-7528-8590-2(1),* Orion) Orion Publishing Group, Ltd. GBR. Dist: Hachette Bk. Group.

Hall, Jennie. The Viking Tales. 2008. 88p. pap. 8.15 *(978-1-60459-529-1(9))* Wilder Pubns., Corp.

Hamme, Van. Giants. Rosinski, illus. 2013. (Thorgal Ser.: 14). (ENG.). 48p. pap. 11.95 *(978-1-84918-156-3(X))* CineBook GBR. Dist: National Bk. Network.

Hapka, Catherine, pseud. How to Train Your Dragon: Meet the Dragons. Grosvenor, Charles & Gerard, Justin, illus. 2010. (I Can Read Book 1 Ser.). 32p. (J). (gr. k-3). pap. 3.99 *(978-0-06-156733-9(7))* HarperCollins Pubs.

Haugaard, Erik Christian. Hakon of Rogen's Saga. Dillon, Leo & Dillon, Diane, illus. 2013. (ENG.). 144p. pap. 11.95 *(978-0-8166-8127-3(9))* Univ. of Minnesota Pr.

Henighan, Tom. Viking Terror. 2006. (ENG.). 180p. (J). pap. 12.99 *(978-1-55002-605-4(4),* Boardwalk Bks.) Dundurn CAN. Dist: Ingram Publisher Services.

Holliday, Susan. Kingsholt. 2015. (ENG.). 120p. (J). (gr. -1-12). pap. 11.95 *(978-1-78279-976-4(1),* Our Street Bks.) Hunt, John Publishing Ltd. GBR. Dist: National Bk. Network.

Hosie, Donna. The Devil's Banshee. 2016. (ENG.). 336p. (YA). 17.95 *(978-0-8234-3650-7(0))* Holiday Hse., Inc.

How to Start a Dragon Academy. 2014. (How to Train Your Dragon TV Ser.). (ENG., Illus.). 32p. (J). (gr. k-2). pap. 3.99 *(978-1-4814-1925-3(0),* Simon Spotlight) Simon Spotlight.

Hulme-Cross, Benjamin. The Viking's Revenge. Rinaldi, Angelo, illus. 2015. (ENG.). 160p. (J). *(978-0-7787-1767-6(4))* Crabtree Publishing Co.

Jacobsen, Annie. Ivar, the Short, but Brave Viking. Hanson, Susan Jo, illus. 2007. (J). lib. bdg. 16.95 *(978-0-9778276-1-9(5))* Pickled Herring Pr.

Jennewein, James & Parker, Tom S. Shield of Odin. 2009. (RuneWarriors Ser.: 1). (ENG.). 336p. (J). (gr. 3-7). pap. 6.99 *(978-0-06-144938-3(5))* HarperCollins Pubs.

—Ship of the Dead. 2010. (RuneWarriors Ser.: 3). (ENG.). 304p. (J). (gr. 3-7). 17.99 *(978-0-06-144942-0(3))* HarperCollins Pubs.

—Sword of Doom. 2009. (RuneWarriors Ser.: 2). (ENG.). 432p. (J). (gr. 3-7). 17.99 *(978-0-06-144939-0(3))* HarperCollins Pubs.

Johnson, Lois Walfrid. The Raider's Promise. 2006. (Viking Quest Ser.: 5). (ENG., Illus.). 304p. (J). (gr. 3-7). per. 8.99 *(978-0-8024-3116-5(X))* Moody Pubs.

Johnson, Vargie. Eric the Red the Fearless: What Made Them Famous? 2006. (J). per. 15.00 *(978-1-931195-94-2(3))* KiwE Publishing, Ltd.

Jones, Terry. The Saga of Erik the Viking. Foreman, Michael, illus. 2017. (ENG.). 168p. (J). (gr. 4-7). pap. 12.99 ***(978-1-84365-314-1(1)***, Pavilion) Pavilion Bks. GBR. Dist: Independent Pubs. Group.

Jones, Terry. The Saga of Erik the Viking. Foreman, Michael, illus. 30th ed. 2013. (ENG.). 250p. (J). (gr. 4-7). 16.99 *(978-1-84365-224-3(2),* Pavilion) Pavilion Bks. GBR. Dist: Independent Pubs. Group.

Judge, Chris. Brian & the Vikings. 2015. (ENG., Illus.). 32p. (J). pap. 13.00 *(978-1-84717-687-5(9))* O'Brien Pr., Ltd., The IRL. Dist: Dufour Editions, Inc.

Kurd, Tariq. Gordon the Goblin in Oh My! Is That a Pork Pie? Robertson, Laura, illus. 2012. 36p. pap. *(978-1-907762-10-9(8))* Malt Publishing.

Langrish, Katherine. Troll Blood. Stevens, Tim & Wyatt, David, illus. 2008. 352p. (gr. 5-8). (ENG.). (J). 16.99 *(978-0-06-111674-2(2))*; (YA). lib. bdg. 17.89 *(978-0-06-111675-9(0),* Eos) HarperCollins Pubs.

—Troll Fell. 2004. (Illus.). 272p. (J). (gr. 5-18). (ENG.). 16.99 *(978-0-06-058304-0(5))*; lib. bdg. 16.89 *(978-0-06-058305-7(3))* HarperCollins Pubs.

—Troll Mill. 2008. (ENG., Illus.). 336p. (YA). (gr. 7). pap. 7.99 *(978-0-06-058309-5(6),* Eos) HarperCollins Pubs.

Leighton-Porter, Wendy. The Shadow of the Norman Arrow. 2013. 270p. pap. *(978-1-909411-07-4(8))* Mauve Square Publishing.

Messner, Kate. Journey Through Ash & Smoke. 2017. (Ranger in Time Ser.: 5). lib. bdg. 16.00 ***(978-0-606-39723-0(X))*** Turtleback Bks.

Nelson, Mary. Catla & the Vikings, 1 vol. 2012. (ENG.). 192p. (J). (gr. 4-7). pap. 9.95 *(978-1-4598-0057-1(5))* Orca Bk. Pubs. USA.

Osborne, Mary Pope. Barcos Vikingos Al Amanecer. Brovelli, Marcela, tr. from ENG. Murdocca, Sal, illus. 2007. (Casa del Arbol Ser.: 15). (SPA.). 73p. (J). per. 5.99 *(978-1-933032-21-4(9))* Lectorum Pubns., Inc.

—Viking Ships at Sunrise. unabr. ed. 2004. (Magic Tree House Ser.: No. 15). 71p. (J). (gr. k-3). pap. 17.00 incl. audio *(978-0-8072-0784-0(5),* LFTR 243 SP, Listening Library) Random Hse. Audio Publishing Group.

Pendergrass, Daphne. Riders of Berk: A Fiery Discovery. 2015. lib. bdg. 13.55 *(978-0-606-36311-2(4))* Turtleback Bks.

Phillips, Dee. Viking, 1 vol., Bk. 8. 2015. (Yesterday's Voices Ser.). (ENG.). 48p. (YA). (gr. 9-12). pap. 8.95 *(978-1-62250-910-2(2))* Saddleback Educational Publishing, Inc.

—Viking: The Story of a Raider. 2015. (Yesterday's Voices Ser.). (YA). lib. bdg. 19.60 *(978-0-606-36676-2(8))* Turtleback Bks.

Rayner, Keith. Torvig's Gift. 2006. 208p. pap. 19.95 *(978-1-4241-1518-1(3))* America Star Bks.

Riel, Jörn & Chodzin, Sherab. The Raiders Vol. 2: The Inuk Quartet. Cann, Helen, illus. 2013. (ENG.). 128p. (J). (gr. 4-6). pap. 9.99 *(978-1-84686-744-6(4))* Barefoot Bks., Inc.

Rosinski & Van Hamme, Jean. Chlid of the Stars. Rosinski, Adolf, illus. 2007. (Thorgal Ser.: 1). (ENG.). 96p. per. 19.95 *(978-1-905460-23-6(6))* CineBook GBR. Dist: National Bk. Network.

Ryan, Carrie. Divide & Conquer. 2015. (Infinity Ring Ser.: 2). (ENG.). 192p. (J). (gr. 3-7). pap. 6.99 *(978-0-545-90017-1(4))* Scholastic, Inc.

Scieszka, Jon. Viking It & Liking It. McCauley, Adam, illus. 2004. (Time Warp Trio Ser.: 12). (ENG.). 96p. (J). (gr. 2-4). pap. 5.99 *(978-0-14-240002-9(5),* Puffin Books) Penguin Young Readers Group.

—Viking It & Liking It. McCauley, Adam, illus. 2004. (Time Warp Trio Ser.: No. 12). 73p. (gr. 2-6). 15.00 *(978-0-7569-2589-5(4))* Perfection Learning Corp.

—Viking It & Liking It. 2004. (Time Warp Trio Ser.: 12). 16.00 *(978-1-4176-3613-6(0),* Turtleback) Turtleback Bks.

Stroud, Jonathan. Heroes of the Valley. 2009. (JPN., Illus.). 587p. (YA). *(978-4-652-07954-6(0))* Fukuinkan Shoten.

—Heroes of the Valley. 2010. (ENG.). 496p. (J). (gr. 5-9). pap. 8.99 *(978-1-4231-0967-9(8))* Hyperion Pr.

Style Guide Staff, illus. Gift of the Night Fury. 2014. (How to Train Your Dragon TV Ser.). (ENG.). 24p. (J). (gr. -1-2). pap. 3.99 *(978-1-4814-0436-5(9),* Simon Spotlight) Simon Spotlight.

Style Guide, Style, illus. A Fiery Discovery. 2015. (How to Train Your Dragon TV Ser.). (ENG.). 24p. (J). (gr. -1-3). pap. 3.99 *(978-1-4814-2768-5(7),* Simon Spotlight) Simon Spotlight.

—How to Defend Your Dragon. 2015. (How to Train Your Dragon TV Ser.). (ENG.). 32p. (J). (gr. k-2). pap. 3.99 *(978-1-4814-3710-3(0),* Simon Spotlight) Simon Spotlight.

Sutcliff, Rosemary. Sword Song. 2005. (ENG., Illus.). 288p. (YA). (gr. 7-12). per. 11.99 *(978-0-374-46984-9(9),* Farrar, Straus & Giroux (BYR)) Farrar, Straus & Giroux.

Testa, Maggie. Gift of the Night Fury. 2014. lib. bdg. 13.55 *(978-0-606-36110-1(3))* Turtleback Bks.

Titan Comics Staff. Underworld, Vol. 6. 2015. (Riders of Berk Ser.). (ENG., Illus.). 64p. (J). (gr. 3-7). pap. 6.99 *(978-1-78276-081-8(4))* Titan Bks. Ltd. GBR. Dist: Penguin Random Hse. LLC.

Van Hamme, Jean. Beyond the Shadows. Rosinski, Grzegorz, illus. 2008. (Thorgal Ser.: 3). (ENG.). 96p. pap. 19.95 *(978-1-905460-45-8(7))* CineBook GBR. Dist: National Bk. Network.

—The Brand of the Exiles. Rosinski, Grzegorz, illus. 2013. (Thorgal Ser.: 12). (ENG.). 48p. (J). (gr. 7-12). pap. 11.95 *(978-1-84918-136-5(5))* CineBook GBR. Dist: National Bk. Network.

—The Cage, Vol. 15. Rosinski, Grzegorz, illus. 2014. (Thorgal Ser.: 15). (ENG.). 48p. pap. 11.95 *(978-1-84918-186-0(1))* CineBook GBR. Dist: National Bk. Network.

—Ogotai's Crown. Rosinski, Grzegorz, illus. 2013. (Thorgal Ser.: 13). (ENG.). 48p. pap. 11.95 *(978-1-84918-142-6(X))* CineBook GBR. Dist: National Bk. Network.

van Hamme, Jean. Thorgal - City of the Lost God, Vol. 6. Rosinski, Grzegorz, illus. 2009. (Thorgal Ser.: 6). (ENG.). 96p. pap. 19.95 *(978-1-84918-001-6(6))* CineBook GBR. Dist: National Bk. Network.

Van Hamme, Jean. The Three Elders of Aran. Rosinski, illus. 2007. (Thorgal Ser.: 2). (ENG.). 96p. (J). (gr. 4-7). pap. 14.99 *(978-1-905460-31-1(7))* CineBook GBR. Dist: National Bk. Network.

Viking Sagas 9 Book Set. 2013. *(978-1-909302-99-0(6))* Abela Publishing.

What Flies Beneath. 2014. (How to Train Your Dragon TV Ser.). (ENG., Illus.). 16p. (J). (gr. -1-2). pap. 5.99 *(978-1-4814-2191-1(3),* Simon Spotlight) Simon Spotlight.

Wilson, Diane Lee. Raven Speak. (ENG.). 256p. (YA). (gr. 7). 2011. pap. 8.99 *(978-1-4169-8654-6(5))* 2010. 16.99 *(978-1-4169-8653-9(7))* McElderry, Margaret K. Bks. (McElderry, Margaret K. Bks.).

Wishinsky, Frieda. Yikes, Vikings! Griffiths, Dean & Owlkids Books Inc. Staff, illus. 2007. (Canadian Flyer Adventures Ser.: 4). (ENG.). 96p. (J). (gr. 1-4). per. 7.95 *(978-1-897066-97-3(X),* Maple Tree Pr.) Owlkids Bks. Inc. CAN. Dist: Publishers Group West (PGW).

VILLAGES

Barber, Nicola. Village Homes. 2007. (Homes Around the World Ser.). (ENG., Illus.). 32p. (J). (gr. 3-7). pap. *(978-0-7787-3558-8(3))*; lib. bdg. *(978-0-7787-3546-5(X))* Crabtree Publishing Co.

Freedman, Jeri. Historical Villages, 01 vols., 1. 2016. (Role-Playing for Fun & Profit Ser.). (ENG.). 48p. (J). pap. 11.75 *(978-1-4994-3724-9(2),* Rosen Central) Rosen Publishing Group, Inc., The.

Gillis, Jennifer Blizin. Restored Villages. 2007. (Field Trips Ser.). (Illus.). 24p. (J). (gr. 2-5). lib. bdg. 27.07 *(978-1-60044-563-7(2))* Rourke Educational Media.

Huebsch, Dave. Village Assignment: True Stories of Humor, Adventure, & Drama in Guatemala's Highland Villages. 2004. (Illus.). 268p. per. 16.95 *(978-0-9741734-0-5(1))* Highlight Publishing.

Kalman, Bobbie. My Community Long Ago. 2010. (My World Ser.). (ENG.). 24p. (J). (gr. k-3). *(978-0-7787-9517-9(9))*; pap. *(978-0-7787-9542-1(X))* Crabtree Publishing Co.

Marsico, Katie. What's It Like to Live Here? Fishing Village. 2014. (Community Connections: What's It Like to Live Here? Ser.). (ENG., Illus.). 24p. (J). (gr. 2-5). 25.64 *(978-1-62431-565-7(8),* 203248) Cherry Lake Publishing.

McDowell, Pamela. Fishing Town. 2015. (Illus.). 24p. (J). pap. *(978-1-4896-3606-5(4))* Weigl Pubs., Inc.

Padrino, Mercedes. Feudalism & Village Life in the Middle Ages. 2005. (World Almanac Library of the Middle Ages). (Illus.). 48p. (gr. 5-12). lib. bdg. 31.00 *(978-0-8368-5894-5(8),* Gareth Stevens Secondary Library) Stevens, Gareth Publishing LLLP.

Popper, Garry & Volke, Gordon. Big World Activity Sticker Book. Johnson, Andi, illus. 2004. 16p. 6.00 *(978-1-84161-082-5(8))* Ravette Publishing, Ltd. GBR. Dist: Parkwest Pubns., Inc.

Schomp, Virginia. The Countryside. 2010. (Life in Victorian England Ser.). 80p. (gr. 6). 34.21 *(978-1-60870-030-1(5))* Marshall Cavendish GBR. Dist: Marshall Cavendish Corp.

Watson, Danielle. The Countryside in Medieval Europe. 2016. (Life in Medieval Europe Ser.). (Illus.). 80p. (J). (gr. 6-6). 35.64 *(978-1-5026-1882-5(6))* Cavendish Square Publishing.

VILLAGES—FICTION

Accord Publishing Staff. The Twelve Days of Christmas. Fang, Jade, illus. 2011. (ENG.). 26p. (J). 17.99 *(978-1-4494-0361-4(1))* Andrews McMeel Publishing.

Aine, Mhari. The Little Children & the Fairies. 2008. 56p. pap. *(978-1-84748-375-1(5))* Athena Pr.

Aisha. Parsley, Sage, Rosemary & Thyme. 2012. 24p. 24.95 *(978-1-4626-5122-1(4))* America Star Bks.

Alcott, Louisa May. Jack & Jill: A Village Story. 2007. 372p. per. 16.45 *(978-1-59462-863-4(7),* Book Jungle) Standard Pubns., Inc.

Alexander, Brad. Antiniak: A Different Kind of Village. 2011. 76p. pap. 15.50 *(978-1-257-10163-4(3))* Lulu Pr., Inc.

Alfaro Sifontes, Manuel Guillermo. Alboroto en un Lugar Remoto. 2005. (Illus.). 32p. (J). *(978-1-58018-052-8(3))* Cambridge BrickHouse, Inc.

Andrade, Marcia. Gust's Maze. 2010. 142p. pap. 11.50 *(978-1-60911-101-4(X),* Eloquent Bks.) Strategic Book Publishing & Rights Agency (SBPRA).

Atinuke. No 1 Car Spotter & the Firebird. Johnson Cadwell, Warwick, illus. 2012. (Fiction Ser.). (ENG.). 112p. (J). pap. 4.99 *(978-1-61067-052-4(3))* Kane Miller.

Balian, Lorna. A Sweetheart for Valentine, 1 vol. Balian, Lorna, illus. 2005. (ENG., Illus.). 32p. (J). 15.95 *(978-1-932065-14-5(8))* Star Bright Bks., Inc.

Barraclough, Lindsey. Long Lankin. (ENG.). 464p. (YA). (gr. 7). 2014. pap. 9.99 *(978-0-7636-6937-9(7))* 2012. (Illus.). 16.99 *(978-0-7636-5808-3(1))* Candlewick Pr.

Blanton, Edwin. Together We Can. 2012. 24p. pap. *(978-1-105-51042-7(5))* Lulu.com.

Bloom, Janice Stitziel. A Grateful Heart under My Bed. Woodcock, Marcy, illus. 2007. 36p. (J). per. 15.99 *(978-1-934643-06-8(8))* Villager Bk. Publishing.

—Wonderfully Made under My Bed. Woodcock, Marcy, illus. 2007. 36p. (J). per. 15.99 *(978-1-934643-00-6(9))* Villager Bk. Publishing.

Bolander, Sharon Miller. Hiram's Song. 2012. 20p. pap. 24.95 *(978-1-4626-6234-0(X))* America Star Bks.

Bourbeau, Julie. The Wednesdays. Beene, Jason, illus. (ENG.). 256p. (J). (gr. 2-5). 2013. pap. 7.99 *(978-0-375-87286-0(8),* Yearling) 2012. 16.99 *(978-0-375-86890-0(9),* Knopf Bks. for Young Readers) Random Hse. Children's Bks.

Bruno, Pep. THE SILLY NANNY GOAT. 2007. (ENG., Illus.). 36p. (J). 17.95 *(978-84-96788-86-2(5))* OQO, Editora ESP. Dist: Baker & Taylor Bks.

Buckham, Derek. The Santa Stories. 2008. 81p. pap. 34.50 *(978-1-4092-4803-3(8))* Lulu Pr., Inc.

Byrne, John Patrick. Donald & Benoit. Byrne, John Patrick, illus. 2011. (ENG., Illus.). 64p. (J). (gr. 2-5). 17.95 *(978-0-7893-2084-1(3))* Universe Publishing.

Cavill, Ian. Elle in the Village. 2010. 56p. pap. 13.49 *(978-1-4490-7822-5(2))* AuthorHouse.

Chandraratna, Bandula. Mirage. 2004. (ENG.). 224p. 24.95 *(978-1-57423-196-0(0))* Godine, David R. Pub.

Cohen, Penny L. Tapuchim & Dvash. Polsky, Beanie, illus. 2012. 36p. pap. 24.95 *(978-1-4626-6667-6(1))* PublishAmerica, Inc.

Coombs, Kate. The Secret-Keeper. Solomon, Heather M., illus. 2006. (ENG.). 32p. (J). (gr. -1-3). 17.99 *(978-0-689-83963-4(4),* Atheneum Bks. for Young Readers) Simon & Schuster Children's Publishing.

Corlett, William. The Tunnel Behind the Waterfall. 2010. (Magician's House Quartet Ser.: 3). (ENG.). 320p. (YA). (gr. 5-8). pap. 14.99 *(978-1-4424-1413-6(8),* Simon Pulse) Simon Pulse.

Crabtree, Zona Mae. White Dove. 2005. (Corn Cave Ser.: 3). (ENG., Illus.). (YA). per. 8.00 *(978-0-9726826-2-6(7))* Owl Hollow Publishing.

Creech, Sharon. The Unfinished Angel. 2013. (ENG.). 160p. (J). (gr. 3-7). pap. 6.99 *(978-0-06-143097-8(8))* HarperCollins Pubs.

Crook, M. J. Village on Crooked Hill. 2008. 168p. pap. 11.99 *(978-1-4389-0486-3(X))* AuthorHouse.

Cunnane, Kelly. For You Are a Kenyan Child. Juan, Ana, illus. 2006. (ENG.). 40p. (J). (gr. -1-3). 17.99 *(978-0-689-86194-9(X)*, Atheneum Bks. for Young Readers) Simon & Schuster Children's Publishing.

Deedy, Carmen Agra. The Rooster Who Would Not Be Quiet! Yelchin, Eugene, illus. 2017. (ENG.). 48p. (J). (gr. -1-3). 17.99 *(978-0-545-72288-9(8)*, Scholastic Pr.) Scholastic, Inc.

Deshpande, Shashi. 3 Novels. 2006. 379p. *(978-0-14-333511-5(1)*, Puffin) Penguin Publishing Group.

Doyle, Malachy & Philpot, Graham. Jack the Giant-Killer. 2009. (Hopscotch Adventures Ser.). (Illus.). 31p. (J). (gr. 1). lib. bdg. 25.65 *(978-1-59771-184-5(5))* Sea-To-Sea Pubns.

Ernestine. Town Girl. 2011. 36p. pap. 21.99 *(978-1-4628-4649-8(1))* Xlibris Corp.

Ferchaud, Steve, illus. Glen Robbie: A Scottish Fairy Tale. 2006. (J). 22.95 *(978-1-58478-013-7(4)*, Highland Children's Pr.) Heather & Highlands Publishing.

Gabriel, Elizabeth P. & Gabriel, Pamela P. Ziccah Blows Her Horn. 2008. 24p. pap. 12.99 *(978-1-4389-2447-2(X))* AuthorHouse.

Garcia Iii, Joe. Dragon Boogers. 2010. 40p. pap. 16.99 *(978-1-4490-5639-1(3))* AuthorHouse.

Gilbert, Harry. Year of Sharing, Level 1. Oxford University Press Staff & Bassett, Jennifer, eds. 3rd ed. 2008. (ENG., Illus.). 64p. 10.00 *(978-0-19-479077-2(0))* Oxford Univ. Pr., Inc.

Goodman-Schneps, Oriana. The Seventh Chime. 2009. 52p. pap. 15.99 *(978-1-4415-2748-6(6))* Xlibris Corp.

Greaves, Margaret. The Mice of Nibbling Village. Pinkney, Jane, illus. 2011. (ENG.). 32p. (J). (gr. -1-k). 14.99 *(978-1-84365-189-5(0))* National Trust, Aylesbury GBR. Dist: Independent Pubs. Group.

Gregory, Steven. The Lion's Drum: A Retelling of an African Folk Tale. Obata, Claudia, illus. 2007. 32p. (J). 13.95 *(978-0-615-15540-1(5))* Words & Music.

Hahn, Molly. Under the Sneep Tree: The Wamboozling of a Village. 2009. pap. *(978-1-61623-907-7(7))* Independent Pub.

Harvey, Sharon M. Legend of the Pumpkin Carver. 2010. 100p. pap. 22.95 *(978-1-4327-1214-3(4))* Outskirts Pr., Inc.

Higgy, M. J. Creator's Dream. 2012. (Illus.). 16p. pap. 18.30 *(978-1-4772-3862-2(X))* AuthorHouse.

Hinwood, Christine. The Returning. 2013. (ENG.). 320p. (YA). (gr. 9). pap. 8.99 *(978-0-14-242477-3(3)*, Speak) Penguin Young Readers Group.

Hiss, Jill. Peppeto's Magic Jelly Bean. 2005. 19.00 *(978-0-8059-9893-1(4))* Dorrance Publishing Co., Inc.

Hoffman, Amalia. Klezmer Bunch. 2009. 36p. 15.95 *(978-965-229-447-0(0))* Gefen Publishing Hse., Ltd ISR. Dist: Strauss Consultants.

Holmqvist, Carin. African Tales. 2010. 64p. pap. 28.70 *(978-0-557-18184-1(4))* Lulu Pr., Inc.

Hudson, Bonnie Rose. The Hidden Village. 2017. (J). **(978-1-62856-311-5(7))** BJU Pr.

Iinuma, Yuuki. Itsuwaribito, Vol. 14. 2015. (ENG.). 192p. pap. 9.99 *(978-1-4215-6525-5(0))* Viz Media.

Izzo, Donna. Frilly Lilly's Candyland Express. 2011. 24p. pap. 15.99 *(978-1-4653-6159-2(6))* Xlibris Corp.

James, Ian. Why the Sky Is Far Away: A Tale from Nigeria. 2006. (J). pap. *(978-1-4108-6172-6(4))* Benchmark Education Co.

Janelle, Nicole & Cholette, Daniel. Naby Recycles. 2012. 32p. pap. 14.60 *(978-1-105-53454-6(5))* Lulu Pr., Inc.

Johnson, Carol V. Somerset Dreams. 2011. (Illus.). 112p. pap. 32.12 *(978-1-4567-9012-7(9))* AuthorHouse.

Jones, Diana Wynne. Enchanted Glass. 304p. (J). (gr. 3-7). 2011. pap. 6.99 *(978-0-06-186685-2(7))* 2010. 16.99 *(978-0-06-186684-5(9))* HarperCollins Pubs. (Greenwillow Bks.).

Jones, T. Llew. Storiau Cwm-Pen-Llo. 2005. (WEL., Illus.). 100p. pap. *(978-0-86381-750-2(5))* Gwasg Carreg Gwalch.

Judge, Chris. The Snow Beast. Judge, Chris, illus. 2015. (ENG., Illus.). 32p. (J). (gr. -1-3). 17.99 *(978-1-4677-9313-1(2))* Andersen Pr. GBR. Dist: Lerner Publishing Group.

Kail, Leanna. The Owl Who Couldn't Whoo. Rottinger, Amy, illus. 2013. 24p. pap. 11.95 *(978-1-61244-129-0(7))* Halo Publishing International.

Kim, JiYu. The Wise Boy. Hwang, YoSeob, illus. 2014. (MySELF Bookshelf Ser.). (ENG.). 32p. (J). (gr. k-2). pap. 11.94 *(978-1-60357-690-1(8))*; lib. bdg. 25.27 *(978-1-59953-655-2(2))* Norwood Hse. Pr.

Knight, Richard. Winter Shadow. Johnson, Richard, illus. 2011. (ENG.). 80p. (J). (gr. 1-5). pap. 9.99 *(978-1-84686-624-1(3))* Barefoot Bks., Inc.

Knight, Richard John & Walker, Richard. Winter Shadow. Johnson, Richard, illus. 2009. (ENG.). 80p. (J). (gr. 3-9). pap. 16.99 *(978-1-84686-116-1(0))* Barefoot Bks., Inc.

Krishnaswami, Uma. Out of the Way! Out of the Way!, 1 vol. Krishnaswamy, Uma, illus. 2012. (ENG.). 28p. (J). (gr. -1-2). 17.95 *(978-1-55498-130-4(1))* Groundwood Bks. CAN. Dist: Publishers Group West (PGW).

Lange, Willem. Favor Johnson: A Christmas Story. Dodson, Bert, illus. 2009. (ENG.). 32p. (J). (gr. 1-3). 16.95 *(978-1-59373-082-6(9))* Bunker Hill Publishing, Inc.

Lederer, Ryan. The Adventures of Captain Candy. 2007. (Illus.). 48p. (J). (gr. 4-7). 15.95 *(978-0-9795852-1-0(X))* Seven Locks Pr.

Lester, Julius. The Girl Who Saved Yesterday. Angel, Carl, illus. 2016. (ENG.). 32p. (J). (gr. -1-4). 16.99 *(978-1-939547-24-8(5))* Creston Bks.

Lincoln, Dallas Ford. The Sawmill Sant. 2011. 36p. pap. 16.95 *(978-1-4626-4335-6(3))* America Star Bks.

Lois, Lowry. Messenger. 2006. (ENG.). 176p. (J). (gr. 3-7). mass mkt. 7.99 *(978-0-440-23912-3(5)*, Laurel Leaf) Random Hse. Children's Bks.

Lord, Jennifer Fallin. Pippersville: And the troll that lost his big Toe. 2011. 32p. pap. 14.50 *(978-1-4670-3820-1(2))* AuthorHouse.

Loveridge, Pamela. The Knife of Blood. 2012. 28p. pap. 32.70 *(978-1-4797-4804-4(8))* Xlibris Corp.

Malton, H. Mel. Pioneer Poltergeist. 2007. (Alan Nearing Mystery Ser.: 2). (ENG.). 208p. (J). pap. 9.95 *(978-1-894917-60-5(X)*, Napoleon & Co.) Dundurn CAN. Dist: Ingram Publisher Services.

Mandla. Garden Green Hills: And Finally Ants Run the Village. 2013. 102p. pap. 15.99 *(978-1-4797-1482-7(8))* Xlibris Corp.

Maruno, Jennifer. Totem, 0 vols. 2014. (ENG.). 168p. (YA). pap. 10.99 *(978-1-4597-1934-7(4)*, 9781459719347) Dundurn CAN. Dist: Ingram Publisher Services.

Matthews, T. J. The Village Safari. Rheburg, Judy, illus. 2005. (J). *(978-0-938978-36-7(5))* Wycliffe Bible Translators.

Mcallister, Bruce. The Village Sang to the Sea. 2013. 172p. pap. *(978-0-9534784-9-1(1))* Aeon Pr.

McDowell, Andrew. Beyond the Forest. 2007. 286p. pap. 16.95 *(978-0-7414-4238-3(8))* Infinity Publishing.

McKinlay, Meg. A Single Stone. 2017. (ENG.). 272p. (J). (gr. 5). 17.99 *(978-0-7636-8837-0(1))* Candlewick Pr.

Medina, Sylvia M. & Ballock-Dixon, Saige J. Jade Elephant. Eagle, Joy, illus. 2012. 36p. pap. 11.49 *(978-0-9836602-4-8(7))* Green Kids Club, Inc.

Mehrlich Iii, Ferdinand Paul. Splugworth Saves the Day, 1 vol. Mehrlich, Cynthia, illus. 2009. 43p. pap. 24.95 *(978-1-60836-765-8(7))* America Star Bks.

Moolenschot, Catherine. A Rough Road. 2008. 142p. pap. 17.96 *(978-1-4092-4153-9(X))* Lulu Pr., Inc.

Moore, Baba Evans. While the Village Sleeps. 2003. 400p. (YA). pap. 14.95 *(978-0-9709762-0-8(8))* Moore, Evans.

Mora, Pat. Doña Flor: A Tall Tale about a Giant Woman with a Great Big Heart. Colón, Raúl, illus. 2010. (ENG & SPA.). 32p. (J). (gr. -1-2). pap. 7.99 *(978-0-375-86144-4(0)*, Dragonfly Bks.) Random Hse. Children's Bks.

Nancy Mann Israel. The Juggler & His Wife. 2009. 24p. pap. 12.95 *(978-1-4389-5334-2(8))* AuthorHouse.

Narsimhan, Mahtab. The Third Eye. 2007. (Tara Trilogy Ser.: 1). (ENG.). 240p. (YA). (gr. 5-7). pap. 12.99 *(978-1-55002-750-1(6)*, Boardwalk Bks.) Dundurn CAN. Dist: Ingram Publisher Services.

Nettrour, Nelani. The Dragonlands Bk. 3: The Village. l.t. ed. 2004. (Illus.). 148p. (J). pap. 19.95 *(978-1-932657-12-8(6))* Third Millennium Pubns.

Olsen, Grant Orrin. Rhino Trouble. Carpenter, Mike, illus. 2015. (J). 14.99 *(978-1-4621-1665-2(5))* Cedar Fort, Inc./CFI Distribution.

Peyo. The Snow Giant. Peyo, illus. 2011. (Smurfs Classic Ser.). (ENG., Illus.). 32p. (J). (gr. k-2). pap. 3.99 *(978-1-4424-2892-8(9)*, Simon Spotlight) Simon Spotlight.

—The Snow Giant. Peyo, illus. 2011. (Smurfs Classic Ser.). (ENG., Illus.). 32p. (J). (gr. k-2). 15.99 *(978-1-4424-3610-7(7)*, Simon Spotlight) Simon Spotlight.

Quirk, Katie. A Girl Called Problem. 2013. (ENG., Illus.). 256p. (J). pap. 8.50 *(978-0-8028-5404-9(4)*, Eerdmans Bks For Young Readers) Eerdmans, William B. Publishing Co.

Reardon, A. C. Galish: The adventure of Isabelle & Eva. 2011. 168p. pap. 14.69 *(978-1-4567-7818-7(8))* AuthorHouse.

Resman, Michael. Liliana Ageiraú. Cayetano, Eldred Roy, tr. Gathigo, Cyrus Ngatia, illus. 2013. 40p. pap. *(978-976-8142-50-4(2))* Producciones de la Hamaca.

Rossignol, Manon Éléonor & Lecor, Tex. Isory Poutch et le Sortilege de Cacouna. 2004. (FRE., Illus.). 398p. (J). *(978-2-9807852-1-4(0)*, Spotlight Poets) Editions le Poutchoman.

Sapre, Reshme. The Unfortunate Tale of Kachuva the Tortoise: As Told by Chukwa Sulcata. Robinson, Jayme, illus. 2012. (ENG.). 40p. 16.95 *(978-0-9829362-0-7(6))* Hathi Chiti Bks. for Kids.

Schott, Elizabeth, illus. Jake & Sam at the Empty Abbey. 2006. 96p. (J). per. 9.95 *(978-0-9724421-1-4(1))* Fountain Square Publishing.

Shah, Idries. The Clever Boy & the Terrible, Dangerous Animal. Santiago, Rose Mary, illus. 2005. 32p. (J). (gr. -1 — 1). pap. 6.99 *(978-1-883536-51-0(0)*, Hoopoe Bks.) I S H K.

—The Clever Boy & the Terrible, Dangerous Animal/el Muchachito Listo y el Terrible y Peligroso Animal. Wirkala, Rita, tr. Santiago, Rose Mary, illus. 2005. 32p. (J). (gr. -1-3). 18.00 *(978-1-883536-39-8(1))*; pap., per. 6.95 *(978-1-883536-40-4(5))* I S H K. (Hoopoe Bks.).

—The Silly Chicken. Jackson, Jeff, illus. 2005. 32p. (J). pap., pap. 6.99 *(978-1-883536-50-3(2)*, Hoopoe Bks.) I S H K.

—The Silly Chicken/el Pollo Bobo. Wirkala, Rita, tr. Jackson, Jeff, illus. 2005. 32p. (J). (gr. -1-3). 18.00 *(978-1-883536-37-4(5)*, Hoopoe Bks.) I S H K.

Sher, Steven. Where the Shouting Began. 2008. (J). *(978-1-932727-08-1(6))* Montemayor Pr.

Shinn, Sharon. The Safe-Keeper's Secret. 2005. (ENG.). 240p. (YA). (gr. 7-7). 7.99 *(978-0-14-240357-0(1)*, Firebird) Penguin Young Readers Group.

Smith, Icy. Mystery of the Giant Mask of Sanxingdui. Roski, Gayle Garner, illus. 2015. (J). *(978-0-9913454-8-9(7))* East West Discovery Pr.

Stiegemeyer, Julie. Under the Baobab Tree, 1 vol. Lewis, E. B., illus. 2012. (ENG.). 32p. (J). 16.99 *(978-0-310-72561-9(5))* Zonderkidz.

Suits, Patti J. Topa & the Path of the Pum. 2008. 112p. pap. 10.99 *(978-1-4343-9520-7(0))* AuthorHouse.

Swanepoel, Sharon. The Adventures of Seek & Save Volume 3: The Village. Locsinto, Lucas, illus. 2011. (J). *(978-0-9772647-6-6(9))* God's Glory Media.

Swarabi, Fatma Abdulla & El Amin, Khalid Hamid. Marim & Her Grandmother. 2010. 28p. pap. 13.99 *(978-1-4490-8156-0(8))* AuthorHouse.

Thomson, Elizabeth & Albert, Sarah. Andros: the Last Villager. 2008. 226p. pap. 17.04 *(978-1-4357-3557-6(9))* Lulu Pr., Inc.

Vickie A. Soman. The Sahara Desert Angel: Education & Nature Folktales 2. 2010. 208p. pap. 14.95 *(978-1-4502-1465-0(7))* iUniverse, Inc.

Vince Crandall, Vince. The Village Baker. 2011. 40p. pap. 16.95 *(978-1-257-16195-9(4))* Lulu Pr., Inc.

Vincent, Patti. The Village Heroes Meet the Dragon. 2008. 44p. pap. 19.95 *(978-1-4389-1764-1(3))* AuthorHouse.

Vogel-Placides, Joan Katherine. The Safe Place. Placides, Del S., illus. 2013. 58p. 13.99 *(978-0-9888718-3-0(1))* DOMINIONHOUSE Publishing & Design.

Waldman, Debby. A Sack Full of Feathers, 1 vol. Revell, Cindy, illus. 2007. (ENG.). 32p. (J). (gr. -1-3). 9.95 *(978-1-55143-863-4(1))* Orca Bk. Pubs. USA.

Wells, H. G. The Invisible Man, 1 vol. Fisher, Eric Scott, illus. 2011. (Calico Illustrated Classics Ser.: No. 3). (ENG.). 112p. (YA). (gr. 3-6). 27.07 *(978-1-61641-103-9(1))* Magic Wagon.

White, Betty. Touring Polka-Dot Village. 2012. 24p. 24.95 *(978-1-4626-5869-5(5))* America Star Bks.

Williamson, Judithe Anne. Princess Kara in Her Village, 1 vol. 2009. 107p. pap. 19.95 *(978-1-60813-817-3(8))* America Star Bks.

Wills, Joseph. The World. 2013. 200p. pap. *(978-1-906954-76-5(3))* Live It Publishing.

Wright, Sky'asia. The Big, Blue Raspberry. 2012. 30p. pap. 5.99 *(978-0-9857095-1-8(0))* RRJ Publishing, Inc.

Yeoman, John. Sixes & Sevens. Blake, Quentin, illus. 2012. (ENG.). 32p. (J). (gr. -1-k). pap. 11.99 *(978-1-84939-308-9(7))* Andersen Pr. GBR. Dist: Independent Pubs. Group.

York, M. J. The Boy at the Dike: A Dutch Folktale. Freeman, Laura, illus. 2012. (Folktales from Around the World Ser.). (ENG.). 24p. (J). (gr. k-3). 28.50 *(978-1-61473-219-8(1)*, 204914) Child's World, Inc., The.

VILLAS

see Architecture, Domestic

VIOLENCE

Agassi, Martine. Hands Are Not for Hitting. Heinlen, Marieka, illus. rev. ed. 2009. (Best Behavior Ser.). (ENG.). 40p. (J). (gr. -1-2). pap. 11.95 *(978-1-57542-308-1(1))* Free Spirit Publishing, Inc.

Agassi, Martine & Verdick, Elizabeth. Las Manos No Son para Pegar. Heinlen, Marieka, illus. 2009. (Best Behavior Ser.).Tr. of Hands Are Not for Hitting. (SPA & ENG.). 40p. (J). (gr. -1-2). pap. 11.95 *(978-1-57542-310-4(3))* Free Spirit Publishing, Inc.

Agassi, Martine, et al. Las Manos No Son para Pegar. Heinlen, Marieka, illus. 2009. (Best Behavior Ser.).Tr. of Hands Are Not for Hitting. (SPA, ENG & MUL.). 24p. (J). (gr. -1 — 1). bds. 7.95 *(978-1-57542-309-8(X))* Free Spirit Publishing, Inc.

Allman, Toney. School Violence. 2016. (Matters of Opinion Ser.). (ENG., Illus.). 64p. (J). (gr. 4-6). lib. bdg. 27.93 *(978-1-59953-757-3(5))* Norwood Hse. Pr.

Andryszewski, Tricia. Terrorism in America. 2003. (Headliners Ser.). (Illus.). 64p. (J). (gr. 5-8). lib. bdg. 25.90 *(978-0-7613-2803-2(3)*, Millbrook Pr.) Lerner Publishing Group.

Apel, Lorelei. Dealing with Weapons at School & at Home. (Conflict Resolution Library). 24p. 2009. (gr. 2-3). 42.50 *(978-1-60853-411-1(1))* 2004. (Illus.). (J). 22.60 *(978-0-8239-6932-6(0))* Rosen Publishing Group, Inc., The. (PowerKids Pr.).

Banks, Delilah & Giacobello, John. Surviving Family Violence, 01 vols., 1. 2016. (Family Issues & You Ser.). (ENG.). 48p. (J). pap. 11.75 *(978-1-4994-3705-8(6)*, Rosen Central) Rosen Publishing Group, Inc., The.

Banks, Jewelene. Don't Give That Boy No Gun. 2010. pap. 12.00 *(978-1-61658-990-5(6))* Independent Pub.

Becnel, Barbara, ed. Gangs & Violence: Stanley Tookie Williams Street Peace Series, 8 bks., Vol. 1, Bk. 3. 2008. 24p. (J). 6.95 *(978-0-9753584-4-3(8))* Damamli Publishing Co.

—Gangs & Weapons: Stanley Tookie Williams Street Peace Series, 8 bks., Vol. 1, Bk. 3. 2008. 24p. (J). *(978-0-9753584-3-6(X))* Damamli Publishing Co.

Berry, Joy. Help Me Be Good about Fighting. 2009. (ENG.). 40p. (J). (gr. k-2). pap. 7.95 *(978-1-60577-128-1(7))* Berry, Joy Enterprises.

Bowen, Shane. Out of the Darkness. 2010. 220p. pap. 21.95 *(978-0-557-26249-6(6))* Lulu Pr., Inc.

Brezina, Corona. Deadly School & Campus Violence. 2008. (Violence & Society Ser.). (Illus.). 64p. (YA). (gr. 9-12). lib. bdg. 31.95 *(978-1-4042-1792-8(4))* Rosen Publishing Group, Inc., The.

Brown, Isobel. Domestic Crime. 2004. (Crime & Detection Ser.). (Illus.). 96p. (YA). (gr. 7-18). lib. bdg. 22.95 *(978-1-59084-370-3(3))* Mason Crest.

Bryfonski, Dedria, ed. Family Violence. 2012. (Current Controversies Ser.). (ENG.). 240p. (gr. 10-12). pap. 28.45 *(978-0-7377-6226-6(8))*; lib. bdg. 40.95 *(978-0-7377-6225-9(X))* Cengage Gale. (Greenhaven Pr., Inc.).

Byers, Ann. Frequently Asked Questions about Gangs & Urban Violence. 2011. (FAQ: Teen Life Ser.). (ENG.). 64p. (YA). lib. bdg. 31.95 *(978-1-4488-1325-4(5))* Rosen Publishing Group, Inc., The.

Cefrey, Holly. Coping with Media Violence. 2005. (Coping Ser.). (Illus.). 192p. (YA). (gr. 7-12). lib. bdg. 34.60 *(978-0-8239-2893-4(4))* Rosen Publishing Group, Inc., The.

Chandler, Matt. Dangerous Times: History's Most Troubled Eras. 2013. (Dangerous History Ser.). (ENG.). 32p. (gr. 3-4). 27.99 *(978-1-4765-0126-0(2)*, Edge Bks.) Capstone Press of Coughlan Cos.

Cobb, Carlene. Coping with an Abusive Relationship. (Coping Ser.). 192p. (gr. 7-12). 2009. 63.90 *(978-1-61511-990-5(6))* 2005. (Illus.). (YA). lib. bdg. 34.60 *(978-0-8239-2822-4(5))* Rosen Publishing Group, Inc., The.

Daniels, Peggy. School Violence. 2008. (Issues That Concern You Ser.). (ENG., Illus.). 144p. (gr. 10-12). lib. bdg. 42.00 *(978-0-7377-4186-5(4)*, LML02109-243090, Greenhaven Pr., Inc.) Cengage Gale.

Dziedzic, Nancy. Family Violence, No. 9. 2009. (Current Controversies Ser.). (ENG., Illus.). 240p. (gr. 10-12). 40.95 *(978-0-7377-3283-2(0))*; 28.45 *(978-0-7377-3284-9(9))* Cengage Gale. (Greenhaven Pr., Inc.).

Edwards, Nicola. Domestic Violence. (Illus.). 32p. (YA). (gr. 1-18). lib. bdg. 27.10 *(978-1-932333-08-4(8))* Chrysalis Education.

Emanuele, Patricia. Coping with Aggression. (Coping Ser.). 192p. (gr. 7-12). 2009. 63.90 *(978-1-61511-989-9(2))* 2005. (Illus.). (YA). lib. bdg. 34.60 *(978-0-8239-3360-0(1))* Rosen Publishing Group, Inc., The.

Etingoff, Kim. Gunman on Campus. Stephens, Ronald, ed. 2014. (Safety First Ser.). (ENG., Illus.). 48p. (J). (gr. 5-18). lib. bdg. 20.95 *(978-1-4222-3047-3(3))* Mason Crest.

Fein, Eric. High Noon: Wild Bill Hickok & the Code of the Old West. 2009. (Great Moments in American History Ser.). 32p. (gr. 3-3). 47.90 *(978-1-61513-145-7(0))* Rosen Publishing Group, Inc., The.

Gerdes, Louise. Gun Violence. 2010. (Opposing Viewpoints Ser.). (ENG.). 240p. pap. 29.45 *(978-0-7377-4967-0(9)*, Greenhaven Pr., Inc.) Cengage Gale.

Gerdes, Louise, ed. Domestic Violence. 2011. (Opposing Viewpoints Ser.). (ENG., Illus.). 224p. (gr. 10-12). 48.80 *(978-0-7377-5719-4(1))*; pap. 33.80 *(978-0-7377-5720-0(5)*, Greenhaven Pr., Inc.) Cengage Gale.

—Violence. 2007. (Opposing Viewpoints Ser.). (ENG.). 234p. (YA). (gr. 7-12). 29.45 *(978-0-7377-3365-5(9))*; (Illus.). pap. 42.95 *(978-0-7377-3364-8(0))* Cengage Gale. (Greenhaven Pr., Inc.).

Giacabello, John. You & Violence in Your Family. 2009. (Family Matters Ser.). 48p. (gr. 5-8). 53.00 *(978-1-61512-484-8(5)*, Rosen Reference) Rosen Publishing Group, Inc., The.

Giacobello, John. You & Violence in Your Family. 2005. (Family Matters Ser.). (Illus.). 48p. (J). (gr. 5-8). lib. bdg. 29.25 *(978-0-8239-3353-2(9))* Rosen Publishing Group, Inc., The.

Gifford, Clive. Violence on the Screen. 2010. (Voices Ser.). (Illus.). 48p. pap. *(978-0-237-54218-4(8))* Evans Brothers, Ltd.

Gitlin, Marty. Helping a Friend in an Abusive Relationship. 2016. (How Can I Help? Friends Helping Friends Ser.). 00064p. (J). (gr. 6-6). pap. 12.95 *(978-1-4994-6436-8(3))* Rosen Publishing Group, Inc., The.

Gordon, Sherri Mabry. Beyond Bruises: The Truth about Teens & Abuse. 2009. (Issues in Focus Today Ser.). (Illus.). 128p. (J). (gr. 6-12). lib. bdg. 33.27 *(978-0-7660-3064-0(4))* Enslow Pubs., Inc.

Hacker, Caryn Sabes. A Bully Grows Up: Erik Meets the Wizard: Adult Guide Edition, 1. Boureau, Silvere, illus. 2006. 34p. (J). tchr. ed. 15.95 *(978-0-9791046-0-2(2))* Caryn Solutions, LLC.

Haugen, David M. Media Violence. 2008. (Opposing Viewpoints Ser.). (ENG., Illus.). 232p. (YA). (gr. 10-12). 29.45 *(978-0-7377-4219-0(4)*, LML02109-243141); pap. 42.95 *(978-0-7377-4218-3(6)*, LML02109-243108) Cengage Gale. (Greenhaven Pr., Inc.).

Henningfeld, Diane Andrews. Family Violence. 2011. (Global Viewpoints Ser.). (ENG., Illus.). 224p. (gr. 10-12). pap. 31.70 *(978-0-7377-5651-7(9)*, Greenhaven Pr., Inc.) Cengage Gale.

Henningfeld, Diane Andrews, ed. Family Violence. 2011. (Global Viewpoints Ser.). (Illus.). 224p. (YA). (gr. 9-12). 40.45 *(978-0-7377-5650-0(0))* Cengage Gale.

Katz, Samuel M. Global Counterstrike: International Counterterrorism. 2005. (Terrorist Dossiers Ser.). (Illus.). 72p. (J). (gr. 6-12). 26.60 *(978-0-8225-1566-1(0))* Lerner Publishing Group.

Kenney, Karen Latchana. Domestic Violence, 1 vol. 2011. (Essential Issues Set 3 Ser.). (ENG., Illus.). 112p. (J). (gr. 6-12). lib. bdg. 35.64 *(978-1-61783-133-1(6))* ABDO Publishing Co.

Kreiner, Anna. Todo lo que necesitas saber sobre la violencia en la escuela (Everything You Need to Know about Violence in School) 2009. (Todo lo que necesitas (the Need to Know Library) Ser.). (SPA.). 64p. (gr. 6-6). 58.50 *(978-1-60854-411-0(7)*, Editorial Buenas Letras) Rosen Publishing Group, Inc., The.

La Bella, Laura. Dating Violence. 2015. (Confronting Violence Against Women Ser.). (ENG.). 64p. (J). (gr. 6-7). 32.95 *(978-1-4994-6030-8(9)*, Rosen Young Adult) Rosen Publishing Group, Inc., The.

—Living in a Violent Household. 2015. (Confronting Violence Against Women Ser.). (ENG.). 64p. (J). (gr. 6-7). 32.95 *(978-1-4994-6034-6(1)*, Rosen Young Adult) Rosen Publishing Group, Inc., The.

Landau, Elaine. Date Violence. 2005. (Life Balance Ser.). (ENG., Illus.). 80p. (J). (gr. 5-8). pap. 6.95 *(978-0-531-16613-0(9)*, Watts, Franklin) Scholastic Library Publishing.

Langwith, Jacqueline. Violence. 2010. (Introducing Issues with Opposing Viewpoints Ser.). (Illus.). 144p. (J). 36.95 *(978-0-7377-4736-2(6)*, Greenhaven Pr., Inc.) Cengage Gale.

Lankford, Ronnie D. Gun Violence. 2010. (Social Issues Firsthand Ser.). (Illus.). 192p. (J). 33.75 *(978-0-7377-4797-3(8)*, Greenhaven Pr., Inc.) Cengage Gale.

Lawrence, Sandra. Murder & Mayhem. 2016. (Hideous History Ser.). (ENG., Illus.). 64p. (J). (gr. 5-9). 11.99 *(978-1-4998-0082-1(7))* Little Bee Books Inc.

Lennon, Liz. I Don't Hit. 2013. (Illus.). (J). 25.65 *(978-1-59771-411-2(9))* Sea-To-Sea Pubns.

Lentini, Rochelle, et al. Tucker the Turtle Takes Time to Tuck & Think. SanGiacomo, Scott, illus. 2016. 16p. (J). pap. *(978-0-87659-705-7(3))* Gryphon Hse., Inc.

Levy, Barrie. In Love & in Danger: A Teen's Guide to Breaking Free of Abusive Relationships. 3rd rev. ed. 2006. (ENG., Illus.). 144p. (Orig.). per. 13.00 *(978-1-58005-187-3(1))* Seal Pr.

McGee, Kathleen M. & Buddenberg, Laura J. Unmasking Sexual Con Games: Helping Teens Avoid Emotional Grooming & Dating Violence. 3rd ed. 2004. (Leader's Guide with Session Plans Ser.). (ENG., Illus.). 199p. pap. 29.95 *(978-1-889322-54-4(7)*, 25-015) Boys Town Pr.

—Unmasking Sexual Con Games Teen's Guide: A Teen's Guide to Avoiding Emotional Grooming & Dating Violence. 3rd ed. 2004. (Leader's Guide with Session Plans Ser.). (ENG.). 79p. pap. 5.95 *(978-1-889322-55-1(5)*, 25-016) Boys Town Pr.

Michaels, Vanessa Lynn & Harrow, Jeremy. Frequently Asked Questions about Family Violence. 2011. (FAQ: Teen Life Ser.). lib. bdg. 31.95 *(978-1-4488-4628-3(5))* Rosen Publishing Group, Inc., The.

Mintzer, Rich. Coping with Random Acts of Violence. 2009. (Coping Ser.). 196p. (gr. 7-12). 63.90 *(978-1-61512-009-3(2))* Rosen Publishing Group, Inc., The.

mooney, carla. Teen Violence. 2013. (ENG.). 96p. (YA). lib. bdg. *(978-1-60152-496-6(X))* ReferencePoint Pr., Inc.

Netzley, Patricia D. How Does Video Game Violence Affect Society? 2013. (Illus.). 96p. (YA). lib. bdg. *(978-1-60152-490-4(0))* ReferencePoint Pr., Inc.

—Video Games, Violence & Crime. 2014. (Video Games & Society Ser.). (ENG., Illus.). 80p. (J). lib. bdg. *(978-1-60152-752-3(7))* ReferencePoint Pr., Inc.

Omnigraphics, Inc. Staff, contrib. by. Abuse & Violence Information for Teens: Health Tips about the Causes &

T U V

Consequences of Abusive & Violent Behavior Including Facts about the Types of Abuse & Violence, the Warning Signs of Abusive & Violent Behavior, Health Concerns of Victims, & Getting Help & Staying Safe. 2nd ed. 2017. (Teen Health Ser.). 440p. (J). 69.00 (978-0-7808-1456-1(8)) Omnigraphics, Inc.

Orr, Tamra. Violence in Our Schools: Halls of Hope, Halls of Fear. 2003. (Single Title: Social Studies Ser.). (ENG., Illus.). 192p. (YA). 30.50 (978-0-531-12268-6(9), Watts, Franklin) Scholastic Library Publishing.

Piano, Doreen. Violence. 2007. (Social Issues Firsthand Ser.). (ENG.). 192p. (gr. 10-12). lib. bdg. 38.30 (978-0-7377-2909-2(0), Greenhaven Pr., Inc.) Cengage Gale.

Powell, Marie. Asking Questions about Violence in Popular Culture. 2015. (21st Century Skills Library: Asking Questions about Media Ser.). (ENG.). 32p. (J). (gr. 4-8). 29.93 (978-1-63362-492-4(7), 206876) Cherry Lake Publishing.

Randolph, Ryan P. Wild West Lawmen & Outlaws. 2009. (Library of the Westward Expansion Ser.). 24p. (gr. 3-4). 42.50 (978-1-60853-944-4(X), PowerKids Pr.) Rosen Publishing Group, Inc., The.

Royston, Angela. Gun Crimes. 2010. (Solve It with Science Ser.). (Illus.). 48p. (YA). (gr. 5-9). lib. bdg. 34.25 (978-1-59920-330-0(8)) Black Rabbit Bks.

Schmermund, Elizabeth, ed. Campus Sexual Violence. 2017. (At Issue Ser.). 128p. (YA). (gr. 10-12). pap. 27.80 (978-1-5345-0037-2(5)); lib. bdg. 39.40 (978-1-5345-0018-1(9)) Greenhaven Publishing LLC. (Greenhaven Publishing).

Slavens, Elaine & James Lorimer and Company Ltd. Staff. Fighting: Without Coming to Blows, 1 vol. Murray, Steven, illus. 2nd ed. 2010. (Lorimer Deal with It Ser.). (ENG.). 32p. (J). (gr. 4-8). pap. 12.95 (978-1-55277-517-2(8), 9781552775172) Lorimer, James & Co., Ltd., Pubs. CAN. Dist: Orca Bk. Pubs. USA.

The Truth about Violence. 2nd rev. ed. 2010. (Truth about Ser.). (Illus.). 224p. (C). (gr. 9). 35.00 (978-0-8160-7644-4(8)) Facts On File, Inc.

The Violence Prevention Library, 6 bks. Incl. Learning How to Be Kind to Others. Kent, Susan. lib. bdg. 22.60 (978-0-8239-5613-5(X)); Learning How to Feel Good about Yourself. Kent, Susan, contrib. by. lib. bdg. 22.60 (978-0-8239-5615-9(6)); Learning How to Say You Are Sorry. Kent, Susan. lib. bdg. 22.60 (978-0-8239-5614-2(8)); Learning How to Stay Safe at School. Kent, Susan. lib. bdg. 22.60 (978-0-8239-5616-6(4)); 24p. (J). (gr. 3). 2001. (Illus.). Set lib. bdg. 103.50 (978-0-8239-7080-3(9), PowerKids Pr.) Rosen Publishing Group, Inc., The.

Watkins, Christi, ed. How Can Gang Violence Be Prevented? 2006. (At Issue Ser.). (ENG., Illus.). 128p. (gr. 10-12). 39.40 (978-0-7377-2380-9(7), Greenhaven Pr., Inc.) Cengage Gale.

Watkins, Christine. How Can Gang Violence Be Prevented? 2006. (At Issue Ser.). (ENG., Illus.). 97p. (J). (gr. 3-7). 24.45 (978-0-7377-2381-6(5), Greenhaven Pr., Inc.) Cengage Gale.

Wilcox, Christine. Understanding Violent Behavior. 2017. (Understanding Psychology Ser.). (ENG.). 80p. (YA). (gr. 5-12). (978-1-68282-283-8(4)) ReferencePoint Pr., Inc.

Wilson, Mike. Domestic Violence. 2008. (Opposing Viewpoints Ser.). (ENG., Illus.). 217p. (YA). (gr. 10-12). pap. 39.70 (978-0-7377-4206-0(2), LML02109-243102, Greenhaven Pr., Inc.) Cengage Gale.

Wingate, Brian. Violence at Sports Events. (Violence & Society Ser.). 64p. 2009. (gr. 6-6). 58.50 (978-1-60854-727-2(2)) 2008. (Illus.). (YA). (gr. 9-12). lib. bdg. 31.95 (978-1-4042-1796-6(7)) Rosen Publishing Group, Inc., The.

Wittekind, Erika. Violence as Entertainment: Why Aggression Sells. 2012. (Exploring Media Literacy Ser.). (ENG.). 80p. (gr. 6-7). pap. 9.10 (978-0-7565-4536-9(6)); lib. bdg. 34.65 (978-0-7565-4520-8(X)) Compass Point Bks. (CPB Grades 4-8).

Worth, Richard. Massacre at Virginia Tech: Disaster & Survival. 2008. (Deadly Disasters Ser.). (Illus.). 48p. (J). (gr. 5-9). lib. bdg. 25.27 (978-0-7660-3274-3(4)) Enslow Pubs., Inc.

Zoldak, Joyce. When Danger Hits Home: Survivors of Domestic Violence. (Survivors Ser.). 2010. 128p. (YA). (gr. 7-12). 24.95 (978-1-4222-0460-3(X)) 2009. (J). pap. 24.95 (978-1-4222-1473-2(7)) Mason Crest.

VIOLENCE—FICTION

Ayarbe, Heidi. Freeze Frame. 2010. (ENG.). 400p. (YA). (gr. 8). pap. 8.99 (978-0-06-135175-4(X), HarperTeen) HarperCollins Pubs.

Baron, Kathi. Shattered. 2009. 262p. (J). (gr. 9-12). 16.95 (978-1-934813-08-9(7)) Westside Bks.

Bilen, Tracy. What She Left Behind. 2012. (ENG.). 256p. (YA). (gr. 9). pap. 9.99 (978-1-4424-3951-1(3), Simon Pulse) Simon Pulse.

Bowler, Tim. Playing Dead. 2010. (Blade Ser.: 1). (ENG.). 256p. (YA). (gr. 9-18). 7.99 (978-0-14-241600-6(2), Speak) Penguin Young Readers Group.

Carmichael, Katrina. Back Together Again. 2008. 20p. pap. 7.95 (978-0-9814650-5-0(6)) G Publishing LLC.

Chessen, Sherri. Gorp's Secret: An Empowering Tale in Pumpernickel Park. Bronson, Linda, illus. 2008. (ENG.). 36p. (J). 16.95 (978-0-9724249-3-6(8)) Gorp Group Pr., The.

Cohen, Joshua C. Leverage. 2012. (ENG.). 432p. (YA). (gr. 9). pap. 8.99 (978-0-14-242086-7(7), Speak) Penguin Young Readers Group.

Connor, Leslie. The Things You Kiss Goodbye. 2014. (ENG.). 368p. (YA). (gr. 9). 17.99 (978-0-06-089091-9(6), Tegen, Katherine Bks) HarperCollins Pubs.

Cummings, Lindsay. The Murder Complex. 2014. (Murder Complex Ser.: 1). (ENG.). 416p. (YA). (gr. 9). 17.99 (978-0-06-222000-4(4), Greenwillow Bks.) HarperCollins Pubs.

Dawson, Delilah S. Strike. 2016. (ENG., Illus.). 480p. (YA). (gr. 9). 17.99 (978-1-4814-2342-7(8), Simon Pulse) Simon Pulse.

Delgado, Alvin. Spirit of the Gang. 2007. 192p. pap. 12.95 (978-1-4303-1334-2(X)) Lulu Pr., Inc.

Destefano, Merrie. Lost Girls. 2017. (ENG.). 360p. (YA). pap. 9.99 (978-1-63375-605-2(X), 9781633756052) Entangled Publishing, LLC.

Doucet, Sharon Arms. Fiddle Fever. 2007. (ENG.). 176p. (J). (gr. 5-7). pap. 12.95 (978-0-618-77682-5(6)) Houghton Mifflin Harcourt Publishing Co.

Dowd, Siobhan. Bog Child. 2010. (ENG.). 336p. (YA). (gr. 7). pap. 9.99 (978-0-375-84135-4(0)) Fickling, David Bks. GBR. Dist: Penguin Random Hse. LLC.

Favole, Robert. Monday Redux. 2003. 200p. (YA). 15.99 (978-1-930826-11-3(7)) Flywheel Publishing Co.

Flake, Sharon G. Bang! 2007. (ENG., Illus.). 304p. (J). (gr. 5-9). pap. 9.99 (978-0-7868-4955-0(X), Jump at the Sun) Hyperion Bks. for Children.

—Bang! 2007. (J). 20.85 (978-1-4177-7952-9(7), Turtleback) Turtleback Bks.

Flinn, Alex. Fade to Black. 2005. 192p. (J). (gr. 8-12). 16.99 (978-0-06-056839-9(9), HarperTeen) HarperCollins Pubs.

Galante, Cecilia. Hershey Herself. 2008. (Mix Ser.). (ENG.). 336p. (J). (gr. 4-8). pap. 15.99 (978-1-4169-5463-7(5), Simon & Schuster/Paula Wiseman Bks.) Simon & Schuster/Paula Wiseman Bks.

Gallagher, Brian. Stormclouds: New Friends. Old Differences. 2014. (ENG.). 224p. (J). 13.95 (978-1-84717-579-3(1)) O'Brien Pr., Ltd., The IRL. Dist: Dufour Editions, Inc.

Giles, Gail. Shattering Glass. 2004. 215p. (J). (gr. 7-18). pap. 37.00 incl. audio (978-1-4000-9013-6(X), Listening Library) Random Hse. Audio Publishing Group.

Goeglein, T. M. Cold Fury. 2013. (Cold Fury Novel Ser.: 1). (ENG.). 336p. (YA). (gr. 7). pap. 9.99 (978-0-14-242631-9(8), Speak) Penguin Young Readers Group.

—Flicker & Burn. 2014. (Cold Fury Novel Ser.: 2). (ENG.). 368p. (YA). (gr. 7). pap. 9.99 (978-0-14-751141-6(0), Speak) Penguin Young Readers Group.

Greg, Neri. Yummy: The Last Days of a Southside Shorty. 2014. (ENG.). 94p. (YA). (gr. k-3). 21.20 (978-1-63245-250-4(2)) Lectorum Pubns., Inc.

Hassan, Michael. Crash & Burn. (ENG.). 544p. (YA). (gr. 9). 2014. pap. 9.99 (978-0-06-211291-0(0)) 2013. 18.99 (978-0-06-211290-3(2)) HarperCollins Pubs.

Heneghan, James. Hit Squad, 1 vol. 2003. (Orca Soundings Ser.). (ENG.). 128p. (YA). (gr. 8-12). pap. 9.95 (978-1-55143-269-4(2)) Orca Bk. Pubs. USA.

—Hit Squad. 2004. (Orca Soundings Ser.). 106p. 19.95 (978-0-7569-4300-4(0)) Perfection Learning Corp.

Houde, Monique. Blinded by Love. 2004. (YA). pap. 14.95 (978-0-9748689-0-5(6)) Choices For Tomorrow.

Houran, Lori Haskins. Too Many Cats. Mathieu, Joe, illus. 2009. (Step into Reading Ser.). (ENG.). 32p. (J). (gr. -1-1). pap. 3.99 (978-0-375-85197-1(6), Random Hse. Bks. for Young Readers) Random Hse. Children's Bks.

Huggins, Peter. In the Company of Owls. Goodman Koz, Paula, illus. 2008. (ENG.). 96p. (J). 15.95 (978-1-58838-036-4(X), NewSouth Bks.) NewSouth, Inc.

Jerry, Spinelli. Wringer. 2014. (ENG.). 256p. (J). (gr. 8-12). 13.24 (978-1-63245-323-5(1)) Lectorum Pubns., Inc.

Jones, Patrick. Taking Sides. 2015. (Locked Out Ser.). (ENG.). 104p. (J). (gr. 6-12). lib. bdg. 27.99 (978-1-4677-5800-0(0)) Lerner Publishing Group.

Jonsberg, Barry. Dreamrider. 2009. (ENG.). 256p. (YA). (gr. 9). pap. 8.99 (978-0-375-84458-4(9), Knopf Bks. for Young Readers) Random Hse. Children's Bks.

Key, Watt. Dirt Road Home. 2011. (Alabama Moon Ser.: 2). (ENG.). 240p. (J). (gr. 5-9). pap. 8.99 (978-0-312-67435-9(X), 9780312674359) Square Fish.

—Fourmile, 1 vol. 2012. (ENG.). 240p. (J). (gr. 4-7). 24.99 (978-0-374-35095-6(7), 9780374350956, Farrar, Straus & Giroux (BYR)) Farrar, Straus & Giroux.

—Fourmile. 2014. (ENG.). 256p. (J). (gr. 4-7). pap. 8.99 (978-1-250-03995-8(9), 9781250039958) Square Fish.

Kinch, Michael. The Fires of New Sun. 2012. (Blending Time Ser.: 2). (ENG.). 288p. (YA). pap. 9.95 (978-0-7387-3076-9(9), Flux) North Star Editions.

—The Rebels of New SUN. 2013. (Blending Time Ser.: 3). (ENG.). 288p. (YA). pap. 9.99 (978-0-7387-3151-3(X), Flux) North Star Editions.

King, A. S. Still Life with Tornado. 2016. (ENG.). 304p. (YA). (gr. 9). 17.99 (978-1-101-99488-7(6), Dutton Books for Young Readers) Penguin Young Readers Group.

Kraus, Daniel. Scowler. 2014. (ENG.). 304p. (YA). (gr. 9). pap. 9.99 (978-0-385-74310-5(6), Ember) Random Hse. Children's Bks.

Lake, Nick. In Darkness. (ENG.). (YA). (gr. 9). 2014. 368p. pap. 10.99 (978-1-61963-122-9(9), 9781619631229) 2012. 352p. 17.99 (978-1-59990-743-7(7), 9781599907437) Bloomsbury Publishing USA. (Bloomsbury USA Childrens).

Lester, Julius. Guardian. 2008. (ENG., Illus.). 144p. (YA). (gr. 9-18). 16.99 (978-0-06-155890-0(7), Amistad) HarperCollins Pubs.

Mac, Carrie. Pain & Wastings, 1 vol. 2008. (Orca Soundings Ser.). (ENG.). (YA). (gr. 8-12). 128p. 16.95 (978-1-55143-906-8(9)); 152p. pap. 9.95 (978-1-55143-904-4(2)) Orca Bk. Pubs. USA.

Marsden, Carolyn. The White Zone. 2014. (ENG.). 192p. (J). (gr. 4-8). pap. 9.95 (978-1-4677-5177-3(4), Carolrhoda Bks.) Lerner Publishing Group.

McDaniel, Lurlene. Red Heart Tattoo. 2013. (ENG.). 224p. (YA). (gr. 7). pap. 8.99 (978-0-440-24019-8(0), Ember) Random Hse. Children's Bks.

Michaels, Rune. Genesis Alpha. 2007. (ENG., Illus.). 208p. (YA). (gr. 7-12). 16.99 (978-1-4169-1886-8(8), Atheneum Bks. for Young Readers) Simon & Schuster Children's Publishing.

Moore, Monica A. Everyday Heroes. 2006. (ENG.). 52p. per. 12.95 (978-1-59800-563-9(4)) Outskirts Pr., Inc.

Moore, Stephanie. Make Something of It. 2014. (Sharp Sisters Ser.: 1). (ENG.). 152p. (YA). (gr. 6-12). pap. 7.95 (978-1-4677-4488-1(3), Darby Creek) Lerner Publishing Group.

Mulder, Michelle. Yeny & the Children for Peace, 1 vol. 2008. (Kids' Power Book Ser.). (ENG., Illus.). 104p. (J). (gr. 3-8). pap. 14.95 (978-1-897187-45-6(9)) Second Story Pr. CAN. Dist: Orca Bk. Pubs. USA.

Myers, Jason. Run the Game: Play or Be Played. 2012. (ENG.). 544p. (YA). (gr. 10). pap. 9.99 (978-1-4424-1432-7(4), Simon Pulse) Simon Pulse.

Myers, Walter Dean. Shooter. 2004. (ENG.). 224p. (J). 15.99 (978-0-06-029519-6(8), HarperTeen) HarperCollins Pubs.

Neri, G. Knockout Games. 2014. (ENG.). 304p. (YA). (gr. 8-12). 17.95 (978-1-4677-3269-7(9), Carolrhoda Lab™) Lerner Publishing Group.

Nijkamp, Marieke. This Is Where It Ends. 2016. (ENG.). 288p. (YA). (gr. 8-12). 17.99 (978-1-4926-2246-8(X), 9781492622468) Sourcebooks, Inc.

—This Is Where It Ends. 2016. lib. bdg. 22.10 (978-0-606-39479-6(0)) 2017. lib. bdg. 22.10 (978-0-606-39992-0(5)) Turtleback Bks.

Oates, Joyce Carol. Freaky Green Eyes. 2005. 341p. (YA). 15.65 (978-0-7569-6308-8(7)) Perfection Learning Corp.

Ostow, Micol. Family. (ENG.). 384p. (J). (gr. 9). 2013. pap. 9.99 (978-1-60684-393-2(1)) 2011. 17.99 (978-1-60684-155-6(6)) Lerner Publishing Group. (Carolrhoda Lab™).

Parrish, Anya. Damage. 2011. (ENG.). 288p. (YA). pap. 9.95 (978-0-7387-2700-4(8), Flux) North Star Editions.

Parsons, Ash. Still Waters. 2015. (ENG.). 320p. (YA). (gr. 9). 17.99 (978-0-399-16847-5(8), Philomel Bks.) Penguin Young Readers Group.

Paulsen, Gary. Paintings from the Cave: Three Novellas. (ENG.). (YA). (gr. 7-7). 2012. 174p. pap. 8.99 (978-0-553-49466-2(X), Ember) 2011. 176p. 15.99 (978-0-385-74684-7(9), Lamb, Wendy Bks.) Random Hse. Children's Bks.

Peters, Julie Anne. Rage: A Love Story. 2010. (ENG.). 306p. (YA). (gr. 9). pap. 9.99 (978-0-375-84411-9(2), Knopf Bks. for Young Readers) Random Hse. Children's Bks.

Phillips, Dee. Fight, 1 vol. unabr. ed. 2011. (Right Now! Ser.). (ENG.). 45p. (YA). (gr. 9-12). pap. 8.95 (978-1-61651-248-4(2)) Saddleback Educational Publishing, Inc.

Posner, Richard. Sweet Pain. 2014. (ENG.). 276p. (J). (gr. 5-12). pap. 16.95 (978-1-59077-318-5(7)) Evans, M. & Co., Inc.

Quick, Matthew. Boy21. 2013. (ENG.). 272p. (YA). (gr. 7-17). pap. 10.99 (978-0-316-12796-7(5)) Little, Brown Bks. for Young Readers.

Quintero, Sofia. Efrain's Secret. 2011. (ENG.). 276p. (YA). (gr. 9). pap. 8.99 (978-0-440-24062-4(X), Ember) Random Hse. Children's Bks.

Scheerger, Sarah Lynn. Are You Still There. 2015. (ENG.). 288p. (YA). (gr. 8-12). 16.99 (978-0-8075-4557-7(0)) Whitman, Albert & Co.

Schraff, Anne E. The Outcasts. 2012. (Urban Underground — Harriet Tubman High School Ser.: 21). (YA). lib. bdg. 20.80 (978-0-606-23794-9(1), Turtleback) Turtleback Bks.

—See No Evil. 2012. (Urban Underground — Harriet Tubman High School Ser.: 22). (YA). lib. bdg. 20.80 (978-0-606-23795-6(X), Turtleback) Turtleback Bks.

Scott, Elizabeth. Living Dead Girl. 2008. (ENG.). 176p. (YA). (gr. 10-18). 17.99 (978-1-4169-6059-1(7), Simon Pulse) Simon Pulse.

Sitomer, Alan Lawrence. Hip-Hop High School. 2006. 368p. (J). (978-0-7868-3831-8(0), Jump at the Sun) Hyperion Bks. for Children.

—Homeboyz. 2008. (ENG.). 304p. (J). (gr. 5-9). pap. 8.99 (978-1-4231-0031-7(X), Jump at the Sun) Hyperion Bks. for Children.

Soto, Gary. Buried Onions. 2006. (ENG., Illus.). 176p. (YA). (gr. 7-12). pap. 6.95 (978-0-15-206265-1(3)) Houghton Mifflin Harcourt Publishing Co.

—Buried Onions. 2006. 149p. 16.95 (978-0-7569-7218-9(3)) Perfection Learning Corp.

Spinelli, Jerry. Wringer. 2004. (ENG.). 256p. (J). (gr. 3-7). pap. 8.99 (978-0-06-059282-0(6), HarperTeen) HarperCollins Pubs.

Strasser, Todd. If I Grow Up. (ENG.). 240p. (YA). (gr. 7). 2010. pap. 9.99 (978-1-4169-9443-5(2)) 2009. 17.99 (978-1-4169-2523-1(6)) Simon & Schuster Bks. For Young Readers. (Simon & Schuster Bks. For Young Readers).

Surviving Southside, 6 vols., Set. Incl. Bad Deal. Korman, Susan. lib. bdg. 27.93 (978-0-7613-6152-7(9)); Beaten. Weyn, Suzanne. lib. bdg. 27.93 (978-0-7613-6150-3(2)); Benito Runs. Fontes, Justine. lib. bdg. 27.93 (978-0-7613-6151-0(0)); Plan B. Simon, Charnan. lib. bdg. 27.93 (978-0-7613-6149-7(9)); Recruited. Weyn, Suzanne. lib. bdg. 27.93 (978-0-7613-6153-4(7)); Shattered Star. Simon, Charnan. lib. bdg. 27.93 (978-0-7613-6154-1(5)); 104p. (YA). (gr. 6-12). (Surviving Southside Ser.). (ENG.). 2011. Set lib. bdg. 335.16 (978-0-7613-6148-0(0), Darby Creek) Lerner Publishing Group.

Tullson, Diane. Lockdown, 1 vol. 2008. (Orca Soundings Ser.). (ENG.). 128p. (YA). (gr. 8-12). pap. 9.95 (978-1-55143-916-7(6)) Orca Bk. Pubs. USA.

van Diepen, Allison. Light of Day. 2017. 336p. (YA). (gr. 9). pap. 9.99 (978-0-06-230348-6(1), HarperTeen) HarperCollins Pubs.

Walsh, Ann. By the Skin of His Teeth. 2005. (Illus.). 144p. (YA). pap., tchr. ed. 6.95 (978-0-88878-448-3(1)) Beach Holme Pubs., Ltd. CAN. Dist: Literary Pr. Group of Canada.

Watkins, Steve. Juvie. 2017. (ENG.). 320p. (YA). (gr. 9). pap. 7.99 (978-0-7636-8756-4(1)) Candlewick Pr.

Weyn, Suzanne. Beaten. (Surviving Southside Ser.). (ENG.). 104p. (YA). (gr. 6-12). 2015. 34.65 (978-1-4677-6007-2(2), Lerner Digital) 2011. lib. bdg. 27.93 (978-0-7613-6150-3(2)) Lerner Publishing Group.

Wilde, Jerry. Peace in the Halls: Stories & Activities to Manage Anger & Prevent School Violence. 2003. 112p. (YA). (gr. 4-12). pap. 9.95 (978-0-9657610-4-8(5)) LGR Publishing, Inc.

Zevin, Gabrielle. Because It Is My Blood, 1 vol. 2012. (Birthright Ser.: 2). (ENG.). 368p. (YA). (gr. 7). 17.99 (978-0-374-38074-8(0), 9780374380748, Farrar, Straus & Giroux (BYR)) Farrar, Straus & Giroux.

—Because It Is My Blood. 2013. (Birthright Ser.: 2). (ENG.). 384p. (YA). (gr. 7). pap. 9.99 (978-1-250-03422-9(1), 9781250034229) Square Fish.

—In the Age of Love & Chocolate. 2014. (Birthright Ser.: 3). (ENG.). 320p. (YA). (gr. 7). pap. 10.99 (978-1-250-05071-7(5), 9781250050717) Square Fish.

VIOLIN

Auh, Yoonil. A Guide to Practicing Repertoire: Level 1, 11 vols. Auh, Yoonil, ed. 2003. (Illus.). 85p. (gr. k-12). pap. 135.00 (978-1-882858-61-3(1)) Yoon-il Auh/Intrepid Pixels.

—A Guide to Practicing Repertoire: Level 2, 11 vols. Auh, Yoonil, ed. 2003. (Illus.). 85p. (gr. k-12). pap. 135.00 (978-1-882858-62-0(X)) Yoon-il Auh/Intrepid Pixels.

—Representation Music. Auh, Yoonil, ed. 2003. (Illus.). 28p. (gr. k-12). pap., instr.'s gde. ed. 25.00 (978-1-882858-55-2(7)) Yoon-il Auh/Intrepid Pixels.

—Representation Music: A New Approch to Creating Sound & Representing Music. Auh, Yoonil, ed. 2003. (Illus.). 45p. (gr. k-12). pap. 17.00 (978-1-882858-54-5(9)) Yoon-il Auh/Intrepid Pixels.

—Singing Hand: Study of Vibrato. Auh, Yoonil, ed. 2003. (Illus.). (gr. k-12). 45p. pap. 16.00 (978-1-882858-60-6(3)); 50p. pap. 16.00 (978-1-882858-59-0(X)) Yoon-il Auh/Intrepid Pixels.

Bennett, Ned. A New Tune a Day Perfomrance Pieces for Flute. 2006. (ENG., Illus.). 48p. pap. 12.95 incl. audio compact disk (978-0-8256-8219-3(3), 0825682193) Music Sales Corp.

—A New Tune a Day Performace Pieces for Cello. 2006. (ENG., Illus.). 48p. pap. 12.95 incl. audio compact disk (978-0-8256-8218-6(5), 0825682185) Music Sales Corp.

—A New Tune a Day Performance Pieces for Trombone. 2006. (ENG., Illus.). 48p. pap. 12.95 incl. audio compact disk (978-0-8256-8220-9(7), 0825682207) Music Sales Corp.

—A New Tune a Day Performance Pieces for Violin. 2006. (ENG., Illus.). 48p. pap. 12.99 incl. audio compact disk (978-0-8256-8217-9(7), 0825682177) Music Sales Corp.

Davey, Peter. Abracadabra Violin, Bk. 1. Hussey, Christopher & Sebba, Jane, eds. Damerum, Kanako & Parks, Paul, illus. 2nd ed. 2004. (Abracadabra Strings Ser.). (ENG.). 64p. (J). pap. 10.95 (978-0-7136-6308-2(1), A&C Black) Bloomsbury Publishing Plc GBR. Dist: Consortium Bk. Sales & Distribution.

—Abracadabra Violin, Bk. 1. 2nd ed. 2003. (Abracadabra Strings Ser.). (ENG., Illus.). 1p. 15.95 (978-0-7136-6309-9(X), A&C Black) Bloomsbury Publishing Plc GBR. Dist: Consortium Bk. Sales & Distribution.

Hal Leonard Corp. Staff, creator. Disney Movie Hits: Violin. 2003. (ENG.). 20p. pap. 12.99 (978-0-634-00099-7(3), 0634000993) Leonard, Hal Corp.

Landau, Elaine. Is the Violin for You? 2010. (Ready to Make Music Ser.). (ENG., Illus.). 40p. (gr. 4-6). lib. bdg. 27.93 (978-0-7613-5423-9(9), Lerner Pubns.) Lerner Publishing Group.

Martin, Iain C., illus. Fun Factory Violin Book. 2004. (ENG.). 32p. pap. 15.99 (978-0-85162-183-8(X), 085162183X) Leonard, Hal Corp.

McCabe, Larry. Easiest Fiddle Tunes for Children, 1 vol. 2007. (Easiest Tunes for Children Ser.). (ENG., Illus.). 32p. 14.95 (978-0-7866-7561-6(6)) Mel Bay Pubns., Inc.

Miles, Lucinda (Cindy). Old-Time Fiddling Gospel Favorites. 2005. (Illus.). 84p. (YA). audio compact disk 19.99 (978-0-9710446-6-1(X)) Miles Music.

Riggs, Kate. Making Music: Violin. 2014. (Making Music Ser.). (ENG.). 24p. (J). (gr. 1-3). pap. 9.99 (978-0-89812-950-2(8), Creative Paperbacks) Creative Co., The.

Roach-Langille, Nancy & Mitchell, Francis G. Fiddle Fantasy: A Selection of Fiddle Tunes by Maritime Composers. Mitchell, Francis G., ed. Roach-Langille, Nancy, illus. 2nd ed. 2004. (ENG., Illus.). 6p. pap. (978-1-895814-28-6(6), NWP103) New World Publishing.

Saari, Holly. Violins. 2010. (Music Makers Ser.). (ENG.). 24p. (J). (gr. -1-2). 27.07 (978-1-60253-358-5(X), 200509) Child's World, Inc., The.

Salzmann, Mary Elizabeth. What in the World Is a Violin?, 1 vol. 2012. (ENG.). 24p. 25.65 (978-1-61783-208-6(1), Super SandCastle) ABDO Publishing Co.

Smith, Melanie. Beginner Violin Theory for Children, Book One, 1 vol. 2005. (ENG., Illus.). 84p. pap. 19.99 (978-0-7866-7087-1(8), 20296) Mel Bay Pubns., Inc.

Wearing, Katie & Richards, Liz. Abracadabra Violin Beginner, 1 vol. rev. ed. 2007. (Abracadabra Ser.). (ENG., Illus.). 32p. (J). pap., stu. ed. 11.95 incl. audio compact disk (978-0-7136-9365-2(7)) HarperCollins Pubs. Ltd. GBR. Dist: Independent Pubs. Group.

White, Cathy Finch. Anna Learns to Play the Violin. 2010. 28p. pap. 12.49 (978-1-4520-5579-4(3)) AuthorHouse.

VIOLIN—INSTRUCTION AND STUDY

Auh, Yoon-Il. Pre-School Virtuoso, Bk. IV. (Auh School of Violin Ser.). 40p. (J). (gr. k-5). stu. ed. 10.00 (978-1-882858-06-4(9)) Yoon-il Auh/Intrepid Pixels.

Hussey, Christopher. Abracadabra Christmas Showsstoppers Violin, 1 vol. 2015. (Abracadabra Ser.). (ENG.). 32p. (J). pap. 22.95 (978-1-4729-2054-6(6)) HarperCollins Pubs. Ltd. GBR. Dist: Independent Pubs. Group.

Scott, Daniel. Classical Greats: Junior Guest Spot. 2003. (ENG., Illus.). 84p. pap. 14.95 incl. audio compact disk (978-0-7119-9145-3(6), 0711991456) Music Sales Corp.

Wohlfahrt, Franz. Easiest Elementary Method for Violin: Op. 38. (Carl Fischer Music Library: No. 1061). 56p. (J). pap. 10.95 (978-0-8258-0053-5(6), L1061) Fischer, Carl LLC.

VIOLINISTS

Frisch, Aaron. Dark Fiddler: The Life & Legend of Nicolo Paganini. Kelley, Gary, illus. 2008. (ENG.). 32p. (J). (gr. 1-3). 17.95 (978-1-56846-200-4(X), Creative Editions) Creative Co., The.

Herbert, Denis & Silver, Joanne. Complément éducatif: Mon Enfance Lilloise Racontée à Ma Fille: Récits D'antan (1950 à 1955) 2010. (978-0-9819417-4-5(5)) Beach Lloyd Pubs., LLC.

Romeu, Emma. El Rey de las Octavas. Moreiro, Enrique S., illus. 2007. (SPA.). 40p. (J). (gr. 3-5). 17.99 (978-1-933032-26-9(X)) Lectorum Pubns., Inc.

Sutryn, Barbara M. Heartstrings: A Biography of Wilmos Csehy. Lt. ed. 2004. (Illus.). 160p. (YA). 21.00 (978-1-892135-33-9(7)) Lamp Post Publishing, Inc.

VIPERS

see Snakes

VIRGIN ISLANDS OF THE UNITED STATES

Burgan, Michael. Puerto Rico y Otras Areas Perifericas. 2004. (World Almanac Ser.).Tr. of Puerto Rico & Other Outlying Areas. (SPA.). 48p. (gr. 4-9). lib. bdg. 31.00 (978-0-8368-5726-9(7), GHS32693, Gareth Stevens Learning Library) Stevens, Gareth Publishing LLLP.

VIRGIN ISLANDS OF THE UNITED STATES—FICTION

Ferguson, Alane & Skurzynski, Gloria. Escape from Fear: A Mystery in Virgin Islands National Park. 2008. (Mysteries in Our National Park Ser.). (ENG., Illus.). 160p. (J). (gr. 3-7).

mass mkt. 4.99 *(978-1-4263-0181-0(2)*, National Geographic Children's Bks.) National Geographic Society.

Hood, Ann & Altmann, Scott. Alexander Hamilton: Little Lion. Kwasney, Karl & Zilber, Denis, illus. 2012. (Treasure Chest Ser.: 2). (ENG.). 224p. (J). (gr. 3-7). pap. 6.99 *(978-0-448-45468-9(8)*, Grosset & Dunlap) Penguin Young Readers Group.

Lewis-Brown, Alscess. Mosquito Get in Trouble Too. Hatfield, Cynthia, illus. 2009. (J). *(978-1-934370-09-4(6))* Editorial Campana.

Sewer, Anecia. Why Transfer Day, Anyway? Samuel, Karen, illus. 2007. 16p. (J). 15.99 *(978-0-9752986-0-2(7))* Research Institute Pr., The.

VIRGIN MARY

see Mary, Blessed Virgin, Saint

VIRGINIA

Barrett, Tracy. Virginia. 2nd rev. ed. 2005. (Celebrate the States Ser.). (Illus.). 144p. (gr. 6-7). lib. bdg. 42.79 *(978-0-7614-1734-7(6)*, Benchmark Bks.) Marshall Cavendish Corp.

Bauer, Marion Dane. Celebrating Virginia & Washington, D. C. 50 States to Celebrate. Canga, C. B., illus. 2013. (Green Light Readers Level 3 Ser.). (ENG.). 40p. (J). (gr. 1-4). 12.99 *(978-0-544-04407-4(X))* Houghton Mifflin Harcourt Publishing Co.

Connors, Kathleen. People of the Chesapeake Bay. 2013. 32p. (J). (gr. 3-6). 26.60 *(978-1-4339-9776-1(2))*; pap. 10.50 *(978-1-4339-9777-8(0))*; pap. 63.00 *(978-1-4339-9778-5(9))* Stevens, Gareth Publishing LLLP.

—Plants & Animals of the Chesapeake Bay. 2013. 32p. (J). (gr. 3-6). 26.60 *(978-1-4339-9780-8(0))*; pap. 10.50 *(978-1-4339-9781-5(9))*; pap. 63.00 *(978-1-4339-9782-2(7))* Stevens, Gareth Publishing LLLP.

Edwards, Pamela Duncan. O Is for Old Dominion: A Virginia Alphabet. Howell, Troy, illus. 2005. (State Ser.). (ENG.). 40p. (J). (gr. -1-3). 17.95 *(978-1-58536-161-8(5))* Sleeping Bear Pr.

Gamble, Adam. Good Night Virginia. Veno, Joe, illus. 2008. (Good Night Our World Ser.). (ENG.). 20p. (J). (gr. k — 1). bds. 9.95 *(978-1-60219-026-9(7))* Good Night Bks.

Kent, Deborah. Virginia. 2014. (America the Beautiful Ser.: 3). (ENG.). 144p. (J). lib. bdg. 40.00 *(978-0-531-24899-7(2))* Scholastic Library Publishing.

King, David C. Virginia. 2004. (It's My State! Ser.). (Illus.). 80p. (J). (gr. 3-7). lib. bdg. 27.07 *(978-0-7614-1827-6(X)*, Benchmark Bks.) Marshall Cavendish Corp.

Mader, Jan. Virginia. 2003. (Rookie Read-About Geography Ser.). (ENG., Illus.). 32p. (J). (gr. 1-2). 20.50 *(978-0-516-22718-4(1)*, Children's Pr.) Scholastic Library Publishing.

Marsh, Carole. Virginia Classic Christmas Trivia. 2005. (Illus.). 32p. (J). (gr. 4-7). pap. 6.95 *(978-0-635-03352-9(6))* Gallopade International.

—Virginia Current Events Projects: 30 Cool, Activities, Crafts, Experiments & More for Kids to Do to Learn about Your State! 2003. (Virginia Experience Ser.). 32p. (gr. k-8). pap. 5.95 *(978-0-635-02064-2(5)*, Marsh, Carole Bks.) Gallopade International.

—Virginia Geography Projects: 30 Cool, Activities, Crafts, Experiments & More for Kids to Do to Learn about Your State! 2003. (Virginia Experience Ser.). 32p. (gr. k-5). pap. 5.95 *(978-0-635-01864-9(0)*, Marsh, Carole Bks.) Gallopade International.

—Virginia Government Projects: 30 Cool, Activities, Crafts, Experiments & More for Kids to Do to Learn about Your State! 2003. (Virginia Experience Ser.). 32p. (gr. k-5). pap. 5.95 *(978-0-635-01965-3(5)*, Marsh, Carole Bks.) Gallopade International.

—Virginia People Projects: 30 Cool, Activities, Crafts, Experiments & More for Kids to Do to Learn about Your State! 2003. (Virginia Experience Ser.). 32p. (gr. k-5). pap. 5.95 *(978-0-635-02015-4(7)*, Marsh, Carole Bks.) Gallopade International.

—Virginia Symbols & Facts Projects: 30 Cool, Activities, Crafts, Experiments & More for Kids to Do to Learn about Your State! 2003. (Virginia Experience Ser.). 32p. (gr. k-5). pap. 5.95 *(978-0-635-01915-8(9)*, Marsh, Carole Bks.) Gallopade International.

Melson, William G. Geology Explained: Virginia's Fort Valley & Massanutten Mountains. 2004. (Illus.). 170p. per. 15.95 *(978-0-9744173-0-1(0)*, Ft. Valley Geology Study Ctr.) InterPress.

Mis, M. S. How to Draw Virginia's Sights & Symbols. 2009. (Kid's Guide to Drawing America Ser.). 32p. (gr. k-k). 50.50 *(978-1-61511-102-2(6)*, PowerKids Pr.) Rosen Publishing Group, Inc., The.

Murray, Julie. Virginia. 1 vol. 2006. (Buddy Book Ser.). (ENG., Illus.). 32p. (gr. 2-4). 27.07 *(978-1-59197-705-6(3)*, Buddy Bks.) ABDO Publishing Co.

Norfolk, Sherry & Norfolk, Bobby. The Virginia Giant: The True Story of Peter Francisco. Brennan, Cait, illus. 2014. (ENG.). 160p. (J). (gr. 4-7). 16.99 *(978-1-62619-117-4(4)*, History Pr., The) Arcadia Publishing.

O'Connell, Kim A. Virginia: A MyReportLinks.com Book. 2003. (States Ser.). (Illus.). 48p. (J). (gr. 4-10). lib. bdg. 25.26 *(978-0-7660-5122-5(6)*, MyReportLinks.com Bks.) Enslow Pubs., Inc.

Parker, Bridget. Virginia. 2016. (States Ser.). (ENG., Illus.). 32p. (gr. 3-4). lib. bdg. 27.32 *(978-1-5157-0434-8(3))* Next Page Pr., The.

Saving the Chesapeake Bay. 2013. (Exploring the Chesapeake Bay Ser.). 32p. (J). (gr. 3-6). pap. 63.00 *(978-1-4339-9786-0(X))* Stevens, Gareth Publishing LLLP.

Shepard, Betty Bruce. Virginia: An Alphabetical Journey Through History. Lederman, Marsha, illus. 2007. 32p. (J). (gr. -1-3). 17.95 *(978-1-893622-14-2(2)*, VSP Bks.) Vacation Spot Publishing.

Sullivan, E. J. V Is for Virginia. Eldredge, Ernie, illus. 2006. 24p. (J). lib. bdg. *(978-1-58173-526-0(X))* Sweetwater Pr.

Way, Jennifer. Virginia. 2009. (Bilingual Library of the United States of America Ser.). (ENG & SPA.). 32p. (gr. 2-2). 47.90 *(978-1-60853-390-9(5)*, Editorial Buenas Letras) Rosen Publishing Group, Inc., The.

White-Adams, Beverly & Adams, Rusty. The Adventures of Rusty: Rusty Goes to Virginia Vol. 1. 2011. 32p. pap. *(978-1-4269-8935-3(0))* Trafford Publishing (UK) Ltd.

VIRGINIA—FICTION

Adrian, Susan. Tunnel Vision: A Novel. 2015. (ENG.). 320p. (YA). (gr. 8-12). 18.99 *(978-1-250-04792-2(7)*, 9781250047922, St. Martin's Griffin) St. Martin's Pr.

Allen, Elaine Ann. Olly's Treasure, 1 vol. Nash, Kelli, illus. 2011. (ENG.). 40p. (J). 16.99 *(978-0-7643-3772-7(6)*, 9780764337727, Schiffer Publishing Ltd) Schiffer Publishing, Ltd.

Altsheler, Joseph A. The Guns of Bull Run: A Story of the Civil War's Eve. 2006. (Civil War Ser.: Vol. 1). 300p. (J). reprint ed. 29.95 *(978-1-4218-1777-4(2))*; pap. 14.95 *(978-1-4218-1877-1(9))* 1st World Publishing, Inc. (1st World Library - Literary Society).

—The Guns of Bull Run: A Story of the Civil War's Eve. 2009. 278p. reprint ed. pap. 14.99 *(978-1-60512-409-4(5))*; (Civil War Ser.: Vol. 1). (J). 27.99 *(978-1-60512-309-7(9))* Akasha Publishing, LLC. (Akasha Classics).

—The Guns of Bull Run: A Story of the Civil War's Eve. l.t. ed. 2007. (Civil War Ser.: Vol. 1). (J). 272p. per. 23.99 *(978-1-4346-7679-5(X))*; (ENG.). 238p. reprint ed. per. 20.99 *(978-1-4346-7678-8(1))* Creative Media Partners, LLC.

—The Guns of Bull Run: A Story of the Civil War's Eve. 2006. (Civil War Ser.: Vol. 1). (J). reprint ed. pap. *(978-1-4065-0812-3(8))* Dodo Pr.

—The Guns of Bull Run: A Story of the Civil War's Eve. 2010. (Civil War Ser.: Vol. 1). (Illus.). 162p. (J). (gr. 4-7). reprint ed. pap. 19.99 *(978-1-153-70504-2(4))* General Bks. LLC.

—The Guns of Bull Run: A Story of the Civil War's Eve. (Civil War Ser.: Vol. 1). (J). reprint ed. 2010. 238p. (gr. 4-7). 33.56 *(978-1-169-29842-2(7))* 2010. 238p. (gr. 4-7). pap. 21.56 *(978-1-162-69670-6(2))* 2010. 41.95 *(978-1-161-46535-8(9))* 2004. pap. 26.95 *(978-1-4191-6519-1(4))* 2004. pap. 1.99 *(978-1-4192-6519-8(9))* Kessinger Publishing, LLC.

—The Guns of Bull Run: A Story of the Civil War's Eve. 2011. (Civil War Ser.: Vol. 1). 256p. (J). (gr. 4-7). reprint ed. pap. *(978-3-8424-5271-8(3))* Tredition GmbH.

—The Guns of Bull Run: A Story of the Civil War's Eve. 2009. (Civil War Ser.: Vol. 1). (YA). (gr. 4-7). reprint ed. pap. 16.95 *(978-1-933573-82-3(1))* Zeezok Publishing, LLC.

—The Scouts of Stonewall: The Story of the Great Valley Campaign. 2006. (Civil War Ser.: Vol. 3). 312p. (J). reprint ed. 29.95 *(978-1-4218-1779-8(9))*; pap. 14.95 *(978-1-4218-1879-5(5))* 1st World Publishing, Inc. (1st World Library - Literary Society).

—The Scouts of Stonewall: The Story of the Great Valley Campaign. l.t. ed. (Civil War Ser.: Vol. 3). (J). reprint ed. 2007. (ENG.). 240p. pap. 22.99 *(978-1-4264-1531-9(1))* 2011. 370p. (gr. 4-7). pap. 32.75 *(978-1-245-65787-7(9))* 2008. 244p. 27.99 *(978-0-554-22030-7(X))* 2008. 244p. 24.99 *(978-0-554-31333-7(2))* 2006. 250p. pap. 20.99 *(978-1-4264-1498-5(6))* Creative Media Partners, LLC.

—The Scouts of Stonewall: The Story of the Great Valley Campaign. 2006. (Civil War Ser.: Vol. 3). (J). reprint ed. pap. *(978-1-4065-0820-8(9))* Dodo Pr.

—The Scouts of Stonewall: The Story of the Great Valley Campaign. 2007. (Civil War Ser.: Vol. 3). 184p. (J). reprint ed. per. *(978-1-4068-1684-6(1))* Echo Library.

—The Scouts of Stonewall: The Story of the Great Valley Campaign. 2010. (Civil War Ser.: Vol. 3). (Illus.). 166p. (J). (gr. 4-7). reprint ed. pap. 19.99 *(978-1-153-72009-0(4))* General Bks. LLC.

—The Scouts of Stonewall: The Story of the Great Valley Campaign. reprint ed. 2010. (Civil War Ser.: Vol. 3). 252p. (J). (gr. 4-7). 33.56 *(978-1-169-30265-5(3))* 2010. (Civil War Ser.: Vol. 3). 252p. (J). (gr. 4-7). pap. 21.56 *(978-1-162-70768-6(2))* 2010. (Civil War Ser.: Vol. 3). 252p. (J). 41.95 *(978-1-161-47632-3(6))* 2004. pap. 26.95 *(978-1-4191-8162-7(9))* 2004. (Civil War Ser.: Vol. 3). (J). pap. 1.99 *(978-1-4192-8162-4(3))* Kessinger Publishing, LLC.

—The Scouts of Stonewall: The Story of the Great Valley Campaign. 2011. (Civil War Ser.: Vol. 3). 278p. (J). (gr. 4-7). reprint ed. pap. *(978-3-8424-6100-0(3))* Tredition GmbH.

—The Shades of the Wilderness: A Story of Lee's Great Stand. 2006. (Civil War Ser.: Vol. 7). 308p. (J). reprint ed. 29.95 *(978-1-4218-2336-2(5))*; pap. 14.95 *(978-1-4218-2436-9(1))* 1st World Publishing, Inc. (1st World Library - Literary Society).

—The Shades of the Wilderness: A Story of Lee's Great Stand. (Civil War Ser.: Vol. 7). 312p. (J). reprint ed. lib. bdg. 25.95 *(978-0-88411-940-1(8))* Amereon Ltd.

—The Shades of the Wilderness: A Story of Lee's Great Stand. l.t. ed. (Civil War Ser.: Vol. 7). (J). reprint ed. 2006. (ENG.). 278p. pap. 23.99 *(978-1-4264-6220-7(4))* 2008. 280p. 28.99 *(978-0-554-24300-9(8))* 2008. 280p. 25.99 *(978-0-554-33603-9(0))* 2006. (ENG.). 250p. pap. 20.99 *(978-1-4264-6165-1(8))* Creative Media Partners, LLC.

—The Shades of the Wilderness: A Story of Lee's Great Stand. 2006. (Civil War Ser.: Vol. 7). (J). reprint ed. pap. *(978-1-4065-0822-2(5))* Dodo Pr.

—The Shades of the Wilderness: A Story of Lee's Great Stand. 2007. (Civil War Ser.: Vol. 7). 180p. (J). reprint ed. per. *(978-1-4068-1686-0(8))* Echo Library.

—The Shades of the Wilderness: A Story of Lee's Great Stand. 2010. (Civil War Ser.: Vol. 7). (Illus.). 162p. (J). (gr. 4-7). reprint ed. pap. 19.99 *(978-1-153-72059-5(0))* General Bks. LLC.

—The Shades of the Wilderness: A Story of Lee's Great Stand. (Civil War Ser.: Vol. 7). (J). reprint ed. 2011. (gr. 4-7). *(978-1-164-50265-4(4))* 2010. 324p. (gr. 4-7). pap. 24.76 *(978-1-163-19558-1(8))* 2008. 324p. 45.95 *(978-1-4366-8424-8(2))* 2007. 324p. per. 30.95 *(978-1-4325-9861-7(9))* Kessinger Publishing, LLC.

—The Shades of the Wilderness: A Story of Lee's Great Stand. 2007. (Civil War Ser.: Vol. 7). 308p. reprint ed. per. 16.45 *(978-1-60424-029-0(6)*, Book Jungle) Standard Pubns., Inc.

—The Shades of the Wilderness: A Story of Lee's Great Stand. 2011. (Civil War Ser.: Vol. 7). 280p. (J). reprint ed. pap. *(978-3-8424-4396-9(X))* Tredition GmbH.

—The Tree of Appomattox: A Story of the Civil War's Close. 2006. (Civil War Ser.: Vol. 8). 324p. (J). reprint ed. 29.95 *(978-1-4218-2338-6(1))*; pap. 14.95 *(978-1-4218-2438-3(8))* 1st World Publishing, Inc. (1st World Library - Literary Society).

—The Tree of Appomattox: A Story of the Civil War's Close. l.t. ed. (Civil War Ser.: Vol. 8). (J). reprint ed. 2007. (ENG.). 298p. pap. 23.99 *(978-1-4346-1261-8(9))* 2008. 300p. 28.99 *(978-0-554-26479-0(X))* 2008. 300p. 25.99 *(978-0-554-35782-9(8))* 2007. (ENG.). 266p. pap. 21.99 *(978-1-4346-1190-1(6))* Creative Media Partners, LLC.

—The Tree of Appomattox: A Story of the Civil War's Close. 2006. (Civil War Ser.: Vol. 8). (J). reprint ed. pap. *(978-1-4065-0828-4(4))* Dodo Pr.

—The Tree of Appomattox: A Story of the Civil War's Close. 2007. (Civil War Ser.: Vol. 8). 192p. (J). reprint ed. per. *(978-1-4068-1693-8(0))* Echo Library.

—The Tree of Appomattox: A Story of the Civil War's Close. 2010. (Civil War Ser.: Vol. 8). (Illus.). 174p. (J). (gr. 4-7). reprint ed. pap. 19.99 *(978-1-153-72402-9(2))* General Bks. LLC.

—The Tree of Appomattox: A Story of the Civil War's Close. Wrenn, Charles L., illus. (Civil War Ser.: Vol. 8). 332p. (J). (gr. 4-7). reprint ed. 2011. 45.95 *(978-1-169-88135-8(1))* 2010. 36.76 *(978-1-163-21361-2(6))* 2010. pap. 24.76 *(978-1-162-78752-7(X))* Kessinger Publishing, LLC.

—The Tree of Appomattox: A Story of the Civil War's Close. 2005. (Civil War Ser.: Vol. 8). (J). reprint ed. pap. 30.95 *(978-1-4179-2071-6(8))* Kessinger Publishing, LLC.

—The Tree of Appomattox: A Story of the Civil War's Close. Wrenn, Charles L., illus. 2005. (Civil War Ser.: Vol. 8). 332p. (J). reprint ed. 45.95 *(978-1-4326-1333-4(2))* Kessinger Publishing, LLC.

—The Tree of Appomattox: A Story of the Civil War's Close. 2011. (Civil War Ser.: Vol. 8). 294p. (J). (gr. 4-7). reprint ed. pap. *(978-3-8424-8485-6(2))* Tredition GmbH.

Amateau, Gigi. Chancey of the Maury River. 2010. (ENG., Illus.). 256p. (J). (gr. 4-7). pap. 6.99 *(978-0-7636-4523-6(0))* Candlewick Pr.

—Come August, Come Freedom: The Bellows, the Gallows, & the Black General Gabriel. (ENG.). (YA). (gr. 7). 2014. 256p. pap. 6.99 *(978-0-7636-6870-9(2))* 2012. (Illus.). 240p. 16.99 *(978-0-7636-4792-6(6))* Candlewick Pr.

—Macadoo of the Maury River. (Horses of the Maury River Ser.). (ENG.). (J). (gr. 4-7). 2015. 208p. pap. 6.99 *(978-0-7636-7670-4(5))* 2013. 192p. 15.99 *(978-0-7636-3766-8(1))* Candlewick Pr.

Armstrong, Alan. Raleigh's Page. Jessell, Tim, illus. 2009. (ENG.). 336p. (J). (gr. 3-7). 7.99 *(978-0-375-83320-5(X)*, Yearling) Random Hse. Children's Bks.

Arnold, Ginger Fudge. Two Tipsy Tots, 1 vol. Crème, Aurora C., illus. 2009. 32p. pap. 24.95 *(978-1-4489-1891-1(X))* America Star Bks.

Aryal, Aimee Sutter. Hello Hokie Bird! Meadows, Sarah, illus. 2003. (J). 18.95 *(978-0-9743442-0-1(6))* Mascot Bks., Inc.

Basham, Tom. Sailing Home. Calvert, Lissa, illus. 2012. 168p. *(978-1-77097-370-1(2))* FriesenPress.

Basham, Tom & Calvert, Lissa. Sailing Home. 2012. 168p. pap. *(978-1-77097-371-8(0))* FriesenPress.

Bayard, Louis. Lucky Strikes. 2016. (ENG., Illus.). 320p. (YA). 16.99 *(978-1-62779-390-2(9)*, 9781627793902, Holt, Henry & Co. Bks. For Young Readers) Holt, Henry & Co.

—Lucky Strikes. 2017. (YA). lib. bdg. 20.85 ***(978-0-606-39951-7(8))*** Turtleback Bks.

The Beach by the Bay: Tanner & Kai Go Surfing. 2007. (Illus.). 24p. (J). 15.95 *(978-0-9796039-0-7(0))* Sandbridge Sons Publishing.

Benedis-Grab, Daphne. Army Brats. 2017. (ENG.). 240p. (J). (gr. 3-7). 17.99 *(978-0-545-93205-9(X)*, Scholastic Pr.) Scholastic, Inc.

Bettino, Teresa Adele. The Adventures of Sugarbabe & Thunder. 2013. 34p. pap. 12.00 *(978-0-9742842-0-0(3))* Bettino, Teresa Adele.

Bradby, Marie. Some Friend. 2007. (ENG.). 240p. (J). (gr. 3-7). pap. 7.99 *(978-1-4169-3452-3(9)*, Atheneum Bks. for Young Readers) Simon & Schuster Children's Publishing.

Bradley, Kimberly Brubaker. Jefferson's Sons: A Founding Father's Secret Children. 2013. (ENG.). 400p. (J). (gr. 3-7). pap. 7.99 *(978-0-14-242184-0(7)*, Puffin Books) Penguin Young Readers Group.

Briggs, Martha Wren. The Little Ferry Travels with Virginia Bk. 6: The Little Ferry Goes to Yorktown. Starbuck-McMillan, Elizabeth, illus. 2007. (The Little Ferry Travels with Virginia Ser.: Vol. 6). 30p. (YA). (gr. 5-8). pap. 6.95 *(978-0-9633240-8-5(X))* Dory Pr.

Brooke, Lauren. All or Nothing. 2007. (Chestnut Hill Ser.: No. 6). 184p. (J). lib. bdg. 15.38 *(978-1-4242-1719-9(9))* Fitzgerald Bks.

—Making Strides. 2005. (Chestnut Hill Ser.: No. 2). 219p. (J). (gr. 4-7). 12.65 *(978-0-7569-6478-8(4))* Perfection Learning Corp.

—The New Class. 2005. (Chestnut Hill Ser.: No. 1). 212p. (J). (gr. 4-7). lib. bdg. 12.65 *(978-0-7569-6479-5(2))* Perfection Learning Corp.

Brown, Cara D. Isabelle's Wish. 2013. 48p. (gr. 2-2). pap. 8.95 *(978-1-4759-7421-8(3))* iUniverse, Inc.

Burgess, Linda, text. Mount Vernon's Magnificent Menagerie: And the Very Mysterious Guest. 2012. (ENG., Illus.). 48p. (J). 15.95 *(978-0-931917-31-8(X))* Mount Vernon Ladies' Assn. of the Union.

Burnham, Niki & Saidens, Amy. Royally Jacked. 2003. (Romantic Comedies Ser.). (ENG.). 208p. (YA). mass mkt. 6.99 *(978-0-689-86668-5(2)*, Simon Pulse) Simon Pulse.

Crane, Stephen. The Red Badge of Courage. (EMC Masterpiece Series Access Editions). (J). 11.99 *(978-0-8219-1981-1(4))* EMC/Paradigm Publishing.

Cromwell, Daisy. Arthur, the Talking Goat. Paxton, Cameron L., illus. 2007. 52p. (J). pap. 18.99 *(978-0-9800675-1-4(0))* Mirror Publishing.

Davis, Catherine Jennings & Thompson, Traci Shirley. Goodnight Cavaliers. 2013. (J). 17.95 *(978-1-62086-038-0(4))* Mascot Bks., Inc.

Dooley, Sarah. Free Verse. 2017. lib. bdg. 19.65 ***(978-0-606-39788-9(4))*** Turtleback Bks.

Earhart, Kristin. Buttercup Mystery. Geddes, Serena, illus. 2015. (Marguerite Henry's Misty Inn Ser.: 2). (ENG.). 128p. (J). (gr. 2-5). pap. 5.99 *(978-1-4814-1416-6(X)*, Aladdin) Simon & Schuster Children's Publishing.

—Finding Luck. Geddess, Serena, illus. 2016. (Marguerite Henry's Misty Inn Ser.: 4). (ENG.). 128p. (J). (gr. 2-5). pap. 5.99 *(978-1-4814-1422-7(4)*, Aladdin) Simon & Schuster Children's Publishing.

—Runaway Pony. Geddess, Serena, illus. 2015. (Marguerite Henry's Misty Inn Ser.: 3). (ENG.). 128p. (J). (gr. 2-5). pap. 5.99 *(978-1-4814-1419-7(4)*, Aladdin) Simon & Schuster Children's Publishing.

—Runaway Pony. 2015. (Marguerite Henry's Misty Inn Ser.: 3). lib. bdg. 16.00 *(978-0-606-37835-2(9))* Turtleback Bks.

—Welcome Home! Geddes, Serena, illus. 2015. (Marguerite Henry's Misty Inn Ser.: 1). (ENG.). 128p. (J). (gr. 2-5). 16.99 *(978-1-4814-1414-2(3)*, Aladdin) Simon & Schuster Children's Publishing.

—Welcome Home! 2015. (Marguerite Henry's Misty Inn Ser.: 1). lib. bdg. 16.00 *(978-0-606-37126-1(5))* Turtleback Bks.

Earhart, Kristin & Geddes, Serena. Welcome Home!; Buttercup Mystery; Runaway Pony; Finding Luck. 2016. (Marguerite Henry's Misty Inn Ser.). (ENG., Illus.). 512p. (J). (gr. 2-5). pap. 23.99 *(978-1-4814-7012-4(4)*, Aladdin) Simon & Schuster Children's Publishing.

Elliott, L. M. Annie, Between the States. 2006. (ENG.). 544p. (YA). (gr. 8-12). per. 9.99 *(978-0-06-001213-7(7)*, Tegen, Katherine Bks) 2004. (Illus.). 496p. (J). (gr. 7-18). 16.99 *(978-0-06-001211-3(0))* HarperCollins Pubs.

Erskine, Kathryn. Mockingbird. (ENG.). (J). (gr. 5-18). 2011. 256p. 7.99 *(978-0-14-241775-1(0)*, Puffin Books) 2010. 240p. 16.99 *(978-0-399-25264-8(9)*, Philomel Bks.) Penguin Young Readers Group.

—Mockingbird. (J). 2012. 1.25 *(978-1-4407-4671-0(0))* 2010. 72.75 *(978-1-4407-4667-3(2))* 2010. 74.75 *(978-1-4407-4665-9(6))* 2010. (SPA.). 62.75 *(978-1-4407-4663-5(X))* 2010. 64.75 *(978-1-4407-4661-1(3))* 2010. 210.75 *(978-1-4407-4662-8(1))* Recorded Bks., Inc.

—Mockingbird. 2011. lib. bdg. 18.40 *(978-0-606-15356-0(X)*, Turtleback) Turtleback Bks.

—Seeing Red. 2013. (YA). *(978-0-545-57645-1(8))*; (ENG.). 352p. (J). (gr. 5-9). 16.99 *(978-0-545-46440-6(4))* Scholastic, Inc. (Scholastic Pr.).

Gourley, Robbin. Bring Me Some Apples & I'll Make You a Pie: A Story about Edna Lewis. (ENG., Illus.). 48p. (J). (gr. -1-3). 2016. pap. 6.99 *(978-0-544-80901-7(7)*, HMH Books For Young Readers) 2008. 17.99 *(978-0-618-15836-2(7))* Houghton Mifflin Harcourt Publishing Co.

Gwaltney, Doris. Homefront. 2009. (ENG.). 320p. (J). (gr. 5-9). pap. 6.99 *(978-1-4169-9572-2(2)*, Simon & Schuster Bks. For Young Readers) Simon & Schuster Bks. For Young Readers.

Hahn, Mary Downing. Closed for the Season. 2010. (ENG.). 192p. (J). (gr. 5-7). pap. 6.99 *(978-0-547-39853-2(0))* Houghton Mifflin Harcourt Publishing Co.

Haislip, Phyllis Hall. Anybody's Hero: The Battle of Old Men & Young Boys. 2004. (Illus.). 220p. (J). pap. 8.95 *(978-1-57249-343-8(7)*, White Mane Kids) White Mane Publishing Co., Inc.

—Lili's Gift: A Civil War Healer's Story. 2008. (ENG., Illus.). 204p. (J). pap. 8.95 *(978-1-57249-392-6(5)*, White Mane Kids) White Mane Publishing Co., Inc.

—Lottie's Courage: A Contraband Slave's Story. 2003. (Illus.). 120p. (J). pap. 7.95 *(978-1-57249-311-7(9)*, White Mane Kids) White Mane Publishing Co., Inc.

Hall, Kate W. Richmond Rocks! 2009. (Illus.). (J). 14.95 *(978-1-61623-975-6(1)*, Richmondmom.com Publishing) Palari Publishing LLP.

Hall, Lucy. From England to Jamestowne: A Journey to Find My Father. 2007. (J). *(978-0-9763706-5-9(4))* Tendril Pr., LLC.

Harris, Teresa E. The Perfect Place. 2014. (ENG.). 272p. (J). (gr. 5-7). 17.99 *(978-0-547-25519-4(5))* Houghton Mifflin Harcourt Publishing Co.

Harvey, Tom. Guido, the Swan with an Attitude. 2011. 44p. (gr. -1). pap. 17.99 *(978-1-4269-6855-6(8))* Trafford Publishing.

Heald, Robin. Liberty Saves the Day! Elkerton, Andy, illus. 2017. (J). ***(978-0-87935-290-5(6))*** Colonial Williamsburg Foundation.

Henry, Marguerite. Cinnabar, the One O'Clock Fox. Dennis, Wesley, illus. (ENG.). 144p. (J). (gr. 3-7). 2015. 19.99 *(978-1-4814-0401-3(6))* 2014. pap. 6.99 *(978-1-4814-0400-6(8))* Simon & Schuster Children's Publishing. (Aladdin).

—Misty of Chincoteague. Dennis, Wesley, illus. 2007. 173p. (gr. 3-7). 17.00 *(978-0-7569-8227-0(8))* Perfection Learning Corp.

—Misty of Chincoteague. Dennis, Wesley, illus. 60th ed. 2006. (ENG.). 176p. (J). (gr. 3-7). pap. 7.99 *(978-1-4169-2783-9(2)*, Aladdin) Simon & Schuster Children's Publishing.

—Sea Star: Orphan of Chincoteague. Dennis, Wesley, illus. 2007. (ENG.). 176p. (J). (gr. 3-7). pap. 7.99 *(978-1-4169-2784-6(0)*, Aladdin) Simon & Schuster Children's Publishing.

—Stormy, Misty's Foal. Dennis, Wesley, illus. (ENG.). (J). (gr. 3-7). 2015. 256p. 19.99 *(978-1-4814-2561-2(7))* 2007. 224p. pap. 6.99 *(978-1-4169-2788-4(3))* Simon & Schuster Children's Publishing. (Aladdin).

Henty, George Alfred. With Lee in Virgini. 2007. 392p. 39.95 *(978-1-4344-8351-5(7))*; per. 24.95 *(978-1-4344-8350-8(9))* Wildside Pr., LLC.

Higgins, Carter. A Rambler Steals Home. 2017. (ENG.). 224p. (J). (gr. 5-7). 16.99 *(978-0-544-60201-4(3)*, HMH Books For Young Readers) Houghton Mifflin Harcourt Publishing Co.

Hollenbeck, Kathleen M. Dancing on the Sand: A Story of an Atlantic Blue Crab. 2005. (ENG., Illus.). 32p. (J). (gr. -1-2). 8.95 *(978-1-59249-234-3(7)*, SC4017) Soundprints.

Holt, Kimberly Willis. Piper Reed, Forever Friend. Davenier, Christine, illus. 2012. (Piper Reed Ser.: 6). (ENG.). 160p. (J). (gr. 3-6). 15.99 *(978-0-8050-9008-6(8)*, 9780805090086, Holt, Henry & Co. Bks. For Young Readers) Holt, Henry & Co.

—Piper Reed, Forever Friend. Davenier, Christine, illus. 2013. (Piper Reed Ser.: 6). (ENG.). 176p. (J). (gr. 3-6). pap. 6.99 *(978-1-250-02725-2(X)*, 9781250027252) Square Fish.

Houston, Julian. New Boy. 2007. 282p. (gr. 7-12). 18.00 *(978-0-7569-8139-6(5))* Perfection Learning Corp.

Hunter, John P. Red Thunder: Secrets, Spies, & Scoundrels at Yorktown. 2006. 234p. (YA). (gr. 6-8). 7.95 *(978-0-87935-231-8(0))* Colonial Williamsburg Foundation.

Jacobs, Lily. The Littlest Bunny in Virginia: An Easter Adventure. Dunn, Robert, illus. 2015. (ENG.). 32p. (J). (-3). 9.99 *(978-1-4926-1228-5(6)*, Sourcebooks Jabberwocky) Sourcebooks, Inc.

James, Eric. A Halloween Scare in Virginia. Le Ray, Marina, illus. 2014. (ENG.). 32p. (J). (-5). 9.99

TUV

(978-1-4926-0636-9(7), 9781492606369, Sourcebooks Jabberwocky) Sourcebooks, Inc.
—Santa's Sleigh Is on Its Way to Virginia. Dunn, Robert, illus. 2015. (ENG.). 32p. (J). (-2). 12.99 (978-1-4926-2754-8(2), Sourcebooks Jabberwocky) Sourcebooks, Inc.
Johnson, Phyllis. Betsy Star Ballerin. 2011. 24p. 16.95 (978-1-4575-0149-4(X)) Dog Ear Publishing, LLC.
Johnston, K. E. M. The Witness Tree & the Shadow of the Noose: Mystery, Lies, & Spies in Manassas. 2009. 111p. (J). (gr. 5-7). pap. 8.95 (978-1-57249-397-1(6), White Mane Kids) White Mane Publishing Co., Inc.
Joyce, Alexandria. Trail of the Caribou: A Tale of Dire Wolves in the Time of the Ice Age. 2011. 216p. (gr. 4-6). pap. 15.95 (978-1-4620-5066-6(2)) iUniverse, Inc.
King, Sarah. The Great Adventures of Piggy the Peruvian Guinea Pig. 2016. (ENG., Illus.). 36p. (J). pap. 10.95 (978-1-63047-568-0(8)) Morgan James Publishing.
Lorenzi, Natalie Dias. Flying the Dragon. (ENG.). 240p. (J). (gr. 4-7). 2014. pap. 8.95 (978-1-58089-435-7(6)) 2012. 16.95 (978-1-58089-434-0(8)) Charlesbridge Publishing, Inc.
Lough, Whitney. Smoke Hole Adventure. Cosner, Jeff, illus. 2013. 36p. (J). 12.00 (978-0-87012-833-2(7)) McClain Printing Co.
Lyne, Jennifer H. Catch Rider. (ENG.). 288p. (YA). (gr. 7). 2014. pap. 8.99 (978-0-544-30182-5(X), HMH Books For Young Readers) 2013. (Illus.). 16.99 (978-0-547-86871-4(5)) Houghton Mifflin Harcourt Publishing Co.
Mack, Stan & Champlin, Susan. Fight for Freedom. 2012. (Cartoon Chronicles of America Ser.). (ENG., Illus.). 128p. (J). (gr. 5-7). pap. 10.99 (978-1-59990-835-9(2), 9781599908359, Bloomsbury USA Childrens) Bloomsbury Publishing USA.
Marsh, Carole. The Mystery at Mount Vernon. Friedlander, Randolyn, illus. 2010. (Real Kids, Real Places Ser.). 32p. pap. 7.99 (978-0-635-07444-7(3), Marsh, Carole Mysteries) Gallopade International.
—The Mystery at Mount Vernon: Home of America's First President George Washington. 2010. (Real Kids, Real Places Ser.). (Illus.). 158p. (J). 18.99 (978-0-635-07443-0(5), Marsh, Carole Mysteries) Gallopade International.
—Pocahontas. (Read-Along Ser.). (J). 7.99 incl. audio (978-1-55723-739-2(5)) Walt Disney Records.
Mathieson, Karen. Duel or Duet: Book Two of the Rosemary Ridge Trilogy. 2013. 160p. (J). pap. 7.99 (978-1-940350-05-9(0)) Portable COO, The.
—Liza, Elizabeth: Book Three of the Rosemary Ridge Trilogy. 2013. 164p. (J). pap. 7.99 (978-1-940350-08-0(5)) Portable COO, The.
McDonald, Megan. Amy Namey in Ace Reporter. Madrid, Erwin, illus. 2014. (Judy Moody Ser.: 3). (ENG.). 64p. (J). (gr. -1-1). 12.99 (978-0-7636-5715-4(8)) Candlewick Pr.
—Judy Moody Saves the World! Reynolds, Peter H., illus. 2004. (Judy Moody Ser.: Bk. 3). 144p. (J). (gr. 1-5). 13.65 (978-0-7569-2588-8(6)) Perfection Learning Corp.
—Judy Moody Saves the World! Reynolds, Peter H., illus. 2010. (Judy Moody Ser.: 3). (ENG.). 160p. (J). (gr. 1-4). 15.99 (978-0-7636-4860-2(4)) Candlewick Pr.
—Judy Moody Saves the World! 2010. (Judy Moody Ser.: 3). lib. bdg. 16.00 (978-0-606-12340-2(7), Turtleback) Turtleback Bks.
—Judy Moody Saves the World!, Bk. 3. Reynolds, Peter H., illus. 2010. (Judy Moody Ser.: 3). (ENG.). 160p. (J). (gr. 1-4). pap. 5.99 (978-0-7636-4859-6(0)) Candlewick Pr.
—Stink & the Great Guinea Pig Express, Bk. 4. Reynolds, Peter H., illus. 2013. (Stink Ser.: 4). (ENG.). (J). (gr. 1-4). 128p. 12.99 (978-0-7636-6391-9(3)); 144p. pap. 4.99 (978-0-7636-6421-3(9)) Candlewick Pr.
—Stink & the Great Guinea Pig Express. Reynolds, Peter H., illus. 2010. (Stink Ser.: No. 4). 128p. (J). (gr. k-4). 24.21 (978-1-59961-683-4(1)) Spotlight.
—Stink & the Great Guinea Pig Express. 2013. (Stink Ser.: 4). lib. bdg. 14.75 (978-0-606-31590-6(X), Turtleback) Turtleback Bks.
McGowen, Julie. Virginia's Voyage. 2007. 48p. per. 16.95 (978-1-4241-6672-5(1)) America Star Bks.
McMahan, Stephanie K. The Mystery of the Golden Rings. 2007. 140p. 21.95 (978-0-595-68451-9(3)); per. 11.95 (978-0-595-43998-0(5)) iUniverse, Inc.
McVicker, Mary. Secret of Belle Meadow, 1 vol. Ramsey, Marcy Dunn, illus. 2009. (ENG.). 152p. (J). per. 9.95 (978-0-87033-554-9(5), 9780870335549, Cornell Maritime Pr./Tidewater Pubs.) Schiffer Publishing, Ltd.
Middleton, William. The Chipmunk Jamboree. 2013. 24p. pap. 12.45 (978-1-4624-0669-2(6), Inspiring Voices) Author Solutions, Inc.
Mills, Charles. The Secret of Scarlett Cove. 2004. (Honors Club Story Ser.: Bk. 3). 127p. (J). 7.99 (978-0-8163-1999-2(5)) Pacific Pr. Publishing Assn.
Moore, Stephanie Perry. True Friends. 2005. (Carmen Browne Ser.: 1). (ENG.). 128p. (YA). pap. 6.99 (978-0-8024-8172-6(8), Lift Every Voice) Moody Pubs.
Mullins, Norman D. Mountain Boy: The Adventures of Orion Saddler. 2004. 104p. (YA). per. 9.95 (978-0-9724867-4-3(7)) Woodland Pr., LLC.
Naylor, Phyllis Reynolds. Alice on Board. 2012. (Alice Ser.: 24). (ENG., Illus.). 288p. (YA). (gr. 9). 16.99 (978-1-4424-4588-8(2), Atheneum Bks. for Young Readers) Simon & Schuster Children's Publishing.
—A Shiloh Christmas. 2015. (Shiloh Quartet Ser.). (ENG., Illus.). 256p. (J). (gr. 3-7). 17.99 (978-1-4814-4151-3(5)) Simon & Schuster Children's Publishing.
Nolen, Jerdine. Calico Girl. 2017. (ENG., Illus.). 192p. (J). (gr. 3-7). 16.99 (978-1-4814-5981-5(3), Simon & Schuster/Paula Wiseman Bks.) Simon & Schuster/Paula Wiseman Bks.
Oladokun, Alexander. Acrux Manor: The Prodigal's Curse (Hardcover) 2013. 206p. 28.50 (978-1-300-68651-4(0)) Lulu Pr., Inc.
Olasky, Susan. *Annie Henry: Adventures in the American Revolution.* 2005. (Illus.). 528p. (J). pap. 16.99 (978-1-58134-521-6(6), Crossway Bibles) Crossway.
—Annie Henry & the Mysterious Stranger. 2003. (Adventures of the American Revolution Ser.: Vol. 3). 144p. (YA). (gr. 3-7). pap. 5.99 (978-0-89107-907-1(6)) Crossway.
—Annie Henry & the Mysterious Stranger. 2011. (J). pap. (978-1-59638-376-0(3)) P & R Publishing.
O'Neill, Elizabeth. Alfred Visits Virginia. 2006. (Illus.). 24p. (J). (gr. -1-3). pap. 12.00 (978-0-9771836-8-5(8)) Global Business Information Strategies, Inc.
Otis, James. Richard of Jamestown: A story of the Virginia Colony. 2007. (Illus.). 140p. (J). per. 9.95 (978-0-9790876-0-8(0)) Living Bks. Pr.
Paterson, Katherine. Bridge to Terabithia. Diamond, Donna, illus. movie tie-in ed. 2006. (ENG.). (J). (gr. 3-7). 176p. pap. 6.99 (978-0-06-122728-8(5)); 208p. pap. 6.99 (978-0-06-125370-6(7)) HarperCollins Pubs. (HarperFestival).
—Bridge to Terabithia. Diamond, Donna, illus. l.t. ed. 2007. (Literacy Bridge Middle Reader Ser.). 187p. (J). (gr. 4-7). 23.95 (978-0-7862-9620-0(8)) Thorndike Pr.
Pistole, Katy. Flying High. 2003. (Illus.). 126p. (J). 7.99 (978-0-8163-1942-8(1)) Pacific Pr. Pubns.
Plehal, Christopher J. Yes, Virginia: There Is a Santa Claus. Bernardin, James, illus. 2010. (ENG.). 32p. (J). (gr. -1-2). 16.99 (978-0-06-200173-3(6)) HarperCollins Pubs.
Porter, Tracey. Lark. 2011. (ENG.). 192p. (YA). (gr. 8-18). 15.99 (978-0-06-112287-3(4), HarperTeen) HarperCollins Pubs.
Powell, Patricia Hruby. Loving vs. Virginia: A Documentary Novel of the Landmark Civil Rights Case. Strickland, Shadra, illus. 2017. (ENG.). 260p. (YA). (gr. 7-12). 21.99 (978-1-4521-2590-9(2)) Chronicle Bks. LLC.
Pyle, Howard. The Story of Jack Ballister's Fortunes: Being the Narrative of the Adventures of a Young Gentleman of Good Family, Who Was Kidnapped in the Year 1719 & Carried to the Plantations of the Continent of Virginia, Where He Fell in with That Famous Pirate Captain Edward Teach, or Blackbeard: of His Escape from the Pirates & the Rescue of a Young Lady from Out Their Hands. unabr. ed. 2012. (Illus.). 436p. 49.99 (978-1-4622-8858-8(8)) Repressed Publishing LLC.
Ransom, Candice. Finding Day's Bottom. 2006. 176p. (J). (gr. 3-7). lib. bdg. 15.95 (978-1-57505-933-4(9), Carolrhoda Bks.) Lerner Publishing Group.
—Iva Honeysuckle Meets Her Match. Ross, Heather, illus. 2014. (Iva Honeysuckle Book Ser.). (ENG.). 192p. (J). (gr. 1-3). pap. 4.99 (978-1-4231-3516-6(4)) Hyperion Bks. for Children.
—Iva Honeysuckle Meets Her Match. Ross, Heather, illus. 2013. (Iva Honeysuckle Book Ser.). (ENG.). 192p. (J). (gr. 2-5). 14.99 (978-1-4231-3514-2(8)) Hyperion Pr.
—Rebel Mckenzie. 2013. (ENG.). 288p. (J). (gr. 3-7). pap. 7.99 (978-1-4231-6388-6(5)) Hyperion Pr.
Ray, Delia. Ghost Girl: A Blue Ridge Mountain Story. 2016. (ENG.). 272p. (J). (gr. 5-7). pap. 6.99 (978-0-544-70633-0(1), HMH Books For Young Readers) Houghton Mifflin Harcourt Publishing Co.
Readler, Blaine C. Under the Radar: The Spy Drone Adventure. 2006. (ENG.). 248p. (J). (gr. 7-12). per. (978-1-933255-18-7(8)) DNA Pr.
Reeder, Carolyn. Moonshiner's Son. O'Brien, Tim, illus. 2003. (ENG.). 208p. (J). (gr. 3-7). pap. 6.99 (978-0-689-85550-4(8), Aladdin) Simon & Schuster Children's Publishing.
Reynolds, Jason. As Brave As You. (ENG.). 432p. (J). (gr. 5). 2017. pap. 7.99 (978-1-4814-1591-0(3), Atheneum Bks. for Young Readers) 2016. (Illus.). 16.99 (978-1-4814-1590-3(5), Atheneum/Caitlyn Dlouhy Books) Simon & Schuster Children's Publishing.
Richmond, Caroline Tung. The Only Thing to Fear. 2014. (ENG.). 288p. (J). (gr. 7). 17.99 (978-0-545-62988-1(8), Scholastic Pr.) Scholastic, Inc.
Riddleburger, Sam & Michael Hemphill. Stonewall Hinkleman & the Battle of Bull Run. 2014. lib. bdg. 18.40 (978-0-606-35709-8(2)) Turtleback Bks.
Rimer, David & Robertson, William P. The Bucktails' Antietam Trials. 2005. (White Mane Kids Ser.: No.14). (Illus.). 175p. (J). (gr. 4-7). per. 7.95 (978-1-57249-337-7(2), White Mane Kids) White Mane Publishing Co., Inc.
Rinaldi, Ann. The Letter Writer. 2010. (ENG., Illus.). 224p. (YA). (gr. 7). pap. 8.99 (978-0-547-32785-3(4)) Houghton Mifflin Harcourt Publishing Co.
—Or Give Me Death. 2004. (Great Episodes Ser.). 226p. (gr. 5-9). 17.00 (978-0-7569-3462-0(1)) Perfection Learning Corp.
—Or Give Me Death: A Novel of Patrick Henry's Family. 2004. (Great Episodes Ser.). (ENG.). 240p. (YA). (gr. 7-8). pap. 6.99 (978-0-15-205076-4(0)) Houghton Mifflin Harcourt Publishing Co.
—Sarah's Ground. 2004. (ENG., Illus.). 192p. (YA). 15.95 (978-0-689-85924-3(4), Simon & Schuster Bks. For Young Readers) Simon & Schuster Bks. For Young Readers.
Robertson, William P. & Rimer, David. The Battling Bucktails at Fredericksburg. 2005. (WM Kids Ser.: Vol. 16). (Illus.). 154p. (J). (gr. 4-7). per. 7.95 (978-1-57249-345-2(3), White Mane Kids) White Mane Publishing Co., Inc.
Roop, Peter & Roop, Connie. An Eye for an Eye. 2004. 168p. (J). lib. bdg. 16.92 (978-1-4242-0772-5(X)) Fitzgerald Bks.
Roy, Ron. The Secret at Jefferson's Mansion. Bush, Timothy, illus. 2009. (Capital Mysteries Ser.: 11). (ENG.). 96p. (J). (gr. 1-4). 4.99 (978-0-375-84533-8(X), Random Hse. Bks. for Young Readers) Random Hse. Children's Bks.
—White House White-Out. Gurney, John Steven, illus. 2008. (A to Z Mysteries Ser.: No. 3). 124p. (gr. 1-4). 15.00 (978-0-7569-8799-2(7)) Perfection Learning Corp.
—White House White-Out. Gurney, John Steven, illus. 2008. (to Z Mysteries Ser.: 3). (ENG.). 144p. (J). (gr. 1-4). 5.99 (978-0-375-84721-9(9), Random Hse. Bks. for Young Readers) Random Hse. Children's Bks.
Rue, Nancy N. Sophie Steps Up, 1 vol. 2009. (Faithgirlz! Ser.: No. 4). (ENG.). 128p. (J). pap. 6.99 (978-0-310-71841-3(4)) Zonderkidz.
—Sophie's Friendship Fiasco. 2009. (Faithgirlz! Ser.: No. 7). (ENG.). 128p. (J). pap. 6.99 (978-0-310-71842-0(2)) Zonderkidz.
Salisbury, Linda. Earthquake Surprise: A Bailey Fish Adventure. Tornatore, Carol, illus. 2012. 192p. (J). pap. 8.95 (978-1-881539-65-0(2)) Tabby Hse. Bks.
Salisbury, Linda G. The Thief at Keswick Inn: A Bailey Fish Adventure. Grotke, Christopher A., illus. 2006. (Bailey Fish Adventures Ser.). 191p. (J). (gr. 3-7). per. 8.95 (978-1-881539-41-4(5)) Tabby Hse. Bks.
—Trouble in Contrary Woods: A Bailey Fish Adventure. Tornatore, Carol, illus. 2009. (J). 8.85 (978-1-881539-46-9(6)) Tabby Hse. Bks.
Seeley, Bonnie L. Chincoteague Daisy Chain. Lidard, Kelly & Seeley, Douglas A., illus. 2003. 32p. (J). bds. 12.95 (978-0-9728380-0-9(7)) Seelcraft Publishing.
Sharpe, Susan. Waterman's Boy. 2007. (ENG.). 176p. (J). (gr. 3-7). pap. 11.95 (978-1-4169-6453-7(3), Simon & Schuster/Paula Wiseman Bks.) Simon & Schuster/Paula Wiseman Bks.
Silvano, Wendi. Love Is All Around Virginia. Czernichowska, Joanna, illus. 2016. (ENG.). 32p. (J). (-6). 12.99 (978-1-4926-2971-9(5), Sourcebooks Jabberwocky) Sourcebooks, Inc.
Siwak, Brenda S. Counting on the Bay. Dodge, Barbara A., illus. 2006. (J). per. 14.95 (978-0-9790906-0-8(1)) Pleasant Plains Pr.
Smallman, Steve. Santa Is Coming to Northern Virginia. Dunn, Robert, illus. 2015. (ENG.). 32p. (J). (-3). 9.99 (978-1-4926-2663-3(5), Sourcebooks Jabberwocky) Sourcebooks, Inc.
—Santa Is Coming to Virginia. Dunn, Robert, illus. 2013. (ENG.). 32p. (J). (-3). 9.99 (978-1-4022-8800-5(X), Sourcebooks Jabberwocky) Sourcebooks, Inc.
—Santa Is Coming to Virginia Beach. Dunn, Robert, illus. 2015. (ENG.). 32p. (J). (-3). 9.99 (978-1-4926-2648-0(1), Sourcebooks Jabberwocky) Sourcebooks, Inc.
Smith, Eunice Geil. Treasure Hunt. 2006. 119p. (J). (gr. 3-7). per. 9.99 (978-0-8361-9332-9(6)) Herald Pr.
Smith, L. J. The Awakening & the Struggle, 2 vols. 2007. (Vampire Diaries: 1). 492p. (YA). (gr. 7). lib. bdg. 20.85 (978-1-4178-2599-8(5), Turtleback) Turtleback Bks.
—Destiny Rising. 2012. (Vampire Diaries: the Hunters Ser.: 3). (ENG.). 400p. (YA). (gr. 9). 17.99 (978-0-06-201773-4(X), HarperTeen) HarperCollins Pubs.
—Moonsong Vol. 9. 2013. (Vampire Diaries: the Hunters Ser.: 2). (ENG.). 416p. (YA). (gr. 9). pap. 10.99 (978-0-06-201771-0(3), HarperTeen) HarperCollins Pubs.
—Phantom. (Vampire Diaries: the Hunters Ser.: 1). (ENG.). (YA). (gr. 9). 2012. 432p. pap. 9.99 (978-0-06-201769-7(1)) 2011. 416p. 17.99 (978-0-06-201768-0(3)) HarperCollins Pubs. (HarperTeen).
Smith, Laverne Byrd. Pokey the Playful Whale: (who wanted to live on Land) 2010. (Illus.). 36p. pap. 25.50 (978-1-4490-7620-7(3)) AuthorHouse.
Smith, Steven K. Summer of the Woods. 2013. 158p. pap. 7.99 (978-0-9893414-1-7(0)) MyBoys3 Pr.
Smolik, Jane Petrlik. Currents. 2015. (ENG., Illus.). 336p. (YA). (gr. 4-7). lib. bdg. 16.95 (978-1-58089-648-1(0)) Charlesbridge Publishing, Inc.
Spain, Susan. The Deep Cut, 0 vols. 2014. (ENG.). 228p. pap. 9.99 (978-1-4778-4768-8(5), 9781477847688, Amazon Children's Publishing) Amazon Publishing.
Spain, Susan Rosson. The Deep Cut, 1 vol. 2006. (ENG., Illus.). 224p. (J). (gr. 5-9). 16.99 (978-0-7614-5316-1(4)) Marshall Cavendish Corp.
Squiers, Connie. The Copper Colt. 2013. 94p. pap. 7.95 (978-1-937829-78-0(2), Total Publishing & Media) Yorkshire Publishing Group.
St. Mark Kindergarten. Kindergarten Goes to Outer Space for the Day. 2009. 28p. pap. 12.49 (978-1-4490-0587-0(X)) AuthorHouse.
Stevens, Bonnie. Fighting Chance. 2015. (ENG.). 326p. (YA). pap. 10.95 (978-1-929345-14-4(3)) Poisoned Pen Pr.
Stone, Phoebe. Deep down Popular. 2010. (ENG.). 288p. (J). (gr. 4-7). 6.99 (978-0-439-80244-4(X), Levine, Arthur A. Bks.) Scholastic, Inc.
Sully, Katherine. Night-Night Virginia. Poole, Helen, illus. 2017. (ENG.). 20p. (J). (-1). bds. 9.99 (978-1-4926-4767-6(5), 9781492647676, Sourcebooks Jabberwocky) Sourcebooks, Inc.
Szymanski, Lois. Wild Colt, 1 vol. Kantjas, Linda, illus. 2012. (ENG.). 40p. (J). 16.99 (978-0-7643-3975-2(3), 9780764339752) Schiffer Publishing, Ltd.
Szymanski, Lois K. The True Story of Sea Feather, 1 vol. 2010. (ENG., Illus.). 48p. (J). pap. 14.99 (978-0-7643-3609-6(6), 9780764336096) Schiffer Publishing, Ltd.
Talley, Robin. Lies We Tell Ourselves. 2016. (ENG.). 416p. pap. 9.99 (978-0-373-21204-0(6), Harlequin Teen) Harlequin Enterprises, Ltd. CAN. Dist: HarperCollins Pubs.
Terry, Chris L. Zero Fade. Knabb, Jacob & Vance, Leonard, eds. 2013. (ENG., Illus.). 294p. (gr. 6). pap. 12.00 (978-0-9884804-3-8(3), 1362831) Curbside Splendor Publishing.
Thomas, Beth. Jack & the Richmond Bubble. 2012. pap. 11.95 (978-0-7414-7495-7(6)) Infinity Publishing.
Thompson, Kimberly. Toulouse Tangled up in Lights. Easey, Chris, illus. 2011. 64p. (J). 19.95 (978-0-9818976-1-5(4)) Little Pigeon Bks.
Tripp, Valerie. Very Funny, Elizabeth! England, Tamara, ed. Andreasen, Dan, illus. 2005. (ENG.). 96p. (gr. 3). pap. 6.95 (978-1-59369-061-8(4), American Girl) American Girl Publishing, Inc.
Tuthill, Louisa C. Hurrah for New England! or the Virginia Boy's Vacation. 2004. reprint ed. pap. 15.95 (978-1-4191-2504-1(4)); pap. 1.99 (978-1-4192-2504-8(9)) Kessinger Publishing, LLC.
Walker, Sally M. Freedom Song: The Story of Henry "Box" Brown. Qualls, Sean, illus. 2012. (ENG.). 40p. (J). (gr. -1-3). 17.99 (978-0-06-058310-1(X)) HarperCollins Pubs.
Walt Disney Company Staff. Pocahontas. 2005. (WEL., Illus.). 24p. (978-1-899877-04-1(5)) Y Ddraig Fach.
Wells, Carolyn. Patty Fairfield. 2011. 166p. (gr. -1-7). 25.95 (978-1-4638-9972-1(6)) Rodgers, Alan Bks.
Wells, Rosemary. Red Moon at Sharpsburg. 2008. (ENG.). 256p. (YA). (gr. 7-18). 7.99 (978-0-14-241205-3(8), Speak) Penguin Young Readers Group.
West, Joseph, Jr. Watching the Hokies with Daddy. 2005. (Illus.). 23p. (J). 18.95 (978-0-9770680-0-5(5)) Titan Publishing.
Westrick, A. B. Brotherhood. 2014. (ENG.). 384p. (J). (gr. 5). pap. 8.99 (978-0-14-242237-3(1), Puffin Books) Penguin Young Readers Group.
Westrick, Anne. Brotherhood. 2013. (ENG., Illus.). 368p. (J). (gr. 5). 17.99 (978-0-670-01439-2(7), Viking Books for Young Readers) Penguin Young Readers Group.
White, Ruth. Belle Prater's Boy. unabr. ed. 2004. 196p. (J). (gr. 5-9). pap. 38.00 incl. audio (978-0-8072-8682-1(6), YA234SP, Listening Library) Random Hse. Audio Publishing Group.
—A Month of Sundays. 2013. (ENG.). 192p. (YA). (gr. 5-9). pap. 6.99 (978-1-250-02730-6(6), 9781250027306) Square Fish.
—The Search for Belle Prater. 2007. 169p. (J). (gr. 4-7). 14.15 (978-0-7569-7274-5(4)) Perfection Learning Corp.
Willis, Cynthia Chapman. Dog Gone. 2009. (ENG.). 240p. (J). (gr. 3-7). pap. 17.99 (978-0-312-56113-0(X), 9780312561130) Square Fish.
Winders, Gertrude Hecker. Jeb Stuart: Boy in the Saddle. Doremus, Robert, illus. 2011. 202p. 44.95 (978-1-258-08155-3(5)) Literary Licensing, LLC.
Wood, D. K. Nightmare at Indian Cave. 2006. pap. 10.00 (978-1-4257-1640-0(7)) Xlibris Corp.
Wood, Michael. Villains in Virginia Beach. 2004. 100p. (YA). per. (978-1-59196-534-3(9)) Instant Pub.

VIRGINIA—HISTORY

Abnett, Dan. The Battle of the Wilderness: Deadly Inferno. (Graphic Civil War Battles Ser.). (ENG.). 48p. 2009. (YA). (gr. 4-5). 58.50 (978-1-61512-901-0(4), Rosen Reference) 2007. (Illus.). (gr. 5-8). pap. 14.05 (978-1-4042-6479-3(5), Rosen Classroom) Rosen Publishing Group, Inc., The.
—The Battle of the Wilderness: Deadly Inferno. Verma, Dheeraj, illus. 2007. (Graphic Battles of the Civil War Ser.). (ENG.). 48p. (YA). (gr. 4-7). lib. bdg. 31.95 (978-1-4042-0780-6(5)) Rosen Publishing Group, Inc., The.
—The Monitor Versus the Merrimac: Ironclads at War. Verma, Dheeraj, illus. 2007. (Graphic Battles of the Civil War Ser.). (ENG.). 48p. (YA). (gr. 4-7). lib. bdg. 31.95 (978-1-4042-0778-3(3)) Rosen Publishing Group, Inc., The.
Abraham, Isaiah. My Great Grandmother's Memorial Service. 2013. (Illus.). 32p. pap. 14.95 (978-1-937829-72-8(3), Total Publishing & Media) Yorkshire Publishing Group.
Adams, Colleen. Pocahontas. 2009. (Reading Room Collection 1 Ser.). 16p. (gr. 2-3). 37.50 (978-1-60851-949-1(X), PowerKids Pr.) Rosen Publishing Group, Inc., The.
—Pocahontas: The Life of an Indian Princess. 2006. (Rosen Publishing Group's Reading Room Collection). (Illus.). 16p. (J). (gr. 3-7). lib. bdg. 17.25 (978-1-4042-3348-5(2), PowerKids Pr.) Rosen Publishing Group, Inc., The.
Bennett, Doraine. Appalachian Plateau. 2011. (Illus.). 32p. (J). (978-1-935884-09-5(3)); pap. (978-1-935884-14-9(X)) State Standards Publishing, LLC.
—Blue Ridge Mountains. 2011. (Illus.). 32p. (J). (978-1-935884-10-1(7)); pap. (978-1-935884-15-6(8)) State Standards Publishing, LLC.
—Coastal Plain (Tidewater) 2011. (Illus.). 32p. (J). (978-1-935884-12-5(3)); pap. (978-1-935884-17-0(4)) State Standards Publishing, LLC.
—Piedmont. 2011. (Illus.). 32p. (978-1-935884-11-8(5)); pap. (978-1-935884-16-3(6)) State Standards Publishing, LLC.
—Valley & Ridge. 2011. (Illus.). 32p. (J). (978-1-935884-13-2(1)); pap. (978-1-935884-18-7(2)) State Standards Publishing, LLC.
Bober, Natalie S. Thomas Jefferson: Draftsman of a Nation. 2008. (ENG., Illus.). 376p. per. 16.95 (978-0-8139-2732-9(3)) University of Virginia Pr.
Boehm Jerome, Kate. Richmond & the State of Virginia: Cool Stuff Every Kid Should Know. 2011. (Arcadia Kids Ser.). (ENG., Illus.). 48p. (J). (gr. 3-6). pap. 9.99 (978-1-4396-0098-6(8)) Arcadia Publishing.
Bridy, Dan & Solomon, Sharon K. Christopher Newport: Jamestown Explorer, 1 vol. 2013. (ENG., Illus.). 32p. (J). (gr. k-3). 16.99 (978-1-4556-1752-4(0)) Pelican Publishing Co., Inc.
Broyles, Janell. A Timeline of the Jamestown Colony. 2009. (Timelines of American History Ser.). 32p. (gr. 4-4). 47.90 (978-1-60854-385-4(4), Rosen Reference) Rosen Publishing Group, Inc., The.
Burrows, Jennifer. Arlington National Cemetery. 2009. (War Memorials Ser.). (Illus.). 32p. (YA). (gr. 3-6). lib. bdg. 29.95 (978-1-60694-425-7(8)) Rourke Educational Media.
Carole Marsh. Virginia Indians. 2004. (Virginia Experience Ser.). 36p. (gr. 3-8). 29.95 (978-0-635-02337-7(7)); pap. 7.95 (978-0-635-02336-0(9)) Gallopade International.
Connors, Kathleen. Visiting the Chesapeake Bay. 2013. 32p. (J). (gr. 3-6). 26.60 (978-1-4339-9788-4(6)); pap. 10.50 (978-1-4339-9789-1(4)) Stevens, Gareth Publishing LLLP.
Cooper, Michael L. Jamestown 1607. 2007. (ENG., Illus.). 112p. (J). (gr. 3-7). 18.95 (978-0-8234-1948-7(7)) Holiday Hse., Inc.
Cunningham, Kevin. The Virginia Colony. 2011. (True Bk Ser.). (ENG., Illus.). 48p. (J). pap. 6.95 (978-0-531-26612-0(5)); lib. bdg. 29.00 (978-0-531-25399-1(6)) Scholastic Library Publishing. (Children's Pr.).
Davidson, Tish. Atlantic: North Carolina, Virginia, West Virginia, Vol. 19. 2015. (Let's Explore the States Ser.). (Illus.). 64p. (J). (gr. 5). 23.95 (978-1-4222-3320-7(0)) Mason Crest.
Dean, Arlan. The Wilderness Trail: From the Shenandoah Valley to the Ohio River. 2009. (Famous American Trails Ser.). 24p. (gr. 3-3). 42.50 (978-1-61512-493-0(4), PowerKids Pr.) Rosen Publishing Group, Inc., The.
DeAngelis, Gina. Virginia. 2009. (From Sea to Shining Sea, Second Ser.). (ENG.). 80p. (J). pap. 7.95 (978-0-531-21144-1(4), Children's Pr.) Scholastic Library Publishing.
Ditchfield, Christin. Exploring the Virginia Colony. 2016. (Exploring the 13 Colonies Ser.). (ENG., Illus.). 48p. (gr. 3-4). lib. bdg. 31.99 (978-1-5157-2229-8(5)) Capstone Press of Coughlan Cos.
Doherty, Craig A. & Doherty, Katherine M. Virginia. 2005. (Thirteen Colonies Ser.). (Illus.). 144p. (gr. 5-8). 35.00 (978-0-8160-5416-9(9)) Facts On File, Inc.
Donohue, Moira Rose. Christopher Newport. 2013. (Illus.). 24p. (J). (978-1-938813-05-4(7)); pap. (978-1-938813-09-2(X)) State Standards Publishing, LLC.
—L. Douglas Wilder. 2012. (Illus.). 32p. (J). (978-1-935884-63-7(8)); pap. (978-1-935884-69-9(7)) State Standards Publishing, LLC.
—Maggie L. Walker. 2012. (Illus.). 32p. (J). (978-1-935884-62-0(X)); pap. (978-1-935884-68-2(9)) State Standards Publishing, LLC.

Dubois, Muriel L. Virginia. 2005. (Portraits of the States Ser.). (Illus.). 32p. (gr. 2-6). pap. 10.50 *(978-0-8368-4655-3(9))*; lib. bdg. 26.00 *(978-0-8368-4636-2(2))* Stevens, Gareth Publishing LLLP. (Gareth Stevens Learning Library).

Espinosa, Rod. Patrick Henry, 1 vol. Espinosa, Rod, illus. 2007. (Bio-Graphics Ser.). (ENG., Illus.). 32p. (gr. 3-6). 28.50 *(978-1-60270-070-3(2)*, Graphic Planet- Nonfiction) ABDO Publishing Co.

Exploring the Chesapeake Bay. 2013. (Exploring the Chesapeake Bay Ser.). 32p. (J). (gr. 3-6). 159.60 *(978-1-4339-9843-0(2))*; pap. 378.00 *(978-1-4339-9845-4(9))*; pap. 63.00 *(978-1-4339-9844-7(0))* Stevens, Gareth Publishing LLLP.

Fradin, Dennis Brindell. Jamestown, Virginia. 2007. (Turning Points in U. S. History Ser.). (Illus.). 48p. (gr. 3-7). lib. bdg. 31.36 *(978-0-7614-2122-1(X)*, Benchmark Bks.) Marshall Cavendish Corp.

Friedman, Robin. The Silent Witness: A True Story of the Civil War. Nivola, Claire A., illus. 2008. (ENG.). 32p. (J). (gr. -1-3). pap. 7.99 *(978-0-547-01436-4(8))* Houghton Mifflin Harcourt Publishing Co.

Gilman, Sarah. Colonial Jamestown. 2016. (Explore Colonial America Ser.). (Illus.). 48p. (J). (gr. 5-4). 27.93 *(978-0-7660-7871-0(X))* Enslow Pubs., Inc.

Gold, Susan Dudley. Parody of Public Figures: Hustler Magazine Inc. V. Falwell. 2013. (J). 42.79 *(978-1-60870-906-9(X))* Marshall Cavendish Corp.

—Parody of Public Figures: Hustler Magazine V. Falwell. 2014. pap. *(978-1-62712-391-4(1))*; lib. bdg. *(978-1-62712-390-7(3))* Cavendish Square Publishing.

Goldsworthy, Steve. Pentagon. 2012. (J). *(978-1-61913-260-3(5))*; (ENG., Illus.). 24p. (gr. 4-7). lib. bdg. 27.13 *(978-1-61913-254-2(0)*, AV2 by Weigl) Weigl Pubs., Inc.

Harkins, Susan Sales & Harkins, William H. Colonial Virginia. 2007. (Building America Ser.). (Illus.). 48p. (J). (gr. 4-8). lib. bdg. 29.95 *(978-1-58415-548-5(5))* Mitchell Lane Pubs., Inc.

The Hatfields & the McCoys. 2014. (Jr. Graphic American Legends Ser.). (Illus.). 24p. (J). (gr. 3-6). lib. bdg. 26.25 *(978-1-4777-7193-8(X)*, PowerKids Pr.) Rosen Publishing Group, Inc., The.

Higgins, Melissa. Jamestown Colony, 1 vol. 2013. (Foundations of Our Nation Ser.). (ENG.). 48p. (J). (gr. 3-6). lib. bdg. 32.79 *(978-1-61783-710-4(5))* ABDO Publishing Co.

History of the Chesapeake Bay. 2013. (Exploring the Chesapeake Bay Ser.). 32p. (J). (gr. 3-6). pap. 63.00 *(978-1-4339-9774-7(6))* Stevens, Gareth Publishing LLLP.

Huey, Lois Miner. American Archaeology Uncovers the Earliest English Colonies. 2009. (American Archaeology Ser.). 64p. (gr. 5-6). 31.36 *(978-0-7614-4264-6(2))* Marshall Cavendish Corp.

Jensen, Niels R. Virginia, 1 vol. 2009. (United States Ser.). (ENG., Illus.). 48p. (YA). (gr. 2-5). 27.07 *(978-1-60453-682-9(9))* ABDO Publishing Co.

Jerome, Kate B. Lucky to Live in Virginia. 2017. (Arcadia Kids Ser.). (ENG., Illus.). 32p. (J). 16.99 ***(978-0-7385-2775-8(0))*** Arcadia Publishing.

—The Wise Animal Handbook Virginia. 2017. (Arcadia Kids Ser.). (ENG., Illus.). 32p. (J). 16.99 ***(978-0-7385-2847-2(1))*** Arcadia Publishing.

Kallio, Jamie. What's Great about Virginia? 2014. (Our Great States Ser.). (ENG., Illus.). 32p. (gr. 2-5). pap. 7.95 *(978-1-4677-4530-7(8))*; lib. bdg. 26.60 *(978-1-4677-3341-0(5)*, Lerner Pubns.) Lerner Publishing Group.

Khalid, Jinnow. Arlington National Cemetery & the Tomb of the Unknown Soldier. 2017. (Landmarks of Democracy: American Institutions Ser.). 24p. (gr. 7-8). 23.60 ***(978-1-5081-6095-3(3)***, PowerKids Pr.) Rosen Publishing Group, Inc., The.

King, David C. & Fitzgerald, Stephanie. Virginia. 2015. (It's My State! Ser.). (ENG.). 80p. (J). (gr. 4-4). 34.21 *(978-1-5026-0019-6(6))* Cavendish Square Publishing.

—Virginia. 2nd rev. ed. 2010. (It's My State! Ser.). 80p. (gr. 3-18). lib. bdg. 31.36 *(978-1-60870-060-8(7))* Marshall Cavendish Corp.

Landau, Elaine. Explore Colonial Jamestown with Elaine Landau. 2006. (Explore Colonial America with Elaine Landau Ser.). (Illus.). 48p. (J). (gr. 3-7). lib. bdg. 25.27 *(978-0-7660-2554-7(3)*, Enslow Elementary) Enslow Pubs., Inc.

Levy, Janey. Life in Jamestown Colony, Vol. 1. 2014. (What You Didn't Know about History Ser.). (ENG.). 24p. (J). (gr. 2-3). 22.60 *(978-1-4824-0586-6(5))* Stevens, Gareth Publishing LLLP.

—Slavery at Mount Vernon. 2016. (Hidden History Ser.). 00032p. (J). pap. 10.50 *(978-1-4824-5802-2(0))* Stevens, Gareth Publishing LLLP.

Lusted, Marcia Amidon. The Jamestown Colony Disaster: A Cause-And-Effect Investigation. 2016. (Cause-And-Effect Disasters Ser.). (ENG., Illus.). 40p. (J). (gr. 4-6). lib. bdg. 30.65 *(978-1-5124-1116-4(7))*; 46.65 *(978-1-5124-1127-0(2)*, Lerner Pubns.) Lerner Publishing Group.

—Virginia: The Old Dominion. (Illus.). 24p. (J). 2010. pap. 8.25 *(978-1-4358-3372-2(4))* 2009. lib. bdg. 22.60 *(978-1-4042-8123-3(1))* Rosen Publishing Group, Inc., The. (PowerKids Pr.).

Marsh, Carole. Exploring Virginia Through Project-Based Learning: Geography, History, Government, Economics & More. 2016. (Virginia Experience Ser.). (ENG.). (J). pap. 9.99 *(978-0-635-12370-1(3))* Gallopade International.

—Virginia History Projects: 30 Cool, Activities, Crafts, Experiments & More for Kids to Do to Learn about Your State! 2003. (Virginia Experience Ser.). 32p. (gr. k-5). pap. 5.95 *(978-0-635-01815-1(2)*, Marsh, Carole Bks.) Gallopade International.

Marsico, Katie. The Chesapeake Bay. 2013. (Explorer Library: Social Studies Explorer Ser.). (ENG.). 32p. (gr. 4-8). pap. 14.21 *(978-1-62431-037-9(0)*, 202505); lib. bdg. 28.50 *(978-1-62431-013-3(3)*, 202503) Cherry Lake Publishing.

McClafferty, Carla Killough. Buried Lives: Slaves of George Washington's Mount Vernon. 2017. (J). ***(978-0-8234-3697-2(7))*** Holiday Hse., Inc.

McNeese, Tim. Jamestown. 2007. (Colonial Settlements in America Ser.). (Illus.). 112p. (YA). (gr. 5-9). lib. bdg. 30.00 *(978-0-7910-9335-1(2))* Facts On File, Inc.

—John Smith. 2010. (Leaders of the Colonial Era Ser.). 128p. (gr. 5-8). 35.00 *(978-1-60413-742-2(8)*, Chelsea Hse.) Facts On File, Inc.

—Williamsburg. 2007. (Colonial Settlements in America Ser.). (Illus.). 112p. (YA). (gr. 5-9). lib. bdg. 30.00 *(978-0-7910-9333-7(6))* Facts On File, Inc.

Miller, Jake. The Colony of Virginia: A Primary Source History. (Primary Source Library of the Thirteen Colonies & the Lost Colony Ser.). 24p. (gr. 3-4). 2009. 42.50 *(978-1-60854-162-1(2))* 2006. (Illus.). (J). lib. bdg. 22.60 *(978-1-4042-3029-3(7))* Rosen Publishing Group, Inc., The. (PowerKids Pr.).

Nagelhout, Ryan. Saving the Chesapeake Bay. 2013. (Exploring the Chesapeake Bay Ser.). (Illus.). 32p. (J). (gr. 3-6). pap. 10.50 *(978-1-4339-9785-3(1))*; (ENG., lib. bdg. 26.60 *(978-1-4339-9784-6(3))* Stevens, Gareth Publishing LLLP.

Nelson, Sheila. The Southern Colonies: The Quest for Prosperity. 2006. (How America Became America Ser.). (Illus.). 96p. (YA). lib. bdg. 22.95 *(978-1-59084-902-6(7))* Mason Crest.

Niver, Heather Moore. Tributaries of the Chesapeake Bay. 2013. (Exploring the Chesapeake Bay Ser.). (Illus.). 32p. (J). (gr. 3-6). pap. 10.50 *(978-1-4339-9793-8(2))*; lib. bdg. 26.60 *(978-1-4339-9792-1(4))* Stevens, Gareth Publishing LLLP.

Parker, Janice. Virginia. 2011. (Guide to American States Ser.). (Illus.). 48p. (J). (gr. 3-6). 29.99 *(978-1-61690-819-5(X))*; 29.99 *(978-1-61690-495-1(X))* Weigl Pubs., Inc.

—Virginia: The Old Dominion. 2016. (J). *(978-1-4896-4956-0(5)*, Berkley) Penguin Publishing Group.

—Virginia: The Old Dominion. 2016. (J). ***(978-1-5105-2097-4(X))*** SmartBook Media, Inc.

Pederson, Charles E. The Jamestown Colony, 1 vol. 2009. (Essential Events Set 3 Ser.). (ENG., Illus.). 112p. (J). (gr. 6-12). lib. bdg. 35.64 *(978-1-60453-515-0(6))* ABDO Publishing Co.

Petrie, Kristin. John Smith, 1 vol. 2007. (Explorers Set 2 Ser.). (ENG., Illus.). 32p. (gr. 4-7). 27.07 *(978-1-59679-751-2(7)*, Checkerboard Library) ABDO Publishing Co.

Pobst, Sandy. Virginia, 1607-1776. 2005. (National Geographic Voices from ColonialAmerica Ser.). (ENG., Illus.). 112p. (J). (gr. 5-9). 32.90 *(978-0-7922-6771-3(0)*, National Geographic Children's Bks.) National Geographic Society.

Pobst, Sandy & Roberts, Kevin D. Virginia, 1607-1776. 2005. (National Geographic Voices from ColonialAmerica Ser.). (ENG., Illus.). 112p. (J). (gr. 5-9). 21.95 *(978-0-7922-6388-3(X)*, National Geographic Children's Bks.) National Geographic Society.

Polette, Nancy. Pocahontas. 2003. (Rookie Biographies Ser.). (ENG., Illus.). 32p. (J). (gr. 1-2). 20.50 *(978-0-516-22859-4(5)*, Children's Pr.) Scholastic Library Publishing.

Porterfield, Jason. Virginia: Past & Present. 2009. 48p. (J). 70.50 *(978-1-4358-5577-9(9))*; pap. 11.75 *(978-1-4358-5576-2(0))*; (ENG., Illus.). lib. bdg. 29.25 *(978-1-4358-5289-1(3))* Rosen Publishing Group, Inc., The. (Rosen Reference).

Pratt, Laura. Virginia: The Old Dominion State. 2012. (J). *(978-1-61913-413-3(6))*; pap. *(978-1-61913-414-0(4))* Weigl Pubs., Inc.

Rossi, Anne. Bright Ideas: The Age of Invention in America 1870-1910. 2005. (Crossroads America Ser.). (ENG., Illus.). 40p. (J). (gr. 5-9). 12.95 *(978-0-7922-8276-1(0)*, National Geographic Children's Bks.) National Geographic Society.

Ruffin, Frances E. Jamestown. 2006. (Places in American History Ser.). (Illus.). 24p. (gr. 1-4). lib. bdg. 22.00 *(978-0-8368-6410-6(7)*, Weekly Reader Leveled Readers) Stevens, Gareth Publishing LLLP.

Schmid, Katie Kelley. Nat Turner & Slave Life on a Southern Plantation. 2013. (Jr. Graphic African American History Ser.). 24p. (J). (gr. 3-6). pap. 63.60 *(978-1-4777-1454-6(5))*; (ENG., Illus.). pap. 10.60 *(978-1-4777-1453-9(7))*; (ENG., Illus.). lib. bdg. 25.25 *(978-1-4777-1314-3(X))* Rosen Publishing Group, Inc., The. (PowerKids Pr.).

Schwartz, Heather E. Pocahontas: Her Life & Legend. 2016. (Primary Source Readers Ser.). (Illus.). 32p. (J). (gr. 4-5). pap. 8.99 *(978-1-4938-3072-5(4))* Teacher Created Materials, Inc.

Shea, Therese. History of the Chesapeake Bay. 2013. 32p. (J). (gr. 3-6). 26.60 *(978-1-4339-9772-3(X))*; pap. 10.50 *(978-1-4339-9773-0(8))* Stevens, Gareth Publishing LLLP.

Stansberry, Don & Cluster Springs Elementary School Staff. Skipping Through the ABC's of History. Barczak, Marliss & Long, Lisa, eds. 2011. (Illus.). 31p. (J). (gr. -1-3). 16.95 *(978-0-929915-50-0(X))* Headline Bks., Inc.

Stefoff, Rebecca. John Brown & Armed Resistance to Slavery. 2015. (Primary Sources of the Abolitionist Movement Ser.). (ENG., Illus.). 64p. (J). (gr. 6-6). 34.21 *(978-1-5026-0534-4(1))* Cavendish Square Publishing.

Sullivan, Laura L., et al. Virginia. 2015. (J). lib. bdg. *(978-1-62712-772-1(0))* Cavendish Square Publishing.

Temple, Bob. Arlington National Cemetery. 2014. (United States Landmarks Ser.). (ENG.). 24p. (J). (gr. 1-4). 27.07 *(978-1-62323-953-4(2)*, 206728) Child's World, Inc., The.

Thomas, Peggy. Farmer George Plants a Nation. Johnson, Layne, illus. 2008. (ENG.). 40p. (J). (gr. 4-6). 17.95 *(978-1-59078-460-0(X)*, Calkins Creek) Boyds Mills Pr.

Tieck, Sarah. Virginia, 1 vol. 2012. (Explore the United States Ser.). (ENG.). 32p. (J). (gr. 2-5). lib. bdg. 28.50 *(978-1-61783-385-4(1)*, Big Buddy Bks.) ABDO Publishing Co.

Tougas, Joe. Virginia. 2009. (This Land Called America Ser.). (Illus.). 32p. (YA). (gr. 3-6). 19.95 *(978-1-58341-799-7(0))* Creative Co., The.

Traylor, Waverley. Indian Legends of the Great Dismal Swamp. Traylor, Margaret, ed. Hancock, Stefanie, illus. 2004. 72p. (gr. 8-18). pap. 9.95 *(978-0-9715068-3-1(3))* Traylor, Waverley Publishing.

Tributaries of the Chesapeake Bay. 2013. (Exploring the Chesapeake Bay Ser.). 32p. (J). (gr. 3-6). pap. 63.00 *(978-1-4339-9794-5(0))* Stevens, Gareth Publishing LLLP.

Vansant, Wayne. Grant vs. Lee: The Graphic History of the Civil War's Greatest Rivals During the Last Year of the War. 2013. (Zenith Graphic Histories Ser.). (ENG., Illus.). 104p. pap. 19.99 *(978-0-7603-4531-3(7)*, 0760345317, Zenith Pr.) Quarto Publishing Group USA.

Visiting the Chesapeake Bay. 2013. (Exploring the Chesapeake Bay Ser.). 32p. (J). (gr. 3-6). pap. 63.00 *(978-1-4339-9790-7(8))* Stevens, Gareth Publishing LLLP.

Walker, Frank S., Jr. Remembering: A History of Orange County, Virginia. 2004. (Illus.). 314p. 30.00 *(978-1-932547-00-9(2))* Orange County Historical Society, Inc.

Way, Jennifer. Virginia. Brusca, Maria Cristina, tr. from ENG. 2006. (Bilingual Library of the United States of America Ser.: Set 2). (ENG & SPA., Illus.). 32p. (J). (gr. 3-6). lib. bdg. 25.25 *(978-1-4042-3112-2(9))* Rosen Publishing Group, Inc., The.

Whiteknact, Sandra. A Primary Source History of the Colony of Virginia. (Primary Sources of the Thirteen Colonies & the Lost Colony Ser.). 64p. 2009. (gr. 5-8). 58.50 *(978-1-60851-890-6(6))* 2006. (Illus.). (YA). (gr. 4-7). lib. bdg. 31.95 *(978-1-4042-0437-9(7))* 2006. (ENG., Illus.). (gr. 4-8). per. 12.95 *(978-1-4042-0678-6(7))* Rosen Publishing Group, Inc., The.

Worth, Richard. Massacre at Virginia Tech: Disaster & Survival. 2008. (Deadly Disasters Ser.). (Illus.). 48p. (J). (gr. 5-9). lib. bdg. 25.27 *(978-0-7660-3274-3(4))* Enslow Pubs., Inc.

VIRTUAL REALITY

Halls, Kelly Milner. Virtual Reality Specialist. 2009. (21st Century Skills Library: Cool Science Careers Ser.). (ENG.). 32p. (gr. 4-8). lib. bdg. 28.50 *(978-1-60279-503-7(7)*, 200307) Cherry Lake Publishing.

Henneberg, Susan, ed. Virtual Reality. 2017. (Opposing Viewpoints Ser.). 224p. (YA). (gr. 10-12). pap. 33.80 ***(978-1-5345-0030-3(8))***; lib. bdg. 48.80 ***(978-1-5345-0026-6(X))*** Greenhaven Publishing LLC. (Greenhaven Publishing).

Hollander, Barbara Gottfried. Bitcoins: Navigating Open Source Currency, 1 vol. 2015. (ENG.). 48p. (YA). 30.25 *(978-1-4777-7930-9(2)*, Rosen Reference) Rosen Publishing Group, Inc., The.

Martin, Brett S. Augmented Reality. 2017. (Tech Bytes Ser.). (ENG.). 48p. (J). (gr. 4-6). 26.60 ***(978-1-59953-886-0(5))***; pap. 13.26 ***(978-1-68404-117-6(1))*** Norwood Hse. Pr.

—Virtual Reality. 2017. (Tech Bytes Ser.). (ENG.). 48p. (J). (gr. 4-6). 26.60 ***(978-1-59953-885-3(7))***; pap. 13.26 ***(978-1-68404-120-6(1))*** Norwood Hse. Pr.

Mooney, Carla. What Is the Future of Virtual Reality? 2016. (ENG.). 80p. (J). (gr. 5-12). lib. bdg. *(978-1-68282-094-0(7))* ReferencePoint Pr., Inc.

Nagle, Jeanne. Getting to Know Alice. 2014. (Code Power: a Teen Programmer's Guide Ser.). (Illus.). 64p. (J). (gr. 5-8). 32.95 *(978-1-4777-7693-3(1)*, Rosen Reference) Rosen Publishing Group, Inc., The.

Rauf, Don. Virtual Reality, 01 vols., 1. 2016. (Digital & Information Literacy Ser.). (ENG.). 48p. (J). pap. 11.75 *(978-1-4994-3781-2(1)*, Rosen Central) Rosen Publishing Group, Inc., The.

Virtual Reality: Individual Title Six-Packs. (Bookweb Ser.). 32p. (gr. 6-18). 34.00 *(978-0-7578-0899-9(9))* Rigby Education.

VIRTUAL REALITY—FICTION

Anderson, Suzette. Cybertreks: Wildest West. 2004. 196p. pap. 13.95 *(978-0-595-30840-8(6))* iUniverse, Inc.

Bond, Gwenda. Fallout. 2016. (Lois Lane Ser.). (ENG.). 304p. (gr. 9-12). pap. 9.95 *(978-1-63079-006-6(0))* Switch Pr.

Brouwer, Sigmund. Counterattack. 2009. (Robot Wars Ser.: 4). (ENG.). 304p. (YA). pap. 6.99 *(978-1-4143-2312-1(3)*, Tyndale Kids) Tyndale Hse. Pubs.

—Final Battle. 2009. (Robot Wars Ser.: 5). (ENG.). 320p. (YA). pap. 7.99 *(978-1-4143-2313-8(1)*, Tyndale Kids) Tyndale Hse. Pubs.

Cole, Steve. Z. Rex. (ENG.). 256p. (J). (gr. 5-18). 2010. 8.99 *(978-0-14-241712-6(2)*, Puffin Books) 2009. 16.99 *(978-0-399-25253-2(3)*, Philomel Bks.) Penguin Young Readers Group.

Dashner, James. The Eye of Minds. 2013. 310p. (YA). *(978-0-385-38370-7(3)*, Delacorte Pr) Random House Publishing Group.

—The Eye of Minds. (Mortality Doctrine Ser.). (ENG.). (YA). (gr. 7). 2014. 342p. pap. 9.99 *(978-0-385-74140-8(5)*, Ember) 2013. 320p. 18.99 *(978-0-385-74139-2(1)*, Delacorte Pr.) Random Hse. Children's Bks.

—The Game of Lives. 2015. (Mortality Doctrine Ser.). (ENG.). 352p. (YA). (gr. 7). lib. bdg. 21.99 *(978-0-375-99003-8(8))*; 18.99 *(978-0-385-74143-9(X))* Random Hse. Children's Bks. (Delacorte Pr.).

—The Rule of Thoughts. (Mortality Doctrine Ser.). (ENG.). (YA). (gr. 7). 2014. 336p. 18.99 *(978-0-385-74141-5(3)*, Delacorte Pr.)Bk. 2. 2016. 352p. pap. 9.99 *(978-0-385-74142-2(1)*, Ember) Random Hse. Children's Bks.

Drake, Raelyn. Realm of Mystics. 2017. (Level Up Ser.). (ENG.). (YA). (gr. 6-12). 120p. pap. 7.99 ***(978-1-5124-5359-1(5))***; lib. bdg. 26.65 ***(978-1-5124-3989-2(4))*** Lerner Publishing Group. (Darby Creek).

Duckro, Rebecca S. Adventures of Charlie KeeperTechnobrat. 2006. 156p. per. 12.95 *(978-0-595-40498-8(7))* iUniverse, Inc.

Durango, Julia. The Leveller. 2015. (ENG.). 256p. (YA). (gr. 8). 17.99 *(978-0-06-231400-0(9)*, HarperTeen) HarperCollins Pubs.

Fields, Jan. Big City Blues: Back to Wonderland, 1 vol. Altmann, Scott, illus. 2013. (Adventures in Extreme Reading Ser.). (ENG.). 112p. (J). (gr. 3-6). 27.07 *(978-1-61641-923-3(7))* Magic Wagon.

—The Calm Before the Storm: A Night in Sleepy Hollow, 1 vol. Altmann, Scott, illus. 2013. (Adventures in Extreme Reading Ser.). (ENG.). 112p. (J). (gr. 3-6). 27.07 *(978-1-61641-920-2(2))* Magic Wagon.

—Hack Attack: A Trip to Wonderland, 1 vol. Altmann, Scott, illus. 2013. (Adventures in Extreme Reading Ser.). (ENG.). 112p. (J). (gr. 3-6). 27.07 *(978-1-61641-919-6(9))* Magic Wagon.

—Lightning Strikes Twice: Escaping Great Expectations, 1 vol. Altmann, Scott, illus. 2013. (Adventures in Extreme Reading Ser.). (ENG.). 112p. (J). (gr. 3-6). 27.07 *(978-1-61641-922-6(9))* Magic Wagon.

—A Novel Nightmare: The Purloined Story, 1 vol. Altmann, Scott, illus. 2013. (Adventures in Extreme Reading Ser.). (ENG.). 112p. (J). (gr. 3-6). 27.07 *(978-1-61641-924-0(5))* Magic Wagon.

—Trapped in Stormy Seas: Sailing to Treasure Island, 1 vol. Altmann, Scott, illus. 2013. (Adventures in Extreme Reading Ser.). (ENG.). 112p. (J). (gr. 3-6). 27.07 *(978-1-61641-921-9(0))* Magic Wagon.

Gabel, Claudia & Klam, Cheryl. Elusion. 2014. (Elusion Ser.: 1). (ENG.). 400p. (YA). (gr. 9). 17.99 *(978-0-06-212241-4(X)*, Tegen, Katherine Bks) HarperCollins Pubs.

—Etherworld. (Elusion Ser.: 2). 352p. (YA). (gr. 9). 2016. pap. 9.99 *(978-0-06-212245-2(2))* 2015. (ENG.). 17.99 *(978-0-06-212244-5(4))* HarperCollins Pubs. (Tegen, Katherine Bks).

Kawahara, Reki. Red Storm Princess, Vol. 2. 2014. (Accel World Ser.: 2). (ENG.). 256p. (YA). (gr. 8-17). pap. 13.00 *(978-0-316-29636-6(8)*, Yen Pr.) Orbit.

Kawahara, Reki & Paul, Stephen. Sword Art Online. Abec, illus. 2014. (YA). ***(978-0-316-39049-1(6)***, Yen Pr.) Orbit.

Keats, Israel. Alien Invasion. 2017. (Level Up Ser.). (ENG.). (J). (gr. 6-12). 120p. pap. 7.99 ***(978-1-5124-5356-0(0))***; lib. bdg. 26.65 ***(978-1-5124-3984-7(3))*** Lerner Publishing Group. (Darby Creek).

—Labyrinth. 2017. (Level Up Ser.). (ENG.). 128p. (YA). (gr. 6-12). 26.65 ***(978-1-5124-3987-8(8))***; pap. 7.99 ***(978-1-5124-5357-7(9))*** Lerner Publishing Group. (Darby Creek).

—The Zephyr Conspiracy. 2017. (Level Up Ser.). (ENG.). (YA). (gr. 6-12). 120p. pap. 7.99 ***(978-1-5124-5361-4(7))***; lib. bdg. 26.65 ***(978-1-5124-3985-4(1))*** Lerner Publishing Group. (Darby Creek).

Keene, Carolyn. Identity Theft. 34th ed. 2009. (Nancy Drew (All New) Girl Detective Ser.: 34). (ENG.). 176p. (J). (gr. 3-7). pap. 5.99 *(978-1-4169-6831-3(8)*, Aladdin) Simon & Schuster Children's Publishing.

Kincaid, S. J. Catalyst. 2014. (Insignia Ser.: 3). (ENG.). 432p. (YA). (gr. 8). 17.99 *(978-0-06-209305-9(3)*, Tegen, Katherine Bks) HarperCollins Pubs.

—Insignia. 2013. (Insignia Ser.: 1). (ENG.). 480p. (YA). (gr. 8). pap. 9.99 *(978-0-06-209300-4(2)*, Tegen, Katherine Bks) HarperCollins Pubs.

—Vortex. 2013. (Insignia Ser.: 2). (ENG.). 400p. (YA). (gr. 8). 17.99 *(978-0-06-209302-8(9)*, Tegen, Katherine Bks) HarperCollins Pubs.

MacHale, D. J. Black Water. 2007. (Pendragon Ser.: 5). (ENG., Illus.). 448p. (J). (gr. 5-9). 18.99 *(978-1-4169-5779-9(0)*, Aladdin) Simon & Schuster Children's Publishing.

—Pendragon: The Merchant of Death; The Lost City of Fear; The Never War; The Reality Bug; Black Water. 2013. (Pendragon Ser.). (ENG., Illus.). 1968p. (J). (gr. 5-9). pap. 49.99 *(978-1-4424-9926-3(5)*, Simon & Schuster/Paula Wiseman Bks.) Simon & Schuster/Paula Wiseman Bks.

Martin, R. Pod Racer. 2017. (Level Up Ser.). (ENG.). (YA). (gr. 6-12). 120p. pap. 7.99 ***(978-1-5124-5358-4(7))***; lib. bdg. 26.65 ***(978-1-5124-3988-5(6))*** Lerner Publishing Group. (Darby Creek).

—Safe Zone. 2017. (Level Up Ser.). (ENG.). (YA). (gr. 6-12). 112p. pap. 7.99 ***(978-1-5124-5360-7(9))***; lib. bdg. 26.65 ***(978-1-5124-3986-1(X))*** Lerner Publishing Group. (Darby Creek).

McGrath, Robin. Livyers World. 2007. (ENG.). 150p. (J). (gr. 4-7). per. *(978-1-897174-15-9(2))* Creative Bk. Publishing.

Seven, John. The Terror of the Tengu, 1 vol. Hans, Stephanie, illus. 2014. (Time-Tripping Faradays Ser.). (ENG.). 192p. (gr. 4-5). 26.65 *(978-1-4342-9173-8(1))* Stone Arch Bks.

Sharpe, Gerald. Parade of Lights. Moya, Patricia, illus. 2007. (What Lies Beneath the Bed Ser.). 487p. (J). per. 11.00 *(978-1-933894-01-0(6))* IJN Publishing, Inc.

Skurzynski, Gloria. Afterwar. 2011. (ENG., Illus.). 528p. (YA). (gr. 7). pap. 9.99 *(978-1-4424-1681-9(5)*, Atheneum Bks. for Young Readers) Simon & Schuster Children's Publishing.

Snow, Carol. Bubble World. 2014. (ENG.). 352p. (YA). (gr. 7). pap. 9.99 *(978-1-250-04441-9(3)*, 9781250044419) Square Fish.

Stokes, Paula. Vicarious. 2016. (Vicarious Ser.). (ENG.). 336p. (YA). 17.99 *(978-0-7653-8094-4(3)*, 9780765380944, Tor Teen) Doherty, Tom Assocs., LLC.

Strange, Jason. Realm of Ghosts, 1 vol. Parks, Phil, illus. 2011. (Jason Strange Ser.). (ENG.). 72p. (gr. 2-3). pap. 6.25 *(978-1-4342-3096-6(1))*; 25.32 *(978-1-4342-2962-5(9))* Stone Arch Bks.

Valentine, Stephen J. The Lazarus Game. 2015. 311p. (YA). pap. 19.99 *(978-1-4621-1554-9(3))* Cedar Fort, Inc./CFI Distribution.

Vande Velde, Vivian. Deadly Pink. (ENG.). 288p. (J). (gr. 5-7). 2013. pap. 6.99 *(978-0-544-02278-2(5))* 2012. 16.99 *(978-0-547-73850-5(1))* Houghton Mifflin Harcourt Publishing Co.

—Heir Apparent. 2004. (ENG., Illus.). 352p. (J). (gr. 5-7). reprint ed. pap. 7.99 *(978-0-15-205125-9(2))* Houghton Mifflin Harcourt Publishing Co.

Watson, Carrie Gordon. Ascending the Boneyard. 2017. (ENG.). 272p. (YA). (gr. 9). pap. 10.99 *(978-1-4814-3185-9(4)*, Simon Pulse) Simon Pulse.

Wayne, Matt. Attack of the Virtual Villains. Moy, Philip, illus. 2012. (Batman: the Brave & the Bold Ser.). (ENG.). 32p. (gr. 2-3). lib. bdg. 22.60 *(978-1-4342-4546-5(2))* Stone Arch Bks.

West, Tracey, adapted by. Jack in! MegaMan! 2006. 59p. (J). *(978-0-439-76837-5(3))* Scholastic, Inc.

Zucker, Jonny. Mission 1: Game On. Woodman, Ned, illus. 2013. (Max Flash Ser.: 1). (ENG.). 144p. (gr. 2-5). pap. 7.95 *(978-1-4677-1465-5(8))*; lib. bdg. 27.93 *(978-1-4677-1207-1(8))* Lerner Publishing Group. (Darby Creek).

VIRUSES

Abramovitz, Melissa. West Nile Virus. (Diseases & Disorders Ser.). (ENG., Illus.). 2013. 128p. (gr. 7-10). lib. bdg. 39.90 *(978-1-4205-0936-6(5))* 2003. 96p. (J). 33.45 *(978-1-59018-343-4(6))* Cengage Gale. (Lucent Bks.).

Berger, Melvin. Germs Make Me Sick! Hafner, Marylin, illus. 2015. (Let's-Read-And-Find-Out Science 2 Ser.). (ENG.). 32p. (J). (gr. -1-3). pap. 6.99 *(978-0-06-238187-3(3))* HarperCollins Pubs.

—Germs Make Me Sick! 2015. (Let's Read & Find Out Science Stage 2 Ser.). (J). lib. bdg. 17.20 *(978-0-606-37742-3(5))* Turtleback Bks.

Berlatsky, Noah. The H1N1 Flu. 2010. (At Issue Ser.). (ENG.). 128p. (gr. 10-12). 39.40 *(978-0-7377-5089-8(8))*; pap. 27.80 *(978-0-7377-5090-4(1))* Cengage Gale. (Greenhaven Pr., Inc.).

TUV

Biskup, Agnieszka. Understanding Viruses with Max Axiom, Super Scientist, 1 vol. 2010. (Graphic Science Ser.). (ENG.). 32p. (gr. 3-4). pap. 8.10 *(978-1-4296-3453-3(7)*, Graphic Library) Capstone Press of Coughlan Cos.

Bringle, Jennifer. Young Women & the HPV Vaccine. 2011. (Girls' Health Ser.). (Illus.). 48p. (YA). (gr. 5-9). lib. bdg. 29.25 *(978-1-4488-4575-0(0))* Rosen Publishing Group, Inc., The.

Brunelle, Lynn & Gave, Marc. Viruses. 2003. (Discovery Channel School Science Ser.). (Illus.). 32p. (gr. 4-8). lib. bdg. 26.00 *(978-0-8368-3375-1(9)*, Gareth Stevens Learning Library) Stevens, Gareth Publishing LLLP.

Bueche, Shelley. The Ebola Virus. 2003. (Parasites Ser.). (ENG., Illus.). 32p. (J). 27.80 *(978-0-7377-1780-8(7)*, Greenhaven Pr., Inc.) Cengage Gale.

Carter, Elizabeth. Everything You Need to Know about Human Papillomavirus. 2009. (Need to Know Library). 64p. (gr. 5-5). 58.50 *(978-1-60854-073-0(1))* Rosen Publishing Group, Inc., The.

Casil, Amy Sterling. Hantavirus. 2004. (Epidemics Ser.). (Illus.). 64p. (YA). (gr. 7-12). lib. bdg. 31.95 *(978-1-4042-0254-2(4))* Rosen Publishing Group, Inc., The.

Chakraborty, Tirtha. Dengue Fever & Other Hemorrhagic Viruses. 2008. (Deadly Diseases & Epidemics Ser.). 102p. (C). (gr. 9). 34.95 *(978-0-7910-8506-6(6)*, Chelsea Hse.) Facts On File, Inc.

Cline-Ransome, Lesa. Germs: Sickness, Bad Breath, & Pizza. Ransome, James, illus. 2017. (ENG.). 40p. (J). 17.99 *(978-0-8050-7915-9(7)*, 9780805079159, Holt, Henry & Co. Bks. For Young Readers) Holt, Henry & Co.

Close, Edward. Germ Warfare, 1 vol., 1. 2014. (Discovery Education: How It Works). (ENG.). 32p. (gr. 3-6). pap. 10.00 *(978-1-4777-6301-8(5)*, PowerKids Pr.) Rosen Publishing Group, Inc., The.

Eaton, Louise & Rogers, Kara. Examining Viruses & Bacteria. 2017. (J). lib. bdg. ***(978-1-5383-0009-1(5))*** Rosen Publishing Group, Inc., The.

Ebola & Marburg Virus. 2nd rev. ed. 2010. (Deadly Diseases & Epidemics Ser.). (Illus.). 104p. (C). (gr. 9). 34.95 *(978-1-60413-252-6(3)*, Chelsea Hse.) Facts On File, Inc.

Goldsmith, Connie. Influenza. 2010. (USA TODAY Health Reports: Diseases & Disorders Ser.). (ENG.). 128p. (gr. 6-12). lib. bdg. 34.60 *(978-0-7613-5881-7(1))* Lerner Publishing Group.

Goldstein, Margaret J. Everything You Need to Know about Multiple Sclerosis. 2009. (Need to Know Library). 64p. (gr. 5-5). 58.50 *(978-1-60854-078-5(2))* Rosen Publishing Group, Inc., The.

Goldstein, Natalie. Viruses. (Germs: the Library of Disease-Causing Organisms Ser.). 48p. 2009. (gr. 5-5). 53.00 *(978-1-61512-719-1(4))* 2004. (Illus.). (gr. 7-12). lib. bdg. 29.25 *(978-0-8239-4496-5(4))* Rosen Publishing Group, Inc., The.

Goldstein, Natalie & Baum, Margaux. Viruses. 2016. (Germs: Disease Causing Organisms Ser.). 48p. (J). (gr. 5-5). pap. 11.75 *(978-1-4777-8855-4(7)*, Rosen Reference) Rosen Publishing Group, Inc., The.

Halvorson, Karin. Inside Your Germs, 1 vol. 2016. (Super Simple Body Set 2 Ser.). (ENG., Illus.). 32p. (J). (gr. k-4). 27.07 *(978-1-62403-944-7(8))* ABDO Publishing Co.

Hirschmann, Kris. The Ebola Virus. 2006. (Diseases & Disorders Ser.). (ENG., Illus.). 104p. (J). (gr. 7-12). lib. bdg. 34.95 *(978-1-59018-672-5(9))* Cengage Gale.

Holt, Rinehart and Winston Staff. Holt Science & Technology Chapter 10: Life Science: Bacteria & Viruses. 5th ed. 2004. (Illus.). pap. 12.86 *(978-0-03-030206-0(4))* Holt McDougal.

Jones, Phill. Viruses. 2011. (Science Foundations Ser.). (Illus.). 138p. (gr. 6-12). lib. bdg. 35.00 *(978-1-60413-341-7(4)*, Chelsea Hse.) Facts On File, Inc.

Leuenroth, Stephanie. Hantavirus Pulmonary Syndrome. 2006. (Deadly Diseases & Epidemics Ser.). (Illus.). 112p. (C). (gr. 9-12). 34.95 *(978-0-7910-8676-6(3)*, Chelsea Hse.) Facts On File, Inc.

Markovics, Joyce L. Tiny Invaders! Deadly Microorganisms, 1 vol. 2013. (Nature's Invaders Ser.). (ENG.). 32p. (gr. 3-4). lib. bdg. 27.99 *(978-1-4765-0142-0(4))* Capstone Press of Coughlan Cos.

May, Suellen. Invasive Microbes. 2007. (Invasive Species Ser.). (Illus.). 100p. (gr. 6-12). lib. bdg. 30.00 *(978-0-7910-9131-9(7)*, Chelsea Hse.) Facts On File, Inc.

Nardo, Don. Human Papillomavirus (HPV) 2007. (Diseases & Disorders Ser.). (ENG., Illus.). 104p. (YA). (gr. 7-12). lib. bdg. 34.95 *(978-1-59018-998-6(1))* Cengage Gale.

Plumb, Jennifer. Everything You Need to Know about Chicken Pox & Shingles. 2009. (Need to Know Library). 64p. (gr. 5-5). 58.50 *(978-1-60854-057-0(X))* Rosen Publishing Group, Inc., The.

Rake, Jody Sullivan. Why Feet Smell & Other Gross Facts about Your Body, 1 vol. 2012. (Gross Me Out Ser.). (ENG.). 24p. (gr. 1-2). pap. 7.29 *(978-1-4296-7955-8(7))*; pap. 41.70 *(978-1-4296-8377-7(5))*; lib. bdg. 25.32 *(978-1-4296-7610-6(8))* Capstone Press of Coughlan Cos. (First Facts).

Romanek, Trudee. Achoo! Cowles, Rose, illus. 2003. (Mysterious You Ser.). (ENG.). 40p. (J). (gr. 4-9). pap. 8.95 *(978-1-55337-451-0(7))* Kids Can Pr., Ltd. CAN. Dist: Hachette Bk. Group.

Shea, John. Combating Computer Viruses. 2012. (Cyberspace Survival Guide Ser.). (Illus.). 32p. (J). (gr. 3-6). 26.60 *(978-1-4339-7212-6(3))*; pap. 10.50 *(978-1-4339-7213-3(1))* Stevens, Gareth Publishing LLLP. (Gareth Stevens Learning Library).

Shea, John M. Viruses up Close. 2013. 32p. (J). (gr. 4-6). 26.60 *(978-1-4339-8354-2(0))*; pap. 11.70 *(978-1-4339-8355-9(9))* Stevens, Gareth Publishing LLLP.

Viruses up Close. 2013. (Under the Microscope Ser.). 32p. (J). (gr. 4-6). pap. 70.20 *(978-1-4339-8356-6(7))* Stevens, Gareth Publishing LLLP.

Yount, Lisa. Luc Montagnier. 2011. (Trailblazers in Science & Technology Ser.). 144p. (gr. 6-12). 35.00 *(978-1-60413-661-6(8)*, Chelsea Hse.) Facts On File, Inc.

VISION

see also Blind; Eye; Optical Illusions

Aloian, Molly. What Is Sight? 2013. (ENG., Illus.). 24p. (J). *(978-0-7787-0969-5(8))*; pap. *(978-0-7787-0996-1(5))* Crabtree Publishing Co.

Appleby, Alex. What I See. 2014. (My Five Senses Ser.). 24p. (J). (gr. k-2). 22.60 *(978-1-4824-0808-9(2))* Stevens, Gareth Publishing LLLP.

Ballard, Carol. Why Do I Need Glasses? Vision, 1 vol. 2011. (Inside My Body Ser.). (ENG.). 32p. (gr. 3-5). 30.65 *(978-1-4109-4010-0(1)*, NA-r) Heinemann-Raintree.

Barnham, Kay. Sight. 2005. (Our Senses Ser.). (Illus.). 24p. (gr. k-3). lib. bdg. 23.00 *(978-0-8368-4407-8(6)*, Gareth Stevens Learning Library) Stevens, Gareth Publishing LLLP.

Barraclough, Sue. What Can I See? 2005. (J). *(978-1-4034-7080-5(4))*; (ENG.). 32p. pap. *(978-1-4034-7086-7(3))* Steck-Vaughn.

Beaumont, Susanna. Baby Senses Sight. 2005. (Baby Senses Ser.). (Illus.). 12p. (gr. -1-k). per., bds. *(978-1-905051-48-9(4))* Make Believe Ideas.

Beckering, Analise. Sight. 2009. (World of Wonder Ser.). (Illus.). 24p. (J). (gr. 2-4). pap. 8.95 *(978-1-60596-053-1(5))* Weigl Pubs., Inc.

Bekkering, Annalise. Sight. 2009. (World of Wonder Ser.). (Illus.). 24p. (J). (gr. 2-4). lib. bdg. 24.45 *(978-1-60596-052-4(7))* Weigl Pubs., Inc.

Bellamy, Adam. What's That I See? 2017. (All about My Senses Ser.). 24p. (J). (gr. k-1). lib. bdg. 22.60 ***(978-0-7660-8605-0(4))*** Enslow Pubs., Inc.

Biskup, Agnieszka. The Science Behind Superman's Sight. 2017. (Science Behind Superman Ser.). (ENG.). 24p. (gr. 1-2). lib. bdg. 25.32 *(978-1-5157-5098-7(1)*, DC Super Heroes) Stone Arch Bks.

—Seeing Through Walls: Superman & the Science of Sight. 2016. (Superman Science Ser.). (ENG., Illus.). 32p. (gr. 3-4). lib. bdg. 27.32 *(978-1-5157-0912-1(4)*, DC Super Heroes) Stone Arch Bks.

Biskup, Agnieszka & Enz, Tammy. Science Behind Superman. 2017. (Science Behind Superman Ser.). (ENG.). 24p. (gr. 1-2). 101.28 *(978-1-5157-5116-8(3)*, DC Super Heroes) Stone Arch Bks.

Boothroyd, Jennifer. Light Helps Me See. 2014. (First Step Nonfiction - Light & Sound Ser.). (Illus.). 24p. (gr. k-2). lib. bdg. 23.93 *(978-1-4677-3911-5(1)*, Lerner Pubns.) Lerner Publishing Group.

—Vision: Nearsightedness, Farsightedness, & More. 2012. (Lightning Bolt Books (tm) — What Traits Are in Your Genes? Ser.). (Illus.). 32p. (gr. k-2). (SPA & ENG.). pap. 7.95 *(978-1-58013-958-8(2))*; (ENG., lib. bdg. 26.60 *(978-0-7613-8940-8(7)*, Lerner Pubns.) Lerner Publishing Group.

—What Is Sight? 2009. (Lightning Bolt Books (tm) — Your Amazing Senses Ser.). (ENG.). 32p. (gr. k-2). 26.60 *(978-0-7613-4248-9(6)*, Lerner Pubns.); pap. 7.95 *(978-0-7613-5015-6(2))* Lerner Publishing Group.

Carr, Aaron. Vista. 2014. (SPA., Illus.). 24p. (J). *(978-1-62127-577-0(9))* Weigl Pubs., Inc.

Caster, Shannon. Eyes. 2010. (Body Works Ser.). (Illus.). 24p. (J). pap. 8.25 *(978-1-4358-9826-4(5)*, PowerKids Pr.) Rosen Publishing Group, Inc., The.

Coan, Sharon. Message Received!, 1 vol. rev. ed. 2014. (Science Readers: Content & Literacy Ser.). (ENG., Illus.). 24p. (gr. 1-1). pap. 8.99 *(978-1-4807-4565-0(0))* Teacher Created Materials, Inc.

Dayton, Connor. Sight. 2014. (Your Five Senses & Your Sixth Sense Ser.). 24p. (J). (gr. k-2). (Illus.). 22.60 *(978-1-4777-2850-5(3))*;1. (ENG.). pap. 8.25 *(978-1-4777-2851-2(1))* Rosen Publishing Group, Inc., The. (PowerKids Pr.).

—La Vista / Sight, 1 vol., 1. De La Vega, Eida, ed. 2014. (Tus Cinco Sentidos y Tu Sexto Sentido / Your Five Senses & Your Sixth Sense Ser.). (SPA & BYN.). 24p. (J). (gr. k-2). 23.60 *(978-1-4777-3265-6(9)*, PowerKids Pr.) Rosen Publishing Group, Inc., The.

Douglas, Lloyd G. My Eyes. 2004. (Wel-My Body Ser.). (J). 19.00 *(978-0-516-24060-2(9)*, Children's Pr.) Scholastic Library Publishing.

Durrie, Karen. Sight. 2012. (J). *(978-1-61913-310-5(5))*; pap. *(978-1-61913-315-0(6))* Weigl Pubs., Inc.

Enslow, Brian. My Eyes. 2010. (All about My Body Ser.). (Illus.). 24p. (J). 22.60 *(978-0-7660-3813-4(0))*; pap. 7.95 *(978-1-59845-169-6(3))* Enslow Pubs., Inc. (Enslow Elementary).

ETA/Cuisenaire Staff. I See. 2003. (SunSprouts Ser.). (ENG.). (gr. -1-3). pap. 4.95 *(978-0-7406-2104-8(1)*, SunSprouts) ETA hand2mind.

Francis, Suzanne, et al. Spy by Night: Stealth & Secrets after Dark. 2007. (Illus.). 32p. (J). pap. *(978-0-545-01557-8(X))* Scholastic, Inc.

Furgang, Kathy. My Eyes. 2009. (My Body Ser.). 24p. (gr. 3-3). 42.50 *(978-1-61514-688-8(1)*, PowerKids Pr.) Rosen Publishing Group, Inc., The.

Ganeri, Anita. Sight. 2013. (Senses Ser.). 24p. (gr. k-3). 28.50 *(978-1-59920-852-7(0))* Black Rabbit Bks.

Gifford, Clive. Eye Benders: The Science of Seeing & Believing. 2014. (ENG.). 64p. (J). (gr. 5-9). pap. 9.99 *(978-1-4380-0366-5(8))* Barron's Educational Series, Inc.

Gray, Susan H. Vision. 2008. (21st Century Skills Innovation Library: Innovation in Medicine Ser.). (ENG., Illus.). 32p. (gr. 4-8). lib. bdg. 28.50 *(978-1-60279-226-5(7)*, 200157) Cherry Lake Publishing.

Hall, Kirsten. Animal Sight. 2005. (Animals & Their Senses Ser.). (Illus.). 24p. (gr. k-3). pap. 8.15 *(978-0-8368-4809-0(8))*; lib. bdg. 22.00 *(978-0-8368-4803-8(9))* Stevens, Gareth Publishing LLLP. (Weekly Reader Leveled Readers).

—Animal Sight: La Vista de los Animales. 2005. (Animals & Their Senses/ Los sentidos de los animales (bilingual) Ser.). (ENG & SPA., Illus.). 24p. (gr. k-3). pap. 8.15 *(978-0-8368-4821-2(7)*, Weekly Reader Leveled Readers) Stevens, Gareth Publishing LLLP.

—Animal Sight/La Vista de los Animales. 2005. (Animals & Their Senses/ Los sentidos de los animales Ser.). (ENG & SPA., Illus.). 24p. (gr. k-3). lib. bdg. 22.00 *(978-0-8368-4815-1(2)*, Weekly Reader Leveled Readers) Stevens, Gareth Publishing LLLP.

Halvorson, Karin. Inside the Eyes, 1 vol. 2013. (Super Simple Your Body Ser.). (ENG.). 32p. (J). (gr. k-4). 27.07 *(978-1-61783-611-4(7))* ABDO Publishing Co.

Hewitt, Sally. Look Here! 2008. (Let's Start Science Ser.). (ENG.). 24p. (J). pap. *(978-0-7787-4059-9(5))* Crabtree Publishing Co.

Hidalgo, Maria. Sight. 2003. 24p. (J). lib. bdg. 21.35 *(978-1-58340-303-7(5))* Black Rabbit Bks.

Huddle, Rusty & Viegas, Jennifer. The Eye in 3D. 2015. (Human Body in 3D Ser.). (ENG., Illus.). 64p. (J). (gr. 5-6). 32.95 *(978-1-4994-3589-4(4)*, Rosen Central) Rosen Publishing Group, Inc., The.

Issa, Joanna. What Can I See?, 1 vol. 2014. (These Are My Senses Ser.). (ENG., Illus.). 24p. (gr. -1-1). pap. 5.99 *(978-1-4846-0431-1(8)*, Acorn) Heinemann-Raintree.

Jacobson, Ryan. Step-by-Step Experiments with Light & Vision. Ostrom, Bob, illus. 2012. (Step-By-Step Experiments Ser.). (ENG.). 32p. (J). (gr. 1-4). lib. bdg. 29.93 *(978-1-60973-588-3(9)*, 201233) Child's World, Inc., The.

Klingel, Cynthia & Noyed, Robert B. Eyes / Los Ojos. 2010. (Let's Read about Our Bodies / Hablemos del cuerpo humano Ser.). (SPA., Illus.). 24p. (gr. k-3). pap. 8.15 *(978-1-4339-3733-0(6))* Stevens, Gareth Publishing LLLP.

Kubler, Annie, illus. What Can I See? 2011. (Small Senses Ser.). (ENG.). 12p. (J). bds. *(978-1-84643-378-8(9))* Child's Play International Ltd.

Lauber, Patricia. What You Never Knew about Beds, Bedrooms, & Pajamas. Manders, John, illus. 2008. (ENG.). 40p. (J). (gr. 1-4). 6.99 *(978-1-4169-6738-5(9)*, Simon & Schuster Bks. For Young Readers) Simon & Schuster Bks. For Young Readers.

Lay, Kathryn. Seeing Their Prey: Animals with an Amazing Sense of Sight, 1 vol. Wald, Christina, illus. 2012. (Sensing Their Prey Ser.). (ENG.). 32p. (J). (gr. -1-4). lib. bdg. 28.50 *(978-1-61641-867-0(2)*, Looking Glass Library) Magic Wagon.

Llewellyn, Claire. Seeing. 2005. (I Know That! Ser.). (Illus.). 24p. (J). (gr. 1-3). lib. bdg. 22.80 *(978-1-932889-48-2(5))* Sea-To-Sea Pubns.

Loria, Laura. The Eyes in Your Body, 1 vol. 2015. (ENG.). 32p. (J). 23.45 *(978-1-62275-648-3(7)*, Britannica Educational Publishing) Rosen Publishing Group, Inc., The.

Lowery, Lawrence F. Look & See: I Wonder Why. 2017. (I Wonder Why Ser.). (ENG., Illus.). 36p. (J). (gr. k-2). pap. 11.95 *(978-1-68140-355-7(2))* National Science Teachers Assn.

Macaulay, David & Keenan, Sheila. Eye: How It Works. 2015. (ENG., Illus.). 32p. (J). (gr. 1-4). 17.99 *(978-1-62672-212-5(9)*, 9781626722125, Macaulay, David Studio) Roaring Brook Pr.

Mandy and Ness Staff, et al. Rosie's Room. 2005. (Senses Ser.). (URD, ENG, TUR, VIE & CHI., Illus.). 16p. (J). (gr. -1-1). pap. 9.95 *(978-1-84059-162-0(5))* Milet Publishing.

Markle, Sandra. Lost Sight. 2010. (Powerful Medicine Ser.). (ENG., Illus.). 48p. (gr. 5-8). lib. bdg. 27.93 *(978-0-8225-8701-9(7))* Lerner Publishing Group.

Meachen Rau, Dana. Look! [Scholastic]: A Book about Sight. Peterson, Rick, illus. 2010. (Amazing Body: the Five Senses Ser.). 24p. pap. 0.56 *(978-1-4048-4390-5(6)*, Nonfiction Picture Bks.) Picture Window Bks.

Milet Publishing Staff. My Bilingual Book - Sight. 2014. (My Bilingual Book Ser.). (ENG & TUR., Illus.). 28p. (J). (gr. -1-k). 9.95 *(978-1-84059-801-8(8))* Milet Publishing.

—My Bilingual Book-Sight. 2014. (My Bilingual Book Ser.). (ENG & KOR., Illus.). 28p. (J). (gr. -1-k). 9.95 *(978-1-84059-795-0(X))* Milet Publishing.

—My Bilingual Book-Sight (English-Bengali) 2014. (My Bilingual Book Ser.). (ENG & BEN., Illus.). 28p. (J). (gr. -1-k). 9.95 *(978-1-84059-789-9(5))* Milet Publishing.

—My Bilingual Book-Sight (English-Chinese) 2014. (My Bilingual Book Ser.). (ENG & CHI., Illus.). 28p. (J). (gr. -1-k). 9.95 *(978-1-84059-790-5(9))* Milet Publishing.

—My Bilingual Book-Sight (English-Farsi) 2014. (My Bilingual Book Ser.). (ENG & PER., Illus.). 28p. (J). (gr. -1-k). 9.95 *(978-1-84059-791-2(7))* Milet Publishing.

—My Bilingual Book-Sight (English-French) 2014. (My Bilingual Book Ser.). (ENG & FRE., Illus.). 28p. (J). (gr. -1-k). 9.95 *(978-1-84059-792-9(5))* Milet Publishing.

—My Bilingual Book-Sight (English-German) 2014. (My Bilingual Book Ser.). (ENG & GER., Illus.). 28p. (J). (gr. -1-k). 9.95 *(978-1-84059-793-6(3))* Milet Publishing.

—My Bilingual Book-Sight (English-Italian) 2014. (My Bilingual Book Ser.). (ENG & ITA., Illus.). 28p. (J). (gr. -1-k). 9.95 *(978-1-84059-794-3(1))* Milet Publishing.

—My Bilingual Book-Sight (English-Polish) 2014. (My Bilingual Book Ser.). (ENG, POL & POR., Illus.). 28p. (J). (gr. -1-k). 9.95 *(978-1-84059-796-7(8))* Milet Publishing.

—My Bilingual Book-Sight (English-Portuguese) 2014. (My Bilingual Book Ser.). (ENG & POR., Illus.). 28p. (J). (gr. -1-k). 9.95 *(978-1-84059-797-4(6))* Milet Publishing.

—My Bilingual Book-Sight (English-Russian) 2014. (My Bilingual Book Ser.). (ENG & RUS., Illus.). 28p. (J). (gr. -1-k). 9.95 *(978-1-84059-798-1(4))* Milet Publishing.

—My Bilingual Book-Sight (English-Somali) 2014. (My Bilingual Book Ser.). (ENG & SOM., Illus.). 28p. (J). (gr. -1-k). 9.95 *(978-1-84059-799-8(2))* Milet Publishing.

—My Bilingual Book-Sight (English-Spanish) 2014. (My Bilingual Book Ser.). (ENG & SPA., Illus.). 28p. (J). (gr. -1-k). 9.95 *(978-1-84059-800-1(X))* Milet Publishing.

—My Bilingual Book-Sight (English-Urdu) 2014. (My Bilingual Book Ser.). (ENG & URD., Illus.). 28p. (J). (gr. -1-k). 9.95 *(978-1-84059-802-5(6))* Milet Publishing.

—My Bilingual Book-Sight (English-Vietnamese) 2014. (My Bilingual Book Ser.). (ENG & VIE., Illus.). 28p. (J). (gr. -1-k). 9.95 *(978-1-84059-803-2(4))* Milet Publishing.

—Sight - English-Arabic. 2014. (My Bilingual Book Ser.). (ENG & ARA., Illus.). 28p. (J). (gr. -1-k). 9.95 *(978-1-84059-788-2(7))* Milet Publishing.

Mlawer, Teresa, tr. What Do I See? / ¿Qué Veo? Kubler, Annie, illus. 2015. (Small Senses Bilingual Ser.: 5). (ENG & SPA.). 12p. (J). bds. *(978-1-84643-725-0(3))* Child's Play International Ltd.

Morgan, Sally. How Sight Works. 2010. (Our Senses Ser.). 24p. (J). (gr. k-2). pap. 8.25 *(978-1-61532-559-7(X)*, PowerKids Pr.); (Illus.). (gr. -1-2). lib. bdg. 22.60 *(978-1-61532-553-5(0))* Rosen Publishing Group, Inc., The.

Morris, Kim Ely. Through the Eyes of Love. 2009. (Illus.). 24p. pap. 14.99 *(978-1-4389-6756-1(X))* AuthorHouse.

Murphy, Patricia J. Sight. 2003. (True Bks.). (ENG.). 48p. (J). 3-5). pap. 6.95 *(978-0-516-26968-9(2)*, Children's Pr.) Scholastic Library Publishing.

Murray, Julie. I Can See, 1 vol. 2016. (ENG., Illus.). 24p. (J). *(978-1-62970-926-0(3)*, 1391207) ABDO Publishing Co.

Nelson, Robin. La Vista. Translations.com Staff, tr. from ENG. 2006. (Mi Primer Paso Al Mundo Real - Los Sentidos (First Step Nonfiction - Senses) Ser.). (SPA., Illus.). 24p. (gr. k-2). lib. bdg. 23.93 *(978-0-8225-6222-1(7)*, Ediciones Lerner) Lerner Publishing Group.

—La Vista (Seeing) 2006. (Mi Primer Paso al Mundo Real Ser.). (Illus.). 23p. (J). (gr. -1-3). per. 5.95 *(978-0-8225-6545-1(5)*, Ediciones Lerner) Lerner Publishing Group.

PatrickGeorge Staff. I See... 2013. (ENG., Illus.). 36p. (J). (gr. -1-k). 12.99 *(978-1-908473-04-2(5))* PatrickGeorge GBR. Dist: Independent Pubs. Group.

Pryor, Kimberley Jane. Seeing. 2003. (Senses Ser.). (Illus.). 32p. (gr. 2-4). 23.00 *(978-0-7910-7555-5(9)*, Chelsea Hse.) Facts On File, Inc.

Randolph, Joanne, ed. The Eyes Have It. 2017. (Amazing Human Body Ser.). 48p. (J). (gr. 6-6). pap. 11.70 ***(978-0-7660-8993-8(2))*** Enslow Pubs., Inc.

Riley, Peter. Light & Seeing. 2007. (Essential Science/Watts Ser.). (Illus.). 32p. (J). (gr. 4-7). lib. bdg. 28.50 *(978-1-59920-028-6(7))* Black Rabbit Bks.

Rotner, Shelley. Whose Eye Am I? Rotner, Shelley, photos by. 2016. (ENG., Illus.). 32p. (J). 16.95 *(978-0-8234-3558-6(X))* Holiday Hse., Inc.

Ruchlis, Hyman. The Wonder of Light: A Picture Story of How & Why We See. Hirsh, Alice, illus. 2011. 160p. 41.95 *(978-1-258-09816-2(4))* Literary Licensing, LLC.

Rustad, Martha E. H. Seeing. 2014. (Illus.). 24p. (J). lib. bdg. 25.65 *(978-1-62031-116-5(X)*, Bullfrog Bks.) Jump! Inc.

Schuh, Mari. The Sense of Sight. 2007. (Senses Ser.). (ENG., Illus.). 24p. (J). (gr. 2-5). lib. bdg. 25.95 *(978-1-60014-071-6(8))* Bellwether Media.

Sheen, Barbara. Artificial Eyes. 2016. (Tech Bytes Ser.). (ENG., Illus.). 48p. (J). (gr. 4-6). lib. bdg. 26.60 *(978-1-59953-761-0(3))* Norwood Hse. Pr.

Sian Revision Vision & Hearing. 2004. (J). *(978-1-59242-079-7(6))* Delta Education, LLC.

Simon, Seymour. Eyes & Ears. 2005. (Illus.). (gr. k-3). 17.00 *(978-0-7569-5398-0(7))* Perfection Learning Corp.

Spilsbury, Louise. Sight, 1 vol. 2012. (Science Behind Ser.). (ENG.). 32p. (gr. 3-3). pap. 8.29 *(978-1-4109-4503-7(0))*; lib. bdg. 30.65 *(978-1-4109-4492-4(1))* Heinemann-Raintree. (Raintree Perspectives).

Stanley, Debbie. Coping with Vision Disorders. (Coping Ser.). 192p. (gr. 7-12). 2009. 63.90 *(978-1-61512-017-8(3))* 2005. (Illus.). (YA). lib. bdg. 34.60 *(978-0-8239-3198-9(6))* Rosen Publishing Group, Inc., The.

—Everything You Need to Know about Vision Disorders. 2005. (Need to Know Library). (Illus.). 64p. (YA). (gr. 7-12). 31.95 *(978-0-8239-3225-2(7))* Rosen Publishing Group, Inc., The.

Stewart, Melissa. The Eyes Have It: The Secrets of Eyes & Seeing. Hamlin, Janet, illus. 2009. (Gross & Goofy Body Ser.). 48p. (gr. 3-4). 29.93 *(978-0-7614-4167-0(0))* Marshall Cavendish Corp.

Tekiela, Stan. Peepers & Peekers, 1 vol. 2013. (Adventure Boardbook Ser.). (ENG.). 22p. (J). (gr. -1-k). bds. 6.95 *(978-1-59193-423-3(0))* Adventure Pubns.

Viegas, Jennifer. The Eye: Learning How We See. 2009. (3-D Library of the Human Body Ser.). 48p. (gr. 5-8). 55.90 *(978-1-60853-321-3(2)*, Rosen Reference) Rosen Publishing Group, Inc., The.

Vogel, Julie. Your Sensational Sense of Sight. Squier, Robert, illus. 2011. (Sensational Senses Ser.). (ENG.). 32p. (J). (gr. k-3). lib. bdg. 27.07 *(978-1-60954-287-0(8)*, 200816) Child's World, Inc., The.

Weiss, Ellen. The Sense of Sight. 2008. (True Book(tm), a — Health & the Human Body Ser.). (ENG., Illus.). 48p. (J). (gr. 2-5). 31.00 *(978-0-531-16871-4(9))* Scholastic Library Publishing.

Wheeler-Toppen, Jodi Lyn. Our Eyes Can See. 2017. (Our Amazing Senses Ser.). (ENG.). 24p. (gr. k-1). lib. bdg. 21.99 ***(978-1-5157-6714-5(0)***, Pebble Bks.) Capstone Press of Coughlan Cos.

Young, Cybèle. The Queen's Shadow: A Story about How Animals See. Young, Cybèle, illus. 2015. (ENG., Illus.). 40p. (J). (gr. 2-6). 16.95 *(978-1-894786-60-7(2))* Kids Can Pr., Ltd. CAN. Dist: Hachette Bk. Group.

VISUAL INSTRUCTION

see Audio-Visual Education

VITAMINS

Centore, Michael. Vitamins & Minerals. 2017. (J). ***(978-1-4222-3745-8(1))*** Mason Crest.

Cohen, Marina. Why We Need Vitamins. 2011. (Science of Nutrition Ser.). (ENG.). 48p. (J). (gr. 5-9). lib. bdg. *(978-0-7787-1690-7(2))*; pap. *(978-0-7787-1697-6(X))* Crabtree Publishing Co.

Ibitokun, Bernadette O. Kids, Know Your Vitamins. 2012. (ENG.). 41p. (J). 30.95 *(978-1-4787-1950-2(8))* Outskirts Pr., Inc.

Sertori, Trisha. Vitamins & Minerals. 2008. (Body Fuel for Healthy Bodies Ser.). 32p. (gr. 4-18). lib. bdg. 18.56 *(978-0-7614-3802-1(5)*, Benchmark Bks.) Marshall Cavendish Corp.

Vitality: Individual Title Six-Packs. (Bookweb Ser.). 32p. (gr. 6-18). 34.00 *(978-0-7578-0906-4(5))* Rigby Education.

Watson, Stephanie. Vitamins & Minerals: Getting the Nutrients Your Body Needs. 2010. (Healthy Habits Ser.). (Illus.). 64p. (YA). (gr. 5-8). pap. 12.95 *(978-1-4488-0613-3(5))*; lib. bdg. 31.95 *(978-1-4358-9443-3(X))* Rosen Publishing Group, Inc., The. (Rosen Reference).

VIVARIUMS

see Terrariums

VOCABULARY

Abrams, Majella. Reading Pals: Short & Long Vowels Gr. K-1. Taylor, Jennifer, ed. Sexton, Brenda, illus. 2007. (J). per. 6.99 *(978-1-59198-436-8(X))* Creative Teaching Pr., Inc.

Ace Academics, ed. English Vocabulary: A Whole Course in a Box! 2007. (Exambusters Ser.). 384p. (gr. 7-18). *(978-1-881374-85-5(8)*, Exambusters) Ace Academics, Inc.

Ackland, Nick. First Words. 2015. (Bright Beginnings Ser.). (ENG.). 20p. (J). (gr. -1 — 1). bds. 6.99 *(978-0-7641-6743-0(X))* Barron's Educational Series, Inc.

Acredolo, Linda & Goodwyn, Susan. My First Spoken Words: Babies. 2007. (My first spoken Words Ser.). (ENG., Illus.). 12p. (gr. -1-k). 12.99 *(978-0-8249-6719-2(4)*, Ideal Pubns.) Worthy Publishing.

Allen, Margaret. Reading Pals: Rhyming Words Using Blends & Digraphs Gr. K-1. Taylor, Jennifer, ed. Sexton, Brenda, illus. 2007. (J). per. 6.99 *(978-1-59198-437-5(8))* Creative Teaching Pr., Inc.
Allen, Molly. Reading Pals: Sight Words Gr. K-1. Taylor, Jennifer, ed. Sexton, Brenda, illus. 2007. (J). per. 6.99 *(978-1-59198-438-2(6))* Creative Teaching Pr., Inc.
Allen, William H., creator. TEH Learns to Read: Primary Words. 2004. (J). 34.95 *(978-0-9745938-2-1(6))* LD Coach, LLC.
Alphasnaps & Snapphonics: Snapphonics Big Book: Eek! Squeak! A Leak! 2003. 36.95 *(978-0-673-60206-0(0))* Celebration Pr.
Alphasnaps & Snapphonics: Snapphonics Big Book: Scat the Cat. 2003. 36.95 *(978-0-673-60207-7(9))* Celebration Pr.
American Heritage Dictionaries Editors, ed. 100 Words Every 4th Grader Should Know. 2014. (100 Words Ser.). (ENG.). 96p. (J). (gr. 2-5). pap. 6.95 *(978-0-544-10611-6(3))* Houghton Mifflin Harcourt Publishing Co.
Amery, H. First Hundred Words. 2004. (ENG.). 32p. (J). pap. 6.95 *(978-0-7945-0002-3(1))* EDC Publishing.
—First Thousand Words. 2004. (J). (SPA.). 70p. pap. 9.99 *(978-0-7945-0463-2(9))*; (FRE.). 64p. 12.99 *(978-0-7945-0283-6(0))*; (HEB & ENG.). 64p. 12.99 *(978-0-7945-0029-0(3))* EDC Publishing.
—First Thousand Words in Spanish IL. rev. ed. 2004. (First Thousand Words Ser.). (SPA.). 64p. (J). lib. bdg. 20.99 *(978-1-58086-564-7(X))* EDC Publishing.
Amery, H. & Cartwright, S. First Spanish Word Book. 2004. (Treasury of Farmyard Tales Ser.). (SPA & ENG.). 48p. (J). 10.95 *(978-0-7945-0476-2(0))* EDC Publishing.
Amery, Heather. Farmyard Tales First Word Book. 2004. (Farmyard Tales Bks.). (ENG., Illus.). 1p. (J). 10.95 *(978-0-7460-4084-3(9))* EDC Publishing.
—First Hundred Words. Tyler, Jenny, ed. Cartwright, Stephen, illus. 2006. (Usborne First Hundred Words Ser.). 32p. (J). (gr. -1). lib. bdg. 14.95 *(978-1-58086-505-0(4))* EDC Publishing.
—First Hundred Words Coloring Book. 2009. (First Hundred Words Ser.). 32p. (J). (gr. k). pap. 5.99 *(978-0-7945-2485-2(0)*, Usborne) EDC Publishing.
—First Thousand Words in English. Irving, Nicole, ed. Cartwright, Stephen, illus. 2003. (First Thousand Words Ser.). 63p. (J). (gr. -1). lib. bdg. 20.95 *(978-1-58086-474-9(0))* EDC Publishing.
—First Thousand Words in Italian. Cartwright, Stephen, illus. rev. ed. 2004. (First Thousand Words Ser.). (ITA & ENG.). 64p. (J). (gr. -1-6). 12.99 *(978-0-7945-0286-7(5))*; lib. bdg. 20.99 *(978-1-58086-560-9(7))* EDC Publishing. (Usborne).
—First Thousand Words in Japanese. Cartwright, Stephen, illus. rev. ed. 2004. (First Thousand Words Ser.). (JPN & ENG.). 64p. (J). (gr. -1-6). 12.95 *(978-0-7945-0480-9(9))*; lib. bdg. 20.95 *(978-1-58086-552-4(6))* EDC Publishing. (Usborne).
—What's Happening on the Farm? Cartwright, Stephen, illus. rev. ed. 2006. (What's Happening? Ser.). 32p. (J). (gr. -1-3). 5.99 *(978-0-7945-1288-0(7)*, Usborne) EDC Publishing.
Amery, Heather & Cartwright, Stephen. First French Word Book. 2004. (Farmyard Tales First Words Ser.). (ENG & FRE., Illus.). 48p. (J). 10.95 *(978-0-7945-0295-9(4)*, Usborne) EDC Publishing.
—First Thousand Words. 2004. (First Thousand Words Ser.). (ENG., Illus.). 63p. (J). 12.99 *(978-0-7945-0282-9(2)*, Usborne) EDC Publishing.
Analogies 1: Grade 7-8 Quiz Book. 2004. (Analogies Ser.). pap. 8.20 *(978-0-8388-2226-5(6))* Educators Publishing Service, Inc.
Analogies & Multiple Meanings (Gr. 2-3) 2003. (J). *(978-1-58232-125-7(6))* ECS Learning Systems, Inc.
Anderson, Jill, ed. Let's Get to Work!/Vamos a Trabajar! Evrard, Gaetan, illus. 2005. (Word Play/Juegos con Pala Ser.). (ENG & SPA.). 20p. (J). (gr. -1-17). bds. 6.95 *(978-1-58728-512-7(6))* Cooper Square Publishing Llc.
—Let's Go on Safari!/Vamos de Safari! Utton, Peter, illus. 2005. (Word Play/Juegos con Pala Ser.). (ENG & SPA.). 20p. (J). (gr. -1-17). bds. 6.95 *(978-1-58728-522-6(3))* Cooper Square Publishing Llc.
—Let's Go!/Vamos a Viajar! Evrard, Gaetan, illus. 2005. (Word Play/Juegos con Pala Ser.). (ENG & SPA.). 20p. (J). (gr. -1-17). bds. 6.95 *(978-1-58728-513-4(4))* Cooper Square Publishing Llc.
Anholt, Catherine & Anholt, Laurence. First Words & Pictures. 2014. (ENG., Illus.). 32p. (J). (gr. -1-k). pap. 8.99 *(978-1-84780-473-0(X)*, Frances Lincoln) Quarto Publishing Group UK GBR. Dist: Hachette Bk. Group.
Animales. (Coleccion Libritos Acordeon). (SPA., Illus.). 10p. (J). pap. 5.50 *(978-950-11-0790-6(6)*, SGM906) Sigmar ARG. Dist: Continental Bk. Co., Inc.
Anness Punlishing. Busy Little People: Fun Pictures & Games for Babies & Toddlers! 2015. (ENG., Illus.). 48p. bds. 9.99 *(978-1-86147-629-6(9)*, Armadillo) Anness Publishing GBR. Dist: National Bk. Network.
Arco Staff. Mastering Vocabulary Skills: Entertaining Instruction & Cool Activities for Students Who Want to Get Wise! 2nd ed. 2003. (ENG., Illus.). 209p. (YA). pap. 12.95 *(978-0-7689-1342-2(X)*, Arco) Peterson's.
Armadillo. Kittens. 2015. (ENG., Illus.). 24p. bds. 6.99 *(978-1-86147-645-6(0)*, Armadillo) Anness Publishing GBR. Dist: National Bk. Network.
—Let's Learn 250 Words: A Very First Reading Book. 2016. (ENG., Illus.). 48p. bds. 9.99 *(978-1-86147-706-4(6)*, Armadillo) Anness Publishing GBR. Dist: National Bk. Network.
Armadillo, Jeffrey. My First Animals: Over 200 Animals to Name & Learn About. Lewis, Jan, illus. 2015. (ENG.). 48p. bds. 9.99 *(978-1-86147-652-4(3)*, Armadillo) Anness Publishing GBR. Dist: National Bk. Network.
Armadillo Press. Dog & Friends! A Box of Exciting Picture Books, 6 vols. 2017. (ENG., Illus.). 54p. (J). (gr. -1-12). bds. 14.99 *(978-1-86147-640-1(X)*, Armadillo) Anness Publishing GBR. Dist: National Bk. Network.
Armadillo Publishing Staff. Words - Let's Look & See. 2015. (ENG., Illus.). 24p. bds. 6.99 *(978-1-86147-485-8(7)*, Armadillo) Anness Publishing GBR. Dist: National Bk. Network.
AstroWord. 2004. (Scott Foresman Reading Ser.). (gr. k-18). cd-rom 69.00 *(978-0-673-64439-8(1))*; (gr. 1-18). cd-rom 69.00 *(978-0-673-62235-8(5))*; (gr. 2-18). cd-rom 69.00 *(978-0-673-62236-5(3))*; (gr. 3-18). cd-rom 69.00 *(978-0-673-62237-2(1))*; (gr. 4-18). cd-rom 69.00 *(978-0-673-62238-9(X))*; (gr. 5-18). cd-rom 69.00 *(978-0-673-62239-6(8))*; (gr. 6-18). cd-rom 69.00 *(978-0-673-62240-2(1))* Addison-Wesley Educational Pubs., Inc.
Austin, Richard, photos by. Pocket Piggies Opposites! Featuring the Teacup Pigs of Pennywell Farm. 2016. (ENG., Illus.). 22p. (J). (gr. -1 — 1). bds. 5.95 *(978-0-7611-8548-2(8))* Workman Publishing Co., Inc.
Baby's First Word Book. 2004. 10p. (J). bds. 4.99 *(978-1-85854-925-5(6))* Brimax Books Ltd. GBR. Dist: Byeway Bks.
Baby's First Words. 2003. (Illus.). (J). bds. 7.98 *(978-0-7525-8651-9(3))* Parragon, Inc.
Badreddine, Delphine. Tell Me about Colors, Shapes, & Opposites. Guillerey, Aurélie, illus. 2012. (ENG.). 72p. (J). (gr. -1-2). 17.95 *(978-1-926973-54-8(2)*, Owlkids) Owlkids Bks. Inc. CAN. Dist: Publishers Group West (PGW).
Baggott, Stella. Baby's Very First Bath Book. 2011. (Baby's Very First Ser.). 10p. (J). 9.99 *(978-0-7945-2972-7(0)*, Usborne) EDC Publishing.
—Baby's Very First Black & White Library. 2012. (Little Black & White Library). 10p. (J). ring bd. 6.99 *(978-0-7945-3241-3(1)*, Usborne) EDC Publishing.
—Baby's Very First Touchy-Feely Animals Book. 2011. (Baby's Very First Ser.). 10p. (J). ring bd. 7.99 *(978-0-7945-2895-9(3)*, Usborne) EDC Publishing.
—Baby's Very First Touchy-Feely Christmas Book. Baggott, Stella, illus. 2010. (Baby's Very First Board Bks). (Illus.). 10p. (J). bds. 6.99 *(978-0-7945-2852-2(X)*, Usborne) EDC Publishing.
—Baby's Very First Touchy-Feely Lift the Flap Play Book. 2013. (Baby's Very First Board Bks). 10p. (J). ring bd. 12.99 *(978-0-7945-3386-1(8)*, Usborne) EDC Publishing.
Baxter, Nicola. My First 200 Words: Learning Is Fun with Teddy the Bear! Lacome, Susie, illus. 2016. (ENG.). 24p. (J). (gr. -1-12). pap. 7.99 *(978-1-86147-759-0(7)*, Armadillo) Anness Publishing GBR. Dist: National Bk. Network.
—My First Words: At Home. Lacome, Susie, illus. 2016. (ENG.). 24p. (J). (gr. -1-12). pap. 7.99 *(978-1-86147-769-9(4)*, Armadillo) Anness Publishing GBR. Dist: National Bk. Network.
—My First Words: Nature. Lacome, Susie, illus. 2016. (ENG.). 24p. (J). (gr. -1-12). pap. 7.99 *(978-1-86147-770-5(8)*, Armadillo) Anness Publishing GBR. Dist: National Bk. Network.
—My First Words: Out & about (Giant Size) Lacome, Susie, illus. 2016. (ENG.). 24p. (J). (gr. -1-12). pap. 7.99 *(978-1-86147-777-4(5)*, Armadillo) Anness Publishing GBR. Dist: National Bk. Network.
—Teddy Bear's Fun to Learn First 1000 Words. Lacome, Susie, illus. 2013. (ENG.). 96p. (J). (gr. -1-k). 12.99 *(978-1-84322-955-1(2))* Anness Publishing GBR. Dist: National Bk. Network.
Baxter, Nicola & Birkinshaw, Marie. A Treasury for Little Ones: Hours of Fun for Babies & Toddlers - Stories & Rhymes, Puzzles to Solve, & Things to Make & Do. Endersby, Frank, illus. 2014. (ENG.). 80p. (J). (gr. -1-6). 14.99 *(978-1-86147-368-4(0)*, Armadillo) Anness Publishing GBR. Dist: National Bk. Network.
Beech, Linda Ward. 180 Essential Vocabulary Words: Independent Learning Packets That Help Students Learn the Most Important Words They Need to Succeed in School. 2009. (ENG.). 80p. pap. 12.99 *(978-0-439-89734-1(3)*, Teaching Resources) Scholastic, Inc.
—240 Vocabulary Words 5th Grade Kids Need to Know: 24 Ready-to-Reproduce Packets That Make Vocabulary Building Fun & Effective. 2003. (240 Vocabulary Words Ser.). (ENG., Illus.). 80p. (gr. 5-5). per. 12.99 *(978-0-439-28045-7(1)*, Teaching Resources) Scholastic, Inc.
—240 Vocabulary Words Kids Need to Know: 24 Ready-to-Reproduce Packets That Make Vocabulary Building Fun & Effective. 2012. (ENG.). 80p. (gr. 5-5). pap. 12.99 *(978-0-545-46865-7(5))*; (Illus.). (gr. 4-4). pap. 12.99 *(978-0-545-46864-0(7))* Scholastic, Inc. (Teaching Resources).
—240 Vocabulary Words Kids Need to Know - Grade 6: 24 Ready-to-Reproduce Packets That Make Vocabulary Building Fun & Effective. 2012. (ENG.). 80p. (gr. 6-6). pap. 12.99 *(978-0-545-46866-4(3)*, Teaching Resources) Scholastic, Inc.
—240 Vocabulary Words Kids Need to Know, Grade 3: 24 Ready-to-Reproduce Packets That Make Vocabulary Building Fun & Effective. 2012. (ENG., Illus.). 80p. (gr. 3-3). pap. 12.99 *(978-0-545-46863-3(9)*, Teaching Resources) Scholastic, Inc.
Benchmark Education Company, LLC Staff, compiled by. High Frequency Word Component Set. 2005. spiral bd. 210.00 *(978-1-4108-4156-8(1))* Benchmark Education Co.
Besson, Agnès. My First 1000 Animals. Surein, Manuel, illus. 2016. (ENG.). 64p. (J). (gr. -1 — 1). 19.95 *(978-1-77085-796-4(6)*, 9781770857964) Firefly Bks., Ltd.
Beyond the Code: Grades 2-3, Bk. 2. 2004. (Beyond the code Ser.). pap. 6.75 *(978-0-8388-2402-3(1))* Educators Publishing Service, Inc.
Bicknell, J. Buby Baby Words_Padded. 2010. 12p. pap. *(978-1-84879-161-9(5))* Make Believe Ideas.
Bicknell, Joanna. Cuddle Buddy: Baby Words. 2006. 10p. (gr. -1). *(978-1-84610-094-9(1))* Make Believe Ideas.
—My First BK of Animals. 2010. 16p. (J). bds. 8.99 *(978-1-84879-361-3(8))* Make Believe Ideas GBR. Dist: Nelson, Thomas Inc.
Bicknell, Joanna, ed. Baby Fun Words. 2005. 12p. *(978-1-905051-16-8(6))* Make Believe Ideas.
Bicknell, Joanna & Phillips, Sarah. Time. 2011. (Illus.). 12p. (J). 7.99 *(978-1-84610-092-5(5))* Make Believe Ideas GBR. Dist: Nelson, Thomas Inc.
Black, Jessica L. & Mullican, Judy. Let's Build a Snowman: Cuddle Book. Crowell, Knox, illus. 6p. (J). (gr. -1-1). bds. 10.95 *(978-1-57332-222-5(9)*, HighReach Learning, Incorporated) Carson-Dellosa Publishing, LLC.
Blackstone, Stella & Scribens, Sunny. Baby's First Words. 2017. (Illus.). 30p. (J). (gr. -1-k). 14.99 **(978-1-78285-321-3(9))** Barefoot Bks., Inc.
Blanchard, Cherie & Plant, Cherie A. Word Roots A2: Learning the Building Blocks of Better Spelling & Vocabulary. 2013. (Word Roots Ser.). 80p. (gr. 5-12). pap. 16.99 *(978-0-89455-865-8(X))* Critical Thinking Co., The.
—Word Roots B2 Bk. 2: Learning the Building Blocks of Better Spelling & Vocabulary. 2005. (Word Roots Ser.). 136p. (gr. 7-12). pap. 16.99 *(978-0-89455-866-5(8))* Critical Thinking Co., The.
Block, Cheryl. Think Analogies A1: Learning to Connect Words & Relationships. 2011. (Think Analogies Books ThinkAnalogy Puzzles Software Ser.). 56p. (gr. 3-5). pap. 11.99 *(978-0-89455-791-0(2))* Critical Thinking Co., The.
Bobby Fling, 6 vols. 8p. (gr. k-1). 21.50 *(978-0-322-02068-9(9))* Wright Group/McGraw-Hill.
Body, Wendy. Minki's Day, 4 vols. 2005. (QEB Readers). (Illus.). 24p. (J). (gr. -1-3). lib. bdg. 15.95 *(978-1-59566-106-7(9))* QEB Publishing Inc.
—Mup's Days of the Week, 4 vols. 2005. (QEB Readers). (Illus.). 24p. (J). (gr. -1-3). lib. bdg. 15.95 *(978-1-59566-104-3(2))* QEB Publishing Inc.
Boehm, Gregory A. Big Big Book of Word Search. 2005. 224p. (YA). mass mkt. *(978-1-59412-000-8(5))* Mud Puddle, Inc.
Bond, G. T. GT Bond's 24 Words Toddlers Can Read in Color. 2007. 60p. pap. 24.95 *(978-0-615-14954-7(5))* S & S Pr.
—60 Words Toddlers Can Read in Black & White. 2007. 140p. pap. 16.95 *(978-0-615-14930-1(8))* S & S Pr.
Bonnett, Rosaline. Very First Words on the Farm. 2011. (Very First Words Board Books Ser.). 12p. (J). ring bd. 6.99 *(978-0-7945-3042-6(7)*, Usborne) EDC Publishing.
Brighter Minds, creator. Animal Sight Words Flashcards. 2006. (PBS Kids Ser.). (J). 9.95 *(978-1-57791-310-8(8))* Brighter Minds Children's Publishing.
Brooks, F. & Litchfield, J. Mis Primeras Palabras. 2004.Tr. of Very First Words. (SPA., Illus.). 10p. (J). 6.95 *(978-0-7460-4823-8(8))* EDC Publishing.
Brooks, Felicity. First Word Book on the Farm. 2015. (My First Word Bks.). (ENG.). 20p. (J). 9.99 *(978-0-7945-3445-5(7)*, Usborne) EDC Publishing.
—Lift-the-Flap Word Book. 2011. (Lift-the-Flap Word Book Ser.). 14p. (J). pap. 11.99 *(978-0-7945-2562-0(8)*, Usborne) EDC Publishing.
—My First Word Book. Bonnet, Rosalinde, illus. 2014. (ENG.). (J). 9.99 *(978-0-7945-3381-6(7)*, Usborne) EDC Publishing.
—Very First Animals Board Book. 2010. (Very First Words Board Bks). 10p. (J). bds. 6.99 *(978-0-7945-2479-1(6)*, Usborne) EDC Publishing.
Brooks, Felicity, et al, eds. Everyday Words. rev. ed. 2006. (Everyday Words Ser.). (Illus.). 47p. (J). (gr. -1-3). pap. 9.99 *(978-0-7945-0120-4(6)*, Usborne) EDC Publishing.
Brownell, Rick. Expressive & Receptive One-Word Picture Vocabulary Tests: EOWPVT-2000 Plates. 3rd rev. ed. (ENG & SPA.). *(978-1-57128-136-4(3))* High Noon Bks.
—Expressive & Receptive One-Word Picture Vocabulary Tests: ROWPVT-2000 Plates. 2nd rev. ed. (ENG & SPA.). *(978-1-57128-140-1(1))* High Noon Bks.
Bruzzone, Catherine & Millar, Louise. My French Sticker Atlas. 2014. (ENG.). 24p. (J). (gr. 1-5). pap. 6.99 *(978-1-4380-0387-0(0))* Barron's Educational Series, Inc.
—My Spanish Sticker Atlas. 2014. (ENG.). 24p. (J). (gr. 1-5). pap. 6.99 *(978-1-4380-0388-7(9))* Barron's Educational Series, Inc.
Bruzzone, Catherine, et al. French-English Picture Dictionary. Comfort, Louise & Dix, Steph, illus. 2011. (First Bilingual Picture Dictionaries Ser.). (FRE & ENG.). 48p. (J). (gr. -1-3). pap. 7.99 *(978-0-7641-4660-2(2))* Barron's Educational Series, Inc.
Buen Viaje Pinguinos! (Coleccion Leo Con Figuras). (SPA., Illus.). 14p. (J). pap. 4.50 *(978-950-11-0929-0(1)*, SGM291) Sigmar ARG. Dist: Continental Bk. Co., Inc.
Burchers, Sam, Jr., et al. Vocabulary Classic Series: The Call of the Wild. 2004. Orig. Title: The Call of the Wild. 216p. (YA). (gr. 6-12). pap. 7.95 *(978-0-9652422-0-2(X))* New Monic Bks.
Butts, Ed. Singing Sight Words, 2 vols. 2008. (Singing Sight Words Ser.: 1). (ENG., Illus.). 48p. (J). Vol. 1. (gr. -1-3). 17.95 *(978-1-55386-088-4(8)*, 1553860888) Vol. 2. 17.95 *(978-1-55386-091-4(8)*, 1553860918) Vol. 3. 17.95 *(978-1-55386-094-5(2)*, 1553860942) Vol. 4. 17.95 *(978-1-55386-097-6(7)*, 1553860977) Jordan, Sara Publishing.
Cáccamo, Pepe. A Cazar Palabras. Fernandez, Maria Xose, illus. (SPA.). 142p. (J). (gr. k-2). *(978-84-95123-36-7(3)*, KA1393) Kalandraka Editora, S.L. ESP. Dist: Lectorum Pubns., Inc.
Callella, Kim. Build-a-Skill Instant Books Short & Long Vowels. Shiotsu, Vicky & Faulkner, Stacey, eds. Campbell, Jenny & Tom, Darcy, illus. 2007. (J). 4.99 *(978-1-59198-412-2(2))* Creative Teaching Pr., Inc.
Callella, Trisha. Greek & Latin Roots: Teaching Vocabulary to Improve Reading Comprehension. Rous, Sheri, ed. Peterson, Barbara, illus. 2004. 144p. pap. 16.99 *(978-0-88160-381-1(3)*, LW-438) Creative Teaching Pr., Inc.
—More Greek & Latin Roots: Teaching Vocabulary to Improve Reading Comprehension. Faulkner, Stacey, ed. Hillam, Corbin, illus. 2006. (J). pap. 18.99 *(978-1-59198-328-6(2))* Creative Teaching Pr., Inc.
—Prefixes & Suffixes: Teaching Vocabulary to Improve Reading Comprehension. Williams, Carolea & Rous, Sheri, eds. Peterson, Barbara, illus. 2004. 144p. pap. 16.99 *(978-0-88160-380-4(5)*, LW-437) Creative Teaching Pr., Inc.
Campanella, Marco, et al. My Day with Billy Brownmouse. 2014. (ENG., Illus.). 10p. (J). pap. 10.00 *(978-1-84135-384-5(1))* Award Pubns. Ltd. GBR. Dist: Parkwest Pubns., Inc.
Campbell, Barbara. Lets Build Something: A Story Book/Coloring Book/Workbook. 2009. 64p. pap. 14.95 *(978-0-692-00349-7(5))* Mumford Institute.
Campbell, Dorthina A. Step Forward Strategies for Struggling Readers: Student Resource Guide. 2005. 59p. (J). stu. ed., per. 8.99 *(978-0-9768208-0-2(3))* Edutech Learning Resource Ctr.
Carey Molter. Ate As in Skate, 1 vol. 2003. (Word Families Set 8 Ser.: Vol. 8). (ENG., Illus.). 24p. (J). (gr. k-3). lib. bdg. 24.21 *(978-1-59197-271-6(X))* ABDO Publishing Co.
Carle, Eric. My Very First Book of Words. Carle, Eric, illus. 2006. (ENG., Illus.). 20p. (J). (gr. -1 — 1). bds. 5.99 *(978-0-399-24510-7(3)*, Philomel Bks.) Penguin Young Readers Group.
—The Very Busy Spider's Favorite Words. Carle, Eric, illus. 2007. (World of Eric Carle Ser.). (ENG., Illus.). 20p. (J). (gr. -1-k). bds. 4.99 *(978-0-448-44703-2(7)*, Grosset & Dunlap) Penguin Young Readers Group.
—The Very Hungry Caterpillar's Favorite Words. Carle, Eric, illus. 2007. (World of Eric Carle Ser.). (ENG., Illus.). 20p. (J). (gr. -1-k). bds. 3.99 *(978-0-448-44704-9(5)*, Grosset & Dunlap) Penguin Young Readers Group.
Carpenter, Tad. I Say, You Say Colors! 2014. (ENG., Illus.). 18p. (J). (gr. -1 — 1). bds. 6.99 *(978-0-316-20072-1(7))* Little, Brown Bks. for Young Readers.
—I Say, You Say Feelings! 2014. (ENG., Illus.). 18p. (J). (gr. -1 — 1). bds. 6.99 *(978-0-316-20074-5(3))* Little, Brown Bks. for Young Readers.
Carson-Dellosa Publishing Staff. Beginning Vocabulary, Grade K. 2010. (Home Workbooks Ser.). (ENG.). 64p. (gr. k-k). pap. 4.49 *(978-1-60418-775-5(1))* Carson-Dellosa Publishing, LLC.
—First Words. 2006. (ENG., Illus.). 54p. (gr. -1-1). 2.99 *(978-0-7696-4719-7(7)*, Brighter Child) Carson-Dellosa Publishing, LLC.
Carson-Dellosa Publishing Staff, compiled by. Beginning Vocabulary, Grade 1. 2010. (Home Workbooks Ser.). (ENG.). 64p. (gr. 1-1). pap. 4.49 *(978-1-60418-789-2(1))* Carson-Dellosa Publishing, LLC.
Cernak, Kim. Build-a-Skill Instant Books Consonant Blends & Digraphs. Shiotsu, Vicky & Faulkner, Stacey, eds. Campbell, Jenny & Tom, Darcy, illus. 2007. (J). 4.99 *(978-1-59198-410-8(6))* Creative Teaching Pr., Inc.
Cernek, Kim & Williams, Rozanne Lanczak. Build-a-Skill Instant Books Color, Shape & Number Words. Shiotsu, Vicky & Faulkner, Stacey, eds. Campbell, Jenny & Tom, Darcy, illus. 2007. (J). 4.99 *(978-1-59198-411-5(4))* Creative Teaching Pr., Inc.
Cestnik, Lisa & Cestnik, Jay. 100 Sight Word Mini-Books: Instant Fill-In Mini-Books That Teach 100 Essential Sight Words. 2005. (ENG.). 112p. (gr. k-2). pap. 15.99 *(978-0-439-38780-4(9)*, Teaching Resources) Scholastic, Inc.
Chambers, Catherine E. DK Adventures: Clash of the Gladiators: Clash of the Gladiators. 2014. (DK Adventures Ser.). (ENG.). 128p. (J). (gr. 3-7). 16.99 *(978-1-4654-1976-7(4)*, DK Children) Dorling Kindersley Publishing, Inc.
Chanko, Pamela. Word Families: 30 Instant Centers with Reproducible Templates & Activities That Help Kids Practice Important Literacy Skills-Independently! 2006. (Shoe Box Learning Centers Ser.). (ENG.). 80p. pap. 12.99 *(978-0-439-53795-7(9)*, Teaching Resources) Scholastic, Inc.
—101 Content-Building Fingerplays, Action Rhymes, & Songs: Easy & Engaging Activities That Build Important Background Knowledge & Enrich Young Learners' Vocabularies. 2009. (ENG.). 112p. (gr. -1-1). pap. 15.99 *(978-0-545-10291-9(X)*, Teaching Resources) Scholastic, Inc.
Chapman, Karen B. The Marino Mission: One Girl, One Mission, One Thousand Words - 1,000 Need-to-Know New SAT Vocabulary Words. 2004. (ENG.). 336p. pap. 15.99 *(978-0-7645-7831-1(6))* Houghton Mifflin Harcourt Publishing Co.
Chapman, Sherill, et al, adapted by. Vocabulary Puzzles. 2003. (Kids Can Learn with Franklin Ser.). (ENG., Illus.). 32p. (J). (gr. 1-3). 3.95 *(978-1-55337-596-8(3))* Kids Can Pr., Ltd. CAN. Dist: Hachette Bk. Group.
Chappell, Jackie. Our School Is Like A Family. 2007. (ENG., Illus.). 16p. (gr. k-2). 28.50 *(978-1-60472-110-2(3))* Rourke Educational Media.
Chedru, Delphine & Duisit, Bernard. This or That? 2017. (Flip Flap Pop-Up Ser.: 0). (ENG., Illus.). 16p. (gr. -1-1). 14.95 *(978-0-500-65093-6(4)*, 565093) Thames & Hudson.
Choosing the Right Word (Gr. 3+) 2003. (J). *(978-1-58232-052-6(7))* ECS Learning Systems, Inc.
Clark, Isobel. My Big Book of Words. Tulip, Jenny, illus. 2009. (ENG.). 48p. (J). (gr. 4-7). 9.99 *(978-0-7548-1941-7(8))* Anness Publishing GBR. Dist: National Bk. Network.
Clarke, Isabel. My Big Book of Words. Tulip, Jenny, illus. 2014. (ENG.). 40p. (J). (gr. -1-k). 12.99 *(978-1-86147-325-7(7)*, Armadillo) Anness Publishing GBR. Dist: National Bk. Network.
Cleary, Brian P. Miss Pell Would Never Misspell & Other Painless Tricks for Memorizing How to Spell & Use Wily Words. Sandy, J. P., illus. 2011. (Adventures in Memory Ser.). (ENG.). 48p. (gr. 4-6). lib. bdg. 26.60 *(978-0-8225-7822-2(0))* Lerner Publishing Group.
—Skin Like Milk, Hair of Silk: What Are Similes & Metaphors? Gable, Brian, illus. 2009. (Words Are CATegorical (r) Ser.). (ENG.). 32p. (gr. 2-5). 16.95 *(978-0-8225-9151-1(0)*, Millbrook Pr.) Lerner Publishing Group.
—Straight & Curvy, Meek & Nervy: More about Antonyms. Gable, Brian, illus. (Words Are CATegorical (r) Ser.). (ENG.). 32p. (gr. 2-5). 2011. pap. 6.95 *(978-1-58013-939-7(6)*, Millbrook Pr.) 2009. 16.95 *(978-0-8225-7878-9(6))* 2008. pap. 39.62 *(978-0-7613-7605-7(4)*, Millbrook Pr.) Lerner Publishing Group.
Clink! Clink! Clink!, 6 vols. 8p. (gr. k-1). 21.50 *(978-0-322-02057-3(3))* Wright Group/McGraw-Hill.
Collins-Matza, Carol. The Palindrome Kids. 2010. 32p. pap. 12.95 *(978-1-60844-513-4(5))* Dog Ear Publishing, LLC.
Collins, Tim & Maples, Mary Jane. Time Zones 1. 2009. (Time Zones: Explore, Discover, Learn Ser.). (ENG.). 144p. (J). pap., stu. ed. 45.95 incl. cd-rom *(978-1-4240-3489-5(2))* Thomson ELT.
Come on into the Rain Forest: Word Study: Plurals, Level C. 2003. ("Plaid" Phonics & Stories Libraries). (gr. 2-3). 38.50 *(978-0-8136-9152-7(4))* Modern Curriculum Pr.
Come to My House: 6 Small Books. (Greetings Ser.: Vol. 3). 24p. (gr. 2-3). 31.00 *(978-0-7635-9418-3(0))* Rigby Education.
Cordier, Séverine & Lacroix, Cynthia, creators. A Day at School. 2013. (ENG., Illus.). 48p. (J). (gr. -1 — 1). 16.95 *(978-1-926973-95-1(X)*, Owlkids) Owlkids Bks. Inc. CAN. Dist: Publishers Group West (PGW).
Corrigan, Kathleen. ABC, 1 vol. 2014. (Canadian Board Bks.). (ENG & FRE.). 20p. bds. 7.99 *(978-1-62370-223-6(2))* Capstone Young Readers of Coughlan Cos.

T
U
V

—My First Colours, 1 vol. 2015. (Maple Leaf Learners Ser.). (ENG.). 20p. bds. 7.99 *(978-1-62370-222-9(4))* Capstone Young Readers of Coughlan Cos.
—My First Shapes, 1 vol. 2015. (Maple Leaf Learners Ser.). (ENG.). 20p. bds. 7.99 *(978-1-62370-221-2(6))* Capstone Young Readers of Coughlan Cos.
—123, 1 vol. 2014. (Canadian Board Bks.). (ENG & FRE.). 20p. bds. 7.99 *(978-1-62370-224-3(0))* Capstone Young Readers of Coughlan Cos.
Cosneau, Olivia & Duisit, Bernard. What's Up? 2017. (Flip Flap Pop-Up Ser.: 0). (ENG., Illus.). 16p. (gr. -1-1). 14.95 *(978-0-500-65092-9(6), 565092)* Thames & Hudson.
Cox, Phil Roxbee & Cartwright, S. Fox on a Box. 2004. (Easy Words to Read Ser.). 16p. (J). (gr. 1-18). pap. 6.95 *(978-0-7945-0443-4(4))* EDC Publishing.
Cox, Phil Roxbee & Cartwright, Stephen. Frog on a Log. 2004. (Illus.). 10p. (J). 4.99 *(978-0-7945-0302-4(0),* Usborne) EDC Publishing.
Crews, G. Ellen G Goes Fishing. marion, designs & proctor, brian, illus. 2007. 28p. pap. 4.99 *(978-0-9795236-0-1(5))* Crews Pubns., LLC.
Daley, Patrick, et al. Amazing Word Power: 100 Words Every 3rd Grader Should Know. 2008. (Amazing Word Power Ser.). (ENG.). 128p. pap. 6.99 *(978-0-545-08706-3(6),* Teaching Resources) Scholastic, Inc.
Data Notes Staff. Word Mapping for Literacy & Language. 2005. 14p. (gr. 11-12). stu. ed., wbk. ed. 25.95 *(978-0-911569-18-6(9))* Prosperity & Profits Unlimited, Distribution Services.
Davidson, Carli, photos by. Heads & Tails. 2017. (ENG., Illus.). 20p. (J). bds. 8.99 *(978-1-4521-5137-3(7))* Chronicle Bks. LLC.
—Shake, Wiggle & Roll. 2017. (ENG., Illus.). 20p. (J). bds. 8.99 *(978-1-4521-5136-6(9))* Chronicle Bks. LLC.
Davis, Caroline. First Opposites. 2012. (ENG., Illus.). 10p. (J). (gr. -1-1). bds. 7.99 *(978-1-84322-844-8(0),* Armadillo) Anness Publishing GBR. Dist: National Bk. Network.
—First Pictures. 2012. (ENG., Illus.). 196p. bds. 7.99 *(978-1-84322-774-8(6),* Armadillo) Anness Publishing GBR. Dist: National Bk. Network.
—First Words. 2012. (ENG., Illus.). 196p. bds. 7.99 *(978-1-84322-842-4(4),* Armadillo) Anness Publishing GBR. Dist: National Bk. Network.
de Brunhoff, Laurent. Babar's ABC. 2012. (ENG., Illus.). 40p. (J). (gr. k-2). 16.95 *(978-1-4197-0382-9(X),* Abrams Bks. for Young Readers) Abrams, Inc.
Deneux, Xavier. TouchThinkLearn: Farm. 2015. (ENG., Illus.). 22p. (J). (gr. -1 — 1). bds. 14.99 *(978-1-4521-4517-4(2))* Chronicle Bks. LLC.
—TouchThinkLearn: Vehicles. 2015. (ENG., Illus.). 22p. (J). (gr. -1 — 1). bds. 14.99 *(978-1-4521-4516-7(4))* Chronicle Bks. LLC.
Diaz-Cubero, Jose H. Practicas de Ortografia: 3 Grado. (SPA & ENG.). (J). (gr. 3). 9.95 *(978-84-357-0127-3(1),* CPR88) Ediciones y Distribuciones Codice, S.A. ESP. Dist: Continental Bk. Co., Inc.
—Practicas de Ortografia: 6 Grado. (SPA & ENG.). (J). (gr. 6). 9.95 *(978-84-357-0124-2(7),* CPR94) Ediciones y Distribuciones Codice, S.A. ESP. Dist: Continental Bk. Co., Inc.
Diktattrainer 5. Klasse. (Duden-Schuelerhilfen Ser.). (GER.). 112p. (J). incl. cd-rom *(978-3-411-71011-9(X))* Bibliographisches Institut & F. A. Brockhaus AG DEU. Dist: International Bk. Import Service, Inc.
Diktattrainer 6. Klasse. (Duden-Schuelerhilfen Ser.). (GER.). 112p. (J). incl. cd-rom *(978-3-411-71021-8(7))* Bibliographisches Institut & F. A. Brockhaus AG DEU. Dist: International Bk. Import Service, Inc.
Disney Book Group. Disney Baby My First Words. Disney Storybook Art Team, illus. 2016. (ENG.). 24p. (J). (gr. -1 — 1). bds. 7.99 *(978-1-4847-5261-6(9))* Disney Pr.
Disney Book Group Staff. Disney Baby My First Words. Disney Storybook Art Team & Houston, Lauren, illus. 2014. (ENG.). 24p. (J). (gr. -1 — 1). bds. 7.99 *(978-1-4847-0915-3(2))* Disney Pr.
Do you Like Rice?, 6 vols. 8p. (gr. k-1). 21.50 *(978-0-322-02058-0(1))* Wright Group/McGraw-Hill.
Donenfeld, Deborah. Baby ABC. 2013. (ENG.). 24p. (J). (— 1). bds. 6.99 *(978-0-8037-3973-4(7),* Dial Bks) Penguin Young Readers Group.
Dooley, Virginia, et al. Amazing Word Power: 100 Words Every 5th Grader Should Know. 2008. (Amazing Word Power Ser.). (ENG.). 128p. pap. 6.99 *(978-0-545-08708-7(2),* Teaching Resources) Scholastic, Inc.
Dorling Kindersley Publishing Staff. Baby First Words! 2013. (ENG.). 16p. (J). (gr. -1 — 1). bds. 6.99 *(978-1-4654-0168-7(7),* DK Children) Dorling Kindersley Publishing, Inc.
—Baby Touch & Feel: First Words. 2016. (Baby Touch & Feel Ser.). (ENG., Illus.). 14p. (J). (— 1). bds. 5.99 *(978-1-4654-5471-3(3),* DK Children) Dorling Kindersley Publishing, Inc.
—Baby Touch & Feel: Halloween. 2017. (Baby Touch & Feel Ser.). (ENG., Illus.). 14p. (J). (— 1). bds. 5.99 ***(978-1-4654-6235-0(X),*** DK Children) Dorling Kindersley Publishing, Inc.
—Big Busy Book - Words. 2013. (ENG.). 14p. (J). (gr. -1 — 1). bds. 9.99 *(978-1-4654-0926-3(2),* DK Children) Dorling Kindersley Publishing, Inc.
—Happy Birthday Sophie! 2014. (ENG., Illus.). 12p. (J). (gr. -1 — 1). bds. 9.99 *(978-1-4654-3256-8(6),* DK Children) Dorling Kindersley Publishing, Inc.
—My First Things That Go. 2016. (ENG., Illus.). 36p. (J). (— 1). bds. 5.99 *(978-1-4654-4490-5(4),* DK Children) Dorling Kindersley Publishing, Inc.
—Sophie la Girafe: Sophie's Big First Word Book. 2016. (ENG., Illus.). 18p. (J). (gr. -1 — 1). bds. 9.99 *(978-1-4654-4494-3(7),* DK Children) Dorling Kindersley Publishing, Inc.
—10 Minutes a Day: Vocabulary, Fourth Grade. 2015. (ENG.). 80p. (J). (gr. 3-4). pap. 9.99 *(978-1-4654-3439-5(9),* DK Children) Dorling Kindersley Publishing, Inc.
Dorling Kindersley Publishing Staff & Bray, Adam. What Makes a Monster? 2014. (DK Adventures Ser.). (ENG.). 128p. (J). (gr. 3-7). pap. 5.99 *(978-1-4654-1991-0(8),* DK Children) Dorling Kindersley Publishing, Inc.
Dorsey, Kathleen. Building Vocabulary with Familiar Songs: A Unique & Fun Way to Motivate Students to Play with Language & Enrich Their Vocabulary. 2007. (ENG., Illus.). 64p. pap. 11.99 *(978-0-439-81311-2(5))* Scholastic, Inc.
Doudna, Kelly. Any Day but Today! 2004. (Sight Words Ser.). (ENG., Illus.). 24p. (J). (gr. k-3). lib. bdg. 24.21 *(978-1-59197-464-2(X))* ABDO Publishing Co.
—Are Buses Big?, 1 vol. (First Words Ser.). (Illus.). (J). (gr. k-3). 2006. (ENG.). 24p. lib. bdg. 24.21 *(978-1-59679-352-1(X),* SandCastle) 2005. 23p. 48.42 *(978-1-59679-353-8(8))* ABDO Publishing Co.
—The Balloons Go up, up, up! 2005. (Illus.). 23p. (J). pap. 48.42 *(978-1-59679-355-2(4))* ABDO Publishing Co.
—Balloons Go up, up, Up!, 1 vol. 2006. (First Words Ser.). (ENG., Illus.). 24p. (J). (gr. k-3). lib. bdg. 24.21 *(978-1-59679-354-5(6),* SandCastle) ABDO Publishing Co.
—Can You Fly?, 1 vol. (First Words Ser.). (Illus.). (J). (gr. k-3). 2006. (ENG.). 24p. lib. bdg. 24.21 *(978-1-59679-358-3(9),* SandCastle) 2005. 23p. pap. 48.42 *(978-1-59679-359-0(7))* ABDO Publishing Co.
—Et As in Jet, 1 vol. 2003. (Word Families Set 2 Ser.). (ENG.). 24p. (J). (gr. k-3). lib. bdg. 24.21 *(978-1-59197-230-3(2),* SandCastle) ABDO Publishing Co.
—Give It a Try! 2004. (Sight Words Ser.). (ENG., Illus.). 24p. (J). (gr. k-3). lib. bdg. 24.21 *(978-1-59197-469-7(0),* SandCastle) ABDO Publishing Co.
—Id As in Squid, 1 vol. 2003. (Word Families Set 3 Ser.). (ENG., Illus.). 24p. (J). (gr. k-3). lib. bdg. 24.21 *(978-1-59197-235-8(3),* SandCastle) ABDO Publishing Co.
—Ig As in Pig, 1 vol. Marx, Monica, ed. 2003. (Word Families Set 3 Ser.). (ENG., Illus.). 24p. (J). (gr. k-3). lib. bdg. 24.21 *(978-1-59197-236-5(1),* SandCastle) ABDO Publishing Co.
—Ill As in Grill, 1 vol. 2003. (Word Families Set 3 Ser.). (ENG., Illus.). 24p. (J). (gr. k-3). lib. bdg. 24.21 *(978-1-59197-237-2(X),* SandCastle) ABDO Publishing Co.
—In As in Twin, 1 vol. 2003. (Word Families Set 3 Ser.). (ENG., Illus.). 24p. (J). (gr. k-3). lib. bdg. 24.21 *(978-1-59197-238-9(8),* SandCastle) ABDO Publishing Co.
—Ip As in Ship, 1 vol. 2003. (Word Families Set 3 Ser.). (ENG., Illus.). 24p. (J). (gr. k-3). lib. bdg. 24.21 *(978-1-59197-239-6(6),* SandCastle) ABDO Publishing Co.
—Is It a Party?, 1 vol. (First Words Ser.). (Illus.). (J). (gr. k-3). 2006. (ENG.). 24p. lib. bdg. 24.21 *(978-1-59679-386-6(4),* SandCastle) 2005. 23p. pap. 48.42 *(978-1-59679-387-3(2))* ABDO Publishing Co.
—Is the TV On?, 1 vol. (First Words Ser.). (Illus.). (J). (gr. k-3). 2006. (ENG.). 24p. lib. bdg. 24.21 *(978-1-59679-388-0(0),* SandCastle) 2005. 23p. pap. 48.42 *(978-1-59679-389-7(9))* ABDO Publishing Co.
—It As in Sit, 1 vol. 2003. (Word Families Set 3 Ser.). (ENG., Illus.). 24p. (J). (gr. k-3). lib. bdg. 24.21 *(978-1-59197-240-2(X),* SandCastle) ABDO Publishing Co.
—It Is My Hat, 1 vol. (First Words Ser.). (Illus.). (J). (gr. k-3). 2006. (ENG.). 24p. lib. bdg. 24.21 *(978-1-59679-392-7(9),* SandCastle) 2005. 23p. pap. 48.42 *(978-1-59679-393-4(7))* ABDO Publishing Co.
—It's My Mission to Make a Definition!, 1 vol. 2007. (Science Made Simple Ser.). (ENG., Illus.). 24p. (J). (gr. k-3). lib. bdg. 24.21 *(978-1-59928-600-6(9),* SandCastle) ABDO Publishing Co.
—Just Make Some Art! 2004. (Sight Words Ser.). (ENG., Illus.). 24p. (J). (gr. k-3). lib. bdg. 24.21 *(978-1-59197-481-9(X),* SandCastle) ABDO Publishing Co.
—My Brother, My Sister, 1 vol. (First Words Ser.). (Illus.). (J). (gr. k-3). 2006. (ENG.). 24p. lib. bdg. 24.21 *(978-1-59679-402-3(X),* SandCastle) 2005. 23p. 48.42 *(978-1-59679-403-0(8))* ABDO Publishing Co.
—My House Is Big!, 1 vol. (First Words Ser.). (Illus.). (J). (gr. k-3). 2006. (ENG.). 24p. lib. bdg. 24.21 *(978-1-59679-404-7(6),* SandCastle) 2005. 23p. 48.42 *(978-1-59679-405-4(4))* ABDO Publishing Co.
—Ow As in Crow, 1 vol. 2003. (Word Families Set 7 Ser.). (ENG., Illus.). 24p. (J). (gr. k-3). lib. bdg. 24.21 *(978-1-59197-265-5(5),* SandCastle) ABDO Publishing Co.
—Sound Words. 2004. (Sound Words Ser.: 5). (ENG.). 24p. (J). (gr. k-3). lib. bdg. 121.05 *(978-1-59197-449-9(6),* SandCastle) ABDO Publishing Co.
—There Are Ants down There! 2004. (Sight Words Ser.). (ENG., Illus.). 24p. (J). (gr. k-3). lib. bdg. 24.21 *(978-1-59197-473-4(9),* SandCastle) ABDO Publishing Co.
—To the Camp!, 1 vol. (First Words Ser.). (Illus.). (J). (gr. k-3). 2006. (ENG.). 24p. lib. bdg. 24.21 *(978-1-59679-420-7(8),* SandCastle) 2005. 23p. pap. 48.42 *(978-1-59679-421-4(6))* ABDO Publishing Co.
—Up the Path, 1 vol. (First Words Ser.). (Illus.). (J). (gr. k-3). 2006. (ENG.). 24p. lib. bdg. 24.21 *(978-1-59679-422-1(4),* SandCastle) 2005. 23p. pap. 48.42 *(978-1-59679-423-8(2))* ABDO Publishing Co.
—Was That Fun? 2004. (Sight Words Ser.). (ENG., Illus.). 24p. (J). (gr. k-3). lib. bdg. 24.21 *(978-1-59197-475-8(5),* SandCastle) ABDO Publishing Co.
—We Can Jump!, 1 vol. (First Words Ser.). (Illus.). (J). (gr. k-3). 2006. (ENG.). 24p. lib. bdg. 24.21 *(978-1-59679-428-3(3),* SandCastle) 2005. 23p. pap. 48.42 *(978-1-59679-429-0(1))* ABDO Publishing Co.
—We Go to the Park, 1 vol. (First Words Ser.). (Illus.). (J). (gr. k-3). 2006. (ENG.). 24p. lib. bdg. 24.21 *(978-1-59679-430-6(5),* SandCastle) 2005. 23p. pap. 48.42 *(978-1-59679-431-3(3))* ABDO Publishing Co.
—When Can You Play Again? 2004. (Sight Words Ser.). (ENG., Illus.). 24p. (J). (gr. k-3). lib. bdg. 24.21 *(978-1-59197-478-9(X),* SandCastle) ABDO Publishing Co.
Dragon's Song: Word Study: Synonyms, Antonyms, Level C. 2003. ("Plaid" Phonics & Stories Libraries). (gr. 2-3). 38.50 *(978-0-8136-9155-8(9))* Modern Curriculum Pr.
Draze, Dianne. Red Hot Root Words Bk. 1: Mastering Vocabulary with Prefixes, Suffixes & Root Words. 2003. (J). pap. 16.95 *(978-1-883055-57-8(1))* Dandy Lion Pubns.
Dubuc, Marianne. In Front of My House. Ghione, Yvette, tr. from FRE. Dubuc, Marianne, illus. 2010. (ENG., Illus.). 120p. (J). (gr. -1-2). 18.95 *(978-1-55453-641-2(3))* Kids Can Pr., Ltd. CAN. Dist: Hachette Bk. Group.
Duncan, Leonard C. Greek Roots J-Ology. Bigelow, Holly, illus. Date not set. 140p. (J). (gr. 6-12). spiral bd. 25.00 *(978-0-941414-01-2(9))* L. C. D.
Dunn, Opal. Un Deux Trois: First French Rhymes. Aggs, Patrice, illus. 2006. (FRE & ENG.). 24p. (J). (gr. k-3). pap. 9.99 *(978-1-84507-623-8(0),* Frances Lincoln Children's Bks.) Quarto Publishing Group UK GBR. Dist: Hachette Bk. Group.
Dupuis, Lynda. Au Pied de la Lettre: Manuel de Lecture de Vocabulaire d'Expression Orale et Ecrite. rev. ed. 2010. (ENG.). 232p. 70.00 *(978-0-7575-7461-0(0))* Kendall Hunt Publishing Co.
Durber, Matt. Backyard. Litchfield, Jo, illus. 2007. (Look & Say Board Bks). 10p. (J). (gr. -1-k). bds. 7.99 *(978-0-7945-1692-5(0),* Usborne) EDC Publishing.
Dyan, Penelope. If You Snooze! Dyan, Penelope, illus. 2012. (Illus.). 34p. pap. 11.95 *(978-1-61477-059-6(X))* Bellissima Publishing, LLC.
—In Gracie's Yard! Dyan, Penelope, illus. 2012. (Illus.). 34p. pap. 11.95 *(978-1-61477-067-1(0))* Bellissima Publishing, LLC.
—Respect! Dyan, Penelope, illus. 2012. (Illus.). 34p. pap. 11.95 *(978-1-61477-058-9(1))* Bellissima Publishing, LLC.
Dyson, Nikki, illus. 1,000 Things to Eat. 2015. (1,000 Pictures Ser.). (ENG.). 34p. (J). (gr. k-5). 14.99 *(978-0-7945-3406-6(6),* Usborne) EDC Publishing.
Eck, Kristin. Colors in My House. (Board Bks.). (gr. k-1). 2009. 16p. 23.90 *(978-1-61511-639-3(7))* 2004. (Illus.). (J). lib. bdg. 8.95 *(978-1-4042-2698-2(2))* Rosen Publishing Group, Inc., The. (PowerKids Pr.).
—Hide-and-Seek Clothes. 2004. (Hide-And-Seek Books). (Illus.). (J). lib. bdg. 21.25 *(978-1-4042-2705-7(9),* PowerKids Pr.) Rosen Publishing Group, Inc., The.
—Hide & Seek Clothes. 2009. (Tough Toddler Bks). 16p. (gr. k-k). 42.50 *(978-1-60854-569-8(5),* PowerKids Pr.) Rosen Publishing Group, Inc., The.
—Shapes in My House. 2004. (Look-And-Learn Books). (Illus.). (J). lib. bdg. 8.95 *(978-1-4042-2699-9(0),* PowerKids Pr.) Rosen Publishing Group, Inc., The.
Education Pub Staff. Code Cards. 2004. pap. 8.05 *(978-0-8388-1788-9(2))* Educators Publishing Service, Inc.
Education.com. Alphabet? Alphabet! A Workbook of Uppercase Letters & Beginning Sounds. 2015. (ENG.). 128p. (J). (gr. -1-k). pap. 7.99 *(978-0-486-80254-1(X))* Dover Pubns., Inc.
Eggleton, Jill. Mrs. Mcfee. Webb, Philip, illus. 2009. 39.95 *(978-0-7664-3147-8(9))* Abrams & Co. Pubs., Inc.
Einhorn, Kama & Beech, Linda. 240 Vocabulary Words Kids Need to Know, Grade 1: 24 Ready-to-Reproduce Packets That Make Vocabulary Building Fun & Effective. 2012. (ENG.). 80p. (gr. 1-1). pap. 12.99 *(978-0-545-46050-7(6),* Teaching Resources) Scholastic, Inc.
Electric Confetti. Neon Baby: Words. 2017. (Neon Baby Ser.). (ENG., Illus.). 20p. (J). (— 1). bds. 12.99 ***(978-1-76012-906-4(2))*** Hardie Grant Egmont Pty, Ltd. AUS. Dist: Independent Pubs. Group.
Emberley, Rebecca. My Big Book of Spanish Words. 2008. (SPA & ENG., Illus.). 14p. (J). (gr. -1-1). bds. 9.99 *(978-0-316-11803-3(6))* Little, Brown Bks. for Young Readers.
EMC-Paradigm Publishing Staff. Discovering Literature: Vocabulary Resource. (J). (gr. 6). *(978-0-8219-2030-5(8))* EMC/Paradigm Publishing.
Enriquece tu Vocabulario: Student & Teacher Support Resources. 2003. (MacMillan/McGraw-Hill. Estudios Sociales Ser.). (ENG & SPA.). (gr. 1-18). *(978-0-02-149765-2(6));* (gr. 2-18). *(978-0-02-149766-9(4));* (gr. 3-18). *(978-0-02-149767-6(2));* (gr. 4-18). *(978-0-02-149976-2(4));* (gr. 5-18). *(978-0-02-149769-0(9))* Macmillan/McGraw-Hill Schl. Div.
Escoffier, Michaël. Have You Seen My Trumpet? Di Giacomo, Kris, illus. 2016. (ENG.). 48p. (J). (gr. -1-3). 17.95 *(978-1-59270-201-5(5))* Enchanted Lion Bks., LLC.
—Take Away the A. Di Giacomo, Kris, illus. 2014. (ENG.). 56p. (J). (gr. -1-3). 17.95 *(978-1-59270-156-8(6))* Enchanted Lion Bks., LLC.
—Where's the Baboon? Di Giacomo, Kris, illus. 2015. (ENG.). 40p. (J). (gr. -1-3). 17.95 *(978-1-59270-189-6(2))* Enchanted Lion Bks., LLC.
Evan-Moor. Vocabulary Centers, Grades 1-2. 2006. (Take It to Your Seat Ser.). (ENG., Illus.). 192p. (J). pap. 24.99 *(978-1-59673-148-6(6),* EMC 3348) Evan-Moor Educational Pubs.
—Vocabulary Centers, Grades 2-3. 2006. (Take It to Your Seat Ser.). (ENG., Illus.). 192p. (J). pap. 24.99 *(978-1-59673-149-3(4),* EMC 3349) Evan-Moor Educational Pubs.
—Vocabulary Centers, Grades 4-5. 2006. (Take It to Your Seat Ser.). (ENG., Illus.). 192p. (J). pap. 24.99 *(978-1-59673-151-6(6),* EMC 3351) Evan-Moor Educational Pubs.
—Vocabulary Centers, Grades K-1. 2006. (Take It to Your Seat Ser.). (ENG., Illus.). 192p. (J). pap. 24.99 *(978-1-59673-147-9(8),* EMC 3347) Evan-Moor Educational Pubs.
Evan-Moor, ed. Daily Academic Vocabulary, Grade 2. 2007. (ENG., Illus.). 160p. (J). pap. 29.99 *(978-1-59673-201-8(6))* Evan-Moor Educational Pubs.
—Daily Academic Vocabulary, Grade 3. 2007. (ENG., Illus.). 160p. (J). pap. 29.99 *(978-1-59673-202-5(4))* Evan-Moor Educational Pubs.
—Daily Academic Vocabulary, Grade 4. 2007. (Evan-Moor Language Skills Ser.). (ENG., Illus.). 160p. (J). pap. 29.99 *(978-1-59673-203-2(2))* Evan-Moor Educational Pubs.
—Daily Academic Vocabulary, Grade 6+ 2007. (ENG., Illus.). 160p. (J). pap. 29.99 *(978-1-59673-205-6(9))* Evan-Moor Educational Pubs.
Evan-Moor Educational Publishers. At the Park: Grades 1-3. 2005. (Look, Listen, & Speak Ser.). (ENG.). 80p. (J). (gr. k-3). cd-rom 29.99 *(978-1-55799-927-6(9),* EMC 2740) Evan-Moor Educational Pubs.
Falletta, Bernadette. We Love to Read Stories Coloring Book & Word Search Puzzles. 2005. 23p. (J). 10.95 *(978-1-4116-6291-9(1))* Lulu Pr., Inc.
Farnsworth, Lauren. Clever Babies Love Art - Wild Animals. 2016. (Clever Babies Love Art Ser.). (ENG., Illus.). 14p. (J). (— 1). bds. 7.99 *(978-1-78055-397-9(8))* O'Mara, Michael Bks., Ltd. GBR. Dist: Independent Pubs. Group.
Fatus, Sophie. My Big, Barefoot Book of Wonderful Words. 2014. (Illus.). (J). pap. *(978-1-78285-168-4(2))* Barefoot Bks., Inc.
Fatus, Sophie & Barefoot Books. My Big Barefoot Book of Wonderful Words. Fatus, Sophie, illus. 2014. (Illus.). 48p. (J). (gr. -1-1). 19.99 *(978-1-78285-092-2(9))* Barefoot Bks., Inc.
Fatus, Sophie & Paris, Mertxe. My Big Barefoot Book of Spanish & English Words. 2016. (SPA & ENG.). (J). pap. *(978-1-78285-275-9(1))* Barefoot Bks., Inc.
Feldman, Jean & Karapetkova, Holly. ABC 123. unabr. ed. 2010. (ENG.). 16p. (gr. -1-k). 12.99 *(978-1-61741-589-0(8))* Rourke Educational Media.
Fernandez, Joyce. Little Bird - Pajarito. 2010. 31p. 15.95 *(978-0-615-23709-1(6))* My Second Language Publishing, USA.
Filipek, Nina. Words. O'Toole, Jeanette, illus. 2009. (Bright Basics Ser.). 12p. (J). (gr. -1-k). bds. 11.40 *(978-1-60754-685-6(X))* Windmill Bks.
Find It, Write It, Read It: Sentences. 2004. (J). pap. 7.95 *(978-1-56911-179-6(0))* Learning Resources, Inc.
Find It, Write It, Read It: Words. 2004. (J). pap. 7.95 *(978-1-56911-178-9(2))* Learning Resources, Inc.
First 100 Words: Busy Day. (Illus.). 12p. (J). *(978-1-902272-36-8(6))* Tucker Slingsby, Ltd.
First Word Book. 2003. (J). (SPA & ENG.). per. *(978-1-884907-31-9(8));* per. *(978-1-884907-29-6(6))* Paradise Pr., Inc.
First Words. 2014. (ENG.). 16p. (J). (gr. -1 — 1). bds. 6.99 *(978-1-4654-1832-6(6),* DK Children) Dorling Kindersley Publishing, Inc.
First Words Sticker Book. 2015. (ENG., Illus.). 56p. (J). (gr. -1-7). pap. *(978-1-78393-830-8(7))* Make Believe Ideas.
Fish, Simon. Silly Shapes. 2012. (ENG.). (J). pap. *(978-1-4675-0898-8(5))* Independent Pub.
Flash Kids Editors, ed. Sight Words: Grade 1 (Flash Skills) 2010. (Flash Skills Ser.). (ENG.). 64p. (J). pap. 3.95 *(978-1-4114-3449-3(8),* Spark Publishing Group) Sterling Publishing Co., Inc.
—Sight Words: Grade 2 (Flash Skills) 2010. (Flash Skills Ser.). (ENG.). 64p. (J). pap. 3.95 *(978-1-4114-3471-4(4),* Spark Publishing Group) Sterling Publishing Co., Inc.
—Vocabulary for the Gifted Student Grade 1 (for the Gifted Student) Challenging Activities for the Advanced Learner. 2011. (For the Gifted Student Ser.). (ENG., Illus.). 192p. (J). pap. 8.95 *(978-1-4114-2767-9(X),* Spark Publishing Group) Sterling Publishing Co., Inc.
—Vocabulary for the Gifted Student Grade 2 (for the Gifted Student) Challenging Activities for the Advanced Learner. 2011. (For the Gifted Student Ser.). (ENG., Illus.). 192p. (J). pap. 8.95 *(978-1-4114-2768-6(8),* Spark Publishing Group) Sterling Publishing Co., Inc.
—Vocabulary for the Gifted Student Grade 3 (for the Gifted Student) Challenging Activities for the Advanced Learner. 2011. (For the Gifted Student Ser.). (ENG., Illus.). 192p. (J). pap. 8.95 *(978-1-4114-2769-3(6),* Spark Publishing Group) Sterling Publishing Co., Inc.
—Vocabulary for the Gifted Student Grade 4 (for the Gifted Student) Challenging Activities for the Advanced Learner. 2011. (For the Gifted Student Ser.). (ENG., Illus.). 192p. (J). pap. 8.95 *(978-1-4114-2770-9(X),* Spark Publishing Group) Sterling Publishing Co., Inc.
—Vocabulary for the Gifted Student Grade 5 (for the Gifted Student) Challenging Activities for the Advanced Learner. 2011. (For the Gifted Student Ser.). (ENG., Illus.). 192p. (J). pap. 8.95 *(978-1-4114-2771-6(8),* Spark Publishing Group) Sterling Publishing Co., Inc.
—Vocabulary for the Gifted Student Grade 6 (for the Gifted Student) Challenging Activities for the Advanced Learner. 2011. (For the Gifted Student Ser.). (ENG., Illus.). 192p. (J). pap. 8.95 *(978-1-4114-2772-3(6),* Spark Publishing Group) Sterling Publishing Co., Inc.
Flora, Sherrill B. Building Essential Vocabulary: Reproducible Photo Cards, Games, & Activities to Build Vocabulary in Any Language. Anderson, Julie, illus. 2005. (ENG.). 96p. (gr. -1-3). per. 13.99 *(978-1-933052-12-0(0),* Key Education Publishing Company, LLC) Carson-Dellosa Publishing, LLC.
Flowerpot Press Staff, contrib. by. Sockheadz: First Words. 2013. (ENG., Illus.). 20p. (J). (gr. -1-k). 6.99 *(978-1-77093-595-2(9))* Flowerpot Children's Pr. Inc. CAN. Dist: Cardinal Pubs. Group.
Foley, Mark. Trivial Matters for Children. 2008. 123p. pap. 12.95 *(978-0-615-19609-1(8))* Foley, Mark.
Forte, Imogene. Ready to Learn: Words & Vocabulary. 2003. (Illus.). 64p. per. 7.95 *(978-0-86530-591-5(9))* Incentive Pubns., Inc.
Foster, Jane. Jane Foster's ABC. 2015. (Jane Foster Bks.). (ENG., Illus.). 26p. (J). (gr. -1 — 1). bds. 8.99 *(978-1-4998-0074-6(6))* Little Bee Books Inc.
—Jane Foster's First Words. 2016. (ENG., Illus.). 26p. (J). (gr. -1 — 1). bds. 7.99 *(978-1-4998-0284-9(6))* Little Bee Books Inc.
Foundations: Early Emergent-Upper Emergent - 1 Each of 25 Student Books: Level E. 124.95 *(978-0-322-02722-0(5))* Wright Group/McGraw-Hill.
Frazier. Time Zones, Vol. 1. 2010. (ENG.). 160p. (J). pap., stu. ed. *(978-1-4240-6008-5(7))* Thomson ELT.
Fried, Miriam. My Jelly Bean Book. 2005. (Illus.). (J). *(978-1-57400-049-8(7))* Data Trace Publishing, Co.
Friedland, Joyce, ed. The Hunger Games: Novel-Ties Teachers Study Guide. 2011. (ENG.). 27p. pupil's gde. ed. 16.95 *(978-0-7675-5352-0(7))* Learning Links Inc.
—Rules: Novel-Ties Study Guide. 2011. 26p. pap. 16.95 *(978-0-7675-4468-9(4))* Learning Links Inc.
Fujikawa, Gyo. Gyo Fujikawa's A to Z Picture Book. 2010. (ENG., Illus.). 72p. (J). (gr. -1-2). 9.95 *(978-1-4027-6818-7(4),* 1318769) Sterling Publishing Co., Inc.
Gallagher, Belinda, ed. Mix & Match: Six Fun Scenes to Search & Find. 2008. (Illus.). 14p. (J). *(978-1-84236-786-5(2))* Miles Kelly Publishing, Ltd.
Ganeri, Anita. Ancient Egypt: The Complete Homework Solution. 2010. (Study Buddies Ser.). (ENG.). 32p. (J). (gr. 4-7). pap. 6.95 *(978-1-84898-183-6(X),* TickTock Books) Octopus Publishing Group GBR. Dist: Independent Pubs. Group.
Geatches, Hazel. Cities, Level 2. 2012. (ENG., Illus.). 40p. pap. 9.38 *(978-0-19-464682-6(3))* Oxford Univ. Pr., Inc.
Geatches, Hazel. At the Beach. 2012. (ENG., Illus.). 32p. 9.38 *(978-0-19-464628-4(9))* Oxford Univ. Pr., Inc.

—Earth. 2012. (ENG., Illus.). 40p. pap., act. bk. ed. 10.00 *(978-0-19-464679-6(3))* Oxford Univ. Pr., Inc.
Geller, Amy. My First Words OUTSIDE, 1 vol. 2013. (ENG., Illus.). 20p. (J). bds. 6.99 *(978-1-59572-332-1(3))* Star Bright Bks., Inc.
Giles, Sophie & Davis, Kate. My First 1000 Words. Peters, Andy & Hewett, Angela, illus. 2014. (ENG.). 125p. 17.50 *(978-1-84135-642-6(5))* Award Pubns. Ltd. GBR. Dist: Parkwest Pubns., Inc.
Gobo, creator. My Magnetic First Words Runaway Cat. 2006. (Illus.). 8p. (J). (gr. -1-3). 9.95 *(978-1-932915-17-4(6))* Sandvik Innovations, LLC.
Gold, Ethel, illus. Outdoor Things. (Picture Bks.: No. S8817-3). 28p. (J). (gr. -1). pap. 3.95 *(978-0-7214-5142-8(X),* Dutton Juvenile) Penguin Publishing Group.
—Things That Go. (Picture Bks.: No. S8817-1). 28p. (J). (gr. -1). pap. 3.95 *(978-0-7214-5140-4(3),* Dutton Juvenile) Penguin Publishing Group.
Gold, Kimberley. Outer Space. (Puzzle Shapes Ser.). (Illus.). 10p. (J). bds. *(978-2-89393-937-7(6))* Phidal Publishing, Inc./Editions Phidal, Inc.
Goldsmith, Mike. Under the Sea. Daubney, Kate, illus. 2015. (I Explore Ser.). (ENG.). 12p. (J). (gr. -1-k). bds. 6.95 *(978-1-4549-1502-7(1))* Sterling Publishing Co., Inc.
Goodwyn, Susan. My First Spoken Words: Animals. 2007. (Smart Kids Talking Bks.). (ENG., Illus.). 12p. (gr. -1-k). bds. 12.99 *(978-0-8249-6718-5(6),* Ideal Pubns.) Worthy Publishing.
Gooly & Campbell Books Staff. Happy Families. Hyun, Kim, illus. 2015. (Chat About Ser.). (ENG.). 22p. (J). (— 1). bds. 9.99 ***(978-1-4472-7729-3(5))*** Pan Macmillan GBR. Dist: Independent Pubs. Group.
Gooly, Gooly, et al. Best Friends. Hyun, Kim, illus. 2015. (Chat About Ser.). (ENG.). 22p. (J). (— 1). bds. 9.99 ***(978-1-4472-7730-9(9))*** Pan Macmillan GBR. Dist: Independent Pubs. Group.
Gordon, Jo Ann. Articulation Tales: Stories for Articulation Remediation. 2006. 136p. pap. 24.00 *(978-1-57128-314-6(5))* Academic Therapy Pubns., Inc.
Gorrell, Gena K. Say What? The Weird & Mysterious Journey of the English Language. 2009. (ENG.). 152p. (J). (gr. 5-9). pap. 10.95 *(978-0-88776-878-1(4),* Tundra Bks.) Tundra Bks. CAN. Dist: Penguin Random Hse. LLC.
Got, Yves. Mi Gran Libro de Las Palabras: Las Vacaciones de Dodo. 2003. (SPA.). 28p. *(978-84-233-3271-7(3),* DS3843) Ediciones Destino ESP. Dist: Lectorum Pubns., Inc.
Gravois, Michael. Fill-In Flip Books for Grammar, Vocabulary, & More, Grades 3-5: 25 Interactive Study AIDS That Kids Fill Out & Use Again & Again to Reinforce Essential Language Arts Content. 2005. (ENG., Illus.). 80p. (gr. 3-5). per. 12.99 *(978-0-439-67682-3(7),* Teaching Resources) Scholastic, Inc.
Grundwortschatz. (Duden-Schuelerhilfen Ser.). (GER.). 80p. (J). (gr. 3-4). *(978-3-411-06342-0(4))* Bibliographisches Institut & F. A. Brockhaus AG DEU. Dist: International Bk. Import Service, Inc.
Gunzi, Christiane. My Favourite Things. 2013. (ENG., Illus.). 6p. (J). bds. 7.95 *(978-1-907604-37-9(5))* Award Pubns. Ltd. GBR. Dist: Parkwest Pubns., Inc.
—My Lovely Day. 2013. (ENG., Illus.). 6p. (J). bds. 7.95 *(978-1-907604-36-2(7))* Award Pubns. Ltd. GBR. Dist: Parkwest Pubns., Inc.
—Words. 2nd rev. ed. 2015. (ENG., Illus.). 34p. (J). 7.99 *(978-1-905503-71-1(7))* Award Pubns. Ltd. GBR. Dist: Parkwest Pubns., Inc.
Gunzi, Christiane. Clothes. 2003. (My Very First Look At Ser.). (SPA & ENG., Illus.). 24p. (J). (gr. -1-k). 9.95 *(978-1-58728-672-8(6));* pap. 5.95 *(978-1-58728-686-5(6))* Cooper Square Publishing Llc.
—My Home. 2003. (My Very First Look At Ser.). (SPA & ENG., Illus.). 24p. (J). (gr. -1-k). pap. 5.95 *(978-1-58728-685-8(8));* 9.95 *(978-1-58728-671-1(8))* Cooper Square Publishing Llc.
—Words. 2003. (My Very First Look At Ser.). (SPA & ENG., Illus.). 24p. (J). (gr. -1-k). 9.95 *(978-1-58728-670-4(X))* Cooper Square Publishing Llc.
Gürth, Per-Henrik. Canada in Words. Gürth, Per-Henrik, illus. 2012. (ENG., Illus.). 32p. (J). (gr. -1-1). 14.95 *(978-1-55453-710-5(X))* Kids Can Pr., Ltd. CAN. Dist: Hachette Bk. Group.
—First Hockey Words. Gürth, Per-Henrik, illus. 2014. (ENG., Illus.). 32p. (J). (gr. -1-k). 15.95 *(978-1-77138-114-7(0))* Kids Can Pr., Ltd. CAN. Dist: Hachette Bk. Group.
Haddon, Jean. Words: A Computer Lesson. Vargo, Sharon Hawkins, illus. 2003. (Silly Millies Ser.). 32p. (J). (gr. -1-1). pap. 4.99 *(978-0-7613-1797-5(X));* lib. bdg. 17.90 *(978-0-7613-2870-4(X))* Lerner Publishing Group. (Millbrook Pr.).
Hahn, Marika, illus. Things to Wear. (Picture Bks.: No. S8817-4). 28p. (J). (gr. -1). pap. 3.95 *(978-0-7214-5143-5(8),* Dutton Juvenile) Penguin Publishing Group.
Hall, Dorothy & Daniel, Marie. Guess the Covered Word for Seasons & Holidays. 2003. (Four Blocks Ser.). 48p. pap. 25.99 *(978-0-88724-125-3(5))* Four Blocks.
Hall, Nancy. Get Set for the Code Book B. 2004. (Explode the code Ser.). pap. 5.95 *(978-0-8388-1782-7(3))* Educators Publishing Service, Inc.
—Go for the Code Book C. 2004. (Explode the code Ser.). pap. 5.95 *(978-0-8388-1784-1(X))* Educators Publishing Service, Inc.
Hambleton, Laura & Turhan, Sedat. Telling Tails: Fun with Homonyms. Hambleton, Laura, illus. 2007. (Milet Wordwise Ser.). (ENG., Illus.). 24p. (J). (gr. k-2). pap. 6.95 *(978-1-84059-498-0(5))* Milet Publishing.
Haney Perez, Jessica. My First 100 Words Book: A Lift-the-Flap, Pull-Tab Learning Book. March, Chloe, illus. 2005. (Learn to Read Ser.). 10p. (J). 10.95 *(978-1-58117-210-2(9),* Intervisual/Piggy Toes) Bendon, Inc.
Hanson, Anders. Can You See Me?, 1 vol. (First Words Ser.). (Illus.). (J). (gr. k-3). 2006. (ENG.). 24p. lib. bdg. 24.21 *(978-1-59679-360-6(0),* SandCastle) 2005. 23p. pap. 48.42 *(978-1-59679-361-3(9))* ABDO Publishing Co.
—Come in & Swim!, 1 vol. (First Words Ser.). (Illus.). (J). (gr. k-3). 2006. (ENG.). 24p. lib. bdg. 24.21 *(978-1-59679-366-8(X),* SandCastle) 2005. 23p. pap. 48.42 *(978-1-59679-367-5(8))* ABDO Publishing Co.
—Go for It!, 1 vol. (First Words Ser.). (Illus.). (J). (gr. k-3). 2006. (ENG.). 24p. lib. bdg. 24.21 *(978-1-59679-372-9(4),* SandCastle) 2005. 23p. pap. 48.42 *(978-1-59679-373-6(2))* ABDO Publishing Co.
—Here Comes the Sun, 1 vol. (First Words Ser.). (Illus.). (J). (gr. k-3). 2006. (ENG.). 24p. lib. bdg. 24.21 *(978-1-59679-376-7(7),* SandCastle) 2005. 23p. pap. 48.42 *(978-1-59679-377-4(5))* ABDO Publishing Co.
—I Like My Family!, 1 vol. (First Words Ser.). (Illus.). (J). (gr. k-3). 2006. (ENG.). 24p. lib. bdg. 24.21 *(978-1-59679-382-8(1),* SandCastle) 2005. 23p. pap. 48.42 *(978-1-59679-383-5(X))* ABDO Publishing Co.
—Little Like Me, 1 vol. (First Words Ser.). (Illus.). (J). (gr. k-3). 2006. (ENG.). 24p. lib. bdg. 24.21 *(978-1-59679-394-1(5),* SandCastle) 2005. 23p. pap. 48.42 *(978-1-59679-395-8(3))* ABDO Publishing Co.
—Seasons Come & Go, 1 vol. (First Words Ser.). (Illus.). (J). (gr. k-3). 2006. (ENG.). 24p. lib. bdg. 24.21 *(978-1-59679-412-2(7),* SandCastle) 2005. 23p. pap. 48.42 *(978-1-59679-413-9(5))* ABDO Publishing Co.
—The Snowman's Clothes, 1 vol. (First Words Ser.). (Illus.). (J). (gr. k-3). 2006. (ENG.). 24p. lib. bdg. 24.21 *(978-1-59679-416-0(X),* SandCastle) 2005. 23p. pap. 48.42 *(978-1-59679-417-7(8))* ABDO Publishing Co.
—We Say Hooray!, 1 vol. (First Words Ser.). (Illus.). (J). (gr. k-3). 2006. (ENG.). 24p. lib. bdg. 24.21 *(978-1-59679-438-2(0),* SandCastle) 2005. 23p. pap. 48.42 *(978-1-59679-439-9(9))* ABDO Publishing Co.
—What Do I Look Like?, 1 vol. (First Words Ser.). (Illus.). (J). (gr. k-3). 2006. (ENG.). 24p. lib. bdg. 24.21 *(978-1-59679-442-9(9),* SandCastle) 2005. 23p. pap. 48.42 *(978-1-59679-443-6(7))* ABDO Publishing Co.
—You & I Can Read!, 1 vol. Craig, Diane, ed. 2006. (First Words Ser.). (ENG., Illus.). 24p. (J). (gr. k-3). lib. bdg. 24.21 *(978-1-59679-444-3(5),* SandCastle) ABDO Publishing Co.
—You & I Can Read! 2005. (Illus.). 23p. (J). pap. 48.42 *(978-1-59679-445-0(3))* ABDO Publishing Co.
Harcourt School Publishers Staff. Decoding & Word Recognition Assessment. 3rd ed. 2003. (Harcourt School Publishers Trophies Ser.). (ENG.). 40p. (gr. k-k). pap. 42.60 *(978-0-15-340340-8(3));* 56p. (gr. 2-2). pap. 43.05 *(978-0-15-340341-5(1))* Harcourt Schl. Pubs.
—Harcourt Language: Vocabulary Power. 2nd ed. 2003. (Harcourt Title I Reading Programs Ser.). (Illus.). (gr. 2-18). pupil's gde. ed. 5.90 *(978-0-15-320608-5(X));* (gr. 3-18). 5.90 *(978-0-15-320609-2(8));* (gr. 4-18). 5.90 *(978-0-15-320610-8(1));* (gr. 5-18). 5.90 *(978-0-15-320611-5(X))* Harcourt Schl. Pubs.
Harpster, Steve, illus. First Word Search: Fun First Words. 2011. (First Word Search Ser.). (ENG.). 64p. (J). pap. 4.95 *(978-1-4027-7807-0(4))* Sterling Publishing Co., Inc.
Harris, Valerie F. & Jones, Eula V. Shaping up for Sight Word Success. Date not set. 30p. (J). (gr. k-6). wbk. ed. *(978-1-889654-03-4(5))* Enricharamics, Inc.
Harry, Pamela. My Body & Me, 1 vol. 2010. 16p. pap. 24.95 *(978-1-4489-6155-9(6))* PublishAmerica, Inc.
Harte, May. 1, 2, 3 in My House. 2004. (Look-And-Learn Books). (Illus.). (J). lib. bdg. 8.95 *(978-1-4042-2823-8(3),* PowerKids Pr.) Rosen Publishing Group, Inc., The.
Haughom, Lisa, illus. People, Places & Things. 2010. (J). *(978-1-58865-541-7(5))* Kidsbooks, LLC.
—Things That Go! 2010. 16p. (J). *(978-1-58865-542-4(3))* Kidsbooks, LLC.
Haydon, Julie. First 1000 Words. 2004. (Illus.). 95p. (J). *(978-1-74121-402-4(5))* Hinkler Bks. Pty. Ltd.
Hayes, Larry E. My Name Starts with S (Library Version) Anderson, Airlie, illus. 2004. (My Name Starts With Ser.). 32p. (J). lib. bdg. 12.95 *(978-0-9725292-8-0(4))* Inspire Pubns.
Hazan, Maurice, creator. El Camino: Practicing Everyday Vocabulary. (SPA.). (J). 124.95 *(978-1-932770-44-5(5),* SG5) Symtalk, Inc.
Heidrich, Delana. Figuratively Speaking: Using Classic Literature to teach 40 Literary Terms, Vol. 1020. Clark, Kim, ed. Armstrong, Beverly & Grayson, Rick, illus. 2004. 136p. (J). (gr. 5-8). pap. 14.99 *(978-0-88160-317-0(1),* LW-1020) Creative Teaching Pr., Inc.
Heinle Childrens Picture Dict-Amer English Sing-Along. 2007. (ENG.). (C). cd-rom 71.95 *(978-1-4240-0942-8(1))* Cengage Heinle.
Helenek, Sophie. My First Book SKY WONDERS: BOOK of the YEAR 2014 for Babies & Toddlers Category by Creative Child Magazine. 2014. (My First Book Ser.). (ENG., Illus.). 16p. (J). (gr. -1 — 1). bds. 5.99 *(978-0-9894505-3-9(8))* Nursery Bks.
Henderson, Meryl. Indoor Things. (Picture Bks.: No. S8817-2). (Illus.). 28p. (J). (gr. -1). pap. 3.95 *(978-0-7214-5141-1(1),* Dutton Juvenile) Penguin Publishing Group.
Hentzell, Brittany, illus. Annie & Arnie's Arduous Afternoon. 2005. spiral bd. 12.95 *(978-0-9773550-0-6(4))* Smartypants Bks.
Herzog, Joyce. Excursion into Words: Student Activity Book. Sinclair, Angie & Sinclair, Dan, eds. 2005. (J). spiral bd. 15.00 *(978-1-887225-46-5(3))* Herzog, Joyce.
Hicks, Diana & Littlejohn, Andrew. American English Primary Colors 2 Vocabulary Cards. 2004. (ENG.). 96p. 33.50 *(978-0-521-60319-5(6))* Cambridge Univ. Pr.
Hiding: KinderWords Individual Title Six-Packs. (Kinderstarters Ser.). 8p. (gr. -1-1). 21.00 *(978-0-7635-8703-1(6))* Rigby Education.
Hills, Tad. Rocket's Mighty Words. 2015. (ENG., Illus.). 22p. (J). (-k). bds. 7.99 *(978-0-553-53866-3(7),* Schwartz & Wade Bks.) Random Hse. Children's Bks.
Hinkler Books, creator. 101 First Words. 2011. (101 First Words Ser.). (Illus.). 16p. (J). (gr. -1). bds. 7.99 *(978-1-74184-816-8(4))* Hinkler Bks. Pty. Ltd. AUS. Dist: Ideals Pubns.
—101 First Words: Animals. 2011. (101 First Words Ser.). (Illus.). 16p. (J). (gr. -1). bds. 7.99 *(978-1-74184-817-5(2))* Hinkler Bks. Pty. Ltd. AUS. Dist: Ideals Pubns.
—101 First Words: At Home. 2011. (101 First Words Ser.). (Illus.). 16p. (J). (gr. -1). bds. 7.99 *(978-1-74184-819-9(9))* Hinkler Bks. Pty. Ltd. AUS. Dist: Ideals Pubns.
—101 First Words: Things That Go. 2011. (101 First Words Ser.). (Illus.). 16p. (J). (gr. -1). bds. 7.99 *(978-1-74184-818-2(0))* Hinkler Bks. Pty. Ltd. AUS. Dist: Ideals Pubns.
Hirschmann, Kris. Feed Me Words. Hindle, James K., illus. 2016. (Scripps National Spelling Bee Ser.). (ENG.). 96p. (J). 17.99 *(978-1-62672-173-9(4),* 9781626721739) Roaring Brook Pr.
Hoban, Tana. Over, under & Through. Hoban, Tana, illus. 2008. (ENG., Illus.). 32p. (J). (gr. -1-2). 8.99 *(978-1-4169-7541-0(1),* Simon & Schuster/Paula Wiseman Bks.) Simon & Schuster/Paula Wiseman Bks.
Hoffmann, Sara E. Ana & the Pet Show. Strange, Katie, illus. 2013. (My Reading Neighborhood: First-Grade Sight Word Stories Ser.). (ENG.). 16p. (gr. -1-1). pap. 5.95 *(978-1-4677-1170-8(5))* Lerner Publishing Group.
—Ana & the Rainy Day. Strange, Katie, illus. 2013. (My Reading Neighborhood: First-Grade Sight Word Stories Ser.). (ENG.). 16p. (gr. -1-1). pap. 5.95 *(978-1-4677-1174-6(8))* Lerner Publishing Group.
—Ben Gives a Gift. Dieterichs, Shelley, illus. 2013. (My Reading Neighborhood: Kindergarten Sight Word Stories Ser.). (ENG.). 16p. (gr. -1-1). pap. 5.95 *(978-1-4677-1164-7(0))* Lerner Publishing Group.
—Fall Fun for Kit. Roraback, Robin, illus. 2013. (My Reading Neighborhood: Kindergarten Sight Word Stories Ser.). (ENG.). 16p. (gr. -1-1). pap. 5.95 *(978-1-4677-1165-4(9))* Lerner Publishing Group.
—Holidays with Joe. Bueno, Lisa, illus. 2013. (My Reading Neighborhood: First-Grade Sight Word Stories Ser.). (ENG.). 16p. (gr. -1-1). pap. 5.95 *(978-1-4677-1169-2(1))* Lerner Publishing Group.
—Nan Swims. Roraback, Robin, illus. 2013. (My Reading Neighborhood: Kindergarten Sight Word Stories Ser.). (ENG.). 16p. (gr. -1-1). pap. 5.95 *(978-1-4677-1166-1(7))* Lerner Publishing Group.
—Nia Bakes Cookies. Strange, Katie, illus. 2013. (My Reading Neighborhood: First-Grade Sight Word Stories Ser.). (ENG.). 16p. (gr. -1-1). pap. 5.95 *(978-1-4677-1172-2(1))* Lerner Publishing Group.
—A Party with Joe. Bueno, Lisa, illus. 2013. (My Reading Neighborhood: First-Grade Sight Word Stories Ser.). (ENG.). 16p. (gr. -1-1). pap. 5.95 *(978-1-4677-1173-9(X))* Lerner Publishing Group.
—A Picnic with Kit. Roraback, Robin, illus. 2013. (My Reading Neighborhood: Kindergarten Sight Word Stories Ser.). (ENG.). 16p. (gr. -1-1). pap. 5.95 *(978-1-4677-1168-5(3))* Lerner Publishing Group.
—Sam Is Six. Dieterichs, Shelley, illus. 2013. (My Reading Neighborhood: Kindergarten Sight Word Stories Ser.). (ENG.). 16p. (gr. -1-1). pap. 5.95 *(978-1-4677-1163-0(2))* Lerner Publishing Group.
—Sam Sees Snow. Dieterichs, Shelley, illus. 2013. (My Reading Neighborhood: Kindergarten Sight Word Stories Ser.). (ENG.). 16p. (gr. -1-1). pap. 5.95 *(978-1-4677-1167-8(5))* Lerner Publishing Group.
—School for Ken. Bueno, Lisa, illus. 2013. (My Reading Neighborhood: First-Grade Sight Word Stories Ser.). (ENG.). 16p. (gr. -1-1). pap. 5.95 *(978-1-4677-1171-5(3))* Lerner Publishing Group.
Hogan, Martina, illus. Dinosaur Big, Dinosaur Small. 2016. (Early Birds Ser.). (ENG.). 12p. (J). (gr. -1 — 1). bds. 6.99 *(978-1-4998-0184-2(X))* Little Bee Books Inc.
Holt, Rinehart and Winston Staff. Elements of Literature: Assessment: Literature, Reading & Vocabulary. 2003. 4th ed. pap. 40.20 *(978-0-03-068518-7(4))* 5th ed. pap. 40.20 *(978-0-03-068517-0(6))* 5th ed. pap. 40.20 *(978-0-03-068519-4(2))* Holt McDougal.
—Elements of Literature: Vocabulary Development. 5th ed. 2003. (Illus.). pap. 30.40 *(978-0-03-073938-5(1));* pap. 30.40 *(978-0-03-073939-2(X))* Holt McDougal.
—Vocabulary Workshop. 2003. (Elements of Language Ser.). (gr. 6-18). 19.20 *(978-0-03-056023-1(3))* Holt McDougal.
Hop, Jog, & Tap: Consonants g, h, j; Short Vowel o word families: Level A, 6 vols. (Wright Skills Ser.). 12p. (gr. k-3). 17.95 *(978-0-322-01449-7(2))* Wright Group/McGraw-Hill.
Hoppner, Gabi. Backyard Fun. 2004. (What A Series of Fun! Ser.). (Illus.). 10p. (J). bds. 3.99 *(978-1-59384-054-9(3))* Parklane Publishing.
—Fun on Wheels. 2004. (What A Series of Fun! Ser.). (Illus.). 10p. (J). bds. 3.99 *(978-1-59384-055-6(1))* Parklane Publishing.
Las Horas. (Coleccion Libritos Acordeon). (SPA., Illus.). 10p. (J). pap. 5.50 *(978-950-11-0827-9(9),* SGM279) Sigmar ARG. Dist: Continental Bk. Co., Inc.
Howard, Linda & Dockray, Tracy Arah, illus. Mi Gran Libro de Palabras Play-Doh. 2006. (SPA.). 10p. (J). (gr. -1-4). reprint ed. 10.00 *(978-1-4223-5586-2(1))* DIANE Publishing Co.
Hudson, Amanda. This Is My Ball. 2008. (Our Toys Ser.). (Illus.). 16p. (gr. -1-2). (J). lib. bdg. 19.00 *(978-0-8368-9252-9(6));* pap. 5.30 *(978-0-8368-9351-9(4))* Stevens, Gareth Publishing LLLP. (Weekly Reader Leveled Readers).
—This Is My Bear. 2008. (Our Toys Ser.). (Illus.). 16p. (gr. -1-2). (J). lib. bdg. 19.00 *(978-0-8368-9253-6(4));* pap. 5.30 *(978-0-8368-9352-6(2))* Stevens, Gareth Publishing LLLP. (Weekly Reader Leveled Readers).
—This Is My Book. 2008. (Our Toys Ser.). (Illus.). 16p. (gr. -1-2). (J). lib. bdg. 19.00 *(978-0-8368-9254-3(2));* pap. 5.30 *(978-0-8368-9353-3(0))* Stevens, Gareth Publishing LLLP. (Weekly Reader Leveled Readers).
—This Is My Book/Este Es Mi Libro. 2008. (Our Toys/Nuestros Juguetes Ser.). (ENG & SPA.). 16p. (gr. -1-2). pap. 5.30 *(978-0-8368-9357-1(5));* (Illus.). (J). lib. bdg. 19.00 *(978-0-8368-9258-1(5))* Stevens, Gareth Publishing LLLP. (Weekly Reader Leveled Readers).
—This Is My Truck. 2008. (Our Toys Ser.). (Illus.). 16p. (gr. -1-2). (J). lib. bdg. 19.00 *(978-0-8368-9255-0(0));* pap. 5.30 *(978-0-8368-9354-0(9))* Stevens, Gareth Publishing LLLP. (Weekly Reader Leveled Readers).
—This Is My Truck (Éste es mi Camión) 2008. (Our Toys/Nuestros Juguetes Ser.). (SPA.). 16p. (gr. -1-2). pap. 5.30 *(978-0-8368-9358-8(1),* Weekly Reader Leveled Readers) Stevens, Gareth Publishing LLLP.
—This Is My Truck/Éste Es Mi Camión. 2008. (Our Toys/Nuestros Juguetes Ser.). (ENG & SPA., Illus.). 16p. (J). (gr. -1-2). lib. bdg. 19.00 *(978-0-8368-9259-8(3),* Weekly Reader Leveled Readers) Stevens, Gareth Publishing LLLP.
Hudson, Amanda & Nations, Susan. This Is My Ball/Ésta es mi Pelota. 2008. (Our Toys/Nuestros Juguetes Ser.). (SPA.). 16p. (gr. -1-2). pap. 5.30 *(978-0-8368-9355-7(7),* Weekly Reader Leveled Readers) Stevens, Gareth Publishing LLLP.
—This Is My Bear: Éste Es Mi Oso. 2008. (Our Toys/Nuestros Juguetes Ser.). (SPA.). 16p. (gr. -1-2). pap. 5.30 *(978-0-8368-9356-4(5),* Weekly Reader Leveled Readers) Stevens, Gareth Publishing LLLP.
—This Is My Bear/Éste Es Mi Oso. 2008. (Our Toys/Nuestros Juguetes Ser.). (SPA & ENG., Illus.). 16p. (J). (gr. -1-2). lib. bdg. 19.00 *(978-0-8368-9257-4(7),* Weekly Reader Leveled Readers) Stevens, Gareth Publishing LLLP.
Hudson, Cheryl Willis. Book of Opposites. Simpson, Howard, illus. (Afro-Bets Ser.). (J). pap. 4.95 *(978-0-940975-11-8(4))* Just Us Bks., Inc.
Hughes, Mónica & Ripley, Frances. 350 Words. 2011. (I Love Reading Book & CD-ROM Packs Ser.). (ENG., Illus.). 96p. (J). (gr. k-2). pap. 16.95 *(978-1-84898-179-9(1),* TickTock Books) Octopus Publishing Group GBR. Dist: Independent Pubs. Group.
Hunsicker, Ranelda Mack. Faerie Gold: A Guide for Teachers & Students. 2005. (Classics for Young Readers Ser.). (Illus.). 64p. (J). 6.99 *(978-0-87552-741-3(8))* P & R Publishing.
—Heidi: A Guide for Teachers & Students. 2006. (Classics for Young Readers Ser.). 51p. (J). (gr. 3). per. 6.99 *(978-0-87552-740-6(X))* P & R Publishing.
—Little Women: A Guide for Teachers & Students. 2003. (Classics for Young Readers Ser.). 64p. (J). 6.99 *(978-0-87552-737-6(X))* P & R Publishing.
Hutchins, J. Spanish First Words (Primeras Palabras en Espanol) 2013. (SPA & ENG.). lib. bdg. 14.75 *(978-0-606-32400-7(3),* Turtleback) Turtleback Bks.
Hynson, Colin. Ancient Rome: The Complete Homework Solution. 2010. (Study Buddies Ser.). (ENG.). 32p. (J). (gr. 4-7). pap. 6.95 *(978-1-84898-182-9(1),* TickTock Books) Octopus Publishing Group GBR. Dist: Independent Pubs. Group.
Ideals Children's Books Staff, creator. My First Words: Fun to Play Bilingual Learning Game! 2007. (Bilingual Builders Ser.). (ENG., Illus.). 10p. (J). (gr. -1-1). bds. 8.99 *(978-0-8249-6696-6(1),* Ideal Pubns.) Worthy Publishing.
Inglés Básico para niños: Edad 7-12, Basic English for Children: ¡Aprenda las 250 Palabras Más Importantes en Inglés!, Learn the 250 Most Important Words in English! 2005. 30.00 *(978-0-9769266-2-7(8))* Weapons of Mass Instruction.
Inside My World. 2015. (Inside My World Ser.). (ENG.). 24p. (J). (gr. k-k). 135.60 *(978-1-4824-1632-9(8))* Stevens, Gareth Publishing LLLP.
Iversen, Sandra. Alphabet Book Aa. 2009. (Quick60 Alphabet Bks.). (ENG., Illus.). 12p. (J). pap. *(978-1-77540-000-4(X))* Iversen Publishing Ltd.
—Alphabet Book Bb. 2009. (Quick60 Alphabet Bks.). (ENG., Illus.). 12p. (J). pap. *(978-1-77540-001-1(8))* Iversen Publishing Ltd.
—Alphabet Book Cc. 2009. (Quick60 Alphabet Bks.). (ENG., Illus.). 12p. (J). pap. *(978-1-77540-002-8(6))* Iversen Publishing Ltd.
—Alphabet Book Dd. 2009. (Quick60 Alphabet Bks.). (ENG., Illus.). 12p. (J). pap. *(978-1-77540-003-5(4))* Iversen Publishing Ltd.
—Alphabet Book Ee. 2009. (Quick60 Alphabet Bks.). (ENG., Illus.). 12p. (J). pap. *(978-1-77540-004-2(2))* Iversen Publishing Ltd.
—Alphabet Book Ff. 2009. (Quick60 Alphabet Bks.). (ENG., Illus.). 12p. (J). pap. *(978-1-77540-005-9(0))* Iversen Publishing Ltd.
—Alphabet Book Gg. 2009. (Quick60 Alphabet Bks.). (ENG., Illus.). 12p. (J). pap. *(978-1-77540-006-6(9))* Iversen Publishing Ltd.
—Alphabet Book Hh. 2009. (Quick60 Alphabet Bks.). (ENG., Illus.). 12p. (J). pap. *(978-1-77540-007-3(7))* Iversen Publishing Ltd.
—Alphabet Book Ii. 2009. (Quick60 Alphabet Bks.). (ENG., Illus.). 12p. (J). pap. *(978-1-77540-008-0(5))* Iversen Publishing Ltd.
—Alphabet Book Jj. 2009. (Quick60 Alphabet Bks.). (ENG., Illus.). 12p. (J). pap. *(978-1-77540-009-7(3))* Iversen Publishing Ltd.
—Alphabet Book Kk. 2009. (Quick60 Alphabet Bks.). (ENG., Illus.). 12p. (J). pap. *(978-1-77540-010-3(7))* Iversen Publishing Ltd.
—Alphabet Book Ll. 2009. (Quick60 Alphabet Bks.). (ENG., Illus.). 12p. (J). pap. *(978-1-77540-011-0(5))* Iversen Publishing Ltd.
—Alphabet Book Mm. 2009. (ENG., Illus.). 12p. (J). pap. *(978-1-77540-012-7(3))* Iversen Publishing Ltd.
—Alphabet Book Nn. 2009. (Quick60 Alphabet Bks.). (ENG., Illus.). 12p. (J). pap. *(978-1-77540-013-4(1))* Iversen Publishing Ltd.
—Alphabet Book Oo. 2009. (Quick60 Alphabet Bks.). (ENG., Illus.). 12p. (J). pap. *(978-1-77540-014-1(X))* Iversen Publishing Ltd.
—Alphabet Book Pp. 2009. (Quick60 Alphabet Bks.). (ENG., Illus.). 12p. (J). pap. *(978-1-77540-015-8(8))* Iversen Publishing Ltd.
—Alphabet Book Zz. 2009. (Quick60 Alphabet Bks.). (ENG., Illus.). 12p. (J). pap. *(978-1-77540-025-7(5))* Iversen Publishing Ltd.
James, Trisha. I Know Things That Go. 2017. (What I Know Ser.). 24p. (J). (gr. k-k). pap. 8.15 ***(978-1-4824-6309-5(1))*** Stevens, Gareth Publishing LLLP.
Jenkins, Emily. Small, Medium, Large, 1 vol. Bogacki, Tomek, illus. 2011. (ENG.). 32p. (J). 19.95 *(978-1-59572-278-2(5))* Star Bright Bks., Inc.
—Small Medium Large, 1 vol. Bogacki, Tomek, illus. 2011. (ENG.). 32p. (J). pap. 12.95 *(978-1-59572-299-7(8))* Star Bright Bks., Inc.
Johnson, Margaret. Gone! Level Starter/Beginner American English. 2010. (ENG., Illus.). 48p. pap. 12.00 *(978-0-521-14904-4(5))* Cambridge Univ. Pr.
Johnson, Paul F. & Halfman, Patti. 50 Quick Play Vocabulary Games. 2004. (YA). per. 34.95 *(978-0-7606-0539-4(4))* LinguiSystems, Inc.
Jones, Stephanie, des. First Words Look & Say Flashcards. 2007. (Look & Say Flashcards Ser.). (Illus.). 30p. (J). (gr. -1-k). 9.99 *(978-0-7945-1497-6(9),* Usborne) EDC Publishing.
Jones, Tammy. I Am Active. 2009. (Sight Word Readers Set A Ser.). (J). *(978-1-60719-139-1(3))* Newmark Learning LLC.

T
U
V

—I Go! 2009. (Sight Word Readers Set A Ser.). (J). 3.49 net. *(978-1-60719-143-8(1))* Newmark Learning LLC.

—I Like the Spring! 2009. (Sight Word Readers Set A Ser.). (J). 3.49 net. *(978-1-60719-138-4(5))* Newmark Learning LLC.

—I Like to Play Sports. 2009. (Sight Word Readers Set A Ser.). (J). 3.49 net. *(978-1-60719-135-3(0))* Newmark Learning LLC.

—Jobs Around Town. 2009. (Sight Word Readers Set A Ser.). (J). 3.49 net. *(978-1-60719-158-2(X))* Newmark Learning LLC.

—Look at the Shapes. 2009. (Sight Word Readers Set A Ser.). (J). 3.49 net. *(978-1-60719-152-0(0))* Newmark Learning LLC.

Juguetes. (Coleccion Libritos Acordeon). (SPA., Illus.). 10p. (J). pap. 5.50 *(978-950-11-0825-5(2)*, SGM252) Sigmar ARG. Dist: Continental Bk. Co., Inc.

Jullien, Jean. Before & After. 2017. (ENG., Illus.). 40p. (gr. -1 — 1). bds. 12.95 ***(978-0-7148-7408-1(6))*** Phaidon Pr., Inc.

Just the Right Word! Classroom Set. (J). (gr. k-3). 109.22 *(978-0-7362-2534-2(X))* CENGAGE Learning.

Kauffman, Dorothy & Apple, Gary. English Dictionary for the Content Areas, Set, Pack. 2nd ed. 2010. (ENG., Illus.). xiii, 196p. (J). pap. 478.50 *(978-0-19-452526-8(0))* Oxford Univ. Pr. GBR. Dist: Oxford Univ. Pr., Inc.

Kauffman, Dorothy, et al. English Dictionary. 2nd ed. 2010. (Oxford Picture Dictionary for the Content Areas 2e Ser.). (ENG., Illus.). 196p. pap. 26.19 *(978-0-19-452500-8(7))* Oxford Univ. Pr., Inc.

—Oxford Picture Dictionary for the Content Areas. 2nd ed. 2010. (Oxford Picture Dictionary for the Content Areas 2e Ser.). (SPA & ENG., Illus.). 216p. pap. 27.00 *(978-0-19-452502-2(3))* Oxford Univ. Pr., Inc.

Kelley, Maria Felicia. Buz Words: Discovering Words in Pairs. Kelley, Maria Felicia, illus. I.t. ed. 2007. (Illus.). 29p. (J). (gr. -1-3). per. 7.95 *(978-0-9650918-2-4(1))* April Arts Press & Productions.

Kelley, Michelle. Rules, Rules, Rules. 2007. (ENG., Illus.). 16p. (gr. k-2). 28.50 *(978-1-60472-111-9(1))* Rourke Educational Media.

Kennard, Philippa. Bunny Island. Fukuda, Yukihiro, photos by. 2015. (ENG., Illus.). 32p. (J). (gr. -1-1). pap. 4.99 *(978-1-77085-657-8(9)*, 9781770856578) Firefly Bks., Ltd.

Kennst du Das? Deine Welt. (Duden Ser.). (GER., Illus.). 16p. (J). *(978-3-411-70431-6(4))* Bibliographisches Institut & F. A. Brockhaus AG DEU. Dist: International Bk. Import Service, Inc.

Kent, Lorna, illus. Baby's First Word Book. 2004. 12p. (J). bds. 7.99 *(978-1-85854-478-6(5))* Brimax Books Ltd. GBR. Dist: Byeway Bks.

—Word Magic: Magnetic Sentence Builder. 8p. (J). bds. *(978-1-58048-382-7(8))* Sandvik Publishing.

Kerrin, Jessica Scott & Kerrin, Jessica. Ready for Takeoff! Kelly, Joseph, illus. 2005. (Martin Bridge Ser.). (ENG.). 120p. (J). (gr. 2-5). 6.95 *(978-1-55337-772-6(9))* Kids Can Pr., Ltd. CAN. Dist: Hachette Bk. Group.

Kindle, Karen. Using Read-Alouds to Teach Vocabulary: Research-Based Strategies & Model Lessons for Using Fiction & Nonfiction Books to Build Children's Vocabulary & Improve Their Reading, Writing, & Speaking Skills. 2011. (ENG.). 128p. (gr. k-2). pap. 18.99 *(978-0-545-16513-6(X)*, Teaching Resources) Scholastic, Inc.

Könnecke, Ole. The Big Book of Words & Pictures. Könnecke, Ole, illus. 2012. (Gecko Press Titles Ser.). (Illus.). 22p. (J). (gr. -1-k). bds. 14.95 *(978-1-877579-05-9(X))* Gecko Pr. NZL. Dist: Lerner Publishing Group.

Kovecses, Anna. One Thousand Things. 2015. (Learn with Little Mouse Ser.). (ENG.). 80p. (J). (gr. -1 — 1). 16.99 *(978-1-84780-702-1(X)*, Wide Eyed Editions) Quarto Publishing Group UK GBR. Dist: Hachette Bk. Group.

—One Thousand Things: Learn to Say Your First Words with Little Mouse. 2015. (Learn with Little Mouse Ser.). (ENG., Illus.). 80p. (J). 16.99 *(978-1-84780-607-9(4)*, Wide Eyed Editions) Quarto Publishing Group UK GBR. Dist: Littlehampton Bk Services, Ltd.

Krause, Claudia. Word Wheels. (Orig.). (J). pap. *(978-0-9655689-0-6(3))* Krause, Claudia.

Ladybird. Minibeasts, Level 3. 2016. (Read It Yourself with Ladybird Ser.). (ENG., Illus.). 48p. (J). (gr. 2-4). pap. 9.99 *(978-0-241-23736-6(X))* Penguin Bks., Ltd. GBR. Dist: Independent Pubs. Group.

—On the Farm. 2016. (Read It Yourself with Ladybird Ser.). (ENG., Illus.). 32p. (J). (gr. 2-4). 5.99 *(978-0-241-23731-1(9))* Penguin Bks., Ltd. GBR. Dist: Independent Pubs. Group.

LaFleur, Richard & Tillery, Brad. Ovid Vocabulary Cards for AP Selections. 2007. 80p. pap. 15.00 *(978-0-86516-657-8(9))* Bolchazy-Carducci Pubs.

Lagonegro, Melissa & Wooster, Devin Ann. Big Dinosaur, Little Dinosaur. Random House Disney Staff, illus. 2016. (Step into Reading Ser.). (ENG.). 24p. (J). (gr. -1-1). 4.99 *(978-0-7364-3247-4(7)*, RH/Disney) Random Hse. Children's Bks.

Lakeshore Learning Materials Staff, contrib. by. The Big Surprise: A Homophone Story, Set of 6 Student Books. 2007. (J). pap. 18.95 *(978-1-59746-028-6(1))* Lakeshore Learning Materials.

—The Big Surprise: A Homophone Story Big Book. 2007. (J). pap. 19.95 *(978-1-59746-024-8(9))* Lakeshore Learning Materials.

—The Game: A Multiple Meaning Story, Set of 6 Student Books. 2007. (J). pap. 18.95 *(978-1-59746-029-3(X))* Lakeshore Learning Materials.

—The Game: A Multiple Meaning Story Big Book. 2007. (J). pap. 19.95 *(978-1-59746-025-5(7))* Lakeshore Learning Materials.

—The Great Race: A Synonym Story Big Book. 2007. (J). pap. 19.95 *(978-1-59746-022-4(2))* Lakeshore Learning Materials.

—Partner Reading Book Set. 2007. (J). pap. 39.95 *(978-1-59746-021-7(4))* Lakeshore Learning Materials.

—Spanish Alphabet Big Book. 2006. (SPA.). (J). pap. 19.95 *(978-1-59746-000-2(1))* Lakeshore Learning Materials.

—A Special Gift: An Antonym Story, Set of 6 Student Books. 2007. (J). pap. 18.95 *(978-1-59746-027-9(3))* Lakeshore Learning Materials.

—A Special Gift: An Antonym Story Big Book. 2007. (J). pap. 19.95 *(978-1-59746-023-1(0))* Lakeshore Learning Materials.

Lamb, Stacey, illus. Wipe Clean First Letters. 2011. (Wipe-Clean Bks). 20p. (J). pap. 7.99 *(978-0-7945-3100-3(8)*, Usborne) EDC Publishing.

LaQuay, Kate & LoGiudice, Carolyn. Spotlight on Vocabulary Antonyms Level 1, 6 vols. 2005. (Illus.). (J). per. 11.95 *(978-0-7606-0586-8(6))* LinguiSystems, Inc.

LaQuay, Kate & Logiudice, Carolyn. Spotlight on Vocabulary Associations Level 1, 6 vols. 2005. (Illus.). per. 11.95 *(978-0-7606-0604-9(8))* LinguiSystems, Inc.

—Spotlight on Vocabulary Attributes Level 1, 6 vols. 2005. (Illus.). (J). per. 11.95 *(978-0-7606-0588-2(2))* LinguiSystems, Inc.

LaQuay, Kate & LoGiudice, Carolyn. Spotlight on Vocabulary Categories Level 1, 6 vols. 2005. (Illus.). (J). per. 11.95 *(978-0-7606-0589-9(0))* LinguiSystems, Inc.

—Spotlight on Vocabulary Concepts Level 1, 6 vols. 2005. (Illus.). (J). per. 11.95 *(978-0-7606-0590-5(4))* LinguiSystems, Inc.

L'Arronge, Lilli & Stratford, Madeleine. Me Tall, You Small. 2017. (ENG., Illus.). 40p. (J). (gr. -1-3). 16.95 *(978-1-77147-194-7(8))* Owlkids Bks. Inc. CAN. Dist: Publishers Group West (PGW).

Lashley, Steven. E. The Buggouts: The Buggouts learning Club. Hunter, Laura E., ed. I.t. ed. 2005. (Illus.). 12p. (J). cd-rom 15.00 *(978-1-59971-244-4(X))* Aardvark Global Publishing.

Laval, Thierry. Look & Find on the Farm. 2017. (Mini Look & Find Ser.). (ENG.). 14p. (J). 9.95 ***(978-0-531-23080-0(5)***, Children's Pr.) Scholastic Library Publishing.

—Look & Find Transportation. 2016. (Look & Find Ser.). (ENG., Illus.). 14p. (J). 18.99 *(978-0-531-22237-9(3)*, Children's Pr.) Scholastic Library Publishing.

—Look & Find Your World. 2016. (Look & Find Ser.). (ENG.). 14p. (J). 18.99 *(978-0-531-22239-3(X)*, Children's Pr.) Scholastic Library Publishing.

Lawrence, Ellen. How We Get Around. 2015. (My World Your World Ser.). (ENG.). 24p. (J). (gr. -1-3). lib. bdg. 23.93 *(978-1-910549-12-4(6))* Bearport Publishing Co., Inc.

Lazarri, Andrea. Vocabulary To Go. 2006. (J). per. 39.95 *(978-0-7606-0663-6(3))* LinguiSystems, Inc.

LD COACH. TEH Learns to Read: Action Words, Volume Five. 2004. (Illus.). 40p. (J). 34.95 *(978-0-9745938-5-2(0))* LD Coach, LLC.

—TEH Learns to Read: Basic Words, Volume Six. 2004. (Illus.). 40p. (J). 34.95 *(978-0-9745938-6-9(9))* LD Coach, LLC.

—TEH Learns to Read: Elementary Words, Volume Seven. 2004. (Illus.). 40p. (J). 34.95 *(978-0-9745938-7-6(7))* LD Coach, LLC.

—TEH Learns to Read: Mixed Sight Words — Group A, Volume Eight. 2004. (Illus.). 40p. (J). 34.95 *(978-0-9745938-8-3(5))* LD Coach, LLC.

—TEH Learns to Read: More Action Words, Volume Nine. 2004. (Illus.). 40p. (J). 34.95 *(978-0-9745938-9-0(3))* LD Coach, LLC.

Le Jars, David. Por Aqui y Por Alli. 2004. (Hablemos Ser.).Tr. of Here & There. (SPA., Illus.). 24p. (J). (gr. -1-k). 9.95 *(978-1-58728-949-1(0))*; pap. 5.95 *(978-1-58728-953-8(9))* T&N Children's Publishing. (Two-Can Publishing).

Learning Company Books Staff, ed. Reader Rabbit: Rhyming Words. 2003. (Illus.). 32p. (J). pap., wbk. ed. *(978-0-7630-7578-1(7))* Magma.

Learning New Words (Gr. K-1) 2003. (J). *(978-1-58232-032-8(2))* ECS Learning Systems, Inc.

Lee, Betsy B. A Funny Dolch Word Book # 1: Un Libro Comico # 1 de la Palabra de Dolch. Davis, Pollyanna S., tr. 2006. (ENG & SPA.). pap. 5.95 *(978-0-9720267-5-8(4))* Learning Abilities Bks.

Lee, Brian, illus. A Castle. 2005. (What's Inside? Ser.). (J). *(978-0-7607-6568-5(5))* backpackbook.

Lengua Espanola: Cuarto Grado. (SPA & ENG.). (J). (gr. 4). 21.95 *(978-84-357-0027-6(5)*, CPR76) Ediciones y Distribuciones Codice, S.A. ESP. Dist: Continental Bk. Co., Inc.

Lengua Espanola: Quinto Grado. (SPA & ENG.). (J). (gr. 5). 22.00 *(978-84-357-0171-6(9)*, CPR78) Ediciones y Distribuciones Codice, S.A. ESP. Dist: Continental Bk. Co., Inc.

Lengua Espanola: Sexto Grado. (SPA & ENG.). (J). (gr. 6). 22.00 *(978-84-357-0170-9(0)*, CPR80) Ediciones y Distribuciones Codice, S.A. ESP. Dist: Continental Bk. Co., Inc.

Let's Read — Word Building. 2003. 16p. (J). 3.79 *(978-1-58792-051-6(4))* Trend Enterprises, Inc.

Levine, Julia Pimsleur. Little Pim: Animals. 2012. (ENG.). 10p. (J). (gr. -1-k). bds. 8.95 *(978-1-4197-0174-0(6))* Abrams, Inc.

—Little Pim: Numbers. 2012. (ENG.). 10p. (J). (gr. -1-k). bds. 8.95 *(978-1-4197-0175-7(4))* Abrams, Inc.

Levitt, Paul M., et al. The Weighty Word Book. Stevens, Janet, illus. 3rd ed. 2009. (ENG.). 96p. (J). 21.95 *(978-0-8263-4555-4(7))* Univ. of New Mexico Pr.

—Weighty Words, Too. Karcz, Katherine, illus. 2009. (ENG.). 96p. (J). (gr. 4-18). 21.95 *(978-0-8263-4558-5(1))* Univ. of New Mexico Pr.

Lewis, Jan. Farm. 2015. (ENG., Illus.). 24p. bds. 6.99 *(978-1-86147-635-7(3)*, Armadillo) Anness Publishing GBR. Dist: National Bk. Network.

—My First Words. 2015. (ENG., Illus.). 24p. bds. 6.99 *(978-1-86147-498-8(9)*, Armadillo) Anness Publishing GBR. Dist: National Bk. Network.

Lewis, Jan, illus. Animals: Turn the Wheels Find the Pictures. 2016. (ENG.). 10p. bds. 14.99 *(978-1-86147-713-2(9)*, Armadillo) Anness Publishing GBR. Dist: National Bk. Network.

—Look & Learn with Little Dino: Action Words. 2014. (ENG.). 24p. (J). (gr. k-2). bds. 6.99 *(978-1-86147-382-0(6)*, Armadillo) Anness Publishing GBR. Dist: National Bk. Network.

—Look & Learn with Little Dino: Busy Day. 2014. (ENG.). 24p. (J). (gr. k-2). bds. 6.99 *(978-1-86147-379-0(6)*, Armadillo) Anness Publishing GBR. Dist: National Bk. Network.

—Love from Santa, 6 vols. 2013. (ENG.). 60p. (J). (gr. -1-2). bds. 7.99 *(978-1-86147-313-4(3)*, Armadillo) Anness Publishing GBR. Dist: National Bk. Network.

—My First Animals. 2014. (ENG.). 24p. (J). (gr. -1-k). bds. 6.99 *(978-1-86147-373-8(7)*, Armadillo) Anness Publishing GBR. Dist: National Bk. Network.

—My First Learning Library: 3 Great Books: First Abc First 123 First Words, 3 vols. 2014. (ENG.). 72p. (J). (gr. -1-1). bds., bds., bds. 9.99 *(978-1-86147-387-5(7)*, Armadillo) Anness Publishing GBR. Dist: National Bk. Network.

—My First Words: Over 300 Everyday Words & Pictures. 2015. (ENG.). 48p. bds. 9.99 *(978-1-86147-627-2(2)*, Armadillo) Anness Publishing GBR. Dist: National Bk. Network.

—Santa's Christmas Box of Books: A Festive Box of Fun Picture Books. 2017. (ENG.). 1p. bds. 14.99 *(978-1-86147-738-5(4)*, Armadillo) Anness Publishing GBR. Dist: National Bk. Network.

—Words: Turn the Wheels, Find the Pictures. 2015. (ENG.). 10p. bds. 14.99 *(978-1-86147-660-9(4)*, Armadillo) Anness Publishing GBR. Dist: National Bk. Network.

Lindsay, Kristine. Basic Vocabulary - 1. 2005. (J). ring bd. 49.95 *(978-1-58804-385-6(1))* P C I Education.

—Basic Vocabulary 2. 2005. (J). ring bd. 49.95 *(978-1-58804-386-3(X))* P C I Education.

Lionni, Leo. What? 2014. (ENG., Illus.). 16p. (J). (— 1). bds. 5.99 *(978-0-385-75406-4(X)*, Knopf Bks. for Young Readers) Random Hse. Children's Bks.

—Where? 2014. (ENG., Illus.). 16p. (J). (— 1). bds. 5.99 *(978-0-385-75407-1(8)*, Knopf Bks. for Young Readers) Random Hse. Children's Bks.

—Who? 2014. (ENG., Illus.). 16p. (J). (— 1). bds. 5.99 *(978-0-385-75405-7(1)*, Knopf Bks. for Young Readers) Random Hse. Children's Bks.

Litchfield & Allman. Los Animales (Animals) 2004. (First Words Board Bks.). (SPA., Illus.). 12p. (J). 4.95 *(978-0-7460-4519-0(0))* EDC Publishing.

Litchfield, Jo. At Home. 2004. (First Words Board Bks.). (SPA & ENG., Illus.). 1p. (J). (gr. -1-18). bds. 4.95 *(978-0-7460-4092-8(X))* EDC Publishing.

—Home. Litchfield, Jo & Allen, Francesca, illus. 2006. (Usborne Look & Say Ser.). 12p. (J). (gr. -1-k). bds. 7.99 *(978-0-7945-1425-9(1)*, Usborne) EDC Publishing.

—Things That Move. 2004. (First Words Board Bks.). (ENG., Illus.). 1p. (J). bds. 4.95 *(978-0-7460-4149-9(7))* EDC Publishing.

—The Usborne Book of Everyday Words. Treays, Rebecca et al, eds. Allman, Howard, photos by. 2006. (Everyday Words Ser.). (Illus.). 48p. (J). (gr. -1). lib. bdg. 15.99 *(978-1-58086-964-5(5))* EDC Publishing.

—The Usborne Book of Everyday Words in French. 2006. (Everyday Words Ser.). (Illus.). 48p. (J). (gr. -1-3). per. 9.99 *(978-0-7945-0882-1(0)*, Usborne) EDC Publishing.

Litchfield, Jo, illus. Baby Sister Look & Say. 2008. (Look & Say Board Bks). 12p. (J). bds. 7.99 *(978-0-7945-2102-8(9)*, Usborne) EDC Publishing.

Litchfield, Jo & Brooks, Felicity. Everyday Words Sticker Book. 2004. (Everyday Words Ser.). (Illus.). 1p. (J). (gr. -1-3). (SPA & ENG.). pap. 8.95 *(978-0-7460-4236-6(1))*; (FRE & ENG., pap. 8.95 *(978-0-7460-4237-3(X))* EDC Publishing.

little bee books, little bee & Seal, Julia. Farm. 2016. (ENG., Illus.). 12p. (J). (gr. -1 — 1). bds. 6.99 *(978-1-4998-0260-3(9))* Little Bee Books Inc.

Litton, Jonathan. Hello World. L'Atelier Cartographik, illus. 2016. (360 Degrees Ser.). (ENG.). 16p. (J). (gr. 3-6). 19.99 *(978-1-944530-00-6(2)*, 360 Degrees) Tiger Tales.

—One, Two, Baa, Moo: A Pop-Up Book of Counting. Verrall, Lisa, illus. 2015. (My Little World Ser.). (ENG.). 12p. (J). bds. 8.99 *(978-1-68010-507-0(8))* Tiger Tales.

Ljungkvist, Laura. A Line Can Be ... 2015. (ENG., Illus.). 24p. (J). (-k). bds. 9.95 *(978-1-57687-753-1(1)*, powerHouse Bks.) powerHouse Cultural Entertainment, Inc.

Llewellyn, Claire. It's Fun to Learn about Words: A Busy Picture Book Full of Fabulous Facts & Things to Do! 2016. (ENG., Illus.). 32p. (J). (gr. -1-12). 9.99 *(978-1-86147-743-9(0)*, Armadillo) Anness Publishing GBR. Dist: National Bk. Network.

Llewellyn, Claire & Holden, Arianne. It's Great to Play & Fun to Learn: A Stimulating Play-And-Learn Book with over 130 Amazing Facts, Exercises & Projects, & More Than 5000 Bright Action-Packed Photographs. 2014. (ENG., Illus.). 256p. (J). (gr. k-4). 16.99 *(978-1-84322-981-0(1)*, Armadillo) Anness Publishing GBR. Dist: National Bk. Network.

Lloyd, Sue & Wernham, Sara. Word Book. Stephen, Lib, illus. 2003. (ENG.). 48p. (J). (gr. k-2). pap. 4.25 *(978-1-84414-028-2(8)*, Jolly Phonics) Jolly Learning, Ltd. GBR. Dist: American International Distribution Corp.

Lluch, Alex A. Baby's First 100 Plus Words. 2012. (ENG.). 22p. (J). bds. 7.95 *(978-1-936061-88-4(0))* WS Publishing.

Loewen, Nancy. She Sells Seashells & Other Tricky Tongue Twisters, 1 vol. Wu, Donald, illus. 2010. (Ways to Say It Ser.). (ENG.). 24p. (gr. 3-5). lib. bdg. 27.99 *(978-1-4048-6273-9(0))* Picture Window Bks.

LoGiudice, Carolyn & LaQuay, Kate. Spotlight on Vocabulary Antonyms Level 2, 6 vols. 2005. (Illus.). (J). per. 11.95 *(978-0-7606-0598-1(X))* LinguiSystems, Inc.

Logiudice, Carolyn & LaQuay, Kate. Spotlight on Vocabulary Associations Level 2, 5 vols. 2005. (Illus.). (J). per. 11.95 *(978-0-7606-0599-8(8))* LinguiSystems, Inc.

London, S. Keith & Osleeb, Rebecca. Defined Mind Vocabulary Accelerator: Music-Driven Vocabulary & Comprehension Tools for School / Test / SAT Prep, 1. 2004. 416p. (YA). pap. 25.00 *(978-0-9763767-0-5(9))* Defined Mind, Inc.

Lonely Planet Publications Staff. Lonely Planet First Words - English, 1 vol. 2017. (Lonely Planet Kids Ser.). (ENG., Illus.). 208p. (J). pap. 12.99 ***(978-1-78701-279-0(4)***, 5716) Lonely Planet Pubns.

Long, Ethan. Ms. Spell. 2015. (ENG., Illus.). 32p. (J). (gr. 1-4). 15.95 *(978-0-8234-3292-9(0))* Holiday Hse., Inc.

Lonsdale, Mary, illus. First Words Sticker Book. 2003. 12p. (J). bds. *(978-1-85854-658-2(3))* Autumn Publishing, Ltd.

Look, Listen, & Speak-at the Mall. 2005. 80p. (gr. k-3). cd-rom 29.99 *(978-1-55799-951-1(1)*, EMC 2745) Evan-Moor Educational Pubs.

Look, Listen, & Speak-at the Supermarket. 2005. 80p. (gr. k-3). cd-rom 29.99 *(978-1-55799-950-4(3)*, EMC 2744) Evan-Moor Educational Pubs.

Look, Listen, & Speak-from Farm to You. 2005. 80p. (gr. k-3). cd-rom 29.99 *(978-1-55799-949-8(X)*, EMC 2743) Evan-Moor Educational Pubs.

Look, Listen, & Speak-Keeping Healthy. 2005. 80p. (gr. k-3). cd-rom 29.99 *(978-1-55799-948-1(1)*, EMC 2742) Evan-Moor Educational Pubs.

Look, Listen, & Speak-Transportation. 2005. 80p. (gr. k-3). cd-rom 29.99 *(978-1-55799-952-8(X)*, EMC 2746) Evan-Moor Educational Pubs.

Lubben, Amy & Williams, Rozanne Lanczak. Build-a-Skill Instant Books Word Families-Long Vowels. Shiotsu, Vicky & Faulkner, Stacey, eds. Campbell, Jenny & Tom, Darcy, illus. 2007. (J). 4.99 *(978-1-59198-409-2(2))* Creative Teaching Pr., Inc.

—Build-a-Skill Instant Books Word Families-Short Vowels. Shiotsu, Vicky & Faulkner, Stacey, eds. Campbell, Jenny & Tom, Darcy, illus. 2007. (J). 4.99 *(978-1-59198-408-5(4))* Creative Teaching Pr., Inc.

Lucero, Jaime. Bilingual Bingo: Easy-to-Make Reproducible Games-in English & Spanish-That Reinforce Key Vocabulary for Emergent Readers & English Language Learners. 2008. (ENG.). 80p. (gr. k-3). pap. 12.99 *(978-0-439-70067-2(1)*, Teaching Resources) Scholastic, Inc.

Lucero, Jamie, et al. Amazing Word Power: 100 Words Every 4th Grader Should Know. 2008. (Amazing Word Power Ser.). (ENG.). 128p. pap. 6.99 *(978-0-545-08707-0(4)*, Teaching Resources) Scholastic, Inc.

Lundquist, Joegil K. & Lundquist, Jeanne L. English from the Roots up, Volume II: Help for Reading, Writing, Spelling & S. A. T. Scores. 2003. (English from the Roots Up Ser.). (Illus.). 107p. (J). (gr. -1-3). 44.95 *(978-1-885942-30-2(3))* Cune Pr., LLC.

—English from the Roots up Volume II: Help for Reading, Writing, Spelling, & S. A. T. Scores, vols. 2, II. 2003. (Illus.). 125p. 29.95 net. *(978-1-885942-31-9(1))* Cune Pr., LLC.

Lunge-Larsen, Lise. Gifts from the Gods: Ancient Words & Wisdom from Greek & Roman Mythology. Hinds, Gareth, illus. 2011. (ENG.). 96p. (J). (gr. 5-7). 18.99 *(978-0-547-15229-5(9))* Houghton Mifflin Harcourt Publishing Co.

Mac, Cola. Rhyming on Time. Bey, Charles, illus. 2011. 20p. pap. 24.95 *(978-1-4560-6940-7(3))* America Star Bks.

MagneTalk Match-Up Adventure Kit (with Barrier) Gb181. 2006. (J). 59.99 *(978-1-58650-616-2(1))* Super Duper Pubns.

MagneTalk Match-Up Adventure Kit (without Barrier) Gb182. 2006. (J). 59.99 *(978-1-58650-653-7(6))* Super Duper Pubns.

Mairi, Mackinnon. Phonics Workbook 1. 2012. (Very First Reading Workbooks Ser.). 36p. (J). pap. 7.99 *(978-0-7945-3115-7(6)*, Usborne) EDC Publishing.

—Phonics Workbook 2. 2012. (Very First Reading Workbooks Ser.). 36p. (J). pap. 7.99 *(978-0-7945-3116-4(4)*, Usborne) EDC Publishing.

Makishi, Cynthia. The Heinle Picture Dictionary for Children - Monkey Puppet. 2007. (ENG.). (C). 19.95 *(978-1-4240-1834-5(X))* Cengage Heinle.

Maldonado, Premier, creator. House-Casa: English-Español. 2004. (SPA., Illus.). 20p. (J). bds. 6.00 *(978-0-9727886-1-8(1))* Osmosis, LLC.

Mancini, Joan. 25 Super Sight Word Songs & Mini-Books: Fun Songs Set to Favorite Tunes with Companion Read & Write Mini-Books That Teach Essential Sight Words. 2009. (ENG.). 112p. (gr. k-2). 20.99 *(978-0-545-10582-8(X)*, Teaching Resources) Scholastic, Inc.

Marrow, Lesley Mandel & Vacca, Richard T. Sadlier Phonics: Level C Grade 3. 2001st ed. 2004. (Sadlier Phonics Reading Program). (Illus.). 336p. (gr. 3-18). pap., tchr. ed. 64.00 net. *(978-0-8215-7013-5(7))* Sadlier, William H. Inc.

Marsh, Carole. Work Words: Job/Business/Career Words & Terms You Need to Know! 2012. (Carole Marsh's Careers Curriculum Ser.). (ENG., Illus.). 58p. (J). pap. 19.99 *(978-0-635-10556-1(X))* Gallopade International.

Marshall, George. The Kingfisher Children's Illustrated Dictionary & Thesaurus. 2nd rev. ed. 2011. (ENG., Illus.). 320p. (J). (gr. 2-5). 16.99 *(978-0-7534-6469-4(1)*, 9780753464694, Kingfisher) Roaring Brook Pr.

Martin, Dayna. The Toddler's Handbook: Bilingual (English / Spanish) (Ingles / Espanol) Numbers, Colors, Shapes, Sizes, ABC Animals, Opposites, & Sounds, with over 100 Words That Every Kid Should Know (Engage Early Readers: Children's Learning Books) Roumanis, A. r., ed. I.t. ed. 2015. (SPA & ENG., Illus.). 48p. (J). pap. *(978-1-77226-225-4(0))* AD Classic.

Martin, John David. A Time to Plant: Workbook. 2005. (Rod & Staff's Readers Ser.). 145p. (gr. 5-18). 4.80 *(978-0-7399-0402-2(7)*, 11521) Rod & Staff Pubs., Inc.

Maskell, Hazell. Very First Words. 2009. (First Words Board Bks). 18p. (J). bds. 6.99 *(978-0-7945-2052-6(9)*, Usborne) EDC Publishing.

Mastering Sight Words (Gr. 1-2) 2003. (J). *(978-1-58232-091-5(8))* ECS Learning Systems, Inc.

McBratney, Sam. Guess How Much I Love You: Look What I Can Do: A First Concepts Book. Jeram, Anita, illus. 2014. (Guess How Much I Love You Ser.). (ENG.). 16p. (J). (— 1). bds. 9.99 *(978-0-7636-7064-1(2))* Candlewick Pr.

McCarty, Diane Bischoff. Copywork for Children: For Grades 1-3. 2004. (Illus.). 63p. (J). *(978-0-9712124-1-1(4))* Angel Heart Children's Pr.

McKay, Sindy. Can You Find? (We Both Read - Level Pk-K) An ABC Book. 2015. (We Both Read - Level Pk -K Ser.). (ENG., Illus.). 41p. (J). 9.95 *(978-1-60115-279-4(5))* Treasure Bay, Inc.

—We Read Phonics-Magic Tricks. Johnson, Meredith, illus. 2011. (We Read Phonics Ser.). 32p. (J). (gr. 1-3). 9.95 *(978-1-60115-337-1(6))*; pap. 4.99 *(978-1-60115-338-8(4))* Treasure Bay, Inc.

—We Read Phonics-Matt & Sid. Reinhart, Larry, illus. 2010. 32p. (J). 9.95 *(978-1-60115-315-9(5))*; pap. 4.99 *(978-1-60115-316-6(3))* Treasure Bay, Inc.

—We Read Phonics-Pat, Cat, & Rat. Johnson, Meredith, illus. 2010. 32p. (J). 9.95 *(978-1-60115-311-1(2))*; pap. 4.99 *(978-1-60115-312-8(0))* Treasure Bay, Inc.

McMahon, Philip & Collins UK Staff. 11+ Vocabulary Results Booster. 2016. (Letts 11+ Success Ser.). (ENG.). 80p. (J). (gr. 5-6). pap. 14.95 *(978-1-84419-899-3(5))* HarperCollins Pubs. Ltd. GBR. Dist: Independent Pubs. Group.

McNamara, Connie. My First IU Words Go Hoosiers. 2012. (ENG.). 16p. 10.99 *(978-0-06-219609-5(X))* HarperCollins Pubs.
—My First Kansas Words Go Jayhawks. 2012. (ENG.). 16p. 10.99 *(978-0-06-219608-8(1))* HarperCollins Pubs.
—My First Michigan State Words Go State. 2012. (ENG.). 16p. 10.99 *(978-0-06-219607-1(3))* HarperCollins Pubs.
—My First Ohio State Words Go Buckeyes. 2012. (ENG.). 16p. 10.99 *(978-0-06-219605-7(7))* HarperCollins Pubs.
—My First Pittsburgh Words Go Pitt. 2012. (ENG.). 16p. 10.99 *(978-0-06-220363-2(0))* HarperCollins Pubs.
—My First U of I Words Go Illini. 2012. (ENG.). 16p. 10.99 *(978-0-06-219610-1(3))* HarperCollins Pubs.
—My First University of Florida Words Go Gators. 2012. (ENG.). 16p. 10.99 *(978-0-06-219611-8(1))* HarperCollins Pubs.
—My First Wisconsin Words Go Badgers. 2012. (ENG.). 16p. 10.99 *(978-0-06-219606-4(5))* HarperCollins Pubs.
McPhail, David. I Get Dressed. 2015. (ENG., Illus.). 12p. (J). (gr. -1 — 1). bds. 5.99 *(978-1-62672-147-0(5),* 9781626721470) Roaring Brook Pr.
—I Play. 2015. (ENG., Illus.). 12p. (J). (gr. -1 — 1). bds. 5.99 *(978-1-62672-148-7(3),* 9781626721487) Roaring Brook Pr.
Meachen Rau, Dana. At the Beach. 2007. (Fun Time Ser.). (Illus.). 24p. (gr. k-1). lib. bdg. 15.95 *(978-0-7614-2609-7(4),* Benchmark Bks.) Marshall Cavendish Corp.
—Baker. 2007. (Jobs in Town Ser.). (SPA., Illus.). 24p. (gr. k-1). lib. bdg. 15.95 *(978-0-7614-2623-3(X),* Benchmark Bks.) Marshall Cavendish Corp.
—Climbing. 2006. (On the Move Ser.). (Illus.). 24p. (gr. k-1). lib. bdg. 15.95 *(978-0-7614-2318-8(4),* Benchmark Bks.) Marshall Cavendish Corp.
—En la Playa. 2007. (¡A Divertimos! Ser.). (SPA., Illus.). 24p. (gr. k-1). lib. bdg. 15.95 *(978-0-7614-2748-3(1),* Benchmark Bks.) Marshall Cavendish Corp.
—Un Panadero. 2007. (En el Trabajo Ser.). (SPA., Illus.). 24p. (gr. k-1). lib. bdg. 15.95 *(978-0-7614-2781-0(3),* Benchmark Bks.) Marshall Cavendish Corp.
—Rolling. 2006. (On the Move Ser.). (Illus.). 24p. (gr. k-1). lib. bdg. 15.95 *(978-0-7614-2314-0(1),* Benchmark Bks.) Marshall Cavendish Corp.
Mein Erstes Woerterbuch: Auf dem Bauernhof. (Duden Ser.). (GER.). 48p. (J). *(978-3-411-71071-3(3))* Bibliographisches Institut & F. A. Brockhaus AG DEU. Dist: International Bk. Import Service, Inc.
Mes 100 Premiers Mots. 2003. (First 100 Words Ser.).Tr. of My First 100 Words. (FRE.). 32p. 5.58 *(978-1-4054-1139-4(2))* Parragon, Inc.
Metsola, Aino-Maija. Colors. 2016. (Learning Garden Ser.). (ENG.). 16p. (J). (gr. -1-k). bds. 9.99 *(978-1-84780-705-2(4),* Wide Eyed Editions) Quarto Publishing Group UK GBR. Dist: Hachette Bk. Group.
—First Words: Art Charts. 2016. (Learning Garden Ser.). (ENG.). 32p. (J). pap. 19.99 *(978-1-84780-820-2(4),* Wide Eyed Editions) Quarto Publishing Group UK GBR. Dist: Littlehampton Bk Services, Ltd.
—First Words - Art Charts: Learn 100 First Words with 12 Decorative Prints to Hang on Your Nursery Wall. 2016. (Learning Garden Ser.). (ENG.). 32p. (J). (gr. -1-k). pap. 19.99 *(978-1-84780-838-7(7),* Wide Eyed Editions) Quarto Publishing Group UK GBR. Dist: Hachette Bk. Group.
Michael, Joan, illus. The Five Senses/Opposites & Position Words, 4 bks., Set. Incl. Let's Play a Five Senses Guessing Game. Miller, Amanda. 18.00 *(978-0-531-14871-6(8));* Let's Talk about Opposites, Morning to Night. Falk, Laine. Larsen, Eric, illus. 18.00 *(978-0-531-14872-3(6));* 24p. (J). (gr. -1-3). 2007. (Let's Find Out Early Learning Bks.). 2007. 72.00 o.p. *(978-0-531-17574-3(X),* Children's Pr.) Scholastic Library Publishing.
Miles Kelly Staff. Mix-Ups. 2003. (Illus.). 14p. 9.95 *(978-1-902947-83-9(5))* Miles Kelly Publishing, Ltd. GBR. Dist: Independent Pubs. Group.
Milet Publishing Staff. Jobs. 2012. (My First Bilingual Book Ser.). (Illus.). 24p. (J). (gr. k — 1). (FRE & ENG.). bds. 7.99 *(978-1-84059-704-2(6));* (ENG & ITA., bds. 7.99 *(978-1-84059-706-6(2));* (ENG & SOM., bds. 7.99 *(978-1-84059-711-0(9))* Milet Publishing.
—Jobs - Berufe. 2012. (My First Bilingual Book Ser.). (ENG & GER., Illus.). 24p. (J). (gr. k — 1). bds. 7.99 *(978-1-84059-705-9(4))* Milet Publishing.
—Jobs - My First Bilingual Book. 2012. (My First Bilingual Book Ser.). (ENG & BEN., Illus.). 24p. (J). (gr. k — 1). bds. 7.99 *(978-1-84059-701-1(1))* Milet Publishing.
—Jobs Empregos. 2012. (My First Bilingual Book Ser.). (ENG & POR., Illus.). 24p. (J). (gr. k — 1). bds. 7.99 *(978-1-84059-709-7(7))* Milet Publishing.
—Jobs Profesiones. 2012. (My First Bilingual Book Ser.). (SPA & ENG., Illus.). 24p. (J). (gr. k — 1). bds. 7.99 *(978-1-84059-712-7(7))* Milet Publishing.
—Music. 2012. (My First Bilingual Book Ser.). (ENG, POL & POR., Illus.). 24p. (J). (gr. k — 1). bds. 7.99 *(978-1-84059-724-0(0));* bds. 7.99 *(978-1-84059-716-5(X));* bds. 7.99 *(978-1-84059-718-9(6))* Milet Publishing.
—Music - English-Spanish. 2012. (My First Bilingual Book Ser.). (SPA & ENG., Illus.). 24p. (J). (gr. k — 1). bds. 7.99 *(978-1-84059-728-8(3))* Milet Publishing.
—Music - My First Bilingual Book. 2012. (My First Bilingual Book Ser.). (ENG & ITA., Illus.). 24p. (J). (gr. k — 1). bds. 7.99 *(978-1-84059-722-6(4));* bds. 7.99 *(978-1-84059-725-7(9))* Milet Publishing.
—La Musique. 2012. (My First Bilingual Book Ser.).Tr. of Music. (FRE & ENG., Illus.). 24p. (J). (gr. k — 1). bds. 7.99 *(978-1-84059-720-2(8))* Milet Publishing.
—My Bilingual Book - Sight. 2014. (My Bilingual Book Ser.). (ENG & TUR., Illus.). 28p. (J). (gr. -1-k). 9.95 *(978-1-84059-801-8(8))* Milet Publishing.
—My Bilingual Book - Smell. 2014. (My Bilingual Book Ser.). (ENG & CHI., Illus.). 28p. (J). (gr. -1-k). 9.95 *(978-1-84059-806-3(9))* Milet Publishing.
—My Bilingual Book-Hearing. 2014. (My Bilingual Book Ser.). (ENG & TUR., Illus.). 28p. (J). (gr. -1-k). 9.95 *(978-1-84059-785-1(2));* 9.95 *(978-1-84059-779-0(8));* 9.95 *(978-1-84059-774-5(7))* Milet Publishing.
—My Bilingual Book-Hearing (English-Arabic) 2014. (My Bilingual Book Ser.). (ENG & ARA., Illus.). 28p. (J). (gr. -1-k). 9.95 *(978-1-84059-772-1(0))* Milet Publishing.
—My Bilingual Book-Hearing (English-Bengali) 2014. (My Bilingual Book Ser.). (ENG & BEN., Illus.). 28p. (J). (gr. -1-k). 9.95 *(978-1-84059-773-8(9))* Milet Publishing.
—My Bilingual Book-Hearing (English-Farsi) 2014. (My Bilingual Book Ser.). (ENG & PER., Illus.). 28p. (J). (gr. -1-k). 9.95 *(978-1-84059-775-2(5))* Milet Publishing.
—My Bilingual Book-Hearing (English-French) 2014. (My Bilingual Book Ser.). (ENG & FRE., Illus.). 28p. (J). (gr. -1-k). 9.95 *(978-1-84059-776-9(3))* Milet Publishing.
—My Bilingual Book-Hearing (English-German) 2014. (My Bilingual Book Ser.). (ENG & GER., Illus.). 28p. (J). (gr. -1-k). 9.95 *(978-1-84059-777-6(1))* Milet Publishing.
—My Bilingual Book-Hearing (English-Italian) 2014. (My Bilingual Book Ser.). (ENG & ITA., Illus.). 28p. (J). (gr. -1-k). 9.95 *(978-1-84059-778-3(X))* Milet Publishing.
—My Bilingual Book-Hearing (English-Polish) 2014. (My Bilingual Book Ser.). (ENG, POL & POR., Illus.). 28p. (J). (gr. -1-k). 9.95 *(978-1-84059-780-6(1))* Milet Publishing.
—My Bilingual Book-Hearing (English-Portuguese) 2014. (My Bilingual Book Ser.). (ENG & POR., Illus.). 28p. (J). (gr. -1-k). 9.95 *(978-1-84059-781-3(X))* Milet Publishing.
—My Bilingual Book-Hearing (English-Russian) 2014. (My Bilingual Book Ser.). (ENG & RUS., Illus.). 28p. (J). (gr. -1-k). 9.95 *(978-1-84059-782-0(8))* Milet Publishing.
—My Bilingual Book-Hearing (English-Somali) 2014. (My Bilingual Book Ser.). (ENG & SOM., Illus.). 28p. (J). (gr. -1-k). 9.95 *(978-1-84059-783-7(6))* Milet Publishing.
—My Bilingual Book-Hearing (English-Urdu) 2014. (My Bilingual Book Ser.). (ENG & URD., Illus.). 28p. (J). (gr. -1-k). 9.95 *(978-1-84059-786-8(0))* Milet Publishing.
—My Bilingual Book-Hearing (English-Vietnamese) 2014. (My Bilingual Book Ser.). (ENG & VIE., Illus.). 28p. (J). (gr. -1-k). 9.95 *(978-1-84059-787-5(9))* Milet Publishing.
—My Bilingual Book-Sight. 2014. (My Bilingual Book Ser.). (ENG & KOR., Illus.). 28p. (J). (gr. -1-k). 9.95 *(978-1-84059-795-0(X))* Milet Publishing.
—My Bilingual Book-Sight (English-Bengali) 2014. (My Bilingual Book Ser.). (ENG & BEN., Illus.). 28p. (J). (gr. -1-k). 9.95 *(978-1-84059-789-9(5))* Milet Publishing.
—My Bilingual Book-Sight (English-Chinese) 2014. (My Bilingual Book Ser.). (ENG & CHI., Illus.). 28p. (J). (gr. -1-k). 9.95 *(978-1-84059-790-5(9))* Milet Publishing.
—My Bilingual Book-Sight (English-Farsi) 2014. (My Bilingual Book Ser.). (ENG & PER., Illus.). 28p. (J). (gr. -1-k). 9.95 *(978-1-84059-791-2(7))* Milet Publishing.
—My Bilingual Book-Sight (English-French) 2014. (My Bilingual Book Ser.). (ENG & FRE., Illus.). 28p. (J). (gr. -1-k). 9.95 *(978-1-84059-792-9(5))* Milet Publishing.
—My Bilingual Book-Sight (English-German) 2014. (My Bilingual Book Ser.). (ENG & GER., Illus.). 28p. (J). (gr. -1-k). 9.95 *(978-1-84059-793-6(3))* Milet Publishing.
—My Bilingual Book-Sight (English-Italian) 2014. (My Bilingual Book Ser.). (ENG & ITA., Illus.). 28p. (J). (gr. -1-k). 9.95 *(978-1-84059-794-3(1))* Milet Publishing.
—My Bilingual Book-Sight (English-Polish) 2014. (My Bilingual Book Ser.). (ENG, POL & POR., Illus.). 28p. (J). (gr. -1-k). 9.95 *(978-1-84059-796-7(8))* Milet Publishing.
—My Bilingual Book-Sight (English-Portuguese) 2014. (My Bilingual Book Ser.). (ENG & POR., Illus.). 28p. (J). (gr. -1-k). 9.95 *(978-1-84059-797-4(6))* Milet Publishing.
—My Bilingual Book-Sight (English-Russian) 2014. (My Bilingual Book Ser.). (ENG & RUS., Illus.). 28p. (J). (gr. -1-k). 9.95 *(978-1-84059-798-1(4))* Milet Publishing.
—My Bilingual Book-Sight (English-Somali) 2014. (My Bilingual Book Ser.). (ENG & SOM., Illus.). 28p. (J). (gr. -1-k). 9.95 *(978-1-84059-799-8(2))* Milet Publishing.
—My Bilingual Book-Sight (English-Spanish) 2014. (My Bilingual Book Ser.). (ENG & SPA., Illus.). 28p. (J). (gr. -1-k). 9.95 *(978-1-84059-800-1(X))* Milet Publishing.
—My Bilingual Book-Sight (English-Urdu) 2014. (My Bilingual Book Ser.). (ENG & URD., Illus.). 28p. (J). (gr. -1-k). 9.95 *(978-1-84059-802-5(6))* Milet Publishing.
—My Bilingual Book-Sight (English-Vietnamese) 2014. (My Bilingual Book Ser.). (ENG & VIE., Illus.). 28p. (J). (gr. -1-k). 9.95 *(978-1-84059-803-2(4))* Milet Publishing.
—My Bilingual Book-Smell. 2014. (My Bilingual Book Ser.). (ENG & SPA., Illus.). 28p. (J). (gr. -1-k). 9.95 *(978-1-84059-816-2(6));* 9.95 *(978-1-84059-811-7(5))* Milet Publishing.
—My Bilingual Book-Smell (English-Arabic) 2014. (My Bilingual Book Ser.). (ENG & ARA., Illus.). 28p. (J). (gr. -1-k). 9.95 *(978-1-84059-804-9(2))* Milet Publishing.
—My Bilingual Book-Smell (English-Bengali) 2014. (My Bilingual Book Ser.). (ENG & BEN., Illus.). 28p. (J). (gr. -1-k). 9.95 *(978-1-84059-805-6(0))* Milet Publishing.
—My Bilingual Book-Smell (English-Farsi) 2014. (My Bilingual Book Ser.). (ENG & PER., Illus.). 28p. (J). (gr. -1-k). 9.95 *(978-1-84059-807-0(7))* Milet Publishing.
—My Bilingual Book-Smell (English-Italian) 2014. (My Bilingual Book Ser.). (ENG & ITA., Illus.). 28p. (J). (gr. -1-k). 9.95 *(978-1-84059-810-0(7))* Milet Publishing.
—My Bilingual Book-Smell (English-Polish) 2014. (My Bilingual Book Ser.). (ENG, POL & POR., Illus.). 28p. (J). (gr. -1-k). 9.95 *(978-1-84059-812-4(3))* Milet Publishing.
—My Bilingual Book-Smell (English-Russian) 2014. (My Bilingual Book Ser.). (ENG & RUS., Illus.). 28p. (J). (gr. -1-k). 9.95 *(978-1-84059-814-8(X))* Milet Publishing.
—My Bilingual Book-Smell (English-Somali) 2014. (My Bilingual Book Ser.). (ENG & SOM., Illus.). 28p. (J). (gr. -1-k). 9.95 *(978-1-84059-815-5(8))* Milet Publishing.
—My Bilingual Book-Smell (English-Turkish) 2014. (My Bilingual Book Ser.). (ENG & TUR., Illus.). 28p. (J). (gr. -1-k). 9.95 *(978-1-84059-817-9(4))* Milet Publishing.
—My Bilingual Book-Smell (English-Urdu) 2014. (My Bilingual Book Ser.). (ENG & URD., Illus.). 28p. (J). (gr. -1-k). 9.95 *(978-1-84059-818-6(2))* Milet Publishing.
—My Bilingual Book-Smell (English-Vietnamese) 2014. (My Bilingual Book Ser.). (ENG & VIE., Illus.). 28p. (J). (gr. -1-k). 9.95 *(978-1-84059-819-3(0))* Milet Publishing.
—My Bilingual Book-Taste (English-Arabic) 2014. (My Bilingual Book Ser.). (ENG & ARA., Illus.). 28p. (J). (gr. -1-k). 9.95 *(978-1-84059-820-9(4))* Milet Publishing.
—My Bilingual Book-Taste (English-Bengali) 2014. (My Bilingual Book Ser.). (ENG & BEN., Illus.). 28p. (J). (gr. -1-k). 9.95 *(978-1-84059-821-6(2))* Milet Publishing.
—My Bilingual Book-Taste (English-Farsi) 2014. (My Bilingual Book Ser.). (ENG & PER., Illus.). 28p. (J). (gr. -1-k). 9.95 *(978-1-84059-823-0(9))* Milet Publishing.
—My Bilingual Book-Taste (English-Italian) 2014. (My Bilingual Book Ser.). (ENG & ITA., Illus.). 28p. (J). (gr. -1-k). 9.95 *(978-1-84059-826-1(3))* Milet Publishing.
—My Bilingual Book-Taste (English-Korean) 2014. (My Bilingual Book Ser.). (ENG & KOR., Illus.). 28p. (J). (gr. -1-k). 9.95 *(978-1-84059-827-8(1))* Milet Publishing.
—My Bilingual Book-Taste (English-Polish) 2014. (My Bilingual Book Ser.). (ENG, POL & POR., Illus.). 28p. (J). (gr. -1-k). 9.95 *(978-1-84059-828-5(X))* Milet Publishing.
—My Bilingual Book-Taste (English-Portuguese) 2014. (My Bilingual Book Ser.). (ENG & POR., Illus.). 28p. (J). (gr. -1-k). 9.95 *(978-1-84059-829-2(8))* Milet Publishing.
—My Bilingual Book-Taste (English-Russian) 2014. (My Bilingual Book Ser.). (ENG & RUS., Illus.). 28p. (J). (gr. -1-k). 9.95 *(978-1-84059-830-8(1))* Milet Publishing.
—My Bilingual Book-Taste (English-Somali) 2014. (My Bilingual Book Ser.). (ENG & SOM., Illus.). 28p. (J). (gr. -1-k). 9.95 *(978-1-84059-831-5(X))* Milet Publishing.
—My Bilingual Book-Taste (English-Turkish) 2014. (My Bilingual Book Ser.). (ENG & TUR., Illus.). 28p. (J). (gr. -1-k). 9.95 *(978-1-84059-833-9(6))* Milet Publishing.
—My Bilingual Book-Taste (English-Urdu) 2014. (My Bilingual Book Ser.). (ENG & URD., Illus.). 28p. (J). (gr. -1-k). 9.95 *(978-1-84059-834-6(4))* Milet Publishing.
—My Bilingual Book-Taste (English-Vietnamese) 2014. (My Bilingual Book Ser.). (ENG & VIE., Illus.). 28p. (J). (gr. -1-k). 9.95 *(978-1-84059-835-3(2))* Milet Publishing.
—My Bilingual Book-Touch. 2014. (My Bilingual Book Ser.). (ENG & KOR., Illus.). 28p. (J). (gr. -1-k). 9.95 *(978-1-84059-843-8(3));* 9.95 *(978-1-84059-848-3(4))* Milet Publishing.
—My Bilingual Book-Touch (English-Arabic) 2014. (My Bilingual Book Ser.). (ENG & ARA., Illus.). 28p. (J). (gr. -1-k). 9.95 *(978-1-84059-836-0(0))* Milet Publishing.
—My Bilingual Book-Touch (English-Bengali) 2014. (My Bilingual Book Ser.). (ENG & BEN., Illus.). 28p. (J). (gr. -1-k). 9.95 *(978-1-84059-837-7(9))* Milet Publishing.
—My Bilingual Book-Touch (English-Chinese) 2014. (My Bilingual Book Ser.). (ENG & CHI., Illus.). 28p. (J). (gr. -1-k). 9.95 *(978-1-84059-838-4(7))* Milet Publishing.
—My Bilingual Book-Touch (English-Farsi) 2014. (My Bilingual Book Ser.). (ENG & PER., Illus.). 28p. (J). (gr. -1-k). 9.95 *(978-1-84059-839-1(5))* Milet Publishing.
—My Bilingual Book-Touch (English-German) 2014. (My Bilingual Book Ser.). (ENG & GER., Illus.). 28p. (J). (gr. -1-k). 9.95 *(978-1-84059-841-4(7))* Milet Publishing.
—My Bilingual Book-Touch (English-Italian) 2014. (My Bilingual Book Ser.). (ENG & ITA., Illus.). 28p. (J). (gr. -1-k). 9.95 *(978-1-84059-842-1(5))* Milet Publishing.
—My Bilingual Book-Touch (English-Portuguese) 2014. (My Bilingual Book Ser.). (ENG & POR., Illus.). 28p. (J). (gr. -1-k). 9.95 *(978-1-84059-845-2(X))* Milet Publishing.
—My Bilingual Book-Touch (English-Russian) 2014. (My Bilingual Book Ser.). (ENG & RUS., Illus.). 28p. (J). (gr. -1-k). 9.95 *(978-1-84059-846-9(8))* Milet Publishing.
—My Bilingual Book-Touch (English-Somali) 2014. (My Bilingual Book Ser.). (ENG & SOM., Illus.). 28p. (J). (gr. -1-k). 9.95 *(978-1-84059-847-6(6))* Milet Publishing.
—My Bilingual Book-Touch (English-Turkish) 2014. (My Bilingual Book Ser.). (ENG & TUR., Illus.). 28p. (J). (gr. -1-k). 9.95 *(978-1-84059-849-0(2))* Milet Publishing.
—My Bilingual Book-Touch (English-Urdu) 2014. (My Bilingual Book Ser.). (ENG & URD., Illus.). 28p. (J). (gr. -1-k). 9.95 *(978-1-84059-850-6(6))* Milet Publishing.
—My Bilingual Book-Touch (English-Vietnamese) 2014. (My Bilingual Book Ser.). (ENG & VIE., Illus.). 28p. (J). (gr. -1-k). 9.95 *(978-1-84059-851-3(4))* Milet Publishing.
—My First Bilingual Book - Jobs. 2012. (My First Bilingual Book Ser.). (ENG, POL & POR., Illus.). 24p. (J). (gr. k — 1). bds. 7.99 *(978-1-84059-708-0(9))* Milet Publishing.
—My First Bilingual Book - Opposites. 2012. (My First Bilingual Book Ser.). (ENG & URD., Illus.). 24p. (J). (gr. k — 1). bds. 8.99 *(978-1-84059-746-2(1));* bds. 7.99 *(978-1-84059-732-5(1))* Milet Publishing.
—My First Bilingual Book-Jobs. 2012. (My First Bilingual Book Ser.). (ENG & PER., Illus.). 24p. (J). (gr. k — 1). bds. 7.99 *(978-1-84059-703-5(8));* bds. 7.99 *(978-1-84059-700-4(3))* Milet Publishing.
—My First Bilingual Book-Jobs (English-Chinese) 2012. (My First Bilingual Book Ser.). (ENG & CHI., Illus.). 24p. (J). (gr. k — 1). bds. 7.99 *(978-1-84059-702-8(X))* Milet Publishing.
—My First Bilingual Book-Jobs (English-Korean) 2012. (My First Bilingual Book Ser.). (ENG & KOR., Illus.). 24p. (J). (gr. k — 1). bds. 7.99 *(978-1-84059-707-3(0))* Milet Publishing.
—My First Bilingual Book-Jobs (English-Russian) 2012. (My First Bilingual Book Ser.). (ENG & RUS., Illus.). 24p. (J). (gr. k — 1). bds. 7.99 *(978-1-84059-710-3(0))* Milet Publishing.
—My First Bilingual Book-Jobs (English-Turkish) 2012. (My First Bilingual Book Ser.). (ENG & TUR., Illus.). 24p. (J). (gr. k — 1). bds. 7.99 *(978-1-84059-713-4(5))* Milet Publishing.
—My First Bilingual Book-Jobs (English-Urdu) 2012. (My First Bilingual Book Ser.). (ENG & URD., Illus.). 24p. (J). (gr. k — 1). bds. 7.99 *(978-1-84059-714-1(3))* Milet Publishing.
—My First Bilingual Book-Jobs (English-Vietnamese) 2012. (My First Bilingual Book Ser.). (ENG & VIE., Illus.). 24p. (J). (gr. k — 1). bds. 7.99 *(978-1-84059-715-8(1))* Milet Publishing.
—My First Bilingual Book-Music. 2012. (My First Bilingual Book Ser.). (ENG & BEN., Illus.). 24p. (J). (gr. k — 1). bds. 7.99 *(978-1-84059-717-2(8))* Milet Publishing.
—My First Bilingual Book-Music (English-Farsi) 2012. (My First Bilingual Book Ser.). (ENG & PER., Illus.). 24p. (J). (gr. k — 1). bds. 7.99 *(978-1-84059-719-6(4))* Milet Publishing.
—My First Bilingual Book-Music (English-German) 2012. (My First Bilingual Book Ser.). (ENG & GER., Illus.). 24p. (J). (gr. k — 1). bds. 7.99 *(978-1-84059-721-9(6))* Milet Publishing.
—My First Bilingual Book-Music (English-Korean) 2012. (My First Bilingual Book Ser.). (ENG & KOR., Illus.). 24p. (J). (gr. k — 1). bds. 7.99 *(978-1-84059-723-3(2))* Milet Publishing.
—My First Bilingual Book-Music (English-Russian) 2012. (My First Bilingual Book Ser.). (ENG & RUS., Illus.). 24p. (J). (gr. k — 1). bds. 7.99 *(978-1-84059-726-4(7))* Milet Publishing.
—My First Bilingual Book-Music (English-Somali) 2012. (My First Bilingual Book Ser.). (ENG & SOM., Illus.). 24p. (J). (gr. k — 1). bds. 7.99 *(978-1-84059-727-1(5))* Milet Publishing.
—My First Bilingual Book-Music (English-Turkish) 2012. (My First Bilingual Book Ser.). (ENG & TUR., Illus.). 24p. (J). (gr. k — 1). bds. 7.99 *(978-1-84059-729-5(1))* Milet Publishing.
—My First Bilingual Book-Music (English-Urdu) 2012. (My First Bilingual Book Ser.). (ENG & URD., Illus.). 24p. (J). (gr. k — 1). bds. 7.99 *(978-1-84059-730-1(5))* Milet Publishing.
—My First Bilingual Book-Music (English-Vietnamese) 2012. (My First Bilingual Book Ser.). (ENG & VIE., Illus.). 24p. (J). (gr. k — 1). bds. 7.99 *(978-1-84059-731-8(3))* Milet Publishing.
—My First Bilingual Book-Opposites. 2012. (My First Bilingual Book Ser.). (ENG & CHI., Illus.). 24p. (J). (gr. k — 1). bds. 7.99 *(978-1-84059-734-9(8));* bds. 7.99 *(978-1-84059-737-0(2));* bds. 7.99 *(978-1-84059-740-0(2))* Milet Publishing.
—My First Bilingual Book-Opposites (English-Bengali) 2012. (My First Bilingual Book Ser.). (ENG & BEN., Illus.). 24p. (J). (gr. k — 1). bds. 7.99 *(978-1-84059-733-2(X))* Milet Publishing.
—My First Bilingual Book-Opposites (English-Korean) 2012. (My First Bilingual Book Ser.). (ENG & KOR., Illus.). 24p. (J). (gr. k — 1). bds. 7.99 *(978-1-84059-739-4(9))* Milet Publishing.
—My First Bilingual Book-Opposites (English-Polish) 2012. (My First Bilingual Book Ser.). (ENG, POL & POR., Illus.). 24p. (J). (gr. k — 1). bds. 7.99 *(978-1-84059-741-7(0))* Milet Publishing.
—My First Bilingual Book-Opposites (English-Russian) 2012. (My First Bilingual Book Ser.). (ENG & RUS., Illus.). 24p. (J). (gr. k — 1). bds. 7.99 *(978-1-84059-742-4(9))* Milet Publishing.
—My First Bilingual Book-Opposites (English-Vietnamese) 2012. (My First Bilingual Book Ser.). (ENG & VIE., Illus.). 24p. (J). (gr. k — 1). bds. 7.99 *(978-1-84059-747-9(X))* Milet Publishing.
—My First Bilingual Book-Sports. 2012. (My First Bilingual Book Ser.). (ENG & TUR., Illus.). 24p. (J). (gr. k — 1). bds. 7.99 *(978-1-84059-761-5(5))* Milet Publishing.
—My First Bilingual Book-Sports (English-Bengali) 2012. (My First Bilingual Book Ser.). (ENG & BEN., Illus.). 24p. (J). (gr. k — 1). bds. 7.99 *(978-1-84059-749-3(6))* Milet Publishing.
—My First Bilingual Book-Sports (English-Farsi) 2012. (My First Bilingual Book Ser.). (ENG & PER., Illus.). 24p. (J). (gr. k — 1). bds. 7.99 *(978-1-84059-751-6(8))* Milet Publishing.
—My First Bilingual Book-Sports (English-German) 2012. (My First Bilingual Book Ser.). (ENG & GER., Illus.). 24p. (J). (gr. k — 1). bds. 7.99 *(978-1-84059-753-0(4))* Milet Publishing.
—My First Bilingual Book-Sports (English-Korean) 2012. (My First Bilingual Book Ser.). (ENG & KOR., Illus.). 24p. (J). (gr. k — 1). bds. 7.99 *(978-1-84059-755-4(0))* Milet Publishing.
—My First Bilingual Book-Sports (English-Polish) 2012. (My First Bilingual Book Ser.). (ENG, POL & POR., Illus.). 24p. (J). (gr. k — 1). bds. 7.99 *(978-1-84059-756-1(9))* Milet Publishing.
—My First Bilingual Book-Sports (English-Russian) 2012. (My First Bilingual Book Ser.). (ENG & RUS., Illus.). 24p. (J). (gr. k — 1). bds. 7.99 *(978-1-84059-758-5(5))* Milet Publishing.
—My First Bilingual Book-Sports (English-Spanish) 2012. (My First Bilingual Book Ser.). (SPA & ENG., Illus.). 24p. (J). (gr. k — 1). bds. 7.99 *(978-1-84059-760-8(7))* Milet Publishing.
—My First Bilingual Book-Sports (English-Urdu) 2012. (My First Bilingual Book Ser.). (ENG & URD., Illus.). 24p. (J). (gr. k — 1). bds. 7.99 *(978-1-84059-762-2(3))* Milet Publishing.
—My First Bilingual Book-Sports (English-Vietnamese) 2012. (My First Bilingual Book Ser.). (ENG & VIE., Illus.). 24p. (J). (gr. k — 1). bds. 7.99 *(978-1-84059-763-9(1))* Milet Publishing.
—Opposites. 2012. (My First Bilingual Book Ser.). (Illus.). 24p. (J). (gr. k — 1). (ENG & SOM.). bds. 7.99 *(978-1-84059-743-1(7));* (FRE & ENG., bds. 7.99 *(978-1-84059-736-3(4));* (ENG & PER., bds. 7.99 *(978-1-84059-735-6(6))* Milet Publishing.
—Opposites - My First Bilingual Book. 2012. (My First Bilingual Book Ser.). (ENG & TUR., Illus.). 24p. (J). (gr. k — 1). bds. 7.99 *(978-1-84059-745-5(3));* bds. 8.99 *(978-1-84059-738-7(0))* Milet Publishing.
—Sight - English-Arabic. 2014. (My Bilingual Book Ser.). (ENG & ARA., Illus.). 28p. (J). (gr. -1-k). 9.95 *(978-1-84059-788-2(7))* Milet Publishing.
—Smell / Das Riechen. 2014. (My Bilingual Book Ser.). (ENG & GER., Illus.). 28p. (J). (gr. -1-k). 9.95 *(978-1-84059-809-4(3))* Milet Publishing.
—Smell (English-French) 2014. (My Bilingual Book Ser.). (ENG & FRE., Illus.). 28p. (J). (gr. -1-k). 9.95 *(978-1-84059-808-7(5))* Milet Publishing.
—Smell O olfato. 2014. (My Bilingual Book Ser.). (ENG & POR., Illus.). 28p. (J). (gr. -1-k). 9.95 *(978-1-84059-813-1(1))* Milet Publishing.
—Sports. 2012. (My First Bilingual Book Ser.). (ENG & CHI., Illus.). 24p. (J). (gr. k — 1). bds. 7.99 *(978-1-84059-750-9(X));* bds. 7.99 *(978-1-84059-757-8(7));* bds. 7.99 *(978-1-84059-748-6(8))* Milet Publishing.
—Sports - My First Bilingual Book. 2012. (My First Bilingual Book Ser.). (Illus.). 24p. (J). (gr. k — 1). (FRE & ENG.). bds. 7.99 *(978-1-84059-752-3(6));* (ENG & SOM., bds. 7.99 *(978-1-84059-759-2(3))* Milet Publishing.
—Sports (English-Italian) 2012. (My First Bilingual Book Ser.). (ENG & ITA., Illus.). 24p. (J). (gr. k — 1). bds. 7.99 *(978-1-84059-754-7(2))* Milet Publishing.
—Taste - My Bilingual Book. 2014. (My Bilingual Book Ser.). (ENG & FRE., Illus.). 28p. (J). (gr. -1-k). 9.95 *(978-1-84059-824-7(7))* Milet Publishing.
—Taste / Das Schmecken. 2014. (My Bilingual Book Ser.). (ENG & GER., Illus.). 28p. (J). (gr. -1-k). 9.95 *(978-1-84059-825-4(5))* Milet Publishing.
—Touch - My Bilingual Book. 2014. (My Bilingual Book Ser.). (ENG & FRE., Illus.). 28p. (J). (gr. -1-k). 9.95 *(978-1-84059-840-7(9))* Milet Publishing.
Miller, Jonathan, illus. When I Grow Up. 2011. 16p. (J). *(978-1-58865-637-7(3))* Kidsbooks, LLC.
Miller, Susan A. My First 1000 Words. 2005. (My First Ser.). (Illus.). 96p. (J). 6.98 *(978-1-4127-1182-1(7),* 1246993) Phoenix International Publications, Inc.

Minden, Cecilia. Up & Down. 2016. (21st Century Basic Skills Library: Animal Opposites Ser.). (ENG., Illus.). 24p. (J). (gr. k-3). 24.21 *(978-1-63470-468-7(1)*, 207603) Cherry Lake Publishing.

Mini My First Book of Words. 2004. (Early Learning Ser.). 18p. (J). bds. 2.99 *(978-1-85854-831-9(4))* Brimax Books Ltd. GBR. Dist: Byeway Bks.

Minsky, Michael. Greenwood Word Lists: One-Syllable Words. 2003. 168p. spiral bd. *(978-1-57035-770-1(6)*, 206WORD1) Cambium Education, Inc.

Mis Primeras 100 Palabras.Tr. of My First 100 Words in Spanish. (FRE & SPA.). 32p. (J). *(978-0-7525-8380-8(8))* Parragon, Inc.

Modéré, Armelle. My First English/Norwegian Dictionary of Sentences. 2008. (NOR & ENG., Illus.). 128p. (J). *(978-1-57534-048-7(8))* Skandisk, Inc.

Modéré, Armelle & Hokenson, Linda. My First English/Swedish Dictionary of Sentences. 2008. (SWE & ENG.). 128p. *(978-1-57534-049-4(6))* Skandisk, Inc.

Modeste, Caroline, illus. My First 1000 Words. 2016. (ENG.). 64p. (J). (gr. -1 — 1). 19.95 *(978-1-77085-797-1(4)*, 9781770857971) Firefly Bks., Ltd.

Molter, Carey. -Ain As in Train, 1 vol. 2003. (Word Families Set 8 Ser.). (ENG., Illus.). 24p. (J). (gr. k-3). lib. bdg. 24.21 *(978-1-59197-272-3(8))* ABDO Publishing Co.

—Ake As in Cake, 1 vol. 2003. (Word Families Set 8 Ser.). (ENG., Illus.). 24p. (J). (gr. k-3). lib. bdg. 24.21 *(978-1-59197-270-9(1))* ABDO Publishing Co.

—Eam As in Ice Cream, 1 vol. 2003. (Word Families Set 8 Ser.). (ENG., Illus.). 24p. (J). (gr. k-3). lib. bdg. 24.21 *(978-1-59197-273-0(6)*, SandCastle) ABDO Publishing Co.

—En As in Pen, 1 vol. 2003. (Word Families Set 2 Ser.). (ENG., Illus.). 24p. (J). (gr. k-3). lib. bdg. 24.21 *(978-1-59197-229-7(9)*, SandCastle) ABDO Publishing Co.

—Ide As in Tide, 1 vol. 2003. (Word Families Set 8 Ser.). (ENG., Illus.). 24p. (J). (gr. k-3). lib. bdg. 24.21 *(978-1-59197-275-4(2)*, SandCastle) ABDO Publishing Co.

—One As in Stone, 1 vol. 2003. (Word Families Set 8 Ser.). (ENG., Illus.). 24p. (J). (gr. k-3). lib. bdg. 24.21 *(978-1-59197-274-7(4)*, SandCastle) ABDO Publishing Co.

—Oon As in Spoon, 1 vol. 2003. (Word Families Set 7 Ser.). (ENG., Illus.). 24p. (J). (gr. k-3). lib. bdg. 24.21 *(978-1-59197-266-2(3)*, SandCastle) ABDO Publishing Co.

Moore, Sonya. Kitchen Talk. 2011. 16p. 9.99 *(978-1-4567-5067-1(4))* AuthorHouse.

Morales, Yuyi. Nino Wrestles the World. 2015. (J). lib. bdg. 18.40 *(978-0-606-37276-3(8))* Turtleback Bks.

The Moves Make the Man: Teaching Unit. 2003. 73p. (YA). ring bd. *(978-1-58049-433-5(1)*, TU4331) Prestwick Hse., Inc.

Muschla, Gary Robert. Exploring Vocabulary, Grades 4-5. 2012. (Practice Makes Perfect Ser.). (ENG.). 224p. pap. 15.00 *(978-0-07-177276-1(6)*, 0071772766) McGraw-Hill Education.

My Community. 2005. (Look, Listen, & Speak Ser.). 80p. (gr. k-3). cd-rom 29.99 *(978-1-55799-928-3(7)*, EMC 2741) Evan-Moor Educational Pubs.

My Community. 2004. cd-rom 89.99 *(978-0-9819585-1-4(6))* Social Skill Builder, Inc.

My Family & Me. 2005. (Look, Listen, & Speak Ser.). 80p. (gr. k-3). cd-rom 29.99 *(978-1-55799-924-5(4)*, EMC 2737) Evan-Moor Educational Pubs.

My First 100 Words. 2003. 32p. (J). 11.95 *(978-0-7525-7767-8(0))* Parragon, Inc.

My First 100 Words in Spanish/English. 2003. 32p. (J). 11.95 *(978-0-7525-7769-2(7))* Parragon, Inc.

My First Sight Words (Gr. K-1) 2003. (J). *(978-1-58232-090-8(X))* ECS Learning Systems, Inc.

My First Word Book about Things That Go. 2017. (My First Word Bks.). (ENG.). (J). bds. 9.99 ***(978-0-7945-3932-0(7)***, Usborne) EDC Publishing.

My First Word Book Large Bd. 2004. 12p. (J). bds. 7.99 *(978-1-85854-467-0(X))* Brimax Books Ltd. GBR. Dist: Byeway Bks.

My First Words. (Punched Foam Book Ser.). 6p. *(978-1-4075-0417-9(7))* Parragon, Inc.

My First Words: English & Spanish Book 1. 2006. (SPA.). (J). bds. *(978-0-9785744-1-3(9))* LTL Media LLC.

My First Words: English & Spanish Book 2. 2006. (SPA.). (J). bds. *(978-0-9785744-2-0(7))* LTL Media LLC.

My Little Box of First Words. Date not set. (Illus.). (J). bds. 6.98 *(978-1-4054-0811-0(1))* Parragon, Inc.

My Nest, 6 vols. 8p. (gr. k-1). 21.50 *(978-0-322-02063-4(8))* Wright Group/McGraw-Hill.

Myers, Connie Ellis. Words to Say out Loud: A Safety Book for Children. 2007. (Illus.). 84p. (J). spiral bd. 19.99 *(978-0-9799127-0-2(9))* Say Out Loud, LLC.

Narváez, Concha López & Salmeron, Carmelo. Tomas Es Distinto a los Demas.Tr. of Tomas Is Different from the Others. (SPA.). 64p. (J). (gr. 2-4). *(978-84-216-3432-5(1))* Bruño, Editorial ESP. Dist: Lectorum Pubns., Inc.

National Geographic Kids Staff. Let's Play! - National Geographic Kids. 2017. (Readers Ser.). (ENG.). 96p. (J). (-k). pap. 7.99 *(978-1-4263-2791-9(9)*, National Geographic Children's Bks.) National Geographic Society.

—Match! 2011. (ENG., Illus.). 24p. (J). (gr. k-k). bds. 6.99 *(978-1-4263-0871-0(X)*, National Geographic Children's Bks.) National Geographic Society.

National Geographic Kids Staff & Neuman, Susan B. Hop, Bunny! 2014. (Readers Ser.). (ENG., Illus.). 24p. (J). (-k). lib. bdg. 13.90 *(978-1-4263-1740-8(9)*, National Geographic Children's Bks.) National Geographic Society.

National Geographic Learning, National Geographic Learning. Avenues PreK Level: Vocabulary Builders Kit. 2004. (Avenues Ser.). (ENG.). (C). (gr. -1-2). 911.95 *(978-0-7362-2396-6(7))* CENGAGE Learning.

Nelson, J. Ron & Marchland-Martella, Nancy. The Multiple Meaning Vocabulary Program: Level I. 2005. (Illus.). 248p. (gr. 4-6). pap., stu. ed., wbk. ed. 10.95 *(978-1-59318-405-6(0)*, 267STU1) Cambium Education, Inc.

—The Multiple Meaning Vocabulary Program: Level II. 2005. (Illus.). 328p. (gr. 4-6). pap., stu. ed., wbk. ed. 10.95 *(978-1-59318-406-3(9))* Cambium Education, Inc.

—The Multiple Meaning Vocabulary Program Instructor's Manual: Level I & Level II. 2005. 64p. *(978-1-59318-422-3(0)*, 267TE) Cambium Education, Inc.

Newmark Learning, compiled by. Complete Fluency Instruction & Practice Set Grades 1-3 with Audio CDs. 2009. (Fluency Instruction Practice Ser.). (gr. 1-3). 107.91 net. *(978-1-60719-099-8(0))* Newmark Learning LLC.

—Sight Word Readers 12 copy set with Rack Set A. 2009. (Sight Word Readers Set A Ser.). (J). 1095.12 net. *(978-1-60719-159-9(8))* Newmark Learning LLC.

Nickelodeon Staff, ed. Words - Dora the Explorer. 2010. (Write, Slide & Learn Ser.). 14p. (J). (gr. -1-1). 9.99 *(978-1-74184-519-8(X)*, Ideal Pubns.) Worthy Publishing.

Nobleman, Marc Tyler. Vocabulary Cartoon of the Day: 180 Reproducible Cartoons That Expand Students' Vocabularies to Help Them Become Better Readers & Writers. 2010. (Vocabulary Cartoon of the Day Ser.). (ENG.). 96p. (gr. 2-3). pap. 14.99 *(978-0-545-14713-2(1)*, Teaching Resources) Scholastic, Inc.

Novelli, Joan & Grundon, Holly. Instant Content Area Vocabulary Packets: 25 Independent Practice Packets That Help Boost Reading Comprehension in Science, Social Studies, & Math - Grades 2-3. 2011. (ENG.). 144p. (gr. 2-3). pap. 18.99 *(978-0-545-23694-2(0)*, Teaching Resources) Scholastic, Inc.

Nunn, Daniel. In Front of or Behind: Where's Eddie?, 1 vol. 2012. (Hide & Seek Ser.). (ENG.). 24p. (gr. -1-k). pap. 9.95 *(978-1-4109-4720-8(3))* Heinemann-Raintree.

—Inside or Outside: Where's Eddie?, 1 vol. 2012. (Hide & Seek Ser.). (ENG.). 24p. (gr. -1-k). pap. 9.95 *(978-1-4109-4719-2(X))*; lib. bdg. 25.32 *(978-1-4109-4713-0(0))* Heinemann-Raintree.

—Left or Right: Where's Eddie?, 1 vol. 2012. (Hide & Seek Ser.). (ENG.). 24p. (gr. -1-k). pap. 9.95 *(978-1-4109-4718-5(1))*; lib. bdg. 25.32 *(978-1-4109-4712-3(2))* Heinemann-Raintree.

—Near or Far: Where's Eddie?, 1 vol. 2012. (Hide & Seek Ser.). (ENG.). 24p. (gr. -1-k). pap. 9.95 *(978-1-4109-4721-5(1))*; lib. bdg. 25.32 *(978-1-4109-4715-4(7))* Heinemann-Raintree.

Nussbaum, Ben. First Words Playtime. 2004. (ENG.). 36p. (J). 12.99 *(978-1-59069-410-7(4)*, 1A109) Studio Mouse LLC.

Orero, Maria Jesus. Nico y Sus Trajes. 2006. (Nico Collection). (SPA & ESP., Illus.). 12p. (gr. -1-2). per., bds. 6.99 *(978-84-272-6152-5(7))* Molino, Editorial ESP. Dist: Santillana USA Publishing Co., Inc.

Organic Baby Sleep. 2008. (Illus.). (J). (gr. -1-3). bds. *(978-0-312-50270-6(2))* Priddy Bks.

Orme, Helen. 800 Words. 2011. (I Love Reading Book & CD-ROM Packs Ser.). (ENG., Illus.). 96p. (J). (gr. k-2). pap. 16.95 *(978-1-84898-180-5(5)*, TickTock Books) Octopus Publishing Group GBR. Dist: Independent Pubs. Group.

Orshoski, Paul. We Read Phonics-Ant in Her Pants. Ebbeler, Jeffrey, illus. 2010. (ENG.). 32p. (J). pap. 4.99 *(978-1-60115-328-9(7))* Treasure Bay, Inc.

—We Read Phonics-Ants in Her Pants. Ebbeler, Jeffrey, illus. 2010. (ENG.). 32p. (J). 9.95 *(978-1-60115-327-2(9))* Treasure Bay, Inc.

—We Read Phonics-Bugs on the Bus. Noiset, Michele, illus. 2010. 32p. (J). 9.95 *(978-1-60115-325-8(2))*; pap. 4.99 *(978-1-60115-326-5(0))* Treasure Bay, Inc.

—We Read Phonics-Sports Dream. Ebbeler, Jeffrey, illus. 2011. (We Read Phonics Ser.). 32p. (J). (gr. 1-3). 9.95 *(978-1-60115-335-7(X))*; pap. 4.99 *(978-1-60115-336-4(8))* Treasure Bay, Inc.

—We Read Phonics-Talent Night. Kulka, Joe, illus. 2011. (We Read Phonics Ser.). 32p. (J). (gr. 1-3). 9.95 *(978-1-60115-339-5(2))*; pap. 4.99 *(978-1-60115-340-1(6))* Treasure Bay, Inc.

O'Sullivan, Jill Korey. The Heinle Picture Dictionary for Children. 2007. (ENG., Illus.). 160p. (C). (gr. 3-7). pap. 23.95 *(978-1-4240-0849-0(2))* Cengage Heinle.

—Picture Dictionary for Children. 2007. (ENG.). 176p. (C). pap. 32.95 *(978-1-4240-0876-6(X))* Cengage Heinle.

O'Toole, Janet & Anness Publishing Staff. First Words: Lift the Flaps to Find Out about Words! Adams, Ben, illus. 2013. (ENG.). 16p. bds. 6.99 *(978-1-84322-795-3(9)*, Armadillo) Anness Publishing GBR. Dist: National Bk. Network.

Ottaiano, Mela & Beech, Linda. 240 Vocabulary Words Kids Need to Know - Grade 2: 24 Ready-to-Reproduce Packets That Make Vocabulary Building Fun & Effective. 2012. (ENG.). 80p. (gr. 2-2). pap. 12.99 *(978-0-545-46051-4(4)*, Teaching Resources) Scholastic, Inc.

Owen, Ruth. 100 Words. 2011. (I Love Reading Book & CD-ROM Packs Ser.). (ENG., Illus.). 96p. (J). (gr. k-2). pap. 16.95 *(978-1-84898-178-2(3)*, TickTock Books) Octopus Publishing Group GBR. Dist: Independent Pubs. Group.

Owlkids Books Inc. Staff. Picture My World. 2012. (ENG., Illus.). 96p. (J). (gr. -1-2). 16.95 *(978-1-926973-56-2(9))* Owlkids Bks. Inc. CAN. Dist: Publishers Group West (PGW).

Paquette, Ammi-Joan. Petey & Pru & the Hullabaloo. Ang, Joy, illus. 2013. (ENG.). 40p. (J). (gr. -1-3). 16.99 *(978-0-544-03888-2(6))* Houghton Mifflin Harcourt Publishing Co.

Paragon Publishing Staff, ed. Words. 2003. (J). per. *(978-1-884907-41-8(5))* Paradise Pr., Inc.

Parragon Staff, ed. Words. Date not set. (Illus.). (J). bds. 5.98 *(978-0-7525-8559-8(2))* Parragon, Inc.

Patterson, James & Patterson, Susan. Big Words for Little Geniuses. Pan, Hsinping, illus. 2017. (ENG.). 32p. (J). (gr. -1-1). 17.99 ***(978-0-316-50293-1(6)***, Jimmy Patterson) Little Brown & Co.

Perret, Fany. ABC Word Play. 2016. (ENG., Illus.). 18p. (J). (gr. -1-k). bds. 19.99 *(978-1-4521-4811-3(2))* Chronicle Bks. LLC.

Peter & the Wolf. 2012. (Collins Big Cat Ser.). (ENG., Illus.). 16p. (J). pap., wbk. ed. 4.99 *(978-0-00-747426-4(1))* HarperCollins Pubs. Ltd. GBR. Dist: Independent Pubs. Group.

Phillips, Dee. First Words. 2009. (Christmas Lift the Flap Ser.). (ENG.). 10p. (J). (gr. -1-k). bds. 5.95 *(978-1-84696-968-3(9)*, TickTock Books) Octopus Publishing Group GBR. Dist: Independent Pubs. Group.

Phillips, Mark. Pinocchio Intermediate Vocabulary Builder. 2004. 326p. pap. 16.95 *(978-0-9727439-2-1(8))* Cornell, A.J. Pubns.

Phonemic Awareness, Level 1. 2003. (Illus.). (J). spiral bd. *(978-1-58605-822-7(3)*, LeapFrog Schl. Hse.) LeapFrog Enterprises, Inc.

Picthall, Chez. Flip Flaps Zoo. 2015. (ENG., Illus.). 18p. (J). 9.99 *(978-1-907604-53-9(7))* Award Pubns. Ltd. GBR. Dist: Parkwest Pubns., Inc.

Picthall, Chez, creator. Flip Flap Colours: A Turn-the-Flap Book! 2014. (ENG., Illus.). 36p. pap. 10.00 *(978-1-906572-79-2(8))* Award Pubns. Ltd. GBR. Dist: Parkwest Pubns., Inc.

—Flip Flaps Shapes. 2014. (ENG., Illus.). 32p. bds. 10.00 *(978-1-906572-80-8(1))* Award Pubns. Ltd. GBR. Dist: Parkwest Pubns., Inc.

Picthall, Chez & Gunzl, Christiane. Words. 2014. (ENG., Illus.). 20p. pap. 8.95 *(978-1-907604-33-1(2))* Award Pubns. Ltd. GBR. Dist: Parkwest Pubns., Inc.

Picture/Word Cards. (gr. -1-12). 75.18 *(978-0-7362-0345-6(1))* CENGAGE Learning.

Pihl, Marshall R. Korean Word Book. 2004. (KOR., Illus.). 112p. pap. 14.95 *(978-1-57306-197-1(2))* Bess Pr., Inc.

Powell, Marie. Dan Can! Cartwright, Amy, illus. 2016. (Word Families Ser.). (ENG.). 16p. (J). (gr. k-3). 17.95 *(978-1-60753-924-7(1))* Amicus Publishing.

—Go to Bed, Ted! Cartwright, Amy, illus. 2016. (Word Families Ser.). (ENG.). 16p. (gr. k-3). 17.95 *(978-1-60753-927-8(6))* Amicus Publishing.

—The Map Trap. Cartwright, Amy, illus. 2016. (Word Families Ser.). (ENG.). 16p. (J). (gr. k-3). 17.95 *(978-1-60753-928-5(4))* Amicus Publishing.

—Stop, Pop! Cartwright, Amy, illus. 2016. (Word Families Ser.). (ENG.). 16p. (gr. k-3). 17.95 *(978-1-60753-925-4(X))* Amicus Publishing.

—When, Jen? Cartwright, Amy, illus. 2016. (Word Families Ser.). (ENG.). 16p. (J). (gr. k-3). 17.95 *(978-1-60753-926-1(8))* Amicus Publishing.

POWer Words Gr. 7-8. 2005. (YA). per. *(978-1-57022-521-5(4))* ECS Learning Systems, Inc.

POWer Words Gr. 9-12. 2005. (YA). per. *(978-1-57022-549-9(4))* ECS Learning Systems, Inc.

Practice Pals Bilingual Practice Book: First Words. 2006. (ENG & FRE., Illus.). 16p. (J). (gr. -1-1). spiral bd. *(978-1-930355-55-2(6))* Bright of America.

Prefixes, Suffixes, & Root Words (Gr. 2-3) 2003. (J). *(978-1-58232-123-3(X))* ECS Learning Systems, Inc.

Preston-Gannon, Frann. My World. Preston-Gannon, Frann, illus. 2017. (ENG., Illus.). 32p. (J). 16.99 *(978-1-62779-530-2(8)*, 9781627795302, Holt, Henry & Co. Bks. For Young Readers) Holt, Henry & Co.

Priddy Books Staff & Priddy, Roger. First Words. rev. ed. 2004. (Bright Baby Ser.).Tr. of Primeras Palabras. (ENG., Illus.). 26p. (J). (gr. -1 — 1). bds. 4.99 *(978-0-312-49388-2(6)*, 9780312493882, Priddy Bks.) St. Martin's Pr.

—My Little Word Book. rev. ed. 2004. (My Little Bks.). (ENG., Illus.). 28p. (J). (gr. -1-k). bds. 9.95 *(978-0-312-49387-5(8)*, 9780312493875, Priddy Bks.) St. Martin's Pr.

Priddy, Roger. Animals. 2013. (Bright Baby Ser.). (ENG., Illus.). 16p. (J). (gr. -1 — 1). bds. 8.99 *(978-0-312-51622-2(3)*, 9780312516222); bds. 4.99 *(978-0-312-51597-3(9)*, 9780312515973) St. Martin's Pr. (Priddy Bks.).

—Baby Basics Animals. 2013. (Baby Basics Ser.). (ENG., Illus.). 10p. (J). (gr. -1 — 1). bds. 4.99 *(978-0-312-51553-9(7)*, 9780312515539, Priddy Bks.) St. Martin's Pr.

—Baby Basics My First Animals. 2013. (Baby Basics Ser.). (ENG., Illus.). 28p. (J). (gr. -1 — 1). bds. 8.99 *(978-0-312-51634-5(7)*, 9780312516345, Priddy Bks.) St. Martin's Pr.

—Baby's First Animals. 2016. (Baby's First Ser.). (ENG., Illus.). 8p. (J). bds. 7.99 *(978-0-312-51952-0(4)*, 9780312519520, Priddy Bks.) St. Martin's Pr.

—Baby's First Words. 2016. (Baby's First Ser.). (ENG., Illus.). 8p. (J). bds. 7.99 *(978-0-312-51950-6(8)*, 9780312519506, Priddy Bks.) St. Martin's Pr.

—Bright Baby 4 Copy Slipcase: Colors; Trucks; First Words; Animals. 2005. (Bright Baby Ser.). (ENG., Illus.). 50p. (J). (gr. -1 — 1). 15.95 *(978-0-312-49447-6(5)*, Priddy Bks.) St. Martin's Pr.

—Faces: A High Contrast Board Book. 2013. (Hello Baby Ser.). (ENG., Illus.). 16p. (J). (gr. -1 — 1). bds. 4.99 *(978-0-312-51600-0(2)*, 9780312516000, Priddy Bks.) St. Martin's Pr.

—First 100 Words. (First 100 Ser.). (ENG., Illus.). (J). 2013. 14p. (gr. -1 — 1). bds. 9.99 *(978-0-312-51689-5(4)*, 9780312516895) 2011. 26p. (— 1). bds. 5.99 *(978-0-312-51078-7(0)*, 9780312510787) 2005. 16p. (gr. -1 — 1). bds. 8.95 *(978-0-312-49541-1(2)*, 9780312495411) St. Martin's Pr. (Priddy Bks.).

—First Farm Words. 2017. (First 100 Ser.). (ENG.). 24p. (J). bds. 5.99 *(978-0-312-52283-4(5)*, 9780312522834, Priddy Bks.) St. Martin's Pr.

—First Words. 2014. (My First Priddy Ser.). (ENG.). 12p. (J). (gr. -1 — 1). bds. 6.99 *(978-0-312-51667-3(3)*, 9780312516673, Priddy Bks.) St. Martin's Pr.

—Happy Baby ABC. rev. ed. 2003. (Happy Baby Ser.). (ENG., Illus.). 28p. (J). (gr. -1 — 1). bds. 6.99 *(978-0-312-49169-7(7)*, 9780312491697, Priddy Bks.) St. Martin's Pr.

—It's Time to Sleep. 2013. (Bright Baby Ser.). (ENG.). 10p. (J). (gr. -1 — 1). bds. 4.99 *(978-0-312-51635-2(5)*, 9780312516352, Priddy Bks.) St. Martin's Pr.

—Learn to Write Your First Words - Cat. 2012. (Wipe Clean Ser.). (ENG., Illus.). 24p. (J). (gr. -1-1). bds. 8.95 *(978-0-312-51393-1(3)*, 9780312513931, Priddy Bks.) St. Martin's Pr.

—My Big Word Book. 2012. (ENG., Illus.). 10p. (J). (gr. -1-k). bds. 8.99 *(978-0-312-51373-3(9)*, 9780312513733, Priddy Bks.) St. Martin's Pr.

—My First Words. 2013. (Baby Basics Ser.). (ENG.). 28p. (J). (gr. -1 — 1). bds. 8.99 *(978-0-312-51633-8(9)*, 9780312516338, Priddy Bks.) St. Martin's Pr.

—My Little Numbers Book. 2012. (My Little Bks.). (ENG., Illus.). 24p. (J). (gr. -1-k). bds. 8.99 *(978-0-312-51463-1(8)*, 9780312514631, Priddy Bks.) St. Martin's Pr.

—My Little Word Book. 2nd rev. ed. 2012. (My Little Bks.). (ENG., Illus.). 24p. (J). (gr. -1-k). bds. 8.99 *(978-0-312-51464-8(6)*, 9780312514648, Priddy Bks.) St. Martin's Pr.

—Simple First Words Let's Talk. 2011. (Simple First Words Ser.). (ENG.). 12p. (J). (gr. -1 — 1). bds. 14.95 *(978-0-312-51421-1(2)*, 9780312514211, Priddy Bks.) St. Martin's Pr.

—Words. (Bright Baby Ser.). (ENG., (J). (gr. -1 — 1). 2013. Illus.). 16p. bds. 8.99 *(978-0-312-51621-5(5)*, 9780312516215) 2008. 12p. bds. 4.95 *(978-0-312-50424-3(1)*, 9780312504243) 2008. (Illus.). 12p. bds. 4.95 *(978-0-312-50216-4(8)*, 9780312502164) St. Martin's Pr. (Priddy Bks.).

—Words: A High Contrast Board Book. 2013. (Hello Baby Ser.). (ENG., Illus.). 16p. (J). (gr. -1 — 1). bds. 4.99 *(978-0-312-51598-0(7)*, 9780312515980, Priddy Bks.) St. Martin's Pr.

—Words Palabras. 2009. (Slide & Find Ser.). (ENG.). 10p. (J). (gr. -1 — 1). bds. 4.95 *(978-0-312-50729-9(1)*, 9780312507299, Priddy Bks.) St. Martin's Pr.

Publications International Ltd. Staff. My First Look & Find Early Learning. 2013. 18p. (gr. -1-1). bds. 7.98 *(978-1-4508-1897-1(8)*, 1450818978) Phoenix International Publications, Inc.

Publications International Ltd. Staff, ed. Baby's Words. 2010. 18p. (J). bds. 7.98 *(978-1-60553-964-5(3))* Publications International, Ltd.

—First Words (Listen & Learn Sound Book) 2011. 19p. (J). bds. 11.98 *(978-1-4508-1441-6(7))* Phoenix International Publications, Inc.

—My First Book Block - First Words. 2011. 12p. (J). bds. 3.75 net. *(978-1-4508-1666-3(5)*, 1450816665) Publications International, Ltd.

Puedo Salir? 2003. (Coleccion Parvulitos). 63.50 *(978-0-8136-8103-0(0))* Modern Curriculum Pr.

Pulse- Fun with Vocabulary & Spelling. 2006. cd-rom 4.99 *(978-1-60245-041-7(2))* GDL Multimedia, LLC.

Quinn, Sarah, tr. from FRE. A Day at the Farm. 2013. (ENG., Illus.). 48p. (J). (gr. -1-k). 16.95 *(978-1-926973-76-0(3)*, Owlkids) Owlkids Bks. Inc. CAN. Dist: Publishers Group West (PGW).

Rabbit's Book of Words. 2004. 12p. (J). bds. 2.99 *(978-1-85997-431-5(7))* Byeway Bks.

Rasinski, Timothy. Starting with Prefixes & Suffixes, 1 vol. rev. ed. 2013. (Building Vocabulary Ser.). (ENG., Illus.). 216p. (gr. 2-4). pap. 24.99 *(978-1-4258-1103-7(5))* Shell Educational Publishing.

—Understanding Word Nuances Level 5, 1 vol. rev. ed. 2014. (Vocabulary Ladders Ser.). (ENG., Illus.). 144p. (gr. 5-5). pap. 15.99 *(978-1-4258-1304-8(6))* Shell Educational Publishing.

—Understanding Word Nuances, Level 6, 1 vol. rev. ed. 2014. (Vocabulary Ladders Ser.). (ENG., Illus.). 144p. (gr. 6-6). pap. 15.99 *(978-1-4258-1305-5(4))* Shell Educational Publishing.

—Vocabulary Ladders: Understanding Word Nuances, Level 4, 1 vol. rev. ed. 2014. (Vocabulary Ladders Ser.). (ENG., Illus.). 144p. (gr. 4-4). pap. 15.99 *(978-1-4258-1303-1(8))* Shell Educational Publishing.

Rasinski, Timothy V. Daily Word Ladders: 150+ Reproducible Word Study Lessons That Help Kids Boost Reading, Vocabulary, Spelling & Phonics Skills! 2008. (Daily Word Ladders Ser.). (ENG.). 176p. (gr. 1-2). pap. 19.99 *(978-0-545-07476-6(2)*, Teaching Resources) Scholastic, Inc.

—100 Reproducible Word Study Lessons That Help Kids Boost Reading, Vocabulary, Spelling & Phonics Skills - Independently! 2005. (Daily Word Ladders Ser.). (ENG., Illus.). 112p. (gr. 4-6). pap. 15.99 *(978-0-439-77345-4(8)*, Teaching Resources) Scholastic, Inc.

—100 Reproducible Word Study Lessons That Help Kids Boost Reading, Vocabulary, Spelling & Phonics Skills — Independently! 2005. (Daily Word Ladders Ser.). (ENG., Illus.). 112p. (gr. 2-3). pap. 15.99 *(978-0-439-51383-8(9)*, Teaching Resources) Scholastic, Inc.

Reaching into Space: Word Study: Suffixes, Level B. 2003. ("Plaid" Phonics & Stories Libraries). (gr. 2-3). 38.50 *(978-0-8136-9153-4(2))* Modern Curriculum Pr.

Reading Rods Prefixes & Suffixes: Instruction & Activity Book. 2003. (J). pap. 12.95 *(978-1-56911-107-9(3))* Learning Resources, Inc.

Reading Rods Prefixes & Suffixes Activity Cards. 2003. (J). pap. 12.95 *(978-1-56911-108-6(1))* Learning Resources, Inc.

Reading Rods Sentence Building Activity Cards, Set 2. 2003. (J). 19.95 *(978-1-56911-116-1(2))* Learning Resources, Inc.

Reading Rods Simple Sentences Activity Cards. 2003. (J). pap. 12.95 *(978-1-56911-111-6(1))* Learning Resources, Inc.

Reading Rods Simple Sentences Activity Cards, Set 2. 2003. (J). pap. 19.95 *(978-1-56911-112-3(X))* Learning Resources, Inc.

Reading Rods Simple Sentences Instruction & Activity Book. 2003. (J). pap. 12.95 *(978-1-56911-110-9(3))* Learning Resources, Inc.

Reading Rods Word Building Activity Book. 2003. (J). pap. 4.95 *(978-1-56911-119-2(7))* Learning Resources, Inc.

Reading Rods Word Building Activity Cards, Set 2. 2003. (J). 19.95 *(978-1-56911-115-4(4))* Learning Resources, Inc.

Reasoner, Charles. Colors in the Garden. Pitt, Sarah, illus. 2009. (3D Board Bks.). 12p. (gr. -1-k). bds. 9.99 *(978-1-934650-40-0(4))* Just For Kids Pr., LLC.

Reeve, Christine E. Functional Vocabulary for Children Ben Likes All Kinds of Sports. 2005. (J). spiral bd. 14.95 *(978-0-7606-0627-8(7))* LinguiSystems, Inc.

—Functional Vocabulary for Children Dontel Learns about Transportation. 2005. (J). spiral bd. 14.95 *(978-0-7606-0625-4(0))* LinguiSystems, Inc.

—Functional Vocabulary for Children Jasmine Sets the Table. 2005. (J). spiral bd. 14.95 *(978-0-7606-0623-0(4))* LinguiSystems, Inc.

—Functional Vocabulary for Children Kira Likes to Go to Schools. 2005. (J). spiral bd. 14.95 *(978-0-7606-0628-5(5))* LinguiSystems, Inc.

—Functional Vocabulary for Children Michelle Goes for a Walk. 2005. (J). spiral bd. 14.95 *(978-0-7606-0624-7(2))* LinguiSystems, Inc.

—Functional Vocabulary for Children Ramon Plays on the Playground. 2005. (J). spiral bd. 14.95 *(978-0-7606-0626-1(9))* LinguiSystems, Inc.

—Functional Vocabulary for Children Sarah Goes to Bed. 2005. (J). spiral bd. 14.95 *(978-0-7606-0620-9(X))* LinguiSystems, Inc.

—Functional Vocabulary for Children Tyler Gets Cleaned Up. 2005. (J). spiral bd. 14.95 *(978-0-7606-0621-6(8))* LinguiSystems, Inc.
—Functional Vocabulary for Children Zoey Uses the Bathroom. 2005. (J). spiral bd. 14.95 *(978-0-7606-0622-3(6))* LinguiSystems, Inc.
Reid, Struan & Stowell, Louie. My First Pirate Book. Allen, Peter, illus. 2012. (My First Book Ser.). 16p. (J). ring bd. 6.99 *(978-0-7945-3228-4(4),* Usborne) EDC Publishing.
Rey, H. A. & Rey, Margret. Curious George's Big Book of Curiosity. Paprocki, Greg, illus. 2005. (Curious George Ser.). (ENG.). 48p. (J). (gr. -1-3). 11.99 *(978-0-618-58338-6(6))* Houghton Mifflin Harcourt Publishing Co.
Reynolds, Edith. Working with Words. 2003. 132p. (YA). pap. 16.95 *(978-1-59330-093-7(X))* Aventine Pr.
Rhyming & Word Families Big Book. 2004. (J). pap. 39.95 *(978-1-56911-175-8(8))* Learning Resources, Inc.
Rhyming Words (Gr. 1-2) 2003. (J). *(978-1-58232-117-2(5)); (978-1-58232-112-7(4))* ECS Learning Systems, Inc.
Rhyming Words in Context (Gr. K-2) 2003. (J). *(978-1-58232-098-4(5))* ECS Learning Systems, Inc.
Rinaldo, Luana & Prasadam-halls, Smriti. Who Am I? This Is My Mouth. 2012. (ENG., Illus.). 12p. (J). (gr. -1-k). 7.99 *(978-1-4083-1509-5(2))* Hodder & Stoughton GBR. Dist: Hachette Bk. Group.
—Who Am I? This Is My Tail. 2012. (ENG., Illus.). 12p. (J). (gr. -1-k). 7.99 *(978-1-4083-1510-1(6))* Hodder & Stoughton GBR. Dist: Hachette Bk. Group.
RiverStream Readers - Pre-1. 2013. (RiverStream Readers Ser.: PK). 124p. (gr. -1-2). 11.49 *(978-1-62588-900-3(3))* Black Rabbit Bks.
Robles, D. & Minquini, Lourdes. Los 100 Mejores Acertijos Matematicos (The One Hundred Best Word Problems) (SPA., Illus.). 151p. (J). (gr. k-6). pap. 7.95 *(978-968-416-820-6(9),* FN8209) Fernandez USA Publishing.
Rofé, April, illus. The SENSEsational Alphabet: See-Read, Touch-Feel, Scratch & Smell, Hear-Learn, Have Fun! 2006. (J). *(978-0-9779189-1-1(2))* Waldenhouse Pubs., Inc.
Roffey, C. My Red Busy Book. 2003. (Illus.). 12p. (J). 6.99 *(978-0-333-65970-0(8))* Macmillan Pubs., Ltd. GBR. Dist: Trafalgar Square Publishing.
Roffey, M. First Words Indoors. 2003. (Illus.). 12p. (J). 3.99 *(978-1-85292-227-6(3),* Campbell Bks.) Pan Macmillan GBR. Dist: Trafalgar Square Publishing.
Rogala, Jennifer. Ways to Say the Words You've Heard. 2006. 28p. (J). per. 11.95 *(978-1-58939-864-1(5))* Virtualbookworm.com Publishing, Inc.
—When My Nose Runs, Where Does It Go? Nicholas, Jacob, illus. 2006. 36p. per. 11.95 *(978-1-58939-866-5(1))* Virtualbookworm.com Publishing, Inc.
Rolbin, Cyrus. Kana-OK! A New Approach to Learning the ABC's of Japanese: Hiragana & Katakana. 2004. (JPN & ENG., Illus.). 128p. pap. 9.95 *(978-4-7700-2988-1(8))* Kodansha International JPN. Dist: Kodansha America, Inc.
Rollason, Jane. Killer Bees Level 2 Elementary/Lower-intermediate American English. 2010. (ENG., Illus.). 64p. pap. 12.00 *(978-0-521-14896-2(0))* Cambridge Univ. Pr.
Rondeau, Amanda. Ed As in Bed, 1 vol. 2003. (Word Families Set 2 Ser.). (ENG., Illus.). 24p. (J). (gr. k-3). lib. bdg. 24.21 *(978-1-59197-228-0(0),* SandCastle) ABDO Publishing Co.
—Ob As in Knob, 1 vol. 2003. (Word Families Set 5 Ser.). (ENG., Illus.). 24p. (J). (gr. k-3). lib. bdg. 24.21 *(978-1-59197-249-5(3),* SandCastle) ABDO Publishing Co.
—Ock As in Block, 1 vol. 2003. (Word Families Set 5 Ser.). (ENG., Illus.). 24p. (J). (gr. k-3). lib. bdg. 24.21 *(978-1-59197-250-1(7),* SandCastle) ABDO Publishing Co.
—Og As in Dog, 1 vol. 2003. (Word Families Set 5 Ser.). (ENG., Illus.). 24p. (J). (gr. k-3). lib. bdg. 24.21 *(978-1-59197-251-8(5),* SandCastle) ABDO Publishing Co.
—Op As in Top, 1 vol. 2003. (Word Families Set 5 Ser.). (ENG., Illus.). 24p. (J). (gr. k-3). lib. bdg. 24.21 *(978-1-59197-252-5(3),* SandCastle) ABDO Publishing Co.
—Ore As in Core, 1 vol. 2003. (Word Families Set 7 Ser.). (ENG., Illus.). 24p. (J). (gr. k-3). lib. bdg. 24.21 *(978-1-59197-267-9(1),* SandCastle) ABDO Publishing Co.
—Ot As in Knot, 1 vol. 2003. (Word Families Set 5 Ser.). (ENG., Illus.). 24p. (J). (gr. k-3). lib. bdg. 24.21 *(978-1-59197-253-2(1),* SandCastle) ABDO Publishing Co.
—Ow As in Cow, 1 vol. 2003. (Word Families Set 5 Ser.). (ENG., Illus.). 24p. (J). (gr. k-3). lib. bdg. 24.21 *(978-1-59197-254-9(X),* SandCastle) ABDO Publishing Co.
Rookie Ready to Learn - First Science: Me & My World, 5 vols., Set. Incl. Germs. Oetting, Judy. Herr, Tad, illus. 40p. lib. bdg. 23.00 *(978-0-531-26500-0(5));* I Love Trees. Meister, Cari. Sirrell, Terry, illus. 40p. lib. bdg. 23.00 *(978-0-531-26501-7(3));* Please, Wind? Greene, Carol. Sharp, Gene, illus. 40p. lib. bdg. 23.00 *(978-0-531-26502-4(1));* Tooth Is Loose. Trumbauer, Lisa. Gray, Steve, illus. 32p. lib. bdg. 23.00 *(978-0-531-26503-1(X));* Water Everywhere! Taylor-Butler, Christine. Manning, Maurie, illus. 40p. lib. bdg. 23.00 *(978-0-531-26504-8(8));* (J). (gr. -1-k). (Rookie Ready to Learn Ser.). 2011. Set lib. bdg. 115.00 *(978-0-531-23850-9(4),* Children's Pr.) Scholastic Library Publishing.
Rookie Ready to Learn - I Can!, 5 vols., Set. Incl. Best Mud Pie. Quinn, Lin. Rooney, Ronnie, illus. 40p. lib. bdg. 23.00 *(978-0-531-26425-6(4));* I Can Do It All. Pearson, Mary E. Shelley, Jeff, illus. 32p. lib. bdg. 23.00 *(978-0-531-26429-4(7));* I'll Do It Later. Ribke, Simone T. White, Lee, illus. 40p. lib. bdg. 23.00 *(978-0-531-26528-4(5));* Splat! Pérez-Mercado, Mary Margaret. Torrey, Rich, illus. 40p. lib. bdg. 23.00 *(978-0-531-26373-0(8));* Willie's Word World. Curry, Don L. Stromoski, Rick, illus. 40p. lib. bdg. 23.00 *(978-0-531-26374-7(6));* (J). (gr. -1-k). (Rookie Ready to Learn Ser.). 2011. Set lib. bdg. 115.00 *(978-0-531-25150-8(0),* Children's Pr.) Scholastic Library Publishing.
Rookie Ready to Learn - My Family & Friends, 5 vols., Set. Incl. Eat Your Peas, Louise! Snow, Pegeen. Venezia, Mike, illus. lib. bdg. 23.00 *(978-0-531-26527-7(7));* I Do Not Want To. Schulz, Kathy. Rescek, Sanja, illus. lib. bdg. 23.00 *(978-0-531-26525-3(0));* Just Like Always. Perry, Anne M. Lyon, Tammie, illus. lib. bdg. 23.00 *(978-0-531-26370-9(3));* Rude Ralph: A Rookie Reader. Fontes, Justine. Jordan, Charles, illus. lib. bdg. 23.00 *(978-0-531-26529-1(3));* So Many Me's. Neasi, Barbara J. Ochoa, Ana, illus. lib. bdg. 23.00 *(978-0-531-26372-3(X));* 40p. (J). (gr. -1-k). (Rookie Ready to Learn Ser.). 2011. Set lib. bdg. 115.00 *(978-0-531-24450-0(4),* Children's Pr.) Scholastic Library Publishing.
Rookie Ready to Learn - Numbers & Shapes, 5 vols., Set. Incl. Balls. Jones, Melanie Davis. Bronson, Linda, illus. 32p. lib. bdg. 23.00 *(978-0-531-26445-4(9));* Circle in the Sky. Wilson, Zachary. Adinolfi, JoAnn, illus. 40p. lib. bdg. 23.00 *(978-0-531-26446-1(7));* Next to an Ant. Rockliff, Mara. Constantin, Pascale, illus. 32p. lib. bdg. 23.00 *(978-0-531-26447-8(5));* Number One Puppy. Wilson, Zachary. Pertile, Paula, illus. 40p. lib. bdg. 23.00 *(978-0-531-26448-5(3));* Too Many Balloons. Matthias, Catherine. Sharp, Gene, illus. 40p. lib. bdg. 23.00 *(978-0-531-26449-2(1));* (J). (gr. -1-k). (Rookie Ready to Learn Ser.). 2011. Set lib. bdg. 115.00 *(978-0-531-24300-8(1),* Children's Pr.) Scholastic Library Publishing.
Rookie Ready to Learn - Out & About: In My Community, 5 vols., Set. Incl. Always Be Safe. Schulz, Kathy. 40p. lib. bdg. 25.00 *(978-0-531-27175-9(7));* Field Day. Jones, Melanie Davis. Molnar, Albert, illus. 40p. lib. bdg. 25.00 *(978-0-531-27176-6(5));* Joshua James Likes Trucks. Petrie, Catherine. Snyder, Joel, illus. 32p. lib. bdg. 25.00 *(978-0-531-27177-3(3));* Work & Play. Meltzer Kleinhenz, Sydnie. Reasor, Mick, illus. 32p. lib. bdg. 25.00 *(978-0-531-27179-7(X));* (J). (gr. -1-k). (Rookie Ready to Learn Ser.). 2011. Set lib. bdg. 115.00 *(978-0-531-25905-4(6),* Children's Pr.) Scholastic Library Publishing.
Rooney, Anne. Working with Words. 2004. (QEB Learn Computing Ser.). (Illus.). 32p. (YA). (gr. 4-7). lib. bdg. 18.95 *(978-1-59566-038-1(0))* QEB Publishing Inc.
Rosa-Mendoza, Gladys. Jobs Around My Neighborhood/Oficios en Mi Vecindario. Iosa, Ann, illus. 2007. (English Spanish Foundations Ser.). 20p. (gr. -1-k). pap. 19.95 *(978-1-931398-81-7(X))* Me+Mi Publishing.
—Let's Go to the Zoo!/Vamos Al Zoologico! Elkerton, Andy, illus. 2007. (English Spanish Foundations Ser.). (ENG & SPA.). 20p. (J). (gr. -1-k). bds. 6.95 *(978-1-931398-20-6(8))* Me+Mi Publishing.
—Lupe Lupita, Where Are You?/Lupe Lupita Donde Estas? Ochoa, Ana, illus. 2007. (English Spanish Foundations Ser.). 20p. (gr. -1-k). pap. 19.95 *(978-1-931398-82-4(8))* Me+Mi Publishing.
—My House/Mi Casa. Borlasca, Hector, illus. (English Spanish Foundations Ser.). (gr. -1-1). 2007. per. 19.95 *(978-1-931398-84-8(4))* 2006. (ENG & SPA.). 20p. (J). bds. 6.95 *(978-1-931398-18-3(6))* Me+Mi Publishing.
—My School/Mi Escuela. Murphy, Terri, illus. 2007. (English Spanish Foundations Ser.). (ENG & SPA.). (J). (gr. -1-k). bds. 6.95 *(978-1-931398-23-7(2))* Me+Mi Publishing.
—My Senses/Mis Sentidos. Merer, Laura, illus. 2007. (English Spanish Foundations Ser.). (ENG & SPA.). 20p. (J). (gr. -1-k). bds. 6.95 *(978-1-931398-21-3(6))* Me+Mi Publishing.
—My Week/Mi Semana. Wesley, Milliana, ed. Grosshauser, Peter, illus. 2007. (English Spanish Foundations Ser.). (gr. -1-k). bds. 6.95 *(978-1-931398-25-1(9))* Me+Mi Publishing.
—Opposites. Cifuentes, Carolina, ed. McGeehan, Dan, illus. 2004. (English-Spanish Foundations Ser.: Vol. 5).Tr. of Opuestos. (ENG & SPA.). 20p. (J). (gr. -1-4). bds. 6.95 *(978-0-9679748-6-6(0))* Me+Mi Publishing.
—Who Lives in the Sea?/Qui'n Vive en el Mar? O'Neil, Sharron, illus. 2007. (English Spanish Foundations Ser.). (ENG & SPA.). 20p. (J). (gr. -1-k). bds. 6.95 *(978-1-931398-24-4(0))* Me+Mi Publishing.
Rowe, Jeanette. First Words. 2016. (I Spy with My Little Eye... Bks.). (ENG.). 16p. (J). (gr. -1-k). bds. 9.99 *(978-0-7641-6816-1(9))* Barron's Educational Series, Inc.
Saddleback Educational Publishing Staff. Lifeskills Vocabulary 1, 1 vol. 2013. (Lifeskills Vocabulary Ser.). (ENG.). 100p. (gr. 6-12). pap. 44.95 *(978-1-62250-028-4(8))* Saddleback Educational Publishing, Inc.
—Lifeskills Vocabulary 2. 2013. (Lifeskills Vocabulary Ser.). (ENG.). 100p. (gr. 6-12). pap. 44.95 *(978-1-62250-029-1(6))* Saddleback Educational Publishing, Inc.
Salzmann, Mary Elizabeth. -Ad As in Dad, 1 vol. 2003. (Word Families Set 1 Ser.). (ENG., Illus.). 24p. (J). (gr. k-3). lib. bdg. 24.21 *(978-1-59197-226-6(4))* ABDO Publishing Co.
—Ag As in Flag, 1 vol. 2003. (Word Families Set 1 Ser.). (ENG., Illus.). 24p. (J). (gr. k-3). lib. bdg. 24.21 *(978-1-59197-225-9(6))* ABDO Publishing Co.
—Am As in Ham, 1 vol. 2003. (Word Families Set 1 Ser.). (ENG., Illus.). 24p. (J). (gr. k-3). lib. bdg. 24.21 *(978-1-59197-223-5(X))* ABDO Publishing Co.
—Am I Happy?, 1 vol. (First Words Ser.). (Illus.). (J). (gr. k-3). 2006. (ENG.). 24p. lib. bdg. 24.21 *(978-1-59679-350-7(3),* SandCastle) 2005. 23p. pap. 48.42 *(978-1-59679-351-4(1))* ABDO Publishing Co.
—Ap As in Cap, 1 vol. 2003. (Word Families Set 1 Ser.). (ENG., Illus.). 24p. (J). (gr. k-3). lib. bdg. 24.21 *(978-1-59197-224-2(8))* ABDO Publishing Co.
—An As in Fan. 2003. (Word Families Set 1 Ser.). (ENG., Illus.). 24p. (J). (gr. k-3). lib. bdg. 24.21 *(978-1-59197-222-8(1))* ABDO Publishing Co.
—At As in Cat, 1 vol. 2003. (Word Families Set 1 Ser.). (ENG., Illus.). 24p. (J). (gr. k-3). lib. bdg. 24.21 *(978-1-59197-221-1(3),* SandCastle) ABDO Publishing Co.
—Ay As in Clay, 1 vol. 2003. (Word Families Set 7 Ser.). (ENG., Illus.). 24p. (J). (gr. k-3). lib. bdg. 24.21 *(978-1-59197-264-8(7))* ABDO Publishing Co.
—Come Home with Me! 2004. (Sight Words Ser.). (ENG., Illus.). 24p. (J). (gr. k-3). lib. bdg. 24.21 *(978-1-59197-465-9(8))* ABDO Publishing Co.
—Did You See One Jump? 2004. (Sight Words Ser.). (ENG., Illus.). 24p. (J). (gr. k-3). lib. bdg. 24.21 *(978-1-59197-466-6(6),* SandCastle) ABDO Publishing Co.
—Ell As in Well, 1 vol. 2003. (Word Families Set 2 Ser.). (ENG., Illus.). 24p. (J). (gr. k-3). lib. bdg. 24.21 *(978-1-59197-231-0(0),* SandCastle) ABDO Publishing Co.
—Here Is a Zoo, 1 vol. (First Words Ser.). (Illus.). (J). (gr. k-3). 2006. (ENG.). 24p. lib. bdg. 24.21 *(978-1-59679-378-1(3),* SandCastle) 2005. 23p. pap. 48.42 *(978-1-59679-379-8(1))* ABDO Publishing Co.
—I Am a Kitten, 1 vol. (First Words Ser.). (Illus.). (J). (gr. k-3). 2006. (ENG.). 24p. lib. bdg. 24.21 *(978-1-59679-380-4(5),* SandCastle) 2005. 23p. pap. 48.42 *(978-1-59679-381-1(3))* ABDO Publishing Co.
—I Had a Great Time! 2004. (Sight Words Ser.). (ENG., Illus.). 24p. (J). (gr. k-3). lib. bdg. 24.21 *(978-1-59197-477-2(1),* SandCastle) ABDO Publishing Co.
—I See a Costume, 1 vol. (First Words Ser.). (Illus.). (J). (gr. k-3). 2006. (ENG.). 24p. lib. bdg. 24.21 *(978-1-59679-384-2(8),* SandCastle) 2005. 23p. pap. 48.42 *(978-1-59679-385-9(6))* ABDO Publishing Co.
—It's Not Good, It's Great! 2003. (Sight Words Ser.). (ENG., Illus.). 24p. (J). (gr. k-3). lib. bdg. 24.21 *(978-1-59197-479-6(8),* SandCastle) ABDO Publishing Co.
—Look at the Playground!, 1 vol. (First Words Ser.). (Illus.). (J). (gr. k-3). 2006. (ENG.). 24p. lib. bdg. 24.21 *(978-1-59679-398-9(8),* SandCastle) 2005. 23p. pap. 48.42 *(978-1-59679-399-6(6))* ABDO Publishing Co.
—No Pigs on the Farm! 2004. (Sight Words Ser.). (ENG., Illus.). 24p. (J). (gr. k-3). lib. bdg. 24.21 *(978-1-59197-471-0(2),* SandCastle) ABDO Publishing Co.
—Out for the Summer! 2004. (Sight Words Ser.). (ENG., Illus.). 24p. (J). (gr. k-3). lib. bdg. 24.21 *(978-1-59197-472-7(0),* SandCastle) ABDO Publishing Co.
—The Parade Is Here!, 1 vol. (First Words Ser.). (Illus.). (J). (gr. k-3). 2006. (ENG.). 24p. lib. bdg. 24.21 *(978-1-59679-406-1(2),* SandCastle) 2005. 23p. pap. 48.42 *(978-1-59679-407-8(0))* ABDO Publishing Co.
—See the Farm!, 1 vol. Craig, Diane, ed. 2006. (First Words Ser.). (ENG., Illus.). 24p. (J). (gr. k-3). lib. bdg. 24.21 *(978-1-59679-414-6(3),* SandCastle) ABDO Publishing Co.
—See the Farm! 2005. (Illus.). 23p. (J). pap. 48.42 *(978-1-59679-415-3(1))* ABDO Publishing Co.
—Snow & More Snow! 2004. (Sight Words Ser.). (ENG., Illus.). 24p. (J). (gr. k-3). lib. bdg. 24.21 *(978-1-59197-470-3(4),* SandCastle) ABDO Publishing Co.
—They Are the Best! 2004. (Sight Words Ser.). (ENG., Illus.). 24p. (J). (gr. k-3). lib. bdg. 24.21 *(978-1-59197-474-1(7),* SandCastle) ABDO Publishing Co.
—Way to Go! 2004. (Sight Words Ser.). (ENG., Illus.). 24p. (J). (gr. k-3). lib. bdg. 24.21 *(978-1-59197-468-0(2),* SandCastle) ABDO Publishing Co.
—We All Like It! 2004. (Sight Words Ser.). (ENG., Illus.). 24p. (J). (gr. k-3). lib. bdg. 24.21 *(978-1-59197-467-3(4),* SandCastle) ABDO Publishing Co.
—We Are at the Park, 1 vol. (First Words Ser.). (Illus.). (J). (gr. k-3). 2006. (ENG.). 24p. lib. bdg. 24.21 *(978-1-59679-424-5(0),* SandCastle) 2005. 23p. pap. 48.42 *(978-1-59679-425-2(9))* ABDO Publishing Co.
—We Are Playing!, 1 vol. (First Words Ser.). (Illus.). (J). (gr. k-3). 2006. (ENG.). 24p. lib. bdg. 24.21 *(978-1-59679-426-9(7),* SandCastle) 2005. 23p. pap. 48.42 *(978-1-59679-427-6(5))* ABDO Publishing Co.
—We Look at Food, 1 vol. (First Words Ser.). (Illus.). (J). (gr. k-3). 2006. (ENG.). 24p. lib. bdg. 24.21 *(978-1-59679-436-8(4),* SandCastle) 2005. 23p. pap. 48.42 *(978-1-59679-437-5(2))* ABDO Publishing Co.
—We See the Beach!, 1 vol. (First Words Ser.). (Illus.). (J). (gr. k-3). 2006. (ENG.). 24p. lib. bdg. 24.21 *(978-1-59679-440-5(2),* SandCastle) 2005. 23p. pap. 48.42 *(978-1-59679-441-2(0))* ABDO Publishing Co.
—What a Day in the Park! 2004. (Sight Words Ser.). (ENG., Illus.). 24p. (J). (gr. k-3). lib. bdg. 24.21 *(978-1-59197-476-5(3),* SandCastle) ABDO Publishing Co.
—Who Is This at the Beach? 2004. (Sight Words Ser.). (ENG., Illus.). 24p. (J). (gr. k-3). lib. bdg. 24.21 *(978-1-59197-480-2(1),* SandCastle) ABDO Publishing Co.
Sanseri, Wanda. Play by the Sea. 2003. (J). 5.00 *(978-1-880045-26-8(5))* Back Home Industries.
Sarkar, Maria. Have Fun with Words. 2014. (ENG., Illus.). 74p. (gr. 4-6). pap. 24.95 *(978-1-84963-497-7(1),* 0c22b27b-089b-48d0-9b8e-3e92976c9dd2) Austin, Stan AUS. Dist: Bookmasters Distribution.
Saviola, Ava. Dinosaur's First Words. 2012. (Dinosaur School Ser.). (Illus.). 24p. (J). (gr. -1-1). pap. 8.15 *(978-1-4339-7156-3(9));* lib. bdg. 22.60 *(978-1-4339-7155-6(0))* Stevens, Gareth Publishing LLLP.
Scarry, Richard. Richard Scarry's Early Words Sticker Book: With 101 Stickers! 2014. (ENG.). 32p. (J). (gr. -1 — 1). pap. 5.99 *(978-1-4380-0412-9(5))* Barron's Educational Series, Inc.
—Richard Scarry's Just Right Word Book! Scarry, Richard, illus. 2015. (ENG., Illus.). 26p. (J). (— 1). bds. 7.99 *(978-0-553-50902-1(0),* Golden Bks.) Random Hse. Children's Bks.
—Richard Scarry's Lowly Worm Word Book. Scarry, Richard, illus. 2014. (Chunky Book(R) Ser.). (ENG., Illus.). 28p. (J). (gr. -1 — 1). bds. 3.99 *(978-0-394-84728-3(8),* Random Hse. Bks. for Young Readers) Random Hse. Children's Bks.
Schaefer, A. Help Me Find Something. 2007. (ENG., Illus.). 16p. (gr. k-2). 28.50 *(978-1-60472-108-9(1))* Rourke Educational Media.
Schecter, Deborah. Sight Word Manipulatives for Reading Success: Wheels, Pull-Throughs, Puzzles, & Dozens of Other Easy-to-Make Manipulatives That Help Kids Read, Write, & Really Learn High-Frequency Words. 2005. (ENG.). 144p. (gr. k-2). pap. 17.99 *(978-0-439-54259-3(6),* Teaching Resources) Scholastic, Inc.
Scheunemann, Pam. -Ack As in Snack, 1 vol. 2003. (Word Families Set 6 Ser.). (ENG., Illus.). 24p. (J). (gr. k-3). lib. bdg. 24.21 *(978-1-59197-261-7(2))* ABDO Publishing Co.
—Ash As in Trash, 1 vol. 2003. (Word Families Set 6 Ser.). (ENG., Illus.). 24p. (J). (gr. k-3). lib. bdg. 24.21 *(978-1-59197-260-0(4))* ABDO Publishing Co.
—Aw As in Paw, 1 vol. 2003. (Word Families Set 7 Ser.). (ENG., Illus.). 24p. (J). (gr. k-3). lib. bdg. 24.21 *(978-1-59197-263-1(9))* ABDO Publishing Co.
—Big Bug, Little Bug, 1 vol. (First Words Ser.). (Illus.). (J). (gr. k-3). 2006. (ENG.). 24p. lib. bdg. 24.21 *(978-1-59679-356-9(2),* SandCastle) 2005. 23p. 48.42 *(978-1-59679-357-6(0))* ABDO Publishing Co.
—Come & See My Game!, 1 vol. (First Words Ser.). (Illus.). (J). (gr. k-3). 2006. (ENG.). 24p. lib. bdg. 24.21 *(978-1-59679-362-0(7),* SandCastle) 2005. 23p. pap. 48.42 *(978-1-59679-363-7(5))* ABDO Publishing Co.
—Come for a Party!, 1 vol. (First Words Ser.). (Illus.). (J). (gr. k-3). 2006. (ENG.). 24p. lib. bdg. 24.21 *(978-1-59679-364-4(3),* SandCastle) 2005. 23p. pap. 48.42 *(978-1-59679-365-1(1))* ABDO Publishing Co.
—The Cow Said Meow!, 1 vol. (First Words Ser.). (Illus.). (J). (gr. k-3). 2006. (ENG.). 24p. lib. bdg. 24.21 *(978-1-59679-368-2(6),* SandCastle) 2005. 23p. pap. 48.42 *(978-1-59679-369-9(4))* ABDO Publishing Co.
—Emma Is Cooking! Word Building with Prefixes & Suffixes, 1 vol. 2012. (Word Building Ser.). (ENG.). 24p. (J). (gr. k-4). 25.65 *(978-1-61714-966-5(7))* ABDO Publishing Co.
—Ent As in Cent, 1 vol. 2003. (Word Families Set 2 Ser.). (ENG., Illus.). 24p. (J). (gr. k-3). lib. bdg. 24.21 *(978-1-59197-233-4(7),* SandCastle) ABDO Publishing Co.
—Ick As in Kick, 1 vol. 2003. (Word Families Set 6 Ser.). (ENG., Illus.). 24p. (J). (gr. k-3). lib. bdg. 24.21 *(978-1-59197-258-7(2),* SandCastle) ABDO Publishing Co.
—Ing As in King, 1 vol. 2003. (Word Families Set 6 Ser.). (ENG., Illus.). 24p. (J). (gr. k-3). lib. bdg. 24.21 *(978-1-59197-256-3(6),* SandCastle) ABDO Publishing Co.
—Ink As in Drink, 1 vol. 2003. (Word Families Set 6 Ser.). (ENG., Illus.). 24p. (J). (gr. k-3). lib. bdg. 24.21 *(978-1-59197-257-0(4),* SandCastle) ABDO Publishing Co.
—Is This a Flower?, 1 vol. (First Words Ser.). (Illus.). (J). (gr. k-3). 2006. (ENG.). 24p. lib. bdg. 24.21 *(978-1-59679-390-3(2),* SandCastle) 2005. 23p. pap. 48.42 *(978-1-59679-391-0(0))* ABDO Publishing Co.
—Look at Me!, 1 vol. (First Words Ser.). (Illus.). (J). (gr. k-3). 2006. (ENG.). 24p. lib. bdg. 24.21 *(978-1-59679-396-5(1),* SandCastle) 2005. 23p. pap. 48.42 *(978-1-59679-397-2(X))* ABDO Publishing Co.
—Meg & I, 1 vol. (First Words Ser.). (Illus.). (J). (gr. k-3). 2006. (ENG.). 24p. lib. bdg. 24.21 *(978-1-59679-400-9(3),* SandCastle) 2005. 23p. 48.42 *(978-1-59679-401-6(1))* ABDO Publishing Co.
—The Puppy Is for Me!, 1 vol. (First Words Ser.). (Illus.). (J). (gr. k-3). 2006. (ENG.). 24p. lib. bdg. 24.21 *(978-1-59679-408-5(9),* SandCastle) 2005. 23p. pap. 48.42 *(978-1-59679-409-2(7))* ABDO Publishing Co.
—Rainy Day, 1 vol. (First Words Ser.). (Illus.). (J). (gr. k-3). 2006. (ENG.). 24p. lib. bdg. 24.21 *(978-1-59679-410-8(0),* SandCastle) 2005. 23p. pap. 48.42 *(978-1-59679-411-5(9))* ABDO Publishing Co.
—The Repainted School: Word Building with Prefixes & Suffixes, 1 vol. 2012. (Word Building Ser.). (ENG.). 24p. (J). (gr. k-4). 25.65 *(978-1-61714-969-6(1))* ABDO Publishing Co.
—Silky Is the Luckiest Cat! Word Building with Prefixes & Suffixes, 1 vol. 2012. (Word Building Ser.). (ENG.). 24p. (J). (gr. k-4). 25.65 *(978-1-61714-970-2(5))* ABDO Publishing Co.
—This Is Not My Dog!, 1 vol. (First Words Ser.). (Illus.). (J). (gr. k-3). 2006. (ENG.). 24p. lib. bdg. 24.21 *(978-1-59679-418-4(6),* SandCastle) 2005. 23p. pap. 48.42 *(978-1-59679-419-1(4))* ABDO Publishing Co.
—Unk As in Skunk, 1 vol. 2003. (Word Families Set 6 Ser.). (ENG., Illus.). 24p. (J). (gr. k-3). lib. bdg. 24.21 *(978-1-59197-259-4(0),* SandCastle) ABDO Publishing Co.
—The Unknown Ballplayer: Word Building with Prefixes & Suffixes, 1 vol. 2012. (Word Building Ser.). (ENG.). 24p. (J). (gr. k-4). 25.65 *(978-1-61714-971-9(3))* ABDO Publishing Co.
—We Like Music!, 1 vol. (First Words Ser.). (Illus.). (J). (gr. k-3). 2006. (ENG.). 24p. lib. bdg. 24.21 *(978-1-59679-432-0(1),* SandCastle) 2005. 23p. pap. 48.42 *(978-1-59679-433-7(X))* ABDO Publishing Co.
—We Like to Play!, 1 vol. (First Words Ser.). (Illus.). (J). (gr. k-3). 2006. (ENG.). 24p. lib. bdg. 24.21 *(978-1-59679-434-4(8),* SandCastle) 2005. 23p. pap. 48.42 *(978-1-59679-435-1(6))* ABDO Publishing Co.
Schmitt, Conrad. ¡Así Se Dice! 2009. (Glencoe Spanish Ser.). (ENG & SPA.). 160p. (gr. 6-12). pap., wbk. ed. 21.84 *(978-0-07-892935-9(0),* 0078929350) McGraw-Hill Education.
—Asi Se Dice 2009, Level 1A. 2009. (Glencoe Spanish Ser.). (ENG & SPA.). 160p. (gr. 6-12). pap., wbk. ed. 21.84 *(978-0-07-892934-2(2),* 0078929342) McGraw-Hill Education.
Scholastic Coach Magazine Staff & Beech, Linda Ward. 180 Essential Vocabulary Words: Independent Learning Packets That Help Students Learn the Most Important Words They Need to Succeed in School. 2009. (ENG.). 80p. pap. 12.99 *(978-0-439-89735-8(1),* Teaching Resources) Scholastic, Inc.
Scholastic Inc, contrib. by. All about Me. 2017. (Words Are Fun Ser.). (ENG.). 12p. (J). bds. 8.95 *(978-0-531-23721-2(4),* Children's Pr.) Scholastic Library Publishing.
—All Around Me. 2017. (Words Are Fun Ser.). (ENG.). 12p. (J). bds. 8.95 *(978-0-531-23724-3(9),* Children's Pr.) Scholastic Library Publishing.
—All Around Me/a Mi Alrededor. 2017. (Words Are Fun/ Diverpalabras (Bilingual) Ser.). (ENG.). 12p. (J). bds. 8.95 *(978-0-531-23074-9(0),* Children's Pr.) Scholastic Library Publishing.
—My Favorite Food. 2017. (Words Are Fun Ser.). (ENG.). 12p. (J). bds. 8.95 *(978-0-531-23723-6(0),* Children's Pr.) Scholastic Library Publishing.
Scholastic Inc. (US) Staff, contrib. by. All about Me/ Todo Sobre Mí. 2017. (Words Are Fun/ Diverpalabras (Bilingual) Ser.). (ENG.). 12p. (J). bds. 8.95 *(978-0-531-23071-8(6),* Children's Pr.) Scholastic Library Publishing.
—Amazing Animals/ Animales Increíbles. 2017. (Words Are Fun/ Diverpalabras (Bilingual) Ser.). (ENG.). 12p. (J). bds. 8.95 *(978-0-531-23072-5(4),* Children's Pr.) Scholastic Library Publishing.
—My Favorite Food/ Mi Comida Favorita. 2017. (Words Are Fun/ Diverpalabras (Bilingual) Ser.). (ENG.). 12p. (J). bds. 8.95 *(978-0-531-23073-2(2),* Children's Pr.) Scholastic Library Publishing.
Scholastic, Inc. Staff. First 100 Words. 2015. (Scholastic Early Learners Ser.). (ENG.). 14p. (J). (— 1). bds. 9.99 *(978-0-545-90315-8(7),* Cartwheel Bks.) Scholastic, Inc.
Scholastic, Inc. Staff, contrib. by. Look Inside. 2016. (Rookie Toddlers Ser.). (ENG.). 12p. (J). bds. 6.95 *(978-0-531-22455-7(4),* Children's Pr.) Scholastic Library Publishing.
Scholastic, Inc. Staff & Beech, Linda Ward. 180 Essential Vocabulary Words: Independent Learning Packets That Help Students Learn the Most Important Words They Need

to Succeed in School. 2009. (ENG.). 80p. pap. 12.99 (978-0-439-89736-5(X), Teaching Resources) Scholastic, Inc.

—180 Essential Vocabulary Words for 6th Grade: Independent Learning Packets That Help Students Learn the Most Important Words They Need to Succeed in School. 2009. (ENG.). 80p. pap. 12.99 (978-0-439-89737-2(8), Teaching Resources) Scholastic, Inc.

Scholastic Library Publishing. Rookie Ready to Learn Español. 2011. (Rookie Ready to Learn Español Ser.). (J). 276.00 (978-0-531-28509-1(X), Children's Pr.) Scholastic Library Publishing.

School Specialty Publishing Staff & Carson-Dellosa Publishing Staff. Sight Words. 2006. (ENG., Illus.). 54p. (gr. -1-2). 2.99 (978-0-7696-6470-5(9), Brighter Child) Carson-Dellosa Publishing, LLC.

School Zone. Wonder Words Flash Action Software. 2007. 128p. pap. 15.99 (978-1-58947-112-2(1)) School Zone Publishing Co.

School Zone Publishing. Vocabulary Puzzles. 2003. (ENG.). cd-rom 19.99 (978-1-58947-931-9(9)) School Zone Publishing Co.

School Zone Publishing Co. Make-A-Word Bingo Game. 2006. (ENG.). (J). 5.99 (978-1-58947-496-3(1)) School Zone Publishing Co.

School Zone Publishing Company Staff. Big Activity Ages 8-Up: Word Searches, Crosswords, Puzzles, & Codes. 2004. (ENG.). 320p. (J). pap. 9.99 (978-1-58947-422-2(8)) School Zone Publishing Co.

—Sight Word Fun! 1. deluxe ed. 2005. (ENG.). 64p. (J). pap., wbk. ed. 3.99 (978-1-58947-338-6(8)) School Zone Publishing Co.

—Vocabulary Puzzles 2. (Illus.). (J). 19.99 incl. audio compact disk (978-0-88743-968-1(3)) School Zone Publishing Co.

School Zone Staff. Bilingual Basic Sight Words. 2004. (ENG.). 54p. (J). 2.99 (978-1-58947-982-1(3)) School Zone Publishing Co.

—Picture Words. 2005. (ENG.). 56p. (J). 2.99 (978-1-58947-480-2(5)) School Zone Publishing Co.

School Zone Staff, ed. My First 100 Magnetic Words. 2006. (ENG.). 14p. (J). (gr. k-2). bds. 15.99 (978-1-58947-318-8(3)) School Zone Publishing Co.

Schumacher, Bev. Critters. 2007. 20p. (J). lib. bdg. 9.95 (978-0-9768706-6-1(5)) Learning Props.

—Critters (Chinese/English) 2012. 20p. (J). pap. 8.95 (978-1-935292-46-3(3)) Learning Props.

—Dress Up. 2007. 20p. (J). lib. bdg. 9.95 (978-0-9768706-4-7(9)) Learning Props.

—Dress Up (Chinese/English) 2012. 20p. (J). pap. 8.95 (978-1-935292-47-0(1)) Learning Props.

—Patterns. 2007. 20p. (J). lib. bdg. 9.95 (978-0-9768706-3-0(0)) Learning Props.

—Where Will You Find Me? 2007. 20p. (J). lib. bdg. 9.95 (978-0-9768706-5-4(7)) Learning Props.

—Where Will You Find Me? / Donde Me Encontraras. 2008. (SPA.). 20p. (J). lib. bdg. 9.95 (978-1-935292-07-4(2)) Learning Props.

—Where Will You Find Me? (Chinese/English) 2012. 20p. (J). pap. 8.95 (978-1-935292-51-7(X)) Learning Props.

Scott, Kimberley, illus. Wipe-Clean First Words. 2014. (ENG.). (J). (gr. k-2). pap. 7.99 (978-0-7945-3331-1(0), Usborne) EDC Publishing.

Scrambled Word Building. 2003. (J). (gr. 1). pap., act. bk. ed. 12.95 (978-1-56911-128-4(6)); (gr. 2). pap., act. bk. ed. 12.95 (978-1-56911-129-1(4)); (gr. 3). pap., act. bk. ed. 12.95 (978-1-56911-130-7(8)) Learning Resources, Inc.

Seeger, Laura Vaccaro. Black? White! Day? Night! A Book of Opposites. 2016. (ENG., Illus.). 20p. (J). 14.99 (978-1-62672-254-5(4), 9781626722545) Roaring Brook Pr.

Seelig, Renate, illus. Mein Kleiner Brockhaus: Erste Woerter. 28p. (J). (gr. -1-18). (978-3-7653-2561-8(9)) Brockhaus, F. A., GmbH DEU. Dist: International Bk. Import Service, Inc.

Sentence Building Activity Cards (OCR) 2004. (J). 14.95 (978-1-56911-195-6(2)) Learning Resources, Inc.

Sevaly, Karen, ed. Beginning Sound Puzzles. 2006. (Scholastic Hands-on Learning Ser.). (ENG.). 12.99 (978-0-439-82387-6(0), Teaching Resources) Scholastic, Inc.

—Sight Word Mats. 2006. (Scholastic Hands-on Learning Ser.). (ENG., Illus.). (gr. k-2). 14.99 (978-0-439-82382-1(X), Teaching Resources) Scholastic, Inc.

Shabanu. (J). pap., stu. ed. (978-0-13-620295-0(0)) Prentice Hall (Schl. Div.).

Shaskan, Trisha Speed. If You Were a Compound Word, 1 vol. Gray, Sara, illus. 2008. (Word Fun Ser.). (ENG.). 24p. (gr. 2-4). pap. 7.95 (978-1-4048-4776-7(6)) Picture Window Bks.

Shaw, Marie-Jose. Jumbo Vocabulary Development Yearbook: Grade 3. (Jumbo Vocabulary Ser.). 96p. (J). (gr. 3). 15.95 (978-0-8209-0052-0(4), B JVDY 3) ESP, Inc.

Sheikh-Miller, Jonathan. Latin Words Sticker Book. Cartwright, Stephen, illus. 2006. (Latin Words Sticker Book Ser.). 16p. (J). (gr. 1). pap. 8.99 (978-0-7945-1145-6(7), Usborne) EDC Publishing.

Shiotsu, Vicky. Build-a-Skill Instant Books Beginning & Ending Consonant Sounds. Faulkner, Stacey, ed. Campbell, Jenny & Tom, Darcy, illus. 2007. (J). 4.99 (978-1-59198-416-0(5)) Creative Teaching Pr., Inc.

Short, Deborah J., et al. PhotoFile Picture Cards. 2003. (Avenues Ser.). (ENG.). (gr. 1-18). pap. 103.95 (978-0-7362-1841-2(6)); (gr. 2-18). pap. 98.95 (978-0-7362-1890-0(4)); (gr. 3-18). pap. 131.95 (978-0-7362-1683-8(9)); (gr. 4-18). pap. 131.95 (978-0-7362-1719-4(3)); (gr. 5-18). pap. 131.95 (978-0-7362-1755-2(X)) CENGAGE Learning.

Shostak, Jerome. Vocabulary Workshop, Student Text, Level A. 2002nd ed. 2005. (Vocabulary Workshop Ser.). 192p. (YA). (gr. 6-18). stu. ed. 6.90 (978-0-8215-7606-9(2)) Sadlier, William H. Inc.

—Vocabulary Workshop, Student Text, Level B. 2002nd ed. 2005. (Vocabulary Workshop Ser.). 192p. (YA). (gr. 7-18). stu. ed. 6.90 (978-0-8215-7607-6(0)) Sadlier, William H. Inc.

—Vocabulary Workshop, Student Text, Level C. 2002nd ed. 2005. (Vocabulary Workshop Ser.). 182p. (YA). (gr. 8-18). stu. ed. 6.90 (978-0-8215-7608-3(9)) Sadlier, William H. Inc.

Shusterman, Danielle. V. 2016. (ICP Beginning Letter Ser.). (ENG., Illus.). 16p. (J). pap. 5.99 (978-1-63437-483-5(5)) American Reading Co.

Sickman, Kari. Rhyming & Sight Words. 2003. (Full-Color Literacy Activities Ser.). (ENG., Illus.). 176p. (gr. -1-1). pap. 24.99 (978-0-7439-3236-3(6)) Teacher Created Resources, Inc.

Siede Preis Photography (Firm) Staff & Brian Warling Photography (Firm) Staff, contrib. by. First Words. 2003. (Lift-A-Flap Ser.). (Illus.). 12p. (J). bds. 12.98 (978-0-7853-8624-7(6), 7188400) Publications International, Ltd.

Sight Word Fun. (Basic Skills Ser.). 48p. (gr. -1-2). 5.99 (978-0-513-02335-2(6), TSD23356) Denison, T. S. & Co., Inc.

Sight Word Rhymes (Gr. K-2) 2003. (J). (978-1-58232-093-9(4)) ECS Learning Systems, Inc.

Sight Word Stories (Gr. K-2) 2003. (J). (978-1-58232-092-2(6)) ECS Learning Systems, Inc.

Sight Words (Gr. 1-2) 2003. (J). (978-1-58232-039-7(X)) ECS Learning Systems, Inc.

Sight Words (Gr. K-1) 2003. (J). (978-1-58232-031-1(4)) ECS Learning Systems, Inc.

Sight Words in Context (Gr. K-2) 2003. (J). (978-1-58232-097-7(7)) ECS Learning Systems, Inc.

Sight Words Word Search (Gr. K-2) 2003. (J). (978-1-58232-094-6(2)) ECS Learning Systems, Inc.

Sight Words/ESL Intro Kit. 2004. (ENG.). (J). 44.99 (978-0-943343-75-4(5)) Learning Wrap-Ups, Inc.

Singhal, Sheetal. Opposites. Sona & Jacob, illus. 2007.Tr. of Vipareet Shabdh. (ENG, HIN, GUJ & PAN.). 32p. (J). pap. 8.00 (978-0-9773645-9-6(3)) MeeraMasi, Inc.

SIPPS Beginning Hand-held Sight Word Cards. 2004. (978-1-57621-457-2(5)) Center for the Collaborative Classroom.

SIPPS Beginning Sight Word Wall Cards. 2004. (978-1-57621-456-5(7)) Center for the Collaborative Classroom.

SIPPS Beginning Sound Wall Cards. 2004. (978-1-57621-454-1(0)) Center for the Collaborative Classroom.

Sirett, Dawn & Dorling Kindersley Publishing Staff. My First Words: Let's Get Talking! Quasha, Jennifer, ed. 2008. (Tab Board Bks.). (ENG., Illus.). 28p. (J). (gr. -1-k). bds. 9.99 (978-0-7566-3431-5(8), DK Children) Dorling Kindersley Publishing, Inc.

Skidmore, Sharon, et al. Balanced Literacy Grade 5. 2008. per. 34.00 (978-1-879097-34-6(6)) Kagan Publishing.

Skultety, Nancy Laney. 101 Words Your Child Will Read by the End of Grade 1. 2006. (Illus.). viii, 151p. (J). (978-0-7641-3305-3(5)) Barron's Educational Series, Inc.

Snyders, Natalie, et al. Vocabulary Quick Take along Mini-Book: Ta230. 2011. (Illus.). 66p. (J). spiral bd. 12.95 net. (978-1-58650-996-5(9)) Super Duper Pubns.

Solotareff, Gregoire. Nieve. 2003. (SPA.). 86p. 21.99 (978-84-8470-039-5(9)) Corimbo, Editorial S.L. ESP. Dist: Lectorum Pubns., Inc.

Spelling & Vocabulary, Set. 2004. (gr. 2). 38.95 (978-0-7403-0219-0(1), Horizons) Alpha Omega Pubns., Inc.

Spigarelli, Jane, et al. Oxford Picture Dictionary: Low Beginning. 3rd ed. 2017. (ENG.). 272p. pap., wbk. ed. 22.00 (978-0-19-451124-7(3)) Oxford Univ. Pr., Inc.

Stamper, Judith Bauer & Keyes, Joan Ross. Monster Parade. 2004. (Oxford Picture Dictionary for Kids Ser.). (ENG., Illus.). 16p. 6.94 (978-0-19-430929-5(0)) Oxford Univ. Pr., Inc.

Stamper, Judith Bauer, et al. Trip to Toy Town. 2004. (Oxford Picture Dictionary for Kids Ser.). (ENG., Illus.). 16p. 6.94 (978-0-19-430930-1(4)) Oxford Univ. Pr., Inc.

Stanek, Robert, pseud. Student's Classroom Handbook for the Kingdoms & the Elves of the Reaches. 2003. (ENG.). 128p. pap. 15.00 (978-1-57545-033-9(X), Ruin Mist Pubns.) RP Media.

Star Bright Books. My First Words at Home, 1 vol. 2011. (ENG.). 20p. (J). (gr. -1). bds. 6.95 (978-1-59572-281-2(5)) Star Bright Bks., Inc.

—My First Words at Home (Burmese Karen/English), 1 vol. 2012. (KAR & ENG., Illus.). 20p. (J). 6.95 (978-1-59572-373-4(0)) Star Bright Bks., Inc.

—My First Words at Home (Burmese/English), 1 vol. 2012. (BUR & ENG., Illus.). 20p. (J). 6.95 (978-1-59572-372-7(2)) Star Bright Bks., Inc.

—My First Words at HOME (Spanish/English), 1 vol. 2011. (ENG.). 32p. (J). bds. 6.95 (978-1-59572-282-9(3)) Star Bright Bks., Inc.

Steck-Vaughn Staff. Vocabulary Connections, Level D. 2004. (Steck-Vaughn Vocabulary Connections Ser.). (ENG., Illus.). 144p. (gr. 4-4). pap., stu. ed. 21.90 (978-0-7398-9171-1(5)) Houghton Mifflin Harcourt Publishing Co.

—Vocabulary Skills. 2003. (Vocabulary Skills Ser.). (ENG.). 96p. (gr. 2-2). pap., wbk. ed. 11.99 (978-0-7398-6901-7(9)) Houghton Mifflin Harcourt Publishing Co.

—Vocabulary Skills, Grade 3. 2003. (Vocabulary Skills Ser.). (ENG.). 96p. (gr. 3-3). pap., wbk. ed. 11.99 (978-0-7398-6902-4(7)) Houghton Mifflin Harcourt Publishing Co.

—Vocabulary Skills, Grade 4. 2003. (Vocabulary Skills Ser.). (ENG.). 96p. (gr. 4-4). pap. 11.99 (978-0-7398-6903-1(5)) Houghton Mifflin Harcourt Publishing Co.

—Vocabulary Skills, Grade 5. 2003. (Vocabulary Skills Ser.). (ENG.). 96p. (gr. 5-5). pap. 11.99 (978-0-7398-6904-8(3)) Houghton Mifflin Harcourt Publishing Co.

—Vocabulary Skills, Grade 6. 2003. (Vocabulary Skills Ser.). (ENG.). 96p. (gr. 6-6). pap. 11.99 (978-0-7398-6905-5(1)) Houghton Mifflin Harcourt Publishing Co.

—Vocabulary Ventures. 2004. (gr. 1-2). pap. 14.99 (978-0-7398-8561-1(8)); (gr. 3-4). pap. 14.99 (978-0-7398-8562-8(6)) Steck-Vaughn.

Steck-Vaughn Staff & Coulter, Barbara. Vocabulary Connections, Level C. 2004. (Steck-Vaughn Vocabulary Connections Ser.). (ENG., Illus.). 144p. (gr. 3-3). pap. 21.90 (978-0-7398-9170-4(7)) Houghton Mifflin Harcourt Publishing Co.

Stella, Gaia. Welcome to My House: A Collection of First Words. 2017. (ENG., Illus.). 48p. (J). (gr. -1-k). 17.99 (978-1-4521-5792-4(8)) Chronicle Bks. LLC.

Sterling Children's, Sterling. My First Basketball Book. 2015. (First Sports Ser.). (ENG., Illus.). 22p. (J). (— 1). bds. 6.95 (978-1-4549-1487-7(4)) Sterling Publishing Co., Inc.

—My First Football Book. 2015. (First Sports Ser.). (ENG., Illus.). 22p. (J). (— 1). bds. 6.95 (978-1-4549-1488-4(2)) Sterling Publishing Co., Inc.

—My First Soccer Book. 2015. (First Sports Ser.). (ENG., Illus.). 22p. (J). (— 1). bds. 6.95 (978-1-4549-1489-1(0)) Sterling Publishing Co., Inc.

Sterling Publishing Co., Inc. Begin Smart(tm) What Does Baby Do? A First Lift-The-Flap Book. 2016. (Begin Smart(tm) Ser.). (ENG., Illus.). 16p. (J). (— 1). bds. 8.95 (978-1-4549-1879-0(9)) Sterling Publishing Co., Inc.

—Begin Smart(tm) What Does Baby Say? A First Lift-The-Flap Book. 2016. (Begin Smart(tm) Ser.). (ENG., Illus.). 16p. (J). (— 1). bds. 8.95 (978-1-4549-1880-6(2)) Sterling Publishing Co., Inc.

—Begin Smart(tm) Woof. 2016. (Begin Smart(tm) Ser.). (ENG., Illus.). 14p. (J). (— 1). bds. 8.95 (978-1-4549-1878-3(0)) Sterling Publishing Co., Inc.

Stones, Brenda & Feldman, Thea. Kingfisher Readers L2 What We Eat. 2014. (Kingfisher Readers Ser.). (ENG., Illus.). 32p. (J). (gr. k-3). 12.99 (978-0-7534-7120-3(5), 9780753471203, Kingfisher) Roaring Brook Pr.

Studio Mouse Staff. First Concepts, Pack. rev. ed. 2003. (ENG., Illus.). 60p. (J). (gr. -1-k). 12.99 (978-1-59069-363-6(9), 1A502) Studio Mouse LLC.

Sunshine TM Word Books Set: 1 Each of 4 Big Books. (gr. k-1). 125.50 (978-0-7802-6930-9(6)); Vol. 2. 125.50 (978-0-7802-6984-2(5)) Wright Group/McGraw-Hill.

Sunshine TM Word Books Set: 1 Each of 4 Student Books. (Sunshine Ser.). (gr. k-1). 19.50 (978-0-7802-3848-0(6)); Vol. 2. 22.95 (978-0-7802-6821-0(0)) Wright Group/McGraw-Hill.

Sunshine TM Word Books Set: 6 Each of 4 Student Books. (Sunshinetm Word Ser.). (gr. k-1). 116.95 (978-0-7802-6820-3(2)); Vol. 2. 150.95 (978-0-7802-6822-7(9)) Wright Group/McGraw-Hill.

Swimow, Linda. What's New at the Zoo? A PhotoPhOnics (c)Reader. 2009. 32p. pap. 12.99 (978-1-4490-2218-1(9)) AuthorHouse.

Tam on Sam: Consonants m, s, t; Short Vowel a; -am, -at word families: Level A, 6 vols. (Wright Skills Ser.). 12p. (gr. k-3). 17.95 (978-0-322-01445-9(X)) Wright Group/McGraw-Hill.

Tat Is Sad: Consonant d: Level A, 6 vols. (Wright Skills Ser.). 12p. (gr. k-3). 17.95 (978-0-322-03105-0(2)) Wright Group/McGraw-Hill.

Teckentrup, Britta, illus. Big & Small. 2013. (ENG.). 14p. (J). (gr. -1-k). bds. 6.99 (978-1-84686-951-8(X)) Barefoot Bks., Inc.

—Fast & Slow. 2013. (ENG.). 14p. (J). (gr. -1-k). bds. 6.99 (978-1-84686-952-5(8)) Barefoot Bks., Inc.

—Grande y Pequeno. 2013. (ENG & SPA.). 14p. (J). (gr. -1-k). bds. 6.99 (978-1-78285-034-2(1)) Barefoot Bks., Inc.

The Learning Company, The Learning. Curious George Adventures in Learning, Grade 1: Story-Based Learning. 2015. (Learning with Curious George Ser.). (ENG., Illus.). 320p. (J). (gr. -1-3). pap. 12.99 (978-0-544-37323-5(5), HMH Books For Young Readers) Houghton Mifflin Harcourt Publishing Co.

—Curious George Adventures in Learning, Kindergarten: Story-Based Learning. 2015. (Learning with Curious George Ser.). (ENG., Illus.). 320p. (J). (gr. k — 1). pap. 12.99 (978-0-544-37263-4(8), HMH Books For Young Readers) Houghton Mifflin Harcourt Publishing Co.

—Curious George Adventures in Learning, Pre-K: Story-Based Learning. 2015. (Learning with Curious George Ser.). (ENG., Illus.). 320p. (J). (gr. -1 — 1). pap. 12.99 (978-0-544-37273-3(5), HMH Books For Young Readers) Houghton Mifflin Harcourt Publishing Co.

Thomas Nelson. First Words. 2015. (ENG., Illus.). 26p. (gr. -1). bds. (978-1-78393-439-3(5)) Make Believe Ideas.

—My First Words Bible, 1 vol. 2016. (God's Little Ones Ser.). (ENG.). 32p. (J). (gr. -1). bds. 8.99 (978-0-7180-8526-1(4)) Nelson, Thomas Inc.

Thome, Pat. My First Word Book. (Illus.). (J). (gr. -1-18). pap. 16.95 (978-0-590-74011-1(3)) Scholastic, Inc.

El Tiempo. (Coleccion Planeta Vivo).Tr. of Weather. (SPA.). (J). (gr. 5-8). 12.00 (978-84-342-1945-8(X)) Parramon Ediciones S.A. ESP. Dist: Distribuidora Norma, Inc.

Tiger Tales, ed. & compiled by. First Words. Tiger Tales, compiled by. 2014. (My First Lift & Learn Ser.). (ENG.). 10p. (J). (gr. -1 — 1). bds. 7.99 (978-1-58925-623-1(9)) Tiger Tales.

Tiger Tales Staff. My First Book of Things to See. 2013. (ENG.). 12p. bds. (978-1-58925-629-3(8)) Tiger Tales.

Tiger Tales Staff, creator. First Colors. 2013. (My First Lift & Learn Ser.). (ENG., Illus.). 10p. (gr. -1). bds. 7.99 (978-1-58925-633-0(6)) Tiger Tales.

—Pets. 2013. (My First Touch & Feel Ser.). (ENG., Illus.). 10p. (gr. -1). bds. 7.99 (978-1-58925-631-6(X)) Tiger Tales.

—100 First Animals. 2013. (My Big Book of Lift & Learn Ser.). (ENG., Illus.). 12p. (gr. -1). bds. 9.99 (978-1-58925-608-8(5)) Tiger Tales.

—100 First Words. 2013. (My Big Book of Lift & Learn Ser.). (ENG., Illus.). 12p. (gr. -1). bds. 9.99 (978-1-58925-607-1(7)) Tiger Tales.

Tilton, Patricia. Reproducible Little Books for Sight Words. 2004. (ENG.). 176p. (gr. k-2). pap. 18.99 (978-0-7439-3225-7(0)) Teacher Created Resources, Inc.

Top That Publishing Staff, ed. Bobby Badgers Box of Books. 2005. (Illus.). 16p. bds. (978-1-84510-542-6(7)) Top That! Publishing PLC.

—First Words. 2004. (Magnetic Play & Learn Ser.). (ENG., Illus.). 8p. (J). (978-1-84510-049-0(2)) Top That! Publishing PLC.

Tucker, Sian. My Book of First Words. Tucker, Sian, illus. 2003. (My Book of. . . Ser.). (Illus.). 48p. (YA). (978-1-85602-439-6(3), Pavilion Children's Books) Pavilion Bks.

Tullet, Hervé. I Am Blop! Stetter, Alexandra, tr. 2013. (ENG., Illus.). 110p. 19.95 (978-0-7148-6533-1(8)) Phaidon Pr., Inc.

Tuminelly, Nancy. -Est As in Nest, 1 vol. 2003. (Word Families Set 2 Ser.). (ENG., Illus.). 24p. (J). (gr. k-3). lib. bdg. 24.21 (978-1-59197-232-7(9), SandCastle) ABDO Publishing Co.

—Ook As in Hook, 1 vol. 2003. (Word Families Set 7 Ser.). (ENG., Illus.). 24p. (J). (gr. k-3). lib. bdg. 24.21 (978-1-59197-268-6(X), SandCastle) ABDO Publishing Co.

—Ub As in Tub, 1 vol. 2003. (Word Families Set 4 Ser.). (ENG., Illus.). 24p. (J). (gr. k-3). lib. bdg. 24.21 (978-1-59197-242-6(6), SandCastle) ABDO Publishing Co.

—Uck As in Duck, 1 vol. 2003. (Word Families Set 4 Ser.). (ENG., Illus.). 24p. (J). (gr. k-3). lib. bdg. 24.21 (978-1-59197-247-1(7), SandCastle) ABDO Publishing Co.

—Uff As in Cuff, 1 vol. 2003. (Word Families Set 4 Ser.). (ENG., Illus.). 24p. (J). (gr. k-3). lib. bdg. 24.21 (978-1-59197-246-4(9), SandCastle) ABDO Publishing Co.

—Ug As in Bug, 1 vol. 2003. (Word Families Set 4 Ser.). (ENG., Illus.). 24p. (J). (gr. k-3). lib. bdg. 24.21 (978-1-59197-243-3(4), SandCastle) ABDO Publishing Co.

—Um As in Drum, 1 vol. Marx, Monica, ed. 2003. (Word Families Set 4 Ser.). (ENG., Illus.). 24p. (J). (gr. k-3). lib. bdg. 24.21 (978-1-59197-244-0(2), SandCastle) ABDO Publishing Co.

—Ump As in Jump, 1 vol. 2003. (Word Families Set 4 Ser.). (ENG., Illus.). 24p. (J). (gr. k-3). lib. bdg. 24.21 (978-1-59197-245-7(0), SandCastle) ABDO Publishing Co.

Turhan, Sedat. Milet Flashwords English. Hagin, Sally, illus. 2005. (Milet Flashwords Ser.). (ENG.). 60p. (J). (gr. 4-7). 8.95 (978-1-84059-455-3(1)) Milet Publishing.

Tuxworth, Nicola. Farm Animals. 2013. (ENG., Illus.). 12p. (J). (gr. -1-12). bds. 6.99 (978-0-7548-2202-8(8)) Anness Publishing GBR. Dist: National Bk. Network.

—Messy. (ENG., (J). (gr. -1-k). 2016. Illus.). 20p. bds. 6.99 (978-1-86147-690-6(6), Armadillo) 2013. 12p. bds. 6.99 (978-0-7548-2209-7(5)) Anness Publishing GBR. Dist: National Bk. Network.

—Mix & Match. 2016. (Learn-a-Word Book Ser.). (ENG., Illus.). 20p. (J). (gr. -1-2). bds. 6.99 (978-1-84322-862-2(9), Armadillo) Anness Publishing GBR. Dist: National Bk. Network.

—Nature. 2015. (ENG., Illus.). 20p. bds. 6.99 (978-1-86147-411-7(3), Armadillo) Anness Publishing GBR. Dist: National Bk. Network.

—Things That Go. 2016. (ENG., Illus.). 20p. bds. 6.99 (978-1-84322-752-6(5), Armadillo) Anness Publishing GBR. Dist: National Bk. Network.

Tyler, Jenny. Baby's Very First Getting Dressed. 2009. (Baby's Very First Board Bks). 10p. (J). (gr. -1). bds. 6.99 (978-0-7945-2609-2(8), Usborne) EDC Publishing.

—Baby's Very First Mealtime Book. 2009. (Baby's Very First Board Bks). 10p. (J). (gr. -1). bds. 6.99 (978-0-7945-2607-8(1), Usborne) EDC Publishing.

Uncle Bill Is Feeling Iii, 6 vols. 8p. (gr. k-1). 21.50 (978-0-322-02078-8(6)) Wright Group/McGraw-Hill.

Under the Clock, 6 vols. 8p. (gr. k-1). 21.50 (978-0-322-02064-1(6)) Wright Group/McGraw-Hill.

University Games Staff. I Have. 2007. 32p. (J). (978-1-57528-888-8(5)) Univ. Games.

Using the Right Words (Gr. 3+) 2003. (J). (978-1-58232-053-3(5)) ECS Learning Systems, Inc.

Valentino, Catherine. Blue Ribbon Spelling & Vocabulary, Level 1. (J). pap. 7.95 (978-0-86651-196-4(2)) Seymour, Dale Pubns.

Vargus, Nanci R. Flying. 2006. (On the Move Ser.). (Illus.). 24p. (gr. k-1). lib. bdg. 15.95 (978-0-7614-2319-5(2), Benchmark Bks.) Marshall Cavendish Corp.

—A Volar! 2006. (En Movimiento Ser.). (SPA & ENG., Illus.). 24p. (gr. k-1). lib. bdg. 15.95 (978-0-7614-2425-3(3), Benchmark Bks.) Marshall Cavendish Corp.

Vaughn, Jim. Jumbo Vocabulary Development Yearbook: Grade 7. (Jumbo Vocabulary Ser.). 96p. (J). (gr. 7-9). 15.95 (978-0-8209-0056-8(7), B JVDY 7) ESP, Inc.

Vickers, Rebecca & Miles, Liz. Find Your Way with Words. 2013. (Find Your Way with Words Ser.). (ENG.). 56p. (gr. 6-7). lib. bdg. 138.60 (978-1-4329-7658-3(3)) Heinemann-Raintree.

Vinopol, Corinne. Spell Well: CD-ROM American Sign Language Spelling Game. 2003. (YA). cd-rom 19.95 (978-0-9752933-0-0(3)) Institute for Disabilities Research & Training, Inc.

VIP Tours. 2014. (VIP Tours Ser.). 48p. (J). (gr. 4-6). 156.80 (978-1-62713-144-5(2)) Cavendish Square Publishing.

VocabuLáminas: VocabuLáminas Kit. (J). (gr. -1-2). 407.79 (978-0-7362-2605-9(2)) CENGAGE Learning.

Vocabulary Centers. 2006. (J). 24.99 (978-1-59673-150-9(8), EMC 3350); 24.99 (978-1-59673-152-3(4), EMC 3352) Evan-Moor Educational Pubs.

Vocabulary Flip Chart. 2004. (Scott Foresman Reading Ser.). (gr. 1-18). suppl. ed. 109.15 (978-0-673-62166-5(9)); (gr. 2-18). suppl. ed. 109.15 (978-0-673-62167-2(7)) Addison-Wesley Educational Pubs., Inc.

Vocabulary from Classical Roots. 2004. (Vocabulary from Classical Roots Ser.). (gr. 10-18). pap. 9.95 (978-0-8388-2258-6(4)); (gr. 11-18). pap. 9.95 (978-0-8388-2260-9(6)); (gr. 7-18). pap. 9.35 (978-0-8388-2252-4(5)); (gr. 8-18). pap. 9.35 (978-0-8388-2254-8(1)); (gr. 9-18). pap. 9.35 (978-0-8388-2256-2(8)) Educators Publishing Service, Inc.

Vocabulary in Action: Level A; Testing Program (BLMs) 2004. (gr. 4-18). (978-0-8294-1333-5(2)) Loyola Pr.

Vocabulary Vocabulary, Level A, Grades 10-11. 2005. (Vocabulary Workshop Ser.). 182p. (YA). (gr. 6-18). tchr. ed. 13.80 (978-0-8215-7616-8(X)) Sadlier, William H. Inc.

Vocabulary Workshop: Test Generator CD-ROM, Level A, (Mac) 2005. (YA). (gr. 6-18). cd-rom 114.00 (978-0-8215-0196-2(8)) Sadlier, William H. Inc.

Vocabulary Workshop: Test Generator CD-ROM, Level B, (Mac) 2005. (YA). (gr. 7-18). cd-rom 114.00 (978-0-8215-0197-9(6)) Sadlier, William H. Inc.

Vocabulary Workshop: Test Generator CD-ROM, Level C, (Mac) 2005. (YA). (gr. 8-18). cd-rom 114.00 (978-0-8215-0198-6(4)) Sadlier, William H. Inc.

Vocabulary Workshop, Level B. annot. ed. 2005. (Vocabulary Workshop Ser.). 182p. (YA). (gr. 7-18). tchr. ed. 13.80 (978-0-8215-7617-5(8)) Sadlier, William H. Inc.

Vocabulary Workshop, Level C. annot. ed. 2005. (Vocabulary Workshop Ser.). 182p. (YA). (gr. 8-18). tchr. ed. 13.80 (978-0-8215-7618-2(6)) Sadlier, William H. Inc.

Vocabulary Workshop Test Generator, Level A, PC Version: 2002. 2005. (Vocabulary Workshop Ser.). (YA). (gr. 6-18). cd-rom 114.00 (978-0-8215-0186-3(0)) Sadlier, William H. Inc.

Vocabulary Workshop Test Generator, Level B, PC Version: 2002. 2005. (Vocabulary Workshop Ser.). (YA). (gr. 7-18). cd-rom 114.00 (978-0-8215-0187-0(9)) Sadlier, William H. Inc.

Vocabulary Workshop Test Generator, Level C, PC Version: 2002. 2005. (Vocabulary Workshop Ser.). (YA). (gr. 8-18). cd-rom 114.00 *(978-0-8215-0188-7(7))* Sadlier, William H. Inc.

Los Volcanes. (Coleccion Planeta Vivo).Tr. of Volcanos. (SPA.). (YA). (gr. 5-8). 10.36 *(978-84-342-1943-4(3))* Parramon Ediciones S.A. ESP. Dist: Lectorum Pubns., Inc.

Wade, Angela. New York City. 2006. (Illus.). 8p. (J). pap. *(978-0-439-74035-7(5))* Scholastic, Inc.

Walden, Libby. Finding First Words & More! Galloway, Fhiona, illus. 2016. (My Little World Ser.). (ENG.). 12p. (J). (gr. -1-k). bds. 12.99 *(978-1-58925-218-9(7))* Tiger Tales.

Wall Words Word Search (Gr. 1-2) 2003. (J). *(978-1-58232-095-3(0))* ECS Learning Systems, Inc.

Watson, Richar, illus. My Book of Letters: For Ages 3+ 2016. (ENG.). (J). pap. ***(978-1-78209-799-0(6))*** Miles Kelly Publishing, Ltd.

Watt, Fiona. Baby's Very First Word Book. 2012. (Baby's Very First Word Book Ser.). 10p. (J). ring bd. 7.99 *(978-0-7945-2979-6(8)*, Usborne) EDC Publishing.

Wernham, Sara & Lloyd, Sue. Dictionary. Stephen, Lib, illus. 2003. (Jolly Grammar Ser.: DICTIONARY). (ENG.). 300p. (J). pap. 13.50 *(978-1-84414-001-5(6)*, JL016, Jolly Learning) Jolly Learning, Ltd. GBR. Dist: American International Distribution Corp.

What a Spelling Test!, 6 Packs. (gr. -1-2). 27.00 *(978-0-7635-9483-1(0))* Rigby Education.

Wheaton, Sheila. Fab Vocab: Greek & Latin Roots: Reproducible Games & Activities That Teach 25 Key Roots. 2017. (Fab Vocab Ser.). (ENG.). 112p. (gr. 3-5). pap. 15.99 ***(978-1-338-15364-4(1))*** Scholastic, Inc.

—Fab Vocab: Prefixes & Suffixes: Reproducible Games & Activities That Teach 50 Key Prefixes & Suffixes. 2017. (Fab Vocab Ser.). (ENG.). 112p. (gr. 3-5). pap. 15.99 ***(978-1-338-15365-1(X))*** Scholastic, Inc.

Wheeler, Kimberly. Emma's Extravagant Expedition. 2012. (ENG.). pap. *(978-1-4675-4236-4(9))* Independent Pub.

Where Do I Live? (Peek A Boo Pockets Ser.). 12p. (J). bds. *(978-2-7643-0108-1(1))* Phidal Publishing, Inc./Editions Phidal, Inc.

Wilbur, Richard. The Pig in the Spigot. Siebold, J. Otto, illus. 2004. (J). reprint ed. pap. 7.00 *(978-0-15-525066-6(3)*, Voyager Books/Libros Viajeros) Harcourt Children's Bks. CAN. Dist: Allen, Thomas & Son, Ltd.

William H. Sadlier Staff. Vocabulary Vocabulary Test Booklets, Level C, Form A. 2005. (Vocabulary Workshop Ser.). 64p. (gr. 8-9). 42.00 net. *(978-0-8215-7628-1(3))* Sadlier, William H. Inc.

—Vocabulary Vocabulary Test Booklets, Level D, Form A. 2002nd ed. 2005. (Vocabulary Workshop Ser.). 64p. (gr. 9-10). 42.00 net. *(978-0-8215-7629-8(1))* Sadlier, William H. Inc.

—Vocabulary Workshop: Test Booklet Form A; Level Purple. 2005. (Vocabulary Workshop 2005 Ser.). (gr. 2-3). 36.00 net. *(978-0-8215-0382-9(0))* Sadlier, William H. Inc.

—Vocabulary Workshop: Test Booklet Form B; Level Purple. 2005. (Vocabulary Workshop 2005 Ser.). (gr. 2-3). 36.00 net. *(978-0-8215-0392-8(8))* Sadlier, William H. Inc.

—Vocabulary Workshop: (with Answer Key to Tests, Forms A & B); Level Purple. annot. ed. 2005. (Vocabulary Workshop 2005 Ser.). (gr. 2-3). 15.00 net. *(978-0-8215-0372-0(3))* Sadlier, William H. Inc.

—Vocabulary Workshop Test Booklets. 2005. (Vocabulary Workshop Ser.). 64p. (gr. 12-18). 42.00 net. *(978-0-8215-7643-4(7))*;Level B, Form B. (gr. 7-8). 42.00 net. *(978-0-8215-7637-3(2))* Sadlier, William H. Inc.

—Vocabulary Workshop, Test Booklets, Cycle 1, Level Blue. 2006. (Vocabulary Workshop Ser.). (gr. 5-6). 42.00 net. *(978-0-8215-0438-3(X))* Sadlier, William H. Inc.

—Vocabulary Workshop, Test Booklets, Cycle 2, Level Blue. 2006. (Vocabulary Workshop Ser.). (gr. 5-6). 42.00 net. *(978-0-8215-0439-0(8))* Sadlier, William H. Inc.

—Vocabulary Workshop Test Booklets, Level A, Form A: 2002. 2005. (Vocabulary Workshop Ser.). 64p. (gr. 6-7). 42.00 net. *(978-0-8215-7626-7(7))* Sadlier, William H. Inc.

—Vocabulary Workshop Test Booklets, Level A, Form B: 2002. 2005. (Vocabulary Workshop Ser.). 64p. (gr. 6-7). 42.00 net. *(978-0-8215-7636-6(4))* Sadlier, William H. Inc.

—Vocabulary Workshop Test Booklets, Level B, Form A. 2005. (Vocabulary Workshop Ser.). 64p. (gr. 7-8). 42.00 net. *(978-0-8215-7627-4(5))* Sadlier, William H. Inc.

—Vocabulary Workshop Test Booklets, Level C, Form B. 2005. (Vocabulary Workshop Ser.). 64p. (gr. 8-9). 42.00 net. *(978-0-8215-7638-0(0))* Sadlier, William H. Inc.

—Vocabulary Workshop Test Booklets, Level E, Form A: 2002. 2005. (Vocabulary Workshop Ser.). 64p. (gr. 10-11). 42.00 net. *(978-0-8215-7630-4(5))* Sadlier, William H. Inc.

—Vocabulary Workshop Test Booklets, Level E, Form B. 2005. (Vocabulary Workshop Ser.). 64p. (gr. 10-11). 42.00 net. *(978-0-8215-7640-3(2))* Sadlier, William H. Inc.

—Vocabulary Workshop Test Booklets, Level F, Form A. 2005. (Vocabulary Workshop Ser.). 64p. (gr. 11-12). 42.00 net. *(978-0-8215-7631-1(3))* Sadlier, William H. Inc.

—Vocabulary Workshop Test Booklets, Level F, Form B. 2005. (Vocabulary Workshop Ser.). 64p. (gr. 11-12). 42.00 net. *(978-0-8215-7641-0(0))* Sadlier, William H. Inc.

—Vocabulary Workshop Test Booklets, Level G, Form A. 2005. (Vocabulary Workshop Ser.). 64p. (gr. 12-18). 42.00 net. *(978-0-8215-7632-8(1))* Sadlier, William H. Inc.

—Vocabulary Workshop Test Booklets, Level G, Form B. 2005. (Vocabulary Workshop Ser.). 64p. (gr. 11-12). 42.00 net. *(978-0-8215-7642-7(9))* Sadlier, William H. Inc.

—Vocabulary Workshop Test Booklets, Level H, Form A. 2005. (Vocabulary Workshop Ser.). 64p. (gr. 12-18). 42.00 net. *(978-0-8215-7633-5(X))* Sadlier, William H. Inc.

—Vocabulary Workshop, Test Booklets Level Orange Cycle 1. 2006. (Vocabulary Workshop Ser.). (gr. 4-18). 42.00 net. *(978-0-8215-0436-9(3))* Sadlier, William H. Inc.

—Vocabulary Workshop, Test Booklets Level Orange, Cycle 2. 2005. (Vocabulary Workshop Ser.). (gr. 4-18). 42.00 net. *(978-0-8215-0437-6(1))* Sadlier, William H. Inc.

—Vocabulary Workshop, TEST PREP Blackline Masters, Level A. 2005. (Vocabulary Workshop Ser.). (gr. 6-7). 29.00 net. *(978-0-8215-7676-2(3))* Sadlier, William H. Inc.

—Vocabulary Workshop TEST PREP Blackline Masters, Level B. 2005. (Vocabulary Workshop Ser.). 64p. (gr. 7-8). 29.00 net. *(978-0-8215-7677-9(1))* Sadlier, William H. Inc.

—Vocabulary Workshop TEST PREP Blackline Masters, Level C. 2005. (Vocabulary Workshop Ser.). 64p. (gr. 8-9). 29.00 net. *(978-0-8215-7678-6(X))* Sadlier, William H. Inc.

—Vocabulary Workshop TEST PREP Blackline Masters, Level D. 2005. (Vocabulary Workshop Ser.). 64p. (gr. 9-10). 29.00 net. *(978-0-8215-7679-3(8))* Sadlier, William H. Inc.

—Vocabulary Workshop TEST PREP Blackline Masters, Level E. 2005. (Vocabulary Workshop Ser.). 64p. (gr. 10-11). 29.00 net. *(978-0-8215-7680-9(1))* Sadlier, William H. Inc.

—Vocabulary Workshop TEST PREP Blackline Masters, Level F. 2005. (Vocabulary Workshop Ser.). 64p. (gr. 10-11). 29.00 net. *(978-0-8215-7681-6(X))* Sadlier, William H. Inc.

—Vocabulary Workshop TEST PREP Blackline Masters, Level G. 2005. (Vocabulary Workshop Ser.). 64p. (gr. 11-12). 29.00 net. *(978-0-8215-7682-3(8))* Sadlier, William H. Inc.

—Vocabulary Workshop Test Booklets, Level D, Form B. 2005. (Vocabulary Workshop Ser.). 64p. (gr. 9-10). 42.00 net. *(978-0-8215-7639-7(6))* Sadlier, William H. Inc.

Williams, Garth. Baby's First Book. Williams, Garth, illus. 2007. (Little Golden Book Ser.). (ENG., Illus.). 24p. (J). (gr. -1-2). 4.99 *(978-0-375-83916-0(X)*, Golden Bks.) Random Hse. Children's Bks.

Williams, Rozanne Lanczak. Build-a-Skill Instant Books Sight Words, Part 1. Faulkner, Stacey, ed. Campbell, Jenny & Tom, Darcy, illus. 2007. (J). 4.99 *(978-1-59198-414-6(9))* Creative Teaching Pr., Inc.

—Build-a-Skill Instant Books Sight Words, Part 2. Faulkner, Stacey, ed. Campbell, Jenny & Tom, Darcy, illus. 2007. (J). 4.99 *(978-1-59198-415-3(7))* Creative Teaching Pr., Inc.

Wilson, P. R. Readle the Reading Beetle: The Journey to Love Read Land. 2007. 26p. pap. 8.95 *(978-0-7414-4318-2(X))* Infinity Publishing.

Wise, Sue. Cómo se Dice... ? Coirault, Christine, illus. 2006. (How I Say That? Ser.). (ENG & SPA.). 32p. (gr. k-4). lib. bdg. 26.00 *(978-0-8368-6259-1(7)*, Gareth Stevens Learning Library) Stevens, Gareth Publishing LLLP.

—How Do I Say That? (¿Cómo se Dice?) Coirault, Christine, illus. 2006. (How Do I Say That?/ Como se dice? Ser.). (ENG & SPA.). 32p. (gr. k-4). pap. 10.50 *(978-0-8368-6583-7(9)*, Gareth Stevens Learning Library) Stevens, Gareth Publishing LLLP.

Wolf, Gita & Ramanathan, Rathna. In the Land of Punctuation. Rao, Sirish, tr. from GER. 2009. (ENG., Illus.). 32p. (gr. 4). 19.95 *(978-81-907546-0-6(2))* Tara Books Agency IND. Dist: Publishers Group West (PGW).

Wong, Benedict Norbert. Lo & Behold: Words That Walk & Run. 2004. (Illus.). 40p. (J). (gr. 1-12). 16.95 *(978-0-9728192-2-0(3))* Taiji Arts Publishing.

Word Building Activity Cards (OCR) 2004. (J). 14.95 *(978-1-56911-194-9(4))* Learning Resources, Inc.

Word Endings in Context (Gr. K-2) 2003. (J). *(978-1-58232-099-1(3))* ECS Learning Systems, Inc.

Word Families Ad Libs. 2004. (J). pap. 10.95 *(978-1-56911-160-4(X))* Learning Resources, Inc.

Word Wall Words. 2004. (gr. k-18). suppl. ed. 39.70 *(978-0-673-62182-5(0))*; (gr. 1-18). suppl. ed. 220.50 *(978-0-673-62183-2(9))*; (gr. 2-18). suppl. ed. 220.50 *(978-0-673-62184-9(7))*; (gr. 3-18). suppl. ed. 220.50 *(978-0-673-62185-6(5))* Addison-Wesley Educational Pubs., Inc.

Wordly Wise: Book 1. 2004. (Wordly Wise Ser.). pap., stu. ed. 8.70 *(978-0-8388-0431-5(4))* Educators Publishing Service, Inc.

Wordly Wise: Book 2. 2004. (Wordly Wise Ser.). pap., stu. ed. 8.70 *(978-0-8388-0432-2(2))* Educators Publishing Service, Inc.

Wordly Wise: Book 3. 2004. (Wordly Wise Ser.). pap., stu. ed. 8.70 *(978-0-8388-0433-9(0))* Educators Publishing Service, Inc.

Wordly Wise: Book 4. 2004. (Wordly Wise Ser.). pap., stu. ed. 8.70 *(978-0-8388-0434-6(9))* Educators Publishing Service, Inc.

Wordly Wise: Book 5. 2004. (Wordly Wise Ser.). pap., stu. ed. 8.70 *(978-0-8388-0435-3(7))* Educators Publishing Service, Inc.

Wordly Wise: Book 6. 2004. (Wordly Wise Ser.). pap., stu. ed. 9.65 *(978-0-8388-0436-0(5))* Educators Publishing Service, Inc.

Wordly Wise: Book 7. 2004. (Wordly Wise Ser.). pap., stu. ed. 9.65 *(978-0-8388-0437-7(3))* Educators Publishing Service, Inc.

Wordly Wise: Book 8. 2004. (Wordly Wise Ser.). pap., stu. ed. 9.65 *(978-0-8388-0438-4(1))* Educators Publishing Service, Inc.

Wordly Wise: Book 9. 2004. (Wordly Wise Ser.). pap., stu. ed. 9.65 *(978-0-8388-0439-1(X))* Educators Publishing Service, Inc.

Wordly Wise: Book A. 2004. (Wordly Wise Ser.). pap., stu. ed. 6.70 *(978-0-8388-0428-5(4))* Educators Publishing Service, Inc.

Wordly Wise: Book B. 2004. (Wordly Wise Ser.). pap., stu. ed. 6.70 *(978-0-8388-0429-2(2))* Educators Publishing Service, Inc.

Wordly Wise: Book C. 2004. (Wordly Wise Ser.). pap., stu. ed. 6.70 *(978-0-8388-0430-8(6))* Educators Publishing Service, Inc.

Wordly Wise 3000: Book 8. 2004. (Wordly Wise 3000 Ser.). pap., stu. ed. 10.62 net. *(978-0-8388-2438-2(2))* Educators Publishing Service, Inc.

Wordly Wise 3000: Book 9. 2004. (Wordly Wise 3000 Ser.). pap., stu. ed. 9.65 *(978-0-8388-2439-9(0))* Educators Publishing Service, Inc.

Wordly Wise 3000: Book A. 2004. (Wordly Wise 3000 Ser.). pap., stu. ed. 6.70 *(978-0-8388-2425-2(0))* Educators Publishing Service, Inc.

Wordly Wise 3000: Book B. 2004. (Wordly Wise 3000 Ser.). pap., stu. ed. 6.70 *(978-0-8388-2426-9(9))* Educators Publishing Service, Inc.

Wordly Wise 3000: Book C. 2004. (Wordly Wise 3000 Ser.). pap., stu. ed. 6.70 *(978-0-8388-2427-6(7))* Educators Publishing Service, Inc.

Words are Fun. 2004. (Play & Learn Pads Ser.). 48p. (J). 3.99 *(978-1-85997-722-4(7))* Byeway Bks.

Words for 3-5 Years. Date not set. (Play & Learn Ser.). (Illus.). 192p. (J). 3.98 *(978-0-7525-6914-7(7))* Parragon, Inc.

Words for 5-7 Years. Date not set. (Play & Learn Ser.). (Illus.). 192p. (J). 3.98 *(978-0-7525-6915-4(5))* Parragon, Inc.

Wordsearch. 2004. (Play & Learn Pads Ser.). 48p. (J). 3.99 *(978-1-85997-716-3(2))* Byeway Bks.

Wordsearch Fun. 2004. (Play & Learn Pads Ser.). 48p. (J). 3.99 *(978-1-85997-723-1(5))* Byeway Bks.

World Book, Inc Staff, contrib. by. Letters to Words: A Supplement to Childcraft — The How & Why Library. 2012. (Illus.). 208p. (J). *(978-0-7166-0627-7(5))* Univ. of Chicago Pr.

Wortgeschichte. (Duden-Schuelerduden Ser.). (GER.). 491p. (YA). 27.95 *(978-3-411-02212-0(4)*, B2212E) Bibliographisches Institut & F. A. Brockhaus AG DEU. Dist: Continental Bk. Co., Inc.

Wotton, Joy. My First Word Book: Pictures & Words to Start Toddlers Reading & to Help Pre-Schoolers Develop Vocabulary Skills. Tulip, Jenny, illus. 2012. (ENG.). 200p. 9.99 *(978-1-84322-617-8(0)*, Armadillo) Anness Publishing GBR. Dist: National Bk. Network.

Write on, Wipe off Writing. 2007. (Early Days: Copy & Learn Ser.). (Illus.). 40p. *(978-1-84666-390-1(3))* Top That! Publishing PLC.

Wyatt, Valerie. Boy Meets Dog: A Word Game Adventure. Whamond, Dave, illus. 2013. (ENG.). 32p. (J). (gr. -1-3). 16.95 *(978-1-55453-824-9(6))* Kids Can Pr., Ltd. CAN. Dist: Hachette Bk. Group.

Wyldeck, Kathi. Grammar & Vocabulary Games for Children. 2007. 83p. pap. 12.95 *(978-1-84799-930-6(1))*; 81p. pap. 12.95 *(978-1-84753-579-5(8))* Lulu Pr., Inc.

Yes I Can Staff. Words Are Everywhere. (J). 29.70 *(978-0-8136-4402-8(X))* Modern Curriculum Pr.

Yoon, Salina, creator. Bug Buddies: A Sparkling Little Colors Book. 2005. (ENG., Illus.). 10p. (J). bds. 5.95 *(978-1-58117-166-2(8)*, Intervisual/Piggy Toes) Bendon, Inc.

Yorke, Jane & Dorling Kindersley Publishing Staff. First Words. Thomson, Maria & Hester, Elizabeth, eds. 2005. (My 1st T&F Picture Cards Ser.). (ENG., Illus.). 16p. (J). (gr. -1 — 1). 9.99 *(978-0-7566-1518-5(6)*, DK Children) Dorling Kindersley Publishing, Inc.

Yoyo Books, creator. Numbers. 2011. (Baby's First Library). (ENG., Illus.). 40p. (gr. -1-k). bds. *(978-94-6033-702-4(3))* YoYo Bks.

Yoyo Books Staff. Words: Mini Baby's First Library. 2005. 42p. bds. *(978-90-5843-803-4(1))* YoYo Bks.

Zakiyyah & Zakiyyah. Chatterworld My Numbers in Spanish/My Numbers in French: MIS Numeros en Espanol/Mes Mombres en Francais. 2006. (Illus.). 40p. (J). (gr. -1-3). 14.99 *(978-0-9777085-0-5(0))* Little Linguists Press.

Ziefert, Harriet. Long Vowels. Roitman, Tanya, illus. 2007. (I'm Going to Read(r) Ser.). (ENG.). 64p. (J). (gr. -1-1). pap. 5.95 *(978-1-4027-5057-1(9))* Sterling Publishing Co., Inc.

—Lower-Case Letters. Kido, Yukiko, illus. 2007. (I'm Going to Read(r) Ser.). (ENG.). 64p. (J). (gr. -1-1). pap. 5.95 *(978-1-4027-5055-7(2))* Sterling Publishing Co., Inc.

—Rhyming Words. Kido, Yukiko, illus. 2007. (I'm Going to Read(r) Ser.). (ENG.). 64p. (J). (gr. -1-1). pap. 5.95 *(978-1-4027-5059-5(5))* Sterling Publishing Co., Inc.

—Short Vowels. Roitman, Tanya, illus. 2007. (I'm Going to Read(r) Ser.). (ENG.). 64p. (J). (gr. -1-1). pap. 5.95 *(978-1-4027-5056-4(0))* Sterling Publishing Co., Inc.

—Sight Words. Roitman, Tanya, illus. 2007. (I'm Going to Read(r) Ser.). (ENG.). 64p. (J). (gr. -1-1). pap. 5.95 *(978-1-4027-5058-8(7))* Sterling Publishing Co., Inc.

—Upper-Case Letters. Kido, Yukiko, illus. 2007. (I'm Going to Read(r) Ser.). (ENG.). 64p. (J). (gr. -1-1). pap. 5.95 *(978-1-4027-5054-0(4))* Sterling Publishing Co., Inc.

Zimic, Lesley, tr. from FRE. Picture My Day. 2012. (ENG., Illus.). 176p. (J). (gr. -1-3). 18.95 *(978-1-926973-30-2(5))* Owlkids Bks. Inc. CAN. Dist: Publishers Group West (PGW).

Zoo-Zológico Bilingual Board Book. 2008. (ENG & SPA., Illus.). (J). pap. 5.99 *(978-0-9727886-8-7(9))* Osmosis, LLC.

VOCABULARY—FICTION

Barnette, Brandon. Word Fanatics. 2012. 32p. pap. 14.50 *(978-1-4669-2942-5(1))* Trafford Publishing.

Battle-Lavert, Gwendolyn. The Barber's Cutting Edge. Holbert, Raymond, illus. 2004. (ENG.). 32p. (J). pap. 7.95 *(978-0-89239-196-7(0))* Lee & Low Bks., Inc.

Benoit-Renard, Anne. Navani from Delhi. Rigaudie, Mylène, illus. 2014. (AV2 Fiction Readalong Ser.: Vol. 133). (ENG.). 32p. (J). (gr. -1-3). lib. bdg. 34.28 *(978-1-4896-2271-6(3)*, AV2 by Weigl) Weigl Pubs., Inc.

Beobi & the Magic Coloring Book ABC First Words. 2005. (J). cd-rom 15.99 *(978-0-9743847-8-8(X))* Cohn, Tricia.

Bizcochitos de Cumpleanos Story Pack. 2003. (Coleccion Parvulitos). (SPA., Illus.). 67.50 *(978-0-8136-8531-1(1))* Modern Curriculum Pr.

Bober, Suzanne & Merberg, Julie. Mama, Baby, & Other First Words. 2010. (ENG.). 22p. (J). bds. 6.99 *(978-1-935703-03-7(X))* Downtown Bookworks.

Boehm, Richard G., et al. Take-Home Review Books. 2003. (Harcourt Brace Social Studies). (gr. 1-18). 6.20 *(978-0-15-310293-6(4))*; (gr. 2-18). 6.20 *(978-0-15-310294-3(2))* Harcourt Schl. Pubs.

Bolger, Kevin. Fun with Ed & Fred. Hodson, Ben, illus. 2016. 40p. (J). (gr. -1-3). 7.99 *(978-0-06-228600-0(5))* HarperCollins Pubs.

Bonnet, Rosalinde, illus. Alphabet Picture Book. 2011. (Alphabet Picture Book Ser.). 26p. (J). ring bd. 11.99 *(978-0-7945-2954-3(2)*, Usborne) EDC Publishing.

Brignaud, Pierre, illus. Caillou: Jobs People Do. 2011. (My First Dictionary Ser.). (ENG.). 16p. (J). (gr. -1-k). bds. 12.95 *(978-2-89450-831-2(X))* Caillouet, Gerry.

Brunetti, Ivan. Wordplay: TOON Level 1. 2017. (ENG., Illus.). 40p. (J). (gr. -1-3). 12.95 *(978-1-943145-17-1(2))* TOON Books / RAW Junior, LLC.

Brus, Mischa & Schlitz, Matt. Little Full Stop. Brus, Mischa, illus. 2012. (ENG., Illus.). 32p. (J). *(978-0-9751837-1-7(0))* Mambooks.

Capucilli, Alyssa Satin. Tulip & Rex Write a Story. Massini, Sarah, illus. 2015. (ENG.). 32p. (J). (gr. -1-3). 17.99 *(978-0-06-209416-2(5))* HarperCollins Pubs.

Cardwell, Michelle. Seeing the World Through Different Eyes. 2009. 32p. pap. 12.99 *(978-1-4389-9776-6(0))* AuthorHouse.

Carol Henson Keesee. The Angry Thunderstorm. Rachel Henson, illus. 2009. 40p. pap. 20.00 *(978-1-4389-4334-3(2))* AuthorHouse.

Carter, David A. B Is for Box — the Happy Little Yellow Box: A Pop-Up Book. Carter, David A., illus. 2014. (ENG., Illus.). 18p. (J). (gr. -1). 12.99 *(978-1-4814-0295-8(1)*, Little Simon) Little Simon.

Claire, Elizabeth. The New Boy Is Lost! An ESL Picture Novel 2004. Orig. Title: Where Is Taro? (Illus.). 70p. stu. ed. 12.00 *(978-0-937630-12-9(8))* Eardley Pubns.

Clayton, Darcy M. Making Mouth Sounds All Day Long. Freeswick, Jill, illus. 2013. 36p. pap. 9.95 *(978-1-889131-90-0(3)*, Castlebridge Bks.) Big Tent Bks.

Cousins, Lucy. Los Alimentos de Maisy. Cousins, Lucy, illus. 2009. (Maisy Ser.). (SPA & ENG., Illus.). 16p. (J). (gr. -1-2). bds. 5.99 *(978-0-7636-4519-9(2))* Candlewick Pr.

—Los Juguetes de Maisy. Cousins, Lucy, illus. 2009. (Maisy Ser.). (SPA & ENG., Illus.). 16p. (J). (gr. -1-2). bds. 5.99 *(978-0-7636-4520-5(6))* Candlewick Pr.

—Maisy's Animals (Los Animales de Maisy) Cousins, Lucy, illus. 2009. (Maisy Ser.). (SPA & ENG., Illus.). 16p. (J). (gr. -1-2). bds. 5.99 *(978-0-7636-4517-5(6))* Candlewick Pr.

—Maisy's Clothes/La Ropa de Maisy. Cousins, Lucy, illus. 2009. (Maisy Ser.). (SPA & ENG., Illus.). 16p. (J). (gr. -1-2). bds. 5.99 *(978-0-7636-4518-2(4))* Candlewick Pr.

Cowley, Joy. Space Aliens in Our School. Ming, Choo Hill, illus. 2004. (ENG.). 8p. (J). (gr. 1-1). pap. 4.67 *(978-1-56270-755-2(8)*, Dominie Elementary) Pearson Schl.

Cox, Phil Roxbee. Fat Cat on a Mat. Tyler, Jenny, ed. Cartwright, Stephen, illus. rev. ed. 2006. (Phonics Readers Ser.). 16p. (J). (gr. -1-3). pap. 6.99 *(978-0-7945-1502-7(9)*, Usborne) EDC Publishing.

Curry, Peter. Millie Goes Shopping. 2004. (First Words with Millie Ser.). (Illus.). 12p. (J). bds. 3.99 *(978-1-85854-505-9(6))* Brimax Books Ltd. GBR. Dist: Byeway Bks.

D'Amico, Christine. Higgledy-Piggledy: Mabel's World. Bell-Myers, Darcy, illus. 2005. (ENG.). 32p. (J). 16.95 *(978-0-9716631-1-4(4))* Avoomba Group Co.

D'Andrea, Deborah, creator. Words. 2006. (Picture Me Ser.). (Illus.). (J). *(978-1-57151-768-5(5))* Playhouse Publishing.

Danylyshyn, Greg. A Crash of Rhinos. Lomp, Stephan, illus. 2016. (ENG.). 40p. (J). (gr. -1-3). 16.99 *(978-1-4814-3150-7(1)*, Little Simon) Little Simon.

Disculpe Usted, Senor. 2003. (SPA., Illus.). stu. ed. 35.50 *(978-0-8136-8033-0(6))* Modern Curriculum Pr.

A Donde Vamos? 2003. (Coleccion Parvulitos). (SPA., Illus.). (J). stu. ed. 35.50 *(978-0-8136-8027-9(1))* Modern Curriculum Pr.

A Donde Vamos? Big Book. 2003. (Coleccion Parvulitos). (SPA., Illus.). 35.50 *(978-0-8136-8029-3(8))* Modern Curriculum Pr.

A Donde Vamos? Story Pack. 2003. (Coleccion Parvulitos). (SPA., Illus.). 67.50 *(978-0-8136-8524-3(9))* Modern Curriculum Pr.

Dorling Kindersley Publishing Staff. My First Words. 2015. (My First Bks.). (ENG., Illus.). 36p. (J). (gr. -1 — 1). bds. 5.99 *(978-1-4654-2899-8(2)*, DK Children) Dorling Kindersley Publishing, Inc.

Duncklee, John. Manchado & His Friends Manchado Y Sus Amigos. 2009. 52p. pap. 9.95 *(978-1-4401-2496-9(5))* iUniverse, Inc.

Emigh, Karen. Bookworm: Discovering Idioms, Sayings & Expressions. Dana, Steve, illus. 2013. (ENG.). 32p. (J). pap. 9.95 *(978-1-935274-88-9(0)*, 9781935274889) Future Horizons, Inc.

farahay, m. l. The BUTTERFLY, the BEE & the SPIDER. 2009. 32p. pap. 6.94 *(978-0-557-14043-5(9))* Lulu Pr., Inc.

—The BUTTERFLY, the BEE & the SPIDER, Sc3. 2009. 32p. pap. 14.94 *(978-0-557-15287-2(9))* Lulu Pr., Inc.

Fleming, Denise. Shout! Shout It Out! Fleming, Denise, illus. 2011. (ENG., Illus.). 40p. (J). (gr. -1-1). 16.99 *(978-0-8050-9237-0(4)*, 9780805092370, Holt, Henry & Co. Bks. For Young Readers) Holt, Henry & Co.

Ford, Adam B. Jam-Bo, Litta-Girl, & the Bullies. Huddleston, Courtney, illus. 2013. 44p. pap. 12.95 *(978-0-9794104-9-9(5))* H Bar Pr.

Forde, Patricia. The List. 2017. (ENG.). 368p. (J). (gr. 5-8). 16.99 *(978-1-4926-4796-6(9)*, 9781492647966, Sourcebooks Jabberwocky) Sourcebooks, Inc.

Frasier, Debra. Miss Alaineus: A Vocabulary Disaster. Frasier, Debra, illus. 2007. (ENG., Illus.). 40p. (J). (gr. -1-3). pap. 7.99 *(978-0-15-206053-4(7))* Houghton Mifflin Harcourt Publishing Co.

Galassi, Isabel. I Want, 1 vol. 2009. 12p. pap. 24.95 *(978-1-61546-535-4(9))* America Star Bks.

Garcia Orihuela, Luis & DIVINCENZO, Sofia & Yoselem. The Army of Words. GARCIA ORIHUELA, Luis, illus. 2012. 24p. pap. 19.99 *(978-1-61196-934-4(4))* Pintos, Yoselem G.

Graham, Mark. Hello, I Am Fiona from Scotland. Sofilas, Mark, illus. 2014. (AV2 Fiction Readalong Ser.: Vol. 128). (ENG.). 32p. (J). (gr. -1-3). lib. bdg. 34.28 *(978-1-4896-2253-2(5)*, AV2 by Weigl) Weigl Pubs., Inc.

Graham, Oakley. When I Dream of 123. 2014. (Illus.). (J). *(978-1-4351-5468-1(1))* Barnes & Noble, Inc.

Grant, Jacob. Little Bird's Bad Word. 2015. (ENG., Illus.). 32p. (J). (gr. -1-2). 16.99 *(978-1-250-05149-3(5)*, 9781250051493) Feiwel & Friends.

Griffith, Christina. Why Jubilee & Ashanti go to the Doctor? 2011. 28p. pap. 13.54 *(978-1-4269-7069-6(2))* Trafford Publishing.

Groeneweg, Nicole. One Word Pearl. Mitchell, Hazel, illus. 2013. (ENG.). 32p. (J). (gr. k-3). 17.95 *(978-1-934133-53-8(1))*; pap. 7.95 *(978-1-934133-54-5(X))* Charlesbridge Publishing, Inc.

Grosset and Dunlap Staff, contrib. by. The World of Dick & Jane Anderson. 2003. (Illus.). (J). 9.97 *(978-0-448-43479-7(2)*, Grosset & Dunlap) Penguin Publishing Group.

Guy, Ginger Foglesong. Bravo! Moreno, Rene King, illus. 2010. (SPA & ENG.). 32p. (J). (gr. -1-k). 16.99 *(978-0-06-173180-8(3)*, Greenwillow Bks.) HarperCollins Pubs.

Hallowell, George & Holub, Joan. Wagons Ho! Avril, Lynne, illus. 2014. (AV2 Fiction Readalong Ser.: Vol. 153). (ENG.). 32p. (J). (gr. -1-3). lib. bdg. 34.28 *(978-1-4896-2389-8(2)*, AV2 by Weigl) Weigl Pubs., Inc.

Hills, Tad. Drop It, Rocket! 2014. (ENG., Illus.). 32p. (J). (gr. 1-4). 12.99 *(978-0-385-37247-3(7)*, Schwartz & Wade Bks.) Random Hse. Children's Bks.

TUV

Howard-Parham, Pam. Caillou Gets in Shape. Gillen, Lisa P., illus. l.t. ed. 2006. (HRL Board Book Ser.). (J). (gr. k-18). pap. 10.95 (978-1-57332-331-4(4), HighReach Learning, Incorporated) Carson-Dellosa Publishing, LLC.

Huisingh, Rosemary. At the Library. 2012. (Illus.). (J). (978-0-7606-1346-7(X)) LinguiSystems, Inc.

—Vocabulary Stories for Toddlers: Getting Ready for Bed. 2012. (Illus.). 10p. (978-0-7606-1345-0(1)) LinguiSystems, Inc.

—Vocabulary Stories for Toddlers: My Body's Just Right for Me. 2012. (Illus.). 10p. (978-0-7606-1347-4(8)) LinguiSystems, Inc.

—Vocabulary Stories for Toddlers: Seasons. 2012. (Illus.). (978-0-7606-1348-1(6)) LinguiSystems, Inc.

Husar, Jaco & Husar, Stephane. Hello, I Am Lily from New York City. Rigaudie, Mylène, illus. 2014. (AV2 Fiction Readalong Ser.: Vol. 129). (ENG.). 32p. (J). (gr. -1-3). lib. bdg. 34.28 (978-1-4896-2259-4(4), AV2 by Weigl) Weigl Pubs., Inc.

Husar, Stephane. Hello, I Am Charlie from London. Robert, Yannick, illus. 2014. (AV2 Fiction Readalong Ser.: Vol. 127). (ENG.). 32p. (J). (gr. -1-3). lib. bdg. 34.28 (978-1-4896-2256-3(X), AV2 by Weigl) Weigl Pubs., Inc.

—Hello, I Am Max from Sydney. Sofilas, Mark, illus. 2014. (AV2 Fiction Readalong Ser.: Vol. 130). (ENG.). 32p. (J). (gr. -1-3). lib. bdg. 34.28 (978-1-4896-2250-1(0), AV2 by Weigl) Weigl Pubs., Inc.

—Paolo from Rome. Le Grand, Claire, illus. 2014. (AV2 Fiction Readalong Ser.: Vol. 134). (ENG.). 32p. (J). (gr. -1-3). lib. bdg. 34.28 (978-1-4896-2274-7(8), AV2 by Weigl) Weigl Pubs., Inc.

James, Tamara. The World Is Your Oyster. SanCartier, Emma, illus. 2010. (ENG.). 50p. (J). (gr. -1-3). 16.95 (978-1-897476-22-2(1)) Simply Read Bks. CAN. Dist: Ingram Publisher Services.

Jansson, Tove. Moomin's Little Book of Words. 2011. (Moomins Ser.). (ENG., Illus.). 16p. (J). (gr. -1 — 1). 7.99 (978-0-374-35048-2(5), 9780374350482, Farrar, Straus & Giroux (BYR)) Farrar, Straus & Giroux.

Jarrell, Pamela R. Time for Bed. Coillen, Lisa P.; illus. l.t. ed. 2005. (HRL Board Book Ser.). (J). (gr. -1-k). pap. 10.95 (978-1-57332-325-3(X), HighReach Learning, Incorporated) Carson-Dellosa Publishing, LLC.

Kelley, Maria Felicia. Buz Words: Discovering Words in Pairs. Kelley, Maria Felicia, illus. 2007. (Illus.). 32p. (J). (gr. -1-3). 14.95 (978-0-9650918-1-7(3)) April Arts Press & Productions.

Kennedy, Kevin. Ten Dollar Words for Kids. Fife, Jay, illus. 2013. 26p. pap. 11.95 (978-1-61244-244-0(7)) Halo Publishing International.

Klise, Kate & Klise, M. Sarah. The Show Must Go On! 2014. (Three-Ring Rascals Ser.: 1). (ENG., Illus.). 160p. (J). (gr. 2-5). pap. 5.95 (978-1-61620-406-8(0), 73406) Algonquin Bks. of Chapel Hill.

Kopley, Richard. The Remarkable David Wordsworth. Fazio, Michael, illus. 2013. 30p. (J). pap. (978-1-936172-67-2(4)) Eifrig Publishing.

Lederer, Susan. I Can Do That. Loehr, Jenny, illus. 2008. 28p. (J). per. 19.95 (978-0-9789347-0-5(9)) Children's Publishing.

Lederer, Suzy. I Can Say That. Loehr, Jenny, illus. l.t. ed. 2006. 32p. (J). (gr. -1-3). 19.95 incl. audio compact disk (978-0-9725803-7-3(9)) Children's Publishing.

Lemke, Donald B. Superman. Ku, Min Sung, illus. 2014. (DC Super Friends Word Adventures Ser.). (ENG.). 12p. (gr. -1 — 1). bds. 6.99 (978-1-4795-5243-6(7)) Picture Window Bks.

—Wonder Woman. Ku, Min Sung, illus. 2014. (DC Super Friends Word Adventures Ser.). (ENG.). 12p. (gr. -1 — 1). bds. 6.99 (978-1-4795-5244-3(5)) Picture Window Bks.

Levis, Caron. May I Have a Word? Rash, Andy, illus. 2017. (ENG.). 40p. (J). 16.99 (978-0-374-34880-9(4), 9780374348809, Farrar, Straus & Giroux (BYR)) Farrar, Straus & Giroux.

Lobato, Arcadio, illus. Volando por las Palabras. 2004.Tr. of Flying through Words. (SPA.). 48p. (J). 10.50 (978-84-263-5018-3(6)) Vives, Luis Editorial (Edelvives) ESP. Dist: Lectorum Pubns., Inc.

Long, Ethan. Up, Tall & High! Long, Ethan, illus. 2012. (ENG., Illus.). 40p. (J). (gr. -1-2). 15.99 (978-0-399-25611-0(3), G.P. Putnam's Sons Books for Young Readers) Penguin Young Readers Group.

MacCuish, Al. Operation Alphabet. Lozano, Luciano, illus. 2011. (Ministry of Letters Ser.: 0). (ENG.). 64p. (J). (gr. -1-k). 19.95 (978-0-500-51584-6(0), 551584) Thames & Hudson.

MacPhail, Catherine. Copycat. 2014. (Read On Ser.). (ENG.). 192p. (J). (gr. 5). 9.99 (978-0-00-754622-0(X)) HarperCollins Pubs. Ltd. GBR. Dist: Independent Pubs. Group.

Malepart, Celine, illus. When Pigs Fly: A Piggy Pop-up Book! 2008. (ENG.). 12p. 16.95 (978-1-58117-671-1(6), Intervisual/Piggy Toes) Bendon, Inc.

Marceau, Fani. In This Book. Jolivet, Joëlle, illus. 2014. (ENG.). 64p. (J). (gr. -1 — 1). 17.99 (978-1-4521-2588-6(0)) Chronicle Bks. LLC.

Matulewicz, Elisabeth Ann. Benny & Marshmallow. Sponaugle, Kim, illus. 2008. 31p. (J). pap. 15.00 (978-0-9786211-7-9(4), Ithaca Pr.) Authors & Artists Publishers of New York, Inc.

Metzger, Steve. The Mixed-Up Alphabet. Ho, Jannie, illus. 2007. (J). (978-0-545-00098-7(X)) Scholastic, Inc.

A Mi Abuelita Le Gusta Correr. 2003. (Coleccion Parvulitos). (SPA., Illus.). stu. ed. 35.50 (978-0-8136-8141-2(3)) Modern Curriculum Pr.

A Mi Abuelita Le Gusta Correr Big Book. 2003. (Coleccion Parvulitos). (SPA., Illus.). 35.50 (978-0-8136-8535-9(4)) Modern Curriculum Pr.

Miller, Jonathan, illus. Winter, Spring, Summer, Fall. 2010. 16p. (J). (978-1-58865-578-3(4)) Kidsbooks, LLC.

Monalisa, DeGross. Donavan's Word Jar. 2014. (Trophy Chapter Bks). (ENG.). 80p. (J). (gr. 2-5). 9.24 (978-1-63245-337-2(1)) Lectorum Pubns., Inc.

Moncure, Jane Belk. *Hop-Skip-Jump-a-Roo Zoo*: A Book about Imitating. Girouard, Patrick, illus. 2013. (Magic Castle Readers Ser.). (ENG.). 32p. (J). (gr. -1-2). 25.64 (978-1-62323-566-6(9), 206300) Child's World, Inc., The.

—Ice Cream Cows & Mitten Sheep: A Book about Farm Animals. Billin-Frye, Paige, illus. 2013. (Magic Castle Readers Ser.). (ENG.). 32p. (J). (gr. -1-2). 25.64 (978-1-62323-583-3(9), 206319) Child's World, Inc., The.

—Mr. Doodle Had a Poodle: A Book about Fun Activities. Regan, Dana, illus. 2013. (Magic Castle Readers Ser.). (ENG.). 32p. (J). (gr. -1-2). 25.64 (978-1-62323-574-1(X), 206310) Child's World, Inc., The.

Muench-Williams, Heather. Adam's Grouchy Day. Meier, Kerry L., illus. l.t. ed. 2005. (HRL Little Book Ser.). (J). (gr. -1-k). pap. 10.95 (978-1-57332-321-5(7)); pap. 10.95 (978-1-57332-320-8(9)) Carson-Dellosa Publishing, LLC. (HighReach Learning, Incorporated).

Mullican, Judy. Caillou & the Storyteller. Storch, Ellen N., illus. l.t. ed. 2006. (HRL Board Book Ser.). (J). (gr. k-18). pap. 10.95 (978-1-57332-330-7(6), HighReach Learning, Incorporated) Carson-Dellosa Publishing, LLC.

Nelson, Mary Beth & Linn, Laurent, illus. Elmo's Big Word Book/el Libro Grande de Palabras de Elmo. Barrett, John E., photos by. 2006. (Elmo's Big Word Book/el Libro Grande de Palabras de Elmo Ser.). (SPA, ENG, MUL & ANG.). 12p. (J). (gr. -1 — 1). bds. 8.95 (978-0-87358-906-2(8)) Cooper Square Publishing Llc.

Niemann, Christoph. Words. Niemann, Christoph, illus. ltd. ed. 2016. (Illus.). 352p. (J). (gr. -1 — 1). 175.00 (978-0-06-266276-7(7), Greenwillow Bks.) HarperCollins Pubs.

Noyce, Pendred. Lost in Lexicon: An Adventure in Words & Numbers. Charles, Joan, illus. 2011. (ENG.). 368p. (J). (gr. 3). pap. 12.95 (978-0-9830219-2-6(9)) Mighty Media Pr.

O'Connor, Jane. Aspiring Artist. Glasser, Robin Preiss, illus. 2011. (Fancy Nancy Ser.). (ENG.). 32p. (J). (gr. -1-2). 12.99 (978-0-06-191526-0(2)) HarperCollins Pubs.

—The Dazzling Book Report. Glasser, Robin Preiss & Enik, Ted, illus. 2009. (I Can Read Level 1 Ser.). (ENG.). 32p. (J). (gr. -1-3). pap. 3.99 (978-0-06-170368-3(0)) HarperCollins Pubs.

—Every Day Is Earth Day. Ivanov, Aleksey et al, illus. 2010. (I Can Read Level 1 Ser.). (ENG.). 32p. (J). (gr. -1-3). 16.99 (978-0-06-187327-0(6)) HarperCollins Pubs.

—Every Day Is Earth Day. Ivanov, Aleksey et al, illus. 2010. (I Can Read Level 1 Ser.). (ENG.). 32p. (J). (gr. -1-3). pap. 3.99 (978-0-06-187326-3(8)) HarperCollins Pubs.

—Every Day Is Earth Day. 2010. (Fancy Nancy - I Can Read! Ser.). (J). lib. bdg. 13.55 (978-0-606-12294-8(X), Turtleback) Turtleback Bks.

—Explorer Extraordinaire! Glasser, Robin Preiss, illus. 2009. (Fancy Nancy Ser.). (ENG.). 32p. (J). (gr. -1-2). 12.99 (978-0-06-168486-9(4)) HarperCollins Pubs.

—Fancy Nancy. Glasser, Robin Preiss, illus. 2009. (Fancy Nancy Ser.). (ENG.). 32p. (J). (gr. -1-3). pap. 24.99 (978-0-06-171944-8(7), HarperFestival) HarperCollins Pubs.

—Fancy Nancy: My Family History. Glasser, Robin Preiss et al, illus. 2010. (I Can Read Level 1 Ser.). (ENG.). 32p. (J). (gr. -1-3). 16.99 (978-0-06-188270-8(4)) HarperCollins Pubs.

—Fancy Nancy: Nancy Clancy, Super Sleuth. 2013. (Nancy Clancy Ser.: 1). (J). lib. bdg. 14.75 (978-0-606-31795-5(3), Turtleback) Turtleback Bks.

—Fancy Nancy: Pajama Day. Drainville, Beth et al, illus. 2009. (I Can Read Level 1 Ser.). (ENG.). 32p. (J). (gr. -1-3). 16.99 (978-0-06-170371-3(0)) HarperCollins Pubs.

—Fancy Nancy: Poison Ivy Expert. Glasser, Robin Preiss & Enik, Ted, illus. 2008. (I Can Read Level 1 Ser.). (ENG.). 32p. (J). (gr. -1-3). 16.99 (978-0-06-123614-3(4)); pap. 3.99 (978-0-06-123613-6(6)) HarperCollins Pubs.

—Fancy Nancy: Tea for Two. Glasser, Robin Preiss, illus. 2012. (Fancy Nancy Ser.). (ENG.). 24p. (J). (gr. -1-3). pap. 3.99 (978-0-06-123597-9(0), HarperFestival) HarperCollins Pubs.

—Fancy Nancy: The Dazzling Book Report. Glasser, Robin Preiss & Enik, Ted, illus. 2009. (I Can Read Level 1 Ser.). (ENG.). 32p. (J). (gr. -1-3). 16.99 (978-0-06-170369-0(9)) HarperCollins Pubs.

—Fancy Nancy: The Dazzling Book Report. Glasser, Robin Preiss & Enik, Ted, illus. 2009. (Fancy Nancy Ser.). 32p. lib. bdg. 14.00 (978-1-60686-531-6(5)) Perfection Learning Corp.

—Fancy Nancy: The Show Must Go On. Glasser, Robin Preiss & Enik, Ted, illus. 2009. (I Can Read Level 1 Ser.). (ENG.). 32p. (J). (gr. -1-3). 16.99 (978-0-06-170373-7(7)) HarperCollins Pubs.

—Fancy Nancy & the Boy from Paris. Enik, Ted & Glasser, Robin Preiss, illus. 2008. (I Can Read Level 1 Ser.). (ENG.). 32p. (J). (gr. -1-3). 16.99 (978-0-06-123610-5(1)); pap. 3.99 (978-0-06-123609-9(8)) HarperCollins Pubs.

—Fancy Nancy & the Delectable Cupcakes. Glasser, Robin Preiss & Enik, Ted, illus. 2010. (I Can Read Level 1 Ser.). (ENG.). 32p. (J). (gr. -1-3). 16.99 (978-0-06-188269-2(0)); pap. 3.99 (978-0-06-188268-5(2)) HarperCollins Pubs.

—Fancy Nancy & the Fabulous Fashion Boutique. Glasser, Robin Preiss, illus. 2010. (Fancy Nancy Ser.). 32p. (J). (gr. -1-3). (ENG.). 17.99 (978-0-06-123592-4(X)); lib. bdg. 18.89 (978-0-06-123593-1(8)) HarperCollins Pubs.

—Fancy Nancy & the Late, Late, Late Night. Glasser, Robin Preiss, illus. 2010. (Fancy Nancy Ser.). (ENG.). 24p. (J). (gr. -1-3). pap. 3.99 (978-0-06-170377-5(X), HarperFestival) HarperCollins Pubs.

—Fancy Nancy & the Late, Late, Late Night. 2010. (Fancy Nancy Picture Bks.). (J). lib. bdg. 13.55 (978-0-606-12312-9(1), Turtleback) Turtleback Bks.

—Fancy Nancy & the Mean Girl. Glasser, Robin Preiss, illus. 2011. (I Can Read Level 1 Ser.). (ENG.). 32p. (J). (gr. -1-3). 16.99 (978-0-06-200178-8(7)); pap. 3.99 (978-0-06-200177-1(9)) HarperCollins Pubs.

—Fancy Nancy & the Mermaid Ballet. Glasser, Robin Preiss & Bracken, Carolyn, illus. 2012. (Fancy Nancy Ser.). (ENG.). 32p. (J). (gr. -1-2). 17.99 (978-0-06-170381-2(8)) HarperCollins Pubs.

—Fancy Nancy & the Sensational Babysitter. Glasser, Robin Preiss et al, illus. 2010. (Fancy Nancy Ser.). (ENG.). 24p. (J). (gr. -1-3). pap. 3.99 (978-0-06-170378-2(8), HarperFestival) HarperCollins Pubs.

—Fancy Nancy & the Sensational Babysitter. 2010. (Fancy Nancy Picture Bks.). (J). lib. bdg. 13.55 (978-0-606-14840-5(X), Turtleback) Turtleback Bks.

—Fancy Nancy & the Too-Loose Tooth. Glasser, Robin Preiss & Enik, Ted, illus. 2012. (I Can Read Level 1 Ser.). (ENG.). 32p. (J). (gr. -1-3). 16.99 (978-0-06-208301-2(5)); pap. 3.99 (978-0-06-208302-9(3)) HarperCollins Pubs.

—Fancy Nancy & the Too-Loose Tooth. 2012. (Fancy Nancy - I Can Read! Ser.). (J). lib. bdg. 13.55 (978-0-606-23551-8(5), Turtleback) Turtleback Bks.

—Fancy Nancy Collector's Quintet. Glasser, Robin Preiss, illus. 2009. (I Can Read Level 1 Ser.). (J). (gr. k-3). pap. 16.99 (978-0-06-171905-9(6)) HarperCollins Pubs.

—Fancy Nancy: Nancy Clancy Seeks a Fortune. Glasser, Robin Preiss & Bracken, Carolyn, illus. 2016. (Nancy Clancy Ser.: 7). 144p. (J). (gr. 1-5). 9.99 (978-0-06-226969-0(0)) HarperCollins Pubs.

—Fancy Nancy: Nancy Clancy, Soccer Mania. Glasser, Robin Preiss, illus. (Nancy Clancy Ser.: 6). (J). (gr. 1-5). 2016. 144p. pap. 4.99 (978-0-06-226966-9(6)) 2015. (ENG.). 128p. 9.99 (978-0-06-226967-6(4)) HarperCollins Pubs.

—Fancy Nancy's Favorite Fancy Words: From Accessories to Zany. Glasser, Robin Preiss, illus. 2008. (Fancy Nancy Ser.). (ENG.). 32p. (J). (gr. -1-2). 12.99 (978-0-06-154923-6(1)) HarperCollins Pubs.

—My Family History. Glasser, Robin Preiss et al, illus. 2010. (I Can Read Level 1 Ser.). (ENG.). 32p. (J). (gr. -1-3). pap. 3.99 (978-0-06-188271-5(2)) HarperCollins Pubs.

—My Family History. 2010. (Fancy Nancy - I Can Read! Ser.). (J). lib. bdg. 13.55 (978-0-606-14988-4(0), Turtleback) Turtleback Bks.

—Nancy Clancy - Super Sleuth. Glasser, Robin Preiss, illus. 2013. (Nancy Clancy Ser.: 1). (ENG.). 144p. (J). (gr. 1-5). pap. 5.99 (978-0-06-208419-4(4)) HarperCollins Pubs.

—Nancy Clancy, Secret Admirer. Glasser, Robin Preiss, illus. 2013. (Nancy Clancy Ser.: 2). (ENG.). 144p. (J). (gr. 1-5). pap. 4.99 (978-0-06-208420-0(8)) HarperCollins Pubs.

—Nancy Clancy, Secret Admirer. 2013. (Nancy Clancy Ser.: 2). (J). lib. bdg. 14.75 (978-0-606-35045-7(4), Turtleback) Turtleback Bks.

O'connor, Jane. Nancy Clancy, Soccer Mania. Glasser, Robin Preiss, illus. 2016. (Nancy Clancy Ser.: 6). (ENG.). 144p. (J). (gr. 1-5). 14.75 (978-0-606-39270-9(X)) Turtleback Bks.

O'Connor, Jane. Nancy Clancy, Star of Stage & Screen. 2016. (Nancy Clancy Ser.: 5). (J). lib. bdg. 14.75 (978-0-606-38153-6(8)) Turtleback Bks.

—Nancy Clancy, Super Sleuth, 3 vols. Glasser, Robin Preiss, illus. 2012. (Nancy Clancy Ser.: 1). (ENG.). 128p. (J). (gr. 1-5). 9.99 (978-0-06-208293-0(0)) HarperCollins Pubs.

—Nancy Clancy's Tres Charming, 3 vols., Set. Glasser, Robin Preiss, illus. 2013. (Fancy Nancy Ser.). (ENG.). 384p. (J). (gr. 1-5). 24.99 (978-0-06-227793-0(6)) HarperCollins Pubs.

—Ooh La La! It's Beauty Day. Glasser, Robin Preiss, illus. 2010. (Fancy Nancy Ser.). (ENG.). 40p. (J). (gr. -1-2). 12.99 (978-0-06-191525-3(4)) HarperCollins Pubs.

—Pajama Day. Drainville, Beth et al, illus. 2009. (I Can Read Level 1 Ser.). (ENG.). 32p. (J). (gr. -1-3). pap. 3.99 (978-0-06-170370-6(2)) HarperCollins Pubs.

—Poison Ivy Expert. Glasser, Robin Preiss & Enik, Ted, illus. 2008. (Fancy Nancy - I Can Read! Ser.). 32p. (J). lib. bdg. 13.55 (978-1-4364-5050-8(0), Turtleback) Turtleback Bks.

—Secret Admirer, 3 vols. Glasser, Robin Preiss, illus. 2013. (Fancy Nancy Ser.: Bk. 2). (ENG.). 128p. (J). (gr. 1-5). 9.99 (978-0-06-208295-4(7)) HarperCollins Pubs.

—The Show Must Go On. Enik, Ted & Glasser, Robin Preiss, illus. 2009. (I Can Read Level 1 Ser.). (ENG.). 32p. (J). (gr. -1-3). pap. 3.99 (978-0-06-170372-0(9)) HarperCollins Pubs.

—Spectacular Spectacles. Glasser, Robin Preiss & Enik, Ted, illus. 2010. (I Can Read Level 1 Ser.). (ENG.). 32p. (J). (gr. -1-3). 16.99 (978-0-06-188263-0(1)) HarperCollins Pubs.

—Spectacular Spectacles, Level 1. Glasser, Robin Preiss & Enik, Ted, illus. 2010. (I Can Read Level 1 Ser.). (ENG.). 32p. (J). (gr. -1-3). pap. 3.99 (978-0-06-188264-7(X)) HarperCollins Pubs.

—Splendid Speller. Glasser, Robin Preiss, illus. 2011. (I Can Read Level 1 Ser.). (ENG.). 32p. (J). (gr. -1-3). 16.99 (978-0-06-200176-4(0)); pap. 3.99 (978-0-06-200175-7(2)) HarperCollins Pubs.

—Splendiferous Christmas. Glasser, Robin Preiss, illus. (Fancy Nancy Ser.). 32p. (J). (gr. -1-2). 2011. (ENG.). 17.99 (978-0-06-123590-0(3)) 2009. lib. bdg. 18.89 (978-0-06-123591-7(1)) HarperCollins Pubs.

—Stellar Stargazer! Glasser, Robin Preiss, illus. 2011. (Fancy Nancy Ser.). (ENG.). 32p. (J). (gr. -1-2). 12.99 (978-0-06-191523-9(8)) HarperCollins Pubs.

—Super Sleuth. Glasser, Robin Preiss, illus. 2015. (Fancy Nancy Ser.). (ENG.). 256p. (J). (gr. 1-5). 12.99 (978-0-06-240364-3(8)) HarperCollins Pubs.

—Tea for Two. Glasser, Robin Preiss, illus. 2012. (Fancy Nancy Picture Bks.). (J). lib. bdg. 13.55 (978-0-606-23577-8(9), Turtleback) Turtleback Bks.

—Tea Parties. Glasser, Robin Preiss, illus. 2009. (Fancy Nancy Ser.). (ENG.). 40p. (J). (gr. -1-2). 12.99 (978-0-06-180174-7(7)) HarperCollins Pubs.

—The 100th Day of School. Glasser, Robin Preiss & Enik, Ted, illus. 2009. (I Can Read Level 1 Ser.). (ENG.). 32p. (J). (gr. -1-3). 16.99 (978-0-06-170375-1(3)); pap. 3.99 (978-0-06-170374-4(5)) HarperCollins Pubs.

Park, Linda Sue. Yaks Yak: Animal Word Pairs. Reinhardt, Jennifer Black, illus. 2016. (ENG.). 40p. (J). (gr. -1-3). 16.99 (978-0-544-39101-7(2), Clarion Bks.) Houghton Mifflin Harcourt Trade & Reference Pubs.

Pecci, Mary. Pecci Reading Series: Primer. 2008. (Pecci Reading Ser.). pap. 9.95 (978-0-943220-16-1(5)) Pecci Educational Pubs.

Priddy, Roger. First 100 Words Sticker Book. 2015. (Play & Learn Ser.). (ENG.). 72p. (J). (gr. -1-1). pap. 9.99 (978-0-312-51899-8(4), 9780312518998, Priddy Bks.) St. Martin's Pr.

Prochovnic, Dawn Babb. Opposites Everywhere: Sign Language for Opposites, 1 vol. Bauer, Stephanie, illus. 2012. (ENG.). 32p. 28.50 (978-1-61641-839-7(7), Looking Glass Library) Magic Wagon.

Pulver, Robin & Reed, Lynn Rowe. Happy Endings: A Story about Suffixes. 2012. (ENG., Illus.). 32p. (J). pap. 7.95 (978-0-8234-2434-4(0)) Holiday Hse., Inc.

Quienes Son Tus Amigos? 2003. (Coleccion Parvulitos). (SPA., Illus.). stu. ed. 35.50 (978-0-8136-8525-0(7)) Modern Curriculum Pr.

Ricci, Christine. Dora in the Deep Sea. Roper, Robert, illus. 2003. (Dora the Explorer Ser.: Vol. 3). (ENG.). 24p. (J). pap. 3.99 (978-0-689-85845-1(0), Simon Spotlight/Nickelodeon) Simon Spotlight/Nickelodeon.

Rosenthal, Marc. Big Bot, Small Bot: A Book of Robot Opposites. 2015. (ENG., Illus.). 20p. (J). (-k). 17.95 (978-1-57687-750-0(7), powerHouse Bks.) powerHouse Cultural Entertainment, Inc.

Rubinger, Ami. I Dream of an Elephant. Rubinger, Ami, illus. 2010. (ENG., Illus.). 28p. (J). (gr. k-k). 13.95 (978-0-7892-1058-6(4), Abbeville Kids) Abbeville Pr., Inc.

Sabatier-Morel, Francoise & Pellegrini, Isabelle. Marie from Paris. Camcam, Princesse, illus. 2014. (AV2 Fiction Readalong Ser.: Vol. 131). (ENG.). 32p. (J). (gr. -1-3). lib. bdg. 34.28 (978-1-4896-2262-4(4), AV2 by Weigl) Weigl Pubs., Inc.

Saroyan, William & Tinkelman, Murray. Me. 2016. (ENG., Illus.). 64p. (gr. 1-3). pap. 9.99 (978-0-486-81066-9(6)) Dover Pubns., Inc.

Scarry, Richard. Richard Scarry's Best Little Word Book Ever! Scarry, Richard, illus. 2016. (Pictureback(R) Ser.). (ENG., Illus.). 24p. (J). (-k). pap. 4.99 (978-0-385-39271-6(0), Random Hse. Bks. for Young Readers) Random Hse. Children's Bks.

Schmidt, Kristina Edelkamp. Miss Flavia & the Cookie Cottage. Cologne, Starla, illus. 2009. 28p. pap. 7.99 (978-1-935125-61-7(3)) Robertson Publishing.

Schotter, Roni. The Boy Who Loved Words. Potter, Giselle, illus. 2006. (ENG.). 40p. (J). (gr. -1-3). 17.99 (978-0-375-83601-5(2), Schwartz & Wade Bks.) Random Hse. Children's Bks.

Seeger, Laura Vaccaro. One Boy. Seeger, Laura Vaccaro, illus. 2016. (ENG., Illus.). 48p. (J). 14.99 (978-1-62672-252-1(8), 9781626722521) Roaring Brook Pr.

Seuss, Dr. Hay un Molillo en Mi Bolsillo! Canetti, Yanitzia, tr. from ENG. 2007.Tr. of There's a Wocket in my Pocket! (SPA., Illus.). 26p. (J). (gr. k-3). 8.99 (978-1-933032-25-2(1)) Lectorum Pubns., Inc.

—Les Oeufs Verts Au Jambon: The French Edition of Green Eggs & Ham. 2009. (FRE & ENG., Illus.). 64p. (J). (gr. -1-3). 12.95 (978-1-56975-688-1(0)) Ulysses Pr.

Shannon, David. Oops! A Diaper David Book. Shannon, David, illus. 2005. (Oops! Ser.). (ENG., Illus.). 12p. (J). (gr. -1-k). bds. 6.99 (978-0-439-68882-6(5), Blue Sky Pr., The) Scholastic, Inc.

Si Yo Tuviera un Cordel... 2003. (Coleccion Parvulitos). (SPA., Illus.). stu. ed. 35.50 (978-0-8136-8530-4(3)) Modern Curriculum Pr.

Snicket, Lemony, pseud. 13 Words. Kalman, Maira, illus. (ENG.). 40p. (J). (gr. -1-3). 2014. pap. 6.99 (978-0-06-166467-0(7)) 2010. 16.99 (978-0-06-166465-6(0)) HarperCollins Pubs.

Stauffacher, Sue & Love, Comfort. Wireman. 2007. (Illus.). 159p. (J). pap. (978-0-9709811-4-1(7)) Grand Valley State Univ.

Steinberg, Laya. Thesaurus Rex. Harter, Debbie, illus. (ENG.). 24p. (J). 2005. (gr. -1-2). pap. 6.99 (978-1-84148-180-7(7)) 2003. 15.99 (978-1-84148-042-8(8)) Barefoot Bks., Inc.

Stihler, Chérie B. Wiggle-Waggle Woof: Counting Sled Dogs in Alaska. Bania, Michael, illus. 2009. (Paws IV Ser.). (ENG.). 32p. (J). (gr. -1-2). pap. 10.99 (978-1-57061-559-7(4), Little Bigfoot) Sasquatch Bks.

Storch, Ellen N. Here We Go! Storch, Ellen N., illus. l.t. ed. 2005. (HRL Board Book Ser.). (Illus.). (J). (gr. -1-k). pap. 10.95 (978-1-57332-322-2(5), HighReach Learning, Incorporated) Carson-Dellosa Publishing, LLC.

Tiger Tales Staff. Things to Learn. 2013. (ENG., Illus.). 12p. (J). bds. (978-1-58925-635-4(2)) Tiger Tales.

Tiger Tales Staff, creator. My Busy Day. 2014. (My First Jumbo Tab Bks.). (ENG., Illus.). 12p. (J). (gr. -1-k). bds. 8.99 (978-1-58925-590-6(9)) Tiger Tales.

—Things That Go. 2014. (My First Jumbo Tab Bks.). (ENG., Illus.). 12p. (J). (gr. -1). bds. 8.99 (978-1-58925-589-0(5)) Tiger Tales.

Tiger Tales Staff, ed. Easter Surprise: My First Lift & Learn. 2014. (ENG.). 10p. (J). bds. 7.99 (978-1-58925-580-7(1)) Tiger Tales.

Tobin, Jim. The Very Inappropriate Word. Coverly, Dave, illus. 2013. (ENG.). 36p. (J). (gr. k-3). 16.99 (978-0-8050-9474-9(1), 9780805094749, Holt, Henry & Co. Bks. For Young Readers) Holt, Henry & Co.

Van Fleet, Matthew. Heads. Van Fleet, Matthew, illus. 2010. (ENG., Illus.). 18p. (J). (gr. -1-1). 19.99 (978-1-4424-0379-6(9), Simon & Schuster/Paula Wiseman Bks.) Simon & Schuster/Paula Wiseman Bks.

Van Slyke, Rebecca. Lexie the Word Wrangler. Hartland, Jessie, illus. 2017. (ENG.). 40p. (J). (gr. k-3). 17.99 (978-0-399-16957-1(1), Nancy Paulsen Books) Penguin Young Readers Group.

Vonthron, Satanta C. Caillou's Community. Storch, Ellen N., illus. l.t. ed. 2006. (HRL Board Book Ser.). (J). (gr. k-18). pap. 10.95 (978-1-57332-332-1(2), HighReach Learning, Incorporated) Carson-Dellosa Publishing, LLC.

Weston, Carol. Ava & Pip. (Ava & Pip Ser.: 1). (ENG.). 224p. (J). (gr. 5-7). 2015. pap. 6.99 (978-1-4926-0183-8(7)) 2014. 15.99 (978-1-4022-8870-8(0), 9781402288708) Sourcebooks, Inc. (Sourcebooks Jabberwocky).

Williams, Garth. Baby's First Book. Williams, Garth, illus. 2011. (Golden Baby Ser.). (ENG., Illus.). 24p. (J). (— 1). bds. 6.99 (978-0-375-85905-2(5), Golden Bks.) Random Hse. Children's Bks.

Wimmer, Sonja. The Word Collector. 2012. (ENG., Illus.). 32p. (J). (gr. k-2). (978-84-15241-34-8(8)) D P & G Military Pubs.

Yamada, Miho. Miyako from Tokyo. Camcam, Princesse, illus. 2014. (AV2 Fiction Readalong Ser.: Vol. 132). (ENG.). 32p. (J). (gr. -1-3). lib. bdg. 34.28 (978-1-4896-2268-6(3), AV2 by Weigl) Weigl Pubs., Inc.

Yoyo. Learning Words. 2005. 40p. bds. (978-90-5843-887-4(2)) YoYo Bks.

VOCAL CULTURE

see Voice

VOCATION, CHOICE OF

see Vocational Guidance

VOCATIONAL GUIDANCE

see also Blind—Education; Counseling; Deaf—Education; Educational Counseling; Job Hunting; Occupations; Professions

also subdivision Vocational Guidance under names of occupations, fields of endeavor, military services, and types of industries

Ames, Michelle. Librarians in Our Community. 2009. (On the Job Ser.). (Illus.). 24p. (J). (ENG.). pap. 8.25 *(978-1-4358-2458-4(X)*, 1300571); lib. bdg. 22.60 *(978-1-4042-8072-4(3)*, 1300571) Rosen Publishing Group, Inc., The. (PowerKids Pr.).

Anonymous. Book of Old-Time Trades & Tools. 2005. (Pictorial Archive Ser.). (ENG., Illus.). 320p. (gr. 3-7). per. 15.95 *(978-0-486-44342-3(6))* Dover Pubns., Inc.

Antill, Sara. 10 Ways I Can Help My Community. 2012. (I Can Make a Difference Ser.). (ENG., Illus.). 24p. (J). (gr. 2-5). pap. 8.25 *(978-1-4488-6363-1(5))*; lib. bdg. 22.60 *(978-1-4488-6202-3(7))* Rosen Publishing Group, Inc., The. (PowerKids Pr.).

Apel, Melanie. Cool Careers Without College for Film & Television Buffs. 2008. (Cool Careers Without College Ser.). (Illus.). 144p. (YA). (gr. 7-12). lib. bdg. 35.95 *(978-1-4042-1429-3(1))* Rosen Publishing Group, Inc., The.

—Cool Careers Without College for Film & TV Buffs. 2009. (Cool Careers Without College Ser.). 144p. (gr. 6-6). 66.50 *(978-1-61511-956-1(6))* Rosen Publishing Group, Inc., The.

Arment Jd, Laura B. Sixteen Things You Should Know about Work Now: A Guide for Young People. 2008. 48p. pap. 11.95 *(978-1-60145-569-7(0))* Booklocker.com, Inc.

Asher, Dana. Epidemiologists: Life Tracking Deadly Diseases. 2005. (Extreme Careers Ser.). (Illus.). 64p. (YA). (gr. 5-8). 31.95 *(978-0-8239-3633-5(3))* Rosen Publishing Group, Inc., The.

Berman, Ron. Future Stars of America. 2006. (Future Stars Ser.). (Illus.). 90p. (gr. 3-8). pap. 9.95 *(978-0-9741997-4-0(5))* Scobre Pr. Corp.

Beyer, Mark. Demolition Experts: Life Blowing Things Up. 2005. (Extreme Careers Ser.). (Illus.). 64p. (YA). (gr. 5-9). 31.95 *(978-0-8239-3365-5(2))* Rosen Publishing Group, Inc., The.

Bickerstaff, Linda. Careers in Nutrition. 2009. (Careers in the New Economy Ser.). 144p. (gr. 7-7). 63.90 *(978-1-61511-818-2(7))* Rosen Publishing Group, Inc., The.

—Oil Power of the Future: New Ways of Turning Petroleum into Energy. 2003. (Library of Future Energy Ser.). (Illus.). 64p. (YA). lib. bdg. 31.95 *(978-0-8239-3662-5(7))* Rosen Publishing Group, Inc., The.

Blackwell, Amy Hackney. Personal Care Services, Fitness & Education. 2008. (Great Careers with a High School Diploma Ser.). 114p. (C). (gr. 9). 32.95 *(978-0-8160-7045-9(8)*, Ferguson Publishing Co.) Facts On File, Inc.

Brezina, Corona. Careers as a Medical Examiner. 2009. (Careers in Forensics Ser.). 64p. (gr. 5-5). 58.50 *(978-1-61511-799-4(7)*, Rosen Reference) Rosen Publishing Group, Inc., The.

—Careers in Nanotechnology. 2009. (Cutting-Edge Careers Ser.). 64p. (gr. 7-7). 55.90 *(978-1-61512-100-7(5))* Rosen Publishing Group, Inc., The.

—Great Decision-Making Skills. (Work Readiness Ser.). 64p. 2009. (gr. 6-6). 58.50 *(978-1-60854-823-1(6))* 2008. (Illus.). (J). (gr. 3-7). lib. bdg. 31.95 *(978-1-4042-1422-4(4))* Rosen Publishing Group, Inc., The.

—Jobs in Sustainable Energy. 2010. (Green Careers Ser.). (Illus.). 80p. (YA). (gr. 7-12). lib. bdg. 33.25 *(978-1-4358-3569-6(7))* Rosen Publishing Group, Inc., The.

Brown, Marty. Webmaster. 2009. (Coolcareers. com Ser.). 48p. (gr. 5-8). 53.00 *(978-1-61511-985-1(X)*, Rosen Reference) Rosen Publishing Group, Inc., The.

Brown, Ruby. I Want to Be ... a Lion Tamer. Coburn, Alisa, illus. 2016. (ENG.). 22p. (J). bds. 8.99 *(978-1-61067-405-8(7))* Kane Miller.

Buell, Tonya. Careers with Successful Dot-Com Companies. 2005. (Library of e-Commerce & Internet Careers Ser.). (Illus.). 64p. (YA). (gr. 7-12). lib. bdg. 31.95 *(978-0-8239-3424-9(1))* Rosen Publishing Group, Inc., The.

—Cool Careers Without College for Web Surfers. (Cool Careers Without College Ser.). 2007. (Illus.). 144p. (J). (gr. 4-7). lib. bdg. 33.25 *(978-1-4042-0871-1(2))* 2005. (YA). (gr. 7-12). 35.95 *(978-1-4042-1092-9(X))* Rosen Publishing Group, Inc., The.

Burnett, Betty. Cool Careers Without College for Math & Science Wizards. 2009. (Cool Careers Without College Ser.). 144p. (gr. 6-6). 66.50 *(978-1-61511-959-2(0))* Rosen Publishing Group, Inc., The.

Burns, Monique. Cool Careers Without College for People Who Love to Make Things Grow. 2009. (Cool Careers Without College Ser.). 144p. (gr. 6-6). 66.50 *(978-1-61511-975-2(2))* Rosen Publishing Group, Inc., The.

Byers, Ann. Jobs As Green Builders & Planners. 2010. (Green Careers Ser.). (Illus.). 80p. (YA). (gr. 7-12). lib. bdg. 33.25 *(978-1-4358-3566-5(2))* Rosen Publishing Group, Inc., The.

Byrd-Hill, Ida. Me & My Big Career, Hill, Karen, ed. Hill, Kevin, illus. 2010. (ENG.). 24p. (J). 14.95 *(978-0-9829610-0-1(6))* Upheaval Media, Inc.

Calling All Innovators: A Career for You (Spring 2016 Set Of 4) 2016. (Calling All Innovators: a Career for You Ser.). (J). lib. bdg. 120.00 *(978-0-531-21679-8(9)*, Children's Pr.) Scholastic Library Publishing.

Caraccilo, Dominic. E-Tailing: Careers Selling over the Web. 2009. (Library of E-Commerce & Internet Careers Ser.). 64p. (gr. 5-5). 58.50 *(978-1-60853-587-3(8))* Rosen Publishing Group, Inc., The.

Career Ideas for Kids Set, 10-Volumes. 2007. (Career Ideas for Kids Ser.). (gr. 4-9). 296.55 *(978-0-8160-7422-8(4)*, Ferguson Publishing Co.) Facts On File, Inc.

Career Ideas for Kids Who Like Adventure & Travel. 2nd rev. ed. 2007. (Career Ideas for Kids Ser.). (Illus.). 208p. (gr. 4-9). 32.95 *(978-0-8160-6547-9(0)*, Checkmark Bks.) Facts On File, Inc.

The Career Resource Library. 2005. (Illus.). (gr. 7-12). lib. bdg. 638.40 *(978-0-8239-3910-7(3))* Rosen Publishing Group, Inc., The.

The Career Resource Library Set 2. 2005. (Illus.). (gr. 7-12). lib. bdg. 159.00 *(978-0-8239-3951-0(0))* Rosen Publishing Group, Inc., The.

The Career Resource Library Set 3. 2005. (Illus.). (gr. 7-12). lib. bdg. 159.00 *(978-0-8239-4066-0(7))* Rosen Publishing Group, Inc., The.

The Career Resource Library Set 4. 2005. (Illus.). (gr. 7-12). lib. bdg. 212.00 *(978-0-8239-3949-7(9))* Rosen Publishing Group, Inc., The.

The Career Resource Library Set 5. 2005. (Illus.). (gr. 7-12). lib. bdg. 238.50 *(978-0-8239-4065-3(9))* Rosen Publishing Group, Inc., The.

Careers in Focus: Personal Services. 2nd rev. ed. 2007. (Careers in Focus Ser.). (Illus.). 192p. (gr. 6-12). 32.95 *(978-0-8160-6592-9(6)*, Ferguson Publishing Co.) Facts On File, Inc.

Careers in the New Economy, 5 bk. set. 2005. (YA). (gr. 7-12). lib. bdg. 159.75 *(978-1-4042-0374-7(5))* Rosen Publishing Group, Inc., The.

Careers Set: Promising Careers, 8 vols. Incl. Careers in Alternative Medicine. Steinfeld, Alan. 192p. (YA). 2000. lib. bdg. 18.95 *(978-0-8239-2963-4(9)*, CAALME); Careers in Coaching. Nagle, Jeanne M. 192p. (YA). 2005. lib. bdg. 31.95 *(978-0-8239-2966-5(3)*, CACOAC); Careers in Starting & Building Franchises. Frisch, Carlienne A. 192p. (YA). 1999. lib. bdg. 34.60 *(978-0-8239-2781-4(4)*, CAFRAN); Careers in the Fashion Industry. Giacobello, John. 122p. (J). 1999. lib. bdg. 18.95 *(978-0-8239-2890-3(X)*, CAFASH); Exploring Careers in Social Work. Simpson, Carolyn & Simpson, Dwain. 192p. (YA). 1999. lib. bdg. 31.95 *(978-0-8239-2879-8(9)*, CASOWO); (gr. 7-12). (Illus.). Set lib. bdg. 135.60 o.p. *(978-0-8239-9085-6(0))* Rosen Publishing Group, Inc., The.

Careers That Count. 2015. (Careers That Count Ser.). (ENG.). 32p. (J). (gr. 4-4). pap., pap., pap. 360.00 *(978-1-4994-1274-1(6)*, PowerKids Pr.) Rosen Publishing Group, Inc., The.

Cassedy, Patrice, tr. Finance. 2003. (Careers for the Twenty-First-Century Ser.). (ENG., Illus.). 112p. (J). 30.85 *(978-1-59018-520-9(X)*, Lucent Bks.) Cengage Gale.

Cefrey, Holly. Career Building Through Machinima: Using Video Games to Make Movies. 2009. (Digital Career Building Ser.). 64p. (gr. 6-6). 58.50 *(978-1-61512-168-7(4))* Rosen Publishing Group, Inc., The.

—Career Building Through Music, Video, & Software Mashups. 2009. (Digital Career Building Ser.). 64p. (gr. 6-6). 58.50 *(978-1-61512-169-4(2))* Rosen Publishing Group, Inc., The.

—Race Car Drivers: Life on the Fast Track. 2005. (Extreme Careers Ser.). (Illus.). 64p. (YA). (gr. 5-8). 31.95 *(978-0-8239-3367-9(9))* Rosen Publishing Group, Inc., The.

Checkmark Books, creator. Communication Skills. 2nd rev. ed. 2007. (Mastering Career Skills Ser.). (Illus.). 144p. per. 12.95 *(978-0-8160-7115-9(2)*, Checkmark Bks.) Facts On File, Inc.

—Organization Skills. 2nd rev. ed. 2007. (Mastering Career Skills Ser.). (Illus.). 144p. per. 12.95 *(978-0-8160-7116-6(0)*, Checkmark Bks.) Facts On File, Inc.

—Research & Information Management. 2nd rev. ed. 2007. (Mastering Career Skills Ser.). (Illus.). 128p. per. 12.95 *(978-0-8160-7118-0(7)*, Checkmark Bks.) Facts On File, Inc.

Christen, Carol & Blomquist, Jean M. What Color Is Your Parachute? for Teens. 2015. lib. bdg. 28.15 *(978-0-606-36433-1(1))* Turtleback Bks.

Chui, David. Choosing a Career in the Post Office. 2005. (World of Work Ser.). (Illus.). 64p. (J). (gr. 7-12). lib. bdg. 31.95 *(978-0-8239-3242-9(7))* Rosen Publishing Group, Inc., The.

Clark, Betty. Choosing a Career in Real Estate. 2005. (World of Work Ser.). (Illus.). 64p. (YA). (gr. 7-12). lib. bdg. 31.95 *(978-0-8239-3246-7(X)*, WWREES) Rosen Publishing Group, Inc., The.

Cool Careers Without College, 8 bks., Set. Incl. Cool Careers Without College for People Who Love Everything Digital. Romano, Amy. lib. bdg. 35.95 *(978-1-4042-0748-6(1))*; Cool Careers Without College for People Who Love Houses. Beco, Alice. lib. bdg. 35.95 *(978-1-4042-0753-0(8))*; Cool Careers Without College for People Who Love Manga, Comics, & Animation. Glass, Sherri & Wentzel, Jim. lib. bdg. 35.95 *(978-1-4042-0754-7(6))*; Cool Careers Without College for People Who Love to Organize, Manage, & Plan. Greenberger, Robert. lib. bdg. 35.95 *(978-1-4042-0752-3(X))*; Cool Careers Without College for People Who Love to Write. Roza, Greg. lib. bdg. 35.95 *(978-1-4042-0750-9(3))*; Cool Careers Without College for People Who Love Video Games. Croce, Nicholas. lib. bdg. 35.95 *(978-1-4042-0747-9(3))*; People Who Love to Buy Things. Santos, Edson. lib. bdg. 35.95 *(978-1-4042-0751-6(1))*; (Illus.). 144p. (YA). (gr. 7-12). 2006. 2006. 266.00 *(978-1-4042-1015-8(6))* Rosen Publishing Group, Inc., The.

Cool Careers Without College: Set 2. 2016. (Cool Careers Without College Ser.). 00104p. (J). (gr. 7-7). 307.60 *(978-1-5081-7360-1(5)*, Rosen Young Adult) Rosen Publishing Group, Inc., The.

Cool Careers Without College: Set 3. 2017. (Cool Careers Without College Ser.). 112p. (gr. 12-12). 230.70 ***(978-1-4994-6632-4(3)***, Rosen Young Adult) Rosen Publishing Group, Inc., The.

Coolcareers.com, 8 bks. Incl. Hardware Engineer. Donelly, Karen. lib. bdg. 29.25 *(978-0-8239-3118-7(8)*, CCHAEN); Multimedia & New Media Developer. Mazor, Barry. lib. bdg. 29.25 *(978-0-8239-3102-6(1)*, CCMEDE); Software Designer. McGinty, Alice B. lib. bdg. 23.95 *(978-0-8239-3149-1(8)*, CCSODE); Web Entrepreneur. Oleksy, Walter. lib. bdg. 29.25 *(978-0-8239-3103-3(X)*, CCWEEN); Webmaster. Brown, Marty. lib. bdg. 23.95 *(978-0-8239-3111-8(0)*, CCWEMA); 48p. (YA). (gr. 5-8). 2000. (Illus.). Set lib. bdg. 191.60 o.p. *(978-0-8239-9089-4(3)*, CCCOCA, Rosen Reference) Rosen Publishing Group, Inc., The.

Coon, Nora. Teen Dream Jobs: How to Find the Job You Really Want Now! 2004. (Illus.). 132p. (YA). (gr. 8-12). per. 9.95 *(978-1-58270-093-9(1))* Beyond Words Publishing, Inc.

Cowan, Carla Romaine. E-Commerce Careers in Multimedia. 2005. (Library of e-Commerce & Internet Careers Ser.). (Illus.). 64p. (YA). (gr. 7-12). lib. bdg. 31.95 *(978-0-8239-3427-0(6))* Rosen Publishing Group, Inc., The.

Cowen, Carla Romaine. E-Commerce: Careers in Multimedia. 2009. (Library of E-Commerce & Internet Careers Ser.). 64p. (gr. 5-5). 58.50 *(978-1-60853-586-6(X))* Rosen Publishing Group, Inc., The.

Craig, Tom. Internet: Technology, People, Process. 2003. (Media Wise Ser.). 64p. (J). lib. bdg. 28.50 *(978-1-58340-257-3(8))* Black Rabbit Bks.

Creative Careers. 2014. (Creative Careers Ser.). 48p. (J). (gr. 4-8). 191.70 *(978-1-4824-1184-3(9))*; pap. 84.30 *(978-1-4824-1557-5(7))* Stevens, Gareth Publishing LLLP.

Croce, Nicholas. Detectives: Life Investigating Crime. 2009. (Extreme Careers Ser.). 64p. (gr. 5-5). 58.50 *(978-1-61512-390-2(3)*, Rosen Reference) Rosen Publishing Group, Inc., The.

—Detectives: Life of Investigating Crime. 2005. (Extreme Careers Ser.). (Illus.). 64p. (YA). (gr. 5-9). 31.95 *(978-0-8239-3796-7(8))* Rosen Publishing Group, Inc., The.

Cutting-Edge Careers, 6 bks., Set. Incl. Careers Creating Search Engines. Levin, Judith. (Illus.). (J). (gr. 3-7). 2007. lib. bdg. 31.95 *(978-1-4042-0957-2(3))*; Careers in Artificial Intelligence. Greenberger, Robert. (Illus.). (YA). (gr. 7-12). 2006. lib. bdg. 31.95 *(978-1-4042-0953-4(0))*; Careers in Biotechnology. Hall, Linley Erin. (Illus.). (J). (gr. 3-7). 2007. lib. bdg. 31.95 *(978-1-4042-0954-1(9)*, 1267025); Careers in Computer Gaming. Robinson, Matthew. (YA). (gr. 7-12). 2006. lib. bdg. 31.95 *(978-1-4042-0958-9(1))*; Careers in Nanotechnology. Brezina, Corona. (Illus.). (J). (gr. 3-7). 2007. lib. bdg. 31.95 *(978-1-4042-0955-8(7))*; Careers in Robotics. Kupperberg, Paul. (Illus.). (gr. 7-12). 2007. lib. bdg. 31.95 *(978-1-4042-0956-5(5))*; 64p. 2007. Set lib. bdg. 167.70 *(978-1-4042-0934-3(4))* Rosen Publishing Group, Inc., The.

Cutting-Edge STEM Careers. 2014. (Cutting-Edge STEM Careers Ser.). 128p. (YA). (gr. 9-12). 142.40 *(978-1-4777-7680-3(X))* Rosen Publishing Group, Inc., The.

Dalton, Sarah, et al, eds. Encyclopedia of Careers & Vocational Guidance, 5 vols., Set. 15th rev. ed. 2010. 4128p. (C). (gr. 9). 249.95 *(978-0-8160-8313-8(4)*, Ferguson Publishing Co.) Facts On File, Inc.

Design. 3rd rev. ed. 2010. (Careers in Focus Ser.). (Illus.). 192p. (gr. 6-12). 32.95 *(978-0-8160-8024-3(0)*, Ferguson Publishing Co.) Facts On File, Inc.

Digital Career Building, 12 vols. 2008. (YA). (gr. 7-12). Set. lib. bdg. 351.00 *(978-1-4042-1497-2(6))*Set 1. lib. bdg. 175.50 *(978-1-4042-1116-2(0))*Set 2. lib. bdg. 175.50 *(978-1-4042-1478-1(X))* Rosen Publishing Group, Inc., The.

Donovan, Sandra. Job Smarts: How to Find Work or Start a Business, Manage Earnings, & More. 2012. (USA TODAY Teen Wise Guides: Time, Money, & Relationships Ser.). (ENG., Illus.). 64p. (gr. 8-12). lib. bdg. 31.93 *(978-0-7613-7015-4(3))* Lerner Publishing Group.

Dorling Kindersley Publishing Staff. Careers. 2015. (ENG.). 320p. (J). (gr. 8-12). pap. 19.99 *(978-1-4654-2973-5(5)*, DK Children) Dorling Kindersley Publishing, Inc.

Draper, Allison Stark. Choosing a Career in the Pulp & Paper Industry. 2005. (World of Work Ser.). (Illus.). 64p. (YA). (gr. 7-12). lib. bdg. 31.95 *(978-0-8239-3333-4(4))* Rosen Publishing Group, Inc., The.

Dunn, Mary R. I Want to Be a Chef. 2009. (Dream Jobs Ser.). (Illus.). 24p. (YA). (gr. 2-5). lib. bdg. 22.60 *(978-1-4042-4471-9(9))* Rosen Publishing Group, Inc., The.

—Quiero Ser Chef. 2009. (Trabajos de Ensueño (Dream Jobs) Ser.).Tr. of I Want to Be a Chef. (SPA & ENG., Illus.). 24p. (J). (gr. 2-4). lib. bdg. 22.60 *(978-1-4042-8156-1(8)*, Editorial Buenas Letras) Rosen Publishing Group, Inc., The.

—Quiero Ser Diseñador de Modas. 2009. (Trabajos de Ensueño (Dream Jobs) Ser.).Tr. of I Want to Be a Fashion Designer. (SPA & ENG., Illus.). 24p. (J). (gr. 2-4). lib. bdg. 22.60 *(978-1-4042-8154-7(1)*, Editorial Buenas Letras) Rosen Publishing Group, Inc., The.

Ellis, Amy, des. Looking at Myself I. 2nd ed. 2003. (J). pap. *(978-1-887481-27-4(3)*, LAM1KIT) CFKR Career Materials, Inc.

—Looking at Myself I Answer Folder. 2nd ed. 2003. (J). pap. *(978-1-887481-28-1(1))* CFKR Career Materials, Inc.

Ellis, Amy, rev. Major-Minor Finder: College to Career Planner. 2nd ed. 2003. (YA). *(978-1-887481-38-0(9))* CFKR Career Materials, Inc.

Environment. 2011. (New Discovering Careers for Your Future Ser.). (Illus.). 128p. (gr. 4-9). 24.95 *(978-0-8160-8050-2(X)*, Ferguson Publishing Co.) Facts On File, Inc.

Extreme Careers Set 2. 2005. (gr. 5-8). 159.00 *(978-0-8239-3884-1(0))* Rosen Publishing Group, Inc., The.

Extreme Careers Set 3. 2005. (gr. 5-8). 159.00 *(978-0-8239-4050-9(0))* Rosen Publishing Group, Inc., The.

Facts on File, Inc. Staff. Adventure. 2010. (New Discovering Careers for Your Future Ser.). (Illus.). 128p. (gr. 4-9). 24.95 *(978-0-8160-8043-4(7)*, Ferguson Publishing Co.) Facts On File, Inc.

—Construction. 2010. (New Discovering Careers for Your Future Ser.). (Illus.). 128p. (gr. 4-9). 24.95 *(978-0-8160-8045-8(3)*, Ferguson Publishing Co.) Facts On File, Inc.

—Top Careers for Economics Graduates. 2004. (Top Careers Ser.). (Illus.). 368p. (gr. 9). pap. 14.95 *(978-0-8160-5566-1(1)*, Checkmark Bks.) Facts On File, Inc.

Facts on File, Inc. Staff, contrib. by. Top Careers for Art Graduates. 2004. (Top Careers Ser.). (Illus.). 368p. (gr. 9). pap. 14.95 *(978-0-8160-5565-4(3)*, Checkmark Bks.) Facts On File, Inc.

Farrell, Courtney. Green Jobs, 1 vol. 2011. (Inside the Industry Ser.). (ENG., Illus.). 112p. (J). (gr. 6-12). lib. bdg. 35.64 *(978-1-61714-801-9(6)*, Essential Library) ABDO Publishing Co.

Federal Forces: Careers As Federal Agents. 2015. (Federal Forces: Careers As Federal Agents Ser.). (ENG.). 32p. (J). (gr. 4-5). pap., pap., pap. 360.00 *(978-1-4994-1291-8(6)*, PowerKids Pr.) Rosen Publishing Group, Inc., The.

Ferguson. Business Managers. 2nd rev. ed. 2009. (Careers in Focus Ser.). 204p. (gr. 6-12). 32.95 *(978-0-8160-7296-5(5)*, Ferguson Publishing Co.) Facts On File, Inc.

—Careers in Focus: Armed Forces. 2008. (Careers in Focus Ser.). 204p. (gr. 6-12). 32.95 *(978-0-8160-7288-0(4)*, Ferguson Publishing Co.) Facts On File, Inc.

—Careers in Focus: Automotives. 2009. (Careers in Focus Ser.). 188p. (gr. 6-12). 32.95 *(978-0-8160-7300-9(7)*, Ferguson Publishing Co.) Facts On File, Inc.

—Careers in Focus: Nonprofit Organizations. 2008. (Careers in Focus Ser.). 188p. (gr. 6-12). 32.95 *(978-0-8160-7289-7(2)*, Ferguson Publishing Co.) Facts On File, Inc.

—Discovering Careers for Your Future: Library & Information Science. 2008. (Discovering Careers for Your Future Ser.). 91p. (gr. 4-9). 21.95 *(978-0-8160-7282-8(5)*, Ferguson Publishing Co.) Facts On File, Inc.

—Sports. 4th rev. ed. 2008. (Careers in Focus Ser.). 204p. (gr. 6-12). 32.95 *(978-0-8160-7287-3(6)*, Ferguson Publishing Co.) Facts On File, Inc.

Ferguson, creator. Earth Science. 2nd rev. ed. 2008. (Careers in Focus Ser.). (Illus.). 188p. (gr. 6-12). 32.95 *(978-0-8160-7272-9(8)*, Ferguson Publishing Co.) Facts On File, Inc.

Ferguson Career Resource Guide Set, 5-Titles: 10-Volumes. 2007. (Ferguson Career Resource Guide Ser.). (C). (gr. 9). 750.00 *(978-0-8160-7237-8(X)*, Ferguson Publishing Co.) Facts On File, Inc.

Ferguson Publishing. Encyclopedia of Careers & Vocational Guidance, 16th Edition, 5-Volume Set, 5 vols. 16th ed. 2014. (ENG., Illus.). 4128p. (J). lib. bdg. 249.95 *(978-0-8160-8503-3(X))* Facts On File, Inc.

Ferguson Publishing Staff. Career Discovery Encyclopedia. 7th rev. ed. 2009. 1728p. (gr. 4-9). 235.00 *(978-0-8160-7931-5(5)*, Ferguson Publishing Co.) Facts On File, Inc.

Ferguson Publishing Staff, contrib. by. Encyclopedia of Careers & Vocational Guidance. 2017. (J). ***(978-0-8160-8514-9(5)***, Ferguson Publishing Co.) Facts On File, Inc.

Ferguson Publishing Staff, creator. Cosmetology. 4th rev. ed. 2008. (Careers in Focus Ser.). (Illus.). 185p. (gr. 6-12). 32.95 *(978-0-8160-7271-2(X)*, Ferguson Publishing Co.) Facts On File, Inc.

—Public Relations. 2007. (Careers in Focus Ser.). (Illus.). 224p. (gr. 6-12). 32.95 *(978-0-8160-6574-5(8)*, Ferguson Publishing Co.) Facts On File, Inc.

Fields, Jennifer. Choosing a Career as a Nurse-Midwife. 2005. (World of Work Ser.). (Illus.). 64p. (YA). (gr. 7-12). lib. bdg. 31.95 *(978-0-8239-3293-1(1))* Rosen Publishing Group, Inc., The.

Fradin, Dennis Brindell & Fradin, Judith Bloom. Earning. 2010. (Money Smart Ser.). 64p. (gr. 4). 32.79 *(978-1-60870-123-0(9))* Marshall Cavendish Corp.

Franks, Katie. Dream Jobs, 6 bks., Set. Incl. I Want to Be a Baseball Player. (J). lib. bdg. 22.60 *(978-1-4042-3622-6(8))*; I Want to Be a Basketball Player. (J). lib. bdg. 22.60 *(978-1-4042-3621-9(X))*; I Want to Be a Movie Star. (YA). lib. bdg. 22.60 *(978-1-4042-3619-6(8))*; I Want to Be a Race Car Driver. (J). lib. bdg. 22.60 *(978-1-4042-3623-3(6))*; (Illus.). 24p. (gr. 2-5). 2007. Set lib. bdg. 127.50 *(978-1-4042-3598-4(1))* Rosen Publishing Group, Inc., The.

—Quiero Ser Beisbolista. 2009. (Trabajos de ensueño (Dream Jobs) Ser.). (SPA & ENG.). 24p. pap. 8.25 *(978-1-4358-3431-6(3))*; (Illus.). 22.60 *(978-1-4042-8159-2(2))* Rosen Publishing Group, Inc., The. (PowerKids Pr.).

Freedman, Jeri. Career Building Through Skinning & Modding. 2009. (Digital Career Building Ser.). 64p. (gr. 6-6). 58.50 *(978-1-61512-171-7(4))* Rosen Publishing Group, Inc., The.

—Careers in Child Care, 1 vol. 2015. (ENG.). 80p. (J). 34.25 *(978-1-4777-7884-5(5)*, Rosen Young Adult) Rosen Publishing Group, Inc., The.

—Careers in Emergency Medical Response Teams' Search & Rescue Units. 2009. (Careers in Search & Rescue Operations Ser.). 64p. (gr. 5-8). 58.50 *(978-1-61511-805-2(5)*, Rosen Reference) Rosen Publishing Group, Inc., The.

Frisch, Carlienne A. Everything You Need to Know about Getting a Job. 2005. (Need to Know Library). (Illus.). 64p. (YA). (gr. 7-12). lib. bdg. 31.95 *(978-0-8239-2961-0(2)*, NTGEJO) Rosen Publishing Group, Inc., The.

Furgang, Kathy. 20 Great Career-Building Activities Using Twitter. 2016. (Social Media Career Building Ser.). 00064p. (J). (gr. 7-7). 34.45 *(978-1-5081-7268-0(4))* Rosen Publishing Group, Inc., The.

Gard, Carolyn. Cool Careers Without College for People Who Love to Sell Things. 2009. (Cool Careers Without College Ser.). 144p. (gr. 6-6). 66.50 *(978-1-61511-979-0(5))* Rosen Publishing Group, Inc., The.

Gerry, Lisa M. 100 Things to Be When You Grow Up. 2017. (ENG., Illus.). 256p. (J). (gr. 3-7). pap. 9.99 *(978-1-4263-2711-7(0)*, National Geographic Children's Bks.) National Geographic Society.

Giacobello, John. Choosing a Career in the Toy Industry. 2005. (World of Work Ser.). (Illus.). 64p. (YA). (gr. 7-12). lib. bdg. 31.95 *(978-0-8239-3438-6(1))* Rosen Publishing Group, Inc., The.

Goetchius, Alex. Career Building Through Social Networking. 2009. (Digital Career Building Ser.). 64p. (gr. 6-6). 58.50 *(978-1-61512-172-4(2))* Rosen Publishing Group, Inc., The.

Goranson, Christopher. Careers as a Webmaster: Maintaining the Site. 2009. (Library of E-Commerce & Internet Careers Ser.). 64p. (gr. 5-5). 58.50 *(978-1-60853-579-8(7))* Rosen Publishing Group, Inc., The.

Gosling, Maureen, et al. You Can Be a Woman Movie Maker. I.t. ed. 2003. (Illus.). 80p. (J). 19.95 incl. DVD *(978-1-880599-64-8(3))*; pap. 14.95 incl. DVD *(978-1-880599-63-1(5))* Cascade Pass, Inc.

Graham, Amy. Be Smart about Your Career: College, Income, & Careers. 2014. (Be Smart about Money & Financial Literacy Ser.). 48p. (J). lib. bdg. 22.60 *(978-0-7660-4286-5(3))* Enslow Pubs., Inc.

Great Careers in the Sports Industry: Set 2. 2014. (Great Careers in the Sports Industry Ser.). 160p. (YA). (gr. 7-12). 245.70 *(978-1-4777-7522-6(6))* Rosen Publishing Group, Inc., The.

Great Careers in the Sports Industry: Sets 1-2. 2014. (Great Careers in the Sports Industry Ser.). 160p. (YA). (gr. 7-12). 409.50 *(978-1-4777-8098-5(X))* Rosen Publishing Group, Inc., The.

Great Careers with a High School Diploma Set, 10-Volumes. 2008. (Great Careers with a High School Diploma Ser.). (C). (gr. 9). 329.50 *(978-0-8160-7836-3(X)*, Ferguson Publishing Co.) Facts On File, Inc.

Greenberger, Robert. Careers in Artificial Intelligence. (Cutting-Edge Careers Ser.). 64p. (gr. 7-7). 2009. 55.90 *(978-1-61512-098-7(X))* 2006. (Illus.). (YA). lib. bdg. 31.95 *(978-1-4042-0953-4(0))* Rosen Publishing Group, Inc., The.

Greene, Meg. Careers in the National Guards' Search & Rescue Units. 2005. (Careers in Search & Rescue Operations Ser.). (Illus.). 64p. (YA). (gr. 5-8). lib. bdg. 31.95 *(978-0-8239-3636-0(0))* Rosen Publishing Group, Inc., The.

T
U
V

Gregory, Josh. Hydrologist. 2013. (21st Century Skills Library: Cool STEM Careers Ser.). (ENG., Illus.). 32p. (J). (gr. 4-8). 28.50 *(978-1-62431-001-0(X)*, 202455); pap. 14.21 *(978-1-62431-025-6(7)*, 202457) Cherry Lake Publishing.

Gustaitis, Joseph Alan. Arctic Trucker. 2010. (Benchmark Rockets: Dirty & Dangerous Jobs Ser.). 32p. (J). (gr. 3-6). 28.50 *(978-1-60870-169-8(7))* Marshall Cavendish Corp.

Haddock, Patricia. Careers in Banking & Finance. 2009. (Career Resource Library). 192p. (gr. 7-12). 63.90 *(978-1-60853-398-5(0))* Rosen Publishing Group, Inc., The.

Haegele, Katie. Cool Careers Without College for Nature Lovers. 2009. (Cool Careers Without College Ser.). 144p. (gr. 6-6). 66.50 *(978-1-61511-961-5(2))*; (Illus.). (J). 35.95 *(978-1-4358-5245-7(1))* Rosen Publishing Group, Inc., The.

—E-Advertising & E-Marketing: Online Opportunities. 2005. (Library of e-Commerce & Internet Careers Ser.). (Illus.). 64p. (YA). (gr. 7-12). lib. bdg. 31.95 *(978-0-8239-3426-3(8))* Rosen Publishing Group, Inc., The.

Hagler, Gina. Money-Making Opportunities for Teens Who Are Artistic. 2013. (Make Money Now! Ser.). (Illus.). 80p. (YA). (gr. 7-12). lib. bdg. 33.25 *(978-1-4488-9387-4(9))* Rosen Publishing Group, Inc., The.

Hall, Linley Erin. Careers in Biotechnology. 2009. (Cutting-Edge Careers Ser.). 64p. (gr. 7-7). 55.90 *(978-1-61512-099-4(8))* Rosen Publishing Group, Inc., The.

Hand, Carol. Getting Paid to Produce Videos. 2016. (Turning Your Tech Hobbies into a Career Ser.). 00080p. (J). (gr. 7-7). 35.75 *(978-1-5081-7292-5(7))* Rosen Publishing Group, Inc., The.

Harbeke, Dan. Get In! How to Market Yourself & Become Successful at a Young Age, Vol. 2003. (ENG.). 128p. pap. 37.00 *(978-1-57886-031-9(8))* Scarecrow Pr., Inc.

Harmon, Daniel E. Careers in Explosives & Arson Investigation. 2009. (Careers in Forensics Ser.). 64p. (gr. 5-5). 58.50 *(978-1-61511-803-8(9)*, Rosen Reference) Rosen Publishing Group, Inc., The.

—Jobs in Environmental Cleanup & Emergency Hazmat Response. 2010. (Green Careers Ser.). (Illus.). 80p. (YA). (gr. 7-12). lib. bdg. 33.25 *(978-1-4358-3570-2(0))* Rosen Publishing Group, Inc., The.

Harrison, Scott & Ross, Allison J. Choosing a Career in Waste Management. 2005. (World of Work Ser.). (Illus.). 64p. (YA). (gr. 7-12). lib. bdg. 31.95 *(978-0-8239-3240-5(0)*, WWWAMA) Rosen Publishing Group, Inc., The.

Hayhurst, Chris. Cool Careers Without College for Animal Lovers. 2009. (Cool Careers Without College Ser.). 144p. (gr. 6-6). 66.50 *(978-1-61511-955-4(8))* Rosen Publishing Group, Inc., The.

Heiman, Diane & Suneby, Liz. See What You Can Be: Explore Careers That Could Be for You! Wood, Tracey, illus. 2009. (ENG.). 108p. (gr. 4-7). spiral bd. 9.95 *(978-1-59369-277-3(3))* American Girl Publishing, Inc.

Heling, Kathryn. Clothesline Clues to Jobs People Do. 2014. 17.95 *(978-1-63419-654-3(6))* Perfection Learning Corp.

Heling, Kathryn & Hembrook, Deborah. Clothesline Clues to Jobs People Do. Davies, Andy Robert, illus. 2012. (ENG.). 40p. (J). (gr. -1-2). 14.95 *(978-1-58089-251-3(5))* Charlesbridge Publishing, Inc.

Henneberg, Susan. Money-Making Opportunities for Teens Who Like Working with Kids. 2013. (Make Money Now! Ser.). (Illus.). 80p. (YA). (gr. 7-12). lib. bdg. 33.25 *(978-1-4488-9385-0(2))* Rosen Publishing Group, Inc., The.

Hinton, Kerry. Cool Careers Without College for People Who Love Food. 2009. (Cool Careers Without College Ser.). 144p. (gr. 6-6). 66.50 *(978-1-61511-966-0(3))*; (Illus.). (J). lib. bdg. 35.95 *(978-1-4358-5246-4(X))* Rosen Publishing Group, Inc., The.

Hovanec, Erin. Careers as a Content Provider for the Web. 2009. (Library of E-Commerce & Internet Careers Ser.). 64p. (gr. 5-5). 58.50 *(978-1-60853-578-1(9))* Rosen Publishing Group, Inc., The.

Hovanec, Erin M. Careers as Content Provider for the Web. 2005. (Library of e-Commerce & Internet Careers Ser.). (Illus.). 64p. (YA). (gr. 7-12). lib. bdg. 31.95 *(978-0-8239-3418-8(7))* Rosen Publishing Group, Inc., The.

Howard, Ayanna. On the Job with an Engineer. 2003. (Adventures in Science Ser.). (J). lib. bdg. *(978-1-58417-059-4(X))* Lake Street Pubs.

Howell, Sara. Chemists at Work. 2017. (Scientists at Work Ser.). 32p. (J). (gr. 6-8). pap. 12.90 ***(978-1-68048-753-4(1)***, Britannica Educational Publishing) Rosen Publishing Group, Inc., The.

Hunt, Christopher. Victory after High School: Survive or Thrive —-You Choose! 2005. 144p. (YA). per. 16.95 *(978-0-9765973-4-6(9))* Adjust Communications.

Infobase Publishing Staff, creator. Writing. 3rd rev. ed. 2007. (Careers in Focus Ser.). (Illus.). 224p. (gr. 6-12). lib. bdg. 32.95 *(978-0-8160-6596-7(9)*, Ferguson Publishing Co.) Facts On File, Inc.

J.G. Ferguson Publishing Company Staff, contrib. by. Publishing. 3rd rev. ed. 2007. (Careers in Focus Ser.). (Illus.). 192p. (gr. 6-12). 32.95 *(978-0-8160-6572-1(1)*, Ferguson Publishing Co.) Facts On File, Inc.

JIST Publishing Editors. Young Person's Occupational Outlook Handbook. 7th ed. 2010. (ENG.). 336p. (J). pap. 19.95 *(978-1-59357-743-8(5)*, JIST Works) JIST Publishing.

JIST Works. Young Person's Occupational Outlook Handbook, Fifth Edition. 5th ed. 2004. (Illus.). 336p. pap. 19.95 *(978-1-59357-125-2(9)*, J1259, JIST Works) JIST Publishing.

Jones, Molly. Top 10 Tips for Planning for a Career. 2012. (Tips for Success Ser.). (ENG., Illus.). 64p. (J). (gr. 7-12). 31.95 *(978-1-4488-6863-6(7))* Rosen Publishing Group, Inc., The.

Jones, Sarah. Film. 2003. (Media Wise Ser.). (Illus.). 64p. (J). lib. bdg. 28.50 *(978-1-58340-256-6(X))* Black Rabbit Bks.

Kallen, Stuart A. Careers If You Like the Outdoors. 2017. (ENG.). 80p. (YA). (gr. 5-12). 39.93 ***(978-1-68282-140-4(4))*** ReferencePoint Pr., Inc.

Kamberg, Mary-Lane. Getting a Job in the IT Industry. 2016. (Job Basics: Getting the Job You Need Ser.). 80p. (J). (gr. 8-8). 35.75 *(978-1-4777-8556-0(6))* Rosen Publishing Group, Inc., The.

Kimbrell, Grady, et al. Entering the World of Work. 4th ed. 2006. (Exploring the World of Work Ser.). (ENG., Illus.). 464p. (gr. 9-12). stu. ed. 88.24 *(978-0-07-861458-3(9)*, 0078614589) McGraw-Hill Education.

Koster, Lorraine. Students Beware: Life Does Not Begin At 21. 2008. 108p. 22.95 *(978-0-595-50442-8(6))*; pap. 12.95 *(978-0-595-47703-6(8))* iUniverse, Inc.

Kupperberg, Paul. Careers in Robotics. 2009. (Cutting-Edge Careers Ser.). 64p. (gr. 7-7). 55.90 *(978-1-61512-101-4(3))* Rosen Publishing Group, Inc., The.

La Bella, Laura. What Degree Do I Need to Pursue a Career in Bookkeeping & Accounting?, 1 vol. 2015. (ENG.). 80p. (YA). 34.60 *(978-1-4777-7861-6(6)*, Rosen Young Adult) Rosen Publishing Group, Inc., The.

Learning a Trade, Preparing for a Career. 2014. (Learning a Trade, Preparing for a Career Ser.). 80p. (YA). (gr. 7-12). 274.00 *(978-1-4777-7738-1(5))* Rosen Publishing Group, Inc., The.

Levin, Judith N. Careers Creating Search Engines. 2009. (Cutting-Edge Careers Ser.). 64p. (gr. 7-7). 55.90 *(978-1-61512-097-0(1))* Rosen Publishing Group, Inc., The.

Levy, Janey. Careers in Criminal Profiling. 2009. (Careers in Forensics Ser.). 64p. (gr. 5-5). 58.50 *(978-1-61511-801-4(2)*, Rosen Reference) Rosen Publishing Group, Inc., The.

Liebman, Dan. Vaquero. 2003. (Quiero Ser.). (SPA., Illus.). 24p. (J). (gr. -1-2). pap. 5.99 *(978-1-55297-747-7(1)*, 9781552977477) Firefly Bks., Ltd.

Liebman, Daniel & Liebman, Dan. Guardian de Zoologico. 2003. (Quiero Ser.). (SPA., Illus.). 24p. (J). (gr. -1-2). pap. 5.99 *(978-1-55297-730-9(7)*, 9781552977309) Firefly Bks., Ltd.

Linn, Dennis, et al. What Is My Song? Miranda, Francisco, illus. 2005. 32p. (J). 16.95 *(978-0-8091-6722-7(0)*, 6722-0) Paulist Pr.

Loh-Hagan, Virginia. Mortician. 2015. (Illus.). 32p. (J). pap. *(978-1-63470-052-8(X))* Cherry Lake Publishing.

Lüsted, Marcia Amidon. The Vo-Tech Track to Success in Human Services. 2014. (Learning a Trade, Preparing for a Career Ser.). 80p. (J). (gr. 7-12). 34.25 *(978-1-4777-7732-9(6))* Rosen Publishing Group, Inc., The.

MacGregor, Lucy. Choosing a Career as an Entrepreneur. 2005. (World of Work Ser.). (Illus.). 64p. (YA). (gr. 7-12). lib. bdg. 31.95 *(978-0-8239-3329-7(6))* Rosen Publishing Group, Inc., The.

Mannino, Stephanie. Cool Careers Without College for People Who Love Crafts. 2004. (Cool Careers Without College Ser.). (Illus.). 144p. (YA). (gr. 7-12). lib. bdg. 35.95 *(978-0-8239-3785-1(2))* Rosen Publishing Group, Inc., The.

Mapua, Jeff. A Career in Customer Service & Tech Support, 1 vol. 2015. (ENG.). 80p. (J). 34.25 *(978-1-4777-7886-9(1)*, Rosen Young Adult) Rosen Publishing Group, Inc., The.

Mara, Wil. Robotics Engineer. 2015. (21st Century Skills Library: Cool STEAM Careers Ser.). (ENG., Illus.). 32p. (J). (gr. 4-7). pap. 14.21 *(978-1-63362-045-2(X)*, 205937) Cherry Lake Publishing.

Marcovitz, Hal. Teens & Career Choices. Developed in Association with the Gallup Organization Staff, ed. 2013. (Gallup Youth Survey: Major Issues & Trends Ser.: 14). 112p. (J). (gr. 7-18). 24.95 *(978-1-4222-2950-7(5))* Mason Crest.

Marlowe, Christie. Presenting Yourself: Business Manners, Personality, & Etiquette. 2013. (Earning $50,000 - $100,000 with a High School Diploma or Less Ser.: 14). 64p. (J). (gr. 7-18). 22.95 *(978-1-4222-2898-2(3))* Mason Crest.

Marsh, Carole. Heroes & Helpers Careers Book. 2003. (Heroes & Helper Ser.). 48p. (J). (gr. 2-8). pap. 9.95 *(978-0-635-01095-7(X))* Gallopade International.

Maybury, Richard J. Uncle Eric Talks about Personal, Career, & Financial Security. Williams, Jane A. & Daniels, Kathryn, eds. 2nd ed. 2004. ("Uncle Eric" Bk.: 1). (ENG., Illus.). 187p. pap. 14.95 *(978-0-942617-38-2(X))* Bluestocking Pr.

McAlpine, Margaret. Working with Children. 2004. (My Future Career Ser.). (Illus.). 64p. (gr. 3-7). lib. bdg. 27.00 *(978-0-8368-4241-8(3)*, Gareth Stevens Learning Library) Stevens, Gareth Publishing LLLP.

McGinty, Alice B. Software Designer. (Coolcareers. com Ser.). 48p. 2009. (gr. 5-8). 53.00 *(978-1-61511-984-4(1)*, Rosen Reference) 2004. (YA). lib. bdg. 29.25 *(978-0-8239-4086-8(1))* Rosen Publishing Group, Inc., The.

McGuire, Kara. All about the Green: The Teens' Guide to Finding Work & Making Money, 1 vol. 2014. (Financial Literacy for Teens Ser.). (ENG.). 64p. (gr. 6-7). lib. bdg. 33.99 *(978-0-7565-4372-3(X)*, CPB Grades 4-8) Compass Point Bks.

Messina, Noreen E. Now Hiring: A Story of Four Teens Finding Their First Jobs. 3rd ed. 2009. (ENG.). 126p. (gr. 6-14). 26.64 *(978-1-60525-177-6(1))* Goodheart-Willcox Pub.

—Teenwork: Four Teens Tell All: A Guide for Finding Jobs. 2005. (Illus.). 126p. (gr. 6-12). per. 12.75 *(978-1-59070-598-8(X))* Goodheart-Willcox Pub.

Meyer, Jared. Working in a War Zone: Military Contractors. 2009. (Extreme Careers Ser.). 64p. (gr. 5-5). 58.50 *(978-1-61512-422-0(5)*, Rosen Reference) Rosen Publishing Group, Inc., The.

Meyer, Susan. Careers As a Bookkeeper & Auditor. 2013. (Essential Careers Ser.). 80p. (YA). (gr. 7-12). 33.25 *(978-1-4777-1792-9(7))* Rosen Publishing Group, Inc., The.

Mezzanotte, Jim. Police. 2010. (Working Animals Ser.). 64p. (gr. 5-18). 28.50 *(978-1-60870-166-7(2))* Marshall Cavendish Corp.

Moore, Elizabeth. Keeping Us Safe, 1 vol. 2011. (Wonder Readers Emergent Level Ser.). (ENG.). (gr. -1-1). 32p. pap. 5.99 *(978-1-4296-7845-2(3))*; 8p. pap. 35.94 *(978-1-4296-8232-9(9))* Capstone Press of Coughlan Cos. (Wonder Readers).

Morkes, Andrew & McKenna, Amy. Nontraditional Careers for Women & Men: More Than 30 Great Jobs for Women & Men with Apprenticeships Through Phds. 2011. (ENG.). (J). pap. 19.95 *(978-0-9745251-9-8(7))* College & Career Pr., LLC.

Mozer, Mindy. Careers As a Commissioned Sales Representative. 2013. (Essential Careers Ser.). 80p. (YA). (gr. 7-12). 33.25 *(978-1-4777-1794-3(3))* Rosen Publishing Group, Inc., The.

Murdico, Suzanne J. Bomb Squad Experts: Life Defusing Explosive Devices. (Extreme Careers Ser.). 64p. (gr. 5-5). 2009. 58.50 *(978-1-61512-386-5(5)*, Rosen Reference) 2004. (Illus.). (YA). lib. bdg. 31.95 *(978-0-8239-3968-8(5))* Rosen Publishing Group, Inc., The.

Nagle, Jeanne M. Careers in Coaching. 2005. (Careers). (Illus.). 192p. (YA). (gr. 7-12). lib. bdg. 31.95 *(978-0-8239-2966-5(3)*, CACOAC) Rosen Publishing Group, Inc., The.

—Careers in Television. 2009. (Career Resource Library). 192p. (gr. 7-12). 63.90 *(978-1-60853-404-3(9))* Rosen Publishing Group, Inc., The.

—Choosing a Career as a Coach. 2005. (World of Work Ser.). (Illus.). 64p. (YA). (gr. 7-12). lib. bdg. 31.95 *(978-0-8239-3285-6(0))* Rosen Publishing Group, Inc., The.

Neale, Vivienne. Keep Your Options Open. (Illus.). x, 134p. (J). pap. 8.99 *(978-0-340-66088-1(0))* Hodder & Stoughton GBR. Dist: Trafalgar Square Publishing.

New Cool Careers Without College. 2013. (New Cool Careers Without College Ser.). 144p. (YA). (gr. 7-12). 215.70 *(978-1-4777-1831-5(1))* Rosen Publishing Group, Inc., The.

Nursing. 2nd rev. ed. 2007. (What Can I Do Now? Ser.). 208p. (YA). (gr. 7-12). 29.95 *(978-0-8160-6028-3(2))* Facts On File, Inc.

O'Donnell, Kerri. Careers in Modeling. 2005. (Career Resource Library). (Illus.). 192p. (YA). (gr. 7-12). lib. bdg. 34.60 *(978-0-8239-3183-5(8))* Rosen Publishing Group, Inc., The.

Olesky, Walter. Choosing a Career in Agriculture. 2005. (World of Work Ser.). (Illus.). 64p. (YA). (gr. 7-12). lib. bdg. 31.95 *(978-0-8239-3332-7(6))* Rosen Publishing Group, Inc., The.

Orr, Tamra B. Money-Making Opportunities for Teens Who Like Working Outside. 2013. (Make Money Now! Ser.). (Illus.). 80p. (YA). (gr. 7-12). lib. bdg. 33.25 *(978-1-4488-9383-6(6))* Rosen Publishing Group, Inc., The.

Owen, Ruth. Building Green Places: Careers in Planning, Designing, & Building. 2009. (Green-Collar Careers Ser.). (ENG., Illus.). 64p. (J). (gr. 5-8). pap. *(978-0-7787-4863-2(4))*; lib. bdg. *(978-0-7787-4852-6(9))* Crabtree Publishing Co.

Parks, Peggy J. Veterinarian. 2004. (EXPLORING CAREERS Ser.). (ENG.). (J). 27.50 *(978-0-7377-2068-6(9)*, Greenhaven Pr., Inc.) Cengage Gale.

—Writer. 2003. (Illus.). 48p. (J). 26.20 *(978-0-7377-2069-3(7)*, Greenhaven Pr., Inc.) Cengage Gale.

Pasternak, Ceel. Cool Careers for Girls in Travel & Hospitality. 2003. (ENG., Illus.). 120p. (YA). (gr. 8-17). pap. 13.95 *(978-1-57023-192-6(3))* Impact Pubns.

Payment, Simone. Cool Careers Without College for People Who Love to Travel. 2009. (Cool Careers Without College Ser.). 144p. (gr. 6-6). 66.50 *(978-1-61511-980-6(9))* Rosen Publishing Group, Inc., The.

Penn, Maya S. You Got This! Unleash Your Awesomeness, Find Your Path, & Change Your World. 2016. (ENG., Illus.). 224p. 15.99 *(978-1-5011-2371-9(8)*, North Star Way) Simon & Schuster.

Penna, Christine. Careers in Network Engineering. 2009. (Library of E-Commerce & Internet Careers Ser.). 64p. (gr. 5-5). 58.50 *(978-1-60853-581-1(9))* Rosen Publishing Group, Inc., The.

Perritano, John. The Most Disgusting Jobs on the Planet, 1 vol. 2012. (Disgusting Stuff Ser.). (ENG., Illus.). 48p. (gr. 3-4). lib. bdg. 31.99 *(978-1-4296-7532-1(2))* Capstone Press of Coughlan Cos.

Petley, Julian. Newspapers & Magazines. 2003. (Media Wise Ser.). (Illus.). 64p. (J). lib. bdg. 28.50 *(978-1-58340-258-0(6))* Black Rabbit Bks.

Rapine, Dawn. Federal Forces: Careers As Federal Agents Set. 2015. (Federal Forces: Careers As Federal Agents Ser.). (ENG.). 32p. (J). (gr. 4-5). 157.50 *(978-1-4994-0772-3(6)*, PowerKids Pr.) Rosen Publishing Group, Inc., The.

Rauf, Don. Working As a Hairstylist in Your Community. 2015. (Careers in Your Community Ser.). (ENG., Illus.). 80p. (J). (gr. 7-8). 34.25 *(978-1-4994-6121-3(6)*, Rosen Young Adult) Rosen Publishing Group, Inc., The.

Reeves, Diane Lindsey. Career Ideas for Kids Who Like Animals & Nature. Bond, Nancy, illus. 2nd rev. ed. 2007. (Career Ideas for Kids Ser.). 208p. (gr. 4-9). 32.95 *(978-0-8160-6539-4(X)*, Ferguson Publishing Co.) Facts On File, Inc.

—Career Ideas for Kids Who Like Math & Money. Bond, Nancy, illus. 2nd rev. ed. 2007. (Career Ideas for Kids Ser.). 208p. (gr. 4-9). 32.95 *(978-0-8160-6545-5(4)*, Ferguson Publishing Co.); per. 16.95 *(978-0-8160-6546-2(2)*, Checkmark Bks.) Facts On File, Inc.

—Career Ideas for Kids Who Like Sports. Bond, Nancy, illus. 2nd rev. ed. 2007. (Career Ideas for Kids Ser.). 208p. (gr. 4-9). lib. bdg. 32.95 *(978-0-8160-6551-6(9)*, Checkmark Bks.) Facts On File, Inc.

—Career Ideas for Kids Who Like Talking. Bond, Nancy, illus. 2nd rev. ed. 2007. (Career Ideas for Kids Ser.). 208p. (gr. 4-9). 32.95 *(978-0-8160-6553-0(5)*, Checkmark Bks.) Facts On File, Inc.

—Find Your Future in Science. 2016. (Bright Futures Press: Find Your Future in STEAM Ser.). (ENG., Illus.). 32p. (J). (gr. 4-6). 29.93 *(978-1-63471-898-1(4)*, 208913) Cherry Lake Publishing.

—Goofy Jobs. 2009. (Way Out Work Ser.). (Illus.). 48p. (gr. 3-5). 29.95 *(978-1-60413-130-7(6)*, Ferguson Publishing Co.) Facts On File, Inc.

—Gross Jobs. 2009. (Way Out Work Ser.). (Illus.). 48p. (gr. 3-5). 29.95 *(978-1-60413-131-4(4)*, Ferguson Publishing Co.) Facts On File, Inc.

—Gutsy Jobs. 2009. (Way Out Work Ser.). (Illus.). 48p. (gr. 3-5). 29.95 *(978-1-60413-133-8(0)*, Ferguson Publishing Co.) Facts On File, Inc.

Reeves, Diane Lindsey & Clasen, Lindsey. Career Ideas for Kids Who Like Writing. Bond, Nancy, illus. 2nd rev. ed. 2007. (Career Ideas for Kids Ser.). 208p. (gr. 4-9). 32.95 *(978-0-8160-6555-4(1)*, Ferguson Publishing Co.) Facts On File, Inc.

Reeves, Diane Lindsey & White, Kelly. Choose Your Own Career Adventure at the White House. 2016. (Bright Futures Press: Choose Your Own Career Adventure Ser.). (ENG., Illus.). 32p. (J). (gr. 4-6). 29.93 *(978-1-63471-916-2(6)*, 208985) Cherry Lake Publishing.

Reeves, Diane Lindsey, et al. Career Ideas for Kids Who Like Computers. Bond, Nancy, illus. 2nd rev. ed. 2007. (Career Ideas for Kids Ser.). 208p. (gr. 4-9). 32.95 *(978-0-8160-6543-1(8)*, Ferguson Publishing Co.) Facts On File, Inc.

Reina, Mary. Earn Money. 2015. (Money & You Ser.). (ENG.). 24p. (gr. k-1). pap. 5.95 *(978-1-4914-2299-1(8)*, Pebble Bks.) Capstone Press of Coughlan Cos.

Riley, Rowan. Great Careers with a High School Diploma: Hospitality, Human Services, & Tourism. 2008. (Great Careers with a High School Diploma Ser.). 93p. (C). (gr. 9). 32.95 *(978-0-8160-7048-0(2)*, Ferguson Publishing Co.) Facts On File, Inc.

Rissman, Rebecca. You're Hired! Business Basics Every Babysitter Needs to Know, 1 vol. 2014. (Babysitter's Backpack Ser.). (ENG., Illus.). 32p. (gr. 3-4). 27.99 *(978-1-4914-0766-0(2)*, Snap Bks.) Capstone Press of Coughlan Cos.

Rocha, Toni L. Careers in Magazine Publishing. 2009. (Career Resource Library). 192p. (gr. 7-12). 63.90 *(978-1-60853-399-2(9))* Rosen Publishing Group, Inc., The.

Roff, Jason T. Careers in E-Commerce: Software Development. 2009. (Library of E-Commerce & Internet Careers Ser.). 64p. (gr. 5-5). 58.50 *(978-1-60853-580-4(0))* Rosen Publishing Group, Inc., The.

Roff, Jason T. & Roff, Kimberly A. Careers in E-Commerce Software Development. 2005. (Library of E-Commerce & Internet Careers). (Illus.). 64p. (YA). (gr. 7-12). lib. bdg. 26.50 *(978-0-8239-3421-8(7))* Rosen Publishing Group, Inc., The.

Rose, Simon. Animal Caretaker. 2014. (J). *(978-1-4896-2982-1(3))* Weigl Pubs., Inc.

Ross, Allison J. Choosing a Career in Desktop Publishing. 2005. (World of Work Ser.). (Illus.). 64p. (YA). (gr. 7-12). lib. bdg. 31.95 *(978-0-8239-3295-5(8)*, WWDEPU) Rosen Publishing Group, Inc., The.

Ross, Allison J. & Harrison, Scott. Choosing a Career in Carpentry. 2005. (World of Work Ser.). (Illus.). 64p. (YA). (gr. 7-12). lib. bdg. 31.95 *(978-0-8239-3294-8(X))* Rosen Publishing Group, Inc., The.

Rowe, Brooke. What's Your Dream Job? 2015. (Illus.). 32p. (J). *(978-1-63470-035-1(X))* Cherry Lake Publishing.

Roza, Greg. Careers in the Military. 2005. (World of Work Ser.). (Illus.). 64p. (YA). (gr. 7-12). lib. bdg. 31.95 *(978-0-8239-3331-0(8))* Rosen Publishing Group, Inc., The.

—Great Networking Skills. (Work Readiness Ser.). 64p. 2009. (gr. 6-6). 58.50 *(978-1-60854-826-2(0))* 2008. (Illus.). (YA). (gr. 8-12). lib. bdg. 31.95 *(978-1-4042-1420-0(8))* Rosen Publishing Group, Inc., The.

Ryan, Jerry & Ryan, Roberta. Preparing for Career Success ExamView(r) Test Generator. 3rd ed. (YA). cd-rom 99.95 *(978-1-59357-211-2(5)*, J2115) JIST Publishing.

—Preparing for Career Success Student Activity Book. 3rd ed. 208p. (YA). pap. 8.95 *(978-1-59357-209-9(3)*, J2093) JIST Publishing.

Ryan, Peter K. Powering up a Career in Robotics. 2015. (Preparing for Tomorrow's Careers Ser.). (ENG., Illus.). 80p. (J). (gr. 7-8). 34.25 *(978-1-4994-6085-8(6)*, Rosen Young Adult) Rosen Publishing Group, Inc., The.

Sanna, Ellyn. Politician. 2004. (Careers with Character Ser.). (Illus.). 96p. (YA). (gr. 7-18). lib. bdg. 22.95 *(978-1-59084-320-8(7))* Mason Crest.

Santos, Edson. Cool Careers Without College for People who Love to Buy Things. 2009. (Cool Careers Without College Ser.). 144p. (gr. 6-6). 66.50 *(978-1-61511-971-4(X))* Rosen Publishing Group, Inc., The.

Sawyer, Sarah. Career Building Through Podcasting. 2009. (Digital Career Building Ser.). 64p. (gr. 6-6). 58.50 *(978-1-61512-170-0(6))* Rosen Publishing Group, Inc., The.

—Careers in DNA Analysis. 2009. (Careers in Forensics Ser.). 64p. (gr. 5-5). 58.50 *(978-1-61511-802-1(0)*, Rosen Reference) Rosen Publishing Group, Inc., The.

Schulz, Christian Dahl. Professional Sports Organizations. 2012. (Career Launcher Ser.). 130p. (C). (gr. 9). 34.95 *(978-0-8160-7964-3(1)*, Ferguson Publishing Co.) Facts On File, Inc.

Schwartz, Tina P. Writing & Publishing: The Ultimate Teen Guide. 2009. (It Happened to Me Ser.: 27). (ENG.). 282p. (gr. 9-18). instr.'s gde. ed. 50.00 *(978-0-8108-5647-9(6))* Scarecrow Pr., Inc.

Sheen, Barbara. Careers in Healthcare. 2014. (Exploring Careers). (ENG., Illus.). 80p. (J). lib. bdg. *(978-1-60152-648-9(2))* ReferencePoint Pr., Inc.

Snyder, Gail. Teen Guide to Starting a Business. 2016. (ENG.). 64p. (J). (gr. 5-12). lib. bdg. *(978-1-68282-088-9(2))* ReferencePoint Pr., Inc.

Sommers, Michael. Wildlife Photographers: Life Through a Lens. 2009. (Extreme Careers Ser.). 64p. (gr. 5-5). 58.50 *(978-1-61512-421-3(7)*, Rosen Reference) Rosen Publishing Group, Inc., The.

Spaulding, Jeffrey. Career Building Through Digital Sampling & Remixing. 2009. (Digital Career Building Ser.). 64p. (gr. 6-6). 58.50 *(978-1-61512-165-6(X))* Rosen Publishing Group, Inc., The.

Stair, Nancy. Choosing a Career in Mortuary Science & the Funeral Industry. 2005. (World of Work Ser.). (Illus.). 64p. (YA). (gr. 7-12). lib. bdg. 31.95 *(978-0-8239-3568-0(X))* Rosen Publishing Group, Inc., The.

Steffora, Tracey. Math on the Job. 2013. (Math on the Job Ser.). (ENG.). 24p. (gr. k-2). pap. 35.94 *(978-1-4329-7164-9(6))*; lib. bdg. 135.90 *(978-1-4329-7157-1(3))* Heinemann-Raintree. (Acorn).

Steinfeld, Alan. Careers in Alternative Medicine. 2009. (Career Resource Library). 192p. (gr. 7-12). 63.90 *(978-1-60853-396-1(4))* Rosen Publishing Group, Inc., The.

Sterngass, Jon. Great Careers with a High School Diploma: Armed Forces. 2008. (Great Careers with a High School Diploma Ser.). 121p. (C). (gr. 9). 32.95 *(978-0-8160-7042-8(3)*, Ferguson Publishing Co.) Facts On File, Inc.

Swaine, Meg. Career Building Through Interactive Online Games. 2009. (Digital Career Building Ser.). 64p. (gr. 6-6). 58.50 *(978-1-61512-167-0(6))* Rosen Publishing Group, Inc., The.

Sylvester, Kevin. Showtime: Meet the People Behind the Scenes. 2013. (ENG., Illus.). 88p. (J). (gr. 5-7). 21.95 *(978-1-55451-487-8(8)*, 9781554514878); pap. 12.95 *(978-1-55451-486-1(X)*, 9781554514861) Annick Pr., Ltd. CAN. Dist: Publishers Group West (PGW).

Syrewicz, Connor. Energizing Energy Markets: Clean Coal, Shale, Oil, Wind, & Solar. 2013. (Earning $50,000 - $100,000 with a High School Diploma or Less Ser.: 14). 64p. (J). (gr. 7-18). 22.95 *(978-1-4222-2894-4(0))* Mason Crest.

—Personal Assistant. 2013. (Earning $50,000 - $100,000 with a High School Diploma or Less Ser.: 14). 64p. (J). (gr. 7-18). 22.95 *(978-1-4222-2897-5(5))* Mason Crest.

Taylor, Allan & Parish, James Robert. Library & Information Science. 2009. (Career Opportunities Ser.). (Illus.). 364p. (C). (gr. 9-18). 49.50 *(978-0-8160-7546-1(8)*, Ferguson Publishing Co.) Facts On File, Inc.

Teen Vogue Staff. The Teen Vogue Handbook: An Insider's Guide to Careers in Fashion. 2009. (ENG., Illus.). 304p. (YA). (gr. 7-18). pap. 24.95 *(978-1-59514-261-0(4)*, Razorbill) Penguin Young Readers Group.

Tobey, Cheryl. Choosing a Career as a Model. 2005. (World of Work Ser.). (Illus.). 64p. (YA). (gr. 7-12). lib. bdg. 31.95 *(978-0-8239-3243-6(5))* Rosen Publishing Group, Inc., The.

Trabajo en Grupo Series, 6 bks., Set. 2003. (Trabajo en Grupo Ser.). (SPA & ENG., Illus.). (J). lib. bdg. 103.50 *(978-0-8239-6915-9(0)*, Editorial Buenas Letras) Rosen Publishing Group, Inc., The.

Turner, Cherie. Adventure Tour Guides: Life on Extreme Outdoor Adventures. 2009. (Extreme Careers Ser.). 64p. (gr. 5-5). 58.50 *(978-1-61512-383-4(0)*, Rosen Reference) Rosen Publishing Group, Inc., The.

—Stunt Performers: Life Before the Camera. 2005. (Extreme Careers Ser.). (Illus.). 64p. (YA). (gr. 5-8). 26.50 *(978-0-8239-3371-6(7))* Rosen Publishing Group, Inc., The.

Uschan, Michael V. Careers If You Like Government & Politics. 2016. (ENG.). 80p. (J). (gr. 5-12). lib. bdg. *(978-1-68282-000-1(9))* ReferencePoint Pr., Inc.

Webber, Diane. Shot & Framed: Photographers at the Crime Scene. 2007. (24/7: Science Behind the Scenes Ser.). (ENG., Illus.). 64p. (YA). (gr. 9-12). 29.00 *(978-0-531-12063-7(5)*, Watts, Franklin) Scholastic Library Publishing.

Weintraub, Aileen. Choosing a Career in Child Care. 2005. (World of Work Ser.). (Illus.). 64p. (YA). (gr. 7-12). lib. bdg. 31.95 *(978-0-8239-3241-2(9)*, WWCHCA) Rosen Publishing Group, Inc., The.

Weiss, Ellen & Fremont, Elenor. Odd Jobs: The Wackiest Jobs You've Never Heard Of. Ross, Damon, photos by. 2012. (ENG., Illus.). 80p. (J). (gr. 4-6). pap. 33.99 *(978-0-689-82934-5(5)*, Simon & Schuster/Paula Wiseman Bks.) Simon & Schuster/Paula Wiseman Bks.

When I Grow Up. 2014. (When I Grow Up Ser.). 24p. (J). (gr. k-2). pap. 48.90 *(978-1-4824-1593-3(3))* Stevens, Gareth Publishing LLLP.

Wilcox, Christine. Careers in Environmental Conservation. 2017. (ENG.). 80p. (YA). (gr. 5-12). ***(978-1-68282-203-6(6))*** ReferencePoint Pr., Inc.

Willett, Edward. Careers in Outer Space: New Business Opportunities. 2009. (Career Resource Library). 192p. (gr. 7-12). 63.90 *(978-1-60853-401-2(4))* Rosen Publishing Group, Inc., The.

Williams, Anna Graf, et al. The Family Guide to the American Workplace. Williams, Anna Graf, ed. 2003. (Illus.). 272p. per. 31.00 *(978-0-9705790-4-1(7)*, 866/332-5905) Learnovation, LLC.

Winning at Work Readiness. 2014. (Winning at Work Readiness Ser.). 64p. (YA). (gr. 9-12). 164.75 *(978-1-4777-7794-7(6))* Rosen Publishing Group, Inc., The.

Winters, Adam. Choosing a Career in the Fishing Industry. 2005. (World of Work Ser.). (Illus.). 64p. (YA). (gr. 7-12). lib. bdg. 31.95 *(978-0-8239-3330-3(X))* Rosen Publishing Group, Inc., The.

Wood, Alix. Explosives Expert, 1 vol., 1. 2014. (World's Coolest Jobs Ser.). (ENG.). 32p. (J). (gr. 3-6). pap. 10.00 *(978-1-4777-6012-3(1))*; lib. bdg. 26.25 *(978-1-4777-6011-6(3))* Rosen Publishing Group, Inc., The. (PowerKids Pr.).

The World of Work. 2005. (Illus.). (gr. 7-12). lib. bdg. 682.20 *(978-0-8239-3909-1(X))* Rosen Publishing Group, Inc., The.

The World of Work Set 1. 2005. (Illus.). (gr. 7-12). lib. bdg. 176.75 *(978-0-8239-9727-5(8))* Rosen Publishing Group, Inc., The.

The World of Work Set 2. 2005. (Illus.). (gr. 7-12). lib. bdg. 202.00 *(978-0-8239-9444-1(9))* Rosen Publishing Group, Inc., The.

The World of Work Set 3. 2005. (Illus.). (gr. 7-12). lib. bdg. 202.00 *(978-0-8239-9443-4(0))* Rosen Publishing Group, Inc., The.

The World of Work Set 4. 2005. (Illus.). (gr. 7-12). lib. bdg. 202.00 *(978-0-8239-9442-7(2))* Rosen Publishing Group, Inc., The.

The World of Work Set 5. 2005. (Illus.). (gr. 7-12). lib. bdg. 126.25 *(978-0-8239-9716-9(2))* Rosen Publishing Group, Inc., The.

Wright, Dixie Lee. Job Smarts: 12 Steps to Job Success. 2nd ed. 2003. 80p. pap., wbk. ed. 13.95 *(978-1-59357-028-6(7)*, JIST Works) JIST Publishing.

—Job Smarts Instructor's Manual: 12 Steps to Job Success for Students with Special Needs. 2nd ed. 2003. 96p. pap., tchr. ed. 29.95 *(978-1-59357-029-3(5)*, JIST Works) JIST Publishing.

Yomtov, Nel. Transportation Planner. 2013. (21st Century Skills Library: Cool STEM Careers Ser.). (ENG.). 32p. (J). (gr. 4-8). 28.50 *(978-1-62431-008-9(7)*, 202483); pap. 14.21 *(978-1-62431-032-4(X)*, 202485) Cherry Lake Publishing.

—Urban Planner. 2015. (21st Century Skills Library: Cool STEAM Careers Ser.). (ENG., Illus.). 32p. (J). (gr. 4-7). 29.93 *(978-1-63362-009-4(3)*, 205948) Cherry Lake Publishing.

VOCATIONS

see Professions

VOICE

see also Phonetics; Public Speaking; Singing; Speech

Comprehending & Verbalizing Visual Clues. 2003. 100p. (J). spiral bd. 28.00 *(978-1-886143-54-8(4))* Great Ideas for Teaching, Inc.

Feierabend, John M. The Book of Pitch Exploration: Can Your Voice Do This? 2004. (First Steps in Music Ser.). (ENG.). 33p. (J). pap. 11.95 *(978-1-57999-242-2(0))*; (Illus.). (gr. -1-2). pap. 12.95 *(978-1-57999-265-1(X)*, G-5276) G I A Pubns., Inc.

Verdick, Elizabeth. Voices Are Not for Yelling. Heinlen, Marieka, illus. 2015. (Best Behavior Ser.). (ENG.). (J). 24p. bds. 7.95 *(978-1-57542-500-9(9))*; 40p. (gr. -1-2). pap. 11.95 *(978-1-57542-501-6(7))* Free Spirit Publishing, Inc.

Verdick, Elizabeth. Voices Are Not for Yelling / la Voz No Es para Gritar. Heinlen, Marieka, illus. 2017. (Best Behavior Ser.). (ENG & SPA.). (J). 24p. bds. 7.95 ***(978-1-63198-194-4(3))***; 40p. (gr. -1-2). pap. 11.95 ***(978-1-63198-191-3(9))*** Free Spirit Publishing, Inc.

VOLCANOES

Anderson, Michael. Investigating Plate Tectonics, Earthquakes, & Volcanoes. 2011. (Illus.). 87p. (J). lib. bdg. 31.70 *(978-1-61530-504-9(1))* Rosen Publishing Group, Inc., The.

Arlon, Penelope. Volcanoes & Other Forces of Nature. 2017. (Lego Ser.). (ENG.). 64p. (J). (gr. 1-3). pap. 8.99 ***(978-1-338-14913-5(X))*** Scholastic, Inc.

Arlon, Penelope & Brown, Laaren. Scholastic Discover More Reader Level 3: Volcanoes. 2013. (Scholastic Discover More Reader Ser.). (ENG.). 32p. (J). (gr. 1-3). pap. 3.99 *(978-0-545-53378-2(3)*, Scholastic Reference) Scholastic, Inc.

Armentrout, David. Volcanoes. 2009. (ENG.). 32p. pap. 3.99 *(978-0-8249-1411-0(2)*, Ideal Pubns.) Worthy Publishing.

Armour, Cy. Volcanoes!, 1 vol. 2nd rev. ed. 2014. (TIME for KIDS(r) Nonfiction Readers Ser.). (ENG., Illus.). 24p. (J). (gr. 2-2). pap. 23.96 *(978-1-4807-1042-9(3))* Shell Educational Publishing.

—Volcanoes!, 1 vol. 2nd rev. ed. 2011. (Nonfiction Readers Ser.). (ENG.). 24p. (J). (gr. 2-2). pap. 6.99 *(978-1-4333-3615-7(4))* Teacher Created Materials, Inc.

Aronin, Miriam. Saving Animals from Volcanoes. 2011. (Rescuing Animals from Disasters Ser.). 32p. (YA). (gr. 2-5). lib. bdg. 25.27 *(978-1-61772-291-2(X))* Bearport Publishing Co., Inc.

Ashworth, William B., Jr. Vulcan's Forge anda Fingal's Cave: Volcanoes, Basalt, & the Discovery of Geological Time. 2004. (Illus.). per. 20.00 *(978-0-9763590-0-5(6))* Linda Hall Library.

Baltzer, Rochelle. Volcanoes, 1 vol. 2011. (Natural Disasters Ser.). (ENG., Illus.). 32p. (J). (gr. 2-5). 28.50 *(978-1-61783-035-8(6))* ABDO Publishing Co.

Bankier, William. The Mount St. Helens Volcano. Miller, Zachary N., ed. Taylor, Marjorie, illus. rev. ed. 2003. (Take Ten Ser.). 45p. (J). (gr. 4-12). pap. 4.95 *(978-1-58659-023-9(5))* Artesian Pr.

Barlow, Dave. Tome of Knowledge; Volcanoes. 2005. (ENG., Illus.). 20p. (YA). per. 4.95 *(978-0-9725230-9-7(X))* Wandering Sage Pubns., LLC.

Barr, Linda. Volcano! When a Mountain Explodes, 6 vols. 2003. (High Five Reading - Red Ser.). (ENG.). 48p. (gr. 3-4). pap. 54.00 *(978-0-7368-2836-9(2))*; (Illus.). per. 9.00 *(978-0-7368-2826-0(5))* Capstone Press of Coughlan Cos. (High Five Reading (RBL)).

Bauer, Marion Dane. Volcano! Wallace, John, illus. 2008. (Natural Disasters Ser.). (ENG.). 32p. (J). (gr. -1-1). pap. 3.99 *(978-1-4169-2549-1(X)*, Simon Spotlight) Simon Spotlight.

Baynard, Kate Holland & Baynard, Holland Callaway. Holland Goes to Pompeii: A brief look at the buried city & its famous volcano named Vesuvius. 2010. 16p. 12.50 *(978-1-4490-4697-2(5))* AuthorHouse.

Benchmark Education Company. Volcanoes (Teacher Guide) Nature's Awesome Power. 2004. *(978-1-4108-2586-5(8))* Benchmark Education Co.

Benoit, Peter. The Krakatau Eruption. 2011. (J). pap. *(978-0-531-29027-9(1))* Children's Pr., Ltd.

—The Krakatau Eruption. 2011. (True Bks.). 48p. (J). (gr. 3-5). 29.00 *(978-0-531-20628-7(9))*; (ENG., Illus.). pap. 6.95 *(978-0-531-28997-6(4))* Scholastic Library Publishing. (Children's Pr.).

Bodden, Valerie. Volcanoes. 2006. (Our World Ser.). (Illus.). 24p. (J). (gr. -1-3). lib. bdg. 16.95 *(978-1-58341-466-8(5)*, Creative Education) Creative Co., The.

Branley, Franklyn M. Volcanoes. Date not set. (J). lib. bdg. 16.89 *(978-0-06-028012-3(3))* HarperCollins Pubs.

Branley, Franklyn M. & Branley. Volcanoes. Lloyd, Megan, illus. 2008. (Let's-Read-And-Find-Out Science 2 Ser.). (ENG.). 40p. (J). (gr. k-4). pap. 5.99 *(978-0-06-445189-5(5))* HarperCollins Pubs.

Bredeson, Carmen. Fiery Volcano: The Eruption of Mount St. Helens. 2012. (Disasters — People in Peril Ser.). (Illus.). 48p. (J). (gr. 5-18). 25.27 *(978-0-7660-4015-1(1))* Enslow Pubs., Inc.

Brooks, Susie. Earthquakes & Volcanoes. 2016. (Where on Earth? Ser.). 32p. (gr. 5-4). 26.25 *(978-1-4994-2256-6(3)*, PowerKids Pr.) Rosen Publishing Group, Inc., The.

Buckwalter, Stephanie. Volcanoes: Disaster & Survival. 2005. (Deadly Disasters Ser.). (Illus.). 48p. (J). (gr. 4-10). lib. bdg. 25.27 *(978-0-7660-2384-0(2))* Enslow Pubs., Inc.

Bulletpoints Volcanoes & Earthquakes. 2005. (Illus.). (J). per. 4.99 *(978-1-933581-06-4(9))* Byeway Bks.

Caplan, Jeremy B., told to. Volcanoes! 2006. (Time for Kids Ser.). (ENG., Illus.). 32p. (J). (gr. 1-3). pap. 3.99 *(978-0-06-078223-8(4))* HarperCollins Pubs.

Chad, Jon. Science Comics: Volcanoes: Fire & Life. Chad, Jon, illus. 2016. (Science Comics Ser.). (ENG., Illus.). 128p. (J). pap. 12.99 *(978-1-62672-360-3(5)*, 9781626723603, First Second Bks.) Roaring Brook Pr.

Challen, Paul. Volcano Alert! 3rd rev. ed. 2011. (ENG., Illus.). 32p. (J). *(978-0-7787-1595-5(7))*; (Disaster Alert! Ser.: No. 19). pap. *(978-0-7787-1628-0(7))* Crabtree Publishing Co.

Claybourne, Anna. Investigating Volcanoes. 2010. (Extreme! Ser.). (ENG.). 32p. (gr. 3-4). pap. 47.70 *(978-1-4296-5132-5(6)*, Fact Finders) Capstone Press of Coughlan Cos.

Close, Edward. Volcanoes: Fire from Below: Rocks & Minerals, 1 vol., 1. 2014. (Discovery Education: Earth & Space Science Ser.). (ENG.). 32p. (gr. 3-6). 26.25 *(978-1-4777-6186-1(1)*, PowerKids Pr.) Rosen Publishing Group, Inc., The.

Cole, Joanna. Volcanoes & Earthquakes. 2014. (Magic School Bus Presents Ser.). lib. bdg. 17.20 *(978-0-606-36333-4(5))* Turtleback Bks.

Cole, Joanna & Jackson, Tom. Volcanoes & Earthquakes. Degen, Bruce & Bracken, Carolyn, illus. 2014. (Magic School Bus Presents Ser.). (ENG.). 32p. (J). (gr. 1-3). pap. 6.99 *(978-0-545-68584-9(2)*, Scholastic Paperbacks) Scholastic, Inc.

Collins. Collins Fascinating Facts - Earthquakes & Volcanoes. rev. ed. 2016. (Collins Fascinating Facts Ser.). (ENG., Illus.). 72p. (J). (gr. 1-3). pap. 10.99 *(978-0-00-816927-5(6))* HarperCollins Pubs. Ltd. GBR. Dist: Independent Pubs. Group.

Cook, Mauliola. Discover Hawaii's Volcanoes: Birth by Fire. Orr, Katherine, illus. rev. ed. 2010. (ENG.). 44p. pap. *(978-1-59700-849-5(4))* Island Heritage Publishing.

Cook, Mauliola & Orr, Katherine. Discover His Birth by Fire Volcanoes. 2010. 44p. 9.95 *(978-1-59700-830-3(3))* Island Heritage Publishing.

Cooper, John. Volcanoes. 2016. (Wise Up Ser.). 32p. (gr. 2-6). 31.35 *(978-1-62588-342-1(0)*, Smart Apple Media) Black Rabbit Bks.

Coss, Lauren. Volcanoes. (Illus.). 48p. (J). 2014. pap. 15.64 *(978-1-62403-007-9(6)*, Core Library) 2013. (ENG., (gr. 3-6). lib. bdg. 32.79 *(978-1-61783-942-9(6))* ABDO Publishing Co.

The Crying Mountain: 6 Small Books. (Greetings Ser.: Vol. 1). 32p. (gr. 3-5). 31.00 *(978-0-7635-1841-7(7))* Rigby Education.

The Crying Mountain: Big Book. (Greetings Ser.: Vol. 1). 32p. (gr. 3-5). 31.00 *(978-0-7635-3222-2(3))* Rigby Education.

Cunningham, Kevin. Volcanologist. 2015. (21st Century Skills Library: Cool STEAM Careers Ser.). (ENG., Illus.). 32p. (J). (gr. 4-7). 29.93 *(978-1-63362-568-6(0)*, 206456) Cherry Lake Publishing.

Dayton, Connor. Volcanic Rocks. (Rocks & Minerals Ser.). 24p. (gr. 2-3). 2009. 42.50 *(978-1-60852-503-4(1)*, PowerKids Pr.) 2007. (Illus.). (YA). lib. bdg. 22.60 *(978-1-4042-3688-2(0))* Rosen Publishing Group, Inc., The.

Dinaberg, Leslie. Volcanoes. 2006. (Reading Rocks! Ser.). (ENG., Illus.). 32p. (J). (gr. 2-5). 28.50 *(978-1-59296-739-1(6)*, 200725) Child's World, Inc., The.

Dobeck, Maryann. Volcanoes Nature's Awesome Power: Set Of 6. 2010. (Navigators Ser.). (J). pap. 50.00 net. *(978-1-4108-2571-1(X))* Benchmark Education Co.

—Volcanoes: Nature's Awesome Power & Volcanes: 6 English, 6 Spanish Adaptations: el poder asombroso de la Naturaleza. 2011. (ENG & SPA.). (J). 101.00 net. *(978-1-4108-5737-8(9))* Benchmark Education Co.

Dodd, Emily. Volcanoes - Collins Big Cat. 2015. (Collins Big Cat Ser.). (ENG., Illus.). 48p. (J). (gr. 3-4). pap. 9.95 *(978-0-00-812786-2(7))* HarperCollins Pubs. Ltd. GBR. Dist: Independent Pubs. Group.

Dorling Kindersley Publishing Staff. Ultimate Sticker Book: Volcano. 2017. (Ultimate Sticker Bks.). (ENG.). 32p. (J). (gr. 1-4). pap. 6.99 *(978-1-4654-5693-9(7)*, DK Children) Dorling Kindersley Publishing, Inc.

—Volcanoes. (DK Find Out! Ser.). (ENG., Illus.). (J). 2016. 64p. (gr. 1-4). pap. 10.99 *(978-1-4654-5425-6(X))* 2013. 56p. (gr. k-4). 10.99 *(978-1-4654-0909-6(2))* Dorling Kindersley Publishing, Inc. (DK Children).

Duffield, Wendell A. What's So Hot about Volcanoes? Black, Bronze, illus. 2011. 96p. (J). pap. 16.00 *(978-0-87842-574-7(8))* Mountain Pr. Publishing Co., Inc.

Duke, Shirley. Volcanoes. 2015. (ENG.). 48p. (gr. 3-6). 35.64 *(978-1-63430-423-8(3))* Rourke Educational Media.

Dwyer, Helen. Volcanoes! 2010. (Eyewitness Disaster Ser.). 32p. (J). (gr. 2-5). 28.50 *(978-1-60870-006-6(2))* Marshall Cavendish Corp.

Dyan, Penelope. It's Hot, Hot, Hot! a Kid's Guide to Hawaiian Volcanoes National Park. Weigand, John D., illus. 2013. 34p. pap. 11.95 *(978-1-61477-118-0(9))* Bellissima Publishing, LLC.

Earth's Crust. 2007. (Illus.). 48p. (J). (gr. 2-5). pap. 8.95 *(978-0-8225-6585-7(4))* Lerner Publishing Group.

Editors of Kingfisher. Violent Volcanoes. 2016. (It's All About... Ser.). (ENG., Illus.). 32p. (J). pap. 5.99 *(978-0-7534-7268-2(6)*, 9780753472682, Kingfisher) Roaring Brook Pr.

Encyclopaedia Britannica, Inc. Staff, compiled by. Britannica Illustrated Science Library: Volcanoes, 16 vols. 2008. (Illus.). (J). 29.95 *(978-1-59339-400-4(4))* Encyclopaedia Britannica, Inc.

Farndon, John. Extreme Volcanoes. 2017. (When Nature Attacks Ser.). (ENG., Illus.). 32p. (J). (gr. 3-6). 26.65 ***(978-1-5124-3220-6(2)***, Hungry Tomato (r)) Lerner Publishing Group.

Farndon, John & Riley, Peter D. Volcanoes & Earthquakes & Other Facts about Planet Earth: Bulletpoints. 2003. (Bulletpoints Ser.). (Illus.). 40p. (J). pap. 6.95 *(978-1-84236-238-9(0))* Miles Kelly Publishing, Ltd. GBR. Dist: Independent Pubs. Group.

Firestone, Mary. Volcanologist. 2005. (Weird Careers in Science Ser.). (Illus.). 80p. (gr. 5-8). lib. bdg. 25.00 *(978-0-7910-8702-2(6)*, Chelsea Hse.) Facts On File, Inc.

Fradin, Judith & Fradin, Dennis Brindell. Volcanoes. 2007. (Witness to Disaster Ser.). (ENG., Illus.). 48p. (J). (gr. 4-7). 16.95 *(978-0-7922-5376-1(0)*, National Geographic Children's Bks.) National Geographic Society.

Furgang, Kathy. Kilauea: Hawaii's Most Active Volcano. 2009. (Volcanoes of the World Ser.). 24p. (gr. 3-3). 42.50 *(978-1-60854-729-6(9)*, PowerKids Pr.) Rosen Publishing Group, Inc., The.

—Krakatoa: History's Loudest Volcano. 2009. (Volcanoes of the World Ser.). 24p. (gr. 3-3). 42.50 *(978-1-60854-730-2(2)*, PowerKids Pr.) Rosen Publishing Group, Inc., The.

—Mount Pelee: The Biggest Volcano Eruption of the 20th Century. 2009. (Volcanoes of the World Ser.). 24p. (gr. 3-3). 42.50 *(978-1-60854-731-9(0)*, PowerKids Pr.) Rosen Publishing Group, Inc., The.

—Mount Vesuvius: Europe's Mighty Volcano of Smoke & Ash. 2009. (Volcanoes of the World Ser.). 24p. (gr. 3-3). 42.50 *(978-1-60854-733-3(7)*, PowerKids Pr.) Rosen Publishing Group, Inc., The.

—Tambora: A Killer Volcamo from Indonesia. 2009. (Volcanoes of the World Ser.). 24p. (gr. 3-3). 42.50 *(978-1-60854-734-0(5)*, PowerKids Pr.) Rosen Publishing Group, Inc., The.

Ganeri, Anita. DK Readers L2: Eruption!: the Story of Volcanoes: Eruption!: the Story of Volcanoes. 2015. (DK Readers Ser.). (ENG., Illus.). 48p. (J). (gr. 1-3). 14.99 *(978-1-4654-3578-1(6)*, DK Children) Dorling Kindersley Publishing, Inc.

—Esos Violentos Volcanes. (Coleccion Esa Horrible Geografia).Tr. of Violent Volcanoes. (SPA., Illus.). 128p. (YA). (gr. 5-8). 9.95 *(978-84-272-2151-2(7)*, ML1621) Molino, Editorial ESP. Dist: Lectorum Pubns., Inc.

—Volcanes y terremotos/Earthquakes & Volcanoes. 2011. 16p. pap. *(978-607-404-319-8(1)*, Silver Dolphin en Español) Advanced Marketing, S. de R. L. de C. V.

—Volcanoes in Action. 2009. (Natural Disasters in Action Ser.). (ENG., Illus.). 48p. (gr. 5-8). pap. 11.75 *(978-1-4358-5134-4(X)*, Rosen Reference) Rosen Publishing Group, Inc., The.

Garbe, Suzanne. The Worst Volcanic Eruptions of All Time. 2012. (Epic Disasters Ser.). (ENG.). 32p. (gr. 3-4). pap. 47.70 *(978-1-4296-8510-8(7))*; pap. 8.29 *(978-1-4296-8016-5(4))*; lib. bdg. 27.99 *(978-1-4296-7658-8(2))* Capstone Press of Coughlan Cos. (Edge Bks.).

Gates, Alexander E. & Ritchie, David. Encyclopedia of Earthquakes & Volcanoes. 3rd rev. ed. 2007. (Science Encyclopedia Ser.). 368p. pap. 21.95 *(978-0-8160-7120-3(9)*, Checkmark Bks.) Facts On File, Inc.

Gedacht, Daniel C. Land & Resources in Ancient Rome. 2009. (Primary Sources of Ancient Civilizations Ser.). 24p. (gr. 3-3). 42.50 *(978-1-60851-559-2(1)*, PowerKids Pr.) Rosen Publishing Group, Inc., The.

George, Michael. Volcanoes: The Fiery Mountains. 2003. (LifeViews Ser.). (Illus.). 32p. (J). lib. bdg. *(978-1-58341-255-8(7)*, Creative Education) Creative Co., The.

Gilkerson, Patricia. My Adventure Inside a Volcano. 2006. 44p. (J). 8.99 *(978-1-59092-443-3(6))* Blue Forge Pr.

Gill, Maria. Volcanic Eruptions. 2009. (ENG., Illus.). 24p. pap. 4.99 *(978-1-59198-699-7(0))* Creative Teaching Pr., Inc.

Giulieri, Anne. Volcano Bubbles, 1 vol. Kreinberg, Sylvia, illus. 2012. (Engage Literacy Blue Ser.). (ENG.). 32p. (gr. k-2). pap. 5.99 *(978-1-4296-8978-6(1)*, Engage Literacy) Capstone Press of Coughlan Cos.

Gonzales, Doreen. Volcanoes. 2012. (Killer Disasters Ser.). (ENG., Illus.). 24p. (J). (gr. 3-6). 22.60 *(978-1-4488-7441-5(6))*; pap. 8.25 *(978-1-4488-7514-6(5))* Rosen Publishing Group, Inc., The. (PowerKids Pr.).

Gray-Wilburn, Renée. Volcanoes! Sotirovski, Aleksandar, illus. 2012. (First Graphics: Wild Earth Ser.). (ENG.). 24p. (gr. 1-2). pap. 35.70 *(978-1-4296-8373-9(2))* Capstone Press of Coughlan Cos.

Gray-Wilburn, Renée & Beehive Illustrations Staff. Volcanoes!, 1 vol. Sotirovski, Aleksandar, illus. 2012. (First Graphics: Wild Earth Ser.). (ENG.). 24p. (gr. 1-2). pap. 6.29 *(978-1-4296-7953-4(0))* Capstone Press of Coughlan Cos.

Green, Emily K. Volcanoes. 2011. (Blastoff! Readers: Learning about the Earth: Level 3 Ser.). (Illus.). 24p. (J). pap. 5.95 *(978-0-531-20845-8(1)*, Children's Pr.) Scholastic Library Publishing.

Green, Jen. Mount St. Helens. 2005. (Disasters Ser.). (Illus.). 32p. (gr. 2-6). lib. bdg. 26.00 *(978-0-8368-4498-6(X)*, Gareth Stevens Learning Library) Stevens, Gareth Publishing LLLP.

—Understanding Volcanoes & Earthquakes. 2008. (Our Earth Ser.). (Illus.). 24p. (YA). (gr. 1-4). lib. bdg. 22.60 *(978-1-4042-4276-0(7))* Rosen Publishing Group, Inc., The.

—Volcanoes Around the World. 2009. (Geography Now! Ser.). (ENG.). 32p. (J). (gr. 4-6). pap. 10.00 *(978-1-4358-2959-6(X)*, PowerKids Pr.); (YA). (gr. 3-6). lib. bdg. 26.50 *(978-1-4358-2873-5(9))* Rosen Publishing Group, Inc., The.

Group/McGraw-Hill, Wright. Forces of Nature: Level K, 6 vols., Vol. 2. (First Explorers Ser.). 24p. (gr. 1-2). 34.95 *(978-0-7699-1458-9(6))* Shortland Pubns. (U. S. A.) Inc.

—Volcanoes: The Hottest Spots on Earth, 6 vols. (Book2WebTM Ser.). (gr. 4-8). 36.50 *(978-0-322-04425-8(1))* Wright Group/McGraw-Hill.

Gullo, Arthur. Volcanoes. 2015. (J). lib. bdg. *(978-1-62713-513-9(8))*; (ENG.). 48p. (gr. 4-4). 31.36 *(978-1-5026-0221-3(0))* Cavendish Square Publishing.

Halpern, Monica. Rivers of Fire: The Story of Volcanoes. 2006. (Science Chapters Ser.). (ENG., Illus.). 48p. (J). (gr. 1-4). lib. bdg. 17.90 *(978-0-7922-5946-6(7)*, National Geographic Children's Bks.) National Geographic Society.

Hamilton, S. L. Volcanoes. 2012. 32p. 27.07 *(978-1-61783-264-2(2))* ABDO Publishing Co.

Harbo, Christopher L. The Explosive World of Volcanoes with Max Axiom, Super Scientist, 1 vol. Smith, Tod, illus. (Graphic Science Ser.). (ENG.). 32p. (gr. 3-4). 2008. pap. 8.10 *(978-1-4296-1770-3(5))* 2007. 30.65 *(978-1-4296-0144-3(2))* Capstone Press of Coughlan Cos. (Graphic Library).

—El Mundo Explosivo de los Volcanes con Max Axiom, Supercientífico. Strictly Spanish, LLC., tr. Smith, Tod G., illus. 2012. (Ciencia Gráfica Ser.). (SPA & ENG.). 32p. (gr. 3-4). lib. bdg. 30.65 *(978-1-4296-9237-3(5))* Capstone Press of Coughlan Cos.

Harper, Kristine. The Mount St. Helens Volcanic Eruption. 2005. (Environmental Disasters Ser.). (Illus.). 112p. (gr. 6-12). 35.00 *(978-0-8160-5757-3(5))* Facts On File, Inc.

Harris, Nicholas & Dennis, Peter. Volcano. 2006. (Illus.). 31p. (J). *(978-0-7607-7530-1(3))* backpackbook.

Harris, Nicolas. Volcanoes Through Time. 2009. (Fast Forward Ser.). 32p. (YA). (gr. 2-5). lib. bdg. 25.25 *(978-1-4358-2800-1(3))* Rosen Publishing Group, Inc., The.

Harris, Terrell. Volcanoes Change the Land. 2013. (InfoMax Readers Ser.). (ENG.). 24p. (J). (gr. 2-3). pap. 49.50 *(978-1-4777-2400-2(1))*; (Illus.). pap. 8.25 *(978-1-4777-2399-9(4))* Rosen Publishing Group, Inc., The. (Rosen Classroom).

Hawkins, John. Volcano Disasters. 2011. (Catastrophe! Ser.). (ENG., Illus.). 48p. (J). (gr. 5-9). lib. bdg. 29.25 *(978-1-4488-6008-1(3))* Rosen Publishing Group, Inc., The.

Hoffman, Steven M. Volcanoes & Earthquakes: Making & Moving Rock. 2011. (Rock It! Ser.). (Illus.). 24p. (J). pap. 8.25 *(978-1-4488-2704-6(3))*; lib. bdg. 22.60 *(978-1-4488-2559-2(8))* Rosen Publishing Group, Inc., The. (PowerKids Pr.).

Holt, Rinehart and Winston Staff. Holt Science & Technology Chapter 9: Earth Science: Volcanoes. 5th ed. 2004. (Illus.). pap. 12.86 *(978-0-03-030306-7(0))* Holt McDougal.

How a Volcano Is Formed: Level M, 6 vols. (Wonder Worldtm Ser.). 16p. 34.95 *(978-0-7802-2913-6(4))* Wright Group/McGraw-Hill.

Jennings, Terry J. Violent Volcanoes. 2009. (Amazing Planet Earth Ser.). 32p. (gr. 4-7). 31.35 *(978-1-59920-374-4(X))* Black Rabbit Bks.

Jerome, Kate Boehm & National Geographic Learning Staff. Volcanoes & Earthquakes. 2007. (Language, Literacy, & Vocabulary - Reading Expeditions Ser.). (ENG., Illus.). 32p. (J). pap. 17.95 *(978-0-7922-8874-9(2))* CENGAGE Learning.

Johnson, Rebecca L. & National Geographic Learning Staff. Surviving Volcanoes & Glaciers. 2007. (Reading Expeditions Ser.). (ENG., Illus.). 32p. (J). pap. 17.95 *(978-0-7922-8448-2(8))* CENGAGE Learning.

T U V

Kalman, Bobbie. Los Volcanes de la Tierra. 2009. (SPA.). 32p. (J). (978-0-7787-8244-5(1)); pap. (978-0-7787-8261-2(1)) Crabtree Publishing Co.

—Les Volcans. 2009. (FRE., Illus.). 32p. (J). pap. 9.95 (978-2-89579-250-5(X)) Bayard Canada Livres CAN. Dist: Crabtree Publishing Co.

Kalman, Bobbie & Aloian, Molly. Volcanoes on Earth. 2008. (Looking at Earth Ser.). (ENG., Illus.). 32p. (J). (gr. 3-7). pap. (978-0-7787-3215-0(0)); lib. bdg. (978-0-7787-3205-1(3)) Crabtree Publishing Co.

Katirgis, Jane & Ingber Drohan, Michele. Volatile Volcanoes. 2015. (Earth's Natural Disasters Ser.). (ENG.). 32p. (J). (gr. 3-4). pap. 10.52 (978-0-7660-6801-8(3)) Enslow Pubs., Inc.

Keedle, Jayne. Volcanoes. 2008. (Ultimate 10 Ser.). 48p. (YA). (gr. 5-9). lib. bdg. 31.00 (978-0-8368-9155-3(4)) Stevens, Gareth Publishing LLLP.

Kerrod, Robin. Exploring Science: Volcanoes & Earthquakes - an Amazing Fact File & Hands-On Project Book. 2014. (ENG., Illus.). 64p. (J). (gr. 3-7). 12.99 (978-1-86147-306-6(0), Armadillo) Anness Publishing GBR. Dist: National Bk. Network.

Koontz, Robin. The Science of a Tsunami. 2015. (21st Century Skills Library: Disaster Science Ser.). (ENG., Illus.). 32p. (J). (gr. 4-8). 29.93 (978-1-63362-483-2(8), 206840) Cherry Lake Publishing.

Kranz, Rachel. Mount St. Helens. 2011. (Early Connections Ser.). (J). (978-1-61672-643-0(1)) Benchmark Education Co.

Landau, Elaine. Volcanoes. 2009. (True Book(tm), a — Earth Science Ser.). (ENG., 48p. (J). Illus.). (gr. 2-5). 31.00 (978-0-531-16886-8(7)); (gr. 3-5). pap. 6.95 (978-0-531-21354-4(4), Children's Pr.) Scholastic Library Publishing.

Latta, Sara L. Lava Scientist: Careers on the Edge of Volcanoes. 2009. (Wild Science Careers Ser.). (Illus.). 128p. (J). (gr. 5-9). lib. bdg. 33.27 (978-0-7660-3049-7(0)) Enslow Pubs., Inc.

—Volcanologists: Examining Active Volcanoes. 2015. (Extreme Science Careers Ser.). (ENG., Illus.). 128p. (J). (gr. 7-7). lib. bdg. 37.27 (978-0-7660-6972-5(9)) Enslow Pubs., Inc.

Law, Felicia. Escape from the Volcano. 2015. (Science to the Rescue Ser.). (ENG., Illus.). 32p. (J). (gr. 3-6). (978-0-7787-1675-4(9)) Crabtree Publishing Co.

Lawrence, Ellen. How Do Volcanoes Make Rock? A Look at Igneous Rock. 2015. (Illus.). 24p. (J). lib. bdg. (978-1-62724-298-1(8)) Bearport Publishing Co., Inc.

Leavitt, Amie Jane. Anatomy of a Volcanic Eruption, 1 vol. 2011. (Disasters Ser.). (ENG.). 48p. (gr. 3-4). pap. 10.95 (978-1-4296-7357-0(5)); pap. 59.70 (978-1-4296-7358-7(3)); lib. bdg. 31.99 (978-1-4296-6022-8(8)) Capstone Press of Coughlan Cos.

Leigh, Autumn. Warning: Volcano! the Story of Mt. St. Helens. 2009. (Reading Room Collection 2 Ser.). 24p. (gr. 3-4). 42.50 (978-1-60852-000-8(5), PowerKids Pr.) Rosen Publishing Group, Inc., The.

Leitten, Emily. Lava. 2009. (Real Life Readers Ser.). 32p. (gr. 4-6). pap. 10.00 (978-1-4358-0231-5(4), Rosen Classroom) Rosen Publishing Group, Inc., The.

Levine, Shar & Johnstone, Leslie. Volcanoes! 2007. (Illus.). 46p. (J). (978-1-60311-062-4(3)) Mud Puddle, Inc.

Levy, Janey. World's Worst Volcanic Eruptions. 2009. (Deadly Disasters Ser.). 24p. (gr. 2-6). pap. 9.40 (978-1-4042-4536-5(7), Rosen Classroom); (gr. 2-3). 42.50 (978-1-61512-153-3(6), PowerKids Pr.); (Illus.). (J). lib. bdg. 22.60 (978-1-4042-4512-9(X)) Rosen Publishing Group, Inc., The.

Levy, Matthys & Salvadori, Mario. Earthquakes, Volcanoes, & Tsunamis: Projects & Principles for Beginning Geologists. 2009. (ENG., Illus.). 160p. (J). (gr. 4). pap. 14.95 (978-1-55652-801-9(9)) Chicago Review Pr., Inc.

Lindop, Laurie. Probing Volcanoes. 2003. (Science on the Edge Ser.). (Illus.). 80p. (gr. 5-18). lib. bdg. 26.90 (978-0-7613-2700-4(2), Twenty-First Century Bks.) Lerner Publishing Group.

Loria, Laura. Volcanic Processes. 2017. (J). **(978-1-5383-0030-5(3))** Rosen Publishing Group, Inc., The.

Lucarelli, Ariana. Volcanoes: Shaping Earth. 2013. (Rosen Readers Ser.). (ENG.). 24p. (J). (gr. 2-3). pap. 8.25 (978-1-4777-2412-5(5)); pap. 49.50 (978-1-4777-2414-9(1)) Rosen Publishing Group, Inc., The. (Rosen Classroom).

Lunis, Natalie. Volcanoes. 2011. (Early Connections Ser.). (J). (978-1-61672-653-9(9)) Benchmark Education Co.

Mallory, Kenneth. Diving to a Deep-Sea Volcano. 2006. (Scientists in the Field Ser.). (ENG., Illus.). 64p. (J). (gr. 5-7). 18.99 (978-0-618-33205-2(7)) Houghton Mifflin Harcourt Publishing Co.

Manatt, Kathleen. Volcanologist. 2007. (21st Century Skills Library: Cool Science Careers Ser.). (ENG.). 32p. (gr. 4-8). pap. 14.21 (978-1-60279-085-8(X), 200646) Cherry Lake Publishing.

Manatt, Kathleen G. Volcanologist. 2007. (21st Century Skills Library: Cool Science Careers Ser.). (ENG., Illus.). 32p. (gr. 4-8). lib. bdg. 28.50 (978-1-60279-050-6(7), 200018) Cherry Lake Publishing.

Mara, Wil. Why Do Volcanoes Erupt? 2009. (Tell Me Why, Tell Me How Ser.). 32p. (gr. 3-18). 29.93 (978-0-7614-3989-9(7)) Marshall Cavendish Corp.

Martin, Claudia. My Little Book of Volcanoes & Earthquakes. 2014. (Illus.). 64p. (J). (978-1-4351-5531-2(9)) Barnes & Noble, Inc.

Masters, Nancy Robinson. Volcanic Eruptions. 2012. (21st Century Skills Library: Real World Math Ser.). (ENG., Illus.). 32p. (J). (gr. 4-8). pap. 14.21 (978-1-61080-414-1(7), 201346); lib. bdg. 28.50 (978-1-61080-328-1(0), 201314) Cherry Lake Publishing.

Mattern, Joanne. Mauna Loa: El volcan en actividad más grande del mundo (Mauna Loa: World's Largest Active Volcano) 2009. (Maravillas naturales (Natures Greatest Hits) Ser.). (SPA.). 24p. (gr. 2-2). 42.50 (978-1-61514-364-1(5), Editorial Buenas Letras) Rosen Publishing Group, Inc., The.

—Mauna Loa: World's Largest Active Volcano. 2009. (Nature's Greatest Hits Ser.). 24p. (gr. 2-2). 42.50 (978-1-61514-841-7(8), PowerKids Pr.) Rosen Publishing Group, Inc., The.

Mayer, Cassie. Volcanoes. 2016. (Landforms Ser.). (ENG.). 24p. (gr. -1-1). pap. 6.29 (978-1-4846-3589-6(2), Acorn) Heinemann-Raintree.

McGlone, Catherine. Visitando Volcanes con una Científica/Visiting Volcanoes with a Scientist. 2008. (I Like Science! Bilingual Ser.). (ENG & SPA., Illus.). 24p. (J). (gr. 1-3). lib. bdg. 22.60 (978-0-7660-2979-8(4), Enslow Elementary) Enslow Pubs., Inc.

—Visiting Volcanoes with a Scientist. 2004. (I Like Science! Ser.). (Illus.). 24p. (J). lib. bdg. 22.60 (978-0-7660-2269-0(2)) Enslow Pubs., Inc.

Meachen Rau, Dana. Los Volcanes. 2007. (Maravillas de la Naturaleza Ser.). (SPA & ENG., Illus.). 31p. (J). (gr. 1-2). lib. bdg. 15.95 (978-0-7614-2808-4(9), Benchmark Bks.) Marshall Cavendish Corp.

—Volcanoes. 2007. (Wonders of Nature Ser.). (SPA & ENG., Illus.). 32p. (gr. 1-2). lib. bdg. 15.95 (978-0-7614-2670-7(1), Benchmark Bks.) Marshall Cavendish Corp.

—Volcanoes/Los Volcanes. 2007. (Wonders of Nature/Maravillas de la Naturaleza Ser.). (SPA & ENG., Illus.). 31p. (J). (gr. 1-2). lib. bdg. 15.95 (978-0-7614-2832-9(1), Benchmark Bks.) Marshall Cavendish Corp.

Meister, Cari. Volcanoes. 2015. (Illus.). 24p. (J). lib. bdg. 25.65 (978-1-62031-227-8(1)) Jump! Inc.

Melin, Jen. Examining Volcanic Eruptions. 2015. (ENG., Illus.). 48p. (J). lib. bdg. 24.95 net. (978-1-934545-68-3(6)) Oliver Pr., Inc.

Moore, David. Expl on Your Own the Island /Formed in 1 Day. 2009. (Explore on Your Own Ser.). (ENG., Illus.). 12p. (J). pap. 7.95 (978-0-7362-5522-6(2)) National Geographic School Publishing, Inc.

Mountains of Fire. 2017. (J). **(978-0-7166-3367-9(1))** World Bk., Inc.

Murray, Peter. Volcanoes. 2015. (Forces of Nature Ser.). (ENG.). 24p. (J). (gr. 2-5). 27.07 (978-1-63143-769-4(0), 208609) Child's World, Inc., The.

Nault, Jennifer. Volcanoes. 2016. (Illus.). 24p. (J). (978-1-5105-1154-5(7)) SmartBook Media, Inc.

—Volcanoes. 2004. (Science Matters Ser.). (Illus.). 24p. (J). lib. bdg. 24.45 (978-1-59036-211-2(X)) Weigl Pubs., Inc.

Nestor, John. Volcanoes. 2009. (21st Century Skills Library: Real World Math Ser.). (ENG.). 32p. (gr. 4-8). lib. bdg. 28.50 (978-1-60279-491-7(X), 200320) Cherry Lake Publishing.

Nuttall, Gina. Volcanoes & Earthquakes. 2004. (QEB Start Writing Ser.). (Illus.). 24p. (J). lib. bdg. 15.95 (978-1-59566-018-3(6)) QEB Publishing Inc.

O'Meara, Donna. Into the Volcano: A Volcano Researcher at Work. O'Meara, Stephen, photos by. 2007. (ENG., Illus.). 56p. (J). (gr. 3-7). 9.95 (978-1-55337-693-4(5)) Kids Can Pr., Ltd. CAN. Dist: Hachette Bk. Group.

O'Neal, Claire. A Project Guide to Volcanoes. 2010. (Earth Science Projects for Kids Ser.). (Illus.). 48p. (J). (gr. 4-7). lib. bdg. 29.95 (978-1-58415-868-4(9)) Mitchell Lane Pubs., Inc.

Oxlade, Chris. Volcanoes, 1 vol. 2014. (Learning about Landforms Ser.). (ENG.). 32p. (gr. 1-3). lib. bdg. 27.32 (978-1-4329-9537-9(5), Heinemann First Library) Heinemann-Raintree.

—Volcanoes. 2010. (Unpredictable Nature Ser.). (Illus.). 48p. (J). (gr. 3-18). lib. bdg. 19.95 (978-1-4222-2007-8(9)) Mason Crest.

Paiva, Johannah Gilman, ed. The Awesome Book of Volcanoes. Various, illus. 2013. (World of Wonder: the Awesome Book Of Ser.). (ENG.). 32p. (J). (gr. 3-7). 7.99 (978-1-77093-778-9(1)) Flowerpot Pr.

Person, Stephen. Devastated by a Volcano! 2010. (Disaster Survivors Ser.). (Illus.). 32p. (YA). (gr. 4-7). lib. bdg. 25.27 (978-1-936087-50-1(2)) Bearport Publishing Co., Inc.

Peterson, Judy Monroe. Braving Volcanoes: Volcanologists. 2009. (Extreme Scientists Ser.). 24p. (gr. 2-3). 42.50 (978-1-61512-449-7(7), PowerKids Pr.); (Illus.). (YA). lib. bdg. 22.60 (978-1-4042-4525-9(1)) Rosen Publishing Group, Inc., The.

Peyrols, Sylvaine, et al. Volcanoes. Peyrols, Sylvaine et al, illus. 2013. (My First Discoveries Ser.). (ENG.). 36p. (J). (-k). 12.99 (978-1-85103-420-8(X)) Moonlight Publishing, Ltd. GBR. Dist: Independent Pubs. Group.

Pierce, Terry. Volcanoes A to Z Coloring Book. Villalobos, Ethel M., illus. 2003. 24p. pap. 4.95 (978-1-57306-123-0(9)) Bess Pr., Inc.

Pirk, Wendy & Super Explorers. Volcanoes, 1 vol. 2017. (Super Explorers Ser.). (ENG., Illus.). 64p. (J). pap. 6.99 **(978-1-926700-70-0(8)**, 9781926700700) Blue Bike Bks. CAN. Dist: Lone Pine Publishing USA.

Prager, Ellen. Earthquakes & Volcanoes. 2008. (Restless Earth Ser.). (Illus.). 120p. (YA). (gr. 5-9). 35.00 (978-0-7910-9705-2(6)) Facts On File, Inc.

Prager, Ellen J. Volcano! Woodman, Nancy, illus. 2007. (Jump into Science Ser.). (ENG.). 32p. (J). (gr. -1-3). per. 6.95 (978-1-4263-0091-2(3), National Geographic Children's Bks.) National Geographic Society.

Prager, Ellen J. & National Geographic Kids Staff. Volcano! Woodman, Nancy, illus. 2016. (Jump into Science Ser.). (ENG.). 32p. (J). (gr. -1-3). pap. 7.99 (978-1-4263-2366-9(2), National Geographic Children's Bks.) National Geographic Society.

PRESS, Celebration. Blast Zone: The Eruption & Recovery of Mount St. Helens. 2003. (ENG.). (J). (gr. 6-8). pap. 37.95 (978-0-7652-3245-8(6), Celebration Pr.) Pearson Schl.

Prokos, Anna. Don't Blow Your Top! A Look Inside Volcanoes. Selivanova, Elena, illus. 2017. (Imagine That! Ser.). (ENG.). 32p. (J). (gr. 2-4). lib. bdg. 26.65 (978-1-63440-148-7(4)); 39.99 **(978-1-63440-160-9(3))** Red Chair Pr.

QEB Start Reading & Writing National Book Stores Edition: Volcanoes & Earthquakes. 2006. (J). per. (978-1-59566-265-1(0)) QEB Publishing Inc.

René, Ellen. Investigating Volcanic Eruptions. 2009. (Science Detectives Ser.). 24p. (gr. 2-3). 42.50 (978-1-60853-014-4(0), PowerKids Pr.); (Illus.). (J). lib. bdg. 22.60 (978-1-4042-4481-8(6)) Rosen Publishing Group, Inc., The.

Rice, William B. Los Volcanes, 1 vol. rev. ed. 2010. (Science Readers: a Closer Look Ser.). (SPA., Illus.). 32p. (J). (gr. 2-3). pap. 8.99 (978-1-4333-2154-2(8)) Shell Educational Publishing.

Riley, Gail Blasser. Volcano! The 1980 Mount St. Helens Eruption. 2006. (X-Treme Disasters That Changed America Ser.). (Illus.). 32p. (J). (gr. 2-5). lib. bdg. 25.27 (978-1-59716-072-8(5)) Bearport Publishing Co., Inc.

Riley, Joelle. Volcanoes. 2008. pap. 40.95 (978-0-8225-9446-8(3)); (ENG., Illus.). 32p. lib. bdg. 22.60 (978-0-8225-7909-0(X), Lerner Pubns.) Lerner Publishing Group.

Rosenberg, Pam. Volcano Explorers, 1 vol. 2011. (Landform Adventurers Ser.). (ENG.). 32p. (gr. 1-2). pap. 8.29 (978-1-4109-4148-0(5)); 29.99 (978-1-4109-4141-1(8)) Heinemann-Raintree. (Read Me!).

Rowe, Brooke. Building a Volcano. Bane, Jeff, illus. 2016. (My Early Library: My Science Fun Ser.). (ENG.). 24p. (J). (gr. k-1). 28.50 (978-1-63471-025-1(8), 208180) Cherry Lake Publishing.

Royston, Angela. The Science of Volcanoes. 2013. (Nature's Wrath: the Science Behind Natural Disasters Ser.). (Illus.). 48p. (gr. 4-6). 31.95 (978-1-4339-8671-0(X)); pap. 14.05 (978-1-4339-8672-7(8)) Stevens, Gareth Publishing LLLP. (Gareth Stevens Learning Library).

Rubin, Ken. Volcanoes & Earthquakes. 2007. (Insiders Ser.). (ENG., Illus.). 64p. (J). (gr. 3-7). 17.99 (978-1-4169-3862-0(1), Simon & Schuster Bks. For Young Readers) Simon & Schuster Bks. For Young Readers.

Rusch, Elizabeth. Eruption! Volcanoes & the Science of Saving Lives. Uhlman, Tom, illus. 2017. (Scientists in the Field Ser.). (ENG.). 80p. (J). (gr. 5-7). pap. 9.99 (978-0-544-93245-6(5), HMH Books For Young Readers) Houghton Mifflin Harcourt Publishing Co.

—Volcano Rising. Swan, Susan, illus. 2013. (ENG.). 32p. (J). (gr. 1-4). 17.95 (978-1-58089-408-1(9)); pap. 7.95 (978-1-58089-409-8(7)) Charlesbridge Publishing, Inc.

—Will It Blow? Lewis, K. E., illus. 2017. (ENG.). 48p. (J). (gr. 1-4). pap. 14.99 (978-1-63217-110-8(4), Little Bigfoot) Sasquatch Bks.

Rustad, Martha E. H. Volcanoes, 1 vol. 2014. (Little Scientist Ser.). (ENG., Illus.). 32p. (gr. 1-2). 6.95 (978-1-4765-5270-5(3)) Capstone Press of Coughlan Cos.

Schreiber, Anne. Volcanoes! 2008. (Readers Ser.). (ENG., Illus.). 32p. (J). (gr. k-3). pap. 3.99 (978-1-4263-0285-5(1)); lib. bdg. 13.90 (978-1-4263-0287-9(8)) National Geographic Society. (National Geographic Children's Bks.).

—Volcanoes (1 Hardcover/1 CD) 2017. (National Geographic Kids Ser.). (ENG.). (J). 29.95 **(978-1-4301-2669-0(8))** Live Oak Media.

—Volcanoes (1 Paperback/1 CD) 2017. (National Geographic Kids Ser.). (ENG.). (J). pap. 19.95 **(978-1-4301-2668-3(X))** Live Oak Media.

—Volcanoes (4 Paperbacks/1 CD), 4 vols. 2017. (National Geographic Kids Ser.). (ENG.). (J). pap., pap. 31.95 **(978-1-4301-2670-6(1))** Live Oak Media.

Schuh, Mari C. Volcanoes. 2016. (Earth in Action Ser.).Tr. of Volcanes. (ENG.). 24p. pap. 6.95 (978-1-5157-6199-0(1), Pebble Plus) Capstone Press of Coughlan Cos.

—Volcanoes. Translation Services Staff & Translations.com Staff, trs. from ENG. 2010. (Tierra en Acción/Earth in Action Ser.).Tr. of Volcanes. (SPA, ENG & MUL.). 24p. (gr. k-1). lib. bdg. 26.65 (978-1-4296-5357-2(4)) Capstone Press of Coughlan Cos.

The Science of a Volcanic Eruption. 2014. (21st Century Skills Library: Disaster Science Ser.). (ENG., Illus.). 32p. (J). (gr. 4-8). 28.50 (978-1-63137-628-3(4), 205295) Cherry Lake Publishing.

Sengupta, Monalisa. Volcanoes & Earthquakes. (Wild Nature Ser.). 48p. 2009. (gr. 4-5). 53.00 (978-1-60854-795-1(7), PowerKids Pr.) 2007. (Illus.). (YA). (gr. 3-6). lib. bdg. 29.25 (978-1-4042-3901-2(4)) Rosen Publishing Group, Inc., The.

Senior, Kathryn. Volcanoes. 2005. (What on Earth? Ser.). (ENG., Illus.). 32p. (J). (gr. 2-4). lib. bdg. 25.50 (978-0-516-25324-4(7), Children's Pr.) Scholastic Library Publishing.

Shone, Rob. Volcanoes. (Graphic Natural Disasters Ser.). (ENG.). 48p. (gr. 5-5). 2009. (YA). 58.50 (978-1-61513-008-5(X), Rosen Reference) 2007. (Illus.). pap. 14.05 (978-1-4042-1975-5(7)) Rosen Publishing Group, Inc., The.

—Volcanoes. Riley, Terry, illus. 2007. (Graphic Natural Disasters Ser.). (ENG.). 48p. (J). (gr. 5-9). lib. bdg. 31.95 (978-1-4042-1988-5(9)) Rosen Publishing Group, Inc., The.

Sillet, Helen. The Awesome Power of Volcanoes & Earthquakes. 2005. (YA). pap. 12.95 (978-1-4105-0421-0(2)); cd-rom (978-1-4105-0423-4(9)) Johnston, Don Inc.

—Understanding Volcanoes & Earthquakes. 2005. (YA). pap. 12.95 (978-1-4105-0417-3(4)); cd-rom (978-1-4105-0419-7(0)) Johnston, Don Inc.

Silverstein, Alvin, et al. Volcanoes: The Science Behind Fiery Eruptions. 2009. (Science Behind Natural Disasters Ser.). (Illus.). 48p. (J). (gr. 5-9). lib. bdg. 25.27 (978-0-7660-2972-9(7)) Enslow Pubs., Inc.

Simon, Seymour. Volcanoes. 2006. (ENG., Illus.). 32p. (J). (gr. k-4). pap. 6.99 (978-0-06-087717-0(0), Collins) HarperCollins Pubs.

—Volcanoes. 2006. (Illus.). 31p. (gr. k-4). 17.00 (978-0-7569-6744-4(9)) Perfection Learning Corp.

Sisk, Maeve T. Mount Terror. 2014. (Scariest Places on Earth Ser.). 24p. (J). (gr. 2-5). 22.60 (978-1-4824-1156-0(3)) Stevens, Gareth Publishing LLLP.

Smith, Kelly. How Hot Is Lava? And Other Questions about Volcanoes. 2016. (Good Question! Ser.). (ENG., Illus.). 40p. (J). (gr. 1). 12.95 (978-1-4549-1600-0(1)) Sterling Publishing Co., Inc.

Smith, Paula. Earthquakes, Eruptions, & Other Events That Change Earth. 2015. (Earth's Processes Close-Up Ser.). (ENG., Illus.). 24p. (J). (gr. k-3). (978-0-7787-1725-6(9)) Crabtree Publishing Co.

Souza, D. M. Volcanoes Inside & Out. Drew-Brook, Deborah & Cormack, Allan, illus. 2006. (On My Own Science Ser.). (ENG.). 48p. (gr. 2-4). per. 6.95 (978-1-57505-853-5(7)) Lerner Publishing Group.

Souza, Dorothy M. Volcanoes Inside & Out. Cormack, Allan & Cormack, Deborah Drew Brook, illus. 2005. (On My Own Science Ser.). 48p. (J). (gr. 3-7). lib. bdg. 25.26 (978-1-57505-761-3(1)) Lerner Publishing Group.

Spilsbury, Louise & Spilsbury, Richard. Violent Volcanoes, 1 vol. 2nd ed. 2010. (Awesome Forces of Nature Ser.). (ENG., Illus.). 32p. (gr. 3-6). 33.32 (978-1-4329-3783-6(9)); pap. 8.29 (978-1-4329-3790-4(1)) Heinemann-Raintree. (Heinemann InfoSearch).

Spilsbury, Richard & Spilsbury, Louise. Escape the Volcano. 2015. (Science Adventures Ser.). (ENG., Illus.). 32p. (J). (gr. 3-7). 31.35 (978-1-62588-146-5(0)) Black Rabbit Bks.

Squire, Ann O. Volcanic Eruptions. 2016. (True Book(tm), a — Extreme Earth Ser.). (ENG., Illus.). 48p. (J). lib. bdg. 31.00 (978-0-531-22299-7(3), Children's Pr.) Scholastic Library Publishing.

Stamper, Judith Bauer. Volcanoes. 2010. (Illus.). 32p. (J). pap. (978-0-545-28543-8(7)) Scholastic, Inc.

—Voyage to the Volcano. Speirs, John, illus. 2003. (Magic School Bus Ser.: 15). (ENG.). 96p. (J). (gr. -1-3). mass mkt. 4.99 (978-0-439-42935-1(8)) Scholastic, Inc.

Stamper, Judith Bauer & Stamper, Judith. Voyage to the Volcano. 2003. (Magic School Bus Chapter Bks.: 15). (gr. 3-6). lib. bdg. 14.75 (978-0-613-63363-5(6), Turtleback) Turtleback Bks.

Steele, Philip & Morris, Neil. Inside Volcanoes. 2006. (Inside Nature's Disasters Ser.). (Illus.). 36p. (gr. 3-7). lib. bdg. 26.00 (978-0-8368-7250-7(9), Gareth Stevens Learning Library) Stevens, Gareth Publishing LLLP.

Steele, Philip, et al. Extreme Planet. 2014. (Illus.). 128p. (J). (978-1-4351-5523-7(8)) Barnes & Noble, Inc.

Stephens, Catherine. Volcanoes. 2007. (Language, Literacy, & Vocabulary - Reading Expeditions Ser.). (ENG., Illus.). 36p. (J). pap. 18.95 (978-0-7922-5434-8(1)) CENGAGE Learning.

Stewart, Melissa. Earthquakes & Volcanoes. 2008. (For Your Information Ser.). (Illus.). 80p. (J). (gr. 3-7). pap. 7.99 (978-0-06-089950-9(6)) HarperCollins Pubs.

—Inside Volcanoes. 2011. (Inside Ser.). (ENG., Illus.). 48p. (J). (gr. 3-5). pap. 9.95 (978-1-4027-8164-3(4)) Sterling Publishing Co., Inc.

Stienecker, David. Blast Zone: The Eruption & Recovery of Mount St. Helens. 2003. (ENG., Illus.). 32p. (J). (gr. 6-8). pap. 7.97 net. (978-0-7652-3265-6(0), Celebration Pr.) Pearson Schl.

Storey, Melinda. Volcanoes: A Comprehensive Hands-on Science Unit. Mitchell, Judy & Lindeen, Mary, eds. Armbrust, Janet, illus. 2007. (Nature's Fury Ser.). 32p. (J). pap. 6.95 (978-1-57310-530-9(9)) Teaching & Learning Co.

Sutherland, Lin. Terremotos y Volcanes. Lopez-Izquierdo, Nieves, tr. 2003. (Exploradores de National Geographic Ser.). (SPA., Illus.). 64p. (gr. 4-7). (978-970-651-716-6(2), 1610) Editorial Oceano De Mexico, S.A. DE C.V.

Tagliaferro, Linda. How Does a Volcano Become an Island? 2016. (How Does It Happen Ser.). (ENG.). 32p. (gr. 3-5). pap. 8.29 (978-1-4109-8530-9(X), Raintree Perspectives) Heinemann-Raintree.

Thoron, Joe. Volcanoes. 2006. (Kaleidoscope Natural Disasters Ser.). (Illus.). 48p. (gr. 3-7). lib. bdg. 20.95 (978-0-7614-2105-4(X), Benchmark Bks.) Marshall Cavendish Corp.

Ticktock Media, Ltd. Staff. Violent Planet. 2008. (ENG.). 128p. (J). (gr. 4-7). pap. 12.95 (978-1-84696-813-6(5), TickTock Books) Octopus Publishing Group GBR. Dist: Independent Pubs. Group.

Time for Kids Magazine Staff, ed. Volcanoes! 2006. (Time for Kids Science Scoops Ser.). (Illus.). 32p. (gr. 1-3). 14.00 (978-0-7569-6984-4(0)) Perfection Learning Corp.

Trueit, Trudi Strain. Detecting Volcanic Eruptions. 2017. (Detecting Disasters (hardcover) Ser.). (ENG., Illus.). 32p. (J). (gr. 4-7). lib. bdg. 28.50 **(978-1-63517-006-1(0)**, Focus Readers) North Star Editions.

Trueno de la Tierra: 6 Small Books. (Saludos Ser.: Vol. 2). (SPA.). (gr. 3-5). 31.00 (978-0-7635-2068-7(3)) Rigby Education.

Tuffen, Hugh & Waldron, Melanie. Volcanologist: The Coolest Jobs on the Planet, 1 vol. HL Studios Staff, illus. 2014. (Coolest Jobs on the Planet Ser.). (ENG.). 48p. (gr. 6-6). 32.65 (978-1-4109-6643-8(7)); pap. 8.99 (978-1-4109-6649-0(6)) Heinemann-Raintree.

Turnbull, Stephanie. Volcanoes. Tudor, Andy, illus. 2006. (Usborne Beginners Ser.). 32p. (J). (gr. 1). lib. bdg. 12.99 (978-1-58086-949-2(1)); 4.99 (978-0-7945-1401-3(4)) EDC Publishing. (Usborne).

—Volcanoes. Tudor, Andy, illus. 2005. 32p. (J). pap. (978-0-439-84610-3(2)) Scholastic, Inc.

U. S. National Geographic Society Staff & Furgang, Kathy. National Geographic Kids Everything Volcanoes & Earthquakes: Earthshaking Photos, Facts, & Fun! 2013. (National Geographic Kids Everything Ser.). (ENG.). 64p. (J). (gr. 3-7). lib. bdg. 21.90 (978-1-4263-1365-3(9), National Geographic Children's Bks.) National Geographic Society.

U. S. National Geographic Society Staff, et al. Everything Volcanoes & Earthquakes: Earthshaking Photos, Facts, & Fun! 2013. (National Geographic Kids Everything Ser.). (ENG., Illus.). 64p. (J). (gr. 3-7). pap. 12.95 (978-1-4263-1364-6(0), National Geographic Children's Bks.) National Geographic Society.

Usborne Books Staff, creator. Volcanoes Kid Kit. 2006. (Kid Kits Ser.). (Illus.). (J). (gr. 1). 15.99 (978-1-58086-981-2(5)) EDC Publishing.

Van Rose, Susanna. Eyewitness Books - Volcano & Earthquake. 2014. (DK Eyewitness Bks.). (ENG., Illus.). 72p. (J). (gr. 3-7). pap. 9.99 (978-1-4654-2618-5(3), DK Children) Dorling Kindersley Publishing, Inc.

Los Volcanes, 6 vols., Vol. 2. (Explorers. Exploradores Nonfiction Sets Ser.).Tr. of Volcanos. (SPA.). 32p. (gr. 3-6). 44.95 (978-0-7699-0645-4(1)) Shortland Pubns. (U. S. A.) Inc.

Volcano & Earthquake. 2014. (DK Eyewitness Bks.). (ENG., Illus.). 72p. (J). (gr. 3-7). lib. bdg. 19.99 (978-1-4654-2622-2(1), DK Children) Dorling Kindersley Publishing, Inc.

Volcanoes: Level O, 6 vols., Vol. 2. (Explorers Ser.). 32p. (gr. 3-6). 44.95 (978-0-7699-0609-6(5)) Shortland Pubns. (U. S. A.) Inc.

Volcanoes of the World. (Illus.). (J). (gr. k-5). 119.70 (978-0-8239-7081-0(7)) Rosen Publishing Group, Inc., The.

Walker, Sally M. Volcanoes. 2008. pap. 52.95 (978-0-8225-9347-8(5)) 2007. (ENG., Illus.). 48p. (gr. 2-5). lib. bdg. 26.60 (978-0-8225-6733-2(4), Lerner Pubns.) Lerner Publishing Group.

Watt, Fiona. Earthquakes & Volcanoes. Stockley, Corinne & Brooks, Felicity, eds. Gower, Jeremy & Shields, Chris, illus. rev. ed. 2007. (Geography Ser.). 32p. (YA). (gr. 8-12). pap. 7.99 (978-0-7945-1531-7(2), Usborne) EDC Publishing.

Webster, Christine. Mauna Loa: The Largest Volcano in the United States. 2004. (Natural Wonders of the U. S. A. Ser.). (Illus.). 32p. (J). (gr. 3-6). per. 9.95 *(978-1-59036-162-7(8))* Weigl Pubs., Inc.
Weil, Ann. Volcanoes, 1 vol. unabr. ed. 2012. (Disasters Ser.). (ENG.). 92p. (YA). (gr. 9-12). 8.95 *(978-1-61651-937-7(1))* Saddleback Educational Publishing, Inc.
Whiting, Jim. The Volcanic Eruption on Santorini, 1650 BCE. 2007. (Natural Disasters Ser.). (Illus.). 32p. (J). (gr. 1-4). lib. bdg. 25.70 *(978-1-58415-568-3(X))* Mitchell Lane Pubs., Inc.
Winchester, Simon. The Day the World Exploded: The Earthshaking Catastrophe at Krakatoa. Chin, Jason, illus. 2008. 96p. (J). (gr. 5-9). lib. bdg. 23.89 *(978-0-06-123983-0(6))* HarperCollins Pubs.
Wiseman, Blaine. Volcanoes. 2014. (J). *(978-1-4896-3276-0(X))* Weigl Pubs., Inc.
Wonders of Creation: Volcanoes & Their. 2004. reprint ed. pap. 15.95 *(978-1-4191-9484-9(4))* Kessinger Publishing, LLC.
Wonders of Creation: Volcanoes & Their Phenomena. 2004. reprint ed. pap. 1.99 *(978-1-4192-9484-6(9))* Kessinger Publishing, LLC.
Woods, Michael & Woods, Mary B. Volcanoes. 2006. (Disasters up Close Ser.). (ENG., Illus.). 64p. (gr. 4-8). lib. bdg. 27.93 *(978-0-8225-4715-0(5)*, Lerner Pubns.) Lerner Publishing Group.
World Book, Inc Staff, contrib. by. Volcanoes. (J). 2007. *(978-0-7166-9815-9(3))* 2nd ed. 2009. (Illus.). 47p. *(978-0-7166-9831-9(5))* World Bk., Inc.
Yomtov, Nel. When Volcanoes Erupt! O'Neill, Sean, illus. 2012. (Adventures in Science Ser.). (ENG.). 32p. (gr. 3-4). pap. 47.70 *(978-1-4296-8468-2(2)*, Graphic Library) Capstone Press of Coughlan Cos.
Yomtov, Nelson. When Volcanoes Erupt!, 1 vol. O'Neill, Sean, illus. 2012. (Adventures in Science Ser.). (ENG.). 32p. (gr. 3-4). pap. 8.10 *(978-1-4296-7990-9(5))*; lib. bdg. 30.65 *(978-1-4296-7547-5(0))* Capstone Press of Coughlan Cos. (Graphic Library).
Zeiger, Jennifer. Measuring Volcanic Activity. 2015. (Explorer Library: Science Explorer Ser.). (ENG., Illus.). 32p. (J). (gr. 4-8). lib. bdg. 29.93 *(978-1-63362-389-7(0)*, 206976) Cherry Lake Publishing.
Zoehfeld, Kathleen Weidner. School of Dragons No. 1: Volcano Escape! Random House, illus. 2016. (Stepping Stone Book(TM) Ser.). (ENG.). 80p. (J). (gr. 2-5). lib. bdg. 12.99 *(978-1-101-93338-1(0)*, Random Hse. Bks. for Young Readers) Random Hse. Children's Bks.
—Volcano Escape! Random House, illus. 2016. (Stepping Stone Book(TM) Ser.). (ENG.). 80p. (J). (gr. 2-5). pap. 7.99 *(978-1-101-93337-4(2)*, Random Hse. Bks. for Young Readers) Random Hse. Children's Bks.

VOLCANOES—FICTION

Avalon, Dawn. Bubbles. A Wet Dragon. 2006. 59p. pap. 8.21 *(978-1-4116-1177-1(2))* Lulu Pr., Inc.
Awdry, W. Thomas & the Volcano. 2015. (Thomas & Friends Step into Reading Ser.). lib. bdg. 14.75 *(978-0-606-36404-1(8))* Turtleback Bks.
Bordiglioni, Stephen & Bordiglioni, Stefano. Volcano! Bertolucci, Federico, illus. 2009. (Dinodino's Dinosaur Adventures Ser.). 56p. (J). (gr. k-4). 27.95 *(978-1-60754-712-9(0))*; pap. 12.85 *(978-1-60754-717-4(1))* Windmill Bks.
Brasch, Nicolas. Escape from Pacaya, 1 vol. 2013. (Fiction Readers Ser.). (ENG., Illus.). 24p. (J). (gr. 2-2). pap. 6.99 *(978-1-4333-5529-5(9))* Shell Educational Publishing.
—Hot Springs & Brown Bears, 1 vol. rev. ed. 2013. (Fiction Readers Ser.). (ENG., Illus.). 32p. (J). (gr. 3-3). pap. 8.99 *(978-1-4333-5637-7(6))* Shell Educational Publishing.
Brunson, Emma. Survivor Spirit Book: Megan's Ark. 2010. 204p. pap. 13.50 *(978-1-60911-834-1(0)*, Eloquent Bks.) Strategic Book Publishing & Rights Agency (SBPRA).
Cook, Sherry & Johnson, Terri. Vinnie Volcano, 26. Kuhn, Jesse, illus. l.t. ed. 2006. (Quirkles — Exploring Phonics through Science Ser.: 22). 32p. (J). 7.99 *(978-1-933815-21-3(3)*, Quirkles, The) Creative 3, LLC.
Coss, Lauren. Volcanoes. 2014. (Illus.). 48p. (J). pap. 15.64 *(978-1-62403-007-9(6)*, Core Library) ABDO Publishing Co.
COX, Margaret. The Emerald-fire. 2010. 166p. pap. 11.50 *(978-1-4461-3379-8(6))* Lulu Pr., Inc.
Crofoot, Betty & Arledge, Roo. The Great Celebration Ceremony - My Genie & Me Series Book 2. 2012. 84p. pap. 8.95 *(978-1-60862-430-0(7))* E-BookTime LLC.
Derubertis, Barbara. Victor Vicuna's Volcano Vacation. Alley, R. W., illus. 2011. (Animal Antics A to Z Set III Ser.). pap. 45.32 *(978-0-7613-8431-1(6))* Kane Press, Inc.
deRubertis, Barbara. Victor Vicuna's Volcano Vacation. Alley, R. W., illus. 2011. (Animal Antics A to Z Ser.). 32p. (J). (ENG.). pap. 7.95 *(978-1-57565-347-1(8))*; lib. bdg. 22.60 *(978-1-57565-355-6(9))* Kane Press, Inc.
deRubertis, Barbara & DeRubertis, Barbara. Victor Vicuna's Volcano Vacation. Alley, R. W., illus. 2012. (Animal Antics A to Z Ser.). 32p. (J). (gr. 2 — 1). cd-rom 7.95 *(978-1-57565-415-7(6))* Kane Press, Inc.
Earhart, Kristin, et al. The Magic School Bus Inside a Volcano. Bracken, Carolyn, illus. 2012. 32p. (J). *(978-0-545-35685-5(7))* Scholastic, Inc.
George, Jean Craighead. Dear Katie, the Volcano Is a Girl. 32p. (J). pap. *(978-0-7868-1178-6(1))* Hyperion Bks. for Children.
Geraghty, Paul. Dinosaur in Danger. 2005. (Illus.). 40p. (J). pap. *(978-0-09-943865-6(8)*, Red Fox) Random House Children's Books.
Giulieri, Anne. The Volcano Sand Hill, 1 vol. Boyer, Susy, illus. 2012. (Engage Literacy Blue Ser.). (ENG.). 32p. (gr. k-2). pap. 5.99 *(978-1-4296-8976-2(5)*, Engage Literacy) Capstone Press of Coughlan Cos.
Greenway, Beth. Una Verdadera Princesa de Hawái. Yee, Tammy, illus. 2017. (SPA.). 32p. (J). (gr. k-3). pap. 9.95 *(978-1-62855-950-7(0))* Arbordale Publishing.
Hayler, Kate. Volcano Alert! Team Mission: A Pop-up Book. Giraffe, Red & Doughty, Clare, illus. 2006. 10p. (J). (gr. k-4). reprint ed. 19.00 *(978-1-4223-5075-1(4))* DIANE Publishing Co.
Hoena, Blake. Can You Survive a Supervolcano Eruption? An Interactive Doomsday Adventure. Vanzo, Filippo, illus. 2016. (You Choose: Doomsday Ser.). (ENG.). 112p. (gr. 3-4). lib. bdg. 31.99 *(978-1-4914-8108-0(0)*, You Choose Bks.) Capstone Press of Coughlan Cos.
Jennings, Terry Catasús. Gopher to the Rescue! A Volcano Recovery Story, 1 vol. O'Keefe, Laurie, illus. 2012. (ENG.). 32p. (J). (gr. -1-4). 17.95 *(978-1-60718-131-6(2))*; pap. 9.95 *(978-1-60718-141-5(X))* Arbordale Publishing.
Kennedy, Marlane. Volcano Blast. 2015. (Disaster Strikes Ser.: 4). (ENG.). 128p. (J). (gr. 2-5). pap. 4.99 *(978-0-545-53047-7(4)*, Scholastic Paperbacks) Scholastic, Inc.
Kerr, P. B., pseud. The Grave Robbers of Genghis Khan. 2011. (Children of the Lamp Ser.: Vol. 7). (ENG.). 448p. (J). (gr. 3-7). 18.99 *(978-0-545-12660-1(6)*, Orchard Bks.) Scholastic, Inc.
Lawrence, Margaret. Earthshakers, Top Blowers & High Rollers. 2012. 170p. pap. 36.95 *(978-1-937600-74-7(2))* Salem Author Services.
Lewis, Paul Owen. Frog Girl. 2004. (Illus.). 38p. (J). tchr. ed., tchr.'s planning gde. ed. 2.95 *(978-1-58246-009-3(4)*, Tricycle Pr.) Ten Speed Pr.
—Frog Girl. (ENG., Illus.). 32p. (J). (gr. -1-5). 18.95 *(978-1-55110-658-8(2))* Whitecap Bks., Ltd. CAN. Dist: Graphic Arts Ctr. Publishing Co.
Locke, Elsie. A Canoe in the Mist. 2005. 224p. *(978-1-86950-568-4(9))* HarperCollins Pubs. Australia.
Mackay, Gregory. Anders & the Volcano. 2017. (Anders Ser.: 2). (ENG.). 176p. (J). (gr. 1-6). pap. 9.99 ***(978-1-76029-003-0(3))*** Allen & Unwin AUS. Dist: Independent Pubs. Group.
Maddox, Jake. Volcano! A Survive! Story. Tiffany, Sean, illus. 2009. (Jake Maddox Sports Stories Ser.). (ENG.). 72p. (gr. 2-3). 25.32 *(978-1-4342-1208-5(4))* Stone Arch Bks.
Marsh, Carole. The Curse of the Ancient Acropolis: Athens, Greece. 2008. (Carole Marsh Mysteries Ser.). 133p. (J). (gr. 3-5). per. 7.99 *(978-0-635-06470-7(7)*, Marsh, Carole Bks.) Gallopade International.
—The Voracious Volcano Mystery. 2008. (Masters of Disasters Ser.). (Illus.). 118p. (J). (gr. 3-5). 14.95 *(978-0-635-06466-0(9))*; per. 5.99 *(978-0-635-06463-9(4))* Gallopade International.
Messner, Kate. Land of Fire & Ice. McMorris, Kelley, illus. 2017. (Ranger in Time Ser.: 5). (ENG.). 160p. (J). (gr. 2-5). pap. 5.99 *(978-0-545-90978-5(3))* Scholastic, Inc.
Milway, Alex. The Magma Conspiracy: Armed, Dangerous & Covered in Fur! Milway, Alex, illus. 2013. (ENG., Illus.). 224p. (J). pap. 5.99 *(978-1-61067-159-0(7))* Kane Miller.
Mullin, Mike. Ashen Winter. (Ashfall Trilogy Ser.). (ENG.). (J). 2013. 580p. (gr. 6). pap. 10.99 *(978-1-933718-98-9(6))* 2012. 594p. (gr. 8). 17.95 *(978-1-933718-75-0(7))* Tanglewood Pr.
—Ashfall. (Ashfall Trilogy Ser.). (ENG.). 476p. (J). 2012. (gr. 8). pap. 10.95 *(978-1-933718-74-3(9))* 2011. (gr. 6). 17.95 *(978-1-933718-55-2(2))* Tanglewood Pr.
—Sunrise. 2014. (Ashfall Trilogy Ser.). (ENG.). 466p. (J). (gr. 8). 17.99 *(978-1-939100-01-6(1))* Tanglewood Pr.
Neff, C. M. The Glue Volcano. 2008. 14p. pap. 24.95 *(978-1-60441-312-0(3))* America Star Bks.
Oplinger, Jon & Cooke, Elizabeth. The Wicked Small People of Whiskey Bridge. 2011. 156p. (gr. 4-6). 22.95 *(978-1-4620-4948-6(6))*; pap. 12.95 *(978-1-4620-4947-9(8))* iUniverse, Inc.
Osborne, Mary Pope. Vacation under the Volcano. unabr. ed. 2004. (Magic Tree House Ser.: No. 13). 74p. (J). (gr. k-3). pap. 17.00 incl. audio *(978-0-8072-0782-6(9)*, LFTR 241 SP, Listening Library) Random Hse. Audio Publishing Group.
Perelman, Helen. Bubble Gum Rescue. Waters, Erica-Jane, illus. 2014. (Candy Fairies Ser.: 8). (ENG.). 128p. (J). (gr. 2-5). 15.99 *(978-1-4424-6496-4(8)*, Simon & Schuster/Paula Wiseman Bks.) Simon & Schuster/Paula Wiseman Bks.
Pugin-Rodas, M. C. The Eight Ball Club: Ocean of Fire. 2007. (ENG., Illus.). 144p. pap. 15.95 *(978-0-9793761-2-2(2))* ESOL Publishing.
Shecter, Vicky Alvear. Curses & Smoke: A Novel of Pompeii. 2014. (ENG.). 336p. (J). (gr. 7). 17.99 *(978-0-545-50993-0(9)*, Levine, Arthur A. Bks.) Scholastic, Inc.
Smith, Roland. Eruption. 2012. (Storm Runners Ser.: 3). (ENG.). 160p. (J). (gr. 3-7). 16.99 *(978-0-545-08174-0(2)*, Scholastic Pr.) Scholastic, Inc.
Snelling, Lauraine. What about Cimmaron? 2008. (J). 8.99 *(978-1-59166-872-5(7))* BJU Pr.
Stamper, Judith. Voyage to the Volcano. Speirs, John, illus. 2010. (Magic School Bus Science Chapter Bks.). (KOR.). 101p. (J). *(978-89-491-5322-3(X))* Biryongso Publishing Co.
—Voyage to the Volcano. Speirs, John, illus. 2003. (Magic School Bus Science Chapter Bks.). 87p. (gr. 3-6). 15.00 *(978-0-7569-1581-0(3))* Perfection Learning Corp.
Stevens, A. P. The Volcano: The Adventures of Antboy & Mr Cricket. Finn, N. K., ed. Deskcube, illus. 2008. (ENG.). 29p. pap. 9.95 *(978-0-9798886-0-1(3))* Mugsy and Sugar Pressed.
Tarshis, Lauren. I Survived the Destruction of Pompeii, 79 A. D. 2014. (I Survived Ser.: No. 10). (ENG.). 112p. (J). (gr. 2-5). pap. 4.99 *(978-0-545-45939-6(7))* Scholastic, Inc.
—I Survived the Destruction of Pompeii, AD 79. Dawson, Scott, illus. 2014. 95p. (J). ***(978-0-545-77568-7(X)***, Scholastic Pr.) Scholastic, Inc.
Tarshis, Lauren. I Survived the Eruption of Mount St. Helens, 1980. 2016. (I Survived Ser.: 14). (ENG.). 112p. (J). (gr. 2-5). pap. 4.99 *(978-0-545-65852-2(7)*, Scholastic Paperbacks) Scholastic, Inc.
Thompson, Gare. Mount St. Helens 1980: Fiery Eruption! Inspiring Tales of Courage & Friendship. 2017. (Great Escapes Ser.). (ENG.). 240p. (J). (gr. 3-7). pap. 7.99 ***(978-1-4380-0972-8(0))*** Barron's Educational Series, Inc.
Troupe, Thomas Kingsley. Volcano: a Fiery Tale of Survival. Fagan, Kirbi, illus. 2016. (Survive! Ser.). (ENG.). 56p. (gr. 4-6). lib. bdg. 25.32 *(978-1-4965-2555-0(8))* Stone Arch Bks.
Turner, Daniel. Cinnamon the Adventurous Guinea Pig Goes to Devil's Island. Skinner, Gayle, illus. 2013. (ENG.). 48p. (J). pap. 10.95 *(978-1-4787-1753-9(X))* Outskirts Pr., Inc.
Verne, Jules. A Journey to the Interior of the Earth. 2006. 196p. per. 13.95 *(978-1-59818-461-7(X))* Aegypan.
—Journey to the Interior of the Earth. 2006. 196p. 26.95 *(978-1-59818-557-7(8))* Aegypan.
—Voyage au Centre de la Terre.Tr. of Voyage to the Center of the Earth. (FRE.). (J). pap. 14.95 *(978-2-07-051437-3(4))* Gallimard, Editions FRA. Dist: Distribooks, Inc.
Westerman, Robert. Alohalani Kalikimaka Auntie: Sheet Music & Lyrics. Westerman, Robert, . 2006. (Illus.). 12p. (J). 6.95 *(978-0-9761992-1-2(1))* Gold Boy Music & Pubn.
Wilson, Wendy. The First Book of Red. 2005. 99p. pap. 19.95 *(978-1-4137-5570-1(4))* America Star Bks.

VOLGA RIVER AND VALLEY

Mattern, Joanne. The Volga River. 2012. (Illus.). 47p. (J). lib. bdg. 29.95 *(978-1-61228-312-8(8))* Mitchell Lane Pubs., Inc.

VOLLEYBALL

Abramovitz, Melissa. Volleyball. Greenhaven Press Editors, ed. 2013. (Science Behind Sports Ser.). (ENG., Illus.). 128p. (J). (gr. 7-10). lib. bdg. 39.40 *(978-1-4205-1157-4(2)*, Lucent Bks.) Cengage Gale.
Ackerman, Jon. Girls' Volleyball, 1 vol. 2013. (Girls' SportsZone Ser.). (ENG., Illus.). 48p. (J). (gr. 3-6). lib. bdg. 32.79 *(978-1-61783-991-7(4)*, SportsZone) ABDO Publishing Co.
Barth, Katrin & Heuchert, Richard. Learning Volleyball. 2006. (Illus.). 152p. (J). (gr. 4-7). pap. 14.95 *(978-1-84126-197-3(1))* Meyer & Meyer Sport, Ltd. GBR. Dist: Cardinal Pubs. Group.
Barth, Katrin & Linkerhand, Antje. Training Volleyball. 2007. (Illus.). 152p. (J). (gr. 4-7). pap. 14.95 *(978-1-84126-211-6(0))* Meyer & Meyer Sport, Ltd. GBR. Dist: Cardinal Pubs. Group.
Crossingham, John & Kalman, Bobbie. Spike It Volleyball. 2008. (Sports Starters Ser.). (ENG., Illus.). 32p. (J). (gr. 3-7). pap. *(978-0-7787-3175-7(8))*; lib. bdg. *(978-0-7787-3143-6(X))* Crabtree Publishing Co.
Dann, Sarah. Le Volleyball. 2011. (FRE., Illus.). 32p. (J). pap. 9.95 *(978-2-89579-413-4(8))* Bayard Canada CAN. Dist: Crabtree Publishing Co.
Derr, Aaron. Volleyball: An Introduction to Being a Good Sport. Angle, Scott, illus. 2017. (Start Smart (tm) — Sports Ser.). (ENG.). 32p. (J). (gr. k-3). lib. bdg. 26.65 *(978-1-63440-134-0(4))*; 39.99 ***(978-1-63440-146-3(8))*** Red Chair Pr.
Doeden, Matt. Volleyball. 2015. (Summer Olympic Sports Ser.). (ENG., Illus.). 32p. (J). (gr. 2-4). 19.95 *(978-1-60753-811-0(3))* Amicus Publishing.
Dolphin, Colleen. Volleyball by the Numbers, 1 vol. 2010. (Team Sports by the Numbers Ser.). (ENG.). 24p. (J). (gr. k-3). lib. bdg. 24.21 *(978-1-60453-772-7(8)*, SandCastle) ABDO Publishing Co.
Douglas, Peter. Volleyball: Approaching the Net. 2017. (Preparing for Game Day Ser.: Vol. 10). (ENG.). (YA). (gr. 7-12). 24.95 ***(978-1-4222-3921-6(7))*** Mason Crest.
Evdokimoff, Natasha. Volleyball. 2010. (In the Zone Ser.). (Illus.). 32p. (J). (gr. 3-5). pap. 11.95 *(978-1-60596-908-4(7))*; lib. bdg. 25.70 *(978-1-60596-907-7(9))* Weigl Pubs., Inc.
Forest, Anne. Girls Play Volleyball. 2016. (Girls Join the Team Ser.). 24p. (J). (gr. 3-3). pap. 8.25 *(978-1-4994-2111-8(7)*, PowerKids Pr.) Rosen Publishing Group, Inc., The.
Getting the Edge: Conditioning, Injuries, & Legal & Illicit Drugs, 14 vols., Set. Incl. Baseball & Softball. Sanna, Gabriel. lib. bdg. 24.95 *(978-1-4222-1730-6(2))*; Basketball. Vanderhoof, Gabrielle. lib. bdg. 24.95 *(978-1-4222-1731-3(0))*; Cheerleading. Vanderhoof, Gabrielle. lib. bdg. 24.95 *(978-1-4222-1732-0(9))*; Extreme Sports. Li, Wenfang. lib. bdg. 24.95 *(978-1-4222-1729-0(9))*; Football. McIntosh, J. S. lib. bdg. 24.95 *(978-1-4222-1733-7(7))*; Gymnastics. McIntosh, J. S. lib. bdg. 24.95 *(978-1-4222-1734-4(5))*; Hockey. Vanderhoof, Gabrielle. lib. bdg. 24.95 *(978-1-4222-1735-1(3))*; Lacrosse. Vanderhoof, Gabrielle. lib. bdg. 24.95 *(978-1-4222-1737-5(X))*; Martial Arts. McIntosh, J. S. lib. bdg. 24.95 *(978-1-4222-1738-2(8))*; Soccer. McIntosh, J. S. lib. bdg. 24.95 *(978-1-4222-1739-9(6))*; Track & Field. Vanderhoof, Gabrielle. lib. bdg. 24.95 *(978-1-4222-1740-5(X))*; Volleyball. Vanderhoof, Gabrielle. lib. bdg. 24.95 *(978-1-4222-1741-2(8))*; Wrestling. McIntosh, J. S. lib. bdg. 24.95 *(978-1-4222-1743-6(4))*; (YA). 2010. (Illus.). 96p. 2011. Set lib. bdg. 349.30 *(978-1-4222-1728-3(0)*, 1317895) Mason Crest.
Grozdanovic, Sava, et al. Volleyball for Boys & Girls. 2004. (Illus.). 168p. pap. 17.95 *(978-1-84126-126-3(2))* Meyer & Meyer Sport, Ltd. GBR. Dist: Cardinal Pubs. Group.
Jensen, Julie. Play-by-Play Volleyball. King, Andy, photos by. 2005. (Play-by-Play Ser.). (Illus.). 80p. (gr. 4-8). pap., lib. bdg. 23.93 *(978-0-8225-9882-4(5))* Lerner Publishing Group.
Kortemeier, Todd. 12 Reasons to Love Volleyball. 2018. (ENG.). 32p. (gr. 3-6). 31.35 ***(978-1-63235-432-7(2)***, 12-Story Library) Pr. Room Editions LLC.
LeBoutillier, Nate. Volleyball. 2012. (Illus.). 48p. (J). 35.65 *(978-1-60818-213-8(4)*, Creative Education) Creative Co., The.
McClellan, Ray. Volleyball. 2010. (My First Sports Ser.). (ENG., Illus.). 24p. (J). (gr. 2-5). lib. bdg. 25.95 *(978-1-60014-464-6(0)*, Blastoff! Readers) Bellwether Media.
McDougall, Chros. Girls Play to Win Volleyball. 2010. (Girls Play to Win Ser.). 64p. (J). (gr. 3-6). lib. bdg. 27.93 *(978-1-59953-392-6(8))* Norwood Hse. Pr.
McIntyre, Abigael & Giddens, Sandra. An Insider's Guide to Volleyball. 2014. (Sports Tips, Techniques, & Strategies Ser.). (Illus.). 48p. (J). (gr. 5-8). pap. 70.50 *(978-1-4777-8598-0(1)*, Rosen Reference) Rosen Publishing Group, Inc., The.
Miller, Kat & Manley, Claudia B. Volleyball: Girls Rocking It, 01 vols., 1. 2016. (Title IX Rocks! Ser.). (ENG., Illus.). 64p. (J). 32.95 *(978-1-5081-7045-7(2)*, Rosen Young Adult) Rosen Publishing Group, Inc., The.
Omoth, Tyler. First Source to Volleyball: Rules, Equipment, & Key Playing Tips. 2017. (First Sports Source Ser.). (ENG.). 24p. (gr. 1-2). lib. bdg. 25.32 ***(978-1-5157-8783-9(4)***, First Facts) Capstone Press of Coughlan Cos.
Saxena, Shalini. Volleyball & Its Greatest Players, 1 vol. 2015. (ENG.). 80p. (YA). 31.70 *(978-1-62275-594-3(4)*, Britannica Educational Publishing) Rosen Publishing Group, Inc., The.
Schwartz, Heather E. Top Volleyball Tips. 2017. (Top Sports Tips Ser.). (ENG., Illus.). 32p. (gr. 3-4). lib. bdg. 27.99 *(978-1-5157-4720-8(4))* Capstone Press of Coughlan Cos.
Slupskiy, Leon. Volleyball with the Family: Fife Steps to Success. Synepolsky, I. & Belomlinsky, M., illus. 2003. 105/35p. (YA). pap. *(978-0-9728301-3-3(8))* Publishing Hse. Gelany.
Vanderhoof, Gabrielle. Volleyball. 2010. (Getting the Edge Ser.). 96p. (YA). lib. bdg. 24.95 *(978-1-4222-1741-2(8))* Mason Crest.
Watson, Stephanie. The Science Behind Soccer, Volleyball, Cycling, & Other Popular Sports. 2016. (Science of the Summer Olympics Ser.). (ENG., Illus.). 32p. (gr. 3-4). lib. bdg. 27.99 *(978-1-4914-8160-8(9)*, Edge Bks.) Capstone Press of Coughlan Cos.

VOLUNTARISM

Ancona, George. Can We Help? Kids Volunteering to Help Their Communities. Ancona, George, illus. 2015. (ENG., Illus.). 48p. (J). (gr. k-3). 16.99 *(978-0-7636-7367-3(6))* Candlewick Pr.
Anderson Lopez, Elizabeth. Fantastic Kids: Helping Others (Level 3) 2017. (Exploring Reading Ser.). (Illus.). 32p. (J). (gr. 3-3). pap. 8.99 ***(978-1-4258-4972-6(5))*** Teacher Created Materials, Inc.
Bartowski, Sara. Gavin Volunteers! 2012. (InfoMax Readers Ser.). (ENG., Illus.). 24p. (J). (gr. 1-2). pap. 8.25 *(978-1-4488-9064-4(0)*, Rosen Classroom) Rosen Publishing Group, Inc., The.
Borus, Audrey. Volunteering. 2011. (Life—a How-To Guide Ser.). (Illus.). 128p. (J). lib. bdg. 33.27 *(978-0-7660-3440-2(2))* Enslow Pubs., Inc.
—Volunteering: A How-to Guide. 2011. (Life—a How-To Guide Ser.). (Illus.). 128p. (J). (gr. 6-18). pap. 10.95 *(978-1-59845-310-2(6))* Enslow Pubs., Inc.
Cane, Ella. Communities in My World, 1 vol. 2013. (My World Ser.). (ENG.). 24p. (gr. k-1). pap. 6.95 *(978-1-4765-3462-6(4)*, Pebble Bks.) Capstone Press of Coughlan Cos.
Clinton, Chelsea. It's Your World: Get Informed, Get Inspired & Get Going! 2015. (ENG., Illus.). 416p. (J). (gr. 5). 18.99 *(978-0-399-17612-8(8)*, Philomel Bks.) Penguin Young Readers Group.
Cohn, Jessica. Hand to Heart: Improving Communities, 1 vol. 2nd rev. ed. 2013. (Nonfiction Readers Ser.). (ENG., Illus.). 48p. (J). (gr. 4-4). pap. 29.96 *(978-1-4807-1118-1(7))* Shell Educational Publishing.
—Hand to Heart: Improving Communities, 1 vol. 2nd rev. ed. 2012. (Nonfiction Readers Ser.). (ENG.). 48p. (J). (gr. 4-4). pap. 9.99 *(978-1-4333-4866-2(7))* Teacher Created Materials, Inc.
—Hand to Paw - Protecting Animals, 1 vol. 2nd rev. ed. 2012. (TIME for KIDS(r) Nonfiction Readers Ser.). (ENG.). 48p. (J). (gr. 4-4). pap. 9.99 *(978-1-4333-4867-9(5))* Teacher Created Materials, Inc.
—Una Mano Al Corazón: Mejorando Las Comunidades. 2017. (TIME for Kids en Español - Level 4 Ser.). (SPA., Illus.). 48p. (gr. 4-4). lib. bdg. 31.99 *(978-1-5157-5147-2(3))* Time for Kids Inc AUS. Dist: Capstone Pub.
Donovan, Sandy. Volunteering Smarts: How to Find Opportunities, Create a Positive Experience, & More. 2012. (USA TODAY Teen Wise Guides: Lifestyle Choices Ser.). (ENG., Illus.). 64p. (gr. 8-12). lib. bdg. 31.93 *(978-0-7613-7021-5(8))* Lerner Publishing Group.
Fischer, James. The Power to Do Good: Money & Charity. 2010. (Junior Library of Money). 64p. (YA). (gr. 7-18). pap. 9.95 *(978-1-4222-1888-4(0))*; lib. bdg. 22.95 *(978-1-4222-1769-6(8))* Mason Crest.
Gerdes, Louise. National Service. 2011. (Opposing Viewpoints Ser.). (ENG.). 224p. (gr. 12-12). lib. bdg. 48.80 *(978-0-7377-5233-5(5)*, Greenhaven Pr., Inc.) Cengage Gale.
Gerdes, Louise I. National Service. 2011. (Opposing Viewpoints Ser.). (ENG.). 224p. (gr. 12-12). pap. 33.80 *(978-0-7377-5234-2(3)*, Greenhaven Pr., Inc.) Cengage Gale.
Gregory, Helen. Team Work, 1 vol. 2011. (Wonder Readers Early Level Ser.). (ENG.). (gr. -1-1). 32p. pap. 5.99 *(978-1-4296-7898-8(4))*; 16p. pap. 35.94 *(978-1-4296-8166-7(7))* Capstone Press of Coughlan Cos. (Wonder Readers).
Hoose, Philip M. It's Our World, Too. 2014. 23.95 *(978-1-63419-712-0(7))* Perfection Learning Corp.
How to Help: A Guide to Giving Back, 8 vols., Set. Incl. Celebrities Giving Back: A Guide to Giving Back. Reusser, Kayleen. lib. bdg. 29.95 *(978-1-58415-922-3(7))*; Volunteering in School: A Guide to Giving Back. O'Neal, Claire. lib. bdg. 29.95 *(978-1-58415-920-9(0))*; Ways to Help after a Natural Disaster: A Guide to Giving Back. Saul, Laya. lib. bdg. 29.95 *(978-1-58415-917-9(0))*; Ways to Help Children with Disabilities: A Guide to Giving Back. Gibson, Karen Bush. lib. bdg. 29.95 *(978-1-58415-916-2(2))*; Ways to Help Chronically Ill Children: A Guide to Giving Back. Gagne, Tammy. lib. bdg. 29.95 *(978-1-58415-919-3(7))*; Ways to Help Disadvantaged Youth: A Guide to Giving Back. Saul, Laya. lib. bdg. 29.95 *(978-1-58415-918-6(9))*; Ways to Help in Your Community: A Guide to Giving Back. O'Neal, Claire. lib. bdg. 29.95 *(978-1-58415-921-6(9))*; Ways to Help the Elderly: A Guide to Giving Back. Orr, Tamra. lib. bdg. 29.95 *(978-1-58415-915-5(4))*; (Illus.). 48p. (J). (gr. 4-8). 2010. 2010. Set lib. bdg. 239.60 *(978-1-58415-923-0(5))* Mitchell Lane Pubs., Inc.
Junior Library of Money, 14 vols., Set. Incl. All about Money: The History, Culture, & Meaning of Modern Finance. Simons, Rae. lib. bdg. 22.95 *(978-1-4222-1760-3(4))*; Banking Basics. Fischer, James. lib. bdg. 22.95 *(978-1-4222-1761-0(2))*; Cost of Living. Thompson, Helen. lib. bdg. 22.95 *(978-1-4222-1762-7(0))*; Earning Money: Jobs. Fischer, James. lib. bdg. 22.95 *(978-1-4222-1763-4(9))*; Entrepreneurship. Simons, Rae. lib. bdg. 22.95 *(978-1-4222-1764-1(7))*; Guide to Teaching Young Adults about Money. Simons, Rae. lib. bdg. 22.95 *(978-1-4222-1765-8(5))*; Investing Money. Thompson, Helen. lib. bdg. 22.95 *(978-1-4222-1766-5(3))*; Money & Relationships. Simons, Rae. lib. bdg. 22.95 *(978-1-4222-1767-2(1))*; Planning for Your Education. Fischer, James. lib. bdg. 22.95 *(978-1-4222-1768-9(X))*; Power to Do Good: Money & Charity. Fischer, James. lib. bdg. 22.95 *(978-1-4222-1769-6(8))*; Spending Money. Simons, Rae. lib. bdg. 22.95 *(978-1-4222-1770-2(1))*; Sustainable Lifestyles in a Changing Economy. Simons, Rae. lib. bdg. 22.95 *(978-1-4222-1771-9(X))*; Understanding Credit. Thompson, Helen. lib. bdg. 22.95 *(978-1-4222-1772-6(8))*; Understanding the Stock Market. Thompson, Helen. lib. bdg. 22.95 *(978-1-4222-1773-3(6))*; (YA). (gr. 7-18). 2010. (Illus.). 64p. 2011. Set lib. bdg. 321.30 *(978-1-4222-1759-7(0))* Mason Crest.

TUV

Kenney, Karen Latchana. Cool School Volunteering: Fun Ideas & Activities to Build School Spirit, 1 vol. 2011. (Cool School Spirit Ser.). (ENG., Illus.). 32p. (J). (gr. 3-6). 28.50 *(978-1-61714-670-1(6)*, Checkerboard Library) ABDO Publishing Co.

Kreisman, Rachelle. Being a Good Citizen: A Kids' Guide to Community Involvement. Haggerty, Tim, illus. 2015. (Start Smart: Community Ser.). (ENG.). 32p. (gr. 1-3). 26.65 *(978-1-937529-50-5(9))* Red Chair Pr.

Laidlaw, Rob. Cat Champions: Caring for Our Feline Friends. (ENG., Illus.). 64p. (J). (gr. 3-7). 2015. pap. 11.95 *(978-1-927485-54-5(1))* 2014. 15.95 *(978-1-927485-31-6(2))* Pajama Pr. CAN. Dist: Ingram Publisher Services.

Lindeen, Mary. Lend a Hand, 1 vol. 2011. (Wonder Readers Fluent Level Ser.). (ENG.). (gr. -1-2). 32p. pap. 5.99 *(978-1-4296-7948-0(4))*; 16p. pap. 35.94 *(978-1-4296-8119-3(5))* Capstone Press of Coughlan Cos. (Wonder Readers).

Marcovitz, Hal. Teens & Voluntarism. 2008. (Gallup Youth Survey, Major Issues & Trends Ser.). (Illus.). 112p. (YA). (gr. 8-12). lib. bdg. 22.95 *(978-1-59084-877-7(2))* Mason Crest.

—Teens & Volunteerism. Developed in Association with the Gallup Organization Staff, ed. 2013. (Gallup Youth Survey: Major Issues & Trends Ser.: 14). 112p. (J). (gr. 7-18). 24.95 *(978-1-4222-2960-6(2))* Mason Crest.

Marsico, Katie. Rotary Clubs. 2016. (Community Connections: How Do They Help? Ser.). (ENG., Illus.). 24p. (J). (gr. 2-5). 27.07 *(978-1-63471-053-4(3)*, 208292) Cherry Lake Publishing.

Mills, Nathan & Pickman, Richard. Let's Volunteer! 2012. (Rosen Readers Ser.). (ENG., Illus.). 24p. (J). (gr. 1-2). pap. 8.25 *(978-1-4488-8851-1(4)*, Rosen Classroom) Rosen Publishing Group, Inc., The.

Nelson, Maria. I Can Volunteer. 2013. (Kids of Character Ser.). 24p. (J). (gr. 1-3). pap. 48.90 *(978-1-4339-9039-7(3))*; (ENG., Illus.). pap. 8.15 *(978-1-4339-9038-0(5))*; (ENG., Illus.). lib. bdg. 22.60 *(978-1-4339-9037-3(7))* Stevens, Gareth Publishing LLLP.

O'Neal, Claire. Volunteering in School: A Guide to Giving Back. 2010. (How to Help Ser.). (Illus.). 48p. (J). (gr. 4-8). lib. bdg. 29.95 *(978-1-58415-920-9(0))* Mitchell Lane Pubs., Inc.

Orr, Tamra & Muschal, Frank. Beyond Government. 2007. (21st Century Skills Library: Citizens & Their Governments Ser.). (ENG., Illus.). 32p. (gr. 4-8). lib. bdg. 28.50 *(978-1-60279-060-5(4)*, 200002) Cherry Lake Publishing.

Parker, Victoria. Helping Family & Friends, 1 vol. 2012. (I Can Make a Difference Ser.). (ENG., Illus.). 32p. (gr. 1-3). pap. 8.29 *(978-1-4329-5949-4(2))*; lib. bdg. 27.32 *(978-1-4329-5944-9(1))* Heinemann-Raintree. (Heinemann First Library).

—Helping in the Community, 1 vol. 2012. (I Can Make a Difference Ser.). (ENG., Illus.). 32p. (gr. 1-3). pap. 8.29 *(978-1-4329-5950-0(6))*; lib. bdg. 27.32 *(978-1-4329-5945-6(X))* Heinemann-Raintree. (Heinemann First Library).

—Helping the Environment, 1 vol. 2012. (I Can Make a Difference Ser.). (ENG., Illus.). 32p. (gr. 1-3). pap. 8.29 *(978-1-4329-5951-7(4)*, Heinemann First Library) Heinemann-Raintree.

Pickman, Richard. Let's Volunteer! 2012. (I'm an American Citizen Ser.). (ENG., Illus.). 24p. (J). (gr. 1-3). 22.60 *(978-1-4488-8589-3(2)*, PowerKids Pr.) Rosen Publishing Group, Inc., The.

Raum, Elizabeth. Helping Others, 1 vol. 2012. (Kids Making a Difference Ser.). (ENG.). 48p. (gr. 3-5). pap. 9.95 *(978-1-4329-6506-8(9))*; lib. bdg. 32.65 *(978-1-4329-6501-3(8))* Heinemann-Raintree. (NA-h).

Rodgers, Kelly. Doing Your Part: Serving Your Community, 1 vol. rev. ed. 2014. (Primary Source Readers Content & Literacy Ser.). (ENG., Illus.). 32p. (gr. 3-3). pap. 8.99 *(978-1-4333-7367-1(X))* Teacher Created Materials, Inc.

Rondeau, Amanda. Do Something in Your City, 1 vol. 2004. (Do Something about It! Ser.). (ENG.). 24p. (J). (gr. k-3). lib. bdg. 24.21 *(978-1-59197-571-7(9)*, SandCastle) ABDO Publishing Co.

—Do Something in Your Community. 2004. (Do Something about It! Ser.). (ENG., Illus.). 24p. (J). (gr. k-3). lib. bdg. 24.21 *(978-1-59197-572-4(7)*, SandCastle) ABDO Publishing Co.

—Do Something in Your Country, 1 vol. 2004. (Do Something about It! Ser.). (ENG., Illus.). 24p. (J). (gr. k-3). lib. bdg. 24.21 *(978-1-59197-573-1(5)*, SandCastle) ABDO Publishing Co.

—Do Something in Your State, 1 vol. 2004. (Do Something about It! Ser.). (ENG., Illus.). 24p. (J). (gr. k-3). lib. bdg. 24.21 *(978-1-59197-575-5(1)*, SandCastle) ABDO Publishing Co.

—Do Something in Your World, 1 vol. 2004. (Do Something about It! Ser.). (ENG., Illus.). 24p. (J). (gr. k-3). lib. bdg. 24.21 *(978-1-59197-576-2(X)*, SandCastle) ABDO Publishing Co.

—Volunteering. 2003. (United We Stand Ser.). (ENG., Illus.). 24p. (J). (gr. k-3). lib. bdg. 24.21 *(978-1-57765-882-5(5)*, SandCastle) ABDO Publishing Co.

Rondeau, Amanda & ABDO Publishing Company Staff. Do Something about It! (Set of 5 Titles) 2004. (Do Something about It! Ser.: 5). (ENG., Illus.). 24p. (J). (gr. k-3). lib. bdg. 121.05 *(978-1-59197-570-0(0)*, SandCastle) ABDO Publishing Co.

Rooney, Anne. Responding to Emergencies, 1 vol. 2012. (Charities in Action Ser.). (ENG.). 64p. (gr. 6-10). pap. 10.95 *(978-1-4329-6395-8(3))*; lib. bdg. 35.99 *(978-1-4329-6388-0(0))* Heinemann-Raintree.

Saul, Laya. Ways to Help after a Natural Disaster: A Guide to Giving Back. 2010. (How to Help Ser.). (Illus.). 48p. (J). (gr. 4-8). lib. bdg. 29.95 *(978-1-58415-917-9(0))* Mitchell Lane Pubs., Inc.

Senker, Cath. Improving Healthcare, 1 vol. 2012. (Charities in Action Ser.). (ENG.). 64p. (gr. 6-10). pap. 10.95 *(978-1-4329-6393-4(7))*; lib. bdg. 35.99 *(978-1-4329-6386-6(4))* Heinemann-Raintree.

Shava, Ryder. Akihiro Volunteers, 01 vols., 1. 2016. (Rosen REAL Readers: Social Studies Nonfiction / Fiction: Family, Community, & the World Ser.). (ENG.). 12p. (J). pap. 6.33 *(978-1-5081-1764-3(0)*, Rosen Classroom) Rosen Publishing Group, Inc., The.

Smith, Paula. Be the Change in the World. 2014. (ENG., Illus.). 24p. (J). *(978-0-7787-0622-9(2))* Crabtree Publishing Co.

Spilsbury, Louise. Protecting & Caring for Children, 1 vol. 2012. (Charities in Action Ser.). (ENG.). 64p. (gr. 6-10). pap. 10.95 *(978-1-4329-6394-1(5))*; lib. bdg. 35.99 *(978-1-4329-6387-3(2))* Heinemann-Raintree.

Volunteering: Do What You Like to Do. 2004. (YA). *(978-1-929888-38-2(4))* National Crime Prevention Council.

Weeldreyer, Laura. Everything You Need to Know about Volunteering. (Need to Know Library). 64p. 2009. (gr. 5-5). 58.50 *(978-1-60854-097-6(9))* 2005. (Illus.). (J). (gr. 7-12). 31.95 *(978-0-8239-3220-7(6)*, NTVOLU) Rosen Publishing Group, Inc., The.

Wheeler, Jill C. Red Cross Volunteers, 1 vol. 2003. (Everyday Heroes Ser.). (ENG., Illus.). 32p. (gr. k-6). 27.07 *(978-1-57765-857-3(4)*, Checkerboard Library) ABDO Publishing Co.

VOLUNTARISM—FICTION

Anderson, Laurie Halse. Helping Hands. 2013. (Vet Volunteers Ser.: 15). (ENG.). 144p. (J). (gr. 3-7). pap. 6.99 *(978-0-14-241677-8(0)*, Puffin Books) Penguin Young Readers Group.

—Left Behind. 2016. (Vet Volunteers Ser.: 17). (ENG.). 128p. (J). (gr. 3-7). 7.99 *(978-0-14-241679-2(7)*, Puffin Books) Penguin Young Readers Group.

—Treading Water. 2014. (Vet Volunteers Ser.: 16). (ENG.). 192p. (J). (gr. 3-7). pap. 6.99 *(978-0-14-241678-5(9)*, Puffin Books) Penguin Young Readers Group.

Fergus, Maureen. Exploits of a Reluctant (but Extremely Goodlooking) Hero. 2007. (ENG.). 216p. (J). (gr. 5-9). 7.95 *(978-1-55453-025-0(3))* Kids Can Pr., Ltd. CAN. Dist: Hachette Bk. Group.

Grimes, Nikki. Almost Zero: A Dyamonde Daniel Book. Christie, R. Gregory, illus. 2010. (Dyamonde Daniel Book Ser.: 3). (ENG.). 128p. (J). (gr. 2-4). 11.99 *(978-0-399-25177-1(4)*, G.P. Putnam's Sons Books for Young Readers) Penguin Young Readers Group.

Grogan, Joy. Into the Fold. 2003. 156p. per. 15.00 *(978-0-9740321-6-0(6))* Open Bk. Publishing.

Gurtler, Janet. The Truth about Us. 2015. (ENG.). 320p. (YA). (gr. 8-12). pap. 9.99 *(978-1-4022-7800-6(4)*, 9781402278006) Sourcebooks, Inc.

Harp, Susan. Evie Goes Clean & Green. Siau, Jon, illus. 2013. 24p. (J). lib. bdg. 14.95 *(978-1-938730-09-2(7))* M.T. Publishing Co., Inc.

—Retrieving with Evie. Siau, John, illus. 2007. (ENG.). 24p. (J). lib. bdg. 12.95 *(978-1-932439-67-0(6))* M.T. Publishing Co., Inc.

Huser, Glen. Skinnybones & the Wrinkle Queen. 2013. 232p. pap. *(978-1-4596-6507-1(4))* ReadHowYouWant.com, Ltd.

Kephart, Beth. The Heart Is Not a Size. 2010. (ENG.). 256p. (YA). (gr. 8-18). 16.99 *(978-0-06-147048-6(1)*, HarperTeen) HarperCollins Pubs.

Krulik, Nancy E. Revenge of the Killer Worms. 2015. (George Brown, Class Clown Ser.: 16). lib. bdg. 14.75 *(978-0-606-37545-0(7))* Turtleback Bks.

Lord, Cynthia. Jelly Bean. McGuire, Erin, illus. 2014. (Shelter Pet Squad Ser.: 1). (ENG.). 128p. (J). (gr. 1-3). 16.99 *(978-0-545-63596-7(9))*; (gr. 2-5). pap. 5.99 *(978-0-545-63597-4(7))* Scholastic, Inc. (Scholastic Pr.).

—Jelly Bean. 2014. (Shelter Pet Squad Ser.: 1). lib. bdg. 16.00 *(978-0-606-36063-0(8))* Turtleback Bks.

—Merlin. McGuire, Erin, illus. 2015. (Shelter Pet Squad Ser.: 2). (ENG.). 128p. (J). (gr. 2-5). 16.99 *(978-0-545-63599-8(3))* Scholastic, Inc.

—Paloma. McGuire, Erin, illus. 2016. (Shelter Pet Squad Ser.: 3). (ENG.). 128p. (J). (gr. 2-5). pap. 5.99 *(978-0-545-63604-9(3))* Scholastic, Inc.

Lyon, George Ella. You & Me & Home Sweet Home. Anderson, Stephanie, illus. 2009. (ENG.). 48p. (J). (gr. -1-3). 17.99 *(978-0-689-87589-2(4)*, Atheneum/Richard Jackson Bks.) Simon & Schuster Children's Publishing.

May, Eleanor. Ty's Triple Trouble. Wummer, Amy, illus. 2007. (Social Studies Connects). 32p. (J). (gr. -1-3). pap. 5.95 *(978-1-57565-237-5(4))* Kane Press, Inc.

Mikkelsen, Jon. The Empty Room. Lueth, Nathan, illus. 2008. (We Are Heroes Ser.). (ENG.). 40p. (gr. 2-3). lib. bdg. 23.99 *(978-1-4342-0791-3(9)*, Keystone Bks.) Stone Arch Bks.

—Kids Against Hunger. Lueth, Nathan, illus. 2008. (We Are Heroes Ser.). (ENG.). 40p. (gr. 2-3). lib. bdg. 23.99 *(978-1-4342-0790-6(0)*, Keystone Bks.) Stone Arch Bks.

Morgan, Melissa J. Freaky Tuesday, 17 vols. 2007. (Camp Confidential Ser.: 17). (ENG.). 160p. (J). (gr. 3-7). pap. 4.99 *(978-0-448-44651-6(0)*, Grosset & Dunlap) Penguin Young Readers Group.

Prentiss, Timothy. Miss Keen Needs Help. 2006. (Early Explorers Ser.). (J). pap. *(978-1-4108-6113-9(9))* Benchmark Education Co.

Randall, Angel. Snow Angels. 2011. (Illus.). 32p. (J). 17.99 *(978-1-60641-046-2(6)*, Shadow Mountain) Shadow Mountain Publishing.

Reinhardt, Dana. How to Build a House. 2009. (ENG.). 240p. (YA). (gr. 9-11). pap. 8.99 *(978-0-375-84454-6(6)*, Ember) Random Hse. Children's Bks.

Rhuday-Perkovich, Olugbemisola. 8th Grade Super Zero. 2011. (ENG.). 336p. (J). (gr. 4-7). pap. 7.99 *(978-0-545-09725-3(8)*, Levine, Arthur A. Bks.) Scholastic, Inc.

Sazaklis, John. The Dangers of Dog Walking. Robinson, Lee, illus. 2016. (Billy Burger, Model Citizen Ser.). (ENG.). 96p. (gr. 2-3). lib. bdg. 22.65 *(978-1-4965-2587-1(6))* Stone Arch Bks.

Schraff, Anne. A Walk in the Park, 1 vol. 2013. (Urban Underground Ser.). (ENG.). 196p. (YA). (gr. 9-12). pap. 9.95 *(978-1-62250-043-7(1))* Saddleback Educational Publishing, Inc.

Schraff, Anne E. A Walk in the Park. 2013. (Urban Underground — Harriet Tubman High School Ser.). (YA). lib. bdg. 20.80 *(978-0-606-31585-2(3)*, Turtleback) Turtleback Bks.

Van Syckle, A. & Schwartz, Josh. The OC: 'twas the Night Before Chrismukkah. 2005. 206p. (YA). *(978-1-4156-3915-3(9))* Scholastic, Inc.

Wallace, Nancy K. Claim to Fame, 1 vol. Chronister, Amanda, illus. 2013. (Abby & the Book Bunch Ser.). (ENG.). 80p. (J). (gr. 2-5). 27.07 *(978-1-61641-912-7(1))* Magic Wagon.

—Movie Mishaps, 1 vol. Chronister, Amanda, illus. 2013. (Abby & the Book Bunch Ser.). (ENG.). 80p. (J). (gr. 2-5). 27.07 *(978-1-61641-914-1(8))* Magic Wagon.

—Out to Lunch, 1 vol. Chronister, Amanda, illus. 2013. (Abby & the Book Bunch Ser.). (ENG.). 80p. (J). (gr. 2-5). 27.07 *(978-1-61641-916-5(4))* Magic Wagon.

Walton, Phillip. Auto-B-Good - Citizen Miles: A Lesson in Citizenship. Rising Star Studios, illus. 2010. 48p. (J). pap. 7.95 *(978-1-936086-52-8(2))*; lib. bdg. 14.95 *(978-1-936086-46-7(8))* Rising Star Studios, LLC.

VON BRAUN, WERNHER, 1912-1977

Peak, Doris-Jean. Wernher Von Braun: Alabama's Rocket Scientist. 2009. (Alabama Roots Biography Ser.). (Illus.). 112p. (J). *(978-1-59421-044-0(6))* Seacoast Publishing, Inc.

Spangenburg, Ray & Moser, Diane Kit. Wernher Von Braun: Out of the Fire, the Stars. 2nd rev. ed. 2008. (Makers of Modern Science Ser.). 192p. (gr. 6-12). 35.00 *(978-0-8160-6179-2(3)*, Chelsea Hse.) Facts On File, Inc.

VOTING

see Elections; Suffrage

VOYAGERS

see Explorers; Travelers

VOYAGES AND TRAVELS

ABDO Publishing Company Staff. Explore the Countries Set 2. 2014. (Explore the Countries Set 2 Ser.: 8). (ENG.). 40p. (gr. 7-11). lib. bdg. 239.44 *(978-1-62403-340-7(7)*, Big Buddy Bks.) ABDO Publishing Co.

Bowen, Richard. Captain James Cook: British Explorer. 2013. (People of Importance Ser.: 21). (Illus.). 32p. (J). (gr. 4-18). 19.95 *(978-1-4222-2843-2(6))* Mason Crest.

Chait, Baruch. The Lost Treasure of Tikkun Hamiddos Island. Pollack, Gadi, illus. (Good Middos Ser.: Vol. 2). 62p. 25.99 *(978-1-58330-478-5(9))* Feldheim Pubs.

Childress, Diana. Marco Polo's Journey to China. 2007. (Pivotal Moments in History Ser.). (ENG.). 160p. (gr. 9-12). lib. bdg. 38.60 *(978-0-8225-5903-0(X))* Lerner Publishing Group.

Claybourne, Anna. The Story of Exploration. McNee, Ian, illus. 2010. (Science Stories Ser.). 103p. (YA). (gr. 3-18). pap. 10.99 *(978-0-7945-2400-5(1)*, Usborne) EDC Publishing.

Claybourne, Anna, et al. Explorer Travel Guides. 2013. (Explorer Travel Guides). (ENG.). 48p. (gr. 3-6). pap. 47.94 *(978-1-4109-5441-1(2))*; lib. bdg. 149.95 *(978-1-4109-5434-3(X))* Heinemann-Raintree. (NA-r).

Collins. Collins Fascinating Facts - Explorers. 2016. (Collins Fascinating Facts Ser.). (ENG., Illus.). 72p. (J). (gr. 1-3). pap. 10.99 *(978-0-00-816926-8(8))* HarperCollins Pubs. Ltd. GBR. Dist: Independent Pubs. Group.

Cooke, Tim. Explore with Marco Polo. 2014. (ENG., Illus.). 32p. (J). *(978-0-7787-1428-6(4))* Crabtree Publishing Co.

—Maps & Exploration. 2010. (Understanding Maps of Our World Ser.). 48p. (YA). (gr. 4-7). lib. bdg. 31.00 *(978-1-4339-3512-1(0))*; (Illus.). (gr. 6-8). pap. 14.05 *(978-1-4339-3513-8(9)*, Gareth Stevens Secondary Library) Stevens, Gareth Publishing LLLP.

Currie, Stephen & National Geographic Learning Staff. Travels to Distant Lands, 1000-1400. 2007. (Nonfiction Reading & Writing Workshops Ser.). (ENG., Illus.). 32p. (J). pap. 17.95 *(978-0-7922-4542-1(3))* CENGAGE Learning.

Diaz, Natalia & Owens, Melissa. A Ticket Around the World. Smith, Kim, illus. 2015. (ENG.). 32p. (J). (gr. 2-5). 16.95 *(978-1-77147-051-3(8)*, Owlkids) Owlkids Bks. Inc. CAN. Dist: Publishers Group West (PGW).

Donovan, Sandra. Deadliest Destinations. 2013. (ShockZone — Deadly & Dangerous Ser.). (ENG.). 32p. (gr. 5-8). lib. bdg. 26.60 *(978-1-4677-0600-1(0)*, Lerner Pubns.) Lerner Publishing Group.

Donovan, Sandy. Deadly Danger Zones. 2013. (ShockZone — Deadly & Dangerous Ser.). (ENG., Illus.). 32p. (gr. 5-8). pap. 8.95 *(978-1-4677-0890-6(9))* Lerner Publishing Group.

Embacher, Eric. Stowed Away, 1 vol. unabr. ed. 2012. (Astonishing Headlines Ser.). (ENG.). 92p. (YA). (gr. 9-12). 8.95 *(978-1-61651-925-4(8))* Saddleback Educational Publishing, Inc.

Enchantment of the World, Second Series, 93 bks., Set. Incl. Belgium. Burgan, Michael. 144p. (J). 2000. 37.00 *(978-0-516-21006-3(8)*, Children's Pr.); Cambodia. Kras, Sara Louise. 144p. (YA). 2005. 39.00 *(978-0-516-23679-7(2))*; Chile. McNair, Sylvia. 144p. (J). 2000. 37.00 *(978-0-516-21007-0(6)*, Children's Pr.); Croatia. Hintz, Martin. 144p. (YA). 2004. 37.00 *(978-0-516-24253-8(9)*, Children's Pr.); Czech Republic. Milivojevic, JoAnn. 144p. (YA). 2004. 37.00 *(978-0-516-24255-2(5)*, Children's Pr.); Enchantment of the World: Tibet. Kummer, Patricia K. 144p. (YA). 2003. 39.00 *(978-0-516-22693-4(2))*; Ethiopia. Heinrichs, Ann & Heinrichs, Anne. 144p. (YA). 2005. 39.00 *(978-0-516-23680-3(6))*; Greenland. Blashfield, Jean F. 144p. (YA). 2005. 39.00 *(978-0-516-23678-0(4))*; Guatemala. Morrison, Marion. 144p. (YA). 2005. 39.00 *(978-0-516-23674-2(1))*; Guyana. Morrison, Marion. 144p. (YA). 2003. 39.00 *(978-0-516-22377-3(1))*; Hungary. Stalcup, Ann. 144p. (YA). 2005. 39.00 *(978-0-516-23683-4(0))*; Iceland. Somervill, Barbara A. 144p. (J). 2003. 37.00 *(978-0-516-22694-1(0)*, Children's Pr.); India. Swan, Erin Pembrey. 144p. (J). 2002. 37.00 *(978-0-516-21121-3(8)*, Children's Pr.); Indonesia. Orr, Tamra & Greenblatt, Miriam. 144p. (YA). 2005. 39.00 *(978-0-516-23684-1(9))*; Ireland. Blashfield, Jean F. & Blashfield, Jean. 144p. (YA). 2002. 39.00 *(978-0-516-21127-5(7))*; Lebanon. Willis, Terri. 144p. (YA). 2005. 39.00 *(978-0-516-23685-8(7))*; Luxembourg. Heinrichs, Ann. 48p. (YA). 2005. 39.00 *(978-0-516-23681-0(4))*; Monaco. Hintz, Martin. 144p. (YA). 2004. 39.00 *(978-0-516-24251-4(2))*; Nicaragua. Morrison, Marion. 144p. (YA). 2002. 37.00 *(978-0-516-20963-0(9)*, Children's Pr.); Panama. Augustin, Byron. 144p. (YA). 2005. 39.00 *(978-0-516-23676-6(8))*; Paraguay. Augustin, Byron. 144p. (YA). 2005. 39.00 *(978-0-516-23675-9(X))*; Portugal. Blauer, Ettagale & Laure, Jason. 144p. (YA). 2002. 37.00 *(978-0-516-21109-1(9)*, Children's Pr.); Scotland. Stein, R. Conrad. 144p. (YA). 2001. 39.00 *(978-0-516-21112-1(9))*; Singapore. Kummer, Patricia K. 144p. (YA). 2003. 39.00 *(978-0-516-22531-9(6))*; Syria. Kummer, Patricia K. 144p. (YA). 2005. 39.00 *(978-0-516-23677-3(6))*; United Arab Emirates. Augustin, Byron. 144p. (YA). 2002. 36.00 *(978-0-516-20473-4(4)*, Children's Pr.); Venezuela. Willis, Terri. 144p. (YA). 2003. 37.00 *(978-0-516-24214-9(8)*, Children's Pr.); Vietnam. Willis, Terri. 144p. (YA). 2002. 39.00 *(978-0-516-22150-2(7))*; Wales. Heinrichs, Ann. 144p. (J). 2003. 37.00 *(978-0-516-22288-2(0)*, Children's Pr.); (gr. 5-9). (Enchantment of the World Ser.). (Illus.). 144p. 2004. Set lib. bdg. 3348.00 o.p. *(978-0-516-20870-1(5)*, Children's Pr.) Scholastic Library Publishing.

Extreme Explorations! [Capstone Sole Source]. 2010. (Extreme Explorations! Ser.). 32p. lib. bdg. 155.94 *(978-1-4296-5856-0(8)*, Fact Finders) Capstone Press of Coughlan Cos.

Feeney, Kathy. Marco Polo: Explorer of China. 2004. (Explorers! Ser.). (Illus.). 48p. (J). lib. bdg. 23.93 *(978-0-7660-2145-7(9))* Enslow Pubs., Inc.

Feinstein, Stephen. Marco Polo: Amazing Adventures in China. 2013. (Great Explorers of the World Ser.). 112p. (gr. 6-12). pap. 10.95 *(978-0-7660-5430-1(6))* Enslow Pubs., Inc.

Feinstein, Stephen. Marco Polo: Amazing Adventures in China. 2009. (Great Explorers of the World Ser.). (Illus.). 112p. (J). (gr. 7-12). lib. bdg. 33.27 *(978-1-59845-103-0(0))* Enslow Pubs., Inc.

Flowers, Pam. Big-Enough Anna. Farnsworth, Bill, illus. 2003. (ENG.). 32p. (J). (gr. -1-18). 15.95 *(978-0-88240-577-3(2))* Graphic Arts Ctr. Publishing Co.

—Big-Enough Anna. Farnsworth, Bill, tr. Farnsworth, Bill, illus. 2003. (ENG.). 32p. (J). pap. 10.99 *(978-0-88240-580-3(2))* Graphic Arts Ctr. Publishing Co.

Flowers, Pam & Farnsworth, Bill. Ellie's Long Walk: The True Story of Two Friends on the Appalachian Trail. 2012. (ENG., Illus.). 32p. (J). (gr. -1-3). pap. 11.99 *(978-0-88240-885-9(2)*, West Winds Pr.) Graphic Arts Ctr. Publishing Co.

Granström, Brita. What Mr Darwin Saw. Manning, Mick, illus. 2014. (ENG.). 48p. (J). (gr. 1-4). pap. 9.95 *(978-1-84780-107-4(2)*, Frances Lincoln) Quarto Publishing Group UK GBR. Dist: Hachette Bk. Group.

Great Journeys - Group 3, 4 bks., Set. 131.14 *(978-0-7614-1320-2(0)*, Benchmark Bks.) Marshall Cavendish Corp.

Hopping, Lorraine Jean. Crossing the Atlantic: One Family's Story. 2004. (ENG., Illus.). 16p. (J). (gr. 2-2). pap. 10.92 *(978-0-7652-5186-2(8)*, Celebration Pr.) Pearson Schl.

Hunter, Nick. New Worlds, 1 vol. 2012. (Explorer Tales Ser.). (ENG.). 32p. (gr. 1-3). pap. 8.29 *(978-1-4109-4788-8(2)*, Read Me!) Heinemann-Raintree.

Journey to the New World: Individual Title Six-Packs. (Action Packs Ser.). 104p. (gr. 3-5). 44.00 *(978-0-7635-3301-4(7))* Rigby Education.

Khanduri, Kamini. The Great World Search. Hancock, David, illus. 2007. (Great Searches (EDC Hardcover) Ser.). 48p. (J). (gr. 3). lib. bdg. 16.99 *(978-1-58086-966-9(1)*, Usborne) EDC Publishing.

Koestler-Grack, Rachel A. Ferdinand Magellan. 2009. (Great Explorers Ser.). (Illus.). 112p. (gr. 6-12). 30.00 *(978-1-60413-422-3(4)*, Chelsea Hse.) Facts On File, Inc.

Lewin, Ted & Lewin, Betsy. How to Babysit a Leopard: And Other True Stories from Our Travels Across Six Continents. 2015. (ENG., Illus.). 144p. (J). (gr. 4-7). 22.99 *(978-1-59643-616-9(6)*, 9781596436169) Roaring Brook Pr.

Malam, John. Extreme Exploration. 2009. (Difficult & Dangerous Ser.). (Illus.). 32p. (J). (gr. 4-7). pap. *(978-1-897563-24-3(8))* Saunders Bk. Co.

McHaffie, Natalie. C-Growl: The Daring Little Airplane. McHaffie, Natalie, illus. 2004. (Illus.). 32p. 14.95 *(978-1-55125-015-1(2))* Vanwell Publishing, Ltd. CAN. Dist: Casemate Pubs. & Bk. Distributors, LLC.

Michels, Dia L. Look What I See! Where Can I Be? Visiting China. Bowles, Michael J. N., photos by. 2005. (Look What I See! Where Can I Be? Ser.: Vol. 5). (ENG., Illus.). 32p. (J). (gr. -1-3). 9.95 *(978-1-930775-15-2(6))* Platypus Media, L.L.C.

Mooney, Carla. Explorers of the New World: Discover the Golden Age of Exploration with 22 Projects. Casteel, Tom, illus. 2011. (Build It Yourself Ser.). (ENG.). 128p. (J). (gr. 3-7). 21.95 *(978-1-936313-44-0(8))*; pap. 15.95 *(978-1-936313-43-3(X))* Open City Bks.

Morley, Jacqueline. You Wouldn't Want to Explore with Marco Polo! A Really Long Trip You'd Rather Not Take. Antram, David, illus. 2009. (You Wouldn't Want to Ser.). (ENG.). 32p. (J). (gr. 3-12). 29.00 *(978-0-531-21327-8(7))*; pap. 9.95 *(978-0-531-20518-1(5))* Scholastic Library Publishing.

Nye, Naomi Shihab. I'll Ask You Three Times, Are You Ok? Tales of Driving & Being Driven. 2007. (YA). 242p. (gr. 7-12). lib. bdg. 16.89 *(978-0-06-085393-8(X))*; (ENG.). 256p. (gr. 8-12). 17.99 *(978-0-06-085392-1(1))* HarperCollins Pubs. (Greenwillow Bks.).

O'Donnell, Kerri. A Trip Around the World: Using Expanded Notation to Represent Numbers. (PowerMath Ser.). 24p. 2009. (gr. 3-4). pap. 8.25 *(978-0-8239-8871-6(6))* 2009. (gr. 3-4). 45.00 *(978-1-60851-377-2(7))* 2004. (J). lib. bdg. 22.50 *(978-0-8239-8966-9(6))* Rosen Publishing Group, Inc., The. (PowerKids Pr.).

Ollhoff, Jim. Marco Polo. 2013. (Great Explorers Ser.). 32p. (J). (gr. 5-9). lib. bdg. 27.07 *(978-1-61783-968-9(X)*, Abdo & Daughters) ABDO Publishing Co.

Orme, David. Great Journeys. 2008. (Trailblazers Ser.). (ENG., Illus.). 36p. pap. *(978-1-84167-653-1(5))* Ransom Publishing Ltd.

Otfinoski, Steven. The Voyages of Christopher Columbus: Text Pairs. 2008. (Bridges/Navigators Ser.). (J). (gr. 5). 89.00 *(978-1-4108-8425-1(2))* Benchmark Education Co.

Reynolds, E. E. Unknown Ways: More Tales of Explorers, Pioneers & Travellers. Tresilian, S., illus. 2011. (ENG.). 126p. pap. 20.99 *(978-1-107-60027-0(8))* Cambridge Univ. Pr.

Rice, Dona Herweck. A Dónde Ir, 1 vol. 2nd rev. ed. 2011. (Nonfiction Readers Ser.). (SPA.). 12p. (J). (gr. 1-1). pap. 4.99 *(978-1-4333-4412-1(2))* Teacher Created Materials, Inc.

Richardson, Gillian. 10 Routes That Crossed the World. Rosen, Kim, illus. 2017. (ENG.). 164p. (J). (gr. 3-7). pap. 12.95 *(978-1-55451-875-3(X))* Annick Pr., Ltd. CAN. Dist: Publishers Group West (PGW).

Ripley's Believe It Or Not! Staff. Prepare to Be Shocked: Epic Endeavors. 2012. (Ripley's Disbelief & Shock Ser.). 36p. (J). (gr. 3-4). 19.95 *(978-1-4222-2568-4(2))* Mason Crest.

Russo, David Anson. Around the World: The Great Treasure Hunt. Russo, David Anson, illus. 2011. (ENG., Illus.). 28p. (J). (gr. 4-6). pap. 14.99 *(978-1-4424-4343-3(X)*, Simon & Schuster Bks. For Young Readers) Simon & Schuster Bks. For Young Readers.

Stewart, David. You Wouldn't Want to Sail on the Titanic! 2013. (You Wouldn't Want To Ser.). lib. bdg. 20.80 (978-0-606-31630-9(2), Turtleback) Turtleback Bks.

Synge, M. B. The Discovery of New Worlds, Book II of the Story of the World. 2007. 224p. 21.99 (978-1-60206-621-2(3)); per. 14.99 (978-1-60206-620-5(5)) Cosimo, Inc.

Trzasko, Cheryl. Around the World in a Cement Boat: A Young Girl's True Adventure. 2013. 202p. (gr. 4-6). pap. 17.95 (978-1-4759-7558-1(9)) iUniverse, Inc.

Turner, Tracey. Hard As Nails Travelers & Explorers. 2015. (Hard As Nails in History Ser.). (ENG., Illus.). 64p. (J). (gr. 3-6). (978-0-7787-1521-4(3)) Crabtree Publishing Co.

Twist, Clint. Marco Polo: History's Great Adventurer. 2011. (Historical Notebooks Ser.). (ENG., Illus.). 30p. (J). (gr. 3-7). 19.99 (978-0-7636-5286-9(5), Templar) Candlewick Pr.

Verhille, Alexandre & Tavernier, Sarah. Legendary Routes of the World. 2015. (ENG., Illus.). 18p. (J). (gr. k-4). 29.99 (978-3-89955-759-6(X)) Die Gestalten Verlag DEU. Dist: Penguin Random Hse. LLC.

Willems, Mo. You Can Never Find a Rickshaw When It Monsoons: The World on One Cartoon a Day. Willems, Mo, illus. 2006. (ENG., Illus.). 408p. (gr. 8-17). pap. 12.99 (978-0-7868-3747-2(0)) Hyperion Pr.

Williams, Megan K. Maddy's Amazing African Birthday, 1 vol. Vallecchi, Alessandro et al, photos by. 2009. (ENG., Illus.). 32p. (J). (gr. 1-4). 12.95 (978-1-897187-47-0(5)) Second Story Pr. CAN. Dist: Orca Bk. Pubs. USA.

Wittmann, Kelly. The Race to Sail Around the World. 2017. (Great Race: Fight to the Finish Ser.). 48p. (gr. 4-5). pap. 84.30 **(978-1-5382-0807-6(5))** Stevens, Gareth Publishing LLLP.

Zannos, Susan. The Life & Times of Marco Polo. 2004. (Biography from Ancient Civilizations Ser.). (Illus.). 48p. (J). (gr. 4-8). lib. bdg. 29.95 (978-1-58415-264-4(8)) Mitchell Lane Pubs., Inc.

VOYAGES AND TRAVELS—FICTION

Abbott, Tony. Becca & the Prisoner's Cross. 2015. (Copernicus Archives Ser.: 2). (ENG.). 208p. (J). (gr. 3-7). pap. 3.99 (978-0-06-231474-1(2), Tegen, Katherine Bks) HarperCollins Pubs.

—The Forbidden Stone. 2014. (Illus.). 423p. (J). (978-0-06-232811-3(5)) HarperCollins Pubs.

—The Forbidden Stone. Perkins, Bill, illus. 2014. (Copernicus Legacy Ser.: 1). (ENG.). 432p. (J). (gr. 3-7). 16.99 (978-0-06-219447-3(X), Tegen, Katherine Bks) HarperCollins Pubs.

—The Golden Vendetta. 2015. (Copernicus Legacy Ser.: 3). (ENG.). 528p. (J). (gr. 3-7). 16.99 (978-0-06-219449-7(6), Tegen, Katherine Bks) HarperCollins Pubs.

—The Golden Vendetta. 2016. (Copernicus Legacy Ser.: 3). (J). lib. bdg. 17.20 (978-0-606-38764-4(1)) Turtleback Bks.

—The Serpent's Curse. 2014. (Illus.). 496p. pap. 9.99 (978-0-06-235159-3(1)) HarperCollins Pubs.

—Wade & the Scorpion's Claw. 2014. (Copernicus Archives Ser.: 1). (ENG.). 224p. (J). (gr. 3-7). pap. 3.99 (978-0-06-231472-7(6), Tegen, Katherine Bks) HarperCollins Pubs.

Acampora, Paul. How to Avoid Extinction. 2016. (ENG.). 208p. (J). (gr. 3-7). 16.99 (978-0-545-89906-2(0), Scholastic Pr.) Scholastic, Inc.

Aiken, Joan. Bridle the Wind. 2007. (ENG., Illus.). 352p. (J). (gr. 5-7). pap. 21.95 (978-0-15-206058-9(8)) Houghton Mifflin Harcourt Publishing Co.

Altman, Joel. Gapper's Grand Tour: A Voyage Through Great American Ball Park. Williams, Tim, illus. 2013. (ENG.). (J). (gr. -1-3). 14.95 (978-1-62086-213-1(1)) Mascot Bks., Inc.

Anaya, Rudolfo A. How Chile Came to New Mexico. Nasario, Garcia, tr. from ENG. Nicolas, Otero, illus. 2014. (SPA & ENG.). 48p. (J). (gr. -1-3). 24.95 (978-1-936744-20-6(1), Rio Grande Bks.) LPD Pr.

Andre, Richard & Snow, William. The Cruise of the Walnut Shell. 2012. (American Antiquarian Society Ser.). (ENG., Illus.). 32p. (gr. 1-7). 24.95 (978-1-4290-9737-6(X)) Applewood Bks.

Andrews, Jane. Each & All: The Seven Little Sisters Prove Their Sisterhood (Yesterday's Classics) 2009. 120p. pap. 8.95 (978-1-59915-308-7(4)) Yesterday's Classics.

Andrews, Julie. Little Bo: The Story of Bonnie Boadicea, No. 2. 2011. (Illus.). (J). lib. bdg. 18.89 (978-0-06-008912-2(1)) HarperCollins Pubs.

Arena, Jen. Lady Liberty's Holiday. Hunt, Matt, illus. 2016. (ENG.). 40p. (J). (gr. k-3). 17.99 (978-0-553-52067-5(9), Knopf Bks. for Young Readers) Random Hse. Children's Bks.

Arends, Donald L. Grandpa Grouper, the Fish with Glasses. 2006. (J). (978-0-9768880-0-0(9)) Mission Manuscripts, Inc.

Arenstam, Peter. Nicholas: A New Hampshire Tale. Holman, Karen Busch, illus. 2009. (Nicholas Northeastern Ser.: 3). (ENG.). 144p. (J). (gr. k-7). 14.95 (978-1-58726-521-1(4), Mitten Pr.) Ann Arbor Editions LLC.

—Nicholas: A Vermont Tale. Holman, Karen Busch, illus. 2010. (Nicholas Northeastern Ser.: 4). (ENG.). 144p. (J). (gr. k-7). 14.95 (978-1-58726-522-8(2), Mitten Pr.) Ann Arbor Editions LLC.

Arnold, David. Kids of Appetite. (ENG.). (YA). (gr. 9). 2017. 368p. pap. 10.99 **(978-0-14-751366-3(9)**, Speak) 2016. 352p. 18.99 (978-0-451-47078-2(8), Viking Books for Young Readers) Penguin Young Readers Group.

—Kids of Appetite. 2017. lib. bdg. 22.10 **(978-0-606-40491-4(0))** Turtleback Bks.

Arnold, David. Mosquitoland. 2015. (ENG.). 352p. (YA). (gr. 7). 17.99 (978-0-451-47077-5(X), Viking Books for Young Readers) Penguin Young Readers Group.

Ashman, Linda. Over the River & Through the Wood: A Holiday Adventure. Smith, Kim, illus. 2015. (ENG.). 32p. (J). (gr. -1). 14.95 (978-1-4549-1024-4(0)) Sterling Publishing Co., Inc.

Avi. The End of the Beginning: Being the Adventures of a Small Snail (and an Even Smaller Ant) Tusa, Tricia, illus. 2008. (ENG.). 144p. (J). (gr. 2-5). pap. 6.95 (978-0-15-205532-5(0)) Houghton Mifflin Harcourt Publishing Co.

—The End of Time. (ENG.). 240p. (J). (gr. 5). 2011. pap. 6.99 (978-0-06-174083-1(7))No. 3. 2010. 16.99 (978-0-06-174080-0(2)) HarperCollins Pubs.

Aviation Publications Staff & National Geographic Learning Staff. Hard Gold: The Colorado Gold Rush of 1859. 2010. (Rise & Shine Ser.). (ENG.). 240p. (C). (gr. 3-7). pap. 10.95 (978-1-4231-0520-6(6)) National Geographic School Publishing, Inc.

Ayarbe, Heidi. Compromised. (ENG.). (YA). (gr. 8). 2011. 480p. pap. 8.99 (978-0-06-172851-8(9)) 2010. 464p. 16.99 (978-0-06-172849-5(7)) HarperCollins Pubs. (HarperTeen).

Baccellia, Kim. Goddesses Can Wait. 2015. (YA). (978-1-61271-297-0(5)) Zumaya Pubns. LLC.

Bakshi, Kelly. Myth-Busting Columbus. 2012. 24p. 18.95 (978-1-61633-316-4(2)); pap. 10.95 (978-1-61633-317-1(0)) Guardian Angel Publishing, Inc.

Ballantyne, R. M. The Crew of the Water Wagtail. 2011. 146p. pap. 12.95 (978-1-60664-550-5(1)) Rodgers, Alan Bks.

—Red Rooney: Or, the Last of the Crew. 2007. (R. M. Ballantyne Collection). (Illus.). 408p. 22.00 (978-1-934554-08-1(1)) Vision Forum, Inc., The.

Ballantyne, Robert Michael. The Battery & the Boiler: Adventures in Laying of Submarine Electric Cables. 2007. 254p. pap. 21.99 (978-1-4346-3754-3(9)); (ENG.). 282p. pap. 23.99 (978-1-4346-3768-0(9)) Creative Media Partners, LLC.

—Red Rooney: The Last of the Crew. 2007. (ENG.). 270p. pap. 21.99 (978-1-4346-3693-5(3)); 302p. pap. 24.99 (978-1-4346-3741-3(7)) Creative Media Partners, LLC.

—The Rover of the Andes: A Tale of Adventure in South America. 2007. (ENG.). 266p. pap. 21.99 (978-1-4346-3753-6(0)); 296p. pap. 23.99 (978-1-4346-3767-3(0)) Creative Media Partners, LLC.

Banks, Kate. City Cat. Castillo, Lauren, illus. 2013. (ENG.). 48p. (J). (gr. -1-2). 17.99 (978-0-374-31321-0(0), 9780374313210, Farrar, Straus & Giroux (BYR)) Farrar, Straus & Giroux.

—The Magician's Apprentice. Sís, Peter, illus. 2012. (ENG.). 224p. (J). (gr. 5-9). 16.99 (978-0-374-34716-1(6), 9780374347161, Farrar, Straus & Giroux (BYR)) Farrar, Straus & Giroux.

Barnhouse, Rebecca. The Book of the Maidservant. 2011. (ENG., Illus.). 240p. (J). (gr. 3-7). pap. 7.99 (978-0-375-85857-4(1), Yearling) Random Hse. Children's Bks.

Barnum, P. T. Dick Broadhead: A Story of Perilous Adve. 2006. pap. 30.95 (978-1-4286-1959-3(3)) Kessinger Publishing, LLC.

Barry, Rick. Kiriath's Quest. 2008. (J). 8.99 (978-1-59166-905-0(7)) BJU Pr.

Baskin, Nora Raleigh. All We Know of Love. 2008. (ENG., Illus.). 208p. (YA). (gr. 9). 16.99 (978-0-7636-3623-4(1)) Candlewick Pr.

Bateman, Rachel. Someone Else's Summer. 2017. (ENG.). 320p. (YA). (gr. 8-17). 17.99 (978-0-7624-6219-3(1), Running Pr.) Running Pr. Bk. Pubs.

Bauer, Sepp. The Christmas Rose. Wenz-Vietor, Else, illus. 2008. 48p. (J). (gr. -1-3). 12.95 (978-1-58089-232-2(9)) Charlesbridge Publishing, Inc.

Bell, Loman. Old Glory. Bell, Loman, illus. 2012. (Illus.). 40p. pap. (978-0-9866065-8-8(8)) Wood Islands Prints.

—Old Glory Faces the Hurricane. Bell, Loman, illus. 2013. (Illus.). 46p. pap. (978-0-9918033-2-3(9)) Wood Islands Prints.

Bencastro, Mario. A Promise to Keep. Giersbach-Rascon, Susan, tr. from SPA. 2005. 134p. (J). (gr. 3-7). pap. 9.95 (978-1-55885-457-4(6), Piñata Books) Arte Publico Pr.

Berk, Sheryl & Berk, Carrie. Royal Icing: The Cupcake Club. 2014. (Cupcake Club Ser.: 6). (ENG.). 144p. (J). (gr. 3-7). pap. 6.99 (978-1-4022-8333-8(4), Sourcebooks Jabberwocky) Sourcebooks, Inc.

Bethell, Zillah. A Whisper of Horses. 2017. (ENG.). 352p. (J). 16.99 (978-1-250-09394-3(5), 9781250093943) Feiwel & Friends.

Bethune, Helen. In a Whirl, 1 vol. 2013. (Fiction Readers Ser.). (ENG., Illus.). 28p. (J). (gr. 2-2). pap. 6.99 (978-1-4333-5561-5(2)) Shell Educational Publishing.

—Sarah's Journal, 1 vol. 2013. (Fiction Readers Ser.). (ENG., Illus.). 28p. (J). (gr. 2-2). pap. 6.99 (978-1-4333-5568-4(X)) Shell Educational Publishing.

Biddulph, Rob. Blown Away. Biddulph, Rob, illus. 2015. (ENG., Illus.). 40p. (J). (gr. -1-3). 17.99 (978-0-06-236724-2(2)) HarperCollins Pubs.

Billet, Marion. Littleland Around the World. Billet, Marion, illus. 2014. (ENG., Illus.). 32p. (J). (-k). 14.99 (978-0-7636-7579-0(2), Nosy Crow) Candlewick Pr.

Billups, Ruth A. No Place for a Horse. 2008. 48p. pap. 16.95 (978-1-60703-118-5(3)) America Star Bks.

Bingham, Jane, retold by. Around the World in Eighty Days. 2004. (Young Reading Gift Books Ser.). 64p. (J). (gr. 2-18). 8.95 (978-0-7945-0826-5(X), Usborne) EDC Publishing.

Bird, Helen. The Balloon Launch. Dimitri, Simona, illus. 2005. 32p. (J). lib. bdg. 9.00 (978-1-4242-0887-6(4)) Fitzgerald Bks.

—Big Yellow Balloon. Dimitri, Simona, illus. 2009. (Get Set Readers Ser.). 32p. (J). (gr. -1-2). lib. bdg. 22.60 (978-1-60754-268-1(4)) Windmill Bks.

Biro, Val. Gumdrop's Magic Journey. (Illus.). 30p. (J). (978-0-340-71455-3(7)) Hodder & Stoughton.

—Magic Journey. (Illus.). 30p. (J). pap. (978-0-340-71441-6(7)) Hodder & Stoughton.

Blackstone, Stella. My Granny Went to Market: A Round-the-World Counting Rhyme. Corr, Christopher, illus. 2005. (ENG.). 24p. (J). 16.99 (978-1-84148-792-2(9)) Barefoot Bks., Inc.

Blackstone, Stella & Corr, Christopher. My Granny Went to Market: A Round-the-World Counting Rhyme. 2006. (ENG., Illus.). 24p. (J). (gr. -1-2). 6.99 (978-1-905236-62-6(X)) Barefoot Bks., Inc.

Blackstone, Stella & Harter, Debbie. Bear Takes a Trip. 2012. (ENG., Illus.). 24p. (J). (gr. -1-1). pap. 6.99 (978-1-84686-756-9(8)) Barefoot Bks., Inc.

Blackstone, Stella & Parker, Elizabeth. L'Ours Fait un Voyage. Harter, Debbie, illus. 2013.Tr. of Bear Takes a Trip. (FRE & ENG.). 24p. (J). (gr. k-1). pap. 6.99 (978-1-84686-946-4(3)) Barefoot Bks., Inc.

Blade, Adam. Vedra & Krimon the Twin Dragons. 2012. (Beast Quest Special Edition Ser.: 2). lib. bdg. 16.00 (978-0-606-26187-6(7), Turtleback) Turtleback Bks.

Block, Francesca Lia. Love in the Time of Global Warming. 2013. (ENG.). 240p. (YA). (gr. 9-13). 16.99 (978-0-8050-9627-9(2), 9780805096279, Holt, Henry & Co. Bks. For Young Readers) Holt, Henry & Co.

Blume, Lesley M. M. The Wondrous Journals of Dr. Wendell Wellington Wiggins. Foote, David, illus. 2013. (ENG.). 256p. (J). (gr. 3-7). pap. 7.99 (978-0-375-87218-1(3), Knopf Bks. for Young Readers) Random Hse. Children's Bks.

Bohner, Charles H. Bold Journey: West with Lewis & Clark. 2004. (ENG.). 192p. (J). (gr. 5-7). pap. 7.99 (978-0-618-43718-4(5)) Houghton Mifflin Harcourt Publishing Co.

Bois, William Pene du. The Twenty-One Balloons. 2005. (Puffin Modern Classics Ser.). (ENG., Illus.). 192p. (J). (gr. 3-7). pap. 7.99 (978-0-14-240330-3(X), Puffin Books) Penguin Young Readers Group.

Bondoux, Anne-Laure. The Princetta. Bell, Anthea, tr. 2008. (ENG.). 448p. (YA). (gr. 6-12). pap. 10.99 (978-1-59990-098-8(X), 9781599900988, Bloomsbury USA Childrens) Bloomsbury Publishing USA.

Bonneval, Gwen de & Smith, Owen. William & the Lost Spirit. Smith, Anne Collins, tr. from FRE. Bonhomme, Matthieu, illus. 2013. (ENG.). 160p. (J). (gr. 8-12). lib. bdg. 30.60 (978-0-7613-8567-7(3), Graphic Universe™) Lerner Publishing Group.

Borgenicht, David & Lurie, Alexander. Deadly Seas: You Decide How to Survive! 2015. (WorstCase Scenario Ultimate Adventure Ser.). (ENG., Illus.). 204p. (gr. 3-8). 47.10 (978-1-59920-981-4(0)) Black Rabbit Bks.

Boutavant, Marc, illus. Around the World with Mouk. 2009. (ENG.). 32p. (J). (gr. 3-17). 17.99 (978-0-8118-6926-3(1)) Chronicle Bks. LLC.

Brahmachari, Sita. Jasmine Skies. 2014. (ENG.). 336p. (J). (gr. 3-7). 16.99 (978-0-8075-3782-4(9)) Whitman, Albert & Co.

Brannon, Tom, illus. Where Are You Going, Charlie Brown? 2014. (Peanuts Great American Adventure Ser.). (ENG.). 40p. (J). (gr. -1). 16.99 (978-1-62157-258-9(7), Little Patriot Pr.) Regnery Publishing, Inc., An Eagle Publishing Co.

Brent, Isabelle. The Christmas Horse & the Three Wise Men. 2016. (ENG., Illus.). 28p. (J). (gr. k-3). 17.95 (978-1-937786-61-8(7), Wisdom Tales) World Wisdom, Inc.

Brown, Jeff. The African Safari Discovery. Pamintuan, Macky, illus. 2010. (Flat Stanley's Worldwide Adventures Ser.: 6). (ENG.). 112p. (J). (gr. 2-5). pap. 4.99 (978-0-06-143000-8(5));No. 6. 15.99 (978-0-06-143001-5(3)) HarperCollins Pubs.

Buck, Alicia. Out of the Ashes. 2015. 281p. (YA). pap. 17.99 (978-1-4621-1727-7(9)) Cedar Fort, Inc./CFI Distribution.

Burnford, Sheila. The Incredible Journey. (J). (gr. 6-8). 18.95 (978-0-88411-099-6(0)) Amereon Ltd.

Campbell, Angus Peter. Archie & the North Wind. 2010. (ENG.). 192p. pap. 17.95 (978-1-906817-38-1(3), 9781906817381) Luath Pr. Ltd. GBR. Dist: Midpoint Trade Bks., Inc.

Carle, Eric. Amigos. Carle, Eric, illus. 2016. (SPA., Illus.). 22p. (J). (— 1). bds. 7.99 (978-0-399-54506-1(9), Philomel Bks.) Penguin Young Readers Group.

—Friends. Carle, Eric, illus. 2013. (ENG., Illus.). 32p. (J). (gr. -1-k). 17.99 (978-0-399-16533-7(9), Philomel Bks.) Penguin Publishing Group.

—Friends. Carle, Eric, illus. 2015. (ENG., Illus.). 24p. (J). (gr. -1-k). bds. 7.99 (978-0-399-17206-9(8), Philomel Bks.) Penguin Young Readers Group.

Carlson, Melody. Notes from a Spinning Planet: Papua New Guinea. 2007. (Notes from a Spinning Planet Ser.: 2). (ENG.). 240p. (YA). (gr. 7-12). per. 12.99 (978-1-4000-7145-6(3), WaterBrook Pr.) Crown Publishing Group.

Carmody, Isobelle. The Farseekers. 2003. (Obernewtyn Chronicles: Bk. 2). (Illus.). 316p. (J). 13.65 (978-0-7569-4608-1(5)) Perfection Learning Corp.

Carrillo, P. S. Desert Passage. 2008. (ENG.). 192p. (YA). (gr. 6-18). pap. 10.95 (978-1-55885-517-5(3), Piñata Books) Arte Publico Pr.

Carter, Caela. My Best Friend, Maybe. 2014. (ENG.). 352p. (YA). (gr. 9). 17.99 (978-1-59990-970-7(7), 9781599909707, Bloomsbury USA Childrens) Bloomsbury Publishing USA.

Carter, Scott William. The Last Great Getaway of the Water Balloon Boys. 2010. (ENG.). 208p. (YA). (gr. 7-18). 16.99 (978-1-4169-7156-6(4), Simon & Schuster Bks. For Young Readers) Simon & Schuster Bks. For Young Readers.

Charles, Norma. The Girl in the Backseat. 2008. (ENG., Illus.). 184p. (YA). (gr. 7-18). per. (978-1-55380-056-9(7)) Ronsdale Pr.

Cheng, Andrea. Shanghai Messenger, 1 vol. Young, Ed, illus. 2005. (ENG.). 40p. (J). (gr. 3-7). 17.95 (978-1-58430-238-4(0)) Lee & Low Bks., Inc.

Cheng, Andrea & Young, Ed. Shanghai Messenger. 2015. (ENG.). 40p. (J). pap. 10.95 (978-1-62014-230-1(9)) Lee & Low Bks., Inc.

Cheng, Jack. See You in the Cosmos. 2017. (ENG.). 320p. (J). (gr. 5-9). 16.99 (978-0-399-18637-0(9), Dial Bks) Penguin Young Readers Group.

Cherry, Alison. For Real. 2016. (ENG.). 304p. (YA). (gr. 7). pap. 9.99 (978-0-385-74296-2(7), Ember) Random Hse. Children's Bks.

Christie, Robert. Into the Outlands. Lang, Deborah, illus. 2016. (Quirk's Quest Ser.). (ENG.). 128p. (J). 16.99 (978-1-62672-233-0(1), 9781626722330, First Second Bks.) Roaring Brook Pr.

Clifton-Brown, Holly. Annie Hoot & the Knitting Extravaganza. Clifton-Brown, Holly, illus. 2010. (Andersen Press Picture Bks). (ENG., Illus.). 32p. (J). (gr. -1-3). 16.95 (978-0-7613-6444-3(7)) Lerner Publishing Group.

Cohagan, Carolyn. The Lost Children. 2011. (ENG.). 320p. (J). (gr. 3-7). pap. 7.99 (978-1-4169-8617-1(0), Aladdin) Simon & Schuster Children's Publishing.

—The Lost Children. 2010. (ENG.). 320p. (J). (gr. 3-7). 16.99 (978-1-4169-8616-4(2), Simon & Schuster/Paula Wiseman Bks.) Simon & Schuster/Paula Wiseman Bks.

Cole, Dina. Meet Eddie the Equator. 2011. 28p. pap. 12.99 (978-1-4634-6023-5(6)) AuthorHouse.

Colfer, Chris. Stranger Than Fanfiction. 2017. (ENG.). (J). 304p. (gr. 10-17). 18.99 (978-0-316-38344-8(9)); 432p. (gr. 9-17). 20.99 (978-0-316-39678-3(8)) Little, Brown Bks. for Young Readers.

Collar, Orpheus & Riordan, Rick. The Throne of Fire. Collar, Orpheus, illus. 2015. (Kane Chronicles Ser.). (ENG., Illus.). 160p. (J). (gr. 5-9). 21.99 (978-1-4847-1490-4(3)) Hyperion Bks. for Children.

Collingwood, Harry. The Cruise of The 'Esmeralda' 2009. 220p. pap. 15.95 (978-1-60664-391-4(6)) Rodgers, Alan Bks.

—The Log of a Privateersman. 2008. 216p. 26.95 (978-1-60664-899-5(3)); pap. 15.95 (978-1-60664-018-0(6)) Aegypan.

Cooney, Barbara. Miss Rumphius. Cooney, Barbara, illus. 2004. (Illus.). 28p. (J). (gr. k-2). reprint ed. pap. 6.00 (978-0-7567-7107-2(2)) DIANE Publishing Co.

Cooper, Elisha. Train. 2013. (ENG., Illus.). 40p. (J). (gr. -1-3). 17.99 (978-0-545-38495-7(8), Orchard Bks.) Scholastic, Inc.

Corder, Zizou. Lionboy. 2004. (ENG., Illus.). 304p. (J). (gr. 3-7). reprint ed. pap. 8.99 (978-0-14-240226-9(5), Puffin Books) Penguin Young Readers Group.

—Lionboy: The Truth. 2006. (ENG., Illus.). 240p. (J). (gr. 3-7). 7.99 (978-0-14-240705-9(4), Puffin Books) Penguin Young Readers Group.

Crawford, Neil. The Journeyers. 2006. (ENG.). 248p. (J). per. (978-0-9778205-4-2(8)) Helm Publishing.

Creech, Sharon. Ruby Holler. 2012. (ENG.). 288p. (J). (gr. 3-7). pap. 6.99 (978-0-06-056015-7(0)) HarperCollins Pubs.

—Ruby Holler. 2004. (Joanna Cotler Bks.). 310p. (gr. 3-7). 17.00 (978-0-7569-1940-5(1)) Perfection Learning Corp.

—Ruby Holler. 2012. (J). (gr. 3-6). 17.20 (978-0-613-86272-1(4), Turtleback) Turtleback Bks.

Cremer, Andrea. The Turncoat's Gambit. 2016. (Inventor's Secret Ser.: 3). (ENG.). 336p. (YA). (gr. 7). 18.99 (978-0-399-16425-5(1), Philomel Bks.) Penguin Young Readers Group.

Crockett, S. D. After the Snow. 2012. (After the Snow Ser.: 1). (ENG.). 304p. (YA). (gr. 7-12). 16.99 (978-0-312-64169-6(9)) Feiwel & Friends.

—After the Snow. 2013. (After the Snow Ser.: 1). (ENG.). 320p. (YA). (gr. 7-12). pap. 9.99 (978-1-250-01676-8(2)) Square Fish.

Crowe, Ellie & Fry, Juliet. HOKU the Stargazer: The Exciting Pirate Adventure! Petosa-Sigel, Kristi, illus. 2009. (ENG.). 28p. (J). (978-1-59700-601-9(7)) Island Heritage Publishing.

Crowley, James. Monsterland. 2017. (ENG.). 384p. (J). (gr. 5). 16.99 (978-0-399-17589-3(X), G.P. Putnam's Sons Books for Young Readers) Penguin Young Readers Group.

Crum, Sally. Race to Moonrise Rev. Carlson, Eric S., illus. 2006. 12.95 (978-1-932738-31-5(2)) Western Reflections Publishing Co.

Cruz, Maria Colleen. Border Crossing. 2003. 128p. (J). pap. 9.95 (978-1-55885-405-5(3), Piñata Books) Arte Publico Pr.

—Border Crossing. 2006. 122p. (gr. 8-12). 19.95 (978-0-7569-6587-7(X)) Perfection Learning Corp.

Culbertson, Kim. Instructions for a Broken Heart. 2011. (ENG.). 304p. (YA). (gr. 7-12). pap. 9.99 (978-1-4022-4302-8(2)) Sourcebooks, Inc.

Culbertson, Kim. The Wonder of Us. 2017. (ENG.). 336p. (J). (gr. 7). 17.99 **(978-0-545-73151-5(8))** Scholastic, Inc.

Cummings, Priscilla. Beetle Boddiker, 1 vol. Ramsey, Marcy Dunn, illus. 2009. (ENG.). 30p. (J). (gr. k-7). 13.95 (978-0-87033-602-7(9), 9780870336027, Cornell Maritime Pr./Tidewater Pubs.) Schiffer Publishing, Ltd.

—The Journey Back. 2013. (ENG.). 272p. (J). (gr. 5). pap. 7.99 (978-0-14-242290-8(8), Puffin Books) Penguin Young Readers Group.

Czekaj, Jef. Austin, Lost in America: A Geography Adventure. Czekaj, Jef, illus. 2015. (ENG., Illus.). 40p. (J). (gr. -1-3). 17.99 (978-0-06-228017-6(1)) HarperCollins Pubs.

Daly, Catherine. The Ghost of Christmas Past. 2012. 162p. (J). (978-0-545-48422-0(7)) Scholastic, Inc.

David, Erica. Anna & Elsa - A Warm Welcome. RH Disney Staff et al, illus. 2015. (Stepping Stone Book(TM) Ser.: 3). (ENG.). 128p. (J). (gr. 1-4). 9.99 (978-0-7364-3289-4(2), RH/Disney) Random Hse. Children's Bks.

—A Warm Welcome, No. 3. RH Disney Staff et al, illus. 2015. (Stepping Stone Book(TM) Ser.: 3). (ENG.). 128p. (J). (gr. 1-4). lib. bdg. 12.99 (978-0-7364-8247-9(4), RH/Disney) Random Hse. Children's Bks.

Day, Jan. The World's Greatest Explorer, 1 vol. Mason, Janeen, illus. 2009. (ENG.). 32p. (J). (gr. k-3). 16.99 (978-1-58980-603-0(4)) Pelican Publishing Co., Inc.

De Bonneval, Gwen. William & the Lost Spirit. Smith, Anne, tr. Bonhomme, Matthieu, illus. 2013. (ENG.). 160p. (YA). (gr. 8-12). pap. 9.95 (978-1-4677-0807-4(0), Graphic Universe™) Lerner Publishing Group.

De la Cruz, Melissa & Johnston, Michael. Frozen. 2014. (Heart of Dread Ser.: 1). (ENG.). 352p. (YA). (gr. 7). pap. 10.99 (978-0-14-751224-6(7), Speak) Penguin Young Readers Group.

—Golden. 2016. (Heart of Dread Ser.: 3). (ENG.). 272p. (YA). (gr. 7). 17.99 (978-0-399-25756-8(X), G.P. Putnam's Sons Books for Young Readers) Penguin Young Readers Group.

Deacon, Alexis. A Place to Call Home. Schwarz, Viviane, illus. 2011. (ENG.). 40p. (J). (gr. -1-2). 16.99 (978-0-7636-5360-6(8)) Candlewick Pr.

DiCamillo, Kate. Where Are You Going, Baby Lincoln? Tales from Deckawoo Drive, Volume Three. Van Dusen, Chris, illus. 2017. (Tales from Deckawoo Drive Ser.: 3). (ENG.). 112p. (J). (gr. 1-4). pap. 5.99 **(978-0-7636-9758-7(3))** Candlewick Pr.

Disney Press Staff, ed. Mickey's New Friend. 2011. (Illus.). 32p. (J). (978-1-4231-4585-1(2)) Disney Pr.

d'Lacey, Chris. The Fire Ascending. (ENG.). 576p. (J). (gr. 3-7). 2013. pap. 9.99 (978-0-545-40293-4(X), Scholastic Paperbacks) 2012. (Last Dragon Chronicles Ser.: 7). 18.99 (978-0-545-40216-3(6), Orchard Bks.) Scholastic, Inc.

—The Fire Ascending. 2013. (Last Dragon Chronicles Ser.: 7). lib. bdg. 20.85 (978-0-606-31958-4(1), Turtleback) Turtleback Bks.

Dockrey Young, Richard & Young, Judy Dockrey. 1492, New World Tales. 2013. (ENG., Illus.). 267p. (J). (gr. 3-5). pap. 16.95 (978-1-939160-73-7(1)) August Hse. Pubs., Inc.

Doktorski, Jennifer Salvato. How My Summer Went up in Flames. 2013. (ENG.). 320p. (YA). (gr. 9). 17.99 (978-1-4424-5940-3(9)); pap. 10.99 (978-1-4424-5939-7(5)) Simon Pulse. (Simon Pulse).

Donaldson, Julia. Jack & the Flumflum Tree. Roberts, David, illus. 2016. (ENG.). 30p. (J). (gr. -1-k). bds. 9.99

(978-1-4472-8549-6(2)) Pan Macmillan GBR. Dist: Independent Pubs. Group.

Doyle, Roddy. A Greyhound of a Girl. 2013. (ENG.). 224p. (YA). (gr. 3-7). pap. 7.95 *(978-1-4197-0798-8(1),* Amulet Bks.) Abrams, Inc.

Dragt, Tonke. The Letter for the King. 2015. (ENG., Illus.). 528p. (J). (gr. 7). 18.99 *(978-0-545-81978-7(4))* Scholastic, Inc.

Draper, Rochelle. The Stone Wall Dragon. Draper, Rochelle, illus. 2007. (ENG., Illus.). 32p. (J). (gr. 1-17). 15.95 *(978-0-89272-690-5(3))* Down East Bks.

Duff, Hilary. Elixir. 2011. (Playaway Young Adult Ser.). (YA). 59.99 *(978-1-4417-7416-3(5))* Findaway World, LLC.

—Elixir. 2011. (Elixir Ser.). (ENG.). 336p. (YA). (gr. 9). pap. 9.99 *(978-1-4424-0854-8(5),* Simon & Schuster Bks. For Young Readers) Simon & Schuster Bks. For Young Readers.

Duff, Hilary & Allen, Elise. Elixir. 2010. (Elixir Ser.). (ENG.). 336p. (YA). (gr. 9-18). 17.99 *(978-1-4424-0853-1(7),* Simon & Schuster Bks. For Young Readers) Simon & Schuster Bks. For Young Readers.

Duggan, Matt. The Royal Woods. 2010. (ENG., Illus.). 244p. (J). (gr. 4-7). pap. *(978-1-55470-060-8(4))* Me to We.

Easton, Kelly. Aftershock. 2007. (ENG.). 176p. (YA). (gr. 7-12). pap. 6.99 *(978-1-4169-0053-5(5),* McElderry, Margaret K. Bks.) McElderry, Margaret K. Bks.

Eboch, M. M. An Artful Escape. 2015. (ENG.). 96p. (gr. 3-6). 31.36 *(978-1-63430-395-8(4))* Rourke Educational Media.

Edwards, Julie Andrews. Little Bo in London, No. 2. Cole, Henry, illus. 2012. (ENG.). 112p. (J). (gr. 1-4). 19.99 *(978-0-06-008911-5(3))* HarperCollins Pubs.

Egan, Tim. Dodsworth in London. Egan, Tim, illus. (Dodsworth Book Ser.). (ENG., Illus.). 48p. (J). 2010. (gr. 2-5). pap. 3.99 *(978-0-547-41440-9(4))* 11th ed. 2009. (gr. 1-4). 15.00 *(978-0-547-13816-9(4))* Houghton Mifflin Harcourt Publishing Co.

—Dodsworth in New York. 2009. (Dodsworth Book Ser.). (ENG., Illus.). 48p. (J). (gr. 2-5). pap. 3.99 *(978-0-547-24831-8(8))* Houghton Mifflin Harcourt Publishing Co.

—Dodsworth in Paris. Egan, Tim, illus. 2010. (Dodsworth Book Ser.). (ENG., Illus.). 48p. (J). (gr. 1-4). pap. 3.99 *(978-0-547-33192-8(4))* Houghton Mifflin Harcourt Publishing Co.

—Dodsworth in Tokyo. Egan, Tim, illus. 2014. (Green Light Readers Level 3 Ser.). (ENG., Illus.). 48p. (J). (gr. 1-4). pap. 3.99 *(978-0-544-33915-6(0),* HMH Books For Young Readers) Houghton Mifflin Harcourt Publishing Co.

Elish, Dan. The School for the Insanely Gifted. 2011. (ENG.). 304p. (J). (gr. 3-7). 15.99 *(978-0-06-113873-7(8))* HarperCollins Pubs.

Elissa, Barbara. The Remarkable Journey of Josh's Kippah. Zaman, Farida, illus. 2010. 32p. (J). (gr. -1-3). pap. 7.95 *(978-0-8225-9933-3(3),* Kar-Ben Publishing) Lerner Publishing Group.

Else, Barbara. The Traveling Restaurant: Jasper's Voyage in Three Parts. 2012. (Gecko Press Titles Ser.). (ENG.). 304p. (J). (gr. 5-8). 17.95 *(978-1-877579-03-5(3))* Gecko Pr. NZL. Dist: Lerner Publishing Group.

Erdrich, Louise. Chickadee. Erdrich, Louise, illus. (Birchbark House Ser.: 4). (Illus.). (J). (gr. 3-7). 2013. (ENG.). 224p. pap. 6.99 *(978-0-06-057792-6(4))* 2012. (ENG., 208p. 16.99 *(978-0-06-057790-2(8))* 2012. 208p. lib. bdg. 17.89 *(978-0-06-057791-9(6))* HarperCollins Pubs.

—The Porcupine Year. Erdrich, Louise, illus. 2010. (Birchbark House Ser.: 3). (Illus.). 224p. (J). (gr. 3-7). pap. 6.99 *(978-0-06-441030-4(7))* HarperCollins Pubs.

Evans, Douglas. MVP. Shelley, John, illus. (ENG.). 232p. (J). (gr. 4-6). 2008. pap. 9.95 *(978-1-59078-625-3(4),* Front Street) 2004. 16.95 *(978-1-932425-13-0(6),* Lemniscaat) Boyds Mills Pr.

Everett Hale, Edward. Last of the Peterkins with Others of the. 2006. pap. *(978-1-4068-1087-5(8))* Echo Library.

Evert, Lori. The Christmas Wish. Breiehagen, Per, illus. Breiehagen, Per, photos by. 2013. (ENG.). 48p. (J). (gr. -1-2). 17.99 *(978-0-449-81681-3(8),* Random Hse. Bks. for Young Readers) Random Hse. Children's Bks.

—The Christmas Wish. Breiehagen, Per, illus. Breiehagen, Per, photos by. 2013. (J). *(978-0-449-81942-5(6))* Random Hse., Inc.

—The Tiny Wish. Breiehagen, Per, illus. 2015. (ENG.). 48p. (J). (gr. -1-2). lib. bdg. 20.99 *(978-0-375-97336-9(2),* Random Hse. Bks. for Young Readers) Random Hse. Children's Bks.

Fabrick, Harriet. Furello Journeys: Furello Questions. Date not set. (Illus.). 200p. (J). (gr. 7-9). wbk. ed. 12.95 *(978-0-9646698-9-5(7))* Wild Flower USA.

Faircloth, Sean. The Enchanted Globe. 2016. (ENG., Illus.). 224p. (J). (gr. 4-7). pap. 12.95 *(978-1-63431-101-4(9))* Pitchstone LLC.

Farrow, G. e. & Farrow, G. E. The Wallypug in London. 2011. 106p. 23.95 *(978-1-4638-9696-6(4))* Rodgers, Alan Bks.

Fayers, Claire. The Voyage to Magical North. 2016. (Accidental Pirates Ser.). (ENG.). 320p. (J). 16.99 *(978-1-62779-420-6(4),* 9781627794206, Holt, Henry & Co. Bks. For Young Readers) Holt, Henry & Co.

Fforde, Jasper. The Eye of Zoltar. 2014. (Chronicles of Kazam Ser.). (ENG.). 416p. (J). (gr. 5-7). 16.99 *(978-0-547-73849-9(8),* HMH Books For Young Readers) Houghton Mifflin Harcourt Publishing Co.

Findlay, Lisa & Swift, Jonathan. Gulliver in Lilliput. Caparó, Antonio Javier, illus. 2010. (Step into Reading Ser.). (ENG.). 48p. (J). (gr. k-3). pap. 3.99 *(978-0-375-86585-5(3),* Random Hse. Bks. for Young Readers) Random Hse. Children's Bks.

Fleischman, Paul. Whirligig. 2010. (ENG.). 144p. (YA). (gr. 7-12). pap. 7.99 *(978-0-312-62911-3(7),* 9780312629113) Square Fish.

Flowers, J. J. Juan Pablo & the Butterflies. 2017. (ENG., Illus.). 224p. (YA). (gr. 9-12). 17.99 *(978-1-5072-0214-2(8),* Simon Pulse) Simon Pulse.

Flusfeder, David. John the Pupil. 2015. 240p. 24.99 *(978-0-06-233918-8(4))* HarperCollins Pubs.

Ford, Sally. Bungee down Under. Dudley, Peter, illus. 2004. 40p. (J). 14.95 *(978-1-931807-26-5(4))* Randall, Peter E. Pub.

Forman, Gayle. Just One Day. 2013. (ENG.). (YA). (gr. 9). 416p. pap. 10.99 *(978-0-14-242295-3(9),* Speak); 384p. 17.99 *(978-0-525-42591-5(8),* Dutton Books for Young Readers) Penguin Young Readers Group.

—Just One Day. 2013. lib. bdg. 22.10 *(978-0-606-34405-0(5),* Turtleback) Turtleback Bks.

—Just One Year. (ENG.). (YA). (gr. 9). 2014. 352p. pap. 10.99 *(978-0-14-242296-0(7),* Speak) 2013. 336p. 17.99 *(978-0-525-42592-2(6),* Dutton Books for Young Readers) Penguin Young Readers Group.

—Just One Year. 2014. lib. bdg. 22.10 *(978-0-606-36190-3(1))* Turtleback Bks.

Fox, Robin C. & Fox, Carol White. The Traveling Adventures of the Robin & the Fox Around the World We Go! A Cruise Through the Mediterranean. 2013. 44p. pap. 20.45 *(978-1-4908-1763-7(8),* WestBow Pr.) Author Solutions, Inc.

Francoise. Fanchette & Jeannot: A Little Story with Pictures. 2011. 26p. 35.95 *(978-1-258-07322-0(6))* Literary Licensing, LLC.

Fraser, Chelsea Curtis. Around the World in Ten Days. 2007. (ENG.). 192p. pap. 19.99 *(978-1-4346-3412-2(4));* 208p. pap. 22.99 *(978-1-4346-3413-9(2))* Creative Media Partners, LLC.

Freer, Dave. Cuttlefish. 2012. (ENG.). 299p. (YA). (gr. 7). 16.95 *(978-1-61614-625-2(7))* Prometheus Bks., Pubs.

Friedman, Laurie. Mallory on Board. Pollak, Barbara, illus. 2008. (Mallory Ser.: 7). (ENG.). 176p. (J). (gr. 2-5). per. 5.95 *(978-0-8225-9023-1(9),* First Avenue Editions) Lerner Publishing Group.

Friesen, Jonathan. Both of Me. 1 vol. 2016. (ENG.). 256p. (J). pap. 9.99 *(978-0-310-73187-0(9))* Blink.

Fromental, Jean-Luc. Oops! Connors, Thomas, tr. from FRE. Jolivet, Joëlle, illus. 2010. (ENG.). 42p. (J). (gr. -1-k). 17.95 *(978-0-8109-8749-4(X))* Abrams, Inc.

Frossard, Claire, illus. Emma's Journey. Frossard, Etienne, photos by. 2010. (ENG.). 56p. (J). (gr. -1-3). 17.95 *(978-1-59270-099-8(3))* Enchanted Lion Bks., LLC.

Gaiman, NEil. Instructions. Vess, Charles, illus. 2010. 40p. (J). (gr. -1-3). (ENG.). 14.99 *(978-0-06-196030-7(6));* lib. bdg. 15.89 *(978-0-06-196031-4(4))* HarperCollins Pubs.

—Instructions. Vess, Charles, illus. 2015. (ENG.). 40p. (J). (gr. -1-3). 8.99 *(978-0-06-196032-1(2))* HarperCollins Pubs.

Gallo, Tina, adapted by. Kung Fu Road Trip. 2014. (Kung Fu Panda TV Ser.). (ENG., Illus.). 32p. (J). (gr. k-2). 16.99 *(978-1-4814-0489-1(X),* Simon Spotlight) Simon Spotlight.

Garfield, Henry. The Lost Voyage of John Cabot. 2007. (ENG., Illus.). 320p. (YA). (gr. 7). pap. 16.95 *(978-1-4169-5460-6(0),* Simon Pulse) Simon Pulse.

Garis, Howard Roger. Uncle Wiggily's Travels. Date not set. 192p. (J). 20.95 *(978-0-8488-2278-1(1))* Amereon Ltd.

Gerstein, Mordicai. How to Bicycle to the Moon to Plant Sunflowers: A Simple but Brilliant Plan in 24 Easy Steps. Gerstein, Mordicai, illus. 2013. (ENG., Illus.). 40p. (J). (gr. -1-2). 16.99 *(978-1-59643-512-4(7),* 9781596435124) Roaring Brook Pr.

Gilligan, Alison. Search for the Black Rhino. 2011. (Illus.). 144p. (J). pap. 6.99 *(978-1-937133-01-6(X))* Chooseco LLC.

Gownley, Jimmy. Her Permanent Record. Gownley, Jimmy, illus. 2012. (Amelia Rules! Ser.). (ENG., Illus.). 160p. (J). (gr. 2-7). 19.99 *(978-1-4169-8615-7(4));* pap. 11.99 *(978-1-4169-8614-0(6))* Simon & Schuster Children's Publishing. (Atheneum Bks. for Young Readers).

—Her Permanent Record. 2012. (Amelia Rules! Ser.: 8). lib. bdg. 23.30 *(978-0-606-26885-1(5),* Turtleback) Turtleback Bks.

Grahame, Kenneth. The Wind in the Willows. Ingpen, Robert R., illus. 2012. (Sterling Illustrated Classics Ser.). (ENG.). 224p. (J). (gr. 2-8). 19.95 *(978-1-4027-8283-1(7))* Sterling Publishing Co., Inc.

Granson, Steven. Zando. 2009. 124p. pap. 10.95 *(978-1-4401-5658-8(1))* iUniverse, Inc.

Gravett, Emily. Meerkat Mail. Gravett, Emily, illus. 2007. (ENG., Illus.). 32p. (J). (gr. -1-3). 17.99 *(978-1-4169-3473-8(1),* Simon & Schuster Bks. For Young Readers) Simon & Schuster Bks. For Young Readers.

Gray, Michael Loyd. King Biscuit. 2013. (J). pap. *(978-1-938237-04-1(8))* Tempest Bk. Shop.

Greenwood, Diana. Insight. 1 vol. 2012. (ENG.). 224p. (YA). pap. 7.99 *(978-0-310-72315-8(9))* Zondervan.

Griggs, Terry. Nieve. L'Hirondelle, Cheryl, illus. 2010. (ENG.). 264p. (J). (gr. 4-10). pap. 14.95 *(978-1-897231-87-6(3))* Biblioasis CAN. Dist: Consortium Bk. Sales & Distribution.

Gutman, Dan. Flashback Four #2: the Titanic Mission. 2017. (Flashback Four Ser.: 2). 240p. (J). (gr. 3-7). 16.99 *(978-0-06-223635-7(0))* HarperCollins Pubs.

—You Only Die Twice. 2013. (Genius Files Ser.: 3). (J). lib. bdg. 17.20 *(978-0-606-35043-3(8),* Turtleback) Turtleback Bks.

Haddix, Margaret Peterson. Torn. (Missing Ser.: 4). (ENG.). (J). (gr. 3-7). 2012. 368p. pap. 8.99 *(978-1-4169-8981-3(1))* 2011. 352p. 17.99 *(978-1-4169-8980-6(3))* Simon & Schuster Bks. For Young Readers. (Simon & Schuster Bks. For Young Readers).

—Torn. l.t. ed. 2011. (Missing Ser.: Bk. 4). (ENG.). 368p. 23.99 *(978-1-4104-4078-5(8))* Thorndike Pr.

—Torn. 2012. (Missing Ser.: 4). lib. bdg. 18.40 *(978-0-606-26333-7(0),* Turtleback) Turtleback Bks.

Hagen, George. Gabriel Finley & the Raven's Riddle. Bakal, Scott, illus. 2014. (ENG.). 384p. (J). (gr. 4-7). 16.99 *(978-0-385-37103-2(9),* Schwartz & Wade Bks.) Random Hse. Children's Bks.

Hale, Lucretia Peabody. The Last of the Peterkins: With Others of Their Kin. 2007. (ENG.). 142p. pap. 18.99 *(978-1-4346-2126-9(X));* 154p. pap. 21.99 *(978-1-4346-2145-0(6))* Creative Media Partners, LLC.

Hall, Lucy. From England to Jamestowne: A Journey to Find My Father. 2007. (J). *(978-0-9763706-5-9(4))* Tendril Pr., LLC.

Hall, Maggie. The Conspiracy of Us. 2015. (Conspiracy of Us Ser.). (ENG.). (YA). 336p. (gr. 7). 17.99 *(978-0-399-16650-1(5));*Pack. 161.91 *(978-0-399-17404-9(4))* Penguin Young Readers Group. (G.P. Putnam's Sons Books for Young Readers).

—The Ends of the World. 2017. (Conspiracy of Us Ser.: 3). (ENG.). 320p. (YA). (gr. 7). 17.99 ***(978-0-399-16652-5(1),*** G.P. Putnam's Sons Books for Young Readers) Penguin Young Readers Group.

Hall, Maggie. Map of Fates. 2016. (Conspiracy of Us Ser.). (ENG.). 320p. (YA). (gr. 7). 17.99 *(978-0-399-16651-8(3),* G.P. Putnam's Sons Books for Young Readers) Penguin Young Readers Group.

Hamilton, Libby & Haworth, Katie. Around the World. Shuttlewood, Craig, illus. 2015. (ENG.). 10p. (J). (gr. -1 — 1). bds. 6.99 *(978-1-4998-0075-3(4))* Little Bee Books Inc.

Hampton, Francesca. Children's Voyage the Long Journey Home. 2010. 222p. pap. 13.96 *(978-0-557-23497-4(2))* Lulu Pr., Inc.

Handford, Martin. The Fantastic Journey. Handford, Martin, illus. deluxe ed. 2013. (Where's Waldo? Ser.). (ENG., Illus.). 32p. (J). (gr. k-12). 16.99 *(978-0-7636-4528-1(1))* Candlewick Pr.

—Where's Waldo? Handford, Martin, illus. (Where's Waldo? Ser.). (ENG., Illus.). (J). (gr. k-4). 2011. 64p. pap. 9.99 *(978-0-7636-5416-0(7))* 2nd ed. 2007. 32p. pap. 7.99 *(978-0-7636-3498-8(0))* 25th anniv. deluxe ed. 2012. 32p. 16.99 *(978-0-7636-4525-0(7))* 30th anniv. ed. 2017. 36p. 7.99 *(978-0-7636-9579-8(3))* Candlewick Pr.

—Where's Waldo? 2007. (Where's Waldo? Ser.). (Illus.). 24p. (gr. 4-7). lib. bdg. 18.40 *(978-1-4178-2424-3(7),* Turtleback) Turtleback Bks.

—Where's Waldo? the Coloring Collection. Handford, Martin, illus. 2017. (Where's Waldo? Ser.). (ENG., Illus.). 80p. (J). (gr. k-12). pap. 12.99 *(978-0-7636-9577-4(7))* Candlewick Pr.

—Where's Waldo? the Fantastic Journey. Handford, Martin, illus. 2007. (Where's Waldo? Ser.). (ENG., Illus.). 32p. (J). (gr. k-4). pap. 7.99 *(978-0-7636-3500-8(6))* Candlewick Pr.

—Where's Waldo? The Great Picture Hunt. Handford, Martin, illus. 2006. (Where's Waldo? Ser.). (ENG., Illus.). 24p. (J). (gr. k-4). 14.99 *(978-0-7636-3043-0(8))* Candlewick Pr.

—Where's Waldo? the Incredible Paper Chase. 2011. (Where's Waldo? Ser.). (ENG., Illus.). 24p. (J). (gr. k-4). pap. 7.99 *(978-0-7636-4725-4(X))* Candlewick Pr.

—Where's Waldo? the Totally Essential Travel Collection. Handford, Martin, illus. 2017. (Where's Waldo? Ser.). (ENG., Illus.). 172p. (J). (gr. k-12). pap. 14.99 *(978-0-7636-9580-4(7))* Candlewick Pr.

—Where's Waldo? the Wonder Book. Handford, Martin, illus. (Where's Waldo? Ser.). (ENG., Illus.). 32p. (J). (gr. k-12). 2014. 16.99 *(978-0-7636-4530-4(3))* 2007. pap. 7.99 *(978-0-7636-3502-2(2))* Candlewick Pr.

—Where's Waldo Now? Handford, Martin, illus. 2007. (Where's Waldo? Ser.). (ENG., Illus.). 32p. (J). (gr. k-4). pap. 7.99 *(978-0-7636-3499-5(9))* Candlewick Pr.

—The Wow Collection: Six Amazing Books & a Puzzle. Handford, Martin, illus. 2012. (Where's Waldo? Ser.). (ENG., Illus.). (J). (gr. k-4). 49.99 *(978-0-7636-6179-3(1))* Candlewick Pr.

Hart, Alison. Emma's River. 1 vol. Bachem, Paul, illus. 2010. (ENG.). 160p. (J). (gr. 2-5). 12.95 *(978-1-56145-524-9(5),* Peachtree Junior) Peachtree Pubs.

Hatton, Libby. Pete Puffin's Wild Ride Cruising Alaska's Currents. Hatton, Libby, illus. 2008. (Illus.). (J). pap. 16.95 *(978-0-930931-92-6(0))* Alaska Geographic Assn.

Helget, Nicole. Wonder at the Edge of the World. 2015. (ENG., Illus.). 384p. (J). (gr. 3-7). 17.00 *(978-0-316-24510-4(0))* Little, Brown Bks. for Young Readers.

Heltzel, Anne. Charlie, Presumed Dead. (ENG.). 272p. (YA). (gr. 9). 2016. pap. 8.99 *(978-0-544-66869-0(3))* 2015. 17.99 *(978-0-544-38849-9(6))* Houghton Mifflin Harcourt Publishing Co. (HMH Books For Young Readers).

Hennessy, B. G. The Once upon a Time Map Book: Take a Tour of Six Enchanted Lands. Joyce, Peter, illus. 2010. (ENG.). 16p. (J). (gr. 1-4). pap. 8.99 *(978-0-7636-2682-2(1))* Candlewick Pr.

Hesse, Karen. Stowaway. unabr. ed. 2004. 328p. (J). (gr. 5-9). pap. 48.00 incl. audio *(978-0-8072-8760-6(1),* LYA 259 SP, Listening Library) Random Hse. Audio Publishing Group.

Hidden. 2014. (ENG., Illus.). 384p. (YA). (gr. 7). 17.99 *(978-1-4424-8300-2(8),* Simon & Schuster/Paula Wiseman Bks.) Simon & Schuster/Paula Wiseman Bks.

Hobbs, Will. Crossing the Wire. (ENG.). 224p. (J). (gr. 5-9). 2007. pap. 7.99 *(978-0-06-074140-2(6))* 2006. (Illus.). 16.99 *(978-0-06-074138-9(4))* HarperCollins Pubs.

—Crossing the Wire. 2007. (Illus.). 216p. (gr. 5-9). 17.00 *(978-0-7569-8053-5(4))* Perfection Learning Corp.

Hobbs, William. Jason's Gold. unabr. ed. 2004. 240p. (J). (gr. 5-9). pap. 38.00 incl. audio *(978-0-8072-8229-8(4),* Listening Library) Random Hse. Audio Publishing Group.

Hollier, Jo. Roary O'Rourke, Quest for the Secret of Bramble Castle. 2004. (J). pap. 9.95 *(978-1-59374-081-8(6))* Whiskey Creek Pr., LLC.

Holmes, Mary Tavener & Harris, John. A Giraffe Goes to Paris. 0 vols. Cannell, Jon, illus. 2010. (ENG.). 32p. (J). (gr. 1-4). 17.99 *(978-0-7614-5595-0(7),* 9780761455950, Amazon Children's Publishing) Amazon Publishing.

Horvath, Polly. Lord & Lady Bunny — Almost Royalty! Blackall, Sophie, illus. 2016. (ENG.). 304p. (J). (gr. 3-7). pap. 8.99 *(978-0-307-98068-7(5),* Yearling) Random Hse. Children's Bks.

Hosford, Kate. How the Queen Found the Perfect Cup of Tea. Swiatkowska, Gabi, illus. 2017. (Carolrhoda Picture Bks.). (ENG.). 40p. (J). (gr. k-3). (J). 9.99 ***(978-1-5124-3273-2(3));*** (J). 38.65 ***(978-1-5124-3272-5(5));*** 38.65 ***(978-1-4677-9563-0(1))*** Lerner Publishing Group. (Carolrhoda Bks.).

Hosford, Kate. The Perfect Cup of Tea. Swiatkowska, Gabi, illus. 2017. (ENG.). 40p. (J). (gr. k-3). 18.99 *(978-1-4677-3904-7(9))* Lerner Publishing Group.

Howard, Chris. Rootless. 2012. (ENG.). 336p. (J). (gr. 9). 17.99 *(978-0-545-38789-7(2))* Scholastic, Inc.

Howard, Jonathan L. Katya's War. 2013. (ENG.). 320p. (YA). (gr. 9). pap. 9.99 *(978-1-908844-19-4(1),* Strange Chemistry) Watkins Media Limited GBR. Dist: Penguin Random Hse. LLC.

Hughes, Devon. Escape from Lion's Head. 2017. (Unnaturals Ser.: 2). 384p. (J). (gr. 3-7). 16.99 *(978-0-06-225757-4(9),* Tegen, Katherine Bks) HarperCollins Pubs.

Hull, Maureen. Rainy Days with Bear. l.t. ed. 2012. 51p. (J). pap. *(978-1-4596-3453-4(5))* ReadHowYouWant.com, Ltd.

Hunter, Derek. Brainwash Escape Victims, Vol. 2. 2006. (ENG., Illus.). 144p. (YA). pap. 12.95 *(978-1-59362-051-6(9),* 9781593620516) Slave Labor Bks.

Hunter, Erin. The Burning Horizon. 2015. (Seekers: Return to the Wild Ser.: 5). (ENG., Illus.). 304p. (J). (gr. 3-7). 16.99 *(978-0-06-199646-7(7))* HarperCollins Pubs.

—Dawn. Richardson, Owen & Stevenson, Dave, illus. 2015. (Warriors: the New Prophecy Ser.: 3). (ENG.). 400p. (J). (gr. 3-7). pap. 7.99 *(978-0-06-236704-4(8))* HarperCollins Pubs.

—River of Lost Bearsrs No. 3. 2013. (Seekers: Return to the Wild Ser.: 3). (ENG., Illus.). 320p. (J). (gr. 3-7). 16.99 *(978-0-06-199640-5(8))* HarperCollins Pubs.

—Warriors Super Edition: Moth Flight's Vision. Barry, James L. & Richardson, Owen, illus. 2016. (Warriors Super Edition Ser.: 8). 544p. (J). (gr. 3-7). pap. 7.99 *(978-0-06-229149-3(1))* HarperCollins Pubs.

Hunter, Erin, et al. Moth Flight's Vision. Barry, James L. & Richardson, Owen, illus. 2015. (Warriors Super Edition Ser.: 8). (ENG.). 528p. (J). (gr. 3-7). 18.99 *(978-0-06-229147-9(5))* HarperCollins Pubs.

Huser, Glen. Skinnybones & the Wrinkle Queen. 2013. 232p. pap. *(978-1-4596-6507-1(4))* ReadHowYouWant.com, Ltd.

Hyde, Catherine Ryan. Becoming Chloe. 2008. (ENG.). 224p. (YA). (gr. 9). pap. 8.99 *(978-0-375-83260-4(2),* Knopf Bks. for Young Readers) Random Hse. Children's Bks.

Ibbotson, Eva. The Abominables. Robinson, Fiona, illus. 2013. (ENG.). 272p. (J). (gr. 3-7). 16.95 *(978-1-4197-0789-6(2),* Amulet Bks.) Abrams, Inc.

—The Abominables. Robinson, Fiona, illus. 2014. (ENG.). 288p. (J). (gr. 3-7). pap. 8.95 *(978-1-4197-1215-9(2),* Amulet Bks.) Abrams, Inc.

—One Dog & His Boy. 2012. (ENG.). 288p. (J). (gr. 3-7). 16.99 *(978-0-545-35196-6(0),* Scholastic Pr.) Scholastic, Inc.

Jackson, Ciandress. Chloe the Jumbo Jet: Fantastic Friends Around the World. 2013. 24p. pap. 9.99 *(978-1-61286-195-1(4))* Avid Readers Publishing Group.

Jahn-Clough, Lisa. Felicity & Cordelia: A Tale of Two Bunnies. Jahn-Clough, Lisa, illus. 2011. (ENG., Illus.). 40p. (J). (gr. -1-3). 16.99 *(978-0-374-32300-4(3),* 9780374323004, Farrar, Straus & Giroux (BYR)) Farrar, Straus & Giroux.

Janisch, Heinz. The Fantastic Adventures of Baron Munchausen. Cooper, Belinda, tr. from GER. Blau, Aljoscha, illus. 2010. (ENG.). 32p. (J). (gr. -1-3). 17.95 *(978-1-59270-091-2(8))* Enchanted Lion Bks., LLC.

Jarman, Julia. The Magic Backpack. Gon, Adriano, illus. 2003. (Flying Foxes Ser.). (ENG.). 48p. (J). lib. bdg. *(978-0-7787-1487-3(X))* Crabtree Publishing Co.

—Stowaway? Oldroyd, Mark, illus. 2007. (Collins Big Cat Ser.). (ENG.). 48p. (J). (gr. 3-4). pap. 8.99 *(978-0-00-723088-4(5))* HarperCollins Pubs. Ltd. GBR. Dist: Independent Pubs. Group.

Jeffers, Oliver. Lost & Found. Jeffers, Oliver, illus. 2005. (ENG., Illus.). 32p. (J). (gr. -1-2). 17.99 *(978-0-399-24503-9(0),* Philomel Bks.) Penguin Young Readers Group.

Jennewein, James & Parker, Tom S. Shield of Odin. 2009. (RuneWarriors Ser.: 1). (ENG.). 336p. (J). (gr. 3-7). pap. 6.99 *(978-0-06-144938-3(5))* HarperCollins Pubs.

—Sword of Doom. 2009. (RuneWarriors Ser.: 2). (ENG.). 432p. (J). (gr. 3-7). 17.99 *(978-0-06-144939-0(3))* HarperCollins Pubs.

Johnson, Maureen. The Last Little Blue Envelope. 2012. (13 Little Blue Envelopes Ser.: 2). (ENG.). 288p. (YA). (gr. 8). pap. 9.99 *(978-0-06-197681-0(4),* HarperTeen) HarperCollins Pubs.

—The Last Little Blue Envelope. 2016. (13 Little Blue Envelopes Ser.: 2). (Illus.). 288p. (YA). (gr. 8). pap. 9.99 *(978-0-06-243912-3(X),* HarperTeen) HarperCollins Pubs.

—13 Little Blue Envelopes. (13 Little Blue Envelopes Ser.: 1). (ENG., Illus.). (YA). (gr. 8-18). 2005. 336p. 17.99 *(978-0-06-054141-5(5))* 2010. 368p. reprint ed. pap. 9.99 *(978-0-06-054143-9(1))* HarperCollins Pubs. (HarperTeen).

—13 Little Blue Envelopes. 2007. 317p. 20.00 *(978-0-7569-7830-3(0))* Perfection Learning Corp.

Johnston, Tony & Mazellan, Ron. The Harmonica. Mazellan, Ron, illus. 2008. (ENG., Illus.). 32p. (J). (gr. 2-5). pap. 7.95 *(978-1-57091-489-8(3))* Charlesbridge Publishing, Inc.

Jolivert, Immaculine. The Lamb Who Counted Clouds. Gillen, Rosemarie, illus. 2013. 24p. pap. 13.75 *(978-1-937260-91-0(7))* Sleepytown Pr.

Jones, Diana Wynne & Jones, Ursula. The Islands of Chaldea. 368p. (J). (gr. 3-7). 2015. pap. 9.99 *(978-0-06-229508-8(X))* 2014. 17.99 *(978-0-06-229507-1(1))* HarperCollins Pubs. (Greenwillow Bks.).

Jones, Frewin. The Enchanted Quest. 2010. (Faerie Path Ser.: 5). (ENG.). 368p. (YA). (gr. 8-18). 16.99 *(978-0-06-087158-1(X),* HarperTeen) HarperCollins Pubs.

Judge, Chris. The Lonely Beast. Judge, Chris, illus. 2011. (Andersen Press Picture Books Ser.). (Illus.). 32p. (J). (gr. -1-4). 16.95 *(978-0-7613-8097-9(3))* Andersen Pr. GBR. Dist: Lerner Publishing Group.

Kargbo, Ms Mariatu. Three Themne Titi Girls. 2013. 24p. (J). pap. 24.95 *(978-1-63004-790-0(2))* America Star Bks.

Kate, Lauren. Atlántida. 2015. (SPA.). 368p. pap. 10.95 *(978-1-101-91062-7(3),* Vintage Espanol) Knopf Doubleday Publishing Group.

Kaufmann, Kelli. Ned Redd, World Traveler: A Search-And-Find Adventure. Boyd, Aaron, illus. 2005. (J). *(978-1-58987-135-9(9))* Kindermusik International.

Kazeroid, Sibylle, tr. from FRE. Liu & the Bird: A Journey in Chinese Calligraphy. Louis, Catherine, illus. 2006. (FRE.). 40p. (J). (gr. -1-3). 16.95 *(978-0-7358-2050-0(3))* North-South Bks., Inc.

Keeling, Annie E. Andrew Golding A Tale of the Great Plague. 2004. reprint ed. pap. 15.95 *(978-1-4191-0694-1(5));* pap. 1.99 *(978-1-4192-0694-8(X))* Kessinger Publishing, LLC.

Kehret, Peg. Runaway Twin. 2011. (ENG.). 208p. (J). (gr. 5-18). 6.99 *(978-0-14-241849-9(8),* Puffin Books) Penguin Young Readers Group.

Kelby, Tom. Nathaniel's Journey: The King's Armory. Yaeger, Mark, illus. 2003. (J). per. *(978-1-930914-04-9(0))* Hands to the Plow, Inc.

Kerby, Mona. Owney, the Mail-Pouch Pooch. Barasch, Lynne, illus. 2008. (ENG.). 40p. (J). (gr. k-3). 17.99 *(978-0-374-35685-9(8),* 9780374356859, Farrar, Straus & Giroux (BYR)) Farrar, Straus & Giroux.

Khanduri, Kamini. Usborne the Great World Search. Hancock, David, illus. rev. ed. 2005. (Great Searches (EDC Paperback) Ser.). 48p. (J). (gr. -1). pap. 8.99 *(978-0-7945-1030-5(2),* Usborne) EDC Publishing.

Kiely, Kevin. SOS Lusitania. 2013. (ENG.). 208p. (J). pap. 12.95 *(978-1-84717-230-3(X))* O'Brien Pr., Ltd., The IRL. Dist: Dufour Editions, Inc.

Kipling, Rudyard. The White Seal. Jones, Chuck, illus. 2006. (ENG.). 32p. (J). (gr. -1-3). 8.95 *(978-0-8249-6598-3(1),* Ideal Pubns.) Worthy Publishing.

Kirby, Matthew J. The Lost Kingdom. 2013. (ENG.). 352p. (J). (gr. 3-7). 18.99 *(978-0-545-27426-5(5),* Scholastic Pr.) Scholastic, Inc.

Kirkpatrick, Katherine. Escape Across the Wide Sea. 2004. (ENG., Illus.). 224p. (J). (gr. 4-6). tchr. ed. 17.95 *(978-0-8234-1854-1(5))* Holiday Hse., Inc.

Kittredge, Caitlin. The Mirrored Shard: the Iron Codex Book Three. 2013. (Iron Codex Ser.). (ENG.). 304p. (YA). (gr. 7). 17.99 *(978-0-385-73833-0(1),* Delacorte Bks. for Young Readers) Random Hse. Children's Bks.

Kono, Erin Eitter. Every Color. 2016. (ENG., Illus.). 32p. (J). (gr. -1-3). 16.99 *(978-0-8037-4132-4(4),* Dial Bks) Penguin Young Readers Group.

Korman, Gordon. Unsinkable, Bk. 1. 2011. (Titanic Ser.: 1). (ENG.). 160p. (J). (gr. 3-7). pap. 6.99 *(978-0-545-12331-0(3),* Scholastic Paperbacks) Scholastic, Inc.

Kotzwinkle, William, et al. Walter the Farting Dog Goes on a Cruise. Coleman, Audrey, illus. 2008. (ENG.). 32p. (J). (gr. k-3). pap. 6.99 *(978-0-14-241142-1(6),* Puffin Books) Penguin Young Readers Group.

LaFaye, A. Walking Home to Rosie Lee. Shepherd, Keith D., illus. 2011. (ENG.). 32p. (J). (gr. 1-6). 16.95 *(978-1-933693-97-2(5))* Cinco Puntos Pr.

Lallemand, Orianne. The Wolf Who Wanted to Travel the World. Thuillier, Eléonore, illus. 2013. (My Little Picture Book Ser.). (ENG.). 32p. (J). (gr. -1). pap. 6.95 *(978-2-7338-2314-9(0))* Auzou, Philippe Editions FRA. Dist: Consortium Bk. Sales & Distribution.

Langen, Annette. Letters from Felix: A Little Rabbit on a World Tour. Droop, Constanza, illus. 2003. 47p. (J). 14.99 *(978-1-59384-034-1(9))* Parklane Publishing.

Langrish, Katherine. Troll Blood. Stevens, Tim & Wyatt, David, illus. 2008. 352p. (gr. 5-8). (ENG.). (J). 16.99 *(978-0-06-111674-2(2));* (YA). lib. bdg. 17.89 *(978-0-06-111675-9(0),* Eos) HarperCollins Pubs.

Larson, Hope. Compass South. Mock, Rebecca, illus. 2016. (Four Points Ser.: 1). (ENG.). 224p. (J). 17.99 *(978-0-374-30043-2(7),* 9780374300432, Farrar, Straus & Giroux (BYR)) Farrar, Straus & Giroux.

Lasky, Kathryn. A Journey to the New World: The Diary of Remember Patience Whipple, Mayflower 1620. 2010. (Dear America Ser.). (ENG.). 192p. (J). (gr. 3-7). 12.99 *(978-0-545-23801-4(3),* Scholastic Pr.) Scholastic, Inc.

—The River of Wind. 2007. (Guardians of Ga'Hoole Ser.: 13). lib. bdg. 17.20 *(978-1-4177-8261-1(7),* Turtleback) Turtleback Bks.

Law, Ingrid. Savvy. 2011. 9.68 *(978-0-7848-3575-3(6),* Everbind) Marco Bk. Co.

—Savvy. (ENG.). (J). (gr. 4-7). 2010. 368p. 7.99 *(978-0-14-241433-0(6),* Puffin Books) 2008. (Illus.). 352p. 18.99 *(978-0-8037-3306-0(2),* Dial Bks) Penguin Young Readers Group.

—Savvy. l.t. ed. 2011. (ENG.). 500p. 23.99 *(978-1-4104-3530-9(X))* Thorndike Pr.

—Savvy. 2010. lib. bdg. 18.40 *(978-0-606-14394-3(7),* Turtleback) Turtleback Bks.

Leth, Kate. Adventure Time Vol. 4. 2014. lib. bdg. 24.50 *(978-0-606-36119-4(7))* Turtleback Bks.

Lisle, Holly. Ruby Key, Bk. 1. 2008. (ENG.). 384p. (J). *(978-0-545-00013-0(0),* Orchard Bks.) Scholastic, Inc.

Little, Kimberley Griffiths. Banished. 2016. (Forbidden Ser.: 2). 416p. (YA). (gr. 9). 17.99 *(978-0-06-219501-2(8))* HarperCollins Pubs.

Little, Penny. Blackest Hole in Space. Vigla, Vincent, illus. 2009. (ENG.). 28p. (J). (gr. -1-k). pap. 8.99 *(978-0-340-94467-7(6))* Hodder & Stoughton GBR. Dist: Hachette Bk. Group.

Lo, Malinda. Huntress. 2012. (ENG.). 416p. (YA). (gr. 10-17). pap. 11.99 *(978-0-316-03999-4(3))* Little, Brown Bks. for Young Readers.

Lofting, Hugh. The Voyages of Doctor Dolittle. 2004. (Dover Children's Classics Ser.). (ENG., Illus.). 224p. (J). (gr. 3-7). pap. 4.95 *(978-0-486-43491-9(5))* Dover Pubns., Inc.

London, Jack. The Mutiny of the ElsinoreApos. 2006. 264p. per. 15.95 *(978-1-59818-834-9(8))* Aegypan.

Ma, Jyoti & Devi, Chandra. Sparkling Together: Starbright & His Earthling Friends. 2004. (ENG., Illus.). 96p. (J). pap. 19.95 *(978-0-932040-54-1(3),* 9780932040541) Integral Yoga Pubns.

Mac Killian, Caroline. Travels of the Zephyr: An Interactive Journey Around the World. 2010. (ENG., Illus.). 88p. (J). (gr. 3-7). 24.95 *(978-0-8109-8974-0(3),* Abrams Bks. for Young Readers) Abrams, Inc.

Malnor, Carol & Fuller, Sandy F. The BLUES Go Extreme Birding, 1 vol. Schroeder, Louise, illus. 2011. (ENG.). 36p. (J). (gr. k-4). 16.95 *(978-1-58469-133-4(6));* pap. 8.95 *(978-1-58469-134-1(4))* Dawn Pubns.

Malnor, Carol L. & Fuller, Sandy F. The BLUES Go Birding at Wild America's Shores, 1 vol. Schroeder, Louise, illus. 2010. (ENG.). 36p. (J). 16.95 *(978-1-58469-131-0(X));* pap. 8.95 *(978-1-58469-132-7(8))* Dawn Pubns.

Mama Doo. Trevor's Adventure in Button Land, 1 vol. 2008. (ENG.). 47p. pap. 24.95 *(978-1-60672-349-4(9))* America Star Bks.

Manzione, Lisa. Let's Visit Jerusalem! Adventures of Bella & Harry. Lucco, Kristine, illus. 2013. (Adventures of Bella & Harry Ser.: 10). (ENG.). 35p. (J). (gr. k-3). 16.95 *(978-1-937616-00-7(2))* Bella & Harry, LLC.

—Let's Visit London! Adventures of Bella & Harry. Lucco, Kristine, illus. 2011. (Adventures of Bella & Harry Ser.: 3). (ENG.). 35p. (J). (gr. k-3). 16.95 *(978-1-937616-03-8(7))* Bella & Harry, LLC.

Marceau, Fani. Panorama: A Foldout Book. Jolivet, Joëlle, illus. 2009. (ENG.). 32p. (J). (gr. -1-k). 21.95 *(978-0-8109-8332-8(X),* Abrams Bks. for Young Readers) Abrams, Inc.

Marillier, Juliet. Raven Flight. (ENG.). 416p. (YA). (gr. 7). 2014. pap. 9.99 *(978-0-375-87197-9(7),* Ember) 2013. 16.99 *(978-0-375-86955-6(7),* Knopf Bks. for Young Readers) Random Hse. Children's Bks.

—Shadowfell. 2013. (ENG.). 416p. (YA). (gr. 7). pap. 10.99 *(978-0-375-87196-2(9),* Ember) Random Hse. Children's Bks.

Marr, Melissa, et al. Enthralled: Paranormal Diversions. 2011. (ENG.). 464p. (YA). (gr. 8). pap. 9.99 *(978-0-06-201578-5(8))* HarperCollins Pubs.

Marsh, Katherine. Jepp, Who Defied the Stars. 2013. (ENG.). 400p. (J). (gr. 5-9). pap. 9.99 *(978-1-4231-3786-3(8))* Hyperion Pr.

Martin, Rafe. Birdwing. 2007. (ENG.). 384p. (J). (gr. 7-12). pap. 7.99 *(978-0-439-21168-0(9),* Levine, Arthur A. Bks.) Scholastic, Inc.

Martinez, David & Benchmark Education Co., LLC. My Whale of a Tale. 2014. (Text Connections Ser.). (J). (gr. 3). *(978-1-4509-9651-8(5))* Benchmark Education Co.

Martínez, Rafael. El Deseo de Aurelio. Martinez, Enrique, illus. 2006. (la Orilla del Viento Ser.). (SPA.). 48p. (J). (gr. 8-10). pap. *(978-968-16-7988-0(1))* Fondo de Cultura Economica.

Mason-Black, Jennifer. Devil & the Bluebird. 2016. (ENG.). 336p. (J). (gr. 8-17). 17.95 *(978-1-4197-2000-0(7),* Amulet Bks.) Abrams, Inc.

Mateboer, Hans. Peter the Cruise Ship. 2007. (Illus.). 32p. (J). 16.95 *(978-0-9759487-1-2(7))* Mateboer, Johannes Aart.

McClintock, Barbara. Adèle & Simon in America. McClintock, Barbara, illus. 2008. (Adele & Simon Ser.). (ENG., Illus.). 40p. (J). (gr. -1-3). 18.99 *(978-0-374-39924-5(7),* 9780374399245, Farrar, Straus & Giroux (BYR)) Farrar, Straus & Giroux.

—Lost & Found: Adèle & Simon in China. 2016. (Adele & Simon Ser.). (ENG., Illus.). 40p. (J). 17.99 *(978-0-374-39923-8(9),* 9780374399238, Farrar, Straus & Giroux (BYR)) Farrar, Straus & Giroux.

McCooke, Valerie J. Grandfather's Chest. 2012. 40p. pap. 32.70 *(978-1-4771-0543-6(3))* Xlibris Corp.

McDonnell, Kathleen. The Shining World, 1 vol. 2003. (Notherland Journeys Ser.: 2). (ENG.). 240p. (YA). (gr. 7-9). pap. 6.95 *(978-1-896764-79-5(7))* Second Story Pr. CAN. Dist: Orca Bk. Pubs. USA.

McMullan, Kate. Get Lost, Odysseus!, 1 vol. 2014. (Myth-O-Mania Ser.). (ENG., Illus.). 240p. (gr. 4-8). 25.32 *(978-1-4342-6016-1(X))* Stone Arch Bks.

Meade, Starr, et al. Keeping Holiday. Gerard, Justin, illus. 2008. 192p. (gr. k). pap. 14.99 *(978-1-4335-0142-5(2))* Crossway.

Melling, O. R. The Book of Dreams. 2009. (Chronicles of Faerie Ser.). (ENG.). 720p. (J). (gr. 2-8). 19.95 *(978-0-8109-8346-5(X),* Amulet Bks.) Abrams, Inc.

—The Light-Bearer's Daughter. 2008. (ENG.). 368p. (YA). (gr. 2-8). pap. 9.95 *(978-0-8109-7123-3(2),* Amulet Bks.) Abrams, Inc.

Meloy, Maile. The Apprentices. Schoenherr, Ian, illus. 2013. (Apothecary Ser.: 2). (ENG.). 416p. (J). (gr. 5). 16.99 *(978-0-399-16245-9(3),* G.P. Putnam's Sons Books for Young Readers) Penguin Young Readers Group.

Melton, Marcia. Joe Henry's Journey. 2014. (Illus.). 169p. (J). pap. 12.00 *(978-1-937849-20-7(1))* Raven Publishing Inc. of Montana.

Meyer, Carolyn. The True Adventures of Charley Darwin. 2011. (ENG., Illus.). 336p. (YA). (gr. 7). pap. 9.99 *(978-0-547-41564-2(8))* Houghton Mifflin Harcourt Publishing Co.

Meyer, Kim Shapiro. The Journey of the Coconut. Shapiro, Pepper, illus. 2012. 36p. pap. 24.95 *(978-1-4626-8641-4(9))* America Star Bks.

Meyer, L. A. Mississippi Jack: Being an Account of the Further Waterborne Adventures of Jacky Faber, Midshipman, Fine Lady, & the Lily of the West. 2nd ed. 2010. (Bloody Jack Adventures Ser.: 5). (ENG., Illus.). 624p. (J). (gr. 7). pap. 8.99 *(978-0-15-206632-1(2))* Houghton Mifflin Harcourt Publishing Co.

Mills, G. Riley. Son of the Sea. 2012. 22.95 *(978-0-7414-7515-2(4));* pap. 11.95 *(978-0-7414-7514-5(6))* Infinity Publishing.

Minshall, Caleigh. Blue: Voyage to the Sky. 2005. 54p. (J). pap. 19.95 net. *(978-1-59975-284-6(0))* Independent Pub.

Morgan, Anna. Daughters of the Ark, 1 vol. 2005. (ENG., Illus.). 200p. (J). (gr. 5-12). pap. 9.95 *(978-1-896764-92-4(4))* Second Story Pr. CAN. Dist: Orca Bk. Pubs. USA.

Morpurgo, Michael. Kensuke's Kingdom. 2004. (ENG.). 176p. (J). (gr. 4-7). mass mkt. 6.99 *(978-0-439-59181-2(3),* Scholastic Paperbacks) Scholastic, Inc.

—El Reino de Kensuke. Aguilar, Carmen, tr. Foreman, Michael, illus. 2006.Tr. of Kensuke's Kingdom. (SPA.). 155p. (J). (gr. 5-8). 16.99 *(978-84-7901-420-9(2))* RBA Libros, S.A. ESP. Dist: Santillana USA Publishing Co., Inc.

—Twist of Gold. 2004. (ENG.). 304p. (J). pap. 8.99 *(978-0-7497-4687-2(4))* Egmont Bks., Ltd. GBR. Dist: Trafalgar Square Publishing.

Moss, Marissa. Amelia's Family Ties. Moss, Marissa, illus. 2013. (Amelia Ser.). (ENG., Illus.). (J). 5.99 *(978-1-4169-1293-4(2),* Simon & Schuster/Paula Wiseman Bks.) Simon & Schuster/Paula Wiseman Bks.

Mull, Brandon. Keys to the Demon Prison. 2010. (Fablehaven Ser.: 5). (ENG., Illus.). 600p. (J). (gr. 3). 21.99 *(978-1-60641-238-1(8),* Shadow Mountain) Shadow Mountain Publishing.

Murdock, Catherine Gilbert. Heaven Is Paved with Oreos. 2013. (ENG.). 208p. (J). (gr. 5-7). 16.99 *(978-0-547-62538-6(3))* Houghton Mifflin Harcourt Publishing Co.

Naylor, Phyllis Reynolds. Emily's Fortune. 2011. (ENG.). 160p. (J). (gr. 3-7). 6.99 *(978-0-375-84492-8(9),* Yearling) Random Hse. Children's Bks.

Newman, Vivian. Ella's Trip to Israel. Nathan, Cheryl & Gutierrez, Akemia, illus. 2011. (Israel Ser.). (ENG.). 24p. (J). (gr. -1 — 1). pap. 8.95 *(978-0-7613-6029-2(8),* Kar-Ben Publishing) Lerner Publishing Group.

Nielson, Kelli S. Stone Mage Wars, Book 1: Journey to the Fringe. 2011. (YA). 17.99 *(978-1-60908-833-0(6))* Deseret Bk. Co.

Nimmo, Jenny. The Stones of Ravenglass. 2012. (Chronicles of the Red King Ser.). (ENG.). 272p. (J). (gr. 3-7). 16.99 *(978-0-439-84674-5(9),* Scholastic Pr.) Scholastic, Inc.

Odgers, Sally. Journey to the Center of the Earth, 1 vol. 2013. (Fiction Readers Ser.). (ENG., Illus.). 24p. (J). (gr. 2-2). pap. 6.99 *(978-1-4333-5527-1(2))* Shell Educational Publishing.

Oliver, Lauren. Liesl & Po. Acedera, Kei, illus. (ENG.). (J). (gr. 3-7). 2012. 336p. pap. 6.99 *(978-0-06-201452-8(8))* 2011. 320p. 16.99 *(978-0-06-201451-1(X))* HarperCollins Pubs.

—Liesl & Po. 2012. (J). lib. bdg. 17.20 *(978-0-606-26853-0(7),* Turtleback) Turtleback Bks.

Oneill, Elizabeth. Alfred Visits Maryland. 2008. 24p. (J). pap. 12.00 *(978-0-9799121-7-7(2))* Global Business Information Strategies, Inc.

—Alfred Visits Oregon. 2008. 24p. pap. 12.00 *(978-0-9799121-8-4(0))* Global Business Information Strategies, Inc.

—Alfred Visits Vermont. 2008. 24p. pap. 12.00 *(978-0-9799121-9-1(9))* Global Business Information Strategies, Inc.

Optic, Oliver, pseud. Outward Bound. 2007. 180p. (gr. 4-7). per. *(978-1-4068-4343-9(1))* Echo Library.

—Outward Bound: Or Young America Afloat. l.t. ed. 2007. (ENG.). 274p. pap. 23.99 *(978-1-4264-9153-5(0))* Creative Media Partners, LLC.

—Sunny Shores; or, Young America in Italy & Austria a Story of Travel & Adventure by William T Adams. 2006. 428p. per. 26.99 *(978-1-4255-4627-4(7))* Michigan Publishing.

Orme, David. Deadly Virus. 2008. (Starchasers Ser.). (ENG., Illus.). 48p. pap. *(978-1-84167-767-5(1))* Ransom Publishing Ltd.

—Galactic Shopping Mall. 2008. (Starchasers Ser.). (ENG., Illus.). 48p. pap. *(978-1-84167-764-4(7))* Ransom Publishing Ltd.

—Jungle Planet. 2008. (Starchasers Ser.). (ENG., Illus.). 48p. pap. *(978-1-84167-768-2(X))* Ransom Publishing Ltd.

—Lost Explorers. 2008. (Starchasers Ser.). (ENG., Illus.). 48p. pap. *(978-1-84167-763-7(9))* Ransom Publishing Ltd.

—Planet of the Vampires. 2008. (Starchasers Ser.). (ENG., Illus.). 48p. pap. *(978-1-84167-765-1(5))* Ransom Publishing Ltd.

Osborne, Mary Pope. Eve of the Emperor Penguin. Murdocca, Sal, illus. 2009. (Magic Tree House Merlin Mission Ser.: No. 12). (ENG.). 144p. (J). (gr. 2-5). 5.99 *(978-0-375-83734-0(5),* Random Hse. Bks. for Young Readers) Random Hse. Children's Bks.

Oso Se Va de Viaje. 2014. (ENG & SPA., Illus.). (J). *(978-1-78285-088-5(0))* Barefoot Bks., Inc.

Oulton, Harry. Heather's Piglets. 2017. (Pig Called Heather Ser.: 3). (ENG., Illus.). 240p. (J). (gr. 4-7). pap. 8.99 ***(978-1-84812-479-0(1))*** Bonnier Publishing GBR. Dist: Independent Pubs. Group.

—A Pig Called Heather. 2015. (ENG.). 192p. (J). (gr. 3-7). 16.95 *(978-0-8234-3290-5(4))* Holiday Hse., Inc.

Oulton, Harry. The Return of a Pig Called Heather. 2017. (Pig Called Heather Ser.: 2). (ENG., Illus.). 192p. (J). (gr. 4-7). pap. 8.99 ***(978-1-84812-473-8(2))*** Bonnier Publishing GBR. Dist: Independent Pubs. Group.

Parker, Emma. Sam the Traveling Snail. 2010. (Illus.). pap. *(978-1-877561-19-1(3))* First Edition Ltd.

Parker, Richard. Voyage to Tasmani. Seward, Prudence, illus. 2011. 128p. 40.95 *(978-1-258-08572-8(0))* Literary Licensing, LLC.

Paulsen, Gary. Tucket's Travels: Francis Tucket's Adventures in the West, 1847-1849. 2003. (Francis Tucket Bks.: Bks. 1-5). (ENG.). 560p. (J). (gr. 3-7). pap. 8.99 *(978-0-440-41967-9(0),* Yearling) Random Hse. Children's Bks.

Paver, Michelle. The Burning Shadow. 2015. (Gods & Warriors Ser.: 2). (ENG.). 320p. (J). (gr. 5). 7.99 *(978-0-14-242285-4(1),* Puffin Books) Penguin Young Readers Group.

—Gods & Warriors. 2013. (Gods & Warriors Ser.: 1). (ENG.). 336p. (J). (gr. 5). pap. 8.99 *(978-0-14-242284-7(3),* Puffin Books) Penguin Young Readers Group.

—HERMANO LOBO: CRÓNICAS DE LA PREHISTORIA I. 2005. (SPA., Illus.). 222p. 17.25 *(978-84-7888-933-4(7))* Emece Editores ESP. Dist: Ediciones Universal.

—Spirit Walker. Taylor, Geoff, illus. 2007. (Chronicles of Ancient Darkness Ser.: 2). 384p. (J). (gr. 5-9). per. 6.99 *(978-0-06-072830-4(2),* Tegen, Katherine Bks) HarperCollins Pubs.

—Warrior Bronze. 2017. (Gods & Warriors Ser.). (ENG.). 272p. (J). (gr. 3-7). 16.99 *(978-0-8037-3884-3(6),* Dial Bks) Penguin Young Readers Group.

—Wolf Brother. Taylor, Geoff, illus. 2006. (Chronicles of Ancient Darkness Ser.: 1). 320p. (J). (gr. 5-9). reprint ed. per. 6.99 *(978-0-06-072827-4(2),* Tegen, Katherine Bks) HarperCollins Pubs.

—Wolf Brother, 6 vols. 2005. (Chronicles of Ancient Darkness Ser.: 1). (J). 89.75 *(978-1-4193-3811-3(0));* 76.75 *(978-1-4193-2628-8(7));* 91.75 *(978-1-4193-3809-0(9));* 73.75 *(978-1-4193-2630-1(9))* Recorded Bks., Inc.

Phelan, Matt. Around the World. Phelan, Matt, illus. 2011. (ENG., Illus.). 240p. (J). (gr. 4-7). 24.99 *(978-0-7636-3619-7(3))* Candlewick Pr.

Pon, Cindy. Silver Phoenix. (Silver Phoenix Ser.: 1). (ENG.). (YA). (gr. 9). 2011. 368p. pap. 8.99 *(978-0-06-173024-5(6))* 2009. 352p. 17.99 *(978-0-06-173021-4(1))* HarperCollins Pubs. (Greenwillow Bks.).

Priceman, Marjorie. How to Make a Cherry Pie & See the U. S. A. 2013. lib. bdg. 18.40 *(978-0-606-32190-7(X),* Turtleback) Turtleback Bks.

Prineas, Sarah. Found. Caparo, Antonio Javier, illus. 2011. (Magic Thief Ser.: 3). (ENG.). 384p. (J). (gr. 5). pap. 7.99 *(978-0-06-137595-8(0))* HarperCollins Pubs.

Pushker, Gloria Teles & Tarman, Mel. Toby Belfer Learns about Heroes & Martyrs, 1 vol. Henriquez, Emile, illus. 2009. (Toby Belfer Ser.). (ENG.). 128p. (J). (gr. 3-7). 14.95 *(978-1-58980-647-4(6))* Pelican Publishing Co., Inc.

Rae, Kristin. Wish You Were Italian. 2014. (If Only... Ser.). (ENG.). 352p. (YA). (gr. 7). 17.99 *(978-1-61963-285-1(3),* 9781619632851, Bloomsbury USA Childrens) Bloomsbury Publishing USA.

—Wish You Were Italian: An If Only Novel. 2014. (If Only... Ser.). (ENG.). 352p. (YA). (gr. 7). pap. 9.99 *(978-1-61963-286-8(1),* 9781619632868, Bloomsbury USA Childrens) Bloomsbury Publishing USA.

Random House Staff. Dora's Big Birthday Adventure (Dora the Explorer) Random House Staff, illus. 2013. (Pictureback(R) Ser.). (ENG.). 24p. (J). (gr. -1-2). pap. 3.99 *(978-0-449-81445-1(9),* Random Hse. Bks. for Young Readers) Random Hse. Children's Bks.

Rapp, Adam. Punkzilla. 2009. (ENG., Illus.). 256p. (YA). (gr. 9). 16.99 *(978-0-7636-3031-7(4))* Candlewick Pr.

Ravin Lodding, Linda. The Queen Is Coming to Tea. von Kitzing, Constanze, illus. 2017. (ENG.). 32p. (J). (-4). 16.99 *(978-1-4926-0757-1(6),* 9781492607571, Sourcebooks Jabberwocky) Sourcebooks, Inc.

Razzell, Mary. Runaway at Sea. unabr. ed. 2005. (ENG., Illus.). 150p. (YA). (gr. 7-9). 9.95 *(978-1-55017-327-7(8))* Harbour Publishing Co., Ltd. CAN. Dist: Midpoint Trade Bks., Inc.

Rees, Celia. Witch Child. unabr. ed. 2004. (Young Adult Cassette Librariestm Ser.). 304p. (J). (gr. 5-9). pap. 40.00 incl. audio *(978-0-8072-1198-4(2),* S YA 343 SP, Listening Library) Random Hse. Audio Publishing Group.

Reese, Jenn. Mirage. 2014. (Above World Ser.). (ENG.). 368p. (J). (gr. 5). pap. 7.99 *(978-0-7636-6929-4(6))* Candlewick Pr.

Reeve, Philip. Cakes in Space. McIntyre, Sarah, illus. 2015. (Not-So-Impossible Tale Ser.). (ENG.). 224p. (J). (gr. 2-5). 12.99 *(978-0-385-38792-7(X),* Random Hse. Bks. for Young Readers) Random Hse. Children's Bks.

Rewa. Molly May on the High Seas. (Illus.). 9.95 *(978-0-9726375-1-0(6))* Little Red Cat Publishing.

RH Disney. Journey to the Lights. RH Disney, illus. deluxe ed. 2016. (Stepping Stone Book Ser.). (ENG., Illus.). 224p. (J). (gr. 3-7). 14.99 *(978-0-7364-3659-5(6),* RH/Disney) Random Hse. Children's Bks.

Riel, Jørn, et al. The Snowstorm. Cann, Helen, illus. 2012. (ENG.). 128p. (J). (gr. 4-6). pap. 9.99 *(978-1-84686-797-2(5))* Barefoot Bks., Inc.

Riggs, Sandy. Joe Boat. Barr, Kristin, illus. 2006. (Reader's Clubhouse Level 2 Reader Ser.). (ENG.). 24p. (J). (gr. 1-4). pap. 3.99 *(978-0-7641-3296-4(2))* Barron's Educational Series, Inc.

Riordan, Rick. The Kane Chronicles Box Set. Rocco, John, illus. 2013. (Kane Chronicles Ser.). (ENG.). 1472p. (J). (gr. 3-7). pap. 26.99 *(978-1-4231-9962-5(6))* Hyperion Bks. for Children.

—The Red Pyramid. 2011. (ENG.). 544p. (J). (gr. 5-17). pap. 9.99 *(978-1-4231-1345-4(4))* Disney Publishing Worldwide.

—The Red Pyramid. 2010. (Kane Chronicles Ser.). (ENG.). 528p. (J). (gr. 5-9). 17.99 *(978-1-4231-1338-6(1))* Hyperion Pr.

—The Red Pyramid, Bk. 1. Collar, Orpheus, illus. 2012. (Kane Chronicles Ser.). (ENG.). 192p. (J). (gr. 5-9). pap. 12.99 *(978-1-4231-5069-5(4))* Hyperion Pr.

—The Red Pyramid. 2009. (Kane Chronicles: Bk. 1). 11.04 *(978-0-7848-3733-7(3),* Everbind) Marco Bk. Co.

—The Red Pyramid. 2012. 20.00 *(978-1-61383-660-6(0))* Perfection Learning Corp.

—The Red Pyramid. 2010. pap. *(978-0-545-40016-9(3))* Scholastic, Inc.

—The Red Pyramid. l.t. ed. 2010. (Kane Chronicles: Bk. 1). (ENG.). 671p. 23.95 *(978-1-4104-2536-2(3))* Thorndike Pr.

—The Red Pyramid. (Kane Chronicles Graphic Novels Ser.: 1). (J). 2012. lib. bdg. 24.50 *(978-0-606-37510-8(4))* 2011. lib. bdg. 20.85 *(978-0-606-39216-7(5))* Turtleback Bks.

—The Serpent's Shadow. (Kane Chronicles Ser.). (ENG.). (gr. 5-17). 2013. 464p. (J). pap. 9.99 *(978-1-4231-4202-7(0))*Bk. 3. 2012. 416p. (YA). 19.99 *(978-1-4231-4057-3(5))* Hyperion Pr.

—The Serpent's Shadow. 2012. 416p. *(978-0-14-133568-1(8),* Puffin) Penguin Bks., Ltd.

—The Serpent's Shadow. l.t. ed. 2012. (Kane Chronicles: Bk. 3). (ENG.). 521p. (gr. 5-12). 23.99 *(978-1-4104-4789-0(8))* Thorndike Pr.

—The Throne of Fire. 2011. (Kane Chronicles: Bk. 2). 452p. (J). pap. *(978-1-4231-5059-6(7))* Disney Pr.

—The Throne of Fire. 2nd ed. 2012. (ENG.). 464p. (YA). (gr. 5-9). pap. 9.99 *(978-1-4231-6703-7(1))* Hyperion Bks. for Children.

—The Throne of Fire, Bk. 2. (ENG.). 464p. (gr. 5-17). 2012. (YA). pap. 9.99 *(978-1-4231-4201-0(2))* 2011. (J). 18.99 *(978-1-4231-4056-6(7))* Hyperion Pr.

—The Throne of Fire. 2011. (Kane Chronicles: Bk. 2). (ENG., Illus.). 451p. 28.25 *(978-0-85757-231-8(8));* 2nd ed. 554p. pap. *(978-0-14-133566-7(1))* Penguin Publishing Group. (Puffin).

—The Throne of Fire. l.t. ed. 2011. (Kane Chronicles: Bk. 2). (ENG.). 591p. 23.99 *(978-1-4104-3607-8(1))* Thorndike Pr.

—The Throne of Fire. (Kane Chronicles Graphic Novels Ser.: 2). 2015. lib. bdg. 24.50 *(978-0-606-37509-2(0))* 2012. (YA). lib. bdg. 20.85 *(978-0-606-39217-4(3))* Turtleback Bks.

Robert, Bulla Clyde & Clyde, Bulla. A Lion to Guard Us. 2014. (Trophy Bk Ser.). (ENG.). 128p. (J). (gr. 3-7). 10.24 *(978-1-63245-324-2(X))* Lectorum Pubns., Inc.

Roberts, Willo Davis. Surviving Summer Vacation. 2015. (ENG., Illus.). 208p. (J). (gr. 3-7). pap. 6.99 *(978-1-4814-3718-9(6),* Aladdin) Simon & Schuster Children's Publishing.

Roman, Dave. Astronaut Academy: Re-Entry. Roman, Dave, illus. 2013. (Astronaut Academy Ser.: 2). (ENG., Illus.). 192p. (J). (gr. 5-9). pap. 9.99 *(978-1-59643-621-3(2),* 9781596436213, First Second Bks.) Roaring Brook Pr.

Rosenberg, Madelyn. Canary in the Coal Mine. 2013. (ENG., Illus.). 192p. (J). (gr. 2-7). 16.95 *(978-0-8234-2600-3(9))* Holiday Hse., Inc.

Rowohlt, Harry & Trier, Walter. The Jolly Steamship. Trier, Walter, illus. 2013. (ENG., Illus.). 32p. (J). (gr. -1-3). 17.95 *(978-0-7358-4127-7(6))* North-South Bks., Inc.

Roy, Philip. Seas of South Africa. 2013. (ENG.). 250p. pap. 11.95 *(978-1-55380-247-1(0))* Ronsdale Pr. CAN. Dist: SPD-Small Pr. Distribution.

—Submarine Outlaw. 2008. (ENG., Illus.). 254p. pap. 10.95 *(978-1-55380-058-3(3))* Ronsdale Pr. CAN. Dist: SPD-Small Pr. Distribution.

Rubalcaba, Jill. The Wadjet Eye. 2006. (ENG.). 160p. (J). (gr. 5-7). pap. 7.99 *(978-0-618-68927-9(3))* Houghton Mifflin Harcourt Publishing Co.

Rushdie, Salman. Luka & the Fire of Life. 2009. 14.75 *(978-0-7848-3731-3(7),* Everbind) Marco Bk. Co.

—Luka & the Fire of Life. 2011. (ENG.). 240p. (J). (gr. 7). pap. 17.00 *(978-0-679-78347-3(4),* Random Hse. Trade Paperbacks) Random House Publishing Group.

Rylant, Cynthia & National Geographic Learning Staff. Tulip Sees America. Desimini, Lisa, illus. 2010. (Rise & Shine Ser.). (ENG.). 32p. (C). (gr. -1-18). pap. 21.95 *(978-0-439-39978-4(5))* National Geographic School Publishing, Inc.

TUV

Said. The Seven Voyages of Sinbad the Sailor. Rashin, illus. 2015. (ENG.). 64p. (J). 19.95 (978-0-7358-4240-3(X)) North-South Bks., Inc.

Sante, Andrew R. The Silver Heart Chronicles: The Voyage. 2012. 50p. 24.99 (978-1-4771-4700-9(4)); pap. 15.99 (978-1-4771-4699-6(7)) Xlibris Corp.

Savedoff, Barbara E. & Elissa, Barbara. The Remarkable Journey of Josh's Kippah. Jamana, Pharida & Zaman, Farida, illus. 2010. (ENG.). 24p. (J). (gr. -1-2). lib. bdg. 7.95 (978-0-8225-9911-1(2), Kar-Ben Publishing) Lerner Publishing Group.

Say, Allen. Grandfather's Journey. Say, Allen, illus. 2008. (ENG., Illus.). 32p. (J). (gr. -1-3). 7.99 (978-0-547-07680-5(0)) Houghton Mifflin Harcourt Publishing Co.

—Grandfather's Journey. 20th anniv. ed. 2013. (ENG., Illus.). 32p. (J). (gr. -1-3). 17.99 (978-0-544-05050-1(9)) Houghton Mifflin Harcourt Publishing Co.

—Grandfather's Journey. 2008. (ENG.). 32p. (J). (gr. -1-3). pap. 7.99 (978-0-547-14178-7(5), Sandpiper) Houghton Mifflin Harcourt Trade & Reference Pubs.

—Grandfather's Journey. 2011. (J). (gr. k-5). 29.95 (978-0-545-10696-2(6)); 18.95 (978-0-545-12708-0(4)) Weston Woods Studios, Inc.

Schaaf, Ron. Tiger's Quest: Rounding Cape Horn. 2007. (J). (978-0-9787555-0-8(2)) Hickory Tales Publishing.

Schomer-Wendel, Gretchen & Schomer, Adam Anthony. Becka Goes to San Francisco. 2009. (Becka & the Big Bubble Ser.). (Illus.). 32p. (J). (gr. -1-2). 22.60 (978-1-60754-107-3(6)); pap. 10.55 (978-1-60754-108-0(4)) Windmill Bks.

Schubert, Dieter. The Umbrella Doodle Book. 2012. (ENG., Illus.). 48p. (J). (gr. -1). 7.95 (978-1-935954-15-6(6), 9781935954156) Lemniscaat USA.

Service, Pamela F. The Wizards of Wyrd World. Gorman, Mike, illus. (Way-Too-Real Aliens Ser.: 3). (ENG.). 112p. (J). (gr. 4-6). 2015. 34.65 (978-1-4677-5962-5(7), Lerner Digital) 2013. pap. 6.95 (978-0-7613-7922-5(3), Darby Creek) 2012. 15.95 (978-0-7613-7920-1(7)) Lerner Publishing Group.

Shan, Darren, pseud. The Thin Executioner. 2011. (ENG.). 512p. (YA). (gr. 10-17). pap. 10.99 (978-0-316-07864-1(6)) Little, Brown Bks. for Young Readers.

Sharp, Margery. The Rescuers. Williams, Garth, illus. 2016. (ENG.). 160p. (J). (gr. 4-7). pap. 9.99 (978-1-68137-007-1(7), NYRB Kids) New York Review of Bks., Inc., The.

Shearer, Alex. Sky Run. 2014. (Cloud Hunters Ser.). (ENG.). 288p. (J). (gr. 2-7). 14.95 (978-1-62873-593-2(7), Sky Pony Pr.) Skyhorse Publishing Co., Inc.

Shepherd, David & Plummer, William K. We Were There at the Driving of the Golden Spike. 2013. (ENG., Illus.). 192p. (J). (gr. 3-8). pap. 6.99 (978-0-486-49259-9(1)) Dover Pubns., Inc.

Shondalae. The Great Giver of Life, No. 8. 2008. 49p. pap. 16.95 (978-1-60672-071-4(6)) America Star Bks.

Sidney, Margaret. Five Little Peppers Abroad. (J). 24.95 (978-0-8488-1475-5(4)) Amereon Ltd.

Silver Phoenix Staff & Pon, Cindy. Fury of the Phoenix. 2011. (Silver Phoenix Ser.: 2). (ENG.). 368p. (YA). (gr. 9-18). 17.99 (978-0-06-173025-2(4), Greenwillow Bks.) HarperCollins Pubs.

Skerwarski, N. D. Freddy Freckles: Friends, Flags, Facts & Fun. Wooten, Neal, illus. 2007. 52p. (J). pap. 16.99 (978-0-9800675-3-8(7)) Mirror Publishing.

Skinner, Daphne. All Aboard! Smath, Jerry, illus. 2007. (Math Matters Ser.). (ENG.). 32p. (J). (gr. -1-3). pap. 5.95 (978-1-57565-239-9(0)) Kane Press, Inc.

Skye, obert. Leven Thumps & the Wrath of Ezra. 2008. (Leven Thumps Ser.: Bk. 4). (Illus.). 388p. (J). 19.95 (978-1-59038-963-8(8), Shadow Mountain) Shadow Mountain Publishing.

—The Ruins of Alder. Sowards, Ben, illus. 2010. (Leven Thumps Ser.: 5). (ENG.). 416p. (J). (gr. 4-9). pap. 9.99 (978-1-4169-9093-2(3), Aladdin) Simon & Schuster Children's Publishing.

—The Wrath of Ezra. Sowards, Ben, illus. 2009. (Leven Thumps Ser.: 4). (ENG.). 464p. (J). (gr. 4-9). pap. 9.99 (978-1-4169-9092-5(5), Aladdin) Simon & Schuster Children's Publishing.

Slanina, Anne Maro. Annie Mouse's Route 66 Adventure: A Photo Journal, vols. 6, vol. 5. Collins, Kelsey, illus. 2011. (ENG.). 48p. (J). pap. 14.99 (978-0-9793379-6-3(8)) Annie Mouse Bks.

SLAY, Jenette. ABBY, the Easter Chicken. 2008. 29p. 13.96 (978-1-4357-1062-7(2)) Lulu Pr., Inc.

Smelcer, John. The Great Death. 2009. (ENG.). 176p. (YA). (gr. 5-9). 17.99 (978-0-8050-8100-8(3), 9780805081008, Holt, Henry & Co. Bks. For Young Readers) Holt, Henry & Co.

Smith, Maggie. Counting Our Way to Maine. 2008. (ENG., Illus.). 32p. (J). (gr. -1-3). 15.95 (978-0-89272-775-9(6)) Down East Bks.

Snell, Gordon. The King of Quizzical Island. McKee, David, illus. 2009. (ENG.). 40p. (J). (gr. -1-3). 16.99 (978-0-7636-3857-3(9)) Candlewick Pr.

Sonberg, Caryn. Six Dogs & a Police Officer. Dorenkamp, Michelle, illus. 2006. 31p. pap. 8.40 (978-1-55501-776-7(2)) Ballard & Tighe Pubs.

Soto, Gary. Pacific Crossing. 2003. (ENG., Illus.). 144p. (J). (gr. 2-5). pap. 6.99 (978-0-15-204696-5(8)) Houghton Mifflin Harcourt Publishing Co.

star, celina. Paw Prints on the Road. 2008. 79p. pap. 9.96 (978-0-557-02420-9(X)) Lulu Pr., Inc.

Stead, Philip C. Jonathan & the Big Blue Boat. Stead, Philip C., illus. 2011. (ENG., Illus.). 32p. (J). (gr. -1-2). 16.99 (978-1-59643-562-9(3), 9781596435629) Roaring Brook Pr.

—Sebastian & the Balloon. Stead, Philip C., illus. 2014. (ENG., Illus.). 40p. (J). (gr. -1-2). 17.99 (978-1-59643-930-6(0), 9781596439306) Roaring Brook Pr.

—Special Delivery. Cordell, Matthew, illus. 2015. (ENG.). 40p. (J). (gr. -1-2). 17.99 (978-1-59643-931-3(9), 9781596439313) Roaring Brook Pr.

Stevenson, Robert Louis. Treasure Island. (Young Collector's Illustrated Classics Ser.). (Illus.). 192p. (J). (gr. 3-7). 9.95 (978-1-56156-456-9(7)) Kidsbooks, LLC.

—Treasure Island: With Story of the Treasure of Normon Island. Date not set. (J). (gr. 5-6). reprint ed. lib. bdg. 22.95 (978-0-89190-236-2(8), American Reprint Co.) Amereon Ltd.

Stilton, Geronimo & Stilton, Thea. Thea Stilton & the Ghost of the Shipwreck. 2010. (Thea Stilton Ser.: 3). lib. bdg. 19.65 (978-0-606-06843-7(0), Turtleback) Turtleback Bks.

Stilton, Thea. The Journey to Atlantis. 2012. (Thea Stilton Special Edition Ser.). (ENG.). 320p. (J). (gr. 2-5). 14.99 (978-0-545-44020-2(3), Scholastic Paperbacks) Scholastic, Inc.

Stockton, Frank Richard. Round-about Rambles in Lands of Fact & Fancy. 2006. pap. (978-1-4068-3083-5(6)) Echo Library.

Stoffels, Karlijn. Heartsinger. 2009. (YA). pap. (978-0-545-06968-7(8), Levine, Arthur A. Bks.) Scholastic, Inc.

—Heartsinger. Watkinson, Laura, tr. from DUT. 2009. (ENG.). 144p. (J). (gr. 7-18). 16.99 (978-0-545-06929-8(7), Levine, Arthur A. Bks.) Scholastic, Inc.

Stoop, Naoko. Red Knit Cap Girl to the Rescue. 2013. (ENG., Illus.). 40p. (J). (gr. -1-3). 17.00 (978-0-316-22885-5(0)) Little, Brown Bks. for Young Readers.

Summers, Susan. The Greatest Gift: The Story of the Other Wise Man. Morris, Jackie, illus. 2011. (ENG.). 30p. (J). 16.99 (978-1-84686-578-7(6)) Barefoot Bks., Inc.

Swift, Jonathan. Gulliver's Travels. Akib, Jamel, illus. 2006. (Classic Starts(tm) Ser.). (ENG.). 160p. (J). (gr. 2-4). 6.95 (978-1-4027-2662-0(7)) Sterling Publishing Co., Inc.

—Gulliver's Travels. Walker, John, illus. 2010. (Stepping Stone Book(TM) Ser.). (ENG.). 112p. (J). (gr. 1-4). 4.99 (978-0-375-86569-5(1), Random Hse. Bks. for Young Readers) Random Hse. Children's Bks.

—Viajes de Gulliver. 2003. (Advanced Reading Ser.). (SPA.). 344p. (J). 11.95 (978-84-670-0095-5(3)) Espasa Calpe, S.A. ESP. Dist: Planeta Publishing Corp.

Taylor, G. P. The Shadowmancer Returns: The Curse of Salamander Street. 2008. (ENG.). 256p. (gr. 7-12). pap. 17.99 (978-1-59979-084-8(X), Realms) Charisma Media.

Taylor, Mark. Henry the Castaway. Booth, Graham, illus. 2010. 48p. (J). (gr. -1-3). 18.95 (978-1-930900-47-9(3)) Purple Hse. Pr.

Thomson, Sarah L. Dragon's Egg. 2007. (ENG.). 272p. (J). (gr. 3-7). 16.99 (978-0-06-128848-7(9), Greenwillow Bks.) HarperCollins Pubs.

Tompert, Ann & Lister, Ralph. Little Fox Goes to the End of the World. 0 vols. Bryant, Laura J., illus. 2010. (ENG.). 32p. (J). (gr. -1-2). 16.99 (978-0-7614-5703-9(8), 9780761457039, Amazon Children's Publishing) Amazon Publishing.

Tonatiuh, Duncan. Pancho Rabbit & the Coyote: A Migrant's Tale. 2013. (ENG., Illus.). 32p. (J). (gr. 1-4). 17.95 (978-1-4197-0583-0(0), Abrams Bks. for Young Readers) Abrams, Inc.

Travis, Lucille. The Far Journey. 2009. 160p. (J). (gr. 4-7). 8.99 (978-1-60682-023-0(0)) BJU Pr.

Troupe, Thomas Kingsley. The Dark Lens. 2014. (ENG.). 96p. (J). (978-1-63235-054-1(8)) Pr. Room Editions LLC.

Twain, Mark, pseud. The Adventures of Huckleberry Finn. Andreasen, Dan, illus. 2006. (Classic Starts(tm) Ser.). (ENG.). 160p. (J). (gr. 2-4). 6.95 (978-1-4027-2499-2(3)) Sterling Publishing Co., Inc.

—The Adventures of Huckleberry Finn: With a Discussion of Friendship. Lauter, Richard, tr. Lauter, Richard, illus. 2003. (Values in Action Illustrated Classics Ser.). (J). (978-1-59203-042-2(4)) Learning Challenge, Inc.

Ungerer, Tomi. Adelaide: The Flying Kangaroo. 2011. (ENG., Illus.). 40p. (J). (gr. -1-3). 16.95 (978-0-7148-6083-1(2)) Phaidon Pr., Inc.

Verne, Jules. Around the World in 80 Days. 2004. (Young Reading Series Two Ser.). 64p. (J). (gr. 2-18). pap. 5.95 (978-0-7945-0741-1(7), Usborne) EDC Publishing.

—Dick Sand. Munro, George, tr. 2008. 296p. 29.95 (978-1-60664-752-3(0)) Rodgers, Alan Bks.

—Dick Sands: The Boy Captain. ELLEN E. FREWER, tr. 2007. (ENG.). 298p. pap. 21.99 (978-1-4264-3403-7(0)) Creative Media Partners, LLC.

—Dick Sands: The Boy Captain. Frewer, Ellen E., tr. Lt. ed. 2007. (ENG.). 328p. pap. 24.99 (978-1-4264-3453-2(7)) Creative Media Partners, LLC.

—The English at the North Pole. 2009. 160p. 24.95 (978-1-60664-684-7(2)); pap. 13.95 (978-1-60664-313-6(4)) Rodgers, Alan Bks.

—The Field of Ice: Part II of the Adventures of Captain Hatteras. 2007. (ENG.). 154p. pap. 19.99 (978-1-4264-3591-1(6)); 170p. pap. 21.99 (978-1-4264-3642-0(4)) Creative Media Partners, LLC.

—Le Tour du Monde en 80 Jours.Tr. of Around the World in 80 Days. (FRE.). (J). pap. 19.95 (978-2-07-051436-6(6)) Gallimard, Editions FRA. Dist: Distribooks, Inc.

—La Vuelta Al Mundo en 80 Dias. 2012. 132p. pap. 9.99 (978-1-60796-466-7(X)) Meirovich, Igal.

Viano, Hannah. Arrow to Alaska: A Pacific Northwest Adventure. 2015. (ENG., Illus.). 32p. (J). (gr. k-4). 16.99 (978-1-57061-949-6(2), Little Bigfoot) Sasquatch Bks.

Viva, Frank. A Long Way Away. 2013. (ENG., Illus.). 40p. (J). (gr. -1-3). 16.99 (978-0-316-22196-2(1)) Little, Brown Bks. for Young Readers.

Voigt, Cynthia. The Tale of Birle. 2015. (Tales of the Kingdom Ser.: 2). (ENG., Illus.). 416p. (YA). (gr. 7). 19.99 (978-1-4424-8356-9(3), Atheneum Bks. for Young Readers) Simon & Schuster Children's Publishing.

Wahl, Jan. Cobweb Castle. 2014. (ENG., Illus.). 32p. (J). 14.95 (978-0-7649-6801-3(7)) Pomegranate Communications, Inc.

—The Long Tall Journey. Gapaillard, Laurent, illus. 2015. (ENG.). 48p. (J). (gr. 1-3). 18.99 (978-1-56846-230-1(1), Creative Editions) Creative Co., The.

Walfish, Miriam. The Jewel & the Journey. 2007. 208p. (J). 16.95 (978-1-932443-81-3(9)) Judaica Pr., Inc., The.

Wallace, Brandon. The Journey Home. (Wilder Boys Ser.). (ENG.). 208p. (J). 2017. (gr. 4-8). pap. 7.99 (978-1-4814-3266-5(4)) 2016. (Illus.). (gr. 3-7). 16.99 (978-1-4814-3267-2(2)) Simon & Schuster Children's Publishing. (Aladdin).

Wallace, Brandon. Wilder Boys. 2017. (Wilder Boys Ser.). (ENG.). 256p. (J). (gr. 4-8). pap. 7.99 (978-1-4814-3263-4(X), Simon & Schuster/Paula Wiseman Bks.) Simon & Schuster/Paula Wiseman Bks.

Wang, Jack, et al. Mark Twain's the Adventures of Huckleberry Finn. 2016. (ENG., Illus.). 24p. (J). (gr. -1 — 1). bds. 9.95 (978-1-4521-5249-3(7)) Chronicle Bks. LLC.

Watson, Jude. Underworld. 2005. (Star Wars Ser.: No. 3). 137p. (J). lib. bdg. 20.00 (978-1-4242-0776-3(2)) Fitzgerald Bks.

Weaver, Anne H. The Voyage of the Beetle: A Journey Around the World with Charles Darwin & the Search for the Solution to the Mystery of Mysteries, As Narrated by Rosie, an Articulate Beetle. Lawrence, George, tr. Lawrence, George, illus. 2004. (Roman Mysteries Ser.). 80p. (J). (gr. 5-8). lib. bdg. 26.90 (978-0-7613-2923-7(4), Millbrook Pr.) Lerner Publishing Group.

Webb, Philip. Where the Rock Splits the Sky. 2014. (ENG.). 272p. (J). (gr. 9). 17.99 (978-0-545-55701-6(1), Chicken Hse., The) Scholastic, Inc.

Webb, Steve. City Kitty Cat. Le Huche, Magali, illus. 2015. (ENG.). 32p. (J). (gr. -1-3). 17.99 (978-1-4814-4331-9(3), Simon & Schuster Bks. For Young Readers) Simon & Schuster Bks. For Young Readers.

Weber, John. Orphan. 2010. 266p. (YA). (gr. 7-18). 16.95 (978-1-934813-38-6(9)) Westside Bks.

Wendel, Gretchen Schomer, et al. All Around Town. Renthrope, Damon, illus. 2007. (ENG.). 32p. (J). (gr. -1-3). 11.99 (978-1-933754-10-9(9)) Waterside Publishing.

Wendel, Gretchen Schomer & Schomer, Adam Anthony. Becka Goes to San Diego. Renthrope, Damon, illus. 2008. (ENG.). 32p. (J). (gr. -1-3). 11.99 (978-1-933754-51-2(6)) Waterside Publishing.

Wendel, Gretchen Schomer & Schomer, Adam Anthony. All Around Town. Renthrope, Damon, illus. 2009. (Becka & the Big Bubble Ser.). 32p. (J). (gr. -1-2). lib. bdg. 22.60 (978-1-60754-104-2(1)) Windmill Bks.

—Becka Goes to Chicago. Renthrope, Damon, illus. 2008. (ENG.). 36p. (J). (gr. -1-3). 11.99 (978-1-933754-52-9(4)) Waterside Publishing.

—Becka Goes to India. Renthrope, Damon, illus. 2009. (Becka & the Big Bubble Ser.). 32p. (J). (gr. -1-2). lib. bdg. 22.60 (978-1-60754-110-3(6)) Windmill Bks.

—Becka Goes to the North Pole. Renthrope, Damon, illus. 2009. (Becka & the Big Bubble Ser.). 32p. (J). (gr. -1-2). lib. bdg. 22.60 (978-1-60754-116-5(5)) Windmill Bks.

Weston Woods Staff, creator. Grandfather's Journey. 2011. 38.75 (978-0-545-12710-3(6)) Weston Woods Studios, Inc.

Whelan, Gloria. Parade of Shadows. 2007. 304p. (J). (gr. 5-18). lib. bdg. 16.89 (978-0-06-089029-2(0)) HarperCollins Pubs.

—Yuki & the One Thousand Carriers. Nascimbene, Yan, illus. 2008. (Tales of the World Ser.). (ENG.). 32p. (J). (gr. -1-3). 17.95 (978-1-58536-352-0(9)) Sleeping Bear Pr.

Where's Waldo: the Complete Set. 2006. (J). 82.94 (978-0-7636-3510-7(3)) Candlewick Pr.

White, E. B. Stuart Little. Date not set. 141p. 18.95 (978-0-8488-2602-4(7)) Amereon Ltd.

—Stuart Little. 2008. (J). 34.99 (978-0-7393-7101-5(0)) Findaway World, LLC.

—Stuart Little. Williams, Garth, illus. 60th anniv. ed. 2005. (Trophy Bk.). (ENG.). 144p. (J). (gr. 3-7). pap. 6.99 (978-0-06-440056-5(5)) HarperCollins Pubs.

—Stuart Little. Williams, Garth & Wells, Rosemary, illus. 60th anniv. ed. 2005. (Stuart-Little Ser.). (ENG.). 144p. (J). (gr. 3-7). pap. 8.99 (978-0-06-441092-2(7)) HarperCollins Pubs.

—Stuart Little. Williams, Garth, illus. 60th anniv. ed. 2005. (Stuart-Little Ser.). (ENG.). 144p. (J). (gr. 3-7). 16.99 (978-0-06-026395-9(4)) HarperCollins Pubs.

—Stuart Little. 131p. (J). pap. 5.95 (978-0-8072-8333-2(9)); 2004. (gr. 3-7). pap. 29.00 incl. audio (978-0-8072-8332-5(0), YA165SP) Random Hse. Audio Publishing Group. (Listening Library).

White, E. B. & White, E. Stuart Little. 2005. (J). (gr. 3-6). lib. bdg. 17.20 (978-0-8085-3806-6(3), Turtleback) Turtleback Bks.

Whitney, A. D. T. Sights & Insights: Patience Strong's Story of over the Way. Vol. 1. 2006. 356p. per. 26.99 (978-1-4255-3625-1(5)) Michigan Publishing.

—Sights & Insights: Patience Strong's Story of over the Way. Vol. 2. 2006. 344p. per. 23.99 (978-1-4255-3480-6(5)) Michigan Publishing.

Wiggins, Bethany. Cured. 2015. (ENG.). 320p. (YA). (gr. 7). pap. 9.99 (978-0-8027-3787-8(0), 9780802737878, Bloomsbury USA Childrens) Bloomsbury Publishing USA.

Wildavsky, Rachel. The Secret of Rover. Caparo, Antonio, illus. (ENG.). 368p. (J). (gr. 3-7). 2015. pap. 7.95 (978-1-4197-1968-4(8)) 2011. 17.95 (978-0-8109-9710-3(X)) Abrams, Inc. (Amulet Bks.).

Wurge, B. B. The Last Notebook of Leonardo. 2010. (LeapKids Ser.). (ENG., Illus.). 154p. (J). (gr. 1-7). pap. 9.95 (978-1-935248-14-9(6)) Leapfrog Pr.

Yaccarino, Dan. Lawn to Lawn. 2010. (ENG.). 40p. (J). (gr. -1-2). 17.99 (978-0-375-85574-0(2), Knopf Bks. for Young Readers) Random Hse. Children's Bks.

Yonge, Charlotte M. Little Lucy's Wonderful Globe. 2008. 152p. 36.95 (978-0-548-97272-4(9)) Kessinger Publishing, LLC.

Yoon, Salina. Penguin's Big Adventure. 2015. (Penguin Ser.). (ENG., Illus.). 40p. (J). (gr. -1-1). 14.99 (978-0-8027-3828-8(1), 9780802738288, Bloomsbury USA Childrens) Bloomsbury Publishing USA.

Young, Rebecca. Teacup. Ottley, Matt, illus. 2016. (ENG.). 40p. (J). (gr. -1-3). 17.99 (978-0-7352-2777-4(2), Dial Bks) Penguin Young Readers Group.

Zahler, Diane. Sleeping Beauty's Daughters. 2013. 216p. (J). lib. bdg. (978-0-06-200497-0(2)) Harper & Row Ltd.

—A True Princess. (ENG.). (J). (gr. 3-7). 2012. 208p. pap. 6.99 (978-0-06-182503-3(4)) 2011. 192p. 15.99 (978-0-06-182501-9(8)) HarperCollins Pubs.

Zarcinas, Scott. The Golden Chalice: A Pilgrim's Chronicle. 2013. 200p. pap. (978-0-9875975-9-5(0)) DoctorZed Publishing.

Zullo, Germano. Line 135. Albertine, illus. 2013. (ENG.). 44p. (J). (gr. -1-1). 18.95 (978-1-4521-1934-2(1)) Chronicle Bks. LLC.

VOYAGES AROUND THE WORLD

see also Adventure and Adventurers; Aeronautics—Flights; Discoveries in Geography; Explorers; Northwest Passage; Overland Journeys to the Pacific; Scientific Expeditions; Seafaring Life; Shipwrecks; Travel; Travelers; Yachts and Yachting also names of countries, continents, etc. with the subdivision Description and Travel (e.g. United States—Description and Travel); also names of regions (e.g. Antarctic Regions)

Ashby, Ruth. Young Charles Darwin & the Voyage of the Beagle, 1 vol. Duranceau, Suzanne, illus. 2009. (ENG.). 128p. (J). (gr. 2-5). 12.95 (978-1-56145-478-5(8), Peachtree Junior) Peachtree Pubs.

Bailey, Katharine. Ferdinand Magellan: Circumnavigating the World. 2005. (In the Footsteps of Explorers Ser.). (ENG., Illus.). 32p. (J). (gr. 4-7). pap. (978-0-7787-2452-0(2)) Crabtree Publishing Co.

Bergreen, Laurence. Over the Edge of the World. 2017. (ENG., Illus.). 224p. (J). (gr. 5-9). 19.99 (978-1-62672-120-3(3), 9781626721203) Roaring Brook Pr.

Big Picture Press, Big Picture. Walk This World at Christmastime. Powell, Debbie, illus. 2016. (ENG.). 24p. (J). (gr. k-3). 17.99 (978-0-7636-8921-6(1), Big Picture Press) Candlewick Pr.

Burnett, Betty. Ferdinand Magellan: The First Voyage Around the World. (Library of Explorers & Exploration Ser.). 112p. (gr. 5-8). 2009. 66.50 (978-1-60853-602-3(5)) 2003. (Illus.). (J). lib. bdg. 34.60 (978-0-8239-3617-5(1)) Rosen Publishing Group, Inc., The. (Rosen Reference).

Butcher, Nancy. It Can't Be Done, Nellie Bly! A Reporter's Race Around the World, 1 vol. Singh, Jen, illus. 2003. (ENG.). 144p. (J). (gr. 2-5). 12.95 (978-1-56145-289-7(0)) Peachtree Pubs.

Castaldo, Nancy F. The Race Around the World (Totally True Adventures) Lowe, Wesley, illus. 2015. (Totally True Adventures Ser.). (ENG.). 112p. (J). (gr. 2-5). 4.99 (978-0-553-52278-5(7), Random Hse. Bks. for Young Readers) Random Hse. Children's Bks.

Connelly, Jack. Ferdinand Magellan: Circumnavigating the Globe. 2015. (Incredible Explorers Ser.). (ENG., Illus.). 64p. (J). (gr. 7-7). 34.21 (978-1-5026-0132-2(X)) Cavendish Square Publishing.

Crompton, Samuel Willard. Ferdinand Magellan & the Quest to Circle the Globe. Goetzmann, William H., ed. 2005. (Explorers of New Lands Ser.). (Illus.). 110p. (J). (gr. 5-8). lib. bdg. 30.00 (978-0-7910-8608-7(9)) Facts On File, Inc.

Dalrymple, Lisa. Explore with James Cook. 2015. (Travel with the Great Explorers Ser.). (ENG., Illus.). 32p. (J). (gr. 3-6). (978-0-7787-1701-0(1)) Crabtree Publishing Co.

Fandel, Jennifer. Ferdinand Magellan. 2003. (Explorers of the Unknown Ser.). (J). (978-1-58417-036-5(0)); pap. (978-1-58417-099-0(9)) Lake Street Pubs.

Feinstein, Stephen. Captain Cook: Great Explorer of the Pacific. 2010. (Great Explorers of the World Ser.). (Illus.). 112p. (J). (gr. 7-12). 33.27 (978-1-59845-102-3(2)) Enslow Pubs., Inc.

Gould, Jane H. Ferdinand Magellan. 2013. (Jr. Graphic Famous Explorers Ser.). (ENG., Illus.). 24p. (J). (gr. 3-6). pap. 10.60 (978-1-4777-0123-2(0)); lib. bdg. 25.25 (978-1-4777-0069-3(2)) Rosen Publishing Group, Inc., The. (PowerKids Pr.).

Hoogenboom, Lynn. Ferdinand Magellan. 2009. (Primary Source Library of Famous Explorers Ser.). 24p. (gr. 4-4). 42.50 (978-1-60854-120-1(7), PowerKids Pr.) Rosen Publishing Group, Inc., The.

—Ferdinand Magellan: A Primary Source Biography. 2006. (Primary Source Library of Famous Explorers Ser.). (Illus.). 24p. (YA). (gr. 2-5). lib. bdg. 22.60 (978-1-4042-3039-2(4)) Rosen Publishing Group, Inc., The.

Justice, William E. Kodoku. Rivera, Hanae, illus. 2012. (ENG.). 32p. (J). 16.95 (978-1-59714-173-4(9)) Heyday.

Kramer, Sydelle. Who Was Ferdinand Magellan? Wolf, Elizabeth & Harrison, Nancy, illus. 2004. (Who Was? Ser.). (ENG.). 112p. (J). (gr. 3-7). pap. 5.99 (978-0-448-43105-5(X), Grosset & Dunlap) Penguin Young Readers Group.

—Who Was Ferdinand Magellan? Wolf, Elizabeth, illus. 2004. (Who Was... ? Ser.). 105p. (J). (gr. 3-7). 12.65 (978-0-7569-4615-9(8)) Perfection Learning Corp.

Lace, William W. Captain James Cook. 2009. (Great Explorers Ser.). (Illus.). 112p. (gr. 6-12). 30.00 (978-1-60413-416-2(X), Chelsea Hse.) Facts On File, Inc.

—Sir Francis Drake. 2009. (Great Explorers Ser.). (Illus.). 112p. (gr. 6-12). 30.00 (978-1-60413-417-9(8), Chelsea Hse.) Facts On File, Inc.

Landau, Elaine. Ferdinand Magellan. 2005. (History Maker Bios Ser.). (Illus.). 48p. (J). (gr. 3-7). lib. bdg. 26.60 (978-0-8225-2942-2(4), Lerner Pubns.) Lerner Publishing Group.

Macdonald, Fiona. Courageous Circumnavigators: True Stories of Around-The-World Adventurers, 1 vol. 2014. (Ultimate Adventurers Ser.). (ENG., Illus.). 48p. (gr. 6-6). lib. bdg. 29.99 (978-1-4109-5416-9(1)) Heinemann-Raintree.

Malam, John. Extreme Exploration. 2009. (Difficult & Dangerous Ser.). (Illus.). 32p. (J). (gr. 4-7). pap. (978-1-897563-24-3(8)) Saunders Bk. Co.

Marsh, Carole. Ferdinand Magellan, World Voyager. 2004. 12p. (gr. k-4). 2.95 (978-0-635-02373-5(3)) Gallopade International.

Meyer, Susan. Ferdinand Magellan. 2016. (Spotlight on Explorers & Colonization Ser.). 48p. (J). (gr. 6-6). pap. 11.75 (978-1-4777-8800-4(X)) Rosen Publishing Group, Inc., The.

Molzahn, Arlene Bourgeois. Ferdinand Magellan: First Explorer Around the World. 2003. (Illus.). 48p. (J). (gr. 1-4). lib. bdg. 23.93 (978-0-7660-2068-9(1)) Enslow Pubs., Inc.

Morriss, Roger. Captain Cook & His Exploration of the Pacific. 2010. (History of Exploration Ser.). 48p. 32.80 (978-1-84898-303-8(4)) Black Rabbit Bks.

Ollhoff, Jim. Ferdinand Magellan. 2013. (Great Explorers Ser.). 32p. (J). (gr. 5-9). lib. bdg. 27.07 (978-1-61783-967-2(1), Abdo & Daughters) ABDO Publishing Co.

Petrie, Kristin. Ferdinand Magellan, 1 vol. 2007. (Explorers Set 2 Ser.). (ENG., Illus.). 32p. (gr. 4-7). 27.07 (978-1-59679-744-4(4), Checkerboard Library) ABDO Publishing Co.

—James Cook, 1 vol. 2004. (Explorers Set 1 Ser.). (ENG., Illus.). 32p. (gr. k-6). 27.07 (978-1-59197-596-0(4), Checkerboard Library) ABDO Publishing Co.

Powell, Marie. Explore with Ferdinand Magellan. 2014. (ENG., Illus.). 32p. (J). (978-0-7787-1425-5(X)) Crabtree Publishing Co.

Rice, Dona Herweck. Lugares del Mundo, 1 vol. 2nd rev. ed. 2012. (Nonfiction Readers Ser.).Tr. of Places Around the World. (SPA.). 20p. (J). (gr. 1-1). pap. 4.99 (978-1-4333-4433-6(5)) Teacher Created Materials, Inc.
—Places Around the World, 1 vol. 2nd rev. ed. 2011. (Nonfiction Readers Ser.). (ENG., Illus.). 20p. (gr. 1-1). pap. 7.96 (978-1-4333-3600-3(6)) Shell Educational Publishing.
Sisk, Siobhan. Would You Dare Sail Around the World? 2016. (Would You Dare? Ser.). 00032p. (J). lib. bdg. 26.60 **(978-1-4824-5828-2(4))** Stevens, Gareth Publishing LLLP.
Thermes, Jennifer. Charles Darwin's Around-The-World Adventure. 2016. (ENG., Illus.). 48p. (J). (gr. k-2). 18.95 (978-1-4197-2120-5(8), Abrams Bks. for Young Readers) Abrams, Inc.
Waldman, Stuart. Magellan's World. Manchess, Gregory, illus. 2007. (Great Explorers Ser.). (ENG.). 48p. (J). (gr. 4-8). 22.95 (978-1-931414-19-7(X), 9781931414197) Mikaya Pr.
Williams, Rachel. Atlas of Adventures: A Collection of Natural Wonders, Exciting Experiences & Fun Festivities from the Four Corners of the Globe. Letherland, Lucy, illus. 2015. (Atlas Of Ser.). (ENG.). 96p. (J). (gr. 2-5). 30.00 (978-1-84780-695-6(3), Wide Eyed Editions) Quarto Publishing Group UK GBR. Dist: Hachette Bk. Group.
Yomtov, Nel. Ferdinand Magellan Sails Around the World. 2015. (Extraordinary Explorers Ser.). (ENG., Illus.). 24p. (J). (gr. 3-7). lib. bdg. 29.95 (978-1-62617-292-0(7), Black Sheep) Bellwether Media.

VOYAGES, IMAGINARY

McNulty, Faith. If You Decide to Go to the Moon. Kellogg, Steven, illus. 2010. (Rise & Shine Ser.). (ENG.). 48p. (C). (gr. -1-3). 30.95 (978-0-590-48359-9(5)) National Geographic School Publishing, Inc.

VOYAGES, IMAGINARY—FICTION

Benton, Jim. The Frandidate, No. 7. Benton, Jim, illus. 2008. (Franny K. Stein, Mad Scientist Ser.: 7). (ENG., Illus.). 128p. (J). (gr. 2-5). 17.99 (978-1-4169-0233-1(3), Simon & Schuster Bks. For Young Readers) Simon & Schuster Bks. For Young Readers.
—Frantastic Voyage, 1 vol. Benton, Jim, illus. 2011. (Franny K. Stein, Mad Scientist Ser.). (ENG., Illus.). 112p. (gr. 3-6). 24.21 (978-1-59961-821-0(4)) Spotlight.
Clark, Eleanor Linton, et al. Dodo's Dream Boat or the Voyage of the Seven Seas. 2008. (Illus.). 45p. (J). (978-0-9816873-2-2(6)) West Barnstable Pr.
Swift, Jonathan. Gulliver's Travels. Date not set. (J). (gr. 5-6). reprint ed. lib. bdg. 26.95 (978-0-89190-845-6(5), American Reprint Co.) Amereon Ltd.
—Gulliver's Travels. 2004. (Young Reading Ser.). (Illus.). 64p. (J). (gr. 2-18). pap. 5.95 (978-0-7945-0329-1(2), Usborne) EDC Publishing.
—Gulliver's Travels. (Young Collector's Illustrated Classics Ser.). (Illus.). 192p. (J). (gr. 3-7). 9.95 (978-1-56156-457-6(5)) Kidsbooks, LLC.
Thorpe, Kiki. A Dandelion Wish/from the Mist (Disney: the Never Girls) Christy, Jana, illus. 2015. (Never Girls Ser.). (ENG.). 256p. (J). (gr. 1-4). 9.99 (978-0-7364-3460-7(7), RH/Disney) Random Hse. Children's Bks.

VOYAGES TO THE MOON

see Space Flight to the Moon

VULTURES

Abbott, Henry. Buzzards, 01 vols., 1. 2016. (Raptors! Ser.). (ENG., Illus.). 24p. (J). pap. 8.25 (978-1-5081-4236-2(X), PowerKids Pr.) Rosen Publishing Group, Inc., The.
Chung, Liz. Vultures, 01 vols., 1. 2016. (Raptors! Ser.). (ENG., Illus.). 24p. (J). pap. 8.25 (978-1-5081-4254-6(8), PowerKids Pr.) Rosen Publishing Group, Inc., The.
Coleman, Miriam. Vultures Eat Rotting Corpses!, 1 vol., 1. 2014. (Disgusting Animal Dinners Ser.). (ENG.). 24p. (J). (gr. k-5). 23.60 (978-1-4777-2886-4(4), PowerKids Pr.) Rosen Publishing Group, Inc., The.
Dunn, Mary R. California Condors. 2015. (Birds of Prey Ser.). (ENG.). 24p. (gr. k-1). pap. 6.95 (978-1-4914-2307-3(2), Pebble Plus) Capstone Press of Coughlan Cos.
—Turkey Vultures. 2015. (Birds of Prey Ser.). (ENG.). 24p. (gr. k-1). pap. 6.95 (978-1-4914-2312-7(9), Pebble Plus) Capstone Press of Coughlan Cos.
Gish, Melissa. Living Wild: Vultures. 2013. (Living Wild Ser.). (ENG., Illus.). 48p. (J). (gr. 4-7). pap. 12.00 (978-0-89812-778-2(5), Creative Paperbacks) Creative Co., The.
—Vultures. 2012. (Living Wild Ser.). (Illus.). 48p. (J). (gr. 5-12). 23.95 (978-1-60818-171-1(5), Creative Education) Creative Co., The.
Gregory, Josh. Vultures. 2016. (Nature's Children Ser.). (ENG., Illus.). 48p. (J). pap. 6.95 (978-0-531-22522-6(4), Children's Pr.) Scholastic Library Publishing.
Kissock, Heather. Vulture. 2015. (Illus.). 24p. (J). (978-1-4896-4125-0(4)) Weigl Pubs., Inc.
Lundgren, Julie. Vultures. 2009. (Illus.). 24p. (J). pap. 7.95 (978-1-60694-774-6(5)) Rourke Educational Media.
Lynch, Wayne. Vultures. Neidigh, Sherry, illus. Lynch, Wayne, photos by. 2005. (Our Wild World Ser.). (ENG.). 48p. (J). (gr. 2-5). pap. 7.95 (978-1-55971-918-6(4)) Cooper Square Publishing Llc.
Lynch, Wayne, contrib. by. Vultures. 2005. (Our Wild World Ser.). (ENG., Illus.). 48p. (J). (gr. 2-5). 10.95 (978-1-55971-917-9(6)) Cooper Square Publishing Llc.
Macken, JoAnn Early. Vultures. 2nd rev. ed. 2009. (Animals That Live in the Desert Ser.). (ENG.). 24p. (J). (gr. -1-3). pap. 8.15 (978-1-4339-2453-8(6)); lib. bdg. 22.60 (978-1-4339-2392-0(0)) Stevens, Gareth Publishing LLLP. (Weekly Reader Leveled Readers).
—Vultures;Buitres. 2nd rev. ed. 2009. (Animals That Live in the Desert/Animales del desierto Ser.). (SPA & ENG.). 24p. (J). (gr. -1-3). pap. 8.15 (978-1-4339-2461-3(7)); lib. bdg. 22.60 (978-1-4339-2424-8(2)) Stevens, Gareth Publishing LLLP. (Weekly Reader Leveled Readers).
Magellan, Marta. Those Voracious Vultures. Weaver, Steve et al, illus. Gersing, James & Magill, Ron, photos by. 2008. (Those Amazing Animals Ser.). (ENG.). 55p. (J). (gr. k-4). 14.95 (978-1-56164-424-7(2)); pap. 8.95 (978-1-56164-425-4(0)) Pineapple Pr., Inc.
Markle, Sandra. Los Buitres. 2007. (Animales carroñeros (Animal Scavengers) Ser.). (SPA., Illus.). (J). (gr. -1-3). 39p. lib. bdg. 25.26 (978-0-8225-7731-7(3)); 40p. per. 7.95 (978-0-8225-7735-5(6)) Lerner Publishing Group. (Ediciones Lerner).
—Los Buitres; Vultures. 2008. pap. 46.95 (978-0-8225-9355-3(6)) Lerner Publishing Group.
—Vultures. (Animal Scavengers Ser.). (Illus.). (gr. 3-7). 2006. 39p. (J). pap. 7.95 (978-0-8225-3471-6(1), First Avenue Editions) 2005. (ENG., 40p. lib. bdg. 25.26 (978-0-8225-3195-1(X), Lerner Pubns.) Lerner Publishing Group.
McCarthy, Cecilia Pinto. Vultures, 1 vol. 2012. (Birds Ser.). (ENG., Illus.). 24p. (gr. 1-2). lib. bdg. 25.32 (978-1-4296-8608-2(1)) Capstone Press of Coughlan Cos.
O'Donnell, Kerri. Vultures. 2009. (Ugly Animals Ser.). 24p. (gr. 2-3). 42.50 (978-1-60854-605-3(5), PowerKids Pr.) Rosen Publishing Group, Inc., The.
Rebman, Renee C. Vultures. 2011. (Animals Animals 12 Ser.). (Illus.). 48p. (J). (gr. 3). 23.95 (978-0-7614-4880-8(2)) Marshall Cavendish Corp.
Riggs, Kate. Amazing Animals: Vultures. 2015. (Amazing Animals Ser.). (ENG.). 24p. (J). (gr. 1-3). pap. 7.99 (978-1-62832-092-3(3), Creative Paperbacks) Creative Co., The.
—Vultures. 2015. (Illus.). 24p. (J). (978-1-60818-492-7(7), Creative Education) Creative Co., The.
Vultures. 2006. (Ugly Animals Ser.). (Illus.). 24p. (J). (gr. 3-7). lib. bdg. 22.60 (978-1-4042-3526-7(4)) Rosen Publishing Group, Inc., The.
Waxman, Laura Hamilton. California Condors: Wide-Winged Soaring Birds. 2016. (Comparing Animal Traits Ser.). (ENG., Illus.). 32p. (J). (gr. 2-4). pap. 8.99 (978-1-4677-9639-2(5)) Lerner Publishing Group.
Wechsler, Doug. Vultures. 2009. (Really Wild Life of Animals Ser.). 24p. (gr. 3-4). 42.50 (978-1-60854-212-3(2), PowerKids Pr.) Rosen Publishing Group, Inc., The.

VULTURES—FICTION

Del Riego, Erica. The Heart of Life. 2010. 36p. pap. 17.75 (978-1-4389-7572-6(4)) AuthorHouse.
Hanson, Jonathan. Victor el Zopilote Renuente! Duffek, Kim Kanoa, illus. 2012. 36p. (J). pap. 16.95 (978-1-886679-46-7(0)) Arizona Sonora Desert Museum Pr.
—Victor, the Reluctant Vulture. Duufek, Kim Kanoa, illus. 2012. 36p. (J). pap. 16.95 (978-1-886679-45-0(2)) Arizona Sonora Desert Museum Pr.
Johnson, Calvin. Buzzy the Vegetarian Vulture. Ciresi-Abremski, M. Kathleen, illus. 2012. 28p. pap. 12.95 (978-1-61493-109-6(7)) Peppertree Pr., The.
McAuliffe, Nichola. Attila, Loolagax & the Eagle. Collins, Ross, tr. Collins, Ross, illus. 2003. (ENG.). 128p. (J). pap. 10.99 (978-0-7475-6499-7(X)) Bloomsbury Publishing Plc GBR. Dist: Independent Pubs. Group.
McDermott, Gerald. Jabutí the Tortoise: A Trickster Tale from the Amazon. 2005. (ENG., Illus.). 32p. (J). (gr. -1-3). pap. 7.99 (978-0-15-205374-1(3)) Houghton Mifflin Harcourt Publishing Co.
Perry, Dakota. Vulture Itus, 1 vol. 2009. 20p. pap. 24.95 (978-1-60836-087-1(3)) America Star Bks.
Pilkey, Dav. The Voodoo Vultures from Venus. Santat, Dan, illus. 2014. (Ricky Ricotta Ser.: 3). (ENG.). 128p. (J). (gr. -1-3). pap. 5.99 (978-0-545-63011-5(8)) Scholastic, Inc.
Willard, Hugh. The Goodwill Vultures Club: No Time for Play. Holjes, Kerry, ed. Eason, D. M., illus. 2013. 140p. pap. 9.99 (978-1-935711-30-8(X)) Peak City Publishing, LLC.
—The Goodwill Vultures Club: The Gift of the Vulture. Dozier, Dolly, ed. Eason, D. M., illus. 2013. 128p. pap. 9.99 (978-1-935711-34-6(2)) Peak City Publishing, LLC.

W

WAGNER, RICHARD, 1813-1883

Getzinger, Donna & Felsenfeld, Daniel. Richard Wagner & German Opera. 2004. (Classical Composers Ser.). (Illus.). 144p. (YA). (gr. 6-12). 26.95 (978-1-931798-24-2(9)) Reynolds, Morgan Inc.
Whiting, Jim. The Life & Times of Richard Wagner. 2004. (Masters of Music Ser.). (Illus.). 48p. (gr. 4-8). lib. bdg. 20.95 (978-1-58415-278-1(8)) Mitchell Lane Pubs., Inc.

WALES

Broomfield, Stuart & Madoc-Jones, Euryn. Turning Points in Welsh History, 1485-1914. 2004. (ENG., Illus.). 176p. pap. 20.00 (978-0-7083-1828-7(2)) Gwasg Prifysgol Cymru / Univ. of Wales Pr. GBR. Dist: Chicago Distribution Ctr.
Colson, Mary. Wales, 1 vol. 2011. (Countries Around the World Ser.). (ENG., Illus.). 48p. (gr. 3-6). pap. 9.95 (978-1-4329-5242-6(0), NA-h) Heinemann-Raintree.
Evans, Robin. Pecyn Lluniau a Llyfr Athrawon. 2005. (WEL., Illus.). 8p. pap. (978-1-85644-873-4(8)) CAA.
Heinrichs, Ann. Wales. 2003. (Enchantment of the World Ser.). (ENG., Illus.). 144p. (J). (gr. 5-9). 37.00 (978-0-516-22288-2(0), Children's Pr.) Scholastic Library Publishing.
Hestler, Anna & Spilling, Jo-Ann. Wales. 2nd rev. ed. 2010. (Cultures of the World Ser.). (Illus.). 144p. (gr. 6-8). lib. bdg. 42.79 (978-1-60870-457-6(2), Cavendish Children's Bks.) Marshall Cavendish Corp.
Lynch, Annabelle. Living in Wales. 2017. (Living in the UK Ser.). (ENG., Illus.). 24p. (J). (gr. 2-4). pap. 11.99 (978-1-4451-4814-4(5), Franklin Watts) Hachette Children's Group GBR. Dist: Hachette Bk. Group.
—Wales. 2016. (Let's Visit Ser.). (ENG., Illus.). 24p. (J). (gr. 1-3). pap. 10.99 (978-1-4451-3706-3(2), Franklin Watts) Hachette Children's Group GBR. Dist: Hachette Bk. Group.
Meirion, Dafydd, et al. Anturio Ar Ynys Mon: Sawl Taith Stori I Ti AC I'R Teulu. 2005. (WEL., Illus.). 84p. pap. (978-0-86381-863-9(3)) Gwasg Carreg Gwalch.
Stevens, Catrin, et al. Yr Oesoedd Canol Cythryblus. 2005. (WEL., Illus.). 144p. pap. 4.99 (978-1-84323-423-4(8)) Gomer Pr. GBR. Dist: Gomer Pr.
Sullivan, Laura L. Black Bart Roberts. 2015. (True-Life Pirates Ser.). (ENG.). 48p. (J). (gr. 3-3). lib. bdg. 31.36 (978-1-5026-0207-7(5)) Cavendish Square Publishing.
Thomas, Dylan. A Child's Christmas in Wales. Raskin, Ellen, illus. 2003. (New Directions Paperbook Ser.: Vol. 972). (ENG.). 32p. reprint ed. pap. 8.00 (978-0-8112-1560-2(1)) New Directions Publishing Corp.

WALES—FICTION

Anrias, Donnan. Targ - the King of Eagles. 2005. 138p. (YA). per. 23.00 (978-1-4116-1923-4(4)) Lulu Pr., Inc.
Armour, Michael C. Orca Song. Lee, Katie, illus. (ENG.). 32p. (J). (gr. -1-2). pap. 6.95 (978-1-59249-479-8(X), S4004) Soundprints.
Billingsley, Franny. Chime. 2011. (Playaway Young Adult Ser.). (YA). 59.99 (978-1-61707-143-0(9)) Findaway World, LLC.
Blyton, Enid. The Mountain of Adventure. Cobb, Rebecca, illus. unabr. ed. 2014. (Adventure Ser.: 5). (ENG.). 288p. (J). (gr. 4-7). pap. 9.99 (978-1-4472-6279-4(4)) Pan Macmillan GBR. Dist: Independent Pubs. Group.
Bond, Nancy. A String in the Harp. 2006. (ENG.). 384p. (J). (gr. 5-9). pap. 8.99 (978-1-4169-2771-6(9), Aladdin) Simon & Schuster Children's Publishing.
Boyce, Frank Cottrell. Framed. (J). (gr. 3). 2008. (Illus.). 320p. per. 8.99 (978-0-06-073404-6(3)) 2006. 306p. lib. bdg. 17.89 (978-0-06-073403-9(5)) HarperCollins Pubs.
—Framed. Lenton, Steven, illus. unabr. ed. 2006. (ENG.). 320p. pap. 15.95 (978-0-330-43425-6(X)) Macmillan Pubs., Ltd. GBR. Dist: Trans-Atlantic Pubns., Inc.
—Framed, 1. Lenton, Steven, illus. 2nd ed. 2008. (ENG.). 336p. 17.95 (978-0-330-45292-2(4), Macmillan) Pan Macmillan GBR. Dist: Trans-Atlantic Pubns., Inc.
Brodien-Jones, Chris. The Glass Puzzle. 2013. (Illus.). 319p. (J). (978-0-385-74298-6(3), Delacorte Pr) Random House Publishing Group.
Brodien-Jones, Christine. The Dreamkeepers. 2009. (ENG.). 148p. (YA). (gr. 7). pap. 8.99 (978-1-4424-0221-8(0), Simon & Schuster Bks. For Young Readers) Simon & Schuster Bks. For Young Readers.
—The Glass Puzzle. 2013. (ENG., Illus.). 336p. (J). (gr. 4-7). 16.99 (978-0-385-74297-9(5), Delacorte Bks. for Young Readers) Random Hse. Children's Bks.
Carpenter, Suzanne. Barti & Bel Whizz Around Wales. 2003. (ENG., Illus.). 32p. pap. 12.95 (978-1-84323-238-4(3)) Beekman Bks., Inc.
Coats, J. Anderson. The Wicked & the Just. (ENG.). 352p. (YA). (gr. 7). 2012. 16.99 (978-0-547-68837-4(7)) 2013. pap. 9.99 (978-0-544-02221-8(1)) Houghton Mifflin Harcourt Publishing Co.
Cooper, Susan. The Dark Is Rising. 2007. (YA). 1.25 (978-1-4193-7923-9(2)) Recorded Bks., Inc.
Davie, Jan. Arthur's Amulet. 2004. 86p. pap. (978-1-84401-228-2(X)) Athena Pr.
Davies, Christie. Dewi the Dragon. 2006. (ENG.). 96p. (J). pap. 9.95 (978-0-86243-770-1(9)) Y Lolfa GBR. Dist: Dufour Editions, Inc.
Davies, Elgan Philip & Ceredigion, Cymdeithas Lyfrau. Olion Hen Elyn. 2005. (WEL.). 200p. pap. (978-1-84512-004-7(3)) Cymdeithas Lyfrau Ceredigion.
Davies, Linda. Longbow Girl. 2016. (ENG.). 336p. (J). (gr. 7). 17.99 (978-0-545-85345-3(1), Chicken Hse., The) Scholastic, Inc.
Eames, Marion. Baner Beca. 2005. (WEL.). 80p. pap. (978-0-86243-729-9(6)) Y Lolfa.
Edwards, Meinir Wyn. Maelgwn, King of Gwynedd. Wade, Gini, illus. 2008. (ENG.). 24p. (J). pap. 4.95 (978-1-84771-024-6(7)) Y Lolfa GBR. Dist: Dufour Editions, Inc.
—Red Bandits of Mawddwy. Wade, Gini, illus. 2008. (ENG.). 24p. (J). pap. 4.95 (978-1-84771-023-9(9)) Y Lolfa GBR. Dist: Dufour Editions, Inc.
—Rhys & Meinir. Wade, Gini, illus. 2007. (ENG.). 24p. (J). pap. 4.95 (978-1-84771-020-8(4)) Y Lolfa GBR. Dist: Dufour Editions, Inc.
—Welsh Folk Stories. Tomos, Morgan, illus. 2012. (WEL & ENG.). 128p. (J). pap. 9.95 (978-1-84771-358-2(0)) Y Lolfa GBR. Dist: Dufour Editions, Inc.
Eynon, Bob & Wen, Dref. Crwydro'r Môr Mawr. 2005. (WEL & ENG.). 80p. pap. (978-1-85596-656-7(5)) Dref Wen.
Fletcher, Chris. Rock Tales. Harrison, Harry, illus. 2012. (ENG.). 72p. (J). pap., pap. 13.95 (978-1-84771-380-3(7)) Y Lolfa GBR. Dist: Dufour Editions, Inc.
Holliday, Susan. Riding the Storm. l.t. ed. 2007. 164p. per. (978-1-905665-22-8(9)) Pollinger In Print.
Huws, Emily & Gomer, Gwasg. CAE Berllan. 2005. (WEL.). 28p. 5.99 (978-1-85902-998-5(1)) Gomer Pr. GBR. Dist: Gomer Pr.
Ifans, Rhiannon. Owain Glyndwr: Prince of Wales. Jones, Margaret, illus. 2003. (WEL & ENG.). 96p. (J). pap. 13.95 (978-0-86243-544-8(7)) Y Lolfa GBR. Dist: Dufour Editions, Inc.
Jenkins, Mike. Child of Dust. 2005. (ENG.). 192p. pap. 15.95 (978-1-84323-491-3(2)) Beekman Bks., Inc.
Jones, Frewin. Destiny's Path. 2009. (Warrior Princess Ser.: 2). (ENG.). 352p. (YA). (gr. 8-18). 16.99 (978-0-06-087146-8(6), HarperTeen) HarperCollins Pubs.
—The Emerald Flame. 2010. (Warrior Princess Ser.: 3). (ENG.). 352p. (YA). (gr. 8-18). 16.99 (978-0-06-087149-9(0), HarperTeen) HarperCollins Pubs.
—Warrior Princess. 2009. (YA). 346p. lib. bdg. 17.89 (978-0-06-087144-4(X)); (ENG.). 352p. (gr. 7-18). 16.99 (978-0-06-087143-7(1)) HarperCollins Pubs. (Eos).
—Warrior Princess #2: Destiny's Path. 2010. (Warrior Princess Ser.: 2). (ENG.). 352p. (YA). (gr. 8). pap. 8.99 (978-0-06-087148-2(2), HarperTeen) HarperCollins Pubs.
Jones, Jac. In Chatter Wood. Jones, Jac, illus. 2004. (ENG., Illus.). 40p. pap. 13.95 (978-1-84323-290-2(1)) Beekman Bks., Inc.
Jones, Margaret. Nat. 2004. (ENG., Illus.). 112p. pap. 13.95 (978-1-84323-327-5(4)) Beekman Bks., Inc.
Jones, T. Llew. Storïau Cwm-Pen-Llo. 2005. (WEL., Illus.). 100p. pap. (978-0-86381-750-2(5)) Gwasg Carreg Gwalch.
Kimmel, Eric A. Moby Dick: Chasing the Great White Whale. Glass, Andrew, illus. 2012. (ENG.). 40p. (J). (gr. k-1). 16.99 (978-0-312-66297-4(1), 9780312662974) Feiwel & Friends.
LaFevers, R. L. The Wyverns' Treasure. 2012. (Nathaniel Fludd, Beastologist Ser.: 3). lib. bdg. 16.00 (978-0-606-24516-6(2), Turtleback) Turtleback Bks.
Lewis, Caryl & Lolfa, Y. Iawn Boi? 2005. (WEL.). 80p. pap. (978-0-86243-699-5(0)) Y Lolfa.
Milway, Alex. Operation Robot Storm: The Mythical 9th Division. Milway, Alex, illus. 2013. (ENG., Illus.). 224p. (J). pap. 5.99 (978-1-61067-074-6(4)) Kane Miller.
Morgan, Gwyn & Owen, Dai. Babi Ben. 2005. (WEL., Illus.). 64p. pap. (978-1-85596-611-6(5)) Dref Wen.
Nimmo, Jenny. Chestnut Soldier. 2009. (Magician Trilogy Ser.). (ENG.). 208p. (J). (gr. 3-7). 5.99 (978-0-545-07127-7(5), Scholastic Paperbacks) Scholastic, Inc.
Nimmo, Jenny & Keating, John. The Snow Spider. 2006. (Magician Trilogy Ser.: Bk. 1). (ENG.). (J). (gr. 3-7). audio compact disk 39.95 (978-0-439-89844-7(7)) Scholastic, Inc.
Orca Song. (Illus.). 32p. (J). (gr. -1-2). 6.95 incl. reel tape (978-1-59249-488-0(9), SC4004) Soundprints.
Orme, David & Baines, Menna. Llanast Llyr. 2005. (WEL., Illus.). 32p. (978-1-901358-16-2(X)) CAMFA.
Orme, Helen. Wet! 2008. (Siti's Sisters Ser.). (ENG., Illus.). 36p. pap. (978-1-84167-688-3(8)) Ransom Publishing Ltd.
Riggs, Ransom. Miss Peregrine's Home for Peculiar Children. (ENG., Illus.). (YA). (gr. 9). 2013. 368p. pap. 10.99 (978-1-59474-603-1(6)) 2011. (Miss Peregrine's Peculiar Children Ser.: 1). 352p. 18.99 (978-1-59474-476-1(9)) 2016. (Miss Peregrine's Peculiar Children Ser.: 1). 392p. pap. 11.99 (978-1-59474-902-5(7)) Quirk Bks.
—Miss Peregrine's Home for Peculiar Children. l.t. ed. 2012. (ENG.). 484p. (J). (gr. 8-12). 23.99 (978-1-4104-5023-4(6)) Thorndike Pr.
—Miss Peregrine's Home for Peculiar Children. 2013. (Miss Peregrine's Peculiar Children Ser.: 1). lib. bdg. 22.10 (978-0-606-32081-8(4), Turtleback) Turtleback Bks.
Riggs, Ransom, et al. Miss Peregrine's Home for Peculiar Children. 2011. pap. (978-1-59474-574-4(9)) Quirk Bks.
Roberts, Esyllt Nest & Owen, Carys Eurwen. Dinas Emrys. 2005. (WEL., Illus.). 36p. pap. (978-0-86381-439-6(5)) Gwasg Carreg Gwalch.
—Rhita Gawr. 2005. (WEL., Illus.). 36p. pap. (978-0-86381-624-6(X)) Gwasg Carreg Gwalch.
Saunders, Karen. Suzy P. & the Trouble with Three. 2014. (Suzy P. Ser.). (ENG.). 352p. (J). (gr. 4-7). pap. 10.99 (978-1-84877-369-1(2)) Bonnier Publishing GBR. Dist: Independent Pubs. Group.
Skuse, C. J. Rockoholic. 2012. (YA). (978-0-545-44251-0(6)); (ENG.). 368p. (J). (gr. 9). 18.99 (978-0-545-42960-3(9)) Scholastic, Inc.
Stevenson, Sarah Jamila. The Truth Against the World. 2014. (ENG.). 360p. (YA). pap. 9.99 (978-0-7387-4058-4(6), Flux) North Star Editions.
Stone, Reuben. Guardians of the Cambrian Lode: An Ancient People - A Timeless Quest. 2005. 254p. (YA). (gr. 8-12). per. 7.99 (978-0-9550034-0-0(7)) Bethania Bks. GBR. Dist: Send The Light Distribution LLC.
Sullivan, Jenny. Magic Apostrophe. 2003. (ENG.). 216p. pap. 19.95 (978-1-85902-116-3(6)) Beekman Bks., Inc.
Swindells, Robert. Blackout. 2011. (ENG.). 224p. (J). (gr. 3-6). pap. 9.99 (978-0-552-56154-9(1)) Transworld Publishers Ltd. GBR. Dist: Independent Pubs. Group.
Thomas, Gwyn. King Arthur. Jones, Margaret, illus. 2006. (ENG.). 144p. (J). pap. 21.95 (978-0-86243-798-5(9)) Y Lolfa GBR. Dist: Dufour Editions, Inc.
Togden, Ra Chel. The Legendary Rabbit of Death - Volume One [Paperback]. 2013. 108p. pap. (978-1-898185-27-7(1)) Aro Bks. worldwide.
Twigg, Aeres. The Green Hawk. 2003. (ENG., Illus.). 88p. (J). pap. 12.95 (978-1-85902-787-5(3)) Beekman Bks., Inc.
Wyn, Dafydd. Hunting the Man in the Moon. 2015. (ENG.). 192p. (J). pap. 13.00 (978-1-84771-833-4(7)) Y Lolfa GBR. Dist: Dufour Editions, Inc.

WALKER, MARY EDWARDS, 1832-1919

Gaines, Alison. Mary Edwards Walker. 2017. (J). **(978-1-5026-2745-2(0))** Cavendish Square Publishing.
Goldsmith, Bonnie Zucker. Dr. Mary Edwards Walker: Civil War Surgeon & Medal of Honor Recipient, 1 vol. 2010. (Military Heroes Ser.). (ENG.). 112p. (J). (gr. 6-12). lib. bdg. 35.64 (978-1-60453-966-0(6)) ABDO Publishing Co.
Harness, Cheryl. Mary Walker Wears the Pants: The True Story of the Doctor, Reformer, & Civil War Hero. Molinari, Carlo, illus. 2013. (ENG.). 32p. (J). (gr. 1-3). 16.99 (978-0-8075-4990-2(8)) Whitman, Albert & Co.

WALKING

see also Hiking

Barraclough, Sue. Move & Run. 2012. (Healthy Habits Ser.). (Illus.). 24p. (gr. 1-3). lib. bdg. 24.25 (978-1-59771-308-5(2)) Sea-To-Sea Pubns.
Benjamin, Tina. Let's Walk in the Woods. 2015. (Let's Go Outdoors! Ser.). (ENG.). 24p. (J). (gr. k-k). lib. bdg. 22.60 (978-1-4824-2635-9(8)); (Illus.). pap. 8.15 (978-1-4824-2633-5(1)) Stevens, Gareth Publishing LLLP.
Bruce, Dan Wingfoot. The Thru-Hiker's Handbook 2004: #1 Guide for Long-Distance Hikes on the Appalachian Trail. 2004. (Illus.). 184p. per. 15.95 (978-0-9707916-5-8(8)) Ctr. for Appalachian Trail Studies.
Caminando: Individual Title Six-Packs. (Literatura 2000 Ser.). (SPA.). (gr. 2-3). 33.00 (978-0-7635-1085-5(8)) Rigby Education.
Meter, Pete O. & Meter, Pete. Walk the Walk: The Kid's Book of Pedometer Challenges. 2008. (ENG., Illus.). 56p. (J). (gr. 4). spiral bd. 12.95 (978-1-60433-048-9(1), Applesauce Pr.) Cider Mill Pr. Bk. Pubs., LLC.
Oregon Center for Applied Science, creator. Walk Smart: Children's Pedestrian Safety Program. 2005. (J). cd-rom 19.95 (978-1-933898-10-0(0)) Oregon Ctr. for Applied Science, Inc.
Rubbino, Salvatore. A Walk in London. Rubbino, Salvatore, illus. 2011. (ENG., Illus.). 40p. (J). (gr. k-3). 16.99 (978-0-7636-5272-2(5)) Candlewick Pr.
Sesame Street Staff, creator. Sesame Street: Elmo & Me! Boxed Set. 2011. 40p. (J). bds. 12.99 (978-1-60745-166-2(2)) Flying Frog Pubs.
Thoreau, Henry. Walking. Clifton Johnson, illus. 2010. 100p. pap. 3.49 (978-1-60386-305-6(2), Watchmaker Publishing) Wexford College Pr.
Tuminelly, Nancy. Super Simple Walk & Run: Healthy & Fun Activities to Move Your Body, 1 vol. 2011. (Super Simple Exercise Ser.). (ENG., Illus.). 32p. (J). (gr. k-3). 27.07 (978-1-61714-964-1(0)) ABDO Publishing Co.
Votry, Kim & Waller, Curt. Out for a Walk. 2003. (Baby's First Signs Bks.). (Illus.). 16p. (J). bds. 6.95 (978-1-56368-146-2(3)) Gallaudet Univ. Pr.

Walking in the City. (J). 26.20 *(978-0-8136-8423-9(4))*; 26.20 *(978-0-8136-8422-2(6))*; (gr. -1-3). 59.50 *(978-0-8136-7966-2(4))* Modern Curriculum Pr.

WALL STREET (NEW YORK, N.Y.)—FICTION

Standish, Burt L. Frank Merriwell in Wall Street. Rudman, Jack, ed. 2003. (Frank Merriwell Ser.). pap. 9.95 *(978-0-8373-9159-5(8))* Merriwell, Frank Inc.

WALLACE, ALFRED RUSSEL, 1823-1913

Colson, Mary. Charles Darwin & Alfred Russel Wallace. 2014. (Dynamic Duos of Science Ser.). 48p. (YA). (gr. 5-8). pap. 84.30 *(978-1-4824-1280-2(2))* Stevens, Gareth Publishing LLLP.

WALLACE, GEORGE C. (GEORGE CORLEY), 1919-1998

Yeager, Alice. George C. Wallace: Alabama Political Power. 2003. (Alabama Roots Biography Ser.). (Illus.). 104p. (J). pap. *(978-1-59421-003-7(9))* Seacoast Publishing, Inc.

WALLACE, LEW, 1827-1905

Boomhower, Ray E. The Sword & the Pen: A Life of Lew Wallace. 2005. (Illus.). x, 164p. (J). 15.95 *(978-0-87195-185-4(1))* Indiana Historical Society.

WALLACE AND GROMIT (FICTITIOUS CHARACTERS)—FICTION

Abnett, Dan. A Pier Too Far. Hansen, Jimmy, illus. 2005. (Wallace & Gromit Ser.). (ENG.). 48p. 12.95 *(978-1-84023-953-9(0)*, Titan Bks.) Titan Bks. Ltd. GBR. Dist: Penguin Random Hse. LLC.

Rimmer, Ian. The Bootiful Game. Hansen, Jimmy & Williamson, Brian, illus. 2005. (Wallace & Gromit Ser.). (ENG.). 48p. pap. 8.95 *(978-1-84023-948-5(4)*, Titan Bks.) Titan Bks. Ltd. GBR. Dist: Penguin Random Hse. LLC.

WALLENBERG, RAOUL, 1912-1947

Borden, Louise W. His Name Was Raoul Wallenberg. 2012. (ENG., Illus.). 144p. (YA). (gr. 7). 18.99 *(978-0-618-50755-9(8))* Houghton Mifflin Harcourt Publishing Co.

Idzikowski, Lisa. Raoul Wallenberg: Rescuer of Hungarian Jews During the Holocaust. 2017. (J). ***(978-1-5383-8118-2(4))***; pap. ***(978-1-5383-8117-5(6))*** Rosen Publishing Group, Inc., The.

Simon, Emma & Streissguth, Thomas. Raoul Wallenberg, 01 vols., 1. 2016. (Holocaust Ser.). (ENG., Illus.). 112p. (J). 35.60 *(978-1-4994-6242-5(5)*, Rosen Young Adult) Rosen Publishing Group, Inc., The.

WALRUSES

Baines, Rebecca, et al. Arctic Tale: Companion to the Major Motion Picture. 2007. (ENG., Illus.). 32p. (J). (gr. -1-3). lib. bdg. 22.90 *(978-1-4263-0085-1(9))*; per. 5.95 *(978-1-4263-0084-4(0))* National Geographic Society. (National Geographic Children's Bks.).

Berger, Melvin & Berger, Gilda. Sea Horses. 2003. (Scholastic Reader Ser.). (Illus.). (J). pap. *(978-0-439-47392-7(6))* Scholastic, Inc.

Bodden, Valerie. Walruses. 2016. (Amazing Animals Ser.). 24p. (J). (ENG.). (gr. 1-3). pap. 8.99 *(978-1-62832-221-7(7)*, Creative Paperbacks); (Illus.). 28.50 *(978-1-60818-615-0(6)*, Creative Education) Creative Co., The.

Drumlin, Sam. Walruses. 2013. (PowerKids Readers: Sea Friends Ser.). (ENG., Illus.). 24p. (J). (gr. k-2). pap. 8.25 *(978-1-4488-9742-1(4))*; lib. bdg. 22.60 *(978-1-4488-9642-4(8))* Rosen Publishing Group, Inc., The. (PowerKids Pr.).

—Walruses: Las Morsas. Alamán, Eduardo, tr. from ENG. 2013. (PowerKids Readers: Sea Friends / Los Amigos Del Mar Ser.). (SPA & ENG., Illus.). 24p. (J). (gr. k-2). lib. bdg. 22.60 *(978-1-4488-9977-7(X)*, PowerKids Pr.) Rosen Publishing Group, Inc., The.

Gish, Melissa. Living Wild: Walruses. 2014. (Living Wild Ser.). (ENG., Illus.). 48p. (J). (gr. 4-7). pap. 12.00 *(978-0-89812-844-4(7)*, Creative Paperbacks) Creative Co., The.

—Walruses. 2013. (Illus.). 46p. (J). 35.65 *(978-1-60818-291-6(6)*, Creative Education) Creative Co., The.

Group/McGraw-Hill, Wright. I am the Walrus: Level N, 6 vols. (Autumn Leaves Ser.). 128p. (gr. 3-6). 36.95 *(978-0-322-06734-9(0))* Wright Group/McGraw-Hill.

Hirschmann, Kris. The Walrus. 2003. (Illus.). 48p. (J). 23.70 *(978-0-7377-1557-6(X)*, Greenhaven Pr., Inc.) Cengage Gale.

Jackson, Tom. Walrus. 2008. (Nature's Children Ser.). (Illus.). 52p. (J). *(978-0-7172-6246-5(4))* Grolier, Ltd.

Jones, Veda Boyd. Jazz Age Poet: A Story about Langston Hughes. Kiwak, Barbara, illus. 2006. (Creative Minds Biographies Ser.). (ENG.). 64p. (gr. 4-8). per. 8.95 *(978-0-8225-3092-3(9))* Lerner Publishing Group.

King, Zelda. Walruses. 2012. (Illus.). 24p. (J). 49.50 *(978-1-4488-5142-3(4)*, PowerKids Pr.); pap. 8.25 *(978-1-4488-5141-6(6)*, PowerKids Pr.); lib. bdg. 22.60 *(978-1-4488-5005-1(3))* Rosen Publishing Group, Inc., The.

Laughlin, Kara L. Walruses. 2017. (In the Deep Blue Sea Ser.). (ENG.). 24p. (J). (gr. k-3). lib. bdg. 27.07 *(978-1-5038-1694-7(X)*, 211528) Child's World, Inc., The.

Macheske, Felicia. Big & Blubbery: Walrus. 2016. (Guess What Ser.). (ENG., Illus.). 24p. (J). (gr. k-2). 28.50 *(978-1-63470-719-0(2)*, 207587) Cherry Lake Publishing.

Markovics, Joyce. My Skin Is Gray & Wrinkly (Walrus) 2014. (Zoo Clues Ser.). 24p. (J). (gr. -1-3). lib. bdg. 23.93 *(978-1-62724-109-0(4))* Bearport Publishing Co., Inc.

Markovics, Joyce L. Mi Piel Es Gris y Arrugada. 2015. (Pistas de Animales Ser.). (SPA.). 24p. (J). (gr. -1-3). lib. bdg. 23.93 *(978-1-62724-585-2(5))* Bearport Publishing Co., Inc.

Meister, Cari. Walruses. 2012. (ENG., Illus.). 24p. (J). lib. bdg. 25.65 *(978-1-62031-013-7(9))* Jump! Inc.

Miller, Sara Swan. Walruses of the Arctic. 2009. (Brrr! Polar Animals Ser.). 24p. (gr. 2-3). 42.50 *(978-1-61511-757-4(1)*, PowerKids Pr.) Rosen Publishing Group, Inc., The.

Murray, Julie. Walruses, 1 vol. (Arctic Animals Ser.). (ENG.). 2013. 32p. (gr. 2-5). lib. bdg. 28.50 *(978-1-61783-802-6(0)*, Big Buddy Bks.) 2003. 24p. (gr. k-4). 25.65 *(978-1-57765-726-2(8)*, Buddy Bks.) ABDO Publishing Co.

Nugent, Samantha. Walrus. 2015. (Illus.). 34p. (J). *(978-1-4896-4129-8(7))* Weigl Pubs., Inc.

Owen, Ruth. Walruses. 2013. (Polar Animals: Life in the Freezer Ser.). (ENG., Illus.). 32p. (J). (gr. k-5). pap. 10.00 *(978-1-4777-0227-7(X))*; lib. bdg. 25.25 *(978-1-4777-0220-8(2))* Windmill Bks.

Paniaq, Herve. Walrus, 1 vol. Shannon, Ben, illus. 2017. (Animals Illustrated Ser.). (ENG.). 32p. (J). (gr. k-2). 15.95 ***(978-1-77227-142-3(X))*** Inhabit Media Inc. CAN. Dist: Independent Pubs. Group.

Person, Stephen. Walrus: Tusk, Tusk. 2011. (Built for Cold Ser.). 32p. (YA). (gr. 1-4). lib. bdg. 25.27 *(978-1-61772-133-5(6))*; (J). (gr. 4-5). lib. bdg., E-Book 49.22 *(978-1-61772-223-3(5))* Bearport Publishing Co., Inc.

Read, Tracy C. Exploring the World of Seals & Walruses. 2011. (Exploring the World Of Ser.). (ENG., Illus.). 24p. (J). (gr. 3-7). 16.95 *(978-1-55407-784-7(2)*, 9781554077847); pap. 6.95 *(978-1-55407-797-7(4)*, 9781554077977) Firefly Bks., Ltd.

Rebman, Renee C. Walruses. 2011. (Animals Animals 12 Ser.). (Illus.). 48p. (J). (gr. 3). 23.95 *(978-0-7614-4881-5(0))* Marshall Cavendish Corp.

Richards, Mose, et al. Arctic Tale: Official Companion to the Major Motion Picture. 2007. (ENG., Illus.). 160p. 30.00 *(978-1-4262-0065-6(X))* National Geographic Society.

Schuetz, Kari. Walruses. 2016. (Ocean Life up Close Ser.). (ENG., Illus.). 24p. (J). (gr. k-3). 25.95 *(978-1-62617-424-5(5)*, Blastoff! Readers) Bellwether Media.

Sexton, Colleen. Walruses. 2007. (Oceans Alive Ser.). (ENG., Illus.). 24p. (J). (gr. k-3). lib. bdg. 25.95 *(978-1-60014-110-2(2))* Bellwether Media.

Soundprints Staff, ed. Oceanic Collection III: Beluga Whale, Harp Seal, Walrus & Lobster Books, 4 micro bks. (Smithsonian Oceanic Collection). (Illus.). 128p. (J). (gr. -1-2). 18.95 *(978-1-56899-633-2(0))* Soundprints.

Varela, Barry, et al. Arctic Tale. movie tie-in ed. 2007. (ENG., Illus.). 132p. (J). (gr. 3-7). per. 4.99 *(978-1-4263-0106-3(5)*, National Geographic Children's Bks.) National Geographic Society.

Weber, Valerie J. Walruses. 2008. (Animals That Live in the Ocean Ser.). (Illus.). 24p. (J). (gr. -1-3). lib. bdg. 22.60 *(978-0-8368-9566-7(5)*, Weekly Reader Leveled Readers) Stevens, Gareth Publishing LLLP.

—Walruses/Morsas. 2008. (Animals That Live in the Ocean/Animales Que Viven en el Oceano Ser.). 24p. (gr. -1-3). (ENG & SPA.). (J). lib. bdg. 22.60 *(978-0-8368-9568-1(1))*; (SPA.). pap. 8.15 *(978-0-8368-9578-0(9))* Stevens, Gareth Publishing LLLP. (Weekly Reader Leveled Readers).

WALRUSES—FICTION

Bradford, Arthur. Benny's Brigade. Hanawalt, Lisa, illus. 2012. (ENG.). 48p. 19.95 *(978-1-936365-61-6(8))* McSweeney's Publishing.

Cook, Sherry & Johnson, Terri. Watery William, 26. Kuhn, Jesse, illus. l.t. ed. 2006. (Quirkles — Exploring Phonics through Science Ser.: 23). 32p. (J). 7.99 *(978-1-933815-22-0(1)*, Quirkles, The) Creative 3, LLC.

Corderoy, Tracey. Lost Little Penguin, 1 vol. Scott, Gavin, illus. 2014. (ENG.). 32p. (gr. -1-2). 14.95 *(978-1-62370-116-1(3))* Capstone Young Readers of Coughlan Cos.

Derrick, Patricia. Mr. Walrus & the Old School Bus. Martinez, J-P Loppo, illus. 2007. 32p. 18.95 incl. audio compact disk *(978-1-933818-13-9(1))* Animalations.

Savage, Stephen. Where's Walrus? Savage, Stephen, illus. 2011. (ENG., Illus.). 32p. (J). (gr. -1-k). 16.99 *(978-0-439-70049-8(3)*, Scholastic Pr.) Scholastic, Inc.

—Where's Walrus? & Penguin? 2015. (ENG., Illus.). 32p. (J). (gr. -1-k). 16.99 *(978-0-545-40295-8(6)*, Scholastic Pr.) Scholastic, Inc.

Simpson, D. C. Closer to the Void: Ozy & Millie 2006-2007. 2008. 127p. pap. 12.45 *(978-1-4357-0504-3(1))* Lulu Pr., Inc.

Walker, Rhonda. Willie Out West. 2013. 24p. pap. 12.95 *(978-1-4497-9848-2(9)*, WestBow Pr.) Author Solutions, Inc.

Wampol, Pam & Woodard, Heather. Oscar's Dreamzz: The Story of Santa's First Elf. 2013. 40p. pap. *(978-1-4602-0414-6(X))* FriesenPress.

Young, Carol. Little Walrus Warning. Stuart, Walter, illus. (Smithsonian Oceanic Collection). (J). 2009. 24.95 incl. audio compact disk *(978-1-59249-667-9(9))* 2005. (ENG.). 32p. (gr. -1-2). 8.95 *(978-1-59249-070-7(0)*, SC4009) 2005. (ENG.). 32p. (gr. -1-3). 6.95 *(978-1-56899-937-1(2)*, S4009) Soundprints.

WANAMAKER, JOHN, 1838-1922

Burt, Olive Woolley. John Wanamaker: Boy Merchant. Lees, Harry H., illus. 2011. 192p. 42.95 *(978-1-258-08290-1(X))* Literary Licensing, LLC.

WAR

see also Aeronautics, Military; Armies; Battles; Disarmament; International Law; Military Art and Science; Military Weapons; Naval Art and Science; Peace; Soldiers; Submarine Warfare

also names of wars, battles, etc., e.g. United States—History—Civil War; Gettysburg, Battle of, 1863

Agnew, Kate, ed. War & Peace: A Collection of Classic Poetry & Prose. 2004. (ENG.). 176p. (J). (gr. 7). 9.95 *(978-1-84046-570-9(0)*, Wizard Books) Icon Bks., Ltd. GBR. Dist: Publishers Group Canada.

Anderson, Judith. War & Conflict. 2010. (Media Power Ser.). 48p. (J). 35.65 *(978-1-60753-116-6(X))* Amicus Publishing.

Anderson, Judith & Flinthart, Dirk. War & Conflict. 2011. (Inside Crime Ser.). 48p. (YA). (gr. 5-9). lib. bdg. 34.25 *(978-1-59920-399-7(5))* Black Rabbit Bks.

Baldwin Kiland, Taylor. Strategic Inventions of the War on Terror. 2016. (Tech in the Trenches Ser.). 112p. (J). lib. bdg. 42.79 *(978-1-5026-2349-2(8))* Cavendish Square Publishing.

Barker, Geoff. War. 2010. (Voices Ser.). (YA). (gr. 5-9). 34.25 *(978-1-59920-278-5(6))* Black Rabbit Bks.

Barnham, Kay. The Fact or Fiction Behind Battles & Wars. 2016. (Fact or Phony? Ser.). (ENG.). 96p. (J). (gr. 5-6). lib. bdg. 33.25 *(978-1-4824-4268-7(X))* Stevens, Gareth Publishing LLLP.

Biographies of War. 2015. (Biographies of War Ser.). (ENG.). 112p. (YA). (gr. 7-8). 329.00 *(978-1-68048-198-3(3)*, Britannica Educational Publishing) Rosen Publishing Group, Inc., The.

Brownell, Richard. War in Afghanistan. 2011. (Hot Topics Ser.). (ENG., Illus.). 128p. (J). (gr. 7-10). lib. bdg. 39.40 *(978-1-4205-0554-2(8))* Cengage Gale.

Broyles, Janell. Chemical Biological Incident Response Force. 2008. (Inside Special Operations Ser.). (Illus.). 54p. (J). lib. bdg. 31.95 *(978-1-4042-1751-5(7))* Rosen Publishing Group, Inc., The.

Carlisle, Rodney P. Afghanistan War. 2010. (America at War Ser.). 958p. (gr. 6-12). 45.00 *(978-0-8160-8119-6(0)*, Chelsea Hse.) Facts On File, Inc.

Chandler, Matt. Dangerous Times: History's Most Troubled Eras. 2013. (Dangerous History Ser.). (ENG.). 32p. (gr. 3-4). 27.99 *(978-1-4765-0126-0(2)*, Edge Bks.) Capstone Press of Coughlan Cos.

Connolly, Sean. War. 2003. (In Time of Need Ser.). (Illus.). 32p. (YA). (gr. 5-9). lib. bdg. 27.10 *(978-1-58340-391-4(4))* Black Rabbit Bks.

DiConsiglio, John. Reporting Live. 2011. (J). *(978-0-531-22552-3(6))* Scholastic, Inc.

Doyle, Bill H. Behind Enemy Lines: Under Fire in the Middle East. 2011. 136p. (J). pap. *(978-0-545-33463-1(2))* Scholastic, Inc.

Early American Wars, 4 vols., Set. Incl. American Revolutionary War. Marston, Daniel & O'Neill, Robert John. lib. bdg. 33.25 *(978-1-4488-1331-5(X))*; Texas War of Independence. Huffines, Alan C. lib. bdg. 33.25 *(978-1-4488-1332-2(8))*; War of 1812: The Fight for American Trade Rights. Benn, Carl. lib. bdg. 33.25 *(978-1-4488-1333-9(6))*; (YA). (gr. 9-18). 2011. (Early American Wars Ser.). (Illus.). 96p. 2011. Set lib. bdg. 127.80 *(978-1-4488-1387-2(5))* Rosen Publishing Group, Inc., The.

Engdahl, Sylvia. War. 2010. (Issues on Trial Ser.). (ENG.). 240p. (gr. 10-12). 48.30 *(978-0-7377-4949-6(0)*, Greenhaven Pr., Inc.) Cengage Gale.

Gray, Leon. Dirty Bombs & Shell Shock: Biology Goes to War. 2017. (STEM on the Battlefield Ser.). (ENG., Illus.). 48p. (J). (gr. 4-6). 31.99 ***(978-1-5124-3928-1(2))*** Lerner Publishing Group.

Green, John. Horses in Battle. 2011. (Dover History Coloring Book Ser.). (ENG., Illus.). 32p. (gr. 3-8). pap. 3.99 *(978-0-486-47608-7(1))* Dover Pubns., Inc.

Haugen, David. War. Greenhaven Press Editors, ed. 2013. (Opposing Viewpoints Ser.). (ENG.). 224p. (gr. 10-12). pap. 33.80 *(978-0-7377-6972-2(6))*; lib. bdg. 48.80 *(978-0-7377-6971-5(8))* Cengage Gale. (Greenhaven Pr., Inc.).

Haulley, Fletcher. Critical Perspectives on 9/11. 2005. (Critical Anthologies of Nonfiction Writing Ser.). 176p. (J). (gr. 7-12). lib. bdg. 37.95 *(978-1-4042-0060-9(6))* Rosen Publishing Group, Inc., The.

History's Greatest Rivals. 2015. (History's Greatest Rivals Ser.). (ENG.). 48p. (J). (gr. 6-8). 191.70 *(978-1-4824-2229-0(8))* Stevens, Gareth Publishing LLLP.

Hoffman, Mary. Lines in the Sand: New Writing on War & Peace. Lassiter, Rhiannon, ed. 2003. (ENG., Illus.). 288p. (J). (gr. 2-18). pap. 8.95 *(978-0-9729529-1-0(8))* Disinformation Co. Ltd., The.

Homer. Classic Starts - The Iliad. Freeberg, Eric, illus. 2014. (Classic Starts(tm) Ser.). (ENG.). 160p. (J). (gr. 2-4). 6.95 *(978-1-4549-0612-4(X))* Sterling Publishing Co., Inc.

Hunt, Jilly. Fight Against War & Terrorism. 2017. (Beyond the Headlines! Ser.). (ENG.). 48p. (gr. 4-6). lib. bdg. 33.32 ***(978-1-4846-4142-2(6)***, Heinemann InfoSearch) Heinemann-Raintree.

Keating, Susan. Native American Rivalries. Johnson, Troy, ed. 2013. (Native American Life Ser.: 15). 64p. (J). (gr. 5-18). 19.95 *(978-1-4222-2975-0(0))* Mason Crest.

Kenney, Karen Latchana. The Spoils of War. 2007. (Shockwave: History & Politics Ser.). (ENG., Illus.). 36p. (J). (gr. 4-6). 25.00 *(978-0-531-17757-0(2)*, Children's Pr.) Scholastic Library Publishing.

Kyi, Tanya Lloyd. Extreme Battlefields: When War Meets the Forces of Nature. Shannon, Drew, illus. 2016. (ENG.). 160p. (J). (gr. 4-8). pap. 14.95 *(978-1-55451-793-0(1))* Annick Pr., Ltd. CAN. Dist: Publishers Group West (PGW).

Lobel, Anita. No Pretty Pictures: A Child of War. 2008. (J). (gr. 5-8). lib. bdg. 18.40 *(978-0-613-28590-2(5)*, Turtleback) Turtleback Bks.

Mapua, Jeff. Weaponizing Poop. 2017. (J). pap. ***(978-0-7660-9093-4(0))*** Enslow Pubs., Inc.

Marsh, Carole. War What Kids Should Know. 2003. 32p. (gr. 2-8). pap. 7.95 *(978-0-635-01715-4(6))* Gallopade International.

Nardo, Don. Invisible Weapons: The Science of Biological & Chemical Warfare, 1 vol. 2010. (Headline Science Ser.). (ENG.). 48p. (gr. 7-8). lib. bdg. 29.32 *(978-0-7565-4217-7(0)*, Headline Science) Compass Point Bks.

Nelson, Sheila & Zoldak, Joyce. In Defense of Our Country: Survivors of Military Conflict. 2009. (J). pap. 24.95 *(978-1-4222-1465-7(6))* Mason Crest.

Nelson, Sheila, et al. In Defense of Our Country: Survivors of Military Conflict. 2010. (Survivors Ser.). 128p. (YA). (gr. 7-12). 24.95 *(978-1-4222-0452-8(9))* Mason Crest.

Parker, Steve. A Brief Illustrated History of Warfare. 2017. (J). pap. *(978-1-4747-2708-2(5))* Capstone Press of Coughlan Cos.

Phillips, Larissa. Cochise: Jefe Apache. de la Vega, Eida, tr. from ENG. 2004. (Grandes Personajes en la Historia de Los Estados Unidos Ser.). (ENG & SPA., Illus.). 32p. (gr. 3-6). pap. 10.00 *(978-0-8239-4223-7(6))* Rosen Publishing Group, Inc., The.

Rivera, Sheila. Rebuilding Iraq. 2004. (War in Iraq Ser.). (Illus.). 48p. (gr. 4-8). 27.07 *(978-1-59197-498-7(4)*, Abdo & Daughters) ABDO Publishing Co.

Road to War: Causes of Conflict, 5 vols., Set. Incl. Causes of the American Revolution. Strum, Richard M. 64p. (J). lib. bdg. 22.95 *(978-1-59556-001-8(7))*; Causes of the Civil War. Epperson, James F. 64p. (J). lib. bdg. 22.95 *(978-1-59556-002-5(5))*; Causes of the Iraq War. Gallagher, Jim. 72p. (J). lib. bdg. 22.95 *(978-1-59556-009-4(2))*; Causes of World War I. Ziff, John. 72p. (J). lib. bdg. 22.95 *(978-1-59556-003-2(3))*; Causes of World War II. Corrigan, Jim. 64p. lib. bdg. 22.95 *(978-1-59556-004-9(1))*; (gr. 4-18). 2005. (Road to War Ser.). (Illus.). 64p. 2005. Set lib. bdg. 114.75 *(978-1-59556-000-1(9))* OTTN Publishing.

Rosenberg, Aaron. The Yom Kippur War. 2004. (War & Conflict in the Middle East Ser.). (Illus.). 64p. (gr. 7-12). lib. bdg. 31.95 *(978-0-8239-4553-5(7))* Rosen Publishing Group, Inc., The.

The Science of War: Strategies, Tactics, & Logistics. 2011. (Britannica Guide to War Ser.). (ENG.). 192p. (YA). (gr. 10-12). 70.50 *(978-1-61530-794-4(X))* Rosen Publishing Group, Inc., The.

Sodaro, Craig. The Dangerous, Disastrous, Unusual History of War, 1 vol. 2012. (Unusual Histories Ser.). (ENG., Illus.). 48p. (gr. 3-4). lib. bdg. 31.99 *(978-1-4296-7536-9(5))* Capstone Press of Coughlan Cos.

Solesbee, Mary Ann. Sal & Amanda Take Morgan's Victory March to the Battle of Cowpens. Waters, Tony, illus. 2014. Orig. Title: Sal & Amanda Take Morgan's Victory March to the Battle of Cowpens. (ENG.). 128p. pap. 12.99 *(978-1-62619-279-9(0)*, History Pr., The) Arcadia Publishing.

Spilsbury, Richard. Geronimo, 1 vol. Faure, Florence, illus. 2013. (Hero Journals). (ENG.). 48p. (gr. 4-6). pap. 9.95 *(978-1-4109-5367-4(X)*, NA-r) Heinemann-Raintree.

—Geronimo, 1 vol. 2013. (Hero Journals). (ENG., Illus.). 48p. (gr. 4-6). 33.32 *(978-1-4109-5360-5(2)*, NA-r) Heinemann-Raintree.

Summers, Elizabeth. Tools of War. 2015. (Tools of War Ser.). (ENG.). 32p. (gr. 1-2). 106.60 *(978-1-4914-6657-5(X)*, Blazers) Capstone Press of Coughlan Cos.

Turner, Tracy. Conquerors. 2015. (Head-To-Head Ser.). (ENG., Illus.). 24p. (gr. 3-8). 28.50 *(978-1-62588-152-6(5))* Black Rabbit Bks.

Urrutia, Maria Cristina, et al. Cinco de Mayo. 2nd ed. 2008. (ENG., Illus.). 32p. (J). (gr. 4). pap. 7.95 *(978-0-88899-877-4(5))* Groundwood Bks. CAN. Dist: Publishers Group West (PGW).

Verrept, Paul. El Pequeno Soldado. Bourgeois, Elodie, tr. Verrept, Paul, illus. 2004. (SPA., Illus.). 26p. (J). (gr. -1-3). 17.99 *(978-84-261-3306-9(1))* Juventud, Editorial ESP. Dist: Lectorum Pubns., Inc.

Voices of War. 2014. (Voices of War Ser.). 48p. (J). (gr. 4-6). 250.88 *(978-1-62713-126-1(4))* Cavendish Square Publishing.

Walker, Niki & Owlkids Books Inc. Staff. Why Do We Fight? Conflict, War, & Peace. 2013. (ENG., Illus.). 80p. (J). (gr. 6-9). 16.95 *(978-1-926973-86-9(0)*, Owlkids) Owlkids Bks. Inc. CAN. Dist: Publishers Group West (PGW).

Walter, Virginia A. War & Peace: A Guide to Literature & New Media, Grades 4-8, 1 vol. 2006. (Children's & Young Adult Literature Reference Ser.). 288p. (C). pap. 45.00 *(978-1-59158-271-7(7)*, LU2717, Libraries Unlimited) ABC-CLIO, LLC.

War on Land. 2011. (Britannica Guide to War Ser.). (ENG.). 160p. (YA). (gr. 10-12). 70.50 *(978-1-61530-799-9(0))* Rosen Publishing Group, Inc., The.

Watkins, Christine. Biological Warfare. 2010. (Opposing Viewpoints Ser.). (Illus.). 240p. (J). 42.95 *(978-0-7377-4757-7(9))*; pap. 29.45 *(978-0-7377-4758-4(7))* Cengage Gale. (Greenhaven Pr., Inc.).

Wheeler, Sherrie Leigh. Defending Americ: A Children's Guide to Understanding the Circumstances & Sacrifices of War. 2012. 32p. pap. 24.95 *(978-1-4626-9758-8(5))* America Star Bks.

Why War Happened. 2016. (Why War Happened Ser.). 48p. (gr. 8-6). pap. 84.30 *(978-1-4824-5329-4(0))*; lib. bdg. 191.70 *(978-1-4824-5119-1(0))* Stevens, Gareth Publishing LLLP.

Willett, Edward. The Iran-Iraq War. 2004. (War & Conflict in the Middle East Ser.). (Illus.). 64p. (gr. 7-12). lib. bdg. 31.95 *(978-0-8239-4547-4(2))* Rosen Publishing Group, Inc., The.

World Book, Inc. Staff, contrib. by. Wooden Spears to Military Drones: A Timeline of Warfare. 2016. (J). *(978-0-7166-3544-4(5))* World Bk.-Childcraft International.

Zullo, Allan. The Secret Agent & Other Spy Kids. 2006. 147p. (J). pap. *(978-0-439-84835-0(0))* Scholastic, Inc.

24/7 Goes to War: On the Battlefield, 4 vols., Set. Incl. Pearl Harbor: The U. S. Enters World War II. Dougherty, Steve. lib. bdg. 29.00 *(978-0-531-25525-4(5))*; Vietnam: The Bloodbath at Hamburger Hill. DiConsiglio, John. lib. bdg. 29.00 *(978-0-531-25526-1(3))*; 64p. (J). (gr. 6-12)., Children's Pr. 2009. Set lib. bdg. 116.00 *(978-0-531-20550-1(9)*, Watts, Franklin) Scholastic Library Publishing.

WAR—FICTION

Alcorn, Anita C. Caught in the Crossfire: A Boy's View of the Battle of Mill Springs, KY. 2006. 48p. pap. 8.95 *(978-0-7414-3581-1(0))* Infinity Publishing.

Almond, David, et al. The Great War: Stories Inspired by Items from the First World War. Kay, Jim, illus. 2015. (ENG.). 304p. (J). (gr. 5). 19.99 *(978-0-7636-7554-7(7))* Candlewick Pr.

Altsheler, Joseph A. The Forest Runners: A Story of the Great War Trail in Early Kentucky. 2006. (Young Trailers Ser.: Vol. 2). (J). reprint ed. pap. *(978-1-4065-0810-9(1))* Dodo Pr.

Appleton, Victor. Tom Swift & his War Tank. 2005. 27.95 *(978-1-4218-1505-3(2)*, 1st World Library - Literary Society) 1st World Publishing, Inc.

Armstrong, Jennifer. Shattered: Stories of Children & War. 2003. (ENG.). 176p. (YA). (gr. 7). mass mkt. 6.99 *(978-0-440-23765-5(3)*, Laurel Leaf) Random Hse. Children's Bks.

Atwater-Rhodes, Amelia. The Shapeshifters: The Kiesha'ra of the Den of Shadows. 2010. (ENG.). 976p. (YA). (gr. 7). pap. 14.99 *(978-0-385-73950-4(8)*, Delacorte Pr.) Random Hse. Children's Bks.

Avery, Pat McGrath. Tommy's War: A Parent Goes to War, 1. Ray, Eric, illus. 2003. 36p. (J). per. 5.95 *(978-0-9663276-8-7(3))* Red Engine Pr.

Bacigalupi, Paolo. The Drowned Cities. 2013. (ENG.). 464p. (J). (gr. 10-17). pap. 10.99 *(978-0-316-05622-9(7))* 2012. 448p. (YA). 17.99 *(978-0-316-20037-0(9))* Little, Brown Bks. for Young Readers.

—The Drowned Cities. 2012. 352p. *(978-1-59606-506-2(0))* Subterranean Pr.

—The Drowned Cities. 2013. (J). lib. bdg. 22.10 *(978-0-606-31749-8(X)*, Turtleback) Turtleback Bks.

Backer, Charles. Fireclaw. 2010. 288p. pap. 15.49 *(978-1-4520-1229-2(6))* AuthorHouse.

Barchers, Suzanne. The Wounded Lion: A Tale from Spain. 2013. pap. 26.60 *(978-1-936163-89-2(6))* Red Chair Pr.

Bates, Gordon. The Khaki Boys over the Top: Doing & Daring for Uncle Sam. 2006. (ENG.). 140p. pap. 18.99 *(978-1-4264-6542-0(4))* Creative Media Partners, LLC.

Bauer, Deidre. Silver Mountain. 2008. 38p. pap. 8.00 *(978-0-8059-7672-4(8))* Dorrance Publishing Co., Inc.

Beacham, Travis, et al. Tales from Year Zero. 2013. (Pacific Rim Ser.). (ENG., Illus.). 128p. (gr. 8-17). 24.99 (978-0-7851-5394-8(2)) Legendary Comics.

Beckwith, Kathy & Lyon, Lea. Playing War, 1 vol. 2005. (ENG., Illus.). 32p. (gr. 2-6). 16.95 (978-0-88448-267-3(7), 884267) Tilbury Hse. Pubs.

Beddor, Frank. ArchEnemy: The Looking Glass Wars, Book Three, 3 vols. 2010. (Looking Glass Wars Ser.: 3). (ENG.). 384p. (YA). (gr. 7-18). 9.99 (978-0-14-241689-1(4), Speak) Penguin Young Readers Group.

—Seeing Redd. (Looking Glass Wars Ser.: 2). (ENG.). (YA). (gr. 7-18). 2008. 400p. 9.99 (978-0-14-241209-1(0), Speak) 2007. (Illus.). 384p. 17.99 (978-0-8037-3155-4(8), Dial Bks) Penguin Young Readers Group.

Beecroft, Simon. Death Star Battles, Level 3. 2010. (DK Readers Ser.). (ENG.). 48p. (J). (gr. 2-4). 3.99 (978-0-7566-6314-8(8), DK Children) Dorling Kindersley Publishing, Inc.

Belanger, Jeff. Ghosts of War: Restless Spirits of Soldiers, Spies, & Saboteurs. 2009. (Haunted: Ghosts & the Paranormal Ser.). 235p. (YA). (gr. 7-12). lib. bdg. 37.95 (978-1-4358-5177-1(3)) Rosen Publishing Group, Inc., The.

Bell, Hilari. The Goblin War. 2011. (ENG.). 304p. (J). (gr. 8). 17.99 (978-0-06-165105-2(2), HarperTeen) HarperCollins Pubs.

Benary-Isbert, Margot. Rowan Farm. 2008. (J). (gr. 5-12). 25.00 (978-0-8446-6475-0(8)) Smith, Peter Pub., Inc.

Bennett, Holly. The Bonemender, 1 vol. 2005. (Bonemender Ser.: 1). (ENG., Illus.). 208p. (YA). (gr. 8-12). per. 9.95 (978-1-55143-336-3(2)) Orca Bk. Pubs. USA.

Berry, Julie. All the Truth That's in Me. 2013. (ENG.). 288p. (YA). (gr. 7). 17.99 (978-0-670-78615-2(2), Viking Books for Young Readers) Penguin Young Readers Group.

—All the Truth That's in Me. 2014. lib. bdg. 20.85 (978-0-606-36191-0(X)) Turtleback Bks.

Birmajer, Marcelo. Una Vida Más: Noticias Extranas IV. 2004. (SPA.). 111p. (J). pap. 9.95 (978-958-04-7081-6(2)) Norma S.A. COL. Dist: Lectorum Pubns., Inc.

Black, Judith. Home Front. (YA). 12.00 (978-0-9701073-7-4(4)) Black, Judith Storyteller.

Blake, Kendare. Mortal Gods. 2014. (Goddess War Ser.: 2). (ENG.). 352p. (YA). (gr. 7-12). 17.99 (978-0-7653-3444-2(5), 9780765334442, Tor Teen) Doherty, Tom Assocs., LLC.

Bobet, Leah. An Inheritance of Ashes. 2015. (ENG.). 400p. (YA). (gr. 7). 17.99 (978-0-544-28111-0(X)) Houghton Mifflin Harcourt Publishing Co.

Bollen, Christine. Flying with the Geese, 1 vol. Matyuschenko, Tanya, illus. 2010. 34p. 24.95 (978-1-4489-4401-9(5)) PublishAmerica, Inc.

Bondoux, Anne-Laure. A Time of Miracles. Maudet, Y., tr. from FRE. 2012. (ENG., Illus.). 192p. (YA). (gr. 7). pap. 7.99 (978-0-375-86036-2(3), Ember) Random Hse. Children's Bks.

Bowen, Carl & Fuentes, Benny. Elite Infantry. Tortosa, Wilson, illus. 2013. (Shadow Squadron Ser.). (ENG.). 224p. pap. 8.95 (978-1-62370-032-4(9)) Capstone Young Readers of Coughlan Cos.

Bowler, Bill. Troy. 2nd ed. 2013. (ENG., Illus.). 40p. pap. 9.38 **(978-0-19-424970-6(0))** Oxford Univ. Pr., Inc.

Bowman, Patrick. Arrow Through the Axes. 2014. (ENG.). 200p. pap. 11.95 (978-1-55380-323-2(X)) Ronsdale Pr. CAN. Dist: SPD-Small Pr. Distribution.

Bowman, Patrick & Homer. Cursed by the Sea God. 2013. (ENG.). 200p. pap. 11.95 (978-1-55380-186-3(5)) Ronsdale Pr. CAN. Dist: SPD-Small Pr. Distribution.

Bradman, Tony & Bradman, Tom. My Brother's Keeper. 2014. (National Archives Ser.). (ENG., Illus.). 112p. (YA). (gr. 7). pap. 10.99 (978-1-4081-9679-3(4), 9781408196793, Bloomsbury USA Childrens) Bloomsbury Publishing USA.

Brennan, Herbie. The Faeman Quest. (Faerie Wars Chronicles Ser.). (ENG.). 368p. (YA). (gr. 7). 2012. pap. 9.99 (978-1-59990-833-5(6), 9781599908335) 2011. 18.99 (978-1-59990-476-4(4), 9781599904764) Bloomsbury Publishing USA. (Bloomsbury USA Childrens).

—Ruler of the Realm. (Faerie Wars Chronicles Ser.). (ENG.). (YA). (gr. 7). 2007. 448p. pap. 9.99 (978-1-59990-149-7(8), 9781599901497) 2006. (Illus.). 432p. 18.95 (978-1-58234-881-0(2), 9781582348810) Bloomsbury Publishing USA. (Bloomsbury USA Childrens).

Brereton, F. S. With Joffre at Verdun: A Story of the Western Front. Webb, Arch, illus. 2012. 240p. (978-1-78139-196-9(3)) Benediction Classics.

Brown, Skila. Caminar. 2014. (ENG.). 208p. (J). (gr. 5). 15.99 (978-0-7636-6516-6(9)) Candlewick Pr.

Brudlos, Christopher. Alpha Shade Chapter One. Brudlos, Joseph, illus. 2005. (YA). per. 24.95 net. (978-0-9768705-0-0(9)) Alpha Shade, Inc.

Buckley, Michael. The Council of Mirrors. 2013. (Sisters Grimm Ser.: 9). (J). lib. bdg. 18.40 (978-0-606-31650-7(7), Turtleback) Turtleback Bks.

—The Everafter War. Ferguson, Peter, illus. (Sisters Grimm Ser.: Bk. 7). (ENG.). (J). (gr. 3-7). 2010. 336p. pap. 8.95 (978-0-8109-8429-5(6))Bk. 7. 2009. 320p. 16.95 (978-0-8109-8355-7(9)) Abrams, Inc. (Amulet Bks.).

—The Everafter War. 2010. (Sisters Grimm Ser.: 7). (J). lib. bdg. 19.60 (978-0-606-12500-0(0), Turtleback) Turtleback Bks.

Bullock, Robert. Sam Marsh & the Battle of the Cloudships: The Sam Marsh Stories - Part 2. 2012. 224p. pap. 13.97 (978-1-61897-348-1(7), Strategic Bk. Publishing) Strategic Book Publishing & Rights Agency (SBPRA).

Bunting, Eve. Gleam & Glow. Sylvada, Peter, illus. 2005. (ENG.). 32p. (J). (gr. -1-3). reprint ed. pap. 7.99 (978-0-15-205380-2(8)) Houghton Mifflin Harcourt Publishing Co.

Caballero, Erica. Mount Mole. 2006. pap. 10.00 (978-1-4257-2301-9(2)) Xlibris Corp.

Calabrese, Diane Marie. My Dad's off to War. Swope, Brenda, illus. 2011. 28p. pap. 24.95 (978-1-4560-0942-7(7)) America Star Bks.

Cali, Davide. The Enemy. Bloch, Serge, illus. 2013. Orig. Title: L'Ennemi. (ENG.). 64p. (J). (gr. 4-7). 24.99 (978-0-9585571-8-4(7)) Wilkins Farago Pty, Ltd. AUS. Dist: Independent Pubs. Group.

Camus, William. Azules Contra Grises. (Barco de Vapor). (SPA.). 200p. (YA). (gr. 5-8). 7.95 (978-84-348-1455-4(2)) SM Ediciones ESP. Dist: AIMS International Bks., Inc.

Cantwell, Michael. The Rising of the Fifth Sun. 2012. 120p. (gr. 4-6). 20.95 (978-1-4620-7203-3(8)); pap. 10.95 (978-1-4620-7201-9(1)) iUniverse, Inc.

Castner, K. D. Daughters of Ruin. 2017. (ENG.). 320p. (YA). (gr. 9). pap. 11.99 (978-1-4814-3666-3(X), McElderry, Margaret K. Bks.) McElderry, Margaret K. Bks.

Chacko, Miss Hannah. The Lie. 2009. 372p. pap. 25.50 (978-0-557-06829-6(0)) Lulu Pr., Inc.

Chapman, Kelly. A Warrior Prince for God. Ebbeler, Jeff, illus. 2010. (ENG.). 32p. (J). (gr. -1-4). 14.99 (978-0-7369-2895-3(2)) Harvest Hse. Pubs.

—A Warrior Prince for God Curriculum Leader's Guide. Ebbeler, Jeff, illus. 2009. pap. 12.99 (978-0-7369-2899-1(5)) Harvest Hse. Pubs.

Chickasaw Adventures: War with the Creeks. 2005. (J). (978-1-4265-0001-5(7)) Layne Morgan Media, Inc.

Chima, Cinda Williams. Shadowcaster. (Shattered Realms Ser.: 2). (YA). (gr. 8). 2018. (ENG.). 576p. pap. 9.99 **(978-0-06-238098-2(2))** 2017. 560p. 18.99 (978-0-06-238097-5(4)) HarperCollins Pubs. (HarperTeen).

Coakley, Lena. Witchlanders. (ENG., Illus.). 416p. (YA). (gr. 7). 2012. pap. 9.99 (978-1-4424-2005-2(7)) 2011. 16.99 (978-1-4424-2004-5(9)) Simon & Schuster Children's Publishing. (Atheneum Bks. for Young Readers).

Cole, Barbara. Anna & Natalie, 1 vol. Himler, Ronald, illus. 2007. (ENG.). 32p. (J). 16.95 (978-1-59572-105-1(3)) Star Bright Bks., Inc.

Colfer, Chris. A Grimm Warning. 2014. (Land of Stories Ser.: Bk. 3). (ENG.). (J). (gr. 3-7). 480p. 19.99 (978-0-316-40681-9(3)); 768p. 32.99 (978-0-316-40964-3(2)) Little, Brown Bks. for Young Readers.

Collingwood, Harry. Across the Spanish Main. 2011. 204p. 26.95 (978-1-4638-9643-0(3)) Rodgers, Alan Bks.

Collins, Suzanne. Gregor & the Code of Claw. 2008. (Underland Chronicles Ser.: 5). (ENG., Illus.). 416p. (J). (gr. 3-7). pap. 7.99 (978-0-439-79144-1(8), Scholastic Paperbacks) Scholastic, Inc.

—Gregor & the Marks of Secret. 2007. (Underland Chronicles Ser.: 4). (ENG., Illus.). 352p. (J). (gr. 3-7). 7.99 (978-0-439-79146-5(4), Scholastic Paperbacks) Scholastic, Inc.

—Gregor & the Marks of Secret. 2007. (Underland Chronicles Ser.: 4). 343p. (gr. 4-7). lib. bdg. 18.40 (978-1-4177-8358-8(3), Turtleback) Turtleback Bks.

Cook, Kajsa. Discoveries in the Shriver Family Attic: How a Woman & Her Children Dealt with the Battle of Gettysburg. 2009. (Illus.). 122p. (J). (gr. 4-8). pap. 8.95 (978-1-57249-398-8(4), White Mane Kids) White Mane Publishing Co., Inc.

Cooney, Caroline B. Goddess of Yesterday. 2009. (ENG.). 272p. (YA). (gr. 7). pap. 8.99 (978-0-385-73865-1(X), Ember) Random Hse. Children's Bks.

Cooper, Michelle. The FitzOsbornes at War. 2013. (Montmaray Journals). (ENG.). 560p. (YA). (gr. 7). pap. 10.99 (978-0-307-93058-3(0), Ember) Random Hse. Children's Bks.

—The FitzOsbornes in Exile. 2012. (Montmaray Journals). (ENG.). 464p. (YA). (gr. 7). pap. 10.99 (978-0-375-85155-1(0), Ember) Random Hse. Children's Bks.

Costa, T. L. Playing Tyler. 2013. (ENG.). 304p. (J). (gr. 9). pap. 9.99 (978-1-908844-61-3(2), Strange Chemistry) Watkins Media Limited GBR. Dist: Penguin Random Hse. LLC.

Cox, Greg. Riese: Kingdom Falling. 2013. (ENG., Illus.). 288p. (YA). (gr. 7). pap. 9.99 (978-1-4424-2970-3(4), Simon & Schuster Bks. For Young Readers) Simon & Schuster Bks. For Young Readers.

D'Adamo, Francesco. My Brother Johnny. 2008. (ENG.). 200p. pap. 16.95 (978-0-9551566-3-2(7)) Aurora Metro Pubns. Ltd. GBR. Dist: Consortium Bk. Sales & Distribution.

Damon, Matt. The Fall of General Custard, or the Overthrow of a Leftover. Kendall, Gideon, illus. 2016. (HumanKIND Project Ser.). (ENG.). 32p. (J). (gr. k-6). 17.95 (978-1-940468-33-4(7)) White Cloud Pr.

Davidson, Halsey. Navy Boys Behind the Big Guns: Or Sinking the German U-Boats. 2007. 144p. pap. 18.99 (978-1-4346-1338-7(0)); (ENG.). 160p. pap. 21.99 (978-1-4346-1390-5(9)) Creative Media Partners, LLC.

—Navy Boys Behind the Big Guns or Sinking the German U-Boats. 2007. 108p. per. (978-1-4068-1847-5(X)) Echo Library.

De la Cruz, Melissa & Johnston, Michael. Stolen Bk. 2: Heart of Dread. 2014. (Heart of Dread Ser.: 2). (ENG.). 304p. (YA). (gr. 7). 17.99 (978-0-399-25755-1(1), G.P. Putnam's Sons Books for Young Readers) Penguin Young Readers Group.

Defoe, Daniel & Perry, John Jasiel. Atalantis Major. 2011. 54p. 15.95 (978-1-4638-9670-6(0)) Rodgers, Alan Bks.

Deforges, Regine. La Bicyclette Bleue, Level C. (FRE.). (YA). (gr. 7-12). 9.95 (978-0-88436-990-5(0), 40304) EMC/Paradigm Publishing.

DiMarco, Carol & Bowman, Sharon. The Tale of Two Kingdoms. 2009. (ENG.). 88p. (J). pap. 10.99 (978-1-59092-170-8(4)) Blue Forge Pr.

DiTerlizzi, Tony. The Battle for WondLa. DiTerlizzi, Tony, illus. 2014. (Search for WondLa Ser.: 3). (ENG., Illus.). 496p. (J). (gr. 5). 17.99 (978-1-4169-8314-9(7), Simon & Schuster Bks. For Young Readers) Simon & Schuster Bks. For Young Readers.

Dixon, Chuck. Airboy, Vol. 1. Truman, Timothy et al, illus. 2014. (Airboy Ser.: 1). (ENG.). 308p. pap. 29.99 (978-1-61377-900-2(3), 9781613779002) Idea & Design Works, LLC.

Dorling Kindersley Publishing Staff & Dowsett, Elizabeth. Attack of the Clones, Level 2. 2013. (DK Readers Ser.). (ENG., Illus.). 32p. (J). (gr. 1-3). pap. 3.99 (978-0-7566-8695-6(4), DK Children) Dorling Kindersley Publishing, Inc.

Driscoll, James R. The Brighton Boys with the Flying Corps. 2005. 152p. pap. 11.95 (978-1-59540-820-4(7), 1st World Library - Literary Society) 1st World Publishing, Inc.

—The Brighton Boys with the Flying Corps. 2006. (ENG.). 128p. pap. 18.99 (978-1-4264-6537-6(8)); 138p. pap. 19.99 (978-1-4264-6596-3(3)) Creative Media Partners, LLC.

Dumas, Alexandre. The Count of Monte Cristo. 2008. (Bring the Classics to Life Ser.). (ENG., Illus.). 72p. (gr. 5-12). pap., act. bk. ed. 10.95 (978-1-55576-359-6(6), EDCTR-509B) EDCON Publishing Group.

Ellis, Deborah. Parvana's Journey, 1 vol. 2015. (Breadwinner Ser.). (ENG., Illus.). 200p. (J). (gr. 4-9). pap. 9.95 (978-1-55498-770-2(9)) Groundwood Bks. CAN. Dist: Publishers Group West (PGW).

Entwistle, Charles. The Promise. 2004. 114p. (YA). per. 9.95 (978-0-9709104-2-4(8)) Hickory Tales Publishing.

Esseltine, Christopher R. Caleb's Quest. 2008. (J). pap. 13.99 (978-1-59955-104-3(7)) Cedar Fort, Inc./CFI Distribution.

Falkner, Brian. The Assault (Recon Team Angel #1) 2013. (Recon Team Angel Ser.: 1). (ENG.). 304p. (YA). (gr. 7). pap. 9.99 (978-0-375-87190-0(X), Ember) Random Hse. Children's Bks.

—Battlesaurus: Rampage at Waterloo. 2016. (Battlesaurus Ser.: 2). (ENG.). 352p. (YA). 17.99 (978-0-374-30077-7(1), 9780374300777, Farrar, Straus & Giroux (BYR)) Farrar, Straus & Giroux.

—Task Force. 2013. (Recon Team Angel Ser.). (ENG., Illus.). 288p. (YA). (gr. 7). 17.99 (978-0-449-81299-0(5), Random Hse. Bks. for Young Readers) Random Hse. Children's Bks.

—Task Force (Recon Team Angel #2) 2014. (Recon Team Angel Ser.). (ENG.). 416p. (YA). (gr. 7). pap. 9.99 (978-0-449-81302-7(9), Ember) Random Hse. Children's Bks.

Fan, Nancy Y. Sword Quest. Rioux, Jo-Anne, illus. 2008. (Swordbird Ser.). 176p. (J). (gr. 3-7). 15.99 (978-0-06-124335-6(3)) HarperCollins Pubs.

Fan, Nancy Yi. Sword Quest. Rioux, Jo-Anne, illus. 2008. (Swordbird Ser.). 288p. (J). (gr. 3-7). lib. bdg. 16.89 (978-0-06-124336-3(1)) HarperCollins Pubs.

—Swordbird. 2008. (J). 54.99 (978-1-60514-800-7(8)) Findaway World, LLC.

Fine, Sarah. The Cursed Queen. 2017. (Impostor Queen Ser.: 2). (ENG., Illus.). 432p. (YA). (gr. 7). 17.99 (978-1-4814-4193-3(0), McElderry, Margaret K. Bks.) McElderry, Margaret K. Bks.

—Of Dreams & Rust. 2016. (ENG.). 304p. (YA). (gr. 9). pap. 11.99 (978-1-4424-8362-0(8), McElderry, Margaret K. Bks.) McElderry, Margaret K. Bks.

Flanagan, John. The Battle for Skandia. (Ranger's Apprentice Ser.: 4). (ENG.). (J). (gr. 5-18). 2008. 304p. 18.99 (978-0-399-24457-5(3), Philomel Bks.)Bk. 4. 2009. 336p. 8.99 (978-0-14-241340-1(2), Puffin Books) Penguin Young Readers Group.

—The Battle for Skandia. 2009. (Ranger's Apprentice Ser.: 4). lib. bdg. 19.65 (978-0-606-02208-8(2), Turtleback) Turtleback Bks.

—The Battle of Hackham Heath. 2016. (Ranger's Apprentice: the Early Years Ser.: 2). (ENG., Illus.). 352p. (J). (gr. 5). 18.99 (978-0-399-16362-3(X), Philomel Bks.) Penguin Young Readers Group.

—The Burning Bridge, Bk. 2. 2007. (Ranger's Apprentice Ser.: 2). (ENG.). 304p. (J). (gr. 5-18). 8.99 (978-0-14-240842-1(5), Puffin Books) Penguin Young Readers Group.

—The Burning Bridge. 2007. (Ranger's Apprentice Ser.: 2). 262p. lib. bdg. 19.65 (978-1-4177-9330-3(9), Turtleback) Turtleback Bks.

—Erak's Ransom, Bk. 7. (Ranger's Apprentice Ser.: 7). (ENG.). (J). (gr. 5-18). 2011. 416p. 8.99 (978-0-14-241525-2(1), Puffin Books) 2010. 384p. 18.99 (978-0-399-25205-1(3), Philomel Bks.) Penguin Young Readers Group.

—The Kings of Clonmel, Bk. 8. 2011. (Ranger's Apprentice Ser.: 8). (ENG.). 400p. (J). (gr. 5-18). 8.99 (978-0-14-241857-4(9), Puffin Books) Penguin Young Readers Group.

—The Lost Stories. (Ranger's Apprentice Ser.: 11). (ENG.). (J). (gr. 5). 2013. 464p. pap. 8.99 (978-0-14-242195-6(2), Puffin Books) 2011. (Illus.). 432p. 18.99 (978-0-399-25618-9(0), Philomel Bks.) Penguin Young Readers Group.

—The Lost Stories. 2013. (Ranger's Apprentice Ser.: 11). lib. bdg. 19.65 (978-0-606-31700-9(7), Turtleback) Turtleback Bks.

—The Siege of Macindaw, Bk. 6. (Ranger's Apprentice Ser.: 6). (ENG.). (J). (gr. 5-18). 2010. 336p. 8.99 (978-0-14-241524-5(3), Puffin Books) 2009. 304p. 18.99 (978-0-399-25033-0(6), Philomel Bks.) Penguin Young Readers Group.

Fontes, Justine & Fontes, Ron. The Trojan Horse: The Fall of Troy [a Greek Myth]. Purcell, Gordon, illus. 2015. (Graphic Myths & Legends Ser.). (ENG.). 48p. (gr. 4-8). 21.32 (978-1-4677-5985-4(6), Lerner Digital) Lerner Publishing Group.

Fontes, Ron, et al. The Trojan Horse: The Fall of Troy. Purcell, Gordon, illus. 2006. (Graphic Myths & Legends Ser.). (ENG.). 48p. (gr. 4-8). 27.93 (978-0-8225-3085-5(6)) Lerner Publishing Group.

Foreman, Michael. El Jardin del Nino: Una Historia de Esperanza. Diego, Rapi & Flores, Martha, illus. 2009. (SPA.). 30p. (J). (gr. 1-3). 14.99 (978-1-933032-56-6(1)) Lectorum Pubns., Inc.

Freedman, Claire. Dinosaurs Love Underpants. Cort, Ben, illus. 2009. (Underpants Bks.). (ENG.). 32p. (J). (gr. -1-2). 16.99 (978-1-4169-8938-7(2), Aladdin) Simon & Schuster Children's Publishing.

Frost, Helen. Crossing Stones. 2009. (ENG., Illus.). 192p. (YA). (gr. 7-18). 18.99 (978-0-374-31653-2(8), 9780374316532, Farrar, Straus & Giroux (BYR)) Farrar, Straus & Giroux.

Fulton-Vengco, Aletha. Felicidad & Her Pen Pal Kamar. 2009. 33p. 13.90 (978-0-578-02728-9(3)) Vengco, Aletha Fulton.

Fussell, Sandy. Owl Ninja. James, Rhian Nest, illus. 2011. (Samurai Kids Ser.: 2). (ENG.). 272p. (J). (gr. 4-7). 15.99 (978-0-7636-5003-2(X)) Candlewick Pr.

Gentry, Nancy. Little Blue, Little Gray. Keaggy, Sarah, illus. 2012. 56p. pap. 10.00 (978-0-9846244-9-2(X)) O'More Publishing.

Geras, Adèle. Ithaka. 2007. (ENG., Illus.). 368p. (YA). (gr. 9-12). pap. 8.99 (978-0-15-206104-3(5)) Houghton Mifflin Harcourt Publishing Co.

—Troy. 2004. 368p. (J). (gr. 8-18). pap. 48.00 incl. audio (978-0-8072-2288-1(7), Listening Library) Random Hse. Audio Publishing Group.

Gilroy, Henry. The Clone Wars: In Service of the Republic Vol. 2: A Frozen Doom!, 1 vol. Hepburn, Scott, illus. 2011. (Star Wars: the Clone Wars Ser.: No. 2). (ENG.). 24p. (J). (gr. 7-12). 24.21 (978-1-59961-839-5(7)) Spotlight.

—The Clone Wars: In Service of the Republic Vol. 3: Blood & Snow, 1 vol. Hepburn, Scott, illus. 2011. (Star Wars: the Clone Wars Ser.: No. 2). (ENG.). 24p. (J). (gr. 7-12). 24.21 (978-1-59961-840-1(0)) Spotlight.

Glessner, Gordon. Water Wars, Secrets Revealed. 2012. 24p. 12.00 (978-0-9859603-0-8(2)) Laughing Rhino Bks.

Goldsmith, Connie. Dogs at War: Military Canine Heroes. 2017. (Nonfiction — Young Adult Ser.). (ENG.). 104p. (YA). (gr. 8-12). 19.99 **(978-1-5124-3905-2(3))**; 53.32 **(978-1-5124-2852-0(3))**; 53.32 **(978-1-5124-3906-9(1))** Lerner Publishing Group. (Twenty-First Century Bks.).

Gonzalez Jensen, Margarita. Botas Negras. Sanchez, Enrique O., illus. (SPA.). (J). (gr. 2-4). 3.96 net. (978-0-590-26842-4(2)) Scholastic, Inc.

Goodman, Alison. The Last Dragoneye. 2012. (ENG.). 672p. (YA). (gr. 7-18). 11.99 (978-0-14-242093-5(X), Firebird) Penguin Young Readers Group.

—The Last Dragoneye. 2012. (Eon Ser.: 2). lib. bdg. 23.30 (978-0-606-23648-5(1), Turtleback) Turtleback Bks.

Grant, Michael. Front Lines. (Front Lines Ser.: 1). (YA). (gr. 9). 2017. 592p. pap. 9.99 (978-0-06-234216-4(9)) 2016. 576p. 18.99 (978-0-06-234215-7(0)) HarperCollins Pubs. (Tegen, Katherine Bks).

Green, Roger Lancelyn. The Tale of Troy. Baynes, Pauline, illus. 2012. (Puffin Classics Ser.). (ENG.). 224p. (J). (gr. 5). pap. 5.99 (978-0-14-134196-5(3), Puffin Books) Penguin Young Readers Group.

Guest, Jacqueline. Belle of Batoche, 1 vol. 2004. (Orca Young Readers Ser.). (ENG., Illus.). 144p. (J). (gr. 3-6). pap. 7.95 (978-1-55143-297-7(8)) Orca Bk. Pubs. USA.

Haar, Jaap Ter & Mearns, Martha. Boris. Poortvliet, Rien, illus. 2009. (J). pap. (978-0-921100-72-0(8)) Inheritance Pubns.

Haddix, Margaret Peterson. The Always War. (ENG.). (YA). (gr. 7). 2012. 224p. pap. 8.99 (978-1-4169-9527-2(7)) 2011. 208p. 16.99 (978-1-4169-9526-5(9)) Simon & Schuster Bks. For Young Readers. (Simon & Schuster Bks. For Young Readers).

—Game Changer. 2012. (ENG.). 256p. (YA). (gr. 7). 16.99 (978-0-689-87380-5(8), Simon & Schuster Bks. For Young Readers) Simon & Schuster Bks. For Young Readers.

Haibara, Yak & Haibara, Yak. Sengoku Basara: Samurai Legends Volume 2: Samurai Legends Volume 2, 2 vols. 2013. (ENG., Illus.). 424p. (YA). pap. 19.99 (978-1-926778-59-4(6), 9781926778594) URON Entertainment Corp. CAN. Dist: Diamond Comic Distributors, Inc.

Halsey, Jacqueline. Peggy's Letters, 1 vol. 2005. (Orca Young Readers Ser.). (ENG., Illus.). 132p. (J). (gr. 3-6). per. 5.95 (978-1-55143-363-9(X)) Orca Bk. Pubs. USA.

Hamley, Dennis. Very Far from Here. 2007. 208p. per. (978-1-904529-33-0(X), Back to Front) Solidus.

—Without Warning: Ellen's Story, 1914-1918. 2007. (ENG., Illus.). 336p. (YA). (gr. 7). 17.99 (978-0-7636-3338-7(0)) Candlewick Pr.

Han, Yu-Mei, illus. The Brave Servant: A Tale from China. 2013. (Tales of Honor Ser.). (ENG.). 32p. (J). (gr. 1-4). pap. 8.95 (978-1-937529-57-4(6)); lib. bdg. 26.60 (978-1-937529-73-4(8)) Red Chair Pr.

Hancock, H. Irving. Uncle Sam's Boys with Pershing's Troops, or Dick Prescott at Grips with the Boche. l.t. ed. 2007. (ENG.). 174p. pap. 21.99 (978-1-4264-9718-6(0)) Creative Media Partners, LLC.

Hand, Elizabeth. A New Threat. 2004. (Star Wars Ser.: Vol. 5). 139p. (J). lib. bdg. 20.00 (978-1-4242-0781-7(9)) Fitzgerald Bks.

Hardy, Janice. A Blue Fire, Bk. 2. 2010. (Healing Wars Ser.: II). (ENG.). 384p. (J). (gr. 5-18). 16.99 (978-0-06-174741-0(6)) HarperCollins Pubs.

—The Healing Wars: Book II: Blue Fire. 2011. (Healing Wars Ser.: II). (ENG.). 400p. (J). (gr. 5). pap. 7.99 (978-0-06-174744-1(0)) HarperCollins Pubs.

—The Shifter. (J). (gr. 5). 2010. (Healing Wars Ser.: I). (ENG.). 400p. pap. 7.99 (978-0-06-174708-3(4)) 2009. (Healing Wars Ser.). 384p. lib. bdg. 17.89 (978-0-06-176177-5(X)) HarperCollins Pubs.

Harrell, Deborah A. Pintos Hope. 2003. 124p. (YA). pap. 10.95 (978-0-595-26514-5(6), Writers Club Pr.) iUniverse, Inc.

Harris, Christine. The Silver Path. (Illus.). (J). (ENG & VIE.). 26p. (978-1-85430-327-1(9), 93381); (CHI & ENG., 32p. (978-1-85430-323-3(6), 93425) Little Tiger Pr. Group.

Hartman, Rachel. Shadow Scale. 2015. (ENG., Illus.). 608p. (J). (gr. 7). 18.99 (978-0-375-86657-9(4), Random Hse. Bks. for Young Readers) Random Hse. Children's Bks.

Hayes, Clair W. The Boy Allies at Verdun or Saving France from the Enemy. 2007. 124p. (gr. -1-7). per. (978-1-4068-1712-6(0)) Echo Library.

—The Boy Allies in the Balkan Campaign or the Struggle to Save a Nation. 2007. 128p. per. (978-1-4068-1714-0(7)) Echo Library.

Haze, Armand. Beautiful Blossom. 2012. 322p. 29.95 (978-1-4626-7056-7(3)) America Star Bks.

Heibel, Dorothy. Message for a Spy. 2004. (Illus.). 94p. (J). pap. (978-1-932663-07-5(X)) History Compass, LLC.

Henty, A. G. With Frederick the Great. 2007. 324p. 98.99 (978-1-4280-7565-8(8)); per. 92.99 (978-1-4280-7566-5(6)) IndyPublish.com.

Henty, George Alfred. By Sheer Pluck: A Tale of the Ashanti War. 2007. (ENG.). 246p. pap. 20.99 (978-1-4264-3065-7(5)) 2006. 272p. pap. 23.99 (978-1-4264-3130-2(9)) Creative Media Partners, LLC.

—For Name & Fame: Or Through Afghan Passes. 2007. (ENG.). 240p. per. 20.99 (978-1-4346-4487-9(1)); 264p. per. 23.99 (978-1-4346-4488-6(X)) Creative Media Partners, LLC.

—No Surrender! A Tale of the Rising in la Vendee. l.t. ed. 2007. 330p. pap. 24.99 (978-1-4346-3575-4(9)) Creative Media Partners, LLC.

—Through Three Campaigns: A Story of Chitral Tirah & Ashanti. 2007. (ENG.). 318p. pap. 23.99 (978-1-4346-4617-0(3)); 356p. pap. 26.99 (978-1-4346-4618-7(1)) Creative Media Partners, LLC.

—True to the Old Flag. 2007. 286p. pap. 21.99 (978-1-4264-4288-9(2)); (ENG.). 318p. pap. 24.99 (978-1-4264-4352-7(8)) Creative Media Partners, LLC.

—True to the Old Flag: A Tale of the American War of Independence. 2004. reprint ed. pap. 1.99

(978-1-4192-9123-4(8)); pap. 27.95 (978-1-4191-9123-7(3)) Kessinger Publishing, LLC.
—With Buller in Natal: Or a Born Leader. 2007. (ENG.). 290p. pap. 21.99 (978-1-4264-9358-4(4)); 324p. pap. 24.99 (978-1-4264-9739-1(3)) Creative Media Partners, LLC.
Hidalgo, Pablo. The Phantom Menace. 2012. (Star Wars Ser.). (ENG.). 64p. (J). (gr. -1-3). 9.99 (978-0-545-38986-0(0)) Scholastic, Inc.
Hinwood, Christine. The Returning. 2013. (ENG.). 320p. (YA). (gr. 9). pap. 8.99 (978-0-14-242477-3(3), Speak) Penguin Young Readers Group.
Holmes, Oliver Wendell, Sr. Grandmother's Story of Bunker Hill Battle. 2009. 45p. pap. 14.80 (978-0-557-05927-0(5)) Lulu Pr., Inc.
Holmes, Sara. Operation Yes. 2009. 234p. (J). pap. (978-0-545-20418-7(6)) Scholastic, Inc.
Homer. The Iliad. Tsilis, Thanos, illus. 2013. (Greek Classics Ser.). (ENG.). 64p. pap. 6.95 (978-1-906230-53-1(6)) Real Reads Ltd. GBR. Dist: Casemate Pubs. & Bk. Distributors, LLC.
Hubble, Miles & Bryant, Justin. Bob & the Fowl War: Book One in the Poultry Series. 2008. 140p. pap. 11.95 (978-1-4401-0857-0(9)) iUniverse, Inc.
Hunter, Erin. Fading Echoes. Richardson, Owen & Douglas, Allen, illus. 2010. (Warriors: Omen of the Stars Ser.: 2). (ENG.). 352p. (J). (gr. 3-7). 16.99 (978-0-06-155512-1(6)) HarperCollins Pubs.
Hunter, John P. Red Thunder: Secrets, Spies, & Scoundrels at Yorktown. 2006. 234p. (YA). (gr. 6-8). 7.95 (978-0-87935-231-8(0)) Colonial Williamsburg Foundation.
Ikeda, Daisaku. The Cherry Tree. McCaughrean, Geraldine, tr. from JPN. Wildsmith, Brian, illus. 2013. 6.95 (978-1-935523-57-4(0)) World Tribune Pr.
Jacques, Brian. The Long Patrol: A Tale from Redwall. Curless, Allan, illus. 2004. (Redwall Ser.). (ENG.). 368p. (J). (gr. 5-3). 8.99 (978-0-14-240245-0(1), Firebird) Penguin Young Readers Group.
Jinks, Catherine. Babylonne. 2008. (ENG., Illus.). 400p. (YA). (gr. 7). 18.99 (978-0-7636-3650-0(9)) Candlewick Pr.
Jones, Carrie. Endure. 2012. (Need Ser.). (ENG.). 272p. (YA). 17.99 (978-1-59990-554-9(X), 9781599905549, Bloomsbury USA Childrens) Bloomsbury Publishing USA.
Jones, Frewin. Destiny's Path. 2009. (Warrior Princess Ser.: 2). (ENG.). 352p. (YA). (gr. 8-18). 16.99 (978-0-06-087146-8(6), HarperTeen) HarperCollins Pubs.
—The Emerald Flame. 2010. (Warrior Princess Ser.: 3). (ENG.). 352p. (YA). (gr. 8-18). 16.99 (978-0-06-087149-9(0), HarperTeen) HarperCollins Pubs.
—Warrior Princess. 2009. (YA). 346p. lib. bdg. 17.89 (978-0-06-087144-4(X)); (ENG.). 352p. (gr. 7-18). 16.99 (978-0-06-087143-7(1)) HarperCollins Pubs. (Eos).
—Warrior Princess #2: Destiny's Path. 2010. (Warrior Princess Ser.: 2). (ENG.). 352p. (YA). (gr. 8). pap. 8.99 (978-0-06-087148-2(2), HarperTeen) HarperCollins Pubs.
Kade, J. V. The Meta-Rise. 2nd ed. 2014. (Bot Wars Ser.). (ENG., Illus.). 304p. (J). (gr. 5). 17.99 (978-0-8037-3861-4(7), Dial Bks) Penguin Young Readers Group.
Keun, Irmgard. Child of All Nations. Hofmann, Michael, tr. from GER. 2008. (ENG.). 208p. (gr. 4-13). 23.95 (978-1-59020-099-5(3), 902099) Overlook Pr., The.
Khanduri, K. Tales of the trojan War. 2005. (Illus.). 144p. (J). pap. 4.95 (978-0-7945-0323-9(3), Usborne) EDC Publishing.
Kincaid, S. J. Catalyst. 2014. (Insignia Ser.: 3). (ENG.). 432p. (YA). (gr. 8). 17.99 (978-0-06-209305-9(3), Tegen, Katherine Bks) HarperCollins Pubs.
—Insignia. (Insignia Ser.: 1). (ENG.). (YA). (gr. 8). 2013. 480p. pap. 9.99 (978-0-06-209300-4(2)) 2012. 464p. 17.99 (978-0-06-209299-1(5)) HarperCollins Pubs. (Tegen, Katherine Bks).
—Vortex. 2013. (Insignia Ser.: 2). (ENG.). 400p. (YA). (gr. 8). 17.99 (978-0-06-209302-8(9), Tegen, Katherine Bks) HarperCollins Pubs.
Krokos, Dan. The Black Stars. 2015. (ENG., Illus.). 304p. (J). (gr. 3-8). pap. 21.99 (978-0-7653-7668-8(7), 9780765376688, Starscape) Doherty, Tom Assocs., LLC.
—False Future. 2014. (False Memory Novel Ser.). (ENG., Illus.). 320p. (YA). (gr. 9-17). 17.99 (978-1-4231-4987-3(4)) Hyperion Bks. for Children.
—The Planet Thieves. (ENG., Illus.). 256p. (J). (gr. 3-7). 2014. pap. 9.99 (978-0-7653-7538-4(9), 9780765375384) 2013. 15.99 (978-0-7653-3428-2(3), 9780765334282) Doherty, Tom Assocs., LLC. (Starscape).
LaFleur, Suzanne. Beautiful Blue World. (ENG., Illus.). (J). (gr. 3-7). 2017. 240p. pap. 6.99 (978-0-307-98032-8(4), Yearling) 2016. 224p. lib. bdg. 19.99 (978-0-375-99089-2(5), Lamb, Wendy Bks.) Random Hse. Children's Bks.
LaFleur, Suzanne. Threads of Blue. 2017. (ENG.). 224p. (J). (gr. 3-7). 16.99 **(978-1-101-93999-4(0))**; lib. bdg. 19.99 **(978-1-101-94000-6(X))** Random Hse. Children's Bks. (Lamb, Wendy Bks.).
LaFleur, Suzanne M. Threads of Blue. 2017. (J). pap. **(978-1-101-94002-0(6)**, Delacorte Pr) Random House Publishing Group.
Lalonde, Carolyn. Hide Tommy Turkey. Lalonde, Johnathan, illus. 2005. 20p. (J). 9.60 (978-1-4120-4893-4(1)) Trafford Publishing.
Landers, Ace. The Padawan Menace. 2012. (Lego Star Wars Ser.). (ENG.). 32p. (J). (gr. 2-5). pap. 3.99 (978-0-545-40450-1(9), Scholastic Paperbacks) Scholastic, Inc.
Lasky, Kathryn. The Shattering. 2004. (Guardians of Ga'hoole Ser.: 5). (ENG., Illus.). 192p. (J). (gr. 3-7). 6.99 (978-0-439-40561-4(0), Scholastic Paperbacks) Scholastic, Inc.
—The Siege. 2004. (Guardians of Ga'hoole Ser.: 4). (ENG., Illus.). 224p. (J). (gr. 3-7). mass mkt. 6.99 (978-0-439-40560-7(2), Scholastic Paperbacks) Scholastic, Inc.
—To Be a King. 2006. (Guardians of Ga'hoole Ser.: 11). (ENG.). 224p. (J). (gr. 3-7). 6.99 (978-0-439-79570-8(2), Scholastic Paperbacks) Scholastic, Inc.
Lawlor, Laurie. Wind on the River. 2004. 156p. (J). lib. bdg. 16.92 (978-1-4242-0771-8(1)) Fitzgerald Bks.
Leicht, Martin & Neal, Isla. Mothership. (Ever-Expanding Universe Ser.: 1). (ENG., Illus.). (YA). (gr. 9). 2013. 336p. pap. 9.99 (978-1-4424-2961-1(5)) 2012. 320p. 16.99 (978-1-4424-2960-4(7)) Simon & Schuster Bks. For Young Readers. (Simon & Schuster Bks. For Young Readers).
—A Stranger Thing. 2013. (Ever-Expanding Universe Ser.: 2). (ENG., Illus.). 288p. (YA). (gr. 9). 17.99 (978-1-4424-2963-5(1), Simon & Schuster Bks. For Young Readers) Simon & Schuster Bks. For Young Readers.
Lesler, Rebecca. The Truth of the Magic Stone, 1 vol. 2009. 107p. pap. 19.95 (978-1-60836-422-0(4)) America Star Bks.
Lindsay, Fitzroy A. My Daddy Came Home Long after the War. 2012. 28p. pap. 19.99 (978-1-4685-6010-7(7)) AuthorHouse.
Littell, William Adams. Guillaume. 2008. 74p. pap. 10.00 (978-0-8059-7757-8(0)) Dorrance Publishing Co., Inc.
Lobel, Anita. Potatoes, Potatoes. 2004. 40p. (J). 15.99 (978-0-06-023927-5(1)); lib. bdg. 16.89 (978-0-06-023928-2(X)) HarperCollins Pubs.
Lon Rogers. The Between Season. 2009. 280p. pap. 17.95 (978-1-4401-8368-3(6)) iUniverse, Inc.
London, C. Alexander. Prisoners of War. 2014. (Dog Tags Ser.: 3). (ENG.). 192p. (J). (gr. 5-9). pap. 5.99 (978-0-545-47706-2(9), Scholastic Paperbacks) Scholastic, Inc.
Lu, Marie. Legend. aut. ltd. collector's ed. 2013. (Legend Trilogy: Bk. 1). (Illus.). 306p. (YA). mass mkt. 100.00 net. (978-1-934267-38-7(4)) Gauntlet, Inc.
—Legend. 2011. (Legend Trilogy: Bk. 1). (ENG.). (YA). (gr. 8-12). 54.99 (978-1-61657-044-6(X), Penguin AudioBooks) Penguin Publishing Group.
—Legend. Kaaris, illus. 2015. (Legend Ser.). (ENG.). 160p. (YA). (gr. 7). pap. 14.99 (978-0-399-17189-5(4), G.P. Putnam's Sons Books for Young Readers) Penguin Young Readers Group.
—Legend. (Legend Ser.: 1). (ENG.). (YA). (gr. 7). 2013. 352p. pap. 9.99 (978-0-14-242207-6(X), Speak) 2011. 320p. 17.99 (978-0-399-25675-2(X), G.P. Putnam's Sons Books for Young Readers) Penguin Young Readers Group.
—Legend. l.t. ed. 2012. (Legend Trilogy: Bk. 1). (ENG.). 394p. (J). (gr. 7-12). 23.99 (978-1-4104-4606-0(9)) Thorndike Pr.
—Legend. (Legend Graphic Novels Ser.: 1). 2015. lib. bdg. 26.95 (978-0-606-38424-7(3)) 2013. lib. bdg. 20.85 (978-0-606-31701-6(5), Turtleback) Turtleback Bks.
—Prodigy. 2013. (Legend Trilogy: Bk. 2). (ENG.). 384p. (YA). (gr. 7). 18.99 (978-0-399-25676-9(8), G.P. Putnam's Sons Books for Young Readers) Penguin Publishing Group.
—Prodigy. 2014. (Legend Ser.: 2). (ENG., Illus.). 416p. (YA). (gr. 7). pap. 10.99 (978-0-14-242755-2(1), Speak) Penguin Young Readers Group.
—Prodigy. l.t. ed. 2013. (Legend Trilogy: Bk. 2). (ENG.). 486p. 23.99 (978-1-4104-5512-3(2)) Thorndike Pr.
—Prodigy. 2014. (Legend Ser.: 2). lib. bdg. 20.85 (978-0-606-35716-6(5)) Turtleback Bks.
—Prodigy: The Graphic Novel. 2016. (Legend Trilogy: Bk. 2). (ENG.). 160p. (YA). (gr. 7). pap. 14.99 (978-0-399-17190-1(8), G.P. Putnam's Sons Books for Young Readers) Penguin Young Readers Group.
Lundquist, Jenny. The Princess in the Opal Mask. 2013. (ENG.). 352p. (YA). (gr. 2-17). pap. 9.95 (978-0-7624-5109-8(2), Running Pr. Kids) Running Pr. Bk. Pubs.
Lynch, Chris. Casualties of War. 2013. (Vietnam Ser.: 4). (ENG.). 192p. (J). (gr. 5-9). pap. 7.99 (978-0-545-27024-3(3), Scholastic Pr.) Scholastic, Inc.
—Free-Fire Zone. 2012. (Vietnam Ser.). (J). (ENG.). 192p. (gr. 5-9). 16.99 (978-0-545-27025-0(1)); 183p. (978-0-545-49427-4(3)) Scholastic, Inc. (Scholastic Pr.).
—Free-Fire Zone. 2013. (Vietnam Ser.: 3). lib. bdg. 18.40 (978-0-606-31963-8(8), Turtleback) Turtleback Bks.
—I Pledge Allegiance. 2011. 183p. (YA). (978-0-545-38415-5(X)) Scholastic, Inc.
—I Pledge Allegiance. 2013. (Vietnam Ser.: 1). lib. bdg. 17.20 (978-0-606-31961-4(1), Turtleback) Turtleback Bks.
—The Liberators. 2015. (World War II Ser.: 4). (ENG.). 192p. (J). (gr. 5-9). 18.99 (978-0-545-52304-2(4), Scholastic Pr.) Scholastic, Inc.
—The Right Fight. 2014. 189p. (YA). (978-0-545-63728-2(7), Scholastic Pr.) Scholastic, Inc.
—Sharpshooter. (J). 2013. (Vietnam Ser.: 2). (ENG.). 192p. (gr. 5-9). pap. 7.99 (978-0-545-27027-4(8)) 2012. (978-0-545-43650-2(8)) Scholastic, Inc. (Scholastic Pr.).
—Sharpshooter. 2013. (Vietnam Ser.: 2). lib. bdg. 18.40 (978-0-606-31962-1(X), Turtleback) Turtleback Bks.
—Walking Wounded, Bk. 5. 2016. (Vietnam Ser.: 5). (ENG.). 208p. (J). (gr. 5-9). pap. 7.99 (978-0-545-64016-9(4), Scholastic Pr.) Scholastic, Inc.
MacHale, D. J. Storm. 2014. (SYLO Chronicles Ser.: 2). (ENG.). (J). (gr. 3-7). 512p. pap. 9.99 (978-1-59514-668-7(7)); 2nd ed. 496p. 17.99 (978-1-59514-667-0(9)) Penguin Young Readers Group. (Razorbill).
Maddox, Joseph & Maddox, Diana. See You in Hell. 2004. 215p. (YA). pap. 14.95 (978-0-7414-1872-2(X)) Infinity Publishing.
Mann, J. Albert. Scar: A Revolutionary War Tale. 2016. (ENG.). 144p. (J). (gr. 3-7). 16.95 (978-1-62979-465-5(1), Calkins Creek) Boyds Mills Pr.
Manning, Matthew K. Go Slow. Lima, Dijjo & Furuzono, Carlos, illus. 2016. (EOD Soldiers Ser.). (ENG.). 40p. (gr. 4-8). lib. bdg. 26.65 (978-1-4965-3109-4(4)) Stone Arch Bks.
—The List. Lima, Rico et al, illus. 2016. (EOD Soldiers Ser.). (ENG.). 40p. (gr. 4-8). lib. bdg. 26.65 (978-1-4965-3110-0(8)) Stone Arch Bks.
—The Mist. Lima, Rico & Bello, Thiago Dal, illus. 2016. (EOD Soldiers Ser.). (ENG.). 40p. (gr. 4-8). lib. bdg. 26.65 (978-1-4965-3108-7(6)) Stone Arch Bks.
—Two Sides. Lima, Dijjo & Furuzono, Carlos, illus. 2016. (EOD Soldiers Ser.). (ENG.). 40p. (gr. 4-8). lib. bdg. 26.65 (978-1-4965-3107-0(8)) Stone Arch Bks.
—U. S. Special Forces: Ghosts of the Night. Enecio, Jeremy, illus. 2016. (U. S. Special Ops Ser.). (ENG.). 96p. (gr. 3-4). lib. bdg. 26.65 (978-1-4965-3475-0(1), Connect) Stone Arch Bks.
—U.S. Special Forces: Ghosts of the Night. Enecio, Jeremy, illus. 2016. (U. S. Special Ops Ser.). (ENG.). 96p. (gr. 3-4). E-Book 26.65 (978-1-4965-3477-4(8), Connect) Stone Arch Bks.
Marsden, Carolyn. The White Zone. 2014. (ENG.). 192p. (J). (gr. 4-8). pap. 9.95 (978-1-4677-5177-3(4), Carolrhoda Bks.) Lerner Publishing Group.
Marsden, John. Tomorrow, When the War Began. 2006. (Tomorrow Ser.: 1). (ENG.). 288p. (J). (gr. 7-12). 9.99 (978-0-439-82910-6(0), Scholastic Paperbacks) Scholastic, Inc.
Mason, Prue. Camel Rider. 2007. (ENG.). 208p. (J). (gr. 5-7). 15.95 (978-1-58089-314-5(7)) Charlesbridge Publishing, Inc.
—Camel Rider. 2011. 9.49 (978-0-7848-3618-7(3), Everbind) Marco Bk. Co.
Massey, David. Torn. 2013. (ENG.). 288p. (J). (gr. 9). 17.99 (978-0-545-49645-2(4)) Scholastic, Inc.
Matson, Erik. Robobattlepets - Home Invasion. 2012. 144p. pap. 7.99 (978-0-9841187-6-2(4)) Asteroid Publishing.
Matthews, L. S. Fish. 2006. 183p. (gr. 5-9). 16.50 (978-0-7569-6626-3(4)) Perfection Learning Corp.
Maxwell, Ruth H. Eighteen Roses Red: A Young Girl's Heroic Mission in the Revolutionary War. 2006. (American Revolution Adventures Ser.). 126p. (J). (gr. 3-7). per. 8.95 (978-1-57249-380-3(1), White Mane Kids) White Mane Publishing Co., Inc.
McCormick, Patricia. Purple Heart. 2009. (ENG.). 208p. (YA). (gr. 8-18). 16.99 (978-0-06-173090-0(4)) HarperCollins Pubs.
McCune, Joshua. Talker 25. 2014. (Talker 25 Ser.: 1). (ENG.). 432p. (YA). (gr. 9). 17.99 (978-0-06-212191-2(X), Greenwillow Bks.) HarperCollins Pubs.
—Talker 25 #2: Invisible Monsters. 2016. (Talker 25 Ser.: 2). 448p. (YA). (gr. 8). pap. 9.99 (978-0-06-212195-0(2), Greenwillow Bks.) HarperCollins Pubs.
McCutcheon, John. Flowers for Sarajevo, 1 vol. Caldwell, Kristy, illus. 2017. (ENG.). 32p. (J). (gr. 2-4). 19.95 (978-1-56145-943-8(7)) Peachtree Pubs.
McDonald, Megan. Judy Moody Predicts the Future. 2010. (Judy Moody Ser.: 4). lib. bdg. 16.00 (978-0-606-12341-9(5), Turtleback) Turtleback Bks.
McElroy, Lisa Tucker. Love, Lizzie: Letters to a Military Mom. Paterson, Diane, illus. (ENG.). 32p. (J). (gr. 1-3). 2009. pap. 6.99 (978-0-8075-4778-6(6)) 2005. lib. bdg. 16.99 (978-0-8075-4777-9(8)) Whitman, Albert & Co.
McKay, Sharon E. Enemy Territory. 2012. (ENG., Illus.). 200p. (YA). (gr. 6-10). 21.95 (978-1-55451-431-1(2), 9781554514311); pap. 12.95 (978-1-55451-430-4(4), 9781554514304) Annick Pr., Ltd. CAN. Dist: Publishers Group West (PGW).
McKee, David. Six Men. 2011. (ENG., Illus.). 44p. (J). (gr. -1-3). 16.95 (978-0-7358-4050-8(4)) North-South Bks., Inc.
McKinty, Adrian. The Lighthouse War. 2007. (ENG.). 414p. (J). (gr. 7-17). 16.95 (978-0-8109-9354-9(6)) Abrams, Inc.
McMullan, Kate. Hit the Road, Helen! 2013. (Myth-O-Mania Ser.: Bk. 9). (ENG.). 240p. (gr. 4-8). 10.95 (978-1-4342-6219-6(7)); lib. bdg. 25.32 (978-1-4342-4990-6(5)) Stone Arch Bks.
McPhail, David. No! McPhail, David, illus. 2009. (ENG., Illus.). 48p. (J). (gr. -1-3). 16.95 (978-1-59643-288-8(8), 9781596432888) Roaring Brook Pr.
Mead, Alice. Year of No Rain. 2005. (Illus.). 129p. (gr. 4-7). 15.50 (978-0-7569-5158-0(5)) Perfection Learning Corp.
Menchen, Antonio Martinez. Fosco. (SPA.). 104p. (YA). (gr. 5-8). (978-84-204-4101-6(5), AF1750) Ediciones Alfaguara ESP. Dist: Lectorum Pubns., Inc.
Merrill, Jean. The Pushcart War. Solbert, Ronni, illus. 50th anniv. ed. 2014. (ENG.). 232p. (J). (gr. 3-7). 15.95 (978-1-59017-819-5(X), NYR Children's Collection) New York Review of Bks., Inc., The.
—The Pushcart War. 2006. (J). 1.25 (978-1-4193-8348-9(5)) Recorded Bks., Inc.
Meyer, Carolyn. Beauty's Daughter: The Story of Hermione & Helen of Troy. 2013. (ENG., Illus.). 352p. (YA). (gr. 7). 16.99 (978-0-544-10862-2(0)) Houghton Mifflin Harcourt Publishing Co.
Mikaelsen, Ben. Tree Girl. 2004. 240p. (J). lib. bdg. 17.89 (978-0-06-009005-0(7), Rayo) HarperCollins Pubs.
Millard, Glenda. A Small Free Kiss in the Dark. 2010. (ENG.). 192p. (YA). (gr. 7-18). pap. 16.95 (978-0-8234-2264-7(X)) Holiday Hse., Inc.
Monsters of Men. 2014. (Chaos Walking Ser.). (ENG., Illus.). (YA). (gr. 9). pap. 10.99 (978-0-7636-7619-3(5)) Candlewick Pr.
Moran, Katy. Bloodline. 2009. (ENG., Illus.). 320p. (YA). (gr. 7). 16.99 (978-0-7636-4083-5(2)) Candlewick Pr.
Morpurgo, Michael. Shadow. 2012. (ENG.). 192p. (J). (gr. 5-9). 16.99 (978-0-312-60659-6(1), 9780312606596) Feiwel & Friends.
Moskowitz, Hannah. A History of Glitter & Blood. 2015. (ENG., Illus.). 280p. (YA). (gr. 9-17). 18.99 (978-1-4521-2942-6(8)) Chronicle Bks. LLC.
Moverley, Richard. The Reluctant Rajput. Dean, David, illus. 2005. (Yellow Go Bananas Ser.). (ENG.). 48p. (J). (gr. 3-4). lib. bdg. (978-0-7787-2723-1(8)) Crabtree Publishing Co.
Muller, Seth. Keepers of the WindClaw Chronicles: The Day of Storms, 3 vols., Vol. 2. Dubay, Tayloe, ed. Whitethorne, Bahe, Jr., illus. 2nd ed. 2010. 224p. (J). pap. 12.95 (978-1-893354-10-4(5)) Salina Bookshelf Inc.
—Keepers of the WindClaw Chronicles: The Mockingbird's Manual. Tayloe, McConnell Dubay, ed. Whitethorne, Bahe, Jr., illus. 2009. (ENG.). 128p. (J). (gr. 4-7). pap. 12.95 (978-1-893354-04-3(0)) Salina Bookshelf Inc.
Myers, Walter Dean. Fallen Angels. 2008. (ENG.). 336p. (J). (gr. 7). pap. 9.99 (978-0-545-05576-5(8), Scholastic Paperbacks) Scholastic, Inc.
—Invasion. 2015. (ENG.). 224p. (J). (gr. 6). pap. 8.99 (978-0-545-38429-2(X)) 2013. (YA). (978-0-545-57659-8(8)) 2013. (ENG.). 224p. (J). (gr. 7). 17.99 (978-0-545-38428-5(1)) Scholastic, Inc. (Scholastic Pr.).
—Patrol: An American Soldier in Vietnam. Grifalconi, Ann, illus. 2005. (ENG.). 40p. (J). (gr. 3-7). pap. 6.99 (978-0-06-073159-5(1)) HarperCollins Pubs.
—Sunrise over Fallujah. 2011. 9.04 (978-0-7848-3413-8(X), Everbind) Marco Bk. Co.
—Sunrise over Fallujah. 2009. (ENG.). 320p. (J). (gr. 7). 8.99 (978-0-439-91625-7(9), Scholastic Pr.) Scholastic, Inc.
—Sunrise over Fallujah. l.t. ed. 2008. 468p. (YA). 23.95 (978-1-4104-1019-1(6)) Thorndike Pr.
Ness, Patrick. Monsters of Men, Bk. 3. 2010. (Chaos Walking Ser.: 3). (ENG., Illus.). 608p. (YA). (gr. 9-18). 18.99 (978-0-7636-4751-3(9)) Candlewick Pr.
Nilsson, Troy, 2nd. Hiroshima Stones: The Shadow Stones of Hiroshima. Nilsson, Troy, 2nd, illus. 2003. (Illus.). 248p. (YA). pap. 9.95 (978-0-9724771-0-9(1), Nilsson, Troy) Nilsson Media.
Optic, Oliver, pseud. Fighting for the Right. 2007. 136p. per. (978-1-4068-3635-6(4)) Echo Library.
—Stand by the Union. 2007. 140p. (gr. 4-7). per. (978-1-4068-4345-3(8)) Echo Library.
—A Victorious Union: The Blue & the Gray-Afloat Book 6. 2007. (ENG.). 208p. pap. 20.99 (978-1-4264-9402-4(5)); 234p. pap. 22.99 (978-1-4264-9783-4(0)) Creative Media Partners, LLC.
—Within the Enemy's Lines. 2007. 132p. (gr. 4-7). per. (978-1-4068-4348-4(2)) Echo Library.
—Within the Enemy's Lines: SERIES: the Blue & the Gray — Afloat. 2007. (ENG.). 196p. per. 19.99 (978-1-4346-2937-1(6)) Creative Media Partners, LLC.
Orzechowski, Shawneen. Sarah's Secret: Civil War Deserter at Fredericksburg. 2011. 104p. (J). pap. 8.95 (978-1-57249-400-8(X), White Mane Kids) White Mane Publishing Co., Inc.
Osborne, Mary Pope. World at War 1944. Murdocca, Sal, illus. 2017. (Magic Tree House (R) Super Edition Ser.: 1). (ENG.). 208p. (J). (gr. 2-5). 6.99 (978-0-553-50885-7(7), Random Hse. Bks. for Young Readers) Random Hse. Children's Bks.
Pacat, C. S. Kings Rising. 2016. (Captive Prince Trilogy Ser.: 3). (ENG., Illus.). 368p. pap. 16.00 (978-0-425-27399-9(7), Berkley) Penguin Publishing Group.
Palmer, W. G. Awaiting Whisperland: The Calling of Galahad Green. 2007. 340p. 29.95 (978-0-595-68248-5(0)); per. 19.95 (978-0-595-43560-9(2)) iUniverse, Inc.
Parker, Robert. Edenville Owls. 2008. 194p. (gr. 4-6). 18.00 (978-0-7569-8920-0(5)) Perfection Learning Corp.
Parry, Rosanne. Heart of a Shepherd. 2010. (ENG.). 176p. (J). (gr. 3-7). pap. 7.99 (978-0-375-84803-2(7), Yearling) Random Hse. Children's Bks.
Patton, Jack. The Butterfly Rebellion. 2016. (Battle Bugs Ser.: 9). (ENG.). 128p. (J). (gr. 2-5). pap. 4.99 (978-0-545-94515-8(1), Scholastic Paperbacks) Scholastic, Inc.
—The Dragonfly Defense. 2016. (Battle Bugs Ser.: 7). (ENG.). 128p. (J). (gr. 2-5). pap. 4.99 (978-0-545-94509-7(7), Scholastic Paperbacks) Scholastic, Inc.
—The Poison Frog Assault (Battle Bugs #3) 2015. (Battle Bugs Ser.: 3). (ENG.). 128p. (J). (gr. 2-5). pap. 4.99 (978-0-545-70744-2(7), Scholastic Paperbacks) Scholastic, Inc.
Penning, L. & Nelson, Marietjie. The Hero of Spionkop. 2006. (Illus.). 166p. (YA). pap. (978-1-894666-92-3(5)) Inheritance Pubns.
—The Lion of Modderspruit. 2004. (Illus.). 142p. (YA). pap. (978-1-894666-91-6(7)) Inheritance Pubns.
Perritano, John. Battle of the Bots, 1 vol. 2014. (Kid Squad Saves the World Ser.). (ENG.). 112p. (J). (gr. 8-12). lib. bdg. 27.07 (978-1-62402-037-7(2), Calico Chapter Bks.) Magic Wagon.
Peyton, Km. Far from Home. 2014. (ENG., Illus.). 183p. (J). (gr. 4-7). pap. 5.99 (978-0-7945-3292-5(6), Usborne) EDC Publishing.
Phillips, Dee. Blast, 1 vol. unabr. ed. 2011. (Right Now! Ser.). (ENG.). 45p. (YA). (gr. 9-12). pap. 8.95 (978-1-61651-245-3(8)) Saddleback Educational Publishing, Inc.
Pierce, Nicola. City of Fate. 2014. (ENG.). 272p. (J). pap. 11.00 **(978-1-84717-337-9(3))** O'Brien Pr., Ltd., The IRL. Dist: Dufour Editions, Inc.
Pochenko. Conspiracy Prophecy II: WWIII & Rumors of WWIV in Revelation. 2003. 230p. (YA). pap. 14.95 (978-0-595-26419-3(0), Writer's Showcase Pr.) iUniverse, Inc.
Porter, Sarah. The Twice Lost. (Lost Voices Trilogy Ser.: 3). (ENG.). 480p. (YA). (gr. 7). 2014. pap. 8.99 (978-0-547-48255-2(8), HMH Books For Young Readers) 2013. 16.99 (978-0-547-48252-1(3)) Houghton Mifflin Harcourt Publishing Co.
Pratchett, Terry. Only You Can Save Mankind. 224p. (J). (gr. 3-7). 2006. (Johnny Maxwell Trilogy Ser.: 1). per. 6.99 (978-0-06-054187-3(3)) 2005. 15.99 (978-0-06-054185-9(7)) HarperCollins Pubs.
—Only You Can Save Mankind. 2006. (Johnny Maxwell Trilogy). 207p. (J). (gr. 3-7). 13.65 (978-0-7569-6933-2(6)) Perfection Learning Corp.
Raether, Erin F. When Auntie Angie Left for Iraq & Remi Came to Stay. 2008. 15p. pap. 24.95 (978-1-4241-8735-5(4)) America Star Bks.
Ransom, Marty. Our Father, Our Soldier, Our Hero. 2011. 36p. pap. 24.95 (978-1-4626-1377-9(2)) America Star Bks.
Reedy, Trent. Burning Nation. 2015. 417p. (YA). (978-0-545-75282-4(5)); (Divided We Fall Ser.: 2). (ENG.). 432p. (J). (gr. 9). 17.99 (978-0-545-54873-1(X), Levine, Arthur A. Bks.) Scholastic, Inc.
—The Last Full Measure. 2016. (Divided We Fall Ser.: 3). (ENG.). 464p. (YA). (gr. 9). 17.99 (978-0-545-54877-9(2), Levine, Arthur A. Bks.) Scholastic, Inc.
Reiter, David P. Las Armas de Fuego. Rosales-Martinez, Guadalupe, tr. from ENG. Murphy, Patrick J., illus. 2010.Tr. of Real Guns. (SPA.). 32p. (YA). (978-1-921479-44-1(2)) Interactive Pubns. Pty, Ltd.
Richards, Elizabeth. Black City. 2013. (Black City Novel Ser.: 1). (ENG., Illus.). 400p. (YA). (gr. 9). pap. 9.99 (978-0-14-242722-4(5), Speak) Penguin Young Readers Group.
—Phoenix. 2nd ed. 2014. (Black City Novel Ser.: 2). (ENG.). 368p. (YA). (gr. 9). pap. 9.99 (978-0-14-751137-9(2), Speak) Penguin Young Readers Group.
Robertson, William P. & Rimer, David. The Battling Bucktails at Fredericksburg. 2005. (WM Kids Ser.: Vol. 16). (Illus.). 154p. (J). (gr. 4-7). per. 7.95 (978-1-57249-345-2(3), White Mane Kids) White Mane Publishing Co., Inc.
Rogers, Lon. The Between Season. 2009. 280p. 27.95 (978-1-4401-8370-6(8)) iUniverse, Inc.
Roop, Peter & Roop, Connie. An Eye for an Eye. 2004. 168p. (J). lib. bdg. 16.92 (978-1-4242-0772-5(X)) Fitzgerald Bks.

Rosenblatt, Darcey. Key to Heaven. 2017. (ENG.). 288p. (J). 16.99 *(978-1-62779-758-0(0)*, 9781627797580, Holt, Henry & Co. Bks. For Young Readers) Holt, Henry & Co.
Rosenblum, Gregg. Fugitive X. 2014. (Revolution 19 Ser.: 2). (ENG.). 272p. (YA). (gr. 8). 17.99 *(978-0-06-212597-2(4)*, HarperTeen) HarperCollins Pubs.
Rosoff, Meg. How I Live Now. (ENG.). (YA). (gr. 7). 2013. 208p. pap. 8.99 *(978-0-449-81960-9(4)*, Ember) 2006. 224p. reprint ed. pap. 8.99 *(978-0-553-37605-0(5)*, Lamb, Wendy Bks.) Random Hse. Children's Bks.
Sanderson, Brandon. Calamity. 2016. (Reckoners Ser.: Bk. 3). (ENG.). 432p. (YA). (gr. 7). lib. bdg. 21.99 *(978-0-375-99123-3(9))*; 18.99 *(978-0-385-74360-0(2))* Random Hse. Children's Bks. (Delacorte Pr.)
—Firefight. 2016. (SPA.). 432p. pap. 28.95 *(978-84-666-5836-2(X))* Ediciones B ESP. Dist: Spanish Pubs., LLC.
—Firefight. (Reckoners Ser.: Bk. 2). (ENG.). (YA). (gr. 7). 2016. 448p. pap. 10.99 *(978-0-385-74359-4(9)*, Ember) 2015. 432p. 18.99 *(978-0-385-74358-7(0)*, Delacorte Pr.) Random Hse. Children's Bks.
—Firefight. 2016. (Reckoners Ser.: 2). lib. bdg. 22.10 *(978-0-606-38447-6(2))* Turtleback Bks.
—The Reckoners, 3 vols. 2016. (ENG.). (YA). (gr. 7). 56.97 *(978-0-399-55168-0(9)*, Delacorte Pr.) Random Hse. Children's Bks.
—Steelheart. (SPA.). 416p. pap. 27.95 *(978-84-666-5296-4(5))*; 2015. pap. 14.95 *(978-84-9070-095-2(8))* Ediciones B ESP. Dist: Spanish Pubs., LLC.
—Steelheart. 2013. 386p. (YA). *(978-0-385-38371-4(1)*, Delacorte Pr) Random House Publishing Group.
—Steelheart. (Reckoners Ser.: 1). (ENG.). (YA). (gr. 7). 2014. 416p. pap. 9.99 *(978-0-385-74357-0(2)*, Ember) 2013. 400p. 18.99 *(978-0-385-74356-3(4)*, Delacorte Pr.) Random Hse. Children's Bks.
—Steelheart. 2014. (Reckoners Ser.: 1). lib. bdg. 20.85 *(978-0-606-36027-2(1))* Turtleback Bks.
Savage, J. Scott. Gears of Revolution. 2016. (Mysteries of Cove Ser.: 2). 342p. (J). 17.99 *(978-1-62972-223-8(5)*, Shadow Mountain) Deseret Bk. Co.
Scheffler, Stephanie. Elise the Patriot: A Revolutionary War Story. 2008. 108p. 20.95 *(978-0-595-51324-6(7))*; pap. 10.95 *(978-0-595-52582-9(2))* iUniverse, Inc.
Shadow, Jak. The F. E. A. R. Agency. 2006. (F. E. A. R. Adventures S. Ser.). (ENG., Illus.). 80p. (J). 4.00 *(978-1-84046-726-0(6)*, Wizard Books) Icon Bks., Ltd. GBR. Dist: Publishers Group Canada.
Shakespeare, William. Henry V: The Graphic Novel. 2010. (Classic Graphic Novel Collection). (ENG.). 160p. (gr. 7-12). 39.40 *(978-1-4205-0371-5(5))* Cengage Gale.
Sherman, M. Zachary. Blood Brotherhood, 1 vol. Casas, Fritz, illus. 2011. (Bloodlines Ser.). (ENG.). 88p. (gr. 4-8). pap. 6.95 *(978-1-4342-3098-0(8))*; 26.65 *(978-1-4342-2559-7(3))* Stone Arch Bks.
—Fighting Phantoms, 1 vol. Casas, Fritz, illus. 2011. (Bloodlines Ser.). (ENG.). 88p. (gr. 4-8). lib. bdg. 26.65 *(978-1-4342-2560-3(7))* Stone Arch Bks.
Sherman, M. Zachary & Iligan, Marlon. Heart of the Enemy, 1 vol. Cage, Josef, illus. 2012. (Bloodlines Ser.). (ENG.). 88p. (gr. 4-8). lib. bdg. 26.65 *(978-1-4342-3767-5(2))* Stone Arch Bks.
Shinn, Sharon. General Winston's Daughter. 2009. (ENG.). 352p. (YA). (gr. 7-18). 7.99 *(978-0-14-241346-3(1)*, Speak) Penguin Young Readers Group.
Singer, Sarah Jane. Two Bullets for Sergeant Franks. 2003. (Illus.). 112p. (YA). pap. 7.99 *(978-0-9721216-9-9(2)*, 0972121692) Computer Classics (R).
Smith, Andrew. The Marbury Lens. 2010. (ENG.). 368p. (YA). (gr. 9-12). 17.99 *(978-0-312-61342-6(3)*, 9780312613426) Feiwel & Friends.
Smith, Mary P. Wells. The Young Puritans in King Philip's War. Bridgman, L. J., illus. 2011. 396p. 54.95 *(978-1-258-05550-9(3))* Literary Licensing, LLC.
Smith, Melinda. Soldiers for Battle. 2008. 192p. 24.50 *(978-1-60693-398-5(1)*, Eloquent Bks.) Strategic Book Publishing & Rights Agency (SBPRA).
Smucker, Barbara. Nubes Negras. (SPA.). (YA). (gr. 5-8). pap. *(978-84-279-3148-0(4)*, NG3493) Noguer y Caralt Editores, S. A. ESP. Dist: Lectorum Pubns., Inc.
Snyder, Maria V. Dawn Study. 2017. (Study Ser.: 6). (ENG.). 480p. pap. 16.99 *(978-0-7783-1985-6(7)*, Mira Bks.) Harlequin Enterprises, Ltd. CAN. Dist: HarperCollins Pubs.
Somper, Justin. Immortal War. 2013. (Vampirates Ser.: 6). (ENG.). 512p. (J). (gr. 3-7). pap. 10.99 *(978-0-316-03325-1(1))* Little, Brown Bks. for Young Readers.
—Immortal War. 2013. (Vampirates Ser.: 6). (J). lib. bdg. 22.10 *(978-0-606-26696-3(8)*, Turtleback) Turtleback Bks.
Speakman, Peter & Galvin, Michael. Rebels of the Lamp, Book 1 Rebels of the Lamp. 2017. (Rebels of the Lamp Ser.). (ENG.). 304p. (J). (gr. 5-9). pap. 7.99 *(978-1-4847-0847-7(4))* Hyperion Bks. for Children.
Spillebeen, Geert. Kipling's Choice. Edelstein, Terese, tr. 2007. (ENG.). 160p. (YA). (gr. 7-9). pap. 12.95 *(978-0-618-80035-3(2))* Houghton Mifflin Harcourt Publishing Co.
—Kipling's Choice. Edelstein, Terese, tr. 2007. 147p. (YA). (gr. 7-9). 15.65 *(978-0-7569-8061-0(5))* Perfection Learning Corp.
Spradlin, Michael P. Into the Killing Seas. 2015. (J). (ENG.). 224p. (gr. 3-7). 16.99 *(978-0-545-72602-3(6)*, Scholastic Pr.); 185p. *(978-0-545-83764-4(2))* Scholastic, Inc.
Star Wars Staff & Valois, Rob. Sticker Storyteller. 2008. (Star Wars). (ENG.). 48p. (J). (gr. 1-3). pap. 12.99 *(978-0-448-45058-2(5))* Penguin Publishing Group.
Steele, William O. The Perilous Road. 2004. (ENG., Illus.). 176p. (J). (gr. 2-5). pap. 6.99 *(978-0-15-205204-1(6))* Houghton Mifflin Harcourt Publishing Co.
Steinlage, Ben. Bird Boy. 2011. 290p. pap. 17.95 *(978-1-4327-6667-2(8))* Outskirts Pr., Inc.
Stevenson, Robert Louis. The Black Arrow. l.t. ed. 2005. 448p. pap. *(978-1-84637-164-6(3))* Echo Library.
Stewart, E. J. The Lyre Birds. 2008. 214p. pap. 16.95 *(978-0-615-18762-4(5))* Leaf & Vine Bks.
Strang, Herbert. With Marlborough to Malplaquet. 2006. pap. *(978-1-4068-3126-9(3))* Echo Library.
Streich, Michel. Grumpy Little King. Streich, Michel, illus. 2012. (ENG., Illus.). 32p. (J). (gr. k-3). 19.99 *(978-1-74237-572-4(3))* Allen & Unwin AUS. Dist: Independent Pubs. Group.
Trout, Robert J. Drumbeat: The Story of a Civil War Drummer Boy. 2007. 190p. (J). (gr. 4-9). pap. 12.95 *(978-1-57249-390-2(9)*, White Mane Kids) White Mane Publishing Co., Inc.
Vaugelade, Anais. The War. Rouffiac, Marie-Christine & Streissguth, Thomas, trs. from FRE. Vaugelade, Anais, illus. 2005. (Picture Bks.). (Illus.). 32p. (J). (gr. k-2). 15.25 *(978-1-57505-562-6(7))* Lerner Publishing Group.
Walker, Alice. Why War Is Never a Good Idea. Vitale, Stefano, illus. 2007. 32p. (J). (gr. -1-3). lib. bdg. 17.89 *(978-0-06-075386-3(2))* HarperCollins Pubs.
Watts, Helen & Thomas, Taffy. The Ghost of the Trenches & Other Stories. 2014. (ENG.). 128p. (YA). (gr. 4-6). pap. 10.99 *(978-1-4729-0787-5(6)*, 9781472907875, Bloomsbury USA Childrens) Bloomsbury Publishing USA.
Wein, Elizabeth. Black Dove, White Raven. 2015. (ENG.). 368p. (YA). (gr. 7-12). 17.99 *(978-1-4231-8310-5(X))* Hyperion Bks. for Children.
Weisleder, Stanley. Wings of the Panther. 2010. (ENG.). 224p. pap. 15.00 *(978-0-936783-38-3(9))* Merril Pr.
Wells, Dan. Ruins. 2014. (Partials Sequence Ser.: 3). (ENG.). 464p. (YA). (gr. 9). 17.99 *(978-0-06-207110-1(6))* HarperCollins Pubs.
Wells, H. G. The War of the Worlds. Wenzel, Paul, illus. 2005. (Reader's Workshop Ser.). (ENG.). 93p. (C). pap. 17.95 *(978-0-7362-2782-7(2))* National Geographic School Publishing, Inc.
Westerfeld, Scott. Behemoth. Thompson, Keith, illus. (Leviathan Trilogy Ser.). (ENG.). (YA). (gr. 7). 2011. 512p. pap. 12.99 *(978-1-4169-7176-4(9))* 2010. 496p. 18.99 *(978-1-4169-7175-7(0))* Simon Pulse. (Simon Pulse).
—Behemoth. Thompson, Keith, illus. l.t. ed. 2010. (Leviathan Trilogy: Bk. 2). (ENG.). 540p. 23.99 *(978-1-4104-3066-3(9))* Thorndike Pr.
—Behemoth. 2011. (Leviathan Ser.: 2). lib. bdg. 24.50 *(978-0-606-22407-9(6)*, Turtleback) Turtleback Bks.
—Goliath, 8 vols. 2011. (YA). 122.75 *(978-1-4618-0617-2(8))*; 124.75 *(978-1-4618-0613-4(5))*; 305.75 *(978-1-4618-0618-9(6))*; 122.75 *(978-1-4618-0614-1(3))*; 1.25 *(978-1-4640-3062-8(6))* Recorded Bks., Inc.
—Goliath. Thompson, Keith, illus. (Leviathan Trilogy Ser.). (ENG.). (YA). (gr. 7). 2012. 576p. pap. 14.99 *(978-1-4169-7178-8(5))* 2011. 560p. 19.99 *(978-1-4169-7177-1(7))* Simon Pulse. (Simon Pulse).
—Goliath. 2012. (Leviathan Ser.: 3). lib. bdg. 24.50 *(978-0-606-26355-9(1)*, Turtleback) Turtleback Bks.
—Leviathan. Thompson, Keith, illus. (Leviathan Trilogy Ser.). (ENG.). (YA). (gr. 7-18). 2010. 464p. pap. 12.99 *(978-1-4169-7174-0(2))* 2009. 448p. 19.99 *(978-1-4169-7173-3(4))* Simon Pulse. (Simon Pulse).
—Leviathan. l.t. ed. 2010. (Leviathan Trilogy: Bk. 1). (ENG.). 526p. 23.95 *(978-1-4104-2572-0(X))* Thorndike Pr.
—Leviathan. 2010. (Leviathan Ser.: 1). lib. bdg. 23.30 *(978-0-606-22393-5(2)*, Turtleback) Turtleback Bks.
Whitley, David. The Canticle of Whispers. 2013. (Agora Trilogy Ser.: 3). (ENG.). 400p. (J). (gr. 6-9). 17.99 *(978-1-59643-615-2(8)*, 9781596436152) Roaring Brook Pr.
Wiechman, Kathy Cannon. Like a River. 2015. (ENG.). 336p. (J). (gr. 3). 17.95 *(978-1-62979-209-5(8)*, Calkins Creek) Boyds Mills Pr.
Wild, Margaret. Let the Celebrations Begin. Vivas, Julie, illus. 2014. (ENG.). 40p. (J). (gr. 2-5). 16.99 *(978-0-7636-7013-9(8))* Candlewick Pr.
Williams, John Joseph. Vak's War. 2013. 102p. (J). pap. *(978-1-78299-323-0(1))* FeedARead.com.
Williams, Mary. Brothers in Hope: The Story of the Lost Boys of Sudan, 1 vol. Christie, R. Gregory, illus. 2013. (ENG.). 32p. (J). 18.95 *(978-1-58430-232-2(1))* Lee & Low Bks., Inc.
Wilson, John. Germania. 2008. (ENG., Illus.). 280p. (YA). (gr. 7-18). *(978-1-55470-112-4(0))* Me to We.
Wolverton, Barry. Neversink. Nielson, Sam, illus. (ENG.). (J). (gr. 3-7). 2013. 320p. pap. 6.99 *(978-0-06-202793-1(X))* 2012. 304p. 16.99 *(978-0-06-202791-7(3))* HarperCollins Pubs. (Waldon Pond Pr.).
—Neversink. Nielson, Sam, illus. 2012. xiii, 287p. (J). *(978-0-06-202792-4(1))* Longman Publishing.
Wright, Pauline. Why Did My Dad Go to War? 2008. 48p. pap. 19.49 *(978-1-4343-4677-3(3))* AuthorHouse.
Yancey, Rick. The Infinite Sea. (5th Wave Ser.: 2). (ENG.). (YA). (gr. 9-12). 2015. 336p. pap. 10.99 *(978-1-101-99698-0(6)*, Speak) 2014. 320p. 18.99 *(978-0-399-16242-8(9)*, G.P. Putnam's Sons Books for Young Readers) Penguin Young Readers Group.
—The Infinite Sea. 2015. (5th Wave Ser.: 2). lib. bdg. 22.10 *(978-0-606-38204-5(6))* Turtleback Bks.
—The Last Star. 2016. (5th Wave Ser.: 3). (ENG.). 352p. (YA). (gr. 9). 18.99 *(978-0-399-16243-5(7)*, G.P. Putnam's Sons Books for Young Readers) Penguin Young Readers Group.
—The Last Star. 2017. (5th Wave Ser.: 3). lib. bdg. 22.10 ***(978-0-606-40098-5(2))*** Turtleback Bks.
Yancey, Rick. The 5th Wave. (5th Wave Ser.: Bk. 1). (ENG.). (YA). (gr. 9). 2015. 512p. pap. 10.99 *(978-0-14-242583-1(4)*, Speak) 2013. 480p. 18.99 *(978-0-399-16241-1(0)*, G.P. Putnam's Sons Books for Young Readers) Penguin Publishing Group.
—The 5th Wave. movie tie-in ed. 2015. (ENG.). (YA). (gr. 9-12). (5th Wave Ser.: 1). 512p. pap. 10.99 *(978-0-14-751908-5(X)*, Speak); (5th Wave Ser.: Bk. 1). 480p. 18.99 *(978-1-101-99651-5(X)*, G.P. Putnam's Sons Books for Young Readers);Set. pap., pap., pap. 21.98 *(978-1-101-99998-1(5)*, Speak) Penguin Young Readers Group.
—The 5th Wave. 2015. (5th Wave Ser.: Vol. 1). (ENG.). (YA). (gr. 9). lib. bdg. 21.60 ***(978-1-62765-623-8(5))*** Perfection Learning Corp.
—The 5th Wave. 2015. (5th Wave Ser.: 1). lib. bdg. 22.10 *(978-0-606-36640-3(7))*; lib. bdg. 22.10 *(978-0-606-37680-8(1))* Turtleback Bks.
Yardi, Robin. The Midnight War of Mateo Martinez. 2016. (ENG.). 184p. (J). (gr. 3-6). 17.99 *(978-1-4677-8306-4(4)*, Carolrhoda Bks.) Lerner Publishing Group.
Yolen, Jane & Stemple, Adam. The Last Changeling. 2014. (Seelie Wars Ser.). (ENG.). 304p. (J). (gr. 3-7). 16.99 *(978-0-670-01435-4(4)*, Viking Books for Young Readers) Penguin Young Readers Group.
—The Seelie King's War. 2016. (Seelie Wars Ser.: 3). (ENG., Illus.). 336p. (J). (gr. 3-7). 17.99 *(978-0-670-01436-1(2)*, Viking Books for Young Readers) Penguin Young Readers Group.
Zerfing, Robert A. The Silencer: A U. N. Conspiracy Novel. 2nd ed. 2003. 326p. (YA). per. 14.95 *(978-0-9747881-0-4(4))* Clawfoot Publishing.
Zug, Mark & Fan, Nancy Yi. Swordbird. Zug, Mark, illus. 2008. (Swordbird Ser.: 1). (ENG., Illus.). 256p. (J). (gr. 3-7). pap. 6.99 *(978-0-06-113101-1(6))* HarperCollins Pubs.

WAR CORRESPONDENTS
see Reporters and Reporting

WAR CRIME TRIALS
Kacer, Kathy. To Look a Nazi in the Eye: A Teen's Account of a War Criminal Trial, 1 vol. 2017. (ENG.). 256p. (YA). (gr. 8-12). pap. 13.95 ***(978-1-77260-040-7(7))*** Second Story Pr. CAN. Dist: Orca Bk. Pubs. USA.
Sachs, Ruth. Adolf Eichmann: Engineer of Death. 2009. (Holocaust Biographies Ser.). 112p. (gr. 7-12). 63.90 *(978-1-61513-380-2(1))* Rosen Publishing Group, Inc., The.

WAR OF 1812
see United States—History—War of 1812

WAR OF 1914
see World War, 1914-1918

WAR OF 1939-1945
see World War, 1939-1945

WAR OF SECESSION, U.S., 1861-1865
see United States—History—Civil War, 1861-1865

WAR OF THE AMERICAN REVOLUTION
see United States—History—Revolution, 1775-1783

WAR POETRY
Dieterman, Nicole. A Child's View of War: A Collection of Poems by Nicole Dieterman. 2003. mass mkt. 12.95 *(978-0-9742472-0-5(0))* Pleiness Publishing.
Greenfield, Eloise. When the Horses Ride By: Children in the Times of War. Gilchrist, Jan Spivey, illus. 2006. (ENG.). (J). 32p. pap. 12.95 *(978-1-60060-454-6(4))*; 40p. (gr. 4-7). 17.95 *(978-1-58430-249-0(6))* Lee & Low Bks., Inc.
Morgan, Gaby. Poems from the First World War: Published in Association with Imperial War Museums. unabr. ed. 2014. (ENG.). 208p. (J). pap. 9.99 *(978-1-4472-4864-4(3))* Pan Macmillan GBR. Dist: Independent Pubs. Group.
Stevens, Roger & Moses, Brian. What Are We Fighting For? New Poems about War. unabr. ed. 2014. (ENG., Illus.). 112p. (J). pap. 7.99 *(978-1-4472-4861-3(9))* Pan Macmillan GBR. Dist: Independent Pubs. Group.
Wade, Stephen. The War Poets: The Secrets of Poems from the Great War. 2003. (Studymates Ser.). (ENG., Illus.). 128p. pap. 27.50 *(978-1-84285-030-5(X))* GLMP Ltd. GBR. Dist: Chicago Distribution Ctr.

WAR SHIPS
see Warships

WARFARE, SUBMARINE
see Submarine Warfare

WARLOCKS
see Witches; Wizards

WARREN, EARL, 1891-1974
Branscomb, Leslie Wolf. Earl Warren. 2011. (Supreme Court Justices Ser.). (Illus.). 112p. 28.95 *(978-1-59935-158-2(7))* Reynolds, Morgan Inc.

WARS
see Military History; Naval History; War

WARSAW (POLAND)
Altman, Linda Jacobs. The Warsaw Ghetto Uprising: Striking a Blow Against the Nazis. 2011. (Holocaust Through Primary Sources Ser.). (Illus.). 128p. (J). (gr. 6-18). pap. 10.95 *(978-1-59845-347-8(5))*; (gr. 9-12). lib. bdg. 33.27 *(978-0-7660-3320-7(1))* Enslow Pubs., Inc.
Beyer, Mark. Emmanuel Ringelblum: Historian of the Warsaw Ghetto. 2009. (Holocaust Biographies Ser.). 112p. (gr. 7-12). 63.90 *(978-1-61513-384-0(4))* Rosen Publishing Group, Inc., The.
Brophy Down, Susan. Irena Sendler: Bringing Life to Children of the Holocaust. 2012. (ENG.). 112p. (J). pap. *(978-0-7787-2556-5(1))*; (Illus.). *(978-0-7787-2553-4(7))* Crabtree Publishing Co.
Callahan, Kerry P. Mordechai Anielewicz: Hero of the Warsaw Ghetto Uprising. 2009. (Holocaust Biographies Ser.). 112p. (gr. 7-12). 63.90 *(978-1-61513-389-5(5))* Rosen Publishing Group, Inc., The.
Freedman, Jeri. The Warsaw Ghetto & Uprising. 2014. (Documentary History of the Holocaust Ser.). 80p. (YA). (gr. 7-12). 34.25 *(978-1-4777-7605-6(2))* Rosen Publishing Group, Inc., The.
Rubin, Susan Goldman. Irena Sendler & the Children of the Warsaw Ghetto. Farnsworth, Bill, illus. 2011. (ENG.). 40p. (J). (gr. 1-5). 18.95 *(978-0-8234-2251-7(8))* Holiday Hse., Inc.
Spielman, Gloria. Janusz Korczak's Children. Archambault, Matthew, illus. 2007. (Kar-Ben for Older Readers Ser.). 40p. (J). (gr. 3-7). lib. bdg. 17.95 *(978-1-58013-255-8(3))*; (ENG.). pap. 7.95 *(978-0-8225-7050-9(5))* Lerner Publishing Group. (Kar-Ben Publishing).
Vaughan, Marcia. Irena's Jars of Secrets, 1 vol. Mazellan, Ron, illus. 2011. (ENG.). 40p. (J). 18.95 *(978-1-60060-439-3(0))* Lee & Low Bks., Inc.

WARSAW (POLAND)—FICTION
Dalager, Stig. David's Story. 2010. (ENG., Illus.). 280p. (J). pap. 18.95 *(978-1-906582-04-3(1))* Aurora Metro Pubns. Ltd. GBR. Dist: Consortium Bk. Sales & Distribution.
Orlev, Uri. Run, Boy, Run. Halkin, Hillel, tr. 10th ed. 2007. (ENG.). 192p. (YA). (gr. 5-18). 7.99 *(978-0-618-95706-4(5))* Houghton Mifflin Harcourt Publishing Co.
Spinelli, Jerry. Milkweed. 2010. (ENG.). 240p. (YA). (gr. 7). pap. 9.99 *(978-0-375-86147-5(5)*, Ember) Random Hse. Children's Bks.

WARSHIPS
see also Aircraft Carriers; Submarines (Ships)
also names of countries with the subhead Navy (e.g. United States—Navy)
Adams, Simon. Warships. 2009. (War Machines Ser.). (YA). (gr. 5-9). 28.50 *(978-1-59920-225-9(5))* Black Rabbit Bks.
Alpert, Barbara. Military Ships. 2012. (Military Machines Ser.). (ENG.). 24p. (J). (gr. k-1). pap. 41.70 *(978-1-4296-8316-6(3))*; lib. bdg. 26.65 *(978-1-4296-7572-7(1))* Capstone Press of Coughlan Cos. (Pebble Plus).
—U. S. Military Warships, 1 vol. 2012. (U. S. Military Technology Ser.). (ENG., Illus.). 32p. (gr. 1-2). lib. bdg. 26.65 *(978-1-4296-8441-5(0))* Capstone Press of Coughlan Cos.
Alpert, Barbara & Shank, Carol. U. S. Military Technology. 2012. (U. S. Military Technology Ser.). (ENG.). 32p. (gr. 1-2). lib. bdg. 106.60 *(978-1-4296-9139-0(5)*, Blazers) Capstone Press of Coughlan Cos.
Alvarez, Carlos. Arleigh Burke Destroyers. 2010. (Military Machines Ser.). (ENG., Illus.). 24p. (J). (gr. 3-7). lib. bdg. 25.95 *(978-1-60014-331-1(8))* Bellwether Media.
—Ticonderoga Cruisers. 2010. (Military Machines Ser.). (ENG., Illus.). 24p. (YA). (gr. 3-7). lib. bdg. 25.95 *(978-1-60014-321-2(0))* Bellwether Media.
Barton, Chris. Dazzle Ships: World War I & the Art of Confusion. Ngai, Victo, illus. 2017. (ENG.). 36p. (J). (gr. 2-5). lib. bdg. 19.99 ***(978-1-5124-1014-3(4)***, Millbrook Pr.) Lerner Publishing Group.
Bodden, Valerie. Battleships. 2012. (J). 25.65 *(978-1-60818-124-7(3)*, Creative Education) Creative Co., The.
—Built for Battle: Battleships. 2012. (Built for Battle Ser.). (ENG., Illus.). 24p. (J). (gr. 1-3). pap. 7.99 *(978-0-89812-699-0(1)*, Creative Paperbacks) Creative Co., The.
Brook, Henry. Warships IR. 2012. (Discovery Adventures Ser.). 80p. (J). pap. 8.99 *(978-0-7945-3289-5(6)*, Usborne) EDC Publishing.
Cohn, Jessica. Military Machines. 2013. (Machines in Motion Ser.). 48p. (J). (gr. 3-5). pap. 84.30 *(978-1-4339-9606-1(5))*; pap. 14.05 *(978-1-4339-9605-4(7))*; (ENG., Illus.). lib. bdg. 31.95 *(978-1-4339-9604-7(9))* Stevens, Gareth Publishing LLLP.
Colson, Rob Scott. Warships. 2013. (Ultimate Machines Ser.). (ENG., Illus.). 24p. (J). (gr. 3-6). pap. 8.25 *(978-1-4777-0113-3(3))*; lib. bdg. 22.60 *(978-1-4777-0064-8(1))* Rosen Publishing Group, Inc., The. (PowerKids Pr.).
Cooke, Tim. Warships. 2012. (Ultimate Military Machines Ser.). (Illus.). 32p. (gr. 4-7). lib. bdg. 31.35 *(978-1-59920-824-4(5))* Black Rabbit Bks.
Dartford, Mark. Warships. 2003. (Military Hardware in Action Ser.). (ENG., Illus.). 48p. (gr. 5-9). lib. bdg. 25.26 *(978-0-8225-4703-7(1))* Lerner Publishing Group.
Dell, Pamela & Delmar, Peter. The Science of Military Vehicles, 1 vol. 2012. (Science of War Ser.). (ENG.). 48p. (gr. 5-6). pap. 9.10 *(978-0-7565-4525-3(0)*, CPB Grades 4-8) Compass Point Bks.
Delmar, Pete. Vehicles of the Civil War, 1 vol. 2013. (War Vehicles Ser.). (ENG.). 32p. (gr. 3-4). 27.99 *(978-1-4296-9912-9(4)*, Edge Bks.) Capstone Press of Coughlan Cos.
Doman, Mary Kate. Big Military Machines. 2011. (All about Big Machines Ser.). (Illus.). 24p. (J). (gr. -1-18). pap. 7.95 *(978-1-59845-243-3(6)*, Enslow Elementary) Enslow Pubs., Inc.
Dougherty, Martin J. Modern Warships up Close, 01 vols., 1. Pearson, Colin, illus. 2016. (Military Technology: Top Secret Clearance Ser.). (ENG.). 224p. (YA). 43.60 *(978-1-5081-7084-6(3)*, Rosen Young Adult) Rosen Publishing Group, Inc., The.
—Sea Warfare. 2010. (Modern Warfare Ser.). (Illus.). 32p. (J). (gr. 2-5). lib. bdg. 26.00 *(978-1-4339-2734-8(9))* Stevens, Gareth Publishing LLLP.
Fighting Ships. 2003. (Illus.). 32p. (YA). pap. *(978-1-904516-33-0(5)*, Pavilion Children's Books) Pavilion Bks.
Finn, Denny Von. Arleigh Burke Destroyers. 2014. (Military Vehicles Ser.). (ENG., Illus.). 24p. (J). (gr. 3-7). lib. bdg. 25.95 *(978-1-62617-080-3(0)*, Epic Bks.) Bellwether Media.
Gilpin, Daniel & Pang, Alex. Modern Warships & Submarines. 2010. (Machines Close-Up Ser.). 32p. (J). (gr. 4-7). 28.50 *(978-0-7614-4-110-0(7))* Marshall Cavendish Corp.
Green, Phillip. Littoral Combat Ships. 2011. (Military Machines Ser.). (ENG., Illus.). 24p. (J). (gr. 3-7). lib. bdg. 25.95 *(978-1-60014-580-3(9)*, Torque Bks.) Bellwether Media.
Hale, Nathan. Big Bad Ironclad! 2012. (Nathan Hale's Hazardous Tales Ser.). (ENG., Illus.). 128p. (J). (gr. 3-7). 12.95 *(978-1-4197-0395-9(1)*, Amulet Bks.) Abrams, Inc.
Hamilton, John. Amphibious Assault Ships. 2012. (Military Ships Ser.). 32p. (J). (gr. 3-9). 27.07 *(978-1-61783-520-9(X)*, A&D Xtreme) ABDO Publishing Co.
—Cruisers. 2012. (Military Ships Ser.). 32p. (J). (gr. 3-9). 27.07 *(978-1-61783-521-6(8)*, A&D Xtreme) ABDO Publishing Co.
—Destroyers. 2012. (Military Ships Ser.). 32p. (J). (gr. 3-9). 27.07 *(978-1-61783-522-3(6)*, A&D Xtreme) ABDO Publishing Co.
—Frigates. 2012. (Military Ships Ser.). 32p. (J). (gr. 3-9). 27.07 *(978-1-61783-523-0(4)*, A&D Xtreme) ABDO Publishing Co.
—United States Navy. 2011. (Armed Forces Ser.). (Illus.). 32p. (YA). (gr. 3-6). 27.07 *(978-1-61783-071-6(2))* ABDO Publishing Co.
Jackson, Kay. Navy Ships in Action. 2009. (Amazing Military Vehicles Ser.). 24p. (gr. 3-5). (Illus.). (J). pap. 8.25 *(978-1-4358-3160-5(8)*, PowerKids Pr.); 42.50 *(978-1-61511-321-7(5)*, PowerKids Pr.); (YA). lib. bdg. 22.60 *(978-1-4358-2750-9(3))* Rosen Publishing Group, Inc., The.
Jackson, Robert. Warships: Inside & Out. 2011. (Weapons of War Ser.). (ENG.). 160p. (YA). (gr. 9-12). lib. bdg. 42.60 *(978-1-4488-5981-8(6))* Rosen Publishing Group, Inc., The.
—101 Great Warships. 2010. (101 Greatest Weapons of All Times Ser.). (Illus.). 112p. (YA). (gr. 9-12). lib. bdg. 34.60 *(978-1-4358-3596-2(4))* Rosen Publishing Group, Inc., The.
Marsico, Katie. Warships. 2016. (True Book(tm) — Engineering Wonders Ser.). (ENG., Illus.). 48p. (J). pap. 6.95 *(978-0-531-22274-4(8)*, Children's Pr.) Scholastic Library Publishing.
Mavrikis, Peter. Battleships, 01 vols., 1. 2016. (What's Inside? Ser.). (ENG.). 48p. (J). pap. 11.75 *(978-1-5081-4603-2(9)*, PowerKids Pr.) Rosen Publishing Group, Inc., The.
—Battleships & Aircraft Carriers. 2014. (Illus.). 48p. (J). *(978-1-4351-5367-7(7))* Barnes & Noble, Inc.

W X Y Z

—Classic Warships. 2014. (Illus.). 48p. (J). (978-1-4351-5368-4(5)) Barnes & Noble, Inc.

—Classic Warships, 01 vols., 1. 2016. (What's Inside? Ser.). (ENG.). 48p. (J). pap. 11.75 (978-1-5081-4607-0(1), PowerKids Pr.) Rosen Publishing Group, Inc., The.

Meister, Cari. Totally Amazing Facts about Military Sea & Air Vehicles. 2017. (Mind Benders Ser.). (ENG., Illus.). 112p. (gr. 1-3). lib. bdg. 23.32 (978-1-5157-4526-6(0)) Capstone Press of Coughlan Cos.

Mighty Military Machines. 2015. (Mighty Military Machines Ser.). (ENG.). 32p. (J). (gr. 1-1). 159.60 (978-1-4824-1649-7(2)) Stevens, Gareth Publishing LLLP.

Mueller, Richard. Naval Warfare of the Future. (Library of Future Weaponry Ser.). 64p. 2009. (gr. 6-6). 58.50 (978-1-60853-640-5(8)) 2005. (Illus.). (J). (gr. 2-7). lib. bdg. 31.95 (978-1-4042-0526-0(8)) Rosen Publishing Group, Inc., The.

Myers, Walter Dean. USS Constellation: Pride of the American Navy. 2004. (ENG., Illus.). 96p. (J). (gr. 4-6). tchr. ed. 16.95 (978-0-8234-1816-9(2)) Holiday Hse., Inc.

Oxlade, Chris. Inside Battleships. Viana, Tatio, illus. 2017. (Inside Military Machines Ser.). (ENG.). (J). (gr. 3-6). lib. bdg. 26.65 **(978-1-5124-3225-1(3))** Lerner Publishing Group.

Parker, Steve. Military Machines. 2010. (How It Works Ser.). 40p. (J). (gr. 3-18). lib. bdg. 19.95 (978-1-4222-1797-9(3)) Mason Crest.

Riggs, Kate. Battleships. 2016. (Seedlings Ser.). (Illus.). 24p. (J). (gr. k-2). (ENG.). pap. 7.99 (978-1-62832-245-3(4)); 28.50 (978-1-60818-660-0(1)) Creative Co., The. (Creative Education).

Ross, David. The World's Most Powerful Battleships. 2016. (World's Most Powerful Machines Ser.). 00224p. (J). (gr. 9-9). 45.10 (978-1-4994-6598-3(X)) Rosen Publishing Group, Inc., The.

Stark, William N. Mighty Military Ships. 2016. (Military Machines on Duty Ser.). (ENG., Illus.). 24p. (gr. 1-2). lib. bdg. 25.32 (978-1-4914-8846-1(8), First Facts) Capstone Press of Coughlan Cos.

Stone, Lynn M. Battleships. 2005. (Fighting Forces Ser.). (Illus.). 32p. (J). (gr. 4-8). lib. bdg. 19.95 (978-1-59515-461-3(2), 1244403) Rourke Educational Media.

War at Sea & in the Air. 2011. (Britannica Guide to War Ser.). (ENG.). 160p. (YA). (gr. 10-12). 70.50 (978-1-61530-798-2(2)) Rosen Publishing Group, Inc., The.

Zuehlke, Jeffrey. Warships. 2005. (Pull Ahead Books-Mighty Movers Ser.). (ENG., Illus.). 32p. (gr. k-3). lib. bdg. 22.60 (978-0-8225-2866-1(5), Lerner Pubns.); per. 7.95 (978-0-8225-2906-4(8)) Lerner Publishing Group.

WARSHIPS—FICTION

Appleton, Victor. Tom Swift & His Aerial Warship or the. 2006. pap. (978-1-4065-0894-9(2)) Dodo Pr.

—Tom Swift & His Aerial Warship or the Naval Terror of the Seas. 2005. reprint ed. pap. 24.95 (978-0-7661-9446-5(9)) Kessinger Publishing, LLC.

—The Tom Swift Omnibus #6: Tom Swift & His Giant Cannon, Tom Swift & His Photo Telephone, Tom Swift & His Aerial Warship. 2007. 296p. per. 12.99 (978-1-60459-108-8(0)) Wilder Pubns., Corp.

O'Connor, Barbara. The Fantastic Secret of Owen Jester. 2010. (ENG.). 176p. (J). (gr. 3-7). 15.99 (978-0-374-36850-0(3), 9780374368500, Farrar, Straus & Giroux (BYR)) Farrar, Straus & Giroux.

WASHINGTON, BOOKER T., 1856-1915

Asim, Jabari. Fifty Cents & a Dream: Young Booker T. Washington. 2012. (ENG., Illus.). 48p. (J). (gr. -1-3). 16.99 (978-0-316-08657-8(6)) Little Brown & Co.

Braun, Eric. Booker T. Washington: Great American Educator, 1 vol. Martin, Cynthia, illus. (Graphic Biographies Ser.). (ENG.). 32p. (gr. 3-4). 2006. per. 8.10 (978-0-7368-6190-8(4)) 2005. 30.65 (978-0-7368-4630-1(1)) Capstone Press of Coughlan Cos. (Graphic Library).

Brimner, Larry Dane. Booker T. Washington: Getting into the Schoolhouse. 2008. (American Heroes Ser.). 48p. (YA). (gr. 3-18). lib. bdg. 29.93 (978-0-7614-3063-6(6), Benchmark Bks.) Marshall Cavendish Corp.

Dunn, Joeming W. Booker T. Washington, 1 vol. Allen, Chris, illus. 2008. (Bio-Graphics Ser.). (ENG.). 32p. 28.50 (978-1-60270-177-9(6), Graphic Planet- Nonfiction) ABDO Publishing Co.

Flynn, Riley. Booker T. Washington, 1 vol. 2014. (Great African-Americans Ser.). (ENG.). 24p. (gr. k-1). lib. bdg. 21.99 (978-1-4765-3952-2(9), Pebble Bks.) Capstone Press of Coughlan Cos.

Haldy, Emma E. Booker T. Washington. Bane, Jeff, illus. 2016. (My Early Library: My Itty-Bitty Bio Ser.). (ENG.). 24p. (J). (gr. k-1). 28.50 (978-1-63471-018-3(5), 208152) Cherry Lake Publishing.

McKissack, Patricia C. & McKissack, Fredrick L. Booker T. Washington: African-American Leader. 2013. (Famous African Americans Ser.). 24p. (J). (gr. k-3). pap. 7.95 (978-1-4644-0194-7(2)); (Illus.). lib. bdg. 22.60 (978-0-7660-4100-4(X)) Enslow Pubs., Inc. (Enslow Elementary).

Schraff, Anne E. Booker T. Washington: Character Is Power. 2006. (African-American Biography Library). (Illus.). 128p. (J). (gr. 3-7). lib. bdg. 33.27 (978-0-7660-2535-6(7)) Enslow Pubs., Inc.

Schroeder, Alan. Booker T. Washington: Educator & Racial Spokesman. 2004. (Black Americans of Achievement Ser.). (Illus.). 112p. (gr. 6-12). 35.00 (978-0-7910-8253-9(9), Chelsea Hse.) Facts On File, Inc.

Slade, Suzanne. With Books & Bricks: How Booker T. Washington Built a School. Tadgell, Nicole, illus. 2014. (ENG.). 32p. (J). (gr. 2-3). 16.99 (978-0-8075-0897-8(7)) Whitman, Albert & Co.

Swain, Gwenyth. A Hunger for Learning: A Story about Booker T. Washington. Johnson, Larry, illus. (Creative Minds Biographies Ser.). (ENG.). 64p. (gr. 4-8). 2006. pap. 8.95 (978-0-8225-3090-9(2)) 2005. lib. bdg. 22.60 (978-1-57505-754-5(9)) Lerner Publishing Group.

Troy, Don. Booker T. Washington. 2009. (Journey to Freedom Ser.). (ENG., Illus.). 32p. (J). (gr. 4-7). 29.93 (978-1-60253-118-5(8), 200384) Child's World, Inc., The.

Whiting, Jim. Booker T. Washington. 2010. (Transcending Race in America Ser.). (Illus.). 64p. (YA). (gr. 4-8). lib. bdg. 22.95 (978-1-4222-1608-8(X)) Mason Crest.

Wukovits, John F. Booker T. Washington & Entrepreneurship. 2008. (Lucent Library of Black History Ser.). (ENG., Illus.). 128p. (gr. 7-10). 39.40 (978-1-4205-0052-3(X), Lucent Bks.) Cengage Gale.

WASHINGTON, GEORGE, 1732-1799

Abbey, Jed. The Life of George Washington. 2012. (InfoMax Readers Ser.). (ENG., Illus.). 24p. (J). (gr. 1-2). pap. 8.25 (978-1-4488-8986-0(3), Rosen Classroom) Rosen Publishing Group, Inc., The.

Abnett, Dan. George Washington & the American Revolution. (Jr. Graphic Biographies Ser.). (ENG.). 24p. 2009. (J). (gr. 2-3). 47.90 (978-1-61513-813-5(7), PowerKids Pr.) 2007. (Illus.). (J). (gr. 2-5). lib. bdg. 25.25 (978-1-4042-3395-9(4)) 2007. (Illus.). (gr. 3-8). pap. 10.60 (978-1-4042-2148-2(4), PowerKids Pr.) Rosen Publishing Group, Inc., The.

—George Washington y la Guerra de Independencia. 2009. (Historietas Juveniles: Biografías (Jr. Graphic Biographies) Ser.). (SPA & ENG., Illus.). 24p. (YA). (gr. 2-5). 25.25 (978-1-4358-8564-6(3)); (gr. 3-8). pap. 10.60 (978-1-4358-3322-7(8)) Rosen Publishing Group, Inc., The.

Abraham, Philip. How to Draw the Life & Times of George Washington. (Kid's Guide to Drawing the Presidents of the United States of America Ser.). 32p. 2009. (gr. 4-4). 50.50 (978-1-61511-140-4(9), PowerKids Pr.) 2005. (Illus.). (YA). (gr. 2-5). 26.50 (978-1-4042-2978-5(7)) Rosen Publishing Group, Inc., The.

Adler, David A. George Washington: An Illustrated Biography. 2004. (ENG., Illus.). 288p. (J). (gr. 4-6). tchr. ed. 24.95 (978-0-8234-1838-1(3)) Holiday Hse., Inc.

—President George Washington. Wallner, John C. & Wallner, John, illus. 2005. (Holiday House Reader, Level 2 Ser.). (ENG.). 32p. (J). 14.95 (978-0-8234-1604-2(6)) Holiday Hse., Inc.

Allen, Thomas B. George Washington, Spymaster: How the Americans Outspied the British & Won the Revolutionary War. Harness, Cheryl, illus. 2007. (ENG.). 192p. (J). (gr. 5-7). per. 7.95 (978-1-4263-0041-7(7), National Geographic Children's Bks.) National Geographic Society.

—Remember Valley Forge: Patriots, Tories, & Redcoats Tell Their Stories. 2015. (ENG., Illus.). 64p. (J). (gr. 5). pap. 7.99 (978-1-4263-2250-1(X), National Geographic Children's Bks.) National Geographic Society.

Ammon, Richard. Valley Forge. Farnsworth, Bill, illus. 2004. (ENG.). 32p. (J). (gr. 4-6). tchr. ed. 17.95 (978-0-8234-1746-9(8)) Holiday Hse., Inc.

Armentrout, David & Armentrout, Patricia. George Washington. 2004. (Discover the Life of an American Legend Ser.). (Illus.). 24p. (J). (gr. 2-5). 20.64 (978-1-58952-662-4(7)) Rourke Educational Media.

Bailer, Darice. George Washington. 2016. (Premier Presidents Ser.). (ENG.). 24p. (J). (gr. 1-4). 27.07 (978-1-5038-0855-3(6), 210705) Child's World, Inc., The.

Baldwin, James. Four Great Americans. 2006. pap. (978-1-4065-0509-2(9)) Dodo Pr.

Benchmark Education Company. George Washington & the American Revolution (Teacher Guide) 2005. (978-1-4108-4681-5(4)) Benchmark Education Co.

Biskup, Agnieszka. George Washington: The Rise of America's First President. Mallea, Cristian, illus. 2012. (American Graphic Ser.). (ENG.). 32p. (gr. 3-4). pap. 47.70 (978-1-4296-9335-6(5)); lib. bdg. 30.65 (978-1-4296-8621-1(9)) Capstone Press of Coughlan Cos. (Graphic Library).

Biskup, Agnieszka Jòzefina. George Washington: The Rise of America's First President, 1 vol. Mallea, Cristian, illus. 2012. (American Graphic Ser.). (ENG.). 32p. (gr. 3-4). pap. 8.10 (978-1-4296-9334-9(7), Graphic Library) Capstone Press of Coughlan Cos.

Botones para el General Washington (Buttons for General Washington) 2006. (J). pap. 6.95 (978-0-8225-6617-5(6), Ediciones Lerner) Lerner Publishing Group.

Boyd, Bentley. George Washington Leads the Way. 2011. (Mount Vernon Comix Ser.). (Illus.). 24p. (J). (gr. 3-9). pap. 6.95 (978-1-933122-44-1(7)) Chester Comix, LLC.

Boyd, Nicole. George Washington: Our First President. 2008. (Rosen Real Readers: Upper Emergent Ser.). (ENG., Illus.). 12p. (gr. 1-2). pap. 5.90 (978-0-8239-8205-9(X)) Rosen Publishing Group, Inc., The.

Brannon, Barbara. Discover George Washington. 2005. (J). pap. (978-1-4108-5158-1(3)) Benchmark Education Co.

Britton, Tamara L. George Washington, 1 vol. 2009. (United States Presidents Ser.). (ENG., Illus.). 40p. (YA). (gr. 3-6). 27.07 (978-1-60453-479-5(6)) ABDO Publishing Co.

Brown, Don. Dolley Madison Saves George Washington. Brown, Don, illus. 2007. (ENG., Illus.). 32p. (J). (gr. -1-3). 16.00 (978-0-618-41199-3(2)) Houghton Mifflin Harcourt Publishing Co.

Calkhoven, Laurie. George Washington: An American Life. 2007. (Sterling Biographies(r) Ser.). (ENG., Illus.). 128p. (J). pap. 5.95 (978-1-4027-3546-2(4)) Sterling Publishing Co., Inc.

Carr, Aaron. Washington Monument. 2013. (J). (978-1-62127-205-2(2)); pap. (978-1-62127-209-0(5)) Weigl Pubs., Inc.

Castrovilla, Selene. Revolutionary Friends: General George Washington & the Marquis de Lafayette. Kozjan, Drazen, illus. 2013. (ENG.). 40p. (J). (gr. 3). 16.95 (978-1-59078-880-6(X), Calkins Creek) Boyds Mills Pr.

Chandra, Deborah & Comora, Madeleine. George Washington's Teeth. Cole, Brock, illus. 2007. (ENG.). 40p. (J). (gr. -1-3). pap. 7.99 (978-0-312-37604-8(9), 9780312376048) Square Fish.

Cheney, Lynne. When Washington Crossed the Delaware: A Wintertime Story for Young Patriots. Fiore, Peter M., illus. 2012. (ENG.). 40p. (J). (gr. k-4). 7.99 (978-1-4424-4423-2(1), Simon & Schuster/Paula Wiseman Bks.) Simon & Schuster/Paula Wiseman Bks.

Cheney, Lynne & Fiore, Peter. When Washington Crossed the Delaware: A Wintertime Story for Young Patriots. 2004. (ENG., Illus.). 32p. (J). (gr. k-4). 19.99 (978-0-689-87043-9(4), Simon & Schuster/Paula Wiseman Bks.) Simon & Schuster/Paula Wiseman Bks.

Coleman, Wim & Perrin, Pat. George Washington: Creating a Nation. 2004. (America's Founding Fathers Ser.). (Illus.). 128p. (J). lib. bdg. 26.60 (978-0-7660-2290-4(0)) Enslow Pubs., Inc.

Collard, Sneed B., III. American Heroes, 6 vols., Group 3. Incl. Cesar Chavez: The Farm Workers' Best Friend. 29.93 (978-0-7614-4055-0(0)); George Washington: Our First President. 29.93 (978-0-7614-4060-4(7)); Jacob Lawrence: A Painter's Story. 29.93 (978-0-7614-4058-1(5)); Lady Bird Johnson: Keeping America Green. 29.93 (978-0-7614-4056-7(9)); Phillis Wheatley: She Loved Words. 29.93 (978-0-7614-4057-4(7)); Sitting Bull: Tatanka-Iyotake. 29.93 (978-0-7614-4059-8(3)); 48p. (gr. 3-18). (American Heroes 3 Ser.). 2009. Set lib. bdg. 179.57 o.p. (978-0-7614-4054-3(2)) Marshall Cavendish Corp.

—George Washington: Our First President. 2009. (American Heroes Ser.). 48p. (gr. 3-18). 29.93 (978-0-7614-4060-4(7)) Marshall Cavendish Corp.

Collier, James Lincoln. The George Washington You Never Knew. Copeland, Greg, illus. 2004. (You Never Knew Ser.). (ENG.). 80p. (J). (gr. 4-6). pap. 6.95 (978-0-516-25833-1(8), Children's Pr.) Scholastic Library Publishing.

Corporate Contibutor Staff & Aloian, Molly. George Washington: Hero of the American Revolution. 2012. (ENG.). 48p. (J). (978-0-7787-0799-8(7)) Crabtree Publishing Co.

Cosson, Jody. George Washington: 1st U. S. President, 1 vol. Soud, illus. 2008. (Beginner Biographies Ser.). (ENG.). 32p. (gr. -1-3). 28.50 (978-1-60270-253-0(5), Looking Glass Library- Nonfiction) Magic Wagon.

Crabtree Staff & Aloian, Molly. George Washington: Hero of the American Revolution. 2012. (ENG., Illus.). 48p. (J). pap. (978-0-7787-0810-0(1)) Crabtree Publishing Co.

Dayton, Connor. Presidents' Day. 2012. (American Holidays Ser.). (ENG., Illus.). 24p. (J). (gr. k-3). pap. 8.25 (978-1-4488-6242-9(6)); lib. bdg. 22.60 (978-1-4488-6142-2(X)) Rosen Publishing Group, Inc., The. (PowerKids Pr.).

Dean, Arlan. Crossing the Delaware: George Washington & the Battle of Trenton. 2009. (Great Moments in American History Ser.). 32p. (gr. 3-3). 47.90 (978-1-61513-140-2(X)) Rosen Publishing Group, Inc., The.

Dean, Sheri. Presidents Day/dia de los Presidentes. 2006. (Our Country's Holidays/ Las fiestas de nuestra nacion Ser.). (SPA., Illus.). 24p. (gr. k-3). lib. bdg. 22.00 (978-0-8368-6522-6(7), Weekly Reader Leveled Readers) Stevens, Gareth Publishing LLLP.

DeRubertis, Barbara. Let's Celebrate Presidents' Day: George Washington & Abraham Lincoln. Griffith, Gershom, illus. 2014. (Holidays & Heroes Ser.). 32p. (J). (gr. 1-3). pap. 7.95 (978-1-57565-649-6(3)) Kane Press, Inc.

Dipiazza, Francesca. When Did George Washington Fight His First Military Battle? And Other Questions about the French & Indian War. 2011. (Six Questions of American History Ser.). (ENG.). 48p. (gr. 4-6). pap. 56.72 (978-0-7613-7643-9(7)) Lerner Publishing Group.

DiPiazza, Francesca Davis. When Did George Washington Fight His First Military Battle? And Other Questions about the French & Indian War. 2011. (Six Questions of American History Ser.). (ENG.). 48p. (gr. 4-6). 30.60 (978-0-7613-5329-4(1)); pap. 9.95 (978-0-7613-7492-3(2)) Lerner Publishing Group.

Doeden, Matt. George Washington: Leading a New Nation. Martin, Cynthia, illus. 2005. (Graphic Biographies Ser.). (ENG.). 32p. (gr. 3-4). 30.65 (978-0-7368-4963-0(7), Graphic Library) Capstone Press of Coughlan Cos.

Dolan, Edward F. George Washington. 2007. (Presidents & Their Times Ser.). (Illus.). 96p. (gr. 6-7). lib. bdg. 34.21 (978-0-7614-2427-7(X), Benchmark Bks.) Marshall Cavendish Corp.

Duling, Kaitlyn. George Washington. 2017. (J). **(978-1-5026-2784-1(1))** Cavendish Square Publishing.

Dyan, Penelope. This Is the House George Built! a Kid's Guide to Mount Vernon. Weigand, John D., photos by. 2009. (Illus.). 44p. pap. 11.95 (978-1-935118-83-1(8)) Bellissima Publishing, LLC.

Earl, Sari. George Washington: Revolutionary Leader & Founding Father, 1 vol. 2010. (Military Heroes Ser.). (ENG.). 112p. (J). (gr. 6-12). lib. bdg. 35.64 (978-1-60453-967-7(4)) ABDO Publishing Co.

Edison, Erin. George Washington, 1 vol. (Presidential Biographies Ser.). (ENG.). 24p. (gr. k-1). 2014. pap. 6.29 (978-1-4765-9631-0(X), Pebble Bks.) 2012. (Illus.). lib. bdg. 26.65 (978-1-4296-8737-9(1), Pebble Plus) Capstone Press of Coughlan Cos.

Edwards, Roberta. Hail to the Chiefs, 5 vols. 2013. (Who Was? Ser.). (ENG.). 560p. (J). (gr. 3-7). pap. 24.95 (978-0-448-48122-7(7), Grosset & Dunlap) Penguin Young Readers Group.

—Who Was George Washington? Kelley, True & Harrison, Nancy, illus. 2009. (Who Was? Ser.). (ENG.). 112p. (J). (gr. 3-7). pap. 5.99 (978-0-448-44892-3(0), Grosset & Dunlap) Penguin Young Readers Group.

—Who Was George Washington? 2009. (Who Was... ? Ser.). lib. bdg. 16.00 (978-0-606-04042-6(0), Turtleback) Turtleback Bks.

Egan, Tracie. George Washington: Padre de la Patria. 2004. (Grandes personajes en la historia de los Estados Unidos Ser.). (SPA.). 32p. (gr. 3-6). pap. 10.00 (978-0-8239-4229-9(5), Rosen Classroom) Rosen Publishing Group, Inc., The.

—George Washington: Padre de la patria (George Washington: Father of the American Nation) 2009. (Grandes personajes en la historia de los Estados Unidos (Famous People in American History) Ser.). (SPA.). 32p. (gr. 2-3). 47.90 (978-1-61512-800-6(X), Editorial Buenas Letras) Rosen Publishing Group, Inc., The.

—George Washington: The Father of the American Nation. (Primary Sources of Famous People in American History Ser.). 32p. 2009. (gr. 2-3). 47.90 (978-1-60851-683-4(0)) 2004. (ENG., Illus.). (gr. 4-8). pap. 10.00 (978-0-8239-4183-4(3)) Rosen Publishing Group, Inc., The.

Espinosa, Rod. George Washington, 1 vol. Espinosa, Rod, illus. 2007. (Bio-Graphics Ser.). (ENG., Illus.). 32p. (gr. 3-7). 28.50 (978-1-60270-067-3(2), Graphic Planet- Nonfiction) ABDO Publishing Co.

Finegan, Jeffrey E., Sr. Colonel Washington & Me: George Washington, His Slave William Lee & Their Incredible Journey Together. Nikolopoulos, Stephanie, ed. 2012. (ENG., Illus.). 32p. (J). 16.95 (978-0-9852819-0-8(1)) Seigle Bks.

Ford, Carin T. George Washington: The First President. 2003. (Heroes of American History Ser.). (Illus.). 32p. (J). (gr. 1-4). lib. bdg. 22.60 (978-0-7660-1999-7(3)) Enslow Pubs., Inc.

Freedman, Russell. Washington at Valley Forge. 2008. (ENG., Illus.). 80p. (J). (gr. 4-7). 24.95 (978-0-8234-2069-8(8)) Holiday Hse., Inc.

Gaff, Jackie. George Washington: The Life of an American Patriot. 2005. (Graphic Nonfiction Biographies Ser.). (ENG., Illus.). 48p. (YA). (gr. 4-7). lib. bdg. 31.95 (978-1-4042-0236-8(6)) Rosen Publishing Group, Inc., The.

Gedacht, Daniel C. George Washington: Leader of a New Nation. (Library of American Lives & Times Ser.). 112p. 2009. (gr. 5-5). 69.20 (978-1-60853-484-5(7)) 2005. (Illus.). (J). (gr. 4-8). lib. bdg. 34.60 (978-0-8239-6622-6(4)) Rosen Publishing Group, Inc., The.

George Washington: A Life of Leadership. 2006. (J). pap. 5.95 (978-0-8225-5696-1(0)) Lerner Publishing Group.

Goddu, Krystyna Poray. George Washington's Presidency. 2016. (Presidential Powerhouses Ser.). (ENG., Illus.). 104p. (J). (gr. 6-12). 35.99 (978-1-4677-7924-1(5)); 53.32 (978-1-4677-8598-3(9), Lerner Pubns.) Lerner Publishing Group.

Gosman, Gillian. George Washington. 2011. (Life Stories Ser.). (Illus.). 24p. (J). pap. 8.25 (978-1-4488-2751-0(5), PowerKids Pr.); (gr. 1-4). lib. bdg. 22.60 (978-1-4488-2581-3(4), PowerKids Pr.); (SPA & ENG., (gr. 1-4). lib. bdg. 22.60 (978-1-4488-3215-6(2)) Rosen Publishing Group, Inc., The.

Gragg, Rod. George Washington: An Interactive Biography, 1 vol. 2012. (ENG., Illus.). 48p. 34.95 (978-1-58980-894-2(0)) Pelican Publishing Co., Inc.

Gregory, Josh. George Washington: The 1st President. 2015. (First Look at America's Presidents Ser.). (ENG.). 24p. (J). (gr. -1-3). lib. bdg. 23.93 (978-1-62724-552-4(9)) Bearport Publishing Co., Inc.

Group/McGraw-Hill, Wright. George Washington: A Quiet Leader, 6 vols. (Book2WebTM Ser.). (gr. 4-8). 36.50 (978-0-322-04461-6(8)) Wright Group/McGraw-Hill.

Haldy, Emma E. George Washington. Bane, Jeff, illus. 2017. (My Early Library: My Itty-Bitty Bio Ser.). (ENG.). 24p. (J). (gr. k-1). lib. bdg. 28.50 (978-1-63472-152-3(7), 209180) Cherry Lake Publishing.

Hamilton, Lynn. Presidents' Day. 2015. (Illus.). 24p. (J). (978-1-5105-0116-4(9)) SmartBook Media, Inc.

—Presidents' Day. (American Celebrations Ser.). (Illus.). 24p. (J). 2010. (gr. 3-5). pap. 11.95 (978-1-60596-931-2(1)) 2010. (gr. 3-5). lib. bdg. 18.99 (978-1-60596-773-8(4)) 2004. (gr. 1-3). lib. bdg. 24.45 (978-1-59036-108-5(3)) 2004. (gr. 1-3). per. 8.95 (978-1-59036-169-6(5)) Weigl Pubs., Inc.

Hansen, Grace. George Washington, 1 vol. 2014. (United States President Biographies Ser.). (ENG.). 24p. (J). (gr. 4-8). lib. bdg. 28.50 (978-1-62970-089-2(4)) ABDO Publishing Co.

—George Washington. 2015. (Biografías de Los Presidentes de Los Estados Unidos Ser.). (SPA., Illus.). 24p. (gr. k-1). pap. 7.95 (978-1-4966-0409-5(1)) Capstone Classroom.

Harness, Cheryl. George Washington. 2006. (ENG., Illus.). 48p. (J). (gr. 4-7). per. 8.99 (978-0-7922-5490-4(2), National Geographic Children's Bks.) National Geographic Society.

Herweck, Dona. George Washington, 1 vol. 2nd rev. ed. 2013. (Nonfiction Readers Ser.). (ENG., Illus.). 28p. (J). (gr. 2-2). pap. 23.96 (978-1-4807-1061-0(X)) Shell Educational Publishing.

—George Washington, 1 vol. 2nd rev. ed. 2011. (Nonfiction Readers Ser.). (ENG.). 28p. (J). (gr. 2-2). pap. 6.99 (978-1-4333-3640-9(5)) Teacher Created Materials, Inc.

Hollar, Sherman, contrib. by. George Washington. 2012. (Pivotal Presidents: Profiles in Leadership Ser.). (ENG.). 80p. (YA). (gr. 7-12). lib. bdg. 32.90 (978-1-61530-939-9(X)); (Illus.). 65.80 (978-1-61530-956-6(X)) Rosen Publishing Group, Inc., The.

Hort, Lenny. George Washington: A Photographic Story of a Life. 2005. (DK Biography Ser.). (ENG., Illus.). 128p. (J). (gr. 5-12). pap. 6.99 (978-0-7566-0835-4(X), DK Children) Dorling Kindersley Publishing, Inc.

Houran, Lori Haskins. My Little Golden Book about George Washington. Garofoli, Viviana, illus. 2016. (Little Golden Book Ser.). (ENG.). 24p. (J). (-k). 4.99 (978-1-101-93969-7(9), Golden Bks.) Random Hse. Children's Bks.

Jeffrey, Gary. George Washington & the Winter at Valley Forge. 2011. (Graphic Heroes of the American Revolution Ser.). 24p. (J). (gr. 3-8). pap. 8.15 (978-1-4339-6014-7(1), Gareth Stevens Learning Library); (Illus.). lib. bdg. 23.95 (978-1-4339-6174-8(1)) Stevens, Gareth Publishing LLLP.

Joseph, Natalie. Visit the Washington Monument. 2012. (Landmarks of Liberty Ser.). (Illus.). 24p. (J). (gr. 2-5). pap. 8.15 (978-1-4339-6406-0(6), Gareth Stevens Learning Library); (ENG., lib. bdg. 22.60 (978-1-4339-6404-6(X)) Stevens, Gareth Publishing LLLP.

Jurmain, Suzanne Tripp. George Did It. Day, Larry, illus. 2007. (ENG.). 40p. (J). (gr. k-4). pap. 6.99 (978-0-14-240895-7(6), Puffin Books) Penguin Young Readers Group.

—George Did It. Day, Larry, illus. 2007. (gr. -1-3). 17.00 (978-0-7569-8161-7(1)) Perfection Learning Corp.

Kaiser, Lori. George Washington. Kaiser, Lori, illus. 2012. (Illus.). 26p. pap. (978-0-9836651-7-5(6)) Roxby Media Ltd.

Katz, Vladimir. A Timeline of the Life of George Washington. 2009. (Timelines of American History Ser.). 32p. (gr. 4-4). 47.90 (978-1-60854-388-5(9), Rosen Reference) Rosen Publishing Group, Inc., The.

Kawa, Katie. 20 Fun Facts about George Washington. 2017. (Fun Fact File: Founding Fathers Ser.). 32p. (gr. 2-3). pap. 63.00 **(978-1-5382-0272-2(7))** Stevens, Gareth Publishing LLLP.

Keating, Frank. George: George Washington, Our Founding Father. Wimmer, Mike, illus. 2012. (Mount Rushmore Presidential Ser.). (ENG.). 32p. (J). (gr. 1-4). 17.99 (978-1-4169-5482-8(1), Simon & Schuster/Paula Wiseman Bks.) Simon & Schuster/Paula Wiseman Bks.

Kirkman, Marissa. The Life & Times of George Washington & the American Revolution. 2016. (Life & Times Ser.). (ENG., Illus.). 24p. (gr. 1-2). lib. bdg. 25.32 (978-1-5157-2476-6(X), First Facts) Capstone Press of Coughlan Cos.

Kraus, Stephanie. George Washington & His Right-Hand Man (Alexander Hamilton) 2017. (Primary Source Readers Focus

On Ser.). (Illus.). 32p. (J). (gr. 4-8). pap. 8.99 ***(978-1-4258-6356-2(6))*** Teacher Created Materials, Inc.

Kravitz, Danny. The Untold Story of Washington's Surprise Attack: The Daring Crossing of the Delaware River. 2015. (What You Didn't Know about the American Revolution Ser.). (ENG.). 64p. (gr. 4-8). 34.65 *(978-0-7565-4973-2(6))* Compass Point Bks.

Krensky, Stephen. George Washington's First Victory. Hearn, Diane Dawson, illus. 2005. (Ready-To-read COFA Ser.). (ENG.). 32p. (J). (gr. k-2). pap. 3.99 *(978-0-689-85942-7(2)*, Simon Spotlight) Simon Spotlight.

Landau, Elaine. General Washington Crosses the Delaware: Would You Join the American Revolution? 2015. (What Would You Do? Ser.). 48p. (J). (gr. 3-4). 25.27 *(978-0-7660-6315-0(1))*; pap. 8.95 *(978-0-7660-6316-7(X)*, Enslow Elementary) Enslow Pubs., Inc.

—George Washington Crosses the Delaware: Would You Risk the Revolution? (What Would You Do? Ser.). (Illus.). 48p. (J). 2010. pap. 8.95 *(978-1-59845-195-5(2))* 2008. (gr. 3-4). lib. bdg. 25.27 *(978-0-7660-2904-0(2))* Enslow Pubs., Inc. (Enslow Elementary).

—The Washington Monument. 2004. (Cornerstones of Freedom Ser.). (ENG.). 48p. (YA). (gr. 4-7). 26.00 *(978-0-516-24238-5(5))* Scholastic Library Publishing.

Leighton, Marian. George Washington. Salvador, Martin, illus. 2005. (Heroes of America Ser.). 239p. (gr. 3-8). 27.07 *(978-1-59679-262-3(0)*, Abdo & Daughters) ABDO Publishing Co.

Levin, Jack E. & Levin, Mark R. George Washington: The Crossing. 2013. (ENG., Illus.). 64p. 18.00 *(978-1-4767-3193-3(4)*, Threshold Editions) Threshold Editions.

Levy, Janey. Slavery at Mount Vernon. 2016. (Hidden History Ser.). 00032p. (J). pap. 10.50 *(978-1-4824-5802-2(0))* Stevens, Gareth Publishing LLLP.

Lusted, Marcia Amidon. Revolution & the New Nation: 1750-Early 1800s. 2007. (Presidents of the United States Ser.). (Illus.). 48p. (J). (gr. 4-7). lib. bdg. 29.05 *(978-1-59036-739-1(1))*; per. 10.95 *(978-1-59036-740-7(5))* Weigl Pubs., Inc.

Malaspina, Ann. Phillis Sings Out Freedom: The Story of George Washington & Phillis Wheatley. Keeter, Susan, illus. 2012. (J). 34.28 *(978-1-61913-149-1(8))* Weigl Pubs., Inc.

Maloof, Torrey. George Washington & the Men Who Shaped America. 2016. (Primary Source Readers Ser.). (Illus.). 32p. (J). (gr. 4-5). pap. 8.99 *(978-1-4938-3081-7(3))* Teacher Created Materials, Inc.

Manolis, Kay & Todd, Anne. George Washington: A Life of Self-Discipline. 2007. (People of Character Ser.). (ENG., Illus.). 24p. (J). (gr. 2-5). lib. bdg. 25.95 *(978-1-60014-094-5(7))* Bellwether Media.

Mara, Wil. George Washington. 2013. (Rookie Biographies(tm) Ser.). (ENG.). 32p. (J). lib. bdg. 25.00 *(978-0-531-24736-5(8))*; pap. 5.95 *(978-0-531-24702-0(3))* Scholastic Library Publishing.

Marcovitz, Hal. Liberty Bell: Let Freedom Ring. 2015. (Illus.). 48p. (J). *(978-1-4222-3117-3(8))* Mason Crest.

—The Washington Monument. 2004. (American Symbols & Their Meanings Ser.). (Illus.). 48p. (J). (gr. 4-18). lib. bdg. 19.95 *(978-1-59084-028-3(3))* Mason Crest.

—Washington Monument: Memorial to a Founding Father. Moreno, Barry, ed. 2014. (Patriotic Symbols of America Ser.: 20). 48p. (J). (gr. 4-18). lib. bdg. 20.95 *(978-1-4222-3137-1(2))* Mason Crest.

Margaret, Amy. Presidents' Day. 2009. (Library of Holidays Ser.). 24p. (gr. 2-3). 42.50 *(978-1-60853-716-7(1)*, PowerKids Pr.) Rosen Publishing Group, Inc., The.

Martin, Justin. Easy Reader Biographies: George Washington: George Washington. 2007. (ENG.). 16p. pap. 2.99 *(978-0-439-92331-6(X)*, Teaching Resources) Scholastic, Inc.

Massie, Elizabeth. George Washington. 2016. (Spring Forward Ser.). (J). (gr. 1). *(978-1-4900-9409-0(1))* Benchmark Education Co.

McClafferty, Carla Killough. Buried Lives: Slaves of George Washington's Mount Vernon. 2017. (J). ***(978-0-8234-3697-2(7))*** Holiday Hse., Inc.

McClafferty, Carla Killough. The Many Faces of George Washington: Remaking a Presidential Icon. 2011. (Exceptional Social Studies Titles for Intermediate Grades). (ENG.). 120p. (gr. 3-6). lib. bdg. 20.95 *(978-0-7613-5608-0(8))* Lerner Publishing Group.

McPherson, Stephanie Sammartino. Martha Washington: Legendary First Lady of the United States. 2015. (Legendary American Biographies Ser.). 96p. (J). (gr. 6-12). 27.94 *(978-0-7660-6475-1(1))* Enslow Pubs., Inc.

Mead, David. Little George Washington Learns about Responsibility: Responsibility. Sharp, Chris, illus. 2004. (American Virtues for Kids Ser.). (J). bds. 6.95 *(978-0-9746440-1-1(3)*, Ideal Pubns.) Worthy Publishing.

Meloche, Renee Taft. Heroes of History for Young Readers - George Washington: America's Patriot. Pollard, Brian, illus. 2006. (Heroes of History Ser.). (ENG.). 32p. 8.99 *(978-1-932096-28-6(0))* Emerald Bks.

—Heroes of History for Young Readers - George Washington Carver: America's Scientist. Pollard, Bryan, illus. 2006. (Heroes for Young Readers Ser.). (ENG.). 32p. (gr. 1-4). 8.99 *(978-1-932096-17-0(5))* Emerald Bks.

Meltzer, Brad. I Am George Washington. Eliopoulos, Christopher, illus. 2016. (Ordinary People Change the World Ser.). (ENG.). 40p. (J). (gr. k-3). 14.99 *(978-0-525-42848-0(8)*, Dial Bks) Penguin Young Readers Group.

Micklos, John. Crossing the Delaware & Valley Forge: Two Wild Winters with Washington. 2008. (Revolutionary War Library). (Illus.). 48p. (J). (gr. 3-4). lib. bdg. 25.27 *(978-0-7660-3017-6(2)*, Enslow Elementary) Enslow Pubs., Inc.

—The Making of the United States from Thirteen Colonies — Through Primary Sources. 2013. (American Revolution Through Primary Sources Ser.). 48p. (J). (gr. 4-18). 25.27 *(978-0-7660-4133-2(6))* Enslow Pubs., Inc.

—The Making of the United States from Thirteen Colonies—Through Primary Sources. 2013. (American Revolution Through Primary Sources Ser.). 48p. (J). (gr. 4-10). pap. 8.95 *(978-1-4644-0191-6(8))* Enslow Pubs., Inc.

—Washington's Crossing the Delaware & the Winter at Valley Forge: Through Primary Sources. 2013. (American Revolution Through Primary Sources Ser.). 48p. (J). (gr. 4-18). 25.27 *(978-0-7660-4132-5(8))* Enslow Pubs., Inc.

—Washington's Crossing the Delaware & the Winter at Valley Forge—Through Primary Sources. 2013. (American Revolution Through Primary Sources Ser.). 48p. (J). (gr. 4-10). pap. 8.95 *(978-1-4644-0190-9(X))* Enslow Pubs., Inc.

Micklos, John & Micklos, John, Jr. From Thirteen Colonies to One Nation. 2008. (Revolutionary War Library). (Illus.). 48p. (J). (gr. 3-7). lib. bdg. 25.27 *(978-0-7660-3015-2(6)*, Enslow Elementary) Enslow Pubs., Inc.

Miller, Brandon Marie. George Washington for Kids: His Life & Times - 21 Activities. 2007. (For Kids Ser.). (ENG., Illus.). 144p. (J). (gr. 4-7). pap. 16.95 *(978-1-55652-655-8(5))* Chicago Review Pr., Inc.

Miller, Chuck. George Washington. 2003. (America's Founders Ser.). (J). pap. *(978-1-58417-080-8(8))*; lib. bdg. *(978-1-58417-017-4(4))* Lake Street Pubs.

Mills, Nathan & Hill, Laura. George Washington Leads the Country. 2012. (Rosen Readers Ser.). (ENG., Illus.). 24p. (J). (gr. 1-2). pap. 8.25 *(978-1-4488-8767-5(4)*, Rosen Classroom) Rosen Publishing Group, Inc., The.

Mooney, Carla. George Washington: 25 Great Projects You Can Build Yourself. Carbaugh, Samuel, illus. 2010. (Build It Yourself Ser.). (ENG.). 128p. (J). (gr. 3-7). 21.95 *(978-1-934670-64-4(2))* Open City Bks.

Murphy, Frank. George Washington & the General's Dog. Walz, Richard, illus. 2015. 48p. pap. 5.00 *(978-1-61003-605-4(0))* Center for the Collaborative Classroom.

—George Washington & the General's Dog. 2003. (J). 1.25 *(978-1-4025-4103-2(1))* Recorded Bks., Inc.

Murphy, Jim. The Crossing: How George Washington Saved the American Revolution. 2016. (ENG.). 96p. (J). (gr. 4-7). pap. 14.99 *(978-0-439-69187-1(7))* Scholastic, Inc.

Murray, Robb. The Washington Monument: Myths, Legends, & Facts, 1 vol. 2014. (Monumental History Ser.). (ENG.). 32p. (gr. 3-4). 27.32 *(978-1-4914-0206-1(7)*, Fact Finders) Capstone Press of Coughlan Cos.

Nagle, Jeanne. How George Washington Fought the Revolutionary War. 2017. (Presidents at War Ser.). 128p. (J). (gr. 8-8). lib. bdg. 37.27 ***(978-0-7660-8523-7(6))*** Enslow Pubs., Inc.

National Geographic Kids Staff & Gilpin, Caroline Crosson. National Geographic Readers: George Washington. 2014. (Readers Bios Ser.). (ENG., Illus.). 32p. (J). (gr. k-3). pap. 3.99 *(978-1-4263-1468-1(X)*, National Geographic Children's Bks.) National Geographic Society.

Nelson, Maria. The Life of George Washington. 2012. (Famous Lives Ser.). (ENG.). 24p. (J). (gr. 1-4). pap. 8.15 *(978-1-4339-6351-3(5))* Stevens, Gareth Publishing LLLP.

—The Life of George Washington / la Vida de George Washington. 2012. (Famous Lives / Vidas extraordinarias Ser.). (ENG & SPA., Illus.). 24p. (J). (gr. k-3). 22.60 *(978-1-4339-6655-2(7))* Stevens, Gareth Publishing LLLP.

Nelson, Robin. George Washington: A Life of Leadership. 2006. (Pull Ahead Bks.). (Illus.). 32p. (J). (gr. 3-7). lib. bdg. 22.60 *(978-0-8225-3474-7(6)*, Lerner Pubns.) Lerner Publishing Group.

—George Washington: Una Vida de Liderazgo. 2006. (Libros para Avanzar Ser.). (ENG & SPA., Illus.). 32p. (J). (gr. 3-7). lib. bdg. 22.60 *(978-0-8225-6235-1(9)*, Ediciones Lerner) Lerner Publishing Group.

—George Washington: Una vida de liderazgo (A Life of Leadership) 2006. (Libros para Avanzar-Biografías (Pull Ahead Books-Biographies Ser.). (Illus.). 32p. (J). (gr. -1-3). per. 6.95 *(978-0-8225-6555-0(2)*, Ediciones Lerner) Lerner Publishing Group.

North, Sterling. George Washington: Frontier Colonel. (Great Leaders & Events Ser.). (ENG.). (J). (gr. 4-8). 2017. 208p. lib. bdg. 35.99 ***(978-1-942875-24-6(X))*** 2016. (Illus.). 175p. pap. 12.99 *(978-0-7603-5229-8(1))* Quarto Publishing Group USA. (Voyageur Pr.).

Norwich, Grace. I Am #5: George Washington. 2012. (I Am Ser.: 5). (ENG.). 128p. (J). (gr. 2-5). pap. 5.99 *(978-0-545-48435-0(9)*, Scholastic Paperbacks) Scholastic, Inc.

Olesen, Andrew. George Washington: The First President of the United States. 2015. (Spotlight on American History Ser.). (ENG., Illus.). 24p. (J). (gr. 4-6). pap. 10.00 *(978-1-4994-1751-7(9)*, PowerKids Pr.) Rosen Publishing Group, Inc., The.

Palazzo-Craig, Janet. The Making of the American Flag: Betsy Ross & George Washington. 2009. (Great Moments in American History Ser.). 32p. (gr. 3-3). 47.90 *(978-1-61513-155-6(8))* Rosen Publishing Group, Inc., The.

Parker, Christi E. George Washington, 1 vol. 2004. (Primary Source Readers Ser.). (ENG.). 24p. (J). (gr. 4-4). pap. 8.99 *(978-0-7439-8749-3(7))* Shell Educational Publishing.

Peacock, Louise. Crossing the Delaware: A History in Many Voices. Krudop, Walter Lyon, illus. 2007. (ENG.). 48p. (J). (gr. 3-7). 12.99 *(978-1-4169-5890-1(8)*, Simon & Schuster/Paula Wiseman Bks.) Simon & Schuster/Paula Wiseman Bks.

Pelleschi, Andrea. George Washington. 2012. (Jr. Graphic Founding Fathers Ser.). (ENG., Illus.). 24p. (J). (gr. 3-6). pap. 10.60 *(978-1-4488-7991-5(4))*; lib. bdg. 25.25 *(978-1-4488-7897-0(7))* Rosen Publishing Group, Inc., The. (PowerKids Pr.).

Pingry, Patricia A. Discover George Washington. 2005. (Discovery Readers Ser.). (ENG.). 32p. (J). pap. 4.35 *(978-0-8249-5505-2(6)*, Ideal Pubns.) Worthy Publishing.

—Meet George Washington. Britt, Stephanie McFetridge, illus. 2009. (ENG.). 32p. (J). pap. 7.99 *(978-0-8249-5612-7(5)*, Ideal Pubns.) Worthy Publishing.

—The Story of George Washington. Britt, Stephanie, illus. 2016. (J). *(978-0-8249-1973-3(4)*, Ideal Pubns.) Worthy Publishing.

Qaiser, Annie. How to Analyze the Works of George Washington, 1 vol. 2013. (Essential Critiques Set 4 Ser.). (ENG.). 112p. (J). (gr. 6-12). lib. bdg. 35.64 *(978-1-61783-645-9(1)*, Essential Library) ABDO Publishing Co.

Rand, Casey. George Washington, 1 vol. Oxford Bible Staff, illus. 2012. (American Biographies Ser.). (ENG.). 48p. (gr. 4-6). lib. bdg. 32.65 *(978-1-4329-6452-8(6)*, NA-h) Heinemann-Raintree.

Ransom, Candice. George Washington & the Story of the U. S. Constitution. Reeves, Jeni, illus. 2011. (History Speaks: Picture Books Plus Reader's Theater Ser.). 48p. pap. 56.72 *(978-0-7613-7632-3(1))*; (ENG.). (gr. 2-4). 27.93 *(978-0-7613-5877-0(3)*, Millbrook Pr.); (ENG.). (gr. 2-4). pap. 9.95 *(978-0-7613-7116-8(8))* Lerner Publishing Group.

Rauf, Don. Washington's Farewell Address. 2016. (Let's Find Out! Primary Sources Ser.). 00032p. (J). (gr. 2-3). lib. bdg. 24.45 *(978-1-5081-0407-0(7))* Rosen Publishing Group, Inc., The.

RJF Publishing Staff & Schaffer, Julia. The Washington Monument. 2009. (Symbols of American Freedom Ser.). 48p. (gr. 4-6). 30.00 *(978-1-60413-517-6(4)*, Chelsea Clubhouse) Facts On File, Inc.

Rockwell, Anne. Big George: How a Shy Boy Became President Washington. Phelan, Matt, illus. 2015. (ENG.). 48p. (J). (gr. 1-4). pap. 8.99 *(978-0-544-58246-0(2)*, HMH Books For Young Readers) Houghton Mifflin Harcourt Publishing Co.

Rockwell, Anne F. Big George: How a Shy Boy Became President Washington. Trueman, Matthew & Phelan, Matt, illus. 2009. (ENG.). 48p. (J). (gr. 1-4). 17.99 *(978-0-15-216583-3(5))* Houghton Mifflin Harcourt Publishing Co.

Roop, Peter & Roop, Connie. Botones Para el General Washington. Hanson, Peter E., illus. 2006. (Yo Solo - Historia (on My Own - History) Ser.).Tr. of Buttons for General Washington. (SPA.). 48p. (gr. 2-4). lib. bdg. 25.26 *(978-0-8225-6261-0(8))* Lerner Publishing Group.

—Buttons for General Washington, 4 bks., Set. unabr. ed. 2007. (Readalongs for Beginning Readers Ser.). (J). (gr. 2-3). pap. 37.95 incl. audio *(978-1-59519-931-7(4))* Live Oak Media.

—Buttons for General Washington, 4 bks., Set. Hanson, Peter E., illus. unabr. ed. 2007. (Readalongs for Beginning Readers Ser.). (J). (gr. 2-3). pap. 39.95 incl. audio compact disk *(978-1-59519-935-5(7))* Live Oak Media.

Saddleback Educational Publishing Staff, ed. George Washington, 1 vol. unabr. ed. 2008. (Graphic Biographies Ser.). (ENG., Illus.). 25p. (YA). (gr. 9-12). pap. 7.95 *(978-1-59905-223-6(7))* Saddleback Educational Publishing, Inc.

Schanzer, Rosalyn. George vs. George: The American Revolution as Seen from Both Sides. 2007. (ENG., Illus.). 64p. (J). (gr. 4-7). per. 6.95 *(978-1-4263-0042-4(5)*, National Geographic Children's Bks.) National Geographic Society.

—George vs. George: The Revolutionary War as Seen by Both Sides. 2004. (ENG., Illus.). 64p. (J). (gr. 4-7). 25.90 *(978-0-7922-6999-1(3))*; 16.95 *(978-0-7922-7349-3(4))* National Geographic Society. (National Geographic Children's Bks.).

Schubert, Barbara. George Washington. 2009. pap. 13.25 *(978-1-60559-060-8(6))* Hameray Publishing Group, Inc.

Smith-Llera, Danielle. The Presidency of George Washington: Inspiring a Young Nation, 1 vol. 2014. (Greatest U. S. Presidents Ser.). (ENG.). 64p. (gr. 5-7). lib. bdg. 33.99 *(978-0-7565-4928-2(0))* Compass Point Bks.

Snyder, Gail. George Washington. 2004. (Childhoods of the Presidents Ser.). (Illus.). 48p. (J). (gr. 4-18). lib. bdg. 17.95 *(978-1-59084-270-6(7))* Mason Crest.

St. George, Judith. Take the Lead, George Washington. Powers, Daniel, illus. 2015. (ENG.). 48p. (J). (gr. 2-4). 8.99 *(978-0-14-751446-2(0)*, Puffin Books) Penguin Young Readers Group.

Stevens, C. M. The Wonderful Story of Washington & Th. 2004. reprint ed. pap. 24.95 *(978-1-4179-2621-3(X))* Kessinger Publishing, LLC.

Strum, Richard. Henry Knox: Washington's Artilleryman. 2006. (Forgotten Heroes of the American Revolution Ser.). (Illus.). 88p. (J). (gr. 5-11). lib. bdg. 23.95 *(978-1-59556-013-1(0))* OTTN Publishing.

Strum, Richard M. Henry Knox: Washington's Artilleryman. 2006. (J). pap. *(978-1-59556-018-6(1))* OTTN Publishing.

Thomas, Peggy. Farmer George Plants a Nation. Johnson, Layne, illus. (ENG.). 40p. (J). (gr. 4-6). 2013. pap. 7.95 *(978-1-62091-029-0(2))* 2008. 17.95 *(978-1-59078-460-0(X))* Boyds Mills Pr. (Calkins Creek).

Venezia, Mike. George Washington. Venezia, Mike, illus. 2005. (Getting to Know the U. S. Presidents Ser.). (ENG., Illus.). 32p. (J). (gr. 3-4). pap. 7.95 *(978-0-516-27475-1(9)*, Children's Pr.) Scholastic Library Publishing.

Wachter, Joanne. George Washington & the American Revolution. 2005. (J). pap. *(978-1-4108-4633-4(4))* Benchmark Education Co.

Wade, Mary Dodson. Presidents' Day. 2016. (Story of Our Holidays Ser.). (Illus.). 32p. (J). pap. 10.52 *(978-0-7660-8345-5(4))* Enslow Pubs., Inc.

Weintraub, Aileen. Lee Sobre George Washington/Read about George Washington. 2006. (I Like Biographies! Bilingual Ser.). (ENG & SPA., Illus.). 24p. (J). (gr. 1-3). lib. bdg. 21.26 *(978-0-7660-2673-5(6)*, Enslow Elementary) Enslow Pubs., Inc.

—Read about George Washington. 2004. (I Like Biographies! Ser.). (Illus.). 24p. (J). lib. bdg. 22.60 *(978-0-7660-2301-7(X))* Enslow Pubs., Inc.

West, David. George Washington: The Life of an American Patriot. 2009. (Graphic Nonfiction Biographies Ser.). (Illus.). 48p. (YA). (gr. 4-5). 58.50 *(978-1-61513-017-7(9)*, Rosen Reference) Rosen Publishing Group, Inc., The.

Weston Woods Staff, creator. George Washington's Mother. 2011. 38.75 *(978-0-439-72669-6(7))*; 18.95 *(978-0-439-72667-2(0))* Weston Woods Studios, Inc.

Williamson, Mary. The Life of George Washington. 2004. (ENG.). 128p. per. 6.95 *(978-1-930367-91-3(0)*, CLP29870) Christian Liberty Pr.

Yoder, Carolyn P., compiled by. George Washington - The Writer: A Treasury of Letters, Diaries, & Public Documents. 2003. (ENG., Illus.). 144p. (J). (gr. 4-2). 16.95 *(978-1-56397-199-0(2))* Boyds Mills Pr.

WASHINGTON, GEORGE, 1732-1799—FICTION

Burgess, Linda, text. Mount Vernon's Magnificent Menagerie: And the Very Mysterious Guest. 2012. (ENG., Illus.). 48p. (J). 15.95 *(978-0-931917-31-8(X))* Mount Vernon Ladies' Assn. of the Union.

Cherry, Jason. Sassafras in the Window, 1 vol. 2009. 44p. pap. 24.95 *(978-1-61582-209-6(7))* America Star Bks.

Cullen, Lynn. Dear Mr. Washington. Carpenter, Nancy, illus. 2015. (ENG.). 32p. (J). (gr. k-3). 16.99 *(978-0-8037-3038-0(1)*, Dial Bks) Penguin Young Readers Group.

Grandpa Dennis, as told by. George Washington's Smallest Army: The Miracle Before Trenton. 2009. 216p. (J). pap. 17.49 *(978-1-4389-3147-0(6))* AuthorHouse.

Heald, Robin. Liberty Saves the Day! Elkerton, Andy, illus. 2017. (J). ***(978-0-87935-290-5(6))*** Colonial Williamsburg Foundation.

Hedstrom-Page, Deborah. From Colonies to Country with George Washington. Martinez, Sergio, illus. 2007. (My American Journey Ser.). 82p. (J). (gr. 3-9). 9.99 *(978-0-8054-3265-7(5))* B&H Publishing Group.

Hemphill, Kris. Ambush in the Wilderness. 2003. (Adventures in America Ser.). (Illus.). 90p. (gr. 4). 14.95 *(978-1-893110-34-2(6))* Silver Moon Pr.

Henry, Marguerite. Cinnabar, the One O'Clock Fox. Dennis, Wesley, illus. (ENG.). 144p. (J). (gr. 3-7). 2015. 19.99 *(978-1-4814-0401-3(6))* 2014. pap. 6.99 *(978-1-4814-0400-6(8))* Simon & Schuster Children's Publishing. (Aladdin).

Hutton, John. Flowers for Mr. President. 2012. (Illus.). (J). *(978-0-9789608-3-4(1))* Salem Academy & College.

Kalb, Deborah. The President & Me: George Washington & the Magic Hat, 1 vol. Lunsford, Robert, illus. 2016. (ENG.). 144p. (J). pap. 12.99 *(978-0-7643-5110-5(9)*, 9780764351105) Schiffer Publishing, Ltd.

Kennedy Center Staff. Chasing George Washington. Hoyt, Ard, illus. 2011. (ENG.). 80p. (J). (gr. 2-5). pap. 5.99 *(978-1-4169-4861-2(9)*, Simon & Schuster Bks. For Young Readers) Simon & Schuster Bks. For Young Readers.

Kidd, Ronald, et al. Chasing George Washington. Hoyt, Ard, illus. 2009. (ENG.). 80p. (J). (gr. 2-5). 12.99 *(978-1-4169-4858-2(9)*, Simon & Schuster Bks. For Young Readers) Simon & Schuster Bks. For Young Readers.

Klimo, Kate. Sweetie, No. 6. Jessell, Tim, illus. 2015. (Dog Diaries: 6). (ENG.). 160p. (J). (gr. 2-5). pap. 7.99 *(978-0-385-39240-2(0)*, Random Hse. Bks. for Young Readers) Random Hse. Children's Bks.

Limbaugh, Rush H., III & Limbaugh, Kathryn Adams. Rush Revere & the Presidency. 2016. (Rush Revere Ser.: 5). (ENG., Illus.). 272p. (gr. 4-7). 19.99 *(978-1-5011-5689-2(6)*, Threshold Editions) Threshold Editions.

McNamara, Margaret. George Washington's Birthday: A Mostly True Tale. Blitt, Barry, illus. 2012. (ENG.). 40p. (J). (gr. -1-3). 17.99 *(978-0-375-84499-7(6)*, Schwartz & Wade Bks.) Random Hse. Children's Bks.

Osborne, Mary Pope. Revolutionary War on Wednesday. unabr. ed. 2004. (Magic Tree House Ser.: No. 22). 69p. (J). (gr. k-3). pap. 17.00 incl. audio *(978-0-8072-0931-8(7)*, S FTR 254 SP, Listening Library) Random Hse. Audio Publishing Group.

Perry, Fred. Time Lincoln, Vol. 1. 2011. (ENG.). 122p. (YA). pap., pap. 19.95 *(978-0-9831823-7-5(X)*, 9780983182375) Antarctic Pr., Inc.

Potter, David. The Left Behinds: the IPhone That Saved George Washington. 2016. (Left Behinds Ser.). (ENG.). 368p. (J). (gr. 3-7). 7.99 *(978-0-385-39059-0(9)*, Yearling) Random Hse. Children's Bks.

Rinaldi, Ann. The Family Greene. 2011. (ENG.). 256p. (YA). (gr. 7). pap. 14.95 *(978-0-547-57723-4(0))* Houghton Mifflin Harcourt Publishing Co.

—Taking Liberty: The Story of Oney Judge, George Washington's Runaway Slave. Dudash, C. Michael, illus. 2004. (ENG.). 272p. (YA). (gr. 7). mass mkt. 7.99 *(978-0-689-85188-9(X)*, Simon Pulse) Simon Pulse.

Roop, Peter & Roop, Connie. The Top-Secret Adventure of John Darragh, Revolutionary War Spy. 2010. pap. 51.02 *(978-0-7613-6923-3(6))* Lerner Publishing Group.

—The Top-Secret Adventure of John Darragh, Revolutionary War Spy. Trover, Zachary, illus. 2010. (History's Kid Heroes Ser.). (ENG.). 32p. (gr. 3-5). lib. bdg. 26.60 *(978-0-7613-6174-9(X))* Lerner Publishing Group.

Scieszka, Jon. Oh Say, I Can't See, No. 15. McCauley, Adam, illus. 2007. (Time Warp Trio Ser.: 15). (ENG.). 80p. (J). (gr. 2-4). 5.99 *(978-0-14-240808-7(5)*, Puffin Books) Penguin Young Readers Group.

Stratemeyer, Edward. With Washington in the West or A Soldier Boy's Battles in the Wilderness. Shute, A. B., illus. 2004. reprint ed. pap. 30.95 *(978-1-4179-2977-1(4))* Kessinger Publishing, LLC.

Turner, Diane D. My Name Is Oney Judge. Massey, Cal, illus. 2010. (J). pap. *(978-0-88378-321-4(5))* Third World Press.

—My Name Is Oney Judge. Massey, Call, illus. 2010. (ENG.). 40p. (J). 19.95 *(978-0-88378-304-7(5))* Third World Press.

WASHINGTON, MARTHA, 1731-1802

Larkin, Tanya. What Was Cooking in Martha Washington's Presidential Mansion? 2009. (Cooking Throughout American History Ser.). 24p. (gr. 3-3). 42.50 *(978-1-61511-953-0(1)*, PowerKids Pr.) Rosen Publishing Group, Inc., The.

Lee, Sally. Martha Washington, 1 vol. 2010. (First Ladies Ser.). (ENG.). 24p. (gr. k-1). pap. 7.29 *(978-1-4296-5605-4(0))*; pap. 41.70 *(978-1-4296-5606-1(9))*; lib. bdg. 26.65 *(978-1-4296-5011-3(7))* Capstone Press of Coughlan Cos. (Pebble Plus).

Manera, Alexandria. Martha Washington. 2003. (Women of the Revolution Ser.). (J). pap. *(978-1-58417-087-7(5))*; lib. bdg. *(978-1-58417-024-2(7))* Lake Street Pubs.

Mattern, Joanne. Martha Washington, 1 vol. 2008. (First Ladies Set 1 Ser.). (ENG., Illus.). 32p. (gr. 1-4). 27.07 *(978-1-59928-801-7(X))* ABDO Publishing Co.

McPherson, Stephanie Sammartino. Martha Washington: Legendary First Lady of the United States. 2015. (Legendary American Biographies Ser.). 96p. (J). (gr. 6-12). 27.94 *(978-0-7660-6475-1(1))* Enslow Pubs., Inc.

Ransom, Candice. Martha Washington. Ritz, Karen, illus. 2003. (On My Own Biographies Ser.). 48p. (J). 25.26 *(978-0-87614-918-8(2))*; (ENG.). (gr. 2-4). per. 6.95 *(978-0-87614-107-6(6))* Lerner Publishing Group. (Carolrhoda Bks.).

WASHINGTON (D.C.)

Alter, Judy. Washington, D. C. A MyReportLinks. Com Book. 2003. (States Ser.). (Illus.). 48p. (J). lib. bdg. 25.26

WXYZ

(978-0-7660-5137-9(4), MyReportLinks.com Bks.) Enslow Pubs., Inc.

Benchmark Education Company. The United States Government (Teacher Guide) 2005. (978-1-4108-4640-2(7)) Benchmark Education Co.

Braithwaite, Jill. The White House. 2003. (Pull Ahead Books-American Symbols Ser.). (ENG., Illus.). 32p. (gr. k-3). pap. 7.95 (978-0-8225-3758-8(3)); lib. bdg. 22.60 (978-0-8225-3800-4(8)) Lerner Publishing Group.

Brown, Vanessa. District of Columbia. 2009. (Bilingual Library of the United States of America Ser.). (ENG & SPA.). 32p. (gr. 2-2). 47.90 (978-1-60853-351-0(4), Editorial Buenas Letras) Rosen Publishing Group, Inc., The.

—District of Columbia/Distrito de Columbia. 2005. (Bilingual Library of the United States of America Ser.: Set 1). (ENG & SPA., Illus.). 32p. (J). (gr. 3-6). lib. bdg. 25.25 (978-1-4042-3072-9(6)) Rosen Publishing Group, Inc., The.

Carr, Aaron. Lincoln Memorial. 2013. (J). (978-1-62127-202-1(8)); pap. (978-1-62127-206-9(0)) Weigl Pubs., Inc.

—Washington Monument. 2013. (J). (978-1-62127-205-2(2)); pap. (978-1-62127-209-0(5)) Weigl Pubs., Inc.

Clark, Diane C., et al. A Kid's Guide to Washington, D. C. Brown, Richard, illus. rev. ed. 2008. (ENG.). 160p. (J). (gr. 1-4). pap. 15.99 (978-0-15-206125-8(8)) Houghton Mifflin Harcourt Publishing Co.

Danis Drouot, Lucile, illus. Washington D. C. Monsters: A Search-And-Find Book. 2017. (ENG.). 22p. (J). (gr. -1). bds. 9.99 **(978-2-924734-06-3(1))** City Monsters Bks. CAN. Dist: Publishers Group West (PGW).

Douglas, Lloyd G. The White House. 2003. (Welcome Bks.). (ENG., Illus.). 24p. (J). (gr. -1-2). pap. 4.95 (978-0-516-27878-0(9), Children's Pr.) Scholastic Library Publishing.

Eldridge, Alison & Eldridge, Stephen. The White House: An American Symbol. 2012. (All about American Symbols Ser.). 24p. (J). (gr. -1-16). 22.60 (978-0-7660-4062-5(3), Enslow Elementary) Enslow Pubs., Inc.

Elish, Dan. Washington, D. C. 2nd rev. ed. 2006. (Celebrate the States Ser.). (Illus.). 144p. (gr. 6-7). lib. bdg. 42.79 (978-0-7614-2352-2(4), Benchmark Bks.) Marshall Cavendish Corp.

Falk, Laine. What's in Washington, D. C. ? 2009. (Scholastic News Nonfiction Readers Ser.). 24p. (J). (ENG.). pap. 6.95 (978-0-531-22429-8(5)); (gr. 1-2). 22.00 (978-0-531-21092-5(8)) Scholastic Library Publishing.

Farris, Christine King. March On! The Day My Brother Martin Changed the World. Ladd, London, illus. 2011. (J). (gr. 2-7). 29.95 (978-0-545-10689-4(3)) Weston Woods Studios, Inc.

Figueroa, Acton. Washington, D. C. 2003. (World Almanac Library of the States). (Illus.). 48p. (gr. 4-9). pap. 14.05 (978-0-8368-5333-9(4)); lib. bdg. 31.00 (978-0-8368-5162-5(5)) Stevens, Gareth Publishing LLLP. (Gareth Stevens Learning Library).

Gamble, Adam. Good Night Washington, DC. Veno, Joe, illus. 2006. (Good Night Our World Ser.). (ENG.). 20p. (J). (gr. k — 1). bds. 9.95 (978-0-9777979-1-2(0)) Good Night Bks.

Gelletly, LeeAnne. The Mid-Atlantic States: Delaware, Maryland, & Washington, D. C. 2015. (Let's Explore the States Ser.). (Illus.). 64p. (J). (gr. 5). 23.95 (978-1-4222-3327-6(8)) Mason Crest.

Group/McGraw-Hill, Wright. Washington D. C. Heartbeat of a Nation, 6 vols. (Book2WebTM Ser.). (gr. 4-8). 36.50 (978-0-322-04457-9(X)) Wright Group/McGraw-Hill.

Hargrove, Julia. Tomb of the Unknowns. 2003. (Historic Monuments Ser.). (Illus.). 48p. (J). pap. 6.95 (978-1-57310-405-0(1)) Teaching & Learning Co.

Hicks, Terry Allan. Washington, D. C. 2006. (It's My State! Ser.). (Illus.). 80p. (J). (gr. 4-7). lib. bdg. 29.93 (978-0-7614-1929-7(2), Benchmark Bks.) Marshall Cavendish Corp.

—Washington D.C. 2014. (J). lib. bdg. (978-1-62712-242-9(7)) Cavendish Square Publishing.

Hicks, Terry Allan & Waring, Kerry Jones. Washington, D. C. 2016. (It's My State! (r) Ser.). 80p. (J). (gr. 4-4). 34.21 (978-1-62713-253-4(8)) Cavendish Square Publishing.

Hill, Isabel. Urban Animals of Washington, D. C. Hill, Isabel, photos by. 2013. (ENG., Illus.). (J). 17.99 (978-1-59572-658-2(6)) Star Bright Bks., Inc.

Horn, Geoffrey M. Washington, D. C. 2006. (Portraits of the States Ser.). (Illus.). 32p. (gr. 2-6). pap. 10.50 (978-0-8368-4695-9(8)); lib. bdg. 26.00 (978-0-8368-4676-8(1)) Stevens, Gareth Publishing LLLP. (Gareth Stevens Learning Library).

Johnson, Etta. The United States Government. 2005. (J). pap. (978-1-4108-4592-4(3)) Benchmark Education Co.

Johnston, Joyce. Washington D. C. 2nd exp. rev. ed. 2003. (Hello U. S. A. Ser.). (Illus.). 84p. (J). (gr. 3-6). 25.26 (978-0-8225-4091-5(6), Lerner Pubns.) Lerner Publishing Group.

—Washington, D.C. 2012. (J). lib. bdg. 25.26 (978-0-7613-4492-6(6), Lerner Pubns.) Lerner Publishing Group.

Kent, Deborah. Washington D. C. rev. ed. 2011. (America the Beautiful, Third Ser.). (ENG.). 144p. (J). pap. 12.95 (978-0-531-22915-6(7), Children's Pr.) Scholastic Library Publishing.

Landolfi, Meghan Ann. Washington, D. C. 2003. (Rosen Real Readers: Upper Emergent Ser.). (ENG., Illus.). 12p. (gr. 1-2). per. 5.90 (978-0-8239-6356-0(X)) Rosen Publishing Group, Inc., The.

Linde, Barbara M. Building Washington, D. C. Measuring the Area of Rectangular Spaces. 2009. (PowerMath Ser.). (Illus.). 32p. (gr. 4-5). pap. 10.00 (978-0-8239-8867-9(8), PowerKids Pr.) Rosen Publishing Group, Inc., The.

—Building Washington, DC: Measuring the Area of Rectangular Shapes. 2004. (PowerMath: Proficiency Ser.). (Illus.). 32p. (YA). (gr. 5-9). lib. bdg. 25.25 (978-0-8239-8980-5(1)) Rosen Publishing Group, Inc., The.

Lusted, Marcia Amidon. The District of Columbia: The Nation's Capital. 2010. (Our Amazing States Ser.). (ENG.). 24p. (J). pap. 8.25 (978-1-4488-0772-7(7)); lib. bdg. 22.60 (978-1-4488-0667-6(4)) Rosen Publishing Group, Inc., The. (PowerKids Pr.).

Marcovitz, Hal. The Lincoln Memorial. 2004. (American Symbols & Their Meanings Ser.). (Illus.). 48p. (J). (gr. 4-18). lib. bdg. 19.95 (978-1-59084-029-0(1)) Mason Crest.

—The Washington Monument. 2004. (American Symbols & Their Meanings Ser.). (Illus.). 48p. (J). (gr. 4-18). lib. bdg. 19.95 (978-1-59084-028-3(3)) Mason Crest.

—The White House. 2004. (American Symbols & Their Meanings Ser.). (Illus.). 48p. (J). (gr. 4-18). lib. bdg. 19.95 (978-1-59084-024-5(0)) Mason Crest.

Mattern, Joanne. Washington, D. C., 1 vol. 2007. (Cities Set 2 Ser.). (ENG., Illus.). 32p. (gr. -1-3). 27.07 (978-1-59679-725-3(8), Checkerboard Library) ABDO Publishing Co.

Melmed, Laura Krauss. Capital! Washington D. C. from A to Z. Lessac, Frané, illus. 2006. (ENG.). 48p. (J). (gr. 1-6). 6.99 (978-0-06-113614-6(X), Collins) HarperCollins Pubs.

Parker, Bridget. Washington, D.C. 2016. (States Ser.). (ENG., Illus.). 32p. (gr. 3-4). lib. bdg. 27.32 (978-1-5157-0436-2(X)) Next Page Pr., The.

Rappoport, Bernice. The Community of Washington, D. C. Set Of 6. 2010. (Navigators Ser.). (J). pap. 44.00 net. (978-1-4108-5094-2(3)) Benchmark Education Co.

—The Community of Washington, D. C. Text Pairs. 2008. (BridgesNavigators Ser.). (J). (gr. 3). 81.00 (978-1-4108-8356-8(6)) Benchmark Education Co.

Ribke, Simone T. Washington, D. C. Hamilton, Harriet, tr. 2006. (Rookie Espanol: Geografia: Estados (Geography: States) Ser.). (SPA., Illus.). 31p. (J). (gr. k-2). per. 5.95 (978-0-516-25049-6(3), Children's Pr.) Scholastic Library Publishing.

—Washington, D. C. 2005. (Rookie Español Geografía Ser.). (ENG & SPA., Illus.). 32p. (J). (gr. k-2). lib. bdg. 19.50 (978-0-516-25248-3(8), Children's Pr.) Scholastic Library Publishing.

Robertson, Charles & Broun, Elizabeth. American Louvre: A History of the Renwick Gallery Building. 2015. (ENG., Illus.). 108p. pap. 24.95 (978-1-907804-81-6(1)) Giles, D. Ltd. GBR. Dist: Consortium Bk. Sales & Distribution.

Segal, Robin. ABC in Washington, DC. 2007. (All 'Bout Cities Ser.). (ENG.). 32p. (J). (gr. k — 1). 12.95 (978-0-9719697-7-3(9)) Murray Hill Bks., LLC.

Slate, Jennifer. The United States Capitol. 2006. (Primary Sources of American Symbols Ser.). (Illus.). 24p. (J). (gr. 4-7). lib. bdg. 22.60 (978-1-4042-2694-4(X)) Rosen Publishing Group, Inc., The.

—The White House. 2006. (Primary Sources of American Symbols Ser.). (Illus.). 24p. (J). (gr. 4-7). lib. bdg. 22.60 (978-1-4042-2695-1(8)) Rosen Publishing Group, Inc., The.

Sterling Children's, Sterling & Schader Lee, Susan. Secrets of Our Nation's Capital: Weird & Wonderful Facts about Washington, DC. 2016. (ENG., Illus.). 160p. (J). (gr. 1-3). 8.95 (978-1-4549-2003-8(3)) Sterling Publishing Co., Inc.

Swain, Gwenyth. Riding to Washington. Geister, David, illus. 2007. (Tales of Young Americans Ser.). (ENG.). 32p. (YA). (gr. 6-12). 17.95 (978-1-58536-324-7(3)) Sleeping Bear Pr.

Weintraub, A. How to Draw District of Columbia's Sights & Symbols. 2009. (Kid's Guide to Drawing America Ser.). 32p. (gr. k-k). 50.50 (978-1-61511-053-7(4), PowerKids Pr.) Rosen Publishing Group, Inc., The.

Zschock, Martha Day. Journey Around Washington D. C. from A to Z. 2004. (Journeys Ser.: Bk. 5). (Illus.). 32p. (J). (gr. 1-6). 17.95 (978-1-889833-62-0(2), Commonwealth Editions) Applewood Bks.

WASHINGTON (D.C.)—CAPITOL

see United States Capitol (Washington, D.C.)

WASHINGTON (D.C.)—FICTION

Ali, Khayyam Esab. The Wormhole Kids Visit President Kennedy. 2004. (ENG., Illus.). 56p. (J). per. 7.95 (978-1-59526-231-8(8)) Aeon Publishing Inc.

Allison, Jennifer. The Dead Drop. (Gilda Joyce Ser.). (ENG.). 320p. (J). (gr. 5-18). 2010. 9.99 (978-0-14-241638-9(X), Puffin Books) 2009. 16.99 (978-0-525-47980-2(5), Dutton Books for Young Readers) Penguin Young Readers Group.

Amato, Mary. Invisible Lines. Caparo, Antonio, illus. 2011. (ENG.). 336p. (gr. 5). 7.99 (978-1-60684-187-7(4), Carolrhoda Bks.) Lerner Publishing Group.

Angleberger, Tom. Emperor Pickletine Rides the Bus. (Origami Yoda Ser.). (ENG., Illus.). (J). (gr. 3-7). 2016. 240p. pap. 7.95 (978-1-4197-2201-1(8)) 2014. 224p. 13.95 (978-1-4197-0933-3(X)) Abrams, Inc. (Amulet Bks.).

—Emperor Pickletine Rides the Bus. 2014. (Origami Yoda Files Ser.: 6). (J). lib. bdg. 25.70 (978-0-606-36168-2(5)) Turtleback Bks.

Barnes, Jennifer Lynn. The Fixer. (ENG.). (YA). 2016. 400p. pap. 9.99 (978-1-61963-598-2(4), 9781619635982) 2015. 384p. (gr. 7). 17.99 (978-1-61963-594-4(1), 9781619635944) Bloomsbury Publishing USA. (Bloomsbury USA Childrens).

Barnes, Peter W. Woodrow, the White House Mouse. Barnes, Cheryl Shaw, illus. 2012. (ENG.). 40p. (J). (gr. k-3). 16.95 (978-1-59698-788-3(X), Little Patriot Pr.) Regnery Publishing, Inc., An Eagle Publishing Co.

Barry, Dave. The Worst Class Trip Ever. 2015. (Class Trip Ser.). (ENG.). 224p. (J). (gr. 3-7). 13.99 (978-1-4847-0849-1(0)) Disney Pr.

Battle, Cleaton D. A Saturday Surprise. Cooper, Emmanuel, illus. 2006. 68p. (J). pap. 11.95 (978-1-59663-504-3(5), Castle Keep Pr.) Rock, James A. & Co. Pubs.

Benchmark Education Co., LLC. A Trip to Washington, D. C. A Capital Idea Teacher's Guide. 2013. (Reader's Theater Word Plays Ser.). (978-1-4509-9037-0(1)) Benchmark Education Co.

Blackwood, Gary L. Second Sight. 2007. (Illus.). 279p. (J). (gr. 5-9). 14.65 (978-0-7569-8132-7(8)) Perfection Learning Corp.

Blackwood, Gary L. & Blackwood, Gary. Second Sight. 2007. (ENG.). 288p. (J). (gr. 5-18). 8.99 (978-0-14-240747-9(X), Speak) Penguin Young Readers Group.

Bond, Thomas A. Mill Creek Kids. 2009. 132p. pap. 14.99 (978-1-60791-634-5(7)) Salem Author Services.

Bowen, Carl. Back Burn. Lee, Marc, illus. 2016. (Firestormers Ser.). (ENG.). 112p. (gr. 4-8). lib. bdg. 26.65 (978-1-4965-3305-0(4)) Stone Arch Bks.

Bradford, Chris. Recruit, Bk. 1. 2017. (Bodyguard Ser.). (ENG.). 272p. (J). (gr. 5). pap. 8.99 (978-1-5247-3697-2(X), Philomel Bks.) Penguin Young Readers Group.

Bradley, F. T. Double Vision - Code Name 711. 2015. (Double Vision Ser.: 2). (ENG.). 272p. (J). (gr. 3-7). pap. 6.99 (978-0-06-210441-0(1)) HarperCollins Pubs.

Brezenoff, Steve. The Ghost Who Haunted the Capitol, 1 vol. Canga, C. B., illus. 2010. (Field Trip Mysteries Ser.). (ENG.). 88p. (gr. 2-3). 25.32 (978-1-4342-2140-7(7)); pap. 6.10 (978-1-4342-2772-0(3)) Stone Arch Bks.

Brown, Jeff. The U. S. Capital Commotion. Pamintuan, Macky, illus. 2011. (Flat Stanley's Worldwide Adventures Ser.: 9). (ENG.). 112p. (J). (gr. 2-5). pap. 4.99 (978-0-06-143019-0(6)) HarperCollins Pubs.

—The US Capital Commotion. Pamintuan, Macky, illus. 2011. (Flat Stanley's Worldwide Adventures Ser.: 9). (ENG.). 112p. (J). (gr. 2-5). 15.99 (978-0-06-157436-8(8)) HarperCollins Pubs.

Cabot, Meg. All-American Girl. 2008. (All-American Girl Ser.: 1). (ENG.). 416p. (YA). (gr. 8). pap. 8.99 (978-0-06-147989-2(6), HarperTeen) HarperCollins Pubs.

—All-American Girl. 2008. (All-American Girl Ser.: Vol. 1). 398p. (YA). (gr. 7-12). 19.65 (978-1-4178-2386-4(0), Turtleback) Turtleback Bks.

—Ready or Not. (All-American Girl Ser.: 2). 2008. (ENG.). 336p. (YA). (gr. 8). pap. 8.99 (978-0-06-147996-0(9), HarperTeen) 2005. (ENG.). 256p. (J). (gr. 7-18). 16.99 (978-0-06-072450-4(1)) 2nd ed. 2005. 256p. (J). (gr. 7-18). lib. bdg. 16.89 (978-0-06-072451-1(X)) HarperCollins Pubs.

Caletti, Deb. The Queen of Everything. Greenberg, Anne, ed. 2008. (ENG.). 352p. (YA). (gr. 7-12). pap. 8.99 (978-1-4169-5781-2(2), Simon Pulse) Simon Pulse.

Cobot, Meg. All-American Girl. 2004. 416p. (J). (gr. 7-18). pap. 44.00 incl. audio (978-0-8072-2281-2(X), Listening Library) Random Hse. Audio Publishing Group.

Cohn, Rachel. You Know Where to Find Me. (ENG.). (YA). (gr. 7). 2009. 224p. pap. 8.99 (978-0-689-87860-2(5)) 2008. 208p. 16.99 (978-0-689-87859-6(1)) Simon & Schuster Bks. For Young Readers. (Simon & Schuster Bks. For Young Readers).

Crawford, Laura. Postcards from Washington D. C./Postales Desde Washington D. C. de La Vega, Eida, tr. Adamson, Bonnie, illus. 2008. (Traveling with Anna Ser.). (ENG.). 32p. (J). (gr. 4-7). 16.95 (978-0-9795477-0-6(9)); per. 7.95 (978-0-9795477-1-3(7)) Continental Sales, Inc. (Raven Tree Pr.,Csi).

Davis, Rachel. My Life at Mapleleaf Cabin. 2nd ed. 2004. (YA). per. 10.00 (978-0-9741176-8-3(4)) Wu Li Turtle Corp.

De Los Heros, Luis & Wilson, Elizabeth. Chifa Chi's Little Adventure in Washington Dc. 2010. 40p. pap. 21.99 (978-0-557-23085-3(3)) Lulu Pr., Inc.

Deflitch, Jennifer L. Delia the Dragonfly's Grand Adventures: Delia Goes to Washington D. C. 2012. 28p. (-18). pap. 24.95 (978-1-62709-290-6(0)) America Star Bks.

DeVillers, Julia. Cleared for Takeoff. Pooler, Paige, illus. 2012. (Liberty Porter, First Daughter Ser.: 3). (ENG.). 224p. (J). (gr. 3-7). pap. 7.99 (978-1-4169-9131-1(X), Simon & Schuster/Paula Wiseman Bks.) Simon & Schuster/Paula Wiseman Bks.

—Liberty Porter, First Daughter. Pooler, Paige, illus. (Liberty Porter, First Daughter Ser.: 1). (ENG.). (J). (gr. 3-7). 2010. 192p. pap. 6.99 (978-1-4169-9127-4(1)) 2009. 176p. 15.99 (978-1-4169-9126-7(3)) Simon & Schuster/Paula Wiseman Bks. (Simon & Schuster/Paula Wiseman Bks.).

—New Girl in Town. Pooler, Paige, illus. 2011. (Liberty Porter, First Daughter Ser.: 2). (ENG.). 224p. (J). (gr. 3-7). pap. 6.99 (978-1-4169-9129-8(8), Simon & Schuster/Paula Wiseman Bks.) Simon & Schuster/Paula Wiseman Bks.

Ehrenberg, Pamela. Ethan, Suspended. 2009. (ENG.). 272p. (J). (gr. 6-9). pap. 8.50 (978-0-8028-5317-2(X)) 2007. 266p. (YA). (gr. 7-18). 16.00 (978-0-8028-5324-0(2), Eerdmans Bks For Young Readers) Eerdmans, William B. Publishing Co.

Elliott, L. M. Suspect Red. 2017. (ENG.). 304p. (J). (gr. 5-9). 16.99 **(978-1-4231-5754-0(0))** Hyperion Bks. for Children.

Emerson, Alice B. Betty Gordon in Washington. 2004. reprint ed. pap. 20.95 (978-1-4191-0977-5(4)); pap. 1.99 (978-1-4192-0977-2(9)) Kessinger Publishing, LLC.

Emmer, E. R. Me, Minerva & the Flying Flora. Huerta, Catherine, illus. 2nd rev. ed. 2003. (Going to Ser.). Orig. Title: Me, Minerva & the Flying Car. (ENG.). 133p. (J). (gr. 4-8). pap. 6.95 (978-1-893577-10-7(4)) Fruitbearer Publishing, LLC.

Evans, Shane W. We March. Evans, Shane W., illus. 2012. (ENG., Illus.). 32p. (J). (gr. -1-3). 16.99 (978-1-59643-539-1(9), 9781596435391) Roaring Brook Pr.

Ewing, Lynne. The Lure. 2014. (ENG.). 288p. (YA). (gr. 9). 17.99 (978-0-06-220688-6(5)) HarperCollins Pubs.

Fisher, Anne. Look What Brains Can Do! 2005. reprint ed. pap. 20.95 (978-1-4179-9453-3(3)) Kessinger Publishing, LLC.

Florence, Leigh Anne. Mr. Dogwood Goes to Washington. Asher, James, illus. 2008. (Woody the Kentucky Wiener Ser.). 56p. (J). (gr. 2-8). pap. 12.95 (978-0-9741417-5-6(5)) HotDiggetyDog Pr.

Flores-Scott, Patrick. Jumped In. 2013. (ENG.). 304p. (YA). (gr. 7). 16.99 (978-0-8050-9514-2(4), 9780805095142, Holt, Henry & Co. Bks. For Young Readers) Holt, Henry & Co.

—Jumped In. 2014. (ENG., Illus.). 304p. (YA). (gr. 7). pap. 10.99 (978-1-250-05398-5(6), 9781250053985) Square Fish.

Frederick, Heather Vogel. The Black Paw. 2013. (Spy Mice Ser.: 1). (ENG., Illus.). 224p. (J). (gr. 3-6). pap. 7.99 (978-1-4424-6701-9(0), Simon & Schuster Bks. For Young Readers) Simon & Schuster Bks. For Young Readers.

Freeman, Don & Freeman, Roy. One More Acorn. 2010. (ENG., Illus.). 32p. (J). (gr. -1-k). 16.99 (978-0-670-01083-7(9), Viking Books for Young Readers) Penguin Young Readers Group.

Freeman, Martha. The Case of the Bug on the Run. 2014. (First Kids Mystery Ser.: 6). (ENG.). 144p. (J). (gr. 2-7). pap. 6.99 (978-0-8234-3188-5(6)) Holiday Hse., Inc.

—The Case of the Bug on the Run: First Kids Mystery #6. 2013. (First Kids Mystery Ser.: 6). (ENG.). 144p. (J). (gr. 2-7). 16.95 (978-0-8234-2872-4(9)) Holiday Hse., Inc.

—The Case of the Diamond Dog Collar. 2nd ed. 2012. (First Kids Mystery Ser.: 2). (ENG., Illus.). 144p. (J). (gr. 3-5). pap. 6.99 (978-0-8234-2642-3(4)) Holiday Hse., Inc.

—The Case of the Missing Dinosaur Egg. Dibley, Glin, illus. 2014. (First Kids Mystery Ser.: 5). (ENG.). 115p. (J). (gr. 3-7). pap. 6.99 (978-0-8234-3061-1(8)) Holiday Hse., Inc.

—The Case of the Missing Dinosaur Egg. 2013. (First Kids Mystery Ser.: 5). (ENG.). 144p. (J). (gr. 3-7). 16.95 (978-0-8234-2523-5(1)) Holiday Hse., Inc.

—The Case of the Piggy Bank Thief. 2012. (First Kids Mystery Ser.: 4). (ENG.). 144p. (J). (gr. 1-5). 16.95 (978-0-8234-2517-4(7)) Holiday Hse., Inc.

—The Case of the Piggy Bank Thief: First Kids Mystery #4. 2013. (First Kids Mystery Ser.: 4). (ENG.). 144p. (J). (gr. 1-5). pap. 6.99 (978-0-8234-2916-5(4)) Holiday Hse., Inc.

—The Case of the Rock 'n' Roll Dog. 2012. (First Kids Mystery Ser.: 1). (ENG.). 128p. (J). (gr. 3-5). pap. 6.99 (978-0-8234-2549-5(5)) Holiday Hse., Inc.

—The Case of the Ruby Slippers. (First Kids Mystery Ser.: 3). (ENG.). 128p. (J). 2013. pap. 6.99 (978-0-8234-2764-2(1)) 2012. 16.95 (978-0-8234-2409-2(X)) Holiday Hse., Inc.

Friedman, Laurie. Red, White, & True Blue Mallory. Kalis, Jennifer, illus. (Mallory Ser.: 11). (ENG.). 184p. (J). (gr. 2-5). 2010. pap. 5.95 (978-0-7613-3946-5(9)) 2009. 15.95 (978-0-8225-8882-5(X)) Lerner Publishing Group. (Carolrhoda Bks.).

Furtney, Charles S. Tryconnel: An Antebellum Adventure along the C & O Canal. 2004. (Illus.). iii, 156p. (J). pap. (978-0-9711835-3-7(8)) Local History Co., The.

Gagnon, Michelle & Gangsei, Jan. Zero Day. 2016. (ENG., Illus.). 364p. (YA). (gr. 7-12). 17.99 (978-1-4847-2226-8(4)) Hyperion Bks. for Children.

Gibbs, Stuart. Spy School Secret Service. 2017. (J). pap. **(978-1-4814-7783-3(8)**, Simon & Schuster Bks. For Young Readers) Simon & Schuster Bks. For Young Readers.

Goguen, Martha. Sissy Goes to Washington. Fowler, Faith, illus. 2013. 36p. pap. (978-1-897435-59-5(2)) Agio Publishing Hse.

Goldsberry, Booty. Scaredy-Cat, I'm Not. 2007. (ENG., Illus.). 40p. (gr. 4-7). pap. 9.95 (978-0-9792875-0-3(2)) Goldsberry, Booty.

Gottesfeld, Jeff. Choices. 2014. (Campus Confessions Ser.: 3). (YA). lib. bdg. 20.80 (978-0-606-34000-7(9), Turtleback) Turtleback Bks.

—Frenemies. 2014. (Campus Confessions Ser.: 2). (YA). lib. bdg. 20.80 (978-0-606-33999-5(X), Turtleback) Turtleback Bks.

Green, S. E. Killer Instinct. 2014. (ENG., Illus.). 272p. (YA). (gr. 9). 17.99 (978-1-4814-0285-9(4), Simon Pulse) Simon Pulse.

—Killer Within. 2015. (ENG.). 304p. (YA). (gr. 9). 17.99 (978-1-4814-0288-0(9), Simon Pulse) Simon Pulse.

Harmon, Michael. Stick. 2015. (ENG.). 240p. (YA). (gr. 9). 17.99 (978-0-385-75436-1(1), Knopf Bks. for Young Readers) Random Hse. Children's Bks.

Harmon, Michael B. Under the Bridge. 2013. (ENG.). 272p. (YA). (gr. 9). pap. 8.99 (978-0-375-85930-4(6), Ember) Random Hse. Children's Bks.

Hicks, Deron R. The Van Gogh Deception. 2017. (ENG.). 320p. (J). (gr. 5-7). 16.99 (978-0-544-75927-5(3), HMH Books For Young Readers) Houghton Mifflin Harcourt Publishing Co.

Hoover, P. J. Tut: The Story of My Immortal Life. 2016. (Tut: My Immortal Life Ser.: 1). (ENG.). 320p. (J). pap. 9.99 (978-0-7653-8372-3(1), 9780765383723, Starscape) Doherty, Tom Assocs., LLC.

Hope, Laura Lee. The Bobbsey Twins in Washington. 2005. 27.95 (978-1-4218-0974-8(5), 1st World Library - Literary Society) 1st World Publishing, Inc.

—The Bobbsey Twins in Washington. 2007. 256p. 29.95 (978-1-4344-8591-5(9)); per. 17.95 (978-1-4344-8590-8(0)) Wildside Pr., LLC.

Horender, Philip M. Homeward Bound: Civil Rights Mouse Leader, 1 vol. Wolek, Guy, illus. 2013. (Maximilian P. Mouse, Time Traveler Ser.). (ENG.). 112p. (J). (gr. 3-6). lib. bdg. 27.07 (978-1-61641-962-2(8), Calico Chapter Bks) Magic Wagon.

Jacobs, Lily. The Littlest Bunny in Washington: An Easter Adventure. 2015. (ENG.). 32p. (J). (-3). 9.99 (978-1-4926-1231-5(6), Sourcebooks Jabberwocky) Sourcebooks, Inc.

—The Littlest Bunny in Washington, DC: An Easter Adventure. Dunn, Robert A., illus. 2015. (ENG.). 32p. (J). (-3). 9.99 (978-1-4926-1234-6(0), Sourcebooks Jabberwocky) Sourcebooks, Inc.

Jacobson, Darlene Beck. Wheels of Change. 2014. (ENG., Illus.). 180p. (J). (gr. 2-8). 12.95 (978-1-939547-13-2(X)) Creston Bks.

James, Eric. A Halloween Scare in Washington. Le Ray, Marina, illus. 2014. (ENG.). 32p. (J). (-5). 9.99 (978-1-4926-0639-0(1), 9781492606390, Sourcebooks Jabberwocky) Sourcebooks, Inc.

—A Halloween Scare in Washington, DC. Le Ray, Marina, illus. 2015. (ENG.). 32p. (J). (-5). 9.99 (978-1-4926-2408-0(X), 9781492624080, Sourcebooks Jabberwocky) Sourcebooks, Inc.

—Santa's Sleigh Is on Its Way to Washington. Dunn, Robert, illus. 2015. (ENG.). 32p. (J). (-2). 12.99 (978-1-4926-2760-9(7), Sourcebooks Jabberwocky) Sourcebooks, Inc.

—Santa's Sleigh Is on Its Way to Washington, D. C. A Christmas Adventure. Dunn, Robert, illus. 2016. (ENG.). 32p. (J). (-2). 12.99 (978-1-4926-4363-0(7), 9781492643630, Sourcebooks Jabberwocky) Sourcebooks, Inc.

Jennings, Terry Catasús. Gopher to the Rescue! A Volcano Recovery Story, 1 vol. O'Keefe, Laurie, illus. 2012. (ENG.). 32p. (J). (gr. -1-4). 17.95 (978-1-60718-131-6(2)); pap. 9.95 (978-1-60718-141-5(X)) Arbordale Publishing.

Johnson, Alaya Dawn. Love Is the Drug. 2014. (YA). pap. (978-0-545-41782-2(1)); (ENG.). 352p. (J). (gr. 9). 17.99 (978-0-545-41781-5(3), Levine, Arthur A. Bks.) Scholastic, Inc.

Keffer, Ann. The Seventh Chair. 2007. 76p. (J). per. 8.95 (978-0-595-45917-9(X)) iUniverse, Inc.

Kehret, Peg & the Cat, Pete. The Stranger Next Door. 2008. (Pete the Cat Ser.). (ENG.). 176p. (J). (gr. 3-7). 5.99 (978-0-14-241248-0(1), Puffin Books) Penguin Young Readers Group.

Kelly, Katy. Here's the Thing about Me. Rex, Adam, illus. 2006. (Lucy Rose Ser.). (ENG.). 160p. (J). (gr. 3-7). reprint ed. per. 6.99 (978-0-440-42026-2(1), Yearling) Random Hse. Children's Bks.

—Melonhead. Johnson, Gillian, illus. 2010. (Melonhead Ser.). (ENG.). 240p. (J). (gr. 3-7). 6.99 (978-0-440-42187-0(X), Yearling) Random Hse. Children's Bks.

—Melonhead & the Big Stink. 2011. (Melonhead Ser.). (ENG.). 224p. (J). (gr. 3-7). 6.99 (978-0-375-84527-7(5), Yearling) Random Hse. Children's Bks.
—Melonhead & the Undercover Operation. Johnson, Gillian, illus. 2012. (Melonhead Ser.). (ENG.). 256p. (J). (gr. 3-7). 7.99 (978-0-375-84528-4(3), Yearling) Random Hse. Children's Bks.
—Melonhead & the Vegalicious Disaster. Johnson, Gillian, illus. 2013. (Melonhead Ser.). (ENG.). 224p. (J). (gr. 3-7). 6.99 (978-0-307-92969-3(8), Yearling) Random Hse. Children's Bks.
—Working Myself to Pieces & Bits. Ferguson, Peter, illus. 2008. (Lucy Rose Ser.). (ENG.). 208p. (J). (gr. 3-7). 6.99 (978-0-440-42186-3(1), Yearling) Random Hse. Children's Bks.
Kogler, Jennifer Anne. The Siren's Cry. 2011. (ENG.). 384p. (YA). (gr. 8). 16.99 (978-0-06-199443-2(X), HarperTeen) HarperCollins Pubs.
Krishnaswami, Uma. The Problem with Being Slightly Heroic. Halpin, Abigail, illus. (ENG.). 288p. (J). (gr. 3-7). 2014. pap. 6.99 (978-1-4424-2329-9(3), Atheneum Bks. for Young Readers) 2013. 16.99 (978-1-4424-2328-2(5)) Simon & Schuster Children's Publishing.
Krulik, Nancy. Go Fetch! Braun, Sebastien, illus. 2014. (Magic Bone Ser.: 5). (ENG.). 128p. (J). (gr. 1-3). 4.99 (978-0-448-48094-7(8), Grosset & Dunlap) Penguin Young Readers Group.
—Go Fetch! 2014. (Magic Bone Ser.: 5). lib. bdg. 14.75 (978-0-606-35701-2(7)) Turtleback Bks.
Labrecque, Candida. A Riverside Walk with Grandma. Labrecque, Candida & Labrecque, Candida, illus. l.t. ed. 2006. (Illus.). 23p. (J). per. 11.95 (978-1-59879-137-2(0)) Lifevest Publishing, Inc.
Larson, Kirby. Audacity Jones to the Rescue. 2016. (Audacity Jones Ser.: 1). (ENG.). 224p. (J). (gr. 3-7). 16.99 (978-0-545-84056-9(2), Scholastic Pr.) Scholastic, Inc.
Leavitt, Lindsey. Have a Mice Flight! Ford, A. G., illus. 2016. (Commander in Cheese Ser.: 3). (ENG.). 112p. (J). (gr. 2-5). 4.99 (978-1-101-93118-9(3), Random Hse. Bks. for Young Readers) Random Hse. Children's Bks.
—Oval Office Escape. Ford, A. G., illus. 2016. (Commander in Cheese Ser.: 2). (ENG.). 112p. (J). (gr. 2-5). 4.99 (978-1-101-93115-8(9), Random Hse. Bks. for Young Readers) Random Hse. Children's Bks.
Lee, Jenny. Elvis & the Underdogs: Secrets, Secret Service, & Room Service. Light, Kelly, illus. 2014. (Elvis & the Underdogs Ser.: 2). (ENG.). 352p. (J). (gr. 3-7). 16.99 (978-0-06-223556-5(7)) HarperCollins Pubs.
Lee, Margaret A. Grandpa, What Are Lasers? 2012. 32p. pap. 19.99 (978-1-4685-6343-6(2)) AuthorHouse.
Leray, Merrill. The House of Lady Chase. 2009. 70p. pap. 15.99 (978-1-4415-4381-3(3)) Xlibris Corp.
Lewis, J. Patrick, et al. First Dog's White House Christmas. Bowers, Tim, illus. 2010. (ENG.). 32p. (J). (gr. 1-4). 15.95 (978-1-58536-503-6(3), 202197) Sleeping Bear Pr.
Lindbergh, Anne M. The People in Pineapple Place. 2011. (ENG.). 176p. (J). pap. 12.95 (978-1-56792-411-4(5)) Godine, David R. Pub.
Marchi, C. You Can Grow Old with Me: A True Story. 2011. 24p. (gr. -1). pap. 12.95 (978-1-4520-3716-5(7)) AuthorHouse.
Marciano, John Bemelmans. Madeline at the White House. (Madeline Ser.). (ENG.). (J). (gr. -1-2). 2016. Illus.). 48p. 8.99 (978-1-101-99780-2(X), Puffin Books) 2011. 45p. 17.99 (978-0-670-01228-2(9), Viking Books for Young Readers) Penguin Young Readers Group.
—Madeline at the White House. 2016. (Madeline Ser.). lib. bdg. 19.65 (978-0-606-38845-0(1)) Turtleback Bks.
Marsh, Carole. The White House Christmas Mystery. 2009. (Real Kids, Real Places Ser.). 146p. (J). 18.99 (978-0-635-06996-2(2), Marsh, Carole Mysteries) Gallopade International.
McCarthy, Peggy & Rivers, Julia. Not for the Meek. 2013. (ENG.). 130p. (J). pap. 10.95 (978-1-4327-9157-5(5)) Outskirts Pr., Inc.
Mcgill, Leslie. Fighter. 2014. (Cap Central Ser.: 1). (YA). lib. bdg. 20.80 (978-0-606-35737-1(8)) Turtleback Bks.
—Hacker. 2014. (Cap Central Ser.: 3). (YA). lib. bdg. 20.80 (978-0-606-35739-5(4)) Turtleback Bks.
—Running Scared. 2014. (Cap Central Ser.: 2). (YA). lib. bdg. 20.80 (978-0-606-35738-8(6)) Turtleback Bks.
McPherson, Missie & O'Neill, Elizabeth. Alfred Visits Washington, D. C. 2005. (ENG., Illus.). 24p. (J). (gr. -1-3). pap. 12.00 (978-0-9771836-1-6(0)) Lipp, G. Douglas & Assocs.
Meddaugh, Susan. White House Dog. 2011. (Martha Speaks Ser.). (ENG., Illus.). 96p. (J). (gr. 1-4). 14.99 (978-0-547-39359-9(8)); pap. 5.99 (978-0-547-21076-6(0)) Houghton Mifflin Harcourt Publishing Co.
Messner, Kate. Capture the Flag. 2013. (ENG.). 240p. (J). (gr. 3-7). pap. 6.99 (978-0-545-41974-1(3), Scholastic Paperbacks) Scholastic, Inc.
—Rolling Thunder. Ruth, Greg, illus. 2017. (ENG.). 32p. (J). (gr. -1-3). 17.99 (978-0-545-47012-4(9), Scholastic Pr.) Scholastic, Inc.
Metivier, Gary. Saluting Grandpa: Celebrating Veterans & Honor Flight. 1 vol. Rath, Robert, illus. 2012. (ENG.). 32p. (J). (gr. k-3). 16.99 (978-1-4556-1748-7(2)) Pelican Publishing Co., Inc.
Monroe, Ella. Truth or Dare. 2013. (Capital Girls Ser.: 3). (ENG.). 304p. (YA). (gr. 8). pap. 20.99 (978-0-312-62304-3(6), 9780312623043, St. Martin's Griffin) St. Martin's Pr.
Myers, Anna. Assassin. 2005. (J). (978-978-080-278-3(9)) Walker & Co.
Nez, John Abbott. The Twelve Days of Christmas in Washington. Nez, John Abbott, illus. 2011. (Twelve Days of Christmas in America Ser.). (ENG., Illus.). 40p. (J). (gr. k-3). 12.95 (978-1-4027-7068-5(5)) Sterling Publishing Co., Inc.
Osborne, Mary Pope. Abe Lincoln at Last! 2013. (Magic Tree House Merlin Missions Ser.: 19). lib. bdg. 16.00 (978-0-606-35563-6(4)) Turtleback Bks.
Patterson, James. Public School Superhero. 2015. (ENG., Illus.). 304p. (J). (gr. 3-7). 13.99 (978-0-316-32214-0(8), Jimmy Patterson) Little Brown & Co.
Patterson, James & Tebbetts, Chris. Public School Superhero. Thomas, Cory, illus. 2016. (ENG.). 304p. (J). (gr. 3-7). pap. 7.99 (978-0-316-26598-0(5), Jimmy Patterson) Little Brown & Co.
Patterson, James, et al. Public School Superhero. 2015. (978-0-316-34231-5(9)) Little, Brown Bks. for Young Readers.
Pellicioli, Anna. Where You End. 2015. (ENG.). 312p. (YA). pap. 9.99 (978-0-7387-4403-2(4), Flux) North Star Editions.
Ponti, James. Framed! 2016. (Framed! Ser.: 1). (ENG., Illus.). 304p. (J). (gr. 3-7). 17.99 (978-1-4814-3630-4(9), Aladdin) Simon & Schuster Children's Publishing.
Powell, Gail. The Adventures of Harold J. Kat. 2008. 40p. pap. 16.99 (978-1-4259-6334-7(X)) AuthorHouse.
Puck. 123 Washington, D. C. 2012. (Cool Counting Bks.). (ENG.). 22p. (J). (gr. k — 1). bds. 8.95 (978-0-9838121-0-4(1)) Duo Pr. LLC.
Ransom, Candice. The Twelve Days of Christmas in Washington, D. C. Hollander, Sarah, illus. 2010. (Twelve Days of Christmas in America Ser.). (ENG.). 40p. (J). (gr. k). 12.95 (978-1-4027-6394-6(8)) Sterling Publishing Co., Inc.
Rosenberg, Madelyn. Nanny X. 2015. (ENG., Illus.). 128p. (J). (gr. 2-5). 16.95 (978-0-8234-3533-3(4)) Holiday Hse., Inc.
Roy, Ron. The Election-Day Disaster. Bush, Timothy, illus. 2008. (Capital Mysteries Ser.: No. 10). 87p. (gr. 1-4). 15.00 (978-0-7569-8802-9(0)) Perfection Learning Corp.
—The Election-Day Disaster. Bush, Timothy, illus. 2008. (Capital Mysteries Ser.: No. 10). (ENG.). 96p. (J). (gr. 1-4). 4.99 (978-0-375-84805-6(3), Random Hse. Bks. for Young Readers) Random Hse. Children's Bks.
—Mystery at the Washington Monument. Bush, Timothy, illus. 2007. (Capital Mysteries Ser.: No. 8). 87p. (gr. 1-4). 15.00 (978-0-7569-7845-7(9)) Perfection Learning Corp.
—Mystery at the Washington Monument. Bush, Timothy, illus. 2007. (Capital Mysteries Ser.: No. 8). (ENG.). 96p. (J). (gr. 1-4). per. 4.99 (978-0-375-83970-2(4), Random Hse. Bks. for Young Readers) Random Hse. Children's Bks.
—The Skeleton in the Smithsonian. Bush, Timothy, illus. 2003. (Capital Mysteries Ser.: No. 3). (ENG.). 96p. (J). (gr. 1-4). 4.99 (978-0-307-26517-3(X), Random Hse. Bks. for Young Readers) Random Hse. Children's Bks.
—A Spy in the White House. Bush, Timothy, tr. Bush, Timothy, illus. 2004. (Capital Mysteries Ser.: No. 4). (ENG.). 96p. (J). (gr. 1-4). 4.99 (978-0-375-82557-6(6), Random Hse. Bks. for Young Readers) Random Hse. Children's Bks.
—A Thief at the National Zoo. Bush, Timothy, illus. 2008. (Capital Mysteries Ser.: No. 9). 87p. (gr. k-3). 15.00 (978-0-7569-8329-1(0)) Perfection Learning Corp.
—Trouble at the Treasury. Bush, Timothy, illus. 2006. (Capital Mysteries Ser.: No. 7). (ENG.). 96p. (J). (gr. 1-4). per. 4.99 (978-0-375-83969-6(0), Random Hse. Bks. for Young Readers) Random Hse. Children's Bks.
—White House White-Out. Gurney, John Steven, illus. 2008. (A to Z Mysteries Ser.: No. 3). 124p. (gr. 1-4). 15.00 (978-0-7569-8799-2(7)) Perfection Learning Corp.
—White House White-Out. Gurney, John Steven, illus. 2008. (to Z Mysteries Ser.: 3). (ENG.). 144p. (J). (gr. 1-4). 5.99 (978-0-375-84721-9(9), Random Hse. Bks. for Young Readers) Random Hse. Children's Bks.
—Who Broke Lincoln's Thumb? Bush, Timothy, illus. 2005. (Capital Mysteries Ser.: No. 5). (ENG.). 96p. (J). (gr. 1-4). per. 4.99 (978-0-375-82558-3(4), Random Hse. Bks. for Young Readers) Random Hse. Children's Bks.
Roy, Ronald. Turkey Trouble on the National Mall. Bush, Timothy, illus. 2012. (Capital Mysteries Ser.: 14). (ENG.). 96p. (J). (gr. 1-4). 4.99 (978-0-307-93220-4(6), Random Hse. Bks. for Young Readers) Random Hse. Children's Bks.
Rutledge, Eddie. Amani's World: Amani Goes to Washington D. C. Anderson, Susan, illus. 2009. 16p. pap. 8.75 (978-1-4490-2095-8(X)) AuthorHouse.
Salazar, L. J. Chin & the Magic Stones: Book One - Becoming Guardians. 2009. 108p. 20.95 (978-0-595-63627-3(6)); pap. 10.95 (978-0-595-53157-8(1)) iUniverse, Inc.
Sauls, Lynn B. Gabriel Goes to Washington: Through Big Brown Eyes; the Adventures of Gabriel the Poodle. Sauls, Lynn B., illus. 2013. (Illus.). 26p. pap. 9.99 (978-0-9893216-1-7(4)) Sauls, Lynn.
Scheffler, Stephanie. Elizabeth & the War of 1812. 2010. 292p. (YA). 28.95 (978-1-4502-3539-6(5)); (ENG.). pap. 18.95 (978-1-4502-3540-2(9)) iUniverse, Inc.
Silvano, Wendi. Love Is All Around Washington, DC. Czernichowska, Joanna, illus. 2016. (ENG.). 32p. (J). (-6). 12.99 (978-1-4926-2973-3(1), Sourcebooks Jabberwocky) Sourcebooks, Inc.
Skewes, John & Fox, Andrew. Larry Gets Lost in Washington, D. C. Skewes, John, illus. 2014. (Larry Gets Lost Ser.). (ENG., Illus.). 32p. (J). (gr. -1-2). 17.99 (978-1-57061-899-4(2), Little Bigfoot) Sasquatch Bks.
Skewes, John & Ode, Eric. Elliott the Otter: The Totally Untrue Story of Elliott Bay. Skewes, John, illus. 2015. (ENG., Illus.). 32p. (J). (gr. -1-2). 16.99 (978-1-57061-952-6(2), Little Bigfoot) Sasquatch Bks.
Slade, Suzanne. The House That George Built. Bond, Rebecca, illus. 2015. (ENG.). 32p. (J). (gr. 1-4). pap. 7.95 (978-1-58089-263-6(9)) Charlesbridge Publishing, Inc.
Smallman, Steve. Santa Is Coming to Washington. Dunn, Robert, illus. 2012. (ENG.). 32p. (J). (-3). 9.99 (978-1-4022-7524-1(2), Sourcebooks Jabberwocky) Sourcebooks, Inc.
—Santa Is Coming to Washington DC. Dunn, Robert, illus. 2013. (ENG.). 32p. (J). (-3). 9.99 (978-1-4022-8833-3(6), Sourcebooks Jabberwocky) Sourcebooks, Inc.
Smith, Lindsay. Skandal. 2015. (Sekret Ser.: Vol. 2). (ENG.). 336p. (YA). (gr. 7-12). 17.99 (978-1-62672-005-3(3), 9781626720053) Roaring Brook Pr.
—Skandal. 2016. (Sekret Ser.: 2). (ENG.). 352p. (YA). pap. 9.99 (978-1-250-07369-3(3), 9781250073693) Square Fish.
Smith, Roland. Beneath. 2015. (ENG., Illus.). 272p. (J). (gr. 4-7). 16.99 (978-0-545-56486-1(7), Scholastic Pr.) Scholastic, Inc.
Smith, Yeardley. I, Lorelei. 2009. 352p. (J). (gr. 3-7). lib. bdg. 17.89 (978-0-06-149345-4(7), Geringer, Laura Book) HarperCollins Pubs.
St. George, Judith. The Ghost, the White House & Me. 2007. (ENG.). 128p. (J). (gr. 4-7). 16.95 (978-0-8234-2045-2(0)) Holiday Hse., Inc.
Stewart, Emma. The Adventures of Fillmore the Gerbil. 2008. 24p. pap. 13.50 (978-1-60693-033-5(8), Eloquent Bks.) Strategic Book Publishing & Rights Agency (SBPRA).
Stinson, Kathy & Petricic, Dusan. The Man with the Violin. 2016. (ENG., Illus.). 32p. (J). (gr. k-3). pap. 9.95 (978-1-55451-564-6(5)) Annick Pr., Ltd. CAN. Dist: Publishers Group West (PGW).
Stossel, Sage. On the Loose in Washington, D. C. 2013. (ENG., Illus.). 28p. (J). (gr. -1-3). 14.95 (978-1-938700-14-9(7), Commonwealth Editions) Applewood Bks.
Sully, Katherine. Night-Night Washington. Poole, Helen, illus. 2017. (ENG.). 20p. (J). (-1). bds. 9.99 (978-1-4926-4766-9(7), 9781492647669, Sourcebooks Jabberwocky) Sourcebooks, Inc.
Sutton, Margaret. The Discovery at Dragon's Mouth, No. 31. Doane, Pelagie, illus. 2008. (Judy Bolton Mysteries Ser.). (ENG.). 196p. (J). (gr. 4-7). pap. 14.95 (978-1-4290-9051-3(0)) Applewood Bks.
—The Whispered Watchword, No. 32. Doane, Pelagie, illus. 2008. (Judy Bolton Mysteries Ser.). (ENG.). 196p. (J). (gr. 4-7). pap. 14.95 (978-1-4290-9052-0(9)) Applewood Bks.
Swain, Gwenyth. Voices for Freedom. Frankenhuyzen, Gijsbert van et al, illus. 2013. (American Adventures Ser.). (ENG.). 72p. (J). (gr. 3-6). 6.99 (978-1-58536-886-0(5), 202900) Sleeping Bear Pr.
Thomson, Melissa. Keena Ford & the Field Trip Mix-Up. 2010. (Keena Ford Ser.). (ENG.). 112p. (J). (gr. 1-3). 5.99 (978-0-14-241572-6(3), Puffin Books) Penguin Young Readers Group.
Trueman, Terry. No Right Turn. 2009. (ENG.). 176p. (YA). (gr. 9). pap. 8.99 (978-0-06-057493-2(3), HarperTeen) HarperCollins Pubs.
Turnage, Cyndy. A Trip to Washington, D. C. A Capital Idea. Fagan, Martin, illus. 2013. (Reader's Theater Word Plays Ser.). (J). (gr. 1-2). (978-1-4509-8941-1(1)) Benchmark Education Co.
Warner, Penny. The Hunt for the Missing Spy. 2016. (Code Busters Club Ser.: 5). (ENG.). 168p. (gr. 3-6). (J). 16.99 (978-1-5124-0304-6(0)); 33.32 (978-1-5124-0305-3(9)) Lerner Publishing Group.
Wildavsky, Rachel. The Secret of Rover. Caparo, Antonio, illus. (ENG.). 368p. (J). (gr. 3-7). 2015. pap. 7.95 (978-1-4197-1968-4(8)) 2011. 17.95 (978-0-8109-9710-3(X)) Abrams, Inc. (Amulet Bks.).
Wiles, Deborah. Countdown. (ENG.). 400p. (J). 2013. (gr. 3-7). pap. 8.99 (978-0-545-10606-1(0), Scholastic Paperbacks) 2010. (gr. 4-7). 19.99 (978-0-545-10605-4(2), Scholastic Pr.) Scholastic, Inc.
Yasso, C. D. The Adventures of Penn & Penelope in Washington, Dc. 2012. 32p. pap. 15.75 (978-1-105-64108-4(2)) Lulu Pr., Inc.
Ziefert, Harriet & National Geographic Learning Staff. I'm Going to Washington to Visit the President. Roitman, Tanya, illus. 2010. (Rise & Shine Ser.). (ENG.). 24p. (C). (gr. -1-k). pap. 6.95 (978-1-4027-3408-3(5)) National Geographic School Publishing, Inc.

WASHINGTON (D.C.)—HISTORY

Aretha, David. The Story of the Civil Rights March on Washington for Jobs & Freedom in Photographs. 2014. (Story of the Civil Rights Movement in Photographs Ser.). 48p. (J). lib. bdg. 25.27 (978-0-7660-4238-4(3)) Enslow Pubs., Inc.
Barger, Jeff. Washington D.C. 2016. (Dropping in On Ser.). (ENG., Illus.). 32p. (gr. 2-4). 32.79 (978-1-68191-405-3(0)) Rourke Educational Media.
Bolden, Tonya. Capital Days: Michael Shiner's Journal & the Growth of Our Nation's Capital. 2015. (ENG., Illus.). 96p. (J). (gr. 3-7). 21.95 (978-1-4197-0733-9(7), Abrams Bks. for Young Readers) Abrams, Inc.
Brown, Don. Dolley Madison Saves George Washington. Brown, Don, illus. 2007. (ENG., Illus.). 32p. (J). (gr. -1-3). 16.00 (978-0-618-41199-3(2)) Houghton Mifflin Harcourt Publishing Co.
Carole Marsh. Washington Dc Coloring & Activity Book. 2004. (City Bks.). 24p. (gr. k-5). pap. 3.95 (978-0-635-02232-5(X)) Gallopade International.
—Washington Indians. 2004. (Washington Experienc Ser.). lib. bdg. 29.95 (978-0-635-02339-1(3)); 36p. (gr. 3-8). pap. 7.95 (978-0-635-02338-4(5)) Gallopade International.
Cunningham, Alvin Robert. Washington Is Burning! The War of 1812. 2003. (Reading Essentials in Social Studies). (Illus.). 48p. (J). 9.00 (978-0-7891-5896-3(5)) Perfection Learning Corp.
Durrie, Karen. District of Columbia: The Nation's Capital. 2012. (J). 27.13 (978-1-61913-337-2(7)); pap. 27.13 (978-1-61913-338-9(5)) Weigl Pubs., Inc.
Dyan, Penelope. Abraham Lincoln Was Here! a Kid's Guide to Washington D C. Weigand, John D., photos by. 2009. (Illus.). 44p. pap. 11.95 (978-1-935118-82-4(X)) Bellissima Publishing, LLC.
Epstein, Brad M. Washington D. C. 101: My First City-Board-book. l.t. ed. 2009. (ENG., Illus.). 24p. (J). 9.95 (978-1-60730-004-5(4), 101 Bk.) Michaelson Entertainment.
Esbaum, Jill. Cherry Blossoms Say Spring. 2012. (ENG., Illus.). (J). (gr. -1-3). pap. 5.95 (978-1-4263-0984-7(8), National Geographic Children's Bks.) National Geographic Society.
Fejtö, Raphaël. Fork. 2016. (Little Inventions Ser.). (ENG., Illus.). 32p. (J). (gr. 3-5). 9.95 (978-1-77085-745-2(1), 9781770857452) Firefly Bks., Ltd.
Figley, Marty Rhodes. Washington Is Burning. Orback, Craig, illus. (On My Own History Ser.). 48p. (gr. 2-4). 2007. (ENG.). per. 6.95 (978-0-8225-6050-0(X), First Avenue Editions) 2006. (J). lib. bdg. 25.26 (978-1-57505-875-7(8)) Lerner Publishing Group.
Fleming, Candace. The Lincolns: A Scrapbook Look at Abraham & Mary. 2008. (ENG., Illus.). 200p. (J). (gr. 5-9). 24.99 (978-0-375-83618-3(7), Schwartz & Wade Bks.) Random Hse. Children's Bks.
Fox, Frances Margaret. Washington D C , the Nation's Capital: Romance, Adventure, Achievement. Vincent, Andrew M. & Higgie, Will K., illus. 2012. 394p. 53.95 (978-1-258-23323-5(1)) Literary Licensing, LLC.
Furman, Elina. Washington, D. C. 2009. (From Sea to Shining Sea, Second Ser.). (ENG.). 80p. (J). pap. 7.95 (978-0-531-21145-8(2), Children's Pr.) Scholastic Library Publishing.
Gaspar, Joe. The White House / la Casa Blanca. Alamn, Eduardo, ed. 2013. (PowerKids Readers: American Symbols / Smbolos de Amrica Ser.). (ENG & SPA.). 24p. (J). (gr. k-2). 22.60 (978-1-4777-1206-1(2), PowerKids Pr.) Rosen Publishing Group, Inc., The.
Gilmore, Frederic. The Lincoln Memorial. 2014. (United States Landmarks Ser.). (ENG.). 24p. (J). (gr. 1-4). 27.07 (978-1-62323-957-2(5), 206732) Child's World, Inc., The.
—The Washington Monument. 2014. (United States Landmarks Ser.). (ENG.). 24p. (J). (gr. 1-4). 27.07 (978-1-62323-959-6(1), 206734) Child's World, Inc., The.
Hamilton, John. Olympic National Park. 2008. (National Parks Set II Ser.). 32p. (gr. 4-9). 27.07 (978-1-60453-093-3(6), Abdo & Daughters) ABDO Publishing Co.
Harper, Kristine. The Mount St. Helens Volcanic Eruption. 2005. (Environmental Disasters Ser.). (Illus.). 112p. (gr. 6-12). 35.00 (978-0-8160-5757-3(5)) Facts On File, Inc.
Herrington, Lisa M. The White House. 2014. (Rookie Read-About(r) American Symbols Ser.). (ENG., Illus.). 32p. (J). pap. 5.95 (978-0-531-21840-2(6)) Scholastic Library Publishing.
Hirsch, Rebecca E. What's Great about Washington, DC? 2015. (Our Great States Ser.). (ENG., Illus.). 32p. (J). (gr. 2-5). pap. 7.95 (978-1-4677-6083-6(8)); lib. bdg. 26.60 (978-1-4677-3859-0(X)) Lerner Publishing Group. (Lerner Pubns.).
Hoena, B. A. Washington, D.C: The U.S. Capital. 2014. (Illus.). 32p. (J). (978-0-531-29158-0(8)) Bellwether Media.
Hoena, Blake. Washington, D. C. 2013. (Exploring the States Ser.). (ENG., Illus.). 32p. (J). (gr. 3-7). lib. bdg. 26.95 (978-1-62617-048-3(7), Blastoff! Readers) Bellwether Media.
Hopkinson, Deborah. Sweet Land of Liberty. 1 vol. Jenkins, Leonard, illus. 2007. (ENG.). 32p. (J). (gr. 1-5). 16.95 (978-1-56145-395-5(1)) Peachtree Pubs.
Jakobsen, Kathy, illus. My Washington, DC. 2016. (ENG.). 40p. (J). (gr. -1-3). 18.99 (978-0-316-12612-0(8)) Little Brown & Co.
Jerome, Kate B. Lucky to Live in Washington. 2017. (Arcadia Kids Ser.). (ENG., Illus.). 32p. (J). 16.99 **(978-0-7385-2774-1(2))** Arcadia Publishing.
—The Wise Animal Handbook Washington. 2017. (Arcadia Kids Ser.). (ENG., Illus.). 32p. (J). 16.99 **(978-0-7385-2848-9(X))** Arcadia Publishing.
Johnson, Robin. March on Washington. 2013. (ENG.). 48p. (J). (978-0-7787-1101-8(3)); pap. (978-0-7787-1121-6(8)) Crabtree Publishing Co.
Kent, Deborah. Washington, DC (Revised Edition) 2014. (America the Beautiful, Third Ser. (Revised Edition) Ser.). (ENG., Illus.). 144p. (J). lib. bdg. 40.00 (978-0-531-28298-4(8)) Scholastic Library Publishing.
Klemm, Rebecca & Rebecca Klemm Charitable Foundation. NumbersAlive! Books for Young Travelers. 2012. (ENG.). pap. 13.95 (978-0-9853667-0-4(2)) NumbersAlive! Pr.
Korrell, Emily B. Awesome Adventures at the Smithsonian: The Official Kids Guide to the Smithsonian Institution. 2013. (ENG., Illus.). 128p. (gr. 2-5). pap. 14.95 (978-1-58834-349-9(9), Smithsonian Bks.) Smithsonian Institution Scholarly Pr.
Krull, Kathleen. What Was the March on Washington? Tomkinson, Tim, illus. 2013. (What Was? Ser.). (ENG.). 112p. (J). (gr. 3-7). pap. 5.99 (978-0-448-46287-5(7), Grosset & Dunlap) Penguin Young Readers Group.
—What Was the March on Washington? 2013. (What Was... ? Ser.). lib. bdg. 16.00 (978-0-606-29974-9(2), Turtleback) Turtleback Bks.
Linde, Barbara M. Building Washington, D. C. Measuring the Area of Rectangular Shapes. 2009. (PowerMath: Proficiency Ser.). 32p. (gr. 4-5). 47.90 (978-1-60851-390-1(4), PowerKids Pr.) Rosen Publishing Group, Inc., The.
Lunis, Natalie & Taylor, Troy. A Haunted Capital. 2015. (Illus.). 32p. (J). lib. bdg. (978-1-62724-243-1(0)) Bearport Publishing Co., Inc.
Maloof, Torrey. You Are There! March on Washington, August 28, 1963. 2nd ed. 2017. (TIME for KIDS(r) Nonfiction Readers Ser.). 32p. (gr. 8-8). 8.99 **(978-1-4938-3929-2(2))** Teacher Created Materials, Inc.
Marcovitz, Hal. Lincoln Memorial: Shrine to an American Hero. Moreno, Barry, ed. 2014. (Patriotic Symbols of America Ser.: 20). (Illus.). 48p. (J). (gr. 4-18). 20.95 (978-1-4222-3127-2(5)) Mason Crest.
Marsh, Carole. Exploring Washington Through Project-Based Learning: Geography, History, Government, Economics & More. 2016. (Washington Experience Ser.). (ENG.). (J). pap. 9.99 (978-0-635-12371-8(1)) Gallopade International.
—I'm Reading about Washington. 2014. (Washington Experience Ser.). (ENG., Illus.). (J). pap., pap. 8.99 (978-0-635-11322-1(8)) Gallopade International.
Mattern, Joanne. National Mall. 2014. (ENG.). 32p. (gr. 3-6). 32.79 (978-1-62717-739-9(6)) Rourke Educational Media.
—Washington, D. C. 2014. (Rookie Read-About(tm) American Symbols Ser.). (ENG., Illus.). 32p. (J). lib. bdg. 25.00 (978-0-531-21569-2(5)); pap. 5.95 (978-0-531-21842-6(2)) Scholastic Library Publishing.
McMenemy, Sarah. Washington D. C. A 3D Keepsake Cityscape. McMenemy, Sarah, illus. 2012. (Panorama Pops Ser.). (ENG., Illus.). 20p. (J). (gr. k-12). 8.99 (978-0-7636-5935-6(5)) Candlewick Pr.
Nelson, Kristin L. The Lincoln Memorial. 2010. (Lightning Bolt Bks.). (Illus.). 32p. (J). (gr. k-2). lib. bdg. 25.26 (978-0-7613-6018-6(2), Lerner Pubns.) Lerner Publishing Group.
—The Washington Monument. (Lightning Bolt Bks.). 32p. (gr. k-2). 2010. (Illus.). (J). lib. bdg. 25.26 (978-0-7613-6019-3(0), Lerner Pubns.) 2010. (ENG.). pap. 7.95 (978-0-7613-6053-7(0)) 2003. (ENG.). pap. 7.95 (978-0-8225-3759-5(1)) 2003. (ENG., Illus.). lib. bdg. 22.60 (978-0-8225-0250-0(X)) Lerner Publishing Group.
O'Connor, Jane. If the Walls Could Talk: Family Life at the White House. Hovland, Gary, illus. 2004. (ENG.). 48p. (J). (gr. 1-4). 17.99 (978-0-689-86863-4(4), Simon & Schuster/Paula Wiseman Bks.) Simon & Schuster/Paula Wiseman Bks.
Ollhoff, Jim. Washington, D. C. 1 vol. 2009. (United States Ser.). (ENG., Illus.). 48p. (YA). (gr. 2-5). 27.07 (978-1-60453-684-3(5)) ABDO Publishing Co.
O'Neal, Claire. Washington, D. C. 2009. (Class Trip Ser.). (Illus.). 48p. (J). (gr. 2-5). lib. bdg. 29.95 (978-1-58415-809-7(3)) Mitchell Lane Pubs., Inc.

Otfinoski, Steven & Benduhn, Tea. Washington. 2015. (It's My State! Ser.). (ENG.). 80p. (J). (gr. 4-4). 34.21 *(978-1-5026-0007-3(2))* Cavendish Square Publishing.

Owens, Tom. Washington, D.C. 2003. (Reading Essentials in Social Studies). (Illus.). 48p. (J). pap. 9.00 *(978-0-7891-5839-0(6))* Perfection Learning Corp.

Panchyk, Richard. Washington, DC History for Kids: The Making of a Capital City, with 21 Activities. 2016. (For Kids Ser.). (ENG., Illus.). 144p. (J). (gr. 4). pap. 16.99 *(978-1-61373-006-5(3))* Chicago Review Pr., Inc.

Publications International Ltd. Staff. Yesterday & Today Seattle. 2008. 192p. 19.95 *(978-1-4127-1577-5(6))* Publications International, Ltd.

Rajczak, Michael. Haunted! the White House. 2013. (History's Most Haunted Ser.). 32p. (J). (gr. 3-6). pap. 63.00 *(978-1-4339-9270-4(1))* Stevens, Gareth Publishing LLLP.

Robinson, Kate. The National Mall: A MyReportLinks.com Book. 2005. (Virtual Field Trips Ser.). (Illus.). 48p. (J). (gr. 4-10). lib. bdg. 26.60 *(978-0-7660-5222-2(2)*, MyReportLinks.com Bks.) Enslow Pubs., Inc.

Rodgers, Kelly. Our Nation's Capital: Washington, DC, 1 vol. rev. ed. 2014. (Primary Source Readers Content & Literacy Ser.). (ENG., Illus.). 32p. (gr. 3-3). pap. 8.99 *(978-1-4333-7362-6(9))* Teacher Created Materials, Inc.

Ruffin, Frances E. The Lincoln Memorial. 2006. (Places in American History Ser.). (Illus.). 24p. (gr. 1-4). pap. 8.15 *(978-0-8368-6418-2(2))*; lib. bdg. 22.00 *(978-0-8368-6411-3(5))* Stevens, Gareth Publishing LLLP. (Weekly Reader Leveled Readers).

Sasek, Miroslav. This Is Washington, D. C. 2011. (ENG., Illus.). 64p. (J). (gr. 2-12). 17.95 *(978-0-7893-2232-6(3))* Universe Publishing.

Silate, Jennifer. The White House. 2009. (Primary Sources of American Symbols Ser.). 24p. (gr. 3-3). 42.50 *(978-1-60851-512-7(5)*, PowerKids Pr.) Rosen Publishing Group, Inc., The.

Silverman, Steve. The Story of the Washington Wizards. 2010. (NBA — A History of Hoops Ser.). 48p. (YA). (gr. 5-18). 23.95 *(978-1-58341-965-6(9)*, Creative Education) Creative Co., The.

Sipperley, Keli. The White House. 2014. (ENG.). 32p. (gr. 3-6). 32.79 *(978-1-62717-744-3(2))* Rourke Educational Media.

Skewes, John. Larry Loves Washington, DC! 2016. (Larry Gets Lost Ser.). (ENG., Illus.). 20p. (J). (— 1). pap. 9.99 *(978-1-63217-048-4(5)*, Little Bigfoot) Sasquatch Bks.

Smith, Charles R., Jr. Brick by Brick. Cooper, Floyd, illus. 2012. (ENG.). 32p. (J). (gr. -1-3). 17.99 *(978-0-06-192082-0(7)*, Amistad) HarperCollins Pubs.

—Brick by Brick. Cooper, Floyd, illus. 2015. (ENG.). 32p. (J). (gr. -1-3). pap. 6.99 *(978-0-06-192084-4(3)*, Amistad) HarperCollins Pubs.

Sonneborn, Liz. District of Columbia: Past & Present. 2010. (United States: Past & Present Ser.). (ENG.). 48p. (YA). pap. 11.75 *(978-1-4358-9528-7(2))*; lib. bdg. 29.25 *(978-1-4358-9501-0(0))* Rosen Publishing Group, Inc., The. (Rosen Reference).

Stine, Megan & dePaola, Tomie. Where Is the White House? Groff, David, illus. 2015. (Where Is? Ser.). (ENG.). 112p. (J). (gr. 3-7). 5.99 *(978-0-448-48355-9(6)*, Grosset & Dunlap) Penguin Young Readers Group.

Sutcliffe, Jane. The White House Is Burning: August 24 1814. Farquharson, Alexander, illus. 2014. (ENG.). 128p. (J). (gr. 4-7). 19.95 *(978-1-58089-656-6(1))* Charlesbridge Publishing, Inc.

Thomas, William. District of Columbia. 2011. (Guide to American States Ser.). (Illus.). 48p. (YA). (gr. 3-6). 29.99 *(978-1-61690-821-8(1))* Weigl Pubs., Inc.

—District of Columbia: The Nation's Capital. 2016. (J). *(978-1-4896-4839-6(9))* Weigl Pubs., Inc.

Tieck, Sarah. Washington DC, 1 vol. 2012. (Explore the United States Ser.). (ENG.). 32p. (J). (gr. 2-5). lib. bdg. 28.50 *(978-1-61783-387-8(8)*, Big Buddy Bks.) ABDO Publishing Co.

WASHINGTON (D.C.)—WHITE HOUSE

see White House (Washington, D.C.)

WASHINGTON (STATE)

Applegate, Katherine. Ivan: the Remarkable True Story of the Shopping Mall Gorilla. Karas, G. Brian, illus. 2014. (ENG.). 40p. (J). (gr. -1-3). 17.99 *(978-0-544-25230-1(6)*, Clarion Bks.) Houghton Mifflin Harcourt Publishing Co.

Boekhoff, P. M. & Brown, Jonatha A. Washington. 2005. (Portraits of the States Ser.). (Illus.). 32p. (gr. 2-6). pap. 10.50 *(978-0-8368-4656-0(7)*, Gareth Stevens Learning Library) Stevens, Gareth Publishing LLLP.

Bredeson, Carmen. Fiery Volcano: The Eruption of Mount St. Helens. 2012. (Disasters — People in Peril Ser.). (Illus.). 48p. (J). (gr. 5-18). 25.27 *(978-0-7660-4015-1(1))* Enslow Pubs., Inc.

Brown, Jonatha A. & Boekhoff, P. M. Washington. 2005. (Portraits of the States Ser.). (Illus.). 32p. (gr. 2-6). lib. bdg. 26.00 *(978-0-8368-4637-9(0)*, Gareth Stevens Learning Library) Stevens, Gareth Publishing LLLP.

Feinstein, Stephen. Washington: A MyReportLinks.com Book. 2003. (States Ser.). (Illus.). 48p. (J). (gr. 4-10). lib. bdg. 25.26 *(978-0-7660-5026-6(2)*, MyReportLinks.com Bks.) Enslow Pubs., Inc.

Green, Jen. Mount St. Helens. 2005. (Disasters Ser.). (Illus.). 32p. (gr. 2-6). lib. bdg. 26.00 *(978-0-8368-4498-6(X)*, Gareth Stevens Learning Library) Stevens, Gareth Publishing LLLP.

Hansen Moench, Megan. Know Your State Activity Book Washington, 1 vol. Padavick, Nate, illus. 2015. (ENG.). 272p. (J). pap. 14.99 *(978-1-4236-4059-2(4))* Gibbs Smith, Publisher.

Harmon, Daniel E. Washington: Past & Present. 2009. (Illus.). 48p. (J). 70.50 *(978-1-4358-5589-2(2))*; pap. 11.75 *(978-1-4358-5588-5(4))*; (ENG., lib. bdg. 29.25 *(978-1-4358-5295-2(8))* Rosen Publishing Group, Inc., The. (Rosen Reference).

Hood, Karen Jean Matsko. Washington State: Activity & Coloring Book. l.t. ed. 2014. (Educational Activity & Coloring Book Ser.). (J). 19.95 *(978-1-930948-56-3(5))* Whispering Pine Pr. International, Inc.

Kranz, Rachel. Mount St. Helens. 2011. (Early Connections Ser.). (J). *(978-1-61672-643-0(1))* Benchmark Education Co.

Labella, Susan. Washington. 2006. (Rookie Read-About Geography Ser.). (ENG., Illus.). 32p. (J). (gr. 1-2). lib. bdg. 20.50 *(978-0-516-24993-3(2)*, Children's Pr.) Scholastic Library Publishing.

Marsh, Carole. Washington Current Events Projects: 30 Cool, Activities, Crafts, Experiments & More for Kids to Do to Learn about Your State! 2003. (Washington Experience Ser.). 32p. (gr. k-8). pap. 5.95 *(978-0-635-02066-6(1)*, Marsh, Carole Bks.) Gallopade International.

—Washington Geography Projects: 30 Cool, Activities, Crafts, Experiments & More for Kids to Do to Learn about Your State! 2003. (Washington Experience Ser.). 32p. (gr. k-5). pap. 5.95 *(978-0-635-01865-6(9)*, Marsh, Carole Bks.) Gallopade International.

—Washington Government Projects: 30 Cool, Activities, Crafts, Experiments & More for Kids to Do to Learn about Your State! 2003. (Washington Experience Ser.). 32p. (gr. k-5). pap. 5.95 *(978-0-635-01966-0(3)*, Marsh, Carole Bks.) Gallopade International.

—Washington People Projects: 30 Cool, Activities, Crafts, Experiments & More for Kids to Do to Learn about Your State! 2003. (Washington Experience Ser.). 32p. (gr. k-5). pap. 5.95 *(978-0-635-02016-1(5)*, Marsh, Carole Bks.) Gallopade International.

—Washington Symbols & Facts Projects: 30 Cool, Activities, Crafts, Experiments & More for Kids to Do to Learn about Your State! 2003. (Washington Experience Ser.). 32p. (gr. k-5). pap. 5.95 *(978-0-635-01916-5(7)*, Marsh, Carole Bks.) Gallopade International.

McConaghy, Lorraine & Bentley, Judy. Free Boy: A True Story of Slave & Master. 2013. (V Ethel Willis White Bks.). (ENG., Illus.). 112p. pap. 18.95 *(978-0-295-99271-6(9))* Univ. of Washington Pr.

McHugh, Erin. Washington. Schrier, Alfred, illus. 2008. (ENG.). 48p. (J). (gr. -1-17). 9.95 *(978-1-57912-775-6(4)*, 81775, Black Dog & Leventhal Pubs. Inc.) Hachette Bks.

Murray, Julie. Washington, 1 vol. 2006. (Buddy Book Ser.). (ENG., Illus.). 32p. (gr. 2-4). 27.07 *(978-1-59197-706-3(1)*, Buddy Bks.) ABDO Publishing Co.

Powell, E. Sandy. Washington. (J). 2012. lib. bdg. 25.26 *(978-0-7613-4562-6(0)*, Lerner Pubns.) 2nd exp. rev. ed. 2003. (Illus.). 84p. (gr. 3-6). pap. 6.95 *(978-0-8225-4155-4(6))* Lerner Publishing Group.

Smith, Roland & Smith, Marie. E Is for Evergreen: A Washington State Alphabet. Holt Ayriss, Linda, illus. 2004. (State Ser.). (ENG.). 40p. (J). 17.95 *(978-1-58536-143-4(7))* Sleeping Bear Pr.

Stefoff, Rebecca. Washington. 2nd rev. ed. 2007. (Celebrate the States Ser.). 144p. (gr. 6). lib. bdg. 42.79 *(978-0-7614-2561-8(6)*, Benchmark Bks.) Marshall Cavendish Corp.

Way, Jennifer. Washington. 2009. (Bilingual Library of the United States of America Ser.). (ENG & SPA.). 32p. (gr. 2-2). 47.90 *(978-1-60853-391-6(3)*, Editorial Buenas Letras) Rosen Publishing Group, Inc., The.

Weintraub, A. How to Draw Washington's Sights & Symbols. 2009. (Kid's Guide to Drawing America Ser.). 32p. (gr. k-k). 50.50 *(978-1-61511-103-9(4)*, PowerKids Pr.) Rosen Publishing Group, Inc., The.

Weintraub, Aileen. Cape Disappointment Light: The First Lighthouse in the Pacific Northwest. 2003. (Great Lighthouses of North America Ser.). (Illus.). 24p. (YA). (gr. 3-6). 22.60 *(978-0-8239-6172-6(9))* Rosen Publishing Group, Inc., The.

Wenatchee High School Staff. W Is for Washington. 2008. (See My State Ser.). (ENG., Illus.). 32p. (J). (gr. -1-3). 13.95 *(978-0-88240-748-7(1)*, West Winds Pr.) Graphic Arts Ctr. Publishing Co.

WASHINGTON (STATE)—FICTION

Alexie, Sherman. The Absolutely True Diary of a Part-Time Indian. Forney, Ellen, illus. (ENG.). (YA). (gr. 7-17). 2009. 288p. pap. 15.99 *(978-0-316-01369-7(2))* 2007. 240p. 20.00 *(978-0-316-01368-0(4))* Little, Brown Bks. for Young Readers.

—The Absolutely True Diary of a Part-Time Indian. 10th anniv. ed. 2017. (ENG., Illus.). 320p. (YA). (gr. 7-17). 20.99 *(978-0-316-50404-1(1))* Little, Brown Bks. for Young Readers.

—The Absolutely True Diary of a Part-Time Indian. 2011. 10.36 *(978-0-7848-3391-9(5))* 2009. 14.44 *(978-0-7848-3800-6(3))* Marco Bk. Co. (Everbind).

—The Absolutely True Diary of a Part-Time Indian. Forney, Ellen, illus. 2008. 230p. 25.00 *(978-1-60686-072-4(0))* Perfection Learning Corp.

—The Absolutely True Diary of a Part-Time Indian. 2008. (YA). 1.25 *(978-1-4281-8291-2(8))*; 78.49 *(978-1-4361-0259-9(6))*; 57.75 *(978-1-4281-8294-3(2))*; 68.75 *(978-1-4281-8300-1(0))*; 55.75 *(978-1-4281-8296-7(9))*; 212.75 *(978-1-4281-8295-0(0))*; 70.75 *(978-1-4281-8298-1(5))* Recorded Bks., Inc.

—The Absolutely True Diary of a Part-Time Indian. Forney, Ellen, illus. l.t. ed. 2008. (Thorndike Literacy Bridge Ser.). (ENG.). 302p. (YA). (gr. 7-12). 23.95 *(978-1-4104-0499-2(4))* Thorndike Pr.

—The Absolutely True Diary of a Part-Time Indian. 2009. (YA). lib. bdg. 28.15 *(978-0-606-07296-0(9)*, Turtleback) Turtleback Bks.

Banerjee, Anjali. Seaglass Summer. 2011. (ENG., Illus.). 176p. (J). (gr. 3-7). pap. 7.99 *(978-0-375-84399-0(X)*, Yearling) Random Hse. Children's Bks.

Birdseye, Tom. Storm Mountain. 2010. (ENG.). 256p. (J). (gr. 3-7). 16.95 *(978-0-8234-2130-5(9))* Holiday Hse., Inc.

Bostic, Megan. Never Eighteen. 2012. (ENG.). 208p. (YA). (gr. 7). pap. 8.99 *(978-0-547-55076-3(6))* Houghton Mifflin Harcourt Publishing Co.

Brainerd, Debbi. The Tree That Came Home: An IslandWood Story Inspired by the True Story of a 92-Foot Beam That Returned to Bainbridge Island, Washington. Zecca, Katherine, illus. 2008. 63p. (J). pap. *(978-0-9821633-0-6(4))* IslandWood.

Brothers, Marilee. Moon Rise. 2009. (YA). pap. 14.95 *(978-0-9821756-9-9(8)*, Bell Bridge Bks.) BelleBks., Inc.

—Moon Spun. 2010. 246p. pap. 14.95 *(978-1-935661-95-5(7)*, Bell Bridge Bks.) BelleBks., Inc.

—Moonstone. 2008. 236p. (YA). pap. 14.95 *(978-0-9802453-4-9(6)*, Bell Bridge Bks.) BelleBks., Inc.

—Shadow Moon. 2011. 230p. (YA). pap. *(978-1-61194-058-9(3))* BelleBks., Inc.

Buckingham, Royce. The Dead Boys. 2010. (ENG.). 208p. (J). (gr. 5-18). 16.99 *(978-0-399-25222-8(3)*, G.P. Putnam's Sons Books for Young Readers) Penguin Young Readers Group.

Caletti, Deb. The Fortunes of Indigo Skye. (ENG.). (YA). (gr. 7). 2009. 320p. pap. 9.99 *(978-1-4169-1008-4(5))* 2008. 304p. 15.99 *(978-1-4169-1007-7(7))* Simon Pulse. (Simon Pulse).

—Love Is All You Need: Wild Roses - The Nature of Jade. 2013. (ENG.). 608p. (YA). (gr. 7-7). pap. 11.99 *(978-1-4424-6636-4(7)*, Simon Pulse) Simon Pulse.

—Stay. (ENG.). (YA). (gr. 7). 2012. 336p. pap. 9.99 *(978-1-4424-0374-1(8))* 2011. 320p. 16.99 *(978-1-4424-0373-4(X))* Simon Pulse. (Simon Pulse).

—Wild Roses. (ENG.). (YA). (gr. 7-12). 2008. 320p. pap. 8.99 *(978-1-4169-5782-9(0))* 2005. (Illus.). 304p. 15.95 *(978-0-689-86766-8(2))* Simon Pulse. (Simon Pulse).

Calhoun, Dia. After the River the Sun. Slater, Kate, illus. 2013. (ENG.). 368p. (J). (gr. 4-7). 16.99 *(978-1-4424-3985-6(8))* Simon & Schuster Children's Publishing.

—Eva of the Farm. Slater, Kate, illus. (ENG.). (J). (gr. 4-7). 2013. 272p. pap. 6.99 *(978-1-4424-1701-4(3))* 2012. 256p. 16.99 *(978-1-4424-1700-7(5))* Simon & Schuster Children's Publishing. (Atheneum Bks. for Young Readers).

Coats, J. Anderson. The Many Reflections of Miss Jane Deming. 2017. (ENG., Illus.). 288p. (J). (gr. 5-7). 16.99 *(978-1-4814-6496-3(5)*, Atheneum Bks. for Young Readers) Simon & Schuster Children's Publishing.

Cook, Eileen. Unraveling Isobel. 2012. (ENG.). (YA). (gr. 9). 320p. pap. 9.99 *(978-1-4424-1328-3(X))*; 304p. 16.99 *(978-1-4424-1327-6(1))* Simon Pulse. (Simon Pulse).

Dashner, James. The Journal of Curious Letters. Beus, Bryan, illus. 2008. (13th Reality Ser.: Bk. 1). 434p. (J). (gr. 4-7). 17.95 *(978-1-59038-831-0(3)*, Shadow Mountain) Shadow Mountain Publishing.

—The Journal of Curious Letters. Beus, Bryan, illus. 2009. (13th Reality Ser.: 1). (ENG.). 528p. (J). (gr. 3-7). pap. 8.99 *(978-1-4169-9152-6(2)*, Aladdin) Simon & Schuster Children's Publishing.

Davis, Heather. The Clearing. 2010. (ENG., Illus.). 224p. (YA). (gr. 9). pap. 8.99 *(978-0-547-26367-0(8))* Houghton Mifflin Harcourt Publishing Co.

Derting, Kimberly. Body Finder. 2011. (Body Finder Ser.: 1). (ENG.). 352p. (YA). (gr. 9). pap. 9.99 *(978-0-06-177983-1(0))* HarperCollins Pubs.

—Desires of the Dead. 2012. (Body Finder Ser.: 2). (ENG.). 384p. (YA). (gr. 9). pap. 8.99 *(978-0-06-177986-2(5))* HarperCollins Pubs.

Deuker, Carl. Gym Candy. 2008. (ENG.). 320p. (YA). (gr. 7). pap. 9.99 *(978-0-547-07631-7(2))* Houghton Mifflin Harcourt Publishing Co.

—Gym Candy. 2008. 313p. 19.00 *(978-1-60686-376-3(2))* Perfection Learning Corp.

Efaw, Amy. After. 2010. (ENG.). 368p. (YA). (gr. 7-18). 8.99 *(978-0-14-241590-0(1)*, Speak) Penguin Young Readers Group.

Emerson, Alice. Betty Gordon in Washington. 2005. pap. 14.95 *(978-1-59605-610-7(X)*, Cosimo Classics) Cosimo, Inc.

Finneyfrock, Karen. Starbird Murphy & the World Outside. 2014. (ENG.). 384p. (YA). (gr. 7). 17.99 *(978-0-670-01276-3(9)*, Viking Books for Young Readers) Penguin Young Readers Group.

Forman, Gayle. I Was Here. l.t. ed. 2015. (ENG.). 420p. 24.99 *(978-1-4104-8255-6(3))* Cengage Gale.

—I Was Here. 2015. (ENG.). 288p. (J). (gr. 9). 18.99 *(978-0-451-47147-5(4)*, Viking Books for Young Readers) Penguin Publishing Group.

—I Was Here. 2016. (ENG.). 304p. (YA). (gr. 9). pap. 10.99 *(978-0-14-751403-5(7)*, Speak) Penguin Young Readers Group.

—I Was Here. 2016. lib. bdg. 22.10 *(978-0-606-38404-9(9))* Turtleback Bks.

Francis, JennaKay. The Ferry Boat. Woodward II, Ed, illus. 2013. 12p. pap. 8.95 *(978-1-61633-426-0(6))* Guardian Angel Publishing, Inc.

Frazier, Sundee T. Brendan Buckley's Universe & Everything in It. 2008. (ENG.). 208p. (J). (gr. 3-7). 6.99 *(978-0-440-42206-8(X)*, Yearling) Random Hse. Children's Bks.

Gamble, Adam & Jasper, Mark. Good Night Washington State. Veno, Joe & Kelly, Cooper, illus. 2012. (Good Night Our World Ser.). (ENG.). 20p. (J). (gr. k — 1). bds. 9.95 *(978-1-60219-072-6(0))* Good Night Bks.

Gemeinhart, Dan. The Honest Truth. 2015. (ENG.). 240p. (J). (gr. 3-7). 16.99 *(978-0-545-66573-5(6)*, Scholastic Pr.) Scholastic, Inc.

—Some Kind of Courage. 2016. (ENG.). 240p. (J). (gr. 3-7). 16.99 *(978-0-545-66577-3(9)*, Scholastic Pr.) Scholastic, Inc.

George, Elisabeth. The Edge of Nowhere. 2014. (Edge of Nowhere Ser.). (ENG.). 464p. (YA). (gr. 7). pap. 10.99 *(978-0-14-242675-3(X)*, Speak) Penguin Young Readers Group.

—The Edge of the Shadows. 2015. (Edge of Nowhere Ser.). (ENG.). 464p. (YA). (gr. 7). 18.99 *(978-0-670-01298-5(X)*, Viking Books for Young Readers) Penguin Young Readers Group.

—The Edge of the Water. 2014. (Edge of Nowhere Ser.). (ENG.). 448p. (YA). (gr. 7). 18.99 *(978-0-670-01297-8(1)*, Viking Books for Young Readers) Penguin Young Readers Group.

George, Elizabeth. The Edge of the Light. 2016. (Edge of Nowhere Ser.). (ENG.). 400p. (YA). (gr. 7). 18.99 *(978-0-670-01299-2(8)*, Viking Books for Young Readers) Penguin Young Readers Group.

—The Edge of the Light. 2017. (Edge of Nowhere Ser.). (ENG.). 416p. (YA). (gr. 7). pap. 10.99 ***(978-0-14-751396-0(0)***, Speak) Penguin Young Readers Group.

George, Elizabeth. The Edge of the Water. 2015. (Edge of Nowhere Ser.). (ENG.). 464p. (YA). (gr. 7). pap. 9.99 *(978-0-14-242674-6(1)*, Speak) Penguin Young Readers Group.

Goode, Suzi. The Lost Wizard Series Bk 1. 2007. pap. 11.95 *(978-1-59374-817-3(5))* Whiskey Creek Pr., LLC.

Grace, Amanda. But I Love Him. 2011. (ENG.). 264p. (YA). (gr. 7-18). pap. 9.95 *(978-0-7387-2594-9(3)*, Flux) North Star Editions.

Gurtler, Janet. If I Tell. 2011. (ENG.). 256p. (YA). (gr. 7-12). pap. 12.99 *(978-1-4022-6103-9(9))* Sourcebooks, Inc.

Hartinger, Brent. Project Sweet Life. 2009. (ENG.). 288p. (YA). (gr. 8-18). 16.99 *(978-0-06-082411-2(5)*, HarperTeen) HarperCollins Pubs.

Hill, Janet Muirhead. Kendall's Storm. Leonhard, Herb, illus. 2011. (J). pap. 12.00 *(978-0-9820893-0-9(9))* Raven Publishing Inc. of Montana.

Holm, Jennifer L. An Adventure. 2010. (Boston Jane Ser.: No. 1). (ENG.). 272p. (J). (gr. 3-7). 7.99 *(978-0-375-86204-5(8)*, Yearling) Random Hse. Children's Bks.

—The Claim. 2010. (Boston Jane Ser.: No. 2). (ENG.). 224p. (J). (gr. 3-7). pap. 7.99 *(978-0-375-86206-9(4)*, Yearling) Random Hse. Children's Bks.

—Our Only May Amelia. unabr. ed. 2004. 253p. (J). (gr. 5-9). pap. 36.00 incl. audio *(978-0-8072-8366-0(5)*, YA191SP, Listening Library) Random Hse. Audio Publishing Group.

—The Trouble with May Amelia. Gustavson, Adam, illus. (ENG.). 224p. (J). (gr. 3-7). 2012. pap. 5.99 *(978-1-4169-1374-0(2))* 2011. 15.99 *(978-1-4169-1373-3(4))* Simon & Schuster Children's Publishing. (Atheneum Bks. for Young Readers).

—Wilderness Days. 2004. (Boston Jane Ser.: No. 2). 256p. (J). (gr. 5-18). pap. 5.99 *(978-0-06-440881-3(7)*, Harper Trophy) HarperCollins Pubs.

—Wilderness Days. unabr. ed. 2004. (Boston Jane Ser.: No. 2). 288p. (J). (gr. 5-9). pap. 38.00 incl. audio *(978-0-8072-0787-1(X)*, S YA 307 SP, Listening Library) Random Hse. Audio Publishing Group.

—Wilderness Days. 2010. (Boston Jane Ser.: No. 2). (ENG.). 256p. (J). (gr. 3-7). pap. 7.99 *(978-0-375-86205-2(6)*, Yearling) Random Hse. Children's Bks.

Holsather, Kent. Henry of York: The Secret of Juan de Vega. Holsather, Bill, illus. 2003. 176p. (YA). (gr. 5-18). 22.95 *(978-0-9729101-0-1(7))*; 2nd ed. per. 12.95 *(978-0-9729101-1-8(5))* Lonejack Mountain Pr.

Hood, Karen Jean Matsko. Washington State: Activity & Coloring Book. 2014. (J). spiral bd. 19.95 *(978-1-59649-434-3(4))* Whispering Pine Pr. International, Inc.

Hubbard, Amanda & Hubbard, Mandy. Everything but the Truth. 2015. (If Only... Ser.). (ENG.). 288p. (YA). (gr. 7). 17.99 *(978-1-61963-659-0(X)*, 9781619636590, Bloomsbury USA Childrens) Bloomsbury Publishing USA.

Johnson, Joy. Harry the Woodpecker's Search for a Home. Johnson, Craig, illus. 2013. 28p. (J). pap. 9.95 *(978-0-9785191-7-9(5))* Orange Spot Publishing.

Johnston, Wayne M. North Fork. 2016. (ENG.). 210p. (YA). (gr. 7-12). pap. 14.95 *(978-1-936364-20-6(4))* Black Heron Pr.

Katcher, Brian. The Improbable Theory of Ana & Zak. (YA). (gr. 8). 2016. 352p. pap. 9.99 *(978-0-06-227278-2(0))* 2015. (ENG.). 336p. 17.99 *(978-0-06-227277-5(2))* HarperCollins Pubs. (Tegen, Katherine Bks).

Kaymer, Lin. Who Is Mackie Spence? 2015. (ENG.). 208p. (YA). 17.99 *(978-1-4405-8460-2(5)*, Simon Pulse) Simon Pulse.

Kehret, Peg. The Ghost's Grave. 2007. 224p. pap. 5.99 *(978-0-14-280819-1(9)*, Puffin) Penguin Publishing Group.

—The Ghost's Grave. 2007. (ENG.). 224p. (J). (gr. 5-18). 6.99 *(978-0-14-240819-3(0)*, Puffin Books) Penguin Young Readers Group.

Kocsis, Konrád Hayward. The Adventures of the Krusaders & the Legend of Wilde Island. 2012. 238p. pap. 16.97 *(978-1-61897-106-7(9)*, Strategic Bk. Publishing) Strategic Book Publishing & Rights Agency (SBPRA).

Larson, Kirby. Dash. (Dogs of World War II Ser.). (ENG.). 256p. (J). (gr. 3-7). 2016. pap. 7.99 *(978-0-545-41636-8(1)*, Scholastic Paperbacks) 2014. 17.99 *(978-0-545-41635-1(3)*, Scholastic Pr.) Scholastic, Inc.

Llewellyn, Tom. The Shadow of Seth: A Seth Anomundy Murder Mystery. 2015. (Seth Anomundy Murder Mysteries Ser.). (ENG.). viii, 174p. (YA). pap. 10.95 *(978-1-929345-18-2(6))* Poisoned Pen Pr.

Mathews, Temple. The Sword of Armaggeddon. 2010. ix, 291p. *(978-1-935618-17-1(2))* BenBella Bks.

McKenzie, Paige. The Haunting of Sunshine Girl. (ENG.). 2016. 320p. (gr. 7-10). pap. 9.99 *(978-1-60286-302-6(4))* 2015. (Haunting of Sunshine Girl Ser.: Bk. 1). 304p. (YA). 16.00 *(978-1-60286-272-2(9))* Perseus Bks. Group. (Weinstein Bks.).

Mentyka, Sharon. Chasing at the Surface. 2016. (ENG., Illus.). 228p. (J). pap. 12.99 *(978-1-943328-60-4(9)*, West Winds Pr.) Graphic Arts Ctr. Publishing Co.

Merrick, Rebecca. Rain Harbor. 2011. 276p. 47.95 *(978-1-258-07693-1(4))* Literary Licensing, LLC.

Meyer, Stephenie. Amanecer. Pallarés, José Miguel & Sánchez, María Jesús, trs. 2008.Tr. of Breaking Dawn. (SPA.). 832p. (gr. 8-12). pap. 19.99 *(978-607-11-0033-7(X)*, Alfaguara Juvenil) Santillana USA Publishing Co., Inc.

—Breaking Dawn. (Twilight Saga Ser.: 4). (ENG.). 768p. (YA). (gr. 7-17). 2012. mass mkt. 7.99 *(978-0-316-22613-4(0))* 2010. pap. 16.99 *(978-0-316-06793-5(8))* 2008. 22.99 *(978-0-316-06792-8(X)*, Tingley, Megan Bks.)Pt. II. 2012. pap. 14.99 *(978-0-316-22642-4(4))* Little, Brown Bks. for Young Readers.

—Breaking Dawn. 2010. (Twilight Saga Ser.: 4). (YA). lib. bdg. 29.40 *(978-0-606-23108-4(0)*, Turtleback) Turtleback Bks.

—Eclipse. 2009. (Twilight Saga Ser.: 3). (ENG.). 640p. (YA). (gr. 7-17). pap. 15.99 *(978-0-316-02765-6(0))* Little Brown & Co.

—Eclipse. 2007. (Twilight Saga Ser.: 3). (ENG.). 640p. (YA). (gr. 7-17). 19.99 *(978-0-316-16020-9(2))* Little, Brown Bks. for Young Readers.

—Eclipse. 2008. 576p. *(978-1-904233-91-6(0)*, Atom Books) Little, Brown Book Group Ltd.

—Eclipse. 2011. (Twilight Saga: Bk. 3). 13.08 *(978-0-7848-3531-9(4)*, Everbind) Marco Bk. Co.

—Eclipse. 2010. (Twilight Saga: Bk. 3). 629p. (YA). (gr. 9-12). 22.10 *(978-1-60686-303-9(7))* Perfection Learning Corp.

—Eclipse. Pallarés, José Miguel & Sánchez, María Jesús, trs. 2007. (SPA.). 870p. (YA). (gr. 8-12). pap. 15.99 *(978-1-60396-022-9(8)*, Punto de Lectura) Santillana USA Publishing Co., Inc.

—Eclipse. 2007. (Twilight Saga Spanish Ser.: 3). (SPA.). 637p. (gr. 7-12). lib. bdg. 28.15 *(978-1-4177-9862-9(9)*, Turtleback) Turtleback Bks.

—Luna Nueva. Pallares, Jose Miguel, tr. from ENG. 2009.Tr. of New Moon. (SPA.). 280p. (YA). (gr. 8-12). pap. 11.99 *(978-1-60396-698-6(6))*, Punto de Lectura) Santillana USA Publishing Co., Inc.

—Luna Nueva. Pallarés, José Miguel & Sánchez, Maria Jesús, trs. from ENG. 2007.Tr. of New Moon. (SPA.). 696p. (YA). (gr. 8-12). per. 15.99 *(978-970-58-0023-8(5))*, Alfaguara) Santillana USA Publishing Co., Inc.

—New Moon. (Twilight Saga Ser.: 2). (ENG.). 608p. (gr. 7-17). 2008. (YA). pap. 15.99 *(978-0-316-02496-9(1))* 2006. (J). 19.99 *(978-0-316-16019-3(9))*, Tingley, Megan Bks.) Little, Brown Bks. for Young Readers.

—New Moon. 2011. (Twilight Saga: Bk. 2). 11.72 *(978-0-7848-3535-7(7))*, Everbind) Marco Bk. Co.

—New Moon. 2008. (Twilight Saga: Bk. 2). 563p. (gr. 9-12). 21.00 *(978-1-60686-336-7(3))* Perfection Learning Corp.

—La Segunda Vida de Bree Tanner. Oliveras, Julio Hermoso, tr. 2010. (SPA.). 240p. (YA). (gr. 8-12). mass mkt. 14.99 *(978-1-61605-142-6(6))*, Alfaguara) Santillana USA Publishing Co., Inc.

—The Short Second Life of Bree Tanner. 2010. (Twilight Saga Ser.). (ENG.). 192p. (YA). (gr. 7-17). 16.00 *(978-0-316-12558-1(X))* Little, Brown Bks. for Young Readers.

—Twilight. 2008. (Twilight Saga: Bk. 1). (CHI.). 375p. (YA). pap. *(978-7-5448-0333-5(3))* Jieli Publishing Hse.

—Twilight. (Twilight Saga Ser.: 1). (ENG.). 544p. (YA). (gr. 7-17). 2005. 19.99 *(978-0-316-16017-9(2))* 2006. reprint ed. pap. 15.99 *(978-0-316-01584-4(9))* Little, Brown Bks. for Young Readers. (Tingley, Megan Bks.).

—Twilight. 2008. 480p. pap. *(978-1-905654-34-5(0))*, Atom Books) Little, Brown Book Group Ltd.

—Twilight. 2009. (Twilight Saga: Bk. 1). 11.72 *(978-0-7848-1934-0(3))*, Everbind) Marco Bk. Co.

—Twilight. (Twilight Saga Ser.: 1). (ENG.). 2012. 224p. (gr. 7-17). pap. 14.99 *(978-0-316-20488-0(9))* 2011. (Illus.). 240p. (gr. 7-17). 19.99 *(978-0-316-13319-7(1))* 2010. (Illus.). 224p. 19.99 *(978-0-7595-2943-4(4))* Orbit. (Yen Pr.).

—Twilight. Kim, Young, illus. collector's ed. 2012. (Twilight Saga Ser.: 0). (ENG.). 464p. (gr. 7-17). 24.99 *(978-0-316-21717-0(4))*, Yen Pr.) Orbit.

—Twilight. (Twilight Saga: Bk. 1). 2010. 498p. (YA). (gr. 9-12). 20.10 *(978-1-60686-352-7(5))* 2006. 21.00 *(978-0-7569-6825-0(9))* Perfection Learning Corp.

—Twilight. (Twilight Ser.: 1). (YA). 2007. 1.25 *(978-1-4193-9974-9(8))* 2006. 87.75 *(978-1-4193-9975-6(6))* Recorded Bks., Inc.

—Twilight. 2006. (Twilight Saga Ser.: 1). (Illus.). 498p. (YA). (gr. 9-12). lib. bdg. 28.15 *(978-1-4177-5591-2(1))*, Turtleback) Turtleback Bks.

Ness, Patrick. The Rest of Us Just Live Here. (YA). 2016. 336p. (gr. 9). pap. 9.99 *(978-0-06-240317-9(6))*, HarperTeen) 2015. (ENG.). 336p. (gr. 9-12). 17.99 *(978-0-06-240316-2(8))*, HarperTeen) 2015. 352p. *(978-1-4063-3116-5(3))* HarperCollins Pubs.

O'Neill, Elizabeth. Alfred Visits Washington State. 2009. 24p. (J). pap. 12.00 *(978-0-9822288-4-5(8))* Global Business Information Strategies, Inc.

Palka, Yvonne. Dragon Fire Ocean Mist. 2009. pap. 12.95 *(978-0-9817668-0-5(3))* Heartrock Pr.

Reed, Amy. Crazy. (ENG.). (YA). (gr. 9). 2013. Illus.). 416p. pap. 9.99 *(978-1-4424-1348-1(4))* 2012. 384p. 16.99 *(978-1-4424-1347-4(6))* Simon Pulse. (Simon Pulse).

Robinson, Gary. Tribal Journey. 2013. (YA). 111p. *(978-1-939053-87-9(0))*; (ENG.). 120p. pap. 9.95 *(978-1-939053-01-5(3))*, 7th Generation) Book Publishing Co.

Rushford, Patricia H. Secrets of Ghost Island. 2007. (J). *(978-88-02-46255-4(0))* Moody Pubs.

Sampson, Jeff. Vesper. 2011. (Deviants Ser.: 1). (ENG.). 304p. (YA). (gr. 8-18). 16.99 *(978-0-06-199276-6(3))* HarperCollins Pubs.

Sargent, Dave & Sargent, Pat. Whiskers: (Roan) Pride & Peace. 30 vols., Vol. 59. Lenoir, Jane, illus. 2003. (Saddle up Ser.: Vol. 59). 42p. (J). pap. 10.95 *(978-1-56763-806-6(6))* Ozark Publishing.

Scott, Mindi. Live Through This. 2012. (ENG.). 304p. (YA). (gr. 9). 17.99 *(978-1-4424-4059-3(7))*; pap. 9.99 *(978-1-4424-4060-9(0))* Simon Pulse. (Simon Pulse).

The Secret of Bunratty Castle: Individual Title Six-Packs. (Action Packs Ser.). 104p. (gr. 3-5). 44.00 *(978-0-7635-3302-1(5))* Rigby Education.

Shaw Wolf, Jennifer. Dead Girls Don't Lie. 2013. 336p. pap. 17.99 *(978-0-8027-3450-1(2))* Walker & Co.

Shepard, Sara. The Good Girls. 2015. (Perfectionists Ser.: 2). (ENG.). 368p. (YA). (gr. 9). 17.99 *(978-0-06-207452-2(0))*, HarperTeen); 341p. (J). *(978-0-06-239115-5(1))* HarperCollins Pubs.

—The Perfectionists. 2014. (Perfectionists Ser.: 1). (ENG.). 336p. (YA). (gr. 9). 17.99 *(978-0-06-207469-0(5))* HarperCollins Pubs.

Silvano, Wendi. Love Is All Around Washington. Czernichowska, Joanna, illus. 2016. (ENG.). 32p. (J). (-6). 12.99 *(978-1-4926-2972-6(3))*, Sourcebooks Jabberwocky) Sourcebooks, Inc.

Smallman, Steve. Santa Is Coming to Bellingham. Dunn, Robert, illus. 2013. (ENG.). 32p. (J). (-3). 9.99 *(978-1-4022-9130-2(2))*, Sourcebooks Jabberwocky) Sourcebooks, Inc.

Snelling, Lauraine. What about Cimmaron? 2008. (J). 8.99 *(978-1-59166-872-5(7))* BJU Pr.

Sullivan, Jacqueline Levering. Annie's War. 2007. (Illus.). 183p. (J). (gr. 3-7). 15.00 *(978-0-8028-5325-7(0))*, Eerdmans Bks For Young Readers) Eerdmans, William B. Publishing Co.

Tarshis, Lauren. I Survived the Eruption of Mount St. Helens, 1980. 2016. (I Survived Ser.: 14). (ENG.). 112p. (J). (gr. 2-5). pap. 4.99 *(978-0-545-65852-2(7))*, Scholastic Paperbacks) Scholastic, Inc.

Thompson, Gare. Mount St. Helens 1980: Fiery Eruption! Inspiring Tales of Courage & Friendship. 2017. (Great Escapes Ser.). (ENG.). 240p. (J). (gr. 3-7). pap. 7.99 ***(978-1-4380-0972-8(0))*** Barron's Educational Series, Inc.

Vaughan, Richard & Crews, Marcia. Three Bears of the Pacific Northwest. Trammell, Jeremiah, illus. 2016. (ENG.). 20p. (J). (— 1). bds. 9.99 *(978-1-63217-076-7(0))*, Little Bigfoot) Sasquatch Bks.

Vaughan, Richard Lee & Vaughan, Marcia. Three Bears of the Pacific Northwest. Trammell, Jeremiah, illus. 2011. (ENG.). 32p. (J). (gr. -1-2). 17.99 *(978-1-57061-684-6(1))*, Little Bigfoot) Sasquatch Bks.

Walton, Rick. 10 Little Monsters Visit Washington. Smiley, Jess Smart, illus. 2015. (ENG.). 32p. (J). 16.95 *(978-1-942672-98-2(5))* Familius LLC.

Wenberg, Michael. Stringz. 2010. 216p. (YA). (gr. 6-10). 16.95 *(978-1-934813-33-1(8))* Westside Bks.

Wilsdon, Christina. On the Trail of Bigfoot in Washington. McCreary, Jane, illus. 2006. 26p. (J). 7.99 *(978-1-59939-012-3(4))* Cornerstone Pr.

Winget, Dianna Dorisi. A Million Ways Home. 2014. (ENG.). 272p. (J). (gr. 3-7). 16.99 *(978-0-545-66706-7(2))*, Scholastic Pr.) Scholastic, Inc.

Wolf, Jennifer Shaw. Dead Girls Don't Lie. 2014. (ENG.). 368p. (YA). (gr. 9). pap. 9.99 *(978-0-8027-3753-3(6))*, 9780802737533, Bloomsbury USA Childrens) Bloomsbury Publishing USA.

WASHINGTON (STATE)—HISTORY

Bauer, Marion Dane. Celebrating Washington State: 50 States to Celebrate. C.B. Canga, C. B., illus. 2014. (Green Light Readers Level 3 Ser.). (ENG.). 40p. (J). (gr. 1-4). pap. 3.99 *(978-0-544-28948-2(X))*, HMH Books For Young Readers) Houghton Mifflin Harcourt Publishing Co.

Conkling, Winifred. Passenger on the Pearl: The True Story of Emily Edmonson's Flight from Slavery. 2016. (ENG., Illus.). 176p. (YA). (gr. 7-10). pap. 10.95 *(978-1-61620-550-8(4))* Algonquin Bks. of Chapel Hill.

Downey, Tika. Washington: The Evergreen State. (Illus.). 24p. (J). 2010. pap. 8.25 *(978-1-4358-3346-3(5))*, 1300532) 2009. lib. bdg. 22.60 *(978-1-4042-8113-4(4))*, 1300532) Rosen Publishing Group, Inc., The. (PowerKids Pr.).

Freedman, Deborah K. & Tacoma Historical Society. Rising up from Tacoma's Twenty-One Disasters & Defeats: Based on Topics Chosen by the 2012-2013 Students of Seabury Middle School. 2015. (Illus.). 48p. (J). pap. 6.99 *(978-0-9846234-4-0(2))* Tacoma Historical Society.

Gish, Melissa. Washington. 2009. (This Land Called America Ser.). 32p. (YA). (gr. 3-6). 19.95 *(978-1-58341-800-0(8))* Creative Co., The.

Hengel, Katherine. The Apple State Treasure Hunt: A Story about Washington, 1 vol. Doucet, Bob, illus. 2011. (Fact & Fable: State Stories Set 3 Ser.). (ENG.). 24p. (J). (gr. -1-2). 25.65 *(978-1-61714-679-4(X))* ABDO Publishing Co.

Kleinmartin, Hex, et al. Washington. 2015. (J). lib. bdg. *(978-1-62712-757-8(7))* Cavendish Square Publishing.

Leigh, Autumn. Warning: Volcano! the Story of Mt. St. Helens. 2009. (Reading Room Collection 2 Ser.). 24p. (gr. 3-4). 42.50 *(978-1-60852-000-8(5))*, PowerKids Pr.) Rosen Publishing Group, Inc., The.

Marsh, Carole. Washington History Projects: 30 Cool, Activities, Crafts, Experiments & More for Kids to Do to Learn about Your State! 2003. (Washington Experience Ser.). 32p. (gr. k-5). pap. 5.95 *(978-0-635-01816-8(0))*, Marsh, Carole Bks.) Gallopade International.

Meinking, Mary. What's Great about Washington? 2015. (Our Great States Ser.). (ENG.). 32p. (gr. 2-5). pap. 7.95 *(978-1-4677-6089-8(7))*; (Illus.). lib. bdg. 26.60 *(978-1-4677-3865-1(4))* Lerner Publishing Group. (Lerner Pubns.).

Ollhoff, Jim. Washington, 1 vol. 2009. (United States Ser.). (ENG., Illus.). 48p. (YA). (gr. 2-5). 27.07 *(978-1-60453-683-6(7))* ABDO Publishing Co.

Otfinoski, Steven & Benduhn, Tea. Washington. 2nd rev. ed. 2010. (It's My State! Ser.). 80p. (gr. 3-18). lib. bdg. 31.36 *(978-1-60870-061-5(5))* Marshall Cavendish Corp.

Parker, Bridget. Washington. 2016. (States Ser.). (ENG., Illus.). 32p. (gr. 3-4). lib. bdg. 27.32 *(978-1-5157-0435-5(1))* Next Page Pr., The.

Pratt, Laura. Washington: The Evergreen State. 2012. (J). *(978-1-61913-415-7(2))*; pap. *(978-1-61913-416-4(0))* Weigl Pubs., Inc.

Stein, R. Conrad. Washington (Revised Edition) 2014. (America the Beautiful, Third Ser. (Revised Edition) Ser.). (ENG., Illus.). 144p. (J). lib. bdg. 40.00 *(978-0-531-28297-7(X))* Scholastic Library Publishing.

Stille, Darlene R. The Capitol Building, 1 vol. Ouren, Todd, illus. 2008. (Our Nation's Pride Ser.). (ENG.). 32p. (gr. -1-3). 28.50 *(978-1-60270-112-0(1))*, Looking Glass Library- Nonfiction) Magic Wagon.

Strudwick, Leslie. Washington. 2011. (Guide to American States Ser.). (Illus.). 48p. (YA). (gr. 3-6). 29.99 *(978-1-61690-820-1(3))* Weigl Pubs., Inc.

—Washington: The Evergreen State. 2016. (J). ***(978-1-5105-2099-8(6))*** SmartBook Media, Inc.

—Washington: The Evergreen State. 2016. (J). *(978-1-4896-4959-1(X))* Weigl Pubs., Inc.

Tieck, Sarah. Washington, 1 vol. 2012. (Explore the United States Ser.). (ENG., Illus.). 32p. (J). (gr. 2-5). lib. bdg. 28.50 *(978-1-61783-386-1(X))*, Big Buddy Bks.) ABDO Publishing Co.

The Washington Journey: New 7th Grade Textbook, 1 vol. l.t. ed. 2009. 281p. (gr. 7-9). 47.95 *(978-1-4236-0622-2(1))* Gibbs Smith, Publisher.

The Washington Journey Program Kit: All program components for the Washington Journey, 1 vol. 2009. 129.95 *(978-1-4236-0735-9(X))* Gibbs Smith, Publisher.

Washington, Our Home: New 4th Grade Textbook, 1 vol. l.t. ed. 2009. 218p. (gr. 4-4). 47.95 *(978-1-4236-0614-7(0))* Gibbs Smith, Publisher.

Washington, Our Home Program Kit: All program components for Washington, Our Home, 1 vol. 2009. (gr. 4-4). 169.95 *(978-1-4236-0734-2(1))* Gibbs Smith, Publisher.

Way, Jennifer. Washington. Brusca, Maria Cristina, tr. from ENG. 2006. (Bilingual Library of the United States of America Ser.: Set 2). (ENG & SPA., Illus.). 32p. (J). (gr. 3-6). lib. bdg. 25.25 *(978-1-4042-3113-9(7))* Rosen Publishing Group, Inc., The.

The Wonderful Washington Events Guide, 2006. 2005. (YA). per. 21.95 *(978-1-881005-49-0(6))* Gail's Guides.

Ziff, John. Northwest: Idaho, Oregon, Washington, Vol. 19. 2015. (Let's Explore the States Ser.). (Illus.). 64p. (J). (gr. 5). 23.95 *(978-1-4222-3331-3(6))* Mason Crest.

WASHINGTON MONUMENT (WASHINGTON, D.C.)

Aboff, Marcie. The Washington Monument. 2016. (Spring Forward Ser.). (J). (gr. 1). *(978-1-4900-6025-5(1))* Benchmark Education Co.

Ashley, Susan. The Washington Monument. 2004. (Weekly Reader Early Learning Library). (Illus.). 24p. (gr. 1-4). pap. 8.15 *(978-0-8368-4151-0(4))*; lib. bdg. 22.00 *(978-0-8368-4144-2(1))* Stevens, Gareth Publishing LLLP. (Weekly Reader Leveled Readers).

Carr, Aaron. Washington Monument. 2013. (J). *(978-1-62127-205-2(2))*; pap. *(978-1-62127-209-0(5))* Weigl Pubs., Inc.

Joseph, Natalie. Visit the Washington Monument. 2012. (Landmarks of Liberty Ser.). (Illus.). 24p. (J). (gr. 2-5). pap. 8.15 *(978-1-4339-6406-0(6))*, Gareth Stevens Learning Library); (ENG., lib. bdg. 22.60 *(978-1-4339-6404-6(X))* Stevens, Gareth Publishing LLLP.

Landau, Elaine. The Washington Monument. 2004. (Cornerstones of Freedom Ser.). (ENG.). 48p. (YA). (gr. 4-7). 26.00 *(978-0-516-24238-5(5))* Scholastic Library Publishing.

Marcovitz, Hal. The Washington Monument. 2004. (American Symbols & Their Meanings Ser.). (Illus.). 48p. (J). (gr. 4-18). lib. bdg. 19.95 *(978-1-59084-028-3(3))* Mason Crest.

—Washington Monument: Memorial to a Founding Father. Moreno, Barry, ed. 2014. (Patriotic Symbols of America Ser.: 20). 48p. (J). (gr. 4-18). lib. bdg. 20.95 *(978-1-4222-3137-1(2))* Mason Crest.

Murray, Julie. Washington Monument, 1 vol. 2005. (Buddy Book Ser.). (ENG., Illus.). 24p. (gr. k-4). 25.65 *(978-1-59197-509-0(3))*, Buddy Bks.) ABDO Publishing Co.

Murray, Robb. The Washington Monument: Myths, Legends, & Facts, 1 vol. 2014. (Monumental History Ser.). (ENG.). 32p. (gr. 3-4). 27.32 *(978-1-4914-0206-1(7))*, Fact Finders) Capstone Press of Coughlan Cos.

Nelson, Kristin L. The Washington Monument. (Lightning Bolt Bks.). (gr. k-2). 2010. (Illus.). 32p. (J). lib. bdg. 25.26 *(978-0-7613-6019-3(0))*, Lerner Pubns.) 2010. pap. 45.32 *(978-0-7613-6994-3(5))* 2010. (ENG.). 32p. pap. 7.95 *(978-0-7613-6053-7(0))* 2003. (ENG.). 32p. pap. 7.95 *(978-0-8225-3759-5(1))* 2003. (ENG., Illus.). 32p. lib. bdg. 22.60 *(978-0-8225-0250-0(X))* Lerner Publishing Group.

RJF Publishing Staff & Schaffer, Julia. The Washington Monument. 2009. (Symbols of American Freedom Ser.). 48p. (gr. 4-6). 30.00 *(978-1-60413-517-6(4))*, Chelsea Clubhouse) Facts On File, Inc.

WASHINGTON NATIONALS (BASEBALL TEAM)

Bodden, Valerie. Bryce Harper: Big Time. 2013. 21p. 23.09 *(978-1-60818-474-3(9))* Creative Co., The.

Connery-Boyd, Peg. Washington Nationals. 2016. (Hawk's Nest Activity Bks.: 0). (ENG.). 64p. (J). (gr. k-3). pap., act. bk. ed. 8.99 *(978-1-4926-3372-3(0))* Sourcebooks, Inc.

Epstein, Brad. Washington Nationals 101. 2008. (My First Team Board Bks.). (ENG., Illus.). 22p. (J). (gr. -1). bds. *(978-1-932530-86-5(X))*, 101 Bk.) Michaelson Entertainment.

Goessling, Ben. Washington Nationals, 1 vol. (Inside MLB Ser.). (ENG., 48p. (gr. 3-6). 2011. Illus.). (YA). lib. bdg. 32.79 *(978-1-61714-063-1(5))* 2014. lib. bdg. 32.79 *(978-1-62403-489-3(6))*, SportsZone) ABDO Publishing Co.

Goodman, Michael E. The Story of the Washington Nationals. 2011. (Baseball: the Great American Game Ser.). (Illus.). 48p. (J). (gr. 5-8). lib. bdg. 34.25 *(978-1-60818-060-8(3))*, Creative Education) Creative Co., The.

Hawkes, Brian. The Story of the Washington Nationals. 2007. (Baseball, the Great American Game Ser.). (Illus.). 48p. (YA). (gr. 4-7). lib. bdg. 32.80 *(978-1-58341-553-5(X))* Creative Co., The.

Raum, Elizabeth. Pro Sports Biographies: Bryce Harper. 2017. (Pro Sports Biographies Ser.). (ENG.). 24p. (J). (gr. 1-3). pap. 8.99 ***(978-1-68152-166-4(0))*** Amicus.

—Pro Sports Biographies: Cam Newton. 2017. (Pro Sports Biographies Ser.). (ENG.). 24p. (J). (gr. 1-3). pap. 8.99 ***(978-1-68152-168-8(7))*** Amicus.

Stewart, Mark. The Washington Nationals. 2012. (Team Spirit Ser.). 48p. (J). (gr. 3-6). lib. bdg. 29.27 *(978-1-59953-501-2(7))* Norwood Hse. Pr.

WASHINGTON REDSKINS (FOOTBALL TEAM)

Basen, Ryan. Washington Redskins, 1 vol. 2010. (Inside the NFL Ser.). (ENG.). 48p. (YA). (gr. 3-6). lib. bdg. 32.79 *(978-1-61714-032-7(5))* ABDO Publishing Co.

Burgess, Zack. Meet the Washington Redskins. 2016. (Big Picture Sports Ser.). (ENG., Illus.). 24p. (J). (gr. k-3). lib. bdg. 22.60 *(978-1-59953-746-7(X))* Norwood Hse. Pr.

Epstein, Brad M. Washington Redskins 101. 2010. (ENG., Illus.). 24p. (J). bds. *(978-1-60730-131-8(8))*, 101 Bk.) Michaelson Entertainment.

Frisch, Aaron. Washington Redskins. 2011. (Super Bowl Champions Ser.). (J). (gr. 1-3). 24.25 *(978-1-60818-030-1(1))* Creative Co., The.

—Washington Redskins. 2014. (Illus.). 24p. (J). 18.95 *(978-1-60818-389-0(0))*, Creative Editions) Creative Co., The.

Gilbert, Sara. NFL Today: Washington Redskins. 2013. (NFL Today Ser.). (ENG.). 48p. (J). (gr. 4-7). pap. 12.00 *(978-0-89812-876-5(5))*, Creative Paperbacks) Creative Co., The.

—The Story of the Washington Redskins. 2013. (Illus.). 48p. (J). 35.65 *(978-1-60818-323-4(8))*, Creative Education) Creative Co., The.

Goodman, Michael E. The History of the Washington Redskins. 2004. (NFL Today Ser.). (Illus.). 32p. (YA). (gr. 5-9). 18.95 *(978-1-58341-317-3(0))* Creative Co., The.

—The Story of the Washington Redskins. 2009. (NFL Today Ser.). 48p. (YA). (gr. 5-9). 22.95 *(978-1-58341-774-4(5))* Creative Co., The.

Mack, Larry. The Washington Redskins Story. 2016. (NFL Teams Ser.). (ENG., Illus.). 32p. (J). (gr. 3-7). lib. bdg. 26.95 *(978-1-62617-386-6(9))*, Torque Bks.) Bellwether Media.

Stewart, Mark. The Washington Redskins. rev. ed. 2012. (Team Spirit Ser.). (ENG.). 48p. (J). (gr. 3-6). lib. bdg. 29.27 *(978-1-59953-543-2(2))* Norwood Hse. Pr.

Temple, Ramey. Washington Redskins. (Illus.). 32p. (J). 2015. pap. *(978-1-4896-0907-6(5))* 2014. (ENG., (gr. 4-7). lib. bdg. 28.55 *(978-1-4896-0906-9(7))*, AV2 by Weigl) Weigl Pubs., Inc.

Wilner, Barry. Washington Redskins. 2015. (Insider's Guide to Pro Football Ser.). (ENG.). 32p. (J). (gr. k-3). 28.50 *(978-1-63407-006-5(2))*, 208841) Child's World, Inc., The.

Zappa, Marcia. Washington Redskins, 1 vol. 2014. (NFL's Greatest Teams Set 2 Ser.). (ENG.). 32p. (gr. 2-5). 28.50 *(978-1-62403-592-0(2))* ABDO Publishing Co.

WASPS

Berne, Emma Carlson. Yellow Jackets. 2014. (Scavengers: Eating Nature's Trash Ser.). (Illus.). 24p. (J). (gr. k-5). pap. 49.50 *(978-1-4777-6594-4(8))*, PowerKids Pr.) Rosen Publishing Group, Inc., The.

Dibble, Traci. Bees & Wasps. 2015. (1G Bugs Ser.). (ENG., Illus.). 24p. (J). pap. 5.99 *(978-1-63437-095-0(3))* American Reading Co.

George, Lynn. Wasps: Nest Builders. 2010. (Animal Architects Ser.). (ENG.). 24p. (J). pap. 8.25 *(978-1-4488-1347-6(6))*; lib. bdg. 22.60 *(978-1-4488-0693-5(3))* Rosen Publishing Group, Inc., The. (PowerKids Pr.).

Green, Jen. Wasps. 2009. (Illus.). 52p. (J). *(978-0-7172-8077-3(2))* Grolier, Ltd.

Harris, Monica. Paper Wasp. 2003. (Bug Bks.). (Illus.). 32p. (J). lib. bdg. 22.79 *(978-1-4034-0767-2(3))* Heinemann-Raintree.

Maclaine, James. Bees & Wasps. 2013. (Beginner's Nature Ser.). 32p. (J). ring bd. 4.99 *(978-0-7945-3360-1(4))*, Usborne) EDC Publishing.

McKinney, Devon. Watch Out for Wasps!, 01 vols., 1. 2016. (Wild Backyard Animals Ser.). (ENG., Illus.). 24p. (J). pap. 8.25 *(978-1-5081-4270-6(X))*, PowerKids Pr.) Rosen Publishing Group, Inc., The.

Morgan, Sally. Bees & Wasps. 2006. (Animal Lives (QEB Publishing) Ser.). (Illus.). 32p. (J). (gr. 4-7). lib. bdg. 19.95 *(978-1-59566-202-6(2))* QEB Publishing Inc.

Morgan, Sally & Teacher Created Resources Staff. Bees & Wasps. 2007. (Animal Lives (QEB Publishing) Ser.). (ENG., Illus.). 32p. (gr. 2-9). pap. 7.99 *(978-1-4206-8112-3(5))* Teacher Created Resources, Inc.

Pallotta, Jerry. Hornet vs. Wasp. Bolster, Rob, illus. 2013. 32p. (J). pap. *(978-0-545-45190-1(6))* Scholastic, Inc.

Perish, Patrick. Wasps. 2017. (Insects up Close Ser.). (ENG., Illus.). 24p. (J). (gr. k-3). lib. bdg. 25.95 ***(978-1-62617-668-3(X))***, Blastoff! Readers) Bellwether Media.

Rockwood, Leigh. Tell Me the Difference Between a Bee & a Wasp. 2013. (How Are They Different? Ser.). (ENG., Illus.). 24p. (J). (gr. k-5). pap. 8.25 *(978-1-4488-9736-0(X))*; lib. bdg. 22.60 *(978-1-4488-9639-4(8))* Rosen Publishing Group, Inc., The. (PowerKids Pr.).

Rustad, Martha E. H. Wasps. 2007. (World of Insects Ser.). (ENG., Illus.). 24p. (J). (gr. k-3). lib. bdg. 25.95 *(978-1-60014-076-1(9))* Bellwether Media.

Scarborough, Kate. A Wasp Builds a Nest. Camm, Martin, illus. 2016. (ENG.). 24p. (J). 12.95 *(978-1-77085-695-0(1))*, 9781770856950) Firefly Bks., Ltd.

Schuh, Mari. Wasps. 2014. (Illus.). 24p. (J). lib. bdg. 25.65 *(978-1-62031-088-5(0))*, Bullfrog Bks.) Jump! Inc.

Silverman, Buffy. Can You Tell a Bee from a Wasp? 2011. (Lightning Bolt Books (tm) — Animal Look-Alikes Ser.). (ENG.). 32p. (gr. k-2). pap. 7.95 *(978-0-7613-7843-3(X))*; (Illus.). lib. bdg. 26.60 *(978-0-7613-6730-7(6))* Lerner Publishing Group.

Taylor, Trace. Wasps. 2009. (2G Bugs Ser.). (ENG.). 12p. (J). (gr. k-2). pap. 5.99 *(978-1-59301-853-5(3))* American Reading Co.

WASTE (ECONOMICS)

Berry, Joy. Help Me Be Good about Being Wasteful. 2009. (Help Me Be Good Ser.). 32p. pap. 7.95 *(978-1-60577-105-2(8))* Berry, Joy Enterprises.

Berry, Joy Wilt. A Book about Being Wasteful. 2005. (Illus.). (J). *(978-0-7172-8587-7(1))* Scholastic, Inc.

Chancellor, Deborah. Food Waste. 2010. (Reduce, Reuse, Recycle! Ser.). 32p. (J). (ENG.). pap. 10.60 *(978-1-61532-240-4(X))*, PowerKids Pr.); (gr. 1-5). E-Book 50.50 *(978-1-4488-0363-7(2))*; (Illus.). (gr. 2-5). lib. bdg. 26.50 *(978-1-61532-233-6(7))* Rosen Publishing Group, Inc., The.

WASTE DISPOSAL

see Refuse and Refuse Disposal; Sewage Disposal; Waste Products

WASTE PRODUCTS

see also Refuse and Refuse Disposal

Bellamy, Rufus. Waste & Pollution. 2010. (Sustaining Our Environment Ser.). 48p. (J). 35.65 *(978-1-60753-139-5(9))* Amicus Publishing.

Bone, Emily & Pratt, Leonie. Recycling Things to Make & Do. 2010. (Activity Book Ser.). 32p. (J). pap. 6.99 *(978-0-7945-2675-7(6))*, Usborne) EDC Publishing.

Green, Jen. Reducing Pollution & Waste, 1 vol. 2011. (Environment Challenge Ser.). (ENG., Illus.). 48p. (gr. 5-6). pap. 9.49 *(978-1-4109-4306-4(2))*, Raintree Freestyle) Heinemann-Raintree.

Holt, Rinehart and Winston Staff. Environmental Science Chptr. 19: Waste. 4th ed. Date not set. pap. 11.20 *(978-0-03-068081-6(6))* Holt McDougal.

Junk: A Journey Through the Dark Matter of the Genome. (Jump Ser.). (Illus.). 36p. (J). (gr. 2-6). pap. *(978-1-882210-37-4(9))* Action Publishing, Inc.

Knighton, Kate. Why Shouldn't I Eat Junk Food? Larkum, Adam, illus. 2008. (Usborne Ser.). 48p. (J). (gr. 4-7). pap. 6.99 *(978-0-7945-1953-7(9))*, Usborne) EDC Publishing.

Llimós Plomer, Anna. Earth-Friendly Christmas Crafts in 5 Easy Steps. 2013. (Earth-Friendly Crafts in 5 Easy Steps Ser.). (Illus.). 32p. (J). lib. bdg. 23.94 *(978-0-7660-4188-2(3))* Enslow Pubs., Inc.

—Earth-Friendly Crafts from Recycled Stuff in 5 Easy Steps. 2013. (Earth-Friendly Crafts in 5 Easy Steps Ser.). (Illus.). 32p. (J). lib. bdg. 23.94 *(978-0-7660-4190-5(5))* Enslow Pubs., Inc.

Scheunemann, Pam. Cool Odds & Ends Projects: Creative Ways to Upcycle Your Trash into Treasure, 1 vol. 2012. (Cool Trash to Treasure Ser.). (ENG.). 32p. (J). (gr. 3-6). 27.07 *(978-1-61783-435-6(1))*, Checkerboard Library) ABDO Publishing Co.

—Cool Paper Projects: Creative Ways to Upcycle Your Trash into Treasure, 1 vol. 2012. (Cool Trash to Treasure Ser.). (ENG.). 32p. (J). (gr. 3-6). 27.07 *(978-1-61783-436-3(X))*, Checkerboard Library) ABDO Publishing Co.

—Cool Plastic Projects: Creative Ways to Upcycle Your Trash into Treasure, 1 vol. 2012. (Cool Trash to Treasure Ser.).

W X Y Z

(ENG.). 32p. (J). (gr. 3-6). 27.07 (978-1-61783-437-0(8), Checkerboard Library) ABDO Publishing Co.

Shea, Jerry. Where Does the Recycling Go? 2012. (Everyday Mysteries Ser.). (ENG., Illus.). 24p. (J). (gr. 2-4). 22.60 (978-1-4339-6333-9(7)); pap. 8.15 (978-1-4339-6335-3(3)) Stevens, Gareth Publishing LLLP.

Walker, Kate. Paper. 2010. (Recycling Ser.). 32p. (gr. 1). 28.50 (978-1-60870-132-2(8)) Marshall Cavendish Corp.

Watson, Stephanie. Making Good Choices about Recycling & Reuse. 2009. (J). 77.70 (978-1-4358-5607-3(4), Rosen Reference); (ENG.). 64p. (YA). pap. 12.95 (978-1-4358-5606-6(6), Rosen Reference); (Illus.). 64p. (YA). (gr. 5-9). lib. bdg. 31.95 (978-1-4358-5312-6(1)) Rosen Publishing Group, Inc., The.

Yanish, Brian. ScrapKins: Junk Re-Thunk: Amazing Creations You Can Build from Junk. Yanish, Brian, illus. 2016. (ENG., Illus.). 80p. (J). pap. 12.99 (978-1-62779-133-5(7), 9781627791335, Holt, Henry & Co. Bks. For Young Readers) Holt, Henry & Co.

WATCHES

see Clocks and Watches

WATER

see also Floods; Fog; Glaciers; Hydraulic Engineering; Ice; Lakes; Ocean; Rain and Rainfall; Rivers; Snow

Ackland, Nick. Splash! Bradley, Jennie, illus. 2016. (Baby Sparkler Ser.). (ENG.). 10p. (J). (gr. -1 — 1). bds. 5.99 (978-0-7641-6847-5(9)) Barron's Educational Series, Inc.

Anderson, Nancy. Water & Life. 2016. (Rosen REAL Readers: STEM & STEAM Collection). 8p. (gr. 1-k). pap. 5.46 (978-1-5081-2380-4(2), Rosen Classroom) Rosen Publishing Group, Inc., The.

Asch, Frank. Water. 2014. 17.00 (978-1-63419-750-2(X)) Perfection Learning Corp.

Atkins, Jill & Dorling Kindersley Publishing Staff. Water Everywhere. 2007. (DK Readers Ser.). (ENG., Illus.). 32p. (J). (gr. 1-3). pap. 3.99 (978-0-7566-2532-0(7), DK Children) Dorling Kindersley Publishing, Inc.

Bailey, Gerry & Way, Steve. Water. 2009. (Simply Science Ser.). (Illus.). 32p. (YA). (gr. 3-6). lib. bdg. 26.00 (978-1-4339-0037-2(8)) Stevens, Gareth Publishing LLLP.

Bailey, Jacqui. A Drop in the Ocean: The Story of Water. Lilly, Matthew, illus. 2004. (Science Works). (ENG.). 32p. (gr. 3-6). per. 7.95 (978-1-4048-1127-0(3)) Picture Window Bks.

Ball, Nate. Let's Investigate with Nate #1: the Water Cycle. Hargis, Wes, illus. 2017. (Let's Investigate with Nate Ser.: 1). 40p. (J). (gr. -1-3). pap. 6.99 (978-0-06-235739-7(5)) HarperCollins Pubs.

Banyard, Antonia & Ayer, Paula. Water Wow! A Visual Exploration. Wuthrich, Belle, illus. 2016. (Visual Exploration Ser.). (ENG.). 64p. (J). (gr. 3-7). pap. 12.95 (978-1-55451-821-0(0)) Annick Pr., Ltd. CAN. Dist: Publishers Group West (PGW).

Barker, Geoff. Water. 2010. (World at Risk Ser.). (YA). (gr. 5-9). 34.25 (978-1-59920-379-9(0)) Black Rabbit Bks.

Bates, Matthew. The Ways We Use Water. 2012. (InfoMax Readers Ser.). (ENG., Illus.). 24p. (J). (gr. 1-2). pap. 8.25 (978-1-4488-9013-2(6), Rosen Classroom) Rosen Publishing Group, Inc., The.

Benchmark Education Company. Water on Earth (Teacher Guide) 2005. (978-1-4108-4637-2(7)) Benchmark Education Co.

Benchmark Education Company, LLC Staff, compiled by. Water. 2006. spiral bd. 375.00 (978-1-4108-6792-6(7)) Benchmark Education Co.

—Water & Weather. 2006. spiral bd. 330.00 (978-1-4108-7018-6(9)) 2006. (J). 206.00 (978-1-4108-7056-8(1)) 2005. (J). spiral bd. 265.00 (978-1-4108-5759-0(X)) Benchmark Education Co.

—Water & Weather: Theme Set. 2006. (J). 215.00 (978-1-4108-7132-9(0)) Benchmark Education Co.

Berne, Emma. From River to Raindrop: The Water Cycle. 2017. (Start to Finish, Second Ser.). (ENG.). (J). (gr. k-3). pap. 6.99 (978-1-5124-5623-3(3)) Lerner Publishing Group.

Berne, Emma Carlson. From River to Raindrop: The Water Cycle. 2017. (Start to Finish, Second Ser.). (ENG.). 24p. (J). (gr. k-3). 23.99 (978-1-5124-3442-2(6)) Lerner Publishing Group.

Bethea, Nikole Brooks. The Water Cycle. 3rd rev. ed. 2011. (Science Foundations Ser.). (Illus.). 118p. (gr. 6-12). 35.00 (978-1-60413-943-3(9), Chelsea Hse.) Facts On File, Inc.

Blokland, Suzanne & Hammer, Randy. God's Blue Earth: Teaching Kids to Celebrate the Sacred Gift of Water. 2013. (Illus.). viii, 134p. (J). (978-0-8298-1941-0(X)) Pilgrim Pr., The/United Church Pr.

Bodden, Valerie. Water Rides. 2012. (Illus.). 24p. (J). 25.65 (978-1-60818-115-5(4), Creative Education) Creative Co., The.

Boelts, Maribeth. A World of Water. 2016. (Spring Forward Ser.). (J). (gr. 2). (978-1-4900-6028-6(6)) Benchmark Education Co.

Bond, Janice & Fiebelkorn, Claire. Water on Earth. 2012. (InfoMax Readers Ser.). (ENG., Illus.). 24p. (J). (gr. 1-2). pap. 8.25 (978-1-4488-9034-7(9), Rosen Classroom) Rosen Publishing Group, Inc., The.

Bourgoing, Pascale De, et al. Water. 2007. (ENG., Illus.). 36p. (J). (gr. k-3). pap. 11.99 (978-1-85103-108-5(1)) Moonlight Publishing, Ltd. GBR. Dist: Independent Pubs. Group.

Brannon, Barbara. Discover Water. 2005. (J). pap. (978-1-4108-5125-3(7)) Benchmark Education Co.

Burgan, Michael. Land & Water. 2004. (Discovery Channel School Science Ser.). (Illus.). 32p. (gr. 4-8). lib. bdg. 26.00 (978-0-8368-3381-2(3), Gareth Stevens Learning Library) Stevens, Gareth Publishing LLLP.

Burstein, John. Outstanding Oils & Wonderful Water. 2009. (Slim Goodbody's Nutrition Edition Ser.). (ENG., Illus.). 24p. (J). (gr. k-3). pap. (978-0-7787-5061-1(2)); lib. bdg. (978-0-7787-5046-8(9)) Crabtree Publishing Co.

Burton, Margie, et al. Water. 2011. (Early Connections Ser.). (J). (978-1-61672-313-2(0)) Benchmark Education Co.

—*Water Goes up! Water Comes Down!* 2011. (Early Connections Ser.). (J). (978-1-61672-510-5(9)) Benchmark Education Co.

—We Use Water. 2011. (Early Connections Ser.). (J). (978-1-61672-274-6(6)) Benchmark Education Co.

Canavan, Roger. You Wouldn't Want to Live Without Clean Water! Antram, David, illus. 2014. (You Wouldn't Want to Live Without... Ser.). (ENG.). 32p. (J). lib. bdg. 29.00 (978-0-531-21219-6(X), Watts, Franklin) Scholastic Library Publishing.

Cardenas, Ernesto A. Bodies of Water. 2009. pap. 4.95 (978-1-60698-062-0(9)) Milo Educational Bks. & Resources.

—Water Cycle. 2009. pap. 4.95 (978-1-60698-096-5(3)) Milo Educational Bks. & Resources.

Centore, Michael. Water. 2017. (J). (978-1-4222-3746-5(X)) Mason Crest.

Claybourne, Anna. Make It Splash!, 1 vol. Scott, Kimberly & Dean, Venetia, illus. 2014. (Whiz Kid Science Ser.). (ENG.). 32p. (gr. 2-4). 29.99 (978-1-4109-6749-7(2), Read Me!) Heinemann-Raintree.

Cobb, Vicki. Squirts & Spurts: Science Fun with Water. Haefele, Steve, illus. 2007. (Science Fun with Vicki Cobb Ser.). 48p. (J). (gr. 4-7). per. 7.95 (978-0-8225-7024-0(6), First Avenue Editions) Lerner Publishing Group.

Cole, Joanna. At the Waterworks. 2004. (Magic School Bus Original Ser.). (gr. k-3). lib. bdg. 17.20 (978-0-8335-1744-9(9), Turtleback) Turtleback Bks.

Cornell, Kari. Water. 2016. (Illus.). 24p. (J). (978-0-87659-700-2(2)) Gryphon Hse., Inc.

Cothran, Helen, ed. Water. 2006. (Fueling the Future Ser.). (ENG., Illus.). 120p. (J). (gr. 3-7). lib. bdg. 39.35 (978-0-7377-3593-2(7), 1256648, Greenhaven Pr., Inc.) Cengage Gale.

Croce, Nicholas, ed. Oceanography & Hydrology. 2016. (Study of Science Ser.). 96p. (gr. 8-8). 72.50 (978-1-68048-234-8(3));1. (ENG.). (J). 36.25 (978-1-68048-235-5(1)) Rosen Publishing Group, Inc., The. (Britannica Educational Publishing).

Danielson, Ethan. Our Water Experiment. 2012. (InfoMax Readers Ser.). (ENG., Illus.). 24p. (J). (gr. 1-2). pap. 8.25 (978-1-4488-9031-6(4), Rosen Classroom) Rosen Publishing Group, Inc., The.

Dawson, Emily C. How Animals Find Water. 2010. (Our Animal World Ser.). 24p. (J). 25.65 (978-1-60753-011-4(2)) Amicus Publishing.

Dayton, Connor. Water. 2014. (Four Elements Ser.). (Illus.). 32p. (J). (gr. k-3). pap. 60.00 (978-1-4777-9265-0(1)) Windmill Bks.

Del Moral, Susana. Agua Por Todas Partes. Zaidi, Nadeem, illus. 2006. (SPA.). 8p. (J). (gr. -1). (978-970-718-452-7(3), Silver Dolphin en Español) Advanced Marketing, S. de R. L. de C. V.

Delaunois, Angèle. Water's Children: Celebrating the Resource That Unites Us All. Woods, Erin, tr. from FRE. Frischeteau, Gérard, illus. 2017. (ENG.). 32p. (J). (gr. k-3). 16.95 (978-1-77278-015-4(4)) Pajama Pr. CAN. Dist: Ingram Publisher Services.

Desonie, Dana. Hydrosphere: Freshwater Systems & Pollution. 2007. (Our Fragile Planet Ser.). (Illus.). 194p. (J). (gr. 7-12). lib. bdg. 35.00 (978-0-8160-6215-7(3)) Facts On File, Inc.

Dickmann, Nancy. The Water Cycle. 2016. (Earth Figured Out Ser.). (ENG.). 32p. (J). (gr. 4-4). pap. 10.58 (978-1-5026-0858-1(8)) Cavendish Square Publishing.

Disney Publishing Staff. The Wonders of Water, 15 vols. 2003. (It's Fun to Learn Ser.). (Illus.). 32p. (J). (gr. -1-3). 3.99 (978-1-57973-137-3(6)) Advance Pubs. LLC.

Ditchfield, Christin. The Story Behind Water, 1 vol. 2011. (True Stories Ser.). (ENG.). 32p. (gr. 3-3). 30.65 (978-1-4329-5440-6(7), NA-h) Heinemann-Raintree.

Doudna, Kelly. Super Simple Things to Do with Water: Fun & Easy Science for Kids, 1 vol. 2011. (Super Simple Science Ser.). (ENG., Illus.). 24p. (J). (gr. k-3). lib. bdg. 25.65 (978-1-61714-677-0(3)) ABDO Publishing Co.

Duke, Shirley. The Earth & the Role of Water. 2012. (ENG.). 48p. (gr. 4-6). pap. 10.95 (978-1-61810-259-1(1)) Rourke Educational Media.

—Step-by-Step Experiments with the Water Cycle. Ostrom, Bob, illus. 2012. (Step-By-Step Experiments Ser.). (ENG.). 32p. (J). (gr. 1-4). lib. bdg. 29.93 (978-1-60973-615-6(X), 201241) Child's World, Inc., The.

Duke, Shirley Smith. The Water Cycle. 2016. (J). (978-1-4896-5298-0(1)) Weigl Pubs., Inc.

Dutton, Michael. The Water Cycle Coloring Book. 2012. (Dover Nature Coloring Book Ser.). (ENG.). 32p. (J). (gr. 2-5). pap. 3.99 (978-0-486-47988-0(9)) Dover Pubns., Inc.

Edison, Erin. Rain, 1 vol. 2011. (Weather Basics Ser.). (ENG.). 24p. (gr. k-1). lib. bdg. 26.65 (978-1-4296-6055-6(4), Pebble Plus) Capstone Press of Coughlan Cos.

Edison, Erin & Saunders-Smith, Gail. Lluvia. Strictly Spanish LLC. Staff, tr. from ENG. 2013. (Lo Básico Sobre el Tiempo/Weather Basics Ser.).Tr. of Rain. (SPA, ENG & MUL.). 24p. (gr. k-1). lib. bdg. 26.65 (978-1-62065-165-0(3)) Capstone Press of Coughlan Cos.

Edom, H. Science Activities, Vol. 1. 2010. (Science Activities Ser.). 72p. (J). 13.99 (978-0-7945-2752-5(3), Usborne) EDC Publishing.

Enz, Tammy. Liquid Planet: Exploring Water on Earth with Science Projects. (Illus.). 32p. 2016. (J). lib. bdg. (978-1-4747-0325-3(9)) 2015. (ENG., (gr. 3-4). lib. bdg. 27.32 (978-1-4914-4817-5(2)) Capstone Press of Coughlan Cos.

Everthing Changes Interactive Packages: Water Changes. (Pebble Soup Explorations Ser.). (gr. -1-18). 52.00 (978-0-7578-5239-8(4)) Rigby Education.

Faucets & Water Sets: 1 Each of 3 Big Books. (Sunshinetm Science Ser.). (gr. 1-2). 111.50 (978-0-7802-2814-6(6)) Wright Group/McGraw-Hill.

Firely, G. M. The Raindrop. Holmes, Joshua D., illus. 2004. 21p. pap. 24.95 (978-1-4137-3388-4(3)) PublishAmerica, Inc.

Flood, Nancy Bo. Water Runs Through This Book. 2015. (ENG., Illus.). 64p. (J). (gr. 3-7). pap. 19.95 (978-1-936218-13-4(5)) Fulcrum Publishing.

Flynn, Claire E. Water World: Earth's Water Cycle. 2009. (Real Life Readers Ser.). 32p. (gr. 5-6). pap. 10.00 (978-1-4358-0193-6(8), Rosen Classroom); 32p. (gr. 5-5). 47.90 (978-1-60853-058-8(2), PowerKids Pr.); (J). pap. 60.00 (978-1-4358-0194-3(6), PowerKids Pr.); (J). lib. bdg. 25.25 (978-1-4358-2999-2(9), PowerKids Pr.) Rosen Publishing Group, Inc., The.

Flynn, James. Water. 2003. (Matter & Materials Ser.). (J). pap. (978-1-58417-167-6(7)); lib. bdg. (978-1-58417-161-4(8)) Lake Street Pubs.

Franklin, Yvonne. Las Charcas, 1 vol. rev. ed. 2010. (Science Readers: a Closer Look Ser.).Tr. of Ponds. (SPA., Illus.). 32p. (J). (gr. 2-3). pap. 8.99 (978-1-4333-2144-3(0)) Shell Educational Publishing.

Fridell, Ron. Protecting Earth's Water Supply. 2015. (Saving Our Living Earth Ser.). (ENG., Illus.). 72p. (gr. 4-7). 30.65 (978-1-5124-1051-8(9), Lerner Pubns.) Lerner Publishing Group.

Furgang, Kathy. Water All Around. 2011. (Early Connections Ser.). (J). (978-1-61672-606-5(7)) Benchmark Education Co.

—Water All Around: Set Of 6. 2011. (Early Connections Ser.). (J). pap. 37.00 net. (978-1-4108-1071-7(2)) Benchmark Education Co.

Galla, Nicole. Water & Ice. 2009. (Real Life Readers Ser.). 8p. (gr. k-1). pap. 5.15 (978-1-4042-7979-7(2), Rosen Classroom) Rosen Publishing Group, Inc., The.

Gallardo, Mary, illus. & as told by. The Tiny Little Raindrop. Gallardo, Mary, as told by. 2007. 32p. (J). 15.99 (978-0-9779763-0-0(0)) Blue Cat Bks.

Garbe, Suzanne. The Science Behind Wonders of the Water: Exploding Lakes, Ice Circles, & Brinicles. 2016. (Science Behind Natural Phenomena Ser.). (ENG., Illus.). 32p. (gr. 3-4). lib. bdg. 27.99 (978-1-5157-0776-9(8), Edge Bks.) Capstone Press of Coughlan Cos.

Gardner, Robert. Earth's Cycles: Great Science Projects about the Water Cycle, Photosynthesis, & More. 2011. (Team Green Science Projects Ser.). (Illus.). 112p. (J). (gr. 5-9). lib. bdg. 33.27 (978-0-7660-3644-4(8)) Enslow Pubs., Inc.

—Science Fair Projects about Water & Soil. 2016. (Hands-On Science Ser.). 48p. (J). pap. 11.70 (978-0-7660-8211-3(3)) Enslow Pubs., Inc.

—Super Science Projects about Earth's Soil & Water. LaBaff, Tom, illus. 2007. (Rockin' Earth Science Experiments Ser.). 48p. (J). (gr. 3-4). lib. bdg. 25.27 (978-0-7660-2735-0(X), Enslow Elementary) Enslow Pubs., Inc.

—Water: Green Science Projects for a Sustainable Planet. 2011. (Team Green Science Projects Ser.). (Illus.). 128p. (J). (gr. 5-9). lib. bdg. 33.27 (978-0-7660-3645-1(6)) Enslow Pubs., Inc.

Goodstein, Madeline P. Water Science Fair Projects, Revised & Expanded Using the Scientific Method. LaBaff, Tom & LaBaff, Stephanie, illus. 2010. (Chemistry Science Projects Using the Scientific Method Ser.). 160p. (J). (gr. 5-18). 35.94 (978-0-7660-3411-2(9)) Enslow Pubs., Inc.

Gordon, Sharon. Mojado Seco. 2006. (Bookworms Ser.). (SPA & ENG., Illus.). 24p. (gr. k-1). lib. bdg. 15.95 (978-0-7614-2370-6(2)) Marshall Cavendish Corp.

—Wet/Dry. 2007. (J). pap. 6.99 (978-0-7614-3285-2(X)) Marshall Cavendish Corp.

—Wet/Dry/Seco/Mojado. 2006. (Bookworms Ser.). (ENG & SPA., Illus.). 24p. (gr. k-1). lib. bdg. 15.95 (978-0-7614-2450-5(4)) Marshall Cavendish Corp.

Green, Jen. How the Water Cycle Works. 2008. (Our Earth Ser.). (Illus.). 24p. (J). (gr. 1-4). lib. bdg. 22.60 (978-1-4042-4273-9(2)) Rosen Publishing Group, Inc., The.

—Water. 2010. (J). pap. 10.60 (978-1-61532-246-6(9), PowerKids Pr.); 32p. (gr. 1-5). E-Book 50.50 (978-1-4488-0368-2(3)); (Illus.). 32p. (gr. 2-5). lib. bdg. 26.50 (978-1-61532-235-0(3)) Rosen Publishing Group, Inc., The.

Greene, Carol. I Love Our Water. 2012. (I Love Our Earth Ser.). (Illus.). 24p. (J). pap. 7.95 (978-1-4644-0138-1(1)); (gr. 3-4). 22.60 (978-0-7660-4042-7(9)) Enslow Pubs., Inc.

Gregoire, Maryellen. What Is Water? 2011. (Wonder Readers Emergent Level Ser.). (ENG.). (gr. -1-1). 8p. pap. 35.94 (978-1-4296-8238-1(8)); 32p. pap. 5.99 (978-1-4296-7849-0(6)) Capstone Press of Coughlan Cos. (Wonder Readers).

Gregory, Josh. Hydrologist. 2013. (21st Century Skills Library: Cool STEM Careers Ser.). (ENG., Illus.). 32p. (J). (gr. 4-8). 28.50 (978-1-62431-001-0(X), 202455); pap. 14.21 (978-1-62431-025-6(7), 202457) Cherry Lake Publishing.

Hamilton, Sue L. Water Parks. 2016. (Illus.). 32p. (J). (978-1-62403-754-2(2), 1391385) ABDO Publishing Co.

Hammersmith, Craig. The Water Cycle, 1 vol. 2011. (Earth & Space Science Ser.). (ENG.). 24p. (gr. k-1). pap. 7.29 (978-1-4296-7142-2(4)); pap. 41.70 (978-1-4296-7146-0(7)); lib. bdg. 26.65 (978-1-4296-6812-5(1)) Capstone Press of Coughlan Cos. (Pebble Plus).

Harman, Rebecca. The Water Cycle: Evaporation, Condensation & Erosion. 2016. (Earth's Processes Ser.). (ENG.). 32p. pap. 8.29 (978-1-4846-3820-0(4), Heinemann InfoSearch) Heinemann-Raintree.

Heitkamp, Kristina Lyn. The Water Cycle. 2017. (978-1-5383-0031-2(1)) Rosen Publishing Group, Inc., The.

Hewitt, Sally. Water. 2008. (Good for Me Ser.). (Illus.). 24p. (J). (gr. k-3). lib. bdg. 22.60 (978-1-4042-4291-3(0), PowerKids Pr.) Rosen Publishing Group, Inc., The.

Higgins, Nadia. Bodies of Water. Infante, Sara, illus. 2017. (Water All Around Us Ser.). (ENG.). 24p. (gr. 1-3). 33.99 (978-1-68410-011-8(9)) Cantata Learning.

—Discover Water. Yamada, Jane, illus. 2014. (Science Around Us Ser.). (ENG.). 24p. (J). (gr. -1-2). 25.64 (978-1-62687-307-0(0), 207148) Child's World, Inc., The.

Higgins, Nadia. Hop on the Water Cycle. Infante, Sara, illus. 2017. (Water All Around Us Ser.). (ENG.). 24p. (gr. 1-3). 33.99 (978-1-68410-035-4(6)) Cantata Learning.

Hill, E. C. Earth: the Water Planet: Text Pairs. 2008. (Bridges/Navigators Ser.). (J). (gr. 5). 94.00 (978-1-4108-8414-5(7)) Benchmark Education Co.

Hodge, Judith. Riches from Earth & Las riquezas de la Tierra: 6 English, 6 Spanish Adaptations. 2011. (ENG & SPA.). (J). 97.00 net. (978-1-4108-5716-3(6)) Benchmark Education Co.

Hollyer, Beatrice. Our World of Water: Children & Water Around the World. 2009. (ENG., Illus.). 48p. (J). (gr. -1-3). 17.99 (978-0-8050-8941-7(1), 9780805089417, Holt, Henry & Co. Bks. For Young Readers) Holt, Henry & Co.

Hooper, Meredith. The Drop in My Drink: The Story of Water on Our Planet. Coady, Chris, illus. 2015. (ENG.). 36p. (J). (gr. 1-4). pap. 9.99 (978-1-84780-714-4(3), Frances Lincoln) Quarto Publishing Group UK GBR. Dist: Hachette Bk. Group.

Hume, Desmond. Earth's Water. 2012. (Exploring Earth & Space Ser.). (ENG., Illus.). 24p. (J). (gr. 1-3). 22.60 (978-1-4488-8568-8(X), PowerKids Pr.) Rosen Publishing Group, Inc., The.

Hutson-Thompson, Holliday & Staggs, Kelley. Water Wonderful: An Activity Book for Grade K-3. 2010. (J). 21.00 (978-1-58321-810-5(6)) American Water Works Assn.

Issues, Evidence & You - Water Mega Module Complete Materials Package. 2003. (Illus.). tchr. ed., ring bd. (978-1-887725-42-2(3)); (YA). tchr. ed., stu. ed., per. (978-1-887725-60-6(1)) Lab-Aids, Inc.

James, Emily. The Simple Science of Water. 2017. (Simply Science Ser.). (ENG.). 32p. (gr. 1-2). lib. bdg. 27.32 (978-1-5157-7080-0(X), Aplus Bks.) Capstone Press of Coughlan Cos.

Johnson, Heather Dornjan. The Itsy Bitsy Water Cycle. 2007. (J). lib. bdg. 19.95 (978-1-933732-21-3(0)) Big Ransom Studio.

—Itsy Bitsy Water Cycle Audiobook. 2007. (J). lib. bdg. 24.95 (978-1-933732-22-0(9)) Big Ransom Studio.

Jones, Tammy. In the Water. 2009. (Sight Word Readers Set A Ser.). (J). 3.49 net. (978-1-60719-142-1(3)) Newmark Learning LLC.

Just Add Water: Individual Title Six-Packs. (Discovery World Ser.). 12p. (gr. k-1). 28.00 (978-0-7635-8451-1(7)) Rigby Education.

Kalman, Bobbie. Hogares de los Seres Vivos. 2008.Tr. of Living Things Need Water. (SPA.). 24p. (J). pap. (978-0-7787-8687-0(0)) Crabtree Publishing Co.

—Rapping about Bodies of Water. 2012. (ENG., Illus.). 24p. (J). (978-0-7787-2795-8(5)); pap. (978-0-7787-2802-3(1)) Crabtree Publishing Co.

—Water Changes. 2011. (ENG.). 16p. (J). (978-0-7787-9559-9(4)); pap. (978-0-7787-9584-1(5)) Crabtree Publishing Co.

Kalman, Bobbie & Sjonger, Rebecca. El Ciclo del Agua. 2006. (Libro de Bobbie Kalman Ser.). (SPA., Illus.). 32p. (J). (gr. 3-7). pap. (978-0-7787-8388-6(X)); lib. bdg. (978-0-7787-8374-9(X)) Crabtree Publishing Co.

—Le Cycle de L'eau. Briere, Marie-Josee, tr. from ENG. rev. ed. 2007. (Petit Monde Vivant Ser.). (FRE., Illus.). 32p. (J). (gr. 1-7). pap. 10.95 (978-2-89579-127-0(9)) Bayard Canada Livres CAN. Dist: Crabtree Publishing Co.

—The Water Cycle. 2006. (Nature's Changes Ser.). (ENG., Illus.). 32p. (J). (gr. 3-7). pap. (978-0-7787-2310-3(0)) Crabtree Publishing Co.

—Water Cycle. 2008. (ENG.). 32p. (J). (978-0-7787-7719-9(7)); (978-0-7787-7720-5(0)) Crabtree Publishing Co.

Kalz, Jill. Water. 2003. 24p. (J). lib. bdg. 21.35 (978-1-58340-302-0(7)) Black Rabbit Bks.

Kids: Healthy Water Healthy People. 2005. (SPA.). (J). 1.00 (978-1-888631-40-1(6)) Project WET Foundation.

Kids: The Water Story. 2004. (J). 1.00 (978-1-888631-31-9(7)) Project WET Foundation.

Kids: Water, Every Drop Counts. 2004. (J). 1.00 (978-1-888631-35-7(X)) Project WET Foundation.

KociendaGenevieve. WATER: VITAL FOR LIFE LOW INTERMEDIATE BOOK WITH ONLINE ACCESS. 2014. (ENG., Illus.). 24p. (J). pap. 9.50 (978-1-107-62251-7(4)) Cambridge Univ. Pr.

Koerner, Sandy, et al. Water Adventures Around the World, 10 vols. 2008. (ENG.). 30p. (J). (gr. 3-5). pap. 25.00 (978-1-58321-558-6(1)) American Water Works Assn.

Koontz, Robin. Water Goes Round: The Water Cycle, 1 vol. Davidson, Chris, illus. 2011. (First Graphics: Nature Cycles Ser.). (ENG.). 24p. (gr. 1-2). pap. 6.29 (978-1-4296-6231-4(X)); pap. 35.70 (978-1-4296-6400-4(2)) Capstone Press of Coughlan Cos.

Koontz, Robin Michal. Water Goes Round: The Water Cycle, 1 vol. Davidson, Chris, illus. 2010. (First Graphics: Nature Cycles Ser.). (ENG.). 24p. (gr. 1-2). lib. bdg. 23.99 (978-1-4296-5364-0(7)) Capstone Press of Coughlan Cos.

Korb, Rena. The Wild Water Cycle, 1 vol. Reibeling, Brandon, illus. 2007. (Science Rocks Ser.). (ENG.). 32p. (gr. -1-4). 28.50 (978-1-60270-041-3(9), Looking Glass Library-Nonfiction) Magic Wagon.

Lawrence, Ellen. Covered in Water. 2016. (Drip, Drip, Drop: Earth's Water Ser.: 6). (ENG., Illus.). 24p. (J). (gr. -1-3). 17.95 (978-1-943553-26-6(2)) Bearport Publishing Co., Inc.

—Everybody Needs Water. 2015. (My World Your World Ser.). (ENG.). 24p. (J). (gr. -1-3). lib. bdg. 23.93 (978-1-910549-08-7(8)) Bearport Publishing Co., Inc.

—Say Hello to H2O. 2016. (Drip, Drip, Drop: Earth's Water Ser.). (ENG., Illus.). 24p. (J). (gr. -1-3). 17.95 (978-1-943553-21-1(1)) Bearport Publishing Co., Inc.

—The Water Beneath Your Feet. 2016. (Drip, Drip, Drop: Earth's Water Ser.). (ENG., Illus.). 24p. (J). (gr. -1-3). 17.95 (978-1-943553-24-2(6)) Bearport Publishing Co., Inc.

—Wet, Blue, & Good for You. 2016. (Drip, Drip, Drop: Earth's Water Ser.). (ENG., Illus.). 24p. (J). (gr. -1-3). 17.95 (978-1-943553-25-9(4)) Bearport Publishing Co., Inc.

—What Is the Water Cycle? 2012. (Weather Wise Ser.). 24p. (J). (gr. -1-3). lib. bdg. 23.93 (978-1-61772-402-2(5)) Bearport Publishing Co., Inc.

—What's So Fresh about Fresh Water? 2016. (Drip, Drip, Drop: Earth's Water Ser.). (ENG., Illus.). 24p. (J). (gr. -1-3). 17.95 (978-1-943553-23-5(8)) Bearport Publishing Co., Inc.

Lawson, Barbara Spilman. Water, Water Everywhere. 2016. (Spring Forward Ser.). (J). (gr. 2). (978-1-4900-9446-5(6)) Benchmark Education Co.

Leake, Diyan. Water, Water Everywhere! (Water, Water Everywhere! Ser.). (ENG.). 24p. 2016. pap. 29.95 (978-1-4846-3868-2(9)) 2014. (gr. -1-1). 90.60 (978-1-4846-0453-3(9)) Heinemann-Raintree. (Acorn).

Lerner, K. Lee, et al. UXL Encyclopedia of Water Science, 3 vols. 2004. (Illus.). xlviii, 510p. (J). (978-0-7876-7674-2(8)); (978-0-7876-7675-9(6)); (978-0-7876-7673-5(X)) Cengage Gale. (UXL).

Levete, Sarah. A Tale of One Well in Malawi. 2010. (Big Picture: Climate Ser.). (ENG.). 24p. (gr. 1-2). pap. 41.70 (978-1-4296-5973-4(4), First Facts) Capstone Press of Coughlan Cos.

Levine, Shar. Bathtub Science. 2003. (Illus.). 80p. pap. 10.95 (978-0-8069-7243-5(2)) Sterling Publishing Co., Inc.

Lilly, Melinda. Water & Ice. (Read & Do Science Ser.). (Illus.). (J). 20.64 (978-1-58952-639-6(2)) Rourke Educational Media.

Linde, Barbara M. The Water Cycle. 2016. (Where's the Water? Ser.). 24p. (J). (gr. 3-2). pap. 8.15 (978-1-4824-4688-3(X)) Stevens, Gareth Publishing LLLP.

—Water on Earth. 2005. (J). pap. *(978-1-4108-4589-4(3))* Benchmark Education Co.
Lindeen, Mary. Water. 2017. (BeginningtoRead Ser.). (ENG.). 32p. (J). (-2). 22.60 ***(978-1-59953-875-4(X))***; pap. 11.94 ***(978-1-68404-094-0(9))*** Norwood Hse. Pr.
Llewellyn, Claire. Water Pink a Band. 2016. (Cambridge Reading Adventures Ser.). (ENG.). 16p. pap. 6.56 *(978-1-107-57584-4(2))* Cambridge Univ. Pr.
Lowery, Lawrence. Clouds, Rain, Clouds Again. 2013. (I Wonder Why Ser.). (ENG., Illus.). 36p. (J). (gr. k-3). pap. 11.95 *(978-1-938946-12-7(X))* National Science Teachers Assn.
Lundberg, Constance. Why We Need Water. 2009. (Real Life Readers Ser.). 12p. (gr. 1-2). pap. 5.90 *(978-1-4042-7915-5(6)*, Rosen Classroom) Rosen Publishing Group, Inc., The.
Madgwick, Wendy. Water Play. 2014. (ENG., Illus.). 270p. (J). (gr. -1-12). 8.99 *(978-1-86147-351-6(6)*, Armadillo) Anness Publishing GBR. Dist: National Bk. Network.
Maloof, Torrey. Water Cycle, 1 vol. rev. ed. 2014. (Science Readers: Content & Literacy Ser.). (ENG.). 32p. (gr. 2-2). pap. 8.99 *(978-1-4807-4612-1(6))* Teacher Created Materials, Inc.
Martineau, Susan. Bubbles in the Bathroom. Noyes, Leighton, illus. 2011. (Everyday Science Experiments Ser.). (ENG.). 24p. (J). (gr. 3-6). pap. 10.60 *(978-1-61533-409-4(2))*; lib. bdg. 25.25 *(978-1-61533-371-4(1))* Windmill Bks.
Masters, Nancy R. How Did That Get to My House? Water. 2009. (Community Connections: How Did That Get to My House? Ser.). (ENG.). 24p. (gr. 2-5). lib. bdg. 25.64 *(978-1-60279-475-7(8)*, 200252) Cherry Lake Publishing.
Maurer, Daniel D. Do You Really Want to Skate on Thin Ice? A Book about States of Matter. Alberini, Teresa, illus. 2016. (Adventures in Science Ser.). (ENG.). 24p. (J). (gr. k-3). 20.95 *(978-1-60753-958-2(6))* Amicus Publishing.
McAllan, Kate. Water Is Precious. 2012. (Discovery Education: the Environment Ser.). (ENG., Illus.). 32p. (J). (gr. 3-6). pap. 10.00 *(978-1-4488-7981-6(7))*; lib. bdg. 25.25 *(978-1-4488-7893-2(4))* Rosen Publishing Group, Inc., The. (PowerKids Pr.).
McGill, Jordan. Water Science Fair Projects. 2011. (J). *(978-1-61690-332-9(5))*; (gr. 3-5). pap. 12.95 *(978-1-61690-656-6(1)*, AV2 by Weigl); (Illus.). 24p. (gr. 3-6). 27.13 *(978-1-61690-652-8(9))* Weigl Pubs., Inc.
McKenzie, Precious. Water World. 2011. (ENG., Illus.). 24p. (gr. k-2). pap. 8.95 *(978-1-61741-971-3(0))* Rourke Educational Media.
McKinney, Barbara Shaw. Water Words Rhymed & Defined. Stich, Carolyn R., illus. 2007. 30p. (J). (gr. 4-7). 19.95 *(978-0-9712692-8-6(9))* EDCO Publishing, Inc.
Meredith, Susan Markowitz. Hooray for Water! 2016. (Spring Forward Ser.). (J). (gr. 2). *(978-1-4900-2250-5(3))* Benchmark Education Co.
Mezzanotte, Jim. Cómo Cambia el Agua. 2006. (Estados de la materia (States of Matter) Ser.). (ENG & SPA., Illus.). 24p. (gr. 1-4). pap. 8.15 *(978-0-8368-7407-5(2))*; lib. bdg. 22.00 *(978-0-8368-7402-0(1))* Stevens, Gareth Publishing LLLP. (Weekly Reader Leveled Readers).
—How Water Changes. 2006. (States of Matter Ser.). 24p. (gr. 1-4). pap. 8.15 *(978-0-8368-6803-6(X))*; (Illus.). lib. bdg. 22.00 *(978-0-8368-6798-5(X))* Stevens, Gareth Publishing LLLP. (Weekly Reader Leveled Readers).
Michele, Tracey. Earth's Land & Water. 2011. (Learn-Abouts Ser.). (Illus.). 16p. (J). pap. 7.95 *(978-1-59920-593-9(9))* Black Rabbit Bks.
Milford, Alison. The Water Cycle. 2016. (ENG., Illus.). 48p. (J). (gr. 3-4). pap. 9.95 *(978-0-00-816388-4(X))* HarperCollins Pubs. Ltd. GBR. Dist: Independent Pubs. Group.
Mills, Nathan & Hume, Desmond. Earth's Water. 2012. (Rosen Readers Ser.). (ENG., Illus.). 24p. (J). (gr. 1-2). pap. 8.25 *(978-1-4488-8818-4(2))*; pap. 49.50 *(978-1-4488-8819-1(0))* Rosen Publishing Group, Inc., The. (Rosen Classroom).
Mills, Nathan & McCann, Margaret. How We Use Water. 2012. (Rosen Readers Ser.). (ENG., Illus.). 24p. (J). (gr. 1-2). pap. 8.25 *(978-1-4488-8794-1(1)*, Rosen Classroom) Rosen Publishing Group, Inc., The.
Modules: Earth Science; Earth's Waters TE. 2005. (gr. 6-12). *(978-0-618-33418-6(1)*, 2-01008) Holt McDougal.
Moonlight Publishing Ltd Staff, et al. Let's Look at the Pond. Sautai, Raoul, illus. 2012. (ENG.). 38p. (J). (gr. 1-4). pap. 11.99 *(978-1-85103-338-6(6))* Moonlight Publishing, Ltd. GBR. Dist: Independent Pubs. Group.
Moore, Rob. Why Does Water Evaporate? 2010. (Solving Science Mysteries Ser.). (Illus.). 24p. (J). pap. 8.25 *(978-1-61531-915-2(8)*, PowerKids Pr.); (YA). (gr. 3-6). lib. bdg. 22.60 *(978-1-61531-892-6(5))* Rosen Publishing Group, Inc., The.
—Why Does Water Evaporate? All about Heat & Temperature. 2010. (Illus.). 24p. (J). 49.50 *(978-1-61531-916-9(6)*, 1307166, PowerKids Pr.) Rosen Publishing Group, Inc., The.
Morgan, Sally. Earth's Water Cycle. 2011. (Earth Cycles Ser.). 32p. (YA). (gr. 3-6). lib. bdg. 28.50 *(978-1-59920-523-6(8))* Black Rabbit Bks.
—The Water Cycle. 2009. (Nature's Cycles Ser.). (J). (ENG.). 32p. (gr. 4-6). pap. 10.00 *(978-1-4358-2950-3(6))*; lib. bdg. 26.50 *(978-1-4358-2868-1(2))* Rosen Publishing Group, Inc., The. (PowerKids Pr.).
Murray, Julie. Water, 1 vol. 2006. (First Science - 12 Titles Ser.). (ENG., Illus.). 24p. (gr. k-4). 25.65 *(978-1-59679-832-8(7)*, Buddy Bks.) ABDO Publishing Co.
Nadeau, Isaac. Learing about the Water Cycle with Graphic Organizers. 2005. (Graphic Organizers in Science Ser.). (Illus.). 24p. (J). lib. bdg. 22.60 *(978-1-4042-2808-5(X)*, PowerKids Pr.) Rosen Publishing Group, Inc., The.
—Learning about the Water Cycle with Graphic Organizers. 2006. (Graphic Organizers in Science Ser.). (ENG., Illus.). 24p. (gr. 4-6). pap. 8.25 *(978-1-4042-5046-8(8)*, PowerKids Pr.) Rosen Publishing Group, Inc., The.
—Water in Glaciers. 2009. (Water Cycle Ser.). 24p. (gr. 4-4). 42.50 *(978-1-60854-268-0(8)*, PowerKids Pr.) Rosen Publishing Group, Inc., The.
—Water in Plants & Animals. (Water Cycle Ser.). 24p. 2009. (gr. 4-4). 42.50 *(978-1-60854-270-3(X))* 2003. (Illus.). (J). lib. bdg. 22.60 *(978-0-8239-6264-8(4))* Rosen Publishing Group, Inc., The. (PowerKids Pr.).
—Water in the Atmosphere. (Water Cycle Ser.). 24p. 2009. (gr. 4-4). 42.50 *(978-1-60854-272-7(6))* 2003. (Illus.). (J). lib. bdg. 22.60 *(978-0-8239-6262-4(8))* Rosen Publishing Group, Inc., The. (PowerKids Pr.).
—Water under Ground. (Water Cycle Ser.). 24p. 2009. (gr. 4-4). 42.50 *(978-1-60854-273-4(4))* 2003. (Illus.). (J). lib. bdg. 22.60 *(978-0-8239-6263-1(6))* Rosen Publishing Group, Inc., The. (PowerKids Pr.).
Nagy, Frances. Science with Water. 2007. (Usborne Science Activities Ser.). (Illus.). 24p. (J). (gr. 1). lib. bdg. 13.99 *(978-1-58086-976-8(9))*; pap. 5.99 *(978-0-7945-1484-6(7))* EDC Publishing. (Usborne).
Nelson, Robin. El Ciclo Del Agua. 2003. (Mi Primer Paso al Mundo Real Ser.). (SPA., Illus.). 24p. (J). (gr. k-2). lib. bdg. 18.60 *(978-0-8225-4866-9(6))* Lerner Publishing Group.
—El Ciclo Del Agua (Earth's Water Cycle) 2012. (Mi Primer Paso Al Mundo Real - Descubriendo Los Ciclos de la Naturaleza (First Step Nonfiction - Discovering Nature's Cycles) Ser.). (Illus.). 24p. (gr. k-2). (ENG & SPA.). pap. 6.95 *(978-0-7613-9348-1(X))*; (SPA., lib. bdg. 23.93 *(978-0-7613-9337-5(4))* Lerner Publishing Group. (Ediciones Lerner).
—¿Dónde Hay Agua? Castañer, Mercedes P. & Fitzpatrick, Julia, trs. 2003. (Mi Primer Paso Al Mundo Real - el Agua (First Step Nonfiction - Water) Ser.). (SPA., Illus.). 24p. (gr. k-2). lib. bdg. 23.93 *(978-0-8225-4868-3(2))* Lerner Publishing Group.
—Earth's Water Cycle. 2010. pap. 33.92 *(978-0-7613-6913-4(9))*; (ENG.). 24p. pap. 6.95 *(978-0-7613-5680-6(0))*; (ENG.). 24p. lib. bdg. 23.93 *(978-0-7613-4581-7(7))* Lerner Publishing Group.
—Flotar y Hundirse. Translations.com Staff, tr. from ENG. 2007. (Mi Primer Paso Al Mundo Real - Fuerzas y Movimiento (First Step Nonfiction - Forces & Motion) Ser.). (SPA., Illus.). 24p. (gr. k-2). lib. bdg. 23.93 *(978-0-8225-7808-6(5)*, Ediciones Lerner) Lerner Publishing Group.
—Freezing & Melting. 2003. (First Step Nonfiction Ser.). (Illus.). 24p. (gr. k-2). (J). lib. bdg. 18.60 *(978-0-8225-4590-3(X))*; (ENG., pap. 6.95 *(978-0-8225-4591-0(8))* Lerner Publishing Group.
—Que Es el Agua? Castañer, Mercedes & Fitzpatrick, Julia, trs. 2003. (Mi Primer Paso Al Mundo Real - el Agua (First Step Nonfiction - Water) Ser.). (SPA., Illus.). 24p. (gr. k-2). lib. bdg. 23.93 *(978-0-8225-4869-0(0))* Lerner Publishing Group.
—Se Congela y Se Derrite. Castañer, Mercedes & Fitzpatrick, Julia, trs. 2003. (Mi Primer Paso Al Mundo Real - el Agua (First Step Nonfiction - Water) Ser.). (SPA., Illus.). 24p. (gr. k-2). lib. bdg. 23.93 *(978-0-8225-4865-2(8))* Lerner Publishing Group.
—Water. 2005. (First Step Nonfiction - Geography Ser.). (ENG.). 8p. (gr. -1-1). pap. 4.95 *(978-0-8225-5390-8(2))*; 24p. (gr. k-2). pap. 6.95 *(978-0-8225-5377-9(5))* Lerner Publishing Group.
—Water: By Robin Nelson. 2005. (First Step Nonfiction Ser.). (Illus.). 23p. (J). (gr. 3-7). lib. bdg. 18.60 *(978-0-8225-2600-1(X)*, Lerner Pubns.) Lerner Publishing Group.
—Water Cycle. 2003. (Illus.). 24p. (J). pap. 5.95 *(978-0-8225-4597-2(7))* Lerner Publishing Group.
—What Is Water? 2003. (First Step Nonfiction Ser.). (Illus.). 24p. (gr. k-2). (J). lib. bdg. 18.60 *(978-0-8225-4588-0(8))*; (ENG., pap. 6.95 *(978-0-8225-4589-7(6))* Lerner Publishing Group.
—Where Is Water? (Illus.). 24p. 2009. 5.95 *(978-0-8225-4593-4(4))* 2003. (J). lib. bdg. 18.60 *(978-0-8225-4592-7(6))* Lerner Publishing Group.
Nunn, Daniel. Water, 1 vol. 2012. (Why Living Things Need Ser.). (ENG.). 24p. (gr. -1-1). pap. 6.29 *(978-1-4329-5923-4(9))*; lib. bdg. 22.65 *(978-1-4329-5917-3(4))* Heinemann-Raintree. (Acorn).
Olien, Rebecca. The Water Cycle at Work. 2016. (Water in Our World Ser.). (ENG.). 24p. (gr. 1-2). lib. bdg. 25.32 *(978-1-4914-8273-5(7)*, First Facts) Capstone Press of Coughlan Cos.
—Water in Our World. 2016. (Water in Our World Ser.). (ENG.). 24p. (gr. 1-2). 101.28 *(978-1-4914-8292-6(3)*, First Facts) Capstone Press of Coughlan Cos.
—Water Sources. 2016. (Water in Our World Ser.). (ENG.). 24p. (gr. 1-2). lib. bdg. 25.32 *(978-1-4914-8277-3(X)*, First Facts) Capstone Press of Coughlan Cos.
Ollhoff, Jim. Water & Ice, 1 vol. 2010. (ABDO & Daughters Ser.). (ENG.). 32p. 27.07 *(978-1-61613-458-7(5)*, Abdo & Daughters) ABDO Publishing Co.
Ostopowich, Melanie. Oceans, Lakes, & Rivers. 2016. ***(978-1-4896-5794-7(0))*** Weigl Pubs., Inc.
Owen, Ruth. Energy from Oceans & Moving Water: Hydroelectric, Wave, & Tidal Power. 2013. (Power: Yesterday, Today, Tomorrow Ser.). (ENG., Illus.). 32p. (J). (gr. 3-6). 25.25 *(978-1-4777-0269-7(5))*; pap. 11.75 *(978-1-4777-0277-2(6))* Rosen Publishing Group, Inc., The. (PowerKids Pr.).
Oxlade, Chris. Experiments with Air & Water, 1 vol. 2015. (ENG., Illus.). 32p. (J). lib. bdg. 27.50 *(978-1-4777-5793-2(7)*, PowerKids Pr.) Rosen Publishing Group, Inc., The.
—Water, 1 vol. 2012. (How Does My Home Work? Ser.). (ENG.). 24p. (gr. k-1). pap. 6.79 *(978-1-4329-6572-3(7))*; lib. bdg. 23.32 *(978-1-4329-6567-9(0))* Heinemann-Raintree. (Heinemann Read & Learn).
Paris, Stephanie. ¡Pop! Presión Del Aire y Del Agua. 2016. (TIME for Kids en Español - Level 5 Ser.). (SPA.). 64p. (gr. 5-5). lib. bdg. 31.99 *(978-1-5157-2931-0(1))* Time for Kids Inc AUS. Dist: Capstone Pub.
Parker, Steve. Tabletop Scientist — the Science of Water: Projects & Experiments with Water Science & Power. 2013. (ENG., Illus.). 32p. (J). (gr. 5). pap. 6.99 *(978-0-486-49262-9(1))* Dover Pubns., Inc.
—Water Power. 2004. (Science Files Ser.). (Illus.). 32p. (gr. 2-6). lib. bdg. 26.00 *(978-0-8368-4033-9(X)*, Gareth Stevens Learning Library) Stevens, Gareth Publishing LLLP.
Paul, Miranda. Water Is Water: A Book about the Water Cycle. Chin, Jason, illus. 2015. (ENG.). 40p. (J). (gr. 1-5). 18.99 *(978-1-59643-984-9(X)*, 9781596439849) Roaring Brook Pr.
Pendergast, George. The Water Cycle at Work. 2015. (Cycles in Nature Ser.). (ENG.). 24p. (J). (gr. 1-2). lib. bdg. 22.60 *(978-1-4824-1670-1(0))* Stevens, Gareth Publishing LLLP.
Perritano, John. Freshwater Resources, Vol. 12. 2015. (North American Natural Resources Ser.). (Illus.). 64p. (J). (gr. 7). lib. bdg. 23.95 *(978-1-4222-3381-8(2))* Mason Crest.
Petersen, Christine. A Project Guide to Earth's Waters. 2010. (Earth Science Projects for Kids Ser.). (Illus.). 48p. (J). (gr. 4-7). lib. bdg. 29.95 *(978-1-58415-871-4(9))* Mitchell Lane Pubs., Inc.
A Pond Ecosystem. 2012. (Nature Trail Ser.). (ENG., Illus.). 32p. (J). (gr. k-5). 23.95 *(978-1-4488-6627-4(8)*, PowerKids Pr.) Rosen Publishing Group, Inc., The.
Proudfit, Benjamin. Why Do Ice Cubes Float? 2016. (Everyday Mysteries Ser.). (ENG.). 24p. (J). (gr. 1-2). pap. 8.15 *(978-1-4824-3852-9(6))* Stevens, Gareth Publishing LLLP.
Purslow, Frances. The Water Cycle. 2015. (Illus.). 24p. (J). *(978-1-5105-0056-3(1))* SmartBook Media, Inc.
—The Water Cycle. 2016. (J). ***(978-1-4896-5800-5(9))*** 2010. (Illus.). 24p. (J). (gr. 3-5). pap. 11.95 *(978-1-61690-009-0(1))* 2010. (Illus.). 24p. (YA). (gr. 3-6). lib. bdg. 25.70 *(978-1-61690-003-8(2))* 2005. (Illus.). 24p. (J). (gr. 3-7). lib. bdg. 24.45 *(978-1-59036-306-5(X)*, 1251285) Weigl Pubs., Inc.
Ranola-Collier, Jean. Living Water. 2013. 24p. pap. *(978-1-4602-0682-9(7))* FriesenPress.
Ransom, Candice. Investigating the Water Cycle. 2015. (ENG.). 40p. (J). (gr. 3-5). 29.32 *(978-1-4677-8055-1(3)*, Lerner Pubns.) Lerner Publishing Group.
Rau, Dana Meachen. Water. 2009. (Bookworms Ser.). 32p. (gr. 1-2). 15.95 *(978-0-7614-4099-4(2))* Marshall Cavendish Corp.
—Water/El Agua. 2009. (Bookworms Ser.). (SPA & ENG.). 32p. (gr. 1-2). lib. bdg. 15.95 *(978-0-7614-4792-4(X))* Marshall Cavendish Corp.
Rees, Peter. Why Do Raindrops Fall? Level 3 Factbook. 2010. (Cambridge Young Readers Ser.). (ENG., Illus.). 16p. pap. 6.00 *(978-0-521-13714-0(4))* Cambridge Univ. Pr.
René, Ellen. Investigating Why It Rains. 2009. (Science Detectives Ser.). 24p. (gr. 2-3). 42.50 *(978-1-60853-016-8(7)*, PowerKids Pr.); (Illus.). (J). lib. bdg. 22.60 *(978-1-4042-4483-2(2))* Rosen Publishing Group, Inc., The.
Rice, Dona. Water Bodies, 1 vol. rev. ed. 2014. (Science Readers: Content & Literacy Ser.). (ENG.). 32p. (gr. 2-2). pap. 8.99 *(978-1-4807-4609-1(6))* Teacher Created Materials, Inc.
Rice, Dona Herweck. Agua, 1 vol. 2nd rev. ed. 2011. (Nonfiction Readers Ser.). (SPA.). 12p. (J). (gr. 1-1). pap. 4.99 *(978-1-4333-4415-2(7))* Teacher Created Materials, Inc.
—Water, 1 vol. 2nd rev. ed. 2013. (Nonfiction Readers Ser.). (ENG., Illus.). 12p. (J). (gr. 1-1). pap. 15.96 *(978-1-4807-1015-3(6))* Shell Educational Publishing.
—Water, 1 vol. 2nd rev. ed. 2011. (Nonfiction Readers Ser.). (ENG.). 12p. (J). (gr. 1-1). pap. 4.99 *(978-1-4333-3576-1(X))* Teacher Created Materials, Inc.
Rice, William B. Water Scientists, 1 vol. 2007. (Science Readers Ser.). (ENG.). 32p. (J). (gr. 3-3). pap. 8.99 *(978-0-7439-0556-5(3))* Shell Educational Publishing.
Rice, William B. Struggle for Survival: Water. 2016. (Time for Kids Nonfiction Readers Ser.). (ENG.). (J). (gr. 5-8). lib. bdg. 20.85 ***(978-0-606-39539-7(3))*** Turtleback Bks.
Richards, Jon. Water & Boats. (Science Factory Ser.). 32p. (gr. 4-5). 2009. 50.50 *(978-1-60853-023-6(X)*, PowerKids Pr.) 2008. (Illus.). (YA). lib. bdg. 26.50 *(978-1-4042-3909-8(X))* Rosen Publishing Group, Inc., The.
Rieger, Linda. Water Party. Bianchi, John, illus. 2008. 20p. (J). *(978-0-9779427-3-2(2))* Pathways into Science.
Rookie Read-About Geography: Bodies of Water, 7 bks., Set. Incl. Lake Tahoe. Zollman, Pam. lib. bdg. 20.50 *(978-0-516-25036-6(1))*; Missouri River. Taylor-Butler, Christine. lib. bdg. 20.50 *(978-0-516-25037-3(X))*; (Illus.). 32p. (J). (gr. 1-2). 2006. 2006. 136.50 o.p. *(978-0-516-25414-2(6)*, Children's Pr.) Scholastic Library Publishing.
Rose, Malcolm. The Adventures of Water. Sims, Sean, illus. 2015. (ENG.). 14p. (J). (gr. 1-3). 23.99 *(978-1-4052-7739-6(4))* Egmont Bks., Ltd. GBR. Dist: Independent Pubs. Group.
Rose, Malcolm. The Water Cycle. Sims, Sean, illus. 2017. (Reading Ladder Ser.). (ENG.). 32p. (J). (gr. 1-3). pap. 7.99 ***(978-1-4052-8493-6(5))*** Egmont Bks., Ltd. GBR. Dist: Independent Pubs. Group.
Rose, Simon. Estuaries. 2014. (Illus.). 32p. (J). *(978-1-62127-485-8(3))* Weigl Pubs., Inc.
Rosenberg, Pam. Waterfall Watchers, 1 vol. 2011. (Landform Adventurers Ser.). (ENG.). 32p. (gr. 1-2). pap. 8.29 *(978-1-4109-4149-7(3))*; 29.99 *(978-1-4109-4142-8(6))* Heinemann-Raintree. (Read Me!).
—Yikes! Icky, Sticky, Gross Stuff Underwater. Ramos, Beatriz Helena, illus. 2007. (Icky, Sticky, Gross-Out Bks.). (ENG.). 24p. (J). (gr. 3-6). 27.07 *(978-1-59296-901-2(1)*, 200358) Child's World, Inc., The.
Roth, Jennifer A. Just Add Water: Science Projects You Can Sink, Squirt, Splash, Sail. 2007. (Experiment with Science Ser.). (ENG., Illus.). 32p. (J). (gr. 3-6). 27.00 *(978-0-531-18545-2(1)*, Children's Pr.) Scholastic Library Publishing.
Royston, Angela. Experiments with Water. 2016. (One-Stop Science Ser.). 32p. (gr. 2-5). 31.35 *(978-1-62588-142-7(8)*, Smart Apple Media) Black Rabbit Bks.
—Water: Let's Look at a Puddle, 1 vol. 2005. (J). (ENG.). 24p. pap. *(978-1-4109-1832-1(7))*; lib. bdg. *(978-1-4109-1823-9(8))* Steck-Vaughn.
Rustad, Martha E. H. Water, 1 vol. 2013. (Little Scientist Ser.). (ENG., Illus.). 32p. (gr. 1-2). 6.95 *(978-1-4765-3543-2(4))*; 27.99 *(978-1-4765-0249-6(8))*; pap. 6.95 *(978-1-4765-3549-4(3))* Capstone Press of Coughlan Cos.
—Why Do Puddles Disappear? Noticing Forms of Water. Schneider, Christine M., illus. 2015. (ENG.). 24p. (gr. k-2). 25.32 *(978-1-4677-8562-4(8)*, Millbrook Pr.) Lerner Publishing Group.
Salas, Laura Purdie. There Goes the Water: A Song about the Water Cycle, 1 vol. De Giorgi, Sergio, illus. 2010. (Science Songs Ser.). (ENG.). 24p. (gr. 1-3). lib. bdg. 26.65 *(978-1-4048-5766-7(4))* Picture Window Bks.
—Water Can Be ... Dabija, Violeta, illus. 2014. (ENG.). 32p. (J). (gr. k-2). 17.95 *(978-1-4677-0591-2(8))*, Millbrook Pr.) Lerner Publishing Group.
Sayre, April Pulley. Raindrops Roll. Sayre, April Pulley, photos by. 2015. (ENG., Illus.). 40p. (J). (gr. -1-3). 17.99 *(978-1-4814-2064-8(X)*, Beach Lane Bks.) Beach Lane Bks.
Schmauss, Judy Kentor. Wicked & Wonderful Water. 2007. (Shockwave: Economics & Geography Ser.). (ENG., Illus.). 36p. (J). (gr. 3-5). 25.00 *(978-0-531-17751-8(3)*, Children's Pr.) Scholastic Library Publishing.
Schomp, Virginia. 24 Hours in a Pond. 2013. 48p. (J). (gr. 4-8). 29.93 *(978-1-60870-894-9(2))* Cavendish Square Publishing.
Selwyn, Josephine. When Does Water Turn into Ice? 2014. (Little Books of Answers: Level F Ser.). (Illus.). 16p. (gr. k-2). pap. 7.95 *(978-1-927136-59-1(8))* Three Crows Media NZL. Dist: RiverStream Publishing.
Sévigny, Eric, illus. Caillou - At the Beach. 2012. (Clubhouse Ser.). (ENG.). 24p. (J). (gr. -1-1). pap. 3.99 *(978-2-89450-942-5(1))* Caillouet, Gerry.
Shookuhi, Aminjon. Where Does the Water Come From? Khodjibaev, Karim & Khodjibaeva, Moukhabbat, trs. Seabaugh, Jan, illus. 2009. 88p. (J). pap. 15.95 *(978-0-9740551-2-1(3))* Smith, Viveca Publishing.
Sian Revision Water Cycle. 2004. (J). *(978-1-59242-081-0(8))* Delta Education, LLC.
Silverman, Buffy. Saving Water: The Water Cycle. 2016. (Do It Yourself Ser.). (ENG.). 48p. (gr. 3-6). pap. 8.99 *(978-1-4846-3695-4(3)*, NA-h) Heinemann-Raintree.
Simon, Chaman & Kazunas, Ariel. Super Cool Science Experiments: Water. 2009. (Explorer Library: Science Explorer Ser.). (ENG., Illus.). 32p. (gr. 4-8). lib. bdg. 28.50 *(978-1-60279-529-7(0)*, 200298) Cherry Lake Publishing.
Simon, Chaman & Kazunis, Ariel. Experiment with Water. 2010. (Explorer Junior Library: Science Explorer Junior Ser.). (ENG.). 32p. (gr. 3-6). lib. bdg. 28.50 *(978-1-60279-838-0(9)*, 200542) Cherry Lake Publishing.
Simon, Seymour. Water. 2017. 40p. (J). (gr. 1-5). pap. 6.99 ***(978-0-06-247054-6(X))*** HarperCollins Pubs.
Slade, Suzanne. A Raindrop's Journey, 1 vol. Conger, Holli, illus. (Follow It! Ser.). (ENG.). 24p. (gr. 1-3). 2011. pap. 7.49 *(978-1-4048-6712-3(0))* 2010. lib. bdg. 26.65 *(978-1-4048-6266-1(8))* Picture Window Bks.
—Water on the Move. (Cycles in Nature Ser.). (gr. 3-3). 2009. 24p. 42.50 *(978-1-61512-117-5(X))* 2007. 28p. pap. 21.25 *(978-1-4358-3829-1(7))* 2007. (Illus.). 24p. (J). lib. bdg. 21.25 *(978-1-4042-3492-5(6))* Rosen Publishing Group, Inc., The. (PowerKids Pr.).
Smith, Michael. It Starts with a Raindrop: Comienza con una Gota de Lluvia. Goley, Jonathon & Alvarenga, Angela, illus. 2016. (ENG.). (J). *(978-0-9973947-1-9(4))* East West Discovery Pr.
Smuskiewicz, Alfred J. Properties of Water. 2007. (Gareth Stevens Vital Science: Earth Science Ser.). (Illus.). 48p. (gr. 5-12). pap. 14.05 *(978-0-8368-7875-2(2))*; lib. bdg. 27.00 *(978-0-8368-7764-9(0))* Stevens, Gareth Publishing LLLP. (Gareth Stevens Secondary Library).
Sohn, Emily & Ash Sullivan, Erin. Weather & the Water Cycle: Will it Rain? 2011. (iScience Readers Ser.). 48p. (J). (gr. 5-6). lib. bdg. 23.94 *(978-1-59953-432-9(0))* Norwood Hse. Pr.
Sohn, Emily & Townsend, Laura. Water: Watch It Change. 2011. (iScience Readers Ser.). 32p. (J). (gr. 3-4). lib. bdg. 22.60 *(978-1-59953-422-0(3))* Norwood Hse. Pr.
Spilsbury, Louise. What Are Rivers, Lakes, & Oceans?, 1 vol., 1. 2014. (Let's Find Out! Ser.). (ENG.). 32p. (gr. 3-6). 23.45 *(978-1-62275-281-2(3))* Rosen Publishing Group, Inc., The.
—What Is the Water Cycle?, 1 vol., 1. 2014. (Let's Find Out! Ser.). (ENG.). 32p. (gr. 3-6). 23.45 *(978-1-62275-261-4(9))* Rosen Publishing Group, Inc., The.
Stearns, Carolyn. Where Did All the Water Go?, 1 vol. Aiken, David, illus. 2009. (ENG.). 30p. (J). (gr. 4-7). 12.95 *(978-0-87033-506-8(5)*, 9780870335068, Cornell Maritime Pr./Tidewater Pubs.) Schiffer Publishing, Ltd.
Stewart, Melissa. Water. 2014. (Readers Ser.). (ENG., Illus.). 48p. (J). (gr. 1-4). pap. 3.99 *(978-1-4263-1474-2(4)*, National Geographic Children's Bks.) National Geographic Society.
Strauss, Rochelle. One Well: The Story of Water on Earth. Woods, Rosemary, illus. 2007. (CitizenKid Ser.). (ENG.). 32p. (J). (gr. 3-7). 18.95 *(978-1-55337-954-6(3))* Kids Can Pr., Ltd. CAN. Dist: Hachette Bk. Group.
Sullivan, Martha. Pitter & Patter, 1 vol. Morrison, Cathy, illus. 2015. (ENG.). 32p. (J). (gr. k-4). pap. 8.95 *(978-1-58469-509-7(9))* Dawn Pubns.
Sundance/Newbridge LLC Staff. Amazing Water. 2007. (Early Science Ser.). (gr. k-3). 18.95 *(978-1-4007-6296-5(0))*; pap. 6.10 *(978-1-4007-6292-7(8))* Sundance/Newbridge Educational Publishing.
Taylor-Butler, Christine. Hydrology: The Study of Water. 2012. (True Book(tm), a — Earth Science Ser.). (ENG., Illus.). 48p. (J). lib. bdg. 31.00 *(978-0-531-24677-1(9))*; pap. 6.95 *(978-0-531-28271-7(6))* Scholastic Library Publishing. (Children's Pr.).
—Water Everywhere! Manning, Maurie, illus. 2011. (Rookie Ready to Learn - First Science Ser.). 40p. (J). (gr. -1-k). lib. bdg. 23.00 *(978-0-531-26504-8(8)*, Children's Pr.) Scholastic Library Publishing.
Taylor, Kim. Water. (Illus.). 32p. (YA). (gr. 3-18). lib. bdg. 27.10 *(978-1-931983-79-2(8))* Chrysalis Education.
Valat, Pierre-Marie. Water. Valat, Pierre-Marie, illus. 2012. (ENG., Illus.). 36p. (J). (gr. -1-k). spiral bd. 14.99 *(978-1-85103-403-1(X))* Moonlight Publishing, Ltd. GBR. Dist: Independent Pubs. Group.
Vogt, Gregory. The Hydrosphere: Agent of Change. 2007. (Earth's Spheres Ser.). (ENG., Illus.). 80p. (gr. 6-8). lib. bdg. 29.27 *(978-0-7613-2839-1(4))* Lerner Publishing Group.
Waldman, Neil. The Snowflake: A Water Cycle Story. Waldman, Neil, illus. 2003. (Illus.). 32p. lib. bdg. 23.90 *(978-0-7613-1762-3(7)*, Millbrook Pr.) Lerner Publishing Group.
Walker, Kate. Water. 2011. (Investigating Earth Ser.). (Illus.). 32p. (J). (gr. 2). 28.50 *(978-1-60870-562-7(5))* Marshall Cavendish Corp.
Walton, Ruth. Let's Drink Some Water. 2013. (Let's Find Out Ser.). (Illus.). 32p. (gr. k-5). 28.50 *(978-1-59771-384-9(8))* Sea-To-Sea Pubns.
Warhol, Tom. Water. 2006. (Earth's Biomes Ser.). (Illus.). 80p. (gr. 6-7). lib. bdg. 34.21 *(978-0-7614-2192-4(0)*, Benchmark Bks.) Marshall Cavendish Corp.
Water. (Jump Ser.). (Illus.). 32p. (J). (gr. 2-7). pap. 4.95 *(978-1-882210-29-9(8))* Action Publishing, Inc.

WXYZ

Water, Vol. 5. 2005. (Our Seasons & Weather Ser.). (YA). (gr. k-3). 178.20 *(978-0-7368-4202-0(0)*, Pebble Bks.) Capstone Press of Coughlan Cos.
Water. 2004. (Illus.). lib. bdg. 7.95 *(978-0-8225-4753-2(8))* Lerner Publishing Group.
Water All Around. 2005. (Water All Around Ser.). (ENG., Illus.). 24p. (gr. 1-2). lib. bdg. 49.30 *(978-0-7368-3811-5(2)*, First Facts) Capstone Press of Coughlan Cos.
The Water Cycle. (Illus.). (J). (gr. k-5). 112.50 *(978-0-8239-7276-0(3))* Rosen Publishing Group, Inc., The.
Webster, Christine. Glaciers. 2015. (Illus.). 24p. (J). *(978-1-5105-0050-1(2))* SmartBook Media, Inc.
—Glaciers. 2016. (J). ***(978-1-4896-5791-6(6))*** Weigl Pubs., Inc.
Der Weg des Wassers.Tr. of Characteristics of Water. (GER., Illus.). (YA). 31.95 *(978-3-411-09131-7(2))* Bibliographisches Institut & F. A. Brockhaus AG DEU. Dist: Continental Bk. Co., Inc.
Wells, Robert E. Did a Dinosaur Drink This Water? 2012. (J). *(978-1-61913-113-2(7))* Weigl Pubs., Inc.
—Did a Dinosaur Drink This Water? Wells, Robert E., illus. 2006. (Wells of Knowledge Science Ser.). (ENG., Illus.). 32p. (J). (gr. -1-3). 7.99 *(978-0-8075-8840-6(7))* Whitman, Albert & Co.
—Why Do Elephants Need the Sun? Wells, Robert E., illus. 2012. (Wells of Knowledge Science Ser.). (ENG., Illus.). 32p. (J). (gr. -1-3). pap. 7.99 *(978-0-8075-9082-9(7))* Whitman, Albert & Co.
Where's the Water? 2016. (Where's the Water? Ser.). 24p. (gr. 3-2). pap. 48.90 *(978-1-4824-5304-1(5))*; lib. bdg. 135.60 *(978-1-4824-4604-3(9))* Stevens, Gareth Publishing LLLP.
Whittaker, Helen. Water. 2011. (Living Green Ser.). 32p. (gr. 3). 28.50 *(978-1-60870-576-4(5))* Marshall Cavendish Corp.
Who Likes Water? KinderWords Individual Title Six-Packs. (Kinderstarters Ser.). 8p. (gr. -1-1). 21.00 *(978-0-7635-8713-0(3))* Rigby Education.
Wilder, Nellie. On Water, 1 vol. (Science Readers: Content & Literacy Ser.). (ENG., Illus.). 24p. (gr. k-k). 2015. (J). 22.96 *(978-1-4938-1143-4(6))* 2014. pap. 8.99 *(978-1-4807-4533-9(2))* Teacher Created Materials, Inc.
Wood, Ira. Water, Ice, & Steam. (Rosen Real Readers Big Bookstm Ser.). (ENG., Illus.). 12p. (gr. 1-2). 2006. 33.50 *(978-1-4042-6215-7(6))* 2003. pap. 5.90 *(978-0-8239-6353-9(5))* Rosen Publishing Group, Inc., The.
World Book, Inc Staff, contrib. by. Fabled Waters. 2017. (J). ***(978-0-7166-3369-3(8))*** World Bk., Inc.
Yanez, Anthony & Guillory, Mike. A Wild Ride on the Water Cycle. 2014. (ENG., Illus.). 28p. (J). (gr. -1-4). 19.95 *(978-1-939055-80-4(6)*, ef1359f7-41d7-4a67-9881-0644ee0049ab) Bright Sky Pr.
Yasuda, Anita. Explore Water! 25 Great Projects, Activities, Experiments. Stone, Bryan, illus. 2011. (Explore Your World Ser.). (ENG.). 96p. (J). (gr. k-4). pap. 12.95 *(978-1-936313-42-6(1))* Open City Bks.
Yates, Irene. Water. 2004. (Activities for 3-5 Year Olds Ser.). (Illus.). 32p. pap. 11.00 *(978-1-897675-25-0(9))* Brilliant Pubns. GBR. Dist: Parkwest Pubns., Inc.
Ylvisake, Anne. Land & Water: World Rivers. (Fact Finders Ser.). (Illus.). (J). (gr. 3-4). lib. bdg. 90.40 *(978-0-7368-2559-7(2))* Capstone Press of Coughlan Cos.
York, M. J. A Pond in Spring. 2017. (Welcome, Spring! Ser.). (ENG.). 24p. (J). (gr. -1-2). lib. bdg. 27.07 *(978-1-5038-1656-5(7)*, 211502) Child's World, Inc., The.
Zappa, Marcia. The Water Cycle, 1 vol. 2010. (Big Buddy Bks.). (ENG.). 32p. (J). (gr. 2-5). 28.50 *(978-1-61613-495-2(X))* ABDO Publishing Co.

WATER—CONSERVATION

see Water Conservation

WATER—POLLUTION

see also Refuse and Refuse Disposal; Sewage Disposal also Petroleum Pollution of Water and similar headings

Benchmark Education Company. Ocean Pollution (Teacher Guide) 2005. *(978-1-4108-4678-5(4))* Benchmark Education Co.
Brannon, Barbara. Discover Ocean Pollution. 2005. (J). pap. *(978-1-4108-5140-6(0))* Benchmark Education Co.
Bullard, Lisa. Watch over Our Water. Xin, Xiao, illus. 2011. (Planet Protectors Ser.). pap. 39.62 *(978-0-7613-8657-5(2)*, Millbrook Pr.); (ENG.). 24p. pap. 6.95 *(978-0-7613-8517-2(7)*, Millbrook Pr.); (ENG.). 24p. lib. bdg. 23.93 *(978-0-7613-6106-0(5))* Lerner Publishing Group.
Castellano, Peter. Water Conservation. 2016. (Where's the Water? Ser.). (Illus.). 24p. (J). (gr. 3-2). pap. 8.15 *(978-1-4824-4692-0(8))* Stevens, Gareth Publishing LLLP.
Farrell, Courtney. Save the Planet: Keeping Water Clean. 2010. (Explorer Library: Language Arts Explorer Ser.). (ENG.). 32p. (gr. 4-8). pap. 14.21 *(978-1-60279-668-3(8)*, 200915); lib. bdg. 28.50 *(978-1-60279-659-1(9)*, 200352) Cherry Lake Publishing.
Faust, Daniel R. Desastres Ecológicos: Los Derrames de Petróleo y el Medio Ambiente = Sinister Sludge: Oil Spills & the Environment. 2009. (Historietas Juveniles: Peligros Del Medioambiente (Jr. Graphic Environmental Dangers) Ser.). (Illus.). 24p. (gr. 3-6). (SPA.). (YA). lib. bdg. 25.25 *(978-1-4358-8468-7(X))*; (ENG & SPA., pap. 10.60 *(978-1-4358-8469-4(8)*, PowerKids Pr.) Rosen Publishing Group, Inc., The.
Feinstein, Stephen. Drying Up: Running Out of Water. 2016. (End of Life As We Know It Ser.). (ENG., Illus.). 144p. (YA). (gr. 7-8). lib. bdg. 37.27 *(978-0-7660-7286-2(X))* Enslow Pubs., Inc.
Feinstein, Stephen & Library. Conserving & Protecting Water: What You Can Do. 2010. (Green Issues in Focus Ser.). (Illus.). 128p. (J). (gr. 7-12). lib. bdg. 33.27 *(978-0-7660-3346-7(5))* Enslow Pubs., Inc.
Fridell, Ron. Protecting Earth's Water Supply. 2009. pap. 58.95 *(978-0-7613-4694-4(5))* 2008. 72p. (YA). (gr. 4-7). lib. bdg. 30.60 *(978-0-8225-7557-3(4))* Lerner Publishing Group.
Goldish, Meish. Poisoned Water: Minamata, Japan. 2017. (Eco-Disasters Ser.). (ENG.). 32p. (J). (gr. 2-7). 19.95 ***(978-1-68402-224-3(X))*** Bearport Publishing Co., Inc.
Greene, Carol. I Love Our Water. 2012. (I Love Our Earth Ser.). (Illus.). 24p. (J). pap. 7.95 *(978-1-4644-0138-1(1))*; (gr. 3-4). 22.60 *(978-0-7660-4042-7(9))* Enslow Pubs., Inc.
Harper, Joel. All the Way to the Ocean. Spusta, Marq, illus. 2006. (J). 14.95 *(978-0-9714254-1-5(8))* Harper, Joel D.
Haynes, Danielle. Chemical Catastrophes. 2017. (Unnatural Disasters Ser.). 32p. (J). (gr. 4-5). pap. 63.00 ***(978-1-5382-0417-7(7))*** Stevens, Gareth Publishing LLLP.
Heos, Bridget. Polluted Water & Your Vital Organs. 2012. (Incredibly Disgusting Environments Ser.). (ENG., Illus.). 48p. (YA). (gr. 5-8). pap. 11.75 *(978-1-4488-8424-7(1))*; lib. bdg. 29.25 *(978-1-4488-8412-4(8))* Rosen Publishing Group, Inc., The.
Hustad, Douglas. How Can We Reduce Manufacturing Pollution? 2016. (Searchlight Books — What Can We Do about Pollution? Ser.). (ENG., Illus.). 40p. (J). (gr. 3-5). 30.65 *(978-1-4677-9518-0(6)*, Lerner Pubns.) Lerner Publishing Group.
Iyer, Rani. Endangered Rivers: Investigating Rivers in Crisis. 2015. (Endangered Earth Ser.). (ENG.). 32p. (gr. 3-4). lib. bdg. 27.32 *(978-1-4914-2040-9(5)*, Fact Finders) Capstone Press of Coughlan Cos.
Kallen, Stuart A. Running Dry: The Global Water Crisis. 2015. (Illus.). 64p. (J). *(978-1-4677-6308-0(X))* Twenty First Century Bks.
—Water, Water Everywhere? Protecting a Diminishing Resource in a Warming World. 2015. (ENG., Illus.). 64p. (J). (gr. 8-12). lib. bdg. 33.32 *(978-1-4677-2646-7(X)*, Twenty-First Century Bks.) Lerner Publishing Group.
La Bella, Laura. Not Enough to Drink: Pollution, Drought, & Tainted Water Supplies. 2009. (Extreme Environmental Threats Ser.). (ENG., Illus.). 64p. (J). (gr. 7-12). pap. 12.95 *(978-1-4358-5376-8(8))*; 64p. (gr. 6-6). 58.50 *(978-1-61512-432-9(2))*; (YA). (gr. 5-9). lib. bdg. 31.95 *(978-1-4358-5020-0(3))* Rosen Publishing Group, Inc., The.
Lawrence, Ellen. Poisoned Rivers & Lakes. 2014. (Science Slam: Green World, Clean World Ser.). 24p. (J). (gr. -1-3). lib. bdg. 23.93 *(978-1-62724-105-2(1))* Bearport Publishing Co., Inc.
Mason, Paul. How Big Is Your Water Footprint? 2009. (Environmental Footprints Ser.). 32p. (gr. 4). 28.50 *(978-0-7614-4417-6(3))* Marshall Cavendish Corp.
Minden, Cecilia. Kids Can Keep Water Clean. 2010. (21st Century Basic Skills Library: Kids Can Ser.). (ENG.). 24p. (gr. k-3). lib. bdg. 22.79 *(978-1-60279-872-4(9)*, 200610) Cherry Lake Publishing.
Newman, Patricia. Plastic, Ahoy! Investigating the Great Pacific Garbage Patch. Crawley, Annie, illus. 2014. (ENG.). 48p. (gr. 3-6). lib. bdg. 30.60 *(978-1-4677-1283-5(3)*, Millbrook Pr.) Lerner Publishing Group.
Ostopowich, Melanie. Water Pollution. 2015. (Illus.). 24p. (J). *(978-1-5105-0058-7(8))* SmartBook Media, Inc.
—Water Pollution. 2016. (J). ***(978-1-4896-5803-6(3))*** 2010. (Illus.). 24p. (J). (gr. 3-5). pap. 11.95 *(978-1-61690-010-6(5))* 2010. (Illus.). 32p. (YA). (gr. k-4). lib. bdg. 25.70 *(978-1-61690-004-5(0))* 2005. (Illus.). 24p. (J). (gr. 3-7). lib. bdg. 24.45 *(978-1-59036-307-2(8))* Weigl Pubs., Inc.
Parsons, Michelle Hyde. Ocean Pollution. 2005. (J). pap. *(978-1-4108-4630-3(X))* Benchmark Education Co.
Price, Sean. Water Pollution. 2008. (Saving Our World Ser.). 32p. (gr. 4-18). lib. bdg. 28.50 *(978-0-7614-3221-0(3)*, Benchmark Bks.) Marshall Cavendish Corp.
Spilsbury, Louise. Threats to Our Water Supply. 2009. (J). 70.50 *(978-1-4358-5481-9(0))*; (ENG.). 48p. (YA). pap. 11.75 *(978-1-4358-5480-2(2))*; (ENG., Illus.). 48p. (J). (gr. 5-9). lib. bdg. 29.25 *(978-1-4358-5352-2(0))* Rosen Publishing Group, Inc., The.

WATER—POLLUTION—FICTION

Allen, Nancy. Trouble in Troublesome Creek. Crawford, K., illus. 2011. (ENG.). 32p. (gr. -1-3). pap. 11.95 *(978-1-933176-36-9(9))* Red Rock Pr., Inc.
Allen, Nancy Kelly. Trouble in Troublesome Creek: A Troublesome Creek Kids Story. Crawford, K. Michael, illus. 2010. (ENG.). 32p. (J). (gr. -1-3). 16.95 *(978-1-933176-32-1(6))* Red Rock Pr., Inc.
Anthony, Fortuna. Tim Tim the River Crayfish. 2011. 40p. (gr. -1). pap. 19.99 *(978-1-4269-6068-0(9))* Trafford Publishing.
Caduto, Michael J. & Pastuchiv, Olga. Riparia's River, 1 vol. 2011. (ENG., Illus.). 32p. (gr. 4-7). 16.95 *(978-0-88448-327-4(4)*, 884327) Tilbury Hse. Pubs.
Covey, Richard D. & Pappas, Diane H. Let's Keep Our Oceans, Rivers, & Lakes Clean. 2009. (Planet Earth Patrol Ser.). (Illus.). (J). *(978-0-545-06105-6(9))* Scholastic, Inc.
Dombek, Jeff. How the Oysters Saved the Bay, 1 vol. 2013. (ENG., Illus.). 32p. (J). 16.99 *(978-0-7643-4283-7(5)*, 9780764342837) Schiffer Publishing, Ltd.
Gordon, Pauline C. The Adventures of the Droplet Twins. 2013. 136p. *(978-1-4602-1343-8(2))*; pap. *(978-1-4602-1344-5(0))* FriesenPress.
Kline, Trish & Donev, Mary. Coming Home: KA Reader 8. 2007. (Illus.). 32p. (J). per. 20.00 *(978-1-934307-01-4(7))* Ghost Hunter Productions.
Lee, WonKyeong. Green River. Yang, HyeWon, illus. 2014. (MySELF Bookshelf Ser.). (ENG.). 32p. (J). (gr. k-2). pap. 11.94 *(978-1-60357-695-6(9))*; lib. bdg. 25.27 *(978-1-59953-660-6(9))* Norwood Hse. Pr.
Meadows, Daisy. Milly the River Fairy. 2014. (Rainbow Magic — the Earth Fairies Ser.). lib. bdg. 14.75 *(978-0-606-35835-4(8))* Turtleback Bks.
Pavanello, Roberto. The Thing in the Sewers, 1 vol. Zeni, Marco, tr. from ITA. Pisapia, Blasco & Brughera, Pamela, illus. 2012. (Echo & the Bat Pack Ser.). (ENG.). 128p. (gr. 2-3). 9.95 *(978-1-4342-4247-1(1))* Stone Arch Bks.
Roddy, Lee. The Ghost Dog of Stoney Ridge. 2008. (D. J. Dillon Adventure Ser.: No. 4). (J). 7.99 *(978-0-88062-268-4(7))* Mott Media.
Shaw, Daniel, illus. Journey to Pansophigus. 2005. (J). per. 9.95 *(978-0-9772168-0-2(2))* Water Lily Pr., Inc.
Taylor-Butler, Christine. Water Everywhere! Manning, Maurie J., illus. 2005. (Rookie Reader Skill Set Ser.). (ENG.). 24p. (J). (gr. 1-2). per. 4.95 *(978-0-516-25285-8(2)*, Children's Pr.) Scholastic Library Publishing.

WATER—PURIFICATION

Evert, Franklin. Water & Other Forces for Good. 2017. (Text Connections Guided Close Reading Ser.). (J). (gr. 2). *(978-1-4900-1833-1(6))* Benchmark Education Co.
Heos, Bridget. Polluted Water & Your Vital Organs. 2012. (Incredibly Disgusting Environments Ser.). (ENG., Illus.). 48p. (YA). (gr. 5-8). pap. 11.75 *(978-1-4488-8424-7(1))*; lib. bdg. 29.25 *(978-1-4488-8412-4(8))* Rosen Publishing Group, Inc., The.
Hicks, Dwayne. Finding Water in the Wild, 01 vols., 1. 2016. (Wilderness Survival Skills Ser.). (ENG., Illus.). 24p. (J). pap. 8.25 *(978-1-5081-4311-6(0)*, PowerKids Pr.) Rosen Publishing Group, Inc., The.
Kallen, Stuart A. Real-World STEM: Global Access to Clean Water. 2017. (ENG.). 80p. (YA). (gr. 5-12). ***(978-1-68282-243-2(5))*** ReferencePoint Pr., Inc.
—Science & Sustainable Water. 2017. (ENG.). 80p. (YA). (gr. 5-12). ***(978-1-68282-257-9(5))*** ReferencePoint Pr., Inc.
Lawrence, Ellen. Poisoned Rivers & Lakes. 2014. (Science Slam: Green World, Clean World Ser.). 24p. (J). (gr. -1-3). lib. bdg. 23.93 *(978-1-62724-105-2(1))* Bearport Publishing Co., Inc.
Olien, Rebecca. Cleaning Water. 2016. (Water in Our World Ser.). (ENG., Illus.). 24p. (gr. 1-2). lib. bdg. 25.32 *(978-1-4914-8278-0(8)*, First Facts) Capstone Press of Coughlan Cos.
Water for the World, 6 Packs. (gr. k-1). 23.00 *(978-0-7635-8852-6(0))* Rigby Education.
Yomtov, Nel. Water/Wastewater Engineer. 2015. (21st Century Skills Library: Cool STEAM Careers Ser.). (ENG.). 32p. (J). (gr. 4-7). pap. 14.21 *(978-1-63362-049-0(2)*, 205953) Cherry Lake Publishing.

WATER ANIMALS

see Freshwater Animals; Marine Animals

WATER BIRDS

Murphy, Julie. Seabirds. 2010. (Weird, Wild, & Wonderful Ser.). 24p. (J). (gr. 2-5). lib. bdg. 22.00 *(978-1-4339-3579-4(1)*, Gareth Stevens Learning Library) Stevens, Gareth Publishing LLLP.

WATERCOLOR PAINTING

Bolte, Mari. Watercolors, 1 vol. Ice, D. C., illus. 2013. (Paint It Ser.). (ENG.). 32p. (gr. 3-4). 27.99 *(978-1-4765-3108-3(0)*, Snap Bks.) Capstone Press of Coughlan Cos.
Burrier, Sara. Watercolor Fairy Art: How to Bring Your Fairy Realm Art to Life. 2014. (ENG.). 128p. pap. 21.99 *(978-1-4380-0436-5(2))* Barron's Educational Series, Inc.
Dutta-Yean, Tutu & Maire, Lucy Bedoya. Twelve Treasures of the East: Legends & Folk Tales from Asia. Dutta-Yean, Tutu, ed. Konatich, James, illus. 2005. (J). per. *(978-0-9768436-0-3(9)*, 20) Maire, Lucy Bedoya.
Giddy Up Staff. Go Diego Go Water Wow! Book. 2009. 4p. (J). 6.99 *(978-1-59524-215-0(5))* Giddy Up, LLC.
Klutz Editors. Watercolor Crush. 2016. (ENG.). 54p. (J). (gr. 3-7). 18.99 *(978-1-338-03756-2(0))* Klutz.
Top That Publishing Staff, ed. Sketching with Watercolor Pencils. 2005. (Illus.). 48p. *(978-1-84510-300-2(9))* Top That! Publishing PLC.
—Watercolor Painting. 2004. (Art Tricks Ser.). (Illus.). 48p. *(978-1-84510-318-7(1))* Top That! Publishing PLC.

WATER CONSERVATION

see also Water-Supply

Bailey, Gerry & Way, Steve. Water. 2009. (Simply Science Ser.). (Illus.). 32p. (YA). (gr. 3-6). lib. bdg. 26.00 *(978-1-4339-0037-2(8))* Stevens, Gareth Publishing LLLP.
Barker, Geoff. Water. 2010. (World at Risk Ser.). (YA). (gr. 5-9). 34.25 *(978-1-59920-379-9(0))* Black Rabbit Bks.
Barnham, Kay. Save Water. 2007. (Rise & Shine Ser.). (ENG., Illus.). 32p. (J). (gr. 3-7). pap. *(978-0-7787-3671-4(7))* Crabtree Publishing Co.
Bodden, Valerie. Water for Life. 2010. (Earth Issues Ser.). 48p. (YA). (gr. 5-18). 23.95 *(978-1-58341-986-1(1)*, Creative Education) Creative Co., The.
Burgan, Michael. Not a Drop to Drink. 2008. (National Geographic Investigates Science Ser.). (ENG., Illus.). 64p. (J). (gr. 5). 17.95 *(978-1-4263-0360-9(2)*, National Geographic Children's Bks.) National Geographic Society.
—Not a Drop to Drink: Water for a Thirsty World. 2008. (National Geographic Investigates Ser.). (ENG., Illus.). 64p. (J). (gr. 5). lib. bdg. 27.90 *(978-1-4263-0267-1(3)*, National Geographic Children's Bks.) National Geographic Society.
Castellano, Peter. Water Conservation. 2016. (Where's the Water? Ser.). (Illus.). 24p. (J). (gr. 3-2). pap. 8.15 *(978-1-4824-4692-0(8))* Stevens, Gareth Publishing LLLP.
Conrad, Steve, intro. Enough Water? A Guide to What We Have & How We Use It. 2016. (ENG., Illus.). 72p. (J). (gr. 4-7). pap. 9.95 *(978-1-77085-818-3(0)*, 9781770858183) Firefly Bks., Ltd.
David, Sarah B. Reducing Your Carbon Footprint at Home. 2009. (Your Carbon Footprint Ser.). 48p. (gr. 5-5). 53.00 *(978-1-60854-910-8(0)*, Rosen Reference) Rosen Publishing Group, Inc., The.
Emoto, Masaru. The Secret of Water: For the Children of the World. 2006. (ENG., Illus.). 32p. (gr. 1-5). 14.95 *(978-1-58270-157-8(1)*, Beyond Words/Atria Bks.) Atria Bks.
Feinstein, Stephen. Drying Up: Running Out of Water. 2016. (End of Life As We Know It Ser.). (ENG., Illus.). 144p. (YA). (gr. 7-8). lib. bdg. 37.27 *(978-0-7660-7286-2(X))* Enslow Pubs., Inc.
Feinstein, Stephen & Library. Conserving & Protecting Water: What You Can Do. 2010. (Green Issues in Focus Ser.). (Illus.). 128p. (J). (gr. 7-12). lib. bdg. 33.27 *(978-0-7660-3346-7(5))* Enslow Pubs., Inc.
Finton, Nancy. Wonders of Water. 2006. (Nonfiction Reading & Writing Workshops Ser.). (ENG., Illus.). 32p. (J). pap. 17.95 *(978-0-7922-4572-8(5))* CENGAGE Learning.
Food and Agriculture Organization of the United Nations Staff, ed. YUNGA Water Challenge Badge. 2013. (ENG., Illus.). 96p. pap. 10.00 *(978-92-5-107536-4(0))* Food & Agriculture Organization of the United Nations ITA. Dist: Rowman & Littlefield Publishers, Inc.
Fridell, Ron. Protecting Earth's Water Supply. 2009. pap. 58.95 *(978-0-7613-4694-4(5))* 2008. 72p. (YA). (gr. 4-7). lib. bdg. 30.60 *(978-0-8225-7557-3(4))* Lerner Publishing Group.
Green, Jen. Saving Water. 2005. (Improving Our Environment Ser.). (Illus.). 32p. (gr. 3-6). lib. bdg. 26.00 *(978-0-8368-4431-3(9)*, Gareth Stevens Learning Library) Stevens, Gareth Publishing LLLP.
—Saving Water. 2011. (Sherlock Bones Looks at the Environment Ser.). (ENG., Illus.). 32p. (YA). (gr. 3-6). lib. bdg. 25.25 *(978-1-61533-347-9(9))* Windmill Bks.
—Why Should I Save Water? Gordon, Mike, illus. 2005. (Why Should I? Bks.). (ENG.). 32p. (J). pap. 6.99 *(978-0-7641-3157-8(5))* Barron's Educational Series, Inc.
Hawes, Alison. Water Wise! 2010. (ENG.). 32p. (J). *(978-0-7787-9904-7(2))*; pap. *(978-0-7787-9925-2(5))* Crabtree Publishing Co.
Heos, Bridget. Follow That Tap Water! A Journey down the Drain. 2016. (Keeping Cities Clean Ser.). (ENG., Illus.). 24p. (J). (gr. k-3). 20.95 *(978-1-60753-962-9(4))* Amicus Publishing.
Hutmacher, Kimberly. The Wonderful Water Cycle. 2012. (ENG.). 24p. (gr. 4-5). pap. 8.95 *(978-1-61810-237-9(0))* Rourke Educational Media.
Kallen, Stuart A. Running Dry: The Global Water Crisis. 2015. (Illus.). 64p. (J). *(978-1-4677-6308-0(X))* Twenty First Century Bks.
—Water, Water Everywhere? Protecting a Diminishing Resource in a Warming World. 2015. (ENG., Illus.). 64p. (J). (gr. 8-12). lib. bdg. 33.32 *(978-1-4677-2646-7(X)*, Twenty-First Century Bks.) Lerner Publishing Group.
Knight, M. J. Why Should I Turn off the Tap? 2009. (One Small Step Ser.). (YA). (gr. 2-5). 28.50 *(978-1-59920-264-8(6))* Black Rabbit Bks.
Lanz, Helen. Wonderful Water. 2012. (Go Green Ser.). (Illus.). 32p. (gr. 3-6). lib. bdg. 28.50 *(978-1-59771-306-1(6))* Sea-To-Sea Pubns.
Llewellyn, Claire. Stop Water Waste. 2005. (Illus.). 32p. (YA). (gr. 1-18). lib. bdg. 27.10 *(978-1-932333-24-4(X))* Chrysalis Education.
Mason, Jennifer. 10 Things You Can Do to Save Water. 2016. (Rookie Star — Make a Difference Ser.). (ENG., Illus.). 32p. (J). lib. bdg. 25.00 *(978-0-531-22651-3(4)*, Children's Pr.) Scholastic Library Publishing.
Mason, Jenny. 10 Cosas Que Puedes Hacer para Ahorrar Aqua. 2017. (Rookie Star — Make a Difference (Spanish Translation) Ser.). (SPA.). 32p. (J). pap. 5.95 ***(978-1-338-18779-3(1))***; lib. bdg. 25.00 ***(978-0-531-22858-6(4))*** Scholastic Library Publishing. (Children's Pr.).
Minden, Cecilia. Kids Can Use Less. 2010. (21st Century Basic Skills Library: Kids Can Ser.). (ENG.). 24p. (gr. k-3). lib. bdg. 22.79 *(978-1-60279-869-4(9)*, 200604) Cherry Lake Publishing.
Mulder, Michelle. Every Last Drop: Bringing Clean Water Home, 1 vol. 2014. (Orca Footprints Ser.). (ENG., Illus.). 48p. (J). (gr. 3-7). 19.95 *(978-1-4598-0223-0(3))* Orca Bk. Pubs. USA.
National Geographic Learning Staff. Why Should I Turn off the Tap? 2010. (ENG., Illus.). 32p. (C). (gr. -1-3). pap. 14.95 *(978-1-897563-49-6(3))* National Geographic School Publishing, Inc.
Olien, Rebecca. Saving Water. 2016. (Water in Our World Ser.). (ENG., Illus.). 24p. (gr. 1-2). lib. bdg. 25.32 *(978-1-4914-8279-7(6)*, First Facts) Capstone Press of Coughlan Cos.
Peterson, Megan Cooley. How Water Gets from Treatment Plants to Toilet Bowls. 2016. (Here to There Ser.). (ENG., Illus.). 24p. (gr. k-1). lib. bdg. 26.65 *(978-1-4914-8435-7(7)*, Pebble Plus) Capstone Press of Coughlan Cos.
Reynolds, Alison. Let's Save Water. Hopgood, Andrew, illus. 2009. (Save Our Planet! Ser.). 12p. (J). (gr. -1-3). bds. 11.40 *(978-1-60754-413-5(X))* Windmill Bks.
Rieger, Linda. Start the Clean Up. Bianchi, John, illus. 2008. 20p. (J). *(978-0-9779427-5-6(9))* Pathways into Science.
Robertson, Joanne. The Water Walker, 1 vol. 2017. (ENG., Illus.). 36p. (J). (gr. 2-6). 16.95 ***(978-1-77260-038-4(5))*** Second Story Pr. CAN. Dist: Orca Bk. Pubs. USA.
Rosenberg, Pam. Watershed Conservation. 2008. (21st Century Skills Library: Global Perspectives Ser.). (ENG.). 32p. (gr. 4-8). lib. bdg. 28.50 *(978-1-60279-131-2(7)*, 200111) Cherry Lake Publishing.
Roza, Greg. Reducing Your Carbon Footprint on Vacation. 2009. (Your Carbon Footprint Ser.). 48p. (gr. 5-5). 53.00 *(978-1-60854-913-9(5)*, Rosen Reference) Rosen Publishing Group, Inc., The.
Sawyer, Ava. Humans & the Hydrosphere: Protecting Earth's Water Sources. 2017. (Humans & Our Planet Ser.). (ENG.). 32p. (gr. 3-4). lib. bdg. 27.32 ***(978-1-5157-7198-2(9)***, Fact Finders) Capstone Press of Coughlan Cos.
Steele, Philip. Saving Water & Energy. 2009. (Now We Know About... Ser.). (ENG., Illus.). 24p. (J). (gr. k-3). pap. *(978-0-7787-4740-6(9))*; lib. bdg. *(978-0-7787-4723-9(9))* Crabtree Publishing Co.
Thomas, Elizabeth. Clean Water. 2011. (Go Green! Ser.). (ENG., Illus.). 32p. (J). (gr. 1-4). lib. bdg. 28.50 *(978-1-60973-171-7(9)*, 201150) Child's World, Inc., The.
Your Carbon Footprint, 6 vols., Set. Incl. On the Move: Green Transportation. Furgang, Kathy & Furgang, Adam. lib. bdg. 29.25 *(978-1-4042-1773-8(8))*; Reducing Your Carbon Footprint at Home. Ganchy, Sally. lib. bdg. 29.25 *(978-1-4042-1772-0(X)*, 1284463); Reducing Your Carbon Footprint at School. Nagle, Jeanne. lib. bdg. 29.25 *(978-1-4042-1774-4(6)*, 1284467); Reducing Your Carbon Footprint in the Kitchen. Hall, Linley Erin. lib. bdg. 29.25 *(978-1-4042-1776-8(2))*; Reducing Your Carbon Footprint on Vacation. Roza, Greg. lib. bdg. 29.25 *(978-1-4042-1777-5(0)*, 1284472); Smart Shopping: Shopping Green. Nagle, Jeanne. lib. bdg. 29.25 *(978-1-4042-1775-1(4)*, 1284468); (Illus.). 48p. (YA). (gr. 5-9). 2008. 2008. Set lib. bdg. 159.00 *(978-1-4042-1880-2(7))* Rosen Publishing Group, Inc., The.

WATER FOWL

see Water Birds

WATER PLANTS

see Marine Plants

WATER POLLUTION

see Water—Pollution

WATER POLO

Egan, Tracie. Water Polo. 2005. (Sports from Coast to Coast Ser.). (Illus.). 48p. (J). (gr. 5-8). lib. bdg. 26.50 *(978-1-4042-0186-6(6))* Rosen Publishing Group, Inc., The.
—Water Polo: Rules, Tips, Strategy, & Safety. 2009. (Sports from Coast to Coast Ser.). 48p. (gr. 6-6). 53.00 *(978-1-60853-132-5(5)*, Rosen Reference) Rosen Publishing Group, Inc., The.

WATER POWER

Bailey, Diane. Hydropower. 2014. (J). *(978-1-60818-410-1(2)*, Creative Education) Creative Co., The.

Benduhn, Tea. Energía del Agua. 2008. (Energía para el presente (Energy for Today) Ser.). (SPA.). 24p. (gr. 2-6). (J). lib. bdg. 22.00 *(978-0-8368-9270-3(4))*; pap. 8.15 *(978-0-8368-9369-4(7))* Stevens, Gareth Publishing LLLP. (Weekly Reader Leveled Readers).

—Water Power. 2008. (Energy for Today Ser.). 24p. (gr. 2-6). (J). lib. bdg. 22.00 *(978-0-8368-9264-2(X))*; pap. 8.15 *(978-0-8368-9363-2(8))* Stevens, Gareth Publishing LLLP. (Weekly Reader Leveled Readers).

Burgan, Michael, et al. Water Power. 2010. (Energy Today Ser.). 48p. (J). (gr. 3-6). 30.00 *(978-1-60413-781-1(9))* Facts On File, Inc.

Currie, Stephen. Hydropower. 2010. (Compact Research Ser.). 96p. (YA). (gr. 7-12). 26.95 *(978-1-60152-122-4(7))* ReferencePoint Pr., Inc.

currie, stephen. What Is the Future of Hydropower? 2012. (Illus.). 80p. (J). lib. bdg. *(978-1-60152-276-4(2)*, 1346139) ReferencePoint Pr., Inc.

Dickmann, Nancy. Energy from Water: Hydroelectric, Tidal, & Wave Power. 2016. (ENG., Illus.). 32p. (J). *(978-0-7787-2380-6(1))* Crabtree Publishing Co.

Doeden, Matt. Finding Out about Hydropower. 2014. (Searchlight Books — What Are Energy Sources? Ser.). (Illus.). 40p. (gr. 3-4). pap. 8.95 *(978-1-4677-4555-0(3))*; (ENG., (J). lib. bdg. 27.93 *(978-1-4677-3659-6(7)*, Lerner Pubns.) Lerner Publishing Group.

Draper, Allison Stark. Hydropower for the Future: New Ways of Turning Water into Energy. 2005. (Library of Future Energy Ser.). (Illus.). 64p. (YA). (gr. 7-12). lib. bdg. 31.95 *(978-0-8239-3664-9(3))* Rosen Publishing Group, Inc., The.

Goodman, Polly. Understanding Water Power. 2010. (World of Energy Ser.). (ENG.). 48p. (J). (gr. 6-8). lib. bdg. 31.95 *(978-1-4339-4130-6(9)*, Gareth Stevens Learning Library) Stevens, Gareth Publishing LLLP.

Grady, Colin. Hydropower. 2016. (Saving the Planet Through Green Energy Ser.). (Illus.). 24p. (J). pap. 9.35 *(978-0-7660-8284-7(9))* Enslow Pubs., Inc.

Graham, Ian. From Falling Water to Electric Car: An Energy Journey Through the World of Electricity. 2015. (Energy Journeys Ser.). (ENG.). 48p. (gr. 3-6). 33.32 *(978-1-4846-0884-5(4)*, Heinemann InfoSearch) Heinemann-Raintree.

Hansen, Amy. Hydropower: Making a Splash! 2010. (Powering Our World Ser.). (ENG.). 24p. (J). pap. 8.25 *(978-1-4358-9746-5(3)*, PowerKids Pr.) Rosen Publishing Group, Inc., The.

Hansen, Amy S. Hydropower: Making a Splash! 2010. (Powering Our World Ser.). 24p. (J). (gr. 2-5). E-Book 42.50 *(978-1-4488-0203-6(2))*; (Illus.). (gr. 1-5). lib. bdg. 22.60 *(978-1-4358-9329-0(8)*, PowerKids Pr.) Rosen Publishing Group, Inc., The.

Harris, William. Water Makes Hydropower. 2003. (From Resource to Energy Source Ser.). (J). *(978-1-58417-286-4(X))*; pap. *(978-1-58417-287-1(8))* Lake Street Pubs.

Mahaney, Ian. Water Power. 2007. 28p. pap. 21.25 *(978-1-4358-3826-0(2)*, PowerKids Pr.) Rosen Publishing Group, Inc., The.

Mahaney, Ian F. Water Power. 2007. (Energy in Action Ser.). (ENG., Illus.). 24p. (gr. 4-6). pap. 7.05 *(978-1-4042-2190-1(5)*, PowerKids Pr.) Rosen Publishing Group, Inc., The.

Morris, Neil. Water Power. 2007. (Energy Sources Ser.). (Illus.). 32p. (YA). (gr. 4-7). lib. bdg. 28.50 *(978-1-58340-909-1(2))* Black Rabbit Bks.

—Water Power: Now & in the Future. 2010. (J). 34.25 *(978-1-59920-343-0(X))* Black Rabbit Bks.

Nagelhout, Ryan. Dams. 2016. (Science on Patrol Ser.). 00048p. (J). pap. 14.05 *(978-1-4824-5988-3(4))* Stevens, Gareth Publishing LLLP.

Newman, Patricia. Water Power. 2013. *(978-1-61080-974-0(2))*; (ENG.). 32p. (gr. 4-8). 28.50 *(978-1-61080-899-6(1)*, 202575); (ENG.). 32p. (gr. 4-8). pap. 14.21 *(978-1-61080-924-5(6)*, 202577) Cherry Lake Publishing.

Ollhoff, Jim. Wind & Water, 1 vol. 2010. (Future Energy Ser.). (ENG., Illus.). 32p. (YA). (gr. 4-7). 27.07 *(978-1-60453-939-4(9))* ABDO Publishing Co.

Orr, Tamra. Hydroelectric Energy. 2007. (21st Century Skills Library: Power Up! Ser.). (ENG., Illus.). 32p. (gr. 4-8). lib. bdg. 28.50 *(978-1-60279-049-0(3)*, 200054) Cherry Lake Publishing.

Paris, Stephanie. Pop! Air & Water Pressure, 1 vol. 2nd rev. ed. 2013. (Nonfiction Readers Ser.). (ENG.). 64p. (J). (gr. 5-5). pap. 10.99 *(978-1-4333-4939-3(6))* Teacher Created Materials, Inc.

Phillips, Cynthia & Priwer, Shana. Dams & Waterways. 2009. (ENG., Illus.). 112p. (C). (gr. 6-18). lib. bdg. 158.00 *(978-0-7656-8122-5(6)*, Y181910) Routledge.

Pipe, Jim. Water Power. 2011. (J). 28.50 *(978-1-59604-216-2(8))* Black Rabbit Bks.

The Power of Water: Individual Title Six-Packs. (gr. k-1). 23.00 *(978-0-7635-8848-9(2))* Rigby Education.

Richards, Julie. Water Energy. 2009. (J). 19.95 *(978-0-7614-4429-9(7))* Marshall Cavendish GBR. Dist: Marshall Cavendish Corp.

Rodger, Marguerite. Hydroelectric Power: Power from Moving Water. 2010. (ENG., Illus.). 32p. (J). pap. *(978-0-7787-2934-1(6))*; lib. bdg. *(978-0-7787-2920-4(6))* Crabtree Publishing Co.

SchreyerKarmel. Water Power: The Greatest Force on Earth. 2014. (ENG., Illus.). 28p. (J). pap. 9.50 *(978-1-107-68897-1(3))* Cambridge Univ. Pr.

Solway, Andrew. Water Power. 2007. (Energy for the Future & Global Warming Ser.). 32p. (gr. 5-8). pap. 11.70 *(978-0-8368-8413-5(2))*; lib. bdg. 27.00 *(978-0-8368-8404-3(3))* Stevens, Gareth Publishing LLLP.

Spilsbury, Louise. Dams & Hydropower. 2011. (Development or Destruction? Ser.). (ENG., Illus.). 48p. (J). (gr. 5-8). 29.25 *(978-1-4488-6990-9(0))*; pap. 11.75 *(978-1-4488-6994-7(3))* Rosen Publishing Group, Inc., The. (Rosen Reference).

Spilsbury, Richard & Spilsbury, Louise. The Pros & Cons of Water Power. 2007. (Energy Debate Ser.). (Illus.). 48p. (YA). (gr. 5-9). lib. bdg. 29.25 *(978-1-4042-3743-8(7))* Rosen Publishing Group, Inc., The.

—Water, Waves, & Tidal Power. 2012. (Let's Discuss Energy Resources Ser.). (Illus.). 32p. (YA). (gr. 4-7). lib. bdg. 26.50 *(978-1-4488-5263-5(3))* Rosen Publishing Group, Inc., The.

Webster, Christine. Water Power. 2015. (Illus.). 24p. (J). *(978-1-5105-0060-0(X))* SmartBook Media, Inc.

—Water Power. 2016. (J). ***(978-1-4896-5806-7(8))*** 2010. (Illus.). 24p. (J). (gr. 3-5). pap. 11.95 *(978-1-61690-011-3(3))* 2010. (Illus.). 24p. (YA). (gr. 3-6). lib. bdg. 25.70 *(978-1-61690-005-2(9))* 2005. (Illus.). 24p. (J). (gr. 3-7). lib. bdg. 24.45 *(978-1-59036-308-9(6))* Weigl Pubs., Inc.

Whiting, Jim. The Science of Lighting a City: Electricity in Action. 2010. (Action Science Ser.). (ENG.). 32p. (gr. 3-4). pap. 47.70 *(978-1-4296-5077-9(X)*, Fact Finders) Capstone Press of Coughlan Cos.

WATER PURIFICATION

see Water—Purification

WATER RESOURCES DEVELOPMENT

see also Irrigation; Water Power; Water-Supply

Bodden, Valerie. Water for Life. 2010. (Earth Issues Ser.). 48p. (YA). (gr. 5-18). 23.95 *(978-1-58341-986-1(1)*, Creative Education) Creative Co., The.

Harris, William. Water Makes Hydropower. 2003. (From Resource to Energy Source Ser.). (J). *(978-1-58417-286-4(X))*; pap. *(978-1-58417-287-1(8))* Lake Street Pubs.

Mulder, Michelle. Every Last Drop: Bringing Clean Water Home, 1 vol. 2014. (Orca Footprints Ser.). (ENG., Illus.). 48p. (J). (gr. 3-7). 19.95 *(978-1-4598-0223-0(3))* Orca Bk. Pubs. USA.

Sawvel, Patty Jo. Water Resource Management. 2008. (Introducing Issues with Opposing Viewpoints Ser.). (ENG., Illus.). 144p. (gr. 10-12). 42.00 *(978-0-7377-3979-4(7)*, Greenhaven Pr., Inc.) Cengage Gale.

WATER SPORTS

see Aquatic Sports

WATER-SUPPLY

see also Dams; Irrigation; Water—Pollution; Water—Purification; Water Conservation

Aldridge, Rebecca. The Hoover Dam. 2009. (Building America Ser.). (Illus.). 120p. (gr. 5-8). 35.00 *(978-1-60413-069-0(5)*, Chelsea Hse.) Facts On File, Inc.

Allyn, Daisy. Where Does the Bathwater Go? 2012. (Everyday Mysteries Ser.). (ENG.). 24p. (J). (gr. 2-4). pap. 8.15 *(978-1-4339-6323-0(X))*; lib. bdg. 22.60 *(978-1-4339-6321-6(3))* Stevens, Gareth Publishing LLLP.

AWWA Staff, compiled by. The Story of Drinking Water - Teacher's Guide. 2011. (ENG.). 70p. (YA). pap. 18.00 *(978-1-58321-820-4(3))* American Water Works Assn.

—Story of Drinking Water (the) 5th ed. 2011. 24p. (J). 22.00 *(978-1-58321-812-9(2))* American Water Works Assn.

Barnham, Kay. Save Water. 2007. (Rise & Shine Ser.). (ENG., Illus.). 32p. (J). (gr. 3-7). pap. *(978-0-7787-3671-4(7))* Crabtree Publishing Co.

Berger, Melvin. Water, Water Everywhere. (Discovery Readers Ser.). (ENG.). 48p. (J). pap. 3.95 *(978-0-8249-5312-6(6)*, Ideal Pubns.) Worthy Publishing.

Berlatsky, Noah. Water. 2011. (Global Viewpoints Ser.). (ENG., Illus.). 224p. (gr. 10-12). pap. 31.70 *(978-0-7377-5667-8(5)*, Greenhaven Pr., Inc.) Cengage Gale.

Bodden, Valerie. Water for Life. 2010. (Earth Issues Ser.). 48p. (YA). (gr. 5-18). 23.95 *(978-1-58341-986-1(1)*, Creative Education) Creative Co., The.

Bowden, Rob. Food & Water. 2010. (Development Without Damage Ser.). (YA). (gr. 5-9). 34.25 *(978-1-59920-248-8(4))* Black Rabbit Bks.

Bright, Michael. From Raindrop to Tap. 2016. (Source to Resource Ser.). (ENG., Illus.). 32p. (J). (gr. 3-6). *(978-0-7787-2708-8(4))* Crabtree Publishing Co.

Bringing Water to People: 6 Small Books. (Greetings Ser.: Vol. 3). 32p. (gr. 3-5). 31.00 *(978-0-7635-1821-9(2))* Rigby Education.

Bringing Water to People: Big Book. (Greetings Ser.: Vol. 3). 32p. (gr. 3-5). 31.00 *(978-0-7635-3269-7(X))* Rigby Education.

Burgan, Michael. Not a Drop to Drink. 2008. (National Geographic Investigates Science Ser.). (ENG., Illus.). 64p. (J). (gr. 5). 17.95 *(978-1-4263-0360-9(2)*, National Geographic Children's Bks.) National Geographic Society.

—Not a Drop to Drink: Water for a Thirsty World. 2008. (National Geographic Investigates Ser.). (ENG., Illus.). 64p. (J). (gr. 5). lib. bdg. 27.90 *(978-1-4263-0267-1(3)*, National Geographic Children's Bks.) National Geographic Society.

Calhoun, Yael. Water in the News. 2007. (Science News Flash Ser.). (Illus.). 105p. (YA). (gr. 7-12). lib. bdg. 31.95 *(978-0-7910-9254-5(2))* Facts On File, Inc.

Cartlidge, Cherese. Water from Air: Water Harvesting Machines. 2009. (Great Idea Ser.). (ENG., Illus.). 48p. (J). (gr. 4-6). lib. bdg. 26.60 *(978-1-59953-196-0(8))* Norwood Hse. Pr.

Casper, Julie Kerr. Water & Atmosphere: The Lifeblood of Natural Systems. 2007. (Natural Resources Ser.). (Illus.). 207p. (YA). (gr. 7-12). lib. bdg. 39.50 *(978-0-8160-6359-8(1))* Facts On File, Inc.

Castellano, Peter. Water Conservation. 2016. (Where's the Water? Ser.). (Illus.). 24p. (J). (gr. 3-2). pap. 8.15 *(978-1-4824-4692-0(8))* Stevens, Gareth Publishing LLLP.

Cherry, Lynne. A River Ran Wild. 2005. 17.00 *(978-0-7569-5231-0(X))* Perfection Learning Corp.

cohen, judith L. & friend, robyn. Future Engineering: The Clean Water Challenge. katz, david A., illus. 2015. 44p. (J). pap. 7.00 *(978-1-935999-08-9(7))* Cascade Pass, Inc.

Cohen, Judith L. & Friend, Robyn. Los Angeles' Water Future. Katz, David A., illus. 2015. 40p. (J). pap. 7.00 *(978-1-935999-11-9(7))* Cascade Pass, Inc.

Cole, Joanna. At the Waterworks. Degen, Bruce, illus. 2004. (Magic School Bus Ser.). (ENG.). 40p. (J). (gr. -1-3). pap. 6.99 *(978-0-590-40360-3(5))* Scholastic, Inc.

Feinstein, Stephen. Drying Up: Running Out of Water. 2016. (End of Life As We Know It Ser.). (ENG., Illus.). 144p. (YA). (gr. 7-8). lib. bdg. 37.27 *(978-0-7660-7286-2(X))* Enslow Pubs., Inc.

Feinstein, Stephen & Library. Conserving & Protecting Water: What You Can Do. 2010. (Green Issues in Focus Ser.). (Illus.). 128p. (J). (gr. 7-12). lib. bdg. 33.27 *(978-0-7660-3346-7(5))* Enslow Pubs., Inc.

Finton, Nancy. Wonders of Water. 2006. (Nonfiction Reading & Writing Workshops Ser.). (ENG., Illus.). 32p. (J). pap. 17.95 *(978-0-7922-4572-8(5))* CENGAGE Learning.

Food and Agriculture Organization of the United Nations Staff, ed. YUNGA Water Challenge Badge. 2013. (ENG., Illus.). 96p. pap. 10.00 *(978-92-5-107536-4(0))* Food & Agriculture Organization of the United Nations ITA. Dist: Rowman & Littlefield Publishers, Inc.

Furgang, Kathy. Zoom in on Water & Sewage Systems. 2017. (Zoom in on Engineering Ser.). 24p. (J). (gr. 2-2). pap. 9.35 ***(978-0-7660-8840-5(5))***; lib. bdg. 22.60 ***(978-0-7660-8714-9(X))*** Enslow Pubs., Inc.

Geiger, Beth. Clean Water. 2009. (Sally Ride Science Ser.). (ENG., Illus.). 40p. (J). (gr. 3-7). pap. 8.99 *(978-1-59643-577-3(1)*, 9781596435773) Roaring Brook Pr.

Goldish, Meish. The Hoover Dam. 2016. (American Places: from Vision to Reality Ser.). (ENG.). 32p. (J). (gr. 2-7). 19.95 *(978-1-944102-45-6(0))* Bearport Publishing Co., Inc.

Green, Jen. Saving Water. 2005. (Improving Our Environment Ser.). (Illus.). 32p. (gr. 3-6). lib. bdg. 26.00 *(978-0-8368-4431-3(9)*, Gareth Stevens Learning Library) Stevens, Gareth Publishing LLLP.

Hawes, Alison. Water Wise! 2010. (ENG.). 32p. (J). *(978-0-7787-9904-7(2))*; pap. *(978-0-7787-9925-2(5))* Crabtree Publishing Co.

Heos, Bridget. Follow That Tap Water! A Journey down the Drain. 2016. (Keeping Cities Clean Ser.). (ENG., Illus.). 24p. (J). (gr. k-3). 20.95 *(978-1-60753-962-9(4))* Amicus Publishing.

Hewitt, Sally. Using Water. 2008. (Green Team Ser.). (ENG., Illus.). 32p. (J). (gr. 3-7). pap. *(978-0-7787-4104-6(4))*; lib. bdg. *(978-0-7787-4097-1(8))* Crabtree Publishing Co.

Higgins, Matt. Clear Choices: The Water You Drink. 2011. (Second Nature Ser.). 48p. (J). (gr. 5-8). lib. bdg. 26.60 *(978-1-59953-450-3(9))* Norwood Hse. Pr.

Hock, Peggy. Saving Water. 2008. (ENG., Illus.). 24p. (J). pap. 6.95 *(978-0-531-20436-8(7)*, Children's Pr.) Scholastic Library Publishing.

Hofer, Charles. How Do Irrigation Systems Work? 2016. (STEM Waterworks Ser.). (Illus.). 32p. (J). (gr. 5-5). pap. 11.75 *(978-1-4994-2007-4(2)*, PowerKids Pr.) Rosen Publishing Group, Inc., The.

Hollyer, Beatrice. Our World of Water: Children & Water Around the World. 2009. (ENG., Illus.). 48p. (J). (gr. -1-3). 17.99 *(978-0-8050-8941-7(1)*, 9780805089417, Holt, Henry & Co. Bks. For Young Readers) Holt, Henry & Co.

How Faucets Work. (Sunshinetm Science Ser.). 24p. (gr. 1-2). 37.50 *(978-0-7802-2778-1(6))* Wright Group/McGraw-Hill.

How Faucets Work: 6 Each of 1 Student Book, 6 vols. (Sunshinetm Science Ser.). 24p. (gr. 1-2). 41.95 *(978-0-7802-2688-3(7))* Wright Group/McGraw-Hill.

Hunter, Rebecca. Water Supply. 2012. (Eco Alert! Ser.). (Illus.). 32p. (gr. 4-6). lib. bdg. 28.50 *(978-1-59771-300-9(7))* Sea-To-Sea Pubns.

Hutmacher, Kimberly. The Wonderful Water Cycle. 2012. (ENG.). 24p. (gr. 4-5). pap. 8.95 *(978-1-61810-237-9(0))* Rourke Educational Media.

Kallen, Stuart A. Real-World STEM: Global Access to Clean Water. 2017. (ENG.). 80p. (YA). (gr. 5-12). ***(978-1-68282-243-2(5))*** ReferencePoint Pr., Inc.

—Running Dry: The Global Water Crisis. 2015. (Illus.). 64p. (J). *(978-1-4677-6308-0(X))* Twenty First Century Bks.

—Science & Sustainable Water. 2017. (ENG.). 80p. (YA). (gr. 5-12). ***(978-1-68282-257-9(5))*** ReferencePoint Pr., Inc.

Kallen, Stuart A. Water, Water Everywhere? Protecting a Diminishing Resource in a Warming World. 2015. (ENG., Illus.). 64p. (J). (gr. 8-12). lib. bdg. 33.32 *(978-1-4677-2646-7(X)*, Twenty-First Century Bks.) Lerner Publishing Group.

Kegley, David E. Where Does Rain Come From? 2009. (Reading Room Collection 2 Ser.). 24p. (gr. 3-4). 42.50 *(978-1-60852-003-9(X)*, PowerKids Pr.) Rosen Publishing Group, Inc., The.

Kerley, Barbara. A Cool Drink of Water. (ENG.). 32p. (J). (gr. -1-3). 2012. 25.95 *(978-1-4263-1329-5(2))* 2006. (Illus.). pap. 7.95 *(978-0-7922-5489-8(9))* National Geographic Society. (National Geographic Children's Bks.).

La Bella, Laura. Not Enough to Drink: Pollution, Drought, & Tainted Water Supplies. 2009. (Extreme Environmental Threats Ser.). (ENG., Illus.). 64p. (J). (gr. 7-12). pap. 12.95 *(978-1-4358-5376-8(8))*; 64p. (gr. 6-6). 58.50 *(978-1-61512-432-9(2))*; (YA). (gr. 5-9). lib. bdg. 31.95 *(978-1-4358-5020-0(3))* Rosen Publishing Group, Inc., The.

Laidlaw, Jill. Water. 2010. (Sustaining Our Environment Ser.). 48p. 35.65 *(978-1-60753-140-1(2))* Amicus Publishing.

Lanz, Helen. Wonderful Water. 2012. (Go Green Ser.). (Illus.). 32p. (gr. 3-6). lib. bdg. 28.50 *(978-1-59771-306-1(6))* Sea-To-Sea Pubns.

Linde, Barbara M. The Water Cycle. 2016. (Where's the Water? Ser.). 24p. (J). (gr. 3-2). pap. 8.15 *(978-1-4824-4688-3(X))* Stevens, Gareth Publishing LLLP.

—What Is Wastewater? 2016. (Where's the Water? Ser.). 24p. (gr. 3-2). pap. 8.15 *(978-1-4824-4696-8(0))* Stevens, Gareth Publishing LLLP.

Mason, Jennifer. 10 Things You Can Do to Save Water. 2016. (Rookie Star — Make a Difference Ser.). (ENG., Illus.). 32p. (J). lib. bdg. 25.00 *(978-0-531-22651-3(4)*, Children's Pr.) Scholastic Library Publishing.

Mason, Jenny. 10 Cosas Que Puedes Hacer para Ahorrar Aqua. 2017. (Rookie Star — Make a Difference (Spanish Translation) Ser.). (SPA.). 32p. (J). pap. 5.95 ***(978-1-338-18779-3(1))***; lib. bdg. 25.00 ***(978-0-531-22858-6(4))*** Scholastic Library Publishing. (Children's Pr.).

Masters, Nancy R. How Did That Get to My House? Water. 2009. (Community Connections: How Did That Get to My House? Ser.). (ENG.). 24p. (gr. 2-5). lib. bdg. 25.64 *(978-1-60279-475-7(8)*, 200252) Cherry Lake Publishing.

Miller, Debra A., ed. Will the World Run Out of Fresh Water? 2007. (At Issue Ser.). (ENG.). (gr. 10-12). 128p. pap. 31.80 *(978-0-7377-3403-4(5))*; 91p. per. 22.50 *(978-0-7377-3404-1(3))* Cengage Gale. (Greenhaven Pr., Inc.).

Nardo, Don. Roman Roads & Aqueducts. 2014. (History's Great Structures). (ENG., Illus.). 80p. (J). lib. bdg. *(978-1-60152-634-2(2))* ReferencePoint Pr., Inc.

Nelson, Robin. Usamos el Agua. 2003. (Primeros Pasos Ser.). (SPA., Illus.). 23p. (J). pap. 6.95 *(978-0-8225-4825-6(9)*, Lerner Pubns.) Lerner Publishing Group.

—We Use Water. 2003. (First Step Nonfiction - Water Ser.). (ENG., Illus.). 24p. (gr. k-2). pap. 6.95 *(978-0-8225-4595-8(0))*; lib. bdg. 23.93 *(978-0-8225-4594-1(2))* Lerner Publishing Group.

Newton, David E. The Global Water Crisis: A Reference Handbook, 1 vol. 2016. (Contemporary World Issues Ser.). (Illus.). 354p. (C). 60.00 *(978-1-4408-3980-1(8)*, A4858C) ABC-CLIO, LLC.

Olien, Rebecca. Cleaning Water. 2016. (Water in Our World Ser.). (ENG., Illus.). 24p. (gr. 1-2). lib. bdg. 25.32 *(978-1-4914-8278-0(8)*, First Facts) Capstone Press of Coughlan Cos.

—Water Sources. 2016. (Water in Our World Ser.). (ENG.). 24p. (gr. 1-2). lib. bdg. 25.32 *(978-1-4914-8277-3(X)*, First Facts) Capstone Press of Coughlan Cos.

Parker, Russ. Water Supplies in Crisis. 2009. (Planet in Crisis Ser.). 32p. (gr. 5-8). (ENG., Illus.). (J). pap. 10.00 *(978-1-4358-0680-1(8))*; (YA). lib. bdg. 25.25 *(978-1-4358-5250-1(8))* Rosen Publishing Group, Inc., The. (Rosen Reference).

Perritano, John. Freshwater Resources, Vol. 12. 2015. (North American Natural Resources Ser.). (Illus.). 64p. (J). (gr. 7). lib. bdg. 23.95 *(978-1-4222-3381-8(2))* Mason Crest.

Peterson, Megan Cooley. How Water Gets from Treatment Plants to Toilet Bowls. 2016. (Here to There Ser.). (ENG., Illus.). 24p. (gr. k-1). lib. bdg. 26.65 *(978-1-4914-8435-7(7)*, Pebble Plus) Capstone Press of Coughlan Cos.

Rieger, Linda. Water in Our House. Bianchi, John, illus. 2008. 20p. (J). *(978-0-9779427-6-3(7))* Pathways into Science.

Rosenberg, Pam. Watershed Conservation. 2008. (21st Century Skills Library: Global Perspectives Ser.). (ENG.). 32p. (gr. 4-8). lib. bdg. 28.50 *(978-1-60279-131-2(7)*, 200111) Cherry Lake Publishing.

Roza, Greg. How Do Aqueducts Work? 2016. (STEM Waterworks Ser.). (Illus.). 32p. (J). (gr. 5-5). pap. 11.75 *(978-1-4994-1991-7(0)*, PowerKids Pr.) Rosen Publishing Group, Inc., The.

Sawyer, Ava. Humans & the Hydrosphere: Protecting Earth's Water Sources. 2017. (Humans & Our Planet Ser.). (ENG.). 32p. (gr. 3-4). lib. bdg. 27.32 ***(978-1-5157-7198-2(9)***, Fact Finders) Capstone Press of Coughlan Cos.

Sévigny, Eric, illus. Every Drop Counts! 2011. (Ecology Club Ser.). (ENG.). 24p. (J). (gr. -1-1). pap. 5.95 *(978-2-89450-772-8(0))* Caillouet, Gerry.

Shaw, Daniel. Southwest Aquatic Habitats: On the Trail of Fish in a Desert. 2013. (Barbara Guth Worlds of Wonder Science Series for Young Readers Ser.). (ENG., Illus.). 112p. (J). 34.95 *(978-0-8263-5309-2(6))* Univ. of New Mexico Pr.

Shea, Therese. How Do Reservoirs Work? 2016. (STEM Waterworks Ser.). (Illus.). 32p. (J). (gr. 5-5). pap. 11.75 *(978-1-4994-2011-1(0)*, PowerKids Pr.) Rosen Publishing Group, Inc., The.

Spilsbury, Louise. Threats to Our Water Supply. 2009. (J). 70.50 *(978-1-4358-5481-9(0))*; (ENG.). 48p. (YA). pap. 11.75 *(978-1-4358-5480-2(2))*; (ENG., Illus.). 48p. (J). (gr. 5-9). lib. bdg. 29.25 *(978-1-4358-5352-2(0))* Rosen Publishing Group, Inc., The.

Stone, Andrew & Bryan, Jessica. Well... What's All That Drilling About? Pender, Rachel, illus. 2007. 40p. (J). 7.95 *(978-0-9641186-3-8(7))* American Ground Water Trust.

Walton, Ruth. Let's Drink Some Water. 2013. (Let's Find Out Ser.). (Illus.). 32p. (gr. k-5). 28.50 *(978-1-59771-384-9(8))* Sea-To-Sea Pubns.

Watching Every Drop, 6 Packs. (gr. k-1). 23.00 *(978-0-7635-8851-9(2))* Rigby Education.

Welton, Jude. Water Supplies. 2005. (Action for the Environment Ser.). (Illus.). 32p. (J). (gr. 4-7). lib. bdg. 27.10 *(978-1-58340-601-4(8)*, 1247299) Black Rabbit Bks.

Why Do We Need Water? 2014. (ENG., Illus.). 24p. (J). *(978-0-7787-0494-2(7))* Crabtree Publishing Co.

Workman, James G. Water. 2009. (Diminishing Resources Ser.). 111p. (J). lib. bdg. 28.95 *(978-1-59935-115-5(3))* Reynolds, Morgan Inc.

World Book, Inc. Staff, contrib. by. Food, Water, & Climate Change. 2015. (Illus.). 48p. (J). *(978-0-7166-2712-8(4))* World Bk., Inc.

WATER-SUPPLY ENGINEERING

Edwards, Erika. Levees & Seawalls. 2016. (Technology Takes on Nature Ser.). 00032p. (J). pap. 10.50 ***(978-1-4824-5775-9(X))*** Stevens, Gareth Publishing LLLP.

WATER WORKS

see Waterworks

WATERGATE AFFAIR, 1972-1974

Archer, Jules. Watergate: A Story of Richard Nixon & the Shocking 1972 Scandal. rev. ed. 2015. (Jules Archer History for Young Readers Ser.). (ENG., Illus.). 344p. (J). (gr. 6). 16.99 *(978-1-63220-606-0(4)*, Sky Pony Pr.) Skyhorse Publishing Co., Inc.

Elish, Dan. The Watergate Scandal. 2004. (Cornerstones of Freedom Ser.). (ENG., Illus.). 48p. (J). 26.00 *(978-0-516-24239-2(3)*, Children's Pr.) Scholastic Library Publishing.

Fremon, David K. The Watergate Scandal in United States History. 2014. (In United States History Ser.). (Illus.). 96p. (J). (gr. 5-12). 27.94 *(978-0-7660-6107-1(8))*; pap. 10.95 *(978-0-7660-6108-8(6))* Enslow Pubs., Inc.

Hillstrom, Kevin. Watergate. 2004. (Defining Moments Ser.). (Illus.). 195p. lib. bdg. 55.00 *(978-0-7808-0769-3(3))* Omnigraphics, Inc.

Noble, William. Presidential Power on Trial: From Watergate to All the President's Men. 2009. (Famous Court Cases That Became Movies Ser.). (Illus.). 128p. (J). (gr. 7-12). lib. bdg. 33.27 *(978-0-7660-3058-9(X))* Enslow Pubs., Inc.

Tracy, Kathleen. The Watergate Scandal. 2006. (Monumental Milestones Ser.). (Illus.). 48p. (YA). (gr. 4-7). lib. bdg. 29.95 *(978-1-58415-470-9(5))* Mitchell Lane Pubs., Inc.

Uschan, Michael V. Watergate. 2009. (American History Ser.). (ENG., Illus.). 104p. 39.40 *(978-1-4205-0135-3(6)*, Lucent Bks.) Cengage Gale.

Van Meter, Larry A. United States V. Nixon: The Question of Executive Privilege. 2007. (Great Supreme Court Decisions Ser.). (Illus.). 112p. (YA). (gr. 5-9). lib. bdg. 32.95 *(978-0-7910-9381-8(6))* Facts On File, Inc.

W
X
Y
Z

Wittekind, Erika & Gerhardt, Michael J. The United States v. Nixon: The Watergate Scandal & Limits to Us Presidential Power, 1 vol. 2012. (Landmark Supreme Court Cases Ser.). (ENG., Illus.). 160p. (J). (gr. 6-12). 37.07 *(978-1-61783-478-3(5))* ABDO Publishing Co.

WATERLOO, BATTLE OF, WATERLOO, BELGIUM, 1815

Roberts, Russell. Battle of Waterloo. 2011. (Technologies & Strategies in Battle Ser.). (Illus.). 48p. (J). (gr. 4-7). lib. bdg. 29.95 *(978-1-61228-076-9(5))* Mitchell Lane Pubs., Inc.

WATERMELONS

Murray, Julie. Watermelon, 1 vol. 2007. (Life Cycles Ser.). (ENG.). 24p. (gr. -1-3). 25.65 *(978-1-59928-712-6(9))*, Buddy Bks.) ABDO Publishing Co.

O'Brady, Terry, et al. Watermelons. 2007. (Language, Literacy, & Vocabulary - Windows on Literacy Ser.). (ENG., Illus.). 8p. pap. 9.95 *(978-0-7922-8455-0(0))* National Geographic School Publishing, Inc.

WATERSHIP DOWN (IMAGINARY PLACE)—FICTION

Adams, Richard. Watership Down. 2005. (ENG., Illus.). 496p. pap. 18.99 *(978-0-7432-7770-9(8))*, Scribner) Scribner.

WATERWAYS

see also Canals; Rivers

Honders, Christine. How Do Canals Work? 2016. (STEM Waterworks Ser.). 32p. (J). (gr. 5-5). pap. 11.75 *(978-1-4994-1995-5(3))*, PowerKids Pr.) Rosen Publishing Group, Inc., The.

Laplante, Walter. Waterways of the Great Lakes. 2014. (Exploring the Great Lakes Ser.). 32p. (J). (gr. 3-6). pap. 63.00 *(978-1-4824-1195-9(4))* Stevens, Gareth Publishing LLLP.

Mitten, Ellen. Aguas Navegables (Waterways) 2009. (Pequeño mundo Geografía (Little World Geography) Ser.). (ENG & SPA., Illus.). 24p. (J). (gr. k-2). lib. bdg. 22.79 *(978-1-60694-587-2(4))* Rourke Educational Media.

—Waterways. 2009. (ENG., Illus.). 24p. (gr. k-2). pap. 8.95 *(978-1-60694-536-0(X))* Rourke Educational Media.

Phillips, Cynthia & Priwer, Shana. Dams & Waterways. 2009. (ENG., Illus.). 112p. (C). (gr. 6-18). lib. bdg. 158.00 *(978-0-7656-8122-5(6))*, Y181910) Routledge.

Radley, Gail. Waterways. Sherlock, Jean & Matheny, Jean, illus. 2005. (Vanishing from Ser.). 32p. (gr. 6-12). lib. bdg. 22.60 *(978-1-57505-408-7(6))* Lerner Publishing Group.

WATERWORKS

see also Water-Supply

Cole, Joanna. At the Waterworks. 2004. (Magic School Bus Original Ser.). (gr. k-3). lib. bdg. 17.20 *(978-0-8335-1744-9(9))*, Turtleback) Turtleback Bks.

Murphy, Kevin. Water for Hartford: The Story of the Hartford Water Works & the Metropolitan District Commission. 2004. (Illus.). xxi, 318p. 29.95 *(978-0-9749352-0-1(4))* Shining Tramp Pr.

STEM Waterworks. 2016. (STEM Waterworks Ser.). 32p. (gr. 5-5). 157.50 *(978-1-4994-1979-5(1))*; pap. 70.50 *(978-1-4994-2459-1(0))* Rosen Publishing Group, Inc., The. (PowerKids Pr.).

WATT, JAMES, 1736-1819

Whiting, Jim. James Watt & the Steam Engine. 2005. (Uncharted, Unexplored, & Unexplained Ser.). (Illus.). 48p. (J). (gr. 4-8). lib. bdg. 29.95 *(978-1-58415-371-9(7))* Mitchell Lane Pubs., Inc.

WAVES

see also Light; Ocean Waves; Radiation

Cain, Marie Mowery. Under the Waves. 2013. (Big Books, Blue Ser.). (ENG & SPA., Illus.). 16p. pap. 33.00 *(978-1-59246-005-2(4))* Big Books, by George!

Dickmann, Nancy. Harnessing Wave & Tidal Energy. 2016. (Future of Power Ser.). 00032p. (J). (gr. 4-5). pap. 10.00 *(978-1-4994-3213-8(5))*, PowerKids Pr.) Rosen Publishing Group, Inc., The.

Gardner, Robert. Light, Sound, & Waves Science Fair Projects: Using Sunglasses, Guitars, CDs, & Other Stuff. 2004. (Physics! Best Science Projects Ser.). (Illus.). 128p. (J). lib. bdg. 27.94 *(978-0-7660-2126-6(2))* Enslow Pubs., Inc.

—Light, Sound, & Waves Science Fair Projects, Revised & Expanded Using the Scientific Method. 2010. (Physics Science Projects Using the Scientific Method Ser.). (Illus.). 160p. (J). (gr. 5-18). 35.94 *(978-0-7660-3416-7(X))* Enslow Pubs., Inc.

Gerdes, Louise I. Wave & Tidal Power. Kiesbye, Stefan, ed. 2010. (At Issue Ser.). (ENG.). 128p. 34.45 *(978-0-7377-4900-7(8))*, Greenhaven Pr., Inc.) Cengage Gale.

Holt, Rinehart and Winston Staff. Holt Science & Technology Chapter 20: Physical Science: The Energy of Waves. 5th ed. 2004. (Illus.). pap. 13.13 *(978-0-03-030431-6(8))* Harcourt Trade Pubs.

Hudak, Heather. Waves & Information Transfer. 2017. (Catch a Wave Ser.). (ENG., Illus.). 32p. (J). pap. ***(978-0-7787-2970-9(2))*** Crabtree Publishing Co.

Hudak, Heather C. What Are Waves? 2017. 32p. (J). ***(978-0-7787-2964-8(8))*** Crabtree Publishing Co.

Ivancic, Linda. What Is a Wave? 2016. (Unseen Science Ser.). (ENG., Illus.). 32p. (J). (gr. 3-3). pap. 10.58 *(978-1-5026-0917-5(7))* Cavendish Square Publishing.

Kenney, Karen Latchana. Sound & Light Waves Investigations. 2017. (Key Questions in Physical Science Ser.). (ENG.). 32p. (J). (gr. 3-6). 27.99 ***(978-1-5124-4004-1(3))*** Lerner Publishing Group.

Mara, Wil. How Do Waves Form? 2010. (Tell Me Why, Tell Me How 4 Ser.). 32p. (gr. 3-5). 29.93 *(978-0-7614-4829-7(2))* Marshall Cavendish Corp.

McPartland, Randall. Understanding Waves & Wave Motion. 2015. (J). lib. bdg. *(978-1-62713-431-6(X))* Cavendish Square Publishing.

Solway, Andrew. Exploring Sound, Light, & Radiation. 2007. (Exploring Physical Science Ser.). (Illus.). 48p. (YA). (gr. 5-9). lib. bdg. 29.25 *(978-1-4042-3746-9(1))* Rosen Publishing Group, Inc., The.

Squire, Ann O. Tsunamis. 2016. (True Book(tm), a — Extreme Earth Ser.). (ENG., Illus.). 48p. (J). lib. bdg. 31.00 *(978-0-531-22298-0(5))*, Children's Pr.) Scholastic Library Publishing.

Thompson, Lisa. Wild Waves. 2003. (Real Deal Ser.). (Illus.). 32p. (J). pap. *(978-0-7608-6690-0(2))* Sundance/Newbridge Educational Publishing.

Wright, Holly. Wave. 2004. (J). *(978-0-9743690-7-5(1))* Britt Allcroft Productions.

WAXES

Murray, Julie. Wax to Crayon, 1 vol. 2006. (Beginning to End Set 1 - 8 Titles Ser.). (ENG., Illus.). 24p. (gr. k-4). 25.65 *(978-1-59679-915-8(3))*, Buddy Bks.) ABDO Publishing Co.

Snyder, Inez. Wax to Crayons. 2003. (Welcome Bks.). (ENG., Illus.). 24p. (J). (gr. -1-2). 19.00 *(978-0-516-24267-5(9))*, Children's Pr.); pap. 4.95 *(978-0-516-24359-7(4))*, Watts, Franklin) Scholastic Library Publishing.

WAYNE, ANTHONY, 1745-1796—FICTION

Rinaldi, Ann. The Family Greene. 2011. (ENG.). 256p. (YA). (gr. 7). pap. 14.95 *(978-0-547-57723-4(0))* Houghton Mifflin Harcourt Publishing Co.

WEAPONS

see also Firearms; Military Weapons

Benoit, Peter. The Nuclear Age. 2012. (Cornerstones of Freedom, Third Ser.). (ENG., Illus.). 64p. (J). pap. 8.95 *(978-0-531-28162-8(0))*; (gr. 4-6). lib. bdg. 30.00 *(978-0-531-23062-6(7))* Scholastic Library Publishing. (Children's Pr.).

Bergin, Mark. Warfare in the 16th to 19th Centuries. 2015. (Warriors Ser.). (Illus.). 48p. (gr. 4-7). 37.10 *(978-1-62588-357-5(9))* Black Rabbit Bks.

Biskup, Agnieszka. Batarangs & Grapnels: The Science Behind Batman's Utility Belt, 1 vol. 2014. (Batman Science Ser.). (ENG.). 32p. (gr. 3-4). 27.32 *(978-1-4765-3943-0(X))*, DC Super Heroes) Stone Arch Bks.

Boos, Ben. Swords: An Artist's Devotion. Boos, Ben, illus. 2008. (ENG., Illus.). 96p. (J). (gr. 5-9). 24.99 *(978-0-7636-3148-2(5))* Candlewick Pr.

Brezina, Corona. Weapons of Mass Destruction: Proliferation & Control. 2009. (Library of Weapons of Mass Destruction Ser.). 64p. (gr. 5-5). 58.50 *(978-1-60853-959-8(8))* Rosen Publishing Group, Inc., The.

Burgan, Michael. Weapons Technology: Science, Technology, & Engineering. 2016. (Calling All Innovators: a Career for You Ser.). (ENG., Illus.). 64p. (J). lib. bdg. 32.00 *(978-0-531-21891-4(0))*, Children's Pr.) Scholastic Library Publishing.

Chambers, Catherine. Tools of Combat. Bustamante, Martín, illus. 2016. (Warriors! Ser.). (ENG.). 32p. (J). (gr. 3-6). 26.65 *(978-1-4677-9355-1(8))* Lerner Publishing Group.

Chapman, Caroline. Battles & Weapons: Exploring History Through Art. 2007. (Picture That Ser.). (ENG., Illus.). 64p. (J). (gr. 3-17). 19.95 *(978-1-58728-588-2(6))* Cooper Square Publishing Llc.

Clarke, Catriona. Armor. McKenna, Terry, illus. 2007. (Usborne Beginners Ser.). 32p. (J). (gr. -1-3). 4.99 *(978-0-7945-1578-2(9))*, Usborne) EDC Publishing.

Clint, Marc. Aztec Warriors. 2011. (History's Greatest Warriors Ser.). (ENG., Illus.). 24p. (J). (gr. 3-7). lib. bdg. 25.95 *(978-1-60014-626-8(0))*, Torque Bks.) Bellwether Media.

Curley, Robert, ed. Weapons of Mass Destruction. 2011. (Britannica Guide to War Ser.). (ENG.). 160p. (YA). (gr. 10-12). lib. bdg. 35.25 *(978-1-61530-687-9(0))* Rosen Publishing Group, Inc., The.

Egan, Tracie. Weapons of Mass Destruction & North Korea. 2004. (Library of Weapons of Mass Destruction Ser.). (Illus.). 64p. (J). lib. bdg. 31.95 *(978-1-4042-0296-2(X))* Rosen Publishing Group, Inc., The.

Fact Atlas: Arms & Armor. 2009. (FACT ATLAS Ser.). 72p. (J). 14.95 *(978-0-8437-1901-7(X))* Hammond World Atlas Corp.

Fowler, Will. The Children's History of Weapons: Ancient & Modern. 2014. (ENG., Illus.). 128p. (J). (gr. -1-12). 14.99 *(978-1-86147-359-2(1))*, Armadillo) Anness Publishing GBR. Dist: National Bk. Network.

—The Story of Ancient Weapons. 2010. (Journey Through History Ser.). (ENG.). 64p. (YA). lib. bdg. 31.95 *(978-1-4488-0623-2(2))*, Rosen Reference) Rosen Publishing Group, Inc., The.

—The Story of Modern Weapons & Warfare. 2011. (Journey Through History Ser.). (J). lib. bdg. 31.95 *(978-1-4488-4793-8(1))* Rosen Publishing Group, Inc., The.

Freese, Susan M. Nuclear Weapons, 1 vol. 2011. (Essential Issues Set 3 Ser.). (ENG., Illus.). 112p. (J). (gr. 6-12). lib. bdg. 35.64 *(978-1-61783-137-9(9))* ABDO Publishing Co.

Gifford, Clive. The Arms Trade. 2004. (World Issues Ser.). (J). lib. bdg. 28.50 *(978-1-59389-154-1(7))* Chrysalis Education.

Hamilton, John. Pirate Ships & Weapons, 1 vol. 2007. (Pirates Ser.). (ENG., Illus.). 32p. (gr. 4-8). 27.07 *(978-1-59928-763-8(3))*, Abdo & Daughters) ABDO Publishing Co.

—Weapons of Science Fiction, 1 vol. 2006. (World of Science Fiction Ser.). (ENG., Illus.). 32p. (gr. 4-7). 27.07 *(978-1-59679-997-4(8))*, Abdo & Daughters) ABDO Publishing Co.

Harris, Ashley Rae. Arms Trade, 1 vol. 2011. (Essential Issues Set 2 Ser.). (ENG., Illus.). 112p. (J). (gr. 6-12). lib. bdg. 35.64 *(978-1-61714-770-8(2))*, Essential Library) ABDO Publishing Co.

Ives, Rob. Break the Siege: Make Your Own Catapults. De Quay, John Paul, illus. 2016. (Tabletop Wars Ser.). (ENG.). 32p. (J). (gr. 3-6). 26.65 *(978-1-5124-0638-2(4))* Lerner Publishing Group.

—Ready, Aim, Launch! Make Your Own Small Launchers. Paul de Quay, John, illus. 2016. (Tabletop Wars Ser.). (ENG.). 32p. (J). (gr. 3-6). lib. bdg. 26.65 *(978-1-5124-0636-8(8))* Lerner Publishing Group.

—Surprise the Enemy: Make Your Own Traps & Triggers. Paul de Quay, John, illus. 2016. (Tabletop Wars Ser.). (ENG.). 32p. (J). (gr. 3-6). lib. bdg. 26.65 *(978-1-5124-0637-5(6))* Lerner Publishing Group.

Jackson, Robert. The 101 Greatest Weapons of All Times, 4 vols., Set. Incl. 101 Great Bombers. lib. bdg. 34.60 *(978-1-4358-3594-8(8))*; 101 Great Fighters. lib. bdg. 34.60 *(978-1-4358-3597-9(2))*; 101 Great Tanks. lib. bdg. 34.60 *(978-1-4358-3595-5(6))*; 101 Great Warships. lib. bdg. 34.60 *(978-1-4358-3596-2(4))*; (YA). (gr. 9-12). 2010. (Illus.). 112p. 2010. Set lib. bdg. 127.80 *(978-1-4358-3604-4(9))* Rosen Publishing Group, Inc., The.

Kevin, Brian. Guns & Special Weapons, 1 vol. 2012. (Gun Education & Safety Ser.). (ENG., Illus.). 32p. (J). 27.07 *(978-1-61783-319-9(3))*, Checkerboard Library) ABDO Publishing Co.

Latno, Mark. The Paper Boomerang Book: Build Them, Throw Them, & Get Them to Return Every Time. 2010. (Science in Motion Ser.). (ENG., Illus.). 160p. (J). (gr. 4-18). pap. 12.95 *(978-1-56976-282-0(1))* Chicago Review Pr., Inc.

The Library of Weapons of Mass Destruction, 6 Bks. 2005. Set 1. (J). 159.00 *(978-1-4042-0382-2(6))*Set 2. (YA). 159.00 *(978-1-4042-0383-9(4))* Rosen Publishing Group, Inc., The.

The Library of Weapons of Mass Destruction: Sets 1 & 2. 2005. (YA). (gr. 7-12). lib. bdg. 239.40 *(978-1-4042-0384-6(2))* Rosen Publishing Group, Inc., The.

Loveless, Antony. Bomb & Mine Disposal Officers. 2009. (World's Most Dangerous Jobs Ser.). (ENG., Illus.). 32p. (J). (gr. 3-6). pap. *(978-0-7787-5109-0(0))*; lib. bdg. *(978-0-7787-5095-6(7))* Crabtree Publishing Co.

Lusted, Marcia Amidon. Ninja Science: Camouflage, Weapons, & Stealthy Attacks. 2016. (Warrior Science Ser.). (ENG., Illus.). 32p. (gr. 3-4). lib. bdg. 27.99 *(978-1-4914-8115-8(3))*, Edge Bks.) Capstone Press of Coughlan Cos.

Marcovitz, Hal. Biological & Chemical Warfare, 1 vol. 2010. (Essential Issues Set 1 Ser.). (ENG.). 112p. (J). (gr. 6-12). lib. bdg. 35.64 *(978-1-60453-951-6(8))*, Essential Library) ABDO Publishing Co.

Nardo, Don. Invisible Weapons: The Science of Biological & Chemical Warfare, 1 vol. 2010. (Headline Science Ser.). (ENG.). 48p. (gr. 7-8). lib. bdg. 29.32 *(978-0-7565-4217-7(0))*, Headline Science) Compass Point Bks.

Owen, Ruth. Ready, Aim, Fire!, 1 vol., 1. 2014. (DIY for Boys Ser.). (ENG.). 32p. (J). (gr. 3-6). 27.50 *(978-1-4777-6286-8(8))*, PowerKids Pr.) Rosen Publishing Group, Inc., The.

Parker, Helen. Weird Weapons Intermediate Book with Online Access. 2014. (ENG., Illus.). 28p. (J). pap. 9.50 *(978-1-107-65200-2(6))* Cambridge Univ. Pr.

Ripley, Tim. Torpedoes, Missiles, & Cannons: Physics Goes to War. 2017. (STEM on the Battlefield Ser.). (ENG., Illus.). 48p. (J). (gr. 4-6). 31.99 ***(978-1-5124-3926-7(6))***, Lerner Pubns.) Lerner Publishing Group.

Rivera, Sheila. Weapons of Mass Destruction. 2003. (World in Conflict-the Middle East Ser.). 32p. (gr. 4-8). 27.07 *(978-1-59197-421-5(6))*, Abdo & Daughters) ABDO Publishing Co.

Staeger, Rob. Native American Tools & Weapons. Johnson, Troy, ed. 2013. (Native American Life Ser.: 15). 64p. (J). (gr. 5-18). 19.95 *(978-1-4222-2977-4(7))* Mason Crest.

Turner, Tracy. Weapons of War. 2015. (Head-To-Head Ser.). (ENG., Illus.). 24p. (gr. 3-8). 28.50 *(978-1-62588-151-9(7))* Black Rabbit Bks.

Weapons & Warfare. 2003. (Illus.). 32p. (YA). pap. *(978-1-904516-31-6(9))*, Pavilion Children's Books) Pavilion Bks.

Weapons of Mass Destruction. 2011. (Britannica Guide to War Ser.). (ENG.). 160p. (YA). (gr. 10-12). 70.50 *(978-1-61530-800-2(8))* Rosen Publishing Group, Inc., The.

The Weapons of World War II. 2014. (True Book(tm), a — World at War Ser.). (ENG.). 48p. (J). lib. bdg. 31.00 *(978-0-531-20495-5(2))* Scholastic Library Publishing.

Wood, Alix. Biological Weapons, 01 vols., 1. 2016. (Today's High-Tech Weapons Ser.). (ENG.). 32p. (J). pap. 10.00 *(978-1-5081-4671-1(3))*, PowerKids Pr.) Rosen Publishing Group, Inc., The.

—Chemical Weapons, 01 vols., 1. 2016. (Today's High-Tech Weapons Ser.). (ENG.). 32p. (J). pap. 10.00 *(978-1-5081-4679-7(9))*, PowerKids Pr.) Rosen Publishing Group, Inc., The.

—Nuclear Weapons, 01 vols., 1. 2016. (Today's High-Tech Weapons Ser.). (ENG.). 32p. (J). pap. 10.00 *(978-1-5081-4687-2(X))*, PowerKids Pr.) Rosen Publishing Group, Inc., The.

Woods, Mary B. & Woods, Michael. Ancient Warfare: From Clubs to Catapults. 2005. (Ancient Technology Ser.). (Illus.). 96p. (gr. 6-12). 25.26 *(978-0-8225-2999-6(8))* Lerner Publishing Group.

Wright, Susan. Weapons of Mass Destruction: Illicit Trade & Trafficking. 2009. (Library of Weapons of Mass Destruction Ser.). 64p. (gr. 5-5). 58.50 *(978-1-60853-960-4(1))* Rosen Publishing Group, Inc., The.

WEASELS

Beer, Amy-Jane. Weasels. 2008. (Nature's Children Ser.). (Illus.). 52p. (J). *(978-0-7172-6263-2(4))* Grolier, Ltd.

Borgert-Spaniol, Megan. Weasels. 2012. (Backyard Wildlife Ser.). (ENG., Illus.). 24p. (J). (gr. k-3). lib. bdg. 25.95 *(978-1-60014-725-8(9))*, Blastoff! Readers) Bellwether Media.

WEASELS—FICTION

Chartrand, Lili. The Smelly Story of Hazel the Weasel. Eid, Jean-Paul, illus. 2009. (Rainy Day Readers Ser.). 32p. (J). (gr. -1-3). 22.60 *(978-1-60754-379-4(6))*; pap. 10.55 *(978-1-60754-380-0(X))* Windmill Bks.

Dolan, Elys. Weasels. Dolan, Elys, illus. 2014. (ENG., Illus.). 32p. (J). (gr. k-3). 17.99 *(978-0-7636-7100-6(2))*, Nosy Crow) Candlewick Pr.

Jackson, Bobby L. Boon the Raccoon & Easel the Weasel. Rodriguez, Christina, illus. 2004. 32p. (J). pap. 11.95 *(978-1-884242-03-8(0))*, BREW2NED); 19.95 *(978-1-884242-02-1(2))*, BREW2NED) Multicultural Pubns.

Marcellino, Fred, illus. The Wainscott Weasel. 2014. (ENG.). 208p. (J). (gr. 2-7). 16.99 *(978-1-4814-1010-6(5))*, Atheneum Bks. for Young Readers) Simon & Schuster Children's Publishing.

Michiko Florence, Debbi. The Disappearing Picnic. Roe, Monika, illus. 2016. (Dorothy & Toto Ser.). (ENG.). 40p. (gr. k-2). lib. bdg. 21.32 *(978-1-4795-8704-9(4))* Capstone Press of Coughlan Cos.

Neumann, Jeanne L. Wendell the Weasel. 2008. 16p. per. 24.95 *(978-1-4241-9922-8(0))* America Star Bks.

Price, Dann. Wesley the Weasel Can't Stop His Sneezel. 2013. 24p. pap. 10.95 *(978-1-4626-9427-3(6))* America Star Bks.

Sabo, J. Train Wrecker. 2011. 28p. pap. 24.95 *(978-1-4626-4379-0(5))* America Star Bks.

Sargent, Dave & Sargent, Pat. Bandit: I Help Others, 56 vols., Vol. 14. Huff, Jeane, illus. 2003. (Animal Pride Ser.: 14). 42p. (J). lib. bdg. 20.95 *(978-1-56763-785-4(X))* Ozark Publishing.

Seidler, Tor. Wainscott Weasel. Marcellino, Fred, illus. 2015. (ENG.). 208p. (J). (gr. 2-7). pap. 8.99 *(978-1-4814-1011-3(3))* Simon & Schuster Children's Publishing.

WEATHER

see also Climate; Meteorology; Rain and Rainfall; Snow; Storms; Weather Control; Winds

ABDO Publishing. This or That? Weather. 2016. (This or That? Weather Ser.: 6). (ENG.). 24p. (J). (gr. k-4). lib. bdg. 153.90 *(978-1-62403-952-2(9))*, Super SandCastle) ABDO Publishing Co.

ABDO Publishing Company Staff & Doudna, Kelly. Weather, 1 vol. 2003. (Weather Ser.: 6). (ENG.). 24p. (J). (gr. k-3). lib. bdg. 145.26 *(978-1-57765-532-9(X))*, SandCastle) ABDO Publishing Co.

Acampora, Courtney & DiPerna, Kaitlyn. Read with Me! Pre, Level 1. 2016. (Smithsonian Readers Ser.). (ENG., Illus.). 200p. (J). (gr. -1). 14.95 *(978-1-62686-571-6(X))*, Silver Dolphin Bks.) Readerlink Distribution Services, LLC.

Adams, Simon. The Best Book of Weather. 2008. (Best Books Of Ser.). (ENG., Illus.). 32p. (J). (gr. k-3). pap. 6.99 *(978-0-7534-6172-3(2))*, 9780753461723, Kingfisher) Roaring Brook Pr.

AIMS Education Foundation. Weather Sense: Moisture. 2008. 272p. (J). pap. 21.95 *(978-1-932093-00-1(1))* AIMS Education Foundation.

Algarra, Alejandro & Bonilla, Rocio. What Causes Weather & Seasons? 2016. (Curious Young Minds Ser.). (ENG.). 36p. (J). (gr. -1-2). pap. 7.99 *(978-1-4380-0892-9(9))* Barron's Educational Series, Inc.

Allaby, Michael. The World's Weather. 2012. (ENG., Illus.). 48p. (J). 15.00 *(978-1-899762-81-1(7))* Award Pubns. Ltd. GBR. Dist: Parkwest Pubns., Inc.

Andersen, Jill. Keeping Track of the Weather. 2016. (Rosen REAL Readers: STEM & STEAM Collection). 12p. (gr. 1-k). pap. 6.33 *(978-1-5081-2422-1(1))*, Rosen Classroom) Rosen Publishing Group, Inc., The.

Anderson, Michael. Investigating Earth's Weather. 2011. (J). lib. bdg. 31.70 *(978-1-61530-499-8(1))* Rosen Publishing Group, Inc., The.

—Investigating the Global Climate. 2011. (Illus.). 87p. (J). lib. bdg. 31.70 *(978-1-61530-496-7(7))* Rosen Publishing Group, Inc., The.

Appleby, Alex. It's Hailing! 2013. (What's the Weather? Ser.). 24p. (J). (gr. k-2). pap. 48.90 *(978-1-4339-9394-7(5))*; pap. 8.15 *(978-1-4339-9393-0(7))*; (ENG., Illus.). lib. bdg. 22.60 *(978-1-4339-9392-3(9))* Stevens, Gareth Publishing LLLP.

—It's Hailing! / Est Granizando! 2013. (What's the Weather? / Qu Tiempo Hace? Ser.). (SPA & ENG., Illus.). 24p. (J). (gr. k-2). 22.60 *(978-1-4339-9462-3(3))* Stevens, Gareth Publishing LLLP.

—It's Rainy! 2013. (What's the Weather? Ser.). (Illus.). 24p. (J). (gr. k-2). pap. 8.15 *(978-1-4339-9397-8(X))*; pap. 48.90 *(978-1-4339-9398-5(8))*; (ENG., lib. bdg. 22.60 *(978-1-4339-9396-1(1))* Stevens, Gareth Publishing LLLP.

—It's Rainy! / Est Lloviendo! 2013. (What's the Weather? / Qu Tiempo Hace? Ser.). (SPA & ENG., Illus.). 24p. (J). (gr. k-2). 22.60 *(978-1-4339-9460-9(7))* Stevens, Gareth Publishing LLLP.

—It's Snowing! 2013. (What's the Weather? Ser.). 24p. (J). (gr. k-2). 22.60 *(978-1-4339-9400-5(3))*; pap. 48.90 *(978-1-4339-9402-9(X))*; pap. 8.15 *(978-1-4339-9401-2(1))* Stevens, Gareth Publishing LLLP.

—It's Snowing! / Est Nevando! 2013. (What's the Weather? / Qu Tiempo Hace? Ser.). (SPA & ENG., Illus.). 24p. (J). (gr. k-2). 22.60 *(978-1-4339-9458-6(5))* Stevens, Gareth Publishing LLLP.

—It's Stormy! 2013. (What's the Weather? Ser.). (Illus.). 24p. (J). (gr. k-2). pap. 48.90 *(978-1-4339-9406-7(2))*; pap. 8.15 *(978-1-4339-9405-0(4))*; (ENG., lib. bdg. 22.60 *(978-1-4339-9404-3(6))* Stevens, Gareth Publishing LLLP.

—It's Stormy!/Es una Tormenta! 2013. (What's the Weather? / Qu Tiempo Hace? Ser.). (ENG & SPA., Illus.). 24p. (J). (gr. k-2). lib. bdg. 22.60 *(978-1-4339-9456-2(9))* Stevens, Gareth Publishing LLLP.

—It's Sunny! 2013. (What's the Weather? Ser.). 24p. (J). (gr. k-2). pap. 8.15 *(978-1-4339-9409-8(7))*; pap. 48.90 *(978-1-4339-9410-4(0))*; (ENG., Illus.). lib. bdg. 22.60 *(978-1-4339-9408-1(9))* Stevens, Gareth Publishing LLLP.

—It's Sunny! / Est Soleado! 2013. (What's the Weather? / Qu Tiempo Hace? Ser.). (SPA & ENG., Illus.). 24p. (J). (gr. k-2). 22.60 *(978-1-4339-9454-8(2))* Stevens, Gareth Publishing LLLP.

—It's Windy! 2013. (Illus.). 24p. (J). (gr. k-2). 22.60 *(978-1-4339-9412-8(7))*; pap. 8.15 *(978-1-4339-9413-5(5))*; pap. 48.90 *(978-1-4339-9414-2(3))* Stevens, Gareth Publishing LLLP.

—It's Windy! / Est Ventoso! 2013. (What's the Weather? / Qu Tiempo Hace? Ser.). (SPA & ENG., Illus.). 24p. (J). (gr. k-2). 22.60 *(978-1-4339-9452-4(6))* Stevens, Gareth Publishing LLLP.

Amer, Elizabeth. Weather Detectives. 2004. (Illus.). (J). (gr. 4-6). 40.00 *(978-1-57336-404-1(5))*, I2065) Interaction Pubs., Inc.

Arnold, Tedd. Fly Guy Presents: Weather. 2016. (Scholastic Reader, Level 2 Ser.). (ENG.). 32p. (J). (gr. k-2). 3.99 *(978-0-545-85187-9(4))* Scholastic, Inc.

—Weather. 2016. (Fly Guy Presents Ser.). (ENG.). 32p. (J). (gr. k-2). 13.55 *(978-0-606-39161-0(4))* Turtleback Bks.

Artell, Mike. Weather Whys. 2nd ed. 2005. (Illus.). 96p. (J). pap. 14.95 *(978-1-59647-001-9(1))* Good Year Bks.

Aspen-Baxter, Linda & Kissock, Heather. Los Arcoiris, with Code. 2012. (Mirando Al Cielo Ser.). (SPA., Illus.). 24p. (J). (gr. k-2). lib. bdg. 27.13 *(978-1-61913-216-0(8))*, AV2 by Weigl) Weigl Pubs., Inc.

Aucoin, Lee. Weather, 1 vol. 2009. (Early Childhood Themes Ser.). (ENG., Illus.). 16p. (J). (gr. -1-2). pap. 6.99 *(978-1-4333-1456-8(8))*; pap. 19.99 *(978-1-4333-1457-5(6))* Shell Educational Publishing.

Baker, Sue. Child's Play Weather. 2011. (Information Bks.). (ENG., Illus.). 14p. (J). (gr. -1-3). *(978-0-85953-929-6(6))* Child's Play International Ltd.

Baker, Theo. Warning: Wild Weather Ahead. 2017. (Penguin Core Concepts Ser.). (ENG.). 32p. (J). (-k). pap. 3.99 *(978-0-448-48873-8(6))*, Grosset & Dunlap) Penguin Young Readers Group.

Baker, Theo. Warning: Wild Weather Ahead. 2017. ***(978-0-515-15895-3(X))***, Grosset & Dunlap) Penguin Young Readers Group.

Barwick. Sail Main5 Weather Alert Nf. 2003. (Rigby Sails Ser.). (ENG.). 32p. (gr. 5-5). pap. 9.50 (978-0-7578-8020-9(7)) Rigby Education.

Basher, Simon & Green, Dan. Weather: Whipping up a Storm! Basher, Simon, illus. 2012. (Basher Basics Ser.). (ENG., Illus.). 64p. (J). (gr. 3-7). pap. 8.99 (978-0-7534-6826-5(3), 9780753468265, Kingfisher) Roaring Brook Pr.

Bassett, John. Experiments with Weather & Climate. 2010. (Cool Science Ser.). 32p. (J). (gr. 5-6). lib. bdg. 28.00 (978-1-4339-3447-6(7)); (Illus.). pap. 10.50 (978-1-4339-3448-3(5)) Stevens, Gareth Publishing LLLP. (Gareth Stevens Learning Library).

Bauer, Marion Dane. Rainbow. Wallace, John, illus. 2016. (Weather Ready-To-Reads Ser.). (ENG.). 32p. (J). (gr. -1-1). pap. 3.99 (978-1-4814-6336-2(5), Simon Spotlight) Simon Spotlight.

Beckett, Sydney. My Favorite Season. 2012. (InfoMax Readers Ser.). (ENG., Illus.). 16 pp.p. (J). (gr. k-1). pap. 7.00 (978-1-4488-8914-3(6), Rosen Classroom) Rosen Publishing Group, Inc., The.

Benchmark Education Company. Weather & Climate (Teacher Guide) 2005. (978-1-4108-4635-8(0)) Benchmark Education Co.

—Weathering & Erosion (Teacher Guide) 2005. (978-1-4108-4648-8(2)) Benchmark Education Co.

Benchmark Education Company, LLC Staff, compiled by. Science Theme: Weather. 2005. spiral bd. 115.00 (978-1-4108-5316-5(0)) Benchmark Education Co.

—Water & Weather. 2006. spiral bd. 330.00 (978-1-4108-7018-6(9)) 2006. (J). 206.00 (978-1-4108-7056-8(1)) 2005. (J). spiral bd. 265.00 (978-1-4108-5759-0(X)) Benchmark Education Co.

—Water & Weather: Theme Set. 2006. (J). 215.00 (978-1-4108-7132-9(0)) Benchmark Education Co.

—Weather & Seasons. 2006. (J). 265.00 (978-1-4108-7031-5(6)) Benchmark Education Co.

Berger, Melvin & Berger, Gilda. Hurricanes Have Eyes but Can't See: And Other Amazing Facts about Wild Weather. 2003. (Illus.). 48p. (J). (978-0-439-54980-6(9)) Scholastic, Inc.

Berry, Joy. Good Answers to Tough Questions Disasters. Bartholomew, illus. 2010. (Good Answers to Tough Questions Ser.). (ENG.). 48p. (J). (gr. k-7). pap. 7.99 (978-1-60577-510-4(X)) Berry, Joy Enterprises.

The Big Picture. 2010. (Big Picture Ser.). (ENG.). 24p. (gr. 1-2). pap. 333.60 (978-1-4296-5829-4(0), First Facts) Capstone Press of Coughlan Cos.

Birch, Robin. How Weather Works. 2009. (Weather & Climate Ser.). 32p. (gr. 3). 28.50 (978-0-7614-4466-4(1)) Marshall Cavendish Corp.

—Living with Weather. 2009. (Weather & Climate Ser.). 32p. (gr. 3). 28.50 (978-0-7614-4465-7(3)) Marshall Cavendish Corp.

Bix, Jasper. Winter Weather. 2016. (Winter Fun Ser.). (ENG., Illus.). 24p. (J). (gr. k-k). pap. 8.15 (978-1-4824-3767-6(8)) Stevens, Gareth Publishing LLLP.

Bliss, Pamela, et al. Introduction to Weather. 2007. (Nonfiction Reading & Writing Workshops Ser.). (ENG., Illus.). 32p. (J). pap. 17.95 (978-0-7922-4800-2(7)) CENGAGE Learning.

Boerger, Kristin & Boyett, Suzi. Let's Read about Rain. 2007. (Let's Read about Weather Ser.). (Illus.). 12p. (gr. -1-2). lib. bdg. 15.00 (978-0-8368-7805-9(1), Weekly Reader Leveled Readers) Stevens, Gareth Publishing LLLP.

—Llueve. 2007. (Que tiempo hace? (Let's Read about Weather) Ser.). (Illus.). 12p. (J). (gr. -1-2). (SPA.). pap. 4.10 (978-0-8368-8118-9(4)); (ENG & SPA., lib. bdg. 15.00 (978-0-8368-8113-4(3)) Stevens, Gareth Publishing LLLP. (Weekly Reader Leveled Readers).

Boothroyd, Jennifer. How Does Weather Change? 2014. (First Step Nonfiction - Let's Watch the Weather Ser.). 24p. (gr. k-2). (Illus.). pap. 6.95 (978-1-4677-4495-9(6)); (ENG.). lib. bdg. 23.93 (978-1-4677-3917-7(0), Lerner Pubns.) Lerner Publishing Group.

—What Is Climate? 2014. (First Step Nonfiction - Let's Watch the Weather Ser.). (ENG.). 24p. (gr. k-2). lib. bdg. 23.93 (978-1-4677-3918-4(9), Lerner Pubns.) Lerner Publishing Group.

—What Is Today's Weather? 2014. (First Step Nonfiction - Let's Watch the Weather Ser.). (Illus.). 24p. (gr. k-2). pap. 6.95 (978-1-4677-4500-0(6)); (ENG., lib. bdg. 23.93 (978-1-4677-3916-0(2), Lerner Pubns.) Lerner Publishing Group.

Boyett, Suzi. Let's Read about Snow. 2007. (Let's Read about Weather Ser.). (Illus.). 12p. (gr. -1-2). lib. bdg. 15.00 (978-0-8368-7806-6(X), Weekly Reader Leveled Readers) Stevens, Gareth Publishing LLLP.

—Nieva. 2007. (Que Tiempo Hace? (Let's Read about Weather) Ser.). (SPA., Illus.). 12p. (J). (gr. -1-2). pap. 4.10 (978-0-8368-8119-6(2)); lib. bdg. 15.00 (978-0-8368-8114-1(1)) Stevens, Gareth Publishing LLLP. (Weekly Reader Leveled Readers).

Brannon, Barbara. Discover Weather. 2005. (J). pap. (978-1-4108-5123-9(0)) Benchmark Education Co.

Brannon, Cecelia H. A Look at Erosion & Weathering. 2016. (Rock Cycle Ser.). (ENG., Illus.). 32p. (J). (gr. 3-4). 25.27 (978-0-7660-7280-0(0)) Enslow Pubs., Inc.

Branson, Sam. Let's Measure the Weather. 2012. (InfoMax Readers Ser.). (ENG., Illus.). 24p. (J). (gr. 1-2). pap. 8.25 (978-1-4488-9019-4(5), Rosen Classroom) Rosen Publishing Group, Inc., The.

Bredeson, Carmen. Weird but True Weather. 2011. (Weird but True Science Ser.). (Illus.). 24p. (J). (gr. k-18). pap. 7.95 (978-1-59845-372-0(6), Enslow Elementary); (gr. 5-9). lib. bdg. 22.60 (978-0-7660-3862-2(9)) Enslow Pubs., Inc.

Bright, Michael. Weather Explained, 1 vol. 2015. (ENG.). 136p. (YA). 38.25 (978-1-4777-8129-6(3), Rosen Young Adult) Rosen Publishing Group, Inc., The.

Bullard, Lisa. Blizzards. 2009. pap. 40.95 (978-0-7613-4767-5(4)) Lerner Publishing Group.

Bundey, Nikki. Drought & People. 2005. (Science of Weather Ser.). (Illus.). 32p. (gr. 4-6). lib. bdg. 21.27 (978-1-57505-498-8(1)) Lerner Publishing Group.

—Drought & the Earth. 2005. (Science of Weather Ser.). (Illus.). 32p. (gr. 4-6). lib. bdg. 21.27 (978-1-57505-473-5(6)) Lerner Publishing Group.

—Storms & People. 2005. (Science of Weather Ser.). (Illus.). 32p. (gr. 4-6). lib. bdg. 21.27 (978-1-57505-499-5(X)) Lerner Publishing Group.

Burton, Margie, et al. Changing Weather. 2011. (Early Connections Ser.). (J). (978-1-61672-517-4(6)) Benchmark Education Co.

—Changing Weather & Cambios en el Clima: 6 English, 6 Spanish Adaptations. 2011. (J). spiral bd. 75.00 net. (978-1-4108-5623-4(2)) Benchmark Education Co.

—Weather. 2011. (Early Connections Ser.). (J). (978-1-61672-275-3(4)) Benchmark Education Co.

Cain, Marie Mowery. It's a Matter of Weather. 2013. (Big Books, Red Ser.). (ENG & SPA., Illus.). 16p. pap. 33.00 (978-1-59246-213-1(8)) Big Books, by George!

Canavan, Roger. You Wouldn't Want to Live Without Extreme Weather! Bergin, Mark, illus. 2015. (You Wouldn't Want to Live Without... Ser.). (ENG.). (J). 40p. pap. 9.95 (978-0-531-21408-4(7)); 32p. lib. bdg. 29.00 (978-0-531-21365-0(X)) Scholastic Library Publishing. (Watts, Franklin).

—You Wouldn't Want to Live Without Extreme Weather! 2015. (You Wouldn't Want to Live Without Ser.). lib. bdg. 20.80 (978-0-606-36711-0(X)) Turtleback Bks.

Cardenas, Ernesto & Saavedra, Patricia. El estado del Tiempo. l.t. ed. 2006. (SPA., Illus.). 16p. pap. 4.95 (978-1-933668-22-2(9)) Milo Educational Bks. & Resources.

Cardenas, Ernesto A. Weather. 2009. pap. 4.95 (978-1-60698-098-9(X)) Milo Educational Bks. & Resources.

—What Is the Weather Like Today? 2009. 23.95 (978-1-60698-053-8(X)); pap. 4.95 (978-1-60698-051-4(3)) Milo Educational Bks. & Resources.

Carson, Mary Kay. Inside Weather. 2011. (Inside Ser.). (ENG., Illus.). 48p. (J). (gr. 3-5). pap. 9.95 (978-1-4027-8948-9(3)) Sterling Publishing Co., Inc.

—Weather Projects for Young Scientists: Experiments & Science Fair Ideas. 2007. (ENG., Illus.). 144p. (J). (gr. 4-7). pap. 16.95 (978-1-55652-629-9(6)) Chicago Review Pr., Inc.

—What Makes a Tornado Twist? And Other Questions about Weather. Mackay, Louis, illus. 2014. (Good Question! Ser.). (ENG.). (J). (gr. 1). 40p. 12.95 (978-1-4549-0682-7(0)); 32p. pap. 5.95 (978-1-4549-0683-4(9)) Sterling Publishing Co., Inc.

Casado, Dami & Casado, Alicia. El Otono. 2005. (Brujita Mo y las Cuatro Estaciones Ser.). (SPA & ESP., Illus.). 14p. (J). per., bds. 7.99 (978-84-272-6236-2(1)) Molino, Editorial ESP. Dist: Santillana USA Publishing Co., Inc.

Challoner, Jack. DK Eyewitness Books: Hurricane & Tornado: Hurricane & Tornado. 2014. (DK Eyewitness Bks.). (ENG., Illus.). 72p. (J). (gr. 3-7). pap. 9.99 (978-1-4654-2053-4(3), DK Children) Dorling Kindersley Publishing, Inc.

Chambers, Catherine. Stickmen's Guide to Earth's Atmosphere in Layers. Dean, Venitia & De Quay, John Paul, illus. 2016. (Stickmen's Guides to This Incredible Earth Ser.). (ENG.). 32p. (J). (gr. 3-6). 26.65 (978-1-5124-0617-7(1)) Lerner Publishing Group.

Chancellor, Deborah & Goldsmith, Mike. The Weather. 2009. (ENG., Illus.). 24p. (J). (gr. k-4). lib. bdg. (978-0-7787-4724-6(7)) Crabtree Publishing Co.

Chancellor, Debroah. The Weather. 2009. (Now We Know About... Ser.). (ENG., Illus.). 24p. (J). (gr. k-3). pap. (978-0-7787-4741-3(7)) Crabtree Publishing Co.

Charlesworth, Liza, ed. Wild Weather: Weather!, Tornadoes!, Blizzards!, Hurricanes!, Floods!, Lightning! 2007. (Science Vocabulary Readers Ser.). (ENG., Illus.). (gr. 1-2). 69.99 (978-0-545-01598-1(7), Teaching Resources) Scholastic, Inc.

Children's Weather Encyclopedia. (Children's Reference Ser.). 224p. (978-1-4054-9554-7(5)); 2008. 256p. (978-1-4075-3206-6(5)) Parragon, Inc.

Cifuentes, Carolina. The Weather. Hullinger, C. D., illus. 2010. (My World Ser.). Orig. Title: El Tiempo. (ENG.). 24p. (J). (gr. -1-1). lib. bdg. 22.60 (978-1-60754-955-0(7)) Windmill Bks.

Cifuentes, Carolina, ed. The Weather. Hullinger, C. D., illus. 2010. (My World Ser.). Orig. Title: El Tiempo. (ENG.). 24p. (J). (gr. -1-1). pap. 8.15 (978-1-61533-043-0(7)) Windmill Bks.

Cipriano, Jeri. El tiempo a Prueba. 2011. (SPA.). 32p. (J). pap. 49.00 net. (978-1-4108-2340-3(7), A23407) Benchmark Education Co.

Clarke, Catriona. Weather. Slane, Andrea & Chen, Kuo Kang, illus. 2006. (Beginners Science: Level 2 Ser.). 32p. (J). (gr. 1-3). 4.99 (978-0-7945-1253-8(4), Usborne) EDC Publishing.

—Weather: Level 7. Chen, Kuo Kang, illus. 2006. (Usborne Beginners Ser.). 32p. (J). (gr. 4-7). lib. bdg. 12.99 (978-1-58086-892-1(4), Usborne) EDC Publishing.

Claybourne, Anna. Extreme Earth. 2014. (100 Facts You Should Know Ser.). 48p. (J). (gr. 4-6). pap. 84.95 (978-1-4824-1262-8(4)) Stevens, Gareth Publishing LLLP.

Close, Edward. All about the Weather, 1 vol., 1. 2014. (Discovery Education: Earth & Space Science Ser.). (ENG.). 32p. (gr. 3-6). 26.25 (978-1-4777-6190-8(X), PowerKids Pr.) Rosen Publishing Group, Inc., The.

Coan, Sharon. Changing Weather. 2015. (TIME for KIDS(r) Nonfiction Readers Ser.). (ENG., Illus.). 12p. (gr. k-k). 4.99 (978-1-4938-2054-2(0)) Teacher Created Materials, Inc.

—El Clima Cambiante (Changing Weather) 2016. (TIME for KIDS(r) Nonfiction Readers Ser.). (SPA., Illus.). 12p. (J). (gr. k-k). 4.99 (978-1-4938-2963-7(7)) Teacher Created Materials, Inc.

Cole, Joanna. Wild Weather. 2014. (Magic School Bus Presents Ser.). lib. bdg. 17.20 (978-0-606-35817-0(X)) Turtleback Bks.

Cole, Joanna, et al. Wild Weather. Degen, Bruce & Bracken, Carolyn, illus. 2014. (Magic School Bus Presents Ser.). (ENG.). 32p. (J). (gr. 1-3). pap. 6.99 (978-0-545-68367-8(X)) Scholastic, Inc.

Collins. Collins Fascinating Facts - Weather. 2016. (Collins Fascinating Facts Ser.). (ENG.). 72p. (J). (gr. 1-3). pap. 10.99 (978-0-00-816921-3(7)) HarperCollins Pubs. Ltd. GBR. Dist: Independent Pubs. Group.

Cortland, D J. A Week of Weather: Learning to Collect & Record Data on a Pictograph. (Math for the Real World: Early Emergent Ser.). (ENG., Illus.). 8p. (gr. k-1). 2009. pap. 5.15 (978-0-8239-8887-7(2)) 2004. 29.95 (978-0-8239-7630-0(0)) Rosen Publishing Group, Inc., The.

Cosgrove, Brian. DK Eyewitness Books: Weather. 2016. (DK Eyewitness Bks.). (ENG., Illus.). 72p. (J). (gr. 3-7). pap. 9.99 (978-1-4654-5180-4(3), DK Children) Dorling Kindersley Publishing, Inc.

—Weather. 2016. (DK Eyewitness Bks.). (ENG., Illus.). 72p. (J). (gr. 3-7). lib. bdg. 19.99 (978-1-4654-5181-1(1), DK Children) Dorling Kindersley Publishing, Inc.

Coss, Lauren. Weird-But-True Facts about Weather. Gallagher-Cole, Mernie, illus. 2013. (Weird-But-True Facts Ser.). (ENG.). 32p. (J). (gr. 2-5). 28.50 (978-1-61473-423-9(2), 205127) Child's World, Inc., The.

Cousins, Lucy. Maisy's Wonderful Weather Book. 2011. (Maisy Ser.). (ENG., Illus.). 16p. (J). (gr. -1-2). 14.99 (978-0-7636-5096-4(X)) Candlewick Pr.

Cox Cannons, Helen. Clouds, 1 vol. 2014. (Weather Wise Ser.). (ENG., Illus.). 24p. (gr. -1-1). 22.65 (978-1-4846-0544-8(6), Acorn) Heinemann-Raintree.

—Rain, 1 vol. 2014. (Weather Wise Ser.). (ENG., Illus.). 24p. (gr. -1-1). pap. 5.99 (978-1-4846-0555-4(1), Acorn) Heinemann-Raintree.

—Snow, 1 vol. 2014. (Weather Wise Ser.). (ENG., Illus.). 24p. (gr. -1-1). pap. 5.99 (978-1-4846-0556-1(X), Acorn) Heinemann-Raintree.

—Sunshine, 1 vol. 2014. (Weather Wise Ser.). (ENG., Illus.). 24p. (gr. -1-1). pap. 5.99 (978-1-4846-0557-8(8), Acorn) Heinemann-Raintree.

Cox-Cannons, Helen. Thunder & Lightning, 1 vol. 2014. (Weather Wise Ser.). (ENG., Illus.). 24p. (gr. -1-1). 22.65 (978-1-4846-0548-6(9), Acorn) Heinemann-Raintree.

Cox Cannons, Helen. Weather Wise, 1 vol. 2014. (Weather Wise Ser.). (ENG.). 24p. (gr. -1-1). 135.90 (978-1-4846-0550-9(0), Acorn) Heinemann-Raintree.

—Wind, 1 vol. 2014. (Weather Wise Ser.). (ENG., Illus.). 24p. (gr. -1-1). pap. 5.99 (978-1-4846-0559-2(4), Acorn) Heinemann-Raintree.

Crook, Jennifer. Mrs. Crook's Kindergarten Sings about the Weather: Musical Colors Series. 2003. (Musical Colors Rhyming Story Coloring Book Ser.). (ENG., Illus.). 21p. (J). spiral bd. 14.95 (978-1-931844-05-5(4), PP1017) Piano Pr.

Cunningham, Kevin. Surviving Droughts & Famines, 1 vol. 2011. (Children's True Stories: Natural Disasters Ser.). (ENG.). 32p. (gr. 3-3). pap. 8.29 (978-1-4109-4101-5(9)); 30.65 (978-1-4109-4094-0(2)) Heinemann-Raintree. (Raintree Perspectives).

D'Aubuisson, Elisabeth. Snowy Days. 2007. (What's the Weather? Ser.). (Illus.). 24p. (J). (gr. 3-7). lib. bdg. 22.60 (978-1-4042-3684-4(8), PowerKids Pr.) Rosen Publishing Group, Inc., The.

d'Aubuisson, Elisabeth. Snowy Days. 2009. (What's the Weather? Ser.). 24p. (gr. 2-3). 42.50 (978-1-60854-776-0(0), PowerKids Pr.) Rosen Publishing Group, Inc., The.

D'Aubuisson, Elisabeth. Sunny Days. 2007. (What's the Weather? Ser.). (Illus.). 24p. (J). (gr. 3-7). lib. bdg. 22.60 (978-1-4042-3685-1(6), PowerKids Pr.) Rosen Publishing Group, Inc., The.

d'Aubuisson, Elisabeth. Sunny Days. 2009. (What's the Weather? Ser.). 24p. (gr. 2-3). 42.50 (978-1-60854-777-7(9), PowerKids Pr.) Rosen Publishing Group, Inc., The.

D'Aubuisson, Elisabeth. What's the Weather?, 4 bks., Set. Incl. Rainy Days. lib. bdg. 22.60 (978-1-4042-3682-0(1)); Snowy Days. lib. bdg. 22.60 (978-1-4042-3684-4(8)); Sunny Days. lib. bdg. 22.60 (978-1-4042-3685-1(6)); Windy Days. lib. bdg. 22.60 (978-1-4042-3683-7(X)); (Illus.). 24p. (J). (gr. 3-7). 2007. 2007. Set lib. bdg. 85.00 (978-1-4042-3609-7(0), PowerKids Pr.) Rosen Publishing Group, Inc., The.

—Windy Days. 2007. (What's the Weather? Ser.). (Illus.). 24p. (J). (gr. 3-7). lib. bdg. 22.60 (978-1-4042-3683-7(X), PowerKids Pr.) Rosen Publishing Group, Inc., The.

d'Aubuisson, Elisabeth. Windy Days. 2009. (What's the Weather? Ser.). 24p. (gr. 2-3). 42.50 (978-1-60854-778-4(7), PowerKids Pr.) Rosen Publishing Group, Inc., The.

Davids, Stacy B. Strange but True Weather, 1 vol. 2010. (Strange but True Ser.). (ENG.). 32p. (gr. 1-2). lib. bdg. 26.65 (978-1-4296-4553-9(9), Blazers) Capstone Press of Coughlan Cos.

Davis, Barbara J. Air & Weather. 2007. (Gareth Stevens Vital Science: Earth Science Ser.). (Illus.). 48p. (gr. 5-12). pap. 14.05 (978-0-8368-7871-4(X)); lib. bdg. 27.00 (978-0-8368-7760-1(8)) Stevens, Gareth Publishing LLLP. (Gareth Stevens Secondary Library).

Daynes, Katie. See Inside Weather & Climate IR. 2015. (See Inside Board Bks.). (ENG.). 16p. (J). (gr. k-5). 14.99 (978-0-7945-2161-5(4), Usborne) EDC Publishing.

DeWitt, Lynda. What Will the Weather Be? Croll, Carolyn, illus. 2015. (Let's-Read-And-Find-Out Science 2 Ser.). (ENG.). 32p. (J). (gr. -1-3). pap. 6.99 (978-0-06-238198-9(9)) HarperCollins Pubs.

Dolphin, Colleen. Advisories to Zero Degrees: Weather from A to Z, 1 vol. 2007. (Let's See A to Z Ser.). (ENG., Illus.). 32p. (gr. -1-3). 27.07 (978-1-59928-879-6(6), Super SandCastle) ABDO Publishing Co.

Donnelly, Karen. Droughts of the Past & the Future. 2009. (Earth's Changing Weather & Climate Ser.). 24p. (gr. 4-4). 42.50 (978-1-61512-244-8(3), PowerKids Pr.) Rosen Publishing Group, Inc., The.

Dorion, Christiane. How the Weather Works: A Hands-On Guide to Our Changing Climate. Young, Beverley, illus. 2011. (Explore the Earth Ser.). (ENG.). 20p. (J). (gr. 2-5). 19.99 (978-0-7636-5262-3(8), Templar) Candlewick Pr.

Dorling Kindersley Publishing Staff. DK Readers L0: Weather: Weather. 2015. (DK Readers Ser.). (ENG.). 32p. (J). (gr. -1-1). pap. 3.99 (978-1-4654-3510-1(7), DK Children) Dorling Kindersley Publishing, Inc.

—Eye Wonder: Weather. 2016. (Eye Wonder Ser.). (ENG., Illus.). 56p. (J). (gr. k-4). 10.99 (978-1-4654-4472-1(6), DK Children) Dorling Kindersley Publishing, Inc.

—Eyewitness Explorer: Weather Watcher. 2015. (ENG., Illus.). 72p. (J). (gr. 3-7). pap. 9.99 (978-1-4654-3503-3(4), DK Children) Dorling Kindersley Publishing, Inc.

Doubleday Entertainment USA - Sun: Weather Watch. 2006. (J). per. 7.95 (978-1-59566-229-3(4)) QEB Publishing Inc.

Earth's Changing Weather. (Illus.). (J). (gr. k-5). 112.50 (978-0-8239-7262-3(3)) Rosen Publishing Group, Inc., The.

Eckart, Edana. Watching the Weather. 2004. (Wel-Watching Nature Ser.). (ENG., Illus.). 24p. (J). (gr. -1-2). pap. 4.95 (978-0-516-25940-6(7), Children's Pr.) Scholastic Library Publishing.

Edison, Erin. Lo Básico Sobre el Tiempo. Strictly Spanish, LLC., tr. 2013. (Lo Básico Sobre el Tiempo/Weather Basics Ser.). (MUL.). 24p. (gr. k-1). lib. bdg. 133.25 (978-1-62065-168-1(8)) Capstone Press of Coughlan Cos.

—Weather Basics. 2011. (Weather Basics Ser.). (ENG.). 24p. (gr. k-1). pap. 250.20 (978-1-4296-7090-6(8)); pap. 43.74 (978-1-4296-7089-0(4)); lib. bdg. 133.25 (978-1-4296-6060-0(0)) Capstone Press of Coughlan Cos. (Pebble Plus).

Editors of Kingfisher. Wild Weather. 2016. (It's All About... Ser.). (ENG., Illus.). 32p. (J). pap. 5.99 (978-0-7534-7269-9(4), 9780753472699, Kingfisher) Roaring Brook Pr.

Encyclopaedia Britannica, Inc. Staff. Britannica Illustrated Science Library Series (18 Title Series), 18 vols. 2010. 599.00 (978-1-61535-423-8(9)) Encyclopaedia Britannica, Inc.

Estigarribia, Diana. Learning about Weather with Graphic Organizers. (Graphic Organizers in Science Ser.). 24p. 2009. (gr. 3-4). 42.50 (978-1-61513-053-5(5)) 2006. (ENG., Illus.). (gr. 4-6). pap. 8.25 (978-1-4042-5036-9(0)) 2005. (Illus.). (J). (gr. 3-7). lib. bdg. 22.60 (978-1-4042-2803-0(9)) Rosen Publishing Group, Inc., The. (PowerKids Pr.).

Evans, Bill. It's Raining Fish & Spiders. 2012. (ENG., Illus.). 240p. (J). (gr. 5). pap. 18.99 (978-0-7653-2132-9(7), 9780765321329, Forge Bks.) Doherty, Tom Assocs., LLC.

Evans, David & Williams, Claudette. Seasons & Weather. (Let's Explore Science Ser.). (Illus.). (J). 12.95 (978-0-590-74592-5(1)) Scholastic, Inc.

Eye on the Sky. 2015. (Eye on the Sky Ser.). (ENG.). 32p. (J). (gr. 3-4). 159.60 (978-1-4824-2551-2(3)); pap., pap., pap. 378.00 (978-1-4824-3460-6(1)) Stevens, Gareth Publishing LLLP.

Felix, Rebecca. How's the Weather in Fall? 2013. (21st Century Basic Skills Library: Let's Look at Fall Ser.). (ENG.). 24p. (J). (gr. k-3). 22.79 (978-1-61080-902-3(5), 202587); pap. 12.79 (978-1-61080-927-6(0), 202589) Cherry Lake Publishing.

—How's the Weather in Fall?/Rebecca Felix. 2013. (J). (978-1-61080-977-1(7)) Cherry Lake Publishing.

—How's the Weather in Summer? 2014. (21st Century Basic Skills Library: Let's Look at Summer Ser.). (ENG.). 24p. (J). (gr. k-3). 22.79 (978-1-63137-596-5(2), 205167) Cherry Lake Publishing.

—How's the Weather in Winter? 2014. (21st Century Basic Skills Library: Let's Look at Winter Ser.). (ENG.). 24p. (J). (gr. k-3). 22.79 (978-1-63137-605-4(5), 205203) Cherry Lake Publishing.

Ferris, Diane J. Weather Watcher. 2009. (Illus.). 20p. pap. 13.00 (978-1-4490-1218-2(3)) AuthorHouse.

Forces of Nature. 2009. (Illus.). 47p. (J). (978-0-7166-9822-7(6)) World Bk., Inc.

Foxxe, Ellen. The Rising Seas: Shorelines under Threat. 2006. (Extreme Environmental Threats Ser.). (Illus.). 64p. (YA). (gr. 5-9). lib. bdg. 31.95 (978-1-4042-0742-4(2)) Rosen Publishing Group, Inc., The.

Franchino, Vicky. Droughts. 2012. (21st Century Skills Library: Real World Math Ser.). (ENG., Illus.). 32p. (J). (gr. 4-8). pap. 14.21 (978-1-61080-407-3(4), 201339); lib. bdg. 28.50 (978-1-61080-322-9(1), 201300) Cherry Lake Publishing.

Fretland VanVoorst, Jenny. El Clima en la Primavera. 2015.Tr. of Weather in Spring. (SPA., Illus.). 24p. (J). lib. bdg. (978-1-62031-252-0(2), Bullfrog Bks.) Jump! Inc.

—Weather in Spring. 2015. (Illus.). 24p. (J). lib. bdg. (978-1-62031-238-4(7), Bullfrog Bks.) Jump! Inc.

Furgang, Kathy. National Geographic Kids Everything Weather: Facts, Photos, & Fun That Will Blow You Away. 2012. (National Geographic Kids Everything Ser.). (ENG., Illus.). 64p. (J). (gr. 3-7). pap. 12.95 (978-1-4263-1058-4(7)); lib. bdg. 25.90 (978-1-4263-1063-8(3)) National Geographic Society. (National Geographic Children's Bks.).

—What Will the Weather Be? Set Of 6. 2010. (Early Connections Ser.). (J). pap. 37.00 net. (978-1-4108-1073-1(9)) Benchmark Education Co.

Gaffney, Timothy R. Storm Scientist: Careers Chasing Severe Weather. 2009. (Wild Science Careers Ser.). (Illus.). 112p. (J). (gr. 5-18). lib. bdg. 33.27 (978-0-7660-3050-3(4)) Enslow Pubs., Inc.

Galiano, Dean. Clouds, Rain & Snow. 2003. (Weather Watchers' Library). (Illus.). 48p. (YA). (gr. 5-8). lib. bdg. 23.95 (978-0-8239-3092-0(0), WECLRA, Rosen Reference) Rosen Publishing Group, Inc., The.

—Thunderstorms & Lightning. (Weather Watcher's Library). 48p. (gr. 5-8). 2009. 53.00 (978-1-60854-275-8(0)) 2003. (Illus.). (YA). lib. bdg. 23.95 (978-0-8239-3093-7(9), WETHLI) Rosen Publishing Group, Inc., The. (Rosen Reference).

Ganeri, Anita. Wild Weather, 1 vol. 2012. (Extreme Nature Ser.). (ENG.). 32p. (gr. 1-3). pap. 8.29 (978-1-4109-4704-8(1)); lib. bdg. 29.99 (978-1-4109-4699-7(1)) Heinemann-Raintree. (Read Me!).

Garbe, Suzanne. Threatening Skies: History's Most Dangerous Weather, 1 vol. 2013. (Dangerous History Ser.). (ENG.). 32p. (gr. 3-4). 27.99 (978-1-4765-0128-4(9), Edge Bks.) Capstone Press of Coughlan Cos.

Gardner, Robert. Easy Genius Science Projects with Weather: Great Experiments & Ideas. 2009. (Easy Genius Science Projects Ser.). (Illus.). 128p. (J). (gr. 5-9). lib. bdg. 33.27 (978-0-7660-2924-8(7)) Enslow Pubs., Inc.

—Experiments with Weather. 2017. (Science Whiz Experiments Ser.). 128p. (J). (gr. 5-5). lib. bdg. 37.27 **(978-0-7660-8686-9(0))** Enslow Pubs., Inc.

—Science Fair Projects about Weather. 2016. (Hands-On Science Ser.). 48p. (J). pap. 11.70 (978-0-7660-8204-5(0)) Enslow Pubs., Inc.

—Weather Science Fair Projects, Revised & Expanded Using the Scientific Method. LaBaff, Tom, illus. 2010. (Earth Science Projects Using the Scientific Method Ser.). 160p. (J). (gr. 5-18). 35.94 (978-0-7660-3424-2(0)) Enslow Pubs., Inc.

—Weather Science Fair Projects Using Sunlight, Rainbows, Ice Cubes, & More. 2005. (Earth Science! Best Science Projects Ser.). (Illus.). 128p. (J). lib. bdg. 27.94 (978-0-7660-2361-1(3)) Enslow Pubs., Inc.

—Wild Science Projects about Earth's Weather. LaBaff, Tom, illus. 2007. (Rockin' Earth Science Experiments Ser.). 48p. (J). (gr. 3-4). lib. bdg. 25.27 (978-0-7660-2734-3(1), Enslow Elementary) Enslow Pubs., Inc.

Gardner, Robert & Tocci, Salvatore. Ace Your Weather Science Project: Great Science Fair Ideas. 2009. (Ace Your

Physics Science Project Ser.). (Illus.). 104p. (J). (gr. 5-18). lib. bdg. 33.27 (978-0-7660-3223-1(X)) Enslow Pubs., Inc.

Geatches, Hazel & Spilsbury, Louise. Sunny & Rainy. 2012. (ENG., Illus.). 40p. pap. 9.38 (978-0-19-464680-2(7)) Oxford Univ. Pr., Inc.

Ghigna, Charles. Raindrops Fall All Around. Watson, Laura, illus. 2015. (Springtime Weather Wonders Ser.). (ENG.). 24p. (gr. -1-2). lib. bdg. 21.99 (978-1-4795-6030-1(8)) Picture Window Bks.

—Springtime Weather Wonders. Watson, Laura, illus. 2015. (Springtime Weather Wonders Ser.). (ENG.). 24p. (gr. -1-2). lib. bdg. 87.96 (978-1-4795-6045-5(6)) Picture Window Bks.

—Sunshine Brightens Springtime. Watson, Laura, illus. 2015. (Springtime Weather Wonders Ser.). (ENG.). 24p. (gr. -1-2). lib. bdg. 21.99 (978-1-4795-6031-8(6)) Picture Window Bks.

—A Windy Day in Spring. Watson, Laura, illus. 2015. (Springtime Weather Wonders Ser.). (ENG.). 24p. (gr. -1-2). lib. bdg. 21.99 (978-1-4795-6032-5(4)) Picture Window Bks.

Gleisner, Jenna Lee. How's the Weather in Spring? 2014. (21st Century Basic Skills Library: Let's Look at Spring Ser.). (ENG., Illus.). 24p. (J). (gr. k-3). pap. 12.79 (978-1-62431-681-4(6), 203129) Cherry Lake Publishing.

Goldsmith, Mike. Flip the Flaps: Weather. Butler, John, illus. 2014. (Flip the Flaps Ser.). (ENG.). 32p. (J). (gr. -1-1). pap. 6.99 (978-0-7534-7132-6(9), 9780753471326, Kingfisher) Roaring Brook Pr.

Goldstein, Natalie. Drought & Heat Waves: A Practical Survival Guide. 2009. (Library of Emergency Preparedness Ser.). 64p. (gr. 6-6). 29.25 (978-1-60853-592-7(4), Rosen Reference) Rosen Publishing Group, Inc., The.

Goodenow, Ellen A. My Weather Journal. 2003. (Shutterbug Bks.). (Illus.). 16p. pap. 4.10 (978-0-7398-7654-1(6)) Steck-Vaughn.

Gosman, Gillian. What Do You Know about Earth's Atmosphere? 2013. (20 Questions: Earth Science Ser.). 24p. (J). (gr. 3-6). pap. 49.50 (978-1-4488-9857-2(9)); pap. 8.25 (978-1-4488-9856-5(0)); lib. bdg. 22.60 (978-1-4488-9699-8(1)) Rosen Publishing Group, Inc., The. (PowerKids Pr.).

—What Do You Know about Weather & Climate? 2013. (20 Questions: Earth Science Ser.). (ENG., Illus.). 24p. (J). (gr. 3-6). pap. 8.25 (978-1-4488-9860-2(9), PowerKids Pr.) Rosen Publishing Group, Inc., The.

Gray-Wilburn, Renée & Rustad, Martha E. H. Weather Aware, 1 vol. 2014. (Weather Aware Ser.). (ENG.). 32p. (gr. 1-2). 109.28 (978-1-4765-9907-6(6), Aplus Bks.) Capstone Press of Coughlan Cos.

Grayson, Augustus. What Is the Weather Today? 2012. (InfoMax Readers Ser.). (ENG., Illus.). 16 pp.p. (J). (gr. k-1). pap. 7.00 (978-1-4488-8968-6(5), Rosen Classroom) Rosen Publishing Group, Inc., The.

Greathead, Helen. Perilous Places. 2016. (What Would You Choose? Ser.). 00032p. (J). pap. 10.50 **(978-1-4824-6116-9(1))** Stevens, Gareth Publishing LLLP.

Greek, Joe. Weather & Climate. 2017. (J). **(978-1-5383-0032-9(X))** Rosen Publishing Group, Inc., The.

Greek, Joe. What Is the Atmosphere & How Does It Circulate?, 1 vol. 2015. (ENG.). 32p. (J). 23.45 (978-1-62275-783-1(1), Britannica Educational Publishing) Rosen Publishing Group, Inc., The.

Green, Jen. Weather & Seasons. 2008. (Our Earth Ser.). (Illus.). 24p. (J). (gr. 1-4). lib. bdg. 22.60 (978-1-4042-4272-2(4)) Rosen Publishing Group, Inc., The.

Group/McGraw-Hill, Wright. Forces of Nature: Level K, 6 vols., Vol. 2. (First Explorers Ser.). 24p. (gr. 1-2). 34.95 (978-0-7699-1458-9(6)) Shortland Pubns. (U. S. A.) Inc.

—Winter Weather: Collection 2. (Storyteller Interactive Writing Cards Ser.). (J). (gr. k-3). (978-0-322-09341-6(4)) Wright Group/McGraw-Hill.

Haddon, Jean. It's a Beautiful Day! Enright, Vicky, illus. 2005. (Silly Millies Ser.). 32p. (J). per. 5.95 (978-0-7613-2397-6(X), First Avenue Editions) Lerner Publishing Group.

—It's a Beautiful Day! Enright, Vicky, tr. Enright, Vicky, illus. 2005. (Silly Millies Level 2 Ser.). (ENG.). 32p. (J). (gr. 1-3). lib. bdg. 21.27 (978-0-7613-2834-6(3), Millbrook Pr.) Lerner Publishing Group.

Haelle, Tara. Seasons, Tides, & Lunar Phases. 2016. (Let's Explore Science Ser.). (ENG., Illus.). 48p. (gr. 5-8). 35.64 (978-1-68191-395-7(X)) Rourke Educational Media.

Hall, Julie. Weather: Grades 2 & 3. (Illus.). (J). pap., wbk. ed. 4.99 (978-0-88743-962-9(4)) School Zone Publishing Co.

Hand, Carol. Science Lab: Weather Patterns. 2011. (Explorer Library: Language Arts Explorer Ser.). (ENG.). 32p. (gr. 4-8). pap. 14.21 (978-1-61080-299-4(3), 201221); lib. bdg. 28.50 (978-1-61080-210-9(1), 201196) Cherry Lake Publishing.

—Weather Myths, Busted! 2017. (Science Myths, Busted! Ser.). (ENG.). 32p. (J). (gr. 3-6). 21.95 (978-1-63235-307-8(5), 12-Story Library) Pr. Room Editions LLC.

—Weather Myths, Busted! 12 Groundbreaking Discoveries. 2016. (Science Myths, Busted! Ser.). (ENG., Illus.). 32p. (J). pap. 9.95 (978-1-63235-357-3(1), 12-Story Library) Pr. Room Editions LLC.

Hansen, Grace. El Clima (Weather) 2015. (Clima Ser.: Vol. 6). (ENG.). 24p. (J). lib. bdg. 171.00 (978-1-68080-349-5(2)) ABDO Publishing Co.

—Wind, 1 vol. 2016. (ENG., Illus.). 24p. (J). (978-1-62970-936-9(0)) ABDO Publishing Co.

Harper, Kathryn. Dressing for the Weather Green Band. Sims, Sean, illus. 2016. (Cambridge Reading Adventures Ser.). (ENG.). 16p. pap. 6.56 (978-1-316-50324-9(0)) Cambridge Univ. Pr.

Harris, Caroline. Discover Science: Weather. 2017. (Discover Science Ser.). (ENG.). 56p. pap. 7.99 (978-0-7534-7336-8(4), 9780753473368, Kingfisher) Roaring Brook Pr.

Heckt, Jackie. What the Clouds Are Telling You. 2013. (Rosen Readers Ser.). (ENG.). 24p. (J). (gr. 2-3). pap. 8.25 (978-1-4777-2309-8(9)); pap. 49.50 (978-1-4777-2310-4(2)) Rosen Publishing Group, Inc., The. (Rosen Classroom).

Herriges, Ann. Clouds. 2006. (Weather Ser.). (ENG., Illus.). 24p. (J). (gr. k-3). lib. bdg. 25.95 (978-1-60014-024-2(6)) Bellwether Media.

—Lightning. 2011. (Blastoff! Readers Ser.). 24p. (J). pap. 5.95 (978-0-531-27621-1(X), Children's Pr.) Scholastic Library Publishing.

—Rain. 2011. (Blastoff! Readers Ser.). 24p. (J). pap. 5.95 (978-0-531-27622-8(8), Children's Pr.) Scholastic Library Publishing.

—Snow. 2011. (Blastoff! Readers Ser.). 24p. (J). pap. 5.95 (978-0-531-27623-5(6), Children's Pr.) Scholastic Library Publishing.

—Sunshine. 2006. (Weather Ser.). (ENG., Illus.). 24p. (J). (gr. k-3). lib. bdg. 25.95 (978-1-60014-028-0(9)) Bellwether Media.

—Wind. 2006. (Weather Ser.). (ENG., Illus.). 24p. (J). (gr. k-3). lib. bdg. 25.95 (978-1-60014-026-6(2)) Bellwether Media.

—Wind. 2011. (Blastoff! Readers Ser.). 24p. (J). pap. 5.95 (978-0-531-27624-2(4), Children's Pr.) Scholastic Library Publishing.

Hewitt, Sally. Weather. 2010. (Starting Geography Ser.). 32p. (J). (gr. 2-5). 28.50 (978-1-60753-130-2(5)) Amicus Publishing.

Hirsch, Rebecca E. Using Climate Maps. 2016. (Searchlight Books (tm) — What Do You Know about Maps? Ser.). (ENG., Illus.). 40p. (J). (gr. 3-5). 30.65 (978-1-5124-0950-5(2)) Lerner Publishing Group.

Hirschmann, Kris & Herndon, Ryan, compiled by. Guinness World Records, up Close. 2007. (Illus.). 47p. (978-0-439-89828-7(5)) Scholastic, Inc.

Hiscock, Bruce. Big Storm. 2008. (ENG.). 32p. (J). (gr. 1-4). pap. 7.95 (978-1-59078-600-0(9)) Boyds Mills Pr.

Hot & Cold Weather, 6 vols. (Sunshinetm Science Ser.). 24p. (gr. 1-2). 37.50 (978-0-7802-1380-7(7)) Wright Group/McGraw-Hill.

Houghton Gosman, Gillian. What Do You Know about Weather & Climate? 2013. (20 Questions: Earth Science Ser.). 24p. (J). (gr. 3-6). 22.60 (978-1-4488-9701-8(7), PowerKids Pr.) Rosen Publishing Group, Inc., The.

Howell, Laura. Introduction to Weather & Climate Change. 2004. (Geography Ser.). (ENG., Illus.). 96p. (J). pap. 14.95 (978-0-7945-0629-2(1)) EDC Publishing.

—Introduction to Weather & Climate Change. Furnival, Keith, illus. 2004. (Geography Ser.). 96p. (J). (gr. 5). lib. bdg. 22.95 (978-1-58086-613-2(1), Usborne) EDC Publishing.

Howell, Laura & Gareth Stevens Editorial Staff. Weather & Climate. 2004. (Discovery Channel School Science Ser.). (Illus.). 32p. (gr. 4-8). lib. bdg. 26.00 (978-0-8368-3386-7(4), Gareth Stevens Learning Library) Stevens, Gareth Publishing LLLP.

How's the Weather? (Discovery Readers Ser.). 48p. (J). pap. 3.95 (978-0-8249-5316-4(9), Ideal Pubns.) Worthy Publishing.

Hynes, Margaret. Navigators: Extreme Weather. 2013. (Navigators Ser.). (ENG., Illus.). 48p. (J). (gr. 4-7). pap. 8.99 (978-0-7534-6954-5(5), 9780753469545, Kingfisher) Roaring Brook Pr.

Jackson, Randy. Get Ready for Hazardous Weather: Learning Through Puzzles, Games & Exercises. 2004. 40p. (YA). 3.50 (978-0-9742794-2-8(0)) HazardousWeather Preparedness Institute.

James, Trisha. I Know the Weather. 2017. (What I Know Ser.). 24p. (J). (gr. k-k). pap. 8.15 **(978-1-4824-6313-2(X))** Stevens, Gareth Publishing LLLP.

Jennings, Terry J. Extreme Weather. 2009. (Amazing Planet Earth Ser.). 32p. (gr. 4-7). 31.35 (978-1-59920-369-0(3)) Black Rabbit Bks.

—The Weather: Rain. 2004. (J). lib. bdg. 27.10 (978-1-59389-143-5(1)) Chrysalis Education.

—The Weather: Wind. 2004. (J). lib. bdg. 27.10 (978-1-59389-146-6(6)) Chrysalis Education.

Johnson, Rebecca L., et al. Weather & Climate. 2006. (Nonfiction Reading & Writing Workshops Ser.). (ENG., Illus.). 32p. (J). pap. 17.95 (978-0-7922-8876-3(9)) CENGAGE Learning.

Johnson, Robin. What Is Weather? 2012. (ENG.). 24p. (J). (978-0-7787-0756-1(3)); (Illus.). pap. (978-0-7787-0763-9(6)) Crabtree Publishing Co.

Jones, Lorraine. Super Science Projects about Weather & Natural Forces. 2005. (Psyched for Science Ser.). (Illus.). 48p. (YA). (gr. 5-8). lib. bdg. 29.25 (978-0-8239-3105-7(6), SCWENA) Rosen Publishing Group, Inc., The.

Jones, Tammy. I Like the Spring! 2009. (Sight Word Readers Set A Ser.). (J). 3.49 net. (978-1-60719-138-4(5)) Newmark Learning LLC.

—Look at the Weather. 2009. (Sight Word Readers Set A Ser.). (J). (978-1-60719-140-7(7)) Newmark Learning LLC.

Kalinowski, Delphine. The Weather Report. 2008. (Real Readers - Upper Emergent Ser.). (ENG., Illus.). 12p. (gr. 1-2). pap. 5.90 (978-0-8239-8207-3(6)) Rosen Publishing Group, Inc., The.

Kallio, Jamie. 12 Things to Know about Wild Weather. 2015. (ENG., Illus.). 32p. (J). (978-1-63235-035-0(1)) Pr. Room Editions LLC.

Kalman, Maira & Handler, Daniel. What the Weather Was Like. Meister, Sarah Hermanson, ed. 2016. (ENG., Illus.). 64p. (gr. -1-2). 17.95 (978-1-63345-014-1(7)) Museum of Modern Art.

Kampff, Joseph. What Are Weather Instruments?, 1 vol. 2015. (ENG.). 32p. (J). 23.45 (978-1-62275-791-6(2), Britannica Educational Publishing) Rosen Publishing Group, Inc., The.

Kauffman, Dorothy. The Weather. 2005. (Oxford Picture Dictionary for the Content Areas Ser.). (ENG., Illus.). 22p. pap. 7.56 (978-0-19-430957-8(6)) Oxford Univ. Pr., Inc.

Kerrod, Robin. Find Out about Weather: With 15 Projects & More Than 260 Pictures. 2013. (ENG., Illus.). 64p. 9.99 (978-1-84322-871-4(8)) Anness Publishing GBR. Dist: National Bk. Network.

Kirmes, William. The Year the Snow Didn't Melt. 2011. 32p. (gr. -1). pap. 12.95 (978-1-4567-5460-0(2)) AuthorHouse.

Kjelle, Marylou Morano. A Project Guide to Wind, Weather, & the Atmosphere. 2010. (Earth Science Projects for Kids Ser.). (Illus.). 48p. (J). (gr. 4-7). lib. bdg. 29.95 (978-1-58415-869-1(7)) Mitchell Lane Pubs., Inc.

Koehler, Susan. El Clima. 2012. (SPA & ENG.). 48p. (gr. 4-8). pap. 10.95 (978-1-61810-469-4(1)) Rourke Educational Media.

Kosara, Tori. Wild Weather Around the World. 2010. (Illus.). 46p. (J). pap. (978-0-545-32147-1(6)) Scholastic, Inc.

Kudlinski, Kathleen V. Boy, Were We Wrong about the Weather! Serra, Sebastià, illus. 2015. (ENG.). 32p. (J). (gr. -1-3). 16.99 (978-0-8037-3793-8(9), Dial Bks) Penguin Young Readers Group.

Ladd, Karol. The Glad Scientist Learn about the Weather. 2004. (Glad Scientist Ser.). pap., act. bk. ed. 6.99 (978-0-8054-0830-0(4)) B&H Publishing Group.

LaFontaine, Bruce. All about the Weather. 2004. (Dover Nature Coloring Book Ser.). (ENG., Illus.). 48p. (J). (gr. 3-8). pap. 4.99 (978-0-486-43036-2(7)) Dover Pubns., Inc.

Langston-George, Rebecca. A Primary Source History of the Dust Bowl. 2015. (Primary Source History Ser.). (ENG., Illus.). 32p. (gr. 3-4). lib. bdg. 27.32 (978-1-4914-1840-6(0)) Capstone Press of Coughlan Cos.

Lanser, Amanda. Adapting to Climate Change, 1 vol. 2014. (Essential Issues Set 4 Ser.). (ENG.). 112p. (J). (gr. 6-12). lib. bdg. 35.64 (978-1-62403-416-9(0), Essential Library) ABDO Publishing Co.

Larrick, Nancy. Rain, Hail, Sleet & Snow. Yap, Weda, illus. 2011. 68p. 36.95 (978-1-258-08878-1(9)) Literary Licensing, LLC.

Law, Felicia & Way, Steve. Weather. 2008. (Simply Science Ser.). (Illus.). 32p. (YA). (gr. 3-6). lib. bdg. 26.00 (978-0-8368-9233-8(X)) Stevens, Gareth Publishing LLLP.

Lawrence, Ellen. Weather. 2016. (FUN-Damental Experiments Ser.). (ENG., Illus.). 24p. (J). (gr. -1-3). 17.95 (978-1-943553-18-1(1)) Bearport Publishing Co., Inc.

—What Is Weather? 2012. (Weather Wise Ser.). 24p. (J). (gr. -1-3). lib. bdg. 23.93 (978-1-61772-405-3(X)) Bearport Publishing Co., Inc.

Lawson, Julia & Goodman, Polly. Weather. 2011. (Little Steps Ser.). (ENG., Illus.). 14p. (J). (gr. -1-k). bds. (978-1-84089-591-9(8)) Zero to Ten, Ltd.

LernerClassroom Editors. First Step Nonfiction-Kinds of Weather Teaching Guide. 2009. pap. 7.95 (978-0-8225-5397-7(X)) Lerner Publishing Group.

—First Step Nonfiction-Weather Teaching Guide. 2009. pap. 7.95 (978-0-8225-5539-1(5)) Lerner Publishing Group.

Levete, Sarah. Catastrophic Weather. 2010. (Protecting Our Planet Ser.). (ENG., Illus.). 32p. (J). (gr. 3-6). (978-0-7787-5210-3(0)); pap. (978-0-7787-5227-1(5)) Crabtree Publishing Co.

Levey, Richard H. Dust Bowl! The 1930s Black Blizzards. 2005. (X-Treme Disasters That Changed America Ser.). 32p. (J). lib. bdg. 25.27 (978-1-59716-007-0(5)) Bearport Publishing Co., Inc.

Life Nature's Fury. 2008. (Time Inc. Home Entertainment Library-Bound Titles Ser.). (ENG.). 144p. (gr. 5-12). lib. bdg. 39.93 (978-0-7613-4051-5(3), Twenty-First Century Bks.) Lerner Publishing Group.

Lilly, Melinda. Hot & Cold. 2005. (ENG.). 24p. (gr. 1-4). pap. 8.95 (978-1-62717-259-2(9)) Rourke Educational Media.

Linde, Barbara M. Weather & Climate. 2005. (J). pap. (978-1-4108-4587-0(7)) Benchmark Education Co.

Lindeen, Mary. Weather near You. 2017. (BeginningtoRead Ser.). (ENG.). 32p. (J). (-2). 22.60 **(978-1-59953-873-0(3))**; pap. 11.94 **(978-1-68404-092-6(2))** Norwood Hse. Pr.

Lindeen, Mary & Kesselring, Susan. Being Safe with Weather. McGeehan, Dan & Moore, David, illus. 2011. (Be Safe Ser.). (ENG.). 24p. (J). (gr. k-3). lib. bdg. 27.07 (978-1-60954-374-7(2), 200085) Child's World, Inc., The.

Litchfield, Jo. Weather. Maynard, Marc, illus. 2008. (Usborne Look & Say Ser.). 12p. (J). (gr. -1-3). bds. 7.99 (978-0-7945-1989-6(X), Usborne) EDC Publishing.

Llewellyn, Claire. The Weather Today Red Band. Jonatronix, illus. 2016. (Cambridge Reading Adventures Ser.). (ENG.). 16p. pap. 6.56 (978-1-107-57676-6(8)) Cambridge Univ. Pr.

Lonsdale, Mary, illus. Whatever the Weather: When the Snow Comes. 2004. (Whatever the Weather Ser.). 10p. (J). bds. 4.99 (978-1-85854-103-7(4)) Brimax Books Ltd. GBR. Dist: Byeway Bks.

—Whatever the Weather: When the Sun Shines. 2004. (Whatever the Weather Ser.). 10p. (J). bds. 4.99 (978-1-85854-105-1(0)) Brimax Books Ltd. GBR. Dist: Byeway Bks.

—Whatever the Weather: When the Wind Blows. 2004. (Whatever the Weather Ser.). 10p. (J). bds. 4.99 (978-1-85854-102-0(6)) Brimax Books Ltd. GBR. Dist: Byeway Bks.

Lowel, Margaret. Weather Tools: A Content Area Reader-science. 2005. (Sadlier Phonics Reading Program). (Illus.). 12p. (gr. k-2). 25.20 (978-0-8215-7814-8(6)) Sadlier, William H. Inc.

Lynn, Saundra. Am I Like the Weather? 2009. 52p. pap. 20.49 (978-1-4490-4510-4(3)) AuthorHouse.

Madgwick, Wendy. Up in the Air: 17 Easy-to-Follow Experiments for Learning Fun - Find Out about Flight & How Weather Works! 2014. (ENG., Illus.). 270p. (J). (gr. -1-12). 8.99 (978-1-86147-350-9(8), Armadillo) Anness Publishing GBR. Dist: National Bk. Network.

Mahaney, Ian F. Weather Maps. (Map It! Ser.). 24p. 2009. (gr. 3-4). 42.50 (978-1-61514-359-7(9), PowerKids Pr.) 2006. (Illus.). (YA). (gr. 2-5). lib. bdg. 22.60 (978-1-4042-3057-6(2)) Rosen Publishing Group, Inc., The.

Make It Work Geography, 4 vol. set. 2003. (gr. 4-8). 59.00 (978-0-7166-5124-6(6)) World Bk., Inc.

Making a Weather Chart: KinderFacts Individual Title Six-Packs. (Kinderstarters Ser.). 8p. (gr. -1-1). 21.00 (978-0-7635-8753-6(2)) Rigby Education.

Malavolti, Angela. You Are a Twisting Tornado. Stiffler, Michael, illus. 2011. 28p. (J). 16.99 (978-0-9834092-0-5(X)) Jungle Wagon Pr.

Malloy, Devin. WeatherTalk: Conversation Cards for the Entire Family. 2008. (Tabletalk Conversation Cards Ser.). (Illus.). (J). (gr. 4-7). 6.00 (978-1-57281-632-9(5)) U.S. Games Systems, Inc.

Maloof, Torrey. Extreme Weather, 1 vol. 2015. (Science Readers: Content & Literacy Ser.). (ENG., Illus.). 32p. (J). (gr. 3-3). pap. 8.99 (978-1-4807-4647-3(9)) Teacher Created Materials, Inc.

—Weathering & Erosion, 1 vol. rev. ed. 2014. (Science Readers: Content & Literacy Ser.). (ENG.). 32p. (gr. 2-2). pap. 8.99 (978-1-4807-4611-4(8)) Teacher Created Materials, Inc.

Manolis, Kay. Blizzards. 2008. (Extreme Weather Ser.). (ENG., Illus.). 24p. (J). (gr. 2-5). lib. bdg. 25.95 (978-1-60014-183-6(8)) Bellwether Media.

Markle, Sandra. Toad Weather, 1 vol. González, Thomas, illus. 2015. (ENG.). 32p. (J). (gr. 1-3). 16.95 (978-1-56145-818-9(X)) Peachtree Pubs.

Marsico, Katie. Weather Math. 2015. (ENG., Illus.). 32p. (J). (gr. 3-4). 26.65 (978-1-4677-1886-8(6)) Lerner Publishing Group.

—Wild Weather Days. 2006. (Scholastic News Nonfiction Readers Ser.). (ENG., Illus.). 24p. (J). (gr. 1-2). lib. bdg. 22.00 (978-0-531-16771-7(2)) Scholastic Library Publishing.

Mattern, Joanne. What Are Weather & Climate?, 1 vol. 2015. (ENG.). 32p. (J). 23.45 (978-1-62275-779-4(3), Britannica Educational Publishing) Rosen Publishing Group, Inc., The.

Maynard, Christopher & Martin, Terry. Why Does Lightning Strike? Questions Children Ask about Weather. (Why Bks.). (Illus.). 24p. (J). pap. 10.99 (978-0-590-24945-4(2)) Scholastic, Inc.

McAneney, Caitie. Precipitation. 2016. (Where's the Water? Ser.). (Illus.). 24p. (J). (gr. 3-2). pap. 8.15 (978-1-4824-4684-5(7)); lib. bdg. 22.60 (978-1-4824-4686-9(3)) Stevens, Gareth Publishing LLLP.

McAneney, Caitlin. Graphing the Weather. 2013. (Rosen Readers Ser.). (ENG.). 24p. (J). (gr. 3-4). pap. 8.25 (978-1-4777-2441-5(9)); pap. 49.50 (978-1-4777-2443-9(5)) Rosen Publishing Group, Inc., The. (Rosen Classroom).

McDonald, Jill. Hello, World! Weather. 2016. (ENG., Illus.). 26p. (J). (— 1). bds. 7.99 (978-0-553-52101-6(2), Doubleday Bks. for Young Readers) Random Hse. Children's Bks.

McDonnell, Rory. Matemáticas con el Tiempo / Math with Weather. de la Vega, Eida, tr. 2016. (¡Matemáticas en Todas Partes! / Math Is Everywhere! Ser.). (ENG & SPA.). 24p. (gr. k-k). lib. bdg. 22.60 (978-1-4824-5212-9(X)) Stevens, Gareth Publishing LLLP.

McHale, Scarlett. Brady Makes a Weather Graph. 2013. (InfoMax Readers Ser.). (ENG., Illus.). 24p. (J). (gr. 3-4). pap. 8.25 (978-1-4777-2460-6(5), Rosen Classroom) Rosen Publishing Group, Inc., The.

McMahon, Michael. Why Does Thunder Clap? 2010. (Solving Science Mysteries Ser.). (Illus.). 24p. (J). pap. 8.25 (978-1-4488-0407-8(8), PowerKids Pr.); (YA). (gr. 3-6). 22.60 (978-1-4488-0406-1(X)) Rosen Publishing Group, Inc., The.

Meachen Rau, Dana. Air. 2008. (Earth Matters Ser.). 32p. (gr. 1-2). lib. bdg. 15.95 (978-0-7614-3042-1(3), Benchmark Bks.) Marshall Cavendish Corp.

—La Airé. 2008. (Planeta Es Importante Ser.). (SPA.). 32p. (gr. 1-2). lib. bdg. 15.95 (978-0-7614-3464-1(X), Benchmark Bks.) Marshall Cavendish Corp.

Mehling, Randi. Weather, & How It Works. 2007. (Scientific American Ser.). (Illus.). 72p. (YA). (gr. 5-9). lib. bdg. 30.00 (978-0-7910-9053-4(1)) Facts On File, Inc.

Meister, Cari. Droughts. 2015. (Illus.). 24p. (J). lib. bdg. 25.65 (978-1-62031-224-7(7)) Jump! Inc.

Meses y Estaciones. (Coleccion Picaros Peluchines). (SPA.). (J). 5.50 (978-950-11-0401-1(X), SGM401) Sigmar ARG. Dist: Continental Bk. Co., Inc.

Michaels, Pat. W Is for Wind: A Weather Alphabet. Rose, Melanie, illus. rev. ed. (Science Ser.). (ENG.). 40p. (J). 2006. (gr. -1-3). pap. 7.95 (978-1-58536-330-8(8)) 2005. 16.95 (978-1-58536-237-0(9)) Sleeping Bear Pr.

Michele, Tracey. Measure the Weather. 2011. (Learn-Abouts Ser.). (Illus.). 16p. (J). pap. 7.95 (978-1-59920-641-7(2)) Black Rabbit Bks.

Milbourne, Anna. The Snowy Day. Temporin, Elena, illus. 2005. 24p. (J). (gr. -1-3). 9.99 (978-0-7945-1147-0(3), Usborne) EDC Publishing.

Mills, Nathan & Frampton, Callie. Tools Tell the Weather. 2012. (Rosen Readers Ser.). (ENG., Illus.). 24p. (J). (gr. 1-2). pap. 8.25 (978-1-4488-8800-9(X), Rosen Classroom) Rosen Publishing Group, Inc., The.

Mills, Nathan & Waters, Grace. The Changing Weather. 2012. (Rosen Readers Ser.). (ENG., Illus.). 16p. (J). (gr. k-1). pap. 7.00 (978-1-4488-8749-1(6), Rosen Classroom) Rosen Publishing Group, Inc., The.

Mogil, H. Michael & Levine, Barbara G. Extreme Weather. 2011. (Insiders Ser.). (ENG.). 64p. (J). (gr. 3-7). 17.99 (978-1-4424-3274-1(8), Simon & Schuster Bks. For Young Readers) Simon & Schuster Bks. For Young Readers.

Montgomery, Sharon, text. Your Invisible Bodies: A Reference Book for Children & Adults about Human Energy Fields. 2011. (Illus.). (978-0-9811089-2-6(X)) Words By Montgomery.

Mooney, Carla. Becoming Invisible: From Camouflage to Cloaks. 2010. (Great Idea Ser.). 48p. (J). (gr. 4-6). lib. bdg. 26.60 (978-1-59953-378-0(2)) Norwood Hse. Pr.

—Climate & Weather. 2012. (ENG.). 48p. (gr. 4-6). pap. 10.95 (978-1-61810-258-4(3)) Rourke Educational Media.

Moore, Philip. What Is Weather? 2014. (Little Books of Answers: Level B Ser.). (Illus.). 16p. (gr. k-2). pap. 7.95 (978-1-927136-16-4(4)) Three Crows Media NZL. Dist: RiverStream Publishing.

Morris, Neil. Weather. 2003. (Knowledge Masters Ser.). (Illus.). 32p. (YA). pap. incl. cd-rom (978-1-903954-52-2(5), Pavilion Children's Books) Pavilion Bks.

National Geographic Kids Staff. Look Outside! - National Geographic Kids. 2017. (Look & Learn Ser.). (ENG., Illus.). 24p. (J). (-k). bds. 6.99 (978-1-4263-2702-5(1), National Geographic Children's Bks.) National Geographic Society.

National Geographic Kids Staff & de Seve, Karen. National Geographic Little Kids First Big Book of Weather. 2017. (ENG., Illus.). 128p. (J). (gr. -1-3). 14.99 (978-1-4263-2719-3(6), National Geographic Children's Bks.) National Geographic Society.

Newson, Lesley & Wadsworth, Pamela. Rhagor Am Greigiau, Pridd a Thywydd. 2005. (WEL., Illus.). 24p. pap. (978-1-85596-238-5(1)) Dref Wen.

Nunn, Daniel. The Weather. 2013. (True or False? Ser.). (ENG.). 24p. (gr. -1-1). lib. bdg. 22.65 (978-1-4109-5070-3(0), NA-r) Heinemann-Raintree.

—The Weather - True or False? 2013. (True or False? Ser.). (ENG.). 24p. (gr. -1-1). pap. 6.29 (978-1-4109-5076-5(X), NA-r) Heinemann-Raintree.

Oard, Michael. The New Weather Book. 2015. (Illus.). 96p. (J). 16.99 (978-0-89051-861-8(0)) Master Bks.

OLIVER, Clare. Weather. 2014. (100 Facts You Should Know Ser.). 48p. (J). (gr. 4-6). pap. 84.95 (978-1-4824-1273-4(X)) Stevens, Gareth Publishing LLLP.

Ord, Michael. The Weather Book. 2006. (Wonders of Creation Ser.). 72p. pap. 3.99 (978-1-893345-59-1(9)) Answers in Genesis Ministries.

Orero, Maria Jesus. Nico y Las Estaciones. 2006. (Nico Collection). (SPA & ESP., Illus.). 12p. (gr. -1-2). per., bds.

6.99 *(978-84-272-6154-9(3))* Molino, Editorial ESP. Dist: Santillana USA Publishing Co., Inc.
Orme, Helen. Weather. 2010. (Science Everywhere! Ser.). 24p. 24.25 *(978-1-84898-293-2(3))* Black Rabbit Bks.
Orr, Tamra B. It Snows. 2015. (Tell Me Why Library). (ENG.). 24p. (J). (gr. 2-5). 27.07 *(978-1-63188-998-1(2),* 205904) Cherry Lake Publishing.
—Super Cool Science Experiments: Weather. 2009. (Explorer Library: Science Explorer Ser.). (ENG., Illus.). 32p. (gr. 4-8). lib. bdg. 28.50 *(978-1-60279-528-0(2),* 200294) Cherry Lake Publishing.
Osborne, Mary Pope. Twisters & Other Terrible Storms: A Nonfiction Companion to Twister on Tuesday. Osborne, Will & Murdocca, Sal, illus. 2003. (Magic Tree House - Fact Tracker Ser.: 8). (ENG.). 128p. (J). (gr. 2-5). 6.99 *(978-0-375-81358-0(6),* Random Hse. Bks. for Young Readers) Random Hse. Children's Bks.
Owen, Ruth. Science & Craft Projects with Weather. 2013. (Get Crafty Outdoors Ser.). (ENG., Illus.). 32p. (J). (gr. k-3). 26.50 *(978-1-4777-0244-4(X));* pap. 11.75 *(978-1-4777-0251-2(2))* Rosen Publishing Group, Inc., The. (PowerKids Pr.).
Oxlade, Chris. Infographics, 1 vol. 2014. (Infographics Ser.). (ENG.). 32p. (gr. 1-3). lib. bdg. 119.96 *(978-1-4109-6220-1(2),* Read Me!) Heinemann-Raintree.
—Weather Infographics, 1 vol. 2014. (Infographics Ser.). (ENG.). 32p. (gr. 1-3). lib. bdg. 29.99 *(978-1-4109-6219-5(9),* Read Me!) Heinemann-Raintree.
—Why Why Why Do Tornadoes Spin. 2008. 32p. pap. *(978-1-84810-004-6(3))* Miles Kelly Publishing, Ltd.
—Why Why Why... Do Tornadoes Spin? 2010. (Why Why Why Ser.). 32p. (J). (gr. 1-3). lib. bdg. 18.95 *(978-1-4222-1586-9(5))* Mason Crest.
—Wild Weather. 2015. (Collins Big Cat Ser.). (ENG.). 32p. (J). (gr. 2-2). pap. 7.95 *(978-0-00-759128-2(4))* HarperCollins Pubs. Ltd. GBR. Dist: Independent Pubs. Group.
Palmer, Kristen. Wild Weather Trivia. 2013. (Ultimate Trivia Challenge Ser.). (Illus.). 32p. (J). (gr. 2-5). pap. 10.50 *(978-1-4339-8305-4(2));* lib. bdg. 25.25 *(978-1-4339-8304-7(4))* Stevens, Gareth Publishing LLLP.
Palmer, Kristin. Wild Weather Trivia. 2013. (Ultimate Trivia Challenge Ser.). 32p. (J). (gr. 2-5). pap. 63.00 *(978-1-4339-8306-1(0))* Stevens, Gareth Publishing LLLP.
Paris, Stephanie. Pop! Air & Water Pressure, 1 vol. 2nd rev. ed. 2013. (Nonfiction Readers Ser.). (ENG., Illus.). 64p. (J). (gr. 5-5). pap. 31.96 *(978-1-4333-7438-8(2))* Teacher Created Materials, Inc.
Parker, Janice. Weather. 2016. (J). ***(978-1-5105-2243-5(3))*** SmartBook Media, Inc.
—Weather. 2008. (Science Q & A Ser.). (Illus.). 48p. (YA). (gr. 5-8). pap. 10.95 *(978-1-59036-953-1(X));* lib. bdg. 29.05 *(978-1-59036-952-4(1))* Weigl Pubs., Inc.
—Weather Q & A. 2013. (J). *(978-1-62127-417-9(9));* pap. *(978-1-62127-423-0(3))* Weigl Pubs., Inc.
Pebble Books: Our Seasons & Weather. 2005. (YA). (gr. k-3). 712.80 *(978-0-7368-4219-8(5),* Pebble Bks.) Capstone Press of Coughlan Cos.
Pendergast, George. A Year of Seasons. 2015. (Cycles in Nature Ser.). (ENG., Illus.). 24p. (J). (gr. 1-2). lib. bdg. 22.60 *(978-1-4824-1654-1(9))* Stevens, Gareth Publishing LLLP.
Peppas, Lynn. How Do Clouds Form? 2012. (ENG.). 24p. (J). pap. *(978-0-7787-4480-1(9))* Crabtree Publishing Co.
—What Are Cirrus Clouds? 2012. (ENG.). 24p. (J). *(978-0-7787-4473-3(6));* pap. *(978-0-7787-4478-8(7))* Crabtree Publishing Co.
—What Are Cumulus Clouds? 2012. (ENG.). 24p. (J). pap. *(978-0-7787-4479-5(5))* Crabtree Publishing Co.
—What Are Stratus Clouds? 2012. (ENG.). 24p. (J). *(978-0-7787-4476-4(0));* pap. *(978-0-7787-4481-8(7))* Crabtree Publishing Co.
Phelan, Glen. Extreme Weather. 2007. (Reading Expeditions Ser.). (ENG., Illus.). 32p. (J). pap. 17.95 *(978-0-7922-4575-9(X))* CENGAGE Learning.
Powell, Jillian. Projects with Weather & Seasons. 2014. (Make & Learn Ser.). (Illus.). 32p. (J). (gr. 3-6). lib. bdg. 27.50 *(978-1-4777-7181-5(6),* PowerKids Pr.) Rosen Publishing Group, Inc., The.
Probst, Jeff. Extreme Weather. 2017. (Challenge Yourself Ser.: 4). (ENG., Illus.). 176p. (J). (gr. 3-7). 8.99 *(978-0-14-751810-1(5),* Puffin Books) Penguin Young Readers Group.
Pugliano-Martin, Carol. Summer to Fall. 2006. (Early Explorers Ser.). (J). pap. *(978-1-4108-6102-3(3))* Benchmark Education Co.
Purdie, Kate. Sunshine & Drought. 2010. (Weatherwise Ser.). 32p. (ENG.). (J). pap. 10.60 *(978-1-61532-278-7(7),* PowerKids Pr.); (Illus.). (YA). (gr. 3-6). lib. bdg. 26.50 *(978-1-61532-266-4(3))* Rosen Publishing Group, Inc., The.
Quin, Caroline & Pearce, Sue. Weather. 2004. (Activities for 3-5 Year Olds Ser.). (Illus.). 32p. pap. 11.00 *(978-1-897675-39-7(9))* Brilliant Pubns. GBR. Dist: Parkwest Pubns., Inc.
Rabe, Tish. Oh Say Can You Say What's the Weather Today? All about Weather. Ruiz, Aristides, illus. 2004. (Cat in the Hat's Learning Library). (ENG.). 48p. (J). (gr. -1-3). 9.99 *(978-0-375-82276-6(3),* Random Hse. Bks. for Young Readers) Random Hse. Children's Bks.
Rain or Shine: Level O, 6 vols. (Explorers Ser.). 32p. (gr. 3-6). 44.95 *(978-0-7699-0596-9(X))* Shortland Pubns. (U. S. A.) Inc.
Randolph, Joanne. What Are the Elements of Weather?, 1 vol. 2015. (ENG., Illus.). 32p. (J). 23.45 *(978-1-62275-775-6(0),* Britannica Educational Publishing) Rosen Publishing Group, Inc., The.
Randolph, Joanne, ed. Air Pressure Driving the Weather! 2017. (Weather Report). 32p. (J). (gr. 3-3). pap. 10.52 ***(978-0-7660-9005-7(1))*** Enslow Pubs., Inc.
—Extreme Weather Ahead! 2017. (Weather Report). 32p. (J). (gr. 3-3). pap. 10.52 ***(978-0-7660-9009-5(4))*** Enslow Pubs., Inc.
—Northern Lights Sighting! 2017. (Weather Report). 32p. (J). (gr. 3-3). pap. 10.52 ***(978-0-7660-9021-7(3))*** Enslow Pubs., Inc.
Rattini, Kristin Baird. National Geographic Readers: Weather. 2013. (Readers Ser.). (ENG., Illus.). 32p. (J). (gr. -1-1). lib. bdg. 13.90 *(978-1-4263-1349-3(7),* National Geographic Children's Bks.) National Geographic Society.
—Weather. 2013. (Readers Ser.). (ENG., Illus.). 32p. (J). (gr. -1-1). pap. 3.99 *(978-1-4263-1348-6(9),* National Geographic Children's Bks.) National Geographic Society.
Rees, Peter. Why Do Raindrops Fall? Level 3 Factbook. 2010. (Cambridge Young Readers Ser.). (ENG., Illus.). 16p. pap. 6.00 *(978-0-521-13714-0(4))* Cambridge Univ. Pr.
Regan, Lisa. A Cool Kid's Field Guide to Weather. Hutchinson, Tim, illus. 2009. (Cool Kid's Field Guide Ser.). 26p. (J). (gr. 1-3). spiral bd. 6.99 *(978-0-8416-7147-8(8))* Hammond World Atlas Corp.
Reilly, Kathleen M. Explore Weather & Climate! With 25 Great Projects. Stone, Bryan, illus. 2012. (Explore Your World Ser.). (ENG.). 96p. (J). (gr. k-4). pap. 12.95 *(978-1-936313-84-6(7))* Open City Bks.
Rice, Dona. ¿Qué Tipo de Tiempo?, 1 vol. rev. ed. 2010. (Early Childhood Themes Ser.). (SPA., Illus.). 16p. (J). (gr. -1-2). pap. 6.99 *(978-1-4333-1498-8(3));* pap. 19.99 *(978-1-4333-1499-5(1))* Shell Educational Publishing.
—What Kind of Weather?, 1 vol. 2009. (Early Childhood Themes Ser.). (ENG., Illus.). 16p. (J). (gr. -1-2). pap. 6.99 *(978-1-4333-1458-2(4))* Teacher Created Materials, Inc.
Rice, Dona Herweck. El Tiempo, 1 vol. 2nd rev. ed. 2011. (Nonfiction Readers Ser.). (SPA.). 12p. (J). (gr. 1-1). pap. 4.99 *(978-1-4333-4414-5(9))* Teacher Created Materials, Inc.
—Weather, 1 vol. 2nd rev. ed. 2013. (Nonfiction Readers Ser.). (ENG., Illus.). 12p. (J). (gr. 1-1). pap. 15.96 *(978-1-4807-1014-6(8))* Shell Educational Publishing.
—Weather, 1 vol. 2nd rev. ed. 2011. (Nonfiction Readers Ser.). (ENG.). 12p. (J). (gr. 1-1). pap. 4.99 *(978-1-4333-3575-4(1))* Teacher Created Materials, Inc.
Riechmann, Annie & Smith, Dawn Suzette. Whatever the Weather: Science Experiments & Art Activities for No Matter What the Day Brings. 2016. (ENG., Illus.). 216p. pap. 19.95 *(978-1-61180-231-3(8),* Roost Books) Shambhala Pubns., Inc.
RIGBY. Look Out the Window: First Grade Big Books. 2003. (Rigby on Our Way to English Ser.). (ENG.). 16p. (gr. 1-1). pap. 50.70 *(978-0-7578-1501-0(4))* Rigby Education.
—What Is the Weather Outside? First Grade Big Books. 2003. (Rigby on Our Way to English Ser.). (ENG.). 16p. (gr. 1-1). pap. 50.70 *(978-0-7578-1507-2(3))* Rigby Education.
Rigby Education Staff. Hot & Cold. (Sails Literacy Ser.). (Illus.). 16p. (gr. 1-2). 27.00 *(978-0-7635-9920-1(4),* 699204C99) Rigby Education.
Robertson, Charmaine. Severe Weather. 2016. (Rosen REAL Readers: STEM & STEAM Collection). 12p. (gr. 1-k). pap. 6.33 *(978-1-5081-2425-2(6),* Rosen Classroom) Rosen Publishing Group, Inc., The.
Rockwell, Lizzy & Fowler, Allan. What's the Weather? 2009. (Rookie Preschool-NEW Ser.). (ENG.). 24p. (J). pap. 6.95 *(978-0-531-24585-9(3));* (gr. -1). lib. bdg. 23.00 *(978-0-531-24410-4(5))* Scholastic Library Publishing.
Rogers, Paul. What Will the Weather Be Like Today? Kazuko, illus. 2011. (Houghton Mifflin Reading Ser.). 38p. (J). pap. 61.35 *(978-0-618-03420-8(X))* Houghton Mifflin Harcourt Trade & Reference Pubs.
Roker, Al. Al Roker's Extreme Weather. 2017. 48p. (J). (gr. 3-7). 16.99 ***(978-0-06-248499-4(0))*** HarperCollins Pubs.
Rookie Ready to Learn - Seasons & Weather, 5 vols., Set. Incl. Animal Babies. Hamsa, Bobbie. Dunnington, Tom, illus. 40p. lib. bdg. 23.00 *(978-0-531-25640-4(5));* Going to the Beach. Kittinger, Jo S. Warren, Shari, illus. 32p. lib. bdg. 23.00 *(978-0-531-25641-1(3));* Pumpkin Fever. Simon, Charnan. Bryan-Hunt, Jan, illus. 40p. lib. bdg. 23.00 *(978-0-531-25643-5(X));* Snow Joe. Greene, Carol. Sharp, Paul, illus. 40p. lib. bdg. 23.00 *(978-0-531-25644-2(8));* (J). (gr. -1-k). (Rookie Ready to Learn Ser.). 2011. Set lib. bdg. 115.00 *(978-0-531-26724-0(5),* Children's Pr.) Scholastic Library Publishing.
Rosa-Mendoza, Gladys. The Weather. Cifuentes, Carolina, ed. Hullinger, C. D., illus. 2004. (English-Spanish Foundations Ser.: Vol. 6). Orig. Title: El Tiempo. (ENG & SPA.). 20p. (J). (gr. -1-4). bds. 6.95 *(978-0-9679748-5-9(2))* Me+Mi Publishing.
Rose, Emma. Warning! Set: Extreme Weather, 6 vols. 2004. (Phonics Readers Books 37-72 Ser.). (ENG.). 8p. (gr. k-1). pap. 35.70 *(978-0-7368-4074-3(5),* Phonics Readers) Capstone Press of Coughlan Cos.
Rosen Publishing Staff. Let's Find Out! Weather, 1 vol. 2015. (Let's Find Out! Ser.). (ENG.). 32p. (J). 140.70 *(978-1-62275-799-2(8),* Britannica Educational Publishing) Rosen Publishing Group, Inc., The.
Ross, Kathy. Crafts for Kids Who Are Learning about Weather. Barger, Jan, illus. 2006. (Crafts for Kids Who Are Learning about Ser.). 47p. (J). (gr. 3-6). lib. bdg. 25.26 *(978-0-7613-2796-7(7))* Lerner Publishing Group.
Rowell, Rebecca. Weather & Climate Through Infographics. Dean, Venitia, illus. 2013. (Super Science Infographics Ser.). (ENG.). 32p. (gr. 3-5). pap. 8.95 *(978-1-4677-1595-9(6));* lib. bdg. 26.60 *(978-1-4677-1292-7(2),* Lerner Pubns.) Lerner Publishing Group.
Royston, Angela. Looking at Weather & Seasons: How Do They Change? 2008. (Looking at Science: How Things Change Ser.). (Illus.). 32p. (J). (gr. 3-7). lib. bdg. 23.94 *(978-0-7660-3093-0(8),* Enslow Elementary) Enslow Pubs., Inc.
Rupp, Rebecca. Weather! A Book about Pink Snow, Fighting Kites, Lightning Rods, Rains of Frogs, Typhoons, Tornadoes, & Ice Balls from Space. Nap, Dug & Sweet, Melissa, illus. 2003. (ENG.). 144p. (J). (gr. 3-8). pap. 14.95 *(978-1-58017-420-6(5),* 67420) Storey Publishing, LLC.
Rustad, Martha E. H. Today Is a Hot Day. 2017. (What Is the Weather Today? Ser.). (ENG., Illus.). 24p. (gr. k-1). lib. bdg. 21.99 *(978-1-5157-4923-3(1),* Pebble Bks.) Capstone Press of Coughlan Cos.
—Today Is a Rainy Day. 2017. (What Is the Weather Today? Ser.). (ENG., Illus.). 24p. (gr. k-1). lib. bdg. 21.99 *(978-1-5157-4921-9(5),* Pebble Bks.) Capstone Press of Coughlan Cos.
—Today Is a Snowy Day. 2017. (What Is the Weather Today? Ser.). (ENG., Illus.). 24p. (gr. k-1). lib. bdg. 21.99 *(978-1-5157-4919-6(3),* Pebble Bks.) Capstone Press of Coughlan Cos.
—Today Is a Sunny Day. 2017. (What Is the Weather Today? Ser.). (ENG., Illus.). 24p. (gr. k-1). lib. bdg. 21.99 *(978-1-5157-4920-2(7),* Pebble Bks.) Capstone Press of Coughlan Cos.
—Today Is a Windy Day. 2017. (What Is the Weather Today? Ser.). (ENG., Illus.). 24p. (gr. k-2). pap. 6.29 *(978-1-4966-0945-8(X),* Pebble Bks.) Capstone Press of Coughlan Cos.
—Weather in Spring. 2012. (All about Spring Ser.). (ENG.). 24p. (gr. k-1). pap. 41.70 *(978-1-4296-9365-3(7));* pap. 7.29 *(978-1-4296-9364-6(9));* (Illus.). lib. bdg. 26.65 *(978-1-4296-8654-9(5))* Capstone Press of Coughlan Cos. (Pebble Plus).
—What Is the Weather Today? 2017. (What Is the Weather Today? Ser.). (ENG.). 24p. (gr. k-2). pap. 45.84 *(978-1-4966-0955-7(7),* Pebble Bks.) Capstone Press of Coughlan Cos.
—When Will It Rain? Noticing Weather Patterns. Conger, Holli, illus. 2015. (ENG.). 24p. (J). (gr. k-2). 25.32 *(978-1-4677-8557-0(1),* Millbrook Pr.) Lerner Publishing Group.
Rustad, Martha E. H. & Kalz, Jill. Droughts: Be Aware & Prepare, 1 vol. 2014. (Weather Aware Ser.). (ENG.). 32p. (gr. 1-2). lib. bdg. 27.32 *(978-1-4765-9905-2(X))* Capstone Press of Coughlan Cos.
Salas, Laura Purdie. Colors of Weather. (Colors All Around Ser.). (ENG.). 32p. (gr. 1-2). 2011. pap. 47.70 *(978-1-4296-6158-4(5))* 2010. lib. bdg. 27.32 *(978-1-4296-5258-2(6))* Capstone Press of Coughlan Cos. (Aplus Bks.).
Scholastic Clubs US Weather Watch Pack (exc. Snow) Weather Watch. 2006. (J). pap. 31.80 *(978-1-59566-320-7(7))* QEB Publishing Inc.
Scholastic, Inc. Staff, contrib. by. What Is the Weather Today? 2014. (Rookie Toddler(r) Ser.). (ENG., Illus.). 12p. (J). bds. 6.95 *(978-0-531-20491-7(X))* Scholastic Library Publishing.
Schuetz, Kristin. Humidity. 2015. (Understanding Weather Ser.). (ENG., Illus.). 24p. (J). (gr. k-3). lib. bdg. 25.95 *(978-1-62617-252-4(8),* Blastoff! Readers) Bellwether Media.
Schuh, Mari. Weather in Fall. 2013. (ENG., Illus.). 24p. (J). lib. bdg. 25.65 *(978-1-62031-061-8(9))* Jump! Inc.
Schuh, Mari C. I Feel Fall Weather. 2016. (First Step Nonfiction — Observing Fall Ser.). (ENG., Illus.). 24p. (J). (gr. k-2). 23.99 *(978-1-5124-0797-6(6))* Lerner Publishing Group.
The Science of Weather. 2004. (Illus.). lib. bdg. 7.95 *(978-0-8225-4341-1(9))* Lerner Publishing Group.
Sengupta, Monalisa. Wild Weather. (Wild Nature Ser.). 48p. 2009. (gr. 4-5). 53.00 *(978-1-60854-796-8(5),* PowerKids Pr.) 2007. (Illus.). (YA). (gr. 3-6). lib. bdg. 29.25 *(978-1-4042-3902-9(2))* Rosen Publishing Group, Inc., The.
Sesame Workshop. Toddler Time Explore Seasons with Cookie Monster. 2011. (J). (gr. k-1). pap. 3.99 *(978-1-59922-883-9(1))* Twin Sisters IP, LLC.
Shea, Therese. Freaky Weather Stories. 2015. (Freaky True Science Ser.). (ENG.). 32p. (J). (gr. 4-5). pap. 10.50 *(978-1-4824-2968-8(3))* Stevens, Gareth Publishing LLLP.
Sherman, Josepha. Amazing Science - Weather, 6 bks. Incl. Flakes & Flurries: A Book about Snow. Yesh, Jeff, illus. 26.65 *(978-1-4048-0098-4(0));* Gusts & Gales: A Book about Wind. Wesley, Omarr, illus. 26.65 *(978-1-4048-0094-6(8));* Shapes in the Sky: A Book about Clouds. Wesley, Omarr, illus. 26.65 *(978-1-4048-0097-7(2));* (gr. -1-3). (Amazing Science: Weather Ser.). (ENG.). 24p. 2003. Set lib. bdg. 159.90 o.p. *(978-1-4048-0092-2(1))* Picture Window Bks.
Shofner, Melissa Raé. Weather & Natural Disasters. 2016. (Spotlight on Earth Science Ser.). 00024p. (J). (gr. 4-6). pap. 10.00 *(978-1-4994-2547-5(3),* PowerKids Pr.) Rosen Publishing Group, Inc., The.
Shulman, Mark. Wicked Weather. 2007. (Illus.). 48p. (J). per. 6.99 *(978-0-696-23689-1(3))* Meredith Bks.
Sian Revision Weather Wise. 2004. (J). *(978-1-59242-085-8(0))* Delta Education, LLC.
Silverstein, Alvin, et al. Weather & Climate. 2007. (Science Concepts, Second Ser.). (Illus.). 96p. (J). (gr. 6-8). lib. bdg. 31.93 *(978-0-8225-6796-7(2),* Twenty-First Century Bks.) Lerner Publishing Group.
Simon, Seymour. Weather. 2006. (ENG., Illus.). 40p. (J). (gr. k-4). pap. 6.99 *(978-0-06-088439-0(8))* HarperCollins Pubs.
Singer, Marilyn. On the Same Day in March. 2014. 17.00 *(978-1-63419-675-8(9))* Perfection Learning Corp.
Slade, Suzanne. How Do Tornadoes Form? And Other Questions Kids Have about Weather, 1 vol. Pillo, Cary, illus. (Kids' Questions Ser.). (ENG.). 24p. (gr. 1-2). 2011. pap. 7.49 *(978-1-4048-6731-4(7))* 2010. lib. bdg. 26.65 *(978-1-4048-6048-3(7))* Picture Window Bks.
Slingerland, Janet. What Causes a Rainbow? 2016. (Everyday Earth Science Ser.). (ENG.). 24p. (J). (gr. k-3). 27.07 *(978-1-5038-0791-4(6),* 210627) Child's World, Inc., The.
—What Makes the Sky Blue? 2016. (Everyday Earth Science Ser.). (ENG.). 24p. (J). (gr. k-3). 27.07 *(978-1-5038-0796-9(7),* 210631) Child's World, Inc., The.
Smith, Alastair & Clarke, Phillip. Weather: With Internet Links. 2006. (Usborne Spotter's Guides). (Illus.). 64p. (J). (gr. 2). lib. bdg. 13.99 *(978-1-58086-915-7(7),* Usborne) EDC Publishing.
Smith, Ben. Who Listens to the Weather Forecast? 2014. (Little Books of Answers: Level d Ser.). (Illus.). 16p. (gr. k-2). pap. 7.95 *(978-1-927136-36-2(9))* Three Crows Media NZL. Dist: RiverStream Publishing.
Sohn, Emily. Experiments in Earth Science & Weather with Toys & Everyday Stuff. 2015. (Fun Science Ser.). (ENG., Illus.). 24p. (gr. 1-2). lib. bdg. 25.32 *(978-1-4914-5035-2(5))* Capstone Press of Coughlan Cos.
Sohn, Emily & Ash Sullivan, Erin. Weather & the Water Cycle: Will it Rain? 2011. (IScience Readers Ser.). 48p. (J). (gr. 5-6). lib. bdg. 23.94 *(978-1-59953-432-9(0))* Norwood Hse. Pr.
Sohn, Emily & Kentor Schmauss, Judy. Air & Weather: Where'd My Hat Go? 2011. (IScience Readers Ser.). 24p. (J). (gr. k-2). lib. bdg. 21.27 *(978-1-59953-403-9(7))* Norwood Hse. Pr.
Spilsbury, Louise. Threats to Our Water Supply. 2009. (J). 70.50 *(978-1-4358-5481-9(0));* (ENG.). 48p. (YA). pap. 11.75 *(978-1-4358-5480-2(2));* (ENG., Illus.). 48p. (J). (gr. 5-9). lib. bdg. 29.25 *(978-1-4358-5352-2(0))* Rosen Publishing Group, Inc., The.
—What Is Weather?, 1 vol., 1. 2014. (Let's Find Out! Ser.). (ENG.). 32p. (gr. 3-6). 23.45 *(978-1-62275-276-8(7))* Rosen Publishing Group, Inc., The.
Spilsbury, Richard. Ask an Expert: Climate Change. 2010. (Crabtree Connections Ser.). (ENG.). 24p. (J). (gr. 3-6). *(978-0-7787-9938-2(7));* pap. *(978-0-7787-9960-3(3))* Crabtree Publishing Co.
Squire, Ann O. Extreme Weather. 2014. (True Book(tm), a — Extreme Science Ser.). (ENG.). 48p. (J). lib. bdg. 31.00 *(978-0-531-20743-7(9))* Scholastic Library Publishing.
Steck-Vaughn Staff. Stormy Weather. 2003. pap. 4.10 *(978-0-7398-7637-4(6))* Steck-Vaughn.
Stein, Paul. Droughts of the Future. 2009. (Library of Future Weather & Climate Ser.). 64p. (gr. 5-5). 58.50 *(978-1-60853-644-3(0))* Rosen Publishing Group, Inc., The.
Steps To Literacy Staff, compiled by. Weather Series: Capv210. 2005. (ENG., Illus.). (J). pap. *(978-1-60015-015-9(2))* Steps To Literacy, LLC.
—What Kind of Day Is It? Collection: Capv204. 2005. (ENG., Illus.). (J). pap. *(978-1-60015-014-2(4))* Steps To Literacy, LLC.
Sterling, Kristin. Lightning Bolt Books: What's the Weather Like?, 5 vols., Set. Incl. It's Cloudy Today. 26.60 *(978-0-7613-4256-4(7));* It's Rainy Today. 26.60 *(978-0-7613-4257-1(5));* It's Snowy Today. 26.60 *(978-0-7613-4258-8(3));* It's Sunny Today. 26.60 *(978-0-7613-4259-5(1));* It's Windy Today. 26.60 *(978-0-7613-4260-1(5));* (Illus.). 32p. (gr. k-2). 2009. Set lib. bdg. 126.30 *(978-0-7613-4255-7(9),* Lerner Pubns.) Lerner Publishing Group.
Stille, Darlene R. Weather, 1 vol. 2012. (Science Behind Ser.). (ENG.). 32p. (gr. 3-3). pap. 8.29 *(978-1-4109-4498-6(0));* lib. bdg. 30.65 *(978-1-4109-4487-0(5))* Heinemann-Raintree. (Raintree Perspectives).
Storad, Conrad J. Studying Weather & Climates. 2011. (ENG., Illus.). 24p. (gr. 2-3). pap. 8.95 *(978-1-61741-951-5(6))* Rourke Educational Media.
—What's the Weather Like Today? 2011. (ENG., Illus.). 24p. (gr. 1-2). pap. 8.95 *(978-1-61741-939-3(7))* Rourke Educational Media.
Stradling, Jan. Erosion & Weathering: Level K, 6 vols., Vol. 2. (First Explorers Ser.). 24p. (gr. 1-2). 34.95 *(978-0-7699-1457-2(8))* Shortland Pubns. (U. S. A.) Inc.
Sundance/Newbridge LLC Staff. Our Sun, Our Weather. 2007. (Early Science Ser.). (gr. k-3). 18.95 *(978-1-4007-6531-7(5));* pap. 6.10 *(978-1-4007-6527-0(7))* Sundance/Newbridge Educational Publishing.
—Who Cares about the Weather? 2007. (Early Science Ser.). (gr. k-3). 18.95 *(978-1-4007-6413-6(0));* pap. 6.10 *(978-1-4007-6409-9(2))* Sundance/Newbridge Educational Publishing.
Thornborough, Kathy. Weather. Petelinsek, Kathleen, illus. 2014. (Talking Hands Ser.). (ENG.). 24p. (J). (gr. k-3). 25.64 *(978-1-62687-324-7(0),* 207164) Child's World, Inc., The.
Time for Kids Editors. TIME for Kids Weather Kit. 2013. (ENG.). 48p. (J). (gr. 3-17). 21.95 *(978-1-61893-011-8(7))* Time Inc. Bks.
Time for Kids Magazine Staff, ed. Storms! 2006. (Time for Kids Science Scoops Ser.). (Illus.). 32p. (gr. 1-3). 14.00 *(978-0-7569-6674-4(4))* Perfection Learning Corp.
Top That Publishing Staff, ed. Weather Watch. 2004. (Fun Kits Ser.). (Illus.). 48p. (J). *(978-1-84510-131-2(6))* Top That! Publishing PLC.
Townsend, John. Is Our Weather Getting Worse? 2010. (Crabtree Connections Ser.). (ENG.). 24p. (J). (gr. 3-6). *(978-0-7787-9957-3(3));* pap. *(978-0-7787-9979-5(4))* Crabtree Publishing Co.
Troupe, Thomas Kingsley. Wild Weather: Science Adventures with Sonny the Origami Bird, 1 vol. Christoph, Jamey, illus. 2014. (Origami Science Adventures Ser.). (ENG.). 24p. (gr. 3-4). lib. bdg. 27.32 *(978-1-4795-2188-3(4))* Picture Window Bks.
Trueit, Trudi Strain. Stormy Days. 2009. (Benchmark Rebus: Weather Watch Ser.). 24p. (gr. k-1). 15.95 *(978-0-7614-4016-1(X))* Marshall Cavendish Corp.
—Windy Days. 2009. (Benchmark Rebus: Weather Watch Ser.). 24p. (gr. k-1). 15.95 *(978-0-7614-4020-8(8))* Marshall Cavendish GBR. Dist: Marshall Cavendish Corp.
Trumbauer, Lisa. Weathering & Erosion. 2005. (J). pap. *(978-1-4108-4600-6(8))* Benchmark Education Co.
Vander Hook, Sue. The Dust Bowl, 1 vol. 2009. (Essential Events Set 3 Ser.). (ENG., Illus.). 112p. (J). (gr. 6-12). lib. bdg. 35.64 *(978-1-60453-512-9(1))* ABDO Publishing Co.
Wadsworth, Pamela. Creigiau, Pridd a Thywydd. 2005. (WEL., Illus.). 24p. pap. *(978-1-85596-237-8(3))* Dref Wen.
Wadsworth, Pamela & Tate, Sylvia. Golwg Gyntaf Ar Greigiau, Pridd a Thywydd. 2005. (WEL., Illus.). 24p. pap. *(978-1-85596-253-8(5))* Dref Wen.
Waldron, Melanie. Mapping the Land & Weather, 1 vol. 2013. (Let's Get Mapping! Ser.). (ENG., Illus.). 32p. (gr. 2-4). 30.65 *(978-1-4109-4902-8(8));* pap. 8.29 *(978-1-4109-4909-7(5))* Heinemann-Raintree. (Raintree Perspectives).
Walker, Kate. Weather. 2011. (Investigating Earth Ser.). 32p. (gr. 2). 28.50 *(978-1-60870-563-4(3))* Marshall Cavendish GBR. Dist: Marshall Cavendish Corp.
Walker, Nan. Weather. 2010. (Illus.). 24p. (J). *(978-0-545-27360-2(9))* Scholastic, Inc.
Wallace, Jessica. Weather: KinderConcepts Individual Title Six-Packs. Ross, Christine, illus. (Kinderstarters Ser.). 8p. (gr. -1-1). 21.00 *(978-0-7635-8725-3(7))* Rigby Education.
Weather. (Jump Ser.). (Illus.). 32p. (J). (gr. 2-7). pap. *(978-1-882210-25-1(5))* Action Publishing, Inc.
Weather. 2005. (Our Seasons & Weather Ser.). (YA). (gr. k-3). 118.80 *(978-0-7368-4198-6(9),* Pebble Bks.) Capstone Press of Coughlan Cos.
Weather, 6 bks., Set. Incl. Sunny Weather Days. Rosenberg, Pam. lib. bdg. 22.00 *(978-0-531-16770-0(4));* Wild Weather Days. Marsico, Katie. lib. bdg. 22.00 *(978-0-531-16771-7(2));* 24p. (J). (gr. 1-2). (Scholastic News Nonfiction Readers Ser.). (Illus.). 2006. 114.00 o.p. *(978-0-531-12473-4(8),* Children's Pr.) Scholastic Library Publishing.
Weather: Individual Title Six-Packs. (Chiquilibros Ser.). (gr. k-1). 23.00 *(978-0-7635-0416-8(5))* Rigby Education.
Weather & Seasons Classroom Library. (gr. k-2). lib. bdg. 128.95 *(978-0-7368-1828-5(6))* Red Brick Learning.
Weather & Seasons Complete Program. (gr. k-2). 642.95 *(978-0-7368-1829-2(4))* Red Brick Learning.
Weather Facts. 2004. (Pocket Guides). 160p. (J). pap. 6.95 *(978-0-328-09817-0(5),* Scott Foresman) Addison Wesley Schl.

W X Y Z

Weather Instructional Guide. 2009. (Grade 8: Science Exit Project Kits Ser.). spiral bd. *(978-1-4042-4024-7(1),* Rosen Classroom) Rosen Publishing Group, Inc., The.

Weather Report. 2012. (Collins Big Cat Ser.). (ENG., Illus.). 16p. (J). pap., wbk. ed. 4.99 *(978-0-00-747290-1(0))* HarperCollins Pubs. Ltd. GBR. Dist: Independent Pubs. Group.

The Weather Report. 2017. (Weather Report). 32p. (gr. 3-3). pap. 63.12 ***(978-0-7660-9036-1(1))***; lib. bdg. 151.62 ***(978-0-7660-9035-4(3))*** Enslow Pubs., Inc.

Weather Sets: 1 Each of 3 Big Books. (Sunshinetm Science Ser.). (gr. 1-2). *(978-0-7802-1451-4(X))* Wright Group/McGraw-Hill.

Weather Sets: 1 Each of 3 Student Books. (Sunshinetm Science Ser.). (gr. 1-2). 20.95 *(978-0-7802-1753-9(5))* Wright Group/McGraw-Hill.

Weather Update [Kaplan]. 2010. (Weather Update Ser.). pap. 41.70 *(978-1-4296-5972-7(6),* Bridgestone Bks.) Capstone Press of Coughlan Cos.

Weather Watching: Level P, 6 vols., Vol. 3. (Explorers Ser.). 32p. (gr. 3-6). 44.95 *(978-0-7699-0618-8(4))* Shortland Pubns. (U. S. A.) Inc.

West, David & Parker, Steve. Natural Disasters. 2011. (ENG., Illus.). 32p. (J). pap. *(978-0-7787-7579-9(8))*; pap. *(978-0-7787-7581-2(X))*; lib. bdg. *(978-0-7787-7576-8(3))* Crabtree Publishing Co.

Wetterer, Margaret K. & Wetterer, Charles M. Caminando Bajo la Nieve; the Snow Walker. 2008. pap. 40.95 *(978-0-8225-9699-8(7))* Lerner Publishing Group.

What a Week!, 6 packs. (gr. -1-2). 23.00 *(978-0-7635-9010-9(X))* Rigby Education.

What Do You Know about Weather & Climate? 2013. (20 Questions: Earth Science Ser.). 24p. (J). (gr. 3-6). pap. 49.50 *(978-1-4488-9861-9(7),* PowerKids Pr.) Rosen Publishing Group, Inc., The.

What Kind of Day Is It?, Vol. 2. 2005. (Our Seasons & Weather Ser.). (YA). (gr. k-3). 178.20 *(978-0-7368-4199-3(7),* Pebble Bks.) Capstone Press of Coughlan Cos.

What's the Weather? 2013. (What's the Weather? Ser.). 24p. (J). (gr. k-2). 135.60 *(978-1-4339-9669-6(3))*; pap. 293.40 *(978-1-4339-9840-9(8))*; pap. 48.90 *(978-1-4339-9839-3(4))* Stevens, Gareth Publishing LLLP.

What's the Weather? / Qu Tiempo Hace? 2013. (What's the Weather? / Qu Tiempo Hace? Ser.). (SPA.). 24p. (J). (gr. k-2). 135.60 *(978-1-4339-9670-2(7))* Stevens, Gareth Publishing LLLP.

What's the Weather Like? 2016. (What's the Weather Like? Ser.). 24p. (gr. 1-1). 118.00 *(978-1-4994-2429-4(9))*; pap. 41.25 *(978-1-4994-2493-5(0))* Rosen Publishing Group, Inc., The. (PowerKids Pr.).

Wilder, Nellie. Changing Weather, 1 vol. (Science Readers: Content & Literacy Ser.). (ENG., Illus.). 24p. (gr. k-k). 2015. (J). 22.96 *(978-1-4938-1141-0(X))* 2014. pap. 8.99 *(978-1-4807-4531-5(6))* Teacher Created Materials, Inc.

—What Is the Weather?, 1 vol. (Science Readers: Content & Literacy Ser.). (ENG., Illus.). 24p. (gr. k-k). 2015. pap. 22.96 *(978-1-4938-1140-3(1))* 2014. pap. 8.99 *(978-1-4807-4530-8(8))* Teacher Created Materials, Inc.

Williams, Judith. Does the Sun Make Weather? 2015. (How Does Weather Happen? Ser.). 24p. (J). (gr. k-3). pap. 7.95 *(978-0-7660-6396-9(8))*; lib. bdg. 22.60 *(978-0-7660-6395-2(X))* Enslow Pubs., Inc. (Enslow Elementary).

—How Does the Sun Make Weather? 2005. (I Like Weather! Ser.). (Illus.). 24p. (J). lib. bdg. 22.60 *(978-0-7660-2317-8(6),* Enslow Elementary) Enslow Pubs., Inc.

Williams, Zella. Experiments on the Weather. (Do-It-Yourself Science Ser.). 24p. (gr. 2-3). 2009. 47.90 *(978-1-61512-188-5(9),* PowerKids Pr.) 2007. (Illus.). (J). lib. bdg. 25.25 *(978-1-4042-3663-9(5))* Rosen Publishing Group, Inc., The.

Woods, Michael. Droughts. 2009. pap. 8.95 *(978-0-8225-6864-3(0))* Lerner Publishing Group.

Workman, James G. Water. 2009. (Diminishing Resources Ser.). 111p. (J). lib. bdg. 28.95 *(978-1-59935-115-5(3))* Reynolds, Morgan Inc.

World Book, Inc Staff, contrib. by. Droughts. 2nd ed. 2009. (Illus.). 47p. (J). *(978-0-7166-9819-7(6))* World Bk., Inc.

—Forces of Nature. 2007. (J). *(978-0-7166-9806-7(4))* World Bk., Inc.

—Learning about Weather. 2011. (J). *(978-0-7166-0235-4(0))* World Bk., Inc.

—Weather. 2007. (J). *(978-0-7166-7732-1(6))* World Bk., Inc.

—Weather & Climate Change. 2015. (Illus.). 47p. (J). *(978-0-7166-2707-4(8))* World Bk., Inc.

Wynne, Patricia J. & Silver, Donald M. My First Book about Weather. 2016. (Dover Children's Science Bks.). (ENG.). 48p. (J). (gr. 3-6). pap. 4.99 *(978-0-486-79872-1(0))* Dover Pubns., Inc.

Zoehfeld, Kathleen Weidner. School of Dragons #3: Storm Approaching! (DreamWorks Dragons) Random House, illus. 2017. (ENG.). 80p. (J). (gr. 2-5). pap. 7.99 *(978-1-101-93343-5(7),* Random Hse. Bks. for Young Readers) Random Hse. Children's Bks.

Zuchora-Walske, Christine. The Dust Bowl: A History Perspectives Book. 2013. (Perspectives Library). (ENG., Illus.). 32p. (J). (gr. 4-8). 28.50 *(978-1-62431-417-9(1),* 202788); pap. 14.21 *(978-1-62431-493-3(7),* 202790) Cherry Lake Publishing.

—Weather Robots. 2014. (Lightning Bolt Books Robots Everywhere! Ser.). (Illus.). 32p. (gr. k-2). pap. 7.95 *(978-1-4677-4511-6(1))* Lerner Publishing Group.

100 Facts You Should Know: Set 3. 2015. (100 Facts You Should Know Ser.). (ENG.). 48p. (J). (gr. 4-5). 191.70 *(978-1-4824-2564-2(5))* Stevens, Gareth Publishing LLLP.

WEATHER—FICTION

Anaya, Rudolfo A. & Anaya, Rudolfo. The First Tortilla: A Bilingual Story. Lamadrid, Enrique R., tr. from ENG. Córdova, Amy, illus. 2007. (SPA & ENG.). 32p. (J). (gr. 4-7). 16.95 *(978-0-8263-4214-0(0))* Univ. of New Mexico Pr.

Bailey, Dawn Wentz. Joey & the Mighty Oak. 2008. 20p. pap. 24.95 *(978-1-60813-377-2(X))* PublishAmerica, Inc.

Barclay, Jane. How Cold Was It? 2004. (Illus.). (J). (gr. k-3). spiral bd. *(978-0-616-01538-4(0))* Canadian National Institute for the Blind/Institut National Canadien pour les Aveugles.

—How Cold Was It? Donato, Janice, illus. 2004. (J). (gr. k-3). spiral bd. *(978-0-616-11862-7(7))* Canadian National Institute for the Blind/Institut National Canadien pour les Aveugles.

Barrett, Judi. Cloudy with a Chance of Meatballs. Barrett, Ronald, illus. 2012. (ENG.). 32p. (J). (gr. -1-3). pap. 9.99 *(978-1-4424-4337-2(5),* Little Simon) Little Simon.

—Cloudy with a Chance of Meatballs. Barrett, Ron, illus. 2011. (Classic Board Bks.). (ENG.). 34p. (J). (gr. -1-k). bds. 7.99 *(978-1-4424-3023-5(0),* Little Simon) Little Simon.

—Cloudy with a Chance of Meatballs. Barrett, Ron, illus. 2009. 9.00 *(978-1-55744-455-4(2),* Everbind) Marco Bk. Co.

—Cloudy with a Chance of Meatballs 3: Planet of the Pies. Mones, Isidre, illus. 2013. (ENG.). 32p. (J). (gr. -1-3). 17.99 *(978-1-4424-9027-7(6),* Atheneum Bks. for Young Readers) Simon & Schuster Children's Publishing.

—Cloudy with a Chance of Meatballs Collection: Cloudy with a Chance of Meatballs; Pickles to Pittsburgh - Cloudy with a Chance of Meatballs 3. Barrett, Ron, illus. 2016. (ENG.). 96p. (J). (gr. -1-3). 53.99 *(978-1-4814-9890-6(8),* Atheneum/Caitlyn Dlouhy Books) Simon & Schuster Children's Publishing.

—Pickles to Pittsburgh: Cloudy with a Chance of Meatballs 2. Barrett, Ronald, illus. (Classic Board Bks.). (ENG.). (J). (gr. -1-k). 2013. 34p. bds. 7.99 *(978-1-4424-6493-3(3))* 2012. 32p. pap. 9.99 *(978-1-4424-4459-1(2))* Little Simon. (Little Simon).

—Pickles to Pittsburgh: The Sequel to Cloudy with a Chance of Meatballs. Barrett, Ron, illus. 2004. 26p. (gr. -1-3). 17.00 *(978-0-7569-4215-1(2))* Perfection Learning Corp.

Batson, Susann. Scaredy: A Cloud Afraid of Thunder. 2010. 16p. pap. 9.95 *(978-1-61633-053-8(8))* Guardian Angel Publishing, Inc.

Bauer, Marion Dane. If Frogs Made the Weather. Donohue, Dorothy, illus. 2005. (ENG.). 32p. (J). 16.95 *(978-0-8234-1622-6(4))* Holiday Hse., Inc.

Becker, Brooke. The Adventures of Sammy Snowflake, Vol. 1. Gentry, Kyle, illus. 2007. (ENG.). 64p. (gr. 4-7). 19.95 *(978-0-9795260-0-8(0))* Courtyard Publishing, LLC.

Bishop, Celeste. Hace Sol / It's Sunny. 2016. (¿Qué Tiempo Hace? / What's the Weather Like? Ser.). (ENG & SPA., Illus.). 24p. (J). (gr. 1-1). lib. bdg. 23.60 *(978-1-4994-2330-3(6),* PowerKids Pr.) Rosen Publishing Group, Inc., The.

—Hace Sol (It's Sunny) 2016. (¿Qué Tiempo Hace? (What's the Weather Like?) Ser.). (ENG & SPA., Illus.). 24p. (J). (gr. 1-1). lib. bdg. 23.60 *(978-1-4994-2326-6(8),* PowerKids Pr.) Rosen Publishing Group, Inc., The.

—Hace Viento / It's Windy. 2016. (¿Qué Tiempo Hace? / What's the Weather Like? Ser.). (ENG & SPA., Illus.). 24p. (J). (gr. 1-1). lib. bdg. 23.60 *(978-1-4994-2337-2(3),* PowerKids Pr.) Rosen Publishing Group, Inc., The.

—Hace Viento (It's Windy) 2016. (¿Qué Tiempo Hace? (What's the Weather Like?) Ser.). (ENG & SPA., Illus.). 24p. (J). (gr. 1-1). lib. bdg. 23.60 *(978-1-4994-2333-4(0),* PowerKids Pr.) Rosen Publishing Group, Inc., The.

—It's Sunny. 2016. (What's the Weather Like? Ser.). 24p. (gr. 1-1). pap. 8.25 *(978-1-4994-2359-4(4),* PowerKids Pr.) Rosen Publishing Group, Inc., The.

Blackstone, Stella & Meza-Riedewald, Leticia. Oso Bajo el Sol. Harter, Debbie, illus. 2009. (SPA & ENG.). 24p. (J). (gr. -1-1). pap. 6.99 *(978-1-84686-389-9(9))* Barefoot Bks., Inc.

Bloom, Jan. You Track it Weather Lab. Free Jenna Staff, ed. 2010. 12p. mass mkt. 14.99 *(978-1-60380-087-7(5))* becker&mayer! books.

Blotnick, Elihu. The Fog Line. Robinson, Barbara J., illus. 2009. (Mr. Blot Ser.: No. 3). (ENG.). 56p. (YA). (gr. 6-18). pap. 9.00 *(978-0-915090-12-9(0),* California Street) Firefall Editions.

Bolton, Nicola Joanne. The WeatherGens. 2010. (ENG.). 89p. pap. 10.50 *(978-1-4452-7936-7(3))* Lulu Pr., Inc.

Bonnell, Kris. Clouds Tell the Weather. 2007. (J). pap. 5.95 *(978-1-933727-47-9(0))* Reading Reading Bks., LLC.

Cameron, Anne. The Lightning Catcher. Jamieson, Victoria, illus. 2075. (Lightning Catcher Ser.). (ENG.). 368p. (J). (gr. 3-7). 7.99 *(978-0-06-211277-4(5),* Greenwillow Bks.) HarperCollins Pubs.

—Secrets of the Storm Vortex. Jamieson, Victoria, illus. 2015. (Lightning Catcher Ser.: 3). (ENG.). 464p. (J). (gr. 3-7). 16.99 *(978-0-06-211283-5(X),* Greenwillow Bks.) HarperCollins Pubs.

—The Storm Tower Thief. Jamieson, Victoria, illus. 2014. (Lightning Catcher Ser.: 2). (ENG.). 432p. (J). (gr. 3-7). 16.99 *(978-0-06-211279-8(1),* Greenwillow Bks.) HarperCollins Pubs.

Celano, June. Dripsy the Cloud. 2008. 28p. per. 24.95 *(978-1-4241-9958-7(1))* America Star Bks.

Cole, Joanna. The Magic School Bus & the Climate Challenge. Degen, Bruce, illus. 2010. (Magic School Bus Ser.). (ENG.). 48p. (J). (gr. 2-5). 16.99 *(978-0-590-10826-3(3),* Scholastic Pr.) Scholastic, Inc.

Conway, David. Lila & the Secret of Rain. Daly, Jude, illus. 2011. (ENG.). 32p. (J). (gr. k-3). pap. 8.95 *(978-1-84780-035-0(1),* Frances Lincoln) Quarto Publishing Group UK GBR. Dist: Hachette Bk. Group.

Costa, Nicoletta. Olga the Cloud. Costa, Nicoletta, illus. 2014. (ENG., Illus.). 32p. (J). (gr. -1-k). 16.95 *(978-0-8234-3051-2(0))* Holiday Hse., Inc.

Cottrell, Kim. Jimmy Has the Bugaloo Zoo Flu. 2009. 32p. pap. 12.99 *(978-1-4389-5209-3(0))* AuthorHouse.

Cousins, Lucy. Maisy's Wonderful Weather Book. Cousins, Lucy, illus. 2006. (Maisy Ser.). (ENG., Illus.). 14p. (J). (gr. -1). 11.99 *(978-0-7636-2987-8(1))* Candlewick Pr.

Crews, Donald. Cloudy Day Sunny Day. 2010. (Rise & Shine Ser.). (ENG., Illus.). 24p. (J). (gr. -1-3). pap. 6.95 *(978-0-15-204850-1(2))* National Geographic School Publishing, Inc.

—Cloudy Day Sunny Day. 2003. (Green Light Readers — Level 1 Ser.). (J). (gr. -1-2). 13.50 *(978-0-613-62277-6(4),* Turtleback) Turtleback Bks.

Crowder, Melanie. Parched. 2013. (ENG.). 160p. (J). (gr. 5-7). 15.99 *(978-0-547-97651-8(8))* Houghton Mifflin Harcourt Publishing Co.

Darlison, Aleesah. Ellabeth's Light Cancelled. Brailsford, Jill, illus. 2017. (Unicorn Riders Ser.). (ENG.). 112p. (gr. 3-5). pap. 5.95 *(978-1-4795-6559-7(6))* Picture Window Bks.

Dean, Janice. Freddy the Frogcaster. 2013. (Freddy the Frogcaster Ser.). (ENG., Illus.). 40p. (J). (gr. -1-3). 16.99 *(978-1-62157-084-4(3),* Regnery Kids) Regnery Publishing, Inc., An Eagle Publishing Co.

—Freddy the Frogcaster & the Big Blizzard. 2014. (Freddy the Frogcaster Ser.). (ENG., Illus.). 40p. (J). (gr. -1-3). 16.99 *(978-1-62157-254-1(4),* Regnery Kids) Regnery Publishing, Inc., An Eagle Publishing Co.

Deutsch, Stacia, adapted by. Cloudy with a Chance of Meatballs 2 Movie Novelization. 2013. (Cloudy with a Chance of Meatballs Movie Ser.). (ENG., Illus.). 128p. (J). (gr. 3-7). pap. 5.99 *(978-1-4424-9551-7(0),* Simon Spotlight) Simon Spotlight.

Doherty, Ellen. Mondo & Gordo Weather the Storm: Set Of 6. 2010. (Early Connections Ser.). (J). pap. 39.00 net. *(978-1-4108-1556-9(0))* Benchmark Education Co.

Durant, Alan & Lucas, Kath. Bird Flies South. 2005. (Illus.). 32p. (J). lib. bdg. 9.00 *(978-1-4242-0888-3(2))* Fitzgerald Bks.

Ellis, Melody A. An Unexpected Hero. 2009. 48p. pap. 16.95 *(978-1-60749-834-6(0))* America Star Bks.

Enderle, Dotti. Crosswire. 2010. (ENG.). 144p. (J). (gr. 4-6). 17.95 *(978-1-59078-751-9(X),* Calkins Creek) Boyds Mills Pr.

Etherly, L. D. Winter Arrives This Summer. 2012. 34p. pap. 12.95 *(978-0-9833877-1-8(0))* Inkspil Publishing.

Evans, Catrin & Evans, Guto. Peiriant y Tywydd. 2005. (WEL., Illus.). 36p. *(978-0-86243-412-0(2))* Y Lolfa.

Falcon, David. Weather or Not? LaGrange, Tiffany, illus. 2009. 28p. pap. 12.95 *(978-1-936051-24-3(9))* Peppertree Pr., The.

Fox, Alex. Windsock Wesley & His Wild & Wonderful Weather MacHine, Living in Cloud. Bazzoni, Lainie M. A., illus. 2010. 48p. pap. 16.50 *(978-1-60911-873-0(1),* Eloquent Bks.) Strategic Book Publishing & Rights Agency (SBPRA).

Fox, Diane. Rain or Shine. Fox, Christyan, illus. 2013. (ENG.). 20p. (J). (gr. -1-k). pap. 9.99 *(978-1-4083-1613-9(7))* Hodder & Stoughton GBR. Dist: Hachette Bk. Group.

Furgang, Kathy. Unlucky Stanley & Stanley no tiene Suerte: 6 English, 6 Spanish Adaptations. 2011. (ENG & SPA.). (J). 75.00 net. *(978-1-4108-5633-3(X))* Benchmark Education Co.

Galloway, Emily Ledford. Nimby the Cloud. 2008. 32p. pap. 24.95 *(978-1-60441-779-1(X))* America Star Bks.

Garcia, Kami & Stohl, Margaret. Beautiful Chaos. (Beautiful Creatures Ser.: 3). (ENG.). 528p. (YA). (gr. 7-17). 2012. pap. 13.99 *(978-0-316-12351-8(X))* 2011. 18.99 *(978-0-316-12352-5(8))* Little, Brown Bks. for Young Readers.

George, Kallie. Fall. Graegin, Stephanie, illus. 2017. (Heartwood Hotel Ser.). (ENG.). 176p. (J). (gr. 2-5). 14.99 ***(978-1-4847-3161-1(1))*** Disney Pr.

George, Olivia. The Weather. Fletcher, Rusty, illus. 2005. (My First Reader Ser.). (ENG.). 32p. (J). (gr. k-1). lib. bdg. 18.50 *(978-0-516-24880-6(4),* Children's Pr.) Scholastic Library Publishing.

Gliori, Debi. Little Bear & the Wish Fish. (Illus.). 32p. (J). (gr. -1-2). pap. *(978-0-7112-0986-2(3))* ReiseArt Buchhandlung GmbH.

Graves, Kassie. Brave Little Sailboat. Graves, Kassie, illus. 2003. (Illus.). 20p. (J). 14.95 *(978-0-9728019-0-4(1))* Bright Eyes Pr.

Gray, P. J. The Lab Book 3, 1 vol. 2015. (Trippin' Ser.). (ENG.). 64p. (YA). (gr. 9-12). pap. 8.95 *(978-1-62250-933-1(1))* Saddleback Educational Publishing, Inc.

Hammond, Rebecca. Winds Cove. 2004. 248p. (YA). pap. 6.99 *(978-1-932307-00-9(1),* Ambassador-Emerald, International) Emerald Hse. Group, Inc.

Harper, Jamie. Miss Mingo Weathers the Storm. Harper, Jamie, illus. (ENG., Illus.). 40p. (J). (gr. -1-3). 2017. 6.99 ***(978-0-7636-9514-9(9))*** 2012. 15.99 *(978-0-7636-4931-9(7))* Candlewick Pr.

Horácek, Petr. A Surprise for Tiny Mouse. Horácek, Petr, illus. 2015. (ENG., Illus.). 16p. (J). (— 1). bds. 8.99 *(978-0-7636-7967-5(4))* Candlewick Pr.

Hoshino, Felicia. Sora & the Cloud. 2012. (JPN & ENG., Illus.). 36p. (J). (gr. -1-3). 15.95 *(978-1-59702-027-5(3))* Immedium.

Howell. Wesley-Hampton Academy - The Weatherman. 2008. 179p. 28.29 *(978-0-615-15346-9(1))* Howell, Steven.

Hughes, Shirley. Alfie Weather. Hughes, Shirley, illus. 2007. (Alfie Ser.). (ENG., Illus.). 48p. (J). (gr. -1-k). pap. 9.99 *(978-0-09-940425-5(7),* Red Fox) Random House Children's Books GBR. Dist: Independent Pubs. Group.

Jackson, Richard. This Beautiful Day. Lee, Suzy, illus. 2017. (ENG.). 40p. (J). (gr. -1-3). 15.99 ***(978-1-4814-4139-1(6),*** Atheneum/Caitlyn Dlouhy Books) Simon & Schuster Children's Publishing.

Jansson, Tove & Jansson, Lars. Moomin & the Comet. 2013. (Moomin Stories Ser.). (J). lib. bdg. 20.80 *(978-0-606-31881-5(X),* Turtleback) Turtleback Bks.

Johnston, Tony. Winter Is Coming. LaMarche, Jim, illus. 2014. (ENG.). 40p. (J). (gr. -1-3). 17.99 *(978-1-4424-7251-8(0),* Simon & Schuster Bks. For Young Readers) Simon & Schuster Bks. For Young Readers.

Kapai, Tommy. Cuzzies Find the Rainbow's End. Henry, Mike, illus. 2004. (Cuzzies Adventures Ser.). (MAO & ENG.). 32p. (J). (gr. -1-3). pap. 9.00 *(978-0-9582517-0-9(3),* Kina) Huia Pubs. NZL. Dist: Univ. of Hawaii Pr.

Kaplan, Madeline. Planet Earth Gets Well. 2008. (ENG.). 24p. pap. 9.99 *(978-1-4196-8986-4(X))* CreateSpace Independent Publishing Platform.

Knowles, Kent. Lucius & the Storm. Knowles, Kent, illus. 2007. (Illus.). 32p. (J). (gr. -1-3). 15.95 *(978-1-60108-005-9(0))* Red Cygnet Pr.

Korba, Joanne. Wild Weather. 2005. (J). pap. *(978-1-4108-4218-3(5))* Benchmark Education Co.

Leblanc, Louise. Leo's Skiing Surprise. Prud'homme, Jules, illus. 2007. (Formac First Novels Ser.). (ENG.). 64p. (J). (gr. 2-5). 14.95 *(978-0-88780-738-1(0),* 9780887807381) Formac Publishing Co., Ltd. CAN. Dist: Casemate Pubs. & Bk. Distributors, LLC.

—Leo's Skiing Surprise, 1 vol. Cummins, Sarah, tr. from FRE. Prud'homme, Jules, illus. 2007. (Formac First Novels Ser.). (ENG.). 64p. (J). (gr. 2-5). 4.95 *(978-0-88780-736-7(4),* 9780887807367) Formac Publishing Co., Ltd. CAN. Dist: Casemate Pubs. & Bk. Distributors, LLC.

Lin, Grace. Ling & Ting: Together in All Weather. 2015. (ENG., Illus.). 48p. (J). (gr. 1-4). 16.00 *(978-0-316-33549-2(5))* Little Brown & Co.

—Ling & Ting: Together in All Weather. 2016. (ENG.). 48p. (J). (gr. 1-4). pap. 4.99 *(978-0-316-33548-5(7))* Little, Brown Bks. for Young Readers.

Look Out the Window: Individual Title Six-Packs. (Story Steps Ser.). (gr. k-2). 29.00 *(978-0-7635-9587-6(X))* Rigby Education.

Maddox, Jake. Blizzard! A Survive! Story, 1 vol. Tiffany, Sean, illus. 2009. (Jake Maddox Sports Stories Ser.). (ENG.). 72p. (gr. 2-3). 25.32 *(978-1-4342-1206-1(8))* Stone Arch Bks.

Mae, Darcie. Sammy & Robert Go Home for the Holidays. 2011. 44p. pap. 24.95 *(978-1-4560-5702-2(2))* America Star Bks.

Malavolti, Angela. You Are a Twisting Tornado. Stiffler, Michael, illus. 2011. 28p. (J). 16.99 *(978-0-9834092-0-5(X))* Jungle Wagon Pr.

Marshall, Rita. Wake up, Weather! Felix, Monique, illus. 2016. (ENG.). 14p. (J). (gr. -1-k). bds. 8.99 *(978-1-56846-286-8(7),* Creative Editions) Creative Co., The.

Mason, Mike. The Blue Umbrella. 2009. (ENG.). 448p. (YA). pap. 10.99 *(978-1-4347-6526-0(1))* Cook, David C.

May, Eleanor. Let's Go, Snow! Pillo, Cary, illus. 2017. (Math Matters (r) Ser.). (ENG.). 32p. (J). (gr. k-3). pap. 5.95 *(978-1-57565-807-0(0))* Kane Press, Inc.

McKee, David. Elmer's Weather. 2010. (Elmer Ser.). (ENG & POL., Illus.). 16p. (J). (gr. k — 1). 8.95 *(978-1-84059-534-5(5))* Milet Publishing.

—Elmer's Weather (Il Tempo di Elmer) Umicini, Roberta, tr. 2004. (Elmer Ser.). (ENG & ITA., Illus.). 14p. (J). (gr. -1). bds. 8.95 *(978-1-84059-405-8(5))* Milet Publishing.

McNeely, Marian Hurd. The Jumping-off Place. Siegel, William, illus. 2008. 321p. (J). 15.95 *(978-0-9798940-4-6(2),* South Dakota State Historical Society Pr.) South Dakota State Historical Society Pr.

Meadows, Daisy. A Fairy Ballet. 2011. (Scholastic Reader, Level 2 Ser.). (ENG.). 32p. (J). (gr. 1-3). pap. 3.99 *(978-0-545-22294-5(X),* Cartwheel Bks.) Scholastic, Inc.

—Hayley the Rain Fairy. 2007. (Rainbow Magic — the Weather Fairies Ser.: 7). (Orig.). lib. bdg. 14.75 *(978-1-4177-7082-3(1),* Turtleback) Turtleback Bks.

Milz, Cynthia A. Waiting for the Last Leaf to Fall. 2008. 20p. per. 24.95 *(978-1-4241-8965-6(9))* America Star Bks.

Montes, Hugo & Montes, Michelle. Young Eagles Armor Academy: Caught in the Storm, V02. 2010. 76p. (J). pap. 5.99 *(978-1-60683-022-2(8))* Harrison House Pubs.

Morrison, Toni & Morrison, Slade. Little Cloud & Lady Wind. Qualls, Sean, illus. 2010. (ENG.). 32p. (J). pap. 7.99 *(978-1-4169-8524-2(7),* Simon & Schuster Bks. For Young Readers) Simon & Schuster Bks. For Young Readers.

—Little Cloud & Lady Wind. Qualls, Sean, illus. 2010. (ENG.). 32p. (J). (gr. -1-3). 16.99 *(978-1-4169-8523-5(9),* Simon & Schuster/Paula Wiseman Bks.) Simon & Schuster/Paula Wiseman Bks.

Narayanan, Manjula. The Grey Grey Cloud. 2010. (Illus.). 32p. pap. 14.49 *(978-1-4490-8507-0(5))* AuthorHouse.

The North Pole Is Sinking! 2005. (J). 9.99 *(978-0-9773674-0-5(1))* Blue State Pr.

Parker, Emma. What Will the Weather Be Today? 2010. (Illus.). pap. *(978-1-877547-90-4(5))* First Edition Ltd.

Parry, Jo. Rainbow Fairies. 2009. (Wow! Bks.). (Illus.). (J). bds. 12.99 *(978-1-934650-25-7(0))* Just For Kids Pr., LLC.

Passey, Marion. Sneezles & Wheezles. Harston, Jerry, illus. 2006. 32p. (J). (gr. -1-3). 15.99 *(978-1-55517-912-0(6))* Cedar Fort, Inc./CFI Distribution.

Pearson, Henrik Barkley de. The Secret of the Rainbow. 2011. 92p. pap. 51.99 *(978-1-4568-1291-1(2))* Xlibris Corp.

Peyo. Smurfs Mini Library: Rise & Shine; Happy Smurfdays; Fun & Games; Making Music; Whatever the Weather. Peyo, illus. 2014. (Smurfs Classic Ser.). (ENG., Illus.). 70p. (J). (gr. -1-2). bds. 6.99 *(978-1-4424-9543-2(X),* Simon Spotlight) Simon Spotlight.

Peysin, Shainy. Whatever the Weather. Rosenfeld, Dina & Leverton, Yossi, eds. Owens, Emily, illus. 2011. 32p. (J). 12.95 *(978-1-929628-56-8(0))* Hachai Publishing.

Phinney, Patty McCoy. Makayla's Rainbow. 2011. 94p. pap. 19.95 *(978-1-4560-7529-3(2))* America Star Bks.

Priddy, Roger. Little Friends: Let's Play. 2014. (Little Friends Ser.). (ENG., Illus.). 8p. (J). (gr. -1 — 1). bds. 8.99 *(978-0-312-51683-3(5),* 9780312516833, Priddy Bks.) St. Martin's Pr.

Quarto Generic Staff. Under the Weather: Stories about Climate Change. Bradman, Tony, ed. 2012. (ENG.). 224p. (J). (gr. 5-8). pap. 8.99 *(978-1-84507-944-4(2),* Frances Lincoln) Quarto Publishing Group UK GBR. Dist: Hachette Bk. Group.

Quinlan, Nigel. The Weatherman. 2015. (ENG.). 320p. (J). (gr. 4-7). 16.99 *(978-1-62672-033-6(9),* 9781626720336) Roaring Brook Pr.

Randolph, Joanne. Stormy: A Storm Cloud's Story. 2009. (Nature Stories Ser.). (Illus.). 24p. (J). (gr. -1-2). pap. 8.15 *(978-1-60754-093-9(2))*; lib. bdg. 22.60 *(978-1-60754-092-2(4))* Windmill Bks.

Ras. Oh No, the Leaves Are Moving! 2011. 24p. pap. 15.99 *(978-1-4568-5030-2(X))* Xlibris Corp.

Rice, Dona. What Kind of Weather?, 1 vol. 2009. (Early Childhood Themes Ser.). (ENG., Illus.). 16p. (J). (gr. -1-2). pap. 19.99 *(978-1-4333-1459-9(2))* Shell Educational Publishing.

Rice, Karen. The Forbidden Sneeze. 2011. 28p. pap. 24.95 *(978-1-4626-3488-0(5))* America Star Bks.

Rider, Cynthia. The Muddy Puddle, 1 vol. Evans, Nicola, illus. 2013. (Start Reading Ser.). (ENG.). 24p. (gr. k-1). pap. 7.95 *(978-1-4765-3195-3(1))*; pap. 41.94 *(978-1-4765-3224-0(9))* Capstone Press of Coughlan Cos.

—A Sunny Day. Evans, Nicola, illus. 2013. (Start Reading Ser.). (ENG.). 24p. (gr. k-1). pap. 41.94 *(978-1-4765-3233-2(8))*; pap. 7.95 *(978-1-4765-3197-7(8))* Capstone Press of Coughlan Cos.

Ross, Fiona. Chilly Milly Moo. 2011. (ENG., Illus.). 32p. (J). (gr. -1-2). 15.99 *(978-0-7636-5693-5(3))* Candlewick Pr.

Ross, Tony. El Tiempo. 2006. (Little Princess Ser.).Tr. of Weather. (SPA.). (J). (gr. -1-k). bds. 7.95 *(978-968-19-1487-5(2),* AT33281) Lectorum Pubns., Inc.

Ruckman, Ivy. Night of the Twisters. 2003. (Trophy Bk.). (ENG.). 160p. (J). (gr. 3-6). reprint ed. pap. 7.99 *(978-0-06-440176-0(6))* HarperCollins Pubs.

Rudolph, Miriam. A Frozen Dream. 2009. 28p. pap. 12.00 (978-1-60693-962-8(9), Eloquent Bks.) Strategic Book Publishing & Rights Agency (SBPRA).

Ruffenach, Jessie, ed. Baby Learns about Weather. Thomas, Peter, tr. from ENG. Blacksheep, Beverly, illus. 2005. (NAV & ENG.). 16p. (J). (gr. 4-7). 7.95 (978-1-893354-62-3(8)) Salina Bookshelf Inc.

Rylant, Cynthia. Gooseberry Park & the Master Plan. Howard, Arthur, illus. 2015. (ENG.). 128p. (J). (gr. 3-7). 16.99 (978-1-4814-0449-5(0), Beach Lane Bks.) Beach Lane Bks.

Schirmer, Jodi L. It Is a Good Day: Clay. 2009. 23p. (J). pap. 11.95 (978-1-4327-4018-4(0)) Outskirts Pr., Inc.

Smith, Gloria. Annie Elf & Bo Bo Robin. 2012. 24p. 24.95 (978-1-62709-650-8(7)) America Star Bks.

Smith, Jennifer E. The Storm Makers. Helquist, Brett, illus. 2013. (ENG.). 384p. (J). (gr. 3-7). pap. 8.00 (978-0-316-17959-1(0)) Little, Brown Bks. for Young Readers.

Spinelli, Eileen. Cold Snap. Priceman, Marjorie, illus. 2012. (ENG.). 40p. (J). (gr. k-3). 17.99 (978-0-375-85700-3(1), Knopf Bks. for Young Readers) Random Hse. Children's Bks.

Stout, Shawn K. Fiona Finkelstein, Big-Time Ballerina!! Martini, Angela, illus. 2010. (ENG.). 192p. (J). pap. 4.99 (978-1-4169-7109-2(2), Simon & Schuster/Paula Wiseman Bks.) Simon & Schuster/Paula Wiseman Bks.

Thompson, Chad. The Itsy Bitsy Spider, 1 vol. 2009. (Early Childhood Themes Ser.). (ENG., Illus.). 16p. (J). (gr. -1-2). pap. 19.99 (978-1-4333-1455-1(X)) Shell Educational Publishing.

Thompson, Kate. Switchers. 220p. (J). (gr. 4-7). pap. 5.99 (978-0-8072-1553-1(8)); 2004. (Switchers Ser.: Vol. 1). (gr. 5-9). pap. 38.00 incl. audio (978-0-8072-8138-3(7), YA115SP) Random Hse. Audio Publishing Group. (Listening Library).

Vischer, Frans. A Very Fuddles Christmas. Vischer, Frans, illus. 2013. (ENG., Illus.). 32p. (J). (gr. -1-2). 15.99 (978-1-4169-9156-4(5), Aladdin) Simon & Schuster Children's Publishing.

Voake, Steve. Daisy Dawson on the Farm. Meserve, Jessica, illus. 2013. (Daisy Dawson Ser.). (ENG.). 96p. (J). (gr. 1-4). pap. 5.99 (978-0-7636-6340-7(9)) Candlewick Pr.

Voght, Victor A. Fun with Huff & Puff, 1 vol. 2009. 15p. pap. 24.95 (978-1-60749-853-7(7)) America Star Bks.

Warren, Jordan L. Jo's Rainy Sad Day. 2011. 28p. pap. 15.99 (978-1-4568-4161-4(0)) Xlibris Corp.

White, Carolyn. Snowff & the Rowdy-Cloudy Bunch. 2006. (Snowff the Snowflake Kid Adventure Ser.). (J). 24.95 (978-1-893563-05-6(7)) AARO Publishing.

—Snowff Visits Razorteeth Village. 2006. (Illus.). 72p. (J). 24.95 (978-1-893563-10-0(3)) AARO Publishing.

—Snowff's MIST.erious Journey (Snowff the Snowflake Kid Adventure, 1) 2006. (J). 24.95 (978-1-893563-00-1(6)) AARO Publishing.

White, Kathryn. Snowshoe the Hare. Rivers, Ruth, illus. 2005. (Red Go Bananas Ser.). (ENG.). 48p. (J). (gr. 2-3). lib. bdg. (978-0-7787-2677-7(0), 1253648) Crabtree Publishing Co.

Wilks, Mike. The Weather Works. Wilks, Mike, illus. 2016. (ENG., Illus.). 32p. (J). 17.95 (978-0-7649-7538-7(2)) Pomegranate Communications, Inc.

Williams, Nate & Snow, Virginia Brimhall. Spring Walk, 1 vol. 2015. (ENG., Illus.). 32p. (J). (gr. 2-3). 16.99 (978-1-4236-3879-7(4)) Gibbs Smith, Publisher.

Yaccarino, Dan. Where the Four Winds Blow. Yaccarino, Dan, illus. 2003. (Illus.). 104p. (J). 17.89 (978-0-06-623627-8(4), Cotler, Joanna Books) HarperCollins Pubs.

Yamashita, Masako. Snow Children, 1 vol. 2012. (ENG., Illus.). 32p. (J). (gr. -1-2). 17.95 (978-1-55498-144-1(1)) Groundwood Bks. CAN. Dist: Publishers Group West (PGW).

Zuchora-Walske, Christine. Weather Robots. 2014. (Lightning Bolt Books Robots Everywhere! Ser.). (ENG., Illus.). 32p. (gr. k-2). lib. bdg. 26.60 (978-1-4677-4057-9(8), Lerner Pubns.) Lerner Publishing Group.

WEATHER CONTROL

Brimner, Larry Dane. The Rain Wizard: The Amazing, Mysterious, True Life of Charles Mallory Hatfield. 2015. (ENG., Illus.). 80p. (J). (gr. 3-7). 16.95 (978-1-59078-990-2(3), Calkins Creek) Boyds Mills Pr.

WEATHER FORECASTING

And Now for the Weather! Individual Title Six-Packs. (Bookweb Ser.). 32p. (gr. 5-18). 34.00 (978-0-7635-3799-9(3)) Rigby Education.

Birch, Robin. Watching Weather. 2009. (Weather & Climate Ser.). 32p. (gr. 3). 28.50 (978-0-7614-4470-1(X)) Marshall Cavendish Corp.

Boothroyd, Jennifer. What Is a Forecast? 2014. (First Step Nonfiction - Let's Watch the Weather Ser.). 24p. (gr. k-2). (Illus.). pap. 6.95 (978-1-4677-4497-3(2)); (ENG.). lib. bdg. 23.93 (978-1-4677-3920-7(0), Lerner Pubns.) Lerner Publishing Group.

Coleman, Miriam. Using the Weather to Learn about Earth. 2015. (Earth Science Detectives Ser.). (ENG., Illus.). 24p. (J). (gr. 3-3). lib. bdg. 23.60 (978-1-4777-5958-5(1), PowerKids Pr.) Rosen Publishing Group, Inc., The.

Davies, Monika. Tracking the Weather, 1 vol. 2015. (Science Readers: Content & Literacy Ser.). (ENG., Illus.). 32p. (J). (gr. 3-3). pap. 8.99 (978-1-4807-4648-0(7)) Teacher Created Materials, Inc.

Davis, Graeme. Floods. 2012. (21st Century Skills Library: Real World Math Ser.). (ENG., Illus.). 32p. (J). (gr. 4-8). lib. bdg. 28.50 (978-1-61080-324-3(8), 201304) Cherry Lake Publishing.

Dixon, Dale. Let's Track the Storm: What Will Happen? 2017. (Computer Science for the Real World Ser.). 8p. (gr. 5-6). pap. 6.20 (**978-1-5383-5059-1(9)**, Rosen Classroom) Rosen Publishing Group, Inc., The.

Felix, Rebecca. How's the Weather in Fall? 2013. (21st Century Basic Skills Library: Let's Look at Fall Ser.). (ENG.). 24p. (J). (gr. k-3). 22.79 (978-1-61080-902-3(5), 202587); pap. 12.79 (978-1-61080-927-6(0), 202589) Cherry Lake Publishing.

—How's the Weather in Fall?/Rebecca Felix. 2013. (J). (978-1-61080-977-1(7)) Cherry Lake Publishing.

Fleisher, Paul. Doppler Radar, Satellites, & Computer Models: The Science of Weather Forecasting. 2010. (Weatherwise Ser.). (Illus.). 48p. (YA). (gr. 4-7). lib. bdg. 29.27 (978-0-8225-7535-1(3)) Lerner Publishing Group.

Franchino, Vicky. Droughts. 2012. (21st Century Skills Library: Real World Math Ser.). (ENG., Illus.). 32p. (J). (gr. 4-8). lib. bdg. 28.50 (978-1-61080-322-9(1), 201300) Cherry Lake Publishing.

Friestad, Kathleen M., et al. The Kids' Book of Weather Forecasting. Kline, Michael, illus. 2008. 160p. (J). 16.99 (978-0-8249-6822-9(0), Ideal Pubns.) Worthy Publishing.

—The Kids' Book of Weather Forecasting. Friestad, Kathleen M. & Kline, Michael, illus. 2008. (ENG.). 160p. (J). pap. 12.99 (978-0-8249-6823-6(9), Ideal Pubns.) Worthy Publishing.

Furgang, Adam. Adapting to Intense Storms. 2012. (Science to the Rescue: Adapting to Climate Change Ser.). (ENG.). 64p. (YA). (gr. 5-8). lib. bdg. 31.95 (978-1-4488-6848-3(3), Rosen Reference) Rosen Publishing Group, Inc., The.

Hirschmann, Kris. Forecasting!, 1 vol. 2008. (What's It Like Out? Ser.). (ENG.). 32p. (gr. k-6). 27.07 (978-1-59928-941-0(5), Checkerboard Library) ABDO Publishing Co.

Hoena, Blake A. If It's Really Cold... & Other Weather Predictions. 2012. (If Bks.). (ENG.). 32p. (gr. 1-2). pap. 47.70 (978-1-4296-9248-9(0), Aplus Bks.); (Illus.). pap. 8.10 (978-1-4296-9247-2(2)) Capstone Press of Coughlan Cos.

Hoyle, Geoffrey. 2011: Living in the Future. Anderson, Alasdair, illus. 2010. (ENG.). 64p. 15.95 (978-1-59583-430-0(3), 9781595834300, Darling & Co.) Laughing Elephant.

Jackson, Randy, et al. Tropical Weather Tracking Book. 2004. (YA). 7.95 (978-0-9742794-1-1(2)) HazardousWeather Preparedness Institute.

Kudlinski, Kathleen V. Boy, Were We Wrong about the Weather! Serra, Sebastià, illus. 2015. (ENG.). 32p. (J). (gr. -1-3). 16.99 (978-0-8037-3793-8(9), Dial Bks) Penguin Young Readers Group.

Lawrence, Ellen. What Is Weather? 2012. (Weather Wise Ser.). 24p. (J). (gr. -1-3). lib. bdg. 23.93 (978-1-61772-405-3(X)) Bearport Publishing Co., Inc.

Maurer, Daniel D. Do You Really Want to Drive in a Blizzard? A Book about Predicting Weather. Alberini, Teresa, illus. 2016. (Adventures in Science Ser.). (ENG.). 24p. (J). (gr. k-3). 20.95 (978-1-60753-959-9(4)) Amicus Publishing.

McAuliffe, Bill. Forecasting. 2017. (J). (**978-1-60818-824-6(8)**, Creative Education) 2010. 47p. (YA). (gr. 4-7). lib. bdg. 23.95 (978-1-58341-927-4(6)) Creative Co., The.

Orr, Tamra B. Forecasting a Flood. 2014. (Explorer Library: Follow the Clues Ser.). (ENG.). 32p. (J). (gr. 4-8). 28.50 (978-1-62431-778-1(2), 203308) Cherry Lake Publishing.

Phelan, Glen. Extreme Weather. 2007. (Reading Expeditions Ser.). (ENG., Illus.). 32p. (J). pap. 17.95 (978-0-7922-4575-9(X)) CENGAGE Learning.

Randolph, Joanne, ed. Tornado Alert! 2017. (Weather Report). 32p. (J). (gr. 3-3). pap. 10.52 (**978-0-7660-9025-5(6)**) Enslow Pubs., Inc.

Rodgers, Alan & Streluk, Angella. Forecasting the Weather. 2016. (Measuring the Weather Ser.). (ENG.). 32p. (gr. 3-5). pap. 7.99 (978-1-4846-3697-8(X), NA-h) Heinemann-Raintree.

Rustad, Martha E. H. & Kalz, Jill. Droughts: Be Aware & Prepare, 1 vol. 2014. (Weather Aware Ser.). (ENG.). 32p. (gr. 1-2). lib. bdg. 27.32 (978-1-4765-9905-2(X)) Capstone Press of Coughlan Cos.

Schuetz, Kristin. Forecasts. 2015. (Understanding Weather Ser.). (ENG., Illus.). 24p. (J). (gr. k-3). lib. bdg. 25.95 (978-1-62617-251-7(X), Blastoff! Readers) Bellwether Media.

Sharkawy, Azza. Predict It! 2014. (ENG., Illus.). 24p. (J). (978-0-7787-0773-8(3)) Crabtree Publishing Co.

Shea, Therese. Freaky Weather Stories. 2015. (Freaky True Science Ser.). (ENG.). 32p. (J). (gr. 4-5). pap. 10.50 (978-1-4824-2968-8(3)) Stevens, Gareth Publishing LLLP.

Sievert, Terri. Forecasting Weather, 1 vol. 2011. (Earth & Space Science Ser.). (ENG.). 24p. (J). (gr. k-1). pap. 7.29 (978-1-4296-7141-5(6)); pap. 41.70 (978-1-4296-7144-6(0)) Capstone Press of Coughlan Cos. (Pebble Plus).

Simpson, Kathleen. Extreme Weather: Science Tackles Global Warming & Climate Change. 2008. (National Geographic Investigates Ser.). (ENG., Illus.). 64p. (J). (gr. 5). lib. bdg. 27.90 (978-1-4263-0281-7(9), National Geographic Children's Bks.) National Geographic Society.

Simpson, Kathleen & National Geographic Kids Staff. Extreme Weather: Science Tackles Global Warming & Climate Change. 2008. (National Geographic Investigates Science Ser.). (ENG., Illus.). 64p. (J). (gr. 5). 17.95 (978-1-4263-0359-3(9), National Geographic Children's Bks.) National Geographic Society.

Somervill, Barbara A. Hurricanes. 2012. (21st Century Skills Library: Real World Math Ser.). (ENG., Illus.). 32p. (J). (gr. 4-8). lib. bdg. 28.50 (978-1-61080-325-0(6), 201302) Cherry Lake Publishing.

Stein, Paul. The Library of Future Weather & Climate, 8 bks. Incl. Droughts of the Future. lib. bdg. 31.95 (978-0-8239-3411-9(X)); Floods of the Future. lib. bdg. 31.95 (978-0-8239-3412-6(8)); Forecasting the Climate of the Future. lib. bdg. 31.95 (978-0-8239-3413-3(6)); Global Warming: A Threat to Our Future. lib. bdg. 31.95 (978-0-8239-3414-0(4)); Ice Ages of the Future. lib. bdg. 31.95 (978-0-8239-3415-7(2)); Oceans of the Future. lib. bdg. 31.95 (978-0-8239-3416-4(0)); Storms of the Future. lib. bdg. 31.95 (978-0-8239-3417-1(9)); 64p. (YA). (gr. 4-6). 2001. (Illus.). Set lib. bdg. 212.00 (978-0-8239-9431-1(7)) Rosen Publishing Group, Inc., The.

Steinberg, Lynnae D. What Is Weather Forecasting?, 1 vol. 2015. (ENG.). 32p. (J). 23.45 (978-1-62275-795-4(5), Britannica Educational Publishing) Rosen Publishing Group, Inc., The.

Sundance/Newbridge LLC Staff. Predicting the Weather. 2004. (Reading PowerWorks Ser.). (gr. 1-3). 37.50 (978-0-7608-9245-9(8)); pap. 6.10 (978-0-7608-9246-6(6)) Sundance/Newbridge Educational Publishing.

Waunsch, John. My Very, Very First Weather Book. 2013. 56p. 23.99 (978-1-62697-903-1(0)); pap. 12.99 (978-1-62697-764-8(X)) Salem Author Services.

Wills, Susan & Wills, Steven R. Meteorology: Predicting the Weather. 2003. (Innovators Ser.: Vol. 12). (Illus.). 144p. (gr. 5-18). lib. bdg. 21.95 (978-1-881508-61-8(7)) Oliver Pr., Inc.

WEATHER SATELLITES

see Meteorological Satellites

WEAVING

see also Basket Making; Beadwork; Textile Industry
also names of woven articles, e.g. Carpets

Howell, Vickie. Finger Knitting Fun: 30 Cute, Clever, & Creative Projects for Kids. 2015. (ENG., Illus.). 96p. pap. 19.99 (978-1-63159-070-2(7), Quarry Books) Quarto Publishing Group USA.

Rodee, Marian. Weaving of the Southwest, 1 vol. 2nd rev. ed. 2003. (ENG., Illus.). 248p. (gr. 10-13). pap. 29.95 (978-0-7643-1854-2(3), 9780764318542) Schiffer Publishing, Ltd.

Switzer, Chris. Projects for Alpaca & Llama. 2004. 16.00 (978-0-9642663-2-2(6)) Switzer Land Enterprises.

Weston Woods Staff, creator. Charlie Needs a Cloak. 2004. 38.75 (978-1-55592-383-9(6)); 18.95 (978-1-55592-382-2(8)) Weston Woods Studios, Inc.

WEB SITES

Anniss, Matt. What Is a Website & How Do I Use It? 2013. (Practical Technology Ser.). 48p. (J). (gr. 5-8). 25.85 (978-1-62275-072-6(1)); pap. 14.05 (978-1-62275-073-3(X)) Rosen Publishing Group, Inc., The.

Anniss, Matthew. Create Your Own Web Site or Blog. 2016. (Media Genius Ser.). (ENG.). 48p. (gr. 5-8). lib. bdg. 33.32 (978-1-4109-8111-0(8)) Heinemann-Raintree.

Bailer, Darice. Will & Wendy Build a Website with Digital Tools. O'Neill, Sean, illus. 2014. (Writing Builders Ser.). (ENG.). 32p. (J). (gr. 2-4). pap. 11.94 (978-1-60357-558-4(8)); lib. bdg. 25.27 (978-1-59953-584-5(X)) Norwood Hse. Pr.

Bingham, Jane, et al. The Usborne Internet-Linked Encyclopedia of World History: Prehistoric, Ancient, Medieval, Last 500 Years. 2004. (World History Ser.). (ENG., Illus.). 1p. (J). (gr. 3-18). 39.95 (978-0-7460-4168-0(3)) EDC Publishing.

Brown, Tracy. Facebook Safety & Privacy. 2013. (21st Century Safety & Privacy Ser.). 64p. (J). (gr. 5-8). 31.95 (978-1-4488-9569-4(3)); pap. 12.95 (978-1-4488-9580-9(4)); pap. 77.70 (978-1-4488-9581-6(2)) Rosen Publishing Group, Inc., The.

Doherty, Gillian. Birds. 2004. (Discovery Program Ser.). (SPA., Illus.). 64p. (J). (gr. 2-18). lib. bdg. 16.95 (978-1-58086-334-6(5)) EDC Publishing.

Ekman, Joseph Anthony. Kids Ultimate Online Homework Resource Guide 2004. 2003. spiral bd. 14.95 (978-0-9745406-0-3(9)) Duke Publishing & Software Corp.

Fontichiaro, Kristin. Blog It! 2012. (Explorer Library: Information Explorer Ser.). (ENG.). 32p. (gr. 4-8). 28.50 (978-1-61080-482-0(1), 202092); pap. 14.21 (978-1-61080-656-5(5), 202266) Cherry Lake Publishing.

Fontichiaro, Kristin & Truesdell, Ann. Learning & Sharing with a Wiki. Petelinsek, Kathleen, illus. 2013. (Explorer Junior Library: Information Explorer Junior Ser.). (ENG.). 24p. (J). (gr. 1-4). 28.50 (978-1-62431-132-1(6), 202848); pap. 12.79 (978-1-62431-264-9(0), 202850) Cherry Lake Publishing.

Fromm, Megan. Gathering & Sharing Digital Information, 1 vol. 2015. (ENG.). 48p. (YA). 30.25 (978-1-4777-8062-6(9), Rosen Reference) Rosen Publishing Group, Inc., The.

Gilbert, Sara. Built for Success: the Story of Facebook. 2013. (Built for Success Ser.). (ENG.). 48p. (J). (gr. 4-7). pap. 12.00 (978-0-89812-761-4(0), Creative Paperbacks) Creative Co., The.

—The Story of Facebook. 2012. (Built for Success Ser.). (Illus.). 48p. (J). (gr. 5-12). 23.95 (978-1-60818-176-6(6), Creative Education) Creative Co., The.

—The Story of Twitter. 2014. 46p. (978-1-60818-398-2(X), Creative Education) Creative Co., The.

Goldsworthy, Steve. Mark Zuckerberg. 2012. (J). (978-1-61913-872-8(7)); pap. (978-1-61913-873-5(5)) Weigl Pubs., Inc.

Gray, Leon. What Is a Blog & How Do I Use It? 2013. (Practical Technology Ser.). 48p. (J). (gr. 5-8). 25.85 (978-1-62275-066-5(7)); pap. 14.05 (978-1-62275-067-2(5)) Rosen Publishing Group, Inc., The.

—What Is a Social Network & How Do I Use It? 2013. (Practical Technology Ser.). 48p. (J). (gr. 5-8). 25.85 (978-1-62275-075-7(6)); pap. 14.05 (978-1-62275-076-4(4)) Rosen Publishing Group, Inc., The.

—What Is a Wiki & How Do I Use It? 2013. (Practical Technology Ser.). 48p. (J). (gr. 5-8). 25.85 (978-1-62275-069-6(1)); pap. 14.05 (978-1-62275-070-2(5)) Rosen Publishing Group, Inc., The.

Green, Julie. Super Smart Information Strategies: Shooting Video to Make Learning Fun. 2010. (Explorer Library: Information Explorer Ser.). (ENG.). 32p. (gr. 4-8). lib. bdg. 28.50 (978-1-60279-955-4(5), 200635) Cherry Lake Publishing.

Hasday, Judy L. Facebook & Mark Zuckerberg. 2012. (Business Leaders Ser.). (Illus.). 112p. (YA). (gr. 7-12). 28.95 (978-1-59935-176-6(5)) Reynolds, Morgan Inc.

Hawthorne, Kate & Sheppard, Daniela. The Young Person's Guide to the Internet: The Essential Website Reference Book for Young People, Parents & Teachers. 2nd ed. 2005. (ENG., Illus.). 224p. (C). (gr. 3-7). per. 38.95 (978-0-415-34505-7(7)) Routledge.

Henneberg, Susan. Twitter Safety & Privacy: A Guide to Microblogging. 2013. (21st Century Safety & Privacy Ser.). 64p. (J). (gr. 5-8). 31.95 (978-1-4488-9572-4(3)); pap. 77.70 (978-1-4488-9589-2(8)); pap. 12.95 (978-1-4488-9588-5(X)) Rosen Publishing Group, Inc., The.

Hillstrom, Laurie. Online Social Networks. 2010. (Technology 360 Ser.). (Illus.). 128p. (YA). (gr. 7-10). lib. bdg. 34.95 (978-1-4205-0167-4(4), LML02109-246079, Lucent Bks.) Cengage Gale.

Kling, Andrew A. Web 2.0: Basiswissen in 50 x 2 Minuten. 2010. (Technology 360 Ser.). (ENG., Illus.). 128p. (gr. 10-10). lib. bdg. 39.90 (978-1-4205-0171-1(2), LML02109-246083, Lucent Bks.) Cengage Gale.

Lent, Colleen Van. Web Design with Html5. 2014. (21st Century Skills Innovation Library: Makers As Innovators Ser.). (ENG., Illus.). 32p. (J). (gr. 4-8). 28.50 (978-1-63137-773-0(6), 205335) Cherry Lake Publishing.

Mark Zuckerberg & Facebook. 2011. (Graphic Nonfiction Biographies Ser.). (ENG.). 48p. (YA). (gr. 5-8). (978-1-4488-5547-6(0), Rosen Reference) Rosen Publishing Group, Inc., The.

Martin, Chris. Build Your Own Web Site. 2013. (Quick Expert's Guide Ser.). 64p. (J). (gr. 5-8). 31.95 (978-1-4777-2823-9(6)); pap. 77.70 (978-1-4777-2826-0(0)); pap. 12.95 (978-1-4777-2825-3(2)) Rosen Publishing Group, Inc., The. (Rosen Reference).

Pascaretti, Vicki & Wilkie, Sara. Super Smart Information Strategies: Team up Online. 2010. (Explorer Library: Information Explorer Ser.). (ENG.). 32p. (gr. 4-8). lib. bdg. 28.50 (978-1-60279-644-7(0), 200347) Cherry Lake Publishing.

Poolos, Jamie. Designing, Building, & Maintaining Web Sites. 2010. (Digital & Information Literacy Ser.). (ENG.). 48p. (YA). pap. 11.75 (978-1-4488-0594-5(5)); lib. bdg. 29.25 (978-1-4358-9424-2(3)) Rosen Publishing Group, Inc., The. (Rosen Reference).

Raatma, Lucia. Blogs. 2010. (21st Century Skills Innovation Library: Innovation in Entertainment Ser.). (ENG.). 32p. (gr. 4-8). lib. bdg. 28.50 (978-1-60279-635-5(1), 200339) Cherry Lake Publishing.

Sack, Rebekah. So You Want to Start a Blog: A Step-By-Step Guide to Starting a Fun & Profitable Blog. 2017. (ENG.). 180p. (YA). (gr. 8-12). lib. bdg. 34.95 (**978-1-62023-230-9(8)**, bdda44f9-2f74-48fd-b4f2-44f05298a0c9) Atlantic Publishing Group, Inc.

Sack, Rebekah & Atlantic Publishing Group. So You Want to Start a Blog: A Step-By-Step Guide to Starting a Fun & Profitable Blog. 2017. (ENG., Illus.). 180p. (YA). pap. 19.95 (978-1-62023-217-0(0), 8a9aa940-2132-4d5b-88d8-e8527614bb16) Atlantic Publishing Group, Inc.

Scott, Celicia. Twitter: How Jack Dorsey Changed the Way We Communicate. 2014. (Wizards of Technology Ser.: 10). 64p. (J). (gr. 7-18). 23.95 (978-1-4222-3187-6(9)) Mason Crest.

Truesdell, Ann. Wonderful Wikis. 2012. (Explorer Library: Information Explorer Ser.). (ENG.). 32p. (gr. 4-8). 28.50 (978-1-61080-480-6(5), 202090); pap. 14.21 (978-1-61080-654-1(9), 202264) Cherry Lake Publishing.

Truesdell, Ann & Fontichiaro, Kristin. Starting Your Own Blog. Petelinsek, Kathleen, illus. 2013. (Explorer Junior Library: Information Explorer Junior Ser.). (ENG.). 24p. (J). (gr. 1-4). 28.50 (978-1-62431-133-8(4), 202852); pap. 12.79 (978-1-62431-265-6(9), 202854) Cherry Lake Publishing.

Van Lent, Colleen. More Web Design with HTML5. 2015. (21st Century Skills Innovation Library: Makers As Innovators Ser.). (ENG., Illus.). 32p. (J). (gr. 4-8). lib. bdg. 29.93 (978-1-63188-868-7(4), 206052) Cherry Lake Publishing.

Waters, Rosa. Pinterest(r): How Ben Silbermann & Evan Sharp Changed the Way We Share What We Love. 2014. (Wizards of Technology Ser.: 10). 64p. (J). (gr. 7-18). 23.95 (978-1-4222-3185-2(2)) Mason Crest.

Wolny, Philip. Foursquare & Other Location-Based Services: Checking in, Staying Safe, & Being Savvy. 2011. (Digital & Information Literacy Ser.). (ENG.). 48p. (YA). (gr. 5-8). pap. 11.75 (978-1-4488-5615-2(9)); lib. bdg. 29.25 (978-1-4488-5554-4(3)) Rosen Publishing Group, Inc., The. (Rosen Reference).

—Google & You: Maximizing Your Google Experience. 2011. (Digital & Information Literacy Ser.). (ENG.). 48p. (YA). (gr. 5-8). pap. 11.75 (978-1-4488-5613-8(2)); lib. bdg. 29.25 (978-1-4488-5553-7(5)) Rosen Publishing Group, Inc., The. (Rosen Reference).

Woog, Adam. Zuckerberg. 2009. (Innovators Ser.). (ENG., Illus.). 64p. (J). 29.95 (978-0-7377-4566-5(5)) Cengage Gale.

WEB SITES—DESIGN

Aho, Kirsti & Underwood, Dale, contrib. by. Town Website Project Using Macromedia Dreamweaver MX 2004: Communicating Information & Ideas on the Web. 2003. (YA). ring bd. 10.00 (978-0-9742273-3-7(1)) Macromedia, Inc.

Amihud, Zohar. Look Mom! I Built My Own Web Site. 2nd ed. 2006. (Illus.). 204p. (YA). (gr. 7). per. 18.95 (978-0-9760111-1-8(5)) BookChamp LLC.

Brown, Marty. Webmaster. 2009. (Coolcareers. com Ser.). 48p. (gr. 5-8). 53.00 (978-1-61511-985-1(X), Rosen Reference) Rosen Publishing Group, Inc., The.

Bussell, Linda. Exploring Solid Figures on the Web. 2008. (Math in Our World - Level 3 Ser.). 24p. (gr. 2-5). (J). lib. bdg. 22.00 (978-0-8368-9287-1(9)); pap. 8.15 (978-0-8368-9386-1(7)) Stevens, Gareth Publishing LLLP. (Weekly Reader Leveled Readers).

Career Building Through Using Search Engine Optimization Techniques. 2013. (Digital Career Building Ser.). 64p. (YA). (gr. 7-12). pap. 77.70 (978-1-4777-1746-2(3)) Rosen Publishing Group, Inc., The.

Endsley, Kezia. Website Design. 2015. (High-Tech Jobs Ser.). (ENG., Illus.). 96p. (J). (gr. 7-7). 42.79 (978-1-5026-0111-7(7)) Cavendish Square Publishing.

Fischer, James. Computer Math. 2013. (Math 24/7 Ser.: 10). 48p. (J). (gr. 5-18). 19.95 (978-1-4222-2904-0(1)) Mason Crest.

Freedman, Jeri. Career Building Through Skinning & Modding. 2009. (Digital Career Building Ser.). 64p. (gr. 6-6). 58.50 (978-1-61512-171-7(4)) Rosen Publishing Group, Inc., The.

Hatter, Clyde & Dojo, Coder. CoderDojo Nano: Building a Website - Create with Code. 2016. (ENG.). 96p. (J). (gr. 3-7). pap. 12.99 (978-1-338-15676-8(4)) Scholastic, Inc.

Hovanec, Erin M. Careers as Content Provider for the Web. 2005. (Library of e-Commerce & Internet Careers Ser.). (Illus.). 64p. (YA). (gr. 7-12). lib. bdg. 31.95 (978-0-8239-3418-8(7)) Rosen Publishing Group, Inc., The.

Oppedisano, Robert & McCoy, Lisa. Internet. 2nd rev. ed. 2011. (Career Launcher Ser.). 160p. (C). (gr. 9). 34.95 (978-0-8160-7951-3(X), Ferguson Publishing Co.) Facts On File, Inc.

Selfridge, Benjamin. A Kid's Guide to Creating Web Pages for Home & School. 2008. 128p. pap. 17.95 (978-1-59363-334-9(3)) Prufrock Pr.

Selfridge, Benjamin & Selfridge, Peter. A Kid's Guide to Creating Web Pages for Home & School. 2004. (Illus.). 128p. (J). (gr. 5-10). pap. 19.95 (978-1-56976-180-9(9), Zephyr Pr.) Chicago Review Pr., Inc.

Souter, Gerry, et al. Bringing Photos, Music, & Video into Your Web Page. 2003. (Internet Library). (Illus.). 64p. (J). (gr. 4-12). lib. bdg. 23.94 (978-0-7660-2082-5(7)) Enslow Pubs., Inc.

—Creating Animation for Your Web Page. 2003. (Internet Library). (Illus.). 64p. (J). (gr. 4-12). lib. bdg. 22.60 (978-0-7660-2083-2(5)) Enslow Pubs., Inc.

—Creating e-Reports & Online Presentations. 2003. (Internet Library). (Illus.). 64p. (J). (gr. 4-12). lib. bdg. 23.94 *(978-0-7660-2080-1(0))* Enslow Pubs., Inc.

Suen, Anastasia. Career Building Through Using Search Engine Optimization Techniques. 2013. (Digital Career Building Ser.). 64p. (YA). (gr. 7-12). 31.95 *(978-1-4777-1726-4(9))*; pap. 12.95 *(978-1-4777-1744-8(7))* Rosen Publishing Group, Inc., The.

Underwood, Dale & Aho, Kirsti. Town Website Project for Macromedia Dreamweaver MX 2004: Communicating Information & Ideas on the Web, 2 bks. Dharkar, Anuja & McCain, Malinda, eds. Morgan, Mark & Gallenson, Ann, illus. 2003. 39p. spiral bd. 10.00 *(978-0-9742273-8-2(2)*, Macromedia Education) Macromedia, Inc.

Vanden-Heuvel, John C., Sr. & Ostrovsky, Andrey. ABCs of the Web. Holmes, Tom, illus. 2016. (ENG.). 28p. (J). (gr. -1-3). bds. 8.99 *(978-1-4998-0312-9(5))* Little Bee Books Inc.

WEBSTER, DANIEL, 1782-1852

Baldwin, James. Four Great Americans. 2006. pap. *(978-1-4065-0509-2(9))* Dodo Pr.

WEBSTER, NOAH, 1758-1843

Ferris, Jeri Chase. Noah Webster & His Words. Kirsch, Vincent X., illus. (ENG.). 32p. (J). (gr. -1-3). 2015. 6.99 *(978-0-544-58242-2(X)*, HMH Books For Young Readers) 2012. 16.99 *(978-0-547-39055-0(6))* Houghton Mifflin Harcourt Publishing Co.

Maurer, Tracy Nelson. Noah Webster's Fighting Words. Catusanu, Mircea, illus. 2017. (ENG.). 40p. (gr. 2-5). 19.99 *(978-1-4677-9410-7(4))*; 30.65 ***(978-1-5124-2839-1(6)***, Millbrook Pr.) Lerner Publishing Group.

Melis, Luisanna Fodde. Noah Webster & the First American Dictionary. 2009. (Library of American Lives & Times Ser.). 112p. (gr. 5-5). 69.20 *(978-1-60853-495-1(2))* Rosen Publishing Group, Inc., The.

Proudfit, Isabel. Noah Webster, Father of the Dictionary. 2008. (Illus.). 224p. (J). pap. 15.95 *(978-0-9801563-0-0(0))* Bradford Pr., Inc.

Reef, Catherine. Noah Webster: Man of Many Words. 2015. (ENG., Illus.). 224p. (J). (gr. 5-7). 18.99 *(978-0-544-12983-2(0)*, Clarion Bks.) Houghton Mifflin Harcourt Trade & Reference Pubs.

Shea, Pegi Deitz. Noah Webster: Weaver of Words. Vachula, Monica, illus. 2009. (ENG.). 40p. (J). (gr. 4-18). 18.95 *(978-1-59078-441-9(3)*, Calkins Creek) Boyds Mills Pr.

WEDDINGS

see Etiquette; Marriage; Marriage Customs and Rites

WEEDS

May, Suellen. Invasive Terrestrial Plants. 2006. (Invasive Species Ser.). (Illus.). 100p. (gr. 6-12). lib. bdg. 30.00 *(978-0-7910-9128-9(7)*, Chelsea Hse.) Facts On File, Inc.

WEIGHT CONTROL

see also Diet; Exercise

Allman, Toney. Food in Schools. rev. ed. 2014. (Matters of Opinion Ser.). (ENG.). 64p. (J). (gr. 4-6). pap. 14.60 *(978-1-60357-584-3(7))* Norwood Hse. Pr.

—Obesity. 2008. (21st Century Skills Library: Health at Risk Ser.). (ENG., Illus.). 32p. (gr. 4-8). lib. bdg. 28.50 *(978-1-60279-285-2(2)*, 200134) Cherry Lake Publishing.

Barraclough, Sue. I Know Someone Who Is Obese, 1 vol. 2011. (Understanding Health Issues Ser.). (ENG.). 32p. (gr. 1-3). 27.32 *(978-1-4329-4566-4(1)*, Heinemann First Library) Heinemann-Raintree.

Bartell, Susan S. Dr. Susan's Girls-Only Weight Loss Guide: The Easy, Fun Way to Look & Feel Good! 2006. (ENG., Illus.). 272p. (J). (gr. 7-12). per. 14.95 *(978-0-9721502-0-0(X))* Parent Positive Pr.

Bauchner, Elizabeth. Weight Management. McDonnell, Mary Ann & Forman, Sara, eds. 2013. (Young Adult's Guide to the Science of Health Ser.: 15). 128p. (J). (gr. 7-18). 24.95 *(978-1-4222-2818-0(5))* Mason Crest.

Boudreau, Helene. Real Mermaids Don't Need High Heels. 2013. (ENG.). 240p. (J). (gr. 4-8). pap. 6.99 *(978-1-4022-6458-0(5)*, Sourcebooks Jabberwocky) Sourcebooks, Inc.

Dickmann, Nancy. What You Need to Know about Obesity. 2016. (Focus on Health Ser.). (ENG., Illus.). 32p. (gr. 3-4). lib. bdg. 27.32 *(978-1-4914-8243-8(5)*, Fact Finders) Capstone Press of Coughlan Cos.

Dru Tecco, Betsy. Food for Fuel: The Connection Between Food & Physical Activity. 2008. (Library of Nutrition Ser.). (Illus.). 48p. (YA). (gr. 8-12). lib. bdg. 29.25 *(978-1-4042-1871-0(8)*, Rosen Reference) Rosen Publishing Group, Inc., The.

Dweck, Joey. Losing for Good. 2005. (YA). per. 19.95 *(978-0-9754448-6-3(7))* Weight Loss Buddy, Inc.

Edwards, Hazel & Alexander, Goldie. Talking about Your Weight. 2010. (Healthy Living Ser.). (Illus.). 32p. (YA). (gr. 3-6). lib. bdg. 26.00 *(978-1-4339-3655-5(0))* Stevens, Gareth Publishing LLLP.

Engdahl, Sylvia. Obesity. Greenhaven Press Staff, ed. 2014. (Opposing Viewpoints Ser.). (ENG.). 224p. (gr. 10-12). lib. bdg. 48.80 *(978-0-7377-7278-4(6)*, Greenhaven Pr., Inc.) Cengage Gale.

Esherick, Joan. Emotions & Eating. Garcia, Victor, ed. 2014. (Understanding Obesity Ser.: 10). 104p. (J). (gr. 7-18). lib. bdg. 24.95 *(978-1-4222-3059-6(7))* Mason Crest.

—Looking & Feeling Good in Your Body. Garcia, Victor, ed. 2014. (Understanding Obesity Ser.: 10). (Illus.). 104p. (J). (gr. 7-18). lib. bdg. 24.95 *(978-1-4222-3063-3(5))* Mason Crest.

Faulkner, Nicholas & Williams, Kara. Conquering Diet Drug Abuse, 01 vols., 1. 2016. (Conquering Eating Disorders Ser.). (ENG.). 64p. (J). 32.95 *(978-1-4994-6197-8(6)*, Rosen Young Adult) Rosen Publishing Group, Inc., The.

Favor, Lesli J. & Massie, Elizabeth. Weighing In: Nutrition & Weight Management. 2009. (Benchmark Rockets Ser.). 32p. (gr. 5-18). 28.50 *(978-0-7614-4367-4(3))* Marshall Cavendish Corp.

Ford, Jean. Health Issues Caused by Obesity. Garcia, Victor, ed. 2014. (Understanding Obesity Ser.: 10). 104p. (J). (gr. 7-18). lib. bdg. 24.95 *(978-1-4222-3062-6(7))* Mason Crest.

Ford, Jean & Libal, Autumn. No Quick Fix: Fad Diets & Weight-Loss Miracles. Garcia, Victor, ed. 2014. (Understanding Obesity Ser.: 10). (Illus.). 104p. (YA). (gr. 7-18). lib. bdg. 24.95 *(978-1-4222-3065-7(1))* Mason Crest.

Friedman, Lauri S. Obesity. 2010. (Introducing Issues with Opposing Viewpoints Ser.). (ENG.). 144p. 36.95 *(978-0-7377-5083-6(9)*, Greenhaven Pr., Inc.) Cengage Gale.

Gay, Kathlyn. Am I Fat? The Obesity Issue for Teens. 2006. (Issues in Focus Today Ser.). (Illus.). 112p. (J). (gr. 8-12). lib. bdg. 33.27 *(978-0-7660-2527-1(6))* Enslow Pubs., Inc.

—Are You Fat? The Obesity Issue for Teens. 2014. (Got Issues? Ser.). (Illus.). 112p. (J). (gr. 6-12). lib. bdg. 33.27 *(978-0-7660-4322-0(3))* Enslow Pubs., Inc.

—Do You Know What to Eat? 2015. (Got Issues? Ser.). (ENG., Illus.). 128p. (J). (gr. 7-7). 37.27 *(978-0-7660-6987-9(7))* Enslow Pubs., Inc.

Gillard, Arthur. Dieting. Greenhaven Press Editors, ed. 2014. (Issues That Concern You Ser.). (ENG., Illus.). 144p. (gr. 7-10). lib. bdg. 42.00 *(978-0-7377-6938-8(6)*, Greenhaven Pr., Inc.) Cengage Gale.

Greene, Meg. Obesity. 2008. (Gallup Major Trends & Events Ser.). (Illus.). 112p. (YA). (gr. 7-18). lib. bdg. 22.95 *(978-1-59084-967-5(1))* Mason Crest.

Griffith, M. Christopher & Griffith, Jeana R. The Tale of Two Athletes: The Story of Jumper & the Thumper a True Story on Understanding & Combating Childhood Obesity. 2012. 60p. pap. 24.99 *(978-1-4685-4014-7(9))* AuthorHouse.

Haerens, Margaret. Obesity. 2011. (Global Viewpoints Ser.). (ENG., Illus.). 224p. (gr. 10-12). pap. 31.70 *(978-0-7377-5661-6(6)*, Greenhaven Pr., Inc.) Cengage Gale.

Haerens, Margaret, ed. Obesity. 2011. (Global Viewpoints Ser.). (Illus.). 224p. (YA). (gr. 9-12). 40.45 *(978-0-7377-5660-9(8))* Cengage Gale.

Harmon, Daniel E. Obesity. (Coping in a Changing World Ser.). 112p. (gr. 7-7). 2009. 63.90 *(978-1-61512-021-5(1))* 2006. (YA). lib. bdg. 34.60 *(978-1-4042-0949-7(2))* Rosen Publishing Group, Inc., The.

Hicks, Terry Allan. Obesity. 2008. (Health Alert Ser.). 64p. (gr. 4-18). lib. bdg. 32.79 *(978-0-7614-2911-1(5)*, Benchmark Bks.) Marshall Cavendish Corp.

Hidalgo-Robert, Alberto. Fat No More: A Teenager's Victory over Obesity. 2012. (J). pap. 16.95 *(978-1-55885-745-2(1)*, Piñata Books) Arte Publico Pr.

Hunt, Jamie. Tired of Being Teased: Obesity & Others. 2010. (Kids & Obesity Ser.). 48p. (YA). lib. bdg. 19.95 *(978-1-4222-1711-5(6))* Mason Crest.

Hunter, William. Nature & Nurture: The Causes of Obesity. 2015. (Illus.). 104p. (YA). *(978-1-4222-3056-5(2))* Mason Crest.

—Nature & Nurture: The Causes of Obesity. Garcia, Victor, ed. 2014. (Understanding Obesity Ser.: 10). 104p. (J). (gr. 7-18). lib. bdg. 24.95 *(978-1-4222-3064-0(3))* Mason Crest.

—Surgery & Medicine for Weight Loss. Garcia, Victor, ed. 2014. (Understanding Obesity Ser.: 10). 104p. (J). (gr. 7-18). lib. bdg. 24.95 *(978-1-4222-3066-4(X))* Mason Crest.

Jimerson, Maxine Newman. Childhood Obesity. 2008. (Diseases & Disorders Ser.). (ENG., Illus.). 112p. (YA). (gr. 7-12). lib. bdg. 34.95 *(978-1-59018-997-9(3)*, LML02109-234912) Cengage Gale.

Juettner, Bonnie. Childhood Obesity. 2009. (In Controversy Ser.). (YA). (gr. 7-12). 25.95 *(978-1-60152-083-8(2))* ReferencePoint Pr., Inc.

Kallen, Stuart. Obesity. 2016. (Matters of Opinion Ser.). (ENG.). 64p. (J). (gr. 4-6). pap. 14.60 *(978-1-60357-859-2(5))* Norwood Hse. Pr.

Kallen, Stuart A. Obesity. 2016. (Matters of Opinion Ser.). (ENG., Illus.). 64p. (J). (gr. 4-6). lib. bdg. 27.93 *(978-1-59953-756-6(7))* Norwood Hse. Pr.

Kern, Merilee A. Making Healthy Choices: A Story to Inspire Fit, Weight-Wise Kids (Boys' Edition) 2007. (J). pap. 11.95 *(978-1-58736-742-7(4))* Wheatmark, Inc.

—Making Healthy Choices: A Story to Inspire Fit, Weight-Wise Kids (Girls' Edition) 2007. (J). pap. 11.95 *(978-1-58736-743-4(2))* Wheatmark, Inc.

Kids & Obesity, 10 vols., Set. Incl. Does Television Make You Fat? Lifestyle & Obesity. Simons, Rae. (Illus.). pap. 7.95 *(978-1-4222-1900-3(3))*; Too Many Sunday Dinners: Family & Diet. Simons, Rae. pap. 7.95 *(978-1-4222-1901-0(1))*; Truth about Diets: What's Right for You? Hunt, Jamie. pap. 7.95 *(978-1-4222-1898-3(8))*; Weighted Down: When Being Overweight makes You Sick. Thompson, Helen. (Illus.). pap. 7.95 *(978-1-4222-1896-9(1))*; 48p. (YA). 2009. 2011. Set pap. 79.50 *(978-1-4222-1893-8(7))*; Set lib. bdg. 199.50 *(978-1-4222-1705-4(1))* Mason Crest.

Langwith, Jacqueline. Childhood Obesity. 2012. (Perspectives on Diseases & Disorders Ser.). (ENG., Illus.). 144p. (gr. 10-12). lib. bdg. 44.30 *(978-0-7377-6350-8(7)*, Greenhaven Pr., Inc.) Cengage Gale.

LeMay, DiDi. Freddy's French Fries Fiasco. 2012. (ENG.). (J). pap. *(978-1-4675-2963-1(X))* Independent Pub.

Libal, Autumn. Discrimination & Prejudice. Garcia, Victor, ed. 2014. (Understanding Obesity Ser.: 10). 104p. (J). (gr. 7-18). lib. bdg. 24.95 *(978-1-4222-3058-9(9))* Mason Crest.

—Fast Food & the Obesity Epidemic. Garcia, Victor, ed. 2014. (Understanding Obesity Ser.: 10). 104p. (J). (gr. 7-18). lib. bdg. 24.95 *(978-1-4222-3061-9(9))* Mason Crest.

—Fats, Sugars, & Empty Calories: The Fast Food Habit. 2007. (Obesity Ser.). (Illus.). 104p. (YA). (gr. 4-7). lib. bdg. 23.95 *(978-1-59084-943-9(4))* Mason Crest.

Lite, Lori. Children's Wellness Curriculum: Lessons, Stories & Techniques Designed to Decrease Bullying, Anxiety, Anger & Obesity While Promoting Self-Esteem & Healthy Food Choices. 2007. (J). (gr. k-5). 89.95 incl. audio compact disk *(978-0-9787781-2-5(X)*, 5) Stress Free Pubs.

Living with Obesity. 2010. (Teen's Guides). 160p. (gr. 6-12). pap. 14.95 *(978-0-8160-7591-1(3))* Facts On File, Inc.

Lluch, Alex A. Lose up to 10 Pounds in 2 Weeks. 2011. (ENG.). 220p. pap., pupil's gde. ed. 11.95 *(978-1-936061-40-2(6))*; 360p. pap. 16.95 *(978-1-936061-17-4(1))* WS Publishing.

Lombardo, Michelle. Balancing the Energy Equation: One Step at a Time! Herron, Mark, illus. 2003. (J). lib. bdg. 17.95 *(978-1-931212-51-9(1))* OrganWise Guys Inc., The.

—Pepto's Place: Where Every Portion Size Is OrganWise! Herron, Mark, illus. 2003. 32p. (J). lib. bdg. 17.95 *(978-1-931212-50-2(3))* OrganWise Guys Inc., The.

Lusted, Marcia Amidon. Obesity & Food Policing, 1 vol. 2008. (Essential Viewpoints Set 2 Ser.). (ENG., Illus.). 112p. (J). (gr. 6-12). lib. bdg. 35.64 *(978-1-60453-058-2(8))* ABDO Publishing Co.

Martin, Don, et al. They Call Me Fat Zoe: Helping Children & Families Overcome Obesity. Voerg, Kathy, illus. 2012. (Let's Talk Ser.). (ENG.). 48p. (J). (gr. -1-2). pap. 9.95 *(978-0-88282-377-5(9))* New Horizon Pr. Pubs., Inc.

Mattern, Joanne. Obesity: Causes & Consequences. 2005. (Behind the News Ser.). (Illus.). 112p. (J). (gr. 5-18). lib. bdg. 24.95 *(978-1-881508-67-0(6))* Oliver Pr., Inc.

McMahon, Christina & Marcovitz, Hal. The Dangers of Diet Drugs. 2017. (Drug Education Library Ser.). 104p. (YA). (gr. 7-7). 37.45 ***(978-1-5345-6005-5(X)***, Lucent Pr.) Greenhaven Publishing LLC.

Murphy, Wendy B. Weight & Health. 2008. (Twenty-First Century Medical Library). (ENG., Illus.). 112p. (gr. 6-12). lib. bdg. 33.26 *(978-0-8225-6784-4(9))* Lerner Publishing Group.

Nakaya, Andrea C. Thinking Critically: Obesity. 2017. (ENG.). 80p. (YA). (gr. 5-12). ***(978-1-68282-267-8(2))*** ReferencePoint Pr., Inc.

Obesity: Modern-Day Epidemic, 10 vols., Set. Incl. Diet & Your Emotions: The Comfort Food Falsehood. Esherick, Joan. (J). 2004. lib. bdg. 23.95 *(978-1-59084-950-7(7))*; Fats, Sugars, & Empty Calories: The Fast Food Habit. Libal, Autumn. (YA). 2007. lib. bdg. 23.95 *(978-1-59084-943-9(4))*; Medications & Surgeries for Weight Loss: When Dieting Isn't Enough. Hunter, William. (YA). 2007. lib. bdg. 23.95 *(978-1-59084-947-7(7))*; (gr. 4-7). (Illus.). 104p. 2005. Set lib. bdg. 239.50 *(978-1-59084-941-5(8))* Mason Crest.

Owens, Peter. Teens Health & Obesity. 2008. (Gallup Youth Survey, Major Issues & Trends Ser.). (Illus.). 112p. (YA). (gr. -1-7). lib. bdg. 22.95 *(978-1-59084-872-2(1))* Mason Crest.

—Teens, Health & Obesity. Developed in Association with the Gallup Organization Staff, ed. 2013. (Gallup Youth Survey: Major Issues & Trends Ser.: 14). 112p. (J). (gr. 7-18). 24.95 *(978-1-4222-2961-3(0))* Mason Crest.

Parsons, William B., Jr. Tough Talk about Fat! How to Reach & Maintain Your Ideal Weight. 2003. 134p. per. 12.95 *(978-0-9662568-9-5(1))* Lilac Pr.

Ritter, Christie Rose. Obesity. 2013. (Healthy Kids Ser.). (ENG.). 24p. (J). (gr. 1-4). 28.50 *(978-1-62323-538-3(3)*, 206273) Child's World, Inc., The.

Robbins, Lynette. How to Deal with Obesity. 2009. (Kids' Health Ser.). 24p. (ENG.). (J). pap. 8.25 *(978-1-4358-3423-1(2)*, PowerKids Pr.); (Illus.). (YA). (gr. 2-5). lib. bdg. 22.60 *(978-1-4042-8143-1(6))* Rosen Publishing Group, Inc., The.

Roberts, Jeremy. Drugs & Dieting. 2009. (Drug Abuse Prevention Library). 64p. (gr. 5-5). 58.50 *(978-1-60853-428-9(6))* Rosen Publishing Group, Inc., The.

Sanna, Ellyn. Big Portions, Big Problems. Garcia, Victor, ed. 2014. (Understanding Obesity Ser.: 10). 104p. (J). (gr. 7-18). lib. bdg. 24.95 *(978-1-4222-3057-2(0))* Mason Crest.

Sartori, Rosanne Sheritz. A New Start: One Child's Struggle with Obesity. 2004. (Illus.). 88p. (J). per. 19.95 *(978-1-931636-33-9(8))* National Ctr. For Youth Issues.

Scherer, Lauri S. Obesity. 2013. (Issues That Concern You Ser.). (ENG., Illus.). 144p. (gr. 7-10). lib. bdg. 42.00 *(978-0-7377-6298-3(5)*, Greenhaven Pr., Inc.) Cengage Gale.

Sheen, Barbara, ed. Childhood Obesity. 2012. (Diseases & Disorders Ser.). (ENG., Illus.). 128p. (J). (gr. 7-10). lib. bdg. 30.95 *(978-1-4205-0723-2(0)*, Lucent Bks.) Cengage Gale.

Simons, Rae. Does Television Make You Fat? Lifestyle & Obesity. (Kids & Obesity Ser.). (Illus.). 48p. (YA). 2010. lib. bdg. 19.95 *(978-1-4222-1712-2(4))* 2009. pap. 7.95 *(978-1-4222-1900-3(3))* Mason Crest.

—I Eat When I'm Sad: Food & Feelings. 2010. (Kids & Obesity Ser.). 48p. (YA). lib. bdg. 19.95 *(978-1-4222-1714-6(0))* Mason Crest.

—Too Many Sunday Dinners: Family & Diet. (Kids & Obesity Ser.). 48p. (YA). 2010. lib. bdg. 19.95 *(978-1-4222-1713-9(2))* 2009. pap. 7.95 *(978-1-4222-1901-0(1))* Mason Crest.

Stettler, Nicolas & Shelly, Susan. Living with Obesity. 2009. (Teen's Guides). 160p. (gr. 6-12). 34.95 *(978-0-8160-7590-4(5))* Facts On File, Inc.

Stewart, Gail. Fat in America. 2007. (Ripped from the Headlines Ser.). 64p. (J). (gr. 7-12). 23.95 *(978-1-60217-002-5(9))* Erickson Pr.

Tecco, Betsy Dru. Food for Fuel: The Connection Between Food & Physical Activity. (Library of Nutrition Ser.). 48p. 2009. (gr. 5-8). 53.00 *(978-1-60853-766-2(8)*, Rosen Reference) 2008. (ENG., Illus.). (gr. 5-8). per. 11.75 *(978-1-4042-1635-8(9))* 2004. (Illus.). (J). lib. bdg. 26.50 *(978-1-4042-0303-7(6))* Rosen Publishing Group, Inc., The.

Thompson, Helen. Weighted Down: When Being Overweight makes You Sick. (Kids & Obesity Ser.). (Illus.). 48p. (YA). 2010. lib. bdg. 19.95 *(978-1-4222-1708-5(6))* 2009. pap. 7.95 *(978-1-4222-1896-9(1))* Mason Crest.

Williams, Kara. Diet Drugs. 2006. (Danger Zone: Dieting & Eating Disorders Ser.). (Illus.). 64p. (YA). (gr. 7-12). lib. bdg. 31.95 *(978-1-4042-1994-6(3))* Rosen Publishing Group, Inc., The.

Zahensky, Barbara. Diet Fads. 2009. (Danger Zone: Dieting & Eating Disorders Ser.). 64p. (gr. 5-6). 55.90 *(978-1-61512-124-3(2))* Rosen Publishing Group, Inc., The.

Zahensky, Barbara A. Diet Fads. 2007. (Danger Zone: Dieting & Eating Disorders Ser.). (Illus.). 64p. (YA). (gr. 7-12). lib. bdg. 31.95 *(978-1-4042-1999-1(4))* Rosen Publishing Group, Inc., The.

WEIGHT CONTROL—FICTION

Babich, Elaine. You Never Called Me Princess. 2012. 210p. pap. 14.00 *(978-1-105-70209-9(X))* Lulu.com GBR. Dist: Lulu Pr., Inc.

Baker, Ken. How I Got Skinny, Famous, & Fell Madly in Love. 2014. (ENG.). 272p. (YA). (gr. 2-17). pap. 9.95 *(978-0-7624-5014-5(2)*, Running Pr. Kids) Running Pr. Bk. Pubs.

Barson, Kelly. 45 Pounds. 2014. (ENG.). 272p. (YA). (gr. 7). pap. 9.99 *(978-0-14-242265-6(7)*, Speak) Penguin Young Readers Group.

—45 Pounds (More or Less) 2013. (ENG.). 272p. (YA). (gr. 7). 16.99 *(978-0-670-78482-0(6)*, Viking Books for Young Readers) Penguin Young Readers Group.

Beck, Nina. This Book Isn't Fat, It's Fabulous. 2009. (ENG.). 256p. (J). (gr. 9). pap. 8.99 *(978-0-545-01704-6(1))* Scholastic, Inc.

Bently, Peter. The Yoga Ogre. Rickerty, Simon, illus. 2012. (ENG.). 32p. (J). 15.99 *(978-1-84738-902-2(3))* Simon & Schuster, Ltd. GBR. Dist: Simon & Schuster, Inc.

Berne, Emma Carlson. Under Pressure. 2013. (Counterattack Ser.). (ENG.). 104p. (YA). (gr. 6-12). pap. 7.95 *(978-1-4677-0718-3(X))*; lib. bdg. 27.93 *(978-1-4677-0303-1(6))* Lerner Publishing Group.

Brown, Gladys. The Adventures of King Flapjack. 2005. 36p. pap. 13.95 *(978-1-4116-2694-2(X))* Lulu Pr., Inc.

Bunting, Eve. My Dog Jack Is Fat, 0 vols. Rex, Michael, illus. 2011. (ENG.). 32p. (J). (gr. -1-3). 16.99 *(978-0-7614-5809-8(3)*, 9780761458098, Amazon Children's Publishing) Amazon Publishing.

Caple, Kathy. Starring Hillary. Caple, Kathy, illus. 2003. (Picture Bks.). (Illus.). 28p. (J). (gr. -1-3). 15.95 *(978-1-57505-261-8(X)*, Carolrhoda Bks.) Lerner Publishing Group.

Capper, Ann. Big Thighs, Tight Jeans (Should Jan Go O. 2005. pap. 11.95 *(978-0-7414-2676-5(5))* Infinity Publishing.

Carter, Catherine. Anna's Choice. Pittman, Gail, illus. 2005. 24p. (J). (gr. 3-7). 12.95 *(978-1-893062-79-5(1))* Quail Ridge Pr., Inc.

Cohn, Rachel. You Know Where to Find Me. (ENG.). (YA). (gr. 7). 2009. 224p. pap. 8.99 *(978-0-689-87860-2(5))* 2008. 208p. 16.99 *(978-0-689-87859-6(1))* Simon & Schuster Bks. For Young Readers. (Simon & Schuster Bks. For Young Readers).

Colbert, June. The King of Large. 2005. 160p. pap. *(978-0-7344-0615-6(0)*, Lothian Children's Bks.) Hachette Australia.

Cooner, Donna. Skinny. 2012. (ENG.). 272p. (J). (gr. 7). 17.99 *(978-0-545-42763-0(0))* Scholastic, Inc.

DeClements, Barthe. Nothing's Fair in Fifth Grade. 2008. (ENG.). 144p. (J). (gr. 3-7). 5.99 *(978-0-14-241349-4(6)*, Puffin Books) Penguin Young Readers Group.

Dionne, Erin. Models Don't Eat Chocolate Cookies. 2009. (ENG.). 256p. (J). (gr. 3-7). pap. 6.99 *(978-0-8037-3296-4(1)*, Dial Bks) Penguin Young Readers Group.

Gonzales Bertrand, Diane. Sofia & the Purple Dress / Sofia y el Vestido Morado. Baeza Ventura, Gabriela, tr. Fields, Lisa, illus. 2012. (SPA & ENG.). (J). 17.95 *(978-1-55885-701-8(X)*, Piñata Books) Arte Publico Pr.

Griffith, Jeana R. The Tale of Two Athletes: the Story of Jumper & the Thumper: Workbook: Steps to Tackle Childhood Obesity. 2012. 68p. pap. 13.95 *(978-1-4772-4086-1(1))* AuthorHouse.

Hardy, Zoey. Everything Changes. 2005. 316p. per. 9.95 *(978-0-9765423-0-8(7))* Eudon Publishing.

Helen, Grace. Santa's Way. 2012. 32p. pap. 24.95 *(978-1-4626-7356-8(2))* America Star Bks.

Jackson, A. Isaiah J. Jiffy: You, You, You. Bully! 2005. 50p. pap. 16.95 *(978-1-4137-8524-1(7))* PublishAmerica, Inc.

Kath, Natalie. The Summer I Lost It, 1 vol. 2012. (Stone Arch Novels Ser.). (ENG.). 128p. (gr. 4-8). pap. 6.95 *(978-1-4342-4067-5(3)*, Stone Arch Novels) Stone Arch Bks.

Kramer, Paul. Maggie Goes on a Diet. 2011. (ENG.). 44p. (J). (gr. 1-7). 15.95 *(978-0-9819745-5-2(4))* Aloha Wellness Pubs.

Lane, Melaina. Chubs. . Another Day at School. 2011. 20p. 9.14 *(978-1-4251-7330-2(6))* Trafford Publishing.

Lang, Diane & Buchanan, Michael. The Fat Boy Chronicles. 2010. (Fat Boy Chronicles Ser.). (ENG.). 224p. (J). (gr. 7-11). pap. 9.95 *(978-1-58536-543-2(2)*, 202220) Sleeping Bear Pr.

Lange, Erin Jade. Butter. 2012. (ENG.). 304p. (YA). (gr. 9-12). 16.99 *(978-1-59990-780-2(1)*, 9781599907802, Bloomsbury USA Childrens) Bloomsbury Publishing USA.

Liberto, Lorenzo. Matt the Rat Fights Back / Ratón Mateo se Defiende. Gomez, Rocio, tr. from ENG. Torres, Irving, illus. 2005. (Matt the Rat Ser. / La Serie de Ratón Mateo). (ENG & SPA.). 32p. (J). lib. bdg. 20.00 *(978-0-9743668-4-5(6))* Harvest Sun Pr., LLC.

Lipsyte, Robert. One Fat Summer. rev. ed. 2004. (ENG.). 240p. (YA). (gr. 8-18). pap. 8.99 *(978-0-06-447073-5(3)*, HarperTeen) HarperCollins Pubs.

Lowry, Brigid. Things You Either Hate or Love. 2006. (ENG.). 179p. (YA). (gr. 7-12). 16.95 *(978-0-8234-2004-9(3))* Holiday Hse., Inc.

—Things You Either Hate or Love. 2007. (ENG.). 192p. (YA). (gr. 8-12). pap. 18.99 *(978-0-312-36308-6(7)*, 9780312363086, St. Martin's Griffin) St. Martin's Pr.

Marino, Peter. Dough Boy. (ENG.). 176p. (YA). (gr. 7-12). 2007. pap. 6.95 *(978-0-8234-2096-4(5))* 2005. 17.95 *(978-0-8234-1873-2(1))* Holiday Hse., Inc.

Mauzy, Barbara E. Don't Be a Schwoe: Fitness, 1 vol. Stuhmer, Bob, illus. 2013. (ENG.). 64p. (J). 16.99 *(978-0-7643-4295-0(9)*, 9780764342950) Schiffer Publishing, Ltd.

May, Eleanor. The Great Shape-up. 2008. pap. 34.95 *(978-1-58013-763-8(6))* Kane Press, Inc.

—The Great Shape-up. Gott, Barry, illus. 2007. (Science Solves It! Ser.). 32p. (J). (gr. -1-3). pap. 5.95 *(978-1-57565-248-1(X))* Kane Press, Inc.

Morgan McKinney Was Portly, Not Skinny: A Christmas Story. 2nd ed. 2003. (Illus.). 50p. (J). per. 59.95 *(978-0-9654843-3-6(5)*, 1) MacGregor, Doug.

Murphy, Julie. Dumplin. (YA). (gr. 8). 2017. 400p. pap. 9.99 *(978-0-06-232719-2(4))* 2015. (ENG.). 384p. 17.99 *(978-0-06-232718-5(6))* HarperCollins Pubs.

—Dumplin. 2017. (YA). lib. bdg. 20.85 ***(978-0-606-39647-9(0))*** Turtleback Bks.

Olsen, Judith K. I Can Hardly Wait. 2006. 100p. (J). pap. 7.95 *(978-1-59800-999-6(0))* Outskirts Pr., Inc.

Paley, Sasha. Huge. 2008. (ENG.). 272p. (YA). (gr. 7-12). pap. 8.99 *(978-1-4169-5795-9(2)*, Simon & Schuster Bks. For Young Readers) Simon & Schuster Bks. For Young Readers.

Perl, Lila. Me & Fat Glenda. 2014. (Fat Glenda Ser.). (ENG.). 200p. (gr. 3). pap. 12.95 *(978-1-939601-03-2(7))* Ig Publishing, Inc.

Potenzone Aliano, Kimberly. Chubby Is Everywhere! 2009. 42p. pap. 16.99 *(978-1-4490-0505-4(5))* AuthorHouse.

Rivera, Lassen. Soy Gordito. Alvarez, Mrinali, illus. 2006. (SPA.). 28p. 8.95 *(978-0-8477-1565-7(5))* Univ. of Puerto Rico Pr.

Sachs, Marilyn. The Fat Girl. 2nd ed. 2007. (ENG.). 240p. (YA). (gr. 8-12). per. 8.95 *(978-0-7387-1000-6(8),* Flux) North Star Editions.
Sackier, Shelley. Dear OPL. 2015. (ENG.). 240p. (J). (gr. 5-8). pap. 7.99 *(978-1-4926-0859-2(9),* 9781492608592) Sourcebooks, Inc.
Sayre, Justin & dePaola, Tomie. Husky. 2015. (ENG.). 272p. (YA). (gr. 5). bds. 16.99 *(978-0-448-48413-6(7),* Grosset & Dunlap) Penguin Young Readers Group.
Schechter, Lynn R. My Big Fat Secret: How Jenna Takes Control of Her Emotions & Eating. Chin, Jason, illus. 2009. 48p. (J). (gr. 3-7). 14.95 *(978-1-4338-0540-0(5));* pap. 9.95 *(978-1-4338-0541-7(3))* American Psychological Assn. (Magination Pr.).
Schraff, Anne. Going for Gold. 2008. 124p. lib. bdg. 13.95 *(978-0-7569-8403-8(3))* Perfection Learning Corp.
Seymour's Weight Loss Challenge! 2004. (J). *(978-0-9777159-2-3(2))* Health New England.
Supplee, Suzanne. Artichoke's Heart. 2009. (ENG.). 288p. (YA). (gr. 7-18). 8.99 *(978-0-14-241427-9(1),* Speak) Penguin Young Readers Group.
Tritt, Adam Byrn. Bud the Spud. Goldacker, "Java John", illus. 2012. (ENG.). 52p. (J). (gr. 3-7). 16.95 *(978-1-60419-062-5(0))* Axios Pr.
Walton, K. M. Empty. 2013. (ENG., (YA). (gr. 9). Illus.). 272p. pap. 10.99 *(978-1-4424-5358-6(3));* 256p. 16.99 *(978-1-4424-5359-3(1))* Simon Pulse. (Simon Pulse).
Whytock, Cherry. My Cup Runneth Over: The Life of Angelica Cookson Potts. Whytock, Cherry, illus. 2012. (ENG., Illus.). 192p. (YA). (gr. 7). pap. 9.99 *(978-1-4424-6055-3(5),* Simon Pulse) Simon Pulse.
—My Scrumptious Scottish Dumplings: The Life of Angelica Cookson Potts. Whytock, Cherry, illus. 2006. (ENG., Illus.). 192p. (YA). mass mkt. 5.99 *(978-0-689-86552-7(X),* Simon Pulse) Simon Pulse.
Willis, Jeanne. Flabby Cat & Slobby Dog. Ross, Tony, illus. 2009. (Andersen Press Picture Bks). (ENG.). 32p. (J). (gr. -1-3). 16.95 *(978-0-7613-5151-1(5),* Carolrhoda Bks.) Lerner Publishing Group.

WEIGHTS AND MEASURES

Here are entered works on a system of standard units of measure. Works on the science of measurement or of weights and measures are entered under Metrology. Works on a quantity taken as a standard of measurement are entered under Units of Measurement. Works on the force exerted by the gravitational field on a body are entered under Weight (Physics).

see also Measurement; Metric System; Metrology

Aboff, Marcie. If You Were an Inch or a Centimeter, 1 vol. Dillard, Sarah, illus. 2009. (Math Fun Ser.). (ENG.). 24p. (gr. 2-4). pap. 7.95 *(978-1-4048-5199-3(2))* Picture Window Bks.
Adamson, Thomas K. & Adamson, Heather. ¿Cómo Mides el Peso? 2011. (Mídelo/Measure It Ser.). (MUL & SPA.). 32p. (gr. 1-2). 27.32 *(978-1-4296-6892-7(X),* A+ Bilingue/Bilingual) Capstone Press of Coughlan Cos.
—¿Cómo Mides los Líquidos? 2011. (Mídelo/Measure It Ser.).Tr. of How Do You Measure Liquids? (MUL & SPA.). 32p. (gr. 1-2). 27.32 *(978-1-4296-6890-3(3),* A+ Bilingue/Bilingual) Capstone Press of Coughlan Cos.
—How Do You Measure Weight?, 1 vol. 2011. (Measure It! Ser.). (ENG.). 32p. (gr. 1-2). pap. 8.10 *(978-1-4296-6333-5(2),* Aplus Bks.) Capstone Press of Coughlan Cos.
Adamson, Thomas K. and Heather. How Do You Measure Weight? 2011. (Measure It! Ser.). (ENG.). 32p. (gr. 1-2). pap. 47.70 *(978-1-4296-6460-8(6),* Aplus Bks.) Capstone Press of Coughlan Cos.
Adamson, Tom & Adamson, Heather. How Do You Measure Weight?, 1 vol. 2010. (Measure It! Ser.). (ENG.). 32p. (gr. 1-2). lib. bdg. 27.32 *(978-1-4296-4458-7(3),* Aplus Bks.) Capstone Press of Coughlan Cos.
Adler, David A. Perimeter, Area, & Volume. Miller, Edward, illus. 2013. (ENG.). 32p. (J). pap. 7.99 *(978-0-8234-2763-5(3))* Holiday Hse., Inc.
—Perimeter, Area, & Volume: A Monster Book of Dimensions. Miller, Edward, illus. 2012. (ENG.). 32p. (J). 17.95 *(978-0-8234-2290-6(9))* Holiday Hse., Inc.
Alvarez, Jordan. Heavy or Light? Describe & Compare Measurable Attributes. 2013. (Rosen Math Readers Ser.). (ENG.). 16p. (J). (gr. k-1). pap. 42.00 *(978-1-4777-1651-9(3));* (Illus.). pap. 7.00 *(978-1-4777-1650-2(5))* Rosen Publishing Group, Inc., The. (Rosen Classroom).
Anderson, Jill. Measuring with Sebastian Pig & Friends on a Road Trip. Huntington, Amy, illus. 2009. (Math Fun with Sebastian Pig & Friends! Ser.). 32p. (J). (gr. k-3). lib. bdg. 23.94 *(978-0-7660-3362-7(7))* Enslow Pubs., Inc.
Arias, Lisa. Marvelous Measurement: Conversions. 2014. (ENG.). 32p. (gr. 3-6). 32.79 *(978-1-62717-712-2(4))* Rourke Educational Media.
Baer, T. H. Measuring Weight. 2016. (Measure It! Ser.). (ENG.). 24p. (J). (gr. 1-2). pap. 8.15 *(978-1-4824-3876-5(3));* lib. bdg. 22.60 *(978-1-4824-3878-9(X))* Stevens, Gareth Publishing LLLP.
Baron, Jessica. What's in the Garden? Learning to Compare Two Sets of Objects. 2009. (Math for the Real World: Early Emergent Ser.). (ENG., Illus.). 8p. (gr. k-1). pap. 5.15 *(978-0-8239-8860-0(0))* Rosen Publishing Group, Inc., The.
Benjamin, Lindsay. Measurement Action! 2005. (Yellow Umbrella Fluent Level Ser.). (ENG., Illus.). 16p. (gr. k-1). pap. 35.70 *(978-0-7368-5322-4(7),* Yellow Umbrella Bks.) Capstone Press of Coughlan Cos.
Bullock, Linda. You Can Use a Balance. 2004. (Rookie Read-About Science Ser.). (ENG., Illus.). 32p. (J). (gr. 1-2). pap. 4.95 *(978-0-516-27899-5(1),* Children's Pr.) Scholastic Library Publishing.
Burton, Margie, et al. Looking Down. 2011. (Early Connections Ser.). (J). *(978-1-61672-260-9(6))* Benchmark Education Co.
—What Can You Measure with A Lollipop? 2011. (Early Connections Ser.). (J). *(978-1-61672-545-7(1))* Benchmark Education Co.
Bussiere, Desirée. What in the World Is a Ton? & Other Weight & Volume Measurements, 1 vol. 2013. (Let's Measure More Ser.). (ENG.). 24p. (J). (gr. -1-3). lib. bdg. 24.21 *(978-1-61783-599-5(4),* SandCastle) ABDO Publishing Co.
Cardenas, Ernesto & Saavedra, Patricia. Medición. l.t. ed. 2006.Tr. of Measurement. (SPA., Illus.). 16p. pap. 4.95 *(978-1-933668-14-7(8))* Milo Educational Bks. & Resources.
Chapman, Joan. Heavy & Light: Learning to Compare Weights of Objects. 2009. (Math for the Real World: Early Emergent Ser.). (ENG., Illus.). 8p. (gr. k-1). pap. 5.15 *(978-0-8239-8844-0(9))* Rosen Publishing Group, Inc., The.
Chrismer, Melanie. Math Tools. 2006. (Rookie Read-About Math Ser.). (ENG., Illus.). 32p. (J). (gr. 1-2). lib. bdg. 20.50 *(978-0-516-24961-2(4),* Children's Pr.) Scholastic Library Publishing.
Chrismer, Melanie & National Geographic Learning Staff. Math Tools. 2010. (Rise & Shine Ser.). (ENG., Illus.). 32p. (C). (gr. 1-2). pap. 19.95 *(978-0-516-25550-7(9))* National Geographic School Publishing, Inc.
Cleary, Brian P. How Long or How Wide? A Measuring Guide. Gable, Brian, illus. 2007. (Math Is CATegorical (r) Ser.). (ENG.). 32p. (gr. k-3). lib. bdg. 16.95 *(978-0-8225-6694-6(X),* Millbrook Pr.) Lerner Publishing Group.
—On the Scale, a Weighty Tale. Gable, Brian, illus. (Math Is CATegorical (r) Ser.). (ENG.). 32p. (gr. k-3). 2010. pap. 6.95 *(978-1-58013-845-1(4),* First Avenue Editions) 2008. 16.95 *(978-0-8225-7851-2(4))* Lerner Publishing Group.
—On the Scale, A Weighty Tale. 2010. pap. 39.62 *(978-0-7613-6997-4(X))* Lerner Publishing Group.
Cobb, Vicki. I Fall Down. Gorton, Julia, illus. 2004. (Science Play Ser.). (ENG.). 40p. (J). (gr. -1-3). 17.99 *(978-0-688-17842-0(1))* HarperCollins Pubs.
Cotugno, Megan. Measure It!, 1 vol., Set. Incl. Distance, Area, & Volume. Somervill, Barbara A. pap. 8.29 *(978-1-4329-3769-0(3));* Mass & Weight. Somervill, Barbara A. pap. 8.29 *(978-1-4329-3771-3(5));* Speed & Acceleration. Somervill, Barbara A. pap. 8.29 *(978-1-4329-3770-6(7));* Temperature. Rand, Casey. pap. 8.29 *(978-1-4329-3773-7(1));* Time. Rand, Casey. pap. 8.29 *(978-1-4329-3772-0(3));* (Illus.). (gr. 3-6). (Measure It! Ser.). (ENG.). 32p. 2010. Set pap. 39.95 *(978-1-4329-3774-4(X),* Heinemann InfoSearch) Heinemann-Raintree.
Dearborne, Hilary. Heavy & Light: Describe & Compare Measurable Attributes. 2013. (InfoMax Math Readers Ser.). (ENG.). 16p. (J). (gr. k-1). pap. 42.00 *(978-1-4777-1941-1(5));* (Illus.). pap. 7.00 *(978-1-4777-1940-4(7))* Rosen Publishing Group, Inc., The. (Rosen Classroom).
Doudna, Kelly. It's My Pleasure to Measure the Treasure!, 1 vol. 2007. (Science Made Simple Ser.). (ENG., Illus.). 24p. (J). (gr. k-3). lib. bdg. 24.21 *(978-1-59928-602-0(5),* SandCastle) ABDO Publishing Co.
—It's Time to Dance, We Can Use a Balance!, 1 vol. 2007. (Science Made Simple Ser.). (ENG., Illus.). 24p. (J). (gr. k-3). lib. bdg. 24.21 *(978-1-59928-608-2(4),* SandCastle) ABDO Publishing Co.
—Let's Be Kids & Measure Liquids!, 1 vol. 2007. (Science Made Simple Ser.). (ENG., Illus.). 24p. (J). (gr. k-3). lib. bdg. 24.21 *(978-1-59928-610-5(6),* SandCastle) ABDO Publishing Co.
Dowdy, Penny. Measurement. 2008. (My Path to Math Ser.). (ENG., Illus.). 24p. (J). (gr. k-3). pap. *(978-0-7787-4359-0(4))* Crabtree Publishing Co.
Elliott, Cathy. How Much Does It Weigh? 2008. (Discovering & Exploring Science Ser.). (Illus.). 16p. (J). (gr. -1-3). lib. bdg. 12.95 *(978-0-7569-8416-8(5))* Perfection Learning Corp.
First, Rachel. Weigh It! Fun with Weight, 1 vol. 2016. (Math Beginnings Ser.). (ENG., Illus.). 24p. (J). (gr. k-3). 24.21 *(978-1-62403-936-2(7))* ABDO Publishing Co.
Fosnot, Catherine Twomey. Measuring for the Art Show: Addition on the Open Number Line. 2008. (ENG.). 80p. (gr. 1-2). pap. 31.25 *(978-0-325-01010-6(2),* E01010, Firsthand) Heinemann.
Franco, Betsy & Key Curriculum Press Staff. English Units of Length, Bk. 1. 2012. (Key To... workbooks Ser.: Bk. 1). (ENG.). 48p. (gr. 6-8). spiral bd. 5.64 *(978-1-55953-021-7(9),* 1559530219) McGraw-Hill Education.
—Measuring Length & Perimeter Using English Units, 2. 2012. (Key To... workbooks Ser.: Bk. 2). (ENG.). 48p. (gr. 6-8). spiral bd. 5.64 *(978-1-55953-022-4(7),* 1559530227) McGraw-Hill Education.
—Measuring Length & Perimeter Using Metric Units, Bk. 2. 2012. (Key To... workbooks Ser.: Bk. 2). (ENG., Illus.). 48p. (gr. 6-8). spiral bd., wbk. ed. 5.64 *(978-1-55953-326-3(9),* 1559533269) McGraw-Hill Education.
Furgang, Kathy. Measuring Length: Set Of 6. 2011. (Early Connections Ser.). (J). pap. 37.00 net. *(978-1-4108-1088-5(7))* Benchmark Education Co.
Gardner, Robert. Heavy-Duty Science Projects with Weight: How Much Does It Weigh? 2003. (Sensational Science Experiments Ser.). (Illus.). 48p. (J). (gr. 1-4). lib. bdg. 23.93 *(978-0-7660-2013-9(4))* Enslow Pubs., Inc.
—How Big Is Big? Science Projects with Volume. 2015. (Hot Science Experiments Ser.). 48p. (J). (gr. 3-4). 25.27 *(978-0-7660-6620-5(7))* Enslow Pubs., Inc.
—How Heavy Is Heavy? Science Projects with Weight. 2015. (Hot Science Experiments Ser.). 48p. (J). (gr. 3-4). 25.27 *(978-0-7660-6600-7(2))* Enslow Pubs., Inc.
—How High Is High? Science Projects with Height & Depth. 2015. (Hot Science Experiments Ser.). 48p. (J). (gr. 3-4). 25.27 *(978-0-7660-6595-6(2))* Enslow Pubs., Inc.
—Super-Sized Science Projects with Volume: How Much Space Does It Take Up? 2003. (Sensational Science Experiments Ser.). (Illus.). 48p. (J). lib. bdg. 25.27 *(978-0-7660-2014-6(2))* Enslow Pubs., Inc.
Guillain, Charlotte. Pesado o Liviano, 1 vol. 2010. (Las Propiedades de Los Materiales Ser.).Tr. of Heavy or Light. (SPA.). 24p. (gr. -1-1). 22.65 *(978-1-4329-4240-3(9));* pap. 6.29 *(978-1-4329-4248-9(4))* Heinemann-Raintree. (Bellota).
Harris, Trudy. The Royal Treasure Measure. Stevanovic, Ivica, illus. 2012. (Math Is Fun! Ser.). (ENG.). 32p. (gr. k-2). lib. bdg. 16.95 *(978-0-7613-6806-9(X),* Millbrook Pr.) Lerner Publishing Group.
Hirschmann, Kris. Is a Paw a Foot? All about Measurement. 2006. (Artist Collection: the Dog Ser.). (ENG., Illus.). 32p. (J). (gr. -1-3). pap. 3.99 *(978-0-439-92213-5(5))* Scholastic, Inc.
Holland, Gini. Light & Heavy. 2007. (I Know Opposites Ser.). 16p. (gr. -1-2). pap. 5.30 *(978-0-8368-8300-8(4));* lib. bdg. 19.00 *(978-0-8368-8295-7(4))* Stevens, Gareth Publishing LLLP. (Weekly Reader Leveled Readers).
—Light & Heavy/ Ligero y Pesado. 2007. (I Know Opposites/ Conceptos contrarios Ser.). (SPA & ENG.). 16p. (gr. -1-3). pap. 5.30 *(978-0-8368-8310-7(1),* Weekly Reader Leveled Readers) Stevens, Gareth Publishing LLLP.
—Light & Heavy/Ligero y Pesado. 2007. (I Know Opposites/Conceptos Contrarios Ser.). (SPA & ENG.). 16p. (gr. -1-3). lib. bdg. 19.00 *(978-0-8368-8305-3(5),* Weekly Reader Leveled Readers) Stevens, Gareth Publishing LLLP.
Ithaca, Sciencenter, NY. How Small Is Nano? 2009. 24p. 11.20 *(978-0-578-00197-5(7))* Sciencenter.
Jeffries, Joyce. Heavy & Light. 2013. (Dinosaur School Ser.). (Illus.). 24p. (gr. -1-1). 22.60 *(978-1-4339-8087-9(8));* pap. 8.15 *(978-1-4339-8088-6(6))* Stevens, Gareth Publishing LLLP.
Kauffman, Dorothy. Measurement All over the World. 2005. (Oxford Picture Dictionary for the Content Areas Ser.). (ENG., Illus.). 22p. pap. 7.56 *(978-0-19-430959-2(2))* Oxford Univ. Pr., Inc.
Kernan, Elizabeth. How Long Is It? Learning to Measure with Nonstandard Units. 2009. (Math for the Real World: Early Emergent Ser.). (ENG., Illus.). 8p. (gr. k-1). pap. 5.15 *(978-0-8239-8843-3(0))* Rosen Publishing Group, Inc., The.
Krech, Bob & Novelli, Joan. 50 Fill-In Math Word Problems - Time & Measurement: Engaging Story Problems for Students to Read, Fill-In, Solve, & Sharpen Their Math Skills. 2009. (50 Fill-in Math Word Problems Ser.). (ENG.). 64p. (gr. 2-3). pap. 11.99 *(978-0-545-07483-4(5),* Teaching Resources) Scholastic, Inc.
Loughran, Donna. A Day at Mini-Golf: What's the Length? 2013. (IMath Ser.). (Illus.). 24p. (J). (gr. k-2). lib. bdg. 21.27 *(978-1-59953-556-2(4))* Norwood Hse. Pr.
Loughran, Donna & Brunner-Jass, Renata. Field of Play: Measuring Distance, Rate, & Time. 2013. (IMath Ser.). (Illus.). 48p. (J). (gr. 5-6). lib. bdg. 23.94 *(978-1-59953-571-5(8))* Norwood Hse. Pr.
Mattern, Joanne. Let's Visit Canada: The Metric System. 2009. (PowerMath Ser.). (Illus.). 24p. (gr. 3-4). pap. 8.25 *(978-0-8239-8872-3(4),* PowerKids Pr.) Rosen Publishing Group, Inc., The.
Metz, Lorijo. Using Scales & Balances. 2013. (Science Tools Ser.). (ENG., Illus.). 24p. (J). (gr. 3-6). 22.60 *(978-1-4488-9686-8(X));* pap. 8.25 *(978-1-4488-9830-5(7))* Rosen Publishing Group, Inc., The. (PowerKids Pr.).
Minden, Cecilia. What Does It Weigh? 2010. (21st Century Basic Skills Library: Measurements Ser.). (ENG.). 24p. (gr. k-3). lib. bdg. 22.79 *(978-1-60279-849-6(4),* 200564) Cherry Lake Publishing.
Murphy, Patricia J. Measuring Puppies & Kittens. 2007. (Puppy & Kitten Math Ser.). (Illus.). 32p. (J). (gr. 1-2). lib. bdg. 23.94 *(978-0-7660-2727-5(9),* Enslow Elementary) Enslow Pubs., Inc.
Murphy, Stuart J. Mighty Maddie. Lum, Bernice, illus. 2004. (MathStart Ser.). 40p. (J). 15.99 *(978-0-06-053159-1(2));* (ENG.). (gr. -1-3). pap. 5.99 *(978-0-06-053161-4(4))* HarperCollins Pubs.
Nsrc. Science & Technology for Children Books: Measuring Time. 2004. (Illus.). 64p. (J). *(978-1-933008-09-7(1))* Smithsonian Science Education Ctr. (SSEC).
O'Hara, Nicholas. Sort It by Weight. 2015. (Sort It Out! Ser.). (ENG., Illus.). 24p. (J). (gr. k-1). pap. 8.15 *(978-1-4824-2585-7(8))* Stevens, Gareth Publishing LLLP.
Pallotta, Jerry. Hershey's Weights & Measures. Bolster, Rob, illus. 2003. (Hershey's Ser.). (ENG.). 32p. (J). 16.99 *(978-0-439-38876-4(7),* Cartwheel Bks.) Scholastic, Inc.
—Weights & Measures. Bolster, Rob, illus. 2008. 32p. (J). pap. *(978-0-545-06448-4(1))* Scholastic, Inc.
Parker, Vic. How Big Is Big? Comparing Plants, 1 vol. 2010. (Measuring & Comparing Ser.). (ENG.). 32p. (gr. 1-3). 27.32 *(978-1-4329-3959-5(9),* Heinemann First Library) Heinemann-Raintree.
—How Small Is Small? Comparing Body Parts, 1 vol. 2010. (Measuring & Comparing Ser.). (ENG.). 32p. (gr. 1-3). 27.32 *(978-1-4329-3960-1(2),* Heinemann First Library) Heinemann-Raintree.
—How Tall Is Tall? Comparing Structures, 1 vol. 2010. (Measuring & Comparing Ser.). (ENG.). 32p. (gr. 1-3). 27.32 *(978-1-4329-3955-7(6),* Heinemann First Library) Heinemann-Raintree.
Rauen, Amy. Vamos a Encontrar lo Más Corto y lo Más Largo. 2008. (Matemáticas para empezar (Getting Started with Math) Ser.). (SPA.). 16p. (gr. -1-2). pap. 5.30 *(978-0-8368-8997-0(5),* Weekly Reader Leveled Readers) Stevens, Gareth Publishing LLLP.
—Vamos a Encontrar lo Más Corto y lo Más Largo. 2008. (Matemáticas para Empezar (Getting Started with Math) Ser.). (SPA., Illus.). 16p. (gr. -1-2). lib. bdg. 19.00 *(978-0-8368-8992-5(4),* Weekly Reader Leveled Readers) Stevens, Gareth Publishing LLLP.
Reinke, Beth Bence. Measuring Weight. Petelinsek, Kathleen, illus. 2014. (Explorer Junior Library: Math Explorer Junior Ser.). (ENG.). 24p. (J). (gr. 1-4). 28.50 *(978-1-62431-652-4(2),* 203120) Cherry Lake Publishing.
Rivera, Sheila. Balance. 2006. (First Step Nonfiction - Simple Tools Ser.). (ENG., Illus.). 8p. (gr. -1-1). pap. 4.95 *(978-0-8225-5716-6(9),* Lerner Pubns.) Lerner Publishing Group.
—Scale. 2007. (First Step Nonfiction - Simple Tools Ser.). (ENG.). 8p. (gr. -1-1). pap. 4.95 *(978-0-8225-6854-4(3))* Lerner Publishing Group.
—Tape Measure. 2007. (First Step Nonfiction - Simple Tools Ser.). (ENG.). 8p. (gr. -1-1). pap. 4.95 *(978-0-8225-6855-1(1))* Lerner Publishing Group.
Roy, Jennifer Rozines & Roy, Gregory. Measuring at Home. 2007. (J). pap. 6.99 *(978-0-7614-3384-2(8))* Marshall Cavendish Corp.
Rustad, Martha E. H. The Highest Places on Earth. 2010. (Extreme Planet Ser.). (ENG.). 24p. (gr. 1-2). lib. bdg. 25.32 *(978-1-4296-3963-7(6),* First Facts) Capstone Press of Coughlan Cos.
Salzmann, Mary Elizabeth. What in the World Is a Cup?, 1 vol. 2009. (Let's Measure Ser.). (ENG., Illus.). 24p. (J). (gr. k-3). lib. bdg. 24.21 *(978-1-60453-162-6(2))* ABDO Publishing Co.
—What in the World Is a Cup? CD & Book. 2010. (Let's Measure CD+Book Ser.). 24p. (gr. k-3). audio compact disk 42.70 *(978-1-61613-313-9(9),* SandCastle) ABDO Publishing Co.
—What in the World Is a Cup? Site CD & Book. 2010. (Let's Measure Site CD+Book Ser.). 24p. (gr. k-3). cd-rom 78.42 *(978-1-61613-285-9(X),* SandCastle) ABDO Publishing Co.
—What in the World Is a Foot?, 1 vol. 2009. (Let's Measure Ser.). (ENG., Illus.). 24p. (J). (gr. k-3). lib. bdg. 24.21 *(978-1-60453-163-3(0))* ABDO Publishing Co.
—What in the World Is a Foot? CD & Book. 2010. (Let's Measure CD+Book Ser.). 24p. (gr. k-3). audio compact disk 42.70 *(978-1-61613-314-6(7),* SandCastle) ABDO Publishing Co.
—What in the World Is a Foot? Site CD & Book. 2010. (Let's Measure Site CD+Book Ser.). 24p. (gr. k-3). cd-rom 78.42 *(978-1-61613-286-6(8),* SandCastle) ABDO Publishing Co.
—What in the World Is a Gallon?, 1 vol. 2009. (Let's Measure Ser.). (ENG., Illus.). 24p. (J). (gr. k-3). lib. bdg. 24.21 *(978-1-60453-164-0(9))* ABDO Publishing Co.
—What in the World Is a Gallon? CD & Book. 2010. (Let's Measure CD+Book Ser.). 24p. (gr. k-3). audio compact disk 42.70 *(978-1-61613-315-3(5),* SandCastle) ABDO Publishing Co.
—What in the World Is a Gallon? Site CD & Book. 2010. (Let's Measure Site CD+Book Ser.). 24p. (gr. k-3). cd-rom 78.42 *(978-1-61613-287-3(6),* SandCastle) ABDO Publishing Co.
—What in the World Is a Pound?, 1 vol. 2009. (Let's Measure Ser.). (ENG., Illus.). 24p. (J). (gr. k-3). lib. bdg. 24.21 *(978-1-60453-165-7(7))* ABDO Publishing Co.
—What in the World Is a Pound? CD & Book. 2010. (Let's Measure CD+Book Ser.). 24p. (gr. k-3). audio compact disk 42.70 *(978-1-61613-316-0(3),* SandCastle) ABDO Publishing Co.
—What in the World Is a Pound? Site CD & Book. 2010. (Let's Measure Site CD+Book Ser.). 24p. (gr. k-3). cd-rom 78.42 *(978-1-61613-288-0(4),* SandCastle) ABDO Publishing Co.
—What in the World Is an Inch?, 1 vol. 2009. (Let's Measure Ser.). (ENG., Illus.). 24p. (J). (gr. k-3). lib. bdg. 24.21 *(978-1-60453-166-4(5))* ABDO Publishing Co.
—What in the World Is an Inch? CD & Book. 2010. (Let's Measure CD+Book Ser.). 24p. (gr. k-3). audio compact disk 42.70 *(978-1-61613-317-7(1),* SandCastle) ABDO Publishing Co.
—What in the World Is an Inch? Site CD & Book. 2010. (Let's Measure Site CD+Book Ser.). 24p. (gr. k-3). cd-rom 78.42 *(978-1-61613-289-7(2),* SandCastle) ABDO Publishing Co.
—What in the World Is an Ounce?, 1 vol. 2009. (Let's Measure Ser.). (ENG., Illus.). 24p. (J). (gr. k-3). lib. bdg. 24.21 *(978-1-60453-167-1(3))* ABDO Publishing Co.
—What in the World Is an Ounce? CD & Book. 2010. (Let's Measure CD+Book Ser.). 24p. (gr. k-3). audio compact disk 42.70 *(978-1-61613-318-4(X),* SandCastle) ABDO Publishing Co.
—What in the World Is an Ounce? Site CD & Book. 2010. (Let's Measure Site CD+Book Ser.). 24p. (gr. k-3). cd-rom 78.42 *(978-1-61613-290-3(6),* SandCastle) ABDO Publishing Co.
Sargent, Brian. How Heavy Is It? 2005. (Rookie Read-About Math Ser.). (ENG., Illus.). 32p. (J). (gr. 1-2). lib. bdg. 20.50 *(978-0-516-25267-4(4),* Children's Pr.) Scholastic Library Publishing.
Schrier, Allyson Valentine. Is It Heavier Than an Elephant? 2008. (Discovering & Exploring Science Ser.). (Illus.). 16p. (J). (gr. -1-3). lib. bdg. 12.95 *(978-0-7569-8438-0(6))* Perfection Learning Corp.
Schwartz, David M. Millions to Measure. Kellogg, Steven, illus. 2006. (ENG.). 40p. (J). (gr. k-7). reprint ed. pap. 6.99 *(978-0-06-084806-4(5))* HarperCollins Pubs.
Schwartz, David M. & Schwartz, David. Millions to Measure. Kellogg, Steven, illus. 2003. (ENG.). 40p. (J). (gr. k-7). 17.99 *(978-0-688-12916-3(1))* HarperCollins Pubs.
Science & Technology for Children Books, Measuring Time Set, 8 vols. 2004. (Illus.). 64p. (J). *(978-1-933008-21-9(0))* Smithsonian Science Education Ctr. (SSEC).
Somervill, Barbara A. Distance, Area, & Volume, 1 vol. 2010. (Measure It! Ser.). (ENG., Illus.). 32p. (gr. 3-6). 33.32 *(978-1-4329-3763-8(4));* pap. 8.29 *(978-1-4329-3769-0(3))* Heinemann-Raintree. (Heinemann InfoSearch).
—Mass & Weight, 1 vol. 2010. (Measure It! Ser.). (ENG., Illus.). 32p. (gr. 3-6). 33.32 *(978-1-4329-3765-2(0));* pap. 8.29 *(978-1-4329-3771-3(5))* Heinemann-Raintree. (Heinemann InfoSearch).
Sullivan, Erin Ash. Measuring Matter: Text Pairs. 2008. (Bridges/Navigators Ser.). (J). (gr. 3). 94.00 *(978-1-4108-8367-4(1))* Benchmark Education Co.
Sullivan, Navin. Weight. 2006. (Measure Up! Ser.). (Illus.). 48p. (gr. 4-7). lib. bdg. 31.36 *(978-0-7614-2324-9(9),* Benchmark Bks.) Marshall Cavendish Corp.
Trumbauer, Lisa. Animal Giants. 2005. (Yellow Umbrella Fluent Level Ser.). (ENG., Illus.). 16p. (gr. k-1). pap. 35.70 *(978-0-7368-5328-6(6),* Yellow Umbrella Bks.) Capstone Press of Coughlan Cos.
—What Is Volume? 2006. (Rookie Read-About Science Ser.). (ENG., Illus.). 32p. (J). (gr. 1-2). pap. 4.95 *(978-0-516-24661-1(5),* Children's Pr.) Scholastic Library Publishing.
Vogel, Julia. Measuring Weight. Marten, Luanne, illus. 2012. (Simple Measurement Ser.). (ENG.). 24p. (J). (gr. -1-2). 27.07 *(978-1-61473-284-6(1),* 204989) Child's World, Inc., The.
Weakland, Mark. How Heavy? Wacky Ways to Compare Weight, 1 vol. Bolton, Bill, illus. 2013. (Wacky Comparisons Ser.). (ENG.). 24p. (gr. -1-2). 27.99 *(978-1-4048-8322-2(3));* pap. 8.95 *(978-1-4795-1912-5(X))* Picture Window Bks.
Woodford, Chris. Weight. 2012. (Measure up Math Ser.). (Illus.). 32p. (J). (gr. 4-6). pap. 10.50 *(978-1-4339-7462-5(2));* lib. bdg. 26.60 *(978-1-4339-7461-8(4))* Stevens, Gareth Publishing LLLP.

WELFARE STATE

see Economic Policy

WELFARE WORK

see Social Service

WELLS, H. G. (HERBERT GEORGE), 1866-1946

Abrams, Dennis. H. G. Wells. 2011. (Who Wrote That? Ser.). (Illus.). 128p. (gr. 6-12). 35.00 *(978-1-60413-770-5(3),* Chelsea Hse.) Facts On File, Inc.
Boerst, William J. Time Machine: The Story of H. G. Wells. 2004. (World Writers Ser.). (Illus.). 112p. (YA). (gr. 6-12).

W X Y Z

23.95 *(978-1-883846-40-4(4)*, First Biographies) Reynolds, Morgan Inc.

H. G. Wells: First Citizen of the Future. 2014. (ENG.). 192p. (J). (gr. 3-7). pap. 13.95 *(978-1-59077-356-7(X))* Evans, M. & Co., Inc.

Saddleback Educational Publishing Staff, ed. War of the Worlds. 2011. (Timeless Classics Ser.). (ENG.). 48p. (YA). (gr. 9-12). pupil's gde. ed. 19.95 incl. cd-rom *(978-1-61651-157-9(5))* Saddleback Educational Publishing, Inc.

WELLS, IDA B., 1862-1931

see Wells-Barnett, Ida B., 1862-1931

WELLS-BARNETT, IDA B., 1862-1931

Dray, Philip. Yours for Justice, Ida B. Wells: The Daring Life of a Crusading Journalist, 1 vol. Alcorn, Stephen, illus. 2008. (ENG.). 48p. (J). (gr. 5-9). 18.95 *(978-1-56145-417-4(6))* Peachtree Pubs.

Hinman, Bonnie. Eternal Vigilance: The Story of Ida B. Wells-Barnett. 2011. (Civil Rights Leaders Ser.). 128p. (gr. 6-10). lib. bdg. 28.95 *(978-1-59935-111-7(0))* Reynolds, Morgan Inc.

McKissack, Patricia C. & McKissack, Fredrick L. Ida B. Wells-Barnett: Fighter for Justice. 2013. (Famous African Americans Ser.). 24p. (J). (gr. k-3). pap. 7.95 *(978-1-4644-0198-5(5)*, Enslow Elementary); (Illus.). 22.60 *(978-0-7660-4108-0(5))* Enslow Pubs., Inc.

Morretta, Alison. Ida B. Wells-Barnett & the Crusade Against Lynching. 2016. (Primary Sources of the Civil Rights Movement Ser.). (Illus.). 64p. (J). (gr. 6-6). 34.21 *(978-1-5026-1874-0(5))* Cavendish Square Publishing.

Myers, Walter Dean. Ida B. Wells: Let the Truth Be Told. Christensen, Bonnie, illus. 2008. (ENG.). 40p. (J). (gr. -1-3). 16.99 *(978-0-06-027705-5(X)*, Amistad) HarperCollins Pubs.

Schraff, Anne E. Ida B. Wells-Barnett: Strike a Blow Against Glaring Evil. 2008. (African-American Biography Library). (Illus.). 128p. (J). (gr. 6-18). lib. bdg. 33.27 *(978-0-7660-2704-6(X))* Enslow Pubs., Inc.

Welch, Catherine A. Ida B. Wells-Barnett: Powerhouse with a Pen. 2005. (Trailblazers Biographies Ser.). (Illus.). 112p. (gr. 5-9). 27.93 *(978-1-57505-352-3(7))* Lerner Publishing Group.

WELLS

see also Petroleum; Water-Supply

Shoveller, Herb. Ryan & Jimmy: And the Well in Africa That Brought Them Together. (CitizenKid Ser.). (ENG., Illus.). 56p. (J). (gr. 3-7). 2008. pap. 9.95 *(978-1-55453-271-1(X))* 2006. 16.95 *(978-1-55337-967-6(5))* Kids Can Pr., Ltd. CAN. Dist: Hachette Bk. Group.

Stone, Andrew & Bryan, Jessica. Well... What's All That Drilling About? Pender, Rachel, illus. 2007. 40p. (J). 7.95 *(978-0-9641186-3-8(7))* American Ground Water Trust.

WELLS—FICTION

Gogarty, Brian. Shamrock Sean & the Wishing Well. Burchartz, Roxanne, illus. 2007. (ENG.). 12p. (J). pap. 7.95 *(978-0-86278-967-1(2))* O'Brien Pr., Ltd., The IRL. Dist: Dufour Editions, Inc.

Jones, Huw Vaughan. Ar ôl y Parti. 2005. (WEL., Illus.). 14p. pap. *(978-1-85644-994-6(7))* CAA.

Kimberly, Anne. Dark Well of Decision. 2007. 136p. per. 7.99 *(978-0-9800356-5-0(1))* Highland Pr. Publishing.

Lin, Joyce, tr. The frog in the Well. Caprio, Pattie, illus. 2008. (ENG & CHI.). 36p. (J). 14.95 *(978-0-9801305-1-5(4))* CE Bilingual Bks. LLC.

Peeler, Gail. Jackson's Magic Wishing Well. 2008. 25p. 35.50 *(978-1-4357-2950-6(1))* Lulu Pr., Inc.

WELLS, FARGO & COMPANY

Moody, Ralph. Wells Fargo. Mays, Victor, illus. 2005. (ENG.). 186p. pap. 13.95 *(978-0-8032-8303-9(2)*, MOOWEX, Bison Bks.) Univ. of Nebraska Pr.

WELSH LANGUAGE

Campbell, Rod. Jyngl: Sefyll-I-Fyny. 2005.Tr. of Pop-Up Jungle. (WEL., Illus.). 14p. *(978-1-85596-166-1(0))* Dref Wen.

Davies, Helen Emanuel & Cooper, Anne Lloyd. Torri Gair. 2005. (WEL., Illus.). 16p. pap. *(978-1-85644-545-0(3))* CAA.

Emlyn, Non ap. Hamddena. 2005. (WEL & ENG., Illus.). 20p. pap. *(978-1-86085-603-7(9))* ICA Video.

—Hamddena - Llyfr 1 Lefel 3/4. 2005. (WEL & ENG., Illus.). 20p. pap. *(978-1-86085-600-6(4))* ICA Video.

—Hamddena - Llyfr 3 Lefel 5/6. 2005. (WEL & ENG., Illus.). 20p. pap. *(978-1-86085-602-0(0))* ICA Video.

Gliori, Debi. Mr. Arth Yn Gwarchod. 2005.Tr. of Mr Bear Babysits. (WEL., Illus.). 32p. pap. *(978-1-85596-139-5(3))* Dref Wen.

Gruffydd, Stella. Haws Dweud: Gweithgareddau Llefaredd, Darllen Ac Ysgrifennu I Blant Cyfnod Allweddol 2. 2005. (WEL., Illus.). 152p. pap. *(978-1-85644-601-3(8))* CAA.

Hughes, Mair Wynn. Y Dewis. 2005. (WEL., Illus.). 16p. pap. *(978-1-85644-747-8(2))* CAA.

Jones, Marlis. Wyn Melangell. 2005. (WEL., Illus.). 16p. pap. *(978-1-85644-744-7(8))* CAA.

Jones, Marlis & Jên, Ruth. Cuddio'r Colur. 2005. (WEL., Illus.). 16p. pap. *(978-1-85644-547-4(X))* CAA.

Lasarus, Gwen. Hud Hen Hanes. 2005. (WEL., Illus.). 16p. pap. *(978-1-85644-745-4(6))* CAA.

Lewis, Siân & Thomas, Rhianedd. Cris Croes. 2005. (WEL., Illus.). 16p. pap. *(978-1-85644-544-3(5))* CAA.

Maelor, Gwawr, et al. Tân Yn y Jyngl. 2005. (WEL., Illus.). 16p. pap. *(978-1-85644-842-0(8))* CAA.

Richards, Aled. Stori Dda. 2005. (WEL., Illus.). 16p. pap. *(978-1-85644-746-1(4))* CAA.

Richards, Aled & Pritchard, Richard Huw. Am y Copa. 2005. (WEL., Illus.). 16p. pap. *(978-1-85644-549-8(6))* CAA.

Roberts, Eirlys. Dweud ein Dweud. 2005. (WEL., Illus.). 72p. pap. *(978-1-85644-906-9(8))* CAA.

Roberts, Heulwen. Anifeiliaid Anwes. 2005. (WEL., Illus.). 16p. pap. *(978-1-85644-778-2(2))* CAA.

University of Wales, Aberystwyth, Centre for Educational Studies Staff, contrib. by. Arch Noa: Casgliad o Sbardunau Ac Ymarferion Ar Thema Creaduriaid. 2005. (WEL., Illus.). 72p. pap. *(978-1-85644-959-5(9))* CAA.

Williams, Carol. Beth Yw'r Gair Am... 2004.Tr. of What's the World For.... (WEL & ENG., Illus.). 126p. (J). pap. 20.00 *(978-0-7083-1736-5(7))* Gwasg Prifysgol Cymru / Univ. of Wales Pr. GBR. Dist: Chicago Distribution Ctr.

WENCESLAS, DUKE OF BOHEMIA, APPROXIMATELY 907-929

Manson, Christopher, illus. Good King Wenceslas. 2004. 25p. (J). (gr. k-4). reprint ed. 15.00 *(978-0-7567-8226-9(0))* DIANE Publishing Co.

WEREWOLVES

Beaumont, Steve. Drawing Werewolves & Other Gothic Ghouls. 2011. (Drawing Legendary Monsters Ser.). (Illus.). 32p. (J). (gr. 3-6). 26.50 *(978-1-4488-3254-5(3)*, PowerKids Pr.) Rosen Publishing Group, Inc., The.

Bennett, Adelaide. Ancient Werewolves & Vampires: The Roots of the Teeth. 2010. (Making of a Monster Ser.). (Illus.). 64p. (YA). (gr. 7-18). pap. 9.95 *(978-1-4222-1955-3(0))*; lib. bdg. 22.95 *(978-1-4222-1802-0(3))* Mason Crest.

—Global Legends & Lore: Vampires & Werewolves Around the World. 2010. (Making of a Monster Ser.). 64p. (YA). (gr. 7-18). pap. 9.95 *(978-1-4222-1963-8(1))* Mason Crest.

Bingham, Jane. Vampires & Werewolves, 1 vol. King, Chris, illus. 2013. (Solving Mysteries with Science Ser.). (ENG.). 48p. (gr. 3-6). pap. 9.95 *(978-1-4109-5507-4(9))* Heinemann-Raintree.

—Vampires & Werewolves, 1 vol. 2013. (Solving Mysteries with Science Ser.). (ENG.). 48p. (gr. 3-6). 29.99 *(978-1-4109-5501-2(X))* Heinemann-Raintree.

Bullard, Lisa. I'm Fearsome & Furry! Meet a Werewolf. Moran, Mike, illus. 2014. (Monster Buddies Ser.). (ENG.). 24p. (gr. k-2). lib. bdg. 23.93 *(978-0-7613-9189-0(4)*, Millbrook Pr.) Lerner Publishing Group.

Castellano, Peter. Werewolves. 2016. (Monsters! Ser.). (ENG., Illus.). 32p. (J). (gr. 1-2). pap. 10.50 *(978-1-4824-4098-0(9))* Stevens, Gareth Publishing LLLP.

Cheatham, Mark. Werewolves! 2012. (Jr. Graphic Monster Stories Ser.). (ENG.). 24p. (J). (gr. 3-6). pap. 10.60 *(978-1-4488-6399-0(6))*; lib. bdg. 25.25 *(978-1-4488-6220-7(5))* Rosen Publishing Group, Inc., The. (PowerKids Pr.).

Collins, Sophie. How to Love a Werewolf. 2010. (ENG., Illus.). 128p. (gr. -1-17). 12.50 *(978-1-84601-368-3(2)*, Spruce) Octopus Publishing Group GBR. Dist: Hachette Bk. Group.

Davis, Graeme. Hunting Werewolves. 2016. (Monster Hunting Ser.). 00088p. (YA). (gr. 8-8). 37.10 *(978-1-4994-6534-1(3)*, Rosen Young Adult) Rosen Publishing Group, Inc., The.

Don, Lari. Serpents & Werewolves: Stories of Shape-Shifters from Around the World. Greenwood, Francesca, illus. 2016. (World of Stories Ser.). (ENG.). 144p. (J). (gr. 2-6). 26.65 *(978-1-5124-1321-2(6))* Lerner Publishing Group.

Etingoff, Kim. Howling at the Moon: Vampires & Werewolves in the New World. 2010. (Making of a Monster Ser.). (Illus.). 64p. (YA). (gr. 7-18). pap. 9.95 *(978-1-4222-1958-4(5))*; lib. bdg. 22.95 *(978-1-4222-1805-1(8))* Mason Crest.

—The Science of the Beast: The Facts Behind the Fangs. 2010. (Making of a Monster Ser.). (Illus.). 64p. (YA). (gr. 7-18). pap. 9.95 *(978-1-4222-1961-4(5))*; lib. bdg. 22.95 *(978-1-4222-1808-2(2))* Mason Crest.

Ferrell, David L. Shape-Shifters!, 1 vol., 1. 2014. (Jr. Graphic Monster Stories Ser.). (ENG.). 24p. (J). (gr. 3-6). 26.25 *(978-1-4777-6219-6(1)*, PowerKids Pr.) Rosen Publishing Group, Inc., The.

Frisch, Aaron. That's Spooky: Werewolves. 2013. (That's Spooky Ser.). (ENG., Illus.). 24p. (J). (gr. 1-3). pap. 7.99 *(978-0-89812-806-2(4)*, Creative Paperbacks) Creative Co., The.

—Werewolves. 2013. (Illus.). 24p. (J). 25.65 *(978-1-60818-249-7(5)*, Creative Education) Creative Co., The.

Hamilton, S. L. Werewolves. 2010. (Xtreme Monsters Ser.). 32p. (gr. 3-9). 27.07 *(978-1-61613-471-6(2)*, A&D Xtreme) ABDO Publishing Co.

Harmon, Daniel E. Werewolves. 2015. (Greatest Movie Monsters Ser.). (ENG., Illus.). 48p. (J). (gr. 5-6). 30.25 *(978-1-4994-3521-4(5)*, Rosen Central) Rosen Publishing Group, Inc., The.

hirschmann, kris. The Werewolf. 2011. 80p. (YA). lib. bdg. 37.27 *(978-1-60152-238-2(X))* ReferencePoint Pr., Inc.

Jeffrey, Gary. Werewolves. 2011. (Graphic Mythical Creatures Ser.). (Illus.). 24p. (J). (gr. 3-5). pap. 8.15 *(978-1-4339-6051-2(6)*, Gareth Stevens Learning Library); 23.95 *(978-1-4339-6049-9(4))* Stevens, Gareth Publishing LLLP.

Jones, Jen. The Girls' Guide to Werewolves: Everything Charming about These Shape-Shifters, 1 vol. 2010. (Girls' Guides to Everything Unexplained Ser.). (ENG.). 32p. (gr. 3-4). lib. bdg. 27.99 *(978-1-4296-5453-1(8)*, Snap Bks.) Capstone Press of Coughlan Cos.

Kallen, Stuart A. Werewolves. 2010. (Mysterious & Unknown Ser.). 104p. (YA). (gr. 7-12). lib. bdg. 25.95 *(978-1-60152-097-5(2))* ReferencePoint Pr., Inc.

Kespert, Deborah. 3-D Chillers: Vampires, Zombies, & Werewolves. 2012. (3-D Chillers Ser.). (ENG.). 48p. (J). (gr. 3-7). pap. 7.99 *(978-0-545-38779-8(5)*, Scholastic Paperbacks) Scholastic, Inc.

Krensky, Stephen. Werewolves. 2006. (Monster Chronicles Ser.). (ENG., Illus.). 48p. (gr. 4-7). lib. bdg. 26.60 *(978-0-8225-5922-1(6))* Lerner Publishing Group.

Lestrade, Ursula & Hachette Children's Group. The Werewolf Hunter's Guide. 2012. (Monster Tracker Ser.). 32p. (gr. 4-6). lib. bdg. 28.50 *(978-1-59771-318-4(X))* Sea-To-Sea Pubns.

Loh-Hagan, Virginia. Werewolves: Magic, Myth, & Mystery. 2016. (Magic, Myth, & Mystery Ser.). (ENG., Illus.). 32p. (J). (gr. 4-8). 29.93 *(978-1-63471-110-4(6)*, 208551, 45th Parallel Press) Cherry Lake Publishing.

Martin, Nicholas. Fighting the Fangs: A Guide to Vampires & Werewolves. 2010. (Making of a Monster Ser.). (Illus.). 64p. (YA). (gr. 7-18). pap. 9.95 *(978-1-4222-1957-7(7))*; lib. bdg. 22.95 *(978-1-4222-1804-4(X))* Mason Crest.

McCollum, Sean. Werewolves: The Truth Behind History's Scariest Shape-Shifters. 2015. (Monster Handbooks Ser.). (ENG., Illus.). 32p. (gr. 3-4). lib. bdg. 27.99 *(978-1-4914-4251-7(4))* Capstone Press of Coughlan Cos.

O'Hearn, Michael. Vampires vs. Werewolves: Battle of the Bloodthirsty Beasts. Kendree, McLean, illus. 2011. (Monster Wars Ser.). (ENG.). 32p. (gr. 3-4). pap. 47.70 *(978-1-4296-7266-5(8))*; lib. bdg. 27.99 *(978-1-4296-6521-6(1))* Capstone Press of Coughlan Cos. (Edge Bks.).

Ollhoff, Jim. Werewolves, 1 vol. 2007. (World of Horror Ser.). (ENG., Illus.). 32p. (gr. 4-8). 27.07 *(978-1-59928-775-1(7)*, Abdo & Daughters) ABDO Publishing Co.

Owen, Ruth. Werewolves & Other Shape-Shifters. 2013. (Not near Normal: the Paranormal Ser.). 32p. (J). (gr. 3-8). lib. bdg. 26.60 *(978-1-61772-695-8(8))* Bearport Publishing Co., Inc.

Peter Pauper Press Staff, et al. Vampires, Werewolves, Zombies: From the papers of Herr Doktor Max Sturm & Baron Ludwig Von Drang. Waldman, Bruce, illus. 2010. 168p. 9.95 *(978-1-59359-647-7(2))* Peter Pauper Pr. Inc.

Rissman, Rebecca. Werewolves, 1 vol. 2010. (Mythical Creatures Ser.). (ENG.). 32p. (gr. 1-2). 29.99 *(978-1-4109-3805-3(0)*, Read Me!) Heinemann-Raintree.

Roby, Cynthia. Werewolves. 2015. (Creatures of Fantasy Ser.). (ENG., Illus.). 64p. (J). (gr. 5-5). 34.21 *(978-1-5026-0510-8(4))* Cavendish Square Publishing.

Sanna, Emily. Pop Monsters: The Modern-Day Craze for Vampires & Werewolves. 2010. (Making of a Monster Ser.). 64p. (YA). (gr. 7-18). pap. 9.95 *(978-1-4222-1959-1(3))* Mason Crest.

Spencer, Liv. Love Bites: The Unofficial Saga of Twilight. 2010. (ENG., Illus.). 203p. (YA). (gr. 7). pap. *(978-1-55022-930-1(3))* Filmer Ltd.

Stefoff, Rebecca. Vampires, Zombies, & Shape-Shifters. 2007. (Secrets of the Supernatural Ser.). (Illus.). 79p. (J). (gr. 4-7). lib. bdg. 32.79 *(978-0-7614-2635-6(3)*, Benchmark Bks.) Marshall Cavendish Corp.

Stewart, Sheila. The Psychology of Our Dark Side: Humans' Love Affair with Vampires & Werewolves. 2010. (Making of a Monster Ser.). (Illus.). 64p. (YA). (gr. 7-18). pap. 9.95 *(978-1-4222-1960-7(7))*; lib. bdg. 22.95 *(978-1-4222-1807-5(4))* Mason Crest.

Ticktock Media, Ltd. Staff. Undead: Zombies, Vampires, Werewolves. 2008. (ENG.). 96p. (J). (gr. 4-7). pap. 9.95 *(978-1-84696-797-9(X)*, TickTock Books) Octopus Publishing Group GBR. Dist: Independent Pubs. Group.

Tieck, Sarah. Werewolves, 1 vol. 2016. (ENG., Illus.). 32p. (J). *(978-1-62403-768-9(2))* ABDO Publishing Co.

Townsend, John. Werewolf Attack. 2008. (ENG., Illus.). 32p. (J). (gr. 5-9). pap. *(978-0-7787-3795-7(0))*; lib. bdg. *(978-0-7787-3773-5(X))* Crabtree Publishing Co.

Weakland, Mark Andrew & Collins, Terry Lee. Scooby Doo Unmasks the Truth Behind Werewolves. 2016. (Illus.). 24p. (J). *(978-1-4062-8896-4(9))* Capstone Press of Coughlan Cos.

West, David & Ganeri, Anita. Werewolves & Other Shape-Shifters. West, David & Ganeri, Anita, illus. 2010. (Dark Side Ser.). (ENG., Illus.). 32p. (J). pap. 10.50 *(978-1-4488-1572-2(X))*; lib. bdg. 26.50 *(978-1-61531-900-8(X))* Rosen Publishing Group, Inc., The. (PowerKids Pr.).

WEREWOLVES—FICTION

Adams, Leon. Jewel of Light. 2008. 182p. pap. 14.00 *(978-1-4357-1538-7(1))* Lulu Pr., Inc.

Amoss, Berthe. The Loup Garou, 1 vol. Amoss, Berthe, illus. 2011. (ENG., Illus.). 48p. (J). (gr. 1-3). pap. 11.99 *(978-1-58980-893-5(2))* Pelican Publishing Co., Inc.

Arcayena-Nguyen, Rachelle. Who Me? a Werewolf: Chronicles of Timothy North. 2011. 138p. pap. 24.95 *(978-1-4560-4234-9(3))* America Star Bks.

Armstrong, Kelley. The Reckoning. 2011. (Darkest Powers Ser.: 3). 416p. (YA). (gr. 8). pap. 9.99 *(978-0-06-145056-3(1))* HarperCollins Pubs.

Barnes, Jennifer Lynn. Raised by Wolves. 2011. (ENG.). 320p. (gr. 7). pap. 9.99 *(978-1-60684-211-9(0))* Lerner Publishing Group.

—Taken by Storm. 2013. (Raised by Wolves Ser.: Bk. 3). (ENG.). 320p. (J). (gr. 7). pap. 9.99 *(978-1-60684-497-7(0)*, Carolrhoda Lab™) Lerner Publishing Group.

—Trial by Fire. 2012. (Raised by Wolves Ser.: Bk. 2). (ENG.). 368p. (J). (gr. 7). pap. 9.99 *(978-1-60684-333-8(8)*, Carolrhoda Lab™) Lerner Publishing Group.

Beastly Boys Staff, et al. Battle of the Zombies. 2012. (Awfully Beastly Business Ser.: 5). (ENG., Illus.). 208p. (J). (gr. 4-7). pap. 8.99 *(978-0-85707-522-2(5))* Simon & Schuster, Ltd. GBR. Dist: Simon & Schuster, Inc.

Bernstein, Nina. Magic by the Book, 4 vols. unabr. ed. 2005. (J). 65.75 *(978-1-4193-3607-2(X)*, 42048) Recorded Bks., Inc.

Blakley-Cartwright, Sarah & Johnson, David Leslie. Red Riding Hood. 2011. (ENG.). 352p. (YA). (gr. 10-17). pap. 9.99 *(978-0-316-17604-0(4)*, Poppy) Little, Brown Bks. for Young Readers.

Carriger, Gail. Waistcoats & Weaponry. 2014. (Finishing School Ser.: 3). (ENG.). 304p. (YA). (gr. 7-17). 18.00 *(978-0-316-19027-5(6))* Little Brown & Co.

—Waistcoats & Weaponry. 2015. (Finishing School Ser.: 3). (ENG.). 320p. (YA). (gr. 7-17). pap. 10.00 *(978-0-316-19025-1(X))* Little, Brown Bks. for Young Readers.

Casanova, Mary. Curse of a Winter Moon. 2014. (ENG.). 144p. pap. 9.95 *(978-0-8166-9207-1(6))* Univ. of Minnesota Pr.

Collins, Tim. Notes from a Hairy-Not-Scary Werewolf. Pinder, Andrew, illus. 2013. (ENG.). 288p. (J). (gr. 5-9). 12.99 *(978-1-4424-8207-4(9)*, Aladdin) Simon & Schuster Children's Publishing.

—Prince of Dorkness: More Notes from a Totally Lame Vampire. Pinder, Andrew, illus. 2011. (ENG.). 336p. (J). (gr. 5-9). 12.99 *(978-1-4424-3388-5(4)*, Aladdin) Simon & Schuster Children's Publishing.

Cremer, Andrea. Bloodrose. 2012. (Nightshade Ser.: 3). (ENG.). 448p. (YA). (gr. 9). pap. 10.99 *(978-0-14-242370-7(X)*, Speak) Penguin Young Readers Group.

—Bloodrose. 2012. (Nightshade Ser.: 3). lib. bdg. 22.10 *(978-0-606-26635-2(6)*, Turtleback) Turtleback Bks.

—Nightshade. (Nightshade Ser.: 1). (ENG.). (YA). (gr. 9-18). 2011. 496p. pap. 9.99 *(978-0-14-241980-9(X)*, Speak) 2010. 464p. 17.99 *(978-0-399-25482-6(X)*, Philomel Bks.) Penguin Young Readers Group.

—Snakeroot. 2014. (Nightshade Ser.: 4). (ENG.). 352p. (YA). (gr. 9). pap. 9.99 *(978-0-14-750860-7(6)*, Speak) Penguin Young Readers Group.

—Wolfsbane. (Nightshade Ser.: 2). (ENG.). (YA). (gr. 9-18). 2012. 432p. 9.99 *(978-0-14-242098-0(0)*, Speak) 2011. 400p. 17.99 *(978-0-399-25483-3(8)*, Philomel Bks.) Penguin Young Readers Group.

Dahl, Michael. Werewolf Skin. Sinkovec, Igor, illus. 2015. (Igor's Lab of Fear Ser.). (ENG.). 40p. (gr. 1-3). lib. bdg. 23.99 *(978-1-4965-0458-6(5))* Stone Arch Bks.

Davis, Heather. Never Cry Werewolf. 2010. (ENG.). 224p. (YA). (gr. 8). pap. 9.99 *(978-0-06-134925-6(9)*, HarperTeen) HarperCollins Pubs.

Delany, Shannon. Destiny & Deception: A 13 to Life Novel. 2012. (13 to Life Ser.: 4). (ENG.). 304p. (YA). (gr. 7). pap. 17.99 *(978-0-312-62446-0(8)*, 9780312624460, St. Martin's Griffin) St. Martin's Pr.

—Rivals & Retribution: A 13 to Life Novel. 2012. (13 to Life Ser.: 5). (ENG.). 320p. (YA). (gr. 8-12). pap. 17.99 *(978-0-312-62518-4(9)*, 9780312625184, St. Martin's Griffin) St. Martin's Pr.

Delany, Shannon & Redgrave, Saoirse. Secrets & Shadows: A 13 to Life Novel. 2011. (13 to Life Ser.: 2). (ENG.). 320p. (YA). (gr. 7-18). pap. 9.99 *(978-0-312-60915-3(9)*, 9780312609153, St. Martin's Griffin) St. Martin's Pr.

Dent, Sue. Never Ceese: Can Two Who Were Wronged Make It Right? 2006. 336p. (YA). lib. bdg. 17.99 *(978-1-59958-017-3(9))* Journey Stone Creations, LLC.

Despain, Bree. The Savage Grace. 2013. (ENG.). 496p. (J). (gr. 7). pap. 9.99 *(978-1-60684-416-8(4)*, Carolrhoda Lab™) Lerner Publishing Group.

Donbavand, Tommy. Attack of the Trolls. 2012. (Scream Street Ser.: 8). (ENG., Illus.). 128p. (J). (gr. 3-7). pap. 5.99 *(978-0-7636-5760-4(3))* Candlewick Pr.

—Attack of the Trolls. 2012. (Scream Street Ser.: 8). lib. bdg. 16.00 *(978-0-606-31471-8(7)*, Turtleback) Turtleback Bks.

—Blood of the Witch: Book 2, 1 vol. Cartoon Saloon, illus. 2012. (ENG.). 120p. (J). 24.21 *(978-1-59961-993-4(8)*, Chapter Bks.) Spotlight.

—Claw of the Werewolf, Bk. 6. Cartoon Saloon Staff, illus. 2010. (Scream Street Ser.: 6). (ENG.). 128p. (J). (gr. 3-7). pap. 5.99 *(978-0-7636-4638-7(5))* Candlewick Pr.

—Claw of the Werewolf: Book 6, 1 vol. Cartoon Saloon, illus. 2012. (ENG.). 120p. (J). 24.21 *(978-1-59961-997-2(0)*, Chapter Bks.) Spotlight.

—Fang of the Vampire. Cartoon Saloon Staff, illus. 2009. (Scream Street Ser.: 1). (ENG.). 160p. (J). (gr. 3-7). pap. 5.99 *(978-0-7636-4608-0(3))* Candlewick Pr.

—Fang of the Vampire: Book 1, 1 vol. Cartoon Saloon, illus. 2012. (ENG.). 129p. (J). 24.21 *(978-1-59961-992-7(X)*, Chapter Bks.) Spotlight.

—Flesh of the Zombie, Bk. 4. Cartoon Saloon Staff, illus. 2010. (Scream Street Ser.: 4). (ENG.). 128p. (J). (gr. 3-7). pap. 5.99 *(978-0-7636-4637-0(7))* Candlewick Pr.

—Flesh of the Zombie: Book 4, 1 vol. Cartoon Saloon, illus. 2012. (ENG.). 120p. (J). 24.21 *(978-1-59961-995-8(4)*, Chapter Bks.) Spotlight.

—Heart of the Mummy, Bk. 3. Cartoon Saloon Staff, illus. 2010. (Scream Street Ser.: 3). (ENG.). 128p. (J). (gr. 3-7). pap. 5.99 *(978-0-7636-4636-3(9))* Candlewick Pr.

—Heart of the Mummy: Book 3, 1 vol. Cartoon Saloon, illus. 2012. (ENG.). 120p. (J). 24.21 *(978-1-59961-994-1(6)*, Chapter Bks.) Spotlight.

—Invasion of the Normals. 2012. (Scream Street Ser.: 7). (ENG., Illus.). 128p. (J). (gr. 3-7). pap. 5.99 *(978-0-7636-5759-8(X))* Candlewick Pr.

—Secret of the Changeling. Donbavand, Tommy, illus. 2015. (Scream Street Ser.: 12). (ENG., Illus.). 128p. (J). (gr. 3-7). pap. 5.99 *(978-0-7636-5764-2(6))* Candlewick Pr.

—Terror of the Nightwatchman. 2014. (Scream Street Ser.: 9). lib. bdg. 16.00 *(978-0-606-35872-9(2))* Turtleback Bks.

—Wolf. 2012. (Stoke Books Titles Ser.). 64p. (J). (gr. 5-8). pap. 45.32 *(978-0-7613-9225-5(4))*; pap. 7.95 *(978-1-78112-034-7(X))*; lib. bdg. 22.60 *(978-1-78112-033-0(1))* Stoke Bks.

Doyle, Bill. The Werewolf at Home Plate. Lee, Jared D., illus. 2012. (Scream Team Ser.: 1). (ENG.). 96p. (J). (gr. 2-5). pap. 4.99 *(978-0-545-34198-1(1)*, Scholastic Paperbacks) Scholastic, Inc.

Dunne, Colin. Werewolf. 128p. (J). pap. 7.95 *(978-0-233-99580-9(3))* Andre Deutsch GBR. Dist: Trans-Atlantic Pubns., Inc.

Epstein, Adam Jay & Jacobson, Andrew. Secrets of the Crown. 2012. (Familiars Ser.: 2). (ENG.). 400p. (J). (gr. 3-7). pap. 6.99 *(978-0-06-196113-7(2))* HarperCollins Pubs.

Evans, Sandra. This Is Not a Werewolf Story. 2016. (ENG., Illus.). 352p. (J). (gr. 4-7). 16.99 *(978-1-4814-4480-4(8)*, Atheneum Bks. for Young Readers) Simon & Schuster Children's Publishing.

Feasey, Steve. Blood Wolf: Wereling Book #3. 2011. (Wereling Ser.: 3). (ENG.). 304p. (YA). (gr. 7). pap. 12.99 *(978-0-312-65352-1(2)*, 9780312653521) Feiwel & Friends.

—Dark Moon. 2011. (Wereling Ser.: 2). (ENG.). 336p. (YA). (gr. 7-18). pap. 18.99 *(978-0-312-64643-1(7)*, 9780312646431) Feiwel & Friends.

Fisher, Rusty. Littlest Werewolf's Story, 1 vol. 2014. (Story Time for Little Monsters Ser.). (ENG.). 24p. (J). (gr. -1-4). lib. bdg. 27.07 *(978-1-62402-021-6(6)*, Looking Glass Library) Magic Wagon.

Fontes, Justine & Fontes, Ron. Casebook: Werewolves. 2009. (Top Secret Graphica Mysteries Ser.). (Illus.). 48p. (YA). (gr. 2-6). 29.25 *(978-1-60754-609-2(4))*; pap. 11.75 *(978-1-60754-611-5(6))* Windmill Bks.

Garfield, Henry. My Father the Werewolf. 2016. (ENG.). 240p. (YA). (gr. 7). pap. 15.99 *(978-1-4814-8808-2(2)*, Atheneum Bks. for Young Readers) Simon & Schuster Children's Publishing.

—Tartabull's Throw. 2015. (ENG., Illus.). 272p. (YA). (gr. 7). pap. 12.99 *(978-1-4814-7510-5(X)*, Atheneum Bks. for Young Readers) Simon & Schuster Children's Publishing.

Gavin, Rohan. Knightley & Son - K-9. 2015. (Knightley & Son Ser.: 2). (ENG., Illus.). 304p. (YA). (gr. 4-6). 16.99 *(978-1-61963-494-7(5)*, 9781619634947, Bloomsbury USA Childrens) Bloomsbury Publishing USA.

Gibbons, Alan. Night Hunger. 2013. (ENG.). 64p. (YA). (gr. 6-12). pap. 6.95 *(978-1-78112-179-5(6))*; lib. bdg. 22.60 *(978-1-78112-178-8(8))* Lerner Publishing Group.

Grant, Tess. Flying in the Dark. 2013. 186p. pap. 10.99 *(978-1-62237-167-9(4))* Turquoise Morning Pr.

Grau, Sheila. Dr. Critchlore's School for Minions. Sutphin, Joe, illus. (Dr. Critchlore's School for Minions Ser.). (ENG.). (J). (gr. 3-7). 2016. 304p. pap. 7.95 *(978-1-4197-2029-1(5))*

2015. 288p. 14.95 *(978-1-4197-1370-5(1))* Abrams, Inc. (Amulet Bks.).
Graves, Judith. Second Skin. 2011. 280p. (J). pap. 16.99 *(978-1-61603-006-3(2))* Leap Bks.
—Under My Skin. Cox, Val, illus. 2010. 328p. (YA). (gr. 8-18). pap. 16.99 *(978-1-61603-000-1(3))* Leap Bks.
Gray, Claudia. Fateful. (ENG.). (YA). (gr. 9). 2012. 352p. pap. 9.99 *(978-0-06-200621-9(5))* 2011. 336p. 17.99 *(978-0-06-200620-2(7))* HarperCollins Pubs. (HarperTeen).
Haesche, Richard, Sr. The Werewolf Syndrome. 3rd ed. 2007. (ENG.). 218p. (YA). pap. 9.95 *(978-0-9798536-0-9(5))* Kreative X-Pressions Pubns.
Haig, Matt. To Be a Cat. Curtis, Stacy, illus. (ENG.). 304p. (J). (gr. 3-7). 2014. pap. 8.99 *(978-1-4424-5406-4(7))* 2013. 16.99 *(978-1-4424-5405-7(9))* Simon & Schuster Children's Publishing.
Hall, Tim. Shadow of the Wolf. 2016. (ENG.). 480p. (J). (gr. 9). pap. 9.99 *(978-1-338-03250-5(X))* Scholastic, Inc.
Hall, Tim K. Shadow of the Wolf. 2015. (ENG.). 480p. (J). (gr. 9). 18.99 *(978-0-545-81664-9(5))* Scholastic, Inc.
Hanford, Juliana. Werewolf Moon. Pillo, Cary, illus. 2009. (Science Solves It! Complete Set Ser.). 32p. (J). (gr. k-7). pap. 5.95 *(978-1-57565-291-7(9))* Kane Press, Inc.
Harrison, Lisi. Where There's a Wolf, There's a Way. 2012. (Monster High Ser.: 3). (ENG., Illus.). 272p. (YA). (gr. 7-17). pap. 9.99 *(978-0-316-18668-1(6),* Poppy) Little, Brown Bks. for Young Readers.
Hawthorne, Rachel. Shadow of the Moon. 2010. (Dark Guardian Ser.: 4). (ENG.). 256p. (YA). (gr. 9-18). pap. 8.99 *(978-0-06-196290-5(2),* HarperTeen) HarperCollins Pubs.
Herman, Gail. Scooby-Doo in up, up, & Away!, 1 vol. 2016. (Scooby-Doo! Set 3 Ser.). (ENG., Illus.). 32p. (J). (gr. k-4). lib. bdg. 24.21 *(978-1-61479-412-7(X))* Spotlight.
Hopkins, Ellen, ed. A New Dawn: Your Favorite Authors on Stephenie Meyer's Twilight Series. 2009. (ENG., Illus.). 200p. (J). (gr. 9-12). pap. 12.95 *(978-1-933771-93-9(3))* BenBella Bks.
Hueller, P. W. Wolf High. 2014. (ENG.). 96p. (J). *(978-1-63235-055-8(6))* Pr. Room Editions LLC.
Hulme-Cross, Benjamin. Wolf Trap. Evergreen, Nelson, illus. 2015. (Dark Hunter Ser.). (ENG.). 64p. (J). (gr. 4-8). pap. 4.99 *(978-1-4677-8086-5(3))* Lerner Publishing Group.
Jobling, Curtis. Nest of Serpents. 2015. (Wereworld Ser.: 4). (ENG.). 512p. (J). (gr. 5). 8.99 *(978-0-14-242193-2(6),* Puffin Books) Penguin Young Readers Group.
—Rage of Lions. 2013. (Wereworld Ser.: 2). (ENG.). 432p. (J). (gr. 5). pap. 8.99 *(978-0-14-242202-1(9),* Puffin Books) Penguin Young Readers Group.
—Rage of Lions. 2013. (Wereworld Ser.: 2). lib. bdg. 19.65 *(978-0-606-30041-4(4),* Turtleback) Turtleback Bks.
—Rise of the Wolf. 2012. (Wereworld Ser.: 1). (ENG.). 432p. (J). (gr. 5-18). pap. 8.99 *(978-0-14-242108-6(1),* Puffin Books) Penguin Young Readers Group.
—Rise of the Wolf. 2012. (Wereworld Ser.: 1). lib. bdg. 19.65 *(978-0-606-26084-8(6),* Turtleback) Turtleback Bks.
—Shadow of the Hawk. 2013. (Wereworld Ser.: 3). (ENG.). 496p. (J). (gr. 5). pap. 8.99 *(978-0-14-242192-5(8),* Puffin Books) Penguin Young Readers Group.
—Shadow of the Hawk. 2013. (Wereworld Ser.: 3). lib. bdg. 19.65 *(978-0-606-30044-5(9),* Turtleback) Turtleback Bks.
—Storm of Sharks. (Wereworld Ser.: 5). (ENG.). 480p. (J). (gr. 5). 2015. 8.99 *(978-0-14-242577-0(X),* Puffin Books) 2013. 16.99 *(978-0-670-78558-2(X),* Viking Books for Young Readers) Penguin Young Readers Group.
Johnson, Christine. Claire de Lune. (ENG.). (YA). (gr. 7). 2011. 368p. pap. 9.99 *(978-1-4424-0766-4(2))* 2010. 352p. 16.99 *(978-1-4169-9182-3(4))* Simon Pulse. (Simon Pulse).
—Nocturne. (ENG.). (YA). (gr. 7). 2012. 384p. pap. 9.99 *(978-1-4424-0777-0(8))* 2011. 368p. 16.99 *(978-1-4424-0776-3(X))* Simon Pulse. (Simon Pulse).
Jones, Carrie. Endure. 2012. (Need Ser.). (ENG.). 272p. (YA). 17.99 *(978-1-59990-554-9(X),* 9781599905549, Bloomsbury USA Childrens) Bloomsbury Publishing USA.
Keswick, Kitty. Freaksville. Cox, Val, illus. 2010. 328p. (YA). (gr. 8-12). pap. 16.99 *(978-1-61603-001-8(1))* Leap Bks.
Klause, Annette Curtis. Blood & Chocolate. 2007. (ENG.). 288p. (YA). (gr. 7). pap. 9.99 *(978-0-385-73421-9(2),* Ember) Random Hse. Children's Bks.
Kovalkova-McKenna, Svetlana & McKenna, Konstantin. Oberon. 2009. 44p. pap. 7.26 *(978-0-557-06114-3(8))* Lulu Pr., Inc.
Kruger, Kat. The Night Has Claws. 2013. 280p. pap. *(978-0-9917937-5-4(7))* Fierce ink Pr. Co-Op, Ltd.
Larbalestier, Justine. Liar. 2010. (ENG.). 384p. (YA). (gr. 9-13). pap. 10.99 *(978-1-59990-519-8(1),* 9781599905198, Bloomsbury USA Childrens) Bloomsbury Publishing USA.
Long, Chad M. The Lycan Journal. 2007. (Illus.). 141p. (YA). per. 12.95 *(978-0-615-15295-0(3))* Long Stories LLC.
Long, Chad Michael, illus. The Lycan Journal. Long, Chad Michael, . 2nd ed. 2007. 141p. (YA). per. 12.95 *(978-0-615-18961-1(X))* Long Stories LLC.
Longmeyer, C. M. My Life As a Third Grade Werewolf. Blanding, Dexter, illus. 2014. (ENG.). (J). (gr. 2-3). pap. 7.99 *(978-0-635-11144-9(6))* Gallopade International.
Luper, Eric. The Haunted Howl. 2016. (Key Hunters Ser.: 3). (ENG., Illus.). 128p. (J). (gr. 2-5). pap. 4.99 *(978-0-545-82211-4(4),* Scholastic Paperbacks) Scholastic, Inc.
Lyons, Jayne. 100% Wolf. Rivas, Victor, illus. (ENG.). 256p. (J). (gr. 2-7). 2010. pap. 7.99 *(978-1-4424-0252-2(0))* 2009. 16.99 *(978-1-4169-7474-1(1))* Simon & Schuster Children's Publishing. (Atheneum Bks. for Young Readers).
Mary-Todd, Jonathan. Lock-In. 2011. (Night Fall Ser.). (ENG.). 112p. (YA). (gr. 6-12). pap. 7.95 *(978-0-7613-7815-0(4));* lib. bdg. 27.93 *(978-0-7613-7743-6(3))* Lerner Publishing Group.
MaryAnn, Aunt. Spooky Journey down Riverside Drive the Night of the Full Moon. 2010. 40p. pap. 15.95 *(978-0-557-31081-4(4))* Lulu Pr., Inc.
McBride, Lish. Hold Me Closer, Necromancer. 2010. (Necromancer Ser.: 1). (ENG.). 352p. (YA). (gr. 9-13). 16.99 *(978-0-8050-9098-7(3),* 9780805090987, Holt, Henry & Co. Bks. For Young Readers) Holt, Henry & Co.
—Necromancing the Stone. 2013. (Necromancer Ser.: 2). (ENG.). 368p. (YA). (gr. 9-13). pap. 9.99 *(978-1-250-03415-1(9),* 9781250034151) Square Fish.
Mercer, Sienna. Cry Wolf!, Vol. 1. 2013. (My Brother the Werewolf Ser.: 1). (ENG.). 256p. (J). (gr. 4-6). pap. 9.99 *(978-1-4052-6438-9(1))* Egmont Bks., Ltd. GBR. Dist: Independent Pubs. Group.
—Puppy Love! 2013. (My Brother the Werewolf Ser.: 2). (ENG.). 240p. (J). (gr. 4-6). pap. 8.99 *(978-1-4052-6439-6(X))* Egmont Bks., Ltd. GBR. Dist: Independent Pubs. Group.
Meyer, Stephenie. Amanecer. Pallarés, José Miguel & Sánchez, María Jesús, trs. 2008.Tr. of Breaking Dawn. (SPA.). 832p. (gr. 8-12). pap. 19.99 *(978-607-11-0033-7(X),* Alfaguara Juvenil) Santillana USA Publishing Co., Inc.
—Breaking Dawn. (Twilight Saga Ser.: 4). (ENG.). 768p. (YA). (gr. 7-17). 2012. mass mkt. 7.99 *(978-0-316-22613-4(0))* 2010. pap. 16.99 *(978-0-316-06793-5(8))* 2008. 22.99 *(978-0-316-06792-8(X),* Tingley, Megan Bks.)Pt. II. 2012. pap. 14.99 *(978-0-316-22642-4(4))* Little, Brown Bks. for Young Readers.
—Breaking Dawn. 2010. (Twilight Saga Ser.: 4). (YA). lib. bdg. 29.40 *(978-0-606-23108-4(0),* Turtleback) Turtleback Bks.
—Eclipse. 2009. (Twilight Saga Ser.: 3). (ENG.). 640p. (YA). (gr. 7-17). pap. 15.99 *(978-0-316-02765-6(0))* Little Brown & Co.
—Eclipse. 2007. (Twilight Saga Ser.: 3). (ENG.). 640p. (YA). (gr. 7-17). 19.99 *(978-0-316-16020-9(2))* Little, Brown Bks. for Young Readers.
—Eclipse. 2008. 576p. *(978-1-904233-91-6(0),* Atom Books) Little, Brown Book Group Ltd.
—Eclipse. 2011. (Twilight Saga: Bk. 3). 13.08 *(978-0-7848-3531-9(4),* Everbind) Marco Bk. Co.
—Eclipse. 2010. (Twilight Saga: Bk. 3). 629p. (YA). (gr. 9-12). 22.10 *(978-1-60686-303-9(7))* Perfection Learning Corp.
—Eclipse. Pallarés, José Miguel & Sánchez, María Jesús, trs. 2007. (SPA.). 870p. (YA). (gr. 8-12). pap. 15.99 *(978-1-60396-022-9(8),* Punto de Lectura) Santillana USA Publishing Co., Inc.
—Eclipse. 2007. (Twilight Saga Spanish Ser.: 3). (SPA.). 637p. (gr. 7-12). lib. bdg. 28.15 *(978-1-4177-9862-9(9),* Turtleback) Turtleback Bks.
—Luna Nueva. Pallares, Jose Miguel, tr. from ENG. 2009.Tr. of New Moon. (SPA.). 280p. (YA). (gr. 8-12). pap. 11.99 *(978-1-60396-698-6(6),* Punto de Lectura) Santillana USA Publishing Co., Inc.
—Luna Nueva. Pallarés, José Miguel & Sánchez, Maria Jesús, trs. from ENG. 2007.Tr. of New Moon. (SPA.). 696p. (YA). (gr. 8-12). per. 15.99 *(978-970-58-0023-8(5),* Alfaguara) Santillana USA Publishing Co., Inc.
—New Moon. (Twilight Saga Ser.: 2). (ENG.). 608p. (gr. 7-17). 2008. (YA). pap. 15.99 *(978-0-316-02496-9(1))* 2006. (J). 19.99 *(978-0-316-16019-3(9),* Tingley, Megan Bks.) Little, Brown Bks. for Young Readers.
—New Moon. 2011. (Twilight Saga: Bk. 2). 11.72 *(978-0-7848-3535-7(7),* Everbind) Marco Bk. Co.
—New Moon. 2008. (Twilight Saga: Bk. 2). 563p. (gr. 9-12). 21.00 *(978-1-60686-336-7(3))* Perfection Learning Corp.
—The Short Second Life of Bree Tanner. 2010. (Twilight Saga Ser.). (ENG.). 192p. (YA). (gr. 7-17). 16.00 *(978-0-316-12558-1(X))* Little, Brown Bks. for Young Readers.
Millar, Martin. Lonely Werewolf Girl. 2008. (ENG.). 560p. per. *(978-0-9796636-6-6(0))* CSA Telltapes, Ltd.
Monstrata, Nessi. Monster High Diaries: Clawdeen Wolf & the Freaky-Fabulous Fashion Show. 2016. (Monster High Diaries: 4). (ENG., Illus.). 160p. (J). (gr. 3-7). 9.99 *(978-0-316-30078-0(0))* Little, Brown Bks. for Young Readers.
Moore, Peter. Red Moon Rising. 2012. (ENG.). 352p. (J). (gr. 5-9). pap. 9.99 *(978-1-4231-1939-5(8))* Hyperion Pr.
North, Laura. Cinderella: The Terrible Truth. Dreidemy, Joëlle, illus. 2014. (ENG.). 32p. (J). *(978-0-7787-1326-5(1))* Crabtree Publishing Co.
O'Callaghan, G. The Eternals. 2007. 376p. per. *(978-1-84693-055-3(3))* Best Global Publishing Ltd.
O'Reilly, Sean. The Wolfboy's Wish, 1 vol. 2011. (Mighty Mighty Monsters Ser.). (ENG.). 48p. (gr. 2-3). lib. bdg. 23.99 *(978-1-4342-3219-9(0))* Stone Arch Bks.
—The Wolfboy's Wish, 1 vol. Arcana Studio Staff, illus. 2012. (Mighty Mighty Monsters Ser.). (ENG.). 48p. (gr. 2-3). pap. 6.10 *(978-1-4342-4613-4(2))* Stone Arch Bks.
O'Shea, M.J. Cold Moon [Library Edition]. 2nd ed. 2014. 180p. pap. 14.99 *(978-1-62798-460-7(7),* Harmony Ink Pr.) Dreamspinner Pr.
Park, Devin & Lee, Claudia. Howl Michigan. 2011. 138p. pap. 24.95 *(978-1-4560-8895-8(5))* America Star Bks.
Peacock, Kathleen. Hemlock. (Hemlock Trilogy Ser.: 1). (ENG.). (YA). (gr. 9). 2013. 432p. pap. 9.99 *(978-0-06-204866-0(X))* 2012. 416p. 17.99 *(978-0-06-204865-3(1))* HarperCollins Pubs. (Tegen, Katherine Bks).
—Thornhill. (Hemlock Trilogy Ser.: 2). (ENG.). (YA). (gr. 9). 2015. 368p. pap. 9.99 *(978-0-06-204869-1(4))* 2013. 352p. 17.99 *(978-0-06-204868-4(6))* HarperCollins Pubs. (Tegen, Katherine Bks).
—Willowgrove. 2015. (Hemlock Trilogy Ser.: 3). (ENG.). 384p. (YA). (gr. 9). 17.99 *(978-0-06-204871-4(6),* Tegen, Katherine Bks) HarperCollins Pubs.
Pearce, Jackson. Sisters Red. 2011. (Fairy Tale Retelling Ser.). (ENG.). 352p. (YA). (gr. 10-17). pap. 10.99 *(978-0-316-06867-3(5))* Little, Brown Bks. for Young Readers.
—Sweetly. 2012. (Fairy Tale Retelling Ser.). (ENG.). 336p. (YA). (gr. 10-17). pap. 8.99 *(978-0-316-06866-6(7))* Little, Brown Bks. for Young Readers.
Perez, Marlene. Dead Is a State of Mind. 2009. (Dead Is Ser.: 2). (ENG., Illus.). 192p. (YA). (gr. 7-18). pap. 7.99 *(978-0-15-206210-1(6))* Houghton Mifflin Harcourt Publishing Co.
—Dead Is Just a Rumor. 2010. (Dead Is Ser.: 4). (ENG., Illus.). 224p. (YA). (gr. 7-18). pap. 7.99 *(978-0-547-34592-5(5))* Houghton Mifflin Harcourt Publishing Co.
Price, Jennifer L. Half Moon: Phases of the Moon: Book 2, 1 vol. 2009. 252p. pap. 27.95 *(978-1-4489-2193-5(7))* PublishAmerica, Inc.
Quin-Harkin, Janet. Friday Night Fright. 2014. (Tgif Ser.: 2). (ENG., Illus.). 128p. (J). (gr. 3-7). pap. 13.99 *(978-1-4814-2880-4(2),* Simon & Schuster/Paula Wiseman Bks.) Simon & Schuster/Paula Wiseman Bks.
Reisz, Kristopher. Unleashed. 2010. (ENG.). 352p. (YA). (gr. 9). pap. 9.99 *(978-1-4424-0637-7(2),* Simon Pulse) Simon Pulse.
Richemont, Enid. The Night of the Were-Boy. 2015. (Race Further with Reading Ser.). (ENG., Illus.). 48p. (J). *(978-0-7787-2087-4(X))* Crabtree Publishing Co.
Riviello, Linda. Werewolves, Vampires & Ghosts... Oh My! 2009. (J). pap. 12.95 *(978-1-61623-088-3(6))* Independent Pub.
Rowleym'Lin. Knights of Right, BK 3: The Warrior's Guard. 2010. 80p. (J). pap. 6.99 *(978-1-60641-240-4(X),* Shadow Mountain) Shadow Mountain Publishing.
Sampson, Jeff. Havoc: A Deviants Novel. 2012. (Deviants Ser.: 2). (ENG.). 352p. (YA). (gr. 8). 17.99 *(978-0-06-199278-0(X))* HarperCollins Pubs.
—Ravage: A Deviants Novel. 2013. (Deviants Ser.: 3). (ENG.). 400p. (YA). (gr. 8). 17.99 *(978-0-06-199280-3(1))* HarperCollins Pubs.
—Vesper. 2011. (Deviants Ser.: 1). (ENG.). 304p. (YA). (gr. 8-18). 16.99 *(978-0-06-199276-6(3))* HarperCollins Pubs.
—Vesper: A Deviants Novel. 2011. (Deviants Ser.: 1). (ENG.). 320p. (YA). (gr. 8). pap. 8.99 *(978-0-06-199277-3(1))* HarperCollins Pubs.
Sander, Sonia. Werewolf Watch. 2012. (Scooby Doo Reader Ser.). lib. bdg. 13.55 *(978-0-606-23961-5(8),* Turtleback) Turtleback Bks.
Schaefer, Peggy. A Haunted Halloween Activity Book. Arif, Tasneem & Reed, Lisa, illus. 2014. 16p. (J). 4.99 *(978-0-8249-5666-0(4),* Ideal Pubns.) Worthy Publishing.
Schreiber, Ellen. Full Moon Kisses. 2013. (Full Moon Ser.: 3). (ENG.). 224p. (YA). (gr. 8). pap. 9.99 *(978-0-06-198654-3(2),* Tegen, Katherine Bks) HarperCollins Pubs.
—Magic of the Moonlight. (Full Moon Ser.: 2). (ENG.). (YA). (gr. 8). 2012. 256p. pap. 9.99 *(978-0-06-198656-7(9))* 2011. 240p. 17.99 *(978-0-06-198657-4(7))* HarperCollins Pubs. (Tegen, Katherine Bks).
—Once in a Full Moon. 2011. (Full Moon Ser.: 1). (ENG.). 320p. (YA). (gr. 8). pap. 8.99 *(978-0-06-198652-9(6),* Tegen, Katherine Bks) HarperCollins Pubs.
Shan, Darren, pseud. Blood Beast. 2008. (ENG.). 224p. (YA). (gr. 10-17). pap. 8.99 *(978-0-316-00378-0(6))* Little, Brown Bks. for Young Readers.
—Dark Calling. 2010. (ENG.). 224p. (YA). (gr. 10-17). pap. 10.00 *(978-0-316-04872-9(0))* Little, Brown Bks. for Young Readers.
—Death's Shadow. 2009. (ENG.). 240p. (YA). (gr. 10-17). pap. 10.00 *(978-0-316-00382-7(4))* Little Brown & Co.
—Demon Apocalypse. 2009. (ENG.). 208p. (YA). (gr. 10-17). pap. 9.99 *(978-0-316-00380-3(8))* Little, Brown Bks. for Young Readers.
—Wolf Island. 2010. (ENG.). 216p. (YA). (gr. 10-17). pap. 10.00 *(978-0-316-04881-1(X))* Little, Brown Bks. for Young Readers.
Shusterman, Neal. Red Rider's Hood. 2006. (Dark Fusion Ser.: 3). (ENG.). 192p. (YA). (gr. 7-18). 6.99 *(978-0-14-240678-6(3),* Speak) Penguin Young Readers Group.
Sinden, David, et al. Bang Goes a Troll, Bk. 3. Duddle, Jonny, illus. 2009. (Awfully Beastly Business Ser.: 3). (ENG.). 208p. (J). (gr. 3-7). 9.99 *(978-1-4169-8651-5(0),* Aladdin) Simon & Schuster Children's Publishing.
—The Jungle Vampire. Duddle, Jonny, illus. 2009. (Awfully Beastly Business Ser.: 4). (ENG.). 208p. (J). (gr. 3-7). 9.99 *(978-1-4169-8652-2(9),* Aladdin) Simon & Schuster Children's Publishing.
—Werewolf Versus Dragon. Duddle, Jonny, illus. 2009. (Awfully Beastly Business Ser.: 1). (ENG.). 192p. (J). (gr. 3-7). 9.99 *(978-1-4169-8649-2(9),* Aladdin) Simon & Schuster Children's Publishing.
Sirod, G. p. & Sirod, G. P. Scabs. 2010. 190p. pap. *(978-1-84923-457-3(4))* YouWriteOn.
Smith, Cynthia Leitich. Blessed. (Tantalize Ser.). (ENG., Illus.). (YA). (gr. 9). 2012. 464p. pap. 8.99 *(978-0-7636-5479-5(5))* 2011. 480p. 17.99 *(978-0-7636-4326-3(2))* Candlewick Pr.
—Diabolical. 2012. (Tantalize Ser.). (ENG., Illus.). 368p. (YA). (gr. 9). 17.99 *(978-0-7636-5118-3(4))* Candlewick Pr.
—Tantalize. 2007. (Tantalize Ser.). (ENG., Illus.). 336p. (YA). (gr. 9-12). 16.99 *(978-0-7636-2791-1(7))* Candlewick Pr.
Sonneborn, Scott. I for an Eye. Banks, Timothy, illus. 2014. (Frankenstein Journals). (ENG.). 80p. (gr. 2-3). 22.65 *(978-1-4342-9000-7(X))* Stone Arch Bks.
Specter, Baron. To Werewolf or Not to Werewolf, 1 vol. Kneupper, Setch, illus. 2012. (Graveyard Diaries Ser.). (ENG.). 128p. (J). (gr. 3-8). 27.07 *(978-1-61641-901-1(6))* Magic Wagon.
Speer, Cindy Lynn. Unbalanced. 2010. pap. *(978-1-934841-90-7(0))* Zumaya Pubns. LLC.
St. Crow, Lili. Betrayals. 2009. (Strange Angels Ser.: 2). (ENG., Illus.). 304p. (YA). (gr. 7-18). 9.99 *(978-1-59514-252-8(5),* Razorbill) Penguin Young Readers Group.
—Betrayals, 10 vols. 2010. (Strange Angels Ser.: 2). (YA). 95.75 *(978-1-4407-7156-9(1))* Recorded Bks., Inc.
—Betrayals. 2009. (Strange Angels Ser.: 2). lib. bdg. 20.85 *(978-0-606-09020-9(7),* Turtleback) Turtleback Bks.
—Jealousy. 2010. (Strange Angels Ser.: 3). (ENG.). 320p. (YA). (gr. 7-18). 9.99 *(978-1-59514-290-0(8),* Razorbill) Penguin Young Readers Group.
—Jealousy, 10 vols. 2010. (Strange Angels Ser.: 3). (J). 86.75 *(978-1-4498-2774-8(8));* 68.75 *(978-1-4498-2773-1(X));* 83.75 *(978-1-4498-2776-2(4));* 1.25 *(978-1-4498-2777-9(2));* 209.75 *(978-1-4498-2772-4(1))* Recorded Bks., Inc.
—Jealousy. 2010. (Strange Angels Ser.: 3). lib. bdg. 20.85 *(978-0-606-14566-4(4),* Turtleback) Turtleback Bks.
—Strange Angels. 2009. (Strange Angels Ser.: 1). (ENG., Illus.). 304p. (YA). (gr. 7-18). pap. 9.99 *(978-1-59514-251-1(7),* Razorbill) Penguin Young Readers Group.
—Strange Angels, 9 vols. 2009. (Strange Angels Ser.: 1). (J). 181.75 *(978-1-4407-6194-2(9));* 117.75 *(978-1-4407-6197-3(3));* 84.75 *(978-1-4407-6195-9(7));* 114.75 *(978-1-4407-6199-7(X));* 87.75 *(978-1-4407-6193-5(0))* Recorded Bks., Inc.
—Strange Angels. 2009. (Strange Angels Ser.: 1). lib. bdg. 20.85 *(978-0-606-08957-9(8),* Turtleback) Turtleback Bks.
Stewart, Paul & Riddell, Chris. Barnaby Grimes: Curse of the Night Wolf. 2012. (Barnaby Grimes Ser.). (ENG.). 224p. (J). (gr. 3-7). 6.99 *(978-0-385-73697-8(5),* Yearling) Random Hse. Children's Bks.
Stine, R. L. Can You Keep a Secret? 2016. (Fear Street Ser.). (ENG.). 272p. (YA). 18.99 *(978-1-250-05894-2(5),* 9781250058942, St. Martin's Griffin) St. Martin's Pr.
—The Werewolf of Fever Swamp. 2009. (Goosebumps Ser.: 11). lib. bdg. 17.20 *(978-0-606-00241-7(3),* Turtleback) Turtleback Bks.
Strange, Jason. Full Moon Horror, 1 vol. Parks, Phil & Dal Lago, Alberto, illus. 2011. (Jason Strange Ser.). (ENG.). 72p. (gr. 2-3). pap. 6.25 *(978-1-4342-3434-6(7));* lib. bdg. 25.32 *(978-1-4342-3235-9(2))* Stone Arch Bks.
Thompson, Paul B. The Battle for the Brightstone: Book III of the Brightstone Saga. 2013. (Brightstone Saga Ser.). 176p. (J). 18.95 *(978-0-7660-3984-1(6))* Enslow Pubs., Inc.
—The Fortune-Teller: Book II of the Brightstone Saga. 2013. (Brightstone Saga Ser.). 160p. (J). (gr. 5-12). pap. 10.95 *(978-1-4644-0265-4(5));* 18.95 *(978-0-7660-3983-4(8))* Enslow Pubs., Inc.
Toft, Di. The Twilight Circus. 2011. (Wolven Ser.: 2). (ENG.). 384p. (J). (gr. 3-7). 17.99 *(978-0-545-29492-8(4),* Chicken Hse., The) Scholastic, Inc.
—Wolven, Bk. 1. 2011. (Wolven Ser.: 1). (ENG.). 352p. (J). (gr. 3-7). pap. 7.99 *(978-0-545-17110-6(5),* Chicken Hse., The) Scholastic, Inc.
Torrey, Michele. The Case of the Terrible T. Rex. Newman, Barbara Johansen, illus. 2010. (Doyle & Fossey, Science Detectives Ser.). (ENG.). 96p. (J). (gr. 3-5). pap. 6.95 *(978-1-4027-4966-7(X))* Sterling Publishing Co., Inc.
Troupe, Thomas Kingsley. The Big Hairy Secret, 1 vol. Gilpin, Stephen, illus. 2013. (Furry & Flo Ser.). (ENG.). 128p. (gr. 2-3). 8.95 *(978-1-62370-033-1(7));* lib. bdg. 25.32 *(978-1-4342-3858-0(X))* Stone Arch Bks.
—The Misplaced Mummy, 1 vol. Gilpin, Stephen, illus. 2014. (Furry & Flo Ser.). (ENG.). 128p. (gr. 2-3). 25.32 *(978-1-4342-6396-4(7))* Stone Arch Bks.
—The Problems with Goblins, 1 vol. Gilpin, Stephen, illus. 2013. (Furry & Flo Ser.). (ENG.). 128p. (gr. 2-3). 8.95 *(978-1-62370-034-8(5));* lib. bdg. 25.32 *(978-1-4342-5042-1(3))* Stone Arch Bks.
—The Skeletons in City Park, 1 vol. Gilpin, Stephen, illus. 2014. (Furry & Flo Ser.). (ENG.). 128p. (gr. 2-3). 25.32 *(978-1-4342-6397-1(5))* Stone Arch Bks.
—The Solemn Golem. Gilpin, Stephen, illus. 2015. (Furry & Flo Ser.). (ENG.). 128p. (gr. 2-3). lib. bdg. 25.32 *(978-1-4342-9646-7(6))* Stone Arch Bks.
—The Voiceless Vampire. Gilpin, Stephen, illus. 2015. (Furry & Flo Ser.). (ENG.). 128p. (gr. 2-3). lib. bdg. 25.32 *(978-1-4342-9645-0(8))* Stone Arch Bks.
VanDervleuten, Robin M. Keepers of the Fairy Moon. 2013. 200p. *(978-1-4602-1429-9(3));* pap. *(978-1-4602-1430-5(7))* FriesenPress.
Viguie, Debbie & Holder, Nancy. Unleashed. 2012. (Wolf Spring Chronicles Ser.). (ENG.). 400p. (YA). (gr. 7). pap. 9.99 *(978-0-385-74099-9(9),* Ember) Random Hse. Children's Bks.
Whiteside, S. K. Inheritance. 2013. 320p. (YA). pap. 12.99 *(978-1-939769-27-5(2))* Crushing Hearts and Black Butterfly Publishing.
Young, Jessica. Howl at the Moon: a Branches Book (Haggis & Tank Unleashed #3) Burks, James, illus. 2017. (Haggis & Tank Unleashed Ser.: 3). (ENG.). 80p. (J). (gr. k-2). pap. 4.99 **(978-1-338-04525-3(3))** Scholastic, Inc.
Zornow, Jeff. Werewolf, 1 vol. Zornow, Jeff, illus. 2007. (Graphic Horror Ser.). (ENG., Illus.). 32p. (gr. 3-7). 28.50 *(978-1-60270-062-8(1),* Graphic Planet- Fiction) ABDO Publishing Co.

WESLEY, JOHN, 1703-1791

Benge, Janet & Benge, Geoff. Christian Heroes - Then & Now - John Wesley: The World, His Parish. 2007. (Christian Heroes Ser.). (ENG.). 192p. (YA). (gr. 3-7). pap. 9.99 *(978-1-57658-382-1(1))* YWAM Publishing.

WEST, JERRY, 1938-

Ramen, Fred. Jerry West. 2009. (Basketball Hall of Famers Ser.). 112p. (gr. 5-8). 63.90 *(978-1-61511-532-7(3),* Rosen Reference) Rosen Publishing Group, Inc., The.

WEST (U.S.)

see also Northwest, Pacific; Pacific States

Allison, Pamela S. Emerald's Journal: A summer with Hatchlings. Cepeda, Joseph C., photos by. 2007. (Illus.). 24p. (J). lib. bdg. 16.95 *(978-0-9793474-1-2(6))* Sand Sage Pr.
Andrews, Barbara. Discover the West Region. 2006. (J). pap. *(978-1-4108-6437-6(5))* Benchmark Education Co.
—The West Region. 2006. (J). pap. *(978-1-4108-6434-5(0))* Benchmark Education Co.
Barkan, Joanne. A Western Activity Book & Libro de actividades del Oeste: 6 English, 6 Spanish Adaptations. 2011. (ENG & SPA.). (J). 101.00 net. *(978-1-4108-5734-7(4))* Benchmark Education Co.
Bodden, Valerie. Through the American West. 2011. (Illus.). 48p. (J). 35.65 *(978-1-60818-065-3(4),* Creative Education) Creative Co., The.
Carlson, Lisa, illus. Calamity Jane. 2007. (On My Own Folklore Ser.). 48p. (J). (gr. -1-3). per. 6.95 *(978-0-8225-6480-5(7),* First Avenue Editions) Lerner Publishing Group.
Criscione, Rachel Damon. The Mustang. 2009. (Library of Horses Ser.). 24p. (gr. 3-3). 42.50 *(978-1-60853-722-8(6),* PowerKids Pr.) Rosen Publishing Group, Inc., The.
Crompton, Samuel Willard. Lewis & Clark. 2009. (Great Explorers Ser.). (Illus.). 120p. (J). (gr. 6-12). 30.00 *(978-1-60413-418-6(6),* Chelsea Hse.) Facts On File, Inc.
Demund, Tom. From Slave to Superstar of the Wild West: The Awesome Story of Jim Beckwourth. 2007. (Illus.). 154p. (J). 18.95 *(978-0-9786904-0-3(0))* Legends of the West Publishing Co.
Drinkard, Lawson. Riding on a Range: Western Activities for Kids. Lee, Fran, illus. 2003. (ENG.). 64p. (YA). pap. 9.99 *(978-1-58685-036-4(9))* Gibbs Smith, Publisher.
Exploring the West Classroom Library. (gr. 2-5). lib. bdg. 49.95 *(978-0-7368-4514-4(3))* Red Brick Learning.
Gilbert, Sara. Calamity Jane. 2005. (Legends of the West (Creative Education) Ser.). (Illus.). 48p. (J). (gr. 5-9). lib. bdg. 21.95 *(978-1-58341-337-1(5),* Creative Education) Creative Co., The.

WXYZ

Glasscock, Sarah. The Western States: Set Of 6. 2011. (Navigators Ser.). (J). pap. 48.00 net. (978-1-4108-6254-9(2)) Benchmark Education Co.

—The Western States: Text Pairs. 2008. (Bridges/Navigators Ser.). (J). (gr. 4). 89.00 (978-1-4108-8398-8(1)) Benchmark Education Co.

Gondosch, Linda. Where Did Sacagawea Join the Corps of Discovery? And Other Questions about the Lewis & Clark Expedition. 2011. (Six Questions of American History Ser.). (ENG.). 48p. (gr. 4-6). pap. 56.72 (978-0-7613-7644-6(5)); pap. 9.95 (978-0-7613-7131-1(1)) Lerner Publishing Group.

Granfield, Linda. Cowboy: An Album. (J). 9.99 (978-1-55054-230-1(3)) Da Capo Pr., Inc.

Green, Carl R. & Sanford, William R. Wild Bill Hickok. rev. ed. 2008. (Outlaws & Lawmen of the Wild West, Revised Edition Ser.). (Illus.). 48p. (J). (gr. 5-18). lib. bdg. 25.27 (978-0-7660-3177-7(2)) Enslow Pubs., Inc.

Johmann, Carol A. The Lewis & Clark Expedition: Join the Corps of Discovery to Explore Uncharted Territory. 2008. (ENG., Illus.). 112p. (J). (gr. 4-6). pap. 14.25 (978-1-885593-73-3(2), Ideal Pubns.) Worthy Publishing.

Jones, Charlotte Foltz. Westward Ho! Eleven Explorers of the American West. 2005. (ENG., Illus.). 240p. (J). (gr. 4-6). tchr. ed. 22.95 (978-0-8234-1586-1(4)) Holiday Hse., Inc.

Knowlton, Laurie Lazzaro. Cowgirl Alphabet, 1 vol. Knowlton, Charlotte & Coates, Kathy, illus. 2011. (ENG.). 32p. (J). (gr. k-3). 16.99 (978-1-58980-669-6(7)) Pelican Publishing Co., Inc.

Krohn, Katherine E. Women of the Wild West. 2003. (Biography Ser.). (Illus.). 112p. (YA). (gr. 6-18). pap. 7.95 (978-0-8225-9690-5(3), Carolrhoda Bks.) Lerner Publishing Group.

Latham, Frank. Jed Smith: Trail Blazer of the West. McHugh, Michael J., ed. Murch, Frank, illus. 2003. 121p. pap. 6.95 (978-1-930367-86-9(4)) Christian Liberty Pr.

Leacock, Elspeth & Schifini, Alfredo. The West. 2007. (Avenues Ser.). (ENG., Illus.). 32p. (J). pap. 17.95 (978-0-7922-8682-0(0)) CENGAGE Learning.

Levy, Janey. Lewis & Clark in Their Own Words, Vol. 1. 2014. (Eyewitness to History Ser.). 32p. (J). (gr. 4-5). (ENG.). pap. 10.50 (978-1-4339-9930-7(7)); 26.60 (978-1-4339-9929-1(3)) Stevens, Gareth Publishing LLLP.

Manheimer, Ann S. James Beckwourth: Legendary Mountain Man. 2005. (Trailblazer Biographies Ser.). (ENG., Illus.). 112p. (gr. 5-9). lib. bdg. 31.93 (978-1-57505-892-4(8), Twenty-First Century Bks.) Lerner Publishing Group.

Marsh, Carole. John C. Fremont. 2004. 12p. (gr. k-4). 2.95 (978-0-635-02380-3(6)) Gallopade International.

Miller, Reagan & Walker, Robert. What's in the the West? Crabtree Publishing Staff, ed. 2011. (ENG.). 32p. (J). (gr. 3-6). pap. (978-0-7787-1833-8(6)) Crabtree Publishing Co.

—What's in the West? 2011. (ENG.). 32p. (J). lib. bdg. (978-0-7787-1827-7(1)) Crabtree Publishing Co.

Miller, Robert H. Reflections of a Black Cowboy: Buffalo Soldiers. 2004. (J). pap. 9.95 (978-0-940975-69-9(6), Sankofa Bks.) Just Us Bks., Inc.

—Reflections of a Black Cowboy: Cowboys. 2004. (J). pap. 9.95 (978-0-940975-70-5(X), Sankofa Bks.) Just Us Bks., Inc.

Moran, Margaret. Cowhands & Cattle Trails & Los vaqueros y el arreo de Ganado: 6 English, 6 Spanish Adaptations. 2011. (ENG & SPA.). (J). 97.00 net. (978-1-4108-5700-2(X)) Benchmark Education Co.

Mulhall, Jill K. Lewis & Clark. 2017. (Primary Source Readers Ser.). (Illus.). 32p. (J). (gr. 4-5). pap. 8.99 (978-1-4938-3886-8(5)) Teacher Created Materials, Inc.

Munro, Roxie. Wild West Trail Ride Maze. 2006. (ENG., Illus.). 50p. (J). (gr. k-2). 16.95 (978-1-931721-67-7(X), c7606323-9d58-4d30-ad89-d1aee1920627) Bright Sky Pr.

Olson, Tod. How to Get Rich on a Texas Cattle Drive: In Which I Tell the Honest Truth about Rampaging Rustlers, Stampeding Steers & Other Fateful Hazards on the Wild Chisolm Trail. Allred, Scott & Proch, Gregory, illus. 2010. (How to Get Rich Ser.). (ENG.). 48p. (J). (gr. 3-7). 27.90 (978-1-4263-0525-2(7), National Geographic Children's Bks.) National Geographic Society.

Osmundson, Linda. How the West Was Drawn: Cowboy Charlie's Art, 1 vol. 2011. (How the West Was Drawn Ser.). (ENG., Illus.). 32p. (J). (gr. k-7). 16.99 (978-1-58980-884-3(3)) Pelican Publishing Co., Inc.

Penn, Sarah. Nat Love: Vaquero Afroamericano. 2004. (Grandes personajes en la historia de los Estados Unidos Ser.). (SPA.). 32p. (gr. 4-8). pap. 10.00 (978-0-8239-4234-3(1), Rosen Classroom) Rosen Publishing Group, Inc., The.

Petrie, Kristin. Lewis & Clark, 1 vol. 2007. (Explorers Set 2 Ser.). (ENG., Illus.). 32p. (gr. 4-7). 27.07 (978-1-59679-743-7(6), Checkerboard Library) ABDO Publishing Co.

Plain, Nancy. Frederic Remington: Artist of the American West. 2003. (Historical American Biographies Ser.). (Illus.). 160p. (J). (gr. 6-12). lib. bdg. 27.94 (978-0-7660-1975-1(6)) Enslow Pubs., Inc.

Pringle, Laurence. American Slave, American Hero: York of the Lewis & Clark Expedition. Van Wright, Cornelius & Hu, Ying-Hwa, illus. 2006. (ENG.). 40p. (J). (gr. 3-3). 19.95 (978-1-59078-282-8(8)) Boyds Mills Pr.

Renehan, Edward J., Jr. The Transcontinental Railroad: The Gateway to the West. 2007. (Milestones in American History Ser.). (Illus.). 120p. (YA). (gr. 7-12). lib. bdg. 35.00 (978-0-7910-9351-1(4)) Facts On File, Inc.

Roop, Peter & Roop, Connie. Explore the West. 2007. (Avenues Ser.). (ENG., Illus.). 36p. (J). pap. 18.95 (978-0-7922-5461-4(9)) CENGAGE Learning.

Ross, Michael Elsohn. Exploring the Earth with John Wesley Powell. Smith, Wendy, illus. 2005. (Naturalist's Apprentice Biographies Ser.). 48p. (gr. 3-6). lib. bdg. 19.93 (978-1-57505-254-0(7)) Lerner Publishing Group.

Sanford, William R. & Green, Carl R. Buffalo Bill Cody: Courageous Wild West Showman. 2012. (Courageous Heroes of the American West Ser.). (Illus.). 48p. (J). pap. 8.95 (978-1-4644-0090-2(3)) Enslow Pubs., Inc.

—Calamity Jane: Courageous Wild West Woman. 2012. (Courageous Heroes of the American West Ser.). (Illus.). 48p. (J). pap. 8.95 (978-1-4644-0093-3(8)) Enslow Pubs., Inc.

Santillo, LuAnn. Wild West, 6 vols. Santillo, LuAnn, ed. 2003. (Half-Pint Kids Readers Ser.). (Illus.). 42p. (J). (gr. -1-1). pap. 6.95 (978-1-59256-077-6(6)) Half-Pint Kids, Inc.

Savage, Candace. Born to Be a Cowgirl: A Spirited Ride Through the Old West. 2004. (Illus.). (978-1-55054-838-9(7)) Da Capo Pr., Inc.

Savage, Jeff. Fearless Scouts: True Tales of the Wild West. 2012. (True Tales of the Wild West Ser.). (Illus.). 48p. (J). (gr. 5-18). lib. bdg. 22.60 (978-0-7660-4024-3(0)) Enslow Pubs., Inc.

—Pioneering Women: True Tales of the Wild West. 2012. (True Tales of the Wild West Ser.). (Illus.). 48p. (J). (gr. 5-18). lib. bdg. 22.60 (978-0-7660-4022-9(4)) Enslow Pubs., Inc.

Sechrist, Darren. Taming the West. 2008. (ENG.). 32p. (J). pap. (978-0-7787-4215-9(6)) Crabtree Publishing Co.

Smith-Llera, Danielle. People & Places of the West. 2016. (United States by Region Ser.). (ENG., Illus.). 32p. (gr. 3-4). lib. bdg. 27.32 (978-1-5157-2441-4(7), Fact Finders) Capstone Press of Coughlan Cos.

Stuckey, Rachel. Go West with Famous Trailblazers. 2016. (ENG.). 32p. (J). (978-0-7787-2324-0(0)) Crabtree Publishing Co.

U. S. National Geographic Society Staff, contrib. by. The West Today. 2007. (Reading Expeditions Ser.). (ENG., Illus.). 32p. (J). pap. 17.95 (978-0-7922-4536-0(9)) CENGAGE Learning.

Urbigkit, Cat. The Shepherd's Trail. 2008. (ENG., Illus.). 32p. (J). (gr. 2-4). 16.95 (978-1-59078-509-6(6)) Boyds Mills Pr.

Vann, Donna. Wild West Adventures. 2006. (Adventure Ser.). (ENG., Illus.). 96p. (J). per. 8.99 (978-1-84550-065-8(2), 9f994332-def5-4d9f-abc1-2f97eaba348d) Christian Focus Pubns. GBR. Dist: Bookmasters Distribution.

Visca, Curt. How to Draw Cartoon Symbols of the Wild West. 2009. (Kid's Guide to Drawing Ser.). 24p. (gr. 3-3). 47.90 (978-1-61511-021-6(6), PowerKids Pr.) Rosen Publishing Group, Inc., The.

Williams, Colleen Madonna Flood. My Adventure in the Wild West. 2007. 44p. (J). 8.99 (978-1-59092-439-6(8)) Blue Forge Pr.

Winter, Jonah. Wild Women of the Wild West. Morgan, Mary & Guevara, Susan, illus. 2011. (ENG.). 40p. (J). 16.95 (978-0-8234-1601-1(1)) Holiday Hse., Inc.

WEST (U.S.)—FICTION

Abnett, Dan. Dragon Frontier. 2015. (Dragon Frontier Ser.). (ENG., Illus.). 330p. (J). (gr. 4). pap. 9.99 (978-0-14-134296-2(X)) Penguin Bks., Ltd. GBR. Dist: Independent Pubs. Group.

Abnett, Dan & Lanning, Andy. Dragon Frontier: Burning Moon. 2nd ed. 2015. (Dragon Frontier Ser.: 2). (ENG.). 352p. (J). (gr. 4). pap. 9.99 (978-0-14-134298-6(6)) Penguin Bks., Ltd. GBR. Dist: Independent Pubs. Group.

Alger, Horatio. Frank & Fearless or the Fortunes of Jasper Kent. 2007. 228p. 20.99 (978-1-4280-7465-1(1)); per. 14.99 (978-1-4280-7470-5(8)) IndyPublish.com.

Anderson, Connie Kingrey. Haunted Cattle Drive. 2013. (Creepers Mysteries Ser.: Bk. 1). (ENG.). 112p. (J). pap. 7.99 (978-1-935793-00-7(4)) Movies for the Ear, LLC.

Anderson, Suzette. Cybertreks: Wildest West. 2004. 196p. pap. 13.95 (978-0-595-30840-8(6)) iUniverse, Inc.

Applegate, Katherine. The Buffalo Storm. Ormerod, Jan, illus. 2014. (ENG.). 32p. (J). (gr. -1-3). pap. 7.99 (978-0-544-33921-7(5), HMH Books For Young Readers) Houghton Mifflin Harcourt Publishing Co.

Arrigan, Mary. Pa Jinglebob - The Fastest Knitter in the West. Paul, Korky, illus. 2005. (Red Bananas Ser.). (ENG.). 48p. (J). lib. bdg. (978-0-7787-1072-1(6)) Crabtree Publishing Co.

—Pa Jinglebob & the Grabble Gang. 2006. (Red Bananas Ser.). (ENG., Illus.). 48p. (J). (gr. -1-3). lib. bdg. (978-0-7787-1074-5(2)) Crabtree Publishing Co.

Arrigan, Mary & Paul, Korky. PA Jinglebob: The Fastest Knitter in the West. 2005. (Red Bananas Ser.). (ENG., Illus.). 48p. (J). (gr. 1-3). (978-0-7787-1088-2(2)) Crabtree Publishing Co.

Asfar, Dan & Banks, Sydney. Dear Liza, 1 vol. rev. ed. 2004. 28. (ENG., Illus.). 88p. 12.95 (978-1-55105-332-5(2), 1551053322) Lone Pine Publishing USA.

ber, Gail. Time of the Cats. 2013. 132p. pap. 11.99 (978-1-4582-1232-0(7), Abbott Pr.) Author Solutions, Inc.

Berenstain, Stan & Berenstain, Jan. The Berenstain Bears Out West. Berenstain, Stan & Berenstain, Jan, illus. 2006. (I Can Read Level 1 Ser.). (ENG., Illus.). 32p. (J). (gr. k-3). pap. 3.99 (978-0-06-058354-5(1)) HarperCollins Pubs.

Bietz, Barbara. The Sundown Kid. 2017. (ENG., Illus.). 32p. (J). (gr. k-2). pap. 8.95 (978-1-939160-94-2(4)) August Hse. Pubs., Inc.

Blakeslee, Ann R. A Different Kind of Hero, 1 vol. 2005. (ENG.). 32p. (YA). pap. 5.95 (978-0-7614-5147-1(1)) Marshall Cavendish Corp.

Blanchet, Deborah A. The Hat. 2009. 122p. 29.99 (978-1-4415-4624-1(3)); pap. 19.99 (978-1-4415-4623-4(5)) Xlibris Corp.

Bloomfield, Susanne George & Reed, Eric Melvin, eds. Adventures in the West: Stories for Young Readers. 2007. (ENG., Illus.). 302p. (gr. 3-7). pap. 19.95 (978-0-8032-5974-4(3), Bison Bks.) Univ. of Nebraska Pr.

Bly, Stephen A. The Lost Wagon Train. 2005. (Retta Barre's Oregon Trail Ser.: Vol. 1). 110p. pap. 5.99 (978-1-58134-391-5(4), Crossway Bibles) Crossway.

Bostick, B. k. Huber Hill & the Dead Man's Treasure. 2011. (J). (978-1-59955-911-7(0), Bonneville Bks.) Cedar Fort, Inc./CFI Distribution.

Bruchac, Joseph. Sacajawea. 2008. (ENG., Illus.). 208p. (YA). (gr. 7). pap. 7.99 (978-0-15-206455-6(9)) Houghton Mifflin Harcourt Publishing Co.

Burgess, Thornton W. Old Mother West Wind's "When" Stories. (J). 21.95 (978-0-8488-0387-2(6)) Amereon Ltd.

Byars, Betsy. Golly Sisters Go West. Truesdell, Sue, illus. 2003. (I Can Read Level 3 Ser.). (ENG.). 64p. (J). (gr. k-3). pap. 3.99 (978-0-06-444132-2(6)) HarperCollins Pubs.

Byars, Betsy & Byars, B. The Golly Sisters Go West. 2003. (I Can Read! Level 3 Ser.). (J). (gr. k-3). lib. bdg. 13.55 (978-0-8335-4709-5(7), Turtleback) Turtleback Bks.

Campbell, Roy. Song of the Jackalope. Bosworth, David, illus. 2nd ed. 2006. 140p. (YA). pap. 12.95 (978-1-933538-04-4(X)) Bridgeway Bks.

Cannon, A. E. Charlotte's Rose. 2011. (ENG., Illus.). 256p. (J). (gr. 4). pap. 9.95 (978-1-60781-141-1(3)) Univ. of Utah Pr.

Casanova, Mary. The Day Dirk Yeller Came to Town. Hoyt, Ard, illus. 2011. (ENG.). 36p. (J). (gr. -1-3). 16.99 (978-0-374-31742-3(9), 9780374317423, Farrar, Straus & Giroux (BYR)) Farrar, Straus & Giroux.

Coren, Alan. Arthur the Kid. 2004. (Illus.). 64p. (978-0-903895-76-7(5), Robson Bks. Ltd.) Pavilion Bks.

—Buffalo Arthur. 2004. (Illus.). 64p. (978-0-903895-75-0(7), Robson Bks. Ltd.) Pavilion Bks.

—Railroad Arthur. 2004. (Illus.). 64p. (978-0-903895-92-7(7), Robson Bks. Ltd.) Pavilion Bks.

Crunk, Tony. Railroad John & the Red Rock Run, 1 vol. Austin, Michael, illus. 2006. (ENG.). 32p. (J). (gr. k-3). 16.95 (978-1-56145-363-4(3)) Peachtree Pubs.

Cushman, Karen. Rodzina. 2016.Tr. of Rodzina. (ENG.). 224p. (J). (gr. 5-7). pap. 6.99 (978-0-544-54029-3(8), HMH Books For Young Readers) Houghton Mifflin Harcourt Publishing Co.

Davies, Robert, adapted by. Lit a Shuck for Texas: Adapted Louis l'Amour Short Stories Series. 2003. (Adapted Louis L'Amour Short Stories Ser.). (Illus.). 56p. (YA). (978-1-57035-983-5(0), 233LIT) Cambium Education, Inc.

—Merrano of the Dry Country: Adapted Louis l'Amour Short Story Series. 2003. (Adapted Louis L'Amour Short Stories Ser.). (Illus.). 60p. (J). (978-1-57035-985-9(7), 233MERRANO) Cambium Education, Inc.

—A Trail to the West: Adapted Louis l'Amour Short Stories Series. 2003. (Adapted Louis L'Amour Short Stories Ser.). (Illus.). 56p. (J). (978-1-57035-984-2(9), 233TRAIL) Cambium Education, Inc.

Disney Book Group. World of Reading: Sheriff Callie's Wild West Callie Asks for Help: Level Pre-1. Disney Storybook Art Team, illus. 2015. (World of Reading Ser.). (ENG.). 32p. (J). (gr. -1-k). pap. 3.99 (978-1-4847-1631-1(0)) Disney Pr.

Disney Book Group Staff. Sheriff Callie's Wild West - The Cat Who Tamed the West. Disney Storybook Art Team, illus. 2015. (ENG.). 40p. (J). (gr. -1-k). 8.99 (978-1-4847-1495-9(4)) Disney Pr.

—Sheriff Callie's Wild West Peck's Trail Mix Mix-Up. Disney Storybook Art Team, illus. 2015. (World of Reading Ser.). (ENG.). 32p. (J). (gr. -1-k). pap. 3.99 (978-1-4847-1566-6(7)) Disney Pr.

Dundy, Melanie Richardson. Westward Ho with Ollie Ox! Date not set. (Illus.). 56p. (J). (gr. k-5). per. 12.95 (978-0-9674491-4-2(6)) M D C T Publishing.

Erickson, John R. The Case of the Black-Hooded Hangmans. Holmes, Gerald L., illus. 2011. (Hank the Cowdog Ser.). (ENG.). 113p. (J). (gr. 3-6). pap. 5.99 (978-1-59188-124-7(2)) Maverick Bks., Inc.

—The Case of the Burrowing Robot. Holmes, Gerald L., illus. 2011. (Hank the Cowdog Ser.). (ENG.). 125p. (J). (gr. 3-6). pap. 5.99 (978-1-59188-142-1(0)) Maverick Bks., Inc.

—The Case of the Car-Barkaholic Dog. Holmes, Gerald L., illus. 2011. (Hank the Cowdog Ser.). (ENG.). 115p. (J). (gr. 3-6). pap. 5.99 (978-1-59188-117-9(X)) Maverick Bks., Inc.

—The Case of the Deadly Ha-Ha Game. Holmes, Gerald L., illus. 2011. (Hank the Cowdog Ser.). (ENG.). 128p. (J). (gr. 3-6). pap. 5.99 (978-1-59188-137-7(4)) Maverick Bks., Inc.

—The Case of the Double Bumblebee Sting. Holmes, Gerald L., illus. 2011. (Hank the Cowdog Ser.: No. 22). (ENG.). 114p. (J). (gr. 3-6). pap. 5.99 (978-1-59188-122-3(6)) Maverick Bks., Inc.

—The Case of the Falling Sky. Holmes, Gerald L., illus. 2011. (Hank the Cowdog Ser.: No. 45). (ENG.). 129p. (J). (gr. 3-6). pap. 5.99 (978-1-59188-145-2(5)) Maverick Bks., Inc.

—The Case of the Fiddle-Playing Fox. Holmes, Gerald L., illus. 2011. (Hank the Cowdog Ser.: No. 12). (ENG.). 118p. (J). (gr. 3-6). pap. 5.99 (978-1-59188-112-4(9)) Maverick Bks., Inc.

—The Case of the Halloween Ghost. Holmes, Gerald L., illus. 2011. (Hank the Cowdog Ser.). (ENG.). 123p. (J). (gr. 3-6). pap. 5.99 (978-1-59188-109-4(9)) Maverick Bks., Inc.

—The Case of the Haystack Kitties. Holmes, Gerald L., illus. 2011. (Hank the Cowdog Ser.). (ENG.). 123p. (J). (gr. 3-6). pap. 5.99 (978-1-59188-130-8(7)) Maverick Bks., Inc.

—The Case of the Hooking Bull. Holmes, Gerald L., illus. 2011. (Hank the Cowdog Ser.). (ENG.). 119p. (J). (gr. 3-6). pap. 5.99 (978-1-59188-118-6(8)) Maverick Bks., Inc.

—The Case of the Kidnapped Collie. Holmes, Gerald L., illus. 2011. (Hank the Cowdog Ser.). (ENG.). 113p. (J). (gr. 3-6). pap. 5.99 (978-1-59188-126-1(9)) Maverick Bks., Inc.

—The Case of the Midnight Rustler. Holmes, Gerald L., illus. 2011. (Hank the Cowdog Ser.: No. 19). (ENG.). 113p. (J). (gr. 3-6). pap. 5.99 (978-1-59188-119-3(6)) Maverick Bks., Inc.

—The Case of the Missing Bird Dog. Holmes, Gerald L., illus. 2011. (Hank the Cowdog Ser.: No. 40). (ENG.). 126p. (J). (gr. 3-6). pap. 5.99 (978-1-59188-140-7(4)) Maverick Bks., Inc.

—The Case of the Missing Cat. Holmes, Gerald L., illus. 2011. (Hank the Cowdog Ser.: No. 15). (ENG.). 114p. (J). (gr. 3-6). pap. 5.99 (978-1-59188-115-5(3)) Maverick Bks., Inc.

—The Case of the Monkey Burglar. Holmes, Gerald L., illus. 2011. (Hank the Cowdog Ser.: No. 48). (ENG.). 129p. (J). (gr. 3-6). pap. 5.99 (978-1-59188-148-3(X)) Maverick Bks., Inc.

—The Case of the Most Ancient Bone. Holmes, Gerald L., illus. 2011. (Hank the Cowdog Ser.). (ENG.). 239p. (J). (gr. 3-6). pap. 5.99 (978-1-59188-150-6(1)) Maverick Bks., Inc.

—The Case of the Night-Stalking Bone Monster. Holmes, Gerald L., illus. 2011. (Hank the Cowdog Ser.). (ENG.). 115p. (J). (gr. 3-6). pap. 5.99 (978-1-59188-127-8(7)) Maverick Bks., Inc.

—The Case of the One-Eyed Killer Stud Horse. Holmes, Gerald L., illus. 2011. (Hank the Cowdog Ser.: No. 8). (ENG.). 120p. (J). (gr. 3-6). pap. 5.99 (978-1-59188-108-7(0)) Maverick Bks., Inc.

—The Case of the Raging Rottweiler. Holmes, Gerald L., illus. 2011. (Hank the Cowdog Ser.). (ENG.). 131p. (J). (gr. 3-6). pap. 5.99 (978-1-59188-136-0(6)) Maverick Bks., Inc.

—The Case of the Saddle House Robbery. Holmes, Gerald L., illus. 2011. (Hank the Cowdog Ser.: No. 35). (ENG.). 125p. (J). (gr. 3-6). pap. 5.99 (978-1-59188-135-3(8)) Maverick Bks., Inc.

—The Case of the Shipwrecked Tree. Holmes, Gerald L., illus. 2011. (Hank the Cowdog Ser.: No. 41). (ENG.). 119p. (J). (gr. 3-6). pap. 5.99 (978-1-59188-141-4(2)) Maverick Bks., Inc.

—The Case of the Tender Cheeping Chickies. Holmes, Gerald L., illus. 2011. (Hank the Cowdog Ser.). (ENG.). 129p. (J). (gr. 3-6). pap. 5.99 (978-1-59188-147-6(1)) Maverick Bks., Inc.

—The Case of the Tricky Trap. Holmes, Gerald L., illus. 2011. (Hank the Cowdog Ser.). (ENG.). 126p. (J). (gr. 3-6). pap. 5.99 (978-1-59188-146-9(3)) Maverick Bks., Inc.

—The Case of the Twisted Kitty. Holmes, Gerald L., illus. 2004. (Hank the Cowdog Ser.: No. 43). 131p. (J). lib. bdg. 17.00 (978-1-4242-1600-0(1)) Fitzgerald Bks.

—The Case of the Twisted Kitty. Holmes, Gerald L., illus. 2011. (Hank the Cowdog Ser.). (ENG.). 131p. (J). (gr. 3-6). pap. 5.99 (978-1-59188-143-8(9)) Maverick Bks., Inc.

—The Case of the Vampire Cat. Holmes, Gerald L., illus. 2011. (Hank the Cowdog Ser.). (ENG.). 115p. (J). (gr. 3-6). pap. 5.99 (978-1-59188-121-6(8)) Maverick Bks., Inc.

—The Case of the Vampire Vacuum Sweeper. Holmes, Gerald L., illus. 2011. (Hank the Cowdog Ser.). (ENG.). 119p. (J). (gr. 3-6). pap. 5.99 (978-1-59188-129-2(3)) Maverick Bks., Inc.

—The Case of the Vanishing Fishhook. Holmes, Gerald L., illus. 2011. (Hank the Cowdog Ser.: No. 31). (ENG.). 124p. (J). (gr. 3-6). pap. 5.99 (978-1-59188-131-5(5)) Maverick Bks., Inc.

—The Curse of the Incredible Priceless Corncob. Holmes, Gerald L., illus. 2011. (Hank the Cowdog Ser.: No. 7). (ENG.). 127p. (J). (gr. 3-6). pap. 5.99 (978-1-59188-107-0(2)) Maverick Bks., Inc.

—The Dungeon of Doom. Holmes, Gerald L., illus. 2004. (Hank the Cowdog Ser.: No. 44). 122p. (J). lib. bdg. 17.00 (978-1-4242-1601-7(X)) Fitzgerald Bks.

—The Dungeon of Doom. Holmes, Gerald L., illus. 2011. (Hank the Cowdog Ser.). (ENG.). 122p. (J). (gr. 3-6). pap. 5.99 (978-1-59188-144-5(7)) Maverick Bks., Inc.

—Every Dog Has His Day. Holmes, Gerald L., illus. 2011. (Hank the Cowdog Ser.). (ENG.). 118p. (J). (gr. 3-6). pap. 5.99 (978-1-59188-110-0(2)) Maverick Bks., Inc.

—Faded Love. Holmes, Gerald L., illus. 2011. (Hank the Cowdog Ser.: No. 5). (ENG.). 125p. (J). (gr. 3-6). pap. 5.99 (978-1-59188-105-6(6)) Maverick Bks., Inc.

—The Fling. Holmes, Gerald L., illus. 2011. (Hank the Cowdog Ser.). (ENG.). 126p. (J). (gr. 3-6). pap. 5.99 (978-1-59188-138-4(2)) Maverick Bks., Inc.

—The Garbage Monster from Outer Space. Holmes, Gerald L., illus. 2011. (Hank the Cowdog Ser.). (ENG.). 126p. (J). (gr. 3-6). pap. 5.99 (978-1-59188-132-2(3)) Maverick Bks., Inc.

—It's a Dog's Life. Holmes, Gerald L., illus. (Hank the Cowdog Ser.: No. 3). (J). 100p. (gr. 2-5). 9.95 (978-0-916941-04-8(3)); 2011. (ENG.). 127p. (gr. 3-6). pap. 5.99 (978-1-59188-103-2(X)) Maverick Bks., Inc.

—Let Sleeping Dogs Lie. Holmes, Gerald L., illus. 2011. (Hank the Cowdog Ser.: No. 6). (ENG.). 129p. (J). (gr. 3-6). pap. 5.99 (978-1-59188-106-3(4)) Maverick Bks., Inc.

—Lost in the Blinded Blizzard. Holmes, Gerald L., illus. 2011. (Hank the Cowdog Ser.). (ENG.). 115p. (J). (gr. 3-6). pap. 5.99 (978-1-59188-116-2(1)) Maverick Bks., Inc.

—Lost in the Dark Unchanted Forest. Holmes, Gerald L., illus. 2011. (Hank the Cowdog Ser.). (ENG.). 124p. (J). (gr. 3-6). pap. 5.99 (978-1-59188-111-7(0)) Maverick Bks., Inc.

—Moonlight Madness. Holmes, Gerald L., illus. 2011. (Hank the Cowdog Ser.: No. 23). (ENG.). 114p. (J). (gr. 3-6). pap. 5.99 (978-1-59188-123-0(4)) Maverick Bks., Inc.

—The Mopwater Files. Holmes, Gerald L., illus. 2011. (Hank the Cowdog Ser.). (ENG.). 111p. (J). (gr. 3-6). pap. 5.99 (978-1-59188-128-5(5)) Maverick Bks., Inc.

—Murder in the Middle Pasture. Holmes, Gerald L., illus. 2011. (Hank the Cowdog Ser.). (ENG.). 120p. (J). (gr. 3-6). pap. 5.99 (978-1-59188-104-9(8)) Maverick Bks., Inc.

—The Original Adventures of Hank the Cowdog. Holmes, Gerald L., illus. (ENG.). 127p. (J). (gr. 3-6). 2012. (Hank the Cowdog Ser.: Vol. 1). 15.99 (978-1-59188-201-5(X)) 2011. (Hank the Cowdog Ser.: No. 1). pap. 5.99 (978-1-59188-101-8(3)) Maverick Bks., Inc.

—The Phantom in the Mirror. Holmes, Gerald L., illus. 2011. (Hank the Cowdog Ser.: No. 20). (ENG.). 114p. (J). (gr. 3-6). pap. 5.99 (978-1-59188-120-9(X)) Maverick Bks., Inc.

—The Quest for the Great White Quail. Holmes, Gerald L., illus. 2011. (Hank the Cowdog Ser.). (ENG.). 123p. (J). (gr. 3-6). pap. 5.99 (978-1-59188-152-0(8)) Maverick Bks., Inc.

—The Return of the Charlie Monsters. Holmes, Gerald L., illus. 2014. 128p. (J). pap. (978-1-59188-163-6(3)) Maverick Bks., Inc.

—The Secret Laundry Monster Files. Holmes, Gerald L., illus. 2011. (Hank the Cowdog Ser.). (ENG.). 128p. (J). (gr. 3-6). pap. 5.99 (978-1-59188-139-1(0)) Maverick Bks., Inc.

—Slim's Good-Bye. Holmes, Gerald L., illus. 2011. (Hank the Cowdog Ser.). (ENG.). 132p. (J). (gr. 3-6). pap. 5.99 (978-1-59188-134-6(X)) Maverick Bks., Inc.

—The Wounded Buzzard on Christmas Eve. Holmes, Gerald L., illus. 2011. (Hank the Cowdog Ser.: No. 13). (ENG.). 112p. (J). (gr. 3-6). pap. 5.99 (978-1-59188-113-1(7)) Maverick Bks., Inc.

Eubanks, Toni. Journey Home: Passage to Womanhood. 2016. (ENG.). 124p. (J). (gr. 2-6). pap. 9.99 (978-1-5040-2728-1(0)) Open Road Integrated Media, Inc.

Fitzgerald, John D. Brave Buffalo Fighter. 2003. (Young Adult Historical Library). 178p. (YA). pap. 11.95 (978-1-883937-59-1(0)) Bethlehem Bks.

Fleischman, Sid. Jim Ugly. Smith, Jos. A., illus. 2003. (ENG.). 144p. (J). (gr. 3-7). pap. 6.99 (978-0-06-052121-9(X), Greenwillow Bks.) HarperCollins Pubs.

Fleming, Candace. Westward Ho, Carlotta! Catrow, David, illus. 2009. (ENG.). 36p. (J). (gr. -1-2). 10.99 (978-1-4424-0218-8(0), Atheneum Bks. for Young Readers) Simon & Schuster Children's Publishing.

Fletcher, Steffi. The Lone Ranger. Dreany, E. Joseph, illus. 2013. (Little Golden Book Ser.). (ENG.). 24p. (J). (-k). 4.99 (978-0-449-81793-3(8), Golden Bks.) Random Hse. Children's Bks.

Frank, John. The Toughest Cowboy: Or How the Wild West Was Tamed. Pullen, Zachary, illus. 2004. (ENG.). 48p. (J). (gr. 1-3). 17.95 (978-0-689-83461-5(6), Simon & Schuster Bks. For Young Readers) Simon & Schuster Bks. For Young Readers.

Garland, Sherry. The Buffalo Soldier, 1 vol. Himler, Ronald, illus. 2006. (ENG.). 32p. (J). (gr. k-3). 16.99 *(978-1-58980-391-6(4))* Pelican Publishing Co., Inc.
Gemeinhart, Dan. Some Kind of Courage. 2016. (ENG.). 240p. (J). (gr. 3-7). 16.99 *(978-0-545-66577-3(9),* Scholastic Pr.) Scholastic, Inc.
Goscinny, René. The Daltons Always on the Run. Morris, illus. 2012. (Lucky Luke Ser.: 34). (ENG.). 48p. (J). (gr. 3-12). pap. 11.95 *(978-1-84918-119-8(5))* CineBook GBR. Dist: National Bk. Network.
—The Wagon Train. Morris, Jean, illus. 2008. (Lucky Luke Ser.: 9). (ENG.). 48p. pap. 11.95 *(978-1-905460-40-3(6))* CineBook GBR. Dist: National Bk. Network.
Goscinny, René & Morris Publishing Company Staff. The Grand Duke. 2011. (Lucky Luke Ser.: 29). (ENG., Illus.). 48p. (gr. 3-17). pap. 11.95 *(978-1-84918-083-2(0))* CineBook GBR. Dist: National Bk. Network.
—The Singing Wire. 2012. (Lucky Luke Ser.: 35). (ENG., Illus.). 48p. (J). (gr. 3-9). pap. 11.95 *(978-1-84918-123-5(3))* CineBook GBR. Dist: National Bk. Network.
Grace & the Guiltless. 2014. (Wanted Ser.). (ENG.). 272p. 16.95 *(978-1-63079-001-1(X))* Switch Pr.
Guzman, Lila & Guzman, Rick. Lorenzo's Revolutionary Quest. 2003. 176p. (J). pap. 9.95 *(978-1-55885-392-8(8),* Piñata Books) Arte Publico Pr.
Heaton, Layce D. The Many Tracks of Lap'n Tap, 1. Heaton, Layce D., illus. 2006. (Illus.). 32p. (J). lib. bdg. 18.95 *(978-0-9761128-3-9(3))* KB Bks. & More.
Hemphill, Helen. The Adventurous Deeds of Deadwood Jones. 2011. (ENG.). 232p. (J). (gr. 6-9). pap. 7.95 *(978-1-59078-896-7(6))* Boyds Mills Pr.
Henry, Marguerite. San Domingo. Lougheed, Robert, illus. 2016. (ENG.). 288p. (J). (gr. 3-7). 19.99 *(978-1-4814-6211-2(3),* Aladdin) Simon & Schuster Children's Publishing.
Henty, George Alfred. Captain Bayley's Heir: A Tale of the California Gold Fields. 2011. 314p. pap. 19.95 *(978-1-61179-115-0(4))* Fireship Pr.
—A Tale of the Western Plains. Pearse, Alfred, illus. 2006. (Dover Children's Classics Ser.). (ENG.). 352p. (YA). (gr. 3-8). per. 8.95 *(978-0-486-45261-6(1))* Dover Pubns., Inc.
Hergé. Land of Black Gold. Orig. Title: Tintin au Pays de l'Or Noir. (Illus.). 62p. (J). 19.95 *(978-0-8288-5048-3(8))* French & European Pubns., Inc.
—Tintin au Pays de l'Or Noir.Tr. of Land of Black Gold. (FRE.). (J). (gr. 7-9). 24.95 *(978-0-8288-5091-9(7))* French & European Pubns., Inc.
—Tintin en el Pais del Oro Negro.Tr. of Land of Black Gold. (SPA., Illus.). 62p. (J). 24.95 *(978-0-8288-4995-1(1))* French & European Pubns., Inc.
Hermes, Patricia. Koda. Sanderson, Ruth, illus. 2009. (Horse Diaries: No. 3). (ENG.). 160p. (J). (gr. 3-7). pap. 7.99 *(978-0-375-85199-5(2),* Random Hse. Bks. for Young Readers) Random Hse. Children's Bks.
Hirsch, Andy. Varmints. 2016. (J). lib. bdg. 29.40 *(978-0-606-39563-2(6))* Turtleback Bks.
Hope, Laura Lee. The Bobbsey Twins in the Great West. 2005. 27.95 *(978-1-4218-0365-4(8),* 1st World Library - Literary Society) 1st World Publishing, Inc.
Horse, Harry. The Last Cowboys. Horse, Harry, illus. 2008. (ENG., Illus.). 128p. (J). (gr. 1-5). 12.95 *(978-1-56145-451-8(6),* Peachtree Junior) Peachtree Pubs.
Hughes, Holly. Hoofbeats of Danger. 2009. (Mysteries Through Time Ser.). 144p. (YA). (gr. 4-8). 31.95 *(978-1-60754-176-9(9));* pap. 15.25 *(978-1-60754-177-6(7))* Windmill Bks.
Ives, David. Scrib. 2005. 208p. (J). (gr. 5-18). lib. bdg. 17.89 *(978-0-06-059842-6(5))* HarperCollins Pubs.
James, Will. Home Ranch. rev. ed. (Tumbleweed Ser.). (Illus.). 302p. (J). (gr. 4). pap. *(978-0-87842-406-1(7),* 802) Mountain Pr. Publishing Co., Inc.
—Look-See with Uncle Bill. rev. ed. (Illus.). 190p. (J). (gr. 4). pap. *(978-0-87842-458-0(X),* 814) Mountain Pr. Publishing Co., Inc.
—Smokey Vol. 1: The Cowhorse. rev. ed. (Tumbleweed Ser.). (Illus.). 260p. (J). (gr. 4-7). 36.00 *(978-0-87842-414-6(8),* 805) Mountain Pr. Publishing Co., Inc.
—Smoky Cowhorse, the Cowhorse. 2011. 9.00 *(978-0-7848-3460-2(1),* Everbind) Marco Bk. Co.
—Smoky the Cowhorse. 2008. (ENG., Illus.). 336p. (J). (gr. 3-7). pap. 8.99 *(978-1-4169-4941-1(0),* Aladdin) Simon & Schuster Children's Publishing.
Johnson, Erin. Her Cold Revenge. 2015. (Wanted Ser.). (ENG.). 272p. 16.95 *(978-1-63079-007-3(9))* Switch Pr.
Karr, Kathleen. The Great Turkey Walk. 2004. 199p. (gr. 4-7). 18.00 *(978-0-7569-4124-6(5))* Perfection Learning Corp.
Kimmel, Eric A. & Korelitz, Jean Hanff. The Great Texas Hamster Drive, 0 vols. Whatley, Bruce, illus. 2007. (ENG.). 40p. (J). (gr. k-3). 16.99 *(978-0-7614-5357-4(1),* 9780761453574, Amazon Children's Publishing) Amazon Publishing.
Langdo, Bryan. Tornado Slim & the Magic Cowboy Hat, 0 vols. 2011. (ENG.). 32p. (J). (gr. k-4). 17.99 *(978-0-7614-5962-0(6),* 9780761459620, Amazon Children's Publishing) Amazon Publishing.
Lee, Stacey. Under a Painted Sky. 2015. (ENG.). 384p. (YA). (gr. 7). 16.99 *(978-0-399-16803-1(6),* G.P. Putnam's Sons Books for Young Readers) Penguin Young Readers Group.
—Under a Painted Sky. 2016. lib. bdg. 22.10 *(978-0-606-38391-2(3))* Turtleback Bks.
McCall, Edith. Stories of American Steamboats. Borja, Robert, illus. 2011. 126p. 40.95 *(978-1-258-10111-4(4))* Literary Licensing, LLC.
McKernan, Victoria. The Devil's Paintbox. (ENG.). (YA). (gr. 9). 2013. 384p. pap. 9.99 *(978-0-449-81655-4(9),* Ember) 2010. 368p. mass mkt. 8.99 *(978-0-440-23962-8(1),* Laurel Leaf) Random Hse. Children's Bks.
McKissack, Patricia C. Away West. James, Gordon C. & James, Gordon, illus. 2006. (Scraps of Time Ser.). (ENG.). 144p. (J). (gr. 3-7). 5.99 *(978-0-14-240688-5(0),* Puffin Books) Penguin Young Readers Group.
Messner, Kate. Rescue on the Oregon Trail. McMorris, Kelley, illus. 2015. (Ranger in Time Ser.: 1). (ENG.). 144p. (J). (gr. 2-5). pap. 5.99 *(978-0-545-63914-9(X),* Scholastic Pr.) Scholastic, Inc.
Miller, Christopher & Miller, Allan. The Legend of Gid the Kid & the Black Bean Bandits, 2 bks., Bk.1. Miller, Christopher & Miller, Allan, illus. 2007. (Heroes of Promise Ser.). (ENG., Illus.). 32p. (J). (gr. 1-5). 12.99 *(978-1-59317-202-2(8))* Warner Pr., Inc.
Morrow, Sherry. Woman of the Mountains. 268p. (YA). pap. 22.00 *(978-1-58982-611-3(6))* American Bk. Publishing Group.
Mortensen, Lori. Cowpoke Clyde Rides the Range. Austin, Michael Allen, illus. 2016. (ENG.). 32p. (J). (gr. -1-3). 16.99 *(978-0-544-37030-2(9))* Houghton Mifflin Harcourt Publishing Co.
Moser, Lisa. Kisses on the Wind. Brown, Kathryn, illus. 2009. (ENG.). 32p. (J). (gr. -1-2). 16.99 *(978-0-7636-3110-9(8))* Candlewick Pr.
Moss, Marissa. Amelia's Are-We-There-Yet Longest Ever Car Trip. Moss, Marissa, illus. (Amelia Ser.). (ENG., Illus.). 40p. (J). (gr. 2-5). 2012. pap. 6.99 *(978-1-4169-1287-3(8))* 2006. 10.99 *(978-1-4169-0906-4(0))* Simon & Schuster/Paula Wiseman Bks. (Simon & Schuster/Paula Wiseman Bks.).
Myers, Walter Dean. The Righteous Revenge of Artemis Bonner. 2003. (J). (gr. 5-18). 23.00 *(978-0-8446-7250-2(5))* Smith, Peter Pub., Inc.
Nayeri, Daniel. Straw House, Wood House, Brick House, Blow: Four Novellas by Daniel Nayeri. Weinberg, James, illus. 2011. (ENG.). 432p. (YA). (gr. 9). 19.99 *(978-0-7636-5526-6(0))* Candlewick Pr.
Naylor, Phyllis Reynolds. Emily & Jackson Hiding Out. 2012. (ENG., Illus.). 176p. (J). (gr. 2-5). 14.99 *(978-0-385-74097-5(2),* Delacorte Bks. for Young Readers) Random Hse. Children's Bks.
—Emily's Fortune. 2011. (ENG.). 160p. (J). (gr. 3-7). 6.99 *(978-0-375-84492-8(9),* Yearling) Random Hse. Children's Bks.
Nell Nugget & the Cow Caper. 2008. (Illus.). 32p. (J). pap. 14.95 *(978-0-9792820-2-7(0))* Toe The Line.
Nislick, June Levitt. Zayda Was a Cowboy. 2005. (ENG.). 88p. pap. 11.95 *(978-0-8276-0817-7(9))* Jewish Pubn. Society.
Nolen, Jerdine. Thunder Rose. Nelson, Kadir, illus. 2007. (ENG.). 32p. (J). (gr. k-3). pap. 7.99 *(978-0-15-206006-0(5))* Houghton Mifflin Harcourt Publishing Co.
—Thunder Rose. Nelson, Kadir, illus. 2007. (gr. k-3). 17.00 *(978-0-7569-8199-0(9))* Perfection Learning Corp.
Novara, Joe. Road Wrangler: Cowboys on Wheels. Lawson, Robert & Spatrisano, Kimberly, illus. 2007. 112p. (J). pap. 8.95 *(978-1-58980-507-1(0))* Pelican Publishing Co., Inc.
O'Hearn, Michael. The el Dorado Map. 2015. (Middle-Grade Novels Ser.). (ENG.). 320p. (gr. 4-7). lib. bdg. 26.65 *(978-1-4965-0158-5(6))* Stone Arch Bks.
Olveira, Luis. The Children of Hope 3. 2009. 56p. pap. 15.49 *(978-0-578-00420-4(8))* Desktop Prepress Services.
Osborne, Mary Pope. Ghost Town at Sundown. unabr. ed. 2004. (Magic Tree House Ser.: No. 10). 73p. (J). (gr. k-3). pap. 17.00 incl. audio *(978-0-8072-0535-8(4),* Listening Library) Random Hse. Audio Publishing Group.
Paulsen, Gary. Tucket's Travels: Francis Tucket's Adventures in the West, 1847-1849. 2003. (Francis Tucket Bks.: Bks. 1-5). (ENG.). 560p. (J). (gr. 3-7). pap. 8.99 *(978-0-440-41967-9(0),* Yearling) Random Hse. Children's Bks.
Payne, Stephen. Teenage Stories of the West. 2011. 252p. 46.95 *(978-1-258-09964-0(0))* Literary Licensing, LLC.
Peck, Jan. Way Out West on My Little Pony, 1 vol. Leonhard, Herb, illus. 2010. (ENG.). 32p. (J). (gr. k-3). 16.99 *(978-1-58980-697-9(2))* Pelican Publishing Co., Inc.
Pierce, Mary E. Permilia: A Western Children's Book. Dobler, Shirley Jean, illus. 2013. 62p. (J). 25.00 *(978-1-936617-15-9(3))* Lemon Pr. LLC.
Pierpoint, Eric. The Last Ride of Caleb O'Toole. 2013. (ENG.). 304p. (J). (gr. 4-7). pap. 7.99 *(978-1-4022-8171-6(4),* 9781402281716, Sourcebooks Jabberwocky) Sourcebooks, Inc.
Platt, Chris. Moon Shadow. 2006. (ENG.). 176p. (J). (gr. 3-7). 14.95 *(978-1-56145-382-5(X))* Peachtree Pubs.
Posner-Sanchez, Andrea. Time to Fly! (Disney Junior: Sheriff Callie's Wild West) Fruchter, Jason, illus. 2015. (Little Golden Book Ser.). (ENG.). 24p. (J). (-k). 4.99 *(978-0-7364-3362-4(7),* Golden/Disney) Random Hse. Children's Bks.
Reeve, Kirk. Sun Father, Corn Mother: A Novel. 2015. 168p. (YA). pap. *(978-1-63293-091-0(9))* Sunstone Pr.
Reid, Mayne. The Boy Hunters or Adventures in Search of a White Buffalo. 2005. reprint ed. pap. 30.95 *(978-1-4179-0412-9(7))* Kessinger Publishing, LLC.
Reynolds, Aaron. Pirates vs. Cowboys. Barneda, David, illus. 2013. (ENG.). 40p. (J). (gr. k-3). 16.99 *(978-0-375-85874-1(1),* Knopf Bks. for Young Readers) Random Hse. Children's Bks.
Roberts, Nancy. Ghosts of the Wild West. Roberts, Bruce, photos by. 2nd fac. ed. 2008. (Illus.). 110p. (J). (gr. 3-7). 24.95 *(978-1-57003-731-3(0))* Univ. of South Carolina Pr.
Rowe, Gordon J. Showdown at Pecos. 2004. (Illus.). 32p. (gr. -1-3). 11.95 *(978-1-57197-192-0(0))* Pentland Pr., Inc.
Rylant, Cynthia. Henry & Mudge & the Tumbling Trip. Bracken, Carolyn, illus. (Henry & Mudge Ser.: 27). (ENG.). 40p. (J). (gr. k-2). 2006. pap. 3.99 *(978-0-689-83452-3(7))* 2005. 16.99 *(978-0-689-81180-7(2))* Simon Spotlight. (Simon Spotlight).
Sargent, Dave & Sargent, Pat. Ginger: (Lilac Roan) Be Likeable, 30 vols., Vol. 27. Lenoir, Jane, illus. 2003. (Saddle up Ser.: Vol. 27). 42p. (J). pap. 10.95 *(978-1-56763-812-7(0));* lib. bdg. 23.60 *(978-1-56763-811-0(2))* Ozark Publishing.
Schaefer, Jack. Stubby Pringle's Christmas. Bjorklund, Lorence, illus. 2017. (ENG.). 48p. pap. 16.95 ***(978-0-8263-5865-3(9))*** Univ. of New Mexico Pr.
Schnetzler, Pattie L. Fast 'n Snappy. Manning, Jane K., tr. Manning, Jane K., illus. 2004. (Carolrhoda Picture Books Ser.). 32p. (J). (gr. k-3). 16.95 *(978-1-57505-539-8(2))* Lerner Publishing Group.
—Widdermaker. Sealock, Rick, illus. 2005. 32p. (gr. k-2). 15.95 *(978-0-87614-647-7(7))* Lerner Publishing Group.
Scieszka, Jon. The Good, the Bad, & the Goofy. Smith, Lane, illus. 2004. (Time Warp Trio Ser.: 3). (ENG.). 80p. (J). (gr. 2-4). pap. 5.99 *(978-0-14-240046-3(7),* Puffin Books) Penguin Young Readers Group.
—The Good, the Bad, & the Goofy. Smith, Lane, illus. 2005. (Time Warp Trio Ser.: No. 3). 70p. (gr. 4-7). 15.00 *(978-0-7569-5876-3(8))* Perfection Learning Corp.
Scillian, Devin & Young, Judy. Westward Journeys. Ellison, Chris et al, illus. 2013. (American Adventures Ser.). (ENG.). 96p. (J). (gr. 3-6). pap. 6.99 *(978-1-58536-860-0(1),* 202367) Sleeping Bear Pr.
Shire, Poppy. Star the Western Pony. Berg, Ron, illus. 2007. (Magic Pony Carousel Ser.: 3). (ENG.). 96p. (J). (gr. 2-5). pap. 3.99 *(978-0-06-083785-3(3))* HarperCollins Pubs.
Simon, Leslie & Kelley, Trevor. Wish You Were Here: An Essential Guide to Your Favorite Music Scenes - From Punk to Indie & Everything in Between. Dobi, Rob, illus. 2009. (ENG.). 256p. pap. 14.99 *(978-0-06-157371-2(X))* HarperCollins Pubs.
Smith, Andrew. Ghost Medicine. 2010. (ENG.). 384p. (YA). (gr. 8-13). pap. 18.99 *(978-0-312-62912-0(5))* Square Fish.
Smith, Roland. The Captain's Dog: My Journey with the Lewis & Clark Tribe. 2008. (ENG., Illus.). 304p. (J). (gr. 5-7). pap. 7.99 *(978-0-15-202696-7(7))* Houghton Mifflin Harcourt Publishing Co.
Sneve, Virginia Driving Hawk. The Chichi Hoohoo Bogeyman. Agard, Nadema, illus. 2nd ed. 2008. (ENG.). 64p. (J). (gr. -1). pap. 9.95 *(978-0-8032-1745-4(5),* Bison Bks.) Univ. of Nebraska Pr.
Sperry, Armstrong. Wagons Westward: The Old Trail to Santa Fe. Sperry, Armstrong, illus. 2005. (Illus.). 200p. (YA). (gr. 6-11). reprint ed. pap. 15.00 *(978-0-7567-9693-8(8))* DIANE Publishing Co.
Steig, Jeanne. Tales from Gizzard's Grill. Turner, Sandy, illus. 2004. 80p. (J). 17.89 *(978-0-06-000960-1(8),* Cotler, Joanna Books) HarperCollins Pubs.
Stein, David Ezra. Cowboy Ned & Andy. Stein, David Ezra, illus. (ENG., Illus.). 32p. (J). (gr. -1-1). 2011. 6.99 *(978-1-4424-3619-0(0))* 2006. 16.99 *(978-1-4169-0041-2(1))* Simon & Schuster/Paula Wiseman Bks. (Simon & Schuster/Paula Wiseman Bks.).
Toni Eubanks. Journey Home. 2010. 52p. pap. 8.95 *(978-1-4401-8246-4(9))* iUniverse, Inc.
Uribe Urbieta, Kirmen & Lete, Nere. Garmendia & the Black Rider. 2015. (Illus.). 93p. (J). pap. *(978-1-935709-64-0(X))* Ctr. for Basque Studies.
Van Dyne, Edith. Aunt Jane's Nieces Out West. 2004. reprint ed. pap. 21.95 *(978-1-4191-0826-6(3))* Kessinger Publishing, LLC.
Vande Velde, Vivian. Ghost of a Hanged Man, 1 vol. 2003. (ENG.). 32p. (J). (gr. 5). pap. 5.95 *(978-0-7614-5154-9(4))* Marshall Cavendish Corp.
Vens, William D. Alias Pecos Bill. 2003. per. 13.95 *(978-1-891929-92-2(5))* Four Seasons Pubs.
Webber, Gail. Time of the Cats. 2013. 132p. 28.95 *(978-1-4582-1233-7(5),* Abbott Pr.) Author Solutions, Inc.
White, Ramy Allison. Sunny Boy in the Far West. Hastings, Howard L., illus. 2011. 216p. 44.95 *(978-1-258-09942-8(X))* Literary Licensing, LLC.
Wilson, Diane Lee. Black Storm Comin' 2006. (ENG.). 240p. (J). (gr. 5-9). pap. 7.99 *(978-0-689-87138-2(4),* McElderry, Margaret K. Bks.) McElderry, Margaret K. Bks.
Wilson, John. Written in Blood, 1 vol. 2010. (Desert Legend Trilogy Ser.: 1). (ENG.). 176p. (YA). (gr. 8-12). pap. 12.95 *(978-1-55469-270-5(9))* Orca Bk. Pubs. USA.
Winfield, Arthur M. The Rover Boys Out West. 2007. 228p. 26.95 *(978-1-4218-4140-3(1));* per. 11.95 *(978-1-4218-4238-7(6))* 1st World Publishing, Inc. (1st World Library - Literary Society).
Wolf, Allan. New Found Land: Lewis & Clark's Voyage of Discovery. 2007. (ENG., Illus.). 512p. (YA). (gr. 7-9). per. 14.99 *(978-0-7636-3288-5(0))* Candlewick Pr.
Woolston, Blythe. Troutzilla. 2012. (Carolrhoda YA Ser.). (ENG.). 216p. (YA). (gr. 9-12). 17.95 *(978-0-7613-7755-9(7),* Carolrhoda Lab™) Lerner Publishing Group.
Wrede, Patricia C. Across the Great Barrier. 2011. (Frontier Magic Ser.: 2). (ENG.). 352p. (J). (gr. 7-7). 16.99 *(978-0-545-03343-5(8),* Scholastic Pr.) Scholastic, Inc.
Yep, Laurence. The Traitor. 2004. (Golden Mountain Chronicles). 310p. (J). (gr. 5). 14.65 *(978-0-7569-3457-6(5))* Perfection Learning Corp.

WEST (U.S.)—HISTORY

Adkins, Jan. What If You Met a Cowboy? Adkins, Jan, illus. 2013. (ENG., Illus.). 48p. (J). (gr. 1-4). 17.99 *(978-1-59643-149-2(0),* 9781596431492) Roaring Brook Pr.
Anderson, Dale. The Civil War in the West (1861-July 1863) 2004. (World Almanac Library of the Civil War). (Illus.). 48p. (gr. 5-12). pap. 14.05 *(978-0-8368-5592-0(2));* lib. bdg. 31.00 *(978-0-8368-5583-8(3))* Stevens, Gareth Publishing LLLP. (Gareth Stevens Secondary Library).
Arnez, Lynda. My Wagon Train Adventure. 2016. (My Place in History Ser.). (ENG., Illus.). 24p. (J). (gr. 2-3). pap. 8.15 *(978-1-4824-4002-7(4))* Stevens, Gareth Publishing LLLP.
Aronin, Miriam. How Many People Traveled the Oregon Trail? And Other Questions about the Trail West. 2012. (Six Questions of American History Ser.). (ENG.). 48p. (gr. 4-6). pap. 56.72 *(978-0-7613-9237-8(8));* pap. 9.95 *(978-0-7613-8566-0(5));* lib. bdg. 30.60 *(978-0-7613-5332-4(1))* Lerner Publishing Group.
Baker, Brynn. Buffalo Soldiers: Heroes of the American West. 2015. (Military Heroes Ser.). (ENG., Illus.). 32p. (gr. 3-4). lib. bdg. 27.32 *(978-1-4914-4838-0(5))* Capstone Press of Coughlan Cos.
Barkan, Joanne. Settling the West 1862-1890: Set Of 6. 2011. (Navigators Ser.). (J). pap. 50.00 net. *(978-1-4108-2566-7(3))* Benchmark Education Co.
—A Western Activity Book: Set Of 6. 2011. (Navigators Ser.). (J). pap. 50.00 net. *(978-1-4108-2579-7(5))* Benchmark Education Co.
Barnett, Tracy. The Buffalo Soldiers. 2004. (History of the Old West Ser.). (Illus.). 64p. (YA). (gr. 5-18). lib. bdg. 19.95 *(978-1-59084-072-6(0))* Mason Crest.
Bearce, Stephanie. Top Secret Files: the Wild West: Secrets, Strange Tales, & Hidden Facts about the Wild West. rev. ed. 2015. (Top Secret Files of History Ser.: 0). (ENG., Illus.). 125p. (J). (gr. 4-7). pap. 8.95 *(978-1-61821-462-1(4))* Prufrock Pr.
Benchmark Education Co., LLC. Gold & the Settling of the West. 2014. (PRIME Ser.). (J). (gr. 6-8). pap. *(978-1-4509-9493-4(8))* Benchmark Education Co.
—Westward Expansion. 2014. (PRIME Ser.). (J). (gr. 6-8). pap. *(978-1-4509-9492-7(X))* Benchmark Education Co.
Benchmark Education Company. Settling the West (Teacher Guide) 1862 To 1890. 2004. *(978-1-4108-2581-0(7))* Benchmark Education Co.
Berman, Ruth. American Bison. rev. ed. 2008. (Nature Watch Ser.). (ENG., Illus.). 48p. (gr. 4-8). 27.93 *(978-0-8225-7513-9(2),* Lerner Pubns.) Lerner Publishing Group.
Bliss, John. Pioneers to the West, 1 vol. 2011. (Children's True Stories: Migration Ser.). (ENG.). 32p. (gr. 3-3). pap. 8.29 *(978-1-4109-4082-7(9),* Raintree Perspectives) Heinemann-Raintree.
Bodden, Valerie. Through the American West. 2012. (Great Expeditions Ser.). (ENG., Illus.). 48p. (J). (gr. 4-7). pap. 12.00 *(978-0-89812-663-1(0),* Creative Paperbacks) Creative Co., The.
Braidich, Victoria. Making History: A Covered Wagon. 2006. (Tony Stead Nonfiction Independent Reading Collection). (ENG.). 24p. (gr. 3-6). pap. 8.85 *(978-1-4042-5589-0(3))* Rosen Publishing Group, Inc., The.
Britton, Arthur K. Life in the Wild West. 2013. (What You Didn't Know about History Ser.). (Illus.). 24p. (J). (gr. 2-5). pap. 8.15 *(978-1-4339-8440-2(7));* lib. bdg. 22.60 *(978-1-4339-8439-6(3))* Stevens, Gareth Publishing LLLP.
Brook, Henry. Wild West. 2008. (True Stories Ser.). 160p. (YA). pap. 4.99 *(978-0-7945-2197-4(5),* Usborne) EDC Publishing.
Brown, Dee. Saga of the Sioux: An Adaptation from Dee Brown's Bury My Heart at Wounded Knee. 2014. (ENG., Illus.). 224p. (J). (gr. 5-9). pap. 12.99 *(978-1-250-05067-0(7),* 9781250050670) Square Fish.
Bryant, Jill. Wagon Train. 2003. (Real Life Stories Ser.). (Illus.). 24p. (J). lib. bdg. 24.45 *(978-1-59036-082-6(6))* Weigl Pubs., Inc.
—Women in the West. 2003. (Real Life Stories Ser.). (Illus.). 24p. (J). lib. bdg. 24.45 *(978-1-59036-083-5(4))* Weigl Pubs., Inc.
Buffalo Bill Cody. 2010. (Legends of the Wild West Ser.). (Illus.). 136p. (gr. 6-12). 35.00 *(978-1-60413-528-2(X),* Chelsea Hse.) Facts On File, Inc.
Burger, James P. Mountain Men of the West. 2009. (Library of the Westward Expansion Ser.). 24p. (gr. 3-4). 42.50 *(978-1-60853-937-6(7),* PowerKids Pr.) Rosen Publishing Group, Inc., The.
Burlingame, Jeff. Jesse James: I Will Never Surrender. 2010. (Americans—the Spirit of a Nation Ser.). (Illus.). 128p. (J). lib. bdg. 33.27 *(978-0-7660-3353-5(8))* Enslow Pubs., Inc.
Byers, Ann. Life As a Homesteader in the American West. 2016. (Life As... Ser.). (Illus.). 32p. (J). (gr. 3-3). 28.50 *(978-1-5026-1787-3(0))* Cavendish Square Publishing.
Calamity Jane. 2010. (Legends of the Wild West Ser.). (Illus.). 128p. (gr. 6-12). 35.00 *(978-1-60413-595-4(6),* Chelsea Hse.) Facts On File, Inc.
Callery, Sean. The Dark History of America's Old West. 2010. (Dark Histories Ser.). 64p. (gr. 5). 32.79 *(978-1-60870-086-8(0))* Marshall Cavendish Corp.
Calvert, Patricia. Kit Carson: He Led the Way. 2006. (Great Explorations Ser.). (Illus.). 80p. (gr. 6-7). lib. bdg. 22.95 *(978-0-7614-2223-5(4),* Benchmark Bks.) Marshall Cavendish Corp.
Christopher, Nick. The Dream of Manifest Destiny: Immigrants & the Westward Expansion, 01 vols., 1. 2016. (Spotlight on Immigration & Migration Ser.). (ENG., Illus.). 24p. (J). pap. 10.00 *(978-1-5081-4071-9(5),* PowerKids Pr.) Rosen Publishing Group, Inc., The.
Clinton, Greg. The Louisiana Purchase. 2016. (Expanding America Ser.). (ENG., Illus.). 96p. (J). (gr. 8-8). lib. bdg. 42.79 *(978-1-5026-0962-5(2))* Cavendish Square Publishing.
Coleman, Wim & Perrin, Pat. What Made the Wild West Wild. 2006. (Wild History of the American West Ser.). (Illus.). 128p. (J). (gr. 4-7). lib. bdg. 34.60 *(978-1-59845-016-3(6),* MyReportLinks.com Bks.) Enslow Pubs., Inc.
Collins, Kathleen. Jesse James: Bank Robber of the American West. 2009. (Primary Sources of Famous People in American History Ser.). 32p. (gr. 2-3). 47.90 *(978-1-60851-690-2(3))* Rosen Publishing Group, Inc., The.
—Jesse James: Bank Robber of the American West / Legendario bandido del oeste Americano. 2009. (Famous People in American History/Grandes personajes en la historia de los Estados Unidos Ser.). (ENG & SPA.). 32p. (gr. 2-3). 47.90 *(978-1-61512-547-0(7),* Editorial Buenas Letras) Rosen Publishing Group, Inc., The.
—Jesse James: Legendario Bandido del Oeste Americano. 2004. (Grandes personajes en la historia de los Estados Unidos Ser.). (SPA.). 32p. (gr. 3-6). pap. 10.00 *(978-0-8239-4230-5(9),* Rosen Classroom) Rosen Publishing Group, Inc., The.
—Jesse James: Legendario bandido del oeste americano (Jesse James: Bank Robber of the American West) 2009. (Grandes personajes en la historia de los Estados Unidos (Famous People in American History) Ser.). (SPA.). 32p. (gr. 2-3). 47.90 *(978-1-61512-801-3(8),* Editorial Buenas Letras) Rosen Publishing Group, Inc., The.
Collins, Terry. Into the West: Causes & Effects of U. S. Westward Expansion, 1 vol. 2013. (Cause & Effect Ser.). (ENG.). 32p. (gr. 3-4). 27.32 *(978-1-4765-0237-3(4));* pap. 8.95 *(978-1-4765-3403-9(9))* Capstone Press of Coughlan Cos. (Fact Finders).
Conant, Susan Sens. Lewis & Clark's Journey of Discovery: A Guide for Young Explorers. Lynn, Rick, illus. 2004. 48p. (J). pap. *(978-0-9725584-1-9(1))* Little Blue Pr.
Cooke, Tim. Butch Cassidy & the Sundance Kid: Notorious Outlaws of the West. 2016. (Wanted! Famous Outlaws Ser.). (ENG., Illus.). 48p. (J). (gr. 6-8). pap. 14.05 *(978-1-4824-4255-7(8))* Stevens, Gareth Publishing LLLP.
—Jesse James: A Notorious Bank Robber of the Wild West. 2016. (Wanted! Famous Outlaws Ser.). (ENG., Illus.). 48p. (J). (gr. 6-8). pap. 14.05 *(978-1-4824-4259-5(0))* Stevens, Gareth Publishing LLLP.
Copeland, Peter F., et al. Big Book of the Old West to Color. 2008. (Dover History Coloring Book Ser.). (ENG., Illus.). 144p. (gr. 3-8). 8.95 *(978-0-486-46679-8(5))* Dover Pubns., Inc.
Corrigan, Jim. Civil War in the West. 2004. (History of the Old West Ser.). (Illus.). 64p. (YA). (gr. 5-18). lib. bdg. 19.95 *(978-1-59084-067-2(4))* Mason Crest.

W X Y Z

Craats, Rennay. Ranching. 2003. (Real Life Stories Ser.). (Illus.). 24p. (J). lib. bdg. 24.45 *(978-1-59036-081-1(8))* Weigl Pubs., Inc.

Crewe, Sabrina & Uschan, Michael V. The Oregon Trail. 2004. (Events That Shaped America Ser.). (Illus.). 32p. (gr. 3-6). lib. bdg. 26.00 *(978-0-8368-3405-5(4)*, Gareth Stevens Learning Library) Stevens, Gareth Publishing LLLP.

Cunningham, Meghan Engsberg. Jesse James. Lapegüe, Matias, illus. 2016. (American Legends & Folktales Ser.). 32p. (J). 28.50 *(978-1-5026-2197-9(5))* Cavendish Square Publishing.

Curtis, Suzanne. John Wesley Powell: American Hero. 2013. (ENG & SPA., Illus.). 78p. (J). pap. 8.95 *(978-0-86541-178-4(6))* Filter Pr., LLC.

Dean, Arlan. The Mormon Pioneer Trail: From Nauvoo, Illinois to the Great Salt Lake, Utah. (Famous American Trails Ser.). 24p. 2009. (gr. 3-3). 42.50 *(978-1-61512-488-6(8))* 2003. (Illus.). (J). lib. bdg. 22.60 *(978-0-8239-6476-5(0))* Rosen Publishing Group, Inc., The. (PowerKids Pr.).

—The Oregon Trail: From Independence, Missouri to Oregon City, Oregon. (Famous American Trails Ser.). 24p. 2009. (gr. 3-3). 42.50 *(978-1-61512-490-9(X))* 2003. (Illus.). (J). lib. bdg. 22.60 *(978-0-8239-6478-9(7))* Rosen Publishing Group, Inc., The. (PowerKids Pr.).

—The Overland Trail: From Atchison, Kansas, to Fort Bridger, Wyoming. 2003. (Famous American Trails Ser.). (Illus.). 24p. (J). lib. bdg. 22.60 *(978-0-8239-6479-6(5)*, PowerKids Pr.) Rosen Publishing Group, Inc., The.

—The Overland Trail: From Atchison, Kansas to Ft. Bridger, Wyoming. 2009. (Famous American Trails Ser.). 24p. (gr. 3-3). 42.50 *(978-1-61512-491-6(8)*, PowerKids Pr.) Rosen Publishing Group, Inc., The.

Ditchfield, Christin. The Lewis & Clark Expedition. 2006. (True Bks.). (ENG., Illus.). 48p. (J). (gr. 3-7). pap. 6.95 *(978-0-516-25222-3(4)*, Children's Pr.) Scholastic Library Publishing.

Domnauer, Teresa. Cornerstones of Freedom, Third Series: the Lewis & Clark Expedition. 2012. (ENG., Illus.). 64p. (J). lib. bdg. 30.00 *(978-0-531-23059-6(7)*, Children's Pr.) Scholastic Library Publishing.

—The Lewis & Clark Expedition. 2012. (Cornerstones of Freedom, Third Ser.). (ENG., Illus.). 64p. (J). pap. 8.95 *(978-0-531-28159-8(0))* Scholastic Library Publishing.

—Life in the West. 2010. (True Book Ser.). (ENG., 48p. (J). Illus.). pap. 6.95 *(978-0-531-21246-2(7))*; (gr. 2-5). 29.00 *(978-0-531-20583-9(5))* Scholastic Library Publishing.

—Westward Expansion. 2010. (True Book Ser.). (ENG., Illus.). 48p. (J). pap. 6.95 *(978-0-531-21249-3(1))*; (gr. 2-5). 29.00 *(978-0-531-20586-0(X))* Scholastic Library Publishing.

Edwards, Judith. The Journey of Lewis & Clark in United States History. 2014. (In United States History Ser.). (Illus.). 96p. (J). (gr. 5-12). 27.94 *(978-0-7660-6058-6(6))* Enslow Pubs., Inc.

Ellis, Edward S. The Life of Kit Carson: Hunter, Trapper, Guide, Indian Agent & Colonel U. S. A. 2007. 176p. per. *(978-1-4065-2477-2(8))* Dodo Pr.

Engle, Stephen Douglas. The Civil War: The Siege of Vicksburg & Other Western Battles, 1861-July 1863. O'Neill, Robert, ed. 2010. (Civil War: Essential Histories Ser.). (ENG.). 96p. (YA). lib. bdg. 33.25 *(978-1-4488-0390-3(X))* Rosen Publishing Group, Inc., The.

Espinosa, Rod. Lewis & Clark, 1 vol. Espinosa, Rod, illus. 2007. (Bio-Graphics Ser.). (ENG., Illus.). 32p. (gr. 3-6). 28.50 *(978-1-60270-069-7(9)*, Graphic Planet- Nonfiction) ABDO Publishing Co.

Evan-Moor. History Pockets: Moving West, Grades 4-6. 2003. (History Pockets Ser.). (ENG., Illus.). 96p. (J). (gr. 4-6). pap., suppl. ed. 14.99 *(978-1-55799-902-3(3)*, EMC 3704) Evan-Moor Educational Pubs.

Expansionism. 2010. (Key Concepts in American History Ser.). (Illus.). 128p. (gr. 6-12). 45.00 *(978-1-60413-221-2(3)*, Chelsea Hse.) Facts On File, Inc.

Favor, Lesli J. A Historical Atlas of America's Manifest Destiny. (United States: Historical Atlases of the Growth of a New Nation Ser.). 64p. 2009. (gr. 5-5). 61.20 *(978-1-60854-250-5(5))* 2005. (Illus.). (J). (gr. 7-12). lib. bdg. 31.95 *(978-1-4042-0201-6(3))* Rosen Publishing Group, Inc., The.

Foran, Jill. Homesteading. 2003. (Real Life Stories Ser.). (Illus.). 24p. (J). lib. bdg. 24.45 *(978-1-59036-079-8(6))* Weigl Pubs., Inc.

Fox, Suzanne G. Meriwether Lewis & William Clark: The Corp of Discovery & the Exploration of the American Frontier. 2009. (Library of American Lives & Times Ser.). 112p. (gr. 5-5). 69.20 *(978-1-60853-493-7(6))* Rosen Publishing Group, Inc., The.

Fradin, Judith Bloom & Fradin, Dennis Brindell. The Lewis & Clark Expedition. 2007. (Turning Points in U. S. History Ser.). (Illus.). 48p. (gr. 3-7). lib. bdg. 31.36 *(978-0-7614-2044-6(4)*, Benchmark Bks.) Marshall Cavendish Corp.

Frazier, Neta. Path to the Pacific: The Story of Sacagawea. 2017. (Great Leaders & Events Ser.). (ENG.). (J). (gr. 4-8). lib. bdg. 35.99 ***(978-1-942875-44-4(4))*** Quarto Publishing Group USA.

Frazier, Neta Lohnes. Path to the Pacific: The Story of Sacagawea. 2016. (Young Voyageur Ser.). (ENG., Illus.). 208p. (J). (gr. 4-9). pap. 12.99 *(978-0-7603-5227-4(5)*, Voyageur Pr.) Quarto Publishing Group USA.

Fredericks, Anthony D. P Is for Prairie Dog: A Prairie Alphabet. Bowles, Doug, illus. 2011. (Sleeping Bear Alphabets Ser.). (ENG.). 32p. (J). (gr. k-6). 16.95 *(978-1-58536-508-1(4))* Sleeping Bear Pr.

Friedman, Mel. The Oregon Trail. 2012. (Cornerstones of Freedom, Third Ser.). (ENG., Illus.). 64p. (J). pap. 8.95 *(978-0-531-28163-5(9))*; lib. bdg. 30.00 *(978-0-531-23063-3(5))* Scholastic Library Publishing.

Frisch, Aaron. Jesse James. 2005. (Legends of the West (Creative Education) Ser.). (Illus.). 48p. (J). (gr. 5-9). lib. bdg. 21.95 *(978-1-58341-338-8(3)*, Creative Education) Creative Co., The.

Ganeri, Anita. On Expedition with Lewis & Clark. 2010. (ENG.). 32p. (J). (gr. 3-5). *(978-0-7787-9896-5(8))*; (Crabtree Connections Ser.: No. 2). pap. *(978-0-7787-9917-7(4))* Crabtree Publishing Co.

Garbe, Suzanne. Ghosts of Alcatraz & Other Hauntings of the West, 1 vol. 2014. (Haunted America Ser.). (ENG.). 32p. (gr. 3-4). lib. bdg. 27.99 *(978-1-4765-3915-7(4)*, Edge Bks.) Capstone Press of Coughlan Cos.

Garland, Sherry. Voices of the Western Frontier, 1 vol. Buckner, Julie Dupre, illus. 2016. (ENG.). 40p. (J). (gr. -1-6). 17.99 *(978-1-4556-1961-0(2))* Pelican Publishing Co., Inc.

George, Enzo. The Expanding Frontier. 2015. (J). lib. bdg. *(978-1-62713-489-7(1))*; (ENG.). 48p. (gr. 4-4). lib. bdg. 31.36 *(978-1-5026-0248-0(2))* Cavendish Square Publishing.

George, Lynn. What Do You Know about Westward Expansion? (20 Questions: History Ser.). 24p. (gr. 2-3). 2009. 42.50 *(978-1-60854-960-3(7)*, PowerKids Pr.) 2008. (Illus.). (J). lib. bdg. 22.60 *(978-1-4042-4189-3(2))* Rosen Publishing Group, Inc., The.

George-Warren, Holly. The Cowgirl Way: Hats off to America's Women of the West. 2015. (ENG., Illus.). 128p. (J). (gr. 5-7). pap. 9.99 *(978-0-544-45595-5(9)*, HMH Books For Young Readers) Houghton Mifflin Harcourt Publishing Co.

Gingrich, Callista. From Sea to Shining Sea. Arciero, Susan, illus. 2014. (Ellis the Elephant Ser.). (ENG.). 40p. (J). (gr. -1-3). 14.99 *(978-1-62157-253-4(6)*, Regnery Kids) Regnery Publishing, Inc., An Eagle Publishing Co.

Graubart, Norman D. Bison in American History. 2014. (How Animals Shaped History Ser.). (Illus.). 24p. (J). (gr. k-5). 23.60 *(978-1-4777-6757-3(6)*, PowerKids Pr.) Rosen Publishing Group, Inc., The.

Green, Carl R. & Sanford, William R. Butch Cassidy. rev. ed. 2008. (Outlaws & Lawmen of the Wild West, Revised Edition Ser.). (Illus.). 48p. (J). (gr. 5-18). lib. bdg. 25.27 *(978-0-7660-3175-3(6))* Enslow Pubs., Inc.

—Wild Bill Hickok. rev. ed. 2008. (Outlaws & Lawmen of the Wild West, Revised Edition Ser.). (Illus.). 48p. (J). (gr. 5-18). lib. bdg. 25.27 *(978-0-7660-3177-7(2))* Enslow Pubs., Inc.

Green, John. Horses of the Old West. 2007. (Dover Nature Coloring Book Ser.). (ENG., Illus.). 32p. (gr. 3-8). 3.99 *(978-0-486-45675-1(7))* Dover Pubns., Inc.

Gregory, Josh. If You Were a Kid on the Oregon Trail. Farré, Lluís, illus. 2016. (If You Were a Kid Ser.). (ENG.). 32p. (J). lib. bdg. 26.00 *(978-0-531-21970-6(4)*, Children's Pr.) Scholastic Library Publishing.

Hamen, Susan E. The Lewis & Clark Expedition, 1 vol. 2008. (Essential Events Set 2 Ser.). (ENG., Illus.). 112p. (J). (gr. 6-12). lib. bdg. 35.64 *(978-1-60453-048-3(0))* ABDO Publishing Co.

Harris, Irene. The Homestead ACT & Westward Expansion: Settling the Western Frontier. 2016. (Spotlight on American History Ser.). (Illus.). 24p. (gr. 6-4). 26.25 *(978-1-5081-4943-9(7)*, PowerKids Pr.) Rosen Publishing Group, Inc., The.

Harrison, Peter. The Amazing History of the Wild West: Find Out about the Brave Pioneers Who Tamed the American Frontier, Shown in 300 Exciting Pictures. 2016. (ENG., Illus.). 64p. (J). (gr. -1-12). 12.99 *(978-1-86147-766-8(X)*, Armadillo) Anness Publishing GBR. Dist: National Bk. Network.

Harrison, Peter & Hunt, Norman Bancroft. The Amazing World of the Wild West: Discover the Trailblazing History of Cowboys, Outlaws & Native Americans. 2010. (ENG., Illus.). 64p. (J). (gr. 4-7). pap. 12.99 *(978-1-84476-609-3(8)*, Hermes House) Anness Publishing GBR. Dist: National Bk. Network.

Harvey, Dan. Rocky Mountain: Colorado, Utah, Wyoming, Vol. 19. 2015. (Let's Explore the States Ser.). (Illus.). 64p. (J). (gr. 5). 23.95 *(978-1-4222-3332-0(4))* Mason Crest.

Hatt, Christine. The American West. 2004. (Questioning History Ser.). (J). lib. bdg. 28.50 *(978-1-58340-443-0(0))* Black Rabbit Bks.

Hicks, Peter. You Wouldn't Want to Live in a Wild West Town! Dust You'd Rather Not Settle. Antram, David, illus. 2013. (ENG.). (J). 32p. 29.00 *(978-0-531-27106-3(4))*; 40p. pap. 9.95 *(978-0-531-23857-8(1))* Scholastic Library Publishing. (Watts, Franklin).

Hill, William E. The California Trail: Yesterday & Today. 2017. ***(978-0-87004-604-9(7))*** Caxton Pr.

Hillstrom, Laurie Collier. The Lewis & Clark Expedition. 2015. (Defining Moments Ser.). (Illus.). 240p. (J). lib. bdg. 60.00 *(978-0-7808-1417-2(7))* Omnigraphics, Inc.

Hooker, Forrestine Cooper. Child of the Fighting Tenth: On the Frontier with the Buffalo Soldiers. Wilson, Steve, ed. 2011. (ENG., Illus.). 296p. pap. 19.95 *(978-0-8061-4080-3(1))* Univ. of Oklahoma Pr.

James, Will. The Will James Cowboy Book, Vol. 1. rev. ed. (Illus.). 128p. (J). (gr. 4). *(978-0-87842-469-6(5)*, 816) Mountain Pr. Publishing Co., Inc.

Jeffrey, Gary. The Oregon Trail. Poluzzi, Allesandro, illus. 2012. (Graphic History of the American West Ser.). (ENG.). 24p. (J). (gr. 3-8). pap. 8.15 *(978-1-4339-6745-0(6)*, Gareth Stevens Learning Library); (gr. 4-7). lib. bdg. 23.95 *(978-1-4339-6743-6(X))* Stevens, Gareth Publishing LLLP.

—The Pony Express. Riley, Terry, illus. 2012. (Graphic History of the American West Ser.). (ENG.). 24p. (J). (gr. 3-8). pap. 8.15 *(978-1-4339-6749-8(9)*, Gareth Stevens Learning Library); (gr. 4-7). lib. bdg. 23.95 *(978-1-4339-6747-4(2))* Stevens, Gareth Publishing LLLP.

Jesse James. 2010. (Legends of the Wild West Ser.). (Illus.). 128p. (gr. 6-12). 35.00 *(978-1-60413-598-5(0)*, Chelsea Hse.) Facts On File, Inc.

Kalman, Bobbie. A Visual Dictionary of the Old West. 2007. (Visual Dictionaries Ser.). (ENG., Illus.). 32p. (J). (gr. 3-7). pap. *(978-0-7787-3523-6(0))*; lib. bdg. *(978-0-7787-3503-8(6))* Crabtree Publishing Co.

Keller, Susanna. The True Story of Lewis & Clark. 2013. (What Really Happened? Ser.). (ENG., Illus.). 24p. (J). (gr. 3-6). pap. 8.25 *(978-1-4488-9846-6(3))*; lib. bdg. 22.60 *(978-1-4488-9694-3(0))* Rosen Publishing Group, Inc., The. (PowerKids Pr.).

Kimmel, Elizabeth Cody. As Far as the Eye Can Reach: Lewis & Clark's Westward Quest. 2005. (Illus.). 119p. (YA). (gr. 4-8). reprint ed. 5.00 *(978-0-7567-9660-0(1))* DIANE Publishing Co.

King, David C. Westward Expansion. 2012. (American Heritage, American Voices Ser.). (ENG.). 144p. (J). (gr. 5-9). pap. 22.95 *(978-1-118-43608-0(3)*, Wiley) Wiley, John & Sons, Inc.

Klar, Jeremy. The Louisiana Purchase & Westward Expansion, 01 vols., 1. 2016. (Early American History Ser.). (ENG., Illus.). 80p. (J). lib. bdg. 32.90 *(978-1-68048-271-3(8)*, Britannica Educational Publishing) Rosen Publishing Group, Inc., The.

Klepeis, Alicia. Lewis & Clark & Exploring the Louisiana Purchase. 2017. (J). ***(978-1-5026-2639-4(X))*** Cavendish Square Publishing.

Kravitz, Danny. Surviving the Journey: The Story of the Oregon Trail, 1 vol. 2014. (Adventures on the American Frontier Ser.). (ENG.). 32p. (gr. 3-4). 27.32 *(978-1-4914-0187-3(7)*, Fact Finders) Capstone Press of Coughlan Cos.

Krohn, Katherine E. Calico Dresses & Buffalo Robes: American West Fashions from the 1840s to the 1890s. 2011. (Dressing a Nation: the History of U. S. Fashion Ser.). (ENG., Illus.). 64p. (gr. 5-12). lib. bdg. 31.93 *(978-0-7613-5890-9(0)*, Twenty-First Century Bks.) Lerner Publishing Group.

LaClair, Teresa. Americans Move West (1846-1860) 2013. (Illus.). 48p. (J). pap. *(978-1-4222-2417-5(1))* Mason Crest.

—Americans Move West (1846-1860) Rakove, Jack N., ed. 2012. (How America Became America Ser.). (Illus.). 48p. (J). (gr. 3-4). 19.95 *(978-1-4222-2403-8(1))* Mason Crest.

Langley, Andrew. 100 Things You Should Know about the Wild West. 2004. (Mosaic of Magical Information Ser.). (Illus.). 48p. (YA). (gr. 3-18). lib. bdg. 19.95 *(978-1-59084-458-8(0))* Mason Crest.

Lassieur, Allison. Westward Expansion: An Interactive History Adventure. 2016. (You Choose: History Ser.). (ENG.). 112p. (gr. 3-4). pap. 6.95 *(978-1-5157-4259-3(8)*, You Choose Bks.) Capstone Press of Coughlan Cos.

Levy, Janey. Life on a Wagon Train. 2003. (Rosen Real Readers Big Bookstm Ser.). (ENG.). 16p. (gr. 2-3). 37.95 *(978-1-4042-6224-9(5))* Rosen Publishing Group, Inc., The.

Lightfoot, D. J. Trail Fever: The Life of a Texas Cowboy. Bobbish, John, illus. exp. ed. 2003. 88p. (J). (gr. 3-18). pap. 12.95 *(978-0-9728768-0-3(4))* Seven Rivers Publishing.

Lusted, Marcia Amidon. The Oregon Trail, 1 vol. 2011. (Essential Events Set 7 Ser.). (ENG., Illus.). 112p. (J). (gr. 6-12). lib. bdg. 35.64 *(978-1-61783-102-7(6))* ABDO Publishing Co.

Lynette, Rachel. Meriwether Lewis & William Clark. 2013. (Pioneer Spirit: the Westward Expansion Ser.). 24p. (J). (gr. 3-6). 22.60 *(978-1-4777-0783-8(2))*; pap. 49.50 *(978-1-4777-0900-9(2))*; (ENG., Illus.). pap. 8.25 *(978-1-4777-0899-6(5))* Rosen Publishing Group, Inc., The. (PowerKids Pr.).

Magoon, Kekla. The Zebulon Pike Expedition, 1 vol. 2009. (Essential Events Set 3 Ser.). (ENG., Illus.). 112p. (J). (gr. 6-12). lib. bdg. 35.64 *(978-1-60453-518-1(0))* ABDO Publishing Co.

Marsh, Carole. Lewis & Clark Go on a Hike. 2003. 32p. (J). (gr. 3-8). pap. 5.95 *(978-0-635-02122-9(6))* Gallopade International.

Maynard, Charles W. Fort Laramie. 2009. (Famous Forts Throughout American History Ser.). 24p. (gr. 3-4). 42.50 *(978-1-61512-516-6(7)*, PowerKids Pr.) Rosen Publishing Group, Inc., The.

—Jedediah Smith: Mountain Man of the American West. 2009. (Famous Explorers of the American West Ser.). 24p. (gr. 3-4). 42.50 *(978-1-61512-501-2(9)*, PowerKids Pr.) Rosen Publishing Group, Inc., The.

—Jim Bridger: Frontiersman & Mountain Guide. (Famous Explorers of the American West Ser.). 24p. 2009. (gr. 3-4). 42.50 *(978-1-61512-502-9(7))* 2003. (Illus.). (J). lib. bdg. 22.60 *(978-0-8239-6288-4(1))* Rosen Publishing Group, Inc., The. (PowerKids Pr.).

—John Charles Fremont: The Pathfinder. 2003. (Famous Explorers of the American West Ser.). (Illus.). 24p. (J). lib. bdg. 22.60 *(978-0-8239-6289-1(X)*, PowerKids Pr.) Rosen Publishing Group, Inc., The.

—Zebulon Pike: Soldier Explorer of the American Southwest. 2003. (Famous Explorers of the American West Ser.). (Illus.). 24p. (J). lib. bdg. 22.60 *(978-0-8239-6286-0(5)*, PowerKids Pr.) Rosen Publishing Group, Inc., The.

—Zebulon Pike: Soldier-Explorer of the American Southwest. 2009. (Famous Explorers of the American West Ser.). 24p. (gr. 3-4). 42.50 *(978-1-61512-506-7(X)*, PowerKids Pr.) Rosen Publishing Group, Inc., The.

McIntosh, Kenneth. Saloons, Shootouts, & Spurs: The Wild West in The 1800's. 2009. (Daily Life in America in the 1800s Ser.). 64p. (YA). (gr. 7-18). pap. 9.95 *(978-1-4222-1862-4(7))*; lib. bdg. 22.95 *(978-1-4222-1789-4(2))* Mason Crest.

McNeese, Tim. The Oregon Trail. 2009. (Milestones in American History Ser.). (Illus.). 152p. (gr. 6-12). 35.00 *(978-1-60413-027-0(X)*, Chelsea Hse.) Facts On File, Inc.

Meachen-Rau, Dana. The West. 2012. (True Book Ser.). (ENG., Illus.). 48p. (J). pap. 6.95 *(978-0-531-28330-1(5)*, Children's Pr.) Scholastic Library Publishing.

Micklos, John, Jr. Bold Riders: The Story of the Pony Express. 2015. (Adventures on the American Frontier Ser.). (ENG., Illus.). 32p. (gr. 3-4). pap. 7.95 *(978-1-4914-4910-3(1))* Capstone Press of Coughlan Cos.

Miller, Brandon Marie. Women of the Frontier: 16 Tales of Trailblazing Homesteaders, Entrepreneurs, & Rabble-Rousers. 2013. (Women of Action Ser.). (ENG., Illus.). 256p. (J). (gr. 7). 19.95 *(978-1-883052-97-3(1))* Chicago Review Pr., Inc.

Monceaux, Morgan & Katcher, Ruth. My Heroes, My People: African Americans & Native Americans in Thewest. Monceaux, Morgan, illus. 2004. (Illus.). 63p. (J). (gr. k-4). reprint ed. 18.00 *(978-0-7567-7868-2(9))* DIANE Publishing Co.

Morley, Jacqueline. You Wouldn't Want to... Be an American Pioneer! Antram, David, illus. rev. ed. 2012. (ENG.). (J). 40p. pap. 9.95 *(978-0-531-28025-6(X))*; 32p. lib. bdg. 29.00 *(978-0-531-27500-9(0))* Scholastic Library Publishing.

—You Wouldn't Want to Explore with Lewis & Clark! An Epic Journey You'd Rather Not Make. Bergin, Mark, illus. 2013. (You Wouldn't Want to... Ser.). (ENG.). 32p. (J). 29.00 *(978-0-531-25942-9(0))*; pap. 9.95 *(978-0-531-23039-8(2))* Scholastic Library Publishing. (Watts, Franklin).

—You Wouldn't Want to Explore with Lewis & Clark! An Epic Journey You'd Rather Not Make. 2013. (You Wouldn't Want To... Ser.). lib. bdg. 20.80 *(978-0-606-31633-0(7)*, Turtleback) Turtleback Bks.

Morretta, Alison. Homesteading & Settling the Frontier. 2017. (J). ***(978-1-5026-2641-7(1))*** Cavendish Square Publishing.

Mountjoy, Shane. Manifest Destiny: Westward Expansion. 2009. (Milestones in American History Ser.). (Illus.). 128p. (gr. 6-12). 35.00 *(978-1-60413-055-3(5)*, Chelsea Hse.) Facts On File, Inc.

Mulhall, Jill K. Expanding the Nation, 1 vol. 2005. (Primary Source Readers Ser.). (ENG.). 24p. (J). (gr. 5-5). pap. 8.99 *(978-0-7439-8905-3(8))* Shell Educational Publishing.

The New South & the Old West, 1866-1890. 2010. (Discovering U. S. History Ser.). (Illus.). 136p. (gr. 5-8). 35.00 *(978-1-60413-354-7(6)*, Chelsea Hse.) Facts On File, Inc.

Nolan, Frederick. Trailblazing the Way West. 2015. (Wild West Ser.). (Illus.). 64p. (J). (gr. 9-12). 39.95 *(978-1-78404-081-9(9))* Arcturus Publishing GBR. Dist: Black Rabbit Bks.

Nolan, Frederick W. Gunslingers & Cowboys. 2015. (Wild West Ser.). (Illus.). 64p. (J). (gr. 9-12). 39.95 *(978-1-78404-078-9(9))* Arcturus Publishing GBR. Dist: Black Rabbit Bks.

—Outlaws & Rebels. 2015. (Wild West Ser.). (Illus.). 64p. (J). (gr. 9-12). 39.95 *(978-1-78404-080-2(0))* Arcturus Publishing GBR. Dist: Black Rabbit Bks.

Oatman, Eric. Cowboys & Cattle Drives: Life on the Western Trail. 2007. (Reading Expeditions Ser.). (ENG., Illus.). 40p. (J). pap. 19.95 *(978-0-7922-4550-6(4))* CENGAGE Learning.

O'Brien, Cynthia. Go West with Miners, Prospectors, & Loggers. 2016. (ENG.). 32p. (J). *(978-0-7787-2328-8(3))* Crabtree Publishing Co.

O'Hara, Megan. Plains Communities Past & Present, 1 vol. 2014. (Who Lived Here? Ser.). (ENG.). 24p. (gr. 1-2). lib. bdg. 25.32 *(978-1-4765-4061-0(6)*, First Facts) Capstone Press of Coughlan Cos.

Olson, Steven. The Oregon Trail: A Primary Source History of the Route to the American West. 2009. (Primary Sources in American History Ser.). 64p. (gr. 5-8). 58.50 *(978-1-60851-501-1(X))* Rosen Publishing Group, Inc., The.

Olson, Tod. How to Get Rich on a Texas Cattle Drive: In Which I Tell the Honest Truth about Rampaging Rustlers, Stampeding Steers & Other Fateful Hazards on the Wild Chisolm Trail. Allred, Scott & Proch, Gregory, illus. 2010. (How to Get Rich Ser.). (ENG.). 48p. (J). (gr. 3-7). 18.95 *(978-1-4263-0524-5(9)*, National Geographic Children's Bks.) National Geographic Society.

O'Neill, Robert John & Glatthaar, Joseph T. The Civil War: Sherman's Capture of Atlanta & Other Western Battles, 1863-1865. 2010. (Civil War: Essential Histories Ser.). (ENG.). 96p. (YA). lib. bdg. 33.25 *(978-1-4488-0389-7(6))* Rosen Publishing Group, Inc., The.

Orr, Tamra. The Lewis & Clark Expedition: A Primary Source History of the Journey of the Corps of Discovery. 2009. (Primary Sources in American History Ser.). 64p. (gr. 5-8). 58.50 *(978-1-60851-498-4(6))* Rosen Publishing Group, Inc., The.

Osmundson, Linda. How the West Was Drawn: Women's Art, 1 vol. 2014. (ENG., Illus.). 32p. (J). (gr. k-7). 16.99 *(978-1-4556-1878-1(0))* Pelican Publishing Co., Inc.

Osmundson, Linda L. Frederic Remington's Art, 1 vol. 2012. (How the West Was Drawn Ser.). (ENG., Illus.). 32p. (J). (gr. k-7). 16.99 *(978-1-4556-1506-3(4))* Pelican Publishing Co., Inc.

Otfinoski, Steven. A Primary Source History of Westward Expansion. 2015. (Primary Source History Ser.). (ENG., Illus.). 32p. (gr. 3-4). lib. bdg. 27.32 *(978-1-4914-1841-3(9))* Capstone Press of Coughlan Cos.

Paprocki, Greg, illus. Wild West Alphabet, 1 vol. 2016. (ENG.). 32p. (J). bds. 9.99 *(978-1-4236-4251-0(1))* Gibbs Smith, Publisher.

Pascal, Janet B. What Was the Wild West? Marchesi, Stephen, illus. 2017. (What Was? Ser.). (ENG.). 112p. (J). (gr. 3-7). 5.99 *(978-0-399-54424-8(0))*; lib. bdg. 15.99 *(978-0-399-54426-2(7))* Penguin Young Readers Group. (Grosset & Dunlap).

—What Was the Wild West? 2017. (What Was... ? Ser.). lib. bdg. 16.00 ***(978-0-606-39775-9(2))*** Turtleback Bks.

Patent, Dorothy Hinshaw. The Lewis & Clark Trail: Then & Now. Muñoz, William, photos by. 2006. (Illus.). 60p. (J). (gr. 4-8). reprint ed. 20.00 *(978-1-4223-5732-3(5))* DIANE Publishing Co.

Patrick, Bethanne Kelly. Forts of the West. 2004. (History of the Old West Ser.). (Illus.). 64p. (YA). (gr. 5-18). lib. bdg. 19.95 *(978-1-59084-071-9(2))* Mason Crest.

Penn, Sarah. Nat Love: African American Cowboy. 2004. (Famous People in American History Ser.). (ENG., Illus.). 32p. (gr. 4-8). pap. 10.00 *(978-0-8239-4188-9(4))* Rosen Publishing Group, Inc., The.

Perritano, John. The Lewis & Clark Expedition. 2010. (True Book Ser.). (ENG.). 48p. (J). (gr. 3-5). pap. 6.95 *(978-0-531-21245-5(9)*, Children's Pr.); (Illus.). (gr. 2-5). 29.00 *(978-0-531-20582-2(7))* Scholastic Library Publishing.

Petrie, Kristin. John C. Fremont, 1 vol. 2004. (Explorers Set 1 Ser.). (ENG., Illus.). 32p. (gr. k-6). 27.07 *(978-1-59197-602-8(2)*, Checkerboard Library) ABDO Publishing Co.

Phillips, Larissa. Wild Bill Hickok: Legend of the American Wild West / Leyenda del oeste Americano. 2009. (Famous People in American History/Grandes personajes en la historia de los Estados Unidos Ser.). (ENG & SPA.). 32p. (gr. 2-3). 47.90 *(978-1-61512-557-9(4)*, Editorial Buenas Letras) Rosen Publishing Group, Inc., The.

—Wild Bill Hickok: Legend of the Wild West. 2009. (Primary Sources of Famous People in American History Ser.). 32p. (gr. 2-3). 47.90 *(978-1-60851-740-4(3))* Rosen Publishing Group, Inc., The.

—Wild Bill Hickok: Leyenda del oeste americano (Wild Bill Hickok: Legend of the American Wild West) 2009. (Grandes personajes en la historia de los Estados Unidos (Famous People in American History) Ser.). (SPA.). 32p. (gr. 2-3). 47.90 *(978-1-61512-810-5(7)*, Editorial Buenas Letras) Rosen Publishing Group, Inc., The.

Porterfield, Jason. The Homestead Act of 1862. 2005. (Primary Sources in American History Ser.). (Illus.). 64p. (J). (gr. 5-8). lib. bdg. 31.95 *(978-1-4042-0178-1(5))* Rosen Publishing Group, Inc., The.

—The Homestead Act Of 1862: A Primary Source History of the Settlement of the American Heartland in the Late 19th Century. 2009. (Primary Sources in American History Ser.). 64p. (gr. 5-8). 58.50 *(978-1-60851-496-0(X))* Rosen Publishing Group, Inc., The.

Quasha, Jennifer. Covered Wagons: Hands-on Projects about America's Westward Expansion. 2009. (Great Social Studies Projects Ser.). 24p. (gr. 3-3). 42.50 *(978-1-61513-208-9(2),* PowerKids Pr.) Rosen Publishing Group, Inc., The.

Raabe, Emily. Buffalo Soldiers & the Western Frontier. 2009. (Westward Ho! Ser.). 24p. (gr. 2-3). 42.50 *(978-1-60854-759-3(0),* PowerKids Pr.) Rosen Publishing Group, Inc., The.

—Pioneers: Life as a Homesteader. (Westward Ho! Ser.). 24p. 2009. (gr. 2-3). 42.50 *(978-1-60854-761-6(2))* 2003. (Illus.). (J). lib. bdg. 22.60 *(978-0-8239-6498-7(1))* Rosen Publishing Group, Inc., The. (PowerKids Pr.).

—Thomas Jefferson & the Louisiana Purchase. 2009. (Westward Ho! Ser.). 24p. (gr. 2-3). 42.50 *(978-1-60854-763-0(9),* PowerKids Pr.) Rosen Publishing Group, Inc., The.

Rae, Thelma. Pioneer Families. 2009. (Reading Room Collection 1 Ser.). 16p. (gr. 2-3). 37.50 *(978-1-60851-948-4(1),* PowerKids Pr.) Rosen Publishing Group, Inc., The.

Rajczak, Kristen. Life on a Wagon Train. 2013. (What You Didn't Know about History Ser.). (Illus.). 24p. (J). (gr. 2-5). pap. 8.15 *(978-1-4339-8445-7(8));* lib. bdg. 22.60 *(978-1-4339-8444-0(X))* Stevens, Gareth Publishing LLLP.

—20 Fun Facts about Pioneer Women. 2015. (Fun Fact File: Women in History Ser.). (ENG., Illus.). 32p. (J). (gr. 2-3). 25.25 *(978-1-4824-2806-3(7))* Stevens, Gareth Publishing LLLP.

Randolph, Ryan. A Bank Robber's End: The Death of Jesse James. 2009. (Great Moments in American History Ser.). 32p. (gr. 3-3). 47.90 *(978-1-61513-138-9(8))* Rosen Publishing Group, Inc., The.

Randolph, Ryan P. Black Cowboys. (Library of the Westward Expansion Ser.). 24p. 2009. (gr. 3-4). 42.50 *(978-1-60853-933-8(4),* PowerKids Pr.) 2003. (Illus.). (J). lib. bdg. 22.60 *(978-0-8239-6294-5(6))* Rosen Publishing Group, Inc., The.

—Frontier Women Who Helped Shape the American West. 2003. (Library of the Westward Expansion Ser.). (Illus.). 24p. (J). lib. bdg. 22.60 *(978-0-8239-6297-6(0),* PowerKids Pr.) Rosen Publishing Group, Inc., The.

—Wild West Lawmen & Outlaws. (Library of the Westward Expansion Ser.). 24p. 2009. (gr. 3-4). 42.50 *(978-1-60853-944-4(X))* 2003. (Illus.). (J). lib. bdg. 22.60 *(978-0-8239-6293-8(8))* Rosen Publishing Group, Inc., The. (PowerKids Pr.).

Ratliff, Thomas. You Wouldn't Want to Be a Pony Express Rider! A Dusty, Thankless Job You'd Rather Not Do. Bergin, Mark, illus. 2012. (You Wouldn't Want to... Ser.). (ENG.). 32p. (J). pap. 9.95 *(978-0-531-20947-9(4),* Watts, Franklin); lib. bdg. 29.00 *(978-0-531-20872-4(9))* Scholastic Library Publishing.

Rau, Dana Meachen. The West. 2012. (True Book Ser.). (ENG., Illus.). 48p. (J). 29.00 *(978-0-531-24855-3(0),* Children's Pr.) Scholastic Library Publishing.

Rice, Dona. Chicas y Chicos Malos Del Lejano Oeste. 2016. (TIME for Kids en Español - Level 5 Ser.). (SPA.). 64p. (gr. 5-5). lib. bdg. 31.99 *(978-1-5157-2954-9(0))* Time for Kids Inc AUS. Dist: Capstone Pub.

Rice, Dona Herweck. Bad Guys & Gals of the Wild West, 1 vol. 2nd rev. ed. 2013. (Nonfiction Readers Ser.). (ENG.). 64p. (J). (gr. 5-5). pap. 10.99 *(978-1-4333-4903-4(5));* (Illus.). pap. 31.96 *(978-1-4333-7426-5(9))* Teacher Created Materials, Inc.

Rice, Katelyn. The Great Leap Westward. 2017. (J). pap. *(978-1-4938-3791-5(5))* Teacher Created Materials, Inc.

Rice, Katelyn. Settling & Unsettling the West (America in The 1800s) 2017. (Primary Source Readers Ser.). (Illus.). 32p. (J). (gr. 4-5). pap. 8.99 ***(978-1-4938-3797-7(4))*** Teacher Created Materials, Inc.

Riddle, John. The Pony Express. 2004. (History of the Old West Ser.). (Illus.). 64p. (YA). (gr. 5-18). lib. bdg. 19.95 *(978-1-59084-061-0(5))* Mason Crest.

Robertson, James. The Wild West: 1804-1890. Kunstler, Mort, illus. 2016. (See American History Ser.). (ENG.). 48p. (J). (gr. 2). 13.95 *(978-0-7892-1260-3(9),* Abbeville Kids) Abbeville Pr., Inc.

Robinson, Kate. Lewis & Clark: Exploring the American West. 2010. (Great Explorers of the World Ser.). (Illus.). 112p. (J). (gr. 7-12). 33.27 *(978-1-59845-124-5(3))* Enslow Pubs., Inc.

Roza, Greg. Westward Expansion. 2011. (Story of America Ser.). (Illus.). 32p. (J). (gr. 4-6). pap. 10.50 *(978-1-4339-4781-0(1));* lib. bdg. 26.60 *(978-1-4339-4780-3(3))* Stevens, Gareth Publishing LLLP. (Gareth Stevens Learning Library).

Sandler, Martin W. Iron Rails, Iron Men, & the Race to Link the Nation: The Story of the Transcontinental Railroad. 2015. (ENG.). 224p. (J). (gr. 5). 22.99 *(978-0-7636-6527-2(4))* Candlewick Pr.

—Who Were the American Pioneers? And Other Questions about Westward Expansion. Barrett, Robert, illus. 2014. (Good Question! Ser.). (ENG.). 32p. (J). pap. 5.95 *(978-1-4027-9047-8(3))* Sterling Publishing Co., Inc.

Sanford, Carl R. & Sanford, William R. Outlaws & Lawmen of the Wild West, 10 bks., Set. (Illus.). (YA). (gr. 4-10). lib. bdg. 169.50 *(978-0-89490-391-5(8))* Enslow Pubs., Inc.

Sanford, William R. & Green, Carl R. Kit Carson: Courageous Mountain Man. 2012. (Courageous Heroes of the American West Ser.). 48p. (J). pap. 8.95 *(978-1-4644-0094-0(6))* Enslow Pubs., Inc.

—Zebulon Pike: Courageous Rocky Mountain Explorer. 2012. (Courageous Heroes of the American West Ser.). (Illus.). 48p. (J). (gr. 5-18). lib. bdg. 22.60 *(978-0-7660-4012-0(7))* Enslow Pubs., Inc.

Savage, Jeff. American Cowboys: True Tales of the Wild West. 2012. (True Tales of the Wild West Ser.). (Illus.). 48p. (J). (gr. 5-18). pap. 8.95 *(978-1-4644-0027-8(X))* Enslow Pubs., Inc.

—Daring Pony Express Riders: True Tales of the Wild West. 2012. (True Tales of the Wild West Ser.). (Illus.). 48p. (J). (gr. 5-18). pap. 8.95 *(978-1-4644-0031-5(8));* lib. bdg. 22.60 *(978-0-7660-4023-6(2))* Enslow Pubs., Inc.

—Fearless Scouts: True Tales of the Wild West. 2012. (True Tales of the Wild West Ser.). (Illus.). 48p. (J). (gr. 5-18). pap. 8.95 *(978-1-4644-0032-2(6))* Enslow Pubs., Inc.

—Quick-Draw Gunfighters: True Tales of the Wild West. 2012. (True Tales of the Wild West Ser.). (Illus.). 48p. (J). (gr. 5-18). pap. 8.95 *(978-1-4644-0029-2(6));* lib. bdg. 22.60 *(978-0-7660-4021-2(6))* Enslow Pubs., Inc.

Schwartz, Heather E. The Foul, Filthy American Frontier: The Disgusting Details about the Journey Out West. 2011. (Disgusting History Ser.). (ENG.). 32p. (gr. 3-4). pap. 47.70 *(978-1-4296-6478-3(9),* Fact Finders) Capstone Press of Coughlan Cos.

—Outlaws, Gunslingers, & Thieves. (ShockZone (tm) — Villains Ser.). (ENG., 32p. (gr. 5-8). 2015. Illus.). 21.32 *(978-1-4677-6004-1(8),* Lerner Digital) 2013. lib. bdg. 26.60 *(978-1-4677-0605-6(1),* Lerner Pubns.) 2013. (Illus.). pap. 8.95 *(978-1-4677-0899-9(2))* Lerner Publishing Group.

Sechrist, Darren. Taming the West. 2008. (ENG.). 32p. (J). lib. bdg. *(978-0-7787-4188-6(5))* Crabtree Publishing Co.

—Westward, Ho! 2008. (ENG.). 32p. (J). pap. *(978-0-7787-4217-3(2))* Crabtree Publishing Co.

Shea, Therese. The Louisiana Purchase & the Lewis & Clark Expedition. 2017. (J). ***(978-1-5383-0013-8(3));*** pap. ***(978-1-68048-790-9(6))*** Rosen Publishing Group, Inc., The. (Britannica Educational Publishing).

Sheinkin, Steve. Which Way to the Wild West? Everything Your Schoolbooks Didn't Tell You about Westward Expansion. 2015. (J). lib. bdg. 20.85 *(978-0-606-37589-4(9))* Turtleback Bks.

Sioux, Tracee. Immigrants & the Westward Expansion. (Primary Sources of Immigration & Migration in America Ser.). 24p. 2009. (gr. 3-4). 42.50 *(978-1-60851-776-3(4))* 2004. (Illus.). (J). lib. bdg. 22.60 *(978-0-8239-6824-4(3))* Rosen Publishing Group, Inc., The. (PowerKids Pr.).

Smalley, Carol Parenzan. Lewis & Clark. 2008. (What's So Great About... ? Ser.). (Illus.). 32p. (YA). (gr. 2-4). lib. bdg. 25.70 *(978-1-58415-725-0(9))* Mitchell Lane Pubs., Inc.

Smith, Jeff. William Clark: Explorer & Diplomat. 2016. (ENG., Illus.). 48p. (J). pap. 27.00 *(978-1-61248-178-4(7))* Truman State Univ. Pr.

Somervill, Barbara A. West. 2011. (Explorer Library: Social Studies Explorer Ser.). (ENG.). 48p. (gr. 4-8). lib. bdg. 31.36 *(978-1-61080-182-9(2),* 201158) Cherry Lake Publishing.

Souza, D. M. John C. Fremont. 2004. (Watts Library). (ENG., Illus.). 64p. (J). (gr. 5-7). pap. 8.95 *(978-0-531-16652-9(X),* Watts, Franklin) Scholastic Library Publishing.

Souza, Dorothy M. John Wesley Powell. 2004. (Watts Library). (ENG., Illus.). 64p. (J). (gr. 5-7). pap. 8.95 *(978-0-531-16653-6(8),* Watts, Franklin) Scholastic Library Publishing.

Spies, Karen Bornemann. Buffalo Bill Cody: Legend of the Wild West. 2015. (Legendary American Biographies Ser.). 96p. (J). (gr. 6-12). 27.94 *(978-0-7660-6450-8(6));* pap. 10.95 *(978-0-7660-6451-5(4))* Enslow Pubs., Inc.

St. George, Judith. What Was the Lewis & Clark Expedition? Foley, Tim, illus. 2014. (What Was? Ser.). (ENG.). 112p. (J). (gr. 3-7). pap. 5.99 *(978-0-448-47901-9(X),* Penguin Workshop) Penguin Young Readers Group.

Staeger, Rob. The Boom Towns. 2004. (History of the Old West Ser.). (Illus.). 64p. (YA). (gr. 5-18). lib. bdg. 19.95 *(978-1-59084-068-9(2))* Mason Crest.

Steele, Christy. Famous Wagon Trails. 2005. (America's Westward Expansion Ser.). (Illus.). 48p. (gr. 5-12). pap. 14.05 *(978-0-8368-5795-5(X));* lib. bdg. 31.00 *(978-0-8368-5788-7(7))* Stevens, Gareth Publishing LLLP. (Gareth Stevens Secondary Library).

—Pioneer Life in the American West. 2005. (America's Westward Expansion Ser.). (Illus.). 48p. (gr. 5-12). pap. 14.05 *(978-0-8368-5797-9(6));* lib. bdg. 31.00 *(978-0-8368-5790-0(9))* Stevens, Gareth Publishing LLLP. (Gareth Stevens Secondary Library).

Stefoff, Rebecca. The Wild West. 2006. (American Voices Ser.). (Illus.). 128p. (gr. 6-7). lib. bdg. 26.95 *(978-0-7614-2170-2(X),* Benchmark Bks.) Marshall Cavendish Corp.

Stille, Darlene R. The Journals of Lewis & Clark, 1 vol. 2012. (Documenting U. S. History Ser.). (ENG.). 48p. (gr. 3-6). pap. 9.95 *(978-1-4329-6763-5(0));* lib. bdg. 32.65 *(978-1-4329-6754-3(1))* Heinemann-Raintree. (NA-h).

Streissguth, Thomas. Perspectives on Westward Expansion. 2018. (ENG.). 32p. (gr. 3-6). ***(978-1-63235-404-4(7),*** 12-Story Library) Pr. Room Editions LLC.

Sullivan, Laura L. Life As an Explorer with Lewis & Clark. 2016. (Life As... Ser.). (ENG., Illus.). 32p. (J). (gr. 3-3). pap. 10.58 *(978-1-5026-1078-2(7))* Cavendish Square Publishing.

Thompson, Gare & National Geographic Learning Staff. The West: Its History & People. 2007. (Nonfiction Reading & Writing Workshops Ser.). (ENG., Illus.). 32p. (J). pap. 17.95 *(978-0-7922-8617-2(0))* CENGAGE Learning.

Torr, James D., ed. Westward Expansion. 2003. (Interpreting American History Through Primary Documents Ser.x). (Illus.). 208p. (J). 32.45 *(978-0-7377-1134-9(5),* Greenhaven Pr., Inc.) Cengage Gale.

The True History of the Wild West. 2015. (True History of the Wild West Ser.). (ENG.). 32p. (J). (gr. 5-5). pap., pap., pap. 360.00 *(978-1-4994-1325-0(4),* PowerKids Pr.) Rosen Publishing Group, Inc., The.

Wadsworth, Ginger. Survival in the Snow. Orback, Craig, illus. 2009. (On My Own History Ser.). (ENG.). 48p. (gr. 2-4). 25.26 *(978-0-8225-7892-5(1))* Lerner Publishing Group.

Walch, Michelle E. & Maddin, John. Letters of the West. Maddin, John, illus. 2014. (Little Naturalist Ser.). (ENG., Illus.). 32p. (J). (gr. -1-k). 17.99 *(978-1-940052-10-6(6))* Craigmore Creations.

Waldman, Stuart. The Last River: John Wesley Powell & the Colorado River Exploring Expedition. Manchess, Gregory, illus. 2015. (ENG.). 48p. (J). (gr. 4-8). pap. 12.95 *(978-1-931414-58-6(0),* 9781931414586) Mikaya Pr.

Walsh, Steve. Zebulon Montgomery Pike: Explorer & Military Officer. 2011. (ENG & SPA., Illus.). 54p. (J). pap. 8.95 *(978-0-86541-123-4(9))* Filter Pr., LLC.

West, David. Lots of Things You Want to Know about Cowboys: ... & Some You Don't! 2015. (Lots of Things You Want to Know About Ser.). (Illus.). 24p. (J). 28.50 *(978-1-62588-089-5(8))* Black Rabbit Bks.

Westward Ho! (Illus.). (J). (gr. 3-6). 103.50 *(978-0-8239-7285-2(2),* Reading Power) Rosen Publishing Group, Inc., The.

White, Katherine. The 2000-2002 Forest Fires in the Western United States. (Tragic Fires Throughout History Ser.). 48p. (gr. 5-8). 2009. 53.00 *(978-1-60854-580-3(6))* 2004. (Illus.). (J). lib. bdg. 29.25 *(978-0-8239-4488-0(3))* Rosen Publishing Group, Inc., The. (Rosen Reference).

Wild Bill Hickok. 2010. (Legends of the Wild West Ser.). (Illus.). 112p. (gr. 6-12). 35.00 *(978-1-60413-593-0(X),* Chelsea Hse.) Facts On File, Inc.

Williams, Jean K. The Perils of the Santa Fe Trail. 2017. (Landmarks in U. S. History Ser.). (ENG.). 32p. (gr. 3-4). lib. bdg. 27.32 ***(978-1-5157-7117-3(2),*** Fact Finders) Capstone Press of Coughlan Cos.

Wiseman, Blaine. The West. 2016. (Illus.). 48p. (J). *(978-1-5105-1144-6(X))* SmartBook Media, Inc.

Yasuda, Anita. Explore the Wild West! With 25 Great Projects. Kim, Alex & Stone, Bryan, illus. 2012. (Explore Your World Ser.). (ENG.). 96p. (J). (gr. k-4). pap. 12.95 *(978-1-936749-71-3(8))* Open City Bks.

WEST INDIES

Duhgam, P. Island Hopping with Anancy. 24p. *(978-976-8184-11-5(6))* LMH Publishing, Ltd.

Hernandez, Romel. The Caribbean Islands: Facts & Figures. (Caribbean Today Ser.). 64p. (YA). 2010. (Illus.). (gr. 9-12). 21.95 *(978-1-4222-0622-5(X))* 2006. (gr. 7-18). pap. 9.95 *(978-1-4222-0689-8(0))* Mason Crest.

Kozleski, Lisa. The Leeward Islands. 2010. (Caribbean Today Ser.). (Illus.). 64p. (YA). (gr. 7-18). 21.95 *(978-1-4222-0627-0(0))* Mason Crest.

Kras, Sara Louise. Antigua & Barbuda. 2007. (Cultures of the World Ser.). 144p. (gr. 6). lib. bdg. 42.79 *(978-0-7614-2570-0(5),* Benchmark Bks.) Marshall Cavendish Corp.

Orr, Tamra. The Windward Islands. (Caribbean Today Ser.). 64p. (YA). 2010. (Illus.). (gr. 9-12). 21.95 *(978-1-4222-0630-0(0))* 2006. (gr. 7-18). pap. 9.95 *(978-1-4222-0697-3(1))* Mason Crest.

Spenceley, Angela. Virgin Islands Coloring Book. 2006. (Illus.). 24p. (J). 2.00 net. *(978-0-9778913-9-9(9))* Coconut Pr., LLC.

WEST INDIES—FICTION

Francis, Claudia Elizabeth Ruth. Island Issues. 2003. 196p. per. 15.00 net. *(978-1-931934-18-3(5))* Back Yard Pub.

Hann, Harry Henry & Johnson, Nancy. Down in the Tropics. Langille, Elaine, illus. 2013. 48p. pap. 14.99 *(978-0-9891323-0-5(7))* Goin' Native, Inc.

Rolt-Wheeler, Francis. Plotting in Pirate Seas. 2007. (ENG.). 166p. pap. 19.99 *(978-1-4346-4415-2(4));* 186p. pap. 21.99 *(978-1-4346-4416-9(2))* Creative Media Partners, LLC.

Sari. Jeanne-Marie Goes to Market: A Story of the West Indies. 2011. 26p. 35.95 *(978-1-258-10346-0(X))* Literary Licensing, LLC.

Spencer, Hannah. With All Best Wishes, Mrs Butterbean. 2008. 28p. pap. 13.50 *(978-1-60693-138-7(5),* Eloquent Bks.) Strategic Book Publishing & Rights Agency (SBPRA).

WEST INDIES—HISTORY

Capek, Michael. Jamaica. 2010. (Country Explorers Ser.). (ENG.). 48p. (gr. 2-4). (J). lib. bdg. 29.27 *(978-1-58013-604-4(4));* pap. 9.95 *(978-0-7613-5545-8(6))* Lerner Publishing Group.

Kozleski, Lisa. Leeward Islands, Vol. 11. Henderson, James D., ed. 2015. (Discovering the Caribbean: History, Politics, & Culture Ser.). (Illus.). 64p. (J). (gr. 7). lib. bdg. 22.95 *(978-1-4222-3314-6(6))* Mason Crest.

Longman Publishing Staff & Norman, Alma. The People Who Came, Bk. 1. 2nd ed. Date not set. (ENG., Illus.). 96p. pap. 9.95 *(978-0-582-76648-8(6))* Addison-Wesley Longman, Ltd. GBR. Dist: Trans-Atlantic Pubns., Inc.

Orr, Tamra. Windward Islands, Vol. 11. Henderson, James D., ed. 2015. (Discovering the Caribbean: History, Politics, & Culture Ser.). (Illus.). 64p. (J). (gr. 7). lib. bdg. 22.95 *(978-1-4222-3318-4(9))* Mason Crest.

WEST POINT (MILITARY ACADEMY)

see United States Military Academy

WEST VIRGINIA

Brown, Jonatha A. West Virginia. 2006. (Portraits of the States Ser.). 32p. (gr. 2-6). pap. 10.50 *(978-0-8368-4728-4(8));* (Illus.). lib. bdg. 26.00 *(978-0-8368-4711-6(3))* Stevens, Gareth Publishing LLLP. (Gareth Stevens Learning Library).

Cribben, Patrick & Heinemann Library Staff. Uniquely West Virginia, 1 vol. 2004. (State Studies). (ENG., Illus.). 48p. pap. 8.99 *(978-1-4034-4734-0(9),* Heinemann State Studies) Heinemann-Raintree.

Di Piazza, Domenica. West Virginia. 2012. (J). lib. bdg. 25.26 *(978-0-7613-4517-6(5),* Lerner Pubns.) Lerner Publishing Group.

Fein, E. How to Draw West Virginia's Sights & Symbols. 2009. (Kid's Guide to Drawing America Ser.). 32p. (gr. k-k). 50.50 *(978-1-61511-104-6(2),* PowerKids Pr.) Rosen Publishing Group, Inc., The.

Fontes, Justine & Fontes, Ron. West Virginia: The Mountain State. 2003. (World Almanac Library of the States). (Illus.). 48p. (gr. 4-9). pap. 14.05 *(978-0-8368-5334-6(2));* lib. bdg. 31.00 *(978-0-8368-5163-2(3))* Stevens, Gareth Publishing LLLP. (Gareth Stevens Learning Library).

Hoffman, Nancy & Hart, Joyce. West Virginia. 2nd rev. ed. 2007. (Celebrate the States Ser.). 144p. (gr. 6). lib. bdg. 42.79 *(978-0-7614-2562-5(4),* Benchmark Bks.) Marshall Cavendish Corp.

Koontz, Robin Michal. West Virginia: The Mountain State. 2010. (Our Amazing States Ser.). (ENG.). 24p. (J). pap. 8.25 *(978-1-4488-0736-9(0));* lib. bdg. 22.60 *(978-1-4488-0652-2(6))* Rosen Publishing Group, Inc., The. (PowerKids Pr.).

Labella, Susan. West Virginia. 2006. (Rookie Read-About Geography Ser.). (ENG., Illus.). 32p. (J). (gr. 1-2). lib. bdg. 20.50 *(978-0-516-24994-0(0),* Children's Pr.) Scholastic Library Publishing.

Marsh, Carole. West Virginia Current Events Projects: 30 Cool, Activities, Crafts, Experiments & More for Kids to Do to Learn about Your State! 2003. (West Virginia Experience Ser.). 32p. (gr. k-8). pap. 5.95 *(978-0-635-02067-3(X),* Marsh, Carole Bks.) Gallopade International.

—West Virginia Government Projects: 30 Cool, Activities, Crafts, Experiments & More for Kids to Do to Learn about Your State! 2003. (West Virginia Experience Ser.). 32p. (gr. k-5). pap. 5.95 *(978-0-635-01967-7(1),* Marsh, Carole Bks.) Gallopade International.

—West Virginia People Projects: 30 Cool, Activities, Crafts, Experiments & More for Kids to Do to Learn about Your State! 2003. (West Virginia Experience Ser.). 32p. (gr. k-5). pap. 5.95 *(978-0-635-02017-8(3),* Marsh, Carole Bks.) Gallopade International.

—West Virginia Symbols & Facts Projects: 30 Cool, Activities, Crafts, Experiments & More for Kids to Do to Learn about Your State! 2003. (West Virginia Experience Ser.). 32p. (gr. k-5). pap. 5.95 *(978-0-635-01917-2(5),* Marsh, Carole Bks.) Gallopade International.

Murray, Julie. West Virginia, 1 vol. 2006. (Buddy Book Ser.). (ENG., Illus.). 32p. (gr. 2-4). 27.07 *(978-1-59197-707-0(X),* Buddy Bks.) ABDO Publishing Co.

Parker, Bridget. West Virginia. 2016. (States Ser.). (ENG., Illus.). 32p. (gr. 3-4). lib. bdg. 27.32 *(978-1-5157-0437-9(8))* Next Page Pr., The.

Petreycik, Rick. West Virginia. 2007. (It's My State! Ser.). (Illus.). 80p. (J). (gr. 3-7). lib. bdg. 21.95 *(978-0-7614-2216-7(1))* Marshall Cavendish GBR. Dist: Marshall Cavendish Corp.

Riehle, Mary Ann McCabe. M Is for Mountain State: A West Virginia Alphabet. Bryant, Laura J., illus. 2004. (State Ser.). (ENG.). 40p. (J). 17.95 *(978-1-58536-151-9(8))* Sleeping Bear Pr.

Somervill, Barbara A. West Virginia. (ENG.). 80p. (J). 2008. pap. 7.95 *(978-0-531-20818-2(4))* 2003. (From Sea to Shining Sea Ser.: 2). (Illus.). 30.50 *(978-0-516-22389-6(5))* Scholastic Library Publishing. (Children's Pr.).

Way, Jennifer. West Virginia. 2009. (Bilingual Library of the United States of America Ser.). (ENG & SPA.). 32p. (gr. 2-2). 47.90 *(978-1-60853-392-3(1),* Editorial Buenas Letras) Rosen Publishing Group, Inc., The.

WEST VIRGINIA—FICTION

Atwell, A. Erika Laura. 2008. 157p. pap. 24.95 *(978-1-60703-006-5(3))* PublishAmerica, Inc.

Bauer, Joan. Close to Famous. 2012. (ENG.). 272p. (J). (gr. 5-18). 7.99 *(978-0-14-242017-1(4),* Puffin Books) Penguin Young Readers Group.

Bolden, Tonya. Finding Family. (ENG., Illus.). 192p. (YA). (gr. 3-12). 2012. pap. 7.99 *(978-1-59990-830-4(1),* 9781599908304) 2010. 15.99 *(978-1-59990-318-7(0),* 9781599903187) Bloomsbury Publishing USA. (Bloomsbury USA Childrens).

Cummings, John Michael. The Night I Freed John Brown. 2016. (ENG.). 256p. pap. 16.99 *(978-1-940425-96-2(4),* Vandalia Pr.) West Virginia Univ. Pr.

—Ugly to Start With. 2011. (ENG.). pap. 16.99 *(978-1-935978-08-4(X),* Vandalia Pr.) West Virginia Univ. Pr.

Dunham, Wendy. Hope Girl. 2016. (ENG.). 144p. (J). (gr. 2-7). pap. 7.99 *(978-0-7369-6495-1(9))* Harvest Hse. Pubs.

—My Name Is River. 2015. (ENG.). 144p. (J). (gr. 2-7). pap. 7.99 *(978-0-7369-6461-6(4))* Harvest Hse. Pubs.

Ehrenberg, Pamela. Tillmon County Fire. 2009. 192p. (YA). (gr. 9-18). pap. 9.00 *(978-0-8028-5345-5(5),* Eerdmans Bks For Young Readers) Eerdmans, William B. Publishing Co.

Faine, Edward Allan. More Little Ned Stories. 2003. 112p. (J). pap. 6.95 *(978-0-9716911-2-4(6))* IM Pr.

Fields, Jan. Meet the Mothman, 1 vol. Brundage, Scott, illus. 2016. (ENG.). 80p. (J). lib. bdg. *(978-1-62402-153-4(0))* Magic Wagon.

Hahn, Mary Downing. Witch Catcher. (ENG.). 240p. (J). (gr. 5-7). 2011. pap. 7.99 *(978-0-547-57714-2(1))* 2006. (Illus.). 16.00 *(978-0-618-50457-2(5))* Houghton Mifflin Harcourt Publishing Co.

Hedrick, Helen Groves. Tails, Trails & Pies: An Appalachian Cattle Drive. Spiker, Sue Ann Maxwell, illus. 2008. 32p. 15.95 *(978-0-929915-87-6(9))* Headline Bks., Inc.

Heidecker, Rosemary. Emmie. 2011. 144p. pap. 17.99 *(978-1-4567-3708-5(2))* AuthorHouse.

Jacobs, Lily. The Littlest Bunny in West Virginia: An Easter Adventure. 2015. (ENG.). 32p. (J). (-3). 9.99 *(978-1-4926-1237-7(5),* Sourcebooks Jabberwocky) Sourcebooks, Inc.

James, Eric. A Halloween Scare in West Virginia. Le Ray, Marina, illus. 2015. (ENG.). 32p. (J). (-5). 9.99 *(978-1-4926-2409-7(8),* 9781492624097, Sourcebooks Jabberwocky) Sourcebooks, Inc.

—Santa's Sleigh Is on Its Way to West Virginia: A Christmas Adventure. Dunn, Robert, illus. 2016. (ENG.). 32p. (J). (-2). 12.99 *(978-1-4926-4364-7(5),* 9781492643647, Sourcebooks Jabberwocky) Sourcebooks, Inc.

Kennedy, Marlane. The Dog Days of Charlotte Hayes. 2009. (ENG., Illus.). 240p. (J). (gr. 3-7). 15.99 *(978-0-06-145241-3(6),* Greenwillow Bks.) HarperCollins Pubs.

Kincaid, Tracy. The Adventures of Casey the Lost Suitcase. 2007. (Illus.). 32p. (J). (gr. -1-3). 16.95 *(978-0-929915-67-8(4))* Headline Bks., Inc.

Laskas, Gretchen Moran. The Miner's Daughter. 2007. (ENG.). 256p. (YA). (gr. 7-12). 17.99 *(978-1-4169-1262-0(2),* Simon & Schuster Bks. For Young Readers) Simon & Schuster Bks. For Young Readers.

Martin, T. Michael. The End Games. (ENG.). (YA). (gr. 9). 2014. 400p. pap. 9.99 *(978-0-06-220181-2(6))* 2013. 384p. 17.99 *(978-0-06-220180-5(8))* HarperCollins Pubs.

Mills, Lauren A. Minna's Patchwork Coat. 2015. (ENG., Illus.). 288p. (J). (gr. 3-7). 17.00 *(978-0-316-40621-5(X))* Little Brown & Co.

Naylor, Phyllis Reynolds. The Girls Take Over. 2004. (Boys Against Girls Ser.: No. 8). 146p. (J). (gr. 4-7). 13.65 *(978-0-7569-2804-9(4))* Perfection Learning Corp.

—Shiloh. 144p. (J). (Shiloh Ser.: No. 1). (gr. 4-7). pap. 4.99 *(978-0-8072-8330-1(4));* No. 1. 2004. (gr. 3-7). pap. 29.00 incl. audio *(978-0-8072-8329-5(0),* YA164SP) Random Hse. Audio Publishing Group. (Listening Library).

—Shiloh Season. unabr. ed. 2004. (Shiloh Ser.: No. 2). 120p. (J). (gr. 3-7). pap. 29.00 incl. audio *(978-0-8072-8707-1(5),* YA242SP, Listening Library) Random Hse. Audio Publishing Group.

Oneill, Elizabeth. Alfred Visits West Virginia. 2009. 24p. (J). pap. 12.00 *(978-0-9822288-2-1(1))* Global Business Information Strategies, Inc.

Rand, Johnathan. American Chillers #23 Wicked Velociraptors of West Virginia. 2008. 208p. (J). pap. 5.99 *(978-1-893699-94-6(3))* AudioCraft Publishing, Inc.

Rosenberg, Madelyn. Canary in the Coal Mine. 2013. (ENG., Illus.). 192p. (J). (gr. 2-7). 16.95 *(978-0-8234-2600-3(9))* Holiday Hse., Inc.

Rylant, Cynthia. Missing May. unabr. ed. 2004. 89p. (J). (gr. 5-9). pap. 29.00 incl. audio *(978-0-8072-8701-9(6),*

W X Y Z

YA240SP, Listening Library) Random Hse. Audio Publishing Group.

—Missing May. 2004. (ENG.). 112p. (J). (gr. 3-7). pap. 5.99 (978-0-439-61383-5(3), Scholastic Paperbacks) Scholastic, Inc.

Shank, Marilyn Sue. Child of the Mountains. 2013. (ENG.). 272p. (J). (gr. 4-7). 6.99 (978-0-375-87331-7(7), Yearling) Random Hse. Children's Bks.

Silvano, Wendi. Love Is All Around West Virginia. Czernichowska, Joanna, illus. 2016. (ENG.). 32p. (J). (-6). 12.99 (978-1-4926-2974-0(X), Sourcebooks Jabberwocky) Sourcebooks, Inc.

Slayton, Fran. When the Whistle Blows. 2010. (ENG.). 176p. (J). (gr. 5-18). 6.99 (978-0-14-241732-4(7), Puffin Books) Penguin Young Readers Group.

Smallman, Steve. Santa Is Coming to West Virginia. Dunn, Robert, illus. 2013. (ENG.). 32p. (J). (-3). 9.99 (978-1-4022-9100-5(0), Sourcebooks Jabberwocky) Sourcebooks, Inc.

Wach, Martin. The Great West Virginia Snow Adventure: Teddy Bear Guardians of the Rain Forest. 2006. (Illus.). 32p. (J). 16.95 (978-0-929915-42-5(9)) Headline Bks., Inc.

Watts, Jeri. A Piece of Home. Yum, Hyewon, illus. 2016. (ENG.). 32p. (J). (gr. k-3). 16.99 (978-0-7636-6971-3(7)) Candlewick Pr.

White, Ruth. The Treasure of Way down Deep. 2013. (ENG.). 176p. (J). (gr. 5-9). 16.99 (978-0-374-38067-0(8), 9780374380670, Farrar, Straus & Giroux (BYR)) Farrar, Straus & Giroux.

—Way down Deep. 2011. (ENG.). 224p. (J). (gr. 5-8). pap. 7.99 (978-0-312-66096-3(0), 9780312660963) Square Fish.

Wyatt, Melissa. Funny How Things Change. 2009. (ENG.). 208p. (YA). (gr. 9-13). 26.99 (978-0-374-30233-7(2), Farrar, Straus & Giroux (BYR)) Farrar, Straus & Giroux.

Yolen, Jane. Snow in Summer. 2013. (ENG.). 272p. (J). (gr. 5). pap. 7.99 (978-0-14-242197-0(9), Puffin Books) Penguin Young Readers Group.

WEST VIRGINIA—HISTORY

Byers, Ann. West Virginia: Past & Present. 2010. (United States: Past & Present Ser.). (ENG.). 48p. (YA). pap. 11.75 (978-1-4358-9526-3(6)); lib. bdg. 29.25 (978-1-4358-9499-0(5)) Rosen Publishing Group, Inc., The. (Rosen Reference).

Carole Marsh. West Virginia Indians. 2004. (West Virginia Experi Ser.). 36p. (gr. 3-8). pap. 7.95 (978-0-635-02340-7(7)) Gallopade International.

Davidson, Tish. Atlantic: North Carolina, Virginia, West Virginia, Vol. 19. 2015. (Let's Explore the States Ser.). (Illus.). 64p. (J). (gr. 5). 23.95 (978-1-4222-3320-7(0)) Mason Crest.

Dillard, Sheri. What's Great about West Virginia? 2015. (ENG., Illus.). 32p. (J). (gr. 2-5). 26.65 (978-1-4677-3877-4(8), Lerner Pubns.) Lerner Publishing Group.

Fluharty, Linda Cunningham. Civil War - West Virginia: Union Lives Lost. 2004. (Illus.). 175p. lib. bdg. 35.00 (978-0-9759097-1-3(1)) Fluharty, Linda Cunningham.

Hallock, Marilyn R. Central Glass Company: The First Thirty Years, 1863-1893, 1 vol. 2003. (ENG., Illus.). 176p. 39.95 (978-0-7643-1762-0(8), 9780764317620) Schiffer Publishing, Ltd.

Hanel, Rachael. West Virginia. 2009. (This Land Called America Ser.). (Illus.). 32p. (YA). (gr. 3-6). 19.95 (978-1-58341-801-7(6)) Creative Co., The.

Heinrichs, Ann. West Virginia (Revised Edition) 2014. (America the Beautiful, Third Ser. (Revised Edition) Ser.). (ENG.). 144p. (J). lib. bdg. 40.00 (978-0-531-28299-1(6)) Scholastic Library Publishing.

Lawton, Val. West Virginia. 2011. (Guide to American States Ser.). (Illus.). 48p. (YA). (gr. 3-6). 29.99 (978-1-61690-822-5(X)); (J). (978-1-61690-497-5(6)) Weigl Pubs., Inc.

—West Virginia: The Mountain State. 2016. (J). (978-1-4896-4962-1(X)) Weigl Pubs., Inc.

Lillard, David. West Virginia: A MyReportLinks. Com Book. 2003. (States Ser.). (Illus.). 48p. (J). lib. bdg. 25.26 (978-0-7660-5143-0(9), MyReportLinks.com Bks.) Enslow Pubs., Inc.

Marsh, Carole. Exploring West Virginia Through Project-Based Learning: Geography, History, Government, Economics & More. 2016. (West Virginia Experience Ser.). (ENG.). (J). pap. 9.99 (978-0-635-12372-5(X)) Gallopade International.

—West Virginia History Projects: 30 Cool, Activities, Crafts, Experiments & More for Kids to Do to Learn about Your State! 2003. (West Virginia Experience Ser.). 32p. (gr. k-5). pap. 5.95 (978-0-635-01817-5(9), Marsh, Carole Bks.) Gallopade International.

—West Virginia Native Americans: A Kid's Look at Our State's Chiefs, Tribes, Reservations, Powwows, Lore & More from the Past & the Present. 2004. (West Virginia Experi Ser.). (Illus.). 36p. (J). (gr. 3-8). 29.95 (978-0-635-02341-4(5)) Gallopade International.

Ollhoff, Jim. West Virginia, 1 vol. 2009. (United States Ser.). (ENG., Illus.). 48p. (YA). (gr. 2-5). 27.07 (978-1-60453-685-0(3)) ABDO Publishing Co.

Owings, Lisa. West Virginia. 2013. (Exploring the States Ser.). (ENG., Illus.). 32p. (J). (gr. 3-7). lib. bdg. 26.95 (978-1-62617-049-0(5), Blastoff! Readers) Bellwether Media.

Petreycik, Rick. West Virginia. 2014. (J). pap. (978-1-62712-486-7(1)); (Illus.). 80p. lib. bdg. (978-1-62712-224-5(9)) Cavendish Square Publishing.

Petreycik, Rick & Boehme, Gerry. West Virginia. 2016. (It's My State! (r) Ser.). 80p. (J). (gr. 4-4). 34.21 (978-1-62713-256-5(2)) Cavendish Square Publishing.

Phillips, Margaret Coull. West Virginia. 2003. (Seeds of a Nation Ser.). (Illus.). 48p. (J). (gr. 3-5). 23.70 (978-0-7377-1567-5(7), Kidhaven) Cengage Gale.

Pratt, Laura. West Virginia: The Mountain State. 2012. (J). (978-1-61913-417-1(9)); pap. (978-1-61913-418-8(7)) Weigl Pubs., Inc.

The Raid on Harpers Ferry: John Brown's Rebellion. 2010. (Milestones in American History Ser.). (Illus.). 136p. (J). (gr. 6-12). 35.00 (978-1-60413-678-4(2), Chelsea Hse.) Facts On File, Inc.

Roxburgh, Ellis. The Raid on Harpers Ferry. 2017. (Rebellions, Revolts, & Uprisings Ser.). 48p. (gr. 5-5). pap. 84.30 **(978-1-5382-0754-3(0))** Stevens, Gareth Publishing LLLP.

Schraff, Anne E. John Brown: We Came to Free the Slaves. 2010. (Americans—the Spirit of a Nation Ser.). (Illus.). 128p. (J). lib. bdg. 33.27 (978-0-7660-3355-9(4)) Enslow Pubs., Inc.

Smucker, Anna. History of West Virginia. 2004. (Illus.). per. 6.95 (978-1-891852-39-8(6)) Quarrier Pr.

Tieck, Sarah. West Virginia, 1 vol. 2012. (Explore the United States Ser.). (ENG.). 32p. (J). (gr. 2-5). lib. bdg. 28.50 (978-1-61783-388-5(6), Big Buddy Bks.) ABDO Publishing Co.

Way, Jennifer. West Virginia/Virginia Occidental. Brusca, Maria Cristina, tr. from ENG. 2006. (Bilingual Library of the United States of America Ser.: Set 2). (ENG & SPA., Illus.). 32p. (J). (gr. 3-6). lib. bdg. 25.25 (978-1-4042-3114-6(5)) Rosen Publishing Group, Inc., The.

Yomtov, Nel. John Brown: Defending the Innocent or Plotting Terror?, 1 vol. 2013. (Perspectives on History Ser.). (ENG.). 32p. (gr. 3-4). 27.32 (978-1-4765-0244-1(7)); pap. 7.95 (978-1-4765-3408-4(X)) Capstone Press of Coughlan Cos. (Fact Finders).

Zaunders, Bo. The Great Bridge-Building Contest. Munro, Roxie, illus. 2006. 30p. (J). (gr. 4-8). reprint ed. 17.00 (978-1-4223-5239-7(0)) DIANE Publishing Co.

WETLAND ECOLOGY

Ake, Anne. Everglades: An Ecosystem Facing Choices & Challenges. 2008. (ENG., Illus.). 110p. (J). (gr. 6-9). 19.95 (978-1-56164-410-0(2)) Pineapple Pr., Inc.

Aloian, Molly & Kalman, Bobbie. Un Hábitat de Pantano. 2007. (Introduction a Los Habitats Ser.). (SPA., Illus.). 32p. (J). (gr. 3-7). lib. bdg. (978-0-7787-8328-2(6)); (gr. k-3). pap. (978-0-7787-8352-7(9)) Crabtree Publishing Co.

—A Wetland Habitat. 2006. (Introducing Habitats Ser.). (ENG., Illus.). 32p. (J). (gr. -1-3). pap. (978-0-7787-2983-9(4)) Crabtree Publishing Co.

Beatty, Richard. Wetlands, 1 vol. 2nd ed. 2010. (Biomes Atlases Ser.). (ENG.). 64p. (gr. 6-9). 34.65 (978-1-4329-4183-3(6)) Heinemann-Raintree.

Bennett, Doraine. Coastal Plain. 2009. (J). (978-1-935077-51-0(1)); pap. (978-1-935077-52-7(X)) State Standards Publishing, LLC.

Benoit, Peter. Wetlands. 2011. (True Bk Ser.). 48p. (J). (ENG.). pap. 6.95 (978-0-531-28100-0(0)); (gr. 3-5). 29.00 (978-0-531-20551-8(7)) Scholastic Library Publishing. (Children's Pr.).

Bosch, Sammy. Super Simple Wetland Critter Crafts: Fun & Easy Animal Crafts. 2016. (ENG., Illus.). 32p. (J). (978-1-68078-164-9(2)) ABDO Publishing Co.

Bow, James. Wetlands Inside Out. 2014. (ENG.). 32p. (J). (978-0-7787-0641-0(9)) Crabtree Publishing Co.

Dunphy, Madeleine. Here Is the Wetland. McLoughlin, Wayne, illus. 2007. (Web of Life Ser.). (ENG.). 32p. (J). (gr. -1-3). 16.95 (978-0-9773795-9-0(0)); pap. 9.95 (978-0-9773795-8-3(2)) Web of Life Children's Bks.

Franchino, Vicky. Florida Wetlands. 2016. (Community Connections: Getting to Know Our Planet Ser.). (ENG., Illus.). 24p. (J). (gr. 2-5). 27.07 (978-1-63470-516-5(5), 207795) Cherry Lake Publishing.

Frisch, Aaron. Wetlands. 2008. (Our World Ser.). (Illus.). 24p. (J). (gr. -1-3). lib. bdg. 24.25 (978-1-58341-575-7(0), Creative Education) Creative Co., The.

Gaarder- Juntti, Oona. What Lives in the Wetlands?, 1 vol. 2008. (Animal Habitats Ser.). (ENG., Illus.). 24p. (J). (gr. k-3). 25.65 (978-1-60453-180-0(0)) ABDO Publishing Co.

Heos, Bridget. Do You Really Want to Visit a Wetland? Fabbri, Daniele, illus. 2014. (Do You Really Want to Visit... ? Ser.). (ENG.). 24p. (J). (gr. 1-4). lib. bdg. 27.10 (978-1-60753-454-9(1)) Amicus Publishing.

Johansson, Philip. Marshes & Swamps: A Wetland Web of Life. 2007. (Wonderful Water Biomes Ser.). (Illus.). 48p. (J). (gr. 3-7). lib. bdg. 25.27 (978-0-7660-2814-2(3), Enslow Elementary) Enslow Pubs., Inc.

Johnson, Robin. Everglades Research Journal. 2017. (Illus.). 32p. (J). **(978-0-7787-3469-7(2))**; pap. **(978-0-7787-3494-9(3))** Crabtree Publishing Co.

Kalman, Bobbie & Bishop, Amanda. Les Terres Humides. 2004. (Petit Monde Vivant Ser.). (FRE., Illus.). 32p. (J). pap. 9.95 (978-2-89579-014-3(0)) Bayard Canada Livres CAN. Dist: Crabtree Publishing Co.

Kalman, Bobbie & Burns, Kylie. Wetland Food Chains. 2006. (Food Chains Ser.). (ENG., Illus.). 32p. (J). (gr. -1-3). pap. (978-0-7787-1999-1(5)) Crabtree Publishing Co.

Lantz, Peggy Sias & Hale, Wendy A. The Wetlands of Florida. 2014. (Florida Water Story Ser.). (ENG., Illus.). 34p. (J). (gr. 4). pap. 6.95 (978-1-56164-705-7(5)) Pineapple Pr., Inc.

Larsen, Laurel. One Night in the Everglades. Turley, Joyce Mihran, illus. 2012. (Long Term Ecological Research Ser.). (ENG.). 32p. (J). (gr. 3-7). 15.95 (978-0-9817700-4-8(5)) Taylor Trade Publishing.

Leeson, Cole. Wetland/Swamp. 2003. (Wild America Habitats Ser.). (Illus.). 24p. (J). 21.20 (978-1-56711-810-0(0), Blackbirch Pr., Inc.) Cengage Gale.

Macken, JoAnn Early & Early Macken, JoAnn. Wetlands: Terrenos Pantanosos. 2005. (Water Habitats/ Habitats acuaticos Ser.). (SPA., Illus.). 24p. (gr. k-3). pap. 8.15 (978-0-8368-6039-9(X), Weekly Reader Leveled Readers) Stevens, Gareth Publishing LLLP.

Marais, Vivian. Life in a Swamp: A Wetlands Habitat. 2009. (Real Life Readers Ser.). 24p. (gr. 3-4). pap. 8.25 (978-1-4358-0141-7(5), Rosen Classroom) Rosen Publishing Group, Inc., The.

McKissack, Fredrick L. & McKissack, Lisa Beringer. Counting in the Wetlands. 2008. (Counting in the Biomes Ser.). (Illus.). 32p. (J). (gr. 1-3). lib. bdg. 23.94 (978-0-7660-2993-4(X), Enslow Elementary) Enslow Pubs., Inc.

Mebane, Jeanie. At the Marsh in the Meadow. Guerlais, Gérald, illus. 2016. (ENG.). 32p. (J). (gr. 1-3). 17.99 (978-1-58536-958-4(6), 204028) Sleeping Bear Pr.

Moore, Peter D. Wetlands. Garratt, Richard, illus. 2nd rev. ed. 2007. (Ecosystems Ser.). 256p. (C). (gr. 9-12). 70.00 (978-0-8160-5931-7(4)) Facts On File, Inc.

Patkau, Karen. Who Needs a Swamp? 2012. (Ecosystem Ser.). (ENG., Illus.). 32p. (J). (gr. 2-5). 17.95 (978-0-88776-991-7(8), Tundra Bks.) Tundra Bks. CAN. Dist: Penguin Random Hse. LLC.

Pettiford, Rebecca. Wetland Food Chains. 2016. (Who Eats What?). 24p. (J). (gr. 2-5). lib. bdg. 25.65 (978-1-62031-305-3(7), Pogo) Jump! Inc.

Pyers, Greg. Biodiversity of Wetlands. 2011. (Biodiversity 2 Ser.). 32p. (gr. 4). 28.50 (978-1-60870-533-7(1)) Marshall Cavendish Corp.

Rivera, Sheila. Wetland. 2005. (Illus.). 24p. (J). pap. 5.95 (978-0-8225-5370-0(8)) Lerner Publishing Group.

Root, Phyllis. Big Belching Bog. Bowen, Betsy, illus. 2010. (ENG.). 40p. (gr. 2-3). 15.95 (978-0-8166-3359-3(2)) Univ. of Minnesota Pr.

Stewart, Melissa. Life in a Wetland. Maka, Stephen, photos by. 2003. (Ecosystems in Action Ser.). (ENG., Illus.). 72p. (gr. 5-9). lib. bdg. 26.60 (978-0-8225-4687-0(6)) Lerner Publishing Group.

Stille, Darlene R. Protecting Land. 2011. (Go Green! Ser.). (ENG., Illus.). 32p. (J). (gr. 1-4). lib. bdg. 28.50 (978-1-60973-175-5(1), 201154) Child's World, Inc., The.

Stone, Lynn M. Wetlands. 2003. (Rourke Discovery Library). (Illus.). 24p. (J). 20.64 (978-1-58952-688-4(0)) Rourke Educational Media.

Sturm, Jeanne. Restoring Wetlands. 2009. (ENG., Illus.). 48p. (gr. 4-8). pap. 10.95 (978-1-60694-527-8(0)) Rourke Educational Media.

Sundance/Newbridge LLC Staff. Wetlands. 2007. (Early Science Ser.). (gr. k-3). 18.95 (978-1-4007-6450-1(5)); pap. 6.10 (978-1-4007-6446-4(7)) Sundance/Newbridge Educational Publishing.

Taylor, Trace & Zorzi, Gina. This Is a Wetland. 2011. (Power 100 - Ecosystems Ser.). 28p. (J). (gr. k-2). pap. 7.95 (978-1-61541-450-5(9)) American Reading Co.

Wallace, Marianne D. America's Wetlands: Guide to Plants & Animals. 2004. (America's Ecosystems Ser.). (ENG., Illus.). 48p. (J). (gr. 3-6). pap. 11.95 (978-1-55591-484-4(5)) Fulcrum Publishing.

Watson, Galadriel Findlay. Wetlands. (J). 2011. (gr. 5-8). pap. 13.95 (978-1-61690-649-8(9), AV2 by Weigl) 2011. (Illus.). 32p. (gr. 2-5). 28.55 (978-1-61690-643-6(X)) 2005. (Illus.). 32p. (gr. 4-6). lib. bdg. 26.00 (978-1-59036-349-2(3)) Weigl Pubs., Inc.

Wechsler, Doug. Marvels in the Muck: Life in the Salt Marshes. 2008. (ENG.). 48p. (J). (gr. 5-18). 17.95 (978-1-59078-588-1(6)) Boyds Mills Pr.

World Book, Inc Staff, contrib. by. Forests & Wetlands. 2008. (J). (978-0-7166-1401-2(4)) World Bk., Inc.

WETLANDS

see also Marshes

Arnold, Quinn M. Wetlands. 2016. (J). (978-1-60818-798-0(5), Creative Education) Creative Co., The.

Benoit, Peter. Wetlands. 2011. (True Bk Ser.). 48p. (J). (ENG.). pap. 6.95 (978-0-531-28100-0(0)); (gr. 3-5). 29.00 (978-0-531-20551-8(7)) Scholastic Library Publishing. (Children's Pr.).

Campbell, Andrew. Protecting Wetlands. 2005. (Protecting Habitats Ser.). (Illus.). 32p. (gr. 4-7). lib. bdg. 26.00 (978-0-8368-4996-7(5), Gareth Stevens Learning Library) Stevens, Gareth Publishing LLLP.

Chambers, Catherine. Threatened Wetlands. 2010. (Protecting Our Planet Ser.). (ENG., Illus.). 32p. (J). (gr. 3-6). (978-0-7787-5214-1(3)); pap. (978-0-7787-5231-8(3)) Crabtree Publishing Co.

Clarke, Penny. Scary Creatures of the Wetlands. 2008. (Scary Creatures Ser.). (ENG.). 32p. (J). 27.00 (978-0-531-21749-8(3), Watts, Franklin) Scholastic Library Publishing.

Endres, Hollie. Wetlands. 2007. (Learning about the Earth Ser.). (ENG., Illus.). 24p. (J). (gr. k-3). lib. bdg. 25.95 (978-1-60014-116-4(1)) Bellwether Media.

Endres, Hollie J. Wetlands. 2011. (Blastoff! Readers: Learning about the Earth: Level 3 Ser.). (Illus.). 24p. (J). pap. 5.95 (978-0-531-26039-5(9), Children's Pr.) Scholastic Library Publishing.

Franklin, Yvonne. Los Pantanos, 1 vol. rev. ed. 2010. (Science Readers: a Closer Look Ser.). (SPA., Illus.). 32p. (J). (gr. 2-3). pap. 8.99 (978-1-4333-2140-5(8)) Shell Educational Publishing.

Gordon, Sharon. Animales de los Humedales. 2008. (Animales Salvajes Ser.). (SPA.). 24p. (gr. k-1). lib. bdg. 15.95 (978-0-7614-3433-7(X), Benchmark Bks.) Marshall Cavendish Corp.

Heos, Bridget. Do You Really Want to Visit a Wetland? Fabbri, Daniele, illus. 2014. (Do You Really Want to Visit... ? Ser.). (ENG.). 24p. (J). (gr. 1-4). lib. bdg. 27.10 (978-1-60753-454-9(1)) Amicus Publishing.

Hodge, Deborah. Wetland Animals. Stephens, Pat, illus. 2008. (Who Lives Here? Ser.). (ENG.). 24p. (J). (gr. -1-2). pap. 5.95 (978-1-55453-046-5(6)) Kids Can Pr., Ltd. CAN. Dist: Hachette Bk. Group.

Howard, Fran. Wetlands, 1 vol. 2006. (Habitats Ser.). (ENG., Illus.). 32p. (gr. -1-3). 27.07 (978-1-59679-783-3(5), Buddy Bks.) ABDO Publishing Co.

Johnson, Rebecca L. A Journey into a Wetland. Saroff, Phyllis V., illus. 2004. (Biomes of North America Ser.). (J). pap. 8.95 (978-0-8225-2047-4(8)); 48p. (gr. 3-6). lib. bdg. 23.93 (978-1-57505-593-0(7)) Lerner Publishing Group.

Kalman, Bobbie & Burns, Kylie. Cadenas Alimentarias de los Pantanos. 2007. (Cadenas Alimentarias Ser.). (SPA., Illus.). 32p. (J). (gr. 3-7). lib. bdg. (978-0-7787-8532-3(7)) Crabtree Publishing Co.

Kanfush, Philip M. Emma's Wetlands Adventure: The Story of the Monastery Run Impovement Project Wetlands at Saint Vincent. 2006. (J). pap. 12.95 (978-0-9708216-9-0(7)) St. Vincent Archabbey Pubns.

Kavanagh, James. My First Wetlands Nature. Leung, Raymond, illus. 2011. (Nature Activity Book Ser.). (ENG.). 32p. (J). (gr. 2-4). act. bk. ed. 6.95 (978-1-58355-591-0(9)) Western National Parks Assn.

Kinsner, Kathy. The Everglades. 2011. (Early Connections Ser.). (J). (978-1-61672-675-1(X)) Benchmark Education Co.

Lantz, Peggy Sias & Hale, Wendy A. The Wetlands of Florida. 2014. (Florida Water Story Ser.). (ENG., Illus.). 34p. (J). (gr. 4). pap. 6.95 (978-1-56164-705-7(5)) Pineapple Pr., Inc.

Leeson, Cole. Wetland/Swamp. 2003. (Wild America Habitats Ser.). (Illus.). 24p. (J). 21.20 (978-1-56711-810-0(0), Blackbirch Pr., Inc.) Cengage Gale.

Looye, Juliette, text. I Live near a Wetland. 2004. (Illus.). 16p. (J). pap. (978-0-7367-1940-7(7)) Zaner-Bloser, Inc.

Mack, Dave. What Lives in a Marsh? 2013. (InfoMax Readers Ser.). (ENG.). 24p. (J). (gr. 3-4). pap. 49.50 (978-1-4777-2580-1(6)); (Illus.). pap. 8.25 (978-1-4777-2579-5(2)) Rosen Publishing Group, Inc., The. (Rosen Classroom).

Macken, JoAnn Early. Wetlands. 2005. (Water Habitats Ser.). (Illus.). 24p. (gr. k-3). pap. 8.15 (978-0-8368-4894-6(2)); lib. bdg. 22.00 (978-0-8368-4887-8(X)) Stevens, Gareth Publishing LLLP. (Weekly Reader Leveled Readers).

Macken, JoAnn Early & Early Macken, JoAnn. Wetlands: Terrenos Pantanosos. 2005. (Water Habitats/ Habitats acuaticos Ser.). (SPA., Illus.). 24p. (gr. k-3). pap. 8.15 (978-0-8368-6039-9(X), Weekly Reader Leveled Readers) Stevens, Gareth Publishing LLLP.

—Wetlands/ Pantanos. 2005. (Water Habitats/ Habitats acuaticos Ser.). (SPA., Illus.). 24p. (gr. k-3). lib. bdg. 22.00 (978-0-8368-6032-0(2), Weekly Reader Leveled Readers) Stevens, Gareth Publishing LLLP.

McKissack, Fredrick L. & McKissack, Lisa Beringer. Counting in the Wetlands. 2008. (Counting in the Biomes Ser.). (Illus.). 32p. (J). (gr. 1-3). lib. bdg. 23.94 (978-0-7660-2993-4(X), Enslow Elementary) Enslow Pubs., Inc.

Mebane, Jeanie. At the Marsh in the Meadow. Guerlais, Gérald, illus. 2016. (ENG.). 32p. (J). (gr. 1-3). 17.99 (978-1-58536-958-4(6), 204028) Sleeping Bear Pr.

Moore, Peter D. Wetlands. Garratt, Richard, illus. 2nd rev. ed. 2007. (Ecosystems Ser.). 256p. (C). (gr. 9-12). 70.00 (978-0-8160-5931-7(4)) Facts On File, Inc.

Pratt-Serafini, Kristin Joy. Salamander Rain: A Lake & Pond Journal. 2004. (Sharing Nature with Children Book Ser.). (Illus.). 32p. (YA). (gr. 4-7). 16.95 (978-1-58469-018-4(6)) Dawn Pubns.

Project WET Foundation, prod. Kids: Celebrate Wetlands Activity Guide. 2003. (ENG.). (J). 1.00 (978-1-888631-25-8(2)) Project WET Foundation.

Rice, William & Franklin, Yvonne. Wetlands, 1 vol. 2009. (Science Readers: a Closer Look Ser.). (ENG.). 32p. (J). (gr. 2-2). pap. 8.99 (978-1-4333-0316-6(7)) Teacher Created Materials, Inc.

Riggs, Kate & Arnold, Quinn M. Wetlands. 2017. (Seedlings Ser.). (ENG.). 24p. (J). (gr. k-2). pap. 7.99 (978-1-62832-351-1(5), Creative Paperbacks) Creative Co., The.

Rivera, Sheila. Wetland. 2005. (First Step Nonfiction Ser.). (Illus.). 23p. (J). (gr. 3-7). lib. bdg. 18.60 (978-0-8225-2598-1(4), Lerner Pubns.) Lerner Publishing Group.

Scrace, Carolyn. Life in the Wetlands. 2005. (What on Earth? Ser.). (ENG., Illus.). 32p. (J). (gr. 2-4). 25.50 (978-0-516-25318-3(2), Children's Pr.) Scholastic Library Publishing.

Sherk, Beth Larson. The Three Sisters. 2012. (Illus.). 35p. (J). 14.95 (978-1-62086-091-5(0)) Mascot Bks., Inc.

Sill, Cathryn. About Habitats-Wetlands, 1 vol. Sill, John, illus. 2008. (About... Ser.). (ENG.). 48p. (J). (gr. k-3). 15.95 (978-1-56145-432-7(X)) Peachtree Pubs.

—Wetlands, 1 vol. Sill, John, illus. 2013. (ENG.). 48p. (J). (gr. -1-2). 7.95 (978-1-56145-689-5(6)) Peachtree Pubs.

Silverman, Buffy. Wetlands, 1 vol. 2012. (Habitat Survival Ser.). (ENG.). 32p. (gr. 2-4). pap. 8.29 (978-1-4109-4610-2(X)); lib. bdg. 30.65 (978-1-4109-4601-0(0)) Heinemann-Raintree. (Raintree Perspectives).

Spilsbury, Richard & Spilsbury, Louise. At Home in the Wetlands, 01 vols., 1. 2016. (Home in the Biome Ser.). (ENG.). 32p. (J). pap. 10.00 (978-1-5081-4569-1(5), PowerKids Pr.) Rosen Publishing Group, Inc., The.

Stone, Lynn M. Wetlands. 2003. (Rourke Discovery Library). (Illus.). 24p. (J). 20.64 (978-1-58952-688-4(0)) Rourke Educational Media.

Taylor, Barbara. Inland Water Habitats. 2006. (Exploring Habitats Ser.). (Illus.). 36p. (gr. 3-7). lib. bdg. 26.00 (978-0-8368-7254-5(1), Gareth Stevens Learning Library) Stevens, Gareth Publishing LLLP.

Walker, Pam & Wood, Elaine. The Saltwater Wetland. 2005. (Life in the Sea Ser.). (Illus.). 152p. (gr. 5-8). 35.00 (978-0-8160-5702-3(8)) Facts On File, Inc.

Wallace, Marianne D. America's Wetlands: Guide to Plants & Animals. 2004. (America's Ecosystems Ser.). (ENG., Illus.). 48p. (J). (gr. 3-6). pap. 11.95 (978-1-55591-484-4(5)) Fulcrum Publishing.

Weaver, Jeanne. Wetlands Journey. 2007. (Science Chapters Ser.). (ENG., Illus.). 48p. (J). (gr. 1-4). lib. bdg. 17.90 (978-1-4263-0185-8(5), National Geographic Children's Bks.) National Geographic Society.

World Book, Inc Staff, contrib. by. Forests & Wetlands. 2008. (J). (978-0-7166-1401-2(4)) World Bk., Inc.

WETLANDS—FICTION

Auer, Chris. The Legend of the Sand Dollar: An Inspirational Story of Hope for Easter, 1 vol. Johnson, Rick, illus. 2005. (ENG.). 32p. (J). 16.99 (978-0-310-70780-6(3)) Zonderkidz.

Jiang, Ji-Li. Lotus & Feather. Downing, Julie, illus. 2016. (ENG.). 40p. (J). (gr. -1-k). 17.99 (978-1-4231-2754-3(4)) Disney Pr.

Szymanski, Lois. Wild Colt, 1 vol. Kantjas, Linda, illus. 2012. (ENG.). 40p. (J). 16.99 (978-0-7643-3975-2(3), 9780764339752) Schiffer Publishing, Ltd.

Ter Haar, Carol. Chris T. Saves the Wetlands. 2008. (J). 20.00 (978-0-9768310-2-0(3)) BIC Alliance.

WHALES

Adamson, Heather. Orcas. 2017. (Ocean Life up Close Ser.). (ENG., Illus.). 24p. (J). (gr. k-3). lib. bdg. 25.95 **(978-1-62617-643-0(4)**, Blastoff! Readers) Bellwether Media.

Adelman, Beth. Killer Whales. 2006. (Reading Rocks! Ser.). (ENG., Illus.). 32p. (J). (gr. 2-5). 28.50 (978-1-59296-732-2(9), 200718) Child's World, Inc., The.

Allen, Judy. Flip the Flaps: Whales & Dolphins. Bostock, Mike, illus. 2011. (Flip the Flaps Ser.). (ENG.). 32p. (J). (gr. -1-1). pap. 6.99 (978-0-7534-6497-7(7), 9780753464977, Kingfisher) Roaring Brook Pr.

Allyn, Daisy. Killer Whales Are Not Whales! 2014. (Confusing Creature Names Ser.). 24p. (J). (gr. 1-3). 22.60 (978-1-4824-0961-1(5)) Stevens, Gareth Publishing LLLP.

Animal Watch: Whales. (J). (gr. 1-3). 75.00 (978-0-669-15103-9(3)); pap. 10.75 (978-0-669-15879-3(8)) Houghton Mifflin Harcourt School Pubs.

Antill, Sara. A Whale's Life. 2012. (Illus.). 24p. (J). 49.50 (978-1-4488-5105-8(X), PowerKids Pr.); pap. 8.25 (978-1-4488-5104-1(1), PowerKids Pr.); lib. bdg. 22.60 (978-1-4488-4978-9(0)) Rosen Publishing Group, Inc., The.

Atlantic, Leonard. 200-Year-Old Bowhead Whales! 2016. (World's Longest-Living Animals Ser.). 00024p. (J). pap. 8.15 **(978-1-4824-5631-8(1))** Stevens, Gareth Publishing LLLP.

Batten, Mary & dePaola, Tomie. Baby Orca. Rallis, Chris, illus. 2016. (ENG.). 32p. (J). (-k). bds. 3.99 *(978-0-448-48839-4(6)*, Grosset & Dunlap) Penguin Young Readers Group.

Battistoni, I. What a Whale! Learning the WH Sound. 2009. (PowerPhonics Ser.). 24p. (gr. 1-1). 39.90 *(978-1-60851-478-6(1)*, PowerKids Pr.) Rosen Publishing Group, Inc., The.

Beaton, Kathryn. Beluga Whales. 2015. (21st Century Basic Skills Library: Splash! Ser.). (ENG., Illus.). 24p. (J). (gr. 2-4). 24.21 *(978-1-63362-596-9(6)*, 206568) Cherry Lake Publishing.

Becker, John E. Gray Whales. 2004. (Returning Wildlife Ser.). (ENG., Illus.). 48p. (J). (gr. 4-7). 27.50 *(978-0-7377-2293-2(2)*, Greenhaven Pr., Inc.) Cengage Gale.

Berger, Melvin & Berger, Gilda. Whales. 2013. (Illus.). 16p. (J). pap. *(978-0-545-35168-3(5))* Scholastic, Inc.

Best, B. J. Humpback Whales. 2016. (Migrating Animals Ser.). 24p. (J). pap. 8.22 *(978-1-5026-2110-8(X))*; lib. bdg. 24.21 *(978-1-5026-2112-2(6))* Cavendish Square Publishing.

Bjorklund, Ruth. Blue Whales. 2013. (ENG.). 48p. (J). 28.00 *(978-0-531-23355-9(3))*; pap. 6.95 *(978-0-531-25153-9(5))* Scholastic Library Publishing.

Blake, Carly. Why Why Why... Do Dolphins Squeak? 2010. (Why Why Why Ser.). 32p. (J). (gr. 1-3). lib. bdg. 18.95 *(978-1-4222-1581-4(4))* Mason Crest.

Block, Cheryl. True Blue Friend. Takeshita, Gene, illus. 2006. 32p. (J). 21.95 *(978-0-9761625-2-0(0))* Block Publishing.

Books Are Fun 8 Title Animal Lives Set: Whales. 2006. (J). *(978-1-59566-308-5(8))* QEB Publishing Inc.

Bowley, Catherine. Giants of the Ocean Gold Band. 2016. (Cambridge Reading Adventures Ser.). (ENG.). 24p. pap. 7.19 *(978-1-107-55165-7(X))* Cambridge Univ. Pr.

Brannon, Cecelia H. Baby Whales at the Zoo. 2016. (All about Baby Zoo Animals Ser.). 24p. (J). (gr. 1-k). 22.60 *(978-0-7660-7563-4(X))* Enslow Pubs., Inc.

Bull, Peter & Ganeri, Anita. Explorers: Whales & Dolphins. 2013. (Explorers Ser.). (ENG., Illus.). 32p. (J). (gr. 2-5). 10.99 *(978-0-7534-6815-9(8)*, 9780753468159, Kingfisher) Roaring Brook Pr.

Burleigh, Robert. Trapped! (1 Hardcover/1 CD) A Whale's Rescue. Minor, Wendell, illus. 2017. (ENG.). (J). (gr. -1-1). 29.95 **(978-1-4301-2684-3(1))** Live Oak Media.

Butterfield, Moira. The Life Cycle of the Orca: Band 16/Sapphire. 2017. (ENG., Illus.). 56p. (J). pap. 8.99 **(978-0-00-820890-5(5))** HarperCollins Pubs. Ltd. GBR. Dist: Independent Pubs. Group.

Camm, Martin, illus. Meyers Buch der Wale und Delfine. (GER.). 48p. *(978-3-411-07451-8(5))* Bibliographisches Institut & F. A. Brockhaus AG DEU. Dist: i. b. d., Ltd.

Cantor, Rachel Anne. Beluga Whale. 2016. (Weird but Cute Ser.). (ENG., Illus.). 24p. (J). (gr. -1-3). 17.95 *(978-1-62724-851-8(X))* Bearport Publishing Co., Inc.

Capone, Lisa. Inland: The True Story of a North Atlantic Humpback Whale. 2011. (ENG., Illus.). 50p. (J). pap. 14.95 *(978-0-945980-92-6(2))* North Country Pr.

Carlson Berne, Emma. Whale Sharks: Bulletproof! 2013. (Animal Superpowers Ser.). 24p. (J). (gr. k-5). 22.60 *(978-1-4777-0749-4(2))*; pap. 8.25 *(978-1-4777-0839-2(1))* Rosen Publishing Group, Inc., The. (PowerKids Pr.).

Carmichael, L. E. Humpback Whale Migration. 2012. (Animal Migrations Ser.). (ENG., Illus.). 32p. (J). (gr. 2-5). lib. bdg. 29.93 *(978-1-60973-622-4(2)*, 201199) Child's World, Inc., The.

—Humpback Whales: A Journey to Warm Waters. 2016. (Illus.). 32p. (J). *(978-1-4896-4519-7(5))* Weigl Pubs., Inc.

Carr, Aaron. Humpback Whale. 2014. (Illus.). 24p. (J). *(978-1-62127-284-7(2))* Weigl Pubs., Inc.

—Narwhal. 2014. (J). *(978-1-4896-2637-0(9))* Weigl Pubs., Inc.

Catt, Thessaly. Migrating with the Humpback Whale. 2011. (Animal Journeys Ser.). (Illus.). 24p. (J). (gr. 1-4). lib. bdg. 22.60 *(978-1-4488-2543-1(1))*; (gr. 2-4). pap. 8.25 *(978-1-4488-2670-4(5)*, PowerKids Pr.) Rosen Publishing Group, Inc., The.

Christopherson, Sara Cohen. Top 50 Reasons to Care about Whales & Dolphins: Animals in Peril. 2010. (Top 50 Reasons to Care about Endangered Animals Ser.). (Illus.). 104p. (J). (gr. 5-9). 33.27 *(978-0-7660-3453-2(4))* Enslow Pubs., Inc.

Claybourne, Anna. Humpback Whales, 1 vol. 2013. (Living in the Wild: Sea Mammals Ser.). (ENG.). 48p. (gr. 4-6). pap. 9.95 *(978-1-4329-7069-7(0))*; lib. bdg. 33.32 *(978-1-4329-7062-8(3))* Heinemann-Raintree. (Heinemann InfoSearch).

—Orcas, 1 vol. 2013. (Animal Abilities Ser.). (ENG.). 32p. (gr. 2-4). 29.99 *(978-1-4109-5239-4(8))*; pap. 8.95 *(978-1-4109-5246-2(0))* Heinemann-Raintree. (Raintree Perspectives).

Coleman, Clara. Whales Work Together. 2017. (Animal Teamwork Ser.). 24p. (J). (gr. 7-8). 23.60 **(978-1-5081-5544-7(5)**, PowerKids Pr.) Rosen Publishing Group, Inc., The.

Cooper, Jason. Great Whale. 2003. (Life Cycles II Ser.). (Illus.). 24p. (J). 25.64 *(978-1-58952-709-6(7))* Rourke Educational Media.

Cooper, Sharon Katz. When Whales Cross the Sea: The Gray Whale Migration. Leonard, Tom, illus. 2015. (Extraordinary Migrations Ser.). (ENG.). 24p. (gr. 2-3). lib. bdg. 26.65 *(978-1-4795-6079-0(0))* Picture Window Bks.

Dahl, Michael. Do Whales Have Wings? A Book about Animal Bodies. D'Antonio, Sandra, illus. 2003. (Animals All Around Ser.). (ENG.). 24p. (gr. -1-2). per. 8.95 *(978-1-4048-0373-2(4))* Picture Window Bks.

Davidson, Susanna. Whales & Dolphins: Internet-Linked. 2009. (Discovery Nature Ser.). 48p. (YA). (gr. 3-18). 8.99 *(978-0-7945-2376-3(5)*, Usborne) EDC Publishing.

Davidson, Susannah. Whales & Dolphins. 2004. (Discovery Program Ser.). (Illus.). 48p. (J). lib. bdg. 16.95 *(978-1-58086-478-7(3))* EDC Publishing.

Davidson, Susannah, et al. Whales & Dolphins. Woodcock, John, illus. 2003. (Usborne Discovery Ser.). 48p. (J). pap. *(978-0-439-57780-9(2))*; pap. *(978-0-439-56060-3(8))* Scholastic, Inc.

Davies, Caroline, illus. Whale. 2013. (Shake & Play Bath Bks.). (ENG.). 8p. (J). (gr. -1 — 1). 5.99 *(978-1-4380-7342-2(9))* Barron's Educational Series, Inc.

Davies, Nicola. Big Blue Whale. Maland, Nick, illus. 2008. (Read, Listen, & Wonder Ser.). (ENG.). 32p. (J). (gr. -1-3). pap. 8.99 *(978-0-7636-3822-1(6))* Candlewick Pr.

—Big Blue Whale. Maland, Nick, illus. 2015. 32p. pap. 7.00 *(978-1-61003-542-2(9))* Center for the Collaborative Classroom.

Desmond, Jenni, creator. The Blue Whale. 2015. (ENG., Illus.). 48p. (J). (gr. -1-4). 17.95 *(978-1-59270-165-0(5))* Enchanted Lion Bks., LLC.

Dorling Kindersley Publishing Staff. Whales & Dolphins. 2013. (Eye Wonder Ser.). (ENG., Illus.). 56p. (J). (gr. k-4). 10.99 *(978-1-4654-0910-2(6)*, DK Children) Dorling Kindersley Publishing, Inc.

Drumlin, Sam. Orcas. 2013. (PowerKids Readers: Sea Friends Ser.). (ENG., Illus.). 24p. (J). (gr. k-2). pap. 8.25 *(978-1-4488-9748-3(3))*; lib. bdg. 22.60 *(978-1-4488-9645-5(2))* Rosen Publishing Group, Inc., The. (PowerKids Pr.).

—Orcas: Las Orcas. Alamán, Eduardo, tr. from ENG. 2013. (PowerKids Readers: Sea Friends / Los Amigos Del Mar Ser.). (SPA & ENG., Illus.). 24p. (J). (gr. k-2). lib. bdg. 22.60 *(978-1-4488-9975-3(3)*, PowerKids Pr.) Rosen Publishing Group, Inc., The.

Dunn, Joeming & Denham, Brian. Shamu: The 1st Killer Whale in Captivity, 1 vol. 2011. (Famous Firsts: Animals Making History Ser.). (ENG., Illus.). 32p. (YA). (gr. 3-6). 28.50 *(978-1-61641-642-3(4))* Magic Wagon.

Fact Atlas: Dolphins & Whales. 2009. (FACT ATLAS Ser.). 72p. (J). 14.95 *(978-0-8437-1865-2(X))* Hammond World Atlas Corp.

Gilkerson, Patricia. My Adventure with Whales. 2009. (ENG.). 44p. (J). 8.99 *(978-1-59092-475-4(4))* Blue Forge Pr.

Gill, Shelley. If I Were a Whale. Brooks, Erik, illus. 2017. (ENG.). 20p. (J). (— 1). bds. 9.99 *(978-1-63217-104-7(X)*, Little Bigfoot) Sasquatch Bks.

Gish, Melissa. Killer Whales. 2017. (J). **(978-1-60818-818-5(3)**, Creative Education) 2011. (ENG.). 48p. (J). (gr. 4-7). pap. 12.00 *(978-0-89812-554-2(5)*, Creative Paperbacks) 2010. 46p. (YA). (gr. 5-18). 23.95 *(978-1-58341-971-7(3)*, Creative Education) Creative Co., The.

Gish, Melissa. Whales. (Living Wild Ser.). (Illus.). (J). 2012. (ENG.). 48p. (gr. 4-7). pap. 12.00 *(978-0-89812-676-1(2)*, Creative Paperbacks) 2011. 46p. 35.65 *(978-1-60818-084-4(0)*, Creative Education) Creative Co., The.

Green, Jen. Whales. 2008. (Nature's Children Ser.). (Illus.). 52p. *(978-0-7172-6264-9(2))* Grolier, Ltd.

Greenberg, Daniel A. & Hess, Nina. Whales. 2009. (Benchmark Rockets Ser.). 24p. (gr. 1-18). 24.21 *(978-0-7614-4346-9(0)*, Benchmark Bks.) Marshall Cavendish Corp.

Gunderson, Megan M. Beluga Whales, 1 vol. 2011. (Whales Set 1 *2011 Ser.). (ENG.). 24p. (J). (gr. 2-5). 25.65 *(978-1-61613-446-4(1))* ABDO Publishing Co.

—Blue Whales, 1 vol. 2011. (Whales Set 1 *2011 Ser.). (ENG.). 24p. (J). (gr. 2-5). 25.65 *(978-1-61613-447-1(X))* ABDO Publishing Co.

—Gray Whales, 1 vol. 2011. (Whales Set 1 *2011 Ser.). (ENG.). 24p. 25.65 *(978-1-61613-448-8(8)*, Checkerboard Library) ABDO Publishing Co.

—Humpback Whales, 1 vol. 2011. (Whales Set 1 *2011 Ser.). (ENG.). 24p. 25.65 *(978-1-61613-449-5(6)*, Checkerboard Library) ABDO Publishing Co.

—Killer Whales, 1 vol. 2011. (Whales Set 1 *2011 Ser.). (ENG.). 24p. 25.65 *(978-1-61613-450-1(X)*, Checkerboard Library) ABDO Publishing Co.

—Sperm Whales, 1 vol. 2011. (Whales Set 1 *2011 Ser.). (ENG.). 24p. 25.65 *(978-1-61613-451-8(8)*, Checkerboard Library) ABDO Publishing Co.

Gustafson, Sarah. Whales, Dolphins, & More Marine Mammals. 2005. (Illus.). 48p. (J). pap. *(978-0-439-71189-0(4))* Scholastic, Inc.

Halfmann, Janet. Narwhal: The Unicorn of the Sea. Petruccio, Steven James, illus. 2008. (ENG.). 32p. (J). (gr. -1-2). 19.95 *(978-1-59249-872-7(8))* Soundprints.

—Narwhal: Unicorn of the Sea. Petruccio, Steven James, illus. 2008. (ENG.). 32p. (J). (gr. -1-2). pap. 9.95 *(978-1-59249-871-0(X))* Soundprints.

Haney, Johannah. Whales. 2008. (Endangered! Ser.). 48p. (gr. 3-18). lib. bdg. 29.93 *(978-0-7614-2990-6(5)*, Benchmark Bks.) Marshall Cavendish Corp.

Hansen, Grace. Whales, 1 vol. 2014. (Ocean Life Ser.). (ENG.). 24p. (J). (gr. 2-4). lib. bdg. 28.50 *(978-1-62970-713-6(9))* ABDO Publishing Co.

Hardyman, Robyn. Whales. 2008. (World of Animals Ser.). 32p. (gr. 2-5). 31.35 *(978-1-933834-34-4(X))* Brown Bear Bks.

Haswell, Peter. Whales. 2009. (Wild Reads Ser.). (ENG., Illus.). 32p. (YA). (gr. k). pap. 4.95 *(978-0-19-911934-9(1))* Oxford Univ. Pr., Inc.

Heos, Bridget. Do You Really Want to Meet an Orca? Fabbri, Daniele, illus. 2017. (Do You Really Want to Meet... Wild Animals? Ser.). (ENG.). 24p. (J). (gr. 1-3). pap. 8.99 *(978-1-68152-118-3(0))* Amicus.

—Do You Really Want to Meet an Orca? Fabbri, Daniele, illus. 2016. (Do You Really Want to Meet... Wild Animals? Ser.). (ENG.). 24p. (J). (gr. k-3). 20.95 *(978-1-60753-947-6(0))* Amicus Publishing.

Herriges, Ann. Whales. 2006. (Oceans Alive Ser.). (ENG., Illus.). 24p. (J). (gr. k-3). lib. bdg. 25.95 *(978-1-60014-023-5(8))* Bellwether Media.

Hirsch, Rebecca E. Humpback Whales: Musical Migrating Mammals. 2015. (Comparing Animal Traits Ser.). (ENG., Illus.). 32p. (gr. 2-4). 39.99 *(978-1-4677-8925-7(9)*, Lerner Digital); (J). pap. 8.99 *(978-1-4677-6062-1(5)*, Lerner Pubns.); (J). lib. bdg. 26.65 *(978-1-4677-5579-5(6)*, Lerner Pubns.) Lerner Publishing Group.

Hodson, Sally. Granny's Clan: A Tale of Wild Orcas. Jones, Ann, illus. 2012. (ENG.). 32p. (J). (gr. k-4). 16.95 *(978-1-58469-171-6(9))*; pap. 8.95 *(978-1-58469-172-3(7))* Dawn Pubns.

Hoyt, Erich. Whale Rescue: Changing the Future for Endangered Wildlife. 2005. (Firefly Animal Rescue Ser.). (ENG., Illus.). 64p. (J). (gr. 5-8). 19.95 *(978-1-55297-601-2(7)*, 9781552976012); pap. 9.95 *(978-1-55297-600-5(9)*, 9781552976005) Firefly Bks., Ltd.

Hutchison, Patricia. Blue Whales. 2015. (Endangered Animals Ser.). (ENG.). 24p. (J). (gr. 1-4). 27.07 *(978-1-63143-966-7(9)*, 208801) Child's World, Inc., The.

Imbriaco, Alison. The Sperm Whale: Help Save This Endangered Species! 2008. (Saving Endangered Species Ser.). (Illus.). 128p. (J). (gr. 3-7). lib. bdg. 34.60 *(978-1-59845-071-2(9)*, MyReportLinks.com Bks.) Enslow Pubs., Inc.

Johnson, Elizabeth R. Beluga Whales. 2016. (Sea Life Ser.). (ENG., Illus.). 24p. (J). (gr. k-1). lib. bdg. 26.65 *(978-1-5157-2081-2(0))* Capstone Press of Coughlan Cos.

—Orcas. 2017. (J). *(978-1-5157-2083-6(7))* 2016. (ENG.). 24p. lib. bdg. 26.65 *(978-1-5157-2079-9(9)*, Pebble Plus) Capstone Press of Coughlan Cos.

Jones, Michael P. Whales — The Gentle Giants: Calendar 1988. (Illus.). (J). 10.00 *(978-0-89904-211-4(2))*; 25.00 *(978-0-89904-213-8(9))* Crumb Elbow Publishing.

Jones, Tracy. Whales & Dolphins. 2011. (Illus.). 16p. (J). *(978-0-545-24793-1(4))* Scholastic, Inc.

Kalman, Bobbie. Wonderful Whales. 2005. (Living Ocean Ser.). (ENG., Illus.). 32p. (J). (gr. 3-4). lib. bdg. *(978-0-7787-1302-9(4))* Crabtree Publishing Co.

Kalman, Bobbie & Thal, Karuna. Les Rorquals. 2005. (Petit Monde Vivant Ser.). (FRE., Illus.). 32p. (J). pap. 9.95 *(978-2-89579-049-5(3))* Bayard Canada Livres CAN. Dist: Crabtree Publishing Co.

Kant, Tanya. The Migration of a Whale. Bergin, Mark, illus. 2008. (Amaze Ser.). (ENG.). 32p. (J). (gr. k-3). 27.00 *(978-0-531-24049-6(5))*; pap. 8.95 *(978-0-531-23803-5(2))* Scholastic Library Publishing. (Children's Pr.).

Katirgis, Jane & Reiter, Chris. Endangered Blue Whales. 2015. (Wildlife at Risk Ser.). (ENG.). 48p. (J). (gr. 6-6). pap. 11.70 *(978-0-7660-6888-9(9))*; (Illus.). 27.93 *(978-0-7660-6890-2(0))* Enslow Pubs., Inc.

Kennedy, Paul E. Fun with Whales Stencils. 2008. (Dover Stencils Ser.). (ENG., Illus.). (J). (gr. -1-5). pap. 1.50 *(978-0-486-46687-3(6))* Dover Pubns., Inc.

Kennington, Tammy. Beluga Whales. 2014. (21st Century Skills Library: Exploring Our Oceans Ser.). (ENG.). 32p. (J). (gr. 3-6). 28.50 *(978-1-62431-603-6(4)*, 203196) Cherry Lake Publishing.

Kerrod, Robin. Exploring Nature: Whales & Dolphins. 2014. (ENG., Illus.). 64p. (J). (gr. 3-7). 12.99 *(978-1-84322-912-4(9)*, Armadillo) Anness Publishing GBR. Dist: National Bk. Network.

—Whales & Dolphins. 2008. (Nature Watch Ser.). (ENG., Illus.). 64p. (J). (gr. 4-7). 14.99 *(978-0-7548-1875-5(6))* Anness Publishing GBR. Dist: National Bk. Network.

Killer Whales, 6 bks. 2005. (Animal Predators Ser.). (Illus.). 40p. (J). (gr. 3-6). pap. 46.95 *(978-0-8225-5492-9(5))* Lerner Publishing Group.

Kinder, Cando. Birth of Whale Read-Along. (J). 7.95 incl. audio *(978-0-8136-0649-1(7))* Modern Curriculum Pr.

King, Zelda. Orcas. 2012. (Illus.). 24p. (J). 49.50 *(978-1-4488-5146-1(7)*, PowerKids Pr.); pap. 8.25 *(978-1-4488-5145-4(9)*, PowerKids Pr.); lib. bdg. 22.60 *(978-1-4488-5335-9(4))* Rosen Publishing Group, Inc., The.

Klepeis, Alicia. Orcas on the Hunt. 2017. (Searchlight Books (tm) — Predators Ser.). (ENG.). (J). (gr. 3-5). pap. 9.99 **(978-1-5124-5609-7(8))**; (Illus.). lib. bdg. 30.65 **(978-1-5124-3398-2(5))** Lerner Publishing Group.

Kluth, Paula & Schwarz, Patrick. Pedro's Whale, 1 vol. 2010. (ENG., Illus.). 32p. (J). 18.95 *(978-1-59857-160-8(5))* Brookes Publishing.

Kops, Deborah. The Humpback Whale: Help Save This Endangered Species! 2006. (Saving Endangered Species Ser.). (Illus.). 128p. (J). (gr. 5-9). lib. bdg. 33.27 *(978-1-59845-036-1(0)*, MyReportLinks.com Bks.) Enslow Pubs., Inc.

Kralovansky, Susan. Whale or Fish?, 1 vol. 2014. (This or That? Ser.). (ENG.). 24p. (J). (gr. 5-10). lib. bdg. 25.65 *(978-1-62403-290-5(7)*, Super SandCastle) ABDO Publishing Co.

Kratt, Chris & Kratt, Martin. Wild Sea Creatures: Sharks, Whales & Dolphins! 2014. (Step into Reading Ser.). (ENG., Illus.). 32p. (J). (gr. -1-1). lib. bdg. 12.99 *(978-0-553-49902-5(5)*, Random Hse. Bks. for Young Readers) Random Hse. Children's Bks.

—Wild Sea Creatures: Sharks, Whales, & Dolphins! 2014. (Step into Reading Ser.). (ENG., Illus.). 32p. (J). (gr. -1-1). 3.99 *(978-0-553-49901-8(7)*, Random Hse. Bks. for Young Readers) Random Hse. Children's Bks.

Landau, Elaine. Beluga Whales. 2010. (Animals of the Snow & Ice Ser.). (Illus.). 32p. (J). (gr. 1-3). lib. bdg. 23.94 *(978-0-7660-3459-4(3))* Enslow Pubs., Inc.

Laughlin, Kara L. Whales. 2017. (In the Deep Blue Sea Ser.). (ENG.). 24p. (J). (gr. k-3). lib. bdg. 27.07 *(978-1-5038-1695-4(8)*, 211529) Child's World, Inc., The.

Leaf, Christina. Humpback Whales. (Humpback Whales Ser.). 24p. (J). (gr. k-3). 2017. pap. 6.99 **(978-1-61891-265-7(8))** 2016. (ENG., Illus.). 25.95 *(978-1-62617-417-7(2))* Bellwether Media. (Blastoff! Readers).

Leaf, Christina. Narwhal. 2014. (Extremely Weird Animals Ser.). (ENG., Illus.). 24p. (J). (gr. 3-8). lib. bdg. 25.95 *(978-1-62617-075-9(4)*, Pilot Bks.) Bellwether Media.

Lee, Justin. How to Draw Whales. 2009. (Kid's Guide to Drawing Ser.). 24p. (gr. 3-3). 47.90 *(978-1-61511-042-1(9)*, PowerKids Pr.) Rosen Publishing Group, Inc., The.

León, Vicki. A Pod of Killer Whales: The Mysterious Life of the Intelligent Orca. Foott, Jeff, photos by. 2nd ed. 2006. (Jean-Michel Cousteau Presents Ser.). (ENG., Illus.). 48p. (J). (gr. 4-9). pap. 9.95 *(978-0-9766134-7-3(6))* London Town Pr.

Lindeen, Carol K. & Lugtu, Carol J. Whales [Scholastic]. 2010. (Under the Sea Ser.). 24p. pap. 0.50 *(978-1-4296-5065-6(6)*, Pebble Plus) Capstone Press of Coughlan Cos.

Lindsey, Marta. Little Gray's Great Migration, 1 vol. Gabriel, Andrea, illus. 2015. (ENG.). 32p. (J). (gr. k-3). 17.95 *(978-1-62855-452-6(5))* Arbordale Publishing.

Little & Large Sticker Activity Whales & Dolphins. 2008. 24p. pap. *(978-1-84810-064-0(7))* Miles Kelly Publishing, Ltd.

Lourie, Peter. Whaling Season: A Year in the Life of an Arctic Whale Scientist. 2015. (Scientists in the Field Ser.). (ENG., Illus.). 80p. (J). (gr. 5-7). pap. 9.99 *(978-0-544-58241-5(1)*, HMH Books For Young Readers) Houghton Mifflin Harcourt Publishing Co.

Lunde, Darrin P. Hello, Baby Beluga. Wynne, Patricia J., illus. 2016. (ENG.). 14p. (J). (— 1). bds. 6.95 *(978-1-58089-525-5(5))* Charlesbridge Publishing, Inc.

Lunde, Darrin P. & Stock, Catherine. Hello, Baby Beluga. Wynne, Patricia J., illus. 2011. (ENG.). 32p. (J). (gr. -1-2). pap. 6.95 *(978-1-57091-740-0(X))* Charlesbridge Publishing, Inc.

Lunis, Natalie. Humpback Whale: The Singer. 2011. (Animal Loudmouths: Noisy Animals Ser.). 24p. (YA). (gr. k-3). lib. bdg. 22.61 *(978-1-61772-280-6(4))* Bearport Publishing Co., Inc.

—Killer Whale: The World's Largest Dolphin. 2010. (More SuperSized! Ser.). (Illus.). 24p. (J). (gr. k-3). lib. bdg. 22.61 *(978-1-936087-27-3(8))* Bearport Publishing Co., Inc.

MacMillan, Dianne M. Humpback Whales. 2003. (Nature Watch Ser.). (ENG., Illus.). 48p. (J). (gr. 4-8). 27.93 *(978-1-57505-347-9(0))* Lerner Publishing Group.

Malam, John. Killer Whales. 2008. (Scary Creatures Ser.). (ENG., Illus.). 32p. (J). (gr. 2-7). 27.00 *(978-0-531-20447-4(2))* Scholastic Library Publishing.

—Killer Whales - Scary Creatures. 2008. (Scary Creatures Ser.). (ENG., Illus.). 32p. (J). (gr. 2-7). pap. 8.95 *(978-0-531-21006-2(5)*, Watts, Franklin) Scholastic Library Publishing.

Markle, Sandra. Killer Whales. (Animal Predators Ser.). 40p. 2005. (J). (gr. 4-6). pap. 7.95 *(978-1-57505-743-9(3))* 2004. (ENG., Illus.). (gr. 3-6). lib. bdg. 26.60 *(978-1-57505-728-6(X))* Lerner Publishing Group.

Markle, Sandra. Ranger Rick: I Wish I Was an Orca. 2017. (I Can Read Level 1 Ser.). 32p. (J). (gr. -1-3). pap. 3.99 **(978-0-06-243207-0(9))** HarperCollins Pubs.

Marsh, Laura. Great Migrations Whales. 2010. (Readers Ser.). (ENG., Illus.). 48p. (J). (gr. 2-4). pap. 3.99 *(978-1-4263-0745-4(4)*, National Geographic Children's Bks.) National Geographic Society.

—Whales. 2010. (Readers Ser.). (ENG., Illus.). 48p. (J). (gr. 2-4). 13.90 *(978-1-4263-0746-1(2)*, National Geographic Children's Bks.) National Geographic Society.

Marsico, Katie. Narwhal, 1 vol. 2011. (Day in the Life: Polar Animals Ser.). (ENG.). 24p. (gr. k-2). pap. 6.79 *(978-1-4329-5339-3(7)*, Heinemann Read & Learn) Heinemann-Raintree.

Matero, Robert. The Birth of a Humpback Whale. Johnson, Pamela, illus. 2014. (ENG.). 64p. (J). (gr. 3-7). 13.99 *(978-1-4814-4460-6(3)*, Simon & Schuster Bks. For Young Readers) Simon & Schuster Bks. For Young Readers.

McDowell, Pamela. Manta Rays. 2014. (J). *(978-1-4896-1074-4(X))* Weigl Pubs., Inc.

McNeill, Michele Babineau. Whales. 2008. (Illus.). 32p. (J). *(978-0-545-08465-9(2))* Scholastic, Inc.

Meachen Rau, Dana. Adivina Quién Caza. 2008. (Adivina Quién Ser.). (SPA.). 32p. (gr. k-2). lib. bdg. 15.95 *(978-0-7614-3461-0(5)*, Benchmark Bks.) Marshall Cavendish Corp.

—La Ballena en el Oceano. 2006. (Naturaleza Ser.). (SPA., Illus.). 24p. (gr. k-1). lib. bdg. 15.95 *(978-0-7614-2412-3(1)*, Benchmark Bks.) Marshall Cavendish Corp.

—The Whale in the Water. 2006. (Nature Ser.). (SPA., Illus.). 24p. (gr. k-1). lib. bdg. 15.95 *(978-0-7614-2307-2(9)*, Benchmark Bks.) Marshall Cavendish Corp.

Meister, Cari. Whales. 2012. (Illus.). 24p. (J). lib. bdg. 25.65 *(978-1-62031-009-0(0))* Jump! Inc.

Miller, Sara Swan. Whales of the Arctic. 2009. (Brrr! Polar Animals Ser.). (Illus.). 24p. (J). pap. 8.25 *(978-1-4358-3147-6(0)*, 1291789, PowerKids Pr.); 24p. (gr. 2-3). 42.50 *(978-1-61511-760-4(1)*, PowerKids Pr.); (J). (gr. k-3). lib. bdg. 22.60 *(978-1-4358-2743-1(0))* Rosen Publishing Group, Inc., The.

Miller-Schroeder, Patricia. Blue Whales. 2013. (Illus.). 48p. (J). *(978-1-61913-423-2(3))* Weigl Pubs., Inc.

—Blue Whales, with Code. 2012. (Animals on the Brink Ser.). (ENG., Illus.). 48p. (J). (gr. 5-9). pap. 14.95 *(978-1-61913-424-9(1)*, AV2 by Weigl) Weigl Pubs., Inc.

Morgan, Sally. Whales. 2015. (ENG.). 24p. (J). (gr. 3-5). 23.99 *(978-1-939581-86-0(9))* QEB Publishing Inc.

Morgan, Sally & Teacher Created Resources Staff. Whales. 2006. (Animal Lives Ser.). (ENG., Illus.). 32p. (gr. -1-3). pap. 7.99 *(978-1-4206-8157-4(5))* Teacher Created Resources, Inc.

Murray, Julie. Beluga Whales, 1 vol. (Arctic Animals Ser.). (ENG.). (J). 2013. 32p. (gr. 2-5). lib. bdg. 28.50 *(978-1-61783-798-2(9)*, Big Buddy Bks.) 2003. 24p. (gr. 1-4). 25.65 *(978-1-57765-709-5(8))* ABDO Publishing Co.

—Blue Whales, 1 vol. 2005. (Animal Kingdom Set Ii Ser.). (ENG., Illus.). 24p. (gr. k-4). 25.65 *(978-1-59197-303-4(1)*, Buddy Bks.) ABDO Publishing Co.

—Gray Whales, 1 vol. 2005. (Animal Kingdom Set Ii Ser.). (ENG., Illus.). 24p. (gr. k-4). 25.65 *(978-1-59197-318-8(X)*, Buddy Bks.) ABDO Publishing Co.

—Humpback Whales, 1 vol. 2003. (Buddy Book Ser.). (ENG., Illus.). 24p. (J). (gr. k-4). 25.65 *(978-1-57765-708-8(X)*, Buddy Bks.) ABDO Publishing Co.

Nagelhout, Ryan. Whales. 2013. (Underwater World Ser.). (Illus.). 24p. (J). (gr. k-2). pap. 8.15 *(978-1-4339-8583-6(7))*; lib. bdg. 22.60 *(978-1-4339-8582-9(9))* Stevens, Gareth Publishing LLLP.

—Whales: Ballenas. 2013. (Underwater World / el Mundo Submarino Ser.). (SPA & ENG., Illus.). 24p. (J). (gr. k-2). lib. bdg. 22.60 *(978-1-4339-8788-5(0))* Stevens, Gareth Publishing LLLP.

Nicklin, Flip, et al. Face to Face with Whales. 2010. (Face to Face with Animals Ser.). (ENG., Illus.). 32p. (J). (gr. 2-5). pap. 6.95 *(978-1-4263-0697-6(0)*, National Geographic Children's Bks.) National Geographic Society.

Norman, Kim & American Museum of Natural History Staff. Whales. Schwartz, Carol, illus. 2012. (Storytime Stickers Ser.). (ENG.). 16p. (J). (gr. k-2). pap. 5.95 *(978-1-4027-7350-1(1))* Sterling Publishing Co., Inc.

Nuzzolo, Deborah & Parham, Donna. Whales K-3, 1. 2003. (Illus.). 28p. (J). (gr. k-3). tchr.'s training gde. ed. 5.99 *(978-1-893698-33-8(5)*, T15) SeaWorld, Inc.

O'Connell, Jennifer. The Eye of the Whale: A Rescue Story, 1 vol. O'Connell, Jennifer, illus. 2013. (Tilbury House Nature Book Ser.: 0). (ENG., Illus.). 32p. (gr. 1-7). 17.95 *(978-0-88448-335-9(5)*, 884335) Tilbury Hse. Pubs.

W X Y Z

Oldfield, Dawn Bluemel. Killer Whale: Water Bullet! 2010. (Blink of an Eye: Superfast Animals Ser.). 24p. (J). (gr. k-3). lib. bdg. 22.61 *(978-1-936087-92-1(8))* Bearport Publishing Co., Inc.

O'Loughlin, Chloe & Borrowman, Mary. The Rescue of Nanoose, 1 vol. Wang, Jacqueline, illus. 2004. (ENG.). 32p. (J). pap. *(978-1-894898-20-1(6))* TouchWood Editions.

Owen, Ruth. Beluga Whales. 2013. (Polar Animals: Life in the Freezer Ser.). (ENG., Illus.). 32p. (gr. k-5). 25.25 *(978-1-4777-0221-5(0))*; pap. 10.00 *(978-1-4777-0229-1(6))* Windmill Bks.

—Blue Whales, 1. 2014. (Dr. Bob's Amazing World of Animals Ser.). (ENG.). 32p. (J). (gr. k-5). 27.50 *(978-1-4777-9028-1(4),* Windmill Bks.) Rosen Publishing Group, Inc., The.

—Orca Calves. 2012. (Water Babies Ser.). 24p. (J). (gr. -1-3). lib. bdg. 21.32 *(978-1-61772-600-2(1))* Bearport Publishing Co., Inc.

Paige, Joy. The Blue Whale: World's Largest Mammal. 2009. (Record-Breaking Animals Ser.). 24p. (gr. 1-1). 42.50 *(978-1-60852-437-2(X),* PowerKids Pr.) Rosen Publishing Group, Inc., The.

Pallotta, Jerry. Killer Whale vs. Great White Shark. Bolster, Rob, illus. 2016. (Who Would Win? Ser.). (ENG.). 32p. (J). (gr. 2-5). pap. 3.99 *(978-0-545-16075-9(8))* Scholastic, Inc.

—Whale vs. Giant Squid. Bolster, Rob, illus. 2016. (Who Would Win? Ser.). (ENG.). 32p. (J). (gr. 1-3). pap. 3.99 *(978-0-545-30173-2(4))* Scholastic, Inc.

Papastavrou, Vassili. Whale. Dorling Kindersley Publishing Staff, ed. 2004. (DK Eyewitness Bks.). (ENG., Illus.). 72p. (J). (gr. 3-7). 16.99 *(978-0-7566-0739-5(6),* DK Children) Dorling Kindersley Publishing, Inc.

Parker, Steve. Wales & Dolphins. 2010. (Remarkable Man & Beast Ser.). (Illus.). 48p. (J). (gr. 3-18). lib. bdg. 19.95 *(978-1-4222-1978-2(X))* Mason Crest.

—Whales & Dolphins. 2015. (100 Facts You Should Know Ser.). (ENG., Illus.). 48p. (J). (gr. 4-5). pap. 14.05 *(978-1-4824-3211-4(0))* Stevens, Gareth Publishing LLLP.

Parker, Steve & Dewan, Ted. Inside the Whale & Other Animals. (Illus.). (J). 18.95 *(978-0-590-73869-9(0))* Scholastic, Inc.

Payment, Simone. Saving the Endangered Blue Whale, 01 vols., 1. 2016. (Conservation of Endangered Species Ser.). (ENG., Illus.). 32p. (J). pap. 12.90 *(978-1-5081-0052-2(7),* Britannica Educational Publishing) Rosen Publishing Group, Inc., The.

Petrie, Kristin. Baird's Beaked Whales, 1 vol. 2006. (Whales Set 2 Ser.). (ENG., Illus.). 24p. (gr. k-6). 25.65 *(978-1-59679-306-4(6),* Checkerboard Library) ABDO Publishing Co.

—Bowhead Whales, 1 vol. 2006. (Whales Set 2 Ser.). (ENG., Illus.). 24p. (gr. k-6). 25.65 *(978-1-59679-307-1(4),* Checkerboard Library) ABDO Publishing Co.

—Dwarf Sperm Whales, 1 vol. 2006. (Whales Set 2 Ser.). (ENG., Illus.). 24p. (gr. k-6). 25.65 *(978-1-59679-308-8(2),* Checkerboard Library) ABDO Publishing Co.

—Fin Whales, 1 vol. 2006. (Whales Set 2 Ser.). (ENG., Illus.). 24p. (gr. k-6). 25.65 *(978-1-59679-309-5(0),* Checkerboard Library) ABDO Publishing Co.

—Minke Whales, 1 vol. 2006. (Whales Set 2 Ser.). (ENG., Illus.). 24p. (gr. k-6). 25.65 *(978-1-59679-310-1(4),* Checkerboard Library) ABDO Publishing Co.

—Pilot Whales, 1 vol. 2006. (Whales Set 2 Ser.). (ENG., Illus.). 24p. (gr. k-6). 25.65 *(978-1-59679-311-8(2),* Checkerboard Library) ABDO Publishing Co.

Pingry, Patricia A. Baby Beluga. Rose, Drew, illus. 2006. (SeaWorld Library: Vol. 6). 26p. (J). (gr. -1-k). bds. 6.95 *(978-0-8249-6643-0(0),* Ideal Pubns.) Worthy Publishing.

Pioch, Melissa. Amazing Animals: Wild Whales: Addition & Subtraction (Grade 3) 2017. (Mathematics Readers Ser.). (Illus.). 32p. (J). (gr. 3-3). pap. 8.99 ***(978-1-4807-5795-0(0))*** Teacher Created Materials, Inc.

Polinsky, Paige V. Humpback Whale: Marvelous Musician. 2016. (ENG., Illus.). 24p. (J). *(978-1-68078-149-6(9))* ABDO Publishing Co.

Portman, Michael. Whales in Danger. 2011. (Animals at Risk Ser.). (Illus.). 24p. (J). (gr. 2-5). 22.60 *(978-1-4339-5814-4(7))*; pap. 8.15 *(978-1-4339-5816-8(3))* Stevens, Gareth Publishing LLLP. (Gareth Stevens Learning Library).

Pringle, Laurence. Whales! Strange & Wonderful. Henderson, Meryl, illus. 2012. (Strange & Wonderful Ser.). (ENG.). 32p. (J). (gr. 2-4). pap. 9.95 *(978-1-59078-917-9(2))* Boyds Mills Pr.

Raff, Courtney Granet. Giant of the Sea: The Story of a Sperm Whale. Gould, Shawn, illus. 2005. (Smithsonian Oceanic Collection). (ENG.). 32p. (J). (gr. -1-2). 15.95 *(978-1-931465-71-7(1),* B4023) Soundprints.

Rake, Jody Sullivan. Beluga Whales up Close [Scholastic]. 2011. (Whales & Dolphins up Close Ser.). 24p. pap. 0.50 *(978-1-4296-6322-9(7),* First Facts) Capstone Press of Coughlan Cos.

—Blue Whales up Close [Scholastic]. 2011. (Whales & Dolphins up Close Ser.). 24p. pap. 0.50 *(978-1-4296-6324-3(3),* First Facts) Capstone Press of Coughlan Cos.

—Killer Whales up Close [Scholastic]. 2011. (Whales & Dolphins up Close Ser.). 24p. pap. 0.50 *(978-1-4296-6323-6(5),* First Facts) Capstone Press of Coughlan Cos.

—Orcas, 1 vol. 2012. (Marine Mammals Ser.). (ENG., Illus.). 24p. (gr. k-1). lib. bdg. 26.65 *(978-1-4296-8717-1(7),* Pebble Plus) Capstone Press of Coughlan Cos.

Rao, Lisa. Whales. 2008. (Smart Animals! Ser.). (Illus.). 32p. (J). (gr. 2-5). lib. bdg. 25.27 *(978-1-59716-579-2(4))* Bearport Publishing Co., Inc.

Rau, Dana Meachen. Guess Who Hunts/Adivina Quién Caza. Victory Productions, Inc. Staff, tr. from ENG. 2007. (Guess Who/Adivina Quién Ser.). (SPA & ENG.). 32p. (gr. k-2). 15.95 *(978-0-7614-3486-3(0))* Marshall Cavendish Corp.

Read, Tracy. Exploring the World of Whales. 2017. (Exploring the World Of Ser.). (ENG., Illus.). 24p. (J). (gr. 3-7). 16.95 ***(978-1-77085-948-7(9),*** 9781770859487); pap. 6.95 ***(978-1-77085-949-4(7),*** 9781770859494) Firefly Bks., Ltd.

Reher, Matt. Blue Whale Babies. 2015. (2G Marine Life Ser.). (ENG., Illus.). 24p. (J). pap. 5.99 *(978-1-63437-084-4(8))* American Reading Co.

Reiter, Chris. The Blue Whale: A MyReportLinks.com Book. 2003. (Endangered & Threatened Animals Ser.). (Illus.). 48p. (J). (gr. 4-10). lib. bdg. 26.60 *(978-0-7660-5055-6(6),* MyReportLinks.com Bks.) Enslow Pubs., Inc.

Rennert, Violette. Little Whales. 2005. (Born to Be Wild Ser.). (Illus.). 24p. (gr. k-3). lib. bdg. 23.00 *(978-0-8368-4740-6(7),* Gareth Stevens Learning Library) Stevens, Gareth Publishing LLLP.

Riehecky, Janet. Killer Whales: On the Hunt. 2016. (Killer Animals Ser.). (ENG.). 32p. (gr. 1-2). pap. 7.95 *(978-1-5157-6240-9(8),* Blazers) Capstone Press of Coughlan Cos.

Riggs, Kate. Amazing Animals: Whales. 2014. (Illus.). 24p. (J). pap. 7.50 *(978-1-60818-351-7(3))* Creative Co., The.

—Amazing Animals: Killer Whales. 2012. (Amazing Animals Ser.). (ENG., Illus.). 24p. (J). (gr. 1-3). pap. 8.99 *(978-0-89812-694-5(0),* Creative Paperbacks) Creative Co., The.

—Amazing Animals: Whales. 2014. (Amazing Animals Ser.). (ENG.). 24p. (J). (gr. 1-3). pap. 8.99 *(978-0-89812-930-4(3),* Creative Paperbacks) Creative Co., The.

—Killer Whales. (J). 2017. ***(978-1-60818-869-7(8))*** 2012. (Illus.). 24p. 25.65 *(978-1-60818-109-4(X))* Creative Co., The. (Creative Education).

—Seedlings: Killer Whales. 2017. (Seedlings Ser.). (ENG.). 24p. (J). (gr. -1-1). pap. 7.99 ***(978-1-62832-484-6(8),*** Creative Paperbacks) Creative Co., The.

—Seedlings: Whales. 2015. (Seedlings Ser.). (ENG.). 24p. (J). (gr. -1-1). pap. 7.99 *(978-1-62832-117-3(2),* Creative Paperbacks) Creative Co., The.

—Whales. 2015. (J). *(978-1-60818-517-7(6),* Creative Education) Creative Co., The.

Ripley's Believe It Or Not! Staff & Ripley's Believe It Or Not! Editors, compiled by. Whales & Dolphins: Believe It or Not! 2014. (Twist Ser.: 11). (ENG., Illus.). 48p. (J). 12.95 *(978-1-60991-114-0(8))* Ripley Entertainment, Inc.

Rose, Simon. Belugas. 2010. (Illus.). 24p. *(978-1-55388-674-7(7))*; pap. *(978-1-55388-675-4(5))* Weigl Educational Pubs. Ltd.

Rosenthal, Sue. Whales. McGinty, Mick, illus. 2003. (Magic School Bus Fact Finder Ser.). (ENG.). 96p. (J). pap. 4.99 *(978-0-439-38174-1(6))* Scholastic, Inc.

Roumanis, Alexis. Blue Marlin. 2014. (J). *(978-1-4896-1086-7(3))* Weigl Pubs., Inc.

Rountree, Monica, tr. Ballenas. 2003. (Zoobooks Ser.). Orig. Title: Whales. (SPA., Illus.). 24p. (J). (gr. 1-7). lib. bdg. 15.95 *(978-1-888153-84-2(9))* Wildlife Education, Ltd.

Royston, Angela. Blue Whales. (Amazing Animals Ser.). (Illus.). 24p. (J). 2009. (gr. 2-4). pap. 8.95 *(978-1-60596-149-1(3))* 2009. (gr. 2-4). lib. bdg. 24.45 *(978-1-60596-148-4(5))* 2003. lib. bdg. 21.35 *(978-1-58340-226-9(8))* Weigl Pubs., Inc.

Ruffin, Fran. Whales / Ballenas. 2009. (My World of Animals / Yo y los animales Ser.). (ENG & SPA.). 24p. (gr. 1-1). 37.50 *(978-1-61514-719-9(5),* Editorial Buenas Letras) Rosen Publishing Group, Inc., The.

Ruffin, Frances E. Whales: Ballenas. Beullens, Nathalie, tr. 2004. (My World of Animals Ser.). (ENG & SPA., Illus.). 24p. (J). (gr. k-1). lib. bdg. 16.00 *(978-1-4042-7520-1(7),* PowerKids Pr.) Rosen Publishing Group, Inc., The.

Sayre, April Pulley. Here Come the Humpbacks! Hogan, Jamie, illus. 2013. (ENG.). 40p. (J). (gr. -1-3). pap. 7.95 *(978-1-58089-406-7(2))*; lib. bdg. 17.95 *(978-1-58089-405-0(4))* Charlesbridge Publishing, Inc.

Scherm, Deedra. The Whale & Jonah: A Story of Obedience & Forgiveness. Dreyer, Laura, illus. 2007. (ENG.). 20p. 7.99 *(978-1-934789-00-1(3))* Lemon Vision Productions.

Schuh, Mari C. Orcas. 2017. (Black & White Animals Ser.). (ENG., Illus.). 24p. (gr. k-1). lib. bdg. 21.99 *(978-1-5157-3373-7(4))* Capstone Press of Coughlan Cos.

Sea 3D Whales& Dolphins. 2008. (Illus.). 24p. (J). spiral bd. 19.95 *(978-0-9759629-1-6(4))* ETN, Inc.

Shaw, Gina. Dolphins & Whales in a Box. 2014. (ENG.). 48p. (J). (gr. k-2). 9.99 *(978-0-545-68163-6(4),* Scholastic Nonfiction) Scholastic, Inc.

Simon, Charnan & Kazunas, Ariel. Killer Whales. 2012. (Nature's Children Ser.). (ENG., Illus.). 48p. (J). pap. 6.95 *(978-0-531-25479-0(8))*; lib. bdg. 28.00 *(978-0-531-26834-6(9))* Scholastic Library Publishing.

Simon, Seymour. Penguins. 2007. (Illus.). 32p. (J). (gr. k-4). lib. bdg. 17.89 *(978-0-06-028396-4(3))* HarperCollins Pubs.

Spilsbury, Louise. Save the Humpback Whale, 1. 2014. (Animal SOS! Ser.). (ENG.). 32p. (J). (gr. k-5). pap. 10.00 *(978-1-4777-6034-5(2),* Windmill Bks.) Rosen Publishing Group, Inc., The.

Spilsbury, Richard & Spilsbury, Louise. Dolphin & Whale Pods. 2013. (Animal Armies Ser.). (ENG., Illus.). 32p. (J). (gr. k-5). pap. 10.00 *(978-1-4777-0332-8(2))*; lib. bdg. 25.25 *(978-1-4777-0305-2(5))* Rosen Publishing Group, Inc., The. (PowerKids Pr.).

Stefoff, Rebecca. Whale Sharks. 2015. (Illus.). 48p. (J). pap. *(978-1-62712-955-8(3))* Musa Publishing.

The Tale of a White Whale: Digraph wh: Level B, 6 vols. (Wright Skills Ser.). 16p. (gr. k-3). 17.95 *(978-0-322-01474-9(3))* Wright Group/McGraw-Hill.

Taylor, Trace & Sánchez, Lucía M. Ballenas: Whales. 2010. (2G Animales Marinos Ser.). (SPA.). 12p. (J). (gr. k-2). pap. 6.99 *(978-1-61541-280-8(8))* American Reading Co.

Taylor, Trace & Sanchez, Lucia M. Ballenas (Whales) 2011. (poder de 100 - Animales marinos Ser.). 12p. pap. 39.62 *(978-1-61541-281-5(6))* American Reading Co.

Terp, Gail. Killer Whales. 2017. (Wild Animal Kingdom Ser.). (ENG., Illus.). 32p. (J). (gr. 3-7). 31.35 ***(978-1-68072-052-5(X),*** Bolt) Black Rabbit Bks.

Thomas, Isabel. Shark vs. Killer Whale. 2017. (Animal Rivals Ser.). (ENG.). 24p. (gr. k-2). lib. bdg. 23.32 ***(978-1-4846-4071-5(3),*** Heinemann Read & Learn) Heinemann-Raintree.

Thomson, Sarah L. Amazing Whales! Wildlife Conservation Society, photos by. 2006. (I Can Read Level 2 Ser.). (ENG., Illus.). 32p. (J). (gr. k-3). pap. 3.99 *(978-0-06-054467-6(8))* HarperCollins Pubs.

—Amazing Whales! 2005. (I Can Read Bks.). (ENG., Illus.). 32p. (J). (gr. k-3). 15.99 *(978-0-06-054465-2(1))* HarperCollins Pubs.

—Amazing Whales! Wildlife Conservation Society, photos by. 2006. (I Can Read Bks.). (Illus.). (gr. -1-3). 14.00 *(978-0-7569-6665-2(5))* Perfection Learning Corp.

Throp, Claire. Orcas, 1 vol. 2013. (Living in the Wild: Sea Mammals Ser.). (ENG., Illus.). 48p. (gr. 4-6). pap. 9.95 *(978-1-4329-7070-3(4),* Heinemann InfoSearch) Heinemann-Raintree.

Tracqui, Valérie. The Whale. 2004. (Animal Close-Ups Ser.). (Illus.). 28p. (J). pap. 6.95 *(978-1-57091-625-0(X))* Charlesbridge Publishing, Inc.

Trapped! a Whale's Rescue. 2015. (ENG., Illus.). 32p. (J). (gr. -1-1). lib. bdg. 17.95 *(978-1-58089-558-3(1))* Charlesbridge Publishing, Inc.

Turnbull, Stephanie. Whale. 2013. (Big Beasts Ser.). (Illus.). 24p. (gr. k-3). 28.50 *(978-1-59920-838-1(5))* Black Rabbit Bks.

Vastola, P. Huge Animals: Learning the Long U Sound. 2009. (PowerPhonics Ser.). 24p. (gr. 1-1). 39.90 *(978-1-60851-445-8(5),* PowerKids Pr.) Rosen Publishing Group, Inc., The.

Waldendorf, Kurt. How Big Is a Blue Whale? 2017. (Comparison Fun Ser.). (ENG.). 24p. (J). (gr. -1-2). lib. bdg. 27.07 *(978-1-5038-1675-6(3),* 211510) Child's World, Inc., The.

Weber, Valerie J. Whales/Ballenas. 2008. (Animals That Live in the Ocean/Animales Que Viven en el Oceano Ser.). (ENG & SPA.). 24p. (J). (gr. -1-3). lib. bdg. 22.60 *(978-0-8368-9569-8(X),* Weekly Reader Leveled Readers) Stevens, Gareth Publishing LLLP.

—Whales/Ballenas. 2008. (Animals That Live in the Ocean/Animales Que Viven en el Oceano Ser.). (SPA.). 24p. (gr. -1-3). pap. 8.15 *(978-0-8368-9579-7(7),* Weekly Reader Leveled Readers) Stevens, Gareth Publishing LLLP.

Weber, Valerie J. & Weber, Valerie J. Whales. 2008. (Animals That Live in the Ocean Ser.). (Illus.). 24p. (J). (gr. -1-3). lib. bdg. 22.60 *(978-0-8368-9567-4(3),* Weekly Reader Leveled Readers) Stevens, Gareth Publishing LLLP.

Weingarten, E. T. Hunting with Killer Whales, Vol. 1. 2014. (Animal Attack! Ser.). (ENG.). 32p. (J). (gr. 2-3). 22.60 *(978-1-4824-0496-8(6))* Stevens, Gareth Publishing LLLP.

Westerskov, Kim, photos by. Whales. 2004. (Illus.). 32p. (J). *(978-0-7685-2109-2(2))* Dominie Pr., Inc.

Wexo, John Bonnett. Whales. rev. ed. 2003. (Illus.). 24p. (J). (gr. 1-7). 10.95 *(978-1-888153-97-2(0),* Zoo Bks.) Wildlife Education, Ltd.

The Whale: Review & Practice Book for Level B, 6 vols. (Wright Skills Ser.). 16p. (gr. k-3). 26.50 *(978-0-322-03100-5(1))* Wright Group/McGraw-Hill.

Whale Sharks: Bulletproof! 2013. (Animal Superpowers Ser.). 24p. (J). (gr. k-5). pap. 49.50 *(978-1-4777-0840-8(5),* PowerKids Pr.) Rosen Publishing Group, Inc., The.

The Whale Watchers, 6, Pack. (gr. 1-2). 22.00 *(978-0-7635-9181-6(5))* Rigby Education.

Whales: Level N, 6 vols. (Wonder Worldtm Ser.). 48p. 34.95 *(978-0-7802-2915-0(0))* Wright Group/McGraw-Hill.

Whales & Dolphins. (Eyes on Nature Ser.). 32p. (J). (gr. 1). pap. *(978-1-882210-56-5(5))* Action Publishing, Inc.

Whales & Dolphins. (Eyes on Nature Ser.). (Illus.). 32p. (J). (gr. 1-18). 7.95 *(978-1-56156-423-1(0))* Kidsbooks, LLC.

Whales & Dolphins. 2014. (Animal Q & A Ser.). (Illus.). 24p. (J). (gr. k-3). lib. bdg. 23.60 *(978-1-4777-9202-5(3))* Windmill Bks.

Whales & Dolphins Pack [Scholastic]. 2011. (Whales & Dolphins up Close Ser.). 24p. pap. 2.00 *(978-1-4296-6325-0(1),* First Facts) Capstone Press of Coughlan Cos.

Whales in American History. 2014. (How Animals Shaped History Ser.). (Illus.). 24p. (J). (gr. k-5). pap. 49.50 *(978-1-4777-6630-9(8),* PowerKids Pr.) Rosen Publishing Group, Inc., The.

Wildlife Education, Ltd Staff, contrib. by. Whales. 2006. (Critters Up Close Ser.). (Illus.). (J). bds. 5.95 *(978-1-932396-17-1(9))* Wildlife Education, Ltd.

Williams, Alwena & Drake, Gwasg Addysgol. Morfilod. 2005. (WEL., Illus.). 20p. *(978-0-86174-101-4(3))* Drake Educational Assocs. Ltd.

Willis, John. Orca. 2015. (Illus.). 24p. (J). *(978-1-4896-4109-0(2))* Weigl Pubs., Inc.

World Book, Inc. Staff, contrib. by. Blue Whales & Other Baleen Whales. 2005. (World Book's Animals of the World Ser.). (Illus.). 64p. (J). *(978-0-7166-1264-3(X))* World Bk., Inc.

A World of Whales, 6 vols. (Book2WebTM Ser.). (gr. 4-8). 36.50 *(978-0-322-02969-9(4))* Wright Group/McGraw-Hill.

Worth, Bonnie. A Whale of a Tale! All about Porpoises, Dolphins, & Whales. Ruiz, Aristides & Mathieu, Joe, illus. 2006. (Cat in the Hat's Learning Library). (ENG.). 48p. (J). (gr. -1-3). 9.99 *(978-0-375-82279-7(8),* Random Hse. Bks. for Young Readers) Random Hse. Children's Bks.

Young, Karen Romano. Whale Quest: Working Together to Save Endangered Species. 2017. (ENG.). 128p. (J). (gr. 8-12). 37.32 *(978-1-4677-9246-2(2),* Twenty-First Century Bks.) Lerner Publishing Group.

Zayarny, Jack. Humpback Whales. 2014. (J). pap. *(978-1-4896-1079-9(0))* Weigl Pubs., Inc.

Zuchora-Walske, Christine. Killer Whales: Built for the Hunt. 2015. (Predator Profiles Ser.). (ENG., Illus.). 24p. (gr. 1-2). lib. bdg. 25.32 *(978-1-4914-5042-0(8))* Capstone Press of Coughlan Cos.

WHALES—FICTION

Al-Ghani, K. I. Baby Blue Has the Blues, 1 vol. Al-Ghani, Haitham, illus. 2011. (ENG.). 32p. (J). 16.99 *(978-0-7643-3732-1(7),* 9780764337321, Schiffer Publishing Ltd) Schiffer Publishing, Ltd.

Aldrich, Sandra D. Lenny Lobster Saves the Day. 2012. 38p. 19.95 *(978-1-4626-9817-2(4))* America Star Bks.

—Trouble in the Park. 2012. 28p. 19.95 *(978-1-4626-8818-0(7))* America Star Bks.

Alexander, Kwame. Surf's Up. Miyares, Daniel, illus. 2016. (ENG.). 32p. (J). 17.95 *(978-0-7358-4220-5(5))* North-South Bks., Inc.

Anderson, M. T. Whales on Stilts! Cyrus, Kurt, illus. 2010. (Pals in Peril Tale Ser.). (ENG.). (J). (gr. 5-9). 208p. 17.99 *(978-1-4424-0695-7(X))*; 224p. pap. 7.99 *(978-1-4424-0701-5(8))* Beach Lane Bks. (Beach Lane Bks.).

—Whales on Stilts! Cyrus, Kurt, illus. 2006. (M. T. Anderson's Thrilling Tales Ser.). 188p. (gr. 5-9). 15.95 *(978-0-7569-7213-4(2))* Perfection Learning Corp.

Anthony, Mike. The Adventures of Henry the Patchwork Whale, 1 vol. 2010. 20p. 24.95 *(978-1-60813-076-4(2))* PublishAmerica, Inc.

Apte, Sunita. Ride the Whale: A Surfer Tall Tale. Reed, Kyle, illus. 2006. 16p. (J). pap. *(978-0-439-74638-0(8))* Scholastic, Inc.

Armstrong, Kim. Petunia in Manhattan. 2009. 50p. pap. 12.99 *(978-1-935436-97-3(X))* Rodaian Pr.

Atkinson, Cale. To the Sea. Atkinson, Cale, illus. 2015. (ENG., Illus.). 48p. (J). (gr. -1-k). 16.99 *(978-1-4847-0813-2(X))* Disney Publishing Worldwide.

Barnett, Mac. Billy Twitters & His Blue Whale Problem. Rex, Adam, illus. 2009. (ENG.). 48p. (J). (gr. -1-2). 16.99 *(978-0-7868-4958-1(4))* Hyperion Pr.

Because of Walter, 6 Packs. (Action Packs Ser.). 104p. (gr. 3-5). 44.00 *(978-0-7635-8402-3(9))* Rigby Education.

Blume, Rebecca. Baby Whales. Blume, Rebecca, illus. 2007. (Illus.). 8p. (J). 5.00 *(978-0-9785427-2-6(X))* Liberty Artists Management.

Bonnell, Kris. The Little Boat. 2006. (J). pap. 5.95 *(978-1-933727-34-9(9))* Reading Reading Bks., LLC.

Botelho, R. J. G. A. R. T. H. Book IV: A Whale of a Tale. 2007. 104p. per. 19.95 *(978-1-4241-8799-7(0))* America Star Bks.

Brown, Joy. Spy Hopping. 2008. 48p. pap. 24.95 *(978-1-60474-525-2(8))* America Star Bks.

Carnavas, Peter. Blue Whale Blues. Carnavas, Peter, illus. 2016. (ENG., Illus.). 32p. (J). 11.99 *(978-1-61067-458-4(8))* Kane Miller.

Case, Julie. Emma & the Whale. White, Lee, illus. 2017. (ENG.). 40p. (J). (gr. -1-3). 17.99 *(978-0-553-53847-2(0),* Schwartz & Wade Bks.) Random Hse. Children's Bks.

Cline-Ransome, Lesa. Whale Trails, Before & Now. Karas, G. Brian, illus. 2015. (ENG.). 40p. (J). (gr. k-4). 17.99 *(978-0-8050-9642-2(6),* 9780805096422, Holt, Henry & Co. Bks. For Young Readers) Holt, Henry & Co.

Collier, Kevin Scott. Journeys of Hope, Pearl of Wisdom. Collier, Kevin Scott, illus. 2006. (Illus.). 28p. (J). E-Book 9.95 incl. cd-rom *(978-1-933090-31-3(6))* Guardian Angel Publishing, Inc.

Cosgrove, Stephen. Pickles & the P-Flock Bullies. James, Robin, illus. 2014. (ENG.). 32p. (J). (gr. k-3). 16.99 *(978-1-57061-887-1(9),* Little Bigfoot) Sasquatch Bks.

Curran, Steven Earl. Whales used to Fly in the Sky. 2005. 9.00 *(978-0-8059-8086-8(5))* Dorrance Publishing Co., Inc.

Dadey, Debby & Dadey, Debbie. Whale of a Tale, 1 vol., Bk. 3. 2015. (Mermaid Tales Ser.). (ENG.). 120p. (J). (gr. 2-4). 24.21 *(978-1-61479-324-3(7),* Spotlight) ABDO Publishing Co.

Dalmatian Press Staff. A Little Whale Tale. 2008. (ENG.). 8p. bds. 4.95 *(978-1-58117-713-8(5),* Intervisual/Piggy Toes) Bendon, Inc.

Dalmatian Press Staff, adapted by. Moby Dick. (J). 9.95 *(978-1-56156-308-1(0))* Kidsbooks, LLC.

David, Jamie. Johann Sebastian Humpbach. David, Jamie, illus. 2009. (Illus.). 167p. pap. 14.95 *(978-0-615-31840-0(1))* Chai Yo Maui Pr.

Davidge, James. Driftwood Saves the Whales. 2009. (ENG., Illus.). 136p. (YA). 10.95 *(978-1-897411-01-8(4))* Bayeux Arts, Inc. CAN. Dist: Chicago Distribution Ctr.

Davies, Benji. The Storm Whale. Davies, Benji, illus. 2014. (ENG., Illus.). 32p. (J). (gr. -1-3). 17.99 *(978-0-8050-9967-6(0),* 9780805099676, Holt, Henry & Co. Bks. For Young Readers) Holt, Henry & Co.

—The Winter Whale. Davies, Benji, illus. 2017. (ENG., Illus.). 32p. (J). 16.99 *(978-1-250-11186-9(2),* 9781250111869, Holt, Henry & Co. Bks. For Young Readers) Holt, Henry & Co.

Davies, Nicola. Whale Boy. 2014. (ENG.). 272p. (J). (gr. 2-4). pap. 8.99 *(978-0-440-87015-9(1))* Transworld Publishers Ltd. GBR. Dist: Independent Pubs. Group.

Davis, Buddy. Whale of a Story: Adventures on the High Seas. 2003. 40p. (J). 14.99 *(978-0-89051-390-3(2))* Master Bks.

Davis, Maggie Steincrohn. A Garden of Whales. O'Connell, Jennifer Barrett, illus. 2008. (ENG.). 32p. (J). (gr. -1-2). reprint ed. pap. 6.95 *(978-0-944475-35-5(3),* 9780944475355) Firefly Bks., Ltd.

Disney Book Group Staff. Doc Mcstuffins Dad's Favorite Toy. Disney Storybook Art Team, illus. 2015. (ENG.). 24p. (J). (gr. -1-k). pap. 4.99 *(978-1-4847-2164-3(0))* Disney Pr.

Donaldson, Julia. The Snail & the Whale. Scheffler, Axel, illus. (ENG.). 32p. (J). (gr. -1-2). 2004. 18.99 *(978-0-8037-2922-3(7),* Dial Bks) 2006. reprint ed. pap. 6.99 *(978-0-14-240580-2(9),* Puffin Books) Penguin Young Readers Group.

Douglas, Babette. Kiss a Me: A Little Whale Watching. Rockwell, Barry, illus. 2006. (Kiss a Me Teacher Creature Stories Ser.). (J). (gr. 3-7). 9.99 *(978-1-890343-08-8(0))* Kiss A Me Productions, Inc.

—Kiss a Me Goes to School. Rockwell, Barry, illus. 2006. (Kiss a Me Teacher Creature Stories Ser.). (J). (gr. -1-3). 9.99 *(978-1-890343-09-5(9))* Kiss A Me Productions, Inc.

—Kiss a Me to the Rescue. Rockwell, Barry, illus. 2006. (Kiss a Me Teacher Creature Stories Ser.). (J). (gr. -1-3). 9.99 *(978-1-890343-11-8(0))* Kiss A Me Productions, Inc.

Dunn, Richard & Sprick, Jessica. Whales: Read Well Level K Unit 18 Storybook. Koontz, Robin Michal, illus. 2003. (Read Well Level K Ser.). 20p. (J). *(978-1-57035-689-6(0),* 55589) Cambium Education, Inc.

Edwardson, Debby Dahl. Whale Snow. Patterson, Annie, illus. 2004. (ENG.). 32p. (J). (gr. -1-3). pap. 7.95 *(978-1-57091-394-5(3))* Charlesbridge Publishing, Inc.

Eisner, Will & Melville, Herman. Moby Dick. 2003. (ENG., Illus.). 32p. (J). pap. 7.95 *(978-1-56163-294-7(5))* NBM Publishing Co.

Elliott, Jenny. Save Me. 2015. (ENG.). 336p. (YA). (gr. 7-12). pap. 9.99 *(978-1-250-06147-8(4),* 9781250061478) Feiwel & Friends.

Evans, Sally. Sea Treasure. Richardson, Linda, illus. 2004. (J). 16.95 *(978-1-59094-073-0(3),* 1590940733, Jawbreakers for Kids) Jawbone Publishing Corp.

Fogliano, Julie. If You Want to See a Whale. Stead, Erin E., illus. 2013. (ENG.). 32p. (J). (gr. -1-2). 17.99 *(978-1-59643-731-9(6),* 9781596437319) Roaring Brook Pr.

Gabriele, Ben. The Tale of a Whale Named Snow. 2014. (ENG.). 18.00 *(978-0-938271-07-9(5))*; pap. 15.00 *(978-0-938271-06-2(7))*; pap. 15.00 *(978-0-938271-08-6(3))*; (J). 18.00 *(978-0-938271-05-5(9))* Press North America.
—The Tale of a Whale Named Snow. 2013. 50p. pap. 31.99 *(978-1-4836-9269-2(8))* Xlibris Corp.
Garner, Alan. The Owl Service. 2006. (Odyssey Classics Ser.). (ENG., Illus.). 240p. (J). (gr. 7-12). pap. 14.95 *(978-0-15-205618-6(1))* Houghton Mifflin Harcourt Publishing Co.
George, Jean Craighead. Ice Whale. Hendrix, John, illus. 2015. (ENG.). 224p. (J). (gr. 4-7). 7.99 *(978-0-14-242741-5(1)*, Puffin Books) Penguin Young Readers Group.
George, Joshua. Tiny Whale. Pinillos, Puy, illus. 2015. (ENG.). 32p. (J). (gr. -1-1). pap. 10.99 *(978-1-78445-287-2(4))* Top That! Publishing PLC GBR. Dist: Independent Pubs. Group.
Ghent, Rena. The Adventures of Billy the Whale. 2009. 28p. pap. 13.99 *(978-1-4490-3456-6(X))* AuthorHouse.
Gill, Shelley. Big Blue. Barrow, Ann, illus. 2005. (ENG.). 32p. (J). (gr. k-3). 7.95 *(978-1-57091-667-0(5))* Charlesbridge Publishing, Inc.
Gleasner, Diana C. Popoki, the Hawaiian Cat: An Amazing Adventure with the Whale. Winton, Andrea Evans, illus. 2004. (J). *(978-0-9651185-7-6(6))* Gleasner, Bill & Diana Inc.
Gray, Rick & Gray, Coral. Evangel Meets Orsen Whale. Headley, Aaron, illus. 2007. (ENG.). 32p. (J). (gr. -1-3). 14.95 *(978-0-9790210-1-5(4))* Evening Star Enterprise, Inc.
Green, Yuko. Naia & Kohola. 2010. 20p. pap. 6.95 *(978-1-59700-803-7(6))* Island Heritage Publishing.
Greenburg, J. C. In the Whale. Reed, Mike, illus. 2003. (Andrew Lost Ser.: 6). (ENG.). 96p. (J). (gr. 1-4). 3.99 *(978-0-375-82524-8(X)*, Random Hse. Bks. for Young Readers) Random Hse. Children's Bks.
Halls, Kelly Milner. Dive into Danger. Parks, Phil, illus. 2016. (Animal Rescues Ser.: 2). (ENG.). 88p. (J). (gr. 4-8). lib. bdg. 25.32 *(978-1-4677-7220-4(8)*, Darby Creek) Lerner Publishing Group.
Hanson, Anders. Whale Tale, 1 vol. 2007. (Critter Chronicles Ser.). (ENG., Illus.). 24p. (J). (gr. k-3). lib. bdg. 24.21 *(978-1-59928-476-7(6)*, SandCastle) ABDO Publishing Co.
Heinz, Brian. Mocha Dick: The Legend & the Fury. Enos, Randall, illus. 2014. (ENG.). 32p. (J). (gr. 1-3). 18.99 *(978-1-56846-242-4(5)*, Creative Editions) Creative Co., The.
Hensley, Annemarie. Freeman Out of Water. 2011. 32p. pap. 14.99 *(978-1-4520-5864-1(4))* AuthorHouse.
Hernandez, Ruben. Elisa Escuchaba el Canto de Las Ballenas. Corichi, Yadhira, illus. rev. ed. 2003. (Castillo de la Lectura Blanca Ser.). (SPA & ENG.). 48p. (J). (gr. 1-3). pap. 6.95 *(978-970-20-0141-6(2))* Castillo, Ediciones, S. A. de C. V. MEX. Dist: Macmillan.
Hicks, Bob. Narvick the Whark (or a Shwale) 2003. (Illus.). cd-rom 9.95 *(978-0-9729703-0-3(4))* Kidderature Publishing.
Hiebert, Elfrieda H. Humpback Whales. (Little Book Practice Reader Ser.). (J). *(978-0-8136-0809-9(0))* Modern Curriculum Pr.
Highley, Rainey Marie. The Long Lost Tale of the Dragon & the Whale. 2013. 28p. pap. 16.95 *(978-1-4808-0151-6(8))* Archway Publishing.
Hill, Ros. Shamoo, a Whale of a Cow. 2013. (Illus.). 34p. pap. 12.95 *(978-1-59687-941-6(6)*, Milk & Cookies) ibooks, Inc.
—Shamooo: A Whale of a Cow. Hill, Ros, illus. 2005. (Illus.). 32p. (J). 15.95 *(978-0-689-04634-6(0)*, Milk & Cookies) ibooks, Inc.
Holden, Pam. Baby Whale's Mistake, 6 pack. Aziz, Lamia, illus. 2009. (Red Rocket Readers Ser.). (ENG.). 16p. (gr. 2-2). pap. *(978-1-877363-87-0(1))* Flying Start Bks.
—Watch Out for Whales, 6 pack. Aziz, Lamia, illus. 2009. (Red Rocket Readers Ser.). (ENG.). 16p. (gr. 2-2). pap. *(978-1-877363-63-4(4)*, Red Rocket Readers) Flying Start Bks.
—Whale Rescue, 6 pack. Aziz, Lamia, illus. 2009. (Red Rocket Readers Ser.). (ENG.). 16p. (gr. 2-2). pap. *(978-1-877363-79-5(0))* Flying Start Bks.
Horácek, Petr. Puffin Peter. Horácek, Petr, illus. 2013. (ENG., Illus.). 40p. (J). (gr. -1-2). 16.99 *(978-0-7636-6572-2(X))* Candlewick Pr.
How the Whale Got His Throat. 2017. (Picture Bks.). (ENG.). (J). 9.99 ***(978-0-7945-3869-9(X)***, Usborne) EDC Publishing.
Ilyas, Adnan. The Tale of Five Whales. 2010. 12p. 8.50 *(978-1-4389-5888-0(9))* AuthorHouse.
Irwin, Bindi & Kunz, Chris. A Whale of a Time. 2011. (Bindi's Wildlife Adventures Ser.: 5). (ENG.). 112p. (J). (gr. 3-6). pap. 4.99 *(978-1-4022-5928-9(X)*, Sourcebooks Jabberwocky) Sourcebooks, Inc.
Jacobson, Bonny B. Whale Fables. 2011. 68p. pap. 31.99 *(978-1-4535-9956-3(8))* Xlibris Corp.
James, Simon. Querido Salvatierra. de la Vega, Eida, tr. from ENG. 2003.Tr. of Dear Mr. Blueberry. (SPA.). (J). (gr. k-2). pap. 7.99 *(978-1-930332-45-4(9))* Lectorum Pubns., Inc.
Johnson, Grace. The Little Fish Who Was Afraid to Swim. 2008. 36p. pap. 15.49 *(978-1-4389-2262-1(0))* AuthorHouse.
Johnston, Johanna. Whale's Way. Weisgard, Leonard, illus. 2015. (ENG.). 48p. 20.00 *(978-1-85124-428-7(X))* Bodleian Library GBR. Dist: Chicago Distribution Ctr.
Jordan, Christina. I Wish I Were a Humpback Whale, 1 vol. Utomo, Gabhor, illus. 2011. (I Wish I Were ... Ser.). (ENG.). 24p. (J). (gr. k-3). 28.50 *(978-1-61641-658-4(0))* Magic Wagon.
Joy, Linda. Little Wave & the Mystery of the Lost Whale. 2011. 28p. pap. 15.99 *(978-1-4628-9711-7(8))* Xlibris Corp.
Judith Anne Moody. Golden Eye & the Killer Cat. 2009. 248p. pap. 19.49 *(978-1-4251-7684-6(4))* Trafford Publishing.
Kita, Suzanne. Three Whales: Who Won the Heart of the World. Sundram, Steve, illus. 2010. (ENG.). 40p. (J). (gr. 3). *(978-1-59700-761-0(7))* Island Heritage Publishing.
Kor, Paul. Flash the Fish. Kor, Paul, illus. 2017. (ENG., Illus.). 32p. (J). (-k). 16.99 *(978-0-7352-2746-0(2)*, Dial Bks) Penguin Young Readers Group.
Lindsey, Marta. Grandes Migraciones de la Ballena Gris, 1 vol. Gabriel, Andrea, illus. 2015. (SPA.). 32p. (J). (gr. k-3). pap. 9.95 *(978-1-62855-468-7(1))* Arbordale Publishing.
Lingemann, Linda. Beluga Passage. Weiman, Jon, illus. 2011. (Smithsonian Oceanic Collection Ser.). (ENG.). 32p. (J). (gr. -1-3). 19.95 *(978-1-60727-645-6(3))* Soundprints.
Loux, Matthew. Salt Water Taffy: Caldera's Revenge! 2011. (ENG., Illus.). 72p. pap. 5.99 *(978-1-934964-62-0(X)*, 9781934964620) Oni Pr., Inc.
—Salt Water Taffy Pt. 2: Caldera's Revenge! 2011. (ENG., Illus.). 80p. pap. 5.99 *(978-1-934964-63-7(8)*, 9781934964637) Oni Pr., Inc.
Lum, Leimomi o. Kamahae Kuamoo Mookini. The Legend of Kuamo'o Mo'okini & Hamumu the Great Whale. Kam, Kathleen, illus. 2004. 24p. (J). 12.95 *(978-1-58178-036-9(2))* Bishop Museum Pr.
Magoon, Scott. Breathe. Magoon, Scott, illus. 2014. (ENG., Illus.). 40p. (J). (gr. -1-3). 17.99 *(978-1-4424-1258-3(5)*, Simon & Schuster/Paula Wiseman Bks.) Simon & Schuster/Paula Wiseman Bks.
Malone, Cheryl Lawton. Dario & the Whale. Masseva, Bistra, illus. 2016. (ENG.). 32p. (J). (gr. -1-3). 16.99 *(978-0-8075-1463-4(2))* Whitman, Albert & Co.
Manning, Sara. Wally the Whale: A Tale about a Whale with Seizures. 2011. 40p. pap. 18.46 *(978-1-4634-4160-9(6))* AuthorHouse.
Marino, Gianna. Following Papa's Song. 2014. (ENG., Illus.). 40p. (J). (gr. -1-k). 16.99 *(978-0-670-01315-9(3)*, Viking Books for Young Readers) Penguin Young Readers Group.
McDonald, Jill, illus. Ghoulish Gang. 2008. (ENG.). 12p. (J). 9.95 *(978-1-58117-782-4(8)*, Intervisual/Piggy Toes) Bendon, Inc.
McKee, David. Elmer & the Whales. McKee, David, illus. 2014. (ENG., Illus.). 32p. (J). (gr. -1-3). 16.95 *(978-1-4677-3453-0(5))* Lerner Publishing Group.
McNulty, Faith & Shiffman, Lena. Le Chant des Baleines. (Hello Reader! Ser.). (FRE., Illus.). 40p. (J). pap. 5.99 *(978-0-590-16027-8(3))* Scholastic, Inc.
MCP Staff. Humpback Whales, 6 bks., set, Level 10, Bk. 36. 2003. (J). (gr. -1-3). 33.50 *(978-0-8136-0808-2(2))* Modern Curriculum Pr.
Meadows, Daisy. Whitney the Whale Fairy. 2011. (Illus.). 64p. (J). *(978-0-545-28876-7(2))* Scholastic, Inc.
Meister, Cari. The Stranded Orca, 1 vol. Harpster, Steve, illus. 2012. (Ocean Tales Ser.). (ENG.). 32p. (gr. 2-4). pap. 6.25 *(978-1-4342-4232-7(3))*; lib. bdg. 22.65 *(978-1-4342-4026-2(6))* Stone Arch Bks.
Melville, Herman. Cities of the Fantastic: Brusel. Eisner, Will, illus. 2003. (Cities of the Fantastic Ser.). (ENG.). 120p. 19.95 *(978-1-56163-291-6(0))* NBM Publishing Co.
—Moby Dick. Eisner, Will, illus. 2003. (ENG.). 32p. (J). (gr. 4-7). 15.95 *(978-1-56163-293-0(7))* NBM Publishing Co.
—Moby Dick. 2008. (Bring the Classics to Life Ser.). (Illus.). 72p. (gr. 5-12). pap., act. bk. ed. 10.95 *(978-1-55576-326-8(X)*, EDCTR-508B) EDCON Publishing Group.
—Moby Dick. 2007. (SPA.). (YA). *(978-987-1129-68-3(8))* Grupo Visor E.A.S.A.
—Moby Dick. 2003. (Historias de Siempre Ser.). (SPA., Illus.). 92p. (J). (gr. 5-8). pap. 9.95 *(978-84-204-5732-1(9))* Santillana USA Publishing Co., Inc.
—Moby-Dick. Freeberg, Eric, illus. 2010. (Classic Starts(tm) Ser.). (ENG.). 160p. (J). (gr. 2-4). 6.95 *(978-1-4027-6644-2(0))* Sterling Publishing Co., Inc.
—Moby Dick: With a Discussion of Determination. 2003. (Values in Action Illustrated Classics Ser.). (Illus.). 190p. (J). *(978-1-59203-033-0(5))* Learning Challenge, Inc.
—Moby Dick, Grades 5-12. adapted ed. pap., tchr. ed. 4.95 *(978-0-8359-0123-9(8))* Globe Fearon Educational Publishing.
—Moby Dick, or the Whale. 2005. (J). Pt. 1. cd-rom *(978-1-4105-0265-0(1))*Pt. 2. pap. 9.95 *(978-1-4105-0267-4(8))* Vol. 1. pap. 9.95 *(978-1-4105-0263-6(5))* Vol. 2. cd-rom *(978-1-4105-0269-8(4))* Johnston, Don Inc.
Melville, Herman & Huth, Michael. Moby Dick. 2004. (Veröffentlichung der Maximilian-Gesellschaft für die Jahre 2004/2005 Ser.). (GER., Illus.). 92p. (J). *(978-3-921743-52-2(4))* Maximilian-Gesellschaft e. V.
Melville, Herman, et al. Moby Dick. (Classics Illustrated Ser.). (Illus.). 52p. (YA). pap. 4.95 *(978-1-57209-003-3(0))* Classics International Entertainment, Inc.
Mentyka, Sharon. Chasing at the Surface. 2016. (ENG., Illus.). 228p. (J). pap. 12.99 *(978-1-943328-60-4(9)*, West Winds Pr.) Graphic Arts Ctr. Publishing Co.
Mikaelsen, Ben. Stranded. 2010. (ENG.). 288p. (J). (gr. 3-7). pap. 5.99 *(978-1-4231-3362-9(5))* Hyperion Pr.
Moniz, Michael. The Boy & the Whale. 2013. (ENG., Illus.). 36p. (J). (gr. -1-3). 16.95 *(978-1-927018-14-9(5))* Simply Read Bks. CAN. Dist: Ingram Publisher Services.
Morpurgo, Michael. Why the Whales Came. 2nd ed. 2017. (ENG., Illus.). 192p. (J). (gr. 5-7). pap. 9.99 ***(978-1-4052-2925-8(X))*** Egmont Bks., Ltd. GBR. Dist: Independent Pubs. Group.
Morris, Dudley. Mike the Monk. 2011. 58p. 36.95 *(978-1-258-02967-8(7))* Literary Licensing, LLC.
Murrow, Vita. The Whale. Murrow, Ethan, illus. 2016. (ENG.). 32p. (J). (gr. -1-3). 17.99 *(978-0-7636-7965-1(8)*, Templar) Candlewick Pr.
Nikolet, C. T. From Bullies to Friends. Howe, Cindy T., illus. 2008. 25p. pap. 24.95 *(978-1-60610-121-6(8))* America Star Bks.
Nosaka, Akiyuki. The Whale That Fell in Love with a Submarine. Takemori, Ginny Tapley, tr. from JPN. 2015. (ENG., Illus.). 192p. (YA). (gr. 3-7). pap. 14.95 *(978-1-78269-027-6(1)*, Pushkin Press) Steerforth Pr.
O'Brien, Kevin J. My Macaroni Whales. 2012. 28p. pap. 15.99 *(978-1-4691-4988-2(5))* Xlibris Corp.
Oppel, Kenneth. Peg & the Whale. 2004. (Illus.). (J). (gr. k-3). spiral bd. *(978-0-616-07245-5(7))* Canadian National Institute for the Blind/Institut National Canadien pour les Aveugles.
Park, Sunny. Bboonk, the Minke Whale. 2012. 20p. pap. 17.99 *(978-1-4685-6363-4(7))* AuthorHouse.
Parks, M. Elizabeth. The Sea Cow. 2013. (Illus.). 44p. pap. 16.95 *(978-0-9824565-2-1(2))* Sibyl Merritt.
Pearl, Barbara. Whale of a Tale. 2005. (Illus.). 32p. (J). 14.95 *(978-0-9647924-7-0(8))* Crane Bks.
Peratrovich, Roy A., Jr. Little Whale: A Story of the Last Tlingit War Canoe. 2016. (ENG., Illus.). 64p. (J). pap. 16.95 *(978-1-60223-295-2(4))* Univ. of Alaska Pr.
Pfister, Marcus. Rainbow Fish Colors. 2013. (Rainbow Fish Ser.). (ENG., Illus.). 12p. (J). (gr. 1-1). bds. 7.95 *(978-0-7358-4147-5(0))* North-South Bks., Inc.
Plumberg, William. The Legend of Peggy Postue: The Girl with the Upturned Nose. 2011. 28p. pap. 15.99 *(978-1-4568-9635-5(0))* Xlibris Corp.
Posner-Sanchez, Andrea. As Big As a Whale (Disney Junior: Doc Mcstuffins) RH Disney Staff, illus. 2014. (Little Golden Book Ser.). (ENG.). 24p. (J). (-k). 4.99 *(978-0-7364-3087-6(3)*, Golden/Disney) Random Hse. Children's Bks.
Postgate, Oliver. Noggin & the Whale. Firmin, Peter, illus. 2016. (Noggin the Nog Ser.: 2). (ENG.). 48p. (J). (gr. 1-3). 8.99 *(978-1-4052-8153-9(7))* Egmont Bks., Ltd. GBR. Dist: Independent Pubs. Group.
Priddy, Roger. Wiggle & the Whale: A Book of Funny Friends. 2016. (Alphaprints Ser.). (ENG.). 32p. (J). 16.99 *(978-0-312-52136-3(7)*, 9780312521363, Priddy Bks.) St. Martin's Pr.
Rae, Lisa. A Distinguished Old Bentley Drove down to the Sea, 1 vol. Pickersgill, Peter, illus. 2007. (ENG.). 28p. (J). (gr. -1-2). pap. 8.95 *(978-1-897174-05-0(5)*, Tuckamore Bks) Creative Bk. Publishing CAN. Dist: Orca Bk. Pubs. USA.
Raschka, Chris. Whaley Whale. 2014. (Thingy Things Ser.). (ENG., Illus.). 24p. (J). (gr. -1-k). 6.95 *(978-1-4197-1058-2(3)*, Abrams Appleseed) Abrams, Inc.
Ratcliff, Charline. The Princess, the Toad & the Whale. 2012. (ENG.). 36p. (J). (-18). pap. 12.95 *(978-1-4787-1672-3(X))* Outskirts Pr., Inc.
Rebal, Tara. Sarah Sue Smith: A Crooked Wharf Adventure. 2010. 52p. pap. 22.49 *(978-1-4520-7165-7(9))* AuthorHouse.
Reed, J. Mac & Briggs-Greenberg, Ruthie. Sea of Echoes. 2015. (ENG., Illus.). 32p. (J). (gr. 3-7). 15.95 *(978-1-63076-107-3(9))* Taylor Trade Publishing.
Riner, Sherry. Wally the Whale Learns How to Be a Winner. Morris, Lillie, illus. 2004. 43p. pap. 24.95 *(978-1-4137-3129-3(5))* PublishAmerica, Inc.
Rml. An Interesting Crew. 2012. 16p. (-18). pap. 15.99 *(978-1-4772-8699-9(3))* AuthorHouse.
Robinson, Fiona. Whale Shines: An Artistic Tale. 2013. (ENG., Illus.). 32p. (J). (gr. k-2). 18.95 *(978-1-4197-0848-0(1)*, Abrams Bks. for Young Readers) Abrams, Inc.
Rylant, Cynthia. The Whale. McDaniels, Preston, illus. 2004. (Lighthouse Family Ser.: 2). (ENG.). 64p. (J). (gr. 1-5). pap. 5.99 *(978-0-689-84883-4(8)*, Simon & Schuster Bks. For Young Readers) Simon & Schuster Bks. For Young Readers.
Scotton, Rob. Splat the Cat: A Whale of a Tale. Scotton, Rob, illus. 2013. (I Can Read Level 1 Ser.). (ENG., Illus.). 32p. (J). (gr. -1-3). 16.99 *(978-0-06-209024-9(0))* HarperCollins Pubs.
—A Whale of a Tale. Scotton, Rob, illus. 2013. (I Can Read Level 1 Ser.). (ENG., Illus.). 32p. (J). (gr. -1-3). pap. 3.99 *(978-0-06-209022-5(4))* HarperCollins Pubs.
—A Whale of a Tale. 2013. (Splat the Cat: I Can Read Ser.). (J). lib. bdg. 13.55 *(978-0-606-31814-3(3)*, Turtleback) Turtleback Bks.
Segal, John. Alistair & Kip's Great Adventure! Segal, John, illus. 2008. (ENG., Illus.). 32p. (J). (gr. -1-3). 17.99 *(978-1-4169-0280-5(5)*, McElderry, Margaret K. Bks.) McElderry, Margaret K. Bks.
Skurzynski, Gloria & Ferguson, Alane. Out of the Deep. 2008. (Mysteries in Our National Park Ser.). (ENG., Illus.). 160p. (J). (gr. 3-7). pap. 4.99 *(978-1-4263-0251-0(7)*, National Geographic Children's Bks.) National Geographic Society.
Smith, John D. H. The Whale Whisperers, 1 vol. Smith, Anne, illus. 2009. 17p. pap. 24.95 *(978-1-60749-211-5(3))* America Star Bks.
Smith, Laverne Byrd. Pokey the Playful Whale: (who wanted to live on Land) 2010. (Illus.). 36p. pap. 25.50 *(978-1-4490-7620-7(3))* AuthorHouse.
Snowden, Gary. Hank & Kale Visit the Aquarium. Smith, William E., illus. 2012. 24p. pap. 8.99 *(978-1-938768-05-7(1))* Gypsy Pubns.
Sommer, Bill & Tilghman, Natalie. A 52-Hertz Whale. 2015. (ENG.). 200p. (YA). (gr. 8-12). 18.99 *(978-1-4677-7917-3(2))* Lerner Publishing Group.
Sommer, Bill & Tilghman, Natalie Haney. A 52-Hertz Whale. 2015. (ENG.). 200p. (YA). (gr. 8-12). 18.99 *(978-1-4677-8811-3(2)*, Carolrhoda Lab™) Lerner Publishing Group.
Speight, Peter. Wally the Whale. 2013. 28p. pap. *(978-1-78222-170-8(0))* Paragon Publishing, Rothersthorpe.
Spinelli, Eileen. Jonah's Whale. Ferri, Giuliano, illus. 2012. (ENG.). 32p. (J). 16.00 *(978-0-8028-5382-0(X)*, Eerdmans Bks For Young Readers) Eerdmans, William B. Publishing Co.
Staake, Bob. Beachy & Me. 2016. (ENG., Illus.). 40p. (J). (gr. -1-2). 16.99 *(978-0-385-37314-2(7))*; lib. bdg. 19.99 *(978-0-375-97198-3(X))* Random Hse. Children's Bks. (Random Hse. Bks. for Young Readers).
Starfall Education. Jake's Tale. Starfall Education, ed. 2004. (ENG., Illus.). 8p. (J). pap. *(978-1-59577-006-6(2))* Starfall Education.
Steig, William. Amos & Boris. 2011. 8.30 *(978-0-7848-3427-5(X)*, Everbind) Marco Bk. Co.
—Amos & Boris. Steig, William, illus. 2009. (ENG., Illus.). 32p. (J). (gr. k-3). pap. 7.99 *(978-0-312-53566-7(X)*, 9780312535667) Square Fish.
—Amos & Boris. 2009. (J). (gr. -1-2). lib. bdg. 18.40 *(978-0-8085-2709-1(6)*, Turtleback) Turtleback Bks.
Stephens, Ann Marie. Scuba Dog. Golden, Jess, illus. 2016. (ENG.). 40p. (J). (gr. -1-3). 17.99 *(978-1-4998-0143-9(2))* Little Bee Books Inc.
Stilton, Geronimo. Save the White Whale! 2011. (ENG.). 128p. (J). (gr. 2-5). pap. 7.99 *(978-0-545-10377-0(0)*, Scholastic Paperbacks) Scholastic, Inc.
Sweeney, Joyce. Waiting for June, 0 vols. 2006. (ENG.). 158p. (YA). (gr. 10-12). pap. 7.99 *(978-0-7614-5329-1(6)*, 9780761453291, Amazon Children's Publishing) Amazon Publishing.
Tate, Suzanne. Katie K. Whale: A Whale of a Tale. Melvin, James, illus. 2000. (Suzanne Tate's Nature Ser.: No. 17). 32p. (J). per. 10.95 *(978-1-878405-47-0(0))* Nags Head Art, Inc.
Thomas, Doris. Through the Eyes of the Orcas. 2010. 146p. pap. 14.90 *(978-3-8391-6582-9(2))* Bks. on Demand.
Thomson, Kerr. Washed Ashore. 2017. (ENG.). 320p. (J). (gr. 7). 17.99 ***(978-0-545-90420-9(X)***, Chicken Hse., The) Scholastic, Inc.
Tobin, Deborah. Tangled in the Bay: The Story of a Baby Right Whale, 1 vol. Domm, Jeffrey, illus. 2003. (ENG.). 33p. (J). (gr. -1-2). pap. 8.95 *(978-1-55109-441-0(X))* Nimbus Publishing, Ltd. CAN. Dist: Orca Bk. Pubs. USA.
Trechsel, Kelli. A Whale Set Sail. Renfroe, Leisa, illus. 2011. 28p. (J). pap. 14.95 *(978-1-936085-42-2(9))* DSA Publishing & Design, Inc.
Van Dusen, Chris. Down to the Sea with Mr. Magee. 2006. (ENG., Illus.). 36p. (J). (gr. -1-7). pap. 6.99 *(978-0-8118-5225-8(3))* Chronicle Bks. LLC.
Van Scoyoc, Pam. I Could Catch a Whale/ Yo Podria Pescar una Ballena. Santillan-Cruz, Sylvia R., tr. Lewis, R. J., illus. l.t. ed. 2005. (ENG & SPA.). 32p. (J). (gr. k-2). lib. bdg. 16.98 *(978-0-9663629-5-4(0))* By Grace Enterprises.
Velmans, Hester. Isabel of the Whales. 2006. (ENG.). 192p. (J). (gr. 3-7). per. 6.99 *(978-0-440-42025-5(3)*, Yearling) Random Hse. Children's Bks.
Verne, Jules. Dick Sand. Munro, George, tr. 2008. 296p. 29.95 *(978-1-60664-752-3(0))* Rodgers, Alan Bks.
—Dick Sands: The Boy Captain. ELLEN E. FREWER, tr. 2007. (ENG.). 298p. pap. 21.99 *(978-1-4264-3403-7(0))* Creative Media Partners, LLC.
—Dick Sands: The Boy Captain. Frewer, Ellen E., tr. l.t. ed. 2007. (ENG.). 328p. pap. 24.99 *(978-1-4264-3453-2(7))* Creative Media Partners, LLC.
—The English at the North Pole. 2009. 160p. 24.95 *(978-1-60664-684-7(2))*; pap. 13.95 *(978-1-60664-313-6(4))* Rodgers, Alan Bks.
Vernick, Audrey. I Won a What? Neubecker, Robert, illus. 2016. (ENG.). 40p. (J). (gr. -1-2). 17.99 *(978-0-553-50993-9(4)*, Knopf Bks. for Young Readers) Random Hse. Children's Bks.
Volke, Gordon. The Little Lost Whale. Bowler, Colin, illus. 2004. 24p. pap. 7.00 *(978-1-84161-118-1(2))* Ravette Publishing, Ltd. GBR. Dist: Parkwest Pubns., Inc.
Wakeham, Kate. Moby-Dick, 1 vol. Tempest, Annabel, illus. 2017. (ENG.). 30p. 12.99 ***(978-1-4236-4784-3(X))*** Gibbs Smith, Publisher.
Wan, Joyce. The Whale in My Swimming Pool. (ENG., Illus.). (J). 2016. 32p. bds. 7.99 *(978-0-374-30188-0(3)*, 9780374301880) 2015. 40p. (gr. -1-1). 17.99 *(978-0-374-30037-1(2)*, 9780374300371) Farrar, Straus & Giroux. (Farrar, Straus & Giroux (BYR)).
Wang, Jack & Wang, Holman. Herman Melville's Moby Dick. 2016. (ENG., Illus.). 24p. (J). (gr. -1 — 1). bds. 9.95 *(978-1-4521-5246-2(2))* Chronicle Bks. LLC.
Waters, Summer. River Rescue, 10. 2010. (Silver Dolphins Ser.: 10). (ENG.). 176p. (J). (gr. 2-4). pap. 7.99 *(978-0-00-736750-4(3)*, HarperCollins Children's Bks.) HarperCollins Pubs. Ltd. GBR. Dist: HarperCollins Pubs.
Westaway, Kylie. A Whale in the Bathtub. Jellett, Tom, illus. 2016. (ENG.). 40p. (J). (gr. -1-3). 16.99 *(978-0-544-53535-0(9))* Houghton Mifflin Harcourt Publishing Co.
Whale Mail. 2003. (J). spiral bd. 9.95 *(978-0-89610-126-5(6))* Island Heritage Publishing.
Wiederhold, Kathryn. Ravenwhale. 2011. 40p. pap. 24.95 *(978-1-4626-2027-2(2))* America Star Bks.
Wilhelm, Hans. Little Whale in Deep Trouble: A Story Inspired by a True Event. 2017. (ENG., Illus.). 32p. (J). (gr. -1-2). 9.99 *(978-0-7641-6851-2(7))* Barron's Educational Series, Inc.
Willems, Mo. A Big Guy Took My Ball! Willems, Mo, illus. 2013. (Elephant & Piggie Ser.). (ENG., Illus.). 64p. (J). (gr. 1-3). 9.99 *(978-1-4231-7491-2(7))* Hyperion Bks. for Children.
Wilson, Bob. Stanley Bagshaw & the Twenty Two Ton Whale. 2006. (Stanley Bagshaw Ser.). (Illus.). 32p. (J). (gr. k-2). pap. 6.95 *(978-1-903015-50-6(2))* Barn Owl Bks, London GBR. Dist: Independent Pubs. Group.
Wishinsky, Frieda. A Whale Tale. Griffiths, Dean & Owlkids Books Inc. Staff, illus. 2008. (Canadian Flyer Adventures Ser.: 8). (ENG.). 96p. (J). (gr. 1-4). pap. 7.95 *(978-1-897349-17-5(3)*, Maple Tree Pr.) Owlkids Bks. Inc. CAN. Dist: Publishers Group West (PGW).
Yolen, Jane. The Stranded Whale. Cataldo, Melanie, illus. 2015. (ENG.). 32p. (J). (gr. k-4). 15.99 *(978-0-7636-6953-9(9))* Candlewick Pr.
Young, Ed. Mighty Moby. 2017. (ENG., Illus.). 40p. (J). (gr. -1-3). 17.99 *(978-0-316-29936-7(7))* Little Brown & Co.
Zalme, Ron, illus. A Humpback Whale Tale. 2006. (Go, Diego, Go! Ser.: Vol. 2). (ENG.). 24p. (J). (gr. -1-2). pap. 3.99 *(978-1-4169-1511-9(7)*, Simon Spotlight/Nickelodeon) Simon Spotlight/Nickelodeon.
Zurchin, Cynthia, et al. The Whale Done School: Transforming a School's Culture by Catching Students Doing Things Right. 2012. 124p. pap. 14.95 *(978-1-4685-9536-9(9))* AuthorHouse.

WHALING

Cook, Peter & Salariya, David. Sail on a 19th-Century Whaling Ship! Grisly Tasks You'd Rather Not Do. Antram, David, illus. 2004. (You Wouldn't Want to Ser.). (ENG.). (J). 29.00 *(978-0-531-12356-0(1))* Scholastic Library Publishing.
Currie, Stephen. Thar She Blows: American Whaling in the Nineteenth Century. 2005. (People's History Ser.). (Illus.). 96p. (gr. 6-18). lib. bdg. 26.60 *(978-0-8225-0646-1(7))* Lerner Publishing Group.
Faiella, Graham. Moby Dick & the Whaling Industry of the 19th Century. 2009. (Looking at Literature Through Primary Sources Ser.). 64p. (gr. 5-8). 58.50 *(978-1-61514-305-4(X))* Rosen Publishing Group, Inc., The.
Herold, Vickey. A Whaling Community: Nantucket. 2006. (J). pap. *(978-1-4108-6426-0(X))* Benchmark Education Co.
Philbrick, Nathaniel. In the Heart of the Sea (Young Readers Edition) 2015. (ENG., Illus.). 208p. (J). (gr. 3-7). 8.99 *(978-1-101-99776-5(1)*, Puffin Books) Penguin Young Readers Group.
Prohibited! Individual Title Six-Packs. (Bookweb Ser.). 32p. (gr. 6-18). 34.00 *(978-0-7578-0908-8(1))* Rigby Education.
Sandler, Martin W. The Impossible Rescue: The True Story of an Amazing Arctic Adventure. 2014. (ENG.). 176p. (J). (gr. 5). pap. 15.99 *(978-0-7636-7093-1(6))* Candlewick Pr.
Whales in American History. 2014. (How Animals Shaped History Ser.). (Illus.). 24p. (J). (gr. k-5). pap. 49.50 *(978-1-4777-6630-9(8)*, PowerKids Pr.) Rosen Publishing Group, Inc., The.

W X Y Z

WHALING—FICTION

Brook, Henry. Moby Dick. 2010. (Usborne Classics Retold Ser.). 144p. (J). 6.99 *(978-0-7945-2761-7(2)*, Usborne) EDC Publishing.

Browne, Susan Chalker. The Land of a Thousand Whales, 1 vol. Keating, Nancy, illus. 2007. (ENG.). 32p. (J). (gr. 3-7). pap. 8.95 *(978-1-897174-08-1(X))* Creative Bk. Publishing CAN. Dist: Orca Bk. Pubs. USA.

Cline-Ransome, Lesa. Whale Trails, Before & Now. Karas, G. Brian, illus. 2015. (ENG.). 40p. (J). (gr. k-4). 17.99 *(978-0-8050-9642-2(6)*, 9780805096422, Holt, Henry & Co. Bks. For Young Readers) Holt, Henry & Co.

Dalmatian Press Staff, adapted by. Moby Dick. (J). 9.95 *(978-1-56156-308-1(0))* Kidsbooks, LLC.

Edwardson, Debby Dahl. Whale Snow. Patterson, Annie, illus. 2004. (ENG.). 32p. (J). (gr. -1-3). pap. 7.95 *(978-1-57091-394-5(3))* Charlesbridge Publishing, Inc.

Eisner, Will & Melville, Herman. Moby Dick. 2003. (ENG., Illus.). 32p. (J). pap. 7.95 *(978-1-56163-294-7(5))* NBM Publishing Co.

Frederick, Heather Vogel. The Voyage of Patience Goodspeed. 2004. (Aladdin Historical Fiction Ser.). 219p. (J). (gr. 3-7). 13.65 *(978-0-7569-2943-5(1))* Perfection Learning Corp.

—The Voyage of Patience Goodspeed. 2004. (ENG., Illus.). 224p. (J). (gr. 3-7). pap. 8.99 *(978-0-689-84869-8(2)*, Simon & Schuster Bks. For Young Readers) Simon & Schuster Bks. For Young Readers.

Hyde, Heidi Smith. Emanuel & the Hanukkah Rescue. Akib, Jamel, illus. 2012. (Hanukkah Ser.). (SPA & ENG.). 32p. (J). (gr. k-3). 7.95 *(978-0-7613-6627-0(X)*, Kar-Ben Publishing) Lerner Publishing Group.

—Emanuel & the Whale Oil Lamp. Akib, Jamel, illus. 2012. (Hanukkah Ser.). (ENG.). 32p. (J). (gr. -1-1). lib. bdg. 17.95 *(978-0-7613-6625-6(3)*, Kar-Ben Publishing) Lerner Publishing Group.

Kassirer, Sue. Thar She Blows! Whaling in The 1860s. Fridell, Pat, illus. 2007. 32p. (J). 15.00 *(978-1-4223-6721-6(5))* DIANE Publishing Co.

Melville, Herman. Cities of the Fantastic: Brusel. Eisner, Will, illus. 2003. (Cities of the Fantastic Ser.). (ENG.). 120p. 19.95 *(978-1-56163-291-6(0))* NBM Publishing Co.

—Moby Dick. Eisner, Will, illus. 2003. (ENG.). 32p. (J). (gr. 4-7). 15.95 *(978-1-56163-293-0(7))* NBM Publishing Co.

—Moby Dick. 2008. (Bring the Classics to Life Ser.). (Illus.). 72p. (gr. 5-12). pap., act. bk. ed. 10.95 *(978-1-55576-326-8(X)*, EDCTR-508B) EDCON Publishing Group.

—Moby Dick. Elphinstone, Katy, illus. 2014. (Travel & Adventure Ser.). (ENG.). 64p. pap. 6.95 *(978-1-906230-72-2(2))* Real Reads Ltd. GBR. Dist: Casemate Pubs. & Bk. Distributors, LLC.

—Moby Dick. 2003. (Historias de Siempre Ser.). (SPA., Illus.). 92p. (J). (gr. 5-8). pap. 9.95 *(978-84-204-5732-1(9))* Santillana USA Publishing Co., Inc.

—Moby-Dick. Freeberg, Eric, illus. 2010. (Classic Starts(tm) Ser.). (ENG.). 160p. (J). (gr. 2-4). 6.95 *(978-1-4027-6644-2(0))* Sterling Publishing Co., Inc.

—Moby Dick: Or, the Whale. 2010. 528p. pap. 12.95 *(978-1-59594-840-3(6)*, Wingspan Pr.) WingSpan Publishing.

—Moby Dick: With a Discussion of Determination. 2003. (Values in Action Illustrated Classics Ser.). (Illus.). 190p. (J). *(978-1-59203-033-0(5))* Learning Challenge, Inc.

—Moby Dick, Grades 5-12. adapted ed. pap., tchr. ed. 4.95 *(978-0-8359-0123-9(8))* Globe Fearon Educational Publishing.

—Moby Dick, or the Whale. 2005. (J). Pt. 1. cd-rom *(978-1-4105-0265-0(1))*Pt. 2. pap. 9.95 *(978-1-4105-0267-4(8))* Vol. 1. pap. 9.95 *(978-1-4105-0263-6(5))* Vol. 2. cd-rom *(978-1-4105-0269-8(4))* Johnston, Don Inc.

Melville, Herman & Huth, Michael. Moby Dick. 2004. (Veröffentlichung der Maximilian-Gesellschaft für die Jahre 2004/2005 Ser.). (GER., Illus.). 92p. (J). *(978-3-921743-52-2(4))* Maximilian-Gesellschaft e. V.

Melville, Herman, et al. Moby Dick. (Classics Illustrated Ser.). (Illus.). 52p. (YA). pap. 4.95 *(978-1-57209-003-3(0))* Classics International Entertainment, Inc.

Prins, Piet. Stefan Derksen's Polar Adventure. 2004. (Illus.). 237p. (J). pap. *(978-1-894666-67-1(4))* Inheritance Pubns.

Rivera, Raquel. Tuk & the Whale, 1 vol. Gerber, Mary Jane, illus. (ENG.). (J). (gr. 2-5). 2009. 88p. pap. 7.95 *(978-0-88899-891-0(0))* 2008. 96p. 15.95 *(978-0-88899-689-3(6))* Groundwood Bks. CAN. Dist: Publishers Group West (PGW).

Roop, Connie & Roop, Peter. Good-Bye for Today: The Diary of a Young Girl at Sea. Allen, Thomas B., illus. 2008. (ENG.). 48p. (J). (gr. 4-6). 11.99 *(978-1-4169-7573-1(X)*, Simon & Schuster/Paula Wiseman Bks.) Simon & Schuster/Paula Wiseman Bks.

Specter, Baron. Chasing Whales Aboard the Charles W. Morgan, 1 vol., Bk. 2. Evans, Dustin, illus. 2010. (Ghostly Graphic Adventures Ser.). (ENG.). 32p. (gr. 4-6). 28.50 *(978-1-60270-771-9(5)*, Graphic Planet- Fiction) ABDO Publishing Co.

Stevenson, Robert Louis. Moby Dick. 2014. (Graphic Classics Ser.). (Illus.). 48p. (gr. 3-6). 37.10 *(978-1-908973-88-7(9))* Book Hse. GBR. Dist: Black Rabbit Bks.

Thompson, Gare. A Whaling Community: Set of 6: New Bedford, Mass. 2011. (Navigators Ser.). (J). pap. 44.00 net. *(978-1-4108-6248-8(8))* Benchmark Education Co.

Wakeham, Kate. Moby-Dick, 1 vol. Tempest, Annabel, illus. 2017. (ENG.). 30p. 12.99 ***(978-1-4236-4784-3(X))*** Gibbs Smith, Publisher.

WHARTON, EDITH, 1862-1937

Wooldridge, Connie Nordhielm. The Brave Escape of Edith Wharton. 2010. (ENG., Illus.). 192p. (YA). (gr. 7-18). 20.00 *(978-0-547-23630-8(1))* Houghton Mifflin Harcourt Publishing Co.

WHEAT

Brannon, Cecelia H. Wheat. 2017. (All about Food Crops Ser.). 24p. (gr. k-1). lib. bdg. 22.60 ***(978-0-7660-8585-5(6))*** Enslow Pubs., Inc.

Etingoff, Kim. Dairy Products. 2013. (J). *(978-1-4222-2741-1(3))* Mason Crest.

Hayes, Amy. Turning Wheat into Bread. 2015. (Step-By-Step Transformations Ser.). (ENG., Illus.). 24p. (J). (gr. 1-1). pap. 8.22 *(978-1-5026-0445-3(0))* Cavendish Square Publishing.

Heos, Bridget. From Wheat to Bread. Coleman, Stephanie Fizer, illus. 2017. (Who Made My Lunch? Ser.). (ENG.). 24p. (gr. 1-4). 20.95 ***(978-1-68151-118-4(5))*** Amicus Publishing.

Lackey, Jennifer. The Biography of Wheat. 2007. (How Did That Get Here? Ser.). (ENG., Illus.). 32p. (J). (gr. 3-7). lib. bdg. *(978-0-7787-2495-7(6))*; (gr. 2-9). pap. *(978-0-7787-2531-2(6))* Crabtree Publishing Co.

Levenson, George. Bread Comes to Life: A Garden of Wheat & a Loaf to Eat. Thaler, Shmuel, photos by. 2008. (ENG., Illus.). 32p. (J). (gr. -1-2). pap. 7.99 *(978-1-58246-273-8(9)*, Tricycle Pr.) Random Hse. Children's Bks.

Nelson, Maria. I'm Allergic to Wheat. 2014. (I'm Allergic Ser.). 24p. (J). (gr. 1-3). 22.60 *(978-1-4824-0989-5(5))* Stevens, Gareth Publishing LLLP.

Owen, Ruth. Bread! Life on a Wheat Farm. 2012. (Food from Farmers Ser.). (ENG.). 32p. (J). (gr. k-3). pap. 11.75 *(978-1-61533-544-2(7))*; lib. bdg. 26.50 *(978-1-61533-532-9(3))* Windmill Bks.

Singer, Jane E. Wheat. 2013. (Feeding the World Ser.: 8). (Illus.). 48p. (J). (gr. 4-18). 19.95 *(978-1-4222-2749-7(9))* Mason Crest.

Taus-Bolstad, Stacy. From Wheat to Bread. 2012. (Start to Finish, Second Series: Food Ser.: No. 2). (ENG., Illus.). 24p. (gr. k-3). pap. 6.95 *(978-1-58013-970-0(1))*; lib. bdg. 23.93 *(978-0-7613-9178-4(9)*, Lerner Pubns.) Lerner Publishing Group.

Welvaert, Scott R. Follow That Crop: From the Farmer's Field to Our Grocery Store. 2003. (From Here to There Ser.). (J). *(978-1-58417-194-2(4))*; pap. *(978-1-58417-195-9(2))* Lake Street Pubs.

WHEATLEY, PHILLIS, 1753-1784

Borland, Kathryn Kilby & Speicher, Helen Ross. Phillis Wheatley: Young Revolutionary Poet, 10 vols. Morrison, Cathy, illus. 2nd rev. ed. 2005. (Young Patriots Ser.: 10). (ENG.). 120p. (J). (gr. 4-7). pap. 9.95 *(978-1-882859-48-1(0)*, Young Patriots Series) Patria Pr., Inc.

Collard, Sneed B., III. American Heroes, 6 vols., Group 3. Incl. Cesar Chavez: The Farm Workers' Best Friend. 29.93 *(978-0-7614-4055-0(0))*; George Washington: Our First President. 29.93 *(978-0-7614-4060-4(7))*; Jacob Lawrence: A Painter's Story. 29.93 *(978-0-7614-4058-1(5))*; Lady Bird Johnson: Keeping America Green. 29.93 *(978-0-7614-4056-7(9))*; Phillis Wheatley: She Loved Words. 29.93 *(978-0-7614-4057-4(7))*; Sitting Bull: Tatanka-Iyotake. 29.93 *(978-0-7614-4059-8(3))*; 48p. (gr. 3-18). (American Heroes 3 Ser.). 2009. Set lib. bdg. 179.57 o.p. *(978-0-7614-4054-3(2))* Marshall Cavendish Corp.

—Phillis Wheatley: She Loved Words. 2009. (American Heroes Ser.). 48p. (gr. 3-18). 29.93 *(978-0-7614-4057-4(7))* Marshall Cavendish Corp.

Corporate Contibutor Staff & Aloian, Molly. Phillis Wheatley: Poet of the Revolutionary Era. 2012. (ENG.). 48p. (J). *(978-0-7787-0803-2(9))*; pap. *(978-0-7787-0814-8(4))* Crabtree Publishing Co.

Doak, Robin S. Phillis Wheatley: The Inspiring Life Story of the American Poet. 2016. (Inspiring Stories Ser.). (ENG., Illus.). 112p. (J). (gr. 5-7). lib. bdg. 35.99 *(978-0-7565-5166-7(8)*, CPB Grades 4-8) Compass Point Bks.

Jarnow, Jesse. Phillis Wheatley. 2004. (Primary Sources of Famous People in American History Ser.). (ENG., Illus.). 32p. (gr. 4-8). pap. 10.00 *(978-0-8239-4191-9(4))* Rosen Publishing Group, Inc., The.

—Phillis Wheatley: African American Poet / Poeta Afroamericana. 2009. (Famous People in American History/Grandes personajes en la historia de los Estados Unidos Ser.). (ENG & SPA.). 32p. (gr. 2-3). 47.90 *(978-1-61512-554-8(X)*, Editorial Buenas Letras) Rosen Publishing Group, Inc., The.

—Phillis Wheatley: Poeta afroamericana (Phillis Wheatley: African American Poet) 2009. (Grandes personajes en la historia de los Estados Unidos (Famous People in American History) Ser.). (SPA.). 32p. (gr. 2-3). 47.90 *(978-1-61512-807-5(7)*, Editorial Buenas Letras) Rosen Publishing Group, Inc., The.

Kent, Deborah. Phillis Wheatley: First Published African-American Poet. 2003. (Our People Ser.). (ENG., Illus.). 32p. (J). (gr. 3-6). 29.93 *(978-1-59296-009-5(X)*, 200649) Child's World, Inc., The.

Kent, Jacqueline C. Phillis Wheatley. 2003. (Women of the Revolution Ser.). (J). pap. *(978-1-58417-089-1(1))*; lib. bdg. *(978-1-58417-026-6(3))* Lake Street Pubs.

Lasky, Kathryn. A Voice of Her Own: A Story of Phillis Wheatley, Slave Poet. 2012. lib. bdg. 14.75 *(978-0-606-26940-7(1)*, Turtleback) Turtleback Bks.

—A Voice of Her Own: The Story of Phillis Wheatley, Slave Poet. Lee, Paul, illus. 2012. (Candlewick Biographies Ser.). (ENG.). 48p. (J). (gr. 3-7). 14.99 *(978-0-7636-6427-5(8))*; pap. 4.99 *(978-0-7636-6091-8(4))* Candlewick Pr.

Malaspina, Ann. Phillis Sings Out Freedom: The Story of George Washington & Phillis Wheatley. Keeter, Susan, illus. 2012. (J). 34.28 *(978-1-61913-149-1(8))* Weigl Pubs., Inc.

Marsh, Carole. Phillis Wheatley. 2003. 12p. (gr. k-4). 2.95 *(978-0-635-02371-1(7))* Gallopade International.

McLeese, Don. Phillis Wheatley. 2004. (Heroes of the American Revolution Ser.). (Illus.). 32p. (J). (gr. -1 — 1). pap. 5.95 *(978-1-59515-320-3(9))* Rourke Educational Media.

McLendon, Jacquelyn. Phillis Wheatley: A Revolutionary Poet. 2009. (Library of American Lives & Times Ser.). 112p. (gr. 5-5). 69.20 *(978-1-60853-499-9(5))* Rosen Publishing Group, Inc., The.

Mclendon, Jacquelyn & Roza, Greg. Katie's Candy. 2006. (Library of American Lives & Timestm Ser.). 12p. (gr. -1-3). pap. 5.90 *(978-1-4042-5750-4(0))* Rosen Publishing Group, Inc., The.

McLendon, Jacquelyn Y. Phillis Wheatley: A Revolutionary Poet. 2005. (Library of American Lives & Times). (Illus.). 112p. (YA). (gr. 4-8). lib. bdg. 34.60 *(978-0-8239-5750-7(0))* Rosen Publishing Group, Inc., The.

Moriarty, J. T. Phillis Wheatley: African American Poet. 2009. (Primary Sources of Famous People in American History Ser.). 32p. (gr. 2-3). 47.90 *(978-1-60851-717-6(9))* Rosen Publishing Group, Inc., The.

Pickford, Susan B. Expectations: The Life of Phillis Wheatley. 18p. (J). (gr. 5-9). pap., wbk. ed. 10.00 *(978-1-878668-67-7(6))* History Compass, LLC.

Roza, Greg. Guide My Pen: The Poems of Phillis Wheatley. 2009. (Great Moments in American History Ser.). 32p. (gr. 3-3). 47.90 *(978-1-61513-133-4(7))* Rosen Publishing Group, Inc., The.

Smith, Emily. Phillis Wheatley (America's Early Years) 2016. (Primary Source Readers Ser.). (Illus.). 32p. (gr. 4-5). pap. 8.99 *(978-1-4938-3882-0(2))* Teacher Created Materials, Inc.

Smith, Emily R. Phillis Wheatley, 1 vol. 2004. (Primary Source Readers Ser.). (ENG.). 24p. (J). (gr. 4-4). pap. 8.99 *(978-0-7439-8743-1(8))* Shell Educational Publishing.

Speicher, Helen Ross & Borland, Kathryn Kilby. Phillis Wheatley: Young Revolutionary Poet. Morrison, Cathy, illus. 2nd rev. ed. 2005. (Young Patriots Ser.: 10). (ENG.). 120p. (J). (gr. 4-7). 15.95 *(978-1-882859-47-4(2))* Patria Pr., Inc.

Watson-Doost, Valeria. Phillis Wheatley. 2008. 35p. pap. 21.50 *(978-0-557-03153-5(2))* Lulu Pr., Inc.

WHEELS

Allyn, Daisy. Wheels & Axles. 2013. (Simple Machine Science Ser.). (Illus.). 24p. (gr. 1-3). 22.60 *(978-1-4339-8156-2(4))*; pap. 8.15 *(978-1-4339-8157-9(2))* Stevens, Gareth Publishing LLLP.

Bailey, Gerry. Rolling Along: Wheels & Axles. 2014. (ENG., Illus.). 32p. (J). *(978-0-7787-0418-8(1))*; pap. *(978-0-7787-0424-9(6))* Crabtree Publishing Co.

Banting, Erinn. Wheels & Axles. 2013. (J). *(978-1-62127-429-2(2))*; pap. *(978-1-62127-435-3(7))* Weigl Pubs., Inc.

Bodden, Valerie. Ferris Wheels. 2012. (Illus.). 24p. (J). 25.65 *(978-1-60818-113-1(8)*, Creative Education) Creative Co., The.

—Wheels & Axles. 2011. (Simple Machine Ser.). 24p. (J). (gr. 1-3). 24.25 *(978-1-60818-013-4(1))*; (ENG.). pap. 8.99 *(978-0-89812-584-9(7)*, Creative Paperbacks) Creative Co., The.

Bourgoing, Pascale De, et al. On Wheels. Kniffke, Sophie, illus. 2006. (ENG.). 38p. (J). (gr. k-3). pap. 11.99 *(978-1-85103-111-5(1))* Moonlight Publishing, Ltd. GBR. Dist: Independent Pubs. Group.

Cardenas, Ernesto A. Wheels & Motors. 2009. 19.95 *(978-1-60698-023-1(8))*; pap. 3.95 *(978-1-60698-021-7(1))* Milo Educational Bks. & Resources.

Challen, Paul. Get to Know Wheels & Axles. 2009. (Get to Know Simple Machines Ser.). (ENG., Illus.). 32p. (J). (gr. 2-4). pap. *(978-0-7787-4488-7(4))*; lib. bdg. *(978-0-7787-4471-9(X))* Crabtree Publishing Co.

Close, Edward. Wheels, Wings, & Motors, 1 vol., 1. 2014. (Discovery Education: How It Works). (ENG.). 32p. (gr. 3-6). 26.25 *(978-1-4777-6313-1(9)*, PowerKids Pr.) Rosen Publishing Group, Inc., The.

Cobb, Annie & Jones, Davy. Ruedas! Jones, Davy, illus. 2003. (Road to Reading Ser.). (Illus.). (J). lib. bdg. 11.99 *(978-0-375-91500-0(1)*, Golden Bks.) Random Hse. Children's Bks.

De Medeiros, Michael & Banting, Erinn. Wheels & Axles. 2009. (Science Matters Ser.). (Illus.). 24p. (J). (gr. 3-5). pap. 8.95 *(978-1-60596-034-0(9))* Weigl Pubs., Inc.

Erinn, Banting. Wheels & Axles. 2009. (Science Matters Ser.). (Illus.). 24p. (J). (gr. 3-5). lib. bdg. 24.45 *(978-1-60596-033-3(0))* Weigl Pubs., Inc.

Feldman, Roseann & Walker, Sally M. Put Wheels & Axles to the Test. 2011. (Searchlight Books (tm) — How Do Simple Machines Work? Ser.). (ENG.). (gr. 3-5). pap. 51.01 *(978-0-7613-8402-1(2))* Lerner Publishing Group.

Feldman, Roseann, et al. Put Wheels & Axles to the Test. 2011. (Searchlight Books (tm) — How Do Simple Machines Work? Ser.). (ENG.). 40p. (gr. 3-5). pap. 8.95 *(978-0-7613-7870-9(7))* Lerner Publishing Group.

Gardner, Robert. Simple Machine Experiments Using Seesaws, Wheels, Pulleys, & More: One Hour or Less Science Experiments. 2012. (Last-Minute Science Projects Ser.). 48p. (J). (gr. 5-18). 25.27 *(978-0-7660-3957-5(9))* Enslow Pubs., Inc.

Goodstein, Madeline P. Wheels! Science Projects with Bicycles, Skateboards, & Skates. 2009. (Score! Sports Science Projects Ser.). (Illus.). 104p. (J). (gr. 5-9). lib. bdg. 33.27 *(978-0-7660-3107-4(1))* Enslow Pubs., Inc.

Gosman, Gillian. Wheels & Axles in Action. 2010. (Simple Machines at Work Ser.). (ENG.). 24p. (J). pap. 8.25 *(978-1-4488-1301-8(8))*; lib. bdg. 22.60 *(978-1-4488-0684-3(4))* Rosen Publishing Group, Inc., The. (PowerKids Pr.).

How Things Work Interactive Packages: Wheels on the Bus. (Pebble Soup Explorations Ser.). (gr. -1-18). 52.00 *(978-0-7578-5244-2(0))* Rigby Education.

LaMachia, Dawn. Wheels & Axles. 2015. (Zoom in on Simple Machines Ser.). (ENG.). 24p. (J). (gr. 2-2). 22.60 *(978-0-7660-6748-6(3))* Enslow Pubs., Inc.

—Wheels & Axles at Work. 2015. (Zoom in on Simple Machines Ser.). (ENG.). 24p. (J). (gr. 2-2). pap. 9.35 *(978-0-7660-6746-2(7))* Enslow Pubs., Inc.

Lindeen, Mary & Kesselring, Susan. Being Safe on Wheels. McGeehan, Dan & Moore, David, illus. 2011. (Be Safe Ser.). (ENG.). 24p. (J). (gr. k-3). lib. bdg. 27.07 *(978-1-60954-371-6(8)*, 200082) Child's World, Inc., The.

Manolis, Kay. Wheels & Axles. 2009. (Simple Machines Ser.). (ENG., Illus.). 24p. (J). (gr. 2-5). lib. bdg. 25.95 *(978-1-60014-347-2(4)*, Blastoff! Readers) Bellwether Media.

Mezzanotte, Jim. Cómo Funcionan Las Ruedas y Los Ejes. 2006. (Como funcionan las maquinas simples (How Simple Machines Work) Ser.). (SPA., Illus.). 24p. (gr. 1-4). pap. 8.15 *(978-0-8368-7451-8(X)*, Weekly Reader Leveled Readers) Stevens, Gareth Publishing LLLP.

—Cómo Funcionan las Ruedas y los Ejes. 2006. (Como funcionan las maquinas simples (How Simple Machines Work) Ser.). (SPA., Illus.). 24p. (gr. 1-4). lib. bdg. 22.00 *(978-0-8368-7446-4(3)*, Weekly Reader Leveled Readers) Stevens, Gareth Publishing LLLP.

—How Wheels & Axles Work. 2006. (How Simple Machines Work Ser.). (Illus.). 24p. (gr. 1-4). pap. 8.15 *(978-0-8368-7355-9(6))*; lib. bdg. 22.00 *(978-0-8368-7350-4(5))* Stevens, Gareth Publishing LLLP. (Weekly Reader Leveled Readers).

Miller, Tim. Wheels & Axles in My Makerspace. 2017. (Simple Machines in My Makerspace Ser.). (ENG., Illus.). 32p. (J). ***(978-0-7787-3375-1(0))*** Crabtree Publishing Co.

Owings, Lisa. Wheels. Butler, Reginald, illus. 2012. (Simple Machines Ser.). (ENG.). 24p. (J). (gr. -1-2). 27.07 *(978-1-61473-278-5(7)*, 204983) Child's World, Inc., The.

Oxlade, Chris. Making Machines with Wheels & Axles. 2015. (Simple Machine Projects Ser.). (ENG.). 32p. (gr. 2-4). 30.65 *(978-1-4109-6804-3(9)*, Raintree Perspectives) Heinemann-Raintree.

—Simple Experiments with Wheels & Axles. 2013. (Science Experiments with Simple Machines Ser.). 32p. (J). (gr. k-3). 26.50 *(978-1-61533-754-5(7))*; pap. 70.50 *(978-1-61533-826-9(8))*; pap. 11.75 *(978-1-61533-825-2(X))* Windmill Bks.

—Wheels. 2009. (Simple Machines (Smart Apple Media Paperback) Ser.). (Illus.). 32p. (J). pap. 7.95 *(978-1-59920-204-4(2))* Black Rabbit Bks.

—Wheels. 2016. (Useful Machines Ser.). (ENG.). 32p. (gr. 1-3). pap. 8.29 *(978-1-4846-3638-1(4)*, Heinemann First Library) Heinemann-Raintree.

Prince, April Jones. ¿Qué Hacen las Ruedas Todo el Día? Laroche, Giles, illus. 2013.Tr. of What Do Wheels Do All Day. (SPA & ENG.). 32p. (J). (— 1). bds. 4.99 *(978-0-547-99625-7(X))* Houghton Mifflin Harcourt Publishing Co.

—What Do Wheels Do All Day? Laroche, Giles, illus. 2006. (ENG.). 32p. (J). (gr. -1-3). 17.99 *(978-0-618-56307-4(5))* Houghton Mifflin Harcourt Publishing Co.

Randolph, Joanne. Wheels & Axles in My World. (Journeys Ser.). 24p. 2007. (ENG.). (gr. k-8). pap. 7.05 *(978-1-4042-8427-2(3)*, Rosen Classroom) 2006. (Illus.). (J). (gr. 3-7). lib. bdg. 18.75 *(978-1-4042-3313-3(X)*, PowerKids Pr.) Rosen Publishing Group, Inc., The.

—Wheels & Axles in My World: Ejes y Ruedas en Mi Mundo. 2006. (My World of Science/ Mi mundo y la Ciencia Ser.). (ENG & SPA.). (J). (gr. k-3). 16.00 *(978-1-4042-3325-6(3))* Rosen Publishing Group, Inc., The.

Rockwell, Anne F. Big Wheels. 2006. (ENG., Illus.). 11p. (J). (gr. -1-1). bds. 7.99 *(978-0-8027-8903-7(X)*, 9780802789037, Bloomsbury USA Childrens) Bloomsbury Publishing USA.

Rosa y el Escarabajo: Individual Title Six-Packs. (Literatura 2000 Ser.). (SPA.). (gr. 2-3). 33.00 *(978-0-7635-1250-7(8))* Rigby Education.

Round & Round, 6 Packs. (gr. k-1). 23.00 *(978-0-7635-9057-4(6))* Rigby Education.

Schuh, Mari C. Hauling a Pumpkin: Wheels & Axles vs. Lever. 2015. (ENG., Illus.). 24p. (J). (gr. k-2). pap. 6.99 *(978-1-4677-8304-0(8)*, Lerner Pubns.) Lerner Publishing Group.

—Holding a Door Open: Wedge vs. Wheels & Axles. 2015. (First Step Nonfiction - Simple Machines to the Rescue Ser.). (ENG., Illus.). 24p. (J). (gr. k-2). 23.99 *(978-1-4677-8303-3(X)*, Lerner Pubns.) Lerner Publishing Group.

Scott, Natalie. Wheels Make it Work. 2009. (Real Life Readers Ser.). 12p. (gr. 1-2). pap. 5.90 *(978-1-4042-7923-0(7)*, Rosen Classroom) Rosen Publishing Group, Inc., The.

ShackletonCaroline. THE WHEEL LOW INTERMEDIATE BOOK WITH ONLINE ACCESS. 2014. (ENG.). 28p. (J). pap. 9.50 *(978-1-107-66739-6(9))* Cambridge Univ. Pr.

Sian Revision Wheels at Work. 2004. (Science in A Nutshell Ser.). (J). *(978-1-59242-087-2(7))* Delta Education, LLC.

Smith, Sian. Wheels & Axles, 1 vol. 2012. (How Toys Work Ser.). (ENG.). 24p. (gr. -1-1). pap. 6.29 *(978-1-4329-6591-4(3))*; lib. bdg. 22.65 *(978-1-4329-6584-6(0))* Heinemann-Raintree. (Acorn).

Taylor, Trace. Wheels. Taylor, Trace, illus. 2012. (1-3Y Getting Around Ser.). (ENG., Illus.). 16p. (J). pap. 5.99 *(978-1-61406-201-1(3))* American Reading Co.

Tieck, Sarah. Wheels & Axles, 1 vol. 2006. (Simple Machines Ser.). (ENG., Illus.). 24p. (gr. -1-3). 25.65 *(978-1-59679-819-9(X)*, Buddy Bks.) ABDO Publishing Co.

Walker, Sally M. & Feldmann, Roseann. Put Wheels & Axles to the Test. 2011. (Searchlight Books (tm) — How Do Simple Machines Work? Ser.). (ENG., Illus.). 40p. (gr. 3-5). lib. bdg. 27.93 *(978-0-7613-5326-3(7))* Lerner Publishing Group.

—Ruedas y Ejes. King, Andy, photos by. 2005. (Libros de Física para Madrugadores (Early Bird Physics) Ser.). (SPA & ENG., Illus.). 48p. (gr. 3-6). lib. bdg. 26.60 *(978-0-8225-2982-8(3)*, Ediciones Lerner) Lerner Publishing Group.

—Wheels & Axles. 2005. (Early Bird Physics Ser.). (Illus.). 48p. (gr. 3-6). lib. bdg. 25.26 *(978-0-8225-2219-5(5))* Lerner Publishing Group.

Weakland, Mark. Los Engranajes Trabajan, las Ruedas Ruedan. 2012. (Comienza la Ciencia/Science Starts Ser.).Tr. of Gears Go, Wheels Roll. (SPA & MUL.). 32p. (gr. 1-2). lib. bdg. 27.32 *(978-1-4296-8258-9(2)*, A+ Bilingue/Bilingual) Capstone Press of Coughlan Cos.

—Fred Flintstone's Adventures with Wheels & Axles: Bedrock & Roll! Brown, Alan, illus. 2016. (Flintstones Explain Simple Machines Ser.). (ENG.). 24p. (gr. k-2). lib. bdg. 27.32 *(978-1-4914-8474-6(8))* Capstone Press of Coughlan Cos.

—Gears Go, Wheels Roll. 2011. (Science Starts Ser.). (ENG.). 32p. (gr. 1-2). pap. 47.70 *(978-1-4296-6144-7(5)*, Aplus Bks.) Capstone Press of Coughlan Cos.

Wells, Robert E. How Do You Lift a Lion? 2012. (J). 34.28 *(978-1-61913-159-0(5))* Weigl Pubs., Inc.

Wheels: Individual Title Six-Packs. (Literatura 2000 Ser.). (gr. k-1). 28.00 *(978-0-7635-0077-1(1))*; 16p. 27.00 *(978-0-7635-4446-1(9))* Rigby Education.

Woods, Michael & Woods, Mary B. Ancient Machine Technology: From Wheels to Forges. 2011. (Technology in Ancient Cultures Ser.). (ENG.). 96p. (gr. 6-12). lib. bdg. 31.93 *(978-0-7613-6523-5(0))* Lerner Publishing Group.

WHISKEY REBELLION, PA., 1794

Schiel, Katy. The Whiskey Rebellion: An Early Challenge to America's New Government. (Life in the New American Nation Ser.). 32p. 2009. (gr. 4-4). 47.90 *(978-1-61514-289-7(4))* 2004. (ENG., Illus.). (gr. 5-8). pap. 10.00 *(978-0-8239-4262-6(7))* Rosen Publishing Group, Inc., The.

WHITE HOUSE (WASHINGTON, D.C.)

Arnold, Tedd. Fly Guy Presents - The White House. Arnold, Tedd, illus. 2016. (Scholastic Reader, Level 2 Ser.). (ENG.,

Illus.). 32p. (J). (gr. k-2). pap. 3.99 *(978-0-545-91737-7(9))* Scholastic, Inc.

Blake, Kevin. The White House. 2016. (American Places: from Vision to Reality Ser.). (ENG.). 32p. (J). (gr. 2-7). lib. bdg. 19.95 *(978-1-944102-42-5(6))* Bearport Publishing Co., Inc.

Braithwaite, Jill. The White House. 2010. pap. 45.32 *(978-0-7613-6995-0(3))*; (ENG.). 32p. pap. 7.95 *(978-0-7613-6054-4(9))*; (ENG.). 32p. lib. bdg. 26.60 *(978-0-7613-6016-2(6)*, Lerner Pubns.) Lerner Publishing Group.

Carr, Aaron. The White House. 2016. (American Icons Ser.). (ENG., Illus.). (J). (gr. k-2). lib. bdg. 27.13 ***(978-1-4896-0532-0(0)**, AV2 by Weigl)* Weigl Pubs., Inc.

Clay, Kathryn. The White House: Introducing Primary Sources. 2017. (Introducing Primary Sources Ser.). (ENG.). 32p. (gr. 1-2). pap. 6.95 ***(978-1-5157-6361-1(7))***; lib. bdg. 27.99 ***(978-1-5157-6356-7(0))*** Capstone Press of Coughlan Cos.

Connors, Kathleen. What's It Like to Live in the White House? 2014. (White House Insiders Ser.). 24p. (J). (gr. 2-5). 22.60 *(978-1-4824-1110-2(5))* Stevens, Gareth Publishing LLLP.

—What's It Like to Work in the White House? 2014. (White House Insiders Ser.). 24p. (J). (gr. 2-5). 22.60 *(978-1-4824-1115-7(6))* Stevens, Gareth Publishing LLLP.

Davidson, Janice. Inside the White House. 2013. (InfoMax Readers Ser.). (ENG.). 24p. (J). (gr. 2-3). pap. 49.50 *(978-1-4777-2270-1(X))*; (Illus.). pap. 8.25 *(978-1-4777-2269-5(6))* Rosen Publishing Group, Inc., The. (Rosen Classroom).

Davis, Gibbs. First Kids. Comport, Sally Wern, illus. 2009. (Step into Reading Ser.). (ENG.). 48p. (J). (gr. 2-4). pap. 3.99 *(978-0-375-82218-6(6)*, Random Hse. Bks. for Young Readers) Random Hse. Children's Bks.

Douglas, Lloyd G. The White House. 2003. (Welcome Bks.). (ENG., Illus.). 24p. (J). (gr. -1-2). pap. 4.95 *(978-0-516-27878-0(9)*, Children's Pr.) Scholastic Library Publishing.

Eldridge, Alison & Eldridge, Stephen. The White House: An American Symbol. 2012. (All about American Symbols Ser.). 24p. (J). (gr. -1-1). (Illus.). pap. 7.95 *(978-1-4644-0050-6(4))*; 22.60 *(978-0-7660-4062-5(3))* Enslow Pubs., Inc. (Enslow Elementary).

Firestone, Mary. The White House, 1 vol. Skeens, Matthew, illus. 2006. (American Symbols Ser.). (ENG.). 24p. (gr. 1-2). 9.95 *(978-1-4048-2223-8(2))*; lib. bdg. 26.65 *(978-1-4048-2217-7(8))* Picture Window Bks.

Freeman, Martha. The Case of the Diamond Dog Collar. 2nd ed. 2011. (First Kids Mystery Ser.: 2). (ENG.). 144p. (J). 16.95 *(978-0-8234-2337-8(9))* Holiday Hse., Inc.

Fuentes, Marco. A Visit to the White House. 2016. (Spring Forward Ser.). (J). (gr. k). *(978-1-4900-3711-0(X))* Benchmark Education Co.

Gaspar, Joe. The White House. 2013. (PowerKids Readers: American Symbols Ser.). (Illus.). 24p. (J). (gr. k-2). pap. 8.25 *(978-1-4777-0817-0(0))*; pap. 49.50 *(978-1-4777-0818-7(9))*; lib. bdg. 22.60 *(978-1-4777-0738-8(7))* Rosen Publishing Group, Inc., The. (PowerKids Pr.).

—The White House / la Casa Blanca. Alamn, Eduardo, ed. 2013. (PowerKids Readers: American Symbols / Smbolos de Amrica Ser.). (ENG & SPA.). 24p. (J). (gr. k-2). 22.60 *(978-1-4777-1206-1(2)*, PowerKids Pr.) Rosen Publishing Group, Inc., The.

Gilbert, H. K. Reporting for Duty: A Day at the White House. 2009. 50p. pap. 9.95 *(978-1-4401-5686-1(7))* iUniverse, Inc.

Gourley, Robbin. First Garden: The White House Garden & How It Grew. 2011. (ENG., Illus.). 48p. (J). (gr. 1-4). 16.99 *(978-0-547-48224-8(8))* Houghton Mifflin Harcourt Publishing Co.

Healy, Nick. The White House. 2003. (J). pap. *(978-1-58417-120-1(0))*; lib. bdg. *(978-1-58417-056-3(5))* Lake Street Pubs.

Herrington, Lisa M. The White House. 2014. (Rookie Read-About(tm) American Symbols Ser.). (ENG., Illus.). 32p. (J). lib. bdg. 25.00 *(978-0-531-21567-8(9))*; pap. 5.95 *(978-0-531-21840-2(6))* Scholastic Library Publishing.

Hess, Deborah. The White House. 2007. (J). pap. 6.99 *(978-0-7614-3394-1(5))* Marshall Cavendish Corp.

Hicks, Terry Allan. Symbols of America Group 2, 6 bks., Set. Incl. Bald Eagle. (J). lib. bdg. 28.50 *(978-0-7614-2133-7(5))*; Capitol. lib. bdg. 20.95 *(978-0-7614-2132-0(7))*; Declaration of Independence. lib. bdg. 20.95 *(978-0-7614-2135-1(1))*; Ellis Island. lib. bdg. 20.95 *(978-0-7614-2134-4(3))*; Pledge of Allegiance. lib. bdg. 20.95 *(978-0-7614-2136-8(X))*; Uncle Sam. lib. bdg. 20.95 *(978-0-7614-2137-5(8))*; (Illus.). 40p. (gr. 3-7). 2006. 2007. Set lib. bdg. 171.00 *(978-0-7614-2130-6(0)*, Benchmark Bks.) Marshall Cavendish Corp.

House, Katherine L. The White House for Kids: A History of a Home, Office, & National Symbol, with 21 Activities. 2014. (For Kids Ser.). (ENG., Illus.). 144p. (J). (gr. 4). pap. 16.95 *(978-1-61374-461-1(7))* Chicago Review Pr., Inc.

Kennedy, Marge. Pets at the White House. 2009. (Scholastic News Nonfiction Readers Ser.). 24p. (J). (gr. 1-2). (ENG.). pap. 6.95 *(978-0-531-22433-5(3))*; (Illus.). 22.00 *(978-0-531-21096-3(0))* Scholastic Library Publishing.

—Scholastic News Nonfiction Readers: Let's Visit the White House, 6 vols., Set. Incl. Having Fun at the White House. Kennedy, Marge M. (Illus.). 22.00 *(978-0-531-21095-6(2))*; Pets at the White House. (Illus.). 22.00 *(978-0-531-21096-3(0))*; See Inside the White House. (Illus.). 22.00 *(978-0-531-21097-0(9))*; Story of the White House. Kennedy, Marge M. (Illus.). 22.00 *(978-0-531-21094-9(4))*; Time to Eat at the White House. 22.00 *(978-0-531-21098-7(7))*; Who Works at the White House? (Illus.). 22.00 *(978-0-531-21099-4(5))*; 24p. (J). (gr. 1-2). 2009. Set lib. bdg. 132.00 *(978-0-531-27902-1(2)*, Children's Pr.) Scholastic Library Publishing.

—See Inside the White House. 2009. (Scholastic News Nonfiction Readers Ser.). (Illus.). 24p. (J). (gr. 1-2). 22.00 *(978-0-531-21097-0(9))* Scholastic Library Publishing.

—The Story of the White House. 2009. (Scholastic News Nonfiction Readers Ser.). (ENG.). 24p. (J). (gr. 1-2). pap. 6.95 *(978-0-531-22431-1(7))* Scholastic Library Publishing.

—Time to Eat at the White House. 2009. (Scholastic News Nonfiction Readers Ser.). 24p. (J). (gr. 1-2). 22.00 *(978-0-531-21098-7(7))*; (ENG.). pap. 6.95 *(978-0-531-22436-6(8))* Scholastic Library Publishing.

—Who Works at the White House? 2009. (Scholastic News Nonfiction Readers Ser.). (Illus.). 24p. (J). (gr. 1-2). 22.00 *(978-0-531-21099-4(5))* Scholastic Library Publishing.

Kennedy, Marge M. & Kennedy, Marge. Having Fun at the White House. 2009. (Scholastic News Nonfiction Readers Ser.). (Illus.). 24p. (J). (gr. 1-2). 22.00 *(978-0-531-21095-6(2))* Scholastic Library Publishing.

—The Story of the White House. 2009. (Scholastic News Nonfiction Readers Ser.). (Illus.). 24p. (J). (gr. 1-2). 22.00 *(978-0-531-21094-9(4))* Scholastic Library Publishing.

Kenney, Karen Latchana. The White House, 1 vol. Hunt, Judith A., illus. 2011. (Our Nation's Pride Set 2 Ser.). (ENG.). 32p. (J). (gr. 1-4). 28.50 *(978-1-61641-154-1(6))* Magic Wagon.

Marcovitz, Hal. The White House. 2004. (American Symbols & Their Meanings Ser.). (Illus.). 48p. (J). (gr. 4-18). lib. bdg. 19.95 *(978-1-59084-024-5(0))* Mason Crest.

—The White House: The Home of the U. S. President. Moreno, Barry, ed. 2014. (Patriotic Symbols of America Ser.: 20). 48p. (J). (gr. 4-18). lib. bdg. 20.95 *(978-1-4222-3134-0(8))* Mason Crest.

Marsh, Carole. The Obama Family - Life in the White House: President Barack Obama, First Lady Michelle Obama, First Children Malia & Sasha. 2008. (Here & Now Ser.). 32p. (J). (gr. 2-9). pap. 8.99 *(978-0-635-07051-7(0))* Gallopade International.

Modifica, Lisa. A Timeline of the White House. 2009. (Timelines of American History Ser.). 32p. (gr. 4-4). 47.90 *(978-1-60854-393-9(5)*, Rosen Reference) Rosen Publishing Group, Inc., The.

Morrison, Jennifer. The White House. 2009. (Structural Wonders Ser.). (Illus.). 32p. (J). (gr. 4-6). lib. bdg. 9.95 *(978-1-60596-664-9(9))*; lib. bdg. 26.00 *(978-1-60596-663-2(0))* Weigl Pubs., Inc.

Morrison, Jessica & Kissock, Heather. The White House. 2012. (J). 27.13 *(978-1-61913-253-5(2))*; pap. 12.95 *(978-1-61913-259-7(1))* Weigl Pubs., Inc.

Murray, Julie. Statue of Liberty, 1 vol. 2003. (Buddy Book Ser.). (ENG., Illus.). 24p. (gr. k-4). 25.65 *(978-1-57765-669-2(5)*, Buddy Bks.) ABDO Publishing Co.

—White House, 1 vol. 2003. (Buddy Book Ser.). (ENG., Illus.). 24p. (gr. k-4). 25.65 *(978-1-57765-668-5(7)*, Buddy Bks.) ABDO Publishing Co.

Nagelhout, Ryan. 20 Fun Facts about the White House. 2013. (Fun Fact File: US History! Ser.). 32p. (J). (gr. 3-6). pap. 10.50 *(978-1-4339-9204-9(3))* Stevens, Gareth Publishing LLLP.

N.C.B.L.A. Our White House: Looking in, Looking Out. 2010. (ENG., Illus.). 256p. (J). (gr. 5). pap. 14.99 *(978-0-7636-4609-7(1))* Candlewick Pr.

Newport, Chelsea. Visiting the White House. 2013. (Rosen Readers Ser.). (ENG.). 24p. (J). (gr. 2-3). pap. 49.50 *(978-1-4777-2247-3(5))*; pap. 8.25 *(978-1-4777-2246-6(7))* Rosen Publishing Group, Inc., The. (Rosen Classroom).

O'Connor, Jane. If the Walls Could Talk: Family Life at the White House. Hovland, Gary, illus. 2004. (ENG.). 48p. (J). (gr. 1-4). 17.99 *(978-0-689-86863-4(4)*, Simon & Schuster/Paula Wiseman Bks.) Simon & Schuster/Paula Wiseman Bks.

Osborne, Mary Pope. Abe Lincoln at Last! Murdocca, Sal, illus. 2013. (Magic Tree House Merlin Mission Ser.: 19). (ENG.). 144p. (J). (gr. 2-5). 5.99 *(978-0-375-86797-2(X)*, Random Hse. Bks. for Young Readers) Random Hse. Children's Bks.

Owings, Lisa. Ghosts in the White House. 2016. (Ghost Stories Ser.). (ENG., Illus.). 24p. (J). (gr. 3-7). 25.95 *(978-1-62617-432-0(6)*, Epic Bks.) Bellwether Media.

Petruccio, Steven James. The History of the White House Coloring Book. 2010. (Dover History Coloring Book Ser.). (ENG.). 32p. (gr. 3-5). pap. 3.99 *(978-0-486-47556-1(5))* Dover Pubns., Inc.

Proudfit, Benjamin. Building the White House. 2015. (What You Didn't Know about History Ser.). (ENG., Illus.). 24p. (J). (gr. 2-3). pap. 8.15 *(978-1-4824-1930-6(0))* Stevens, Gareth Publishing LLLP.

Rajczak, Michael. Haunted! The White House. 2013. (History's Most Haunted Ser.). (Illus.). 32p. (J). (gr. 3-6). pap. 10.50 *(978-1-4339-9269-8(8))*; lib. bdg. 26.60 *(978-1-4339-9268-1(X))* Stevens, Gareth Publishing LLLP.

—Haunted! the White House. 2013. (History's Most Haunted Ser.). 32p. (J). (gr. 3-6). pap. 63.00 *(978-1-4339-9270-4(1))* Stevens, Gareth Publishing LLLP.

Reeves, Diane Lindsey & White, Kelly. Choose Your Own Career Adventure at the White House. 2016. (Bright Futures Press: Choose Your Own Career Adventure Ser.). (ENG., Illus.). 32p. (J). (gr. 4-6). 29.93 *(978-1-63471-916-2(6)*, 208985) Cherry Lake Publishing.

Sabuda, Robert. The White House: A Pop-Up of Our Nation's Home. Sabuda, Robert, illus. 2015. (ENG., Illus.). 12p. (J). (gr. 1-3). bds. 29.99 *(978-0-545-54089-6(5)*, Orchard Bks.) Scholastic, Inc.

Silate, Jennifer. The White House. (Primary Sources of American Symbols Ser.). 24p. 2009. (gr. 3-3). 42.50 *(978-1-60851-512-7(5)*, PowerKids Pr.) 2006. (Illus.). (J). (gr. 4-7). lib. bdg. 22.60 *(978-1-4042-2695-1(8))* Rosen Publishing Group, Inc., The.

Sipperley, Keli. The White House. 2014. (ENG.). 32p. (gr. 3-6). 32.79 *(978-1-62717-744-3(2))* Rourke Educational Media.

Slade, Suzanne. The House That George Built. Bond, Rebecca, illus. 2012. (ENG.). 32p. (J). (gr. 1-4). 16.95 *(978-1-58089-262-9(0))* Charlesbridge Publishing, Inc.

Smith, A. g. & Smith, A. G. The White House Cut & Assemble. 2010. (Dover Children's Activity Bks.). (ENG., Illus.). 20p. (J). (gr. 3-6). pap. 9.99 *(978-0-486-47681-0(2))* Dover Pubns., Inc.

Smith, Charles R., Jr. Brick by Brick. Cooper, Floyd, illus. 2012. (ENG.). 32p. (J). (gr. -1-3). 17.99 *(978-0-06-192082-0(7)*, Amistad) HarperCollins Pubs.

—Brick by Brick. 2015. (J). lib. bdg. 17.20 *(978-0-606-37371-5(3))* Turtleback Bks.

Stevens, Stewart, Sr. The White House Chandeliers: My Experiences While Working for Seven U. S. Presidents. 2016. (ENG., Illus.). xi, 127p. (gr. 6-17). pap. 25.00 *(978-0-9974925-0-7(3))* Lightning Fast Bk. Publishing.

Stine, Megan. Where Is the White House? 2015. (Where Is... ? Ser.). lib. bdg. 16.00 *(978-0-606-36591-8(5))* Turtleback Bks.

Stine, Megan & dePaola, Tomie. Where Is the White House? Groff, David, illus. 2015. (Where Is? Ser.). (ENG.). 112p. (J). (gr. 3-7). 5.99 *(978-0-448-48355-9(6)*, Grosset & Dunlap) Penguin Young Readers Group.

Sutcliffe, Jane. The White House Is Burning: August 24 1814. Farquharson, Alexander, illus. 2014. (ENG.). 128p. (J). (gr. 4-7). 19.95 *(978-1-58089-656-6(1))* Charlesbridge Publishing, Inc.

Waters, Kate. Curious about the White House. 2016. (Smithsonian Ser.). (ENG., Illus.). 32p. (J). (gr. 1-3). pap. 3.99 *(978-0-399-54145-2(4)*, Grosset & Dunlap) Penguin Young Readers Group.

White House Insiders. 2014. (White House Insiders Ser.). 24p. (J). (gr. 2-5). 135.60 *(978-1-4824-1089-1(3))*; pap. 41.70 *(978-1-4824-1595-7(X))* Stevens, Gareth Publishing LLLP.

Wilson, Jon. The White House. 2014. (United States Landmarks Ser.). (ENG.). 24p. (J). (gr. 1-4). 27.07 *(978-1-62323-960-2(5)*, 206735) Child's World, Inc., The.

20 Fun Facts about the White House. 2013. (Fun Fact File: US History! Ser.). 32p. (J). (gr. 3-6). pap. 63.00 *(978-1-4339-9205-6(1))* Stevens, Gareth Publishing LLLP.

WHITMAN, MARCUS, 1802-1847—FICTION

Frazier, Neta. The Stout-Hearted Seven: Orphaned on the Oregon Trail. 2017. (Great Leaders & Events Ser.). (ENG.). (J). (gr. 4-8). lib. bdg. 35.99 ***(978-1-942875-43-7(6))*** Quarto Publishing Group USA.

Frazier, Neta Lohnes. The Stout-Hearted Seven: Orphaned on the Oregon Trail. 2016. (Young Voyageur Ser.). (ENG., Illus.). 224p. (J). (gr. 4-9). pap. 12.99 *(978-0-7603-5224-3(0)*, Voyageur Pr.) Quarto Publishing Group USA.

—The Stout-Hearted Seven: Orphaned on the Oregon Trail. 2006. (Sterling Point Books(r) Ser.). (ENG., Illus.). 208p. (J). (gr. 4-7). pap. 6.95 *(978-1-4027-3617-9(7))* Sterling Publishing Co., Inc.

WHITMAN, NARCISSA (PRENTISS), 1808-1847

Harness, Cheryl. The Tragic Tale of Narcissa Whitman & a Faithful History of the Oregon Trail. Harness, Cheryl, illus. 2006. (Cheryl Harness Histories Ser.). (ENG., Illus.). 144p. (J). (gr. 5-9). 16.95 *(978-0-7922-5920-6(3))*; lib. bdg. 25.90 *(978-0-7922-5921-3(1))* National Geographic Society. (National Geographic Children's Bks.).

WHITMAN, WALT, 1819-1892

Beene, Alex. Reading & Interpreting the Works of Walt Whitman. 2017. (Lit Crit Guides). 160p. (J). (gr. 8-8). lib. bdg. 39.93 ***(978-0-7660-8495-7(7))*** Enslow Pubs., Inc.

Kerley, Barbara. Walt Whitman: Words for America. Selznick, Brian, illus. 2004. (ENG.). 56p. (J). (gr. 2-5). 17.99 *(978-0-439-35791-3(8)*, Scholastic Pr.) Scholastic, Inc.

Llanas, Sheila Griffin. Walt Whitman, 1 vol. 2013. (Great American Authors Ser.). (ENG.). 48p. (J). (gr. 3-6). lib. bdg. 32.79 *(978-1-61783-720-3(2))* ABDO Publishing Co.

Loewen, Nancy. Walt Whitman. Day, Rob, illus. 2014. 47p. 35.65 *(978-1-60818-329-6(7)*, Creative Education) Creative Co., The.

Riggs, Thomas, ed. Democracy in the Poetry of Walt Whitman. 2012. (Social Issues in Literature Ser.). (ENG., Illus.). 224p. (gr. 10-12). pap. 28.45 *(978-0-7377-6378-2(7))*; lib. bdg. 40.95 *(978-0-7377-6377-5(9))* Cengage Gale. (Greenhaven Pr., Inc.).

Whiting, Jim & Loewen, Nancy. Voices in Poetry: Walt Whitman. Day, Rob, illus. 2015. (Voices in Poetry Ser.). (ENG.). 48p. (J). (gr. 5-8). pap. 12.00 *(978-1-62832-057-2(5)*, Creative Paperbacks) Creative Co., The.

WHITNEY, ELI, 1765-1825

Bethea, Nikole Brooks. The Invention of the Cotton Gin. 2017. (Engineering That Made America Ser.). (ENG.). 32p. (J). (gr. 3-6). lib. bdg. 28.50 *(978-1-5038-1642-8(7)*, 211158) Child's World, Inc., The.

Cefrey, Holly. The Inventions of Eli Whitney: The Cotton Gin. (19th Century American Inventors Ser.). 24p. 2009. (gr. 2-3). 42.50 *(978-1-60854-951-1(8))* 2003. (ENG., Illus.). (J). (gr. 3-6). lib. bdg. 22.60 *(978-0-8239-6443-7(4))* Rosen Publishing Group, Inc., The. (PowerKids Pr.).

Davis, Marc & Santella, Andrew. The Wright Brothers: Inventors & Aviators. 2003. (Our People Ser.). (ENG., Illus.). 32p. (J). (gr. 3-6). 29.93 *(978-1-56766-369-3(9)*, 200657) Child's World, Inc., The.

Garcia, Tracy J. Eli Whitney. 2013. (Jr. Graphic American Inventors Ser.). (ENG., Illus.). 24p. (J). (gr. 3-6). pap. 10.60 *(978-1-4777-0135-5(4))*; lib. bdg. 25.25 *(978-1-4777-0075-4(7))* Rosen Publishing Group, Inc., The. (PowerKids Pr.).

Gibson, Karen Bush. Eli Whitney. 2006. (Profiles in American History Ser.). (Illus.). 48p. (J). (gr. 3-7). lib. bdg. 29.95 *(978-1-58415-434-1(9))* Mitchell Lane Pubs., Inc.

Gunderson, Jessica Sarah, et al. Eli Whitney & the Cotton Gin, 1 vol. Acerno, Gerry, illus. 2007. (Inventions & Discovery Ser.). (ENG.). 32p. (gr. 3-4). per. 8.10 *(978-0-7368-7895-1(5)*, Graphic Library) Capstone Press of Coughlan Cos.

—Eli Whitney & the Cotton Gin, 1 vol. Acerno, Gerry et al, illus. 2007. (Inventions & Discovery Ser.). (ENG.). 32p. (gr. 3-4). 30.65 *(978-0-7368-6843-3(7)*, Graphic Library) Capstone Press of Coughlan Cos.

Huff, Regan A. Eli Whitney: The Cotton Gin & American Manufacturing. 2009. (Library of American Lives & Times Ser.). 112p. (gr. 5-5). 69.20 *(978-1-60853-478-4(2))* Rosen Publishing Group, Inc., The.

Mitchell, Barbara. Maker of Machines: A Story about Eli Whitney. Jones, Jan Naimo, tr. Jones, Jan Naimo, illus. 2004. (Creative Minds Biographies Ser.). (ENG.). 64p. (gr. 4-8). 22.60 *(978-1-57505-603-6(8)*, Carolrhoda Bks.); pap. 8.95 *(978-1-57505-634-0(8))* Lerner Publishing Group.

Welch, Catherine A. Eli Whitney: History Maker Bios Set. 2008. pap. 52.95 *(978-0-8225-9388-1(2))* Lerner Publishing Group.

WHITTIER, JOHN GREENLEAF, 1807-1892

Cody, Sherwin. Four American Poets. 2009. 198p. pap. 14.14 *(978-0-217-47860-1(3))* General Bks. LLC.

WHITTINGTON, RICHARD, 1358-1423

Potter, Melisande, illus. Dick Whittington & His Cat. 2006. (ENG.). 32p. (J). (gr. -1-3). 16.95 *(978-0-8234-1987-6(8))* Holiday Hse., Inc.

WHITTLING

see Wood-Carving

WIESEL, ELIE, 1928-2016

Bayer, Linda N. Elie Wiesel: Spokesman for Remembrance. 2005. (Holocaust Biographies Ser.). (Illus.). 112p. (J). (gr. 7-12). lib. bdg. 34.60 *(978-0-8239-3306-8(7)*, HBWIES) Rosen Publishing Group, Inc., The.

Dakers, Diane. Elie Wiesel: Holocaust Survivor & Messenger for Humanity. 2012. (ENG., Illus.). 112p. (J). *(978-0-7787-2552-7(9))*; pap. *(978-0-7787-2555-8(3))* Crabtree Publishing Co.

Elie Wiesel's Night. 2009. (Bloom's Guides). 136p. (C). (gr. 9-18). 30.00 *(978-1-60413-198-7(5)*, Chelsea Hse.) Facts On File, Inc.

Houghton, Sarah. Elie Wiesel: A Holocaust Survivor Cries Out for Peace. 2003. (High Five Reading - Green Ser.). (ENG., Illus.). 48p. (J). (gr. 3-4). per. 9.00 *(978-0-7368-2833-8(8)*, High Five Reading (RBL)) Capstone Press of Coughlan Cos.

—Elie Wiesel Set: A Holocaust Survivor Cries Out for Peace, 6. 2003. (High Five Reading - Green Ser.). (ENG.). 48p. (gr. 3-4). pap. 54.00 *(978-0-7368-2843-7(5)*, High Five Reading (RBL)) Capstone Press of Coughlan Cos.

Koestler-Grack, Rachel. Elie Wiesel: Witness for Humanity. 2009. (Life Portraits Ser.). (Illus.). 112p. (J). (gr. 7-12). lib. bdg. 36.00 *(978-1-4339-0054-9(8)*, 1293616) Stevens, Gareth Publishing LLLP.

Moore, Lisa. Elie Wiesel: Surviving the Holocaust, Speaking Out Against Genocide. 2005. (Holocaust Heroes & Nazi Criminals Ser.). (Illus.). 160p. (J). (gr. 7-12). lib. bdg. 27.93 *(978-0-7660-2576-9(4))* Enslow Pubs., Inc.

Silverman, Jean. Elie Wiesel, 01 vols., 1. 2016. (Holocaust Ser.). (ENG., Illus.). 112p. (J). 35.60 *(978-1-4994-6250-0(6)*, Rosen Young Adult) Rosen Publishing Group, Inc., The.

Wagner, Heather Lehr. Elie Wiesel: Messenger of Peace. 2007. (Modern Peacemakers Ser.). (Illus.). 112p. (YA). (gr. 9-12). lib. bdg. 30.00 *(978-0-7910-9220-0(8))* Facts On File, Inc.

WIESENTHAL, SIMON, 1908-2005

Rubin, Susan Goldman. The Anne Frank Case: Simon Wiesenthal's Search for the Truth. Farnsworth, Bill, illus. 2009. (ENG.). 40p. (J). (gr. 5-18). 18.95 *(978-0-8234-2109-1(0))* Holiday Hse., Inc.

WIGMAKERS

Sullivan, Laura L. The Colonial Wigmaker. 2015. (Colonial People Ser.). (ENG.). 48p. (J). (gr. 4-4). 31.36 *(978-1-5026-0480-4(9))* Cavendish Square Publishing.

WILBERFORCE, WILLIAM, 1759-1833

Belmonte, Kevin. Travel with William Wilberforce: The Friend of Humanity. 2006. (Travel With... Ser.). (Illus.). 128p. per. 15.00 *(978-1-84625-027-9(7))* DayOne Pubns. GBR. Dist: Send The Light Distribution LLC.

Benge, Janet & Benge, Geoff. William Wilberforce: Take up the Fight. 2015. (ENG.). 201p. (YA). pap. 9.99 *(978-1-62486-057-7(5))* Emerald Bks.

Edwards, Andrew & Thornton, Fleur. Wilberforce: an Activity Book: 24 Ready to Use Lesson Plans. 2007. (Illus.). 32p. (J). (gr. 3-7). pap. 6.99 *(978-0-89221-672-7(7))* New Leaf Pub. Group.

WILD ANIMALS

see Animals

WILD BOAR

Avett, Harper. Wild Boars. 2016. (Creatures of the Forest Habitat Ser.). 00024p. (J). (gr. 3-3). pap. 8.25 *(978-1-4994-2718-9(2)*, PowerKids Pr.) Rosen Publishing Group, Inc., The.

Somervill, Barbara & Gray, Susan H. Wild Boar. 2009. (21st Century Skills Library: Animal Invaders Ser.). (ENG.). 32p. (gr. 4-8). lib. bdg. 28.50 *(978-1-60279-329-3(8)*, 200225) Cherry Lake Publishing.

Thatcher, Henry. Wild Boars & Teacup Pigs, 1 vol., 1. 2014. (Big Animals, Small Animals Ser.). (ENG.). 32p. (J). (gr. k-5). 26.25 *(978-1-4777-6097-0(0)*, PowerKids Pr.) Rosen Publishing Group, Inc., The.

WILD BOAR—FICTION

Rosoff, Meg. Meet Wild Boars. Blackall, Sophie, illus. 2008. (Wild Boars Ser.). (ENG.). 40p. (J). (gr. k-3). pap. 7.99 *(978-0-312-37963-6(3)*, 9780312379636) Square Fish.

WILD FLOWERS

Bredeson, Carmen & Cousins, Lindsey. Can You Find These Flowers? 2012. (All about Nature Ser.). 24p. (J). (gr. -1-16). 22.60 *(978-0-7660-3976-6(5))* Enslow Pubs., Inc.

Cooke, Arthur O. Flowers of the Farm. 2007. (ENG., Illus.). 80p. per. *(978-1-4065-1515-2(9))* Dodo Pr.

Forey, Pamela. Wild Flowers of the United States & Canada. 2004. (World Book's Science & Nature Guides Ser.). (Illus.). 80p. (J). *(978-0-7166-4220-6(4))* World Bk., Inc.

Green, Jen. Wild Flowers, 01 vols., 1. 2016. (Adventures in Nature Ser.). (ENG.). 32p. (J). pap. 10.00 *(978-1-5081-4594-3(6)*, PowerKids Pr.) Rosen Publishing Group, Inc., The.

Green, John. Wildflowers GemGlow Stained Glass Coloring Book. 2009. (Dover Nature Stained Glass Coloring Book Ser.). (ENG., Illus.). 32p. (J). (gr. 1-5). pap. 7.99 *(978-0-486-47148-8(9))* Dover Pubns., Inc.

Kavanagh, James. Hawaii Trees & Wildflowers: A Folding Pocket Guide to Familiar Species. Leung, Raymond, illus. 2010. (Pocket Naturalist Guide Ser.). (ENG.). 1p. 6.95 *(978-1-58355-509-5(9))* Western National Parks Assn.

Kershaw, Linda. Alberta Wayside Wildflowers, 1 vol. Kershaw, Linda, illus. rev. ed. 2003. (ENG., Illus.). 160p. (gr. 4). pap. 16.95 *(978-1-55105-350-9(0)*, 1551053500) Lone Pine Publishing USA.

Kershaw, Linda J. Manitoba Wayside Wildflowers, 1 vol. rev. ed. 2003. (ENG., Illus.). 160p. (gr. 4). pap. 16.95 *(978-1-55105-352-3(7)*, 1551053527) Lone Pine Publishing USA.

Kukolax, Andy. Ultralight Wildflower Guide to the Central Montana Rocky Mountains: Wildflower Montana. 2003. (Illus.). 64p. pap. 19.95 *(978-0-9729940-0-2(9))* Diamond Springs Pr.

Ruggiero, M. Wild Flowers of North America. rev. ed. 2004. (Spotter's Guides). (ENG.). 64p. (J). pap. 5.95 *(978-0-7945-0256-0(3))* EDC Publishing.

Tenenbaum, Frances & Peterson, Roger Tory. Wildflowers. Peterson, Roger Tory, ed. Savage, Virginia, illus. 2013. (Peterson Field Guide Color-In Bks.). (ENG.). 64p. (J). 8.95

W X Y Z

(978-0-544-02697-1(7)) Houghton Mifflin Harcourt Publishing Co.

Voake, Charlotte. A Little Guide to Wild Flowers. 2007. (ENG., Illus.). 80p. (J). (gr. -1-2). pap. 16.99 *(978-1-903919-11-8(8))* Transworld Publishers Ltd. GBR. Dist: Independent Pubs. Group.

Wildflowers. (Color & Learn Ser.). 36p. (J). (gr. 1-5). pap. *(978-1-882210-02-2(6))* Action Publishing, Inc.

WILD FOWL

see Water Birds

WILD LIFE CONSERVATION

see Wildlife Conservation

WILDEBEESTS

see Gnus

WILDER, LAURA INGALLS, 1867-1957

Alter, Judy & Alter, Judy. Laura Ingalls Wilder: Pioneer & Author. 2003. (Our People Ser.). (ENG., Illus.). 32p. (J). (gr. 3-6). 29.93 *(978-1-59296-007-1(3)*, 200644) Child's World, Inc., The.

Anderson, William. Laura Ingalls Wilder: A Biography. 2007. (Little House Nonfiction Ser.). (ENG., Illus.). 256p. (J). (gr. 3-7). pap. 6.99 *(978-0-06-088552-6(1)*, Collins) HarperCollins Pubs.

—Laura's Album. 2017. (Little House Nonfiction Ser.). 80p. (J). (gr. 3-7). 21.99 *(978-0-06-245934-3(1))* HarperCollins Pubs.

Benge, Janet & Benge, Geoff. Heroes of History - Laura Ingalls Wilder: A Storybook Life. 2005. (Heroes of History Ser.). (ENG., Illus.). 196p. (YA). (gr. 4-7). pap. 9.99 *(978-1-932096-32-3(9))* Emerald Bks.

Bennett, Doraine. Laura Ingalls Wilder: Little World Biographies. 2013. (ENG.). 24p. (gr. k-3). pap. 8.95 *(978-1-61810-293-5(1))* Rourke Educational Media.

Berne, Emma Carlson. Laura Ingalls Wilder, 1 vol. 2007. (Essential Lives Set 1 Ser.). (ENG., Illus.). 112p. (J). (gr. 6-12). lib. bdg. 35.64 *(978-1-59928-843-7(5))* ABDO Publishing Co.

Collins, Carolyn Strom & Eriksson, Christina Wyss. The World of Little House. Williams, Garth & Maze, Deborah, illus. 2015. (Little House Nonfiction Ser.). (ENG.). 160p. (J). (gr. 3). 29.99 *(978-0-06-243049-6(1))* HarperCollins Pubs.

Demuth, Patricia Brennan. Who Was Laura Ingalls Wilder? 2013. (Who Was? Ser.). (ENG., Illus.). 112p. (J). (gr. 3-7). 5.99 *(978-0-448-46706-1(2)*, Grosset & Dunlap) Penguin Young Readers Group.

—Who Was Laura Ingalls Wilder? 2013. (Who Was... ? Ser.). lib. bdg. 16.00 *(978-0-606-32134-1(9)*, Turtleback) Turtleback Bks.

Ford, Carin T. Laura Ingalls Wilder: Real-Life Pioneer of the Little House Books. 2003. (People to Know Ser.). (Illus.). 112p. (J). lib. bdg. 26.60 *(978-0-7660-2105-1(X))* Enslow Pubs., Inc.

Giff, Patricia Reilly. Laura Ingalls Wilder. 2014. (Women of Our Time Ser.). (ENG., Illus.). 80p. (J). (gr. 3-7). pap. 7.99 *(978-0-14-751364-9(2)*, Puffin Books) Penguin Young Readers Group.

Herweck Rice, Dona. Laura Ingalls Wilder: Pioneer Woman (America in The 1800s) 2017. (Primary Source Readers Ser.). (Illus.). 32p. (J). (gr. 4-5). pap. 8.99 ***(978-1-4938-3798-4(2))*** Teacher Created Materials, Inc.

Hill, Pamela Smith. Laura Ingalls Wilder: A Writer's Life. 2007. (South Dakota Biography Ser.). (Illus.). 244p. per. *(978-0-9777955-6-7(X)*, South Dakota State Historical Society Pr.) South Dakota State Historical Society Pr.

Ingalls, Laura. Aquellos Años Dorado. 2003. (SPA., Illus.). 222p. (gr. 5-8). pap. 12.99 *(978-84-279-3255-5(3))* Noguer y Caralt Editores, S. A. ESP. Dist: Lectorum Pubns., Inc.

Leaf, Christina. Laura Ingalls Wilder. 2015. (Children's Storytellers Ser.). (ENG., Illus.). 24p. (J). (gr. 2-5). lib. bdg. 25.95 *(978-1-62617-269-2(2)*, Blastoff! Readers) Bellwether Media.

Mara, Wil. Laura Ingalls Wilder. 2003. (Rookie Biographies Ser.). (ENG., Illus.). 32p. (J). (gr. 1-2). 20.50 *(978-0-516-22855-6(2)*, Children's Pr.) Scholastic Library Publishing.

Mara, Wil & National Geographic Learning Staff. Laura Ingalls Wilder. 2010. (Rise & Shine Ser.). (ENG.). 32p. (C). (gr. 1-2). pap. 7.95 *(978-0-516-27840-7(1))* National Geographic School Publishing, Inc.

Parker, Christi E. Laura Ingalls Wilder, 1 vol. 2005. (Primary Source Readers Ser.). (ENG.). 24p. (J). (gr. 4-4). pap. 8.99 *(978-0-7439-8910-7(4))* Shell Educational Publishing.

Rajczak, Kristen. Laura Ingalls Wilder in Her Own Words. 2016. (Eyewitness to History Ser.). (ENG.). 32p. (J). (gr. 4-5). pap. 10.50 *(978-1-4824-4070-6(9))* Stevens, Gareth Publishing LLLP.

Scraper, Katherine. Laura Ingalls Wilder. 2011. (Early Connections Ser.). (J). *(978-1-61672-555-6(9))* Benchmark Education Co.

—Laura Ingalls Wilder & Laura Ingalls Wilder (Spanish) 6 English, 6 Spanish Adaptations. 2011. (ENG & SPA.). (J). 75.00 net. *(978-1-4108-5620-3(8))* Benchmark Education Co.

Sickels, Amy. Laura Ingalls Wilder. 2007. (Who Wrote That? Ser.). (Illus.). 126p. (gr. 6-12). lib. bdg. 35.00 *(978-0-7910-9525-6(8)*, Chelsea Hse.) Facts On File, Inc.

Stone, Tanya Lee & Dorling Kindersley Publishing Staff. Laura Ingalls Wilder. 2009. (DK Biography Ser.). (ENG.). 128p. (J). (gr. 5-12). 6.99 *(978-0-7566-4508-3(5)*, DK Children) Dorling Kindersley Publishing, Inc.

Wilder, Laura Ingalls. A Little House Traveler: Writings from Laura Ingalls Wilder's Journeys Across America. 2011. (Little House Nonfiction Ser.). (ENG., Illus.). 368p. (J). (gr. 5). pap. 7.99 *(978-0-06-072492-4(7)*, Collins) HarperCollins Pubs.

WILDERNESS SURVIVAL

Awa, Solomon. Igluvigaliurniq Qamusiurnirlu: How to Build an Iglu & a Qamutiik, 1 vol. Breithaupt, Andrew, illus. 2013. (ENG.). 32p. (J). (gr. 3-6). 9.95 *(978-1-927095-31-7(X))* Inhabit Media Inc. CAN. Dist: Independent Pubs. Group.

Bailey, Diane. Survival Skills, Vol. 10. 2016. (Great Outdoors! Ser.). (Illus.). 48p. (J). (gr. 5). 20.95 *(978-1-4222-3574-4(2))* Mason Crest.

Bath, Louella. Making Fire in the Wild, 01 vols., 1. 2016. (Wilderness Survival Skills Ser.). (ENG., Illus.). 24p. (J). pap. 8.25 *(978-1-5081-4320-8(X)*, PowerKids Pr.) Rosen Publishing Group, Inc., The.

Bell, Samantha. How to Survive in the Wilderness. 2015. (Survival Guides). (ENG.). 24p. (J). (gr. 2-5). 27.07 *(978-1-60973-160-1(3)*, 208796) Child's World, Inc., The.

—How to Survive on a Deserted Island. 2015. (Survival Guides). (ENG.). 24p. (J). (gr. 2-5). 27.07 *(978-1-60973-162-5(X)*, 208797) Child's World, Inc., The.

Bowman, Chris. Survive in the Mountains. 2016. (Survival Zone Ser.). (ENG., Illus.). 24p. (J). (gr. 3-7). 25.95 *(978-1-62617-446-7(6)*, Torque Bks.) Bellwether Media.

—Survive in the Woods. 2016. (Survival Zone Ser.). (ENG., Illus.). 24p. (J). (gr. 3-7). 25.95 *(978-1-62617-447-4(4)*, Torque Bks.) Bellwether Media.

Brown, Alex. Mountain Adventures. 2009. (Difficult & Dangerous Ser.). (J). 28.50 *(978-1-59920-157-3(7))* Black Rabbit Bks.

—Mountain Adventures. 2009. (Difficult & Dangerous Ser.). (Illus.). 32p. (J). pap. *(978-1-897563-25-0(6))* Saunders Bk. Co.

Brush, Jim & Scarborough, Kate. Extreme Survival. 2012. (Fast Facts Ser.). (Illus.). 32p. (gr. 4-6). pap. 28.50 *(978-1-59771-325-2(2))* Sea-To-Sea Pubns.

Champion, Neil. Finding Your Way. 2010. (Survive Alive Ser.). 32p. (J). (gr. 3-6). 28.50 *(978-1-60753-038-1(4))* Amicus Publishing.

—Finding Your Way. 2012. (Illus.). 32p. (gr. 3-7). pap. 8.95 *(978-1-926722-56-6(6))* Saunders Bk. Co. CAN. Dist: RiverStream Publishing.

—Making Shelter. 2010. (Survive Alive Ser.). 32p. (YA). (gr. 3-6). 28.50 *(978-1-60753-041-1(4))* Amicus Publishing.

—Making Shelter. 2012. (Illus.). 32p. (gr. 3-7). pap. 8.95 *(978-1-926722-59-7(0))* Saunders Bk. Co. CAN. Dist: RiverStream Publishing.

—Tools & Crafts. 2010. (Survive Alive Ser.). 32p. (J). (gr. 3-6). 28.50 *(978-1-60753-042-8(2))* Amicus Publishing.

—Tools & Crafts. 2012. (Illus.). 32p. (gr. 3-7). pap. 8.95 *(978-1-926722-60-3(4))* Saunders Bk. Co. CAN. Dist: RiverStream Publishing.

Champion, Neil & Ganeri, Anita. Finding Food & Water. 2011. (How the World Makes Music Ser.). 32p. (gr. 4-7). lib. bdg. 31.35 *(978-1-59920-478-9(9))* Black Rabbit Bks.

—Making Shelter. 2011. (How the World Makes Music Ser.). 32p. (gr. 4-7). lib. bdg. 31.35 *(978-1-59920-477-2(0))* Black Rabbit Bks.

—Tools & Crafts. 2011. (How the World Makes Music Ser.). 32p. (gr. 4-7). lib. bdg. 31.35 *(978-1-59920-481-9(9))* Black Rabbit Bks.

Decker, William. Getting Rescued in the Wild, 01 vols., 1. 2016. (Wilderness Survival Skills Ser.). (ENG., Illus.). 24p. (J). pap. 8.25 *(978-1-5081-4315-4(3)*, PowerKids Pr.) Rosen Publishing Group, Inc., The.

Doeden, Matt. Can You Survive the Wilderness? An Interactive Survival Adventure, 1 vol. 2012. (You Choose: Survival Ser.). (ENG.). 112p. (gr. 3-4). pap. 6.95 *(978-1-4296-7996-1(4))*; pap. 41.70 *(978-1-4296-8480-4(1))*; lib. bdg. 31.99 *(978-1-4296-7542-0(X))* Capstone Press of Coughlan Cos. (You Choose Bks.).

Donovan, Sandra. Deadliest Destinations. 2013. (ShockZone — Deadly & Dangerous Ser.). (ENG.). 32p. (gr. 5-8). lib. bdg. 26.60 *(978-1-4677-0600-1(0)*, Lerner Pubns.) Lerner Publishing Group.

Donovan, Sandy. Deadly Danger Zones. 2013. (ShockZone — Deadly & Dangerous Ser.). (ENG., Illus.). 32p. (gr. 5-8). pap. 8.95 *(978-1-4677-0890-6(9))* Lerner Publishing Group.

Erwin, Wesley. Boundary Waters ABC, 1 vol. Kemp, Kathie, illus. 2014. (ENG.). 64p. (J). (gr. -1-k). 12.95 *(978-1-59193-498-1(2))* Adventure Pubns.

Flynn, Mike. The Science of Survival: The Ultimate Survival Guide. unabr. ed. 2010. (Science Of... Ser.). (ENG., Illus.). 144p. (J). (gr. 2-6). 13.95 *(978-0-330-46725-4(5))* Macmillan Pubs., Ltd. GBR. Dist: Independent Pubs. Group.

Goldish, Meish. Lost in the Woods. 2015. (Illus.). 32p. (J). lib. bdg. *(978-1-62724-293-6(7))* Bearport Publishing Co., Inc.

Green, Jen. Extreme Survival. 2010. (Unpredictable Nature Ser.). (Illus.). 48p. (J). (gr. 3-18). lib. bdg. 19.95 *(978-1-4222-1999-7(2))* Mason Crest.

Hanel, Rachael. Can You Survive Antarctica? An Interactive Survival Adventure, 1 vol. 2011. (You Choose: Survival Ser.). (ENG.). 112p. (gr. 3-4). pap. 6.95 *(978-1-4296-7345-7(1))*; pap. 41.70 *(978-1-4296-7346-4(X))*; lib. bdg. 31.99 *(978-1-4296-6589-6(0))* Capstone Press of Coughlan Cos. (You Choose Bks.).

Hicks, Dwayne. Finding Water in the Wild, 01 vols., 1. 2016. (Wilderness Survival Skills Ser.). (ENG., Illus.). 24p. (J). pap. 8.25 *(978-1-5081-4311-6(0)*, PowerKids Pr.) Rosen Publishing Group, Inc., The.

Jankowski, Susan & Library. True Wilderness Rescue Stories. 2010. (True Rescue Stories Ser.). 48p. (J). lib. bdg. 22.60 *(978-0-7660-3666-6(9))* Enslow Pubs., Inc.

King, Vickie. Search Dogs & You, a Wilderness Safety Guide from American Search Dogs. 2009. 32p. pap. 13.00 *(978-1-60860-105-9(6)*, Strategic Bk. Publishing) Strategic Book Publishing & Rights Agency (SBPRA).

Lassieur, Allison. Can You Survive Being Lost at Sea? An Interactive Survival Adventure, 1 vol. 2013. (You Choose: Survival Ser.). (ENG., 112p. (gr. 3-4). Illus.). pap. 6.95 *(978-1-62065-711-9(2))*; pap. 41.70 *(978-1-62065-712-6(0))*; (Illus.). lib. bdg. 31.99 *(978-1-4296-6861-3(X))* Capstone Press of Coughlan Cos. (You Choose Bks.).

Lewis, Brenda Ralph. Wilderness Rescue with the U. S. Search & Rescue Task Force. 2004. (Rescue & Prevention Ser.). (Illus.). 96p. (YA). (gr. 7-18). lib. bdg. 22.95 *(978-1-59084-404-5(1))* Mason Crest.

Mack, Dave. Making Shelter in the Wild, 01 vols., 1. 2016. (Wilderness Survival Skills Ser.). (ENG., Illus.). 24p. (J). pap. 8.25 *(978-1-5081-4323-9(4)*, PowerKids Pr.) Rosen Publishing Group, Inc., The.

Marciniak, Kristin. Surviving in the Wilderness. 2014. (Shockzone: True Survival Stories Ser.). (ENG., Illus.). 32p. (gr. 5-8). lib. bdg. 26.60 *(978-1-4677-1437-2(2)*, Lerner Pubns.) Lerner Publishing Group.

Mathias, Adeline. How a Young Brave Survived. Hamilton, Penny, ed. Auld, Francis & Joseph, Debbie, illus. 2009. (ENG.). 30p. (J). pap. 5.95 *(978-1-934594-04-9(0))* Salish Kootenia College Pr.

McNab, Chris. Survival in the Wilderness. Carney, John, ed. 2014. (Extreme Survival in the Military Ser.: 12). 64p. (J). (gr. 7-18). lib. bdg. 23.95 *(978-1-4222-3087-9(2))* Mason Crest.

Nickens, T. Eward. Field & Stream's Guide to Outdoor Survival. 2015. (Field & Stream's Guide to the Outdoors Ser.). (ENG.). 96p. (J). (gr. 6-8). 35.95 *(978-1-4824-2304-4(9))* Stevens, Gareth Publishing LLLP.

O'DellKathryn. SURVIVAL GUIDE: LOST IN THE MOUNTAINS LOW INTERMEDIATE BOOK WITH ONLINE ACCESS. 2014. (ENG.). 28p. (J). pap. 9.50 *(978-1-107-64328-4(7))* Cambridge Univ. Pr.

Owen, Ruth. Desert Survival Guide. 2010. (ENG., Illus.). 32p. (J). pap. *(978-0-7787-7554-6(2))*; lib. bdg. *(978-0-7787-7532-4(1))* Crabtree Publishing Co.

—Roughing It, 1 vol., 1. 2014. (DIY for Boys Ser.). (ENG.). 32p. (J). (gr. 3-6). 27.50 *(978-1-4777-6278-3(7)*, PowerKids Pr.) Rosen Publishing Group, Inc., The.

Phillips, Georgina. Ouch! Extreme Feats of Human Endurance, 1. unabr. ed. 2010. (Science Of... Ser.). (ENG., Illus.). 96p. (J). (gr. 2-6). pap. 5.99 *(978-0-330-45405-6(6))* Macmillan Pubs., Ltd. GBR. Dist: Independent Pubs. Group.

Pipe, Jim. Survivors: Into the Wilderness. 2012. (Mission Impossible Ser.). 32p. (gr. 4-8). lib. bdg. 31.35 *(978-1-936333-27-1(9))* Brown Bear Bks.

Piper, Ross. Survival! Staying Alive in the Wild, 1 vol. 2009. (Extreme! Ser.). (ENG.). 32p. (gr. 3-4). pap. 7.95 *(978-1-4296-3130-3(9)*, Fact Finders) Capstone Press of Coughlan Cos.

Puri, Devi. Making Tools in the Wild, 01 vols., 1. 2016. (Wilderness Survival Skills Ser.). (ENG., Illus.). 24p. (J). pap. 8.25 *(978-1-5081-4327-7(7)*, PowerKids Pr.) Rosen Publishing Group, Inc., The.

Rice, William & Herweck Rice, Dona. ¡Supervivencia! Jungla. 2017. (TIME for Kids en Español - Level 4 Ser.). (SPA., Illus.). 48p. (J). (gr. 4-4). lib. bdg. 31.99 *(978-1-5157-5125-0(2))* Time for Kids Inc AUS. Dist: Capstone Pub.

Rice, William B. Survival! Desert, 1 vol. 2nd rev. ed. 2012. (Nonfiction Readers Ser.). (ENG., Illus.). 48p. (J). (gr. 4-4). pap. 9.99 *(978-1-4333-4818-1(7))* Teacher Created Materials, Inc.

—Survival! Jungle, 1 vol. 2nd rev. ed. 2012. (Nonfiction Readers Ser.). (ENG., Illus.). 48p. (J). (gr. 4-4). pap. 9.99 *(978-1-4333-4820-4(9))* Teacher Created Materials, Inc.

—Survival! Ocean, 1 vol. 2nd rev. ed. 2012. (Nonfiction Readers Ser.). (ENG., Illus.). 48p. (J). (gr. 4-4). pap. 9.99 *(978-1-4333-4819-8(5))* Teacher Created Materials, Inc.

Shone, Rob. Defying Death in the Mountains. Spender, Nik, illus. 2010. (Graphic Survival Stories Ser.). 48p. (YA). (ENG.). pap. 14.05 *(978-1-61532-866-6(1))*; (gr. 5-8). 31.95 *(978-1-4358-3532-0(8))* Rosen Publishing Group, Inc., The. (Rosen Reference).

—Defying Death in the Wilderness. Field, James, illus. 2010. (Graphic Survival Stories Ser.). 48p. (YA). 58.50 *(978-1-4488-0068-1(4))*; (ENG.). pap. 14.05 *(978-1-61532-865-9(3))*; (gr. 5-8). 31.95 *(978-1-4358-3531-3(X))* Rosen Publishing Group, Inc., The. (Rosen Reference).

Smith, L. Survival Skills. 2008. (Survival Skills Ser.). 48p. (J). pap. 5.99 *(978-0-7945-2218-6(1)*, Usborne) EDC Publishing.

Spilsbury, Louise. How to Survive in the Arctic & Antarctica. 2012. (Tough Guides). (ENG., Illus.). 32p. (J). (gr. 4-6). pap. 10.00 *(978-1-4488-7931-1(0))*; lib. bdg. 25.25 *(978-1-4488-7866-6(7))* Rosen Publishing Group, Inc., The. (PowerKids Pr.).

—How to Survive in the Ocean. 2012. (Tough Guides). (ENG., Illus.). 32p. (J). (gr. 4-6). pap. 10.00 *(978-1-4488-7933-5(7))*; lib. bdg. 25.25 *(978-1-4488-7868-0(3))* Rosen Publishing Group, Inc., The. (PowerKids Pr.).

—How to Survive on a Mountain. 2012. (Tough Guides). (ENG., Illus.). 32p. (J). (gr. 4-6). pap. 10.00 *(978-1-4488-7936-6(1))*; lib. bdg. 25.25 *(978-1-4488-7871-0(3))* Rosen Publishing Group, Inc., The. (PowerKids Pr.).

Turnbull, Stephanie. Cold! 2015. (Survival Challenge Ser.). (Illus.). 24p. (gr. 3-6). 28.50 *(978-1-62588-213-4(0))* Black Rabbit Bks.

—Cold! 2015. (ENG., Illus.). 24p. (J). pap. 8.95 *(978-1-77092-238-9(5))* RiverStream Publishing.

—Emergency! 2015. (Survival Challenge Ser.). (Illus.). 24p. (gr. 3-6). 28.50 *(978-1-62588-214-1(9))* Black Rabbit Bks.

—Emergency! 2015. (ENG., Illus.). 24p. (J). pap. 8.95 *(978-1-77092-239-6(3))* RiverStream Publishing.

—Hungry! 2015. (Survival Challenge Ser.). 24p. (gr. 3-6). 28.50 *(978-1-62588-215-8(7))* Black Rabbit Bks.

—Hungry! 2015. (ENG., Illus.). 24p. (J). pap. 8.95 *(978-1-77092-240-2(7))* RiverStream Publishing.

—Lost! 2015. (Survival Challenge Ser.). 24p. (gr. 3-6). 28.50 *(978-1-62588-216-5(5))* Black Rabbit Bks.

—Lost! 2015. (ENG., Illus.). 24p. (J). pap. 8.95 *(978-1-77092-241-9(5))* RiverStream Publishing.

—Stranded! 2015. (Survival Challenge Ser.). 24p. (gr. 3-6). 28.50 *(978-1-62588-217-2(3))* Black Rabbit Bks.

—Stranded! 2015. (ENG., Illus.). 24p. (J). pap. 8.95 *(978-1-77092-242-6(3))* RiverStream Publishing.

—Thirsty! 2015. (Survival Challenge Ser.). 24p. (gr. 3-6). 28.50 *(978-1-62588-218-9(1))* Black Rabbit Bks.

—Thirsty! 2015. (ENG., Illus.). 24p. (J). pap. 8.95 *(978-1-77092-243-3(1))* RiverStream Publishing.

Wadsworth, Ginger. Survival in the Snow. Orback, Craig, illus. 48p. 2011. (J). pap. 6.95 *(978-0-7613-3941-0(8)*, First Avenue Editions) 2009. (ENG.). (gr. 2-4). 25.26 *(978-0-8225-7892-5(1))* Lerner Publishing Group.

Wilson, Patrick. Survival Equipment. Carney, John, ed. 2014. (Extreme Survival in the Military Ser.: 12). 64p. (J). (gr. 7-18). lib. bdg. 23.95 *(978-1-4222-3085-5(6))* Mason Crest.

—Surviving by Trapping, Fishing, & Eating Plants. Carney, John, ed. 2014. (Extreme Survival in the Military Ser.: 12). (Illus.). 64p. (J). (gr. 7-18). lib. bdg. 23.95 *(978-1-4222-3088-6(0))* Mason Crest.

Zoldak, Joyce. Danger in the Deep: Survivors of Shark Attacks. 2009. (J). pap. 25.95 *(978-1-4222-1475-6(3))* Mason Crest.

WILDERNESS SURVIVAL—FICTION

Armstrong, Kelley. The Calling. 2012. (Darkness Rising Ser.: Bk. 2). 336p. pap. *(978-1-907410-47-5(3))* Atom Pr.

—The Calling. (Darkness Rising Ser.: 2). (YA). (gr. 8). 2013. 352p. pap. 9.99 *(978-0-06-179706-4(5))* 2012. 336p. 17.99 *(978-0-06-179705-7(7))* HarperCollins Pubs.

Bates, Sonya Spreen. Marsh Island, 1 vol. Charko, Kasia, illus. 2009. (Orca Echoes Ser.). (ENG.). 64p. (J). (gr. 2-3). pap. 6.95 *(978-1-55469-117-3(6))* Orca Bk. Pubs. USA.

Daher, Anita. On the Trail of the Bushman, 1 vol. 2009. (Orca Young Readers Ser.). (ENG.). 128p. (J). (gr. 3-6). pap. 7.95 *(978-1-55469-013-8(7))* Orca Bk. Pubs. USA.

Eustache, Harold. Shuswap Journey. 2004. (Shuswap Journey Ser.). (ENG.). 176p. pap. 15.95 *(978-1-894778-15-2(4))* Theytus Bks., Ltd. CAN. Dist: Univ. of Toronto Pr.

Gaetz, Dayle Campbell. Spoiled Rotten. 2006. (Orca Currents Ser.). 103p. (gr. 5-9). 19.95 *(978-0-7569-6875-5(5))* Perfection Learning Corp.

George, Jean Craighead. My Side of the Mountain. l.t. ed. 2003. (LRS Large Print Cornerstone Ser.). 205p. (J). lib. bdg. 32.95 *(978-1-58118-114-2(0))* LRS.

—My Side of the Mountain. 2004. (Puffin Modern Classics Ser.). (ENG., Illus.). 192p. (J). (gr. 3-7). 7.99 *(978-0-14-240111-8(0)*, Puffin Books) Penguin Young Readers Group.

Gilliland, Hap. Alone in the Wilderness. 2003. (Illus.). 160p. (YA). (gr. 6-10). pap. 14.95 *(978-0-87961-257-3(6))* Naturegraph Pubs., Inc.

Goerzen, Christy. Explore, 1 vol. 2009. (Orca Currents Ser.). (ENG.). (J). (gr. 5-9). 112p. 16.95 *(978-1-55469-120-3(6))*; 128p. pap. 9.95 *(978-1-55469-119-7(2))* Orca Bk. Pubs. USA.

Goodspeed, Betsy. The Reluctant Mountaineer. 2004. 230p. (YA). per. *(978-1-59196-617-3(5))* Instant Pub.

Gutman, Dan. Getting Air. (ENG.). 240p. (J). (gr. 3-7). 2008. pap. 5.99 *(978-0-689-87681-3(5))* 2007. 16.99 *(978-0-689-87680-6(7))* Simon & Schuster Bks. For Young Readers. (Simon & Schuster Bks. For Young Readers).

Hobbs, Will & Hobbs, William. Wild Man Island. 2003. (ENG.). 192p. (J). (gr. 5-18). pap. 5.99 *(978-0-380-73310-1(2))* HarperCollins Pubs.

Holmes, Kathryn. The Distance Between Lost & Found. 2016. 320p. (YA). (gr. 8). pap. 9.99 *(978-0-06-231727-8(X)*, HarperTeen) HarperCollins Pubs.

Hughey, Sue C. Herby's Secret Formula. Hughey, Sue C., illus. 2013. (Illus.). 232p. pap. 11.95 *(978-0-9840358-1-6(8))* Associated Arts Pub.

Hunter, Erin. The Apprentice's Quest. 2017. (Warriors — a Vision of Shadows Ser.: 1). (J). lib. bdg. 18.40 ***(978-0-606-39643-1(8))*** Turtleback Bks.

Hunter, Erin. Warriors: a Vision of Shadows #1: the Apprentice's Quest. (Warriors: a Vision of Shadows Ser.: 1). (J). (gr. 3-7). 2017. 352p. pap. 7.99 *(978-0-06-238639-7(5))* 2016. (ENG., Illus.). 336p. 16.99 *(978-0-06-238637-3(9))* 2016. (Illus.). 336p. lib. bdg. 17.89 *(978-0-06-238638-0(7))* HarperCollins Pubs.

Key, Watt. Alabama Moon. (Alabama Moon Ser.: 1). (ENG.). (J). (gr. 5-9). 2008. 304p. pap. 8.99 *(978-0-312-38428-9(9)*, 9780312384289) 2010. 320p. pap. 8.99 *(978-0-312-64480-2(9)*, 9780312644802) Square Fish.

London, Jonathan. Grizzly Peak. London, Sean, illus. 2017. (Aaron's Wilderness Ser.). (ENG.). 174p. (YA). 24.99 ***(978-1-943328-85-7(4)***, West Winds Pr.) Graphic Arts Ctr. Publishing Co.

Maddox, Jake. Volcano! A Survive! Story. Tiffany, Sean, illus. 2009. (Jake Maddox Sports Stories Ser.). (ENG.). 72p. (gr. 2-3). 25.32 *(978-1-4342-1208-5(4))* Stone Arch Bks.

McCabe, James Dabney, Jr. Planting the Wilderness or, the Pioneer Boys: a Story of Frontier Life. 2007. pap. 27.95 *(978-1-4304-8187-4(0))* Kessinger Publishing, LLC.

Mills, Charles. Storm on Shadow Mountain. 2003. 127p. (J). 7.99 *(978-0-8163-1993-0(6))* Pacific Pr. Publishing Assn.

Monninger, Joseph. Stay Alive #1: Crash. 2014. (Stay Alive Ser.: 1). (ENG.). 208p. (J). (gr. 3-7). pap. 5.99 *(978-0-545-56348-2(8)*, Scholastic Paperbacks) Scholastic, Inc.

Osborne, Mary Pope. Adaline Falling Star. unabr. ed. 2004. (Middle Grade Cassette Librariestm Ser.). 176p. (J). (gr. 3-7). pap. 29.00 incl. audio *(978-0-8072-1195-3(8)*, S YA 319 SP, Listening Library) Random Hse. Audio Publishing Group.

Patterson, James & Tebbetts, Chris. Save Rafe! Park, Laura, illus. 2014. (Middle School Ser.: 6). (ENG.). 288p. (J). (gr. 3-7). 13.99 *(978-0-316-32212-6(1)*, Jimmy Patterson) Little Brown & Co.

Paulsen, Gary. Brian's Return. unabr. ed. 2004. (Middle Grade Cassette Librariestm Ser.). 115p. (J). (gr. 5-9). pap. 29.00 incl. audio *(978-0-8072-0658-4(X)*, S YA 292 SP, Listening Library) Random Hse. Audio Publishing Group.

—Hatchet. 2006. (ENG.). 192p. (J). (gr. 5-9). pap. 7.99 *(978-1-4169-3647-3(5)*, Simon & Schuster Bks. For Young Readers) Simon & Schuster Bks. For Young Readers.

—Hatchet. Willis, Drew, illus. 20th anniv. ed. 2007. (ENG.). 192p. (J). (gr. 5-9). 19.99 *(978-1-4169-2508-8(2)*, Simon & Schuster Bks. For Young Readers) Simon & Schuster Bks. For Young Readers.

—Hatchet. 2006. (ENG., Illus.). 208p. (YA). (gr. 7-9). mass mkt. 7.99 *(978-1-4169-3646-6(7)*, Simon Pulse) Simon Pulse.

—The River. unabr. ed. 2004. (Middle Grade Cassette Librariestm Ser.). 132p. (J). (gr. 5-9). pap. 29.00 incl. audio *(978-0-8072-8704-0(0)*, S YA 241 SP, Listening Library) Random Hse. Audio Publishing Group.

Petersen, P. J. Wild River. 2013. (ENG.). 128p. (J). (gr. 4-7). 6.99 *(978-0-375-84624-3(7)*, Yearling) Random Hse. Children's Bks.

Rock, Jonathan. Out of Bounds Bk. 1, Bk. 1. 2013. (Survival Squad Ser.: 1). (ENG., Illus.). 272p. (J). (gr. 4-7). pap. 8.99 *(978-1-86230-965-4(5)*, Red Fox) Random House Children's Books GBR. Dist: Independent Pubs. Group.

—Search & Rescue Bk. 2, Bk. 2. 2013. (Survival Squad Ser.: 2). (ENG., Illus.). 256p. (J). (gr. 4-7). pap. 12.99 *(978-1-86230-966-1(3)*, Red Fox) Random House Children's Books GBR. Dist: Independent Pubs. Group.

Roddy, Lee. Escape down the Raging Rapids. 2008. (D. J. Dillon Adventure Ser.: No. 10). (J). 7.99 *(978-0-88062-274-5(1))* Mott Media.

—The Legend of the White Raccoon. 2008. (D. J. Dillon Adventure Ser.: No. 6). (J). 7.99 *(978-0-88062-270-7(9))* Mott Media.

—Mad Dog of Lobo Mountain. 2008. (D. J. Dillon Adventure Ser.: No. 5). (J). 7.99 *(978-0-88062-269-1(5))* Mott Media.

Rorby, Ginny. Lost in the River of Grass. (Carolrhoda YA Ser.). (ENG.). 264p. (YA). (gr. 7-12). 2012. pap. 9.95

(978-0-7613-8498-4(7)) 2011. 17.95 *(978-0-7613-5685-1(1))* Lerner Publishing Group. (Carolrhoda Lab™).

Schwarz, S. L. Treasure at Lure Lake. 2016. (Illus.). 185p. (J). ***(978-1-4621-2600-2(6))*** Cedar Fort, Inc./CFI Distribution.

Troupe, Thomas Kingsley. Lost: a Wild Tale of Survival. Fagan, Kirbi, illus. 2016. (Survive! Ser.). (ENG.). 56p. (gr. 4-6). lib. bdg. 25.32 *(978-1-4965-2557-4(4))* Stone Arch Bks.

Turnbull, Ann. Maroo of the Winter Caves. 20th anniv. ed. 2004. (ENG., Illus.). 144p. (J). (gr. 2-5). pap. 6.95 *(978-0-618-44299-7(5))* Houghton Mifflin Harcourt Publishing Co.

VanRiper, Gary & VanRiper, Justin. Escape from Black Bear Mountain. 2008. (Adirondack Kids Ser.: Vol. 8). 70p. (J). (gr. 2-7). pap. 9.95 *(978-0-9707044-8-1(8))* Adirondack Kids Pr.

Weaver, Will. Memory Boy. 2012. Orig. Title: The Boy on Platform One. (ENG.). 240p. (YA). (gr. 8). pap. 8.99 *(978-0-06-201814-4(0),* HarperTeen) HarperCollins Pubs.

—The Survivors. 2012. (ENG.). 320p. (YA). (gr. 8). 17.99 *(978-0-06-009476-8(1),* HarperTeen) HarperCollins Pubs.

Wedekind, Annie. Samirah's Ride: The Story of an Arabian Filly. 2010. (Breyer Horse Collection: 3). (ENG.). 128p. (J). (gr. 4-7). pap. 14.99 *(978-0-312-62268-8(6),* 9780312622688) Feiwel & Friends.

Wheeler, Jordan & Jackson, Dennis. Christmas at Wapos Bay, 1 vol. 2005. (From Many Peoples Ser.). (ENG.). 152p. (J). (gr. 4-7). per. 7.95 *(978-1-55050-324-1(3))* Coteau Bks. CAN. Dist: Orca Bk. Pubs. USA.

Withers, Pam. Camp Wild, 1 vol. 2006. (Orca Currents Ser.). (ENG.). 112p. (J). (gr. 5-9). 14.95 *(978-1-55143-557-2(8))* Orca Bk. Pubs. USA.

—Camp Wild. 2006. (Orca Currents Ser.). 104p. (gr. 5-9). lib. bdg. 19.95 *(978-0-7569-6878-6(X))* Perfection Learning Corp.

Wyss, Johann. Swiss Family Robinson. 2003. (Saddleback Classics Ser.). (Illus.). 79p. (J). per. 6.95 *(978-1-56254-531-4(0),* SP5310) Saddleback Educational Publishing, Inc.

WILDLIFE CONSERVATION

see also Birds—Protection; Endangered Species; Forests and Forestry; Game Protection; National Parks and Reserves

Aitken, Stephen. Fever on the Land, 1 vol. 2011. (Climate Change Ser.). (ENG., Illus.). 32p. (J). (gr. k-3). 28.50 *(978-1-61641-673-7(4))* Magic Wagon.

Allgor, Marie. Endangered Animals of Africa. 2011. (Save Earth's Animals! Ser.). 24p. (J). (ENG.). pap. 8.25 *(978-1-4488-2640-7(3));* (Illus.). (gr. 3-4). lib. bdg. 22.60 *(978-1-4488-2528-8(8))* Rosen Publishing Group, Inc., The. (PowerKids Pr.).

—Endangered Animals of Antarctica & the Arctic. 2011. (Save Earth's Animals! Ser.). (Illus.). 24p. (J). pap. 8.25 *(978-1-4488-2652-0(7));* (gr. 3-4). lib. bdg. 22.60 *(978-1-4488-2534-9(2))* Rosen Publishing Group, Inc., The. (PowerKids Pr.).

—Endangered Animals of Asia. 2011. (Save Earth's Animals! Ser.). 24p. (J). (ENG.). pap. 8.25 *(978-1-4488-2642-1(X));* (Illus.). (gr. 3-4). lib. bdg. 22.60 *(978-1-4488-2529-5(6))* Rosen Publishing Group, Inc., The. (PowerKids Pr.).

—Endangered Animals of Australia. 2011. (Save Earth's Animals! Ser.). 24p. (J). (ENG.). pap. 8.25 *(978-1-4488-2644-5(6));* (Illus.). (gr. 3-4). lib. bdg. 22.60 *(978-1-4488-2530-1(X))* Rosen Publishing Group, Inc., The. (PowerKids Pr.).

—Endangered Animals of Europe. 2011. (Save Earth's Animals! Ser.). (Illus.). 24p. (J). pap. 8.25 *(978-1-4488-2646-9(2));* (gr. 3-4). 22.60 *(978-1-4488-2531-8(8))* Rosen Publishing Group, Inc., The. (PowerKids Pr.).

—Endangered Animals of North America. 2011. (Save Earth's Animals! Ser.). (Illus.). 24p. (J). pap. 8.25 *(978-1-4488-2648-3(9));* (gr. 3-4). 22.60 *(978-1-4488-2532-5(6))* Rosen Publishing Group, Inc., The. (PowerKids Pr.).

—Endangered Animals of South America. 2011. (Save Earth's Animals! Ser.). 24p. (J). (ENG.). pap. 8.25 *(978-1-4488-2650-6(0));* (Illus.). (gr. 3-4). lib. bdg. 22.60 *(978-1-4488-2533-2(4))* Rosen Publishing Group, Inc., The. (PowerKids Pr.).

—Endangered Desert Animals. 2012. (Save Earth's Animals! Ser.). (ENG., Illus.). 24p. (J). (gr. k-5). 22.60 *(978-1-4488-7423-1(8));* pap. 8.25 *(978-1-4488-7496-5(3))* Rosen Publishing Group, Inc., The. (PowerKids Pr.).

—Endangered Forest Animals. 2012. (Save Earth's Animals! Ser.). (ENG., Illus.). 24p. (J). (gr. k-5). pap. 8.25 *(978-1-4488-7497-2(1));* lib. bdg. 22.60 *(978-1-4488-7424-8(6))* Rosen Publishing Group, Inc., The. (PowerKids Pr.).

—Endangered Grassland Animals. 2012. (Save Earth's Animals! Ser.). (ENG., Illus.). 24p. (J). (gr. k-5). pap. 8.25 *(978-1-4488-7498-9(X));* lib. bdg. 22.60 *(978-1-4488-7425-5(4))* Rosen Publishing Group, Inc., The. (PowerKids Pr.).

—Endangered Rain Forest Animals. 2012. (Save Earth's Animals! Ser.). (ENG., Illus.). 24p. (J). (gr. k-5). pap. 8.25 *(978-1-4488-7495-8(5));* lib. bdg. 22.60 *(978-1-4488-7422-4(X))* Rosen Publishing Group, Inc., The. (PowerKids Pr.).

—Endangered Tundra Animals. 2012. (Save Earth's Animals! Ser.). (ENG., Illus.). 24p. (J). (gr. k-5). pap. 8.25 *(978-1-4488-7494-1(7));* lib. bdg. 22.60 *(978-1-4488-7421-7(1))* Rosen Publishing Group, Inc., The. (PowerKids Pr.).

Animals on the Edge, 1 vol. 2010. (Animals on the Edge Ser.). (ENG.). 32p. (gr. 3-4). lib. bdg. 81.96 *(978-1-4296-4535-5(0),* Fact Finders) Capstone Press of Coughlan Cos.

Bailey, Diane. Battling Wildlife Poachers: The Fight to Save Elephants, Rhinos, Lions, Tigers, & More. 2017. (J). ***(978-1-4222-3874-5(1))*** Mason Crest.

—Saving Marine Mammals: Whales, Dolphins, Seals, & More. 2017. (J). ***(978-1-4222-3878-3(4))*** Mason Crest.

Baillie, Marilyn, et al. How to Save a Species. 2014. (ENG.). 48p. (J). (gr. 3-7). 17.95 *(978-1-77147-063-6(1),* Owlkids) Owlkids Bks. Inc. CAN. Dist: Publishers Group West (PGW).

Bath, Louella. Saving Endangered Animals. 2016. (Global Guardians Ser.). 00024p. (J). (gr. 3-3). 23.60 *(978-1-4994-2936-7(3));* pap. 8.25 *(978-1-4994-2753-0(0))* Rosen Publishing Group, Inc., The. (PowerKids Pr.).

Becker, John E. Frenemies for Life: Cheetahs & Anatolian Shepherd Dogs. 2010. 56p. (YA). (gr. 5-8). pap. 8.95 *(978-0-9841554-1-5(4));* lib. bdg. 18.95 *(978-0-9841554-0-8(6))* Columbus Zoo & Aquarium, The.

Bell, Samantha S. 12 Amphibians Back from the Brink. 2015. (ENG., Illus.). 32p. (J). pap. 9.95 *(978-1-63235-060-2(2))* RiverStream Publishing.

—12 Insects Back from the Brink. 2014. (ENG., Illus.). 32p. (J). *(978-1-63235-002-2(5))* Pr. Room Editions LLC.

—12 Reptiles Back from the Brink. 2014. (ENG., Illus.). 32p. (J). *(978-1-63235-005-3(X))* Pr. Room Editions LLC.

Blewett, Ashlee Brown. National Geographic Kids Chapters: Hoot, Hoot, Hooray! And More True Stories of Amazing Animal Rescues. 2015. (NGK Chapters Ser.). (ENG., Illus.). 112p. (J). (gr. 2-5). pap. 5.99 *(978-1-4263-2054-5(X),* National Geographic Children's Bks.) National Geographic Society.

Bow, James. Saving Endangered Plants & Animals. 2008. (Science Solves It Ser.). (ENG., Illus.). 32p. (J). (gr. 3-7). pap. *(978-0-7787-4177-0(X),* 1286291) Crabtree Publishing Co.

Brown, Vinson. The Californian Wildlife Region. 3rd rev. ed. 2003. (Illus.). 302p. (J). pap. 14.95 *(978-0-87961-201-6(0))* Naturegraph Pubs., Inc.

Bruchac, Joseph. Buffalo Song. Farnsworth, Bill, illus. 2008. (J). Lee & Low Bks., Inc.

Burroughs, Caleb. Animal Rescue Adventure. 2006. (Illus.). (J). pap. 24.98 *(978-1-4127-6491-9(2))* Publications International, Ltd.

Burton, L. DeVere. Fish & Wildlife: Principles of Zoology & Ecology. 3rd ed. 2009. (ENG.). 416p. (C). 197.95 *(978-1-4354-1963-6(4))* Delmar Cengage Learning.

Capstone Press. Animals on the Edge. 2010. (Animals on the Edge Ser.). (ENG.). 32p. lib. bdg. 103.96 *(978-1-4296-5923-9(8),* Fact Finders) Capstone Press of Coughlan Cos.

Carson, Mary Kay. Emi & the Rhino Scientist. Uhlman, Tom, photos by. 2010. (Scientists in the Field Ser.). (ENG., Illus.). 64p. (J). (gr. 5-7). pap. 9.99 *(978-0-547-40850-7(1))* Houghton Mifflin Harcourt Publishing Co.

Centore, Michael. Saving Ocean Animals: Sharks, Turtles, Coral, & Fish. 2017. (J). ***(978-1-4222-3879-0(2))*** Mason Crest.

Christian, Peggy. Chocolate, a Glacier Grizzly. Cottone-Kolthoff, Carol, illus. (Humane Society of the United States Animal Tales Ser.). 32p. (J). (gr. 1-5). 34.95 incl. audio *(978-1-882728-64-0(5));* pap. 9.95 incl. audio *(978-1-882728-67-1(X));* pap. 19.95 incl. audio *(978-1-882728-69-5(6))* Benefactory, Inc., The.

Clendening, John. Wildlife Preserves. 2014. (Animal Rescue Ser.). (Illus.). 32p. (J). (gr. 3-6). 26.25 *(978-1-4777-7015-3(1),* PowerKids Pr.) Rosen Publishing Group, Inc., The.

Coey, Julia. Animal Hospital: Rescuing Urban Wildlife. 2015. (ENG., Illus.). 64p. (J). (gr. 4-7). 19.95 *(978-1-77085-572-4(6),* 9781770855724) Firefly Bks., Ltd.

Cohn, Jessica. Hand to Paw - Protecting Animals, 1 vol. 2nd rev. ed. 2012. (TIME for KIDS(r) Nonfiction Readers Ser.). (ENG.). 48p. (J). (gr. 4-4). pap. 9.99 *(978-1-4333-4867-9(5))* Teacher Created Materials, Inc.

Cram101 Textbook Reviews Staff & L. DeVere Burton. Studyguide for Fish & Wildlife: Principles of Zoology & Ecology by L. Devere Burton, Isbn 9781435419636. 3rd ed. 2014. (ENG.). 216p. (C). pap. 30.95 *(978-1-4784-1055-3(8))* Cram101 Inc.

Crum, Anna-Maria. Animal Behaviorists & Conductistas de Animales: 6 English, 6 Spanish Adaptations. 2011. (ENG & SPA.). (J). 89.00 net. *(978-1-4108-5679-1(8))* Benchmark Education Co.

Crump, Marty. Amphibians & Reptiles: An Introduction to Their Natural History & Conservation, 1 vol. 2011. (ENG., Illus.). 272p. (J). 29.95 *(978-1-935778-20-2(X))* McDonald & Woodward Publishing Co., The.

Curtis, Jennifer Keats. Animal Helpers: Raptor Centers, 1 vol. 2015. (Animal Helpers Ser.). (ENG., Illus.). 32p. (J). (gr. 2-5). 17.95 *(978-1-62855-447-2(9))* Arbordale Publishing.

deMarin, Layne. Save the Animals, 1 vol. (Wonder Readers: Science Ser.). (ENG.). (gr. -1-2). 2012. 20p. lib. bdg. 22.65 *(978-1-4296-9612-8(5))* 2011. 32p. pap. 5.99 *(978-1-4296-7941-1(7))* 2011. 16p. pap. 35.94 *(978-1-4296-8144-5(6))* Capstone Press of Coughlan Cos. (Wonder Readers).

Discover Series: Science, Nature, Wildlife, 11 bks. (Illus.). (J). (gr. 3-6). lib. bdg. 175.45 *(978-1-56674-935-0(2))* Forest Hse. Publishing Co., Inc.

Doak, Robin S. Jane Goodall: Chimpanzee Protector, 1 vol. 2014. (Women in Conservation Ser.). (ENG., Illus.). 48p. (gr. 3-6). pap. 8.99 *(978-1-4846-0474-8(1),* Heinemann InfoSearch) Heinemann-Raintree.

Dunne, Abbie. Endangered & Threatened Animals. 2016. (Life Science Ser.). (ENG., Illus.). 24p. (gr. k-1). lib. bdg. 26.65 *(978-1-5157-0945-9(0),* Pebble Plus) Capstone Press of Coughlan Cos.

Eszterhas, Suzi. Koala Hospital. 2015. (Wildlife Rescue Ser.: 1). (ENG., Illus.). 44p. (J). (gr. 2-5). 17.95 *(978-1-77147-140-4(9),* Owlkids) Owlkids Bks. Inc. CAN. Dist: Publishers Group West (PGW).

Faust, Daniel R. Desastres Ecológicos: Los Derrames de Petróleo y el Medio Ambiente = Sinister Sludge: Oil Spills & the Environment. 2009. (Historietas Juveniles: Peligros Del Medioambiente (Jr. Graphic Environmental Dangers) Ser.). (Illus.). 24p. (gr. 3-6). (SPA.). (YA). lib. bdg. 25.25 *(978-1-4358-8468-7(X));* (ENG & SPA., pap. 10.60 *(978-1-4358-8469-4(8),* PowerKids Pr.) Rosen Publishing Group, Inc., The.

French, Jess & The Born Free Foundation. Chimp Rescue: A True-Life Story. 2017. (Born Free... Bks.). (ENG.). 112p. (J). (gr. 2-6). pap. 6.99 *(978-1-4380-0985-8(2))* Barron's Educational Series, Inc.

Furstinger, Nancy. 12 Mammals Back from the Brink. 2014. (ENG., Illus.). 32p. (J). *(978-1-63235-003-9(3))* Pr. Room Editions LLC.

—12 Marine Animals Back from the Brink. 2014. (ENG., Illus.). 32p. (J). *(978-1-63235-004-6(1))* Pr. Room Editions LLC.

Gagne, Tammy. Day by Day with Bindi Sue Irwin. 2012. 32p. (J). (gr. -1-2). lib. bdg. 25.70 *(978-1-61228-326-5(8))* Mitchell Lane Pubs., Inc.

Gazlay, Suzy. Managing Green Spaces: Careers in Wilderness & Wildlife Management. 2009. (Green-Collar Careers Ser.). (ENG., Illus.). 64p. (J). (gr. 5-8). pap. *(978-0-7787-4866-3(9));* lib. bdg. *(978-0-7787-4855-7(3))* Crabtree Publishing Co.

Gibson, Brylee. Wildlife Detectives. 2007. (Connectors Ser.). (gr. 2-5). pap. *(978-1-877453-18-2(8))* Global Education Systems Ltd.

Goldish, Meish. Wildlife Rehabilitators to the Rescue. 2013. (Work of Heroes: First Responders in Action Ser.). 32p. (J). (gr. 1-6). lib. bdg. 25.27 *(978-1-61772-748-1(2))* Bearport Publishing Co., Inc.

Greene, Carol. I Love Our Animals. 2012. (I Love Our Earth Ser.). (Illus.). 24p. (J). pap. 7.95 *(978-1-4644-0139-8(X));* (gr. 3-4). 22.60 *(978-0-7660-4038-0(0))* Enslow Pubs., Inc. (Enslow Elementary).

Hamilton, Garry. Rhino Rescue: Changing the Future for Endangered Wildlife. 2006. (Firefly Animal Rescue Ser.). (ENG., Illus.). 64p. (J). (gr. 5-12). 19.95 *(978-1-55297-912-9(1),* 9781552979129); pap. 9.95 *(978-1-55297-910-5(5),* 9781552979105) Firefly Bks., Ltd.

Hemstock, Annie Wendt. Hunting Laws & Safety. 2014. (Open Season Ser.). 32p. (J). (gr. 4-6). lib. bdg. 26.25 *(978-1-4777-6725-2(8),* PowerKids Pr.) Rosen Publishing Group, Inc., The.

Hibbert, Clare. Elephant Orphans, 1 vol. 2015. (ENG.). 32p. (J). pap. 10.00 *(978-1-4777-5896-0(8),* PowerKids Pr.) Rosen Publishing Group, Inc., The.

—Save the Animals, 1 vol. 2015. (Save the Animals Ser.). (ENG.). 32p. (J). 60.00 *(978-1-4994-0316-9(X),* PowerKids Pr.) Rosen Publishing Group, Inc., The.

Hickman, Pamela. Birds of Prey Rescue: Changing the Future for Endangered Wildlife. 2006. (Firefly Animal Rescue Ser.). (ENG., Illus.). 64p. (J). (gr. 5-12). 19.95 *(978-1-55407-145-6(3),* 9781554071456); pap. 9.95 *(978-1-55407-144-9(5),* 9781554071449) Firefly Bks., Ltd.

Hopkins, Andy & Potter, Joc. Animals in Danger, Level 1. Lindop, Christine, ed. 3rd ed. 2008. (ENG., Illus.). 64p. pap. 9.38 *(978-0-19-423379-8(0))* Oxford Univ. Pr., Inc.

Houston, Dick. Bulu: African Wonder Dog. 2011. (ENG.). 336p. (J). (gr. 3-7). 7.99 *(978-0-375-84724-0(3),* Yearling) Random Hse. Children's Bks.

Hunter, Rebecca. Saving Wildlife. 2012. (Eco Alert! Ser.). (Illus.). 32p. (gr. 4-6). lib. bdg. 28.50 *(978-1-59771-298-9(1))* Sea-To-Sea Pubns.

Jackson, Donna M. The Wildlife Detectives: How Forensic Scientists Fight Crimes Against Nature. Shattil, Wendy & Rozinski, Bob, photos by. 2005. (Scientists in the Field Ser.). (Illus.). 47p. (gr. 3-7). 20.00 *(978-0-7569-5191-7(7))* Perfection Learning Corp.

Jazynka, Kitson & National Geographic Kids Staff. Panda Rescue: All about Pandas & How to Save Them. 2016. (NG Kids Mission: Animal Rescue Ser.). (ENG., Illus.). 112p. (J). (gr. 5). pap. 12.99 *(978-1-4263-2088-0(4),* National Geographic Children's Bks.) National Geographic Society.

Jenkins, Martin. Can We Save the Tiger? White, Vicky, illus. 2014. (ENG.). 56p. (J). (gr. k-3). 9.99 *(978-0-7636-7378-9(1))* Candlewick Pr.

Kalman, Bobbie. Big Challenges That Animals Face. 2016. (ENG., Illus.). 32p. (J). lib. bdg. *(978-0-7787-2781-1(5))* Crabtree Publishing Co.

Kavanagh, James. Grasslands Wildlife: A Folding Pocket Guide to Familiar Species Found in Prairie Grasslands. Leung, Raymond, illus. 2010. (Pocket Naturalist Guide Ser.). (ENG.). 1p. 6.95 *(978-1-58355-510-1(2))* Western National Parks Assn.

Kenyon, Linda. Rainforest Bird Rescue: Changing the Future for Endangered Wildlife. 2006. (Firefly Animal Rescue Ser.). (ENG., Illus.). 64p. (J). (gr. 5-12). 19.95 *(978-1-55407-153-1(4),* 9781554071531); pap. 9.95 *(978-1-55407-152-4(6),* 9781554071524) Firefly Bks., Ltd.

Kinsner, Kathy. Doomed to Disappear? Endangered Species & Condenadas a desaparecer? Especies en peligro de Extinción: 6 English, 6 Spanish Adaptations. 2011. (ENG & SPA.). (J). 97.00 net. *(978-1-4108-5698-2(4))* Benchmark Education Co.

Kirk, Daniel. Rhino in the House: The Story of Saving Samia. 2017. (ENG., Illus.). 40p. (J). (gr. -1-3). 17.95 *(978-1-4197-2316-2(2),* Abrams Bks. for Young Readers) Abrams, Inc.

Kortemeier, Todd. Saving Endangered Species. 2017. (Illus.). 32p. (J). *(978-1-62143-520-4(2))* Pr. Room Editions LLC.

Kortemeier, Todd & Smibert, Angie. Saving Endangered Species. 2016. (Science Frontiers Ser.). (ENG., Illus.). 32p. (J). pap. 9.95 *(978-1-63235-396-2(2))* Pr. Room Editions LLC.

Lasky, Kathryn. Interrupted Journey: Saving Endangered Sea Turtles. Knight, Christopher G., photos by. 2006. (ENG., Illus.). 48p. (J). (gr. 1-4). 6.99 *(978-0-7636-2883-3(2))* Candlewick Pr.

Leaman, Louisa & The Born Free Foundation. Elephant Rescue: A True-Life Story. 2017. (Born Free... Bks.). (ENG.). 96p. (J). (gr. 2-6). pap. 6.99 *(978-1-4380-0987-2(9))* Barron's Educational Series, Inc.

Levete, Sarah. Habitats & Wildlife in Danger. 2010. (Protecting Our Planet Ser.). (ENG., Illus.). 32p. (J). (gr. 3-6). *(978-0-7787-5213-4(5));* pap. *(978-0-7787-5230-1(5))* Crabtree Publishing Co.

Lourie, Peter. The Manatee Scientists: Saving Vulnerable Species. 2016. (Scientists in the Field Ser.). (ENG., Illus.). 80p. (J). (gr. 5-7). pap. 9.99 *(978-0-544-22529-9(5),* HMH Books For Young Readers) Houghton Mifflin Harcourt Publishing Co.

Machajewski, Sarah. The Return of the Mountain Gorilla. 2017. (Bouncing Back from Extinction Ser.). 32p. (J). (gr. 9-10). 60.00 ***(978-1-5081-5603-1(4),*** PowerKids Pr.) Rosen Publishing Group, Inc., The.

Malnor, Carol L. & Malnor, Bruce. Earth Heroes, Champions of Wild Animals, 1 vol. Hovemann, Anisa Claire, illus. 2010. (ENG.). 144p. (J). pap. 11.95 *(978-1-58469-123-5(9))* Dawn Pubns.

Markle, Sandra. The Great Leopard Rescue: Saving the Amur Leopards. 2016. (ENG., Illus.). 48p. (J). (gr. 4-6). 30.65 *(978-1-4677-9247-9(0));* 46.65 *(978-1-4677-9755-9(3))* Lerner Publishing Group. (Millbrook Pr.).

Marsico, Katie. Elephants. 2017. (True Book(tm) — The Most Endangered Ser.). (ENG., Illus.). 48p. (J). lib. bdg. 31.00 *(978-0-531-22727-5(8),* Children's Pr.) Scholastic Library Publishing.

—World Wildlife Fund. 2016. (Community Connections: How Do They Help? Ser.). (ENG., Illus.). 24p. (J). (gr. 2-5). 27.07 *(978-1-63471-055-8(X),* 208300) Cherry Lake Publishing.

Meissner, David. Habitat Rescue & Rescate del Hábitat: 6 English, 6 Spanish Adaptations. 2011. (ENG & SPA.). (J). 89.00 net. *(978-1-4108-5676-0(3))* Benchmark Education Co.

Montgomery, Sy. The Great White Shark Scientist. Ellenbogen, Keith, photos by. 2016. (Scientists in the Field Ser.). (ENG., Illus.). 80p. (J). (gr. 5-7). 18.99 *(978-0-544-35298-8(X),* HMH Books For Young Readers) Houghton Mifflin Harcourt Publishing Co.

Nagelhout, Ryan. Saving the Chesapeake Bay. 2013. (Exploring the Chesapeake Bay Ser.). (Illus.). 32p. (J). (gr. 3-6). pap. 10.50 *(978-1-4339-9785-3(1));* (ENG., lib. bdg. 26.60 *(978-1-4339-9784-6(3))* Stevens, Gareth Publishing LLLP.

Nagle, Jeanne. Endangered Wildlife: Habitats in Peril. 2009. (Extreme Environmental Threats Ser.). 64p. (gr. 6-6). 58.50 *(978-1-61512-429-9(2))* Rosen Publishing Group, Inc., The.

Nagle, Jeanne M. Endangered Wildlife: Habitats in Peril. 2009. (Extreme Environmental Threats Ser.). (ENG., Illus.). 64p. (J). (gr. 7-12). pap. 12.95 *(978-1-4358-5375-1(X));* (YA). (gr. 5-9). lib. bdg. 31.95 *(978-1-4358-5019-4(X))* Rosen Publishing Group, Inc., The.

National Geographic Kids & Hogan, Zeb. Monster Fish: True Stories of Adventures with Animals. 2017. (NGK Chapters Ser.). (ENG., Illus.). 112p. (J). (gr. 2-5). pap. 5.99 *(978-1-4263-2703-2(X),* National Geographic Children's Bks.) National Geographic Society.

National Geographic Learning. Habitat Preservation. 2012. (Global Issues Ser.). (ENG., Illus.). 32p. (J). pap. 12.95 *(978-0-7362-9778-3(2))* National Geographic School Publishing, Inc.

Navarro, Dominique & Baha El Din, Sherif. Wildlife of the Holy Land: An AUC Press Nature Foldout. 2015. (ENG., Illus.). 8p. pap. 6.95 *(978-977-416-674-7(4))* American Univ. in Cairo Pr.

Newland, Sonya. Desert Animals. 2011. (Saving Wildlife Ser.). 32p. (YA). (gr. 3-6). lib. bdg. 28.50 *(978-1-59920-655-4(2))* Black Rabbit Bks.

—Ocean Animals. 2011. (Saving Wildlife Ser.). 32p. (YA). (gr. 3-6). lib. bdg. 28.50 *(978-1-59920-658-5(7))* Black Rabbit Bks.

—Polar Animals. 2011. (Saving Wildlife Ser.). 32p. (gr. 4-7). lib. bdg. 31.35 *(978-1-59920-659-2(5))* Black Rabbit Bks.

—Rain Forest Animals. 2011. (Saving Wildlife Ser.). 32p. (gr. 4-7). lib. bdg. 31.35 *(978-1-59920-660-8(9))* Black Rabbit Bks.

Newman, Patricia. Zoo Scientists to the Rescue. Crawley, Annie, photos by. 2017. (ENG., Illus.). (J). (gr. 4-8). lib. bdg. 33.32 ***(978-1-5124-1571-1(5),*** Millbrook Pr.) Lerner Publishing Group.

O'Connell, Jennifer. The Eye of the Whale: A Rescue Story, 1 vol. O'Connell, Jennifer, illus. 2013. (Tilbury House Nature Book Ser.: 0). (ENG., Illus.). 32p. (gr. 1-7). 17.95 *(978-0-88448-335-9(5),* 884335) Tilbury Hse. Pubs.

O'Connor, Karen. Animals on the Verge of Extinction. 2013. (Animal 911: Environmental Threats Ser.). 48p. (J). (gr. 3-5). pap. 14.05 *(978-1-4339-9715-0(0));* pap. 84.30 *(978-1-4339-9716-7(9));* (ENG., Illus.). lib. bdg. 31.95 *(978-1-4339-9714-3(2))* Stevens, Gareth Publishing LLLP.

O'Neal, Claire. Threat to the Bengal Tiger. 2008. (On the Verge of Extinction Ser.). (Illus.). 32p. (J). (gr. 1-5). lib. bdg. 25.70 *(978-1-58415-688-8(0))* Mitchell Lane Pubs., Inc.

Orr, Tamra B. Battling Extinction. 2014. (Explorer Library: Follow the Clues Ser.). (ENG., Illus.). 32p. (J). (gr. 4-8). 28.50 *(978-1-62431-780-4(4),* 203316) Cherry Lake Publishing.

Parker, Russ. Wildlife Crisis. 2009. (Planet in Crisis Ser.). 32p. (gr. 5-8). (ENG., Illus.). (J). pap. 10.00 *(978-1-4358-0685-6(9));* (YA). lib. bdg. 25.25 *(978-1-4358-5255-6(9))* Rosen Publishing Group, Inc., The. (Rosen Reference).

Patent, Dorothy Hinshaw. The Call of the Osprey. Muñoz, William, illus. Muñoz, William, photos by. 2015. (Scientists in the Field Ser.). (ENG.). 80p. (J). (gr. 5-7). 18.99 *(978-0-544-23268-6(2),* HMH Books For Young Readers) Houghton Mifflin Harcourt Publishing Co.

Patterson, Virginia Sharpe. Dickey Downy: The Autobiography of a Bird. 2007. 106p. pap. 10.99 *(978-1-4346-2478-9(1));* 116p. pap. 11.99 *(978-1-4346-2479-6(X))* Creative Media Partners, LLC.

Pobst, Sandra. Animals on the Edge: Science Races to Save Species Threatened with Extinction. 2008. (National Geographic Investigates Science Ser.). (ENG., Illus.). 64p. (J). (gr. 5). 17.95 *(978-1-4263-0358-6(0));* lib. bdg. 27.90 *(978-1-4263-0265-7(7))* National Geographic Society. (National Geographic Children's Bks.).

Posewitz, James. Rifle in Hand: How Wild America Was Saved. 2004. (Illus.). 128p. per. 9.95 *(978-1-931832-41-0(2),* 8667872363) Riverbend Publishing.

Rice, William. Animales de la Jungla en Peligro. 2016. (TIME for Kids en Español - Level 5 Ser.). (SPA.). 64p. (gr. 5-5). lib. bdg. 31.99 *(978-1-5157-2933-4(8))* Time for Kids Inc AUS. Dist: Capstone Pub.

—Animales Del Desierto en Peligro. 2016. (TIME for Kids en Español - Level 5 Ser.). (SPA.). 64p. (gr. 5-5). lib. bdg. 31.99 *(978-1-5157-2934-1(6))* Time for Kids Inc AUS. Dist: Capstone Pub.

Rich, Mari. Rescuing Primates: Gorillas, Chimps, & Monkeys. 2017. (J). ***(978-1-4222-3877-6(6))*** Mason Crest.

Robinson, Jill & Bekoff, Marc. Jasper's Story: Saving Moon Bears. Frankenhuyzen, Gijsbert van, illus. 2013. (ENG.). 40p. (J). (gr. 1-4). 16.99 *(978-1-58536-798-6(2),* 202359) Sleeping Bear Pr.

Rose, Deborah Lee. Jimmy the Joey: The True Story of an Amazing Koala Rescue. Rose, Deborah Lee, photos by. 2013. (ENG., Illus.). 32p. (J). (gr. -1-3). lib. bdg. 25.90 *(978-1-4263-1372-1(1),* National Geographic Children's Bks.) National Geographic Society.

Rose, Deborah Lee & Kelly, Susan. Jimmy the Joey: The True Story of an Amazing Koala Rescue. Kelly, Susan, photos by. 2013. (ENG., Illus.). 32p. (J). (gr. -1-3). 16.95 *(978-1-4263-1371-4(3),* National Geographic Children's Bks.) National Geographic Society.

Rosen Publishing Staff. Save the Animals, 1 vol. 2015. (Save the Animals Ser.). (ENG.). 32p. (J). 157.50

W
X
Y
Z

(978-1-4777-5726-0(0), PowerKids Pr.) Rosen Publishing Group, Inc., The.

Royston, Angela. Desert Food Chains, 1 vol. 2014. (Food Chains & Webs Ser.). (ENG., Illus.). 32p. (gr. 1-3). 27.32 (978-1-4846-0521-9(7), Heinemann First Library) Heinemann-Raintree.

—Grassland Food Chains, 1 vol. 2014. (Food Chains & Webs Ser.). (ENG., Illus.). 32p. (gr. 1-3). 27.32 (978-1-4846-0522-6(5), Heinemann First Library) Heinemann-Raintree.

—Mountain Food Chains, 1 vol. 2014. (Food Chains & Webs Ser.). (ENG., Illus.). 32p. (gr. 1-3). 27.32 (978-1-4846-0519-6(5), Heinemann First Library) Heinemann-Raintree.

—Ocean Food Chains, 1 vol. 2014. (Food Chains & Webs Ser.). (ENG., Illus.). 32p. (gr. 1-3). 27.32 (978-1-4846-0517-2(9), Heinemann First Library) Heinemann-Raintree.

—Rain Forest Food Chains, 1 vol. 2014. (Food Chains & Webs Ser.). (ENG., Illus.). 32p. (gr. 1-3). 27.32 (978-1-4846-0518-9(7), Heinemann First Library) Heinemann-Raintree.

Salmansohn, Pete & Kress, Stephen W. Saving Birds: Heroes Around the World, 1 vol. 2005. (ENG., Illus.). 40p. (gr. 3-6). 16.95 (978-0-88448-237-6(5)) Tilbury Hse. Pubs.

Saving the Chesapeake Bay. 2013. (Exploring the Chesapeake Bay Ser.). 32p. (J). (gr. 3-6). pap. 63.00 (978-1-4339-9786-0(X)) Stevens, Gareth Publishing LLLP.

Shepherd, Jodie. Jane Goodall. 2015. (Rookie Biographies(tm) Ser.). (ENG.). 32p. (J). lib. bdg. 25.00 (978-0-531-21413-8(3), Children's Pr.) Scholastic Library Publishing.

Shields, Amy. National Geographic Readers: Saving Animal Babies. 2013. (Readers Ser.). (ENG., Illus.). 32p. (J). (gr. k-3). lib. bdg. 13.90 (978-1-4263-1041-6(2), National Geographic Children's Bks.) National Geographic Society.

—Saving Animal Babies. 2013. (Readers Ser.). (ENG., Illus.). 32p. (J). (gr. k-3). pap. 3.99 (978-1-4263-1040-9(4), National Geographic Children's Bks.) National Geographic Society.

Simpson, Phillip. How Can We Save the Cheetah? A Problem & Solution Text, 1 vol. 2014. (Text Structures Ser.). (ENG.). 32p. (gr. 1-3). pap. 7.99 (978-1-4846-0415-1(6), Heinemann First Library) Heinemann-Raintree.

Slade, Suzanne. What Can We Do about Endangered Animals? 2009. (J). 49.50 (978-1-4358-2478-2(4), PowerKids Pr.); (ENG.). 24p. (J). pap. 8.25 (978-1-4358-2477-5(6), PowerKids Pr.); (ENG., Illus.). 24p. (YA). (gr. 2-5). lib. bdg. 22.60 (978-1-4042-8080-9(4)) Rosen Publishing Group, Inc., The.

Smith van Frankenhuyzen, Robbyn. Saving Samantha: A True Story. van Frankenhuyzen, Gijsbert, illus. 2004. (Hazel Ridge Farm Stories Ser.). (ENG.). 32p. (J). 17.95 (978-1-58536-220-2(4)) Sleeping Bear Pr.

Snyder, Trish. Alligator & Crocodile Rescue: Changing the Future for Endangered Wildlife. 2006. (Firefly Animal Rescue Ser.). (ENG., Illus.). 64p. (J). (gr. 5-12). 19.95 (978-1-55297-920-4(2), 9781552979204); pap. 9.95 (978-1-55297-919-8(9), 9781552979198) Firefly Bks., Ltd.

Stamper, Judith Bauer. Eco Dogs. 2016. (Dog Heroes Ser.). (ENG.). 32p. (J). (gr. 2-7). pap. 8.95 (978-1-944998-63-9(2)) Bearport Publishing Co., Inc.

Starbuck, Sara & The Born Free Foundation. Lion Rescue: A True-Life Story. 2017. (Born Free... Bks.). (ENG.). 112p. (J). (gr. 2-6). pap. 6.99 (978-1-4380-0989-6(5)) Barron's Educational Series, Inc.

Stetson, Emily. Create a Wildlife Habitat for Urban & Suburban Small Spaces. 2004. (ENG., Illus.). 128p. (J). pap. 12.95 (978-0-8249-8665-0(2), Ideal Pubns.) Worthy Publishing.

Swanson, Diane. Why Seals Blow Their Noses: Canadian Wildlife in Fact & Fiction, 1 vol. Penhale, Douglas, illus. (ENG.). 80p. (J). pap. 12.95 (978-1-55110-038-8(X)) Whitecap Bks., Ltd. CAN. Dist: Graphic Arts Ctr. Publishing Co.

Thomas, Keltie. Bear Rescue: Changing the Future for Endangered Wildlife. 2006. (Firefly Animal Rescue Ser.). (ENG., Illus.). 64p. (J). (gr. 5-12). 19.95 (978-1-55297-922-8(9), 9781552979228); pap. 9.95 (978-1-55297-921-1(0), 9781552979211) Firefly Bks., Ltd.

Tieck, Sarah. Bindi Irwin: Star of Bindi the Jungle Girl, 1 vol. 2008. (Big Buddy Biographies Ser.). (ENG.). 32p. (J). (gr. 2-5). 28.50 (978-1-60453-122-0(3)) ABDO Publishing Co.

Todino, Grace. Tina the Turtle. Keeble, Susan, illus. 2013. (ENG.). 58p. (J). (gr. k). 19.95 (978-1-908531-00-1(2)) Gilgamesh Publishing GBR. Dist: Consortium Bk. Sales & Distribution.

Torres, John. Threat to the Giant Panda. 2008. (On the Verge of Extinction Ser.). (Illus.). 32p. (YA). (gr. 2-5). lib. bdg. 25.70 (978-1-58415-689-5(9)) Mitchell Lane Pubs., Inc.

Trueit, Trudi Strain. Wildlife Conservationist. 2014. 64p. pap. 34.21 (978-1-62712-467-6(5)) Cavendish Square Publishing.

Tupper, Susan. Fran & Frederick Hamerstrom: Wildlife Conservation Pioneers. 2016. (Badger Biographies Ser.). (Illus.). 136p. (J). (gr. 4-6). pap. 12.95 (978-0-87020-732-7(6)) Wisconsin Historical Society.

Watkins, Sue. Getting Involved! A Guide to Hunting & Conservation for Kids. 2011. (ENG.). 128p. pap. 12.95 (978-1-57157-377-3(1)) Safari Pr., Inc.

Weitzman, Elizabeth. 10 Cosas Que Puedes Hacer para Proteger a Los Animales. 2017. (Rookie Star — Make a Difference (Spanish Translation) Ser.). (SPA.). 32p. (J). pap. 5.95 **(978-1-338-18778-6(3))**; lib. bdg. 25.00 **(978-0-531-22857-9(6))** Scholastic Library Publishing. (Children's Pr.).

Weitzman, Elizabeth. 10 Things You Can Do to Protect Animals. 2016. (Rookie Star — Make a Difference Ser.). (ENG., Illus.). 32p. (J). lib. bdg. 25.00 (978-0-531-22652-0(2), Children's Pr.) Scholastic Library Publishing.

Wells, Robert E. Can We Share the World with Tigers? Wells, Robert E., illus. 2012. (Wells of Knowledge Science Ser.). (ENG., Illus.). 32p. (J). (gr. 1-3). 16.99 (978-0-8075-1055-1(6)) Whitman, Albert & Co.

Wildlife at Risk. 2015. (Wildlife at Risk Ser.). (ENG.). 48p. (J). (gr. 6-6). 167.58 (978-0-7660-6688-5(6)); pap., pap., pap. 421.20 (978-0-7660-6689-2(4)) Enslow Pubs., Inc.

Williams, Judith. Saving Endangered Animals with a Scientist. 2004. (I Like Science! Ser.). (Illus.). 24p. (J). (gr. 2-4). lib. bdg. 21.26 (978-0-7660-2276-8(5)) Enslow Pubs., Inc.

World Book, Inc Staff, contrib. by. Code Red: Animals in Peril: A Supplement to Childcraft-The How & Why Library. 2011. (Illus.). 206p. (J). (978-0-7166-0626-0(7)) World Bk., Inc.

World Book, Inc. Staff, contrib. by. Endangered Animals of Europe. 2014. (J). (978-0-7166-5624-1(8)) World Bk., Inc.

Yomtov, Nelson. Poachers. 2016. (True Book(tm), a — The New Criminals Ser.). (ENG., Illus.). 48p. (J). lib. bdg. 31.00 (978-0-531-21467-1(2), Children's Pr.) Scholastic Library Publishing.

WILDLIFE CONSERVATION—FICTION

Ball Sr., Frank J. Bryanna Global Warrior: Attack of the Alaska Aerial Wolf Hunters, 1 vol. Pelton, Bonnie L., illus. 2009. 23p. pap. 24.95 (978-1-61582-587-5(8)) America Star Bks.

Barr, Brady & Curtis, Jennifer Keats. Hasta la Vista, Cocodrilo: El Diario de Alexa. Detwiler, Susan, illus. 2016. (SPA.). 32p. (J). (gr. k-3). pap. 9.95 (978-1-62855-836-4(9)) Arbordale Publishing.

Beckhorn, Susan Williams. Moose Power! Muskeg Saves the Day. Huntington, Amy, illus. 2010. (ENG.). 40p. (J). (gr. -1-3). 16.95 (978-0-89272-762-9(4)) Down East Bks.

Blake, Quentin. Loveykins. Blake, Quentin, illus. 2003. (Illus.). 32p. (J). (gr. k-3). 15.95 (978-1-56145-282-8(3)) Peachtree Pubs.

Bowen, Carl. Hot Spot. Lee, Marc, illus. 2016. (Firestormers Ser.). (ENG.). 112p. (gr. 4-8). lib. bdg. 26.65 (978-1-4965-3307-4(0)) Stone Arch Bks.

Brooks, John. Balloons, Sea Creatures, & Me. 2006. 34p. (J). 14.58 (978-0-9661789-3-7(9)) Lulu Pr., Inc.

Burchett, Jan & Vogler, Sara. Earthquake Escape, 1 vol. Le Feyer, Diane, illus. 2012. (Wild Rescue Ser.). (ENG.). 152p. (gr. 3-6). lib. bdg. 25.32 (978-1-4048-6891-5(7)) Picture Window Bks.

—Poacher Panic, 1 vol. Le Feyer, Diane, illus. 2012. (Wild Rescue Ser.). (ENG.). 152p. (gr. 3-6). 9.95 (978-1-4342-4593-9(4)); lib. bdg. 25.32 (978-1-4342-3286-1(7)) Stone Arch Bks.

—Polar Meltdown, 1 vol. Le Feyer, Diane, illus. 2012. (Wild Rescue Ser.). (ENG.). 152p. (gr. 3-6). 9.95 (978-1-4342-4594-6(2)); lib. bdg. 25.32 (978-1-4342-3769-9(9)) Stone Arch Bks.

—Safari Survival, 1 vol. Le Feyer, Diane & Kennedy, Sam, illus. 2012. (Wild Rescue Ser.). (ENG.). 152p. (gr. 3-6). lib. bdg. 25.32 (978-1-4342-3770-5(2)) Stone Arch Bks.

Chapman, Karen B. The Marino Mission: One Girl, One Mission, One Thousand Words - 1,000 Need-to-Know New SAT Vocabulary Words. 2004. (ENG.). 336p. pap. 15.99 (978-0-7645-7831-1(6)) Houghton Mifflin Harcourt Publishing Co.

Cochard, David, illus. The Legend of Honey Hollow. 2008. 46p. (J). 16.99 (978-0-9799444-0-6(6)) Joey Publishing.

Cohn, Diana. Crane Boy. 2015. (ENG., Illus.). 40p. (J). (gr. 2-5). 17.95 (978-1-941026-16-8(8)) Cinco Puntos Pr.

Collins, Yvonne & Rideout, Sandy. The Black Sheep. 2007. 348p. (J). (978-1-4287-4665-7(X)) Hyperion Pr.

Cry of the Falcon. 2006. 208p. (J). pap. 9.95 (978-0-9788541-0-2(1)) m.d. hughes.

Curtis, Jennifer Keats. Baby Owl's Rescue, 1 vol. Jacques, Laura, illus. 2009. (ENG.). 32p. (J). (gr. -1-3). 16.95 (978-1-934359-95-2(5), 9781934359952) Arbordale Publishing.

Davies, Nicola. The Lion Who Stole My Arm. Wright, Annabel, illus. 2014. (Heroes of the Wild Ser.). (ENG.). 96p. (J). (gr. 2-5). 14.99 (978-0-7636-6620-0(3)) Candlewick Pr.

Dillard, Mary Gregory. Jeepers Creepers! The Squirrels Are Coming. 2007. 85p. pap. 19.95 (978-1-4241-9951-8(4)) America Star Bks.

Doerr, Bonnie J. Kenzie's Key. Aberle, Xylena Apotheloz, illus. 2003. 211p. (J). 16.95 (978-0-9619155-6-8(0)) Laurel & Herbert, Inc.

Draper, Sharon M. The Backyard Animal Show. Watson, Jesse Joshua, illus. 2012. (Clubhouse Mysteries Ser.: 5). (ENG.). 128p. (J). (gr. 3-7). pap. 5.99 (978-1-4424-5022-6(3), Aladdin) Simon & Schuster Children's Publishing.

—The Backyard Animal Show. Watson, Jesse Joshua, illus. 2012. (Clubhouse Mysteries Ser.: 5). (ENG.). 128p. (J). (gr. 3-7). 15.99 (978-1-4424-5023-3(1), Simon & Schuster/Paula Wiseman Bks.) Simon & Schuster/Paula Wiseman Bks.

Dunlap, Jim. Sam Snake Says. Holland, Kathy, illus. 2008. 35p. pap. 24.95 (978-1-60672-709-6(5)) America Star Bks.

French, Lisa S. A Planet Called Home: Eco-Pig's Animal Protection, 1 vol. Gott, Barry, illus. 2009. (Eco-Pig Ser.). (ENG.). 32p. (J). (gr. -1-2). 28.50 (978-1-60270-662-0(X)) ABDO Publishing Co.

George, Jean Craighead. Frightful's Mountain. 2014. (ENG.). 272p. (J). (gr. 4-8). 11.24 (978-1-63245-351-8(7)) Lectorum Pubns., Inc.

Graham, Bob. How to Heal a Broken Wing. Graham, Bob, illus. 2008. (ENG., Illus.). 40p. (J). (gr. -1-2). 16.99 (978-0-7636-3903-7(6)) Candlewick Pr.

Graham, Bob. How to Heal a Broken Wing. Graham, Bob, illus. 2017. (ENG., Illus.). 40p. (J). (gr. -1-2). 7.99 **(978-0-7636-9841-6(5))** Candlewick Pr.

Grindley, Sally. Paw Prints in the Snow. Frost, Adam, illus. 2012. (ENG.). 112p. (J). (gr. 3-5). pap. 11.99 (978-1-4088-1945-6(7), 9781408819456, Bloomsbury USA Childrens) Bloomsbury Publishing USA.

Harlow, Patty Fayerweather. Rock with Rodney and, Party with Perky to Preserve Wildlife. 2006. (Illus.). 96p. (J). per. 16.95 (978-1-60002-002-5(X), 3583) Mountain Valley Publishing, LLC.

Hay, Jerry M. & Pollema-Cahill, Phyllis. A Goose Named Gilligan. 2004. (ENG., Illus.). 32p. (J). 15.95 (978-1-932073-09-6(4)) Kramer, H.J. Inc.

Henry, Marguerite. Mustang: Wild Spirit of the West. Lougheed, Robert, illus. 2016. (ENG.). 240p. (J). (gr. 3-7). 19.99 (978-1-4814-5222-9(3), Simon & Schuster/Paula Wiseman Bks.) Simon & Schuster/Paula Wiseman Bks.

Hiaasen, Carl. Scat. 2011. 10.54 (978-0-7848-3574-6(8), Everbind) Marco Bk. Co.

—Scat. (ENG.). (J). (gr. 5). 2012. 400p. 7.99 (978-0-440-42104-7(7), Yearling) 2010. 384p. pap. 8.99 (978-0-375-83487-5(7), Ember) 2009. 384p. 16.99 (978-0-375-83486-8(9), Knopf Bks. for Young Readers) Random Hse. Children's Bks.

—Scat. 2012. lib. bdg. 18.40 (978-0-606-26532-4(5), Turtleback) Turtleback Bks.

Irwin, Bindi & Kunz, Chris. Croc Capers: Bindi Wildlife Adventures. 2012. (Bindi's Wildlife Adventures Ser.: 7). (ENG.). 112p. (J). (gr. 3-6). pap. 4.99 (978-1-4022-7373-5(8), Sourcebooks Jabberwocky) Sourcebooks, Inc.

Knight, Richard John & Walker, Richard. Winter Shadow. Johnson, Richard, illus. 2009. (ENG.). 80p. (J). (gr. 3-9). pap. 16.99 (978-1-84686-116-1(0)) Barefoot Bks., Inc.

Lamperd, Laurel. Battle for Boodicuttup Creek. 2008. 64p. pap. (978-1-84923-238-8(5)) YouWriteOn.

Lewis, J. M. The Adventures of Gabby & Coyote Girl. 2007. 64p. per. 7.95 (978-1-4327-1511-3(9)) Outskirts Pr., Inc.

Lumry, Amanda & Hurwitz, Laura. Riddle of the Reef. 2009. (Illus.). 32p. (J). (978-0-545-06848-2(7), Scholastic Pr.) Scholastic, Inc.

—Tigers in Terai. McIntyre, Sarah, illus. 2nd rev. ed. 2007. (Adventures of Riley (Unnumberd) Ser.). 36p. (J). (gr. -1-3). 15.95 (978-1-60040-003-2(5)) Centro Bks., LLC.

—Tigers in Terai. McIntyre, Sarah, illus. 2nd ed. 2007. 36p. (978-0-9748411-6-8(1)) Eaglemont Pr.

Lyle-Soffe, Shari. Trouble Finds Rooter & Snuffle. Collier, Kevin Scott, illus. 2008. 20p. pap. 9.95 (978-1-933090-72-6(3)) Guardian Angel Publishing, Inc.

Malone, Geoffrey. Tiger! 2006. (ENG.). 304p. (J). (gr. 4-6). pap. 10.95 (978-0-340-89358-6(3)) Hachette Children's Group GBR. Dist: Hachette Bk. Group.

Messer, Celeste M. Forever & Always. Hoeffner, Deb, illus. 2004. 82-92p. 4.95 (978-0-9710145-0-3(7)) AshleyAlan Enterprises.

Meunier, Sylvain. Raffi's Animal Rescue. Cummins, Sarah, tr. from FRE. Eudes-Pascal, Elisabeth, illus. 2007. (ENG.). 64p. (J). (gr. 2-5). (978-0-88780-742-8(9)) Formac Publishing Co., Ltd.

Mikaelsen, Ben. Stranded. 2010. (ENG.). 288p. (J). (gr. 3-7). pap. 5.99 (978-1-4231-3362-9(5)) Hyperion Pr.

Perry, Phyllis. Stand up & Whistle. Grochalska, Agnieszka, illus. 2016. (ENG.). 164p. (J). pap. 7.99 (978-0-9972377-5-7(9)) Amberjack Publishing Co.

Poke-A-Dot: Wheels on the Bus. 2017. (ENG.). (J). 15.99 **(978-1-60169-420-1(2))** Innovative Kids.

Prager, Ellen. The Shark Rider. Caparo, Antonio Javier, illus. 2015. (Tristan Hunt & the Sea Guardians Ser.: 2). (ENG.). 326p. (J). (gr. 3-7). pap. 9.95 (978-1-938063-51-0(1), Mighty Media Junior Readers) Mighty Media Pr.

—Stingray City. Caparo, Antonio Javier, illus. 2016. (Tristan Hunt & the Sea Guardians Ser.: 3). (ENG.). 292p. (J). (gr. 2-7). pap. 9.95 (978-1-938063-70-1(8), Mighty Media Junior Readers) Mighty Media Pr.

Ralph, Donna J. Critter Chronicles: Stories of Critters in a Colorado Wildlife Rehabilitator's Life. 2007. 200p. per. 16.95 (978-0-595-47858-3(1)) iUniverse, Inc.

Reed, Lynn Rowe. Roscoe & the Pelican Rescue. Reed, Lynn Rowe, illus. 2011. (ENG., Illus.). 32p. (J). (gr. -1-3). 14.95 (978-0-8234-2352-1(2)) Holiday Hse., Inc.

Smith, Lauren. Ashley Enright & the Mystery at Miller's Pond. 2006. (ENG.). 60p. per. 16.95 (978-1-4241-5268-1(2)) America Star Bks.

St. John, Lauren. Dolphin Song. 2009. (ENG.). 272p. (J). (gr. 3-7). 7.99 (978-0-14-241375-3(5), Puffin Books) Penguin Young Readers Group.

—The Elephant's Tale. 2011. (ENG.). 240p. (J). (gr. 3-7). 6.99 (978-0-14-241879-6(X), Puffin Books) Penguin Young Readers Group.

—The White Giraffe. 2008. (ENG., Illus.). 208p. (J). (gr. 2-5). 7.99 (978-0-14-241152-0(3), Puffin Books) Penguin Young Readers Group.

Stauffacher, Sue. Special Delivery! Lamont, Priscilla, illus. 2010. (Animal Rescue Team Ser.: No. 2). (ENG.). 176p. (J). (gr. 3-7). 12.99 (978-0-375-85848-2(2), Knopf Bks. for Young Readers) Random Hse. Children's Bks.

Taylor, Theodore. The Weirdo. 2006. (Illus.). 292p. (gr. 7-12). 18.00 (978-0-7569-6752-9(X)) Perfection Learning Corp.

Taylor, Theodore & Taylor, Theodore. The Weirdo. 2006. (ENG., Illus.). 304p. (YA). (gr. 7-12). pap. 8.99 (978-0-15-205666-7(1)) Houghton Mifflin Harcourt Publishing Co.

Thompson, Jolene & Thompson, Justin K. Faraway Fox. Thompson, Jolene & Thompson, Justin K., illus. 2016. (ENG., Illus.). 32p. (J). (gr. -1-3). 17.99 (978-0-544-70711-5(7), HMH Books For Young Readers) Houghton Mifflin Harcourt Publishing Co.

Townsend, Wendy. Blue Iguana. 2014. 188p. 18.95 (978-1-60898-157-1(6)) namelos llc.

Van Frankenhuyzen, Robbyn Smith. Kelly of Hazel Ridge. van Frankenhuyzen, Gijsbert, illus. 3rd rev. ed. 2006. (Hazel Ridge Farm Stories Ser.). (ENG.). 32p. (J). (gr. k-5). 17.95 (978-1-58536-268-4(9)) Sleeping Bear Pr.

Wildsmith, Brian. Hunter & His Dog, 1 vol. Wildsmith, Brian, illus. 2008. (ENG., Illus.). 32p. (J). 16.95 (978-1-59572-123-5(1)) Star Bright Bks., Inc.

Wilson, Anna. Monkey Business, 1. unabr. ed. 2014. (ENG., Illus.). 256p. (J). (gr. 2-4). pap. 7.99 (978-0-330-50928-2(4)) Pan Macmillan GBR. Dist: Independent Pubs. Group.

Wyss, Tyan. African Dream. Immelman, Sarita, illus. 2006. 48p. (J). pap. 15.95 (978-1-58939-915-0(3)) Virtualbookworm.com Publishing, Inc.

WILLIAM I, KING OF ENGLAND, 1027 OR 1028-1087

Abbott, Jacob. History of William the Conqueror. 2003. 291p. 89.00 (978-0-7950-4508-0(5)) New Library Press LLC.

Hamilton, Janice. The Norman Conquest of England. 2007. (Pivotal Moments in History Ser.). (ENG., Illus.). 160p. (J). (gr. 9-12). lib. bdg. 38.60 (978-0-8225-5902-3(1)) Lerner Publishing Group.

Harkins, Susan Sales & Harkins, William H. The Life & Times of William the Conqueror. 2008. (Biography from Ancient Civilizations Ser.). (Illus.). 48p. (J). (gr. 4-8). lib. bdg. 29.95 (978-1-58415-700-7(3)) Mitchell Lane Pubs., Inc.

Hilliam, Paul. William the Conqueror: First Norman King of England. (Leaders of the Middle Ages Ser.). 112p. 2009. (gr. 5-8). 66.50 (978-1-61513-903-3(6), Rosen Reference) 2004. (Illus.). (J). lib. bdg. 34.60 (978-1-4042-0166-8(1)) Rosen Publishing Group, Inc., The.

McGowen, Tom. William the Conqueror: Last Invader of England. 2007. (Rulers of the Middle Ages Ser.). (Illus.). 160p. (YA). (gr. 6-12). lib. bdg. 35.94 (978-0-7660-2713-8(9)) Enslow Pubs., Inc.

Ross, Stewart. Will's Dream. Shields, Susan, illus. 28p. pap. 9.99 (978-0-7502-2965-4(9)) Hodder & Stoughton GBR. Dist: Trafalgar Square Publishing.

William the Conqueror: a Ladybird Adventure from History Book. 2016. (Ladybird Histories Ser.). (ENG., Illus.). 56p. (J). (gr. k-3). 10.99 **(978-0-241-24947-5(3))** Penguin Bks., Ltd. GBR. Dist: Independent Pubs. Group.

WILLIAMS, HANK, 1923-1953

Bailey, Tom. Hank Williams Sr. Country Music Legend. 2008. (Illus.). 104p. (J). (978-1-59421-043-3(8)) Seacoast Publishing, Inc.

WILLIAMS, ROGER, 1604?-1683

Marsh, Carole. Roger Williams. 2003. 12p. (gr. k-4). 2.95 (978-0-635-02361-2(X)) Gallopade International.

The Puritans, Algonkians & Roger Williams (NCHS) (J). (gr. 5-8). spiral bd., tchr.'s planning gde. ed. 13.50 (978-0-382-44447-0(7)) Cobblestone Publishing Co.

The Puritans, Algonkians & Roger Williams (NCHS) Grades 5-8. (J). tchr. ed. 18.00 (978-0-382-44537-8(6)) Cobblestone Publishing Co.

WILLIAMS, SERENA, 1981-

Anniss, Matt. Venus & Serena Williams in the Community, 1 vol., 1. 2014. (Making a Difference: Athletes Who Are Changing the World Ser.). (ENG.). 48p. (J). (gr. 5-8). 25.85 (978-1-62275-170-9(1)) Rosen Publishing Group, Inc., The.

Bailey, Diane. Venus & Serena Williams: Tennis Champions. 2010. (Sports Families Ser.). 48p. (ENG.). (J). pap. 11.75 (978-1-4358-8520-2(1), Rosen Reference); (YA). (gr. 5-8). lib. bdg., E-Book 53.00 (978-1-4488-0124-4(9)); (Illus.). (YA). (gr. 4-7). lib. bdg. 29.25 (978-1-4358-3552-8(2)) Rosen Publishing Group, Inc., The.

Boehme, Gerry. Serena Williams: Setting New Standards. 2017. (J). **(978-1-5026-2762-9(0))** Cavendish Square Publishing.

Brown, Jonatha A. Venus & Serena Williams. 2005. (People to Know Ser.). (Illus.). 24p. (gr. 1-4). pap. 8.15 (978-0-8368-4477-1(7)); lib. bdg. 22.00 (978-0-8368-4470-2(X)) Stevens, Gareth Publishing LLLP. (Weekly Reader Leveled Readers).

—Venus y Serena Williams. 2005. (Gente que hay que conocer (People We Should Know- Spanish) Ser.).Tr. of Venus & Serena Williams. (SPA.). 24p. (gr. 1-4). lib. bdg. 22.00 (978-0-8368-4586-0(2), Weekly Reader Leveled Readers) Stevens, Gareth Publishing LLLP.

Christopher, Matt. Serena Williams: Legends in Sports. 2017. (ENG., Illus.). 144p. (J). (gr. 3-7). pap. 6.99 **(978-0-316-47180-0(1))** Little, Brown Bks. for Young Readers.

Donaldson, Madeline. Venus & Serena Williams. (Amazing Athletes Ser.). 32p. 2007. (Illus.). (J). (gr. -1-3). per. 6.95 (978-0-8225-8857-3(9), First Avenue Editions) 2005. (Illus.). (gr. 3-4). lib. bdg. 22.60 (978-0-8225-3316-0(2)) 2nd rev. ed. 2011. (J). pap. 45.32 (978-0-7613-7654-5(2)) 2nd rev. ed. 2011. (ENG., Illus.). (J). (gr. 2-5). pap. 7.95 (978-0-7613-7463-3(9)) Lerner Publishing Group.

—Venus & Serena Williams. rev. ed. 2007. (Amazing Athletes Ser.). (ENG., Illus.). 32p. (J). (gr. 2-5). lib. bdg. 25.26 (978-0-8225-7595-5(7)) Lerner Publishing Group.

Dorrie, Roxanne. Venus & Serena Williams: The Smashing Sisters, 6 vols. 2003. (High Five Reading - Red Ser.). (ENG.). 48p. (gr. 3-4). pap. 54.00 (978-0-7368-2837-6(0)); (Illus.). per. 9.00 (978-0-7368-2827-7(3)) Capstone Press of Coughlan Cos. (High Five Reading (RBL)).

Fishman, Jon M. Serena Williams. 2016. (Amazing Athletes Ser.). (ENG., Illus.). 32p. (J). (gr. 2-5). 26.65 (978-1-5124-1334-2(8)) Lerner Publishing Group.

Marcovitz, Hal. Venus & Serena Williams. 2012. (Role Model Athletes Ser.). 64p. (J). (gr. 7). 22.95 (978-1-4222-2714-5(6)) Mason Crest.

Morgan, Terri. Venus & Serena Williams: Grand Slam Sisters. (Sports Achievers Biographies Ser.). (Illus.). 2005. 80p. (gr. 7-12). lib. bdg. 22.60 (978-0-8225-3684-0(6)) 2003. 64p. (J). (gr. 4-9). pap. 5.95 (978-0-8225-9866-4(3), Carolrhoda Bks.) Lerner Publishing Group.

Nagelhout, Ryan. Serena Williams. 2016. (Sports MVPs Ser.). (Illus.). 24p. (J). (gr. 2-1). 22.60 (978-1-4824-4642-5(1)) Stevens, Gareth Publishing LLLP.

Peters, Gregory N. Serena & Venus Williams Tennis Stars, 1 vol. 2014. (Sports & Recreation Ser.). (ENG.). 48p. (gr. 4-12). 31.99 (978-1-4765-8075-3(8)) Capstone Press of Coughlan Cos.

Pina, Andrew & Uschan, Michael. Serena Williams: Tennis Ace. 2017. (People in the News Ser.). 104p. (YA). (gr. 7-7). lib. bdg. 39.40 **(978-1-5345-6027-7(0)**, Lucent Pr.) Greenhaven Publishing LLC.

Porter, Esther. Serena Williams. 2016. (Women in Sports Ser.). (ENG., Illus.). 24p. (gr. k-1). pap. 6.95 (978-1-4914-8569-9(8), Pebble Plus) Capstone Press of Coughlan Cos.

Rajczak Nelson, Kristen. Serena Williams: Tennis Star. 2016. (Junior Biographies Ser.). (Illus.). 24p. (J). pap. 9.35 (978-0-7660-8181-9(8)) Enslow Pubs., Inc.

Raum, Elizabeth. Pro Sports Biographies: Serena Williams. 2017. (Pro Sports Biographies Ser.). (ENG.). 24p. (J). (gr. 1-3). pap. 8.99 **(978-1-68152-170-1(9))** Amicus.

—Serena Williams. 2017. (Pro Sports Biographies Ser.). (ENG.). 24p. (gr. 1-4). 20.95 **(978-1-68151-139-9(8))** Amicus Publishing.

Roza, Greg. Venus & Serena Williams: The Sisters of Tennis. 2006. (Tony Stead Nonfiction Independent Reading Collection). (ENG.). 24p. (gr. 3-6). pap. 8.85 (978-1-4042-5537-1(0)) Rosen Publishing Group, Inc., The.

Shepherd, Jodie. Serena Williams: A Champion on & off the Court. 2016. (Rookie Biographies(tm) Ser.). (ENG., Illus.). 32p. (J). lib. bdg. 25.00 (978-0-531-21684-2(5), Children's Pr.) Scholastic Library Publishing.

Shoup, Kate & Cunningham, Meghan Engsberg. Serena Williams: International Tennis Superstar. 2016. (Leading Women Ser.). 112p. (J). (gr. 7-7). 39.93 (978-1-5026-2014-9(6)) Cavendish Square Publishing.

Swanson, June. Venus & Serena Williams. Burke, Susan S., illus. 2003. (You Must Be Joking! Riddle Bks.). 32p. (J). (gr. 2-5). pap. 5.95 (978-0-8225-9842-8(6)) Lerner Publishing Group.

Todd, Anne M. Venus & Serena Williams. 2009. (Women of Achievement Ser.). (Illus.). 144p. (gr. 6-12). 35.00 (978-1-60413-461-2(5), Chelsea Hse.) Facts On File, Inc.
Uschan, Michael V. Serena Williams. 2011. (People in the News Ser.). (ENG.). 128p. (gr. 10-10). lib. bdg. 39.40 (978-1-4205-0488-0(6), Lucent Bks.) Cengage Gale.
Venus & Serena Williams. 2015. (Quotes from the Greatest Athletes Ser.). (ENG.). (J). lib. bdg. 12.95 (978-1-4896-3385-9(5)); lib. bdg. 28.55 (978-1-4896-3384-2(7)) Weigl Pubs., Inc. (AV2 by Weigl).
Watson, Galadriel Findlay. Venus & Serena Williams. 2005. (Great African American Women for Kids Ser.). (Illus.). 24p. (J). (gr. 2-3). lib. bdg. 24.45 (978-1-59036-332-4(9)); (gr. 3-7). per. 8.95 (978-1-59036-338-6(8)) Weigl Pubs., Inc.

WILLIAMS, TENNESSEE, 1914-1983

Hermann, Spring. Reading & Interpreting the Works of Tennessee Williams. 2016. (Lit Crit Guides). 176p. (J). lib. bdg. 39.93 (978-0-7660-8346-2(2)) Enslow Pubs., Inc.
—A Student's Guide to Tennessee Williams. 2007. (Understanding Literature Ser.). (Illus.). 160p. (YA). (gr. 8-12). lib. bdg. 29.27 (978-0-7660-2706-0(6)) Enslow Pubs., Inc.
Novel Units, Inc. Staff, creator. A Streetcar Named Desire Student Packet. 2007. (YA). 12.99 (978-1-58130-951-5(1)) Novel Units, Inc.
Tracy, Kathleen. Tennessee Williams. 2007. (Poets & Playwrights Ser.). (Illus.). 112p. (J). (gr. 3-7). lib. bdg. 37.10 (978-1-58415-427-3(6)) Mitchell Lane Pubs., Inc.

WILLIAMS, TED, 1918-2002

Bowen, Fred. No Easy Way: The Story of Ted Williams & the Last .400 Season. Pyle, Charles S. & Pyle, Chuck, illus. 2010. (ENG.). 32p. (J). (gr. k-3). 16.99 (978-0-525-47877-5(9), Dutton Books for Young Readers) Penguin Young Readers Group.
McCormack, Shaun. Ted Williams. (Baseball Hall of Famers Ser.). 112p. (gr. 5-8). 2009. 63.90 (978-1-61511-517-4(X)) 2004. (Illus.). (J). lib. bdg. 34.60 (978-0-8239-3783-7(6)) Rosen Publishing Group, Inc., The. (Rosen Reference).
Tavares, Matt. There Goes Ted Williams: The Greatest Hitter Who Ever Lived. Tavares, Matt, illus. (Candlewick Biographies Ser.). (ENG., Illus.). (J). (gr. 1-4). 2015. 48p. 14.99 (978-0-7636-7655-1(1)) 2012. 40p. 16.99 (978-0-7636-2789-8(5)) Candlewick Pr.

WILLIAMS, VENUS, 1980-

Anniss, Matt. Venus & Serena Williams in the Community. 1 vol., 1. 2014. (Making a Difference: Athletes Who Are Changing the World Ser.). (ENG.). 48p. (J). (gr. 5-8). 25.85 (978-1-62275-170-9(1)) Rosen Publishing Group, Inc., The.
Bailey, Diane. Venus & Serena Williams: Tennis Champions. 2010. (Sports Families Ser.). 48p. (ENG.). (J). pap. 11.75 (978-1-4358-8520-2(1), Rosen Reference); (YA). (gr. 5-8). lib. bdg., E-Book 53.00 (978-1-4488-0124-4(9)); (Illus.). (YA). (gr. 4-7). lib. bdg. 29.25 (978-1-4358-3552-8(2)) Rosen Publishing Group, Inc., The.
Brown, Jonatha A. Venus & Serena Williams. 2005. (People to Know Ser.). (Illus.). 24p. (gr. 1-4). pap. 8.15 (978-0-8368-4477-1(7)); lib. bdg. 22.00 (978-0-8368-4470-2(X)) Stevens, Gareth Publishing LLLP. (Weekly Reader Leveled Readers).
—Venus y Serena Williams. 2005. (Gente que hay que conocer (People We Should Know- Spanish) Ser.).Tr. of Venus & Serena Williams. (SPA.). 24p. (gr. 1-4). lib. bdg. 22.00 (978-0-8368-4586-0(2), Weekly Reader Leveled Readers) Stevens, Gareth Publishing LLLP.
Donaldson, Madeline. Venus & Serena Williams. (Amazing Athletes Ser.). 32p. 2007. (Illus.). (J). (gr. -1-3). per. 6.95 (978-0-8225-8857-3(9), First Avenue Editions) 2005. (Illus.). (gr. 3-4). lib. bdg. 22.60 (978-0-8225-3316-0(2)) 2nd rev. ed. 2011. (J). pap. 45.32 (978-0-7613-7654-5(2)) 2nd rev. ed. 2011. (ENG., Illus.). (J). (gr. 2-5). pap. 7.95 (978-0-7613-7463-3(9)) Lerner Publishing Group.
—Venus & Serena Williams. rev. ed. 2007. (Amazing Athletes Ser.). (ENG., Illus.). 32p. (gr. 2-5). lib. bdg. 25.26 (978-0-8225-7595-5(7)) Lerner Publishing Group.
Dorrie, Roxanne. Venus & Serena Williams: The Smashing Sisters, 6 vols. 2003. (High Five Reading - Red Ser.). (ENG.). 48p. (gr. 3-4). pap. 54.00 (978-0-7368-2837-6(0)); (Illus.). per. 9.00 (978-0-7368-2827-7(3)) Capstone Press of Coughlan Cos. (High Five Reading (RBL)).
Feldman, Heather. Venus Williams: Campeona de Tenis (Tennis Champion) 2009. (Superestrellas del Deporte (Superstars of Sports) Ser.). (SPA.). 24p. (gr. 1-2). 42.50 (978-1-60853-229-2(1), Editorial Buenas Letras) Rosen Publishing Group, Inc., The.
—Venus Williams: Tennis Champion. 2009. (Sports Superstars Ser.). 24p. (gr. 1-1). 42.50 (978-1-60853-183-7(X), PowerKids Pr.) Rosen Publishing Group, Inc., The.
—Venus Williams: Tennis Champion / Campeona de Tenis. 2009. (Superstars of Sports/Superestrellas del deporte Ser.). (ENG & SPA.). 24p. (gr. 1-2). 42.50 (978-1-60853-241-4(0), Editorial Buenas Letras) Rosen Publishing Group, Inc., The.
—Venus Williams, Tennis Champion/Campeona de Tenis. De Leon, Mauricio Velzaquez, tr. 2008. (Reading Power Ser.). (ENG., Illus.). 24p. (gr. 1-6). per. 8.85 (978-0-8239-6212-9(1)) Rosen Publishing Group, Inc., The.
Franzen, Lenore. Venus Williams. 2003. (Ovations Ser.). (Illus.). 32p. (J). (978-1-58341-249-7(2), Creative Education) Creative Co., The.
Marcovitz, Hal. Venus & Serena Williams. 2012. (Role Model Athletes Ser.). 64p. (J). (gr. 7). 22.95 (978-1-4222-2714-5(6)) Mason Crest.
Morgan, Terri. Venus & Serena Williams: Grand Slam Sisters. (Sports Achievers Biographies Ser.). (Illus.). 2005. 80p. (gr. 7-12). lib. bdg. 22.60 (978-0-8225-3684-0(6)) 2003. 64p. (J). (gr. 4-9). pap. 5.95 (978-0-8225-9866-4(3), Carolrhoda Bks.) Lerner Publishing Group.
Peters, Gregory N. Serena & Venus Williams Tennis Stars, 1 vol. 2014. (Sports & Recreation Ser.). (ENG.). 48p. (gr. 4-12). 31.99 (978-1-4765-8075-3(8)) Capstone Press of Coughlan Cos.
Roza, Greg. Venus & Serena Williams: The Sisters of Tennis. 2006. (Tony Stead Nonfiction Independent Reading Collection). (ENG.). 24p. (gr. 3-6). pap. 8.85 (978-1-4042-5537-1(0)) Rosen Publishing Group, Inc., The.
Sandler, Michael. Tennis: Victory for Venus Williams. 2006. (Upsets & Comebacks Ser.). (Illus.). 32p. (J). (gr. 3-6). lib. bdg. 25.27 (978-1-59716-170-1(5)) Bearport Publishing Co., Inc.
Swanson, June. Venus & Serena Williams. Burke, Susan S., illus. 2003. (You Must Be Joking! Riddle Bks.). 32p. (J). (gr. 2-5). pap. 5.95 (978-0-8225-9842-8(6)) Lerner Publishing Group.
Todd, Anne M. Venus & Serena Williams. 2009. (Women of Achievement Ser.). (Illus.). 144p. (gr. 6-12). 35.00 (978-1-60413-461-2(5), Chelsea Hse.) Facts On File, Inc.
Venus & Serena Williams. 2015. (Quotes from the Greatest Athletes Ser.). (ENG.). (J). lib. bdg. 12.95 (978-1-4896-3385-9(5)); lib. bdg. 28.55 (978-1-4896-3384-2(7)) Weigl Pubs., Inc. (AV2 by Weigl).
Watson, Galadriel Findlay. Venus & Serena Williams. 2005. (Great African American Women for Kids Ser.). (Illus.). 24p. (J). (gr. 2-3). lib. bdg. 24.45 (978-1-59036-332-4(9)); (gr. 3-7). per. 8.95 (978-1-59036-338-6(8)) Weigl Pubs., Inc.
Wilson, Mike. The Williams Sisters: Venus & Serena. 2005. (ENG., Illus.). 32p. pap. 8.50 (978-0-340-84876-0(6)) Cambridge Univ. Pr.

WILLIAMSBURG (VA.)

Chorao, Kay. D Is for Drums: A Colonial Williamsburg ABC. 2004. (ENG., Illus.). 32p. (J). (gr. -1-1). 16.95 (978-0-8109-4927-0(X)) Abrams, Inc.
McNeese, Tim. Williamsburg. 2007. (Colonial Settlements in America Ser.). (Illus.). 112p. (YA). (gr. 5-9). lib. bdg. 30.00 (978-0-7910-9333-7(6)) Facts On File, Inc.
Rudolph, Ellen K. Willi Gets a History Lesson: In Virginia's Historic Triangle. Rudolph, Ellen K., photos by. 2007. (ENG., Illus.). 80p. pap. 24.00 (978-0-9791348-0-7(3)) EKR Pubns.

WILLIAMSBURG (VA.)—FICTION

Elliott, L. M. Give Me Liberty. 2008. (ENG., Illus.). 384p. (J). (gr. 4-7). per. 7.99 (978-0-06-074423-6(5), Tegen, Katherine Bks) HarperCollins Pubs.
Nixon, Joan Lowery. Ann's Story, 1747. 2004. (J). (978-0-87935-198-4(5)) Colonial Williamsburg Foundation.
—Caesar's Story, 1759. 2004. (J). (978-0-87935-199-1(3)) Colonial Williamsburg Foundation.
—John's Story, 1775. 2004. (J). (978-0-87935-228-8(0)) Colonial Williamsburg Foundation.
—Maria's Story, 1773. 2004. (J). (978-0-87935-227-1(2)) Colonial Williamsburg Foundation.
—Nancy's Story, 1765. 2004. (J). (978-0-87935-225-7(6)) Colonial Williamsburg Foundation.
—Will's Story, 1771. 2004. (J). (978-0-87935-226-4(4)) Colonial Williamsburg Foundation.
Tripp, Valerie. Felicity Story Collection. Andreasen, Dan, illus. 2008. (ENG.). 404p. (J). 29.95 (978-1-59369-452-4(0)) American Girl Publishing, Inc.
Trumbore, Cindy. Three Cheers for Liberty! Elkerton, Andy, illus. 2016. (J). pap. (978-0-87935-287-5(6)) Colonial Williamsburg Foundation.

WILLIAMSBURG (VA.)—HISTORY

Bauley, Thomas K. Williamsburg A-Z: An Alphabetical Journey, 1 vol. 2010. (ENG., Illus.). 32p. 19.99 (978-0-7643-3671-3(1), 9780764336713) Schiffer Publishing, Ltd.
Chorao, Kay. D Is for Drums: A Colonial Williamsburg A. B. C. 2004. (J). 16.95 (978-0-87935-197-7(7)) Colonial Williamsburg Foundation.
—D Is for Drums: A Colonial Williamsburg ABC. 2004. (ENG., Illus.). 32p. (J). (gr. -1-1). 16.95 (978-0-8109-4927-0(X)) Abrams, Inc.
—D Is for Drums: A Colonial Williamsburg ABC. Chorao, Kay, illus. 2006. (Illus.). 30p. (J). (gr. k-4). reprint ed. 17.00 (978-1-4223-5240-3(4)) DIANE Publishing Co.
Coleman, Wim & Perrin, Pat. Colonial Williamsburg: A MyReportLinks.com Book. 2005. (Virtual Field Trips Ser.). (Illus.). 48p. (J). (gr. 4-10). lib. bdg. 26.60 (978-0-7660-5220-8(6), MyReportLinks.com Bks.) Enslow Pubs., Inc.
Kostyal, Karen & Colonial Williamsburg Foundation Staff. 1776: A New Look at Revolutionary Williamsburg. Epstein, Lori, photos by. 2009. (ENG., Illus.). 48p. (J). (gr. 3-7). 27.90 (978-1-4263-0518-4(4), National Geographic Children's Bks.) National Geographic Society.
—1776: A New Look at Revolutionary Williamsburg. Epstein, Lori, photos by. 2009. (ENG., Illus.). 48p. (J). (gr. 3-7). 17.95 (978-1-4263-0517-7(6), National Geographic Children's Bks.) National Geographic Society.
Varela, Barry. The Young Patriots' Guide to Colonial Williamsburg's Historic Area. 2010. (J). pap. (978-0-87935-245-5(0)) Colonial Williamsburg Foundation.
Zschock, Martha Day. Hello Williamsburg! 2013. (ENG., Illus.). 16p. (J). (gr. -1-k). bds. 9.95 (978-1-933212-03-6(9), Commonwealth Editions) Applewood Bks.

WILLOW—FICTION

Hegamin, Tonya Cherie. Willow. 2014. (ENG.). 384p. (YA). (gr. 9). 16.99 (978-0-7636-5769-7(7)) Candlewick Pr.
Miller, Stanley W. Wishing Willow: A Young People's Story for All Ages. 2007. (YA). per. 10.95 (978-0-9748884-6-0(X)) Little Thoughts For Little Ones Publishing, Inc.
The Willow Pattern: Individual Title Six-Packs. (Action Packs Ser.). 104p. (gr. 3-5). 44.00 (978-0-7635-2996-3(6)) Rigby Education.

WILLS—FICTION

Diggle, David Mark. Sammy: Leaves His Mark. Diggle, Daniel James, illus. 2011. 24p. (J). pap. (978-0-9871657-3-2(9)) Diggle de Doo Productions Pty, Ltd.
Keene, Carolyn. The Bungalow Mystery, No. 3. 2014. (Nancy Drew Ser.: 3). (ENG.). 192p. (J). (gr. 3-7). 7.99 (978-0-448-47971-2(0), Grosset & Dunlap) Penguin Young Readers Group.
—The Hidden Staircase, No. 2. 2014. (Nancy Drew Ser.: 2). (ENG.). 192p. (J). (gr. 3-7). 7.99 (978-0-448-47970-5(2), Grosset & Dunlap) Penguin Young Readers Group.
—The Mystery at Lilac Inn. 2014. (Nancy Drew Ser.: 4). (ENG.). 192p. (J). (gr. 3-7). 7.99 (978-0-448-47972-9(9), Grosset & Dunlap) Penguin Young Readers Group.
—The Secret of the Old Clock, Bk. 1. 2014. (Nancy Drew Ser.: 1). (ENG.). 192p. (J). (gr. 3-7). 7.99 (978-0-448-47969-9(9), Grosset & Dunlap) Penguin Young Readers Group.

WILSON, SAMUEL, 1766-1854

Friesen, Helen Lepp. Uncle Sam with Code. 2012. (AV2 American Icons Ser.). (ENG., Illus.). 24p. (J). (gr. -1-3). pap. 12.95 (978-1-61913-304-4(0), AV2 by Weigl) Weigl Pubs., Inc.
Hicks, Terry Allan. Uncle Sam. (Symbols of America Ser.). (Illus.). 40p. 2007. (J). (gr. -1-3). pap. 6.99 (978-0-7614-3379-8(1), Cavendish Children's Bks.) 2006. (gr. 3-7). lib. bdg. 20.95 (978-0-7614-2137-5(8), Benchmark Bks.) Marshall Cavendish Corp.
Marcovitz, Hal. Uncle Sam: International Symbol of America. Moreno, Barry, ed. 2014. (Patriotic Symbols of America Ser.: 20). 48p. (J). (gr. 4-18). lib. bdg. 20.95 (978-1-4222-3135-7(6)) Mason Crest.
Monroe, Tyler. Uncle Sam, 1 vol. 2013. (U. S. Symbols Ser.). (ENG.). 24p. (gr. k-1). 26.65 (978-1-4765-3086-4(6)); pap. 7.95 (978-1-4765-3535-7(3)) Capstone Press of Coughlan Cos. (Pebble Plus).

WILSON, WOODROW, 1856-1924

Aronin, Miriam. Woodrow Wilson. 2016. (First Look at America's Presidents Ser.). (ENG., Illus.). 24p. (J). (gr. -1-3). 17.95 (978-1-943553-30-3(0)) Bearport Publishing Co., Inc.
Ashby, Ruth. Woodrow & Edith Wilson. 2005. (Presidents & First Ladies Ser.). (Illus.). 48p. (gr. 5-12). lib. bdg. 31.00 (978-0-8368-5759-7(3), World Almanac Library) Stevens, Gareth Publishing LLLP.
Crompton, Samuel Willard. How Woodrow Wilson Fought World War I. 2017. (Presidents at War Ser.). 128p. (J). (gr. 8-8). lib. bdg. 37.27 (978-0-7660-8529-9(5)) Enslow Pubs., Inc.
Dommermuth-Costa, Carol. Woodrow Wilson. 2003. (Presidential Leaders Ser.). (Illus.). 112p. (J). 29.27 (978-0-8225-0094-0(9), Lerner Pubns.) Lerner Publishing Group.
Frith, Margaret & dePaola, Tomie. Who Was Woodrow Wilson? Thomson, Andrew & Harrison, Nancy, illus. 2015. (Who Was? Ser.). (ENG.). 112p. (J). (gr. 3-7). 5.99 (978-0-448-48428-0(5), Grosset & Dunlap) Penguin Young Readers Group.
Harmon, Daniel E. Woodrow Wilson. 2004. (Childhoods of the Presidents Ser.). (Illus.). 48p. (J). (gr. 4-18). lib. bdg. 17.95 (978-1-59084-277-5(4)) Mason Crest.
Holden, Henry M. Woodrow Wilson: A MyReportLinks.com Book. 2003. (Presidents Ser.). (Illus.). 48p. (J). (gr. 4-10). lib. bdg. 25.26 (978-0-7660-5123-2(4), MyReportLinks.com Bks.) Enslow Pubs., Inc.
Huddle, Lorena. Woodrow Wilson. 2017. (Pivotal Presidents: Profiles in Leadership Ser.). 80p. (gr. 12-13). lib. bdg. 33.90 (978-1-68048-635-3(7), Britannica Educational Publishing) Rosen Publishing Group, Inc., The.
Lukes, Bonnie L. Woodrow Wilson & the Progressive Era. 2006. (World Leaders Ser.). (Illus.). 192p. (J). (gr. 6-10). lib. bdg. 26.95 (978-1-931798-79-2(6)) Reynolds, Morgan Inc.
Marsico, Katie. Woodrow Wilson. 2010. (Presidents & Their Times 4 Ser.). 96p. (gr. 6). 34.21 (978-0-7614-4815-0(2)) Marshall Cavendish Corp.
Mis, M. S. How to Draw the Life & Times of Woodrow Wilson. 2009. (Kid's Guide to Drawing the Presidents of the United States of America Ser.). 32p. (gr. 4-4). 50.50 (978-1-61511-168-8(9), PowerKids Pr.) Rosen Publishing Group, Inc., The.
Mis, Melody S. How to Draw the Life & Times of Woodrow Wilson. 2007. (Kid's Guide to Drawing the Presidents of the United States of America Ser.). (Illus.). 32p. (YA). (gr. 2-5). 26.50 (978-1-4042-3004-0(1)) Rosen Publishing Group, Inc., The.
Rumsch, BreAnn. Woodrow Wilson, 1 vol. 2009. (United States Presidents Ser.). (ENG., Illus.). 40p. (YA). (gr. 3-6). 27.07 (978-1-60453-480-1(X)) ABDO Publishing Co.
Schwartz, Eric. A World Contender. 2006. (How America Became America Ser.). (Illus.). 96p. (YA). lib. bdg. 22.95 (978-1-59084-911-8(6)) Mason Crest.
Venezia, Mike. Woodrow Wilson: Twenty-Eighth President. Venezia, Mike, illus. 2007. (Getting to Know the U. S. Presidents Ser.). (Illus.). 32p. (J). (gr. 3-7). pap. 7.95 (978-0-516-25462-3(6), Children's Pr.) Scholastic Library Publishing.
Waxman, Laura Hamilton. Woodrow Wilson. 2006. (History Maker Biographies Ser.). (ENG., Illus.). 48p. (gr. 3-6). lib. bdg. 27.93 (978-0-8225-6053-1(4), Lerner Pubns.) Lerner Publishing Group.
York, M. J. Woodrow Wilson. 2017. (Premier Presidents Ser.). (ENG.). 24p. (J). (gr. 1-4). lib. bdg. 27.07 (978-1-5038-1650-3(8), 211493) Child's World, Inc., The.
Zamosky, Lisa. Woodrow Wilson, 1 vol. 2007. (Primary Source Readers Ser.). (ENG.). 32p. (J). (gr. 4-4). pap. 8.99 (978-0-7439-0665-4(9)) Shell Educational Publishing.

WIND

see Winds

WIND INSTRUMENTS

see also Bands (Music)

Fraser, Dot & Fraser, Noel. Abracadabra Brass: The Way to Learn Through Songs & Tunes. Shulman, Dee & Tinkler, Dennis, illus. 2005. (Abracadabra Ser.). (ENG.). 64p. (J). pap. 13.95 (978-0-7136-7184-1(X)) HarperCollins Pubs. Ltd. GBR. Dist: Independent Pubs. Group.
Ganeri, Anita. Brass Instruments. 2011. (ENG., Illus.). 32p. (J). pap. 10.95 (978-1-77092-029-3(3)) Saunders Bk. Co. CAN. Dist: RiverStream Publishing.
—Wind Instruments. 2011. (ENG., Illus.). 32p. (J). pap. 10.95 (978-1-77092-034-7(X)) Saunders Bk. Co. CAN. Dist: RiverStream Publishing.
Hussey, Christopher. Abracadabra Christmas Showstoppers Clarinet, 1 vol. 2015. (Abracadabra Ser.). (ENG.). 32p. (J). (gr. k-4). pap. 22.95 (978-1-4729-2053-9(8)) HarperCollins Pubs. Ltd. GBR. Dist: Independent Pubs. Group.
—Abracadabra Christmas Showstoppers Trumpet, 1 vol. 2015. (Abracadabra Ser.). (ENG.). 32p. (J). pap. 22.95 (978-1-4729-2052-2(X)) HarperCollins Pubs. Ltd. GBR. Dist: Independent Pubs. Group.
Jolly, Hattie & Steynor, Ali. Get Set Flute Tutor Book 2. 2017. (Get Set! Ser.). (ENG., Illus.). 48p. (J). (gr. 4-7). pap. 14.95 (978-1-4729-3086-6(X)) HarperCollins Pubs. Ltd. GBR. Dist: Independent Pubs. Group.
Landau, Elaine. Is the Clarinet for You? 2010. (Ready to Make Music Ser.). (ENG.). 40p. (gr. 4-6). lib. bdg. 27.93 (978-0-7613-5421-5(2), Lerner Pubns.) Lerner Publishing Group.
Nunn, Daniel. Brass, 1 vol. 2011. (Instruments & Music Ser.). (ENG.). 24p. (gr. -1-1). pap. 6.29 (978-1-4329-5065-1(7), Acorn) Heinemann-Raintree.
—Woodwind, 1 vol. 2011. (Instruments & Music Ser.). (ENG.). 24p. (gr. -1-1). pap. 6.29 (978-1-4329-5070-5(3)); 22.65 (978-1-4329-5063-7(0)) Heinemann-Raintree. (Acorn).
Pollock, Malcolm & Hussey, Christopher. Abracadabra Flute Technique, 1 vol. 2015. (Abracadabra Ser.). (ENG.). 48p. (J). (gr. 1-3). pap. 15.95 (978-1-4081-9344-0(2)) HarperCollins Pubs. Ltd. GBR. Dist: Independent Pubs. Group.
Salzmann, Mary Elizabeth. What in the World Is a Clarinet?, 1 vol. 2012. (ENG.). 24p. 25.65 (978-1-61783-203-1(0), Super SandCastle) ABDO Publishing Co.
Shaskan, Trisha Speed. The Brass Family on Parade!, 1 vol. Meganck, Robert & Communication Design (Firm) Staff, illus. 2010. (Musical Families Ser.). (ENG.). 24p. (gr. 2-3). lib. bdg. 25.32 (978-1-4048-6041-4(X)) Picture Window Bks.
—Opening Night with the Woodwind Family!, 1 vol. Meganck, Robert & Communication Design (Firm) Staff, illus. 2010. (Musical Families Ser.). (ENG.). 24p. (gr. 2-3). lib. bdg. 25.32 (978-1-4048-6042-1(8)) Picture Window Bks.
Steynor, Ali & Jolly, Hattie. Get Set! Flute Pieces Book 1 with Cd, 1 vol. 2015. (Get Set! Ser.). (ENG.). 48p. (J). (gr. k-4). pap. 15.95 (978-1-4729-0909-1(7)) HarperCollins Pubs. Ltd. GBR. Dist: Independent Pubs. Group.
—Get Set! Flute Tutor Book 1 with Cd, 1 vol. 2015. (Get Set! Ser.). (ENG., Illus.). 48p. (J). pap. 15.95 (978-1-4729-0908-4(9)) HarperCollins Pubs. Ltd. GBR. Dist: Independent Pubs. Group.
Storey, Rita. The Recorder & Other Wind Instruments. 2010. (J). 28.50 (978-1-59920-213-6(1)) Black Rabbit Bks.

WIND POWER

Allen, Kathy. Wind Power. 2013. (J). (978-1-61080-975-7(0)); (ENG.). 32p. (gr. 4-8). 28.50 (978-1-61080-900-9(9), 202579); (ENG.). 32p. (gr. 4-8). pap. 14.21 (978-1-61080-925-2(4), 202581) Cherry Lake Publishing.
Armentrout, David & Armentrout, Patricia. Energía Del Viento. 2012. (SPA & ENG.). 48p. (gr. 4-8). pap. 10.95 (978-1-61810-474-8(8)) Rourke Educational Media.
Bailey, Diane. Harnessing Energy: Wind Power. 2015. (Harnessing Energy Ser.). (ENG.). 48p. (J). (gr. 5-8). pap. 12.00 (978-0-89812-999-1(0), Creative Paperbacks) Creative Co., The.
—Wind Power. 2014. (Harnessing Energy Ser.). lib. bdg. 35.65 (978-1-60818-413-2(7), Creative Education) Creative Co., The.
Benduhn, Tea. Energía del Viento. 2008. (Energía para el presente (Energy for Today) Ser.). (SPA.). 24p. (gr. 2-6). (J). lib. bdg. 22.00 (978-0-8368-9271-0(2)); pap. 8.15 (978-0-8368-9370-0(0)) Stevens, Gareth Publishing LLLP. (Weekly Reader Leveled Readers).
—Wind Power. 2008. (Energy for Today Ser.). 24p. (gr. 2-6). (J). lib. bdg. 22.00 (978-0-8368-9265-9(8)); pap. 8.15 (978-0-8368-9364-9(5)) Stevens, Gareth Publishing LLLP. (Weekly Reader Leveled Readers).
Dickmann, Nancy. Harnessing Wind Energy. 2016. (Future of Power Ser.). 00032p. (J). (gr. 4-5). pap. 10.00 (978-1-4994-3215-2(1), PowerKids Pr.) Rosen Publishing Group, Inc., The.
Dobson, Clive. Wind Power: 20 Projects to Make with Paper. 2010. (ENG., Illus.). 96p. (J). (gr. 5-12). 24.95 (978-1-55407-659-8(5), 9781554076598); pap. 12.95 (978-1-55407-749-6(4), 9781554077496) Firefly Bks., Ltd.
Doeden, Matt. Finding Out about Wind Energy. 2014. (Searchlight Books — What Are Energy Sources? Ser.). (ENG., Illus.). 40p. (gr. 3-5). lib. bdg. 27.93 (978-1-4677-3656-5(2), Lerner Pubns.) Lerner Publishing Group.
Drummond, Allan. Energy Island: How One Community Harnessed the Wind & Changed Their World. Drummond, Allan, illus. 2011. (ENG., Illus.). 40p. (J). (gr. 1-5). 18.99 (978-0-374-32184-0(1), 9780374321840, Farrar, Straus & Giroux (BYR)) Farrar, Straus & Giroux.
—Energy Island: How One Community Harnessed the Wind & Changed Their World. Drummond, Allan, illus. 2015. (ENG., Illus.). 40p. (J). (gr. 1-5). 8.99 (978-1-250-05676-4(4), 9781250056764) Square Fish.
Fitzgerald, Stephanie, et al. Wind Power. 2010. (Energy Today Ser.). 48p. (J). (gr. 3-6). 30.00 (978-1-60413-780-4(0)) Facts On File, Inc.
Francis, Amy. Wind Farms. 2015. (At Issue Ser.). (ENG.). 128p. (gr. 10-12). pap. 27.80 (978-0-7377-7204-3(2), Greenhaven Pr., Inc.) Cengage Gale.
Goodman, Polly. Understanding Wind Power. 2010. (World of Energy Ser.). (ENG.). 48p. (J). (gr. 6-8). lib. bdg. 31.95 (978-1-4339-4133-7(3), Gareth Stevens Learning Library) Stevens, Gareth Publishing LLLP.
Grady, Colin. Wind Energy. 2016. (Saving the Planet Through Green Energy Ser.). 24p. (J). pap. 9.35 (978-0-7660-8296-0(2)) Enslow Pubs., Inc.
Hansen, Amy. Wind Energy: Blown Away! 2010. (Powering Our World Ser.). (ENG.). 24p. (J). pap. 8.25 (978-1-4358-9742-7(0), PowerKids Pr.) Rosen Publishing Group, Inc., The.
Hansen, Amy S. Wind Energy: Blown Away! 2010. (Powering Our World Ser.). 24p. (J). (gr. 2-5). E-Book 42.50 (978-1-4488-0199-2(0)); (Illus.). lib. bdg. 22.60 (978-1-4358-9327-6(1), PowerKids Pr.) Rosen Publishing Group, Inc., The.
Hirsch, Rebecca E. Birds vs. Blades? Offshore Wind Power & the Race to Protect Seabirds. 2016. (ENG., Illus.). 48p. (gr. 4-6). 33.32 (978-1-4677-9520-3(8)); 50.65 (978-1-5124-1111-9(6)) Lerner Publishing Group. (Millbrook Pr.).
Iwinski, Melissa. The Wind at Work. 2007. (Shockwave: Technology & Manufacturing Ser.). (ENG., Illus.). 36p. (J). (gr. 3-5). 25.00 (978-0-531-17586-6(3), Children's Pr.) Scholastic Library Publishing.
Johnson, Anne. Catch the Wind. 2008. (Illus.). (J). 11.50 (978-1-59298-258-5(1)) Beaver's Pond Pr., Inc.
Kopp, Megan. Energy from Wind: Wind Farming. 2015. (Next Generation Energy Ser.). (ENG., Illus.). 32p. (J). (978-0-7787-1983-0(9)) Crabtree Publishing Co.
Land-Sailing Venus Rover: Meet NASA Inventor Geoffrey Landis & His Team's. 2017. (J). (978-0-7166-6160-3(8)) World Bk., Inc.

Mara, Wil. Wind Turbine Service Technician. 2013. (21st Century Skills Library: Cool STEM Careers Ser.). (ENG.). 32p. (J). (gr. 4-8). 28.50 (978-1-62431-003-4(6), 202463); pap. 14.21 (978-1-62431-027-0(3), 202465) Cherry Lake Publishing.

McCann, Shawn, illus. Catch the Wind. 2008. 38p. (J). pap. (978-1-59298-244-8(1)) Beaver's Pond Pr., Inc.

Morris, Neil. Wind Power. 2010. (J). 34.25 (978-1-59920-344-7(8)) 2007. (Illus.). 32p. (YA). (gr. 4-7). lib. bdg. 28.50 (978-1-58340-910-7(6)) Black Rabbit Bks.

Muschal, Frank. Energy from Wind, Sun, & Tides. 2007. (21st Century Skills Library: Power Up! Ser.). (ENG.). 32p. (gr. 4-8). pap. 14.21 (978-1-60279-096-4(5), 200657); (Illus.). lib. bdg. 28.50 (978-1-60279-046-9(9), 200052) Cherry Lake Publishing.

Nazzaro, Robin M. Wind Power: Impacts on Wildlife & Government Responsibilities for Regulating Development & Protecting Wildlife. 2006. (Illus.). 59p. (C). pap. 20.00 (978-1-4223-0354-2(3)) DIANE Publishing Co.

Ollhoff, Jim. Wind & Water, 1 vol. 2010. (Future Energy Ser.). (ENG., Illus.). 32p. (YA). (gr. 4-7). 27.07 (978-1-60453-939-4(9)) ABDO Publishing Co.

O'Neal, Claire. How to Use Wind Power to Light & Heat Your Home. 2009. (Tell Your Parents Ser.). (Illus.). 48p. (J). (gr. 4-7). lib. bdg. 29.95 (978-1-58415-762-5(3)) Mitchell Lane Pubs., Inc.

Owen, Ruth. Energy from the Wind: Generating Power with Wind Turbines. 2013. (Power: Yesterday, Today, Tomorrow Ser.). (ENG., Illus.). 32p. (J). (gr. 3-6). 25.25 (978-1-4777-0271-0(7)); pap. 11.75 (978-1-4777-0281-9(4)) Rosen Publishing Group, Inc., The. (PowerKids Pr.).

Parks, Peggy J. Wind Power. 2009. (Compact Research Ser.). 96p. (YA). (gr. 7-12). 25.95 (978-1-60152-080-7(8)) ReferencePoint Pr., Inc.

Pipe, Jim. Wind Power. 2010. (J). 28.50 (978-1-59604-212-4(5)) Black Rabbit Bks.

Pluckrose, Henry. Air. 2007. (Let's Explore: Elements Ser.). (Illus.). 32p. (J). (gr. 4-7). lib. bdg. 27.10 (978-1-59771-033-6(4)) Sea-To-Sea Pubns.

Richards, Julie. Wind Energy. 2009. (J). 19.95 (978-0-7614-4430-5(0)) Marshall Cavendish GBR. Dist: Marshall Cavendish Corp.

Saunders, Nigel. Wind Power. 2007. (Energy for the Future & Global Warming Ser.). (Illus.). 32p. (J). (gr. 5-8). pap. 11.70 (978-0-8368-8414-2(0)); lib. bdg. 27.00 (978-0-8368-8405-0(1)) Stevens, Gareth Publishing LLLP.

Spilsbury, Richard & Spilsbury, Louise. The Pros & Cons of Wind Power. 2007. (Energy Debate Ser.). (Illus.). 48p. (YA). (gr. 5-9). lib. bdg. 29.25 (978-1-4042-3745-2(3)) Rosen Publishing Group, Inc., The.

—Wind Power. 2012. (Let's Discuss Energy Resources Ser.). (Illus.). 32p. (J). (gr. 4-7). lib. bdg. 26.50 (978-1-4488-5264-2(1)) Rosen Publishing Group, Inc., The.

Sterling, Kristin. It's Windy Today. 2009. (Lightning Bolt Books — What's the Weather Like? Ser.). (ENG., Illus.). 32p. (gr. k-2). 26.60 (978-0-7613-4260-1(5), Lerner Pubns.); pap. 7.95 (978-0-7613-5023-1(3)) Lerner Publishing Group.

Walker, Niki. Generating Wind Power. 2006. (Energy Revolution Ser.). (ENG., Illus.). 32p. (J). (gr. 3-7). pap. (978-0-7787-2927-3(3)) Crabtree Publishing Co.

WINDMILLS

Cartlidge, Cherese. Home Windmills. 2009. (Great Idea Ser.). (ENG., Illus.). 48p. (J). (gr. 4-6). lib. bdg. 26.60 (978-1-59953-192-2(5)) Norwood Hse. Pr.

Doeden, Matt. Finding Out about Wind Energy. 2014. (Searchlight Books — What Are Energy Sources? Ser.). (Illus.). 40p. (gr. 3-4). pap. 8.95 (978-1-4677-4558-1(8)) Lerner Publishing Group.

Friedman, Mark. What Does It Do? Windmill. 2011. (Community Connections: What Does It Do? Ser.). (ENG.). 24p. (gr. 2-5). lib. bdg. 25.64 (978-1-61080-118-8(0), 201126) Cherry Lake Publishing.

Kamkwamba, William. The Boy Who Harnessed the Wind: Creating Currents of Electricity & Hope. 2009. 14.44 (978-0-7848-3872-3(0), Everbind) Marco Bk. Co.

—The Boy Who Harnessed the Wind: Creating Currents of Electricity & Hope. Hymas, Anna, illus. 2015. (ENG.). 304p. (J). (gr. 5). 18.99 (978-0-8037-4080-8(8), Dial Bks) Penguin Young Readers Group.

Kamkwamba, William & Mealer, Bryan. The Boy Who Harnessed the Wind: Young Readers Edition. Zunon, Elizabeth, illus. (ENG.). (J). 2016. 304p. (gr. 5). 8.99 (978-0-14-751042-6(2), Puffin Books) 2012. 32p. (gr. 1-3). 17.99 (978-0-8037-3511-8(1), Dial Bks) Penguin Young Readers Group.

McCook, William. Windmills of the World. Harris, Coy F., ed. 2003. (Illus.). 109p. (YA). reprint ed. pap. 24.95 (978-0-9679480-1-0(0)) American Wind Power Ctr.

Woelfle, Gretchen. The Wind at Work: An Activity Guide to Windmills. 2nd ed. 2013. (ENG., Illus.). 160p. (J). (gr. 4). pap. 16.95 (978-1-61374-100-9(6)) Chicago Review Pr., Inc.

WINDOWS, STAINED GLASS

see Glass Painting and Staining

WINDS

see also Hurricanes; Storms; Tornadoes

Appleby, Alex. It's Windy! 2013. (Illus.). 24p. (J). (gr. k-2). 22.60 (978-1-4339-9412-8(7)); pap. 48.90 (978-1-4339-9414-2(3)); pap. 8.15 (978-1-4339-9413-5(5)) Stevens, Gareth Publishing LLLP.

—It's Windy! / Est Ventoso! 2013. (What's the Weather? / Qu Tiempo Hace? Ser.). (SPA & ENG., Illus.). 24p. (J). (gr. k-2). 22.60 (978-1-4339-9452-4(6)) Stevens, Gareth Publishing LLLP.

Bauer, Marion Dane. Wind. Wallace, John, illus. 2005. (Ready-to-Read Ser.). 32p. (gr. -1-1). 14.00 (978-0-7569-5622-6(6)) Perfection Learning Corp.

—Wind. Wallace, John, illus. 2003. (Weather Ready-To-Reads Ser.). (ENG.). 32p. (J). (gr. -1-1). pap. 3.99 (978-0-689-85443-9(9), Simon Spotlight) Simon Spotlight.

Benchmark Education Co., LLC. The Wind Big Book. 2014. (Shared Reading Foundations Ser.). (J). (gr. -1). (978-1-4509-9441-5(5)) Benchmark Education Co.

Berkes, Marianne. Daisylocks, 1 vol. Morrison, Cathy, illus. 2014. (ENG.). 32p. (J). (gr. -1-3). pap. 9.95 (978-1-62855-215-7(8)) Arbordale Publishing.

Berkes, Marianne Collins, et al. La Plantita Margarita, 1 vol. Morrison, Cathy, illus. 2014. (SPA.). 32p. (J). (gr. -1-3). pap. 9.95 (978-1-62855-224-9(7)) Arbordale Publishing.

Blaisdell, Molly. Can You See the Wind? 2008. (Discovering & Exploring Science Ser.). (Illus.). 16p. (J). (gr. -1-3). lib. bdg. 12.95 (978-0-7569-8412-0(2)) Perfection Learning Corp.

Boerger, Kristin. Hace Viento. 2007. (Que tiempo hace? (Let's Read about Weather) Ser.). (ENG & SPA., Illus.). 12p. (J). (gr. -1-2). pap. 4.10 (978-0-8368-8117-2(6)); lib. bdg. 15.00 (978-0-8368-8112-7(5)) Stevens, Gareth Publishing LLLP. (Weekly Reader Leveled Readers).

—Let's Read about Wind. 2007. (Let's Read about Weather Ser.). (Illus.). 12p. (gr. -1-2). pap. 4.10 (978-0-8368-7813-4(2)); lib. bdg. 15.00 (978-0-8368-7808-0(6)) Stevens, Gareth Publishing LLLP. (Weekly Reader Leveled Readers).

Bundey, Nikki. Wind & People. 2005. (Science of Weather Ser.). (Illus.). 32p. (gr. 4-6). lib. bdg. 21.27 (978-1-57505-495-7(7)) Lerner Publishing Group.

Cain, Marie Mowery. Air Power. 2013. (Big Books, Red Ser.). (ENG & SPA., Illus.). 16p. pap. 33.00 (978-1-59246-210-0(3)) Big Books, by George!

Canizares, Susan & Chessen, Betsey. Wind: El Viento. 2005. (Illus.). (J). (978-0-439-66391-5(1)) Scholastic, Inc.

Capeci, Anne & Cole, Joanna. The Magic School Bus Rides the Wind, Level 2. Bracken, Carolyn, illus. 2007. (Magic School Bus Science Reader Ser.). (ENG.). 32p. (J). (gr. -1-3). pap. 4.99 (978-0-439-80108-9(7), Cartwheel Bks.) Scholastic, Inc.

Cardenas, Ernesto A. Wind. 2009. 19.95 (978-1-60698-026-2(2)); pap. 3.95 (978-1-60698-024-8(6)) Milo Educational Bks. & Resources.

Clark, Stacy. When the Wind Blows. Sneed, Brad, illus. 2015. (ENG.). 32p. (J). (gr. -1-3). 16.95 (978-0-8234-3069-7(3)) Holiday Hse., Inc.

Cobb, Vicki. I Face the Wind. Gorton, Julia, illus. 2003. (Science Play Ser.). (ENG.). 40p. (J). (gr. -1-3). 16.99 (978-0-688-17840-6(5)) HarperCollins Pubs.

Cox Cannons, Helen. Wind, 1 vol. 2014. (Weather Wise Ser.). (ENG., Illus.). 24p. (gr. -1-1). pap. 5.99 (978-1-4846-0559-2(4), Acorn) Heinemann-Raintree.

D'Aubuisson, Elisabeth. Windy Days. 2007. (What's the Weather? Ser.). (Illus.). 24p. (J). (gr. 3-7). lib. bdg. 22.60 (978-1-4042-3683-7(X), PowerKids Pr.) Rosen Publishing Group, Inc., The.

d'Aubuisson, Elisabeth. Windy Days. 2009. (What's the Weather? Ser.). 24p. (gr. 2-3). 42.50 (978-1-60854-778-4(7), PowerKids Pr.) Rosen Publishing Group, Inc., The.

Eckart, Edana. Watching the Wind. 2004. (Welcome Bks.). (ENG., Illus.). 24p. (J). (gr. -1-2). pap. 4.95 (978-0-516-25941-3(5), Children's Pr.) Scholastic Library Publishing.

Edison, Erin. Wind, 1 vol. 2011. (Weather Basics Ser.). (ENG.). 24p. (gr. k-1). pap. 7.29 (978-1-4296-7082-1(7)); pap. 41.70 (978-1-4296-7086-3(6)) Capstone Press of Coughlan Cos. (Pebble Plus).

Edison, Erin & Saunders-Smith, Gail. Viento. Strictly Spanish LLC. Staff, tr. from ENG. 2013. (Lo Básico Sobre el Tiempo/Weather Basics Ser.).Tr. of Wind. (SPA, ENG & MUL.). 24p. (gr. k-1). lib. bdg. 26.65 (978-1-62065-167-4(X)) Capstone Press of Coughlan Cos.

Eggleton, Jill. The Wonder of the Wind. 2007. (Connectors Ser.). (gr. 2-5). pap. (978-1-877453-19-9(6)) Global Education Systems Ltd.

Ganeri, Anita. Wind. 2004. (Weather Around You Ser.). (Illus.). 24p. (gr. 1-4). lib. bdg. 22.00 (978-0-8368-4302-6(9), Weekly Reader Leveled Readers) Stevens, Gareth Publishing LLLP.

Ghigna, Charles. A Windy Day in Spring. Watson, Laura, illus. 2015. (Springtime Weather Wonders Ser.). (ENG.). 24p. (gr. -1-2). lib. bdg. 21.99 (978-1-4795-6032-5(4)) Picture Window Bks.

Hansen, Grace. El Viento. 2016. (Clima Ser.). (SPA.). 24p. (J). (gr. 1-6). pap. 7.95 (978-1-4966-0697-6(3)) Capstone Classroom.

—Wind, 1 vol. 2016. (ENG., Illus.). 24p. (J). (978-1-62970-936-9(0)) ABDO Publishing Co.

Hardyman, Robyn. Wind & Storms. 2010. (Weatherwise Ser.). 32p. (ENG.). (J). pap. 10.60 (978-1-61532-282-4(5), PowerKids Pr.); (Illus.). (YA). (gr. 3-6). lib. bdg. 26.50 (978-1-61532-267-1(1)) Rosen Publishing Group, Inc., The.

Herriges, Ann. Wind. 2006. (Weather Ser.). (ENG., Illus.). 24p. (J). (gr. k-3). lib. bdg. 25.95 (978-1-60014-026-6(2)) Bellwether Media.

—Wind. 2011. (Blastoff! Readers Ser.). 24p. (J). pap. 5.95 (978-0-531-27624-2(4), Children's Pr.) Scholastic Library Publishing.

Hirschmann, Kris. It's Windy!, 1 vol. 2008. (What's It Like Out? Ser.). (ENG.). 32p. (gr. k-6). 27.07 (978-1-59928-945-8(8), Checkerboard Library) ABDO Publishing Co.

Ikids Staff. Why Does the Wind Blow? Science Made Simple! Pérez, Sara Rojo, illus. 2009. (ENG.). 20p. (J). (gr. -1-1). 9.99 (978-1-58476-934-7(3)) Innovative Kids.

Ivancic, Linda. What Is Wind? 2016. (Unseen Science Ser.). (ENG., Illus.). 32p. (J). (gr. 3-3). pap. 10.58 (978-1-5026-0923-6(1)) Cavendish Square Publishing.

Jennings, Terry J. The Weather: Wind. 2004. (J). lib. bdg. 27.10 (978-1-59389-146-6(6)) Chrysalis Education.

Johnson, Robin. What Is Wind? 2012. (ENG., Illus.). 24p. (J). pap. (978-0-7787-0764-6(4)) Crabtree Publishing Co.

Kjelle, Marylou Morano. A Project Guide to Wind, Weather, & the Atmosphere. 2010. (Earth Science Projects for Kids Ser.). (Illus.). 48p. (J). (gr. 4-7). lib. bdg. 29.95 (978-1-58415-869-1(7)) Mitchell Lane Pubs., Inc.

Lonsdale, Mary, illus. Whatever the Weather: When the Wind Blows. 2004. (Whatever the Weather Ser.). 10p. (J). bds. 4.99 (978-1-85854-102-0(6)) Brimax Books Ltd. GBR. Dist: Byeway Bks.

Lowery, Lawrence F. How Does the Wind Blow? 2013. (I Wonder Why Ser.). (ENG., Illus.). 36p. (J). (gr. k-3). pap. 11.95 (978-1-938946-13-4(8)) National Science Teachers Assn.

Murphy, Patricia J. How Does the Wind Blow? 2006. (Tell Me Why, Tell Me How Ser.). (Illus.). 32p. (J). (gr. 3-7). lib. bdg. 29.93 (978-0-7614-2107-8(6), Benchmark Bks.) Marshall Cavendish Corp.

Naff, Clay Farris, ed. Wind. 2006. (Fueling the Future Ser.). (ENG., Illus.). 120p. (gr. 10-12). lib. bdg. 44.60 (978-0-7377-3580-2(5), Greenhaven Pr., Inc.) Cengage Gale.

Nelson, Robin. Un Día Con Viento. Translations.com Staff, tr. from ENG. 2006. (Mi Primer Paso Al Mundo Real - el Estado Del Tiempo (First Step Nonfiction - Weather) Ser.).Tr. of Windy Day. (SPA., Illus.). 24p. (gr. k-2). lib. bdg. 23.93 (978-0-8225-6214-6(6), Ediciones Lerner) Lerner Publishing Group.

—Un Día con Viento (A Windy Day) 2006. (Mi Primer Paso al Mundo Real Ser.). (Illus.). 23p. (J). (gr. -1-3). per. 5.95 (978-0-8225-6549-9(8), Ediciones Lerner) Lerner Publishing Group.

—Windy. (First Step Nonfiction - Kinds of Weather Ser.). (ENG., Illus.). 8p. (gr. -1-1). 2015. 11.99 (978-1-5124-1040-2(3)) 2005. pap. 4.95 (978-0-8225-5364-9(3), Lerner Pubns.) Lerner Publishing Group.

O'Mara, Mary. Monsoon! an Extreme Weather Season. 2009. (Real Life Readers Ser.). 32p. (gr. 4-5). pap. 10.00 (978-1-4358-0159-2(8), Rosen Classroom); 47.90 (978-1-60853-038-0(8), PowerKids Pr.) Rosen Publishing Group, Inc., The.

Orr, Tamra B. The Wind Blows. 2015. (Tell Me Why Library). (ENG., Illus.). 24p. (J). (gr. 2-5). 27.07 (978-1-63362-618-8(0), 206656) Cherry Lake Publishing.

Randolph, Joanne, ed. Jet Stream Steering the Winds! 2017. (Weather Report). 32p. (J). (gr. 3-3). pap. 10.52 **(978-0-7660-9017-0(5))** Enslow Pubs., Inc.

Raum, Elizabeth. Wind Energy. 2016. (Fueling the Future Ser.). (ENG.). 32p. (gr. 3-6). pap. 8.29 (978-1-4846-3692-3(9), Heinemann InfoSearch) Heinemann-Raintree.

Roy, Jennifer Rozines & Roy, Gregory. How Does the Wind Blow? 2007. (J). pap. 6.99 (978-0-7614-3363-7(5)) Marshall Cavendish Corp.

Rustad, Martha E. H. Today Is a Windy Day. 2017. (What Is the Weather Today? Ser.). (ENG., Illus.). 24p. (gr. k-2). pap. 6.29 (978-1-4966-0945-8(X), Pebble Bks.) Capstone Press of Coughlan Cos.

Sánchez, Lucía M. Viento. Taylor, Trace, illus. 2012. (1B el Tiempo Ser.). (SPA.). 40p. (J). pap. 6.99 (978-1-61406-207-3(2)) American Reading Co.

Sherman, Josepha. Gusts & Gales: A Book about Wind, 1 vol. Wesley, Omarr, illus. 2003. (Amazing Science: Weather Ser.). (ENG.). 24p. (gr. -1-3). per. 8.95 (978-1-4048-0338-1(6)) Picture Window Bks.

—Gusts & Gales: A Book about Wind. Wesley, Omarr, illus. 2003. (Amazing Science: Weather Ser.). (ENG.). 24p. (gr. -1-3). 26.65 (978-1-4048-0094-6(8)) Picture Window Bks.

Sherman, Josepha & Picture Window Books Staff. Sopla y Silba: Un Libro Sobre el Viento, 1 vol. Robledo, Sol, tr. from ENG. Wesley, Omarr, illus. 2007. (Ciencia Asombrosa: el Tiempo Ser.). (SPA.). 24p. (gr. -1-3). 26.65 (978-1-4048-3217-6(3)) Picture Window Bks.

Sterling, Kristin. It's Windy Today. 2009. (Lightning Bolt Books — What's the Weather Like? Ser.). (ENG., Illus.). 32p. (gr. k-2). 26.60 (978-0-7613-4260-1(5), Lerner Pubns.); pap. 7.95 (978-0-7613-5023-1(3)) Lerner Publishing Group.

Trueit, Trudi Strain. Windy Days. 2009. (Benchmark Rebus: Weather Watch Ser.). 24p. (gr. k-1). 15.95 (978-0-7614-4020-8(8)) Marshall Cavendish GBR. Dist: Marshall Cavendish Corp.

Williams, Judith. How Come It's Windy? 2015. (How Does Weather Happen? Ser.). 24p. (J). (gr. k-3). pap. 7.95 (978-0-7660-6391-4(7)); lib. bdg. 22.60 (978-0-7660-6390-7(9)) Enslow Pubs., Inc. (Enslow Elementary).

—Why Is It Windy? 2005. (I Like Weather! Ser.). (Illus.). 24p. (J). (gr. 1-3). lib. bdg. 22.60 (978-0-7660-2320-8(6), Enslow Elementary) Enslow Pubs., Inc.

The Wind: Level D, 6 vols. (Wonder Worldtm Ser.). 16p. 24.95 (978-0-7802-1057-8(3)) Wright Group/McGraw-Hill.

Wind & Storms: 6 Each of 1 Student Book, 6 vols. (Sunshinetm Science Ser.). 24p. (gr. 1-2). 41.95 (978-0-7802-1376-0(9)) Wright Group/McGraw-Hill.

Wind & Storms: Big Book. (Sunshinetm Science Ser.). 24p. (gr. 1-2). 37.50 (978-0-7802-1377-7(7)) Wright Group/McGraw-Hill.

WINDS—FICTION

Aesop. The Wind & the Sun. 2012. (J). 29.99 (978-1-61913-108-8(0)) Weigl Pubs., Inc.

Andrade, Marcia. Gust's Maze. 2010. 142p. pap. 11.50 (978-1-60911-101-4(X), Eloquent Bks.) Strategic Book Publishing & Rights Agency (SBPRA).

Asch, Frank & Asch, Devin. Like a Windy Day. 2008. (ENG., Illus.). 32p. (J). (gr. -1-3). pap. 7.99 (978-0-15-206403-7(6)) Houghton Mifflin Harcourt Publishing Co.

Bauer, Marion Dane. The Longest Night. Lewin, Ted, illus. 2009. (ENG.). 40p. (J). (gr. -1-3). 17.95 (978-0-8234-2054-4(X)) Holiday Hse., Inc.

Birdsall, Jeanne. Flora's Very Windy Day. Phelan, Matt, illus. 2013. (ENG.). 32p. (J). (gr. -1-3). pap. 6.99 (978-0-547-99485-7(0)) Houghton Mifflin Harcourt Publishing Co.

Bishop, Celeste. It's Windy. 2016. (What's the Weather Like? Ser.). 24p. (gr. 1-1). pap. 8.25 (978-1-4994-2363-1(2), PowerKids Pr.) Rosen Publishing Group, Inc., The.

Busy Little Breezie. 2006. (J). per. 7.95 (978-0-9742714-2-2(X)) I C Creative, Inc.

Cepeda, Joe. Up. Cepeda, Joe, illus. 2016. (I Like to Read(r) Ser.). (ENG., Illus.). 24p. (J). 6.99 (978-0-8234-3689-7(6)); 14.95 (978-0-8234-3655-2(1)) Holiday Hse., Inc.

Collins, Terry. The Wind Blows. 2010. 33p. pap. 15.95 (978-0-557-48340-2(9)) Lulu Pr., Inc.

Cowley, Joy. Big Bear & Little Bear: Wind. Lam, Amy, illus. 2013. (ENG.). 8p. pap. (978-1-927186-20-6(X), Joy Cowley Club) Flying Start Bks.

—Smarty No Pants. 2009. pap. 8.25 (978-1-60559-239-8(0)) Hameray Publishing Group, Inc.

Del Negro, Janice M. & Del Negro. Willa & the Wind, 1 vol. Solomon, Heather M., illus. 2005. (ENG.). 32p. (J). (gr. k-3). 16.95 (978-0-7614-5232-4(X)) Marshall Cavendish Corp.

Derby, Sally. Whoosh Went the Wind!, 0 vols. 2013. (ENG.). 32p. (J). (gr. k-3). pap. 9.99 (978-1-4778-1677-6(1), 9781477816776, Amazon Children's Publishing) Amazon Publishing.

di Chiara, Francesca, illus. The Sun & the Wind. 2007. (First Reading Level 1 Ser.). 32p. (J). (gr. -1-3). 8.99 (978-0-7945-1811-0(7), Usborne) EDC Publishing.

Disney Publishing Staff. Blow, Wind, Blow, 15 vols. 2003. (It's Fun to Learn Ser.). (Illus.). 32p. (J). (gr. -1-3). 3.99 (978-1-57973-134-2(1)) Advance Pubs. LLC.

Dixon, Pamela. A Windy Day Walk. Homer, Maree, illus. 2016. (ENG.). 32p. (J). (gr. 1-4). (978-0-473-34486-3(6)) Lizzy Web Bks.

Dwyer, Mindy. Just Close Your Eyes. 2005. (J). (978-0-88240-592-6(6)); pap. (978-0-88240-593-3(4)) Graphic Arts Ctr. Publishing Co. (Alaska Northwest Bks.).

Ehlert, Lois. Leaf Man. (ENG., Illus.). 40p. (J). (gr. -1-3). 2014. 26.99 (978-0-544-33916-3(9), HMH Books For Young Readers) 2005. 17.99 (978-0-15-205304-8(2)) Houghton Mifflin Harcourt Publishing Co.

Erin, Bethany. The Wind & the Blows. 2010. 24p. pap. 11.99 (978-1-4490-7569-9(X)) AuthorHouse.

Farber, Erica. Richard Scarry's Readers (Level 1): Get That Hat! Scarry, Huck, illus. 2015. (Richard Scarry's Great Big Schoolhouse Ser.). (ENG.). 24p. (J). (gr. -1-k). pap. 3.95 (978-1-4027-9919-8(5)) Sterling Publishing Co., Inc.

Felix, Monique. The Wind. 2012. (Mouse Book Ser.). (ENG.). 32p. (J). (gr. -1-k). 12.99 (978-1-56846-227-1(1), Creative Editions) Creative Co., The.

Gibbins, Desiree. The Book Keeper's Oracle. 2008. 212p. pap. 14.49 (978-1-4389-0791-8(5)) AuthorHouse.

Grahame, Kenneth. The Wind in the Willows. Rackham, Arthur, illus. 2012. (ENG.). 280p. (978-1-904919-51-3(0), Collector's Library, The) Pan Macmillan.

—The Wind in the Willows. Grahame, Kenneth & McKowen, Scott, illus. 2005. (Sterling Unabridged Classics Ser.). (ENG.). 208p. (J). (gr. 5-9). 9.95 (978-1-4027-2505-0(1)) Sterling Publishing Co., Inc.

Greene, Carol. Please, Wind? Sharp, Gene, illus. 2011. (Rookie Ready to Learn - First Science Ser.). 40p. (J). (gr. -1-k). lib. bdg. 23.00 (978-0-531-26502-4(1), Children's Pr.) Scholastic Library Publishing.

Hancock, Susan G. The Wind & Little Cloud. Simmons, Robert, illus. 2006. (J). (ENG.). 40p. spiral bd. 17.95 (978-0-9741743-3-4(5)); 48p. (gr. -1-3). per. 10.95 (978-0-9741743-0-3(0)) Perlycross Pubs.

Herbauts, Anne, creator. What Color Is the Wind? 2016. (ENG., Illus.). 48p. (J). (gr. k). pap. 19.95 (978-1-59270-221-3(X)) Enchanted Lion Bks., LLC.

Jacobsen, Laura, illus. The Boy & the North Wind: A Tale from Norway. 2013. (Tales of Honor Ser.). (ENG.). 32p. (J). (gr. 1-4). pap. 8.95 (978-1-937529-56-7(8)) Red Chair Pr.

Jacobsen, Laura, illus. & retold by. The Boy & the North Wind: A Tale from Norway. Jacobsen, Laura, retold by. 2013. (Tales of Honor (Red Chair Press) Ser.). (ENG.). 32p. (J). (gr. 1-4). lib. bdg. 26.60 (978-1-937529-72-7(X)) Red Chair Pr.

Joseph, O'Day E. I Like Wind! Foster, Ron, illus. 2007. 28p. (J). (gr. -1-3). (978-1-929039-42-5(5)) Ambassador Bks., Inc.

Leibenkop, T. The Sovereign of the Northern Winds. 2009. 30p. pap. 13.50 (978-1-60693-847-8(9), Eloquent Bks.) Strategic Book Publishing & Rights Agency (SBPRA).

Levine, Gail Carson. Ever. 2011. (ENG.). 288p. (J). (gr. 3-7). pap. 6.99 (978-0-06-122964-0(4)) HarperCollins Pubs.

Mattern, Carrie. Papa, Why Does the Wind Blow? 2009. 24p. pap. 15.95 (978-1-4490-0809-3(7)) AuthorHouse.

Mencio, Anna. The Day the Wind Changed. 2012. 24p. pap. 28.03 (978-1-4691-8232-2(7)) Xlibris Corp.

Messenger, Shannon. Let the Sky Fall. 2013. (Sky Fall Ser.: 1). (ENG., Illus.). 432p. (YA). (gr. 7). pap. 10.99 (978-1-4424-5042-4(8), Simon Pulse) Simon Pulse.

—Let the Storm Break. 2014. (Sky Fall Ser.: 2). (ENG., Illus.). 400p. (YA). (gr. 7). 17.99 (978-1-4424-5044-8(4), Simon Pulse) Simon Pulse.

—Let the Wind Rise. (Sky Fall Ser.: 3). (ENG., Illus.). (YA). (gr. 7). 2017. 432p. pap. 10.99 (978-1-4814-4655-6(X)) 2016. 416p. 17.99 (978-1-4814-4654-9(1)) Simon Pulse. (Simon Pulse).

Michaels, Fern, et al. Silver Bells. l.t. ed. 2008. (YA). 34.95 (978-1-59722-823-7(0)) Thorndike Pr.

Milbourne, Anna. The Windy Day. Temporin, Elena, illus. 2007. (Picture Bks). 24p. (J). (gr. -1-3). 9.99 (978-0-7945-1616-1(5), Usborne) EDC Publishing.

Montgomery, L. M. Ana la de Alamos Ventosos. Fantín de Bellocq, Constanza, tr. (Ana la de Tejas Verdes Ser.: 4).Tr. of Anne of Windy Poplars. (SPA.). 288p. (J). (gr. 5-8). (978-84-7888-636-4(2), SAL3944) Emece Editores ESP. Dist: Lectorum Pubns., Inc.

Morrison, Toni & Morrison, Slade. Little Cloud & Lady Wind. Qualls, Sean, illus. 2010. (ENG.). 32p. (J). pap. 7.99 (978-1-4169-8524-2(7), Simon & Schuster Bks. For Young Readers) Simon & Schuster Bks. For Young Readers.

—Little Cloud & Lady Wind. Qualls, Sean, illus. 2010. (ENG.). 32p. (J). (gr. -1-3). 16.99 (978-1-4169-8523-5(9), Simon & Schuster/Paula Wiseman Bks.) Simon & Schuster/Paula Wiseman Bks.

Nana, Old. Just Right. 2013. 24p. pap. 11.50 (978-1-62857-212-4(4), Strategic Bk. Publishing) Strategic Book Publishing & Rights Agency (SBPRA).

Nash, Margaret. Hetty's New Hat. Impey, Martin, illus. 2005. (Reading Corner Ser.). 24p. (J). (gr. k-3). lib. bdg. 22.80 (978-1-59771-007-7(5)) Sea-To-Sea Pubns.

Noble, Trinka Hakes. The Legend of Michigan. Van Frankenhuyzen, Gijsbert, illus. 2006. (Legend (Sleeping Bear) Ser.). (ENG.). 40p. (J). (gr. -1-3). 17.95 (978-1-58536-278-3(6)) Sleeping Bear Pr.

Oberman, Sheldon. The Wind That Wanted to Rest. Waldman, Neil, illus. 2012. (ENG.). 32p. (J). (gr. k-2). 17.95 (978-1-59078-858-5(3)) Boyds Mills Pr.

peddi, radhika. Kichkide. 2010. 44p. pap. 19.70 (978-0-557-16435-6(4)) Lulu Pr., Inc.

Ras. Oh No, the Leaves Are Moving! 2011. 24p. pap. 15.99 (978-1-4568-5030-2(X)) Xlibris Corp.

Reyes, Yazmin. Fairies vs. Wizards: The Last Battle, 1 vol. 2009. 48p. pap. 16.95 (978-1-4489-9527-1(2)) America Star Bks.

Rhema, Dan. Bluegrass Breeze. Leonard, Michael, illus. 2004. (J). per. 19.95 (978-0-9729835-1-8(1)) Mesquite Tress Pr., LLC.

Rice, T. F. The Wind Being. 2007. 28p. 15.95 (978-0-615-17173-9(7)) Hidden Valley Farm Pub.

Rider, Cynthia. What a Windy Day! Evans, Nicola, illus. 2013. (Start Reading Ser.). (ENG.). 24p. (gr. k-1). pap. 41.94 (978-1-4765-3234-9(6)); pap. 7.95 (978-1-4765-3198-4(6)) Capstone Press of Coughlan Cos.

Rink, Cynthia A. Where Does the Wind Blow? Rink, Cynthia A., illus. 2004. (Sharing Nature with Children Book Ser.). (Illus.). 32p. (J). (gr. k-5). 16.95 (978-1-58469-041-2(0)) Dawn Pubns.

Rink, Cynthia A., illus. Where Does the Wind Blow? 2004. (Sharing Nature with Children Book Ser.). 32p. (J). pap. 7.95 (978-1-58469-040-5(2)) Dawn Pubns.

Ritz, Lee F. The Sun & the Wind. Hale, Randy, illus. 2013. 62p. 23.99 (978-1-940840-00-0(7)) Ritz, Lee Pubns.

Roller, Pat Kellogg. Pink Hat's Adventure with Kites. Salazar, Riana, illus. Roller, John, photos by. 2009. 36p. pap. 10.95 (978-1-59858-957-3(1)) Dog Ear Publishing, LLC.

Salzano, Tammi J. One Windy Day. Wood, Hannah, illus. 2012. (ENG.). 24p. (J). bds. (978-1-58925-875-4(4)) Tiger Tales.

Spalding, Andrea. Sarah May & the New Red Dress. 2004. (Illus.). (J). (gr. k-3). spiral bd. (978-0-616-01782-1(0)) Canadian National Institute for the Blind/Institut National Canadien pour les Aveugles.

Spurr, Elizabeth. In the Wind, 1 vol. Oliphant, Manelle, illus. 2016. (In the Weather Ser.). (ENG.). 22p. (J). (gr. -1-k). bds. 6.95 (978-1-56145-854-7(6)) Peachtree Pubs.

Stephens, Jane. Katie's Too-Big Coat. 2014. (ENG., Illus.). 32p. (J). (gr. -1-3). 16.99 (978-1-4814-2532-2(3), Simon & Schuster Bks. For Young Readers) Simon & Schuster Bks. For Young Readers.

Teague, David. The Red Hat. Portis, Antoinette, illus. 2015. (ENG.). 36p. (J). (gr. -1-k). 16.99 (978-1-4231-3411-4(7)) Hyperion Bks. for Children.

The Library Fairy. The Magical Tree & Musical Wind. Faust, Laurie A., illus. 2008. 32p. pap. 16.95 (978-1-59858-604-6(1)) Dog Ear Publishing, LLC.

Thompson, Carol. Wind! 2014. (Whatever the Weather Ser.). (ENG., Illus.). 12p. (J). (gr. k-k). bds. (978-1-84643-682-6(6)) Child's Play International Ltd.

Thompson, Lauren. Mouse's First Fall. Erdogan, Buket, illus. 2010. (Classic Board Bks.). (ENG.). 34p. (J). (gr. -1 — 1). bds. 7.99 (978-1-4169-9477-0(7), Little Simon) Little Simon.

—Mouse's First Fall. Erdogan, Buket, illus. 2006. (ENG.). 32p. (J). (gr. -1-1). 15.99 (978-0-689-85837-6(X), Simon & Schuster Bks. For Young Readers) Simon & Schuster Bks. For Young Readers.

—Mouse's First Spring. Erdogan, Buket, illus. 2012. (Classic Board Bks.). (ENG.). 34p. (J). (gr. -1-3). bds. 7.99 (978-1-4424-3431-8(7), Little Simon) Little Simon.

—Mouse's First Spring. Erdogan, Buket, illus. 2005. (ENG.). 32p. (J). (gr. -1-3). 17.99 (978-0-689-85838-3(8), Simon & Schuster Bks. For Young Readers) Simon & Schuster Bks. For Young Readers.

Westall, Robert. Voces en el Viento. (SPA.). 9.95 (978-958-04-4700-9(4)) Norma S.A. COL. Dist: Distribuidora Norma, Inc.

White, Loricia. Little Tail's Rhyming Roots. 2012. 74p. pap. 19.95 (978-1-4626-6885-4(2)) America Star Bks.

Willems, Ashley. The Boy & the Wind. 2013. 52p. pap. 20.99 (978-1-4525-8369-3(2), Balboa Pr.) Author Solutions, Inc.

Wolff, Ferida. It Is the Wind. Ransome, James E., illus. Date not set. (ENG.). 32p. (J). (gr. -1-1). pap. 5.99 (978-0-06-443530-7(X)) HarperCollins Pubs.

Wright, Maureen. Sneeze, Big Bear, Sneeze!, 0 vols. Hillenbrand, Will, illus. 2011. (ENG.). 32p. (J). (gr. -1-3). 16.99 (978-0-7614-5959-0(6), 9780761459590, Amazon Children's Publishing) Amazon Publishing.

Yildirim, Rabia. Wind, Rain & Snow. 2013. (ENG., Illus.). 53p. (J). (gr. k-1). pap. 9.95 (978-1-59784-284-6(2)) Tughra Bks.

Zolotow, Charlotte. When the Wind Stops. 2004. (Illus.). (J). (gr. 2-4). spiral bd. (978-0-616-01823-1(1)); spiral bd. (978-0-616-01822-4(3)) Canadian National Institute for the Blind/Institut National Canadien pour les Aveugles.

WINE AND WINE MAKING

Blumenthal, Karen. Bootleg: Murder, Moonshine, & the Lawless Years of Prohibition. 2013. (ENG., Illus.). 176p. (YA). (gr. 7-12). pap. 13.99 (978-1-250-03427-4(2), 9781250034274) Square Fish.

Johnston, Jack. The Vineyard Book. Manion, Moira, illus. 2005. 48p. (J). 25.00 (978-0-9629880-0-4(6)) ACME Pr.

WINFREY, OPRAH, 1954-

Alter, Judy. Oprah Winfrey. 2007. (21st Century Skills Library: Life Skills Biographies Ser.). (ENG., Illus.). 48p. (gr. 4-8). lib. bdg. 31.36 (978-1-60279-069-8(8), 200045) Cherry Lake Publishing.

Blashfield, Jean F. Oprah Winfrey. 2003. (Trailblazers of the Modern World Ser.). (ENG & SPA., Illus.). 48p. (gr. 5-12). pap. 14.05 (978-0-8368-5247-9(8), Gareth Stevens Secondary Library) Stevens, Gareth Publishing LLLP.

Brown, Jonatha A. Oprah Winfrey. 2004. (People We Should Know Ser.). (Illus.). 24p. (gr. 1-4). pap. 8.15 (978-0-8368-4319-4(3)); (ENG & SPA., pap. 8.15 (978-0-8368-4361-3(4)); lib. bdg. 22.00 (978-0-8368-4312-5(6)) Stevens, Gareth Publishing LLLP. (Weekly Reader Leveled Readers).

—Oprah Winfrey. Acosta, Tatiana & Gutierrez, Guillermo, trs. 2004. (Gente Que Hay Que Conocer Ser.). (SPA., Illus.). 24p. (gr. 1-4). lib. bdg. 22.00 (978-0-8368-4354-5(1), Weekly Reader Leveled Readers) Stevens, Gareth Publishing LLLP.

Dakers, Diane. Oprah Winfrey: Media Legend & Inspiration to Millions. 2015. (Crabtree Groundbreaker Biographies Ser.). (ENG., Illus.). 112p. (J). (gr. 5-8). (978-0-7787-2559-6(6)) Crabtree Publishing Co.

Feinstein, Stephen. Oprah Winfrey. 2007. (African-American Heroes Ser.). (Illus.). 24p. (J). (gr. 1-3). lib. bdg. 22.60 (978-0-7660-2764-0(3), Enslow Elementary) Enslow Pubs., Inc.

Hudak, Heather C. Oprah Winfrey. (Remarkable People Ser.). (Illus.). 24p. (J). 2009. (gr. 4-6). pap. 8.95 (978-1-60596-631-1(2)) 2009. (gr. 4-6). lib. bdg. 24.45 (978-1-60596-630-4(4)) 2005. (gr. 2-3). lib. bdg. 24.45 (978-1-59036-335-5(3)) 2005. (gr. 3-7). per. 8.95 (978-1-59036-341-6(8)) Weigl Pubs., Inc.

Jeffrey, Gary. Oprah Winfrey: The Life of a Media Superstar. (Graphic Nonfiction Biographies Ser.). (ENG.). 48p. 2009. (YA). (gr. 4-5). 58.50 (978-1-61513-024-5(1), Rosen Reference) 2007. (Illus.). (gr. 5-8). pap. 14.05 (978-1-4042-0925-1(5)) Rosen Publishing Group, Inc., The.

Jones, Jen. Oprah Winfrey: Celebrity with Heart. 2010. (Celebrities with Heart Ser.). (Illus.). 128p. (J). pap. 10.95 (978-1-59845-206-8(1)); (gr. 7-12). 33.27 (978-0-7660-3406-8(2)) Enslow Pubs., Inc.

Keedle, Jayne. Oprah Winfrey. 2008. (Today's Superstars). (Illus.). 32p. (J). (gr. 4-7). lib. bdg. 31.95 (978-0-8368-9238-3(0)) Stevens, Gareth Publishing LLLP.

Krohn, Katherine E. Oprah Winfrey. (Just the Facts Biographies Ser.). (Illus.). 112p. 2004. (ENG.). (gr. 5-12). lib. bdg. 27.93 (978-0-8225-2472-4(4)) 2003. (J). (gr. 6-18). pap. 7.95 (978-0-8225-5000-6(8)) Lerner Publishing Group.

—Oprah Winfrey: Global Media Leader. 2008. (USA TODAY Lifeline Biographies Ser.). (ENG.). 112p. (gr. 6-12). lib. bdg. 34.60 (978-1-58013-571-9(4)) Lerner Publishing Group.

Lee, T. S. The Oprah Winfrey Story: The First Oprah Winfrey Comic Biography. 2010. 190p. (J). pap. 14.95 (978-0-9819542-6-4(X)) DASANBOOKS.

Lies, Anne. Oprah Winfrey: Media Mogul, 1 vol. 2011. (Essential Lives Set 6 Ser.). (ENG., Illus.). 112p. (J). (gr. 6-12). lib. bdg. 35.64 (978-1-61714-786-9(9), Essential Library) ABDO Publishing Co.

Oprah Winfrey. 2004. (Illus.). 112p. pap. 9.95 (978-0-8225-5320-5(1)) Lerner Publishing Group.

Paprocki, Sherry. Oprah Winfrey. 2008. (Black Americans of Achievement: Legacy Edition Ser.). 112p. (gr. 6-12). pap. 11.95 (978-1-60413-326-4(0), Checkmark Bks.) Facts On File, Inc.

Westen, Robin. Oprah Winfrey: A Biography of a Billionaire Talk Show Host. 2013. (African-American Icons Ser.). 104p. (J). (gr. 6-12). pap. 10.95 (978-1-59845-394-2(7)); lib. bdg. 27.94 (978-0-7660-3991-9(9)) Enslow Pubs., Inc.

Woog, Adam. Oprah Winfrey. 2009. (People in the News Ser.). (ENG., Illus.). 128p. (gr. 7-12). lib. bdg. 39.40 (978-1-4205-0128-5(3), LML02109-245442) Cengage Gale.

WINNIE-THE-POOH (FICTITIOUS CHARACTER)—FICTION

Bendon Publishing International Staff. Pooh Workbook Bindup #1040. 2004. pap. 9.99 (978-1-59394-323-3(7)) Bendon, Inc.

Benedictus, David. Return to the Hundred Acre Wood. Burgess, Mark, illus. 2009. (Winnie-The-Pooh Ser.). (ENG.). 216p. (J). (gr. 3-7). 19.99 (978-0-525-42160-3(2), Dutton Books for Young Readers) Penguin Young Readers Group.

Bergner, Bobby. Why kitty Is afraid of Poo: A cautionary Tale. Bergner, Bobby, illus. 2008. (Illus.). 20p. 12.99 (978-0-615-21301-9(4)) Bergner, Bobby.

Canfield, Nancy Lee. A Rose for My Mother: A Memoir. Grey, Andrew, illus. 2010. (ENG.). 300p. pap. 21.95 (978-1-4502-3123-7(3)) iUniverse, Inc.

Classic Sticker Stories: Winnie-the-Pooh. (Illus.). 80p. (J). pap. 14.95 (978-0-525-46782-3(3)) Penguin Publishing Group.

de Alba, Arlette, tr. Musica en Casa: Libro de Cuentos. 2005. (Disney Winnie the Pooh (SilverDolphin) Ser.). (SPA., Illus.). 38p. (J). (gr. -1-7). incl. audio compact disk (978-970-718-290-5(3), Silver Dolphin en Español) Advanced Marketing, S. de R. L. de C. V.

—Winnie Pooh Tesoros para Llevar. 2006. (Disney Winnie the Pooh (SilverDolphin) Ser.). (Illus.). 24p. (J). (gr. -1-k). bds. (978-970-718-358-2(6), Silver Dolphin en Español) Advanced Marketing, S. de R. L. de C. V.

Disney Book Group. Disney Baby Peek-a-Boo Winnie the Pooh. Disney Storybook Art Team, illus. 2016. (ENG.). 10p. (J). (gr. -1 — 1). bds. 8.99 (978-1-4847-7824-1(3)) Disney Pr.

Disney Book Group Staff. The Easter Egg Hunt. 2010. (Read-Along Storybook & CD Ser.). (ENG.). 32p. (J). (gr. -1-2). pap. 6.99 (978-1-4231-2087-2(6)) Disney Pr.

Disney Staff. Winnie the Pooh. (FRE.). 96p. (J). (gr. k-5). pap. 9.95 (978-0-7859-8848-9(3)) French & European Pubns., Inc.

Dorling Kindersley Publishing Staff. Winnie the Pooh. (Ultimate Sticker Bks.). (ENG.). 16p. (J). (gr. k-4). 2011. pap. 6.99 (978-0-7566-7212-6(0)) 2004. pap. 6.99 (978-0-7894-9996-7(7)) Dorling Kindersley Publishing, Inc. (DK Children).

Ferguson, Don. Winnie the Pooh's A to ZZZZ. Wakeman, Bill & Langley, Bill, illus. 2009. 32p. (gr. -1-2). pap. 4.99 (978-0-7868-4094-6(3)) Disney Pr.

Gaines, Isabel & Milne, A. A. Pooh's Leaf Pile. Rigol, Francesc, illus. 2012. (J). (978-1-4351-4190-2(3)) Disney Pr.

Galvin, Laura. Pooh & Friends Colors & Shapes. 2008. (ENG.). 24p. (J). (gr. -1). 4.99 (978-1-59069-736-8(7)) Studio Mouse LLC.

Galvin, Laura Gates. Best Book of Pooh, Ever: Reading to Grow. rev. ed. 2005. (Reading to Grow Ser.). (ENG., Illus.). 40p. (J). (gr. -1-3). 12.99 (978-1-59069-450-3(3), 1A701) Studio Mouse LLC.

—Pooh's Counting Fun. 2009. (Leanring Anywhere Pooh & Friends Ser.). 24p. (J). (gr. -1). pap. 7.99 (978-1-59069-859-4(2)) Studio Mouse LLC.

—Winnie the Pooh Bedtime ABCs. 2008. (ENG.). 20p. (J). (gr. -1-3). 9.99 (978-1-59069-656-9(5)) Studio Mouse LLC.

Galvin, Laura Gates & Studio Mouse Staff. Write-with-Me Alphabet. Giblin, Brian E., ed. 2011. (Write-with-Me Ser.). (Illus.). 28p. (J). 15.99 (978-1-59069-921-8(1)) Studio Mouse LLC.

Hapka, Catherine, pseud & Disney Book Group Staff. Pooh's Secret Garden. Disney Storybook Art Team, illus. 2012. (ENG.). 24p. (J). (gr. -1-k). pap. 4.99 (978-1-4231-4845-6(2)) Disney Pr.

—Sweet Dreams, Roo. Disney Storybook Art Team, illus. 2012. (ENG.). 24p. (J). (gr. -1-k). bds. 6.99 (978-1-4231-4843-2(6)) Disney Pr.

Hapka, Cathy, pseud, et al. Pooh's Halloween Pumpkin. Disney Storybook Artists Staff, illus. 2013. (ENG.). 10p. (J). (gr. -1-k). bds. 5.99 (978-1-4231-6767-9(8)) Disney Pr.

Here Comes Winter! 2003. (J). per. (978-1-57657-967-1(0)) Paradise Pr., Inc.

Hinkler Studios Staff., ed. Winnie the Pooh: ABC & First Words. 2011. 12p. 9.99 (978-1-74183-872-5(X)) Hinkler Bks. Pty, Ltd. AUS. Dist: Ideals Pubns.

Izquierdo, Ana, tr. Caritas Felices: Winnie-the-Pooh. 2007. (Disney Winnie the Pooh (SilverDolphin) Ser.). (SPA., Illus.). 10p. (J). (gr. -1). bds. (978-970-718-393-3(4), Silver Dolphin en Español) Advanced Marketing, S. de R. L. de C. V.

LeapFrog Staff. Lots & Lots of Honeypots. 2003. (Illus.). (J). spiral bd. 14.99 (978-1-59319-002-6(6)) LeapFrog Enterprises, Inc.

Little Red Riding Pooh: A Fairy Tale Friend a Board Book & Plush Figure. 2004. (Pooh's Fairy Tale Theater Ser.). 12p. (J). 6.99 (978-0-7364-2239-0(0), RH/Disney) Random Hse. Children's Bks.

Mattick, Lindsay. Finding Winnie: The True Story of the World's Most Famous Bear. Blackall, Sophie, illus. 2015. (ENG.). 56p. (J). (gr. -1-1). 18.00 (978-0-316-32490-8(6)) Little Brown & Co.

Miller, Sara F. A Gift for Pooh. 2012. (ENG.). 24p. (J). (gr. -1-1). pap. 4.99 (978-1-4231-3592-0(X)) Disney Pr.

—Pooh's Honey Trouble. 2012. (ENG.). 16p. (J). (gr. -1-1). bds. 6.99 (978-1-4231-3579-1(2)) Disney Pr.

Milne, A. A. In Which a House Is Built at Pooh Corner for Eeyore. Shepard, Ernest H., illus. unabr. ed. (Classic Pooh Treasury Ser.). (J). incl. audio (978-1-57375-527-6(3), 71394) Audioscope.

—In Which Christopher Robin Gives Pooh a Party. Shepard, Ernest H., illus. unabr. ed. (Winnie-the-Pooh Ser.). (J). incl. audio (978-1-57375-046-2(8), 70554) Audioscope.

—In Which Pooh Goes Visiting & Gets into a Tight Place & in Which Pooh & Piglet Go Hunting & Nearly Catch a Woozle. Shepard, Ernest H., illus. unabr. ed. (Winnie-the-Pooh Ser.). (J). incl. audio (978-1-57375-001-1(8), 70014) Audioscope.

—In Which Tigger Is Unbounced. Shepard, Ernest H., illus. unabr. ed. (Classic Pooh Treasury Ser.). (J). incl. audio (978-1-57375-528-3(1), 71404) Audioscope.

—In Which We Are Introduced to Winnie the Pooh & Some Bees, & the Stories Begin. Shepard, Ernest H., illus. unabr. ed. (Winnie-the-Pooh Ser.). (J). incl. audio (978-1-57375-000-4(X), 70004) Audioscope.

—Positively Pooh: Timeless Wisdom from Pooh. Shepard, Ernest H., illus. 2008. (Winnie-The-Pooh Ser.). (ENG.). 120p. (J). (gr. 3-7). 22.00 (978-0-525-47931-4(7), Dutton Books for Young Readers) Penguin Young Readers Group.

—Pu Baut ein Haus.Tr. of Pooh Builds a House. (GER.). (J). pap. 12.95 (978-3-423-07395-0(0)) Deutscher Taschenbuch Verlag GmbH & Co KG DEU. Dist: Distribooks, Inc.

—A Smackerel of Pooh: Ten Favorite Stories & Poems. Shepard, Ernest H., illus. 2006. 79p. (J). (gr. k-4). 16.00 (978-1-4223-5283-0(8)) DIANE Publishing Co.

—Winnie Puh. Meddemmen, John, tr. Shepard, Ernest H., illus.Tr. of Winnie the Pooh. (ITA.). 164p. pap. 29.95 (978-88-7782-278-9(3)) Salani ITA. Dist: Distribooks, Inc.

—Winnie-the-Pooh. Shepard, Ernest H., illus. 2005. (Winnie-The-Pooh Ser.). (ENG.). 176p. (J). (gr. 3-7). 6.99 (978-0-14-240467-6(5), Puffin Books) Penguin Young Readers Group.

—Winnie-the-Pooh. Shepard, Ernest H., illus. 80th anniv. deluxe ed. 2009. (Winnie-The-Pooh Ser.). (ENG.). 176p. (J). (gr. 3-7). 19.99 (978-0-525-47768-6(3), Dutton Books for Young Readers) Penguin Young Readers Group.

—Winnie the Pooh & When We Were Young. Shepard, Ernest H., illus. 32p. (J). Boxed set. pap. incl. audio compact disk (978-1-57375-583-2(4), 71512)Set. pap. incl. audio (978-1-57375-652-5(0), 71514) Audioscope.

—Winnie the Pooh's 1,2,3. Shepard, Ernest H., illus. 2009. (Winnie-The-Pooh Ser.). (ENG.). 18p. (J). (gr. -1 — 1). bds. 6.99 (978-0-525-42084-2(3), Dutton Books for Young Readers) Penguin Young Readers Group.

—Winnie the Pooh's Colors. Shepard, Ernest H., illus. 2009. (Winnie-The-Pooh Ser.). (ENG.). 20p. (J). (gr. -1 — 1). bds. 6.99 (978-0-525-42083-5(5), Dutton Books for Young Readers) Penguin Young Readers Group.

—The World of Pooh: The Complete Winnie-the-Pooh & the House at Pooh Corner. Shepard, Ernest H., illus. 2010. (Winnie-The-Pooh Ser.). (ENG.). 384p. (J). (gr. 3-7). 25.99 (978-0-525-44447-3(5), Dutton Books for Young Readers) Penguin Young Readers Group.

Mouse Works Staff. Winnie the Pooh's Touch & Feel Book. 2nd ed. 2005. 10p. (J). 6.99 (978-0-7364-1021-2(X)) Hyperion Pr.

Parragon Staff. Celebrate the Year with Winnie the Pooh. 2010. (Disney Diecut Classics). 72p. (J). (gr. -1-1). (978-1-4075-8902-2(4)) Parragon, Inc.

—My Book of Winnie the Pooh. 2010. (Disney Diecut Classics). (Illus.). 72p. (J). (gr. -1-1). (978-1-4075-8904-6(0)) Parragon, Inc.

—Once upon a Time with Winnie the Pooh. 2010. (Disney Diecut Classics). 72p. (J). (gr. -1-1). (978-1-4075-8905-3(9)) Parragon, Inc.

Pooh & Friends Numbers & Counting. 2007. (ENG., Illus.). 26p. (J). (gr. -1-1). 16.99 (978-1-59069-502-9(X), 1A1000) Studio Mouse LLC.

Publications International Ltd. Staff. My 1St Libraries Winnie the Pooh. 2011. 10p. (J). bds. 13.98 (978-1-4508-0870-5(0)) Phoenix International Publications, Inc.

Publications International Ltd. Staff, creator. Pooh Surprise Sing-along. 2007. (Surprise Mirror Book Ser.). (Illus.). (gr. -1-k). 15.98 (978-1-4127-7418-5(7)) Publications International, Ltd.

Publications International Ltd. Staff, ed. My First Look & Find Winnie The Pooh. 2011. 18p. (J). bds. 9.98 (978-1-4508-0734-0(8)) Phoenix International Publications, Inc.

—My Friends Tigger & Pooh. 2008. (J). bds. 5.98 (978-1-4127-8483-2(2)) Publications International, Ltd.

—Play a Sound 10 Stories Winnie the Pooh. 2009. 24p. (J). 17.98 (978-1-4127-5370-8(8), PIL Kids) Publications International, Ltd.

—Pooh's Heffalump Movie. 2004. (Illus.). 24p. (J). 15.98 (978-1-4127-3555-1(6), 7259300) Publications International, Ltd.

—A Ring-A-Ling Day! 2009. 12p. (J). bds. 11.98 (978-1-4127-9614-9(8), PIL Kids) Publications International, Ltd.

—Winnie the Pooh. 2007. (J). 15.98 (978-1-4127-8351-4(8)) Publications International, Ltd.

—Winnie the Pooh: I Love You Winnie the Pooh. 2011. 12p. (J). bds. 10.98 (978-1-4508-0767-8(4)) Phoenix International Publications, Inc.

—Winnie the Pooh: Super Look & Find Activity Pad. 2011. 64p. (J). 10.98 (978-1-4508-1866-7(8)) Publications International, Ltd.

—Winnie the Pooh: Super Look & Find Activity Pad with Stickers. 2011. 64p. (J). 10.98 (978-1-4508-0869-9(7)) Publications International, Ltd.

—Winnie the Pooh Drum Sound. 2011. 14p. (J). bds. 20.98 (978-1-4508-0911-5(1)) Phoenix International Publications, Inc.

—Winnie the Pooh (Find-A-Friend Book) 2011. 14p. (J). bds. 17.98 (978-1-4508-0694-7(5)) Phoenix International Publications, Inc.

—Winnie the Pooh Large Look & Find Activity Pad. 2011. 64p. (J). (978-1-4508-0868-2(9)) Publications International, Ltd.

—Winnie The Pooh Large Play A Sound. 2011. 24p. (J). 12.98 (978-1-4508-0570-4(1)) Publications International, Ltd.

—9 Button Record Story Pooh Friends & Fun. 2011. 18p. 19.98 (978-1-4508-1994-7(X)) Publications International, Ltd.

Studio Mouse, ed. Disney Time to Learn with Pooh: Flat Learn & Carry 4 Board Books & CD. rev. ed. 2007. (ENG.). 12.99 (978-1-59069-626-2(3)) Studio Mouse LLC.

Studio Mouse Staff. Pooh & Eeyore. 2008. (ENG., Illus.). 36p. (J). (gr. -1). 7.99 (978-1-59069-418-3(X)) Studio Mouse LLC.

—Pooh & Eeyore, Pooh & Tigger. rev. ed. 2004. (Friends Collection). (ENG., Illus.). 36p. (J). (gr. -1-3). 15.99 (978-1-59069-390-2(6), 1A302) Studio Mouse LLC.

—Pooh & Friends ABCs & 123s: First Concepts. rev. ed. 2007. (ENG., Illus.). 24p. (J). (gr. -1-3). 4.99 (978-1-59069-606-4(9)) Studio Mouse LLC.

—Pooh & Piglet. 2008. (ENG., Illus.). 36p. (J). (gr. -1). 7.99 (978-1-59069-419-0(8)) Studio Mouse LLC.

—Pooh & Roo. 2008. (ENG., Illus.). 36p. (J). (gr. -1). 7.99 (978-1-59069-420-6(1)) Studio Mouse LLC.

—Pooh & Tigger. 2008. (ENG., Illus.). 36p. (J). (gr. -1). 7.99 (978-1-59069-417-6(1)) Studio Mouse LLC.

—Winnie Pooh y sus amigos Ejercicios: Puffy Book with CD. rev. ed. 2007. (ESP & ENG.). 36p. (J). 14.99 (978-1-59069-528-9(3)) Studio Mouse LLC.

ToyBox Innovations, creator. Disney's Winnie the Pooh: Winnie the Pooh Springtime with Roo/Pooh's Huffalump Movie/Piglet's Big Movie. unabr. ed. 2005. (Disney's Read along Collection Ser.). (ENG.). (J). pap. (978-0-7634-1147-3(7)) Walt Disney Records.

Willis, Jeanne, et al. The Best Bear in All the World. Burgess, Mark, illus. 2016. (Winnie-The-Pooh Ser.). (ENG.). 128p. (J). (gr. 3-7). 21.99 (978-0-399-18747-6(2), Dutton Books for Young Readers) Penguin Young Readers Group.

Winnie the Pooh. The Close-up Day. 2010. 16p. 5.99 (978-1-4231-3096-3(0)) Disney Pr.

—Goodbye, Honeypot! 2010. 12p. 6.99 (978-1-4231-3098-7(7)) Disney Pr.

—Spring Cleaning. 2010. 32p. pap. 4.99 (978-1-4231-3072-7(3)) Disney Pr.

—Winnie the Pooh Nature's True Colors. 2009. 10.95 (978-1-4231-3097-0(9)) Disney Pr.

Winnie the Pooh. (Sing-Along Ser.). (J). 11.99 incl. audio (978-1-55723-933-4(9)) Walt Disney Records.

Winnie the Pooh: Party in the Wood. 2011. 32p. pap. 4.99 (978-1-4231-5386-3(3)) Disney Pr.

Winnie the Pooh & a Day for Eeyore (Read-Along Ser.). (J). 7.99 incl. audio (978-1-55723-176-5(1)) Walt Disney Records.

Zolotow, Charlotte. Growing up Stories for 5-6 Year Olds. 114p. (J). (gr. -1-17). 19.99 (978-0-7868-0519-8(6)) Disney Pr.

WINNING AND LOSING—FICTION

Banks, Jane Whelen. Liam Wins the Game, Sometimes: A Story about Losing with Grace. 2008. (ENG., Illus.). 32p. 12.95 (978-1-84310-898-6(4), 5374) Kingsley, Jessica Pubs. GBR. Dist: Macmillan Distribution Ltd.

Bowen, Fred. Playoff Dreams, 1 vol. 2009. (All-Star Sports Story Ser.). (ENG., Illus.). 112p. (J). pap. 5.95 (978-1-56145-507-2(5)) Peachtree Pubs.

Catalanotto, Peter. Emily's Art. Catalanotto, Peter, illus. 2006. (ENG., Illus.). 32p. (J). (gr. k-3). 7.99 (978-1-4169-2688-7(7), Atheneum Bks. for Young Readers) Simon & Schuster Children's Publishing.

Chaconas, Dori. Good Sports. McCue, Lisa, illus. 2010. (Cork & Fuzz Ser.: 3). (ENG.). 32p. (J). (gr. 1-3). mass mkt. 3.99 (978-0-14-241713-3(0), Penguin Young Readers) Penguin Young Readers Group.

Christopher, Matt. Body Check. 2003. (ENG.). 144p. (J). (gr. 3-7). pap. 5.99 (978-0-316-13405-7(8)) Little, Brown Bks. for Young Readers.

—Body Check. 2004. (Matt Christopher Sports Ser.). 138p. (gr. 3-7). 15.00 (978-0-7569-2984-8(9)) Perfection Learning Corp.

Cooper, Ann Goode. Zebordee Goes to the Races. Jessee, Diana, illus. 2005. 32p. (J). (gr. -1-3). (978-1-933251-01-1(8)) Parkway Pubs., Inc.

Gilman, Grace. Dixie Wins the Race. Rogers, Jacqueline, illus. 2012. (I Can Read Level 1 Ser.). (ENG.). 32p. (J). (gr. -1-3). 16.99 (978-0-06-208618-1(9)); pap. 3.99 (978-0-06-208614-3(6)) HarperCollins Pubs.

Krensky, Stephen. I Can Do It Myself! Gillingham, Sara, illus. 2012. (Empowerment Ser.). (ENG.). 12p. (J). (gr. -1 — 1). bds. 6.95 (978-1-4197-0400-0(1), Abrams Appleseed) Abrams, Inc.

Krosoczka, Jarrett J. Max for President. 2008. (ENG.). 40p. (J). (gr. -1-2). pap. 6.99 (978-0-440-41789-7(9), Dragonfly Bks.) Random Hse. Children's Bks.

Lupica, Mike. Shoot-Out. (Comeback Kids Ser.). (ENG.). 176p. (J). (gr. 3-7). 2011. 6.99 (978-0-14-241844-4(7), Puffin Books) 2010. 10.99 (978-0-399-24718-7(1), Philomel Bks.) Penguin Young Readers Group.

—Shoot-Out, 1 vol. 2012. (Comeback Kids Ser.). (ENG.). 176p. (J). (gr. 4-8). lib. bdg. 27.07 (978-1-59961-178-5(3)) Spotlight.

Magee, Helen. What's French for Help, George? l.t. ed. 2007. pap. (978-1-905665-68-6(7)) Pollinger In Print.

Martin, R. Pod Racer. 2017. (Level Up Ser.). (ENG.). (YA). (gr. 6-12). 120p. pap. 7.99 **(978-1-5124-5358-4(7))**; lib. bdg. 26.65 **(978-1-5124-3988-5(6))** Lerner Publishing Group. (Darby Creek).

Marwood, Lorraine. Jamie Wins Again. Hocking, Geoff, illus. 2004. iv, 36p. (J). pap. (978-0-7608-6743-3(7)) Sundance/Newbridge Educational Publishing.

Mazeroski, Kelly. Maz, You're Up! Lauso, Judith, illus. 2010. 24p. (J). pap. 12.95 (978-0-936340-18-0(5)) Historical Society of Western Pennsylvania.

Miles, Brenda & Sweet, Susan D. Chicken or Egg: Who Comes First? 2017. (J). **(978-1-4338-2719-8(0))** American Psychological Assn.
Mills, Claudia. Simon Ellis, Spelling Bee Champ. Shepperson, Rob, illus. 2015. (Franklin School Friends Ser.: 4). (ENG.). 144p. (J). (gr. 2-5). 15.99 (978-0-374-30221-4(9), 9780374302214, Farrar, Straus & Giroux (BYR)) Farrar, Straus & Giroux.
Paley, Daniel & Boyd, Aaron. Luigi & the Barefoot Races, 1 vol. 2015. (ENG., Illus.). 32p. (gr. -1-2). 16.95 (978-0-88448-397-7(5), 884397) Tilbury Hse. Pubs.
Park, Barbara. Dumb Bunny. Brunkus, Denise, illus. 2009. (Junie B. Jones Ser.). (ENG.). 128p. (J). (gr. 1-4). 4.99 (978-0-375-83810-1(4), Random Hse. Bks. for Young Readers) Random Hse. Children's Bks.
Purciello, Gerard. The Year They Won: A Tale of the Boston Red Sox. 2005. 112p. (J). (gr. 5-9). per. (978-0-9746481-5-6(9)) Brown Barn Bks.
Rayner, Robert. Miss Little's Losers, 1 vol. 2003. (Lorimer Sports Stories Ser.). (ENG.). 128p. (J). (gr. 4-8). 16.95 (978-1-55028-811-7(3), 9781550288117) Lorimer, James & Co., Ltd., Pubs. CAN. Dist: Casemate Pubs. & Bk. Distributors, LLC.
Ross, Tony. I Want to Win! Ross, Tony, illus. 2012. (Andersen Press Picture Bks). (ENG., Illus.). 32p. (J). (gr. -1-3). 16.95 (978-0-7613-8993-4(8)) Lerner Publishing Group.
Shea, Bob. Cheetah Can't Lose. Shea, Bob, illus. 2013. (ENG., Illus.). 40p. (J). (gr. -1-3). 17.99 (978-0-06-173083-2(1)) HarperCollins Pubs.
Simon, Charnan. Me Gusta Ganar! Translations.com Staff, tr. from ENG. Handelman, Dorothy, photos by. 2007. (Lecturas para niños de Verdad - Nivel 1 (Real Kids Readers - Level 1) Ser.).Tr. of I Like to Win! (SPA., Illus.). 32p. (gr. k-2). per. 5.95 (978-0-8225-7801-7(8), Ediciones Lerner) Lerner Publishing Group.
—Me Gusta Ganar; I Like to Win. 2008. pap. 34.95 (978-0-8225-9499-4(4)) Lerner Publishing Group.
Steers, Billy. Tractor Mac You're a Winner. 2015. (Tractor Mac Ser.). (ENG., Illus.). 32p. (J). (gr. -1-k). 8.99 (978-0-374-30104-0(2), 9780374301040, Farrar, Straus & Giroux (BYR)) Farrar, Straus & Giroux.
—You're a Winner. 2016. (Tractor Mac Ser.). (ENG.). 24p. (J). (gr. -1-k). 14.75 (978-0-606-39283-9(1)) Turtleback Bks.
Suen, Anastasia. A Prize Inside: A Robot & Rico Story, 1 vol. Laughead, Mike, illus. 2009. (Robot & Rico Ser.). (ENG.). 32p. (gr. 1-2). pap. 6.25 (978-1-4342-1749-3(3)) Stone Arch Bks.
Warner, Sally. Excellent Emma. Harper, Jamie, illus. 2010. (Emma Ser.). (ENG.). 144p. (J). (gr. 3-7). 6.99 (978-0-14-241569-6(3), Puffin Books) Penguin Young Readers Group.
Warner, Sally & Harper, Jamie. Excellent Emma. Harper, Jamie, illus. 2009. (Emma Ser.). (ENG., Illus.). 144p. (J). (gr. 3-7). 14.99 (978-0-670-06310-9(X), Viking Books for Young Readers) Penguin Young Readers Group.
Wong, Janet S. Alex & the Wednesday Chess Club. Schuett, Stacey, illus. 2004. (ENG.). 40p. (J). (gr. -1-3). 17.99 (978-0-689-85890-1(6), McElderry, Margaret K. Bks.) McElderry, Margaret K. Bks.

WINTER

Abeel, Samantha. My Thirteenth Winter: A Memoir. 2005. (ENG., Illus.). 208p. (J). (gr. 3-7). pap. 6.99 (978-0-439-33905-6(7), Scholastic Paperbacks) Scholastic, Inc.
Aloian, Molly. How Do We Know It Is Winter? 2013. (ENG., Illus.). 24p. (J). (978-0-7787-0962-6(0)) Crabtree Publishing Co.
—How Do We Know It's Winter? 2013. (ENG., Illus.). 24p. (J). pap. (978-0-7787-0966-4(3)) Crabtree Publishing Co.
Amoroso, Cynthia & Noyed, Robert B. Winter. 2014. (Seasons of the Year Ser.). (ENG.). 24p. (J). (gr. -1-2). 25.64 (978-1-62687-028-4(4), 206827) Child's World, Inc., The.
Anderson, Maxine. Explore Winter! 25 Great Ways to Learn about Winter. Frederick-Frost, Alexis, illus. 2007. (Explore Your World Ser.). (ENG.). 96p. (J). (gr. k-4). pap. 12.95 (978-0-9785037-5-8(9)) Octavio Publishing.
Anderson, Sheila. Are You Ready for Winter? 2010. (Lightning Bolt Books (tm) — Our Four Seasons Ser.). (ENG.). 32p. (gr. k-2). lib. bdg. 26.60 (978-0-7613-4583-1(3)); (Illus.). pap. 7.95 (978-0-7613-5669-1(X), 1306419, Lerner Pubns.) Lerner Publishing Group.
Appleby, Alex. Qu Sucede en Invierno? / What Happens in Winter?, Vol. 1. 2014. (Cuatro Estaciones Estupendas / Four Super Seasons Ser.). (SPA & BYN.). 24p. (J). (gr. k-k). 22.60 (978-1-4824-0132-5(0)) Stevens, Gareth Publishing LLLP.
Barklem, Jill. Cuento de Invierno.Tr. of Winter Story. (SPA.). 32p. (J). 8.95 (978-84-233-2617-4(9)) Ediciones Destino ESP. Dist: Planeta Publishing Corp.
Barnham, Kay. Winter. 2010. (Seasons Ser.). (ENG.). 24p. (J). lib. bdg. 22.60 (978-1-61532-568-9(9), PowerKids Pr.) Rosen Publishing Group, Inc., The.
Berger, Melvin. What Do Animals Do in Winter? (Discovery Readers Ser.). (ENG.). 48p. (J). pap. 3.95 (978-0-8249-5314-0(2), Ideal Pubns.) Worthy Publishing.
Berger, Melvin & Berger, Gilda. Cold Weather. 2010. (Illus.). 16p. (J). (978-0-545-16084-1(7)) Scholastic, Inc.
Bix, Jasper. Winter Holidays. 2016. (Winter Fun Ser.). (ENG., Illus.). 24p. (J). (gr. k-k). pap. 8.15 (978-1-4824-3763-8(5)) Stevens, Gareth Publishing LLLP.
—Winter Weather. 2016. (Winter Fun Ser.). (ENG., Illus.). 24p. (J). (gr. k-k). pap. 8.15 (978-1-4824-3767-6(8)) Stevens, Gareth Publishing LLLP.
Brode, Robyn. December. 2nd rev. ed. 2009. (Months of the Year Ser.). 24p. (J). (gr. -1-3). pap. 8.15 (978-1-4339-2105-6(7)); lib. bdg. 22.00 (978-1-4339-1928-2(1)) Stevens, Gareth Publishing LLLP. (Weekly Reader Leveled Readers).
—December/diciembre. 2009. (Months of the Year/Meses del año Ser.). (ENG & SPA.). 24p. (J). (gr. -1-3). pap. 8.15 (978-1-4339-2117-9(0), Weekly Reader Leveled Readers) Stevens, Gareth Publishing LLLP.
—December/Diciembre. 2009. (Months of the Year/Meses del año Ser.). (ENG & SPA.). 24p. (J). (gr. -1-3). lib. bdg. 22.00 (978-1-4339-1940-4(0), Weekly Reader Leveled Readers) Stevens, Gareth Publishing LLLP.
—February/febrero. 2009. (Months of the Year/Meses del año Ser.). (ENG & SPA.). 24p. (J). (gr. -1-3). pap. 8.15 (978-1-4339-2107-0(3), Weekly Reader Leveled Readers) Stevens, Gareth Publishing LLLP.
—February/Febrero. 2009. (Months of the Year/Meses del año Ser.). (ENG & SPA.). 24p. (J). (gr. -1-3). lib. bdg. 22.00 (978-1-4339-1930-5(3), Weekly Reader Leveled Readers) Stevens, Gareth Publishing LLLP.
—January/enero. 2009. (Months of the Year/Meses del año Ser.). (ENG & SPA.). 24p. (J). (gr. -1-3). pap. 8.15 (978-1-4339-2106-3(5), Weekly Reader Leveled Readers) Stevens, Gareth Publishing LLLP.
—January/Enero. 2009. (Months of the Year/Meses del año Ser.). (ENG & SPA.). 24p. (J). (gr. -1-3). lib. bdg. 22.00 (978-1-4339-1929-9(X), Weekly Reader Leveled Readers) Stevens, Gareth Publishing LLLP.
Brode, Robyn & Nations, Susan. February. 2nd rev. ed. 2009. (Months of the Year Ser.). (ENG.). 24p. (J). (gr. -1-3). pap. 8.15 (978-1-4339-2095-0(6)); lib. bdg. 22.00 (978-1-4339-1918-3(4)) Stevens, Gareth Publishing LLLP. (Weekly Reader Leveled Readers).
—January. 2nd rev. ed. 2009. (Months of the Year Ser.). (ENG.). 24p. (J). (gr. -1-3). pap. 8.15 (978-1-4339-2094-3(8)); lib. bdg. 22.00 (978-1-4339-1917-6(6)) Stevens, Gareth Publishing LLLP. (Weekly Reader Leveled Readers).
Bryant, Margaret A., et al. Learning about Winter with Children's Literature. 2006. (ENG., Illus.). 160p. (J). (gr. k-3). pap. 14.95 (978-1-56976-205-9(8), Zephyr Pr.) Chicago Review Pr., Inc.
Butterworth Moira. Winter. James, Helen, illus. 2005. (Seasons (Smart Apple Media) Ser.). 32p. (YA). (gr. 2-4). lib. bdg. 27.10 (978-1-58340-617-5(4)) Black Rabbit Bks.
Carlson-Voiles, Polly. Someone Walks By. 2008. 32p. (J). (gr. 1-2). 18.95 (978-0-9801045-5-4(6)) Raven Productions, Inc.
—Someone Walks By: The Wonders of Winter Wildlife. 2008. 32p. (J). (gr. 1-2). pap. 9.95 (978-0-9801045-6-1(4)) Raven Productions, Inc.
Carole, Bonnie. Black & White in Winter. 2015. (SPA.). 24p. (gr. -1-1). pap. 8.95 (978-1-63430-081-0(5)) Rourke Educational Media.
Carr, Aaron. Winter. 2013. pap. 17.95 (978-1-62127-495-7(0)) Weigl Pubs., Inc.
Casado, Dami & Casado, Alicia. El Invierno. 2005. (Brujita Mo y las Cuatro Estaciones Ser.). (ESP., Illus.). 14p. (J). per., bds. 7.99 (978-84-272-6237-9(X)) Molino, Editorial ESP. Dist: Santillana USA Publishing Co., Inc.
Charron, Ashley. Hello Green Mountains: It's a Winter Wonderland. 2013. 26p. 21.95 (978-1-4787-2416-2(1)) Outskirts Pr., Inc.
Coleman, Karlyn. Where Are All the Minnesotans? Hartman, Carrie, illus. 2017. (ENG.). 32p. (J). 16.95 **(978-1-68134-040-1(2))** Minnesota Historical Society Pr.
Collinson, Clare. Winter. 2010. (Thinking about the Seasons Ser.). 32p. 28.50 (978-1-59771-262-0(0)) Sea-To-Sea Pubns.
DeGezelle, Terri. Exploring Winter, 1 vol. 2012. (Exploring the Seasons Ser.). (ENG.). 24p. (gr. k-1). pap. 7.29 (978-1-4296-7916-9(6)); pap. 41.70 (978-1-4296-8353-1(8)); lib. bdg. 26.65 (978-1-4296-7699-1(X)) Capstone Press of Coughlan Cos. (Pebble Plus).
Dolphin, Colleen. Signs of Winter, 1 vol. 2012. (Signs of the Seasons Ser.). (ENG.). 24p. (J). (gr. k-3). lib. bdg. 24.21 (978-1-61783-395-3(9), SandCastle) ABDO Publishing Co.
Don, Lari. Fire & Ice: Stories of Winter from Around the World. Greenwood, Francesca, illus. 2016. (World of Stories Ser.). (ENG.). 120p. (J). (gr. 2-6). 26.65 (978-1-5124-1320-5(8)) Lerner Publishing Group.
Enslow, Brian. Winter Colors. 2011. (All about Colors of the Seasons Ser.). (Illus.). 24p. (J). (gr. -1-18). pap. 7.95 (978-1-59845-268-6(1), Enslow Elementary) Enslow Pubs., Inc.
Esbaum, Jill. Winter Wonderland. 2010. (ENG., Illus.). 16p. (J). (gr. -1-3). pap. 5.95 (978-1-4263-0714-0(4), National Geographic Children's Bks.) National Geographic Society.
Felix, Rebecca. How's the Weather in Winter? 2014. (21st Century Basic Skills Library: Let's Look at Winter Ser.). (ENG.). 24p. (J). (gr. k-3). 22.79 (978-1-63137-605-4(5), 205203) Cherry Lake Publishing.
—We Celebrate Hanukkah in Winter. 2014. (21st Century Basic Skills Library: Let's Look at Winter Ser.). (ENG.). 24p. (J). (gr. k-3). 22.79 (978-1-63137-610-8(1), 205223) Cherry Lake Publishing.
—We See Snowflakes in Winter. 2014. (21st Century Basic Skills Library: Let's Look at Winter Ser.). (ENG., Illus.). 24p. (J). (gr. k-3). 22.79 (978-1-63137-612-2(8), 205231) Cherry Lake Publishing.
—What Do People Do in Winter? 2014. (21st Century Basic Skills Library: Let's Look at Winter Ser.). (ENG.). 24p. (J). (gr. k-3). 22.79 (978-1-63137-606-1(3), 205207) Cherry Lake Publishing.
—What Happens to Plants in Winter? 2014. (21st Century Basic Skills Library: Let's Look at Winter Ser.). (ENG.). 24p. (J). (gr. k-3). 22.79 (978-1-63137-608-5(X), 205215) Cherry Lake Publishing.
Flatt, Lizann. Sizing up Winter. Barron, Ashley & Owlkids Books Inc. Staff, illus. 2013. (Math in Nature Ser.: 3). (ENG.). 32p. (J). (gr. k-3). 15.95 (978-1-926973-82-1(8), Owlkids) Owlkids Bks. Inc. CAN. Dist: Publishers Group West (PGW).
Fowler, Allan. How Do You Know It's Winter? 2013. (Rookie Read-About Science Ser.). (gr. k-3). 15.95 (978-0-613-37393-7(6), Turtleback) Turtleback Bks.
George, Jean Craighead. Winter Moon. 2003. (J). (gr. 3-7). 20.75 (978-0-8446-7244-1(0)) Smith, Peter Pub., Inc.
Ghigna, Charles. Count by 10 To 100. Saburi, Misa, illus. 2017. (Winter Math Ser.). (ENG.). 24p. (gr. k-2). 33.99 **(978-1-68410-017-0(8))** Cantata Learning.
—Making 10. Saburi, Misa, illus. 2017. (Winter Math Ser.). (ENG.). 24p. (gr. k-2). 33.99 **(978-1-68410-037-8(2))** Cantata Learning.
Glaser, Rebecca. Winter. 2012. (ENG., Illus.). 24p. (J). lib. bdg. 25.65 (978-1-62031-017-5(1)) Jump! Inc.
Goldstone, Bruce. Wonderful Winter. Goldstone, Bruce, photos by. 2016. (ENG., Illus.). 48p. (J). 17.99 (978-0-8050-9981-2(6), 9780805099812, Holt, Henry & Co. Bks. For Young Readers) Holt, Henry & Co.
Group/McGraw-Hill, Wright. Winter Weather: Collection 2: (Storyteller Interactive Writing Cards Ser.). (J). (gr. k-3). (978-0-322-09341-6(4)) Wright Group/McGraw-Hill.
Hedlund, Stephanie. Winter. Bauer, Stephanie, illus. 2013. (Seasons Ser.). 24p. (J). (gr. k-4). lib. bdg. 27.07 (978-1-61641-995-0(4), Looking Glass Library- Nonfiction) Magic Wagon.
Herriges, Ann. Winter. 2006. (Seasons Ser.). (ENG., Illus.). 24p. (J). (gr. k-3). lib. bdg. 25.95 (978-1-60014-030-3(0)) Bellwether Media.
—Winter. 2011. (Blastoff! Readers: Seasons: Level 3 Ser.). (Illus.). 24p. (J). pap. 5.95 (978-0-531-26249-8(9), Children's Pr.) Scholastic Library Publishing.
Herrington, Lisa M. How Do You Know It's Winter? 2013. (ENG.). 32p. (J). 23.00 (978-0-531-29949-4(X)); pap. 5.95 (978-0-531-22578-3(X)) Scholastic Library Publishing.
Highlights for Children Editorial Staff, creator. All about Winter. 2016. (Highlights(tm) All about Activity Bks.). (ENG.). 32p. (J). (gr. -1-k). pap. 4.99 (978-1-62979-695-6(6), Highlights) Boyds Mills Pr.
Jackson, Ellen B. The Winter Solstice. Ellis, Jan Davey, illus. 2003. (Traditions of the Seasons Ser.). (ENG.). 32p. (J). (gr. 3-6). pap. 7.95 (978-0-7613-0297-1(2), Millbrook Pr.) Lerner Publishing Group.
Jeffries, Joyce. Dinosaurs in the Winter. 2014. (Dinosaur School Ser.). 24p. (J). (gr. -1-1). 22.60 (978-1-4824-0717-4(5)) Stevens, Gareth Publishing LLLP.
Jones, Jennifer Berry. Who Lives in the Snow? Powell, Consie, illus. 2012. (ENG.). 32p. (J). (gr. -1-3). pap. 8.95 (978-1-57098-444-0(1)) Rinehart, Roberts Pubs.
Kalz, Jill. Winter. 2005. (My First Look at Seasons Ser.). (Illus.). 24p. (J). (gr. k-3). lib. bdg. 15.95 (978-1-58341-365-4(0), Creative Education) Creative Co., The.
Kramer, Nash. Why Do You Change in Winter? 2014. (Little Books of Answers: Level F Ser.). (Illus.). 16p. (gr. k-2). pap. 7.95 (978-1-927136-57-7(1)) Three Crows Media NZL. Dist: RiverStream Publishing.
Lapenta, Marilyn. Winter Punches to Nut Crunches. 2013. (Yummy Tummy Recipes: Seasons Ser.). 24p. (J). (gr. 1-6). lib. bdg. 23.93 (978-1-61772-743-6(1)) Bearport Publishing Co., Inc.
Latta, Sara L. ¿Qué Pasa en el Invierno? What Happens in Winter? 2010. (SPA.). (J). 23.94 (978-0-7660-3244-6(2), Enslow Elementary) Enslow Pubs., Inc.
—What Happens in Winter? 2006. (I Like the Seasons! Ser.). (Illus.). 24p. (J). (gr. 1-3). lib. bdg. 22.60 (978-0-7660-2418-2(0), Enslow Elementary) Enslow Pubs., Inc.
—Why Is It Winter? 2012. (Why Do We Have Seasons? Ser.). (Illus.). 24p. (J). (gr. k-18). pap. 7.95 (978-1-59845-391-1(2), Enslow Elementary); 22.60 (978-0-7660-3988-9(9)) Enslow Pubs., Inc.
Lim, Annalees. 10-Minute Seasonal Crafts for Winter. 2014. (10-Minute Seasonal Crafts Ser.). (Illus.). 24p. (J). (gr. k-3). lib. bdg. 26.25 (978-1-4777-9218-6(X)) Windmill Bks.
Lindeen, Mary. Winter! 2015. (BeginningtoRead Ser.). (ENG., Illus.). 32p. (J). (gr. k-2). lib. bdg. 22.60 (978-1-59953-682-8(X)) Norwood Hse. Pr.
—Winter. 2015. (BeginningtoRead Ser.). (ENG., Illus.). 32p. (J). (gr. k-2). pap. 11.94 (978-1-60357-742-7(4)) Norwood Hse. Pr.
Lowrie, Paul. Hooray for Minnesota Winters. 2008. 19.95 (978-0-9755801-9-6(1)) Questmarc Publishing.
MacDonald, Margaret. What Do People Do in Winter? 2011. (Learn-Abouts: Level 10 Ser.). (Illus.). 16p. (J). pap. 7.95 (978-1-59920-601-1(3)) Black Rabbit Bks.
Macken, JoAnn Early. Winter. 2006. (Seasons of the Year Ser.). (Illus.). 16p. (gr. -1-2). pap. 5.30 (978-0-8368-6361-1(5)); lib. bdg. 19.00 (978-0-8368-6356-7(9)) Stevens, Gareth Publishing LLLP. (Weekly Reader Leveled Readers).
—Winter (Invierno) 2006. (Seasons of the Year/ Las estaciones del ano Ser.). (SPA.). 16p. (gr. -1-2). pap. 5.30 (978-0-8368-6540-0(5), Weekly Reader Leveled Readers) Stevens, Gareth Publishing LLLP.
Macken, JoAnn Early & Early Macken, JoAnn. Winter/Invierno. 2006. (Seasons of the Year/Las Estaciones del Ano Ser.). (ENG & SPA., Illus.). 16p. (gr. -1-2). lib. bdg. 19.00 (978-0-8368-6535-6(9), Weekly Reader Leveled Readers) Stevens, Gareth Publishing LLLP.
McCarroll, Tolbert. A Winter Walk. Beebee, Dorothy, illus. 2006. (ENG.). 160p. 14.95 (978-0-8245-2416-6(0)) Crossroad Publishing Co., The.
McGee, Randel. Fun & Festive Winter Crafts: Snow Globes, Groundhog Puppets, & Fairy Masks. 2014. (Fun & Festive Crafts for the Seasons Ser.). (Illus.). 48p. (J). (gr. 3-4). lib. bdg. 25.27 (978-0-7660-4317-6(7), Enslow Elementary) Enslow Pubs., Inc.
Meister, Cari. Winter Is Wonderful, 1 vol. Lingenfelter, Jim, illus. 2010. (First Graphics: Seasons Ser.). (ENG.). 24p. (gr. 1-2). pap. 6.29 (978-1-4296-5624-5(7)); pap. 35.70 (978-1-4296-5695-5(6)); lib. bdg. 23.99 (978-1-4296-4732-8(9)) Capstone Press of Coughlan Cos.
Moon, Walt K. ¡El Invierno Es Divertido! 2017. (Bumba Books (tm) en Español — Diviértete con Las Estaciones (Season Fun) Ser.). (SPA., Illus.). 24p. (J). (gr. -1-1). 25.32 (978-1-5124-2863-6(9)) Lerner Publishing Group.
—Winter Is Fun! 2016. (Bumba Books (tm) — Season Fun Ser.). (ENG., Illus.). 24p. (J). (gr. -1-1). lib. bdg. 25.32 (978-1-5124-1410-3(7)) Lerner Publishing Group.
Moskal, G. I Like Winter: Learning the ER Sound. 2009. (PowerPhonics Ser.). 24p. (gr. 1-1). 39.90 (978-1-60851-451-9(X), PowerKids Pr.) Rosen Publishing Group, Inc., The.
Muller, Gerda. Winter, 1 vol. 2004. (ENG., Illus.). 12p. (J). 10.00 (978-0-86315-192-7(2)) Floris Bks. GBR. Dist: SteinerBooks, Inc.
Murray, Julie. El Invierno. 2016. (Las Estaciones Ser.). (SPA.). 24p. (J). (gr. k-5). pap. 7.95 (978-1-4966-0713-3(9)) Capstone Classroom.
Murray, Julie. Winter, 1 vol. 2016. (ENG., Illus.). 24p. **(978-1-62970-922-2(0))**, 1391203) ABDO Publishing Co.
Owen, Ruth. How Do You Know It's Winter? (Signs of the Seasons Ser.). 24p. (J). 2016. (ENG.). (gr. k-3). pap. 7.95 (978-1-944998-51-6(9)) 2012. (gr. -1-3). lib. bdg. 23.93 (978-1-61772-397-1(5)) Bearport Publishing Co., Inc.
Pfeffer, Wendy. The Shortest Day: Celebrating the Winter Solstice. Reisch, Jesse, illus. (ENG.). 40p. (J). (gr. 1-4). 2014. 8.99 (978-0-14-751284-0(0), Puffin Books) 2003. 17.99 (978-0-525-46968-1(0), Dutton Books for Young Readers) Penguin Young Readers Group.
Posner, Renee & Quinton, Sasha. Suzy Season Loves Winter. D'Argo, Laura, illus. 2003. (Be Mine Bears Ser.). (J). bds. 4.99 (978-1-58209-353-6(9)) Bks. Are Fun, Ltd.
Preparing for Winter, Vol. 3. 2005. (Our Seasons & Weather Ser.). (YA). (gr. k-3). 118.80 (978-0-7368-4200-6(4), Pebble Bks.) Capstone Press of Coughlan Cos.
Priddy, Roger. Bright Baby Touch & Feel Winter. 2011. (Bright Baby Touch & Feel Ser.). (ENG., Illus.). 12p. (J). (gr. -1 — 1). bds. 4.95 (978-0-312-50976-7(6), 9780312509767, Priddy Bks.) St. Martin's Pr.
Rau, Dana Meachen. Creating Winter Crafts. Petelinsek, Kathleen, illus. 2013. (How-To Library). (ENG.). 32p. (J). (gr. 3-6). 28.50 (978-1-62431-150-5(4), 202920); pap. 14.21 (978-1-62431-282-3(9), 202922) Cherry Lake Publishing.
Rustad, Martha E. H. All about Animals in Winter. 2015. (Celebrate Winter Ser.). (ENG., Illus.). 24p. (gr. k-1). lib. bdg. 21.99 (978-1-4914-6005-4(9), Pebble Bks.) Capstone Press of Coughlan Cos.
—Animales en Invierno/Animals in Winter, 1 vol. 2012. (Todo Sobre el Invierno/All about Winter Ser.). (SPA, ENG & MUL.). 24p. (gr. k-1). lib. bdg. 26.65 (978-1-4296-8239-8(6)) Capstone Press of Coughlan Cos.
—Animals in Fall: Preparing for Winter. Enright, Amanda, illus. 2011. (Fall's Here! Ser.). pap. 39.62 (978-0-7613-8643-8(2), Millbrook Pr.); (ENG.). 24p. (J). lib. bdg. 23.93 (978-0-7613-5066-8(7)); (ENG.). 24p. pap. 6.95 (978-0-7613-8506-6(1), Millbrook Pr.) Lerner Publishing Group.
—Todo Sobre el Invierno. 2012. (Todo Sobre el Invierno/All about Winter Ser.).Tr. of All about Winter. (MUL.). 24p. (gr. k-1). lib. bdg. 53.30 (978-1-4296-8243-5(4)) Capstone Press of Coughlan Cos.
Rustad, Martha E. H. & Clay, Kathryn. Celebrate Winter. 2015. (Celebrate Winter Ser.). (ENG.). 24p. (gr. k-1). 87.96 (978-1-4914-6918-7(8), Pebble Bks.) Capstone Press of Coughlan Cos.
Sabuda, Robert. Winter's Tale: An Original Pop-Up Journey. 2005. (ENG., Illus.). 12p. (J). (gr. -1-3). 39.99 (978-0-689-85363-0(7), Little Simon) Little Simon.
Sams, Carl R., II & Stoick, Jean. Happy Bird Day! Sams, Carl R., II & Stoick, Jean, photos by. 2012. (ENG., Illus.). 14p. (J). bds. 7.95 (978-0-9827625-2-3(6)) Sams, II, Carl R. Photography, Inc.
Sayre, April Pulley. Best in Snow. Sayre, April Pulley, photos by. 2016. (ENG., Illus.). 40p. (J). (gr. -1-3). 17.99 (978-1-4814-5916-7(3), Beach Lane Bks.) Beach Lane Bks.
Shepherd, Jodie. Crayola Winter Colors. 2017. (Crayola (r) Seasons Ser.). (ENG.). 24p. (J). (gr. -1-3). 26.65 **(978-1-5124-3293-0(8))** Lerner Publishing Group.
Smith, Sian. What Can You See in Winter?, 1 vol. 2014. (Seasons Ser.). (ENG.). 24p. (gr. -1-1). pap. 5.99 (978-1-4846-0356-7(7), Acorn) Heinemann-Raintree.
Sterling, Kristin. It's Snowy Today. 2009. (Lightning Bolt Books — What's the Weather Like? Ser.). (ENG., Illus.). 32p. (gr. k-2). 26.60 (978-0-7613-4258-8(3), Lerner Pubns.); pap. 7.95 (978-0-7613-5021-7(7)) Lerner Publishing Group.
Stewart, Mark. Blizzards & Winter Storms. 2008. (Ultimate 10 Ser.). 48p. (YA). (gr. 5-9). lib. bdg. 31.00 (978-0-8368-9150-8(3)) Stevens, Gareth Publishing LLLP.
Turnbull, Stephanie. Winter. 2013. (Seasons Ser.). (Illus.). 24p. (gr. 1-4). 25.65 (978-1-59920-850-3(4)) Black Rabbit Bks.
Wearing, Judy. Winter: WOW Study of Day & Seasons. 2010. (J). (978-1-60596-765-3(3)); pap. (978-1-60596-769-1(6)) Weigl Pubs., Inc.
Wearing, Judy & Diemer, Lauren. Winter. 2010. (Illus.). 24p. (J). pap. 9.95 (978-1-61690-049-6(0)); (gr. 2-4). lib. bdg. 25.70 (978-1-61690-045-8(8)) Weigl Pubs., Inc.
Winter Sunshine: Level P, 6 vols. (Wonder Worldtm Ser.). 48p. 39.95 (978-0-7802-7080-0(0)) Wright Group/McGraw-Hill.
Winter Survival: Individual Title Six-Packs. (Action Packs Ser.). 104p. (gr. 3-5). 44.00 (978-0-7635-8400-9(2)) Rigby Education.
World Book, Inc. Staff, contrib. by. Winter Celebrations. 2003. (World Book's Celebrations & Rituals Around the World Ser.). (Illus.). 46p. (J). (978-0-7166-5013-3(4)) World Bk., Inc.

WINTER—FICTION

Abbott, Jacob. Jonas on a Farm in Winter (Illustrated E. 2006. pap. (978-1-4065-0358-6(4)) Dodo Pr.
Albrecht, Sally K., et al. Snow Way Out! A Vacation in Winter's Wonderland: A Mini-Musical for Unison & 2-Part Voices. 2009. (ENG.). 68p. pap. 34.99 (978-0-7390-5835-0(5)) Alfred Publishing Co., Inc.
Alcott, Louisa May. Jack & Jill. 2005. 29.95 (978-1-4218-1069-0(7)); 320p. pap. 14.95 (978-1-4218-1169-7(3)) 1st World Publishing, Inc. (1st World Library - Literary Society).
—Jack & Jill. Date not set. 352p. (YA). 25.95 (978-0-8488-2671-0(X)) Amereon Ltd.
—Jack & Jill. 2012. (ENG., Illus.). 368p. (J). (gr. 3-9). pap. 17.95 (978-1-4290-9310-1(2)) Applewood Bks.
—Jack & Jill. 2007. (ENG.). 252p. pap. 21.99 (978-1-4346-2587-8(7)); 276p. pap. 23.99 (978-1-4346-2665-3(2)) Creative Media Partners, LLC.
—Jack & Jill. 2005. pap. (978-1-4065-0100-1(X)) Dodo Pr.
—Jack & Jill. 2013. (Works of Louisa May Alcott). 425p. reprint ed. lthr. 79.00 (978-0-7812-1638-8(9)) Reprint Services Corp.
Allison, Samuel Buel. An American Robinson Crusoe. 2006. pap. (978-1-4065-0803-1(9)) Dodo Pr.
Anbinder, Adrienne. Clarence Blooms in Winter. Pickman, Marian, illus. 2009. 40p. pap. 16.99 (978-1-4389-7028-8(5)) AuthorHouse.
Atkinson, Elizabeth. Lisa's Totally Unforgettable Winter. 2006. (ENG.). 56p. per. 16.95 (978-1-4241-6249-9(1)) America Star Bks.
Ayaz, Huda. Freeze-Land: A New Beginning. 2013. 110p. pap. 11.99 (978-1-4808-0267-4(0)) Archway Publishing.
Badoe, Adwoa. Nana's Cold Days, 1 vol. Junaid, Bushra, illus. 2009. (ENG.). 24p. (J). (gr. k-k). pap. 6.95 (978-0-88899-937-5(2)) Groundwood Bks. CAN. Dist: Publishers Group West (PGW).
Bak, Robyn. Lucky Little Bison. 2012. 12p. pap. 15.99 (978-1-4685-4734-4(8)) AuthorHouse.

Baker, Keith. No Two Alike. Baker, Keith, illus. 2011. (ENG., Illus.). 40p. (J). (gr. -1-2). 16.99 *(978-1-4424-1742-7(0),* Beach Lane Bks.) Beach Lane Bks.
Bauer, Marion Dane. Winter Dance. Jones, Richard, illus. 2017. (ENG.). 40p. (J). (gr. -1-3). 16.99 ***(978-0-544-31334-7(8),*** HMH Books For Young Readers) Houghton Mifflin Harcourt Publishing Co.
Berenstain, Jan & Berenstain, Mike. The Berenstain Bears' Winter Wonderland. Berenstain, Jan & Berenstain, Mike, illus. 2011. (Berenstain Bears Ser.). (ENG., Illus.). 16p. (J). (gr. -1-1). pap. 6.99 *(978-0-06-057427-7(5),* HarperFestival) HarperCollins Pubs.
Berger, Carin. Finding Spring. Berger, Carin, illus. 2015. (ENG., Illus.). 40p. (J). (gr. -1-3). 17.99 *(978-0-06-225019-3(1),* Collins Design) HarperCollins Pubs.
Biggs, Brian. Henry Goes Skating. Abbott, Simon, illus. 2012. (My First I Can Read Ser.). (J). lib. bdg. 13.55 *(978-0-606-26852-3(9),* Turtleback) Turtleback Bks.
Birney, Betty G. Winter According to Humphrey. 2013. (Humphrey Ser.: 9). (ENG.). 176p. (J). (gr. 3-7). pap. 5.99 *(978-0-14-242759-0(4),* Puffin Books) Penguin Young Readers Group.
—Winter According to Humphrey. 2013. (According to Humphrey Ser.: 9). lib. bdg. 16.00 *(978-0-606-32138-9(1),* Turtleback) Turtleback Bks.
Blackaby, Susan. Brownie Groundhog & the February Fox. Segovia, Carmen, illus. 2011. (ENG.). 32p. (J). (gr. -1-2). 14.95 *(978-1-4027-4336-8(X))* Sterling Publishing Co., Inc.
—Brownie Groundhog & the Wintry Surprise. Segovia, Carmen, illus. 2013. (ENG.). 32p. (J). (gr. -1). 14.95 *(978-1-4027-9836-8(9))* Sterling Publishing Co., Inc.
Bogart, Mike. Ice Warriors, 1 vol. 2010. 72p. pap. 19.95 *(978-1-4489-3885-8(6))* America Star Bks.
Bratun, Katy. Gingerbread Mouse. Bratun, Katy, illus. 2007. (ENG., Illus.). 32p. (J). (gr. -1-3). per. 6.99 *(978-0-06-009082-1(0))* HarperCollins Pubs.
Brett, Jan. The Night Before Christmas. Brett, Jan, illus. 2011. (ENG., Illus.). 32p. (J). (gr. -1-k). 20.00 *(978-0-399-25670-7(9),* G.P. Putnam's Sons Books for Young Readers) Penguin Young Readers Group.
Brooks, Amy. Princess Polly's Gay Winter. 2004. reprint ed. pap. 1.99 *(978-1-4192-4299-1(7));* pap. 15.95 *(978-1-4191-4299-4(2))* Kessinger Publishing, LLC.
Cammuso, Frank. Frozen Fiasco. 2015. (Misadventures of Salem Hyde Ser.: 5). (J). lib. bdg. 17.15 *(978-0-606-37433-0(7))* Turtleback Bks.
Campbell, Mari & Jennings, Randy. Maggiemoosetracks: Christmas Star. 2013. 106p. pap. 21.00 *(978-0-9895205-4-6(4))* MaggieMooseTracks.
Caple, Kathy. Hillary to the Rescue. Caple, Kathy, illus. 2003. (Picture Bks.). (Illus.). 32p. (J). (gr. -1-3). 15.95 *(978-1-57505-420-9(5),* Carolrhoda Bks.) Lerner Publishing Group.
Carlstrom, Nancy White. Mama, Will It Snow Tonight? Tong, Paul, illus. 2009. (ENG.). 32p. (J). (gr. k-3). 16.95 *(978-1-59078-562-1(2))* Boyds Mills Pr.
Carnesi, Mônica. Sleepover with Beatrice & Bear. Carnesi, Mônica, illus. 2014. (ENG., Illus.). 32p. (J). (gr. -1-k). 15.99 *(978-0-399-25667-7(9),* Nancy Paulsen Books) Penguin Young Readers Group.
Carr, Annie Roe. Nan Sherwood's Winter Holidays. 2007. 124p. per. *(978-1-4068-4397-2(0))* Echo Library.
—Nan Sherwoods Winter Holidays or Rescuin. 2007. pap. *(978-1-4065-1296-0(6))* Dodo Pr.
Carriger, Candace. Inside My Garden. Allen, Cassandra, illus. 2011. 46p. (J). pap. 11.95 *(978-0-9816047-5-6(7))* Sadie Bks.
Carter, David A. Snow Bugs: A Wintery Pop-Up Book. Carter, David A., illus. 2009. (David Carter's Bugs Ser.). (ENG., Illus.). 20p. (J). (gr. -1-3). 11.99 *(978-1-4169-5054-7(0),* Little Simon) Little Simon.
—Winter. 2015. (Seasons Pop-Up Ser.). (ENG., Illus.). 12p. (J). (gr. -1-k). 14.95 *(978-1-4197-1823-6(1),* Abrams Appleseed) Abrams, Inc.
Caviezel, Giovanni. Little Snowman. Mesturini, C., illus. 2014. (Mini People Shape Bks.). (ENG.). 10p. (J). (gr. -1-2). bds. 4.99 *(978-0-7641-6737-9(5))* Barron's Educational Series, Inc.
Chernesky, Felicia Sanzari. Sugar White Snow & Evergreens: A Winter Wonderland of Color. Swan, Susan, illus. 2014. (ENG.). 32p. (J). (gr. -1-3). 16.99 *(978-0-8075-7234-4(9))* Whitman, Albert & Co.
Child's Play Staff. Winter. Busby, Ailie, illus. 2015. (Seasons Ser.: 4). (ENG.). 12p. (J). (gr. 1-1). bds. *(978-1-84643-745-8(8))* Child's Play International Ltd.
Christensen, Gerda & Evans, Carol. Troll Peter & His Family Prepare for Winter & Other Stories: Troll Peter's Adventures Book 4. 2011. 40p. pap. *(978-1-4269-7312-3(8))* Trafford Publishing (UK) Ltd.
Christiansen, Candace. The Mitten Tree. Greenstein, Elaine, illus. 2008. (ENG.). 32p. pap. 7.95 *(978-1-55591-698-5(8))* Fulcrum Publishing.
Clark, Catherine. Icing on the Lake. 2005. (ENG.). 368p. (YA). (gr. 9-12). pap. 5.99 *(978-0-06-081534-9(5),* HarperTeen) HarperCollins Pubs.
Conforto, Lisa. The Very Compromising Adventures of Thumby Blackstone, 1 vol. 2010. 34p. 24.95 *(978-1-4512-0270-0(9))* PublishAmerica, Inc.
Cooper, Mimi. Me Versus Snow. 2006. 17p. 9.99 *(978-1-4116-8257-3(2))* Lulu Pr., Inc.
Corum, Stephanie J. Goats with Coats. 2008. 32p. pap. 12.99 *(978-1-4343-9302-9(X))* AuthorHouse.
Cotten, Cynthia. Snow Ponies. Cockcroft, Jason, illus. 2013. (ENG.). 32p. (J). (gr. -1-1). 6.99 *(978-1-250-03429-8(9),* 9781250034298) Square Fish.
Crandall, Janet. Winter on the Farm. 2006. (J). per. 9.95 *(978-1-59872-612-1(9))* Instant Pub.
Crane, Christine E. It's Winter the First Day of Spring on Summer Street. 2009. 20p. pap. 14.00 *(978-1-4490-1099-7(7))* AuthorHouse.
Crockett, S. D. After the Snow. 2012. (After the Snow Ser.: 1). (ENG.). 304p. (YA). (gr. 7-12). 16.99 *(978-0-312-64169-6(9))* Feiwel & Friends.
—After the Snow. 2013. (After the Snow Ser.: 1). (ENG.). 320p. (YA). (gr. 7-12). pap. 9.99 *(978-1-250-01676-8(2))* Square Fish.
Currie, Robin. Tuktuk: Un Cuento Sobre la Tundra. Saroff, Phyllis, illus. 2016. (SPA.). 32p. (J). (gr. k-3). pap. 9.95 *(978-1-62855-881-4(4))* Arbordale Publishing.
Czajak, Paul. Monster Needs a Christmas Tree. Grieb, Wendy, illus. 2014. (Monster & Me Ser.). (ENG.). 32p. (J). (-k). 16.95 *(978-1-938063-46-6(5),* Mighty Media Kids) Mighty Media Pr.
Daniel, Noel, ed. A Treasury of Wintertime Tales. 2014. (ENG.). 324p. 39.99 *(978-3-8365-4400-9(8))* TASCHEN DEU. Dist: Ingram Publisher Services.
Debowski, Sharon. The Snowman, the Owl, & the Groundhog. 2007. (J). lib. bdg. 15.95 *(978-1-60227-468-6(1));* (Illus.). 32p. (gr. -1-4). 14.95 *(978-1-60227-470-9(3))* Above the Clouds Publishing.
DePrisco, Dorothea. Mini Snowbears Winter Day. 2006. (ENG.). 10p. (J). 4.95 *(978-1-58117-506-6(X),* Intervisual/Piggy Toes) Bendon, Inc.
Disney Editors. Anna's Act of Love. 2013. (Frozen 8X8 Ser.). lib. bdg. 14.75 *(978-0-606-32204-1(3),* Turtleback) Turtleback Bks.
Disney Frozen Melt My Heart. 2014. (Hugs Book Ser.). (ENG.). 10p. (J). (gr. -1-k). bds. 10.99 *(978-0-7944-3266-9(2),* Reader's Digest Children's Bks.) Studio Fun International.
Doyle, Brian. Spud in Winter, 1 vol. 2nd ed. 2006. (ENG.). 140p. (J). (gr. 2-7). pap. 5.95 *(978-0-88899-755-5(8))* Groundwood Bks. CAN. Dist: Publishers Group West (PGW).
Doyle, Eugenie. Sleep Tight Farms: A Farm Prepares for Winter. Stadtlander, Becca, illus. 2016. (ENG.). 36p. (J). (gr. -1-k). 16.99 *(978-1-4521-2901-3(0))* Chronicle Bks. LLC.
Duncan Gurley, Ann. Esbe's Halo. 2009. 108p. (J). pap. 15.95 *(978-1-4327-3453-4(9))* Outskirts Pr., Inc.
Dunn, Hunter S. A Winter's Dream. Ellis, Joey, illus. 2004. 65p. (J). 19.95 *(978-0-9761732-0-5(4))* Dunn, Hunter.
Dunshee, Gloria Fjare. Will & the Magic Snowman. 2010. 32p. pap. 11.95 *(978-0-9828231-1-8(8))* WillGo Pr.
Eastman, P. D. Aaron Is Cool. 2015. (Step into Reading Ser.). (ENG., Illus.). 32p. (J). (gr. -1-1). 12.99 *(978-0-553-51238-0(2),* Random Hse. Bks. for Young Readers) Random Hse. Children's Bks.
Emerson, Carl. The Cold Winter Day, 1 vol. Doerrfeld, Cori, illus. 2008. (Read-It! Readers: Science Ser.). (ENG.). 32p. (gr. k-2). lib. bdg. 21.32 *(978-1-4048-2627-4(0),* Easy Readers) Picture Window Bks.
Evans, Clay Bonnyman. The Winter Witch. Bender, Robert, illus. 2005. (ENG.). 32p. (J). (gr. -1-3). 16.95 *(978-0-8234-1615-8(1))* Holiday Hse., Inc.
Fleming, Denise. The First Day of Winter. Fleming, Denise, illus. rev. ed. 2005. (ENG., Illus.). 32p. (J). (gr. -1-1). 18.99 *(978-0-8050-7384-3(1),* 9780805073843, Holt, Henry & Co. Bks. For Young Readers) Holt, Henry & Co.
Fordham, Walter. Ilian. Krizmanic, Tatjana, illus. 2012. 42p. pap. *(978-0-9813889-5-3(7))* Publish Yourself.
Frampton, Caytie. Bernard's Winter Nap. 2004. 21p. pap. 24.95 *(978-1-4137-3083-8(3))* PublishAmerica, Inc.
Fraser, Christine Marion. Rhanna. (Illus.). 320p. (J). (gr. k-6). pap. 11.95 *(978-0-340-76565-4(8))* Hodder & Stoughton GBR. Dist: Trafalgar Square Publishing.
Freedman, Claire. Little Bear's Special Friend. Kolanovic, Dubravka, illus. 2007. (J). *(978-0-545-06757-7(X))* Scholastic, Inc.
Freedman, Claire & Cabban, Vanessa. Gooseberry Goose. 2003. (Illus.). 32p. (J). (gr. -1-2). tchr. ed. 15.95 *(978-1-58925-030-7(3))* Tiger Tales.
Friedman, Becky. Daniel's Winter Adventure. Fruchter, Jason, illus. 2016. (Daniel Tiger's Neighborhood 8X8 Ser.). (ENG.). 24p. (gr. -1-2). 13.55 *(978-0-606-39247-1(5))* Turtleback Bks.
Gavin, Ciara. Bear Is Not Tired. 2016. (ENG., Illus.). 32p. (J). (gr. -1-2). 16.99 *(978-0-385-75476-7(0),* Knopf Bks. for Young Readers) Random Hse. Children's Bks.
George, Kallie. The Greatest Gift. 2017. (Heartwood Hotel Ser.: 2). (J). lib. bdg. 16.00 ***(978-0-606-39967-8(4))*** Turtleback Bks.
—Heartwood Hotel, Book 2 the Greatest Gift. Graegin, Stephanie, illus. 2017. (Heartwood Hotel Ser.). (ENG.). 176p. (J). (gr. 2-5). 14.99 ***(978-1-4847-3234-2(0));*** pap. 5.99 ***(978-1-4847-4639-4(2))*** Hyperion Bks. for Children.
Ghigna, Charles. I See Winter, 1 vol. Jatkowska, Ag, illus. 2011. (I See Ser.). (ENG.). 24p. (gr. -1 — 1). pap. 6.10 *(978-1-4048-6850-2(X));* lib. bdg. 22.65 *(978-1-4048-6588-4(8))* Picture Window Bks. (I See).
—Snow Wonder. Woolf, Julia, illus. 2008. (Step into Reading Ser.: Vol. 2). (ENG.). 24p. (J). (gr. -1-1). 3.99 *(978-0-375-85586-3(6),* Random Hse. Bks. for Young Readers) Random Hse. Children's Bks.
—Veo el Invierno. Jatkowska, Ag, illus. 2012. (Bilingual I See Ser.).Tr. of I See Winter. (ENG, SPA & MUL.). 24p. (gr. -1 — 1). lib. bdg. 22.65 *(978-1-4048-7310-0(4),* I See) Picture Window Bks.
Graire, Virginie, illus. Snowman. 2016. (ENG.). 12p. (J). (gr. -1 — 1). bds. 6.99 *(978-1-4998-0344-0(3))* Little Bee Books Inc.
Grandma Sue. Bubba the Bear. 2010. 12p. pap. 8.49 *(978-1-4490-1813-9(0))* AuthorHouse.
Green, Poppy. Winter's No Time to Sleep! Bell, Jennifer A., illus. 2015. (Adventures of Sophie Mouse Ser.: 6). (ENG.). 128p. (J). (gr. k-4). pap. 5.99 *(978-1-4814-4199-5(X),* Little Simon) Little Simon.
Hadcroft, Will. Anne Droyd & the Ghosts of Winter Hill. 2013. 210p. pap. *(978-0-9560537-2-5(6))* Nordic.
Hader, Berta and Elmer. The Big Snow & Other Stories: A Treasury of Caldecott Award Winning Tales. 2015. (ENG., Illus.). 160p. (J). (gr. 1-4). pap. 14.99 *(978-0-486-78163-1(1))* Dover Pubns., Inc.
Hallwood, Cheri L. Winter's First Snowflake. Rose, Patricia M., illus. Lt. ed. 2006. (ENG.). 32p. (J). 15.99 *(978-0-9774422-0-1(9))* Forever Young Pubs.
Hamilton, Pamela Greenhalgh. Snow Day. 2011. 34p. (J). pap. 18.95 *(978-1-4327-5743-4(1))* Outskirts Pr., Inc.
Hannan, Peter. The Greatest Snowman in the World! Hannan, Peter, illus. 2010. (ENG., Illus.). 32p. (J). (gr. -1-3). 16.99 *(978-0-06-128480-9(7))* HarperCollins Pubs.
Hapka, Catherine, pseud. Walking with Dinosaurs: the Winter Ground. 2013. (I Can Read Level 2 Ser.). (ENG., Illus.). 32p. (J). (gr. -1-3). 16.99 *(978-0-06-223284-7(3))* HarperCollins Pubs.
Hartley Bellows, Carol. Icabog Bear. 2009. 24p. pap. 15.50 *(978-1-4389-3856-1(X))* AuthorHouse.
Hawley, Mabel C. Four Little Blossoms & Their Winter Fun. 2007. (ENG.). 100p. per. 16.99 *(978-1-4346-4265-3(8));* 116p. per. 19.99 *(978-1-4346-4266-0(6))* Creative Media Partners, LLC.
—Four Little Blossoms & Their Winter Fun. 2007. 96p. per. *(978-1-4068-1705-8(8))* Echo Library.
Hayes, Karel. The Winter Visitors. 2007. (ENG., Illus.). 32p. (J). (gr. -1-3). 17.95 *(978-0-89272-750-6(0))* Down East Bks.
Heinz, Brian J. A Coming of Winter in the Adirondacks. Healy, Maggie, illus. 2011. 32p. (J). 19.95 *(978-1-59531-038-5(X))* North Country Bks., Inc.
Here Comes Winter! 2003. (J). per. *(978-1-57657-967-1(0))* Paradise Pr., Inc.
Herring, Bruce D. The Wizard of Wonderland, 1 vol. 2010. 192p. pap. 24.95 *(978-1-4489-5844-3(X))* America Star Bks.
Hest, Amy. You Can Do It, Sam. Jeram, Anita, illus. 2007. (Sam Bks.). (ENG.). 32p. (J). (gr. -1-k). pap. 4.99 *(978-0-7636-3688-3(5))* Candlewick Pr.
Hillert, Margaret. Feliz Navidad, Querido Dragón. Pullan, Jack, illus. 2017. (BeginningtoRead Ser.).Tr. of Merry Christmas, Dear Dragon. (ENG & SPA.). 32p. (J). (-2). 22.60 ***(978-1-59953-838-9(5))*** Norwood Hse. Pr.
—It's Winter, Dear Dragon. Schimmell, David, illus. 2009. (BeginningtoRead Ser.). 32p. (J). (gr. k-2). lib. bdg. 22.60 *(978-1-59953-314-8(6))* Norwood Hse. Pr.
—Merry Christmas, Dear Dragon. Pullan, Jack, illus. 2016. (BeginningtoRead Ser.). (ENG.). 32p. (J). (-2). lib. bdg. 22.60 *(978-1-59953-775-7(3))* Norwood Hse. Pr.
Huizenga, Nathaniel. Justice in Winter: Justice the Dog Series. 2009. 28p. pap. 13.99 *(978-1-4389-7361-6(6))* AuthorHouse.
Hurley, Wes. How the Winter Frog Came to Was: Or, How to Get a Nice Surprise on Thanksgiving! Lee, Susan, illus. 2007. 36p. per. 24.95 *(978-1-4241-8395-1(2))* America Star Bks.
ImageBooks Staff & Chronicle Books Editors. Little Turkey. 2010. (Little Finger Puppet Board Bks.). (ENG., Illus.). 12p. (J). (gr. -1 — 1). bds. 6.99 *(978-0-8118-7513-4(X))* Chronicle Bks. LLC.
Iwamura, Kazuo. Seven Little Mice Have Fun on the Ice. 2011. (ENG., Illus.). 32p. (J). (gr. -1-2). 16.95 *(978-0-7358-4048-5(2))* North-South Bks., Inc.
Jakobs, D. Holly, Jolly Harmony. 2013. (Passport to Reading Level 2 Ser.). (J). lib. bdg. 14.75 *(978-0-606-32276-8(0),* Turtleback) Turtleback Bks.
Jansson, Tove. Moominland Midwinter. Warburton, Thomas, tr. Jansson, Tove, illus. 2010. (Moomins Ser.: 5). (ENG., Illus.). 160p. (J). (gr. 4-7). pap. 7.99 *(978-0-312-62541-2(3),* 9780312625412) Square Fish.
—Moomin's Winter Follies. 2012. (Moomin Ser.). (ENG., Illus.). 48p. (J). (gr. 4-7). pap. 9.95 *(978-1-77046-098-0(5),* 9781770460980) Drawn & Quarterly Pubns. CAN. Dist: Macmillan.
—Moominvalley in November. Hart, Kingsley, tr. Jansson, Tove, illus. 2010. (Moomins Ser.: 8). (ENG., Illus.). 208p. (J). (gr. 4-7). pap. 7.99 *(978-0-312-62544-3(8),* 9780312625443) Square Fish.
Jeffries, Joyce. It's Winter. 2016. (Four Seasons Ser.). (ENG., Illus.). 24p. (gr. 1-1). pap. 8.25 *(978-1-5081-5191-3(1),* PowerKids Pr.) Rosen Publishing Group, Inc., The.
Jenkins, Emily. Lemonade in Winter: A Book about Two Kids Counting Money. Karas, G. Brian, illus. 2012. (ENG.). 40p. (J). (gr. -1-2). 16.99 *(978-0-375-85883-3(0),* Schwartz & Wade Bks.) Random Hse. Children's Bks.
Jocelyn, Marthe. Ready for Winter. 2008. (ENG., Illus.). 16p. (J). (gr. -1-k). bds. 7.95 *(978-0-88776-848-4(2),* Tundra Bks.) Tundra Bks. CAN. Dist: Penguin Random Hse. LLC.
Johnson, Andi. Hailey Snowstorm. 2004. (Illus.). 16p. 9.00 *(978-1-84161-113-6(1))* Ravette Publishing, Ltd. GBR. Dist: Parkwest Pubns., Inc.
Johnson, Christine. Deep in Alaska. Johnson, Gary R., illus. 2013. 42p. pap. 12.95 *(978-1-60223-215-0(6))* Univ. of Alaska Pr.
Johnson, Crockett. Time for Spring. Johnson, Crockett, illus. 2016. (Illus.). 40p. (J). (gr. -1-3). 14.99 *(978-0-06-243033-5(5))* HarperCollins Pubs.
Jones, Janey Louise. Violet the Velvet Rabbit. Poh, Jennie, illus. 2016. (Superfairies Ser.). (ENG.). 56p. (gr. k-3). lib. bdg. 23.99 *(978-1-4795-8644-8(7))* Picture Window Bks.
Jordan, Apple J. Winter Wishes. Marrucchi, Elisa, illus. 2006. (Step into Reading Ser.). (ENG.). 32p. (J). (gr. k-3). per. 3.99 *(978-0-7364-2409-7(1),* RH/Disney) Random Hse. Children's Bks.
Joyce, William. Jack Frost. Joyce, William, illus. 2015. (Guardians of Childhood Ser.). (ENG., Illus.). 48p. (J). (gr. -1-3). 17.99 *(978-1-4424-3043-3(5),* Atheneum Bks. for Young Readers) Simon & Schuster Children's Publishing.
Judge, Chris. The Snow Beast. Judge, Chris, illus. 2015. (ENG., Illus.). 32p. (J). (gr. -1-3). 17.99 *(978-1-4677-9313-1(2))* Andersen Pr. GBR. Dist: Lerner Publishing Group.
Katz, Karen. Baby Loves Winter! A Karen Katz Lift-The-Flap Book. Katz, Karen, illus. 2013. (ENG., Illus.). 14p. (J). (gr. -1 — 1). bds. 6.99 *(978-1-4424-5213-8(7),* Little Simon) Little Simon.
Kelley, Marty, illus. Winter Woes. 2003. 32p. (J). 12.95 *(978-1-55933-306-1(5))* Zino Pr. Children's Bks.
Kemp, Michelle. Flutter by Butterfly. 2012. 28p. pap. 24.95 *(978-1-4626-6181-7(5))* America Star Bks.
Keyes, Diane. Spirit of the Snowpeople. Stevens, Helen, illus. 2008. (ENG.). 32p. (J). (gr. -1-3). 15.95 *(978-0-89272-710-0(1))* Down East Bks.
Kirby, Matthew J. Icefall. (ENG.). 336p. (J). (gr. 3-7). 2013. pap. 6.99 *(978-0-545-27425-8(7),* Scholastic Paperbacks) 2011. 17.99 *(978-0-545-27424-1(9),* Scholastic Pr.) Scholastic, Inc.
Kohara, Kazuno. Here Comes Jack Frost. Kohara, Kazuno, illus. 2011. (ENG., Illus.). 32p. (J). (gr. -1-1). pap. 7.99 *(978-0-312-60446-2(7),* 9780312604462) Square Fish.
Krensky, Stephen. Chaucer's First Winter. Cole, Henry, illus. (ENG.). 32p. (J). (gr. -1-1). 2010. 9.99 *(978-1-4424-1658-1(0))* 2009. 17.99 *(978-1-4169-9026-0(7))* Simon & Schuster Bks. For Young Readers. (Simon & Schuster Bks. For Young Readers).
Kroll, Linda. Winter, Awake! Lieberherr, Ruth, illus. rev. ed. 2003. (ENG.). 32p. (J). pap. 11.95 *(978-0-88010-528-6(3))* SteinerBooks, Inc.
Lagonegro, Melissa. A Tale of Two Sisters. Random House Disney Staff, illus. 2013. (Step into Reading Ser.). (ENG.). 32p. (J). (gr. -1-1). 3.99 *(978-0-7364-3120-0(9),* RH/Disney) Random Hse. Children's Bks.
Landis, Mary M. Winter Days with the Treelo Triplets. 2012. (Illus.). 218p. (J). *(978-0-7399-2447-1(8))* Rod & Staff Pubs., Inc.
Lasky, Kathryn. The River of Wind. 2007. (Guardians of Ga'hoole Ser.: 13). (ENG., Illus.). 224p. (J). (gr. 3-7). 6.99 *(978-0-439-88807-3(7))* Scholastic, Inc.
Laughing Elephant Staff, ed. The Truth about Snow People. 2005. (ENG., Illus.). 32p. (J). (gr. -1-3). 9.95 *(978-1-59583-052-4(9),* 9781595830524) Laughing Elephant.
Levine, Rhoda. Arthur. Aison, Everett, illus. 2015. (ENG.). 48p. (J). (gr. -1-2). 15.95 *(978-1-59017-935-2(8),* NYR Children's Collection) New York Review of Bks., Inc., The.
Little Bee Books Staff. Snowflake. Graire, Virginie, illus. 2015. (ENG.). 12p. (J). (gr. -1 — 1). 6.99 *(978-1-4998-0148-4(3))* Little Bee Books Inc.
Luciani, Brigitte. Peace & Quiet. Burrell, Carol, tr. Tharlet, Eve, illus. 2012. (Mr. Badger & Mrs. Fox Ser.: 4). (ENG.). 32p. (J). (gr. k-3). pap. 6.95 *(978-0-8225-9163-4(4));* lib. bdg. 25.26 *(978-0-7613-8520-2(7))* Lerner Publishing Group. (Graphic Universe™).
Lyons, Fergus. Muckeen & the Big Freeze. 2012. (Pandas Ser.: 39). (ENG., Illus.). 64p. (J). pap. 9.95 *(978-1-84717-243-3(1))* O'Brien Pr., Ltd., The IRL. Dist: Dufour Editions, Inc.
Mackall, Dandi. Wonderful Gifts of Winter. Blackmore, Katherine, illus. (Seasons Ser.). (ENG.). 32p. (gr. -1-3). 2017. (J). pap. 3.99 ***(978-1-4627-4524-1(5))*** 2014. 9.99 *(978-1-4336-8239-1(7))* B&H Publishing Group. (B&H Kids).
MacLean, Kerry Lee, creator. Pigs Ski over Colorado: The Top Ten Reasons Winter Is the Piggies Favorite Season. 2005. (J). per. 15.95 *(978-0-9652998-7-9(2))* On the Spot! Bks.
Maclear, Kyo. The Wish Tree. Turnham, Chris, illus. 2016. (ENG.). 40p. (J). (gr. -1 — 1). 16.99 *(978-1-4521-5065-9(6))* Chronicle Bks. LLC.
Marie, Barbara. Snowy & Felix Find Christmas. 2009. 24p. pap. 11.49 *(978-1-4389-7392-0(6))* AuthorHouse.
Marino Walters, Jennifer. Wonderful Winter. Nez, John, illus. 2016. (Seasons Ser.). (ENG.). 24p. (J). (gr. -1-1). lib. bdg. 25.32 *(978-1-63440-046-6(1))* Red Chair Pr.
Marshall, Natalie. Millie-Mae: In Winter. 2014. (Illus.). (J). *(978-1-4351-5613-5(7))* Barnes & Noble, Inc.
Mason, Jane B. & Stephens, Sarah Hines. Snowfall Surprise. 2009. (Candy Apple Ser.: 21). (ENG.). 144p. (J). (gr. 3-7). 5.99 *(978-0-545-10067-0(4),* Scholastic Paperbacks) Scholastic, Inc.
Matthews, Caitlin & Barefoot Books. Fireside Stories: Tales for a Winter's Eve. Cann, Helen, illus. 2015. 96p. (J). (gr. 2-6). 19.99 *(978-1-78285-251-3(4))* Barefoot Bks., Inc.
Matthews, Caitlin, et al. Fireside Stories: Tales for a Winter's Eve. 2007. (ENG., Illus.). 96p. (J). (gr. -1-5). 19.99 *(978-1-84686-065-2(2))* Barefoot Bks., Inc.
McAllister, Angela. Winter's Child. Baker-Smith, Grahame, illus. 2015. (ENG.). 40p. (J). (gr. -1-2). 16.99 *(978-0-7636-7964-4(X),* Templar) Candlewick Pr.
McCollum, Kimberly. Gloves in a Hat. 2011. 16p. (gr. -1). pap. 8.32 *(978-1-4567-3430-5(X))* AuthorHouse.
McCracken, Harold. Pirate of the North. Tonk, Ernest, illus. 2011. 224p. 44.95 *(978-1-258-09631-1(5))* Literary Licensing, LLC.
McCue, Lisa. Quiet Bunny & Noisy Puppy. (ENG., Illus.). (J). 2013. 30p. (gr. -1 — 1). bds. 7.95 *(978-1-4549-0860-9(2))* 2011. 32p. 14.95 *(978-1-4027-8559-7(3))* Sterling Publishing Co., Inc.
McDonald, Megan. Ant & Honey Bee: A Pair of Friends in Winter. Karas, G. Brian, illus. (Candlewick Sparks Ser.). (ENG.). 64p. (J). (gr. k-4). 2014. pap. 3.99 *(978-0-7636-6862-4(1))* 2013. 14.99 *(978-0-7636-5712-3(3))* Candlewick Pr.
McEwen, Katharine. Bear Hug. McEwen, Katharine, illus. 2014. (ENG., Illus.). 32p. (J). (gr. -1-2). 15.99 *(978-0-7636-6630-9(0),* Templar) Candlewick Pr.
McGregor, John. Daisy & Her Autumn & Winter Adventures. 2012. (Illus.). 77p. pap. 13.50 *(978-1-78035-482-8(7),* Fastprint Publishing) Upfront Publishing Ltd. GBR. Dist: Printondemand-worldwide.com.
Menear, Linda. The Little Groundhog Discovers the True Meaning of Christmas. 2011. 24p. pap. 24.95 *(978-1-4626-3288-6(2))* America Star Bks.
Meschenmoser, Sebastian. Waiting for Winter. Meschenmoser, Sebastian, illus. 2015. (ENG., Illus.). 58p. (J). (gr. k-3). 10.99 *(978-1-61067-435-5(9))* Kane Miller.
Messner, Kate. Over & under the Snow. Neal, Christopher Silas, illus. 2014. (ENG.). 44p. (J). (gr. k-3). 7.99 *(978-1-4521-3646-2(7))* Chronicle Bks. LLC.
Milligan, Bryce. Comanche Captive. 2005. (Illus.). 168p. (YA). (gr. 7). per. *(978-1-57168-849-1(8))* Eakin Pr.
Miska & the Long, Cold Winter. 2004. (Literacy Think-Togethers Ser.). 16-24p. (gr. 2-3). pap. 31.50 *(978-0-322-06357-0(4))* Wright Group/McGraw-Hill.
Mitton, Tony. Snowy Bear. Brown, Alison, illus. (ENG.). (J). 2016. 26p. bds. 7.99 *(978-1-68119-084-6(2),* 9781681190846) 2015. 32p. (gr. -1-1). 16.99 *(978-1-61963-905-8(X),* 9781619639058) Bloomsbury Publishing USA. (Bloomsbury USA Childrens).
Moulton, Mark Kimball. The Annual Snowman's Ball. Good, Karen Hillard, illus. 2007. (ENG.). 32p. (J). (gr. -1-3). 14.99 *(978-0-8249-5564-9(1),* Ideal Pubns.) Worthy Publishing.
Muench-Williams, Heather. A Cold Winter Day. Crowell, Knox, illus. Lt. ed. 2006. (HRL Board Book Ser.). (J). (gr. -1-k). pap. 10.95 *(978-1-57332-326-0(8),* HighReach Learning, Incorporated) Carson-Dellosa Publishing, LLC.
Muller, Marie. 'Twas the Night Before Winter. 2009. 24p. pap. 12.99 *(978-1-4389-6984-8(8))* AuthorHouse.
Na, Il Sung. Snow Rabbit, Spring Rabbit: A Book of Changing Seasons. 2011. (ENG.). 24p. (J). (gr. -1-2). 15.99 *(978-0-375-86786-6(4),* Knopf Bks. for Young Readers) Random Hse. Children's Bks.
Neubecker, Robert. Winter Is for Snow. Neubecker, Robert, illus. 2013. (ENG., Illus.). 32p. (J). (gr. -1-k). 16.99 *(978-1-4231-7831-6(9))* Hyperion Pr.
Nicholas, Nicki. Peter & Lil on a Winter's Day. 2011. 24p. pap. 12.99 *(978-1-4269-7316-1(0))* Trafford Publishing (UK) Ltd.

WXYZ

Nolan, Allia Zobel. God's Winter Wonderland. Mitchell, Melanie, illus. 2006. 10p. (J). bds. 8.99 *(978-0-8254-5526-1(X))* Kregel Pubns.

Nona Theresa Perez - Bayanin. Nadia Mei's First Winter in the Forest & Meeting with First Friends. 2012. 28p. pap. 21.99 *(978-1-4771-0596-2(4))* Xlibris Corp.

Norman, Kimberly. If It's Snowy & You Know It, Clap Your Paws! Woodruff, Liza, illus. 2013. (ENG.). 26p. (J). (gr. -1). 14.95 *(978-1-4549-0384-0(8))* Sterling Publishing Co., Inc.

Nuzum, K. A. The Leanin' Dog. (ENG.). 256p. (J). (gr. 3-7). 2010. pap. 6.99 *(978-0-06-113936-9(X))* 2008. 15.99 *(978-0-06-113934-5(3))* HarperCollins Pubs.

Oberman, Sheldon. The Wind That Wanted to Rest. Waldman, Neil, illus. 2012. (ENG.). 32p. (J). (gr. k-2). 17.95 *(978-1-59078-858-5(3))* Boyds Mills Pr.

Oceanak, Karla. Hotdogger. Spanjer, Kendra, illus. 2013. (Aldo Zelnick Comic Novel Ser.: 8). (ENG.). 160p. (J). (gr. 3-7). 12.95 *(978-1-934649-37-4(6))* Bailiwick Pr.

Oeslchlager, Vanita. Big Blue. Blackwood, Kristin, illus. 2008. (ENG.). 32p. (J). (gr. -1-3). 17.95 *(978-0-9800162-5-3(8))* VanitaBooks.

Off to School: Individual Title Six-Packs. (Story Steps Ser.). (gr. k-2). 29.00 *(978-0-7635-9577-7(2))* Rigby Education.

On a Cold, Cold Day: 6 Small Books. (gr. k-3). 24.00 *(978-0-7635-6231-1(9))* Rigby Education.

O'Reilly, Sean. The Abominable Snow Kid, 1 vol. 2012. (Mighty Mighty Monsters Ser.). (ENG.). 48p. (gr. 2-3). lib. bdg. 23.99 *(978-1-4342-3892-4(X))* Stone Arch Bks.

—Abominable Snow Kid. 2013. (Mighty Mighty Monsters Ser.). (ENG., Illus.). 48p. (gr. 2-3). pap. 6.10 *(978-1-4342-4227-3(7))* Stone Arch Bks.

Orsi, Tea. Tinker Bell & the Secret of the Wings. 2014. (Disney Fairies Graphic Novels Ser.: 15). (J). lib. bdg. 18.40 *(978-0-606-35533-9(2))* Turtleback Bks.

Osborne, M. D. The Rescue of Mr. Goldsmith. l.t. ed. 2005. (Illus.). 40p. (J). 12.95 *(978-0-9762852-1-2(5))* Wooden Shoe Pr.

Pak, Kenard. Goodbye Autumn, Hello Winter. Pak, Kenard, illus. 2017. (ENG., Illus.). 32p. (J). 17.99 ***(978-1-62779-416-9(6)***, 9781627794169, Holt, Henry & Co. Bks. For Young Readers) Holt, Henry & Co.

Palmer, Deokie Savie. My Little Baby Sister & I, on a Cold Winter Day. 2007. 38p. 17.95 *(978-1-4303-2061-6(3))* Lulu Pr., Inc.

Partridge, Helen L. Blinky: The Bear Who Wouldn't Hibernate. 2008. 32p. per. 24.95 *(978-1-4241-9261-8(7))* America Star Bks.

Paulsen, Gary. Brian's Winter. 2012. (Hatchet Adventure Ser.). (ENG.). 176p. (YA). (gr. 5). pap. 9.99 *(978-0-307-92958-7(2)*, Ember) Random Hse. Children's Bks.

—Brian's Winter. 2012. lib. bdg. 20.85 *(978-0-606-23879-3(4)*, Turtleback) Turtleback Bks.

Potter, Beatrix. A Winter's Tale. 2009. (Peter Rabbit Ser.). (ENG.). 32p. (J). (gr. k-3). 21.99 *(978-0-7232-6381-4(7)*, Warne) Penguin Young Readers Group.

Pratchett, Terry. Wintersmith. (YA). 2015. (Tiffany Aching Ser.: 3). (ENG.). 416p. (gr. 8). pap. 9.99 *(978-0-06-243528-6(0))* 2007. (Tiffany Aching Ser.: 3). 464p. (gr. 8-12). per. 8.99 *(978-0-06-089033-9(9))* 2006. (Discworld Novels Ser.). 323p. (gr. 7-12). 16.99 *(978-0-06-089031-5(2)*, HarperTeen) 2006. (Discworld Novels Ser.). 323p. (gr. 7-12). lib. bdg. 17.89 *(978-0-06-089032-2(0)*, HarperTeen) HarperCollins Pubs.

—Wintersmith. 2007. 450p. (gr. 7). 19.00 *(978-0-7569-8091-7(7))* Perfection Learning Corp.

Princess Rosa's Winter: Level M, 6 vols. 128p. (gr. 2-3). 49.95 *(978-0-7699-0986-8(8))* Shortland Pubns. (U. S. A.) Inc.

Purdy, Rebekah L. The Winter People. 2014. (Entangled Teen Ser.). (ENG.). 320p. (YA). (gr. 7-12). 16.99 *(978-1-62266-368-2(3)*, 9781622663682) Entangled Publishing, LLC.

Rabe, Tish. Big Snowman, Little Snowman. Random House Disney Staff, illus. 2013. (Step into Reading Ser.). (ENG.). 32p. (J). (gr. -1-1). 3.99 *(978-0-7364-3119-4(5)*, RH/Disney) Random Hse. Children's Bks.

Random House Disney Staff. Anna's Act of Love - Elsa's Icy Magic, 2 bks. in 1. Random House Disney Staff, illus. 2013. (Pictureback(R) Ser.). (ENG., Illus.). 24p. (J). (gr. -1-2). 4.99 *(978-0-7364-3061-6(X)*, RH/Disney) Random Hse. Children's Bks.

Ravera, Giuseppe. Snowflake. 2014. (ENG., Illus.). 10p. (J). (gr. -1 — 1). bds. 6.99 *(978-0-7641-6719-5(7))* Barron's Educational Series, Inc.

Reasoner, Charles. Let It Snow. Jones, Anna, illus. 2013. (Charles Reasoner Holiday Bks.). (ENG.). 10p. (gr. -1 — 1). bds. 9.99 *(978-1-4048-8147-1(6))* Picture Window Bks.

Rey, H. A. Three Tales for a Winter's Night. 2012. (Curious George Ser.). (ENG., Illus.). 72p. (J). (gr. -1-3). pap. 7.99 *(978-0-547-83936-3(7))* Houghton Mifflin Harcourt Publishing Co.

—Windy Delivery. 2014. (Curious George Ser.). (ENG., Illus.). 24p. (J). (gr. -1-3). 12.99 *(978-0-544-32075-8(1))*; pap. 4.99 *(978-0-544-32076-5(X))* Houghton Mifflin Harcourt Publishing Co. (HMH Books For Young Readers).

—A Winter's Nap. 2010. (Curious George Ser.). (ENG., Illus.). 24p. (J). (gr. -1-3). pap. 3.99 *(978-0-547-23590-5(9))* Houghton Mifflin Harcourt Publishing Co.

Rey, H. A. & Rey, Margret. Three Tales for a Winter's Night. 2012. (Curious George TV Tie-In 8x8 Ser.). lib. bdg. 18.40 *(978-0-606-26603-1(8)*, Turtleback) Turtleback Bks.

RH Disney Staff & Rabe, Tish. Frozen - Big Snowman, Little Snowman. RH Disney Staff, illus. 2013. (Step into Reading Ser.). (ENG., Illus.). 32p. (J). (gr. -1-1). lib. bdg. 12.99 *(978-0-7364-8130-4(3)*, RH/Disney) Random Hse. Children's Bks.

Rohmann, Eric, creator. My Friend Rabbit & the Snow Geese. 2013. (My Readers Ser.). (ENG., Illus.). 32p. (J). (gr. -1-1). pap. 3.99 *(978-1-250-01661-4(4)*, 9781250016614) Square Fish.

Rollins, Walter & Nelson, Steve. Frosty the Snowman. Williams, Sam, illus. 2013. (ENG.). 16p. (J). (gr. -1-k). bds. 9.99 *(978-0-545-45005-8(5)*, Cartwheel Bks.) Scholastic, Inc.

Rose, Andrea. A Home for Abby. 2011. 24p. pap. 12.79 *(978-1-4634-2121-2(4))* AuthorHouse.

Rudolph, Miriam. A Frozen Dream. 2009. 28p. pap. 12.00 *(978-1-60693-962-8(9)*, Eloquent Bks.) Strategic Book Publishing & Rights Agency (SBPRA).

Russell-Gilmer, Phyllis A. Where Do Crickets Go When Winter Comes? Jones, Chamira, illus. 2009. 32p. (J). 16.95 *(978-1-934363-10-2(3))* Zoe Life Publishing.

Rylant, Cynthia. Annie & Snowball & the Wintry Freeze. Stevenson, Sucie, illus. (Annie & Snowball Ser.: 8). (ENG.). 40p. (J). (gr. k-2). 2011. pap. 3.99 *(978-1-4169-7206-8(4))* 2010. 16.99 *(978-1-4169-7205-1(6))* Simon Spotlight. (Simon Spotlight).

—Little Penguins. Robinson, Christian, illus. 2016. (ENG.). 40p. (J). (gr. -1-2). 17.99 *(978-0-553-50770-6(2)*, Schwartz & Wade Bks.) Random Hse. Children's Bks.

—Mr. Putter & Tabby Hit the Slope. Howard, Arthur, illus. 2016. (Mr. Putter & Tabby Ser.). (ENG.). 40p. (J). (gr. 1-4). 14.99 *(978-0-15-206427-3(3)*, HMH Books For Young Readers) Houghton Mifflin Harcourt Publishing Co.

—Poppleton in Winter. Teague, Mark, illus. 2008. 48p. (gr. -1-3). 14.00 *(978-0-7569-8910-1(8))* Perfection Learning Corp.

—Poppleton in Winter, Level 3. Teague, Mark, illus. 2008. (Scholastic Reader Level 3 Ser.). (ENG.). 56p. (J). (gr. -1-3). pap. 3.99 *(978-0-545-06823-9(1)*, Cartwheel Bks.) Scholastic, Inc.

Sabuda, Robert. Winter in White: A Mini Pop-Up Treat. Sabuda, Robert, illus. 2007. (ENG., Illus.). 18p. (J). (gr. -1-3). 17.99 *(978-0-689-85365-4(3)*, Little Simon) Little Simon.

Sams II, Carl R. A Magical Winter. 2016. (ENG., Illus.). (J). 19.95 *(978-0-9827625-8-5(5))* Sams, II, Carl R. Photography, Inc.

Sander, Sonia, adapted by. Dragon's Snowy Day. 2005. (Scholastic Reader Ser.). (Illus.). 32p. (J). pap. *(978-0-439-80163-8(X))* Scholastic, Inc.

Sanrio Company, LTD. Hello Kitty, Hello Winter! Hirashima, Jean, illus. 2013. (ENG.). 14p. (J). (gr. -1 — 1). bds. 7.95 *(978-1-4197-0797-1(3)*, Abrams Appleseed) Abrams, Inc.

Sapp, Karen. Who Is Sleeping? 2009. (Rookie Preschool-NEW Ser.). (ENG.). 24p. (J). pap. 6.95 *(978-0-531-24586-6(1))*; (gr. -1). lib. bdg. 23.00 *(978-0-531-24411-1(3))* Scholastic Library Publishing. (Children's Pr.).

Sargent, Dave. Sammy's First Winter #10, 10 vols. 2007. (Little Stinker Ser.: 10). (J). lib. bdg. 23.60 *(978-1-59381-300-0(7))* Ozark Publishing.

—Sammy's First Winter #10 (PB), 10 vols. 2007. (Little Stinker Ser.: 10). (J). pap. 10.95 *(978-1-59381-301-7(5))* Ozark Publishing.

Scotton, Rob. And the Snowy Day Surprise. Scotton, Rob, illus. 2014. (Splat the Cat Ser.). (ENG., Illus.). 16p. (J). (gr. -1-3). pap. 6.99 *(978-0-06-197864-7(7)*, HarperFestival) HarperCollins Pubs.

Shaw, Gina. Waiting for Snow. Barton, Patrice, illus. 2010. 48p. (J). pap. *(978-0-545-24385-8(8))* Scholastic, Inc.

Sherman, Marcia A. The Splendid, Blended Family. 2007. 24p. 13.95 *(978-0-615-17159-3(1))* Pumpkin Seeds Pr.

Smith, Danna. Arctic White. White, Lee, illus. 2016. (ENG.). 32p. (J). (gr. -1-3). 17.99 *(978-1-62779-104-5(3)*, 9781627791045, Holt, Henry & Co. Bks. For Young Readers) Holt, Henry & Co.

Smith, John D. H. The Whale Whisperers, 1 vol. Smith, Anne, illus. 2009. 17p. pap. 24.95 *(978-1-60749-211-5(3))* America Star Bks.

Smith, Richard B. & Bernard, Felix. Walking in a Winter Wonderland. Hopgood, Tim, illus. 2016. (ENG.). 32p. (J). 17.99 *(978-1-62779-304-9(6)*, 9781627793049, Holt, Henry & Co. Bks. For Young Readers) Holt, Henry & Co.

Snow Rabbit, Spring Rabbit: a Book of Changing Seasons. 2013. (ENG.). 24p. (J). (gr. -1 — 1). bds. 6.99 *(978-0-307-97790-8(0)*, Knopf Bks. for Young Readers) Random Hse. Children's Bks.

Sommer, Cindy. Saving Kate's Flowers, 1 vol. Klein, Laurie Allen, illus. 2016. (ENG & SPA.). 32p. (J). (gr. k-3). 17.95 *(978-1-62855-870-8(9))* Arbordale Publishing.

Spinelli, Eileen. Now It Is Winter. DePalma, Mary Newell, illus. 2004. 32p. (J). 16.00 *(978-0-8028-5244-1(0))* Eerdmans, William B. Publishing Co.

Stoick, Jean & Sams, Carl R., II, photos by. First Snow in the Woods. 2007. (ENG., Illus.). 49p. (J). (gr. -1-3). 19.95 *(978-0-9770108-6-8(4))* Sams, II, Carl R. Photography, Inc.

Stones, Yvonne. Olivia's Magical Moment. 2010. 36p. pap. 16.99 *(978-1-4490-8045-7(6))* AuthorHouse.

Strange, Jason. Zombie Winter, 1 vol. Parks, Phil, illus. 2011. (Jason Strange Ser.). (ENG.). 72p. (gr. 2-3). pap. 6.25 *(978-1-4342-3095-9(3))* Stone Arch Bks.

—Zombie Winter, 1 vol. Soleiman, Serg & Parks, Phil, illus. 2011. (Jason Strange Ser.). (ENG.). 72p. (gr. 2-3). lib. bdg. 25.32 *(978-1-4342-2964-9(5))* Stone Arch Bks.

Stringer, Lauren. Winter Is the Warmest Season. 2006. (ENG., Illus.). 40p. (J). (gr. -1-3). 16.99 *(978-0-15-204967-6(3))* Houghton Mifflin Harcourt Publishing Co.

Swenson, Jamie. Woof & Quack in Winter (reader) Sias, Ryan, illus. 2017. (Green Light Readers Level 1 Ser.). (ENG.). 32p. (J). (gr. -1-3). 12.99 ***(978-0-544-95949-1(3)***, HMH Books For Young Readers) Houghton Mifflin Harcourt Publishing Co.

Teckentrup, Britta. Sleep Tight, Little Bear. 2014. (ENG., Illus.). 40p. (J). 17.95 *(978-0-7358-4180-2(2))* North-South Bks., Inc.

Thomas, Patricia. Red Sled. Demarest, Chris L., illus. 2013. (ENG.). 32p. (J). (gr. -1-1). pap. 6.95 *(978-1-62091-592-9(8))* Boyds Mills Pr.

Thompson, Lauren. Mouse's First Snow. Erdogan, Buket, illus. 2011. (Classic Board Bks.). (ENG.). 34p. (J). (gr. -1 — 1). bds. 7.99 *(978-1-4424-2651-1(9)*, Little Simon) Little Simon.

Thornhill, Jan. Winter's Coming: A Story of Seasonal Change. Bisaillon, Josée, illus. 2014. (ENG.). 32p. (J). (gr. k-4). 16.95 *(978-1-77147-002-5(X)*, Owlkids) Owlkids Bks. Inc. CAN. Dist: Publishers Group West (PGW).

Trimble, Irene. Winter Fun for Everyone! (Disney Princess) RH Disney Staff, illus. 2015. (Pictureback(R) Ser.). (ENG.). 16p. (J). (gr. -1-2). 5.99 *(978-0-7364-3416-4(X)*, RH/Disney) Random Hse. Children's Bks.

Urbanovic, Jackie. Duck at the Door. Urbanovic, Jackie, illus. 2011. (Max the Duck Ser.: 1). (ENG., Illus.). 32p. (J). (gr. -1-2). pap. 6.99 *(978-0-06-121440-0(X))* HarperCollins Pubs.

van Genechten, Guido. Little Snowman Stan. 2011. (ENG., Illus.). 32p. (J). (gr. -1-k). 16.95 *(978-1-60537-108-5(4))* Cobblestone Publishing Co.

Van Stockum, Hilda. A Day on Skates: The Story of a Dutch Picnic. Van Stockum, Hilda, illus. 2007. (Illus.). 40p. (J). (gr. 1). 19.95 *(978-0-9721-18-0(7))* Bethlehem Bks.

Vance, Colleen. The Flip Flop Family. Kinra, Richa, illus. 2013. (ENG.). (J). (gr. -1-3). 14.95 *(978-1-62086-275-9(1))* Mascot Bks., Inc.

Vaughan, Garth. Tommy's New Block Skates, 1 vol. Smith, David Preston, illus. 2007. (ENG.). 32p. (J). (gr. -1-3). pap. 12.95 *(978-1-55109-620-9(X))* Nimbus Publishing, Ltd. CAN. Dist: Orca Bk. Pubs. USA.

Vogel, Vin. The Thing about Yetis. 2015. (ENG., Illus.). 32p. (J). (gr. -1-k). 16.99 *(978-0-8037-4170-6(7)*, Dial Bks) Penguin Young Readers Group.

Vojta, Pat Stemper. Mr. Groundhog Wants the Day Off/El Señor Marmota Quiere el Día Libre. Leviskiy, Olga, illus. 2010. (ENG & SPA.). 32p. (J). (gr. 4-7). 16.95 *(978-1-934960-77-6(2)*, Raven Tree Pr.,Csi) Continental Sales, Inc.

Wahman, Joe. Snowboy 1, 2, 3. Wahman, Wendy, illus. 2012. (ENG.). 32p. (J). (gr. -1-1). 14.99 *(978-0-8050-8732-1(X)*, 9780805087321, Holt, Henry & Co. Bks. For Young Readers) Holt, Henry & Co.

Waits, Kristine. Sweet Sam Shares. 2008. 36p. pap. 14.98 *(978-0-557-01679-2(7))* Lulu Pr., Inc.

Waldron, Kathleen Cook. Five Stars for Emily, 1 vol. 2004. (Orca Young Readers Ser.). (ENG., Illus.). 144p. (J). (gr. 3-6). pap., tchr. ed. 4.99 *(978-1-55143-296-0(X)*, 1234541) Orca Bk. Pubs. USA.

Wilder, Laura Ingalls. The Long Winter. Williams, Garth, illus. 2008. (Little House Ser.: 6). (ENG.). 352p. (J). (gr. 3-7). pap. 8.99 *(978-0-06-440006-8(9))* HarperCollins Pubs.

Willard, Nancy. A Starlit Snowfall. Pinkney, Jerry, illus. 2011. (ENG.). 32p. (J). (gr. -1-3). 6.99 *(978-0-316-18366-6(0))* Little Brown & Co.

Williamson, Greg. How Do I Cure This Cold? Popko, Wendy, illus. 2005. (J). 7.99 *(978-0-9666076-4-2(3))* Peerless Publishing, L.L.C.

Wilson, CeCe. Snow Much Fun! 2015. (Rosen REAL Readers: STEM & STEAM Collection). (ENG.). 8p. pap. 5.46 *(978-1-4994-9551-5(X)*, Rosen Classroom) Rosen Publishing Group, Inc., The.

Wilson, Karma. Dormouse Dreams. Liwska, Renata, illus. 2017. (ENG.). 40p. (J). (gr. -1-k). 16.99 *(978-1-4231-7874-3(2))* Disney Pr.

Wingart, Ramona A. Where Is Brother Beaver?, 1 vol. 2010. 30p. 24.95 *(978-1-4489-4773-7(1))* PublishAmerica, Inc.

Winter Beauty. 2005. (J). 8.00 *(978-0-9769843-0-6(X))* Simmons, Kristina.

Winter Recess. 2003. (J). *(978-1-58453-113-5(4))* Pioneer Valley Bks.

Wolff, Ashley. Baby Bear Counts One. Wolff, Ashley, illus. 2013. (Baby Bear Ser.). (ENG., Illus.). 40p. (J). (gr. -1-1). 16.99 *(978-1-4424-4158-3(5)*, Beach Lane Bks.) Beach Lane Bks.

Woods, Emily. Thingamafig B Quaxindehouse: Best Friends. 2011. 24p. pap. 12.99 *(978-1-4634-4853-0(8))* AuthorHouse.

Woodward, Caroline. Singing Away the Dark. Morstad, Julie, illus. 2011. (ENG.). 36p. (J). (gr. -1-3). 16.95 *(978-1-897476-41-3(8))* Simply Read Bks. CAN. Dist: Ingram Publisher Services.

Worcester, Daryl D. Traves Travislot's Going South for the Winter. 2011. 46p. pap. 16.95 *(978-1-4626-1091-4(9))* America Star Bks.

Wright, Maureen. Sleep, Big Bear, Sleep!, 0 vols. Hillenbrand, Will, illus. 2009. (ENG.). 32p. (J). (gr. -1-3). 16.99 *(978-0-7614-5560-8(4)*, 9780761455608, Amazon Children's Publishing) Amazon Publishing.

Yeoman, John. Bear's Winter House. Blake, Quentin, illus. 2010. (ENG.). 32p. (J). (gr. k-k). pap. 12.99 *(978-1-84270-916-0(X))* Andersen Pr. GBR. Dist: Independent Pubs. Group.

Yolen, Jane & Stemple, Heidi E. Y. Sleep, Black Bear, Sleep. Dyer, Brooke, illus. 2007. 32p. (J). (gr. -1-1). (ENG.). 15.99 *(978-0-06-081560-8(4))*; lib. bdg. 16.89 *(978-0-06-081561-5(2))* HarperCollins Pubs.

WINTER—POETRY

Hines, Anna Grossnickle. Winter Lights: A Season in Poems & Quilts. Hines, Anna Grossnickle, illus. 2005. (Illus.). 32p. (J). lib. bdg. 17.89 *(978-0-06-000818-5(0))* HarperCollins Pubs.

Prelutsky, Jack. It's Snowing! It's Snowing! Abolafia, Yossi, illus. 2007. (I Can Read Bks.). 48p. (gr. -1-3). 14.00 *(978-0-7569-8057-3(7))* Perfection Learning Corp.

Whipple, Laura. A Snowflake Fell: Poems about Winter. Hori, Hatsuki, illus. 2003. 40p. (J). 16.99 *(978-1-84148-033-6(9))* Barefoot Bks., Inc.

WINTER SPORTS

see also Hockey; Skating; Skis and Skiing

Adams, C. On My Sled: Learning the SL Sound. 2009. (PowerPhonics Ser.). 24p. (gr. 1-1). 39.90 *(978-1-60851-465-6(X)*, PowerKids Pr.) Rosen Publishing Group, Inc., The.

Bix, Jasper. Let's Go Sledding! 2016. (Winter Fun Ser.). (ENG., Illus.). 24p. (J). (gr. k-k). pap. 8.15 *(978-1-4824-3759-1(7))* Stevens, Gareth Publishing LLLP.

Butler, Erin K. Extreme Snow & Ice Sports. 2017. (Sports to the Extreme Ser.). (ENG.). 32p. (gr. 3-4). lib. bdg. 27.99 ***(978-1-5157-7859-2(2)***, Edge Bks.) Capstone Press of Coughlan Cos.

Dymock, Melissa. Sliding in the Snow: Winter Activities for Kids, 1 vol. Lee, Frances Cook, illus. 2015. (ENG.). 64p. (J). pap. 9.99 *(978-1-4236-3893-3(X))* Gibbs Smith, Publisher.

Hamilton, S. L. Iditarod. 2013. (Xtreme Races Ser.). 32p. (J). (gr. 3-9). lib. bdg. 27.07 *(978-1-61783-693-0(1)*, Abdo & Daughters) ABDO Publishing Co.

Johnson, Robin. Bobsleigh, Luge, & Skeleton. 2009. (Winter Olympic Sports Ser.). (ENG., Illus.). 32p. (J). (gr. 3-6). lib. bdg. *(978-0-7787-4024-7(2))*; (gr. 4-6). pap. *(978-0-7787-4043-8(9))* Crabtree Publishing Co.

—Ice Hockey & Curling. 2009. (Winter Olympic Sports Ser.). (ENG., Illus.). 32p. (J). (gr. 3-6). lib. bdg. *(978-0-7787-4023-0(4))* Crabtree Publishing Co.

Luke, Andrew. Snow Sports. 2017. 48p. (J). ***(978-1-4222-3708-3(7))*** Mason Crest.

Marsh, Carole. I'm Reading about the Iditarod. 2016. (I'm Reading about Ser.). (ENG., Illus.). 24p. (J). pap. 7.99 ***(978-0-635-12204-9(9))*** Gallopade International.

McClellan, Ray. Snocross. 2008. (Action Sports Ser.). (ENG., Illus.). 24p. (J). (gr. 3-7). lib. bdg. 25.95 *(978-1-60014-143-0(9))* Bellwether Media.

McKinney, John & Bailey, Diane. Snow Sports, Vol. 10. 2016. (Great Outdoors! Ser.). (Illus.). 48p. (J). (gr. 5). 20.95 *(978-1-4222-3573-7(4))* Mason Crest.

McNeil, Niki, et al. HOCPP 1143 Winter Sports. 2007. spiral bd. 14.00 *(978-1-60308-143-6(7))* In the Hands of a Child.

Rajczak, Kristen. Racing the Iditarod. 2014. (Illus.). 32p. (J). *(978-1-4824-3292-3(7)*, 1368191) Stevens, Gareth Publishing LLLP.

Rigby Education Staff. Gliders & Sliders. (Sails Literacy Ser.). (Illus.). 16p. (gr. 1-2). 27.00 *(978-0-7635-9922-5(0)*, 699220C99) Rigby Education.

Salzmann, Mary Elizabeth. Boards, Skis & Skates, 1 vol. 2012. (Sports Gear Ser.). (ENG., Illus.). 24p. (J). (gr. k-3). lib. bdg. 24.21 *(978-1-61714-824-8(5))* ABDO Publishing Co.

Sommers, Michael A. Snowmobiling: Have Fun, Be Smart. 2005. (Explore the Outdoors Ser.). (Illus.). 64p. (YA). (gr. 7-12). lib. bdg. 31.95 *(978-0-8239-3761-5(5))* Rosen Publishing Group, Inc., The.

Sticker Winter Sports. 2017. (Sticker Dressing Ser.). (ENG.). (J). pap. 9.99 ***(978-0-7945-3937-5(8)***, Usborne) EDC Publishing.

Throp, Claire. Curling, 1 vol. 2013. (Winter Sports Ser.). (ENG., Illus.). 48p. (gr. 3-6). pap. 6.95 *(978-1-4109-5455-8(2))*; 32.65 *(978-1-4109-5449-7(8))* Heinemann-Raintree.

Throp, Claire, et al. Winter Sports. 2013. (Winter Sports Ser.). (ENG.). 48p. (gr. 3-6). pap. 34.75 *(978-1-4109-5460-2(9))*; lib. bdg. 130.60 *(978-1-4109-5454-1(4))* Heinemann-Raintree.

Waxman, Laura Hamilton. Bobsled & Luge. 2017. (Winter Olympic Sports Ser.). (ENG.). 32p. (J). (gr. 2-5). pap. 9.99 *(978-1-68152-181-7(4))* Amicus.

—Bobsled & Luge. 2017. (Winter Olympic Sports Ser.). (ENG.). 32p. (gr. 1-4). 20.95 *(978-1-68151-150-4(9))* Amicus Publishing.

—Figure Skating. 2017. (Winter Olympic Sports Ser.). (ENG.). 32p. (gr. 1-4). 20.95 *(978-1-68151-148-1(7))* Amicus Publishing.

—Ice Hockey & Curling. 2017. (Winter Olympic Sports Ser.). (ENG.). 32p. (J). (gr. 2-5). pap. 9.99 *(978-1-68152-180-0(6))* Amicus.

—Ice Hockey & Curling. 2017. (Winter Olympic Sports Ser.). (ENG.). 32p. (gr. 1-4). 20.95 *(978-1-68151-149-8(5))* Amicus Publishing.

Whitelaw, Ian & Dorling Kindersley Publishing Staff. Snow Dogs! Racers of the North Level 4. 2008. (DK Readers Ser.). (ENG.). 48p. (J). (gr. 3-7). 3.99 *(978-0-7566-4081-1(4)*, DK Children) Dorling Kindersley Publishing, Inc.

WINTER SPORTS—FICTION

Blake, Robert J. Akiak: A Tale from the Iditarod. Blake, Robert J., illus. 2004. (ENG., Illus.). 40p. (J). (gr. k-3). reprint ed. pap. 7.99 *(978-0-14-240185-9(4)*, Puffin Books) Penguin Young Readers Group.

Bowes, Lisa. Lucy Tries Luge, 1 vol. Hearne, James, illus. 2015. (Lucy Tries Sports Ser.). (ENG.). 32p. (J). (gr. -1-3). pap. 12.95 *(978-1-4598-1019-8(8))* Orca Bk. Pubs. USA.

Brown, Jeff. The Intrepid Canadian Expedition. Pamintuan, Macky, illus. 2009. (Flat Stanley's Worldwide Adventures Ser.: 4). (ENG.). 112p. (J). (gr. 2-5). 15.99 *(978-0-06-142997-2(X))* HarperCollins Pubs.

—The Intrepid Canadian Expedition Vol. 4. Pamintuan, Macky, illus. 2009. (Flat Stanley's Worldwide Adventures Ser.: 4). (ENG.). 112p. (J). (gr. 2-5). pap. 4.99 *(978-0-06-142996-5(1))* HarperCollins Pubs.

Bunting, Eve. Snowboarding on Monster Mountain. Ritz, Karen, illus. 2003. (ENG.). 64p. (J). 15.95 *(978-0-8126-2704-6(0))* Cricket Bks.

Christopher, Matt. Snowboard Champ. 2004. (ENG.). 160p. (J). (gr. 3-7). pap. 16.99 *(978-0-316-79643-9(3)*, Tingley, Megan Bks.) Little, Brown Bks. for Young Readers.

Farnes, Catherine. Snowblind. 2004. 108p. (J). *(978-1-59166-329-4(6))* BJU Pr.

Ferguson, Donald. The Chums of Scranton High at Ice Hockey. 2007. 124p. per. *(978-1-4065-2361-4(5))* Dodo Pr.

—Chums of Scranton High at Ice Hockey. 2006. 25.95 *(978-1-4218-2936-4(3))*; pap. 10.95 *(978-1-4218-3036-0(1))* 1st World Publishing, Inc.

Gürth, Per-Henrik. Snowy Sports: Ready, Set, Play! Gürth, Per-Henrik, illus. 2009. (ENG., Illus.). 24p. (J). (gr. -1-2). 14.95 *(978-1-55337-367-4(7))* Kids Can Pr., Ltd. CAN. Dist: Hachette Bk. Group.

Holm, Jennifer L. & Holm, Matthew. Extreme Babymouse. Holm, Jennifer L. & Holm, Matthew, illus. 2013. (Babymouse Ser.: 17). (ENG., Illus.). 96p. (J). (gr. 2-5). lib. bdg. 12.99 *(978-0-375-97096-2(7)*, Random Hse. Bks. for Young Readers) Random Hse. Children's Bks.

Kiefer, Kit. Jake the Grizz & the World's Fastest Snowboard. 2010. (ENG.). (J). pap. *(978-0-9774802-9-6(1))* Cornerstone Pr.

Klein, Abby. Ready, Set, Snow! McKinley, John, illus. 2009. (Ready, Freddy! Ser.: 16). (ENG.). 96p. (J). (gr. -1-3). pap. 5.99 *(978-0-439-89596-5(0))* Scholastic, Inc.

Krensky, Stephen. The Three Little Pigs' Sledding Adventure. Shortley, Michele, illus. 2011. 28p. (J). pap. *(978-0-7680-3486-8(8))* SAE Intl.

Lester, Helen. Tacky & the Winter Games. Munsinger, Lynn, illus. 2007. (Tacky the Penguin Ser.). (ENG.). 32p. (J). (gr. -1-3). 6.95 *(978-0-618-95674-6(3))* Houghton Mifflin Harcourt Publishing Co.

Maddox, Jake. Half-Pipe Prize, 1 vol. Mourning, Tuesday, illus. 2009. (Jake Maddox Girl Sports Stories Ser.). (ENG.). 72p. (gr. 2-3). 25.32 *(978-1-4342-1607-6(1))* Stone Arch Bks.

Ritchey, Kate. Goofy's Sledding Contest. 2013. (Mickey & Friends World of Reading Ser.). (J). lib. bdg. 13.55 *(978-0-606-32293-5(0)*, Turtleback) Turtleback Bks.

Shaw, Gina. Waiting for Snow. Barton, Patrice, illus. 2010. 48p. (J). pap. *(978-0-545-24385-8(8))* Scholastic, Inc.

Sherman, M. Zachary. Fall Line, Vol. 3. Majado, Caio & Emery, Thomas, illus. 2011. (Tony Hawk's 900 Revolution Ser.). (ENG.). 128p. (gr. 3-4). pap. 7.19 *(978-1-4342-3453-7(3))*; lib. bdg. 26.65 *(978-1-4342-3204-5(2))* Stone Arch Bks. (Tony Hawk's 900 Revolution).

WIRE

Swanson, Jennifer. The Shocking Truth about Electricity. Lum, Bernice, illus. 2012. (LOL Physical Science Ser.). (ENG.).

32p. (gr. 3-4). pap. 47.70 *(978-1-4296-9301-1(0),* Fact Finders) Capstone Press of Coughlan Cos.

WISCONSIN

Apps, Jerry. Tents, Tigers & the Ringling Brothers. 2006. (Badger Biographies Ser.). (ENG., Illus.). 128p. (J). (gr. 3-7). per. 12.95 *(978-0-87020-374-9(6))* Wisconsin Historical Society.

Blashfield, Jean F. Wisconsin. 2014. (America the Beautiful Ser.: 3). (ENG.). 144p. (J). lib. bdg. 40.00 *(978-0-531-24874-4(7))* Scholastic Library Publishing.

Bratvold, Gretchen. Wisconsin. 2012. (J). lib. bdg. 25.26 *(978-0-7613-4518-3(3),* Lerner Pubns.) Lerner Publishing Group.

Cohen, Sheila & Terman Cohen, Sheila. Mai Ya's Long Journey. 2005. (Badger Biographies Ser.). (ENG., Illus.). 96p. (J). (gr. 3-7). per. 12.95 *(978-0-87020-365-7(7))* Wisconsin Historical Society.

Dornfeld, Margaret & Hantula, Richard. Wisconsin. 2014. (It's My State! (r) Ser.). 80p. (J). (gr. 4-8). lib. bdg. 34.21 *(978-1-62712-760-8(7))* Cavendish Square Publishing.

Flatt, Lizann. Life in a Farming Community. 2009. (Learn about Rural Life Ser.). (ENG., Illus.). 32p. (J). (gr. 3-6). pap. *(978-0-7787-5084-0(1))* Crabtree Publishing Co.

Gamble, Adam & Jasper, Mark. Count to Sleep Wisconsin. Veno, Joe, illus. 2014. (Count to Sleep Ser.). (ENG.). 20p. (J). (— 1). bds. 7.95 *(978-1-60219-328-4(2))* Good Night Bks.

Hart, Joyce & Zeinert, Karen. Wisconsin. 2nd rev. ed. 2006. (Celebrate the States Ser.). (Illus.). 144p. (gr. 6-7). lib. bdg. 42.79 *(978-0-7614-2157-3(2),* Benchmark Bks.) Marshall Cavendish Corp.

Holden, Henry M. Wisconsin: A MyReportLinks. Com Book. 2003. (States Ser.). (Illus.). 48p. (J). lib. bdg. 25.26 *(978-0-7660-5125-6(0),* MyReportLinks.com Bks.) Enslow Pubs., Inc.

Jacobson, Bob. Ole Evinrude & His Outboard Motor. 2009. (Badger Biographies Ser.). (ENG., Illus.). 78p. (J). (gr. 3-7). pap. 12.95 *(978-0-87020-420-3(3))* Wisconsin Historical Society.

Kono, Erin Eitter, illus. The Twelve Days of Christmas in Wisconsin. (Twelve Days of Christmas in America Ser.). (ENG.). (J). 2017. 22p. (— 1). bds. 7.95 ***(978-1-4549-2286-5(9))*** 2007. 40p. (gr. -1-3). 12.95 *(978-1-4027-3815-9(3))* Sterling Publishing Co., Inc.

Lantier, Patricia. Wisconsin. 2005. (Portraits of the States Ser.). (Illus.). 32p. (gr. 2-6). pap. 10.50 *(978-0-8368-4657-7(5),* Gareth Stevens Learning Library) Stevens, Gareth Publishing LLLP.

Lantier-Sampon, Patricia. Wisconsin. 2005. (Portraits of the States Ser.). (Illus.). 32p. (gr. 2-6). lib. bdg. 26.00 *(978-0-8368-4638-6(9),* Gareth Stevens Learning Library) Stevens, Gareth Publishing LLLP.

Malone, Bobbie, et al. Wisconsin: Our State, Our Story. 2016. (Illus.). x, 252p. (J). *(978-0-87020-796-9(2))* Wisconsin Historical Society.

Marsh, Carole. My First Book about Wisconsin. 2004. (Wisconsin Experience! Ser.). (Illus.). 32p. (J). (gr. k-4). pap. 7.95 *(978-0-7933-9539-2(9))* Gallopade International.

—Wisconsin Current Events Projects: 30 Cool, Activities, Crafts, Experiments & More for Kids to Do to Learn about Your State! 2003. (Wisconsin Experience Ser.). 32p. (gr. k-8). pap. 5.95 *(978-0-635-02068-0(8),* Marsh, Carole Bks.) Gallopade International.

—The Wisconsin Experience Pocket Guide. 2004. (Wisconsin Experience! Ser.). (Illus.). 96p. (J). (gr. 3-8). pap. 6.95 *(978-0-7933-9538-5(0))* Gallopade International.

—Wisconsin Geography Projects: 30 Cool, Activities, Crafts, Experiments & More for Kids to Do to Learn about Your State! 2003. (Wisconsin Experience Ser.). 32p. (gr. k-5). pap. 5.95 *(978-0-635-01867-0(5),* Marsh, Carole Bks.) Gallopade International.

—Wisconsin Government Projects: 30 Cool, Activities, Crafts, Experiments & More for Kids to Do to Learn about Your State! 2003. (Wisconsin Experience Ser.). 32p. (gr. k-5). pap. 5.95 *(978-0-635-01968-4(X),* Marsh, Carole Bks.) Gallopade International.

—Wisconsin Jeopardy! Answers & Questions about Our State! 2004. (Wisconsin Experience! Ser.). (Illus.). 32p. (J). (gr. 3-8). pap. 7.95 *(978-0-7933-9540-8(2))* Gallopade International.

—Wisconsin "Jography" A Fun Run Thru Our State! 2004. (Wisconsin Experience! Ser.). (Illus.). 32p. (J). (gr. 3-8). pap. 7.95 *(978-0-7933-9541-5(0))* Gallopade International.

—Wisconsin People Projects: 30 Cool, Activities, Crafts, Experiments & More for Kids to Do to Learn about Your State! 2003. (Wisconsin Experience Ser.). 32p. (gr. k-5). pap. 5.95 *(978-0-635-02018-5(1),* Marsh, Carole Bks.) Gallopade International.

—Wisconsin Symbols & Facts Projects: 30 Cool, Activities, Crafts, Experiments & More for Kids to Do to Learn about Your State! 2003. (Wisconsin Experience Ser.). 32p. (gr. k-5). pap. 5.95 *(978-0-635-01918-9(3),* Marsh, Carole Bks.) Gallopade International.

—Wisconsin's Big Activity Book. 2004. (Wisconsin Experience! Ser.). (Illus.). 96p. (J). (gr. 2-6). pap. 9.95 *(978-0-7933-9542-2(9))* Gallopade International.

—The Wonderful Wisconsin Coloring Book. 2004. (Wisconsin Experience! Ser.). (Illus.). 32p. (J). (gr. k-2). pap. 3.95 *(978-0-7933-9543-9(7))* Gallopade International.

Murray, Julie. Wisconsin, 1 vol. 2006. (Buddy Book Ser.). (ENG., Illus.). 32p. (gr. 2-4). 27.07 *(978-1-59197-708-7(8),* Buddy Bks.) ABDO Publishing Co.

Obregón, José María. Wisconsin. 2009. (Bilingual Library of the United States of America Ser.). (SPA.). 32p. (gr. 2-2). 47.90 *(978-1-60853-393-0(X),* Editorial Buenas Letras) Rosen Publishing Group, Inc., The.

Parker, Bridget. Wisconsin. 2016. (States Ser.). (ENG., Illus.). 32p. (gr. 3-4). lib. bdg. 27.32 *(978-1-5157-0438-6(6))* Next Page Pr., The.

Peters, S. True. How to Draw Wisconsin's Sights & Symbols. 2009. (Kid's Guide to Drawing America Ser.). 32p. (gr. k-k). 50.50 *(978-1-61511-105-3(0),* PowerKids Pr.) Rosen Publishing Group, Inc., The.

Rechner, Amy. Wisconsin. 2013. (Exploring the States Ser.). (ENG., Illus.). 32p. (J). (gr. 3-7). lib. bdg. 26.95 *(978-1-62617-050-6(9),* Blastoff! Readers) Bellwether Media.

Rosebrough, Amy & Malone, Bobbie. Water Panthers, Bears, & Thunderbirds: Exploring Wisconsin's Effigy Mounds. 2003. (New Badger History Ser.). (ENG., Illus.). 48p. (J). (gr. 4-7). pap. 9.95 *(978-0-87020-357-2(6))* Wisconsin Historical Society.

Trumbauer, Lisa. Wisconsin. 2003. (Rookie Read-About Geography Ser.). (ENG., Illus.). 32p. (J). 20.50 *(978-0-516-22745-0(9),* Children's Pr.) Scholastic Library Publishing.

Wargin, Kathy-jo. B Is for Badger: A Wisconsin Alphabet. Graef, Renee, illus. 2004. (Discover America State by State Ser.). (ENG.). 40p. (J). 17.95 *(978-1-58536-135-9(6))* Sleeping Bear Pr.

Wittekind, Erika. What's Great about Wisconsin? 2014. (Our Great States Ser.). (Illus.). 32p. (J). (gr. 2-5). lib. bdg. 26.60 *(978-1-4677-3390-8(3),* Lerner Pubns.) Lerner Publishing Group.

WISCONSIN—FICTION

Addy, Sharon. In Grandpa's Woods. Akins, Tamlyn, illus. 2004. (J). *(978-1-931599-42-9(4),* Trails Bks.) Bower Hse.

Alger, Horatio. Strive & Succeed. 2007. 172p. 24.95 *(978-1-4344-8359-1(2));* per. 14.95 *(978-1-4344-8358-4(4))* Wildside Pr., LLC.

Anderson, Jodi Lynn. The Vanishing Season. 2014. (ENG.). 272p. (YA). (gr. 9). 17.99 *(978-0-06-200327-0(5),* HarperTeen) HarperCollins Pubs.

Aryal, Aimee. Go, Pack, Go! De Angel, Miguel, illus. 2007. 24p. (J). (gr. -1-3). 14.95 *(978-1-932888-94-2(2))* Mascot Bks., Inc.

Atkinson, Elizabeth. I, Emma Freke. (Exceptional Reading & Language Arts Titles for Intermediate Grades Ser.). (ENG.). 240p. (J). (gr. 4-7). 2012. 9.95 *(978-0-7613-8500-4(2))* 2010. 16.95 *(978-0-7613-5604-2(5))* Lerner Publishing Group. (Carolrhoda Bks.).

Baker, Amanda, illus. The Cheesehead Night Before Christmas. 2007. 40p. (J). per. 19.95 *(978-0-9797781-0-0(7))* Dreams 2 Wings LLC.

Berenato, Dave. Medlocks: The Peractio Blackout. 2011. 284p. (gr. 10-12). 27.95 *(978-1-4620-5219-6(3));* pap. 17.95 *(978-1-4620-5217-2(7))* iUniverse, Inc.

Bick, Ilsa J. Draw the Dark. (Carolrhoda YA Ser.). (ENG.). 344p. (YA). (gr. 9-12). 2011. pap. 9.95 *(978-0-7613-8131-0(7))* 2010. 16.95 *(978-0-7613-5686-8(X))* Lerner Publishing Group. (Carolrhoda Lab™).

—The Sin-Eater's Confession. Elyum Studio, illus. 2014. (ENG.). 296p. (YA). (gr. 9-12). pap. 9.95 *(978-1-4677-3705-0(4),* Carolrhoda Lab™) Lerner Publishing Group.

—The Sin-Eater's Confession. 2013. (ENG.). 296p. (YA). (gr. 9-12). 17.95 *(978-0-7613-5687-5(8))* Lerner Publishing Group.

Birdsall, Bridget. Double Exposure. 2014. (ENG.). 304p. (J). (gr. 6). 16.95 *(978-1-62914-606-5(4),* Sky Pony Pr.) Skyhorse Publishing Co., Inc.

Bjornson, Nancy. Sleds, Skins & Snow. 2007. (J). *(978-1-930596-83-2(9))* Amherst Pr.

Brink, Carol Ryrie. Caddie Woodlawn. 2006. (ENG., Illus.). 288p. (J). (gr. 3-7). pap. 7.99 *(978-1-4169-4028-9(6),* Aladdin) Simon & Schuster Children's Publishing.

Brookins, Cara. Doris Free. Barrow, Ann, illus. 2006. 127p. (J). pap. *(978-1-59336-333-8(8))* Mondo Publishing.

Busteed, Kerri J. Will's Bow Hunting Adventure. Byers, Leon, illus. 2012. 108p. pap. 30.00 *(978-1-61897-207-1(3),* Strategic Bk. Publishing) Strategic Book Publishing & Rights Agency (SBPRA).

Cameron, Ann. The Secret Life of Amanda K. Woods. 2014. (ENG.). 208p. (J). (gr. 5-9). pap. 6.99 *(978-1-250-04419-8(7),* 9781250044198) Square Fish.

Carter, Alden R. Up Country. 2004. (ENG.). 256p. (YA). (gr. 7-5). 7.99 *(978-0-14-240243-6(5),* Speak) Penguin Young Readers Group.

—Walkaway. 2008. (ENG.). 192p. (YA). (gr. 7-18). 16.95 *(978-0-8234-2106-0(6))* Holiday Hse., Inc.

Charbonneau, Joelle. Need. 2017. (ENG.). 352p. (YA). (gr. 7). pap. 9.99 *(978-0-544-93883-0(6),* HMH Books For Young Readers) Houghton Mifflin Harcourt Publishing Co.

Clarissa - Evaluation Guide: Evaluation Guide. 2006. (J). *(978-1-55942-402-8(8))* Witcher Productions.

Cumbie, Patricia. Where People Like Us Live. 2008. 224p. (YA). (gr. 7-18). lib. bdg. 17.89 *(978-0-06-137598-9(5),* Geringer, Laura Book) HarperCollins Pubs.

Daly, Maureen. Seventeenth Summer. 2010. (ENG.). 384p. (YA). (gr. 7). pap. 9.99 *(978-1-4169-9463-3(7),* Simon Pulse) Simon Pulse.

Enright, Elizabeth. Thimble Summer. 2006. 21.75 *(978-0-8446-7281-6(5))* Smith, Peter Pub., Inc.

—Thimble Summer. Enright, Elizabeth, illus. 2008. (ENG., Illus.). 144p. (J). (gr. 3-7). pap. 6.99 *(978-0-312-38002-1(X),* 9780312380021) Square Fish.

Erdrich, Louise. The Porcupine Year. Erdrich, Louise, illus. 2010. (Birchbark House Ser.: 3). (Illus.). 224p. (J). (gr. 3-7). pap. 6.99 *(978-0-06-441030-4(7))* HarperCollins Pubs.

Farrey, Brian. With or Without You. 2011. (ENG., Illus.). 368p. (YA). (gr. 11-18). pap. 8.99 *(978-1-4424-0699-5(2),* Simon Pulse) Simon Pulse.

Fleming, Vicki & Dipietro, Kara. North Woods Numbers. 2010. 28p. pap. 13.99 *(978-1-4490-8420-2(6))* AuthorHouse.

Freeman, Meryl. The Voyages of Galley Cat. 2008. 36p. pap. 24.95 *(978-1-60474-632-7(7))* America Star Bks.

Gliori, Debi. No Matter What. 2017. (ENG., Illus.). 24p. (J). (— 1). bds. 8.99 *(978-0-544-91584-8(4),* HMH Books For Young Readers) Houghton Mifflin Harcourt Publishing Co.

Goodman, Gabriel. Plague Riders. 2012. (After the Dust Settled Ser.). (ENG.). 112p. (YA). (gr. 6-12). pap. 7.95 *(978-0-8225-9033-0(6),* Darby Creek); lib. bdg. 27.93 *(978-0-7613-8330-7(1))* Lerner Publishing Group.

Groethe, Kd. The Virtual Adventures of Megan & Timmy. 2012. 230p. (gr. 4-6). 27.99 *(978-1-4685-5050-4(0));* pap. 16.95 *(978-1-4685-5049-8(7))* AuthorHouse.

Hannigan, Katherine. Ida B: ... And Her Plans to Maximize Fun, Avoid Disaster, & (Possibly) Save the World. 2004. 256p. (gr. 4-18). lib. bdg. 16.89 *(978-0-06-073025-3(0));* (ENG.). (J). 17.99 *(978-0-06-073024-6(2),* Greenwillow Bks.) HarperCollins Pubs.

—Ida B: And Her Plans to Maximize Fun Avoid Disaster, & (Possibly) Save the World. 2011. (ENG.). 272p. (J). (gr. 5-9). reprint ed. pap. 6.99 *(978-0-06-073026-0(9),* Greenwillow Bks.) HarperCollins Pubs.

Hawke, Jay Jordan. Onwaachige the Dreamer. 2016. (ENG., Illus.). (YA). 24.99 ***(978-1-63533-058-8(0),*** Harmony Ink Pr.) Dreamspinner Pr.

Henkes, Kevin. Bird Lake Moon. (ENG.). 192p. (J). (gr. 3-7). 2010. pap. 5.99 *(978-0-06-147079-0(1))* 2008. 17.99 *(978-0-06-147076-9(7))* HarperCollins Pubs. (Greenwillow Bks.).

Henkes, Kevin. The Year of Billy Miller. Henkes, Kevin, illus. 2013. (Illus.). 240p. (J). (gr. 3-7). (ENG.). 16.99 *(978-0-06-226812-9(0));* lib. bdg. 17.89 *(978-0-06-226813-6(9))* HarperCollins Pubs. (Greenwillow Bks.).

—The Year of Billy Miller. Henkes, Kevin, illus. 2015. (ENG., Illus.). (J). (gr. 3-7). lib. bdg. 17.60 ***(978-1-62765-762-4(2))*** Perfection Learning Corp.

—The Year of Billy Miller. 2015. (J). lib. bdg. 17.20 *(978-0-606-36977-0(5))* Turtleback Bks.

Hijuelos, Oscar. Dark Dude. 2009. (ENG., Illus.). 464p. (YA). (gr. 8-18). pap. 12.99 *(978-1-4169-4945-9(3),* Atheneum Bks. for Young Readers) Simon & Schuster Children's Publishing.

Hijuelos, Óscar & Óscar, Hijuelos. Dark Dude. Roja, Alberto Jimenez, tr. 2010. (SPA.). 430p. (YA). (gr. 9-18). 19.99 *(978-84-441-4316-3(2))* Everest Editora ESP. Dist: Lectorum Pubns., Inc.

Hysen, Sylvia. A Very Dairy Christmas. 2005. 290p. 24.95 *(978-0-9763365-6-3(1))* 1st Impression Publishing.

Jacobs, Lily. The Littlest Bunny in Wisconsin: An Easter Adventure. 2015. (ENG.). 32p. (J). (-3). 9.99 *(978-1-4926-1240-7(5),* Sourcebooks Jabberwocky) Sourcebooks, Inc.

James, Eric. A Halloween Scare in Wisconsin. Le Ray, Marina, illus. 2014. (ENG.). 32p. (J). (-5). 9.99 *(978-1-4926-0642-0(1),* 9781492606420, Sourcebooks Jabberwocky) Sourcebooks, Inc.

—Santa's Sleigh Is on Its Way to Wisconsin. Dunn, Robert, illus. 2015. (ENG.). 32p. (J). (-2). 12.99 *(978-1-4926-2755-5(0),* Sourcebooks Jabberwocky) Sourcebooks, Inc.

James, Steven. Blur, 0 vols. 2014. (Blur Trilogy Ser.: 1). (ENG.). 368p. (YA). (gr. 7-12). pap. 9.99 *(978-1-4778-4727-5(8),* 9781477847275, Amazon Children's Publishing) Amazon Publishing.

Johnson, Lois Walfrid. The Creeping Shadows. 2009. (Orig.). (J). 8.99 *(978-0-88062-277-6(6))* Mott Media.

—Disaster on Windy Hill. 2009. (J). 8.99 *(978-0-88062-284-4(9))* Mott Media.

—Grandpa's Stolen Treasure. 2009. (Orig.). (J). 8.99 *(978-0-88062-281-3(4))* Mott Media.

—The Runaway Clown. 2009. (Orig.). (J). 8.99 *(978-0-88062-282-0(2))* Mott Media.

—Trouble at Wild River. 2009. (J). 8.99 *(978-0-88062-279-0(2))* Mott Media.

Kopetz, Mark. Red Herrings at Rock Island: A Door County Mystery. 2005. 15.00 *(978-0-940473-42-3(9))* Caxton, Wm Ltd.

LaBree Stute, Lela. The Sunnyset Pugs. 2010. 34p. pap. 19.99 *(978-0-557-41751-3(1))* Lulu Pr., Inc.

Liebig, Nelda Johnson. Carrie & the Boarding House. 2005. 127p. (J). (gr. 3-7). 10.95 *(978-1-883953-35-5(9))* Great Lakes Literary, LLC.

Maddox, Jake. Snowboard Struggle. 2016. (Jake Maddox JV Ser.). (ENG., Illus.). 96p. (gr. 3-4). lib. bdg. 25.99 *(978-1-4965-3980-9(X))* Stone Arch Bks.

Maxwell, William. The Heavenly Tenants. Karasz, Ilonka, illus. 2017. (ENG.). 64p. 16.95 *(978-0-486-81529-9(3))* Dover Pubns., Inc.

Meaney, Flynn. The Boy Recession. 2012. (ENG.). 256p. (YA). (gr. 10-17). 17.99 *(978-0-316-10213-1(X),* Poppy) Little, Brown Bks. for Young Readers.

Merkel, Ruth Vitrano. Ann: 1833-1897. 2006. (Hannah's Girls Ser.). (Illus.). 112p. (J). (gr. 4-7). per. 9.99 *(978-0-8280-1951-4(7))* Review & Herald Publishing Assn.

—Grace: 1890-1973, 6. 2006. (Hannah's Girls Ser.). (Illus.). 128p. (J). (gr. 4-7). per. 9.99 *(978-0-8280-1953-8(3))* Review & Herald Publishing Assn.

—Marilla 1851-1916, 6 bks. 2006. (Hannah's Girls Ser.). (Illus.). 144p. (J). (gr. 4-7). per. 9.99 *(978-0-8280-1952-1(5))* Review & Herald Publishing Assn.

—Ruthie: Born 1931. 2007. (Hannah's Girls Ser.). (Illus.). 144p. (J). (gr. 4-7). per. 9.99 *(978-0-8280-1954-5(1))* Review & Herald Publishing Assn.

Miller-Lachmann, Lyn. Gringolandia. 2009. (ENG.). 288p. (YA). (gr. 9-18). 18.95 *(978-1-931896-49-8(6))* Curbstone Pr.

Murdock, Catherine Gilbert. Front & Center. 2011. (ENG.). 288p. (YA). (gr. 7). pap. 8.99 *(978-0-547-40305-2(4))* Houghton Mifflin Harcourt Publishing Co.

—Heaven Is Paved with Oreos. (ENG.). 208p. (J). (gr. 5-7). 2015. pap. 6.99 *(978-0-544-43932-0(5),* HMH Books For Young Readers) 2013. 16.99 *(978-0-547-62538-6(3))* Houghton Mifflin Harcourt Publishing Co.

Nation, Kay. Jamie Learns to Love. 2006. pap. 10.00 *(978-1-4257-0534-3(0))* Xlibris Corp.

Nelson, Bruce. Captain Black Licorice. 2004. (Illus.). 60p. (J). per. 7.95 *(978-1-59466-026-9(3))* Port Town Publishing.

Olin, Sean. Killing Britney. 2005. (ENG.). 240p. (YA). (gr. 9-12). pap. 9.99 *(978-0-689-87778-0(1),* Simon Pulse) Simon Pulse.

Oliver, Andrew. Haunted Hill. 2006. (Sam & Stephanie Mystery Ser.). 268p. (J). (gr. 5-9). per. 12.95 *(978-0-9661009-7-6(2))* Adams-Pomeroy Pr.

—If Photos Could Talk. 2005. (Sam & Stephanie Mystery Ser.). 264p. (J). per. 12.95 *(978-0-9661009-6-9(4))* Adams-Pomeroy Pr.

—Scrambled. 2007. 288p. (J). per. 12.95 *(978-0-9661009-8-3(0))* Adams-Pomeroy Pr.

Paulsen, Gary. The Island. 2006. (Point Ser.). 202p. (gr. 7-12). 16.00 *(978-0-7569-6382-8(6))* Perfection Learning Corp.

Pellowski, Anne. First Farm in the Valley: Anna's Story. Sharpe, Roseanne, illus. 2008. 194p. (J). pap. 12.95 *(978-1-932350-24-1(1))* Bethlehem Bks.

Pferdehirt, Julia. Wisconsin Forest Tales. 2004. (Illus.). vii, 152p. (J). *(978-1-931599-47-4(5),* Trails Bks.) Bower Hse.

Qualey, Marsha. Thin Ice. 2007. (YA). *(978-0-9793444-0-4(9))* Quercus Pr.

Riordan, Robert. Medicine for Wildcat: A Story of the Friendship between a Menominee Indian & Frontier Priest Samuel Mazzuchelli. 2006. (Illus.). 132p. (YA). per. 14.95 *(978-0-9774934-0-1(7))* Sinsinawa Dominicans, Inc.

Rousselow, Jeff. Bury the Dead. 2009. 244p. pap. 15.26 *(978-0-557-07129-6(1))* Lulu Pr., Inc.

Sales, Leila. Once Was a Time: An Alliteration Adventure. 2016. (ENG., Illus.). 272p. (J). (gr. 5-17). 16.99 *(978-1-4521-4009-4(X))* Chronicle Bks. LLC.

Schaefer, Laura. The Secret Ingredient. Rim, Sujean, illus. (ENG.). 240p. (J). (gr. 4-8). 2012. pap. 6.99 *(978-1-4424-1960-5(1))* 2011. 15.99 *(978-1-4424-1959-9(8))* Simon & Schuster/Paula Wiseman Bks. (Simon & Schuster/Paula Wiseman Bks.).

—The Teashop Girls. Rim, Sujean, illus. 2009. (ENG.). 272p. (J). (gr. 4-9). pap. 6.99 *(978-1-4169-6794-1(X),* Simon & Schuster/Paula Wiseman Bks.) Simon & Schuster/Paula Wiseman Bks.

Silvano, Wendi. Love Is All Around Wisconsin. Czernichowska, Joanna, illus. 2016. (ENG.). 32p. (J). (-6). 12.99 *(978-1-4926-2975-7(8),* Sourcebooks Jabberwocky) Sourcebooks, Inc.

Smallman, Steve. Santa Is Coming to Green Bay. Dunn, Robert, illus. 2013. (ENG.). 32p. (J). (-3). 9.99 *(978-1-4022-9112-8(4),* Sourcebooks Jabberwocky) Sourcebooks, Inc.

—Santa Is Coming to the Wisconsin Dells. Dunn, Robert, illus. 2015. (ENG.). 32p. (J). (-3). 9.99 *(978-1-4926-2661-9(9),* Sourcebooks Jabberwocky) Sourcebooks, Inc.

—Santa Is Coming to Wisconsin. Dunn, Robert, illus. 2012. (ENG.). 32p. (J). (-3). 9.99 *(978-1-4022-7533-3(1),* Sourcebooks Jabberwocky) Sourcebooks, Inc.

Smith, Jennifer E. The Storm Makers. Helquist, Brett, illus. 2013. (ENG.). 384p. (J). (gr. 3-7). pap. 8.00 *(978-0-316-17959-1(0))* Little, Brown Bks. for Young Readers.

Soileau, Hodges, illus. The Mystery of the Runaway Ghost. 2004. (Boxcar Children Mysteries Ser.: 98). (ENG.). 144p. (J). (gr. 1-5). pap. 5.99 *(978-0-8075-5551-4(7))* Whitman, Albert & Co.

Stanton, Angie. Rock & a Hard Place. 2013. (Jamieson Brothers Ser.: 1). (ENG.). 304p. (YA). (gr. 9). pap. 9.99 *(978-0-06-227254-6(3),* HarperTeen) HarperCollins Pubs.

—Snapshot. 2013. (Jamieson Brothers Ser.: 2). (ENG.). 416p. (YA). (gr. 9). pap. 9.99 *(978-0-06-227256-0(X),* HarperTeen) HarperCollins Pubs.

—Under the Spotlight. 2015. (Jamieson Brothers Ser.: 3). (ENG.). 400p. (YA). (gr. 8). pap. 9.99 *(978-0-06-227260-7(8),* HarperTeen) HarperCollins Pubs.

—Waking in Time. 2017. (ENG.). 360p. (gr. 9-12). 17.95 *(978-1-63079-070-7(2))* Switch Pr.

Sully, Katherine. Night-Night Wisconsin. Kolanovic, Dubravka & Poole, Helen, illus. 2016. (ENG.). 20p. (J). (-1). bds. 9.99 *(978-1-4926-4217-6(7),* 9781492642176, Sourcebooks Jabberwocky) Sourcebooks, Inc.

Timberlake, Amy. One Came Home. (ENG., Illus.). 272p. (J). 2014. (gr. 5-7). 7.99 *(978-0-375-87345-4(7),* Yearling) 2013. (gr. 4-7). 16.99 *(978-0-375-86925-9(5),* Knopf Bks. for Young Readers) Random Hse. Children's Bks.

Tougas, Shelley. Finders Keepers. 2015. (ENG.). 288p. (J). (gr. 3-7). 16.99 *(978-1-59643-990-0(4),* 9781596439900) Roaring Brook Pr.

—Finders Keepers. 2016. (ENG.). 304p. (J). (gr. 3-7). 18.40 *(978-0-606-39290-7(4))* Turtleback Bks.

Wargin, Kathy-jo. The Legend of Old Abe: A Civil War Eagle. Caple, Laurie, illus. 2006. (Legend (Sleeping Bear) Ser.). (ENG.). 40p. (J). (gr. 3-7). 17.95 *(978-1-58536-232-5(8))* Sleeping Bear Pr.

Wilder, Laura Ingalls. Little House in the Big Woods. Williams, Garth, illus. 2008. (Little House Ser.: 1). (ENG.). 256p. (J). (gr. 3-7). pap. 7.99 *(978-0-06-440001-5(8))* HarperCollins Pubs.

—Little House in the Big Woods. 2007. (Little House Ser.). 224p. (J). (gr. 3-7). pap. 6.99 *(978-0-06-088537-3(8),* Harper Trophy) HarperCollins Pubs.

Wilkes, Maria D. Little House in Brookfield. abr. ed. 2007. (Little House Ser.). (ENG.). 144p. (J). (gr. 3-7). pap. 6.99 *(978-0-06-114821-7(0))* HarperCollins Pubs.

—Little Town at the Crossroads. 2007. (Little House Ser.). 159p. (J). (gr. 3-7). per. 5.99 *(978-0-06-114822-4(9),* Harper Trophy) HarperCollins Pubs.

Wright, Betty Ren. Crandalls' Castle. 2005. (ENG.). 184p. (YA). (gr. 4-6). tchr. ed. 17.95 *(978-0-8234-1726-1(3))* Holiday Hse., Inc.

WISCONSIN—HISTORY

Ball, Jacqueline A. Wildfire! The 1871 Peshtigo Firestorm. 2005. (X-Treme Disasters That Changed America Ser.). 32p. (J). lib. bdg. 25.27 *(978-1-59716-011-7(3))* Bearport Publishing Co., Inc.

Bollow, Ludmilla. Lulu's Christmas Story: A True Story of Faith & Hope During the Great Depression. 2014. (ENG.). 256p. 22.95 *(978-0-9911938-5-1(7))* Titletown Publishing, LLC.

Carole Marsh. Wisconsin Indians. 2004. (Wisconsin Experience Ser.). 36p. (gr. 3-8). 29.95 *(978-0-635-02343-8(1));* pap. 7.95 *(978-0-635-02342-1(3))* Gallopade International.

Davis, Susan Burdick. Old Forts & Real Folks. 2006. pap. 31.95 *(978-1-4286-5582-9(4))* Kessinger Publishing, LLC.

Dornfeld, Margaret & Hantula, Richard. Wisconsin. 2nd rev. ed. 2010. (It's My State! Ser.). 80p. (gr. 3-18). lib. bdg. 31.36 *(978-1-60870-062-2(3))* Marshall Cavendish Corp.

Galiano, Dean. Wisconsin. Brusca, Maria Cristina, tr. from ENG. 2006. (Bilingual Library of the United States of America Ser.: Set 2). (ENG & SPA., Illus.). 32p. (J). (gr. 3-6). lib. bdg. 25.25 *(978-1-4042-3115-3(3))* Rosen Publishing Group, Inc., The.

Gamble, Jasper, et al. Good Night Wisconsin. Jasper, Mark & Kelly, Cooper, illus. 2012. (Good Night Our World Ser.). (ENG.). 20p. (J). (gr. k — 1). bds. 9.95 *(978-1-60219-064-1(X))* Good Night Bks.

Henry, Marcia. Madeline Island ABC Coloring Book. Parsons, Sally, illus. 2008. (ENG.). 32p. (J). (gr. k-6). pap. 6.95 *(978-0-9817723-0-1(7))* Univ. of Wisconsin Pr.

Henry, Marcia Kierland. Madeline Island ABC Book. Parsons, Sally, illus. 2008. (ENG.). 32p. (J). (gr. -1-4). pap. 18.95 *(978-1-4243-3753-8(4))* Univ. of Wisconsin Pr.

W X Y Z

Heos, Bridget. Wisconsin: Past & Present. 2009. (J). 70.50 (978-1-4358-5585-4(X)); pap. 11.75 (978-1-4358-5584-7(1)); (ENG., Illus.). 48p. lib. bdg. 29.25 (978-1-4358-5293-8(1)) Rosen Publishing Group, Inc., The. (Rosen Reference).

Holliday, Diane Young & Malone, Bobbie. Digging & Discovery: Wisconsin Archaeology. 2nd ed. 2006. (New Badger History Ser.). (Illus.). 120p. (gr. 2-7). pap. 15.95 (978-0-87020-376-3(2)) Wisconsin Historical Society.

Holtz, Monica Stauber. Behind the Zoo: Find Out What the Animals Eat & Do at Irvine Park Zoo, Chippewa Falls, Wisconsin. Opatz, Shane, illus. Opatz, Shane, photos by. 2011. (J). (978-0-9837617-1-6(X)) Holtz Creative Enterprises.

Hunt, Nancy Nye & Bradley, Nina Leopold. Aldo Leopold's Shack: Nina's Story. 2011. (Center for American Places - Center Books on American Places Ser.). (ENG., Illus.). 88p. 29.95 (978-1-935195-17-7(4)) Ctr. for American Places, Inc.

Jerome, Kate B. Lucky to Live in Wisconsin. 2017. (Arcadia Kids Ser.). (ENG., Illus.). 32p. (J). 16.99 (978-0-7385-2787-1(4)) Arcadia Publishing.

—The Wise Animal Handbook Wisconsin. 2017. (Arcadia Kids Ser.). (ENG., Illus.). 32p. (J). 16.99 (978-0-7385-2849-6(8)) Arcadia Publishing.

Knickelbine, Scott. The Great Peshtigo Fire: Stories & Science from America's Deadliest Fire. 2012. (ENG., Illus.). 88p. (J). pap. 15.95 (978-0-87020-499-9(8)) Wisconsin Historical Society.

Loew, Patty, et al. Native People of Wisconsin, Rev. TG & Student Materials. 2016. (New Badger History Ser.). (ENG.). (J). (gr. 4-6). cd-rom 49.95 (978-0-87020-749-5(0)) Wisconsin Historical Society.

Lorbiecki, Marybeth. Things Natural, Wild, & Free: The Life of Aldo Leopold. 2011. (ENG., Illus.). 112p. (J). (gr. 4-7). pap. 12.95 (978-1-55591-474-5(8)) Fulcrum Publishing.

Lusted, Marcia Amidon. Wisconsin: The Badger State. (Illus.). 24p. (J). 2010. pap. 8.25 (978-1-4358-3366-1(X)) 2009. lib. bdg. 22.60 (978-1-4042-8120-2(7)) Rosen Publishing Group, Inc., The. (PowerKids Pr.).

Malone, Bobbie. Learning from the Land: Wisconsin Land Use. 2nd ed. 2011. (New Badger History Ser.). (ENG.). 160p. (J). pap. 15.95 (978-0-87020-464-7(5)) Wisconsin Historical Society.

—Wisconsin: Our State, Our Story. 2008. (J). pap. (978-0-87020-396-1(7)) Wisconsin Historical Society.

Malone, Bobbie & Oberle, Kori. Wisconsin: Our State, Our Story. 2008. (Illus.). x, 246p. (J). (978-0-87020-512-5(9)) Wisconsin Historical Society.

Manger, Barbara & Smith, Janine. Mary Nohl: A Lifetime in Art. 2013. (Badger Biographies Ser.). (ENG., Illus.). 128p. (J). pap. 12.95 (978-0-87020-577-4(3)) Wisconsin Historical Society.

Marsh, Carole. Exploring Wisconsin Through Project-Based Learning: Geography, History, Government, Economics & More. 2016. (Wisconsin Experience Ser.). (ENG.). (J). pap. 9.99 (978-0-635-12373-2(8)) Gallopade International.

—Wisconsin History Projects: 30 Cool, Activities, Crafts, Experiments & More for Kids to Do to Learn about Your State! 2003. (Wisconsin Experience Ser.). 32p. (gr. k-5). pap. 5.95 (978-0-635-01818-2(7), Marsh, Carole Bks.) Gallopade International.

Ollhoff, Jim. Wisconsin, 1 vol. 2009. (United States Ser.). (ENG., Illus.). 48p. (YA). (gr. 2-5). 27.07 (978-1-60453-686-7(1)) ABDO Publishing Co.

O'Neill, Elizabeth. Alfred Visits Wisconsin. 2009. 24p. (J). pap. 12.00 (978-0-9841507-0-0(6)) Lipp, G. Douglas & Assocs.

Parker, Janice. Wisconsin. 2011. (Guide to American States Ser.). (Illus.). 48p. (YA). (gr. 3-6). 29.99 (978-1-61690-823-2(8)); (978-1-61690-498-2(4)) Weigl Pubs., Inc.

Parker, Janice. Wisconsin: The Badger State. 2016. (J). (978-1-5105-2101-8(1)) SmartBook Media, Inc.

—Wisconsin: The Badger State. 2016. (J). (978-1-4896-4965-2(4)) Weigl Pubs., Inc.

Peterson, Sheryl. Wisconsin. 2009. (This Land Called America Ser.). (Illus.). 32p. (YA). (gr. 3-6). 19.95 (978-1-58341-802-4(4)) Creative Co., The.

Pferdehirt, Julia. Freedom Train North: Stories of the Underground Railroad in Wisconsin. Butler, Jerry, illus. Date not set. (J). (gr. 3-8). pap. 10.00 (978-0-9664925-0-7(1)) Living History Pr.

Pratt, Laura. Wisconsin: The Badger State. 2012. (J). (978-1-61913-419-5(5)); pap. (978-1-61913-420-1(9)) Weigl Pubs., Inc.

Tieck, Sarah. Wisconsin, 1 vol. 2012. (Explore the United States Ser.). (ENG.). 32p. (J). (gr. 2-5). lib. bdg. 28.50 (978-1-61783-389-2(4), Big Buddy Bks.) ABDO Publishing Co.

Uschan, Michael V. Wisconsin. 2003. (Seeds of a Nation Ser.). (Illus.). 48p. (J). (gr. 3-5). 23.70 (978-0-7377-1481-4(6), Kidhaven) Cengage Gale.

Wargin, Kathy-jo. Little Wisconsin. 2012. (My Little State Ser.). (ENG., Illus.). 20p. (J). (gr. k-3). 9.95 (978-1-58536-209-7(3)) Sleeping Bear Pr.

Wittekind, Erika. What's Great about Wisconsin? 2014. (Our Great States Ser.). (ENG., Illus.). 32p. (gr. 2-5). pap. 7.95 (978-1-4677-4540-6(5)) Lerner Publishing Group.

Ziff, John. Western Great Lakes: Illinois, Minnesota, Wisconsin, Vol. 19. 2015. (Let's Explore the States Ser.). (Illus.). 64p. (J). (gr. 5). 23.95 (978-1-4222-3338-2(3)) Mason Crest.

WISHBONE (FICTITIOUS CHARACTER)—FICTION

Williamson, Barbara. Wishbone. 2007. (Illus.). 24p. (J). per. 12.95 (978-1-60002-197-8(2), 4216) Mountain Valley Publishing, LLC.

Worley, Roger. The Wishbone Journal. 2003. 173p. pap. 24.95 (978-1-4137-0101-2(9)) America Star Bks.

WIT AND HUMOR

see also Comedy; Humorists; Nonsense Verses; Satire
also American Wit and Humor; English Wit and Humor

Aalgaard, Wendy. Venezuela in Pictures. 2nd ed. 2004. (Visual Geography Series, Second Ser.). (ENG., Illus.). 80p. (gr. 5-12). lib. bdg. 31.93 (978-0-8225-1172-4(X)) Lerner Publishing Group.

ABDO Publishing Company. Jokes, 6 vols. 2004. (Jokes Ser.). (gr. k-4). 205.20 (978-1-59197-619-6(7), Buddy Bks.) ABDO Publishing Co.

ABDO Publishing Company Staff. Jokes & More Jokes! Set Of 8. 2005. (More Jokes! Ser.). (Illus.). (gr. k-4). 205.20 (978-1-59197-869-5(6), Buddy Bks.) ABDO Publishing Co.

Andreu Iglesias, Cesar & Hernández, Juan A. A Mal Tiempo, Buena Cara: El Humor en el Periodismo Puertorriqueño. I.t. ed. 2003. (SPA., Illus.). 48p. pap. (978-0-9743102-0-6(4)) Casa de Periodistas Editorial.

Angleberger, Tom. To Kick a Corpse: The Qwikpick Papers. 2017. (Qwikpick Papers). (ENG., Illus.). 176p. (J). (gr. 3-7). pap. 6.95 (978-1-4197-2376-6(6), Amulet Bks.) Abrams, Inc.

Applesauce Press, Applesauce. Stump the Grown-Up. 2016. (ENG.). 256p. (J). (gr. 2). pap. 10.95 (978-1-60433-656-6(0), Applesauce Pr.) Cider Mill Pr. Bk. Pubs., LLC.

Applesauce Press Staff, et al. Gut Busters! Over 600 Jokes That Pack a Punch... ; Line! 2012. (ENG.). 160p. (J). (gr. 3). pap. 5.95 (978-1-60433-273-5(5), Applesauce Pr.) Cider Mill Pr. Bk. Pubs., LLC.

—Side Splitters: Over 600 Funtastic Jokes & Riddles. 2012. (ENG.). 160p. (J). (gr. 3). pap. 5.95 (978-1-60433-274-2(3), Applesauce Pr.) Cider Mill Pr. Bk. Pubs., LLC.

Arcturus Publishing. The Big Book of Kids Jokes. 2016. (ENG.). 128p. (J). pap. 12.95 (978-1-78599-812-6(9), 9781785998126) Arcturus Publishing GBR. Dist: Bookmasters Distribution.

ARISE Foundation Staff. Life Skills Curriculum: ARISE Life Isn't Fair (Instructor's Manual) 2011. 78p. (J). pap. 29.95 (978-1-58614-296-4(8)) Arise Foundation.

Artell, Mike. Ten-Second Tongue Twisters. Jones, Buck, illus. 2010. (ENG.). 96p. (J). pap. 4.95 (978-1-4027-7858-2(9)) Sterling Publishing Co., Inc.

Austen, Catherine. 26 Tips for Surviving Grade 6, 1 vol. 2011. (ENG., Illus.). 168p. (J). (gr. 5-7). 16.95 (978-1-55277-925-5(4), 9781552779255); pap. 9.95 (978-1-55277-924-8(6), 9781552779248) Lorimer, James & Co., Ltd., Pubs. CAN. Dist: Casemate Pubs. & Bk. Distributors, LLC.

Balestier, Courtney. Would You Rather... ? Super Secrets! Over 300 Fiercely Fascinating Questions to Ask Your Friends. Heimberg, Justin & Gomberg, David, eds. 2011. (Would You Rather... ? Ser.). (ENG.). 192p. (gr. 4-9). pap. 9.95 (978-1-934734-69-8(1)) Seven Footer Pr.

Barfield, Mike. The Ultimate Wisecrack Generator: Over 60 Million Hilarious Zingers & Stingers. 2017. (ENG.). 100p. (J). (gr. 1-4). 14.99 (978-1-78627-030-6(7)) King, Laurence Publishing GBR. Dist: Hachette Bk. Group.

Barlow, Steve L. & Skidmore, Steve. The Lost Title of Shakespeare's Ghost Play. 2011. (ENG., Illus.). 128p. (J). pap. 7.99 (978-0-00-694588-8(0), HarperCollins Children's Bks.) HarperCollins Pubs. Ltd. GBR. Dist: HarperCollins Pubs.

Barnham, Kay & Connolly, Sean. The Laugh Out Loud Joke Book. 2012. (ENG., Illus.). 128p. (J). pap. 9.95 (978-1-84858-106-7(8)) Arcturus Publishing GBR. Dist: Bookmasters Distribution.

Barrett, Judi. Animals Should Definitely Not Wear Clothing. Barrett, Ron, illus. 2012. (Classic Board Bks.). (ENG.). 36p. (J). (gr. -1 — 1). bds. 7.99 (978-1-4424-3334-2(5), Little Simon) Little Simon.

—Animals Should Definitely Not Wear Clothing. Barrett, Ron, illus. 2006. (ENG.). 32p. (J). (gr. -1-2). 4.99 (978-1-4169-1232-3(0), Simon & Schuster/Paula Wiseman Bks.) Simon & Schuster/Paula Wiseman Bks.

Bathroom Readers' Institute Staff. Funniest Joke Book Ever! 2016. (ENG., Illus.). 128p. (J). (gr. 1). pap. 4.99 (978-1-62686-584-6(1), Portable Pr.) Readerlink Distribution Services, LLC.

—The Grossest Joke Book Ever! 2016. (ENG., Illus.). 128p. (J). (gr. 1). pap. 4.99 (978-1-62686-585-3(X), Portable Pr.) Readerlink Distribution Services, LLC.

—Uncle John's Smell-O-Scopic Bathroom Reader for Kids Only! 2013. (ENG., Illus.). 288p. (J). (gr. 2-7). pap. 12.95 (978-1-60710-780-4(5), Portable Pr.) Readerlink Distribution Services, LLC.

—Uncle John's Top Secret Bathroom Reader for Kids Only! Collectible Edition. 2014. (ENG., Illus.). 288p. (J). (gr. 2-7). 14.95 (978-1-62686-047-6(5), Portable Pr.) Readerlink Distribution Services, LLC.

—Uncle John's Totally Quacked Bathroom Reader for Kids Only! 2014. (ENG., Illus.). 288p. (J). (gr. 2-7). 14.95 (978-1-62686-175-6(7), Portable Pr.) Readerlink Distribution Services, LLC.

Bathroom Readers' Institute Staff, creator. Uncle John's Bathroom Reader for Kids Only! Collectible Edition. 2014. (ENG., Illus.). 288p. (J). (gr. 2-7). 14.95 (978-1-62686-045-2(9), Portable Pr.) Readerlink Distribution Services, LLC.

—Uncle John's Electrifying Bathroom Reader for Kids Only! 2014. (ENG., Illus.). 288p. (J). (gr. 2-7). 14.95 (978-1-62686-046-9(7), Portable Pr.) Readerlink Distribution Services, LLC.

Behnke, Alison. South Korea in Pictures. 2nd ed. 2005. (Visual Geography Ser.). (Illus.). 80p. (YA). (gr. 7-12). 27.93 (978-0-8225-1174-8(6)) Lerner Publishing Group.

Bender, Mike & Chernack, Doug. Everything Is Awkward. 2016. (ENG.). 40p. (J). (gr. k-4). 14.99 (978-0-399-54984-7(6), Crown Books For Young Readers) Random Hse. Children's Bks.

Berne, Emma Carlson. World's Best (and Worst) Animal Jokes. 2017. (J). (978-1-5124-8351-2(6)) Lerner Publishing Group.

Besley, Adrian. How to Fart at School — And Get Away with It! 2012. (ENG., Illus.). 144p. (J). (gr. 2-5). pap. 12.99 (978-1-85375-872-0(8)) Prion GBR. Dist: Independent Pubs. Group.

Bird, Benjamin. A Baby's Guide to Surviving Dad. Americo, Tiago, illus. 2016. (Baby Survival Guides). (ENG.). 24p. (gr. -1-1). 6.95 (978-1-62370-610-4(6)) Capstone Young Readers of Coughlan Cos.

—A Baby's Guide to Surviving Mom. Americo, Tiago, illus. 2016. (Baby Survival Guides). (ENG.). 24p. (gr. -1-1). 6.95 (978-1-62370-611-1(4)) Capstone Young Readers of Coughlan Cos.

Bird, Nicky. Knock Knock Jokes: Bird Brains, 1 vol. 2016. (Knock-Knock Jokes Ser.: 1). (ENG., Illus.). 64p. (J). pap. 6.99 (978-1-926677-96-5(X), 9781926677965) Folklore Publishing CAN. Dist: Lone Pine Publishing USA.

—Knock Knock Jokes: Bug Brains, 1 vol. 2016. (Knock-Knock Jokes Ser.: 3). (ENG., Illus.). 64p. (J). pap. 6.99 (978-1-926677-98-9(6), 9781926677989) Folklore Publishing CAN. Dist: Lone Pine Publishing USA.

—Knock Knock Jokes: Monkey Madness, 1 vol. 2016. (Knock-Knock Jokes Ser.: 2). (ENG., Illus.). 64p. (J). pap. 6.99 (978-1-926677-97-2(8), 9781926677972) Folklore Publishing CAN. Dist: Lone Pine Publishing USA.

Birtles. Dumb Jokes For Smart Kids. (Illus.). 96p. (J). pap. 5.95 (978-1-85479-649-3(6)) O'Mara, Michael Bks., Ltd. GBR. Dist: Trans-Atlantic Pubns., Inc.

Blank, Eva, et al. Jokelopedia: The Biggest, Best, Silliest, Dumbest Joke Book Ever! Wright, Mike, illus. 3rd ed. 2016. (ENG.). 288p. (J). (gr. 2-7). pap. 9.95 (978-0-7611-8997-8(1)) Workman Publishing Co., Inc.

Books, Macmillan Children's. Match! Joke Book. 2016. (ENG., Illus.). 224p. (J). (gr. 2-9). 9.99 (978-1-5098-2499-1(5)) Pan Macmillan GBR. Dist: Independent Pubs. Group.

Borgenicht, David. Monkeyfarts! Wacky Jokes Every Kid Should Know. 2012. (ENG., Illus.). 96p. (J). (gr. 1-4). 8.99 (978-1-59474-605-5(2)) Quirk Bks.

Boyer, Crispin. That's Gross! Icky Facts That Will Test Your Gross-Out Factor. 2012. (ENG., Illus.). 176p. (J). (gr. 3-7). lib. bdg. 21.95 (978-1-4263-1127-7(3), National Geographic Children's Bks.) National Geographic Society.

Boyer, Crispin & National Geographic Kids Staff. That's Gross! Icky Facts That Will Test Your Gross-Out Factor. 2012. (ENG., Illus.). 176p. (J). (gr. 3-7). pap. 12.95 (978-1-4263-1066-9(8), National Geographic Children's Bks.) National Geographic Society.

Bozzo, Linda. Corny Thanksgiving Jokes to Tickle Your Funny Bone. 2013. (Funnier Bone Jokes Ser.). 48p. (J). (gr. 3-4). pap. 8.95 (978-1-4644-0178-7(0), Enslow Elementary); lib. bdg. 22.60 (978-0-7660-4120-2(4)) Enslow Pubs., Inc.

—Food Jokes to Tickle Your Funny Bone. (Funny Bone Jokes Ser.). (Illus.). 48p. (J). (gr. 3-4). 2013. pap. 8.95 (978-0-7660-5986-3(3)) 2011. lib. bdg. 22.60 (978-0-7660-3541-6(7)) Enslow Pubs., Inc. (Enslow Elementary).

—Funny Valentine's Day Jokes to Tickle Your Funny Bone. 2013. (Funnier Bone Jokes Ser.). (Illus.). 48p. (J). (gr. 3-4). 22.60 (978-0-7660-4119-6(0)); pap. 8.95 (978-1-4644-0177-0(2), Enslow Elementary) Enslow Pubs., Inc.

—Gross Body Jokes to Tickle Your Funny Bone. (Funny Bone Jokes Ser.). (Illus.). 48p. (J). (gr. 3-4). 2013. pap. 8.95 (978-0-7660-5987-0(1)) 2011. lib. bdg. 22.60 (978-0-7660-3540-9(9)) Enslow Pubs., Inc. (Enslow Elementary).

—Kooky Halloween Jokes to Tickle Your Funny Bone. 2013. (Funnier Bone Jokes Ser.). 48p. (J). (gr. 3-4). 22.60 (978-0-7660-4118-9(2)); pap. 8.95 (978-1-4644-0176-3(4), Enslow Elementary) Enslow Pubs., Inc.

Brandreth, Gyles. The Super Joke Book. Berringer, Nick, illus. 2009. (ENG.). 112p. (J). (gr. 2-7). pap. 4.95 (978-1-4027-4713-7(6)) Sterling Publishing Co., Inc.

Brewer, Paul. You Must Be Joking! Lots of Cool Jokes, Plus 17 1/2 Tips for Remembering, Telling, & Making up Your Own Jokes. 2003. (ENG., Illus.). 128p. (J). 17.95 (978-0-8126-2661-2(3)) Cricket Bks.

—You Must Be Joking, Two! Even Cooler Jokes, Plus 11 1/2 Tips for Laughing Yourself into Your Own Stand-Up Comedy Routine. Brewer, Paul, illus. 2007. (ENG., Illus.). 128p. (J). (gr. k-5). 17.95 (978-0-8126-2752-7(0)) Cricket Bks.

Brown, Peggy. The Little Golden Book of Jokes & Riddles. Sheldon, David, illus. 2013. (Little Golden Book Ser.). (ENG.). 24p. (J). (-k). 4.99 (978-0-307-97916-2(4), Golden Bks.) Random Hse. Children's Bks.

Browning. Mega Joke Book For Kids. (Illus.). 162p. (J). pap. 9.95 (978-1-85479-249-5(0)) O'Mara, Michael Bks., Ltd. GBR. Dist: Trans-Atlantic Pubns., Inc.

The Bunty Annual 2005. 2004. (Illus.). 128p. (J). 9.95 (978-0-85116-849-4(3)) Thomson, D.C. & Co., Ltd. GBR. Dist: APG Sales & Distribution Services.

Burns, Diane L. Horsing Around: Jokes to Make Ewe Smile. Gable, Brian, illus. 2005. (Make Me Laugh! Ser.). 32p. (J). (gr. k-3). lib. bdg. 19.93 (978-1-57505-662-3(3)) Lerner Publishing Group.

Burns, Diane L. & Scholten, Dan. Horsing Around: Jokes to Make Ewe Smile. Gable, Brian, illus. 2004. (Make Me Laugh! Ser.). 32p. (J). (gr. -1-3). per. 4.95 (978-1-57505-737-8(9)) Lerner Publishing Group.

Burns, Diane L., et al. Backyard Beasties: Jokes to Snake You Smile. Gable, Brian, illus. 2004. (Make Me Laugh! Ser.). 32p. (J). (gr. k-3). lib. bdg. 19.93 (978-1-57505-646-3(1)) Lerner Publishing Group.

—Jordan in Pictures. Gable, Brian, illus. 2nd ed. 2005. (Visual Geography Series, Second Ser.). (ENG.). 80p. (gr. 5-12). 31.93 (978-0-8225-1173-1(8)) Lerner Publishing Group.

Capstone Press. Joke Books. 2010. (Joke Bks.). (ENG.). 32p. lib. bdg. 123.90 (978-1-4296-5942-0(4), Pebble Bks.) Capstone Press of Coughlan Cos.

Carbone, Courtney. Disney Princess Joke Book (Disney Princess) RH Disney Staff et al, illus. 2015. (Stepping Stone Book(TM) Ser.). (ENG.). 64p. (J). (gr. -1-2). 5.99 (978-0-7364-3414-0(3), RH/Disney) Random Hse. Children's Bks.

Cartoon Nation, Set. 2009. (Cartoon Nation Ser.). (ENG., Illus.). 32p. (gr. 3-4). lib. bdg. 61.30 (978-1-4296-3687-2(4), Graphic Library) Capstone Press of Coughlan Cos.

Charney, Steve. Hocus-Jokus: 50 Funny Magic Tricks Complete with Jokes. 2003. (Illus.). ix, 132p. (J). (978-0-88166-376-1(X)) Meadowbrook Pr.

Chirp Magazine Editors. Joking Around with Chirp: More Than 130 Feather-Ruffling Jokes, Riddles, & Tongue Twisters! Kain, Bob & Owlkids Books Inc. Staff, illus. 2013. (ENG.). 96p. (J). (gr. -1-3). pap. 8.95 (978-1-926973-65-4(8)) Owlkids Bks. Inc. CAN. Dist: Publishers Group West (PGW).

Chmielewski, Gary. The Animal Zone. Caputo, Jim, illus. rev. ed. 2007. (Funny Zone Ser.). (ENG.). 24p. (J). (gr. 2-4). pap. 11.94 (978-1-60357-677-2(0)) Norwood Hse. Pr.

—Animal Zone. Caputo, Jim, illus. rev. ed. 2007. (Funny Zone Ser.). (ENG.). 24p. (J). (gr. 2-4). lib. bdg. 22.60 (978-1-59953-139-7(9)) Norwood Hse. Pr.

—The Classroom Zone. Caputo, Jim, illus. rev. ed. 2007. (Funny Zone Ser.). (ENG.). 24p. (J). (gr. 2-4). pap. 11.94 (978-1-60357-680-2(0)) Norwood Hse. Pr.

—Classroom Zone. Caputo, Jim, illus. rev. ed. 2007. (Funny Zone Ser.). (ENG.). 24p. (J). (gr. 2-4). lib. bdg. 22.60 (978-1-59953-145-8(3)) Norwood Hse. Pr.

—The Computer Zone. Caputo, Jim, illus. rev. ed. 2009. (Funny Zone Ser.). (ENG.). 24p. (J). (gr. 2-4). pap. 11.94 (978-1-60357-684-0(3)) Norwood Hse. Pr.

—The Computer Zone: Jokes, Riddles, Tongue Twisters & Daffynitions. Caputo, Jim, illus. rev. ed. 2009. (Funny Zone Ser.). (ENG.). 24p. (J). (gr. 2-4). lib. bdg. 22.60 (978-1-59953-300-1(6)) Norwood Hse. Pr.

—The Fright Zone. Caputo, Jim, illus. rev. ed. 2009. (Funny Zone Ser.). (ENG.). 24p. (J). (gr. 2-4). pap. 11.94 (978-1-60357-685-7(1)) Norwood Hse. Pr.

—The Fright Zone: Jokes, Riddles, Tongue Twisters & Daffynitions. Caputo, Jim, illus. rev. ed. 2009. (Funny Zone Ser.). (ENG.). 24p. (J). (gr. 2-4). lib. bdg. 22.60 (978-1-59953-298-1(0)) Norwood Hse. Pr.

—The Ghost Zone. Caputo, Jim, illus. rev. ed. 2009. (Funny Zone Ser.). (ENG.). 24p. (J). (gr. 2-4). pap. 11.94 (978-1-60357-686-4(X)) Norwood Hse. Pr.

—The Ghost Zone: Jokes, Riddles, Tongue Twisters & Daffynitions. Caputo, Jim, illus. rev. ed. 2009. (Funny Zone Ser.). (ENG.). 24p. (J). (gr. 2-4). lib. bdg. 22.60 (978-1-59953-297-4(2)) Norwood Hse. Pr.

—The History Zone. Caputo, Jim, illus. rev. ed. 2007. (Funny Zone Ser.). (ENG.). 24p. (J). (gr. 2-4). pap. 11.94 (978-1-60357-678-9(9)) Norwood Hse. Pr.

—History Zone. Caputo, Jim, illus. rev. ed. 2007. (Funny Zone Ser.). (ENG.). 24p. (J). (gr. 2-4). lib. bdg. 22.60 (978-1-59953-141-0(0)) Norwood Hse. Pr.

—Let's Eat in the Funny Zone. Caputo, Jim, illus. rev. ed. 2007. (Funny Zone Ser.). (ENG.). 24p. (J). (gr. 2-4). pap. 11.94 (978-1-60357-681-9(9)) Norwood Hse. Pr.

—Let's Eat in the Funny Zone: Jokes, Riddles, Tongue Twisters & Daffynitions. Caputo, Jim, illus. rev. ed. 2007. (Funny Zone Ser.). (ENG.). 24p. (J). (gr. 2-4). lib. bdg. 22.60 (978-1-59953-181-6(X)) Norwood Hse. Pr.

—Let's Go in the Funny Zone. Caputo, Jim, illus. rev. ed. 2007. (Funny Zone Ser.). (ENG.). 24p. (J). (gr. 2-4). pap. 11.94 (978-1-60357-682-6(7)) Norwood Hse. Pr.

—Let's Go in the Funny Zone: Jokes, Riddles, Tongue Twisters & Daffynitions. Caputo, Jim, illus. rev. ed. 2007. (Funny Zone Ser.). (ENG.). 24p. (J). (gr. 2-4). lib. bdg. 22.60 (978-1-59953-182-3(8)) Norwood Hse. Pr.

—The Medical Zone. Caputo, Jim, illus. rev. ed. 2009. (Funny Zone Ser.). (ENG.). 24p. (J). (gr. 2-4). pap. 11.94 (978-1-60357-687-1(8)) Norwood Hse. Pr.

—The Medical Zone: Jokes, Riddles, Tongue Twisters & Daffynitions. Caputo, Jim, illus. rev. ed. 2009. (Funny Zone Ser.). (ENG.). 24p. (J). (gr. 2-4). lib. bdg. 22.60 (978-1-59953-299-8(9)) Norwood Hse. Pr.

—The Science Zone. Caputo, Jim, illus. rev. ed. 2007. (Funny Zone Ser.). (ENG.). 24p. (J). (gr. 2-4). pap. 11.94 (978-1-60357-683-3(5)) Norwood Hse. Pr.

—The Science Zone: Jokes, Riddles, Tongue Twisters & Daffynitions. Caputo, Jim, illus. rev. ed. 2007. (Funny Zone Ser.). (ENG.). 24p. (J). (gr. 2-4). lib. bdg. 22.60 (978-1-59953-183-0(6)) Norwood Hse. Pr.

—The Sports Zone. Caputo, Jim, illus. rev. ed. 2007. (Funny Zone Ser.). (ENG.). 24p. (J). (gr. 2-4). pap. 11.94 (978-1-60357-679-6(7)); lib. bdg. 22.60 (978-1-59953-144-1(5)) Norwood Hse. Pr.

Christopher, Clara. Animal Jokes, Riddles, & Games. 2016. (ENG., Illus.). 32p. (J). (978-0-7787-2387-5(9)) Crabtree Publishing Co.

Churchill, E. Richard. Tricks & Pranks. 2007. (ENG., Illus.). 352p. (J). (gr. 2-6). pap. 6.95 (978-1-4027-4977-3(5)) Sterling Publishing Co., Inc.

Clark, Brian D. & Sloan, Price Stern. Stoned off Our Mad Libs. 2015. (Adult Mad Libs Ser.). (ENG.). 48p. (gr. 13). bds. 4.99 (978-0-8431-8330-6(6), Mad Libs) Penguin Young Readers Group.

Cleary, Brian P. Chips & Cheese & Nana's Knees: What Is Alliteration? Goneau, Martin, illus. 2017. (Words Are CATegorical (r) Ser.). (ENG.). 32p. (J). (gr. 2-5). 6.95 (978-1-5124-3421-7(3), Millbrook Pr.) Lerner Publishing Group.

Cliff Road Books Staff & Sweetwater Press Staff, contrib. by. Jokes & Riddles for Kids of All Ages, 3 vols. 2004. (Illus.). (978-1-60261-115-3(7)); (978-1-58173-312-9(7)); (978-1-58173-313-6(5)) Cliff Road Bks.

Cole, William. Monster Knock Knocks. 2012. (ENG.). 112p. (Orig.). (J). (gr. 3-6). pap. 6.99 (978-1-4424-7438-3(6), Simon Pulse) Simon Pulse.

Cole, William Edward. Cole's Funny Picture Book No. 2011. 976p. (978-1-84902-480-8(4)) Benediction Classics.

Connolly, Sean. The Fun on the Farm Joke Book. 2013. (Laugh Out Loud Ser.). (ENG., Illus.). 32p. (J). (gr. 1-5). pap. 11.75 (978-1-61533-654-8(0)); lib. bdg. 26.50 (978-1-61533-644-9(3)) Windmill Bks.

—The Hysterical History Joke Book. 2013. (Laugh Out Loud Ser.). (ENG., Illus.). 32p. (gr. 1-5). pap. 11.75 (978-1-61533-656-2(7)); lib. bdg. 26.50 (978-1-61533-645-6(1)) Windmill Bks.

—The Jolly Jungle Joke Book. 2013. (Laugh Out Loud Ser.). (ENG., Illus.). 32p. (J). (gr. 1-5). pap. 11.75 (978-1-61533-658-6(3)); lib. bdg. 26.50 (978-1-61533-646-3(X)) Windmill Bks.

—Laugh Out Loud: The Silly Spells Joke Book. 2013. (Laugh Out Loud Ser.). (ENG., Illus.). 32p. (J). (gr. 1-5). pap. 11.75 (978-1-61533-662-3(1)); lib. bdg. 26.50 (978-1-61533-648-7(6)) Windmill Bks.

—The Out to Sea Joke Book. 2013. (Laugh Out Loud Ser.). (ENG., Illus.). 32p. (J). (gr. 1-5). pap. 11.75 (978-1-61533-660-9(5)); lib. bdg. 26.50 (978-1-61533-647-0(8)) Windmill Bks.

Connolly, Sean & Barnham, Kay. The Animal Antics Joke Book. 2011. (Laugh Out Loud Ser.). (ENG., Illus.). 32p. (J). (gr. 1-5). pap. 11.75 (978-1-61533-400-1(9)); lib. bdg. 26.50 (978-1-61533-362-2(2)) Windmill Bks.

—The Funny Food Joke Book. 2011. (Laugh Out Loud Ser.). (ENG., Illus.). 32p. (J). (gr. 1-5). pap. 11.75 (978-1-61533-403-2(3)); lib. bdg. 26.50 (978-1-61533-365-3(7)) Windmill Bks.

—The Monster Fun Joke Book. 2011. (Laugh Out Loud Ser.). (ENG., Illus.). 32p. (J). (gr. 1-5). pap. 11.75

(978-1-61533-398-1(3), 1328741); lib. bdg. 26.50 *(978-1-61533-360-8(6)*, 1328741) Windmill Bks.
—The Outer Space Joke Book. 2011. (Laugh Out Loud Ser.). (ENG., Illus.). 32p. (J). (gr. 1-5). pap. 11.75 *(978-1-61533-402-5(5))*; lib. bdg. 26.50 *(978-1-61533-364-6(9))* Windmill Bks.
—The School's Cool Joke Book. 2011. (Laugh Out Loud Ser.). (ENG., Illus.). 32p. (J). (gr. 1-5). pap. 11.75 *(978-1-61533-401-8(7))*; lib. bdg. 26.50 *(978-1-61533-363-9(0))* Windmill Bks.
—The Silly Safari Joke Book. 2011. (Laugh Out Loud Ser.). (ENG., Illus.). 32p. (J). (gr. 1-5). pap. 11.75 *(978-1-61533-399-8(1))*; lib. bdg. 26.50 *(978-1-61533-361-5(4))* Windmill Bks.
Connolly, Sean & Harris, Joe. The Crazy Computers Joke Book. 2013. (Laugh Out Loud Ser.). (ENG., Illus.). 32p. (J). (gr. 1-5). pap. 11.75 *(978-1-61533-652-4(4))*; lib. bdg. 26.50 *(978-1-61533-643-2(5))* Windmill Bks.
Corchin, Dj. The Marching Band Nerds Handbook. Dougherty, Dan, illus. 2012. 136p. 22.95 *(978-0-9834876-7-8(7))*; pap. 12.95 *(978-0-9819645-7-7(5))* phazelFOZ Co., LLC., The.
Coster, Patience. Really Horrible History Jokes, 1. 2014. (Really Horrible Jokes Ser.). (ENG.). 32p. (J). (gr. k-3). pap. 10.00 *(978-1-4777-9083-0(7)*, Windmill Bks.) Rosen Publishing Group, Inc., The.
—Really Horrible Science Jokes, 1. 2014. (Really Horrible Jokes Ser.). (ENG.). 32p. (J). (gr. k-3). pap. 10.00 *(978-1-4777-9087-8(X)*, Windmill Bks.) Rosen Publishing Group, Inc., The.
Coster, Patience & King, Karen. Really Horrible History Jokes, 1. 2014. (Really Horrible Jokes Ser.). (ENG.). 32p. (J). (gr. k-3). 26.25 *(978-1-4777-9082-3(9)*, Windmill Bks.) Rosen Publishing Group, Inc., The.
Crosbie, Duncan & Potter, Tony, compiled by. Irish Jokes. 2003. (Illus.). 60p. 11.95 *(978-0-7171-3532-5(2))* M.H. Gill & Co. U. C. IRL. Dist: Dufour Editions, Inc.
Crotts, Barbara. Gemini Cricket: John Glenn - First Person to Orbit the Earth. Khory, Emil, illus. 2011. 56p. pap. 10.03 *(978-1-4269-6213-4(4))* Trafford Publishing.
Crowe, Sharon. Daniel & the Big Belly Button. 2009. 23p. (J). pap. 17.95 *(978-1-4327-1549-6(6))* Outskirts Pr., Inc.
Dahl, Michael. Animal Jokes! 2013. (Laff-O-Tronic Joke Books! Ser.). (ENG., Illus.). 96p. (gr. k-3). pap. 4.95 *(978-1-4342-6190-8(5))* Stone Arch Bks.
—Knock Your Socks Off: A Book of Knock-Knock Jokes, 1 vol. Haugen, Ryan & Jensen, Brian, illus. 2010. (Michael Dahl Presents Super Funny Joke Bks.). (ENG.). 80p. (gr. k-3). 25.32 *(978-1-4048-5774-2(5))* Picture Window Bks.
—Laff-O-Tronic Animal Jokes! Holgate, Douglas & Collins, Daryll, illus. 2013. (Laff-O-Tronic Joke Books! Ser.). (ENG.). 96p. (gr. k-3). pap. 29.70 *(978-1-4342-6238-7(3))* Stone Arch Bks.
—Laff-O-Tronic Animal Jokes!, 1 vol. Collins, Daryll et al, illus. 2013. (Laff-O-Tronic Joke Books! Ser.). (ENG.). 96p. (gr. k-3). 25.32 *(978-1-4342-6020-8(8))* Stone Arch Bks.
—Laff-O-Tronic Joke Books. Collins, Daryll & Holgate, Douglas, illus. 2013. (Laff-O-Tronic Joke Books! Ser.). (ENG.). 96p. (gr. k-3). pap. 19.80 *(978-1-4342-6224-0(3))* Stone Arch Bks.
—Laff-O-Tronic Monster Jokes! Collins, Daryll & Holgate, Douglas, illus. 2013. (Laff-O-Tronic Joke Books! Ser.). (ENG.). 96p. (gr. k-3). pap. 29.70 *(978-1-4342-6239-4(1))* Stone Arch Bks.
—Laff-O-Tronic Monster Jokes!, 1 vol. Collins, Daryll et al, illus. 2013. (Laff-O-Tronic Joke Books! Ser.). (ENG.). 96p. (gr. k-3). 25.32 *(978-1-4342-6021-5(6))* Stone Arch Bks.
—Laff-O-Tronic School Jokes! Holgate, Douglas & Collins, Daryll, illus. 2013. (Laff-O-Tronic Joke Books! Ser.). (ENG.). 96p. (gr. k-3). pap. 29.70 *(978-1-4342-6240-0(5))* Stone Arch Bks.
—Laff-O-Tronic School Jokes!, 1 vol. Collins, Daryll et al, illus. 2013. (Laff-O-Tronic Joke Books! Ser.). (ENG.). 96p. (gr. k-3). 25.32 *(978-1-4342-6022-2(4))* Stone Arch Bks.
—Laff-O-Tronic Sports Jokes! Holgate, Douglas & Collins, Daryll, illus. 2013. (Laff-O-Tronic Joke Books! Ser.). (ENG.). 96p. (gr. k-3). pap. 29.70 *(978-1-4342-6241-7(3))* Stone Arch Bks.
—Laff-O-Tronic Sports Jokes!, 1 vol. Collins, Daryll et al, illus. 2013. (Laff-O-Tronic Joke Books! Ser.). (ENG.). 96p. (gr. k-3). 25.32 *(978-1-4342-6023-9(2))* Stone Arch Bks.
—Monster Jokes! 2013. (Laff-O-Tronic Joke Books! Ser.). (ENG., Illus.). 96p. (gr. k-3). pap. 4.95 *(978-1-4342-6191-5(3))* Stone Arch Bks.
—School Jokes! 2013. (Laff-O-Tronic Joke Books! Ser.). (ENG., Illus.). 96p. (gr. k-3). pap. 4.95 *(978-1-4342-6192-2(1))* Stone Arch Bks.
—Scooby-Doo Animal Jokes. Jeralds, Scott, illus. 2015. (Scooby-Doo Joke Bks.). (ENG.). 64p. (gr. 2-3). lib. bdg. 22.65 *(978-1-4342-9683-2(0))* Stone Arch Bks.
—Scooby-Doo! Food Jokes! Jeralds, Scott, illus. 2015. (Scooby-Doo Joke Bks.). (ENG.). 64p. (gr. 2-3). lib. bdg. 22.65 *(978-1-4342-9682-5(2))* Stone Arch Bks.
—Scooby-Doo Monster Jokes. Jeralds, Scott, illus. 2015. (Scooby-Doo Joke Bks.). (ENG.). 64p. (gr. 2-3). lib. bdg. 22.65 *(978-1-4342-9681-8(4))* Stone Arch Bks.
—Scooby-Doo on the Go Jokes. Jeralds, Scott, illus. 2015. (Scooby-Doo Joke Bks.). (ENG.). 64p. (gr. 2-3). lib. bdg. 22.65 *(978-1-4342-9684-9(9))* Stone Arch Bks.
—Scooby-Doo's Laugh-Out-Loud Jokes! Jeralds, Scott, illus. 2015. (Scooby-Doo Joke Bks.). (ENG.). 224p. (gr. 2-3). pap. 9.95 *(978-1-62370-182-6(1))* Capstone Press of Coughlan Cos.
—Sports Jokes! 2013. (Laff-O-Tronic Joke Books! Ser.). (ENG., Illus.). 96p. (gr. k-3). pap. 4.95 *(978-1-4342-6193-9(X))* Stone Arch Bks.
Dahl, Michael & Collins, Daryll. Laff-O-Tronic Joke Books. Holgate, Douglas, illus. 2013. (Laff-O-Tronic Joke Books! Ser.). (ENG.). 96p. (gr. k-3). 101.28 *(978-1-4342-6325-4(8))* Stone Arch Bks.
Dahl, Michael & Moore, Mark. Screaming with Laughter: Jokes about Ghosts, Ghouls, Zombies, Dinosaurs, Bugs, & Other Scary Creatures, 1 vol. Haberstroh, Anne & Reibeling, Brandon, illus. 2010. (Michael Dahl Presents Super Funny Joke Bks.). (ENG.). 80p. (gr. k-3). 25.32 *(978-1-4048-6101-5(7))* Picture Window Bks.
Dahl, Michael & Ziegler, Mark. Laughs for a Living: Jokes about Doctors, Teachers, Firefighters, & Other People Who Work, 1 vol. Haugen, Ryan & Jensen, Brian, illus. 2010. (Michael Dahl Presents Super Funny Joke Bks.). (ENG.). 80p. (gr. k-3). 25.32 *(978-1-4048-5771-1(0))* Picture Window Bks.
Davies, Bronwen, illus. Scholastic Reader Level 1: Get the Giggles: A First Joke Book. 2014. (Scholastic Reader Level 1 Ser.). (ENG.). 32p. (J). (gr. -1-2). pap. 3.99 *(978-0-545-54087-2(9))* Scholastic, Inc.
Davis, James (Jim) W. Out-takes of 55 Years of Camping 2004. (Illus.). 168p. (YA). per. 5.95 *(978-0-9760960-0-9(5))* Davis, James (Jim).
Degen, Bruce. Snow Joke. 2014. 24p. pap. *(978-0-8234-3223-3(8))* Holiday Hse., Inc.
deGroat, Diane. April Fool! Watch Out at School! deGroat, Diane, illus. 2009. (Gilbert Ser.). (Illus.). 32p. (J). (gr. -1-3). lib. bdg. 18.89 *(978-0-06-143043-5(9))* HarperCollins Pubs.
DeTellis, Luc. Who's There: 101 Knock Knock Jokes for Kids. 2003. pap. 5.95 *(978-0-9722774-1-9(2))* Muscatello Publishing.
—Who's There Again? 101 More Knock Knock Jokes for Kids. 2004. 108p. (J). per. 6.99 *(978-0-9722774-3-3(9))* Muscatello Publishing.
Dewin, Howard & Barba, M. J. Scooby-Doo! A to Z Ultimate Joke Book. 2011. (Illus.). 63p. (J). pap. *(978-0-545-37944-1(X))* Scholastic, Inc.
Dinneen, John. The Practical Joker's Handbook. (ENG., Illus.). 80p. (J). pap. 4.95 *(978-0-330-34634-4(2)*, Pan) Pan Macmillan GBR. Dist: Trafalgar Square Publishing.
—The Practical Joker's Handbook 2. Maddison, Lucy, illus. (ENG.). 80p. (J). pap. 4.95 *(978-0-330-35524-7(4)*, Pan) Pan Macmillan GBR. Dist: Trafalgar Square Publishing.
Dipiazza, Francesca. Turkey in Pictures. 2nd ed. 2004. (Visual Geography Series, Second Ser.). (ENG., Illus.). 80p. (gr. 5-12). 31.93 *(978-0-8225-1169-4(X))* Lerner Publishing Group.
Disney Book Group. Puppy Dog Pals Rolly & Bingo's Jokes & Riddles. Disney Storybook Art Team & Premise Entertainment Staff, illus. 2017. (ENG.). 48p. (J). (gr. -1-k). pap. 4.99 ***(978-1-368-00617-0(5))*** Disney Pr.
Doering, Jennie Spray. Beach Riddles. Pica, Steve, illus. 2006. (Silly Millies Level 3 Ser.). (ENG.). 32p. (gr. 1-3). lib. bdg. 21.27 *(978-0-7613-2885-8(8)*, Millbrook Pr.) Lerner Publishing Group.
Dreams that Lye Within. 2005. (YA). *(978-1-59872-101-0(1))* Instant Pub.
Dunn, S. K., compiled by. Just Joking! 1001 Jokes to Crack You Up. 2007. (Illus.). 208p. (J). *(978-0-545-03271-1(7))* Scholastic, Inc.
Eliot, Jan. Road Kill in the Closet No. 4. 2004. (Illus.). 192p. pap. 13.95 *(978-0-9674102-3-4(1))* Four Panel Pr.
Elliott, Rob. The Complete Laugh-Out-Loud Jokes for Kids: A 4-In-1 Collection. 2016. (ENG.). 256p. 12.99 *(978-0-8007-2829-8(7))* Revell.
—Laugh-Out-Loud Animal Jokes for Kids. 2014. (ENG.). 128p. (J). pap. 4.99 *(978-0-8007-2375-0(9))* Revell.
—Laugh-Out-Loud Awesome Jokes for Kids. Gearbox Studios Staff, illus. 2017. (Laugh-Out-Loud Jokes for Kids Ser.). 128p. (J). (gr. 1-5). pap. 4.99 *(978-0-06-249795-6(2))* HarperCollins Pubs.
—Laugh-Out-Loud Holiday Jokes for Kids: 2-In-1 Collection of Spooky Jokes & Christmas Jokes. 2016. (Laugh-Out-Loud Jokes for Kids Ser.). 272p. (J). (gr. 1-5). 10.99 *(978-0-06-256976-9(7))* HarperCollins Pubs.
—Laugh-Out-Loud Jokes for Kids Christmas Joke Book. 2016. (Laugh-Out-Loud Jokes for Kids Ser.). 144p. (J). (gr. 1-5). pap. 5.99 *(978-0-06-249791-8(X))* HarperCollins Pubs.
—Laugh-Out-Loud Road Trip Jokes for Kids. Gearbox, illus. 2017. (Laugh-Out-Loud Jokes for Kids Ser.). 128p. (J). (gr. 1-5). pap. 4.99 *(978-0-06-249793-2(6))* HarperCollins Pubs.
—Laugh-Out-Loud Spooky Jokes for Kids. 2016. (Laugh-Out-Loud Jokes for Kids Ser.). (Illus.). 128p. (J). (gr. 1-5). pap. 4.99 *(978-0-06-249788-8(X))* HarperCollins Pubs.
—Laugh-Out-Loud Spooky Jokes for Kids () 2016. (Laugh-Out-Loud Jokes for Kids Ser.). 128p. (J). (gr. 1-5). pap. 4.99 ***(978-0-06-266105-0(1))*** HarperCollins Pubs.
—Laugh-Out-Loud Ultimate Jokes for Kids. Gearbox, illus. 2017. (Laugh-Out-Loud Jokes for Kids Ser.). 256p. (J). (gr. 1-5). 10.99 *(978-0-06-256977-6(5))* HarperCollins Pubs.
—More Laugh-Out-Loud Jokes for Kids. 2014. (ENG.). 128p. (J). pap. 4.99 *(978-0-8007-8821-6(4))* Revell.
Ephron, Delia. Do I Have to Say Hello? Aunt Delia's Manners Quiz for Kids & Their Grownups. Koren, Edward, illus. rev. ed. 2015. (ENG.). 144p. 24.95 *(978-1-101-98307-2(8)*, Blue Rider Pr.) Penguin Publishing Group.
Ertner, Jim & Lederer, Richard. Wild & Wacky Animal Jokes. 2011. (Animal Cracker Uppers Ser.). (ENG.). 96p. (J). (gr. 4-7). pap. 7.95 *(978-1-933338-89-7(X))* Marion Street Pr., LLC.
Eshleman, William & Kimball, Paige. Prank & Pray You Get Away! over 60 Fun Jokes to Play on Your Sibling. 2012. 154p. pap. 13.95 *(978-0-9849322-0-7(8))* Find Your Way Publishing, Inc.
Figglehorn, Fred & Fisher, J. J. Fred-Tastically Funny Jokes. 2012. (Illus.). 64p. (J). pap. *(978-0-545-35603-9(2))* Scholastic, Inc.
Fitch, Sheree. There Were Monkeys in My Kitchen. braille ed. 2004. (Illus.). (J). (gr. k-3). spiral bd. *(978-0-616-01639-8(5))* Canadian National Institute for the Blind/Institut National Canadien pour les Aveugles.
Fleischman, Sid. Jim Ugly. Smith, Jos. A., illus. 2003. (ENG.). 144p. (J). (gr. 3-7). pap. 6.99 *(978-0-06-052121-9(X)*, Greenwillow Bks.) HarperCollins Pubs.
Friedman, Sharon. Grin & Bear It: Zoo Jokes to Make You Roar. Gable, Brian, illus. 2005. (Make Me Laugh! Ser.). 32p. (J). (gr. k-3). lib. bdg. 19.93 *(978-1-57505-660-9(7))* Lerner Publishing Group.
Fuhrer, David & Silbermintz, Marvin. Backwords: The Secret Language of Talking Backwards ... & More Incredible Games, Stunts & Mind-Bending Word Fun! 2007. (ENG., Illus.). 96p. (J). (gr. 2-7). pap. 12.95 *(978-0-9788178-7-9(7))* Seven Footer Pr.
Gallo, Tina. Lettuce In! And Other Knock-Knock Jokes. Chollat, Emilie, illus. 2011. (Little Simon Sillies Ser.). (ENG.). 20p. (J). (gr. -1-1). 5.99 *(978-1-4424-1404-4(9)*, Little Simon) Little Simon.
Gatacre, Sophie. Please Don't Call Me Mad! 2005. Orig. Title: Don't Call Me Mad. (YA). pap. 9.99 *(978-0-9746697-1-7(7))* Three Cents Publishing.
Gibeau, Claire Janvier. Homonyms. 2009. 40p. pap. 16.99 *(978-1-4490-3367-5(9))* AuthorHouse.
Gogol, Nikolai. The Nose. 2011. (ENG.). 42p. (gr. 4-7). pap. 7.95 *(978-1-60664-520-8(X))* Rodgers, Alan Bks.
Gonzales, Doreen. Silly Cat Jokes to Tickle Your Funny Bone. 2014. (Funniest Bone Animal Jokes Ser.). 48p. (J). (gr. 3-4). 14.95 *(978-0-7660-5991-7(X))*; (Illus.). pap. 8.95 *(978-0-7660-5992-4(8)*, Enslow Elementary) Enslow Pubs., Inc.
Goode, Ben. The Fine Art of Worrying: The Official Guide Book for Worry Warts. 2003. (YA). per. 9.95 *(978-1-885027-21-4(4))* Apricot Pr.
Goodman, Susan E. It's a Dog's Life: How Man's Best Friend Sees, Hears, & Smells the World. Slonim, David, illus. 2012. (ENG.). 32p. (J). (gr. 1-4). 16.99 *(978-1-59643-448-6(1)*, 9781596434486) Roaring Brook Pr.
Green, Rod. Mr Bean's Joke Book. 25th ed. 2015. (ENG., Illus.). 144p. (J). (gr. 2-6). pap. 7.99 *(978-1-78312-137-3(8))* Carlton Bks., Ltd. GBR. Dist: Independent Pubs. Group.
Griffiths, Andy. What Body Part Is That? A Wacky Guide to the Funniest, Weirdest, & Most Disgustingest Parts of Your Body. Denton, Terry, illus. 2013. (ENG.). 208p. (J). (gr. 3-7). pap. 7.99 *(978-1-250-03406-9(X)*, 9781250034069) Square Fish.
Gross, Peter. 101 Ways to Amaze & Entertain. 2017. (101 Ser.). (ENG., Illus.). 144p. (J). (gr. 3-5). lib. bdg. 33.32 ***(978-1-942875-14-7(2)*** , Walter Foster Jr) Quarto Publishing Group USA.
Gross, Peter & Walter Foster Jr. Creative Team. 101 Ways to Amaze & Entertain: Amazing Magic & Hilarious Jokes to Try on Your Friends & Family. 2015. (101 Things Ser.). (ENG., Illus.). 144p. (J). (gr. 3-7). pap. 12.95 *(978-1-63322-042-3(7))* Quarto Publishing Group USA.
Grossman, Bill. Cowboy Ed. Wint, Florence, illus. 2004. 28p. (J). (gr. -1-3). reprint ed. *(978-0-7567-7851-4(4))* DIANE Publishing Co.
Guess, Alison. No Bones about It, Skeleton Jokes. White, David, illus. 2008. 88p. pap. 9.95 *(978-0-9817572-4-7(3))* Peppertree Pr., The.
Gumm, Merry L. Help! I'm in Middle School... How Will I Survive? 2005. (Illus.). 80p. (J). per. 9.95 *(978-0-9761724-5-1(3)*, B-HMS) NSR Pubns.
Hall, Katy, pseud & Eisenberg, Lisa. Dino Riddles. Rubel, Nicole, illus. 2003. (Easy-to-Read Ser.). 40p. (J). (gr. -1-3). 11.65 *(978-0-7569-2823-0(0))* Perfection Learning Corp.
Hample, Stuart E. & Hample, Stoo. The Silly Book. Hample, Stoo, illus. 2004. (ENG., Illus.). 32p. (J). (gr. k-12). 15.99 *(978-0-7636-2256-5(7))* Candlewick Pr.
Hargrave, John. Mischief Maker's Manual. 2009. (ENG., Illus.). 272p. (J). (gr. 3-7). 15.99 *(978-0-448-44982-1(X)*, Grosset & Dunlap) Penguin Young Readers Group.
—Sir John Hargrave's Mischief Maker's Manual. 2011. (ENG.). 272p. (J). (gr. 3-7). pap. 8.99 *(978-0-448-45606-5(0)*, Grosset & Dunlap) Penguin Young Readers Group.
Healy, Shay. Beastly Jokes. 2005. (ENG., Illus.). 96p. (J). pap. 10.00 *(978-0-86278-923-7(0))* O'Brien Pr., Ltd., The IRL. Dist: Dufour Editions, Inc.
—More Beastly Jokes. 2005. (ENG., Illus.). 96p. (J). pap. 10.00 *(978-0-86278-924-4(9))* O'Brien Pr., Ltd., The IRL. Dist: Dufour Editions, Inc.
Heap, Sue, illus. The Giggle-a-Day Joke Book. 2011. (ENG.). 112p. (J). pap. 7.99 *(978-0-00-711591-4(1)*, HarperCollins Children's Bks.) HarperCollins Pubs. Ltd. GBR. Dist: HarperCollins Pubs.
Heimberg, Justin & Gomberg, David. Radically Repulsive: Over 400 Crazy Questions! 2010. (Would You Rather... ? Ser.). (ENG., Illus.). 216p. (J). (gr. 2-18). pap. 9.95 *(978-1-934734-42-1(X))* Seven Footer Pr.
—Would You Rather... ? Terrifically Twisted: Over 300 Crazy Questions! 2012. (Would You Rather... ? Ser.). (ENG., Illus.). 224p. pap. 9.95 *(978-1-934734-25-4(X))* Seven Footer Pr.
—Would You Rather... ? Wonderfully Weird: Over 400 Crazy Questions! 2013. (Would You Rather... ? Ser.). (ENG.). 224p. (gr. 2-7). pap. 9.95 *(978-1-934734-92-6(6))* Seven Footer Pr.
Heimberg, Justin & Gomberg, David, eds. Would You Rather... ? LOL: Over 300 Intensely Intriguing Questions to Ask Your Friends. 2011. (Would You Rather... ? Ser.). (ENG.). 192p. (gr. 7-18). pap. 9.95 *(978-1-934734-26-1(8))* Seven Footer Pr.
Highlights for Children Editorial Staff. Animal Crackups: 1,001 Beastly Riddles, Jokes, & Tongue Twisters from Highlights. Powell, Rich, illus. 2015. (Highlights(tm) Laugh Attack! Joke Bks.). (ENG.). 256p. (J). (gr. k). pap. 5.95 *(978-1-62979-426-6(0)*, Highlights) Boyds Mills Pr.
—Laugh It Up! 501 Super-Silly Jokes, Riddles, & Cartoons from Highlights. Coulson, David, illus. 2013. (Highlights(tm) Laugh Attack! Joke Bks.). (ENG.). 256p. (J). (gr. k). pap. 5.95 *(978-1-62091-071-9(3))* Boyds Mills Pr.
—Wack-A-Doodle School: 1,001 Grade-A Riddles, Jokes, & Tongue Twisters from Highlights. Whitehead, Pete, illus. 2015. (Highlights(tm) Laugh Attack! Joke Bks.). (ENG.). 256p. (J). (gr. k). pap. 5.95 *(978-1-62979-427-3(9)*, Highlights) Boyds Mills Pr.
Highlights Staff, compiled by. Highlights Laugh Attack! The Biggest, Best Joke Book Ever. 2016. (Highlights(tm) Laugh Attack! Joke Bks.). (ENG.). 352p. (J). (gr. k-4). pap. 9.99 *(978-1-62979-553-9(4)*, Highlights) Boyds Mills Pr.
Hollow, Michele C. Animal Jokes to Tickle Your Funny Bone. (Funny Bone Jokes Ser.). (Illus.). 48p. (J). (gr. 3-4). 2013. pap. 8.95 *(978-0-7660-5985-6(5))* 2011. lib. bdg. 22.60 *(978-0-7660-3544-7(1))* Enslow Pubs., Inc. (Enslow Elementary).
Hollow, Michele C., et al. Booby Traps, Bombs, Boo-Boos, & More. 2016. (Jokes for Minecrafters Ser.). (ENG., Illus.). 176p. (J). (gr. k). pap. 7.99 *(978-1-5107-0633-0(X)*, Sky Pony Pr.) Skyhorse Publishing Co., Inc.
—Mobs, Creepers, Skeletons, & More. 2016. (Jokes for Minecrafters Ser.). (ENG., Illus.). 176p. (J). (gr. k). pap. 7.99 *(978-1-5107-0632-3(1)*, Sky Pony Pr.) Skyhorse Publishing Co., Inc.
Horsfall, Jacqueline. Kids' Silliest Jokes. Jones, Buck, illus. 2003. (ENG.). 96p. (J). pap. 4.95 *(978-1-4027-0598-4(0))* Sterling Publishing Co., Inc.
Horsfall, Jacqueline & Pierce, Terry. Laughin' Jammin' Slammin' Jokefest. 2007. (ENG., Illus.). 352p. (J). (gr. 3-7). pap. 6.95 *(978-1-4027-4991-9(0))* Sterling Publishing Co., Inc.
Howard, Martin. How to Cook Children: A Grisly Recipe Book for Gruesome Witches. Stimpson, Colin, illus. 2011. (ENG.). 80p. (J). (gr. 4-7). pap. 10.99 *(978-1-84365-179-6(3)*, Pavilion) Pavilion Bks. GBR. Dist: Independent Pubs. Group.
Howell, Laura. Hundreds of Silly Jokes. 2008. (Activity Cards Ser.). (Illus.). 50p. (J). 9.99 *(978-0-7945-2384-8(6)*, Usborne) EDC Publishing.
Howell, Laura, ed. Animal Jokes. Rolland, Leonard Le, illus. 2004. (Jokes Ser.). 96p. (J). pap. 6.95 *(978-0-7945-0655-1(0)*, Usborne) EDC Publishing.
—Jokes. 2009. (Kid Kits Ser.). 50p. (J). 15.99 *(978-1-60130-161-1(8)*, Usborne) EDC Publishing.
—The Usborne Book of Really Awful Jokes: About School & Other Stuff. Le Rolland, Leonard, illus. 2005. (Usborne Ser.). 288p. (J). (gr. -1-7). per. 10.95 *(978-0-7945-0578-3(3)*, Usborne) EDC Publishing.
—The Usborne Book of Silly Jokes. Le Rolland, Leonard, illus. 2003. (Jokes Ser.). 96p. (J). (gr. 4-7). pap. 6.95 *(978-0-7945-0395-6(0)*, Usborne) EDC Publishing.
Hughes, Emily C. Plants vs. Zombies - Brain Busters. 2013. (Plants vs. Zombies Ser.). (ENG.). 224p. (J). (gr. 1-5). 10.99 *(978-0-06-222844-4(7)*, HarperFestival) HarperCollins Pubs.
Isler, Linda Germano. It's Elementary, Funny Things Kids Say in School. Santitoro, Theresa & Tumminello, Giovanna, illus. 2010. 32p. pap. 9.95 *(978-1-936343-00-3(2))* Peppertree Pr., The.
Joke Books, 1 vol. 2010. (Joke Bks.). (ENG.). 24p. (gr. k-1). lib. bdg. 109.95 *(978-1-4296-4488-4(5)*, Pebble Bks.) Capstone Press of Coughlan Cos.
Jumbo Shrimp, the Ultimate Oxymoron Book. 2003. per. 19.95 *(978-0-9745049-0-2(4))* Fein, Bruce.
Just Joking. 2016. (Just Joking Ser.). 48p. (gr. 3-2). 187.50 *(978-1-4994-8094-8(6))*; pap. 70.50 *(978-1-5081-9277-0(4))* Rosen Publishing Group, Inc., The. (Windmill Bks.).
Just Kidding! 2014. (Just Kidding! Ser.). 24p. (J). (gr. 2-3). pap. 48.90 *(978-1-4824-1545-2(3))* Stevens, Gareth Publishing LLLP.
Keating, Eliza. Folk of Feodora's Lane: There Is a Lane... ... . 2010. 68p. pap. 11.95 *(978-1-4327-5659-8(1))* Outskirts Pr., Inc.
Keller, Charles. Knock-Knocks. Hoffman, Sanford, illus. 2007. (ENG.). 352p. (J). (gr. 2-5). pap. 6.95 *(978-1-4027-4970-4(8))* Sterling Publishing Co., Inc.
Keller, Charles & Rosenbloom, Joseph. The Gigantic Book of Giggles. 2004. (Illus.). 255p. (J). pap. 4.98 *(978-1-4027-1535-8(8)*, Sterling/Main St.) Sterling Publishing Co., Inc.
Kennedy, Kelly, illus. Who's There? 501 Side-Splitting Knock-Knock Jokes from Highlights. 2012. (Highlights(tm) Laugh Attack! Joke Bks.). (ENG.). 256p. (J). (gr. k). pap. 5.95 *(978-1-59078-918-6(0))* Boyds Mills Pr.
King, Joe. The Funniest Animal Joke Book Ever. Baines, Nigel, illus. 2015. (ENG.). 96p. (J). pap. 9.99 *(978-1-78344-233-1(6))* Andersen Pr. GBR. Dist: Independent Pubs. Group.
—The Funniest Space Joke Book Ever. 2017. (ENG., Illus.). 64p. (J). (gr. 2-4). pap. 8.99 ***(978-1-78344-503-5(3))*** Andersen Pr. GBR. Dist: Independent Pubs. Group.
—The Little Book of Christmas Jokes. Baines, Nigel, illus. 2016. (ENG.). 128p. (J). (gr. k-2). pap. 6.95 ***(978-1-78344-487-8(8))*** Andersen Pr. GBR. Dist: Independent Pubs. Group.
King, Karen. Really Horrible Animal Jokes, 1. 2014. (Really Horrible Jokes Ser.). (ENG.). 32p. (J). (gr. k-3). 26.25 *(978-1-4777-9074-8(8)*, Windmill Bks.) Rosen Publishing Group, Inc., The.
—Really Horrible Body Jokes, 1. 2014. (Really Horrible Jokes Ser.). (ENG.). 32p. (J). (gr. k-3). 26.25 *(978-1-4777-9078-6(0)*, Windmill Bks.) Rosen Publishing Group, Inc., The.
Kingfisher Editors. A Joke a Day: 365 Guaranteed Giggles. Trimmer, Tony & Chatterton, Martin, illus. 2007. (Sidesplitters Ser.). (ENG.). 64p. (J). (gr. 1-5). pap. 6.99 *(978-0-7534-6128-0(5)*, 9780753461280, Kingfisher) Roaring Brook Pr.
Kirby, Robert. Kirby Soup for the Soul. Bagley, Pat, illus. 2003. 127p. per. 9.95 *(978-0-9744860-2-4(7))* White Horse Bks.
Klutz Editors. Scratch Off Carabiners: Punch Lines; Truth or Dare; Your Future. 2005. (ENG.). 40p. (J). (gr. 1-18). 3.95 *(978-1-57054-878-9(1))* Klutz.
Kowitt, Holly. Off-The-Hook Big Book of Really Dumb School Jokes. 2007. (Illus.). (J). *(978-0-439-93335-3(8))* Scholastic, Inc.
—Too Funny! 234 Laugh-Out-Loud Jokes. 2008. (Illus.). 63p. (J). pap. *(978-0-439-67172-9(8))* Scholastic, Inc.
Krieger, Emily & National Geographic Kids Staff. Real or Fake? Far-Out Fibs, Fishy Facts, & Phony Photos to Test for the Truth. 2016. (ENG., Illus.). 208p. (J). (gr. 3-7). pap. 7.99 *(978-1-4263-2405-5(7)*, National Geographic Children's Bks.) National Geographic Society.
Krull, Kathleen & Brewer, Paul. The Beatles Were Fab (and They Were Funny) Innerst, Stacy, illus. 2013. (ENG.). 40p. (J). (gr. 1-4). lib. bdg. 16.99 *(978-0-547-50991-4(X))* Houghton Mifflin Harcourt Publishing Co.
—Lincoln Tells a Joke: How Laughter Saved the President (and the Country) Innerst, Stacy, illus. 2010. (ENG.). 40p. (J). (gr. 1-4). 17.99 *(978-0-15-206639-0(X))* Houghton Mifflin Harcourt Publishing Co.
Laffin, Ima. Knock-Knock Jokes, 1 vol. 2004. (Jokes Ser.). (ENG.). 24p. (gr. k-4). 25.65 *(978-1-59197-622-6(7)*, Buddy Bks.) ABDO Publishing Co.
—Monster Jokes, 1 vol. 2004. (Jokes Ser.). (ENG.). 24p. (gr. k-4). 25.65 *(978-1-59197-623-3(5)*, Buddy Bks.) ABDO Publishing Co.
—More Monster Jokes, 1 vol. 2005. (More Jokes! Ser.). (ENG., Illus.). 24p. (gr. k-4). 25.65 *(978-1-59197-874-9(2)*, Buddy Bks.) ABDO Publishing Co.
LaRoche, Amelia. Amusing Animal Jokes to Tickle Your Funny Bone. 2014. (Funniest Bone Animal Jokes Ser.). 48p. (J). (gr. 3-4). 14.95 *(978-0-7660-5968-9(5))*; (Illus.). pap. 8.95 *(978-0-7660-5969-6(3)*, Enslow Elementary) Enslow Pubs., Inc.

—April Fool's Day Jokes to Tickle Your Funny Bone. 2013. (Funnier Bone Jokes Ser.). 48p. (J). (gr. 3-4). pap. 8.95 *(978-1-4644-0180-0(2)*, Enslow Elementary); lib. bdg. 22.60 *(978-0-7660-4122-6(0))* Enslow Pubs., Inc.

—Fowl Chicken Jokes to Tickle Your Funny Bone. 2014. (Funniest Bone Animal Jokes Ser.). (Illus.). 48p. (J). (gr. 3-4). 14.95 *(978-0-7660-5963-4(4)*, Enslow Elementary) Enslow Pubs., Inc.

—Ho-Ho-Ho Christmas Jokes to Tickle Your Funny Bone. 2013. (Funnier Bone Jokes Ser.). 48p. (J). (gr. 3-4). 22.60 *(978-0-7660-4123-3(9))*; pap. 8.95 *(978-1-4644-0181-7(0)*, Enslow Elementary) Enslow Pubs., Inc.

Laughter. 2004. per. 9.95 *(978-0-9760484-0-4(X))* Dennison, Donna.

Laughter Is the Best Medicine: Individual Title Six-Packs. (Action Packs Ser.). 120p. (gr. 3-5). 44.00 *(978-0-7635-8433-7(9))* Rigby Education.

Le Rolland, L. & Smith, Alastair. Classroom Jokes. 2004. (What's Happening Ser.). (ENG.). 96p. (J). pap. 6.95 *(978-0-7945-0391-8(8))* EDC Publishing.

Lederer, Richard & Ertner, Jim. Animal Cracker Uppers Jr. 2013. (Animal Cracker Uppers Ser.). (ENG., Illus.). 96p. (J). (gr. k-2). pap. 7.95 *(978-1-936863-50-1(2))* Marion Street Pr., LLC.

—Cleverly Comical Animal Jokes. 2012. (Animal Cracker Uppers Ser.). (ENG.). 96p. (J). (gr. 4-7). pap. 7.95 *(978-1-936863-15-0(4))* Marion Street Pr., LLC.

—Rip Roaring Animal Jokes. 2012. (Animal Cracker Uppers Ser.). (ENG.). 96p. (J). (gr. 4-7). pap. 7.95 *(978-1-936863-16-7(2))* Marion Street Pr., LLC.

Lederer, Richard & Kegel, Stan. Hilarious Holiday Humor. 2013. (ENG., Illus.). 96p. (J). (gr. 4-7). pap. 7.95 *(978-1-936863-51-8(0))* Marion Street Pr., LLC.

Lee, Cyl. Really Silly Jokes, 1 vol. 2004. (Jokes Ser.). (ENG.). 24p. (gr. k-4). 25.65 *(978-1-59197-624-0(3)*, Buddy Bks.) ABDO Publishing Co.

—Ridiculous Riddles, 1 vol. 2004. (Jokes Ser.). (ENG.). 24p. (gr. k-4). 25.65 *(978-1-59197-625-7(1)*, Buddy Bks.) ABDO Publishing Co.

Leet, Karen M. Gross Pranks, 1 vol. 2013. (Gross Guides). (ENG., Illus.). 32p. (gr. 3-4). 27.99 *(978-1-4296-9922-8(1))* Capstone Press of Coughlan Cos.

Lewis, J. Patrick. Just Joking Animal Riddles. 2015. (ENG., Illus.). 208p. (J). (gr. 2-5). pap. 7.99 *(978-1-4263-1869-6(3)*, National Geographic Children's Bks.) National Geographic Society.

Lewis, J. Patrick & Yolen, Jane. Last Laughs: Animal Epitaphs. Timmins, Jeffrey Stewart, illus. 2012. (ENG.). 32p. (J). (gr. 2-5). 16.95 *(978-1-58089-260-5(4))* Charlesbridge Publishing, Inc.

Li, Amanda. Hotdogs & Dinosnores: A First Animal Joke Book. Eccles, Jane, illus. unabr. ed. 2014. (ENG.). 80p. (J). pap. 7.99 *(978-1-4472-5373-0(6))* Pan Macmillan GBR. Dist: Independent Pubs. Group.

Lindley, Sally. Stellar Space Jokes. 2016. (Just Joking Ser.). (ENG., Illus.). 48p. (J). (gr. 3-2). lib. bdg. 31.25 *(978-1-5081-9258-9(8)*, Windmill Bks.) Rosen Publishing Group, Inc., The.

Lisboa, David M. The World Best Jokes. 2004. 160p. 12.00 *(978-0-9752740-0-2(7))* Lisboa, David.

Little Bee Books Staff. The Gross Book of Jokes. 2015. (ENG., Illus.). 144p. (J). (gr. 2-4). pap. 7.99 *(978-1-4998-0162-0(9))* Little Bee Books Inc.

MacLennan, David. Christmas Jokes for Kids, 1 vol. 2013. (ENG.). 240p. (J). pap. 14.95 *(978-1-926677-91-0(9)*, 9781926677910) Folklore Publishing CAN. Dist: Lone Pine Publishing USA.

MacLennan, David. Jokes for Canadian Kids, 1 vol. 2011. (ENG.). 168p. (J). pap. 14.95 ***(978-1-926677-45-3(5)***, 1926677455) Folklore Publishing CAN. Dist: Lone Pine Publishing USA.

Macmillan Children's Books Staff. Football Jokes: Fantastically Funny Jokes for Football Fanatics, 1. unabr. ed. 2014. (ENG., Illus.). 112p. (J). pap. 7.99 *(978-1-4472-5461-4(9))* Pan Macmillan GBR. Dist: Independent Pubs. Group.

Mad Libs Staff. Diary of a Wimpy Kid Mad Libs. 2015. (Mad Libs Ser.). (ENG.). 48p. (J). (gr. 3-7). pap. 4.99 *(978-0-8431-8353-5(5)*, Mad Libs) Penguin Young Readers Group.

—SEC Mad Libs. 2015. (Mad Libs Ser.). (ENG.). 48p. (J). (gr. 3-7). 4.99 *(978-0-8431-8325-2(X)*, Mad Libs) Penguin Young Readers Group.

—Uncle Grandpa Mad Libs. 2015. (Uncle Grandpa Ser.). (ENG.). 48p. (J). (gr. 3-7). 3.99 *(978-0-8431-8285-9(7)*, Mad Libs) Penguin Young Readers Group.

Manushkin, Fran. Katie Woo's Crazy Critter Jokes. 2017. (Katie Woo's Joke Bks.). (ENG., Illus.). 32p. (gr. k-2). pap. 5.95 *(978-1-5158-0975-3(7))*; lib. bdg. 20.65 *(978-1-5158-0971-5(4))* Picture Window Bks.

—Katie Woo's Funny Friends & Family Jokes. 2017. (Katie Woo's Joke Bks.). (ENG., Illus.). 32p. (gr. k-2). lib. bdg. 20.65 *(978-1-5158-0973-9(0))* Picture Window Bks.

—Katie Woo's Hilarious Holiday Jokes. 2017. (Katie Woo's Joke Bks.). (ENG.). 32p. (gr. k-2). lib. bdg. 20.65 *(978-1-5158-0972-2(2))* Picture Window Bks.

—Katie Woo's Joke Books. 2017. (Katie Woo's Joke Bks.). (ENG.). 32p. (gr. k-2). pap. 23.80 *(978-1-5158-0992-0(7))* Picture Window Bks.

—Katie Woo's Silly School Jokes. 2017. (Katie Woo's Joke Bks.). (ENG., Illus.). 32p. (gr. k-2). pap. 5.95 *(978-1-5158-0978-4(1))*; lib. bdg. 20.65 *(978-1-5158-0974-6(9))* Picture Window Bks.

Matheis, Mickie & Sloan, Price Stern. Edward Scissorhands Mad Libs. 2015. (Mad Libs Ser.). (ENG.). 48p. (J). (gr. 3-7). bds. 3.99 *(978-0-8431-8308-5(X)*, Mad Libs) Penguin Young Readers Group.

Mayer, Kristin. Alvin & the Chipmunks: Joke Book. 2012. 48p. *(978-0-545-48121-2(X))* Scholastic, Inc.

McCarthy, Rebecca. Laugh Your Rabbids Off! A Rabbids Joke Book. Ruiz, Fernando, illus. 2014. (Rabbids Invasion Ser.). (ENG.). 48p. (J). (gr. 2-5). pap. 3.99 *(978-1-4814-0040-4(1)*, Simon Spotlight) Simon Spotlight.

McCourt, Richard & Wood, Dominic. Dick & Dom's Big Fat & Very Silly Joke Book. unabr. ed. 2014. (ENG., Illus.). 368p. (J). pap. 11.99 *(978-1-4472-5637-3(9))* Pan Macmillan GBR. Dist: Independent Pubs. Group.

—Dick & Dom's Christmas Jokes, Nuts & Stuffing! 2015. (ENG., Illus.). 208p. (J). (gr. 4-6). pap. 10.99 *(978-1-4472-8497-0(6))* Pan Macmillan GBR. Dist: Independent Pubs. Group.

Mcky, Katie. It All Began with a Bean. Hill, Tracy, illus. 2004. (ENG.). 32p. (J). (gr. -1-3). 14.95 *(978-0-9749303-0-5(X))* Tanglewood Pr.

Merrell, Patrick. iFlush - Plunging into Mystery Bathroom Reader for Kids Only! 2014. (ENG., Illus.). 96p. (J). (gr. 1-6). 12.95 *(978-1-62686-042-1(4)*, Portable Pr.) Readerlink Distribution Services, LLC.

—iFlush- Hunting for Heroes. 2014. (ENG., Illus.). 96p. (J). (gr. 1-6). 12.95 *(978-1-62686-041-4(6)*, Portable Pr.) Readerlink Distribution Services, LLC.

Mitchell, Susan K. Humorous Small Critter Jokes to Tickle Your Funny Bone. 2014. (Funniest Bone Animal Jokes Ser.). (Illus.). 48p. (J). (gr. 3-4). 14.95 *(978-0-7660-6032-6(2)*, Enslow Elementary) Enslow Pubs., Inc.

Moore, Hugh. Bug Jokes, 1 vol. 2005. (More Jokes! Ser.). (ENG., Illus.). 24p. (gr. k-4). 25.65 *(978-1-59197-870-1(X)*, Buddy Bks.) ABDO Publishing Co.

—School Jokes, 1 vol. 2004. (Jokes Ser.). (ENG.). 24p. (gr. k-4). 25.65 *(978-1-59197-626-4(X)*, Buddy Bks.) ABDO Publishing Co.

—Sports Jokes, 1 vol. 2004. (Jokes Ser.). (ENG.). 24p. (gr. k-4). 25.65 *(978-1-59197-627-1(8)*, Buddy Bks.) ABDO Publishing Co.

Mutchnick, Brenda & Casden, Ron. A Noteworthy Tale. Penney, Ian, illus. 2004. 30p. (J). (gr. k-4). reprint ed. 19.00 *(978-0-7567-7654-1(6))* DIANE Publishing Co.

Myers, Robert. 365 Knock-Knock Jokes. Toohey, Eileen N., illus. 2006. (ENG.). 128p. (J). (gr. 1-4). per. 4.95 *(978-1-4027-4108-1(1))* Sterling Publishing Co., Inc.

Namm, Diane. Laugh Out Loud Jokes. Becker, Wayne, illus. 2004. (Laugh-A-Long Readers Ser.). (J). *(978-0-7607-5281-4(8))* Barnes & Noble, Inc.

—Slithery Squirmy Jokes. Becker, Wayne, illus. 2004. (Laugh-A-Long Readers Ser.). (J). *(978-0-7607-5282-1(6))* Barnes & Noble, Inc.

National Geographic Editors & Pattison, Rosie Gowsell. 300 Hilarious Jokes about Everything, Including Tongue Twisters, Riddles, & More! 2013. (Just Joking Ser.). (ENG., Illus.). 208p. (J). (gr. 2-5). pap. 7.95 *(978-1-4263-1378-3(0)*, National Geographic Children's Bks.) National Geographic Society.

National Geographic Kids. National Geographic Kids Funny Fill-In: My Amazing Earth Adventures. 2015. (NG Kids Funny Fill In Ser.). (ENG.). 144p. (J). (gr. 3-7). pap. 10.99 *(978-1-4263-2026-2(4)*, National Geographic Children's Bks.) National Geographic Society.

—National Geographic Kids Funny Fill-In: My Amusement Park Adventure. 2015. (NG Kids Funny Fill In Ser.). (ENG.). 48p. (J). (gr. 3-7). pap. 4.99 *(978-1-4263-1897-9(9)*, National Geographic Children's Bks.) National Geographic Society.

—National Geographic Kids Funny Fill-In: My Far-Out Adventures. 2015. (NG Kids Funny Fill In Ser.). (ENG.). 144p. (J). (gr. 3-7). pap. 10.99 *(978-1-4263-2025-5(6)*, National Geographic Children's Bks.) National Geographic Society.

—National Geographic Kids Funny Fill-In: My Flying Adventure. 2015. (NG Kids Funny Fill In Ser.). (ENG.). 48p. (J). (gr. 3-7). pap. 4.99 *(978-1-4263-2065-1(5)*, National Geographic Children's Bks.) National Geographic Society.

—National Geographic Kids Funny Fill-In: My Haunted House Adventure. 2015. (NG Kids Funny Fill In Ser.). (ENG.). 48p. (J). (gr. 3-7). pap. 4.99 *(978-1-4263-2064-4(7)*, National Geographic Children's Bks.) National Geographic Society.

—National Geographic Kids Funny Fill-In: My Rain Forest Adventure. 2015. (NG Kids Funny Fill In Ser.). (ENG.). 48p. (J). (gr. 3-7). pap. 4.99 *(978-1-4263-1898-6(7)*, National Geographic Children's Bks.) National Geographic Society.

—National Geographic Kids Funny Fill-In: My Time Travel Adventure. 2015. (NG Kids Funny Fill In Ser.). (ENG.). 48p. (J). (gr. 3-7). pap. 4.99 *(978-1-4263-1899-3(5)*, National Geographic Children's Bks.) National Geographic Society.

—National Geographic Kids Funny Fill-In: My Wild West Adventure. 2015. (NG Kids Funny Fill In Ser.). (ENG.). 48p. (J). (gr. 3-7). pap. 4.99 *(978-1-4263-1900-6(2)*, National Geographic Children's Bks.) National Geographic Society.

National Geographic Kids. National Geographic Kids Just Joking LOL. 2017. (Just Joking Ser.). (ENG.). 208p. (J). (gr. 2-5). lib. bdg. 17.90 ***(978-1-4263-2846-6(X)***, National Geographic Children's Bks.) National Geographic Society.

National Geographic Kids Staff. Ha! - National Geographic Kids. 2016. (Just Joking Ser.). (ENG., Illus.). 208p. (J). (gr. 2-5). pap. 7.99 *(978-1-4263-2327-0(1)*, National Geographic Children's Bks.) National Geographic Society.

—Just Joking: 300 Hilarious Jokes, Tricky Tongue Twisters, & Ridiculous Riddles. 2012. (ENG., Illus.). 208p. (J). (gr. 2-5). pap. 7.95 *(978-1-4263-0930-4(9)*, National Geographic Children's Bks.) National Geographic Society.

—Just Joking Gross. 2017. (ENG., Illus.). 208p. (J). (gr. 2-5). pap. 7.99 *(978-1-4263-2717-9(X)*, National Geographic Children's Bks.) National Geographic Society.

—Just Joking Lol! 2017. (Just Joking Ser.). (ENG., Illus.). 208p. (J). (gr. 2-5). pap. 7.99 ***(978-1-4263-2845-9(1)***, National Geographic Children's Bks.) National Geographic Society.

—National Geographic Kids Just Joking 2: 300 Hilarious Jokes about Everything, Including Tongue Twisters, Riddles, & More! 2012. (Just Joking Ser.). (ENG., Illus.). 208p. (J). (gr. 2-5). lib. bdg. 15.90 *(978-1-4263-1017-1(X)*, National Geographic Children's Bks.) National Geographic Society.

—300 Hilarious Jokes, about Eerything, Including Tongue Twisters, Riddles, & More! 2014. (Just Joking Ser.). (ENG., Illus.). 208p. (J). (gr. 2-5). pap. 7.99 *(978-1-4263-1735-4(2)*, National Geographic Children's Bks.) National Geographic Society.

—300 Hilarious Jokes about Everything, Including Tongue Twisters, Riddles, & More! (Just Joking Ser.). (ENG., Illus.). 208p. (J). (gr. 2-5). 2014. pap. 7.99 *(978-1-4263-1504-6(X))* 2012. pap. 7.95 *(978-1-4263-1016-4(1))* National Geographic Society. (National Geographic Children's Bks.).

—900 Hilarious Jokes. 2013. (Just Joking Ser.). (ENG., Illus.). 624p. (J). (gr. 2-5). pap., pap., pap. 23.95 *(978-1-4263-1614-2(3)*, National Geographic Children's Bks.) National Geographic Society.

National Geographic Kids Staff & Musgrave, Ruth A. Just Joking 3 - National Geographic Kids: 300 Hilarious Jokes about Everything, Including Tongue Twisters, Riddles, & More! 2013. (Just Joking Ser.). (ENG., Illus.). 208p. (J). (gr. 2-5). pap. 7.95 *(978-1-4263-1098-0(6)*, National Geographic Children's Bks.) National Geographic Society.

—National Geographic Kids Just Joking 3: 300 Hilarious Jokes about Everything, Including Tongue Twisters, Riddles, & More! 2013. (Just Joking Ser.). (ENG., Illus.). 208p. (J). (gr. 2-5). lib. bdg. 14.90 *(978-1-4263-1099-7(4)*, National Geographic Children's Bks.) National Geographic Society.

National Geographic Kids Staff & Pattison, Rosie Gowsell. Just Joking 4: 300 Hilarious Jokes about Everything, Including Tongue Twisters, Riddles, & More! 2013. (Just Joking Ser.). (ENG.). 208p. (J). (gr. 2-5). lib. bdg. 15.90 *(978-1-4263-1379-0(9)*, National Geographic Children's Bks.) National Geographic Society.

National Geographic Society (U.S.) Staff, contrib. by. Just Joking: 300 Hilarious Jokes, Tricky Tongue Twisters, & Ridiculous Riddles. 2012. (ENG.). 208p. (J). (gr. 2-5). lib. bdg. 14.90 *(978-1-4263-0944-1(9)*, National Geographic Children's Bks.) National Geographic Society.

Nelson, Maria. Jokes & More about Bees. 2014. (Just Kidding! Ser.). (Illus.). 24p. (J). (gr. 2-5). 22.60 *(978-1-4824-0538-5(5))* Stevens, Gareth Publishing LLLP.

—Jokes & More about Dogs. 2014. (Illus.). 24p. (J). (gr. 2-5). pap. 8.15 *(978-1-4824-0542-2(3))* Stevens, Gareth Publishing LLLP.

—Jokes & More about Fish. 2014. (Illus.). 24p. (J). (gr. 2-5). pap. 8.15 *(978-1-4824-0546-0(6))* Stevens, Gareth Publishing LLLP.

—Jokes & More about Horses. 2014. (Just Kidding! Ser.). 24p. (J). (gr. 2-5). 22.60 *(978-1-4824-0548-4(2))* Stevens, Gareth Publishing LLLP.

—Jokes & More about Monkeys & Apes. 2014. (Just Kidding! Ser.). (Illus.). 24p. (J). (gr. 2-5). 22.60 *(978-1-4824-0550-7(4))* Stevens, Gareth Publishing LLLP.

—Jokes & More about Snakes. 2014. (Just Kidding! Ser.). (Illus.). 24p. (J). (gr. 2-5). 22.60 *(978-1-4824-0554-5(7))* Stevens, Gareth Publishing LLLP.

Niven, Felicia Lowenstein. Brainless Birthday Jokes to Tickle Your Funny Bone. 2013. (Funnier Bone Jokes Ser.). 48p. (J). (gr. 3-4). pap. 8.95 *(978-1-4644-0179-4(9)*, Enslow Elementary); lib. bdg. 22.60 *(978-0-7660-4121-9(2))* Enslow Pubs., Inc.

—Ha-Ha Holiday Jokes to Tickle Your Funny Bone. (Funny Bone Jokes Ser.). (Illus.). 48p. (J). (gr. 3-4). 2013. pap. 8.95 *(978-0-7660-5988-7(X))* 2011. lib. bdg. 22.60 *(978-0-7660-3542-3(5))* Enslow Pubs., Inc. (Enslow Elementary).

—Hilarious Huge Animal Jokes to Tickle Your Funny Bone. 2014. (Funniest Bone Animal Jokes Ser.). (Illus.). 48p. (J). (gr. 3-4). 14.95 *(978-0-7660-5948-1(0)*, Enslow Elementary) Enslow Pubs., Inc.

—Hysterical Dog Jokes to Tickle Your Funny Bone. 2014. (Funniest Bone Animal Jokes Ser.). (Illus.). 48p. (J). (gr. 3-4). 14.95 *(978-0-7660-5958-0(8))*; pap. 8.95 *(978-0-7660-5959-7(6)*, Enslow Elementary) Enslow Pubs., Inc.

—Weird Science Jokes to Tickle Your Funny Bone. (Funny Bone Jokes Ser.). (Illus.). 48p. (J). (gr. 3-4). 2013. pap. 8.95 *(978-0-7660-5990-0(1))* 2011. lib. bdg. 22.60 *(978-0-7660-3543-0(3))* Enslow Pubs., Inc. (Enslow Elementary).

Nuevas Adivinanzas. 2003. (SPA.). (J). pap. *(978-956-13-1304-0(9)*, AB8001) Bello, Andres CHL. Dist: Lectorum Pubns., Inc.

O'Brien, Daniel. Your Presidential Fantasy Dream Team. Rowntree, Winston, illus. 2016. (ENG.). 272p. (J). (gr. 5). pap. 13.99 *(978-0-553-53747-5(4)*, Crown Books For Young Readers) Random Hse. Children's Bks.

Oscar's New Home. 12p. (J). bds. *(978-2-7643-0050-3(6))* Phidal Publishing, Inc./Editions Phidal, Inc.

Pallotta, Jerry. A Giraffe Did One Way up High. 2012. (ENG., Illus.). 32p. (J). (gr. k-3). 15.95 *(978-1-58536-641-5(2))* Sleeping Bear Pr.

Parr, Todd. The Underwear Book. 2012. (ENG., Illus.). 32p. (J). (gr. -1-1). pap. 7.99 *(978-0-316-18831-9(X))* Little, Brown Bks. for Young Readers.

Pastis, Stephan. Suit Your Selfie: A Pearls Before Swine Collection. 2017. (Pearls Before Swine Kids Ser.: 5). (ENG.). 176p. (J). pap. 9.99 ***(978-1-4494-8375-3(5))*** Andrews McMeel Publishing.

Paxton, Rain. Children's Joke Book. 2012. 12p. pap. 12.68 *(978-1-4669-2312-6(1))* Trafford Publishing.

Peirce, Lincoln. Big Nate Boredom Buster. Peirce, Lincoln, illus. 2014. (Big Nate Activity Book Ser.: 1). (ENG., Illus.). 224p. (J). (gr. 3-7). pap. 6.99 *(978-0-06-233800-6(5))* HarperCollins Pubs.

Pellowski, Michael J. Joke & Riddle Bonanza. Hoffman, Sanford, illus. 2017. (ENG.). 96p. (J). (gr. k-8). pap. 6.95 ***(978-1-4549-2247-6(8))*** Sterling Publishing Co., Inc.

—Joke & Riddle Jackpot. 2017. (ENG., Illus.). 96p. (J). (gr. k-7). pap. 6.95 *(978-1-4549-2228-5(1))* Sterling Publishing Co., Inc.

—Lunchroom Laughs Joke Book. Davis, Tim, illus. 2005. (ENG.). 128p. (J). (gr. 2-6). per. 3.99 *(978-1-58196-032-7(8)*, Darby Creek) Lerner Publishing Group.

—Out of This World Jokes & Riddles. 2017. (ENG., Illus.). 96p. (J). (gr. k-7). pap. 6.95 ***(978-1-4549-2257-5(5))*** Sterling Publishing Co., Inc.

—Scared Silly Jokes & Riddles. 2017. (ENG., Illus.). 96p. (J). (gr. k-7). pap. 6.95 ***(978-1-4549-2256-8(7))*** Sterling Publishing Co., Inc.

Pellowski, Michael J. Wild & Wacky Pet Jokes & Riddles. 2017. (ENG., Illus.). 96p. (J). (gr. k-7). pap. 6.95 *(978-1-4549-2248-3(6))* Sterling Publishing Co., Inc.

Pellowski, Michael J., et al. Belly Achers: 500 Clean, Never Mean, Good for Your Bean, Funniest Jokes You've Ever Seen. 2012. (ENG.). 160p. (J). (gr. 3). pap. 5.95 *(978-1-60433-276-6(X)*, Applesauce Pr.) Cider Mill Pr. Bk. Pubs., LLC.

—Knock-Knock Madness: Over 600 Jokes & Riddles. 2012. (ENG., Illus.). 160p. (J). (gr. 3). pap. 5.95 *(978-1-60433-275-9(1)*, Applesauce Pr.) Cider Mill Pr. Bk. Pubs., LLC.

—The Most Ginormous Joke Book in the Universe! More Laughs for Everyone! More Jokes for Every Occasion! More Jokes for Every Situation! More, More, More! 2nd rev. ed. 2012. (ENG., Illus.). 528p. (J). (gr. 7). pap. 14.95 *(978-1-60433-265-0(4)*, Applesauce Pr.) Cider Mill Pr. Bk. Pubs., LLC.

Peterson, Scott K. Let the Fun Begin: Nifty Knock-Knocks, Playful Puns, & More. Gable, Brian, illus. 2005. (Make Me Laugh! Ser.). 32p. (J). (gr. k-3). lib. bdg. 19.93 *(978-1-57505-661-6(5))* Lerner Publishing Group.

Phillips, Bob. All-Time Awesome Collection of Good Clean Jokes for Kids. 2006. (Illus.). 366p. (J). (gr. 3-12). per. 10.99 *(978-0-7369-1777-3(2))* Harvest Hse. Pubs.

—Awesome Knock-Knock Jokes for Kids. 2006. (ENG.). 112p. (J). (gr. 4-7). per. 4.99 *(978-0-7369-1714-8(4))* Harvest Hse. Pubs.

—The Best Ever Knock-Knock Jokes for Kids. 2010. (ENG.). 112p. (J). pap. 4.99 *(978-0-7369-2772-7(7))* Harvest Hse. Pubs.

—Flat-Out Awesome Knock-Knock Jokes for Kids. 2008. (ENG.). 112p. (J). mass mkt. 4.99 *(978-0-7369-2404-7(3))* Harvest Hse. Pubs.

—Slam Dunk Jokes for Kids. 2004. 160p. (J). pap. 4.99 *(978-0-7369-1346-1(7))* Harvest Hse. Pubs.

—Super Duper Knock-Knock Jokes for Kids. 2014. (ENG.). 112p. (J). pap. 4.99 *(978-0-7369-5863-9(0))* Harvest Hse. Pubs.

Phillips, Bob & Russo, Steve. Fabulous & Funny Clean Jokes for Kids. 2nd ed. 2004. 176p. (YA). reprint ed. pap. 4.99 *(978-0-7369-1365-2(3))* Harvest Hse. Pubs.

Phunny, U. R. Animal Jokes, 1 vol. 2004. (Jokes Ser.). (ENG.). 24p. (gr. k-4). 25.65 *(978-1-59197-620-2(0)*, Buddy Bks.) ABDO Publishing Co.

—Dinosaur Jokes, 1 vol. 2004. (Jokes Ser.). (ENG.). 24p. (gr. k-4). 25.65 *(978-1-59197-621-9(9)*, Buddy Bks.) ABDO Publishing Co.

—More Animal Jokes, 1 vol. 2005. (More Jokes! Ser.). (ENG., Illus.). 24p. (gr. k-4). 25.65 *(978-1-59197-872-5(6)*, Buddy Bks.) ABDO Publishing Co.

Portable Press, Editors of. The Funniest Knock Knock Jokes Ever. 2017. (ENG., Illus.). 128p. (J). (gr. k). pap. 4.99 *(978-1-62686-365-1(2)*, Portable Pr.) Readerlink Distribution Services, LLC.

—The Wackiest Joke Book Ever! 2017. (ENG., Illus.). 128p. (J). (gr. k). pap. 4.99 *(978-1-62686-380-4(6)*, Portable Pr.) Readerlink Distribution Services, LLC.

Practical Pranks. 2004. (Formula Fun Ser.). (Illus.). 48p. (J). *(978-1-84229-579-3(9))* Top That! Publishing PLC.

Press & Sky Pony Editors. Belly Laugh Riddles & Puns for Kids: 350 Hilarious Riddles & Puns. Straker, Bethany, illus. 2016. (ENG.). 144p. (J). (gr. k). 9.99 *(978-1-5107-1198-3(8)*, Sky Pony Pr.) Skyhorse Publishing Co., Inc.

Quackenbush, Robert. Henry's Awful Mistake. Quackenbush, Robert, illus. rev. deluxe ed. 2005. (Illus.). 40p. (J). (gr. k-2). reprint ed. 12.95 *(978-0-9712757-0-6(X))* Quackenbush, Robert Studios.

Ransford, Sandy. Jokes & Pranks, 3 vols. 2003. (Wicked Wallets Ser.). (Illus.). 24p. (YA). *(978-1-84347-040-3(3)*, Pavilion Children's Books) Pavilion Bks.

—2001 A Joke Odyssey: The Millennium Joke Book. 2003. (ENG., Illus.). 288p. (J). pap. 8.99 *(978-0-330-34988-8(0)*, Pan) Pan Macmillan GBR. Dist: Trafalgar Square Publishing.

Rayner, Shoo. Monster Joke Book. Rayner, Shoo, illus. 2007. (Collins Big Cat Ser.). (ENG., Illus.). 32p. (J). (gr. 2-4). pap. 7.99 *(978-0-00-723075-4(3))* HarperCollins Pubs. Ltd. GBR. Dist: Independent Pubs. Group.

Read, Howard & Chantler, Chris. Little Howard's Big Book. 2011. (ENG., Illus.). 128p. (J). pap. 15.99 *(978-0-00-739125-7(0))* HarperCollins Pubs. Ltd. GBR. Dist: Independent Pubs. Group.

Regan, Lisa. Lunchtime Riddles. 2014. (Riddle Me This! Ser.). 32p. (J). (gr. 1-5). lib. bdg. 27.50 *(978-1-4777-9165-3(5))* Rosen Publishing Group, Inc., The.

—Underwater Riddles. 2014. (Riddle Me This! Ser.). 32p. (J). (gr. 1-5). lib. bdg. 27.50 *(978-1-4777-9177-6(9))* Windmill Bks.

Reid, Alastair. Ounce, Dice, Trice. Shahn, Ben, illus. 2009. (ENG.). 64p. (J). (gr. k-4). 15.95 *(978-1-59017-320-6(1)*, NYR Children's Collection) New York Review of Bks., Inc., The.

RH Disney. The Unforgettable Joke Book. RH Disney, illus. 2016. (Joke Book Ser.). (ENG., Illus.). 80p. (J). (gr. 1-4). 4.99 *(978-0-7364-3611-3(1)*, RH/Disney) Random Hse. Children's Bks.

Richards, Kitty. Phineas & Ferb Laughapalooza Joke Book. 2011. (ENG., Illus.). (J). (-3). pap. *(978-1-4075-8486-7(3))* Parragon Bk. Service Ltd.

Riddles at Home. 2014. (Riddle Me This! Ser.). 32p. (gr. 1-5). lib. bdg. 27.50 *(978-1-4777-9169-1(8))* Windmill Bks.

Riddles at School. 2014. (Riddle Me This! Ser.). 32p. (gr. 1-5). lib. bdg. 27.50 *(978-1-4777-9173-8(6))* Windmill Bks.

Ristas. Chistes para Ninos, Vol. II.Tr. of Jokes for Children. (SPA.). (J). 6.98 *(978-970-643-265-0(5))* Selector, S.A. de C.V. MEX. Dist: AIMS International Bks., Inc.

Robinson, Barbara. The Best School Year Ever. 2005. (Trophy Bk.). (ENG.). 176p. (J). (gr. 3-18). pap. 5.99 *(978-0-06-440492-1(7))* HarperCollins Pubs.

Robinson, Sir Tony. Joke Book: Hysterical, Historical Jokes & Facts. 2017. (ENG., Illus.). 160p. (J). (gr. 4-7). pap. 8.99 ***(978-1-5098-3880-6(5))*** Pan Macmillan GBR. Dist: Independent Pubs. Group.

Rocks, Tim, illus. Bathroom Jokes: For Kids of All Ages. 2006. 288p. pap. *(978-1-58173-601-4(0))* Sweetwater Pr.

—Gross-Out Jokes: For Kids of All Ages. 2006. 288p. pap. *(978-1-58173-602-1(9))* Sweetwater Pr.

—Knock-Knock Jokes: For Kids of All Ages. 2006. 288p. pap. *(978-1-58173-600-7(2))* Sweetwater Pr.

Rodger, Anne-Marie. Sports Jokes, Riddles, & Games. 2016. (ENG., Illus.). 32p. (J). *(978-0-7787-2390-5(9))* Crabtree Publishing Co.

Rodger, Ellen. Monster & Creepy-Crawly Jokes, Riddles, & Games. 2016. (ENG., Illus.). 32p. (J). *(978-0-7787-2389-9(5))* Crabtree Publishing Co.

Rodger, Marguerite. Around the World in Jokes, Riddles, & Games. 2016. (ENG., Illus.). 32p. (J). *(978-0-7787-2388-2(7))* Crabtree Publishing Co.

Rogers, J. Ellen. Hairy Legs & Wagon Wheels. 2011. 28p. pap. 15.99 *(978-1-4628-7819-2(9))* Xlibris Corp.

Romain, Trevor. Bullying Is a Pain in the Brain. Romain, Trevor & Mark, Steve, illus. rev. ed. 2016. (Laugh & Learn(r) Ser.). (ENG.). 128p. (J). pap. 8.95 *(978-1-63198-065-7(3))* Free Spirit Publishing, Inc.

Roop, Peter & Roop, Connie. Holiday Howlers: Jokes for Punny Parties. Gable, Brian, illus. 2004. (Make Me Laugh! Ser.). 32p. (J). (gr. k-3). lib. bdg. 19.93 *(978-1-57505-645-6(3))* Lerner Publishing Group.

Rosenberg, Pam. Baseball Jokes. Ostrom, Bob, illus. 2014. (Laughing Matters Ser.). (ENG.). 24p. (J). (gr. 1-4). 27.07 *(978-1-62323-993-0(1)*, 206782) Child's World, Inc., The.

—Bug Jokes. Ostrom, Bob, illus. 2014. (Laughing Matters Ser.). (ENG.). 24p. (J). (gr. 1-4). 27.07 *(978-1-62323-994-7(X)*, 206783) Child's World, Inc., The.

—Dinosaur Jokes. Ostrom, Bob, illus. 2014. (Laughing Matters Ser.). (ENG.). 24p. (J). (gr. 1-4). 27.07 *(978-1-62323-995-4(8)*, 206784) Child's World, Inc., The.

—Eek! Icky, Sticky, Gross Stuff in Your Food. Ramos, Beatriz Helena, illus. 2007. (Icky, Sticky, Gross-Out Bks.). (ENG.). 24p. (J). (gr. 3-6). 27.07 *(978-1-59296-895-4(3)*, 200354) Child's World, Inc., The.

—Gross-Out Jokes. Ostrom, Bob, illus. 2014. (Laughing Matters Ser.). (ENG.). 24p. (J). (gr. 1-4). 27.07 *(978-1-62323-996-1(6)*, 206785) Child's World, Inc., The.

—Monster Jokes. Ostrom, Bob, illus. 2014. (Laughing Matters Ser.). (ENG.). 24p. (J). (gr. 1-4). 27.07 *(978-1-62323-998-5(2)*, 206787) Child's World, Inc., The.

—School Jokes. Ostrom, Bob, illus. 2014. (Laughing Matters Ser.). (ENG.). 24p. (J). (gr. 1-4). 27.07 *(978-1-62323-999-2(0)*, 206788) Child's World, Inc., The.

Rosenbloom, Joseph. Jokes. Hoffman, Sanford, illus. 2007. (ENG.). 352p. (J). (gr. 2-5). pap. 6.95 *(978-1-4027-4973-5(2))* Sterling Publishing Co., Inc.

Rosenbloom, Joseph & Artell, Mike. Tongue Twisters. Artell, Mike & Kendrick, D., illus. 2007. (ENG.). 352p. (J). (gr. 2-5). pap. 6.95 *(978-1-4027-4974-2(0))* Sterling Publishing Co., Inc.

Rothman, Joel & Stein, Frank N. Shut up & Straighten the Bolt in Your Neck: For Monster Kids Ages 7-11. 2007. (Illus.). 80p. (J). (gr. 2-6). pap. 6.95 *(978-1-930596-71-9(5))* Amherst Pr.

Santini, Nicky. Christes y Sorpresas prar Ninos.Tr. of Jokes & Surprises for Kids. (SPA.). (J). 6.98 *(978-968-403-937-7(9))* Selector, S.A. de C.V. MEX. Dist: AIMS International Bks., Inc.

Scanlon, Allison. Great Grilled Cheese! My Sandwich Is on Fire! 2010. 36p. (J). 15.49 *(978-1-4490-5634-6(2))* AuthorHouse.

Scheunemann, Pam. Ape Cape, 1 vol. 2004. (Rhyming Riddles Ser.). (ENG., Illus.). 24p. (J). (gr. k-3). lib. bdg. 24.21 *(978-1-59197-457-4(7)*, SandCastle) ABDO Publishing Co.

—Chipper Flipper, 1 vol. 2004. (Rhyming Riddles Ser.). (ENG., Illus.). 24p. (J). (gr. k-3). lib. bdg. 24.21 *(978-1-59197-458-1(5)*, SandCastle) ABDO Publishing Co.

—Cooler Ruler, 1 vol. 2004. (Rhyming Riddles Ser.). (ENG., Illus.). 24p. (J). (gr. k-3). lib. bdg. 24.21 *(978-1-59197-459-8(3)*, SandCastle) ABDO Publishing Co.

—Loud Crowd, 1 vol. 2004. (Rhyming Riddles Ser.). (ENG., Illus.). 24p. (J). (gr. k-3). lib. bdg. 24.21 *(978-1-59197-461-1(5)*, SandCastle) ABDO Publishing Co.

—Overdue Kangaroo, 1 vol. 2004. (Rhyming Riddles Ser.). (ENG., Illus.). 24p. (J). (gr. k-3). lib. bdg. 24.21 *(978-1-59197-462-8(3)*, SandCastle) ABDO Publishing Co.

Scholastic, Inc. Staff. Corny Jokes & Riddles. 2016. (Shopkins Ser.). (ENG.). 48p. (J). (gr. -1-3). pap. 4.99 *(978-0-545-94049-8(4))* Scholastic, Inc.

Schultz, Sam. Don't Kid Yourself: Relatively Great (Family) Jokes. Gable, Brian, illus. 2004. (Make Me Laugh! Ser.). 32p. (J). (gr. k-3). lib. bdg. 19.93 *(978-1-57505-641-8(0))* Lerner Publishing Group.

—Ivan to Make You Laugh: Jokes about Novel, Nifty, & Notorious Names. Gable, Brian, illus. 2005. (Make Me Laugh! Ser.). 32p. (J). (gr. k-3). lib. bdg. 19.93 *(978-1-57505-659-3(3))* Lerner Publishing Group.

—Monster Mayhem: Jokes to Scare You Silly. Gable, Brian, illus. 2004. (Make Me Laugh! Ser.). 32p. (J). (gr. k-3). lib. bdg. 19.93 *(978-1-57505-642-5(9))* Lerner Publishing Group.

—Schoolyard Snickers: Classy Jokes That Make the Grade. Gable, Brian, illus. 2004. (Make Me Laugh! Ser.). 32p. (J). (gr. k-3). lib. bdg. 19.93 *(978-1-57505-643-2(7))* Lerner Publishing Group.

Schwartz, Joel. Noses are Red. 2006. pap. *(978-0-9785885-0-2(9))* Schwartz, Joel.

Scott, Jerry & Borgman, Jim. Extra Cheesy Zits: A Zits Treasury. 2016. (Zits Ser.: 33). (ENG., Illus.). 208p. pap. 18.99 *(978-1-4494-7982-4(0))* Andrews McMeel Publishing.

Seaburn, Paul. Jestercises & Gamestorms. 2004. (J). pap. 5.50 *(978-1-931334-39-6(0))* Pieces of Learning.

Searight Dibert, Tracy. Detective Pancake. 2010. 24p. pap. 12.99 *(978-1-4490-2264-8(2))* AuthorHouse.

Seed, Andy. The Silly Book of Sidesplitting Stuff. Garrett, Scott, illus. 2015. (ENG.). 160p. (J). (gr. 2-4). pap. 9.99 *(978-1-61963-794-8(4)*, 9781619637948, Bloomsbury USA Childrens) Bloomsbury Publishing USA.

Shores, Erika L. More Funny Knock-Knock Jokes, 1 vol. 2012. (Joke Bks.). (ENG.). 24p. (gr. k-1). lib. bdg. 21.99 *(978-1-4296-7564-2(0)*, Pebble Bks.) Capstone Press of Coughlan Cos.

—Silly Classroom Jokes, 1 vol. 2012. (Joke Bks.). (ENG.). 24p. (gr. k-1). lib. bdg. 21.99 *(978-1-4296-7563-5(2)*, Pebble Bks.) Capstone Press of Coughlan Cos.

Simon, Francesca. Horrid Henry's Joke Book. Ross, Tony, illus. 2010. (Horrid Henry Ser.: 0). (ENG.). 112p. (J). (gr. 2-5). pap. 6.99 *(978-1-4022-4425-4(8)*, 9781402244254, Sourcebooks Jabberwocky) Sourcebooks, Inc.

Singleton, Glen. Crazy Book of Gross Jokes. 2004. (Illus.). 192p. pap. *(978-1-74121-544-1(7))* Hinkler Bks. Pty, Ltd.

—1001 Even More Cool Jokes. (Illus.). 208p. pap. *(978-1-86515-868-6(2))* Hinkler Bks. Pty, Ltd.

Sky Pony Editors, Sky Pony. Belly Laugh Jokes for Kids. Straker, Bethany, illus. 2015. (ENG.). 144p. (J). (gr. k). 9.99 *(978-1-63450-156-9(X)*, Sky Pony Pr.) Skyhorse Publishing Co., Inc.

—Belly Laugh Knock-Knock Jokes for Kids. Straker, Bethany, illus. 2015. (ENG.). 144p. (J). (gr. k). 9.99 *(978-1-63220-437-0(1)*, Sky Pony Pr.) Skyhorse Publishing Co., Inc.

Sloan, Price Stern & Mad Libs Staff. Mad Libs Mania. 2015. (Mad Libs Ser.). (ENG.). 240p. (J). (gr. 3-7). bds. 6.99 *(978-0-8431-8289-7(X)*, Mad Libs) Penguin Young Readers Group.

—Meow Libs. 2015. (Mad Libs Ser.). (ENG.). 48p. (J). (gr. 3-7). pap. 4.99 *(978-0-8431-8292-7(X)*, Mad Libs) Penguin Young Readers Group.

Sloan, Price Stern & Marchesani, Laura. Teachers Rule! Mad Libs. 2015. (Mad Libs Ser.). (ENG.). 48p. (J). (gr. 3-7). bds. 4.99 *(978-0-8431-8334-4(9)*, Mad Libs) Penguin Young Readers Group.

Snider, Brandon T. How to Be Annoying: A Joke Book. 2013. (Annoying Orange Ser.). (ENG., Illus.). 112p. (J). (gr. 1-5). pap. 7.99 *(978-0-06-223615-9(6))* HarperCollins Pubs.

—This or That? 2017. (ENG., Illus.). 208p. (J). (gr. 3-5). pap. 8.95 *(978-1-4549-2102-8(1))* Sterling Publishing Co., Inc.

Spinelli, Jerry. Tooter Pepperday. 2004. (Stepping Stone Book Ser.). (ENG., Illus.). 96p. (J). (gr. 1-4). 3.99 *(978-0-679-84702-1(2)*, Random Hse. Bks. for Young Readers) Random Hse. Children's Bks.

Stewart, Melissa. Creepy, Crawly Jokes about Spiders & Other Bugs: Laugh & Learn about Science. Kelley, Gerald, illus. 2012. (Super Silly Science Jokes Ser.). 48p. (J). (gr. 3-4). pap. 8.95 *(978-1-4644-0167-1(5)*, Enslow Elementary) Enslow Pubs., Inc.

—Dino-Mite Jokes about Prehistoric Life: Laugh & Learn about Science. Kelley, Gerald, illus. 2012. (Super Silly Science Jokes Ser.). 48p. (J). (gr. 3-4). pap. 8.95 *(978-1-4644-0164-0(0)*, Enslow Elementary); E-Book *(978-1-4645-1071-7(7))* Enslow Pubs., Inc.

—Mountains of Jokes about Rocks, Minerals, & Soil: Laugh & Learn about Science. Kelley, Gerald, illus. 2012. (Super Silly Science Jokes Ser.). 48p. (J). (gr. 3-4). pap. 8.95 *(978-1-4644-0165-7(9))*; 25.27 *(978-0-7660-3969-8(2))* Enslow Pubs., Inc. (Enslow Elementary).

—Out of This World Jokes about the Solar System: Laugh & Learn about Science. Kelley, Gerald, illus. 2012. (Super Silly Science Jokes Ser.). 48p. (J). (gr. 3-4). pap. 8.95 *(978-1-4644-0166-4(7))*; 25.27 *(978-0-7660-3970-4(6))* Enslow Pubs., Inc. (Enslow Elementary).

—Shockingly Silly Jokes about Electricity & Magnetism: Laugh & Learn about Science. Kelley, Gerald, illus. 2012. (Super Silly Science Jokes Ser.). 48p. (J). (gr. 3-4). pap. 8.95 *(978-1-4644-0163-3(2)*, Enslow Elementary); (J). (gr. 3-4). 25.27 *(978-0-7660-3967-4(6)*, Enslow Elementary); E-Book *(978-1-4645-1070-0(9))* Enslow Pubs., Inc.

—Wacky Weather & Silly Season Jokes: Laugh & Learn about Science. Kelley, Gerald, illus. 2012. (Super Silly Science Jokes Ser.). 48p. (J). (gr. 3-4). pap. 8.95 *(978-1-4644-0168-8(3))*; 25.27 *(978-0-7660-3971-1(4))* Enslow Pubs., Inc. (Enslow Elementary).

Strecker, Michael. Young Comic's Guide to Telling Jokes, Bk. 1. 2017. (ENG., Illus.). 96p. (J). (gr. k-7). pap. 6.95 *(978-1-4549-2130-1(7))* Sterling Publishing Co., Inc.

Streissguth, Tom. Costa Rica in Pictures. 2nd ed. 2005. (Visual Geography Ser.). (Illus.). 80p. (YA). (gr. 7-12). 27.93 *(978-0-8225-1168-7(1))* Lerner Publishing Group.

Swanson, June. Punny Places: Jokes That Go the Extra Mile. Gable, Brian, illus. 2004. (Make Me Laugh! Ser.). 32p. (J). (gr. k-3). lib. bdg. 19.93 *(978-1-57505-647-0(X))* Lerner Publishing Group.

Swift, Jonathan. Gulliver's Travels. 2008. (Bring the Classics to Life Ser.). (Illus.). 72p. (gr. 4-12). pap., act. bk. ed. 10.95 *(978-1-55576-065-6(1)*, EDCTR-404B) EDCON Publishing Group.

Tait, Chris. Ridiculous Tongue Twisters. Jones, Buck, illus. 2010. (ENG.). 96p. (J). pap. 4.95 *(978-1-4027-7854-4(6))* Sterling Publishing Co., Inc.

Tait, Chris & Horsfall, Jacqueline. Super Colossal Knock-Knocks. 2007. (ENG., Illus.). 352p. (J). (gr. 3-7). pap. 6.95 *(978-1-4027-4993-3(7))* Sterling Publishing Co., Inc.

Temko, Florence. Funny Money. Davis, Tim, illus. 2005. 48p. (J). (gr. -1-3). per. 4.99 *(978-1-58196-037-2(9)*, Darby Creek) Lerner Publishing Group.

Thaler, Mike. Bible Knock Knock Jokes from the Back Pew, 1 vol. Lee, Jared, illus. 2010. (Tales from the Back Pew Ser.). (ENG.). 32p. (J). pap. 3.99 *(978-0-310-71598-6(9))* Zonderkidz.

—In the Big Inning Bible Riddles from the Back Pew. Lee, Jared, illus. 2010. (Tales from the Back Pew Ser.). (ENG.). 32p. (J). pap. 4.99 *(978-0-310-71597-9(0))* Zonderkidz.

—Oinkers Away. 2014. (ENG.). 96p. (J). (gr. 3-7). pap. 13.99 *(978-1-4814-2542-1(0)*, Simon Pulse) Simon Pulse.

—School Riddles from the Black Lagoon. Lee, Jared, illus. 2007. (J). pap. *(978-0-545-01758-9(0))* Scholastic, Inc.

Thomas, Marian. Comedy Writer. (Illus.). 48p. (J). (gr. 3-6). pap. *(978-1-875739-84-4(X))* Wizard Bks.

Thornley, Stew. Sports Jokes to Tickle Your Funny Bone. (Funny Bone Jokes Ser.). (Illus.). 48p. (J). (gr. 3-4). 2013. pap. 8.95 *(978-0-7660-5989-4(8))* 2011. lib. bdg. 22.60 *(978-0-7660-3545-4(X))* Enslow Pubs., Inc. (Enslow Elementary).

Tize W. Clark. Street Jokes: 1st Edition. 2012. (ENG.). 150p. (YA). per. 14.95 *(978-0-9766770-2-4(4))* BAU Publishing Group.

Top That Publishing Staff, ed. Practical Jokes. 2004. (I-Quest Ser.). (Illus.). 48p. (J). per. *(978-1-84510-194-7(4))* Top That! Publishing PLC.

Veillé, Éric. My Pictures after the Storm. Veillé, Éric, illus. 2017. (ENG., Illus.). 32p. (gr. -1-k). 16.99 *(978-1-77657-104-8(5))* Gecko Pr. NZL. Dist: Lerner Publishing Group.

Vernon, Steve. Maritime Monsters, 1 vol. Solway, Jeff, illus. 2010. (ENG.). 32p. (J). (gr. 3-7). 12.95 *(978-1-55109-727-5(3))* Nimbus Publishing, Ltd. CAN. Dist: Orca Bk. Pubs. USA.

Vilsaint, Fequiere. Jokes, Riddles & Proverbs: In Haitian Creole. Date not set. 28p. (J). (gr. 3-6). wbk. ed. 2.50 *(978-1-881839-54-5(0))* Educa Vision Inc.

Wagner, Kathi. The Jokiest Joking Joke Book Ever Written ... No Joke! 2,001 Brand New Side-Splitters That Will Keep You Laughing Out Loud. 2015. (ENG., Illus.). 368p. (J). pap. 9.99 *(978-1-250-08615-0(9)*, 9781250086150) St. Martin's Pr.

Walton, Rick. The Sky's the Limit: Naturally Funny Jokes. Gable, Brian, illus. 2005. (Make Me Laugh! Ser.). 32p. (J). (gr. k-3). lib. bdg. 19.93 *(978-1-57505-663-0(1))* Lerner Publishing Group.

Walton, Rick & Walton, Ann. Can You Match This? Jokes about Unlikely Pairs. Hanson, Joan, illus. (Make Me Laugh! Joke Bks.). 36p. (J). reprint ed. pap. 2.95 *(978-0-8225-9565-6(6)*, Lerner Pubns.) Lerner Publishing Group.

—Foul Play: Sports Jokes That Won't Strike Out. Gable, Brian, illus. 2005. (Make Me Laugh! Ser.). 32p. (J). (gr. k-3). lib. bdg. 19.93 *(978-1-57505-666-1(6))* Lerner Publishing Group.

—Kiss a Frog! Jokes about Fairy Tales, Knights, & Dragons. Hanson, Joan, illus. 40p. (J). (gr. 1-4). reprint ed. pap. 2.95 *(978-0-8225-9566-3(4)*, Lerner Pubns.) Lerner Publishing Group.

—Magical Mischief: Jokes That Shock & Amaze. Gable, Brian, illus. 2005. (Make Me Laugh! Ser.). 32p. (J). (gr. k-3). lib. bdg. 19.93 *(978-1-57505-664-7(X))* Lerner Publishing Group.

Walton, Rick, et al. Real Classy: Silly School Jokes. Gable, Brian, illus. 2005. (Make Me Laugh! Ser.). 32p. (J). (gr. k-3). lib. bdg. 19.93 *(978-1-57505-665-4(8))* Lerner Publishing Group.

Weitzman, Et Al. & Weitzman, Ilana. Jokelopedia: The Biggest, Best, Silliest, Dumbest Joke Book Ever! 2016. lib. bdg. 20.80 *(978-0-606-39012-5(X))* Turtleback Bks.

West, Mira. If Beaumont Could Speak. 2009. 28p. pap. 9.99 *(978-1-60693-447-0(3)*, Eloquent Bks.) Strategic Book Publishing & Rights Agency (SBPRA).

West, Tracey. 365 Silly Jokes for Kids. West, Simon, ed. Stroud, Joanne, illus. 2013. 100p. pap. *(978-1-910094-05-1(6))* Magic Oxygen.

Wilcox, Jean K. & Cameron, E. Jane. AbuLLard's ABC's of Branding: 26 Concepts That Capture the Essence of Good Brand Management Koppervas, Gary & Hanes, Don, illus. unabr. ed. 2003. 64p. 19.95 *(978-0-9745612-0-2(7)*, CPN-BMS-001) CattLeLogos Brand Management Systems.

Winn, Whee. Lots of Knock-Knock Jokes for Kids, 1 vol. 2016. (ENG., Illus.). 128p. (J). pap. 3.99 *(978-0-310-75062-8(8))* Zonderkidz.

Winter, Judy A. Joke Books, 8 vols., Set. Incl. Jokes about Animals. lib. bdg. 21.99 *(978-1-4296-4466-2(4))*; Jokes about Bugs. lib. bdg. 21.99 *(978-1-4296-4997-1(6))*; Jokes about Monsters. lib. bdg. 21.99 *(978-1-4296-4998-8(4))*; Jokes about School. lib. bdg. 21.99 *(978-1-4296-4467-9(2))*; Jokes about Sports. lib. bdg. 21.99 *(978-1-4296-5270-4(5))*; Knock-Knock Jokes. lib. bdg. 21.99 *(978-1-4296-4468-6(0))*; (gr. k-1). 2010. (Joke Bks.). (ENG.). 24p. 2010. Set lib. bdg. 131.94 *(978-1-4296-5272-8(1)*, Pebble Bks.) Capstone Press of Coughlan Cos.

—Jokes about Animals, 1 vol. 2010. (Joke Bks.). (ENG.). 24p. (gr. k-1). lib. bdg. 21.99 *(978-1-4296-4466-2(4)*, Pebble Bks.) Capstone Press of Coughlan Cos.

—Jokes about Bugs, 1 vol. 2010. (Joke Bks.). (ENG.). 24p. (gr. k-1). lib. bdg. 21.99 *(978-1-4296-4997-1(6)*, Pebble Bks.) Capstone Press of Coughlan Cos.

—Jokes about Monsters, 1 vol. 2010. (Joke Bks.). (ENG.). 24p. (gr. k-1). lib. bdg. 21.99 *(978-1-4296-4998-8(4)*, Pebble Bks.) Capstone Press of Coughlan Cos.

—Jokes about School, 1 vol. 2010. (Joke Bks.). (ENG.). 24p. (gr. k-1). lib. bdg. 21.99 *(978-1-4296-4467-9(2)*, Pebble Bks.) Capstone Press of Coughlan Cos.

—Jokes about Sports, 1 vol. 2010. (Joke Bks.). (ENG.). 24p. (gr. k-1). lib. bdg. 21.99 *(978-1-4296-5270-4(5)*, Pebble Bks.) Capstone Press of Coughlan Cos.

—Knock-Knock Jokes, 1 vol. 2010. (Joke Bks.). (ENG.). 24p. (gr. k-1). lib. bdg. 21.99 *(978-1-4296-4468-6(0)*, Pebble Bks.) Capstone Press of Coughlan Cos.

Winter, Judy A. & Shores, Erika L. Joke Books. 2012. (Joke Bks.). (ENG.). 24p. (gr. k-1). lib. bdg. 175.92 *(978-1-4296-8109-4(8))*; lib. bdg. 43.98 *(978-1-4296-8108-7(X))* Capstone Press of Coughlan Cos. (Pebble Bks.).

Winterbottom, Julie. Pranklopedia: The Funniest, Grossest, Craziest, Not-Mean Pranks on the Planet! 2016. lib. bdg. 20.80 *(978-0-606-39013-2(8))* Turtleback Bks.

Wodehouse, P. G. Mike at Wrykyn. 2013. 189p. reprint ed. lthr. 69.00 *(978-0-7426-3265-3(2))* Classic Bks.

Wood, Dominic & McCourt, Richard. Dick & Dom's Whoopee Book of Practical Jokes. Chapman, David, illus. 2015. (ENG.). 240p. (J). (gr. 4-6). pap. 10.99 *(978-1-4472-8495-6(X))* Pan Macmillan GBR. Dist: Independent Pubs. Group.

Wullie, Oor. Oor Wullie's Big Bucket of Laughs Joke Book. 2015. (ENG., Illus.). 192p. (J). (gr. 4-7). pap. 9.95 *(978-1-910230-00-8(6))* Black and White Publishing Ltd. GBR. Dist: Independent Pubs. Group.

Wynne-Jones, Tim. Mischief City. (J). 16.95 *(978-0-88899-049-5(9)*, Libros Tigrillo) Groundwood Bks. CAN. Dist: Publishers Group West (PGW).

Yates, Philip & Rissinger, Matt. Laughs - Little Giant(r) Book. 2007. (ENG., Illus.). 352p. (J). (gr. 3-7). pap. 6.95 *(978-1-4027-4979-7(1))* Sterling Publishing Co., Inc.

Z, Elena Dianna. 102 Awesome School Jokes. 2008. 48p. pap. 13.95 *(978-1-4327-1356-0(6))* Outskirts Pr., Inc.

Ziegler, Mark & Dahl, Michael. The Funny Farm: Jokes about Dogs, Cats, Ducks, Snakes, Bears, & Other Animals, 1 vol. Haberstroh, Anne et al, illus. 2010. (Michael Dahl Presents Super Funny Joke Bks.). (ENG.). 80p. (gr. k-3). 25.32 *(978-1-4048-5772-8(9))* Picture Window Bks.

Zuehlke, Jeffrey. Ethiopia in Pictures. 2nd ed. 2004. (Visual Geography Series, Second Ser.). (ENG., Illus.). 80p. (gr. 5-12). 31.93 *(978-0-8225-1170-0(3))* Lerner Publishing Group.

Zullo, Allan. Worlds Dumbest Crooks 2: True Tales of Goofs, Giggles & Gaffes. 2009. 127p. (J). pap. *(978-0-545-11664-0(3))* Scholastic, Inc.

WIT AND HUMOR, PICTORIAL

Archie Superstars Staff. Archie's Even Funnier Kids' Joke Book. 2013. (Archie's Joke Bks.: 2). (ENG., Illus.). 192p. (J). (gr. 4-7). 6.99 *(978-1-936975-67-9(X))* Archie Comic Pubns., Inc.

Esos Prodigiosos Actores. 2003. (Coleccion Esa Gran Cultura).Tr. of Dreadful Drama. (SPA., Illus.). (YA). pap. 7.96 *(978-84-272-2138-3(X))* Molino, Editorial ESP. Dist: Lectorum Pubns., Inc.

Frazee, Marla. Why Did the Chicken Cross the Road? 2006. (Illus.). 32p. (J). lib. bdg. 16.99 *(978-0-8037-3203-2(1)*, Dial) Penguin Publishing Group.

Gervais, Ricky. Flanimals Pop-Up. Steen, Rob, illus. 2010. (ENG.). 14p. (J). (gr. k-4). 19.99 *(978-0-7636-4781-0(0))* Candlewick Pr.

Lyne, Alison Davis & Burrows, Mark. Little Things Aren't Little ... When You're Little, 1 vol. Lyne, Alison Davis, illus. 2013. (ENG., Illus.). 32p. (J). (gr. -1-k). 16.99 *(978-1-4556-1791-3(1))* Pelican Publishing Co., Inc.

O'Hare, J. The Highlights Big Book of Fun: An Amazing Collection of Jokes, Riddles, Puzzles, & More! 2003. (ENG., Illus.). 96p. (YA). (gr. k-7). pap., act. bk. ed. 9.95 *(978-1-59078-006-0(X))* Boyds Mills Pr.

Outcault, R. F. My Resolutions, by Buster Brown. 2010. (ENG., Illus.). 64p. pap. 14.95 *(978-1-59583-391-4(9)*, 9781595833914, Green Tiger Pr.) Laughing Elephant.

Pastis, Stephan. The Croc Ate My Homework. 2014. (Pearls Before Swine Kids Ser.: 2). (ENG., Illus.). 224p. (J). pap. 9.99 *(978-1-4494-3636-0(6))* Andrews McMeel Publishing.

Peirce, Lincoln. Epic Big Nate. 2016. (ENG.). 472p. 50.00 *(978-1-4494-7195-8(1))* Andrews McMeel Publishing.

Smith, Elwood. How to Draw with Your Funny Bone. Smith, Elwood, illus. 2015. (ENG., Illus.). 40p. (J). (gr. 1-3). 17.99 *(978-1-56846-243-1(3)*, Creative Editions) Creative Co., The.

Snider, Brandon T. Spider-Man Presents the Marvel Joke Book. Marvel Press Artist Staff, illus. 2017. (ENG.). 128p. (J). (gr. 3-7). pap. 4.99 ***(978-1-368-00066-6(5)**,* Marvel Pr.) Disney Publishing Worldwide.

Thaler, Richard. Catzilla: Cat Riddles, Cat Jokes, & Cartoons. 2014. (ENG.). 128p. (J). (gr. 3-7). pap. 13.99 *(978-1-4814-2543-8(9)*, Simon Pulse) Simon Pulse.

Thebo, Patricia J. Uncle Looker & the Hurricane. 2003. (Illus.). 50p. (J). (gr. k-9). 16.50 *(978-0-9725706-0-2(8))* Seaforth Publishing.

120 Ways to Annoy Your Mother (and Influence People) 2014. (ENG., Illus.). 224p. (gr. 6-9). pap. 19.95 *(978-0-500-29146-7(2)*, 529146) Thames & Hudson.

WITCHCRAFT

see also Charms; Occultism

Aronson, Marc. Witch-Hunt: Mysteries of the Salem Witch Trials. 2005. (Illus.). 272p. (YA). (gr. 7-12). 16.65 *(978-0-7569-5659-2(5))* Perfection Learning Corp.

Benoit, Peter. The Salem Witch Trials. 2013. (ENG.). 64p. (J). 30.00 *(978-0-531-28206-9(6))*; pap. 8.95 *(978-0-531-27671-6(6))* Scholastic Library Publishing.

Ceanadach, Siusaidh. Let's Talk about Pagan Festivals. 2012. (ENG., Illus.). 59p. pap. 9.95 *(978-1-78099-463-5(X)*, Moon Bks.) Hunt, John Publishing Ltd. GBR. Dist: National Bk. Network.

Crewe, Sabrina & Uschan, Michael V. The Salem Witch Trials. 2004. (Events That Shaped America Ser.). (Illus.). 32p. (gr. 3-6). lib. bdg. 26.00 *(978-0-8368-3406-2(2)*, Gareth Stevens Learning Library) Stevens, Gareth Publishing LLLP.

Dellaccio, Tanya & Nardo, Don. The Salem Witch Trials: A Crisis in Puritan New England. 2017. (American History Ser.). 104p. (YA). (gr. 7-7). lib. bdg. 39.40 ***(978-1-5345-6039-0(4)**,* Lucent Pr.) Greenhaven Publishing LLC.

Doeden, Matt. The Salem Witch Trials: An Interactive History Adventure, 1 vol. 2011. (You Choose: History Ser.). (ENG.). 112p. (gr. 3-4). pap. 6.95 *(978-1-4296-6272-7(7)*, You Choose Bks.) Capstone Press of Coughlan Cos.

Dowswell, Paul. The Amazing History of Wizards & Witches: Discover a World of Magic & Mystery, with over 340 Exciting Pictures. 2016. (ENG., Illus.). 64p. (J). (gr. -1-12). 12.99 *(978-1-86147-731-6(7))* Anness Publishing, Inc.

Dowswell, Paul & Greenwood, Susan. The Amazing World of Witches: Discover the Spellbinding History of Witches, Wizardry, Magic & Mystery. 2010. (ENG., Illus.). 64p. (J). (gr. 4-7). pap. 12.99 *(978-1-84476-669-7(1))* Anness Publishing GBR. Dist: National Bk. Network.

Dunn, Joeming W. The Salem Witch Trials, 1 vol. Martin, Cynthia, illus. 2008. (Graphic History Ser.). (ENG.). 32p. 28.50 *(978-1-60270-186-1(5)*, Graphic Planet- Nonfiction) ABDO Publishing Co.

Ellis, Stacy. A Wiccan ABC Book for Babies. 2005. (Illus.). (J). pap. 13.00 *(978-0-9773731-2-3(6))* MaestroMedia Pr.

Fradin, Judith Bloom & Fradin, Dennis Brindell. The Salem Witch Trials. 2008. (Turning Points in U. S. History Ser.). 48p. (gr. 3-18). lib. bdg. 31.36 *(978-0-7614-3013-1(X)*, Benchmark Bks.) Marshall Cavendish Corp.

Fremon, David K. The Salem Witchcraft Trials in United States History. 2015. (In United States History Ser.). 96p. (J). (gr. 5-12). 27.94 *(978-1-910230-6340-2(2))* Enslow Pubs., Inc.

Giordano, Geraldine. Everything You Need to Know about Wicca: Ancient Beliefs for a Modern World. 2009. (Need to Know Library). 64p. (gr. 5-5). 58.50 *(978-1-60854-098-3(7))* Rosen Publishing Group, Inc., The.

Graves, Lisa. History's Witches. Graves, Lisa, illus. 2013. (Illus.). 32p. 19.99 *(978-1-62395-516-8(5))* Xist Publishing.

Gregson, Susan R. Investigating Demons, Possessions, & Exorcisms, 1 vol. 2010. (Unexplained Phenomena Ser.). (ENG.). 48p. (gr. 3-4). lib. bdg. 31.99 *(978-1-4296-4815-8(5))* Capstone Press of Coughlan Cos.

Guiley, Rosemary Ellen. Witches & Wiccans. 2009. (Mysteries, Legends, & Unexplained Phenomena Ser.). 120p. (gr. 6-12). pap. 10.95 *(978-0-7910-9896-7(6)*, Checkmark Bks.) Facts On File, Inc.

Hill, Raine. Growing up Pagan: A Workbook for Wiccan Families, 1 vol. Pearce, Gillian M., illus. 2009. (ENG.). 64p. pap., wbk. ed. 19.99 *(978-0-7643-3143-5(4)*, 9780764331435) Schiffer Publishing, Ltd.

Hinds, Maurene J. Witchcraft on Trial: From the Salem Witch Hunts to the Crucible. 2009. (Famous Court Cases That Became Movies Ser.). (Illus.). 104p. (J). (gr. 7-12). lib. bdg. 33.27 *(978-0-7660-3055-8(5))* Enslow Pubs., Inc.

Holub, Joan. What Were the Salem Witch Trials? 2015. (What Was... ? Ser.). lib. bdg. 16.00 *(978-0-606-36761-5(6))* Turtleback Bks.

Holub, Joan & dePaola, Tomie. What Were the Salem Witch Trials? Putra, Dede & McVeigh, Kevin, illus. 2015. (What Was? Ser.). (ENG.). 112p. (J). (gr. 3-7). 5.99 *(978-0-448-47905-7(2)*, Grosset & Dunlap) Penguin Young Readers Group.

W X Y Z

Horne, Fiona. Witchin' A Handbook for Teen Witches. 2003. (Illus.). 224p. pap. (978-0-00-713695-7(1), HarperThorsons) HarperCollins Pubs. Ltd.

Kent, Deborah. Witchcraft Trials: Fear, Betrayal, & Death in Salem. 2009. (America's Living History Ser.). (Illus.). 128p. (J). (gr. 5-9). lib. bdg. 33.27 (978-0-7660-2906-4(9)) Enslow Pubs., Inc.

Landau, Elaine. The Salem Witchcraft Trials: Would You Join the Madness? 2014. (What Would You Do? Ser.). (Illus.). 48p. (J). (gr. 3-4). lib. bdg. 25.27 (978-0-7660-4224-7(3), Enslow Elementary) Enslow Pubs., Inc.

—Witness the Salem Witchcraft Trials. 2006. (Explore Colonial America with Elaine Landau Ser.). (Illus.). 48p. (J). (gr. 3-4). lib. bdg. 25.27 (978-0-7660-2558-5(6), Enslow Elementary) Enslow Pubs., Inc.

Loh-Hagan, Virginia. Witches: Magic, Myth, & Mystery. 2016. (Magic, Myth, & Mystery Ser.). (ENG., Illus.). 32p. (J). (gr. 4-8). 29.93 (978-1-63471-112-8(2), 208559, 45th Parallel Press) Cherry Lake Publishing.

MacBain, Jenny. The Salem Witch Trials: A Primary Source History of the Witchcraft Trials in Salem, Massachusetts. (Primary Sources in American History Ser.). 64p. (gr. 5-8). 2009. 58.50 (978-1-60851-503-5(6)) 2003. (Illus.). lib. bdg. 31.95 (978-0-8239-3683-0(X), Rosen Reference) Rosen Publishing Group, Inc., The.

Magoon, Kekla. The Salem Witch Trials, 1 vol. 2008. (Essential Events Set 2 Ser.). (ENG., Illus.). 112p. (J). (gr. 6-12). lib. bdg. 35.64 (978-1-60453-049-0(9)) ABDO Publishing Co.

Manoy, Laureen. Where to Park Your Broomstick: A Teen's Guide to Witchcraft. 2004. (Illus.). 311p. (YA). (gr. 7-11). reprint ed. pap. 13.00 (978-0-7567-7048-8(3)) DIANE Publishing Co.

Martin, Michael. The Salem Witch Trials, 1 vol. Bascle, Brian, illus. 2005. (Graphic History Ser.). (ENG.). 32p. (gr. 3-4). per. 8.10 (978-0-7368-5246-3(8), Graphic Library) Capstone Press of Coughlan Cos.

Martin, Michael & Martin, Michael J. The Salem Witch Trials, 1 vol. Kamerer, Justin & Bascle, Brian, illus. 2005. (Graphic History Ser.). (ENG.). 32p. (gr. 3-4). 30.65 (978-0-7368-3847-4(3), Graphic Library) Capstone Press of Coughlan Cos.

Mills, J. Elizabeth. Witches in America. 2011. (America's Supernatural Secrets Ser.). (ENG.). 48p. (YA). (gr. 5-8). pap. 11.75 (978-1-4488-5580-3(2)); lib. bdg. 29.25 (978-1-4488-5531-5(4)) Rosen Publishing Group, Inc., The.

Olivares, Katie Lydon. ABC Book of Shadows. l.t. ed. 2005. (Illus.). 30p. (J). bds. 9.99 (978-0-9768573-0-3(8)) Itty Bitty Witch Works.

Parks, Peggy J. Witches. 2007. (Mysterious & Unknown Ser.). (Illus.). 96p. (YA). (gr. 7-12). lib. bdg. 25.95 (978-1-60152-031-9(X)) ReferencePoint Pr., Inc.

Pipe, Jim. Be a Salem Witch! Bizarre Accusations You'd Rather Not Face. 2009. (You Wouldn't Want to Ser.). (ENG., Illus.). 32p. (J). (gr. 3-18). 29.00 (978-0-531-20821-2(4), Watts, Franklin) Scholastic Library Publishing.

—You Wouldn't Want to Be a Salem Witch! 2009. (You Wouldn't Want To Ser.). lib. bdg. 20.80 (978-0-606-04265-9(2), Turtleback) Turtleback Bks.

—You Wouldn't Want to Be a Salem Witch! Bizarre Accusations You'd Rather Not Face. 2009. (You Wouldn't Want to... Ser.). (ENG., Illus.). 32p. (J). pap. 9.95 (978-0-531-21047-5(2), Children's Pr.) Scholastic Library Publishing.

Pizer, Carol. Witchcraft. 2015. (Red Rhino Nonfiction Ser.). (J). lib. bdg. 20.80 (978-0-606-37205-3(9)) Turtleback Bks.

Rieth, Velvet. My First Little Workbook of Wicca: A Child's Guide to Wicca Through Interactive Play. 2007. (J). per. 16.95 (978-0-9794533-0-4(5), Full Circle Pr.) WillowTree Pr., L.L.C.

Roby, Cynthia. Witches. 2016. (Creatures of Fantasy Ser.). (ENG., Illus.). 64p. (J). (gr. 6-6). 34.21 (978-1-5026-0930-4(4)) Cavendish Square Publishing.

Roleff, Tamara L., ed. Black Magic & Witches. 2003. (Illus.). 127p. (J). pap. 18.70 (978-0-7377-1319-0(4), Greenhaven Pr., Inc.) Cengage Gale.

Scholastic, Inc. Staff, contrib. by. Harry Potter: Hogwarts: A Cinematic Yearbook. 2017. (Harry Potter Ser.). (ENG.). 64p. (J). (gr. 3). 12.99 (978-1-338-14924-1(5)) Scholastic, Inc.

Slavicek, Louise Chipley. The Salem Witch Trial: Hysteria in Colonial America. 2011. (Milestones in American History Ser.). (Illus.). 124p. (gr. 6-12). 35.00 (978-1-60413-763-7(0), Chelsea Hse.) Facts On File, Inc.

Smith, Andrea P. The Salem Witch Trials. 2012. (Illus.). 24p. 63.60 (978-1-4488-5215-4(3)); pap. 10.60 (978-1-4488-5214-7(5)); lib. bdg. 25.25 (978-1-4488-5188-1(2)) Rosen Publishing Group, Inc., The. (PowerKids Pr.).

Solotareff, Gregoire. Dictionary of Witches. 2017. (ENG., Illus.). 192p. (J). (gr. 7-12). pap. 14.95 (978-1-77085-995-1(0), 9781770859951) Firefly Bks., Ltd.

Stefoff, Rebecca. Witches & Witchcraft. 2007. (Secrets of the Supernatural Ser.). (Illus.). 80p. (J). (gr. 4-7). lib. bdg. 32.79 (978-0-7614-2637-0(X), Benchmark Bks.) Marshall Cavendish Corp.

Stern, Steven L. Witchcraft in Salem. 2010. (HorrorScapes Ser.). 32p. (YA). (gr. 4-7). lib. bdg. 25.27 (978-1-936088-00-3(2)) Bearport Publishing Co., Inc.

Teen Spirit Wicca. 2014. (ENG., Illus.). 221p. (YA). (gr. 8-17). pap. 22.95 (978-1-78279-059-4(4), Soul Rocks Bks.) Hunt, John Publishing Ltd. GBR. Dist: National Bk. Network.

von Zumbusch, Amelie. The True Story of the Salem Witch Hunts. 2009. (What Really Happened? Ser.). 24p. (gr. 2-3). 42.50 (978-1-60854-770-8(1), PowerKids Pr.) Rosen Publishing Group, Inc., The.

Wallis, Jeffrey. Trials in Salem. 2005. (Houghton Mifflin Social Studies Leveled Readers). (Illus.). 16p. (J). pap. (978-0-618-56037-0(8)) Houghton Mifflin Harcourt Publishing Co.

Wood, Alix. Witch Trials. Wood, Alix, illus. 2013. (Illus.). 32p. (J). (gr. 4-6). 26.60 (978-1-4339-9592-7(1)); pap. 10.50 (978-1-4339-9593-4(X)); pap. 63.00 (978-1-4339-9594-1(8)) Stevens, Gareth Publishing LLLP.

WITCHCRAFT—FICTION

Angelini, Josephine. Trail of Tears. 2015. (Worldwalker Trilogy Ser.: 2). (SPA & ENG.). 352p. (YA). (gr. 7). 17.99 (978-1-250-05090-8(1), 9781250050908) Feiwel & Friends.

Anonymous. Jay's Journal. Sparks, Beatrice, ed. (ENG.). 240p. (YA). 2012. (gr. 9). 17.99 (978-1-4424-8094-0(7)) 2010. (gr. 7). pap. 10.99 (978-1-4424-1993-3(8)) Simon Pulse. (Simon Pulse).

Armstrong, Kelley. The Gathering. (Darkness Rising Ser.: 1). (YA). (gr. 8). 2012. 384p. pap. 9.99 (978-0-06-179703-3(0)) 2011. 368p. 17.99 (978-0-06-179702-6(2)) HarperCollins Pubs.

—The Gathering. (Darkness Rising Ser.: Bk. 1). (YA). 1.25 (978-1-4498-6189-6(X)); 100.75 (978-1-4498-6186-5(5)); 2013. 102.75 (978-1-4498-6184-1(9)) Recorded Bks., Inc.

Balian, Lorna. Humbug Witch, 1 vol. 2004. (ENG., Illus.). 32p. (J). pap. 4.95 (978-1-59572-009-2(X)) Star Bright Bks., Inc.

—Humbug Witch, 1 vol. Balian, Lorna, illus. 2003. (ENG., Illus.). 32p. (J). 12.95 (978-1-932065-32-9(6), 1-718-784-9112) Star Bright Bks., Inc.

Bolger, Kevin. Zombiekins 2. Blecha, Aaron, illus. 2011. (J). 10.99 (978-1-59514-432-4(3), Razorbill) Penguin Publishing Group.

Bolte, Marissa. Arrested for Witchcraft! Nickolas Flux & the Salem Witch Trials, 1 vol. Ginevra, Dante, illus. 2014. (Nickolas Flux History Chronicles Ser.). (ENG.). (gr. 3-4). 40p. pap. 7.95 (978-1-4765-5151-7(0)); 32p. lib. bdg. 30.65 (978-1-4765-3947-8(2)) Capstone Press of Coughlan Cos. (Graphic Library).

Bow, Erin. Plain Kate. (ENG.). 320p. (J). (gr. 7-7). 2012. pap. 9.99 (978-0-545-16665-2(9)) 2010. 17.99 (978-0-545-16664-5(0)) Scholastic, Inc. (Levine, Arthur A. Bks.).

Breslin, Theresa. Whispers in the Graveyard. 2016. (Egmont Modern Classics Ser.). (ENG.). 224p. (J). (gr. 3-5). pap. 8.99 (978-1-4052-8181-2(2)) Egmont Bks., Ltd. GBR. Dist: Independent Pubs. Group.

Brian, Kate, pseud. The Book of Spells. 2011. (Private Ser.). (ENG.). 320p. (YA). (gr. 9). pap. 9.99 (978-1-4424-1237-8(2), Simon & Schuster Bks. For Young Readers) Simon & Schuster Bks. For Young Readers.

Burg, Shana & Coombs, Patricia. Laugh with the Moon. Coombs, Patricia, illus. 2013. (ENG., Illus.). 256p. (J). (gr. 5-6). pap. 6.99 (978-0-440-42210-5(8), Yearling) Random Hse. Children's Bks.

Burge, Constance M. Seasons of the Witch, Vol. 1. Simon and Schuster Children's Staff, ed. 2003. (Charmed Ser.). (ENG.). 192p. (YA). pap. (978-0-689-86545-9(7)) Gallery Pr., The.

Burgis, Stephanie. Renegade Magic. 2012. (Kat, Incorrigible Ser.: 2). (ENG., Illus.). 336p. (J). (gr. 5-9). 16.99 (978-1-4169-9449-7(1), Atheneum Bks. for Young Readers) Simon & Schuster Children's Publishing.

Burtenshaw, Jenna. Winterveil. 2013. (Secrets of Wintercraft Ser.: 3). (ENG.). 304p. (YA). (gr. 8). 17.99 (978-0-06-202646-0(1), Greenwillow Bks.) HarperCollins Pubs.

Cabot, Meg. Jinx. 2007. (gr. 7-12). 262p. (YA). lib. bdg. 17.89 (978-0-06-083765-5(9)); (ENG.). 272p. (J). 16.99 (978-0-06-083764-8(0)) HarperCollins Pubs. (HarperTeen).

Clement-Moore, Rosemary. Texas Gothic. 2012. (ENG.). 416p. (YA). (gr. 9). pap. 10.99 (978-0-385-73694-7(0), Ember) Random Hse. Children's Bks.

Curley, Marianne. Old Magic. 2009. (ENG.). 400p. (YA). (gr. 7-18). pap. 9.99 (978-1-4169-8991-2(9), Simon Pulse) Simon Pulse.

Dahl, Roald. Las Brujas. Date not set.Tr. of Witches. (SPA.). 208p. 15.95 (978-84-204-3655-5(0)) Ediciones Alfaguara ESP. Dist: Santillana USA Publishing Co., Inc.

—Las Brujas. Blake, Quentin, illus. 2003.Tr. of Witches. (SPA.). 200p. (YA). (gr. 5-8). pap. 12.95 (978-958-24-0100-9(1)) Santillana USA Publishing Co., Inc.

DeKeyser, Stacy. The Brixen Witch. Nickle, John, illus. (ENG.). 208p. (J). (gr. 3-7). 2013. pap. 6.99 (978-1-4424-3329-8(9)) 2012. 15.99 (978-1-4424-3328-1(0)) McElderry, Margaret K. Bks. (McElderry, Margaret K. Bks.).

DeLuca, Laura. Destiny. 2011. (ENG.). 276p. (YA). pap. 12.95 (978-0-9826747-2-7(4)) Free Focus Publishing.

Duble, Kathleen Benner. The Sacrifice. 2007. (ENG.). 224p. (J). (gr. 5-9). pap. 7.99 (978-0-689-87651-6(3), McElderry, Margaret K. Bks.) McElderry, Margaret K. Bks.

Duce, Gillian. Magic & Mayhem. 2006. (ENG.). 212p. per. (978-1-894936-64-4(7)) Saga Bks.

Duncan, Lois. Summer of Fear. 2011. (ENG.). 256p. (YA). (gr. 7-17). pap., pap. 9.99 (978-0-316-09907-3(4)) Little, Brown Bks. for Young Readers.

Elfgren, Sara B. & Strandberg, Mats. The Circle: The Engelsfors Trilogy — Book 1. 2013. (Engelsfors Trilogy Ser.: 1). (ENG.). 608p. (gr. 9-13). 18.99 (978-1-4683-0658-3(8), 460658) Overlook Pr., The.

Elliott, Jenny. Save Me. 2015. (ENG.). 336p. (YA). (gr. 7-12). pap. 9.99 (978-1-250-06147-8(4), 9781250061478) Feiwel & Friends.

Gallagher, Diana G. & Burge, Constance M. Trickery Treat. 2008. (Charmed Ser.). (ENG.). 208p. (YA). (gr. 8-12). mass mkt. 6.99 (978-1-4169-3670-1(X)) Pocket Books.

Gibbs, Gretchen. The Book of Maggie Bradstreet. 2012. (Bradstreet Chronicles). (ENG.). 183p. (YA). pap. 9.99 (978-0-9852948-0-9(9)) Glenmere Pr.

Gold, Maya. Spellbinding. 2013. (ENG.). 272p. (J). (gr. 7). pap. 8.99 (978-0-545-43380-8(0)) Scholastic, Inc.

Greenburg, Dan. It's Itchcraft!, 30 vols. Davis, Jack E., illus. 2003. (Zack Files Ser.: 30). (ENG.). 128p. (J). (gr. 2-5). pap. 4.99 (978-0-448-42888-8(1), Grosset & Dunlap) Penguin Young Readers Group.

—It's Itchcraft! Davis, Jack E., illus. 2004. (Zack Files Ser.). 118p. lib. bdg. 15.00 (978-0-7569-2238-2(0)) Perfection Learning Corp.

Hansen, Lynne. A Time for Witches. 2007. (YA). (978-1-4114-9671-2(X), Spark Publishing Group) Sterling Publishing Co., Inc.

Hearn, Julie. The Minister's Daughter. 2006. (ENG.). 272p. (YA). (gr. 7-12). pap. 7.99 (978-0-689-87691-2(2), Atheneum Bks. for Young Readers) Simon & Schuster Children's Publishing.

Hemphill, Stephanie. Wicked Girls: A Novel of the Salem Witch Trials. (YA). 2013. (ENG.). 432p. (gr. 8). pap. 9.99 (978-0-06-185330-2(5)) 2010. 336p. (gr. 7-18). lib. bdg. 17.89 (978-0-06-185329-6(1)) 2010. (ENG.). 416p. (gr. 8-18). 17.99 (978-0-06-185328-9(3)) HarperCollins Pubs.

Hightman, J. P. Spirit. 2008. 224p. (gr. 7-18). (ENG.). (J). 16.99 (978-0-06-085063-0(9)); (YA). lib. bdg. 17.89 (978-0-06-085064-7(7)) HarperCollins Pubs. (HarperTeen).

Hoffman, Alice. Nightbird. (ENG., Illus.). 208p. (J). (gr. 5). 2016. pap. 7.99 (978-0-385-38961-7(2), Yearling) 2015. 16.99 (978-0-385-38958-7(2), Lamb, Wendy Bks.) Random Hse. Children's Bks.

—Nightbird. 2016. lib. bdg. 18.40 (978-0-606-38451-3(0)) Turtleback Bks.

Hoffman, Judy. The Art of Flying: A Novel. Graegin, Stephanie, illus. 2014. (ENG.). 320p. (J). (gr. 3-7). pap. 7.99 (978-1-4231-5907-0(1)) Hyperion Bks. for Children.

Hulme-Cross, Benjamin. The Stone Witch. Evergreen, Nelson, illus. 2015. (Dark Hunter Ser.). (ENG.). 64p. (J). (gr. 4-8). pap. 4.99 (978-1-4677-8089-6(8)) Lerner Publishing Group.

Hunter, Mollie. The Thirteenth Member. 2008. (J). (gr. 6-9). 24.75 (978-0-8446-6362-3(X)) Smith, Peter Pub., Inc.

Jobin, Matthew. The Nethergrim. 2014. (Nethergrim Ser.: 1). (ENG.). 368p. (J). (gr. 5). 17.99 (978-0-399-15998-5(3), Philomel Bks.) Penguin Young Readers Group.

Jones, Diana Wynne. The Chronicles of Chrestomanci. (Chronicles of Chrestomanci Ser.: Nos. 1-2). (YA). (gr. 8-12). Vol. 1. 2007. 608p. pap. 8.99 (978-0-06-447268-5(X)) Vol. 2. 2007. 560p. pap. 8.99 (978-0-06-447269-2(8)) Vol. 3. 2008. 688p. pap. 8.99 (978-0-06-114832-3(6)) HarperCollins Pubs. (Greenwillow Bks.).

—The Chronicles of Chrestomanci Vol. 1: Charmed Life; The Lives of Christopher Chant, Vol. 1. 2007. (Chrestomanci Ser.). (YA). (gr. 5-8). lib. bdg. 19.65 (978-0-613-31070-3(5), Turtleback) Turtleback Bks.

—Conrad's Fate. 2006. (ENG., Illus.). 352p. (978-0-00-719087-4(5)) HarperCollins Children's Bks.

—Conrad's Fate. (J). 2006. (Chronicles of Chrestomanci Ser.: 3). 400p. (gr. 3-7). per. 6.99 (978-0-06-074745-9(5), Greenwillow Bks.) 2005. (Chrestomanci Ser.: No. 5). 384p. (gr. k-17). lib. bdg. 17.89 (978-0-06-074744-2(7)) 2005. (Chrestomanci Ser.: No. 5). 384p. (gr. 5-18). 16.99 (978-0-06-074743-5(9)) HarperCollins Pubs.

—Conrad's Fate: Read-Along/Homework Pack, 6 vols. 2005. (Chrestomanci Ser.: No. 5). (J). (gr. 5-8). 86.75 (978-1-4193-3551-8(0), 42039) Recorded Bks., Inc.

—The Pinhoe Egg. (J). 2007. (Chronicles of Chrestomanci Ser.: 6). 480p. (gr. 3-7). per. 7.99 (978-0-06-113126-4(1), Greenwillow Bks.) 2006. (Chrestomanci Ser.: No. 6). 528p. lib. bdg. 18.89 (978-0-06-113125-7(3)) HarperCollins Pubs.

Karmaniolos, Ellie. Groomilda, the Witch. 2016. (ENG., Illus.). 24p. (J). pap. 24.19 (978-1-5245-1857-8(3)) Xlibris Corp.

Konigsburg, E. L. Jennifer, Hecate, Macbeth, William McKinley, & Me, Elizabeth. (J). (gr. 3-6). 177p. pap. 4.99 (978-0-8072-1524-1(4)); 117p. pap. 4.99 (978-0-8072-1417-6(5)) Random Hse. Audio Publishing Group. (Listening Library).

—Jennifer, Hecate, Macbeth, William Mckinley, & Me, Elizabeth. 2007. (ENG., Illus.). 128p. (J). (gr. 3-7). pap. 7.99 (978-1-4169-3396-0(4), Atheneum Bks. for Young Readers) Simon & Schuster Children's Publishing.

Lachtman, Ofelia Dumas. The Trouble with Tessa. 2005. 122p. (J). (gr. 3-7). per. 9.95 (978-1-55885-448-2(7), Piñata Books) Arte Publico Pr.

Laird, Elizabeth. The Betrayal of Maggie Blair. 2011. (ENG.). 432p. (YA). (gr. 7-18). 16.99 (978-0-547-34126-2(1)) Houghton Mifflin Harcourt Publishing Co.

MacHale, D.j. Black Moon Rising. 2017. (J). pap. (978-1-101-93260-5(0)) Random Hse., Inc.

Magaziner, Lauren. The Only Thing Worse Than Witches. 2014. (ENG.). 272p. (J). (gr. 3-7). 16.99 (978-0-8037-3918-5(4), Dial Bks) Penguin Young Readers Group.

Martinez, Roland L. The Evil Leaf. 2009. 232p. 24.99 (978-1-4490-0916-8(6)); pap. 14.90 (978-1-4490-0917-5(4)) AuthorHouse.

Mather, Adriana. How to Hang a Witch. 2016. (ENG.). 368p. (YA). (gr. 7). 17.99 (978-0-553-53947-9(7), Knopf Bks. for Young Readers) Random Hse. Children's Bks.

McAllister, Margaret. High Crag Linn. 2008. (ENG.). 224p. (YA). (gr. 7-18). pap. 8.95 (978-0-7459-6062-3(6)) Lion Hudson PLC GBR. Dist: Independent Pubs. Group.

McGann, Erika. The Broken Spell. 2014. (Demon Notebook Ser.: 2). (ENG.). 352p. (J). (gr. 4-8). pap. 6.99 (978-1-4926-0296-5(5), Sourcebooks Jabberwocky) Sourcebooks, Inc.

—The Demon Notebook. 2014. (Demon Notebook Ser.: 1). (ENG.). 288p. (J). (gr. 3-6). pap. 6.99 (978-1-4022-9538-6(3), 9781402295386, Sourcebooks Jabberwocky) Sourcebooks, Inc.

McNeil, Gretchen. Possess. (ENG.). (YA). (gr. 8). 2012. 400p. pap. 9.99 (978-0-06-206072-3(4)) 2011. 384p. 17.99 (978-0-06-206071-6(6)) HarperCollins Pubs.

Moore, Daniel. Abdallah Jones & the DisappearingDust. 2006. 168p. pap. 17.00 (978-0-615-13570-0(6)) Ecstatic Exchange, The.

Myracle, Lauren. Rhymes with Witches. (ENG.). (YA). (gr. 8-17). 2006. 272p. pap. 7.95 (978-0-8109-9215-3(9)) 2005. 224p. 16.95 (978-0-8109-5859-3(7), Amulet Bks.) Abrams, Inc.

Naifeh, Ted. Courtney Crumrin & the Prince of Nowhere. Nozemack, Joe & Beaton, Jill, eds. 2008. (Illus.). 54p. (J). pap. 5.95 (978-1-932664-86-7(6)) Oni Pr., Inc.

—Courtney Crumrin Volume 1: The Night Things Special Edition. 2012. (ENG., Illus.). 144p. (YA). 19.99 (978-1-934964-77-4(8), 9781934964774) Oni Pr., Inc.

Naylor, Phyllis Reynolds. The Witch Returns. 2005. (Witch Ser.: No. 6). 186p. (J). (gr. 3-7). 12.65 (978-0-7569-5504-5(1)) Perfection Learning Corp.

—Witch Weed. 2004. (ENG., Illus.). 192p. (J). (gr. 3-7). pap. 9.99 (978-0-689-85381-4(5), Simon & Schuster/Paula Wiseman Bks.) Simon & Schuster/Paula Wiseman Bks.

Nix, Garth. The Ragwitch. 2004. (ENG., Illus.). 400p. (YA). (gr. 8-18). pap. 8.99 (978-0-06-050807-4(8), HarperTeen) HarperCollins Pubs.

Ocelot, Michel. Kirikou et la Soriciere. pap. 14.95 (978-2-01-321877-1(X)) Hachette Groupe Livre FRA. Dist: Distribooks, Inc.

Papineau, Lucie. Baby Witch, Yuck! 2004. (Illus.). (J). (gr. -1-18). spiral bd. (978-0-616-03052-3(5)); spiral bd. (978-0-616-04560-2(3)) Canadian National Institute for the Blind/Institut National Canadien pour les Aveugles.

Preussler, Otfried. Krabat & the Sorcerer's Mill. Bell, Anthea, tr. from GER. 2014. (ENG.). 264p. (J). (gr. 3-7). 17.95 (978-1-59017-778-5(9), NYR Children's Collection) New York Review of Bks., Inc., The.

Rinaldi, Ann. A Break with Charity: A Story about the Salem Witch Trials. 2003. (Great Episodes Ser.). (ENG.). 320p. (YA). (gr. 7-8). pap. 8.99 (978-0-15-204682-8(8)) Houghton Mifflin Harcourt Publishing Co.

Rowling, J. K. Harry Potter à l'École des Sorciers. Menard, Jean-François, tr. from ENG. 2007. (Harry Potter Ser.: Year 1).Tr. of Harry Potter & the Sorcerer's Stone. 311p. (J). per. 14.95 (978-2-07-061236-9(8)) Gallimard, Editions FRA. Dist: Distribooks, Inc.

Shutter. 2015. (ENG.). 384p. (YA). (gr. 8-12). 17.99 (978-1-250-04467-9(7)) Feiwel & Friends.

Smith, L. J. The Captive Part II & the Power. 2012. (Secret Circle Ser.: Vols. 1-2). (ENG.). 416p. (YA). (gr. 8). pap. 9.99 (978-0-06-167135-7(5), HarperTeen) HarperCollins Pubs.

—The Hunt, Vol. 5. 2012. (Secret Circle Ser.: 5). (ENG.). 288p. (YA). (gr. 8). 17.99 (978-0-06-213042-6(0), HarperTeen) HarperCollins Pubs.

—The Initiation & the Captive. movie tie-in ed. 2011. (Secret Circle Ser.). (ENG.). 416p. (YA). (gr. 8). pap. 9.99 (978-0-06-211900-1(1), HarperTeen) HarperCollins Pubs.

—The Secret Circle Vol.4: The Divide. 2012. (Secret Circle Ser.: 4). (ENG.). 304p. (YA). (gr. 8). 17.99 (978-0-06-213039-6(0), HarperTeen) HarperCollins Pubs.

Snyder, Zilpha Keatley. The Witches of Worm. 2009. 9.00 (978-0-7848-3612-5(4), Everbind) Marco Bk. Co.

—The Witches of Worm. Raible, Alton, illus. 2009. (ENG.). (J). (gr. 3-7). 192p. 16.99 (978-1-4169-9531-9(5)); 208p. pap. 7.99 (978-1-4169-9053-6(4)) Simon & Schuster Children's Publishing. (Atheneum Bks. for Young Readers).

—The Witches of Worm. 2006. 22.75 (978-0-8446-7290-8(4)) Smith, Peter Pub., Inc.

Speare, Elizabeth George. The Witch of Blackbird Pond. 2011. (ENG.). 272p. (J). (gr. 5-7). pap. 7.99 (978-0-547-55029-9(4)) Houghton Mifflin Harcourt Publishing Co.

—The Witch of Blackbird Pond. Random House Publishing Group.

—The Witch of Blackbird Pond. 2004. 223p. (J). (gr. 4-7). pap., tchr.'s planning gde. ed. 38.00 incl. audio (978-0-8072-0862-5(0), Listening Library) Random Hse. Audio Publishing Group.

Spence, Craig. Josh & the Magic Vial. 2006. (ENG.). 396p. (J). per. 17.95 (978-1-897235-10-2(0)) Thistledown Pr., Ltd. CAN. Dist: Univ. of Toronto Pr.

Stolarz, Laurie Faria. Red Is for Remembrance. 2005. (Stolarz Ser.: 4). (ENG.). 336p. (YA). pap. 11.99 (978-0-7387-0760-0(0), Flux) North Star Editions.

—Red Is for Remembrance. l.t. ed. 2008. (Blue Is for Nightmares Ser.: Bk. 4). 385p. (YA). (gr. 7). 22.95 (978-1-4104-0339-1(4)) Thorndike Pr.

—Silver Is for Secrets. 2005. (Stolarz Ser.: 3). (ENG.). 288p. (YA). pap. 11.99 (978-0-7387-0631-3(0), Flux) North Star Editions.

—White Is for Magic. Karre, Andrew, ed. 2004. (Stolarz Ser.: 2). (ENG.). 312p. (YA). pap. 11.99 (978-0-7387-0443-2(1), Flux) North Star Editions.

Stone, Kelsey. The Predahil Chronicles. 2005. (YA). per. 6.49 (978-1-59196-995-2(6)) Instant Pub.

Thompson, Paul B. The Devil's Door: A Salem Witchcraft Story. 2010. (Historical Fiction Adventures (HFA) Ser.). (Illus.). 160p. (J). pap. 10.95 (978-1-59845-214-3(2)); (gr. 3-6). 29.27 (978-0-7660-3387-0(2)) Enslow Pubs., Inc.

Tiernan, Cate. A Chalice of Wind - A Circle of Ashes - A Feather of Stone - A Necklace of Water. 2011. (Balefire Ser.). (ENG.). 976p. (YA). (gr. 7-18). 9.99 (978-1-59514-411-9(0), Razorbill) Penguin Young Readers Group.

—Awakening. 2007. (Sweep Ser.: 5). (ENG.). 192p. (YA). (gr. 7-18). pap. 7.99 (978-0-14-241020-2(9), Speak) Penguin Young Readers Group.

—Book of Shadows, Bk. 1. 2007. (Sweep Ser.: 1). (ENG.). 192p. (YA). (gr. 7-18). pap. 7.99 (978-0-14-240986-2(3), Speak) Penguin Young Readers Group.

—The Calling, Bk. 7. 2008. (Sweep Ser.: 7). (ENG.). 192p. (YA). (gr. 7-18). 7.99 (978-0-14-241022-6(5), Speak) Penguin Young Readers Group.

—Changeling, Bk. 8. 2008. (Sweep Ser.: 8). (ENG.). 192p. (YA). (gr. 7-18). 7.99 (978-0-14-241023-3(3), Speak) Penguin Young Readers Group.

—Dark Magick, Bk. 4. 2007. (Sweep Ser.: 4). (ENG.). 192p. (YA). (gr. 7-18). 7.99 (978-0-14-240989-3(8), Speak) Penguin Young Readers Group.

—Dark Magick - Awakening - Spellbound, 2 vols., Vol. 2. 2010. (Sweep Ser.: 2). (ENG.). 576p. (YA). (gr. 7-18). pap. 9.99 (978-0-14-241897-0(8), Speak) Penguin Young Readers Group.

—Spellbound. 2007. (Sweep Ser.: 6). (ENG.). 192p. (YA). (gr. 7-18). 7.99 (978-0-14-241021-9(7), Speak) Penguin Young Readers Group.

—Sweep Vol. 3: The Calling - Changeling - Strife, 3 vols. 2011. (Sweep Ser.: 3). (ENG.). 576p. (YA). (gr. 7-18). 9.99 (978-0-14-241955-7(9), Speak) Penguin Young Readers Group.

Vande Velde, Vivian. Dragon's Bait. 2003. (ENG., Illus.). 208p. (YA). (gr. 7-12). pap. 13.95 (978-0-15-216663-2(7)) Houghton Mifflin Harcourt Publishing Co.

—Magic Can Be Murder. 2009. (ENG.). 208p. (YA). (gr. 7). pap. 12.99 (978-0-547-25872-0(0)) Houghton Mifflin Harcourt Publishing Co.

Vega, Danielle. The Merciless. 2014. (Merciless Ser.: 1). (ENG.). 288p. (YA). (gr. 9). 17.99 (978-1-59514-722-6(5), Razorbill) Penguin Young Readers Group.

Walton, Rick. Pig Pigger Piggest. Holder, Jimmy, illus. 2003. (ENG.). 32p. (J). (gr. 1). reprint ed. pap. 6.99 (978-1-58685-318-1(X)) Gibbs Smith, Publisher.

Whipple, Natalie. House of Ivy & Sorrow. 2014. (ENG.). 368p. (YA). (gr. 8). pap. 9.99 (978-0-06-212018-2(2), HarperTeen) HarperCollins Pubs.

White, Paul. Jungle Doctor Spots a Leopard. 2008. (Flamingo Fiction 9-13s Ser.). (ENG., Illus.). 176p. (J). (gr. 5-7). per. 8.99 (978-1-84550-301-7(5), 6c36bf51-d79e-4a21-bb4f-54dc3b30085b) Christian Focus Pubns. GBR. Dist: Bookmasters Distribution.

—Jungle Doctor's Enemies. 2011. (Flamingo Fiction 9-13s Ser.). (ENG., Illus.). 160p. (J). (gr. 5-7). pap. 8.99 *(978-1-84550-300-0(7)*, c2552503-49be-450c-84cc-9ec522751da8) Christian Focus Pubns. GBR. Dist: Bookmasters Distribution.

Wigington, Patti. Summer's Ashes. 2007. (ENG.). 208p. (gr. 8-12). per. 15.00 *(978-0-9766805-9-8(9))* Keene Publishing.

Wrede, Patricia C. Snow White & Rose Red. 2009. (ENG.). 288p. (YA). (gr. 7-18). 8.99 *(978-0-14-241121-6(3)*, Firebird) Penguin Young Readers Group.

WITCHES

Alexander, Audrey. Witches & Wicca. 2015. (J). *(978-1-61900-072-8(5))* Eldorado Ink.

Beaumont, Steve. How to Draw Witches & Wizards. (Drawing Fantasy Art Ser.). 32p. (gr. 4-5). 2009. 50.50 *(978-1-61512-195-3(1)*, PowerKids Pr.) 2007. (Illus.). (J). lib. bdg. 26.50 *(978-1-4042-3857-2(3))* Rosen Publishing Group, Inc., The.

—How to Draw Wizards, Warriors, Orcs & Elves. 2007. (Illus.). 143p. pap. 7.99 *(978-0-7858-2345-2(X)*, Chartwell) Book Sales, Inc.

Braun, Eric. The Truth about Witches, 1 vol. Squier, Robert, illus. 2010. (Fairy-Tale Superstars Ser.). (ENG.). 32p. (gr. 1-3). lib. bdg. 27.32 *(978-1-4048-6160-2(2))* Picture Window Bks.

Brinker, Spencer. The Witch's Things: A Counting to 20 Rhyme. 2015. (Illus.). 32p. (J). lib. bdg. *(978-1-62724-333-9(X))* Bearport Publishing Co., Inc.

Broutin, Christian & Delafosse, Claude. Let's Look at Fairies, Witches, Giants & Dragons. 2012. (ENG., Illus.). 38p. (J). (gr. k-3). pap. 11.99 *(978-1-85103-358-4(0))* Moonlight Publishing, Ltd. GBR. Dist: Independent Pubs. Group.

Bullard, Lisa. I'M Casting a Spell!! Meet a Fairy-Tale Witch. Diaz, Diego, illus. 2014. (Monster Buddies Ser.). (ENG.). 24p. (gr. k-2). lib. bdg. 23.93 *(978-0-7613-9192-0(4)*, Millbrook Pr.) Lerner Publishing Group.

Castellano, Peter. Witches. 2016. (Monsters! Ser.). (ENG.). 32p. (J). (gr. 1-2). pap. 10.50 *(978-1-4824-4102-4(0))* Stevens, Gareth Publishing LLLP.

Cheatham, Mark. Witches! 2012. (Jr. Graphic Monster Stories Ser.). (ENG.). 24p. (J). (gr. 3-6). pap. 10.60 *(978-1-4488-6407-2(0))*; lib. bdg. 25.25 *(978-1-4488-6224-5(8))* Rosen Publishing Group, Inc., The. (PowerKids Pr.).

Frisch, Aaron. That's Spooky: Witches. 2013. (That's Spooky Ser.). (ENG., Illus.). 24p. (J). (gr. 1-3). pap. 7.99 *(978-0-89812-807-9(2)*, Creative Paperbacks) Creative Co., The.

—Witches. 2013. (Illus.). 24p. (J). 25.65 *(978-1-60818-250-3(9)*, Creative Education) Creative Co., The.

Graves, Lisa. History's Witches. Graves, Lisa, illus. 2013. (Illus.). 32p. 19.99 *(978-1-62395-516-8(5))* Xist Publishing.

Guiley, Rosemary Ellen. Witches & Wiccans. 2009. (Mysteries, Legends, & Unexplained Phenomena Ser.). 120p. (gr. 6-12). pap. 10.95 *(978-0-7910-9896-7(6)*, Checkmark Bks.) Facts On File, Inc.

Hamilton, John. Witches, 1 vol. 2007. (World of Horror Ser.). (ENG., Illus.). 32p. (gr. 4-8). 27.07 *(978-1-59928-776-8(5)*, Abdo & Daughters) ABDO Publishing Co.

—Wizards & Witches, 1 vol. 2004. (Fantasy & Folklore Ser.). (ENG., Illus.). 32p. (gr. 4-8). 27.07 *(978-1-59197-716-2(9)*, Abdo & Daughters) ABDO Publishing Co.

Hill, Raine. Growing up Pagan: A Workbook for Wiccan Families, 1 vol. Pearce, Gillian M., illus. 2009. (ENG.). 64p. pap., wbk. ed. 19.99 *(978-0-7643-3143-5(4)*, 9780764331435) Schiffer Publishing, Ltd.

Kerns, Ann. Wizards & Witches. 2009. (Fantasy Chronicles Ser.). (ENG., Illus.). 48p. (gr. 4-7). lib. bdg. 27.93 *(978-0-8225-9983-8(X))* Lerner Publishing Group.

Leblanc, Catherine. How to Outwit Witches. Garrigue, Roland, illus. 2013. (ENG.). 32p. (J). (gr. -1). 14.99 *(978-1-60887-193-3(2))* Insight Editions.

Loh-Hagan, Virginia. Witches: Magic, Myth, & Mystery. 2016. (Magic, Myth, & Mystery Ser.). (ENG., Illus.). 32p. (J). (gr. 4-8). 29.93 *(978-1-63471-112-8(2)*, 208559, 45th Parallel Press) Cherry Lake Publishing.

Lynette, Rachel. Witches. 2006. (Mysterious Encounters Ser.). (ENG., Illus.). 48p. (J). (gr. 4-8). lib. bdg. 27.50 *(978-0-7377-3643-4(7)*, LML02109-229793, Kidhaven) Cengage Gale.

Marsico, Katie. Magic Monsters: From Witches to Goblins. 2017. (Monster Mania Ser.). (ENG.). 32p. (J). (gr. 2-5). 12.99 ***(978-1-5124-3821-5(9)***, Lerner Pubns.); 39.99 ***(978-1-5124-2815-5(9)***, Lerner Pubns.); 39.99 ***(978-1-5124-3822-2(7)***, Lerner Pubns.); (Illus.). 26.65 *(978-1-5124-2595-6(8))* Lerner Publishing Group.

Narayan, Natasha. Witches, Wizards & Warlocks of London. 2004. (Of London Ser.). (ENG., Illus.). 96p. (J). pap. 8.99 *(978-1-904153-12-2(7))* Watling St., Ltd. GBR. Dist: Independent Pubs. Group.

Netzley, Patricia D. Do Witches Exist? 2015. (ENG., Illus.). 80p. (J). lib. bdg. *(978-1-60152-862-9(0))* ReferencePoint Pr., Inc.

O'Hearn, Michael. Ghosts vs. Witches: Tussle of the Tricksters. Moffet, Patricia, illus. 2011. (Monster Wars Ser.). (ENG.). 32p. (gr. 3-4). pap. 47.70 *(978-1-4296-7262-7(5))*; lib. bdg. 27.99 *(978-1-4296-6522-3(X))* Capstone Press of Coughlan Cos. (Edge Bks.).

Parks, Peggy J. Witches. 2007. (Mysterious & Unknown Ser.). (Illus.). 96p. (YA). (gr. 7-12). lib. bdg. 25.95 *(978-1-60152-031-9(X))* ReferencePoint Pr., Inc.

Rawson, Christopher. Stories of Witches. Cartwright, Stephen, illus. 2004. (Young Reading Ser.: Vol. 1). 48p. (J). (gr. 2-18). lib. bdg. 13.95 *(978-1-58086-630-9(1)*, Usborne) EDC Publishing.

Roby, Cynthia. Witches. 2016. (Creatures of Fantasy Ser.). (ENG., Illus.). 64p. (J). (gr. 6-6). 34.21 *(978-1-5026-0930-4(4))* Cavendish Square Publishing.

Solotareff, Gregoire. Dictionary of Witches. 2017. (ENG., Illus.). 192p. (J). (gr. 7-12). pap. 14.95 ***(978-1-77085-995-1(0)***, 9781770859951) Firefly Bks., Ltd.

Steffoff, Rebecca. Witches & Witchcraft. 2007. (Secrets of the Supernatural Ser.). (Illus.). 80p. (J). (gr. 4-7). lib. bdg. 32.79 *(978-0-7614-2637-0(X)*, Benchmark Bks.) Marshall Cavendish Corp.

Stemple, Heidi E. Y. Witch Haunts. 2016. (Scary Places Ser.). (ENG.). 32p. (J). (gr. 4-8). 19.95 *(978-1-944102-39-5(6))* Bearport Publishing Co., Inc.

Susaeta, Equipo. LAS BRUJAS. (SPA.). (J). 3.48 *(978-84-305-9406-1(X))* Susaeta Ediciones, S.A. ESP. Dist: AIMS International Bks., Inc.

Tieck, Sarah. Witches, 1 vol. 2016. (ENG.). 32p. (J). *(978-1-62403-769-6(0))* ABDO Publishing Co.

Turner, Queen of England Patrenia. Queen Patrenialla - A Canadian Story Poem. Turner, Keeng of England Troyius, ed. 2015. (Illus.). pap. *(978-0-578-18000-7(6))* Royalty Patrenia Turner Publications.

West, David & Ganeri, Anita. Witches & Warlocks. West, David & Ganeri, Anita, illus. 2010. (Dark Side Ser.). (ENG., Illus.). 32p. (J). lib. bdg. 26.50 *(978-1-61531-901-5(8)*, PowerKids Pr.) Rosen Publishing Group, Inc., The.

Witch Sticker Book. 2003. (Illus.). 16p. (J). 2.98 *(978-1-84273-117-8(3)*, Exclusive Editions) Parragon, Inc.

WITCHES—FICTION

Adams, Adrienne. A Woggle of Witches. Adams, Adrienne, illus. 2017. (ENG., Illus.). 32p. (J). (gr. -1-3). 13.99 ***(978-1-5344-1246-0(8)***, Aladdin) Simon & Schuster Children's Publishing.

Adams, Denise H. Itchy the Witch. Adams, Denise H., illus. 2007. (Illus.). 32p. (J). (gr. -1-3). 13.99 *(978-1-59879-385-7(3))* Lifevest Publishing, Inc.

Aikins, Dave, illus. Dora Saves the Snow Princess. 2008. (Dora the Explorer Ser.: 27). (ENG.). 24p. (J). (gr. -1-2). pap. 3.99 *(978-1-4169-5866-6(5)*, Simon Spotlight/Nickelodeon) Simon Spotlight/Nickelodeon.

Alcántara, Ricardo. Huy, Que Miedo! 13th ed. 2003. (SPA., Illus.). 44p. *(978-84-236-2559-8(1)*, ED6263) Edebé ESP. Dist: Lectorum Pubns., Inc.

Alexander, R. C. Unfamiliar Magic. 2011. (ENG.). 368p. (J). (gr. 3-7). pap. 8.99 *(978-0-375-85855-0(5)*, Yearling) Random Hse. Children's Bks.

Alexander, Susanne L. Adventures of the Pixies of Penny Brook Village: Reeza's Revenge. 2007. 174p. (J). pap. 12.95 *(978-0-7414-4292-5(2))* Infinity Publishing.

Almeida, Jose-Gabriel. Lodiville: Adventure Land. 2008. 52p. pap. 16.95 *(978-1-60563-989-5(3))* America Star Bks.

Alton, Steve. The Firehills. 2005. (ENG.). 192p. (YA). (gr. 5-12). 15.95 *(978-1-57505-798-9(0)*, Carolrhoda Bks.) Lerner Publishing Group.

—The Malifex. 2003. (Middle Readers Ser.). (Illus.). 182p. (J). (gr. 3-7). 14.95 *(978-0-8225-0959-2(8))* Lerner Publishing Group.

Anderson, Al. Adventures with Bingo Borden. Agora Publications Staff, tr. Kurzyca, Krystyna Emilia, illus. 2010. 77p. (J). pap. 9.50 *(978-1-887250-46-7(8))* Agora Pubns., Inc.

Anderson, Clay. Mary Margaret Hammersmith & the Lady of the Roundtable, 1 vol. 2009. 134p. pap. 24.95 *(978-1-4489-1892-8(8))* America Star Bks.

Andrews, Nina. Ciara's Witch. 2004. 272p. (YA). pap. 22.50 *(978-1-920731-62-5(8))* Fremantle Pr. AUS. Dist: Independent Pubs. Group.

Anholt, Laurence. Hansel & Gretel & the Space Witch. 2016. (Seriously Silly: Scary Fairy Tales Ser.). (ENG., Illus.). 48p. (J). (gr. k-17). pap. 6.99 *(978-1-4083-2960-3(3)*, Orchard Bks.) Hachette Children's Group GBR. Dist: Hachette Bk. Group.

Argyle, Amber. Winter Queen. 2013. 256p. 21.99 *(978-0-9857394-4-7(4))* Starling Publishing.

Arthur, Jenny. Little Witch. Arthur, Jenny, illus. 2012. (Spooky Sounds Ser.). (ENG., Illus.). 10p. (J). (gr. k — 1). 7.99 *(978-0-230-74487-5(7))* Macmillan Pubs., Ltd. GBR. Dist: Independent Pubs. Group.

Ashby, Mandy Anne. Mindy's Adventure with the Pussycat Witches: Playing in the Rain. 2011. (Illus.). 28p. pap. 20.66 *(978-1-4567-8788-2(8))* AuthorHouse.

Ashby, Norman. Magic Fireplace. 2003. (Illus.). 50p. pap. *(978-1-84401-066-0(X))* Athena Pr.

Asquith, Ros. Trixie Gets the Witch Factor. 2007. (Trixie Ser.). (ENG., Illus.). 176p. (J). (gr. 3-6). pap. 13.95 *(978-0-00-725910-6(7))* HarperCollins Pubs. Ltd. GBR. Dist: Independent Pubs. Group.

Attia, Stephan. Other Christmas Stories. 2009. 42p. pap. 19.68 *(978-0-557-11189-3(7))* Lulu Pr., Inc.

Atwater-Rhodes, Amelia. Persistence of Memory. 2010. (Den of Shadows Ser.: Bk. 4). (ENG.). 224p. (YA). (gr. 7). pap. 8.99 *(978-0-440-24004-4(2)*, Delacorte Pr.) Random Hse. Children's Bks.

Baeten, Lieve. The Clever Little Witch. Fossey, Wietse, illus. 2012. (ENG.). 32p. (J). (gr. -1-1). 16.95 *(978-0-7358-4079-9(2))* North-South Bks., Inc.

—The Curious Little Witch. 2010. (ENG., Illus.). 32p. (gr. -1-3). 16.95 *(978-0-7358-2305-1(7))* North-South Bks., Inc.

—Curious Little Witch Board Book. 2012. (ENG., Illus.). 14p. (J). (gr. -1 — 1). bds. 9.95 *(978-0-7358-4102-4(0))* North-South Bks., Inc.

—Up & Away with the Little Witch. 2011. (ENG., Illus.). 32p. (J). (gr. -1-2). 16.95 *(978-0-7358-4004-1(0))* North-South Bks., Inc.

Baker, E. D. Dragon's Breath: Read-Along/Homework Pack, 6 vols. unabr. ed. 2005. (Frog Princess Ser.: 2). (SPA.). (J). (gr. 5-8). 78.75 *(978-1-4193-3563-1(4)*, 42041) Recorded Bks., Inc.

—A Question of Magic. 2015. (ENG.). 288p. (YA). (gr. 3-6). pap. 8.99 *(978-1-61963-437-4(6)*, 9781619634374, Bloomsbury USA Childrens) Bloomsbury Publishing USA.

Barnhill, Kelly. The Girl Who Drank the Moon. 2016. (ENG.). 400p. (J). (gr. 5-9). 17.95 *(978-1-61620-567-6(9))* Algonquin Bks. of Chapel Hill.

—The Witch's Boy. 2014. (ENG.). 384p. (J). (gr. 4). 17.95 *(978-1-61620-351-1(X)*, 73351) Algonquin Bks. of Chapel Hill.

Barraclough, Lindsey. The Mark of Cain. 2016. (ENG.). 496p. (YA). (gr. 9). 17.99 *(978-0-7636-7864-7(3))* Candlewick Pr.

Bateson Hill, Margaret. Masha & the Firebird. Wilson, Anne, illus. 2005. (Folk Tales Ser.: 1). (RUS & ENG.). 32p. (J). pap. *(978-1-84089-201-7(3))* Zero to Ten, Ltd.

Batham, Matthew. Lightsleep. 2006. 167p. pap. *(978-1-904623-39-7(5))* WritersPrintShop.

Baum, L. Frank. 8 Books In: L. Frank Baum's Oz Series, volume 2 of 2. Little Wizard Stories of Oz, Tik-Tok of Oz, the Scarecrow of Oz, Rinkitink in Oz, the Lost P. 2008. 812p. pap. *(978-1-905921-09-6(8))* Shoes & Ships & Sealing Wax Ltd.

Baxter, Nicola. Witches, Wizards & Magicians. Morton, Ken, illus. 2012. (ENG.). 80p. (J). (gr. k-4). pap. 9.99 *(978-1-84322-807-3(6))* Anness Publishing GBR. Dist: National Bk. Network.

Begler, Peter. The Fearless Travelers' Guide to Wicked Places. 2017. (ENG., Illus.). 384p. (gr. 4-8). 14.95 *(978-1-62370-799-6(4))* Capstone Young Readers of Coughlan Cos.

Bell, Hilari. The Goblin Gate. (ENG.). (YA). (gr. 8). 2011. 400p. pap. 8.99 *(978-0-06-165104-5(4))* 2010. 384p. 16.99 *(978-0-06-165102-1(8))* HarperCollins Pubs. (HarperTeen).

—The Goblin Wood. 2004. (Illus.). 371p. (J). (gr. 5-9). 14.65 *(978-0-7569-3253-4(X))* Perfection Learning Corp.

Bennett, Anna Elizabeth. Little Witch. Stone, Helen, illus. 60th anniv. ed. 2013. (ENG.). 128p. (J). (gr. k-3). pap. 12.95 *(978-1-61608-964-1(4)*, 608964, Sky Pony Pr.) Skyhorse Publishing Co., Inc.

Berger, Samantha. Boo-La-La Witch Spa. Roxas, Isabel, illus. 2015. (ENG.). 32p. (J). (gr. -1-k). 16.99 *(978-0-8037-3886-7(2)*, Dial Bks) Penguin Young Readers Group.

BeSwitched. 2004. (YA). mass mkt. 7.99 *(978-0-9759784-0-5(3))* Breezy Reads.

Biederman, Ashley. The Witches Keys. 2012. 250p. 28.99 *(978-1-105-52163-8(X))* Lulu Pr., Inc.

Bishop, Debbie. MYST of the Lost Shadow Boys. 2008. (ENG.). 228p. (J). (gr. 4-9). pap. 6.99 *(978-1-932431-79-7(9))* Left Field Angel Gate.

Blacker, Terence & Ross, Tony. En la Carcel. 2003. (Serafina the Little Witch Ser.). (SPA., Illus.). 72p. (J). 7.95 *(978-84-8453-011-4(6))* Ediciones del Bronce ESP. Dist: Planeta Publishing Corp.

—Estrella de la Tele. 2003. (Serafina the Little Witch Ser.). (SPA.). 80p. (J). 7.95 *(978-84-8453-066-4(3))* Ediciones del Bronce ESP. Dist: Planeta Publishing Corp.

—Fuera de Control. 2003. (Serafina the Little Witch Ser.). (SPA., Illus.). 72p. (J). 7.95 *(978-84-8453-049-7(3))* Ediciones del Bronce ESP. Dist: Planeta Publishing Corp.

—Una Intrusa en el Hospital. 2003. (Serafina the Little Witch Ser.). (SPA., Illus.). 72p. (J). 7.95 *(978-84-8453-010-7(8))* Ediciones del Bronce ESP. Dist: Planeta Publishing Corp.

—Un Mundo de Problemas. 2003. (Serafina the Little Witch Ser.). (SPA.). 80p. (J). 7.95 *(978-84-8453-009-1(4))* Ediciones del Bronce ESP. Dist: Planeta Publishing Corp.

Blevins, Wiley. Hansel & Gretel & the Haunted Hut. Cox, Steve, illus. 2016. (Scary Tales Retold Ser.). (ENG.). 24p. (gr. k-3). pap. 6.99 *(978-1-63440-097-8(6))* Red Chair Pr.

—Hansel & Gretel & the Haunted Hut. Cox, Steve, illus. 2016. (Scary Tales Retold Ser.). (ENG.). 24p. (gr. k-3). lib. bdg. 23.99 *(978-1-63440-096-1(8))* Red Chair Pr.

Bloom, Ira. Hearts & Other Body Parts. 2017. (ENG.). 352p. (J). (gr. 9). 17.99 *(978-1-338-03073-0(6)*, Scholastic Pr.) Scholastic, Inc.

Bredin, Henrietta & McEwen, Priscilla. The Prince & the Goosegirl: A Story with Activities Based on the Opera by Humperdinck. 2006. (Illus.). 30p. (J). (gr. k-4). reprint ed. pap. 17.00 *(978-1-4223-5538-1(1))* DIANE Publishing Co.

Brezenoff, Steve. Witch Mayor, 1 vol. Percival, Tom, illus. 2012. (Ravens Pass Ser.). (ENG.). 96p. (gr. 2-3). pap. 6.15 *(978-1-4342-4212-9(9))*; lib. bdg. 25.32 *(978-1-4342-3791-0(5))* Stone Arch Bks.

Brignull, Irena. The Hawkweed Prophecy. 2017. (Hawkweed Ser.: 1). (ENG.). 384p. (gr. 7-17). pap. 10.99 ***(978-1-60286-313-2(X)***, Weinstein Bks.) Perseus Bks. Group.

Briley, Randy. Mr Underneath. 2013. 134p. pap. 12.99 *(978-0-9896269-0-3(3))* Raven Mad Studios.

Brinkerhoff, Phillip. To the Magical Pond. 2004. 116p. (YA). pap. 11.95 *(978-0-7414-1982-8(3))* Infinity Publishing.

Brinson, Julie L. Princess Olivia & the Leap Frog, 1 vol. Brinson, Connor J., illus. 2009. 22p. pap. 24.95 *(978-1-60813-802-9(X))* America Star Bks.

Broadribb, Donald. Marcia. 2009. 423p. 39.47 *(978-1-4092-6754-6(7))* Lulu Pr., Inc.

Brokamp, Elizabeth. Back to School, Picky Little Witch!, 1 vol. Welling, Peter, illus. 2014. (ENG.). 32p. (J). (gr. k-3). 16.99 *(978-1-4556-1887-3(X))* Pelican Publishing Co., Inc.

—The Picky Little Witch, 1 vol. Riti, Marsha, illus. 2011. (ENG.). 32p. (J). (gr. k-3). 16.99 *(978-1-58980-882-9(7))* Pelican Publishing Co., Inc.

Brothers, Marilee. Moon Rise. 2009. (YA). pap. 14.95 *(978-0-9821756-9-9(8)*, Bell Bridge Bks.) BelleBks., Inc.

—Moon Spun. 2010. 246p. pap. 14.95 *(978-1-935661-95-5(7)*, Bell Bridge Bks.) BelleBks., Inc.

—Moonstone. 2008. 236p. (YA). pap. 14.95 *(978-0-9802453-4-9(6)*, Bell Bridge Bks.) BelleBks., Inc.

—Shadow Moon. 2011. 230p. (YA). pap. *(978-1-61194-058-9(3))* BelleBks., Inc.

Brown, Anne. The Dumari Chronicles: Year One: Year One. 2007. 376p. (YA). per. 20.95 *(978-0-595-45725-0(8))* iUniverse, Inc.

Brown, Lisa. Vampire Boy's Good Night. Brown, Lisa, illus. 2010. (ENG., Illus.). 32p. (J). (gr. -1-2). 16.99 *(978-0-06-114011-2(2))* HarperCollins Pubs.

Brunn Emmanuele, Susan. Brooms Are Out! 2009. 24p. pap. 12.99 *(978-1-4490-2227-3(8))* AuthorHouse.

Bryant, Ann. The Lost Broomstick. 2011. (Tadpoles Ser.: No. 37). (ENG., Illus.). 24p. (J). (gr. k-3). pap. *(978-0-7787-0594-9(3))* Crabtree Publishing Co.

Buckmaster, Heath L. Box of Hair: A Fairy Tale, 3 bks., Bk. 1. (Illus.). (YA). 2007. 102p. pap. 12.99 *(978-0-9771802-5-7(5))* 2008. 108p. lib. bdg. 25.00 *(978-0-9771802-4-0(7))* Transaltar Publishing.

—Box of Hair: A Fairy Tale. 2008. 104p. pap. 12.50 *(978-1-4357-2690-1(1))* Lulu Pr., Inc.

Burge, Constance M. Seasons of the Witch, Vol. 1. Simon and Schuster Children's Staff, ed. 2003. (Charmed Ser.). (ENG.). 192p. (YA). pap. *(978-0-689-86545-9(7))* Gallery Pr., The.

Burge, Constance M., creator. The Warren Witches. 2005. (Charmed Ser.). (ENG.). 320p. (YA). pap. *(978-0-689-87876-3(1))* Gallery Pr., The.

Burns, A. M. Witches. 2016. (ENG., Illus.). (J). 24.99 ***(978-1-63477-996-8(7)***, Harmony Ink Pr.) Dreamspinner Pr.

Busch, Jean. Alden & the Frog Prince, 1 vol. 2009. 48p. pap. 16.95 *(978-1-60836-892-1(0))* America Star Bks.

Butler, Erin. Blood Hex. 2013. 260p. pap. *(978-1-77130-351-4(4))* Evernight Publishing.

Cammuso, Frank. Big Birthday Bash. 2014. (Misadventures of Salem Hyde Ser.). (ENG., Illus.). 96p. (J). (gr. 1-4). 14.95 *(978-1-4197-1025-4(7)*, Amulet Bks.) Abrams, Inc.

—Cookie Catastrophe. 2014. (Misadventures of Salem Hyde Ser.: 3). (J). lib. bdg. 17.15 *(978-0-606-36149-1(9))* Turtleback Bks.

—The Misadventures of Salem Hyde: Cookie Catastrophe. 2014. (Misadventures of Salem Hyde Ser.). (ENG., Illus.). 96p. (J). (gr. 1-4). 14.95 *(978-1-4197-1198-5(9)*, Amulet Bks.) Abrams, Inc.

—The Misadventures of Salem Hyde: Spelling Trouble. 2013. (Misadventures of Salem Hyde Ser.: 1). (J). lib. bdg. 17.15 *(978-0-606-33440-2(8)*, Turtleback) Turtleback Bks.

Campana, Augustine. The Last Fairy. 2008. 204p. (gr. -1 — 1). 24.95 *(978-0-595-50892-1(8))*; pap. 14.95 *(978-0-595-52086-2(3))* iUniverse, Inc.

Canfield, Andrea. Sassy the Seahag. Hallinan, Susan, illus. 2003. Orig. Title: Sassy the Seahag. (J). per. *(978-0-9721327-3-2(2))* Bad Choices Media.

Cardwell, Helen. Amber Janusson: Protector of the Magic Lands. 2003. 136p. pap. 11.95 *(978-0-595-29436-7(7))* iUniverse, Inc.

Carretero, Mónica. Witches Handbook. 2012. (ENG., Illus.). 32p. (J). (gr. k-2). *(978-84-15241-06-5(2))* D P & G Military Pubs.

Carter, Amy. The Not So Wicked, Wicked Witch! 2009. 24p. pap. 15.95 *(978-1-4327-3781-8(3))* Outskirts Pr., Inc.

Catalano, Nikki. Mitsu: The Dark Witch & the Dream Wilderness. 2010. 88p. pap. 25.13 *(978-1-4251-7411-8(6))* Trafford Publishing.

Chapman, Lara. Accidentally Evil. 2015. (Mix Ser.). (ENG., Illus.). 240p. (J). (gr. 4-8). pap. 7.99 *(978-1-4814-0110-4(6)*, Aladdin) Simon & Schuster Children's Publishing.

—The XYZs of Being Wicked. 2014. (ENG., Illus.). 272p. (J). (gr. 4-8). pap. 6.99 *(978-1-4814-0107-4(6)*, Aladdin) Simon & Schuster Children's Publishing.

—The XYZs of Being Wicked. 2014. (ENG., Illus.). 272p. (J). (gr. 4-8). 17.99 *(978-1-4814-0108-1(4)*, Simon & Schuster/Paula Wiseman Bks.) Simon & Schuster/Paula Wiseman Bks.

Chew, Ruth. A Matter-of-Fact Magic Book: The Would-Be Witch. 2014. (Matter-Of-Fact Magic Book Ser.). (ENG., Illus.). 144p. (J). (gr. 2-5). 15.99 *(978-0-449-81567-0(6)*, Random Hse. Bks. for Young Readers) Random Hse. Children's Bks.

—No Such Thing as a Witch. 2013. (Matter-Of-Fact Magic Book Ser.). (ENG., Illus.). 128p. (J). (gr. 2-5). 5.99 *(978-0-449-81562-5(5))*; 15.99 *(978-0-449-81559-5(5))* Random Hse. Children's Bks. (Random Hse. Bks. for Young Readers).

—The Wednesday Witch. 2015. (Matter-Of-Fact Magic Book Ser.). (ENG., Illus.). 144p. (J). (gr. 2-5). pap. 5.99 *(978-0-449-81556-4(0)*, Random Hse. Bks. for Young Readers) Random Hse. Children's Bks.

—Witch's Broom. 2015. (Matter-Of-Fact Magic Book Ser.). (ENG., Illus.). 144p. (J). (gr. 2-5). pap. 5.99 *(978-0-449-81578-6(1)*, Random Hse. Bks. for Young Readers) Random Hse. Children's Bks.

Christian, Cheryl. Witches, 1 vol. Williams, Wish, illus. 2011. (ENG.). 32p. (J). pap. 5.95 *(978-1-59572-283-6(1))* Star Bright Bks., Inc.

Chupeco, Rin. The Bone Witch. 2017. (Bone Witch Ser.: 1). (ENG.). 432p. (YA). (gr. 7-12). 17.99 *(978-1-4926-3582-6(0)*, 9781492635826) Sourcebooks, Inc.

Cinebook. Halloween. Jeffrey, Erica, tr. from FRE. 2007. (Melusine Ser.: 2). (ENG., Illus.). 48p. (J). (gr. 4-7). pap. 11.95 *(978-1-905460-34-2(1))* CineBook GBR. Dist: National Bk. Network.

Clark, Isabelle. The Enchanted Forest of Hope. 2009. 44p. pap. 18.50 *(978-1-4389-7781-2(6))* AuthorHouse.

Clarke, Jane. Creaky Castle. Fox, Christyan, illus. 2013. *(978-1-4351-4951-9(3))* Barnes & Noble, Inc.

Coakley, Lena. Witchlanders. (ENG., Illus.). 416p. (YA). (gr. 7). 2012. pap. 9.99 *(978-1-4424-2005-2(7))* 2011. 16.99 *(978-1-4424-2004-5(9))* Simon & Schuster Children's Publishing. (Atheneum Bks. for Young Readers).

Cochran, Molly. Legacy. (Legacy Ser.). (ENG.). (YA). (gr. 9). 2012. 448p. pap. 9.99 *(978-1-4424-1740-3(4))* 2011. 432p. 17.99 *(978-1-4424-1739-7(0))* Simon & Schuster/Paula Wiseman Bks. (Simon & Schuster/Paula Wiseman Bks.).

—Poison. (Legacy Ser.). (ENG., 368p. (YA). (gr. 9). 2014. Illus.). pap. 9.99 *(978-1-4424-5051-6(7))* 2012. 17.99 *(978-1-4424-5050-9(9))* Simon & Schuster/Paula Wiseman Bks. (Simon & Schuster/Paula Wiseman Bks.).

Cochrane, Ian. Shian & the Corryvreckan. 2013. (Illus.). 96p. pap. *(978-1-909465-09-1(7))* Cloister Hse. Pr., The.

Coe, Mary. The Prince of Betherland. 2007. 100p. pap. 9.95 *(978-1-4303-2521-5(6))* Lulu Pr., Inc.

Coe, Mary E. The Prince of Betherland. 2008. 117p. 24.95 *(978-0-557-03112-2(5))* Lulu Pr., Inc.

Cohen, Caron Lee. Broom, Zoom! Ruzzier, Sergio, illus. 2010. (ENG.). 32p. (J). (gr. -1-3). 14.99 *(978-1-4169-9113-7(1)*, Simon & Schuster Bks. For Young Readers) Simon & Schuster Bks. For Young Readers.

Coll, Ivar Da. Medias Dulces. (SPA.). (J). (gr. 3-5). 7.95 *(978-958-04-3398-9(4)*, NR7686) Norma S.A. COL. Dist: Distribuidora Norma, Inc., Lectorum Pubns., Inc.

Columbus, Chris & Vizzini, Ned. Battle of the Beasts. 2014. (House of Secrets Ser.: 2). (ENG.). 480p. (J). (gr. 3-7). 17.99 *(978-0-06-219249-3(3))* HarperCollins Pubs.

Condenzio, John. Cocoa the Witch Cat. 2013. 20p. pap. 24.95 *(978-1-62709-264-7(1))* America Star Bks.

Connolly, MarcyKate. Ravenous. 2016. (Illus.). 416p. (J). (gr. 3-7). 16.99 *(978-0-06-227274-4(8))* HarperCollins Pubs.

Connolly, Tina. Seriously Shifted. 2016. (Seriously Wicked Ser.). (ENG.). 240p. (YA). 17.99 *(978-0-7653-8375-4(6)*, 9780765383754, Tor Teen) Doherty, Tom Assocs., LLC.

—Seriously Wicked. 2015. (ENG.). 208p. (YA). (gr. 8-12). 17.99 *(978-0-7653-7516-2(8)*, 9780765375162, Tor Teen) Doherty, Tom Assocs., LLC.

—Seriously Wicked. 2016. (YA). lib. bdg. 20.85 *(978-0-606-38783-5(8))* Turtleback Bks.

Connor, Lexi. B Magical #5: the Chocolate Meltdown. 2011. (B Magical Ser.: 5). (ENG.). 144p. (J). (gr. 3-7). pap. 5.99

W X Y Z

(978-0-545-11740-1(2), Scholastic Paperbacks) Scholastic, Inc.

—The Runaway Spell. 2011. (B Magical Ser.: 3). (ENG.). 144p. (J). (gr. 3-7). pap. 5.99 *(978-0-545-26552-2(5)*, Scholastic Paperbacks) Scholastic, Inc.

Coombes, Patrick. The Witch's Assistant. 2013. 34p. pap. *(978-1-909593-74-9(5))* Legend Pr.

Cooney, Caroline B. Enter Three Witches: A Story of MacBeth. 2008. (ENG.). 288p. (J). (gr. 7). pap. 6.99 *(978-0-439-71157-9(6)*, Scholastic Paperbacks) Scholastic, Inc.

Cooper, Bernice Soroka. The Little Elf-Frog. 2012. 24p. pap. 17.99 *(978-1-4772-9525-0(9))* AuthorHouse.

Corderoy, Tracey. The Great Granny Cake Contest! Hubble Bubble. Berger, Joe, illus. 2017. (ENG.). 128p. (J). (gr. 1-4). pap. 6.99 *(978-0-7636-8849-3(5)*, Nosy Crow) Candlewick Pr.

—Hubble Bubble, Granny Trouble. Berger, Joe, illus. 2012. (ENG.). 32p. (J). (gr. -1-2). 14.99 *(978-0-7636-5904-2(5)*, Nosy Crow) Candlewick Pr.

Córdova, Zoraida. Labyrinth Lost. (Brooklyn Brujas Ser.: 1). (ENG.). (YA). (gr. 8-12). 2017. 352p. pap. 10.99 *(978-1-4926-2316-8(4))* 2016. 336p. 17.99 *(978-1-4926-2094-5(7)*, 9781492620945) Sourcebooks, Inc.

Coughlin, Jennie Rose. The Purple Scarf. Howes, Bryan Arthur, illus. 2008. 20p. per. 24.95 *(978-1-60441-733-3(1))* America Star Bks.

Coven, Wanda. Heidi Heckelbeck & the Big Mix-Up. Burris, Priscilla, illus. 2016. (Heidi Heckelbeck Ser.: 18). (ENG.). 128p. (J). (gr. k-4). pap. 5.99 *(978-1-4814-7169-5(4)*, Little Simon) Little Simon.

—Heidi Heckelbeck & the Christmas Surprise. Burris, Priscilla, illus. 2013. (Heidi Heckelbeck Ser.: 9). (ENG.). 128p. (J). (gr. k-2). 16.99 *(978-1-4424-8125-1(0))*; pap. 4.99 *(978-1-4424-8124-4(2))* Little Simon. (Little Simon).

—Heidi Heckelbeck & the Christmas Surprise. 2013. (Heidi Heckelbeck Ser.: 9). lib. bdg. 14.75 *(978-0-606-32325-3(2)*, Turtleback) Turtleback Bks.

—Heidi Heckelbeck & the Cookie Contest. Burris, Priscilla, illus. 2012. (Heidi Heckelbeck Ser.: 3). (ENG.). 128p. (J). (gr. k-2). 16.99 *(978-1-4424-4166-8(6))*; pap. 5.99 *(978-1-4424-4165-1(8))* Little Simon. (Little Simon).

—Heidi Heckelbeck & the Cookie Contest. 2012. (Heidi Heckelbeck Ser.: 3). lib. bdg. 16.00 *(978-0-606-26328-3(4)*, Turtleback) Turtleback Bks.

—Heidi Heckelbeck & the Magic Puppy. Burris, Priscilla, illus. 2017. (Heidi Heckelbeck Ser.: 20). (ENG.). 128p. (J). (gr. k-4). pap. 5.99 ***(978-1-4814-9521-9(6)***, Little Simon) Little Simon.

—Heidi Heckelbeck & the Never-Ending Day. Burris, Priscilla, illus. 2017. (Heidi Heckelbeck Ser.: 21). (ENG.). 128p. (J). (gr. k-4). 16.99 ***(978-1-4814-9525-7(9))***; pap. 5.99 ***(978-1-4814-9524-0(0))*** Little Simon. (Little Simon).

—Heidi Heckelbeck & the Secret Admirer. Burris, Priscilla, illus. 2012. (Heidi Heckelbeck Ser.: 6). (ENG.). 128p. (J). (gr. k-4). 16.99 *(978-1-4424-4175-0(5))*; pap. 5.99 *(978-1-4424-4174-3(7))* Little Simon. (Little Simon).

—Heidi Heckelbeck & the Secret Admirer. 2012. (Heidi Heckelbeck Ser.: 6). lib. bdg. 16.00 *(978-0-606-26905-6(3)*, Turtleback) Turtleback Bks.

—Heidi Heckelbeck & the Tie-Dyed Bunny. 2014. (Heidi Heckelbeck Ser.: 10). lib. bdg. 16.00 *(978-0-606-35429-5(8))* Turtleback Bks.

—Heidi Heckelbeck Casts a Spell. Burris, Priscilla, illus. 2012. (Heidi Heckelbeck Ser.: 2). (ENG.). 128p. (J). (gr. k-4). 16.99 *(978-1-4424-4088-3(0))*; pap. 5.99 *(978-1-4424-3567-4(4))* Little Simon. (Little Simon).

—Heidi Heckelbeck Casts a Spell. 2012. (Heidi Heckelbeck Ser.: 2). lib. bdg. 16.00 *(978-0-606-26327-6(6)*, Turtleback) Turtleback Bks.

—The Heidi Heckelbeck Collection: A Bewitching Four-Book Boxed Set: Heidi Hecklebeck Has a Secret; Heidi Hecklebeck Casts a Spell; Heidi Hecklebeck & the Cookie Contest; Heidi Hecklebeck in Disguise. Burris, Priscilla, illus. 2013. (Heidi Heckelbeck Ser.). (ENG.). 512p. (J). (gr. k-4). pap. 23.99 *(978-1-4424-8976-9(6)*, Little Simon) Little Simon.

—Heidi Heckelbeck Gets Glasses. Burris, Priscilla, illus. 2012. (Heidi Heckelbeck Ser.: 5). (ENG.). 128p. (J). (gr. k-2). pap. 5.99 *(978-1-4424-4171-2(2))*; 15.99 *(978-1-4424-4172-9(0))* Little Simon. (Little Simon).

—Heidi Heckelbeck Gets Glasses. 2012. (Heidi Heckelbeck Ser.: 5). lib. bdg. 16.00 *(978-0-606-26888-2(X)*, Turtleback) Turtleback Bks.

—Heidi Heckelbeck Goes to Camp! Burris, Priscilla, illus. 2013. (Heidi Heckelbeck Ser.: 8). (ENG.). 128p. (J). (gr. k-2). 15.99 *(978-1-4424-6481-0(X))*; pap. 5.99 *(978-1-4424-6480-3(1))* Little Simon. (Little Simon).

—Heidi Heckelbeck Goes to Camp! 2013. (Heidi Heckelbeck Ser.: 8). lib. bdg. 16.00 *(978-0-606-32031-3(8)*, Turtleback) Turtleback Bks.

—Heidi Heckelbeck Has a Secret. Burris, Priscilla, illus. 2012. (Heidi Heckelbeck Ser.: 1). (ENG.). 128p. (J). (gr. k-4). 16.99 *(978-1-4424-4087-6(2))*; pap. 5.99 *(978-1-4424-3565-0(8))* Little Simon. (Little Simon).

—Heidi Heckelbeck Has a Secret. 2012. (Heidi Heckelbeck Ser.: 1). lib. bdg. 16.00 *(978-0-606-26326-9(8)*, Turtleback) Turtleback Bks.

—Heidi Heckelbeck Has a Secret - Heidi Heckelbeck Casts a Spell - Heidi Heckelbeck & the Cookie Contest. Burris, Priscilla, illus. 2014. (Heidi Heckelbeck Ser.). (ENG.). 384p. (J). (gr. k-4). pap. 8.99 *(978-1-4814-2771-5(7)*, Little Simon) Little Simon.

—Heidi Heckelbeck in Disguise. Burris, Priscilla, illus. 2012. (Heidi Heckelbeck Ser.: 4). (ENG.). 128p. (J). (gr. k-2). 16.99 *(978-1-4424-4169-9(0))*; pap. 5.99 *(978-1-4424-4168-2(2))* Little Simon. (Little Simon).

—Heidi Heckelbeck in Disguise. 2012. (Heidi Heckelbeck Ser.: 4). lib. bdg. 16.00 *(978-0-606-26329-0(2)*, Turtleback) Turtleback Bks.

—Heidi Heckelbeck Is a Flower Girl. Burris, Priscilla, illus. 2014. (Heidi Heckelbeck Ser.: 11). (ENG.). 128p. (J). (gr. k-2). pap. 4.99 *(978-1-4814-0498-3(9)*, Little Simon) Little Simon.

—Heidi Heckelbeck Is Not a Thief! Burris, Priscilla, illus. 2015. (Heidi Heckelbeck Ser.: 13). (ENG.). 128p. (J). (gr. k-4). pap. 5.99 *(978-1-4814-2324-3(X)*, Little Simon) Little Simon.

—Heidi Heckelbeck Is Ready to Dance! Burris, Priscilla, illus. 2013. (Heidi Heckelbeck Ser.: 7). (ENG.). 128p. (J). (gr. k-2). pap. 5.99 *(978-1-4424-5191-9(2))*; 17.99 *(978-1-4424-5192-6(0))* Little Simon. (Little Simon).

—Heidi Heckelbeck Is Ready to Dance! 2013. (Heidi Heckelbeck Ser.: 7). lib. bdg. 16.00 *(978-0-606-27033-5(7)*, Turtleback) Turtleback Bks.

—Heidi Heckelbeck Is the Bestest Babysitter! Burris, Priscilla, illus. 2015. (Heidi Heckelbeck Ser.: 16). (ENG.). 128p. (J). (gr. k-4). pap. 5.99 *(978-1-4814-4630-3(4)*, Little Simon) Little Simon.

—Heidi Heckelbeck Makes a Wish. 2016. (Heidi Heckelbeck Ser.: 17). lib. bdg. 16.00 *(978-0-606-38962-4(8))* Turtleback Bks.

—Heidi Heckelbeck Makes a Wish: Super Special! Burris, Priscilla, illus. 2016. (Heidi Heckelbeck Ser.: 17). (ENG.). 160p. (J). (gr. k-4). pap. 5.99 *(978-1-4814-6613-4(5)*, Little Simon) Little Simon.

—Heidi Heckelbeck Might Be Afraid of the Dark. Burris, Priscilla, illus. 2015. (Heidi Heckelbeck Ser.: 15). (ENG.). 128p. (J). (gr. k-4). pap. 5.99 *(978-1-4814-4627-3(4)*, Little Simon) Little Simon.

—Heidi Heckelbeck Says "Cheese!" Burris, Priscilla, illus. 2015. (Heidi Heckelbeck Ser.: 14). (ENG.). 128p. (J). (gr. k-4). pap. 5.99 *(978-1-4814-2327-4(4)*, Little Simon) Little Simon.

—Heidi Heckelbeck Tries Out for the Team. Burris, Priscilla, illus. 2017. (Heidi Heckelbeck Ser.: 19). (ENG.). 128p. (J). (gr. k-4). pap. 5.99 *(978-1-4814-7172-5(4)*, Little Simon) Little Simon.

Crenshaw, Glenda. Friends of the Enchanted Forest: How they Save Christmas. 2011. 28p. pap. 15.47 *(978-1-4520-0512-6(5))* AuthorHouse.

Crommett, Lora. The Blue Witch Who Dared to Be Different. 2013. 64p. 14.99 *(978-1-62951-025-5(4))* Mockingbird Lane Pr.

Crum, Shutta. William & the Witch's Riddle. 2016. (ENG., Illus.). 288p. (J). (gr. 3-7). 16.99 *(978-1-101-93269-8(4)*, Knopf Bks. for Young Readers) Random Hse. Children's Bks.

Crump, Fred, Jr. Ebonita & the Seven Boyz. 2010. 32p. (J). 12.95 *(978-1-934056-71-4(5))* UMI (Urban Ministries, Inc.).

Cummins, Molly. The Jewel of Fez. 2006. 141p. pap. 24.95 *(978-1-4241-1044-5(0))* PublishAmerica, Inc.

Cunliffe, Ian. I Want to Be a Witch. Cunliffe, Ian, illus. (ENG., Illus.). 32p. (J). (gr. -1-2). 2016. mass mkt. 3.99 *(978-1-58925-495-4(3))* 2014. 16.99 *(978-1-58925-159-5(8))* Tiger Tales.

Dahl, Roald. The Witches. Blake, Quentin, illus. 30th ed. 2013. (ENG.). 240p. (J). (gr. 3-6). 21.99 *(978-0-374-38459-3(2)*, 9780374384593, Farrar, Straus & Giroux (BYR)) Farrar, Straus & Giroux.

—The Witches. Blake, Quentin, illus. 2007. (ENG.). 224p. (J). (gr. 3-7). 7.99 *(978-0-14-241011-0(X)*, Puffin Books) Penguin Young Readers Group.

—The Witches. Blake, Quentin, illus. 2007. 206p. (gr. 4-7). 17.00 *(978-0-7569-8229-4(4))* Perfection Learning Corp.

Daily, Lorrie Ann. The Castlewood Twins, the Magic Begins. 2008. 196p. pap. 12.95 *(978-0-9820479-8-9(3))* Peppertree Pr., The.

Daines, Julie. Unraveled: A Tale of True Love. 2014. 192p. (J). pap. 14.99 *(978-1-62108-627-7(5))* Covenant Communications, Inc.

D'Angelo, Elaina R. The Magic Book of E, 1 vol. 2010. 48p. pap. 16.95 *(978-1-4489-3949-7(6))* America Star Bks.

Davies, Anna. Wrecked. (ENG., Illus.). 336p. (YA). (gr. 9). 2013. pap. 9.99 *(978-1-4424-3279-6(9))* 2012. 16.99 *(978-1-4424-3278-9(0))* Simon & Schuster Bks. For Young Readers. (Simon & Schuster Bks. For Young Readers).

Dawson, James. Hollow Pike. 2012. (ENG.). 320p. (YA). (gr. 7-17). 8.99 *(978-1-78062-128-9(0)*, Orion Children's Bks.) Hachette Children's Group GBR. Dist: Hachette Bk. Group.

De Blumenthal, Verra X. K. Folk Tales from the Russian. 2008. 88p. pap. 8.95 *(978-1-60664-152-1(2))* Aegypan.

De la Cruz, Melissa. Double Eclipse. 2016. (Summer on East End Ser.). (ENG.). 336p. (YA). (gr. 7). 17.99 *(978-0-399-17356-1(0)*, G.P. Putnam's Sons Books for Young Readers) Penguin Young Readers Group.

de Las Casas, Dianne. The House That Witchy Built, 1 vol. Stone-Barker, Holly, illus. 2011. (ENG.). 32p. (J). (gr. k-k). 16.99 *(978-1-58980-965-9(3))* Pelican Publishing Co., Inc.

Deane, Nancy Lou. Meg's Secret. 2011. 148p. (gr. 4-6). pap. 14.69 *(978-1-4567-8884-1(1))* AuthorHouse.

deGroat, Diane. Trick or Treat, Smell My Feet. deGroat, Diane, illus. 2008. (Illus.). (J). (gr. -1-7). pap. 16.95 incl. audio *(978-1-4301-0425-4(2))* Live Oak Media.

del Rio, Tania. Sabrina the Teenage Witch: the Magic Within 1. 2013. (Sabrina Manga Ser.). (ENG., Illus.). 256p. (J). (gr. 4-7). 10.99 *(978-1-936975-39-6(4)*, Archie Comics) Archie Comic Pubns., Inc.

—Sabrina the Teenage Witch: the Magic Within 3. 2013. (Sabrina Manga Ser.: 3). (ENG., Illus.). 256p. (J). (gr. 4-7). pap. 10.99 *(978-1-936975-60-0(2)*, Archie Comics) Archie Comic Pubns., Inc.

—Sabrina the Teenage Witch: the Magic Within 4. 2014. (Sabrina Manga Ser.: 4). (ENG., Illus.). 272p. (J). (gr. 4-7). pap. 10.99 *(978-1-936975-76-1(9)*, Archie Comics) Archie Comic Pubns., Inc.

Delaney, Joseph. Attack of the Fiend. Arrasmith, Patrick, illus. 2009. (Last Apprentice Ser.: 4). (ENG.). 576p. (YA). (gr. 8-18). pap. 9.99 *(978-0-06-089129-9(7)*, Greenwillow Bks.) HarperCollins Pubs.

—A Coven of Witches. Arrasmith, Patrick, illus. (Last Apprentice Short Fiction Ser.: 2). 240p. (YA). (gr. 8). 2011. (ENG.). pap. 9.99 *(978-0-06-196040-6(3))* 2010. lib. bdg. 17.89 *(978-0-06-196039-0(X))* 2010. (ENG.). 16.99 *(978-0-06-196038-3(1))* HarperCollins Pubs. (Greenwillow Bks.).

—Curse of the Bane. Arrasmith, Patrick, illus. (Last Apprentice Ser.: 2). (YA). (gr. 8-9). 2007. (ENG.). 496p. pap. 9.99 *(978-0-06-076623-8(9))* 2006. (ENG.). 480p. 17.99 *(978-0-06-076621-4(2))*Bk. 2. 2006. 480p. lib. bdg. 19.89 *(978-0-06-076622-1(0))* HarperCollins Pubs. (Greenwillow Bks.).

—Grimalkin the Witch Assassin, Bk. 9. Arrasmith, Patrick, illus. 2013. (Last Apprentice Ser.: 9). (ENG.). 416p. (YA). (gr. 8). pap. 9.99 *(978-0-06-208208-4(6)*, Greenwillow Bks.) HarperCollins Pubs.

—Grimalkin the Witch Assassin Bk. 9, Bk. 9. Arrasmith, Patrick, illus. 2012. (Last Apprentice Ser.: 9). (ENG.). 400p. (YA). (gr. 8). 17.99 *(978-0-06-208207-7(8)*, Greenwillow Bks.) HarperCollins Pubs.

—The Last Apprentice Bk. 8: Rage of the Fallen. Arrasmith, Patrick, illus. 2012. (Last Apprentice Ser.: 8). (ENG.). 416p. (YA). (gr. 8). pap. 9.99 *(978-0-06-202758-0(1)*, Greenwillow Bks.) HarperCollins Pubs.

—The Last Apprentice - Revenge of the Witch, Bk. 1. Arrasmith, Patrick, illus. 2006. (Last Apprentice Ser.: 1). (ENG.). 384p. (YA). (gr. 8). reprint ed. pap. 9.99 *(978-0-06-076620-7(4)*, Greenwillow Bks.) HarperCollins Pubs.

—A New Darkness. 2014. (ENG.). 352p. (YA). (gr. 8). 17.99 *(978-0-06-233453-4(0)*, Greenwillow Bks.) HarperCollins Pubs.

—Night of the Soul Stealer, Bk. 3. 2008. (Last Apprentice Ser.: 3). (ENG.). 528p. (YA). (gr. 8-18). pap. 9.99 *(978-0-06-076626-9(3)*, Greenwillow Bks.) HarperCollins Pubs.

—Night of the Soul Stealer Bk. 3. Arrasmith, Patrick, illus. 2007. (Last Apprentice Ser.: 3). (ENG.). 512p. (YA). (gr. 8-9). 17.99 *(978-0-06-076624-5(7)*, Greenwillow Bks.) HarperCollins Pubs.

—Rage of the Fallen, Bk. 8. Arrasmith, Patrick, illus. 2011. (Last Apprentice Ser.: 8). (ENG.). 416p. (YA). (gr. 8-18). 17.99 *(978-0-06-202756-6(5)*, Greenwillow Bks.) HarperCollins Pubs.

—Revenge of the Witch, Bk. 1. Arrasmith, Patrick, illus. 2005. (Last Apprentice Ser.: 1). (ENG.). 368p. (YA). (gr. 8). 17.99 *(978-0-06-076618-4(2)*, Greenwillow Bks.) HarperCollins Pubs.

—Rise of the Huntress, Bk. 7. Arrasmith, Patrick, illus. 2010. (Last Apprentice Ser.: 7). (ENG.). 448p. (YA). (gr. 8-18). 17.99 *(978-0-06-171510-5(7)*, Greenwillow Bks.) HarperCollins Pubs.

—Rise of the Huntress Bk. 7, Bk. 7. Arrasmith, Patrick, illus. 2011. (Last Apprentice Ser.: 7). (ENG.). 464p. (YA). (gr. 8). pap. 9.99 *(978-0-06-171512-9(3)*, Greenwillow Bks.) HarperCollins Pubs.

—The Spook's Tale - And Other Horrors. 2010. (Last Apprentice Short Fiction Ser.: 1). (ENG.). 176p. (YA). (gr. 8-18). pap. 8.99 *(978-0-06-173031-3(9)*, Greenwillow Bks.) HarperCollins Pubs.

—The Spook's Tale & Other Horrors. 2009. (Last Apprentice Short Fiction Ser.: 1). (ENG.). 176p. (YA). (gr. 8-18). 16.99 *(978-0-06-173028-3(9)*, Greenwillow Bks.) HarperCollins Pubs.

—The Spook's Tale-And Other Horrors. 2009. (Last Apprentice Short Fiction Ser.: 1). 176p. (YA). (gr. 8). lib. bdg. 14.89 *(978-0-06-173030-6(0)*, Greenwillow Bks.) HarperCollins Pubs.

—Wrath of the Bloodeye. (Last Apprentice Ser.: 5). (ENG.). (YA). (gr. 8-18). 2009. 544p. pap. 9.99 *(978-0-06-134461-9(3))*Bk. 5. 2008. 528p. 17.99 *(978-0-06-134459-6(1))* HarperCollins Pubs. (Greenwillow Bks.).

Demolin, G. The Blaue Hexe. 2010. (Illus.). 44p. pap. 21.22 *(978-1-4520-5516-9(5))* AuthorHouse.

Dennard, Susan. Truthwitch. (ENG.). (YA). 2017. (Witchlands Ser.: 1). 432p. pap. 9.99 *(978-0-7653-7929-0(5)*, 9780765379290) 2016. (Witchlands Ser.: Vol. 1). (gr. 8-12). pap. 12.99 ***(978-0-7653-9022-6(1))*** 2016. (Illus.). 416p. (gr. 9-12). 18.99 *(978-0-7653-7928-3(7)*, 9780765379283) Doherty, Tom Assocs., LLC. (Tor Teen).

—Truthwitch. 2017. (Witchlands Ser.: 1). (YA). lib. bdg. 20.85 ***(978-0-606-39586-1(5))*** Turtleback Bks.

Dennard, Susan. Windwitch. 2017. (ENG., Illus.). (Witchlands Ser.). 380p. (J). (gr. 8-12). pap. 12.99 ***(978-0-7653-9579-5(7))***; (Witchlands Ser.: 2). 384p. (YA). 18.99 *(978-0-7653-7930-6(9)*, 9780765379306) Doherty, Tom Assocs., LLC. (Tor Teen).

dePaola, Tomie. Strega Nona Does It Again. dePaola, Tomie, illus. 2013. (ENG., Illus.). 40p. (J). (gr. -1-3). 17.99 *(978-0-399-25781-0(0)*, Nancy Paulsen Books) Penguin Young Readers Group.

—Strega Nona Does It Again. 2017. lib. bdg. 19.65 ***(978-0-606-39784-1(1))*** Turtleback Bks.

—Strega Nona Takes a Vacation. dePaola, Tomie, illus. 2003. (ENG., Illus.). 32p. (J). (gr. -1-3). pap. 5.99 *(978-0-14-250076-7(3)*, Puffin Books) Penguin Young Readers Group.

—Strega Nona Takes a Vacation. dePaola, Tomie, illus. 2003. (Illus.). (J). (gr. -1-3). 13.65 *(978-0-7569-1469-1(8))* Perfection Learning Corp.

—Strega Nona's Gift. dePaola, Tomie, illus. 2011. (ENG., Illus.). 32p. (J). (gr. -1-3). 17.99 *(978-0-399-25649-3(0)*, Nancy Paulsen Books) Penguin Young Readers Group.

—Strega Nona's Harvest. dePaola, Tomie, illus. (ENG., Illus.). 32p. (J). (gr. -1-3). 2012. mass mkt. 7.99 *(978-0-14-242338-7(6)*, Puffin Books) 2009. 16.99 *(978-0-399-25291-4(6)*, G.P. Putnam's Sons Books for Young Readers) Penguin Young Readers Group.

Deutsch, Barry. Hereville: How Mirka Got Her Sword. 2012. (Hereville Ser.). (ENG., Illus.). 144p. (J). (gr. 3-7). pap. 9.95 *(978-1-4197-0619-6(5)*, Amulet Bks.) Abrams, Inc.

—Hereville: How Mirka Met a Meteorite. 2012. (Hereville Ser.). (ENG., Illus.). 128p. (J). (gr. 3-7). 17.95 *(978-1-4197-0398-0(6)*, Amulet Bks.) Abrams, Inc.

Devlin, Wende. Old Black Witch! Devlin, Harry, illus. 2012. (ENG.). 32p. (J). (gr. -1-3). 18.95 *(978-1-930900-62-2(7))* Purple Hse. Pr.

Dietrich, Sean, illus. Hansel & Gretel: The Graphic Novel, 1 vol. 2008. (Graphic Spin Ser.). (ENG.). 40p. (gr. 1-3). 25.32 *(978-1-4342-0767-8(6)*, Graphic Revolve) Stone Arch Bks.

Disney Book Group Staff. Sofia's Cup of Tea. Disney Storybook Art Team, illus. 2015. (ENG.). 10p. (J). (gr. -1-k). bds. 7.99 *(978-1-4847-0646-6(3))* Disney Pr.

Ditchfield, Lily K. & Zielski, Juile A. The Witches That Saved the Dogs. 2009. 26p. pap. 12.95 *(978-1-60264-494-6(2))* Virtualbookworm.com Publishing, Inc.

Dixon, Joyce Ann. The Witches' Cat, 1 vol. 2010. 48p. pap. 16.95 *(978-1-4489-7030-8(X))* America Star Bks.

Dokey, Cameron & Burge, Constance M. Truth & Consequences. 2003. (Charmed Ser.). (ENG., Illus.). 208p. (YA). mass mkt. 6.99 *(978-0-689-85791-1(8))* Pocket Books.

Donaldson, Julia. Room on the Broom. Scheffler, Axel, illus. 2003. (ENG.). 32p. (J). (gr. -1-2). pap. 6.99 *(978-0-14-250112-2(3)*, Puffin Books) Penguin Young Readers Group.

Donaldson, Julia & Robertson, James. Room on the Broom in Scots. Scheffler, Axel, illus. 2014. (ENG.). 32p. (J). (-k). pap. 10.99 *(978-1-84502-753-7(1))* Black and White Publishing Ltd. GBR. Dist: Independent Pubs. Group.

Donbavand, Tommy. Blood of the Witch. 2009. (Scream Street Ser.: 2). (ENG., Illus.). 128p. (J). (gr. 3-7). pap. 5.99 *(978-0-7636-4607-3(5))* Candlewick Pr.

—Claw of the Werewolf, Bk. 6. Cartoon Saloon Staff, illus. 2010. (Scream Street Ser.: 6). (ENG.). 128p. (J). (gr. 3-7). pap. 5.99 *(978-0-7636-4638-7(5))* Candlewick Pr.

—Claw of the Werewolf: Book 6, 1 vol. Cartoon Saloon, illus. 2012. (ENG.). 120p. (J). 24.21 *(978-1-59961-997-2(0)*, Chapter Bks.) Spotlight.

Dowell, Frances O'Roark. Falling In. 2012. (ENG., Illus.). 256p. (J). (gr. 3-7). pap. 8.99 *(978-1-4424-2205-6(X)*, Atheneum Bks. for Young Readers) Simon & Schuster Children's Publishing.

Doyen, Denise. The Pomegranate Witch. Wheeler, Eliza, illus. 2017. (ENG.). 40p. (J). (gr. k-3). 16.99 ***(978-1-4521-4589-1(X))*** Chronicle Bks. LLC.

—The Pomegranate Witch. Moser, Barry, illus. 2013. (J). *(978-0-375-87057-6(1))*; lib. bdg. *(978-0-375-97057-3(6))* Random Hse., Inc.

Doyle, Marissa. Betraying Season. 2010. (ENG.). 336p. (YA). (gr. 9-13). pap. 19.99 *(978-0-312-62916-8(8)*, 9780312629168) Square Fish.

—Courtship & Curses. 2013. (ENG.). 368p. (YA). (gr. 9-13). pap. 10.99 *(978-1-250-02744-3(6))* Square Fish.

Dyer, Jill. The Plant of the Zorks. 2005. 11p. 6.65 *(978-1-4116-6641-2(0))* Lulu Pr., Inc.

EDCON Publishing Group Staff. Jack & the Beanstalk - The Stubborn Witch - Rapunzel - Betsy - The Magic Bus. l.t. ed. 2008. (Classic Children's Tales Ser.). 32p. (gr. k-4). pap. 8.95 *(978-1-55576-551-4(3))* EDCON Publishing Group.

Edgson, Alison & Stockham, Jessica. Hansel & Gretel. Petrlik, Andrea, illus. 2006. (Flip-Up Fairy Tales Ser.). (ENG.). 24p. (J). (gr. 1-2). *(978-1-904550-73-0(8))* Child's Play International Ltd.

Edwards, Marnie. Pets & Parties. Hodgkinson, Leigh, illus. 2013. (Magical Mix-Ups Ser.). (ENG.). 96p. (J). (gr. 2-5). pap. 6.99 *(978-0-7636-6371-1(9)*, Nosy Crow) Candlewick Pr.

Egan, Catherine. Shade & Sorceress Bk. 1: The Last Days of Tian Di, 1 vol. 2012. (Last Days of Tian Di Ser.: 1). (ENG., Illus.). 352p. (J). (gr. 4-8). pap. 12.95 *(978-1-55050-514-6(9))* Coteau Bks. CAN. Dist: Orca Bk. Pubs. USA.

Egan, Kate, adapted by. World's Apart. 2005. (W. I. T. C. H. Ser.: Bk. 14). 134p. (J). lib. bdg. 16.92 *(978-1-4242-0788-6(6))* Fitzgerald Bks.

Ele, Delores. Horse Bones: The Adventures of Daisy & Maisy. 2012. 56p. pap. 15.99 *(978-1-4771-4113-7(8))* Xlibris Corp.

Elgert, C. J. The Elder Brothers & the Dragon's Portal. 2011. 236p. (gr. 4-6). 25.95 *(978-1-4620-1467-5(4))*; pap. 15.95 *(978-1-4620-1466-8(6))* iUniverse, Inc.

Elliot, Rachel. The Friendly Witch. Broadley, Leo, illus. 2015. (ENG.). 28p. (J). (gr. -1-3). 7.99 *(978-1-85733-725-9(5))* Lerner Publishing Group.

Epstein, Alex. The Circle Cast, 1 vol. 2011. (ENG., Illus.). 304p. (YA). (gr. 2-4). pap. 12.95 *(978-1-896580-63-0(7))* Tradewind Bks. CAN. Dist: Orca Bk. Pubs. USA.

Evans, Catrin & Evans, Guto. Peiriant y Tywydd. 2005. (WEL., Illus.). 36p. *(978-0-86243-412-0(2))* Y Lolfa.

Evans, Robert J. Dorothy's Mystical Adventures in Oz. 2004. reprint ed. pap. 1.99 *(978-1-4192-1658-9(9))* Kessinger Publishing, LLC.

Falkner, Brian. Maddy West & the Tongue Taker, 1 vol. Bixley, Donovan, illus. 2014. (ENG.). 256p. (gr. 4-8). 12.95 *(978-1-62370-084-3(1))* Capstone Young Readers of Coughlan Cos.

Falter, Laury. Residue. 2013. 306p. pap. 12.99 *(978-0-9855110-0-5(1))* Falter, Laury.

Fisher, Rusty. Littlest Witch's Story, 1 vol. 2014. (Story Time for Little Monsters Ser.). (ENG., Illus.). 24p. (J). (gr. -1-4). lib. bdg. 27.07 *(978-1-62402-022-3(4)*, Looking Glass Library) Magic Wagon.

Fliess, Sue. Goblin Hood. Thibodeau, Piper, illus. 2016. (ENG.). 32p. (J). (gr. -1-k). pap. 3.99 *(978-0-448-48933-9(3)*, Grosset & Dunlap) Penguin Young Readers Group.

Flinn, Alex. Bewitching: Beastly Was Just One of Her Curses. 2012. (Kendra Chronicles Ser.: 2). (ENG.). 352p. (YA). (gr. 8). 17.99 *(978-0-06-202414-5(0)*, HarperTeen) HarperCollins Pubs.

—Bewitching: The Kendra Chronicles. 2013. (Kendra Chronicles Ser.: 2). (ENG.). 368p. (YA). (gr. 8). pap. 9.99 *(978-0-06-202416-9(7)*, HarperTeen) HarperCollins Pubs.

—A Kiss in Time. (ENG.). (YA). (gr. 8-18). 2010. 400p. pap. 9.99 *(978-0-06-087421-6(X))* 2009. 384p. 17.99 *(978-0-06-087419-3(8))* HarperCollins Pubs. (HarperTeen).

—Mirrored. 2015. (Kendra Chronicles Ser.: 3). (ENG.). 384p. (YA). (gr. 8). 17.99 *(978-0-06-213451-6(5))* HarperCollins Pubs.

Flood, Heather. Mousey Mousey & the Witches' Revenge. 2012. 220p. pap. *(978-1-909359-03-1(3))* My Voice Publishing.

Foxlee, Karen. A Most Magical Girl. (ENG.). 304p. (J). (gr. 3-7). 2017. 7.99 ***(978-0-553-51288-5(9)***, Yearling) 2016. 16.99 *(978-0-553-51285-4(4)*, Knopf Bks. for Young Readers) 2016. lib. bdg. 19.99 *(978-0-553-51286-1(2)*, Knopf Bks. for Young Readers) Random Hse. Children's Bks.

Freeman, David. The Whispery Witch. Beers, Robert Lee, illus. 2012. 24p. pap. 24.95 *(978-1-4137-9620-9(6))* PublishAmerica, Inc.

Freese, Thomas & Riddell, Fran. Halloween Sleepwalker, 1 vol. 2013. (ENG., Illus.). 64p. (J). 16.99 *(978-0-7643-4399-5(8)*, 9780764343995) Schiffer Publishing, Ltd.

French, Vivian. The Bag of Bones: The Second Tale from the Five Kingdoms. Collins, Ross, illus. 2009. (Tales from the Five Kingdoms Ser.: 2). (ENG.). 256p. (J). (gr. 3-7). 14.99 *(978-0-7636-4255-6(X))* Candlewick Pr.

Friel, Maeve. Brewing Up, Vol. 4. Reed, Nathan, illus. 2011. (Witch-In-Training Ser.: 4). (ENG.). 96p. (J). pap. 5.99 *(978-0-00-713344-4(8))* HarperCollins Pubs. Ltd. GBR. Dist: HarperCollins Pubs.

—Broomstick Battles. Reed, Nathan, illus. 2011. (Witch-In-Training Ser.: 5). (ENG.). 96p. (J). pap. 5.99 *(978-0-00-718524-5(3))* HarperCollins Pubs. Ltd. GBR. Dist: HarperCollins Pubs.

—The Broomstick Collection, Bks 1-4. Reed, Nathan, illus. 2006. (Witch-In-Training Ser.). (ENG.). 368p. (J). (gr. 2-4). pap., pap., pap. 11.99 *(978-0-00-724072-2(4))* HarperCollins Pubs. Ltd. GBR. Dist: HarperCollins Pubs.

—Charming or What?, Vol. 3. Reed, Nathan, illus. 2011. (Witch-In-Training Ser.: 3). (ENG.). 96p. (J). pap. 5.99 *(978-0-00-713343-7(X))* HarperCollins Pubs. Ltd. GBR. Dist: HarperCollins Pubs.

—Flying Lessons, Vol. 1. Reed, Nathan, illus. 2011. (Witch-In-Training Ser.: 1). (ENG.). 96p. (J). pap. 5.99 *(978-0-00-713341-3(3),* HarperCollins Children's Bks.) HarperCollins Pubs. Ltd. GBR. Dist: HarperCollins Pubs.

—The Last Task. Reed, Nathan, illus. 2011. (Witch-In-Training Ser.: 8). (ENG.). 96p. (J). (gr. 4-7). pap. 5.99 *(978-0-00-718527-6(8),* HarperCollins Children's Bks.) HarperCollins Pubs. Ltd. GBR. Dist: HarperCollins Pubs.

—Moonlight Mischief. Reed, Nathan, illus. 2011. (Witch-In-Training Ser.: 7). (ENG.). 96p. (J). per. 5.99 *(978-0-00-718526-9(X))* HarperCollins Pubs. Ltd. GBR. Dist: HarperCollins Pubs.

—Watch-in-Train Vol. 2: Spelling Trouble. Reed, Nathan, illus. 2011. (Witch-In-Training Ser.: 2). (ENG.). 96p. (J). pap. 5.99 *(978-0-00-713342-0(1))* HarperCollins Pubs. Ltd. GBR. Dist: HarperCollins Pubs.

—Witch Switch. Reed, Nathan, illus. 2011. (Witch-In-Training Ser.: 6). (ENG.). 96p. (J). pap. 5.99 *(978-0-00-718525-2(1))* HarperCollins Pubs. Ltd. GBR. Dist: HarperCollins Pubs.

Gaichies, Sarah. Angela & the Prince. 2011. (FRE & ENG., Illus.). 96p. pap. 32.26 *(978-1-4567-8999-2(6))* AuthorHouse.

Gardner, Sally. Operation Bunny. Roberts, David, illus. 2014. (Wings & Co Ser.: 1). (ENG.). 192p. (J). (gr. 2-5). 12.99 *(978-0-8050-9892-1(5),* 9780805098921, Holt, Henry & Co. Bks. For Young Readers) Holt, Henry & Co.

—Operation Bunny. Roberts, David, illus. 2014. (Wings & Co Ser.: 1). (ENG.). 208p. (J). (gr. 2-5). pap. 6.99 *(978-1-250-05053-3(7),* 9781250050533) Square Fish.

Garza, Xavier & Villarroel, Carolina. Zulema & the Witch Owl/Zulema y la Bruja Lechuza. Garza, Xavier, illus. 2009. (SPA & ENG., Illus.). 32p. (J). (gr. -1-4). 16.95 *(978-1-55885-515-1(7),* Piñata Books) Arte Publico Pr.

George, Ben W. Wanda the Witch's Broom: How an Old School Witch Learns New Tricks. 2011. 24p. pap. 12.99 *(978-1-4634-4380-1(3))* AuthorHouse.

George, Jessica Day. Princess of Glass. (Twelve Dancing Princesses Ser.). (ENG.). 272p. (YA). (gr. 7). 2011. pap. 9.99 *(978-1-59990-659-1(7),* 9781599906591) 2010. 16.99 *(978-1-59990-478-8(0),* 9781599904788) Bloomsbury Publishing USA. (Bloomsbury USA Childrens).

Geragotelis, Brittany. Life's a Witch. 2013. (Life's a Witch Ser.). (ENG., Illus.). 320p. (YA). (gr. 9). 16.99 *(978-1-4424-6655-5(3),* Simon & Schuster Bks. For Young Readers) Simon & Schuster Bks. For Young Readers.

—What the Spell. (Life's a Witch Ser.). (ENG., Illus.). (YA). (gr. 9). 2014. 352p. pap. 9.99 *(978-1-4424-6707-1(X))* 2013. 336p. 16.99 *(978-1-4424-6815-3(7))* Simon & Schuster Bks. For Young Readers. (Simon & Schuster Bks. For Young Readers).

—The Witch Is Back. 2014. (Life's a Witch Ser.). (ENG., Illus.). 352p. (YA). (gr. 9). 17.99 *(978-1-4424-6688-3(X),* Simon & Schuster Bks. For Young Readers) Simon & Schuster Bks. For Young Readers.

—The Witch Is Back: A Life's a Witch Book. 2015. (Life's a Witch Ser.). (ENG., Illus.). 352p. (YA). (gr. 9). pap. 11.99 *(978-1-4424-6691-3(X))* Simon & Schuster Children's Publishing.

Gerber, Carole. 10 Busy Brooms. Fleming, Michael, illus. 2016. (ENG.). 32p. (J). (gr. -1-2). 12.99 *(978-0-553-53341-5(X),* Doubleday Bks. for Young Readers) Random Hse. Children's Bks.

Gibbs, Gretchen. The Book of Maggie Bradstreet. 2012. (Bradstreet Chronicles). (ENG.). 183p. (YA). pap. 9.99 *(978-0-9852948-0-9(9))* Glenmere Pr.

Gilbert, Julie. Into the Storm: A Mermaid's Journey. Fagan, Kirbi, illus. 2017. (Dark Waters Ser.). (ENG.). 160p. (gr. 2-4). pap. 6.95 *(978-1-4965-4175-8(8));* lib. bdg. 26.65 *(978-1-4965-4171-0(5))* Stone Arch Bks.

Gill, David Macinnis. Uncanny. 2017. 544p. (YA). (gr. 9). 17.99 ***(978-0-06-229016-8(9)**,* Greenwillow Bks.) HarperCollins Pubs.

Gilson. Melusine Vol. 3: The Vampires' Ball. 2008. (Melusine Ser.: 3). (ENG., Illus.). 48p. (J). (gr. 4-7). pap. 11.95 *(978-1-905460-69-4(4))* CineBook GBR. Dist: National Bk. Network.

—Melusine - Hocus Pocus. Clarke & Clarke, illus. 2007. (Melusine Ser.: 1). (ENG.). 48p. (J). (gr. -1-12). per. 9.99 *(978-1-905460-20-5(1))* CineBook GBR. Dist: National Bk. Network.

Glassman, Miriam. Halloweena. Roberts, Victoria, illus. 2015. (ENG.). 40p. (J). (gr. -1-3). 13.99 *(978-1-4814-7996-7(2),* Atheneum Bks. for Young Readers) Simon & Schuster Children's Publishing.

Gliori, Debi. Witch Baby & Me. 2010. (ENG., Illus.). 256p. (J). (gr. 2-4). pap. 12.99 *(978-0-552-55676-7(9))* Transworld Publishers Ltd. GBR. Dist: Independent Pubs. Group.

—Witch Baby & Me after Dark, No. 3. 2010. (ENG., Illus.). 304p. (J). (gr. 2-4). pap. 11.99 *(978-0-552-55678-1(5))* Transworld Publishers Ltd. GBR. Dist: Independent Pubs. Group.

Gliori, Debi & Hurst, Kelly. Witch Baby & Me on Stage. Gliori, Debi, illus. 2011. (ENG., Illus.). 336p. (J). (gr. 2-4). pap. 7.99 *(978-0-552-55679-8(3))* Transworld Publishers Ltd. GBR. Dist: Independent Pubs. Group.

Gogonya, Carol. The African Mermaid & Other Stories. 2011. 40p. pap. 32.70 *(978-1-4568-5416-4(X))* Xlibris Corp.

Goodman, John. Percy's Magical Adventures. 2005. (Illus.). 170p. pap. *(978-1-84401-556-6(4))* Athena Pr.

Gore, Jim. Witch Snatchit & Mr Grabbit. 2005. (Illus.). 80p. pap. *(978-1-84401-486-6(X))* Athena Pr.

Gormley, Greg. Fairy Tale Frankie & the Tricky Witch. Lenton, Steven, illus. 2016. (ENG.). 32p. (J). (gr. -1-1). 17.99 *(978-1-4814-6625-7(9),* Aladdin) Simon & Schuster Children's Publishing.

Granata, Nancy. The Perfect Porch for Witch Watching. 2008. 52p. pap. 22.49 *(978-1-4389-0107-7(0))* AuthorHouse.

Grandoit, Jean. In the Quest for Inshalla: Simbies of the Caribbean at the World Under. 2010. 68p. pap. 25.49 *(978-1-4520-3900-8(3))* AuthorHouse.

Grant, Holly. The Witch's Glass. 2017. (League of Beastly Dreadfuls Ser.: Bk. 3). (ENG., Illus.). 320p. (J). (gr. 3-7). 16.99 ***(978-1-101-93366-4(6)**,* Random Hse. Bks. for Young Readers) Random Hse. Children's Bks.

Gray, Claudia. Sorceress. 2015. (Spellcaster Ser.: 3). (ENG.). 352p. (YA). (gr. 8). 17.99 *(978-0-06-196124-3(8),* HarperTeen) HarperCollins Pubs.

—Spellcaster. 2013. (Spellcaster Ser.: 1). (ENG.). 400p. (YA). (gr. 8). 17.99 *(978-0-06-196120-5(5),* HarperTeen) HarperCollins Pubs.

—Steadfast. (Spellcaster Ser.: 2). (ENG.). (YA). (gr. 8). 2015. 368p. pap. 9.99 *(978-0-06-196123-6(X))* 2014. 352p. 17.99 *(978-0-06-196122-9(1))* HarperCollins Pubs. (HarperTeen).

Gray, Rev. Maxine A. Children's Lessons on Morality: Don't Use Your Friends. 2013. 24p. pap. 14.99 *(978-1-4669-8831-6(2))* Trafford Publishing.

Greban, Tanguy. Sarah So Small. Greban, Quentin, illus. 2004. (ENG.). 32p. (J). (gr. 4-7). 16.95 *(978-1-59687-179-3(2))* IBks., Inc.

—Sarah So Small. Greban, Quentin, illus. 2004. 32p. (J). 16.95 *(978-0-689-03594-4(2),* Milk & Cookies) ibooks, Inc.

Green, Sally. Half Bad. (ENG.). (YA). 2015. (Half Bad Trilogy Ser.: 1). 432p. (gr. 7). pap. 9.99 *(978-0-14-751146-1(1),* Speak) 2014. (Half Bad Trilogy Ser.: 1). 416p. (gr. 7). 18.99 *(978-0-670-01678-5(0),* Viking Books for Young Readers)Pack. 2015. pap. 89.91 *(978-0-14-751591-9(2),* Speak) Penguin Young Readers Group.

—Half Wild. 2015. (Half Bad Trilogy Ser.: 2). (ENG.). 432p. (YA). (gr. 7). 18.99 *(978-0-670-01713-3(2),* Viking Books for Young Readers) Penguin Young Readers Group.

Gregory, Caroline. Puppy Stew. Suorsa, Michael, illus. 2009. (ENG.). 28p. (J). pap. 8.99 *(978-0-9772025-9-1(3))* Sortis Publishing.

Grimm, Jacob & Grimm, Wilhelm K. Hansel & Gretel. Price, Margaret Evans, illus. 2005. (Shape Bks.). (ENG.). 16p. (J). (gr. -1-3). 9.95 *(978-1-59583-012-8(X),* 9781595830128, Green Tiger Pr.) Laughing Elephant.

Gripari, Pierre. Le Gentil Petit Diable: Et Autres Contes de la Rue Broca. Rosado, Puig, illus. 2007. (Folio Junior Ser.). 142p. (J). per. *(978-2-07-061255-0(4))* National Round Table on the Environment & the Economy (NRTEE)/Table ronde nationale sur l'environnement et l'economie (TRNEE).

Gritton, Steve. The Kandy Witch. 2007. (Illus.). (J). 18.95 *(978-0-9795361-0-6(3))* Bad Frog Art/SMG Bks.

Guerin, F. A. The Witch at NO46: Verbrola. 2011. (Illus.). 140p. pap. 14.69 *(978-1-4567-7118-8(3))* AuthorHouse.

Guerrera, Jeannette D. The Christmas Witch. 2012. 24p. pap. 17.99 *(978-1-4685-6226-2(6))* AuthorHouse.

Gummelt, Donna & Melchiorre, Dondino. Michelina the Magical Musical Good Witch of the Forest. Wall, Randy Hugh, ed. Varela, Juan D., tr. Varela, Juan D., illus. 2006. (SPA.). 34p. (J). 14.95 *(978-0-9764798-6-4(9))* Story Store Collection Publishing.

Gutenberg, S. R. Abby Longbotham & the Quilt. 2008. 28p. pap. 24.95 *(978-1-4241-9428-5(8))* America Star Bks.

Hahn, Mary Downing. Took: A Ghost Story. 2016. (ENG.). 272p. (J). (gr. 5-7). pap. 7.99 *(978-0-544-81310-6(3),* HMH Books For Young Readers) Houghton Mifflin Harcourt Publishing Co.

—Witch Catcher. (ENG.). 240p. (J). (gr. 5-7). 2011. pap. 7.99 *(978-0-547-57714-2(1))* 2006. (Illus.). 16.00 *(978-0-618-50457-2(5))* Houghton Mifflin Harcourt Publishing Co.

Hardie, Samantha. Samantha's Oracle: A Fortune Teller for Teenage Witches. (Illus.). 80p. 12.95 *(978-1-55285-282-8(2))* Whitecap Bks., Ltd. CAN. Dist: Graphic Arts Ctr. Publishing Co.

Hargreaves, Roger & Hargreaves, Adam. Little Miss Sunshine & the Wicked Witch. Hargreaves, Adam, illus. 2007. (Mr. Men & Little Miss Ser.). (ENG., Illus.). 32p. (J). (gr. -1-2). mass mkt. 4.99 *(978-0-8431-2490-3(3),* Price Stern Sloan) Penguin Young Readers Group.

Harper, Benjamin. Hansel & Gretel & Zombies: a Graphic Novel. Cano, Fern, illus. 2016. (Far Out Fairy Tales Ser.). (ENG.). 40p. (gr. 3-4). lib. bdg. 25.32 *(978-1-4965-2509-3(4),* Far Out Fairy Tales) Stone Arch Bks.

Harris, Christine. Four Tails: An Anthology of Four Tales for Children. 2011. (Illus.). 92p. (gr. -1). pap. 12.10 *(978-1-4520-7643-0(X))* AuthorHouse.

Hartley, James. Berlina's Quest. Legge, Barbara, ed. Kelsey, Amanda, illus. 2013. 146p. (J). pap. 17.99 *(978-1-61572-948-7(8))* Damnation Bks.

Harvey, Alyxandra. A Breath of Frost. 2014. (Lovegrove Legacy Ser.). (ENG.). 512p. (YA). (gr. 7). pap. 10.99 *(978-0-8027-3444-0(8),* 9780802734440, Bloomsbury USA Childrens) Bloomsbury Publishing USA.

—Whisper the Dead. 2014. (Lovegrove Legacy Ser.: Bk. 2). (ENG.). 408p. (YA). (gr. 7). 17.99 *(978-0-8027-3750-2(1),* 9780802737502, Bloomsbury USA Childrens) Bloomsbury Publishing USA.

Harvey, Damian. Whizzy Witch. Dumortier, Marjorie, illus. 2008. (Reading Corner Ser.). (ENG.). 24p. (J). (gr. k-2). pap. 6.99 *(978-0-7496-7699-5(X),* Franklin Watts) Hachette Children's Group GBR. Dist: Hachette Bk. Group.

Hautzig, Deborah. Little Witch Learns to Read. Wickstrom, Sylvie K., illus. 2003. (Step into Reading Ser.). (ENG.). 48p. (J). (gr. k-3). pap. 3.99 *(978-0-375-82179-0(1),* Random Hse. Bks. for Young Readers) Random Hse. Children's Bks.

Havard, Amanda. The Survivors. 2011. (ENG.). (YA). 294p. 21.99 *(978-0-9833190-0-9(6));* 300p. pap. 11.99 *(978-0-9833190-2-3(2))* Chafie Pr., LLC.

Hawkins, Rachel. Demonglass. 2012. (ENG.). 384p. (YA). (gr. 6-17). pap. 8.99 *(978-1-4231-2844-1(3))* Hyperion Pr.

—Hex Hall, Bk. 1. 2010. (ENG.). 336p. (J). (gr. 7-17). 16.99 *(978-1-4231-2130-5(9))* Hyperion Pr.

Hayden, Jeanne. Last Minute Wilma & Her Toad Soup. 2009. 24p. pap. 14.95 *(978-1-4327-3857-0(7))* Outskirts Pr., Inc.

Haynes, Lori. The Wallenda Witches Flying School. 2005. (Illus.). 24p. (J). pap. 13.13 *(978-0-9746959-4-5(7),* 2000) Falcon Publishing LTD.

Healy, Christopher. The Hero's Guide to Saving Your Kingdom. Harris, Todd, illus. (Hero's Guide Ser.: 1). (ENG.). (J). (gr. 3-7). 2013. 480p. pap. 7.99 *(978-0-06-211745-8(9))* 2012. 448p. 16.99 *(978-0-06-211743-4(2))* HarperCollins Pubs. (Waldon Pond Pr.).

Heible, Beverly. A Christmas Party on River Row. 2012. 98p. 22.95 *(978-1-62709-018-6(5))* America Star Bks.

Heidi Heckelbeck Gets the Sniffles. 2014. (Heidi Heckelbeck Ser.: 12). (ENG., Illus.). 128p. (J). (gr. k-4). pap. 5.99 *(978-1-4814-1362-6(7),* Little Simon) Little Simon.

Henderson, Jason. The Triumph of Death. 2012. (Alex Van Helsing Ser.: 3). (ENG.). 320p. (YA). (gr. 8). 17.99 *(978-0-06-195103-9(X),* HarperTeen) HarperCollins Pubs.

Henry, James. The Cabinet of Curiosities. 2010. 240p. pap. 21.50 *(978-0-9559851-0-2(2))* Blue Cat GBR. Dist: Lulu Pr., Inc.

Heppermann, Christine & Koertge, Ron. Jess's Story. Marcero, Deborah, illus. 2016. (Backyard Witch Ser.: 2). 192p. (J). (gr. 3-7). 16.99 *(978-0-06-233841-9(2),* Greenwillow Bks.) HarperCollins Pubs.

Heppermann, Christine & Koertge, Ron. Maya's Story. Marcero, Deborah, illus. 2017. (Backyard Witch Ser.: 3). 192p. (J). (gr. 3-7). 16.99 ***(978-0-06-233844-0(7)**,* Greenwillow Bks.) HarperCollins Pubs.

Heppermann, Christine & Koertge, Ronald. Sadie's Story. Marcero, Deborah, illus. 2015. (Backyard Witch Ser.: 1). (ENG.). 176p. (J). (gr. 3-7). 16.99 *(978-0-06-233838-9(2),* Greenwillow Bks.) HarperCollins Pubs.

Higgins, Nadia. Hansel & Gretel & the Cheddar Trail, 1 vol. Johnson, Meredith, illus. 2009. (Fiona & Frieda's Fairy-Tale Adventures Ser.). (ENG.). 80p. (J). (gr. 2-5). 27.07 *(978-1-60270-574-6(7))* Magic Wagon.

Hillert, Margaret. The Witch Who Went for a Walk. Gallagher-Cole, Mernie, illus. 2016. (BeginningtoRead Ser.). (ENG.). 32p. (J). (gr. -1-2). pap. 11.94 *(978-1-60357-951-3(6));* (gr. 1-2). 22.60 *(978-1-59953-810-5(5))* Norwood Hse. Pr.

Hoena, Blake. Witch's Brew. Bardin, Dave, illus. 2016. (Monster Heroes Ser.). (ENG.). 32p. (gr. 1-2). lib. bdg. 21.32 *(978-1-4965-3756-0(4))* Stone Arch Bks.

Hoepfner, John P. The Tale of Magic Pixie Dust. 2011. 34p. pap. 16.95 *(978-1-4560-6811-0(3))* PublishAmerica, Inc.

Holder, Nancy & Viguié, Debbie. Legacy & Spellbound. 2008. (Wicked Ser.). (ENG.). 672p. (YA). (gr. 9). pap. 8.99 *(978-1-4169-7117-7(3),* Simon Pulse) Simon Pulse.

—Resurrection. 2009. (Wicked Ser.). (ENG.). 416p. (YA). (gr. 9-18). pap. 9.99 *(978-1-4169-7227-3(7),* Simon Pulse) Simon Pulse.

—Wicked: Witch & Curse. 2008. (Wicked Ser.). (ENG.). 672p. (YA). (gr. 9). pap. 9.99 *(978-1-4169-7119-1(X),* Simon Pulse) Simon Pulse.

Holder, Nancy & Viguie, Debbie. Wicked: Witch & Curse. 2009. *(978-1-4351-2000-6(0))* Barnes & Noble, Inc.

Horn, Emily. Excuse Me... Are You a Witch? Pawlak, Pawel, illus. 2004. (ENG.). 32p. (J). (gr. -1-2). pap. 7.95 *(978-1-58089-103-5(9))* Charlesbridge Publishing, Inc.

Horowitz, Anthony. Raven's Gate. 2006. (Gatekeepers Ser.: 1). (ENG.). 272p. (J). (gr. 3-7). pap. 8.99 *(978-0-439-68009-7(3),* Scholastic Paperbacks) Scholastic, Inc.

—Raven's Gate. 2005. 288p. pap. *(978-1-84428-619-5(3))* Walker Bks., Ltd.

Howard, Martin. Wickedest Witch. Stimpson, Colin, illus. 2011. (Witches at War! Ser.: 1). (ENG.). 216p. (J). (gr. 3-7). 12.99 *(978-1-84365-131-4(9),* Pavilion) Pavilion Bks. GBR. Dist: Independent Pubs. Group.

—The Wild Winter. Stimpson, Colin, illus. 2012. (Witches at War! Ser.: 3). (ENG.). 214p. (J). (gr. 3-7). 12.99 *(978-1-84365-180-2(7),* Pavilion Children's Books) Pavilion Bks. GBR. Dist: Independent Pubs. Group.

Howell, Robert. Third Times the Charm. 2007. (ENG.). 224p. (gr. 4-7). per. 12.95 *(978-1-897235-20-1(8))* Thistledown Pr., Ltd. CAN. Dist: Univ. of Toronto Pr.

Human, Deborah. Pinky Promise. 2009. 40p. (J). pap. 11.99 *(978-0-9818374-0-6(9))* Writing Bench LLC., The.

Hume, Maureen. The Pizza Gang: Facing the Witch. 2009. 80p. pap. 9.95 *(978-1-60860-337-4(7),* Eloquent Bks.) Strategic Book Publishing & Rights Agency (SBPRA).

Hurd, Pamela. Switch Witch: An Old Fashioned Witch Learns a New Trick. 2011. 20p. pap. 11.99 *(978-1-4634-4587-4(3))* AuthorHouse.

Hurley, Crystal. The Witch with an Itch. 2008. 24p. pap. 24.95 *(978-1-60703-339-4(9))* America Star Bks.

Hutchings, Paul. Halloween Tails. 2012. 24p. pap. 24.95 *(978-1-4626-7106-9(3))* America Star Bks.

Ibbotson, Eva. Not Just a Witch. Hawkes, Kevin, illus. 2004. (ENG.). 192p. (J). (gr. 3-7). pap. 5.99 *(978-0-14-240232-0(X),* Puffin Books) Penguin Young Readers Group.

Impey, Rose. The Very Wicked Witch, Bk. 6. McEwen, Katharine, illus. 2017. (Sir Lance-A-Little Ser.). (ENG.). 32p. (J). (gr. k-2). 9.99 *(978-1-4083-2525-4(X),* Orchard Bks.) Hachette Children's Group GBR. Dist: Hachette Bk. Group.

Isbell, Shaun. The Mouse & the Witch, 1 vol. 2009. 56p. pap. 16.95 *(978-1-61546-892-8(7))* PublishAmerica, Inc.

Jablonski, Carla. Shadow of the Sphinx. 2007. (Charmed Ser.). (ENG.). 192p. (YA). pap. 14.95 *(978-1-4169-6756-9(7),* Gallery Bks.) Gallery Bks.

Jensen, Danielle L. Stolen Songbird. 2014. (Malediction Trilogy Ser.: 1). (ENG.). 480p. (YA). (gr. 9). pap. 9.99 *(978-1-908844-96-5(5),* Angry Robot, Limited) Watkins Media Limited GBR. Dist: Penguin Random Hse. LLC.

Jessup, VonDa. Wanda the Witch at the Happy Haunted House. 2008. (Illus.). 44p. pap. 18.50 *(978-1-60693-149-3(0),* Eloquent Bks.) Strategic Book Publishing & Rights Agency (SBPRA).

Johansen, K. V. Treason in Eswy, 1 vol. 2008. (ENG., Illus.). 192p. (YA). (gr. 7-12). pap. 9.95 *(978-1-55143-888-7(7))* Orca Bk. Pubs. USA.

—Warden of Greyrock, 1 vol. 2009. (ENG.). 256p. (YA). (gr. 7-12). pap. 9.95 *(978-1-55469-005-3(6))* Orca Bk. Pubs. USA.

Jolley, Dan. Wrapped up in You. Nourigat, Natalie, illus. 2012. (My Boyfriend Is a Monster Ser.: 6). (ENG.). 128p. (YA). (gr. 7-12). pap. 9.95 *(978-0-8225-9425-3(0));* lib. bdg. 29.27 *(978-0-7613-6856-4(6))* Lerner Publishing Group. (Graphic Universe™).

Jones, Chris. Cameron Jack & the Key to the Universe. 2010. (Illus.). 136p. pap. 10.99 *(978-1-4490-6547-8(3))* AuthorHouse.

Jones, Diana Wynne. Earwig & the Witch. Zelinsky, Paul O., illus. 2012. 128p. (J). (gr. 3-7). 15.99 *(978-0-06-207511-6(X),* Greenwillow Bks.) HarperCollins Pubs.

Jones, J. J. Flute Tudor & the Secret Order. 2012. 304p. 22.95 *(978-1-4575-1302-2(1))* Dog Ear Publishing, LLC.

Jordan, Annie Laurie. Bogwaddle Pond. La Grange, Myrtle, illus. 2004. 25p. pap. 24.95 *(978-1-4137-2013-6(7))* PublishAmerica, Inc.

Jordan, Jennifer. Silly Tilly Witch: And Other Stories. Guile, Gill, illus. 2004. (Early Learning Ser.). 18p. (J). bds. 2.99 *(978-1-85854-825-8(X))* Brimax Books Ltd. GBR. Dist: Byeway Bks.

Joyce, Rita. Wandawillie. 2005. (J). lib. bdg. 17.95 *(978-1-59094-095-2(4))* Jawbone Publishing Corp.

Kaaberbøl, Lene. Heartbreak Island. 2005. (W. I. T. C. H. Adventures Ser.: Bk. 3). (Illus.). 105p. (J). lib. bdg. 11.00 *(978-1-4242-0786-2(X))* Fitzgerald Bks.

Kakinouchi, Narumi. My Codename Is Charmer, Vol. 3. 208p. pap. 12.95 *(978-1-932575-08-8(1))* International Comics & Entertainment L.L.C.

Kane, Gillian. The Witch Who Liked to Wear Pink. Povey, Andrea, illus. 2013. 24p. pap. 11.50 *(978-1-62516-315-8(0),* Strategic Bk. Publishing) Strategic Book Publishing & Rights Agency (SBPRA).

Kats, Jewel. Hansel & Gretel: A Fairy Tale with a Down Syndrome Twist. Lenart, Claudia, illus. 2014. 37p. (J). *(978-1-61599-251-5(0))* Loving Healing Pr., Inc.

Kayser, Megan. Finishing What I Didn't Start. 2006. 108p. pap. 19.95 *(978-1-4241-1271-5(0))* PublishAmerica, Inc.

Kidwell, Justina. The Enchanted Garden & the Curse of the Evil Witch: The Kent Boys' Adventures. 2009. 68p. pap. 19.95 *(978-1-60749-163-7(X))* America Star Bks.

Kimmel, Elizabeth Cody. ParaNormaN. 2012. (ENG.). (J). (gr. 4-7). 64.99 *(978-1-61969-450-7(6))* Findaway World, LLC.

—ParaNorman: A Novel. 2013. (ENG., Illus.). 256p. (J). (gr. 3-7). pap. 6.99 *(978-0-316-20987-8(2))* Little, Brown Bks. for Young Readers.

Kladstrup, Kristin. Garden Princess. 2015. (ENG.). 272p. (J). (gr. 5). pap. 7.99 *(978-0-7636-7668-1(3))* Candlewick Pr.

Kohara, Kazuno. Ghosts in the House! Kohara, Kazuno, illus. 2012. (ENG., Illus.). 26p. (J). (gr. -1 — 1). bds. 7.99 *(978-1-59643-725-8(1),* 9781596437258) Roaring Brook Pr.

—Ghosts in the House! Kohara, Kazuno, illus. 2010. (ENG., Illus.). 32p. (J). (gr. -1-1). pap. 7.99 *(978-0-312-60886-6(1),* 9780312608866) Square Fish.

Kok, Gemma. Explore. 2008. 44p. pap. 18.50 *(978-1-4092-2058-9(3))* Lulu Pr., Inc.

—Explore (Printed in black & White) 2008. 44p. pap. 8.00 *(978-1-4092-2530-0(5))* Lulu Pr., Inc.

Konigsburg, E. L. Jennifer, Hecate, Macbeth, William McKinley, & Me, Elizabeth. 2011. 8.32 *(978-0-7848-3469-5(5),* Everbind) Marco Bk. Co.

Kontis, Alethea. Hero. 2013. (Woodcutter Sisters Ser.: 2). (ENG.). 304p. (YA). (gr. 7). 17.99 *(978-0-544-05677-0(9))* Houghton Mifflin Harcourt Publishing Co.

Korba, Joanna. Sleepless Beauty. 2006. (J). pap. *(978-1-4108-7171-8(1))* Benchmark Education Co.

Kovalkova-McKenna, Svetlana. Vasilisa & the Queen of Asps. 2009. 63p. pap. 8.02 *(978-0-557-05710-8(8))* Lulu Pr., Inc.

Krulik, Nancy. Witch Switch. John and Wendy, illus. 2006. (Katie Kazoo, Switcheroo Ser.: No. 4). (ENG.). 160p. (J). (gr. 2-4). pap. 4.99 *(978-0-448-44330-0(9),* Grosset & Dunlap) Penguin Young Readers Group.

Krys, Michelle. Hexed. 2014. (ENG.). 384p. (YA). (gr. 7). 17.99 *(978-0-385-74337-2(8),* Delacorte Pr.) Random Hse. Children's Bks.

Kuiper, Kendall. Drift & Dagger. 2015. (ENG.). 368p. (YA). (gr. 7-17). 18.00 *(978-0-316-40453-2(5))* Little, Brown Bks. for Young Readers.

—Salt & Storm. 2014. (YA). *(978-0-316-40456-3(X))* Little Brown & Co.

Lagron, Camille. Tatian. 2012. 302p. pap. 12.99 *(978-0-9856698-0-5(2))* Camas Pr.

Laky, Esther. Just Fairy Tales. 2010. 95p. pap. 11.80 *(978-0-557-01926-7(5))* Lulu Pr., Inc.

Lanagan, Margo. The Brides of Rollrock Island. (ENG.). (YA). (gr. 9). 2013. 318p. pap. 9.99 *(978-0-375-87336-2(8),* Ember) 2012. 320p. 17.99 *(978-0-375-86919-8(0),* Knopf Bks. for Young Readers) Random Hse. Children's Bks.

Lane, Leonie. The Retford Witch Catchers. 2005. 144p. per. *(978-1-84667-002-2(0))* Derwent Pr., The.

Lansdale, John L., et al. Something Wicca This Way Comes, No. 7. Romberger, James et al, illus. 7th ed. 2009. (Tales from the Crypt Graphic Novels Ser.: 7). (ENG.). 96p. (J). (gr. 5-12). 12.95 *(978-1-59707-151-2(X),* 9781597071512) Papercutz.

Larson, M. A. Pennyroyal Academy. 2014. (Pennyroyal Academy Ser.: 1). (ENG.). 320p. (J). (gr. 5). 16.99 *(978-0-399-16324-1(7),* G.P. Putnam's Sons Books for Young Readers) Penguin Young Readers Group.

Laughlin, Florence. The Little Leftover Witch. 2013. (ENG.). 96p. (J). (gr. 3-7). 15.99 *(978-1-4424-8677-5(5));* pap. 5.99 *(978-1-4424-8672-0(4))* Simon & Schuster Bks. For Young Readers. (Simon & Schuster Bks. For Young Readers).

Launchbury, Jane. Witch & Wizard Stories. 2012. (ENG., Illus.). 64p. (J). 9.95 *(978-1-84135-103-2(2))* Award Pubns. Ltd. GBR. Dist: Parkwest Pubns., Inc.

Laura Grey Wahl. The Magic Town of Stuart Easterly. 2009. 16p. pap. 15.00 *(978-1-4389-4703-7(8))* AuthorHouse.

Lawlor, Ashley. Ashley & the First Day of School. 2012. 24p. pap. 24.95 *(978-1-4626-6518-1(7))* America Star Bks.

Layboum, Emma. Dungeon Dragon. 2008. (ENG.). 156p. (J). (gr. 3-6). pap. 9.95 *(978-1-84270-736-4(1))* Andersen Pr. GBR. Dist: Independent Pubs. Group.

LeGette, M. L. The Unicorn Girl. 2008. (ENG.). 416p. pap. 10.00 *(978-1-4196-8696-2(8))* CreateSpace Independent Publishing Platform.

Legrand, Claire. Foxheart. Zollars, Jaime, illus. 2016. 480p. (J). (gr. 3-7). 16.99 *(978-0-06-242773-1(3),* Greenwillow Bks.) HarperCollins Pubs.

W X Y Z

Lemire, Lillie. A Young Witch's Magical Adventure. 2006. (ENG.). 48p. per. 16.95 (978-1-4241-5413-5(8)) America Star Bks.

Lenagh, Cecilia. La Brujita Fregona. (Raton de Biblioteca Coleccion). (SPA., Illus.). 64p. (J). (gr. 3-5). 7.95 (978-84-88061-83-6(8)) Serres, Ediciones, S. L. ESP. Dist: Lectorum Pubns., Inc.

Lenhard, Elizabeth. Different Path. 2004. (W. I. T. C. H. Ser.: Bk. 13). 158p. (J). lib. bdg. 16.92 (978-1-4242-0791-6(6)) Fitzgerald Bks.

Lewis, C. S. The Lion, the Witch & the Wardrobe. 2008. (Chronicles of Narnia Ser.: 2). (J). 18.40 (978-0-613-94066-5(0), Turtleback) Turtleback Bks.

Loewen, Nancy. Trust Me, Hansel & Gretel Are SWEET! The Story of Hansel & Gretel As Told by the Witch. Bock, Janna, illus. 2016. (Other Side of the Story Ser.). (ENG.). 24p. (gr. 2-3). lib. bdg. 27.32 (978-1-4795-8623-3(4)) Picture Window Bks.

Losure, Mary. Backwards Moon. 2014. (ENG.). 144p. (J). (gr. 2-5). 16.95 (978-0-8234-3160-1(6)) Holiday Hse., Inc.

Lou, Rachel. The Bridge. 2016. (ENG., Illus.). (YA). (gr. 8-12). 24.99 **(978-1-63477-964-7(9)**, Harmony Ink Pr.) Dreamspinner Pr.

Lowe, Natasha. The Courage of Cat Campbell. 2015. (Poppy Pendle Ser.). (ENG., Illus.). 288p. (J). (gr. 3-7). 16.99 (978-1-4814-1870-6(X), Simon & Schuster/Paula Wiseman Bks.) Simon & Schuster/Paula Wiseman Bks.

—The Marvelous Magic of Miss Mabel. 2016. (Poppy Pendle Ser.). (ENG., Illus.). 288p. (J). (gr. 3-7). 16.99 (978-1-4814-6533-5(3), Simon & Schuster/Paula Wiseman Bks.) Simon & Schuster/Paula Wiseman Bks.

—The Power of Poppy Pendle. (Poppy Pendle Ser.). (ENG., 272p. (J). (gr. 3-7). 2013. Illus.). pap. 7.99 (978-1-4424-4926-8(8)) 2012. 16.99 (978-1-4424-4679-3(X)) Simon & Schuster/Paula Wiseman Bks. (Simon & Schuster/Paula Wiseman Bks.).

Lubar, David. The Unwilling Witch: A Monsterrific Tale. 2013. (Monsterrific Tales Ser.). (ENG.). 158p. (J). (gr. 3-7). 15.99 (978-0-7653-3078-9(4), 9780765330789, Starscape) Doherty, Tom Assocs., LLC.

Luberto, Bradley. Clide & Druce: A Repulsive Tale of Trolls & Tax Money. 2006. (ENG.). 48p. per. 16.95 (978-1-4241-5012-0(4)) PublishAmerica, Inc.

Lück, Stefanie. Carla's Worlds. 2010. 222p. pap. 20.90 (978-3-8391-4857-0(X)) Bks. on Demand.

Lucke, Deb. Knee-Deep in Niceness. 2016. (Lunch Witch Ser.: 2). (ENG.). 180p. (J). (gr. 2-5). 26.95 (978-0-606-39301-0(3)) Turtleback Bks.

Lyle, Patrice. The Case of the Invisible Witch. 2013. 194p. pap. 9.99 (978-1-61603-034-6(8)) Leap Bks.

MacCullough, Carolyn. Once a Witch. 2010. (ENG.). 320p. (YA). (gr. 7). pap. 8.99 (978-0-547-41730-1(6)) Houghton Mifflin Harcourt Publishing Co.

MacDonald, George. Stephen Archer & Other Tales. 2008. 212p. 26.95 (978-1-60664-985-5(X)) Aegypan.

Magaziner, Lauren. The Only Thing Worse Than Witches. 2015. (ENG., Illus.). 272p. (J). (gr. 3-7). 7.99 (978-0-14-242442-1(0), Puffin Books) Penguin Young Readers Group.

Mahoney, Karen. The Wood Queen: An Iron Witch Novel. 2012. (Iron Witch Ser.: 2). (ENG.). 336p. (YA). pap. 9.95 (978-0-7387-2662-5(1), Flux) North Star Editions.

Mahy, Margaret. Aunt Nasty. Mould, Chris, illus. 2016. (Early Reader Ser.). (ENG.). 80p. (J). (gr. k-2). 6.99 (978-1-4440-1442-6(0), Orion Children's Bks.) Hachette Children's Group GBR. Dist: Hachette Bk. Group.

Manning, Jane. Cat Nights. Manning, Jane, illus. 2008. (Illus.). 32p. (J). lib. bdg. 17.89 (978-0-06-113889-8(4), Greenwillow Bks.) HarperCollins Pubs.

Manning, Matthew K. The Salem Witch Showdown. Neely, Scott, illus. 2017. (You Choose Stories: Scooby-Doo Ser.). (ENG.). 112p. (gr. 2-3). lib. bdg. 32.65 (978-1-4965-4334-9(3), You Choose Bks.) Capstone Press of Coughlan Cos.

Marciano, John Bemelmans. The All Powerful Ring. Blackall, Sophie, illus. 2016. (Witches of Benevento Ser.: 2). (ENG.). 144p. (J). (gr. 2-5). 13.99 (978-0-451-47180-2(6), Viking Books for Young Readers) Penguin Young Readers Group.

—Mischief Season. Blackall, Sophie, illus. 2016. (Witches of Benevento Ser.: 1). (ENG.). 128p. (J). (gr. 2-5). 13.99 (978-0-451-47181-9(4), Viking Books for Young Readers) Penguin Young Readers Group.

—Respect Your Ghosts. Blackall, Sophie, illus. 2017. (Witches of Benevento Ser.: 4). (ENG.). 128p. (J). (gr. 2-5). 13.99 (978-0-451-47183-3(0), Viking Books for Young Readers) Penguin Young Readers Group.

Mariotte, Jeff. Dark Vengeance Vol. 2: Winter, Spring. 2012. (ENG.). 448p. (YA). (gr. 9). pap. 10.99 (978-1-4424-2976-5(3), Simon Pulse) Simon Pulse.

—Fall. (Witch Season Ser.). (ENG.). 320p. (YA). (gr. 9). 2011. pap. 14.99 (978-1-4424-3099-0(0)) 2004. mass mkt. 5.99 (978-0-689-86724-8(7)) Simon Pulse. (Simon Pulse).

Marlow, Layn. The Witch with a Twitch. Dreidemy, Joëlle, illus. (Tiger Tales Ser.). (J). (gr. -1-2). 2006. 28p. pap. 6.95 (978-1-58925-400-8(7)) 2005. 32p. 15.95 (978-1-58925-052-9(4)) Tiger Tales.

Marsh, Katherine. The Door by the Staircase. 2016. (ENG., Illus.). 284p. (J). (gr. 3-7). 16.99 (978-1-4231-3499-2(0)) Disney Pr.

—The Door by the Staircase. Murphy, Kelly, illus. 2017. (ENG.). 288p. (J). (gr. 5-9). pap. 7.99 (978-1-4231-3785-6(X)) Hyperion Bks. for Children.

Martin, W. Lyon. Aidan's First Full Moon Circle: A Magical Child Story. Martin, W. Lyon, illus. 2008. (Illus.). 32p. (J). (gr. -1-1). lib. bdg. 16.95 (978-0-9796834-4-2(0)) Shades of White.

Martinez, Roland L. The Evil Leaf. 2009. 232p. 24.99 (978-1-4490-0916-8(6)); pap. 14.90 (978-1-4490-0917-5(4)) AuthorHouse.

Masters, H. Pink Feathers,Murky Pools & a Witch: A Lellaland Adventure. Lie, Vivian, illus. 2003. 52p. pap. (978-1-84401-098-1(8)) Athena Pr.

Mayo, Jason. Do Witches Make Fishes? 2010. 36p. pap. 16.99 (978-1-4520-6944-9(1)) AuthorHouse.

Mc Shane, Mary. Karena the Fairy & the Bat Colony. 2011. 344p. (gr. 4-6). pap. 19.95 (978-1-4620-5295-0(9)) iUniverse, Inc.

McCafferty, Catherine. Rapunzel. Spong, Clive, illus. 2008. (Keepsake Stories Ser.). (ENG & SPA.). 32p. (gr. -1-3). pap. 3.99 (978-0-7696-5418-8(5), Brighter Child) Carson-Dellosa Publishing, LLC.

McClymer, Kelly. Competition's a Witch. 2007. (ENG.). 256p. (YA). (gr. 7-18). pap. 8.99 (978-1-4169-1645-1(8), Simon Pulse) Simon Pulse.

—The Salem Witch Tryouts. 2006. (ENG.). 272p. (YA). (gr. 7-12). pap. 12.99 (978-1-4169-1644-4(X), Simon Pulse) Simon Pulse.

McCoola, Marika. Baba Yaga's Assistant. 2015. (ENG., Illus.). 136p. (J). (gr. 5). 16.99 (978-0-7636-6961-4(X)) Candlewick Pr.

Mcghee, Alison. Only a Witch Can Fly. Yoo, Taeeun, illus. movie tie-in ed. 2009. (ENG.). 32p. (J). (gr. -1-3). 16.99 (978-0-312-37503-4(4), 9780312375034) Feiwel & Friends.

—The Sweetest Witch Around. Bliss, Harry, illus. 2014. (ENG.). 32p. (J). (gr. -1-3). 15.99 (978-1-4424-7833-6(0), Simon & Schuster/Paula Wiseman Bks.) Simon & Schuster/Paula Wiseman Bks.

—A Very Brave Witch. Bliss, Harry, illus. 2007. (J). (gr. -1-3). 24.95 incl. audio (978-0-545-04268-0(2)) Scholastic, Inc.

—A Very Brave Witch. Bliss, Harry, illus. (ENG.). 32p. (J). (gr. -1-3). 2011. 7.99 (978-0-689-86731-6(X)) 2009. 9.99 (978-1-4169-8670-6(7)) 2006. 17.99 (978-0-689-86730-9(1)) Simon & Schuster/Paula Wiseman Bks. (Simon & Schuster/Paula Wiseman Bks.).

—A Very Brave Witch. 2011. (J). (gr. -1-3). 29.95 (978-0-545-04267-3(4)) Weston Woods Studios, Inc.

McGowan, Keith. The Witch's Curse. Tanaka, Yoko, illus. 2013. (ENG.). 304p. (J). (gr. 4-7). 16.99 (978-0-8050-9324-7(9), 9780805093247, Holt, Henry & Co. Bks. For Young Readers) Holt, Henry & Co.

—The Witch's Guide to Cooking with Children. Tanaka, Yoko, illus. 2011. (ENG.). 192p. (J). (gr. 4-7). pap. 8.99 (978-0-312-67486-1(4), 9780312674861) Square Fish.

McGrath, Barbara Barbieri. The Little Green Witch. Alexander, Martha, illus. (ENG.). 32p. (J). (gr. -1-2). 2006. pap. 7.95 (978-1-58089-153-0(5)) 2005. 15.95 (978-1-58089-042-7(3)) Charlesbridge Publishing, Inc.

Mckenzie, Riford. The Witches of Dredmoore Hollow, 0 vols. unabr. ed. 2013. (ENG.). 274p. (J). (gr. 5-7). pap. 9.99 (978-1-4778-1702-5(6), 9781477817025, Amazon Children's Publishing) Amazon Publishing.

McLean, Matthew. A Bewitching Summer, 1 vol. 2009. 100p. pap. 19.95 (978-1-60836-686-6(3)) America Star Bks.

McMullan, Kate. Sir Lancelot, Where Are You? Basso, Bill, illus. 2003. (Dragon Slayers' Academy Ser.: 6). (ENG.). 112p. (J). (gr. 2-5). pap. 5.99 (978-0-448-43278-6(1), Grosset & Dunlap) Penguin Young Readers Group.

Meadows, Daisy. Bella Tabbypaw in Trouble. 2015. (Magic Animal Friends Ser.: 4). (ENG., Illus.). 112p. (J). (gr. 2-5). pap. 4.99 (978-0-545-68648-8(2), Scholastic Paperbacks) Scholastic, Inc.

—Chloe Slipperside's Secret. 2016. (Magic Animal Friends Ser.: 11). (ENG., Illus.). 112p. (J). (gr. 2-5). pap. 4.99 (978-0-545-94078-8(8), Scholastic Paperbacks) Scholastic, Inc.

—Chloe Slipperslide's Secret. 2016. (Magic Animal Friends Ser.: 11). lib. bdg. 14.75 (978-0-606-38801-6(X)) Turtleback Bks.

—Ellie Featherbill All Alone. 2015. (Magic Animal Friends Ser.: 3). (ENG.). 112p. (J). (gr. 2-5). pap. 4.99 (978-0-545-68646-4(6), Scholastic Paperbacks) Scholastic, Inc.

—Emily Prickleback's Clever Idea. 2016. (Magic Animal Friends Ser.: 6). (ENG.). 112p. (J). (gr. 2-5). pap. 4.99 (978-0-545-90743-9(8), Scholastic Paperbacks) Scholastic, Inc.

—Evie Scruffypup's Big Surprise. 2016. (Magic Animal Friends Ser.: 1). (ENG., Illus.). 112p. (J). (gr. 2-5). pap. 4.99 (978-0-545-94077-1(X), Scholastic Paperbacks) Scholastic, Inc.

—Evie Scruffypup's Surprise. 2016. (Magic Animal Friends Ser.: 10). lib. bdg. 14.75 (978-0-606-38800-9(1)) Turtleback Bks.

—Grace Woollyhop's Musical Mystery. 2016. (Magic Animal Friends Ser.: 12). lib. bdg. 14.75 (978-0-606-38802-3(8)) Turtleback Bks.

—Grace Woollyhop's Musical Mystery (Magic Animal Friends #12) 2016. (Magic Animal Friends Ser.: 12). (ENG., Illus.). 112p. (J). (gr. 2-5). pap. 4.99 (978-0-545-94079-5(6), Scholastic Paperbacks) Scholastic, Inc.

—Lucy Longwhiskers Gets Lost. 2015. (Magic Animal Friends Ser.: 1). (ENG., Illus.). 112p. (J). (gr. 2-5). pap. 4.99 (978-0-545-68642-6(3), Scholastic Paperbacks) Scholastic, Inc.

—Magic Animal Friends - Poppy Muddlepup's Daring Rescue. 2015. (Magic Animal Friends Ser.: 1). (ENG., Illus.). 176p. (J). (gr. 2-5). pap. 6.99 (978-0-545-90750-7(0)) Scholastic, Inc.

—Molly Twinkletail Runs Away. 2015. (Magic Animal Friends Ser.: 2). (ENG.). 112p. (J). (gr. 2-5). pap. 4.99 (978-0-545-68644-0(X), Scholastic Paperbacks) Scholastic, Inc.

—Rosie Gigglepip's Lucky Escape. 2016. (Magic Animal Friends Ser.: 8). (ENG., Illus.). 112p. (J). (gr. 2-5). pap. 4.99 (978-0-545-90747-7(0), Scholastic Paperbacks) Scholastic, Inc.

—Ruby Fuzzybrush's Star Dance. 2016. (Magic Animal Friends Ser.: 7). (ENG., Illus.). 112p. (J). (gr. 2-5). pap. 4.99 (978-0-545-90745-3(4), Scholastic Paperbacks) Scholastic, Inc.

—Sophie Flufftail's Brave Plan. 2016. (Magic Animal Friends Ser.: 5). (ENG., Illus.). 112p. (J). (gr. 2-5). pap. 4.99 (978-0-545-90741-5(1), Scholastic Paperbacks) Scholastic, Inc.

Meddaugh, Susan. The Witches' Supermarket. 2014. (Martha Speaks Ser.). (ENG., Illus.). 32p. (J). (gr. -1-3). pap. 4.99 (978-0-544-32358-2(0), HMH Books For Young Readers) Houghton Mifflin Harcourt Publishing Co.

Meroto, Tina. The Tooth Gnashing Witch. 2007. (ENG., Illus.). 48p. (J). 18.95 (978-84-96788-82-4(2)) OQO, Editora ESP. Dist: Baker & Taylor Bks.

Miceli, Mary Anne. Boston North Shore's ... Salem's Golden Broomstick. 2013. 44p. pap. 20.00 (978-0-9888654-0-2(8)) Miceli, Mary Anne.

Milburn, Trish. White Witch. 2012. 188p. pap. 12.95 (978-1-61194-083-1(4), Bell Bridge Bks.) BelleBks., Inc.

Miyazaki, Hayao. Kiki's Delivery Service, Vol. 3. 2006. (Kiki's Delivery Service Film Comics Ser.: 3). (ENG., Illus.). 208p. pap. 9.99 (978-1-59116-784-6(1)) Viz Media.

—Kiki's Delivery Service Film Comic, Vol. 4. 2006. Orig. Title: Majo No Takkyubin. (ENG., Illus.). 208p. pap. 9.99 (978-1-4215-0595-4(9)) Viz Media.

—Kiki's Delivery Service Picture Book, Vol. 1. 2006. (ENG., Illus.). 208p. pap. 19.99 (978-1-4215-0596-1(7)) Viz Media.

Mlynowski, Sarah. Frogs & French Kisses. 2007. (Magic in Manhattan Ser.: No. 2). (ENG.). 304p. (YA). (gr. 7). pap. 8.99 (978-0-385-73185-0(X), Delacorte Pr.) Random Hse. Children's Bks.

—Parties & Potions. 2010. (Magic in Manhattan Ser.: No. 4). (ENG., Illus.). 368p. (YA). (gr. 7). pap. 10.99 (978-0-385-73646-6(0), Ember) Random Hse. Children's Bks.

—Spells & Sleeping Bags. 2008. (Magic in Manhattan Ser.: No. 3). (ENG.). 320p. (YA). (gr. 7-12). pap. 8.99 (978-0-385-73388-5(7), Delacorte Pr.) Random Hse. Children's Bks.

—Sugar & Spice. 2016. (Whatever After Ser.: 10). (ENG.). 176p. (J). (gr. 3-7). 14.99 (978-0-545-85106-0(8), Scholastic Pr.) Scholastic, Inc.

Moore, Victor L. The Pentacle of Northumbria. 2013. 432p. pap. (978-1-78222-073-2(9)) Paragon Publishing, Rothersthorpe.

Moriarty, Chris. The Inquisitor's Apprentice. Geyer, Mark Edward, illus. (ENG.). 352p. (J). (gr. 5-7). 2013. pap. 7.99 (978-0-547-85084-9(0)) 2011. 16.99 (978-0-547-58135-4(1)) Houghton Mifflin Harcourt Publishing Co.

Morrison, Megan. Grounded: The Tale of Rapunzel. 2015. (Illus.). 374p. (J). (978-0-545-75468-2(2)) Scholastic, Inc.

Moss, Ronald. The Wizard Next Door. 2009. 198p. pap. 14.95 (978-1-60911-077-2(3), Eloquent Bks.) Strategic Book Publishing & Rights Agency (SBPRA).

Mould, Chris. Pip & the Wood Witch Curse: A Spindlewood Tale, Bk. 1. 2012. (Spindlewood Tales Ser.: Book 1). (ENG.). 176p. (J). (gr. 3-7). 12.99 (978-0-8075-6548-3(2)) Whitman, Albert & Co.

Muncaster, Harriet. Happy Halloween, Witch's Cat! Muncaster, Harriet, illus. 2015. (ENG., Illus.). 32p. (J). (gr. -1-3). 15.99 (978-0-06-222916-8(8)) HarperCollins Pubs.

—I Am a Witch's Cat. Muncaster, Harriet, illus. 2014. (ENG., Illus.). 32p. (J). (gr. -1-3). 15.99 (978-0-06-222914-4(1)) HarperCollins Pubs.

Murphy, Jill. A Bad Spell for the Worst Witch. Murphy, Jill, illus. 2014. (Worst Witch Ser.). (ENG., Illus.). 128p. (J). (gr. 3-7). pap. 5.99 (978-0-7636-7252-2(1)) Candlewick Pr.

—The Worst Witch & the Wishing Star. Murphy, Jill, illus. 2015. (Worst Witch Ser.). (ENG., Illus.). 208p. (J). (gr. 3-7). 14.99 (978-0-7636-7000-9(6)) Candlewick Pr.

—The Worst Witch Saves the Day. Murphy, Jill, illus. 2014. (Worst Witch Ser.). (ENG., Illus.). 160p. (J). (gr. 3-7). pap. 5.99 (978-0-7636-7255-3(6)) Candlewick Pr.

—The Worst Witch to the Rescue. Murphy, Jill, illus. (Worst Witch Ser.). (ENG., Illus.). 176p. (J). (gr. 3-7). 2015. pap. 5.99 (978-0-7636-7862-3(7)) 2014. 14.99 (978-0-7636-6999-7(7)) Candlewick Pr.

Murray, Diana. Grimelda & the Spooktacular Pet Show. Ross, Heather, illus. 2017. 40p. (J). (gr. -1-3). 16.99 **(978-0-06-226449-7(4)**, Tegen, Katherine Bks) HarperCollins Pubs.

Murray, Diana. Grimelda: the Very Messy Witch. Ross, Heather, illus. 2016. 32p. (J). (gr. -1-3). 16.99 (978-0-06-226448-0(6), Tegen, Katherine Bks) HarperCollins Pubs.

Naifeh, Ted & Wucinich, Warren. Courtney Crumrin Volume 5: the Witch Next Door: The Witch Next Door. 2014. (ENG., Illus.). 144p. (J). 24.99 (978-1-934964-96-5(4), 9781934964965) Oni Pr., Inc.

Nardone, Frank. Something's Brewing in Salem. 2013. 164p. pap. 9.99 (978-0-9884024-1-6(6)) Dragon Tree Bks.

Neff, Henry H. The Fiend & the Forge. 2011. (Tapestry Ser.). (ENG., Illus.). 560p. (J). (gr. 3-7). 7.99 (978-0-375-83899-6(6), Yearling) Random Hse. Children's Bks.

—The Maelstrom: Book Four of the Tapestry. Neff, Henry H., illus. 2013. (Tapestry Ser.). (ENG., Illus.). 480p. (J). (gr. 3-7). 7.99 (978-0-375-87148-1(9), Yearling) Random Hse. Children's Bks.

—The Second Siege. 2010. (Tapestry Ser.). (ENG., Illus.). 512p. (J). (gr. 3-7). 7.99 (978-0-375-83897-2(X), Yearling) Random Hse. Children's Bks.

Niemann, Christoph. The Pet Dragon: A Story about Adventure, Friendship, & Chinese Characters. Niemann, Christoph, illus. 2008. (ENG., Illus.). 40p. (J). (gr. -1-3). 16.99 (978-0-06-157776-5(6), Greenwillow Bks.) HarperCollins Pubs.

North, Laura. Hansel & Gretel & the Green Witch. Jevons, Chris, illus. 2015. (ENG.). 32p. (J). (978-0-7787-1928-1(6)) Crabtree Publishing Co.

North, Lynne. Gerties Gets It Right. 2008. 204p. pap. (978-1-84923-231-9(8)) YouWriteOn.

Novak, Matt. No Zombies Allowed. Novak, Matt, illus. 2014. (ENG., Illus.). 32p. (J). (gr. -1-1). 16.99 (978-1-4814-2540-7(4), Atheneum Bks. for Young Readers) Simon & Schuster Children's Publishing.

Nowicki, Colin J. Lamia High: Moon of Destiny, 1 vol. 2010. 186p. pap. 24.95 (978-1-4512-8561-1(2)) America Star Bks.

Oakes, Cory Putman. Witchtown. 2017. (ENG.). 320p. (YA). (gr. 7). 17.99 (978-0-544-76557-3(5), HMH Books For Young Readers) Houghton Mifflin Harcourt Publishing Co.

O'Connor, Jane. Lulu & the Witch Baby. Sinclair, Bella, illus. 2014. (I Can Read Level 2 Ser.). (ENG.). 48p. (J). (gr. -1-3). pap. 3.99 (978-0-06-230516-9(6)) HarperCollins Pubs.

—Lulu Goes to Witch School. Sinclair, Bella, illus. 2013. (I Can Read Level 2 Ser.). (ENG.). 48p. (J). (gr. -1-3). 16.99 (978-0-06-223351-6(3)); pap. 3.99 (978-0-06-223350-9(5)) HarperCollins Pubs.

Olin, Marilyn. Mom, Mac & Cheese, Please! Pantic, Dunja, illus. 2013. (ENG.). 28p. (J). (gr. -1-k). 16.95 (978-1-62087-995-5(6), 620995, Sky Pony Pr.) Skyhorse Publishing Co., Inc.

Oliver, Ilanit. Ten Flying Brooms. Poling, Kyle, illus. 2015. (J). (ENG.). 24p. (gr. -1-k). 3.99 (978-0-545-81336-5(0)); (978-1-4844-5738-2(2)) Scholastic, Inc. (Cartwheel Bks.).

Oram, Hiawyn. My Unwilling Witch Gets a Makeover. Warburton, Sarah, illus. 2010. (Rumblewick's Diary Ser.: 4). (ENG.). 112p. (J). (gr. 1-4). 7.99 (978-0-316-03462-3(2)) Little, Brown Bks. for Young Readers.

—My Unwilling Witch Goes to Ballet School. Warburton, Sarah, illus. 2009. (Rumblewick's Diary Ser.: 1). (ENG.). 112p. (J). (gr. 1-4). 7.99 (978-0-316-03472-2(X)) Little, Brown Bks. for Young Readers.

O'Reilly, Sean. Homesick Witch, 1 vol. (Mighty Mighty Monsters Ser.). (ENG., 48p. (gr. 2-3). 2013. Illus.). pap. 6.10 (978-1-4342-4225-9(0)) 2012. lib. bdg. 23.99 (978-1-4342-3893-1(8)) Stone Arch Bks.

Owen, Sarah. The Enchanted Tales. 2009. 39p. pap. 26.50 (978-1-4452-5948-2(6)) Lulu Pr., Inc.

Paige, Danielle. Dorothy Must Die. (Dorothy Must Die Ser.: 1). (ENG.). (gr. 9). 2015. 480p. (J). pap. 9.99 (978-0-06-228068-8(6)) 2014. 464p. (YA). 17.99 (978-0-06-228067-1(8), HarperTeen) HarperCollins Pubs.

—Dorothy Must Die. 2015. (Dorothy Must Die Ser.: 1). (YA). lib. bdg. 20.85 (978-0-606-36510-9(9)) Turtleback Bks.

—Dorothy Must Die 2-Book Box Set: Dorothy Must Die, the Wicked Will Rise. 2016. (Dorothy Must Die Ser.). 800p. (YA). (gr. 9). pap. 19.98 (978-0-06-256982-0(1)) HarperCollins Pubs.

—Dorothy Must Die Stories: No Place Like Oz - The Witch Must Burn; the Wizard Returns. 2015. (Dorothy Must Die Novella Ser.). (ENG., Illus.). 416p. (YA). (gr. 9). pap. 9.99 (978-0-06-228079-4(1)) HarperCollins Pubs.

—Dorothy Must Die Stories: No Place Like Oz, the Witch Must Burn, the Wizard Returns. 2015. (Dorothy Must Die Ser.). (YA). lib. bdg. 20.85 (978-0-606-37248-0(2)) Turtleback Bks.

—Dorothy Must Die Stories Volume 2. 2016. (Dorothy Must Die Novella Ser.). 336p. (YA). (gr. 9). pap. 9.99 (978-0-06-240397-1(4)) HarperCollins Pubs.

—The Wicked Will Rise. (Dorothy Must Die Ser.: 2). (YA). (gr. 9). 2016. 320p. pap. 9.99 (978-0-06-228071-8(6)) 2015. (ENG.). 304p. 17.99 (978-0-06-228070-1(8)) HarperCollins Pubs.

—The Wicked Will Rise. 2016. (Dorothy Must Die Ser.: 2). (YA). lib. bdg. 20.85 (978-0-606-38170-3(8)) Turtleback Bks.

—Yellow Brick War. 2016. (Dorothy Must Die Ser.: 3). (ENG.). 288p. (YA). (gr. 9-12). 18.99 (978-0-06-228073-2(2)) HarperCollins Pubs.

Palatini, Margie. Piggie Pie!, 1 vol. Fine, Howard, illus. 2008. (Read along Book & CD Ser.). (ENG.). 32p. (J). (gr. -1-3). audio compact disk 10.99 (978-0-547-18178-3(7)) Houghton Mifflin Harcourt Publishing Co.

Palmer, Jennie. The Wompananny Witches Make One Mean Pizza. 2017. (ENG., Illus.). 40p. (J). (gr. -1-2). 16.95 **(978-1-4197-2642-2(0)**, Abrams Bks. for Young Readers) Abrams, Inc.

Pardoe, David. Jasper Tippett's Amazing Journey to Page 42. 2006. (Illus.). 132p. pap. (978-1-84401-785-0(0)) Athena Pr.

Parker, Emma. The Wickedest Witch. 2010. (Illus.). pap. (978-1-877561-17-7(7)) First Edition Ltd.

Pascual, P. V. The Beautiful Witch. 2004. (J). per. 28.95 (978-1-58939-603-6(0)) Virtualbookworm.com Publishing, Inc.

Patterson, James. The Fire. 2011. (Playaway Children Ser.). (ENG.). (YA). (gr. 8-12). 59.99 (978-1-61113-385-1(8)) Hachette Audio.

—The Gift. 2010. (Witch & Wizard Ser.: No. 2). (J). 59.99 (978-1-60941-012-4(2)) Findaway World, LLC.

—The Gift. 2014. lthr. 79.00 (978-1-62715-523-6(6)) Leatherbound Bestsellers.

—Witch & Wizard. 2014. lthr. 79.00 (978-1-62715-529-8(5)) Leatherbound Bestsellers.

—Witch & Wizard. 2010. (Witch & Wizard Ser.: 1). (ENG.). 336p. (YA). (gr. 5-17). pap. 10.00 (978-0-316-03834-8(2), Jimmy Patterson) Little Brown & Co.

—Witch & Wizard. 2010. (Witch & Wizard Ser.: 1). (YA). lib. bdg. 20.85 (978-0-606-15119-1(2), Turtleback) Turtleback Bks.

Patterson, James & Charbonnet, Gabrielle. Witch & Wizard. 2011. (Witch & Wizard Ser.: 1). (ENG.). 368p. mass mkt. 8.00 (978-0-446-56243-0(2), Jimmy Patterson) Little Brown & Co.

—Witch & Wizard. 2011. (Witch & Wizard Ser.: 1). lib. bdg. 18.45 (978-0-606-26452-5(3), Turtleback) Turtleback Bks.

Patterson, James & Dembowski, Jill. The Fire. 2011. (Witch & Wizard Ser.: 3). (ENG.). 352p. (YA). (gr. 5-17). 17.99 (978-0-316-10190-5(7), Jimmy Patterson) Little Brown & Co.

—The Kiss. 2013. (Witch & Wizard Ser.: 4). (ENG.). 384p. (YA). (gr. 7-17). pap. 10.00 (978-0-316-10176-9(1), Jimmy Patterson) Little Brown & Co.

—The Kiss. 2013. (Witch & Wizard Ser.: 4). (YA). lib. bdg. 20.85 (978-0-606-32281-2(7), Turtleback) Turtleback Bks.

Patterson, James & Raymond, Emily. The Lost. 2014. (YA). (Witch & Wizard Ser.: 5). (ENG.). 384p. (gr. 7-17). 18.00 (978-0-316-20770-6(5), Jimmy Patterson); 355p. (978-0-316-24266-0(7)) Little Brown & Co.

Patterson, James & Rust, Ned. The Gift. (Witch & Wizard Ser.: 2). (ENG.). 2012. 352p. mass mkt. 7.99 (978-0-446-56245-4(9)) 2011. 400p. (gr. 5-17). pap. 9.99 (978-0-316-03835-5(0)) 2010. 352p. (gr. 5-17). 17.99 (978-0-316-03625-2(0)) Little Brown & Co. (Jimmy Patterson).

—The Gift. 2012. (Witch & Wizard Ser.: 2). lib. bdg. 18.40 (978-0-606-26451-8(5), Turtleback) Turtleback Bks.

Pau Pau. The Princess' Adventure. 2007. 52p. pap. 16.95 (978-1-60441-069-3(8)) America Star Bks.

Paulk, William. The Creatures of Vision City: Pokie's Party, Book One. 2009. 48p. pap. 10.99 (978-1-4389-5659-6(2)) AuthorHouse.

Pavanello, Roberto. The Midnight Witches, 1 vol. Zeni, Marco, tr. from ITA. Pisapia, Blasco & Brughera, Pamela, illus. 2012. (Echo & the Bat Pack Ser.). (ENG.). 128p. (gr. 2-3). 9.95 (978-1-4342-4246-4(3)); lib. bdg. 25.32 (978-1-4342-3822-1(9), Echo & the Bat Pack) Stone Arch Bks.

PC Treasures Staff, prod. Hansel & Gretel. 2007. (J). (978-1-60072-030-7(7)) PC Treasures, Inc.

Peace, Bob. The Wicked Witch Pop Quiz. Rasheed, M., illus. 2013. 132p. pap. 12.95 *(978-0-9824741-4-3(8))* Sojourner Publishing, Inc.
Pearce, Jackson. Sweetly. 2012. (Fairy Tale Retelling Ser.). (ENG.). 336p. (YA). (gr. 10-17). pap. 8.99 *(978-0-316-06866-6(7))* Little, Brown Bks. for Young Readers.
Pearce, Margaret. A Belinda Robinson Novel Book 1: Belinda & the Witch's Cat. 2013. 82p. pap. *(978-1-922066-58-9(3))* Writers Exchange E-Publishing.
Pearson, Kimberly Ann. Mystling Glen Book I: The Tale of A Prince. 2009. 207p. pap. 14.95 *(978-1-4327-4169-3(1))* Outskirts Pr., Inc.
Perkins, T. J. Four Little Witches, 1 vol. Pinero, Eimi, illus. 2015. (ENG.). 40p. (J). 12.99 *(978-0-7643-4943-0(0),* 9780764349430) Schiffer Publishing, Ltd.
Perry, Pete. The Secret of Bedside Manor. 2009. (Illus.). 140p. pap. 36.49 *(978-1-4389-6668-7(7))* AuthorHouse.
Petrlik, Andrea, illus. Hansel & Gretel. 2007. (Flip-Up Fairy Tales Ser.). (ENG.). 24p. (J). (gr. -1-2). audio compact disk *(978-1-84643-090-9(9))* Child's Play International Ltd.
Philpot, Graham, illus. Hansel & Gretel. 2007. (First Fairy Tales Ser.). 32p. (J). (gr. -1-3). lib. bdg. 28.50 *(978-1-59771-075-6(X))* Sea-To-Sea Pubns.
Pierce, Meredith Ann. The Pearl of the Soul of the World. 2008. (Darkangel Trilogy Ser.: Bk. 3). (ENG.). 256p. (YA). (gr. 7-17). per. 7.99 *(978-0-316-06724-9(5))* Little, Brown Bks. for Young Readers.
Pike, Christopher, pseud. Black Knight. 2014. (Witch World Ser.: 2). (ENG., Illus.). 464p. (YA). (gr. 9). 19.99 *(978-1-4424-6733-0(9))*; pap. 11.99 *(978-1-4424-6734-7(7))* Simon Pulse. (Simon Pulse).
—Red Queen. 2014. (Witch World Ser.: 1). (ENG., Illus.). 560p. (YA). (gr. 9). pap. 9.99 *(978-1-4424-3029-7(X),* Simon Pulse) Simon Pulse.
—Witch World. 2012. (Witch World Ser.: 1). (ENG.). 528p. (YA). (gr. 9). 17.99 *(978-1-4424-3028-0(1),* Simon Pulse) Simon Pulse.
—The Witch's Revenge. 2015. (Spooksville Ser.: 6). (ENG., Illus.). 128p. (J). (gr. 3-7). pap. 6.99 *(978-1-4814-1069-4(5),* Aladdin) Simon & Schuster Children's Publishing.
Pinkwater, Daniel M. The Yggyssey: How Iggy Wondered What Happened to All the Ghosts, Found Out Where They Went, & Went There. 2010. (ENG., Illus.). 256p. (J). (gr. 5-7). pap. 6.99 *(978-0-547-32865-2(6))* Houghton Mifflin Harcourt Publishing Co.
Plourde, Paulette. Smitty Moose, Petey & Me - Episode One, the Witch. Golen, Jessica, illus. l.t. ed. 2005. 32p. (J). per. 9.95 *(978-1-59879-038-2(2))* Lifevest Publishing, Inc.
Popper, Garry. Worm's Eye View: A Witch's Tale. Forshaw, John, illus. 2004. 48p. 7.00 *(978-1-84161-025-2(9))* Ravette Publishing, Ltd. GBR. Dist: Parkwest Pubns., Inc.
Pounder, Sibéal. Witch Switch. Anderson, Laura Ellen, illus. 2017. (Witch Wars Ser.). (ENG.). 272p. (J). 16.99 *(978-1-61963-984-3(X),* 9781619639843, Bloomsbury USA Childrens) Bloomsbury Publishing USA.
—Witch Wars. Anderson, Laura Ellen, illus. 2016. (Witch Wars Ser.). (ENG.). 272p. (J). 16.99 *(978-1-61963-925-6(4),* 9781619639256, Bloomsbury USA Childrens) Bloomsbury Publishing USA.
—Witch Wars. Anderson, Laura Ellen, illus. 2017. (Witch Wars Ser.). (ENG.). 288p. (J). pap. 7.99 *(978-1-68119-296-3(9),* 9781681192963, Bloomsbury USA Childrens) Bloomsbury Publishing USA.
Powell, J. Frederick. Puffy & the Witch's Revenge. 2004. (Illus.). 96p. pap. *(978-1-84401-326-6(4))* Athena Pr.
Powell, Laura. Burn Mark. (ENG.). (YA). (gr. 9). 2013. 432p. pap. 9.99 *(978-1-61963-119-9(9),* 9781619631199) 2012. 416p. 17.99 *(978-1-59990-843-4(3),* 9781599908434) Bloomsbury Publishing USA. (Bloomsbury USA Childrens).
—Witch Fire. 2013. (ENG.). 336p. (YA). (gr. 7). 17.99 *(978-1-61963-006-2(0),* 9781619630062, Bloomsbury USA Childrens) Bloomsbury Publishing USA.
Pratchett, Terry. A Hat Full of Sky. (Tiffany Aching Ser.: 2). (YA). (gr. 8). 2015. (ENG.). 400p. pap. 9.99 *(978-0-06-243527-9(2))* 2004. 288p. 17.99 *(978-0-06-058660-7(5))* HarperCollins Pubs.
—A Hat Full of Sky. 2005. 407p. (gr. 7). 19.00 *(978-0-7569-5126-9(7))* Perfection Learning Corp.
—A Hat Full of Sky. 2005. (Discworld Ser.: 32). 407p. (YA). 19.65 *(978-1-4177-2658-5(X),* Turtleback) Turtleback Bks.
—I Shall Wear Midnight. (Tiffany Aching Ser.: 4). (YA). (gr. 8). 2015. (ENG.). 464p. pap. 9.99 *(978-0-06-243529-3(9))* 2011. 368p. pap. 9.99 *(978-0-06-143306-1(3))* 2010. 368p. 16.99 *(978-0-06-143304-7(7))* HarperCollins Pubs.
—The Wee Free Men. (Tiffany Aching Ser.: 1). (YA). (gr. 8). 2015. (ENG.). 352p. pap. 9.99 *(978-0-06-243526-2(4))* 2010. 576p. pap. 9.99 *(978-0-06-201217-3(7))* 2006. 400p. reprint ed. pap. 8.99 *(978-0-06-001238-0(2))* HarperCollins Pubs.
—The Wee Free Men. 2004. 19.00 *(978-0-7569-3252-7(1))* Perfection Learning Corp.
—The Wee Free Men. 2006. (Discworld Ser.: 28). (YA). 19.65 *(978-1-4176-2764-6(6),* Turtleback) Turtleback Bks.
—Wintersmith. (YA). 2015. (Tiffany Aching Ser.: 3). (ENG.). 416p. (gr. 8). pap. 9.99 *(978-0-06-243528-6(0))* 2007. (Tiffany Aching Ser.: 3). 464p. (gr. 8-12). per. 8.99 *(978-0-06-089033-9(9))* 2006. (Discworld Novels Ser.). 323p. (gr. 7-12). 16.99 *(978-0-06-089031-5(2),* HarperTeen) 2006. (Discworld Novels Ser.). 323p. (gr. 7-12). lib. bdg. 17.89 *(978-0-06-089032-2(0),* HarperTeen) HarperCollins Pubs.
—Wintersmith. 2007. 450p. (gr. 7). 19.00 *(978-0-7569-8091-7(7))* Perfection Learning Corp.
Preble, Joy. Dreaming Anastasia. 2009. (ENG.). 320p. (YA). (gr. 7-12). pap. 13.99 *(978-1-4022-1817-0(6),* Sourcebooks Jabberwocky) Sourcebooks, Inc.
—Haunted. 2011. (ENG.). 304p. (YA). (gr. 7-12). pap. 9.99 *(978-1-4022-4468-1(1))* Sourcebooks, Inc.
Preussler, Otfried. The Little Witch. Bell, Anthea, tr. from GER. Gebhardt-Gayler, Winnie, illus. 2015. (ENG.). 144p. (J). (gr. k-4). 15.95 *(978-1-59017-934-5(X),* NYR Children's Collection) New York Review of Bks., Inc., The.
The Princess & the Magic Locket. (My Tooth Is Loose!). (Illus.). 32p. (J). *(978-1-4054-1022-9(1))* Parragon, Inc.
Pullman, Philip. Lyra's Oxford. Lawrence, John, illus. 2007. (His Dark Materials Ser.). (ENG.). 64p. (J). (gr. 5-12). per. 6.99 *(978-0-375-84369-3(8),* Knopf Bks. for Young Readers) Random Hse. Children's Bks.
Pyykkonen, Carrie & Washington, Linda. Secrets of the Wee Free Men & Discworld: The Myths & Legends of Terry Pratchett's Multiverse. 2008. (ENG., Illus.). 288p. (YA). (gr. 8-13). pap. 21.99 *(978-0-312-37243-9(4),* 9780312372439, St. Martin's Griffin) St. Martin's Pr.
Randall, Thomas. The Waking: A Winter of Ghosts. 2011. (YA). pap. 9.99 *(978-1-59990-252-4(4),* Bloomsbury USA Childrens) Bloomsbury Publishing USA.
RavenWolf, Silver. Jóvenes y Brujas. 2004. (SPA.). 352p. pap. *(978-84-7720-753-5(4))* Ediciones Obelisco.
Rawson, C. Stories of Witches. 2004. (Young Reading Ser.: Vol. 1). 48p. (J). (gr. 2-18). pap. 5.95 *(978-0-7945-0647-6(X))* EDC Publishing.
Rees, Celia. Witch Child. unabr. ed. 2004. (Young Adult Cassette Librariestm Ser.). 304p. (J). (gr. 5-9). pap. 40.00 incl. audio *(978-0-8072-1198-4(2),* S YA 343 SP, Listening Library) Random Hse. Audio Publishing Group.
Reid, Isabelle. Serafina Moon. 2009. 48p. pap. *(978-1-84923-771-0(9))* YouWriteOn.
Riding, Will. Ebenezer's Tale. 2008. (Illus.). 188p. pap. 14.49 *(978-1-4343-9694-5(0))* AuthorHouse.
Riveros, Gabriela. El Encargo de Fernanda. Castillo, Jesus, illus. rev. ed. 2006. (Castillo de la Lectura Blanca Ser.). (SPA & ENG.). 64p. (J). (gr. k-2). pap. 6.95 *(978-970-20-0126-3(9))* Castillo, Ediciones, S. A. de C. V. MEX. Dist: Macmillan.
Roberts, Roxanne. Angel Wings, Faery Dust & Other Magical Things: A Story about Witches, Warlocks & Such. 2011. 24p. pap. 11.50 *(978-1-61204-072-1(1),* Eloquent Bks.) Strategic Book Publishing & Rights Agency (SBPRA).
Robertson, M. P. The Great Dragon Rescue. 2009. (ENG., Illus.). 32p. (J). (gr. -1-2). pap. 8.95 *(978-1-84507-379-4(7),* Frances Lincoln) Quarto Publishing Group UK GBR. Dist: Hachette Bk. Group.
Rockley, Frank. Tinderbox Cottage. 2010. 136p. pap. 10.99 *(978-1-4490-3120-6(X))* AuthorHouse.
Rogers, Bud & Martin, Gary. The Witch of Endor, 1 vol. Cariello, Sergio, illus. 2008. (Z Graphic Novels / Son of Samson Ser.). (ENG.). 160p. (J). pap. 6.99 *(978-0-310-71283-1(1))* Zonderkidz.
Rojo, Sara, illus. Baba Yaga: the Flying Witch. 2008. (Usborne First Reading: Level 4 Ser.). 48p. (J). 8.99 *(978-0-7945-2078-6(2),* Usborne) EDC Publishing.
Rose, Alice. Maria Dracula: A Fantasy Novel for Children. 2007. (Illus.). 191p. pap. 13.50 *(978-0-615-15099-4(3))* DUENDE Bks.
Rowling, J. K. The Tales of Beedle the Bard. GrandPré, Mary, illus. 2008. (ENG.). 128p. *(978-0-7475-9987-6(4))* Bloomsbury Publishing Plc.
—The Tales of Beedle the Bard. GrandPré, Mary, illus. collector's ed. 2008. 184p. *(978-0-9560109-0-2(3))* Children's High Level Group.
—The Tales of Beedle the Bard. 2017. (Harry Potter Ser.). (ENG.). 128p. (J). (gr. 3-3). 12.99 *(978-1-338-12568-9(0),* Levine, Arthur A. Bks.) Scholastic, Inc.
—The Tales of Beedle the Bard. 2017. (ENG.). (J). (gr. 3). lib. bdg. 24.50 ***(978-0-606-39695-0(0))*** Turtleback Bks.
Roy, Lauren M. The Fire Children. 2015. (ENG.). 272p. (YA). (gr. 8-13). mass mkt. 9.99 *(978-1-78108-353-6(3),* Ravenstone) Rebellion GBR. Dist: Simon & Schuster, Inc.
Sage, Angie. Todhunter Moon: Starchaser. Zug, Mark, illus. 2016. (World of Septimus Heap Ser.: 3). 496p. (J). (gr. 3-7). 17.99 *(978-0-06-227251-5(9),* Tegen, Katherine Bks) HarperCollins Pubs.
Samwell, Cynthia A. Witches Anonymous. 2006. (Illus.). 84p. pap. *(978-1-84401-660-0(9))* Athena Pr.
Sandoval, John. The Witches of Ruidoso. 2013. (ENG.). 120p. (YA). pap. 12.95 *(978-1-55885-766-7(4),* Piñata Books) Arte Publico Pr.
Santoro, Scott. Which Way to Witch School? Santoro, Scott, illus. (ENG., Illus.). 32p. (J). (gr. -1-2). 2012. pap. 5.99 *(978-0-06-078183-5(1))* 2010. 16.99 *(978-0-06-078181-1(5))* HarperCollins Pubs.
Saunders, Kate. The Curse of the Chocolate Phoenix: A Companion to the Whizz Pop Chocolate Shop. 2015. (ENG.). 272p. (J). (gr. 5). 19.99 *(978-0-375-99183-7(2),* Delacorte Bks. for Young Readers) Random Hse. Children's Bks.
Scary Stories Treasury Lenticular Cover. 2007. 80p. *(978-1-4054-9871-5(4))* Parragon, Inc.
Schaefer, Peggy. A Haunted Halloween Activity Book. Arif, Tasneem & Reed, Lisa, illus. 2014. 16p. (J). 4.99 *(978-0-8249-5666-0(4),* Ideal Pubns.) Worthy Publishing.
Scharf, J. L. Grace & the Ice Prince: The Diamond Heart Quest. 2006. (ENG.). 262p. (J). per. 16.95 *(978-1-897235-09-6(7))* Thistledown Pr., Ltd. CAN. Dist: Univ. of Toronto Pr.
Schliewen, Richard. Paulina's Teddy Bear Journey. Visaya, Artemio, illus. 2012. 104p. 24.95 *(978-1-62709-055-1(X))* America Star Bks.
Schlitz, Laura Amy. Splendors & Glooms. (ENG.). 400p. (J). 2014. (gr. 5-9). pap. 8.99 *(978-0-7636-6926-3(1))* 2012. (Illus.). (gr. 4-7). 17.99 *(978-0-7636-5380-4(2))* Candlewick Pr.
—Splendors & Glooms. 2014. (ENG.). (J). (gr. 4-7). lib. bdg. 18.60 ***(978-1-62765-443-2(7))*** Perfection Learning Corp.
—Splendors & Glooms. 2014. lib. bdg. 18.40 *(978-0-606-35170-6(1))* Turtleback Bks.
Schwartz, Alvin. More Scary Stories to Tell in the Dark. Helquist, Brett, illus. 2010. (Scary Stories Ser.). (ENG.). 128p. (J). (gr. 4-18). 16.99 *(978-0-06-083521-7(4))*; pap. 5.99 *(978-0-06-083522-4(2))* HarperCollins Pubs.
—Scary Stories Box Set, 3 vols. Helquist, Brett, illus. 2011. (Scary Stories Ser.). (ENG.). 128p. (J). (gr. 4). pap. 14.99 *(978-0-06-198093-0(5))* HarperCollins Pubs.
Seduction. 2014. (Legacy Ser.). (ENG., Illus.). 416p. (YA). (gr. 9). 17.99 *(978-1-4814-0023-7(1),* Simon & Schuster/Paula Wiseman Bks.) Simon & Schuster/Paula Wiseman Bks.
Seever, Berni. A Supernatural Tale. 2007. 62p. pap. 20.00 *(978-1-4196-7788-5(8))* CreateSpace Independent Publishing Platform.
Selfors, Suzanne. Kiss & Spell. 2015. (Ever after High Ser.: Bk. 2). (ENG., Illus.). 224p. (J). (gr. 3-7). 13.99 *(978-0-316-40131-9(5))* Little, Brown Bks. for Young Readers.
Serafin, Jordan. Bella: The Crooked Hat Witch. Rubino, Alisa A., illus. 2004. (J). *(978-0-932991-57-7(2))* Place In The Woods, The.
Serrano, Tomas. Salfon el Limpiador de Tejados. (SPA.). 48p. (J). (gr. 1-3). pap. *(978-84-264-3746-4(X))* Editorial Lumen ESP. Dist: Lectorum Pubns., Inc.
Shannon, George. A Very Witchy Spelling Bee. Fearing, Mark, illus. 2013. (ENG.). 32p. (J). (gr. -1-3). 16.99 *(978-0-15-206696-3(9))* Houghton Mifflin Harcourt Publishing Co.
Sharratt, Nick. What's in the Witch's Kitchen? Sharratt, Nick, illus. 2011. (ENG., Illus.). 20p. (J). (gr. -1-2). 12.99 *(978-0-7636-5224-1(5))* Candlewick Pr.
Shepherd, Audrey. Morgana the Recession Witch. 2010. (ENG., Illus.). 48p. pap. *(978-1-84748-783-4(1))* Athena Pr.
Shields, Gillian. Eternal. (Immortal Ser.: 3). (ENG.). (YA). (gr. 8). 2012. 384p. pap. 9.99 *(978-0-06-200040-8(3))* 2011. 368p. 16.99 *(978-0-06-200039-2(X))* HarperCollins Pubs. (Tegen, Katherine Bks).
—Immortal. 2010. (Immortal Ser.: 1). (ENG.). 384p. (YA). (gr. 8). pap. 8.99 *(978-0-06-137583-5(7),* Tegen, Katherine Bks) HarperCollins Pubs.
Shults, Sylvia. Double Double Love & Trouble. 2013. 150p. pap. 12.99 *(978-0-9848931-3-3(X))* Dark Continents Publishing.
Shurtliff, Liesl. Red: the True Story of Red Riding Hood. (ENG.). 256p. (J). (gr. 3-7). 2017. 7.99 *(978-0-385-75586-3(4),* Yearling) 2016. 16.99 *(978-0-385-75583-2(X),* Knopf Bks. for Young Readers) Random Hse. Children's Bks.
Simmons, H. Two Tales from Our Corner Lot. 2004. 68p. pap. 19.95 *(978-1-4137-5251-9(9))* America Star Bks.
Simpson, C. E. & Smith, C. E. Eighth Grade Witch. Utomo, Gabhor, illus. 2014. (ENG.). 144p. (J). mass mkt. 6.99 *(978-1-937133-45-0(1))* Chooseco LLC.
Skye, Evelyn. The Crown's Fate. (Crown's Game Ser.: 2). (ENG.). 432p. (YA). (gr. 8). 2018. pap. 9.99 ***(978-0-06-242262-0(6),*** Balzer & Bray) 2017. 17.99 *(978-0-06-242261-3(8))* HarperCollins Pubs.
Skye Toggles. Bella the Witch & Her Worries. 2010. 36p. pap. 16.99 *(978-1-4490-6803-5(0))* AuthorHouse.
Sleigh, Barbara. Carbonel & Calidor: Being the Further Adventures of a Royal Cat. Front, Charles, illus. 2009. (ENG.). 224p. (J). (gr. 4-7). 17.95 *(978-1-59017-333-6(3),* NYR Children's Collection) New York Review of Bks., Inc., The.
Sloat, Teri. Zip! Zoom! on a Broom. Bonnet, Rosalinde, illus. 2017. (ENG.). 40p. (J). (gr. -1-3). 16.99 ***(978-0-316-25673-5(0))*** Little Brown & Co.
Smith, Ann Pierce. Esmereida Hedgepath's First Date. 2010. 16p. 12.50 *(978-1-4520-3493-5(1))* AuthorHouse.
Smith, Audrey. The Halloween Misfits. 2004. 23p. (J). pap. 9.95 incl. audio compact disk *(978-0-9722673-4-2(4))* Audrey Productions.
Smith, Cleveland W. Billabongo. 2008. 172p. pap. *(978-1-84923-100-8(1))* YouWriteOn.
Smith, L. J. Dark Angel - The Chosen - Soulmate, 3 vols. 2008. (Night World Ser.: 2). (ENG.). 688p. (YA). (gr. 9). pap. 9.99 *(978-1-4169-7451-2(2),* Simon Pulse) Simon Pulse.
—The Divide, Vol. 4. 2013. (Secret Circle Ser.: 4). (ENG.). 320p. (YA). (gr. 8). pap. 10.99 *(978-0-06-213041-9(2),* HarperTeen) HarperCollins Pubs.
—The Hunt. 2013. (Secret Circle Ser.: 5). (ENG.). 288p. (YA). (gr. 8). pap. 9.99 *(978-0-06-213043-3(9),* HarperTeen) HarperCollins Pubs.
—Huntress, Black Dawn, Witchlight, 3 vols. 2009. (Night World Ser.: 3). (ENG., Illus.). 752p. (YA). (gr. 9). pap. 9.99 *(978-1-4169-7452-9(0),* Simon Pulse) Simon Pulse.
—The Initiation & the Captive, Pt. 1. 2012. (Secret Circle Ser.: Vols. 1 - 2). (ENG.). 416p. (YA). (gr. 8). pap. 10.99 *(978-0-06-167085-5(5),* HarperTeen) HarperCollins Pubs.
—Night World: Secret Vampire; Daughters of Darkness; Spellbinder. 2008. (Night World Ser.: 1). (ENG.). 752p. (YA). (gr. 9). pap. 9.99 *(978-1-4169-7450-5(4),* Simon Pulse) Simon Pulse.
—The Temptation. (Secret Circle Ser.: 6). (ENG.). (YA). (gr. 8). 2014. 304p. pap. 9.99 *(978-0-06-213045-7(5))* Vol. 6. 2013. 288p. 17.99 *(978-0-06-213047-1(1))* HarperCollins Pubs. (HarperTeen).
Smith, L. J. & Williamson, Kevin. The Compelled. 2012. (Vampire Diaries: Stefan's Diaries: 6). (ENG.). 256p. (YA). (gr. 9). pap. 10.99 *(978-0-06-211398-6(4),* HarperTeen) HarperCollins Pubs.
Snowe, Olivia. Dandelion & the Witch, 1 vol. Lamoreaux, Michelle, illus. 2014. (Twicetold Tales Ser.). (ENG.). 128p. (gr. 3-4). 25.32 *(978-1-4342-9147-9(2))* Stone Arch Bks.
—The Girl & the Seven Thieves, 1 vol. Lamoreaux, Michelle, illus. (Twicetold Tales Ser.). (ENG.). 128p. (gr. 3-4). 2014. pap. 5.95 *(978-1-4342-9555-2(9))* 2013. 8.95 *(978-1-4342-6280-6(4))* 2013. lib. bdg. 25.32 *(978-1-4342-6018-5(6))* Stone Arch Bks.
—Hansen & Gracie, 1 vol. Lamoreaux, Michelle, illus. 2014. (Twicetold Tales Ser.). (ENG.). 128p. (gr. 3-4). pap. 5.95 *(978-1-4342-9150-9(2))* Stone Arch Bks.
Sobat, Gail Sidonie. A Winter's Tale. 2004. (Ingamald Ser.: 2). (ENG.). 176p. pap. 16.95 *(978-1-894283-45-8(7))* Great Plains Pubns. CAN. Dist: Publishers Group Canada.
Sobel, Gerrie. Jacob & His Magical Flying Bears, a Halloween Story. Torres, Dottie, illus. 2009. 32p. pap. 12.95 *(978-1-936051-42-7(7))* Peppertree Pr., The.
Soper, Stuart A. The P. U'Trid & S. Pooky Pickles Company. 2013. 400p. (J). pap. 21.50 *(978-1-61204-724-9(6),* Strategic Bk. Publishing) Strategic Book Publishing & Rights Agency (SBPRA).
Sorenson, Jack R. Eibhlin & Her Dragon, 1 vol. 2009. 131p. pap. 24.95 *(978-1-60749-634-2(8))* America Star Bks.
Spotswood, Jessica. Born Wicked. 2013. (Cahill Witch Chronicles Ser.: 1). (ENG.). 352p. (YA). (gr. 7). pap. 10.99 *(978-0-14-242187-1(1),* Speak) Penguin Young Readers Group.
—Born Wicked. 2013. lib. bdg. 22.10 *(978-0-606-26729-8(8),* Turtleback) Turtleback Bks.
Spurr, Elizabeth. Halloween Sky Ride. Long, Ethan, illus. 2005. (ENG.). 32p. (J). (gr. -1-3). 16.95 *(978-0-8234-1870-1(7))* Holiday Hse., Inc.
Stadelmann, Amy Marie. The Not-So Itty-Bitty Spiders. 2015. (Olive & Beatrix Ser.: 1). (ENG., Illus.). 80p. (J). (gr. k-2). pap. 4.99 *(978-0-545-81480-5(4))* Scholastic, Inc.
—The Super-Smelly Moldy Blob. Stadelmann, Amy Marie, illus. 2016. (Olive & Beatrix Ser.: 2). (ENG., Illus.). 80p. (J). (gr. k-2). 15.99 *(978-0-545-81485-0(5))* Scholastic, Inc.
Stanley, Pauline. The Children & the Witches Magic. 2010. (Illus.). 48p. pap. 10.49 *(978-1-4490-9544-4(5))* AuthorHouse.
Steig, William. Wizzil. Blake, Quentin, illus. 2014. 32p. pap. 8.00 *(978-1-61003-221-6(7))* Center for the Collaborative Classroom.
—Wizzil. 2015. (J). lib. bdg. 18.40 *(978-0-606-36445-4(5))* Turtleback Bks.
Stephens, Helen. Witchety Sticks & the Magic Buttons. Stephens, Helen, illus. 2010. (ENG., Illus.). 32p. (J). (gr. -1-k). pap. 8.99 *(978-1-4169-1107-4(3),* Simon & Schuster Children's) Simon & Schuster, Ltd. GBR. Dist: Simon & Schuster, Inc.
Stewart, Mary. The Little Broomstick. pap. *(978-0-440-44897-6(2))* Random Hse. Children's Bks.
Stilton, Geronimo. The Search for Treasure. 2014. (ENG.). 320p. (J). (gr. 2-5). 14.99 *(978-0-545-65604-7(4),* Scholastic Paperbacks) Scholastic, Inc.
Stone Arch Books (Firm: Afton, Minn.) Staff. Hansel & Gretel: The Graphic Novel, 1 vol. Dietrich, Sean, illus. 2008. (Graphic Spin Ser.). (ENG.). 40p. (gr. 1-3). pap. 5.95 *(978-1-4342-0863-7(X),* Graphic Revolve) Stone Arch Bks.
Storm, Falcon. Natalie the Not-So-Nasty: Tales from upon A Time Series. 2013. (ENG.). 82p. pap. 9.95 *(978-1-62253-072-4(1))* Evolved Publishing.
Strega Nona. 2005. (J). *(978-1-59564-834-1(8))* Steps To Literacy, LLC.
Stuart, Lisa Marie. The Little Cat, the Wonderful Witch, & the Clever Mouse. Potter, Lori, illus. 2008. 60p. pap. 21.95 *(978-1-59858-691-6(2))* Dog Ear Publishing, LLC.
Sundstrom, Dainel H. The Return of Oz. 2007. pap. 10.00 *(978-0-8059-8944-1(7))* Dorrance Publishing Co., Inc.
Symes, Ruth. Bella Donna: Too Many Spells. Lindsay, Marion, illus. 2016. (ENG.). 192p. (J). (gr. 1-5). pap. 7.99 *(978-1-63450-155-2(1),* Sky Pony Pr.) Skyhorse Publishing Co., Inc.
Tagg, Christine. Who Will You Meet on Scary Street? Nine Pop-up Nightmares! Fuge, Charles, illus. 2004. 20p. (J). reprint ed. 15.00 *(978-0-7567-8003-6(9))* DIANE Publishing Co.
Tatcheva, Eva. Witch Zelda's Birthday Cake: A Wild & Wicked Pop-up, Pull-the-Tab Book. Tatcheva, Eva, illus. 2004. (Illus.). 12p. (J). (gr. k-3). reprint ed. 18.00 *(978-0-7567-7225-3(7))* DIANE Publishing Co.
Tate, N. F. The Witch of Hambone: Books 1 And 2. 2009. (Illus.). 120p. pap. 33.49 *(978-1-4490-0621-1(3))* AuthorHouse.
Tenney, Shawna J. C., illus. Brunhilda's Backwards Day. 2016. (ENG.). 32p. (J). (gr. -1-k). 16.99 *(978-1-63450-691-5(X),* Sky Pony Pr.) Skyhorse Publishing Co., Inc.
Thame, Val. Witches in Secret. l.t. ed. 2007. 100p. per. *(978-1-905665-26-6(1))* Pollinger In Print.
Thomas, Valerie. Winnie's Big Bad Robot. Paul, Korky, illus. 2015. (ENG.). 32p. ***(978-0-19-273874-5(7))*** Oxford Univ. Pr.
Thompson, Colin. The Floods #2: School Plot. Scrambly, Crab, illus. 2008. (Floods Ser.). (J). (ENG.). 224p. 15.99 *(978-0-06-113861-4(4))*; 256p. lib. bdg. 16.89 *(978-0-06-113855-3(X))* HarperCollins Pubs.
—The Floods Family Files. Thompson, Colin, illus. 2012. (Floods Ser.: 1). (ENG., Illus.). 32p. (J). (gr. 4-7). pap. 12.99 *(978-1-86471-942-0(7))* Random Hse. Australia AUS. Dist: Independent Pubs. Group.
—Good Neighbors. Scrambly, Crab, illus. 2008. (Floods Ser.: No. 1). 214p. (J). (gr. 3-7). 15.99 *(978-0-06-113196-7(2))* HarperCollins Pubs.
Thompson, Jill. Magic Trixie. Thompson, Jill, illus. 2008. (ENG., Illus.). 96p. (J). (gr. 3-7). pap. 8.99 *(978-0-06-117045-4(3))* HarperCollins Pubs.
—Magic Trixie & the Dragon. Thompson, Jill, illus. 2009. (ENG., Illus.). 96p. (J). (gr. 3-7). pap. 7.99 *(978-0-06-117050-8(X))* HarperCollins Pubs.
Tiernan, Cate. Awakening. 2007. (Sweep Ser.: 5). (ENG.). 192p. (YA). (gr. 7-18). pap. 7.99 *(978-0-14-241020-2(9),* Speak) Penguin Young Readers Group.
—Sweep Vol. 3: The Calling - Changeling - Strife, 3 vols. 2011. (Sweep Ser.: 3). (ENG.). 576p. (YA). (gr. 7-18). 9.99 *(978-0-14-241955-7(9),* Speak) Penguin Young Readers Group.
Tiger Tales Staff & Mantle, Ben. Five Little Pumpkins. Tiger Tales Staff, ed. 2010. (ENG., Illus.). 24p. (J). (gr. -1-k). bds. 8.95 *(978-1-58925-856-3(8))* Tiger Tales.
Tomos, Angharad. Ceridwen. 2005. (WEL., Illus.). 48p. pap. 1.95 *(978-0-86243-066-5(6))* Y Lolfa GBR. Dist: Dufour Editions, Inc.
—Cosyn. 2005. (WEL., Illus.). 24p. pap. *(978-0-86243-566-0(8))* Y Lolfa.
—Rala Rwdins. Tomos, Angharad, illus. 2005. (WEL., Illus.). 48p. pap. 1.95 *(978-0-86243-065-8(8))* Y Lolfa GBR. Dist: Dufour Editions, Inc.
Town, Vicky. The Runaway Pumpkin Pie Man, 1 vol. Baird, Roberta, illus. 2015. (ENG.). 32p. (J). (gr. k-3). 16.99 *(978-1-4556-2025-8(4))* Pelican Publishing Co., Inc.
Tozier, Christopher. Olivia Brophie & the Pearl of Tagelus. 2012. (ENG.). 208p. (J). pap. 12.95 *(978-1-56164-519-0(2))* Pineapple Pr., Inc.
Trent, Tiffany. The Unnaturalists. (ENG., (YA). (gr. 7). 2013. Illus.). 336p. pap. 9.99 *(978-1-4424-2207-0(6))* 2012. 320p. 16.99 *(978-1-4424-2206-3(8))* Simon & Schuster Bks. For Young Readers. (Simon & Schuster Bks. For Young Readers).
Trotter, Bob. The Curious Tale of Marmalade Tuttle. 2008. 116p. pap. 12.95 *(978-1-60693-014-4(1),* Eloquent Bks.) Strategic Book Publishing & Rights Agency (SBPRA).
Troulis, Jennifer. Penelope & Priscilla & the City of the Banished. 2007. (J). per. 14.95 *(978-0-9768602-1-1(X))* Twin Monkeys Pr.
Tyrrell, Melissa. Hansel & Gretel. McMullen, Nigel, illus. 2005. (Fairytale Friends Ser.). 12p. (J). bds. 5.95 *(978-1-58117-152-5(8),* Intervisual/Piggy Toes) Bendon, Inc.

W X Y Z

Umansky, Kaye. Clover Twig & the Perilous Path. Wright, Johanna, illus. 2013. (ENG.). 272p. (J). (gr. 3-7). pap. 7.99 *(978-1-250-02727-6(6)*, 9781250027276) Square Fish.
—Pongwiffy. Smedley, Chris, illus. 2007. (ENG.). 192p. (J). (gr. 3-7). pap. 10.95 *(978-1-4169-6832-0(6)*, Simon & Schuster/Paula Wiseman Bks.) Simon & Schuster/Paula Wiseman Bks.
Valentino, Serena. Poor Unfortunate Soul: A Tale of the Sea Witch. Disney Storybook Art Team, illus. 2016. (Villains Ser.: 3). (ENG.). 208p. (J). (gr. 5-9). 17.99 *(978-1-4847-2405-7(4))* Disney Pr.
Van Eekhout, Greg. Kid vs. Squid. 2010. (ENG.). 208p. (YA). (gr. 3-6). 16.99 *(978-1-59990-489-4(6)*, 9781599904894, Bloomsbury USA Childrens) Bloomsbury Publishing USA.
Van Nostrand, Michele. The Little Witch. 2013. 24p. pap. 13.00 *(978-1-4525-8329-7(3)*, Balboa Pr.) Author Solutions, Inc.
Vance, Alexander. Behind the Canvas. 2016. (ENG.). 336p. (J). 16.99 *(978-1-250-02970-6(8)*, 9781250029706) Feiwel & Friends.
Vande Velde, Vivian. Three Good Deeds. 2007. (ENG., Illus.). 160p. (J). (gr. 5-7). pap. 7.99 *(978-0-15-205455-7(3))* Houghton Mifflin Harcourt Publishing Co.
—Witch Dreams, 0 vols. 2008. (ENG.). 128p. (YA). (gr. 5-9). pap. 7.99 *(978-0-7614-5460-1(8)*, 9780761454601, Amazon Children's Publishing) Amazon Publishing.
Vandepeer, Helen. Gifts. 2008. 76p. pap. 35.80 *(978-0-557-03191-7(5))* Lulu Pr., Inc.
Vant, Jeanie. The Witch's Cat. Vant, Tim, illus. 2010. 24p. pap. 11.50 *(978-1-60976-051-9(4)*, Eloquent Bks.) Strategic Book Publishing & Rights Agency (SBPRA).
Vernon, Ursula. Castle Hangnail. (ENG., Illus.). 384p. (J). (gr. 3-7). 2016. 8.99 *(978-0-14-751273-4(5)*, Puffin Books) 2015. 16.99 *(978-0-8037-4129-4(4)*, Dial Bks) Penguin Young Readers Group.
Viz Media. Fairy Dreams. 2013. (Winx Club Ser.: 5). lib. bdg. 17.20 *(978-0-606-26987-2(8)*, Turtleback) Turtleback Bks.
VIZ Media Staff & Staffi, Iginio. WINX Club, Vol. 5. 2013. (ENG.). 96p. (J). pap. 6.99 *(978-1-4215-4163-1(7))* Viz Media.
Wadsworth, Peter. The Wicked Witch of the Woods. 2012. (Illus.). 28p. pap. 8.49 *(978-1-78035-481-1(9)*, Fastprint Publishing) Upfront Publishing Ltd. GBR. Dist: Printondemand-worldwide.com.
Walker, Chris, creator. Collision Course Goad by Zombienose. 2005. (Illus.). 60p. (YA). 13.95 *(978-0-9768670-0-5(1))* Icecat Bks.
Walker, Sally M. Druscilla's Halloween. White, Lee, illus. 2009. (Carolrhoda Picture Bks.). (ENG.). 32p. (J). (gr. k-3). 16.95 *(978-0-8225-8941-9(9))* Lerner Publishing Group.
Wallace Ii, James C. & Wallace, Amanda D. The Emerald Slippers of Oz. 2013. 156p. pap. 14.99 *(978-0-578-12511-4(0))* Scientia Est Vox Pr.
Wallace, Jessica. The Present 6 Packs. KinderConcepts. Gardner, Marjory, illus. (Kinderstarters Ser.). 8p. (gr. -1-1). 21.00 *(978-0-7635-8720-8(6))* Rigby Education.
Watson, Sally. Witch of the Glens. 2004. (YA). pap. 12.95 *(978-1-59511-001-5(1)*, 800-691-7779) Image Cascade Publishing.
Wax, Wendy. City Witch, Country Switch, 0 vols. Gibala-Broxholm, Scott, illus. 2013. (ENG.). 42p. (J). (gr. -1-3). pap. 9.99 *(978-1-4778-1676-9(3)*, 9781477816769, Amazon Children's Publishing) Amazon Publishing.
Webb, Holly. Rose. 2013. (Rose Ser.: 1). (ENG.). 240p. (J). (gr. 3-6). pap. 6.99 *(978-1-4022-8581-3(7)*, 9781402285813, Sourcebooks Jabberwocky) Sourcebooks, Inc.
Weston Woods Staff, creator. Hansel & Gretel. 2011. 38.75 *(978-0-439-80425-7(6))* Weston Woods Studios, Inc.
Wetherby, Mark. The Tales of Mossy Dell. 2009. (Illus.). 88p. pap. 10.49 *(978-1-4389-7726-3(3))* AuthorHouse.
Weyn, Suzanne. The Invisible World. 2012. (ENG.). 240p. (J). (gr. 9-9). 17.99 *(978-0-545-33486-0(1)*, Scholastic Pr.) Scholastic, Inc.
Whalen, Erin T. Charlie Gets Spooked, 3 vols. 2004. (Illus.). 32p. (J). (gr. k-3). 16.95 *(978-1-929265-04-6(2))*; pap. 8.95 *(978-1-929265-05-3(0))* Lily & Co. Publishing.
White, J. A. The Thickety: a Path Begins. Offermann, Andrea, illus. 2017. (Thickety Ser.: 4). 512p. (J). (gr. 5). 16.99 *(978-0-06-238139-2(3)*, Tegen, Katherine Bks) HarperCollins Pubs.
—Well of Witches. Offermann, Andrea, illus. 2017. (Thickety Ser.: 3). 528p. (J). (gr. 5). pap. 7.99 *(978-0-06-225731-4(5)*, Tegen, Katherine Bks) HarperCollins Pubs.
Wilde, Terry Lee. The Vampire... in My Dreams. 2008. (ENG.). 244p. (YA). (gr. 7-12). pap. 13.00 *(978-1-59998-837-5(2))* Samhain Publishing, LTD.
Williams, Guana Dunbar. The Wacky Winter Witch. William, Iceberg Dunbar, illus. 2003. (J). per. *(978-0-9740673-1-5(8))* Graphix Network.
Williams, John Joseph. The Frightened Garden. 2013. 98p. (J). pap. *(978-1-78299-167-0(0))* FeedARead.com.
Wilson, N. D. The Door Before (100 Cupboards Prequel) 2017. (ENG.). 240p. (J). (gr. 3-7). lib. bdg. 19.99 *(978-0-449-81678-3(8)*, Random Hse. Bks. for Young Readers) Random Hse. Children's Bks.
Wilson, W. Shane. Little Monsters. 2009. 99p. pap. 11.96 *(978-0-557-20687-2(1))* Lulu Pr., Inc.
Winters, Ben H. Literally Disturbed No. 1: Tales to Keep You up at Night. Watkins, Adam F., illus. 2013. (ENG.). 64p. (J). (gr. 3-7). 9.99 *(978-0-8431-7194-5(4)*, Price Stern Sloan) Penguin Young Readers Group.
Wrede, Patricia C. Searching for Dragons. unabr. ed. 2004. (Enchanted Forest Chronicles: Bk. 2). 242p. (J). (gr. 5-18). pap. 38.00 incl. audio *(978-0-8072-0670-6(9)*, Listening Library) Random Hse. Audio Publishing Group.
Yolen, Jane. Baba Yaga. Date not set. 32p. (J). (gr. -1-1). pap. 5.99 *(978-0-06-443599-4(7))* HarperCollins Pubs.
—The Flying Witch. Vagin, Vladimir, illus. 2003. 40p. (J). (gr. -1-1). 15.99 *(978-0-06-028536-4(2))* HarperCollins Pubs.
Yolen, Jane & Stemple, Heidi E. Y. The Salem Witch Trials: An Unsolved Mystery from History. Roth, Roger, Sr., illus. 2004. (Unsolved Mystery from History Ser.). (ENG.). 32p. (J). (gr. 1-5). 17.99 *(978-0-689-84620-5(7)*, Simon & Schuster Bks. For Young Readers) Simon & Schuster Bks. For Young Readers.
Yorinks, Arthur. The Witch's Child. Smith, Jos. A., illus. 2007. (ENG.). 34p. (J). (gr. 1-4). 17.95 *(978-0-8109-9349-5(X)*, Abrams Bks. for Young Readers) Abrams, Inc.
Zera, Beata. Little Puppy Swifty & Elle. 2008. 64p. pap. 21.99 *(978-1-4257-6703-7(6))* Xlibris Corp.
Ziefert, Harriet. Two Little Witches: A Halloween Counting Story. Taback, Simms, illus. 2007. (ENG.). 32p. (J). (gr. k-k). pap. 3.99 *(978-0-7636-3309-7(7))* Candlewick Pr.
Ziegler, Argentina Palacios, tr. Dora y la Princesa de la Nieve (Dora Saves the Snow Princess) Aikins, Dave, illus. 2008. (Dora la Exploradora Ser.). (SPA.). 24p. (J). (gr. -1-2). pap. 3.99 *(978-1-4169-5870-3(3)*, Libros Para Ninos) Libros Para Ninos.

WIZARDS

Beahm, George. The Whimsic Alley Book of Spells: Mythical Incantations for Wizards of All Ages. Goldin, Stan, ed. 2007. (ENG., Illus.). 192p. (YA). pap. 14.95 *(978-1-57174-535-4(1))* Hampton Roads Publishing Co., Inc.
Beaumont, Steve. How to Draw Witches & Wizards. (Drawing Fantasy Art Ser.). 32p. (gr. 4-5). 2009. 50.50 *(978-1-61512-195-3(1)*, PowerKids Pr.) 2007. (Illus.). (J). lib. bdg. 26.50 *(978-1-4042-3857-2(3))* Rosen Publishing Group, Inc., The.
—How to Draw Wizards, Warriors, Orcs & Elves. 2007. (Illus.). 143p. pap. 7.99 *(978-0-7858-2345-2(X)*, Chartwell) Book Sales, Inc.
Doherty, Gillian. 1001 Wizard Things to Spot. Gower, Teri, illus. 2008. (Usborne 1001 Things to Spot Ser.). 31p. (J). (gr. 4-7). 9.99 *(978-0-7945-1860-8(5)*, Usborne) EDC Publishing.
Dooling, Sandra. Sorcerers, Spells, & Magic!, 1 vol., 1. 2014. (Jr. Graphic Monster Stories Ser.). (ENG.). 24p. (J). (gr. 3-6). 26.25 *(978-1-4777-6211-0(6)*, PowerKids Pr.) Rosen Publishing Group, Inc., The.
Hamilton, John. Wizards & Witches, 1 vol. 2004. (Fantasy & Folklore Ser.). (ENG., Illus.). 32p. (gr. 4-8). 27.07 *(978-1-59197-716-2(9)*, Abdo & Daughters) ABDO Publishing Co.
Jones, Jen. The Girls' Guide to Wizards: Everything Magical about These Spellbinders. 2010. (Girls' Guides to Everything Unexplained Ser.). (ENG.). 32p. (gr. 3-4). lib. bdg. 27.99 *(978-1-4296-5454-8(6)*, Snap Bks.) Capstone Press of Coughlan Cos.
Kerns, Ann. Wizards & Witches. 2009. (Fantasy Chronicles Ser.). (ENG., Illus.). 48p. (gr. 4-7). lib. bdg. 27.93 *(978-0-8225-9983-8(X))* Lerner Publishing Group.
Lee, Puck Hee. The Wizard Monk of Kamayut & Six Other True Stories. 2005. 48p. per. 10.00 *(978-1-4134-8216-4(3))* Xlibris Corp.
Lehotsky, Chris. Wizards. 2016. (Creatures of Fantasy Ser.). (Illus.). 64p. (J). (gr. 6-6). 34.21 *(978-1-5026-1856-6(7))* Cavendish Square Publishing.
McIntee, David A. & McIntee, Lesley. Wizards. 2015. (Heroes & Legends Ser.). (ENG., Illus.). 80p. (J). (gr. 7-8). 35.60 *(978-1-4994-6176-3(3)*, Rosen Young Adult) Rosen Publishing Group, Inc., The.
Merlin, Master. Wizardology: A Guide to Wizards of the World. Steer, Dugald A., ed. 2007. (Ologies Ser.). (ENG., Illus.). 40p. (J). (gr. 3-7). 14.99 *(978-0-7636-3710-1(6))* Candlewick Pr.
Narayan, Natasha. Witches, Wizards & Warlocks of London. 2004. (Of London Ser.). (ENG., Illus.). 96p. (J). pap. 8.99 *(978-1-904153-12-2(7))* Watling St., Ltd. GBR. Dist: Independent Pubs. Group.
Savage, Candace & Savage, C. Wizards: An Amazing Journey Through the Last Great Age of Magic. 2003. (ENG., Illus.). 80p. (J). (gr. 4-7). 17.95 *(978-1-55054-943-0(X))* Greystone Books Ltd. CAN. Dist: Publishers Group West (PGW).
Wizard Sticker Book. (Creepy Sticker Ser.). (Illus.). 16p. (J). *(978-1-84273-118-5(1)*, Exclusive Editions) Parragon, Inc.

WIZARDS—FICTION

Alton, Steve. The Firehills. 2005. (ENG.). 192p. (YA). (gr. 5-12). 15.95 *(978-1-57505-798-9(0)*, Carolrhoda Bks.) Lerner Publishing Group.
—The Malifex. 2003. (Middle Readers Ser.). (Illus.). 182p. (J). (gr. 3-7). 14.95 *(978-0-8225-0959-2(8))* Lerner Publishing Group.
Ambrosio, Stefano. Mouse Magic. Pastrovicchio, Lorenzo, illus. 2010. (ENG.). 112p. (J). 24.99 *(978-1-60886-550-5(9))*; Vol. 1. pap. 9.99 *(978-1-60886-541-3(X))* Boom! Studios.
—Wizards of Mickey - Grand Tournament, Vol. 2. Pastrovicchio, Lorenzo & Magic Eye Studios, illus. 2010. (Wizards of Mickey Ser.). (ENG.). 128p. (J). (gr. 3-6). pap. 9.99 *(978-1-60886-564-2(9))* Boom! Studios.
Anderson, Scoular. Bubble Trouble. Anderson, Scoular, illus. 2010. (Wizzbang Wizard Ser.: 2). (ENG., Illus.). 96p. (J). (gr. 2-4). pap. 5.99 *(978-0-00-719006-5(9))* HarperCollins Pubs. Ltd. GBR. Dist: HarperCollins Pubs.
—Dragon Danger / Grasshopper Glue. Anderson, Scoular, illus. 2011. (Wizzbang Wizard Ser.). (ENG., Illus.). 192p. (J). (gr. 2-4). pap. 7.99 *(978-0-00-719007-2(7))* HarperCollins Pubs. Ltd. GBR. Dist: HarperCollins Pubs.
—Super Slosh. Anderson, Scoular, illus. 2011. (Wizzbang Wizard Ser.: 1). (ENG., Illus.). 96p. (J). (gr. 2-4). pap. 5.99 *(978-0-00-719005-8(0))* HarperCollins Pubs. Ltd. GBR. Dist: HarperCollins Pubs.
Anfuso, Dennis & Lindsay, Alan. Oz House. 2012. (ENG.). 321p. pap. 19.95 *(978-1-57433-041-0(1))* Interset Pr.
Appleton, Victor. Tom Swift Omnibus #5: Tom Swift in Captivity, Tom Swift & His Wizard Camera, Tom Swift & His Great Searchlight. 2007. 312p. 24.95 *(978-1-60459-106-4(4))*; per. 12.99 *(978-1-60459-105-7(6))* Wilder Pubns., Corp.
Baker, E. D. A Prince among Frogs. 2nd ed. 2015. (Tales of the Frog Princess Ser.). (ENG.). 240p. (YA). (gr. 3-6). pap. 8.99 *(978-1-61963-624-8(7)*, 9781619636248, Bloomsbury USA Childrens) Bloomsbury Publishing USA.
Banerjee, Anjali. The Silver Spell. Fiegenshuh, Emily, illus. 2005. (Knights of the Silver Dragon Ser.: Bk. 8). 174p. (J). *(978-1-4156-1645-1(0)*, Mirrorstone) Wizards of the Coast.
Barrera, F. M. Tales of the Blue Wizard: The Children of Jamomere. 2005. (Illus.). 180p. (YA). (gr. 4-9). per. 10.99 *(978-0-9670848-1-7(4))* Talisman Pr.
Barron, T. A. The Book of Magic, 12 vols., Bk. 12. Hall, August, illus. 2011. (Merlin Saga Ser.: 12). (ENG.). 160p. (J). (gr. 5-18). 17.99 *(978-0-399-24741-5(6)*, Philomel Bks.) Penguin Young Readers Group.
—Doomraga's Revenge, 7 vols., Bk. 7. 2011. (Merlin Saga Ser.: 7). (ENG.). 272p. (J). (gr. 5-18). 8.99 *(978-0-14-241925-0(7)*, Puffin Books) Penguin Young Readers Group.
—The Dragon of Avalon, Bk. 6. 2011. (Merlin Saga Ser.: 6). (ENG.). 336p. (J). (gr. 5-18). 8.99 *(978-0-14-241924-3(9)*, Puffin Books) Penguin Young Readers Group.
—The Eternal Flame: Book 11, 11 vols. 2011. (Merlin Saga Ser.: 11). (ENG.). 416p. (J). (gr. 5-18). 8.99 *(978-0-14-241929-8(X)*, Puffin Books) Penguin Young Readers Group.
—The Lost Years, Bk. 1. 2011. (Merlin Saga Ser.: 1). (ENG.). 352p. (J). (gr. 5-18). 8.99 *(978-0-14-241889-5(7)*, Puffin Books) Penguin Young Readers Group.
—The Lost Years of Merlin. unabr. ed. 2004. (Lost Years of Merlin Ser.: Bk. 1). 284p. (J). (gr. 5-9). pap. 46.00 incl. audio *(978-0-8072-8766-8(0)*, YA261SP, Listening Library) Random Hse. Audio Publishing Group.
—The Raging Fires, Bk. 3. 2011. (Merlin Saga Ser.: 2). (ENG.). 288p. (J). (gr. 5-18). 8.99 *(978-0-14-241921-2(4)*, Puffin Books) Penguin Young Readers Group.
—The Seven Songs, Bk. 2. 2011. (Merlin Saga Ser.: 2). (ENG.). 336p. (J). (gr. 5-18). 8.99 *(978-0-14-241920-5(6)*, Puffin Books) Penguin Young Readers Group.
—Ultimate Magic, 8 vols., Bk. 8. 2011. (Merlin Saga Ser.: 8). (ENG.). 256p. (J). (gr. 5-18). 8.99 *(978-0-14-241926-7(5)*, Puffin Books) Penguin Young Readers Group.
—The Wizard's Wings, Bk. 5. 2011. (Merlin Saga Ser.: 5). (ENG.). 384p. (J). (gr. 5-18). 8.99 *(978-0-14-241923-6(0)*, Puffin Books) Penguin Young Readers Group.
Bartholomeusz, James. The White Fox. 2011. (Seven Stars Trilogy Ser.: 1). (ENG.). 472p. (YA). (gr. 6). pap. 9.95 *(978-1-60542-462-0(5))* Medallion Pr., Inc.
Batham, Matthew. Lightsleep. 2006. 167p. pap. *(978-1-904623-39-7(5))* WritersPrintShop.
Baum, Frank. The Wonderful Wizard of Oz. 2008. (Oxford World's Classics Ser.). (ENG., Illus.). 336p. pap. 13.95 *(978-0-19-954064-8(0))* Oxford Univ. Pr., Inc.
Baum, L. Frank. Adventures in Oz: Dorothy & the Wizard in Oz, the Road to Oz, the Emerald City of Oz. 2007. 296p. 24.95 *(978-1-60459-017-3(3))*; per. 12.95 *(978-1-60459-016-6(5))* Wilder Pubns., Corp.
—Adventures in Oz: The Patchwork Girl of Oz, Little Wizard Stories of Oz, Tik-Tok of Oz. 2007. 268p. 24.95 *(978-1-60459-019-7(X))*; per. 12.99 *(978-1-60459-018-0(1))* Wilder Pubns., Corp.
—Complete Book of Oz: The Wonderful Wizard of Oz, the Marvelous Land of Oz, & Ozma of Oz, Vol. 1. 2009. 268p. (J). 24.95 *(978-1-60459-711-0(9))* Wilder Pubns., Corp.
—Dorothy & the Wizard of Oz. 2005. pap. *(978-1-4065-0075-2(5))* Dodo Pr.
—Dorothy & the Wizard of Oz. 2004. (Twelve-Point Ser.). lib. bdg. 24.00 *(978-1-58287-273-5(2))*; lib. bdg. 25.00 *(978-1-58287-769-3(6))* North Bks.
—Glinda of Oz. 2007. 108p. 22.95 *(978-1-60312-591-8(4))* Aegypan.
—Large Hardback 1: L. Frank Baum's Original Oz Series. Wonderful Wizard of Oz, Marvelous Land of Oz, Ozma of Oz, Dorothy & the Wizard I. 2011. 1194p. *(978-1-905921-22-5(5))* Shoes & Ships & Sealing Wax Ltd.
—Little Wizard Stories of Oz. Neill, John R., illus. 2011. (Dover Children's Classics Ser.). (ENG.). 160p. (J). (gr. 3-5). pap. 14.99 *(978-0-486-47644-5(8))* Dover Pubns., Inc.
—Michael Foreman's the Wonderful Wizard of Oz. Foreman, Michael, illus. 2010. (ENG.). 160p. (J). (gr. 2-7). 19.99 *(978-1-84365-157-4(2)*, Pavilion Children's Books) Pavilion Bks. GBR. Dist: Independent Pubs. Group.
—La Mirinda Sorchisto de Oz. Broadribb, Donald, tr. Denslow, W. W., illus. 2012. 278p. pap. 24.00 *(978-1-59569-245-0(2))* Mondial.
—The Treasury of Oz. 2007. 784p. 49.99 *(978-1-60459-028-9(9))* Wilder Pubns., Corp.
—The Tresury of Oz: The Wonderful Wizard of Oz, the Marvelous Land of Oz, Ozma of Oz, Dorothy & the Wizard in Oz, the Road to Oz, the Emerald City Of. 2007. 548p. per. 19.49 *(978-1-60459-029-6(7))* Wilder Pubns., Corp.
—The Wizard of Oz. Evangelista, Mauro, illus. 2007. (Usborne Young Reading: Series Two Ser.). 64p. (J). (gr. 3-7). 8.99 *(978-0-7945-1457-0(X)*, Usborne) EDC Publishing.
—The Wizard of Oz. 2004. reprint ed. pap. 19.95 *(978-1-4191-8832-9(1))* Kessinger Publishing, LLC.
—The Wizard of Oz. Denslow, W. W., illus. 2012. (Stepping Stone Book Ser.). (ENG.). 112p. (J). (gr. 1-4). 4.99 *(978-0-375-86994-5(8)*, Random Hse. Bks. for Young Readers) Random Hse. Children's Bks.
—The Wizard of Oz: And Other Wonderful Books of Oz - The Emerald City of Oz & Glinda of Oz. Sumpter, Rachell, illus. deluxe ed. 2012. (Penguin Classics Deluxe Edition Ser.). (ENG.). 432p. (gr. 5). pap. 17.00 *(978-0-14-310663-0(5)*, Penguin Classics) Penguin Publishing Group.
—The Wonderful Wizard of Oz. 2005. 180p. 26.95 *(978-1-4218-0652-5(5)*, 1st World Library - Literary Society) 1st World Publishing, Inc.
—The Wonderful Wizard of Oz. 2007. (ENG.). 134p. pap. 19.99 *(978-1-4264-4884-3(8))*; 374p. pap. 18.99 *(978-1-4264-4841-6(4))* Creative Media Partners, LLC.
—The Wonderful Wizard of Oz. Denslow, W. W. & Menten, Ted, illus. 2010. (Dover Read & Listen Ser.). (ENG.). 112p. (J). (gr. 1-5). pap. 14.99 *(978-0-486-47725-1(8))* Dover Pubns., Inc.
—The Wonderful Wizard of Oz: A Classic Story about Cooperation. 2003. (Illus.). 32p. per. 3.95 *(978-0-9747133-5-9(X)*, Values to Live By Classic Stories) Thomas, Frederic Inc.
Baum, L. Frank & Zwerger, Lisbeth. The Wizard of Oz. 2011. (ENG., Illus.). 160p. (J). (gr. 4-3). 22.95 *(978-0-7358-4042-3(3))* North-South Bks., Inc.
Baxter, Nicola. Witches, Wizards & Magicians. Morton, Ken, illus. 2012. (ENG.). 80p. (J). (gr. k-4). pap. 9.99 *(978-1-84322-807-3(6))* Anness Publishing GBR. Dist: National Bk. Network.
Benjamin, A. H. Shamwood. 2006. 140p. pap. 24.95 *(978-1-4137-9193-8(X))* PublishAmerica, Inc.
Bennett, Jeffrey. El Mago Que Salvo el Mundo. Collier-Morales, Roberta, illus. 2011. (SPA.). 32p. (J). (gr. 2-4). 15.00 *(978-0-9721819-5-2(4))* Big Kid Science.
—The Wizard Who Saved the World. Collier-Morales, Roberta, illus. 2011. (ENG.). 32p. (J). (gr. 2-4). 15.00 *(978-0-9721819-4-5(6))* Big Kid Science.
Bergsma, Jody. Wizard. 2nd ed. 2008. (Illus.). 32p. (J). 15.95 *(978-0-9740190-9-3(7))* Illumination Arts Publishing Co., Inc.
Birney, Betty G. The Princess & the Peabodys. 2007. (ENG.). 256p. (J). (gr. 5-9). 15.99 *(978-0-06-084720-3(4))* HarperCollins Pubs.
Bishop, Desmond. The Wizard of Zee. 2012. 194p. pap. 14.95 *(978-1-61897-447-1(5)*, Strategic Bk. Publishing) Strategic Book Publishing & Rights Agency (SBPRA).
Blackwood, Sage. Jinx. (Jinx Ser.: 3). 400p. (J). (gr. 3-7). 2016. pap. 7.99 *(978-0-06-212997-0(X))* 2015. (ENG.). 16.99 *(978-0-06-212996-3(1))* 2014. (ENG.). 16.99 *(978-0-06-212993-2(7))* HarperCollins Pubs. (Tegen, Katherine Bks).
Blade, Adam. The Dagger of Doom. 2014. (Beast Quest Ser.). (ENG., Illus.). 128p. (J). (gr. 2-4). 5.99 *(978-1-4083-1406-7(1))* Hodder & Stoughton GBR. Dist: Hachette Bk. Group.
—Fang: The Bat Fiend. 2015. (Beast Quest Ser.). (ENG., Illus.). 144p. (J). (gr. 2-4). pap. 5.99 *(978-1-4083-0725-0(1))* Hodder & Stoughton GBR. Dist: Hachette Bk. Group.
—Komodo Bk. 31: The Lizard King. 2015. (Beast Quest Ser.). (ENG., Illus.). 144p. (J). (gr. 2-4). pap. 5.99 *(978-1-4083-0723-6(5))* Hodder & Stoughton GBR. Dist: Hachette Bk. Group.
—Murk: The Swamp Man. 2015. (Beast Quest Ser.). (ENG., Illus.). 144p. (J). (gr. 2-4). pap. 5.99 *(978-1-4083-0726-7(X))* Hodder & Stoughton GBR. Dist: Hachette Bk. Group.
—Muro: The Rat Monster. 2015. (Beast Quest Ser.). (ENG., Illus.). 144p. (J). (gr. 2-4). pap. 5.99 *(978-1-4083-0724-3(3))* Hodder & Stoughton GBR. Dist: Hachette Bk. Group.
—The Pirate's Curse. 2016. (Beast Quest Ser.). (ENG., Illus.). 144p. (J). (gr. 2-4). pap. 5.99 *(978-1-4083-1840-9(7))* Hodder & Stoughton GBR. Dist: Hachette Bk. Group.
—Vedra & Krimon the Twin Dragons. 2012. (Beast Quest Special Edition Ser.: 2). lib. bdg. 16.00 *(978-0-606-26187-6(7)*, Turtleback) Turtleback Bks.
—Vespick Bk. 36: The Wasp Queen. 2015. (Beast Quest Ser.). (ENG., Illus.). 144p. (J). (gr. 2-4). pap. 5.99 *(978-1-4083-0728-1(6))* Hodder & Stoughton GBR. Dist: Hachette Bk. Group.
Blashfield, Jean F. Realm of the Enchanter. 2007. (Paths of Doom Ser.). (Illus.). 127p. (J). per. 4.99 *(978-1-931567-73-2(5))* Margaret Weis Productions, Ltd.
Blossom, Maggie. Wizard of Oz. Pearse, Asha, illus. 2014. (ENG.). 16p. (J). (gr. -1-4). 7.99 *(978-1-4867-0009-7(8))* Flowerpot Children's Pr. Inc. CAN. Dist: Cardinal Pubs. Group.
Blunden, Alan. Tommy & the Garden Shed. 2008. 104p. pap. *(978-1-84923-111-4(7))* YouWriteOn.
Brittain, Bill. The Wizards & the Monster. Date not set. 96p. (J). (gr. 2-5). pap. 4.25 *(978-0-06-442003-7(5))* HarperCollins Pubs.
Brodhead, Kimberly. Gaden's Tower: Book One. 2007. 164p. per. 24.95 *(978-1-60441-038-9(8))* America Star Bks.
Brown, Ruth E. The Goontoff Kingdom Chronicles: The Bogus King. 2011. 46p. pap. 16.95 *(978-1-4560-8346-5(5))* America Star Bks.
Bucay, Jorge. The King & the Magician. Gusti, illus. 2014. (ENG.). 52p. (J). (gr. -1). 14.95 *(978-0-7892-1204-7(8)*, Abbeville Kids) Abbeville Pr., Inc.
Busiek, Kurt. Wizard's Tale. 2013. (ENG., Illus.). 144p. pap. 19.99 *(978-1-61377-593-6(8)*, 9781613775936) Idea & Design Works, LLC.
Card, Orson Scott. Stonefather. Kidd, Tom, illus. 2008. 112p. 35.00 *(978-1-59606-194-1(4))* Subterranean Pr.
Carter, Grant Matthew. The Disaster Caster. Morling, Donovan, illus. 2012. 38p. pap. 16.00 *(978-1-4349-8432-6(X)*, RoseDog Bks.) Dorrance Publishing Co., Inc.
Catipon, Atreyu. The Wizard's Magic Hat. 2012. 26p. 16.00 *(978-1-61863-390-3(2))* Bookstand Publishing.
Chima, Cinda Williams. The Crimson Crown. (Seven Realms Novel Ser.). (ENG.). (J). (gr. 5-9). 2013. 624p. pap. 9.99 *(978-1-4231-5214-9(X))* 2012. 608p. 18.99 *(978-1-4231-4433-5(3))* Hyperion Pr.
—The Demon King. 2010. (ENG.). 528p. (J). (gr. 5-6). pap. 9.99 *(978-1-4231-2136-7(8))* Hyperion Pr.
—The Dragon Heir. 2009. (Heir Chronicles Ser.). (ENG., Illus.). 528p. (J). (gr. 5-9). pap. 9.99 *(978-1-4231-1071-2(4))* Hyperion Pr.
—The Enchanter Heir. 2013. 464p. 18.99 *(978-1-4231-8789-9(X))* Disney Pr.
—The Enchanter Heir. 2013. (Heir Chronicles Ser.). (ENG.). 464p. (YA). (gr. 7-17). 18.99 *(978-1-4231-4434-2(1))* Hyperion Pr.
—The Exiled Queen. 2011. (Seven Realms Novel Ser.). (ENG.). 608p. (J). (gr. 5-17). pap. 9.99 *(978-1-4231-2137-4(6))* Hyperion Pr.
—The Gray Wolf Throne. 2012. (ENG.). 544p. (YA). (gr. 7-17). pap. 9.99 *(978-1-4231-2138-1(4))* Hyperion Pr.
—The Seven Realms Box Set. 2013. (Seven Realms Novel Ser.). (ENG.). 2272p. (YA). (gr. 7-12). pap. 37.99 *(978-1-4231-9961-8(8))* Hyperion Bks. for Children.
—The Sorcerer Heir. (Heir Chronicles Ser.). (ENG.). 560p. 2016. (J). (gr. 5-9). pap. 9.99 *(978-1-4231-9475-0(6))* 2014. (YA). (gr. 7-12). 18.99 *(978-1-4231-4435-9(X))* Hyperion Bks. for Children.
—The Warrior Heir. 2007. (Heir Chronicles Ser.). (ENG.). 448p. (J). (gr. 5-9). pap. 9.99 *(978-0-7868-3917-9(1))* Hyperion Pr.
—The Warrior Heir. 2006. (Heir Chronicles: No. 1). 1.00 *(978-1-4294-0323-8(3))* Recorded Bks., Inc.
—The Wizard Heir. 2008. (Heir Chronicles Ser.). (ENG.). 480p. (J). (gr. 5-9). pap. 9.99 *(978-1-4231-0488-9(9))* Hyperion Pr.
Clark, Platte F. Bad Unicorn. 2013. (Bad Unicorn Trilogy Ser.: 1). (ENG., Illus.). 432p. (J). (gr. 3-7). 15.99 *(978-1-4424-5012-7(6)*, Aladdin) Simon & Schuster Children's Publishing.
—Good Ogre. 2015. (Bad Unicorn Trilogy Ser.: 3). (ENG., Illus.). 384p. (J). (gr. 3-7). 17.99 *(978-1-4424-5018-9(5)*, Aladdin) Simon & Schuster Children's Publishing.
Cole, Bob. Power Reading: Chapter Books/Wizard of OZ. Sirrell, Terri, illus. 2004. 94p. (J). (gr. 3-4). vinyl bd. 39.95 *(978-1-883186-64-7(1)*, PPCL1) National Reading Styles Institute, Inc.
—Power Reading: Comic Book/Wizard of OZ. Sirrell, Terri, illus. 2005. 60p. (J). (gr. 3-4). vinyl bd. 39.95 *(978-1-883186-80-7(3)*, PPCLC1) National Reading Styles Institute, Inc.

Coleboum, Craig. The Knights of Videnland: Passing the Torch. 2007. 428p. per. 23.95 *(978-0-595-46989-5(2))* iUniverse, Inc.

Connolly, MarcyKate. Monstrous. Young, Skottie, illus. (J). (gr. 3-7). 2016. 448p. pap. 7.99 *(978-0-06-227272-0(1))* 2015. (ENG.). 432p. 16.99 *(978-0-06-227271-3(3))* HarperCollins Pubs.

—Monstrous. 2016. (J). lib. bdg. 18.40 *(978-0-606-38136-9(8))* Turtleback Bks.

Cook, Jeremy. The Illusion Stick. 2008. 115p. pap. 19.95 *(978-1-60474-705-8(6))* America Star Bks.

Coonan, Candace N. The Darkest Hour: Tales from Fadreama: Book 1. 2012. 328p. (gr. 4-6). pap. 19.11 *(978-1-4669-3565-5(0))* Trafford Publishing.

Cormier, Shawn P. Nomadin. 2003. 296p. (YA). per. 12.95 *(978-0-9740151-0-1(5))* Pine View Pr.

Cox, R. The Lonely Wizard Named Wizzy: The Apprentice. 2009. 16p. pap. 8.49 *(978-1-4490-2236-5(7))* AuthorHouse.

Croggon, Alison. The Singing: Book Four of Pellinor. 2017. (Pellinor Ser.). (ENG.). 496p. (J). (gr. 7). pap. 9.99 *(978-0-7636-9446-3(0))* Candlewick Pr.

Curley, Marianne. Key. 2011. (Guardians of Time Ser.). (ENG.). 416p. (YA). (gr. 7). pap. 9.99 *(978-1-59990-545-7(0)*, 9781599905457, Bloomsbury USA Childrens) Bloomsbury Publishing USA.

Daily, Lorrie Ann. The Castlewood Twins, the Magic Begins. 2008. 196p. pap. 12.95 *(978-0-9820479-8-9(3))* Peppertree Pr., The.

Darlison, Aleesah. Ellabeth's Light Cancelled. Brailsford, Jill, illus. 2017. (Unicorn Riders Ser.). (ENG.). 112p. (gr. 3-5). pap. 5.95 *(978-1-4795-6559-7(8))* Picture Window Bks.

Davis, Graeme. Re-Read Harry Potter & the Chamber of Secrets Today! an Unauthorized Guide. 2008. 112p. pap. 15.49 *(978-1-934840-72-6(6))* Nimble Bks. LLC.

Disney Press Staff. School's Out. 2010. 128p. pap. 4.99 *(978-1-4231-2677-5(7))* Disney Pr.

Dokey, Cameron. Golden: A Retelling of Rapunzel. 2007. (Once upon a Time Ser.). (ENG.). 192p. (YA). (gr. 7-9). mass mkt. 7.99 *(978-1-4169-3926-9(1)*, Simon Pulse) Simon Pulse.

Dolamore, Jaclyn. Magic under Glass. (Magic under Glass Ser.). (ENG.). (YA). (gr. 7). 2011. 256p. pap. 8.99 *(978-1-59990-587-7(6)*, 9781599905877) 2010. 240p. 16.99 *(978-1-59990-430-6(6)*, 9781599904306) Bloomsbury Publishing USA. (Bloomsbury USA Childrens).

—Magic under Stone. 2012. (Magic under Glass Ser.). (ENG.). 304p. (YA). 16.99 *(978-1-59990-643-0(0)*, 9781599906430, Bloomsbury USA Childrens) Bloomsbury Publishing USA.

Donaldson, Julia. Superworm. Scheffler, Axel, illus. 2014. (ENG.). 32p. (J). (gr. -1-3). 16.99 *(978-0-545-59176-8(7)*, Levine, Arthur A. Bks.) Scholastic, Inc.

Downer, Ann. The Dragon of Never-Was. Rayyan, Omar, illus. 2008. (ENG.). 320p. (J). (gr. 3-6). pap. 14.99 *(978-1-4169-5453-8(8)*, Atheneum Bks. for Young Readers) Simon & Schuster Children's Publishing.

—Hatching Magic. Rayyan, Omar, illus. 2004. 242p. 16.00 *(978-0-7569-3481-1(8))* Perfection Learning Corp.

Dozier, Kim. The Backwards Wizard. Dozier, Ashlyn McCauley & Dozier, Makenna Joy, illus. l.t. ed. 2005. (ENG.). 28p. (J). 10.00 *(978-0-9745839-4-5(4)*, Fun to Read Bks. with Royally Good Morals) MKADesigns.

Drischel, Candy L. Restless with the Dark Moon Rising. 2008. 105p. pap. 19.95 *(978-1-60610-421-7(7))* America Star Bks.

Duane, Diane. Games Wizards Play. (Young Wizards Ser.: 10). (ENG.). 640p. (YA). (gr. 7). 2017. pap. 8.99 *(978-0-544-81323-6(5))* 2016. 17.99 *(978-0-547-41806-3(X))* Houghton Mifflin Harcourt Publishing Co. (HMH Books For Young Readers).

—High Wizardry, 7 vols. (Young Wizards Ser.: 3). (J). 2006. 90.75 *(978-1-4025-9917-0(X))* 2004. 93.75 *(978-1-4025-8355-1(9))* Recorded Bks., Inc.

—A Wizard Alone. 2003. (Young Wizards Ser.: 6). (ENG.). 352p. (J). (gr. 5-7). pap. 8.99 *(978-0-15-204911-9(8))* Houghton Mifflin Harcourt Publishing Co.

—A Wizard of Mars Bk. 9. 2011. (Young Wizards Ser.: 9). (ENG.). 560p. (YA). (gr. 7-9). pap. 8.99 *(978-0-15-205449-6(9))* Houghton Mifflin Harcourt Publishing Co.

—Wizards at War Bk. 8. 2007. (Young Wizards Ser.: 8). (ENG., Illus.). 560p. (YA). (gr. 7-9). pap. 8.99 *(978-0-15-205223-2(2))* Houghton Mifflin Harcourt Publishing Co.

—Wizard's Holiday. 2005. (Young Wizards Ser.: 7). (ENG.). 448p. (J). (gr. 5-7). pap. 8.99 *(978-0-15-205207-2(0))* Houghton Mifflin Harcourt Publishing Co.

Dunn, Edward Grieves. Crinkles Academy for Wizards. 2008. 424p. pap. *(978-1-906210-98-4(5))* Grosvenor Hse. Publishing Ltd.

Edwards, Garth. The Blue Wizard. Stasyuk, Max, illus. 2011. (Adventures of Titch & Mitch Ser.). (J). pap. *(978-0-9567449-9-0(0))* Inside Pocket Publishing, Ltd.

—The #05 Blue Wizard. Stasyuk, Max, illus. 2011. (Adventures of Titch & Mitch, the Ser.). (J). pap. *(978-0-7613-8425-0(1))* Inside Pocket Publishing, Ltd.

Elgert, C. J. The Elder Brothers & the Dragon's Portal. 2011. 236p. (gr. 4-6). 25.95 *(978-1-4620-1467-5(4))*; pap. 15.95 *(978-1-4620-1466-8(6))* iUniverse, Inc.

Eliotte, Lisa J. The Adventures of Derby Doodle. 2009. 640p. pap. 25.99 *(978-1-4389-3058-9(5))* AuthorHouse.

Epstein, Adam Jay & Jacobson, Andrew. Circle of Heroes. (Familiars Ser.: 3). (ENG.). 336p. (J). (gr. 3-7). 2013. pap. 6.99 *(978-0-06-196116-8(7))* 2012. (Illus.). 16.99 *(978-0-06-196114-4(0))* HarperCollins Pubs.

—The Familiars. 2011. (Familiars Ser.: 1). (ENG.). 384p. (J). (gr. 3-7). pap. 6.99 *(978-0-06-196110-6(8))* HarperCollins Pubs.

—The Familiars. Chiu, Bobby, illus. 2010. (Familiars Ser.: 1). (ENG.). 368p. (J). (gr. 3-7). 16.99 *(978-0-06-196108-3(6))* HarperCollins Pubs.

—Secrets of the Crown. (Familiars Ser.: 2). (ENG.). (J). (gr. 3-7). 2012. 400p. pap. 6.99 *(978-0-06-196113-7(2))* 2011. 384p. 16.99 *(978-0-06-196111-3(6))* HarperCollins Pubs.

Eubank, Patricia Reeder. The Princess & the Snarls. Eubank, Patricia Reeder, illus. 2006. (ENG., Illus.). 32p. (J). (gr. k-3). 16.95 *(978-0-8249-5536-6(6)*, Ideal Pubns.) Worthy Publishing.

Feasey, Steve. Dark Moon. 2011. (Wereling Ser.: 2). (ENG.). 336p. (YA). (gr. 7-18). pap. 18.99 *(978-0-312-64643-1(7)*, 9780312646431) Feiwel & Friends.

Fernandez, David R. Lady Godiva & the Legend of the Black Rose. 2008. (Illus.). 32p. (J). pap. 8.99 *(978-0-9817521-4-3(4))* Mirror Publishing.

Fisch, Sholly. Wanted - The Super Friends. McKenny, Stewart & Moy, Philip, illus. 2012. (DC Super Friends Ser.). (ENG.). 32p. (gr. 1-2). lib. bdg. 22.60 *(978-1-4342-4543-4(8))* Stone Arch Bks.

Fischer, David. Heir to Oswyn. 2011. 66p. pap. 19.95 *(978-1-4626-2581-9(9))* America Star Bks.

Flannigan, Liz. Cara & the Wizard, 2 vols. Docampo, Valeria, illus. 2013. (Magic Stories Ser.). (ENG.). 48p. (J). (gr. 1-4). pap. 8.99 *(978-1-84686-780-4(0))* Barefoot Bks., Inc.

Fletcher, Pamela. Who Is Freddy Farlittle? 2011. 40p. pap. 16.99 *(978-1-4634-1086-5(7))* AuthorHouse.

Flood, Tony. Jody Richards & the Secret Potion. 2nd ed. 2012. 146p. pap. *(978-0-9569682-9-6(5))* My Voice Publishing.

Fodi, Lee Edward. Kendra Kandlestar & the Crack in Kazah. Fodi, Lee Edward, illus. 2011. (ENG., Illus.). 282p. (J). (gr. 4-7). 16.95 *(978-1-61254-018-4(X))* Brown Books Publishing Group.

Forman, M. L. Adventurers Wanted, Book 1: Slathbog's Gold. 2011. 400p. mass mkt. 7.99 *(978-1-60641-681-5(2))* Deseret Bk. Co.

—Adventurers Wanted, Book 2: The Horn of Moran. 2012. (J). pap. 7.99 *(978-1-60908-911-5(1))* 2011. 400p. 39.99 *(978-1-60641-255-8(8))* Deseret Bk. Co.

—Adventurers Wanted, Book 3: Albrek's Tomb. 2013. (Adventurers Wanted Ser.: 3). (ENG.). 504p. (J). (gr. 5). pap. 9.99 *(978-1-60907-339-8(8)*, Shadow Mountain) Shadow Mountain Publishing.

—Adventurers Wanted, Book 4: Sands of Nezza. 2013. (Adventurers Wanted Ser.: 4). (ENG.). 400p. (J). (gr. 5). 19.99 *(978-1-60907-329-9(0)*, Shadow Mountain) Shadow Mountain Publishing.

—Adventures Wanted, Book 3: Albrek's Tomb. 2012. (YA). 19.99 *(978-1-60908-892-7(1))* Deseret Bk. Co.

Forman, Mark. The Horn of Moran. 2011. 400p. (YA). (gr. 3-18). 18.99 *(978-1-60641-226-8(4)*, Shadow Mountain) Shadow Mountain Publishing.

—Slathbog's Gold. 2009. (Adventurers Wanted Ser.: Bk. 1). 432p. (J). 17.95 *(978-1-60641-029-5(6)*, Shadow Mountain) Shadow Mountain Publishing.

Forward, Toby. Doubleborn: A Dragonborn Novel. 2016. (Dragonborn Ser.: 3). (ENG.). 352p. (J). pap. 8.99 *(978-1-61963-921-8(1)*, 9781619639218, Bloomsbury USA Childrens) Bloomsbury Publishing USA.

—Dragonborn. (Dragonborn Ser.: 1). (ENG.). (YA). (gr. 3-6). 2013. 368p. pap. 8.99 *(978-1-59990-983-7(9)*, 9781599909837) 2012. 352p. 16.99 *(978-1-59990-724-6(0)*, 9781599907246) Bloomsbury Publishing USA. (Bloomsbury USA Childrens).

—Fireborn. 2015. (Dragonborn Ser.: 2). (ENG.). 448p. (YA). (gr. 5-8). pap. 8.99 *(978-1-61963-439-8(2)*, 9781619634398, Bloomsbury USA Childrens) Bloomsbury Publishing USA.

—Starborn: A Dragonborn Novel. (Dragonborn Ser.). (ENG.). 448p. (J). 2017. pap. 9.99 *(978-1-68119-277-2(2)*, 9781681192772) 2016. 16.99 *(978-1-61963-842-6(8)*, 9781619638426) Bloomsbury Publishing USA. (Bloomsbury USA Childrens).

Foxlee, Karen. A Most Magical Girl. (ENG.). 304p. (J). (gr. 3-7). 2017. 7.99 ***(978-0-553-51288-5(9)***, Yearling) 2016. 16.99 *(978-0-553-51285-4(4)*, Knopf Bks. for Young Readers) 2016. lib. bdg. 19.99 *(978-0-553-51286-1(2)*, Knopf Bks. for Young Readers) Random Hse. Children's Bks.

Foxlee, Karen. Ophelia & the Marvelous Boy. 2014. (ENG.). 240p. (J). (gr. 3-7). 16.99 *(978-0-385-75354-8(3)*, Knopf Bks. for Young Readers) Random Hse. Children's Bks.

Frost, C. Amethyst. Mourning under the Bridge. 2012. 280p. pap. 9.99 *(978-0-9847236-2-1(5))* Frost, C. A.

Gallego García, Laura & Peden, Margaret Sayers. The Valley of the Wolves. 2006. 247p. (J). pap. *(978-0-439-58554-5(6)*, Levine, Arthur A. Bks.) Scholastic, Inc.

Garner, Alan. The Moon of Gomrath: A Tale of Alderley. 2006. (ENG., Illus.). 216p. (J). (gr. 4-8). pap. 13.95 *(978-0-15-205630-8(0))* Houghton Mifflin Harcourt Publishing Co.

—The Weirdstone of Brisingamen: A Tale of Alderley. 2006. (ENG., Illus.). 288p. (J). (gr. 4-8). pap. 16.95 *(978-0-15-205636-0(X))* Houghton Mifflin Harcourt Publishing Co.

George, Jessica Day. Fridays with the Wizards. 2016. (Tuesdays at the Castle Ser.: 4). (ENG.). 240p. (YA). 16.99 *(978-1-61963-429-9(5)*, 9781619634299, Bloomsbury USA Childrens) Bloomsbury Publishing USA.

Geronimo Stilton Staff. The Wizard's Wand. 2016. (ENG.). 320p. (J). (gr. 2-5). 14.99 *(978-1-338-03291-8(7)*, Scholastic Paperbacks) Scholastic, Inc.

Gogonya, Carol. The African Mermaid & Other Stories. 2011. 40p. pap. 32.70 *(978-1-4568-5416-4(X))* Xlibris Corp.

Goodyear-Brown, Paris. Gabby the Gecko. 2003. per. *(978-1-932203-54-7(0))* Sundog, Ltd.

Gordon, Sylvia. Further Adventures of the Potty Wizard & His Cat, Muddles. 2009. (Illus.). 60p. pap. 10.49 *(978-1-4389-6819-3(1))* AuthorHouse.

Grace, N. B. Rev It Up! 9th ed. 2010. (Wizards of Waverly Place Ser.: No. 9). 128p. (J). (gr. 3-7). pap. 4.99 *(978-1-4231-2676-8(9))* Disney Pr.

Graham, Deborah. The Magic Comes Back: A Max & Sam Adventure. 2012. 66p. (gr. 2-4). pap. 8.95 *(978-1-4759-4758-8(5))* iUniverse, Inc.

Grove, Malachai. The Return of Malachai. 2011. 24p. pap. 14.99 *(978-1-4567-6257-5(5))* AuthorHouse.

Haining, Peter. Magicians' Circle. 2012. 348p. (-18). pap. *(978-1-4596-4365-9(8))* ReadHowYouWant.com, Ltd.

Haining, Peter, ed. Magician's Circle: More Spellbinding Stories of Wizards & Wizardry. 2004. (ENG., Illus.). 256p. (J). (gr. 5). 19.95 *(978-0-285-63681-1(2))* Souvenir Pr. Ltd. GBR. Dist: Independent Pubs. Group.

Hamley, Dennis. Hawk's Vision. 2006. 116p. per. *(978-1-904529-20-0(8)*, Back to Front) Solidus.

Helm, Julie G. Merlin for Sherman. Cary, Debbi G., photos by. 2010. (Illus.). 84p. pap. 26.49 *(978-1-4520-5183-3(6))* AuthorHouse.

Henderson, Hugh. VanDland. 2012. 112p. pap. 10.95 *(978-1-61204-859-8(5)*, Strategic Bk. Publishing) Strategic Book Publishing & Rights Agency (SBPRA).

Hook, Carol A. Before There Were Stars: An Orange Dragon. 2009. 48p. pap. 8.95 *(978-1-4401-5475-1(9))* iUniverse, Inc.

Hounam, Donald. A Dangerous Magic. 2017. (ENG.). 352p. (YA). (gr. 5-12). 17.99 ***(978-1-5124-3232-9(6))*** Lerner Publishing Group.

James, Kari, adapted by. Barbie & the Magic of Pegasus: A Junior Novelization. 2005. (Illus.). 72p. pap. *(978-0-439-78542-6(1))* Scholastic, Inc.

Joe Thomson-Swift. The Magic Stone. 2011. 92p. pap. *(978-1-908105-83-7(6))* Grosvenor Hse. Publishing Ltd.

Johansen, K. V. The Shadow Road, 1 vol. 2010. (ENG., Illus.). 240p. (YA). (gr. 7-12). pap. 9.95 *(978-1-55469-165-4(6))* Orca Bk. Pubs. USA.

—Warden of Greyrock, 1 vol. 2009. (ENG.). 256p. (YA). (gr. 7-12). pap. 9.95 *(978-1-55469-005-3(6))* Orca Bk. Pubs. USA.

Jones, Diana Wynne. House of Many Ways. 2008. 404p. (J). 9.99 *(978-0-06-147798-0(2)*, Greenwillow Bks.) HarperCollins Pubs.

—House of Many Ways. 2009. (J). 1.25 *(978-1-4361-6123-7(1))*; 79.75 *(978-1-4361-6128-2(2))*; 100.75 *(978-1-4361-6132-9(0))*; 245.75 *(978-1-4361-6127-5(4))*; 102.75 *(978-1-4361-6130-5(4))* Recorded Bks., Inc.

—Howl's Moving Castle. 2008. (World of Howl Ser.: 1). (ENG.). 448p. (J). (gr. 3-7). pap. 7.99 *(978-0-06-147878-9(4)*, Greenwillow Bks.) HarperCollins Pubs.

—Howl's Moving Castle. 2009. 9.00 *(978-0-7848-2484-9(3)*, Everbind) Marco Bk. Co.

—Howl's Moving Castle, 8 vols. 2008. (YA). 101.75 *(978-1-4361-5953-1(9))*; 104.75 *(978-1-4361-5951-7(2))*; 179.75 *(978-1-4361-5948-7(2))*; 1.25 *(978-1-4361-5944-9(X))*; 78.75 *(978-1-4361-5947-0(4))*; 75.75 *(978-1-4361-5949-4(0))* Recorded Bks., Inc.

Jones, J. J. Flute Tudor & the Secret Order. 2012. 304p. 22.95 *(978-1-4575-1302-2(1))* Dog Ear Publishing, LLC.

Jones, Marcia Thornton & Dadey, Debbie. Wizards Do Roast Turkeys. Dreidemy, Joëlle, illus. 2007. 64p. (J). pap. *(978-0-545-00235-6(4))* Scholastic, Inc.

Joyce, William. E. Aster Bunnymund & the Warrior Eggs at the Earth's Core!, Bk. 2. Joyce, William, illus. 2012. (Guardians Ser.: 2). (ENG., Illus.). 272p. (J). (gr. 2-6). 15.99 *(978-1-4424-3050-1(8)*, Atheneum Bks. for Young Readers) Simon & Schuster Children's Publishing.

Joyce, William & Geringer, Laura. Nicholas St. North & the Battle of the Nightmare King, Bk. 1. Joyce, William, illus. 2011. (Guardians Ser.: 1). (ENG., Illus.). 240p. (J). (gr. 2-6). 15.99 *(978-1-4424-3048-8(6)*, Atheneum Bks. for Young Readers) Simon & Schuster Children's Publishing.

Kent, Elizabeth. The Enchanted Adventures of the Caroline Kemps. 2007. 148p. pap. 24.95 *(978-1-4241-9915-0(8))* America Star Bks.

Kent, Jaden. #1: the Cave of Aaaaah! Doom! Bodnaruk, Iryna, illus. 2017. (Ella & Owen Ser.: 1). (ENG.). 112p. (J). (gr. 1-3). pap. 5.99 *(978-1-4998-0368-6(0))* Little Bee Books Inc.

Kilgore, Lee. Widga's Quest, 1 vol. 2009. 48p. pap. 16.95 *(978-1-4489-2517-9(7))* America Star Bks.

King, J. R. Arianna Kelt & the Renegades of Time: Deluxe Edition, Wizards of Skyhall Book 2. 2008. (ENG.). 252p. (YA). per. 15.95 *(978-1-57545-120-6(4))* RP Media.

—Arianna Kelt & the Renegades of Time: Signature Edition, Wizards of Skyhall Book 2. 2008. (ENG.). 256p. (J). 18.95 *(978-1-57545-165-7(4)*, Reagent Pr. Echo) RP Media.

—Arianna Kelt & the Wizards of Skyhall. (J). 2008. (ENG.). 200p. 18.95 *(978-1-57545-164-0(6)*, Reagent Pr. Echo) 2006. (Illus.). 200p. pap. 11.95 *(978-1-57545-115-2(8))* 2006. (Illus.). 148p. per. 18.95 *(978-1-57545-106-0(9)*, Reagent Pr. Echo) RP Media.

—Arianna Kelt & the Wizards of Skyhall: Deluxe Edition, Wizards of Skyhall Book 1. 2008. (ENG.). 200p. (YA). per. 14.95 *(978-1-57545-170-1(0))* RP Media.

Kinton, P. D. Wishing for Wizards & Chips for Te. 2010. 28p. pap. *(978-1-907211-26-3(8))* Grosvenor Hse. Publishing Ltd.

Klett, David E. Rachel & the Wizard of Lake Lure: The Lake Lure Chronicles - Book 2. 2006. (Illus.). (J). lib. bdg. 17.95 *(978-0-9779325-1-1(6))* Five Oaks Pr.

Koller, Jackie French. A Wizard Named Nell. Guay, Rebecca, illus. 2003. (ENG.). 208p. (J). (gr. 3-7). pap. 11.95 *(978-0-689-85591-7(5)*, Aladdin) Simon & Schuster Children's Publishing.

—The Wizard's Apprentice. Guay, Rebecca, illus. 2003. (ENG.). 192p. (J). (gr. 3-7). pap. 9.99 *(978-0-689-85592-4(3)*, Aladdin) Simon & Schuster Children's Publishing.

—The Wizard's Scepter. 2012. (ENG., Illus.). 176p. (J). (gr. 3-7). pap. 9.99 *(978-0-689-85593-1(1)*, Aladdin) Simon & Schuster Children's Publishing.

Korczak, Janusz. Kaytek the Wizard. Lloyd-Jones, Antonia, tr. from POL. 2012. (ENG.). 272p. (J). (gr. 4-7). 17.95 *(978-0-9838685-0-7(6))* Flashlight Pr.

Kositsky, Lynne. Minerva's Voyage. 2009. (ENG., Illus.). 240p. (YA). (gr. 6-18). pap. 10.99 *(978-1-55488-439-1(X)*, Dundurn Pr.) Dundurn CAN. Dist: Ingram Publisher Services.

Lacle, Tony. A Man Called Avalon. 2006. 156p. per. 15.63 *(978-1-4120-5609-0(8))* Trafford Publishing.

Lamb, Enelle. Christopher Collin & the True Okemus - the Adventure Begins. 2009. 123p. pap. 13.00 *(978-0-557-05783-2(3))* Lulu Pr., Inc.

Landy, Derek. Dark Days, 4. (ENG.). 416p. pap. *(978-0-00-732597-9(5))* HarperCollins Children's Bks.

—The Faceless Ones. (Skulduggery Pleasant Ser.: 3). (ENG.). 432p. (J). (gr. 5). 2010. pap. 7.99 *(978-0-06-124093-5(1))* 2009. 16.99 *(978-0-06-124091-1(5))* HarperCollins Pubs.

—Playing with Fire. (Skulduggery Pleasant Ser.: 2). (ENG.). (J). (gr. 5). 2009. 416p. pap. 7.99 *(978-0-06-124090-4(7))* 2008. 400p. 16.99 *(978-0-06-124088-1(5))* HarperCollins Pubs.

—Scepter of the Ancients. Percival, Tom, illus. 2008. (Skulduggery Pleasant Ser.: 1). (ENG.). 416p. (J). (gr. 5). pap. 7.99 *(978-0-06-123117-9(7))* HarperCollins Pubs.

Launchbury, Jane. Witch & Wizard Stories. 2012. (ENG., Illus.). 64p. (J). 9.95 *(978-1-84135-103-2(2))* Award Pubns. Ltd. GBR. Dist: Parkwest Pubns., Inc.

Le Guin, Ursula K. Tehanu. 2012. (Earthsea Cycle Ser.: 4). (ENG., Illus.). 320p. (YA). (gr. 7). pap. 9.99 *(978-1-4424-5996-0(4)*, Atheneum Bks. for Young Readers) Simon & Schuster Children's Publishing.

Le Guin, Ursula K. A Wizard of Earthsea. 2012. (Earthsea Cycle Ser.: Vol. 1). (ENG.). (YA). (gr. 7). lib. bdg. 19.60 ***(978-1-68065-210-9(9))*** Perfection Learning Corp.

—A Wizard of Earthsea. 2012. (Earthsea Ser.: 1). lib. bdg. 19.65 *(978-0-606-26624-6(0)*, Turtleback) Turtleback Bks.

Lee, Brian. Bouncey the Elf & Friends - Bedtime St. 2005. (ENG., Illus.). 53p. pap. *(978-0-7552-1023-7(9))* Authors OnLine, Ltd.

Lehane, Pearse. The Train That Never Came. 2008. 328p. pap. *(978-1-84923-249-4(0))* YouWriteOn.

Levine, Gail Carson. The Two Princesses of Bamarre. (J). 2012. (ENG.). 272p. (gr. 3-7). pap. 6.99 *(978-0-06-440966-7(X))* 2004. (Illus.). 304p. (gr. 7-18). reprint ed. pap. 6.99 *(978-0-06-057580-9(8))* HarperCollins Pubs.

Levinson, Marilyn. Rufus & Magic Run Amok, 1 vol. 2005. (ENG.). 32p. (YA). pap. 5.95 *(978-0-7614-5176-1(5))* Marshall Cavendish Corp.

Lobel, Arnold. The Arnold Lobel Treasury. 2014. (ENG., Illus.). 160p. (J). (gr. 1-4). pap. 14.99 *(978-0-486-78078-8(3))* Dover Pubns., Inc.

Loiske, Jennifer, et al. Tales of an Old Wizard. 2013. 116p. pap. 10.58 *(978-1-291-30601-9(3))* Lulu Pr., Inc.

Lubar, David. Wizards of the Game. 2004. (ENG.). 176p. (J). (gr. 3-7). 6.99 *(978-0-14-240215-3(X)*, Puffin Books) Penguin Young Readers Group.

Luberto, Bradley. Clide & Druce: A Repulsive Tale of Trolls & Tax Money. 2006. (ENG.). 48p. per. 16.95 *(978-1-4241-5012-0(4))* PublishAmerica, Inc.

Lutz II, William. Seeking Mason. 2009. 212p. pap. 14.00 *(978-0-557-03737-7(9))* Lulu Pr., Inc.

Malaspina, Ann. The Mouse & the Wizard: A Hindu Folktale. Sylvaine, Jenny, illus. 2013. (Folktales from Around the World Ser.). (ENG.). 24p. (J). (gr. k-3). 28.50 *(978-1-62323-633-5(9)*, 206384) Child's World, Inc., The.

Malchow, Hal & Malchow, Alex. The Sword of Darrow. 2011. (ENG.). (gr. 3-7). 372p. pap. 12.99 *(978-1-935618-47-8(4))*; 532p. 17.99 *(978-1-935618-46-1(6))* BenBella Bks.

Malloy, Chris. Wizard Academies - A Special Kind of Talent. 2008. 142p. pap. 19.95 *(978-0-615-18505-7(3))* Wizard Academies, LLC.

Martin, Dick. The Ozmapolitan of Oz. 2006. (J). 24.95 *(978-1-930764-11-8(1))* International Wizard of Oz Club, The.

McCullough, Karen. Wizard's Bridge. 2004. pap. 13.75 *(978-0-9759653-0-6(1)*, ImaJinn Bks.) BelleBks., Inc.

McDonald, John. The Tempest: The Graphic Novel. Gale Editor, ed. 2011. (Classic Graphic Novel Collection). (ENG.). 160p. (gr. 7-10). lib. bdg. 39.40 *(978-1-4205-0632-7(3))* Cengage Gale.

McDowell, Andrew. Beyond the Forest. 2007. 286p. pap. 16.95 *(978-0-7414-4238-3(8))* Infinity Publishing.

McGowan, Maureen. Cinderella: Ninja Warrior. 2010. 320p. pap. 8.95 *(978-1-60747-778-5(5)*, Pickwick Pr.) Phoenix Bks., Inc.

McGraw, Eloise Jarvis & McGraw, Lauren Lynn. The Forbidden Fountain of Oz. 2006. (J). 24.95 *(978-1-930764-12-5(X))* International Wizard of Oz Club, The.

McKillip, Patricia A. The Forgotten Beasts of Eld. 2006. (ENG., Illus.). 352p. (YA). (gr. 7-12). pap. 16.95 *(978-0-15-205536-3(3))* Houghton Mifflin Harcourt Publishing Co.

McMullan, Kate. Danger! Wizard at Work, No. 11. Basso, Bill, illus. 2004. (Dragon Slayers' Academy Ser.: 11). (ENG.). 112p. (J). (gr. 2-5). pap. 4.99 *(978-0-448-43529-9(2)*, Grosset & Dunlap) Penguin Young Readers Group.

—Pig Latin — Not Just for Pigs!, 1 vol. Basso, Bill, illus. 2006. (Dragon Slayers' Academy Ser.: No. 14). (ENG.). 112p. (gr. 1-7). 24.21 *(978-1-59961-127-3(9))* Spotlight.

Memling, Carl. The Sword in the Stone (Disney) Random House Disney Staff, illus. 2015. (Little Golden Book Ser.). (ENG.). 24p. (J). (-k). 4.99 *(978-0-7364-3374-7(0)*, Golden/Disney) Random Hse. Children's Bks.

Mertz, Alyssa. The Lucky Farm Boy, 1 vol. Crum, A. M., illus. 2009. 28p. pap. 24.95 *(978-1-60813-892-0(5))* PublishAmerica, Inc.

Metz, Diana. Brinn & the Dragons of Pallan Cliffs. 2003. 352p. (J). pap. *(978-0-9718431-2-7(0))* M.O.T.H.E.R. Publishing Co., Inc., The.

Mitchell, N. J. W. Saraly & the Dragons. 2003. 124p. pap. 10.95 *(978-0-595-30264-2(5))* iUniverse, Inc.

Mlynowski, Sarah. Genie in a Bottle (Whatever After #9) 2016. (Whatever After Ser.: 9). (ENG.). 176p. (J). (gr. 3-7). 14.99 *(978-0-545-85102-2(5)*, Scholastic Pr.) Scholastic, Inc.

Moffitt, Sara. Merlin & the Frog Meet Chatly & Noble. 2011. 25p. (J). pap. 18.95 *(978-1-4327-5921-6(3))* Outskirts Pr., Inc.

Mongredien, Sue. Oliver Moon & the Broomstick Battle. 2011. (Oliver Moon Ser.). 94p. (J). pap. 4.99 *(978-0-7945-3038-9(9)*, Usborne) EDC Publishing.

—Oliver Moon & the Dragon Disaster. 2011. (Oliver Moon Ser.). 94p. (J). pap. 4.99 *(978-0-7945-3036-5(2)*, Usborne) EDC Publishing.

—Oliver Moon & the Monster Mystery. 2011. (Oliver Moon Ser.). 89p. (J). pap. 4.99 *(978-0-7945-3095-2(8)*, Usborne) EDC Publishing.

—Oliver Moon & the Nipperbat Nightmare. 2011. (Oliver Moon Ser.). 94p. (J). pap. 4.99 *(978-0-7945-3037-2(0)*, Usborne) EDC Publishing.

—Oliver Moon & the Spell Off. 2011. (Oliver Moon Ser.). 93p. (J). pap. 4.99 *(978-0-7945-3093-8(1)*, Usborne) EDC Publishing.

—Oliver Moon's Fangtastic Sleepover. 2011. (Oliver Moon Ser.). 92p. (J). pap. 4.99 *(978-0-7945-3094-5(X)*, Usborne) EDC Publishing.

Morpurgo, Michael. Toto: The Dog-Gone Amazing Story of the Wizard of Oz. Chichester Clark, Emma, illus. 2017. (ENG.). 284p. (J). 17.99 ***(978-0-00-825256-4(4)***, HarperCollins Children's Bks.) HarperCollins Pubs. Ltd. GBR. Dist: HarperCollins Pubs.

Morris, J. S. The Jewel. 2007. 204p. pap. 22.95 *(978-1-4357-0140-3(2))* Lulu Pr., Inc.

WXYZ

Morrissey, Dean & Krensky, Stephen. The Wizard Mouse. Morrissey, Dean, illus. 2011. (ENG., Illus.). 32p. (J). (gr. k-4). 16.99 *(978-0-06-008066-2(3))* HarperCollins Pubs.

Moss, Ronald. The Wizard Next Door. 2009. 198p. pap. 14.95 *(978-1-60911-077-2(3)*, Eloquent Bks.) Strategic Book Publishing & Rights Agency (SBPRA).

Mulholland, Marie. A Study Guide for the Necklace of Terrersylvanous. 2007. 38p. (J). ring bd. 11.95 *(978-0-9797715-0-7(1))* Sonic Sword Productions.

Mull, Brandon. Chasing the Prophecy. (Beyonders Ser.: 3). (ENG.). (J). (gr. 3-7). 2014. 528p. pap. 8.99 *(978-1-4169-9797-9(0))* 2013. 512p. 19.99 *(978-1-4169-9796-2(2))* Simon & Schuster Children's Publishing. (Aladdin).

—Seeds of Rebellion. (Beyonders Ser.: 2). (ENG., Illus.). (J). (gr. 3-7). 2013. 528p. pap. 8.99 *(978-1-4169-9795-5(4))* 2012. 512p. 19.99 *(978-1-4169-9794-8(6))* Simon & Schuster Children's Publishing. (Aladdin).

—Seeds of Rebellion. 2012. (Beyonders Ser.: Bk. 2). (ENG., Illus.). 512p. (J). pap. 10.99 *(978-1-4424-4965-7(9)*, Simon & Schuster/Paula Wiseman Bks.) Simon & Schuster/Paula Wiseman Bks.

—Seeds of Rebellion. 2013. (Beyonders Ser.: 2). lib. bdg. 19.65 *(978-0-606-27030-4(2)*, Turtleback) Turtleback Bks.

—A World Without Heroes. (J). 2011. (Beyonders Ser.: 1). 1.25 *(978-1-4640-0920-4(1))* (Beyonders Ser.: 1). 92.75 *(978-1-4618-0338-6(1))* 2011. (Beyonders Ser.: 1). 124.75 *(978-1-4618-0353-9(5))* 2011. 122.75 *(978-1-4618-0363-8(2))* Recorded Bks., Inc.

—A World Without Heroes. (Beyonders Ser.: 1). (ENG.). (J). (gr. 3-7). 2012. 496p. pap. 8.99 *(978-1-4169-9793-1(8))* 2011. 464p. 19.99 *(978-1-4169-9792-4(X))* Simon & Schuster Children's Publishing. (Aladdin).

—A World Without Heroes. 2011. (Beyonders Ser.: Bk. 1). (ENG.). 464p. (J). pap. 10.99 *(978-1-4424-3530-8(5)*, Simon & Schuster/Paula Wiseman Bks.) Simon & Schuster/Paula Wiseman Bks.

—A World Without Heroes. 2012. (Beyonders Ser.: 1). lib. bdg. 19.65 *(978-0-606-23675-1(9)*, Turtleback) Turtleback Bks.

—A World Without Heroes; Seeds of Rebellion; Chasing the Prophecy, Set. 2013. (Beyonders Ser.). (ENG., Illus.). 1456p. (J). (gr. 3-7). 59.99 *(978-1-4424-8593-8(0)*, Aladdin) Simon & Schuster Children's Publishing.

Negrin, Fabian, illus. Wizard Tales. 2003. 96p. 19.95 *(978-1-55285-558-4(9))* Whitecap Bks., Ltd. CAN. Dist: Graphic Arts Ctr. Publishing Co.

Nguyen, Thao. Consequences: A Chance for Hope. 2012. 60p. pap. 15.99 *(978-1-4691-8794-5(9))* Xlibris Corp.

Nix, Garth. Frogkisser! 2017. (ENG.). 384p. (J). (gr. 7). 18.99 *(978-1-338-05208-4(X)*, Scholastic Pr.) Scholastic, Inc.

Ogilvy, Ian. Measle & the Dragodon. 2006. 344p. (J). (gr. 3-8). per. 6.99 *(978-0-06-058690-4(7)*, Harper Trophy) HarperCollins Pubs.

—Measle & the Wrathmonk. 2004. 224p. (J). (gr. 4-6). 15.99 *(978-0-06-058685-0(0))* HarperCollins Pubs.

Okugas, Juanaiga. The tales of Mew the Cat. 2011. 92p. pap. 35.30 *(978-1-4567-3480-0(6))* AuthorHouse.

O'Neal, Eilis. The False Princess. 2012. (ENG.). 336p. (J). (gr. 7). pap. 8.99 *(978-1-60684-392-5(3)*, Carolrhoda Lab™) Lerner Publishing Group.

Osborne, Mary Pope. El Invierno Del Hechicero Del Hielo. 2015. (Casa De árbol Ser.: 32). (SPA., Illus.). 144p. (J). (gr. 2-4). pap. 5.99 *(978-1-63245-535-2(8))* Lectorum Pubns., Inc.

Parsons, Colin. Wizards' Kingdom. 2005. (ENG., Illus.). 117p. pap. *(978-1-84401-522-1(X))* Athena Pr.

Patterson, James. The Fire. 2011. (Playaway Children Ser.). (ENG.). (YA). (gr. 8-12). 59.99 *(978-1-61113-385-1(8))* Hachette Audio.

—The Gift. 2010. (Witch & Wizard Ser.: No. 2). (J). 59.99 *(978-1-60941-012-4(2))* Findaway World, LLC.

—The Gift. 2014. lthr. 79.00 *(978-1-62715-523-6(6))* Leatherbound Bestsellers.

—Witch & Wizard. 2014. lthr. 79.00 *(978-1-62715-529-8(5))* Leatherbound Bestsellers.

—Witch & Wizard. 2010. (Witch & Wizard Ser.: 1). (ENG.). 336p. (YA). (gr. 5-17). pap. 10.00 *(978-0-316-03834-8(2)*, Jimmy Patterson) Little Brown & Co.

—Witch & Wizard. 2010. (Witch & Wizard Ser.: 1). (YA). lib. bdg. 20.85 *(978-0-606-15119-1(2)*, Turtleback) Turtleback Bks.

Patterson, James & Charbonnet, Gabrielle. Witch & Wizard. 2011. (Witch & Wizard Ser.: 1). (ENG.). 368p. mass mkt. 8.00 *(978-0-446-56243-0(2)*, Jimmy Patterson) Little Brown & Co.

—Witch & Wizard. 2011. (Witch & Wizard Ser.: 1). lib. bdg. 18.45 *(978-0-606-26452-5(3)*, Turtleback) Turtleback Bks.

Patterson, James & Dembowski, Jill. The Fire. 2011. (Witch & Wizard Ser.: 3). (ENG.). 352p. (YA). (gr. 5-17). 17.99 *(978-0-316-10190-5(7)*, Jimmy Patterson) Little Brown & Co.

—The Kiss. 2013. (Witch & Wizard Ser.: 4). (ENG.). 384p. (YA). (gr. 7-17). pap. 10.00 *(978-0-316-10176-9(1)*, Jimmy Patterson) Little Brown & Co.

—The Kiss. 2013. (Witch & Wizard Ser.: 4). (YA). lib. bdg. 20.85 *(978-0-606-32281-2(7)*, Turtleback) Turtleback Bks.

Patterson, James & Raymond, Emily. The Lost. 2014. (YA). (Witch & Wizard Ser.: 5). (ENG.). 384p. (gr. 7-17). 18.00 *(978-0-316-20770-6(5)*, Jimmy Patterson); 355p. *(978-0-316-24266-0(7))* Little Brown & Co.

Patterson, James & Rust, Ned. The Gift. (Witch & Wizard Ser.: 2). (ENG.). 2012. 352p. mass mkt. 7.99 *(978-0-446-56245-4(9))* 2011. 400p. (gr. 5-17). pap. 9.99 *(978-0-316-03835-5(0))* 2010. 352p. (gr. 5-17). 17.99 *(978-0-316-03625-2(0))* Little Brown & Co. (Jimmy Patterson).

—The Gift. 2012. (Witch & Wizard Ser.: 2). lib. bdg. 18.40 *(978-0-606-26451-8(5)*, Turtleback) Turtleback Bks.

Paul, Donita K. Two Renegade Realms, 1 vol. 2014. (Realm Walkers Ser.). (ENG.). 416p. (YA). pap. 13.99 *(978-0-310-73581-6(5))* Zondervan.

Perry, Pete. The Secret of Bedside Manor. 2009. (Illus.). 140p. pap. 36.49 *(978-1-4389-6668-7(7))* AuthorHouse.

Pickering, Sean & Morrill, Scott. The Adventures of Danny & Spike: Underground. 2007. 92p. per. 9.95 *(978-0-595-44365-9(6))* iUniverse, Inc.

Pierce, Tamora. Battle Magic. (ENG.). 464p. (J). (gr. 7). 2015. pap. 10.99 *(978-0-439-84298-3(0))* 2013. 17.99 *(978-0-439-84297-6(2)*, Scholastic Pr.) Scholastic, Inc.

—In the Hand of the Goddess. 2014. (Song of the Lioness Ser.: 2). (ENG., Illus.). 272p. (YA). (gr. 7). 19.99 *(978-1-4814-3960-2(X)*, Atheneum Bks. for Young Readers) Simon & Schuster Children's Publishing.

Plourde, Lynn. The Blizzard Wizard. Aardema, John, illus. 2010. (ENG.). 32p. (J). (gr. -1-3). 16.95 *(978-0-89272-789-6(6))* Down East Bks.

Price, Nick, illus. The Wonderful Wizard of Oz. 2009. (ENG.). 12p. (J). 8.95 *(978-1-58117-856-2(5)*, Intervisual/Piggy Toes) Bendon, Inc.

Princess Madeline & the Dragon. 2013. (Illus.). 118p. (YA). pap. 5.99 *(978-1-62375-070-1(9)*, Caliburn Bks.) MQuills Publishing.

Prineas, Sarah. Found. Caparo, Antonio Javier, illus. 2011. (Magic Thief Ser.: 3). (ENG.). 384p. (J). (gr. 5). pap. 7.99 *(978-0-06-137595-8(0))* HarperCollins Pubs.

—Lost. Caparo, Antonio Javier, illus. 2009. (Magic Thief Ser.: 2). (ENG.). 400p. (J). (gr. 5-18). 17.99 *(978-0-06-137589-7(6))* HarperCollins Pubs.

—Lost. 2009. (Magic Thief Ser.: 2). (J). 88.75 *(978-1-4407-3133-4(0))*; 130.75 *(978-1-4407-3129-7(2))*; 1.25 *(978-1-4407-3131-0(4))*; 112.75 *(978-1-4407-3123-5(3))*; 110.75 *(978-1-4407-3125-9(X))*; 132.75 *(978-1-4407-3127-3(6))*; (SPA.). 265.75 *(978-1-4407-3124-2(1))* Recorded Bks., Inc.

—The Magic Thief. Caparo, Antonio Javier, illus. (Magic Thief Ser.: 1). (ENG.). (J). (gr. 5). 2009. 448p. pap. 7.99 *(978-0-06-137590-3(X))* 2008. 432p. 16.99 *(978-0-06-137587-3(X))* HarperCollins Pubs.

—The Magic Thief - Found. Caparo, Antonio Javier, illus. 2010. (Magic Thief Ser.: 3). (ENG.). 368p. (J). (gr. 5-18). 16.99 *(978-0-06-137593-4(4))* HarperCollins Pubs.

—The Magic Thief - Home. Caparo, Antonio Javier, illus. 2015. (Magic Thief Ser.: 4). (ENG.). 416p. (J). (gr. 3-7). pap. 7.99 *(978-0-06-220956-6(6))* HarperCollins Pubs.

—The Magic Thief - Lost. Caparo, Antonio Javier, illus. 2010. (Magic Thief Ser.: 2). (ENG.). 416p. (J). (gr. 5). pap. 7.99 *(978-0-06-137592-7(6))* HarperCollins Pubs.

—The Magic Thief: Home. Caparo, Antonio Javier, illus. 2014. (Magic Thief Ser.: 4). (ENG.). 416p. (J). (gr. 3-7). 17.99 *(978-0-06-220954-2(X))* HarperCollins Pubs.

Pritchard, G. Rosemary Sage & the Man in Black. 2005. 78p. pap. 16.95 *(978-1-4137-9809-8(8))* PublishAmerica, Inc.

Rawson, C. Wizards. 2004. (Young Reading Ser.). (Illus.). 48p. (J). (gr. 2-18). pap. 5.95 *(978-0-7945-0328-4(4)*, Usborne) EDC Publishing.

Rayment, Carolynn. Buster Batey & Mops. 2009. (Illus.). 16p. pap. 8.49 *(978-1-4490-4163-2(9))* AuthorHouse.

Reardon, A. C. Galish: The adventure of Isabelle & Eva. 2011. 168p. pap. 14.69 *(978-1-4567-7818-7(8))* AuthorHouse.

Reyes, Laurisa White. The Rock of Ivanore. 2012. (Celestine Chronicles Ser.: 1). (ENG., Illus.). 356p. (J). (gr. 2-7). 16.95 *(978-1-933718-60-6(9))* Tanglewood Pr.

Roberts, Roxanne. Angel Wings, Faery Dust & Other Magical Things: A Story about Witches, Warlocks & Such. 2011. 24p. pap. 11.50 *(978-1-61204-072-1(1)*, Eloquent Bks.) Strategic Book Publishing & Rights Agency (SBPRA).

Robinson, Robin, illus. L. Frank Baum's Wizard of Oz. 2013. (Penguin Young Readers, Level 4 Ser.). (ENG.). 48p. (J). (gr. 3-4). mass mkt. 3.99 *(978-0-448-45588-4(9)*, Penguin Young Readers) Penguin Young Readers Group.

Rodda, Emily. The Wizard of Rondo. 2009. (ENG.). 400p. (J). (gr. 3-7). 16.99 *(978-0-545-11516-2(7)*, Scholastic Pr.) Scholastic, Inc.

Rodriguez, AJ. Theodore Da Baer. 2004. 113p. pap. 19.95 *(978-1-4137-5247-2(0))* America Star Bks.

—Theodore Da Baer Ii: A New Beginning. 2006. 207p. pap. 24.95 *(978-1-4241-1125-1(0))* America Star Bks.

Rose, Christine & Rose, Ethan. Rowan of the Wood. 2008. 240p. (YA). pap. 14.95 *(978-0-9817443-1-5(1))* Dalton Publishing GBR. Dist: Midpoint Trade Bks., Inc.

Round, Suzanne. The Dragonfire Crystal. 2011. 154p. pap. *(978-0-7552-1359-7(9))* Authors OnLine, Ltd.

Rowe, W. W. The Wizard's Wayward Wand. 2010. (ENG.). 99p. (J). (gr. 3-7). pap. 12.95 *(978-0-9843754-0-0(6))* Sanctuary Publishing, Inc.

Rowling, J. K. Fantastic Beasts & Where to Find Them. 2017. (Harry Potter Ser.). (ENG.). 128p. (J). (gr. 3). 12.99 *(978-1-338-13231-1(8))* Scholastic, Inc.

—Harrius Potter et Camera Secretorum. Needham, Peter, tr. from ENG. 2007. (Harry Potter Ser.).Tr. of Harry Potter & the Chamber of Secrets. (LAT & ENG., Illus.). 288p. (YA). (gr. 5). 23.95 *(978-1-59990-067-4(X)*, 9781599900674, Bloomsbury USA Childrens) Bloomsbury Publishing USA.

—Harrius Potter et Philosophi Lapis. Needham, Peter, tr. from ENG. 2003. (Harry Potter Ser.).Tr. of Harry Potter & the Philosopher's Stone. (LAT & ENG., Illus.). 256p. (YA). (gr. 7). 29.99 *(978-1-58234-825-4(1)*, 9781582348254, Bloomsbury USA Childrens) Bloomsbury Publishing USA.

—Harry Potter à l'École des Sorciers. Menard, Jean-François, tr. from ENG. 2007. (Harry Potter Ser.: Year 1).Tr. of Harry Potter & the Sorcerer's Stone. 311p. (J). per. 14.95 *(978-2-07-061236-9(8))* Gallimard, Editions FRA. Dist: Distribooks, Inc.

—Harry Potter & the Chamber of Secrets. 2009. 9.64 *(978-0-7848-1444-4(9)*, Everbind) Marco Bk. Co.

—Harry Potter & the Chamber of Secrets. unabr. ed. 2004. (Harry Potter Ser.: Year 2). 352p. (J). (gr. 3-18). pap. 46.00 incl. audio *(978-0-8072-8207-6(3)*, S YA 137 SP, Listening Library) Random Hse. Audio Publishing Group.

—Harry Potter & the Chamber of Secrets. (Harry Potter Ser.: 2). (J). 2006. 1.25 *(978-1-4193-8079-2(6))* 2003. 78.75 *(978-1-4025-6698-1(0))* Recorded Bks., Inc.

—Harry Potter & the Chamber of Secrets. (Harry Potter Ser.: Year 2). (RUS., Illus.). 28.95 *(978-5-8451-0947-7(7))* Rosmen-Izdat RUS. Dist: Distribooks, Inc.

—Harry Potter & the Chamber of Secrets. Kay, Jim, illus. 2016. (Harry Potter Ser.: 2). (ENG.). 272p. (J). (gr. 3). 39.99 *(978-0-545-79132-8(4))*; 275.00 *(978-1-338-11986-2(9))* Scholastic, Inc. (Levine, Arthur A. Bks.).

—Harry Potter & the Chamber of Secrets. l.t. ed. 2003. (Harry Potter Ser.: Year 2). (ENG.). 466p. pap. 13.95 *(978-1-59413-001-4(9))* Thorndike Pr.

—Harry Potter & the Chamber of Secrets. 2013. (Harry Potter (Kazu Kibuishi Illustrations) Ser.: 2). lib. bdg. 24.50 *(978-0-606-32346-8(5)*, Turtleback) Turtleback Bks.

—Harry Potter & the Deathly Hallows. (Illus.). 2008. 832p. pap. *(978-0-7475-9586-1(0))* 2007. (ENG., 608p. *(978-0-7475-9106-1(7))* Bloomsbury Publishing Plc.

—Harry Potter & the Deathly Hallows. braille ed. 2007. (Harry Potter Ser.: Year 7). (J). (gr. 4-7). 34.99 *(978-0-939173-57-0(3))* National Braille Pr.

—Harry Potter & the Deathly Hallows. 2010. 25.00 *(978-1-60686-882-9(9))* Perfection Learning Corp.

—Harry Potter & the Deathly Hallows, 17 vols. 2007. (Harry Potter Ser.: 7). (YA). 129.79 *(978-1-4281-6654-7(8))*; 131.75 *(978-1-4281-6652-3(1))* Recorded Bks., Inc.

—Harry Potter & the Deathly Hallows. GrandPré, Mary, illus. (Harry Potter Ser.: 7). (ENG.). (J). 2009. 784p. (gr. 4-7). pap. 14.99 *(978-0-545-13970-0(8)*, Levine, Arthur A. Bks.) 2007. 784p. (gr. 5-9). 34.99 *(978-0-545-01022-1(5))* 2007. 816p. (gr. 4-7). 65.00 *(978-0-545-02937-7(6)*, Levine, Arthur A. Bks.) Scholastic, Inc.

—Harry Potter & the Deathly Hallows. l.t. ed. 2009. (ENG.). 970p. pap. 14.95 *(978-1-59413-355-8(7)*, Large Print Pr.) 2007. (Harry Potter Ser.: Year 7). (Illus.). 969p. (J). (gr. 4-7). 34.95 *(978-0-7862-9665-1(8))* Thorndike Pr.

—Harry Potter & the Deathly Hallows. (Harry Potter (Kazu Kibuishi Illustrations) Ser.: 7). 2013. lib. bdg. 29.40 *(978-0-606-32351-2(1))* 2009. lib. bdg. 26.95 *(978-0-606-00420-6(3))* Turtleback Bks. (Turtleback).

—Harry Potter & the Deathly Hallows. Bar-hillel, Gili, tr. from ENG. 2007. (Harry Potter Ser.: Year 7). (HEB., Illus.). 568p. (J). (gr. 4-7). pap. *(978-965-482-635-8(6))* Yediot Aharonot Bks., Miscal.

—Harry Potter & the Goblet of Fire. 2009. 10.24 *(978-0-7848-1587-8(9)*, Everbind) Marco Bk. Co.

—Harry Potter & the Goblet of Fire. (Harry Potter Ser.: 4). (J). 2006. 1.25 *(978-1-4193-8531-5(3))* 2003. 101.75 *(978-1-4025-6702-5(2))* Recorded Bks., Inc.

—Harry Potter & the Goblet of Fire. GrandPré, Mary, illus. l.t. ed. 2003. (Harry Potter Ser.: Vol. 4). (ENG.). 936p. pap. 11.66 *(978-1-59413-003-8(5))* Thorndike Pr.

—Harry Potter & the Goblet of Fire. 2013. (Harry Potter (Kazu Kibuishi Illustrations) Ser.: 4). lib. bdg. 26.95 *(978-0-606-32348-2(1)*, Turtleback) Turtleback Bks.

—Harry Potter & the Half-Blood Prince. 2005. (ENG.). cd-rom *(978-0-7475-8258-8(0))* Bloomsbury Publishing Plc.

—Harry Potter & the Half-Blood Prince, 9 vols. braille ed. 2005. (Harry Potter Ser.: Year 6). (J). (gr. 4-8). 29.99 *(978-0-939173-39-6(5)*, HALF) National Braille Pr.

—Harry Potter & the Half-Blood Prince. GrandPré, Mary, illus. 2006. (Harry Potter Ser.: Year 6). 652p. (gr. 4-8). 23.00 *(978-0-7569-6765-9(1))* Perfection Learning Corp.

—Harry Potter & the Half-Blood Prince. (Harry Potter Ser.: 6). (J). 2007. 1.25 *(978-1-4193-5430-4(2))* 2006. 110.75 *(978-1-4193-5436-6(1))* 2006. 193.75 *(978-1-4193-5432-8(9))* 2005. 113.75 *(978-1-4193-5434-2(5))* Recorded Bks., Inc.

—Harry Potter & the Half-Blood Prince. GrandPré, Mary, illus. (Harry Potter Ser.: 6). (ENG.). 672p. (J). (gr. 4-8). 2005. 29.99 *(978-0-439-78454-2(9))* 2006. reprint ed. per. 12.99 *(978-0-439-78596-9(0))* Scholastic, Inc. (Levine, Arthur A. Bks.).

—Harry Potter & the Half-Blood Prince. (Illus.). (J). (gr. 4-7). 2007. (ENG.). 832p. per. 14.95 *(978-1-59413-221-6(6))* 2005. (Harry Potter Ser.: Year 6). 831p. 29.95 *(978-0-7862-7745-2(9))* Thorndike Pr. (Large Print Pr.).

—Harry Potter & the Half-Blood Prince. 2013. (Harry Potter (Kazu Kibuishi Illustrations) Ser.: 6). lib. bdg. 26.95 *(978-0-606-32350-5(3)*, Turtleback) Turtleback Bks.

—Harry Potter & the Half Blood Prince - Chinese Language. 2005. (Harry Potter Ser.: Year 6). (CHI.). 496p. (YA). (gr. 4-8). pap. 28.95 *(978-7-02-005323-0(8)*, HAP06) People's Literature Publishing Hse. CHN. Dist: Chinasprout, Inc.

—Harry Potter & the Order of the Phoenix. (ENG.). 768p. (J). (gr. 6-10). pap. *(978-0-7475-6107-1(9))* Bloomsbury Publishing Plc.

—Harry Potter & the Order of the Phoenix. 2008. *(978-977-14-2697-4(4))* Nahdat Misr Bkshop for Printing and Pubs.

—Harry Potter & the Order of the Phoenix, 13 vols. braille ed. 2003. (Harry Potter Ser.: Year 5). (YA). 29.99 *(978-0-939173-38-9(7))* National Braille Pr.

—Harry Potter & the Order of the Phoenix. 2003. (Harry Potter Ser.: Year 5). (CHI.). 575p. (YA). pap. 26.95 *(978-7-02-004327-9(5)*, HAP05) People's Literature Publishing Hse. CHN. Dist: Chinasprout, Inc.

—Harry Potter & the Order of the Phoenix. 2004. (Harry Potter Ser.). 870p. (gr. 4-6). 16.49 *(978-0-7569-4163-5(6))* Perfection Learning Corp.

—Harry Potter & the Order of the Phoenix. 2003. (ENG.). 768p. *(978-1-55192-570-7(2))* Raincoast Bk. Distribution.

—Harry Potter & the Order of the Phoenix. GrandPré, Mary, illus. (Harry Potter Ser.: 5). (ENG.). (J). (gr. 3-7). 2004. 896p. mass mkt. 12.99 *(978-0-439-35807-1(8)*, Scholastic Paperbacks) 2003. 870p. 29.99 *(978-0-439-35806-4(X))* Scholastic, Inc.

—Harry Potter & the Order of the Phoenix. l.t. ed. 2003. (Harry Potter Ser.: Year 5). 1093p. 29.95 *(978-0-7862-5778-2(4)*, Large Print Pr.) Thorndike Pr.

—Harry Potter & the Order of the Phoenix. GrandPré, Mary, illus. l.t. ed. 2003. (Thorndike Young Adult Ser.). (ENG.). 1232p. (J). (gr. 4-7). per. 14.95 *(978-1-59413-112-7(0)*, Large Print Pr.) Thorndike Pr.

—Harry Potter & the Order of the Phoenix. (Harry Potter (Kazu Kibuishi Illustrations) Ser.: 5). 2013. lib. bdg. 26.95 *(978-0-606-32349-9(X))* 2004. lib. bdg. 24.50 *(978-0-613-99916-8(9))* Turtleback Bks. (Turtleback).

—Harry Potter & the Philosopher's Stone. 2014. (ENG., Illus.). 352p. *(978-1-4088-5589-8(5))* Bloomsbury Publishing Plc.

—Harry Potter & the Prisoner of Azkaban. 2009. 9.64 *(978-0-7848-1542-7(9)*, Everbind) Marco Bk. Co.

—Harry Potter & the Prisoner of Azkaban. 2005. (Harry Potter Ser.: Year 3). (CHI.). 260p. (YA). pap. 16.95 *(978-7-02-003345-4(8)*, HAP03) People's Literature Publishing Hse. CHN. Dist: Chinasprout, Inc.

—Harry Potter & the Prisoner of Azkaban, 10 vols. 2003. (Harry Potter Ser.: 3). (J). 84.75 *(978-1-4025-6700-1(6))* Recorded Bks., Inc.

—Harry Potter & the Prisoner of Azkaban. l.t. ed. 2003. (Harry Potter Ser.: Year 3). (ENG.). 592p. pap. 13.95 *(978-1-59413-002-1(7)*, Large Print Pr.) Thorndike Pr.

—Harry Potter & the Prisoner of Azkaban. 2013. (Harry Potter (Kazu Kibuishi Illustrations) Ser.: 3). lib. bdg. 24.50 *(978-0-606-32347-5(3)*, Turtleback) Turtleback Bks.

—Harry Potter & the Sorcerer's Stone. 2014. (ENG.). lthr. 79.00 *(978-1-62715-772-8(7))* Leatherbound Bestsellers.

—Harry Potter & the Sorcerer's Stone. 2009. 8.44 *(978-0-7848-2438-2(X))*; 10.84 *(978-0-7848-1357-7(4))* Marco Bk. Co. (Everbind).

—Harry Potter & the Sorcerer's Stone. 2003. (Harry Potter Ser.: Year 1). (CHI.). 191p. (YA). pap. 14.95 *(978-7-02-003343-0(1)*, HAP01) People's Literature Publishing Hse. CHN. Dist: Chinasprout, Inc.

—Harry Potter & the Sorcerer's Stone. (Harry Potter Ser.: 1). (J). 2004. 1.25 *(978-1-4025-6757-5(X))* 2003. 80.75 *(978-1-4025-6696-7(4))* Recorded Bks., Inc.

—Harry Potter & the Sorcerer's Stone. Kay, Jim, illus. 2015. (Harry Potter Ser.: 1). (ENG.). 256p. (J). (gr. 3). 39.99 *(978-0-545-79035-2(2)*, Levine, Arthur A. Bks.) Scholastic, Inc.

—Harry Potter & the Sorcerer's Stone, Bk. 1. 2013. (Harry Potter Ser.: 1). (ENG., Illus.). 336p. (J). (gr. 4). pap. 12.99 *(978-0-545-58288-9(1))* Scholastic, Inc.

—Harry Potter & the Sorcerer's Stone. 2013. (Harry Potter (Kazu Kibuishi Illustrations) Ser.: 1). lib. bdg. 24.50 *(978-0-606-32345-1(7)*, Turtleback) Turtleback Bks.

—Harry Potter e a Camara Secreta. (Harry Potter Ser.: Year 2).Tr. of Harry Potter & the Chamber of Secrets. (POR.). pap. 28.95 *(978-85-325-1166-9(X))* Rocco, Editora, Ltda BRA. Dist: Distribooks, Inc.

—Harry Potter e a Pedra Filosofal. (Harry Potter Ser.: Year 1).Tr. of Harry Potter & the Philospher's Stone. (POR.). pap. 28.95 *(978-85-325-1101-0(5))* Rocco, Editora, Ltda BRA. Dist: Distribooks, Inc.

—Harry Potter e a Prisioneiro de Azkaban. (Harry Potter Ser.: Year 3).Tr. of Harry Potter & the Prisioner of Azkaban. (POR.). pap. 29.95 *(978-85-325-1206-2(2))* Rocco, Editora, Ltda BRA. Dist: Distribooks, Inc.

—Harry Potter e il Prigioniero di Azkaban. (Harry Potter Ser.: Year 3).Tr. of Harry Potter & the Prisioner of Azkaban. (ITA.). pap. 32.95 *(978-88-7782-852-1(8))* Salani ITA. Dist: Distribooks, Inc.

—Harry Potter e o Cálice de Fogo. (Harry Potter Ser.: Year 4).Tr. of Harry Potter & the Goblet of Fire. (POR.). pap. 38.95 *(978-85-325-1252-9(6))* Rocco, Editora, Ltda BRA. Dist: Distribooks, Inc.

—Harry Potter et la Coupe de Feu. (Harry Potter Ser.: Year 4).Tr. of Harry Potter & the Goblet of Fire. (FRE., Illus.). 766p. pap. 19.95 *(978-2-07-054351-9(X))* Gallimard, Editions FRA. Dist: Distribooks, Inc.

—Harry Potter y el Prisionero de Azkaban. 2004. (Harry Potter Ser.: Year 3).Tr. of Harry Potter & the Prisioner of Azkaban. (SPA., Illus.). 360p. (gr. 3-18). 17.95 *(978-84-7888-519-0(6)*, SAL1889) Emece Editores ESP. Dist: Lectorum Pubns., Inc.

—Harry Potter y el Prisionero de Azkaban. 2015. (Harry Potter Spanish Ser.: 3).Tr. of Harry Potter & the Prisioner of Azkaban. (SPA.). (gr. 3-6). lib. bdg. 28.10 *(978-0-613-35958-0(5)*, Turtleback) Turtleback Bks.

—Harry Potter y la Camara Secreta. 2004. (Harry Potter Ser.: Year 2).Tr. of Harry Potter & the Chamber of Secrets. (SPA., Illus.). 288p. (YA). (gr. 3-18). 15.95 *(978-84-7888-495-7(5)*, SAL4595) Emece Editores ESP. Dist: Lectorum Pubns., Inc.

—Harry Potter y la Piedra Filosofal. 2004. (Harry Potter Ser.: Year 1).Tr. of Harry Potter & the Sorcerer's Stone. (SPA., Illus.). 256p. (YA). (gr. 7-18). 15.95 *(978-84-7888-445-2(9)*, SAL2819) Emece Editores ESP. Dist: Lectorum Pubns., Inc.

—The Tales of Beedle the Bard. GrandPré, Mary, illus. 2008. (ENG.). 128p. *(978-0-7475-9987-6(4))* Bloomsbury Publishing Plc.

—The Tales of Beedle the Bard. GrandPré, Mary, illus. collector's ed. 2008. 184p. *(978-0-9560109-0-2(3))* Children's High Level Group.

—The Tales of Beedle the Bard. 2017. (Harry Potter Ser.). (ENG.). 128p. (J). (gr. 3-3). 12.99 *(978-1-338-12568-9(0)*, Levine, Arthur A. Bks.) Scholastic, Inc.

—The Tales of Beedle the Bard. 2017. (ENG.). (J). (gr. 3). lib. bdg. 24.50 ***(978-0-606-39695-0(0))*** Turtleback Bks.

Rowling, J. K. & Scholastic, Inc. Staff. Harry Potter. 2007. (Harry Potter Ser.: Years 1-7). (ENG.). (J). (gr. 3-7). 205.93 *(978-0-545-04425-7(1)*, Levine, Arthur A. Bks.) Scholastic, Inc.

Rowntree, G. M. Wizards Spell Magic in the Legends of Mere Leander. 2010. 291p. pap. 32.50 *(978-1-4452-6812-5(4))* Lulu Pr., Inc.

—Wizards Spell Magic in the Legends of Mere Leander - US Trade Size. 2010. 291p. pap. 24.95 *(978-1-4452-9266-3(1))* Lulu Pr., Inc.

Ruth, Nick. The Dark Dreamweaver. Concannon, Sue, illus. 2007. (Remin Chronicles: 1). (ENG.). 256p. (J). (gr. 4-7). per. 11.95 *(978-0-9745603-5-9(9))* Imaginator Pr.

Ryan, Brittney. The Legend of Holly Claus. Long, Laurel, illus. 2004. (Julie Andrews Collection). 544p. (J). (gr. 4-18). 16.99 *(978-0-06-058511-2(0))*; lib. bdg. 17.89 *(978-0-06-058514-3(5))* HarperCollins Pubs. (Julie Andrews Collection).

Ryan, Carrie & Davis, John Parke. The Map to Everywhere. 2014. (Map to Everywhere Ser.: Bk. 1). (ENG., Illus.). 448p. (J). (gr. 3-7). 17.00 *(978-0-316-24077-2(X))* Little Brown & Co.

—The Map to Everywhere. 2015. (Map to Everywhere Ser.: 1). (J). lib. bdg. 18.45 *(978-0-606-37521-4(X))* Turtleback Bks.

Sage, Angie. Darke. Zug, Mark, illus. (Septimus Heap Ser.: 6). 656p. (J). (gr. 4). 2012. (ENG.). pap. 7.99 *(978-0-06-124244-1(6))* 2011. lib. bdg. 18.89 *(978-0-06-124243-4(8))*Bk. 6. 2011. (ENG.). 17.99 *(978-0-06-124242-7(X))* HarperCollins Pubs. (Tegen, Katherine Bks).

—Darke, 12 vols. (Septimus Heap Ser.: 6). (J). 297.75 *(978-1-4498-6217-6(9))*; 131.75 *(978-1-4498-6218-3(7))*; 1.25 *(978-1-4498-6226-8(8))*; 2013. 92.75 *(978-1-4498-6225-1(X))*; 2011. 133.75 *(978-1-4498-6220-6(9))*; 2011. 131.75 *(978-1-4498-6222-0(5))* Recorded Bks., Inc.

—Darke. Zug, Mark, illus. 2012. (Septimus Heap Ser.: 6). (J). lib. bdg. 18.40 (978-0-606-26264-4(4), Turtleback) Turtleback Bks.

—Flyte. Zug, Mark, illus. (Septimus Heap Ser.: 2). (ENG.). 544p. (J). (gr. 4-7). 2007. pap. 7.99 (978-0-06-057736-0(3)) 2006. 17.99 (978-0-06-057734-6(7)) HarperCollins Pubs. (Tegen, Katherine Bks).

—Flyte. (Septimus Heap Ser.: 2). (J). 2009. 84.49 (978-1-4361-5831-2(1)) 2008. 1.25 (978-1-4193-9383-9(9)) 2006. 114.75 (978-1-4193-9386-0(3)) 2006. 133.75 (978-1-4193-9390-7(1)) 2006. 131.75 (978-1-4193-9392-1(8)) 2006. 111.75 (978-1-4193-9388-4(X)) 2006. 282.75 (978-1-4193-9387-7(1)) Recorded Bks., Inc.

—Fyre. Zug, Mark, illus. 2013. (J). (Septimus Heap Ser.: 7). (ENG.). 720p. (gr. 3-7). 17.99 (978-0-06-124245-8(4), Tegen, Katherine Bks); 702p. (978-0-06-224697-4(6)) HarperCollins Pubs.

—Fyre. 2014. (Septimus Heap Ser.: 7). (J). lib. bdg. 18.40 (978-0-606-35067-9(5), Turtleback) Turtleback Bks.

—Magyk. Zug, Mark, illus. (Septimus Heap Ser.: 1). (J). (gr. 4-18). 2005. (ENG.). 576p. 17.99 (978-0-06-057731-5(2)) 2005. 576p. lib. bdg. 18.89 (978-0-06-057732-2(0)) 2006. (ENG.). 608p. reprint ed. pap. 7.99 (978-0-06-057733-9(9)) HarperCollins Pubs. (Tegen, Katherine Bks).

—Magyk. Zug, Mark, illus. 2007. (Septimus Heap Ser.: Bk. 1). 564p. (gr. 4-7). 18.00 (978-0-7569-7760-3(6)) Perfection Learning Corp.

—Magyk. (Septimus Heap Ser.: 1). (J). 2008. 79.75 (978-1-4361-0584-2(6)) 2007. 1.25 (978-1-4193-2619-6(8)) 2006. 123.75 (978-1-4193-3807-6(2)) 2005. 106.75 (978-1-4193-2622-6(8)) 2005. 126.75 (978-1-4193-3805-2(6)) 2005. 103.75 (978-1-4193-2624-0(4)) Recorded Bks., Inc.

—Magyk. 2006. (Septimus Heap Ser.: 1). (J). lib. bdg. 18.40 (978-1-4177-3321-7(7), Turtleback) Turtleback Bks.

—Physik. Zug, Mark, illus. (Septimus Heap Ser.: 3). (ENG.). (J). (gr. 4-7). 2007. 560p. 17.99 (978-0-06-057737-7(1))Bk. 3. 2008. 576p. pap. 7.99 (978-0-06-057739-1(8)) HarperCollins Pubs. (Tegen, Katherine Bks).

—Physik, 11 vols. 2007. (Septimus Heap Ser.: 3). (J). 113.75 (978-1-4281-4576-4(1)); 133.75 (978-1-4281-4580-1(X)); (SPA.). 131.75 (978-1-4281-4582-5(6)); 277.75 (978-1-4281-4577-1(X)); 111.75 (978-1-4281-4578-8(8)); 1.25 (978-1-4281-4573-3(7)) Recorded Bks., Inc.

—Physik. 2008. (Septimus Heap Ser.: 3). (J). lib. bdg. 18.40 (978-1-4178-1565-4(5), Turtleback) Turtleback Bks.

—Queste. Zug, Mark, illus. (Septimus Heap Ser.: 4). (ENG.). (J). (gr. 4). 2009. 624p. pap. 7.99 (978-0-06-088209-9(3)) 2008. 608p. 17.99 (978-0-06-088207-5(7)) HarperCollins Pubs. (Tegen, Katherine Bks).

—Queste. Zug, Mark, illus. 2009. (Septimus Heap Ser.: 4). 596p. (J). lib. bdg. 18.40 (978-0-606-02607-9(X), Turtleback) Turtleback Bks.

—Sandrider. 2015. (World of Septimus Heap Ser.: 2). (ENG., Illus.). 480p. (J). (gr. 3-7). 17.99 (978-0-06-227248-5(9), Tegen, Katherine Bks) HarperCollins Pubs.

—Septimus Heap, Set. Zug, Mark, illus. 2007. (Septimus Heap Ser.: Bks. 1-2). (J). (gr. 4). pap. 15.99 (978-0-06-136195-1(X), Tegen, Katherine Bks) HarperCollins Pubs.

—Septimus Heap - Todhunter Moon. Zug, Mark, illus. 2014. (World of Septimus Heap Ser.: 1). (ENG.). 480p. (J). (gr. 3-7). 17.99 (978-0-06-227245-4(4), Tegen, Katherine Bks) HarperCollins Pubs.

—Syren. Zug, Mark, illus. (Septimus Heap Ser.: 5). (J). (gr. 4). 2011. (ENG.). 656p. pap. 7.99 (978-0-06-088212-9(3)) 2009. 640p. lib. bdg. 18.89 (978-0-06-088211-2(5)) 2009. (ENG.). 640p. 17.99 (978-0-06-088210-5(7)) HarperCollins Pubs. (Tegen, Katherine Bks).

—Todhunter Moon: Starchaser. Zug, Mark, illus. 2016. (World of Septimus Heap Ser.: 3). 496p. (J). (gr. 3-7). 17.99 (978-0-06-227251-5(9), Tegen, Katherine Bks) HarperCollins Pubs.

Santillo, LuAnn. Look at Me. Santillo, LuAnn, ed. 2003. (Half-Pint Kids Readers Ser.). (Illus.). 7p. (J). (gr. -1-1). pap. 1.00 (978-1-59256-052-3(0)) Half-Pint Kids, Inc.

Santore, Charles, illus. The Wizard of Oz Coloring Book. 2017. (ENG.). 96p. (J). pap. 10.99 **(978-1-60433-706-8(0)**, Applesauce Pr.) Cider Mill Pr. Bk. Pubs., LLC.

Sarrasin, Alex. The Guardians of Neoegypti: Book One. 2007. 300p. per. 18.95 (978-0-595-45710-6(X)) iUniverse, Inc.

Shapiro D., Brian. Plaquetooth. 2008. 28p. pap. 13.99 (978-1-4343-8913-8(8)) AuthorHouse.

Shaw, Stephanie. Schnitzel: A Cautionary Tale for Lazy Louts. Barry, Kevin, illus. 2016. (ENG.). 32p. (J). (gr. k-3). 16.99 (978-1-58536-957-7(8), 204104) Sleeping Bear Pr.

Shi, Charleston. The Quest of the Phoenix: Book 1, the Phoenix & the Yeti. 2009. 168p. pap. 14.95 (978-1-60844-173-0(3)) Dog Ear Publishing, LLC.

—The Quest of the Phoenix: Book Two, Storm of the Kraken. 2010. 180p. pap. 14.95 (978-1-60844-352-9(3)) Dog Ear Publishing, LLC.

Shue, Jenna. Animal Island. Herzog, Inge, illus. 2005. 27p. (J). (gr. -1-3). per. 14.95 (978-1-4259-0039-7(9)) AuthorHouse.

Simon, Elizabeth. Tyler Adams & the Adventures of Bravura: the First Quest. 2009. 49p. pap. 19.95 (978-0-557-06290-4(X)) Lulu Pr., Inc.

Simon, Morris. Wizards Keep. 2007. 124p. pap. 4.99 (978-1-931567-67-1(0)) Margaret Weis Productions, Ltd.

Smith, M. a. & Smith, M. A. A Boy & His Wizard. Freeland, Devon & Contreras-Freeland, Gina, illus. 2009. 32p. pap. 8.95 (978-1-60076-152-2(6)) StoneGarden.net Publishing.

Sonneborn, Scott. Prisoner of the Ring, 1 vol. Schoening, Dan, illus. 2011. (Green Lantern Ser.). (ENG.). 56p. (gr. 2-3). pap. 4.95 (978-1-4342-3410-0(X)); lib. bdg. 26.65 (978-1-4342-2624-2(7)) Stone Arch Bks. (DC Super Heroes).

Speakman, Peter & Galvin, Michael M. B. Finders Keepers. 2017. (Rebels of the Lamp Ser.). (ENG.). 288p. (J). (gr. 5-9). 16.99 (978-1-4231-8040-1(2)) Disney Pr.

St-Onge, Donna Na-Tasa Katherine. The Eye of Isis, 1 vol. 2009. 155p. pap. 24.95 (978-1-60836-986-7(2)) America Star Bks.

St-Onge, Julie-Ann. Passage to Fairywell. 2008. 80p. pap. 19.95 (978-1-60441-172-0(4)) America Star Bks.

Stanek, Robert, pseud. The Kingdoms & the Elves of the Reaches: Signature, Keeper Martin's Tales, Bk. 1. 2007. (Illus.). 240p. (YA). 35.00 (978-1-57545-128-2(X)) RP Media.

—The Kingdoms & the Elves of the Reaches II: Keeper Martin's Tales, Book 2. 2008. (Keeper Martin's Tales (Playaway) Ser.). (J). 54.99 (978-1-60514-649-2(8)) Findaway World, LLC.

—The Kingdoms & the Elves of the Reaches II: Signature, Keeper Martin's Tales, Bk. 2. 2007. (Illus.). 244p. (J). (gr. 4-7). 35.00 (978-1-57545-129-9(8)) RP Media.

—The Kingdoms & the Elves of the Reaches III: Signature, Keeper Martin's Tales, Bk. 3. 2008. (Illus.). 244p. (J). (gr. 4-7). 35.00 (978-1-57545-130-5(1)) RP Media.

Stanley, P. "Olivia". The Dreadful Noises of Landoshar. 2008. 44p. pap. 12.26 (978-0-557-02381-3(5)) Lulu Pr., Inc.

Stansberry, Don. Inky & the Missing Gold. 2007. (Illus.). 128p. (YA). per. 15.95 (978-0-929915-10-4(0), Publisher Page) Headline Bks., Inc.

Stevermer, Caroline. Magic below Stairs. 2011. (ENG.). 208p. (J). (gr. 3-7). 6.99 (978-0-14-241871-0(4), Puffin Books) Penguin Young Readers Group.

Stilton, Geronimo & Dami, Elisabetta. The Enchanted Charms: The Seventh Adventure in the Kingdom of Fantasy. Barozzi, Danilo, illus. 2015. (ENG.). 320p. (J). (gr. 2-5). 14.99 (978-0-545-74615-1(9)) Scholastic, Inc.

Stine, R. L. Wizard of Ooze. 2010. (Goosebumps Horrorland Ser.: 17). (ENG.). 160p. (J). (gr. 3-7). pap. 6.99 (978-0-545-16198-5(3), Scholastic Paperbacks) Scholastic, Inc.

Strickland, Brad. The House Where Nobody Lived. 2006. (Lewis Barnavelt Ser.). (ENG.). 176p. (J). (gr. 3-7). 16.99 (978-0-8037-3148-6(5), Dial Bks) Penguin Young Readers Group.

Strings Magazine Staff. The Wizard's Den: Spellbinding Stories of Magic & Magicians. Haining, Peter, ed. 2003. (ENG., Illus.). 320p. (J). (gr. 3-7). 22.95 (978-0-285-63628-6(6)) Souvenir Pr. Ltd. GBR. Dist: Independent Pubs. Group.

Stroud, Jonathan. The Amulet of Samarkand, Bk. 1. 2003. (Bartimaeus Novel Ser.). (ENG., Illus.). 464p. (J). (gr. 5-9). 17.99 (978-0-7868-1859-4(X)) Disney Publishing Worldwide.

—Bartimaeus, 3 vols., Set. 2010. (ENG.). 1552p. (J). (gr. 5-6). pap. 24.99 (978-1-4231-3682-8(9)) Disney Pr.

Sturm, James, et al. Hocus Focus. 2017. (Adventures in Cartooning Ser.). (ENG., Illus.). 40p. (J). 14.99 (978-1-59643-654-1(9), 9781596436541, First Second Bks.) Roaring Brook Pr.

Sutton, S. A. A Hero for Quale. 2009. 72p. pap. 9.99 (978-1-60860-189-9(7), Strategic Bk. Publishing) Strategic Book Publishing & Rights Agency (SBPRA).

Sykes, Julie. Beware the Werepup & Other Stories. Reed, Nathan, illus. unabr. ed. 2014. (ENG.). 384p. (J). (gr. 2-4). pap. 8.99 (978-1-4472-1961-3(9)) Pan Macmillan GBR. Dist: Independent Pubs. Group.

Terry, Frederick H. Gingerbread for All Seasons. 2009. 32p. pap. 14.95 (978-1-4490-4476-3(X)) AuthorHouse.

Terry Lowey's Children's Stories Staff. The Secret of the Wizard's Wand. 2007. (Illus.). 24p. (J). 18.95 (978-0-9792695-0-9(4)) Terry Lowey's Children's Stories, LLC.

Thomas, Sherry. The Immortal Heights. 2015. (Elemental Trilogy Ser.: 3). (ENG.). 448p. (YA). (gr. 9). 17.99 (978-0-06-220735-7(0)) HarperCollins Pubs.

—The Perilous Sea. 2015. (Elemental Trilogy Ser.: 2). (ENG.). 448p. (YA). (gr. 9). pap. 9.99 (978-0-06-220733-3(4)) HarperCollins Pubs.

Thompson, Colin. The Floods #2: School Plot. Scrambly, Crab, illus. 2008. (Floods Ser.). (J). (ENG.). 224p. 15.99 (978-0-06-113861-4(4)); 256p. lib. bdg. 16.89 (978-0-06-113855-3(X)) HarperCollins Pubs.

—The Floods Family Files. Thompson, Colin, illus. 2012. (Floods Ser.: 1). (ENG., Illus.). 32p. (J). (gr. 4-7). pap. 12.99 (978-1-86471-942-0(7)) Random Hse. Australia AUS. Dist: Independent Pubs. Group.

—Good Neighbors. Scrambly, Crab, illus. 2008. (Floods Ser.: No. 1). 214p. (J). (gr. 3-7). 15.99 (978-0-06-113196-7(2)) HarperCollins Pubs.

Thompson, Paul B. The Battle for the Brightstone: Book III of the Brightstone Saga. 2013. (Brightstone Saga Ser.). 176p. (J). 18.95 (978-0-7660-3984-1(6)) Enslow Pubs., Inc.

Thompson, Ruth Plumly. The Enchanted Island of Oz. 2006. (J). 24.95 (978-1-930764-10-1(3)) International Wizard of Oz Club, The.

—The Wonder Book. 2006. (J). 24.95 (978-1-930764-15-6(4)) International Wizard of Oz Club, The.

—Yankee in Oz. 2006. (J). 24.95 (978-1-930764-13-2(8)) International Wizard of Oz Club, The.

Tillworth, Mary. Dragon in the School (Dora & Friends) Goddard, Brenda & Haskett, Dan, illus. 2015. (Little Golden Book Ser.). (ENG.). 24p. (J). (gr. -1-2). 4.99 (978-0-553-52089-7(X), Golden Bks.) Random Hse. Children's Bks.

Titelman, Becky. The Wonky Witch & the Witching Well. 2009. 364p. pap. 19.99 (978-1-4490-2673-8(7)) AuthorHouse.

Toby Forward Staff. Doubleborn. 2015. (Dragonborn Ser.: 3). (ENG.). 336p. (YA). (gr. 5-8). 16.99 (978-1-61963-528-9(3), 9781619635289, Bloomsbury USA Childrens) Bloomsbury Publishing USA.

—Fireborn. 2013. (Dragonborn Ser.: 2). (ENG.). 432p. (YA). (gr. 5-6). 16.99 (978-1-59990-889-2(1), 9781599908892, Bloomsbury USA Childrens) Bloomsbury Publishing USA.

Tulien, Sean. The Not-So-Evil Wizard. Cunyat, Pol, illus. 2016. (Thud & Blunder Ser.). (ENG.). 56p. (gr. 2-4). pap. 4.95 (978-1-4965-3225-1(2)); lib. bdg. 23.99 (978-1-4965-3221-3(X)) Stone Arch Bks.

Vande Velde, Vivian. Wizard at Work. 2004. (ENG., Illus.). 144p. (J). (gr. 5-7). pap. 10.95 (978-0-15-205309-3(3)) Houghton Mifflin Harcourt Publishing Co.

Vande Velde, Vivian & Bash, Barbara. The Book of Mordred. 2007. (ENG.). 352p. (YA). (gr. 7-12). pap. 8.99 (978-0-618-80916-5(3)) Houghton Mifflin Harcourt Publishing Co.

Wallace Ii, James C. & Wallace, Amanda D. The Emerald Slippers of Oz. 2013. 156p. pap. 14.99 (978-0-578-12511-4(0)) Scientia Est Vox Pr.

Wasson, Christopher. Quest for Adlaremzee Molair Nopeeoh. 2003. 120p. pap. 19.95 (978-1-4137-0117-3(5)) America Star Bks.

Waterfield, Susan. Spunkie's Magical Garden. 2012. 32p. pap. 14.95 (978-1-257-77576-7(6)) Lulu Pr., Inc.

West, Tracey. Flight of the Moon Dragon. Jones, Damien, illus. 2016. (Dragon Masters Ser.: 6). (ENG.). 96p. (J). (gr. 1-3). pap. 4.99 (978-0-545-91392-8(6)) Scholastic, Inc.

—Power of the Fire Dragon. Howells, Graham, illus. 2015. (Dragon Masters Ser.: No. 4). (ENG.). 96p. (J). (gr. 1-3). pap. 4.99 (978-0-545-64631-4(6)) Scholastic, Inc.

—Rise of the Earth Dragon. Howells, Graham, illus. 2014. (Dragon Masters Ser.: 1). (ENG.). 96p. (J). (gr. 1-3). 15.99 (978-0-545-64624-6(3)); pap. 4.99 (978-0-545-64623-9(5)) Scholastic, Inc.

—Rise of the Earth Dragon. 2014. (Dragon Masters Ser.: 1). lib. bdg. 14.75 (978-0-606-36050-0(6)) Turtleback Bks.

—Roar of the Thunder Dragon: a Branches Book. Jones, Damien, illus. 2017. (Dragon Masters Ser.: 8). (ENG.). 96p. (J). (gr. 1-3). lib. bdg. 15.99 **(978-1-338-04293-1(9))**; pap. 4.99 **(978-1-338-04292-4(0))** Scholastic, Inc.

—Saving the Sun Dragon. Howells, Graham & Jones, Damien, illus. 2014. (Dragon Masters Ser.: 2). (ENG.). 96p. (J). (gr. 1-3). 15.99 (978-0-545-64626-0(X)); pap. 4.99 (978-0-545-64625-3(1)) Scholastic, Inc.

—Saving the Sun Dragon. 2014. (Dragon Masters Ser.: 2). lib. bdg. 14.75 (978-0-606-36051-7(4)) Turtleback Bks.

—Search for the Lightning Dragon: a Branches Book (Dragon Masters #7) Jones, Damien, illus. 2017. (Dragon Masters Ser.: 7). (ENG.). 96p. (J). (gr. 1-3). pap. 4.99 (978-1-338-04288-7(2)) Scholastic, Inc.

—Secret of the Water Dragon. Howells, Graham & Jones, Damien, illus. 2015. (Dragon Masters Ser.: 3). (ENG.). 96p. (J). (gr. 1-3). pap. 4.99 (978-0-545-64628-4(6)) Scholastic, Inc.

Wexler, Django. The Forbidden Library. 2015. (ENG., Illus.). 400p. (J). (gr. 5). 8.99 (978-0-14-242681-4(4), Puffin Books) Penguin Young Readers Group.

—The Mad Apprentice. Jansson, Alexander, illus. 2015. (Forbidden Library). (ENG.). 352p. (J). (gr. 5). 16.99 (978-0-8037-3976-5(1), Kathy Dawson Books) Penguin Young Readers Group.

Whisp, Kennilworthy, pseud. Quidditch Through the Ages. 2017. (Harry Potter Ser.). (ENG.). 128p. (J). (gr. 3-3). 12.99 (978-1-338-12574-0(5), Levine, Arthur A. Bks.) Scholastic, Inc.

—Quidditch Through the Ages. 2017. (ENG.). (J). (gr. 3). lib. bdg. 24.50 **(978-0-606-39694-3(2))** Turtleback Bks.

Willow, Tirissa & the Necklace of Nulidor. 2009. 338p. pap. 17.95 (978-1-4327-4013-9(X)) Outskirts Pr., Inc.

Wilson, Karma. Baby Cakes. Williams, Sam, illus. 2006. (ENG.). 32p. (J). (gr. -1 — 1). bds. 7.99 (978-1-4169-0289-8(9), Little Simon) Little Simon.

Wilson, Wendy. The First Book of Red. 2005. 99p. pap. 19.95 (978-1-4137-5570-1(4)) America Star Bks.

Wind, Chuck T. The Test of Love. 2011. 24p. pap. 24.95 (978-1-4626-2398-3(0)) America Star Bks.

Wizard Academies I: The Heart of Darkness. 2006. 658p. pap. 24.96 (978-1-4116-7787-6(0)) Lulu Pr., Inc.

The Wizard of OZ. 2008. (Charm Book Classics Ser.). 32p. (978-1-4075-1582-3(9)) Parragon, Inc.

Wizards of Waverly Place Insider's Guide. 2009. 128p. pap. 8.99 (978-1-4231-2473-3(1)) Disney Pr.

Wrede, Patricia C. Talking to Dragons. unabr. ed. 2004. (Enchanted Forest Chronicles: Bk. 4). 255p. (J). (gr. 6-18). pap. 38.00 incl. audio (978-0-8072-0983-7(X), S YA 385 SP, Listening Library) Random Hse. Audio Publishing Group.

Yagmin, Daniel, Jr., illus. Norton B. Nice. 2009. (J). (978-1-60108-018-9(2)) Red Cygnet Pr.

Yolen, Jane. Wizard's Hall. 144p. (J). (gr. 3-5). pap. 6.00 (978-0-8072-1544-9(9), Listening Library) Random Hse. Audio Publishing Group.

Zahler, Diane. Baker's Magic. Price, Mina, illus. 2016. (Middle-Grade Novels Ser.). (ENG.). 336p. (gr. 4-7). lib. bdg. 26.65 (978-1-4965-2724-0(0)) Stone Arch Bks.

Zimmerman, Diana S. Kandide & the Secret of the Mists, Bk. 1. Gadd, Maxine, illus. 2008. (Calabiyau Chronicles Ser.). 289p. (J). (gr. 4-7). pap. 9.99 (978-0-9794328-2-8(0)) Noesis Publishing.

WOLFE, THOMAS, 1900-1938

Boffa, Laura. Writing Home: The Story of Author Thomas Wolfe. 2016. (ENG., Illus.). 32p. (J). 15.95 (978-1-63076-133-2(8)) Taylor Trade Publishing.

WOLVERINE

Borgert-Spaniol, Megan. Wolverines. (Illus.). 24p. (J). 2014. (978-0-531-21818-1(X)) 2013. (ENG., lib. bdg. 25.95 (978-1-60014-916-0(2), Blastoff! Readers) Bellwether Media.

Carr, Aaron. Wolverine. 2014. (J). (978-1-4896-2645-5(X)) Weigl Pubs., Inc.

Gish, Melissa. Living Wild: Wolverines. 2015. (Living Wild Ser.). (ENG., Illus.). 48p. (J). (gr. 5-8). pap. 12.00 (978-1-62832-007-7(9), Creative Paperbacks) Creative Co., The.

—Wolverines. 2014. 46p. (978-1-60818-421-7(8), Creative Education) Creative Co., The.

Markle, Sandra. Los Glotones. 2007. (Animales carroñeros (Animal Scavengers) Ser.). (SPA., Illus.). (J). (gr. -1-3). 39p. lib. bdg. 25.26 (978-0-8225-7732-4(1)); 40p. per. 7.95 (978-0-8225-7736-2(4)) Lerner Publishing Group. (Ediciones Lerner).

—Los Glotones; Wolverines. 2008. pap. 46.95 (978-0-8225-9453-6(6)) Lerner Publishing Group.

—Wolverines. 2005. (Animal Scavengers Ser.). (ENG., Illus.). 40p. (J). (gr. 3-6). lib. bdg. 25.26 (978-0-8225-3198-2(4), Lerner Pubns.) Lerner Publishing Group.

Markovics, Joyce L. Wolverine: Super Strong. 2011. (Built for Cold Ser.). 32p. (YA). (gr. 1-4). lib. bdg. 25.27 (978-1-61772-131-1(X)); (J). (gr. 4-5). lib. bdg., E-Book 49.22 (978-1-61772-224-0(3)) Bearport Publishing Co., Inc.

McIntyre, Sandra. Wolverines. 2010. (Illus.). 24p. (978-1-55388-671-6(2)); pap. (978-1-55388-672-3(0)) Weigl Educational Pubs. Ltd.

Pallotta, Jerry. Wolverine vs. Tasmanian Devil. Bolster, Rob, illus. 2009. 32p. (J). pap. (978-0-545-45189-5(2)) Scholastic, Inc.

Polinsky, Paige V. Wolverine: Powerful Predator. 2016. (ENG., Illus.). 24p. (J). (978-1-68078-151-9(0)) ABDO Publishing Co.

WOLVERINE—FICTION

Caballero, Erica. Mount Mole. 2006. pap. 10.00 (978-1-4257-2301-9(2)) Xlibris Corp.

Jacques, Brian. Rakkety Tam. Elliot, David, illus. 2006. (Redwall Ser.). (ENG.). 384p. (J). (gr. 5-18). 8.99 (978-0-14-240683-0(X), Firebird) Penguin Young Readers Group.

—Rakkety Tam. 2004. (Redwall Ser.). 1.00 (978-1-4175-5517-8(3)) Recorded Bks., Inc.

McCracken, Harold. Pirate of the North. Tonk, Ernest, illus. 2011. 224p. 44.95 (978-1-258-09631-1(5)) Literary Licensing, LLC.

McIntyre, Sandra. Les Carcajous: Les Animaux du Canada. Karvonen, Tanjah, tr. from ENG. 2011. (FRE.). 24p. (gr. 3-6). (978-1-77071-417-5(0)) Weigl Educational Pubs. Ltd.

Skurzynski, Gloria & Ferguson, Alane. Buried Alive. 2003. (Mysteries in Our National Park Ser.: No. 12). (ENG.). 160p. (J). (gr. 3-7). 15.95 (978-0-7922-6966-3(7), National Geographic Children's Bks.) National Geographic Society.

—Buried Alive! 2008. (Mysteries in Our National Park Ser.). (ENG., Illus.). 160p. (J). (gr. 3-7). pap. 4.99 (978-1-4263-0252-7(5), National Geographic Children's Bks.) National Geographic Society.

WOLVES

American Museum of Natural History. Wolf Pups Join the Pack. 2017. (First Discoveries Ser.). (ENG., Illus.). 32p. (J). (gr. -1). 14.95 **(978-1-4549-2237-7(0))** Sterling Publishing Co., Inc.

Animal Watch: Wolves. (J). (gr. 1-3). 75.00 (978-0-669-15881-6(X)) Houghton Mifflin Harcourt School Pubs.

Barnes, Julia. The Secret Lives of Wolves. 2007. (Secret Lives of Animals Ser.). (Illus.). 32p. (gr. 2-6). lib. bdg. 26.00 (978-0-8368-7660-4(1), Gareth Stevens Learning Library) Stevens, Gareth Publishing LLLP.

Bergeron, Alain M., et al. Les Loups. 2008. (FRE., Illus.). 64p. (J). pap. 8.95 (978-2-89435-375-2(8)) Quintin Pubs./Editions Michel Quintin CAN. Dist: Crabtree Publishing Co.

Bjorklund, Ruth. Wolves. 2008. (Endangered! Ser.). 48p. (gr. 3-18). lib. bdg. 29.93 (978-0-7614-2993-7(X), Benchmark Bks.) Marshall Cavendish Corp.

Black, Robyn Hood. Wolves. Howard, Colin, illus. 2008. (ENG.). 24p. (J). (gr. 3-18). 19.95 (978-1-58117-817-3(4), Intervisual/Piggy Toes) Bendon, Inc.

Borgert-Spaniol, Megan. Jackals. 2013. (Animal Safari Ser.). (ENG., Illus.). 24p. (J). (gr. k-3). lib. bdg. 25.95 (978-1-60014-910-8(3), Blastoff! Readers) Bellwether Media.

Brandenburg, Jim & National Geographic Kids Staff. Face to Face with Wolves. 2010. (Face to Face with Animals Ser.). (ENG., Illus.). 32p. (J). (gr. 2-5). pap. 6.95 (978-1-4263-0698-3(9), National Geographic Children's Bks.) National Geographic Society.

Brannon, Cecelia H. Baby Wolves at the Zoo. 2016. (All about Baby Zoo Animals Ser.). (ENG., Illus.). 24p. (J). (gr. k-1). pap. 9.35 (978-0-7660-7162-9(6)) Enslow Pubs., Inc.

Butz, Christopher. Red Wolves. 2003. (Endangered Plants & Animals of North America Ser.). (J). pap. (978-1-58417-213-0(4)); lib. bdg. (978-1-58417-212-3(6)) Lake Street Pubs.

Carmichael, L. E. Fox Talk. Bronson, Jody, illus. 2013. 62p. (978-0-9881638-5-0(3)) Ashby-BP Publishing.

Carter, James. The Story of the Wolf: Band 17/Diamond. 2017. (ENG., Illus.). 56p. (J). pap. 8.99 **(978-0-00-820896-7(4))** HarperCollins Pubs. Ltd. GBR. Dist: Independent Pubs. Group.

Christopher, Nick. Arctic Wolves of the Tundra. 2017. (J). **(978-1-5345-2215-2(8)**, KidHaven Publishing) Greenhaven Publishing LLC.

Clark, Willow. Wolves: Life in the Pack. 2011. (Animal Families Ser.). 24p. (J). (ENG.). pap. 8.25 (978-1-4488-2616-2(0)); (Illus.). lib. bdg. 22.60 (978-1-4488-2515-8(6)) Rosen Publishing Group, Inc., The. (PowerKids Pr.).

—Wolves: Lobos: Life in the Pack: Vida en la Manada. 2011. (Animal Families / Familias de animales Ser.). (SPA & ENG., Illus.). 24p. lib. bdg. 22.60 (978-1-4488-3141-8(5), PowerKids Pr.) Rosen Publishing Group, Inc., The.

Clarke, Penny. Wolves. Hersey, Bob, illus. 2004. (Scary Creatures Ser.). (ENG.). 32p. (J). (gr. 2-4). pap. 6.95 (978-0-531-16749-6(6), Watts, Franklin) Scholastic Library Publishing.

Claybourne, Anna. A Pack of Wolves: And Other Canine Groups, 1 vol. 2012. (Animals in Groups Ser.). (ENG.). 48p. (gr. 4-6). pap. 9.95 (978-1-4329-6489-4(5)); lib. bdg. 33.32 (978-1-4329-6482-5(8)) Heinemann-Raintree. (Heinemann InfoSearch).

Clever Coyote & other Wild Dogs: Level L, 6 vols. 128p. (gr. 2-3). 40.50 (978-0-7699-1033-8(5)) Shortland Pubns. (U. S. A.) Inc.

Cohn, Scotti. One Wolf Howls, 1 vol. Detwiler, Susan, illus. 2009. (ENG.). 32p. (J). (gr. -1-3). 16.95 (978-1-934359-92-1(0)) Arbordale Publishing.

Curtis, Jennifer Keats. La Camada con Suerte: Cachorros de Lobo Rescatados de un Incendio Forestal, 1 vol. Gomes, John, illus. 2015. (ENG & SPA.). 32p. (J). (gr. 2-5). pap. 9.95 (978-1-62855-720-6(6)) Arbordale Publishing.

—The Lucky Litter: Wolf Pups Rescued from Wildfire, 1 vol. Gomes, John, illus. 2015. (ENG.). 32p. (J). (gr. 2-5). 17.95 (978-1-62855-718-3(4)) Arbordale Publishing.

Dahl, Michael. Wolves, 1 vol. 2012. (North American Animals Ser.). (ENG.). 24p. (gr. k-1). pap. 7.29 (978-1-4296-7925-1(5)); pap. 41.70 (978-1-4296-8361-6(9)); lib. bdg. 26.65 (978-1-4296-7701-1(5)) Capstone Press of Coughlan Cos. (Pebble Plus).

DeLallo, Laura. Arctic Wolf: The High Arctic. 2011. (Built for Cold Ser.). 32p. (YA). (gr. 1-4). lib. bdg. 25.27 (978-1-61772-132-8(8)); (J). (gr. 4-5). lib. bdg., E-Book 49.22 (978-1-61772-219-6(7)) Bearport Publishing Co., Inc.

Dibble, Traci. Wolves. 2011. (Predator Animals Ser.). 16p. pap. 39.62 (978-1-61541-364-5(2)) American Reading Co.

Dibble, Traci & Sanchez, Lucia M. Lobos: Wolves. 2011. (Animales depredadores (Predator Animals) Ser.). (SPA.). 16p. (J). pap. 6.95 (978-1-61541-365-2(0)) American Reading Co.

Dibble, Traci & Washington, Joi. Wolves. Washington, Joi, illus. 2010. (1-3Y Animals Ser.). (ENG., Illus.). 16p. (J). (gr. k-2). pap. 5.99 (978-1-61541-363-8(4)) American Reading Co.

W X Y Z

Doudna, Kelly. It's a Baby Gray Wolf!, 1 vol. 2008. (Baby Mammals Ser.). (ENG., Illus.). 24p. (J). (gr. k-3). lib. bdg. 24.21 (978-1-60453-024-7(3)) ABDO Publishing Co.

Dutcher, Jim & Dutcher, Jamie. A Friend for Lakota. 2015. (ENG., Illus.). 32p. (J). (gr. -1-3). 16.99 (978-1-4263-2082-8(5), National Geographic Children's Bks.) National Geographic Society.

—Living with Wolves! True Stories of Adventures with Animals. 2016. (NGK Chapters Ser.). (ENG., Illus.). 112p. (J). (gr. 2-5). pap. 5.99 (978-1-4263-2563-2(0), National Geographic Children's Bks.) National Geographic Society.

Field, Nancy & Karasov, Corliss. Discovering Wolves. Hunkel, Cary, illus. 2011. (Discovering Nature Library). (ENG.). 40p. (J). (gr. 3-8). pap. 6.95 (978-0-941042-39-0(1)) Dog-Eared Pubns.

Fleischer, Jayson. These Are Wolves. Washington, Joi, illus. 2011. (2G Predator Animals Ser.). (ENG.). 28p. (J). (gr. k-2). pap. 5.99 (978-1-61541-508-3(4)) American Reading Co.

Gangemi, Alphia. Hunting with Wolves. 2012. (Animal Attack! Ser.). (Illus.). 24p. (J). (gr. 2-5). 22.60 (978-1-4339-7083-2(X)); pap. 8.15 (978-1-4339-7084-9(8)) Stevens, Gareth Publishing LLLP. (Gareth Stevens Learning Library).

Gardner, Jane P. Jackals. 2013. (Wild Canine Pups Ser.). 24p. (J). (gr. -1-3). lib. bdg. 21.32 (978-1-61772-929-4(9)) Bearport Publishing Co., Inc.

Gareth Stevens Editorial Staff. Wolves. 2004. (All about Wild Animals Ser.). (Illus.). 32p. (gr. k-4). lib. bdg. 26.00 (978-0-8368-4124-4(7), Gareth Stevens Learning Library) Stevens, Gareth Publishing LLLP.

George, Jean Craighead. Autumn Moon. 2003. (J). (gr. 3-7). 20.75 (978-0-8446-7241-0(6)) Smith, Peter Pub., Inc.

—The Wolves Are Back. 2008. (J). (gr. 1-4). 28.95 incl. audio compact disk (978-1-4301-0594-7(1)) Live Oak Media.

—The Wolves Are Back. Minor, Wendell, illus. 2008. (J). (gr. 1-4). 25.95 incl. audio (978-1-4301-0591-6(7)) Live Oak Media.

—The Wolves Are Back. Minor, Wendell, illus. 2008. (ENG.). 32p. (J). (gr. -1-3). 16.99 (978-0-525-47947-5(3), Dutton Books for Young Readers) Penguin Young Readers Group.

Gilbert, Sara. Dire Wolves. 2017. (Illus.). 24p. (J). (978-1-60818-765-2(9), Creative Education) Creative Co., The.

Gilbert, Sara. Ice Age Mega Beasts: Dire Wolves. 2017. (Ice Age Mega Beasts Ser.). (ENG., Illus.). 24p. (J). (gr. 1-3). pap. 8.99 **(978-1-62832-373-3(6)**, Creative Paperbacks) Creative Co., The.

Gilkerson, Patricia. My Adventure with Wolves. 2009. (ENG.). 44p. (J). 8.99 (978-1-59092-476-1(2)) Blue Forge Pr.

Godkin, Celia. The Wolves Return. Godkin, Celia, illus. 2017. (ENG., Illus.). 32p. (J). (gr. 1-3). 17.95 (978-1-77278-011-6(1)) Pajama Pr. CAN. Dist: Ingram Publisher Services.

Goecke, Michael P. Dire Wolf, 1 vol. 2003. (Prehistoric Animals Ser.). (ENG.). 24p. (gr. k-4). 25.65 (978-1-57765-966-2(X), Buddy Bks.) ABDO Publishing Co.

Goldish, Meish. Gray Wolves: Return to Yellowstone. 2016. (America's Animal Comebacks Ser.). (ENG.). 32p. (J). (gr. 2-7). pap. 8.95 **(978-1-944998-72-1(1))** Bearport Publishing Co., Inc.

Goldish, Meish. Red Wolves: And Then There Were (Almost) None. 2007. (America's Animal Comebacks Ser.). (Illus.). 32p. (YA). (gr. 2-5). lib. bdg. 25.27 (978-1-59716-742-0(8)) Bearport Publishing Co., Inc.

Green, Emily. Wolves. 2011. (Backyard Wildlife Ser.). (ENG., Illus.). 24p. (J). (gr. k-3). lib. bdg. 25.95 (978-1-60014-563-6(9), Blastoff! Readers) Bellwether Media.

—Wolves. 2011. (Backyard Wildlife Ser.). 24p. (J). (gr. k-1). lib. bdg. 22.00 (978-0-531-20489-4(8), Children's Pr.) Scholastic Library Publishing.

Green, Jen. Exploring Nature: Examine the Wonderful World of Wolves, Jackals, Coyotes, Foxes & Other Wild Dogs, Shown in 190 Exciting Images: Wolves - Life in the Wild. 2015. (ENG., Illus.). 64p. (J). (gr. 3-7). 12.99 (978-1-86147-395-0(8), Armadillo) Anness Publishing GBR. Dist: National Bk. Network.

—Wolves. 2010. (Amazing Animal Hunters Ser.). 32p. (J). 28.50 (978-1-60753-050-3(3)) Amicus Publishing.

—Wolves. 2008. (Nature's Children Ser.). (Illus.). 52p. pap. (978-0-7172-6266-3(9)) Grolier, Ltd.

—Wolves. 2012. (Illus.). 32p. (gr. 3-5). pap. 8.95 (978-1-926722-54-2(X)) Saunders Bk. Co. CAN. Dist: RiverStream Publishing.

Green, Jen & Martineau, Susan. Wolves. 2011. (Positive Steps Ser.). 32p. (gr. 2-5). lib. bdg. 31.35 (978-1-59920-490-1(8)) Black Rabbit Bks.

Gregory, Josh. Red Wolves. 2014. (Nature's Children Ser.). (ENG.). 48p. (J). lib. bdg. 28.00 (978-0-531-21227-1(0)) Scholastic Library Publishing.

Halfpenny, James C. Yellowstone Wolves in the Wild. 2003. (Illus.). 104p. per. 19.95 (978-1-931832-26-7(9), 8667872363) Riverbend Publishing.

Hamilton, S. L. Wolves. 2010. (Xtreme Predators Ser.). 32p. (gr. 3-9). 27.07 (978-1-60453-995-0(X), A&D Xtreme) ABDO Publishing Co.

Harrington, Fred H. The Ethiopian Wolf. 2009. (Library of Wolves & Wild Dogs Ser.). 24p. (gr. 3-3). 42.50 (978-1-60853-972-7(5), PowerKids Pr.) Rosen Publishing Group, Inc., The.

—The Red Wolf. 2009. (Library of Wolves & Wild Dogs Ser.). 24p. (gr. 3-3). 42.50 (978-1-60853-974-1(1), PowerKids Pr.) Rosen Publishing Group, Inc., The.

Harris, Tim, ed. Wolves. 2012. (Animal Families Ser.). (ENG., Illus.). 32p. (gr. 2-5). 31.35 (978-1-78121-006-2(3), Brown Bear Bks.) Windmill Bks. Ltd. GBR. Dist: Black Rabbit Bks.

Havard, Christian. The Wolf: Night Howler. Jacana Agency, photos by. 2006. (Animal Close-Ups Ser.). (Illus.). 28p. (Orig.). (J). (gr. -1-3). pap. 6.95 (978-1-57091-630-4(6)) Charlesbridge Publishing, Inc.

Heinz, Brian. The Wolves. Fuchs, Bernie, illus. 2005. 32p. (J). lib. bdg. 15.99 (978-0-936335-11-7(4)) Ballyhoo BookWorks, Inc.

Heos, Bridget. Do You Really Want to Meet a Wolf? Fabbri, Daniele, illus. 2017. (Do You Really Want to Meet... Wild Animals? Ser.). (ENG.). 24p. (J). (gr. 1-3). pap. 8.99 (978-1-68152-120-6(2)) Amicus.

—Do You Really Want to Meet a Wolf? Fabbri, Daniele, illus. 2016. (Do You Really Want to Meet... Wild Animals? Ser.). (ENG.). 24p. (J). (gr. k-3). 20.95 (978-1-60753-949-0(7)) Amicus Publishing.

Hirsch, Rebecca E. Gray Wolves: Howling Pack Mammals. 2015. (Comparing Animal Traits Ser.). (ENG., Illus.). 32p. (gr. 2-4). 39.99 (978-1-4677-8923-3(2), Lerner Digital); (J). pap. 8.99 (978-1-4677-6060-7(9), Lerner Pubns.); (J). lib. bdg. 26.65 (978-1-4677-5577-1(X), Lerner Pubns.) Lerner Publishing Group.

Hudak, Heather C. Wolves. 2008. (Backyard Animals Ser.). (Illus.). 24p. (J). (gr. 4-7). lib. bdg. 24.45 (978-1-60596-005-0(5)) Weigl Pubs., Inc.

Hudak, Heather C., ed. Wolves. 2008. (Backyard Animals Ser.). (Illus.). 24p. (J). (gr. 4-7). pap. 8.95 (978-1-60596-011-1(X)) Weigl Pubs., Inc.

Imbriaco, Alison. The Red Wolf: Help Save This Endangered Species! 2007. (Saving Endangered Species Ser.). (Illus.). 128p. (J). (gr. 5-9). lib. bdg. 34.60 (978-1-59845-038-5(7), MyReportLinks.com Bks.) Enslow Pubs., Inc.

Jazynka, Kitson. Wolf Rescue - National Geographic Kids Mission: All about Wolves & How to Save Them. Raven-Ellison, Daniel, ed. 2014. (ENG., Illus.). 128p. (J). (gr. 5). pap. 12.99 (978-1-4263-1494-0(9), National Geographic Children's Bks.) National Geographic Society.

Johnson, Jinny. Gray Wolf. 2014. (North American Mammals Ser.). 24p. (gr. 2-5). 28.50 (978-1-62588-038-3(3)) Black Rabbit Bks.

—Gray Wolf. 2014. (North American Mammals Ser.). (ENG., Illus.). 24p. (J). (gr. -1-4). pap. 8.95 (978-1-77092-173-3(7)) Saunders Bk. Co. CAN. Dist: RiverStream Publishing.

Kalman, Bobbie. Baby Wolves. 2010. (Fun to Learn about Baby Animals Ser.). (ENG.). 24p. (J). (gr. k-3). (978-0-7787-4895-3(2)); pap. (978-0-7787-4900-4(2)) Crabtree Publishing Co.

—Endangered Wolves. 2004. (Earth's Endangered Animals Ser.). (ENG., Illus.). 32p. (J). pap. (978-0-7787-1900-7(6)) Crabtree Publishing Co.

—Wolf Family Adventures. 2016. (ENG., Illus.). 32p. (J). (978-0-7787-2234-2(1)) Crabtree Publishing Co.

Kissock, Heather. Wolves. 2016. (J). **(978-1-4896-5402-1(X))** Weigl Pubs., Inc.

Lawrence, Ellen. A Wolf's Life. 2012. (Science Slam: Animal Diaries-Life Cycles Ser.). 24p. (J). (gr. -1-3). lib. bdg. 23.93 (978-1-61772-597-5(8)) Bearport Publishing Co., Inc.

Lawton, Carol L. Votive Reliefs. 2017. (ENG., Illus.). 248p. 150.00 (978-0-87661-238-5(9)) American Schl. of Classical Studies at Athens.

Leaf, Christina. Gray Wolves. 2015. (North American Animals Ser.). (ENG., Illus.). 24p. (J). (gr. k-3). lib. bdg. 25.95 (978-1-62617-188-6(2), Blastoff! Readers) Bellwether Media.

Leblanc, Catherine. How to Ward off Wolves. Garrigue, Roland, illus. 2013. (ENG.). 32p. (J). (gr. -1). 14.99 (978-1-60887-194-0(0)) Insight Editions.

Linde, Barbara. Coyotes & Wolves Are Not Pets! 2013. (When Pets Attack! Ser.). 32p. (J). (gr. 3-6). pap. 63.00 (978-1-4339-9295-7(7)); pap. 10.50 (978-1-4339-9294-0(9)) Stevens, Gareth Publishing LLLP.

Linde, Barbara & Linde, Barbara M. Coyotes & Wolves Are Not Pets! 2013. 32p. (J). (gr. 3-6). 26.60 (978-1-4339-9293-3(0)) Stevens, Gareth Publishing LLLP.

Llanas, Sheila Griffin. Gray Wolves, 1 vol. 2013. (Animal Icons Ser.). (ENG.). 32p. (J). (gr. 3-6). lib. bdg. 27.07 (978-1-61783-571-1(4), Checkerboard Library) ABDO Publishing Co.

Los Lobos (Wolves) 2006. (J). pap. 7.95 (978-0-8225-6626-7(5), Ediciones Lerner) Lerner Publishing Group.

Los Lobos: Individual Title Six-Packs. (Literatura 2000 Ser.). (SPA.). (gr. 2-3). 33.00 (978-0-7635-1262-0(1)) Rigby Education.

MacLaine, James. Wolves. Francis, John & Scott, Kimberley, illus. 2013. (Usborne Beginners Ser.). (ENG.). 32p. (J). 4.99 (978-0-7945-3402-8(3), Usborne) EDC Publishing.

Malam, John. Hyenas. 2008. (Scary Creatures Ser.). (ENG., Illus.). 32p. (J). (gr. 2-4). pap. 8.95 (978-0-531-21900-3(3), Watts, Franklin) Scholastic Library Publishing.

Markle, Sandra. Los Lobos. Translations.com Staff, tr. from ENG. 2006. (Animales Depredadores (Animal Predators) Ser.). (SPA., Illus.). 40p. (gr. 3-6). lib. bdg. 25.26 (978-0-8225-6489-8(0), Ediciones Lerner) Lerner Publishing Group.

—Los Lobos; Wolves. 2008. pap. 46.95 (978-0-8225-7090-5(4)) Lerner Publishing Group.

—Wolves. (Animal Predators Ser.). (ENG.). (gr. 3-6). 2005. 39p. pap. 7.95 (978-1-57505-748-4(4)) 2004. (Illus.). 40p. lib. bdg. 26.60 (978-1-57505-732-3(8)) Lerner Publishing Group.

Marquardt, Meg. Wolves on the Hunt. 2017. (Searchlight Books (tm) — Predators Ser.). (ENG.). (J). (gr. 3-5). pap. 9.99 **(978-1-5124-5614-1(4))**; (Illus.). lib. bdg. 30.65 **(978-1-5124-3399-9(3))** Lerner Publishing Group.

Marsh, Laura. National Geographic Readers: Wolves. 2012. (Readers Ser.). (ENG., Illus.). 32p. (J). (gr. k-3). lib. bdg. 13.90 (978-1-4263-0914-4(7), National Geographic Children's Bks.) National Geographic Society.

—Wolves. 2012. (Readers Ser.). (ENG., Illus.). 32p. (J). (gr. k-3). pap. 3.99 (978-1-4263-0913-7(9), National Geographic Children's Bks.) National Geographic Society.

Martin, Patricia A. Fink. Gray Wolves. 2003. (True Bks.). (ENG., Illus.). 48p. (J). (gr. 3-5). pap. 6.95 (978-0-516-27472-0(4), Children's Pr.) Scholastic Library Publishing.

McDowell, Pamela. Lobos. 2013. (Animales en Mi Patio Ser.). (SPA., Illus.). 24p. (J). (gr. -1-3). lib. bdg. 27.13 (978-1-62127-599-2(X), AV2 by Weigl) Weigl Pubs., Inc.

—Wolves. 2012. (J). pap. 12.95 (978-1-61913-274-0(5)); 27.13 (978-1-61913-270-2(2)) Weigl Pubs., Inc.

McLeese, Don. Gray Wolves. 2010. (ENG., Illus.). 24p. (gr. 3-6). pap. 8.95 (978-1-61590-511-9(1)) Rourke Educational Media.

Meinking, Mary. Gray Wolves. 2013. (Wild Canine Pups Ser.). 24p. (J). (gr. -1-3). lib. bdg. 21.32 (978-1-61772-926-3(4)) Bearport Publishing Co., Inc.

—Wolf vs. Elk, 1 vol. 2011. (Predator vs. Prey Ser.). (ENG., Illus.). 32p. (gr. 1-2). pap. 8.29 (978-1-4109-3950-0(2), Read Me!) Heinemann-Raintree.

Meister, Cari. Wolves. 2015. (J). lib. bdg. 25.65 (978-1-62031-170-7(4), Bullfrog Bks.) Jump! Inc.

Miller, Sara Swan. Wolves. (Paws & Claws Ser.). 24p. 2009. (gr. 2-3). 42.50 (978-1-60851-155-6(3)) 2008. (Illus.). (J). (gr. 3-7). lib. bdg. 22.60 (978-1-4042-4161-9(2)) Rosen Publishing Group, Inc., The. (PowerKids Pr.).

Montardre, Hélène. Little Wolves. Castile, Muriel, tr. from FRE. 2005. (Born to Be Wild Ser.). (Illus.). 24p. (J). (gr. k-3). lib. bdg. 23.00 (978-0-8368-4440-5(8), Gareth Stevens Learning Library) Stevens, Gareth Publishing LLLP.

Moore Niver, Heather. Wolves after Dark. 2016. (Animals of the Night Ser.). (ENG.). 32p. (J). (gr. 3-3). pap. 10.52 (978-0-7660-7416-3(1)) Enslow Pubs., Inc.

Niver, Heather Moore. Wolves after Dark. 2016. (Animals of the Night Ser.). (ENG., Illus.). 32p. (J). (gr. 3-3). 25.27 (978-0-7660-7418-7(8)) Enslow Pubs., Inc.

Olson, Bethany. Baby Wolves. 2013. (Super Cute! Ser.). (ENG., Illus.). 24p. (J). (gr. k-3). lib. bdg. 25.95 (978-1-60014-934-4(0), Blastoff! Readers) Bellwether Media.

Owen, Ruth. Wolves. 2012. (Dr. Bob's Amazing World of Animals Ser.). (Illus.). 32p. (J). (gr. k-5). pap. 11.75 (978-1-61533-558-9(7)); lib. bdg. 26.50 (978-1-61533-549-7(8)) Windmill Bks.

Patent, Dorothy Hinshaw. When the Wolves Returned: Restoring Nature's Balance in Yellowstone. Hartman, Dan, illus. Hartman, Cassie & Hartman, Dan, photos by. 2008. (ENG.). 40p. (J). (gr. 1-4). 19.99 (978-0-8027-9686-8(9), 9780802796868, Bloomsbury USA Childrens) Bloomsbury Publishing USA.

Pfeffer, Wendy & American Museum of Natural History Staff. Wolf Pup, Level 1. 2011. (Amer Museum of Nat History Easy Readers Ser.: 4). (ENG., Illus.). 32p. (J). (gr. -1-k). pap. 3.95 (978-1-4027-7785-1(X)) Sterling Publishing Co., Inc.

Polydoros, Lori. Wolves: On the Hunt. 2016. (Killer Animals Ser.). (ENG.). 32p. (gr. 1-2). pap. 7.95 (978-1-5157-6227-0(0), Blazers) Capstone Press of Coughlan Cos.

Read, Nicholas. The Sea Wolves: Living Wild in the Great Bear Rainforest, 1 vol. McAllister, Ian, photos by. 2010. (ENG., Illus.). 128p. (J). (gr. 3-7). pap. 19.95 (978-1-55469-206-4(7)) Orca Bk. Pubs. USA.

Read, Tracy C. Exploring the World of Wolves. 2010. (Exploring the World Of Ser.). (ENG., Illus.). 24p. (J). (gr. 4-7). 16.95 (978-1-55407-646-8(3), 9781554076468); pap. 6.95 (978-1-55407-655-0(2), 9781554076550) Firefly Bks., Ltd.

Reher, Matt. Orcas: The Wolves of the Seas. 2016. (1B Animal Behaviors Ser.). (ENG., Illus.). 28p. (J). pap. 5.99 **(978-1-63437-587-0(4))** American Reading Co.

—When the Wolves Came Back. 2015. (2B Wild Animals Ser.). (ENG., Illus.). 32p. (J). pap. 5.99 (978-1-63437-201-5(8)) American Reading Co.

—Wolf Babies Eat. 2016. (1G Predator Animals Ser.). (ENG., Illus.). 28p. (J). pap. 5.99 **(978-1-63437-572-6(6))** American Reading Co.

Reher, Matt. Wolves Eat. 2015. (1G Predator Animals Ser.). (ENG., Illus.). 24p. (J). pap. 5.99 (978-1-63437-013-4(9)) American Reading Co.

Reiter, Chris. The Gray Wolf: A MyReportLinks.com Book. 2003. (Endangered & Threatened Animals Ser.). (Illus.). 48p. (J). (gr. 4-10). lib. bdg. 26.60 (978-0-7660-5056-3(4), MyReportLinks.com Bks.) Enslow Pubs., Inc.

Riggs, Kate. Amazing Animals - Wolves. 2011. (Amazing Animals Ser.). (J). (gr. 2-5). 24.25 (978-1-58341-991-5(8)) Creative Co., The.

—Seedlings: Wolves. 2014. (Seedlings Ser.). (ENG.). 24p. (J). (gr. -1-k). pap. 7.99 (978-0-89812-890-1(0), Creative Paperbacks) Creative Co., The.

—Wolves. (J). 2013. 25.65 (978-1-60818-345-6(9), Creative Education) 2011. (ENG.). 24p. (gr. 1-3). pap. 8.99 (978-0-89812-564-1(2), Creative Paperbacks) Creative Co., The.

—Wolves. 2010. (ENG., Illus.). 24p. (J). 8.95 (978-1-926853-71-0(7)) Saunders Bk. Co. CAN. Dist: Creative Co., The.

Royston, Angela. Wolf. 2013. (Top of the Food Chain Ser.). 32p. (J). (gr. k-5). 25.25 (978-1-61533-738-5(5)); pap. 10.00 (978-1-61533-793-4(8)) Rosen Publishing Group, Inc., The. (PowerKids Pr.).

—Wolves. (Amazing Animals Ser.). (Illus.). 24p. (J). 2009. (gr. 2-4). pap. 8.95 (978-1-60596-157-6(4)) 2009. (gr. 2-4). lib. bdg. 24.45 (978-1-60596-156-9(6)) 2003. lib. bdg. 24.45 (978-1-58340-228-3(4)) Weigl Pubs., Inc.

Rue, Leonard Lee. Wolves - Pb: A Portrait of the Animal World. 2013. (Portrait of the Animal World Ser.). (Illus.). 80p. pap. 9.95 (978-1-59764-326-9(2)) New Line Bks.

Saxena, Shalini. Saving the Endangered Gray Wolf, 01 vols., 1. 2016. (Conservation of Endangered Species Ser.). (ENG., Illus.). 32p. (J). pap. 12.90 (978-1-5081-0055-3(1), Britannica Educational Publishing) Rosen Publishing Group, Inc., The.

Scieszka, Jon. The True Story of the 3 Little Pigs. Smith, Lane, illus. 2011. (J). (gr. -1-3). 29.95 (978-0-545-09457-3(7)); 18.95 (978-0-545-09459-7(3)) Weston Woods Studios, Inc.

Searl, Duncan. Wolves. 2007. (Smart Animals! Ser.). (Illus.). 32p. (J). (gr. 2-5). lib. bdg. 25.27 (978-1-59716-370-5(8), 1265961) Bearport Publishing Co., Inc.

Seymour, Simon. Wolves. 2014. (ENG.). 32p. (J). (gr. k-4). 11.24 (978-1-63245-273-3(1)) Lectorum Pubns., Inc.

Shea, Abigail. Wolves in Danger. 2013. (Animals at Risk Ser.). 24p. (J). (gr. 2-5). pap. 8.15 (978-1-4339-9179-0(9)) Stevens, Gareth Publishing LLLP.

Shea, Adele. Wolves in Danger. 2013. (Animals at Risk Ser.). (ENG., Illus.). 24p. (J). (gr. 2-5). lib. bdg. 22.60 (978-1-4339-9178-3(0)) Stevens, Gareth Publishing LLLP.

Silverman, Buffy. Can You Tell a Coyote from a Wolf? 2012. (Animal Look-Alikes Ser.). 32p. (gr. k-2). pap. 45.32 (978-0-7613-9253-8(X)); (ENG.). pap. 7.95 (978-0-7613-8557-8(6)); (ENG., Illus.). lib. bdg. 26.60 (978-0-7613-6739-0(X), Lerner Pubns.) Lerner Publishing Group.

Simon, Charnan. Wolves. 2012. (Nature's Children Ser.). (ENG., Illus.). 48p. (J). pap. 6.95 (978-0-531-21084-0(7)); (gr. 3-5). lib. bdg. 28.00 (978-0-531-20909-7(1)) Scholastic Library Publishing. (Children's Pr.).

Simon, Seymour. Wolves. 2009. (ENG., Illus.). 32p. (J). (gr. k-4). pap. 6.99 (978-0-06-162657-9(0), Collins) HarperCollins Pubs.

Sisk, Maeve T. Arctic Wolves. 2010. (Animals That Live in the Tundra Ser.). (ENG.). 24p. (J). (gr. -1-3). pap. 8.15 (978-1-4339-3894-8(4)); lib. bdg. 22.60 (978-1-4339-3893-1(6)) Stevens, Gareth Publishing LLLP.

Slade, Suzanne. What If There Were No Gray Wolves? A Book about the Temperate Forest Ecosystem, 1 vol. Schwartz, Carol, illus. 2010. (Food Chain Reactions Ser.). (ENG.). 24p. (gr. 2-4). pap. 9.95 (978-1-4048-6395-8(8)) Picture Window Bks.

Spilsbury, Richard & Spilsbury, Louise. Wolf Packs. 2013. (Animal Armies Ser.). (ENG., Illus.). 32p. (J). (gr. k-5). pap. 10.00 (978-1-4777-0336-6(5)); lib. bdg. 25.25 (978-1-4777-0307-6(1)) Rosen Publishing Group, Inc., The. (PowerKids Pr.).

Stone, Lynn M. Gray Wolves. 2004. (Early Bird Nature Bks.). (Illus.). 47p. (J). 25.26 (978-0-8225-3050-3(3), Lerner Pubns.) Lerner Publishing Group.

Strauss, Holden. Wolves. 2016. (Wild Canines Ser.). (Illus.). 24p. (J). (gr. 3-3). pap. 8.25 (978-1-4994-2023-4(4), PowerKids Pr.) Rosen Publishing Group, Inc., The.

Tanner, S. The Wild Wolf: Learning the W Sound. 2009. (PowerPhonics Ser.). 24p. (gr. 1-1). 39.90 (978-1-60851-473-1(0), PowerKids Pr.) Rosen Publishing Group, Inc., The.

Terp, Gail. Gray Wolves. 2017. (Wild Animal Kingdom Ser.). (ENG., Illus.). 32p. (J). (gr. 3-7). 31.35 **(978-1-68072-051-8(1)**, Bolt) Black Rabbit Bks.

Troupe, Thomas Kingsley. The Legend of the Werewolf, 1 vol. Ice, D. C., illus. 2010. (Legend Has It Ser.). (ENG.). 32p. (gr. 2-4). lib. bdg. 27.32 (978-1-4048-6033-9(9)) Picture Window Bks.

Wallace, Karen. Wolves. 2009. (Wild Reads Ser.). (ENG., Illus.). 32p. (YA). (gr. k). pap. 4.95 (978-0-19-911935-6(X)) Oxford Univ. Pr., Inc.

Washington, Joi & Fleischer, Jayson. These Are Wolves. 2011. (ARC Press / Power 100 - Predator Animals Ser.). pap. 45.32 (978-1-61541-509-0(2)) American Reading Co.

Wexo, John Bonnett. Wolves. rev. ed. 2003. (Illus.). 24p. (J). (gr. 1-7). 10.95 (978-1-932396-01-0(2), Zoo Bks.) Wildlife Education, Ltd.

Wildlife Education. Wolves. 2007. (Illus.). 10p. (J). pap. (978-1-932396-33-1(0), Critters Up Close) Wildlife Education, Ltd.

Wilsdon, Christina. Wolves. 2006. (J). 7.99 (978-1-59939-031-4(0)) Cornerstone Pr.

—Wolves. 2010. (Amazing Animals Ser.). (ENG.). 48p. (J). (gr. 2-6). pap. 10.50 (978-1-4339-4032-3(9)); lib. bdg. 28.00 (978-1-4339-4031-6(0)) Stevens, Gareth Publishing LLLP. (Gareth Stevens Learning Library).

Wimmer, Teresa. Wolves. 2009. (Living Wild Ser.). (Illus.). 48p. (J). 22.95 (978-1-58341-744-7(3), Creative Education) Creative Co., The.

Wolf: Killer King of the Forest. 2013. (Top of the Food Chain Ser.). 32p. (J). (gr. k-5). pap. 60.00 (978-1-61533-794-1(6), PowerKids Pr.) Rosen Publishing Group, Inc., The.

Wolves: Easyreads - Level 1, 6 bks. 2005. (Animal Predators Ser.). (Illus.). 40p. (J). (gr. 3-6). pap. 46.95 (978-0-8225-5494-3(1)) Lerner Publishing Group.

Wolves: Easyreads - Level 1, 6 Packs. (Literatura 2000 Ser.). (gr. 2-3). 33.00 (978-0-7635-0271-3(5)) Rigby Education.

Wolves & Coyotes. (Eyes on Nature Ser.). 32p. (J). (gr. 1). pap. (978-1-882210-57-2(3)) Action Publishing, Inc.

Wolves & Coyotes. (Eyes on Nature Ser.). (Illus.). 32p. (J). (gr. 1-18). 7.95 (978-1-56156-424-8(9)) Kidsbooks, LLC.

Wolves in Danger. 2013. (Animals at Risk Ser.). 24p. (J). (gr. 2-5). pap. 48.90 (978-1-4339-9180-6(2)) Stevens, Gareth Publishing LLLP.

World Book, Inc. Staff, contrib. by. Harry the Wolf. 2017. (J). **(978-0-7166-3522-2(4))** World Bk., Inc.

Zeiger, Jennifer. Coyotes. 2013. (ENG.). 48p. (J). 28.00 (978-0-531-23356-6(1)); pap. 6.95 (978-0-531-25154-6(3)) Scholastic Library Publishing.

WOLVES—FICTION

Adams, Elizabeth. The Boy Who Cried Wolf. 2012. (ENG., Illus.). 24p. (J). pap. (978-0-7787-7902-5(5)) Crabtree Publishing Co.

Aesop. The Sheperd Boy & the Wolf. 2012. (J). 29.99 (978-1-61913-107-1(2)) Weigl Pubs., Inc.

—The Wolf in Sheep's Clothing: A Tale about Appearances. 2006. (J). (978-1-59939-086-4(8), Reader's Digest Young Families, Inc.) Studio Fun International.

Afanasyev, Alexander. The Tale of Tsarevich Ivan, the Firebird, & the Grey Wolf. Bilibin, Ivan, illus. 2013. 28p. pap. (978-1-909115-50-7(9)) Planet, The.

Alexis, André. Ingrid & the Wolf. 2005. (ENG.). 168p. (J). (gr. 3-7). pap. 8.95 (978-0-88776-691-6(9), Tundra Bks.) Tundra Bks. CAN. Dist: Penguin Random Hse. LLC.

Alily, Joseph. Untold- the Never Ending Tales: The Boy & the Wolf - Children's Story. 2006. 10.00 (978-0-8059-8133-9(0)) Dorrance Publishing Co., Inc.

Alley, Zoe. There's a Wolf at the Door. Alley, R. W. & Alley, R., illus. 2008. (ENG.). 40p. (J). (gr. -1-3). 21.99 (978-1-59643-275-8(6), 9781596432758) Roaring Brook Pr.

Anderson, Derek. Ten Hungry Pigs: An Epic Lunch Adventure. Anderson, Derek, illus. 2016. (ENG., Illus.). 40p. (J). (gr. -1-k). 16.99 (978-0-545-16848-9(1)) Scholastic, Inc.

Anderson, Max Elliot. Legend of the White Wolf. 2005. (Illus.). 125p. (J). (gr. -1-7). pap. 10.95 (978-0-9752880-3-0(2)) Baker Trittin Pr.

Andrews, Julie & Hamilton, Emma Walton. Dragon. 2004. (Julie Andrews Collection). 192p. (J). (gr. 4-18). 16.99 (978-0-06-057119-1(5)); lib. bdg. 17.89 (978-0-06-057120-7(9)) HarperCollins Pubs. (Julie Andrews Collection).

Anónimo. Juguemos en el Bosque. Bergna, Monica, illus. 2004. (SPA.). 28p. (J). (gr. k-18). pap. 6.50 (978-980-257-282-3(9)) Ekare, Ediciones VEN. Dist: Iaconi, Mariuccia Bk. Imports.

Ansley, Frank & Wheeler, Lisa. Who's Afraid of Granny Wolf? Ansley, Frank, tr. 2004. (Fitch & Chip Ser.: 3). (ENG., Illus.). 48p. (J). (gr. 1-3). 16.99 (978-0-689-84952-7(4), Simon Spotlight) Simon Spotlight.

Archer, Dosh. Big Bad Wolf. Archer, Dosh, illus. (Urgency Emergency! Ser.). (ENG., Illus.). 48p. (J). (gr. -1-3). 2015. pap. 9.99 (978-0-8075-8351-7(0)) 2013. 12.99 (978-0-8075-8352-4(9)) Whitman, Albert & Co.

Armo, Nancy. A Friend for Mole, 1 vol. Armo, Nancy, illus. 2016. (ENG., Illus.). 32p. (J). (gr. -1-k). 16.95 *(978-1-56145-865-3(1))* Peachtree Pubs.
Asch, Frank. Happy Birthday, Big Bad Wolf. Asch, Frank, illus. 2011. (ENG., Illus.). 32p. (J). (gr. -1-2). 16.95 *(978-1-55337-368-1(5))* Kids Can Pr., Ltd. CAN. Dist: Hachette Bk. Group.
Atwater-Rhodes, Amelia. Wolfcry. 2008. (Kiesha'ra Ser.: Bk. 4). (ENG.). 208p. (YA). (gr. 9-12). pap. 7.99 *(978-0-440-23886-7(2)*, Delacorte Pr.) Random Hse. Children's Bks.
Austin, Jeanne J. Unlikely Friends. 2009. 24p. pap. 14.99 *(978-1-4343-2348-4(X))* AuthorHouse.
Avi. The Good Dog. 2003. 243p. (gr. 3-7). 17.00 *(978-0-7569-1389-2(6))* Perfection Learning Corp.
—Old Wolf. Floca, Brian, illus. 2015. (ENG.). 160p. (J). (gr. 3-7). 16.99 *(978-1-4424-9921-8(4))* Simon & Schuster Children's Publishing.
Aylesworth, Jim. Goldilocks & the Three Bears. McClintock, Barbara, illus. 2003. (ENG.). 32p. (J). (gr. -1-3). 17.99 *(978-0-439-39545-8(3)*, Scholastic Pr.) Scholastic, Inc.
Bad Boys. 2007. (J). (gr. k-3). 29.95 incl. audio compact disk *(978-0-8045-4179-4(5))*; 27.95 incl. audio *(978-0-8045-6956-9(8))* Spoken Arts, Inc.
Baker, Olaf. Dusty Star. 2011. (Illus.). 168p. pap. 12.99 *(978-1-61203-233-7(8))* Bottom of the Hill Publishing.
Bargach, Naim. Wolfen: Beware, even, of little Wolves... 2008. 56p. per. 8.95 *(978-1-4327-1802-2(9))* Outskirts Pr., Inc.
Bauer, Marion Dane. Runt. 2004. 138p. (gr. 4-7). 17.00 *(978-0-7569-3203-9(3))* Perfection Learning Corp.
—Runt. 2004. (ENG.). 144p. (J). (gr. 3-7). reprint ed. 6.99 *(978-0-440-41978-5(6)*, Yearling) Random Hse. Children's Bks.
Beckhorn, Susan Williams. The Wolf's Boy. 2016. (ENG., Illus.). 236p. (J). (gr. 3-7). 16.99 *(978-1-4847-2553-5(0))* Disney Pr.
Bedard, Michael. The Wolf of Gubbio. 2004. (Illus.). (J). (gr. k-3). spiral bd. *(978-0-616-07213-4(9))* Canadian National Institute for the Blind/Institut National Canadien pour les Aveugles.
Belloni, Giulia. Anything Is Possible. Trevisan, Marco, illus. 2013. (ENG.). 32p. (J). (gr. -1-3). 16.95 *(978-1-926973-91-3(7)*, Owlkids) Owlkids Bks. Inc. CAN. Dist: Publishers Group West (PGW).
Bentley, Sue. Cloud Capers, 3 vols. Swan, Angela & Farley, Andrew, illus. 2009. (Magic Puppy Ser.: 3). (ENG.). 128p. (J). (gr. 1-3). pap. 5.99 *(978-0-448-45046-9(1)*, Grosset & Dunlap) Penguin Young Readers Group.
—A Forest Charm. 2008. (ENG., Illus.). 128p. (J). pap. *(978-0-14-132380-0(9)*, Puffin) Penguin Bks., Ltd.
—New Beginning, No. 1. Swan, Angela & Farley, Andrew, illus. 2009. (Magic Puppy Ser.: 1). (ENG.). 128p. (J). (gr. 1-3). pap. 5.99 *(978-0-448-45044-5(5)*, Grosset & Dunlap) Penguin Young Readers Group.
—Party Dreams. 5th ed. 2008. (ENG., Illus.). 128p. (J). pap. *(978-0-14-132379-4(5)*, Puffin) Penguin Bks., Ltd.
—Snowy Wishes. 2013. (Magic Puppy Ser.). lib. bdg. 16.00 *(978-0-606-32124-2(1)*, Turtleback) Turtleback Bks.
Bently, Peter. The Great Sheep Shenanigans. Matsuoka, Mei, illus. 2012. (Andersen Press Picture Bks). (ENG.). 32p. (J). (gr. -1-3). 16.95 *(978-0-7613-8990-3(3))* Lerner Publishing Group.
Bergren, Lisa Tawn. God Gave Us Thankful Hearts. Hohn, David, illus. 2016. (ENG.). 40p. (J). (gr. -1-2). 10.99 *(978-1-60142-874-5(X)*, WaterBrook Pr.) Crown Publishing Group.
Bernard, Greg. Alpha Summer. 2005. (YA). per. 12.95 *(978-0-926147-21-8(8))* Loonfeather Pr.
Bevis, Mary. Wolf Song. Powell, Consie, illus. 2007. 32p. (gr. 1-2). 18.95 *(978-0-9794202-0-7(2))*; pap. 12.95 *(978-0-9794202-1-4(0))* Raven Productions, Inc.
Biddle, Charles, Jr. The Three Little Pigs. Malak, Annabel, illus. 2011. 16p. (J). pap. 12.95 *(978-2-89558-409-4(5))* Editions Alexandre Stanke CAN. Dist: Bookmasters Distribution.
Black, Holly & Clare, Cassandra. The Copper Gauntlet. (Magisterium Ser.: 2). (ENG.). 272p. (J). 2016. (gr. 4-7). pap. 7.99 *(978-0-545-52229-8(3))* 2015. (gr. 3-7). 17.99 *(978-0-545-52228-1(5)*, Scholastic Pr.) Scholastic, Inc.
Blackford, Andy. The Three Little Pigs & the New Neighbor. 2014. (ENG., Illus.). 32p. (J). *(978-0-7787-0447-8(5))*; pap. *(978-0-7787-0482-9(3))* Crabtree Publishing Co.
Blair, Eric. The Boy Who Cried Wolf, 1 vol. Silverman, Dianne, illus. 2011. (My First Classic Story Ser.). (ENG.). 24p. (gr. k-3). pap. 7.10 *(978-1-4048-7364-3(3)*, My First Classic Story) Picture Window Bks.
—El Lobo y los Siete Cabritos. Abello, Patricia, tr. from ENG. Petrusek, Brett, illus. 2006. (Read-It! Readers en Español: Cuentos de Hadas Ser.). (SPA.). 32p. (gr. k-3). 21.32 *(978-1-4048-1645-9(3)*, Easy Readers) Picture Window Bks.
Blair, Eric & Aesop Enterprise Inc. Staff. The Boy Who Cried Wolf: A Retelling of Aesop's Fable, 1 vol. Silverman, Dianne, illus. 2011. (My First Classic Story Ser.). (ENG.). 24p. (gr. k-3). lib. bdg. 22.65 *(978-1-4048-6507-5(1)*, My First Classic Story) Picture Window Bks.
Blanco, César. Hoky the Caring Wolf. 2013. (ENG., Illus.). 32p. (J). (gr. k-2). 15.95 *(978-84-15241-92-8(5))* Eastern National.
Blevins, Wiley. Little Dead Riding Hood. Cox, Steve, illus. 2016. (Scary Tales Retold Ser.). (ENG.). 24p. (gr. k-3). lib. bdg. 23.99 *(978-1-63440-102-9(6))* Red Chair Pr.
Bradford, Karleen. Ghost Wolf. Cormack, Allan & Drew-Brook, Deborah, illus. 2005. 59p. (J). lib. bdg. 20.00 *(978-1-4242-1254-5(5))* Fitzgerald Bks.
—Ghost Wolf, 1 vol. Cormack, Allan & Drew-Brook, Deborah, illus. 2005. (Orca Echoes Ser.). (ENG.). 64p. (J). (gr. 2-3). per. 6.95 *(978-1-55143-341-7(9))* Orca Bk. Pubs. USA.
Bradman, Tony. Mr. Wolf Bounces Back, 1 vol. Warburton, Sarah, illus. 2009. (After Happily Ever After Ser.). (ENG.). 56p. (gr. 2-3). 25.32 *(978-1-4342-1306-8(4)*, After Happily Ever After) Stone Arch Bks.
—Mr. Wolf Bounces Back [Scholastic]. Warburton, Sarah, illus. 2009. (After Happily Ever After Ser.). (ENG.). 56p. (gr. 2-3). pap. 4.99 *(978-1-4342-1676-2(4)*, After Happily Ever After) Stone Arch Bks.
Brave M.A., Kathryn A. & Lavin, Paul J. A Fit ting Fairy Tale. 2006. 60p. pap. 16.95 *(978-1-4241-2992-8(3))* PublishAmerica, Inc.
Brightwood, Laura, illus. Wolf under the Bed. Brightwood, Laura, . 2007. (J). DVD *(978-1-934409-04-6(9))* 3-C Institute for Social Development.
Broach, Elise. The Wolf Keepers. Ratterree, Alice, illus. 2016. (ENG.). 352p. (J). 16.99 *(978-0-8050-9899-0(2)*, 9780805098990, Holt, Henry & Co. Bks. For Young Readers) Holt, Henry & Co.
Brown, Carron, ed. The Three Little Pigs & Little Red Riding Hood: Two Tales & Their Histories. 2009. (World of Fairy Tales Ser.). (Illus.). 32p. (J). (gr. -1-2). pap. 10.55 *(978-1-60754-641-2(8))*; lib. bdg. 22.60 *(978-1-60754-640-5(X))* Windmill Bks.
Brown, Ken. What's the Time, Grandma Wolf?, 1 vol. Brown, Ken, illus. 2015. (ENG., Illus.). 32p. (J). (gr. -1-2). pap. 7.95 *(978-1-56145-891-2(0))* Peachtree Pubs.
Brun-Cosme, Nadine. Big Wolf & Little Wolf. Bedrick, Claudia Z., tr. from FRE. Tallec, Olivier & Sorman, Joy, illus. 2009. (ENG.). 32p. (J). (gr. -1-2). 16.95 *(978-1-59270-084-4(5))* Enchanted Lion Bks., LLC.
—Big Wolf & Little Wolf: The Little Leaf That Wouldn't Fall. Tallec, Olivier & Sorman, Joy, illus. 2009. (ENG.). 32p. (J). (gr. -1-2). 16.95 *(978-1-59270-088-2(8))* Enchanted Lion Bks., LLC.
—Big Wolf & Little Wolf, Such a Beautiful Orange! Tallec, Olivier & Sorman, Joy, illus. 2011. (ENG.). 32p. (J). (gr. -1-3). 16.95 *(978-1-59270-106-3(X))* Enchanted Lion Bks., LLC.
Bryant, Ann. Tag. 2009. (ENG., Illus.). 24p. (J). pap. *(978-0-7787-3900-5(7))*; lib. bdg. *(978-0-7787-3869-5(8))* Crabtree Publishing Co.
Burgess, Mark. Where Teddy Bears Come From. Ayto, Russell, illus. 2009. 32p. (J). (gr. -1-3). 16.95 *(978-1-56145-487-7(7))* Peachtree Pubs.
Burgess, Melvin. The Cry of the Wolf. 2012. (ENG.). 160p. (YA). (gr. 7). pap. 12.99 *(978-1-84939-375-1(3))* Andersen Pr. GBR. Dist: Independent Pubs. Group.
Burgess, Thornton W. The Adventures of Danny Meadow Mouse. 2009. (gr. 4-7). 108p. 22.95 *(978-1-60664-649-6(4))*; 104p. pap. 9.95 *(978-1-60664-274-0(X))* Rodgers, Alan Bks.
Burks, James. Bird & Squirrel on the Edge! 2015. (Bird & Squirrel Ser.). (ENG., Illus.). 144p. (J). (gr. 2-5). 18.99 *(978-0-545-80425-7(6)*, Graphix) Scholastic, Inc.
Butler, Dori. A Sheep in Wolf's Clothing. 2006. (J). pap. *(978-1-4108-6185-6(6))* Benchmark Education Co.
Caballero, Erica. Mount Mole. 2006. pap. 10.00 *(978-1-4257-2301-9(2))* Xlibris Corp.
The Call of the Wild Guide. 16.47 *(978-0-13-425968-0(8))* Prentice Hall PTR.
Campbell, Mari. Maggiemoosetracks: Making Friends. Katsumoto, Sayaka, tr. Jennings, Randy, illus. 2013. 108p. pap. 21.99 *(978-0-9895205-6-0(0))* MaggieMooseTracks.
—Maggiemoosetracks: Wolf Pack. Jennings, Randy, illus. 2013. 106p. pap. 21.00 *(978-0-9895205-5-3(2))* MaggieMooseTracks.
Campos, Jacqueline. The Adventures of Lil' Wolf, Twinkie, to. 2005. 63p. pap. 16.95 *(978-1-4137-8494-7(1))* PublishAmerica, Inc.
Carbone, Elisa. The Pack. 2006. (ENG.). 160p. (YA). (gr. 7-18). per. 6.99 *(978-0-14-240535-2(3)*, Puffin Books) Penguin Young Readers Group.
Carey, Lorraine. Cinderella's Stepsister & the Big Bad Wolf. Blanco, Migy, illus. 2015. (ENG.). 32p. (J). (gr. -1-2). 15.99 *(978-0-7636-8005-3(2)*, Nosy Crow) Candlewick Pr.
Carlson-Voiles, Polly. Summer of the Wolves. 2013. (ENG.). 352p. (J). (gr. 5-7). pap. 7.99 *(978-0-544-02276-8(9))* Houghton Mifflin Harcourt Publishing Co.
Carter, Aimée. Simon Thorn & the Wolf's Den. 2017. (Simon Thorn Ser.: 1). (J). lib. bdg. 18.40 ***(978-0-606-39595-3(4))*** Turtleback Bks.
Carter, Anne Laurel, et al. The Shepherd's Granddaughter, 1 vol. 2010. (ENG.). 224p. (J). (gr. 8-8). pap. 8.95 *(978-0-88899-903-0(8))* Groundwood Bks. CAN. Dist: Publishers Group West (PGW).
Casanova, Mary. Wolf Shadows. 2nd ed. 2009. (J). *(978-0-9793444-1-7(7))* Quercus Press.
Chapman, Jared. Steve, Raised by Wolves. 2015. (ENG., Illus.). 40p. (J). (gr. -1-3). 17.00 *(978-0-316-25390-1(1))* Little Brown & Co.
Child, Lauren. Beware of the Storybook Wolves. Child, Lauren, illus. 2012. (ENG., Illus.). 32p. (J). (gr. -1-k). pap. 9.99 *(978-1-4083-1480-7(0))* Hodder & Stoughton GBR. Dist: Hachette Bk. Group.
—Cuidado con los Cuentos de Lobos. 2004. (SPA., Illus.). 36p. (J). (gr. -1-3). 17.99 *(978-84-95040-80-0(8))* Serres, Ediciones, S. L. ESP. Dist: Lectorum Pubns., Inc.
Clanton, Connie, illus. The Boy Who Cried Wolf: The Boy Who Cried Wolf. 2012. (SGN, ARA, BOS, CHI & ENG.). 32p. (J). pap. 19.95 incl. DVD *(978-0-9818139-1-2(7))* ASL Tales.
Clark, Anthony & Whybrow, Ian. Little Wolf's Book of Badness. 2008. (ENG.). 96p. (J). pap. 18.95 *(978-1-84002-823-2(8))* Oberon Bks., Ltd. GBR. Dist: Consortium Bk. Sales & Distribution.
Clement-Davies, David. Fell. 2009. (ENG.). 544p. (YA). (gr. 7-11). pap. 10.95 *(978-0-8109-7266-7(2)*, Amulet Bks.) Abrams, Inc.
Cleveland, Marie. Prowlers in Peril: A Storybook Land Adventure, 1 vol. 2010. 52p. pap. 16.95 *(978-1-4489-5204-5(2))* America Star Bks.
Clish, Marian L. A Wolf's Tale. Anderson, Jan, illus. unabr. l.t. ed. (J). (gr. k-5). pap. 14.95 incl. audio compact disk *(978-1-928632-01-6(7))* Writers Marketplace:Consulting, Critiquing & Publishing.
Collins, Lynette. Margie & Wolf: The Series. 2016. 260p. (gr. 1-1). 40.31 *(978-1-5245-1645-1(7))*; pap. 24.19 *(978-1-5245-1644-4(9))* Xlibris Corp.
Collins, Lynette. Margie & Wolf: When They Were Free. 2017. (ENG., Illus.). pap. 32.25 ***(978-1-5245-2168-4(X))*** Xlibris Corp.
Connelly, Erin. Watch Out for Wolves! 2017. (Text Connections Guided Close Reading Ser.). (J). (gr. 1). *(978-1-4900-1820-1(4))* Benchmark Education Co.
Connolly, Brian A. Hawk. 2007. 156p. 20.95 *(978-1-60264-030-6(0))*; 160p. per. 13.95 *(978-1-60264-029-0(7))* Virtualbookworm.com Publishing, Inc.
—Wolf Journal: A Novel. 2005. 164p. 20.95 *(978-1-58939-795-8(9))*; 168p. per. 13.95 *(978-1-58939-794-1(0))* Virtualbookworm.com Publishing, Inc.
Constable, Cathryn. The Wolf Princess. (ENG.). 320p. (J). (gr. 5-9). 2014. pap. 6.99 *(978-0-545-52841-2(0))* 2013. 16.99 *(978-0-545-52839-9(9))* Scholastic, Inc. (Chicken Hse., The).
Conway, David. The Great Fairy Tale Disaster. Williamson, Melanie, illus. 2012. (ENG.). 32p. (J). *(978-1-58925-111-3(3))* Tiger Tales.
Cordell, Matthew. Wolf in the Snow. 2017. (ENG., Illus.). 48p. (J). 17.99 *(978-1-250-07636-6(6)*, 9781250076366) Feiwel & Friends.
Corentin, Philippe. Chafl 2005. (SPA.). (J). 9.95 *(978-84-8470-131-6(X))* Corimbo, Editorial S.L. ESP. Dist: Iaconi, Mariuccia Bk. Imports.
—El Ogro, el Lobo, la Niña y el Pastel. 2004. (SPA.). 32p. (J). (gr. k-2). 19.99 *(978-84-8470-157-6(3))* Corimbo, Editorial S.L. ESP. Dist: Lectorum Pubns., Inc.
Costamagna, Beatrice, illus. Wolf Crunch! 2016. (Crunchy Board Bks.). (ENG.). 12p. (J). (gr. -1-1). bds. 6.99 *(978-1-4998-0200-9(5))* Little Bee Books Inc.
Crabtree, Zona Mae. White Dove. 2005. (Corn Cave Ser.: 3). (ENG., Illus.). (YA). per. 8.00 *(978-0-9726826-2-6(7))* Owl Hollow Publishing.
Crayton, Tina Lorice. The Lost Sheep. 2010. 20p. 10.50 *(978-1-4490-7707-5(2))* AuthorHouse.
Crayton, Tina Lorice (Anderson). The Wolf in Sheep's Clothing: The Impostor. 2011. 20p. 10.50 *(978-1-4567-3011-6(8))* AuthorHouse.
Cresswell, Helen. Sophie & the Seawolf. (Illus.). 32p. (J). *(978-0-340-65608-2(5))* Hodder & Stoughton.
Cummins, Amanda Lynn. The Wolf: The Untold Story. 2005. (Illus.). 32p. (J). (gr. 5-6). 10.00 *(978-0-9670947-7-9(1))* Green Sheet Inc., The.
Dance, Jennifer. Red Wolf. 2014. (ENG., Illus.). 256p. (YA). pap. 12.99 *(978-1-4597-0810-5(5)*, 9781459708105) Dundurn CAN. Dist: Ingram Publisher Services.
Dawson, Willow. The Wolf-Birds. 2015. (ENG., Illus.). 40p. (J). (gr. k-4). 17.95 *(978-1-77147-054-4(2)*, Owlkids) Owlkids Bks. Inc. CAN. Dist: Publishers Group West (PGW).
De Luca, Daniela. Harry the Wolf. 2008. (It's a Wildlife, Buddy! Ser.). (ENG., Illus.). 30p. (J). (gr. -1-1). 12.95 *(978-88-89272-60-2(0))* McRae Bks. Srl ITA. Dist: Independent Pubs. Group.
De Velasco, Miguel Martin Fernandez. Pabluras y Gris. (SPA.). 112p. (YA). (gr. 5-8). *(978-84-279-3178-7(6)*, NG3679) Noguer y Caralt Editores, S. A. ESP. Dist: Lectorum Pubns., Inc.
deRubertis, Barbara. Lana Llama's Little Lamb. Alley, R. W., illus. 2011. (Animal Antics A to Z Ser.). 32p. (J). pap. 45.32 *(978-0-7613-7658-3(5))*; (ENG.). lib. bdg. 22.60 *(978-1-57565-333-4(8))*; (gr. -1-3). pap. 7.95 *(978-1-57565-324-2(9))* Kane Press, Inc.
deRubertis, Barbara & DeRubertis, Barbara. Lana Llama's Little Lamb. Alley, R. W., illus. 2012. (Animal Antics A to Z Ser.). 32p. (J). (gr. 2 — 1). cd-rom 7.95 *(978-1-57565-405-8(9))* Kane Press, Inc.
Devlin, Ivy. Low Red Moon. 2010. (ENG., Illus.). 256p. (YA). (gr. 7-18). 16.99 *(978-1-59990-510-5(8)*, 9781599905105, Bloomsbury USA Childrens) Bloomsbury Publishing USA.
Dewolfe, Jeannee'. The Adventures of Billy Chicken Toes & the Wolf: Add Your Own Art Children's Books. 2012. 56p. pap. 11.97 *(978-1-61204-921-2(4)*, Strategic Bk. Publishing) Strategic Book Publishing & Rights Agency (SBPRA).
Dodd, Emma. Wish. Dodd, Emma, illus. 2015. (Emma Dodd's Love You Bks.). (ENG., Illus.). 24p. (J). (-k). 12.99 *(978-0-7636-8009-1(5)*, Nosy Crow) Candlewick Pr.
Don, Lari. The Hungry Wolf: A Story from North America. Williamson, Melanie, illus. 2013. (Animal Stories Ser.). (ENG.). 48p. (J). (gr. 1-4). pap. 8.99 *(978-1-84686-872-6(6))* Barefoot Bks., Inc.
Donovan, Kevin. Billy & His Friends Tame a Wild Wolf. 2003. (Illus.). 32p. 10.95 *(978-0-9641338-1-5(4))* Billy the Bear & His Friends, Inc.
Dudley, Maywill. The Story of Little Red Riding Hood. 2005. reprint ed. pap. 15.95 *(978-1-4191-5430-0(3))* Kessinger Publishing, LLC.
Dyckman, Ame. Wolfie the Bunny. OHora, Zachariah, illus. 2015. (ENG.). 40p. (J). (gr. -1-1). 17.99 *(978-0-316-22614-1(9))* Little, Brown Bks. for Young Readers.
Early, Alan. Arthur Quinn & the Fenris Wolf. 2013. (Father of Lies Chronicles Ser.: 02). (ENG.). 384p. (J). pap. 14.95 *(978-1-85635-998-6(0))* Mercier Pr., Ltd., The IRL. Dist: Dufour Editions, Inc.
Eash, Sara. Adeline. 2011. 28p. pap. 15.99 *(978-1-4568-7099-7(8))* Xlibris Corp.
Edwards, Julie Andrews & Hamilton, Emma Walton. Dragon: Hound of Honor. 2005. (ENG.). 208p. (J). (gr. 4-18). pap. 6.99 *(978-0-06-057121-4(7))* HarperCollins Pubs.
Eichler, Ken. Swift Eagle's Vision Quest, 1 vol. 2009. 95p. pap. 19.95 *(978-1-60703-649-4(5))* America Star Bks.
Escoffier, Michaël. Rabbit & the Not-So-Big-Bad Wolf. Di Giacomo, Kris, illus. 2013. (ENG.). 32p. (J). (gr. -1-3). 16.95 *(978-0-8234-2813-7(3))* Holiday Hse., Inc.
Evans, Sandra. This Is Not a Werewolf Story. 2016. (ENG., Illus.). 352p. (J). (gr. 4-7). 16.99 *(978-1-4814-4480-4(8)*, Atheneum Bks. for Young Readers) Simon & Schuster Children's Publishing.
Faria, N. K. The Little Smart Rabbit & the Greedy Wolf: Finding Carrots. 2009. (Illus.). 24p. pap. 11.49 *(978-1-4490-1004-1(0))* AuthorHouse.
Farrell, Liam. The Return of the Big Bad Wolf. Myler, Terry, illus. 2004. (ENG.). 64p. (J). pap. 10.95 *(978-1-901737-48-6(9))* Anvil Bks., Ltd. IRL. Dist: Dufour Editions, Inc.
—The True Story of the Three Little Pigs & the Big Bad Wolf. 2nd rev. ed. 2012. (ENG.). 192p. (J). pap. 13.95 *(978-1-85635-955-9(7))* Mercier Pr., Ltd., The IRL. Dist: Dufour Editions, Inc.
—True Story of the Three Little Pigs & the Big Bad Wolf. Myler, Terry, illus. 2nd rev. ed. 2012. (ENG.). 192p. (J). pap. 13.95 *(978-1-85635-682-4(5))* Mercier Pr., Ltd., The IRL. Dist: Dufour Editions, Inc.
Farrow, Stephanie, ed. Blue Wolf & Friends Storybook, 1 Vol., Units 1-4. l.t. ed. 2004. (Illus.). 93p. *(978-0-9758759-2-6(2))* Progressive Language, Inc.
Farshtey, Greg. Beware of the Wolves. 2013. (LEGO Legends of Chima Chapter Bks.: 2). lib. bdg. 14.75 *(978-0-606-32014-6(8)*, Turtleback) Turtleback Bks.
Fearnley, Jan. Mr Wolf & the Enormous Turnip. Fearnley, Jan, illus. 2005. (ENG., Illus.). 40p. (J). (gr. k-2). pap. 10.99 *(978-1-4052-1580-0(1))* Egmont Bks., Ltd. GBR. Dist: Independent Pubs. Group.
—Mr Wolf's Pancakes. 2008. (ENG., Illus.). 32p. (J). (gr. -1-2). 12.95 *(978-1-4052-3872-4(0))* Egmont Bks., Ltd. GBR. Dist: Independent Pubs. Group.
Ferrier, Charlotte. Little Red Riding Hood. 2016. (Fairytale Cottages Ser.). (ENG.). 12p. (J). (gr. -1-k). bds. 8.99 *(978-0-7641-6818-5(5))* Barron's Educational Series, Inc.
Flaxman, Andrew. Little Red Riding Hood: The Classic Grimm's Fairy Tale. Delisa, Patricia, illus. 2006. 32p. (J). (gr. -1-3). 14.95 *(978-0-88010-571-2(2)*, Bell Pond Bks.) SteinerBooks, Inc.
Forward, Toby. The Wolf's Story: What Really Happened to Little Red Riding Hood. Cohen, Izhar, illus. 2005. (ENG.). 32p. (J). (gr. -1-3). 17.99 *(978-0-7636-2785-0(2))* Candlewick Pr.
Fraser, W. A. The Gold Wolf. 2004. reprint ed. pap. 1.99 *(978-1-4192-6404-7(4))* Kessinger Publishing, LLC.
Freitag, Fred. On Hills & Meadows by the River. 2013. 28p. pap. 24.95 *(978-1-63000-584-9(3))* America Star Bks.
Frontiera, Deborah K. Eric & the Enchanted Leaf / Eric y la Hoja Encantada: A Visit with Canis Lupis / una Visita con Canis Lupis. Santillan-Cruz, Silvia R., tr. Scott, Korey, illus. 2nd l.t. ed. 2005. (SPA & ENG.). 32p. (J). lib. bdg. 16.95 *(978-0-9663629-8-5(5))* By Grace Enterprises.
Gaichies, Sarah. Mirabelle the Lost Kitten. 2010. (Illus.). 76p. pap. 24.99 *(978-1-4490-5593-6(1))* AuthorHouse.
Gaiman, NEil. Los Lobos de la Pared. McKean, Dave, illus. 2006.Tr. of Wolves in the Wall. (SPA.). 64p. 22.95 *(978-1-59497-222-5(2))* Public Square Bks.
—The Wolves in the Walls. McKean, Dave, illus. 2003. (ENG.). 56p. (J). (gr. k). 17.99 *(978-0-380-97827-4(X))* HarperCollins Pubs.
Gangloff, Sylviane, illus. Zulka the Wolf. 2015. (Talking Back Ser.). (ENG.). 36p. (J). (gr. -1-2). 7.95 *(978-0-7892-1245-0(5)*, Abbeville Kids) Abbeville Pr., Inc.
George, Jean Craighead. Julie of the Wolves. Schoenherr, John, illus. (Julie of the Wolves Ser.: 1). (ENG.). (J). (gr. 8-18). 2016. 224p. pap. 6.99 *(978-0-06-440058-9(1))* 2003. 208p. pap. 8.99 *(978-0-06-054095-1(8)*, HarperTeen) HarperCollins Pubs.
—Julie of the Wolves. l.t. ed. 2004. (Beeler Mystery Ser.). 32.95 *(978-1-58118-121-0(3))* LRS.
—Julie y los Lobos. 26th ed. 2003.Tr. of Julie & the Wolves. (SPA., Illus.). 184p. (J). (gr. 5-8). pap. 12.95 *(978-84-204-4887-9(7)*, AF0842) Santillana USA Publishing Co., Inc.
Goetze, Jutta. Howl. 2007. 96p. (YA). pap. *(978-1-4207-0740-3(X))* Sundance/Newbridge Educational Publishing.
Golden, Christopher & Lebbon, Tim. The Wild. Ruth, Greg, illus. 2011. (Secret Journeys of Jack London Ser.: 1). (ENG.). 368p. (YA). (gr. 5-18). 15.99 *(978-0-06-186317-2(3)*, HarperTeen) HarperCollins Pubs.
Goldsack, Gaby & Kolanovic, Dubravka, illus. Little Red Riding Hood. 2015. (J). *(978-1-4723-3139-7(7))* Parragon Bk. Service Ltd.
Gordon, Mike, illus. Little Red Riding Hood. 2007. (Picture Book Classics Ser.). 24p. (J). (gr. 1-4). 9.99 *(978-0-7945-1787-8(0)*, Usborne) EDC Publishing.
Grant, V. F. Stories from Grimley Forest. 2011. 48p. (gr. 1-2). pap. 19.50 *(978-1-4567-4709-1(6))* AuthorHouse.
Gravett, Emily. Wolf Won't Bite! Gravett, Emily, illus. 2012. (ENG., Illus.). 32p. (J). (gr. -1-1). 16.99 *(978-1-4424-2763-1(9)*, Simon & Schuster Bks. For Young Readers) Simon & Schuster Bks. For Young Readers.
—Wolves. Gravett, Emily, illus. 2006. (ENG., Illus.). 40p. (J). (gr. k-3). 17.99 *(978-1-4169-1491-4(9)*, Simon & Schuster Bks. For Young Readers) Simon & Schuster Bks. For Young Readers.
Grimm, Jacob & Grimm, Wilhelm K. Little Red Riding Hood: Caperucita Roja. Surges, James, tr. Estrada, Pau, illus. 2006. 22p. (J). (gr. k-4). reprint ed. 15.00 *(978-0-7567-9994-6(5))* DIANE Publishing Co.
Grimm, Wilhelm K. & Grimm, Jacob. Little Red Cap. Zwerger, Lisbeth, illus. 37p. (J). (gr. k-2). pap. 5.95 *(978-0-8072-1285-1(7)*, Listening Library) Random Hse. Audio Publishing Group.
Grotholt, Yannick. Wings for a Lion. 2015. (LEGO Legends of Chima Graphic Novels Ser.: 5). (J). lib. bdg. 18.40 *(978-0-606-37293-0(8))* Turtleback Bks.
Guillain, Charlotte. Red Riding Hood Meets the Three Bears. West, Karl, illus. 2016. (Fairy Tale Mix-Ups Ser.). (ENG.). 24p. (gr. k-2). lib. bdg. 23.32 *(978-1-4109-8304-6(8))* Heinemann-Raintree.
Gunderson, Jessica. No Lie, Pigs (and Their Houses) CAN Fly! The Story of the Three Little Pigs As Told by the Wolf. Bernardini, Cristian, illus. 2016. (Other Side of the Story Ser.). (ENG.). 24p. (gr. 2-3). lib. bdg. 27.32 *(978-1-4795-8621-9(8))* Picture Window Bks.
Haesche, Richard, Sr. Ghost Wolf. 2007. (ENG.). 207p. (YA). 10.99 *(978-0-9798536-5-4(6))* Kreative X-Pressions Pubns.
Hahm, Ji-seul. Prokofiev's Peter & the Wolf. Lupton, David, illus. 2016. (Music Storybooks Ser.). (ENG.). 44p. (gr. 3-6). 26.65 *(978-1-925247-39-8(2)*, Big and SMALL) ChoiceMaker Pty. Ltd., The AUS. Dist: Lerner Publishing Group.
Harrell, Rob. The Troll Who Cried Wolf. 2015. (Life of Zarf Ser.: 2). (ENG., Illus.). 272p. (J). (gr. 3-7). 14.99 *(978-0-8037-4104-1(9)*, Dial Bks) Penguin Young Readers Group.
Harrison, Paul. Three Blind Mice Team up with the Three Little Pigs. Epelbaum, Mariano, illus. 2016. (Fairy Tale Mix-Ups Ser.). (ENG.). 24p. (gr. k-2). lib. bdg. 23.32 *(978-1-4109-8301-5(3))* Heinemann-Raintree.
Hart, Caryl & Lord, Leonie. Whiffy Wilson: The Wolf Who Wouldn't Go to Bed. 2016. (ENG., Illus.). 32p. (J). (gr. -1-k). pap. 8.99 *(978-1-4380-0863-9(5))* Barron's Educational Series, Inc.
—The Wolf Who Wouldn't Go to School. 2015. (ENG.). 32p. (J). (gr. -1-k). pap. 8.99 *(978-1-4380-0620-8(9))* Barron's Educational Series, Inc.

W
X
Y
Z

Hartman, Bob. The Sheep in Wolf's Clothing. Raglin, Tim, illus. 2014. (ENG.). 28p. (J). (gr. k-2). 16.99 (978-0-7459-6515-4(6)) Lion Hudson PLC GBR. Dist: Independent Pubs. Group.

—The Wolf Who Cried Boy. Raglin, Tim, illus. 2004. (ENG.). 32p. (J). (gr. k-3). pap. 7.99 (978-0-14-240159-0(5), Puffin Books) Penguin Young Readers Group.

—The Wolf Who Cried Boy. Raglin, Tim, illus. 2004. (Picture Puffins Ser.). (gr. k-3). 17.00 (978-0-7569-2950-3(4)) Perfection Learning Corp.

—The Wolf Who Cried Boy. Rayla, Tim, illus. 2004. (J). (gr. 1-3). spiral bd. (978-0-616-14574-6(8)) Canadian National Institute for the Blind/Institut National Canadien pour les Aveugles.

Hartnett, Sonya. Stripes of the Sidestep Wolf. 2005. (ENG.). 208p. (YA). (gr. 7-18). 16.99 (978-0-7636-2644-0(9)) Candlewick Pr.

Heede, Sylvia Vanden. What Dog Knows. Tolman, Marije, illus. 2016. 128p. (J). pap. 19.99 (978-1-77657-037-9(5)) Gecko Pr. NZL. Dist: Lerner Publishing Group.

Helakoski, Leslie. Big Chickens. Cole, Henry, illus. 2008. (ENG.). 32p. (J). (gr. -1-k). pap. 6.99 (978-0-14-241057-8(8), Puffin Books) Penguin Young Readers Group.

Hennessy, B. G. The Boy Who Cried Wolf. Kulikov, Boris, illus. 2006. (ENG.). 40p. (J). (gr. -1-3). 17.99 (978-0-689-87433-8(2), Simon & Schuster Bks. For Young Readers) Simon & Schuster Bks. For Young Readers.

—The Boy Who Cried Wolf. Kulikov, Boris, illus. 2011. (J). (gr. -1-2). 29.95 (978-0-545-09452-8(6)) Weston Woods Studios, Inc.

Herrold. City & Village Planning & Zon. 2013. (Fesler-Lampert Minnesota Heritage Ser.). (ENG.). 136p. pap. 9.95 (978-0-8166-9031-2(6)) Univ. of Minnesota Pr.

Hillert, Margaret. Little Red Riding Hood. (Illus.). (J). 6.00 (978-0-87895-680-7(8)) Modern Curriculum Pr.

—Wolves: For the Earliest Reader. Starfall Education, ed. Sloan, Monty, photos by. 2006. (ENG., Illus.). 32p. (J). (978-1-59577-037-0(2)); pap. (978-1-59577-038-7(0)) Starfall Education.

Hobbs, Valerie. Wolf. 2013. (ENG.). 128p. (J). (gr. 3-7). 15.99 (978-0-374-31575-7(2), 9780374315757, Farrar, Straus & Giroux (BYR)) Farrar, Straus & Giroux.

Hobson, Mary Daniel & Rauh, Anna Isabel. The Wolf Who Ate the Sky. Hobson, Charles, illus. 2015. (J). (978-1-59714-298-4(0)) Heyday.

Holden, Pam. The Big Bad Wolf, 6 pack. Hawley, Kelvin, illus. 2009. (Red Rocket Readers Ser.). (ENG.). 16p. (gr. 2-2). pap. (978-1-877363-56-6(1), Red Rocket Readers) Flying Start Bks.

—Don't Cry Wolf. Hatam, Samer, illus. 2015. (ENG.). 16p. (-1). pap. (978-1-77654-130-0(8), Red Rocket Readers) Flying Start Bks.

Holdren, Mark W. Spirit Wolf. 2004. (Illus.). 158p. reprint ed. pap. 13.95 (978-0-9760648-0-0(4)) Powell Hill Pr.

Holmes, Sara. The Wolf Hour. 2017. (J). pap. **(978-0-545-10798-3(9)**, Levine, Arthur A. Bks.) Scholastic, Inc.

Hoover, Helen. Great Wolf & the Good Woodsman. Bowen, Betsy, illus. 2005. (Fesler-Lampert Minnesota Heritage Ser.). 40p. (J). (gr. -1-7). 14.95 (978-0-8166-4445-2(4)) Univ. of Minnesota Pr.

Hopkins, Suzette. Little Wolf's Christmas. Taylor, Jill, illus. 2004. (Little Wolf & Friends Ser.). 19p. (J). 12.95 (978-1-932133-72-1(0)) Writers' Collective, The.

Howker, Janni. Walk with a Wolf: Read, Listen & Wonder. Fox-Davies, Sarah, illus. 2008. (Read, Listen, & Wonder Ser.). (ENG.). 32p. (J). (gr. -1-3). pap. 8.99 (978-0-7636-3875-7(7)) Candlewick Pr.

Hub, Ulrich & Ragg-Kirkby, Helena. Becoming the Wolf. Mühle, Jörg, illus. 2012. (ENG.). 64p. (YA). 12.00 (978-0-8028-5409-4(5), Eerdmans Bks For Young Readers) Eerdmans, William B. Publishing Co.

Impey, Rose. The Big Bad Wolf. McEwen, Katharine, illus. 2017. (Sir Lance-A-Little Ser.). (ENG.). 32p. (J). (gr. k-2). pap. 9.99 **(978-1-4083-2526-1(8)**, Orchard Bks.) Hachette Children's Group GBR. Dist: Hachette Bk. Group.

Irvin-Marston, Hope. My Little Book of Timber Wolves. Magdalena-Brown, Maria, illus. 2nd ed. 2004. 32p. (J). pap. 7.95 (978-0-89317-052-3(6), WW-0526, Windward Publishing) Finney Co., Inc.

Jakubsen, Ryan. Portals III , Band of Rogues. 2011. 128p. pap. 10.00 (978-0-9846320-0-8(X)) Alabaster Bk. Pub.

Jarman, Julia. Little Bad Riding Hood. 2014. (ENG., Illus.). 32p. (J). (978-0-7787-0442-3(4)); pap. (978-0-7787-0450-8(5)) Crabtree Publishing Co.

Johnson, Sandi. White Wolf at Dawn. Johnson, Britt, ed. Sturgen, Bobbi, illus. 2014. (ENG.). 30p. (J). (gr. k-5). pap. 12.99 (978-1-929063-72-7(5), 171) Moons & Stars Publishing For Children.

Jones, Noah Z. Little Red Quacking Hood. 2014. (Princess Pink & the Land of Fake-Believe Ser.: 2). (ENG.). 80p. (J). (gr. k-2). 15.99 (978-0-545-63842-5(9)) Scholastic, Inc.

—Little Red Quacking Hood. Jones, Noah Z., illus. 2014. (Princess Pink & the Land of Fake-Believe Ser.: 2). (ENG., Illus.). 80p. (J). (gr. k-2). pap. 4.99 (978-0-545-63841-8(0)) Scholastic, Inc.

—Little Red Quacking Hood. 2014. (Princess Pink & the Land of Fake-Believe Ser.: 2). lib. bdg. 14.75 (978-0-606-36048-7(4)) Turtleback Bks.

—The Three Little Pugs. 2015. (ENG., Illus.). 80p. (J). (gr. k-2). pap. 4.99 (978-0-545-84857-2(1)) Scholastic, Inc.

Jungman, Ann. Lucy & the Big Bad Wolf. Littlewood, Karin, illus. 2005. 120p. (J). (gr. -1-6). pap. 4.95 (978-1-903015-39-1(1)) Barn Owl Bks, London GBR. Dist: Independent Pubs. Group.

Kantner, Seth. Pup & Pokey. Hill, Beth, illus. 2014. 48p. pap. 14.95 (978-1-60223-241-9(5)) Univ. of Alaska Pr.

Kasza, Keiko. The Dog Who Cried Wolf. Kasza, Keiko, illus. 2009. (ENG., Illus.). 32p. (J). (gr. -1-2). pap. 6.99 (978-0-14-241305-0(4), Puffin Books) Penguin Young Readers Group.

Kellum, Rebecca L. The Conceited Little Girl. 2007. 24p. per. 24.95 (978-1-4241-9810-8(0)) America Star Bks.

Keough, Rob. Wolf Summer. 2009. (Gem Lakes Ser.: 2). (ENG.). 192p. pap. 14.95 (978-1-894283-87-8(2), Great Plains Teen Fiction) Great Plains Pubns. CAN. Dist: Publishers Group Canada.

Kim, Cecil. The Three Pig Sisters. Park, Keun, illus. 2014. (MySELF Bookshelf Ser.). (ENG.). 32p. (J). (gr. k-2). lib. bdg. 25.27 (978-1-59953-654-5(4)) Norwood Hse. Pr.

Kimmel, Eric A. Little Red Hot, 0 vols. Huliska-Beith, Laura, illus. 2013. (ENG.). 32p. (J). (gr. -1-3). 17.99 (978-1-4778-1638-7(0), 9781477816387, Amazon Children's Publishing) Amazon Publishing.

—The Three Little Tamales, 0 vols. Docampo, Valeria, illus. 2009. (ENG.). 32p. (J). (gr. -1-3). 17.99 (978-0-7614-5519-6(1), 9780761455196, Amazon Children's Publishing) Amazon Publishing.

Kimura & North, Lucy. One Stormy Night. Abe, Hiroshi, illus. 2005. 48p. (J). (gr. 1-3). 16.00 (978-4-7700-2970-6(5)) Kodansha International JPN. Dist: Cheng & Tsui Co.

—One Sunny Day, 2 vols., Vol. 2. Abe, Hiroshi, illus. 2005. 48p. (J). 16.00 (978-4-7700-2971-3(3)) Kodansha International JPN. Dist: Cheng & Tsui Co.

Kitamura, Satoshi. Por el Hilo se Saca el Ovillo. Kitamura, Satoshi, illus. 2003. (Picture Books Collection). (SPA., Illus.). 32p. (J). (gr. k-3). 14.95 (978-84-372-2357-5(1)) Altea, Ediciones, S.A. - Grupo Santillana ESP. Dist: Santillana USA Publishing Co., Inc.

Knapman, Timothy. Time Now to Dream. Oxenbury, Helen, illus. 2017. (ENG.). 32p. (J). (gr. -1-2). 16.99 (978-0-7636-9078-6(3)) Candlewick Pr.

Knight, Richard. Winter Shadow. Johnson, Richard, illus. 2011. (ENG.). 80p. (J). (gr. 1-5). pap. 9.99 (978-1-84686-624-1(3)) Barefoot Bks., Inc.

Knight, Richard John & Walker, Richard. Winter Shadow. Johnson, Richard, illus. 2009. (ENG.). 80p. (J). (gr. 3-9). pap. 16.99 (978-1-84686-116-1(0)) Barefoot Bks., Inc.

Knopp, Sue, creator. Study Guide for Wolf Journal: A Novel. 2005. 60p. per. 7.95 (978-1-58939-827-6(0)) Virtualbookworm.com Publishing, Inc.

Knox nee Ramsamugh, Lorna. Fire the Wolf & His Magical Kingdom, 1 vol. 2010. 24p. pap. 24.95 (978-1-4489-6677-6(9)) PublishAmerica, Inc.

Koch, Claus. The Three Little Wolves & the Big Bad Boar. 2011. 68p. pap. 9.99 (978-1-4520-5321-9(9)) AuthorHouse.

Kramer, Alan. The Three Little Pigs Wise up & the Princess Prince & the Vegetables. 2011. (Navigators Ser.). (J). pap. (978-1-61672-962-2(7)) Benchmark Education Co.

Krensky, Stephen. Big Bad Wolves at School. Sneed, Brad, illus. 2007. (ENG.). 32p. (J). (gr. -1-3). 18.99 (978-0-689-83799-9(2), Simon & Schuster Bks. For Young Readers) Simon & Schuster Bks. For Young Readers.

—Big Bad Wolves at School. 2008. (J). (gr. k-3). 27.95 incl. audio (978-0-8045-6966-8(5)) Spoken Arts, Inc.

—The Three Little Pigs' Sledding Adventure. Shortley, Michele, illus. 2011. 28p. (J). pap. (978-0-7680-3486-8(8)) SAE Intl.

Kubler, Annie, illus. What's the Time, Mr. Wolf? 2003. (Finger Puppet Bks.). (ENG.). 24p. (J). (gr. 1-1). (978-0-85953-944-9(X)) Child's Play International Ltd.

Kvasnosky, Laura McGee. Little Wolf's First Howling. Kvasnosky, Laura McGee & McGee, Kate Harvey, illus. 2017. (ENG.). 32p. (J). (gr. -1-2). 15.99 (978-0-7636-8971-1(8)) Candlewick Pr.

Lallemand, Orianne. The Wolf Who Didn't Want to Walk. Thuillier, Eléonore, illus. 2012. (My Little Picture Book Ser.). (ENG.). 32p. (J). 6.95 (978-2-7338-2149-7(0)) Auzou, Philippe Editions FRA. Dist: Consortium Bk. Sales & Distribution.

—The Wolf Who Wanted to Change His Color. Thuillier, Eléonore, illus. 2012. (My Little Picture Book Ser.). (ENG.). 32p. (J). (gr. -1-2). pap. 6.95 (978-2-7338-1945-6(3)) Auzou, Philippe Editions FRA. Dist: Consortium Bk. Sales & Distribution.

Langton, Jane P. Saint Francis & the Wolf. Plume, Ilse, illus. 2007. (ENG.). 32p. (J). (gr. -1-3). 16.95 (978-1-56792-320-9(8)) Godine, David R. Pub.

Lasky, Kathryn. Frost Wolf. (Wolves of the Beyond Ser.: 4). (ENG.). (J). (gr. 3-7). 2012. 256p. pap. 6.99 (978-0-545-09317-0(1)) 2011. 288p. 17.99 (978-0-545-09316-3(3)) Scholastic, Inc. (Scholastic Pr.).

—Frost Wolf. 2012. (Wolves of the Beyond Ser.: 4). lib. bdg. 17.20 (978-0-606-26739-7(5), Turtleback) Turtleback Bks.

—Lone Wolf. 2011. (Wolves of the Beyond Ser.: 1). (ENG.). 240p. (J). (gr. 3-7). pap. 6.99 (978-0-545-09311-8(2)) Scholastic, Inc.

—Lost Tales of Ga'Hoole. Huang, Kathryn, illus. 2010. (Guardians of Ga'hoole Ser.). (ENG.). 192p. (J). (gr. 3-7). 6.99 (978-0-545-10244-5(8), Scholastic Paperbacks) Scholastic, Inc.

—Shadow Wolf. 2011. (Wolves of the Beyond Ser.: 2). (ENG.). 288p. (J). (gr. 3-7). pap. 6.99 (978-0-545-09313-2(9), Scholastic Pr.) Scholastic, Inc.

—Spirit Wolf. Cowdrey, Richard, illus. 2013. (Wolves of the Beyond Ser.: 5). (ENG.). 240p. (J). (gr. 3-7). pap. 6.99 (978-0-545-27971-0(2), Scholastic Pr.) Scholastic, Inc.

—Spirit Wolf. 2012. (Wolves of the Beyond Ser.: 5). (ENG.). 240p. (J). (gr. 3-7). 16.99 (978-0-545-27961-1(5), Scholastic Pr.) Scholastic, Inc.

—Star Wolf. (Wolves of the Beyond Ser.: 6). (ENG.). 256p. (J). (gr. 3-7). 2014. pap. 6.99 (978-0-545-27972-7(0), Scholastic Paperbacks) 2013. (Illus.). 16.99 (978-0-545-27962-8(3), Scholastic Pr.) Scholastic, Inc.

—Watch Wolf. (Wolves of the Beyond Ser.: 3). (ENG.). 240p. (J). (gr. 3-7). 2012. pap. 6.99 (978-0-545-09315-6(5)) 2011. 17.99 (978-0-545-09314-9(7), Scholastic Pr.) Scholastic, Inc.

Laurel Carter, Anne. The Shepherd's Granddaughter. 2013. 236p. pap. (978-1-4596-6490-6(6)) ReadHowYouWant.com, Ltd.

Lee, George Douglas. The Wolf Who Cried Boy. Lee, Brenda Donaloio, ed. Lee, George Douglas, illus. 2012. (Illus.). 46p. pap. 15.95 (978-0-9848486-2-1(2)) Electric Theatre Radio Hour.

Lee, Ji-yeong. Tchaikovsky's Swan Lake. Pacheco, Gabriel, illus. 2016. (Music Storybooks Ser.). (ENG.). 44p. (gr. 3-6). pap. 9.99 (978-1-925247-11-4(2), Big and SMALL) ChoiceMaker Pty. Ltd., The AUS. Dist: Lerner Publishing Group.

Lefèvre, A. M. Hugan Fach Goch. 2005. (WEL., Illus.). 10p. (978-0-86381-645-1(2)) Gwasg Carreg Gwalch.

Lester, Helen. The Sheep in Wolf's Clothing. Munsinger, Lynn, illus. 2014. (Laugh-Along Lessons Ser.). (ENG.). 32p. (J). (gr. -1-3). 8.99 (978-0-544-23300-3(X), HMH Books For Young Readers) Houghton Mifflin Harcourt Publishing Co.

Levine, Gail Carson. Betsy Red Hoodie. Nash, Scott, illus. 2010. (ENG.). 40p. (J). (gr. -1-3). 16.99 (978-0-06-146870-4(3)) HarperCollins Pubs.

—Betsy Who Cried Wolf. Nash, Scott, illus. 2005. (ENG.). 40p. (J). (gr. -1-3). reprint ed. pap. 6.99 (978-0-06-443640-3(3)) HarperCollins Pubs.

Little Bear, Shena. How the lone wolf got her Name. 2008. 80p. pap. 9.95 (978-0-578-00171-5(3)) Stone Castle Publishing.

Little Red Riding Hood: 6 Small Books. (gr. k-2). 23.00 (978-0-7635-8510-5(6)) Rigby Education.

Little Red Riding Hood: Individual Title Six-Packs. (Story Steps Ser.). (gr. k-2). 32.00 (978-0-7635-9841-9(0)) Rigby Education.

Little Red Riding Hood, Level 2. 2016. (Ladybird Readers Ser.). (ENG.). 48p. (J). (gr. 2-4). pap. 9.99 (978-0-241-25446-2(9)) Penguin Bks., Ltd. GBR. Dist: Independent Pubs. Group.

Liz, Pichon. Three Horrid Little Pigs. Liz, Pichon, illus. 2010. (ENG., Illus.). 32p. (J). pap. 7.95 (978-1-58925-423-7(6)) Tiger Tales.

Loewen, Nancy & Gunderson, Jessica. The Other Side of the Story. Bernardini, Cristian & Guerlais, Gérald, illus. 2013. (Other Side of the Story Ser.). (ENG.). 24p. (gr. 2-3). lib. bdg. 109.28 (978-1-4048-8077-1(1)) Picture Window Bks.

Loewen, Nancy, et al. The Other Side of the Story. Guerlais, Gérald & Bernardini, Cristian, illus. 2013. (Other Side of the Story Ser.). (ENG.). 24p. (gr. 2-3). pap. 69.50 (978-1-4795-2004-6(7)); pap. 27.80 (978-1-4795-2006-0(3)); lib. bdg. 273.20 (978-1-4048-8079-5(8)) Picture Window Bks.

—The Other Side of the Story. Avakyan, Tatevik et al, illus. 2013. (Other Side of the Story Ser.). (ENG.). 24p. (gr. 2-3). 99.50 (978-1-4795-2007-7(1)) Picture Window Bks.

Lomba, Ana. Le Petit Chaperon Rouge. Wenzel, Dominique, tr. Cornejo, Santiago, illus. 2006.Tr. of Little Red Riding Hood/The Fun Way to Learn 50 New French Words! (ENG & FRE.). 48p. (gr. -1-3). 17.00 incl. audio compact disk (978-0-07-146167-2(1), 0071461671) McGraw-Hill Cos., The.

London, Jack. The Call of the Wild. 2014. iv, 96p. (J). pap. (978-1-4677-4602-1(9), First Avenue Editions) Lerner Publishing Group.

—The Call of the Wild, 1 vol. VanArsdale, Anthony, illus. 2011. (Calico Illustrated Classics Ser.). (ENG.). 112p. (YA). (gr. 3-6). 27.07 (978-1-60270-742-9(1)) Magic Wagon.

—The Call of the Wild. 2003. (Aladdin Classics Ser.). (ENG.). 160p. (J). (gr. 4-7). mass mkt. 6.99 (978-0-689-85674-7(1), Aladdin) Simon & Schuster Children's Publishing.

—The Call of the Wild. Clift, Eva, tr. Clift, Eva, illus. 2003. (Values in Action Illustrated Classics Ser.). (J). (978-1-59203-047-7(5)) Learning Challenge, Inc.

—The Call of the Wild. Corvino, Lucy, illus. 2005. (Classic Starts(tm) Ser.). (ENG.). 160p. (J). (gr. 2-4). 6.95 (978-1-4027-1274-6(X)) Sterling Publishing Co., Inc.

—The Call of the Wild & White Fang. McKowen, Scott, illus. 2004. (Sterling Unabridged Classics Ser.). (ENG.). 312p. (J). (gr. 5). 9.95 (978-1-4027-1455-9(6)) Sterling Publishing Co., Inc.

—Colmillo Blanco. 2003. (Advanced Reading Ser.: Vol. 56).Tr. of White Fang. (SPA., Illus.). 268p. (J). (gr. 4-7). 11.95 (978-84-239-9030-6(3)) Espasa Calpe, S.A. ESP. Dist: Planeta Publishing Corp.

—Colmillo Blanco.Tr. of White Fang. (SPA.). (J). 8.00 (978-958-04-7143-1(6)) Norma S.A. COL. Dist: Distribuidora Norma, Inc.

—Colmillo Blanco. 2006. (Clasicos Juveniles Ser.).Tr. of White Fang. (SPA., Illus.). 279p. pap. 13.95 (978-84-263-5246-0(4)) Vives, Luis Editorial (Edelvives) ESP. Dist: Lectorum Pubns., Inc.

—White Fang. 2005. 28.95 (978-1-4218-1472-8(2)); 276p. pap. 13.95 (978-1-4218-1572-5(9)) 1st World Publishing, Inc. (1st World Library - Literary Society).

—White Fang. 2005. (ENG.). 176p. (gr. 3-7). per. 14.95 (978-1-59818-531-7(4)) Aegypan.

—White Fang. Guillope, Antoine, illus. 2013. (ENG.). 40p. (J). (gr. 2). 14.95 (978-2-7338-2145-9(8)) Auzou, Philippe Editions FRA. Dist: Consortium Bk. Sales & Distribution.

—White Fang. 2005. 120p. per. 5.95 (978-1-4209-2246-2(7)) Digireads.com Publishing.

—White Fang. 2006. (Aladdin Classics Ser.). (ENG., Illus.). 368p. (J). (gr. 4-7). pap. 7.99 (978-1-4169-1414-3(5), Aladdin) Simon & Schuster Children's Publishing.

—White Fang. Andreasen, Dan, illus. 2006. (Classic Starts(tm) Ser.). (ENG.). 160p. (J). (gr. 2-4). 6.95 (978-1-4027-2500-5(0)) Sterling Publishing Co., Inc.

—White Fang, 1 vol. VanArsdale, Anthony, illus. 2011. (Calico Illustrated Classics Ser.: No. 3). (ENG.). 112p. (J). (gr. 3-6). 27.07 (978-1-61641-112-1(0)) Magic Wagon.

—White Fang. 2004. reprint ed. pap. 22.95 (978-1-4191-9386-6(4)); pap. 1.99 (978-1-4192-9386-3(9)) Kessinger Publishing, LLC.

—White Fang: With a Discussion of Resilience. Walker, Karen, illus. 2003. (Values in Action Illustrated Classics Ser.). 191p. (J). (978-1-59203-038-5(6)) Learning Challenge, Inc.

—White Fang Study Guide. 2003. (Saddleback Classics Ser.). (Illus.). 48p. (J). (gr. 4-7). per. 17.95 (978-1-56254-536-9(1), SP5361) Saddleback Educational Publishing, Inc.

London, Jonathan. The Eyes of Gray Wolf. Van Zyle, Jon, illus. 2016. (ENG.). 30p. (J). pap. 10.99 (978-1-943328-72-7(2), West Winds Pr.) Graphic Arts Ctr. Publishing Co.

—The Seasons of Little Wolf. Van Zyle, Jon, illus. (ENG.). 32p. (J). 2016. (gr. -1-3). pap. 10.99 (978-1-941821-74-9(X)) 2014. 16.99 (978-1-941821-06-0(5)) Graphic Arts Ctr. Publishing Co. (West Winds Pr.).

Machado, Ana Maria. Wolf Wanted, 1 vol. Amado, Elisa, tr. from POR. Cardon, Laurent, illus. 2010. (ENG.). 40p. (J). (gr. -1-2). 18.95 (978-0-88899-880-4(5)) Groundwood Bks. CAN. Dist: Publishers Group West (PGW).

Mackinnon, Mairi. The Boy Who Cried Wolf. 2009. (First Reading Level 3 Ser.). 48p. (J). 6.99 (978-0-7945-2472-2(9), Usborne) EDC Publishing.

Markle, Sandra. Family Pack. Marks, Alan, illus. 2011. (ENG.). 32p. (J). (gr. -1-3). 15.95 (978-1-58089-217-9(5)) Charlesbridge Publishing, Inc.

Martín Fernández de Velasco, Miguel. Pabluras. (SPA.). 120p. (YA). (gr. 5-8). (978-84-279-3146-6(8), NG3678) Noguer y Caralt Editores, S. A. ESP. Dist: Lectorum Pubns., Inc.

Martin, Nicole. The Werewolf. 2006. 146p. pap. 14.99 (978-1-4120-8802-2(X)) Trafford Publishing.

Mawhinney, Art, illus. Diego's Wolf Pup Rescue. 2006. (Go, Diego, Go! Ser.: 1). (ENG.). 24p. (J). (gr. -1-2). pap. 3.99 (978-1-4169-1559-1(1), Simon Spotlight/Nickelodeon) Simon Spotlight/Nickelodeon.

Mazula, Derek. A Drifen's Tale. 2009. 48p. pap. 24.99 (978-1-4490-2782-7(2)) AuthorHouse.

McCleery, William. Wolf Story. Chappell, Warren, illus. 2012. (ENG.). 88p. (J). (gr. k-4). 15.95 (978-1-59017-589-7(1), NYR Children's Collection) New York Review of Bks., Inc., The.

McKy, Katie. Wolf Camp. Leick, Bonnie, illus. 2009. (ENG.). 32p. (J). (gr. -1-3). pap. 8.95 (978-1-933718-25-5(0)) Tanglewood Pr.

McMullan, Kate. Knight for a Day, 1 vol. Basso, Bill, illus. 2007. (Dragon Slayers' Academy Ser.: No. 5). (ENG.). 109p. (gr. 2-5). 24.21 (978-1-59961-377-2(8)) Spotlight.

McNaughton, Colin. Gôl! Williams, Dylan, tr. from ENG. McNaughton, Colin, illus. 2005.Tr. of Goal! (WEL., Illus.). 30p. (978-0-948930-79-9(9)) Cymdeithas Lyfrau Ceredigion.

—M. W. S. G. Williams, Dylan, tr. 2005.Tr. of S. W. A. L. K. (WEL., Illus.). 32p. (978-1-902416-62-5(7)) Cymdeithas Lyfrau Ceredigion.

McNaughton, Colin, et al. Wps! 2005.Tr. of Oops! (WEL., Illus.). 28p. (978-1-902416-29-8(5)) Cymdeithas Lyfrau Ceredigion.

Mcwilliams, Ronnie. The Leaf People: Philip & the Wolf. 2011. 16p. (gr. 1-2). pap. 9.36 (978-1-4567-6583-5(3)) AuthorHouse.

Mejuto, Eva. Run Pumpkin, Run. 2007. (ENG., Illus.). 36p. (J). 17.95 (978-84-96788-88-6(1)) OQO, Editora ESP. Dist: Baker & Taylor Bks.

Menard, Michele R. Who Do I Think You Are? 2013. 26p. pap. 10.95 (978-0-9887969-5-9(3)) Four Menards, The.

Milani, Mino. El Ultimo Lobo. (Barco de Vapor).Tr. of Last Wolf. (SPA.). 144p. (YA). (gr. 5-8). (978-84-348-4520-6(2)) SM Ediciones.

Milhander, Laura Aron. Not for All the Hamantaschen in Town. Chernyak, Inna, illus. 2016. (ENG.). 32p. (gr. -1-3). 17.99 (978-1-4677-5928-1(7), Kar-Ben Publishing) Lerner Publishing Group.

Mortimer, Rachael. Red Riding Hood & the Sweet Little Wolf. Pichon, Liz, illus. 2013. (ENG.). 32p. 12.95 (978-1-58925-117-5(2)) Tiger Tales.

Murphy, Jill. On the Way Home. Murphy, Jill, illus. 2nd rev. ed. 2007. (ENG., Illus.). 32p. (J). (gr. k-2). pap. 11.95 (978-0-230-01584-5(0)) Pan Macmillan GBR. Dist: Independent Pubs. Group.

Murray, Donna. Mottsie, Wolf of Great Price. 2003. 80p. pap. 19.95 (978-1-4137-0080-0(2)) America Star Bks.

Night, P. J. You Can't Come in Here!, 1 vol. 2013. (You're Invited to a Creepover Ser.). (ENG.). 160p. (J). (gr. 3-6). lib. bdg. 24.21 (978-1-61479-066-2(3), Essential Library) ABDO Publishing Co.

—You Can't Come in Here! 2011. (You're Invited to a Creepover Ser.: 2). (ENG.). 160p. (J). (gr. 3-7). pap. 6.99 (978-1-4424-2095-3(2), Simon Spotlight) Simon Spotlight.

Nobisso, Josephine. Francis Woke up Early. Hyde, Maureen, illus. 2011. (ENG.). 32p. (J). (gr. k-2). 17.95 (978-0-940112-20-9(5)); pap. 9.95 (978-0-940112-22-3(1)) Gingerbread Hse.

Norris-Gooding, S. M. The Legend of Kerloup. 2011. 340p. (gr. -1). pap. 23.03 (978-1-4343-5229-3(3)) AuthorHouse.

North, Laura. The Big Bad Wolf & the Robot Pig. 2014. (ENG., Illus.). 32p. (J). (978-0-7787-1291-6(5)) Crabtree Publishing Co.

Nosy Crow Staff. Little Red Riding Hood: a Nosy Crow Fairy Tale. Bryan, Ed, illus. 2017. (ENG.). 32p. (J). (gr. -1-2). 9.99 (978-0-7636-9331-2(6), Nosy Crow) Candlewick Pr.

Numeroff, Laura Joffe. The Chicken Sisters. Collicott, Sharleen, illus. abr. ed. 2003. (J). (gr. -1-2). 28.95 incl. audio compact disk (978-1-59112-533-4(2)) Live Oak Media.

O'Byrne, Nicola. Use Your Imagination. O'Byrne, Nicola, illus. 2015. (ENG., Illus.). 36p. (J). (gr. -1-2). 15.99 (978-0-7636-8001-5(X), Nosy Crow) Candlewick Pr.

Once upon a Time Spanish Version-Little Red Riding Hood. 2005. (J). (978-1-57022-562-8(1)) ECS Learning Systems, Inc.

Once upon a Time Spanish Version-the Boy Who Cried Wolf. 2005. (J). (978-1-57022-557-4(5)) ECS Learning Systems, Inc.

Palatini, Margie. Bad Boys. Cole, Henry, illus. 40p. (J). (gr. -1-2). 2003. lib. bdg. 16.89 (978-0-06-000103-2(8)) 2003. (ENG.). 15.99 (978-0-06-000102-5(X), Tegen, Katherine Bks) 2006. (ENG.). reprint ed. 6.99 (978-0-06-000104-9(6), Tegen, Katherine Bks) HarperCollins Pubs.

—Bad Boys Get Cookie! Cole, Henry, illus. 2006. 32p. (J). (gr. -1-3). 18.89 (978-0-06-074437-3(5)); (ENG.). 17.99 (978-0-06-074436-6(7), Tegen, Katherine Bks) HarperCollins Pubs.

—Bad Boys Get Cookie! 2007. (J). (gr. k-3). 29.95 incl. audio compact disk (978-0-8045-4180-0(9)); 27.95 incl. audio compact disk (978-0-8045-6957-6(6)) Spoken Arts, Inc.

—Bad Boys Get Henpecked! Cole, Henry, illus. 2009. (ENG.). 32p. (J). (gr. -1-2). 17.99 (978-0-06-074433-5(2), Tegen, Katherine Bks) HarperCollins Pubs.

Parker, Emma. Litttle Red Riding Hood. 2010. (Illus.). pap. (978-1-877561-01-6(0)) First Edition Ltd.

Parker, Vic, ed. The Wolf & His Shadow & Other Fables. 2014. (Aesop's Fables Ser.). 40p. (J). (gr. 2-5). pap. 84.95 (978-1-4824-0793-8(0)) Stevens, Gareth Publishing LLLP.

—The Wolf in Sheep's Clothing & Other Fables. 2014. (Aesop's Fables Ser.). 40p. (J). (gr. 2-5). pap. 84.95 (978-1-4824-1261-1(6)) Stevens, Gareth Publishing LLLP.

Paver, Michelle. HERMANO LOBO: CRÓNICAS DE LA PREHISTORIA I. 2005. (SPA., Illus.). 222p. 17.25 (978-84-7888-933-4(7)) Emece Editores ESP. Dist: Ediciones Universal.

—Soul Eater. Taylor, Geoff, illus. 2008. (Chronicles of Ancient Darkness Ser.: 3). 352p. (J). (gr. 5). pap. 6.99 (978-0-06-072833-5(7), Tegen, Katherine Bks) HarperCollins Pubs.

—Spirit Walker. Taylor, Geoff, illus. 2007. (Chronicles of Ancient Darkness Ser.: 2). 384p. (J). (gr. 5-9). per. 6.99 (978-0-06-072830-4(2), Tegen, Katherine Bks) HarperCollins Pubs.
—Wolf Brother. Taylor, Geoff, illus. 2006. (Chronicles of Ancient Darkness Ser.: 1). 320p. (J). (gr. 5-9). reprint ed. per. 6.99 (978-0-06-072827-4(2), Tegen, Katherine Bks) HarperCollins Pubs.
—Wolf Brother, 6 vols. 2005. (Chronicles of Ancient Darkness Ser.: 1). (J). 89.75 (978-1-4193-3811-3(0)); 91.75 (978-1-4193-3809-0(9)); 76.75 (978-1-4193-2628-8(7)); 73.75 (978-1-4193-2630-1(9)) Recorded Bks., Inc.
Pennart, Geoffroy de. EL LOBO SENTIMENTAL. 2004. (SPA.). 36p. (J). (gr. k-2). 20.99 (978-84-8470-120-0(4)) Corimbo, Editorial S.L. ESP. Dist: Lectorum Pubns., Inc.
Percival, Tom. The Magic Looking Glass. 2017. (Little Legends Ser.: 4). (ENG.). 192p. (J). (gr. 2-5). 14.99 **(978-1-4926-4667-9(9))**; pap. 5.99 **(978-1-4926-4259-6(2))** Sourcebooks, Inc. (Sourcebooks Jabberwocky).
Perret, Delphine. The Big Bad Wolf & Me. 2006. (ENG., Illus.). 64p. (J). (gr. -1-3). 9.95 (978-1-4027-3725-1(4)) Sterling Publishing Co., Inc.
Peter & the Wolf. 2016. (Ladybird Tales Ser.). (ENG., Illus.). 48p. (J). (gr. k-2). 9.99 (978-0-7232-9448-1(8)) Penguin Bks., Ltd. GBR. Dist: Independent Pubs. Group.
Peter L. Ward. Freya & the Fenris-Wolf. 2010. 184p. 24.50 (978-1-4269-2511-5(5)); pap. 14.50 (978-1-4269-2510-8(7)) Trafford Publishing.
Pichon, Liz. The Three Horrid Little Pigs. Pichon, Liz, illus. 2008. (Illus.). 32p. (J). (gr. -1-2). 15.95 (978-1-58925-077-2(X)) Tiger Tales.
Pilney, Dovie. Charlie the Cocky Rooster: Another Adventure. 2008. 52p. pap. 20.95 (978-1-4389-3517-1(X)) AuthorHouse.
Ponting, Susan. The Revenge of BB Wolf. 2011. 140p. (gr. -1). 28.98 (978-1-4567-7528-5(6)); (Illus.). pap. 17.23 (978-1-4567-7011-2(X)) AuthorHouse.
Poole, Stephanie. Adopted by Wolves. 2009. 52p. pap. 15.99 (978-1-4415-1032-7(X)) Xlibris Corp.
Porter, Harry. Wolf. Stites, Theresa, illus. 2012. 28p. pap. 14.99 (978-0-9838018-5-6(1)) 4RV Publishing, LLC.
Power, Timothy. The Boy Who Howled. 2012. (ENG.). 272p. (YA). (gr. 3-12). pap. 7.99 (978-1-59990-852-6(2), 9781599908526, Bloomsbury USA Childrens) Bloomsbury Publishing USA.
Publications International Ltd. Staff. Sweet Dreams Padded Treasury. 2013. 320p. (J). bds. (978-1-4127-6333-2(9), 1412763339) Phoenix International Publications, Inc.
Quiller-Couch, Arthur Thomas. The White Wolf & Other Fireside Tales. l.t. ed. 2007. (ENG.). 286p. pap. 23.99 (978-1-4346-5046-7(4)) Creative Media Partners, LLC.
Raines, Kristy. Grizzer the Goofy Wolf. Raines, Morgan, illus. 2007. (ENG.). 80p. per. 11.95 (978-1-59594-132-9(0), Wingspan Pr.) WingSpan Publishing.
Ramadier, Cédric. Help! the Wolf Is Coming! Burgess, Linda, tr. from FRE. Bourgeau, Vincent, illus. 2015.Tr. of Au Secours, Voila le Loup! (ENG.). 22p. (J). (gr. -1 — 1). bds. 14.99 (978-1-927271-84-1(3)) Gecko Pr. NZL. Dist: Lerner Publishing Group.
Rameaka, T. Mystery of Wolf Den Cave. 2005. 74p. pap. 19.95 (978-1-4137-5551-0(8)) America Star Bks.
Ramos, Mario. I Am So Handsome. 2012. (ENG., Illus.). 32p. (gr. -1-4). 17.95 (978-1-877579-19-6(X)) Gecko Pr. NZL. Dist: Lerner Publishing Group.
Ransom, Jeanie Franz. Big Red & the Little Bitty Wolf: A Tale about Bullies. Zivoin, Jennifer, illus. 2016. 32p. (J). (978-1-4338-2048-9(X), Magination Pr.) American Psychological Assn.
Redmond, Diane. Peter & the Wolf: Band 09/Gold. Bendall-Brunello, John, illus. 2007. (Collins Big Cat Ser.). (ENG.). 24p. (J). (gr. 1-2). pap. 7.99 (978-0-00-718674-7(6)) HarperCollins Pubs. Ltd. GBR. Dist: Independent Pubs. Group.
Reilly, Carmel & Miesen, Christina. The Call of the Wolf. 2008. (Rigby Focus Forward: Level H Ser.). (Illus.). 24p. (J). (gr. 4-7). pap. (978-1-4190-3722-1(6), Rigby) Pearson Education Australia.
Richards, Pat. Bardolph Bedivere Wolf Returns. Richards, Charles, illus. 2007. 42p. (J). (978-0-9790796-4-1(0)) PJR Assocs., Ltd.
Rigby Education Staff. Red Riding Hood: Jumbled Tumble. (gr. k-2). 26.00 (978-0-7635-2416-6(6)) Rigby Education.
Rimmington, Natasha, illus. The Wolf & the Seven Little Kids. 2014. (Flip-Up Fairy Tales Ser.). (ENG.). 24p. (J). (978-1-84643-656-7(7)) Child's Play International Ltd.
Robberecht, Thierry. The Wolf Who Fell Out of a Book, 1 vol. 2017. (ENG.). 24p. (J). 14.99 **(978-1-4236-4797-3(1))** Gibbs Smith, Publisher.
Robinson, Hilary. Goldilocks & the Wolf. Sanfilippo, Simona, illus. 2012. (ENG.). 32p. (J). (978-0-7787-8023-6(6)); pap. (978-0-7787-8034-2(1)) Crabtree Publishing Co.
—Three Pigs & a Gingerbread Man. Sanfilippo, Simona, illus. 2012. (ENG.). 32p. (J). (978-0-7787-8026-7(0)); pap. (978-0-7787-8037-3(6)) Crabtree Publishing Co.
Roddy, Lee. Tracked by the Wolf Pack. 2006. (Ladd Family Adventure Ser.: Vol. 15). (J). 7.99 (978-0-88062-264-6(4)) Mott Media.
Romeu, Emma. Here Comes the Grey Wolf. Vigil, Luis Gerardo Sanchez & Broeck, Fabricio Vanden, illus. 2004. (Colección Animales de América / Animals of the Americas Ser.). (SPA.). 32p. (gr. 3-5). pap. 11.95 (978-1-59437-843-0(6)) Santillana USA Publishing Co., Inc.
Roy, Ron. The White Wolf. Gurney, John Steven, tr. Gurney, John Steven, illus. 2004. (to Z Mysteries Ser.: No. 23). (ENG.). 96p. (J). (gr. 1-4). pap. 4.99 (978-0-375-82480-7(4), Random Hse. Bks. for Young Readers) Random Hse. Children's Bks.
Rozanski, Bonnie. Borderline. 2007. (ENG.). 208p. (YA). (gr. 10). pap. 22.95 (978-0-88984-293-9(0)) Porcupine's Quill, Inc. CAN. Dist: Univ. of Toronto Pr.
Rueda, Claudia. Huff & Puff: Can You Blow down the Houses of the Three Little Pigs? 2012. (ENG., Illus.). 32p. (J). (gr. -1-k). 15.95 (978-1-4197-0170-2(3), Abrams Appleseed) Abrams, Inc.
Rundell, Katherine. The Wolf Wilder. 2015. (ENG., Illus.). 240p. (J). (gr. 3-7). 16.99 (978-1-4814-1942-0(0), Simon & Schuster Bks. For Young Readers) Simon & Schuster Bks. For Young Readers.
Sanders, Alex. Un Lobo! (SPA.). 36p. (978-84-95150-34-9(4)) Corimbo, Editorial S.L.
—Un Lobo! (SPA.). 36p. 16.95 (978-84-95150-24-0(7)) Corimbo, Editorial S.L. ESP. Dist: Distribooks, Inc.
Sarfatti, Esther, tr. Caperucita Roja. Rovira, Francesc, illus. 2006. (Bilingual Tales Ser.). (SPA & ENG.). 24p. (J). (gr. -1-3). pap. 3.99 (978-0-439-77375-1(X), Scholastic en Espanol) Scholastic, Inc.
Sargent, Dave & Sargent, Pat. Bo Bo's Big Imagination, 10 vols., Vol. 13. Robinson, Laura, illus. 2004. (Learn to Read Ser.: 10).Tr. of Gran Imaginacion de Bo Bo. 18p. (J). pap. 10.95 (978-1-56763-822-6(8)) Ozark Publishing.
Sargent, Pat L. Topper: Son of Barney, 8. Lenoir, Jane, illus. 2007. (Barney the Bear Killer Ser.: 7). 147p. (YA). lib. bdg. 25.25 (978-1-56763-425-9(7)) Ozark Publishing.
—Topper, Son of Barney #7, 6 vols. 2007. (Barney the Bear Killer Ser.: 7). (YA). pap. 9.95 (978-1-56763-426-6(5)); lib. bdg. 26.25 (978-1-59381-609-4(X)) Ozark Publishing.
Schwartz, Corey Rosen. Ninja Red Riding Hood. Santat, Dan, illus. 2014. (ENG.). 40p. (J). (gr. k-3). 16.99 (978-0-399-16354-8(9), G.P. Putnam's Sons Books for Young Readers) Penguin Young Readers Group.
Scieszka, Jon. ¡La Verdadera Historia de los Tres Cerditos! 2009. (ENG & SPA.). 64p. (J). (gr. k-3). pap. 8.99 (978-0-14-241447-7(6), Puffin Books) Penguin Young Readers Group.
Scott, Victoria. Hear the Wolves. 2017. (ENG.). 240p. (J). (gr. 3-7). 16.99 (978-1-338-04358-7(7), Scholastic Pr.) Scholastic, Inc.
Scraper, Katherine. The Boy Who Cried Wolf: An Aesop's Fable. 2006. (J). pap. (978-1-4108-6166-5(X)) Benchmark Education Co.
Scuderi. Lo Que el Lobo le Conto a la Luna. 2004.Tr. of What the Wolf Told the Moon. (SPA., Illus.). (J). 20.99 (978-84-261-3275-8(8)) Juventud, Editorial ESP. Dist: Lectorum Pubns., Inc.
Seidler, Tor. Firstborn. Sheban, Chris, illus. 2015. (ENG.). 240p. (J). (gr. 4-9). 16.99 (978-1-4814-1017-5(2), Atheneum Bks. for Young Readers) Simon & Schuster Children's Publishing.
Sesame Street Staff. Fairly Furry 2 bk Big Red Riding Hood 3 Little Grouches. 2007. 15.99 (978-1-59069-625-5(5)) Studio Mouse LLC.
Shireen, Nadia. Good Little Wolf. 2011. (ENG.). 32p. (J). (gr. -1-2). 16.99 (978-0-375-86904-4(2), Knopf Bks. for Young Readers) Random Hse. Children's Bks.
Shurtliff, Liesl. Red: the True Story of Red Riding Hood. (ENG.). 256p. (J). (gr. 3-7). 2017. 7.99 (978-0-385-75586-3(4), Yearling) 2016. 16.99 (978-0-385-75583-2(X), Knopf Bks. for Young Readers) Random Hse. Children's Bks.
Sierra, Judy. Tell the Truth, B. B. Wolf. Seibold, J. Otto, illus. 2010. (ENG.). 40p. (J). (gr. -1-2). 16.99 (978-0-375-85620-4(X), Knopf Bks. for Young Readers) Random Hse. Children's Bks.
Simmons, Kristen. The Glass Arrow. 2015. (ENG.). 336p. (YA). (gr. 8-12). 17.99 (978-0-7653-3661-3(8), 9780765336613, Tor Teen) Doherty, Tom Assocs., LLC.
Simone, Yve. Little Valentine. 2013. 72p. pap. 28.99 (978-1-4817-0496-0(6)) AuthorHouse.
Singh, Jay. Once upon a Time in a Forest Far Away. 2009. 394p. pap. 33.12 (978-1-4251-9122-1(3)) Trafford Publishing.
Smallman, Steve. The Lamb Who Came for Dinner. Dreidemy, Joëlle, illus. 2007. 32p. (J). (gr. -1-2). 15.95 (978-1-58925-067-3(2)) Tiger Tales.
Smith, Carrie. The Boy Who Cried Wolf: Classic Tales Edition. Kelley, Gerald, illus. 2011. (Classic Tales Ser.). (J). (978-1-936258-59-8(5)) Benchmark Education Co.
Smith, Emma Bland. Journey: The Most Famous Wolf in the West. James, Robin, illus. 2016. (ENG.). 32p. (J). (gr. k-4). 17.99 (978-1-63217-065-1(5), Little Bigfoot) Sasquatch Bks.
Smith, Lynda Faye. The Revenge of the Big Bad Wolf. 2012. pap. 9.95 (978-0-7414-6529-0(9)) Infinity Publishing.
Smith, Sherry. The Wolf & the Shield: An Adventure with Saint Patrick. McNally, Nicholas, illus. 2016. 118p. (J). pap. (978-0-8198-8356-8(5)) Pauline Bks. & Media.
Smith, Stephanie & Smith, Stephanie A. Gray Wolf Pup's Adventure. Hynes, Robert, illus. 2nd ed. 2003. (ENG.). 32p. (J). (gr. 1-3). 12.95 (978-1-931465-43-4(6), PS2077) Soundprints.
Snell, Roy J. Triple Spies. 2008. 112p. (gr. -1-7). 22.95 (978-1-60664-743-1(1)) Rodgers, Alan Bks.
Sommer, Carl. No One Will Ever Know. Budwine, Greg, illus. 2014. (J). pap. (978-1-57537-962-3(7)) Advance Publishing, Inc.
—No One Will Ever Know. 2003. (Another Sommer-Time Story Ser.). (Illus.). 48p. (J). (gr. 1-4). 16.95 incl. audio (978-1-57537-555-7(9)) Advance Publishing, Inc.
—No One Will Ever Know. Westbrook, Dick, illus. 2003. (Another Sommer-Time Story Ser.). (ENG.). 48p. (J). (gr. 1-4). 16.95 incl. audio compact disk (978-1-57537-506-9(0)) Advance Publishing, Inc.
—No One Will Ever Know(Nadie Se Va a Enterar) Westbrook, Dick, illus. 2009. (Another Sommer-Time Story Bilingual Ser.). (SPA & ENG.). 48p. (J). lib. bdg. 16.95 (978-1-57537-163-4(4)) Advance Publishing, Inc.
Soni, Parwinder Singh, illus. Little Red Riding Hood. 2010. (J). (978-1-60617-132-5(1)) Teaching Strategies, LLC.
Stewart, Paul. In the Dark of the Night. Vyner, Tim, illus. 2009. (ENG.). 40p. (J). (gr. -1-2). (978-1-84507-764-8(4)) Rough Guides, Ltd.
Stiefvater, Maggie. Forever. (Shiver Ser.: 3). (ENG.). (J). (gr. 9). 2014. 416p. pap. 9.99 (978-0-545-68280-0(0)) 2011. 400p. 17.99 (978-0-545-25908-8(8), Scholastic Pr.) Scholastic, Inc.
—Forever. l.t. ed. 2011. (Shiver Trilogy: Bk. 3). (ENG.). 598p. 23.99 (978-1-4104-3606-1(3)) Thorndike Pr.
—Forever. 2014. (Wolves of Mercy Falls Ser.: 3). lib. bdg. 20.85 (978-0-606-36649-6(0)) Turtleback Bks.
—Hunted, Bk. 2. 2014. (Spirit Animals Ser.: 2). (ENG., Illus.). 192p. (J). (gr. 3-7). 12.99 (978-0-545-52244-1(7)) Scholastic, Inc.
—Linger. 2014. (Shiver Ser.). (ENG.). (YA). (gr. 9). lib. bdg. 20.60 **(978-1-68065-091-4(2))** Perfection Learning Corp.
—Linger. (Shiver Ser.: 2). (ENG.). (J). (gr. 9). 2014. 384p. pap. 9.99 (978-0-545-68279-4(7)) 2010. 368p. 17.99 (978-0-545-12328-0(3), Scholastic Pr.) Scholastic, Inc.
—Linger. l.t. ed. 2011. (Shiver Trilogy: Bk. 2). (ENG.). 488p. 23.99 (978-1-4104-3447-0(8)) Thorndike Pr.
—Shiver. 2011. (Shiver Trilogy: Bk. 1). 9.64 (978-0-7848-3572-2(1), Everbind) Marco Bk. Co.
—Shiver. (ENG.). (gr. 9). 2014. (Shiver Ser.). (YA). lib. bdg. 20.60 **(978-1-68065-090-7(4))** 2010. (Shiver Trilogy: Bk. 1). 392p. 20.00 (978-1-60686-750-1(4)) Perfection Learning Corp.
—Shiver. (Shiver Ser.: 1). (ENG.). (J). 2014. 416p. (gr. 9). pap. 9.99 (978-0-545-68278-7(9)) 2009. 400p. (gr. 7-18). 17.99 (978-0-545-12326-6(7), Scholastic Pr.) Scholastic, Inc.
—Shiver. l.t. ed. 2010. (Shiver Trilogy: Bk. 1). (ENG.). 506p. 23.95 (978-1-4104-2667-3(X)) Thorndike Pr.
—Shiver. 2014. (Wolves of Mercy Falls Ser.: 1). lib. bdg. 20.85 (978-0-606-36647-2(4)) Turtleback Bks.
—Sinner. 2015. (Shiver Ser.). (ENG.). 368p. (J). (gr. 9). pap. 10.99 (978-0-545-65459-3(9)) Scholastic, Inc.
Stiefvater, Maggie & Scholastic, Inc. Staff. Shiver; Linger; Forever. 2011. (Shiver Ser.). (ENG.). (J). (gr. 9-9). 52.97 (978-0-545-32686-5(9), Scholastic Pr.) Scholastic, Inc.
Stine, Faye. Wolf: A Story of the Wild. 2012. (ENG.). 64p. pap. 10.95 (978-1-4787-2054-6(9)) Outskirts Pr., Inc.
Stockham, Jess, illus. The Boy Who Cried Wolf. 2011. (Flip-Up Fairy Tales Ser.). (ENG.). 24p. (J). audio compact disk (978-1-84643-407-5(6)); (gr. 2-2). (978-1-84643-368-9(1)) Child's Play International Ltd.
Stockham, Jessica, illus. Little Red Riding Hood. 2005. (Flip-Up Fairy Tales Ser.). (ENG.). 24p. (J). pap. (978-1-904550-22-8(3)) Child's Play International Ltd.
Storr, Catherine. The Complete Polly & the Wolf. Watts, Marjorie Anne & Bennett, Jill, illus. 2016. (ENG.). 304p. (J). (gr. 3-7). 17.95 (978-1-68137-001-9(8), NYR Children's Collection) New York Review of Bks., Inc., The.
Talbott, Hudson. From Wolf to Woof. Talbott, Hudson, illus. 2016. (ENG., Illus.). 40p. (J). (gr. k-3). 16.99 (978-0-399-25404-8(8), Nancy Paulsen Books) Penguin Young Readers Group.
Taplin, Sam. Little Red Riding Hood. 2008. (First Fairytales Look & Say Ser.). 12p. (J). (gr. -1). bds. 9.99 (978-0-7945-2199-8(1), Usborne) EDC Publishing.
Taylor, Christine. Red Riding Hood & the Toad. 2009. (Illus.). 44p. (gr. -1 — 1). 18.49 (978-1-4389-3483-9(1)) AuthorHouse.
Taylor, Sean. Small Bad Wolf. Lewis, Jan, illus. 2004. (I Am Reading Ser.). 45p. (J). (gr. -1-3). 11.60 (978-0-7569-5400-0(2)) Perfection Learning Corp.
Teague, Mark. The Three Little Pigs & the Somewhat Bad Wolf. 2013. (ENG., Illus.). 48p. (J). (gr. -1-k). 17.99 (978-0-439-91501-4(5), Orchard Bks.) Scholastic, Inc.
Thuillier, Eléonore, illus. Wolf, Are You There? Learn How to Get Dressed with the Little Wolf. 2012. (ENG.). 14p. (J). (gr. -1). bds. 14.99 (978-2-7338-1952-4(6)) Auzou, Philippe Editions FRA. Dist: Consortium Bk. Sales & Distribution.
Toliver, Wendy. Once upon a Time: Red's Untold Tale. 2015. (ENG., Illus.). 410p. (YA). (gr. 7-12). 16.99 (978-1-4847-2746-1(0)) Hyperion Bks. for Children.
Tong, Reia D. The Lonely Gourmet: Juan the Vegetarian Wolf. 2010. 44p. pap. 16.99 (978-1-4490-9466-9(X)) AuthorHouse.
Tow, Jack. Up All Night with Howie. Tow, Jack, illus. 2012. (ENG., Illus.). 48p. 16.99 (978-88-89854-93-8(6)) Officina Libraria srl ITA. Dist: National Bk. Network.
Tremblay, Marc. Le Petit Frere du Chaperon Rouge. Fil et al, illus. 2004. (était une Fois Ser.). (FRE.). 24p. (J). (gr. -1). pap. (978-2-89021-698-3(5)) Diffusion du livre Mirabel (DLM).
Trivizas, Eugene. The Three Little Wolves & the Big Bad Pig. Oxenbury, Helen, illus. 2004. (ENG.). 16p. (J). 24.95 (978-1-4052-0669-3(1)) Egmont Bks., Ltd. GBR. Dist: Trafalgar Square Publishing.
—The Three Little Wolves & the Big Bad Pig: A Pop-up Storybook. Oxenbury, Helen, illus. 2006. 16p. (J). (gr. k-4). reprint ed. 27.00 (978-0-7567-9913-7(9)) DIANE Publishing Co.
—Los Tres Lobitos y el Cochino Feroz. Oxenbury, Helen, illus. 2003. (SPA.). 32p. (J). (gr. k-3). pap. 12.99 (978-980-257-246-5(2), EK1366) Ekare, Ediciones VEN. Dist: Kane Miller, Lectorum Pubns., Inc.
Tsaliovich, Anatoly. Of Wolves & Lambs & Others. Burke, Daniel, illus. 2005. 73p. (YA). pap. 12.99 (978-0-9773816-0-9(9)) ATInternational Pubs.
Tucker, Stephen. Little Red Riding Hood, 2 vols. Sharratt, Nick, illus. 2017. (Lift-The-Flap Fairy Tales Ser.). (ENG.). 24p. (J). (gr. -1-1). 10.99 **(978-1-5098-2815-9(X))** Pan Macmillan GBR. Dist: Independent Pubs. Group.
Tyler, William H. The Little Wolf Cubs' Christmas Gift. 2011. 48p. pap. (978-1-4269-7443-4(4)) Trafford Publishing (UK) Ltd.
Vanalstine, Carrie. Frizzy Izzy Yelp! 2012. 32p. pap. 11.95 (978-1-4685-4609-5(0)) AuthorHouse.
Vanden Heede, Sylvia. Wolf & Dog. Nagelkerke, Bill, tr. from DUT. Tolman, Marije, illus. 2013. (ENG.). 96p. (978-1-877579-47-9(5)) Gecko Pr.
Velez, Walter, illus. Little Red Riding Hood: A Tale about Staying Safe. 2006. (J). 6.99 (978-1-59939-021-5(3)) Cornerstone Pr.
Vidal, Séverine. Mega Wolf. Barroux, Stephane, illus. 2015. (Mega Hero Bks.). (ENG.). 28p. (J). (gr. k-2). 12.95 (978-1-77085-637-0(4), 9781770856370) Firefly Bks., Ltd.
Visconti, Guido. El Lobo con Correa. Vignoli, Daniella, illus. 2006. (Wolf on a Leash (Spanish) Ser.). (SPA.). 24p. (gr. k-3). lib. bdg. 24.00 (978-0-8368-6262-1(7), Gareth Stevens Learning Library) Stevens, Gareth Publishing LLLP.
Wallace, R. Mike. Saunter. 2009. 36p. pap. 10.75 (978-1-60693-994-9(7), Strategic Bk. Publishing) Strategic Book Publishing & Rights Agency (SBPRA).
Weston Woods Staff, creator. Red Riding Hood. 2011. 18.95 (978-0-439-72882-9(7)); 29.95 (978-0-439-73518-6(1)); 38.75 (978-0-439-72883-6(5)) Weston Woods Studios, Inc.
—The True Story of the 3 Little Pigs. 2011. 38.75 (978-0-545-09460-3(7)) Weston Woods Studios, Inc.
Whatley, Bruce & Whatley. Wait! No Paint! Whatley, Bruce, illus. 2005. (ENG., Illus.). 32p. (J). (gr. -1-3). pap. 7.99 (978-0-06-443546-8(6)) HarperCollins Pubs.
Wheeler, Lisa. Invasion of the Pig Sisters. Ansley, Frank, illus. 2006. (Fitch & Chip Ser.: 4). (ENG.). 48p. (J). (gr. 1-3). 16.99 (978-0-689-84953-4(2)); pap. 3.99 (978-0-689-84958-9(3)) Simon Spotlight. (Simon Spotlight).
—New Pig in Town. Ansley, Frank, illus. 2003. (Fitch & Chip Ser.: 1). (ENG.). 48p. (J). (gr. 1-3). 16.99 (978-0-689-84950-3(8), Atheneum/Richard Jackson Bks.) Simon & Schuster Children's Publishing.
—Who's Afraid of Granny Wolf? Ansley, Frank, illus. 2006. (Fitch & Chip Ser.: 3). (ENG.). 48p. (J). (gr. 1-3). pap. 3.99 (978-0-689-84957-2(5), Simon Spotlight) Simon Spotlight.
White, Kathy. Little Green Riding Hood. 2006. (J). pap. (978-1-4108-6182-5(1)) Benchmark Education Co.
White, Mark. The Wolf in Sheep's Clothing: A Retelling of Aesop's Fable, 1 vol. Pérez, Sara Rojo, illus. 2013. (My First Classic Story Ser.). (ENG.). 24p. (gr. k-3). pap. 7.10 (978-1-4795-1857-9(3), My First Classic Story) Picture Window Bks.
White, Mark & Aesop Enterprise Inc. Staff. The Wolf in Sheep's Clothing: A Retelling of Aesop's Fable, 1 vol. Pérez, Sara Rojo, illus. 2011. (My First Classic Story Ser.). (ENG.). 24p. (gr. k-3). lib. bdg. 22.65 (978-1-4048-6509-9(8), My First Classic Story) Picture Window Bks.
White, Matthew & Sanderson, Ana. Little Red Riding Hood & the Wolf: A Howling Hilarious Musical, 1 vol. Baiton, Janice, ed. Eccles, Jane, illus. 2005. (and C Black Musicals Ser.). (ENG.). 56p. (J). (gr. 2-6). pap. 42.95 incl. cd-rom **(978-0-7136-6958-9(6))** HarperCollins Pubs. Ltd. GBR. Dist: Independent Pubs. Group.
Whybrow, Ian. Dear Little Wolf. Ross, Tony, illus. 2005. (Little Wolf Adventures Ser.). 64p. (gr. 3-6). pap., lib. bdg. 14.95 (978-0-87614-902-7(6)) Lerner Publishing Group.
—Little Wolf, Forest Detective. Ross, Tony, illus. 2005. (Middle Grade Fiction Ser.). 112p. (J). (gr. 3-6). 14.95 (978-1-57505-413-1(2)); pap. 6.95 (978-1-57505-829-0(4)) Lerner Publishing Group.
—Little Wolf, Pack Leader. Ross, Tony, illus. 2005. (Little Wolf Adventures Ser.). 126p. (gr. 3-6). 14.95 (978-1-57505-400-1(0)) Lerner Publishing Group.
—Little Wolf, Terror of the Shivery Sea. Ross, Tony, illus. 2004. (Little Wolf Adventures Ser.). (ENG.). 144p. (J). (gr. 3-6). 14.95 (978-1-57505-629-6(1)) Lerner Publishing Group.
—Little Wolf's Book of Badness. Ross, Tony, illus. 2005. (Middle Grade Fiction Ser.). 132p. (gr. 3-6). 14.95 (978-1-57505-410-0(8)) Lerner Publishing Group.
—Little Wolf's Diary of Daring Deeds. Ross, Tony, illus. (Middle Grade Fiction Ser.). 132p. (gr. 3-6). 2005. 14.95 (978-1-57505-411-7(6)) 2003. (J). pap. 6.95 (978-0-87614-536-4(5), Carolrhoda Bks.) Lerner Publishing Group.
—Little Wolf's Handy Book of Poems. Ross, Tony, illus. 2005. (Little Wolf Adventures Ser.). 80p. (gr. 3-6). pap., lib. bdg. 14.95 (978-0-87614-927-0(1)) Lerner Publishing Group.
—Little Wolf's Haunted Hall for Small Horrors. Ross, Tony, illus. (Middle Grade Fiction Ser.). (J). 2005. 132p. (gr. 3-6). 14.95 (978-1-57505-412-4(4)) 2004. 125p. (gr. 4-7). per. 6.95 (978-1-57505-794-1(8)) Lerner Publishing Group.
—Lobito Aprende a Ser Malo. Azaola, Miguel, tr. from ENG. Ross, Tony, illus. 2007. (Ediciones Lerner Single Titles Ser.). (SPA.). 136p. (J). (gr. 3-6). per. 6.95 (978-0-8225-8644-9(4), Ediciones Lerner) Lerner Publishing Group.
—Malicia para Principiantes: Una Aventura de Lobito y Apestosito. Quintana, Joela, tr. Ross, Tony, illus. 2005. (Libros Ilustrados (Picture Bks.)). (SPA.). 32p. (J). (gr. k-2). 16.95 (978-0-8225-3211-8(5), Ediciones Lerner) Lerner Publishing Group.
—What's the Time, Little Wolf? A Little Wolf & Smellybreff Adventure. Ross, Tony, illus. 2006. 32p. (J). (gr. -1-3). lib. bdg. 15.95 (978-1-57505-939-6(8), Carolrhoda Bks.) Lerner Publishing Group.
Whybrow, Ian & Ross, Tony. Badness for Beginners: A Little Wolf & Smellybreff Adventure. 2005. (Illus.). 32p. (J). (gr. -1-3). 16.95 (978-1-57505-861-0(8), Carolrhoda Bks.) Lerner Publishing Group.
Williams, M. J. Alora & the Howling Guff. 2010. 132p. pap. 10.68 (978-1-4520-3207-8(6)) AuthorHouse.
Williamson, Melanie. El magnifico plan de Lobo/ Wolf's Magnificent Plan. Williamson, Melanie, illus. 2008. (SPA., Illus.). 29p. 20.95 (978-84-263-6837-9(9)) Vives, Luis Editorial (Edelvives) ESP. Dist: Baker & Taylor Bks.
Wilson, W. Shane. War for Ice. 2010. 158p. pap. 13.99 (978-0-557-23572-8(3)) Lulu Pr., Inc.
Winter, Milo, illus. The Three Little Pigs. 2008. (Shape Bks.). (ENG.). 16p. (J). (gr. -1-3). per. 9.95 (978-1-59583-265-8(3), 9781595832658, Green Tiger Pr.) Laughing Elephant.
Wisnewski, Andrea. Little Red Riding Hood. 2006. (ENG., Illus.). 32p. (J). (gr. 3-7). 18.95 (978-1-56792-303-2(8)) Godine, David R. Pub.
Wood, Maryrose. The Incorrigible Children of Ashton Place Bk. IV: The Interrupted Tale. Wheeler, Eliza, illus. 2013. (Incorrigible Children of Ashton Place Ser.: 4). (ENG.). 400p. (J). (gr. 3-7). 16.99 (978-0-06-179122-2(9)) HarperCollins Pubs.
Woodington, Artie. Elroy, the Big Bad Wolf: The product of his Environment. 2011. 48p. pap. 16.95 (978-1-4560-7229-2(3)) America Star Bks.
Woollvin, Bethan. Little Red, 1 vol. Woollvin, Bethan, illus. 2016. (ENG., Illus.). 32p. (J). (gr. k-4). 16.95 (978-1-56145-917-9(8)) Peachtree Pubs.
Yanez-Arellano, Katherine. The Gunny Wolf Story. 2009. 28p. pap. 12.95 (978-1-4269-1594-9(2)) Trafford Publishing.
Young, Ed. Lon Po Po: A Red-Riding Hood Story from China. unabr. ed. 2006. (J). (gr. k-4). 18.95 (978-0-439-87366-6(5), WPCD690); (Illus.). 29.95 (978-0-439-87367-3(3), WHCD690) Weston Woods Studios, Inc.
Zuill, Andrea. Wolf Camp. 2016. (ENG., Illus.). 40p. (J). (gr. -1-3). 16.99 (978-0-553-50912-0(8), Schwartz & Wade Bks.) Random Hse. Children's Bks.

WOMBATS

Arnold, Caroline. A Wombat's World, 1 vol. Arnold, Caroline, illus. 2008. (Caroline Arnold's Animals Ser.). (ENG., Illus.). 24p. (gr. k-2). lib. bdg. 27.99 (978-1-4048-3986-1(0)) Picture Window Bks.
Fishman, Jon. Meet a Baby Wombat. 2017. (Lightning Bolt Books (tm) — Baby Australian Animals Ser.). (ENG.). (J). (gr. 1-3). pap. 6.99 **(978-1-5124-5592-2(X))** Lerner Publishing Group.

Fishman, Jon M. Meet a Baby Wombat. 2017. (Lightning Bolt Books (tm) — Baby Australian Animals Ser.). (ENG.). 24p. (J). (gr. 1-3). 25.32 **(978-1-5124-3387-6(X))** Lerner Publishing Group.

Gates, Margo. Wombats. 2013. (Animal Safari Ser.). (ENG., Illus.). 24p. (J). (gr. k-3). lib. bdg. 25.95 *(978-1-60014-917-7(0),* Blastoff! Readers) Bellwether Media.

George, Lynn. Wombats: Burrow Builders. 2010. (Animal Architects Ser.). (ENG.). 24p. (J). pap. 8.25 *(978-1-4488-1355-1(7));* lib. bdg. 22.60 *(978-1-4488-0697-3(6))* Rosen Publishing Group, Inc., The. (PowerKids Pr.).

Murray, Julie. Wombats, 1 vol. 2011. (Australian Animals Ser.). (ENG., Illus.). 32p. (J). (gr. 2-5). 28.50 *(978-1-61783-015-0(1))* ABDO Publishing Co.

Petrie, Kristin. Wombats, 1 vol. 2010. (Nocturnal Animals Ser.). (ENG.). 24p. (YA). (gr. 3-6). 25.65 *(978-1-60453-740-6(X))* ABDO Publishing Co.

Phillips, Dee. Wombat's Burrow. 2014. (Science Slam: the Hole Truth Ser.). 24p. (J). (gr. -1-3). lib. bdg. 23.93 *(978-1-62724-091-8(8))* Bearport Publishing Co., Inc.

WOMBATS—FICTION

Chambers, Susannah. The Snow Wombat. Jackson, Mark, illus. 2016. (ENG.). 32p. (J). (gr. -1-1). 16.99 *(978-1-76011-381-0(6))* Allen & Unwin AUS. Dist: Independent Pubs. Group.

Churchill, Vicki & Fuge, Charles. Sometimes I Like to Curl up in a Ball. 2003. (ENG., Illus.). 22p. (J). (gr. -1-k). bds. 5.95 *(978-1-4027-0870-1(X))* Sterling Publishing Co., Inc.

French, Jackie. Christmas Wombat. Whatley, Bruce, illus. 2012. (ENG.). 32p. (J). (gr. -1-3). 16.99 *(978-0-547-86872-1(3))* Houghton Mifflin Harcourt Publishing Co.

—Diary of a Baby Wombat. Whatley, Bruce, illus. 2010. (ENG.). 32p. (J). (gr. -1-3). 16.99 *(978-0-547-43005-8(1))* Houghton Mifflin Harcourt Publishing Co.

—Diary of a Wombat. Whatley, Bruce, illus. 2007. 16p. (J). bds. *(978-0-7322-8662-0(X))* HarperCollins Pubs. Australia.

—Diary of a Wombat. Whatley, Bruce, illus. 2009. (ENG.). 32p. (J). (gr. -1-3). pap. 6.99 *(978-0-547-07669-0(X))* Houghton Mifflin Harcourt Publishing Co.

Lester, Helen. Batter up Wombat. Munsinger, Lynn, illus. 2006. (ENG.). 32p. (J). (gr. k-3). 24.80 *(978-1-4287-0160-1(5),* Follettbound) Follett School Solutions.

McAllister, Angela. Dyna Lle'r Wyt Ti! Williams, Dylan & Jones, Gwen Angharad, trs. from ENG. 2005.Tr. of Found You, Little Wombat! (WEL., Illus.). 24p. *(978-1-902416-90-8(2))* Cymdeithas Lyfrau Ceredigion.

Shields, Carol Diggory. Wombat Walkabout. Blackall, Sophie, illus. 2009. (ENG.). 32p. (J). (gr. -1-k). 16.99 *(978-0-525-47865-2(5),* Dutton Books for Young Readers) Penguin Young Readers Group.

Treml, Renee. Once I Heard a Little Wombat. Treml, Renee, illus. 2016. (ENG., Illus.). 24p. (J). (gr. -1-k). bds. 12.99 *(978-0-85798-739-6(9))* Random Hse. Australia AUS. Dist: Independent Pubs. Group.

WOMEN

see also Girls; Mothers

Angelou, Maya. My Painted House, My Friendly Chicken, & Me. Courtney-Clarke, Margaret, illus. 2003. (ENG.). 48p. (J). (gr. -1-2). pap. 7.99 *(978-0-375-82567-5(3),* Crown Books For Young Readers) Random Hse. Children's Bks.

—My Painted House, My Friendly Chicken, & Me. 2003. (gr. k-3). lib. bdg. 18.40 *(978-0-613-71911-7(5),* Turtleback) Turtleback Bks.

Bevis, Mary. Old Woman Winter. Powell, Consie, illus. 2010. 32p. (J). (gr. 1-2). pap. 9.95 *(978-0-9819307-6-3(X))* Raven Productions, Inc.

Butterfield, Moira. Lady of the Manor. 2009. (Medieval Lives Ser.). 32.80 *(978-1-59920-169-6(0))* Black Rabbit Bks.

Chatterjee. With Our Own Minds: Women Organizing & Developing on Indian Plantation. 2010. (Gender, Culture, & Global Politics Ser.: 10). (gr. 13). 85.00 *(978-0-8153-3701-0(9))* Routledge.

Dinaberg, Leslie. Women in Charge. 2007. (Reading Rocks! Ser.). (ENG., Illus.). 32p. (J). (gr. 2-5). 28.50 *(978-1-59296-870-1(8),* 200753) Child's World, Inc., The.

Esherick, Joan. Women in the World of Africa. 2006. (Women's Issues Ser.). (Illus.). 112p. (YA). lib. bdg. 22.95 *(978-1-59084-857-9(8))* Mason Crest.

Frisch, Aaron. Witches. 2013. (Illus.). 24p. (J). 25.65 *(978-1-60818-250-3(9),* Creative Education) Creative Co., The.

Hamilton, John. Princesses & Heroines, 1 vol. 2006. (Fantasy & Folkore Set 2 Ser.). (ENG., Illus.). 32p. (gr. 4-8). 27.07 *(978-1-59679-339-2(2),* Abdo & Daughters) ABDO Publishing Co.

Henningfeld, Diane Andrews. Should Women Be Allowed to Serve in Combat in the U. S. Armed Forces? 2007. (At Issue Ser.). (ENG., Illus.). 116p. (gr. 10-12). 24.45 *(978-0-7377-3939-8(8),* Greenhaven Pr., Inc.) Cengage Gale.

—Women in Islam. 2010. (At Issue Ser.). (ENG.). 128p. (gr. 10-12). pap. 27.80 *(978-0-7377-4905-2(9),* Greenhaven Pr., Inc.) Cengage Gale.

Jensen, Kelly, ed. Here We Are: Feminism for the Real World. 2017. (ENG., Illus.). 240p. (YA). (gr. 9-12). pap. 16.95 *(978-1-61620-586-7(5))* Algonquin Bks. of Chapel Hill.

Johnson, Claudia. Women's Issues in Alice Walker's the Color Purple. 2011. (Social Issues in Literature Ser.). (Illus.). 224p. (ENG.). (gr. 12-12). lib. bdg. 46.40 *(978-0-7377-5270-0(X));* (J). pap. 28.45 *(978-0-7377-5271-7(8))* Cengage Gale. (Greenhaven Pr., Inc.).

Katz, Naomi. Beautiful-Being an Empowered Young Woman. 2016. (ENG., Illus.). 154p. (J). pap. 16.95 *(978-1-59687-441-1(4),* ipicturebooks) ibooks, Inc.

Langston-George, Rebecca, et al. Encounter. 2015. (Encounter Ser.). (ENG.). (gr. 3-4). 118.61 *(978-1-4914-6920-0(X))* Encounter Bks.

Lewis, Anna M. Women of Steel & Stone: 22 Inspirational Architects, Engineers, & Landscape Designers. 2014. (Women of Action Ser.). (ENG., Illus.). 272p. (YA). (gr. 7). 19.95 *(978-1-61374-508-3(7))* Chicago Review Pr., Inc.

Libal, Autumn. Women in the Hispanic World. 2006. (Women's Issues, Global Trends Ser.). (Illus.). 112p. (YA). lib. bdg. 22.95 *(978-1-59084-858-6(6))* Mason Crest.

Lowery, Zoe & Bezdecheck, Bethany. Women in Relationships. 2017. (Women in the World Ser.). 112p. (gr. 12-11). 37.10 **(978-1-5081-7443-1(1),** Rosen Young Adult) Rosen Publishing Group, Inc., The.

Lowery, Zoe & Mills, J. Elizabeth. Social Roles & Stereotypes. 2017. (Women in the World Ser.). 112p. (gr. 12-11). 37.10 **(978-1-5081-7441-7(5),** Rosen Young Adult) Rosen Publishing Group, Inc., The.

Marriott, Emma. Violence Against Women. 2016. (Illus.). 48p. (J). *(978-0-7787-2590-9(1))* Crabtree Publishing Co.

Martz, Sandra, ed. When I Am an Old Woman I Shall Wear Purple: Petite Version. 2nd gif. rev. ed. 2006. (Illus.). 64p. (C). pap. 47.70 *(978-1-57601-093-8(7))* Nodin Pr.

Nyman, Debbie & Wortzman, Ricki. The 10 Most Notable Elected Female Leaders. 2008. 14.99 *(978-1-55448-527-7(4))* Scholastic Library Publishing.

Phelps, Ethel Johnston, ed. Kamala: Feminist Folktales from Around the World. Boynton, Suki, illus. 2016. (Feminist Folktales Ser.: 2). (ENG.). 120p. (J). (gr. 2-7). pap. 14.95 *(978-1-55861-940-1(2))* Feminist Pr. at The City Univ. of New York.

—Sea Girl: Feminist Folktales from Around the World. Boynton, Suki, illus. 2017. (Feminist Folktales Ser.: 3). (ENG.). 200p. (J). (gr. 2-7). pap. 14.95 *(978-1-55861-418-5(4))* Feminist Pr. at The City Univ. of New York.

Pitman, Gayle E. Feminism from A to Z. 2017. (J). pap. **(978-1-4338-2721-1(2),** Magination Pr.) American Psychological Assn.

Rajczak, Kristen. Women in Business. 2015. (Women Groundbreakers Ser.). (ENG.). 32p. (J). (gr. 4-5). pap. 10.00 *(978-1-4994-1040-2(9),* PowerKids Pr.) Rosen Publishing Group, Inc., The.

—20 Fun Facts about Women in Ancient Egypt. 2015. (Fun Fact File: Women in History Ser.). (ENG., Illus.). 32p. (J). (gr. 2-3). pap. 10.50 *(978-1-4824-2812-4(1))* Stevens, Gareth Publishing LLLP.

Rauf, Don. Female Serial Killers. 2016. (Psychology of Serial Killers Ser.). (ENG.). 128p. (J). (gr. 9-9). lib. bdg. 37.27 *(978-0-7660-7288-6(6))* Enslow Pubs., Inc.

Robertson, David. Betty: The Helen Betty Osborne Story, 1 vol. Henderson, Scott B., illus. 2016. (ENG.). 32p. (YA). (gr. 9-12). pap. 16.00 *(978-1-55379-544-5(X),* 155379544X, HighWater Pr.) Portage & Main Pr. CAN. Dist: Orca Bk. Pubs. USA.

Sideman, Jill, intro. Women in Science. 2005. (Women in Science Ser.). (Illus.). 112p. (gr. 6-12). 120.00 *(978-0-7910-7250-9(9),* Chelsea Hse.) Facts On File, Inc.

Stewart, Sheila. Sometimes My Mom Drinks Too Much. (Kids Have Troubles Too Ser.). (Illus.). 48p. (YA). (gr. 5-18). 2010. lib. bdg. 19.95 *(978-1-4222-1704-7(3))* 2009. pap. 7.95 *(978-1-4222-1917-1(8))* Mason Crest.

Tougas, Shelley & Phillips, Jennifer. Girls Rock!, 1 vol. 2014. (Girls Rock! Ser.). (ENG.). 64p. (gr. 4-5). lib. bdg. 69.30 *(978-1-4765-4650-6(9))* Capstone Press of Coughlan Cos.

Waters, Sophie. Seeing the Gynecologist. 2007. (Girls' Health Ser.). (Illus.). 48p. (YA). (gr. 7-12). lib. bdg. 29.25 *(978-1-4042-1948-9(X))* Rosen Publishing Group, Inc., The.

Weatherford, Carole Boston. Dorothea Lange. Green, Sarah, illus. 2017. (ENG.). 32p. (J). (gr. -1-3). 16.99 *(978-0-8075-1699-7(6))* Whitman, Albert & Co.

Wolfe, Helen. Terrific Women Teachers, 1 vol. 2011. (Women's Hall of Fame Ser.). (ENG., Illus.). 112p. (J). (gr. 4-8). pap. 10.95 *(978-1-897187-86-9(6))* Second Story Pr. CAN. Dist: Orca Bk. Pubs. USA.

WOMEN—BIOGRAPHY

Abbott, L. A. House by the Side of the Road: Stories of 20th Century Farm Life beside Illinois' Lincoln Highway. Abbott Gidel, Susan & Abbott Landow, Jan, eds. 2005. (Illus.). 120p. (YA). per. 14.95 *(978-0-9766820-0-4(1))* Pines Publishing.

Abirached, Zeina. I Remember Beirut. 2014. (ENG.). 96p. pap. 9.95 *(978-1-4677-4458-4(1),* Graphic Universe™) Lerner Publishing Group.

Abrams, Dennis. Julia Child. 2011. (Women of Achievement Ser.). (Illus.). 128p. (gr. 6-12). 35.00 *(978-1-60413-912-9(9),* Chelsea Hse.) Facts On File, Inc.

Acker, Kerry. Nina Simone. 2003. (Women in the Arts Ser.). (Illus.). 112p. (gr. 6-12). 30.00 *(978-0-7910-7456-5(0),* Chelsea Hse.) Facts On File, Inc.

Adams, Colleen. The Courage of Helen Keller. 2009. (Reading Room Collection 2 Ser.). 24p. (gr. 3-4). 42.50 *(978-1-60851-992-7(9),* PowerKids Pr.) Rosen Publishing Group, Inc., The.

—The True Story of Pocahontas. 2009. (What Really Happened? Ser.). (Illus.). 24p. (J). (gr. 3-6). lib. bdg. 22.60 *(978-1-4042-4475-7(1))* Rosen Publishing Group, Inc., The.

Adiletta, Dawn. Elizabeth Cady Stanton: Women's Suffrage & the First Vote. (Library of American Lives & Times Ser.). 112p. 2009. (gr. 5-5). 69.20 *(978-1-60853-479-1(0))* 2005. (Illus.). (J). (gr. -1-3). lib. bdg. 34.60 *(978-1-4042-2647-0(8))* Rosen Publishing Group, Inc., The.

Adler, David A. Harriet Tubman & the Underground Railroad. 2012. (ENG.). 144p. (J). 18.95 *(978-0-8234-2365-1(4))* Holiday Hse., Inc.

—Helen Keller. Wallner, John, illus. 2006. (ENG.). 32p. (J). (gr. -1-3). 4.95 *(978-0-8234-2042-1(6))* Holiday Hse., Inc.

Agins, Donna Brown. Jacqueline Kennedy Onassis: Legendary First Lady. 2004. (People to Know Ser.). (Illus.). 128p. (J). lib. bdg. 26.60 *(978-0-7660-2186-0(6))* Enslow Pubs., Inc.

Alagna, Magdalena. Mae Jemison: The First African American Woman in Space. 2009. (Women Hall of Famers in Mathematics & Science Ser.). 112p. (gr. 5-8). 63.90 *(978-1-60854-813-2(9),* Rosen Reference) Rosen Publishing Group, Inc., The.

Aldridge, Rebecca. Stella Mccartney. 2011. (Famous Fashion Designers Ser.). (Illus.). 112p. (gr. 6-12). 35.00 *(978-1-60413-982-2(X),* Chelsea Hse.) Facts On File, Inc.

Allen, Kathy. Girls Race! Amazing Tales of Women in Sports, 1 vol. 2013. (Girls Rock! Ser.). (ENG.). 64p. (gr. 4-5). 34.65 *(978-1-4765-0233-5(1))* Capstone Press of Coughlan Cos.

Aller, Susan Bivin. Anne Hutchinson. 2010. (History Maker Biographies Ser.). (ENG.). 48p. (gr. 3-6). lib. bdg. 27.93 *(978-0-7613-5208-2(2),* Lerner Pubns.) Lerner Publishing Group.

Allman, Toney. Women Scientists & Inventors. 2016. (ENG.). 80p. (YA). (gr. 5-12). *(978-1-68282-032-2(7))* ReferencePoint Pr., Inc.

Anita Roddick. 2010. (Women of Achievement Ser.). (Illus.). 120p. (gr. 6-12). 35.00 *(978-1-60413-688-3(X),* Chelsea Hse.) Facts On File, Inc.

Ardagh, Philip. Marie Curie. 7th ed. 2003. (ENG., Illus.). 64p. (J). pap. 6.99 *(978-0-330-37571-9(7),* Pan) Pan Macmillan GBR. Dist: Trafalgar Square Publishing.

Bach, Nancy. Maria Montessori & Her Quiet Revolution: A Picture Book about Maria Montessori & Her School Method. Lätti, Leo, illus. 2013. 24p. pap. *(978-1-938712-10-4(2))* Roxby Media Ltd.

Ball, Heather. Astonishing Women Artists, 1 vol. 2007. (Women's Hall of Fame Ser.). (ENG., Illus.). 120p. (J). (gr. 4-8). pap. 10.95 *(978-1-897187-23-4(8))* Second Story Pr. CAN. Dist: Orca Bk. Pubs. USA.

—Remarkable Women Writers, 1 vol. 2006. (Women's Hall of Fame Ser.). (ENG., Illus.). 100p. (J). (gr. 4-8). pap. 10.95 *(978-1-897187-08-1(4))* Second Story Pr. CAN. Dist: Orca Bk. Pubs. USA.

—Women Leaders Who Changed the World. 2011. (Great Women of Achievement Ser.). (ENG., Illus.). 112p. (YA). (gr. 5-8). lib. bdg. 34.60 *(978-1-4488-6000-5(8))* Rosen Publishing Group, Inc., The.

Bankston, John. Missy Elliott: Hip-Hop Superstar. l.t. ed. 2004. (Blue Banner Biography Ser.). (Illus.). 32p. (J). (gr. 3-8). lib. bdg. 25.70 *(978-1-58415-219-4(2))* Mitchell Lane Pubs., Inc.

—Shirley Temple. l.t. ed. 2003. (Real-Life Reader Biography Ser.). (Illus.). 32p. (J). (gr. 3-8). lib. bdg. 25.70 *(978-1-58415-172-2(2))* Mitchell Lane Pubs., Inc.

Bates, Marni. Marni: My True Story of Stress, Hair-Pulling, & Other Obsessions. 2009. (Louder Than Words Ser.). (ENG.). 168p. (YA). (gr. 7-18). pap. 7.95 *(978-0-7573-1412-4(0),* HCI Teens) Health Communications, Inc.

Baum, Margaux & Hopkins, Andrea. The Lives of Women. 2016. (Life in the Middle Ages Ser.). 00064p. (J). (gr. 5-5). 34.45 *(978-1-4994-6466-5(5),* Rosen Central) Rosen Publishing Group, Inc., The.

Becker, Cynthia S. Chipeta: Ute Peacemaker. 2008. (Now You Know Bio Ser.: 11). (Illus.). 98p. (J). pap. 8.95 *(978-0-86541-091-6(7))* Filter Pr., LLC.

Benatar, Raquel & Rubio, Adrian. Go, Milka, Go! The Life of Milka Duno. Benatar, Raquel & Rubio, Adrian, illus. 2008.Tr. of Corre, Milka, Corre! (SPA & ENG., Illus.). 32p. (J). 19.95 *(978-1-56492-360-8(6))* Laredo Publishing Co., Inc.

Benavidez, Barbara. My School Years: Kindergarten Through Graduation. (Illus.). (J). (gr. 5-12). 24.95 *(978-0-9619463-0-2(X))* Barmarie Pubns.

Benge, Janet & Benge, Geoff. Christian Heroes - Then & Now - Lillian Trasher: The Greatest Wonder in Egypt. 2003. (Christian Heroes Ser.). (ENG.). 190p. (YA). pap. 9.99 *(978-1-57658-305-0(8))* YWAM Publishing.

Benjamin, Michelle & Mooney, Maggie. Nobel's Women of Peace, 1 vol. 2008. (Women's Hall of Fame Ser.). (ENG., Illus.). 120p. (J). (gr. 4-8). pap. 10.95 *(978-1-897187-38-8(6))* Second Story Pr. CAN. Dist: Orca Bk. Pubs. USA.

Benson, Michael. Gloria Estefan. 2005. (Biography Ser.). (Illus.). 112p. (gr. 6-12). lib. bdg. 27.93 *(978-0-8225-4982-6(4))* Lerner Publishing Group.

Bjorklund, Ruth. Aung San Suu Kyi. 2013. 112p. (J). (gr. 7-12). 39.93 *(978-0-7614-4957-7(4))* Cavendish Square Publishing.

Bodden, Valerie. Rihanna. 2013. (Illus.). 24p. (J). *(978-1-60818-479-8(X),* Creative Education) Creative Co., The.

Bohannon, Lisa Frederiksen. Failure Is Impossible: The Story of Susan B. Anthony. 2004. (Feminist Voices Ser.). (Illus.). 112p. (YA). (gr. 6-12). 23.95 *(978-1-883846-77-0(3),* First Biographies) Reynolds, Morgan Inc.

Borden, Louise & Kroeger, Mary Kay. Fly High! The Story of Bessie Coleman. Flavin, Teresa, illus. 2004. (ENG.). 40p. (J). (gr. 3-7). 7.99 *(978-0-689-86462-9(0),* Simon & Schuster/Paula Wiseman Bks.) Simon & Schuster/Paula Wiseman Bks.

Boutet de Monvel, Maurice. The Story of Joan of Arc. 2010. (Dover Children's Classics Ser.). (ENG., Illus.). 64p. (J). (gr. 4-7). pap. 14.99 *(978-0-486-47026-9(1))* Dover Pubns., Inc.

Brackett, Virginia. A Home in the Heart: The Story of Sandra Cisneros. 2004. (World Writers Ser.). (Illus.). 112p. (J). (gr. 6-12). 23.95 *(978-1-931798-42-6(7))* Reynolds, Morgan Inc.

—Restless Genius: The Story of Virginia Woolf. 2004. (World Writers Ser.). (Illus.). 144p. (YA). (gr. 6-12). 23.95 *(978-1-931798-37-2(0))* Reynolds, Morgan Inc.

Braun, Sandra. Women Inventors Who Changed the World. 2011. (Great Women of Achievement Ser.). (ENG., Illus.). 112p. (YA). (gr. 5-8). lib. bdg. 34.60 *(978-1-4488-5996-2(4),* Rosen Reference) Rosen Publishing Group, Inc., The.

Bridges, Shirin Yim. Agrippina: "Atrocious & Ferocious" Malone, Peter, illus. 2011. (Thinking Girl's Treasury of Dastardly Dames Ser.). (ENG.). 32p. (J). (gr. 3-8). 18.95 *(978-0-9834256-1-8(2))* Goosebottom Bks. LLC.

—Agrippina: "Atrocious & Ferocious" 2011. 18.95 *(978-0-938425-65-6(X));* 18.95 *(978-0-938425-61-8(7))* Goosebottom Bks. LLC.

Bridges, Shirin Yim & Yim Bridges, Shirin. Qutlugh Terkan Khatun of Kirman. Nguyen, Albert, illus. 2010. (Thinking Girl's Treasury of Real Princesses Ser.). (ENG.). 24p. (J). (gr. 3-8). 18.95 *(978-0-9845098-3-6(6))* Goosebottom Bks. LLC.

Brown, Don. Uncommon Traveler: Mary Kingsley in Africa. 2003. (ENG., Illus.). 32p. (J). (gr. -1-3). 7.99 *(978-0-618-36916-4(3))* Houghton Mifflin Harcourt Publishing Co.

—A Voice from the Wilderness: The Story of Anna Howard Shaw. 2010. 32p. (J). (gr. k-3). pap. 5.95 *(978-0-618-58544-1(3))* Houghton Mifflin Harcourt Trade & Reference Pubs.

Bruchac, Joseph & Locker, Thomas. Rachel Carson: Preserving a Sense of Wonder. 2009. (ENG., Illus.). 32p. (gr. 3-5). pap. 12.95 *(978-1-55591-695-4(3))* Fulcrum Publishing.

Bryant, Jill. Phenomenal Female Entrepreneurs, 1 vol. 2013. (Women's Hall of Fame Ser.). (ENG.). 128p. (J). (gr. 6-8). pap. 10.95 *(978-1-927583-12-8(8))* Second Story Pr. CAN. Dist: Orca Bk. Pubs. USA.

Bryant, Jill & Second Story Press Staff. Dazzling Women Designers, 1 vol. 2010. (Women's Hall of Fame Ser.). (ENG., Illus.). 128p. (J). (gr. 3-5). pap. 10.95 *(978-1-897187-82-1(3))* Second Story Pr. CAN. Dist: Orca Bk. Pubs. USA.

Buckley, Carol. Travels with Tarra, 1 vol. 2005. (ENG., Illus.). 40p. (J). (gr. 3-7). 16.95 *(978-0-88448-241-3(3))* Tilbury Hse. Pubs.

Buffalohead, Julie & Erdrich, Liselotte. Sacagawea. Buffalohead, Julie, illus. 2003. (ENG., Illus.). 40p. (J). (gr. 3-6). 17.95 *(978-0-87614-646-0(9),* Carolrhoda Bks.) Lerner Publishing Group.

Burling, Alexis. Aung San Suu Kyi: Burmese Politician & Activist for Democracy. 2017. (J). **(978-1-5383-8070-3(6))** Rosen Publishing Group, Inc., The.

Butler, Mary. Sojourner Truth: From Slave to Activist for Freedom. 2009. (Library of American Lives & Times Ser.). 112p. (gr. 5-5). 69.20 *(978-1-60853-505-7(3))* Rosen Publishing Group, Inc., The.

Butts, Ed. She Dared: True Stories of Heroines, Scoundrels, & Renegades. Collins, Heather, illus. 2005. (ENG.). 128p. (J). (gr. 5-9). pap. 8.95 *(978-0-88776-718-0(4),* Tundra Bks.) Tundra Bks. CAN. Dist: Penguin Random Hse. LLC.

Butzer, Anna & Colich, Abby. Great Women in History, 1 vol. 2014. (Great Women in History Ser.). (ENG.). 24p. (gr. k-1). 65.97 *(978-1-4914-0556-7(2),* Pebble Bks.) Capstone Press of Coughlan Cos.

Büyüksahin, Mehmet, et al. Khadija Bint Khuwaylid. 2016. (Age of Bliss Ser.). (ENG.). v, 80p. (J). (gr. 4-8). pap. 5.95 *(978-1-59784-375-1(X))* Tughra Bks.

Campbell, Cassie. H. E. A. R. T. 2007. (ENG., Illus.). 108p. (J). (gr. 2-9). pap. *(978-1-55168-315-7(6))* Me to We.

Caravantes, Peggy. Daughters of Two Nations. Flores, Carolyn Dee, illus. 2013. 144p. (J). pap. 14.00 *(978-0-87842-610-2(8))* Mountain Pr. Publishing Co., Inc.

Carey, Nicolette & Bryant, Jill. Women Athletes Who Changed the World. 2011. (Great Women of Achievement Ser.). (ENG., Illus.). 112p. (YA). (gr. 5-8). lib. bdg. 34.60 *(978-1-4488-6001-2(6))* Rosen Publishing Group, Inc., The.

Carlson, Lisa, illus. Calamity Jane. 2007. (On My Own Folklore Ser.). 48p. (J). (gr. -1-3). per. 6.95 *(978-0-8225-6480-5(7),* First Avenue Editions) Lerner Publishing Group.

Cefrey, Holly. The Inventions of Amanda Jones: The Vacuum Method of Canning & Food Preservation. 2009. (19th Century American Inventors Ser.). 24p. (gr. 2-3). 42.50 *(978-1-60854-950-4(X),* PowerKids Pr.) Rosen Publishing Group, Inc., The.

Cheney, Lynne. A Is for Abigail: An Almanac of Amazing American Women. Glasser, Robin Preiss, illus. 2003. (ENG.). 48p. (J). (gr. 1-7). 19.99 *(978-0-689-85819-2(1),* Simon & Schuster Bks. For Young Readers) Simon & Schuster Bks. For Young Readers.

Chin-Lee, Cynthia. Amelia to Zora: Twenty-Six Women Who Changed the World. Halsey, Megan & Addy, Sean, illus. 2008. (ENG.). 32p. (J). (gr. 3-7). pap. 7.95 *(978-1-57091-523-9(7))* Charlesbridge Publishing, Inc.

Colbert, David. Anne Frank. 2008. (10 Days Ser.). (ENG., Illus.). 160p. (J). (gr. 3-8). pap. 7.99 *(978-1-4169-6445-2(2),* Aladdin) Simon & Schuster Children's Publishing.

Cole, Peter. Ben Fletcher: The Life & Times of a Black Wobbly: Including Fellow Worker Fletcher's Writings & Speeches. 10th annot. ed. 2006. (Labor Classics Ser.). (Illus.). 149p. per. 15.00 *(978-0-88286-311-5(8))* Kerr, Charles H. Publishing Co.

Collins, Ellen. A Biography: My Life As a Basset Hound (2005. 51p. pap. 16.95 *(978-1-4137-8776-4(2))* America Star Bks.

Collins, Kathleen. Sojourner Truth: Equal Rights Advocate. 2009. (Primary Sources of Famous People in American History Ser.). 32p. (gr. 2-3). 47.90 *(978-1-60851-727-5(6))* Rosen Publishing Group, Inc., The.

Collins, Lily. Unfiltered: No Shame, No Regrets, Just Me. 2017. 240p. (YA). (gr. 9). 18.99 *(978-0-06-247301-1(8))* HarperCollins Pubs.

Conlan, Kathy & Canadian Museum of Nature Staff. Under the Ice: A Marine Biologist at Work. 2004. (ENG., Illus.). 56p. (J). (gr. 4-6). 11.95 *(978-1-55337-060-4(0))* Kids Can Pr., Ltd. CAN. Dist: Hachette Bk. Group.

Connors, Kathleen. The Life of Florence Nightingale, Vol. 1. 2014. (Famous Lives Ser.). (ENG.). 24p. (J). (gr. 1-2). 22.60 *(978-1-4824-0405-0(2))* Stevens, Gareth Publishing LLLP.

Cooperman, Stephanie H. Chien-Shiung Wu: Pioneering Physicist & Atomic Researcher. 2009. (Women Hall of Famers in Mathematics & Science Ser.). 112p. (gr. 5-8). 63.90 *(978-1-60854-810-1(4),* Rosen Reference) Rosen Publishing Group, Inc., The.

Cregan, Elizabeth R. C. Marie Curie: Pioneering Physicist, 1 vol. 2007. (Science Readers Ser.). (ENG., Illus.). 32p. (J). (gr. 3-3). pap. 8.99 *(978-0-7439-0570-1(9))* Shell Educational Publishing.

Croll, Jennifer. Bad Girls of Fashion: Style Rebels Through the Ages. Buchholc, Ada, illus. 2016. (ENG.). 208p. (J). pap. 14.95 *(978-1-55451-785-5(0))* Annick Pr., Ltd. CAN. Dist: Publishers Group West (PGW).

Crysdale, Joy. Courageous Women Rebels, 1 vol. 2013. (Women's Hall of Fame Ser.). (ENG.). 128p. (J). (gr. 6-8). pap. 10.95 *(978-1-926920-99-3(6))* Second Story Pr. CAN. Dist: Orca Bk. Pubs. USA.

Cullen, J. Heather. Barbara McClintock. 2003. (Women in Science Ser.). (Illus.). 112p. (gr. 6-12). 30.00 *(978-0-7910-7248-6(7),* Chelsea Hse.) Facts On File, Inc.

Cummins, Julie. Women Daredevils. Harness, Cheryl, illus. 2015. (ENG.). 48p. (J). (gr. 2-5). 8.99 *(978-0-14-751737-1(0),* Puffin Books) Penguin Young Readers Group.

Cummins, Julie & Cummins, Julia. Women Daredevils: Thrills, Chills, & Frills. Harness, Cheryl, illus. 2008. (ENG.). 48p. (J). (gr. 2-5). 17.99 *(978-0-525-47948-2(1),* Dutton Books for Young Readers) Penguin Young Readers Group.

Darraj, Susan Muaddi. Mairead Corrigan & Betty Williams: Partners in Peace in Northern Ireland. 2006. (Modern Peacemakers Ser.). (Illus.). 106p. (J). (gr. 9-12). lib. bdg. 30.00 *(978-0-7910-9001-5(9))* Facts On File, Inc.

Davis, Rebecca Henry. Fanny Crosby: Queen of Gospel Songs. 2003. (Illus.). 107p. (J). 6.49 *(978-1-57924-970-0(1))* BJU Pr.

DeFord, Diane. Sacagawea. 2009. pap. 13.25 *(978-1-60559-069-1(X))* Hameray Publishing Group, Inc.

Devillier, Christy. Clara Barton, 1 vol. 2004. (First Biographies Set Iv Ser.). (ENG., Illus.). 32p. (gr. k-4). 27.07 *(978-1-59197-511-3(5),* Buddy Bks.) ABDO Publishing Co.

—Helen Keller, 1 vol. 2004. (First Biographies Set Iv Ser.). (ENG., Illus.). 32p. (gr. k-4). 27.07 *(978-1-59197-514-4(X)*, Buddy Bks.) ABDO Publishing Co.
Ditchfield, Christin. Clara Barton: Founder of the American Red Cross. 2004. (Great Life Stories Ser.). (ENG., Illus.). 111p. (J). 30.50 *(978-0-531-12276-1(X)*, Watts, Franklin) Scholastic Library Publishing.
DiVito, Anna. Annie Oakley Saves the Day. DiVito, Anna, illus. 2004. (Ready-To-read COFA Ser.). (ENG., Illus.). 32p. (J). (gr. k-2). pap. 3.99 *(978-0-689-86520-6(1)*, Simon Spotlight) Simon Spotlight.
Doak, Robin S., et al. Extraordinary Women, 1 vol. 2014. (Extraordinary Women Ser.). (ENG.). 48p. (gr. 6-6). lib. bdg. 163.25 *(978-1-4109-5947-8(3))* Heinemann-Raintree.
Domenico, Kelly Di. Women Scientists Who Changed the World. 2011. (Great Women of Achievement Ser.). (ENG., Illus.). 112p. (YA). (gr. 5-8). lib. bdg. 34.60 *(978-1-4488-5999-3(9))* Rosen Publishing Group, Inc., The.
Donohue, Moira Rose. Maggie L. Walker. 2012. (Illus.). 32p. (J). *(978-1-935884-62-0(X))*; pap. *(978-1-935884-68-2(9))* State Standards Publishing, LLC.
Drimmer, Stephanie Warren. The Book of Heroines: Tales of History's Gutsiest Gals. 2016. (ENG., Illus.). 176p. (J). (gr. 3-7). 14.99 *(978-1-4263-2557-1(6)*, National Geographic Children's Bks.) National Geographic Society.
Dublin, Anne. Dynamic Women Dancers, 1 vol. 2009. (Women's Hall of Fame Ser.). (ENG., Illus.). 120p. (J). (gr. 4-8). pap. 10.95 *(978-1-897187-56-2(4))* Second Story Pr. CAN. Dist: Orca Bk. Pubs. USA.
Dzidrums, Christine. Yuna Kim: Ice Queen. Rendon, Leah, ed. Dzidrums, Joseph et al, photos by. 2011. (Skate Stars Ser.: Vol. 2). (Illus.). 72p. (YA). pap. 10.99 *(978-0-9826435-9-4(4))* Creative Media Publishing.
Dzidrums, Christine & Rendon, Leah. Joannie Rochette: Canadian Ice Princess. Allison, Elizabeth, ed. Adeff, Jay & Mittan, J. Barry, photos by. 2nd exp. rev. ed. 2010. (Skate Stars Ser.: Vol. 1). (Illus.). 100p. (YA). pap. 12.99 *(978-0-9826435-0-1(0))* Creative Media Publishing.
Earl, C. F. Alicia Keys. 2012. (Superstars of Hip-Hop Ser.). (Illus.). 48p. (J). (gr. 3-4). 19.95 *(978-1-4222-2521-9(6))* Mason Crest.
Eddy, Susan. Mother Teresa. 2004. (Rookie Biographies Ser.). (ENG., Illus.). 32p. (J). (gr. 1-2). pap. 4.95 *(978-0-516-27922-0(X)*, Children's Pr.) Scholastic Library Publishing.
Edge, Laura. Tad Lucas: Trick-Riding Rodeo Cowgirl, 1 vol. Ford, Stephanie, illus. 2017. 32p. (J). (gr. k-3). 16.99 *(978-1-4556-2277-1(X))* Pelican Publishing Co., Inc.
Edison, Erin. Great Women in History, 1 vol. (Great Women in History Ser.). (ENG.). 24p. (gr. k-1). 2014. pap. 23.80 *(978-1-4765-7100-3(7))* 2013. pap. 35.70 *(978-1-62065-867-3(4))* 2013. pap. 214.20 *(978-1-62065-868-0(2))* 2013. lib. bdg. 109.95 *(978-1-62065-077-6(0))* Capstone Press of Coughlan Cos. (Pebble Bks.).
—Jane Goodall, 1 vol. 2013. (Great Women in History Ser.). (ENG.). 24p. (gr. k-1). pap. 6.29 *(978-1-4765-0144-4(0))*; pap. 35.70 *(978-1-4765-0145-1(9))*; lib. bdg. 21.99 *(978-1-4765-0143-7(2))* Capstone Press of Coughlan Cos. (Pebble Bks.).
Edwards, Laurie J. Rihanna. 2009. (People in the News Ser.). (ENG., Illus.). 128p. (YA). (gr. 7-12). lib. bdg. 33.95 *(978-1-4205-0129-2(1)*, LML02109-245443) Cengage Gale.
Edwards, Roberta. Who Is Jane Goodall? Marchesi, Stephen et al, illus. 2012. (Who Was? Ser.). (ENG.). 112p. (J). (gr. 3-7). 5.99 *(978-0-448-46192-2(7)*, Grosset & Dunlap) Penguin Young Readers Group.
—Who Is Jane Goodall? 2012. (Who Is... ? Ser.). lib. bdg. 16.00 *(978-0-606-26651-2(8)*, Turtleback) Turtleback Bks.
Egan, Tracie. Cynthia Ann Parker: Cautiva de los Comanches. Gonzalez, Tomas, tr. 2004. (Grandes Personajes en la Historia de Los Estados Unidos Ser.). (ENG & SPA.). 32p. (gr. 3-6). pap. 10.00 *(978-0-8239-4225-1(2))* Rosen Publishing Group, Inc., The.
—Francisca Alavez, the Angel of Goliad. 2004. (Famous People in American History Ser.). (ENG., Illus.). 32p. (gr. 4-8). pap. 10.00 *(978-0-8239-4181-0(7))* Rosen Publishing Group, Inc., The.
—Francisca Alvarez: El ángel de Goliad (Francisca Alvarez: the Angel of Goliad) 2009. (Grandes personajes en la historia de los Estados Unidos (Famous People in American History) Ser.). (SPA.). 32p. (gr. 2-3). 47.90 *(978-1-61512-798-6(4)*, Editorial Buenas Letras) Rosen Publishing Group, Inc., The.
—Francisca Alvarez: The Angel of Goliad. 2009. (Primary Sources of Famous People in American History Ser.). 32p. (gr. 2-3). 47.90 *(978-1-60851-675-9(X))* Rosen Publishing Group, Inc., The.
—Francisca Alvarez: The Angel of Goliad / el ángel de Goliad. 2009. (Famous People in American History/Grandes personajes en la historia de los Estados Unidos Ser.). (ENG & SPA.). 32p. (gr. 2-3). 47.90 *(978-1-61512-544-9(2)*, Editorial Buenas Letras) Rosen Publishing Group, Inc., The.
Emery, Joanna. Caring for a Colony: The Story of Jeanne Mance. Thompson, Allister, ed. Wysotski, Chrissie, illus. 2005. (Stories of Canada Ser.: 8). (ENG.). 72p. (J). (gr. 4-7). 18.95 *(978-1-894917-07-0(3)*, Napoleon & Co.) Dundurn CAN. Dist: Ingram Publisher Services.
Engle, Margarita. Enchanted Air: Two Cultures, Two Wings: A Memoir. Rodriguez, Edel, illus. (ENG.). (YA). (gr. 7). 2016. 224p. pap. 10.99 *(978-1-4814-3523-9(X))* 2015. 208p. 18.99 *(978-1-4814-3522-2(1))* Simon & Schuster Children's Publishing.
Ernest, Brother. Angel of the Poor: A Story of Mother Emmelie Gamelin. Jagodits, Carolyn Lee, illus. 2011. 96p. 38.95 *(978-1-258-06652-9(1))* Literary Licensing, LLC.
Etingoff, Kim. Women Who Built Our Scientific Foundations. Lee-Karlon, Ann, ed. 2013. (Major Women in Science Ser.: 10). 64p. (J). (gr. 7-18). 22.95 *(978-1-4222-2933-0(5))* Mason Crest.
Eva Peron. 2010. (Great Hispanic Heritage Ser.). (Illus.). 104p. (gr. 6-12). 35.00 *(978-1-60413-729-3(0)*, Chelsea Hse.) Facts On File, Inc.
Extraordinary Women. (Illus.). (gr. 6-12). pap. *(978-0-7910-8050-4(1))*; lib. bdg. 688.50 *(978-0-7910-8416-8(7))* Facts On File, Inc. (Chelsea Hse.).
Favilli, Elena & Cavallo, Fran. Good Night Stories for Rebel Girls. 2016. (ENG.). 35.00 *(978-0-9978958-1-0(0))* Timbuktu Labs, Inc.
Favor, Lesli J. Eva Perón. 2010. (Leading Women Ser.). 96p. (gr. 6). 39.93 *(978-0-7614-4962-1(0))* Marshall Cavendish Corp.
Feinstein, Stephen. Read about Sacagawea. 2004. (I Like Biographies! Ser.). (Illus.). 24p. (J). lib. bdg. 22.60 *(978-0-7660-2297-3(8))* Enslow Pubs., Inc.
Feldman, Heather. Valentina Tereshkova: The First Woman in Space. (Space Firsts Ser.). 24p. 2009. (gr. 3-4). 42.50 *(978-1-60853-114-1(7))* 2003. (Illus.). (J). lib. bdg. 22.60 *(978-0-8239-6246-4(6))* Rosen Publishing Group, Inc., The. (PowerKids Pr.).
Fern, Tracey E. Dare the Wind: The Record-Breaking Voyage of Eleanor Prentiss & the Flying Cloud. McCully, Emily Arnold, illus. 2014. (ENG.). 540p. (J). (gr. k-3). 17.99 *(978-0-374-31699-0(6)*, 9780374316990, Farrar, Straus & Giroux (BYR)) Farrar, Straus & Giroux.
Ferris, Jeri Chase. Demanding Justice: A Story about Mary Ann Shadd Cary. Smith, Kimanne, illus. 2003. (Creative Minds Biographies Ser.). (ENG.). 64p. (gr. 4-8). 22.60 *(978-1-57505-177-2(X))*; pap. 8.95 *(978-0-87614-928-7(X)*, Carolrhoda Bks.) Lerner Publishing Group.
Ferry, Joseph. Maria Goeppert Mayer. 2003. (Women in Science Ser.). (Illus.). 112p. (gr. 6-12). 30.00 *(978-0-7910-7247-9(9)*, Chelsea Hse.) Facts On File, Inc.
Findley, Violet. Easy Reader Biographies: Harriet Tubman: Follow the North Star. 2007. (ENG.). 16p. pap. 2.99 *(978-0-439-92330-9(1)*, Teaching Resources) Scholastic, Inc.
Fitzpatrick, Anne. Mother Teresa. 2005. (Genius Ser.). (Illus.). 48p. (J). (gr. 5-9). lib. bdg. 21.95 *(978-1-58341-330-2(8)*, Creative Education) Creative Co., The.
Flynn, Jean. Texas Women Who Dared to Be First. 2004. (Illus.). 144p. (gr. 4-7). 18.95 *(978-1-57168-232-1(5))* Eakin Pr.
Ford, Carin T. Pocahontas: American Indian Princess. 2006. (Heroes of American History Ser.). (Illus.). 32p. (J). (gr. 4-7). lib. bdg. 23.94 *(978-0-7660-2604-9(3)*, Enslow Elementary) Enslow Pubs., Inc.
—Sacagawea: Meet an American Legend. 2003. (Meeting Famous People Ser.). (Illus.). 32p. (J). lib. bdg. 22.60 *(978-0-7660-2004-7(5))* Enslow Pubs., Inc.
Ford, Gabrielle & Thomson, Sarah. Gabe & Izzy: Standing up for America's Bullied. 2014. (ENG., Illus.). 192p. (J). (gr. 5). pap. 8.99 *(978-0-14-750994-9(7)*, Puffin Books) Penguin Young Readers Group.
Fournel, Kelly. Native Women of Courage, 1 vol. 2007. (Native Trailblazers Ser.). (ENG., Illus.). 96p. (J). (gr. 3-12). per. 9.95 *(978-0-9779183-2-4(7)*, 7th Generation) Book Publishing Co.
Frank, Mary Kate. Rihanna. 2009. (Today's Superstars Ser.). 48p. (J). (gr. 5-8). pap. 14.05 *(978-1-4339-2375-3(0))*; lib. bdg. 31.95 *(978-1-4339-2379-1(3))* Stevens, Gareth Publishing LLLP.
Franklin, Virgil. The Story of Sacagawea. 2009. (Reading Room Collection 2 Ser.). 24p. (gr. 3-4). 42.50 *(978-1-60851-997-2(X)*, PowerKids Pr.) Rosen Publishing Group, Inc., The.
Freedman, Russell. The Voice That Challenged a Nation: Marian Anderson & the Struggle for Equal Rights. 2004. (ENG., Illus.). 128p. (J). (gr. 5-7). tchr. ed. 18.00 *(978-0-618-15976-5(2))* Houghton Mifflin Harcourt Publishing Co.
Fryar, Jane L. Hero of Faith - Katharina Von Bora. 2011. 64p. pap. 7.99 *(978-0-7586-2827-5(7))* Concordia Publishing Hse.
Gabourel, Harriet. True to Her Faith: A Story of France at the Time of the Huguenots. 2006. (ENG., Illus.). 224p. (J). per. 7.99 *(978-1-84550-220-1(5)*, 9d879b33-bec0-477a-a976-afb79bfae58a) Christian Focus Pubns. GBR. Dist: Bookmasters Distribution.
Gertner, Sheina Sachar. The Tree Stood Still. 2006. 96p. per. 9.95 *(978-1-58939-886-3(6))* Virtualbookworm.com Publishing, Inc.
Gilbert, Sara. Calamity Jane. 2005. (Legends of the West (Creative Education) Ser.). (Illus.). 48p. (J). (gr. 5-9). lib. bdg. 21.95 *(978-1-58341-337-1(5)*, Creative Education) Creative Co., The.
Glavich, Mary Kathleen. Blessed Teresa of Calcutta: Missionary of Charity. Kiwak, Barbara, tr. Kiwak, Barbara, illus. 2003. (Encounter the Saints Ser.: Vol. 17). 136p. (J). pap. 7.95 *(978-0-8198-1160-8(2)*, 332-024) Pauline Bks. & Media.
—Saint Therese of Lisieux: The Way of Love. Esquinaldo, Virginia, tr. Esquinaldo, Virginia, illus. 2003. (Encounter the Saints Ser.). 132p. (J). pap. 5.95 *(978-0-8198-7074-2(9)*, 332-370) Pauline Bks. & Media.
Golden, Nancy. Life with the Comanches: The Kidnapping of Cynthia Ann Parker. 2009. (Great Moments in American History Ser.). 32p. (gr. 3-4). 47.90 *(978-1-61513-146-4(9))* Rosen Publishing Group, Inc., The.
Gordon, Fernando. Marie Curie, 1 vol. 2016. (ENG., Illus.). 24p. (J). 25.65 *(978-1-68078-154-0(5))* ABDO Publishing Co.
Gosling, Maureen, et al. You Can Be a Woman Movie Maker. I.t. ed. 2003. (Illus.). 80p. (J). 19.95 incl. DVD *(978-1-880599-64-8(3))*; pap. 14.95 incl. DVD *(978-1-880599-63-1(5))* Cascade Pass, Inc.
Gueldenpfennig, Sonia. Women in Space Who Changed the World. 2011. (Great Women of Achievement Ser.). (ENG., Illus.). 112p. (YA). (gr. 5-8). lib. bdg. 34.60 *(978-1-4488-5998-6(0)*, Rosen Reference) Rosen Publishing Group, Inc., The.
Gutowski, Eva. My Life As Eva: Advice from Me to You. 2017. (Illus.). 199p. (J). pap. ***(978-1-5011-4672-5(6)***, Gallery Bks.) Gallery Bks.
Haldy, Emma E. Jane Goodall. Bane, Jeff, illus. 2016. (My Early Library: My Itty-Bitty Bio Ser.). (ENG.). 24p. (J). (gr. k-1). 28.50 *(978-1-63471-022-0(3)*, 208168) Cherry Lake Publishing.
Hally, Ashleigh. Lugenia Burns Hope. 2012. (Illus.). 24p. (J). lib. bdg. *(978-1-935884-76-7(X))* State Standards Publishing, LLC.
—Martha Berry. 2012. (Illus.). 24p. (J). *(978-1-935884-73-6(5))*; pap. *(978-1-935884-79-8(4))* State Standards Publishing, LLC.
Harkins, Susan Sales & Harkins, William H. Pochantas. 2008. (What's So Great About... ? Ser.). (Illus.). 32p. (J). (gr. 2-4). lib. bdg. 25.70 *(978-1-58415-682-6(1))* Mitchell Lane Pubs., Inc.
Harness, Cheryl. Remember the Ladies: 100 Great American Women. Harness, Cheryl, illus. 2003. (ENG., Illus.). 64p. (J). (gr. 3-18). pap. 8.99 *(978-0-06-443869-8(4))* HarperCollins Pubs.
Harris, Laurie Lanzen. Biography for Beginners: Women Who Made a Difference. 2011. (J). lib. bdg. 49.00 *(978-1-931360-43-2(X))* Favorable Impressions.
Hart, Phillip S. Bessie Coleman. 2005. (Just the Facts Biographies Ser.). (ENG., Illus.). 112p. (gr. 5-12). 27.93 *(978-0-8225-2469-4(4))* Lerner Publishing Group.
Hasday, Judy L. Marie Curie: Pioneer on the Frontier of Radioactivity. 2004. (Nobel Prize-Winning Scientists Ser.). (Illus.). 112p. (J). lib. bdg. 27.94 *(978-0-7660-2440-3(7))* Enslow Pubs., Inc.
Havemeyer, Janie. Catherine de' Medici: "The Black Queen" Malone, Peter, illus. 2011. (Thinking Girl's Treasury of Dastardly Dames Ser.). (ENG.). 32p. (J). (gr. 3-8). 18.95 *(978-0-9834256-3-2(9))* Goosebottom Bks. LLC.
Heroes of the Women's Suffrage Movement. 2016. (Heroes of the Women's Suffrage Movement Ser.). 128p. (gr. 6-6). lib. bdg. 223.62 *(978-0-7660-7507-8(9))* Enslow Pubs., Inc.
Hill, Anne E. Michelle Kwan. 2004. (Sports Heroes & Legends Ser.). (ENG., Illus.). 112p. (J). (gr. 5-12). lib. bdg. 30.60 *(978-0-8225-1795-5(7))* Lerner Publishing Group.
Hilliam, David. Eleanor of Aquitaine: The Richest Queen in Medieval Europe. 2009. (Leaders of the Middle Ages Ser.). 112p. (gr. 5-8). 66.50 *(978-1-61513-897-5(8)*, Rosen Reference) Rosen Publishing Group, Inc., The.
—Joan of Arc: Heroine of France. 2004. (Leaders of the Middle Ages Ser.). (Illus.). 112p. (J). lib. bdg. 34.60 *(978-1-4042-0164-4(5))* Rosen Publishing Group, Inc., The.
Hockinson, Liz. Marie Antoinette "Madame Deficit" Malone, Peter, illus. 2011. (Thinking Girl's Treasury of Dastardly Dames Ser.). (ENG.). 32p. (J). (gr. 3-8). 18.95 *(978-0-9834256-4-9(7))* Goosebottom Bks. LLC.
Holden, Henry M. American Women of Flight: Pilots & Pioneers. 2003. (Collective Biographies Ser.). (Illus.). 112p. (J). (gr. 6-12). lib. bdg. 26.60 *(978-0-7660-2005-4(3))* Enslow Pubs., Inc.
Hollingsworth, Tamara. Helen Keller: A New Vision, 1 vol. 2nd rev. ed. 2013. (Nonfiction Readers Ser.). (ENG., Illus.). 48p. (J). (gr. 4-4). pap. 29.96 *(978-1-4807-1115-0(2))* Shell Educational Publishing.
—Helen Keller: Una Nueva Visión. 2017. (TIME for Kids en Español - Level 4 Ser.). (SPA & ENG., Illus.). 48p. (gr. 4-4). lib. bdg. 31.99 *(978-1-5157-5144-1(9))* Time for Kids Inc AUS. Dist: Capstone Pub.
Homan, Lynn M. & Reilly, Thomas. Women Who Fly, 1 vol. Shepherd, Rosalie M., illus. 2004. (ENG.). 104p. (J). (gr. 3-7). 14.95 *(978-1-58980-160-8(1))* Pelican Publishing Co., Inc.
Howat, Irene. Ten Girls Who Changed the World. 2015. (Lightkeepers Ser.). (ENG.). 160p. (J). pap. 8.99 *(978-1-85792-649-1(8)*, 88e5376b-86d8-4202-a61d-050c2649c1e9) Christian Focus Pubns. GBR. Dist: Bookmasters Distribution.
—Ten Girls Who Made a Difference. 2012. (Lightkeepers Ser.). (ENG.). 160p. (J). pap. 8.99 *(978-1-85792-776-4(1)*, abd5e7d9-3bf4-428b-a3a7-b8ae57c254d2) Christian Focus Pubns. GBR. Dist: Bookmasters Distribution.
—Ten Girls Who Used Their Talents. 2014. (Lightkeepers Ser.). (ENG., Illus.). 160p. (J). (gr. 3-7). per. 8.99 *(978-1-84550-147-1(0)*, de728062-6bc3-4bf7-87b9-a97ebd0810fb) Christian Focus Pubns. GBR. Dist: Bookmasters Distribution.
Hoyt, Megan. Hildegard's Gift. Hill, David, illus. 2014. (ENG.). 32p. (J). pap. 15.99 *(978-1-61261-358-1(6))* Paraclete Pr., Inc.
Hunsaker, Joyce Badgley. They Call Me Sacagawea. 2003. (ENG., Illus.). 48p. pap. 9.95 *(978-0-7627-2580-9(X)*, TwoDot) Globe Pequot Pr., The.
Hunter, Nick. Women in World War I, 1 vol. 2013. (Remembering World War I Ser.). (ENG.). 48p. (gr. 4-6). 33.32 *(978-1-4329-8084-9(X))*; pap. 9.95 *(978-1-4329-8089-4(0))* Heinemann-Raintree. (Heinemann InfoSearch).
Hunter, Ryan Ann. In Disguise! Stories of Real Women Spies. 2004. (Illus.). 133p. (J). (gr. 4-7). per. 9.95 *(978-1-58270-095-3(8))* Beyond Words Publishing, Inc.
Ignotofsky, Rachel. Women in Science. (ENG., Illus.). 2017. 100p. 20.00 *(978-0-60774-981-3(5)*, Clarkson Potter) 2016. 128p. (gr. 5). 16.99 *(978-1-60774-976-9(9)*, Ten Speed Pr.) Potter/TenSpeed/Harmony.
Ignotofsky, Rachel. Women in Sports: 50 Fearless Athletes Who Played to Win. 2017. (ENG., Illus.). 128p. (gr. 5-12). 16.99 ***(978-1-60774-978-3(5)***, Ten Speed Pr.) Potter/TenSpeed/Harmony.
Indovino, Shaina. Women in Physics. Lee-Karlon, Ann, ed. 2013. (Major Women in Science Ser.: 10). 64p. (J). (gr. 7-18). 22.95 *(978-1-4222-2930-9(0))* Mason Crest.
—Women in the Environmental Sciences. Lee-Karlon, Ann, ed. 2013. (Major Women in Science Ser.: 10). 64p. (J). (gr. 7-18). 22.95 *(978-1-4222-2927-9(0))* Mason Crest.
Jane Addams, 34 bks., Set. Incl. Air Pollution. Lopez, Gary. 32p. (gr. 2-12). 1992. lib. bdg. *(978-0-88682-427-3(3))*; Cells. George, Michael. 40p. (gr. 2-7). 1992. lib. bdg. 23.95 *(978-0-88682-437-2(0))*; Clouds. Markert, Jenny. 40p. (gr. 2-12). 1997. lib. bdg. 23.95 *(978-0-88682-435-8(4))*; Coral Reef. George, Michael. 32p. (gr. 2-12). 1992. lib. bdg. *(978-0-88682-430-3(3))*; Deserts. George, Michael. 40p. (gr. 2-12). 1992. lib. bdg. 23.95 *(978-0-88682-434-1(6))*; Earthquakes. George, Michael. 30p. (gr. 2-12). 1997. lib. bdg. 23.95 *(978-0-88682-709-0(4))*; Fungi. Rotter, Charles M. 40p. (gr. 2-12). 1993. lib. bdg. 23.95 *(978-0-88682-593-5(8))*; Galaxies. George, Michael. 40p. (gr. 2-12). 1993. lib. bdg. 23.95 *(978-0-88682-433-4(8))*; Glaciers. George, Michael. 32p. (gr. 2-12). 1992. lib. bdg. *(978-0-88682-401-3(X))*; Life. George, Michael. 32p. (gr. 2-12). 1994. lib. bdg. *(978-0-88682-602-4(0))*; Mars. George, Michael. 32p. (gr. 3-7). 1992. lib. bdg. *(978-0-88682-432-7(X))*; Moon. George, Michael. 40p. (gr. 2-12). 1993. lib. bdg. 23.95 *(978-0-88682-436-5(2))*; Mountains. Rotter, Charles M. 40p. (gr. 2-12). 1994. lib. bdg. 23.95 *(978-0-88682-596-6(2))*; Ocean Resources. Markert, Jenny. 40p. (gr. 2-12). 1994. lib. bdg. 23.95 *(978-0-88682-599-7(7))*; Prairie. Rotter, Charles M. 40p. (gr. 2-12). 1994. lib. bdg. 17.95 *(978-0-88682-598-0(9))*; Rain Forest. George, Michael. 40p. (gr. 2-12). 1992. lib. bdg. 23.95 *(978-0-88682-483-9(4))*; Sequoias. George, Michael. 32p. (gr. 2-12). 1992. lib. bdg. *(978-0-88682-482-2(6))*; Space Exploration. George, Michael. 32p. (gr. 2-12). 1993. lib. bdg. *(978-0-88682-481-5(8))*; Stars. George, Michael. 40p. (gr. 2-12). 1992. lib. bdg. 17.95 *(978-0-88682-400-6(1))*; Sun. George, Michael. 40p. (gr. 2-12). 1992. lib. bdg. 23.95 *(978-0-88682-402-0(8))*; Volcanoes. George, Michael. 32p. (gr. 3-12). 1992. lib. bdg. *(978-0-88682-403-7(6))*; Water. Markert, Jenny. 32p. (gr. 2-12). 1992. lib. bdg. *(978-0-88682-431-0(1))*; (Illus.). (J). (Women of America Ser.). 32p. Set lib. bdg. 576.30 o.p. *(978-0-88682-165-4(7)*, Creative Education) Creative Co., The.
Jenner, Caryn. Pocahontas, Level 2. 2009. (DK Readers Ser.). (ENG.). 32p. (J). (gr. 1-3). 3.99 *(978-0-7566-5611-9(7)*, DK Children) Dorling Kindersley Publishing, Inc.
Johnson, Jen Cullerton. Seeds of Change. Sadler, Sonia Lynn, illus. 2013. (ENG.). 40p. (J). (gr. 1-6). 18.95 *(978-1-60060-367-9(X))* Lee & Low Bks., Inc.
Jordan-Fenton, Christy & Pokiak-Fenton, Margaret. Fatty Legs: A True Story. Amini-Holmes, Liz, illus. 9th ed. 2010. (ENG.). 112p. (J). (gr. 4-7). pap. 12.95 *(978-1-55451-246-1(8)*, 9781554512461) Annick Pr., Ltd. CAN. Dist: Publishers Group West (PGW).
—Not My Girl. Grimard, Gabrielle, illus. 2014. (ENG.). 36p. (J). (gr. 1-4). 21.95 *(978-1-55451-625-4(0)*, 9781554516254); pap. 9.95 *(978-1-55451-624-7(2)*, 9781554516247) Annick Pr., Ltd. CAN. Dist: Publishers Group West (PGW).
—A Stranger at Home: A True Story. Amini-Holmes, Liz, illus. 2011. (ENG.). 112p. (J). (gr. 3-7). 21.95 *(978-1-55451-362-8(6)*, 9781554513628); 3rd ed. pap. 12.95 *(978-1-55451-361-1(8)*, 9781554513611) Annick Pr., Ltd. CAN. Dist: Publishers Group West (PGW).
—When I Was Eight. Grimard, Gabrielle, illus. 2nd ed. 2013. (ENG.). 32p. (J). (gr. 1-4). 21.95 *(978-1-55451-491-5(6)*, 9781554514915); pap. 9.95 *(978-1-55451-490-8(8)*, 9781554514908) Annick Pr., Ltd. CAN. Dist: Publishers Group West (PGW).
Jordan-Fenton, Christy, et al. Fatty Legs: A True Story. Amini-Holmes, Liz, illus. 8th ed. 2010. (ENG.). 112p. (J). (gr. 4-7). 21.95 *(978-1-55451-247-8(6)*, 9781554512478) Annick Pr., Ltd. CAN. Dist: Publishers Group West (PGW).
Kalman, Bobbie & Aloian, Molly. Famous Native North Americans. 2003. (Native Nations of North America Ser.). (ENG., Illus.). 32p. (J). (gr. 5). pap. *(978-0-7787-0471-3(8))*; lib. bdg. *(978-0-7787-0379-2(7))* Crabtree Publishing Co.
Keating, Susan K. Isadora Duncan: American Dancer. 2004. (Great Names Ser.). (Illus.). 32p. (J). (gr. 3-18). lib. bdg. 19.95 *(978-1-59084-144-0(1))* Mason Crest.
Kemeny, Esther. On the Shores of Darkness: The Memoir of Esther Kemeny Haller, Heather, ed. 2003. (Illus.). 144p. per. *(978-0-9743961-7-0(6))* Haller Company, The.
Kent, Deborah. Frida Kahlo: An Artist Celebrates Life. 2004. (Proud Heritage: the Hispanic Library). (ENG., Illus.). 40p. (J). (gr. 3-6). 29.93 *(978-1-59296-167-2(3)*, 200008) Child's World, Inc., The.
Kepnes, Caroline. Stephen Crane. 2004. (Classic Storytellers Ser.). (Illus.). 48p. (J). (gr. 4-8). lib. bdg. 29.95 *(978-1-58415-272-9(9))* Mitchell Lane Pubs., Inc.
Kernan, Elizabeth. Harriet Tubman: A Lesson in Bravery. 2009. (Reading Room Collection 2 Ser.). 24p. (gr. 3-4). 42.50 *(978-1-60851-966-8(X)*, PowerKids Pr.) Rosen Publishing Group, Inc., The.
Kimmel, Elizabeth Cody. Ladies First: 40 Daring American Women Who Were Second to None. 2006. (ENG., Illus.). 192p. (J). (gr. 5). 18.95 *(978-0-7922-5393-8(0)*, National Geographic Children's Bks.) National Geographic Society.
—Ladies First: 40 Daring Women Who Were Second to None. 2006. (ENG., Illus.). 192p. (J). (gr. 5). lib. bdg. 27.90 *(978-0-7922-5394-5(9)*, National Geographic Children's Bks.) National Geographic Society.
Kishel, Ann-Marie. Elizabeth Blackwell: A Life of Diligence. 2007. (Pull Ahead Bks.). (Illus.). 32p. (J). (gr. 3-7). lib. bdg. 22.60 *(978-0-8225-6459-1(9)*, Lerner Pubns.) Lerner Publishing Group.
Kite, L. Patricia. Maya Angelou. 2006. (Just the Facts Biographies Ser.). (Illus.). 112p. (J). (gr. 3-7). pap. 9.95 *(978-0-8225-5997-9(8))*; (ENG., (gr. 5-12). lib. bdg. 27.93 *(978-0-8225-3426-6(6))* Lerner Publishing Group. (Lerner Pubns.).
Kjelle, Marylou. Katherine Paterson. 2004. (Classic Storytellers Ser.). (Illus.). 48p. (J). (gr. 4-8). lib. bdg. 29.95 *(978-1-58415-268-2(0))* Mitchell Lane Pubs., Inc.
Klein, Emily. Bethany Mota Unauthorized Bio. 2015. (ENG., Illus.). 48p. (J). (gr. 1-3). pap. 4.99 *(978-0-545-87572-1(2))* Scholastic, Inc.
Koestler-Grack, Rachel A. Marie Curie: Scientist. 2009. (Women of Achievement Ser.). (Illus.). 136p. (gr. 6-12). 35.00 *(978-1-60413-086-7(5)*, Chelsea Hse.) Facts On File, Inc.
Kops, Deborah. Alice Paul & the Fight for Women's Rights: From the Vote to the Equal Rights Amendment. 2017. (ENG.). 216p. (J). (gr. 5). 17.95 *(978-1-62979-323-8(X)*, Calkins Creek) Boyds Mills Pr.
Kovatch, Sarah & Crumpler, Rebecca Lee. Rebecca Lee Crumpler. 2005. (Illus.). 16p. (J). *(978-0-7367-2891-1(0))* Zaner-Bloser, Inc.
Kramer, Barbara. Mahalia Jackson: The Voice of Gospel & Civil Rights. 2003. (African-American Biographies Ser.). (Illus.). 128p. (J). lib. bdg. 26.60 *(978-0-7660-2115-0(7))* Enslow Pubs., Inc.
Krasner, Barbara. Goldie Takes a Stand! Golda Meir's First Crusade. Garrity-Riley, Kelsey, illus. 2014. (ENG.). 32p. (J). (gr. k-4). 17.95 *(978-1-4677-1200-2(0))* Lerner Publishing Group.
—Goldie Takes a Stand: Golda Meir's First Crusade. Garrity-Riley, Kelsey, illus. 2014. (ENG.). 32p. (J). (gr. k-4). 7.95 *(978-1-4677-1201-9(9)*, Kar-Ben Publishing) Lerner Publishing Group.
Krensky, Stephen. Calamity Jane. Carlson, Lisa, illus. 2006. (On My Own Folklore Ser.). (ENG.). 48p. (gr. 2-4). lib. bdg.

W
X
Y
Z

25.26 *(978-1-57505-886-3(3)*, Millbrook Pr.) Lerner Publishing Group.

Kudlinski, Kathleen. Joan of Arc. 2008. (DK Biography Ser.). (ENG., Illus.). 128p. (J). (gr. 5-12). pap. 6.99 *(978-0-7566-3526-8(8)*, DK Children) Dorling Kindersley Publishing, Inc.

Labrecque, Ellen. Maria Beasley & Life Rafts. 2017. (21st Century Junior Library: Women Innovators Ser.). (ENG., Illus.). 24p. (J). (gr. 2-5). lib. bdg. 27.07 *(978-1-63472-179-0(9)*, 209288) Cherry Lake Publishing.

—Yvonne Brill & Satellite Propulsion. 2017. (21st Century Junior Library: Women Innovators Ser.). (ENG., Illus.). 24p. (J). (gr. 2-5). lib. bdg. 27.07 *(978-1-63472-184-4(5)*, 209308) Cherry Lake Publishing.

Laidlaw, Jill A. Frida Kahlo. 2003. (Artists in Their Time Ser.). (ENG., Illus.). 48p. (J). (gr. 5-7). pap. 6.95 *(978-0-531-16642-0(2)*, Watts, Franklin) Scholastic Library Publishing.

Lakin, Patricia, et al. Amelia Earhart: More Than a Flier. Daniel, Alan & Daniel, Lea, illus. 2003. (Ready-To-read SOFA Ser.). (ENG.). 48p. (J). (gr. 1-3). pap. 3.99 *(978-0-689-85575-7(3)*, Simon Spotlight) Simon Spotlight.

Larkin, Tanya. What Was Cooking in Abigail Adams' White House? 2009. (Cooking Throughout American History Ser.). 24p. (gr. 3-3). 42.50 *(978-1-61511-949-3(3)*, PowerKids Pr.) Rosen Publishing Group, Inc., The.

—What Was Cooking in Dolley Madison's White House? 2009. (Cooking Throughout American History Ser.). 24p. (gr. 3-3). 42.50 *(978-1-61511-950-9(7)*, PowerKids Pr.) Rosen Publishing Group, Inc., The.

—What Was Cooking in Edith Roosevelt's White House? 2009. (Cooking Throughout American History Ser.). 24p. (gr. 3-3). 42.50 *(978-1-61511-951-6(5)*, PowerKids Pr.) Rosen Publishing Group, Inc., The.

—What Was Cooking in Martha Washington's Presidential Mansion? 2009. (Cooking Throughout American History Ser.). 24p. (gr. 3-3). 42.50 *(978-1-61511-953-0(1)*, PowerKids Pr.) Rosen Publishing Group, Inc., The.

Lasky, Kathryn. A Voice of Her Own: A Story of Phillis Wheatley, Slave Poet. 2012. lib. bdg. 14.75 *(978-0-606-26940-7(1)*, Turtleback) Turtleback Bks.

Latta, Sara L. The Woman Who Invented Windshield Wipers: Mary Anderson & Her Wonderful Invention. 2014. (Inventors at Work! Ser.). 48p. (J). pap. 8.95 *(978-1-4644-0349-1(X)*, Enslow Elementary) Enslow Pubs., Inc.

Lawlor, Laurie. Rachel Carson & Her Book That Changed the World. Beingessner, Laura, illus. 2014. (ENG.). 32p. (J). (gr. k-5). 7.99 *(978-0-8234-3193-9(2))* Holiday Hse., Inc.

—Super Women: Six Scientists Who Changed the World. 2017. (ENG.). 48p. (J). (gr. 3-7). 17.95 *(978-0-8234-3675-0(6))* Holiday Hse., Inc.

Leading Women (Group 3) 2014. (Leading Women Ser.). 112p. (YA). (gr. 7-11). 239.85 *(978-1-62713-138-4(8))* Cavendish Square Publishing.

Leon, Georgina Lazaro. Conoce a Gabriela Mistral: Get to Know Gabriela Mistral. Palacios, Sara Helena, illus. 2014. (Personajes Del Mundo Hispnico Ser.). (ENG & SPA.). 32p. (J). (gr. -1-3). 15.95 *(978-1-61435-351-5(4)*, Alfaguara) Santillana USA Publishing Co., Inc.

Leslie, Roger. Isak Dinesen: Gothic Storyteller. 2004. (World Writers Ser.). (Illus.). 128p. (YA). (gr. 6-12). 23.95 *(978-1-931798-17-4(6))* Reynolds, Morgan Inc.

Lew, Kristi. ADA Lovelace: Mathematician & First Programmer. 2017. (J). ***(978-1-5383-0022-0(2))*** Rosen Publishing Group, Inc., The.

Literature Connections English: So Far from the Bamboo Grove. 2004. (gr. 6-12). *(978-0-395-77138-9(2)*, 2-70216) Holt McDougal.

Litmanovich, Ellina. Ronda Rousey: Champion Mixed Martial Arts Star. 2017. (Sports Star Champions Ser.). 48p. (J). (gr. 5-6). lib. bdg. 27.93 ***(978-0-7660-8696-8(8))*** Enslow Pubs., Inc.

Love, D. Anne. Of Numbers & Stars: The Story of Hypatia. Paparone, Pamela & Paparone, Pam, illus. 2006. (ENG.). 32p. (J). (gr. 4-8). 16.95 *(978-0-8234-1621-9(6))* Holiday Hse., Inc.

Lynette, Rachel. Sacagawea. 2013. (Pioneer Spirit: the Westward Expansion Ser.). 24p. (J). (gr. 3-6). 22.60 *(978-1-4777-0782-1(4))*; pap. 49.50 *(978-1-4777-0898-9(7))*; (ENG., Illus.). pap. 8.25 *(978-1-4777-0897-2(9))* Rosen Publishing Group, Inc., The. (PowerKids Pr.).

Lyon, George Ella & Catalanotto, Peter. Mother to Tigers. 2003. (ENG., Illus.). 32p. (J). (gr. k-3). 18.99 *(978-0-689-84221-4(X)*, Atheneum/Richard Jackson Bks.) Simon & Schuster Children's Publishing.

MacLeod, Elizabeth. The Kids Book of Great Canadian Women. Mantha, John, illus. 2006. (Kids Book Of Ser.). (ENG.). 64p. (J). (gr. 3-7). 19.95 *(978-1-55337-820-4(2))* Kids Can Pr., Ltd. CAN. Dist: Hachette Bk. Group.

—Marie Curie. Mantha, John, illus. 2009. (Kids Can Read Ser.). (ENG.). 32p. (J). (gr. 1-3). 3.95 *(978-1-55453-297-1(3))*; 14.95 *(978-1-55453-296-4(5))* Kids Can Pr., Ltd. CAN. Dist: Hachette Bk. Group.

Majher, Patricia. Great Girls in Michigan History. 2015. (Great Lakes Books Ser.). (ENG., Illus.). 192p. (J). pap. 14.99 *(978-0-8143-4073-8(3)*, 3653) Wayne State Univ. Pr.

Marsh, Carole. Marie Curie, Nobel Prize Winning Scientist. 2004. 12p. (gr. k-4). 2.95 *(978-0-635-02374-2(1))* Gallopade International.

Martin, Carol. Catharine Parr Traill: Backwoods Pioneer. 2004. (ENG., Illus.). 128p. (YA). pap. *(978-0-88899-495-0(8)*, Libros Tigrillo) Groundwood Bks. CAN. Dist: Publishers Group West (PGW).

Martin, Claudia. Malala Yousafzai: Education Campaigner. 2017. (Inspirational Lives Ser.). (ENG., Illus.). 32p. (J). (gr. 4-6). pap. 12.99 ***(978-0-7502-9314-3(4)***, Wayland) Hachette Children's Group GBR. Dist: Hachette Bk. Group.

Mattern, Joanne. Elizabeth Cady Stanton & Susan B. Anthony: Fighting Together for Women's Rights. 2009. (Women Who Shaped History Ser.). 24p. (gr. 2-3). 42.50 *(978-1-60854-818-7(X)*, PowerKids Pr.) Rosen Publishing Group, Inc., The.

—Katharine Graham & 20th Century American Journalism. 2003. (Women Who Shaped History Ser.). 24p. (J). lib. bdg. 22.60 *(978-0-8239-6500-7(7)*, PowerKids Pr.) Rosen Publishing Group, Inc., The.

Mattern, Joanne & Brandt, Keith. Marie Curie, Brave Scientist. Dugan, Karen, illus. 2005. 45p. (J). *(978-0-439-80153-9(2))* Scholastic, Inc.

McAllister, Margaret. Women of the Bible. Massari, Alida, illus. 2013. (ENG.). 48p. (J). 16.99 *(978-1-61261-372-7(1))* Paraclete Pr., Inc.

Mccann, Michelle Roehm & Welden, Amelie. Girls Who Rocked the World: From Anne Frank to Natalie Portman. 2012. lib. bdg. 22.10 *(978-0-606-26898-1(7)*, Turtleback) Turtleback Bks.

McCarney, Rosemary. Dear Malala, We Stand with You. 2014. (ENG.). 32p. (J). (gr. -1-3). lib. bdg. 19.99 *(978-0-553-52121-4(7))*; 16.99 *(978-0-553-52120-7(9))* Random Hse. Children's Bks. (Crown Books For Young Readers).

McCully, Emily Arnold. Caroline's Comets: A True Story. 2017. (ENG.). 40p. (J). (gr. -1-3). 16.95 *(978-0-8234-3664-4(0))* Holiday Hse., Inc.

McDonnell, Patrick. Me... Jane. 2011. (ENG., Illus.). 40p. (J). (gr. -1-3). 17.99 *(978-0-316-04546-9(2))* Little, Brown Bks. for Young Readers.

—Me... Jane. 2011. (J). *(978-1-4618-4349-8(9))* Recorded Bks., Inc.

McDonnell, Peter. The Last Princess. 2005. (Illus.). 16p. *(978-0-7367-2910-9(0))* Zaner-Bloser, Inc.

McDonough, Yona Zeldis. Who Was Harriet Tubman? Harrison, Nancy, illus. 2003. (Who Was... ? Ser.). 106p. (gr. 4-7). 15.00 *(978-0-7569-1590-2(2))* Perfection Learning Corp.

McGinty, Alice B. Meet Jane Yolen. 2003. (About the Author Ser.). (Illus.). 24p. (J). lib. bdg. 22.60 *(978-0-8239-6407-9(8)*, PowerKids Pr.) Rosen Publishing Group, Inc., The.

McIlroy, Michelle. Sophie Scholl: Student Resister & Anti-Nazi Political Activist. 2017. (J). ***(978-1-5383-8108-3(7))*** Rosen Publishing Group, Inc., The.

McKown, Robin. Marie Curie. Rethi, Lili, illus. 2012. 128p. 40.95 *(978-1-258-23532-1(3))*; pap. 25.95 *(978-1-258-24675-4(9))* Literary Licensing, LLC.

McLean, Jacqueline. Victoria Woodhull: First Woman Presidential Candidate. 2004. (Feminist Voices Ser.). (Illus.). 112p. (YA). (gr. 6-12). 23.95 *(978-1-883846-47-3(1)*, First Biographies) Reynolds, Morgan Inc.

—Women of Adventure. 2003. (Profiles Ser.). (Illus.). 160p. (gr. 5-18). lib. bdg. 19.95 *(978-1-881508-73-1(0))* Oliver Pr., Inc.

Meltzer, Milton. Emily Dickinson: A Biography. 2006. (Literary Greats Ser.). (ENG.). 128p. (gr. 7-12). lib. bdg. 33.26 *(978-0-7613-2949-7(8)*, Millbrook Pr.) Lerner Publishing Group.

Miklowitz, Gloria. Anne Frank. 2009. pap. 13.25 *(978-1-60559-053-0(3))* Hameray Publishing Group, Inc.

Miklowitz, Gloria D. Jane Goodall. 2004. (ENG., Illus.). 28p. (J). (gr. 2-5). pap. 7.33 *(978-0-7685-1218-2(2)*, Dominie Elementary) Pearson Schl.

Miller, Calvin Craig. Spirit Like a Storm: The Story of Mary Shelley. 2nd rev. ed. 2004. (World Writers Ser.). (Illus.). 144p. (YA). (gr. 6-12). 23.95 *(978-1-931798-08-2(7))* Reynolds, Morgan Inc.

Mills, Cliff. Virginia Woolf. 2003. (Women in the Arts Ser.). (Illus.). 112p. (gr. 6-12). 30.00 *(978-0-7910-7459-6(5)*, Chelsea Hse.) Facts On File, Inc.

Mitchell, Saundra. 50 Unbelievable Women & Their Fascinating (and True!) Stories. 2016. (They Did What? Ser.). (ENG., Illus.). 288p. (J). (gr. 5). 8.99 *(978-0-14-751812-5(1)*, Puffin Books) Penguin Young Readers Group.

Morrison, John. Mathilde Krim. 2004. (Women in Medicine Ser.). (Illus.). 112p. (YA). (gr. 6-12). 30.00 *(978-0-7910-8026-9(9)*, Chelsea Hse.) Facts On File, Inc.

Murphy, Patricia J. Grace Hopper: Computer Pioneer. 2004. (Famous Inventors Ser.). (Illus.). 32p. (J). lib. bdg. 22.60 *(978-0-7660-2273-7(0))* Enslow Pubs., Inc.

Naden, Corinne J. & Blue, Rose. Mae Jemison: Out of This World. 2003. (Gateway Biography Ser.: 4). (Illus.). 48p. lib. bdg. 23.90 *(978-0-7613-2570-3(0)*, Millbrook Pr.) Lerner Publishing Group.

Nagle, Jeanne, ed. Top 101 Remarkable Women, 1 vol., 1. 2014. (People You Should Know Ser.). (ENG.). 176p. (YA). (gr. 7-12). 35.25 *(978-1-62275-126-6(4))* Rosen Publishing Group, Inc., The.

Nelson, Maria. The Life of Sacagawea. 2012. (Famous Lives Ser.). (ENG., Illus.). 24p. (J). (gr. k-3). lib. bdg. 22.60 *(978-1-4339-6357-5(4))*; (gr. 1-4). pap. 8.15 *(978-1-4339-6359-9(0))* Stevens, Gareth Publishing LLLP.

Nelson, S. D. Buffalo Bird Girl: A Hidatsa Story. 2012. (ENG., Illus.). 56p. (J). (gr. 1-4). 21.95 *(978-1-4197-0355-3(2)*, Abrams Bks. for Young Readers) Abrams, Inc.

Nichols, Catherine. Madam C.J. Walker. 2005. (Scholastic News Nonfiction Readers Ser.). (Illus.). 24p. (J). pap. 6.95 *(978-0-516-24784-7(0)*, Children's Pr.) Scholastic Library Publishing.

Nivola, Claire A. Planting the Trees of Kenya: The Story of Wangari Maathai. Nivola, Claire A., illus. 2008. (ENG., Illus.). 32p. (J). (gr. k-3). 18.99 *(978-0-374-39918-4(2)*, 9780374399184, Farrar, Straus & Giroux (BYR)) Farrar, Straus & Giroux.

Noland, Thelma. Annie Sweet Annie. 2004. 174p. (J). pap. 13.95 *(978-0-595-31138-5(5))* iUniverse, Inc.

O'Connell, Diane. People Person: The Story of Sociologist Marta Tienda. 2005. (Women's Adventures in Science Ser.). (ENG., Illus.). 120p. (YA). (gr. 5-9). lib. bdg. 31.50 *(978-0-531-16781-6(X))* Scholastic Library Publishing.

O'Keefe, Sherry. Aung San Suu Kyi. 2012. (Champion of Freedom Ser.). (J). (gr. 7-12). 28.95 *(978-1-59935-168-1(4))* Reynolds, Morgan Inc.

—From China to America: The Story of Amy Tan. 2011. (World Writers Ser.). 112p. (gr. 7-18). lib. bdg. 28.95 *(978-1-59935-138-4(2))* Reynolds, Morgan Inc.

Orgill, Roxane. Shout, Sister, Shout! Ten Girl Singers Who Shaped a Century. 2007. (ENG.). 160p. (YA). (gr. 7). pap. 12.95 *(978-1-4169-6391-2(X)*, McElderry, Margaret K. Bks.) McElderry, Margaret K. Bks.

Orr, Tamra. Marie Curie. 2003. (World Was Never the Same Ser.). (J). pap. *(978-1-58417-263-5(0))*; lib. bdg. *(978-1-58417-262-8(2))* Lake Street Pubs.

Ottaviani, Jim. Primates: The Fearless Science of Jane Goodall, Dian Fossey, & Biruté Galdikas. Wicks, Maris, illus. 2013. (ENG.). 144p. (YA). (gr. 7). 21.99 *(978-1-59643-865-1(7)*, 9781596438651, First Second Bks.) Roaring Brook Pr.

—Primates: The Fearless Science of Jane Goodall, Dian Fossey, & Biruté Galdikas. Wicks, Maris, illus. 2015. (ENG.). 144p. (YA). (gr. 7). pap. 12.99 *(978-1-250-06293-2(4)*, 9781250062932) Square Fish.

Pack, Mary Fisk. Cleopatra: "Serpent of the Nile" Malone, Peter, illus. 2011. (Thinking Girl's Treasury of Dastardly Dames Ser.). (ENG.). 32p. (J). (gr. 3-8). 18.95 *(978-0-9834256-0-1(4))* Goosebottom Bks. LLC.

The Padded Girdle: The Unbelievable True Story of Overcoming Adversity Again, & Again, & Again. . . 2003. (Illus.). 198p. pap. 19.95 *(978-0-9745860-0-7(5))* Eaglesquest Publishing.

Paige, Joy. Ellen Ochoa: The First Hispanic Woman in Space. 2009. (Library of Astronaut Biographies Ser.). 112p. (gr. 5-8). 63.90 *(978-1-60853-520-0(7)*, Rosen Reference) Rosen Publishing Group, Inc., The.

Paprocki, Sherry Beck. Diana, Princess of Wales. 2nd rev. ed. 2009. (Women of Achievement Ser.). (Illus.). 144p. (gr. 6-12). 35.00 *(978-1-60413-463-6(1)*, Chelsea Hse.) Facts On File, Inc.

Parish, James Robert. Gloria Estefan Singer: Singer. 2006. (Ferguson Career Biographies Ser.). (Illus.). 122p. (gr. 6-12). 25.00 *(978-0-8160-5833-4(4)*, Ferguson Publishing Co.) Facts On File, Inc.

Parker-Rock, Michelle. Alma Flor Ada: An Author Kids Love. 2008. (Authors Kids Love Ser.). (Illus.). 48p. (J). (gr. 3-4). lib. bdg. 25.27 *(978-0-7660-2760-2(0)*, Enslow Elementary) Enslow Pubs., Inc.

Patrick, Jean L. S. The Baseball Adventure of Jackie Mitchell, Girl Pitcher vs. Babe Ruth. Hammond, Ted & Carbajal, Richard, illus. 2011. (History's Kid Heroes Ser.). (ENG.). 32p. (gr. 3-5). pap. 8.95 *(978-0-7613-7072-7(2)*, Graphic Universe™) Lerner Publishing Group.

—La Nina Que Poncho A Babe Ruth. Reeves, Jeni, illus. 2007. (Yo Solo - Historia (on My Own - History) Ser.). 48p. (J). (gr. 4-7). per. 6.95 *(978-0-8225-7788-1(7))* Lerner Publishing Group.

—La Niña Que Ponchó a Babe Ruth. Translations.com Staff, tr. from ENG. Reeves, Jeni, illus. 2007. (Yo Solo - Historia (on My Own - History) Ser.).Tr. of Girl Who Struck Out Babe Ruth. (SPA.). 48p. (gr. 2-4). lib. bdg. 25.26 *(978-0-8225-7785-0(2))* Lerner Publishing Group.

—La Nina Que Poncho a Babe Ruth; the Girl Who Struck Out Babe Ruth. 2008. pap. 40.95 *(978-0-8225-9725-4(X))* Lerner Publishing Group.

Patteson, Nelda. Adina de Zavala: "Angel of the Alamo" Her Life Story Presented Through the Clothes She Wore. Patteson, Nelda, illus. 2003. (Women of Texas Ser.: Vol. 3). Orig. Title: Angel of the Alamo. (Illus.). 32p. (J). (gr. 4-8). pap. 14.95 *(978-0-9629001-2-9(5))* Smiley Co.

Perry, Phyllis Jean. Bold Women in Colorado History. 2012. (J). pap. *(978-0-87842-584-6(5))* Mountain Pr. Publishing Co., Inc.

Petrick, Neila S. Katherine Stinson Otero: High Flyer, 1 vol. Wallace, Daggi, illus. 2006. (ENG.). 32p. (J). (gr. k-3). 16.99 *(978-1-58980-368-8(X))* Pelican Publishing Co., Inc.

Pferdehirt, Julia. Caroline Quarlls & the Underground Railroad. 2008. (Badger Biographies Ser.). (ENG., Illus.). 120p. (J). (gr. 3-7). per. 12.95 *(978-0-87020-388-6(6))* Wisconsin Historical Society.

Phillips, Larissa. Women Civil War Spies of the Confederacy. 2004. (American Women at War Ser.). (Illus.). 112p. (gr. 7-12). lib. bdg. 34.60 *(978-0-8239-4451-4(4))* Rosen Publishing Group, Inc., The.

Phillips, Robin. Who in the World Was the Acrobatic Empress? The Story of Theodora. unabr. ed. 2010. (ENG.). 1p. audio compact disk 12.95 *(978-1-933339-39-9(X)*, 333939) Well-Trained Mind Pr.

Pimm, Nancy Roe. The Jerrie Mock Story: The First Woman to Fly Solo Around the World. 2016. (Biographies for Young Readers Ser.). (ENG., Illus.). 168p. (J). (gr. 1-6). 28.95 *(978-0-8214-2215-1(4))* Ohio Univ. Pr.

Polcovar, Jane. Rosalind Franklin & the Structure of Life. 2006. (Profiles in Science Ser.). (Illus.). 144p. (J). (gr. 3-7). lib. bdg. 27.95 *(978-1-59935-022-6(X))* Reynolds, Morgan Inc.

Polette, Nancy. Mae Jemison. 2003. (Rookie Biographies Ser.). (ENG., Illus.). 32p. (J). (gr. 1-2). 20.50 *(978-0-516-22856-3(0)*, Children's Pr.) Scholastic Library Publishing.

Pomeroy, Sarah B. & Kathirithamby, Jeyaraney. Maria Sibylla Merian: Artist, Scientist, Adventurer. 2017. (J). ***(978-1-60606-555-6(6)***, J. Paul Getty Museum) Getty Pubns.

Randolph, Ryan. Betsy Ross: The American Flag, & Life in a Young America. 2009. (Library of American Lives & Times Ser.). 112p. (gr. 5-5). 69.20 *(978-1-60853-473-9(1))* Rosen Publishing Group, Inc., The.

Rappoport, Ken. Ladies First: Women Athletes Who Made a Difference, 1 vol. 2005. (ENG., Illus.). 192p. (J). (gr. 3-7). 14.95 *(978-1-56145-338-2(2))* Peachtree Pubs.

Rausch, Monica. Harriet Tubman. 2007. (Great Americans Ser.). (Illus.). 24p. (gr. 1-4). lib. bdg. 22.00 *(978-0-8368-7686-4(5)*, Weekly Reader Leveled Readers) Stevens, Gareth Publishing LLLP.

Reed, Jennifer. Computer Scientist Jean Bartik. 2016. (STEM Trailblazer Bios Ser.). (ENG., Illus.). 32p. (J). (gr. 2-5). 26.65 *(978-1-5124-0789-1(5))* Lerner Publishing Group.

Reid, Jamie. Diana Krall. 2004. 224p. pap. 17.95 *(978-1-894997-07-2(7))* Kingston Pr. CAN. Dist: SCB Distributors.

Reynolds, Toby & Calver, Paul. Fearless Women: Courageous Females Who Refused to Be Denied. 2017. (Real Lives Ser.). (ENG., Illus.). 64p. (J). (gr. 4-10). 8.99 *(978-0-7641-6886-4(X))* Barron's Educational Series, Inc.

Rice, William B. Jane Goodall, 1 vol. 2nd rev. ed. 2014. (TIME for KIDS(r) Nonfiction Readers Ser.). (ENG., Illus.). 32p. (J). (gr. 3-3). pap. 25.96 *(978-1-4807-1093-1(8))* Shell Educational Publishing.

—Jane Goodall, 1 vol. 2nd rev. ed. 2012. (TIME for KIDS(r) Nonfiction Readers Ser.). (ENG.). 32p. (J). (gr. 3-3). pap. 8.99 *(978-1-4333-3684-3(7))* Teacher Created Materials, Inc.

Rinaldo, Denise. Jane Goodall: With a Discussion of Responsibility. 2003. (Values in Action Ser.). (J). *(978-1-59203-062-0(9))* Learning Challenge, Inc.

Riner, Dax. Annika Sorenstam. 2007. (Sports Heroes & Legends Ser.). (YA). (gr. 7-12). lib. bdg. 30.60 *(978-0-8225-7160-5(9))* Twenty First Century Bks.

Rivera, Ursula. Aretha Franklin. 2006. (Rock & Roll Hall of Famers Ser.). (Illus.). 112p. (YA). (gr. 5-8). lib. bdg. 34.60 *(978-0-8239-3639-7(2))* Rosen Publishing Group, Inc., The.

—The Supremes. (Rock & Roll Hall of Famers Ser.). 112p. (gr. 5-8). 2009. 63.90 *(978-1-60852-479-2(5)*, Rosen Reference) 2006. (Illus.). (YA). lib. bdg. 34.60 *(978-0-8239-3527-7(2))* Rosen Publishing Group, Inc., The.

Robbins, Trina. Florence Nightingale: Lady with the Lamp, 1 vol. Timmons, Anne, illus. 2007. (Graphic Biographies Ser.). (ENG.). 32p. (gr. 3-4). per. 8.10 *(978-0-7368-7902-6(1)*, 1264942, Graphic Library) Capstone Press of Coughlan Cos.

Roberts, Russell. Sally Field. l.t. ed. 2003. (Billboard Biography Ser.). (Illus.). 32p. (J). (gr. 3-8). lib. bdg. 25.70 *(978-1-58415-183-8(8))* Mitchell Lane Pubs., Inc.

Robinson, Ella May. Stars in Her Heart. 2005. 127p. per. 10.95 *(978-1-57258-318-4(5))* TEACH Services, Inc.

Robinson, Fiona. Ada's Ideas: The Story of Ada Lovelace, the World's First Computer Programmer. 2016. (ENG., Illus.). 40p. (J). (gr. 1-4). 17.95 *(978-1-4197-1872-4(X)*, Abrams Bks. for Young Readers) Abrams, Inc.

Rolfe, Helen Y. & Rolfe, Helen. Women Explorers: 100 Years of Mountain Adventure. 2007. (Amazing Stories Ser.). (ENG., Illus.). 96p. (J). (gr. 4-5). pap. 9.95 *(978-1-55439-709-9(X)*, 9781554397099) Lorimer, James & Co., Ltd., Pubs. CAN. Dist: Casemate Pubs. & Bk. Distributors, LLC.

Rooney, Frances. Exceptional Women Environmentalists, 1 vol. 2007. (Women's Hall of Fame Ser.). (ENG., Illus.). 120p. (J). (gr. 4-8). pap. 10.95 *(978-1-897187-22-7(X))* Second Story Pr. CAN. Dist: Orca Bk. Pubs. USA.

—Extraordinary Women Explorers, 1 vol. 2005. (Women's Hall of Fame Ser.). (ENG., Illus.). 110p. (J). (gr. 4-8). pap. 10.95 *(978-1-896764-98-6(3))* Second Story Pr. CAN. Dist: Orca Bk. Pubs. USA.

Rose, Mary Catherine. Clara Barton: Soldier of Mercy. Johnson, E. Harper, illus. 2011. 80p. 37.95 *(978-1-258-07364-0(1))* Literary Licensing, LLC.

Ross, Michael Elsohn. Fish Watching with Eugenie Clark. Smith, Wendy, illus. 2005. (Naturalist's Apprentice Biographies Ser.). 48p. (gr. 3-6). lib. bdg. 19.93 *(978-1-57505-384-4(5))* Lerner Publishing Group.

Ross, Nancy Wilson. Joan of Arc. 2003. vii, 182p. pap. 29.00 *(978-0-7581-5017-2(2))* Textbook Pubs.

Ryan, Pam Muñoz. When Marian Sang: The True Recital of Marian Anderson. Selznick, Brian, illus. pap. 16.95 incl. audio *(978-1-59112-943-1(5))*; pap. incl. audio *(978-1-59112-945-5(1))*; pap. 18.95 incl. audio compact disk *(978-1-59112-947-9(8))*; pap. incl. audio compact disk *(978-1-59112-949-3(4))* Live Oak Media.

Sabin, Francene & Macken, JoAnn Early. Elizabeth Blackwell, the First Woman Doctor. Toulmin-Rothe, Ann, illus. 2007. 53p. (J). *(978-0-439-66044-0(0))* Scholastic, Inc.

Saddleback Educational Publishing Staff. Beyonce, 1 vol. 2015. (Hip-Hop Biographies Ser.). (ENG.). 48p. (YA). (gr. 9-12). 11.95 *(978-1-62250-927-0(7))* Saddleback Educational Publishing, Inc.

Sakany, Lois. Women Civil War Spies of the Union. 2004. (American Women at War Ser.). (Illus.). 112p. (gr. 7-12). lib. bdg. 34.60 *(978-0-8239-4450-7(6))* Rosen Publishing Group, Inc., The.

Sally Ride Science Editors, Sally Ride Science. What Do You Want to Be? Explore Earth Sciences. 2004. (J). 6.00 *(978-0-9753920-2-7(6))* Sally Ride Science.

—What Do You Want to Be? Explore Health Sciences. 2004. (J). 6.00 *(978-0-9753920-3-4(4))* Sally Ride Science.

Salzmann, Mary Elizabeth. Alcott to Zaharias: Famous Women from A to Z, 1 vol. 2008. (Let's Look A to Z Ser.). (ENG., Illus.). 32p. (gr. k-4). 27.07 *(978-1-60453-010-0(3)*, Super SandCastle) ABDO Publishing Co.

Sanchez Vegara, Isabel & Albero, Ana. Coco Chanel. 2016. (Little People, Big Dreams Ser.). (ENG.). 32p. (J). (gr. k-3). 14.99 *(978-1-84780-784-7(4))*; (Illus.). 14.99 *(978-1-84780-771-7(2))* Quarto Publishing Group UK GBR. (Frances Lincoln Children's Bks.). Dist: Hachette Bk. Group, Littlehampton Bk Services, Ltd.

Sanchez Vegara, Isabel & Fan, Eng Gee. Frida Kahlo. 2016. (Little People, Big Dreams Ser.). (ENG., Illus.). 32p. (J). 14.99 *(978-1-84780-770-0(4)*, Frances Lincoln Children's Bks.) Quarto Publishing Group UK GBR. Dist: Littlehampton Bk Services, Ltd.

Savage, Candace. Born to Be a Cowgirl: A Spirited Ride Through the Old West. 2004. (Illus.). *(978-1-55054-838-9(7))* Da Capo Pr., Inc.

Sawyer, Sarah. Avril Lavigne. (Illus.). 48p. 2009. (gr. 7-12). pap. 11.75 *(978-1-4358-5128-3(5)*, Rosen Classroom) 2008. (J). lib. bdg. 29.25 *(978-1-4042-1820-8(3))* Rosen Publishing Group, Inc., The.

Schatz, Kate & Stahl, Miriam Klein. Rad Women Worldwide: Artists & Athletes, Pirates & Punks, & Other Revolutionaries Who Shaped History. 2016. (ENG., Illus.). 112p. (gr. 5-12). 15.99 *(978-0-399-57886-1(2)*, Ten Speed Pr.) Potter/TenSpeed/Harmony.

Schott, Jane A. Dian Fossey & the Mountain Gorillas. Ramstad, Ralph L., illus. 2005. (On My Own Biographies Ser.). 48p. (gr. 2-5). lib. bdg. 23.93 *(978-1-57505-082-9(X))* Lerner Publishing Group.

Schraff, Anne. Wilma Rudolph: The Greatest Woman Sprinter in History. 2004. (African-American Biographies Ser.). (Illus.). 112p. (J). lib. bdg. 26.60 *(978-0-7660-2291-1(9))* Enslow Pubs., Inc.

Schwartz, Heather. Little Mix: Singers with X-Tra Success. 2014. (Pop Culture Bios Ser.). (Illus.). 32p. (J). (gr. 3-6). lib. bdg. 26.60 *(978-1-4677-3668-8(6)*, Lerner Pubns.) Lerner Publishing Group.

—Lizzie Johnson: Texan Cowgirl, 1 vol. 2012. (Primary Source Readers Ser.). (ENG.). 32p. (J). (gr. 3-3). pap. 8.99 *(978-1-4333-5051-1(3))* Teacher Created Materials, Inc.

Schwartz, Heather E. Girls Rebel! Amazing Tales of Women Who Broke the Mold, 1 vol. 2013. (Girls Rock! Ser.). (ENG.). 64p. (gr. 4-5). 34.65 *(978-1-4765-0232-8(3))* Capstone Press of Coughlan Cos.

Senker, Cath. J. K. Rowling: Creator of Harry Potter. 2011. (Famous Lives Ser.). (Illus.). 32p. (YA). (gr. 3-6). lib. bdg.

26.50 (978-1-4488-3288-0(8)) Rosen Publishing Group, Inc., The.

Serrano, Francisco. La Malinche: The Princess Who Helped Cortés Conquer the Aztec Empire, 1 vol. Ouriou, Susan, tr. from SPA. Serrano, Pablo, illus. 2012. (ENG.). 36p. (J). (gr. 3-7). 18.95 (978-1-55498-111-3(5)) Groundwood Bks. CAN. Dist: Publishers Group West (PGW).

Sexton, Colleen. J. K. Rowling. 2008. pap. 52.95 (978-1-57505-984-6(3)) Lerner Publishing Group.

Shannon, Chelsey. Chelsey: My True Story of Murder, Loss, & Starting Over. 2009. (Louder Than Words Ser.). (ENG.). 168p. (YA). (gr. 7-18). pap. 7.95 (978-0-7573-1413-1(9), HCI Teens) Health Communications, Inc.

Shapiro, Marc. J. K. Rowling: The Wizard Behind Harry Potter. 4th ed. 2007. (ENG., Illus.). 288p. pap. 20.99 (978-0-312-37697-0(9), 9780312376970, St. Martin's Griffin) St. Martin's Pr.

Shaw, Maura D. Dorothy Day: A Catholic Life of Action. Marchesi, Stephen, illus. 2004. (ENG.). 32p. (J). 12.99 (978-1-59473-011-5(3), 9781594730115, Skylight Paths Publishing) LongHill Partners, Inc.

Sheafer, Silvia Anne. Aimee Semple McPherson. 2004. (Spiritual Leaders & Thinkers Ser.). (Illus.). 120p. (C). (gr. 9-13). 30.00 (978-0-7910-7867-9(1), Chelsea Hse.) Facts On File, Inc.

Sheen, Barbara. Danica Patrick. 2009. (People in the News Ser.). (ENG.). 128p. (gr. 7-12). 39.40 (978-1-4205-0155-1(0)) Cengage Gale.

Shepherd, Jodie. Jane Goodall. 2015. (Rookie Biographies(tm) Ser.). (ENG.). 32p. (J). lib. bdg. 25.00 (978-0-531-21413-8(3), Children's Pr.) Scholastic Library Publishing.

Shone, Rob. Harriet Tubman: The Life of an African-American Abolitionist. 2009. (Graphic Nonfiction Biographies Ser.). (ENG.). 48p. (YA). (gr. 4-5). 58.50 (978-1-61513-018-4(7), Rosen Reference) Rosen Publishing Group, Inc., The.

Shuckburgh, Emily & Chambers, Catherine. Polar Scientist: The Coolest Jobs on the Planet, 1 vol. HL Studios Staff, illus. 2014. (Coolest Jobs on the Planet Ser.). (ENG.). 48p. (gr. 6-6). pap. 8.99 (978-1-4109-6648-3(8)) Heinemann-Raintree.

Shull, Jodie A. Georgia O'Keeffe: Legendary American Painter. 2003. (People to Know Ser.). (Illus.). 112p. (J). lib. bdg. 27.94 (978-0-7660-2104-4(1)) Enslow Pubs., Inc.

Silate, Jennifer. Betsy Ross: Creadora de la bandera estadounidense (Betsy Ross: Creator of the American Flag) 2009. (Grandes personajes en la historia de los Estados Unidos (Famous People in American History) Ser.). (SPA.). 32p. (gr. 2-3). 47.90 (978-1-61512-791-7(7), Editorial Buenas Letras) Rosen Publishing Group, Inc., The.

—Betsy Ross: Creator of the American Flag. 2009. (Primary Sources of Famous People in American History Ser.). 32p. (gr. 2-3). 47.90 (978-1-60851-657-5(1)) Rosen Publishing Group, Inc., The.

—Betsy Ross: Creator of the American Flag / Creadora de la bandera Estadounidense. 2009. (Famous People in American History/Grandes personajes en la historia de los Estados Unidos Ser.). (ENG & SPA.). 32p. (gr. 2-3). 47.90 (978-1-61512-539-5(6), Editorial Buenas Letras) Rosen Publishing Group, Inc., The.

—Little Sure Shot: Annie Oakley & Buffalo Bill's Wild West Show. 2009. (Great Moments in American History Ser.). 32p. (gr. 3-3). 47.90 (978-1-61513-147-1(7)) Rosen Publishing Group, Inc., The.

Sita, Lisa. Pocahontas: The Powhatan Culture & the Jamestown Colony. 2009. (Library of American Lives & Times Ser.). 112p. (gr. 5-5). 69.20 (978-1-60853-500-2(2)) Rosen Publishing Group, Inc., The.

Skelton, Renee. A Woman of Courage. 2005. (Time for Kids Ser.). (ENG., Illus.). 48p. (J). (gr. 2-4). pap. 3.99 (978-0-06-057607-3(3)) HarperCollins Pubs.

Skelton, Renee & Time for Kids Editors. Time for Kids: A Woman of Courage. 2005. (Time for Kids Ser.). (ENG., Illus.). 48p. (J). 16.99 (978-0-06-057608-0(1)) HarperCollins Pubs.

Somervill, Barbara A. Mary McLeod Bethune: African-American Educator. 2003. (Our People Ser.). (ENG., Illus.). 32p. (J). (gr. 3-6). 29.93 (978-1-59296-008-8(1), 200647) Child's World, Inc., The.

St. George, Judith. Sacagawea. 2006. pap. 8.75 (978-0-15-365175-5(X)) Harcourt Schl. Pubs.

Stanley, Phyllis M. Elizabeth Terwilliger - Someone Special: A Biography of the Celebrated Naturalist. 2003. (ENG., Illus.). 110p. (J). (gr. 4-10). pap. 17.95 (978-1-878044-54-9(0)) Mayhaven Publishing, Inc.

Stanton, Sue. Great Women of Faith: Inspiration for Action. 2003. (Illus.). 128p. (J). 12.95 (978-0-8091-4123-4(X), 4123-x) Paulist Pr.

Stathis, Roberta & Blanch, Gregory. Women Who Ruled. 2003. (Explore the Ages Ser.). (Illus.). 79p. 17.00 (978-1-55501-592-3(1)) Ballard & Tighe Pubs.

Sterling, Kristin. Jane Goodall: A Life of Loyalty. 2008. (Pull Ahead Bks.). (Illus.). 32p. (J). (gr. -1-3). lib. bdg. 22.60 (978-0-8225-8727-9(0), Lerner Pubns.) Lerner Publishing Group.

Stewart, Mark. Maria Sharapova. 2009. (Today's Superstars Ser.). 48p. (J). (gr. 5-8). pap. 14.05 (978-1-4339-2160-5(X)); lib. bdg. 31.95 (978-1-4339-1967-1(2)) Stevens, Gareth Publishing LLLP.

Stoinich, Elisabetta, illus. Good Night Stories for Rebel Girls: Coloring Book. 2016. (ENG.). pap. 9.00 **(978-0-9978958-0-3(2))** Timbuktu Labs, Inc.

Sullivan, Anne Marie. Mother Theresa: Religious Humanitarian. 2004. (Great Names Ser.). (Illus.). 32p. (J). (gr. 3-18). lib. bdg. 19.95 (978-1-59084-142-6(5)) Mason Crest.

Sutcliffe, Jane. Amelia Earhart. 2003. (History Maker Bios Ser.). (Illus.). 48p. (J). (gr. 3-5). lib. bdg. 26.60 (978-0-8225-0396-5(4)) Lerner Publishing Group.

Terp, Gail. Demi Lovato. 2017. (Women Who Rock Ser.). (ENG.). 32p. (gr. 3-7). 31.35 **(978-1-68072-066-2(X))** Black Rabbit Bks.

Thatcher Murcia, Rebecca. What Its Like to Be Marta Vieira. de la Vega, Eida, tr. 2010. (What It's Like to Be/Que se Siente al Ser Ser.). (ENG & SPA., Illus.). 32p. (J). (gr. -1-2). lib. bdg. 25.70 (978-1-58415-852-3(2)) Mitchell Lane Pubs., Inc.

—What It's Like to Be Shakira. de la Vega, Eida, tr. from SPA. 2010. (What It's Like to Be/Que se Siente al Ser Ser.). (ENG & SPA., Illus.). 32p. (J). (gr. -1-2). lib. bdg. 25.70 (978-1-58415-851-6(4)) Mitchell Lane Pubs., Inc.

Thiel, Kristin. Joan of Arc. 2017. (J). **(978-1-5026-2791-9(4))** Cavendish Square Publishing.

Tougas, Shelley. Girls Rule! Amazing Tales of Female Leaders, 1 vol. 2013. (Girls Rock! Ser.). (ENG.). 64p. (gr. 4-5). 34.65 (978-1-4765-0235-9(8)) Capstone Press of Coughlan Cos.

Townsley, Janet Howe. Dakota Dreams: Fannie Sabra Howe's Own Story, 1881-1884. 2003. (Illus.). 77p. (J). 19.95 (978-0-9715171-4-1(2)) South Dakota State Historical Society Pr.

Tracy, Kathleen. Orianthi. 2010. (Blue Banner Biography Ser.). (Illus.). 32p. (YA). (gr. 4-7). lib. bdg. 25.70 (978-1-58415-913-1(8)) Mitchell Lane Pubs., Inc.

Trouvé, Marianne Lorraine. Saint Catherine Labouré: And Our Lady of the Miraculous Medal. 2011. (ENG.). (J). pap. 7.95 (978-0-8198-7224-1(5)) Pauline Bks. & Media.

UNESCO. Wangari Maathai. 2016. (ENG., Illus.). 112p. (J). (gr. 3-7). 13.95 (978-0-00-814935-2(6)) HarperCollins Pubs. Ltd. GBR. Dist: Independent Pubs. Group.

Valentine, Emily. Mother Teresa: With a Discussion of Compassion. 2004. (Values in Action Ser.). (J). (978-1-59203-070-5(X)) Learning Challenge, Inc.

Van Allsburg, Chris. Queen of the Falls. 2011. (ENG., Illus.). 40p. (J). (gr. 1-4). 18.99 (978-0-547-31581-2(3)) Houghton Mifflin Harcourt Publishing Co.

Van Haeringen, Annmarie. Coco & the Little Black Dress. 2015. (ENG., Illus.). 32p. (J). 16.95 (978-0-7358-4239-7(6)) North-South Bks., Inc.

Vargas, Constanza Orozco. Coco Chanel: Una Mujer Salida del Molde. 2005. (100 Personajes Ser.). (SPA.). 152p. (YA). (978-958-30-1765-0(5)) Panamericana Editorial.

Vegetarians of Washington Staff. Vegetarian Pacific Northwest: A Guide to Restaurants & Shopping. 2008. (ENG., Illus.). 128p. (gr. 4-7). pap. 14.95 (978-1-57067-211-8(3)) Book Publishing Co.

Venezia, Mike. Jane Goodall: Researcher Who Champions Chimps. 2010. (Getting to Know the World's Greatest Inventors & Scientists Ser.). 32p. (J). (gr. 3-4). pap. 6.95 (978-0-531-22352-9(3), Children's Pr.) Scholastic Library Publishing.

—Lise Meitner: Had the Right Vision about Nuclear Fission. Venezia, Mike, illus. 2010. (Getting to Know the World's Greatest Inventors & Scientists Ser.). (ENG., Illus.). 32p. (J). (gr. 3-4). pap. 6.95 (978-0-531-20776-5(5), Children's Pr.) Scholastic Library Publishing.

—Marie Curie: Scientist Who Made Glowing Discoveries. Venezia, Mike, illus. (Getting to Know the World's Greatest Inventors & Scientists Ser.). (ENG., Illus.). 32p. (J). 2009. (gr. 3-4). pap. 6.95 (978-0-531-22208-9(X), Children's Pr.) 2008. (gr. 2-5). 28.00 (978-0-531-14977-5(3)) Scholastic Library Publishing.

Vinberger, Naftali Yehiel ben Shelomoh Avraham, et al. The Story of Rebbetzin Kanievsky: A Biography for Young Readers. 2012. (Illus.). 204p. (J). (978-1-4226-1333-7(X)) Mesorah Pubns., Ltd.

Volovar, Vivian. Lobster Lady. 2007. (Illus.). 32p. (J). pap. 14.95 (978-0-9773725-8-4(8)) Flat Hammock Pr.

Wade, Mary Dodson. Joan Lowery Nixon: Masterful Mystery Writer. 2004. (Authors Teens Love Ser.). (Illus.). 128p. (J). lib. bdg. 27.94 (978-0-7660-2194-5(7)) Enslow Pubs., Inc.

Walker, Sally M. Mary Anning: Fossil Hunter. Saroff, Phyllis V., illus. 2007. (On My Own Biographies Ser.). 48p. (J). (gr. 2-5). per. 6.95 (978-1-57505-457-5(4), First Avenue Editions) Lerner Publishing Group.

Ward, S. Meet J. K. Rowling. 2003. (About the Author Ser.). 24p. (J). lib. bdg. 18.75 (978-0-8239-6808-4(1), PowerKids Pr.) Rosen Publishing Group, Inc., The.

Waxman, Laura Hamilton. Marie Curie. 2003. (History Maker Biographies Ser.). (ENG., Illus.). 48p. (gr. 3-6). 27.93 (978-0-8225-0300-2(X), Lerner Pubns.) Lerner Publishing Group.

Webster, Christine. Sandra Cisneros: My Favorite Writer. 2008. (J). 29.05 (978-1-59036-933-3(5)) Weigl Pubs., Inc.

Weinberger, Kimberly. Let's Read About — Pocahontas. Marchesi, Stephen, illus. 2003. (Scholastic First Biographies Ser.). (J). pap. (978-0-439-56148-8(5)) Scholastic, Inc.

Wenzel, Angela & Schuelmann, Bettina. 13 Women Artists Children Should Know. 2009. (ENG., Illus.). 48p. (J). (gr. 3-7). 14.95 (978-3-7913-4333-4(5)) Prestel Verlag GmbH & Co KG. DEU. Dist: Penguin Random Hse. LLC.

Wheeler, Jill C. Gertrude Chandler Warner, 1 vol. 2005. (Children's Authors Set 3 Ser.). (ENG.). 24p. (gr. k-6). 25.65 (978-1-59197-609-7(X), Checkerboard Library) ABDO Publishing Co.

White, Katherine. Sylvia Earle: Deep Sea Explorer & Ocean Activist. (Women Hall of Famers in Mathematics & Science Ser.). 112p. (gr. 5-8). 2009. 63.90 (978-1-60854-814-9(7)) 2004. (Illus.). lib. bdg. 34.60 (978-0-8239-3879-7(4)) Rosen Publishing Group, Inc., The. (Rosen Reference).

Wilkinson, Philip. Joan of Arc: The Teenager Who Saved Her Nation. 2007. (National Geographic World History Biographies Ser.). (ENG., Illus.). 64p. (J). (gr. 3-7). 17.95 (978-1-4263-0116-2(2)); lib. bdg. 27.90 (978-1-4263-0117-9(0)) National Geographic Society. (National Geographic Children's Bks.).

Willen, Janet & Gann, Marjorie. Speak a Word for Freedom: Women Against Slavery. 2015. (ENG., Illus.). 208p. (J). (gr. 7). 21.99 (978-1-77049-651-4(3), Tundra Bks.) Tundra Bks. CAN. Dist: Penguin Random Hse. LLC.

Williams, Suzanne. China's Daughters. MacLean, Amber, illus. 2011. (J). (978-1-881896-34-0(X)) Pacific View Pr.

Wilson, Antoine. S. E. Hinton. 2009. (Library of Author Biographies Ser.). (gr. 5-8). 63.90 (978-1-60853-553-8(3), Rosen Reference) Rosen Publishing Group, Inc., The.

Winegarten, Debra L. Katherine Stinson: The Flying Schoolgirl. 2004. (Illus.). 133p. (gr. 4-7). 26.95 (978-1-57168-459-2(X)) Eakin Pr.

Winter, Jeanette. My Name Is Georgia. 2003. (ENG., Illus.). 48p. (J). (gr. -1-3). pap. 7.99 (978-0-15-204597-5(X)) Houghton Mifflin Harcourt Publishing Co.

—The Watcher: Jane Goodall's Life with the Chimps. Winter, Jeanette, illus. 2011. (ENG., Illus.). 48p. (J). (gr. -1-3). 17.99 (978-0-375-86774-3(0), Schwartz & Wade Bks.) Random Hse. Children's Bks.

Winter, Jonah. Wild Women of the Wild West. Morgan, Mary & Guevara, Susan, illus. 2011. (ENG.). 40p. (J). 16.95 (978-0-8234-1601-1(1)) Holiday Hse., Inc.

Women Explorers. (J). pap. 4.95 (978-0-88388-203-0(5)) Bellerophon Bks.

Women Who Changed History. 2017. (Women Who Changed History Ser.). 48p. (gr. 10-12). 161.10 **(978-1-5081-0550-3(2))**; pap. 84.30 **(978-1-5081-0552-7(9))** Rosen Publishing Group, Inc., The. (Britannica Educational Publishing).

Wood, Susan. Vaccine Innovators Pearl Kendrick & Grace Eldering. 2016. (STEM Trailblazer Bios Ser.). (ENG., Illus.). 32p. (J). (gr. 2-5). 26.65 (978-1-5124-0790-7(9)) Lerner Publishing Group.

Woods, Bob. Racer Girls. 2016. (Illus.). 32p. (J). (978-1-4896-4781-8(3)) Weigl Pubs., Inc.

Yolen, Jane. Sea Queens: Women Pirates Around the World. Pratt, Christine Joy, illus. (ENG.). 112p. (J). (gr. 2-5). 2010. pap. 9.95 (978-1-58089-132-5(2)) 2008. 18.95 (978-1-58089-131-8(4)) Charlesbridge Publishing, Inc.

Yolen, Jane & Stemple, Heidi E. Y. Bad Girls: Sirens, Jezebels, Murderesses, Thieves & Other Female Villains. 2015. lib. bdg. 20.80 (978-0-606-37602-0(X)) Turtleback Bks.

Zachry, Juanita Daniel. Katy O'Neil: She Found a Way or Made One. 2004. 224p. per. 14.95 (978-0-9749725-1-0(7)); bds. 24.95 (978-0-9749725-0-3(9)) LoneStar Abilene Publishing, LLC.

Zhang, Gui Jie. The Bamboo Forest: I Truly Love You, & God Loves You Too, 1 vol. 2009. 47p. pap. 24.95 (978-1-60836-292-9(2)) America Star Bks.

WOMEN—CLOTHING

see Clothing and Dress

WOMEN—DRESS

see Clothing and Dress; Costume

WOMEN—EDUCATION

Aretha, David. Malala Yousafzai & the Girls of Pakistan. 2014. (ENG.). (J). 27.45 (978-1-59935-454-5(3)) Reynolds, Morgan Inc.

Bakarat, Ibtisam. Balcony on the Moon: Growing up in Palestine. 2016. (ENG.). 240p. (J). 17.99 (978-0-374-30251-1(0), 9780374302511, Farrar, Straus & Giroux (BYR)) Farrar, Straus & Giroux.

Brown, Dinah. Who Is Malala Yousafzai? Thomson, Andrew, illus. 2015. 105p. (J). (978-1-4844-6131-0(2), Grosset & Dunlap) Penguin Publishing Group.

—Who Is Malala Yousafzai? 2015. (Who Is... ? Ser.). lib. bdg. 16.00 (978-0-606-37551-1(1)) Turtleback Bks.

Corey, Shana. Malala: A Hero for All. Sayles, Elizabeth, illus. 2016. (Step into Reading Ser.). (ENG.). 48p. (J). (gr. 2-4). pap. 3.99 (978-0-553-53761-1(X), Random Hse. Bks. for Young Readers) Random Hse. Children's Bks.

Doeden, Matt. Malala Yousafzai: Shot by the Taliban, Still Fighting for Equal Education. 2014. (Gateway Biographies Ser.). (ENG., Illus.). 48p. (gr. 4-8). lib. bdg. 26.60 (978-1-4677-4907-7(9), Lerner Pubns.) Lerner Publishing Group.

Gagliardi, Tina. School Survival: Keeping Your Cool at School, 1 vol. 2008. (Essential Health: Strong Beautiful Girls Set 1 Ser.). (ENG.). 112p. (J). (gr. 6-12). lib. bdg. 35.64 (978-1-60453-104-6(5)) ABDO Publishing Co.

Hansen, Grace. Malala Yousafzai: Education Activist, 1 vol. 2014. (History Maker Biographies Ser.). (ENG.). 24p. (J). (gr. 2-4). lib. bdg. 28.50 (978-1-62970-703-7(1)) ABDO Publishing Co.

Herweck Rice, Dona. Fantastic Kids: Malala Yousafzai (Level 5) 2017. (Exploring Reading Ser.). (Illus.). 48p. (J). (gr. 5-5). pap. 10.99 **(978-1-4258-4988-7(1))** Teacher Created Materials, Inc.

Langston-George, Rebecca. For the Right to Learn: Malala Yousafzai's Story. Bock, Janna, illus. (Encounter: Narrative Nonfiction Picture Bks.). (ENG.). 40p. (gr. 3-4). 2016. pap. 7.95 (978-1-4914-6556-1(5)) 2015. lib. bdg. 28.65 (978-1-4914-6071-9(7)) Encounter Bks.

Lew, Kristi. Cool Biology Activities for Girls, 1 vol. 2012. (Girls Science Club Ser.). (ENG.). 32p. (gr. 3-4). pap. 8.19 (978-1-4296-8019-6(9)); pap. 47.70 (978-1-4296-8517-7(4)); lib. bdg. 27.99 (978-1-4296-7676-2(0)) Capstone Press of Coughlan Cos. (Snap Bks.).

Malala, a Brave Girl from Pakistan/Iqbal, a Brave Boy from Pakistan. 2014. (ENG., Illus.). 40p. (J). (gr. 1-5). 17.99 (978-1-4814-2294-9(4), Beach Lane Bks.) Beach Lane Bks.

Manion, Jennifer. Safia AMA Jan. 2011. (J). lib. bdg. (978-0-8225-9038-5(7)) Twenty First Century Bks.

McCarney, Rosemary. Dear Malala, We Stand with You. 2014. (ENG.). 32p. (J). (gr. -1-3). lib. bdg. 19.99 (978-0-553-52121-4(7)); 16.99 (978-0-553-52120-7(9)) Random Hse. Children's Bks. (Crown Books For Young Readers).

—Every Day Is Malala Day, 1 vol. 2014. (ENG., Illus.). 32p. (J). (gr. 3-5). 18.95 (978-1-927583-31-9(4)) Second Story Pr. CAN. Dist: Orca Bk. Pubs. USA.

Montalbano, Julie Williams. Middle School. 2014. (Smart Girl's Guide Ser.). lib. bdg. 24.50 (978-0-606-35213-0(9)) Turtleback Bks.

Niver, Heather Moore. Malala Yousafzai, 01 vols., 1. 2016. (Britannica Beginner Bios Ser.). (ENG., Illus.). 32p. (J). lib. bdg. 23.45 (978-1-68048-253-9(X), Britannica Educational Publishing) Rosen Publishing Group, Inc., The.

Peters, Elisa. Malala Yousafzai: Pakistani Activist for Female Education. 2017. (J). **(978-1-5081-7749-4(X))** Rosen Publishing Group, Inc., The.

Rowell, Rebecca & Llanas, Sheila Griffin. Malala Yousafzai: Education Activist, 1 vol. 2013. (Essential Lives Set 8 Ser.). (ENG., Illus.). 112p. (J). (gr. 6-12). lib. bdg. 35.64 (978-1-61783-897-2(7), Essential Library) ABDO Publishing Co.

Schwartz, Heather E. Cool Engineering Activities for Girls, 1 vol. 2012. (Girls Science Club Ser.). (ENG.). 32p. (gr. 3-4). Illus.). pap. 8.19 (978-1-4296-8021-9(0)); pap. 47.70 (978-1-4296-8519-1(0)); lib. bdg. 27.99 (978-1-4296-7677-9(9)) Capstone Press of Coughlan Cos. (Snap Bks.).

Slade, Suzanne. Cool Physics Activities for Girls, 1 vol. 2012. (Girls Science Club Ser.). (ENG.). 32p. (gr. 3-4). pap. 8.19 (978-1-4296-8022-6(9)); pap. 47.70 (978-1-4296-8520-7(4)) Capstone Press of Coughlan Cos. (Snap Bks.).

Speregen, Debra Newberger. Got Class? A GF's Guide to School Style. 2008. (Illus.). 48p. (J). (978-0-545-04092-1(2)) Scholastic, Inc.

Stone, Tanya Lee. Girl Rising: Changing the World One Girl at a Time. 2017. (ENG.). 208p. (YA). (gr. 9). 22.99 (978-0-553-51146-8(7), Lamb, Wendy Bks.) Random Hse. Children's Bks.

Throp, Claire. Malala Yousafzai. 2015. (Against the Odds Biographies Ser.). (ENG., Illus.). 48p. (gr. 3-6). 33.32 (978-1-4846-2464-7(5)) Heinemann-Raintree.

Wang, Andrea. Malala Yousafzai: Nobel Peace Prize Winner & Education Activist, 1 vol. 2014. (Newsmakers Ser.). (ENG.). 48p. (gr. 3-6). lib. bdg. 32.79 (978-1-62403-646-0(5)) ABDO Publishing Co.

Wheeler-Toppen, Jodi. Cool Chemistry Activities for Girls, 1 vol. 2012. (Girls Science Club Ser.). (ENG., 32p. (gr. 3-4). Illus.). pap. 8.19 (978-1-4296-8020-2(2)); pap. 47.70 (978-1-4296-8518-4(2)); (Illus.). lib. bdg. 27.99 (978-1-4296-7674-8(4)) Capstone Press of Coughlan Cos. (Snap Bks.).

Wheeler-Toppen, Jodi, et al. Girls Science Club. 2012. (Girls Science Club Ser.). (ENG.). 32p. (gr. 3-4). pap. 31.80 (978-1-4296-8521-4(2)); pap. 190.80 (978-1-4296-8522-1(0)) Capstone Press of Coughlan Cos. (Snap Bks.).

Winter, Jeanette. Nasreen's Secret School: A True Story from Afghanistan. Winter, Jeanette, illus. 2009. (ENG., Illus.). 40p. (J). (gr. 1-4). 17.99 (978-1-4169-9437-4(8), Beach Lane Bks.) Beach Lane Bks.

Yousafzai, Malala. I Am Malala: The Girl Who Stood up for Education & Was Shot by the Taliban. (ENG.). (J). 2016. 256p. 98.91 (978-0-316-30398-9(4)) 2016. (Illus.). 256p. (gr. 5-17). pap. 10.99 (978-0-316-32791-6(3)) 2014. 256p. 153.00 (978-0-316-33917-9(2)) 2014. (Illus.). 240p. (gr. 5-17). 17.99 (978-0-316-32793-0(X)) 2015. 240p. (gr. 5-17). 17.00 (978-0-316-31119-9(7)) Little, Brown Bks. for Young Readers.

—I Am Malala: The Girl Who Stood up for Education & Was Shot by the Taliban. 2016. (J). lib. bdg. 22.10 (978-0-606-37164-3(8)) Turtleback Bks.

Yousafzai, Malala & McCormick, Patricia. I Am Malala: The Girl Who Stood up for Education & Was Shot by the Taliban. Lt. ed. 2017. (ENG., Illus.). 302p. 22.99 **(978-1-4104-9916-5(2))** Cengage Gale.

WOMEN—EDUCATION—FICTION

Lyons, Wendy Ackerman. The Girl Who Reached for the Star. Sayles, John, illus. 2007. (J). (978-0-696-23982-3(5)) Meredith Bks.

WOMEN—EMPLOYMENT

Berlatsky, Noah. Working Women. 2015. (Opposing Viewpoints Ser.). (ENG.). 224p. (J). (gr. 10-12). 48.80 (978-0-7377-7302-6(2), Greenhaven Pr., Inc.) Cengage Gale.

Campbell, Candy. My Mom Is A Nurse, 1 vol. 2010. (ENG.). 208p. pap., pap. 27.95 (978-0-578-02360-1(1)) New Year Publishing.

Dorman, Jennifer. Are Women Paid Fairly? 2012. (At Issue Ser.). (ENG.). 128p. (gr. 10-12). pap. 27.80 (978-0-7377-6154-2(7)); lib. bdg. 39.40 (978-0-7377-6153-5(9)) Cengage Gale. (Greenhaven Pr., Inc.).

Edge, Laura Bufano. We Stand As One: The International Ladies Garment Workers' Strike, New York, 1909. 2010. (Civil Rights Struggles around the World Ser.). (ENG., Illus.). 160p. (gr. 9-12). lib. bdg. 38.60 (978-0-7613-4609-8(0)) Lerner Publishing Group.

Fisanick, Christina, ed. Working Women. 2007. (Opposing Viewpoints Ser.). (ENG., Illus.). 186p. (gr. 10-12). lib. bdg. 46.45 (978-0-7377-3771-4(9), LML02109-234440, Greenhaven Pr., Inc.) Cengage Gale.

Lowery, Zoe & Freedman, Jeri. Women's Rights at Work. 2017. (Women in the World Ser.). 112p. (J). (gr. 12-11). 37.10 **(978-1-5081-7451-6(2)**, Rosen Young Adult) Rosen Publishing Group, Inc., The.

MacDonald, Fiona. Equal Opportunities. (World Issues Ser.). (Illus.). 57p. (J). lib. bdg. 28.50 (978-1-931983-30-3(5)) Chrysalis Education.

Morkes, Andrew & McKenna, Amy. Nontraditional Careers for Women & Men: More Than 30 Great Jobs for Women & Men with Apprenticeships Through Phds. 2011. (ENG.). (J). pap. 19.95 (978-0-9745251-9-8(7)) College & Career Pr., LLC.

Petersen, Christine. Rosie the Riveter. 2008. (Cornerstones of Freedom Ser.). (ENG.). 48p. (J). pap. 5.95 (978-0-531-20840-3(0), Children's Pr.) Scholastic Library Publishing.

Women in the World: Set 1. 2017. (Women in the World Ser.). 112p. (gr. 12-11). 222.60 **(978-1-4994-6639-3(0)**, Rosen Young Adult) Rosen Publishing Group, Inc., The.

WOMEN—EMPLOYMENT—FICTION

Finnan, Kristie. Mommy's High Heel Shoes. Achilles, Pat, illus. 2008. 32p. (J). 16.99 (978-0-9817565-2-3(2)) Mommy Workshop Bks.

WOMEN—ENFRANCHISEMENT

see Women—Suffrage

WOMEN—FICTION

Anderson, Erin. Repulsive. 2008. 16p. pap. 24.95 (978-1-4241-9429-2(6)) America Star Bks.

Anderson, Jessica Lee. Calli. 2011. (ENG.). 198p. (J). (gr. 6). 16.95 (978-1-57131-702-5(3)); pap. 8.00 (978-1-57131-699-8(X)) Milkweed Editions.

Anderson, William. Little Woman. Date not set. 32p. (J). (gr. 2-5). pap. 5.99 (978-0-06-443574-1(1)) HarperCollins Pubs.

Arroyo, Madeline. Calie's Gift. Vavak, S. Dean, illus. 2003. 32p. (gr. 2-5). 16.95 (978-0-9740061-0-9(6), 1234106) Stairway Pubns.

Asai, Carrie. The Book of the Shadow. Alarcao, Renato, illus. 2013. (Samurai Girl Ser.: 2). (ENG.). 224p. (YA). (gr. 11). pap. 13.99 (978-1-4814-1540-8(9), Simon Pulse) Simon Pulse.

Austen, Jane. Pride & Prejudice. 2003. (Saddleback Classics Ser.). (Illus.). 48p. (J). stu. ed., per. 17.95 (978-1-56254-530-7(2), SP5302); 80p. (YA). (gr. 8-12). per.

WXYZ

6.95 (978-1-56254-529-1(9), SP5299) Saddleback Educational Publishing, Inc.
Berry, Erick. Valiant Captive. 2011. 204p. 44.95 (978-1-258-06194-4(5)) Literary Licensing, LLC.
Bertola, Ann Marie, et al, contrib. by. Four in the Afternoon. 2003. 118p. pap. 11.99 (978-0-9743661-0-4(2)) Circle Pr.
Bloom, Deb-b. The Bird Who Could Fly. 2008. 24p. pap. 24.95 (978-1-60441-383-0(2)) America Star Bks.
Burnett, Frances Hodgson. A Lady of Quality. 2011. 190p. 26.95 (978-1-4638-9631-7(X)) Rodgers, Alan Bks.
Chadwick, Katie. Meet Miss Molly. 2012. 44p. pap. (978-1-84961-134-3(3)) RealTime Publishing.
Chopin, Kate. The Story of an Hour. (Illus.). 32p. 3.30 (978-0-7891-5479-8(X)) Perfection Learning Corp.
Clark, K. M. Beautiful Disaster. 2013. 106p. 24.99 (978-1-4797-6506-5(6)); pap. 15.99 (978-1-4797-6505-8(8)) Xlibris Corp.
Colandro, Lucille. There Was an Old Lady Who Swallowed Some Leaves! Lee, Jared, illus. 2010. (ENG.). 32p. (J). (gr. -1-k). pap. 6.99 (978-0-545-24198-4(7), Cartwheel Bks.) Scholastic, Inc.
Davies, Kate, ed. Old Woman Who Swallowed a Fly. Home, Sarah, illus. 2009. (First Reading Level 3 Ser.). 48p. (J). (gr. 2). 6.99 (978-0-7945-2267-4(X), Usborne) EDC Publishing.
Dee, Katya. Orna Puella, 1 vol. 2009. 194p. pap. 24.95 (978-1-61582-195-2(3)) PublishAmerica, Inc.
d'Lacey, Chris. The Fire Eternal. 2010. (Last Dragon Chronicles Ser.: 4). (ENG.). 512p. (J). (gr. 3-7). 8.99 (978-0-545-05164-4(9), Orchard Bks.) Scholastic, Inc.
Dokey, Cameron. Kissed: Belle; Sunlight & Shadow; Winter's Child. 2013. (ENG.). 624p. (YA). (gr. 7). pap. 9.99 (978-1-4424-7220-4(0), Simon Pulse) Simon Pulse.
Dolbeck, Andrew. Fever Jenny, Bk. 1. 2006. 120p. pap. 10.99 (978-1-59092-324-5(3)) Blue Forge Pr.
Durkee, Noura. Yunus & the Whale. Durkee, Noura, illus. 2007. (ENG., Illus.). 28p. (J). (gr. k-5). 16.00 (978-1-879402-60-7(2)) Tahrike Tarsile Quran, Inc.
Dyan, Penelope. Eve. Dyan, Penelope, illus. 2011. (Illus.). 34p. pap. 11.95 (978-1-935630-95-1(4)) Bellissima Publishing, LLC.
Edwards, Jo. Go Figure. 2007. (ENG.). 288p. (YA). (gr. 9-12). pap. 13.99 (978-1-4169-2492-0(2), Simon Pulse) Simon Pulse.
Finley, Martha. Elsie Dinsmore, Vol. 1. 320p. (gr. 7-12). pap. 5.95 (978-1-58182-064-5(X), Cumberland Hse.) Sourcebooks, Inc.
—Elsie's Girlhood, Vol. 3. 320p. (gr. 7-12). pap. 5.95 (978-1-58182-066-9(6), Cumberland Hse.) Sourcebooks, Inc.
—Elsie's Holidays at Roselands, Vol. 2. 320p. (gr. 7-12). pap. 5.95 (978-1-58182-065-2(8), Cumberland Hse.) Sourcebooks, Inc.
—Elsie's Widowhood, Vol. 1. 320p. (gr. 7-12). pap. 5.95 (978-1-58182-070-6(4), Cumberland Hse.) Sourcebooks, Inc.
—Elsie's Womanhood, Vol. 4. 320p. (gr. 7-12). pap. 5.95 (978-1-58182-067-6(4), Cumberland Hse.) Sourcebooks, Inc.
—Grandmother Elsie, Vol. 8. 320p. (gr. 7-12). pap. 5.95 (978-1-58182-071-3(2), Cumberland Hse.) Sourcebooks, Inc.
Flake, Sharon G. The Skin I'm In. Disney Press Staff, illus. rev. ed. 2007. (ENG.). 176p. (J). (gr. 5-9). pap. 8.99 (978-1-4231-0385-1(8), Jump at the Sun) Hyperion Bks. for Children.
Follet, René. The Fascinating Madame Tussaud. Duchateau, illus. 2008. (Expresso Collection). (ENG.). 104p. pap. 19.95 (978-1-905460-36-6(8)) CineBook GBR. Dist: National Bk. Network.
Fosberry, Jennifer. My Name Is Not Isabella. Litwin, Mike, illus. 2008. 32p. (J). (gr. -1-3). lib. bdg. 19.99 (978-0-9802000-7-2(5)) Monkey Barrel Pr.
—My Name Is Not Isabella: Just How Big Can a Little Girl Dream? Litwin, Mike, illus. 2010. (ENG.). 32p. (J). (gr. k-3). 16.99 (978-1-4022-4395-0(2), Sourcebooks Jabberwocky) Sourcebooks, Inc.
Fraustino, Lisa Rowe, ed. Don't Cramp My Style: Stories about That Time of the Month. 2004. (ENG., Illus.). 304p. (YA). 15.95 (978-0-689-85882-6(5), Simon & Schuster Bks. For Young Readers) Simon & Schuster Bks. For Young Readers.
Frost, Helen. Crossing Stones. 2009. (ENG., Illus.). 192p. (YA). (gr. 7-18). 18.99 (978-0-374-31653-2(8), 9780374316532, Farrar, Straus & Giroux (BYR)) Farrar, Straus & Giroux.
Fuerst, Jeffrey B. The Old Woman Who Lived in a Shoe. Greenhead, Bill, illus. 2010. (Rising Readers Ser.). (J). 3.49 (978-1-60719-703-4(0)) Newmark Learning LLC.
Godbersen, Anna. Envy. 2009. (Luxe Ser.: 3). (ENG.). 432p. (YA). (gr. 9). pap. 9.99 (978-0-06-134574-6(1)) HarperCollins Pubs.
Guttentag, Devora. Saving Soraya. 236p. (YA). 18.99 (978-1-56871-256-7(1)) Targum Pr., Inc.
Haddix, Margaret Peterson. Turnabout. 2007. (ENG.). 240p. (YA). (gr. 7-12). mass mkt. 7.99 (978-1-4169-3653-4(X), Simon Pulse) Simon Pulse.
Hearn, Julie. Hazel: A Novel. 2010. (ENG.). 416p. (YA). (gr. 7). pap. 8.99 (978-1-4169-2505-7(8), Atheneum Bks. for Young Readers) Simon & Schuster Children's Publishing.
Hoblin, Paul & Hueller, Patrick. Archenemy. 2013. (Counterattack Ser.). (ENG.). 112p. (YA). (gr. 6-12). lib. bdg. 27.93 (978-1-4677-0306-2(0)) Lerner Publishing Group.
House, Silas. Eli the Good. 2009. (ENG., Illus.). 304p. (YA). (gr. 7). 16.99 (978-0-7636-4341-6(6)) Candlewick Pr.
James, Henry. The Ambassadors. 1stWorld Library, ed. 2007. 516p. (YA). (gr. 12). pap. 20.95 (978-1-4218-2714-8(X), 1st World Library - Literary Society) 1st World Publishing, Inc.
—The Ambassadors. 312p. reprint ed. pap. 99.00 (978-1-4047-3431-9(7)) Classic Textbooks.
—The Ambassadors. 2008. 368p. (YA). (gr. 13). pap. 20.99 (978-1-59547-714-9(4)) NuVision Pubns., LLC.
—The Ambassadors. 2008. 376p. (YA). (gr. 12). 35.00 (978-1-4344-7145-1(4)); pap. 19.95 (978-1-4344-7144-4(6)) Wildside Pr., LLC.
Keene, Carolyn. Dangerous Plays. 16th ed. 2006. (Nancy Drew (All New) Girl Detective Ser.: 16). (ENG.). 160p. (J). (gr. 3-7). pap. 6.99 (978-1-4169-0605-6(3), Aladdin) Simon & Schuster Children's Publishing.
—Wedding Day Disaster. Pamintuan, Macky, illus. 2008. (Nancy Drew & the Clue Crew Ser.: 17). (ENG.). 96p. (J). (gr. 1-4). pap. 5.99 (978-1-4169-6778-1(8), Aladdin) Simon & Schuster Children's Publishing.
Komada, Yoshihiro, et al. Flesh for the Beast. Pannone, Frank, ed. Ohtsuka, Tommy et al, illus. 2004. 132p. pap. 9.99 (978-1-58655-556-6(1), SSNOV-0419) Media Blasters, Inc.
Leslie, Emma. From Bondage to Freedom: A Tale of the Times of Mohammed. Symmons, Sheeres, illus. 2007. 308p. 24.95 (978-1-934671-10-8(X)) Salem Ridge Press LLC.
Llewellyn, Claire. Boudica. 2016. (ENG.). 48p. (J). (gr. 3-4). pap. 9.95 (978-0-00-816391-4(X)) HarperCollins Pubs. Ltd. GBR. Dist: Independent Pubs. Group.
Man-Kong, Mary. Barbie in a Mermaid Tale. Golden Books Staff, illus. 2010. (Pictureback(R) Ser.). (ENG.). 16p. (J). (gr. -1-2). pap. 3.99 (978-0-375-85735-5(4), Random Hse. Bks. for Young Readers) Random Hse. Children's Bks.
Marlo's Rainbow Pony. 2004.Tr. of Marlo'w Rainbow Pony. (Illus.). 12p. (J). 5.95 net. (978-0-9728871-0-6(5)) Rainbow Pony Publishing.
Martin, Ann M. Needle & Thread. Andreasen, Dan, illus. 2007. 205p. (J). pap. (978-0-545-03660-3(7)) Scholastic, Inc.
Martinez, Alejandro Cruz. La Mujer que Brillaba Aun Mas Que el Sol. 2004. (SPA.). (J). (gr. k-3). spiral bd. (978-0-616-07278-3(3)) Canadian National Institute for the Blind/Institut National Canadien pour les Aveugles.
McDavid-Jones, Elizabeth. Secrets on 26th Street. 2009. (Mysteries Through Time Ser.). 144 - 176p. (YA). (gr. 4-8). 31.95 (978-1-60754-200-1(5)); pap. 15.25 (978-1-60754-201-8(3)) Windmill Bks.
McDougal-Littell Publishing Staff, creator. Picture Bride & Related Readings. 2006. (Literature Connections Ser.). 314p. (gr. 6-12). (978-0-395-77540-0(X), 2-80109) Holt McDougal.
McLaren, Clemence. Aphrodite's Blessing. 2008. (ENG.). 208p. (YA). (gr. 7). pap. 10.99 (978-1-4169-7860-2(7), Simon Pulse) Simon Pulse.
McOmber, Rachel B., ed. McOmber Phonics Storybooks: Miss Vie. rev. ed. (Illus.). (J). (978-0-944991-48-0(3)) Swift Learning Resources.
Michaelis, Antonia. Tiger Moon. 2009. (ENG.). 480p. (YA). (gr. 7-11). pap. 9.95 (978-0-8109-4499-2(5), Amulet Bks.) Abrams, Inc.
Montgomery, L. M. Rilla of Ingleside. 2014. (ENG.). 352p. (J). (gr. 4-7). 10.99 (978-0-349-00451-8(X), Virago Press) Little, Brown Book Group Ltd. GBR. Dist: Hachette Bk. Group.
Moore, Stephanie. Make Something of It. 2014. (Sharp Sisters Ser.: 1). (ENG.). 152p. (YA). (gr. 6-12). pap. 7.95 (978-1-4677-4488-1(3), Darby Creek) Lerner Publishing Group.
Mora, Pat. Doña Flor: A Tall Tale about a Giant Woman with a Great Big Heart. Colón, Raúl, illus. 2005. (ENG & SPA.). 40p. (J). (gr. -1-2). 15.95 (978-0-375-82337-4(9), Knopf Bks. for Young Readers) Random Hse. Children's Bks.
Munro, Alice. Runaway. 2011. 14.75 (978-0-7848-3510-4(1), Everbind) Marco Bk. Co.
Murphy, Claire Rudolf. Marching with Aunt Susan: Susan B. Anthony & the Fight for Women's Suffrage, 1 vol. Schuett, Stacey, illus. 2017. (ENG.). 36p. (J). (gr. 1-5). pap. 7.95 (978-1-56145-979-7(8)) Peachtree Pubs.
Murray, Kirsty. Vulture's Wake. 2010. (ENG.). 256p. (YA). (gr. 7-18). pap. 17.95 (978-0-8234-2282-1(8)) Holiday Hse., Inc.
Murray, Victoria Christopher. Diamond. 2008. (Divas Ser.). (ENG.). 256p. (gr. 8-12). pap. 11.00 (978-1-4165-6216-0(8), Gallery Bks.) Gallery Bks.
O'Brien, Robert C. La Senora Frisby y las Ratas de NIMH. (Barco de Vapor). (SPA., Illus.). 200p. (J). (gr. 4-7). 6.36 (978-84-348-1601-5(6), SM2855) SM Ediciones ESP. Dist: Lectorum Pubns., Inc.
Ostow, Micol. Family. 2011. (ENG.). 384p. (J). (gr. 9). 17.99 (978-1-60684-155-6(6), Carolrhoda Lab™) Lerner Publishing Group.
Page, P. K. The Old Woman & the Hen. Westergard, Jim, illus. 2008. (ENG.). 32p. (J). pap. 10.95 (978-0-88984-309-7(0)) Porcupine's Quill, Inc. CAN. Dist: Univ. of Toronto Pr.
Parker, Jeff. Medieval Women. Santacruz, Juan, illus. 2012. (Avengers Set 3 Ser.). 24p. (J). (gr. 2-6). lib. bdg. 24.21 (978-1-61479-016-7(7)) Spotlight.
Peters, Julie Anne. Rage: A Love Story. 2010. (ENG.). 306p. (YA). (gr. 9). pap. 9.99 (978-0-375-84411-9(2), Knopf Bks. for Young Readers) Random Hse. Children's Bks.
Pinkney, Andrea Davis. Sojourner Truth's Step-Stomp Stride. Pinkney, Brian, illus. 2009. (ENG.). 32p. (J). (gr. k-4). 16.99 (978-0-7868-0767-3(9), Jump at the Sun) Hyperion Bks. for Children.
Rigby Education Staff. Birdwoman Interview. (Sails Literacy Ser.). (Illus.). 16p. (gr. 2-3). 27.00 (978-0-7635-9953-9(0), 699530C99) Rigby Education.
Riley, Lehman & Austin, Megan. The Life of Babe Didrikson: "Greatness Is Never Forgotten" Wallace, Joshua, illus. 2005. 47p. (J). pap. (978-0-9760523-2-6(6)) Matter of Africa America Time.
Rohner, Dorothia, illus. Effie's Image. 2006. 32p. (J). (gr. -1-3). 17.95 (978-0-9759829-5-2(8)) Prairieland Pr.
Rueda, Claudia, illus. I Know an Old Lady Who Swallowed a Fly. 2005. 14p. (J). 12.95 (978-1-58117-267-6(2), Intervisual/Piggy Toes) Bendon, Inc.
San Souci, Robert D. Cut from the Same Cloth: American Women of Myth, Legend, & Tall Tale. Pinkney, Brian, illus. 2005. 140p. 17.00 (978-0-7569-6284-5(6)) Perfection Learning Corp.
Scandora, Julie. Rules Are Rules. 2008. (ENG., Illus.). 32p. (gr. -1). 17.95 (978-1-887542-64-7(7)) Scandora.
Siegel, R. V. The Son of Olympia. 2005. 20p. 7.43 (978-1-4116-2888-5(8)) Lulu Pr., Inc.
Silverberg, Selma Kritzer. Naomi's Song. 2009. (ENG.). 142p. (gr. 7-18). pap. 14.00 (978-0-8276-0886-3(1)) Jewish Pubn. Society.
Smith, Sherri L. Flygirl. 2010. (ENG.). 304p. (YA). (gr. 7-18). 9.99 (978-0-14-241725-6(4), Speak) Penguin Young Readers Group.
—Flygirl. 2010. lib. bdg. 19.65 (978-0-606-14999-0(6), Turtleback) Turtleback Bks.
Souhami, Jessica, illus. No Dinner! The Story of the Old Woman & the Pumpkin. 2012. (ENG.). 32p. (J). (gr. -1-2). pap. 8.99 (978-1-84507-818-8(7), Frances Lincoln) Quarto Publishing Group UK GBR. Dist: Hachette Bk. Group.
Stockton, Frank Richard. Kate Bonnet: The Romance of a Pirate's Daughter. reprint ed. pap. 28.00 (978-1-4047-8937-1(5)) Classic Textbooks.
—Kate Bonnet: The Romance of a Pirate's Daughter. 2007. 364p. (J). (gr. -1-7). 46.95 (978-0-548-02295-5(X)) Kessinger Publishing, LLC.
—Kate Bonnet: The Romance of a Pirate's Daughter. 2005. 29.95 (978-1-59818-254-5(4)) Wildside Pr., LLC.
Sutton, Margaret. The Yellow Phantom: A Judy Bolton Mystery. Doane, Pelagie, illus. 2011. 222p. 44.95 (978-1-258-10044-5(4)) Literary Licensing, LLC.
Thomas, Jacquelin. Divine Match-Up. 2008. (ENG., Illus.). 304p. (gr. 8-12). pap. 19.99 (978-1-4165-5145-4(X), Gallery Bks.) Gallery Bks.
Turner, Morrie. Super Sistahs: Featuring the Accomplishments of African-American Women. 2005. (Illus.). 112p. pap. 14.95 (978-0-9656739-5-2(2)) BYE Publishing Services.
Vanasse, Deb. Cold Spell. 2014. (Alaska Literary Ser.). 224p. pap. 15.95 (978-1-60223-242-6(3)) Univ. of Alaska Pr.
Vanderhoop, Jannette, illus. The Legend of Katama: The Creation Story of Dolphins, A Wampanoag Legend of Martha's Vineyard. 2004. 80p. (J). lib. bdg. 18.95 (978-0-9755605-0-1(6)) Island Moon Pr.
Veronique, Catel. Bluesy Lucy - the Existential Chronicles of a Thirtysomething. 2013. (Bluesy Lucy - the Existential Chronicles of a Thirtysomething Ser.). (ENG., Illus.). 120p. 24.95 (978-1-59465-048-2(9), 9781594650482) Humanoids, Inc.
Whitney, A. D. T. The Other Girls. l.t. ed. 2007. (ENG.). 398p. pap. 26.99 (978-1-4346-0103-2(X)) Creative Media Partners, LLC.

WOMEN—HISTORY

Adiletta, Dawn. Elizabeth Cady Stanton: Women's Suffrage & the First Vote. 2005. (Library of American Lives & Times). (Illus.). 112p. (J). (gr. -1-3). lib. bdg. 34.60 (978-1-4042-2647-0(8)) Rosen Publishing Group, Inc., The.
Baum, Margaux & Hopkins, Andrea. The Lives of Women in the Middle Ages. 2016. (J). (978-1-4994-6467-2(3)) Rosen Publishing Group, Inc., The.
Eastwood, Kay. Women & Girls in the Middle Ages. 2003. (Medieval World Ser.). (ENG., Illus.). 32p. (J). (gr. 5). pap. (978-0-7787-1378-4(4)) Crabtree Publishing Co.
Fun Fact File: Women in History. 2015. (Fun Fact File: Women in History Ser.). (ENG.). 32p. (J). (gr. 2-3). 151.50 (978-1-4824-2548-2(3)); pap., pap., pap. 63.00 (978-1-4824-3474-3(1)) Stevens, Gareth Publishing LLLP.
Furbee, Mary Rodd. Outrageous Women of Civil War Times. 2003. (Outrageous Women Ser.: 7). (ENG., Illus.). 132p. (J). (gr. 5-9). pap. 14.95 (978-0-471-22926-1(1), Jossey-Bass) Wiley, John & Sons, Inc.
Hopkins, Andrea. Damsels Not in Distress: The Lives of Medieval Women. 2004. (Library of the Middle Ages Ser.). (Illus.). 64p. (YA). (gr. 5-9). lib. bdg. 31.95 (978-0-8239-3992-3(8)) Rosen Publishing Group, Inc., The.
—Damsels Not in Distress: The True Story of Women in Medieval Times. 2009. (Library of the Middle Ages Ser.). 64p. (gr. 5-8). 58.50 (978-1-60853-898-0(2), Rosen Reference) Rosen Publishing Group, Inc., The.
Hubbard, Ben, et al. Women's Stories from History. 2015. (Women's Stories from History Ser.). (ENG.). 112p. lib. bdg. 127.96 (978-1-4846-0867-8(4)) Heinemann-Raintree.
Huntley, Theresa. Women in the Renaissance. 2009. (ENG., Illus.). 32p. (J). (gr. 5-7). (978-0-7787-4598-3(8)); (gr. 6-9). pap. (978-0-7787-4618-8(6)) Crabtree Publishing Co.
Kramer, Ann. Women & War. 2009. (J). 24.25 (978-1-59771-142-5(X)) Sea-To-Sea Pubns.
Langley, Andrew. Stories of Women in World War II: We Can Do It! 2015. (Women's Stories from History Ser.). (ENG., Illus.). 112p. (gr. 6-11). 31.99 (978-1-4846-0865-4(8)) Heinemann-Raintree.
Levy, Janey. 20 Fun Facts about Women of the Middle Ages. 2015. (Fun Fact File: Women in History Ser.). (ENG., Illus.). 32p. (J). (gr. 2-3). pap. 10.50 (978-1-4824-2824-7(5)) Stevens, Gareth Publishing LLLP.
Libal, Autumn. Women in the World of Russia. 2006. (Women's Issues, Global Trends Ser.). (Illus.). 112p. (YA). lib. bdg. 22.95 (978-1-59084-866-1(7)) Mason Crest.
Micklos, John. The Brave Women & Children of the American Revolution. 2008. (Revolutionary War Library). (Illus.). 48p. (J). (gr. 3-4). lib. bdg. 25.27 (978-0-7660-3019-0(9), Enslow Elementary) Enslow Pubs., Inc.
Morrison, Jessica. Women's Issues. 2010. (Illus.). 48p. (978-1-55388-689-1(5)); pap. (978-1-55388-694-5(1)) Weigl Educational Pubs. Ltd.
Perry, Phyllis Jean. Bold Women in Colorado History. 2012. (J). pap. (978-0-87842-584-6(5)) Mountain Pr. Publishing Co., Inc.
Rajczak, Kristen. 20 Fun Facts about Women in Ancient Greece & Rome. 2015. (Fun Fact File: Women in History Ser.). (ENG., Illus.). 32p. (J). (gr. 2-3). 25.25 (978-1-4824-2818-6(0)) Stevens, Gareth Publishing LLLP.
Schatz, Kate & Stahl, Miriam Klein. Rad Women Worldwide: Artists & Athletes, Pirates & Punks, & Other Revolutionaries Who Shaped History. 2016. (ENG., Illus.). 112p. (gr. 5-12). 15.99 (978-0-399-57886-1(2), Ten Speed Pr.) Potter/TenSpeed/Harmony.
Sharp, Anne Wallace. Women of Ancient Egypt. 2005. (Women in History Ser.). (ENG., Illus.). 112p. (YA). (gr. 7-10). lib. bdg. 33.45 (978-1-59018-361-8(4), Lucent Bks.) Cengage Gale.
Simpson, Kathleen. Women in the Renaissance: Set Of 6. 2011. (Navigators Ser.). (J). pap. 50.00 net. (978-1-4108-6266-2(6)) Benchmark Education Co.
—Women in the Renaissance: Text Pairs. 2008. (Bridges/Navigators Ser.). (J). (gr. 6). 89.00 (978-1-4108-8449-7(X)) Benchmark Education Co.
Swisher, Clarice. Women of Victorian England. 2004. (Women in History Ser.). (ENG., Illus.). 112p. (YA). (gr. 7-12). lib. bdg. 33.45 (978-1-59018-571-1(4), Lucent Bks.) Cengage Gale.
Thomson, Melissa & Dean, Ruth. Women of the Renaissance. 2004. (Women in History Ser.). (ENG., Illus.). 128p. (YA). (gr. 7-10). lib. bdg. 33.45 (978-1-59018-473-8(4), Lucent Bks.) Cengage Gale.
The Trail West. 2004. (Illus.). lib. bdg. 7.95 (978-0-8225-4283-4(8)) Lerner Publishing Group.
Women Groundbreakers. 2015. (Women Groundbreakers Ser.). (ENG.). 32p. (J). (gr. 4-5). pap., pap., pap. 360.00 (978-1-4994-1331-1(9), PowerKids Pr.) Rosen Publishing Group, Inc., The.

WOMEN—OCCUPATIONS

see Women—Employment

WOMEN—POLITICAL ACTIVITY

Aung San Suu Kyi. 2014. (Making a Difference: Leaders Who Are Changing the World Ser.). 48p. (J). (gr. 5-8). 25.85 (978-1-62275-430-4(1)) Rosen Publishing Group, Inc., The.
Benoit, Peter. Women's Right to Vote. 2014. (Cornerstones of Freedom Ser.: 3). (ENG.). 64p. (J). lib. bdg. 30.00 (978-0-531-21333-9(1)) Scholastic Library Publishing.
Bjorklund, Ruth. Aung San Suu Kyi. 2013. 112p. (gr. 7-12). (J). 39.93 (978-0-7614-4957-7(4)); (YA). pap. 19.99 (978-1-62712-115-6(3)) Cavendish Square Publishing.
Clapper, Kathryn N. Irma Rangel, 1 vol. 2014. (Great Women in History Ser.). (ENG., Illus.). 24p. (gr. k-1). lib. bdg. 21.99 (978-1-4914-0538-3(4), Pebble Bks.) Capstone Press of Coughlan Cos.
Coleman, Miriam. Mujeres en la Politica (Women in Politics) 2015. (Ellas Abrieron Camino (Women Groundbreakers) Ser.). (ENG & SPA.). 32p. (J). (gr. 4-5). 26.25 (978-1-4994-0547-7(2), PowerKids Pr.) Rosen Publishing Group, Inc., The.
—Women in Politics. 2015. (Women Groundbreakers Ser.). (ENG., Illus.). 32p. (J). (gr. 4-5). 26.25 (978-1-4994-1084-6(0), PowerKids Pr.) Rosen Publishing Group, Inc., The.
Cooper, Ilene. A Woman in the House (and Senate) How Women Came to the United States Congress, Broke down Barriers, & Changed the Country. Baddeley, Elizabeth, illus. 2014. (ENG.). 144p. (J). (gr. 3-7). 24.95 (978-1-4197-1036-0(2), Abrams Bks. for Young Readers) Abrams, Inc.
Cooper, Meghan. The Women's Suffrage Movement. 2017. (J). **(978-1-5026-2711-7(6))** Cavendish Square Publishing.
Crysdale, Joy. Courageous Women Rebels, 1 vol. 2013. (Women's Hall of Fame Ser.). (ENG.). 128p. (J). (gr. 6-8). pap. 10.95 (978-1-926920-99-3(6)) Second Story Pr. CAN. Dist: Orca Bk. Pubs. USA.
Cunningham, Anne C. Women Political Leaders. 2016. (Defying Convention: Women Who Changed the Rules Ser.). 128p. (J). 37.27 (978-0-7660-8141-3(9)) Enslow Pubs., Inc.
Doak, Robin S. Hillary Clinton. 2013. (True Book™—Biographies Ser.). (ENG., Illus.). 48p. (J). pap. 6.95 (978-0-531-23877-6(6)); lib. bdg. 29.00 (978-0-531-21906-5(2)) Scholastic Library Publishing.
Friedman, Lita. Mary Robinson: Fighter for Human Rights. 2004. (Avisson Young Adult Ser.). (Illus.). 142p. (YA). pap. 19.95 (978-1-888105-65-0(8)) Avisson Pr., Inc.
Furstinger, Nancy. Women & Leadership. 2012. (Young Woman's Guide to Contemporary Issues Ser.). (ENG., Illus.). 112p. (YA). (gr. 9-12). lib. bdg. 34.60 (978-1-4488-8402-5(0)) Rosen Publishing Group, Inc., The.
Guernsey, Joann Bren. Hillary Rodham Clinton: Secretary of State. 2009. (USA TODAY Lifeline Biographies Ser.). (ENG.). 112p. (gr. 6-12). lib. bdg. 34.60 (978-0-7613-5122-1(1)) Lerner Publishing Group.
Hanson-Harding, Alexandra. Activism: Taking on Women's Issues. 2012. (Young Woman's Guide to Contemporary Issues Ser.). (ENG., Illus.). 112p. (YA). (gr. 9-12). lib. bdg. 34.60 (978-1-4488-8401-8(2)) Rosen Publishing Group, Inc., The.
Henneberg, Susan, ed. Gender Politics. 2017. (At Issue Ser.). 128p. (YA). (gr. 10-12). pap. 27.80 **(978-1-5345-0041-9(3))**; lib. bdg. 39.40 **(978-1-5345-0014-3(6))** Greenhaven Publishing LLC. (Greenhaven Publishing).
Hurt, Avery Elizabeth. Women in Politics. 2017. (Women in the World Ser.). 112p. (gr. 12-11). 37.10 **(978-1-5081-7449-3(0)**, Rosen Young Adult) Rosen Publishing Group, Inc., The.
Kaiser, Lisbeth. Emmeline Pankhurst. Sanfelippo, Ana, illus. 2017. (Little People, Big Dreams Ser.). (ENG.). 32p. (J). (gr. k-3). 14.99 **(978-1-78603-020-7(9)**, Frances Lincoln Children's Bks.) Quarto Publishing Group UK GBR. Dist: Hachette Bk. Group.
Koya, Lena & Hanson-Harding, Alexandra. Female Activists. 2017. (J). **(978-1-5081-7720-3(1))** Rosen Publishing Group, Inc., The.
Krull, Kathleen. A Woman for President: The Story of Victoria Woodhull. Dyer, Jane, illus. 2006. (J). (gr. 2-7). 14.60 (978-0-7569-8179-2(4)) Perfection Learning Corp.
Manion, Jennifer. Safia AMA Jan. 2011. (J). lib. bdg. (978-0-8225-9038-5(7)) Twenty First Century Bks.
Marsh, Carole. The First Woman President of the U. S. 2007. 48p. pap. 7.95 (978-0-635-06404-2(9)) Gallopade International.
McElroy, Lisa Tucker. Nancy Pelosi. 2008. pap. 52.95 (978-0-8225-9477-2(3)) Lerner Publishing Group.
Miller, Debra A. Women in Politics. 2012. (Current Controversies Ser.). (ENG.). 224p. (gr. 10-12). pap. 32.00 (978-0-7377-6250-1(0)); lib. bdg. 46.40 (978-0-7377-6249-5(7)) Cengage Gale. (Greenhaven Pr., Inc.).
Naden, Corinne J. Benazir Bhutto. 2010. (Leading Women Ser.). 96p. (YA). (gr. 7-12). 39.93 (978-0-7614-4952-2(3)) Marshall Cavendish Corp.
Nivola, Claire A. Planting the Trees of Kenya: The Story of Wangari Maathai. Nivola, Claire A., illus. 2008. (ENG., Illus.). 32p. (J). (gr. k-3). 18.99 (978-0-374-39918-4(2), 9780374399184, Farrar, Straus & Giroux (BYR)) Farrar, Straus & Giroux.
Raatma, Lucia. Barbara Jordan. 2013. 96p. (YA). (gr. 7-12). 39.93 (978-0-7614-4956-0(6)) Cavendish Square Publishing.
Ross, Michael Elsohn. She Takes a Stand: 16 Fearless Activists Who Have Changed the World. 2015. (Women of Action Ser.). (ENG., Illus.). 208p. (YA). (gr. 7). 19.95 (978-1-61373-026-3(8)) Chicago Review Pr., Inc.
Shepherd, Jodie. Hillary Clinton. 2015. (Rookie Biographies(r) Ser.). (ENG., Illus.). 32p. (J). lib. bdg. 23.00 (978-0-531-20592-1(4)) Scholastic Library Publishing.
Sherman, Jill. Donald Trump: Outspoken Personality & President. 2017. (Gateway Biographies Ser.). (ENG., Illus.). 48p. (J). (gr. 4-8). lib. bdg. 26.65 (978-1-5124-2596-3(6)) Lerner Publishing Group.
Somervill, Barbara A. Votes for Women! The Story of Carrie Chapman Catt. 2004. (Feminist Voices Ser.). (Illus.). 128p.

(YA). (gr. 6-12). 23.95 *(978-1-883846-96-1(X),* First Biographies) Reynolds, Morgan Inc.

Thimmesh, Catherine. Madam President: The Extraordinary, True (and Evolving) Story of Women in Politics. Jones, Douglas B., illus. 2008. (ENG.). 80p. (J). (gr. 1-4). pap. 8.95 *(978-0-618-97143-5(2))* Houghton Mifflin Harcourt Publishing Co.

Tracy, Kathleen. The Historic Fight for the 2008 Democratic Presidential Nomination: The Clinton View. 2009. (Monumental Milestones Ser.). (Illus.). 48p. (YA). (gr. 4-7). lib. bdg. 29.95 *(978-1-58415-731-1(3))* Mitchell Lane Pubs., Inc.

Winter, Jeanette. Wangari's Trees of Peace: A True Story from Africa. Winter, Jeanette, illus. 2008. (ENG., Illus.). 32p. (J). (gr. -1-3). 17.99 *(978-0-15-206545-4(8))* Houghton Mifflin Harcourt Publishing Co.

Women in Politics. 2005. (Women in Politics Ser.). 112p. (gr. 6-12). 120.00 *(978-0-7910-7730-6(6),* Chelsea Hse.) Facts On File, Inc.

WOMEN—SUFFRAGE

see also Suffragists

Adiletta, Dawn. Elizabeth Cady Stanton: Women's Suffrage & the First Vote. (Library of American Lives & Times Ser.). 112p. 2009. (gr. 5-5). 69.20 *(978-1-60853-479-1(0))* 2005. (Illus.). (J). (gr. -1-3). lib. bdg. 34.60 *(978-1-4042-2647-0(8))* Rosen Publishing Group, Inc., The.

Bailey Association Staff & Senker, Cath. Women Claim the Vote. 2011. (Cultural History of Women in America Ser.). (Illus.). 64p. (gr. 6-12). 35.00 *(978-1-60413-930-3(7),* Chelsea Hse.) Facts On File, Inc.

Barber, Lynnae. Champions for Women's Rights: Matilda Joslyn Gage, Julia Ward Howe, Lucretia Mott, & Lucy Stone. 2016. (Heroes of the Women's Suffrage Movement Ser.). (Illus.). 128p. (J). (gr. 6-6). 37.27 *(978-0-7660-7891-8(4))* Enslow Pubs., Inc.

Bardhan-Quallen, Sudipta. Ballots for Belva: The True Story of a Woman's Race for the Presidency. Martin, Courtney A., illus. 2015. (ENG.). 32p. (J). (gr. k-2). 9.95 *(978-1-4197-1627-0(1),* Abrams Bks. for Young Readers) Abrams, Inc.

Bausum, Ann. With Courage & Cloth: Winning the Fight for a Woman's Right to Vote. 2004. (ENG., Illus.). 112p. (J). (gr. 5). 21.95 *(978-0-7922-7647-0(7),* National Geographic Children's Bks.) National Geographic Society.

Benoit, Peter. Women's Right to Vote. 2014. (Cornerstones of Freedom Ser.: 3). (ENG.). 64p. (J). lib. bdg. 30.00 *(978-0-531-21333-9(1))* Scholastic Library Publishing.

Bjornlund, Lydia D. Women of the Suffrage Movement. 2003. (Women in History Ser.). (ENG., Illus.). 112p. (J). 33.45 *(978-1-59018-173-7(5),* Lucent Bks.) Cengage Gale.

Bozonelis, Helen Koutras. A Look at the Nineteenth Amendment: Women Win the Right to Vote. 2008. (Constitution of the United States Ser.). (Illus.). 128p. (J). (gr. 5-9). lib. bdg. 34.60 *(978-1-59845-067-5(0))* Enslow Pubs., Inc.

Carson, Mary Kay. Who Was Susan B. Anthony Vote? And Other Questions about Women's Suffrage. 2015. (Good Question! Ser.). (ENG., Illus.). 32p. (J). (gr. 2). pap. 5.95 *(978-1-4549-1242-2(1))* Sterling Publishing Co., Inc.

—Why Couldn't Susan B. Anthony Vote? And Other Questions about Women's Suffrage. 2015. (Good Question! Ser.). (ENG., Illus.). 40p. (J). (gr. 2). 12.95 *(978-1-4549-1241-5(3))* Sterling Publishing Co., Inc.

Ching, Jacqueline. Abigail Adams: A Revolutionary Woman. 2009. (Library of American Lives & Times Ser.). 112p. (gr. 5-5). 69.20 *(978-1-60853-469-2(3))* Rosen Publishing Group, Inc., The.

Collins, Terry. Women's Right to Vote, 1 vol. Bascle, Brian, illus. 2009. (Cartoon Nation Ser.). (ENG.). 32p. (gr. 3-4). lib. bdg. 30.65 *(978-1-4296-2341-4(1),* Graphic Library) Capstone Press of Coughlan Cos.

Cooper, Meghan. The Women's Suffrage Movement. 2017. (J). ***(978-1-5026-2711-7(6))*** Cavendish Square Publishing.

Day, Meredith & Adams, Colleen. A Primary Source Investigation of Women's Suffrage. 2015. (Uncovering American History Ser.). (ENG., Illus.). 64p. (J). (gr. 5-6). 32.95 *(978-1-4994-3519-1(3),* Rosen Central) Rosen Publishing Group, Inc., The.

DeAngelis, Therese. Women's Rights on the Frontier. 2012. (J). pap. *(978-1-4222-2369-7(8))* Mason Crest.

—Women's Rights on the Frontier. Harrington, A. Page, ed. 2012. (Finding a Voice: Women's Fight for Equality in U. S. Society Ser.). 64p. (J). (gr. 5). 22.95 *(978-1-4222-2359-8(0))* Mason Crest.

Fredericks, Carrie. Amendment XIX: Grating Women the Right to Vote. 2009. (Constitutional Amendments Ser.). (ENG., Illus.). 160p. (gr. 10-12). lib. bdg. 43.20 *(978-0-7377-4127-8(9),* LML02109-243016) Cengage Gale.

Gelletly, LeeAnne. Seeking Th Right to Vote. 2012. (J). pap. *(978-1-4222-2364-2(7))* Mason Crest.

—Seeking Th Right to Vote. Harrington, A. Page, ed. 2012. (Finding a Voice: Women's Fight for Equality in U. S. Society Ser.). 64p. (J). (gr. 5). 22.95 *(978-1-4222-2354-3(X))* Mason Crest.

Goddu, Krystyna Poray. What's Your Story, Susan B. Anthony? 2016. (Cub Reporter Meets Famous Americans Ser.). (ENG.). 32p. (J). (gr. k-3). 26.65 *(978-1-4677-8785-7(X),* Lerner Pubns.) Lerner Publishing Group.

Goodman, Susan E. & Smith, Michael W., Jr. Women Work for Change. 2006. (Hampton-Brown Edge: Reading, Writing, & Language (c)2009 Ser.). (ENG., Illus.). 36p. (J). pap. 18.95 *(978-0-7922-5456-0(2))* CENGAGE Learning.

Guillain, Charlotte. Stories of Women's Suffrage: Votes for Women! 2015. (Women's Stories from History Ser.). (ENG.). 112p. (gr. 6-11). 31.99 *(978-1-4846-0864-7(X))* Heinemann-Raintree.

Hicks, Peter. Documenting Women's Suffrage. 2010. (Documenting History Ser.). (Illus.). 48p. (J). pap. 11.75 *(978-1-4358-9675-8(0),* Rosen Reference); (YA). (gr. 5-9). lib. bdg. 29.25 *(978-1-4358-9672-7(6))* Rosen Publishing Group, Inc., The.

Hollihan, Kerrie Logan. Rightfully Ours: How Women Won the Vote, 21 Activities. 2012. (For Kids Ser.). (ENG., Illus.). 144p. (J). (gr. 4). pap. 16.95 *(978-1-883052-89-8(0))* Chicago Review Pr., Inc.

Isecke, Harriet. Women's Suffrage: Fighting for Women's Rights, 1 vol. 2011. (Primary Source Readers Ser.). (ENG.). 32p. (J). (gr. 5-5). pap. 8.99 *(978-1-4333-1507-7(6))* Teacher Created Materials, Inc.

Kent, Deborah. Elizabeth Cady Stanton: Founder of the Women's Suffrage Movement. 2016. (Heroes of the Women's Suffrage Movement Ser.). 128p. (J). (gr. 6-6). 37.27 *(978-0-7660-7889-5(2))* Enslow Pubs., Inc.

Keppeler, Jill. Women's Suffrage Movement. 2016. (Civic Participation: Working for Civil Rights Ser.). 00032p. (J). (gr. 5-5). pap. 10.00 *(978-1-4994-2685-4(2),* PowerKids Pr.) Rosen Publishing Group, Inc., The.

Kops, Deborah. Alice Paul & the Fight for Women's Rights: From the Vote to the Equal Rights Amendment. 2017. (ENG.). 216p. (J). (gr. 5). 17.95 *(978-1-62979-323-8(X),* Calkins Creek) Boyds Mills Pr.

Lusted, Marcia Amidon. The Fight for Women's Suffrage, 1 vol. 2011. (Essential Events Set 7 Ser.). (ENG., Illus.). 112p. (J). (gr. 6-12). lib. bdg. 35.64 *(978-1-61783-099-0(2))* ABDO Publishing Co.

Macbain-Stephens, Jennifer. Women's Suffrage: Giving the Right to Vote to All Americans. 2004. (Progressive Movement, 1900-1920 Ser.). (Illus.). 32p. (YA). (gr. 5-9). lib. bdg. 22.50 *(978-1-4042-0199-6(8))* Rosen Publishing Group, Inc., The.

MacBain-Stephens, Jennifer. Women's Suffrage: Giving the Right to Vote to All Americans. 2009. (Progressive Movement 1900-1920: Efforts to Reform America's New Industrial Society Ser.). (gr. 3-4). 47.90 *(978-1-60854-175-1(4))* Rosen Publishing Group, Inc., The.

MacDonald, Fiona. Be a Suffragist! A Protest Movement That's Rougher Than You Expected. Antram, David, illus. 2008. (You Wouldn't Want to...: History of the World Ser.). (ENG.). 32p. (J). (gr. 3-12). 29.00 *(978-0-531-20701-7(3),* Watts, Franklin) Scholastic Library Publishing.

—You Wouldn't Want to Be a Suffragist! A Protest Movement That's Rougher Than You Expected. Antram, David, illus. 2008. (You Wouldn't Want to...: History of the World Ser.). (ENG.). 32p. (J). (gr. 3-18). pap. 9.95 *(978-0-531-21911-9(9),* Watts, Franklin) Scholastic Library Publishing.

Malaspina, Ann. Heart on Fire: Susan B. Anthony Votes for President. James, Steven, illus. 2012. (ENG.). 32p. (J). (gr. 1-3). 16.99 *(978-0-8075-3188-4(X))* Whitman, Albert & Co.

McConnell, Robert L., contrib. by. The Split History of the Women's Suffrage Movement: A Perspectives Flip Book, 1 vol. 2014. (Perspectives Flip Bks.). (ENG.). 64p. (gr. 5-6). pap. 8.95 *(978-0-7565-4791-2(1),* CPB Grades 4-8) Compass Point Bks.

McConnell, Robert L. & Baxter, Kathleen, contrib. by. The Split History of the Women's Suffrage Movement: A Perspectives Flip Book, 1 vol. 2014. (Perspectives Flip Bks.). (ENG.). 64p. (gr. 5-6). lib. bdg. 33.99 *(978-0-7565-4735-6(0),* CPB Grades 4-8) Compass Point Bks.

Metz, Lorijo. El Movimiento Por el Sufragio Femenino / the Women's Suffrage Movement, 1 vol., 1. Beullens-Maoui, Nathalie, ed. 2014. (¡Celebremos la Libertad! / Let's Celebrate Freedom! Ser.). (SPA & BYN.). 24p. (J). (gr. 3-6). 23.60 *(978-1-4777-3250-2(0),* PowerKids Pr.) Rosen Publishing Group, Inc., The.

—The Women's Suffrage Movement, 1 vol., 1. 2014. (Let's Celebrate Freedom! Ser.). (ENG., Illus.). 24p. (J). (gr. 3-6). 23.60 *(978-1-4777-2898-7(8),* PowerKids Pr.) Rosen Publishing Group, Inc., The.

Mosley, Shelley & Charles, John. The Suffragists in Literature for Youth: The Fight for the Vote, Vol. annot. ed. 2006. (Literature for Youth Ser.: 10). (ENG.). 342p. (gr. 3-7). per. 70.00 *(978-0-8108-5372-0(8))* Scarecrow Pr., Inc.

Nadin, Joanna. The Story of the Suffragettes: Band 17/Diamond. 2017. (ENG., Illus.). 56p. (J). pap. 8.99 ***(978-0-00-820894-3(8))*** HarperCollins Pubs. Ltd. GBR. Dist: Independent Pubs. Group.

Nash, Carol Rust. Women Winning the Right to Vote in United States History. 2014. (In United States History Ser.). (Illus.). 96p. (J). (gr. 5-12). pap. 10.95 *(978-0-7660-6074-6(8))* Enslow Pubs., Inc.

Peppas, Lynn. Women's Suffrage. 2015. (Uncovering the Past: Analyzing Primary Sources Ser.). (ENG.). 48p. (J). (gr. 5-8). *(978-0-7787-1720-1(8))* Crabtree Publishing Co.

Rice, Dona Herwick & Sugarman, Dorothy. Women's Suffrage, 1 vol. 2009. (Building Fluency Through Reader's Theater Ser.). (ENG., Illus.). 32p. (J). (gr. 3-5). pap. 7.99 *(978-1-4333-0550-4(X))* Teacher Created Materials, Inc.

Robbins, Dean. Miss Paul & the President: The Creative Campaign for Women's Right to Vote. Zhang, Nancy, illus. 2016. (ENG.). 40p. (J). (gr. -1-3). 17.99 *(978-1-101-93720-4(3),* Knopf Bks. for Young Readers) Random Hse. Children's Bks.

Todd, Anne M. Susan B. Anthony: Activist. 2009. (Women of Achievement Ser.). (Illus.). 128p. (gr. 6-12). 35.00 *(978-1-60413-087-4(3),* Chelsea Hse.) Facts On File, Inc.

Van Meter, Larry A. Women Win the Vote: The Hard-Fought Battle for Women's Suffrage. 2009. (America's Living History Ser.). (Illus.). 128p. (J). (gr. 5-9). lib. bdg. 33.27 *(978-0-7660-2940-8(9))* Enslow Pubs., Inc.

Weidt, Maryann N. Fighting for Equal Rights: A Story about Susan B. Anthony. Sartor, Amanda, tr. Sartor, Amanda, illus. (Creative Minds Biography Ser.). 64p. 2004. (J). 22.60 *(978-1-57505-181-9(8),* Carolrhoda Bks.) 2003. (ENG.). (gr. 4-8). pap. 8.95 *(978-1-57505-609-8(7))* Lerner Publishing Group.

White, Linda Arms. I Could Do That! Esther Morris Gets Women the Vote. Carpenter, Nancy, illus. 2005. (ENG.). 40p. (J). (gr. 2-4). 18.99 *(978-0-374-33527-4(3),* 9780374335274, Farrar, Straus & Giroux (BYR)) Farrar, Straus & Giroux.

—I Could Do That! Esther Morris Gets Women the Vote. unabr. ed. 2006. (J). (gr. 2-4). 29.95 *(978-0-439-90582-4(6),* WHCD692) Weston Woods Studios, Inc.

Winter, Barbara. Fight for Rights. Kostic, Dimitri, illus. 2007. 48p. (J). lib. bdg. 23.08 *(978-1-4242-1636-9(2))* Fitzgerald Bks.

Women Winning the Right to Vote in United States History. 2014. (In United States History Ser.). 96p. (J). (gr. 5-12). 27.94 *(978-0-7660-6073-9(X))* Enslow Pubs., Inc.

Women's Right to Vote. 2010. (J). *(978-0-7166-1508-8(8))* World Bk., Inc.

WOMEN—UNITED STATES

see also Presidents' Spouses

Bailey Association Staff & Gorman, Jacqueline Laks. The Modern Feminist Movement. 2011. (Cultural History of Women in America Ser.). (Illus.). 64p. (gr. 6-12). 35.00 *(978-1-60413-935-8(8),* Chelsea Hse.) Facts On File, Inc.

Bailey Association Staff & Senker, Cath. Strength in Numbers. 2011. (Cultural History of Women in America Ser.). (Illus.). 64p. (gr. 6-12). 35.00 *(978-1-60413-931-0(5),* Chelsea Hse.) Facts On File, Inc.

—Women Claim the Vote. 2011. (Cultural History of Women in America Ser.). (Illus.). 64p. (gr. 6-12). 35.00 *(978-1-60413-930-3(7),* Chelsea Hse.) Facts On File, Inc.

Bailey Association Staff, et al. Women of Today. 2011. (Cultural History of Women in America Ser.). (Illus.). 64p. (gr. 6-12). 35.00 *(978-1-60413-936-5(6),* Chelsea Hse.) Facts On File, Inc.

Bausum, Ann. With Courage & Cloth: Winning the Fight for a Woman's Right to Vote. 2004. (ENG., Illus.). 112p. (J). (gr. 5). 21.95 *(978-0-7922-7647-0(7),* National Geographic Children's Bks.) National Geographic Society.

Benoit, Peter. Women's Right to Vote. 2014. (Cornerstones of Freedom Ser.: 3). (ENG.). 64p. (J). lib. bdg. 30.00 *(978-0-531-21333-9(1))* Scholastic Library Publishing.

Bjornlund, Lydia D. Women in Colonial America. 2003. (Women in History Ser.). (ENG., Illus.). 112p. (J). 33.45 *(978-1-59018-470-7(X),* Lucent Bks.) Cengage Gale.

Brill, Marlene Targ. Annie Shapiro & the Clothing Workers' Strike. Akib, Jamel, illus. 2010. (History Speaks: Picture Books Plus Reader's Theater Ser.). (ENG.). 48p. (gr. 2-4). pap. 9.95 *(978-0-7613-6132-9(4));* lib. bdg. 27.93 *(978-1-58013-672-3(9),* Millbrook Pr.) Lerner Publishing Group.

Carosella, Melissa. Still Marching Strong: Women in Modern America, 1 vol. 2011. (Primary Source Readers Ser.). (ENG.). 32p. (J). (gr. 5-5). pap. 8.99 *(978-1-4333-1509-1(2))* Teacher Created Materials, Inc.

Casey, Susan. Women Heroes of the American Revolution: 20 Stories of Espionage, Sabotage, Defiance, & Rescue. (Women of Action Ser.). (ENG.). 240p. (YA). (gr. 7). 2017. pap. 12.99 ***(978-1-61373-831-3(5))*** 2015. (Illus.). 19.95 *(978-1-61374-583-0(4))* Chicago Review Pr., Inc.

Clifford, Mary Louise & Clifford, J. Candace. Mind the Light, Katie: The History of Thirty-Three Female Lighthouse Keepers. 2006. (YA). per. 12.95 *(978-0-9636412-7-4(1))* Cypress Communications.

Cole, Peter. Ben Fletcher: The Life & Times of a Black Wobbly: Including Fellow Worker Fletcher's Writings & Speeches. 10th annot. ed. 2006. (Labor Classics Ser.). (Illus.). 149p. per. 15.00 *(978-0-88286-311-5(8))* Kerr, Charles H. Publishing Co.

Coster, Patience & Walker, Pamela. A New Deal for Women. 2011. (Cultural History of Women in America Ser.). (Illus.). 64p. (gr. 6-12). 35.00 *(978-1-60413-934-1(X),* Chelsea Hse.) Facts On File, Inc.

Daily Life in America in the 1800s, 15 vols., Set. Incl. America at War: Military Conflicts, Home & Abroad in the 1800s. Strange, Matthew. pap. 9.95 *(978-1-4222-1851-8(1));* Bleeding, Blistering, & Purging: Health & Medicine in The 1800s. Strange, Matthew. pap. 9.95 *(978-1-4222-1848-8(1));* Buggies, Bicycles & Iron Horses: Transportation in the 1800s. McIntosh, Kenneth. pap. 9.95 *(978-1-4222-1849-5(X));* Cornmeal & Cider: Food & Drink in the 1800s. Chastain, Zachary. pap. 9.95 *(978-1-4222-1850-1(3));* From the Parlor to the Altar: Romance & Marriage in The 1800s. Chastain, Zachary. pap. 9.95 *(978-1-4222-1852-5(X));* Guardians of the Home: Women's Lives in The 1800s. Strange, Matthew. pap. 9.95 *(978-1-4222-1853-2(8));* Home Sweet Home: Around the House in the 1800s. Chastain, Zachary. pap. 9.95 *(978-1-4222-1854-9(6));* Jump Ropes, Jacks, & Endless Chores: Children's Lives in The 1800s. Strange, Matthew. pap. 9.95 *(978-1-4222-1855-6(4));* Outlaws & Lawmen: Crime & Punishment in the 1800s. McIntosh, Kenneth. pap. 9.95 *(978-1-4222-1857-0(0));* Passing the Time: Entertainment in The 1800s. Chastain, Zachary. pap. 9.95 *(978-1-4222-1858-7(9));* Reviving the Spirit, Reforming Society: Religion in The 1800s. McIntosh, Kenneth. pap. 9.95 *(978-1-4222-1856-3(2));* Rooting for the Home Team: Sports in The 1800s. Chastain, Zachary. pap. 9.95 *(978-1-4222-1859-4(7));* Saloons, Shootouts, & Spurs: The Wild West in The 1800's. McIntosh, Kenneth. pap. 9.95 *(978-1-4222-1862-4(7));* Scandals & Glory: Politics in The 1800s. Chastain, Zachary. pap. 9.95 *(978-1-4222-1860-0(0));* Sweat of Their Brow: Occupations in the 1800s. Chastain, Zachary. pap. 9.95 *(978-1-4222-1861-7(9));* (YA). (gr. 7-18). 2009. (Illus.). 64p. 2011. Set pap. 149.25 *(978-1-4222-1847-1(3),* 1317825); Set lib. bdg. 344.25 *(978-1-4222-1774-0(4),* 1317825) Mason Crest.

DeAngelis, Therese. Women's Rights on the Frontier. 2012. (J). pap. *(978-1-4222-2369-7(8))* Mason Crest.

—Women's Rights on the Frontier. Harrington, A. Page, ed. 2012. (Finding a Voice: Women's Fight for Equality in U. S. Society Ser.). 64p. (J). (gr. 5). 22.95 *(978-1-4222-2359-8(0))* Mason Crest.

Facts on File, Inc. Staff, creator. A to Z of Women Set, 9-Volumes. 2007. (A to Z of Women Ser.). (Illus.). 464p. (C). (gr. 9). 240.00 *(978-0-8160-7433-4(X))* Facts On File, Inc.

Florida's Women's Heritage Trail. (Heritage Trail Ser.). (J). (gr. -1-7). pap. 2.40 *(978-1-889030-19-7(8))* Florida Div. of Historical Resources.

Friedman, Michael & Friedman, Brett. Settlement Houses: Improving the Social Welfare of America's Immigrants. 2006. (Progressive Movement, 1900-1920 — Efforts to Reform America's New Industrial Society Ser.). (ENG., Illus.). 32p. (gr. 4-8). pap. 10.00 *(978-1-4042-0859-9(3))* Rosen Publishing Group, Inc., The.

Gelletly, LeeAnne. Seeking Th Right to Vote. 2012. (J). pap. *(978-1-4222-2364-2(7))* Mason Crest.

—Seeking Th Right to Vote. Harrington, A. Page, ed. 2012. (Finding a Voice: Women's Fight for Equality in U. S. Society Ser.). 64p. (J). (gr. 5). 22.95 *(978-1-4222-2354-3(X))* Mason Crest.

—A Woman's Place in Early America. 2012. (J). pap. *(978-1-4222-2365-9(5))* Mason Crest.

—A Woman's Place in Early America. Harrington, A. Page, ed. 2012. (Finding a Voice: Women's Fight for Equality in U. S. Society Ser.). 64p. (J). (gr. 5). 22.95 *(978-1-4222-2355-0(8))* Mason Crest.

Goldberg, Judy. Samantha's World: A Girl's-Eye View of the Turn of the 20th Century. Andreasen, Dan, illus. 2009. 30p. (YA). (gr. 3-18). 24.95 *(978-1-59369-554-5(3))* American Girl Publishing, Inc.

Hall, Brianna. Great Women of the American Revolution. 2012. (Story of the American Revolution Ser.). (ENG.). 32p. (gr. 3-4). pap. 47.70 *(978-1-4296-9285-4(5),* Fact Finders) Capstone Press of Coughlan Cos.

Hicks, Peter. Documenting Women's Suffrage. 2010. (Documenting History Ser.). (Illus.). 48p. (J). pap. 11.75 *(978-1-4358-9675-8(0),* Rosen Reference); (YA). (gr. 5-9). lib. bdg. 29.25 *(978-1-4358-9672-7(6))* Rosen Publishing Group, Inc., The.

Isecke, Harriet. Women's Suffrage: Fighting for Women's Rights, 1 vol. 2011. (Primary Source Readers Ser.). (ENG.). 32p. (J). (gr. 5-5). pap. 8.99 *(978-1-4333-1507-7(6))* Teacher Created Materials, Inc.

Jerome, Janice. A Dust of Flour. . . Beyond the Family Tree. 2003. spiral bd. 20.00 *(978-0-9729741-0-3(5))* Jerome, Janice.

Kamma, Anne. If You Lived When Women Won Their Rights. Johnson, Pamela, illus. 2008. (If You... Ser.). (ENG.). 64p. (J). (gr. 2-5). pap. 7.99 *(978-0-439-74869-8(0),* Scholastic Reference) Scholastic, Inc.

Kent, Deborah. The Seneca Falls Convention: Working to Expand Women's Rights. 2016. (Heroes of the Women's Suffrage Movement Ser.). (Illus.). 128p. (J). (gr. 6-6). 37.27 *(978-0-7660-7892-5(2))* Enslow Pubs., Inc.

Lusted, Marcia Amidon. The Fight for Women's Suffrage, 1 vol. 2011. (Essential Events Set 7 Ser.). (ENG., Illus.). 112p. (J). (gr. 6-12). lib. bdg. 35.64 *(978-1-61783-099-0(2))* ABDO Publishing Co.

Lyman Schremmer, Patty. Women of the Green Mountain State: 25 Vermont Women You Should Know. Greenleaf, Lisa, illus. 2012. 136p. (J). pap. 16.00 *(978-0-9842549-5-8(1))* Apprentice Shop Bks., LLC.

Malaspina, Ann. Heart on Fire: Susan B. Anthony Votes for President. James, Steven, illus. 2012. (ENG.). 32p. (J). (gr. 1-3). 16.99 *(978-0-8075-3188-4(X))* Whitman, Albert & Co.

Mayr, Diane & Sisters, Write. Women of the Constitution State: 25 Connecticut Women You Should Know. Greenleaf, Lisa, illus. 2012. 136p. (J). pap. 16.00 *(978-0-9842549-1-0(9))* Apprentice Shop Bks., LLC.

McConnell, Robert L., contrib. by. The Split History of the Women's Suffrage Movement: A Perspectives Flip Book, 1 vol. 2014. (Perspectives Flip Bks.). (ENG.). 64p. (gr. 5-6). pap. 8.95 *(978-0-7565-4791-2(1),* CPB Grades 4-8) Compass Point Bks.

McConnell, Robert L. & Baxter, Kathleen, contrib. by. The Split History of the Women's Suffrage Movement: A Perspectives Flip Book, 1 vol. 2014. (Perspectives Flip Bks.). (ENG.). 64p. (gr. 5-6). lib. bdg. 33.99 *(978-0-7565-4735-6(0),* CPB Grades 4-8) Compass Point Bks.

Metz, Lorijo. The Women's Suffrage Movement, 1 vol., 1. 2014. (Let's Celebrate Freedom! Ser.). (ENG., Illus.). 24p. (J). (gr. 3-6). 23.60 *(978-1-4777-2898-7(8),* PowerKids Pr.) Rosen Publishing Group, Inc., The.

Micklos, John. Courageous Children & Women of the American Revolution: Through Primary Sources. 2013. (American Revolution Through Primary Sources Ser.). 48p. (J). (gr. 4-18). 25.27 *(978-0-7660-4131-8(X))* Enslow Pubs., Inc.

Miller, Brandon Marie. Good Women of a Well-Blessed Land: Women's Lives in Colonial America. 2003. (People's History Ser.). (Illus.). 96p. (J). 29.27 *(978-0-8225-0032-2(9))* Lerner Publishing Group.

Miller, Debra A. Women in Politics. 2012. (Current Controversies Ser.). (ENG.). 224p. (gr. 10-12). pap. 32.00 *(978-0-7377-6250-1(0));* lib. bdg. 46.40 *(978-0-7377-6249-5(7))* Cengage Gale. (Greenhaven Pr., Inc.).

Nyman, Debbie & Wortzman, Ricki. The 10 Most Outstanding Women. 2007. 14.99 *(978-1-55448-468-3(5))* Scholastic Library Publishing.

Roppelt, Donna. Women Go to Work, 1941-1945. 2012. (J). pap. *(978-1-4222-2367-3(1))* Mason Crest.

—Women Go to Work, 1941-1945. Harrington, A. Page, ed. 2012. (Finding a Voice: Women's Fight for Equality in U. S. Society Ser.). 64p. (J). (gr. 5). 22.95 *(978-1-4222-2357-4(4))* Mason Crest.

Rossi, Ann & National Geographic Learning Staff. Votes for Women. 2007. (Language, Literacy, & Vocabulary - Reading Expeditions Ser.). (ENG., Illus.). 40p. (J). pap. 19.95 *(978-0-7922-8626-4(X))* CENGAGE Learning.

Sanford, William R. & Green, Carl R. Calamity Jane: Courageous Wild West Woman. 2012. (Courageous Heroes of the American West Ser.). (Illus.). 48p. (J). pap. 8.95 *(978-1-4644-0093-3(8))* Enslow Pubs., Inc.

Savage, Jeff. Pioneering Women: True Tales of the Wild West. 2012. (True Tales of the Wild West Ser.). (Illus.). 48p. (J). (gr. 5-18). lib. bdg. 22.60 *(978-0-7660-4022-9(4))* Enslow Pubs., Inc.

Schwartz, Heather. Zendaya: Capturing the Stage, Screen, & Modeling Scene. 2014. (Pop Culture Bios Ser.). (ENG., Illus.). 32p. (gr. 3-6). pap. 7.95 *(978-1-4677-4548-2(0))* Lerner Publishing Group.

Silvey, Anita. I'll Pass for Your Comrade: Women Soldiers in the Civil War. 2008. (ENG., Illus.). 128p. (J). (gr. 5-7). 19.99 *(978-0-618-57491-9(3))* Houghton Mifflin Harcourt Publishing Co.

Strange, Matthew. Guardians of the Home: Women's Lives in The 1800s. 2009. (Daily Life in America in the 1800s Ser.). 64p. (YA). (gr. 7-18). pap. 9.95 *(978-1-4222-1853-2(8));* lib. bdg. 22.95 *(978-1-4222-1780-1(9))* Mason Crest.

Swisher, Clarice. Women of the Roaring Twenties. 2005. (Women in History Ser.). (ENG., Illus.). 112p. (YA). (gr. 7-10). lib. bdg. 33.45 *(978-1-59018-363-2(0),* Lucent Bks.) Cengage Gale.

Walsh, Francis. Daring Women of the American Revolution. 2009. (American History Flashpoints! Ser.). 32p. (gr. 4-4). 47.90 *(978-1-61511-367-5(3),* PowerKids Pr.) Rosen Publishing Group, Inc., The.

Women Who Shaped History. (Illus.). (J). (gr. 3-6). 103.50 *(978-0-8239-7286-9(0),* Reading Power) Rosen Publishing Group, Inc., The.

W X Y Z

Women Winning the Right to Vote in United States History. 2014. (In United States History Ser.). 96p. (J). (gr. 5-12). 27.94 (978-0-7660-6073-9(X)) Enslow Pubs., Inc.

Zourelias, Diana. First Ladies Fascinating Facts. 2012. (Dover History Coloring Book Ser.). (ENG.). 48p. (J). (gr. 3-5). pap. 4.99 (978-0-486-49832-4(8)) Dover Pubns., Inc.

WOMEN—UNITED STATES—BIOGRAPHY

Abrams, Dennis. Rachael Ray: Food Entrepreneur. 2009. (Women of Achievement Ser.). (Illus.). 136p. (YA). (gr. 7-12). 35.00 (978-1-60413-078-2(4)) Facts On File, Inc.

—Sandra Day O'Connor: U. S. Supreme Court Justice. 2009. (Women of Achievement Ser.). (Illus.). 136p. (gr. 6-12). 35.00 (978-1-60413-337-0(6), Chelsea Hse.) Facts On File, Inc.

Acker, Kerry. Dorothea Lange. 2003. (Women in the Arts Ser.). (Illus.). 112p. (gr. 6-12). 30.00 (978-0-7910-7460-2(9), Chelsea Hse.) Facts On File, Inc.

Adams, Colleen. The True Story of Pocahontas. 2009. (What Really Happened? Ser.). 24p. (gr. 2-3). 42.50 (978-1-60854-765-4(5), PowerKids Pr.) Rosen Publishing Group, Inc., The.

Adler, David A. A Picture Book of Amelia Earhart. Fisher, Jeff, illus. 2015. 32p. pap. 8.00 (978-1-61003-403-6(1)) Center for the Collaborative Classroom.

—A Picture Book of Rosa Parks. Casilla, Robert, illus. 2004. (J). (gr. -1-2). 28.95 incl. audio compact disk (978-1-59112-762-8(9)) Live Oak Media.

Allen, Audrey. Jennifer Lawrence. 2013. 32p. (J). (gr. 3-6). 25.25 (978-1-4339-8977-3(8)); pap. 10.50 (978-1-4339-8978-0(6)) Stevens, Gareth Publishing LLLP.

Allen, Nancy Kelly. Barreling over Niagara Falls, 1 vol. Fields, Lisa, illus. 2013. (ENG.). 40p. (J). (gr. k-3). 17.99 (978-1-4556-1766-1(0)) Pelican Publishing Co., Inc.

Aller, Susan Bivin. Juliette Low. 2007. (History Maker Biographies Ser.). (Illus.). 48p. (J). (gr. 3-7). lib. bdg. 26.60 (978-0-8225-6580-2(3), Lerner Pubns.) Lerner Publishing Group.

—Madam C. J. Walker. 2007. (History Maker Biographies Ser.). (ENG., Illus.). 48p. (gr. 3-6). lib. bdg. 27.93 (978-0-8225-6582-6(X), Lerner Pubns.) Lerner Publishing Group.

Alter, Judy & Alter, Judy. Laura Ingalls Wilder: Pioneer & Author. 2003. (Our People Ser.). (ENG., Illus.). 32p. (J). (gr. 3-6). 29.93 (978-1-59296-007-1(3), 200644) Child's World, Inc., The.

Anderson, Jameson. Danica Patrick, 1 vol. 2014. (Awesome Athletes Ser.). (ENG., Illus.). 32p. (J). (gr. 8-12). lib. bdg. 27.07 (978-1-62403-339-1(3), Checkerboard Library) ABDO Publishing Co.

—Gabby Douglas, 1 vol. 2014. (Awesome Athletes Ser.). (ENG.). 32p. (gr. 8-12). lib. bdg. 27.07 (978-1-62403-338-4(5), Checkerboard Library) ABDO Publishing Co.

Anderson, Jane. My Name Is Deborah Samson. 2005. (J). pap. (978-1-4108-4225-1(8)) Benchmark Education Co.

Anderson, Jennifer Joline. Miley Cyrus: Pop Princess, 1 vol. 2014. (Contemporary Lives Set 4 Ser.). (ENG., Illus.). 112p. (J). (gr. 6-12). lib. bdg. 35.64 (978-1-62403-544-9(2), Essential Library) ABDO Publishing Co.

Anderson, Laurie Halse. Independent Dames: What You Never Knew about the Women & Girls of the American Revolution. Faulkner, Matt, illus. 2008. (ENG.). 40p. (J). (gr. 1-5). 17.99 (978-0-689-85808-6(6), Simon & Schuster Bks. For Young Readers) Simon & Schuster Bks. For Young Readers.

Anema, Durlynn. Ynes Mexia: Botanist & Adventurer. 2005. (Women Adventurers Ser.). (Illus.). 144p. (J). (gr. 3-7). lib. bdg. 26.95 (978-1-931798-67-9(2)) Reynolds, Morgan Inc.

Annie Oakley. 2010. (Legends of the Wild West Ser.). (Illus.). 104p. (gr. 6-12). 35.00 (978-1-60413-594-7(8), Chelsea Hse.) Facts On File, Inc.

Apel, Melanie Ann. Virginia Apgar: Innovative Female Physician & Inventor of the Apgar Score. 2009. (Women Hall of Famers in Mathematics & Science Ser.). 112p. (gr. 5-8). 63.90 (978-1-60854-815-6(5), Rosen Reference) Rosen Publishing Group, Inc., The.

Auch, Allison. Women Who Dared & Mujeres que se Atrevieron: 6 English, 6 Spanish Adaptations. 2011. (ENG & SPA.). (J). 97.00 net. (978-1-4108-5692-0(5)) Benchmark Education Co.

Bailey, Diane. Venus & Serena Williams: Tennis Champions. 2010. (Sports Families Ser.). 48p. (YA). (gr. 5-8). lib. bdg., E-Book 53.00 (978-1-4488-0124-4(9)) Rosen Publishing Group, Inc., The.

Bankston, John. Abby Wambach. 2013. (ENG.). 32p. (gr. 4-8). lib. bdg. 25.70 (978-1-61228-465-1(5)) Mitchell Lane Pubs., Inc.

Banting, Erinn. Rosa Parks. 2005. (Great African American Women for Kids Ser.). (Illus.). 24p. (J). (gr. 2-3). lib. bdg. 26.00 (978-1-59036-336-2(1)); (gr. 3-7). per. 8.95 (978-1-59036-342-3(6)) Weigl Pubs., Inc.

Barasch, Lynne. Hiromi's Hands. 2015. (ENG.). (J). pap. 10.95 (978-1-62014-251-6(1)) Lee & Low Bks., Inc.

—Hiromi's Hands, 1 vol. Barasch, Lynne, illus. 2007. (ENG., Illus.). 40p. (J). (gr. k-6). 18.95 (978-1-58430-275-9(5)) Lee & Low Bks., Inc.

Barbara Jordan. 2004. 12p. (gr. k-4). 2.95 (978-0-635-02616-3(3)) Gallopade International.

Barbara Walters. 2010. (Women of Achievement Ser.). (Illus.). 128p. (J). (gr. 6-12). 35.00 (978-1-60413-686-9(3), Chelsea Hse.) Facts On File, Inc.

Barghoorn, Linda. Dolores Huerta: Advocate for Women & Workers. 2017. (Illus.). 32p. (J). **(978-0-7787-3418-5(8))** Crabtree Publishing Co.

—Mae Jemison: Trailblazing Astronaut, Doctor, & Teacher. 2016. (Remarkable Lives Revealed Ser.). (ENG., Illus.). 32p. (J). (gr. 2-5). (978-0-7787-2693-7(2)) Crabtree Publishing Co.

—Temple Grandin: Pioneer for Animal Rights & Autism Awareness. 2016. (Remarkable Lives Revealed Ser.). (ENG., Illus.). 32p. (J). (gr. 2-5). (978-0-7787-2688-3(6)) Crabtree Publishing Co.

Barron, Patricia. Meet Judge Patricia Barron. Barron, Robert, photos by. 2006. (Illus.). 40p. per. 14.95 (978-1-59858-301-4(8)) Dog Ear Publishing, LLC.

Bates, Martine G. Heather Whitestone: Inspirational Miss America. 2007. (Illus.). 104p. (J). pap. (978-1-59421-029-7(2)) Seacoast Publishing, Inc.

Baumann, Susan K. Harriet Tubman. 2013. (Jr. Graphic African American History Ser.). 24p. (J). (gr. 3-6). 25.25 (978-1-4777-1312-9(3)); pap. 10.60 (978-1-4777-1449-2(9)) Rosen Publishing Group, Inc., The. (PowerKids Pr.).

—Harriet Tubman: Conductor of the Underground Railroad. 2013. (Jr. Graphic African American History Ser.). 24p. (J). (gr. 3-6). pap. 63.60 (978-1-4777-1450-8(2), PowerKids Pr.) Rosen Publishing Group, Inc., The.

Bausum, Ann. With Courage & Cloth: Winning the Fight for a Woman's Right to Vote. 2004. (ENG., Illus.). 112p. (J). (gr. 5-17). lib. bdg. 32.90 (978-0-7922-6996-0(9), National Geographic Children's Bks.) National Geographic Society.

Beauregarde, Madelyn & Kelly, David M. Jennifer Lawrence: Academy Award-Winning Actress. 2016. (Leading Women Ser.). 112p. (gr. 7-7). 39.93 (978-1-5026-1985-3(7)) Cavendish Square Publishing.

Benson, Michael. Gloria Estefan. 2003. (Biography Ser.). (Illus.). 112p. (YA). (gr. 6-18). pap. 7.95 (978-0-8225-9692-9(X), Carolrhoda Bks.) Lerner Publishing Group.

Berne, Emma Carlson & Hodge, Marie. Helen Keller: Courage in Darkness. 2009. (Sterling Biographies(r) Ser.). (ENG., Illus.). 128p. (J). (gr. 5-18). pap. 5.95 (978-1-4027-5147-9(8)) Sterling Publishing Co., Inc.

Bert, Ruth J. Everyone Called Her Sister Sarah. Westbeld, Kristine, illus. 2004. (ENG.). 32p. (J). (gr. -1-3). pap. 4.99 (978-1-928915-62-1(0)) Evangel Publishing Hse.

Biery, Martha. Josephine Aspinwall Roche: Humanitarian. 2011. (ENG & SPA., Illus.). 66p. (J). pap. 8.95 (978-0-86541-119-7(0)) Filter Pr., LLC.

Bindi, Paulo. Sally Ride: The Sky's the Limit. 2013. (InfoMax Readers Ser.). (ENG.). 24p. (J). (gr. 2-3). pap. 49.50 (978-1-4777-2452-1(4)); (Illus.). pap. 8.25 (978-1-4777-2451-4(6)) Rosen Publishing Group, Inc., The. (Rosen Classroom).

Black, Donnette. Madam C. J. Walker's Road to Success. 2010. 36p. pap. 17.50 (978-1-4520-2443-1(X)) AuthorHouse.

Blair, Eric. Annie Oakley, 1 vol. Silverman, Dianne, illus. 2011. (My First Classic Story Ser.). (ENG.). 32p. (gr. k-3). lib. bdg. 22.65 (978-1-4048-6577-8(2), My First Classic Story) Picture Window Bks.

Blakely, Gloria. Condoleezza Rice. 2003. (African American Leaders Ser.). (Illus.). 112p. (gr. 6-12). 30.00 (978-0-7910-7683-5(0), Chelsea Hse.) Facts On File, Inc.

Blashfield, Jean F. Hillary Clinton. 2010. (Leading Women Ser.). 96p. (YA). (gr. 7-12). 39.93 (978-0-7614-4954-6(X)) Marshall Cavendish Corp.

—Oprah Winfrey. 2003. (Trailblazers of the Modern World Ser.). (ENG & SPA., Illus.). 48p. (gr. 5-12). pap. 14.05 (978-0-8368-5247-9(8), Gareth Stevens Secondary Library) Stevens, Gareth Publishing LLLP.

Blumenthal, Karen. Hillary Rodham Clinton: A Woman Living History. 2016. (ENG., Illus.). 448p. (J). 18.99 (978-1-250-06014-3(1), 9781250060143) Feiwel & Friends.

Bodden, Valerie. Hillary Clinton: Historic Leader, 1 vol. 2009. (Essential Lives Set 4 Ser.). (ENG., Illus.). 112p. (J). (gr. 6-12). lib. bdg. 35.64 (978-1-60453-699-7(3)) ABDO Publishing Co.

—Michelle Obama: First Lady & Role Model, 1 vol. 2009. (Essential Lives Set 4 Ser.). (ENG., Illus.). 112p. (J). (gr. 6-12). lib. bdg. 35.64 (978-1-60453-703-1(5)) ABDO Publishing Co.

—Nuclear Physicist Chien-Shiung Wu. 2016. (STEM Trailblazer Bios Ser.). (ENG., Illus.). 32p. (J). (gr. 2-5). 26.65 (978-1-5124-0786-0(0)) Lerner Publishing Group.

Bodie, Idella. Heroines of the American Revolution. 2003. (Illus.). 99p. (J). pap. 6.95 (978-0-87844-170-9(0)) Sandlapper Publishing Co., Inc.

Bohannon, Lisa Frederiksen. Woman's Work: The Story of Betty Friedan. 2004. (Illus.). 144p. (YA). (gr. 6-12). 23.95 (978-1-931798-41-9(9)) Reynolds, Morgan Inc.

Bolden, Tonya. Searching for Sarah Rector: The Richest Black Girl in America. 2014. (ENG., Illus.). 80p. (J). (gr. 3-7). 21.95 (978-1-4197-0846-6(5), Abrams Bks. for Young Readers) Abrams, Inc.

Books, Golson & Purdy, Elizabeth. Celebrating Women in American History, 5 vols., Set. 2011. (Celebrating Women in American History Ser.). 1280p. (gr. 6-12). 315.00 (978-0-8160-7878-3(5)) Facts On File, Inc.

Bowdish, Lynea. With Courage: Seven Women Who Changed America. 2004. (Illus.). 48p. (J). 6.95 (978-1-59336-280-5(3)) Mondo Publishing.

Bozzuti-Jones, Mark Francisco. The Miter Fits Just Fine: A Story about the Rt. Rev. Barbara Clementine Harris, Suffragan Bishop, Diocese of Massachusetts. 2003. (ENG.). 86p. pap. 10.95 (978-1-56101-220-6(3)) Cowley Pubns.

Brainard, Cecilia Manguerra. Cecilia's Diary 1962-1969. 2003. (YA). per. 15.95 (978-0-9719458-1-4(0)) PALH.

Braun, Eric. Loretta Lynch: First African American Woman Attorney General. 2016. (Gateway Biographies Ser.). (ENG., Illus.). 48p. (J). (gr. 4-8). 39.99 (978-1-5124-0587-3(6), Lerner Pubns.) Lerner Publishing Group.

Brean, Alta. Dear Grandchildren: Growing up on the Frontier. 2003. (Illus.). 144p. 18.95 (978-0-9726360-0-1(5), (408) 718-5654) Alta Omnimedia.

Bredeson, Carmen. The Chocolate Chip Cookie Queen: Ruth Wakefield & Her Yummy Invention. 2014. (Inventors at Work! Ser.). 48p. (J). lib. bdg. 25.27 (978-0-7660-4242-1(1), Enslow Elementary) Enslow Pubs., Inc.

Bregoli, Jane. The Goat Lady. Bregoli, Jane, illus. 2008. (ENG., Illus.). 32p. (gr. 2-6). pap. 8.95 (978-0-88448-309-0(6), 884309) Tilbury Hse. Pubs.

Brennan, Linda Crotta. Women of the Ocean State: 25 Rhode Island Women You Should Know. Greenleaf, Lisa, illus. 2012. 136p. (J). pap. 16.00 (978-0-9842549-7-2(8)) Apprentice Shop Bks., LLC.

Briere-Haquet, Alice. Nina. 2017. 40p. (J). (-2). 13.99 **(978-958-30-5461-7(5))** Panamericana Editorial COL. Dist: Lectorum Pubns., Inc.

Brooks, Riley. Taylor Swift: Fearless Star. 2010. (Illus.). 48p. (J). (978-0-545-30382-8(6)) Scholastic, Inc.

Brown, Anne K. & Burns, Jan. Gwen Stefani. 2009. (People in the News Ser.). (ENG., Illus.). 128p. (gr. 7-12). lib. bdg. 39.40 (978-1-4205-0126-1(7), LML02109-245440) Cengage Gale.

Brown, Jonatha A. Eleanor Roosevelt. 2005. (People We Should Know Ser.). (Illus.). 24p. (gr. 1-4). pap. 8.15 (978-0-8368-4475-7(0)); lib. bdg. 22.00 (978-0-8368-4468-9(8)) Stevens, Gareth Publishing LLLP. (Weekly Reader Leveled Readers).

—Rosa Parks. 2005. (Gente que hay que conocer (People We Should Know- Spanish edition) Ser.). (Illus.). 24p. (gr. 1-4). (ENG & SPA.). pap. 8.15 (978-0-8368-4769-7(5)); pap. 8.15 (978-0-8368-4755-0(5)); (ENG & SPA., lib. bdg. 22.00 (978-0-8368-4762-8(8)); lib. bdg. 22.00 (978-0-8368-4748-2(2)) Stevens, Gareth Publishing LLLP. (Weekly Reader Leveled Readers).

Brown, Tami Lewis. Soar, Elinor! Roca, François, illus. 2010. (ENG.). 40p. (J). (gr. -1-3). 16.99 (978-0-374-37115-9(6), 9780374371159, Farrar, Straus & Giroux (BYR)) Farrar, Straus & Giroux.

Buckley, Annie. Ellen Ochoa. 2007. (21st Century Skills Library: Life Skills Biographies Ser.). (ENG., Illus.). 48p. (gr. 4-8). lib. bdg. 31.36 (978-1-60279-075-9(2), 200041) Cherry Lake Publishing.

Buckley, James. Katie Ledecky. 2017. (Amazing Americans: Olympians Ser.). (ENG.). 24p. (J). (gr. -1-3). 17.95 **(978-1-68402-240-3(1))** Bearport Publishing Co., Inc.

Buell, Janet & Sisters, Write. Women of the Granite State: 25 New Hampshire Women You Should Know. Greenleaf, Lisa, illus. 2012. 136p. (J). pap. 16.00 (978-0-9842549-8-9(6)) Apprentice Shop Bks., LLC.

Burke, John. Amelia Earhart: Flying Solo. 2017. (Great Leaders & Events Ser.). (ENG.). (J). (gr. 4-8). lib. bdg. 35.99 **(978-1-942875-45-1(2))** Quarto Publishing Group USA.

Burlingame, Jeff. Hillary Clinton: A Life in Politics. 2008. (People to Know Today Ser.). (Illus.). 112p. (J). (gr. 3-7). lib. bdg. 33.27 (978-0-7660-2892-0(5)) Enslow Pubs., Inc.

—Taylor Swift: Music Superstar. 2011. (Hot Celebrity Biographies Ser.). (Illus.). 48p. (J). (gr. 5-18). pap. 8.95 (978-1-59845-286-0(X)) Enslow Pubs., Inc.

Butler, Darren J. Helen Keller: Leader Without Sight or Sound. 2012. (Illus.). 108p. (J). pap. (978-1-59421-083-9(7)) Seacoast Publishing, Inc.

Butler, Mary G. Sojourner Truth: From Slave to Activist for Freedom. 2005. (Library of American Lives & Times). (Illus.). 112p. (YA). (gr. 4-8). lib. bdg. 34.60 (978-0-8239-5736-1(5)) Rosen Publishing Group, Inc., The.

Byman, Jeremy. Madam Secretary: The Story of Madeleine Albright. rev. exp. ed. 2004. (Notable Americans Ser.). (Illus.). 128p. (YA). (gr. 6-12). 23.95 (978-1-931798-34-1(6)) Reynolds, Morgan Inc.

Calamity Jane. 2010. (Legends of the Wild West Ser.). (Illus.). 128p. (gr. 6-12). 35.00 (978-1-60413-595-4(6), Chelsea Hse.) Facts On File, Inc.

Calkhoven, Laurie. Women Who Changed the World: 50 Amazing Americans. Castelao, Patricia, illus. 2015. (ENG.). 96p. (J). (gr. 2-5). pap. 8.99 (978-0-545-88962-9(6), Scholastic Paperbacks) Scholastic, Inc.

—Women Who Launched the Computer Age. Petersen, Alyssa, illus. 2016. (You Should Meet Ser.). (ENG.). 48p. (J). (gr. 1-3). pap. 3.99 (978-1-4814-7046-9(9), Simon Spotlight) Simon Spotlight.

Cameron, Charles. Why Lizzie Johnson Matters to Texas. 2014. (Illus.). 32p. (J). lib. bdg. 26.25 (978-1-4777-0908-5(8)) Rosen Publishing Group, Inc., The.

Cantwell, Lois. Women Winners: Then & Now. 2009. (Sports Illustrated for Kids Bks.). 176p. (gr. 7-12). 63.90 (978-1-60853-157-8(0)) Rosen Publishing Group, Inc., The.

Cantwell, Lois & Smith, Pohla. Women Winners: Then & Now. 2005. (Sports Illustrated for Kids Books Ser.). (Illus.). 176p. (YA). (gr. 7-12). lib. bdg. 33.25 (978-0-8239-3695-3(3)) Rosen Publishing Group, Inc., The.

—Women Winners: Then & Now. (J). (gr. 3-9). pap. 3.99 (978-1-930623-09-5(7)) Sports Illustrated For Kids.

Caravantes, Peggy. Petticoat Spies: Six Women Spies of the US Civil War. 2004. (Notable Americans Ser.). (Illus.). 112p. (YA). (gr. 6-12). 23.95 (978-1-883846-88-6(9), First Biographies) Reynolds, Morgan Inc.

—Waging Peace: The Story of Jane Addams. 2004. (Illus.). 144p. (YA). (gr. 6-12). 23.95 (978-1-931798-40-2(0)) Reynolds, Morgan Inc.

Carosella, Melissa. Founding Mothers: Women Who Shaped America, 1 vol. 2011. (Primary Source Readers Ser.). (ENG.). 32p. (J). (gr. 5-5). pap. 8.99 (978-1-4333-1505-3(X)) Teacher Created Materials, Inc.

Carson, Mary Kay. Who Was the Hair-Care Millionaire? Madam C. J. Walker. 2012. (I Like Inventors! Ser.). (Illus.). 24p. (J). (gr. k-3). pap. 7.95 (978-1-4644-0133-6(0), Enslow Elementary) Enslow Pubs., Inc.

Cartlidge, Cherese. Jennifer Lopez. Greenhaven Press Staff, ed. 2012. (People in the News Ser.). (ENG., Illus.). 128p. (gr. 7-10). lib. bdg. 39.40 (978-1-4205-0755-3(9), Lucent Bks.) Cengage Gale.

Castaldo, Nancy F. The Race Around the World (Totally True Adventures) Lowe, Wesley, illus. 2015. (Totally True Adventures Ser.). (ENG.). 112p. (J). (gr. 2-5). 4.99 (978-0-553-52278-5(7), Random Hse. Bks. for Young Readers) Random Hse. Children's Bks.

Cefrey, Holly. The Inventions of Martha Coston: Signal Flares That Save Sailors' Lives. 2009. (19th Century American Inventors Ser.). 24p. (gr. 2-3). 42.50 (978-1-60854-953-5(4), PowerKids Pr.) Rosen Publishing Group, Inc., The.

—Taylor Swift. 2011. (Megastars Ser.). (Illus.). 48p. (YA). (gr. 5-8). 29.25 (978-1-4358-3575-7(1), Rosen Reference) Rosen Publishing Group, Inc., The.

Cheney, Lynne. A Is for Abigail: An Almanac of Amazing American Women. Glasser, Robin Preiss, illus. 2003. (ENG.). 48p. (J). (gr. 1-7). 19.99 (978-0-689-85819-2(1), Simon & Schuster Bks. For Young Readers) Simon & Schuster Bks. For Young Readers.

Ching, Jacqueline. Abigail Adams: A Revolutionary Woman. 2009. (Library of American Lives & Times Ser.). 112p. (gr. 5-5). 69.20 (978-1-60853-469-2(3)) Rosen Publishing Group, Inc., The.

Clinton, Chelsea. She Persisted: 13 American Women Who Changed the World. Boiger, Alexandra, illus. 2017. (ENG.). 32p. (J). (gr. -1-3). 17.99 **(978-1-5247-4172-3(8)**, Philomel Bks.) Penguin Young Readers Group.

Cohen, Della. Eleanor Roosevelt: Proud & Tall. 2005. (Illus.). 16p. (J). pap. (978-0-7367-2879-9(1)) Zaner-Bloser, Inc.

Cohen, Sheila & Terman Cohen, Sheila. Mai Ya's Long Journey. 2005. (Badger Biographies Ser.). (ENG., Illus.). 96p. (J). (gr. 3-7). per. 12.95 (978-0-87020-365-7(7)) Wisconsin Historical Society.

Coleman, Miriam. Women in the Military. 2015. (Women Groundbreakers Ser.). (ENG.). 32p. (J). (gr. 4-5). pap. 10.00 (978-1-4994-1052-5(2), PowerKids Pr.) Rosen Publishing Group, Inc., The.

Collins, Kathleen. Sojourner Truth: Defensora de los derechos Civiles. 2004. (Grandes personajes en la historia de los Estados Unidos Ser.). (SPA.). 32p. (gr. 3-6). pap. 10.00 (978-0-8239-4239-8(2), Rosen Classroom) Rosen Publishing Group, Inc., The.

—Sojourner Truth: Defensora de los derechos civiles (Sojourner Truth: Equal Rights Advocate) 2009. (Grandes personajes en la historia de los Estados Unidos (Famous People in American History) Ser.). (SPA.). 32p. (gr. 2-3). 47.90 (978-1-61512-808-2(5), Editorial Buenas Letras) Rosen Publishing Group, Inc., The.

—Sojourner Truth: Equal Rights Advocate. 2004. (Famous People in American History Ser.). (ENG., Illus.). 32p. (gr. 4-8). pap. 10.00 (978-0-8239-4193-3(0)) Rosen Publishing Group, Inc., The.

—Sojourner Truth: Equal Rights Advocate / Defensora de los derechos Civiles. 2009. (Famous People in American History/Grandes personajes en la historia de los Estados Unidos Ser.). (ENG & SPA.). 32p. (gr. 2-3). 47.90 (978-1-61512-556-2(6), Editorial Buenas Letras) Rosen Publishing Group, Inc., The.

Colson, Mary. Beyoncé: A Life in Music. 2010. (Culture in Action Ser.). (ENG.). 32p. (gr. 3-6). 30.65 (978-1-4109-3914-2(6), NA-r) Heinemann-Raintree.

Corey, Shana. Hillary Clinton: the Life of a Leader. Gustavson, Adam, illus. 2016. (Step into Reading Ser.). (ENG.). 48p. (J). (gr. k-3). 3.99 (978-1-101-93235-3(X), Random Hse. Bks. for Young Readers) Random Hse. Children's Bks.

Crawford, Ann Fears. Rosa: A German Woman on the Texas Frontier. Fain, Cheryl, illus. l.t. ed. 2003. 60p. (J). (gr. 3-8). 16.95 (978-1-931823-09-8(X)) Halcyon Pr.

Crowley Conn, Kathe. Juliette Kinzie: Frontier Storyteller. 2015. (Badger Biographies Ser.). (ENG., Illus.). 123p. (J). (gr. 4-6). pap. 12.95 (978-0-87020-701-3(6)) Wisconsin Historical Society.

Cummins, Julie. Flying Solo: How Ruth Elder Soared into America's Heart. Laugesen, Malene R., illus. 2013. (ENG.). 32p. (J). (gr. 1-3). 17.99 (978-1-59643-509-4(7), 9781596435094) Roaring Brook Pr.

Cunningham, Kevin. Condoleezza Rice. 2009. (Journey to Freedom Ser.). (ENG., Illus.). 32p. (J). (gr. 4-7). 29.93 (978-1-60253-120-8(X), 200386) Child's World, Inc., The.

Curran, Abbey & Kaye, Elizabeth. The Courage to Compete: Living with Cerebral Palsy & Following My Dreams. 2015. (ENG., Illus.). 272p. (YA). (gr. 8-7). 17.99 (978-0-06-236391-6(3)) HarperCollins Pubs.

Currie-McGhee, L. K. Miley Cyrus. 2009. (People in the News Ser.). (ENG., Illus.). 128p. (gr. 7-12). lib. bdg. 39.40 (978-1-4205-0127-8(5), LML02109-245441) Cengage Gale.

Dakers, Diane. Vera Wang: A Passion for Bridal & Lifestyle Design. 2010. (Crabtree Groundbreaker Biographies Ser.). (ENG., Illus.). 112p. (J). pap. (978-0-7787-2544-2(8)); (gr. 5-8). lib. bdg. (978-0-7787-2535-0(9)) Crabtree Publishing Co.

Daly, Ruth. Rosa Parks. 2014. (J). (978-1-4896-2452-9(X)) Weigl Pubs., Inc.

Daniel, Susanna. Paula Fox. 2009. (Library of Author Biographies Ser.). 112p. (gr. 5-8). 63.90 (978-1-60853-550-7(9), Rosen Reference) Rosen Publishing Group, Inc., The.

Darragh, Marty & Pitkin, Jo. Women of the Prairie State: 25 Illinois Women You Should Know. Greenleaf, Lisa, illus. 2012. 136p. (J). pap. 16.00 (978-0-9842549-2-7(7)) Apprentice Shop Bks., LLC.

Darraj, Susan Muaddi. Anna Sui. 2009. (Asian Americans of Achievement Ser.). (Illus.). 120p. (YA). (gr. 7-12). 35.00 (978-1-60413-570-1(0)) Facts On File, Inc.

De Capua, Sarah. Sandra Day O'Connor. 2013. 96p. (YA). (gr. 7-12). 39.93 (978-0-7614-4961-4(2)) Cavendish Square Publishing.

DeFord, Diane. Harriet Tubman. 2009. pap. 13.25 (978-1-60559-061-5(4)) Hameray Publishing Group, Inc.

Devillier, Christy. Helen Keller, 1 vol. 2004. (First Biographies Set Iv Ser.). (ENG., Illus.). 32p. (gr. k-4). 27.07 (978-1-59197-514-4(X), Buddy Bks.) ABDO Publishing Co.

DeVillier, Christy. Molly Pitcher, 1 vol. 2004. (First Biographies Set Iv Ser.). (ENG., Illus.). 32p. (gr. k-4). 27.07 (978-1-59197-515-1(8), Buddy Bks.) ABDO Publishing Co.

Di Piazza, Domenica. NASA Computer Scientist Margaret Hamilton. 2017. (STEM Trailblazer Bios Ser.). (ENG.). 32p. (J). (gr. 2-5). 26.65 **(978-1-5124-3450-7(7))** Lerner Publishing Group.

Diamond, Cheryl. Model: A Memoir. 2008. (ENG., Illus.). 368p. (YA). (gr. 9-18). pap. 11.99 (978-1-4169-5904-5(1), Simon Pulse) Simon Pulse.

Dickmann, Nancy. Rachel Carson: Environmental Crusader. 2015. (Superheroes of Science Ser.). (ENG., Illus.). 48p. (J). (gr. 6-6). pap. 14.05 (978-1-4824-3149-0(1)) Stevens, Gareth Publishing LLLP.

Ditchfield, Christin. Condoleezza Rice: America's Leading Stateswoman. 2006. (Great Life Stories Ser.). (ENG., Illus.). 112p. (J). (gr. 6-8). lib. bdg. 30.50 (978-0-531-13874-8(7), Watts, Franklin) Scholastic Library Publishing.

Doak, Robin S. Amelia Earhart, 1 vol. 2012. (American Biographies Ser.). (ENG.). 48p. (gr. 4-6). pap. 9.95 (978-1-4329-6462-7(3), NA-h) Heinemann-Raintree.

—Dian Fossey: Friend to Africa's Gorillas, 1 vol. 2014. (Women in Conservation Ser.). (ENG., Illus.). 48p. (gr. 3-6). 33.32 (978-1-4846-0468-7(7)); pap. 8.99 (978-1-4846-0473-1(3)) Heinemann-Raintree. (Heinemann InfoSearch).

—Eleanor Roosevelt, 1 vol. 2012. (American Biographies Ser.). (ENG.). 48p. (gr. 4-6). pap. 9.95 (978-1-4329-6461-0(5), NA-h) Heinemann-Raintree.

Doeden, Matt. Ivanka Trump: A Brand of Her Own. 2017. (Gateway Biographies Ser.). (ENG., Illus.). (J). (gr. 4-8). lib. bdg. 26.65 **(978-1-5124-8624-7(8))** Lerner Publishing Group.

Doeden, Matt. Michele Bachmann: Tea Party Champion. 2011. (Gateway Biographies Ser.). (YA). (gr. 4-7). lib. bdg. 26.60 *(978-0-7613-9074-9(X))* Lerner Publishing Group.

Donaldson, Chelsea. Christine Sinclair, 1 vol. 2014. (Canadian Biographies Ser.). (ENG.). 24p. (gr. k-1). 26.65 *(978-1-4914-1959-5(8),* Pebble Plus) Capstone Press of Coughlan Cos.

Donaldson, Madeline. Venus & Serena Williams. (Amazing Athletes Ser.). 32p. 2005. (Illus.). (gr. 3-4). lib. bdg. 22.60 *(978-0-8225-3316-0(2))* 2nd rev. ed. 2011. (J). pap. 45.32 *(978-0-7613-7654-5(2))* Lerner Publishing Group.

Donelly, Karen. American Women Pilots of World War II. 2009. 112p. (YA). (gr. 7-12). pap. 12.95 *(978-1-4358-3274-9(4))* Rosen Publishing Group, Inc., The.

Dorrie, Roxanne. Venus & Serena Williams: The Smashing Sisters. 2003. (High Five Reading - Red Ser.). (ENG., Illus.). 48p. (gr. 3-4). per. 9.00 *(978-0-7368-2827-7(3),* High Five Reading (RBL)) Capstone Press of Coughlan Cos.

Dubowski, Cathy East. Rosa Parks: Don't Give In! 2005. (Defining Moments Ser.). (Illus.). 32p. (J). (gr. 2-5). lib. bdg. 25.27 *(978-1-59716-078-0(4))* Bearport Publishing Co., Inc.

Dudley Gold, Susan. The Women's Rights Movement & Abolitionism. 2015. (Primary Sources of the Abolitionist Movement Ser.). (ENG., Illus.). 64p. (J). (gr. 6-6). lib. bdg. 34.21 *(978-1-5026-0536-8(8))* Cavendish Square Publishing.

Dunn, L. Kerr. Dreaming with Animals: Anna Hyatt Huntington & Brookgreen Gardens. Wyrick, Monica, illus. 2017. (Young Palmetto Bks.). (ENG.). 40p. (J). 18.99 *(978-1-61117-820-3(7))* Univ. of South Carolina Pr.

Dunn, Mary R. & David, Rose. Michelle Wie. 2016. (Women in Sports Ser.). (ENG., Illus.). 24p. (gr. k-1). lib. bdg. 26.65 *(978-1-4914-7976-6(0),* Pebble Plus) Capstone Press of Coughlan Cos.

Dunn, Mary R. & Davin, Rose. Candace Parker. 2016. (Women in Sports Ser.). (ENG., Illus.). 24p. (gr. k-1). lib. bdg. 26.65 *(978-1-4914-7975-9(2),* Pebble Plus) Capstone Press of Coughlan Cos.

Dzidrums, Christine. Kelly Clarkson: Behind Her Hazel Eyes. 2013. 104p. pap. 9.99 *(978-1-938438-19-6(1))* Creative Media Publishing.

—Missy Franklin: Swimming Sensation. 2013. 72p. pap. 9.99 *(978-1-938438-23-3(X))* Creative Media Publishing.

Dzidrums, Christine & Rendon, Leah. Jennie Finch. Dzidrums, Joseph, photos by. 2013. (Illus.). 72p. pap. 9.99 *(978-1-938438-13-4(2))* Creative Media Publishing.

Earl, C. F. Alicia Keys. 2012. (J). pap. *(978-1-4222-2547-9(X))* Mason Crest.

Earl, C. F. & Hill, Z. B. Rihanna. 2012. (Superstars of Hip-Hop Ser.). 48p. (J). (gr. 3-4). pap. 9.95 *(978-1-4222-2552-3(6));* (Illus.). 19.95 *(978-1-4222-2526-4(7))* Mason Crest.

Edgar, Susan E. & Edgar, Kathleen J. 50 American Women of Courage & Vision. 2007. (Illus.). 288p. (J). *(978-1-58865-391-8(9))* Kidsbooks, LLC.

Edge, Laura Bufano. Laura Bush: Portrait of a First Lady. 2006. (People to Know Today Ser.). (Illus.). 128p. (J). (gr. 6). lib. bdg. 31.93 *(978-0-7660-2629-2(9))* Enslow Pubs., Inc.

Edgers, Geoff & Hempel, Carlene. Who Was Julia Child? Putra, Dede, illus. 2015. 105p. (J). ***(978-1-4844-6776-3(0),*** Grosset & Dunlap) Penguin Publishing Group.

—Who Was Julia Child? 2015. (Who Was... ? Ser.). lib. bdg. 16.00 *(978-0-606-37555-9(4))* Turtleback Bks.

Edgers, Geoff, et al. Who Was Julia Child? Harrison, Nancy & Putra, Dede, illus. 2015. (Who Was? Ser.). (ENG.). 112p. (J). (gr. 3-7). 5.99 *(978-0-448-48297-2(5),* Grosset & Dunlap) Penguin Young Readers Group.

Edison, Erin. Clara Barton, 1 vol. 2013. (Great Women in History Ser.). (ENG., Illus.). 24p. (gr. k-1). lib. bdg. 21.99 *(978-1-62065-076-9(2),* Pebble Bks.) Capstone Press of Coughlan Cos.

—Helen Keller, 1 vol. 2014. (Great Women in History Ser.). (ENG.). 24p. (gr. k-1). lib. bdg. 21.99 *(978-1-4765-4217-1(1),* Pebble Bks.) Capstone Press of Coughlan Cos.

—Pocahontas, 1 vol. 2013. (Great Women in History Ser.). (ENG.). 24p. (gr. k-1). pap. 6.29 *(978-1-62065-861-1(5));* pap. 35.70 *(978-1-62065-862-8(3))* Capstone Press of Coughlan Cos. (Pebble Bks.).

—Rosa Parks. 2013. (Great Women in History Ser.). (ENG.). 24p. (gr. k-1). pap. 35.70 *(978-1-62065-864-2(X));* pap. 6.29 *(978-1-62065-863-5(1))* Capstone Press of Coughlan Cos. (Pebble Bks.).

—Sally Ride, 1 vol. 2014. (Great Women in History Ser.). (ENG.). 24p. (gr. k-1). lib. bdg. 21.99 *(978-1-4765-4215-7(5),* Pebble Bks.) Capstone Press of Coughlan Cos.

—Susan B. Anthony, 1 vol. 2013. (Great Women in History Ser.). (ENG., Illus.). 24p. (gr. k-1). lib. bdg. 21.99 *(978-1-62065-075-2(4),* Pebble Bks.) Capstone Press of Coughlan Cos.

Edwards, Roberta. Michelle Obama: Primera Dama y Primera Mama. Call, Ken, illus. 2010. (SPA.). 48p. (gr. 3-5). pap. 9.99 *(978-1-60396-946-8(2))* Santillana USA Publishing Co., Inc.

Egan, Tracie. Cynthia Ann Parker: Cautiva de los comanches (Cynthia Ann Parker: Comanche Captive) 2009. (Grandes personajes en la historia de los Estados Unidos (Famous People in American History) Ser.). (SPA.). 32p. (gr. 2-3). 47.90 *(978-1-61512-796-2(8),* Editorial Buenas Letras) Rosen Publishing Group, Inc., The.

—Cynthia Ann Parker: Comanche Captive. 2009. (Primary Sources of Famous People in American History Ser.). 32p. (gr. 2-3). 47.90 *(978-1-60851-667-4(9))* Rosen Publishing Group, Inc., The.

—Cynthia Ann Parker: Comanche Captive / Cautiva de los Comanches. 2009. (Famous People in American History/Grandes personajes en la historia de los Estados Unidos Ser.). (ENG & SPA.). 32p. (gr. 2-3). 47.90 *(978-1-61512-542-5(6),* Editorial Buenas Letras) Rosen Publishing Group, Inc., The.

—Francisca Alvarez: El angel de Goliad. 2004. (Grandes personajes en la historia de los Estados Unidos Ser.). (SPA.). 32p. (gr. 3-6). pap. 10.00 *(978-0-8239-4227-5(9),* Rosen Classroom) Rosen Publishing Group, Inc., The.

Ehrlich, Amy. Rachel: The Story of Rachel Carson. Minor, Wendell, illus. 2008. (ENG.). 32p. (J). (gr. -1-3). pap. 7.99 *(978-0-15-206324-5(2))* Houghton Mifflin Harcourt Publishing Co.

Enander, Glen. Elisabeth Schussler Fiorenza. 2005. (Spiritual Leaders & Thinkers Ser.). (Illus.). 120p. (C). (gr. 9-13). 30.00 *(978-0-7910-8105-1(2),* Chelsea Hse.) Facts On File, Inc.

Epstein, Dwayne. Hillary Clinton. 2010. (People in the News Ser.). (Illus.). 128p. (J). 33.95 *(978-1-4205-0268-8(9),* Lucent Bks.) Cengage Gale.

—Nancy Pelosi. 2008. (People in the News Ser.). (ENG., Illus.). 104p. (YA). (gr. 7-10). lib. bdg. 33.95 *(978-1-4205-0057-8(0),* LML02109-240045, Lucent Bks.) Cengage Gale.

Fabiny, Sarah. Who Is Gloria Steinem? Hergenrother, Max & Harrison, Nancy, illus. 2014. (Who Was? Ser.). (ENG.). 112p. (J). (gr. 3-7). 5.99 *(978-0-448-48238-5(X),* Grosset & Dunlap) Penguin Young Readers Group.

—Who Is Gloria Steinem? 2014. (Who Is... ? Ser.). (Illus.). 105p. (J). lib. bdg. 16.00 *(978-0-606-36182-8(0))* Turtleback Bks.

Faust, Daniel R. Ibtihaj Muhammad: Muslim American Champion Fencer & Olympian. 2017. (Breakout Biographies Ser.). 32p. (gr. 9-10). 26.25 ***(978-1-5081-6060-1(0),*** PowerKids Pr.) Rosen Publishing Group, Inc., The.

Favor, Lesli J. Women Doctors & Nurses of the Civil War. 2009. (American Women at War Ser.). 112p. (gr. 8-8). 63.90 *(978-1-61511-404-7(1))* Rosen Publishing Group, Inc., The.

Favor, Leslie. Women Doctors & Nurses of the Civil War. 2009. 112p. (YA). (gr. 7-12). pap. 12.95 *(978-1-4358-3273-2(6))* Rosen Publishing Group, Inc., The.

Fedyszyn, Kirra. Molly Brown. 2014. (Jr. Graphic American Legends Ser.). (Illus.). 24p. (J). (gr. 3-6). pap. 10.60 *(978-1-4777-7201-0(4),* PowerKids Pr.) Rosen Publishing Group, Inc., The.

—Molly Pitcher. 2014. (Jr. Graphic American Legends Ser.). 24p. (J). (gr. 3-6). lib. bdg. 26.25 *(978-1-4777-7205-8(7),* PowerKids Pr.) Rosen Publishing Group, Inc., The.

Feinberg, Barbara Silberdick. Eleanor Roosevelt: Everything She Could Be. 2003. (Gateway Biography Ser.: 4). (Illus.). 48p. lib. bdg. 23.90 *(978-0-7613-2623-6(5),* Millbrook Pr.) Lerner Publishing Group.

Feldman, Heather. Marion Jones: Atleta de Categoría Internacional (World-Class Runner) 2009. (Superestrellas del Deporte (Superstars of Sports) Ser.). (SPA.). 24p. (gr. 1-2). 42.50 *(978-1-60853-227-8(5),* Editorial Buenas Letras) Rosen Publishing Group, Inc., The.

—Marion Jones: World Class Runner. 2009. (Sports Superstars Ser.). 24p. (gr. 1-1). 42.50 *(978-1-60853-179-0(1),* PowerKids Pr.) Rosen Publishing Group, Inc., The.

—Mia Hamm: Soccer Superstar. 2009. (Sports Superstars Ser.). 24p. (gr. 1-1). 42.50 *(978-1-60853-180-6(5),* PowerKids Pr.) Rosen Publishing Group, Inc., The.

—Mia Hamm: Soccer/Soccer Superstar/Superestrella del Fútbol. 2009. (Superstars of Sports/Superestrellas del deporte Ser.). (ENG & SPA.). 24p. (gr. 1-2). 42.50 *(978-1-60853-240-7(2),* Editorial Buenas Letras) Rosen Publishing Group, Inc., The.

—Mia Hamm: Superestrella del Fútbol Soccer (Soccer Superstar. 2009. (Superestrellas del Deporte (Superstars of Sports) Ser.). (SPA.). 24p. (gr. 1-2). 42.50 *(978-1-60853-228-5(3),* Editorial Buenas Letras) Rosen Publishing Group, Inc., The.

—Mia Hamm, Soccer Superstar/Superestrella del Futbol Soccer. De Leon, Mauricio Velzaquez, tr. 2008. (Reading Power Ser.). (ENG., Illus.). 24p. (gr. 1-6). pap. 8.85 *(978-1-4042-7543-0(6))* Rosen Publishing Group, Inc., The.

—Venus Williams: Campeona de Tenis (Tennis Champion) 2009. (Superestrellas del Deporte (Superstars of Sports) Ser.). (SPA.). 24p. (gr. 1-2). 42.50 *(978-1-60853-229-2(1),* Editorial Buenas Letras) Rosen Publishing Group, Inc., The.

—Venus Williams: Tennis Champion. 2009. (Sports Superstars Ser.). 24p. (gr. 1-1). 42.50 *(978-1-60853-183-7(X),* PowerKids Pr.) Rosen Publishing Group, Inc., The.

—Venus Williams: Tennis Champion / Campeona de Tenis. 2009. (Superstars of Sports/Superestrellas del deporte Ser.). (ENG & SPA.). 24p. (gr. 1-2). 42.50 *(978-1-60853-241-4(0),* Editorial Buenas Letras) Rosen Publishing Group, Inc., The.

—Venus Williams, Tennis Champion/Campeona del Tenis. De Leon, Mauricio Velzaquez, tr. 2008. (Reading Power Ser.). (ENG., Illus.). 24p. (gr. 1-6). per. 8.85 *(978-0-8239-6212-9(1))* Rosen Publishing Group, Inc., The.

Ferguson, Amanda. American Women of the Vietnam War. 2009. (American Women at War Ser.). 112p. (gr. 8-8). 63.90 *(978-1-61511-395-8(9))* Rosen Publishing Group, Inc., The.

Ferguson, Isabel, et al. A World More Bright: The Life of Mary Baker Eddy. 2013. (Illus.). vi, 279p. (J). *(978-0-87510-494-2(0))* Christian Science Publishing Society.

Fertig, Dennis. Sylvia Earle: Ocean Explorer, 1 vol. 2014. (Women in Conservation Ser.). (ENG., Illus.). 48p. (gr. 3-6). 33.32 *(978-1-4846-0470-0(9));* pap. 8.99 *(978-1-4846-0475-5(X))* Heinemann-Raintree. (Heinemann InfoSearch).

Fillion, Susan. Miss Etta & Dr. Claribel: Bringing Matisse to America. 2011. (Illus.). 92p. (YA). (gr. 5-18). 18.95 *(978-1-56792-434-3(4))* Godine, David R. Pub.

Fine, Edith Hope. Rosa Parks: Meet a Civil Rights Hero. 2004. (Meeting Famous People Ser.). (Illus.). 32p. (J). lib. bdg. 23.94 *(978-0-7660-2099-3(1))* Enslow Pubs., Inc.

Fiorelli, June Estep. Fannie Lou Hamer: A Voice for Freedom. 2004. (Avisson Young Adult Ser.). (Illus.). 117p. (J). pap. 19.95 *(978-1-888105-62-9(3))* Avisson Pr., Inc.

First Ladies. 2010. (First Ladies Ser.). (ENG.). 24p. (gr. k-1). lib. bdg. 133.25 *(978-1-4296-5329-9(9),* Pebble Plus) Capstone Press of Coughlan Cos.

Fishman, Jon M. Simone Biles. 2017. (Sports All-Stars Ser.). (ENG.). 32p. (J). (gr. 2-5). 12.99 ***(978-1-5124-4901-3(6),*** Lerner Pubns.); 39.99 ***(978-1-5124-4900-6(8),*** Lerner Pubns.); 39.99 ***(978-1-5124-4899-3(0),*** Lerner Pubns.); (Illus.). lib. bdg. 26.65 *(978-1-5124-4897-9(4))* Lerner Publishing Group.

Fleming, Candace. Amelia Lost: The Life & Disappearance of Amelia Earhart. 2011. (ENG., Illus.). 128p. (J). (gr. 3-7). 19.99 *(978-0-375-84198-9(9));* lib. bdg. 21.99 *(978-0-375-94598-4(9))* Random Hse. Children's Bks. (Schwartz & Wade Bks.).

Flynn, Jean. Annie Oakley: Sharpshooter & Entertainer. 2015. (J). pap. *(978-0-7660-6441-6(7))* Enslow Pubs., Inc.

Ford, Carin T. Clara Barton: Brave Nurse. 2006. (Heroes of American History Ser.). (Illus.). 32p. (J). (gr. 3-7). lib. bdg. 23.94 *(978-0-7660-2602-5(7),* Enslow Elementary) Enslow Pubs., Inc.

—Laura Ingalls Wilder: Real-Life Pioneer of the Little House Books. 2003. (People to Know Ser.). (Illus.). 112p. (J). lib. bdg. 26.60 *(978-0-7660-2105-1(X))* Enslow Pubs., Inc.

Frank, Mary Kate. Carrie Underwood. 2009. (Today's Superstars Ser.). 48p. (J). (gr. 5-8). pap. 14.05 *(978-1-4339-2377-7(7));* lib. bdg. 31.95 *(978-1-4339-2381-4(5))* Stevens, Gareth Publishing LLLP.

Franzen, Lenore. Venus Williams. 2003. (Ovations Ser.). (Illus.). 32p. (J). *(978-1-58341-249-7(2),* Creative Education) Creative Co., The.

Freedman, Jeri. Elizabeth Warren: Democratic Senator from Massachusetts. 2017. (J). ***(978-1-5026-2699-8(3))*** Cavendish Square Publishing.

Freedman, Jeri. Hillary Rodham Clinton: Profile of a Leading Democrat. (Career Profiles Ser.). 112p. 2009. (gr. 9-10). 63.90 *(978-1-61511-794-9(6))* 2007. (YA). (gr. 7-12). lib. bdg. 34.60 *(978-1-4042-1910-6(2))* Rosen Publishing Group, Inc., The.

Freedman, Lew. All about Amelia Earhart. 2015. (ENG., Illus.). 128p. (J). pap. 4.99 *(978-1-935628-44-6(5))* Blue River Pr.

Freedman, Russell. Babe Didrikson Zaharias: The Making of a Champion. 2014. (ENG., Illus.). 192p. (J). (gr. 5-7). pap. 10.99 *(978-0-544-10491-4(9))* Houghton Mifflin Harcourt Publishing Co.

—The Voice That Challenged a Nation: Marian Anderson & the Struggle for Equal Rights. 2011. (ENG., Illus.). 128p. (J). (gr. 5-7). pap. 10.99 *(978-0-547-48034-3(2))* Houghton Mifflin Harcourt Publishing Co.

Freistadt, Margo. Kate Spade. 2011. (Profiles in Fashion Ser.). (Illus.). 112p. 28.95 *(978-1-59935-154-4(4))* Reynolds, Morgan Inc.

French, Martin, illus. Stompin' at the Savoy: The Story of Norma Miller. 2006. (ENG.). 64p. (J). (gr. 4-7). 15.99 *(978-0-7636-2244-2(3))* Candlewick Pr.

Frey, Wendy. Citizen Heroes. 2007. (Illus.). 68p. (J). *(978-1-4105-0887-4(0)); (978-1-4105-0888-1(9))* Johnston, Don Inc.

Friend, Robyn C. The Women of Apollo. Katz, David Arthur, illus. l.t. ed. 2006. 80p. (J). 17.95 *(978-1-880599-80-8(5));* pap. 12.95 *(978-1-880599-79-2(1))* Cascade Pass, Inc.

Fromowitz, Lori. Louisa May Alcott, 1 vol. 2013. (Great American Authors Ser.). (ENG.). 48p. (J). (gr. 3-6). lib. bdg. 32.79 *(978-1-61783-715-9(6))* ABDO Publishing Co.

Fry, Erin. The Power of Friendship. 2005. (Illus.). 16p. (J). pap. *(978-0-7367-2920-8(8))* Zaner-Bloser, Inc.

Furbee, Mary Rodd. Outrageous Women of Civil War Times. 2003. (Outrageous Women Ser.: 7). (ENG., Illus.). 132p. (J). (gr. 5-9). pap. 14.95 *(978-0-471-22926-1(1),* Jossey-Bass) Wiley, John & Sons, Inc.

Garza, Carmen Lomas, illus. Cuadros de Familia. 2nd anniv. ed. 2013.Tr. of Family Pictures. (ENG & SPA.). 32p. (J). pap. 9.95 *(978-0-89239-207-0(X))* Lee & Low Bks., Inc.

Gaskill, Rachel. Agnes de Mille. 2009. (Library of American Choreographers Ser.). 48p. (gr. 5-8). 53.00 *(978-1-60853-454-8(5),* Rosen Reference) Rosen Publishing Group, Inc., The.

Gay, Kathlyn. Mother Jones. 2006. (American Workers Ser.). (Illus.). 144p. (J). (gr. 3-7). lib. bdg. 28.95 *(978-1-59935-016-5(5))* Reynolds, Morgan Inc.

Gayle, Sharon. Harriet Tubman & the Freedom Train. Marshall, Felicia, illus. 2003. (Ready-To-read SOFA Ser.). (ENG.). 32p. (J). (gr. 1-3). pap. 3.99 *(978-0-689-85480-4(3),* Simon Spotlight) Simon Spotlight.

Giff, Patricia Reilly. Laura Ingalls Wilder. 2014. (Women of Our Time Ser.). (ENG., Illus.). 80p. (J). (gr. 3-7). pap. 7.99 *(978-0-14-751364-9(2),* Puffin Books) Penguin Young Readers Group.

Glaser, Jason. Danica Patrick. 2008. (Sports Idols Ser.). (Illus.). 24p. (J). (gr. 2-5). lib. bdg. 22.60 *(978-1-4042-4180-0(9))* Rosen Publishing Group, Inc., The.

—Molly Pitcher: Young American Patriot, 1 vol. Smith, Tod G. et al, illus. 2006. (Graphic Biographies Ser.). (ENG.). 32p. (gr. 3-4). 30.65 *(978-0-7368-5486-3(X),* Graphic Library) Capstone Press of Coughlan Cos.

Glass, Maya. Abigail Adams: Destacada Primera Dama (Abigail Adams: Famous First Lady) 2009. (Grandes personajes en la historia de los Estados Unidos (Famous People in American History) Ser.). (SPA.). 32p. (gr. 2-3). 47.90 *(978-1-61512-787-0(9),* Editorial Buenas Letras) Rosen Publishing Group, Inc., The.

—Abigail Adams: Famous First Lady / Destacada Primera Dama. 2009. (Famous People in American History/Grandes personajes en la historia de los Estados Unidos Ser.). (ENG & SPA.). 32p. (gr. 2-3). 47.90 *(978-1-61512-535-7(3),* Editorial Buenas Letras) Rosen Publishing Group, Inc., The.

Gold, Susan Dudley. Sofia Coppola. 2014. (Great Filmmakers Ser.). 80p. (YA). (gr. 8-11). lib. bdg. 35.64 *(978-1-62712-945-9(6))* Cavendish Square Publishing.

Goldsmith, Bonnie Zucker. Dr. Mary Edwards Walker: Civil War Surgeon & Medal of Honor Recipient, 1 vol. 2010. (Military Heroes Ser.). (ENG.). 112p. (J). (gr. 6-12). lib. bdg. 35.64 *(978-1-60453-966-0(6))* ABDO Publishing Co.

Goldsworthy, Steve. Sarah Palin. 2010. (Remarkable People Ser.). (Illus.). 24p. (J). (gr. 4-6). pap. 11.95 *(978-1-61690-167-5(9));* lib. bdg. 25.70 *(978-1-61690-166-0(7))* Weigl Pubs., Inc.

Golio, Gary. Strange Fruit: Billie Holiday & the Power of a Protest Song. Riley-Webb, Charlotte, illus. 2017. (Millbrook Picture Bks.). (ENG.). 40p. (gr. 3-6). 30.65 ***(978-1-5124-2837-7(X),*** Millbrook Pr.) Lerner Publishing Group.

Gomez, Rebecca. Sally Ride, 1 vol. 2003. (First Biographies Ser.). (ENG., Illus.). 32p. (gr. k-4). 27.07 *(978-1-57765-948-8(1),* Buddy Bks.) ABDO Publishing Co.

Gomez, Selena. Selena Gomez Style Guide. 2010. 14.99 *(978-1-4231-2976-9(8))* Hyperion Bks. for Children.

Goodridge, Catherine. Michelle Kwan & Michelle Kwan (Spanish) 6 English, 6 Spanish Adaptations. 2011. (ENG & SPA.). (J). 79.00 net. *(978-1-4108-5659-3(3))* Benchmark Education Co.

—Michelle Kwan (Spanish) 2011. (SPA.). (J). pap. 40.00 net. *(978-1-4108-2428-8(4),* A24284) Benchmark Education Co.

Gourley, Catherine. Who Is Maria Tallchief? Taylor, Val Paul, illus. 2003. (Who Was... ? Ser.). 103p. 15.00 *(978-0-7569-1592-6(9))* Perfection Learning Corp.

Graubart, Norman D. Laila Ali. 2015. (Exceptional African Americans Ser.). (ENG., Illus.). 24p. (J). (gr. 3-4). 22.60 *(978-0-7660-6656-4(8))* Enslow Pubs., Inc.

Graves, Charles P. Annie Oakley: The Shooting Star. Cary, illus. 2011. 80p. (gr. 4-7). 37.95 *(978-1-258-01390-5(8))* Literary Licensing, LLC.

Graves, Jeseca, illus. Bessie Coleman: The Story of an Aviation Pioneer. 2007. 24p. (J). *(978-0-9745294-1-7(9))* San Diego County Regional Airport Authority.

Grayson, Robert. Estée Lauder: Businesswoman & Cosmetics Pioneer, 1 vol. 2013. (Essential Lives Set 8 Ser.). (ENG.). 112p. (J). (gr. 6-12). lib. bdg. 35.64 *(978-1-61783-892-7(6),* Essential Library) ABDO Publishing Co.

Green, Carl R. & Sanford, William R. Belle Starr. rev. ed. 2008. (Outlaws & Lawmen of the Wild West, Revised Edition Ser.). (Illus.). 48p. (J). (gr. 5-18). lib. bdg. 25.27 *(978-0-7660-3176-0(4))* Enslow Pubs., Inc.

Green, Mary. Sarah Winnemucca: The Inspiring Life Story of the Activist & Educator. 2016. (Inspiring Stories Ser.). (ENG., Illus.). 112p. (gr. 5-7). lib. bdg. 35.99 *(978-0-7565-5167-4(6),* CPB Grades 4-8) Compass Point Bks.

Greenberg, Michael. Sword of a Champion: The Sharon Monplaisir Story. 2003. (Anything You Can Do. . .Ser.: Vol. 2). (Illus.). 96p. (J). (gr. 2-5). pap. 9.95 *(978-1-930546-39-4(4))* Wish Publishing.

Greenberger, Robert. Christina Aguilera. 2009. (Contemporary Musicians & Their Music Ser.). (Illus.). 48p. (gr. 7-12). pap. 11.75 *(978-1-4358-5124-5(2),* Rosen Classroom) Rosen Publishing Group, Inc., The.

Griffin, Lydia. Susan Anderson: Colorado's Doc Susie. 2010. (ENG., Illus.). 72p. (J). pap. 8.95 *(978-0-86541-108-1(5))* Filter Pr., LLC.

Guzmán, Lila & Guzmán, Rick. Ellen Ochoa: First Latina Astronaut. 2006. (Famous Latinos Ser.). (Illus.). 32p. (J). (gr. 4-7). lib. bdg. 23.94 *(978-0-7660-2642-1(6),* Enslow Elementary) Enslow Pubs., Inc.

Haldy, Emma E. Helen Keller. Bane, Jeff, illus. 2016. (My Early Library: My Itty-Bitty Bio Ser.). (ENG.). 24p. (J). (gr. k-1). 28.50 *(978-1-63471-020-6(7),* 208160) Cherry Lake Publishing.

Hall, Brianna. Great Women of the American Revolution, 1 vol. 2012. (Story of the American Revolution Ser.). (ENG., Illus.). 32p. (gr. 3-4). pap. 8.10 *(978-1-4296-9284-7(7));* lib. bdg. 27.32 *(978-1-4296-8451-4(8),* Fact Finders) Capstone Press of Coughlan Cos.

Hally, Ashleigh. Jackie Cochran. 2012. (Illus.). 24p. (J). *(978-1-935884-75-0(1));* pap. *(978-1-935884-81-1(6))* State Standards Publishing, LLC.

—Juliette Gordon Low. 2012. (Illus.). 24p. (J). *(978-1-935884-77-4(8));* pap. *(978-1-935884-83-5(2))* State Standards Publishing, LLC.

—Rosalynn Carter. 2012. (Illus.). 24p. (J). *(978-1-935884-74-3(3));* pap. *(978-1-935884-80-4(8))* State Standards Publishing, LLC.

Hamen, Susan E. Clara Barton: Civil War Hero & American Red Cross Founder, 1 vol. 2010. (Military Heroes Ser.). (ENG.). 112p. (J). (gr. 6-12). lib. bdg. 35.64 *(978-1-60453-960-8(7))* ABDO Publishing Co.

Harkins, Susan Sales & Harkins, William H. Betsy Ross. 2006. (Profiles in American History Ser.). (Illus.). 48p. (J). (gr. 3-7). lib. bdg. 29.95 *(978-1-58415-446-4(2))* Mitchell Lane Pubs., Inc.

Harmon, Daniel E. Amelia Earhart: Aviation Pioneer. 2017. (J). ***(978-1-5383-0020-6(6))*** Rosen Publishing Group, Inc., The.

Harness, Cheryl. Remember the Ladies: 100 Great American Women. 2003. (J). (gr. 3-6). 19.65 *(978-0-613-61843-4(2),* Turtleback) Turtleback Bks.

Harris, Lois V. Lotta Crabtree: Gold Rush Fairy Star, 1 vol. 2017. (ENG., Illus.). 80p. (J). (gr. 3-7). 17.99 *(978-1-4556-2230-6(3))* Pelican Publishing Co., Inc.

Hartland, Jessie. Bon Appétit! The Delicious Life of Julia Child. Hartland, Jessie, illus. 2012. (ENG., Illus.). 48p. (J). (gr. k-12). 20.99 *(978-0-375-96944-7(6));* 17.99 *(978-0-375-86944-0(1))* Random Hse. Children's Bks. (Schwartz & Wade Bks.).

Harvey, Bonnie C. Jane Addams: Social Worker & Nobel Peace Prize Winner. 2015. (Legendary American Biographies Ser.). 96p. (J). (gr. 6-12). pap. 10.95 *(978-0-7660-6461-4(1))* Enslow Pubs., Inc.

Harvey, Bonnie Carman. Jane Addams: Social Worker & Nobel Peace Prize Winner. 2015. (Legendary American Biographies Ser.). 96p. (J). (gr. 6-12). 27.94 *(978-0-7660-6460-7(3))* Enslow Pubs., Inc.

Hasday, Judy L. Agnes de Mille. 2003. (Women in the Arts Ser.). (Illus.). 112p. (gr. 6-12). 30.00 *(978-0-7910-7457-2(9),* Chelsea Hse.) Facts On File, Inc.

Heatley, Michael. Katy Perry. 2015. (Pop Icons Ser.). (Illus.). 64p. (J). (gr. 7). lib. bdg. 23.95 *(978-1-4222-3248-4(4))* Mason Crest.

Heatley, Michael & Gent, Mike. Taylor Swift. 2015. (Pop Icons Ser.). (Illus.). 64p. (J). (gr. 7). lib. bdg. 23.95 *(978-1-4222-3250-7(6))* Mason Crest.

Hernandez, Laurie. I Got This: To Gold & Beyond. 240p. (J). (gr. 3-7). 2018. (ENG.). pap. 8.99 ***(978-0-06-267732-7(2))*** 2017. 17.99 ***(978-0-06-267731-0(4))*** HarperCollins Pubs.

Herweck Rice, Dona. Laura Ingalls Wilder: Pioneer Woman (America in The 1800s) 2017. (Primary Source Readers Ser.). (Illus.). 32p. (J). (gr. 4-5). pap. 8.99 ***(978-1-4938-3798-4(2))*** Teacher Created Materials, Inc.

Herwick Rice, Dona & Greathouse, Lisa. Annie Oakley, 1 vol. 2009. (Building Fluency Through Reader's Theater Ser.). (ENG.). 24p. (J). (gr. 2-4). pap. 6.99 *(978-1-4333-0997-7(1))* Teacher Created Materials, Inc.

Hill, Christine M. Gwendolyn Brooks: Poetry Is Life Distilled. 2005. (African-American Biography Library). (Illus.). 128p. (J). (gr. 6-12). lib. bdg. 33.27 *(978-0-7660-2292-8(7))* Enslow Pubs., Inc.

Hill, Z. B. Beyoncé. 2012. (J). pap. *(978-1-4222-2536-3(4));* (Illus.). 48p. (gr. 3-4). 19.95 *(978-1-4222-2510-3(0))* Mason Crest.

Hillery, Louise. Bold Women in Indiana History. 2016. (Illus.). 212p. (J). pap. *(978-0-87842-655-3(8))* Mountain Pr. Publishing Co., Inc.

WXYZ

Hinds, Maurene. Emily Dickinson, 1 vol. 2013. (Great American Authors Ser.). (ENG.). 48p. (J). (gr. 3-6). lib. bdg. 32.79 *(978-1-61783-716-6(4))* ABDO Publishing Co.

Hirsch, Jesse. Tina Fey, 01 vols., 1. 2016. (Giants of Comedy Ser.). (ENG.). 112p. (J). 35.60 *(978-1-4994-6256-2(5),* Rosen Young Adult) Rosen Publishing Group, Inc., The.

Hitchcock, Susan Tyler. Karen Horney: Pioneer of Feminine Psychology. 2004. (Women in Medicine Ser.). (Illus.). 112p. (gr. 6-12). 30.00 *(978-0-7910-8025-2(0),* Chelsea Hse.) Facts On File, Inc.

Hoffman, Megan Mills. Ivanka Trump: Businesswoman & First Daughter. 2017. (J). ***(978-1-5026-2701-8(9))*** Cavendish Square Publishing.

Holden, Henry M. Pioneering Astronaut Sally Ride: A MyReportLinks. com Book. 2004. (Space Flight Adventures & Disasters Ser.). (Illus.). 48p. (J). lib. bdg. 26.60 *(978-0-7660-5169-0(2),* MyReportLinks.com Bks.) Enslow Pubs., Inc.

Hollihan, Kerrie Logan. Reporting under Fire: 16 Daring Women War Correspondents & Photojournalists. 2014. (Women of Action Ser.). (ENG., Illus.). 256p. (YA). (gr. 7). 19.95 *(978-1-61374-710-0(1))* Chicago Review Pr., Inc.

Hoobler, Thomas & Hoobler, Dorothy. Real American Girls Tell Their Own Stories: Messages from the Heart & Heartland. 2012. (ENG.). 112p. (J). (gr. 5-9). pap. 6.99 *(978-1-4424-6043-0(1),* Simon & Schuster Bks. For Young Readers) Simon & Schuster Bks. For Young Readers.

Hoose, Phillip. Claudette Colvin: Twice Toward Justice. 2010. (ENG., Illus.). 160p. (YA). (gr. 8-12). pap. 9.99 *(978-0-312-66105-2(3),* 9780312661052) Square Fish.

Hopkins, H. Joseph. The Tree Lady: The True Story of How One Tree-Loving Woman Changed a City Forever. McElmurry, Jill, illus. 2013. (ENG.). 32p. (J). (gr. k-5). 17.99 *(978-1-4424-1402-0(2),* Beach Lane Bks.) Beach Lane Bks.

Hopkinson, Deborah. Annie & Helen. Colón, Raúl, illus. 2012. (ENG.). 48p. (J). (gr. -1-3). 17.99 *(978-0-375-85706-5(0),* Schwartz & Wade Bks.) Random Hse. Children's Bks.

—Michelle. Ford, A. G., illus. 2009. 32p. (J). (gr. -1-2). 17.99 *(978-0-06-182739-6(8))* HarperCollins Pubs.

Hopping, Lorraine Jean. Bone Detective: The Story of Forensic Anthropologist Diane France. 2005. (Women's Adventures in Science Ser.). (ENG., Illus.). 128p. (YA). (gr. 5-9). 31.50 *(978-0-531-16776-2(3))* Scholastic Library Publishing.

Horn, Geoffrey M. Laila Ali. 2006. (Today's Superstars). (Illus.). 32p. (gr. 5-8). lib. bdg. 31.95 *(978-0-8368-6181-5(7))* Stevens, Gareth Publishing LLLP.

—Margaret Mead. 2004. (Trailblazers of the Modern World Ser.). (Illus.). 48p. (gr. 5-12). pap. 14.05 *(978-0-8368-5259-2(1));* lib. bdg. 31.00 *(978-0-8368-5099-4(8))* Stevens, Gareth Publishing LLLP. (Gareth Stevens Secondary Library).

—Nancy Pelosi. 2009. (People We Should Know Ser.). 32p. (J). (gr. 3-5). pap. 10.50 *(978-1-4339-0162-1(5));* lib. bdg. 31.00 *(978-1-4339-0021-1(1))* Stevens, Gareth Publishing LLLP. (Gareth Stevens Learning Library).

Houts, Michelle. When Grandma Gatewood Took a Hike. Magnus, Erica, illus. 2016. (ENG.). 32p. (J). 17.95 *(978-0-8214-2235-9(9))* Ohio Univ. Pr.

Hull, Mary. Mary Todd Lincoln: Civil War's First Lady. 2015. (Legendary American Biographies Ser.). 96p. (J). (gr. 6-12). pap. 10.95 *(978-0-7660-6481-2(6))* Enslow Pubs., Inc.

Hull, Mary E. Mary Todd Lincoln: Civil War's First Lady. 2015. (Legendary American Biographies Ser.). 96p. (J). (gr. 6-12). 27.94 *(978-0-7660-6480-5(8))* Enslow Pubs., Inc.

Isbell, Hannah. Rihanna: Pop Star. 2017. (Junior Biographies Ser.). 24p. (gr. 3-4). lib. bdg. 22.60 ***(978-0-7660-8674-6(7))*** Enslow Pubs., Inc.

Jackson, Constance L. Over the River: Life of Lydia Maria Child, Abolitionist for Freedom, 1802-1880. 2008. (Illus.). 160p. pap. 18.95 *(978-0-9818204-0-8(9))* Permanent Productions Publishing.

Jackson, Garnet N. Shirley Chisholm, Congresswoman. 2012. (ENG., Illus.). (J). (gr. 1-4). pap. 7.47 net. *(978-0-8136-5247-4(2),* Modern Curriculum Pr.) Pearson Schl.

Jarrow, Jesse. Phillis Wheatley: African American Poet / Poeta Afroamericana. 2009. (Famous People in American History/Grandes personajes en la historia de los Estados Unidos Ser.). (ENG & SPA.). 32p. (gr. 2-3). 47.90 *(978-1-61512-554-8(X),* Editorial Buenas Letras) Rosen Publishing Group, Inc., The.

—Phillis Wheatley: Poeta afroamericana (Phillis Wheatley: African American Poet) 2009. (Grandes personajes en la historia de los Estados Unidos (Famous People in American History) Ser.). (SPA.). 32p. (gr. 2-3). 47.90 *(978-1-61512-807-5(7),* Editorial Buenas Letras) Rosen Publishing Group, Inc., The.

Jazynka, Kitson. Helen Keller. 2017. (Readers Bios Ser.). (ENG., Illus.). 32p. (J). (gr. k-3). pap. 3.99 *(978-1-4263-2669-1(6),* National Geographic Children's Bks.) National Geographic Society.

Jennifer Lawrence. 2013. (Rising Stars Ser.). 32p. (J). (gr. 3-6). pap. 63.00 *(978-1-4339-8979-7(4))* Stevens, Gareth Publishing LLLP.

Johnson, Robin. Kristen Stewart. 2010. (Superstars! Ser.). (ENG.). 32p. (J). pap. *(978-0-7787-7257-6(8))* Crabtree Publishing Co.

—Rihanna. 2013. (ENG., Illus.). 32p. (J). *(978-0-7787-1051-6(3));* pap. *(978-0-7787-1055-4(6))* Crabtree Publishing Co.

Johnston, Johanna. They Led the Way: 14 American Women. Hollinger, Deanne, illus. 2004. (ENG.). 128p. (J). (gr. 3-7). 5.99 *(978-0-14-240057-9(2),* Speak) Penguin Young Readers Group.

Jökulsson, Illugi. Alex Morgan. 2015. (World Soccer Legends Ser.). (ENG., Illus.). 64p. (J). (gr. 1). 13.95 *(978-0-7892-1216-0(1),* Abbeville Kids) Abbeville Pr., Inc.

Jones, Carrie. Sarah Emma Edmonds Was a Great Pretender: The True Story of a Civil War Spy. Oldroyd, Mark, illus. 2011. (Carolrhoda Picture Bks.). (ENG.). 32p. (J). (gr. 2-5). 17.95 *(978-0-7613-5399-7(2))* Lerner Publishing Group.

Jones, Jen. Oprah Winfrey: Celebrity with Heart. 2010. (Celebrities with Heart Ser.). (Illus.). 128p. (J). pap. 10.95 *(978-1-59845-206-8(1))* Enslow Pubs., Inc.

Jones, Joyce Adams. Remembering the Marches in Selma, Alabama. 2006. 8.00 *(978-0-8059-7237-5(4))* Dorrance Publishing Co., Inc.

Jordin Sparks. 2013. (Rising Stars Ser.). 32p. (J). (gr. 3-6). pap. 63.00 *(978-1-4339-8983-4(2))* Stevens, Gareth Publishing LLLP.

Juarez, Christine. Ellen Ochoa. 2016. (Great Hispanic & Latino Americans Ser.). (ENG.). 24p. (gr. k-1). lib. bdg. 21.99 *(978-1-5157-1888-8(3),* Pebble Bks.) Capstone Press of Coughlan Cos.

Kanefield, Teri. The Extraordinary Suzy Wright: A Colonial Woman on the Frontier. 2016. (ENG., Illus.). 64p. (J). (gr. 3-7). 19.95 *(978-1-4197-1866-3(5),* Abrams Bks. for Young Readers) Abrams, Inc.

—The Girl from the Tar Paper School: Barbara Rose Johns & the Advent of the Civil Rights Movement. 2014. (ENG., Illus.). 56p. (J). (gr. 3-7). 19.95 *(978-1-4197-0796-4(5),* Abrams Bks. for Young Readers) Abrams, Inc.

Kann, Bob. Cordelia Harvey: Civil War Angel. 2011. (Badger Biographies Ser.). (ENG., Illus.). 128p. (J). pap. 12.95 *(978-0-87020-458-6(0))* Wisconsin Historical Society.

—A Recipe for Success: Lizzie Kander & Her Cookbook. 2006. (Badger Biographies Ser.). (ENG., Illus.). 144p. (J). (gr. 3-7). per. 12.95 *(978-0-87020-373-2(8))* Wisconsin Historical Society.

Katirgis, Jane. Celebrating First Lady Michelle Obama in Pictures. 2009. (Obama Family Photo Album Ser.). (Illus.). 32p. (J). (gr. 2-5). lib. bdg. 23.94 *(978-0-7660-3652-9(9))* Enslow Pubs., Inc.

Kennon, Michou. Beyoncé. 2011. (Hip-Hop Headliners Ser.). (Illus.). 32p. (gr. 3-8). pap. 10.50 *(978-1-4339-4789-6(7));* (J). lib. bdg. 25.25 *(978-1-4339-4788-9(9))* Stevens, Gareth Publishing LLLP.

Kent, Deborah. Elizabeth Cady Stanton: Woman Knows the Cost of Life. 2010. (Americans—the Spirit of a Nation Ser.). (Illus.). 128p. (J). lib. bdg. 33.27 *(978-0-7660-3357-3(0))* Enslow Pubs., Inc.

Kerley, Barbara. What to Do about Alice? How Alice Roosevelt Broke the Rules, Charmed the World, & Drove Her Father Teddy Crazy! Fotheringham, Edwin, illus. 2008. (ENG.). 48p. (J). (gr. 2-5). 16.99 *(978-0-439-92231-9(3),* Scholastic Pr.) Scholastic, Inc.

Kessel, Kristin. Martha Graham. 2009. (Library of American Choreographers Ser.). 48p. (gr. 5-8). 53.00 *(978-1-60853-460-9(X),* Rosen Reference) Rosen Publishing Group, Inc., The.

King, David C. Dorothea Lange: Photographer of the People. 2009. (ENG., Illus.). 88p. (C). (gr. 6-18). lib. bdg. 158.00 *(978-0-7656-8154-6(4),* Y181941) Routledge.

Kirkpatrick, Rob. Mia Hamm: Soccer Star. 2009. (Great Record Breakers in Sports Ser.). 24p. (gr. 3-3). 42.50 *(978-1-61513-189-1(2),* PowerKids Pr.) Rosen Publishing Group, Inc., The.

—Tara Lipinski: Super Ice-Skater. 2009. (Great Record Breakers in Sports Ser.). 24p. (gr. 3-3). 42.50 *(978-1-61513-191-4(4),* PowerKids Pr.) Rosen Publishing Group, Inc., The.

Kishel, Ann-Marie. Jane Addams: A Life of Cooperation. (Pull Ahead Books-Biographies Ser.). 32p. 2007. (ENG.). (gr. k-3). pap. 7.95 *(978-0-8225-6436-2(X))* 2006. (Illus.). (J). (gr. 3-7). lib. bdg. 22.60 *(978-0-8225-6382-2(7),* Lerner Pubns.) Lerner Publishing Group.

—Rosa Parks: A Life of Courage. 2006. (Pull Ahead Books-Biographies Ser.). (ENG., Illus.). 32p. (gr. k-3). lib. bdg. 22.60 *(978-0-8225-3478-5(9),* Lerner Pubns.) Lerner Publishing Group.

Klepeis, Alicia. Calamity Jane: Frontierswoman. Lapegüe, Matias, illus. 2016. (American Legends & Folktales Ser.). 32p. (J). pap. 10.58 *(978-1-5026-2200-6(9));* lib. bdg. 28.50 *(978-1-5026-2202-0(5))* Cavendish Square Publishing.

Kovatch, Sarah. Record Breaking Woman. 2005. (Voices Reading Ser.). (Illus.). 16p. (J). *(978-0-7367-2914-7(3))* Zaner-Bloser, Inc.

Kraft, Betsy Harvey. Mother Jones: One Woman's Fight for Labor. 2006. (Illus.). 116p. (YA). (gr. 6-10). reprint ed. 17.00 *(978-1-4223-5443-8(1))* DIANE Publishing Co.

Krass. Sojourner Truth. 2004. (Black Americans of Achievement Ser.). (Illus.). 112p. (gr. 6-12). 35.00 *(978-0-7910-8165-5(6),* Chelsea Hse.) Facts On File, Inc.

Krebs, Laurie. A Day in the Life of a Colonial Indigo Planter. 2009. (Library of Living & Working in Colonial Times Ser.). 24p. (gr. 3-3). 42.50 *(978-1-60853-732-7(3),* PowerKids Pr.) Rosen Publishing Group, Inc., The.

Krensky, Stephen. Calamity Jane. 2008. pap. 40.95 *(978-0-8225-9291-4(6))* Lerner Publishing Group.

Krohn, Katherine E. Madam C. J. Walker & New Cosmetics, 1 vol. Dominguez, Richard et al, illus. 2006. (Inventions & Discovery Ser.). (ENG.). 32p. (gr. 3-4). 8.10 *(978-0-7368-9647-4(3),* Graphic Library) Capstone Press of Coughlan Cos.

—Oprah Winfrey. 2003. (Biography Ser.). (Illus.). 112p. (J). (gr. 6-18). pap. 7.95 *(978-0-8225-5000-6(8))* Lerner Publishing Group.

—Vera Wang. 2007. (Biography Ser.). (Illus.). 112p. (J). (gr. 3-7). lib. bdg. 29.27 *(978-0-8225-6612-0(5),* Twenty-First Century Bks.) Lerner Publishing Group.

—Vera Wang: Enduring Style. 2008. (USA TODAY Lifeline Biographies Ser.). (ENG.). 112p. (gr. 6-12). lib. bdg. 34.60 *(978-1-58013-572-6(2))* Lerner Publishing Group.

—Women of the Wild West. 2003. (Biography Ser.). (Illus.). 112p. (YA). (gr. 6-18). pap. 7.95 *(978-0-8225-9690-5(3),* Carolrhoda Bks.) Lerner Publishing Group.

Krull, Kathleen. Dolley Madison: Parties Can Be Patriotic! Fancher, Lou & Johnson, Steve, illus. 2015. (Women Who Broke the Rules Ser.). (ENG.). 48p. (J). (gr. 1-4). 16.99 *(978-0-8027-3793-9(5),* 9780802737939, Bloomsbury USA Childrens) Bloomsbury Publishing USA.

—A Kids' Guide to America's First Ladies. DiVito, Anna, illus. 2017. (Kids' Guide to American History Ser.: 1). 256p. (J). (gr. 3-7). pap. 6.99 *(978-0-06-238106-4(7))* HarperCollins Pubs.

—A Woman for President: The Story of Victoria Woodhull. Dyer, Jane, illus. 2006. (J). (gr. 2-7). 14.60 *(978-0-7569-8179-2(4))* Perfection Learning Corp.

Kudlinski, Kathleen. Sojourner Truth: Voice for Freedom. Wooden, Lenny, illus. 2003. (Childhood of Famous Americans Ser.). (ENG.). 160p. (Orig.). (J). (gr. 3-7). mass mkt. 7.99 *(978-0-689-85274-9(6),* Simon & Schuster/Paula Wiseman Bks.) Simon & Schuster/Paula Wiseman Bks.

Kudlinski, Kathleen V. Rebel with a Cause: The Daring Adventure of Dicey Langston, Girl Spy of the American Revolution. Faber, Rudy, illus. 2015. (Encounter: Narrative Nonfiction Picture Bks.). (ENG.). 40p. (gr. 3-4). lib. bdg. 28.65 *(978-1-4914-6073-3(3))* Encounter Bks.

Kulling, Monica. In the Bag! Margaret Knight Wraps It Up. Parkins, David, illus. 2011. (Great Idea Ser.). (ENG.). 32p. (J). (gr. k-3). 17.95 *(978-1-77049-239-4(9),* Tundra Bks.) Tundra Bks. CAN. Dist: Penguin Random Hse. LLC.

—Spic-and-Span! Lillian Gilbreth's Wonder Kitchen. Parkins, David, illus. 2016. (Great Idea Ser.). (ENG.). 32p. (J). (gr. k-3). pap. 6.99 *(978-1-101-91843-2(8),* Tundra Bks.) Tundra Bks. CAN. Dist: Penguin Random Hse. LLC.

Kunstler, James Howard. Annie Oakley, 1 vol. Warter, Fred, illus. 2004. (Rabbit Ears-A Classic Tale Ser.). (ENG.). 36p. (gr. k-5). 25.65 *(978-1-59197-759-9(2))* Spotlight.

Labrecque, Ellen. Gertrude B. Elion & Pharmacology. 2017. (21st Century Junior Library: Women Innovators Ser.). (ENG., Illus.). 24p. (J). (gr. 2-5). lib. bdg. 27.07 *(978-1-63472-182-0(9),* 209300) Cherry Lake Publishing.

—Mary Anderson & Windshield Wipers. 2017. (21st Century Junior Library: Women Innovators Ser.). (ENG., Illus.). 24p. (J). (gr. 2-5). lib. bdg. 27.07 *(978-1-63472-178-3(0),* 209284) Cherry Lake Publishing.

Lakin, Patricia. Abigail Adams: First Lady of the American Revolution. Bandelin, Debra & Dacey, Bob, illus. 2006. 48p. (J). lib. bdg. 15.00 *(978-1-4242-1560-7(9))* Fitzgerald Bks.

Lang, Glenna & Wunsch, Marjory. Genius of Common Sense: Jane Jacobs & the Story of the Death & Life of Great American Cities. 2012. pap. 15.95 *(978-1-56792-456-5(5))* Godine, David R. Pub.

Lang, Glenna W. & Wunsch, Marjory. Genius of Common Sense: Jane Jacobs & the Story of the Death & Life of Great American Cities. 2009. (ENG., Illus.). 128p. (YA). (gr. 5-18). 17.95 *(978-1-56792-384-1(4))* Godine, David R. Pub.

Lang, Heather. Queen of the Track: Alice Coachman, Olympic High-Jump Champion. Cooper, Floyd, illus. 2012. (ENG.). 40p. (J). (gr. k). 16.95 *(978-1-59078-850-9(8))* Boyds Mills Pr.

Lantier, Patricia. Harriet Tubman: Conductor on the Underground Railroad. 2009. (Voices for Freedom Ser.). (ENG., Illus.). 64p. (J). (gr. 5-8). pap. *(978-0-7787-4838-0(3));* lib. bdg. *(978-0-7787-4822-9(7))* Crabtree Publishing Co.

Larkin, Tanya. What Was Cooking in Julia Grant's White House? 2009. (Cooking Throughout American History Ser.). 24p. (gr. 3-3). 42.50 *(978-1-61511-952-3(3),* PowerKids Pr.) Rosen Publishing Group, Inc., The.

Lasky, Kathryn. Vision of Beauty: The Story of Sarah Breedlove Walker. Bennett, Nneka, illus. 2012. (Candlewick Biographies Ser.). (ENG.). 56p. (J). (gr. 3-7). 14.99 *(978-0-7636-6428-2(6));* pap. 4.99 *(978-0-7636-6092-5(2))* Candlewick Pr.

Lassieur, Allison. Eleanor Roosevelt: Activist for Social Change. 2006. (Great Life Stories Ser.). (ENG., Illus.). 112p. (J). (gr. 6-8). lib. bdg. 30.50 *(978-0-531-13871-7(2),* Watts, Franklin) Scholastic Library Publishing.

Latham, Donna. Norah Jones. (Sharing the American Dream Ser.). 64p. (YA). (gr. 7-12). 2009. 22.95 *(978-1-4222-0590-7(8))* 2007. pap. 9.95 *(978-1-4222-0751-2(X))* Mason Crest.

Lauber, Leah F. Soccer Dreams: My True Adventure Following the U. S. Women's National Soccer Team, As a Fan & 12-Year Old Junior Reporter for the St. Petersburg Times During the History-Making 1999 FIFA Women's World Cup! 2003. (Illus.). 96p. (YA). per. 19.99 *(978-0-9745480-0-5(6))* WCI Pr.

Leavitt, Amie Jane. Nancy Pelosi. 2007. (Blue Banner Biography Ser.). (Illus.). 32p. (YA). (gr. 4-7). lib. bdg. 25.70 *(978-1-58415-613-0(9))* Mitchell Lane Pubs., Inc.

—What It's Like to Be Miley Cyrus. Vega, Eida de la, tr. 2009. (What It's Like to Be/Que se Siente al Ser Ser.). (SPA & ENG., Illus.). 32p. (J). (gr. -1-2). lib. bdg. 25.70 *(978-1-58415-841-7(7))* Mitchell Lane Pubs., Inc.

Lee, Sally. Eleanor Roosevelt, 1 vol. 2010. (First Ladies Ser.). (ENG.). 24p. (gr. k-1). pap. 7.29 *(978-1-4296-5603-0(4));* pap. 41.70 *(978-1-4296-5604-7(2))* Capstone Press of Coughlan Cos. (Pebble Plus).

—Hillary Clinton, 1 vol. 2010. (First Ladies Ser.). (ENG.). 24p. (gr. k-1). lib. bdg. 26.65 *(978-1-4296-5327-5(2),* Pebble Plus) Capstone Press of Coughlan Cos.

—Martha Washington, 1 vol. 2010. (First Ladies Ser.). (ENG.). 24p. (gr. k-1). pap. 7.29 *(978-1-4296-5605-4(0),* Pebble Plus) Capstone Press of Coughlan Cos.

Letters of a Woman Homesteader. 2003. (Our American Heritage Ser.). (J). pap. 62.00 incl. audio compact disk *(978-1-58472-527-5(3),* In Audio) Sound Room Pubs., Inc.

Lew, Kristi. Laurie Halse Anderson. 2013. (All about the Author Ser.). 112p. (YA). (gr. 7-12). 34.60 *(978-1-4777-1764-6(1))* Rosen Publishing Group, Inc., The.

Lewis, Meharry H. Mary Lena Lewis Tate - Vision! The Woman Who Compassed a Man 2005. (Illus.). 484p. 74.95 *(978-0-910003-08-7(4))* New & Living Way Publishing Co.

Linde, Barbara M. Taylor Swift. 2010. (Today's Superstars Ser.). (ENG.). 48p. (J). (gr. 5-8). pap. 14.05 *(978-1-4339-4002-6(7));* lib. bdg. 31.95 *(978-1-4339-4001-9(9))* Stevens, Gareth Publishing LLLP.

Litwin, Laura Baskes. Dorothea Lange: A Life in Pictures. 2007. (People to Know Today Ser.). (Illus.). 128p. (J). (gr. 3-7). lib. bdg. 33.27 *(978-0-7660-2697-1(3))* Enslow Pubs., Inc.

Lloyd, Carli & Coffey, Wayne. All Heart: My Dedication & Determination to Become One of Soccer's Best. 2016. (ENG., Illus.). 304p. (J). (gr. 5-7). 16.99 *(978-0-544-97869-0(2),* HMH Books For Young Readers) Houghton Mifflin Harcourt Publishing Co.

Lobb, Nancy. 16 Extraordinary Americans with Disabilities. 2nd ed. 2007. (16 Extraordinary Ser.). (Illus.). 139p. (J). (gr. 3-7). tchr. ed., per. 25.00 *(978-0-8251-6278-7(5))* Walch Education.

Lobby, Mackenzie. Babe Didrikson Zaharias: Groundbreaking All-Around Athlete, 1 vol. 2011. (Legendary Athletes Ser.). (ENG., Illus.). 112p. (YA). (gr. 7-12). 34.22 *(978-1-61714-755-5(9))* ABDO Publishing Co.

Lohse, Joyce B. Unsinkable: The Molly Brown Story. 2006. (Now You Know Bio Ser.). (Illus.). 76p. (J). pap. 8.95 *(978-0-86541-081-7(X))* Filter Pr., LLC.

Lowery, Linda. Aunt Clara Brown: Official Pioneer. Porter, Janice Lee, illus. 2006. (On My Own Biographies Ser.). 48p. 16.95 *(978-0-7569-6699-7(X))* Perfection Learning Corp.

—Tía Clara Brown: Pionera Oficial. Porter, Janice Lee, illus. 2005. (Yo Solo Biografías Ser.). (SPA.). 48p. (J). (gr. 2-4). per. 6.95 *(978-0-8225-3129-6(1))* Lerner Publishing Group.

Lynette, Rachel. Julia Butterfly Hill: Saving the Ancient Redwoods. 2007. (Young Heros Ser.). (ENG., Illus.). 48p. (J). (gr. 4-7). lib. bdg. 30.50 *(978-0-7377-3628-1(3),* Kidhaven) Cengage Gale.

MacBain, Jennifer. Gertrude Elion: Nobel Prize Winner in Physiology & Medicine. 2009. (Women Hall of Famers in Mathematics & Science Ser.). 112p. (gr. 5-8). 63.90 *(978-1-60854-811-8(2),* Rosen Reference) Rosen Publishing Group, Inc., The.

Mack, Lorna B. Lorna's Whale. 2011. 56p. pap. 26.12 *(978-1-4634-1610-2(5))* AuthorHouse.

MacLeod, Elizabeth. Helen Keller: A Determined Life. 2004. (Snapshots: Images of People & Places in History Ser.). (ENG., Illus.). 32p. (J). (gr. 3-7). 7.95 *(978-1-55337-509-8(2))* Kids Can Pr., Ltd. CAN. Dist: Hachette Bk. Group.

Macy, Sue. Basketball Belles: How Two Teams & One Scrappy Player Put Women's Hoops on the Map. Collins, Matt & Matt, Collins, illus. 2011. (ENG.). 32p. (J). (gr. 1-5). 17.95 *(978-0-8234-2163-3(5))* Holiday Hse., Inc.

—Bull's Eye: A Photobiography of Annie Oakley. 2015. (Photobiographies Ser.). (ENG.). 64p. (J). (gr. 5). pap. 7.99 *(978-1-4263-2218-1(6),* National Geographic Children's Bks.) National Geographic Society.

—Bylines: A Photobiography of Nellie Bly. 2009. (Photobiographies Ser.). (ENG., Illus.). 64p. (J). (gr. 5). 28.90 *(978-1-4263-0514-6(1));* 19.95 *(978-1-4263-0513-9(3))* National Geographic Society. (National Geographic Children's Bks.).

—Miss Mary Reporting. Payne, C. F., illus. 2016. (ENG.). 40p. (J). (gr. k-3). 17.99 *(978-1-4814-0120-3(3),* Simon & Schuster Bks. For Young Readers) Simon & Schuster Bks. For Young Readers.

Mah, Adeline Yen. Chinese Cinderella. 2010. (ENG.). 240p. (YA). (gr. 7). pap. 9.99 *(978-0-385-74007-4(7),* Ember) Random Hse. Children's Bks.

Maher, Jack. Animal Instincts. 2011. (J). pap. *(978-0-531-22560-8(7))* Scholastic, Inc.

Maimone, Sofia Z. Mary J. Blige. 2011. (Hip-Hop Headliners Ser.). (Illus.). 32p. (J). (gr. 3-8). 25.25 *(978-1-4339-4804-6(4));* pap. 10.50 *(978-1-4339-4805-3(2))* Stevens, Gareth Publishing LLLP.

Malaspina, Ann. Harriet Tubman. 2009. (Leaders of the Civil War Era Ser.). (Illus.). 120p. (gr. 6-12). 35.00 *(978-1-60413-303-5(1),* Chelsea Hse.) Facts On File, Inc.

Mallory, Mark. Amelia Earhart: Queen of the Sky. 2009. (Real Life Readers Ser.). 16p. (gr. 2-3). pap. 7.05 *(978-1-4358-0053-3(2),* Rosen Classroom) Rosen Publishing Group, Inc., The.

Maloof, Torrey. Mary Musgrove: Bringing People Together. 2016. (Primary Source Readers Ser.). (Illus.). 32p. (gr. 2-2). 8.99 *(978-1-4938-2557-8(7))* Teacher Created Materials, Inc.

Manzano, Sonia. Becoming Maria: Love & Chaos in the South Bronx. 2015. (ENG.). 272p. (J). (gr. 7). 17.99 *(978-0-545-62184-7(4),* Scholastic Pr.) Scholastic, Inc.

Mapua, Jeff. Hillary Clinton, 1 vol. 2015. (ENG., Illus.). 32p. (J). 23.45 *(978-1-62275-689-6(4),* Britannica Educational Publishing) Rosen Publishing Group, Inc., The.

Mara, Wil. Amelia Earhart. 2014. (Rookie Biographies(tm) Ser.). (ENG.). 32p. (J). lib. bdg. 25.00 *(978-0-531-21059-8(6))* Scholastic Library Publishing.

—Laura Bush. 2003. (Rookie Biographies Ser.). (ENG., Illus.). 32p. (J). (gr. 1-2). 20.50 *(978-0-516-22854-9(4),* Children's Pr.) Scholastic Library Publishing.

—Laura Ingalls Wilder. 2003. (Rookie Biographies Ser.). (ENG., Illus.). 32p. (J). (gr. 1-2). 20.50 *(978-0-516-22855-6(2),* Children's Pr.) Scholastic Library Publishing.

—Rosa Parks. (Rookie Biographies Ser.). (ENG., Illus.). 32p. (J). (gr. 1-2). 2004. pap. 4.95 *(978-0-516-27916-9(5))* 2007. pap. 4.95 *(978-0-531-12592-2(0))* Scholastic Library Publishing. (Children's Pr.).

—Rosa Parks: Mother of the Civil Rights Movement. 2014. (Rookie Biographies(r) Ser.). (ENG.). 32p. (J). pap. 5.95 *(978-0-531-21204-2(1))* Scholastic Library Publishing.

Mara, Wil & National Geographic Learning Staff. Laura Ingalls Wilder. 2010. (Rise & Shine Ser.). (ENG.). 32p. (C). (gr. 1-2). pap. 7.95 *(978-0-516-27840-7(1))* National Geographic School Publishing, Inc.

Marcovitz, Hal. Venus & Serena Williams. 2012. (Role Model Athletes Ser.). 64p. (J). (gr. 7). 22.95 *(978-1-4222-2714-5(6))* Mason Crest.

Markarian, Margie. Hilary Duff: Life in the Spotlight. 2009. (Hot Celebrity Biographies Ser.). (Illus.). 48p. (J). (gr. 5-9). pap. 8.95 *(978-0-7660-3626-0(X))* Enslow Pubs., Inc.

Markel, Michelle. Hillary Rodham Clinton: Some Girls Are Born to Lead. Pham, LeUyen, illus. 2016. 40p. (J). (gr. -1-3). 17.99 *(978-0-06-238122-4(9))* HarperCollins Pubs.

Marlgorz, Juliet. Elizabeth Cady Stanton & the Fight for Equal Rights. 2009. (Real Life Readers Ser.). 32p. (gr. 4-6). pap. 10.00 *(978-1-4358-0233-9(0),* Rosen Classroom) Rosen Publishing Group, Inc., The.

Marsh, Carole. Abigail Adams. 2004. 12p. (gr. k-4). 2.95 *(978-0-635-02372-8(5))* Gallopade International.

—Amelia Earhart. 2003. 12p. (gr. k-4). 2.95 *(978-0-635-02131-1(5))* Gallopade International.

—Antonia C. Novello: First Female U. S. Surgeon General: First Female U. S. Surgeon General. 2003. 12p. (gr. k-4). 2.95 *(978-0-635-02139-7(0))* Gallopade International.

—Carol Moseley Braun. 2003. 12p. (gr. k-4). 2.95 *(978-0-635-02384-1(9))* Gallopade International.

—Clara Barton. 2003. 12p. (gr. k-4). 2.95 *(978-0-635-02353-7(9))* Gallopade International.

—Condoleezza Rice. 2003. 12p. (gr. k-4). 2.95 *(978-0-635-02385-8(7))* Gallopade International.

—Ellen Ochoa: First Hispanic American Woman in Space: First Hispanic American Woman in Space. 2003. 12p. (gr. k-4). 2.95 *(978-0-635-02138-0(2))* Gallopade International.

—Harriet Beecher Stowe. 2003. 12p. (gr. k-4). 2.95 *(978-0-635-02356-8(3))* Gallopade International.

—Meet Shirley Franklin, Mayor of Atlanta! 2003. 32p. (gr. 3-8). 21.95 *(978-0-635-01141-1(7))* Gallopade International.

—Molly Pitcher. 2004. 12p. (gr. k-4). 2.95 *(978-0-635-02375-9(X))* Gallopade International.
—Phillis Wheatley. 2003. 12p. (gr. k-4). 2.95 *(978-0-635-02371-1(7))* Gallopade International.
—Rachel Carson: Excellent Ecologist. 2004. (1000 Readers Ser.). (Illus.). 14p. (J). (gr. k-4). pap. 2.95 *(978-0-635-02524-1(8))* Gallopade International.
—Sacagawea: Native American Heroine: Native American Heroine. 2003. 12p. (gr. k-4). 2.95 *(978-0-635-02143-4(9))* Gallopade International.
—Sojourner Truth. 2003. 12p. (gr. k-4). 2.95 *(978-0-635-02355-1(5))* Gallopade International.
Martin, Isabel. Wilma Rudolph, 1 vol. 2014. (Great African-Americans Ser.). (ENG., Illus.). 24p. (gr. k-1). lib. bdg. 21.99 *(978-1-4914-0503-1(1),* Pebble Bks.) Capstone Press of Coughlan Cos.
Marx, Trish. Jeannette Rankin: First Lady of Congress. Andreasen, Dan, illus. 2013. (ENG.). 48p. (J). (gr. 2-5). 19.99 *(978-1-4424-9618-7(5),* McElderry, Margaret K. Bks.) McElderry, Margaret K. Bks.
Mattern, Joanne. Coretta Scott King: Civil Rights Activist. 2003. (Reading Power Ser.). (Illus.). 24p. (J). lib. bdg. 19.95 *(978-0-8239-6504-5(X),* PowerKids Pr.) Rosen Publishing Group, Inc., The.
—Eleanor Roosevelt: More Than a First Lady. (Women Who Shaped History Ser.). 24p. 2009. (gr. 2-3). 42.50 *(978-1-60854-817-0(1))* 2003. (Illus.). (J). lib. bdg. 22.60 *(978-0-8239-6501-4(5))* Rosen Publishing Group, Inc., The. (PowerKids Pr.).
—Elizabeth Cady Stanton & Susan B. Anthony: Fighting Together for Women's Rights. 2003. (Women Who Shaped History Ser.). (Illus.). 24p. (J). lib. bdg. 22.60 *(978-0-8239-6503-8(1),* PowerKids Pr.) Rosen Publishing Group, Inc., The.
—Helen Keller. 2015. (Rookie Biographies(r) Ser.). (ENG., Illus.). 32p. (J). pap. 5.95 *(978-0-531-20995-0(4))* Scholastic Library Publishing.
—Kim Kardashian: Reality TV Star, 1 vol. 2012. (Contemporary Lives Set 1 Ser.). (ENG.). 112p. (J). (gr. 6-12). lib. bdg. 35.64 *(978-1-61783-326-7(6))* ABDO Publishing Co.
—Sojourner Truth: Early Abolitionist. (Women Who Shaped History Ser.). 24p. 2009. (gr. 2-3). 42.50 *(978-1-60854-821-7(X))* 2003. (Illus.). (J). lib. bdg. 22.60 *(978-0-8239-6502-1(3))* Rosen Publishing Group, Inc., The. (PowerKids Pr.).
—What's So Great about Michelle Obama. 2009. (What's So Great About... ? Ser.). 32p. (J). (gr. 2-4). lib. bdg. 25.70 *(978-1-58415-833-2(6))* Mitchell Lane Pubs., Inc.
Mayo, Edith P., ed. The Smithsonian Book of the First Ladies. 2004. (J). 29.95 *(978-0-8050-7272-3(1),* Holt, Henry & Co. Bks. For Young Readers) Holt, Henry & Co.
McAneney, Caitie. Simone Biles: Greatest Gymnast of All Time. 2017. (Breakout Biographies Ser.). 32p. (J). (gr. 9-10). 26.25 ***(978-1-5081-6072-4(4))***; pap. 10.00 ***(978-1-5081-6070-0(8))*** Rosen Publishing Group, Inc., The. (PowerKids Pr.).
McAneney, Caitie. 20 Fun Facts about Native American Women. 2015. (Fun Fact File: Women in History Ser.). (ENG., Illus.). 32p. (J). (gr. 2-3). 25.25 *(978-1-4824-2810-0(5))* Stevens, Gareth Publishing LLLP.
McCarthy, Meghan. Daredevil: The Daring Life of Betty Skelton. McCarthy, Meghan, illus. 2013. (ENG., Illus.). 48p. (J). (gr. -1-3). 17.99 *(978-1-4424-2262-9(9),* Simon & Schuster/Paula Wiseman Bks.) Simon & Schuster/Paula Wiseman Bks.
McCully, Emily Arnold. Queen of the Diamond: The Lizzie Murphy Story. 2015. (ENG., Illus.). 32p. (J). (gr. k-3). 17.99 *(978-0-374-30007-4(0),* 9780374300074, Farrar, Straus & Giroux (BYR)) Farrar, Straus & Giroux.
McDaniel, Jequita Potts. Mardy Murie Did! Grandmother of Conservation. Van Zyle, Jon, illus. 2011. (J). *(978-1-58979-525-9(3))* Taylor Trade Publishing.
McDaniel, Jequite Po & Van Zyle, Jon. Mardi Murie Did! Grandmother of Conservation. 2011. (ENG., Illus.). 32p. (J). (gr. -1-2). 15.95 *(978-1-58979-565-5(2))* Taylor Trade Publishing.
McDonough, Yona Zeldis. Little Author in the Big Woods: A Biography of Laura Ingalls Wilder. Thermes, Jennifer, illus. 2014. (ENG.). 176p. (J). (gr. 3-7). 16.99 *(978-0-8050-9542-5(X),* 9780805095425, Holt, Henry & Co. Bks. For Young Readers) Holt, Henry & Co.
—Who Was Rosa Parks? Harrison, Nancy & Marchesi, Stephen, illus. 2010. (Who Was? Ser.). (ENG.). 112p. (J). (gr. 3-7). pap. 5.99 *(978-0-448-45442-9(4),* Grosset & Dunlap) Penguin Young Readers Group.
McGintry, Alice B. Cynthia Rylant. 2009. (Library of Author Biographies Ser.). 112p. (gr. 5-8). 63.90 *(978-1-60853-530-9(4),* Rosen Reference) Rosen Publishing Group, Inc., The.
McGinty, Alice B. Meet Eve Bunting. 2009. (About the Author Ser.). 24p. (gr. 4-4). 42.50 *(978-1-61511-248-7(0),* PowerKids Pr.) Rosen Publishing Group, Inc., The.
—Meet Jane Yolen. 2009. (About the Author Ser.). 24p. (gr. 4-4). 42.50 *(978-1-61511-252-4(9),* PowerKids Pr.) Rosen Publishing Group, Inc., The.
—Sharon Creech. 2009. (Library of Author Biographies Ser.). 112p. (gr. 5-8). 63.90 *(978-1-60853-555-2(X),* Rosen Reference) Rosen Publishing Group, Inc., The.
McKissack, Patricia C. & McKissack, Fredrick, Jr. Sojourner Truth: Ain't I a Woman? 2003. (Illus.). 186p. (gr. 4-7). 17.20 *(978-0-7857-2515-2(6),* Turtleback) Turtleback Bks.
McLendon, Jacquelyn. Phillis Wheatley: A Revolutionary Poet. 2009. (Library of American Lives & Times Ser.). 112p. (gr. 5-5). 69.20 *(978-1-60853-499-9(5))* Rosen Publishing Group, Inc., The.
Meade, Marion. Free Woman: The Life & Times of Victoria Woodhull. 2011. 176p. pap. 15.95 *(978-1-61756-052-1(9))* Open Road Integrated Media, Inc.
Medearis, Angela Shelf. Coretta Scott King: Dare to Dream. Rich, Anna, illus. 2014. (Women of Our Time Ser.). (ENG.). 96p. (J). (gr. 3-7). 7.99 *(978-0-14-751363-2(4),* Puffin Books) Penguin Young Readers Group.
Mello, Tara Baukus. Danica Patrick. 2007. (Race Car Legends Ser.). (Illus.). 71p. (YA). (gr. 5-9). lib. bdg. 25.00 *(978-0-7910-9126-5(0))* Facts On File, Inc.
Meltzer, Brad. I Am Helen Keller. Eliopoulos, Christopher, illus. 2015. (Ordinary People Change the World Ser.). (ENG.). 40p. (J). (gr. k-3). 14.99 *(978-0-525-42851-0(8),* Dial Bks) Penguin Young Readers Group.
Michelle Obama. 2009. (Political Profiles Ser.). 112p. (YA). (gr. 5-9). lib. bdg. 28.95 *(978-1-59935-090-5(4))* Reynolds, Morgan Inc.
Miklowitz, Gloria D. Amelia Earhart. 2004. (ENG., Illus.). 31p. (J). (gr. 2-5). pap. 7.33 *(978-0-7685-1213-7(1),* Dominie Elementary) Pearson Schl.
Miller, Brandon Marie. Women of Colonial America: 13 Stories of Courage & Survival in the New World. 2016. (Women of Action Ser.). (ENG., Illus.). 256p. (YA). (gr. 7). 19.95 *(978-1-55652-487-5(0))* Chicago Review Pr., Inc.
Miller, Connie Colwell. Danica Patrick, 1 vol. 2013. (NASCAR Heroes Ser.). (ENG.). 32p. (J). (gr. 3-9). lib. bdg. 27.07 *(978-1-61783-666-4(4),* SportsZone) ABDO Publishing Co.
—Mother Jones: Labor Leader, 1 vol. Erwin, Steve & Barnett, Charles, III, illus. 2006. (Graphic Biographies Ser.). (ENG.). 32p. (gr. 3-4). per. 8.10 *(978-0-7368-9662-7(7),* Graphic Library) Capstone Press of Coughlan Cos.
Miller, Dean & Talbot, Jeffrey. Annie Oakley. 2014. (Illus.). 32p. (J). 28.50 *(978-1-62712-286-3(9))* Cavendish Square Publishing.
Miller, Debra A. Dolores Huerta: Labor Leader. 2006. (Twentieth Century's Most Influential Hispanics Ser.). (ENG., Illus.). 104p. (YA). (gr. 7-12). lib. bdg. 34.80 *(978-1-59018-971-9(X))* Cengage Gale.
Miller, Kat. I Love Taylor Swift. 2010. (Fan Club Ser.). (ENG.). 24p. (J). (gr. 3-6). lib. bdg. 22.60 *(978-1-61533-051-5(8))*; (Illus.). pap. 8.15 *(978-1-61533-052-2(6))* Windmill Bks.
Mills, Nathan & Peck, Audrey. Helen Keller: Miracle Child. 2012. (Rosen Readers Ser.). (ENG., Illus.). 24p. (J). (gr. 1-2). pap. 8.25 *(978-1-4488-8824-5(7),* Rosen Classroom) Rosen Publishing Group, Inc., The.
Miriam Colon, Actriz y Fundadora de Teatro. 2003. 94.95 *(978-0-8136-9219-7(9))*; pap. 48.95 *(978-0-8136-9207-4(5))* Modern Curriculum Pr.
Moore, Kaitlin. Kerri Strug & & the Magnificent Seven. 2016. (Totally True Adventures Ser.). (ENG., Illus.). 112p. (J). (gr. 1-4). pap. 4.99 *(978-0-553-52174-0(8),* Random Hse. Bks. for Young Readers) Random Hse. Children's Bks.
Morales, Leslie. Esther Dyson: Internet Visionary. 2003. (Internet Biographies Ser.). (Illus.). 48p. (J). (gr. 4-10). lib. bdg. 23.93 *(978-0-7660-1973-7(X))* Enslow Pubs., Inc.
Morgan, Terri. Venus & Serena Williams: Grand Slam Sisters. (Sports Achievers Biographies Ser.). (Illus.). 2005. 80p. (gr. 7-12). lib. bdg. 22.60 *(978-0-8225-3684-0(6))* 2003. 64p. (J). (gr. 4-9). pap. 5.95 *(978-0-8225-9866-4(3),* Carolrhoda Bks.) Lerner Publishing Group.
Morganelli, Adrianna. Wilma Rudolph: Track & Field Champion. 2016. (Remarkable Lives Revealed Ser.). (ENG.). 32p. (J). (gr. 2-5). *(978-0-7787-2689-0(4))* Crabtree Publishing Co.
Moriarty, J. T. Phillis Wheatley: African American Poet. 2009. (Primary Sources of Famous People in American History Ser.). 32p. (gr. 2-3). 47.90 *(978-1-60851-717-6(9))* Rosen Publishing Group, Inc., The.
Morretta, Alison. Ida B. Wells-Barnett & the Crusade Against Lynching. 2016. (Primary Sources of the Civil Rights Movement Ser.). (Illus.). 64p. (J). (gr. 6-6). 34.21 *(978-1-5026-1874-0(5))* Cavendish Square Publishing.
Morris, Roz. Rosa Parks: Mother of the Civil Rights Movement. 2003. (Alabama Roots Biography Ser.). (Illus.). 109p. (J). *(978-1-878561-57-2(X))* Seacoast Publishing, Inc.
Moss, Marissa. Brave Harriet. Payne, C. F., illus. 2015. 32p. pap. 8.00 *(978-1-61003-492-0(9))* Center for the Collaborative Classroom.
—The Bravest Woman in America. U'Ren, Andrea, illus. 2011. (ENG.). 32p. (J). (gr. k-3). 16.99 *(978-1-58246-369-8(7),* Tricycle Pr.) Random Hse. Children's Bks.
—Mighty Jackie: The Strike-Out Queen. Payne, C. F., tr. Payne, C. F., illus. 2004. (ENG.). 32p. (J). (gr. k-3). 18.99 *(978-0-689-86329-5(2),* Simon & Schuster/Paula Wiseman Bks.) Simon & Schuster/Paula Wiseman Bks.
—Nurse, Soldier, Spy: The Story of Sarah Edmonds, a Civil War Hero. Hendrix, John, illus. 2011. (ENG.). 48p. (J). (gr. 3-7). 19.95 *(978-0-8109-9735-6(5),* Abrams Bks. for Young Readers) Abrams, Inc.
Mueller, Marilyn J. Thank You God for Everything! Gracias a Dios por Todo. 2007. pap. 11.00 *(978-0-8059-8648-8(0))* Dorrance Publishing Co., Inc.
Mueller, Pamela Bauer. Aloha Crossing. 2008. (Aloha Set Ser.: 2). (ENG., Illus.). 176p. (J). (gr. 3-7). pap. 8.99 *(978-0-9685097-9-1(7))* Pinata Publishing CAN. Dist: Midpoint Trade Bks., Inc.
Murphy, Andrea & Ray, Joyce. Women of the Pine Tree State: 25 Maine Women You Should Know. Greenleaf, Lisa, illus. 2012. 136p. (J). pap. 16.00 *(978-0-9842549-6-5(X))* Apprentice Shop Bks., LLC.
Murphy, Claire Rudolf & Haigh, Jane G. Gold Rush Women. 12th ed. 2012. (Illus.). 128p. pap. 16.95 *(978-0-9627530-5-3(X))* Hillside Pr.
Murphy, Maggie. Taylor Swift: Country Music Star. 2010. (Reading Power). (Illus.). 24p. (J). pap. 8.85 *(978-1-4488-1803-7(6),* PowerKids Pr.) Rosen Publishing Group, Inc., The.
Murphy, Sage. Sally Ride: Female Astronaut. 2013. (Rosen Readers Ser.). (ENG.). 24p. (J). (gr. 2-3). pap. 49.50 *(978-1-4777-2307-4(2))*; pap. 8.25 *(978-1-4777-2306-7(4))* Rosen Publishing Group, Inc., The. (Rosen Classroom).
Mussari, Mark. Amy Tan. 2010. (Today's Writers & Their Works). 128p. (gr. 7-18). 42.79 *(978-0-7614-4127-4(1))* Marshall Cavendish Corp.
Nagelhout, Ryan. Abby Wambach. 2016. (Sports MVPs Ser.). (Illus.). 24p. (J). (gr. 2-1). 22.60 *(978-1-4824-4639-5(1))* Stevens, Gareth Publishing LLLP.
Nelson, Robin. Taylor Swift: Country Pop Hit Maker. 2012. (Pop Culture Bios Ser.). (ENG., Illus.). 32p. (gr. 3-6). lib. bdg. 26.60 *(978-0-7613-4143-7(9),* Lerner Pubns.) Lerner Publishing Group.
Nichols, Joan Kane. Civil War Heroines. 2005. (ENG., Illus.). 16p. (J). (gr. 5-5). pap. 7.47 net. *(978-0-328-14901-8(2),* Scott Foresman) Pearson Schl.
—The Civil War Sisterhood: Women Who Made a Difference. 2005. (ENG., Illus.). 16p. (J). (gr. 5-5). pap. 7.47 net. *(978-0-328-14902-5(0),* Scott Foresman) Pearson Schl.
—Women of the Civil War. 2005. (ENG., Illus.). 16p. (J). (gr. 5-5). pap. 7.47 net. *(978-0-328-14900-1(4),* Scott Foresman) Pearson Schl.
Nivola, Claire A. Life in the Ocean: The Story of Oceanographer Sylvia Earle, 1 vol. Nivola, Claire A., illus. 2012. (ENG., Illus.). 32p. (J). (gr. -1-3). 18.99 *(978-0-374-38068-7(6),* 9780374380687, Farrar, Straus & Giroux (BYR)) Farrar, Straus & Giroux.
Norgren, Jill. Belva Lockwood: The Woman Who Would Be President. 2007. (ENG., Illus.). 311p. 89.00 *(978-0-8147-5834-2(7))* New York Univ. Pr.
Norwich, Grace. I Am #6: Harriet Tubman. 2013. (I Am Ser.: 6). (ENG.). 128p. (J). (gr. 2-5). pap. 5.99 *(978-0-545-48436-7(7),* Scholastic Paperbacks) Scholastic, Inc.
—I Am Harriet Tubman. Simon, Ute, illus. 2013. 127p. (J). *(978-0-545-61344-6(2))* Scholastic, Inc.
Nothing Stood in Her Way, Captain Julie Clark. 2004. 232p. 24.95 *(978-0-9749190-0-3(4))* Women in Aviation, International.
Noyes, Deborah. Ten Days a Madwoman: The Daring Life & Turbulent Times of the Original Girl Reporter Nellie Bly. 2016. (ENG., Illus.). 144p. (J). (gr. 5). 18.99 *(978-0-8037-4017-4(4),* Viking Books for Young Readers) Penguin Young Readers Group.
O'Brien, John A. Who Was Helen Keller? Harrison, Nancy, illus. 2003. (Who Was... ? Ser.). 107p. (J). (gr. 3-7). 12.65 *(978-0-7569-1596-4(1))* Perfection Learning Corp.
Orr, Tamra B. Abby Wambach. 2007. (No Hands Allowed Ser.). (Illus.). 32p. (J). (gr. 2-4). lib. bdg. 25.70 *(978-1-58415-601-7(5))* Mitchell Lane Pubs., Inc.
—Amelia Earhart. 2015. (ENG., Illus.). 48p. (J). pap. 6.95 *(978-0-531-21207-3(6),* Orchard Bks.) Scholastic Library Publishing.
O'Shaughnessy, Tam. Sally Ride: A Photobiography of America's Pioneering Woman in Space. 2015. (ENG., Illus.). 160p. (J). (gr. 5-8). 19.99 *(978-1-59643-994-8(7),* 9781596439948) Roaring Brook Pr.
Paprocki, Sherry Beck. Ellen Degeneres: Entertainer. 2009. (Women of Achievement Ser.). (Illus.). 136p. (gr. 6-12). 35.00 *(978-1-60413-082-9(2),* Chelsea Hse.) Facts On File, Inc.
Parks, Deborah A. Nature's Machines: The Story of Biomechanist Mimi Koehl. 2006. (ENG., Illus.). 128p. (gr. 7-9). per. 19.95 *(978-0-309-09559-4(X),* Joseph Henry Pr.) National Academies Pr.
Pastan, Amy. First Ladies. 2017. (Illus.). 72p. (J). ***(978-1-5364-0121-9(8))*** Dorling Kindersley Publishing, Inc.
Patterson, Marie. Pocahontas, 1 vol. 2004. (Primary Source Readers Ser.). (ENG.). 24p. (J). (gr. 4-4). pap. 8.99 *(978-0-7439-8745-5(4))* Shell Educational Publishing.
Payment, Simone. American Women Spies of World War II. 2009. (American Women at War Ser.). 112p. (gr. 8-8). 63.90 *(978-1-61511-399-6(1))* Rosen Publishing Group, Inc., The.
Peck, Audrey. Helen Keller: Miracle Child. 2012. (Beginning Biographies Ser.). (ENG., Illus.). 24p. (J). (gr. 1-3). 22.60 *(978-1-4488-8593-0(0),* PowerKids Pr.) Rosen Publishing Group, Inc., The.
Pelleschi, Andrea. Mathematician & Computer Scientist Grace Hopper. 2016. (STEM Trailblazer Bios Ser.). (ENG., Illus.). 32p. (J). (gr. 2-5). 26.65 *(978-1-5124-0785-3(2))* Lerner Publishing Group.
Peppas, Lynn. Miley Cyrus. 2010. (Superstars! Ser.). (ENG.). 32p. (J). pap. *(978-0-7787-7259-0(4))* Crabtree Publishing Co.
—Taylor Swift. 2010. (Superstars! Ser.). (ENG.). 32p. (J). pap. *(978-0-7787-7261-3(6))* Crabtree Publishing Co.
Petrick, Neila Skinner. Jane Wilkinson Long: Texas Pioneer, 1 vol. Haynes, Joyce, illus. 2004. (ENG.). 32p. (J). (gr. k-3). 16.99 *(978-1-58980-147-9(4))* Pelican Publishing Co., Inc.
Petrillo, Lisa. Vera Wang. 2011. (Profiles in Fashion Ser.). (Illus.). 112p. 28.95 *(978-1-59935-150-6(1))* Reynolds, Morgan Inc.
Pettinella, Amy. Queen Latifah: Award-Winning Actress & Hip-Hop Activist. 2014. (Leading Women Ser.). 112p. (J). (gr. 7-11). lib. bdg. 39.93 *(978-1-62712-984-8(7))* Cavendish Square Publishing.
Phillips, Larissa. Women Civil War Spies of the Confederacy. 2009. (American Women at War Ser.). 112p. (gr. 8-8). 63.90 *(978-1-61511-402-3(5))* Rosen Publishing Group, Inc., The.
Pingry, Patricia A. The Story of Coretta Scott King. Walker, Steven, illus. 2007. (ENG.). 26p. (J). (gr. 3-7). bds. 7.69 *(978-0-8249-6717-8(8),* Ideal Pubns.) Worthy Publishing.
Polacco, Patricia. Betty Doll. 2004. 18.00 *(978-0-7569-3208-4(4))* Perfection Learning Corp.
Polette, Nancy. Biography, by Golly! 2004. (J). pap. 7.50 *(978-1-931334-49-5(8))* Pieces of Learning.
—The Spy with the Wooden Leg: The Story of Virginia Hall. 2012. (ENG.). 160p. (J). pap. 12.95 *(978-1-934617-16-8(4))*; 16.95 *(978-1-934617-15-1(6))* Elva Resa Publishing, LLC. (Alma Little).
Pollack, Pamela D. & Meg Belviso. Who Was Lucille Ball? 2017. (Who Was... ? Ser.). lib. bdg. 16.00 ***(978-0-606-39781-0(7))*** Turtleback Bks.
Porter, Esther. Abby Wambach. 2016. (Women in Sports Ser.). (ENG., Illus.). 24p. (gr. k-1). lib. bdg. 26.65 *(978-1-4914-7974-2(4),* Pebble Plus) Capstone Press of Coughlan Cos.
Porterfield, Jason. Annie Oakley: Tiradora del Lejano Oeste (Annie Oakley: Wild West Sharpshooter) 2009. (Grandes personajes en la historia de los Estados Unidos (Famous People in American History) Ser.). 32p. (gr. 2-3). 47.90 *(978-1-61512-789-4(5),* Editorial Buenas Letras) Rosen Publishing Group, Inc., The.
—Annie Oakley: Wild West Sharpshooter. 2009. (Primary Sources of Famous People in American History Ser.). 32p. (gr. 2-3). 47.90 *(978-1-60851-651-3(2))* Rosen Publishing Group, Inc., The.
—Annie Oakley: Wild West Sharpshooter / Tiradora del Lejano Oeste. 2009. (Famous People in American History/Grandes personajes en la historia de los Estados Unidos Ser.). 32p. (gr. 2-3). 47.90 *(978-1-61512-537-1(X),* Editorial Buenas Letras) Rosen Publishing Group, Inc., The.
PRESS, Celebration. Ellen Ochoa: Reaching for the Stars. 2003. (ENG.). (J). (gr. 2-5). pap., stu. ed. 34.95 *(978-0-673-62081-1(6),* Celebration Pr.) Pearson Schl.
Priscilla, Marie. L' il Bitty Book. 2007. 130p. (J). pap. 13.95 *(978-0-7414-4343-4(0))* Infinity Publishing.
Purdy, Elizabeth Rholetter. Celebrating Women in American History. 2011. (J). *(978-0-8160-7883-7(1))*; *(978-0-8160-7882-0(3))*; *(978-0-8160-7881-3(5))*; *(978-0-8160-7880-6(7))*; *(978-0-8160-7879-0(3))* Facts On File, Inc.
Raatma, Lucia. Barbara Jordan. 2013. 96p. (YA). (gr. 7-12). 39.93 *(978-0-7614-4956-0(6))* Cavendish Square Publishing.
—Jacqueline Kennedy, 1 vol. 2010. (First Ladies Ser.). (ENG.). 24p. (gr. k-1). pap. 7.29 *(978-1-4296-5601-6(8))*; pap. 41.70 *(978-1-4296-5602-3(6))* Capstone Press of Coughlan Cos. (Pebble Plus).
—Shirley Chisholm. 2010. (Leading Women Ser.). 96p. (YA). (gr. 7-12). 39.93 *(978-0-7614-4953-9(1))* Marshall Cavendish Corp.
Rand, Carol. Lydia Darragh: Quaker Patriot. Marshall, Dan, illus. (J). 15.95 *(978-0-945912-33-0(1))* Pippin Pr.
Randolph, Jennifer & Benchmark Education Co. Staff. Women of the Civil War. 2014. (Text Connections Ser.). (J). (gr. 5). *(978-1-4900-1377-0(6))* Benchmark Education Co.
Randolph, Joanne. The Angel of Goliad: Francisca Alvarez & the Texas War for Independence. 2009. (Great Moments in American History Ser.). 32p. (gr. 3-3). 47.90 *(978-1-61513-151-8(5))* Rosen Publishing Group, Inc., The.
Randolph, Ryan P. Frontier Women Who Helped Shape the American West. (Library of the Westward Expansion Ser.). 24p. 2009. (gr. 3-4). 42.50 *(978-1-60853-936-9(9))* 2003. (Illus.). (J). lib. bdg. 22.60 *(978-0-8239-6297-6(0))* Rosen Publishing Group, Inc., The. (PowerKids Pr.).
Ransom, Candice. Maggie L. Walker: Pioneering Banker & Community Leader. 2008. (Trailblazer Biographies Ser.). (ENG.). 112p. (gr. 5-9). lib. bdg. 31.93 *(978-0-8225-6611-3(7))* Lerner Publishing Group.
Rappaport, Doreen. Eleanor, Quiet No More. Kelley, Gary, illus. 2009. (ENG.). 48p. (J). (gr. 1-3). 16.99 *(978-0-7868-5141-6(4))* Hyperion Pr.
—Helen's Big World: The Life of Helen Keller. Tavares, Matt, illus. 2017. (Big Words Ser.). (ENG.). 48p. (J). (gr. 1-3). pap. 8.99 *(978-1-4847-4960-9(X))* Hyperion Bks. for Children.
—Helen's Big World: The Life of Helen Keller. Tavares, Matt, illus. 2012. (Big Words Ser.). (ENG.). 48p. (J). (gr. 1-3). 17.99 *(978-0-7868-0890-8(X))* Hyperion Pr.
Raum, Elizabeth. Carli Lloyd. 2017. (Pro Sports Biographies Ser.). (ENG.). 24p. (gr. 1-4). 20.95 ***(978-1-68151-132-0(0))*** Amicus Publishing.
—Chloe Kim. 2017. (Pro Sports Biographies Ser.). (ENG.). 24p. (J). (gr. 1-4). 20.95 ***(978-1-68151-134-4(7),*** Amicus High Interest) Amicus Publishing.
—Pro Sports Biographies: Carli Lloyd. 2017. (Pro Sports Biographies Ser.). (ENG.). 24p. (J). (gr. 1-3). pap. 8.99 ***(978-1-68152-163-3(6))*** Amicus.
—Pro Sports Biographies: Chloe Kim. 2017. (Pro Sports Biographies Ser.). (ENG.). 24p. (J). (gr. 1-3). pap. 8.99 ***(978-1-68152-165-7(2))*** Amicus.
—Pro Sports Biographies: Maya Moore. 2017. (Pro Sports Biographies Ser.). (ENG.). 24p. (J). (gr. 1-3). pap. 8.99 ***(978-1-68152-164-0(4))*** Amicus.
Rausch, Monica. Sacagawea. 2007. (Grandes personajes (Spanish- Great Americans) Ser.). (SPA.). 24p. (gr. 1-4). pap. 8.15 *(978-0-8368-7991-9(0),* Weekly Reader Leveled Readers) Stevens, Gareth Publishing LLLP.
Rausch, Monica L. Sacagawea. 2007. (Grandes personajes (Great Americans) Ser.). (SPA., Illus.). 24p. (gr. 1-4). lib. bdg. 22.00 *(978-0-8368-7984-1(8),* Weekly Reader Leveled Readers) Stevens, Gareth Publishing LLLP.
Ray, Deborah Kogan. Paiute Princess: The Story of Sarah Winnemucca, 1 vol. Ray, Deborah Kogan, illus. 2012. (ENG., Illus.). 48p. (J). (gr. 3-7). 17.99 *(978-0-374-39897-2(6),* 9780374398972, Farrar, Straus & Giroux (BYR)) Farrar, Straus & Giroux.
Reed, Jennifer. Elizabeth Bloomer: Child Labor Activist. 2006. (Young Heroes Ser.). (ENG., Illus.). 48p. (J). (gr. 3-7). lib. bdg. 30.50 *(978-0-7377-3615-1(1),* Kidhaven) Cengage Gale.
Reusser, Kayleen. Day by Day with Taylor Swift. 2010. (Randy's Corner Ser.). (Illus.). 32p. (J). (gr. -1-2). lib. bdg. 25.70 *(978-1-58415-857-8(3))* Mitchell Lane Pubs., Inc.
—Taylor Swift. 2008. (Blue Banner Biography Ser.). (Illus.). 32p. (YA). (gr. 4-7). lib. bdg. 25.70 *(978-1-58415-675-8(9))* Mitchell Lane Pubs., Inc.
Rey, Carol. Iris Wall, Cracker Cowgirl, 1 vol. Lux, Eldon, illus. 2012. (ENG.). 32p. (J). (gr. k-3). 16.99 *(978-1-4556-1525-4(0))* Pelican Publishing Co., Inc.
Rhynes, Martha E. Gwendolyn Brooks: Poet from Chicago. 2004. (World Writers Ser.). (Illus.). 112p. (YA). (gr. 6-12). 23.95 *(978-1-931798-05-1(2))* Reynolds, Morgan Inc.
Riddolls, Tom. Sally Ride: The First American Woman in Space. 2010. (Crabtree Groundbreaker Biographies Ser.). (ENG., Illus.). 112p. (J). pap. *(978-0-7787-2550-3(2))*; (gr. 5-8). lib. bdg. *(978-0-7787-2541-1(3))* Crabtree Publishing Co.
Riddolls, Tom & Wearing, Judy. Hillary Clinton. 2009. (Remarkable People Ser.). (Illus.). 24p. (J). (gr. 4-6). pap. 8.95 *(978-1-60596-621-2(5))*; lib. bdg. 24.45 *(978-1-60596-620-5(7))* Weigl Pubs., Inc.
Rieken, Ethel Plaep. Growing Pains: A Childhood on Bear Creek. Zander, Julie McDonald, ed. Slavens, Rick, photos by. 2004. (Illus.). 140p. (YA). per. 23.00 *(978-0-9740348-2-9(7),* Special Editions — Customized Biographies) Slavens Enterprises, LLC.
Riley, John B. Jane Addams: A Photo Biography. l.t. ed. 2004. (First Biographies Ser.). (Illus.). 24p. (YA). (gr. 5-18). 16.95 *(978-1-883846-61-9(7),* First Biographies) Reynolds, Morgan Inc.
Rinaldo, Denise. Amelia Earhart: With a Discussion of Courage. 2004. (Values in Action Ser.). (J). *(978-1-59203-068-2(8))* Learning Challenge, Inc.
—Eleanor Roosevelt: With a Discussion of Respect. 2003. (Values in Action Ser.). (J). *(978-1-59203-063-7(7))* Learning Challenge, Inc.
—Rosa Parks: With a Discussion of Courage. 2003. (Values in Action Ser.). (J). *(978-1-59203-061-3(0))* Learning Challenge, Inc.

W
X
Y
Z

Rivera, Ursula. Aretha Franklin. 2009. (Rock & Roll Hall of Famers Ser.). 112p. (gr. 5-8). 63.90 *(978-1-60852-467-9(1),* Rosen Reference) Rosen Publishing Group, Inc., The.

Robbins, Dean. Miss Paul & the President: The Creative Campaign for Women's Right to Vote. Zhang, Nancy, illus. 2016. (ENG.). 40p. (J). (gr. -1-3). 17.99 *(978-1-101-93720-4(3),* Knopf Bks. for Young Readers) Random Hse. Children's Bks.

Robbins, Trina. Hedy Lamarr & a Secret Communication System, 1 vol. Martin, Cynthia, illus. 2006. (Inventions & Discovery Ser.). (ENG.). 32p. (gr. 3-4). 8.10 *(978-0-7368-9641-2(4),* Graphic Library) Capstone Press of Coughlan Cos.

Roberts, Cokie. Founding Mothers: Remembering the Ladies. Goode, Diane, illus. 2014. 40p. (J). (gr. 2-7). (ENG.). 17.99 *(978-0-06-078002-9(9));* lib. bdg. 18.89 *(978-0-06-078003-6(7))* HarperCollins Pubs.

Roberts, Pauline. When I Was Just a Pea in a Pod: A True Story. 2012. 24p. pap. 13.50 *(978-1-4669-1401-8(7))* Trafford Publishing.

Robson, David. Soledad O'Brien. (Transcending Race in America: Biographies of Biracial Achievers Ser.). (Illus.). 64p. (J). (gr. 5-18). 2010. lib. bdg. 22.95 *(978-1-4222-1617-0(9))* 2009. pap. 9.95 *(978-1-4222-1631-6(4))* Mason Crest.

Roby, Cynthia A. Zora Neale Hurston. 2016. (Artists of the Harlem Renaissance Ser.). (ENG.). 128p. (J). (gr. 9-9). lib. bdg. 45.64 *(978-1-5026-1038-6(8))* Cavendish Square Publishing.

Rock, Meghan. Rachel Carson: Marine Biologist & Winner of the National Book Award. 2016. (Women in Science Ser.). 128p. (J). 45.64 *(978-1-5026-2319-5(6))* Cavendish Square Publishing.

Rodriguez, Gaby. The Pregnancy Project: A Memoir. 2013. (ENG., Illus.). 240p. (YA). (gr. 9). pap. 10.99 *(978-1-4424-4623-6(4),* Simon & Schuster Bks. For Young Readers) Simon & Schuster Bks. For Young Readers.

Roland, James. Ruth Bader Ginsburg: Iconic Supreme Court Justice. 2016. (Gateway Biographies Ser.). (ENG., Illus.). 48p. (J). (gr. 4-8). 26.65 *(978-1-5124-0596-5(5));* 39.99 *(978-1-5124-0597-2(3))* Lerner Publishing Group. (Lerner Pubns.).

Roop, Peter & Roop, Connie. The Stormy Adventure of Abbie Burgess, Lighthouse Keeper. Trover, Zachary, illus. 2010. (History's Kid Heroes Ser.). (ENG.). 32p. (gr. 3-5). pap. 8.95 *(978-0-7613-6191-6(X),* Graphic Universe™) Lerner Publishing Group.

Rose, Katherine. Annie Oakley. 2014. (Illus.). 32p. (J). pap. *(978-1-62712-287-0(7))* Cavendish Square Publishing.

Rosenstock, Barb. Dorothea's Eyes: Dorothea Lange Photographs the Truth. DuBois, Gerard, illus. 2016. (ENG.). 40p. (J). (gr. 2-7). 16.95 *(978-1-62979-208-8(X),* Calkins Creek) Boyds Mills Pr.

Ross, Michael Elsohn. Pond Watching with Ann Morgan. Smith, Wendy, illus. 2005. (Naturalist's Apprentice Biographies Ser.). 48p. (gr. 3-6). lib. bdg. 19.93 *(978-1-57505-385-1(3))* Lerner Publishing Group.

Roycroft, Mitch. Jennifer Harman. (Superstars of Poker Ser.). (Illus.). 64p. (YA). 2009. (gr. 3-7). lib. bdg. 22.95 *(978-1-4222-0227-2(5))* 2007. pap. 7.95 *(978-1-4222-0373-6(5))* Mason Crest.

Roza, Greg. Guide My Pen: The Poems of Phillis Wheatley. 2009. (Great Moments in American History Ser.). 32p. (gr. 3-3). 47.90 *(978-1-61513-133-4(7))* Rosen Publishing Group, Inc., The.

Ruffin, Frances E. Annie Oakley. 2009. (American Legends Ser.). 24p. (gr. 3-3). 42.50 *(978-1-61511-378-1(9),* PowerKids Pr.) Rosen Publishing Group, Inc., The.

—Clara Barton. 2009. (American Legends Ser.). 24p. (gr. 3-3). 42.50 *(978-1-61511-379-8(7),* PowerKids Pr.) Rosen Publishing Group, Inc., The.

—Her Story, Her Words: The Narrative of Sojourner Truth. (Great Moments in American History Ser.). 32p. 2009. (gr. 3-3). 47.90 *(978-1-61513-144-0(2))* 2004. (Illus.). (gr. 4-8). lib. bdg. 22.50 *(978-0-8239-4387-6(9),* Rosen Reference) Rosen Publishing Group, Inc., The.

—Meet Patricia MacLachlan. 2009. (About the Author Ser.). 24p. (gr. 4-4). 42.50 *(978-1-61511-257-9(X),* PowerKids Pr.) Rosen Publishing Group, Inc., The.

—Molly Pitcher. 2009. (American Legends Ser.). 24p. (gr. 3-3). 42.50 *(978-1-61511-384-2(3),* PowerKids Pr.) Rosen Publishing Group, Inc., The.

—Sally Hemings. 2009. (American Legends Ser.). 24p. (gr. 3-3). 42.50 *(978-1-61511-386-6(X),* PowerKids Pr.) Rosen Publishing Group, Inc., The.

—Sojourner Truth: Early Abolitionist. 2009. (American Legends Ser.). 24p. (gr. 3-3). 42.50 *(978-1-61511-387-3(8),* PowerKids Pr.) Rosen Publishing Group, Inc., The.

—Unsinkable Molly Brown. 2009. (American Legends Ser.). 24p. (gr. 3-3). 42.50 *(978-1-61511-377-4(0),* PowerKids Pr.) Rosen Publishing Group, Inc., The.

Russell, Greta. Olive Boone: Frontier Woman. Hare, John, illus. 2014. (Notable Missourians Ser.). (ENG.). 48p. (J). lib. bdg. 24.00 *(978-1-61248-118-0(3))* Truman State Univ. Pr.

Ryan, Bernard. Hillary Rodham Clinton: First Lady & Senator. 2004. (Ferguson Career Biographies Ser.). (Illus.). 160p. (gr. 6-12). 25.00 *(978-0-8160-5544-9(0),* Ferguson Publishing Co.) Facts On File, Inc.

Sabin, Francene & Macken, JoAnn Early. Abigail Adams: Young Patriot. Miyake, Yoshi, illus. 2007. 55p. (J). pap. *(978-0-439-88003-9(3))* Scholastic, Inc.

Sabin, Francene & Mattern, Joanne. Helen Keller, Girl of Courage. Meyer, Jean, illus. 2006. 56p. (J). *(978-0-439-66043-3(2))* Scholastic, Inc.

Saddleback Educational Publishing. Rihanna, 1 vol. 2013. (Hip-Hop Biographies Ser.). (ENG.). 48p. (YA). (gr. 9-12). 11.95 *(978-1-62250-011-6(3))* Saddleback Educational Publishing, Inc.

Sakany, Lois. Women Civil War Spies of the Union. 2009. (American Women at War Ser.). 112p. (gr. 8-8). 63.90 *(978-1-61511-403-0(3))* Rosen Publishing Group, Inc., The.

Salazar, Sam. Jordin Sparks. 2013. (Rising Stars Ser.). 32p. (J). (gr. 3-6). pap. 10.50 *(978-1-4339-8982-7(4))* Stevens, Gareth Publishing LLLP.

Salazar, Sam & Kennon, Michou. Jordin Sparks. 2013. 32p. (J). (gr. 3-6). 25.25 *(978-1-4339-8981-0(6))* Stevens, Gareth Publishing LLLP.

Sanchez Vegara, Ma Isabel. Amelia Earhart. Mariadiamantes, illus. 2016. (Little People, Big Dreams Ser.). (ENG.). 32p. (J). (gr. k-3). 14.99 *(978-1-84780-888-2(3),* Frances Lincoln Children's Bks.) Quarto Publishing Group UK GBR. Dist: Hachette Bk. Group.

Savage, Jeff. Danica Patrick. (Amazing Athletes Ser.). 32p. (gr. 2-5). 2006. (Illus.). (J). lib. bdg. 23.93 *(978-0-8225-5954-2(4),* Lerner Pubns.) 2010. (ENG.). pap. 7.95 *(978-0-7613-5760-5(2))* 2010. (ENG.). lib. bdg. 25.26 *(978-0-7613-5750-6(5),* Lerner Pubns.) Lerner Publishing Group.

—Marion Jones. 2005. (J). pap. 5.95 *(978-0-8225-2040-5(0),* First Avenue Editions); (Illus.). (gr. 3-4). lib. bdg. 22.60 *(978-0-8225-3657-4(9))* Lerner Publishing Group.

—Maya Moore. 2012. (Amazing Athletes Ser.). 32p. (gr. 2-5). (J). pap. 45.32 *(978-0-7613-9316-0(1));* (ENG., Illus.). lib. bdg. 25.26 *(978-0-7613-8637-7(8))* Lerner Publishing Group.

Sawyer, Kem Knapp. Harriet Tubman - A Photographic Story of a Life. 2010. (DK Biography Ser.). (ENG.). 128p. (J). (gr. 5-12). 6.99 *(978-0-7566-5806-9(3),* DK Children) Dorling Kindersley Publishing, Inc.

Schatz, Kate. Rad American Women A-Z: Rebels, Trailblazers, & Visionaries Who Shaped Our History ... & Our Future! Stahl, Miriam Klein, illus. 2015. (City Lights/Sister Spit Ser.). (ENG.). 64p. (J). (gr. 2-11). 14.95 *(978-0-87286-683-6(1))* City Lights Bks.

Schiffman, Jessica, illus. Sybil Ludington: Freedom's Brave Rider. 2005. 32p. (J). pap. *(978-0-7367-2931-4(3))* Zaner-Bloser, Inc.

Schraff, Anne E. Rosa Parks: Tired of Giving In. 2005. (African-American Biography Library). (Illus.). 128p. (J). (gr. 6-12). lib. bdg. 33.27 *(978-0-7660-2463-2(6))* Enslow Pubs., Inc.

Schulte, Mary. Helen Greiner: Cofounder of iRobot Corporation. 2009. (Innovators Ser.). (ENG., Illus.). 48p. (gr. 4-8). lib. bdg. 34.60 *(978-0-7377-4404-0(9),* LML02109-245405, Kidhaven) Cengage Gale.

Schuman, Michael A. Angelina Jolie: Celebrity with Heart. 2010. (Celebrities with Heart Ser.). (Illus.). 128p. (J). pap. 10.95 *(978-1-59845-203-7(7))* Enslow Pubs., Inc.

—Halle Berry: Beauty Is Not Just Physical. 2006. (African-American Biography Library). (Illus.). 112p. (J). (gr. 6-12). lib. bdg. 33.27 *(978-0-7660-2467-0(9))* Enslow Pubs., Inc.

—Tina Fey: TV Comedy Superstar. 2011. (People to Know Today Ser.). (Illus.). 112p. (J). (gr. 7-12). lib. bdg. 33.27 *(978-0-7660-3557-7(3))* Enslow Pubs., Inc.

Schwartz, Heather. Lizzie Johnson: Vaquera Texana. 2013. (Primary Source Readers Ser.). (SPA.). lib. bdg. 19.65 *(978-0-606-31871-6(2),* Turtleback) Turtleback Bks.

Schweitzer, Karen. Sheryl Swoopes. (Role Model Athletes Ser.). 64p. 2012. (J). (gr. 7). 22.95 *(978-1-4222-2712-1(X))* 2010. (Illus.). (YA). (gr. 7-12). 22.95 *(978-1-4222-0491-7(X))* 2007. (Illus.). (YA). pap. 9.95 *(978-1-4222-0778-9(1))* Mason Crest.

Segovia, Patty. Skate Girls. 2006. (Reading Rocks! Ser.). (ENG., Illus.). 32p. (J). (gr. 2-5). 28.50 *(978-1-59296-748-3(5),* 200734) Child's World, Inc., The.

Seguin, Marilyn. Young & Courageous: American Girls Who Made History. 2012. (J). pap. *(978-0-8283-2463-2(6))* Branden Bks.

Shapiro, Marc & Ooten, Tara Broeckel. Selena Gomez - Fame. 2012. (ENG., Illus.). 40p. (YA). pap. 7.99 *(978-1-4507-6679-1(X))* Bluewater Productions, Inc.

Sharp, Anne Wallace. Nancy Lopez. 2008. (Twentieth Century's Most Influencial Hispanics Ser.). (ENG., Illus.). 96-128p. (gr. 7-10). 34.80 *(978-1-4205-0060-8(0),* Lucent Bks.) Cengage Gale.

—Women Civil Rights Leaders. 2012. (Lucent Library of Black History Ser.). (ENG., Illus.). 128p. (J). (gr. 7-10). 39.40 *(978-1-4205-0880-2(6),* Lucent Bks.) Cengage Gale.

Shea, Mary Molly. Taylor Swift. 2010. (Country Music Stars Ser.). (Illus.). 32p. (J). (gr. 3-8). pap. 10.50 *(978-1-4339-3611-1(9));* lib. bdg. 25.25 *(978-1-4339-3610-4(0))* Stevens, Gareth Publishing LLLP.

Shea, Molly. Alicia Keys. 2011. (Hip-Hop Headliners Ser.). (Illus.). 32p. (gr. 3-8). pap. 10.50 *(978-1-4339-4785-8(4));* (J). 25.25 *(978-1-4339-4784-1(6))* Stevens, Gareth Publishing LLLP.

Sheen, Barbara. Janet Guthrie: Racing Pioneer. 2010. (Innovators Ser.). (Illus.). 64p. (J). 29.95 *(978-0-7377-5050-8(2),* Kidhaven) Cengage Gale.

Sheen, Barbara, ed. Natalie Coughlin. 2013. (People in the News Ser.). (ENG., Illus.). 128p. (gr. 7-10). lib. bdg. 39.40 *(978-1-4205-0998-4(5),* Lucent Bks.) Cengage Gale.

Shepherd, Jodie. Hillary Clinton. 2015. (Rookie Biographies(r) Ser.). (ENG., Illus.). 32p. (J). lib. bdg. 23.00 *(978-0-531-20592-1(4))* Scholastic Library Publishing.

Sherrard, Valerie. Vanessa Hudgens. 2010. (Superstars! Ser.). (ENG., Illus.). 32p. (J). pap. *(978-0-7787-7262-0(4))* Crabtree Publishing Co.

Shetterly, Margot Lee. Hidden Figures. Freeman, Laura, illus. 2018. (ENG.). 40p. (J). (gr. -1-3). 17.99 ***(978-0-06-274246-9(9))*** HarperCollins Pubs.

—Hidden Figures. 2016. 240p. (J). (gr. 3-7). 16.99 *(978-0-06-266238-5(4));* (Illus.). pap. 7.99 *(978-0-06-266237-8(6))* HarperCollins Pubs.

—Hidden Figures. 2016. (Illus.). 231p. (J). lib. bdg. 18.40 ***(978-0-606-39623-3(3))*** Turtleback Bks.

Shichtman, Sandra H. Nancy Pelosi. 2008. (Political Profiles Ser.). (Illus.). 112p. (YA). (gr. 5-9). lib. bdg. 27.95 *(978-1-59935-049-3(1))* Reynolds, Morgan Inc.

Shoup, Kate & Spence, Kelly. Ellen DeGeneres: Television Comedian & Gay Rights Activist. 2016. (Leading Women Ser.). 112p. (gr. 7-7). 39.93 *(978-1-5026-1989-1(X))* Cavendish Square Publishing.

Shulman, Holly. Dolley Madison: Her Life, Letters, & Legacy. 2009. (Library of American Lives & Times Ser.). 112p. (gr. 5-5). 69.20 *(978-1-60853-477-7(4))* Rosen Publishing Group, Inc., The.

Silate, Jennifer. Betsy Ross: Creadora de la bandera Estadounidense. 2004. (Grandes personajes en la historia de los Estados Unidos Ser.). (SPA.). 32p. (gr. 3-6). pap. 10.00 *(978-0-8239-4222-0(8),* Rosen Classroom) Rosen Publishing Group, Inc., The.

Silverman, Erica. Liberty's Voice: The Story of Emma Lazarus. Schuett, Stacey, illus. 2014. (ENG.). 32p. (J). (gr. 1-3). 8.99 *(978-0-14-751174-4(7),* Puffin Books) Penguin Young Readers Group.

Simon, Charnan. Rachel Carson: Author & Environmentalist. 2003. (Our People Ser.). (ENG., Illus.). 32p. (J). (gr. 3-6). 29.93 *(978-1-59296-011-8(1),* 200650) Child's World, Inc., The.

Slade, Suzanne. Dangerous Jane, 1 vol. Ratterree, Alice, illus. 2017. (ENG.). 40p. (J). (gr. 1-5). 17.95 *(978-1-56145-913-1(5))* Peachtree Pubs.

Slavicek, Louise Chipley. Anne Hutchinson. 2010. (Leaders of the Colonial Era Ser.). 120p. (gr. 5-8). 35.00 *(978-1-60413-741-5(X),* Chelsea Hse.) Facts On File, Inc.

Small, Cathleen. Barbara Mcclintock: Cytogeneticist & Discoverer of Mobile Genetic Elements. 2016. (Women in Science Ser.). 128p. (J). lib. bdg. 45.64 *(978-1-5026-2311-9(0))* Cavendish Square Publishing.

Small, Cathleen. Bessie Coleman: First African American & Native American Pilot. 2017. (J). ***(978-1-5026-2753-7(1))*** Cavendish Square Publishing.

Snow, Kevin. Ronda Rousey: Conquering New Ground. 2017. (J). ***(978-1-5026-2832-9(5))*** Cavendish Square Publishing.

Solo, Hope. Hope Solo - My Story. 2013. (ENG.). 256p. (J). (gr. 3-7). pap. 5.99 *(978-0-06-222066-0(7))* HarperCollins Pubs.

Solomon, Sharon. Cathy Williams, Buffalo Soldier, 1 vol. Lorenzetti, Doreen, illus. 2010. (ENG.). 32p. (J). (gr. k-3). 16.99 *(978-1-58980-801-0(0))* Pelican Publishing Co., Inc.

Somervill, Barbara A. Votes for Women! The Story of Carrie Chapman Catt. 2004. (Feminist Voices Ser.). (Illus.). 128p. (YA). (gr. 6-12). 23.95 *(978-1-883846-96-1(X),* First Biographies) Reynolds, Morgan Inc.

Sonneborn, Liz. Wilma Mankiller. 2010. (Leading Women Ser.). 96p. (YA). (gr. 7-12). 39.93 *(978-0-7614-4959-1(0))* Marshall Cavendish Corp.

Spangenburg, Ray, et al. Chien-Shiung Wu: The Elegance of Experiment. 2009. (Makers of Modern Science Ser.). (Illus.). 144p. (gr. 6-12). 35.00 *(978-0-8160-6177-8(7),* Chelsea Hse.) Facts On File, Inc.

Spence, Kelly. Taylor Swift: Pop Music Superstar. 2016. (Leading Women Ser.). (Illus.). 112p. (J). (gr. 7-7). 39.93 *(978-1-5026-1991-4(1))* Cavendish Square Publishing.

Spinner, Stephanie. Who Was Annie Oakley? Day, Larry, illus. 2003. (Who Was... ? Ser.). 109p. (gr. 4-7). 15.00 *(978-0-7569-1588-9(5))* Perfection Learning Corp.

—Who Was Clara Barton? 2014. (Who Was... ? Ser.). lib. bdg. 16.00 *(978-0-606-35695-4(9))* Turtleback Bks.

Staley, Erin. Maggie Stiefvater. 2013. (All about the Author Ser.). 112p. (YA). (gr. 7-12). 34.60 *(978-1-4777-1762-2(5))* Rosen Publishing Group, Inc., The.

Stein, R. Conrad. Harriet Tubman: On My Underground Railroad I Never Ran My Train off the Track. 2010. (Americans—the Spirit of a Nation Ser.). (Illus.). 128p. (J). lib. bdg. 33.27 *(978-0-7660-3481-5(X))* Enslow Pubs., Inc.

Sterling, Kristin. Jane Goodall: A Life of Loyalty. 2008. (Pull Ahead Books-Biographies Ser.). (ENG.). 32p. (gr. k-3). pap. 7.95 *(978-0-8225-8728-6(9))* Lerner Publishing Group.

Stewart, Gail B. Stephanie Kwolek: Creator of Kevlar. 2008. (Innovators Ser.). (ENG., Illus.). 48p. (J). (gr. 4-8). lib. bdg. 29.95 *(978-0-7377-4040-0(X),* LML02109-239897, Kidhaven) Cengage Gale.

Stille, Darlene R. Madam C. J. Walker: The Inspiring Life Story of the Hair Care Entrepreneur. 2016. (Inspiring Stories Ser.). (ENG., Illus.). 112p. (gr. 5-7). lib. bdg. 35.99 *(978-0-7565-5165-0(X),* CPB Grades 4-8) Compass Point Bks.

Stine, Megan. Who Is Michelle Obama? 2013. (Who Is... ? Ser.). lib. bdg. 14.75 *(978-0-606-32131-0(4),* Turtleback) Turtleback Bks.

Stock, Catherine. Vinnie & Abraham. unabr. ed. 2008. (J). (gr. 2-5). 29.95 incl. audio compact disk *(978-0-8045-4190-9(6));* 27.95 incl. audio *(978-0-8045-6967-5(3))* Spoken Arts, Inc.

Stone, Tanya Lee. Almost Astronauts: 13 Women Who Dared to Dream. 2009. (ENG., Illus.). 144p. (J). (gr. 5). 24.99 *(978-0-7636-3611-1(8))* Candlewick Pr.

—The House That Jane Built: A Story about Jane Addams. Brown, Kathryn, illus. 2015. (ENG.). 32p. (J). (gr. 1-4). 17.99 *(978-0-8050-9049-9(5),* 9780805090499, Holt, Henry & Co. Bks. For Young Readers) Holt, Henry & Co.

Stone, Tanya Lee & Dorling Kindersley Publishing Staff. Amelia Earhart. 2007. (DK Biography Ser.). (ENG., Illus.). 128p. (J). (gr. 5-12). pap. 6.99 *(978-0-7566-2552-8(1),* DK Children) Dorling Kindersley Publishing, Inc.

Stout, Glenn. Baseball Heroes. 2010. (Good Sports Ser.). (ENG., Illus.). 128p. (J). (gr. 2-5). pap. 6.99 *(978-0-547-41708-0(X))* Houghton Mifflin Harcourt Publishing Co.

Streissguth, Tom. Wilma Rudolph. 2006. (Sports Heroes & Legends Ser.). (ENG., Illus.). 120p. (gr. 5-12). lib. bdg. 30.60 *(978-0-8225-5958-0(7))* Lerner Publishing Group.

Stumpff, April D. & Messersmith, Patrick. Ann Richards: A Woman's Place Is in the Dome. 2006. (Stars of Texas Ser.: 6). (ENG., Illus.). 80p. (gr. 4-7). 14.95 *(978-1-933337-12-8(5))* State Hse. Pr.

Summers, Kimberly Dillon. Miley Cyrus: A Biography, 1 vol. 2009. (Greenwood Biographies Ser.). 156p. (C). 39.00 *(978-0-313-37847-8(9),* GR7847, Greenwood) ABC-CLIO, LLC.

Sutcliffe, Jane. Helen Keller. 2009. (History Maker Biographies Ser.). (gr. k-2). 27.93 *(978-0-7613-4223-6(0),* Lerner Pubns.) Lerner Publishing Group.

—Helen Keller. Verstraete, Elaine, illus. 2003. (On My Own Biographies Ser.). 48p. (J). (gr. 1-3). 6.95 *(978-0-87614-903-4(4),* Carolrhoda Bks.) Lerner Publishing Group.

—Sacagawea. 2009. (History Maker Biographies Ser.). (ENG.). 48p. (gr. 3-6). 27.93 *(978-0-7613-4222-9(2),* Lerner Pubns.) Lerner Publishing Group.

Sutton, A. Trevor. Dr. Bessie Rehwinkel. Pierce, Linda, illus. 2012. (Hero of Faith Ser.). (ENG.). 47p. (J). pap. 7.99 *(978-0-7586-3078-0(6))* Concordia Publishing Hse.

Swain, Gwenyth. Sojourner Truth. Archambault, Matthew, illus. 2005. (On My Own Biography Ser.). 48p. (J). (gr. 1-3). pap. 6.95 *(978-1-57505-827-6(8))* Lerner Publishing Group.

—Sojourner Truth. 2005. (On My Own Biography Ser.). (Illus.). 48p. (J). 25.26 *(978-1-57505-651-7(8),* Carolrhoda Bks.) Lerner Publishing Group.

Swanson, June. Venus & Serena Williams. Burke, Susan S., illus. 2003. (You Must Be Joking! Riddle Bks.). 32p. (J). (gr. 2-5). pap. 5.95 *(978-0-8225-9842-8(6))* Lerner Publishing Group.

Tafolla, Carmen & Tenayuca, Sharyll. That's Not Fair! - ¡No es Justo! Emma Tenayuca's Struggle for Justice - La Lucha de Emma Tenayuca Por la Justicia. Ybáñez, Terry, illus. 2008. (ENG & SPA.). 40p. (J). (gr. k-2). 19.95 *(978-0-916727-33-8(5))* Wings Pr.

Taylor Swift. 2011. (Megastars Ser.). (Illus.). 48p. (YA). pap. 11.75 *(978-1-4488-2261-4(0),* Rosen Reference) Rosen Publishing Group, Inc., The.

Terp, Gail. Misty Copeland. 2017. (Women Who Rock Ser.). (ENG.). 32p. (gr. 3-7). 31.35 ***(978-1-68072-065-5(1))*** Black Rabbit Bks.

—Taylor Swift. 2017. (Women Who Rock Ser.). (ENG.). 32p. (gr. 3-7). 31.35 ***(978-1-68072-069-3(4))*** Black Rabbit Bks.

Thiel, Kristin. Amelia Earhart: First Woman to Fly Solo Across the Atlantic. 2017. (J). ***(978-1-5026-2749-0(3))*** Cavendish Square Publishing.

Thompson, Gare. Who Was Eleanor Roosevelt? Wolf, Elizabeth, illus. 2004. (Who Was... ? Ser.). 106p. (gr. 3-7). 15.00 *(978-0-7569-2829-2(X))* Perfection Learning Corp.

Thornton, Jeremy. Famous Women of the American Revolution. 2009. (Building America's Democracy Ser.). 24p. (gr. 3-3). 42.50 *(978-1-61511-763-5(6),* PowerKids Pr.) Rosen Publishing Group, Inc., The.

Tieck, Sarah. Emma Stone: Talented Actress, 1 vol. 2013. (Big Buddy Biographies Set 10 Ser.). (ENG.). 32p. (J). (gr. 2-5). lib. bdg. 28.50 *(978-1-61783-861-3(6),* Big Buddy Bks.) ABDO Publishing Co.

—Gabby Douglas: Historic Olympic Champion, 1 vol. 2013. (Big Buddy Biographies Set 9 Ser.). (ENG., Illus.). 32p. (J). (gr. 2-5). lib. bdg. 28.50 *(978-1-61783-748-7(2),* Big Buddy Bks.) ABDO Publishing Co.

—Hillary Rodham Clinton, 1 vol. 2010. (First Biographies Set 6 Ser.). (ENG.). 32p. (J). (gr. 1-4). 27.07 *(978-1-60453-983-7(6))* ABDO Publishing Co.

—Kelly Clarkson: Original American Idol, 1 vol. 2014. (Big Buddy Biographies Set 11 Ser.). (ENG., Illus.). 32p. (gr. 2-5). 28.50 *(978-1-62403-196-0(X))* ABDO Publishing Co.

—Taylor Swift: Country Music Star, 1 vol. 2009. (Big Buddy Biographies Set 3 Ser.). (ENG., Illus.). 32p. (J). (gr. 2-5). 28.50 *(978-1-60453-712-3(4))* ABDO Publishing Co.

—Taylor Swift: Country Music Star CD & Book. 2010. (Big Buddy Biographies CD+Book Ser.). 32p. (gr. 2-5). audio compact disk 57.00 *(978-1-61613-311-5(2),* Big Buddy Bks.) ABDO Publishing Co.

—Taylor Swift: Country Music Star Site CD & Book. 2010. (Big Buddy Biographies Site CD+Book Ser.). 32p. (gr. 2-5). cd-rom 85.57 *(978-1-61613-283-5(3),* Big Buddy Bks.) ABDO Publishing Co.

Time for Kids Editors. Rosa Parks: Civil Rights Pioneer. 2007. (Time for Kids Biographies Ser.). (Illus.). 44p. (gr. 2-4). 14.00 *(978-0-7569-8110-5(7))* Perfection Learning Corp.

Tina Fey. 2010. (Women of Achievement Ser.). (Illus.). 136p. (J). (gr. 6-12). 35.00 *(978-1-60413-709-5(6),* Chelsea Hse.) Facts On File, Inc.

Todd, Anne M. Susan B. Anthony: Activist. 2009. (Women of Achievement Ser.). (Illus.). 128p. (gr. 6-12). 35.00 *(978-1-60413-087-4(3),* Chelsea Hse.) Facts On File, Inc.

Todd, Kim D. Jean Jennings Bartik: Computer Pioneer. 2015. (Notable Missourians Ser.). (ENG., Illus.). 48p. (J). pap. 24.00 *(978-1-61248-145-6(0))* Truman State Univ. Pr.

Tol, Alex Van & National Geographic Learning Staff. Dolores Huerta: Voice for the Working Poor. 2010. (ENG., Illus.). 112p. (J). pap. *(978-0-7787-2545-9(6))* Crabtree Publishing Co.

Tourville, Jacqueline & Guglielmo, Amy. Pocket Full of Colors: The Magical World of Mary Blair. Barrager, Brigette, illus. 2017. (ENG.). 48p. (J). (gr. -1-3). 17.99 *(978-1-4814-6131-3(1))* Simon & Schuster Children's Publishing.

Tremblay, E. A. Rachel Carson. 2003. (Women in Science Ser.). (Illus.). 112p. (gr. 6-12). 30.00 *(978-0-7910-7244-8(4),* Chelsea Hse.) Facts On File, Inc.

Trusdell, Brian. US Women Win the World Cup, 1 vol. 2014. (Greatest Events in Sports History Ser.). (ENG., Illus.). 48p. (J). (gr. 3-6). lib. bdg. 32.79 *(978-1-62403-599-9(X),* SportsZone) ABDO Publishing Co.

Turner, Ann. My Name Is Truth: The Life of Sojourner Truth. Ransome, James, illus. 2015. 40p. (J). (gr. 1-5). (ENG.). 17.99 *(978-0-06-075898-1(8));* lib. bdg. 18.89 *(978-0-06-075899-8(6))* HarperCollins Pubs.

Uschan, Michael V. Michelle Obama. 2010. (People in the News Ser.). (Illus.). 128p. (YA). (gr. 8-10). 33.95 *(978-1-4205-0209-1(3),* Lucent Bks.) Cengage Gale.

Valentin, Jean. The Bravery of Amelia Earhart. 2012. (InfoMax Readers Ser.). (ENG., Illus.). 24p. (J). (gr. 1-2). pap. 8.25 *(978-1-4488-9067-5(5),* Rosen Classroom) Rosen Publishing Group, Inc., The.

Van Steenwyk, Elizabeth. How Kate Warne Saved President Lincoln. Belloni, Valentina, illus. 2016. (ENG.). 32p. (J). (gr. -1-3). 16.99 *(978-0-8075-4117-3(6))* Whitman, Albert & Co.

Van Tol, Alex. Dolores Huerta: Voice for the Working Poor. 2010. (Crabtree Groundbreaker Biographies Ser.). (ENG., Illus.). 112p. (J). (gr. 5-8). lib. bdg. *(978-0-7787-2536-7(7))* Crabtree Publishing Co.

Van Vleet, Carmella & Sullivan, Kathy. To the Stars! The First American Woman to Walk in Space. Wong, Nicole, illus. 2016. (ENG.). 40p. (J). (gr. k-3). lib. bdg. 16.95 *(978-1-58089-644-3(8))* Charlesbridge Publishing, Inc.

Venezia, Mike. Georgia O'Keefe. Venezia, Mike, illus. 2015. (Getting to Know the World's Greatest Artists Ser.). (ENG., Illus.). 40p. (J). pap. 7.95 *(978-0-531-21291-2(2))* Scholastic Library Publishing.

—Mary Cassatt. Venezia, Mike, illus. rev. ed. 2015. (Getting to Know the World's Greatest Artists Ser.). (ENG., Illus.). 40p. (J). pap. 7.95 *(978-0-531-21292-9(0))* Scholastic Library Publishing.

Wade, Linda R. Condoleezza Rice. 2004. (Illus.). 32p. (J). lib. bdg. 25.70 *(978-1-58415-332-0(6))* Mitchell Lane Pubs., Inc.

Wade, Mary Dodson. Amazing Olympic Athlete Wilma Rudolph. 2013. (Amazing Americans Ser.). (Illus.). 24p. (J). (gr. k-3). pap. 7.95 *(978-0-7660-5978-8(2),* Enslow Elementary) Enslow Pubs., Inc.

—Condoleezza Rice. rev. ed. 2005. (Gateway Biography Ser.). (Illus.). 48p. (J). (gr. 4-7). pap. 8.95 *(978-0-7613-9549-2(0),* First Avenue Editions) Lerner Publishing Group.
—Condoleezza Rice: Being the Best. 2003. (Gateway Biography Ser.: 4). 48p. lib. bdg. 23.90 *(978-0-7613-2619-9(7));* (Illus.). (gr. 2-4). pap. 8.95 *(978-0-7613-1927-6(1))* Lerner Publishing Group. (Millbrook Pr.).
—Henrietta King: Loving the Land. Farnsworth, Bill, illus. 2011. (ENG.). 24p. 16.95 *(978-1-933979-64-9(X),* dcf39346-020e-471d-9505-349b26473e11) Bright Sky Pr.
Wallner, Alexandra. Abigail Adams. 2005. (ENG., Illus.). 32p. (J). pap. 6.95 *(978-0-8234-1942-5(8))* Holiday Hse., Inc.
—Susan B. Anthony. Wallner, Alexandra, illus. 2012. (ENG., Illus.). 32p. (J). 16.95 *(978-0-8234-1953-1(3))* Holiday Hse., Inc.
Walsh, Barbara. The Poppy Lady: Moina Belle Michael & Her Tribute to Veterans. Johnson, Layne, illus. 2012. (ENG.). 40p. (J). (gr. 2-4). 16.95 *(978-1-59078-754-0(4),* Calkins Creek) Boyds Mills Pr.
Walsh, Francis. Daring Women of the American Revolution. 2009. (Real Life Readers Ser.). 32p. (gr. 4-5). pap. 10.00 *(978-1-4358-0177-6(6),* Rosen Classroom); (J). (gr. 3-4). lib. bdg. 25.25 *(978-1-4358-2994-7(8),* PowerKids Pr.) Rosen Publishing Group, Inc., The.
Wambach, Abby. Forward: Young Reader's Edition. 224p. (J). (gr. 3-7). 2017. pap. 6.99 *(978-0-06-245793-6(4))* 2016. 16.99 *(978-0-06-245792-9(6))* HarperCollins Pubs.
Warner, Emily B. Dottie Lamm: A Friend to Families. 2007. (Now You Know Bio Ser.: 8). (J). pap. 8.95 *(978-0-86541-085-5(2))* Filter Pr., LLC.
Warren, Sarah E. Dolores Huerta: A Hero to Migrant Workers, 0 vols. Casilla, Robert, illus. 2012. (ENG.). 32p. (J). (gr. 2-5). 17.99 *(978-0-7614-6107-4(8),* 9780761461074, Amazon Children's Publishing) Amazon Publishing.
Washington, Shirley. A Gift for Girls: Words of Wisdom from Successful Women. 2005. (Illus.). 124p. (YA). (gr. 7). per. 12.95 *(978-1-933285-06-1(0))* Brown Books Publishing Group.
Watson-Doost, Valeria. Phillis Wheatley. 2008. 35p. pap. 21.50 *(978-0-557-03153-5(2))* Lulu Pr., Inc.
Watson, Marilyn Myrick. Rose Mofford: State Greats Arizona. 2007. (Acacia Biographies Ser.). (Illus.). 28p. (J). (gr. 3-7). lib. bdg. 16.95 *(978-0-9788283-5-6(6));* (gr. 4-7). per. 6.95 *(978-0-9790826-1-0(7))* Acacia Publishing, Inc.
Watson, Stephanie. Amy Poehler. Greenhaven Press Editors, ed. 2013. (People in the News Ser.). (ENG., Illus.). 128p. (gr. 7-10). lib. bdg. 39.40 *(978-1-4205-0883-3(0),* Lucent Bks.) Cengage Gale.
Watts, Franklin. Fifth Harmony: The Dream Begins ... Now! 2014. (ENG., Illus.). 48p. (J). (gr. -1-7). 12.99 *(978-1-4451-2690-6(7))* Hodder & Stoughton GBR. Dist: Hachette Bk. Group.
Waxman, Laura Hamilton. Aerospace Engineer Aprille Ericsson. 2015. (STEM Trailblazer Bios Ser.). (ENG., Illus.). 32p. (J). (gr. 2-5). lib. bdg. 26.60 *(978-1-4677-5793-5(4),* Lerner Pubns.) Lerner Publishing Group.
—Computer Engineer Ruchi Sanghvi. 2015. (STEM Trailblazer Bios Ser.). (ENG.). 32p. (J). (gr. 2-5). pap. 7.95 *(978-1-4677-6119-2(2));* lib. bdg. 26.60 *(978-1-4677-5794-2(2))* Lerner Publishing Group. (Lerner Pubns.).
—Sojourner Truth. 2008. (History Maker Biographies Ser.). (ENG., Illus.). 48p. (gr. 3-6). lib. bdg. 27.93 *(978-0-8225-7172-8(2),* Lerner Pubns.) Lerner Publishing Group.
Weakland, Mark. When Amelia Earhart Built a Roller Coaster. Grivina, Oksana, illus. 2017. 31p. (J). *(978-1-5158-0142-9(X))* Picture Window Bks.
—When Wilma Rudolph Played Basketball. Duncan, Daniel, illus. 2016. (Leaders Doing Headstands Ser.). (ENG.). 32p. (gr. 2-3). lib. bdg. 27.99 *(978-1-4795-9684-3(1))* Picture Window Bks.
Wearing, Judy. Amelia Earhart. 2010. pap. 9.95 *(978-1-61690-060-1(1));* 24p. (J). (gr. 2-4). lib. bdg. 25.70 *(978-1-61690-059-5(8))* Weigl Pubs., Inc.
Weber, Rebecca. Ellen Ochoa. 2011. (Early Connections Ser.). (J). *(978-1-61672-550-1(8))* Benchmark Education Co.
Weber, Terri Smith. Jennifer Lopez: Realizando Los Suenos. 2003. (SPA.). (J). pap. *(978-0-9740180-4-1(X));* lib. bdg. *(978-0-9740180-3-4(1))* Panda Publishing, L.L.C. (Bios for Kids).
Webster, Gayle. I Can Still Remember ..., 1 vol. 2010. 146p. pap. 24.95 *(978-1-61546-175-2(2))* America Star Bks.
Weerts, Christine. Hero of Faith - Rosa Young. 2011. 64p. pap. 7.99 *(978-0-7586-2830-5(7))* Concordia Publishing Hse.
Weidt, Maryann N. Harriet Tubman. 2003. (History Maker Bios Ser.). (Illus.). 47p. (J). 26.60 *(978-0-8225-4676-4(0),* Lerner Pubns.) Lerner Publishing Group.
—Rosa Parks. (History Maker Bios Ser.). (Illus.). (J). 2004. 48p. pap. 8.95 *(978-0-8225-4805-8(4))* 2003. 47p. 26.60 *(978-0-8225-4673-3(6))* Lerner Publishing Group. (Lerner Pubns.).
Wells, Peggy Sue. Fergie. 2007. (Blue Banner Biography Ser.). (Illus.). 32p. (YA). (gr. 4-7). lib. bdg. 25.70 *(978-1-58415-521-8(3))* Mitchell Lane Pubs., Inc.
Westen, Robin. Oprah Winfrey: I Don't Believe in Failure. 2005. (African-American Biography Library). (Illus.). 128p. (J). (gr. 6-12). lib. bdg. 33.27 *(978-0-7660-2462-5(8))* Enslow Pubs., Inc.
Weston Woods Staff, creator. Ella Fitzgerald. 2011. 38.75 *(978-0-545-02763-2(2));* 18.95 *(978-0-545-02761-8(6))* Weston Woods Studios, Inc.
Wheeler, Irvin, illus. Justina's Dream. 2005. 30p. (J). *(978-1-887302-12-8(3))* Western Images Pubns., Inc.
Wheeler, Jill C. Abigail Adams, 1 vol. 2010. (First Ladies Set 2 Ser.). (ENG., Illus.). 32p. (YA). (gr. 1-4). 27.07 *(978-1-60453-629-4(2))* ABDO Publishing Co.
—Chien-Shiung Wu: Phenomenal Physicist, 1 vol. 2012. (Women in Science Ser.). (ENG., Illus.). 32p. (J). (gr. 3-6). lib. bdg. 27.07 *(978-1-61783-451-6(3),* Checkerboard Library) ABDO Publishing Co.
—Edith Wilson, 1 vol. 2010. (First Ladies Set 2 Ser.). (ENG., Illus.). 32p. (YA). (gr. 1-4). 27.07 *(978-1-60453-634-8(9))* ABDO Publishing Co.
—Harriet Tubman. 2003. (Breaking Barriers Ser.). (Illus.). 64p. (gr. 3-8). 27.07 *(978-1-57765-908-2(2),* Abdo & Daughters) ABDO Publishing Co.
—Hillary Rodham Clinton. 2003. (Breaking Barriers Ser.). 64p. (gr. 3-8). 27.07 *(978-1-57765-741-5(1),* Abdo & Daughters) ABDO Publishing Co.
—Joanne Simpson: Magnificent Meteorologist, 1 vol. 2012. (Women in Science Ser.). (ENG., Illus.). 32p. (J). (gr. 3-6). lib. bdg. 27.07 *(978-1-61783-449-3(1),* Checkerboard Library) ABDO Publishing Co.
—Judy Blume, 1 vol. 2005. (Children's Authors Set 3 Ser.). (ENG., Illus.). 24p. (J). (gr. 2-5). 25.65 *(978-1-59197-604-2(9))* ABDO Publishing Co.
—Mae Jemison: Awesome Astronaut, 1 vol. 2012. (Women in Science Ser.). (ENG., Illus.). 32p. (J). (gr. 3-6). lib. bdg. 27.07 *(978-1-61783-447-9(5),* Checkerboard Library) ABDO Publishing Co.
—Mamie Eisenhower, 1 vol. 2010. (First Ladies Set 2 Ser.). (ENG., Illus.). 32p. (YA). (gr. 1-4). 27.07 *(978-1-60453-630-0(6))* ABDO Publishing Co.
—Marjorie Weinman Sharmat, 1 vol. 2005. (Children's Authors Set 3 Ser.). (ENG., Illus.). 24p. (gr. k-6). 25.65 *(978-1-59197-608-0(1),* Checkerboard Library) ABDO Publishing Co.
—Patricia Nixon, 1 vol. 2010. (First Ladies Set 2 Ser.). (ENG., Illus.). 32p. (YA). (gr. 1-4). 27.07 *(978-1-60453-632-4(2))* ABDO Publishing Co.
—Rosa Parks, Set II. 2003. (Breaking Barriers Ser.). 64p. (gr. 3-8). 27.07 *(978-1-57765-640-1(7),* Abdo & Daughters) ABDO Publishing Co.
Whitaker, Suzanne George. The Daring Miss Quimby. Stock, Catherine, illus. 2009. (ENG.). 32p. (J). (gr. -1-3). 16.95 *(978-0-8234-1996-8(7))* Holiday Hse., Inc.
Whiting, Jim. Annie Oakley. 2006. (What's So Great About... ? Ser.). (Illus.). 32p. (J). (gr. 2-4). lib. bdg. 25.70 *(978-1-58415-477-8(2))* Mitchell Lane Pubs., Inc.
Wills, Chuck. Annie Oakley. 2007. (DK Biography Ser.). (ENG., Illus.). 128p. (J). (gr. 5-12). per. 6.99 *(978-0-7566-2997-7(7),* DK Children) Dorling Kindersley Publishing, Inc.
Winget, Mary. Eleanor Roosevelt. (Biography Ser.). (Illus.). 2005. 112p. (gr. 6-12). lib. bdg. 27.93 *(978-0-8225-4985-7(9))* 2003. 48p. (J). pap. 8.95 *(978-0-8225-4801-0(1),* Lerner Pubns.) 2003. 48p. (J). (gr. 3-5). lib. bdg. 26.60 *(978-0-8225-4675-7(2))* Lerner Publishing Group.
Winter, Jonah. Ruth Bader Ginsburg: The Case of R. B. G. vs. Inequality. Innerst, Stacy, illus. 2017. (ENG.). 48p. (J). (gr. 1-4). 18.95 ***(978-1-4197-2559-3(9),*** Abrams Bks. for Young Readers) Abrams, Inc.
Wishinsky, Frieda. Profiles #4: Freedom Heroines. 2012. (Profiles Ser.). (ENG.). 144p. (J). (gr. 5-9). pap. 6.99 *(978-0-545-42518-6(2),* Scholastic Paperbacks) Scholastic, Inc.
Woelfle, Gretchen. Write on, Mercy! The Secret Life of Mercy Otis Warren. Wallner, Alexandra, illus. 2012. (ENG.). 40p. (J). (gr. 3). 16.95 *(978-1-59078-822-6(2),* Calkins Creek) Boyds Mills Pr.
Wojahn, Rebecca Hogue & Wojahn, Rebecca. Dr. Kate: Angel on Snowshoes. 2009. (Badger Biographies Ser.). (ENG., Illus.). 104p. (J). (gr. 3-7). pap. 12.95 *(978-0-87020-421-0(1))* Wisconsin Historical Society.
Wolff, Marion. Shedding Skins. 2004. pap. 12.00 *(978-1-930401-27-3(2))* Central Coast Bks./Pr.
Women in Science. 2016. (Women in Science Ser.). 128p. (YA). lib. bdg. 273.84 *(978-1-5026-2439-0(7))* Cavendish Square Publishing.
Women of the American Revolution (NCHS) Grades 5-8. 58p. (J). tchr. ed. 29.45 *(978-0-382-40934-9(5))* Cobblestone Publishing Co.
Wood, Ramona. The Goat Woman of Smackover: An Arkansas Legend. Wood, Ramona, . 2006. (Illus.). 32p. (J). 11.00 *(978-0-9758622-1-6(9))* ABC Pr.
Worth, Richard. Eva Longoria: Actress, Activist, & Entrepreneur. 2015. (Influential Latinos Ser.). (ENG., Illus.). 128p. (J). (gr. 7-7). 37.27 *(978-0-7660-6993-0(1))* Enslow Pubs., Inc.
Wukovits, John F. Ellen Ochoa, First Female Hispanic Astronaut. 2006. (Twentieth Century's Most Influential Hispanics Ser.). (ENG., Illus.). 104p. (YA). (gr. 7-12). lib. bdg. 34.80 *(978-1-59018-976-4(0),* 1256844) Cengage Gale.
Wyckoff, Edwin Brit. Hair-Care Millionaire: Madam C.J. Walker & Her Amazing Business. 2010. (Genius at Work! Great Inventor Biographies Ser.). 32p. (J). (gr. 2-5). 23.94 *(978-0-7660-3449-5(6))* Enslow Pubs., Inc.
—Stopping Bullets with a Thread: Stephanie Kwolek & Her Incredible Invention. 2008. (Genius at Work! Great Inventor Biographies Ser.). (Illus.). 32p. (J). (gr. 3-7). lib. bdg. 23.94 *(978-0-7660-2850-0(X),* Enslow Elementary) Enslow Pubs., Inc.
Yasuda, Anita. Lady Bird Johnson. 2010. (My Life Ser.). 24p. (J). (gr. 2-4). lib. bdg. 25.70 *(978-1-61690-062-5(8))* Weigl Pubs., Inc.
—Lady Bird Johnson: My Life. 2010. pap. 9.95 *(978-1-61690-063-2(6))* Weigl Pubs., Inc.
—Taylor Swift. 2010. (Remarkable People Ser.). (Illus.). 24p. (J). (gr. 4-6). pap. 11.95 *(978-1-61690-158-5(6));* lib. bdg. 25.70 *(978-1-61690-157-8(8))* Weigl Pubs., Inc.
Yim, Natasha. Sacajawea of the Shoshone. Nguyen, Albert, illus. 2012. (Thinking Girl's Treasury of Real Princesses Ser.). (ENG.). 32p. (J). (gr. 3-8). 18.95 *(978-0-9845098-6-7(0))* Goosebottom Bks. LLC.
Young, Jeff C. Michelle Wie. 2012. (Xtreme Athletes Ser.). (Illus.). 112p. (YA). (gr. 7-12). 28.95 *(978-1-59935-187-2(0))* Reynolds, Morgan Inc.
Younger, Barbara. Purple Mountain Majesties: The Story of Katharine Lee Bates & America the Beautiful. Schuett, Stacey, illus. 2005. 29p. (J). reprint ed. 16.00 *(978-0-7567-8984-8(2))* DIANE Publishing Co.

WOMEN ARTISTS

Abirached, Zeina. I Remember Beirut. 2014. (ENG.). 96p. pap. 9.95 *(978-1-4677-4458-4(1),* Graphic Universe™) Lerner Publishing Group.
Ball, Heather. Astonishing Women Artists, 1 vol. 2007. (Women's Hall of Fame Ser.). (ENG., Illus.). 120p. (J). (gr. 4-8). pap. 10.95 *(978-1-897187-23-4(8))* Second Story Pr. CAN. Dist: Orca Bk. Pubs. USA.
Manes, Cara & Ramos, Fatinha. Sonia Delaunay: A Life of Color. 2017. (ENG., Illus.). 36p. (J). 19.95 *(978-1-63345-024-0(4))* Museum of Modern Art.
O'Connor, Jane. Mary Cassatt: Family Pictures. Kalis, Jennifer, illus. 2003. (Smart about Art Ser.). (ENG.). 32p. (J). (gr. k-4). mass mkt. 5.99 *(978-0-448-43152-9(1),* Grosset & Dunlap) Penguin Young Readers Group.
Osmundson, Linda. How the West Was Drawn: Women's Art, 1 vol. 2014. (ENG., Illus.). 32p. (J). (gr. k-7). 16.99 *(978-1-4556-1878-1(0))* Pelican Publishing Co., Inc.
Rembert, Winfred. Don't Hold Me Back: My Life & Art. Rembert, Winfred, illus. 2003. (ENG., Illus.). 48p. (J). 19.95 *(978-0-8126-2703-9(2))* Cricket Bks.
Singh, Rina. Pitseolak Ashoona: Une Artiste Inuite. 2004. (FRE., Illus.). (J). *(978-2-7650-0741-8(1))* Les Editions de la Cheneliere, Inc.
Spinner, Stephanie. Who Was Annie Oakley? Day, Larry, illus. 2003. (Who Was...? Ser.). 109p. (gr. 4-7). 15.00 *(978-0-7569-1588-9(0))* Perfection Learning Corp.
Terp, Gail. Taylor Swift. 2017. (Women Who Rock Ser.). (ENG.). 32p. (gr. 3-7). 31.35 ***(978-1-68072-069-3(4))*** Black Rabbit Bks.
Wenzel, Angela & Schuelmann, Bettina. 13 Women Artists Children Should Know. 2009. (ENG., Illus.). 48p. (J). (gr. 3-7). 14.95 *(978-3-7913-4333-4(5))* Prestel Verlag GmbH & Co KG. DEU. Dist: Penguin Random Hse. LLC.

WOMEN ATHLETES

Adler, David A. America's Champion Swimmer: Gertrude Ederle. Widener, Terry, illus. 2005. (ENG.). 32p. (J). (gr. -1-3). reprint ed. pap. 7.99 *(978-0-15-205251-5(8))* Houghton Mifflin Harcourt Publishing Co.
Allen, Kathy. Girls Race! Amazing Tales of Women in Sports, 1 vol. 2013. (Girls Rock! Ser.). (ENG.). 64p. (gr. 4-5). 34.65 *(978-1-4765-0233-5(1))* Capstone Press of Coughlan Cos.
Anderson, Jameson. Gabby Douglas, 1 vol. 2014. (Awesome Athletes Ser.). (ENG.). 32p. (gr. 8-12). lib. bdg. 27.07 *(978-1-62403-338-4(5),* Checkerboard Library) ABDO Publishing Co.
Blumenthal, Karen. Let Me Play: The Story of Title IX - The Law That Changed the Future of Girls in America. 2005. (ENG., Illus.). 160p. (J). (gr. 3-7). 22.99 *(978-0-689-85957-1(0),* Atheneum Bks. for Young Readers) Simon & Schuster Children's Publishing.
Braun, Eric. Lindsey Vonn. 2017. (Sports All-Stars Ser.). (ENG.). 32p. (J). (gr. 2-5). 12.99 ***(978-1-5124-3786-7(7),*** Lerner Pubns.); 39.99 ***(978-1-5124-3785-0(9),*** Lerner Pubns.); (Illus.). 26.65 *(978-1-5124-2580-2(X));* (Illus.). 39.99 ***(978-1-5124-2825-4(6),*** Lerner Pubns.) Lerner Publishing Group.
Buckley, James. Katie Ledecky. 2017. (Amazing Americans: Olympians Ser.). (ENG.). 24p. (J). (gr. -1-3). 17.95 ***(978-1-68402-240-3(1))*** Bearport Publishing Co., Inc.
Cantwell, Lois. Women Winners: Then & Now. 2009. (Sports Illustrated for Kids Bks). 176p. (gr. 7-12). 63.90 *(978-1-60853-157-8(0))* Rosen Publishing Group, Inc., The.
Carey, Nicolette & Bryant, Jill. Women Athletes Who Changed the World. 2011. (Great Women of Achievement Ser.). (ENG., Illus.). 112p. (YA). (gr. 5-8). lib. bdg. 34.60 *(978-1-4488-6001-2(6))* Rosen Publishing Group, Inc., The.
Carroll, Myrna & Manley, Claudia B. Track & Field: Girls Rocking It, 01 vols., 1. 2016. (Title IX Rocks! Ser.). (ENG., Illus.). 64p. (J). 32.95 *(978-1-5081-7043-3(6),* Rosen Young Adult) Rosen Publishing Group, Inc., The.
Douglas, Gabrielle & Burford, Michelle. Raising the Bar, 1 vol. 2013. (ENG.). 144p. (J). 19.99 *(978-0-310-74070-4(3))* Zondervan.
Dzidrums, Christine. Missy Franklin: Swimming Sensation. 2013. 72p. pap. 9.99 *(978-1-938438-23-3(X))* Creative Media Publishing.
Dzidrums, Christine & Rendon, Leah. Jennie Finch. Dzidrums, Joseph, photos by. 2013. (Illus.). 72p. pap. 9.99 *(978-1-938438-13-4(2))* Creative Media Publishing.
Faust, Daniel R. Ibtihaj Muhammad: Muslim American Champion Fencer & Olympian. 2017. (Breakout Biographies Ser.). 32p. (gr. 9-10). 26.25 ***(978-1-5081-6060-1(0),*** PowerKids Pr.) Rosen Publishing Group, Inc., The.
Feldman, Heather. Marion Jones: Atleta de Categoría Internacional (World-Class Runner) 2009. (Superestrellas del Deporte (Superstars of Sports) Ser.). (SPA.). 24p. (gr. 1-2). 42.50 *(978-1-60853-227-8(5),* Editorial Buenas Letras) Rosen Publishing Group, Inc., The.
—Marion Jones: World Class Runner. 2009. (Sports Superstars Ser.). 24p. (gr. 1-1). 42.50 *(978-1-60853-179-0(1),* PowerKids Pr.) Rosen Publishing Group, Inc., The.
Fishman, Jon M. Simone Biles. 2017. (Sports All-Stars Ser.). (ENG.). 32p. (J). (gr. 2-5). 12.99 ***(978-1-5124-4901-3(6),*** Lerner Pubns.); 39.99 ***(978-1-5124-4899-3(0),*** Lerner Pubns.); 39.99 ***(978-1-5124-4900-6(8),*** Lerner Pubns.); (Illus.). lib. bdg. 26.65 *(978-1-5124-4897-9(4))* Lerner Publishing Group.
Freedman, Russell. Babe Didrikson Zaharias: The Making of a Champion. 2014. (ENG., Illus.). 192p. (J). (gr. 5-7). pap. 10.99 *(978-0-544-10491-4(9))* Houghton Mifflin Harcourt Publishing Co.
Green, Michelle Y. A Strong Right Arm: The Story of Mamie Peanut Johnson. Nelson, Kadir, illus. 2004. (ENG.). 128p. (J). (gr. 3-7). 5.99 *(978-0-14-240072-2(6),* Puffin Books) Penguin Young Readers Group.
Guillermo-Newton, Judith. Competitive Tennis for Girls. 2005. (SportsGirl Ser.). (Illus.). 64p. (YA). (gr. 5-9). lib. bdg. 31.95 *(978-0-8239-3407-2(1))* Rosen Publishing Group, Inc., The.
Guillermo-Newton, Judy. Competitive Tennis for Girls. 2009. (SportsGirl Ser.). 64p. (gr. 5-8). 58.50 *(978-1-60853-194-3(5),* Rosen Reference) Rosen Publishing Group, Inc., The.
Hernandez, Laurie. I Got This: To Gold & Beyond. 240p. (J). (gr. 3-7). 2018. (ENG.). pap. 8.99 ***(978-0-06-267732-7(2))*** 2017. 17.99 ***(978-0-06-267731-0(4))*** HarperCollins Pubs.
Ignotofsky, Rachel. Women in Sports: 50 Fearless Athletes Who Played to Win. 2017. (ENG., Illus.). 128p. (gr. 5-12). 16.99 ***(978-1-60774-978-3(5),*** Ten Speed Pr.) Potter/TenSpeed/Harmony.
Jones, Emma. Girls Play Rugby. 2016. (Girls Join the Team Ser.). 24p. (J). (gr. 3-3). pap. 8.25 *(978-1-4994-2105-7(2),* PowerKids Pr.) Rosen Publishing Group, Inc., The.
Kawa, Katie. Women in Sports. 2015. (Women Groundbreakers Ser.). (ENG., Illus.). 32p. (J). (gr. 4-5). pap. 10.00 *(978-1-4994-1051-8(4),* PowerKids Pr.) Rosen Publishing Group, Inc., The.
Kirkpatrick, Rob. Florence Griffith Joyner: Olympic Runner. 2009. (Great Record Breakers in Sports Ser.). 24p. (gr. 3-3). 42.50 *(978-1-61513-187-7(6),* PowerKids Pr.) Rosen Publishing Group, Inc., The.
Koya, Lena & La Bella, Laura. Women Athletes. 2017. (J). ***(978-1-5081-7718-0(X))*** Rosen Publishing Group, Inc., The.
La Bella, Laura. Women & Sports. 2012. (Young Woman's Guide to Contemporary Issues Ser.). (ENG., Illus.). 112p. (YA). (gr. 9-12). lib. bdg. 34.60 *(978-1-4488-8398-1(9))* Rosen Publishing Group, Inc., The.
Lang, Heather. Queen of the Track: Alice Coachman, Olympic High-Jump Champion. Cooper, Floyd, illus. 2012. (ENG.). 40p. (J). (gr. k). 16.95 *(978-1-59078-850-9(8))* Boyds Mills Pr.
Lloyd, Carli & Coffey, Wayne. All Heart: My Dedication & Determination to Become One of Soccer's Best. 2016. (ENG., Illus.). 304p. (J). (gr. 5-7). 16.99 *(978-0-544-97869-0(2),* HMH Books For Young Readers) Houghton Mifflin Harcourt Publishing Co.
Lobby, Mackenzie. Babe Didrikson Zaharias: Groundbreaking All-Around Athlete, 1 vol. 2011. (Legendary Athletes Ser.). (ENG., Illus.). 112p. (YA). (gr. 7-12). 34.22 *(978-1-61714-755-5(9))* ABDO Publishing Co.
Mabry-Gordon, Sherri. Women Athletes. 2016. (Defying Convention: Women Who Changed the Rules Ser.). (Illus.). 128p. (J). 37.27 *(978-0-7660-8147-5(8))* Enslow Pubs., Inc.
Macy, Sue. Roller Derby Rivals. Collins, Matt, illus. 2014. (ENG.). 32p. (J). (gr. k-5). 16.95 *(978-0-8234-2923-3(7))* Holiday Hse., Inc.
—Trudy's Big Swim: How Gertrude Ederle Swam the English Channel & Took the World by Storm. Collins, Matt, illus. 2017. (ENG.). 40p. (J). (gr. 1-5). 16.95 *(978-0-8234-3665-1(9))* Holiday Hse., Inc.
Manley, Claudia B. Competitive Track & Field for Girls. (SportsGirl Ser.). 64p. (gr. 5-8). 2009. 58.50 *(978-1-60853-195-0(3),* Rosen Reference) 2005. (Illus.). (YA). lib. bdg. 31.95 *(978-0-8239-3408-9(X))* Rosen Publishing Group, Inc., The.
McDougall, Chros. Girls Play to Win Figure Skating. 2010. (Girls Play to Win Ser.). 64p. (J). (gr. 3-6). lib. bdg. 27.93 *(978-1-59953-389-6(8))* Norwood Hse. Pr.
—Girls Play to Win Volleyball. 2010. (Girls Play to Win Ser.). 64p. (J). (gr. 3-6). lib. bdg. 27.93 *(978-1-59953-392-6(8))* Norwood Hse. Pr.
McMahon, Dave. Girls Play to Win Hockey. 2010. (Girls Play to Win Ser.). 64p. (J). (gr. 3-6). lib. bdg. 27.93 *(978-1-59953-390-2(1))* Norwood Hse. Pr.
Moore, Kaitlin. Kerri Strug & & the Magnificent Seven. 2016. (Totally True Adventures Ser.). (ENG., Illus.). 112p. (J). (gr. 1-4). pap. 4.99 *(978-0-553-52174-0(8),* Random Hse. Bks. for Young Readers) Random Hse. Children's Bks.
Moss, Marissa. Mighty Jackie: The Strike-Out Queen. Payne, C. F., tr. Payne, C. F., illus. 2004. (ENG.). 32p. (J). (gr. k-3). 18.99 *(978-0-689-86329-5(2),* Simon & Schuster/Paula Wiseman Bks.) Simon & Schuster/Paula Wiseman Bks.
Nagelhout, Ryan. Beth Phoenix. 2013. (Superstars of Wrestling Ser.). (Illus.). 32p. (J). (gr. 3-6). pap. 10.50 *(978-1-4339-8513-3(6));* lib. bdg. 25.25 *(978-1-4339-8512-6(8))* Stevens, Gareth Publishing LLLP.
Nicholson, Lorna Schultz. Pink Power: The First Women's Hockey World Champions. 2007. (Recordbooks Ser.). (ENG., Illus.). 128p. (YA). (gr. 3-8). *(978-1-55028-989-3(6))* Lorimer, James & Co., Ltd., Pubs. CAN. Dist: Casemate Pubs. & Bk. Distributors, LLC.
—Winning Gold: Canada's Incredible 2002 Olympic Victory in Women's Hockey, 1 vol. (Lorimer Recordbooks Ser.). (ENG., Illus.). 112p. (J). (gr. 8-12). 2010. 16.95 *(978-1-55277-473-1(2),* 9781552774731) 2009. pap. 9.95 *(978-1-55277-472-4(4),* 9781552774724) Lorimer, James & Co., Ltd., Pubs. CAN. Dist: Casemate Pubs. & Bk. Distributors, LLC.
Offutt, Jason. Helen Stephens: The Fulton Flash. Hare, John, illus. 2014. (ENG.). 48p. (J). lib. bdg. 24.00 *(978-1-61248-114-2(0))* Truman State Univ. Pr.
Paul, Caroline. The Gutsy Girl: Escapades for Your Life of Epic Adventure. MacNaughton, Wendy, illus. 2016. (ENG.). 160p. (gr. 5-8). 18.00 *(978-1-63286-123-8(2),* 9781632861238) Bloomsbury Publishing USA.
Rappoport, Ken. Ladies First: Women Athletes Who Made a Difference, 1 vol. 2005. (ENG., Illus.). 192p. (J). (gr. 3-7). 14.95 *(978-1-56145-338-2(2))* Peachtree Pubs.
—Ladies First: Women Athletes Who Made a Difference, 1 vol. 2010. (ENG., Illus.). 192p. (J). pap. 8.95 *(978-1-56145-534-8(2))* Peachtree Pubs.
Riner, Dax & Savage, Jeff. Annika Sorenstam. 2008. (Sports Heroes & Legends Ser.). (ENG.). (gr. 5-12). pap. 56.72 *(978-0-8225-9397-3(1))* Lerner Publishing Group.
Robinson, Tom. Girls Play to Win Basketball. 2010. (Girls Play to Win Ser.). 64p. (J). (gr. 3-6). lib. bdg. 27.93 *(978-1-59953-388-9(X))* Norwood Hse. Pr.
Savage, Jeff. Maya Moore. 2012. (Amazing Athletes Ser.). (ENG.). 32p. (gr. 2-5). pap. 7.95 *(978-0-7613-8666-7(1))* Lerner Publishing Group.
Schultz Nicholson, Lorna. Pink Power: The First Women's Hockey World Champions, 1 vol. 2007. (Lorimer Recordbooks Ser.). (ENG., Illus.). 128p. (J). (gr. 3-8). 9.95 *(978-1-55028-987-9(X),* 9781550289879) Lorimer, James & Co., Ltd., Pubs. CAN. Dist: Casemate Pubs. & Bk. Distributors, LLC.
Segovia, Patty. Skate Girls. 2016. (Illus.). 32p. (J). *(978-1-4896-4783-2(X))* Weigl Pubs., Inc.
Trusdell, Brian. US Women Win the World Cup, 1 vol. 2014. (Greatest Events in Sports History Ser.). (ENG., Illus.). 48p. (J). (gr. 3-6). lib. bdg. 32.79 *(978-1-62403-599-9(X),* SportsZone) ABDO Publishing Co.
Wade, Mary Dodson. Amazing Olympic Athlete Wilma Rudolph. 2013. (Amazing Americans Ser.). (Illus.). 24p. (J). (gr. k-3). pap. 7.95 *(978-0-7660-5978-8(2),* Enslow Elementary) Enslow Pubs., Inc.
Wills, Chuck. Annie Oakley. 2007. (DK Biography Ser.). (ENG., Illus.). 128p. (J). (gr. 5-12). per. 6.99 *(978-0-7566-2997-7(7),* DK Children) Dorling Kindersley Publishing, Inc.

W X Y Z

Young, Jeff C. Michelle Wie. 2012. (Xtreme Athletes Ser.). (Illus.). 112p. (YA). (gr. 7-12). 28.95 *(978-1-59935-187-2(0))* Reynolds, Morgan Inc.

WOMEN AUTHORS

Abrams, Dennis. Maxine Hong Kingston. 2009. (Asian Americans of Achievement Ser.). (Illus.). 128p. (YA). (gr. 7-12). 35.00 *(978-1-60413-568-8(9))* Facts On File, Inc.

Ball, Heather. Women Writers Who Changed the World. 2011. (Great Women of Achievement Ser.). (ENG., Illus.). 112p. (YA). (gr. 5-8). lib. bdg. 34.60 *(978-1-4488-5997-9(2),* Rosen Reference) Rosen Publishing Group, Inc., The.

Bennett, Doraine. Laura Ingalls Wilder: Little World Biographies. 2013. (ENG.). 24p. (gr. k-3). pap. 8.95 *(978-1-61810-293-5(1))* Rourke Educational Media.

Berne, Emma Carlson. Laura Ingalls Wilder, 1 vol. 2007. (Essential Lives Set 1 Ser.). (ENG., Illus.). 112p. (J). (gr. 6-12). lib. bdg. 35.64 *(978-1-59928-843-7(5))* ABDO Publishing Co.

Burton, Zisca Isabel. Bloom's How to Write about Toni Morrison. 2008. (Bloom's How to Write about Literature Ser.). 212p. (C). (gr. 9-12). 45.00 *(978-0-7910-9548-5(7),* Chelsea Hse.) Facts On File, Inc.

Butler, Erin. Writers. 2016. (Uncommon Women Ser.). (ENG., Illus.). 48p. (gr. 3-8). 27.99 *(978-1-62920-581-6(8))* Scobre Pr. Corp.

Capaldi, Gina & Pearce, Q. L. Red Bird Sings: The Story of Zitkala-Sa, Native American Author, Musician, & Activist. Capaldi, Gina, illus. 2011. (Exceptional Social Studies Titles for Intermediate Grades). (ENG., Illus.). 32p. (J). (gr. 3-6). lib. bdg. 17.95 *(978-0-7613-5257-0(0))* Lerner Publishing Group.

Castor, Harriet & Collins UK Staff. Charlotte Bronte. 2016. (ENG.). 80p. (J). (gr. 5-6). pap. 9.95 *(978-0-00-816405-8(3))* HarperCollins Pubs. Ltd. GBR. Dist: Independent Pubs. Group.

Colbert, David. Maya Angelou. 2009. (10 Days Ser.). (ENG.). 160p. (J). pap. 6.99 *(978-1-4169-6804-7(0),* Simon & Schuster/Paula Wiseman Bks.) Simon & Schuster/Paula Wiseman Bks.

Demuth, Patricia Brennan. Who Was Laura Ingalls Wilder? 2013. (Who Was...? Ser.). lib. bdg. 16.00 *(978-0-606-32134-1(9),* Turtleback) Turtleback Bks.

Dubois, Muriel L. To My Countrywomen: The Life of Sarah Josepha Hale. 2006. 16.00 *(978-0-9723410-1-1(3))* Apprentice Shop Bks., LLC.

Eason, Sarah. Malorie Blackman. 2016. (Real-Life Stories Ser.). (ENG., Illus.). 32p. (J). (gr. 4-6). pap. 11.99 *(978-0-7502-9045-6(5),* Wayland) Hachette Children's Group GBR. Dist: Hachette Bk. Group.

Engle, Margarita. Enchanted Air: Two Cultures, Two Wings: A Memoir. Rodriguez, Edel, illus. (ENG.). (YA). (gr. 7). 2016. 224p. pap. 10.99 *(978-1-4814-3523-9(X))* 2015. 208p. 18.99 *(978-1-4814-3522-2(1))* Simon & Schuster Children's Publishing.

—Enchanted Air: Two Cultures, Two Wings: A Memoir. 2016. lib. bdg. 20.85 *(978-0-606-38989-1(X))* Turtleback Bks.

Fabiny, Sarah & dePaola, Tomie. Who Was Beatrix Potter? Lacey, Mike & Harrison, Nancy, illus. 2015. (Who Was? Ser.). (ENG.). 112p. (J). (gr. 3-7). 5.99 *(978-0-448-48305-4(X),* Grosset & Dunlap) Penguin Young Readers Group.

Ferguson, Isabel, et al. A World More Bright: The Life of Mary Baker Eddy. 2013. (Illus.). vi, 279p. (J). *(978-0-87510-494-2(0))* Christian Science Publishing Society.

Ferguson, Melissa. Suzanne Collins: Author of the Hunger Games Trilogy. 2016. (Famous Female Authors Ser.). (ENG., Illus.). 32p. (gr. 3-4). lib. bdg. 27.99 *(978-1-5157-1326-5(1),* Snap Bks.) Capstone Press of Coughlan Cos.

Fromowitz, Lori. Louisa May Alcott. 2013. (ENG.). 48p. (J). pap. 15.64 *(978-1-61783-765-4(2));* (gr. 3-6). lib. bdg. 32.79 *(978-1-61783-715-9(6))* ABDO Publishing Co.

Griffiths, Katie. Harriet Beecher Stowe. 2016. (Great American Thinkers Ser.). (ENG.). 128p. (J). (gr. 9-9). 45.64 *(978-1-5026-1930-3(X))* Cavendish Square Publishing.

Griskey, Michele. Beverly Cleary. 2006. (Classic Storytellers Ser.). (Illus.). 48p. (J). (gr. 4-7). lib. bdg. 29.95 *(978-1-58415-457-0(8),* 1259543) Mitchell Lane Pubs., Inc.

Hagler, Gina. Sarah Dessen. 2013. (All about the Author Ser.). 112p. (YA). (gr. 7-12). 34.60 *(978-1-4777-1768-4(4))* Rosen Publishing Group, Inc., The.

Haugen, Brenda. Harriet Beecher Stowe: The Inspiring Life Story of the Abolition Advocate. 2016. (Inspiring Stories Ser.). (ENG., Illus.). 112p. (gr. 5-7). lib. bdg. 35.99 *(978-0-7565-5164-3(1),* CPB Grades 4-8) Compass Point Bks.

Herweck Rice, Dona. Stepping into Louisa May Alcott's World (Grade 7) 2017. (TIME for KIDS(r) Nonfiction Readers Ser.). (Illus.). 48p. (J). (gr. 7-7). pap. 9.99 ***(978-1-4938-3619-2(6))*** Teacher Created Materials, Inc.

Hoover, Elizabeth. Suzanne Collins. 2012. (People in the News Ser.). (ENG., Illus.). 128p. (gr. 7-10). lib. bdg. 39.40 *(978-1-4205-0762-1(1),* Lucent Bks.) Cengage Gale.

Hunsicker, Jennifer, et al. Famous Female Authors. 2016. (Famous Female Authors Ser.). (ENG.). 32p. (gr. 3-4). 111.96 *(978-1-5157-1351-7(2),* Snap Bks.) Capstone Press of Coughlan Cos.

Hunter, Nick. Suzanne Collins, 1 vol. 2014. (Extraordinary Women Ser.). (ENG.). 48p. (gr. 6-6). lib. bdg. 32.65 *(978-1-4109-5944-7(9))* Heinemann-Raintree.

Johanson, Paula. Women Writers. 2016. (Defying Convention: Women Who Changed the Rules Ser.). 128p. (J). 37.27 *(978-0-7660-8145-1(1))* Enslow Pubs., Inc.

Kamberg, Mary-Lane. Margaret Peterson Haddix. 2013. (All about the Author Ser.). 112p. (YA). (gr. 7-12). 34.60 *(978-1-4777-1765-3(X))* Rosen Publishing Group, Inc., The.

Kite, L. Patricia. Maya Angelou. 2006. (Just the Facts Biographies Ser.). (Illus.). 112p. (J). (gr. 3-7). pap. 9.95 *(978-0-8225-5997-9(8),* Lerner Pubns.) Lerner Publishing Group.

Lasky, Kathryn. A Voice of Her Own: The Story of Phillis Wheatley, Slave Poet. Lee, Paul, illus. 2012. (Candlewick Biographies Ser.). (ENG.). 48p. (J). (gr. 3-7). 14.99 *(978-0-7636-6427-5(8));* pap. 4.99 *(978-0-7636-6091-8(4))* Candlewick Pr.

Lazaro, Georgina. Juana Ines. Preza, Bruno Gonzalez, illus. 2007. (SPA.). 32p. (J). (gr. 3-5). 14.99 *(978-1-930332-57-7(2))* Lectorum Pubns., Inc.

Leaf, Christina. Laura Ingalls Wilder. 2015. (Children's Storytellers Ser.). (ENG., Illus.). 24p. (J). (gr. 2-5). lib. bdg. 25.95 *(978-1-62617-269-2(2),* Blastoff! Readers) Bellwether Media.

Macy, Sue. Miss Mary Reporting. Payne, C. F., illus. 2016. (ENG.). 40p. (J). (gr. k-3). 17.99 *(978-1-4814-0120-3(3),* Simon & Schuster Bks. For Young Readers) Simon & Schuster Bks. For Young Readers.

Marcovitz, Hal. Pat Mora. 2007. (Who Wrote That? Ser.). (Illus.). 135p. (gr. 6-12). lib. bdg. 35.00 *(978-0-7910-9528-7(2),* Chelsea Hse.) Facts On File, Inc.

Marsh, Carole. Harriet Beecher Stowe. 2003. 12p. (gr. k-4). 2.95 *(978-0-635-02356-8(3))* Gallopade International.

O'Keefe, Sherry. From China to America: The Story of Amy Tan. 2011. (World Writers Ser.). 112p. (gr. 7-18). lib. bdg. 28.95 *(978-1-59935-138-4(2))* Reynolds, Morgan Inc.

Rau, Dana Meachen & dePaola, Tomie. Who Was Harriet Beecher Stowe? Harrison, Nancy & Copeland, Gregory, illus. 2015. (Who Was? Ser.). (ENG.). 112p. (J). (gr. 3-7). 5.99 *(978-0-448-48301-6(7),* Grosset & Dunlap) Penguin Young Readers Group.

Reef, Catherine. The Brontë Sisters: The Brief Lives of Charlotte, Emily, & Anne. (ENG., Illus.). 240p. (J). (gr. 5-7). 2015. pap. 9.99 *(978-0-544-45590-0(8),* HMH Books For Young Readers) 2012. 18.99 *(978-0-547-57966-5(7))* Houghton Mifflin Harcourt Publishing Co.

Reiff, Rachel Haugrud. Sandra Cisneros. 2013. (Today's Writers & Their Works Ser.). (ENG.). 144p. (YA). (gr. 7-12). pap. 22.34 *(978-1-62712-145-3(5))* Cavendish Square Publishing.

Rice, Dona Herweck. Stepping into Louisa May Alcott's World. 2017. (Time for Kids Nonfiction Readers Ser.). lib. bdg. 20.85 ***(978-0-606-40262-0(4))*** Turtleback Bks.

Sanchez Vegara, Isabel. Agatha Christie. 2017. (Little People, Big Dreams Ser.). (ENG., Illus.). (J). (gr. k-3). 14.99 ***(978-1-84780-960-5(X),*** Frances Lincoln Children's Bks.) Quarto Publishing Group UK GBR. Dist: Hachette Bk. Group.

Sanderson, Caroline. Jane Austen: Novelist. 2016. (History Makers Ser.). 128p. (YA). lib. bdg. 45.64 *(978-1-5026-2445-1(1))* Cavendish Square Publishing.

Sapet, Kerrily. Suzanne Collins. 2012. (Illus.). 112p. (J). *(978-1-59935-346-3(6))* Reynolds, Morgan Inc.

Sexton, Colleen A. & Cosgrove, Martha. J. K. Rowling. 2006. (Just the Facts Biographies Ser.). (Illus.). 112p. (J). pap. 9.95 *(978-0-8225-5995-5(1),* Lerner Pubns.) Lerner Publishing Group.

Smith, Emily R. Phillis Wheatley, 1 vol. 2004. (Primary Source Readers Ser.). (ENG.). 24p. (J). (gr. 4-4). pap. 8.99 *(978-0-7439-8743-1(8))* Shell Educational Publishing.

Staley, Erin. Maggie Stiefvater. 2013. (All about the Author Ser.). 112p. (YA). (gr. 7-12). 34.60 *(978-1-4777-1762-2(5))* Rosen Publishing Group, Inc., The.

Sullivan, Laura L. Jacqueline Woodson. 2014. (Spotlight on Children's Authors Ser.). (Illus.). 48p. (J). (gr. 4-6). lib. bdg. 29.93 *(978-1-62712-855-1(7))* Cavendish Square Publishing.

Undset, Sigrid. Happy Times in Norway. 2013. (ENG., Illus.). 240p. pap. 16.95 *(978-0-8166-7827-3(8))* Univ. of Minnesota Pr.

Wilson, Jacqueline & Carey, Joanna. Interview with Jacqueline Wilson. (Illus.). 96p. pap. 5.50 *(978-1-4052-0055-4(3))* Egmont Bks., Ltd. GBR. Dist: Trafalgar Square Publishing.

WOMEN IN AERONAUTICS

Barton, Jen. What's Your Story, Amelia Earhart? 2016. (Cub Reporter Meets Famous Americans Ser.). (ENG., Illus.). 32p. (J). (gr. k-3). pap. 8.99 *(978-1-4677-9645-3(X))* Lerner Publishing Group.

Burke, John. Amelia Earhart: Flying Solo. 2017. (Great Leaders & Events Ser.). (ENG.). (J). (gr. 4-8). lib. bdg. 35.99 ***(978-1-942875-45-1(2))*** Quarto Publishing Group USA.

Dell, Pamela. The Soviet Night Witches: Brave Women Bomber Pilots of World War II. 2017. (Women & War Ser.). (ENG.). 32p. (gr. 3-4). lib. bdg. 27.99 ***(978-1-5157-7938-4(6),*** Snap Bks.) Capstone Press of Coughlan Cos.

Friend, Robyn C. The Women of Apollo. Katz, David Arthur, illus. l.t. ed. 2006. 80p. (J). 17.95 *(978-1-880599-80-8(5));* pap. 12.95 *(978-1-880599-79-2(1))* Cascade Pass, Inc.

Gibson, Karen Bush. Women Aviators: 26 Stories of Pioneer Flights, Daring Missions, & Record-Setting Journeys. 2013. (Women of Action Ser.). (ENG., Illus.). 240p. (YA). (gr. 7). 19.95 *(978-1-61374-540-3(0))* Chicago Review Pr., Inc.

Homan, Lynn M. & Reilly, Thomas. Women Who Fly, 1 vol. Shepherd, Rosalie M., illus. 2004. (ENG.). 104p. (J). (gr. 3-7). 14.95 *(978-1-58980-160-8(1))* Pelican Publishing Co., Inc.

Klingel, Cynthia Fitterer & Klingel, Cynthia. Amelia Earhart: Aviation Pioneer. 2003. (Our People Ser.). (ENG., Illus.). 32p. (J). (gr. 3-6). 29.93 *(978-1-59296-000-2(6),* 200627) Child's World, Inc., The.

Lakin, Patricia, et al. Amelia Earhart: More Than a Flier. Daniel, Alan & Daniel, Lea, illus. 2003. (Ready-To-read SOFA Ser.). (ENG.). 48p. (J). (gr. 1-3). pap. 3.99 *(978-0-689-85575-7(3),* Simon Spotlight) Simon Spotlight.

Langley, Wanda. Women of the Wind: Early Women Aviators. 2006. (Women Adventurers Ser.). (Illus.). 160p. (J). (gr. 6-12). lib. bdg. 26.95 *(978-1-931798-81-5(8))* Reynolds, Morgan Inc.

Lukesh, Jean A. Sky Rider: Story of Evelyn Sharp, World War II WASP. 2011. (Noteworthy Americans Young Readers Biography Book Ser.). (ENG., Illus.). 161p. (J). pap. 14.95 *(978-0-9647586-3-6(6))* Field Mouse Productions.

Micklos, John & Micklos, John, Jr. Unsolved: What Really Happened to Amelia Earhart? 2006. (Prime (Middle/Senior) Ser.). (Illus.). 144p. (J). (gr. 5-9). lib. bdg. 34.60 *(978-0-7660-2365-9(6))* Enslow Pubs., Inc.

Montgomery, Christine. Marie Meyer Fower: Barnstormer. 2015. (ENG., Illus.). 48p. (J). 24.00 *(978-1-61248-149-4(3))* Truman State Univ. Pr.

Pflueger, Lynda. Amelia Earhart: Legend of Flight. 2003. (Historical American Biographies Ser.). (Illus.). 128p. (J). lib. bdg. 27.94 *(978-0-7660-1976-8(4))* Enslow Pubs., Inc.

Reyburn, Susan. Amelia Earhart. 2006. (Women Who Dare Ser.). (Illus.). 64p. 12.95 *(978-0-7649-3545-9(3),* A111) Pomegranate Communications, Inc.

Rinaldo, Denise. Amelia Earhart: With a Discussion of Courage. 2004. (Values in Action Ser.). (J). *(978-1-59203-068-2(8))* Learning Challenge, Inc.

Simons, Lisa M. Bolt. The U. S. WASP: Trailblazing Women Pilots of World War II. 2017. (Women & War Ser.). (ENG.). 32p. (gr. 3-4). pap. 8.19 ***(978-1-5157-7944-5(0));*** lib. bdg. 27.99 ***(978-1-5157-7937-7(8))*** Capstone Press of Coughlan Cos. (Snap Bks.).

Smith, Matthew Clark. Lighter Than Air: Sophie Blanchard, the First Woman Pilot. Tavares, Matt, illus. 2017. (ENG.). 32p. (J). (gr. 1-4). 16.99 *(978-0-7636-7732-9(9))* Candlewick Pr.

Weakland, Mark. When Amelia Earhart Built a Roller Coaster. Grivina, Oksana, illus. 2016. (Leaders Doing Headstands Ser.). (ENG.). 32p. (gr. 2-3). pap. 7.95 *(978-1-5158-0138-2(1))* Picture Window Bks.

WOMEN IN INDUSTRY

see Women—Employment

WOMEN IN POLITICS

see Women—Political Activity

WOMEN IN THE BIBLE

Bader, Joanne. The Widow's Offering. 2008. (Arch Bks.). 16p. (J). (gr. k-4). pap. 1.99 *(978-0-7586-1451-3(9))* Concordia Publishing Hse.

Green, John. Women of the Bible. 2006. (Dover Classic Stories Coloring Book Ser.). (ENG., Illus.). 32p. (J). (gr. 3-8). 3.99 *(978-0-486-45193-0(3))* Dover Pubns., Inc.

Holmes, Andy. My Princess Bible. Eliseev, Sergey, illus. 2010. (ENG.). 66p. (J). bds. 12.99 *(978-1-4143-3324-3(2))* Tyndale Hse. Pubs.

Krishna, McArthur & Spalding, Bethany Brady. Girls Who Choose God. Peterson, Kathleen, illus. 2014. (J). 17.99 *(978-1-60907-882-9(9),* Ensign Peak) Shadow Mountain Publishing.

Larsen, Carolyn. Princess Stories: Real Bible Stories of God's Princesses. Eliseev, Sergey, illus. 2012. (ENG.). 128p. (J). 14.99 *(978-1-4143-4811-7(8),* Tyndale Kids) Tyndale Hse. Pubs.

Lo, Monica. Old Testament Heroines of the Faith. Diehl, Nichole, illus. 2007. 82p. per. 17.99 *(978-1-59879-224-9(5),* Lifevest) Lifevest Publishing, Inc.

MacKenzie, Carine. Hannah: The Mother Who Prayer. McLaren, Duncan, illus. 2013. (Bible Time Ser.). (ENG.). 32p. (J). (gr. -1-2). pap. 3.99 *(978-1-84550-163-1(2),* 42f83b3d-91f5-4654-9c10-9ee2c9829c4b) Christian Focus Pubns. GBR. Dist: Bookmasters Distribution.

Mackenzie, Carine. Rebekah: The Mother of Twins. McLaren, Duncan, illus. 2012. (Bible Time Ser.). (ENG.). 32p. (J). (gr. -1-2). pap. 3.99 *(978-1-84550-172-3(1),* b1353d62-4998-4e7b-b65b-f625dabff4e3) Christian Focus Pubns. GBR. Dist: Bookmasters Distribution.

Nellis, Glenys. Girls' Love Letters from God: Bible Stories for a Girl's Heart, 1 vol. 2017. (Love Letters from God Ser.). (ENG., Illus.). 32p. (J). 16.99 *(978-0-310-75328-5(7))* Zonderkidz.

Rivadeneira, Caryn. Grit & Grace. Betz, Katy, illus. 2017. (ENG.). 144p. (J). (gr. 4-6). pap. 9.99 ***(978-1-5064-2495-8(3),*** Sparkhouse Family) Augsburg Fortress, Pubs.

Sasso, Sandy Eisenberg. But God Remembered: Stories of Women from Creation to the Promised Land. Andersen, Bethane, illus. 2008. (ENG.). 32p. (J). pap. 8.99 *(978-1-58023-372-9(4),* 9781580233729, Jewish Lights Publishing) LongHill Partners, Inc.

Thomas Nelson Publishing Staff. Brave Girls Bible Stories, 1 vol. 2014. (ENG.). 224p. (J). 16.99 *(978-0-529-10898-2(4))* Nelson, Thomas Inc.

Ward, Elaine M. Old Testament Women. 2003. (ENG., Illus.). 32p. (J). (gr. 3-9). 18.95 *(978-1-59270-011-0(X))* Enchanted Lion Bks., LLC.

WOMEN JOURNALISTS

Butcher, Nancy. It Can't Be Done, Nellie Bly! A Reporter's Race Around the World, 1 vol. Singh, Jen, illus. 2003. (ENG.). 144p. (J). (gr. 2-5). 12.95 *(978-1-56145-289-7(0))* Peachtree Pubs.

Crysdale, Joy & Second Story Press Staff. Fearless Female Journalists, 1 vol. 2010. (Women's Hall of Fame Ser.). (ENG., Illus.). 128p. (J). (gr. 3-8). pap. 10.95 *(978-1-897187-71-5(8))* Second Story Pr. CAN. Dist: Orca Bk. Pubs. USA.

Hinman, Bonnie. Eternal Vigilance: The Story of Ida B. Wells-Barnett. 2011. (Civil Rights Leaders Ser.). 128p. (gr. 6-10). lib. bdg. 28.95 *(978-1-59935-111-7(0))* Reynolds, Morgan Inc.

Hollihan, Kerrie Logan. Reporting under Fire: 16 Daring Women War Correspondents & Photojournalists. 2014. (Women of Action Ser.). (ENG., Illus.). 256p. (YA). (gr. 7). 19.95 *(978-1-61374-710-0(1))* Chicago Review Pr., Inc.

Macy, Sue. Bylines: A Photobiography of Nellie Bly. 2009. (Photobiographies Ser.). (ENG., Illus.). 64p. (J). (gr. 5). 19.95 *(978-1-4263-0513-9(3));* 28.90 *(978-1-4263-0514-6(1))* National Geographic Society. (National Geographic Children's Bks.).

Myers, Walter Dean. Ida B. Wells: Let the Truth Be Told. Christensen, Bonnie, illus. 2008. (ENG.). 40p. (J). (gr. -1-3). 16.99 *(978-0-06-027705-5(X),* Amistad) HarperCollins Pubs.

Robson, David. Soledad O'Brien. 2010. (Transcending Race in America: Biographies of Biracial Achievers Ser.). (Illus.). 64p. (J). (gr. 5-18). lib. bdg. 22.95 *(978-1-4222-1617-0(9))* Mason Crest.

WOMEN PHYSICIANS

Apel, Melanie Ann. Virginia Apgar: Innovative Female Physician & Inventor of the Apgar Score. (Women Hall of Famers in Mathematics & Science Ser.). 112p. (gr. 5-8). 2009. 63.90 *(978-1-60854-815-6(5))* 2004. (Illus.). lib. bdg. 34.60 *(978-0-8239-3880-3(8))* Rosen Publishing Group, Inc., The. (Rosen Reference).

Bailey, Diane. Physics. 2017. (Illus.). 64p. (J). *(978-1-4222-3554-6(8))* Mason Crest.

Crayton, Lisa A. Elizabeth Blackwell: Doctor & Advocate for Women in Medicine. 2016. (Heroes of the Women's Suffrage Movement Ser.). (Illus.). 128p. (J). (gr. 6-6). 37.27 *(978-0-7660-7890-1(6))* Enslow Pubs., Inc.

Etingoff, Kim. Women in Medicine. Karlon, Ann Lee, ed. 2013. (Major Women in Science Ser.: 10). 64p. (J). (gr. 7-18). 22.95 *(978-1-4222-2929-3(7))* Mason Crest.

Favor, Lesli J. Women Doctors & Nurses of the Civil War. 2009. (American Women at War Ser.). 112p. (gr. 8-8). 63.90 *(978-1-61511-404-7(1))* Rosen Publishing Group, Inc., The.

Favor, Leslie. Women Doctors & Nurses of the Civil War. 2009. 112p. (YA). (gr. 7-12). pap. 12.95 *(978-1-4358-3273-2(6))* Rosen Publishing Group, Inc., The.

Gaines, Alison. Mary Edwards Walker. 2017. (J). ***(978-1-5026-2745-2(0))*** Cavendish Square Publishing.

Goldsmith, Bonnie Zucker. Dr. Mary Edwards Walker: Civil War Surgeon & Medal of Honor Recipient, 1 vol. 2010. (Military Heroes Ser.). (ENG.). 112p. (J). (gr. 6-12). lib. bdg. 35.64 *(978-1-60453-966-0(6))* ABDO Publishing Co.

James, Emily. Elizabeth Blackwell. 2017. (Great Scientists & Inventors Ser.). (ENG., Illus.). 24p. (gr. k-1). lib. bdg. 26.65 *(978-1-5157-3882-4(5))* Capstone Press of Coughlan Cos.

Kishel, Ann-Marie. Elizabeth Blackwell: A Life of Diligence. 2007. (Pull Ahead Bks.). (Illus.). 32p. (J). (gr. 3-7). lib. bdg. 22.60 *(978-0-8225-6459-1(9),* Lerner Pubns.) Lerner Publishing Group.

Klobuchar, Lisa. Elizabeth Blackwell: With Profiles of Elizabeth Garrett Anderson & Susan la Flesche Picotte. 2006. (Biographical Connections Ser.). (Illus.). 112p. *(978-0-7166-1826-3(5))* World Bk., Inc.

Kovatch, Sarah & Crumpler, Rebecca Lee. Rebecca Lee Crumpler. 2005. (Illus.). 16p. (J). *(978-0-7367-2891-1(0))* Zaner-Bloser, Inc.

Leavitt, Amie Jane. Elizabeth Blackwell. 2007. (What's So Great About...? Ser.). (Illus.). 32p. (J). (gr. 1-5). lib. bdg. 25.70 *(978-1-58415-579-9(5))* Mitchell Lane Pubs., Inc.

Mah, Adeline Yen. Chinese Cinderella. 2010. (ENG.). 240p. (YA). (gr. 7). pap. 9.99 *(978-0-385-74007-4(7),* Ember) Random Hse. Children's Bks.

Rich, Mari. Medicine, Vol. 10. Gilmore, Malinda & Pouson, Mel, eds. 2016. (Black Achievement in Science Ser.). (Illus.). 64p. (J). (gr. 7). 23.95 *(978-1-4222-3561-4(0))* Mason Crest.

Robbins, Trina. Elizabeth Blackwell: America's First Woman Doctor. Martin, Cynthia & Timmons, Anne, illus. 2006. (Graphic Biographies Ser.). (ENG.). 32p. (gr. 3-4). 30.65 *(978-0-7368-6497-8(0));* per. 8.10 *(978-0-7368-9660-3(0))* Capstone Press of Coughlan Cos. (Graphic Library).

Somervill, Barbara A. Elizabeth Blackwell: America's First Female Doctor. 2009. (Life Portraits Ser.). (Illus.). 112p. (YA). (gr. 7-12). lib. bdg. 36.00 *(978-1-4339-0055-6(6))* Stevens, Gareth Publishing LLLP.

Sutton, A. Trevor. Dr. Bessie Rehwinkel. Pierce, Linda, illus. 2012. (Hero of Faith Ser.). (ENG.). 47p. (J). pap. 7.99 *(978-0-7586-3078-0(6))* Concordia Publishing Hse.

Thomas, Isabel. Collins Big Cat - The World's First Women Doctors: Elizabeth Blackwell & Elizabeth Garrett Anderson: Band 16/Sapphire. 2015. (Collins Big Cat Ser.). (ENG., Illus.). 56p. (J). (gr. 4-5). pap. 9.95 *(978-0-00-812789-3(1))* HarperCollins Pubs. Ltd. GBR. Dist: Independent Pubs. Group.

Wheeler, Jill C. Antonia Novello: Fantastic Physician, 1 vol. 2012. (Women in Science Ser.). (ENG., Illus.). 32p. (J). (gr. 3-6). lib. bdg. 27.07 *(978-1-61783-448-6(3),* Checkerboard Library) ABDO Publishing Co.

Wojahn, Rebecca Hogue & Wojahn, Rebecca. Dr. Kate: Angel on Snowshoes. 2009. (Badger Biographies Ser.). (ENG., Illus.). 104p. (J). (gr. 3-7). pap. 12.95 *(978-0-87020-421-0(1))* Wisconsin Historical Society.

Women in Medicine. 2005. (Extraordinary Women Ser.). (Illus.). 112p. (gr. 6-12). 180.00 *(978-0-7910-8418-2(3),* Chelsea Hse.) Facts On File, Inc.

WOMEN PIRATES

Sharp, Anne Wallace. Daring Pirate Women. 2005. (Biography Ser.). (Illus.). 112p. (gr. 6-12). 27.93 *(978-0-8225-0031-5(0))* Lerner Publishing Group.

Yolen, Jane. Sea Queens: Women Pirates Around the World. Pratt, Christine Joy, illus. (ENG.). 112p. (J). (gr. 2-5). 2010. pap. 9.95 *(978-1-58089-132-5(2))* 2008. 18.95 *(978-1-58089-131-8(4))* Charlesbridge Publishing, Inc.

WOMEN SCIENTISTS

Allman, Toney. Women Scientists & Inventors. 2016. (ENG.). 80p. (YA). (gr. 5-12). *(978-1-68282-032-2(7))* ReferencePoint Pr., Inc.

Anniss, Matt. Jane Goodall & Mary Leakey. 2014. (Dynamic Duos of Science Ser.). 48p. (YA). (gr. 5-8). pap. 84.30 *(978-1-4824-0822-5(8))* Stevens, Gareth Publishing LLLP.

Ardagh, Philip. Marie Curie. 7th ed. 2003. (ENG., Illus.). 64p. (J). pap. 6.99 *(978-0-330-37571-9(7),* Pan) Pan Macmillan GBR. Dist: Trafalgar Square Publishing.

Barghoorn, Linda. Temple Grandin: Pioneer for Animal Rights & Autism Awareness. 2016. (Remarkable Lives Revealed Ser.). (ENG., Illus.). 32p. (J). (gr. 2-5). *(978-0-7787-2688-3(6))* Crabtree Publishing Co.

Coleman, Miriam. Women in Science. 2015. (Women Groundbreakers Ser.). (ENG., Illus.). 32p. (J). (gr. 4-5). pap. 10.00 *(978-1-4994-1047-1(6),* PowerKids Pr.) Rosen Publishing Group, Inc., The.

Conkling, Winifred. Radioactive! How Irene Curie & Lise Meitner Revolutionized Science & Changed the World. 2016. (ENG., Illus.). 240p. (J). (gr. 5-9). 17.95 *(978-1-61620-415-0(X))* Algonquin Bks. of Chapel Hill.

Dickmann, Nancy. Rachel Carson: Environmental Crusader. 2015. (Superheroes of Science Ser.). (ENG., Illus.). 48p. (J). (gr. 6-6). pap. 14.05 *(978-1-4824-3149-0(1))* Stevens, Gareth Publishing LLLP.

Doak, Robin S., et al. Women in Conservation, 1 vol. 2014. (Women in Conservation Ser.). (ENG.). 48p. (gr. 3-6). 133.28 *(978-1-4846-0472-4(5),* Heinemann InfoSearch) Heinemann-Raintree.

Domenico, Kelly Di. Women Scientists Who Changed the World. 2011. (Great Women of Achievement Ser.). (ENG., Illus.). 112p. (YA). (gr. 5-8). lib. bdg. 34.60 *(978-1-4488-5999-3(9))* Rosen Publishing Group, Inc., The.

Etingoff, Kim. Women Who Built Our Scientific Foundations. Lee-Karlon, Ann, ed. 2013. (Major Women in Science Ser.: 10). 64p. (J). (gr. 7-18). 22.95 *(978-1-4222-2933-0(5))* Mason Crest.

Faulkner, Nicholas, ed. 101 Women of STEM. 2016. (People You Should Know Ser.). 184p. (J). (gr. 8-8). lib. bdg. 36.25 *(978-1-68048-511-0(3))* Rosen Publishing Group, Inc., The.

Fertig, Dennis. Sylvia Earle: Ocean Explorer, 1 vol. 2014. (Women in Conservation Ser.). (ENG., Illus.). 48p. (gr. 3-6). 33.32 (978-1-4846-0470-0(9)); pap. 8.99 (978-1-4846-0475-5(X)) Heinemann-Raintree. (Heinemann InfoSearch).

Guidi, Victoria. Who on Earth Is Jane Goodall? Champion for the Chimpanzees. 2009. (Scientists Saving the Earth Ser.). (Illus.). 112p. (J). (gr. 5-9). lib. bdg. 33.27 (978-1-59845-119-1(7)) Enslow Pubs., Inc.

Haldy, Emma E. Jane Goodall. Bane, Jeff, illus. 2016. (My Early Library: My Itty-Bitty Bio Ser.). (ENG.). 24p. (J). (gr. k-1). 28.50 (978-1-63471-022-0(3), 208168) Cherry Lake Publishing.

Hustad, Douglas. Animal Scientist & Activist Jane Goodall. 2016. (STEM Trailblazer Bios Ser.). (ENG., Illus.). 32p. (J). (gr. 2-5). 26.65 (978-1-5124-0788-4(7)) Lerner Publishing Group.

Ignotofsky, Rachel. I Love Science: A Journal for Self-Discovery & Big Ideas. 2017. (ENG., Illus.). 192p. 14.99 (978-1-60774-980-6(7), Ten Speed Pr.) Potter/TenSpeed/Harmony.

Indovino, Shaina. Women in the Environmental Sciences. Lee-Karlon, Ann, ed. 2013. (Major Women in Science Ser.: 10). 64p. (J). (gr. 7-18). 22.95 (978-1-4222-2927-9(0)) Mason Crest.

Juarez, Christine. Ellen Ochoa. 2016. (Great Hispanic & Latino Americans Ser.). (ENG.). 24p. (gr. k-1). lib. bdg. 21.99 (978-1-5157-1888-8(3), Pebble Bks.) Capstone Press of Coughlan Cos.

Klein, Rebecca T. Careers for Tech Girls in Science. 2015. (Tech Girls Ser.). (ENG., Illus.). 80p. (J). (gr. 7-8). 34.25 (978-1-4994-6103-9(8), Rosen Young Adult) Rosen Publishing Group, Inc., The.

Labrecque, Ellen. Gertrude B. Elion & Pharmacology. 2017. (21st Century Junior Library: Women Innovators Ser.). (ENG., Illus.). 24p. (J). (gr. 2-5). lib. bdg. 27.07 (978-1-63472-182-0(9), 209300) Cherry Lake Publishing.

Lawlor, Laurie. Super Women: Six Scientists Who Changed the World. 2017. (ENG.). 48p. (J). (gr. 3-7). 17.95 (978-0-8234-3675-0(6)) Holiday Hse., Inc.

Lindeen, Mary. Jane Goodall: Friend of the Apes, 1 vol. Soud, illus. 2008. (Beginner Biographies Ser.). (ENG.). 32p. (gr. -1-3). 28.50 (978-1-60270-249-3(7), Looking Glass Library-Nonfiction) Magic Wagon.

—Marie Curie: Scientist, 1 vol. Soud, illus. 2008. (Beginner Biographies Ser.). (ENG.). 32p. (gr. -1-3). 28.50 (978-1-60270-248-6(9), Looking Glass Library- Nonfiction) Magic Wagon.

MacBain, Jennifer. Gertrude Elion: Nobel Prize Winner in Physiology & Medicine. 2009. (Women Hall of Famers in Mathematics & Science Ser.). 112p. (gr. 5-8). 63.90 (978-1-60854-811-8(2), Rosen Reference) Rosen Publishing Group, Inc., The.

Marsh, Carole. Rachel Carson: Excellent Ecologist. 2004. (1000 Readers Ser.). (Illus.). 14p. (J). (gr. k-4). pap. 2.95 (978-0-635-02524-1(8)) Gallopade International.

McAneney, Caitlin. Women in Space. 2015. (Women Groundbreakers Ser.). (ENG., Illus.). 32p. (J). (gr. 4-5). pap. 10.00 (978-1-4994-1048-8(4), PowerKids Pr.) Rosen Publishing Group, Inc., The.

McDonnell, Patrick. Me... Jane. 2011. (ENG., Illus.). 40p. (J). (gr. -1-3). 17.99 (978-0-316-04546-9(2)) Little, Brown Bks. for Young Readers.

—Me... Jane. 2011. (J). (978-1-4618-4349-8(9)) Recorded Bks., Inc.

Niver, Heather Moore. Careers for Tech Girls in Computer Science. 2015. (Tech Girls Ser.). (ENG., Illus.). 80p. (J). (gr. 7-8). 34.25 (978-1-4994-6105-3(4), Rosen Young Adult) Rosen Publishing Group, Inc., The.

Nivola, Claire A. Life in the Ocean: The Story of Oceanographer Sylvia Earle, 1 vol. Nivola, Claire A., illus. 2012. (ENG., Illus.). 32p. (J). (gr. -1-3). 18.99 (978-0-374-38068-7(6), 9780374380687, Farrar, Straus & Giroux (BYR)) Farrar, Straus & Giroux.

—Life in the Ocean: The Story of Oceanographer Sylvia Earle. 2012. (J). 38.75 (978-1-4703-0113-2(X)) Recorded Bks., Inc.

Ottaviani, Jim. Primates: The Fearless Science of Jane Goodall, Dian Fossey, & Biruté Galdikas. Wicks, Maris, illus. 2013. (ENG.). 144p. (YA). (gr. 7). 21.99 (978-1-59643-865-1(7), 9781596438651, First Second Bks.) Roaring Brook Pr.

—Primates: The Fearless Science of Jane Goodall, Dian Fossey, & Biruté Galdikas. Wicks, Maris, illus. 2015. (ENG.). 144p. (YA). (gr. 7). pap. 12.99 (978-1-250-06293-2(4), 9781250062932) Square Fish.

Phillips, Jennifer. Girls Research! Amazing Tales of Female Scientists, 1 vol. 2014. (Girls Rock! Ser.). (ENG.). 64p. (gr. 4-5). lib. bdg. 34.65 (978-1-4765-4056-6(X)) Capstone Press of Coughlan Cos.

Reichard, Susan E. Who on Earth Is Sylvia Earle? Undersea Explorer of the Ocean. 2009. (Scientists Saving the Earth Ser.). (Illus.). 112p. (J). (gr. 5-9). lib. bdg. 33.27 (978-1-59845-118-4(9)) Enslow Pubs., Inc.

Rice, William. Jane Goodall. 2017. (TIME for Kids en Español - Level 3 Ser.). (SPA.). 32p. (gr. 3-3). lib. bdg. 31.99 **(978-1-5157-5191-5(0))** Time for Kids Inc AUS. Dist: Capstone Pub.

Robbins, Dean. Margaret & the Moon: How Margaret Hamilton Saved the First Lunar Landing. Knisley, Lucy, illus. 2017. (ENG.). 40p. (J). (gr. -1-3). 17.99 (978-0-399-55185-7(9), Knopf Bks. for Young Readers) Random Hse. Children's Bks.

Rooney, Frances. Exceptional Women Environmentalists, 1 vol. 2007. (Women's Hall of Fame Ser.). (ENG., Illus.). 120p. (J). (gr. 4-8). pap. 10.95 (978-1-897187-22-7(X)) Second Story Pr. CAN. Dist: Orca Bk. Pubs. USA.

Saddleback Educational Publishing Staff, ed. Marie Curie, 1 vol. unabr. ed. 2008. (Graphic Biographies Ser.). (ENG., Illus.). 25p. (YA). (gr. 9-12). pap. 7.95 (978-1-59905-226-7(1)) Saddleback Educational Publishing, Inc.

Sally Ride Science Editors, Sally Ride Science. What Do You Want to Be? Explore Earth Sciences. 2004. (J). 6.00 (978-0-9753920-2-7(6)) Sally Ride Science.

Sanchez Vegara, Isabel. Marie Curie. Isa, Frau, illus. 2017. (Little People, Big Dreams Ser.). (ENG.). 32p. (J). (gr. k-3). 14.99 **(978-1-84780-962-9(6)**, Frances Lincoln Children's Bks.) Quarto Publishing Group UK GBR. Dist: Hachette Bk. Group.

Schwartz, Heather E. Astronaut Ellen Ochoa. 2017. (STEM Trailblazer Bios Ser.). (ENG.). 32p. (J). (gr. 2-5). pap. 8.99 **(978-1-5124-5627-1(6))**; (Illus.). 26.65 **(978-1-5124-3449-1(3)**, Lerner Pubns.) Lerner Publishing Group.

Shuckburgh, Emily & Chambers, Catherine. Polar Scientist: The Coolest Jobs on the Planet, 1 vol. HL Studios Staff, illus. 2014. (Coolest Jobs on the Planet Ser.). (ENG.). 48p. (gr. 6-6). pap. 8.99 (978-1-4109-6648-3(8)) Heinemann-Raintree.

Silvey, Anita & National Geographic Kids Staff. Untamed: The Wild Life of Jane Goodall. 2015. (ENG., Illus.). 96p. (J). (gr. 3-7). 18.99 (978-1-4263-1518-3(X), National Geographic Children's Bks.) National Geographic Society.

Snedden, Robert. Mary Anning: Fossil Hunter. 2015. (Superheroes of Science Ser.). (ENG., Illus.). 48p. (J). (gr. 6-6). pap. 14.05 (978-1-4824-3145-2(9)) Stevens, Gareth Publishing LLLP.

Steele, Philip. Marie Curie: The Woman Who Changed the Course of Science. 2008. (National Geographic World History Biographies Ser.). (ENG., Illus.). 64p. (J). (gr. 3-7). pap. 7.99 (978-1-4263-0249-7(5), National Geographic Children's Bks.) National Geographic Society.

Stux, Erica. The Achievers: Great Women in the Biological Sciences. 2005. (Avisson Young Adult Ser.). (Illus.). 148p. (J). (978-1-888105-70-4(4)) Avisson Pr., Inc.

Swaby, Rachel. Trailblazers: 33 Women in Science Who Changed the World. (ENG.). 208p. (J). (gr. 5). 2017. 6.99 **(978-0-399-55418-6(1)**, Yearling) 2016. 15.99 (978-0-399-55396-7(7), Delacorte Bks. for Young Readers) Random Hse. Children's Bks.

Thimmesh, Catherine. The Sky's the Limit: Stories of Discovery by Women & Girls. Sweet, Melissa, illus. 2005. 73p. (J). (gr. 4-8). reprint ed. 16.00 (978-0-7567-9631-0(8)) DIANE Publishing Co.

Van Vleet, Carmella & Sullivan, Kathy. To the Stars! The First American Woman to Walk in Space. Wong, Nicole, illus. 2016. (ENG.). 40p. (J). (gr. k-3). lib. bdg. 16.95 (978-1-58089-644-3(8)) Charlesbridge Publishing, Inc.

Venezia, Mike. Jane Goodall: Researcher Who Champions Chimps. Venezia, Mike, illus. 2010. (Getting to Know the World's Greatest Inventors & Scientists Ser.). (ENG., Illus.). 32p. (J). (gr. 3-4). 28.00 (978-0-531-23731-1(1)) Scholastic Library Publishing.

—Lise Meitner: Had the Right Vision about Nuclear Fission. Venezia, Mike, illus. 2009. (Getting to Know the World's Greatest Inventors & Scientists Ser.). (ENG., Illus.). 32p. (J). (gr. 2-5). 28.00 (978-0-531-23702-1(8)) Scholastic Library Publishing.

Welty, Tara. Jane Goodall. 2011. (Conservation Heroes Ser.). (Illus.). 128p. (gr. 6-12). 35.00 (978-1-60413-952-5(8), Chelsea Hse.) Facts On File, Inc.

Wheeler, Jill C. Hayat Sindi: Brilliant Biochemist, 1 vol. 2012. (Women in Science Ser.). (ENG., Illus.). 32p. (J). (gr. 3-6). lib. bdg. 27.07 (978-1-61783-450-9(5), Checkerboard Library) ABDO Publishing Co.

—Joanne Simpson: Magnificent Meteorologist, 1 vol. 2012. (Women in Science Ser.). (ENG., Illus.). 32p. (J). (gr. 3-6). lib. bdg. 27.07 (978-1-61783-449-3(1), Checkerboard Library) ABDO Publishing Co.

White, Katherine. Sylvia Earle: Deep Sea Explorer & Ocean Activist. (Women Hall of Famers in Mathematics & Science Ser.). 112p. (gr. 5-8). 2009. 63.90 (978-1-60854-814-9(7)) 2004. (Illus.). lib. bdg. 34.60 (978-0-8239-3879-7(4)) Rosen Publishing Group, Inc., The. (Rosen Reference).

Women in Science. 2016. (Women in Science Ser.). 128p. (YA). lib. bdg. 273.84 (978-1-5026-2439-0(7)) Cavendish Square Publishing.

Wood, Susan. Vaccine Innovators Pearl Kendrick & Grace Eldering. 2016. (STEM Trailblazer Bios Ser.). (ENG., Illus.). 32p. (J). (gr. 2-5). 26.65 (978-1-5124-0790-7(9)) Lerner Publishing Group.

Yasuda, Anita. Astronomy: Cool Women in Space. 2015. (Girls in Science Ser.). (ENG., Illus.). 112p. (gr. 3-7). 19.95 (978-1-61930-326-3(4)) Open City Bks.

Yount, Lisa. Rosalind Franklin. 2011. (Trailblazers in Science & Technology Ser.). 152p. (gr. 6-12). 35.00 (978-1-60413-660-9(X), Chelsea Hse.) Facts On File, Inc.

WOMEN'S CLOTHING

see Clothing and Dress

WOMEN'S RIGHTS

Adiletta, Dawn. Elizabeth Cady Stanton: Women's Suffrage & the First Vote. (Library of American Lives & Times Ser.). 112p. 2009. (gr. 5-5). 69.20 (978-1-60853-479-1(0)) 2005. (Illus.). (J). (gr. -1-3). lib. bdg. 34.60 (978-1-4042-2647-0(8)) Rosen Publishing Group, Inc., The.

Alter, Judy. Women's Rights. 2008. (21st Century Skills Library: Global Perspectives Ser.). (ENG.). 32p. (gr. 4-8). lib. bdg. 28.50 (978-1-60279-133-6(3), 200112) Cherry Lake Publishing.

Anderson, Dale. The Seneca Falls Women's Rights Convention. 2004. (Landmark Events in American History Ser.). (Illus.). 48p. (J). (gr. 5-12). lib. bdg. 31.00 (978-0-8368-5389-6(X), Gareth Stevens Secondary Library) Stevens, Gareth Publishing LLLP.

Anderson, Jennifer Joline. Women's Rights Movement, 1 vol. 2013. (Essential Library of Social Change Ser.). (ENG.). 112p. (J). (gr. 6-12). lib. bdg. 35.64 (978-1-61783-889-7(6), Essential Library) ABDO Publishing Co.

The Antebellum Women's Movement, 1820-1860. (YA). (gr. 6-9). spiral bd., tchr.'s planning gde. ed. 12.00 (978-0-382-44465-4(5)) Cobblestone Publishing Co.

Bailey Association Staff & Gorman, Jacqueline Laks. The Modern Feminist Movement. 2011. (Cultural History of Women in America Ser.). (Illus.). 64p. (gr. 6-12). 35.00 (978-1-60413-935-8(8), Chelsea Hse.) Facts On File, Inc.

Bailey Association Staff & Senker, Cath. Strength in Numbers. 2011. (Cultural History of Women in America Ser.). (Illus.). 64p. (gr. 6-12). 35.00 (978-1-60413-931-0(5), Chelsea Hse.) Facts On File, Inc.

Bakshi, Kelly. Perspectives on the Women's Rights Movement. 2018. (ENG.). 32p. (gr. 3-6). **(978-1-63235-405-1(5)**, 12-Story Library) Pr. Room Editions LLC.

Barber, Lynnae. Champions for Women's Rights: Matilda Joslyn Gage, Julia Ward Howe, Lucretia Mott, & Lucy Stone. 2016. (Heroes of the Women's Suffrage Movement Ser.). (Illus.). 128p. (J). (gr. 6-6). 37.27 (978-0-7660-7891-8(4)) Enslow Pubs., Inc.

Bausum, Ann. With Courage & Cloth: Winning the Fight for a Woman's Right to Vote. 2004. (ENG., Illus.). 112p. (J). (gr. 5-17). lib. bdg. 32.90 (978-0-7922-6996-0(9), National Geographic Children's Bks.) National Geographic Society.

Bjornlund, Lydia D. Women of the Suffrage Movement. 2003. (Women in History Ser.). (ENG., Illus.). 112p. (J). 33.45 (978-1-59018-173-7(5), Lucent Bks.) Cengage Gale.

Bohannon, Lisa Frederiksen. Women's Rights & Nothing Less: The Story of Elizabeth Cady Stanton. 2004. (Feminist Voices Ser.). (Illus.). 112p. (YA). (gr. 6-12). 23.95 (978-1-883846-66-4(8), First Biographies) Reynolds, Morgan Inc.

Bohannon, Lisa Frederiksen. Failure Is Impossible: The Story of Susan B. Anthony. 2004. (Feminist Voices Ser.). (Illus.). 112p. (YA). (gr. 6-12). 23.95 (978-1-883846-77-0(3), First Biographies) Reynolds, Morgan Inc.

Boothroyd, Jennifer. Susan B. Anthony: A Life of Fairness. 2006. (Pull Ahead Bks.). (Illus.). 32p. (J). (gr. 3-7). lib. bdg. 22.60 (978-0-8225-3479-2(7), Lerner Pubns.) Lerner Publishing Group.

—Susan B. Anthony: Una Vida de Igualdad. Translations.com Staff, tr. 2006. (Libros para Avanzar-Biografías (Pull Ahead Books-Biographies) Ser.). (ENG & SPA., Illus.). 32p. (gr. k-3). lib. bdg. 22.60 (978-0-8225-6234-4(0)) Lerner Publishing Group.

Carson, Mary Kay. Who Was Susan B. Anthony Vote? And Other Questions about Women's Suffrage. 2015. (Good Question! Ser.). (ENG., Illus.). 32p. (J). (gr. 2). pap. 5.95 (978-1-4549-1242-2(1)) Sterling Publishing Co., Inc.

—Why Couldn't Susan B. Anthony Vote? And Other Questions about Women's Suffrage. 2015. (Good Question! Ser.). (ENG., Illus.). 40p. (J). (gr. 2). 12.95 (978-1-4549-1241-5(3)) Sterling Publishing Co., Inc.

Ching, Jacqueline. Women's Rights. 2009. (Individual Rights & Civic Responsibility Ser.). 128p. (gr. 7-12). 63.90 (978-1-61513-518-9(9)) Rosen Publishing Group, Inc., The.

Confronting Violence Against Women. 2015. (Confronting Violence Against Women Ser.). (ENG.). 64p. (J). (gr. 6-7). pap., pap., pap. 466.20 (978-1-4994-6148-0(8), Rosen Young Adult) Rosen Publishing Group, Inc., The.

Connors, Kathleen. The Life of Susan B. Anthony, Vol. 1. 2014. (Famous Lives Ser.). (ENG.). 24p. (J). (gr. 1-2). 22.60 (978-1-4824-0425-8(7)) Stevens, Gareth Publishing LLLP.

Crewe, Sabrina & Anderson, Dale. The Seneca Falls Women's Rights Convention. 2004. (Events That Shaped America Ser.). (Illus.). 32p. (J). (gr. 3-6). lib. bdg. 26.00 (978-0-8368-3408-6(9), Gareth Stevens Learning Library) Stevens, Gareth Publishing LLLP.

DeAngelis, Therese. Women's Rights on the Frontier. 2012. (J). pap. (978-1-4222-2369-7(8)) Mason Crest.

—Women's Rights on the Frontier. Harrington, A. Page, ed. 2012. (Finding a Voice: Women's Fight for Equality in U. S. Society Ser.). 64p. (J). (gr. 5). 22.95 (978-1-4222-2359-8(0)) Mason Crest.

Donelly, Karen. American Women Pilots of World War II. 2009. 112p. (YA). (gr. 7-12). pap. 12.95 (978-1-4358-3274-9(4)) Rosen Publishing Group, Inc., The.

Dowdy, Penny. The Famous Five: Defining Moments in Canadian History/Graphic Novels. 2010. (Illus.). 32p. (978-1-77071-616-2(5)) Weigl Educational Pubs. Ltd.

Dudley Gold, Susan. The Women's Rights Movement & Abolitionism. 2015. (Primary Sources of the Abolitionist Movement Ser.). (ENG., Illus.). 64p. (J). (gr. 6-6). lib. bdg. 34.21 (978-1-5026-0536-8(8)) Cavendish Square Publishing.

Edison, Erin. Susan B. Anthony, 1 vol. 2013. (Great Women in History Ser.). (ENG., Illus.). 24p. (gr. k-1). lib. bdg. 21.99 (978-1-62065-075-2(4), Pebble Bks.) Capstone Press of Coughlan Cos.

Frey, Wendy. Citizen Heroes. 2007. (Illus.). 68p. (J). (978-1-4105-0887-4(0)); (978-1-4105-0888-1(9)) Johnston, Don Inc.

Fry, Erin. The Power of Friendship. 2005. (Illus.). 16p. (J). pap. (978-0-7367-2920-8(8)) Zaner-Bloser, Inc.

Gelletly, LeeAnne. The Equal Rights Amendment. 2012. (J). pap. (978-1-4222-2361-1(2)) Mason Crest.

—The Equal Rights Amendment. Harrington, A. Page, ed. 2012. (Finding a Voice: Women's Fight for Equality in U. S. Society Ser.). 64p. (J). (gr. 5). 22.95 (978-1-4222-2351-2(5)) Mason Crest.

—Origins of the Women's Rights Movement. 2012. (Illus.). 64p. (J). pap. (978-1-4222-2363-5(9)) Mason Crest.

—Origins of the Women's Rights Movement. Harrington, A. Page, ed. 2012. (Finding a Voice: Women's Fight for Equality in U. S. Society Ser.). (Illus.). 64p. (J). (gr. 5). 22.95 (978-1-4222-2353-6(1)) Mason Crest.

—A Woman's Place in Early America. 2012. (J). pap. (978-1-4222-2365-9(5)) Mason Crest.

—A Woman's Place in Early America. Harrington, A. Page, ed. 2012. (Finding a Voice: Women's Fight for Equality in U. S. Society Ser.). 64p. (J). (gr. 5). 22.95 (978-1-4222-2355-0(8)) Mason Crest.

Glenn, Avery, et al. The Women's Rights Movement. Javier, Emmanuel Xerx & Burton, Daniel, illus. 2007. (Jt Am Hist Graph Novel Ser.). (ENG.). 24p. (gr. 6-12). spiral bd. 12.72 (978-0-07-878025-7(X), 007878025X) McGraw-Hill Cos., The.

Goddu, Krystyna Poray. What's Your Story, Susan B. Anthony? 2016. (Cub Reporter Meets Famous Americans Ser.). (ENG.). 32p. (J). (gr. k-3). 26.65 (978-1-4677-8785-7(X), Lerner Pubns.) Lerner Publishing Group.

Gold, Susan Dudley. Roberts v. Jaycees: Women's Rights. 2008. (Supreme Court Milestones Ser.). 128p. (gr. 7-18). lib. bdg. 42.79 (978-0-7614-2952-4(2), Benchmark Bks.) Marshall Cavendish Corp.

Gordon, Minette, et al. Understanding Women's Rights. 2011. (Personal Freedom & Civic Duty Ser.). (J). lib. bdg. 35.95 (978-1-4488-4671-9(4)) Rosen Publishing Group, Inc., The.

Hanson-Harding, Alexandra. Activism: Taking on Women's Issues. 2012. (Young Woman's Guide to Contemporary Issues Ser.). (ENG., Illus.). 112p. (YA). (gr. 9-12). lib. bdg. 34.60 (978-1-4488-8401-8(2)) Rosen Publishing Group, Inc., The.

Haughton, Emma. Equality of the Sexes? 2005. (Viewpoints (Sea to Sea) Ser.). (Illus.). 32p. (YA). (gr. 5-9). lib. bdg. 27.10 (978-1-932889-58-1(2)) Sea-To-Sea Pubns.

Hawker, Louise. Womens Rights. 2010. (Global Viewpoints Ser.). (ENG., Illus.). 224p. (J). pap. 40.45 (978-0-7377-4474-3(X)) Cengage Gale.

Hawker, Louise, ed. Womens Rights. 2010. (Global Viewpoints Ser.). (ENG., Illus.). 224p. (gr. 10-12). pap. 31.70 (978-0-7377-4475-0(8)) Cengage Gale.

Hermann, Spring. The Struggle for Equality: Women & Minorities in America. 2006. (American Saga Ser.). (Illus.). 128p. (J). (gr. 5-9). lib. bdg. 33.27 (978-0-7660-2573-8(X)) Enslow Pubs., Inc.

Herweck, Dona. Susan B. Anthony, 1 vol. 2nd rev. ed. 2014. (TIME for KIDS(r) Nonfiction Readers Ser.). (ENG., Illus.). 28p. (J). (gr. 2-2). pap. 23.96 (978-1-4807-1063-4(6)) Shell Educational Publishing.

Hollihan, Kerrie Logan. Rightfully Ours: How Women Won the Vote, 21 Activities. 2012. (For Kids Ser.). (ENG., Illus.). 144p. (J). (gr. 4). pap. 16.95 (978-1-883052-89-8(0)) Chicago Review Pr., Inc.

Hopkinson, Deborah. Susan B. Anthony: Fighter for Women's Rights. Bates, Amy, illus. 2005. 32p. (J). lib. bdg. 15.00 (978-1-4242-1563-8(3)) Fitzgerald Bks.

—Susan B. Anthony: Fighter for Women's Rights. Bates, Amy June, illus. 2005. (Ready-To-read SOFA Ser.). (ENG.). 32p. (J). (gr. 1-3). pap. 3.99 (978-0-689-86909-9(6), Simon Spotlight) Simon Spotlight.

Howard, Melanie A. Civil Rights Marches, 1 vol. 2004. (American Moments Ser.). (ENG.). 48p. (gr. 4-8). 27.07 (978-1-59197-282-2(5), Abdo & Daughters) ABDO Publishing Co.

Isecke, Harriet. Women's Suffrage: Fighting for Women's Rights, 1 vol. 2011. (Primary Source Readers Ser.). (ENG.). 32p. (J). (gr. 5-5). pap. 8.99 (978-1-4333-1507-7(6)) Teacher Created Materials, Inc.

Jennings, Terry Catasús. The Women's Liberation Movement, 1960-1990. 2012. (J). pap. (978-1-4222-2368-0(X)) Mason Crest.

—The Women's Liberation Movement, 1960-1990. Harrington, A. Page, ed. 2012. (Finding a Voice: Women's Fight for Equality in U. S. Society Ser.). 64p. (J). (gr. 5). 22.95 (978-1-4222-2358-1(2)) Mason Crest.

Johnson, Jen Cullerton. Seeds of Change. Sadler, Sonia Lynn, illus. 2013. (ENG.). 40p. (J). (gr. 1-6). 18.95 (978-1-60060-367-9(X)) Lee & Low Bks., Inc.

Kamma, Anne. If You Lived When Women Won Their Rights. Johnson, Pamela, illus. 2008. (If You... Ser.). (ENG.). 64p. (J). (gr. 2-5). pap. 7.99 (978-0-439-74869-8(0), Scholastic Reference) Scholastic, Inc.

Kendall, Martha E. Failure Is Impossible! The History of American Women's Rights. 3rd ed. 2005. (People's History Ser.). (Illus.). 96p. (gr. 6-12). lib. bdg. 26.60 (978-0-8225-1744-3(2)) Lerner Publishing Group.

Kent, Deborah. The Seneca Falls Convention: Working to Expand Women's Rights. 2016. (Heroes of the Women's Suffrage Movement Ser.). (Illus.). 128p. (J). (gr. 6-6). 37.27 (978-0-7660-7892-5(2)) Enslow Pubs., Inc.

Kops, Deborah. Alice Paul & the Fight for Women's Rights: From the Vote to the Equal Rights Amendment. 2017. (ENG.). 216p. (J). (gr. 5). 17.95 (978-1-62979-323-8(X), Calkins Creek) Boyds Mills Pr.

Koya, Lena & Hanson-Harding, Alexandra. Female Activists. 2017. (J). **(978-1-5081-7720-3(1))** Rosen Publishing Group, Inc., The.

Litwin, Laura Baskes. Susan. B. Anthony: Social Reformer & Feminist. 2016. (Heroes of the Women's Suffrage Movement Ser.). (Illus.). 128p. (J). (gr. 6-6). 37.27 (978-0-7660-7888-8(4)) Enslow Pubs., Inc.

Lowery, Zoe & Bickerstaff, Linda. Gender-Based Violence & Women's Rights. 2017. (Women in the World Ser.). 112p. (J). (gr. 12-11). 37.10 **(978-1-5081-7447-9(4)**, Rosen Young Adult) Rosen Publishing Group, Inc., The.

Lowery, Zoe & Bringle, Jennifer. Reproductive Health & Women's Rights. 2017. (Women in the World Ser.). 112p. (J). (gr. 12-11). 37.10 **(978-1-5081-7445-5(8)**, Rosen Young Adult) Rosen Publishing Group, Inc., The.

Margiorz, Juliet. Elizabeth Cady Stanton & the Fight for Equal Rights. 2009. (Real Life Readers Ser.). 32p. (gr. 4-6). pap. 10.00 (978-1-4358-0233-9(0), Rosen Classroom) Rosen Publishing Group, Inc., The.

Mattern, Joanne. Elizabeth Cady Stanton & Susan B. Anthony: Fighting Together for Women's Rights. (Women Who Shaped History Ser.). 24p. 2009. (gr. 2-3). 42.50 (978-1-60854-818-7(X)) 2003. (Illus.). (J). lib. bdg. 22.60 (978-0-8239-6503-8(1)) Rosen Publishing Group, Inc., The. (PowerKids Pr.).

McPherson, Stephanie Sammartino. Susan B. Anthony. 2006. (History Maker Bios Ser.). (Illus.). 48p. (J). (gr. 3-7). lib. bdg. 26.60 (978-0-8225-5938-2(2), Lerner Pubns.) Lerner Publishing Group.

Mountjoy, Shane. The Women's Rights Movement: Moving Toward Equality. 2007. (Reform Movements in American History Ser.). (Illus.). 156p. (YA). (gr. 7-12). lib. bdg. 32.50 (978-0-7910-9505-8(3)) Facts On File, Inc.

Nash, Carol Rust. Women Winning the Right to Vote in United States History. 2014. (In United States History Ser.). (Illus.). 96p. (J). (gr. 5-12). pap. 10.95 (978-0-7660-6074-6(8)) Enslow Pubs., Inc.

Pollack, Pamela D. & Belviso, Meg. Who Was Susan B. Anthony? Lacey, Mike & Harrison, Nancy, illus. 2014. (Who Was? Ser.). (ENG.). 112p. (J). (gr. 3-7). 5.99 (978-0-448-47963-7(X), Grosset & Dunlap) Penguin Young Readers Group.

Rappaport, Doreen. Elizabeth Started All the Trouble. Faulkner, Matt, illus. 2016. (ENG.). 40p. (J). (gr. 1-3). 17.99 (978-0-7868-5142-3(2)) Disney Pr.

Robbins, Dean. Miss Paul & the President: The Creative Campaign for Women's Right to Vote. Zhang, Nancy, illus. 2016. (ENG.). 40p. (J). (gr. -1-3). 17.99 (978-1-101-93720-4(3), Knopf Bks. for Young Readers) Random Hse. Children's Bks.

Ross, Michael Elsohn. She Takes a Stand: 16 Fearless Activists Who Have Changed the World. 2015. (Women of Action Ser.). (ENG., Illus.). 208p. (YA). (gr. 7). 19.95 (978-1-61373-026-3(8)) Chicago Review Pr., Inc.

W X Y Z

Rossi, Ann. Created Equal: Women Campaign for the Right to Vote 1840 - 1920. 2005. (Crossroads America Ser.). (ENG., Illus.). 40p. (J). (gr. 5-9). 12.95 *(978-0-7922-8275-4(2))*; 21.90 *(978-0-7922-8285-3(X))* National Geographic Society. (National Geographic Children's Bks.).

Rossi, Ann & National Geographic Learning Staff. Votes for Women. 2007. (Language, Literacy, & Vocabulary - Reading Expeditions Ser.). (ENG., Illus.). 40p. (J). pap. 19.95 *(978-0-7922-8626-4(X))* CENGAGE Learning.

Schomp, Virginia. American Voices from the Women's Movement. 2006. (American Voices Ser.). (Illus.). 128p. (gr. 6-7). lib. bdg. 26.95 *(978-0-7614-2171-9(8)*, Benchmark Bks.) Marshall Cavendish Corp.

Todd, Anne M. Susan B. Anthony: Activist. 2009. (Women of Achievement Ser.). (Illus.). 128p. (gr. 6-12). 35.00 *(978-1-60413-087-4(3)*, Chelsea Hse.) Facts On File, Inc.

Wallner, Alexandra. Susan B. Anthony. Wallner, Alexandra, illus. 2012. (ENG., Illus.). 32p. (J). 16.95 *(978-0-8234-1953-1(3))* Holiday Hse., Inc.

Weidt, Maryann N. Fighting for Equal Rights: A Story about Susan B. Anthony. Sartor, Amanda, tr. Sartor, Amanda, illus. (Creative Minds Biography Ser.). 64p. 2004. (J). 22.60 *(978-1-57505-181-9(8)*, Carolrhoda Bks.) 2003. (ENG.). (gr. 4-8). pap. 8.95 *(978-1-57505-609-8(7))* Lerner Publishing Group.

Women Winning the Right to Vote in United States History. 2014. (In United States History Ser.). 96p. (J). (gr. 5-12). 27.94 *(978-0-7660-6073-9(X))* Enslow Pubs., Inc.

Women's Right to Vote. 2010. (J). *(978-0-7166-1508-8(8))* World Bk., Inc.

WOMEN'S RIGHTS—FICTION

Deborah, Ellis. The Breadwinner. 2014. (ENG.). 176p. (J). 13.20 *(978-1-63245-145-3(X))* Lectorum Pubns., Inc.

Dublin, Anne. 44 Hours or Strike!, 1 vol. 2015. (ENG., Illus.). 112p. (J). (gr. 6-8). pap. 11.95 *(978-1-927583-76-0(4))* Second Story Pr. CAN. Dist: Orca Bk. Pubs. USA.

Ellis, Deborah. The Breadwinner. 2013. 164p. pap. *(978-1-4596-6483-8(3))* ReadHowYouWant.com, Ltd.

Grimes, Nikki. Chasing Freedom: The Life Journeys of Harriet Tubman & Susan B. Anthony, Inspired by Historical Facts. Wood, Michele, illus. 2015. (ENG.). 56p. (J). (gr. 2-5). 18.99 *(978-0-439-79338-4(6)*, Orchard Bks.) Scholastic, Inc.

Immel, Mary Blair. Giant Steps: Suffragettes & Soldiers. 2016. (J). pap. ***(978-0-87195-406-0(0))*** Indiana Historical Society.

Murphy, Claire Rudolf. Marching with Aunt Susan: Susan B. Anthony & the Fight for Women's Suffrage, 1 vol. Schuett, Stacey, illus. 2011. (ENG.). 36p. (J). (gr. 1-5). 16.95 *(978-1-56145-593-5(8)*, Peachtree Junior) Peachtree Pubs.

Newbery, Linda. Polly's March. 2009. (Historical House Ser.). 192p. (YA). (gr. 5-18). pap. 5.99 *(978-0-7945-2336-7(6)*, Usborne) EDC Publishing.

Penson, Mary E. Martha Mary Overstreet, M. D. 2007. (Chaparral Bks.). (ENG.). 142p. (J). per. 11.95 *(978-0-87565-345-7(6))* Texas Christian Univ. Pr.

Robbins, Dean. Two Friends: Susan B. Anthony & Frederick Douglass: Susan B. Anthony & Frederick Douglass. Qualls, Sean & Alko, Selina, illus. 2016. (ENG.). 32p. (J). (gr. -1-3). 17.99 *(978-0-545-39996-8(3)*, Orchard Bks.) Scholastic, Inc.

Schwabach, Karen. The Hope Chest. 2010. (ENG.). 288p. (J). (gr. 3-7). 7.99 *(978-0-375-84096-8(6)*, Yearling) Random Hse. Children's Bks.

Sheth, Kashmira. Keeping Corner. 2009. (ENG.). 304p. (J). (gr. 7-17). pap. 7.99 *(978-0-7868-3860-8(4))* Hyperion Pr.

WONDER WOMAN (FICTITIOUS CHARACTER)—FICTION

Aptekar, Devan. Darkseid's Revenge. Gordon, Eric A. & Gordon, Steven E., illus. 2012. (ENG.). 24p. (J). (gr. -1-3). pap. 3.99 *(978-0-06-188533-4(9)*, HarperFestival) HarperCollins Pubs.

—Darkseid's Revenge. Gordon, Eric A. & Gordon, Steven E., illus. 2012. (Justice League Classic 8X8 Ser.). (J). lib. bdg. 13.55 *(978-0-606-23566-2(3)*, Turtleback) Turtleback Bks.

Bardugo, Leigh. Wonder Woman: Warbringer. 2017. (DC Icons Ser.). (ENG.). 384p. (YA). (gr. 7). 18.99 *(978-0-399-54973-1(0)*, Random Hse. Bks. for Young Readers) Random Hse. Children's Bks.

Bright, J. E. & Sutton, Laurie S. Wonder Woman vs. Circe, 1 vol. Vecchio, Luciano, illus. 2013. (DC Super Heroes Ser.). (ENG.). 56p. (gr. 2-3). lib. bdg. 26.65 *(978-1-4342-6014-7(3))* Stone Arch Bks.

Carbone, Courtney. Flower Power! (DC Super Friends) Schoening, Dan, illus. 2014. (Little Golden Book Ser.). (ENG.). 24p. (J). (-k). 4.99 *(978-0-385-37396-8(1)*, Golden Bks.) Random Hse. Children's Bks.

—Wonder Woman. Random House, illus. 2017. (Pictureback(R) Ser.). (ENG.). 24p. (J). (gr. -1-2). pap. 4.99 *(978-0-399-55844-3(6)*, Random Hse. Bks. for Young Readers) Random Hse. Children's Bks.

—Wonder Woman to the Rescue! 2016. (Step into Reading Level 2 Ser.). lib. bdg. 14.75 *(978-0-606-38476-6(6))* Turtleback Bks.

—Wonder Woman to the Rescue! (DC Super Friends) Doescher, Erik & Random House, illus. 2016. (Step into Reading Ser.). (ENG.). 24p. (J). (gr. -1-1). 4.99 *(978-1-101-93308-4(9)*, Random Hse. Bks. for Young Readers) Random Hse. Children's Bks.

Cosentino, Ralph. Wonder Woman: The Story of the Amazon Princess. Cosentino, Ralph, illus. 2011. (ENG., Illus.). 40p. (J). (gr. -1-2). 16.99 *(978-0-670-06256-0(1)*, Viking Books for Young Readers) Penguin Young Readers Group.

Dahl, Michael. Be a Star, Wonder Woman! Lozano, Omar, illus. 2017. (DC Super Heroes Ser.). (ENG.). 32p. (gr. -1-2). 15.95 ***(978-1-62370-875-7(3)***, DC Super Heroes) Stone Arch Bks.

Fisch, Sholly, et al. The Bride & the Bold. 2015. (All-New Batman: the Brave & the Bold Ser.). (ENG., Illus.). 32p. (gr. 2-3). lib. bdg. 22.60 *(978-1-4342-9661-0(X))* Stone Arch Bks.

Hutton, Laurie S. & Marsham, Liz. Wonder Woman Classic - A Hero for All. Hood, Josh et al, illus. 2017. 24p. (J). (gr. -1-3). pap. 3.99 *(978-0-06-236081-6(7)*, HarperFestival) HarperCollins Pubs.

Katz, David Bar. My First Wonder Woman Book: Touch & Feel. 2011. (DC Super Heroes Ser.). (ENG.). 12p. (J). (gr. -1). bds. 11.99 *(978-1-935703-13-6(7))* Downtown Bookworks.

Korte, Steve. Wonder Woman - I Am an Amazon Warrior. Ferguson, Lee, illus. 2017. (I Can Read Level 2 Ser.). 32p. (J). (gr. -1-3). pap. 3.99 ***(978-0-06-268184-3(2))*** HarperCollins Pubs.

—Wonder Woman & the Heroes of Myth. Altmann, Scott, illus. 2017. (Wonder Woman Mythology Ser.). (ENG.). 32p. (gr. 3-4). lib. bdg. 26.65 *(978-1-5157-4585-3(6)*, DC Super Heroes) Stone Arch Bks.

—Wonder Woman & the Monsters of Myth. Altmann, Scott, illus. 2017. (Wonder Woman Mythology Ser.). (ENG.). 32p. (gr. 3-4). lib. bdg. 26.65 *(978-1-5157-4583-9(X)*, DC Super Heroes) Stone Arch Bks.

—Wonder Woman & the Villains of Myth. Altmann, Scott, illus. 2017. (Wonder Woman Mythology Ser.). (ENG.). 32p. (gr. 3-4). lib. bdg. 26.65 *(978-1-5157-4584-6(8)*, DC Super Heroes) Stone Arch Bks.

—Wonder Woman & the World of Myth. Altmann, Scott, illus. 2017. (Wonder Woman Mythology Ser.). (ENG.). 32p. (gr. 3-4). lib. bdg. 26.65 *(978-1-5157-4582-2(1)*, DC Super Heroes) Stone Arch Bks.

—Wonder Woman Movie Deluxe Junior Novel. 2017. 144p. (J). (gr. 1-5). 9.99 ***(978-0-06-268190-4(7)***, HarperFestival) HarperCollins Pubs.

—Wonder Woman Movie ICR #2. Ferguson, Lee & Roberts, Jeremy, illus. 2017. (I Can Read Level 2 Ser.). 32p. (J). (gr. -1-3). pap. 3.99 ***(978-0-06-268186-7(9))*** HarperCollins Pubs.

—Wonder Woman Movie Junior Novel. 2017. 144p. (J). (gr. 1-5). pap. 6.99 ***(978-0-06-268188-1(5)***, HarperFestival) HarperCollins Pubs.

Korte, Steve. Wonder Woman Mythology. 2017. (Wonder Woman Mythology Ser.). (ENG.). 32p. (gr. 3-4). 106.60 *(978-1-5157-4586-0(4)*, DC Super Heroes) Stone Arch Bks.

Lemke, Donald B. Wonder Woman. Ku, Min Sung, illus. 2014. (DC Super Friends Word Adventures Ser.). (ENG.). 12p. (gr. -1 — 1). bds. 6.99 *(978-1-4795-5244-3(5))* Picture Window Bks.

Manning, Matthew K. Wonder Woman Wrestles Circe's Sorcery. Beavers, Ethen, illus. 2017. (DC Super Hero Stories Ser.). (ENG.). 56p. (gr. 1-3). lib. bdg. 25.32 *(978-1-4965-4635-7(0)*, DC Super Heroes) Stone Arch Bks.

Marsham, Liz. DK Readers L3: DC Comics Wonder Woman: Warrior for Justice! 2017. (DK Readers Ser.). (ENG.). 64p. (J). (gr. 2-4). 14.99 *(978-1-4654-6065-3(9)*, DK Children) Dorling Kindersley Publishing, Inc.

—Wonder Woman: Maze of Magic. 2017. (I Can Read! Level 2 Ser.). lib. bdg. 13.55 ***(978-0-606-40057-2(5))*** Turtleback Bks.

—Wonder Woman Classic: Maze of Magic. Ferguson, Lee, illus. 2017. (I Can Read Level 2 Ser.). 32p. (J). (gr. -1-3). pap. 3.99 ***(978-0-06-236093-9(0))*** HarperCollins Pubs.

Rau, Zachary. The Incredible Shrinking Super Hero! With Wonder Woman. Gordon, Steven E., illus. 2009. (ENG.). 24p. (J). (gr. -1-3). pap. 3.99 *(978-0-06-187855-8(3)*, HarperFestival) HarperCollins Pubs.

Sazaklis, John. Wonder Woman: An Origin Story. Baltazar, Art & Vecchio, Luciano, illus. 2015. (DC Super Heroes Origins Ser.). (ENG.). 48p. (gr. k-2). lib. bdg. 23.99 *(978-1-4342-9729-7(2))* Stone Arch Bks.

Stein, Erin K. I Am Wonder Woman. Farley, Rick, illus. 2010. (I Can Read Level 2 Ser.). (ENG.). 32p. (J). (gr. -1-3). pap. 3.99 *(978-0-06-188517-4(7))* HarperCollins Pubs.

Stewart, Yale. Alien Superman!, 1 vol. Stewart, Yale, illus. 2014. (Amazing Adventures of Superman! Ser.). (ENG., Illus.). 32p. (gr. k-2). lib. bdg. 25.32 *(978-1-4795-5733-2(1)*, DC Super Heroes) Stone Arch Bks.

Stone Arch Books & Fisch, Sholly. DC Super Friends, 1 vol. 2014. (DC Super Friends Ser.). (ENG.). 32p. (gr. 1-2). 90.40 *(978-1-4342-9526-2(5))* Stone Arch Bks.

Sutton, Laurie S. Cheetah & the Purrfect Crime, 1 vol. Vecchio, Luciano, illus. 2012. (DC Super-Villains Ser.). (ENG.). 56p. (gr. 2-3). pap. 5.95 *(978-1-4342-3900-6(4))*; lib. bdg. 26.65 *(978-1-4342-3799-6(0))* Stone Arch Bks. (DC Super-villains).

Teitelbaum, Michael. Meet the Super Heroes. 2009. (Justice League Classic: I Can Read! Ser.). (J). lib. bdg. 13.55 *(978-0-606-06941-0(0)*, Turtleback) Turtleback Bks.

Tillworth, Mary. Wonder Woman. Golden Books & Doescher, Erik, illus. 2017. (Big Golden Book Ser.). (ENG.). 32p. (J). (gr. -1-2). 9.99 *(978-1-5247-1840-4(8)*, Golden Bks.) Random Hse. Children's Bks.

Vivinetto, Gina. With Superman & Wonder Woman. Farley, Rick & Tripp, Kanila, illus. 2011. (ENG.). 24p. (J). (gr. -1-3). pap. 3.99 *(978-0-06-188531-0(2)*, HarperFestival) HarperCollins Pubs.

Wrecks, Billy. Batman's Hero Files (DC Super Friends) Random House Editors et al, illus. 2015. (Step into Reading Ser.). (ENG.). 24p. (J). (gr. -1-1). 4.99 *(978-0-553-50808-6(3)*, Random Hse. Bks. for Young Readers) Random Hse. Children's Bks.

—Wonder Woman & Her Super Friends! (DC Super Friends) Random House, illus. 2016. (Tabbed Board Book Ser.). (ENG.). 16p. (J). (-k). bds. 7.99 *(978-1-101-93992-5(3)*, Random Hse. Bks. for Young Readers) Random Hse. Children's Bks.

Yee, Lisa. Wonder Woman at Super Hero High. Random House Disney Staff, illus. 2016. (ENG.). 240p. (J). (gr. 3-7). 13.99 *(978-1-101-94059-4(X)*, Random Hse. Bks. for Young Readers) Random Hse. Children's Bks.

WOOD

see also Forests and Forestry; Lumber and Lumbering; Woodwork

also kinds of wood, e.g. Oak

Cardenas, Ernesto A. Wood or Paper? 2009. 23.95 *(978-1-60698-059-0(9))*; pap. 4.95 *(978-1-60698-057-6(2))* Milo Educational Bks. & Resources.

Colich, Abby. Wood, 1 vol. 2013. (Exploring Materials Ser.). (ENG.). 24p. (gr. -1-1). 22.65 *(978-1-4329-8020-7(3))*; pap. 6.95 *(978-1-4329-8028-3(9))* Heinemann-Raintree. (Acorn).

Hoffmann, Sara. Made of Wood. 2012. (First Step Nonfiction - Exploring Materials Ser.). (ENG., Illus.). 8p. (gr. -1-1). pap. 4.95 *(978-1-4677-0504-2(7)*, Lerner Pubns.) Lerner Publishing Group.

Jennings, Terry. Wood. 2006. (Illus.). 32p. (YA). (gr. 1-18). lib. bdg. 27.10 *(978-1-932333-00-8(2))* Chrysalis Education.

Langley, Andrew. Wood. 2008. (Everyday Materials Ser.). (ENG., Illus.). 24p. (J). (gr. k-3). pap. *(978-0-7787-4137-4(0))* Crabtree Publishing Co.

Llewellyn, Claire. Wood. 2005. (I Know That! Ser.). (Illus.). 24p. (J). (gr. 1-3). lib. bdg. 22.80 *(978-1-932889-51-2(5))* Sea-To-Sea Pubns.

Mitchell, Melanie S. Wood. 2003. (First Step Nonfiction - Materials Ser.). (ENG., Illus.). 24p. (gr. k-2). lib. bdg. 23.93 *(978-0-8225-4618-4(3))* Lerner Publishing Group.

Morris, Neil. Wood. 2010. (Materials That Matter Ser.). 32p. (YA). (gr. 4-7). 28.50 *(978-1-60753-070-1(8))* Amicus Publishing.

Rae, Alison. Trees & Timber Products. 2010. (Development Without Damage Ser.). (YA). (gr. 5-9). 34.25 *(978-1-59920-247-1(6))* Black Rabbit Bks.

Randolph, Joanne. Wedges in My World. 2007. (Journeys Ser.). (ENG.). 24p. (gr. k-8). pap. 7.05 *(978-1-4042-8426-5(5)*, Rosen Classroom) Rosen Publishing Group, Inc., The.

Rau, Dana Meachen. Wood. 2011. (Bookworms Chapter Books: Use It! Reuse It! Ser.). 24p. (gr. 2-3). 22.79 *(978-1-60870-519-1(6))* Marshall Cavendish Corp.

Ridley, Sarah. A Wooden Chair. 2006. (How It's Made Ser.). (Illus.). 32p. (gr. 1-4). lib. bdg. 26.00 *(978-0-8368-6296-6(1)*, Gareth Stevens Learning Library) Stevens, Gareth Publishing LLLP.

Rooney, Anne. Infectious Diseases. 2011. (Mapping Global Issues Ser.). 48p. (J). (gr. 7-9). lib. bdg. 34.25 *(978-1-59920-510-6(6))* Black Rabbit Bks.

Royston, Angela. Wood: Let's Look at a Sports Bat. 2005. (J). *(978-1-4109-1819-2(X))*; (ENG.). 24p. pap. *(978-1-4109-1828-4(9))* Steck-Vaughn.

Shah, Nupur. In the Woods. Shah, Nupur, illus. rev. ed. 2011. (1-3Y Ecosystems Ser.). (ENG., Illus.). 12p. (J). (gr. k-1). pap. 5.99 *(978-1-61541-458-1(4))* American Reading Co.

Tiner, John Hudson. Wood. 2003. (Matter & Materials Ser.). (J). *(978-1-58417-160-7(X))*; pap. *(978-1-58417-166-9(9))* Lake Street Pubs.

Wallace, Holly. Wood. 2007. (How We Use Materials/Watts Ser.). (Illus.). 30p. (J). (gr. 4-7). lib. bdg. 28.50 *(978-1-59920-007-1(4))* Black Rabbit Bks.

WOOD BLOCK PRINTING

see Wood-Engraving

WOOD-CARVING

Dorling Kindersley Publishing Staff. Woodcarving. 2009. 72p. (J). (gr. 5-18). 12.99 *(978-0-7566-3507-7(1))* Dorling Kindersley Publishing, Inc.

Tiede, Karen. Carve Smart. 2004. 189p. (YA). pap. 19.95 *(978-0-7414-2093-0(7))* Infinity Publishing.

Trudel, Robin Edward. Carving for Kids: An Introduction to Woodcarving. 2006. (ENG., Illus.). 94p. 16.95 *(978-1-933502-02-1(9))* Linden Publishing Co., Inc.

Waltner, Elma. Carving Animal Caricatures. 2012. (Dover Woodworking Ser.). (ENG., Illus.). 104p. (gr. 7-12). pap. 22.95 *(978-0-486-22813-6(4))* Dover Pubns., Inc.

WOOD-ENGRAVING

Noble, Marty. Color Your Own Japanese Woodblock Prints. 2011. (Dover Art Coloring Book Ser.). (ENG., Illus.). 32p. (gr. 3-8). pap. 4.99 *(978-0-486-47651-3(0))* Dover Pubns., Inc.

WOOD WIND INSTRUMENTS

see Wind Instruments

WOODCHUCK

Beer, Amy-Jane. Woodchucks. 2008. (Nature's Children Ser.). (Illus.). 52p. (J). *(978-0-7172-6267-0(7))* Grolier, Ltd.

Cella, Clara. Groundhog Day. 2012. (Let's Celebrate Ser.). (ENG.). 24p. (gr. k-1). pap. 41.70 *(978-1-4296-9387-5(8)*, Pebble Plus) Capstone Press of Coughlan Cos.

Gibbons, Gail. Groundhog Day! Gibbons, Gail, illus. 2007. (ENG., Illus.). 32p. (J). (gr. -1-3). pap. 7.99 *(978-0-8234-2116-9(3))* Holiday Hse., Inc.

Gillenwater, Chadwick. Groundhogs, 1 vol. 2012. (North American Animals Ser.). (ENG., Illus.). 24p. (gr. k-1). lib. bdg. 26.65 *(978-1-4296-8673-0(1)*, Pebble Plus) Capstone Press of Coughlan Cos.

Lindeen, Mary. Groundhog Day. 2015. (BeginningtoRead Ser.). (ENG.). 32p. (J). (gr. k-2). pap. 11.94 *(978-1-60357-748-9(3))* Norwood Hse. Pr.

McNeil, Niki, et al. HOCPP 1146 Mr. Groundhog. 2007. spiral bd. 15.50 *(978-1-60308-146-7(1))* In the Hands of a Child.

Meister, Cari. Groundhogs. 2015. (J). lib. bdg. 25.65 *(978-1-62031-167-7(4)*, Bullfrog Bks.) Jump! Inc.

Peppas, Lynn. Groundhog Day. 2010. (Celebrations in My World Ser.). (ENG.). 32p. (J). (gr. k-3). *(978-0-7787-4926-4(6))*; pap. *(978-0-7787-4933-2(9))* Crabtree Publishing Co.

Phillips, Dee. Groundhog's Burrow. 2012. (Hole Truth! Underground Animal Life Ser.). 24p. (J). (gr. -1-3). lib. bdg. 23.93 *(978-1-61772-410-7(6))* Bearport Publishing Co., Inc.

Schuetz, Kari. Groundhogs. 2014. (Backyard Wildlife Ser.). (ENG., Illus.). 24p. (J). (gr. k-3). lib. bdg. 25.95 *(978-1-62617-057-5(6)*, Blastoff! Readers) Bellwether Media.

WOODCHUCK—FICTION

Arno, Iris Hiskey. The Secret of the First One Up. Graef, Renee, illus. 2003. (ENG.). 32p. (J). (gr. k-3). 15.95 *(978-1-55971-867-7(6))* Cooper Square Publishing Llc.

Balian, Lorna. A Garden for a Groundhog, 1 vol. Balian, Lorna, illus. 2011. (ENG., Illus.). 32p. (J). pap. 6.95 *(978-1-59572-296-6(3))* Star Bright Bks., Inc.

—A Garden for a Groundhog, 1 vol. 2004. (ENG., Illus.). 32p. (J). 15.95 *(978-1-932065-38-1(5))* Star Bright Bks., Inc.

Bell, Cece. Chuck & Woodchuck. Bell, Cece, illus. 2016. (ENG., Illus.). 32p. (J). (gr. -1-3). 15.99 *(978-0-7636-7524-0(5))* Candlewick Pr.

Biedrzycki, David. Groundhog's Runaway Shadow. Biedrzycki, David, illus. 2016. (ENG., Illus.). 32p. (J). (gr. -1-3). 16.95 *(978-1-58089-734-1(7))* Charlesbridge Publishing, Inc.

Blackaby, Susan. Brownie Groundhog & the February Fox. Segovia, Carmen, illus. 2011. (ENG.). 32p. (J). (gr. -1-2). 14.95 *(978-1-4027-4336-8(X))* Sterling Publishing Co., Inc.

—Brownie Groundhog & the Wintry Surprise. Segovia, Carmen, illus. 2013. (ENG.). 32p. (J). (gr. -1). 14.95 *(978-1-4027-9836-8(9))* Sterling Publishing Co., Inc.

Canady, Mary Monica. Why Is My Name Sam? Papeo, Maria Eugenia & Saumell, Marina, illus. 2008. 24p. pap. 24.95 *(978-1-60474-028-8(0))* America Star Bks.

Clover. Groundhogs & Golfers. 2011. 24p. pap. 11.50 *(978-1-4634-2909-6(6))* AuthorHouse.

Cox, Judy. Go to Sleep, Groundhog. Meisel, Paul, illus. 2003. (ENG.). 32p. (gr. k-3). tchr. ed. 17.95 *(978-0-8234-1645-5(3))* Holiday Hse., Inc.

Dalton, Kippy. Groundhog & the Sun. Czernichowska, Joanna, illus. 2016. (Spring Forward Ser.). (J). (gr. 1). *(978-1-4900-9369-7(9))* Benchmark Education Co.

Debowski, Sharon. The Snowman, the Owl, & the Groundhog. 2007. (J). lib. bdg. 15.95 *(978-1-60227-468-6(1))*; (Illus.). 32p. (gr. -1-4). 14.95 *(978-1-60227-470-9(3))* Above the Clouds Publishing.

Elish, Dan. The Attack of the Frozen Woodchucks. Call, Greg, illus. 2008. (ENG.). 256p. (J). (gr. 3-7). 16.99 *(978-0-06-113870-6(3)*, Geringer, Laura Book) HarperCollins Pubs.

Freeman, Don. Gregory's Shadow. Freeman, Don, illus. 2003. (Illus.). pap. 39.95 incl. audio compact disk *(978-1-59112-536-5(7))* Live Oak Media.

Graffius, Richard. The Great Groundhog Caper. 2007. pap. 9.00 *(978-0-8059-8423-1(2))* Dorrance Publishing Co., Inc.

Higginson, Hadley. Keeker & the Springtime Surprise. Perrett, Lisa, illus. 2007. (Keeker & the Sneaky Pony Ser.: KEEK). (ENG.). 58p. (J). (gr. k-3). per. 4.99 *(978-0-8118-5599-0(6))* Chronicle Bks. LLC.

Hillert, Margaret. It's Ground Hog Day Dear Dragon. Schimmell, David, illus. 2012. (BeginningtoRead Ser.). 32p. (J). (-2). lib. bdg. 22.60 *(978-1-59953-504-3(1))* Norwood Hse. Pr.

—It's Groundhog Day, Dear Dragon. Schimmell, David, illus. 2012. (BeginningtoRead Ser.). 32p. (J). (-2). pap. 11.94 *(978-1-60357-384-9(4))* Norwood Hse. Pr.

Holub, Joan. Groundhog Weather School. Sorra, Kristin, illus. 2009. (ENG.). 32p. (J). (gr. k-3). 16.99 *(978-0-399-24659-3(2)*, G.P. Putnam's Sons Books for Young Readers) Penguin Young Readers Group.

—Groundhog Weather School: Fun Facts about Weather & Groundhogs. Sorra, Kristin, illus. 2013. (ENG.). 32p. (J). (gr. k-3). 6.99 *(978-0-14-750945-1(9)*, Puffin Books) Penguin Young Readers Group.

Hondel, Gary. Pudgee Woodchuck. Hondel, Gary, illus. 2007. (Illus.). 36p. per. 14.95 *(978-1-59858-323-6(9))* Dog Ear Publishing, LLC.

Jenkins, Emily. A Greyhound, a Groundhog. Appelhans, Chris, illus. 2017. (ENG.). 32p. (J). (gr. -1-2). 17.99 *(978-0-553-49805-9(3))*; lib. bdg. 20.99 *(978-0-553-49806-6(1))* Random Hse. Children's Bks. (Schwartz & Wade Bks.).

Johnson, Crockett. Will Spring Be Early? or Will Spring Be Late? Johnson, Crockett, illus. 2016. (Illus.). 48p. (J). (gr. -1-3). 14.99 *(978-0-06-243037-3(8))* HarperCollins Pubs.

Korman, Susan. Groundhog at Evergreen Road. 2005. (Smithsonian's Backyard Ser.). (ENG., Illus.). 32p. (J). (gr. -1-2). 9.95 *(978-1-59249-028-8(X)*, PB5074) Soundprints.

—Groundhog at Evergreen Road. Bond, Higgins, illus. (Smithsonian's Backyard Ser.). (ENG.). 32p. (J). (gr. -1-2). 2005. 15.95 *(978-1-59249-022-6(0)*, B5024) 2003. 19.95 *(978-1-59249-025-7(5)*, BC5024) 2003. 8.95 *(978-1-59249-061-5(1)*, SC5024) 2003. 4.95 *(978-1-59249-023-3(9)*, B5074) 2003. 6.95 *(978-1-59249-024-0(7)*, S5024) Soundprints.

Lamm, C. Drew. Woodchuck at Blackberry Road. Davis, Allen, illus. 2011. (Smithsonian's Backyard Ser.). (ENG.). 32p. (J). (gr. -1-3). 19.95 *(978-1-60727-644-9(5))* Soundprints.

Landry, Leo. What's up, Chuck? 2016. (ENG., Illus.). 48p. (J). (gr. k-3). lib. bdg. 12.95 *(978-1-58089-698-6(7))* Charlesbridge Publishing, Inc.

McArthur, Cathy E. The Adventures of Elvis the Groundhog: The Golden Glow. 2005. 9.00 *(978-0-8059-8154-4(3))* Dorrance Publishing Co., Inc.

Mean Margaret. 2014. (ENG., Illus.). 176p. (J). (gr. 2-7). 16.99 *(978-1-4814-1014-4(8)*, Atheneum Bks. for Young Readers) Simon & Schuster Children's Publishing.

Menear, Linda. The Little Groundhog Discovers the True Meaning of Christmas. 2011. 24p. pap. 24.95 *(978-1-4626-3288-6(2))* America Star Bks.

Miller, Jean. Curious Chucky. 2013. 32p. pap. 16.00 *(978-1-939615-05-3(4))* Perfect Bound Marketing.

Miller, Pat. Substitute Groundhog. Ember, Kathi, illus. 2012. (J). *(978-1-61913-133-0(1))* Weigl Pubs., Inc.

—Substitute Groundhog, 1 vol. Ember, Kathi, illus. 2010. (ENG.). 32p. (J). (gr. k-3). pap. 6.99 *(978-0-8075-7644-1(1))* Whitman, Albert & Co.

Pearlman, Robb. Groundhog's Day Off. Helquist, Brett, illus. 2015. (ENG.). 40p. (J). (gr. -1-1). 16.99 *(978-1-61963-289-9(6)*, 9781619632899, Bloomsbury USA Childrens) Bloomsbury Publishing USA.

Remenar, Kristen. Groundhog's Dilemma. Faulkner, Matt, illus. 2015. (ENG.). 32p. (J). (gr. -1-2). lib. bdg. 16.95 *(978-1-58089-600-9(6))* Charlesbridge Publishing, Inc.

Roberts, Bethany. Double Trouble Groundhog Day. Cauley, Lorinda Bryan, illus. 2011. (ENG.). 40p. (J). (gr. -1-3). pap. 6.99 *(978-0-312-55350-0(1)*, 9780312553500) Square Fish.

Ruelle, Karen Gray. Great Groundhogs! (ENG., Illus.). 32p. (J). pap. 4.95 *(978-0-8234-1964-7(9))* Holiday Hse., Inc.

—Great Groundhogs! A Harry & Emily Adventure. Ruelle, Karen Gray, illus. 2005. (Holiday House Readers: Level 2 Ser.). (ENG., Illus.). 32p. (J). (gr. k-3). 14.95 *(978-0-8234-1930-2(4))* Holiday Hse., Inc.

Sargent, Dave & Sargent, Pat. Greta Groundhog: I'm Special!, 20 vols., Vol. 20. Huff, Jeane, illus. 2nd rev. ed. 2003. (Animal Pride Ser.: 20). 42p. (J). pap. 10.95 *(978-1-56763-798-4(1))*; lib. bdg. 20.95 *(978-1-56763-797-7(3))* Ozark Publishing.

Schories, Pat. Pants for Chuck. 2014. (I Like to Read(r) Ser.). (ENG., Illus.). 24p. (J). (gr. -1-3). 14.95 *(978-0-8234-3066-6(9))* Holiday Hse., Inc.

Swallow, Pamela Curtis & Swallow, Pamela C. Groundhog Gets a Say. Bunkus, Denise, illus. 2007. (ENG.). 40p. (J). (gr. k-3). pap. 6.99 *(978-0-14-240896-4(4)*, Puffin Books) Penguin Young Readers Group.

Travers, Georgia. The Wily Woodchucks. Gag, Flavia, illus. 2009. (Fesler-Lampert Minnesota Heritage Ser.). (ENG.). 32p. 14.95 *(978-0-8166-6548-8(6))* Univ. of Minnesota Pr.

Vogel, Rob & Azarov, Max. Garry the Groundhog l.t. ed. 2005. (Illus.). 10p. (J). spiral bd. 19.95 incl. DVD *(978-0-9768455-0-8(4)*, N/A) Vogel, Robert.

Vojta, Pat Stemper. Mr. Groundhog Wants the Day Off/El Senor Marmota Quiere el Dia Libre. Leviskiy, Olga, illus. 2010. (ENG & SPA.). 32p. (J). (gr. 4-7). 16.95 *(978-1-934960-77-6(2)*, Raven Tree Pr.,Csi) Continental Sales, Inc.

WOODCUTS

see Wood-Engraving

WOODPECKERS

Caez, Joshua, illus. To Find an Ivory-billed Woodpecker. Lt. ed. 2005. 21p. (YA). 9.95 net. *(978-0-9771752-0-8(0))* Harrison, Bobby.

Carr, Aaron. Woodpeckers. 2014. (J). *(978-1-4896-2950-0(5))* Weigl Pubs., Inc.

Elora, Grace. A Bird Watcher's Guide to Woodpeckers. 2017. (Backyard Bird Watchers Ser.). 32p. (J). (gr. 2-3). pap. 10.50 ***(978-1-5382-0331-6(6))*** Stevens, Gareth Publishing LLLP.

Gish, Melissa. Living Wild: Woodpeckers. 2013. (Living Wild Ser.). (ENG., Illus.). 48p. (J). (gr. 4-7). pap. 12.00 *(978-0-89812-779-9(3),* Creative Paperbacks) Creative Co., The.

—Woodpeckers. 2012. (Living Wild Ser.). (Illus.). 48p. (J). (gr. 5-12). 23.95 *(978-1-60818-172-8(3),* Creative Education) Creative Co., The.

Gregory, Josh. From Woodpeckers to... Helmets. 2012. (21st Century Skills Innovation Library: Innovations from Nature Ser.). (ENG.). 32p. (gr. 4-8). 28.50 *(978-1-61080-495-0(3),* 202105); pap. 14.21 *(978-1-61080-669-5(7),* 202279) Cherry Lake Publishing.

Hoose, Phillip. The Race to Save the Lord God Bird. rev. ed. 2014. (ENG., Illus.). 224p. (YA). (gr. 7-12). 24.99 *(978-0-374-30035-7(6),* Farrar, Straus & Giroux (BYR)) Farrar, Straus & Giroux.

Kalz, Jill. Woodpeckers. 2003. (Birds Ser.). (Illus.). 24p. (J). lib. bdg. 21.35 *(978-1-58340-132-3(X))* Black Rabbit Bks.

Mara, Wil. Woodpeckers. 2014. (Backyard Safari Ser.). 32p. (J). (gr. 3-5). 28.50 *(978-1-62712-837-7(9))* Cavendish Square Publishing.

Murray, Julie. Woodpeckers, 1 vol. 2005. (Animal Kingdom Set Ii Ser.). (ENG., Illus.). 24p. (gr. k-4). 25.65 *(978-1-59197-340-9(6),* Buddy Bks.) ABDO Publishing Co.

Phillips, Dee. Woodpecker. 2013. (Science Slam: Treed-Animal Life in the Trees Ser.). 24p. (J). (gr. -1-3). lib. bdg. 23.93 *(978-1-61772-913-3(2))* Bearport Publishing Co., Inc.

Riggs, Kate. Amazing Animals: Woodpeckers. 2014. (Amazing Animals Ser.). (ENG.). 24p. (J). (gr. 1-3). pap. 7.99 *(978-0-89812-931-1(1),* Creative Paperbacks) Creative Co., The.

—Woodpeckers. 2014. (Illus.). 24p. (J). 25.65 *(978-1-60818-352-4(1),* Creative Education) Creative Co., The.

Sayre, April Pulley. Woodpecker Wham! Jenkins, Steve, illus. 2015. (ENG.). 40p. (J). (gr. -1-3). 17.99 *(978-0-8050-8842-7(3),* 9780805088427, Holt, Henry & Co. Bks. For Young Readers) Holt, Henry & Co.

Schuetz, Kari. Woodpeckers. 2011. (Backyard Wildlife Ser.). (ENG., Illus.). 24p. (J). (gr. k-3). lib. bdg. 25.95 *(978-1-60014-599-5(X),* Blastoff! Readers) Bellwether Media.

Soffer, Ruth. Woodpeckers Stickers. 2006. (Dover Little Activity Books Stickers Ser.). (ENG., Illus.). 4p. (gr. -1-5). pap. 1.50 *(978-0-486-44841-1(X))* Dover Pubns., Inc.

Waxman, Laura Hamilton. Pileated Woodpeckers. 2016. (Comparing Animal Traits Ser.). (ENG., Illus.). 32p. (J). (gr. 2-4). pap. 8.99 *(978-1-4677-9637-8(9),* Lerner Pubns.) Lerner Publishing Group.

—Pileated Woodpeckers: Insect-Hunting Birds. 2016. (Comparing Animal Traits Ser.). (ENG., Illus.). 32p. (J). (gr. 2-4). 39.99 *(978-1-4677-9638-5(7),* Lerner Pubns.) Lerner Publishing Group.

WOODS, TIGER, 1975-

Brown, Jonatha A. Tiger Woods. 2004. (People We Should Know Ser.). (SPA.). 24p. (gr. 1-4). pap. 8.15 *(978-0-8368-4362-0(2),* GHS33881, Weekly Reader Leveled Readers) Stevens, Gareth Publishing LLLP.

—Tiger Woods. Acosta, Tatiana & Gutierrez, Guillermo, trs. 2004. (Gente Que Hay Que Conocer Ser.). (SPA.). 24p. (gr. 1-4). lib. bdg. 22.00 *(978-0-8368-4355-2(X),* Weekly Reader Leveled Readers) Stevens, Gareth Publishing LLLP.

Brown, Jonatha A. & Raatma, Lucia. Tiger Woods. 2004. (People We Should Know Ser.). (Illus.). 24p. (gr. 1-4). pap. 8.15 *(978-0-8368-4320-0(7));* lib. bdg. 22.00 *(978-0-8368-4313-2(4))* Stevens, Gareth Publishing LLLP. (Weekly Reader Leveled Readers).

Doeden, Matt. Tiger Woods. 2005. (Sports Heroes & Legends Ser.). (ENG., Illus.). 112p. (gr. 5-12). lib. bdg. 30.60 *(978-0-8225-3082-4(1))* Lerner Publishing Group.

Feinstein, Stephen. Lee Sobre Tiger Woods/Read about Tiger Woods. 2006. (I Like Biographies! Bilingual Ser.). (ENG & SPA., Illus.). 24p. (J). (gr. 1-3). lib. bdg. 22.60 *(978-0-7660-2743-5(0),* Enslow Elementary) Enslow Pubs., Inc.

Gallagher, Jim. Tiger Woods. 2008. (Pop Culture Ser.). (Illus.). 64p. (YA). (gr. 3-7). lib. bdg. 22.95 *(978-1-4222-0211-1(9))* Mason Crest.

Glaser, Jason. Tiger Woods. (Sports Idols Ser.). 24p. (gr. 2-3). 2009. 42.50 *(978-1-60853-143-1(0),* PowerKids Pr.) 2008. (Illus.). (J). lib. bdg. 22.60 *(978-1-4042-4179-4(5))* Rosen Publishing Group, Inc., The.

Goodman, Michael E. Tiger Woods. 2003. (Ovations Ser.). (Illus.). 32p. (J). *(978-1-58341-246-6(8),* Creative Education) Creative Co., The.

Goodridge, Catherine. Tiger Woods. 2004. (SPA.). (J). pap. 5.00 *(978-1-4108-2427-1(6),* A24276) Benchmark Education Co.

—Tiger Woods & Tiger Woods (Spanish) 6 English, 6 Spanish Adaptations. 2011. (ENG & SPA.). (J). 76.00 net. *(978-1-4108-5660-9(7))* Benchmark Education Co.

Hasday, Judy. Tiger Woods. 2008. (Black Americans of Achievement: Legacy Edition Ser.). (Illus.). 112p. (gr. 6-12). pap. 11.95 *(978-1-60413-327-1(9),* Checkmark Bks.) Facts On File, Inc.

Hasday, Judy L. Tiger Woods. 2008. (Black Americans of Achievement Ser.). (Illus.). 95p. (YA). (gr. 7-12). 35.00 *(978-0-7910-9714-4(5))* Facts On File, Inc.

Raatma, Lucia. Tiger Woods. 2007. (21st Century Skills Library: Life Skills Biographies Ser.). (ENG., Illus.). 48p. (gr. 4-8). lib. bdg. 31.36 *(978-1-60279-076-6(0),* 200048) Cherry Lake Publishing.

Riddolls, Tom & Wearing, Judy. Tiger Woods. 2009. (Remarkable People Ser.). (Illus.). 24p. (J). (gr. 4-6). pap. 8.95 *(978-1-60596-623-6(1));* lib. bdg. 24.45 *(978-1-60596-622-9(3))* Weigl Pubs., Inc.

Roberts, Jeremy. Tiger Woods. 2008. pap. 52.95 *(978-0-8225-5238-3(8))* 2007. (Illus.). 112p. (J). (gr. 4-7). per. 7.95 *(978-0-8225-8563-3(4),* First Avenue Editions) Lerner Publishing Group.

—Tiger Woods: Golf's Master. 2008. (USA TODAY Lifeline Biographies Ser.). (ENG.). 112p. (gr. 6-12). lib. bdg. 34.60 *(978-1-58013-569-6(2))* Lerner Publishing Group.

Savage, Jeff. Tiger Woods. (Amazing Athletes Ser.). 32p. 2005. (Illus.). (gr. 3-4). lib. bdg. 22.60 *(978-0-8225-1337-7(4))* rev. ed. 2007. (ENG., Illus.). (gr. 2-5). per. 7.95 *(978-0-8225-6890-2(X),* First Avenue Editions) 2nd rev. ed. 2009. (ENG.). (gr. 2-5). 25.26 *(978-0-7613-4921-1(9))* 2nd rev. ed. 2009. (ENG.). (gr. 2-5). pap. 7.95 *(978-0-7613-4923-5(5),* First Avenue Editions) Lerner Publishing Group.

Tieck, Sarah. Tiger Woods: Famous Golfer, 1 vol. 2008. (Big Buddy Biographies Ser.). (ENG.). 32p. (J). (gr. 2-5). 28.50 *(978-1-60453-127-5(4))* ABDO Publishing Co.

Williams, Doug. Tiger Woods Makes Masters History, 1 vol. 2014. (Greatest Events in Sports History Ser.). (ENG., Illus.). 48p. (J). (gr. 3-6). lib. bdg. 32.79 *(978-1-62403-598-2(1),* SportsZone) ABDO Publishing Co.

Woods, Earl & Tiger Woods Foundation Staff. Start Something: You Can Make a Difference. 2006. (ENG., Illus.). 144p. (gr. 4-7). pap. 14.00 *(978-1-4165-3704-5(X))* Simon & Schuster.

WOODS

see Forests and Forestry

WOODSON, CARTER GODWIN, 1875-1950

Durden, Robert F. The Life of Carter G. Woodson: Father of African-American History. 2014. (Legendary African Americans Ser.). (Illus.). 96p. (J). (gr. 6-12). pap. 10.95 *(978-0-7660-6123-1(X))* Enslow Pubs., Inc.

Durden, Robert Franklin. The Life of Carter G.Woodson: Father of African-American History. 2014. (Legendary African Americans Ser.). 96p. (J). (gr. 6-12). 27.94 *(978-0-7660-6122-4(1))* Enslow Pubs., Inc.

McKissack, Patricia C. & McKissack, Fredrick L. Carter G. Woodson: Black History Pioneer. 2013. (Famous African Americans Ser.). 24p. (J). (gr. k-3). pap. 7.95 *(978-1-4644-0195-4(0));* (Illus.). lib. bdg. 22.60 *(978-0-7660-4109-7(3))* Enslow Pubs., Inc. (Enslow Elementary).

WOODWORK

see also Cabinetwork; Carpentry; Furniture; Wood-Carving

Beeby, Betty. Great Granny's Sturdy Stable Picnic Tables. 2004. (Illus.). 32p. (J). *(978-0-9674525-2-4(X))* Pearl Pr.

Braithwaite, Jill. From Tree to Table. 2003. (Start to Finish Ser.). (ENG., Illus.). 24p. (gr. k-3). 19.93 *(978-0-8225-0947-9(4),* Lerner Pubns.) Lerner Publishing Group.

Dorling Kindersley Publishing Staff. Woodworking. 2009. 72p. (J). (gr. 5-18). 12.99 *(978-0-7566-3506-0(3))* Dorling Kindersley Publishing, Inc.

Felix, Rebecca. Cool Woodworking Projects: Fun & Creative Workshop Activities. 2016. (ENG., Illus.). 32p. (J). *(978-1-68078-130-4(8))* ABDO Publishing Co.

Levete, Sarah. Maker Projects for Kids Who Love Woodworking. 2016. (Be a Maker! Ser.). (ENG., Illus.). 32p. (J). (gr. 5-8). *(978-0-7787-2579-4(0))* Crabtree Publishing Co.

Llimós, Anna. Earth-Friendly Wood Crafts in 5 Easy Steps. 2013. (Earth-Friendly Crafts in 5 Easy Steps Ser.). 32p. (J). (gr. 3-4). pap. 7.95 *(978-1-4644-0317-0(1),* Enslow Elementary) Enslow Pubs., Inc.

Llimós Plomer, Anna. Earth-Friendly Wood Crafts in 5 Easy Steps. 2013. (Earth-Friendly Crafts in 5 Easy Steps Ser.). (Illus.). 32p. (J). lib. bdg. 23.94 *(978-0-7660-4193-6(X))* Enslow Pubs., Inc.

Llimos Plomer, Anna & Llimós, Anna. Madera y Corcho. Casanova, Jose Maria, illus. 2003. (Coleccion Ivamos a Crear!). (SPA.). 32p. (J). (gr. 2). 12.00 *(978-84-342-2344-8(9))* Parramon Ediciones S.A. ESP. Dist: Lectorum Pubns., Inc.

Llimos Plomer, Anna & Parramon's Editorial Team Staff. Wood & Cork. 2003. (Let's Create! Ser.). (Illus.). 32p. (gr. 1-4). lib. bdg. 26.00 *(978-0-8368-3749-0(5),* Gareth Stevens Learning Library) Stevens, Gareth Publishing LLLP.

McGuire, Kevin. The All-New Woodworking for Kids. 2008. (ENG., Illus.). 144p. (J). pap. 14.95 *(978-1-60059-035-1(7))* Lark Bks.

Riley, Margaret. Awesome Woodlets: Wooden Cut-Out Projects for Every Season. 2012. (ENG., Illus.). 16p. pap. 8.99 *(978-1-57421-354-6(7),* 9781574213546, Design Originals) Fox Chapel Publishing Co., Inc.

Robertson, Craig & Robertson, Barbara. The Kids' Building Workshop: 15 Woodworking Projects for Kids & Parents to Build Together. 2004. (ENG., Illus.). 144p. (J). (gr. 3-8). pap. 14.95 *(978-1-58017-488-6(4),* 67488) Storey Publishing, LLC.

Sullivan, Laura L. The Colonial Woodworker. 2015. (Colonial People Ser.). (ENG.). 48p. (J). (gr. 4-4). 31.36 *(978-1-5026-0484-2(1))* Cavendish Square Publishing.

WOOL

see also Dyes and Dyeing

Blaxland, Wendy. Sweaters. 2009. (How Are They Made? 2 Ser.). 32p. (gr. 4). lib. bdg. 18.56 *(978-0-7614-4756-6(3))* Marshall Cavendish GBR. Dist: Marshall Cavendish Corp.

Ditchfield, Christin. The Story Behind Wool, 1 vol. 2011. (True Stories Ser.). (ENG.). 32p. (gr. 3-3). 30.65 *(978-1-4329-5436-9(9),* NA-h) Heinemann-Raintree.

Gibbons, Gail. From Sheep to Sweater. Date not set. (J). *(978-0-8234-1885-5(5))* Holiday Hse., Inc.

Gleason, Carrie. The Biography of Wool. 2007. (How Did That Get Here? Ser.). (ENG., Illus.). 32p. (J). (gr. 3-7). lib. bdg. *(978-0-7787-2496-4(4));* (gr. 2-9). pap. *(978-0-7787-2532-9(4))* Crabtree Publishing Co.

Langley, Andrew. Wool. 2008. (Everyday Materials Ser.). (ENG., Illus.). 24p. (J). (gr. k-3). pap. *(978-0-7787-4138-1(9))* Crabtree Publishing Co.

Levete, Sarah. Wool. 2006. (Material Matters Ser.). (J). *(978-1-59389-274-6(8))* Chrysalis Education.

Murray, Julie. Sheep to Sweater, 1 vol. 2006. (Beginning to End Set 1 - 8 Titles Ser.). (ENG., Illus.). 24p. (gr. k-4). 25.65 *(978-1-59679-914-1(5),* Buddy Bks.) ABDO Publishing Co.

Nelson, Robin. From Sheep to Sweater. 2003. (Start to Finish Ser.). (Illus.). 24p. (J). 18.60 *(978-0-8225-0716-1(1),* Lerner Pubns.) Lerner Publishing Group.

Weston Woods Staff, creator. Charlie Needs a Cloak. 2004. 38.75 *(978-1-55592-383-9(6));* 18.95 *(978-1-55592-382-2(8))* Weston Woods Studios, Inc.

WORD GAMES

Amery, Heather & Cartwright, Stephen. First One Hundred Words Sticker Book. 2004. (First Hundred Words Ser.). (ENG., Illus.). 1p. (J). pap. 8.95 *(978-0-7945-0190-7(7),* Usborne) EDC Publishing.

Andrews McMeel Publishing, LLC Staff. Go Fun! Big Book of Word Search. 2014. (Go Fun! Ser.: 4). (ENG.). 144p. (J). pap. 8.99 *(978-1-4494-6487-5(4))* Andrews McMeel Publishing.

—Go Fun! Big Book of Word Search 2. 2015. (Go Fun! Ser.: 10). (ENG.). 128p. (J). pap. 8.99 *(978-1-4494-7232-0(X))* Andrews McMeel Publishing.

Barbara Jordan. 2004. 12p. (gr. k-4). 2.95 *(978-0-635-02616-3(3))* Gallopade International.

Berthel, Alice H. Power Puzzles: John. 2007. (J). per. 12.95 *(978-1-59352-193-6(6))* Christian Services Publishing.

—Power Puzzles: Luke. 2007. (J). per. 12.95 *(978-1-59352-192-9(8))* Christian Services Publishing.

—Power Puzzles: Mark. 2007. (J). per. 12.95 *(978-1-59352-191-2(X))* Christian Services Publishing.

—Power Puzzles: Matthew. 2006. (J). per. 12.95 *(978-1-59352-174-5(X))* Christian Services Publishing.

Black, Howard & Parks, Sandra. Dr. Funster's Word Benders B1: Thinking & Vocabulary Fun! 2003. (Dr. Funster's Ser.). 30p. (gr. 5-6). pap. 4.99 *(978-0-89455-813-9(7))* Critical Thinking Co., The.

—Dr. Funster's Word Benders C1: Thinking & Vocabulary Fun! 2003. (Dr. Funster's Ser.). 30p. (gr. 7-12). pap. 4.99 *(978-0-89455-814-6(5))* Critical Thinking Co., The.

Booth, Karon. Aslan Is on the Move: Romp in Narnia with Study Helps, Art & Play. 2003. (Illus.). 196p. (J). per. *(978-0-941367-13-4(4))* Peach Blossom Pubns.

Burns, Walter. Steven Universe Mad Libs. 2015. (Steven Universe Ser.). (ENG.). 48p. (J). (gr. 3-7). pap. 3.99 *(978-0-8431-8309-2(8),* Mad Libs) Penguin Young Readers Group.

Carole Marsh. California Indians. 2004. (California Experienc Ser.). 36p. (gr. 3-8). pap. 7.95 *(978-0-635-02254-7(0))* Gallopade International.

Carson-Dellosa Publishing Staff. Puzzles & Games: Word Play. 2010. (Home Workbooks Ser.). (ENG.). 64p. (gr. k-1). pap. 4.49 *(978-1-60418-782-3(4))* Carson-Dellosa Publishing, LLC.

—Word Play, Grades K - 1: Rhyming. 2010. (Home Workbooks Ser.). (ENG.). 64p. (gr. k-1). pap. 4.49 *(978-1-60418-781-6(6))* Carson-Dellosa Publishing, LLC.

Carson-Dellosa Publishing Staff, compiled by. Puzzles & Games, Grade 2: Word Play. 2010. (Home Workbooks Ser.). (ENG.). 64p. (gr. 2-2). pap. 4.49 *(978-1-60418-796-0(4))* Carson-Dellosa Publishing, LLC.

Chamberlain, Kim. The Five-Minute Brain Workout for Kids: 365 Amazing, Fabulous, & Fun Word Puzzles. Chamberlain, Jon, illus. 2015. (ENG.). 416p. (J). (gr. 1). pap. 14.99 *(978-1-63450-159-0(4),* Sky Pony Pr.) Skyhorse Publishing Co., Inc.

Charlip, Remy. Arm in Arm: A Collection of Connections, Endless Tales, Reiterations, & Other Echolalia. 2010. (ENG., Illus.). 48p. (J). (gr. 1-4). pap. 8.99 *(978-1-58246-368-1(9),* Tricycle Pr.) Random Hse. Children's Bks.

Chronicle Books Staff. 75 Word Puzzles. 2005. (Genius Decks Ser.: GENI). (ENG., Illus.). (gr. 8-17). 13.95 *(978-0-8118-5196-1(6))* Chronicle Bks. LLC.

Cleary, Brian. Madam & Nun And 1001: What Is a Palindrome? Gable, Brian, illus. 2014. (Words Are CATegorical (r) Ser.). (ENG.). 32p. (gr. 2-5). pap. 6.95 *(978-1-4677-2628-3(1),* Millbrook Pr.) Lerner Publishing Group.

Cloutier, Toni Lynn. Word Search USA. 2010. (ENG., Illus.). 128p. (J). (gr. 3-6). spiral bd. 6.95 *(978-1-4027-6905-4(9))* Sterling Publishing Co., Inc.

Danna, Mark. Word Searches. 2008. (ENG.). 352p. (J). pap. 6.95 *(978-1-4027-4667-3(9))* Sterling Publishing Co., Inc.

DeNinno, Joanne & Gill, Kim. The Question Challenge Card Game Fun Sheets. 2012. 34.95 net. *(978-1-60723-023-6(2))* Super Duper Pubns.

Dompierre, Judith. Read It Whichever Direction You Want. 2012. 50p. 29.95 *(978-1-4626-3524-5(5))* America Star Bks.

Dompierre, Judith E. Read It Whichever Direction You Want. 2012. 38p. pap. 24.95 *(978-1-4626-9324-5(5))* America Star Bks.

DynaNotes Lab Measurement & Equipment Workbook. 2007. (J). pap. *(978-1-933854-72-4(3))* DynaStudy, Inc.

Findley, Violet. Word Family Bingo Ladders: Fun-and-Easy Reproducible Games That Teach Kids the Top 25 Word Families. 2009. (ENG.). 96p. pap. 12.99 *(978-0-545-09440-5(2),* Teaching Resources) Scholastic, Inc.

Gardner, Martin. Mind-Boggling Word Puzzles. Myers, V. G., illus. 2010. (Dover Children's Activity Bks.). (ENG.). 96p. (J). (gr. 3-5). pap. 4.99 *(978-0-486-47496-0(8))* Dover Pubns., Inc.

Geatches, Hazel. Cities, Level 2. 2012. (ENG., Illus.). 40p. pap. 9.38 *(978-0-19-464682-6(3))* Oxford Univ. Pr., Inc.

Geatches, Hazel, ed. At the Beach. 2012. (ENG., Illus.). 32p. 9.38 *(978-0-19-464628-4(9))* Oxford Univ. Pr., Inc.

—Earth. 2012. (ENG., Illus.). 40p. pap., act. bk. ed. 10.00 *(978-0-19-464679-6(3))* Oxford Univ. Pr., Inc.

Grimes, Nikki. Words with Wings. 2013. (ENG., Illus.). 96p. (J). (gr. 3). 16.95 *(978-1-59078-985-8(7),* Wordsong) Boyds Mills Pr.

Harpster, Steve, illus. First Word Search: Easy First Words. 2011. (First Word Search Ser.). (ENG.). 64p. (J). (gr. -1-1). pap. 4.95 *(978-1-4027-7808-7(2))* Sterling Publishing Co., Inc.

—First Word Search: Fun First Phonics. 2011. (First Word Search Ser.). (ENG.). 64p. (J). pap. 4.95 *(978-1-4027-7806-3(6))* Sterling Publishing Co., Inc.

—First Word Search: Fun First Words. 2011. (First Word Search Ser.). (ENG.). 64p. (J). pap. 4.95 *(978-1-4027-7807-0(4))* Sterling Publishing Co., Inc.

—First Word Search: Reading Made Easy. 2011. (First Word Search Ser.). (ENG.). 64p. (J). (gr. -1-1). pap. 4.95 *(978-1-4027-7802-5(3))* Sterling Publishing Co., Inc.

Highlights for Children Editorial Staff, creator. Word Searches. 2015. (Highlights(tm) Puzzlemania(r) Puzzle Pads Ser.). (ENG.). 64p. (J). (gr. k). pap. 4.99 *(978-1-62979-423-5(6),* Highlights) Boyds Mills Pr.

Hirschmann, Kris. Feed Me Words. Hindle, James K., illus. 2016. (Scripps National Spelling Bee Ser.). (ENG.). 96p. (J). 17.99 *(978-1-62672-173-9(4),* 9781626721739) Roaring Brook Pr.

Hoffman, Joan. Word Search People & Places. 2004. (ENG.). 32p. (J). pap. 2.99 *(978-1-58947-388-1(4),* 02193) School Zone Publishing Co.

HOP, LLC. Hooked on Phonics Word Games. 2006. 64p. 3.79 *(978-1-933863-93-1(5))* HOP, LLC.

Kellaher, Karen. Grammar Games & Activities Kids Can't Resist! 40 Super-Cool Crosswords, Codes, Mazes & More That Teach the Essential Rules of Grammar. 2003. (ENG., Illus.). 64p. (J). pap. 10.95 *(978-0-439-07756-9(7))* Scholastic, Inc.

Kline, Michael. Wordplay Cafe: Cool Codes, Priceless Punzles & Phantastic Phonetic Phun. Kline, Michael, illus. 2008. (ENG., Illus.). 128p. (J). (gr. 4-7). per. 12.95 *(978-0-8249-6753-6(4),* Ideal Pubns.) Worthy Publishing.

Kurchan, Rodolfo, et al. Giant Book of Hard-to-Solve Word Puzzles/Giant Book of Hard-to-Solve Mind Puzzles: Flip Book. Sterling Publishing Company Staff, ed. (Illus.). 512p. pap. 9.98 *(978-1-4027-0285-3(X))* Sterling Publishing Co., Inc.

LaCoste, Gary, illus. First Word Search: Phonics Word Search. 2011. (First Word Search Ser.). (ENG.). 64p. (J). (gr. -1-1). pap. 4.95 *(978-1-4027-7801-8(5))* Sterling Publishing Co., Inc.

—First Word Search: Words to Learn. 2011. (First Word Search Ser.). (ENG.). 64p. (J). (gr. -1-1). pap. 4.95 *(978-1-4027-7809-4(0))* Sterling Publishing Co., Inc.

—Phonics Fun. 2011. (First Word Search Ser.). (ENG.). 64p. (J). (gr. -1-1). pap. 4.95 *(978-1-4027-8391-3(4))* Sterling Publishing Co., Inc.

Laval, Thierry. Look & Find Transportation. 2016. (Look & Find Ser.). (ENG., Illus.). 14p. (J). 18.99 *(978-0-531-22237-9(3),* Children's Pr.) Scholastic Library Publishing.

—Look & Find Your World. 2016. (Look & Find Ser.). (ENG.). 14p. (J). 18.99 *(978-0-531-22239-3(X),* Children's Pr.) Scholastic Library Publishing.

Lee, Betsy B. A Funny Dolch Word Book # 1: Un Libro Comico # 1 de la Palabra de Dolch. Davis, Pollyanna S., tr. 2006. (ENG & SPA.). pap. 5.95 *(978-0-9720267-5-8(4))* Learning Abilities Bks.

Levin, Freddie. Outer Space Activity Book. 2009. (Dover Little Activity Bks.). (ENG.). 64p. (J). (gr. k-3). pap. 1.99 *(978-0-486-47389-5(9))* Dover Pubns., Inc.

Mad Libs Staff. Mad Scientist Mad Libs. 2014. (Mad Libs Ser.). (ENG.). 48p. (J). (gr. 3-7). 4.99 *(978-0-8431-8057-2(9),* Mad Libs) Penguin Young Readers Group.

Marsh, Carole. Abigail Adams. 2004. 12p. (gr. k-4). 2.95 *(978-0-635-02372-8(5))* Gallopade International.

—Albert Einstein. 2003. 12p. (gr. k-4). 2.95 *(978-0-635-02352-0(0))* Gallopade International.

—Alexander Graham Bell. 2003. 12p. (gr. k-4). 2.95 *(978-0-635-02354-4(7))* Gallopade International.

—Alvar Nunez Cabeza de Vaca:Explorer & Survivor: Explorer & Survivor. 2003. 12p. (gr. k-4). 2.95 *(978-0-635-02135-9(8))* Gallopade International.

—Amelia Earhart. 2003. 12p. (gr. k-4). 2.95 *(978-0-635-02131-1(5))* Gallopade International.

—Andrew Jackson. 2003. 12p. (gr. k-4). 2.95 *(978-0-635-02360-5(1))* Gallopade International.

—Anne Hutchinson. 2004. 12p. (gr. k-4). 2.95 *(978-0-635-02370-4(9))* Gallopade International.

—Antonia C. Novello: First Female U. S. Surgeon General: First Female U. S. Surgeon General. 2003. 12p. (gr. k-4). 2.95 *(978-0-635-02139-7(0))* Gallopade International.

—Ben Nighthorse Campbell. 2003. 12p. (gr. k-4). 2.95 *(978-0-635-02383-4(0))* Gallopade International.

—Benjamin Banneker. 2003. 12p. (gr. k-4). 2.95 *(978-0-635-02129-8(3))* Gallopade International.

—Carol Moseley Braun. 2003. 12p. (gr. k-4). 2.95 *(978-0-635-02384-1(9))* Gallopade International.

—Charles Drew: Dedicated Doctor. 2004. (1000 Readers Ser.). (Illus.). 12p. (J). (gr. k-4). per. 2.95 *(978-0-635-02528-9(0))* Gallopade International.

—Charles Kettering: Patent Giant. 2004. (1000 Readers Ser.). (Illus.). 14p. (J). (gr. k-4). pap. 2.95 *(978-0-635-02525-8(6))* Gallopade International.

—Charles Lindbergh. 2003. 12p. (gr. k-4). 2.95 *(978-0-635-02130-4(7))* Gallopade International.

—Charles W. Dryden: Tuskegee Airman. 2004. (1000 Readers Ser.). (Illus.). 12p. (J). (gr. k-4). pap. 2.95 *(978-0-635-02493-0(4))* Gallopade International.

—Clara Barton. 2003. 12p. (gr. k-4). 2.95 *(978-0-635-02353-7(9))* Gallopade International.

—Crazy Horse. 2003. 12p. (gr. k-4). 2.95 *(978-0-635-02382-7(2))* Gallopade International.

—Dick Cheney: U. S. Vice President. 2004. (1000 Readers Ser.). (Illus.). 14p. (J). (gr. k-4). pap. 2.95 *(978-0-635-02670-5(8))* Gallopade International.

—Diego Rivera: Acclaimed Mural Painter: Acclaimed Mural Painter. 2003. 12p. (gr. k-4). 2.95 *(978-0-635-02137-3(4))* Gallopade International.

—Ellen Ochoa: First Hispanic American Woman in Space: First Hispanic American Woman in Space. 2003. 12p. (gr. k-4). 2.95 *(978-0-635-02138-0(2))* Gallopade International.

—Father Junipero Serra: California Missions Founder: California Missions Founder. 2003. 12p. (gr. k-4). 2.95 *(978-0-635-02136-6(6))* Gallopade International.

—Ferdinand Magellan, World Voyager. 2004. 12p. (gr. k-4). 2.95 *(978-0-635-02373-5(3))* Gallopade International.

—Frederick Douglass. 2003. 12p. (gr. k-4). 2.95 *(978-0-635-02125-0(0))* Gallopade International.

—Garrett Morgan, Innovative Inventor. 2004. 12p. (gr. k-4). 2.95 *(978-0-635-02526-5(4))* Gallopade International.

W X Y Z

—General Colin Powell. 2003. 12p. (gr. k-4). 2.95 *(978-0-635-02359-9(8))* Gallopade International.
—Geronimo. 2003. 12p. (gr. k-4). 2.95 *(978-0-635-02381-0(4))* Gallopade International.
—Granville Woods: Excellent Inventor. 2004. (1000 Readers Ser.). (Illus.). 14p. (J). (gr. k-4). pap. 2.95 *(978-0-635-02527-2(2))* Gallopade International.
—Harriet Beecher Stowe. 2003. 12p. (gr. k-4). 2.95 *(978-0-635-02356-8(3))* Gallopade International.
—John C. Fremont. 2004. 12p. (gr. k-4). 2.95 *(978-0-635-02380-3(6))* Gallopade International.
—John Edwards: Vice Presidential Hopeful. 2004. (Did You Know... ? Ser.). (Illus.). 12p. (J). (gr. k-4). pap. 2.95 *(978-0-635-02671-2(6))* Gallopade International.
—King George III. 2004. 12p. (gr. k-4). 2.95 *(978-0-635-02364-3(4))* Gallopade International.
—Marco Polo. 2004. 12p. (gr. k-4). 2.95 *(978-0-635-02376-6(8))* Gallopade International.
—Meriwether Lewis & William Clark: Explorers of the Uncharted West: Explorers of the Uncharted West. 2003. 12p. (gr. k-4). 2.95 *(978-0-635-02133-5(1))* Gallopade International.
—Roberto Clemente: Baseball Hero & Humanitarian: Baseball Hero & Humanitarian. 2003. 12p. (gr. k-4). 2.95 *(978-0-635-02140-3(4))* Gallopade International.
—Sacagawea: Native American Heroine: Native American Heroine. 2003. 12p. (gr. k-4). 2.95 *(978-0-635-02143-4(9))* Gallopade International.
—Sequoyah. 2003. 12p. (gr. k-4). 2.95 *(978-0-635-02363-6(6))* Gallopade International.
—Sitting Bull. 2003. 12p. (gr. k-4). 2.95 *(978-0-635-02378-0(4))* Gallopade International.
—Theodore Roosevelt. 2004. 12p. (gr. k-4). 2.95 *(978-0-635-02362-9(8))* Gallopade International.
—Thomas Paine. 2004. 12p. (gr. k-4). 2.95 *(978-0-635-02369-8(5))* Gallopade International.
—William Penn. 2003. 12p. (gr. k-4). 2.95 *(978-0-635-02358-2(X))* Gallopade International.
Martorana, Cherie. Made You Laugh for Kids: Wacky Word Searches. 2005. (Kids Made You Laugh Ser.). (ENG., Illus.). pap. 5.95 *(978-1-57528-926-7(1))* Univ. Games.
Matheis, Mickie. Peanuts Mad Libs. 2015. (Mad Libs Ser.). (ENG.). 48p. (J). (gr. 3-7). pap. 4.99 *(978-0-8431-8331-3(4),* Mad Libs) Penguin Young Readers Group.
McCowan Nevills, Jennifer. Have You Ever? Part 2. 2008. (Illus.). 31p. (YA). pap. 17.99 *(978-0-9655792-4-7(7))* Don Paul Publishing, LLC.
—Have You Ever? Part 3. 2008. (Illus.). 31p. (YA). pap. 17.99 *(978-0-9655792-5-4(5))* Don Paul Publishing, LLC.
—Have You Ever? Part 4. 2008. (Illus.). 33p. (YA). pap. 17.99 *(978-0-9655792-6-1(3))* Don Paul Publishing, LLC.
Nicholas, Mother Andrea, compiled by. My Little Orthodox Christian Feast Days Activity Book. 2005. (J). spiral bd. 6.95 *(978-0-9773579-0-1(2))* St. Nicholas Monastery.
Nye, Mark Aaron. Scriptureable Game Book - Bible King James Version. 2003. 88p. (YA). spiral bd. 13.95 *(978-0-9746665-1-8(3))* Nye Products.
—Scriptureable Game Book - LDS Version. 2003. 194p. (YA). spiral bd. 17.95 *(978-0-9746665-0-1(5))* Nye Products.
Parker, Sherri. God's Word Ages 4-10, Bk. 2. 2004. (J). spiral bd. 5.18 net. *(978-1-56870-554-5(9))* Hewell Publishing.
Plant, Cherie A. Word Roots A1: Learning the Building Blocks of Better Spelling & Vocabulary. 2013. (Word Roots Ser.). 72p. (gr. 5-12). pap. 15.99 *(978-0-89455-804-7(8))* Critical Thinking Co., The.
—Word Roots B1: Learning the Building Blocks of Better Spelling & Vocabulary. 2012. (Word Roots Ser.). 112p. (gr. 7-12). pap. 15.99 *(978-0-89455-805-4(6))* Critical Thinking Co., The.
Price, Roger & Mad Libs Staff. I Love Seattle Mad Libs. 2015. (Mad Libs Ser.). (ENG.). 48p. (J). (gr. 3-7). bds. 4.99 *(978-0-8431-8268-2(7),* Mad Libs) Penguin Young Readers Group.
Price, Roger & Stern, Leonard. Best of Mad Libs. 2008. (Mad Libs Ser.). (ENG.). 288p. (J). (gr. 3-7). pap. 6.99 *(978-0-8431-2698-3(1),* Mad Libs) Penguin Young Readers Group.
—Diva Girl Mad Libs. 2004. (Mad Libs Ser.). (ENG.). 48p. (J). (gr. 3-7). mass mkt. 4.99 *(978-0-8431-0837-8(1),* Mad Libs) Penguin Young Readers Group.
—Family Tree Mad Libs. 2007. (Mad Libs Ser.). (ENG., Illus.). 48p. (J). (gr. 3-7). 4.99 *(978-0-8431-1643-4(9),* Mad Libs) Penguin Young Readers Group.
—Gobble Gobble Mad Libs. 2013. (Mad Libs Ser.). (ENG.). 48p. (J). (gr. 3-7). 4.99 *(978-0-8431-7292-8(4),* Mad Libs) Penguin Young Readers Group.
—Happily Ever Mad Libs. 2010. (Mad Libs Ser.). (ENG.). 48p. (J). (gr. 3-7). 4.99 *(978-0-8431-9962-8(8),* Mad Libs) Penguin Young Readers Group.
—Letters from Camp Mad Libs. 2006. (Mad Libs Ser.). (ENG., Illus.). 48p. (J). (gr. 3-7). 4.99 *(978-0-8431-1827-8(X),* Mad Libs) Penguin Young Readers Group.
—Sleepover Party Mad Libs. 2008. (Mad Libs Ser.). (ENG.). 48p. (J). (gr. 3-7). 4.99 *(978-0-8431-2699-0(X),* Mad Libs) Penguin Young Readers Group.
Price, Roger & Stern, Leonard, creators. WWE Mad Libs. 2011. (Wwe Ser.). (ENG.). 48p. (J). (gr. 3-7). bds. 3.99 *(978-0-8431-9882-9(6),* Mad Libs) Penguin Young Readers Group.
Priddy, Roger. Priddy Learning: Word Fun. 2017. (ENG., Illus.). 32p. (J). pap. 4.99 *(978-0-312-52204-9(5),* 9780312522049, Priddy Bks.) St. Martin's Pr.
Puzzle Society Staff. Girl Hangman 2: 100 Puzzles. 2011. (ENG.). 112p. pap. 7.99 *(978-1-4494-0733-9(1))* Andrews McMeel Publishing.
—Pocket Posh Girl Word Search 2 Vol. 2: 100 Puzzles. 2011. (ENG.). 128p. pap. 7.99 *(978-1-4494-0740-7(4))* Andrews McMeel Publishing.
Puzzler's Giant Book of Word Games. 2003. (YA). Vol. 10. per. 9.45 *(978-1-55956-870-8(4))* Vol. 11. per. 9.45 *(978-1-55956-873-9(9))* Penny Pubns., LLC. (Penny Pr.).
Puzzler's Giant Book of Word Seeks. 2003. (YA). 10. per. 9.45 *(978-1-55956-871-5(2))*11. per. 9.45 *(978-1-55956-874-6(7))* Penny Pubns., LLC. (Penny Pr.).
Rosenthal, Amy Krouse. Wumbers. Lichtenheld, Tom, illus. 2015. (ENG.). 40p. (J). (gr. k-3). 7.99 *(978-1-4521-4122-0(3))* Chronicle Bks. LLC.
—Wumbers. 2015. (J). lib. bdg. 18.40 *(978-0-606-36988-6(0))* Turtleback Bks.
Rubins, Diane Teitel & Daste, Larry. Nature Search-a-Words. 2005. (Dover Children's Activity Bks.). (ENG., Illus.). 48p. (J). (gr. 1-3). per. 4.99 *(978-0-486-44291-4(8))* Dover Pubns., Inc.
Sastrías, Martha. Lecto-Juego-Acertijos: Para Motivar a los Niños a Leer el Mundo Natural. 2005. (SPA & ENG., Illus.). 200p. (gr. 4-7). per. 16.95 *(978-968-860-725-1(8))* Editorial Pax MEX. Dist: Independent Pubs. Group.
School Zone Publishing. Spelling Puzzles. 2003. (Language Arts Ser.). (ENG.). cd-rom 19.99 *(978-1-58947-914-2(9))* School Zone Publishing Co.
—Vocabulary Puzzles. 2003. (ENG.). cd-rom 19.99 *(978-1-58947-931-9(9))* School Zone Publishing Co.
—Word Search Challenges. 2006. (ENG.). 32p. (J). pap. 2.99 *(978-1-58947-392-8(2),* 02194) School Zone Publishing Co.
Schujer, Silvia. Palabras para Jugar (Word Play) (SPA.). (J). pap. *(978-950-07-0664-3(4))* Editorial Sudamericana S.A.
Schulz, Charles. The Peanuts Guide to the Seasons: A Jumbo Activity Book. Bennett, Elizabeth, illus. 2003. (Peanuts Club with Charlie Brown & Friends Ser.). 144p. (J). *(978-0-439-46826-8(4))* Scholastic, Inc.
Schulz, Charles & Bennett, Elizabeth. The Peanuts Guide to Sports: A Jumbo Activity Book. 2003. (Peanuts Club with Charlie Brown & Friends Ser.). (Illus.). 144p. (J). *(978-0-439-46824-4(8))* Scholastic, Inc.
Sevaly, Karen & Scholastic, Inc. Staff. Word Family Words Mats. 2007. (ENG.). (J). (gr. k-2). 14.99 *(978-0-439-92036-0(1))* Scholastic, Inc.
Simpson, Dana. Rainy Day Unicorn Fun: Phoebe & Her Unicorn. 2017. (ENG.). 144p. (J). pap., act. bk. ed. 8.99 ***(978-1-4494-8725-6(4))*** Andrews McMeel Publishing.
Skeete, D. C., creator. Hip Hop Wordsearch. 2005. (YA). pap. 3.99 *(978-0-9769012-0-4(X),* 0-9769012) Skeete, D.
Sloan, Price Stern & Mad Libs Staff. The Amazing World of Gumball Mad Libs. 2014. (Amazing World of Gumball Ser.). (ENG.). 48p. (J). (gr. 3-7). 4.99 *(978-0-8431-7999-6(6),* Mad Libs) Penguin Young Readers Group.
—History of the World Mad Libs. 2015. (Mad Libs Ser.). (ENG.). 48p. (J). (gr. 3-7). bds. 4.99 *(978-0-8431-8075-6(7),* Mad Libs) Penguin Young Readers Group.
So, Patty. So Simple Sightwords At-Home: 31 Fun Sightword Activities. 2007. 36p. (J). spiral bd. *(978-0-9772158-3-6(0))* So Simple Learning.
—So Simple Sightwords at-Home Volume 1. 2007. (Illus.). 124p. (J). spiral bd. *(978-0-9772158-1-2(4))* So Simple Learning.
—So Simple Sightwords at-Home Volume 2. 2007. (Illus.). 132p. (J). spiral bd. *(978-0-9772158-2-9(2))* So Simple Learning.
—So Simple Sightwords at-Home Volume 3. So, Patty, illus. 2008. (Illus.). 117p. (J). spiral bd. *(978-0-9772158-4-3(9))* So Simple Learning.
Steig, William. C D B! Steig, William, illus. 2003. (ENG., Illus.). 48p. (J). (gr. k-3). pap. 8.99 *(978-0-689-85706-5(3),* Aladdin) Simon & Schuster Children's Publishing.
—C D C ? Steig, William, illus. 2008. (ENG., Illus.). 64p. (J). (gr. 1-4). pap. 9.99 *(978-0-312-38012-0(7),* 9780312380120) Square Fish.
Stern, Leonard. School Rules! Mad Libs Junior. 2004. (Mad Libs Junior Ser.). (ENG., Illus.). 48p. (J). (gr. k-3). 4.99 *(978-0-8431-0853-8(3),* Mad Libs) Penguin Young Readers Group.
Stern, Leonard & Price, Roger. Luck of the Mad Libs. 2014. (Mad Libs Ser.). (ENG.). 48p. (J). (gr. 3-7). 4.99 *(978-0-8431-8005-3(6),* Mad Libs) Penguin Young Readers Group.
—More Best of Mad Libs. 2009. (Mad Libs Ser.). (ENG.). 288p. (J). (gr. 3-7). 6.99 *(978-0-8431-2549-8(7),* Mad Libs) Penguin Young Readers Group.
—You've Got Mad Libs. 2004. (Mad Libs Ser.). (ENG., Illus.). 48p. (J). (gr. 3-7). pap. 4.99 *(978-0-8431-0855-2(X),* Mad Libs) Penguin Young Readers Group.
Stern, Leonard, et al. Animals, Animals, Animals. 2004. (Mad Libs Junior Ser.). (ENG.). 48p. (J). (gr. k-3). 4.99 *(978-0-8431-0951-1(3),* Mad Libs) Penguin Young Readers Group.
Sun Staff. Sun Wordsearch, Bk. 1. 2015. (ENG.). 368p. 10.95 *(978-0-00-812767-1(0))* HarperCollins Pubs. Ltd. GBR. Dist: Independent Pubs. Group.
Sylvan Learning Staff. Kindergarten Word Games (Sylvan Fun on the Run Series) 2012. (Sylvan Fun on the Run Series, Language Arts Ser.). (ENG.). 32p. (J). (gr. -1-2). pap. 3.99 *(978-0-307-47947-1(1),* Sylvan Learning Publishing) Random Hse. Children's Bks.
Tallarico, Tony J., Jr. Eco-Logical Brain Games. 2009. (Dover Children's Activity Bks.). (ENG., Illus.). 48p. (J). (gr. 3-8). pap. 4.99 *(978-0-486-46840-2(2))* Dover Pubns., Inc.
Vigia, Vincent, illus. My Magnetic Word Puzzles: Let's Make Words. 2006. (Magnix Learning Fun Ser.). 12p. (J). (gr. -1-3). 9.95 *(978-1-932915-19-8(2))* Sandvik Innovations, LLC.
Whelon, Chuck. Word Play - Write Your Own Crazy Comics, No. 1. 2013. (BOOST Educational Ser.). (ENG.). 64p. (J). (gr. 3-5). pap. 5.99 *(978-0-486-49441-8(1))* Dover Pubns., Inc.
Word Games. 2004. (Play & Learn Pads Ser.). 48p. (J). 3.99 *(978-1-85997-719-4(7))* Byeway Bks.
Word Puzzles. Date not set. (Illus.). 96p. (J). 2.98 *(978-0-7525-7520-9(1))* Parragon, Inc.
Words are Fun. 2004. (Play & Learn Pads Ser.). 48p. (J). 3.99 *(978-1-85997-722-4(7))* Byeway Bks.
Wordsearch. 2004. (Play & Learn Pads Ser.). 48p. (J). 3.99 *(978-1-85997-716-3(2))* Byeway Bks.
Wordsearch Fun. 2004. (Play & Learn Pads Ser.). 48p. (J). 3.99 *(978-1-85997-721-7(9))* Byeway Bks.
Zamazing, Cherie. ComicQuest Adventure Island. 2010. (Dover Children's Activity Bks.). (ENG., Illus.). 48p. (J). (gr. 2-5). pap. 4.99 *(978-0-486-47829-6(7))* Dover Pubns., Inc.

WORD GAMES—FICTION

Banks, Kate. Max's Words. Kulikov, Boris, illus. 2006. (Max's Words Ser.: 1). (ENG.). 32p. (J). (gr. -1-3). 17.99 *(978-0-374-39949-8(2),* 9780374399498, Farrar, Straus & Giroux (BYR)) Farrar, Straus & Giroux.
Brown, J. Darrell. I Play with Words! 2009. 24p. pap. 14.95 *(978-1-60844-050-4(8))* Dog Ear Publishing, LLC.
Handford, Martin. Where's Waldo? the Search for the Lost Things. Handford, Martin, illus. 2012. (Where's Waldo? Ser.). (ENG., Illus.). 104p. (J). (gr. 2-5). pap. 12.99 *(978-0-7636-5832-8(4))* Candlewick Pr.
Lezin, Katya. Knight Swam. 2010. 138p. pap. 14.99 *(978-0-557-20384-0(8))* Lulu Pr., Inc.
Lubar, David. Punished! (Darby Creek Exceptional Titles Ser.). (ENG.). 96p. (J). (gr. 2-5). 2007. per. 4.99 *(978-1-58196-063-1(8))* 2006. 15.95 *(978-1-58196-042-6(5))* Lerner Publishing Group. (Darby Creek).
Mathis, Pamela. Sound Town the Story of Words. 2010. 32p. pap. 15.99 *(978-1-4389-9194-8(0))* AuthorHouse.
Parish, Peggy. Good Work, Amelia Bedelia. Sweat, Lynn, illus. 2003. (I Can Read Level 2 Ser.). (ENG.). 64p. (J). (gr. k-3). pap. 3.99 *(978-0-06-051115-9(X),* Greenwillow Bks.) HarperCollins Pubs.
—Good Work, Amelia Bedelia. 2003. (Amelia Bedelia: I Can Read! Ser.: 6). (J). (gr. k-3). lib. bdg. 13.55 *(978-0-613-68343-2(9),* Turtleback) Turtleback Bks.
Perlman, Rhea. Born to Drive. Santat, Dan, illus. 2006. (Otto Undercover Ser.). 127p. (J). (gr. 4-7). 14.99 *(978-0-06-075496-9(6),* Tegen, Katherine Bks) HarperCollins Pubs.
—Canyon Catastrophe. Santat, Dan, illus. 2006. (Otto Undercover Ser.). 128p. (J). (gr. 4-7). 14.99 *(978-0-06-075498-3(2))* HarperCollins Pubs.
Petrey, Ashley. The Abc's Game. 2013. 36p. pap. 24.95 *(978-1-62709-707-9(4))* America Star Bks.
Solomon, Sharon. A Walk With Grandpa/Un Paseo con el Abuelo. Del Risco, Eida, tr. Barcita, Pamela, illus. 2009. (ENG & SPA.). 32p. (J). (gr. -1-3). 16.95 *(978-1-932748-91-8(1),* Raven Tree Pr.,Csi) Continental Sales, Inc.
Solomon, Sharon K. A Walk with Grandpa. Barcita, Pamela, illus. 2009. (ENG.). 32p. (J). (gr. -1-3). 16.95 *(978-1-934960-11-0(X),* Raven Tree Pr.,Csi) Continental Sales, Inc.

WORD PROCESSING

Dalton, James. The Computer Classroom: Word Processing. (Illus.). (J). (gr. 5-6). pap. *(978-1-876973-01-8(3))* Wizard Bks.
Gilpin, Rebecca. An Introduction to Word Processing: Using Microsoft Word 2000 or Microsoft Office 2000. 2004. (Computer Guides Ser.). (SPA., Illus.). 64p. (J). (gr. 5-18). lib. bdg. 18.95 *(978-1-58086-310-0(8))* EDC Publishing.
Greek, Joseph. Writing Term Papers with Cool New Digital Tools. 2013. (Way Beyond PowerPoint: Making 21st Century Presentations Ser.). (Illus.). 48p. (J). (gr. 5-8). 29.95 *(978-1-4777-1835-3(4));* pap. 11.75 *(978-1-4777-1853-7(2))* Rosen Publishing Group, Inc., The. (Rosen Reference).
Howell, Sara. How to Plan, Revise, & Edit Your Text, 1 vol., 1. 2014. (Core Writing Skills Ser.). (ENG.). 24p. (J). (gr. 3-4). 23.60 *(978-1-4777-2910-6(0),* PowerKids Pr.) Rosen Publishing Group, Inc., The.
—How to Use Technology to Write & Publish, 1 vol., 1. 2014. (Core Writing Skills Ser.). (ENG.). 24p. (J). (gr. 3-4). 23.60 *(978-1-4777-2911-3(9),* PowerKids Pr.) Rosen Publishing Group, Inc., The.
Oleck, Joan. Graphic Design & Desktop Publishing. 2010. (Digital & Information Literacy Ser.). (ENG.). 48p. (YA). pap. 11.75 *(978-1-4488-0593-8(7));* lib. bdg. 29.25 *(978-1-4358-9425-9(1))* Rosen Publishing Group, Inc., The. (Rosen Reference).
Ross, Allison J. Choosing a Career in Desktop Publishing. 2009. (World of Work Ser.). 64p. (gr. 5-5). 58.50 *(978-1-60854-331-1(5))* Rosen Publishing Group, Inc., The.
Southall, Margo. Differentiated Small-Group Reading Lessons: Scaffolded & Engaging Lessons for Word Recognition, Fluency, & Comprehension That Help Every Reader Grow. 2009. (ENG.). 160p. pap. 20.99 *(978-0-439-83920-4(3),* Teaching Resources) Scholastic, Inc.
Wanniarachchi, Ruwan. Early Childhood Computer Learning Workbook - Level 1. 2007. 79p. pap. 18.50 *(978-0-615-17026-8(9))* Wanniarachchige, Somiruwan.
Writing Term Papers with Cool New Digital Tools. 2013. (Way Beyond PowerPoint: Making 21st Century Presentations Ser.). (Illus.). 48p. (J). (gr. 5-8). pap. 70.50 *(978-1-4777-1854-4(0),* Rosen Reference) Rosen Publishing Group, Inc., The.
Zocchi, Judy. Dear Principal Petunia: Word Processing. Bird, Nikolai, illus. 2005. (Click & Squeak Ser.). 32p. (J). pap. 9.95 *(978-1-59646-111-6(X))* Dingles & Co.

WORDS

see Vocabulary

WORK

Here are entered works on the physical or mental exertion of individuals to produce or accomplish something. Works on the collective human activities involved in the production and distribution of goods and services are entered under Labor.

see also Labor

Ancona, George. Mis Quehaceres - My Chores. 2005. (Somos Latinos (We Are Latinos) Ser.). (ENG & SPA., Illus.). 32p. (J). (gr. 1-3). lib. bdg. 21.00 *(978-0-516-25291-9(7),* Children's Pr.) Scholastic Library Publishing.
Boothroyd, Jennifer. From Assembly Lines to Home Offices: How Work Has Changed. 2011. (Comparing Past & Present Ser.). pap. 45.32 *(978-0-7613-8389-5(1));* pap. 7.95 *(978-0-7613-7842-6(1));* (ENG., Illus.). 32p. lib. bdg. 26.60 *(978-0-7613-6748-2(9))* Lerner Publishing Group.
Bullard, Lisa. Ella Earns Her Own Money. Moran, Mike, illus. 2013. (Cloverleaf Books — Money Basics Ser.). (ENG.). 24p. (gr. k-2). pap. 6.95 *(978-1-4677-1511-9(5),* Millbrook Pr.) Lerner Publishing Group.
—Ella Earns Her Own Money. Moran, Michael, illus. 2013. (Cloverleaf Books — Money Basics Ser.). (ENG.). 24p. (gr. k-2). lib. bdg. 23.93 *(978-1-4677-0761-9(9),* Millbrook Pr.) Lerner Publishing Group.
Fischer, James. Earning Money: Jobs. 2010. (Junior Library of Money). 64p. (YA). (gr. 7-18). pap. 9.95 *(978-1-4222-1882-2(1));* lib. bdg. 22.95 *(978-1-4222-1763-4(9))* Mason Crest.
Harcourt School Publishers Staff. People & Work Big Book No. 6. 2nd ed. 2003. (Illus.). pap. 139.70 *(978-0-15-337571-2(X))* Harcourt Schl. Pubs.
Harper, Reggie. Honeybees Work Together: Working As a Team. 2017. (Computer Science for the Real World Ser.). 12p. (gr. 6-7). pap. 7.05 ***(978-1-5383-5156-7(0),*** Rosen Classroom) Rosen Publishing Group, Inc., The.
Hinman, Bonnie. The Scoop on School & Work in Colonial America, 1 vol. 2012. (Life in the American Colonies Ser.). (ENG.). 32p. (gr. 3-4). pap. 8.10 *(978-1-4296-7986-2(7),* Fact Finders) Capstone Press of Coughlan Cos.
La Plante, Clare. A Teen's Guide to Working. 2003. (Illus.). 60p. (J). 11.60 net. *(978-0-7398-5171-5(3))* Steck-Vaughn.
Markarian, Margie. Wild Work, 1 vol., Set. Incl. Who Cleans Dinosaur Bones? Working at a Museum. (ENG.). 32p. (gr. 1-2). 2010. pap. 8.29 *(978-1-4109-3857-2(3),* Read Me!); (Wild Work Ser.). (ENG.). 32p. 2010. Set pap. 16.58 o.p. *(978-1-4109-3865-7(4),* Read Me!) Heinemann-Raintree.
Murphy, Patricia J. Earning Money. 2005. (How Economics Works). (Illus.). 48p. (J). (gr. 3-7). lib. bdg. 25.26 *(978-0-8225-2149-5(0),* Lerner Pubns.) Lerner Publishing Group.
Nelson, Robin. Jobs. 2004. (First Step Nonfiction - Basic Human Needs Ser.). (ENG., Illus.). 8p. (gr. -1-1). pap. 4.95 *(978-0-8225-3929-2(2),* Lerner Pubns.) Lerner Publishing Group.
—Working Then & Now. 2008. pap. 34.95 *(978-0-8225-9486-4(2));* (ENG., Illus.). 24p. lib. bdg. 23.93 *(978-0-8225-8604-3(5))* Lerner Publishing Group.
Thornborough, Kathy. Work. Petelinsek, Kathleen, illus. 2014. (Talking Hands Ser.). (ENG.). 24p. (J). (gr. k-3). 25.64 *(978-1-62687-325-4(9),* 207165) Child's World, Inc., The.
Walker, Sally M. & Feldmann, Roseann. Trabajo. King, Andy, photos by. 2005. (Libros de Física para Madrugadores (Early Bird Physics) Ser.). (SPA & ENG., Illus.). 48p. (gr. 3-6). lib. bdg. 26.60 *(978-0-8225-2984-2(X),* Ediciones Lerner) Lerner Publishing Group.
Whittaker, Helen. How Toys Slide. 2012. (Toys & Forces Ser.). 32p. (gr. 1-4). lib. bdg. 28.50 *(978-1-59920-466-6(5))* Black Rabbit Bks.

WORK—FICTION

Banks, Kate. The Night Worker. Hallensleben, Georg, illus. 2007. (ENG.). 40p. (J). (gr. -1-1). 8.99 *(978-0-374-40000-2(8),* 9780374400002) Square Fish.
—Night Worker. 2014. 19.00 *(978-1-63419-674-1(0))* Perfection Learning Corp.
Barkley, Brad & Hepler, Heather. Dream Factory. 2009. (ENG.). 272p. (YA). (gr. 7-18). 8.99 *(978-0-14-241298-5(8),* Speak) Penguin Young Readers Group.
Bilan Hochenberg, Nerissa. Mommy Works. Bilan, Edgar, illus. 2013. 24p. pap. *(978-1-4602-2602-5(X))* FriesenPress.
Brody, Jessica. 52 Reasons to Hate My Father. 2013. (ENG.). 368p. (YA). (gr. 7-12). pap. 10.99 *(978-1-250-02459-6(5),* 9781250024596) Square Fish.
Brunel, Aude. Let's Go to Work. Mancek, Marjan, illus. 2007. 32p. (J). (ARA & ENG.). pap. 16.95 *(978-1-60195-089-5(6));* (POL & ENG.). pap. 16.95 *(978-1-60195-101-4(9))* International Step by Step Assn.
Buzo, Laura. Love & Other Perishable Items. (ENG.). 256p. (YA). (gr. 9). 2013. pap. 8.99 *(978-0-307-92974-7(4),* Ember) 2012. 17.99 *(978-0-375-87000-2(8),* Knopf Bks. for Young Readers) Random Hse. Children's Bks.
Capucilli, Alyssa Satin. Katy Duck Goes to Work. Cole, Henry, illus. 2014. (Katy Duck Ser.). (ENG.). 24p. (J). (gr. -1-1). pap. 3.99 *(978-1-4424-7281-5(2),* Simon Spotlight) Simon Spotlight.
—Katy Duck Goes to Work. 2014. (Simon & Schuster Ready-To-Read Level 1 Ser.). lib. bdg. 13.55 *(978-0-606-35455-4(7))* Turtleback Bks.
Carlson, Nancy. Loudmouth George Earns His Allowance. Carlson, Nancy, illus. (ENG., Illus.). 32p. (J). (gr. k-2). 2013. 9.95 *(978-1-4677-0865-4(8))* 2007. 15.95 *(978-0-8225-6560-4(9))* Lerner Publishing Group. (Carolrhoda Bks.).
Clark, Eleanor. Eleanor Jo: The Farmer's Daughter. 2007. (Eleanor Ser.: Bk. 5). (Illus.). 193p. 14.99 *(978-0-9788726-1-8(4))* HonorNet.
Clark, Ruth. Airport Mouse Works the Nightshift. 2008. (ENG.). 32p. (J). 15.95 *(978-0-9792963-3-8(1))* Hollywood Operating System.
Cushman, Jean, et al. Little Golden Book Mommy Stories. Wilkin, Eloise & Meisel, Paul, illus. 2015. (Little Golden Book Favorites Ser.). (ENG.). 80p. (J). (-k). 6.99 *(978-0-385-39273-0(7),* Golden Bks.) Random Hse. Children's Bks.
Dalrymple, Marilyn. Bartholomew's Buttons. 2006. 18p. (J). 9.73 *(978-1-4116-9200-8(4))* Lulu Pr., Inc.
De Jong, Riet M. W. I. Little Freebie & All His Friends. 2011. 124p. pap. 42.75 *(978-1-4269-5243-2(0))* Trafford Publishing.
DeSpain, Christine. And Please Take the Banana off Your Head. 2003. (Illus.). 34p. (J). (gr. 1-3). pap. 6.95 *(978-0-9678030-1-2(2))* Caribbean Scene.
Douglas, Ryke. Tock a Tick. 2007. 32p. per. 11.95 *(978-1-59800-756-5(4))* Outskirts Pr., Inc.
Floyd, Gina. Can Daddy Stay Home & Play? Scott, Judy, illus. 2011. 28p. pap. 12.99 *(978-1-4567-1373-7(6))* AuthorHouse.
Gallagher, Diana G. Advice about Work & Play: Claudia Cristina Cortez Uncomplicates Your Life. Garvey, Brann, illus. 2010. (Claudia Cristina Cortez Ser.). (ENG.). 80p. (gr. 2-3). pap. 6.10 *(978-1-4342-2253-4(5));* 26.65 *(978-1-4342-1908-4(9))* Stone Arch Bks. (Claudia Cristina Cortez).
Gardner, Lindsey, et al. Pan Fydd Popi a Macs yn Fawr. 2005. (WEL., Illus.). 20p. *(978-1-902416-45-8(7))* Cymdeithas Lyfrau Ceredigion.
Goldman, Leslie. On the Job. 2004. 138p. (J). lib. bdg. 16.92 *(978-1-4242-0674-2(X))* Fitzgerald Bks.
Goodrich, C. C. Barnabee: Goes to Work. 2009. (Illus.). 32p. pap. 13.99 *(978-1-4389-8461-2(8))* AuthorHouse.
Green, Melissa J. & G., Melissa J. Mona Whine'ona: (the List) G., Ashley R., illus. 2007. 20p. per. 24.95 *(978-1-4241-8451-4(7))* PublishAmerica, Inc.
Greene, Stephanie. Owen Foote, Money Man. Weston, Martha, illus. 2003. 88p. (gr. 2-4). 14.95 *(978-0-7569-1559-9(7))* Perfection Learning Corp.
Heim, Robert. The Squeaking Earl. 2009. 32p. pap. 16.50 *(978-1-60693-711-2(1),* Strategic Bk. Publishing) Strategic Book Publishing & Rights Agency (SBPRA).

Jones, Patrick. Bridge. 2014. (Alternative Ser.). (ENG.). 96p. (YA). (gr. 6-12). lib. bdg. 27.93 *(978-1-4677-3903-0(0))* Lerner Publishing Group.

Jordan, Terry W. Carson Goes to Work with Dad. 2012. 28p. pap. 24.95 *(978-1-4626-8892-0(6))* America Star Bks.

Katherine, Paterson. Lyddie. 2014. (Puffin Modern Classics Ser.). (ENG.). 192p. (J). (gr. 1-4). 11.24 *(978-1-63245-222-1(7))* Lectorum Pubns., Inc.

Keilbart, L. S. One. Benson, Barbara, illus. 2007. (ENG.). 76p. (J). (gr. k-k). per. *(978-1-85756-610-9(6))* Janus Publishing Co.

Kessler, Ethel & Kessler, Leonard. Night Story. 2008. (ENG.). 52p. (J). (gr. -1-3). 10.99 *(978-1-4169-9030-7(5)*, Simon & Schuster Bks. For Young Readers) Simon & Schuster Bks. For Young Readers.

Kiernan, Tim. Liams Luck & Finnegans Fortune. 2009. (ENG.). 144p. pap. 10.95 *(978-1-933916-48-4(6)*, Ferne Pr.) Nelson Publishing & Marketing.

Liwska, Renata. The Red Wagon. Liwska, Renata, illus. 2011. (ENG., Illus.). 32p. (J). (gr. -1-k). 16.99 *(978-0-399-25237-2(1)*, Philomel Bks.) Penguin Young Readers Group.

—Red Wagon. Liwska, Renata, illus. 2013. (ENG., Illus.). 32p. (J). (gr. -1 — 1). 6.99 *(978-0-399-16239-8(9)*, Philomel Bks.) Penguin Young Readers Group.

Lovett, Darrell F. Darrell's Lake Franklin. 2007. 13.00 *(978-0-8059-8807-9(6))* Dorrance Publishing Co., Inc.

Mighty Mike, 6 vols., Set. Incl. Mighty Mike Builds a Ball Field. Lynch, Casey. Lynch, Kelly, illus. 28.50 *(978-1-61641-128-2(7))*; Mighty Mike Builds a Library. Lynch, Casey. Lynch, Kelly, illus. 28.50 *(978-1-61641-129-9(5))*; Mighty Mike Builds a Nature Trail. Lynch, Kelly. Lynch, Casey, illus. 28.50 *(978-1-61641-130-5(9))*; Mighty Mike Does What's Right! Lynch, Kelly. Lynch, Casey, illus. 28.50 *(978-1-61641-131-2(7))*; Mighty Mike Repairs a Playground. Lynch, Casey. Lynch, Kelly, illus. 28.50 *(978-1-61641-132-9(5))*; Mighty Mike Saves a School Bus. Lynch, Casey. Lynch, Kelly, illus. 28.50 *(978-1-61641-133-6(3))*; (gr. -1-2). (Mighty Mike Ser.). 32p. 2011. 171.00 *(978-1-61641-127-5(9)*, Looking Glass Library) ABDO Publishing Co.

Montes, Marisa. Juan Bobo Busca Trabajo, 1 vol. Cepeda, Joe, illus. 2006. (SPA.). 32p. (J). (gr. -1-4). pap. 6.99 *(978-0-06-113681-8(6)*, Rayo) HarperCollins Pubs.

Naoshi. Ice Cream Work. Naoshi, illus. 2015. (ENG & JPN., Illus.). 40p. (J). 14.99 *(978-0-9834917-3-6(9))* Overcup Pr.

Patrick, B. Blob's Odd Jobs. Torre, Attilio, illus. 2006. (ENG.). 48p. (J). (gr. -1-3). 16.95 *(978-0-9741319-3-1(8))* 4N Publishing LLC.

Pearson, Betty Jean. Learn with Ladee: A Service Dog. 2008. 30p. pap. 24.95 *(978-1-4241-9507-7(1))* America Star Bks.

Petty, Colin, illus. The Three Little Pigs: A Tale about Working Hard. 2006. (J). 6.99 *(978-1-59939-016-1(7))* Cornerstone Pr.

Pittar, Gill. Milly, Molly & Aunt Maude. 2004. 28p. *(978-1-86972-014-8(8))* Milly Molly Bks.

Reichert, Amy. Take Your Mama to Work Today. Boiger, Alexandra, illus. 2012. (ENG.). 40p. (J). (gr. -1-8). 16.99 *(978-1-4169-7095-8(9)*, Atheneum Bks. for Young Readers) Simon & Schuster Children's Publishing.

Reynolds, Peter H. So Few of Me. Reynolds, Peter H., illus. 2006. (ENG., Illus.). 32p. (J). (gr. k-12). 15.00 *(978-0-7636-2623-5(6))* Candlewick Pr.

Roth, Carol. Here Comes the Choo Choo! Cushman, Doug, illus. 2007. (J). *(978-0-15-205582-0(7))* Harcourt Trade Pubs.

Santillo, LuAnn. Rags. Santillo, LuAnn, ed. 2003. (Half-Pint Kids Readers Ser.). (Illus.). 7p. (J). (gr. -1-1). pap. 1.00 *(978-1-59256-073-8(3))* Half-Pint Kids, Inc.

—Ted's Job. Santillo, LuAnn, ed. 2003. (Half-Pint Kids Readers Ser.). (Illus.). 7p. (J). (gr. -1-1). pap. 1.00 *(978-1-59256-060-8(1))* Half-Pint Kids, Inc.

Sommer, Carl. No Longer a Dilly Dally. James, Kennon, illus. 2014. (J). pap. *(978-1-57537-961-6(9))* Advance Publishing, Inc.

—No Longer a Dilly Dally, 1 bk. 2003. (Another Sommer-Time Story Ser.). (Illus.). 48p. (J). 16.95 incl. audio *(978-1-57537-550-2(8))* Advance Publishing, Inc.

—No Longer a Dilly Dally, 11 vols. James, Kennon, illus. 2003. (Another Sommer-Time Story Ser.). (ENG.). 48p. (J). (gr. 1-4). 16.95 incl. audio compact disk *(978-1-57537-501-4(X))* Advance Publishing, Inc.

—No Longer a Dilly Dally(Nunca Mas a Troche y Moche) James, Kennon, illus. 2009. (Another Sommer-Time Story Bilingual Ser.). (SPA & ENG.). 48p. (J). lib. bdg. 16.95 *(978-1-57537-162-7(6))* Advance Publishing, Inc.

—Your Job Is Easy. James, Kennon, illus. (J). 2014. pap. *(978-1-57537-973-9(2))* 2003. (ENG.). 48p. (gr. -1-4). 9.95 *(978-1-57537-018-7(2))* 2003. (ENG.). 48p. (gr. 1-4). 16.95 incl. audio compact disk *(978-1-57537-517-5(6))* 2003. (ENG.). 48p. (gr. 2-4). lib. bdg. 16.95 *(978-1-57537-067-5(0))* Advance Publishing, Inc.

—Your Job Is Easy. 2003. (Another Sommer-Time Story Ser.). (Illus.). 48p. (J). (gr. 1-4). 16.95 incl. audio *(978-1-57537-566-3(4))* Advance Publishing, Inc.

—Your Job Is Easy(Tu Trabajo Es Facil) James, Kennon, illus. 2009. (Another Sommer-Time Story Bilingual Ser.). (SPA & ENG.). 48p. (J). lib. bdg. 16.95 *(978-1-57537-173-3(1))* Advance Publishing, Inc.

Stanek, Robert, pseud. Visit Dad & Mom at Work. 2008. (ENG., Illus.). 28p. (J). pap. 5.29 *(978-1-57545-187-9(5))* RP Media.

Staunton, Ted. Morgan Makes a Deal. Slavin, Bill, illus. 2005. 60p. (J). lib. bdg. 12.00 *(978-1-4242-1205-7(7))* Fitzgerald Bks.

Steers, Billy. Tractor Mac Builds a Barn. 2015. (Tractor Mac Ser.). (ENG., Illus.). 32p. (J). (gr. -1-2). 8.99 *(978-0-374-30105-7(0)*, 9780374301057, Farrar, Straus & Giroux (BYR)) Farrar, Straus & Giroux.

Studio Mouse Staff. Sesame Street Bert & Ernie Work Together. rev. ed. 2008. (ENG.). 24p. 4.99 *(978-1-59069-620-0(4))* Studio Mouse LLC.

Sweeney, Kathleen. Matty Monster Truck. 2008. 14p. pap. 24.95 *(978-1-60672-865-9(2))* America Star Bks.

Swerling, Lisa & Lazar, Ralph. Flying Memos & Other Office Antics. 2004. (Illus.). 64p. 9.95 *(978-1-84072-605-3(9))* M Q Pubns.

Tarver, Whitney B. When Mommy Went Back to Work. 2011. 20p. (gr. 1-2). pap. 13.95 *(978-1-4269-6833-4(7))* Trafford Publishing.

Wagler, Elizabeth. Sojourn in Africa. 2003. (Travels with Aunt Laura Ser.: Vol. 1). (Illus.). v, 256p. (J). *(978-0-87813-607-0(X))* Christian Light Pubns., Inc.

WORKING CLASS

Here are entered works on the social class composed of persons who work for wages, generally excluding managers, professionals, and those not at the lower end of the educational and economic scale.

see also Labor

Bair, Sheila. The Bullies of Wall Street: How Greedy Adults Messed up Our Economy. 2016. (ENG.). 288p. (YA). (gr. 7). pap. 11.99 *(978-1-4814-0086-2(X)*, Simon & Schuster Bks. For Young Readers) Simon & Schuster Bks. For Young Readers.

—The Bullies of Wall Street: This Is How Greedy Adults Messed up Our Economy. 2015. (ENG., Illus.). 272p. (YA). (gr. 7). 17.99 *(978-1-4814-0085-5(1)*, Simon & Schuster Bks. For Young Readers) Simon & Schuster Bks. For Young Readers.

Barber, Nicola. Ancient Roman Jobs. 2010. (Ancient Communities: Roman Life Ser.). (Illus.). 32p. (J). pap. 10.60 *(978-1-61532-317-3(1))*; (gr. 3-6). lib. bdg. 26.50 *(978-1-61532-307-4(4))* Rosen Publishing Group, Inc., The. (PowerKids Pr.).

Gunderson, Jessica. The Triangle Shirtwaist Factory Fire. Miller, Phil & Barnett III, Charles, illus. 2006. (Disasters in History Ser.). (ENG.). 32p. (gr. 3-4). pap. 47.70 *(978-0-7368-6999-7(9)*, Graphic Library) Capstone Press of Coughlan Cos.

Gunderson, Jessica Sarah. The Triangle Shirtwaist Factory Fire. Miller, Phil & Barnett, Charles, III, illus. 2006. (Disasters in History Ser.). (ENG.). 32p. (gr. 3-4). per. 8.10 *(978-0-7368-6878-5(X)*, Graphic Library) Capstone Press of Coughlan Cos.

McNeese, Tim. The Labor Movement: Unionizing America. 2007. (Reform Movements in American History Ser.). (Illus.). 168p. (YA). (gr. 7-12). lib. bdg. 32.50 *(978-0-7910-9503-4(7))* Facts On File, Inc.

Michele, Tracey. People Who Work for the City. 2011. (Learn-Abouts Ser.). (Illus.). 16p. (J). pap. 7.95 *(978-1-59920-640-0(4))* Black Rabbit Bks.

Skurzynski, Gloria. Sweat & Blood: A History of U. S. Labor Unions. 2008. (People's History Ser.). (ENG.). 112p. (gr. 5-12). lib. bdg. 33.26 *(978-0-8225-7594-8(9))* Lerner Publishing Group.

WORKING CLASS—FICTION

Almond, David. The Tightrope Walkers. 2016. (ENG.). 336p. (YA). (gr. 9). pap. 9.99 *(978-0-7636-9104-2(6))* Candlewick Pr.

Kurstedt, Rosanne. And I Thought about You. Carletta-Vietes, Lisa, illus. 2012. (J). 14.95 *(978-1-937406-65-3(2))* Mascot Bks., Inc.

WORKING CLASSES

see Working Class

WORKING GIRLS

see Child Labor

WORKING WOMEN

see Women—Employment

WORKINGMEN'S INSURANCE

see Social Security

WORKSHOP COUNCILS

see Management—Employee Participation

WORLD

see Earth (Planet)

WORLD ECONOMICS

see Economic Geography; Economic History; Economic Policy

WORLD, END OF THE

see end of the World

WORLD GOVERNMENT

see International Organization

WORLD HEALTH ORGANIZATION

Connolly, Sean. The World Health Organization. 2009. (Global Organizations Ser.). (Illus.). 46p. (J). (gr. 4-7). pap. *(978-1-897563-39-7(6))* Saunders Bk. Co.

Marsico, Katie. The World Health Organization. 2014. (Community Connections: How Do They Help? Ser.). (ENG., Illus.). 24p. (J). (gr. 2-5). 25.64 *(978-1-63188-030-8(6)*, 205527) Cherry Lake Publishing.

WORLD HISTORY

see also Geography; History, Ancient; History, Modern

ABDO Publishing Company Staff. Countries of the World Set 2, 1 vol. 2013. (Countries of the World Set 2 Ser.: 16). (ENG.). 144p. (J). (gr. 6-12). lib. bdg. 593.12 *(978-1-61783-624-4(9)*, Essential Library) ABDO Publishing Co.

—Essential Events. 2007. (Essential Events Set 1 Ser.: 8). (ENG.). (J). (gr. 6-12). lib. bdg. 285.12 *(978-1-59928-847-5(8)*, Essential Library) ABDO Publishing Co.

—Essential Events Set 2-Set Of 8. 2008. (Essential Events Set 2 Ser.: 8). (ENG., Illus.). 112p. (J). (gr. 6-12). lib. bdg. 285.12 *(978-1-60453-043-8(X)*, Essential Library) ABDO Publishing Co.

Abraham, Henry & Pfeffer, Irwin. Enjoying Global History. rev. ed. 2005. 600p. (gr. 10-12). pap. *(978-0-87720-890-7(5)*, R625P) AMSCO Schl. Pubns., Inc.

Adams, Simon. The Kingfisher Atlas of World History: A Pictorial Guide to the World's People & Events, 10000BCE-Present. 2016. (ENG.). 192p. (J). 24.99 *(978-0-7534-7294-1(5)*, 9780753472941, Kingfisher) Roaring Brook Pr.

Adamson, Lynda G. Literature Links to World History, K-12: Resources to Enhance & Entice, 1 vol. 2010. (Children's & Young Adult Literature Reference Ser.). 684p. (C). 70.00 *(978-1-59158-470-4(1)*, LU4701, Libraries Unlimited) ABC-CLIO, LLC.

Adcock, Michael. Cambridge Checkpoints VCE History - Revolutions 2005. 2004. (Cambridge Checkpoints Ser.). (ENG.). 144p. pap., stu. ed. 12.00 *(978-0-521-61225-8(X))* Cambridge Univ. Pr.

Aftermath of History, 8 vols., Set. Incl. Aftermath of the Anglo-Zulu War. Weltig, Matthew Scott. (gr. 9-12). 2008. lib. bdg. 38.60 *(978-0-8225-7599-3(X))*; Aftermath of the Chinese Nationalist Revolution. Gay, Kathlyn. (Illus.). (J). (gr. 9-12). 2008. lib. bdg. 38.60 *(978-0-8225-7601-3(5))*; Aftermath of the French Defeat in Vietnam. Cunningham, Mark E. & Zwier, Lawrence. (gr. 9-12). 2009. 38.60 *(978-0-8225-9093-4(X))*; Aftermath of the French Revolution. Arnold, James R. (gr. 9-12). 2008. lib. bdg. 38.60 *(978-0-8225-7598-6(1))*; Aftermath of the Mexican Revolution. Beller, Susan Provost. (gr. 9-12). 2008. lib. bdg. 38.60 *(978-0-8225-7600-6(7))*; Aftermath of the Russian Revolution. Gay, Kathlyn. (gr. 9-12). 2009. 38.60 *(978-0-8225-9092-7(1))*; Aftermath of the Sandinista Revolution. Kallen, Stuart A. (YA). (gr. 7-12). 2009. 38.60 *(978-0-8225-9091-0(3))*; Aftermath of the Wars Against the Barbary Pirates. January, Brendan. (gr. 9-12). 2009. 38.60 *(978-0-8225-9094-1(8))*; 160p. (Aftermath of History Ser.). (ENG.). 2008. Set lib. bdg. 47.26 *(978-0-8225-7597-9(3)*, Twenty-First Century Bks.) Lerner Publishing Group.

All about My World. 2016. (All about My World Ser.). 24p. (J). lib. bdg. 135.60 *(978-0-7660-8361-5(6))* Enslow Pubs., Inc.

Allen, Mark, ed. New Tales of Euterpe: The Star of India as a British Emigrant Ship. unabr. ed. 2003. (Mains'L Haul Special Publications). (Illus.). 68p. (J). pap. *(978-0-944580-13-4(0))* Maritime Museum Assn. of San Diego.

Ancient World History: Patterns of Interaction. 2005. (gr. 6-12). tchr. ed. *(978-0-618-37681-0(X)*, 2-00462) Holt McDougal.

Ancient World History: Patterns of Interaction: EEdition Plus Online. (gr. 6-12). 2005. *(978-0-618-42268-5(4)*, 2-00681) 2003. *(978-0-618-19413-1(4)*, 2-70055) Holt McDougal.

Ancient World History: Patterns of Interaction: EEdition Plus Online with purchase of print Pupil's Edition-1 Year. 2005. (gr. 6-12). *(978-0-618-42278-4(1)*, 2-00683) Holt McDougal.

Anon. The Great Men & Women That Shaped Our World - a Selection of Articles from a Classic Children's Encyclopedi. 2012. 504p. pap. 32.95 *(978-1-4474-6903-2(8))* Audubon Pr. & Christian Bk. Service.

Around the World Series, 5 bks., Set. 149.64 *(978-0-7614-1083-6(X)*, Benchmark Bks.) Marshall Cavendish Corp.

Atlas de los Animales. (Coleccion Atlas del Saber). (SPA., Illus.). (YA). (gr. 4-18). 20.95 *(978-950-11-0886-6(4)*, SGM64) Sigmar ARG. Dist: Continental Bk. Co., Inc.

Barber, Nicola, et al. Primary Source Detectives, 1 vol. 2014. (Primary Source Detectives Ser.). (ENG.). 64p. (gr. 7-8). lib. bdg. 215.94 *(978-1-4329-9608-6(8))* Heinemann-Raintree.

Bauer, Susan Wise. Ancient Times Vol. 1: From the Earliest Nomads to the Last Roman Emperor. 2003. (Story of the World: Vol. 1). (ENG., Illus.). 1p. (J). 21.95 *(978-0-9714129-6-5(0))* Well-Trained Mind Pr.

—Early Modern Times Bk. 3: From Elizabeth the First to the Forty-Niners. Martirosian, Patty Ann et al, illus. 2004. (Story of the World Ser.: 0). (ENG.). 412p. pap., act. bk. ed. 38.95 *(978-0-9728603-2-1(0)*, 86032) Well-Trained Mind Pr.

—Early Modern Times Vol. 3: From Elizabeth the First to the Forty-Niners. Martirosian, Patty Ann et al, illus. 2004. (Story of the World Ser.: 0). (ENG.). 400p. 24.95 *(978-0-9728603-0-7(4)*, 86030) Well-Trained Mind Pr.

—Early Modern Times Vol. 3: From Elizabeth the First to the Forty-Niners. 2004. (Story of the World Ser.: 0). (ENG., Illus.). 420p. (gr. 3-6). pap. 17.95 *(978-0-9714129-9-6(5)*, 41299) Well-Trained Mind Pr.

—The Modern Age Bk. 4: Victoria's Empire to the End of the USSR. Park, Charlie & Wise Bauer, Susan, eds. 2005. (Story of the World Ser.: 0). (ENG., Illus.). 275p. pap., act. bk. ed. 38.95 *(978-0-9728603-5-2(5)*, 86035) Well-Trained Mind Pr.

—The Modern Age Vol. 4: From Victoria's Empire to the End of the USSR. 2005. (Story of the World Ser.: 0). (ENG., Illus.). 512p. 24.95 *(978-0-9728603-4-5(7)*, 86034) Well-Trained Mind Pr.

—The Modern Age Vol. 4: From Victoria's Empire to the End of the USSR. Park, Sarah, illus. 2005. (Story of the World Ser.: 0). (ENG.). 512p. (gr. 4-8). per. 17.95 *(978-0-9728603-3-8(9)*, 86033) Well-Trained Mind Pr.

Bauer, Susan Wise & Johnson, Barbara Allen. The Story of the World: History for the Classical Child. unabr. ed. 2005. (ENG.). 1p. 55.95 *(978-0-9742391-2-5(7))* Open Texture.

Bauer, Susan Wise & Weiss, Jim. Early Modern Times Vol. 3: From Elizabeth the First to the Forty-Niners. 2nd unabr. ed. 2008. (Story of the World Ser.: 0). (ENG.). 1p. cd-rom 49.95 *(978-1-933339-17-7(9)*, 333917) Well-Trained Mind Pr.

Beck, Roger B. Modern World History: Patterns of Interaction: Pupil's Edition. l.t. ed. 2005. (YA). (gr. 9-12). 83.76 *(978-0-618-37711-4(5)*, 2-00492) Holt McDougal.

Beck, Roger B., et al. Modern World History: Patterns of Interaction. 2006. (Illus.). 716p. (gr. 6-12). *(978-0-618-10820-6(3)*, 2-81212) Holt McDougal.

—World History: Patterns of Interaction. 2006. (Illus.). 1082p. (gr. 6-12). *(978-0-395-87274-1(X)*, 2-80400) Holt McDougal.

Benchmark Education Co., LLC. Becoming a World Power: 1890-1918. 2014. (PRIME Ser.). (J). (gr. 6-8). pap. *(978-1-4509-9497-2(0))* Benchmark Education Co.

Benchmark Education Company, LLC Staff, compiled by. Eve Bunting's World of Stories & Citizenship. 2005. spiral bd. 225.00 *(978-1-4108-5807-8(3))* Benchmark Education Co.

—20th Century History: Theme Set. 2006. (J). 183.00 *(978-1-4108-7144-2(4))* Benchmark Education Co.

Berlatsky, Noah. Stalin's Great Purge. 2012. (Perspectives on Modern World History Ser.). (ENG., Illus.). 224p. (gr. 10-12). lib. bdg. 47.80 *(978-0-7377-6371-3(X)*, Greenhaven Pr., Inc.) Cengage Gale.

Berndl, Klaus & Hattstein, Markus. The Contemporary World: From 1945 to the 21st Century. 2012. (Witness to History: A Visual Chronicle of the World Ser.). (ENG., Illus.). 200p. (J). (gr. 7-12). 46.50 *(978-1-4488-7225-1(1))* Rosen Publishing Group, Inc., The.

Berne, Emma Carlson & Burgan, Michael. Captured World History, 1 vol. 2014. (Captured World History Ser.). (ENG.). 64p. (gr. 5-7). lib. bdg. 138.60 *(978-0-7565-4810-0(1)*, CPB Grades 4-8) Compass Point Bks.

Billings. History of Our World 2003. 2003. (Steck-Vaughn History of Our World Ser.). (ENG., Illus.). 592p. (gr. 6-12). 72.15 *(978-0-7398-6087-8(9))* Houghton Mifflin Harcourt Publishing Co.

Bingham, Jane. Encyclopedia of World History: Prehistoric, Ancient, Medieval, Last 500 Years. 2004. (World History Ser.). (Illus.). 415p. (J). pap. 19.99 *(978-0-7945-0332-1(2)*, Usborne) EDC Publishing.

Bingham, Jane, et al. Encyclopedia of World History: Prehistoric, Ancient, Medieval, Last 500 Years. 2004. (World History Ser.). (Illus.). 415p. (J). (gr. 3-18). lib. bdg. 47.95 *(978-1-58086-336-0(1))* EDC Publishing.

—The Usborne Internet-Linked Encyclopedia of World History: Prehistoric, Ancient, Medieval, Last 500 Years. 2004. (World History Ser.). (ENG., Illus.). 1p. (J). (gr. 3-18). 39.95 *(978-0-7460-4168-0(3))* EDC Publishing.

Biography from Ancient Civilizations: Legends, Folklore, & Stories of Ancient Worlds, 20 vols., Set. Incl. Life & Times of Alexander the Great. Bankston, John. (gr. 4-8). 2005. lib. bdg. 29.95 *(978-1-58415-283-5(4))*; Life & Times of Archimedes. Zannos, Susan. (gr. 4-8). 2004. lib. bdg. 29.95 *(978-1-58415-242-2(7))*; Life & Times of Augustus Caesar. Whiting, Jim. (gr. -1-7). 2005. lib. bdg. 29.95 *(978-1-58415-336-8(9))*; Life & Times of Buddha. Gedney, Mona K. (gr. -1-7). 2005. lib. bdg. 29.95 *(978-1-58415-342-9(3))*; Life & Times of Catherine the Great. Gibson, Karen Bush. (gr. 4-7). 2005. lib. bdg. 29.95 *(978-1-58415-347-4(4))*; Life & Times of Charlemagne. Whiting, Jim. (gr. 4-8). 2005. lib. bdg. 29.95 *(978-1-58415-346-7(6))*; Life & Times of Cleopatra. Adams, Michelle Medlock. (gr. 4-8). 2005. lib. bdg. 29.95 *(978-1-58415-335-1(0))*; Life & Times of Confucius. Tracy, Kathleen. (gr. 4-8). 2004. lib. bdg. 29.95 *(978-1-58415-246-0(X))*; Life & Times of Constantine. Tracy, Kathleen. (gr. 4-8). 2005. lib. bdg. 29.95 *(978-1-58415-343-6(1))*; Life & Times of Genghis Khan. Whiting, Jim. (gr. 4-8). 2005. lib. bdg. 29.95 *(978-1-58415-348-1(2))*; Life & Times of Hammurabi. Bryant, Tamera. (gr. -1-7). 2005. lib. bdg. 29.95 *(978-1-58415-338-2(5)*, 1244807); Life & Times of Homer. Tracy, Kathleen. (gr. 4-8). 2004. lib. bdg. 29.95 *(978-1-58415-260-6(5))*; Life & Times of Joan of Arc. Whiting, Jim. (gr. 4-8). 2005. lib. bdg. 29.95 *(978-1-58415-345-0(8))*; Life & Times of Julius Caesar. Whiting, Jim. (gr. -1-7). 2005. lib. bdg. 29.95 *(978-1-58415-337-5(7))*; Life & Times of Marco Polo. Zannos, Susan. (gr. 4-8). 2004. lib. bdg. 29.95 *(978-1-58415-264-4(8))*; Life & Times of Moses. Whiting, Jim. (gr. -1-7). 2005. lib. bdg. 29.95 *(978-1-58415-340-5(7))*; Life & Times of Nero. Whiting, Jim. (gr. 5-8). 2005. lib. bdg. 29.95 *(978-1-58415-349-8(0))*; Life & Times of Pericles. Whiting, Jim. (gr. -1-7). 2005. lib. bdg. 29.95 *(978-1-58415-339-9(3))*; Life & Times of Rameses the Great. Whiting, Jim. (gr. 5-8). 2005. lib. bdg. 29.95 *(978-1-58415-341-2(5))*; Life & Times of Socrates. Zannos, Susan. (gr. 4-8). 2004. lib. bdg. 29.95 *(978-1-58415-282-8(6))*; (Illus.). 48p. (J). 2005. lib. bdg. *(978-1-58415-407-5(1))* Mitchell Lane Pubs., Inc.

Boardworks Learning Centers: Where in the World? 2006. (J). bds. *(978-0-9755252-6-5(3))* Evergreen Pr. of Brainerd, LLC.

Body, Robert J. Bob. I Survived the Bataan Death March. 2003. 2003p. per. 14.95 net. *(978-1-931934-21-3(5))* Back Yard Pub.

Boehm, Richard G., et al. The World & Its People. 2nd ed. 2004. (GEOGRAPHY: WORLD & ITS PEOPLE Ser.). (ENG., Illus.). 904p. (gr. 6-9). stu. ed. 119.16 *(978-0-07-860976-3(3)*, 0078609763) McGraw-Hill Education.

Brasier, Michael. The World Through A Child's Eyes: A View of Various Countries & Global Cultures from a Child's Perspective. 2005. 110p. (J). per. 29.95 *(978-0-9772591-0-6(2))* Around The World Pubns., LLC.

Broida, Marian. Hands-On History, 5 bks., Group 2. Incl. Projects about Nineteenth-Century European Immigrants. lib. bdg. *(978-0-7614-1980-8(2))*; Projects about the American Revolution. lib. bdg. *(978-0-7614-1981-5(0))*; (Illus.). 48p. (J). (gr. 3-7). 2005. *(978-0-7614-1977-8(2)*, Benchmark Bks.) Marshall Cavendish Corp.

Brookes, Olivia. Uncover History. Kent, Peter, illus. 2009. (Hide-and-Seek Visual Adventures Ser.). 24p. (J). (gr. 2-5). lib. bdg. 22.60 *(978-1-60754-653-5(1))* Windmill Bks.

Burgan, Michael & Berne, Emma Carlson. Captured History. 2017. (Captured History Ser.). (ENG.). 64p. (gr. 5-7). 415.80 ***(978-0-7565-5627-3(9)***, CPB Grades 4-8) Compass Point Bks.

Capstone Press. Disgusting History. 2010. (Disgusting History Ser.). (ENG.). 32p. lib. bdg. 155.94 *(978-1-4296-5932-1(7)*, Fact Finders) Capstone Press of Coughlan Cos.

—Unusual Histories. 2010. (Unusual Histories Ser.). (ENG.). 32p. lib. bdg. 122.60 *(978-1-4296-5899-7(1))* Capstone Press of Coughlan Cos.

Carnagie, Julie. U-X-L World Eras, 10 vols. 2016. (U-X-L World Eras Ser.). (ENG., Illus.). 2400p. (J). (gr. 5-8). 819.00 *(978-1-57302-967-4(X))* Cengage Gale.

Cawthorne, Nigel. Notorious Tyrants. 2012. (Great People in History Ser.). (ENG., Illus.). 128p. (YA). (gr. 8-12). lib. bdg. 34.60 *(978-1-4777-0406-6(X))* Rosen Publishing Group, Inc., The.

Celebrate! Set, 8-Volumes. 2009. (Celebrate! Ser.). (gr. 4-6). 224.00 *(978-1-60413-600-5(6)*, Chelsea Clubhouse) Facts On File, Inc.

Chandler, F. First Encyclopedia of History. 2004. (First Encyclopedias Ser.). (Illus.). 64p. (J). lib. bdg. 17.99 *(978-1-58086-518-0(6))* EDC Publishing.

Chandler, Fiona. Ancient world - internet Linked. McCaffrey, Susie, illus. rev. ed. 2004. 96p. (J). pap. 14.95 *(978-0-7945-0816-6(2)*, Usborne) EDC Publishing.

—Encyclopedia of World History. rev. ed. 2011. (World History Ser.). 416p. (J). ring bd. 39.99 *(978-0-7945-2688-7(8)*, Usborne) EDC Publishing.

Chin-Lee, Cynthia. Akira to Zoltan: Twenty-Six Men Who Changed the World. Addy, Sean & Halsey, Megan, illus. 2008. (ENG.). 32p. (J). (gr. 3-7). pap. 7.95 *(978-1-57091-580-2(6))* Charlesbridge Publishing, Inc.

Chinese Kites: Level A, 6 vols. 8p. 20.95 *(978-0-322-00627-0(9))* Wright Group/McGraw-Hill.

Chisholm, Jane. Timelines of World History. 2004. (World History Ser.). (Illus.). (J). 128p. 7.95 *(978-0-7945-0358-1(6)*, Usborne); (ENG., 1p. (gr. 3-18). 19.95 *(978-0-7460-4103-1(9))*; 128p. (gr. 3-18). lib. bdg. 27.95 *(978-1-58086-329-2(9))* EDC Publishing.

W X Y Z

Clarke, Evelyn. Crisis. 2007. (Steck-Vaughn BOLDPRINT Anthologies Ser.). (ENG., Illus.). 48p. (gr. 9-12). pap. 16.90 *(978-1-4190-4034-4(0))* Houghton Mifflin Harcourt Publishing Co.

Class, Michael S. Anthony & the Magic Picture Frame: The Story of the Boy Who Traveled into the Past by Stepping into the Picture Frame on His Bedroom Wall & Returned to See His Own Time in A New Light. 2005. (Illus.). 225p. (YA). (gr. 6-12). 35.00 *(978-0-9749269-0-2(6))* Magic Picture Frame Studio, LLC.

Cole, Sonja. Booktalking Around the World: Great Global Reads for Ages 9-14. 2010. (ENG.). 178p. E-Book *(978-1-59884-614-0(0)*, Libraries Unlimited) ABC-CLIO, LLC.

Cribb, John T. E., Jr., et al. The Human Odyssey, 2 vols. 2004. (Illus.). *(978-1-931728-53-9(4))*; *(978-1-60153-018-9(8))*; *(978-1-931728-56-0(9))* K12.

Cultures of the World Group 11, 6 bks., Set. 2nd ed. Incl. Afghanistan. Ali, Sharifah Enayat. (gr. 6-7). lib. bdg. 42.79 *(978-0-7614-2064-4(9))*; Belgium. Pateman, Robert & Elliott, Mark. (J). (gr. 6-7). lib. bdg. 42.79 *(978-0-7614-2059-0(2))*; Bolivia. Pateman, Robert & Cramer, Marcus. (gr. 6-7). lib. bdg. 42.79 *(978-0-7614-2066-8(5))*; Norway. Kagda, Sakina & Cooke, Barbara. (gr. 6-7). lib. bdg. 42.79 *(978-0-7614-2067-5(3))*; Peru. Falconer, Kieran & Quek, Lynette. (J). (gr. 6-7). lib. bdg. 42.79 *(978-0-7614-2068-2(1))*; Taiwan. Moiz, Azra & Wu, Janice. (J). (gr. 3-7). lib. bdg. 39.93 *(978-0-7614-2069-9(X))*; (Illus.). 144p. 2006. 2007. Set lib. bdg. 239.57 *(978-0-7614-2057-6(6)*, Benchmark Bks.) Marshall Cavendish Corp.

Cultures of the World Group 12, 6 bks., Set. 2nd rev. ed. Incl. Cambodia. Sheehan, Sean & Cooke, Barbara. lib. bdg. 42.79 *(978-0-7614-2071-2(1))*; Ethiopia. Gish, Steven. lib. bdg. 42.79 *(978-0-7614-2025-5(8))*; Finland. Tan, Chung Lee. lib. bdg. 42.79 *(978-0-7614-2073-6(8))*; Iceland. Wilcox, Jonathan & Latif, Zawiah Abdul. lib. bdg. 42.79 *(978-0-7614-2074-3(6))*; Panama. Hassig, Susan M. & Quek, Lynette. lib. bdg. 42.79 *(978-0-7614-2028-6(2))*; Tibet. Levy, Patricia & Bosco, Don. lib. bdg. 42.79 *(978-0-7614-2076-7(2))*; (Illus.). 144p. (gr. 6). (Cultures of the World 12 Ser.). 2006. Set lib. bdg. 256.74 *(978-0-7614-2070-5(3)*, Benchmark Bks.) Marshall Cavendish Corp.

Cultures of the World Group 25, 6 bks., Set. Incl. Benin. Kneib, Martha. (J). (gr. 3-7). 2007. lib. bdg. 39.93 *(978-0-7614-2328-7(1))*; Botswana. LeVert, Suzanne. (J). (gr. 3-7). 2007. lib. bdg. 39.93 *(978-0-7614-2330-0(3))*; Chad. Kneib, Martha. (gr. 6-7). 2006. lib. bdg. 42.79 *(978-0-7614-2327-0(3))*; Mozambique. King, David C. (gr. 6-7). 2006. lib. bdg. 42.79 *(978-0-7614-2331-7(1))*; Rwanda. King, David C. (gr. 6-7). 2006. lib. bdg. 42.79 *(978-0-7614-2333-1(8))*; Sierra Leone. LeVert, Suzanne. (gr. 6-7). 2006. lib. bdg. 42.79 *(978-0-7614-2334-8(6))*; (Illus.). 144p. 2007. Set lib. bdg. 239.57 *(978-0-7614-2326-3(5)*, Benchmark Bks.) Marshall Cavendish Corp.

Dalby, Elizabeth. World History Sticker Atlas. Larkum, Adam, illus. 2006. (Sticker Atlases Ser.). 24p. (J). (gr. 1-4). pap. 8.99 *(978-0-7945-1244-6(5)*, Usborne) EDC Publishing.

Dawson, Ian & Wilson, Maggie. SHP History Year 7. 2006. (Illus.). 228p. (YA). pap., stu. ed. *(978-0-340-90733-7(9))* Hodder & Stoughton.

Dawson, Ian, et al. SHP History Elearning Activities. 2006. (YA). cd-rom *(978-0-340-90735-1(5))* Hodder & Stoughton.

DBQ Practice: World History. 2003. spiral bd. 19.95 *(978-1-56004-145-0(5))* Social Studies Schl. Service.

Deary, Terry. Blood-Curdling Box, 20 vols. Brown, Martin, illus. 2008. 2880p. pap. *(978-1-4071-0815-5(8)*, Scholastic) Scholastic, Inc.

Decades of the 20th & 21st Centuries. 2015. (Decades of the 20th & 21st Centuries Ser.). (ENG.). 96p. (J). (gr. 7-7). 380.60 *(978-0-7660-6693-9(2))* Enslow Pubs., Inc.

Dickmann, Nancy & Throp, Claire. Deadly History. 2017. (Deadly History Ser.). (ENG.). 48p. (gr. 3-4). 133.28 ***(978-1-4846-4186-6(8)***, Heinemann InfoSearch) Heinemann-Raintree.

Discovering Cultures Group 6, 6 bks., Set. Incl. Austria. Grahame, Deborah A. (J). (gr. 3-7). lib. bdg. 28.50 *(978-0-7614-1984-6(5))*; Chile. Meachen Rau, Dana. (J). (gr. 3-7). lib. bdg. 28.50 *(978-0-7614-1988-4(8))*; Haiti. Mara, Wil. (J). (gr. 3-7). lib. bdg. 28.50 *(978-0-7614-1987-7(X))*; Iran. Mara, Wil. lib. bdg. 28.50 *(978-0-7614-1986-0(1))*; Sweden. Grahame, Deborah A. (J). (gr. 3-7). lib. bdg. 28.50 *(978-0-7614-1985-3(3))*; Thailand. Meachen Rau, Dana. (J). (gr. 3-7). lib. bdg. 28.50 *(978-0-7614-1989-1(6))*; (Illus.). 48p. 2006. 2007. Set lib. bdg. 171.00 *(978-0-7614-1983-9(7)*, Benchmark Bks.) Marshall Cavendish Corp.

Disgusting History. (Disgusting History Ser.). (ENG.). 32p. (gr. 3-4). 2011. pap. 286.20 *(978-1-4296-6481-3(9))* 2010. pap. 32.40 *(978-1-4296-6355-7(3))* 2010. lib. bdg. 163.92 *(978-1-4296-5408-1(2))* 2010. lib. bdg. 54.64 *(978-1-4296-5407-4(4))* 2010. lib. bdg. 109.28 *(978-1-4296-4735-9(3))* Capstone Press of Coughlan Cos. (Fact Finders).

Diwmod i'r Brenin: Chwaraeon, Hamdden a Thwristiaeth Er 1900. 2005. *(978-1-902346-01-4(7))* Addysg Y Cyfryngau Cymru.

Documenting History, 4 vols., Set. Incl. Documenting Slavery & Civil Rights. Steele, Philip. lib. bdg. 29.25 *(978-1-4358-9671-0(8))*; Documenting the Industrial Revolution. Hicks, Peter. lib. bdg. 29.25 *(978-1-4358-9670-3(X))*; Documenting Women's Suffrage. Hicks, Peter. lib. bdg. 29.25 *(978-1-4358-9672-7(6))*; Documenting World War I. Steele, Philip. lib. bdg. 29.25 *(978-1-4358-9673-4(4))*; (YA). (gr. 5-9). 2010. (Illus.). 48p. 2010. Set lib. bdg. 106.00 *(978-1-4358-9705-2(6)*, Rosen Reference) Rosen Publishing Group, Inc., The.

Dorling Kindersley Publishing Staff. It Can't Be True! 2013. (ENG.). 192p. (J). (gr. 2-5). 19.99 *(978-1-4654-1422-9(3)*, DK Children) Dorling Kindersley Publishing, Inc.

—100 Events That Made History. 2016. (ENG., Illus.). 128p. (J). (gr. 3-7). 16.99 *(978-1-4654-4426-4(2)*, DK Children) Dorling Kindersley Publishing, Inc.

Doty, Eldon, illus. Truth & Rumors, 4 vols., Set. Incl. Mummies: Truth & Rumors. Montgomery, Heather L. lib. bdg. 27.99 *(978-1-4296-3950-7(4))*; Titanic: Truth & Rumors. Burgan, Michael. lib. bdg. 27.99 *(978-1-4296-3951-4(2))*; U. S. Presidents: Truth & Rumors. Price, Sean Stewart. lib. bdg. 27.99 *(978-1-4296-3952-1(0))*; (Illus.). (gr. 3-4). (Truth & Rumors Ser.). (ENG.). 32p. 2010. Set lib. bdg. 83.97 *(978-1-4296-4444-0(3)*, Edge Bks.) Capstone Press of Coughlan Cos.

Drimmer, Stephanie Warren. The Book of Heroines: Tales of History's Gutsiest Gals. 2016. (ENG., Illus.). 176p. (J). (gr. 3-7). 14.99 *(978-1-4263-2557-1(6)*, National Geographic Children's Bks.) National Geographic Society.

Dupré, Judith. De las pirámides a los Rascacielos. 2011. (SPA.). 32p. (J). pap. 49.00 net. *(978-1-4108-2338-0(5)*, A23385) Benchmark Education Co.

Eaton, Gale & Hoose, Phillip. A History of Civilization in 50 Disasters, 1 vol. 2015. (History In 50 Ser.: 0). (ENG., Illus.). 240p. (gr. 6-12). 24.95 *(978-0-88448-383-0(5)*, 884383) Tilbury Hse. Pubs.

Enchantment of the World & Trade 2013, Set. 2013. (Enchantment of the World™, Second Ser.). (J). 240.00 *(978-0-531-26700-4(8)*, Children's Pr.) Scholastic Library Publishing.

Enchantment of the World, Second Series, 6 vols., Set. Incl. Afghanistan. Willis, Terri. 39.00 *(978-0-531-18483-7(8))*; Iran. Milivojevic, JoAnn. 39.00 *(978-0-531-18484-4(6)*, Children's Pr.); (Illus.). 144p. (J). (gr. 5-9). 2008. Set lib. bdg. 222.00 o.p. *(978-0-531-20409-2(X))*; 216.00 o.p. *(978-0-516-25407-4(3))* Scholastic Library Publishing. (Children's Pr.).

Enchantment of the World, Second Series Spring 2012 Set Of 6. 2012. (Enchantment of the World, Second Ser.). 234.00 *(978-0-531-25818-7(1)*, Children's Pr.) Scholastic Library Publishing.

Encyclopedia of World History. (Children's Reference Ser.). (Illus.). 256p. (J). *(978-1-4054-1702-0(1))* Parragon, Inc.

Essential Events, 8 vols., Set 3. Incl. Bolshevik Revolution. O'Neill, Joseph R. lib. bdg. 35.64 *(978-1-60453-511-2(3))*; Dust Bowl. Vander Hook, Sue. lib. bdg. 35.64 *(978-1-60453-512-9(1))*; Great Wall of China. O'Neill, Joseph R. lib. bdg. 35.64 *(978-1-60453-513-6(X))*; Irish Potato Famine. O'Neill, Joseph R. lib. bdg. 35.64 *(978-1-60453-514-3(8))*; Jamestown Colony. Pederson, Charles E. lib. bdg. 35.64 *(978-1-60453-515-0(6))*; Operation Desert Storm. Gitlin, Martin. lib. bdg. 35.64 *(978-1-60453-516-7(4))*; Pearl Harbor. Hamen, Susan E. lib. bdg. 35.64 *(978-1-60453-517-4(2))*; Zebulon Pike Expedition. Magoon, Kekla. lib. bdg. 35.64 *(978-1-60453-518-1(0))*; (J). (gr. 6-12). (Essential Events Set 3 Ser.: 8). (ENG., Illus.). 112p. 2009. Set lib. bdg. 285.12 *(978-1-60453-510-5(5)*, Essential Library) ABDO Publishing Co.

Essential Histories: War & Conflict in Modern Times, 6 vols., Set. Incl. Arab-Israeli Conflict: The 1948 War. Karsh, Efraim. lib. bdg. 33.25 *(978-1-4042-1842-0(4))*; Korean War. Malkasian, Carter. lib. bdg. 33.25 *(978-1-4042-1834-5(3))*; (Illus.). 96p. (YA). (gr. 9-12). 2008. 2008. Set lib. bdg. 191.70 *(978-1-4042-1894-9(7))* Rosen Publishing Group, Inc., The.

Evans, Charlotte. Historia (Enciclopedias Everst Internacional) (SPA.). 804p. (YA). (gr. 5-8). 39.99 *(978-84-241-9403-1(9))* Everest Editora ESP. Dist: Lectorum Pubns., Inc.

Exploration Into.. 2005. (Exploration into... Ser.). 48p. (gr. 6-12). 200.00 *(978-0-7910-6027-8(6)*, Chelsea Hse.) Facts On File, Inc.

Eyewitness to History: Sets 1-2. 2014. (Eyewitness to History Ser.). 32p. (J). (gr. 4-6). pap. 126.00 *(978-1-4824-1601-5(8))* Stevens, Gareth Publishing LLLP.

Facts on File, Inc. Staff, et al. World History on File, 4 vols., Set. Chapman, Victoria L. & Lindroth, David, eds. 2nd rev. ed. 2006. (World History on File Ser.). (gr. 6-12). 560.00 *(978-0-8160-6372-7(9))* Facts On File, Inc.

Farman, John. Shockingly Short History Of Absolutely Everything. (ENG., Illus.). 110p. (J). pap. 8.99 *(978-0-330-34904-8(X))* Pan Macmillan GBR. Dist: Trafalgar Square Publishing.

Farndon, John. A History of Civilization Illustrated History Encyclopedia: The Great Landmarks in the Development of Mankind. 2006. (Illus.). 256p. (gr. 7-10). reprint ed. pap. 22.00 *(978-1-4223-5514-5(4))* DIANE Publishing Co.

Fisher, Douglas & Glencoe McGraw-Hill Staff. Journey Across Time: World History - Active Reading & Note-Taking Guide. 2nd ed. 2007. (MS Wh Jat Full Survey Ser.). (ENG., Illus.). 466p. (gr. 6-9). per. 12.08 *(978-0-07-878949-6(4)*, 0078789494) McGraw-Hill Education.

Fisher, Douglas & McGraw-Hill - Jamestown Education Staff. World History. 2nd ed. 2004. (Human Experience - Modern Era Ser.). (ENG., Illus.). 432p. (gr. 6-9). stu. ed., per. 12.28 *(978-0-07-867561-4(8)*, 0078675618) McGraw-Hill Higher Education.

Fisher, Douglas & McGraw-Hill Staff. Glencoe World History. 2nd ed. 2004. (World History (hs) Ser.). (ENG., Illus.). 568p. (gr. 6-9). stu. ed., per. 12.80 *(978-0-07-867553-9(7)*, 0078675537) McGraw-Hill Education.

Fleming, F. & Dowswell, P. Shock Horror History! 2004. (Illus.). 128p. (YA). (gr. 5-18). 22.95 *(978-0-7460-3369-2(9))* EDC Publishing.

Fuhr, Ute & Sautai, Raoul. Let's Look for Lost Treasure. 2012. (ENG., Illus.). 38p. (J). (gr. k-3). pap. 11.99 *(978-1-85103-291-4(6))* Moonlight Publishing, Ltd. GBR. Dist: Independent Pubs. Group.

Gale Research Inc Staff, contrib. by. Global Events: Milestone Events Throughout History. 2014. (Illus.). (J). *(978-1-4144-9133-2(6))* Gale Research International, Ltd.

Ganeri, Anita. The Top Ten Events That Changed the World. 2009. (Top Ten Ser.). 32p. (ENG.). (J). pap. 10.00 *(978-1-4358-9162-3(7)*, PowerKids Pr.); (Illus.). (YA). (gr. 3-6). 26.50 *(978-1-4358-9161-6(9))* Rosen Publishing Group, Inc., The.

—The Top Ten Leaders That Changed the World. 2009. (J). 60.00 *(978-1-4358-9166-1(X)*, PowerKids Pr.); (ENG., Illus.). 32p. (J). pap. 10.00 *(978-1-4358-9165-4(1)*, PowerKids Pr.); (Illus.). 32p. (YA). (gr. 3-6). 26.50 *(978-1-4358-9164-7(3))* Rosen Publishing Group, Inc., The.

George, Enzo. The Modern Age. 2016. (Primary Sources in World History Ser.). (ENG.). 48p. (YA). (gr. 6-6). 31.36 *(978-1-5026-1828-3(1))* Cavendish Square Publishing.

George, Lynn. 20 Questions: History, 6 vols., Set. 2008. (J). (gr. 2-4). lib. bdg. 127.50 *(978-1-4042-4242-5(2))* Rosen Publishing Group, Inc., The.

Gibbons, David, ed. Timechart History of the World: 6000 Years of World History Unfolded. 2004. (ENG., Illus.). 34p. 14.98 *(978-0-7607-6534-0(0))* Barnes & Noble, Inc.

Gifford, Clive. Killer History: A Gruesome & Grisly Trip Through the Past. 2012. 143p. (J). *(978-1-62145-031-3(7))* Reader's Digest Assn., Ltd.

Glencoe McGraw-Hill Staff. Journey Across Time. 2nd ed. 2007. (MS Wh Jat Full Survey Ser.). (ENG.). (gr. 6-9). cd-rom 155.60 *(978-0-07-878158-2(2)*, 0078781582); (Illus.). 56p. stu. ed., spiral bd., act. bk. ed. 7.20 *(978-0-07-878954-0(0)*, 0078789540) McGraw-Hill Education.

—Journey Across Time, Early Ages, Reading Essentials & Study Guide, Workbook. 2nd ed. 2007. (MS Wh Jat Full Survey Ser.). (ENG.). (gr. 6-9). pap. 12.08 *(978-0-07-878923-6(0)*, 0078789230) McGraw-Hill Education.

—World History. 2007. (World History (hs) Ser.). (ENG., Illus.). 64p. (gr. 6-9). pap., stu. ed. 8.08 *(978-0-07-878230-5(9)*, 0078782309) McGraw-Hill Education.

Glencoe McGraw-Hill Staff, creator. Glencoe world history StudentWorks Plus. 2nd ed. 2005. (World History (hs) Ser.). (ENG.). (gr. 6-9). stu. ed. 163.72 *(978-0-07-865380-3(0)*, 0078653800) McGraw-Hill Higher Education.

—Journey Across Time - The Early Ages. 2004. (MS World History Ser.). (ENG., Illus.). 400p. (gr. 6-9). stu. ed., per., wbk. ed. 12.72 *(978-0-07-860318-1(8)*, 0078603188) McGraw-Hill Higher Education.

Glencoe McGraw-Hill Staff & McGraw-Hill Education Editors. Exploring Our World: People, Places, & Culture. 2007. (WORLD & ITS PEOPLE EASTERN Ser.). (ENG., Illus.). 216p. (gr. 6-8). per. 23.20 *(978-0-07-877602-1(3)*, 0078776023) McGraw-Hill Education.

Glencoe McGraw-Hill Staff & McGraw-Hill Education Staff. Journey Across Time, Early Ages, Active Reading & Note-Taking Guide. 2nd ed. 2007. (MS Wh Jat Full Survey Ser.). (ENG.). 384p. (gr. 6-9). pap. 12.08 *(978-0-07-878926-7(5)*, 0078789265) McGraw-Hill Education.

—Journey Across Time, Early Ages, Activity Workbook, Student Edition. 2nd ed. 2007. (MS Wh Jat Full Survey Ser.). (ENG.). (gr. 6-9). pap. 7.20 *(978-0-07-878931-1(1)*, 0078789311) McGraw-Hill Education.

Global Hotspots, 6 bks., Set. Incl. Afghanistan. Downing, David & Cavendish, Marshall. lib. bdg. 18.56 *(978-0-7614-3177-0(2))*; Indian Subcontinent. Mason, Paul & Cavendish, Marshall. lib. bdg. 18.56 *(978-0-7614-3178-7(0))*; Iran. Downing, David & Marshall Cavendish Corporation Staff. lib. bdg. 18.56 *(978-0-7614-3179-4(9))*; Iraq. Mason, Paul & Marshall Cavendish Corporation Staff. lib. bdg. 18.56 *(978-0-7614-3180-0(2))*; Israel & Palestine. Mason, Paul & Marshall Cavendish Staff. lib. bdg. 18.56 *(978-0-7614-3181-7(0))*; Sudan. Barker, Geoff & Marshall Cavendish Corporation Staff. lib. bdg. 18.56 *(978-0-7614-3182-4(9))*; 32p. (gr. 5-18). (Global Hotspots Ser.). 2008. Set lib. bdg. 111.36 *(978-0-7614-3175-6(6)*, Benchmark Bks.) Marshall Cavendish Corp.

Goes, Peter. Timeline: A Visual History of Our World. Goes, Peter, illus. 2016. (ENG., Illus.). 80p. (gr. 5-12). 29.99 *(978-1-77657-069-0(3))* Gecko Pr. NZL. Dist: Lerner Publishing Group.

Goes, Peter. Timeline: Activity Book Create Your Own Journey Through Time. Goes, Peter, illus. 2017. (ENG., Illus.). 72p. (gr. 5-12). 12.99 ***(978-1-77657-128-4(2))*** Gecko Pr. NZL. Dist: Lerner Publishing Group.

Goldman, Phyllis, ed. Monkeyshines on Mysteries in History. 2003. (Illus.). 92p. per. 32.95 *(978-1-888325-20-1(8))* Allosaurus Pubs.

Gombrich, E. H. A Little History of the World. Mustill, Caroline, tr. from GER. Harper, Clifford, illus. 2008. (Little Histories Ser.). (ENG.). 304p. pap. 15.00 *(978-0-300-14332-4(X))* Yale Univ. Pr.

—A Little History of the World. Mustill, Caroline, tr. from GER. Harper, Clifford, illus. 2005. (Little Histories Ser.). (ENG.). 304p. 25.00 *(978-0-300-10883-5(4))* Yale Univ. Pr.

—A Little History of the World. 2011. (Little Histories Ser.). (ENG., Illus.). 304p. 29.95 *(978-0-300-17614-8(7))* Yale Univ. Pr.

—A Little History of the World: Illustrated Edition. 2013. (Little Histories Ser.). (ENG., Illus.). 304p. pap. 25.00 *(978-0-300-19718-1(7))* Yale Univ. Pr.

Gorman, Joe & Trammell, Jack. Conversations in History: 9 Important Historical Events & the People Who Starred in Them. 2004. (Illus.). 80p. (J). pap. 6.50 *(978-1-931334-30-3(7))* Pieces of Learning.

Gray, Dee. Po Cats (9 Lives) Cultural Adventure Series: 2 Low-Income Felines Share Their Musings on Travel, Colonialism, & Geopolitics, 4 bks., Set. 2003. (Illus.). per. 200.00 *(978-0-9742007-0-5(0))* Poor Magazine.

Great Battles Through the Ages. (Illus.). (gr. 6-12). pap. *(978-0-7910-8043-6(9)*, Chelsea Hse.) Facts On File, Inc.

Greathouse, Lisa E. & Kuligowski, Stephanie. ¡Sin Resolver! Lugares Misteriosos. 2017. (TIME for Kids en Español - Level 4 Ser.). (SPA.). 48p. (gr. 4-4). lib. bdg. 31.99 *(978-1-5157-5133-5(3))* Time for Kids Inc AUS. Dist: Capstone Pub.

Green, Janessa. Perimeters of the Ancient World: Recognize Perimeter, 1 vol. 2015. (InfoMax Common Core Math Readers Ser.). (ENG.). 24p. (J). pap. 8.25 *(978-1-4777-4585-4(8)*, Rosen Classroom) Rosen Publishing Group, Inc., The.

Gritzner, Charles F., ed. Modern World Nations. (Illus.). (J). 848.30 *(978-0-7910-7272-1(X)*, Chelsea Hse.) Facts On File, Inc.

Hands-On History Group 3, 5 bks., Set. Incl. Projects about Ancient China. Bjorklund, Ruth. lib. bdg. 21.95 *(978-0-7614-2257-0(9))*; Projects about Ancient Egypt. King, David C. lib. bdg. 21.95 *(978-0-7614-2258-7(7))*; Projects about Ancient Greece. Broida, Marian. lib. bdg. 21.95 *(978-0-7614-2259-4(5))*; Projects about Ancient Rome. Frankel, Karen. lib. bdg. 21.95 *(978-0-7614-2260-0(9))*; Projects about the Ancient Aztecs. King, David C. lib. bdg. 21.95 *(978-0-7614-2256-3(0))*; (Illus.). 48p. (gr. 3-7). 2006. 2007. Set lib. bdg. 156.79 *(978-0-7614-2255-6(2)*, Benchmark Bks.) Marshall Cavendish Corp.

Harcourt School Publishers Staff. Beginnings 1877. 3rd ed. 2003. (Harcourt School Publishers Horizons Ser.). (ENG.). 728p. (gr. 4-5). stu. ed., pupil's gde. ed. 85.65 *(978-0-15-321349-6(3))* Harcourt Schl. Pubs.

—World History, 5 Packs. 3rd ed. (Horizons Ser.). 2004. pap. 7.30 *(978-0-15-338611-4(8))* 2003. pap. 38.10 *(978-0-15-338635-0(5))*Bk. 2. 2004. pap. 7.30 *(978-0-15-338612-1(6))*Bk. 2. 2003. pap. 38.10 *(978-0-15-338636-7(3))*Bk. 3. 2004. pap. 7.30 *(978-0-15-338613-8(4))*Bk. 3. 2003. pap. 38.10 *(978-0-15-338637-4(1))*Bk. 4. 2004. pap. 7.30 *(978-0-15-338614-5(2))*Bk. 5. 2004. pap. 7.30 *(978-0-15-338615-2(0))*Bk. 5. 2003. pap. 38.10 *(978-0-15-338639-8(8))*Bk. 6. 2004. pap. 7.30 *(978-0-15-338616-9(9))*Bk. 6. 2003. pap. 38.10 *(978-0-15-338640-4(1))*Bk. 7. 2004. pap. 7.30 *(978-0-15-338617-6(7))*Bk. 7. 2003. pap. 38.10 *(978-0-15-338641-1(X))*Bk. 8. 2004. pap. 7.30 *(978-0-15-338618-3(5))*Bk. 8. 2003. pap. 38.10 *(978-0-15-338642-8(8))*Bk. 9. 2004. pap. 7.30 *(978-0-15-338619-0(3))*Bk. 9. 2003. pap. 38.10 *(978-0-15-338643-5(6))*Bk. 10. 2004. pap. 7.30 *(978-0-15-338620-6(7))*Bk. 10. 2003. pap. 38.10 *(978-0-15-338644-2(4))*Bk. 11. 2004. pap. 7.30 *(978-0-15-338621-3(5))*Bk. 11. 2003. pap. 38.10 *(978-0-15-338645-9(2))*Bk. 12. 2004. pap. 7.30 *(978-0-15-338622-0(3))*Bk. 12. 2003. pap. 38.10 *(978-0-15-338646-6(0))*Bk. 13. 2004. pap. 7.30 *(978-0-15-338623-7(1))*Bk. 13. 2003. pap. 38.10 *(978-0-15-338647-3(9))*Bk. 14. 2004. pap. 7.30 *(978-0-15-338624-4(X))*Bk. 14. 2003. pap. 38.10 *(978-0-15-338648-0(7))*Bk. 15. 2004. pap. 7.30 *(978-0-15-338625-1(8))*Bk. 15. 2003. pap. 38.10 *(978-0-15-338649-7(5))*Bk. 16. 2004. pap. 7.30 *(978-0-15-338626-8(6))*Bk. 16. 2003. pap. 38.10 *(978-0-15-338650-3(9))*Bk. 17. 2004. pap. 7.30 *(978-0-15-338627-5(4))*Bk. 17. 2003. pap. 38.10 *(978-0-15-338651-0(7))*Bk. 18. 2004. pap. 7.30 *(978-0-15-338628-2(2))*Bk. 18. 2003. pap. 38.10 *(978-0-15-338652-7(5))*Bk. 19. 2004. pap. 7.30 *(978-0-15-338629-9(0))*Bk. 19. 2003. pap. 38.10 *(978-0-15-338653-4(3))*Bk. 20. 2004. pap. 7.30 *(978-0-15-338630-5(4))*Bk. 20. 2003. pap. 38.10 *(978-0-15-338654-1(1))*Bk. 21. 2004. pap. 7.30 *(978-0-15-338631-2(2))*Bk. 21. 2003. pap. 38.10 *(978-0-15-338655-8(X))*Bk. 22. 2004. pap. 7.30 *(978-0-15-338632-9(0))*Bk. 22. 2003. pap. 38.10 *(978-0-15-338656-5(8))*Bk. 23. 2004. pap. 7.30 *(978-0-15-338633-6(9))*Bk. 23. 2003. pap. 38.10 *(978-0-15-338657-2(6))*Bk. 24. 2004. pap. 7.30 *(978-0-15-338634-3(7))*Bk. 24. 2003. pap. 38.10 *(978-0-15-338658-9(4))* Harcourt Schl. Pubs.

—World History: The Civil War to the Present. 3rd ed. 2003. (Harcourt Horizons Ser.). (ENG., Illus.). 680p. (gr. 5-6). stu. ed. 89.15 *(978-0-15-339621-2(0))* Harcourt Schl. Pubs.

—World History: Time for Kids Reader 5-Pack, Bk. 4. 3rd ed. 2003. (Horizons Ser.). pap. 38.10 *(978-0-15-338638-1(X))* Harcourt Schl. Pubs.

Hardyman, Robyn. Lost Kings & Kingdoms. 2016. (Mystery Hunters Ser.). 00048p. (J). lib. bdg. 31.95 ***(978-1-4824-6009-4(2))*** Stevens, Gareth Publishing LLLP.

—Tombs & Cursed Treasure. 2016. (Mystery Hunters Ser.). 00048p. (J). pap. 14.05 ***(978-1-4824-6011-7(4))*** Stevens, Gareth Publishing LLLP.

Hawkins, Jay. Really Horrible History Facts. 2013. (Really Horrible Facts Ser.). 32p. (J). (gr. k-3). 25.25 *(978-1-61533-746-0(6))* Windmill Bks.

Hay, Jeff. Japanese American Internment. Wukovits, John, ed. 2012. (World History Ser.). (ENG., Illus.). 128p. (gr. 7-10). lib. bdg. 39.90 *(978-1-4205-0824-6(5)*, Lucent Bks.) Cengage Gale.

Healey, Tim. The 1960s. 2005. (Picture History of the 20th Century Ser.). (Illus.). 48p. (YA). (gr. 7-12). lib. bdg. 29.95 *(978-1-932889-74-1(4))* Sea-To-Sea Pubns.

Herweck Rice, Dona. ¡Sin Resolver! Misterios de la Historia. 2017. (TIME for Kids en Español - Level 4 Ser.). (SPA., Illus.). 48p. (gr. 4-4). lib. bdg. 31.99 *(978-1-5157-5134-2(1))* Time for Kids Inc AUS. Dist: Capstone Pub.

Hirschmann, Kris & Herndon, Ryan. Test Your Smarts! 2009. (Illus.). 80p. (J). *(978-0-545-12042-5(X))* Scholastic, Inc.

Historia y Geografia del Mundo: Del Renacimiento al Siglo XX. (SPA., Illus.). (J). 40.00 *(978-958-04-3807-6(2))* Norma S.A. COL. Dist: Distribuidora Norma, Inc.

History & Geography. 2004. (Switched on Schoolhouse Ser.). (YA). (gr. 7). cd-rom 69.95 *(978-0-7403-0587-0(5))*;Set. (Illus.). (gr. 5). tchr. ed., stu. ed. 47.95 *(978-1-58095-651-2(3)*, HIS05015, Lifepac) Alpha Omega Pubns., Inc.

History & Geography: Government & Economics. 2004. (Illus.). (gr. 12). tchr. ed., stu. ed. 47.95 *(978-1-58095-672-7(6)*, HIS1215, Lifepac) Alpha Omega Pubns., Inc.

History & Geography: U. S. History, 12 vols., Set. 2004. (Illus.). (gr. 11-12). tchr. ed., stu. ed. 47.95 *(978-1-58095-669-7(6)*, HIS1115, Lifepac) Alpha Omega Pubns., Inc.

History of the World 8-Book Set. 2014. (Primary Source Readers Ser.). (ENG., Illus.). 32p. (gr. 4-5). spiral bd. 71.92 *(978-1-4938-0840-3(0))* Teacher Created Materials, Inc.

History's Fearless Fighters. 2015. (History's Fearless Fighters Ser.). (ENG.). 48p. (J). (gr. 5-6). pap., pap., pap. 505.80 *(978-1-4824-3480-4(6))* Stevens, Gareth Publishing LLLP.

Hogan, Maggie S. Student History Notebook of America. 2007. (Illus.). 111p. per. 12.95 *(978-0-9663722-3-6(9))* Coffee Hse. Ink.

Hollingsworth, Tamara. Noticias Que Marcaron la Historia. 2016. (TIME for Kids en Español - Level 5 Ser.). (SPA.). 64p. (gr. 5-5). lib. bdg. 31.99 *(978-1-5157-2943-3(5))* Time for Kids Inc AUS. Dist: Capstone Pub.

HOLT, RINEHART AND WINSTON. World History: People & Nations. 2003. (Holt World History: People & a Nation Ser.). (ENG.). 1040p. (gr. 9-9). 187.85 *(978-0-03-053359-4(7))* Houghton Mifflin Harcourt Publishing Co.

Holt, Rinehart and Winston Staff. The Human Journey: Online Edition. 3rd ed. 2003. 77.13 *(978-0-03-072542-5(9))* Holt McDougal.

—The Human Journey: The Modern World: Online Edition. 3rd ed. 2003. 75.93 *(978-0-03-072541-8(0))* Holt McDougal.

—World History: The Human Journey: Online Edition. 5th ed. 2004. (gr. 1). 17.26 *(978-0-03-038134-8(7))*; (gr. 6). 78.60 *(978-0-03-038136-2(3))* Holt McDougal.
—World History: The Human Journey: Online Edition Plus. 3rd ed. 2003. 17.26 *(978-0-03-037423-4(5))*; 17.26 *(978-0-03-037424-1(3))*; 17.26 *(978-0-03-037426-5(X))* Holt McDougal.
—World History & Doc-B's Questions: New York Edition. 3rd ed. 2003. (Holt World History Ser.). (J). pap. 8.40 *(978-0-03-070236-5(4))* Holt, Rinehart & Winston of Canada, Ltd. CAN. Dist: Harcourt Canada, Ltd.
Hoose, Phillip & Eaton, Gale. A History in Civilization in 50 Disasters. 2015. (History In 50 Ser.: 0). (ENG., Illus.). 240p. (gr. 6-12). pap. 16.95 *(978-0-88448-489-9(0)*, 884489) Tilbury Hse. Pubs.
Hyde, Natalie. History Mysteries Revealed. 2010. (ENG., Illus.). 32p. (J). pap. *(978-0-7787-7429-7(5))*; (gr. 4-7). lib. bdg. *(978-0-7787-7414-3(7))* Crabtree Publishing Co.
I, Senator James, ed. Arbitrary Borders: Political Boundaries in World History Set, 18-Volumes. 2007. (Arbitrary Borders Ser.). 172p. (C). (gr. 9). 595.00 *(978-0-7910-9450-1(2)*, Chelsea Hse.) Facts On File, Inc.
Images of War. (Illus.). 192p. (J). *(978-0-7835-0153-6(6))* Time-Life Education, Inc.
In World History, 26 bks., Set. Incl. Cinque of the Amistad & the Slave Trade in World History. Worth, Richard. 112p. (J). 2001. lib. bdg. 26.60 *(978-0-7660-1460-2(6))*; Commodore Perry Opens Japan to Trade in World History. Gaines, Ann Graham. 128p. (YA). 2000. lib. bdg. 26.60 *(978-0-7660-1462-6(2))*; Cortes & the Conquest of the Aztec Empire in World History. Flowers, Charles. 128p. (J). 2001. lib. bdg. 26.60 *(978-0-7660-1395-7(2))*; Julius Caesar & Ancient Rome in World History. Barter, James. 128p. (J). 2001. lib. bdg. 26.60 *(978-0-7660-1461-9(4))*; King Henry VIII & the Reformation in World History. Worth, Richard. 112p. (J). 2001. lib. bdg. 26.60 *(978-0-7660-1615-6(3))*; Lenin & the Russian Revolution in World History. Edwards, Judith. 128p. (J). 2001. lib. bdg. 26.60 *(978-0-7660-1464-0(9))*; Leonardo da Vinci & the Renaissance in World History. Lassieur, Allison. 128p. (YA). 2000. lib. bdg. 26.60 *(978-0-7660-1401-5(0))*; Mahatma Gandhi & India's Independence in World History. Malaspina, Ann. 128p. (YA). 2000. lib. bdg. 26.60 *(978-0-7660-1398-8(7))*; Nelson Mandela & Apartheid in World History. Gaines, Ann Graham. 128p. (J). 2001. lib. bdg. 27.94 *(978-0-7660-1463-3(0))*; Philip II & Alexander the Great Unify Greece in World History. Nardo, Don. 112p. (J). 2000. lib. bdg. 26.60 *(978-0-7660-1399-5(5))*; Pizarro & the Conquest of the Incan Empire in World History. Worth, Richard. 128p. (YA). 2000. lib. bdg. 26.60 *(978-0-7660-1396-4(0))*; Robespierre & the French Revolution in World History. McGowen, Tom. 128p. (YA). 2000. lib. bdg. 26.60 *(978-0-7660-1397-1(9))*; Stanley & Livingstone & the Exploration of Africa in World History. Worth, Richard. 128p. (J). 2000. lib. bdg. 27.94 *(978-0-7660-1400-8(2))*; (gr. 5-12). (Illus.). Set lib. bdg. 544.70 *(978-0-7660-1604-0(8))* Enslow Pubs., Inc.
Incas Mayas Aztecs: Mr Donn & Maxie's World History Series. 2006. spiral bd. 29.95 net. *(978-1-56004-244-0(3))* Social Studies Schl. Service.
Johnson, Terri, creator. Blackline Maps of World History: The Complete Set - Revised, 4 sets. 2nd rev. ed. 2004. (Illus.). 250p. (J). ring bd. 39.95 *(978-1-932786-16-3(3))* Knowledge Quest.
—Wonders of Old: A Blank Timeline Book of World History. 2007. (Illus.). 96p. 21.95 *(978-1-932786-10-1(4))* Knowledge Quest.
Kemp, Ellwood W. Streams of History. 2008. 64p. pap. 7.95 *(978-1-59915-260-8(6))* Yesterday's Classics.
Kingfisher Editors. The Kingfisher History Encyclopedia. 3rd ed. 2012. (Kingfisher Encyclopedias Ser.). (ENG., Illus.). 496p. (J). (gr. 4-9). 32.99 *(978-0-7534-6875-3(1)*, 9780753468753, Kingfisher) Roaring Brook Pr.
Knapp-Fisher, H. C. Outline of World History: For Boys & Girls. (J). 25.00 *(978-0-8196-2798-8(4))* Biblo & Tannen Booksellers & Pubs., Inc.
Knebel, Arthur & Udelhoven, Hermann-Josef. The Modern Era through World War II: From the 18th Century To 1945. 2012. (Witness to History: A Visual Chronicle of the World Ser.). (ENG., Illus.). 200p. (J). (gr. 7-12). 46.50 *(978-1-4488-7224-4(3))* Rosen Publishing Group, Inc., The.
Knight, Margy Burns. Talking Walls: Discover Your World. O'Brien, Anne Sibley, illus. 2014. (ENG.). 64p. (gr. 2-7). 18.95 *(978-0-88448-356-4(8)*, 884356) Tilbury Hse. Pubs.
Layton, Neal. The Story of Things: From the Stone Age to the Modern Age in 10 Pop-Up Spreads. 2010. (ENG., Illus.). 24p. (J). (gr. k-2). 15.99 *(978-0-340-94532-2(X)*, Hodder Children's Books) Hachette Children's Group GBR. Dist: Hachette Bk. Group.
Leaders of the Ancient World: Set 1. 2016. (Leaders of the Ancient World Ser.). 00112p. (J). (gr. 6-6). 296.80 *(978-1-5081-7358-8(3)*, Rosen Young Adult) Rosen Publishing Group, Inc., The.
Leaders of the Ancient World: Set 2. 2017. (Leaders of the Ancient World Ser.). 112p. (gr. 12-11). 296.80 ***(978-1-4994-6629-4(3)***, Rosen Young Adult) Rosen Publishing Group, Inc., The.
LernerClassroom Editors. Count Your Way Teaching Guide. 2009. pap. 7.95 *(978-0-8225-6886-5(1))* Lerner Publishing Group.
El Libro de los Acertijos Historicos. (Coleccion Acertijos). (SPA.). (YA). (gr. 5-8). pap. *(978-950-724-249-6(X)*, LMA8235) Lumen ARG. Dist: Lectorum Pubns., Inc.
Long, David. Diary of a Time Traveller. Stevenson, Nicholas, illus. 2015. (ENG.). 64p. (J). 22.99 *(978-1-84780-636-9(8)*, Wide Eyed Editions) Quarto Publishing Group UK GBR. Dist: Littlehampton Bk Services, Ltd.
Looking at Countries, 6 vols., Set. Incl. Looking at Canada. Pohl, Kathleen. lib. bdg. 26.00 *(978-0-8368-8168-4(0))*; Looking at China. Powell, Jillian. lib. bdg. 26.00 *(978-0-8368-8169-1(9))*; Looking at Great Britain. Powell, Jillian. lib. bdg. 26.00 *(978-0-8368-8170-7(2))*; Looking at Japan. Powell, Jillian. lib. bdg. 26.00 *(978-0-8368-8171-4(0))*; Looking at Mexico. Pohl, Kathleen. lib. bdg. 26.00 *(978-0-8368-8172-1(9))*; Looking at Russia. Powell, Jillian. lib. bdg. 26.00 *(978-0-8368-8173-8(7))*; (Illus.). 32p. (gr. 1-5). 2007., Gareth Stevens Learning Library 2007. Set lib. bdg. 151.62 o.p. *(978-0-8368-8167-7(2))* Stevens, Gareth Publishing LLLP.
Lubawy, Susan. World View: A Global Study of Geography, History & Culture, Bk. 1. (J). stu. ed. 8.95 *(978-0-916591-30-4(1))* Linmore Publishing, Inc.
Macdonald, Fiona. The World in the Time Of... 2005. (World in the Time of... Ser.). 48p. (gr. 5-8). 137.70 *(978-0-7910-8407-6(8)*, Chelsea Hse.) Facts On File, Inc.
MacLeod, Elizabeth, et al. A History of Just about Everything: 180 Events, People & Inventions That Changed the World. Leng, Qin, illus. 2013. (ENG.). 124p. (J). (gr. 3-7). 21.95 *(978-1-55453-775-4(4))* Kids Can Pr., Ltd. CAN. Dist: Hachette Bk. Group.
McDougal-Littell Publishing Staff. Modern World History: Patterns of Interaction. 2004. (Modern World History: Patterns of Interaction Ser.). (ENG.). 240p. (gr. 9-12). pap., pupil's gde. ed. 4.90 *(978-0-618-40991-4(2)*, 2-00647) Great Source Education Group, Inc.
—Modern World History: Patterns of Interaction - Reading Study Guide. 2004. (McDougal Littell World History: Patterns of Interaction Ser.). (SPA.). 240p. (gr. 9-12). pap. 4.90 *(978-0-618-40992-1(0)*, 2-00648) Great Source Education Group, Inc.
—World History: Patterns of Interaction. 2004. (World History: Patterns of Interaction Ser.). (ENG.). 160p. (gr. 9-12). pap., wbk. ed. 7.40 *(978-0-618-40938-9(6)*, 2-00619) Great Source Education Group, Inc.
—World History - Patterns of Interaction. 2004. (World History: Patterns of Interaction Ser.). (ENG.). 384p. (gr. 9-12). pap. 7.40 *(978-0-618-40933-4(5)*, 2-00614) Great Source Education Group, Inc.
—World History - Patterns of Interaction: Reading Study Guide. 2004. (McDougal Littell World History: Patterns of Interaction Ser.). (SPA.). 384p. (gr. 9-12). pap. 7.40 *(978-0-618-40934-1(3)*, 2-00615) Great Source Education Group, Inc.
McGraw-Hill Education. Human Heritage: A World History. 3rd ed. 2005. (Merrill Human Heritage Ser.). (ENG.). (gr. 6-9). cd-rom 142.12 *(978-0-07-873136-5(4)*, 0078731364) McGraw-Hill Higher Education.
McGraw-Hill Education Editors. Journey Across Time, Early Ages. 2007. (MS Wh Jat Full Survey Ser.). (ENG.). (gr. 6-9). cd-rom 147.72 *(978-0-07-878150-6(7)*, 0078781507) McGraw-Hill Education.
—World History: Modern Times: Spanish Reading Essentials & Note-Taking Guide. 2007. (World History (hs) Ser.). (ENG & SPA., Illus.). 252p. (gr. 6-9). per. 11.56 *(978-0-07-878270-1(8)*, 0078782708) McGraw-Hill Education.
McGraw-Hill Education Staff. Exploring Our World Standardized Test Practice: People, Places, & Cultures. 2007. (WORLD & ITS PEOPLE EASTERN Ser.). (ENG., Illus.). 128p. (gr. 6-8). spiral bd., wbk. ed. 6.88 *(978-0-07-877605-2(8)*, 0078776058) McGraw-Hill Education.
—Glencoe World History. 2007. (World History (hs) Ser.). (ENG.). (gr. 6-9). cd-rom 107.12 *(978-0-07-878250-3(3)*, 0078782503) McGraw-Hill Education.
—Glencoe World History: Modern Times. 2nd ed. 2005. (Human Experience - Modern Era Ser.). (ENG.). (gr. 6-9). stu. ed. 155.72 *(978-0-07-865302-5(9)*, 0078653029) McGraw-Hill Higher Education.
McGraw-Hill-Glencoe Staff. Exploring Our World. 2nd ed. 2007. (WORLD & ITS PEOPLE EASTERN Ser.). (ENG.). (gr. 6-8). stu. ed. 120.04 *(978-0-07-874576-8(4)*, 0078745764) McGraw-Hill Education.
McGraw-Hill Staff. Human Heritage, Spanish Reading Essentials & Study Guide, Student Edition. 2005. pap. 18.00 *(978-0-07-869627-5(5))* Glencoe/McGraw-Hill.
—Journey Across Time - The Early Ages: Standardized Test Skills Practice Workbook. 2004. (MS World History Ser.). (ENG., Illus.). 48p. (gr. 6-9). stu. ed., spiral bd. 6.88 *(978-0-07-868191-2(X)*, 007868191X) McGraw-Hill Education.
—Journey Across Time, Early Ages. 2005. (MS World History Ser.). (ENG.). (gr. 6-9). stu. ed. 138.12 *(978-0-07-867415-0(8)*, 0078674158) McGraw-Hill Higher Education.
—Journey Across Time, Early Ages, Active Reading Note-Taking Strategies. 2004. (MS World History Ser.). (ENG.). (gr. 6-9). pap., stu. ed. 12.28 *(978-0-07-868132-5(4)*, 0078681324) McGraw-Hill Higher Education.
McGraw-Hill Staff, creator. The World & Its People. 2004. (GEOGRAPHY: WORLD & ITS PEOPLE Ser.). (ENG., Illus.). 59p. (gr. 6-9). pap., stu. ed., wbk. ed. 7.40 *(978-0-07-865502-9(1)*, 0078655021) McGraw-Hill Education.
—The World & Its People: Standardized Test Skills Practice. 2004. (GEOGRAPHY: WORLD & ITS PEOPLE Ser.). (ENG., Illus.). 59p. (gr. 6-9). pap., stu. ed., wbk. ed. 7.20 *(978-0-07-865523-4(4)*, 0078655234) McGraw-Hill Education.
—World History: Modern Times. 2007. (World History (hs) Ser.). (ENG., Illus.). 50p. (gr. 6-9). stu. ed., per., wbk. ed. 7.76 *(978-0-07-878261-9(9)*, 0078782619) McGraw-Hill Education.
—World History - Journey Across Time, the Early Ages. 2004. (MS World History Ser.). (SPA., Illus.). 390p. (gr. 6-9). stu. ed., per., wbk. ed. 12.28 *(978-0-07-868194-3(4)*, 0078681944) McGraw-Hill Higher Education.
McGraw-Hill Staff & Glencoe McGraw-Hill Staff. Journey Across Time, Early Ages, Interactive Tutor. 2nd ed. 2007. (MS Wh Jat Full Survey Ser.). (ENG.). (gr. 6-9). cd-rom 107.12 *(978-0-07-878941-0(9)*, 0078789419) McGraw-Hill Education.
McNeese, Tim, ed. Rivers in World History. 2005. (Rivers in World History Ser.). (Illus.). 120p. (C). (gr. 9-13). 195.00 *(978-0-7910-8473-1(6)*, Chelsea Hse.) Facts On File, Inc.
McNeill, William H., et al, eds. Berkshire Encyclopedia of World History, 5 vols. 2005. (Illus.). 2500p. lib. bdg. 575.00 *(978-0-9743091-0-1(9))* Berkshire Publishing Group.
Millard, A. World History. 2009. (World History Ser.). 192p. (YA). (gr. 3-18). 24.99 *(978-0-7945-2478-4(8)*, Usborne) EDC Publishing.
Miller, Adam. Research It!, 5 vols., Set. Incl. Industrial Revolution. Morris, Neil. lib. bdg. 34.65 *(978-1-4329-3497-2(X))*; Medieval Europe. Ross, Stewart. lib. bdg. 34.65 *(978-1-4329-3498-9(8))*; Slavery & the Slave Trade. Spilsbury, Richard. lib. bdg. 34.65 *(978-1-4329-3495-8(3))*; World War I. Ross, Stewart. lib. bdg. 34.65 *(978-1-4329-3494-1(5))*; World War II. Langley, Andrew. lib. bdg. 34.65 *(978-1-4329-3493-4(7))*; (Illus.). (gr. 6-9). (Research It! Ser.). (ENG.). 56p. 2010. Set lib. bdg. 207.90 *(978-1-4329-3499-6(6)*, NA-h) Heinemann-Raintree.
Miller, Olive Beaupre & Baum, Harry Neal. A Picturesque Tale of Progress. 2009. (J). *(978-1-59731-396-4(3))*; *(978-1-59731-397-1(1))*; *(978-1-59731-398-8(X))*; *(978-1-59731-399-5(8))*; *(978-1-59731-395-7(5))*; *(978-1-59731-364-3(5))*; *(978-1-59731-394-0(7))*; *(978-1-59731-374-2(2))* Perennis, Sophia.
—A Picturesque Tale of Progress: Beginnings I. 2009. (Illus.). 282p. (J). pap. 14.95 *(978-1-59731-365-0(3)*, Dawn Chorus Pr.) Perennis, Sophia.
—A Picturesque Tale of Progress: Beginnings I-II. 2009. (Illus.). 540p. (J). pap. 19.95 *(978-1-59731-389-6(0)*, Dawn Chorus Pr.) Perennis, Sophia.
—A Picturesque Tale of Progress: Beginnings II. 2009. (Illus.). 304p. (J). pap. 14.95 *(978-1-59731-366-7(1)*, Dawn Chorus Pr.) Perennis, Sophia.
—A Picturesque Tale of Progress: Conquests III. 2009. (Illus.). 348p. (J). pap. 15.95 *(978-1-59731-367-4(X)*, Dawn Chorus Pr.) Perennis, Sophia.
—A Picturesque Tale of Progress: Conquests III-IV. 2009. (Illus.). 544p. (J). pap. 19.95 *(978-1-59731-390-2(4)*, Dawn Chorus Pr.) Perennis, Sophia.
—A Picturesque Tale of Progress: Conquests IV. 2009. (Illus.). 264p. (J). pap. 14.95 *(978-1-59731-368-1(8)*, Dawn Chorus Pr.) Perennis, Sophia.
—A Picturesque Tale of Progress: Explorations VII. 2009. (Illus.). 340p. (J). pap. 15.95 *(978-1-59731-371-1(8)*, Dawn Chorus Pr.) Perennis, Sophia.
—A Picturesque Tale of Progress: Explorations VII-VIII. 2009. 568p. (J). pap. 19.95 *(978-1-59731-392-6(0)*, Dawn Chorus Pr.) Perennis, Sophia.
—A Picturesque Tale of Progress: Explorations VIII. 2009. (Illus.). 292p. (J). pap. 14.00 *(978-1-59731-372-8(6)*, Dawn Chorus Pr.) Perennis, Sophia.
—A Picturesque Tale of Progress: Index. 2009. 238p. (J). pap. 13.95 *(978-1-59731-393-3(9)*, Dawn Chorus Pr.) Perennis, Sophia.
—A Picturesque Tale of Progress: Index IX. 2009. 238p. (J). pap. 12.95 *(978-1-59731-373-5(4)*, Dawn Chorus Pr.) Perennis, Sophia.
—A Picturesque Tale of Progress: New Nations V. 2009. (Illus.). 296p. (J). pap. 14.95 *(978-1-59731-369-8(6)*, Dawn Chorus Pr.) Perennis, Sophia.
—A Picturesque Tale of Progress: New Nations V-VI. 2009. (Illus.). 540p. (J). pap. 19.95 *(978-1-59731-391-9(2))* Perennis, Sophia.
—A Picturesque Tale of Progress: New Nations VI. 2009. (Illus.). 308p. (J). pap. 14.95 *(978-1-59731-370-4(X)*, Dawn Chorus Pr.) Perennis, Sophia.
Modern World History: Patterns of Interaction: EEdition Plus Online. (gr. 6-12). 2005. *(978-0-618-41039-2(2)*, 2-00657) 2003. *(978-0-618-19414-8(2)*, 2-70056) Holt McDougal.
Modern World History: Patterns of Interaction: EEdition Plus Online with purchase of print Pupil's Edition-1 Year. (gr. 6-12). 2005. *(978-0-618-41042-2(2)*, 2-00660) 2003. *(978-0-618-25845-1(0)*, 2-10037) Holt McDougal.
Modern World History: Patterns of Interaction: Reading Study Guide Answer Key. 2005. (gr. 6-12). *(978-0-618-40994-5(7)*, 2-00649) Holt McDougal.
Mooney, Brian. Great Leaders. 2012. (Great People in History Ser.). (ENG., Illus.). 128p. (YA). (gr. 8-12). lib. bdg. 34.60 *(978-1-4777-0403-5(5))* Rosen Publishing Group, Inc., The.
Moore, Christopher. From Then to Now: A Short History of the World. Krystoforski, Andrej, illus. 2011. (ENG.). 192p. (J). (gr. 5-18). 25.95 *(978-0-88776-540-7(8)*, Tundra Bks.) Tundra Bks. CAN. Dist: Penguin Random Hse. LLC.
Morter, Peter. Atlas Visual de los Descubrimientos. (SPA., Illus.). 412p. (YA). (gr. 5-8). *(978-84-216-1814-1(8)*, BU4892) Bruño, Editorial ESP. Dist: Lectorum Pubns., Inc.
National Geographic Learning Staff. Famous Landmarks, Level 3. 2011. (World Windows Ser.). (ENG.). 16p. stu. ed. 9.95 *(978-1-133-56616-8(2))* Cengage Heinle.
Nineteen Sixty-Eight (World History) (Illus.). 192p. (J). *(978-0-7835-0152-9(8))* Time-Life Education, Inc.
Notgrass, Ray. Exploring World History. 2014. (Illus.). *(978-1-60999-061-9(7))* Notgrass Co.
Omoth, Tyler, et al. Top Secret Files. 2017. (Top Secret Files Ser.). (ENG.). 32p. (gr. 3-4). 111.96 *(978-1-5157-4163-3(X)*, Edge Bks.) Capstone Press of Coughlan Cos.
O'Neill, Elizabeth. The World's Story. 2013. 394p. 39.95 *(978-0-9885106-3-0(4))* Hillside Education.
Otfinoski, Steven. World War II. 2017. (Step into History(tm) Ser.). (ENG., Illus.). 144p. (J). lib. bdg. 36.00 *(978-0-531-22572-1(0))* Scholastic Library Publishing.
Otfinoski, Steven & Burgan, Michael. You Choose: History: An Interactive History Adventure. 2015. (You Choose: History Ser.). (ENG.). 112p. (gr. 3-4). lib. bdg. 63.98 *(978-1-4914-1810-9(9)*, You Choose Bks.) Capstone Press of Coughlan Cos.
Otfinoski, Steven, et al. Tangled History. 2017. (Tangled History Ser.). (ENG.). 112p. (gr. 3-4). 383.88 *(978-1-5157-3640-0(7))* Capstone Press of Coughlan Cos.
Pak, Amy. History Through the Ages - Napoleon to Now: Historical Timeline Figures (1750 AD - Present) Pak, Amy, illus. 2003. (Illus.). (J). pap. 19.95 *(978-0-9720265-3-6(3))* Home Schl. in the Woods.
Phan, Sandy. Imperialism: Expanding Empires, 1 vol. 2012. (Primary Source Readers Ser.). (ENG.). 32p. (J). (gr. 5-5). pap. 8.99 *(978-1-4333-5015-3(7))* Teacher Created Materials, Inc.
A Political & Diplomatic History of the Modern World. 2016. (Political & Diplomatic History of the Modern World Ser.). 224p. (gr. 10-10). 184.00 *(978-1-5081-0228-1(7)*, Britannica Educational Publishing) Rosen Publishing Group, Inc., The.
Primary Sources in World History. 2016. (Primary Sources in World History Ser.). 48p. (gr. 6-6). lib. bdg. 188.16 *(978-1-5026-1825-2(7))* Cavendish Square Publishing.
Primary Sources of Countries of the World: Set 1, 6 bks, Set. 2003. (Illus.). (J). 117.00 *(978-0-8239-8487-9(7)*, PowerKids Pr.) Rosen Publishing Group, Inc., The.
Primary Sources of Countries of the World: Set 2, 6 bks., Set. 2003. (Illus.). (J). 117.00 *(978-0-8239-7277-7(1)*, PowerKids Pr.) Rosen Publishing Group, Inc., The.
Quick Revision KS3 History Staff. Quick Revision KS3 History. 2007. pap. 9.95 *(978-0-340-94309-0(2)*, Hodder Education) Hodder Education Group GBR. Dist: Trans-Atlantic Pubns., Inc.
Raum, Elizabeth & Collins, Terry. You Choose: Historical Eras. 2012. (You Choose: Historical Eras Ser.). (ENG.). 112p. (gr. 3-4). pap. 333.60 *(978-1-4296-9477-3(7))*; pap. 13.90 *(978-1-4296-9492-6(0))* Capstone Press of Coughlan Cos. (You Choose Bks.).
Raum, Elizabeth, et al. You Choose: Historical Eras. 2012. (You Choose: Historical Eras Ser.). (ENG.). 112p. (gr. 3-4). 63.98 *(978-1-4296-4782-3(5)*, You Choose Bks.) Capstone Press of Coughlan Cos.
Reformation: PowerPoint Presentation in World History. 2005. cd-rom 49.95 net. *(978-1-56004-216-7(8))* Social Studies Schl. Service.
Reid, Scott. The Great Society. Greenhaven Press Staff, ed. 2015. (Perspectives on Modern World History Ser.). (ENG., Illus.). 224p. (gr. 10-12). lib. bdg. 47.80 *(978-0-7377-7308-8(1)*, Greenhaven Pr., Inc.) Cengage Gale.
Rigby Education Staff. Discovery World. (Illus.). 68.00 *(978-0-7635-8444-3(4))* Rigby Education.
—Discovery World Orange Encyclopedia: Tiny Big Book. (Discovery World Ser.). 12p. (gr. 1-2). 27.00 *(978-0-7635-2702-0(5))* Rigby Education.
Rissman, Rebecca. Comparing Past & Present, 1 vol. 2014. (Comparing Past & Present Ser.). (ENG.). 24p. (gr. -1-1). lib. bdg. 135.90 *(978-1-4329-9022-0(5)*, Acorn) Heinemann-Raintree.
Road to War: Causes of Conflict, 5 vols., Set. Incl. Causes of the American Revolution. Strum, Richard M. 64p. (J). lib. bdg. 22.95 *(978-1-59556-001-8(7))*; Causes of the Civil War. Epperson, James F. 64p. (J). lib. bdg. 22.95 *(978-1-59556-002-5(5))*; Causes of the Iraq War. Gallagher, Jim. 72p. (J). lib. bdg. 22.95 *(978-1-59556-009-4(2))*; Causes of World War I. Ziff, John. 72p. (J). lib. bdg. 22.95 *(978-1-59556-003-2(3))*; Causes of World War II. Corrigan, Jim. 64p. lib. bdg. 22.95 *(978-1-59556-004-9(1))*; (gr. 4-18). 2005. (Road to War Ser.). (Illus.). 64p. 2005. Set lib. bdg. 114.75 *(978-1-59556-000-1(9))* OTTN Publishing.
Rountree, Elizabeth & Bauer, Susan Wise. The Modern Age Vol. 4: From Victoria's Empire to the End of the USSR. 2007. (Story of the World Ser.: 0). (ENG., Illus.). 176p. per. 14.95 *(978-1-933339-02-3(0)*, 333902) Well-Trained Mind Pr.
Rupert, Matthews. Visual Factfinder HIST Timelines. 2008. 512p. pap. *(978-1-84810-077-0(9))* Miles Kelly Publishing, Ltd.
Scholastic Library Publishing. Enchantment of the World. 2012. (Second Ser.). (J). 240.00 *(978-0-531-23525-6(4)*, Children's Pr.) Scholastic Library Publishing.
Schwartz, Heather E. & Salzano, Tammi. Around the World: An Amazing World. 2009. (Illus.). 48p. (J). pap. *(978-0-545-17229-5(2))* Scholastic, Inc.
Scientific Revolution: PowerPoints in World History. 2005. cd-rom 49.95 net. *(978-1-56004-215-0(X))* Social Studies Schl. Service.
Selmes, Caroline & Dickmann, Nancy. Sticky History of the World. 2017. (Magma for Laurence King Ser.). (ENG., Illus.). 32p. (J). (gr. 1-4). pap. 14.99 ***(978-1-78627-037-5(4))*** King, Laurence Publishing GBR. Dist: Hachette Bk. Group.
Shukin, Barbara. Modern History Portfolio: A History of America & the World from the 17th to the 21st Centuries. 2004. (J). ring bd. 29.95 *(978-0-9762918-3-1(5))* Homeschool Journey.
Sloan, Price Stern & Mad Libs Staff. History of the World Mad Libs. 2015. (Mad Libs Ser.). (ENG.). 48p. (J). (gr. 3-7). bds. 4.99 *(978-0-8431-8075-6(7)*, Mad Libs) Penguin Young Readers Group.
Smith, David J. If: A Mind-Bending New Way of Looking at Big Ideas & Numbers. Adams, Steve, illus. 2014. (ENG.). 40p. (J). (gr. 3-7). 18.95 *(978-1-894786-34-8(3))* Kids Can Pr., Ltd. CAN. Dist: Hachette Bk. Group.
Smith-Llera, Danielle & Burgan, Michael. Captured World History. 2016. (Captured World History Ser.). (ENG.). 64p. (gr. 5-7). 207.90 *(978-0-7565-5450-7(0)*, CPB Grades 4-8) Compass Point Bks.
Spielvogel, Jackson J. & McGraw-Hill Editors. Glencoe World History. 2nd ed. 2004. (World History (hs) Ser.). (ENG., Illus.). 1136p. (gr. 6-9). stu. ed. 131.96 *(978-0-07-860702-8(7)*, 0078607027) McGraw-Hill Education.
Spielvogel, Jackson J. & McGraw-Hill Education Editors. Glencoe World History. 2007. (World History (hs) Ser.). (ENG., Illus.). 1248p. (gr. 6-9). stu. ed. 137.20 *(978-0-07-874525-6(X)*, 007874525X) Glencoe/McGraw-Hill.
Spielvogel, Jackson J. & McGraw-Hill Education Staff. World History: Modern Times. 2nd ed. 2004. (Human Experience - Modern Era Ser.). (ENG., Illus.). 912p. (gr. 6-9). stu. ed. 125.24 *(978-0-07-860705-9(1)*, 0078607051) McGraw-Hill Education.
Spielvogel, Jackson J., et al. Glencoe World History: Modern Times. 2007. (World History (hs) Ser.). (ENG., Illus.). 992p. (gr. 6-9). stu. ed. 128.60 *(978-0-07-874527-0(6)*, 0078745276) McGraw-Hill Education.
—Journey Across Time. 2nd ed. 2006. (MS Wh Jat Full Survey Ser.). (ENG., Illus.). 1096p. (gr. 6-9). stu. ed. 126.08 *(978-0-07-875050-2(4)*, 0078750504) McGraw-Hill Education.
Steck-Vaughn Staff. History of Our World. 2003. (Steck-Vaughn History of Our World Ser.). (ENG.). 624p. (gr. 6-12). pap., tchr. ed. 120.80 *(978-0-7398-6088-5(7))* Houghton Mifflin Harcourt Publishing Co.
Steele, Philip, et al. Weird & Wacky History Book Box: Find Out What Is Fact or Fantasy in 8 Amazing Books, 8 vols. 2012. (ENG., Illus.). 200p. (J). (gr. -1-12). pap. 20.00 *(978-1-84322-797-7(5)*, Armadillo) Anness Publishing GBR. Dist: National Bk. Network.
Stewart, David. World of Wonder, 3 vols., Set. Incl. Dinosaurs. Hewetson, Nick, illus. 29.00 *(978-0-531-20450-4(2))*; Ocean Life. Franklin, Carolyn. Franklin, Carolyn, illus. 29.00 *(978-0-531-20451-1(0))*; Rain Forest Animals. Franklin, Carolyn. Franklin, Carolyn, illus. 29.00 *(978-0-531-20452-8(9))*; (Illus.). 32p. (J). (gr. 1-4). 2008. Set

W X Y Z

lib. bdg. 203.00 *(978-0-531-21004-8(9)*, Children's Pr.) Scholastic Library Publishing.

Synge, M. B. The Discovery of New Worlds, Book II of the Story of the World. 2007. 224p. 21.99 *(978-1-60206-621-2(3))*; per. 14.99 *(978-1-60206-620-5(5))* Cosimo, Inc.

—The Discovery of New Worlds (Yesterday's Classics) Synge, E. M., illus. l.t. ed. 2006. 252p. (J). per. *(978-1-59915-014-7(X))* Yesterday's Classics.

—The Struggle for Sea Power, Book Iv of the Story of the World. 2007. 248p. 21.99 *(978-1-60206-625-0(6))*; per. 14.99 *(978-1-60206-624-3(8))* Cosimo, Inc.

—The Struggle for Sea Power (Yesterday's Classics) Synge, E. M., illus. l.t. ed. 2006. 276p. (J). per. 11.95 *(978-1-59915-016-1(6))* Yesterday's Classics.

Tames, Richard. Tell Me Why Didn't Mummies Have Brains? And More about History. 2004. (Illus.). 32p. (J). pap. *(978-1-84458-059-0(8)*, Pavilion Children's Books) Pavilion Bks.

Taylor, Trace. One World Single Copy Set. 2010. pap. 46.22 *(978-0-7613-7046-8(3))* American Reading Co.

Thunder from Above. (Illus.). 192p. (J). *(978-0-7835-0155-0(2))* Time-Life Education, Inc.

Timelines of World History. 2017. (World History Ser.). (ENG.). (J). 19.99 ***(978-0-7945-3921-4(1)***, Usborne) EDC Publishing.

Trembinski, Donna. Medieval Myths, Legends & Songs. 2005. (Medieval World Ser.). (ENG., Illus.). 32p. (J). (gr. 4-9). pap. *(978-0-7787-1391-3(1))* Crabtree Publishing Co.

Truth & Rumor [Capstone Sole Source]. 2010. (Truth & Rumors Ser.). 32p. lib. bdg. 106.60 *(978-1-4296-5886-7(X)*, Edge Bks.) Capstone Press of Coughlan Cos.

Turner, Tracey. Hard As Nails Kings & Queens. 2015. (Hard As Nails in History Ser.). (ENG., Illus.). 64p. (J). (gr. 3-6). lib. bdg. *(978-0-7787-1519-1(1))* Crabtree Publishing Co.

Turner, Tracey & Kindberg, Sally. The Comic Strip Big Fat Book of Knowledge. 2012. (ENG., Illus.). 288p. (J). (gr. 6-9). pap. 18.99 *(978-1-4088-0824-5(2)*, 9781408808245, Bloomsbury USA Childrens) Bloomsbury Publishing USA.

Turning Points in History, 4 vols., Set. Incl. Britannica Guide to Explorers & Explorations That Changed the Modern World. Pletcher, Kenneth. 352p. lib. bdg. 45.00 *(978-1-61530-028-0(7))*; Britannica Guide to Inventions That Changed the Modern World. Curley, Robert, ed. 392p. lib. bdg. 45.00 *(978-1-61530-020-4(1))*; (YA). (gr. 9-12). (Turning Points in History Ser.). (Illus.). 392p. 2009. Set lib. bdg. 180.00 *(978-1-61530-034-1(1))* Rosen Publishing Group, Inc., The.

Understanding History: Concepts & Skills. 2006. 19.50 net. *(978-1-56004-263-1(X))* Social Studies Schl. Service.

Understanding People in the Past, 5 bks., Set 1. (J). (gr. 4-6). lib. bdg. 135.35 *(978-1-57572-891-9(5))* Heinemann-Raintree.

Unexplained Phenomena, 4 vols., Set. Incl. Investigating Demons, Possessions, & Exorcisms. Gregson, Susan R. lib. bdg. 31.99 *(978-1-4296-4815-8(5))*; Investigating Hauntings, Ghosts, & Poltergeists. Doak, Robin S. lib. bdg. 31.99 *(978-1-4296-4814-1(7))*; Tracking Sea Monsters, Bigfoot, & Other Legendary Beasts. Yomtov, Nelson. lib. bdg. 31.99 *(978-1-4296-4817-2(1))*; (gr. 3-4). (Unexplained Phenomena Ser.). (ENG.). 48p. 2010. Set lib. bdg. 95.97 *(978-1-4296-4818-9(X))* Capstone Press of Coughlan Cos.

Unglik, Richard. Adventures in History. 2016. (Playmobil Ser.). (ENG., Illus.). 96p. (J). (gr. 1-7). 19.95 *(978-1-63322-185-7(7)*, Walter Foster Jr) Quarto Publishing Group USA.

Unusual Histories, 1 vol. 2010. (Unusual Histories Ser.). (ENG.). 48p. (gr. 3-4). lib. bdg. 63.98 *(978-1-4296-4793-9(0))* Capstone Press of Coughlan Cos.

Van Loon, Hendrik Willem. The Story of Mankind. 2006. 31.95 *(978-1-59605-956-6(7)*, Cosimo Classics) Cosimo, Inc.

—The Story of Mankind. 2007. 382p. pap. 25.99 *(978-1-4346-3848-9(0))*; (ENG.). 412p. pap. 28.99 *(978-1-4346-3847-2(2))* Creative Media Partners, LLC.

—The Story of Mankind. 2003. xxiv, 548p. pap. 29.00 *(978-0-7581-9568-5(0))* Textbook Pubs.

Van Loon, Hendrik Willem, et al. The Story of Mankind. 2013. (Liveright Classics Ser.: 0). (ENG., Illus.). 736p. (gr. 5-9). 35.00 *(978-0-87140-715-3(9)*, 40715) Liveright Publishing Corp.

Visions of History SPICE. 115p. (YA). (gr. 5-9). spiral bd., tchr.'s planning gde. ed. 39.95 *(978-0-382-40952-3(3))* Cobblestone Publishing Co.

Visions of History SPICE: Grades 5-9. 115p. (YA). (gr. 5-9). tchr. ed. 48.95 *(978-0-382-40953-0(1))* Cobblestone Publishing Co.

A Visual History of the World. 2016. (Visual History of the World Ser.). 00096p. (YA). (gr. 8-8). 259.70 *(978-1-4994-6561-7(0)*, Rosen Young Adult) Rosen Publishing Group, Inc., The.

Welch, Laura & Hodge, Bodie, eds. Big Book of History: A 15' Fold-Out Time-line from Creation to Modern Computers. 2011. (J). lib. bdg. 21.99 *(978-0-89051-623-2(5))* Master Bks.

A Wicked History, 4 vols., Set. Incl. Ivan the Terrible: Tsar of Death. Price, Sean. (gr. 3-7). 31.00 *(978-0-531-12597-7(1))*; Leopold II: Butcher of the Congo. Olson, Tod. (gr. 8-12). 31.00 *(978-0-531-18552-0(4))*; (Illus.). 128p. (J)., Children's Pr. 2008. Set lib. bdg. 120.00 o.p. *(978-0-531-20417-7(0)*, Watts, Franklin) Scholastic Library Publishing.

Wijesinha, Rajiva. Foundations of Modern Society. 2004. 75p. pap. *(978-81-7596-244-6(5))* Cambridge Univ. Pr. India Pvt. Ltd.

Williams, Brian. History. 2010. (What About... Ser.). (Illus.). 40p. (J). (gr. 6-8). lib. bdg. 19.95 *(978-1-4222-1559-3(8))* Mason Crest.

—History: Biggest & Best. 2004. (Biggest & Best Ser.). (Illus.). 40p. (J). pap. 7.95 *(978-1-84236-065-1(5))* Miles Kelly Publishing, Ltd. GBR. Dist: Independent Pubs. Group.

—Natural World: Biggest & Best. 2004. (Biggest & Best Ser.). (Illus.). 40p. (J). pap. 7.95 *(978-1-84236-061-3(2))* Miles Kelly Publishing, Ltd. GBR. Dist: Independent Pubs. Group.

—What about HIST. 2008. 40p. pap. *(978-1-84810-068-8(X))* Miles Kelly Publishing, Ltd.

—What about People & Places. 2008. 40p. pap. *(978-1-84810-072-5(8))* Miles Kelly Publishing, Ltd.

World Book, Inc Staff, contrib. by. Explore & Learn — People in Place & Time. 2008. (J). *(978-0-7166-3020-3(6))* World Bk., Inc.

World History - Patterns of Interaction: Reading Study Guide. 2003. (SPA.). (gr. 6-12). *(978-0-618-18291-6(8)*, 2-01372) Holt McDougal.

World History: Patterns of Interaction. 2005. (gr. 6-12). tchr. ed. *(978-0-618-37774-9(3)*, 2-00552) Holt McDougal.

World History: Patterns of Interaction: EEdition Plus Online. (gr. 6-12). 2005. *(978-0-618-40923-5(8)*, 2-00604) 2003. *(978-0-618-19415-5(0)*, 2-70057) Holt McDougal.

World History: Patterns of Interaction: EEdition Plus Online with purchase of print Pupil's Edition-1 Year. 2005. (gr. 6-12). *(978-0-618-40925-9(4)*, 2-00606) Holt McDougal.

World History: Patterns of Interaction: EEdition Plus Online with Purchase of Print Pupil's Edition-1 Year. 2003. (gr. 6-12). *(978-0-618-25863-5(9)*, 2-01416) Holt McDougal.

World History: Patterns of Interaction: Electronic Library of Primary Sources. (gr. 6-12). 2005. cd-rom *(978-0-618-42871-7(2)*, 2-00770) 2003. cd-rom *(978-0-618-18619-8(0)*, 2-01392) Holt McDougal.

World History: Patterns of Interaction: Reading Study Guide Answer Key. (gr. 6-12). 2005. *(978-0-618-40932-7(7)*, 2-00613) 2003. *(978-0-618-18288-6(8)*, 2-01370) Holt McDougal.

World History: Patterns of Interaction: World History: Patterns of Interaction Workbook Answer Key. 2005. (gr. 6-12). *(978-0-618-40939-6(4)*, 2-00620) Holt McDougal.

World History: Patterns of Interaction: World History Workbook Answer Key. 2003. (gr. 6-12). *(978-0-395-95208-5(5)*, 2-81094) Holt McDougal.

World View: A Global Study of Geography, History & Culture, Bk. 2. stu. ed. 21.95 *(978-0-916591-45-8(X))* Linmore Publishing, Inc.

Yomtov, Nel, et al. 24-Hour History, 1 vol. 2014. (24-Hour History Ser.). (ENG.). 48p. (gr. 3-5). lib. bdg. 166.60 *(978-1-4329-9297-2(X)*, NA-h) Heinemann-Raintree.

You Choose: Historical Eras Spring 2011. 2010. (You Choose: Historical Eras Ser.). (ENG.). 112p. (gr. 3-4). 63.98 *(978-1-4296-5982-6(3)*, You Choose Bks.) Capstone Press of Coughlan Cos.

You Choose: History. 2011. (You Choose: History Ser.). (ENG.). 112p. (gr. 3-4). pap. 1000.80 *(978-1-4296-6442-4(8)*, You Choose Bks.) Capstone Press of Coughlan Cos.

You Choose Assortment [Levy]. 2010. (You Choose Bks.). 37.56 *(978-1-4296-5882-9(7)*, You Choose Bks.) Capstone Press of Coughlan Cos.

You Choose Books [Capstone Sole Source]. 2010. (You Choose Bks.). 112p. 858.20 *(978-1-4296-5892-8(4)*, You Choose Bks.) Capstone Press of Coughlan Cos.

You Choose: Historical Eras. 2010. (You Choose: Historical Eras Ser.). (ENG.). 112p. (gr. 3-4). pap. 13.90 *(978-1-4296-6278-9(6)*, You Choose Bks.) Capstone Press of Coughlan Cos.

You Choose: Historical Eras Classroom Collection. 2011. (You Choose: Historical Eras Ser.). (ENG.). 112p. (gr. 3-4). pap. 250.20 *(978-1-4296-6443-1(6)*, You Choose Bks.) Capstone Press of Coughlan Cos.

You Choose: History. 2010. (You Choose: History Ser.). (ENG.). 112p. (gr. 3-4). 63.98 *(978-1-4296-5482-1(1)*, You Choose Bks.) Capstone Press of Coughlan Cos.

You Choose History Assortment [Levy]. 2010. (You Choose Bks.). pap. 6.95 *(978-1-4296-5182-0(2)*, You Choose Bks.) Capstone Press of Coughlan Cos.

You Choose Pack 1 [Levy]. 2010. (You Choose Bks.). pap. 3.13 *(978-1-4296-5830-0(4)*, You Choose Bks.) Capstone Press of Coughlan Cos.

You Choose Pack 2 [Levy]. 2010. (You Choose Bks.). pap. 3.13 *(978-1-4296-5831-7(2)*, You Choose Bks.) Capstone Press of Coughlan Cos.

You Choose Pack 3 [Levy]. 2010. (You Choose Bks.). pap. 3.13 *(978-1-4296-5832-4(0)*, You Choose Bks.) Capstone Press of Coughlan Cos.

You Choose Pack 4 [Levy]. 2010. (You Choose Bks.). pap. 3.13 *(978-1-4296-5833-1(9)*, You Choose Bks.) Capstone Press of Coughlan Cos.

You Choose Pack 5 [Levy]. 2010. (You Choose Bks.). pap. 3.13 *(978-1-4296-5834-8(7)*, You Choose Bks.) Capstone Press of Coughlan Cos.

You Choose Pack 6 [Levy]. 2010. (You Choose Bks.). pap. 3.13 *(978-1-4296-5835-5(5)*, You Choose Bks.) Capstone Press of Coughlan Cos.

Zacharias, Gary. Events That Changed the World - 1900-1920. 2003. (Illus.). 224p. pap. 22.45 *(978-0-7377-1753-2(X))* Cengage Gale.

19th Century Nationalism. 2003. spiral bd. 16.95 *(978-1-56004-171-9(4))* Social Studies Schl. Service.

WORLD ORGANIZATION

see International Organization

WORLD POLITICS

see also International Organization; International Relations; World War, 1939-1945

also names of countries with the subdivisions Foreign Relations and Politics and Government, e.g. United States—Foreign Relations; United States—Politics and Government

ABDO Publishing Company Staff. Essential Viewpoints Set 2 (Set Of 8) 2008. (Essential Viewpoints Set 2 Ser.: 8). (ENG., Illus.). 112p. (J). (gr. 6-12). lib. bdg. 285.12 *(978-1-60453-052-0(9)*, Essential Library) ABDO Publishing Co.

America's Role in a Changing World. 2010. (Global Connections Ser.). (Illus.). 120p. (gr. 5-8). 35.00 *(978-1-60413-287-8(6)*, Chelsea Hse.) Facts On File, Inc.

Aronson, Marc. The Real Revolution: The Global Story of American Independence. 2005. (ENG., Illus.). 256p. (YA). (gr. 7-12). 22.00 *(978-0-618-18179-7(2))* Houghton Mifflin Harcourt Publishing Co.

Baker, Lawrence W. Cold War Reference Library Cumulative Index. 2003. (Cold War Reference Library). (ENG.). 85p. (J). 5.00 *(978-0-7876-7667-4(5)*, UXL) Cengage Gale.

—Immigration & Migration Reference. 2004. (US Immigration & Migration Reference Library). (ENG.). (J). 5.00 *(978-0-7876-7734-3(5)*, UXL) Cengage Gale.

Beyer, Mark. Nuclear Weapons & the Cold War. (Library of Weapons of Mass Destruction Ser.). 64p. 2009. (gr. 5-5). 58.50 *(978-1-60853-953-6(9))* 2005. (Illus.). (J). lib. bdg. 31.95 *(978-1-4042-0290-0(0))* Rosen Publishing Group, Inc., The.

Block, Marta Segal. Graphing Global Politics, 1 vol. 2010. (Real World Data Ser.). (ENG., Illus.). 32p. (gr. 3-5). lib. bdg. 29.99 *(978-1-4329-2624-3(1)*, NA-h) Heinemann-Raintree.

Byers, Ann. The Legacy of the Cold War. 2017. (J). ***(978-1-5026-2865-7(1))*** Cavendish Square Publishing.

Cotugno, Megan. Real World Data, 4 vols., Set. Incl. Graphing Natural Disasters. Somervill, Barbara A. pap. 8.95 *(978-1-4329-2631-1(4))*; Graphing War & Conflict. Solway, Andrew. pap. 8.95 *(978-1-4329-2629-8(2))*; (Illus.). (gr. 3-5). (Real World Data Ser.). (ENG.). 32p. 2010. Set pap. 17.90 *(978-1-4329-2634-2(9))*; Set lib. bdg. 239.92 *(978-1-4329-2625-0(X))* Heinemann-Raintree. (NA-h).

Crawford, Steve. Cold War. 2010. (FAYFT: Modern Military History Ser.). 64p. (gr. 4-10). 39.95 *(978-1-933834-52-8(8))* Brown Bear Bks.

Day, Meredith, ed. The Cold War. 2016. (Political & Diplomatic History of the Modern World Ser.). 224p. (J). (gr. 10-10). 46.00 *(978-1-68048-358-1(7))* Rosen Publishing Group, Inc., The.

DeMarco, Neil & Aylett, J. F. Cold War & After. 2nd rev. ed. 2005. (Illus.). 64p. pap. 32.50 *(978-0-340-81479-6(9))* Hodder Education Group GBR. Dist: Trans-Atlantic Pubns., Inc.

Duling, Kaitlyn. Nuclear Proliferation, the Military-Industrial Complex, & the Arms Race. 2017. (J). ***(978-1-5026-2730-8(2))*** Cavendish Square Publishing.

Egan, Tracie. Weapons of Mass Destruction & North Korea. (Library of Weapons of Mass Destruction Ser.). 64p. 2009. (gr. 5-5). 58.50 *(978-1-60853-961-1(X))* 2004. (Illus.). (J). lib. bdg. 31.95 *(978-1-4042-0296-2(X))* Rosen Publishing Group, Inc., The.

Frankfeldt, Gwen & Fleischman, Paul. Dateline - Troy. Frankfeldt, Gwen & Morrow, Glenn, illus. 2006. (ENG.). 80p. (J). (gr. 7-10). pap. 8.99 *(978-0-7636-3084-3(5))* Candlewick Pr.

Gale Editors, ed. Worldmark Conflict & Diplomacy: 2 Volume Set, 2 vols. 2014. (Worldmark Conflict & Diplomacy Ser.). (ENG.). 1000p. 329.00 *(978-1-57302-726-7(X))* Cengage Gale.

George, Enzo. The Cold War. 2015. (Primary Sources in U. S. History Ser.). (ENG., Illus.). 48p. (J). (gr. 4-4). 31.36 *(978-1-5026-0498-9(1))* Cavendish Square Publishing.

Gottfried, Ted. The Cold War. Reim, Melanie, illus. 2003. (Rise & Fall of the Soviet Union Ser.). (ENG.). 160p. (gr. 7-12). lib. bdg. 29.20 *(978-0-7613-2560-4(3)*, Twenty-First Century Bks.) Lerner Publishing Group.

Grahame-Smith, Deborah, contrib. by. Countdown to Catastrophe. 2010. (World War Ii Ser.). 128p. (gr. 6-9). 35.64 *(978-0-7614-4944-7(2))* Marshall Cavendish GBR. Dist: Marshall Cavendish Corp.

Grant, R. G. The Great Depression. 2005. (How Did It Happen? Ser.). (ENG., Illus.). 48p. (YA). (gr. 7-10). lib. bdg. 32.10 *(978-1-59018-606-0(0)*, Lucent Bks.) Cengage Gale.

Grapes, Bryan J. Events That Changed the World - 1980-2000. 2003. (EVENTS THAT CHANGED the WRLD Ser.). (ENG., Illus.). 187p. lib. bdg. 38.45 *(978-0-7377-1760-0(2))* Cengage Gale.

The Great Depression 1929-1938. 2010. (Discovering U. S. History Ser.). (Illus.). 136p. (gr. 5-8). 35.00 *(978-1-60413-357-8(0)*, Chelsea Hse.) Facts On File, Inc.

Gunderson, Cory Gideon. The Need for Oil. 2003. (World in Conflict-the Middle East Ser.). 32p. (gr. 4-8). 27.07 *(978-1-59197-417-8(8)*, Abdo & Daughters) ABDO Publishing Co.

Hanes, Sharon M., et al. Cold War: Almanac, 2 vols. 2003. (Cold War Reference Library). (Illus.). (J). 200p. 55.00 *(978-0-7876-7662-9(4))*; *(978-0-7876-9087-8(2))*; (ENG., 376p. lib. bdg. 191.00 *(978-0-7876-9089-2(9))* Cengage Gale. (UXL).

—Cold War - Primary Sources. 2003. (Cold War Reference Library). (ENG., Illus.). 400p. (J). 106.00 *(978-0-7876-7666-7(7)*, UXL) Cengage Gale.

—Cold War Reference Library: Includes Cumulative Index, 5.0. Incl. Cold War: Almanac. 200p. 55.00 *(978-0-7876-7662-9(4))*; Cold War: Biographies. 474p. 191.00 *(978-0-7876-7663-6(2))*; Cold War - Primary Sources. 400p. 106.00 *(978-0-7876-7666-7(7))*; (J). (Cold War Reference Library). (ENG., Illus.). 800p. 2003. Set lib. bdg. 458.00 *(978-0-7876-7609-4(8)*, UXL) Cengage Gale.

Harrison, Paul. The Cold War. 2005. (How Did It Happen? Ser.). (ENG., Illus.). 48p. (YA). (gr. 7-10). lib. bdg. 32.10 *(978-1-59018-603-9(6)*, Lucent Bks.) Cengage Gale.

—Why Did the Cold War Happen? 2010. (Moments in History Ser.). 48p. (ENG.). (J). (gr. 6-8). pap. 14.05 *(978-1-4339-4167-2(8)*, Gareth Stevens Secondary Library); (Illus.). (YA). (gr. 5-9). lib. bdg. 31.95 *(978-1-4339-4166-5(X))* Stevens, Gareth Publishing LLLP.

Hasan, Tahara. Anthrax Attacks Around the World. (Terrorist Attacks Ser.). 64p. 2009. (gr. 5-5). 58.50 *(978-1-60853-307-7(7))* 2005. (Illus.). (YA). (gr. 7-12). lib. bdg. 31.95 *(978-0-8239-3859-9(X))* Rosen Publishing Group, Inc., The.

Johnson, Cynthia. Worldmark Conflict & Diplomacy. 2014. (J). *(978-1-57302-727-4(8))* Cengage Gale.

Levering, Ralph B. The Cold War, 1945-1991. Eisenstadt, Abraham S. & Franklin, John Hope, eds. 2003. (American History Ser.). (Illus.). 200p. (J). (gr. 11-12). pap. 13.95 *(978-0-88295-912-2(3))* Davidson, Harlan Inc.

Link, Theodore. Communism: A Primary Source Analysis. 2009. (Primary Sources of Political Systems Ser.). 64p. (gr. 5-8). 58.50 *(978-1-60851-835-7(3))* Rosen Publishing Group, Inc., The.

MacDonald, Fiona & Weaver, Clare. Human Rights. 2003. (World Issues Ser.). (Illus.). 57p. (J). (gr. 5-18). lib. bdg. 29.95 *(978-1-931983-82-2(8))* Chrysalis Education.

Marciniak, Kristin. The Revolutionary War: Why They Fought. 2015. (What Were They Fighting For? Ser.). (ENG., Illus.). 64p. (gr. 5-9). lib. bdg. 34.65 *(978-0-7565-5169-8(2))* Compass Point Bks.

Mason, Paul. Did Anything Good Come Out of the Cold War?, 01 vols., 1. 2016. (Innovation Through Adversity Ser.). (ENG.). 48p. (J). 30.25 *(978-1-5081-7066-2(5)*, Rosen Young Adult) Rosen Publishing Group, Inc., The.

Maybury, Richard J. World War II: The Rest of the Story & How It Affects You Today, 1930 to September 11 2001. Williams, Jane A., ed. rev. ed. 2003. ("Uncle Eric" Bk.: 11). (ENG., Illus.). 349p. pap. 19.95 *(978-0-942617-43-6(6))* Bluestocking Pr.

McCarthy, Rose. Dictatorship: A Primary Source Analysis. 2009. (Primary Sources of Political Systems Ser.). 64p. (gr. 5-8). 58.50 *(978-1-60851-837-1(X))* Rosen Publishing Group, Inc., The.

Nelson, Sheila. The Birth of the un, Decolonization & Building Strong Nations, Vol. 10. Russett, Bruce, ed. 2015. (United Nations: Leadership & Challenges in a Global World Ser.). (Illus.). 88p. (J). (gr. 7). lib. bdg. 24.95 *(978-1-4222-3430-3(4))* Mason Crest.

—Decolonization: Dismantling Empires & Building Independence. 2008. (United Nations Ser.). (Illus.). 88p. (YA). (gr. 5-18). lib. bdg. 21.95 *(978-1-4222-0066-7(3))* Mason Crest.

Olson, Steven P. The International Atomic Energy Agency. (Library of Weapons of Mass Destruction Ser.). 64p. 2009. (gr. 5-5). 58.50 *(978-1-60853-957-4(1))* 2004. (Illus.). (J). lib. bdg. 31.95 *(978-1-4042-0294-8(3))* Rosen Publishing Group, Inc., The.

Perritano, John. Education, Poverty, & Inequality. 2017. (Illus.). 64p. (J). *(978-1-4222-3634-5(X))* Mason Crest.

Phillips, Tracy A. Weapons of Mass Destruction: The Threat of Chemical, Biological, & Nuclear Weapons. 2007. (Issues in Focus Today Ser.). (Illus.). 104p. (J). (gr. 6-12). lib. bdg. 33.27 *(978-0-7660-2685-8(X))* Enslow Pubs., Inc.

Piddock, Charles. The Cold War. 2016. (Illus.). 48p. (J). *(978-1-5105-1282-5(9))* SmartBook Media, Inc.

Porterfield, Jason. Communism: A Primary Source Analysis. 2003. (Primary Sources of Political Systems Ser.). (Illus.). 64p. (YA). (gr. 5-9). 31.95 *(978-0-8239-4517-7(0))* Rosen Publishing Group, Inc., The.

Richardson, Erik. NATO, the Warsaw Pact, & the Iron Curtain. 2017. (J). ***(978-1-5026-2727-8(2))*** Cavendish Square Publishing.

Riggs, Kate. The End of the Cold War. 2016. (Illus.). 48p. (J). *(978-1-60818-748-5(9)*, Creative Education) Creative Co., The.

Rivera, Sheila. Weapons of Mass Destruction. 2003. (World in Conflict-the Middle East Ser.). 32p. (gr. 4-8). 27.07 *(978-1-59197-421-5(6)*, Abdo & Daughters) ABDO Publishing Co.

Roxburgh, Ellis. John F. Kennedy vs. Nikita Khrushchev. 2015. (History's Greatest Rivals Ser.). (ENG., Illus.). 48p. (J). (gr. 6-8). lib. bdg. 31.95 *(978-1-4824-2221-4(2))* Stevens, Gareth Publishing LLLP.

Sheehan, Sean. The Cold War. 2003. (Questioning History Ser.). (Illus.). 64p. (J). (gr. 5). lib. bdg. 28.50 *(978-1-58340-266-5(7))* Black Rabbit Bks.

Sherman, Josepha. The Cold War. 2004. (Chronicle of America's Wars Ser.). (Illus.). 96p. (J). (gr. 5-12). 27.93 *(978-0-8225-0150-3(3))* Lerner Publishing Group.

Spalding, Frank. Nuclear Annihilation. 2010. (Doomsday Scenarios: Separating Fact from Fiction Ser.). 64p. (YA). (ENG.). pap. 12.95 *(978-1-4358-8522-6(8)*, Rosen Reference); (gr. 5-8). E-Book 58.50 *(978-1-4488-1208-0(9))*; (Illus.). (gr. 5-8). lib. bdg. 31.95 *(978-1-4358-3560-3(3)*, Rosen Reference) Rosen Publishing Group, Inc., The.

Stanley, George Edward. An Emerging World Power, 1900-1929. 2005. (Primary Source History of the United States Ser.). (Illus.). 48p. (gr. 5-12). pap. 14.05 *(978-0-8368-5837-2(9))*; lib. bdg. 31.00 *(978-0-8368-5828-0(X))* Stevens, Gareth Publishing LLLP. (Gareth Stevens Secondary Library).

Stites, Bill. Democracy: A Primary Source Analysis. (Primary Sources of Political Systems Ser.). 64p. (gr. 5-8). 2009. 58.50 *(978-1-60851-836-4(1))* 2003. (Illus.). (YA). lib. bdg. 31.95 *(978-0-8239-4518-4(9))* Rosen Publishing Group, Inc., The.

Strum, Richard M. Causes of the American Revolution. 2005. (Road to War Ser.). (Illus.). 64p. (J). pap. 12.95 *(978-1-59556-005-6(X))*; (gr. 4-18). lib. bdg. 22.95 *(978-1-59556-001-8(7))* OTTN Publishing.

Van Dijk, Ruud. The Making of the Modern World: 1945 to the Present: Governance & the Quest for Security, Vol. 9. 2016. (Making of the Modern World: 1945 to the Present Ser.: Vol. 9). (ENG., Illus.). 64p. (J). (gr. 7-12). 23.95 *(978-1-4222-3638-3(2))* Mason Crest.

Wilson, John. Failed Hope: The Story of the Lost Peace. 2012. (Stories of Canada Ser.: 14). (ENG., Illus.). 120p. (J). pap. 18.99 *(978-1-4597-0345-2(6))* Dundurn CAN. Dist: Ingram Publisher Services.

—Failed Hope: The Story of the Lost Peace (Large Print 16pt) 2013. 180p. pap. *(978-1-4596-6314-5(4))* ReadHowYouWant.com, Ltd.

WORLD POLITICS—FICTION

Levithan, David. Love Is the Higher Law. 2010. (ENG.). 176p. (YA). (gr. 7). pap. 9.99 *(978-0-375-83469-1(9)*, Knopf Bks. for Young Readers) Random Hse. Children's Bks.

O'Donnell, Liam. Power Play, 1 vol. Deas, Mike, illus. 2011. (Graphic Guides). (ENG.). 64p. (J). (gr. 3-7). pap. 9.95 *(978-1-55469-069-5(2))* Orca Bk. Pubs. USA.

WORLD RECORDS

Adamson, Heather, et al. Wow! 2013. (Wow! Ser.). (ENG.). 24p. (gr. k-1). lib. bdg. 79.95 *(978-1-4765-0465-0(2)*, Pebble Plus) Capstone Press of Coughlan Cos.

Adamson, Thomas K. & Adamson, Heather. The World's Tallest House of Cards & Other Number Records, 1 vol. 2013. (Wow! Ser.). (ENG.). 24p. (gr. k-1). lib. bdg. 26.65 *(978-1-4765-0240-3(4)*, Pebble Plus) Capstone Press of Coughlan Cos.

Amazing Me! for Boys: A Book of Your Own World Records. 2014. (ENG.). 96p. (J). (gr. 3-7). pap. 9.99 *(978-0-7944-3217-1(4)*, Reader's Digest Children's Bks.) Studio Fun International.

Amazing Me! for Girls: A Book of Your Own World Records. 2014. (ENG.). 96p. (J). (gr. 3-7). pap. 9.99 *(978-0-7944-3216-4(6)*, Reader's Digest Children's Bks.) Studio Fun International.

Brill, Calista. Guinness World Records: Wacky & Wild! 2016. (J). lib. bdg. 24.50 *(978-0-606-38194-9(5))* Turtleback Bks.

Brill, Calista & Glass, Calliope. Officially Amazing - Extraordinary & Outrageous! 2016. (Guinness World Records Ser.). (Illus.). 176p. (J). (gr. 3-7). pap. 12.99 *(978-0-06-234176-1(6))* HarperCollins Pubs.

Burnham, Molly B. Almost a World Record Breaker. 2016. (Teddy Mars Ser.: 1). (J). lib. bdg. 17.20 *(978-0-606-38132-1(5))* Turtleback Bks.

Finnegan, Delphine. Guinness World Records: Remarkable Robots. 2017. (I Can Read Level 2 Ser.). 32p. (J). (gr. -1-3). pap. 3.99 *(978-0-06-234191-4(X))* HarperCollins Pubs.

Forest, Christopher, et al. Library of Weird. 2015. (Library of Weird Ser.). (ENG.). 32p. (gr. 3-4). lib. bdg. 167.94 *(978-1-4914-2550-3(4)*, Edge Bks.) Capstone Press of Coughlan Cos.

Gilpin, Daniel. Record-Breaking Buildings. 2012. (Record Breakers Ser.). 32p. (J). lib. bdg. 26.50 *(978-1-4488-5288-8(9)*, PowerKids Pr.) Rosen Publishing Group, Inc., The.

—Record-Breaking Cars. 2012. (Record Breakers Ser.). (Illus.). 32p. (J). lib. bdg. 26.50 *(978-1-4488-5289-5(7)*, PowerKids Pr.) Rosen Publishing Group, Inc., The.

Gilpin, Daniel & Pang, Alex. Record Breakers. 2010. (Machines Close-Up Ser.). 32p. (J). (gr. 4-7). 28.50 *(978-1-60870-113-1(1))* Marshall Cavendish Corp.

Grove, Tim. First Flight Around the World: The Adventures of the American Fliers Who Won the Race. 2015. (ENG., Illus.). 96p. (J). (gr. 5-9). 21.95 *(978-1-4197-1482-5(1))* Abrams, Inc.

Guinness Editors. Guinness World Records 2016, Gamers Edition. 2015. lib. bdg. 26.95 *(978-0-606-38494-0(4))* Turtleback Bks.

Hansen, Grace. World Records to Wow You!, 1 vol. 2014. (Seeing Is Believing Ser.). (ENG., Illus.). 24p. (J). lib. bdg. 28.50 *(978-1-62970-736-5(8))* ABDO Publishing Co.

Herndon, Ryan, compiled by. 3-D Extreme! 2006. (Illus.). 31p. (J). pap. *(978-0-439-79190-8(1))* Scholastic, Inc.

Hirschmann, Kris & Herndon, Ryan, compiled by. Guinness World Records. 2011. (Illus.). 80p. (J). *(978-0-545-30851-9(8))* Scholastic, Inc.

—Guinness World Records: Records of Overwhelming Size. 2007. (Illus.). 90p. (J). pap. *(978-0-439-89829-4(3))* Scholastic, Inc.

—Guinness World Records, up Close. 2007. (Illus.). 47p. *(978-0-439-89828-7(5))* Scholastic, Inc.

Lemke, Donald. Guinness World Records: Super Humans! 2016. (J). lib. bdg. 24.50 *(978-0-606-38193-2(7))* Turtleback Bks.

—Guinness World Records: Man-Made Marvels! 2016. (Guinness World Records Ser.). 176p. (J). (gr. 3-7). pap. 12.99 *(978-0-06-234180-8(4))* HarperCollins Pubs.

—Officially Amazing - Super Humans! 2016. (Guinness World Records Ser.). (Illus.). 176p. (J). (gr. 3-7). pap. 12.99 *(978-0-06-234173-0(1))* HarperCollins Pubs.

Mattern, Joanne & Herndon, Ryan, compiled by. Guinness World Records: Extraordinary Records of Unusual Facts & Feats. 2005. (Illus.). 90p. (J). pap. *(978-0-439-79192-2(8))* Scholastic, Inc.

McCollum, Sean. The World's Most Daring Stunts. 2016. (World Record Breakers Ser.). (ENG., Illus.). 32p. (gr. 3-4). lib. bdg. 27.99 *(978-1-4914-8179-0(X)*, Edge Bks.) Capstone Press of Coughlan Cos.

Meister, Cari. Guinness World Records: Daring Dogs. 2016. (I Can Read Level 2 Ser.). 32p. (J). (gr. -1-3). pap. 3.99 *(978-0-06-234182-2(0))* HarperCollins Pubs.

—Guinness World Records: Wacky Wheels. 2016. (I Can Read Level 2 Ser.). (Illus.). 32p. (J). (gr. -1-3). pap. 3.99 *(978-0-06-234185-3(5))* HarperCollins Pubs.

Mitchell, Susan K. The Longest Bridges. 2007. (Megastructures Ser.). (Illus.). 32p. (gr. 5-8). lib. bdg. 26.00 *(978-0-8368-8364-0(0))* Stevens, Gareth Publishing LLLP.

Morse, Jenifer Corr. Scholastic Book of World Records. 2008. (Scholastic Book of World Records Ser.). (Illus.). 304p. (J). (gr. 4-7). 17.65 *(978-0-7569-8839-5(X))* Perfection Learning Corp.

—Scholastic Book of World Records, 2008. 2007. (Illus.). 304p. (J). *(978-1-4287-5691-5(4)*, Scholastic Reference) Scholastic, Inc.

—Scholastic Book of World Records 2014. 2013. (ENG.). 320p. (J). (gr. 3-7). pap. 10.99 *(978-0-545-56262-1(7)*, Scholastic Paperbacks) Scholastic, Inc.

—Scholastic Book of World Records 2015. 2014. (ENG.). 320p. (J). (gr. 3-7). pap. 10.99 *(978-0-545-67950-3(8)*, Scholastic Paperbacks) Scholastic, Inc.

—Scholastic Book of World Records 2016. 2015. lib. bdg. 22.10 *(978-0-606-37751-5(4))* Turtleback Bks.

Price, Sean Stewart, et al. World Record Breakers. 2016. (World Record Breakers Ser.). (ENG.). 32p. (gr. 3-4). 111.96 *(978-1-4914-8192-9(7)*, Edge Bks.) Capstone Press of Coughlan Cos.

Ripley Entertainment. Life in the Fast Lane. 2010. (Ripley's Believe It or Not Ser.). 36p. (YA). (gr. 3-18). lib. bdg. 19.95 *(978-1-4222-1538-6(5))* Mason Crest.

Ripley's Believe It Or Not! Staff. Awesome Feats. 2012. (Ripley's Disbelief & Shock Ser.). 36p. (J). (gr. 3-4). 19.95 *(978-1-4222-2562-2(3))* Mason Crest.

—World Wonders. 2012. (Ripley's Disbelief & Shock Ser.). 36p. (J). (gr. 3-4). 19.95 *(978-1-4222-2576-9(3))* Mason Crest.

Roberts, Christa. Guinness World Records: Amazing Body Records! 100 Mind-Blowing Body Records from Around the World! 2016. (J). lib. bdg. 16.00 *(978-0-606-38192-5(9))* Turtleback Bks.

—Guinness World Records: Incredible Animals: Amazing Animals & Their Awesome Feats! 2016. (J). lib. bdg. 16.00 *(978-0-606-38191-8(0))* Turtleback Bks.

—Guinness World Records: Awesome Entertainers! 2016. (Guinness World Records Ser.). (Illus.). 112p. (J). (gr. 1-5). pap. 5.99 *(978-0-06-234169-3(3))* HarperCollins Pubs.

—Paws, Claws, & More: Amazing Animals & Their Awesome Feats! 2016. (Guinness World Records Ser.). 112p. (J). (gr. 1-5). pap. 5.99 *(978-0-06-234167-9(7))* HarperCollins Pubs.

Rooney, Anne. Space Record Breakers. 2014. (ENG., Illus.). 128p. (J). (gr. 3). pap. 14.95 *(978-1-78312-072-7(X))* Carlton Bks., Ltd. GBR. Dist: Sterling Publishing Co., Inc.

Rustad, Martha E. H. World's Longest Snake & Other Animal Records. 2013. (Wow! Ser.). (ENG.). 24p. (gr. k-1). 26.65 *(978-1-4765-0258-8(7)*, Pebble Plus) Capstone Press of Coughlan Cos.

Webster, Christy. Guinness World Records: Biggest & Smallest! 2016. (J). lib. bdg. 24.50 *(978-0-606-38195-6(3))* Turtleback Bks.

—Guinness World Records: Fun with Food. 2016. (I Can Read Level 2 Ser.). (Illus.). 32p. (J). (gr. -1-3). pap. 3.99 *(978-0-06-234188-4(X))* HarperCollins Pubs.

—Officially Amazing - Biggest & Smallest! 2016. (Guinness World Records Ser.). (Illus.). 176p. (J). (gr. 3-7). pap. 12.99 *(978-0-06-234178-5(2))* HarperCollins Pubs.

WORLD SERIES (BASEBALL)

Cho, Alan. World Series. (J). 2012. *(978-1-61913-063-0(7))* 2012. pap. *(978-1-61913-625-0(2))* 2007. (Illus.). 32p. (gr. 4-6). lib. bdg. 26.00 *(978-1-59036-699-8(9))* 2007. (Illus.). 32p. (gr. 4-7). per. 9.95 *(978-1-59036-700-1(6))* Weigl Pubs., Inc.

Doeden, Matt. The World Series: Baseball's Biggest Stage. 2014. (Spectacular Sports Ser.). (Illus.). 64p. (gr. 5-12). lib. bdg. 33.27 *(978-1-4677-1896-7(3)*, Millbrook Pr.) Lerner Publishing Group.

Garcia, Tom & Naga, Karun. Daddy's Heroes: Gibby's Homer: the 1988 World Series. Donnelly, Jenifer, illus. 2007. (1988 World Ser.). 32p. (J). (gr. -1-3). pap. 9.95 *(978-0-9792111-0-2(7))* Daddy's Heroes, Inc.

Herman, Gail & dePaola, Tomie. What Is the World Series? Anderson, Scott, illus. 2015. (What Was? Ser.). (ENG.). 112p. (J). (gr. 3-7). 5.99 *(978-0-448-48406-8(4)*, Penguin Workshop) Penguin Young Readers Group.

Hetrick, Hans. The World Series: All about Pro Baseball's Biggest Event. 2012. (Winner Takes All Ser.). (ENG.). 32p. (gr. 3-4). pap. 41.70 *(978-1-4296-9445-2(9))*; (Illus.). lib. bdg. 27.99 *(978-1-4296-6574-2(2))* Capstone Press of Coughlan Cos.

Sandler, Michael. David Eckstein & the St. Louis Cardinals: 2006 World Series. 2008. (World Series Superstars). (Illus.). 24p. (J). (gr. 1-4). lib. bdg. 22.61 *(978-1-59716-636-2(7))* Bearport Publishing Co., Inc.

—Mike Lowell & the Boston Red Sox: 2007 World Series. 2008. (World Series Superstars). (Illus.). 24p. (J). (gr. 1-4). lib. bdg. 22.61 *(978-1-59716-739-0(8)*, 1284374) Bearport Publishing Co., Inc.

—Randy Johnson & the Arizona Diamondbacks: 2001 World Series. 2008. (World Series Superstars). (Illus.). 24p. (J). (gr. 1-4). lib. bdg. 22.61 *(978-1-59716-638-6(3))* Bearport Publishing Co., Inc.

—Troy Glaus & the Anaheim Angels: 2002 World Series. 2008. (World Series Superstars). (Illus.). 24p. (J). (gr. 1-4). lib. bdg. 22.61 *(978-1-59716-640-9(5))* Bearport Publishing Co., Inc.

Winters, Jaime. For the Win: The World Series. 2015. (ENG., Illus.). 32p. (J). *(978-0-7787-1477-4(2))* Crabtree Publishing Co.

WORLD WAR, 1914-1918

ABDO Publishing. Essential Library of World War I. 2016. (Essential Library of World War I Ser.: 10). (ENG.). 112p. (J). (gr. 6-12). lib. bdg. 356.40 *(978-1-62403-920-1(0)*, Essential Library) ABDO Publishing Co.

ABDO Publishing Company Staff. World War I. 2004. (World War I Ser.). (gr. 4-8). 162.42 *(978-1-57765-911-2(2)*, Abdo & Daughters) ABDO Publishing Co.

Adams, Simon. World War I. 2014. (DK Eyewitness Bks.). (ENG.). 72p. (J). (gr. 3-7). pap. 9.99 *(978-1-4654-2058-9(4)*, DK Children) Dorling Kindersley Publishing, Inc.

Adamson, Thomas K. World War I. 2015. (Wars in U. S. History Ser.). (ENG.). 32p. (J). (gr. 2-5). 28.50 *(978-1-63143-708-3(9)*, 208541) Child's World, Inc., The.

Baldwin, Douglas & Kissock, Heather. World War I. 2010. (Illus.). 48p. *(978-1-55388-719-5(0))*; pap. *(978-1-55388-723-2(9))* Weigl Educational Pubs. Ltd.

Barber, Nicola. World War I, 1 vol. 2012. (Living Through... Ser.). (ENG.). 80p. (gr. 7-8). lib. bdg. 37.32 *(978-1-4329-6001-8(6))* Heinemann-Raintree.

Barton, Chris. Dazzle Ships: World War I & the Art of Confusion. Ngai, Victo, illus. 2017. (ENG.). 36p. (J). (gr. 2-5). lib. bdg. 19.99 ***(978-1-5124-1014-3(4)***, Millbrook Pr.) Lerner Publishing Group.

Batten, Jack. The War to End All Wars: The Story of World War I. 2009. (ENG., Illus.). 160p. (J). (gr. 5-18). 22.95 *(978-0-88776-879-8(2)*, Tundra Bks.) Tundra Bks. CAN. Dist: Penguin Random Hse. LLC.

Bausum, Ann. Stubby the War Dog: The True Story of World War I's Bravest Dog. 2014. (ENG., Illus.). 80p. (J). (gr. 5). 17.99 *(978-1-4263-1486-5(8)*, National Geographic Children's Bks.) National Geographic Society.

Bearce, Stephanie. World War I: Spies, Secret Missions, & Hidden Facts from World War I. 2014. (Top Secret Files of History Ser.: 0). (ENG.). 125p. (J). (gr. 4-7). pap. 8.95 *(978-1-61821-241-2(9))* Prufrock Pr.

Beller, Susan Provost. The Doughboys over There: Soldiering in World War I. 2007. (Soldiers on the Battlefront Ser.). (ENG., Illus.). 112p. (J). (gr. 6-8). lib. bdg. 33.26 *(978-0-8225-6295-5(2))* Lerner Publishing Group.

Benjamin, Andrew. World War I: The War to End All Wars. 2014. (J). pap. *(978-1-62712-862-9(X))* Cavendish Square Publishing.

Benjamin, Andrew & George, Enzo. World War I: The War to End All Wars. 2014. (Voices of War Ser.). 48p. (J). (gr. 4-6). lib. bdg. 31.36 *(978-1-62712-861-2(1))* Cavendish Square Publishing.

Brocklehurst, Ruth & Brook, Henry. First World War. Chisholm, Jane, ed. 2007. (World Wars Ser.). (Illus.). 128p. (J). (gr. 4-7). 19.99 *(978-0-7945-1455-6(3)*, Usborne) EDC Publishing.

—The Usborne Introduction to the First World War. 2007. (Illus.). 128p. (J). pap. *(978-0-545-03901-7(0))* Scholastic, Inc.

Brouwer, Sigmund. Innocent Heroes. 2017. (ENG., Illus.). 208p. (J). (gr. 4-7). 16.99 *(978-1-101-91846-3(2)*, Tundra Bks.) Tundra Bks. CAN. Dist: Penguin Random Hse. LLC.

Burgan, Michael. Spies of World War I: An Interactive History Adventure. 2015. (You Choose: Spies Ser.). (ENG., Illus.). 112p. (gr. 3-4). pap. 6.95 *(978-1-4914-5933-1(6)*, You Choose Bks.) Capstone Press of Coughlan Cos.

—Split History of World War I. 2013. (Perspectives Flip Bks.). (ENG.). 64p. (gr. 5-6). 33.99 *(978-0-7565-4694-6(X))*; pap. 8.95 *(978-0-7565-4700-4(8))* Compass Point Bks. (CPB Grades 4-8).

Clarke, Gordon. Canada in World War I: Outstanding Victories Create a Nation. 2014. (ENG.). 48p. (J). *(978-0-7787-0327-3(4))* Crabtree Publishing Co.

Conway, John Richard. World War I: A MyReportLinks. Com Book. 2003. (U.S. Wars Ser.). (Illus.). 48p. (J). lib. bdg. 26.60 *(978-0-7660-5142-3(0))* Enslow Pubs., Inc.

Cooke, Tim. World War I on the Front Lines, 1 vol. 2014. (Life on the Front Lines Ser.). (ENG., Illus.). 32p. (gr. 3-4). 27.99 *(978-1-4914-0843-8(X)*, Edge Bks.) Capstone Press of Coughlan Cos.

Cox Cannons, Helen. The Remembrance Day & the Poppy. 2016. (Important Events in History Ser.). (ENG., Illus.). 24p. (gr. 1-3). lib. bdg. 23.32 *(978-1-4846-2707-5(5)*, Heinemann Read & Learn) Heinemann-Raintree.

Dell, Pamela. A World War I Timeline, 1 vol. 2014. (War Timelines Ser.). (ENG.). 48p. (gr. 4-6). lib. bdg. 34.65 *(978-1-4765-4159-4(0))* Capstone Press of Coughlan Cos.

Dickmann, Nancy. The Horrors of World War I. 2017. (Deadly History Ser.). (ENG.). 48p. (gr. 3-4). lib. bdg. 33.32 ***(978-1-4846-4168-2(X)***, Heinemann InfoSearch) Heinemann-Raintree.

Doeden, Matt. Weapons of World War I. 2017. (Weapons of War Ser.). (ENG.). 32p. (gr. 2-3). lib. bdg. 26.65 ***(978-1-5157-7907-0(6))*** Capstone Press of Coughlan Cos.

Dowswell, Paul. First World War - Internet Referenced. rev. ed. 2007. (True Stories Ser.). 137p. (J). pap. 4.99 *(978-0-7945-1979-7(2)*, Usborne) EDC Publishing.

—The Story of the First World War. 2014. (ENG., Illus.). 95p. (J). (gr. 4-7). pap. 10.99 *(978-0-7945-2974-1(7)*, Usborne) EDC Publishing.

—True Stories of the First World War. (True Adventure Stories Ser.). (Illus.). (J). 2004. 137p. (gr. 5). lib. bdg. 12.95 *(978-1-58086-652-1(2))* 2011. 144p. pap. 4.99 *(978-0-7945-0721-3(2))* EDC Publishing. (Usborne).

—War Stories. rev. ed. 2012. (True Stories Ser.). 432p. (J). pap. 12.99 *(978-0-7945-3221-5(7)*, Usborne) EDC Publishing.

Dowswell, Paul, et al. The World Wars: An Introduction to the First & Second World Wars. Chisholm, Jane, ed. 2007. (World Wars Ser.). (Illus.). 256p. (J). (gr. 4-7). 25.99 *(978-0-7945-1971-1(7)*, Usborne) EDC Publishing.

Endrulat, Harry & Innes, Stephanie. A Bear in War. Deines, Brian, illus. 2009. (ENG.). 40p. (J). (gr. k-3). *(978-1-55470-097-4(3))* Me to We.

Fein, Eric. Weapons, Gear, & Uniforms of World War I, 1 vol. 2012. (Equipped for Battle Ser.). (ENG.). 32p. (gr. 3-4). lib. bdg. 27.99 *(978-1-4296-7649-6(3)*, Edge Bks.) Capstone Press of Coughlan Cos.

Feldman, Ruth Tenzer. World War I. 2004. (Chronicle of America's Wars Ser.). (Illus.). 88p. (gr. 5-12). lib. bdg. 27.93 *(978-0-8225-0148-0(1))* Lerner Publishing Group.

First World War. 2013. (Ladybird Histories Ser.). (ENG., Illus.). 64p. (J). (gr. 2-4). pap. 13.99 ***(978-0-7232-7085-0(6))*** Penguin Bks., Ltd. GBR. Dist: Independent Pubs. Group.

Freedman, Russell. The War to End All Wars: World War I. (ENG., Illus.). 192p. (YA). (gr. 7). 2013. pap. 10.99 *(978-0-544-02171-6(1))* 2010. 22.00 *(978-0-547-02686-2(2))* Houghton Mifflin Harcourt Publishing Co.

Gail, Margaret. Moggie Grows up, 1939-1945. 2006. (ENG., Illus.). 74p. pap. *(978-0-7552-0227-0(9))* Authors OnLine, Ltd.

George, Enzo. World War I. 2015. (J). lib. bdg. *(978-1-62713-493-4(X))*; (ENG.). 48p. (gr. 4-4). lib. bdg. 31.36 *(978-1-5026-0252-7(0))* Cavendish Square Publishing.

Goodman, Michael. World War I Spies. 2015. (Illus.). 48p. (J). *(978-1-60818-602-0(4)*, Creative Education) Creative Co., The.

Goodman, Michael E. World War I Spies: Wartime Spies. 2016. (Wartime Spies Ser.). (ENG., Illus.). 48p. (J). (gr. 5-9). pap. 12.00 *(978-1-62832-207-1(1)*, Creative Paperbacks) Creative Co., The.

Gould, Jane. World War I: 1914-1916 — a Terrible New Warfare Begins. 2014. (ENG.). 48p. (J). *(978-0-7787-0325-9(8))* Crabtree Publishing Co.

Grahame-Smith, Deborah, contrib. by. Countdown to Catastrophe. 2010. (World War Ii Ser.). 128p. (gr. 6-9). 35.64 *(978-0-7614-4944-7(2))* Marshall Cavendish GBR. Dist: Marshall Cavendish Corp.

Grant, R. G. Moments in History - Why Did World War I Happen? 2010. (Moments in History Ser.). 48p. (ENG.). (J). (gr. 6-8). pap. 14.05 *(978-1-4339-4182-5(1)*, Gareth Stevens Secondary Library); (Illus.). (YA). (gr. 5-9). lib. bdg. 31.95 *(978-1-4339-4181-8(3))* Stevens, Gareth Publishing LLLP.

—World War I. 2005. (How Did It Happen? Ser.). (ENG., Illus.). 48p. (YA). (gr. 7-10). lib. bdg. 32.10 *(978-1-59018-605-3(2)*, Lucent Bks.) Cengage Gale.

Greene, Robert. World War I. 2007. (World History Ser.). (ENG., Illus.). 104p. (J). (gr. 7-10). lib. bdg. 34.95 *(978-1-4205-0025-7(2)*, Lucent Bks.) Cengage Gale.

Gregory, Josh. World War I. 2012. (Cornerstones of Freedom, Third Ser.). (ENG., Illus.). 64p. (J). pap. 8.95 *(978-0-531-28168-0(X))*; (gr. 4-6). lib. bdg. 30.00 *(978-0-531-23068-8(6))* Scholastic Library Publishing. (Children's Pr.).

Hale, Nathan. Treaties, Trenches, Mud, & Blood. 2014. (Nathan Hale's Hazardous Tales Ser.). (ENG., Illus.). 128p. (J). (gr. 3-7). 12.95 *(978-1-4197-0808-4(2)*, Amulet Bks.) Abrams, Inc.

—Treaties, Trenches, Mud, & Blood. 2017. (Nathan Hale's Hazardous Tales Ser.). (J). lib. bdg. 24.45 ***(978-0-606-40707-6(3))*** Turtleback Bks.

Hamilton, John. Aircraft of World War I, 1 vol. 2004. (World War I Ser.). (ENG.). 32p. (gr. 4-8). 27.07 *(978-1-57765-912-9(0)*, Abdo & Daughters) ABDO Publishing Co.

—Battles of World War I, 1 vol. 2004. (World War I Ser.). (ENG.). 32p. 27.07 *(978-1-57765-913-6(9)*, Abdo & Daughters) ABDO Publishing Co.

—Weapons of World War I, 1 vol. 2004. (World War I Ser.). (ENG.). 32p. (gr. 4-8). 27.07 *(978-1-57765-917-4(1)*, Abdo & Daughters) ABDO Publishing Co.

Hardyman, Robyn. What Caused World War I? 2016. (Why War Happened Ser.). 48p. (gr. 8-6). lib. bdg. 31.95 *(978-1-4824-5182-5(4))* Stevens, Gareth Publishing LLLP.

Heinrichs, Ann. Voices of World War I: Stories from the Trenches, 1 vol. 2010. (Voices of War Ser.). (ENG., 32p. (gr. 3-4). Illus.). pap. 8.29 *(978-1-4296-5626-9(3))*; pap. 47.70 *(978-1-4296-5701-3(4))* Capstone Press of Coughlan Cos. (Edge Bks.).

Hinman, Bonnie. World War I: 12 Things to Know. 2017. (America at War Ser.). (ENG., Illus.). 32p. (gr. 3-6). 21.95 *(978-1-63235-270-5(2))* Pr. Room Editions LLC.

Hoena, Blake. Stubby the Dog Soldier: World War I Hero, 1 vol. 2014. (Animal Heroes Ser.). (ENG., Illus.). 32p. (gr. k-2). 28.65 *(978-1-4795-5461-4(8))* Picture Window Bks.

Hosch, William L. World War I: People, Politics, & Power. 2009. (America at War Ser.). (ENG.). 240p. (YA). 98.00 *(978-1-61530-092-1(9))* Rosen Publishing Group, Inc., The.

Hosch, William L., ed. World War I: People, Politics, & Power. 2009. (America at War Ser.). (Illus.). 240p. (YA). (gr. 9-12). lib. bdg. 49.00 *(978-1-61530-013-6(9))* Rosen Publishing Group, Inc., The.

Hosein, Ann, ed. Key Figures of World War I. 2015. (Biographies of War Ser.). (ENG.). 112p. (YA). (gr. 7-8). 65.80 *(978-1-68048-055-9(3)*, Britannica Educational Publishing) Rosen Publishing Group, Inc., The.

Howell, Izzi. Edith Cavell. 2016. (Fact Cat: History Ser.). (ENG., Illus.). 24p. (J). (gr. k-2). 14.99 *(978-0-7502-9772-1(7)*, Wayland) Hachette Children's Group GBR. Dist: Hachette Bk. Group.

Hunter, Nick. Campaigns of World War I, 1 vol. 2013. (Remembering World War I Ser.). (ENG.). 48p. (gr. 4-6). 33.32 *(978-1-4329-8081-8(5))*; pap. 9.95 *(978-1-4329-8086-3(6))* Heinemann-Raintree. (Heinemann InfoSearch).

—Home Fronts in World War I. 2013. (Remembering World War I Ser.). (ENG.). 48p. (gr. 4-6). 33.32 *(978-1-4329-8083-2(1))*; pap. 9.95 *(978-1-4329-8088-7(2))* Heinemann-Raintree. (Heinemann InfoSearch).

—Remembering World War I. 2013. (Remembering World War I Ser.). (ENG.). 48p. (gr. 4-6). pap. 35.96 *(978-1-4329-8090-0(4))*; lib. bdg. 133.28 *(978-1-4329-8085-6(8))* Heinemann-Raintree. (Heinemann InfoSearch).

—World War I: Frontline Soldiers & Their Families. 2015. (Frontline Families Ser.). (ENG., Illus.). 48p. (J). (gr. 5-6). pap. 14.05 *(978-1-4824-3065-3(7))* Stevens, Gareth Publishing LLLP.

—World War I - Unclassified: Secrets Revealed! 2014. (ENG., Illus.). 64p. (J). (gr. 2-4). 18.99 *(978-1-4729-0525-3(3)*, 9781472905253, Bloomsbury USA Childrens) Bloomsbury Publishing USA.

Hyde, Natalie. World War I: The Cause for War. 2014. (ENG.). 48p. (J). *(978-0-7787-0387-7(8))* Crabtree Publishing Co.

Innes, Stephanie & Endrulat, Harry. A Bear in War, 1 vol. Deines, Brian, illus. 2013. (ENG.). 40p. (J). (gr. k-4). 19.95 *(978-1-927485-12-5(6))* Pajama Pr. CAN. Dist: Ingram Publisher Services.

Kenney, Karen L. National Geographic Kids Everything World War I. 2014. (National Geographic Kids Everything Ser.). (ENG., Illus.). 64p. (J). (gr. 3-7). pap. 12.99 *(978-1-4263-1715-6(8)*, National Geographic Children's Bks.) National Geographic Society.

Lanser, Amanda. World War I by the Numbers. 2015. (America at War by the Numbers Ser.). (ENG., Illus.). 32p. (gr. 3-4). lib. bdg. 27.99 *(978-1-4914-4296-8(4))* Capstone Press of Coughlan Cos.

Lassieur, Allison. At Battle in World War I: An Interactive Battlefield Adventure. 2015. (You Choose: Battlefields Ser.). (ENG., Illus.). 112p. (gr. 3-4). lib. bdg. 31.99 *(978-1-4914-2151-2(7)*, You Choose Bks.) Capstone Press of Coughlan Cos.

—Courageous Spies & International Intrigue of World War I. 2017. (Spies! Ser.). (ENG., Illus.). 64p. (gr. 5-6). lib. bdg. 33.99 *(978-0-7565-5499-6(3)*, CPB Grades 4-8) Compass Point Bks.

Lassieur, Allison, et al. You Choose: Battlefields. 2015. (You Choose: Battlefields Ser.). (ENG.). 112p. (gr. 3-4). lib. bdg. 127.96 *(978-1-4914-2630-2(6)*, You Choose Bks.) Capstone Press of Coughlan Cos.

Lawson, J. C. The Litany of the Elves. 2013. (ENG.). 36p. pap. 15.99 *(978-1-107-68397-6(1))* Cambridge Univ. Pr.

Lewis, J. Patrick. And the Soldiers Sang. Kelley, Gary, illus. 2014. (ENG.). 32p. (J). (gr. 1-3). pap. 9.99 *(978-0-89812-975-5(3)*, Creative Paperbacks) Creative Co., The.

—Harlem Hellfighters. Kelley, Gary, illus. 2014. (ENG.). 32p. (J). (gr. 4-7). 19.99 *(978-1-56846-246-2(8)*, Creative Editions) Creative Co., The.

Long, David. War School for Dogs: Band 16/Sapphire. 2017. (ENG., Illus.). 56p. (J). pap. 8.99 ***(978-0-00-820891-2(3))*** HarperCollins Pubs. Ltd. GBR. Dist: Independent Pubs. Group.

Malam, John. World War I: Armistice Day. 2003. 45p. (J). lib. bdg. 28.50 *(978-1-58340-410-2(4))* Black Rabbit Bks.

Mason, Conrad. The First World War. 2014. (Usborne Young Reading: Series Three Ser.). (ENG., Illus.). 63p. (J). (gr. 4-7). 6.99 *(978-0-7945-2092-2(8)*, Usborne) EDC Publishing.

Matthews, Rupert. The World Wars. 2008. (Timelines Ser.). (Illus.). 96p. (J). pap. *(978-1-84236-809-1(5))* Miles Kelly Publishing, Ltd.

Maybury, Richard J. World War I: The Rest of the Story & How It Affects You Today, 1870 To 1935. Williams, Jane A., ed. rev. ed. 2003. ("Uncle Eric" Bk.: 10). (ENG., Illus.). 253p. pap. 17.95 *(978-0-942617-42-9(8))* Bluestocking Pr.

McCollum, Sean. Secrets of World War I. 2017. (Top Secret Files Ser.). (ENG., Illus.). 32p. (gr. 3-4). lib. bdg. 27.99 *(978-1-5157-4139-8(7)*, Edge Bks.) Capstone Press of Coughlan Cos.

McNeil, Niki, et al. HOCPP 1086 World War I. 2006. spiral bd. 19.50 *(978-1-60308-086-6(4))* In the Hands of a Child.

Miller, Derek L. Minority Soldiers Fighting in World War I. 2017. (J). ***(978-1-5026-2663-9(2))*** Cavendish Square Publishing.

Morgan, Elizabeth & Green, Robert. World War I & the Rise of Global Conflict. 2017. (World History Ser.). 104p. (J). (gr. 7-7). lib. bdg. 39.90 ***(978-1-5345-6058-1(0)***, Lucent Pr.) Greenhaven Publishing LLC.

Myers, Walter Dean & Miles, Bill. The Harlem Hellfighters: When Pride Met Courage. 2014. (ENG.). 160p. (J). (gr. 3-7). pap. 9.99 *(978-0-06-001138-3(6)*, Amistad) HarperCollins Pubs.

Myers, Walter Dean & William Miles. The Harlem Hellfighters: When Pride Met Courage. 2014. (J). lib. bdg. 20.85 *(978-0-606-35507-0(3))* Turtleback Bks.

W X Y Z

Nardo, Don. Cause & Effect: World War I. 2017. (ENG.). 80p. (YA). (gr. 5-12). **(978-1-68282-172-5(2))** ReferencePoint Pr., Inc.

Nelson, Sheila. A Nation Is Born: World War I & Independence, 1910-1929. 2007. (How Canada Became Canada Ser.). (Illus.). 87p. (YA). (gr. 3-7). lib. bdg. 21.95 *(978-1-4222-0006-3(X),* 1247972) Mason Crest.

Oakes, John. Kitchener's Lost Boys: From the Playing Fields to the Killing Fields. 2009. (ENG., Illus.). 192p. 38.95 *(978-0-7524-4930-2(3))* History Pr. Ltd., The GBR. Dist: Independent Pubs. Group.

Otfinoski, Steven. World War I. 2017. (Step into History(tm) Ser.). (ENG., Illus.). 144p. (J). lib. bdg. 36.00 *(978-0-531-22571-4(2),* Children's Pr.) Scholastic Library Publishing.

Perritano, John. World War I. 2010. (America at War Ser.). 32p. (J). pap. 8.95 *(978-0-531-24912-3(3),* Watts, Franklin) Scholastic Library Publishing.

Powell, Jillian. The First World War. 2014. (Collins Big Cat Progress Ser.). (ENG., Illus.). 32p. (J). (gr. 4-5). pap. 7.99 *(978-0-00-751936-1(2))* HarperCollins Pubs. Ltd. GBR. Dist: Independent Pubs. Group.

—War Art. 2014. (Collins Big Cat Progress Ser.). (ENG., Illus.). 32p. (J). (gr. 5-6). pap. 7.99 *(978-0-00-751930-9(3))* HarperCollins Pubs. Ltd. GBR. Dist: Independent Pubs. Group.

Pratt, Mary K. World War I, 1 vol. 2013. (Essential Library of American Wars Ser.). (ENG.). 112p. (J). (gr. 6-12). lib. bdg. 35.64 *(978-1-61783-881-1(0),* Essential Library) ABDO Publishing Co.

Rasmussen, R. Kent. World War I for Kids: A History with 21 Activities. 2014. (For Kids Ser.). (ENG., Illus.). 192p. (J). (gr. 4). pap. 17.95 *(978-1-61374-556-4(7))* Chicago Review Pr., Inc.

Ridley, Sarah. Remembering the Fallen of the First World War. 2016. (ENG., Illus.). 48p. (J). (gr. 6-11). 18.99 *(978-1-4451-4250-0(3),* Franklin Watts) Hachette Children's Group GBR. Dist: Hachette Bk. Group.

Roberts, Steven & Gould, Jane H. The United States in World War I: America's Entry Ensures Victory. 2014. (ENG.). 48p. (J). *(978-0-7787-0389-1(4))* Crabtree Publishing Co.

Robinson, Tony. World War I. unabr. ed. 2013. (Weird World of Wonders Ser.). (ENG., Illus.). 160p. (J). (gr. 2-5). pap. 9.99 *(978-1-4472-2771-7(9))* Pan Macmillan GBR. Dist: Independent Pubs. Group.

Robson, Pam. The First World War. 2nd ed. 2003. (All about Ser.). (Illus.). 48p. pap. *(978-0-7500-1936-1(0),* Wayland) Hachette Children's Group.

Roby, Cynthia. Strategic Inventions of World War I. 2016. (Tech in the Trenches Ser.). (ENG., Illus.). 112p. (J). (gr. 9-9). lib. bdg. 42.79 *(978-1-5026-1024-9(8))* Cavendish Square Publishing.

Ross, Stewart. World War I, 1 vol. 2010. (Research It! Ser.). (ENG., Illus.). 56p. (gr. 6-9). lib. bdg. 34.65 *(978-1-4329-3494-1(5),* NA-h) Heinemann-Raintree.

—World War I. 2004. (Atlas of Conflicts Ser.). (Illus.). 64p. (gr. 6-12). pap. 14.05 *(978-0-8368-5675-0(9));* lib. bdg. 34.00 *(978-0-8368-5668-2(6))* Stevens, Gareth Publishing LLLP. (Gareth Stevens Secondary Library).

Rothstein, Evelyn. Clara's Great War. Uhlig, Elizabeth, illus. 2011. 88p. (J). pap. 12.95 *(978-0-9815345-9-6(7))* Marble Hse. Editions.

Royce, Ruth. The Children of France. 2007. 88p. per. *(978-1-4068-4064-3(5))* Echo Library.

Ryles, Briony & Hall, Derek. The Early 20th Century. 2010. (CC: Technology Through the Ages Ser.). 112p. (gr. 6-12). 42.80 *(978-1-933834-87-0(0))* Brown Bear Bks.

Samuels, Charlie. Machines & Weaponry of World War I. 2013. (Machines That Won the War Ser.). (Illus.). 48p. (J). (gr. 5-8). pap. 14.05 *(978-1-4339-8604-8(3));* lib. bdg. 31.95 *(978-1-4339-8603-1(5))* Stevens, Gareth Publishing LLLP.

Schaub, Michelle. Vehicles of World War I, 1 vol. 2013. (War Vehicles Ser.). (ENG.). 32p. (gr. 3-4). 27.99 *(978-1-4296-9911-2(6),* Edge Bks.) Capstone Press of Coughlan Cos.

Scherer, Glenn & Fletcher, Marty. Primary Source Accounts of World War I. 2006. (America's Wars Through Primary Sources Ser.). (Illus.). 128p. (J). (gr. 4-7). lib. bdg. 33.27 *(978-1-59845-008-6(5),* MyReportLinks.com Bks.) Enslow Pubs., Inc.

Scott, Janine. The Two Great Wars. 2007. (Shockwave: History & Politics Ser.). (ENG., Illus.). 36p. (J). (gr. 4-6). lib. bdg. 25.00 *(978-0-531-17756-3(4),* Children's Pr.) Scholastic Library Publishing.

Steele, Philip. Did Anything Good Come Out of World War I?, 01 vols., 1. 2016. (Innovation Through Adversity Ser.). (ENG.). 48p. (J). 30.25 *(978-1-5081-7068-6(1),* Rosen Young Adult) Rosen Publishing Group, Inc., The.

Summers, Elizabeth. Weapons & Vehicles of World War I. 2015. (Tools of War Ser.). (ENG., Illus.). 32p. (gr. 1-2). lib. bdg. 26.65 *(978-1-4914-4095-7(3))* Capstone Press of Coughlan Cos.

Swain, Gwenyth. World War I: An Interactive History Adventure, 1 vol. 2012. (You Choose: History Ser.). (ENG., 112p. (gr. 3-4). Illus.). pap. 6.95 *(978-1-4296-7997-8(2));* pap. 41.70 *(978-1-4296-8484-2(4));* (Illus.). lib. bdg. 31.99 *(978-1-4296-6020-4(1))* Capstone Press of Coughlan Cos. (You Choose Bks.).

Swayze, Alan. The End of World War I: The Treaty of Versailles & Its Tragic Legacy. 2014. (ENG.). 48p. (J). *(978-0-7787-0388-4(6))* Crabtree Publishing Co.

Torres, Jennifer. Alan Jackson. 2006. (Blue Banner Biography Ser.). (Illus.). 32p. (YA). (gr. 4-7). lib. bdg. 25.70 *(978-1-58415-504-1(3),* 1259609) Mitchell Lane Pubs., Inc.

The Treaty of Versailles. 2010. (Milestones in World History Ser.). (Illus.). 120p. (C). (gr. 9-18). 35.00 *(978-1-60413-277-9(9),* Chelsea Hse.) Facts On File, Inc.

Turner, Jason. World War I. 2008. (Wars Day by Day Ser.). 48p. (gr. 5-9). 37.10 *(978-1-933834-40-5(4))* Brown Bear Bks.

Wagner, Heather Lehr. The Division of the Middle East: The Treaty of Sevres. 2004. (Arbitrary Borders Ser.). (Illus.). 120p. (C). (gr. 9-13). 35.00 *(978-0-7910-7831-0(0),* Chelsea Hse.) Facts On File, Inc.

Walker, Robert. World War I: 1917-1918 — the Turning of the Tide. 2014. (ENG.). 48p. (J). *(978-0-7787-0326-6(6))* Crabtree Publishing Co.

Westwell, Ian. World War I. 2010. (FAYFT: Modern Military History Ser.). 64p. (gr. 4-10). 39.95 *(978-1-933834-49-8(8))* Brown Bear Bks.

Whiting, Jim. An Overview of World War I. 2006. (Monumental Milestones Ser.). (Illus.). 48p. (YA). (gr. 4-7). lib. bdg. 29.95 *(978-1-58415-471-6(3))* Mitchell Lane Pubs., Inc.

Wiest, Andrew. World War I. 2016. (Primary Sources in World Warfare Ser.). 256p. (YA). lib. bdg. 55.00 *(978-1-5026-2470-3(2))* Cavendish Square Publishing.

Wilson, John. Desperate Glory: The Story of WWI. 2008. (Stories of Canada Ser.: 12). (ENG., Illus.). 96p. (J). (gr. 6-18). 20.95 *(978-1-894917-42-1(1),* Napoleon & Co.) Dundurn CAN. Dist: Ingram Publisher Services.

World War I: PowerPoint Presentations in World History. 2005. cd-rom 49.95 net. *(978-1-56004-208-2(7))* Social Studies Schl. Service.

Zaboly, Gary. Story of World War I. 2013. (Dover History Coloring Book Ser.). (ENG.). 48p. (gr. 3-12). pap. 4.99 *(978-0-486-49791-4(7))* Dover Pubns., Inc.

Zamosky, Lisa. World War I, 1 vol. 2007. (Primary Source Readers Ser.). (ENG.). 32p. (J). (gr. 5-5). pap. 8.99 *(978-0-7439-0664-7(0))* Shell Educational Publishing.

Ziff, John. The American Revolution. 2015. (Illus.). 64p. (J). *(978-1-4222-3352-8(9))* Mason Crest.

—World War I, Vol. 11. Musteen, Jason R., ed. 2015. (Major U. S. Historical Wars Ser.). (Illus.). 64p. (J). (gr. 7). lib. bdg. 23.95 *(978-1-4222-3362-7(6))* Mason Crest.

Zullo, Allan. World War I Heroes. 2014. 162p. (J). pap. **(978-0-545-67533-8(2))** Scholastic, Inc.

WORLD WAR, 1914-1918—AERIAL OPERATIONS

Adams, Simon. Warplanes. 2009. (J). 28.50 *(978-1-59920-223-5(9))* Black Rabbit Bks.

Jeffrey, Gary. War in the Air. 2013. (ENG., Illus.). 48p. (J). *(978-0-7787-0914-5(0));* pap. *(978-0-7787-0924-4(8))* Crabtree Publishing Co.

Myhra, David. The Horten Ho 9/Ho 229 Vol. 1: Retrospective, 1 vol. 2003. (ENG., Illus.). 224p. (gr. 10-13). 49.95 *(978-0-7643-1666-1(4),* 9780764316661) Schiffer Publishing, Ltd.

Orr, Tamra. What's So Great about the Tuskegee Airmen. 2009. (What's So Great About... ? Ser.). 32p. (J). (gr. 2-4). lib. bdg. 25.70 *(978-1-58415-832-5(8))* Mitchell Lane Pubs., Inc.

Purcell, Martha Sias. Pioneer Pilots & Flying Aces of World War I. 2003. (Reading Essentials in Social Studies). (Illus.). 48p. (J). 9.00 *(978-0-7891-5881-9(7))* Perfection Learning Corp.

Vansant, Wayne. The Red Baron: The Graphic History of Richthofen's Flying Circus & the Air War in WWI. Vansant, Wayne, illus. 2015. (Graphic Histories Ser.). (ENG., Illus.). 104p. (J). (gr. 8-12). 34.65 *(978-1-939581-80-8(X))* Quarto Publishing Group USA.

—The Red Baron: The Graphic History of Richthofen's Flying Circus & the Air War in WWI. 2014. (Zenith Graphic Histories Ser.). (ENG., Illus.). 104p. pap. 19.99 *(978-0-7603-4602-0(X),* 076034602X, Zenith Pr.) Quarto Publishing Group USA.

Watson, Marilyn Myrick. Frank Luke, the Arizona Balloon Buster. 2007. *(978-0-9790826-3-4(3));* *(978-0-9790826-4-1(1))* Acacia Publishing, Inc.

WORLD WAR, 1914-1918—BIOGRAPHY

Batten, Jack. Silent in an Evil Time: The Brave War of Edith Cavell. 2007. (ENG., Illus.). 144p. (J). (gr. 5-18). pap. 16.95 *(978-0-88776-737-1(0),* Tundra Bks.) Tundra Bks. CAN. Dist: Penguin Random Hse. LLC.

Brooker, Marion Fargey. Hold the Oxo! A Teenage Soldier Writes Home. 2011. (Canadians at War Ser.: 6). (ENG., Illus.). 144p. (YA). pap. 14.99 *(978-1-55488-870-2(0))* Dundurn CAN. Dist: Ingram Publisher Services.

Hosein, Ann. Key Figures of World War I. 2015. (Biographies of War Ser.). (ENG., Illus.). 112p. (J). (gr. 7-8). 32.90 *(978-1-68048-054-2(5),* Britannica Educational Publishing) Rosen Publishing Group, Inc., The.

Hunter, Nick. Women in World War I, 1 vol. 2013. (Remembering World War I Ser.). (ENG.). 48p. (gr. 4-6). 33.32 *(978-1-4329-8084-9(X));* pap. 9.95 *(978-1-4329-8089-4(0))* Heinemann-Raintree. (Heinemann InfoSearch).

Purcell, Martha Sias. Pioneer Pilots & Flying Aces of World War I. 2003. (Reading Essentials in Social Studies). (Illus.). 48p. (J). 9.00 *(978-0-7891-5881-9(7))* Perfection Learning Corp.

Raum, Elizabeth, et al. Stories of War. 2012. (Stories of War Ser.). (ENG.). 32p. (gr. 3-4). lib. bdg. 122.60 *(978-1-4296-9164-2(6),* Graphic Library) Capstone Press of Coughlan Cos.

Smith, Rupert. Poets of World War I, 1 vol. 2014. (ENG., Illus.). 64p. (gr. 7-8). lib. bdg. 35.99 *(978-1-4329-9645-1(2))* Heinemann-Raintree.

Williams, Brian. Heroes of the Battlefield. 2015. (Heroes of World War II Ser.). (ENG., Illus.). 48p. (gr. 4-6). 32.65 *(978-1-4109-8048-9(0))* Heinemann-Raintree.

Yomtov, Nel. True Stories of World War I. Proctor, Jon, illus. 2012. (Stories of War Ser.). (ENG.). 32p. (gr. 3-4). pap. 47.70 *(978-1-4296-9345-5(2),* Graphic Library) Capstone Press of Coughlan Cos.

Yomtov, Nel, et al. Stories of War. 2012. (Stories of War Ser.). (ENG.). 32p. (gr. 3-4). pap. 31.80 *(978-1-4296-9348-6(7));* pap. 190.80 *(978-1-4296-9349-3(5))* Capstone Press of Coughlan Cos. (Graphic Library).

Yomtov, Nelson. True Stories of World War I, 1 vol. Proctor, Jon, illus. 2012. (Stories of War Ser.). (ENG.). 32p. (gr. 3-4). pap. 8.10 *(978-1-4296-9344-8(4));* lib. bdg. 30.65 *(978-1-4296-8625-9(1))* Capstone Press of Coughlan Cos. (Graphic Library).

WORLD WAR, 1914-1918—CAMPAIGNS

see also Somme, 1st Battle of the, France, 1916

Burnett, Allan. World War I: Scottish Tales of Adventure. 2016. (ENG., Illus.). 112p. (gr. 4-7). pap. 9.99 *(978-1-84158-932-9(2))* Birlinn, Ltd. GBR. Dist: Casemate Pubs. & Bk. Distributors, LLC.

Feldman, Ruth Tenzer. World War I. 2004. (Chronicle of America's Wars Ser.). (Illus.). 88p. (gr. 5-12). lib. bdg. 27.93 *(978-0-8225-0148-0(1))* Lerner Publishing Group.

Greenwood, Mark. The Donkey of Gallipoli: A True Story of Courage in World War I. Lessac, Frané, illus. 2008. (ENG.). 32p. (J). (gr. 1-4). 16.99 *(978-0-7636-3913-6(3))* Candlewick Pr.

Hamilton, John. Final Years of World War I, 1 vol. 2004. (World War I Ser.). (ENG.). 32p. (gr. 4-8). 27.07 *(978-1-57765-915-0(5),* Abdo & Daughters) ABDO Publishing Co.

—Trench Fighting of World War I, 1 vol. 2004. (World War I Ser.). (ENG.). 32p. (gr. 4-8). 27.07 *(978-1-57765-916-7(3),* Abdo & Daughters) ABDO Publishing Co.

Hunter, Nick. Life on the Western Front, 1 vol. 2013. (Remembering World War I Ser.). (ENG.). 48p. (gr. 4-6). 33.32 *(978-1-4329-8082-5(3));* pap. 9.95 *(978-1-4329-8087-0(4))* Heinemann-Raintree. (Heinemann InfoSearch).

Jeffrey, Gary. Gallipoli & the Southern Theaters. 2013. (ENG., Illus.). 48p. (J). pap. *(978-0-7787-0917-6(5))* Crabtree Publishing Co.

—Lawrence of Arabia & the Middle East & Africa. 2013. (ENG., Illus.). 48p. (J). *(978-0-7787-0912-1(4));* pap. *(978-0-7787-0918-3(3))* Crabtree Publishing Co.

—On the Eastern Front. 2013. (ENG., Illus.). 48p. (J). *(978-0-7787-0910-7(8));* pap. *(978-0-7787-0916-9(7))* Crabtree Publishing Co.

—On the Western Front. 2013. (ENG., Illus.). 48p. (J). *(978-0-7787-0909-1(4));* pap. *(978-0-7787-0915-2(9))* Crabtree Publishing Co.

—War in the Air. 2013. (ENG., Illus.). 48p. (J). *(978-0-7787-0914-5(0));* pap. *(978-0-7787-0924-4(8))* Crabtree Publishing Co.

Kalman, Bobbie & Jeffrey, Gary. Gallipoli & the Southern Theaters. 2013. (ENG.). 48p. (J). *(978-0-7787-0911-4(6))* Crabtree Publishing Co.

Long, David & Collins UK Staff. The Battle of Passchendaele. 2016. (ENG.). 80p. (J). (gr. 5-6). pap. 9.95 *(978-0-00-816406-5(1))* HarperCollins Pubs. Ltd. GBR. Dist: Independent Pubs. Group.

Malam, John. Hitler Invades Poland. 2007. (Dates with History Ser.). (ENG., Illus.). 48p. (J). pap. 9.99 *(978-1-84234-535-1(4))* Evans Brothers, Ltd. GBR. Dist: Independent Pubs. Group.

Murphy, Jim. Truce. 2009. (ENG., Illus.). 128p. (J). (gr. 4-7). 19.99 *(978-0-545-13049-3(2),* Scholastic Pr.) Scholastic, Inc.

Peyton, Katherine & George, Enzo. World War II in Europe & North Africa: Preserving Democracy. 2014. (Voices of War Ser.). 48p. (J). (gr. 4-6). lib. bdg. 31.36 *(978-1-62712-864-3(6))* Cavendish Square Publishing.

Samuels, Charlie. Timeline of World War I. 2011. (Americans at War: a Gareth Stevens Timeline Ser.). 48p. (J). (gr. 6-8). pap. 14.05 *(978-1-4339-5928-8(3));* lib. bdg. 31.95 *(978-1-4339-5926-4(7))* Stevens, Gareth Publishing LLLP. (Gareth Stevens Secondary Library).

WORLD WAR, 1914-1918—CAUSES

Bodden, Valerie. The Assassination of Archduke Ferdinand. 2009. (Days of Change Ser.). 48p. (YA). (gr. 4-7). 22.95 *(978-1-58341-731-7(1))* Creative Co., The.

Feldman, Ruth Tenzer. World War I. 2004. (Chronicle of America's Wars Ser.). (Illus.). 88p. (gr. 5-12). lib. bdg. 27.93 *(978-0-8225-0148-0(1))* Lerner Publishing Group.

Hamilton, John. Events Leading to World War I, 1 vol. 2004. (World War I Ser.). (ENG.). 32p. (gr. 4-8). 27.07 *(978-1-57765-914-3(7),* Abdo & Daughters) ABDO Publishing Co.

Maybury, Richard J. World War I: The Rest of the Story & How It Affects You Today, 1870 To 1935. Williams, Jane A., ed. rev. ed. 2003. ("Uncle Eric" Bk.: 10). (ENG., Illus.). 253p. pap. 17.95 *(978-0-942617-42-9(8))* Bluestocking Pr.

Rissman, Rebecca. World War I: Why They Fought. 2015. (What Were They Fighting For? Ser.). (ENG., Illus.). 64p. (gr. 5-9). 34.65 *(978-0-7565-5170-4(6))* Compass Point Bks.

WORLD WAR, 1914-1918—FICTION

Aaron, Chester. Alex, Who Won His War. 2014. 225p. (YA). *(978-1-936144-26-6(3))* Zumaya Pubns. LLC.

Almond, David, et al. The Great War: Stories Inspired by Items from the First World War. Kay, Jim, illus. 2015. (ENG.). 304p. (J). (gr. 5). 19.99 *(978-0-7636-7554-7(7))* Candlewick Pr.

Altsheler, Joseph A. The Complete 'Great War' Series: The Guns of Europe, the Forest of Swords & the Hosts of the Air. 2010. (Great War Ser.). 576p. (J). (gr. 4-7). reprint ed. *(978-0-85706-344-1(8));* pap. *(978-0-85706-343-4(X))* Leonaur Ltd.

—The Forest of Swords: A Story of Paris & the Marne. 2006. (World War I Ser.: Vol. 3). 284p. (J). reprint ed. 28.95 *(978-1-4218-1772-9(1));* pap. 13.95 *(978-1-4218-1872-6(8))* 1st World Publishing, Inc. (1st World Library - Literary Society).

—The Forest of Swords: A Story of Paris & the Marne. 2004. (World War I Ser.: Vol. 3). (J). reprint ed. 32.95 *(978-0-8488-3005-2(9))* Amereon Ltd.

—The Forest of Swords: A Story of Paris & the Marne. l.t. ed. (World War I Ser.: Vol. 3). (J). 2007. (ENG.). 252p. pap. 23.99 *(978-1-4264-8960-0(9))* 2008. 256p. reprint ed. 28.99 *(978-0-554-25416-6(6))* 2008. 256p. reprint ed. 25.99 *(978-0-554-34719-6(9))* 2007. (ENG.). 226p. reprint ed. pap. 20.99 *(978-1-4264-8902-0(1))* Creative Media Partners, LLC.

—The Forest of Swords: A Story of Paris & the Marne. 2006. (World War I Ser.: Vol. 3). (J). reprint ed. pap. *(978-1-4065-0809-3(8))* Dodo Pr.

—The Forest of Swords: A Story of Paris & the Marne. 2006. (World War I Ser.: Vol. 3). (J). reprint ed. pap. *(978-1-4068-0742-4(7))* Echo Library.

—The Forest of Swords: A Story of Paris & the Marne. 2010. (World War I Ser.: Vol. 3). (Illus.). 150p. (J). (gr. 4-7). reprint ed. pap. 19.99 *(978-1-153-70289-8(4))* General Bks. LLC.

—The Forest of Swords: A Story of Paris & the Marne. 2010. (World War I Ser.: Vol. 3). 216p. (J). reprint ed. pap. *(978-1-4076-1521-9(1))* HardPr.

—The Forest of Swords: A Story of Paris & the Marne. 2011. (World War I Ser.: Vol. 3). 252p. (J). (gr. 4-7). reprint ed. pap. *(978-3-8424-7930-2(1))* Tredition GmbH.

—The Guns of Europe. Date not set. reprint ed. lib. bdg. 39.95 *(978-0-8488-1860-9(1),* 204) Amereon Ltd.

—The Guns of Europe. 2009. 174p. (J). pap. *(978-1-150-78710-2(4))* Books LLC.

—The Guns of Europe. 2010. (World War I Ser.: Vol. 1). 342p. pap. 31.75 *(978-1-148-38046-9(9),* Nabu Pr.) 2009. 339p. pap. 23.99 *(978-1-113-15368-5(7),* BiblioLife) 2009. (World War I Ser.: Vol. 1). 340p. (J). (gr. 3-7). 32.99 *(978-1-113-15374-6(1))* 2009. (World War I Ser.: Vol. 1). 340p. (J). (gr. 3-7). pap. 30.75 *(978-1-113-15371-5(7))* 2009. (World War I Ser.: Vol. 1). 339p. (J). (gr. 3-7). pap. 24.99 *(978-1-113-15369-2(5),* BiblioLife) 2011. (World War I Ser.: Vol. 1). 344p. (J). (gr. 4-7). reprint ed. pap. 32.75 *(978-1-175-98804-1(9))* 2010. (World War I Ser.: Vol. 1). (ENG.). 346p. (J). (gr. 4-7). reprint ed. pap. 32.75 *(978-1-176-64128-0(X))* 2009. (ENG.). 330p. (J). reprint ed. 36.99 *(978-1-117-70555-2(2))* 2009. 332p. (J). reprint ed. pap. 30.75 *(978-1-117-70556-9(0))* 2009. (World War I Ser.: Vol. 1). 330p. (J). (gr. 4-7). reprint ed. pap. 23.99 *(978-1-117-70557-6(9),* BiblioLife) Creative Media Partners, LLC.

—The Guns of Europe. 2010. (World War I Ser.: Vol. 1). (J). reprint ed. 144p. (gr. 4-7). pap. 19.99 *(978-1-153-65770-9(8));* (gr. 5-7). 15.89 *(978-1-154-98722-5(1));* (gr. 5-7). 19.99 *(978-1-154-72171-3(X))* General Bks. LLC.

—The Guns of Europe. 2012. (World War I Ser.: Vol. 1). 352p. (J). reprint ed. pap. *(978-1-290-02432-7(4))* HardPr.

—The Guns of Europe. Wrenn, Charles, illus. (World War I Ser.: Vol. 1). (J). reprint ed. 2010. 338p. (gr. 4-7). 36.76 *(978-1-164-35775-9(1))* 2010. 338p. (gr. 4-7). pap. 24.76 *(978-1-163-97980-8(5))* 2008. 336p. 45.95 *(978-0-548-98692-9(4))* 2007. 340p. per. 30.95 *(978-0-548-66038-6(7))* Kessinger Publishing, LLC.

—The Hosts of the Air: The Story of a Quest in the Great War. 2006. (World War I Ser.: Vol. 2). 288p. (J). reprint ed. 28.95 *(978-1-4218-1773-6(X));* pap. 13.95 *(978-1-4218-1873-3(6))* 1st World Publishing, Inc. (1st World Library - Literary Society).

—The Hosts of the Air: The Story of a Quest in the Great War. (World War I Ser.: Vol. 2). 327p. (J). reprint ed. lib. bdg. 25.95 *(978-0-88411-947-0(5))* Amereon Ltd.

—The Hosts of the Air: The Story of a Quest in the Great War. 2010. 352p. pap. 32.75 *(978-1-142-69983-3(8))* 2007. (World War I Ser.: Vol. 2). 258p. (J). reprint ed. pap. 23.99 *(978-1-4264-9850-3(0))* 2010. (World War I Ser.: Vol. 2). 356p. (J). (gr. 3-7). reprint ed. pap. 32.75 *(978-1-149-41015-8(9),* Nabu Pr.) 2008. (World War I Ser.: Vol. 2). 260p. (J). reprint ed. 28.99 *(978-0-554-25738-9(6))* 2008. (World War I Ser.: Vol. 2). 260p. (J). reprint ed. 25.99 *(978-0-554-35041-7(6))* 2007. (World War I Ser.: Vol. 2). 232p. (J). reprint ed. pap. 20.99 *(978-1-4264-9469-7(6))* Creative Media Partners, LLC.

—The Hosts of the Air: The Story of a Quest in the Great War. 2006. (World War I Ser.: Vol. 2). (Illus.). (J). reprint ed. pap. *(978-1-4065-0814-7(4))* Dodo Pr.

—The Hosts of the Air: The Story of a Quest in the Great War. 2007. (World War I Ser.: Vol. 2). 168p. (J). reprint ed. per. *(978-1-4068-1679-2(5))* Echo Library.

—The Hosts of the Air: The Story of a Quest in the Great War. (World War I Ser.: Vol. 2). (J). reprint ed. 2010. 152p. (gr. 4-7). pap. 19.99 *(978-1-4432-1323-3(3))* 2009. 170p. pap. 9.39 *(978-1-150-51448-7(5))* General Bks. LLC.

—The Hosts of the Air: The Story of a Quest in the Great War. Wrenn, Charles, illus. (World War I Ser.: Vol. 2). (J). reprint ed. 2010. 346p. (gr. 4-7). 37.56 *(978-1-164-36346-0(8))* 2010. 346p. (gr. 4-7). pap. 25.56 *(978-1-163-98051-4(X))* 2008. 344p. 46.95 *(978-0-548-98763-6(7))* 2007. 348p. per. 31.95 *(978-0-548-65961-8(3))* Kessinger Publishing, LLC.

—The Hosts of the Air: The Story of a Quest in the Great War. 2011. (World War I Ser.: Vol. 2). 252p. (J). (gr. 4-7). reprint ed. pap. *(978-3-8424-7804-6(6))* Tredition GmbH.

Angus, Sam. Soldier Dog. 2014. (ENG.). 272p. (J). (gr. 4-7). pap. 7.99 *(978-1-250-04417-4(0),* 9781250044174) Square Fish.

Autio, Karen. Saara's Passage, 1 vol. 2009. (ENG.). 256p. (J). (gr. 4-12). pap. 10.95 *(978-1-55039-168-8(2))* Sono Nis Pr. CAN. Dist: Orca Bk. Pubs. USA.

—Sabotage, 1 vol. 2014. (ENG.). 293p. (J). (gr. 4-8). pap. 10.95 *(978-1-55039-208-1(5))* Sono Nis Pr. CAN. Dist: Orca Bk. Pubs. USA.

Barroux. Line of Fire: Diary of an Unknown Soldier. Ardizzone, Sarah, tr. from FRE. 2014. (ENG., Illus.). 96p. (J). (gr. 5-8). pap. 16.99 *(978-1-907912-39-9(8))* Phoenix Yard Bks. GBR. Dist: Independent Pubs. Group.

Black, Robert. Liberty Girl. (YA). pap. 9.99 *(978-0-88092-488-7(8))* Royal Fireworks Publishing Co.

Boyne, John. Stay Where You Are & Then Leave. Jeffers, Oliver, illus. 2014. (ENG.). 256p. (J). (gr. 4-7). 16.99 *(978-1-62779-031-4(4),* 9781627790314, Holt, Henry & Co. Bks. For Young Readers) Holt, Henry & Co.

Bradman, Tony & Bradman, Tom. My Brother's Keeper. 2014. (National Archives Ser.). (ENG., Illus.). 112p. (YA). (gr. 7). pap. 10.99 *(978-1-4081-9679-3(4),* 9781408196793, Bloomsbury USA Childrens) Bloomsbury Publishing USA.

Brown, Teri. Velvet Undercover. 2015. (ENG.). 336p. (YA). (gr. 8). 17.99 *(978-0-06-232127-5(7))* HarperCollins Pubs.

Burnett, Frances Hodgson. Robin. 2008. 236p. pap. 15.95 *(978-1-60664-143-9(3))* Aegypan.

Carroll, Emma. In Darkling Wood. 2017. (ENG.). 240p. (J). (gr. 5). 16.99 *(978-0-399-55601-2(X),* Delacorte Bks. for Young Readers) Random Hse. Children's Bks.

Cary, Kate. Bloodline. 2006. (ENG.). 352p. (YA). (gr. 7-12). 9.99 *(978-1-59514-078-4(6),* Razorbill) Penguin Young Readers Group.

Cheaney, J. B. I Don't Know How the Story Ends. 2015. (ENG.). 288p. (J). (gr. 4-7). 16.99 *(978-1-4926-0944-5(7),* 9781492609445, Sourcebooks Jabberwocky) Sourcebooks, Inc.

Cowsill, Alan. World War One, 1914-1918. Sharma, Lalit Kumar, illus. 2014. (Campfire Graphic Novels Ser.). (ENG.). 114p. (YA). (gr. 8-12). pap. 12.99 *(978-93-80741-85-7(5),* Campfire) Steerforth Pr.

Crew, Gary. Memorial. Tan, Shaun, illus. 32p. *(978-0-85091-983-7(5),* Lothian Children's Bks.) Hachette Australia.

Daviess, Maria Thompson. The Golden Bird. 2007. 92p. per. *(978-1-4068-1853-6(4))* Echo Library.

Deary, Terry. The War Game. 2014. (World War I Tales Ser.). (ENG., Illus.). 64p. (J). pap. 9.99 *(978-1-4081-9174-3(1),* 9781408191743, Bloomsbury USA Childrens) Bloomsbury Publishing USA.

Drake, Ensign Robert L. The Boy Allies with Uncle Sams Cruisers. 2004. reprint ed. pap. 21.95 *(978-1-4191-5495-9(8))* Kessinger Publishing, LLC.

Drake, Robert L. The Boy Allies at Jutland. 2005. 28.95 *(978-1-4218-0384-5(4))*; 264p. pap. 13.95 *(978-1-4218-0484-2(0))* 1st World Publishing, Inc. (1st World Library - Literary Society).

—The Boy Allies at Jutland. 2004. reprint ed. pap. 22.95 *(978-1-4191-5492-8(3))*; pap. 1.99 *(978-1-4192-5492-5(8))* Kessinger Publishing, LLC.

—The Boy Allies at Jutland: Or, the Greatest Naval Battle of History. l.t. ed. 2007. (ENG.). 346p. pap. 24.99 *(978-1-4264-3984-1(9))*; 166p. pap. 19.99 *(978-1-4264-3926-1(1))* Creative Media Partners, LLC.

—The Boy Allies under the Sea. 2005. 27.95 *(978-1-4218-1083-6(2))*; 244p. pap. 12.95 *(978-1-4218-1183-3(9))* 1st World Publishing, Inc. (1st World Library - Literary Society).

—The Boy Allies under Two Flags. 2005. 28.95 *(978-1-4218-0383-8(6))*; 256p. pap. 13.95 *(978-1-4218-0483-5(2))* 1st World Publishing, Inc. (1st World Library - Literary Society).

—The Boy Allies under Two Flags. 2006. 162p. pap. 19.99 *(978-1-4264-4925-3(9))*; 184p. pap. 21.99 *(978-1-4264-5226-0(8))* Creative Media Partners, LLC.

—The Boy Allies under Two Flags. 2004. reprint ed. pap. 1.99 *(978-1-4192-5493-2(6))* Kessinger Publishing, LLC.

—The Boy Allies with the Victorious Fleet. 2005. 236p. pap. 12.95 *(978-1-4218-1182-6(0)*, 1st World Library - Literary Society) 1st World Publishing, Inc.

—The Boy Allies with the Victorious Fleets. 2005. 27.95 *(978-1-4218-1082-9(4)*, 1st World Library - Literary Society) 1st World Publishing, Inc.

—The Boy Allies with Uncle Sams Cruisers. 2005. 27.95 *(978-1-4218-1081-2(6))*; 212p. pap. 12.95 *(978-1-4218-1181-9(2))* 1st World Publishing, Inc. (1st World Library - Literary Society).

—The Boy Allies with Uncle Sams Cruisers. 2004. reprint ed. pap. 1.99 *(978-1-4192-5495-6(2))* Kessinger Publishing, LLC.

Driscoll, James R. The Brighton Boys with the Flying Corps. 2005. 26.95 *(978-1-59540-818-1(5)*, 1st World Library - Literary Society) 1st World Publishing, Inc.

—The Brighton Boys with the Submarine Fleet. 2005. 26.95 *(978-1-59540-819-8(3)*, 1st World Library - Literary Society) 1st World Publishing, Inc.

Dunn, Joeming. Armistice Day. Dunn, Ben, illus. 2016. (Graphic Warfare Ser.). (ENG.). 32p. (J). (gr. 3-8). 28.50 *(978-1-61641-978-3(4))* Magic Wagon.

Durston, George. Boy Scouts' Victory. 2005. pap. 26.95 *(978-1-885529-58-9(9))* Stevens Publishing.

Emerson, Alice B. Ruth Fielding at the War Front. 2007. 148p. per. *(978-1-4065-2538-0(3))* Dodo Pr.

Farenhorst, Christine. A Cup of Cold Water: The Compassion of Nurse Edith Cavell. 2007. 222p. (J). (gr. 3-7). per. 11.99 *(978-1-59638-026-4(8))* P & R Publishing.

Fiske, James. The Belgians to the Front. 2007. (ENG.). 120p. pap. 18.99 *(978-1-4264-8476-6(3))*; 126p. pap. 19.99 *(978-1-4264-8253-3(1))* Creative Media Partners, LLC.

Fitzgugh, Percy Keese. Tom Slade with the Boys over There. 2007. (ENG.). 140p. pap. 18.99 *(978-1-4264-9511-3(0))*; 150p. pap. 19.99 *(978-1-4264-9892-3(6))* Creative Media Partners, LLC.

Fitzhugh, Percy K. Tom Slade: Motorcycle Dispatch Bearer. 2005. pap. 26.95 *(978-1-4191-6253-4(5))* Kessinger Publishing, LLC.

—Tom Slade with the Boys over There. 2005. (Illus.). pap. 24.95 *(978-1-885529-89-3(9))* Stevens Publishing.

—Tom Slade with the Flying Corps. 2005. (Illus.). pap. 27.95 *(978-1-885529-87-9(2))* Stevens Publishing.

Foreman, Michael. War Game (Special 100th Anniversary of WW1 Ed.) 100th ed. 2014. (ENG., Illus.). 96p. (J). (gr. 3-5). 17.99 *(978-1-84365-178-9(5)*, Pavilion) Pavilion Bks. GBR. Dist: Independent Pubs. Group.

French, Jackie. A Rose for the Anzac Boys. 2008. (Illus.). 304p. pap. *(978-0-7322-8540-1(2))* HarperCollins Pubs. Australia.

French, Moira. The Swingewood Stories. 2009. 36p. pap. 16.99 *(978-1-4490-4777-1(7))* AuthorHouse.

Frost, Helen. Crossing Stones. 2009. (ENG., Illus.). 192p. (YA). (gr. 7-18). 18.99 *(978-0-374-31653-2(8)*, 9780374316532, Farrar, Straus & Giroux (BYR)) Farrar, Straus & Giroux.

Goodman, Carol & Wells, Rosemary. Hawthorn. 2015. (Blythewood Novel Ser.). (ENG.). 416p. (YA). (gr. 7). bds. 17.99 *(978-0-670-78478-3(8)*, Viking Books for Young Readers) Penguin Young Readers Group.

Hagar, Erin. Doing Her Bit: A Story about the Women's Land Army of America. Hill, Jen, illus. 2016. (ENG.). 32p. (J). (gr. 1-4). lib. bdg. 16.95 *(978-1-58089-646-7(4))* Charlesbridge Publishing, Inc.

Hahn, Mary Downing. One for Sorrow: A Ghost Story. 2017. (ENG.). 304p. (J). (gr. 5-7). 16.99 *(978-0-544-81809-5(1))* Houghton Mifflin Harcourt Publishing Co.

Hancock, H. Irving. Uncle Sam's Boys with Pershing's Troops. 2006. 27.95 *(978-1-4218-2944-9(4))*; pap. 12.95 *(978-1-4218-3044-5(2))* 1st World Publishing, Inc.

Harrison, Charles. Generals Die in Bed: 100th Anniversary of World War I Special Edition. 100th ed. 2014. (ENG., Illus.). 168p. (YA). (gr. 9-18). pap. 11.95 *(978-1-55451-692-6(7)*, 9781554516926) Annick Pr., Ltd. CAN. Dist: Publishers Group West (PGW).

Hart, Alison. Darling, Mercy Dog of World War I, 1 vol. Montgomery, Michael G., illus. (Dog Chronicles Ser.: 5). (ENG.). (J). (gr. 2-5). 2017. 170p. pap. 7.95 *(978-1-56145-981-0(X))* 2013. 160p. 12.95 *(978-1-56145-705-2(1))* Peachtree Pubs.

Hartnett, Sonya. The Silver Donkey. Powers, Don, illus. 2014. (ENG.). 272p. (J). (gr. 5). 16.99 *(978-0-7636-7211-9(4))* Candlewick Pr.

—The Silver Donkey. Spudvilas, Anne, illus. 2004. viii, 193p. (J). *(978-0-670-04240-1(4)*, Viking Adult) Penguin Publishing Group.

Hayes, Clair W. The Boy Allies at Verdun. 2005. 28.95 *(978-1-4218-0324-1(0))*; 264p. pap. 13.95 *(978-1-4218-0424-8(7))* 1st World Publishing, Inc. (1st World Library - Literary Society).

—The Boy Allies at Verdun. 2007. 200p. per. *(978-1-4065-4393-3(4))* Dodo Pr.

—The Boy Allies at Verdun or Saving France from the Enemy. 2007. 124p. (gr. -1-7). per. *(978-1-4068-1712-6(0))* Echo Library.

—The Boy Allies in Great Peril. 2007. 200p. per. *(978-1-4065-4394-0(2))* Dodo Pr.

—The Boy Allies in the Balkan Campaign. 2007. 208p. per. *(978-1-4065-4395-7(0))* Dodo Pr.

—The Boy Allies in the Balkan Campaign or the Struggle to Save a Nation. 2007. 128p. per. *(978-1-4068-1714-0(7))* Echo Library.

—The Boy Allies in the Trenches. 2007. 192p. per. *(978-1-4065-4396-4(9))* Dodo Pr.

—The Boy Allies on the Firing Line. 2007. 188p. per. *(978-1-4065-4397-1(7))* Dodo Pr.

—The Boy Allies on the Firing Line or Twelve Days Battle along the Marne. 2007. 120p. per. *(978-1-4068-1716-4(3))* Echo Library.

—The Boy Allies with Haig in Flanders. 2007. 172p. per. *(978-1-4065-4398-8(5))* Dodo Pr.

—The Boy Allies with Haig in Flanders. 2004. reprint ed. pap. 21.95 *(978-1-4191-5494-2(X))*; pap. 1.99 *(978-1-4192-5494-9(4))* Kessinger Publishing, LLC.

Hayes, Clair Wallace. The Boy Allies at Verdun: Saving France from the Enemy. 2007. (ENG.). 174p. pap. 19.99 *(978-1-4264-7694-5(9))*; 190p. pap. 21.99 *(978-1-4264-7752-2(X))* Creative Media Partners, LLC.

Hendrix, John, illus. Shooting at the Stars: The Christmas Truce of 1914. 2014. (ENG.). 40p. (J). (gr. 3-7). 18.95 *(978-1-4197-1175-6(X)*, Abrams Bks. for Young Readers) Abrams, Inc.

Herwick Rice, Dona & Sugarman, Dorothy. World War I: In Flanders Fields, 1 vol. 2009. (Building Fluency Through Reader's Theater Ser.). (ENG.). 32p. (J). (gr. 3-5). pap. 7.99 *(978-1-4333-0551-1(8))* Teacher Created Materials, Inc.

Hooper, Mary. Poppy. 2016. (ENG.). 288p. (YA). 17.99 *(978-1-61963-496-1(1)*, 9781619634961, Bloomsbury USA Childrens) Bloomsbury Publishing USA.

Hopkinson, Deborah. Knit Your Bit. Guarnaccia, Steven, illus. 2013. (ENG.). 32p. (J). (gr. k-3). 16.99 *(978-0-399-25241-9(X)*, G.P. Putnam's Sons Books for Young Readers) Penguin Young Readers Group.

Huggins-Cooper, Lynn & Hayward, Ian Benfold. One Boy's War. 2014. (ENG., Illus.). 32p. (J). (gr. 2-6). pap. 8.99 *(978-1-84780-126-5(9)*, Frances Lincoln) Quarto Publishing Group UK GBR. Dist: Hachette Bk. Group.

Jorgenson, Norman. In Flanders Fields. Harrison-Lever, Brian, illus. 2010. (ENG.). 32p. (J). (gr. -1-3). pap. 9.95 *(978-1-894965-83-5(3))* Simply Read Bks. CAN. Dist: Ingram Publisher Services.

Kassel, Roger de. Mr P & the Red Poppy. 2013. (Illus.). 22p. pap. 8.75 *(978-1-78035-707-2(9)*, Fastprint Publishing) Upfront Publishing Ltd. GBR. Dist: Printondemand-worldwide.com.

Keenan, Sheila. Dogs of War. Fox, Nathan, illus. 2013. (ENG.). 176p. (J). (gr. 3-7). pap. 12.99 *(978-0-545-12888-9(9)*, Graphix) Scholastic, Inc.

Klimo, Kate. Stubby. Jessell, Tim, illus. 2015. (Dog Diaries: 7). (ENG.). 160p. (J). (gr. 2-5). lib. bdg. 12.99 *(978-0-385-39244-0(3)*, Random Hse. Bks. for Young Readers) Random Hse. Children's Bks.

Lalana, Fernando & Almarcegui, Jose Maria. La Bomba. 2003. (SPA.). 144p. *(978-84-216-1540-9(8)*, BU5058) Bruño, Editorial ESP. Dist: Lectorum Pubns., Inc.

Landsberry, Belinda. Anzac Ted. 2016. (ENG., Illus.). 32p. (J). (gr. -1-5). 17.99 *(978-1-921966-56-9(4)*, EK Bks.) Exisle Publishing Pty Ltd. AUS. Dist: Hachette Bk. Group.

Larson, Kirby. Hattie Big Sky. (ENG.). (YA). (gr. 7-7). 2008. 304p. 7.99 *(978-0-385-73595-7(2)*, Yearling) 2007. 320p. pap. 8.99 *(978-0-440-23941-3(9)*, Ember) Random Hse. Children's Bks.

—Hattie Big Sky. l.t. ed. 2007. (Literacy Bridge Young Adult Ser.). 381p. (YA). (gr. 7-12). 23.95 *(978-0-7862-9697-2(6))* Thorndike Pr.

Lewis, J. Patrick. And the Soldiers Sang. Kelley, Gary, illus. 2011. (ENG.). 32p. (J). (gr. 4-7). 19.99 *(978-1-56846-220-2(4)*, Creative Editions) Creative Co., The.

MacLeod, Elizabeth. Bunny the Brave War Horse: Based on a True Story. Lafrance, Marie, illus. 2014. (ENG.). 32p. (J). (gr. 1-3). 16.95 *(978-1-77138-024-9(1))* Kids Can Pr., Ltd. CAN. Dist: Hachette Bk. Group.

McCutcheon, John. Christmas in the Trenches, 1 vol. Sorensen, Henri, illus. 2006. (ENG.). 32p. (J). (gr. 1-5). 18.95 *(978-1-56145-374-0(9))* Peachtree Pubs.

McDavid-Jones, Elizabeth. The Night Flyers. 2009. (Mysteries Through Time Ser.). 144 - 176p. (YA). (gr. 4-8). 31.95 *(978-1-60754-197-4(1))*; pap. 15.25 *(978-1-60754-198-1(X))* Windmill Bks.

McDonough, Yona Zeldis. The Doll Shop Downstairs. Maione, Heather, illus. 2011. (ENG.). 128p. (J). (gr. 2-5). 5.99 *(978-0-14-241691-4(6)*, Puffin Books) Penguin Young Readers Group.

Millard, Glenda. Once a Shepherd. Lesnie, Phil, illus. 2014. (ENG.). 32p. (J). (gr. -1-3). 16.99 *(978-0-7636-7458-8(3))* Candlewick Pr.

Miller, Sarah. The Lost Crown. (ENG., Illus.). 448p. (gr. 7). 2012. (YA). pap. 9.99 *(978-1-4169-8341-5(4))* 2011. (J). 17.99 *(978-1-4169-8340-8(6))* Simon & Schuster Children's Publishing. (Atheneum Bks. for Young Readers).

Montgomery, L. M. Rilla of Ingleside. 2007. (ENG.). 284p. pap. 21.99 *(978-1-4346-5285-0(8))*; 314p. pap. 24.99 *(978-1-4346-5286-7(6))* Creative Media Partners, LLC.

—Rilla of Ingleside. 2004. 224p. (YA). pap. 10.95 *(978-1-57646-891-3(7))* Quiet Vision Publishing.

—Rilla of Ingleside. 2006. 384p. pap. 25.45 *(978-1-59462-427-8(5)*, Book Jungle) Standard Pubns., Inc.

Morpurgo, Michael. The Best Christmas Present in the World. Foreman, Michael, illus. 2004. (ENG.). 48p. (J). (gr. k-4). 9.99 *(978-1-4052-1518-3(6))* Egmont Bks., Ltd. GBR. Dist: Independent Pubs. Group.

—Listen to the Moon. 2015. (ENG.). 352p. (J). (gr. 5-9). 16.99 *(978-1-250-04204-0(6)*, 9781250042040) Feiwel & Friends.

—Private Peaceful. 2006. 18.00 *(978-0-7569-6630-0(2))* Perfection Learning Corp.

—Private Peaceful. 2006. (YA). 1.25 *(978-1-4193-2976-0(6))* Recorded Bks., Inc.

—Private Peaceful. 2006. (After Words Ser.). (ENG., Illus.). 224p. (J). (gr. 7-12). per. 7.99 *(978-0-439-63653-7(1)*, Scholastic Paperbacks) Scholastic, Inc.

—War Horse. 2nd ed. 2013. (ENG., Illus.). 72p. pap. 9.38 *(978-0-19-424982-9(4))* Oxford Univ. Pr., Inc.

—War Horse. 2010. (ENG.). 176p. (J). (gr. 3-7). pap. 7.99 *(978-0-439-79664-4(4)*, Scholastic Pr.) Scholastic, Inc.

Myers, Walter Dean. Invasion. (ENG.). 224p. (J). 2015. (gr. 6). pap. 8.99 *(978-0-545-38429-2(X))* 2013. (gr. 7). 17.99 *(978-0-545-38428-5(1))* Scholastic, Inc. (Scholastic Pr.).

O'Brien, Johnny. Day of the Assassins. Hardcastle, Nick, illus. 2010. (Jack Christie Adventure Ser.: 1). (ENG.). 224p. (J). (gr. 4-7). pap. 6.99 *(978-0-7636-4995-1(3)*, Templar) Candlewick Pr.

—Day of the Assassins: A Jack Christie Novel. Hardcastle, Nick, illus. 2009. (Jack Christie Adventure Ser.: 1). (ENG.). 224p. (J). (gr. 4-7). 15.99 *(978-0-7636-4595-3(8)*, Templar) Candlewick Pr.

Pickett, Anola. Callahan Crossroads. 2015. (ENG.). 192p. (J). pap. 12.99 *(978-1-4621-1715-4(5)*, Sweetwater Bks.) Cedar Fort, Inc./CFI Distribution.

Plamer, Anthony. Soldier's Gift. 2017. (ENG., Illus.). 44p. (J). (gr. 3-7). 14.99 **(978-0-14-350716-1(8))** Penguin Books Australia AUS. Dist: Independent Pubs. Group.

Randall, Homer. Army Boys in the French Trenches: Or, Hand to Hand Fighting with the Enemy. 2007. (ENG.). 140p. pap. 18.99 *(978-1-4264-3679-6(3))*; 230p. pap. 22.99 *(978-1-4264-3736-6(6))* Creative Media Partners, LLC.

Reid, Charles. Ghost of Heroes Past. 2010. (ENG., Illus.). 170p. pap. 10.95 *(978-1-55380-102-3(4))* Ronsdale Pr. CAN. Dist: SPD-Small Pr. Distribution.

Remarque, Erich Maria. All Quiet on the Western Front. Wimperis, Sarah, illus. 2014. (World War I Ser.). (ENG.). 64p. pap. 6.95 *(978-1-906230-66-1(8))* Real Reads Ltd. GBR. Dist: Casemate Pubs. & Bk. Distributors, LLC.

Remarque, Erich-Maria. All Quiet on the Western Front: With Related Readings. Wheen, A. W., tr. from GER. 2003. (EMC Masterpiece Series Access Editions). (Illus.). xxv, 249p. (YA). 13.99 *(978-0-8219-2420-4(6))* EMC/Paradigm Publishing.

Robert L. Drake. The Boy Allies with the Victorious Fleets: The Fall of the German Navy. l.t. ed. 2007. 384p. pap. 21.99 *(978-1-4264-8195-6(0))* Creative Media Partners, LLC.

Salten, Felix. Renni the Rescuer. Kaufman, Kenneth C., tr. from GER. 2013. (Bambi's Classic Animal Tales Ser.). (ENG., Illus.). 384p. (J). (gr. 3-7). pap. 6.99 *(978-1-4424-8273-9(7)*, Aladdin) Simon & Schuster Children's Publishing.

—Renni the Rescuer. Kaufman, Kenneth C., tr. from GER. 2013. (Bambi's Classic Animal Tales Ser.). (ENG., Illus.). 384p. (J). (gr. 3-7). 16.99 *(978-1-4424-8274-6(5)*, Simon & Schuster/Paula Wiseman Bks.) Simon & Schuster/Paula Wiseman Bks.

Saunders, Kate & Nesbit, E. Five Children on the Western Front. 2016. (J). *(978-0-553-49785-4(5)*, Delacorte Pr) Random House Publishing Group.

Searching for Silverheels. 2014. (ENG., Illus.). 304p. (J). (gr. 5-9). 16.99 *(978-1-4814-0029-9(0)*, McElderry, Margaret K. Bks.) McElderry, Margaret K. Bks.

Skrypuch, Marsha Forchuk. Dance of the Banished, 1 vol. 2015. (ENG., Illus.). 288p. (YA). (gr. 7-11). pap. 12.95 *(978-1-927485-65-1(7))* Pajama Pr. CAN. Dist: Ingram Publisher Services.

Skurzynski, Gloria. Good-Bye, Billy Radish. 2013. (ENG., Illus.). 152p. (J). (gr. 3-7). pap. 13.99 *(978-1-4814-0158-6(0)*, Simon & Schuster Bks. For Young Readers) Simon & Schuster Bks. For Young Readers.

Spillebeen, Geert. Kipling's Choice. Edelstein, Terese, tr. 2007. (ENG.). 160p. (YA). (gr. 7-9). pap. 12.95 *(978-0-618-80035-3(2))* Houghton Mifflin Harcourt Publishing Co.

—Kipling's Choice. Edelstein, Terese, tr. 2007. 147p. (YA). (gr. 7-9). 15.65 *(978-0-7569-8061-0(5))* Perfection Learning Corp.

Thompson, Emma. Nanny Mcphee Returns, Vol. 2. 2010. (ENG., Illus.). 304p. (J). (gr. 3-6). pap. 7.99 *(978-1-59990-472-6(1)*, 9781599904726, Bloomsbury USA Childrens) Bloomsbury Publishing USA.

Trottier, Maxine. Forget-Me-Not, 1 vol. Keating, Nancy, illus. 2008. (ENG.). 32p. (J). (gr. 1-8). pap. 10.95 *(978-1-897174-24-1(1)*, Tuckamore Bks.) Creative Bk. Publishing CAN. Dist: Orca Bk. Pubs. USA.

Van Dyne, Edith. Aunt Jane's Nieces in the Red Cross. rev. ed. 2006. 180p. 26.95 *(978-1-4218-1724-8(1))*; pap. 11.95 *(978-1-4218-1824-5(8))* 1st World Publishing, Inc. (1st World Library - Literary Society).

Watts, Helen & Thomas, Taffy. The Ghost of the Trenches & Other Stories. 2014. (ENG.). 128p. (YA). (gr. 4-6). pap. 10.99 *(978-1-4729-0787-5(6)*, 9781472907875, Bloomsbury USA Childrens) Bloomsbury Publishing USA.

Watts, Julia. Secret City. 2013. (ENG.). 264p. (gr. 7). pap. 11.95 *(978-1-59493-390-5(1))* Bella Bks., Inc.

Wilson, John. And in the Morning. 2010. (ENG.). 200p. (YA). (gr. 7-18). pap. *(978-1-55470-264-0(X))* Me to We.

Winters, Cat. In the Shadow of Blackbirds. 2013. (ENG., Illus.). 400p. (YA). (gr. 7-17). 17.95 *(978-1-4197-0530-4(X)*, Amulet Bks.) Abrams, Inc.

WORLD WAR, 1914-1918—NAVAL OPERATIONS

Jeffrey, Gary. War at Sea. 2013. (ENG., Illus.). 48p. (J). *(978-0-7787-0913-8(2))*; pap. *(978-0-7787-0923-7(X))* Crabtree Publishing Co.

Otfinoski, Steven. The Sinking of the Lusitania: An Interactive History Adventure, 1 vol. 2014. (You Choose: History Ser.). (ENG.). 112p. (gr. 3-4). 31.99 *(978-1-4765-4186-0(8)*, You Choose Bks.) Capstone Press of Coughlan Cos.

Preston, Diana. Remember the Lusitania! 2004. (Illus.). 112p. (J). (gr. 3-7). 21.85 *(978-0-8027-8847-4(5))* Walker & Co.

WORLD WAR, 1914-1918—PERSONAL NARRATIVES

Allan, Robert Marshall, et al. War Diaries. 2014. (Text Connections Ser.). (J). (gr. 5). *(978-1-4900-1386-2(5))* Benchmark Education Co.

Brooker, Marion Fargey. Hold the Oxo! A Teenage Soldier Writes Home. 2011. (Canadians at War Ser.: 6). (ENG., Illus.). 144p. (YA). pap. 14.99 *(978-1-55488-870-2(0))* Dundurn CAN. Dist: Ingram Publisher Services.

Rabjohn, R. H. & Wilson, John. A Soldier's Sketchbook: The Illustrated First World War Diary of R.H. Rabjohn. 2017. (ENG., Illus.). 112p. (J). (gr. 5). 16.99 *(978-1-77049-854-9(0)*, Tundra Bks.) Tundra Bks. CAN. Dist: Penguin Random Hse. LLC.

Zullo, Allan. World War I Heroes. 2015. (Ten True Tales Ser.). (ENG.). 176p. (J). (gr. 3-7). pap. 5.99 *(978-0-545-83751-4(0))* Scholastic, Inc.

WORLD WAR, 1914-1918—REGIMENTAL HISTORIES

Dowdy, Penny. The Battle of Vimy Ridge: Defining Moments in Canadian History/Graphic Novels. 2010. (Illus.). 32p. *(978-1-77071-615-5(7))* Weigl Educational Pubs. Ltd.

Raven, Margot Theis. Rags Hero Dog of WWI: A True Story. Brown, Petra, illus. 2014. (ENG.). 32p. (J). (gr. 2-5). 16.99 *(978-1-58536-258-5(1)*, 203672) Sleeping Bear Pr.

WORLD WAR, 1914-1918—UNITED STATES

Bausum, Ann. Unraveling Freedom: The Battle for Democracy on the Homefront During World War I. 2010. (ENG., Illus.). 96p. (J). (gr. 5-18). 19.95 *(978-1-4263-0702-7(0))*; 28.90 *(978-1-4263-0703-4(9))* National Geographic Society. (National Geographic Children's Bks.).

Bosco, Peter. World War I. 2nd rev. ed. 2010. (America at War Ser.). 200p. (gr. 6-12). 45.00 *(978-0-8160-8188-2(3))* Facts On File, Inc.

Crompton, Samuel Willard. How Woodrow Wilson Fought World War I. 2017. (Presidents at War Ser.). 128p. (J). (gr. 8-8). lib. bdg. 37.27 **(978-0-7660-8529-9(5))** Enslow Pubs., Inc.

Dunn, Joeming & Dunn, Ben. Cher Ami: WWI Homing Pigeon, 1 vol. 2011. (Famous Firsts: Animals Making History Ser.). (ENG., Illus.). 32p. (YA). (gr. 3-6). 28.50 *(978-1-61641-639-3(4))* Magic Wagon.

Feldman, Ruth Tenzer. World War I. 2004. (Chronicle of America's Wars Ser.). (Illus.). 88p. (gr. 5-12). lib. bdg. 27.93 *(978-0-8225-0148-0(1))* Lerner Publishing Group.

Fisher, Douglas & McGraw-Hill Staff. The American Journey to World War 1, Active Reading Note-Taking Guide Student Workbook. 2005. (MS Wh Jat Building America Ser.). (ENG., Illus.). 350p. (gr. 6-8). per. 12.28 *(978-0-07-870384-3(0)*, 0078703840) McGraw-Hill Education.

Gitlin, Marty. World War I. 2016. (Illus.). 48p. (J). *(978-1-5105-1294-8(2))* SmartBook Media, Inc.

Goldsworthy, Steve. World War I: 1914-1918. 2014. (Illus.). 48p. (J). *(978-1-62127-657-9(0))* Weigl Pubs., Inc.

Hamilton, John. Final Years of World War I, 1 vol. 2004. (World War I Ser.). (ENG.). 32p. (gr. 4-8). 27.07 *(978-1-57765-915-0(5)*, Abdo & Daughters) ABDO Publishing Co.

Haugen, David M. War in Hemingway's a Farewell to Arms. Gale, ed. 2014. (Social Issues in Literature Ser.). (ENG., Illus.). 224p. (gr. 7-12). lib. bdg. 46.40 *(978-0-7377-6395-9(7)*, Greenhaven Pr., Inc.) Cengage Gale.

Kent, Zachary. World War I: From the Lusitania to Versailles. 2011. (United States at War Ser.). (Illus.). 128p. (J). (gr. 5-18). lib. bdg. 33.27 *(978-0-7660-3641-3(3))* Enslow Pubs., Inc.

McGraw-Hill Education Staff. The American Journey to World War 1, Reading Essentials. 2005. (MS Wh Jat Building America Ser.). (ENG.). (gr. 6-9). pap., stu. ed., wbk. ed. 11.92 *(978-0-07-873198-3(4)*, 0078731984) McGraw-Hill Higher Education.

—The American Journey to World War 1, StudentWorks Plus! 2005. (MS Wh Jat Building America Ser.). (ENG.). (gr. 6-9). cd-rom 149.36 *(978-0-07-873445-8(2)*, 0078734452) McGraw-Hill Higher Education.

Micklos, John, Jr. Harlem Hellfighters: African-American Heroes of World War I. 2017. (Military Heroes Ser.). (ENG., Illus.). 32p. (gr. 3-4). lib. bdg. 27.32 *(978-1-5157-3348-5(3))* Capstone Press of Coughlan Cos.

Osborne, Linda Barrett. Come on in, America: The United States in World War I. 2017. (ENG., Illus.). 176p. (J). (gr. 5-17). 17.95 *(978-1-4197-2378-0(2)*, Abrams Bks. for Young Readers) Abrams, Inc.

Price, Sean Stewart. Yanks in World War I: Americans in the Trenches, 1 vol. 2008. (American History Through Primary Sources Ser.). (ENG., Illus.). 32p. (gr. 2-2). 29.99 *(978-1-4109-3110-8(2)*, Raintree Fusion) Heinemann-Raintree.

Raven, Margot Theis. Rags Hero Dog of WWI: A True Story. Brown, Petra, illus. 2014. (ENG.). 32p. (J). (gr. 2-5). 16.99 *(978-1-58536-258-5(1)*, 203672) Sleeping Bear Pr.

Rissman, Rebecca. World War I: Why They Fought. 2015. (What Were They Fighting For? Ser.). (ENG., Illus.). 64p. (gr. 5-9). 34.65 *(978-0-7565-5170-4(6))* Compass Point Bks.

Vander Hook, Sue. The United States Enters World War I, 1 vol. 2010. (Essential Events Set 4 Ser.). (ENG.). 112p. (J). (gr. 6-12). lib. bdg. 35.64 *(978-1-60453-947-9(X))* ABDO Publishing Co.

World War I & the Roaring Twenties, 1914-1928. 2010. (Discovering U. S. History Ser.). (Illus.). 136p. (J). (gr. 5-8). 35.00 *(978-1-60413-356-1(2)*, Chelsea Hse.) Facts On File, Inc.

Worth, Richard. America in World War I. 2006. (Wars That Changed American History Ser.). (Illus.). 48p. (gr. 5-12). lib. bdg. 31.00 *(978-0-8368-7292-7(4)*, Gareth Stevens Secondary Library) Stevens, Gareth Publishing LLLP.

WORLD WAR, 1939-1945

ABDO Publishing Company Staff. World War II, 1 vol. 2011. (World War II Ser.). (ENG., Illus.). 32p. 162.42 *(978-1-61783-058-7(5)*, Abdo & Daughters) ABDO Publishing Co.

Adams, Simon. World War II. 2014. (DK Eyewitness Bks.). (ENG.). 72p. (J). (gr. 3-7). pap. 9.99 *(978-1-4654-2059-6(2)*, DK Children) Dorling Kindersley Publishing, Inc.

—50 Thing You Should Know about the Second World War. 2015. (50 Things You Should Know About Ser.). (ENG., Illus.). 80p. (J). (gr. 4-7). pap. 15.95 *(978-1-60992-770-7(2))* QEB Publishing Inc.

Adamson, Thomas K. World War II. 2015. (Wars in U. S. History Ser.). (ENG.). 32p. (J). (gr. 2-5). 28.50 *(978-1-63143-709-0(7)*, 208542) Child's World, Inc., The.

Allen, John. Cause & Effect World War II: World War II. 2015. (ENG., Illus.). 80p. (J). lib. bdg. *(978-1-60152-798-1(5))* ReferencePoint Pr., Inc.

Altman, Linda Jacobs. Warsaw, Lodz, Vilna: The Holocaust Ghettos. 2014. (Remembering the Holocaust Ser.). 96p. (J). (gr. 6-12). pap. 10.95 *(978-0-7660-6208-5(2))* Enslow Pubs., Inc.

W X Y Z

Amis, Nancy. The Orphans of Normandy: A True Story of World War II Told Through Drawings by Children. 2016. (ENG., Illus.). 48p. (J). (gr. 3-7). pap. 13.99 (978-1-4814-9470-0(8), Atheneum Bks. for Young Readers) Simon & Schuster Children's Publishing.

Anderson, M. T. Symphony for the City of the Dead: Dmitri Shostakovich & the Siege of Leningrad. 2015. (ENG., Illus.). 464p. (YA). (gr. 9). 25.99 (978-0-7636-6818-1(4)) Candlewick Pr.

Atwood, Kathryn J. Women Heroes of World War II: The Pacific Theater - 15 Stories of Resistance, Rescue, Sabotage, & Survival. 2016. (Women of Action Ser.). (ENG., Illus.). 240p. (YA). (gr. 9). 19.99 (978-1-61373-168-0(X)) Chicago Review Pr., Inc.

Bailey, Rachel A. The Japanese Internment Camps: A History Perspectives Book. 2014. (Perspectives Library). (ENG., Illus.). 32p. (J). (gr. 4-8). 28.50 (978-1-62431-666-1(2), 203228) Cherry Lake Publishing.

Bains, Alisha, ed. World War II. 2016. (Political & Diplomatic History of the Modern World Ser.). 224p. (J). (gr. 10-10). 46.00 (978-1-68048-360-4(9)) Rosen Publishing Group, Inc., The.

Baldwin, Douglas & Baldwin, Patricia. World War II. 2010. (Illus.). 48p. (978-1-55388-720-1(4)) Weigl Educational Pubs. Ltd.

Baldwin, Douglas & Baldwin, Patricia L. World War II. 2010. (Illus.). 48p. pap. (978-1-55388-724-9(7)) Weigl Educational Pubs. Ltd.

Barber, Nicola. Who Broke the Wartime Codes?, 1 vol. 2014. (Primary Source Detectives Ser.). (ENG., Illus.). 64p. (gr. 7-8). lib. bdg. 35.99 (978-1-4329-9606-2(1)) Heinemann-Raintree.

Barlow, Cassie B. & Norrod, Sue Hill. Saluting Our Grandmas: Women of World War II, 1 vol. 2017. (ENG., Illus.). 176p. (YA). (gr. 7-12). pap. 18.95 (**978-1-4556-2319-8(9)**) Pelican Publishing Co., Inc.

Bascomb, Neal. The Nazi Hunters: How a Team of Spies & Survivors Captured the World's Most Notorious Nazi. 2013. (ENG., Illus.). 256p. (J). (gr. 7). 17.99 (978-0-545-43099-9(2), Levine, Arthur A. Bks.) Scholastic, Inc.

—Sabotage: The Mission to Destroy Hitler's Atomic Bomb. 2016. (ENG., Illus.). 320p. (J). (gr. 7). 17.99 (978-0-545-73243-7(3), Levine, Arthur A. Bks.) Scholastic, Inc.

Bearce, Stephanie. World War II: Spies, Secret Missions, & Hidden Facts from World War II. 2014. (Top Secret Files of History Ser.: 0). (ENG.). 125p. (J). (gr. 4-7). pap. 8.95 (978-1-61821-244-3(3)) Prufrock Pr.

Becker, Peggy Daniels. Japanese-American Internment During World War II. 2013. (Defining Moments Ser.). 240p. lib. bdg. 55.00 (978-0-7808-1333-5(2)) Omnigraphics, Inc.

Bell-Rehwoldt, Sheri. Great World War II Projects: You Can Build Yourself. 2006. (Build It Yourself Ser.). (ENG., Illus.). 128p. (J). (gr. 3-7). pap. 15.95 (978-0-9771294-1-6(1)) Northern Trails Pr.

Benchmark Education Co., LLC. The Aftermath of World War II. 2014. (PRIME Ser.). (J). (gr. 6-8). pap. (978-1-4509-9501-6(2)) Benchmark Education Co.

Benchmark Education Company. World War II (Teacher Guide) By the Numbers. 2004. (978-1-4108-2589-6(2)) Benchmark Education Co.

Bingham, Jane. World War II. 2017. (Explore! Ser.). (ENG., Illus.). 32p. (J). (gr. 4-6). pap. 11.99 (978-0-7502-8883-5(3), Wayland) Hachette Children's Group GBR. Dist: Hachette Bk. Group.

Black, Hermann. World War II. 2008. (Wars Day by Day Ser.). 48p. (gr. 5-9). 37.10 (978-1-933834-41-2(2)) Brown Bear Bks.

Blohm, Craig E. Holocaust Camps & Killing Centers. 2015. (ENG., Illus.). 80p. (J). lib. bdg. (978-1-60152-842-1(6)) ReferencePoint Pr., Inc.

—Holocaust Resistance. 2015. (ENG., Illus.). 80p. (J). lib. bdg. (978-1-60152-846-9(9)) ReferencePoint Pr., Inc.

Booth, Owen & Walton, John. World War II. 2016. (Primary Sources in World Warfare Ser.). 256p. (YA). lib. bdg. 55.00 (978-1-5026-2472-7(9)) Cavendish Square Publishing.

Braun, Eric. Trapped Behind Enemy Lines: The Story of the U. S. Army Air Force 807th Medical Evacuation Squadron. 2016. (Encounter: Narrative Nonfiction Stories Ser.). (ENG., Illus.). 224p. (gr. 4-6). lib. bdg. 32.65 (978-1-4914-8042-7(4), 1400082) Encounter Bks.

Brook, Henry. D-Day. rev. ed. 2008. (True Stories Ser.). 160p. (J). pap. 4.99 (978-0-7945-1840-0(0), Usborne) EDC Publishing.

Burgan, Michael. Raising the Flag: How a Photograph Gave a Nation Hope in Wartime, 1 vol. 2011. (Captured History Ser.). (ENG.). 64p. (gr. 5-7). pap. 9.10 (978-0-7565-4449-2(1)); lib. bdg. 34.65 (978-0-7565-4395-2(9)) Compass Point Bks. (CPB Grades 4-8).

—Weapons, Gear, & Uniforms of World War II, 1 vol. 2012. (Equipped for Battle Ser.). (ENG.). 32p. (gr. 3-4). lib. bdg. 27.99 (978-1-4296-7650-2(7), Edge Bks.) Capstone Press of Coughlan Cos.

Burgan, Michael, et al. Equipped for Battle. 2012. (Equipped for Battle Ser.). (ENG.). 32p. (gr. 3-4). lib. bdg. 167.94 (978-1-4296-8191-9(8), Edge Bks.) Capstone Press of Coughlan Cos.

Burian, Boris & Zhizhenko, V. A. Nekogda Ne Zabudem: Rasskazy Belorusskikh Rebiat o Dniakh Velikoi Otechestvennoi Voiny. 2010. (RUS., Illus.). 330p. (J). (978-985-02-1082-1(6)) Mastackaja litaratura, Vydavectva.

Burrell, Bill. The Path to Glory. 2011. 24p. pap. (978-1-4269-9427-2(3)) Trafford Publishing (UK) Ltd.

Burrows, Terry. Codes, Ciphers, & Cartography: Math Goes to War. 2017. (STEM on the Battlefield Ser.). (ENG., Illus.). 48p. (J). (gr. 4-6). 31.99 (**978-1-5124-3927-4(4)**, Lerner Pubns.) Lerner Publishing Group.

Byers, Ann. Auschwitz, Bergen-Belsen, Treblinka: The Holocaust Camps. 2014. (Remembering the Holocaust Ser.). 96p. (J). (gr. 6-12). 27.94 (978-0-7660-6212-2(0)); pap. 10.95 (978-0-7660-6213-9(9)) Enslow Pubs., Inc.

Chandler, Matt. Behind Enemy Lines: The Escape of Robert Grimes with the Comet Line Ginevra, Dante, illus. 2017. (Great Escapes of World War II Ser.). (ENG.). 32p. (gr. 3-4). lib. bdg. 30.65 (978-1-5157-3530-4(3), Graphic Library) Capstone Press of Coughlan Cos.

Chant, Christopher. The Allied Powers Fight Back. 2017. (World War II Ser.: Vol. 5). (ENG.). (YA). (gr. 7-12). 24.95 (**978-1-4222-3895-0(4)**) Mason Crest.

Chrisp, Peter. The Story of the Second World War for Children. 2016. (ENG., Illus.). 64p. (J). (gr. 5). 17.95 (978-1-78312-115-1(7)) Carlton Kids GBR. Dist: Sterling Publishing Co., Inc.

Clare, John D. Vietnam, 1939-75. 2nd rev. ed. 2004. (Hodder 20th Century History Ser.). (Illus.). 48p. (YA). pap. 26.50 (978-0-340-81476-5(4), Hodder Education) Hodder Education Group GBR. Dist: Trans-Atlantic Pubns., Inc.

Conway, John Richard. Primary Source Accounts of World War II. 2006. (America's Wars Through Primary Sources Ser.). (Illus.). 128p. (J). (gr. 4-7). lib. bdg. 34.60 (978-1-59845-002-6(6), MyReportLinks.com Bks.) Enslow Pubs., Inc.

Cooke, Tim. Behind the Lines. 2015. (World War II: the Full Story Ser.). (Illus.). 48p. (gr. 4-8). 37.10 (978-1-78121-234-9(1)) Brown Bear Bks.

—Causes & Outbreak. 2015. (World War II: the Full Story Ser.). (Illus.). 48p. (gr. 4-8). 37.10 (978-1-78121-229-5(5)) Brown Bear Bks.

—Home Fronts. 2015. (World War II: the Full Story Ser.). (Illus.). 48p. (gr. 4-8). 37.10 (978-1-78121-232-5(5)) Brown Bear Bks.

—Life in the War. 2015. (World War II: the Full Story Ser.). (Illus.). 48p. (gr. 4-8). 37.10 (978-1-78121-233-2(3)) Brown Bear Bks.

—War in the Pacific (1941-1945) 2015. (World War II: the Full Story Ser.). (Illus.). 48p. (gr. 4-8). 37.10 (978-1-78121-231-8(7)) Brown Bear Bks.

—World War II on the Front Lines, 1 vol. 2014. (Life on the Front Lines Ser.). (ENG., Illus.). 32p. (gr. 3-4). lib. bdg. 27.99 (978-1-4914-0844-5(8)) Capstone Press of Coughlan Cos.

Copeland, Peter F. Story of World War II. 2004. (Dover History Coloring Book Ser.). (ENG., Illus.). 48p. (gr. 3-8). pap. 4.99 (978-0-486-43695-1(0)) Dover Pubns., Inc.

Corrigan, Jim. World War II, Vol. 11. Musteen, Jason R., ed. 2015. (Major U. S. Historical Wars Ser.). (Illus.). 64p. (J). (gr. 7). lib. bdg. 23.95 (978-1-4222-3363-4(4)) Mason Crest.

Darman, Peter, ed. The Home Fronts: Allied & Axis Life During World War II. 2012. (World War II Ser.). (ENG., Illus.). 64p. (J). (gr. 7-12). lib. bdg. 31.95 (978-1-4488-9236-5(8)) Rosen Publishing Group, Inc., The.

Deem, James M. The Prisoners of Breendonk: Personal Histories from a World War II Concentration Camp. 2015. (ENG., Illus.). 352p. (YA). (gr. 9). 18.99 (978-0-544-09664-6(9), HMH Books For Young Readers) Houghton Mifflin Harcourt Publishing Co.

DeLibero, Nicholas & Benchmark Education Co. Staff. The Cadence of War. 2014. (Text Connections Ser.). (J). (gr. 5). (978-1-4900-1379-4(2)) Benchmark Education Co.

Dickmann, Nancy. The Horrors of World War II. 2017. (Deadly History Ser.). (ENG.). 48p. (gr. 3-4). lib. bdg. 33.32 (**978-1-4846-4165-1(5)**, Heinemann InfoSearch) Heinemann-Raintree.

Dickson, Keith D. World War II Almanac, 2 vols., Set. Facts on File, Inc. Staff, ed. 2008. (Almanacs of American Wars Ser.). 608p. (C). (gr. 9-18). 150.00 (978-0-8160-6297-3(8)) Facts On File, Inc.

Doeden, Matt. At Battle in World War II: An Interactive Battlefield Adventure. 2015. (You Choose: Battlefields Ser.). (ENG., Illus.). 112p. (gr. 3-4). lib. bdg. 31.99 (978-1-4914-2152-9(5), You Choose Bks.) Capstone Press of Coughlan Cos.

Doeden, Matt. Weapons of World War II. 2017. (Weapons of War Ser.). (ENG.). 32p. (gr. 2-3). lib. bdg. 26.65 (**978-1-5157-7906-3(8)**) Capstone Press of Coughlan Cos.

Dooling, Sandra. Japanese Internment: Defining Moments in Canadian History. 2011. (Illus.). 32p. (gr. 5-8). (978-1-77071-688-9(2)) Weigl Educational Pubs. Ltd.

Dorling Kindersley Publishing Staff. World War II: Visual Encyclopedia. 2015. (ENG., Illus.). 208p. (J). (gr. 4-7). 16.99 (978-1-4654-4027-3(5), DK Children) Dorling Kindersley Publishing, Inc.

Dorling Kindersley Publishing Staff & Matthews, Rupert. Battle in the Air. 2014. (DK Adventures Ser.). (ENG.). 128p. (J). (gr. 3-7). pap. 5.99 (978-1-4654-2839-4(9), DK Children) Dorling Kindersley Publishing, Inc.

Dougherty, Martin J. Tanks of World War II up Close, 01 vols., 1. Pearson, Colin, illus. 2016. (Military Technology: Top Secret Clearance Ser.). (ENG.). 224p. (YA). 43.60 (978-1-5081-7086-0(X), Rosen Young Adult) Rosen Publishing Group, Inc., The.

Dowswell, Paul. The Second World War. rev. ed. 2007. (True Stories Ser.). (Illus.). 169p. (YA). pap. 4.99 (978-0-7945-1841-7(9), Usborne) EDC Publishing.

—Second world war - internet Linked. Le, Leonard Rolland, illus. 2005. 128p. (J). 19.99 (978-0-7945-1044-2(2), Usborne) EDC Publishing.

—Story of Second World War. 2012. (Science Stories Ser.). 96p. (J). pap. 10.99 (978-0-7945-3247-5(0), Usborne) EDC Publishing.

—True Stories of the Second World War. 2004. (True Adventure Stories Ser.). 144p. (J). pap. 4.95 (978-0-7945-0599-8(6)) EDC Publishing.

—True Stories of the Second World War. 2004. (True Adventure Stories Ser.). (Illus.). 169p. (J). (gr. 5). lib. bdg. 12.95 (978-1-58086-615-6(8), Usborne) EDC Publishing.

—War Stories. rev. ed. 2012. (True Stories Ser.). 432p. (J). pap. 12.99 (978-0-7945-3221-5(7), Usborne) EDC Publishing.

Dowswell, Paul, et al. The World Wars: An Introduction to the First & Second World Wars. Chisholm, Jane, ed. 2007. (World Wars Ser.). (Illus.). 256p. (J). (gr. 4-7). 25.99 (978-0-7945-1971-1(7), Usborne) EDC Publishing.

Ellis, Catherine, ed. Key Figures of World War II. 2015. (Biographies of War Ser.). (ENG.). 112p. (YA). (gr. 7-8). 65.80 (978-1-68048-058-0(8), Britannica Educational Publishing) Rosen Publishing Group, Inc., The.

Emert, Phyllis Raybin. World War II: The European Theater. 2nd ed. 2005. (Perspectives on History Ser.). (ENG.). 64p. (YA). pap. 7.95 (978-1-932663-12-9(6)) History Compass, LLC.

Fein, Eric. Vehicles of World War II, 1 vol. 2013. (War Vehicles Ser.). (ENG.). 32p. (gr. 3-4). 27.99 (978-1-4296-9915-0(9), Edge Bks.) Capstone Press of Coughlan Cos.

Feinstein, Stephen. The 1940s from World War II to Jackie Robinson. rev. ed. 2006. (Decades of the 20th Century in Color Ser.). (Illus.). 64p. (J). (gr. 4-7). lib. bdg. 29.27 (978-0-7660-2634-6(5)) Enslow Pubs., Inc.

Fletcher, Robert A. Jeeps at War. Naples, Thomas R. et al, eds. Fletcher, Robert A., illus. 2008. (Illus.). 36p. (J). 19.95 (978-0-9722961-1-3(5)) Iron Mountain Pr.

Foster, Jo. Why Would a Dog Need a Parachute? Questions & Answers about the Second World. 2014. (ENG., Illus.). 160p. (J). (gr. 2-4). pap. 8.99 (978-1-4472-2618-5(6)) Pan Macmillan GBR. Dist: Independent Pubs. Group.

Freedman, Jeri. Strategic Inventions of World War II. 2016. (Tech in the Trenches Ser.). (ENG., Illus.). 112p. (J). (gr. 9-9). lib. bdg. 42.79 (978-1-5026-1026-3(4)) Cavendish Square Publishing.

George, Enzo. World War II. 2015. (Primary Sources in U. S. History Ser.). (ENG., Illus.). 48p. (J). (gr. 4-4). 31.36 (978-1-5026-0492-7(2)) Cavendish Square Publishing.

Gerdes, Louise I. World War II. 2004. (gr. 10-12). 17.45 (978-0-7377-2536-0(2), Greenhaven Pr., Inc.) Cengage Gale.

Gitlin, Martin. World War II on the Home Front: An Interactive History Adventure. 2012. (You Choose: History Ser.). (ENG.). 112p. (gr. 3-4). pap. 41.70 (978-1-4296-8483-5(6), You Choose Bks.) Capstone Press of Coughlan Cos.

Goldstein, Margaret J. World War II: Europe. 2004. (Chronicle of America's Wars Ser.). (Illus.). 96p. (J). (gr. 5-12). 27.93 (978-0-8225-0139-8(2)) Lerner Publishing Group.

Group/McGraw-Hill, Wright. History: World War II, 6 vols. (Book2WebTM Ser.). (gr. 4-8). 36.50 (978-0-322-04455-5(3)) Wright Group/McGraw-Hill.

Gutner, Howard. America's Secret Weapon: The Navajo Code Talkers of World War II. 2003. (ENG., Illus.). 32p. (J). (gr. 6-8). pap. 7.97 net. (978-0-7652-3266-3(9), Celebration Pr.) Pearson Schl.

Hamen, Susan E. World War II, 1 vol. 2013. (Essential Library of American Wars Ser.). (ENG., Illus.). 112p. (J). (gr. 6-12). lib. bdg. 35.64 (978-1-61783-882-8(9), Essential Library) ABDO Publishing Co.

Hamilton, John. World War II: Early Battles, 1 vol. 2011. (World War II Ser.). (ENG., Illus.). 32p. (YA). (gr. 5-9). 27.07 (978-1-61783-059-4(3)) ABDO Publishing Co.

—World War II: The Final Years, 1 vol. 2011. (World War II Ser.). (ENG., Illus.). 32p. (YA). (gr. 5-9). 27.07 (978-1-61783-060-0(7)) ABDO Publishing Co.

—World War II: Weapons, 1 vol. 2011. (World War II Ser.). (ENG., Illus.). 32p. (YA). (gr. 5-9). 27.07 (978-1-61783-064-8(X)) ABDO Publishing Co.

Heinrichs, Ann. The Japanese-American Internment: Innocence, Guilt, & Wartime Justice. 2010. (Perspectives on 2 Ser.). 112p. (gr. 7-10). 39.93 (978-0-7614-4983-6(3)) Marshall Cavendish Corp.

Hosch, William L. World War II: People, Politics, & Power. 2009. (America at War Ser.). 264p. (YA). (ENG.). 98.00 (978-1-61530-093-8(7)); (Illus.). (gr. 9-12). lib. bdg. 49.00 (978-1-61530-008-2(2)) Rosen Publishing Group, Inc., The.

Huey, Lois Miner. Voices of World War II: Stories from the Front Lines. 2010. (Voices of War Ser.). (ENG.). 32p. (gr. 3-4). pap. 47.70 (978-1-4296-5702-0(2), Edge Bks.) Capstone Press of Coughlan Cos.

Hunter, Nick. World War II: Frontline Soldiers & Their Families. 2015. (Frontline Families Ser.). (ENG., Illus.). 48p. (J). (gr. 5-6). pap. 14.05 (978-1-4824-3069-1(X)) Stevens, Gareth Publishing LLLP.

Hutchison, Patricia. World War II: 12 Things to Know. 2017. (America at War Ser.). (ENG., Illus.). 32p. (J). (gr. 3-6). 21.95 (978-1-63235-271-2(0)) Pr. Room Editions LLC.

Jones, Rob Lloyd. See Inside the Second World War. Pritelli, Maria Cristina, illus. 2012. (See Inside Board Bks). 16p. (J). ring bd. 13.99 (978-0-7945-3085-3(0), Usborne) EDC Publishing.

Kaelberer, Angie Peterson. Eyewitness to World War II. 2017. (Eyewitness to World War II Ser.). (ENG.). 112p. (gr. 5-7). 143.96 (**978-0-7565-5606-8(6)**, CPB Grades 4-8) Compass Point Bks.

Kaelberer, Angie Peterson & Burgan, Michael. Japanese American Internment. 2017. (Eyewitness to World War II Ser.). (ENG.). 112p. (gr. 5-7). pap. 8.95 (**978-0-7565-5585-6(X)**, CPB Grades 4-8) Compass Point Bks.

Keyes, Anna. World War II: 6 English, 6 Spanish Adaptations: by the Numbers & Los números de la Segunda Guerra Mundial. 2011. (ENG & SPA.). (J). 101.00 net. (978-1-4108-5736-1(0)) Benchmark Education Co.

—World War II by the Numbers: Set Of 6. 2011. (Navigators Ser.). (J). pap. 50.00 net. (978-1-4108-2574-2(4)) Benchmark Education Co.

Klar, Jeremy & Lily, Henrietta M. Josef Mengele, 01 vols., 1. 2016. (Holocaust Ser.). (ENG., Illus.). 112p. (J). 35.60 (978-1-5081-7047-1(9), Rosen Young Adult) Rosen Publishing Group, Inc., The.

Kramer, Ann. Women & War. 2009. (J). 24.25 (978-1-59771-142-5(X)) Sea-To-Sea Pubns.

Langley, Andrew. Stories of Women in World War II: We Can Do It! 2015. (Women's Stories from History Ser.). (ENG., Illus.). 112p. (gr. 6-11). 31.99 (978-1-4846-0865-4(8)) Heinemann-Raintree.

—World War II, 1 vol. (Living Through... Ser.). (ENG.). 2012. 80p. (gr. 7-8). lib. bdg. 37.32 (978-1-4329-6002-5(4)) 2010. (Illus.). 56p. (gr. 6-9). lib. bdg. 34.65 (978-1-4329-3493-4(7), NA-h) Heinemann-Raintree.

Lanier, Wendy H. Life During World War II, 1 vol. 2014. (Daily Life in US History Ser.). (ENG., Illus.). 48p. (J). (gr. 3-6). lib. bdg. 32.79 (978-1-62403-629-3(5)) ABDO Publishing Co.

Lanser, Amanda. World War II by the Numbers. 2015. (America at War by the Numbers Ser.). (ENG., Illus.). 32p. (gr. 3-4). lib. bdg. 27.99 (978-1-4914-4297-5(2)) Capstone Press of Coughlan Cos.

Lewis, J. Patrick. The Navajo Code Talkers. Kelley, Gary, illus. 2016. (ENG.). 32p. (J). (gr. 2-4). 18.99 (978-1-56846-295-0(6), Creative Editions) Creative Co., The.

Lombardo, Jennifer & Robson, David. The Horrors of Auschwitz. 2017. (World History Ser.). 104p. (YA). (gr. 7-7). 39.90 (**978-1-5345-6054-3(8)**, Lucent Pr.) Greenhaven Publishing LLC.

Lukesh, Jean A. Sky Rider: Story of Evelyn Sharp, World War II WASP. 2011. (Noteworthy Americans Young Readers Biography Book Ser.). (ENG., Illus.). 161p. (J). pap. 14.95 (978-0-9647586-3-6(6)) Field Mouse Productions.

Malam, John. You Wouldn't Want to Be a Secret Agent During World War II! A Perilous Mission Behind Enemy Lines. 2010. (You Wouldn't Want to... Ser.). 32p. (J). 29.00 (978-0-531-20474-0(X)); (ENG.). (gr. 3-18). pap. 9.95 (978-0-531-13783-3(X)) Scholastic Library Publishing. (Watts, Franklin).

Marchione, Margherita. Pope Pius XII: Bilingual Coloring Book. Elliott, John, illus. 2004. (SPA & ENG.). 32p. 1.00 (978-0-8091-6721-0(2), 6721-2) Paulist Pr.

Marcovitz, Hal. Cause & Effect: World War II. 2017. (ENG.). 80p. (YA). (gr. 5-12). (**978-1-68282-174-9(9)**) ReferencePoint Pr., Inc.

Marrin, Albert. FDR & the American Crisis. 2016. (ENG.). 336p. (YA). (gr. 7). pap. 15.99 (978-0-385-75362-3(4), Ember) Random Hse. Children's Bks.

—Uprooted: The Japanese American Experience During World War II. 2016. (ENG., Illus.). 256p. (YA). (gr. 7). 17.99 (978-0-553-50936-6(5), Knopf Bks. for Young Readers) Random Hse. Children's Bks.

Marriott, Emma. Did Anything Good Come Out of World War II?, 01 vols., 1. 2016. (Innovation Through Adversity Ser.). (ENG.). 48p. (J). 30.25 (978-1-5081-7070-9(3), Rosen Young Adult) Rosen Publishing Group, Inc., The.

Marsh, Carole. World War II: Reproducible Activity Book. 2004. (Illus.). 28p. (J). (gr. 4-12). pap. 5.95 (978-0-635-02678-1(3)) Gallopade International.

—World War II Reproducible Activity Book (HC) 2004. 28p. (gr. 4-12). 29.95 (978-0-635-02679-8(1)) Gallopade International.

Marshall Cavendish. The Attack on Pearl Harbor. 2011. (Perspectives on 3 Ser.). (Illus.). 112p. (J). (gr. 7). 39.93 (978-1-60870-448-4(3)) Marshall Cavendish Corp.

Mason, Paul. Reports from the Front in WWII. 2010. (ENG.). 32p. (J). (978-0-7787-9905-4(0)); pap. (978-0-7787-9926-9(3)) Crabtree Publishing Co.

Maybury, Richard J. World War II: The Rest of the Story & How It Affects You Today, 1930 to September 11 2001. Williams, Jane A., ed. rev. ed. 2003. ("Uncle Eric" Bk.: 11). (ENG., Illus.). 349p. pap. 19.95 (978-0-942617-43-6(6)) Bluestocking Pr.

McGowen, Tom. D-Day. 2017. (J). (978-0-531-22093-1(1), Orchard Bks.) Scholastic, Inc.

McNeil, Niki, et al. HOCPP 1089 World War II. 2006. spiral bd. 24.50 (978-1-60308-089-7(9)) In the Hands of a Child.

Meyer, Susan. Nazi Concentration Camps: A Policy of Genocide. 2014. (Documentary History of the Holocaust Ser.). (Illus.). 80p. (J). (gr. 7-12). 34.25 (978-1-4777-7603-2(6)) Rosen Publishing Group, Inc., The.

Miller, Terry. D-Day at Omaha Beach: Turning the Tide of World War II. 2011. (J). (978-0-545-32945-3(0)) Scholastic, Inc.

Moss, Marissa. Barbed Wire Baseball. Shimizu, Yuko, illus. 2013. (ENG.). 48p. (J). (gr. 1-4). 19.95 (978-1-4197-0521-2(0), Abrams Bks. for Young Readers) Abrams, Inc.

Murray, Stuart. World War II. 2009. (FACT ATLAS Ser.). 72p. (J). (gr. 3-7). pap. 13.99 (978-0-8416-1093-4(2)) Hammond World Atlas Corp.

Murray, Stuart A. P. World War II: Step into the Action & Behind Enemy Lines from Hitler's Rise to Japan's Surrender. 2015. (Fact Atlas Ser.). (ENG., Illus.). 72p. (J). (gr. 2-7). 14.99 (978-1-63220-433-2(9), Sky Pony Pr.) Skyhorse Publishing Co., Inc.

Nardo, Don. Nazi War Criminals. 2015. (Illus.). 80p. (J). (978-1-60152-850-6(7)) ReferencePoint Pr., Inc.

Nelson, Peter. Left for Dead. 2003. (ENG.). 224p. (YA). (gr. 7-7). pap. 8.95 (978-0-385-73091-4(8), Delacorte Bks. for Young Readers) Random Hse. Children's Bks.

Norton, James. The Holocaust: Jews, Germany, & the National Socialists. 2009. (Genocide in Modern Times Ser.). 64p. (gr. 6-6). 58.50 (978-1-61512-677-4(5)) Rosen Publishing Group, Inc., The.

Norton, James R. The Holocaust: Jews, Germany, & the National Socialists. 2008. (Genocide in Modern Times Ser.). (Illus.). 64p. (YA). (gr. 9-12). lib. bdg. 31.95 (978-1-4042-1821-5(1)) Rosen Publishing Group, Inc., The.

Ohlin, Nancy. Blast Back! World War II. Larkum, Adam & Simo, Roger, illus. 2016. (Blast Back! Ser.). (ENG.). 112p. (J). (gr. 2-5). pap. 5.99 (978-1-4998-0275-7(7)) Little Bee Books Inc.

O'Neill, Robert John. World War II: Essential Histories, 6 vols., Set. Incl. World War II: Europe, 1944-1945. Havers, R. P. W. lib. bdg. 33.25 (978-1-4358-9130-2(9)); World War II: Northwest Europe, 1944-1945. Hart, R. & Hart, S. lib. bdg. 33.25 (978-1-4358-9129-6(5)); World War II: The Eastern Front 1941-1945. Jukes, Geoffrey. lib. bdg. 33.25 (978-1-4358-9134-0(1)); World War II: The Mediterranean 1940-1945. Collier, Paul H. lib. bdg. 33.25 (978-1-4358-9132-6(5)); World War II: The Pacific. Homer, D. M. lib. bdg. 33.25 (978-1-4358-9133-3(3)); World War II: The War at Sea. Grove, Philip D. & Grove, Mark J. lib. bdg. 33.25 (978-1-4358-9131-9(7)); (YA). (gr. 9-12). 2010. (Illus.). 96p. 2010. Set lib. bdg. 191.70 (978-1-4358-9135-7(X)) Rosen Publishing Group, Inc., The.

Oppenheim, Joanne F. Dear Miss Breed: True Stories of the Japanese American Incarceration During World War II & a Librarian Who Made a Difference. 2006. (ENG., Illus.). 288p. (J). (gr. 7-12). 22.99 (978-0-439-56992-7(3)) Scholastic, Inc.

Osborne, Mary Pope & Boyce, Natalie Pope. World War II: A Nonfiction Companion to Magic Tree House Super Edition #1: World at War 1944. Molinari, Carlo, illus. 2017. (Magic Tree House (R) Fact Tracker Ser.: 36). (ENG.). 144p. (J). (gr. 4-7). 6.99 (978-1-101-93639-9(8), Random Hse. Bks. for Young Readers) Random Hse. Children's Bks.

Osborne, Mary Pope & Natalie Pope Boyce. World War II: A Nonfiction Companion to Magic Tree House Super Edition #1 World at War 1944. 2017. (Magic Tree House Fact Trackers Ser.). lib. bdg. 17.20 (**978-0-606-39849-7(X)**) Turtleback Bks.

Oshiro, Beverly & Sachs, Ruth. Adolf Eichmann, 01 vols., 1. 2016. (Holocaust Ser.). (ENG., Illus.). 112p. (J). 35.60 (978-1-4994-6246-3(8), Rosen Young Adult) Rosen Publishing Group, Inc., The.

Page, Andrea. The Sioux Code Talkers of World War II, 1 vol. 2017. (Illus.). 136p. (J). (gr. 3-7). 14.95 (978-1-4556-2243-6(5)) Pelican Publishing Co., Inc.

Parsons, Martin. Women's War. (Illus.). 31p. (YA). pap. *(978-0-7502-2845-9(8),* Wayland) Hachette Children's Group.

Perritano, John. Health & Medicine, Vol. 9. van Dijk, Ruud, ed. 2016. (Making of the Modern World: 1945 to the Present Ser.). (Illus.). 64p. (J). (gr. 7). 23.95 *(978-1-4222-3639-0(0))* Mason Crest.

—The Making of the Modern World: 1945 to the Present: Migration & Refugees, Vol. 9. van Dijk, Ruud, ed. 2016. (Making of the Modern World: 1945 to the Present Ser.: Vol. 9). (ENG.). 64p. (J). (gr. 7-12). 23.95 *(978-1-4222-3640-6(4))* Mason Crest.

PRESS, Celebration. America's Secret Weapon: The Navajo Code Talkers of World War II. 2003. (ENG.). (J). (gr. 6-8). pap. 37.95 *(978-0-7652-3246-5(4),* Celebration Pr.) Pearson Schl.

Prins, Marcel & Steenhuis, Peter Henk. Hidden Like Anne Frank. Watkinson, Laura, tr. from DUT. 2014. (ENG., Illus.). 240p. (J). (gr. 7). 18.99 *(978-0-545-54362-0(2),* Levine, Arthur A. Bks.) Scholastic, Inc.

Ramen, Fred. Hermann Goering: Hitler's Second in Command. 2005. (Holocaust Biographies Ser.). (Illus.). 112p. (YA). (gr. 7-12). lib. bdg. 34.60 *(978-0-8239-3307-5(5),* HBGORI) Rosen Publishing Group, Inc., The.

—Hermann Goring: Hitler's Second-in-Command. 2009. (Holocaust Biographies Ser.). 112p. (gr. 7-12). 63.90 *(978-1-61513-387-1(9))* Rosen Publishing Group, Inc., The.

Raum, Elizabeth. Stealing Nazi Secrets in World War II: An Interactive Espionage Adventure. 2015. (You Choose: Spies Ser.). (ENG., Illus.). 112p. (gr. 3-4). pap. 6.95 *(978-1-4914-5934-8(4),* You Choose Bks.) Capstone Press of Coughlan Cos.

—World War II: An Interactive History Adventure, 1 vol. (You Choose: History Ser.). (ENG.). 112p. (gr. 3-4). 2010. pap. 6.95 *(978-1-4296-3457-1(X))* 2009. 31.99 *(978-1-4296-2344-5(6))* Capstone Press of Coughlan Cos. (You Choose Bks.).

—A World War II Timeline, 1 vol. 2014. (War Timelines Ser.). (ENG.). 48p. (gr. 4-6). pap. 8.95 *(978-1-4765-5178-4(2));* lib. bdg. 34.65 *(978-1-4765-4158-7(2))* Capstone Press of Coughlan Cos.

Reynoldson, Fiona. The Home Front. (Illus.). 48p. (J). pap. *(978-0-7502-2696-7(X),* Wayland) Hachette Children's Group.

Robertson, David. The Scout: Tommy Prince. Henderson, Scott B., illus. 2014. (Tales from Big Spirit Ser.: 6). (ENG.). 32p. (J). (gr. 4-6). pap. *(978-1-55379-478-3(8),* 78912685-2d85-4153-9f88-b7d8feb31ffe, HighWater Pr.) Portage & Main Pr.

Robinson, Tony. World War II. unabr. ed. 2013. (Weird World of Wonders Ser.). (ENG., Illus.). 160p. (J). (gr. 2-5). pap. 9.99 *(978-1-4472-2768-7(9))* Pan Macmillan GBR. Dist: Independent Pubs. Group.

Rose, Simon. The Split History of World War II: A Perspectives Flip Book, 1 vol. 2012. (Perspectives Flip Bks.). (ENG.). 64p. (gr. 5-6). pap. 8.95 *(978-0-7565-4598-7(6));* lib. bdg. 33.99 *(978-0-7565-4569-7(2))* Compass Point Bks.

Rosenberg, Aaron. World War II. 2011. (Profiles Ser.: 2). (ENG.). 160p. (J). (gr. 5-9). pap. 6.99 *(978-0-545-31655-2(3),* Scholastic Paperbacks) Scholastic, Inc.

Ross, Stewart. The Home Front in World War II. (Illus.). 32p. 22.99 *(978-0-7502-4184-7(5))* Hodder & Stoughton GBR. Dist: Trafalgar Square Publishing.

Roxburgh, Ellis. Adolf Hitler vs. Winston Churchill: Foes of World War II. 2015. (History's Greatest Rivals Ser.). (ENG.). 48p. (J). (gr. 6-8). lib. bdg. 31.95 *(978-1-4824-2205-4(0))* Stevens, Gareth Publishing LLLP.

Rubin, Susan Goldman. The Flag with Fifty-Six Stars: A Gift from the Survivors of Mauthausen. Farnsworth, Bill, illus. 2005. (ENG.). 40p. (J). (gr. 1-5). 17.95 *(978-0-8234-1653-0(4))* Holiday Hse., Inc.

Ryles, Briony & Hall, Derek. The Early 20th Century. 2010. (CC: Technology Through the Ages Ser.). 112p. (gr. 6-12). 42.80 *(978-1-933834-87-0(0))* Brown Bear Bks.

Sachs, Ruth. Adolf Eichmann: Engineer of Death. 2009. (Holocaust Biographies Ser.). 112p. (gr. 7-12). 63.90 *(978-1-61513-380-2(1))* Rosen Publishing Group, Inc., The.

Samuels, Charlie. Home Front. 2012. (World War II Sourcebook Ser.). (Illus.). 48p. (gr. 5-12). lib. bdg. 37.10 *(978-1-936333-22-6(8))* Brown Bear Bks.

—Machines & Weaponry of World War II. 2013. (Machines That Won the War Ser.). (Illus.). 48p. (J). (gr. 5-8). pap. 14.05 *(978-1-4339-8608-6(6));* lib. bdg. 31.95 *(978-1-4339-8607-9(8))* Stevens, Gareth Publishing LLLP.

—Propaganda. 2012. (World War II Sourcebook Ser.). (Illus.). 48p. (gr. 5-12). lib. bdg. 37.10 *(978-1-936333-23-3(6))* Brown Bear Bks.

—Soldiers. 2012. (World War II Sourcebook Ser.). (Illus.). 48p. (gr. 5-12). lib. bdg. 37.10 *(978-1-936333-24-0(4))* Brown Bear Bks.

—Soldiers. 2017. (World War II Sourcebook Ser.). (ENG., Illus.). 48p. (J). (gr. 4-6). pap. 11.99 *(978-0-7502-8884-2(1),* Wayland) Hachette Children's Group GBR. Dist: Hachette Bk. Group.

Sandler, Martin W. Why Did the Whole World Go to War? And Other Questions about... World War II. Barrett, Robert, illus. 2013. (Good Question! Ser.). (ENG.). 32p. (J). (gr. 2). pap. 5.95 *(978-1-4027-9044-7(9))* Sterling Publishing Co., Inc.

—Why Did the Whole World Go to War? And Other Questions About... World War II. Barrett, Robert, illus. 2013. (Good Question! Ser.). (ENG.). 40p. (J). (gr. 2). 12.95 *(978-1-4027-9621-0(8))* Sterling Publishing Co., Inc.

Santella, Andrew. Navajo Code Talkers. 2005. (Reader's Workshop Ser.). (ENG., Illus.). 45p. (C). pap. 21.95 *(978-0-7362-2794-0(6))* National Geographic School Publishing, Inc.

Scott, Janine. The Two Great Wars. 2007. (Shockwave: History & Politics Ser.). (ENG., Illus.). 36p. (J). (gr. 4-6). lib. bdg. 25.00 *(978-0-531-17756-3(4),* Children's Pr.) Scholastic Library Publishing.

Second World War. 2014. (Ladybird Histories Ser.). (ENG., Illus.). 64p. (J). (gr. 2-4). pap. 13.99 ***(978-0-7232-7727-9(3))*** Penguin Bks., Ltd. GBR. Dist: Independent Pubs. Group.

Seidlitz, Lauri. The Legacy of World War II. 2015. (ENG., Illus.). 48p. (J). *(978-0-7787-2117-8(5))* Crabtree Publishing Co.

Senker, Cath. Why Did World War II Happen? 2010. (Moments in History Ser.). 48p. (ENG.). (J). (gr. 6-8). pap. 14.05 *(978-1-4339-4185-6(6),* Gareth Stevens Secondary Library); (Illus.). (YA). (gr. 5-9). lib. bdg. 31.95 *(978-1-4339-4184-9(8))* Stevens, Gareth Publishing LLLP.

—World War II. 2005. (How Did It Happen? Ser.). (ENG., Illus.). 48p. (YA). (gr. 7-10). lib. bdg. 32.10 *(978-1-59018-604-6(4),* Lucent Bks.) Cengage Gale.

Setterington, Ken. Branded by the Pink Triangle, 1 vol. 2013. (ENG.). 196p. (YA). (gr. 8-10). pap. 15.95 *(978-1-926920-96-2(1))* Second Story Pr. CAN. Dist: Orca Bk. Pubs. USA.

Shaw, Antony. World War II. 2010. (Facts at Your Fingertips: Modern Military History Ser.). 64p. (YA). (gr. 9-12). 35.65 *(978-1-933834-50-4(1))* Brown Bear Bks.

Sheehan, Sean. From Jessie Owens to Hiroshima: The Mid 1930s to 1945. 2005. (Modern Eras Uncovered Ser.). (Illus.). 56p. (J). pap. *(978-1-4109-1795-9(9))* Steck-Vaughn.

—Modern Eras Uncovered: From Jesse Owens to Hiroshima. 2005. (Modern Eras Uncovered Ser.). (Illus.). 56p. (J). *(978-1-84443-962-1(3)); (978-1-84443-952-2(6))* Steck-Vaughn.

Simons, Lisa M. Bolt. The U. S. WASP: Trailblazing Women Pilots of World War II. 2017. (Women & War Ser.). (ENG.). 32p. (gr. 3-4). pap. 8.19 ***(978-1-5157-7944-5(0),*** Snap Bks.) Capstone Press of Coughlan Cos.

Spilsbury, Richard & Spilsbury, Louise. WWII Survival Tips. 2010. (ENG.). 32p. (J). *(978-0-7787-9898-9(4));* pap. *(978-0-7787-9919-1(0))* Crabtree Publishing Co.

Stalcup, Ann. America's Secret Weapon: Navajo Code Talkers of World War II. 2017. (J). pap. ***(978-1-63293-176-4(1))*** Sunstone Pr.

Stein, R. Conrad. World War II. 2012. (Cornerstones of Freedom, Third Ser.). (ENG., Illus.). 64p. (J). pap. 8.95 *(978-0-531-28169-7(8));* (gr. 4-6). lib. bdg. 30.00 *(978-0-531-23069-5(4))* Scholastic Library Publishing. (Children's Pr.).

Stephens, Chris S. A Wartime Scrapbook. 2004. (ENG., Illus.). 32p. pap. 14.95 *(978-1-84323-285-8(5))* Beekman Bks., Inc.

Streissguth, Tom. Adolf Eichmann: Executing the Final Solution. 2005. (Holocaust Heroes & Nazi Criminals Ser.). (Illus.). 160p. (YA). (gr. 7-13). lib. bdg. 29.27 *(978-0-7660-2575-2(6))* Enslow Pubs., Inc.

Summers, Elizabeth. Weapons & Vehicles of World War II. 2015. (Tools of War Ser.). (ENG., Illus.). 32p. (gr. 1-2). lib. bdg. 26.65 *(978-1-4914-4080-3(5))* Capstone Press of Coughlan Cos.

Thompson, Ben. World War II. Butzer, C. M., illus. 2016. 372p. (J). *(978-0-316-32199-0(0))* Little Brown & Co.

Throp, Claire. Heroes of World War Two. 2015. (Heroes of World War II Ser.). (ENG.). 48p. (gr. 4-6). lib. bdg. 130.60 *(978-1-4109-8049-6(9))* Heinemann-Raintree.

Townsend, John. Army. 2016. (Action Force: World War II Ser.). 32p. (gr. 3-7). 31.35 *(978-1-59920-982-1(9),* Smart Apple Media) Black Rabbit Bks.

—Special Operations. 2016. (Action Force: World War II Ser.). 32p. (gr. 3-7). 31.35 *(978-1-59920-983-8(7),* Smart Apple Media) Black Rabbit Bks.

A True Book(tm) — World at War (Set Of 5) 2014. (True Book — World War II Ser.). (J). lib. bdg. 145.00 *(978-0-531-24356-5(7))* Scholastic Library Publishing.

Tucker, Spencer C. & Roberts, Priscilla Mary, eds. World War II Set. Vol. 1: A Student Encyclopedia, 5 vols. 2005. (Illus.). 1795p. (C). 439.00 *(978-1-85109-857-6(7),* WW2SCH1C) ABC-CLIO, LLC.

Watts, Ana Dearborn & Dearborn, Dorothy. The Pony Princess. Taylor, Carol, illus. 2008. (ENG.). 32p. pap. 6.00 *(978-1-896543-32-1(4))* DreamCatcher Publishing CAN. Dist: Univ. of Toronto Pr.

The Weapons of World War II. 2014. (True Book(tm), a — World at War Ser.). (ENG.). 48p. (J). lib. bdg. 31.00 *(978-0-531-20495-5(2))* Scholastic Library Publishing.

Wehrertuchtigungslager der Hitler-Jugend, 1942-1945. (GER.). *(978-3-928379-00-7(3))* Verein zur Fordenrung der Umweltforschung.

Welky, Ali. A Captive Audience: Voices of Japanese American Youth in World War II Arkansas. 2015. (ENG., Illus.). 124p. pap. 21.95 *(978-1-935106-86-9(4))* Butler Ctr. for Arkansas Studies.

Williams, Brenda & Williams, Brian. Saving the Persecuted. 2015. (Heroes of World War II Ser.). (ENG., Illus.). 48p. (gr. 4-6). 32.65 *(978-1-4109-8046-5(4))* Heinemann-Raintree.

Wilson, John. Bitter Ashes: The Story of WW II. 2010. (ENG., Illus.). 96p. (J). (gr. 6-9). 20.95 *(978-1-894917-90-2(1),* Napoleon & Co.) Dundurn CAN. Dist: Ingram Publisher Services.

Wood, Douglas. Franklin & Winston: A Christmas That Changed the World. Moser, Barry, illus. 2011. (ENG.). 40p. (J). (gr. 1-4). 16.99 *(978-0-7636-3383-7(6))* Candlewick Pr.

World War II: PowerPoint Presentations in World History. 2005. cd-rom 49.95 net. *(978-1-56004-209-9(5))* Social Studies Schl. Service.

World War II Instructional Guide. 2009. (Grade 8: Social Studies Exit Project Kits Ser.). spiral bd. *(978-1-4042-4039-1(X),* Rosen Classroom) Rosen Publishing Group, Inc., The.

Worth, Richard. Heinrich Himmler: Murderous Architect of the Holocaust. 2005. (Holocaust Heroes & Nazi Criminals Ser.). (Illus.). 160p. (YA). (gr. 7-13). lib. bdg. 27.93 *(978-0-7660-2532-5(2))* Enslow Pubs., Inc.

Wukovits, John F. World War II in Europe. 2004. (World History Ser.). (ENG., Illus.). 112p. (gr. 7-10). 34.95 *(978-1-59018-185-0(9),* Lucent Bks.) Cengage Gale.

WWII Airplanes. (Color & Learn Ser.). 36p. (J). (gr. 1-5). pap. *(978-1-882210-01-5(8))* Action Publishing, Inc.

Yomtov, Nel. Great Escapes of World War II. 2017. (Great Escapes of World War II Ser.). (ENG.). 32p. (gr. 3-4). 122.60 *(978-1-5157-3533-5(8),* Graphic Library) Capstone Press of Coughlan Cos.

Zamosky, Lisa & Conklin, Wendy. World War II, 1 vol. 2007. (Primary Source Readers Ser.). (ENG.). 32p. (J). (gr. 5-5). pap. 8.99 *(978-0-7439-0668-5(3))* Shell Educational Publishing.

WORLD WAR, 1939-1945—AERIAL OPERATIONS

Adams, Simon. Warplanes. 2009. (J). 28.50 *(978-1-59920-223-5(9))* Black Rabbit Bks.

Asso, B. & Bergese, F. Cinebook Recounts: Battle of Britain. movie tie-in ed. 2010. (Cinebook Recounts Ser.). (ENG., Illus.). 48p. pap. 11.95 *(978-1-84918-025-2(3))* CineBook GBR. Dist: National Bk. Network.

Asso, Bernard & Bergèse, Francis. Battle of Britain. 2008. (ENG., Illus.). 48p. pap. 11.95 *(978-1-905460-39-7(2))* CineBook GBR. Dist: National Bk. Network.

Baker, Brynn. Tuskegee Airmen: Freedom Flyers of World War II. 2015. (Military Heroes Ser.). (ENG., Illus.). 32p. (gr. 3-4). lib. bdg. 27.32 *(978-1-4914-4839-7(3))* Capstone Press of Coughlan Cos.

Barnes, Pete. Richard Bong: World War II Flying Ace. 2009. (Badger Biographies Ser.). (ENG., Illus.). 128p. (J). (gr. 2-7). pap. 12.95 *(978-0-87020-434-0(3))* Wisconsin Historical Society.

Benge, Janet & Benge, Geoff. Jacob Deshazer: Forgive Your Enemies. 2009. (ENG.). 224p. (YA). pap. 9.99 *(978-1-57658-475-0(5))* YWAM Publishing.

Brook, Henry. True Stories of the Blitz. McNee, Ian, illus. 2006. (True Adventure Stories Ser.). 160p. (J). (gr. 4-7). per. 4.99 *(978-0-7945-1245-3(3),* Usborne) EDC Publishing.

Burgan, Michael. World War II Pilots, 1 vol. 2013. (You Choose: World War II Ser.). (ENG., Illus.). 112p. (gr. 3-4). pap. 6.95 *(978-1-62065-718-8(X),* You Choose Bks.) Capstone Press of Coughlan Cos.

—World War II Pilots: An Interactive History Adventure. 2013. (You Choose: World War II Ser.). (ENG.). 112p. (gr. 3-4). pap. 41.70 *(978-1-62065-719-5(8));* lib. bdg. 31.99 *(978-1-4296-9899-3(3))* Capstone Press of Coughlan Cos. (You Choose Bks.).

Burgan, Michael, et al. You Choose: World War II. 2013. (You Choose: World War II Ser.). (ENG.). 112p. (gr. 3-4). 127.96 *(978-1-4296-9970-9(1));* pap. 166.80 *(978-1-62065-725-6(2));* pap. 27.80 *(978-1-62065-724-9(4))* Capstone Press of Coughlan Cos. (You Choose Bks.).

Dell, Pamela. The Soviet Night Witches: Brave Women Bomber Pilots of World War II. 2017. (Women & War Ser.). (ENG.). 32p. (gr. 3-4). lib. bdg. 27.99 ***(978-1-5157-7938-4(6),*** Snap Bks.) Capstone Press of Coughlan Cos.

Donelly, Karen. American Women Pilots of World War II. 2009. 112p. (YA). (gr. 7-12). pap. 12.95 *(978-1-4358-3274-9(4))* Rosen Publishing Group, Inc., The.

Dorling Kindersley Publishing Staff & Matthews, Rupert. Battle in the Air. 2014. (DK Adventures Ser.). (ENG.). 128p. (J). (gr. 3-7). 16.99 *(978-1-4654-2838-7(0),* DK Children) Dorling Kindersley Publishing, Inc.

Garstecki, Julia. Tuskegee Airmen. 2017. (All-American Fighting Forces Ser.). (ENG.). 32p. (gr. 3-7). 31.35 ***(978-1-68072-004-4(X),*** Bolt) Black Rabbit Bks.

Graham, Ian. You Wouldn't Want to Be a World War II Pilot! Air Battles You Might Not Survive. Antram, David, illus. 2009. (You Wouldn't Want to Ser.). (ENG.). 32p. (J). 29.00 *(978-0-531-21326-1(9));* (gr. 3-18). pap. 9.95 *(978-0-531-20517-4(7))* Scholastic Library Publishing.

Group/McGraw-Hill, Wright. Al Ataque!, 6 vols. (First Explorers. Primeros Exploradores Nonfiction Sets Ser.). (SPA.). (gr. 1-2). 29.95 *(978-0-7699-1477-0(2))* Shortland Pubns. (U. S. A.) Inc.

Hamilton, John. World War II: War in the Air, 1 vol. 2011. (World War II Ser.). (ENG., Illus.). 32p. (YA). (gr. 5-9). 27.07 *(978-1-61783-063-1(1))* ABDO Publishing Co.

Hillenbrand, Laura. Unbroken: An Olympian's Journey from Airman to Castaway to Captive. 2014. (ENG., Illus.). 320p. (YA). (gr. 7). 19.99 *(978-0-385-74251-1(7));* lib. bdg. 22.99 *(978-0-375-99062-5(3))* Random Hse. Children's Bks. (Delacorte Pr.).

Horn, Bernd. Men of Steel: Canadian Paratroopers in Normandy 1944. 2010. (Canadians at War Ser.: 2). (ENG., Illus.). 120p. (YA). (gr. 6). pap. 19.99 *(978-1-55488-708-8(9))* Dundurn CAN. Dist: Ingram Publisher Services.

Jackson, Robert. Warplanes of World War II up Close, 01 vols., 1. Pearson, Colin, illus. 2016. (Military Technology: Top Secret Clearance Ser.). (ENG.). 224p. (YA). 43.60 *(978-1-5081-7078-5(9),* Rosen Young Adult) Rosen Publishing Group, Inc., The.

Mullaney, Patricia E. Documentary of an Airman' Tour with the Eighth 1944-1945. 2003. (Illus.). 355p. cd-rom 34.99 *(978-1-893767-02-7(7))* E-Booksgen.

Murray, Aaron R. Aircraft of World War II. 2014. (Illus.). 48p. (J). *(978-1-4351-5366-0(9))* Barnes & Noble, Inc.

—Aircraft of World War II, 01 vols., 1. 2016. (What's Inside? Ser.). (ENG.). 48p. (J). pap. 11.75 *(978-1-5081-4599-8(7),* PowerKids Pr.) Rosen Publishing Group, Inc., The.

Nicholson, Dorinda Makanaōnalani. The School the Aztec Eagles Built, 1 vol. Nicholson, Dorinda Makanaōnalani, photos by. 2016. (ENG., Illus.). 48p. (J). 18.95 *(978-1-60060-440-9(4))* Lee & Low Bks., Inc.

Olson, Tod. Lost in the Pacific, 1942: Not a Drop to Drink. 2016. (Lost Ser.: 1). (ENG., Illus.). 176p. (J). (gr. 4-7). 12.99 *(978-0-545-92811-3(7),* Scholastic Nonfiction) Scholastic, Inc.

Otfinoski, Steven. Pilots in Peril! The Untold Story of U. S. Pilots Who Braved the Hump in World War II. (Encounter: Narrative Nonfiction Stories Ser.). (ENG.). 232p. (gr. 3-4). 2016. pap. 9.95 *(978-1-4914-5166-3(1))* 2015. 16.95 *(978-1-62370-318-9(2))* Encounter Bks.

—Pilots in Peril! The Untold Story of U.S. Pilots Who Braved "The Hump" in World War II. 2015. (Encounter: Narrative Nonfiction Stories Ser.). (ENG., Illus.). 232p. (gr. 3-4). lib. bdg. 33.99 *(978-1-4914-5156-4(4))* Encounter Bks.

Parsons, Martin. The History Detective Investigates: Air Raids in World War II. 2017. (History Detective Investigates Ser.). (ENG., Illus.). 32p. (J). (gr. 4-6). pap. 11.99 *(978-0-7502-9651-9(8),* Wayland) Hachette Children's Group GBR. Dist: Hachette Bk. Group.

Prien, Jochen & Stemmer, Gerhard. Jagdgeschwader 3 Udet in World War II: II. /JG 3 in Action with the Messerschmitt Bf 109, 1 vol. 2003. (ENG., Illus.). 464p. (gr. 10-13). 69.95 *(978-0-7643-1774-3(1),* 9780764317743) Schiffer Publishing, Ltd.

Sears, Stephen W. Air War Against Hitler's Germany. 2007. (ENG., Illus.). 176p. pap. 9.95 *(978-1-59687-004-8(4))* IBks., Inc.

Shea, John M. The Tuskegee Airmen. 2015. (Heroes of Black History Ser.). (ENG., Illus.). 32p. (J). (gr. 3-4). 26.60 *(978-1-4824-2918-3(7))* Stevens, Gareth Publishing LLLP.

Simons, Lisa M. Bolt. The U. S. WASP: Trailblazing Women Pilots of World War II. 2017. (Women & War Ser.). (ENG.). 32p. (gr. 3-4). lib. bdg. 27.99 ***(978-1-5157-7937-7(8),*** Snap Bks.) Capstone Press of Coughlan Cos.

Townsend, John. Air Force. 2016. (Action Force: World War II Ser.). 32p. (gr. 3-7). 31.35 *(978-1-59920-985-2(3),* Smart Apple Media) Black Rabbit Bks.

—Air Force. 2017. (EDGE - Action Force Ser.). (ENG., Illus.). 32p. (J). (gr. 4-6). pap. 9.99 *(978-1-4451-2630-2(3),* Franklin Watts) Hachette Children's Group GBR. Dist: Hachette Bk. Group.

WORLD WAR, 1939-1945—AFRICAN AMERICANS

Baker, Brynn. Tuskegee Airmen: Freedom Flyers of World War II. 2015. (Military Heroes Ser.). (ENG., Illus.). 32p. (gr. 3-4). lib. bdg. 27.32 *(978-1-4914-4839-7(3))* Capstone Press of Coughlan Cos.

Fleischman, John. Black & White Airmen: Their True History. 2007. (ENG., Illus.). 160p. (J). (gr. 5-12). 28.80 *(978-1-4287-3953-6(X),* Follettbound) Follett School Solutions.

—Black & White Airmen: Their True History. 2007. (ENG., Illus.). 160p. (J). (gr. 5-7). 20.00 *(978-0-618-56297-8(4))* Houghton Mifflin Harcourt Publishing Co.

Lang, Matt. Minority Soldiers Fighting in World War II. 2017. (J). ***(978-1-5026-2664-6(0))*** Cavendish Square Publishing.

Orr, Tamra. What's So Great About the Tuskegee Airmen. 2009. (What's So Great About...? Ser.). 32p. (J). (gr. 2-4). lib. bdg. 25.70 *(978-1-58415-832-5(8))* Mitchell Lane Pubs., Inc.

Sheinkin, Steve. The Port Chicago 50: Disaster, Mutiny, & the Fight for Civil Rights. 2014. (ENG., Illus.). 208p. (J). (gr. 5-9). 19.99 *(978-1-59643-796-8(0),* 9781596437968) Roaring Brook Pr.

WORLD WAR, 1939-1945—BATTLES

see World War, 1939-1945—Campaigns

WORLD WAR, 1939-1945—BIOGRAPHY

Atwood, Kathryn J. Women Heroes of World War II: 26 Stories of Espionage, Sabotage, Resistance, & Rescue. (Women of Action Ser.). (ENG.). 272p. (gr. 7). 2013. (YA). pap. 14.95 *(978-1-61374-523-6(0))* 2011. (Illus.). (J). 19.95 *(978-1-55652-961-0(9))* Chicago Review Pr., Inc.

Boomhower, Ray E. The Soldier's Friend: A Life of Ernie Pyle. 2006. (Illus.). 134p. 17.95 *(978-0-87195-200-4(9))* Indiana Historical Society.

Bozuwa, Titia. In the Shadow of the Cathedral: Growing up in Holland During WW II. 2004. (ENG & DUT., Illus.). 199p. 22.95 *(978-0-9754825-0-6(5));* 212p. per. 15.95 *(978-0-9754825-1-3(3))* Triple Tulip Pr.

Bryant, Jen. Music for the End of Time. Peck, Beth, illus. 2005. 32p. (J). (gr. 4-5). 17.00 *(978-0-8028-5229-8(7))* Eerdmans, William B. Publishing Co.

Byers, Ann. Saving Children from the Holocaust: The Kindertransport. 2011. (Holocaust Through Primary Sources Ser.). (Illus.). 128p. (J). (gr. 6-18). pap. 10.95 *(978-1-59845-344-7(0));* (gr. 9-12). lib. bdg. 33.27 *(978-0-7660-3323-8(6))* Enslow Pubs., Inc.

Collins, Terry. True Stories of World War II, 1 vol. Kinsella, Pat, illus. 2012. (Stories of War Ser.). (ENG.). 32p. (gr. 3-4). pap. 8.10 *(978-1-4296-9346-2(0));* pap. 47.70 *(978-1-4296-9347-9(9));* lib. bdg. 30.65 *(978-1-4296-8623-5(5))* Capstone Press of Coughlan Cos. (Graphic Library).

Dolan, Sean. Adolf Eichmann: Engineer of Death. 2005. (Holocaust Biographies Ser.). (Illus.). 112p. (YA). (gr. 7-12). lib. bdg. 34.60 *(978-0-8239-3308-2(3),* HBEICH) Rosen Publishing Group, Inc., The.

Ellis, Catherine. Key Figures of World War II. 2015. (Biographies of War Ser.). (ENG., Illus.). 112p. (J). (gr. 7-8). 32.90 *(978-1-68048-057-3(X),* Britannica Educational Publishing) Rosen Publishing Group, Inc., The.

Gifford, Clive. World War II: True Stories. (Illus.). 128p. (J). pap. *(978-0-340-80497-1(1),* Hodder Children's Books) Hachette Children's Group.

Hamilton, John. World War II: Leaders & Generals, 1 vol. 2011. (World War II Ser.). (ENG., Illus.). 32p. (YA). (gr. 5-9). 27.07 *(978-1-61783-061-7(5))* ABDO Publishing Co.

Hardin, Travis. Called to Serve. 2007. (Young Writers Ser.). 95p. (YA). (gr. 8-14). per. 5.99 *(978-1-58158-108-9(4))* McDougal Publishing Co.

Hawes, Alison. Who's Who in WWII. 2010. (ENG.). 32p. (J). *(978-0-7787-9912-2(3));* (gr. 3-6). pap. *(978-0-7787-9933-7(6))* Crabtree Publishing Co.

Huey, Lois Miner. Voices of World War II: Stories from the Front Lines, 1 vol. 2010. (Voices of War Ser.). (ENG., 32p. (gr. 3-4). Illus.). pap. 8.29 *(978-1-4296-5627-6(1));* lib. bdg. 27.99 *(978-1-4296-4738-0(8))* Capstone Press of Coughlan Cos. (Edge Bks.).

Hyde, Natalie. Significant People of World War II. 2015. (ENG., Illus.). 48p. (J). *(978-0-7787-2115-4(9))* Crabtree Publishing Co.

Jones, Tina C. Mothballs, Mothballs All in the Hall: Memories of a Great World War II Hero. Jones, Tina C. & Balogh, Jared, illus. 2012. 48p. pap. 24.95 *(978-1-4560-7483-8(0))* America Star Bks.

Knapp, Ron. Fighting U. S. Generals of World War II. 2013. (Inspiring Collective Biographies Ser.). 112p. (J). (gr. 5-12). pap. 10.95 *(978-1-4644-0249-4(3));* 33.27 *(978-0-7660-4164-6(6))* Enslow Pubs., Inc.

Lukesh, Jean A. Lucky Ears: The True Story of Ben Kuroki, World War II Hero. 2010. (Noteworthy Americans Young Readers Biography Book Ser.). (ENG., Illus.). 140p. (J). pap. 9.99 *(978-0-9647586-2-9(8))* Field Mouse Productions.

Raum, Elizabeth, et al. Stories of War. 2012. (Stories of War Ser.). (ENG.). 32p. (gr. 3-4). lib. bdg. 122.60 *(978-1-4296-9164-2(6),* Graphic Library) Capstone Press of Coughlan Cos.

—The World War II Soldiers' Experience. 2014. (You Choose: World War II Ser.). (ENG.). 328p. (gr. 3-4). pap. 14.95 *(978-1-4914-1514-6(2),* You Choose Bks.) Capstone Press of Coughlan Cos.

Rubin, Susan Goldman. Irena Sendler & the Children of the Warsaw Ghetto. Farnsworth, Bill, illus. 2016. (ENG.). 40p. (J). (gr. 4-7). pap. 8.99 *(978-0-8234-2595-2(9))* Holiday Hse., Inc.

Ruelle, Karen Gray. Hidden on the Mountain: Stories of Children Sheltered from the Nazis in le Chambon. DeSaix,

Deborah Durland, illus. 2007. (ENG.). 272p. (J). (gr. 5-18). 24.95 *(978-0-8234-1928-9(2))* Holiday Hse., Inc.

Welter, Anni. Child of War: How We Lived & Survived under the Third Reich. 2nd ed. 2003. Orig. Title: Child of the Third Reich: How We Lived & Survived. 160p. (YA). per. 14.95 *(978-0-9741434-0-8(5))* A H W Publishing.

Yomtov, Nel, et al. Stories of War. 2012. (Stories of War Ser.). (ENG.). 32p. (gr. 3-4). pap. 190.80 *(978-1-4296-9349-3(5))*; pap. 31.80 *(978-1-4296-9348-6(7))* Capstone Press of Coughlan Cos. (Graphic Library).

WORLD WAR, 1939-1945—CAMPAIGNS

see also Ardennes, Battle Of The, 1944-1945; Britain, Battle of, Great Britain, 1940; Guadalcanal, Battle of, Solomon Islands, 1942-1943; Iwo Jima, Battle of, Japan, 1945; Leyte Gulf, Battle of, Philippines, 1944; Midway, Battle Of, 1942; Stalingrad, Battle of, Volgograd, Russia, 1942-1943

Archer, Jules. Jungle Fighters: A Firsthand Account of the Forgotten New Guinea Campaign. 2016. (Jules Archer History for Young Readers Ser.). (ENG., Illus.). 224p. (J). (gr. 6). 16.99 *(978-1-63450-175-0(6))*, Sky Pony Pr.) Skyhorse Publishing Co., Inc.

Barber, Nicola. The Western Front. 2003. (Questioning History Ser.). (J). lib. bdg. 28.50 *(978-1-58340-268-9(3))* Black Rabbit Bks.

Benchmark Education Co., LLC. The Battles of World War II. 2014. (PRIME Ser.). (J). (gr. 6-8). pap. *(978-1-4509-9500-9(4))* Benchmark Education Co.

Benge, Janet & Benge, Geoff. Jacob Deshazer: Forgive Your Enemies. 2009. (ENG.). 224p. (YA). pap. 9.99 *(978-1-57658-475-0(5))* YWAM Publishing.

Big Battles of World War II. 2014. (ENG.). 48p. (J). lib. bdg. 29.00 *(978-0-531-20494-8(4))* Scholastic Library Publishing.

Bliven, Bruce, Jr. & Bliven, Bruce. Invasion: The Story of D-Day. 2007. (Sterling Point Books(r) Ser.). (ENG., Illus.). 176p. (J). (gr. 7). pap. 6.95 *(978-1-4027-4141-8(3))* Sterling Publishing Co., Inc.

Cochrane, Kelly. Significant Battles of World War II. 2015. (ENG., Illus.). 48p. (J). *(978-0-7787-2114-7(0))* Crabtree Publishing Co.

Collier, Paul H. & O'Neill, Robert John. World War II: The Mediterranean 1940-1945. 2010. (World War II: Essential Histories Ser.). (Illus.). 96p. (YA). (gr. 9-12). lib. bdg. 33.25 *(978-1-4358-9132-6(5))* Rosen Publishing Group, Inc., The.

D-Day & the Liberation of France. 2010. (Milestones in World History Ser.). (Illus.). 136p. (C). (gr. 9-18). 35.00 *(978-1-60413-280-9(9))*, Chelsea Hse.) Facts On File, Inc.

Darman, Peter, ed. The Battle of the Atlantic: Naval Warfare From 1939-1945. 2012. (World War II Ser.). (ENG., Illus.). 64p. (YA). (gr. 7-12). 31.95 *(978-1-4488-9237-2(6))* Rosen Publishing Group, Inc., The.

Demuth, Patricia Brennan & dePaola, Tomie. What Was D-Day? Kenyon, David Grayson & Anderson, Scott, illus. 2015. (What Was? Ser.). (ENG.). 112p. (J). (gr. 3-7). 5.99 *(978-0-448-48407-5(2))*, Penguin Workshop) Penguin Young Readers Group.

dePaola, Tomie. I'm Still Scared. 2007. (26 Fairmount Avenue Bks.). (Illus.). 83p. (gr. 2-5). 17.00 *(978-0-7569-8150-1(6))* Perfection Learning Corp.

Drez, Ronald J. Remember D-Day: The Plan, the Invasion, Survivor Stories. 2004. (Remember Ser.). (ENG., Illus.). 64p. (J). (gr. 5). 17.95 *(978-0-7922-6666-2(8))*; 27.90 *(978-0-7922-6965-6(9))* National Geographic Society. (National Geographic Children's Bks.).

Gitlin, Martin. George S. Patton: World War II General & Military Innovator, 1 vol. 2010. (Military Heroes Ser.). (ENG.). 112p. (J). (gr. 6-12). lib. bdg. 35.64 *(978-1-60453-964-6(X))* ABDO Publishing Co.

Grahame-Smith, Deborah, contrib. by. The First Bloody Battles. 2010. (World War Ii Ser.). 128p. (gr. 6-9). 35.64 *(978-0-7614-4946-1(9))* Marshall Cavendish GBR. Dist: Marshall Cavendish Corp.

—Horrific Invasions. 2010. (World War Ii Ser.). 128p. (gr. 6-9). 35.64 *(978-0-7614-4947-8(7))*, Benchmark Bks.) Marshall Cavendish Corp.

Grant, Reg. World War II: Europe. 2004. (Atlas of Conflicts Ser.). (Illus.). 64p. (gr. 6-12). lib. bdg. 34.00 *(978-0-8368-5669-9(4))*, Gareth Stevens Secondary Library) Stevens, Gareth Publishing LLLP.

Hachette Children's Group. The Western Front in World War I. (Illus.). 32p. *(978-0-7502-4183-0(7))*, Wayland) Hachette Children's Group.

Hamilton, John. World War II: Turning Points, 1 vol. 2011. (World War II Ser.). (ENG., Illus.). 32p. (YA). (gr. 5-9). 27.07 *(978-1-61783-062-4(3))* ABDO Publishing Co.

Havers, R. P. W. & O'Neill, Robert John. World War II: Europe, 1944-1945. 2010. (World War II: Essential Histories Ser.). (Illus.). 96p. (YA). (gr. 9-12). lib. bdg. 33.25 *(978-1-4358-9130-2(9))* Rosen Publishing Group, Inc., The.

Horn, Bernd. Men of Steel: Canadian Paratroopers in Normandy 1944. 2010. (Canadians at War Ser.: 2). (ENG., Illus.). 120p. (YA). (gr. 6). pap. 19.99 *(978-1-55488-708-8(9))* Dundurn CAN. Dist: Ingram Publisher Services.

Horner, D. M. & O'Neill, Robert John. World War II: The Pacific. 2010. (World War II: Essential Histories Ser.). (Illus.). 96p. (YA). (gr. 9-12). lib. bdg. 33.25 *(978-1-4358-9133-3(3))* Rosen Publishing Group, Inc., The.

Jeffrey, Gary. Battle for the Atlantic. 2012. (ENG., Illus.). 48p. (J). *(978-0-7787-4192-3(3))*; pap. *(978-0-7787-4199-2(0))* Crabtree Publishing Co.

—The Eastern Front. 2012. (ENG., Illus.). 48p. (J). *(978-0-7787-4194-7(X))*; pap. *(978-0-7787-4201-2(6))* Crabtree Publishing Co.

—North Africa & the Mediterranean. 2012. (ENG., Illus.). 48p. (J). *(978-0-7787-4193-0(1))*; pap. *(978-0-7787-4200-5(8))* Crabtree Publishing Co.

—War in the Pacific. 2012. (ENG., Illus.). 48p. (J). *(978-0-7787-4197-8(4))*; pap. *(978-0-7787-4204-3(0))* Crabtree Publishing Co.

Jukes, Geoffrey & O'Neill, Robert John. World War II: The Eastern Front 1941-1945. 2010. (World War II: Essential Histories Ser.). (Illus.). 96p. (YA). (gr. 9-12). lib. bdg. 33.25 *(978-1-4358-9134-0(1))* Rosen Publishing Group, Inc., The.

Lessman, Steve. D-Day: American Character. 2010. (Illus.). 32p. (J). lib. bdg. 15.95 *(978-1-58107-181-8(7))* New Forums Pr.

Marshall Cavendish Corporation Staff. The Final Victories. 2010. (World War Ii Ser.). 128p. (gr. 6-9). lib. bdg. 35.64 *(978-0-7614-4950-8(7))* Marshall Cavendish GBR. Dist: Marshall Cavendish Corp.

—Global Chaos. 2010. (World War Ii Ser.). 128p. (gr. 6-9). lib. bdg. 35.64 *(978-0-7614-4948-5(5))* Marshall Cavendish Corp.

—Terror & Triumph. 2010. (World War Ii Ser.). 128p. (gr. 6-9). lib. bdg. 35.64 *(978-0-7614-4949-2(3))* Marshall Cavendish Corp.

McGowen, Tom & Mcgowen, Tom. D-Day. 2008. (Cornerstones of Freedom Ser.). (ENG.). 48p. (J). (gr. 4-6). pap. 5.95 *(978-0-531-20831-1(1))*, Children's Pr.) Scholastic Library Publishing.

McNeese, Tim. Battle of the Bulge. 2003. (Great Battles Through the Ages Ser.). (Illus.). 112p. (gr. 6-12). 30.00 *(978-0-7910-7435-0(8))*, Chelsea Hse.) Facts On File, Inc.

Nicholson, Dorinda Makanaōnalani. The School the Aztec Eagles Built, 1 vol. Nicholson, Dorinda Makanaōnalani, photos by. 2016. (ENG., Illus.). 48p. (J). 18.95 *(978-1-60060-440-9(4))* Lee & Low Bks., Inc.

O'Neill, Robert John, et al. World War II: Northwest Europe, 1944-1945. 2010. (World War II: Essential Histories Ser.). (Illus.). 96p. (YA). (gr. 9-12). lib. bdg. 33.25 *(978-1-4358-9129-6(5))* Rosen Publishing Group, Inc., The.

O'Reilly, Bill. The Day the World Went Nuclear: Dropping the Atom Bomb & the End of World War II in the Pacific. 2017. (ENG., Illus.). 320p. (J). 19.99 ***(978-1-250-12033-5(0))***, 9781250120335, Holt, Henry & Co. Bks. For Young Readers) Holt, Henry & Co.

O'Reilly, Bill. Hitler's Last Days: The Death of the Nazi Regime & the World's Most Notorious Dictator. 2015. (Illus.). 320p. (J). pap. 19.99 *(978-1-62779-455-8(7))*; (ENG., (gr. 5-9). 19.99 *(978-1-62779-396-4(8))*, 9781627793964, Holt, Henry & Co. Bks. For Young Readers) Holt, Henry & Co.

—Hitler's Last Days: The Death of the Nazi Regime & the World's Most Notorious Dictator. Barcellona, Christine, ed. 2017. (ENG.). 336p. (J). pap. 12.99 *(978-1-250-08859-8(3))*, 9781250088598) Square Fish.

Orr, Tamra. What's So Great about the Tuskegee Airmen. 2009. (What's So Great About... ? Ser.). 32p. (J). (gr. 2-4). lib. bdg. 25.70 *(978-1-58415-832-5(8))* Mitchell Lane Pubs., Inc.

Peyton, Katherine & George, Enzo. World War II in the Pacific: War with Japan. 2014. (Voices of War Ser.). (Illus.). 48p. (J). (gr. 4-6). lib. bdg. 31.36 *(978-1-62712-867-4(0))* Cavendish Square Publishing.

Rice, Earle, Jr. Blitzkrieg! Hitler's Lightning War. 2007. (Monumental Milestones Ser.). (Illus.). 48p. (YA). (gr. 4-7). lib. bdg. 29.95 *(978-1-58415-542-3(6))* Mitchell Lane Pubs., Inc.

Samuels, Charlie. World War II. 2011. (Americans at War: a Gareth Stevens Timeline Ser.). 48p. (J). (gr. 6-8). pap. 14.05 *(978-1-4339-5935-6(6))*; pap. 14.05 *(978-1-4339-5932-5(1))*; lib. bdg. 31.95 *(978-1-4339-5934-9(8))*; lib. bdg. 31.95 *(978-1-4339-5930-1(5))* Stevens, Gareth Publishing LLLP. (Gareth Stevens Secondary Library).

Sheehan, Sean. World War II: The Pacific. 2004. (Atlas of Conflicts Ser.). (Illus.). 64p. (gr. 6-12). lib. bdg. 34.00 *(978-0-8368-5670-5(8))*, Gareth Stevens Secondary Library) Stevens, Gareth Publishing LLLP.

Stanley, George E. George S. Patton: War Hero. Henderson, Meryl, illus. 2007. (Childhood of Famous Americans Ser.). (ENG.). 192p. (J). (gr. 3-7). pap. 6.99 *(978-1-4169-1547-8(8))*, Simon & Schuster/Paula Wiseman Bks.) Simon & Schuster/Paula Wiseman Bks.

Stein, R. Conrad. World War II in the Pacific: From Pearl Harbor to Nagasaki. 2011. (United States at War Ser.). (Illus.). 128p. (J). (gr. 5-18). lib. bdg. 33.27 *(978-0-7660-3640-6(5))* Enslow Pubs., Inc.

Stone, Tanya Lee. Courage Has No Color - The True Story of the Triple Nickles: America's First Black Paratroopers. 2013. (ENG., Illus.). 160p. (J). (gr. 5). pap. 17.99 *(978-0-7636-6548-7(7))*; 24.99 *(978-0-7636-5117-6(6))* Candlewick Pr.

Wallace, Karen & Platt, Richard. D-Day Landings, Level 4: The Story of the Allied Invasion. 2004. (DK Readers Ser.). (ENG., Illus.). 32p. (J). (gr. 3-7). pap. 3.99 *(978-0-7566-0275-8(0))*, DK Children) Dorling Kindersley Publishing, Inc.

Williams, Brian. The Normandy Beaches. 2011. (Place in History Ser.). 48p. (YA). (gr. 5-9). lib. bdg. 34.25 *(978-1-84837-675-5(8))* Arcturus Publishing GBR. Dist: Black Rabbit Bks.

WORLD WAR, 1939-1945—CAMPAIGNS—FRANCE—NORMANDY

Atkinson, Rick. D-Day: The Invasion of Normandy 1944. 2014. (ENG., Illus.). 224p. (J). (gr. 3-7). 18.99 *(978-1-62779-111-3(6))*, 9781627791113, Holt, Henry & Co. Bks. For Young Readers) Holt, Henry & Co.

Benoit, Peter. D-Day. 2014. (ENG.). 48p. (J). lib. bdg. 29.00 *(978-0-531-20498-6(7))* Scholastic Library Publishing.

Biskup, Agnieszka. D-Day: June 6 1944, 1 vol. 2014. (24-Hour History Ser.). (ENG.). 48p. (gr. 3-5). pap. 8.95 *(978-1-4329-9301-6(1))*; (Illus.). lib. bdg. 33.32 *(978-1-4329-9295-8(3))* Heinemann-Raintree. (NA-h).

Bliven, Bruce. Invasion: The Story of D-Day. 2017. (Young Voyageur Ser.). (ENG.). 176p. (YA). (gr. 4-8). pap. 12.99 ***(978-0-7603-5436-0(7))***, Voyageur Pr.) Quarto Publishing Group USA.

Burgan, Michael. Turning Point: The Story of the d-Day Landings. 2017. (Tangled History Ser.). (ENG., Illus.). 112p. (gr. 3-4). lib. bdg. 31.99 *(978-1-5157-3607-3(5))* Capstone Press of Coughlan Cos.

Challen, Paul C. Surviving D-Day. 2015. (Surviving Disaster Ser.). (ENG., Illus.). 48p. (J). (gr. 5-6). 30.25 *(978-1-4994-3653-2(X))*, Rosen Central) Rosen Publishing Group, Inc., The.

Darman, Peter, ed. The Allied Invasion of Europe. 2012. (World War II Ser.). (ENG., Illus.). 64p. (YA). (gr. 7-12). 31.95 *(978-1-4488-9234-1(1))* Rosen Publishing Group, Inc., The.

Donohue, Moira Rose. The Invasion of Normandy: Epic Battle of World War II. 2017. (Major Battles in US History (paperback) Ser.). (ENG., Illus.). 32p. (J). (gr. 4-7). pap. 9.95 ***(978-1-63517-080-1(X))***, Focus Readers) North Star Editions.

Drez, Ronald J. Remember D-Day: The Plan, the Invasion, Survivor Stories. 2015. (ENG., Illus.). 64p. (J). (gr. 5). pap. 7.99 *(978-1-4263-2245-7(3))*, National Geographic Children's Bks.) National Geographic Society.

Otfinoski, Steven. World War II Infantrymen: An Interactive History Adventure. 2013. (You Choose: World War II Ser.). (ENG.). 112p. (gr. 3-4). Illus.). pap. 6.95 *(978-1-62065-716-4(3))*; pap. 41.70 *(978-1-62065-717-1(1))*; lib. bdg. 31.99 *(978-1-4296-9964-8(7))* Capstone Press of Coughlan Cos. (You Choose Bks.).

Samuels, Charlie. D-Day, Vol. 1. 2014. (Turning Points in US Military History Ser.). (ENG.). 48p. (J). (gr. 5-6). 31.95 *(978-1-4824-0432-6(X))* Stevens, Gareth Publishing LLLP.

Sepahban, Lois. 12 Incredible Facts about the d-Day Invasion. 2015. (Turning Points in US History Ser.). (ENG., Illus.). 32p. (J). (gr. 3-5). pap. *(978-1-63235-171-5(4))*, 12-Story Library) Pr. Room Editions LLC.

—12 Incredible Facts about the D-Day Invasion. 2015. (Turning Points in US History Ser.). (ENG., Illus.). 32p. (J). (gr. 3-5). *(978-1-63235-128-9(5))*, 12-Story Library) Pr. Room Editions LLC.

Zaloga, Steven J. The Most Daring Raid of World War II: D-Day — Pointe-Du-Hoc. 2011. (Most Daring Raids in History Ser.). (Illus.). 64p. (YA). (gr. 7-12). lib. bdg. 31.95 *(978-1-4488-1867-9(2))* Rosen Publishing Group, Inc., The.

WORLD WAR, 1939-1945—CAUSES

Benchmark Education Co., LLC. The Causes of World War II. 2014. (PRIME Ser.). (J). (gr. 6-8). pap. *(978-1-4509-9499-6(7))* Benchmark Education Co.

Corrigan, Jim. Causes of World War II. 2005. (Road to War Ser.). (Illus.). 64p. (gr. 4-18). lib. bdg. 22.95 *(978-1-59556-004-9(1))* OTTN Publishing.

Darman, Peter, ed. Attack on Pearl Harbor: America Enters World War II. 2012. (World War II Ser.). (ENG., Illus.). 64p. (J). (gr. 7-12). lib. bdg. 31.95 *(978-1-4488-9233-4(3))*, Rosen Reference) Rosen Publishing Group, Inc., The.

—World War II Begins. 2012. (World War II Ser.). (ENG., Illus.). 64p. (J). (gr. 7-12). lib. bdg. 31.95 *(978-1-4488-9232-7(5))* Rosen Publishing Group, Inc., The.

Davenport, John C. The Attack on Pearl Harbor: The United States Enters World War II. 2008. (Milestones in American History Ser.). (Illus.). 128p. (YA). (gr. 7-12). 35.00 *(978-1-60413-010-2(5))* Facts On File, Inc.

Dougherty, Steve. Attack on Pearl Harbor: World War II Strikes Home in the USA. 2011. (J). pap. *(978-0-545-32930-9(2))* Scholastic, Inc.

Freed, Kira. Surviving Pearl Harbor. 2015. (Surviving Disaster Ser.). (ENG., Illus.). 48p. (J). (gr. 5-6). 30.25 *(978-1-4994-3649-5(1))*, Rosen Central) Rosen Publishing Group, Inc., The.

Grahame-Smith, Deborah, contrib. by. Countdown to Catastrophe. 2010. (World War Ii Ser.). 128p. (gr. 6-9). 35.64 *(978-0-7614-4944-7(2))* Marshall Cavendish GBR. Dist: Marshall Cavendish Corp.

Johnson, Robin. Pearl Harbor. 2014. (ENG., Illus.). 48p. (J). *(978-0-7787-1367-8(9))* Crabtree Publishing Co.

Lassieur, Allison. The Attack on Pearl Harbor [Scholastic]: An Interactive History Adventure. 2009. (You Choose: History Ser.). 112p. (gr. 3-4). pap. 0.86 *(978-1-4296-4046-6(4))*, You Choose Bks.) Capstone Press of Coughlan Cos.

Marcovitz, Hal. Cause & Effect: World War II. 2017. (ENG.). 80p. (YA). (gr. 5-12). ***(978-1-68282-174-9(9))*** ReferencePoint Pr., Inc.

Marsico, Katie. World War II: Why They Fought. 2015. (What Were They Fighting For? Ser.). (ENG., Illus.). 64p. (gr. 5-9). 34.65 *(978-0-7565-5171-1(4))* Compass Point Bks.

Offord, Alexander. The Causes of World War II. 2015. (ENG., Illus.). 48p. (J). *(978-0-7787-2116-1(7))* Crabtree Publishing Co.

Pierce, Alan. Bombing of Pearl Harbor, 1 vol. 2005. (American Moments Set Ii Ser.). (ENG., Illus.). 48p. (gr. 4-8). 27.07 *(978-1-59197-729-2(0))*, Abdo & Daughters) ABDO Publishing Co.

Ross, Stewart & Woodward, Joe. Pearl Harbor. 2011. (Place in History Ser.). (Illus.). 48p. (YA). (gr. 5-9). lib. bdg. 34.25 *(978-1-84837-676-2(6))* Arcturus Publishing GBR. Dist: Black Rabbit Bks.

Samuels, Charlie. The Attack on Pearl Harbor, Vol. 1. 2014. (Turning Points in US Military History Ser.). (ENG.). 48p. (J). (gr. 5-6). 31.95 *(978-1-4824-0409-8(5))* Stevens, Gareth Publishing LLLP.

Uschan, Michael V. The Bombing of Pearl Harbor. 2003. (Landmark Events in American History Ser.). (Illus.). 48p. (gr. 5-12). lib. bdg. 31.00 *(978-0-8368-5373-5(3))*, Gareth Stevens Secondary Library) Stevens, Gareth Publishing LLLP.

Woog, Adam. Pearl Harbor. 2013. (Illus.). 96p. (J). lib. bdg. *(978-1-60152-486-7(2))* ReferencePoint Pr., Inc.

Wukovits, John F. The Bombing of Pearl Harbor. 2011. (World History Ser.). (ENG.). 128p. (gr. 10-10). lib. bdg. 39.90 *(978-1-4205-0330-2(8))*, Lucent Bks.) Cengage Gale.

Yomtov, Nel. The Attack on Pearl Harbor: December 7 1941, 1 vol. 2014. (24-Hour History Ser.). (ENG.). 48p. (gr. 3-5). pap. 8.95 *(978-1-4329-9299-6(6))*; (Illus.). lib. bdg. 33.32 *(978-1-4329-9293-4(7))* Heinemann-Raintree. (NA-h).

WORLD WAR, 1939-1945—CHILDREN

Alma, Ann. Brave Deeds: How One Family Saved Many from the Nazis. 2008. (ENG., Illus.). 96p. (J). (gr. 3-7). 17.95 *(978-0-88899-791-3(4))* Groundwood Bks. CAN. Dist: Publishers Group West (PGW).

Altman, Linda Jacobs. Escape-Teens on the Run: Primary Sources from the Holocaust. 2010. (True Stories of Teens in the Holocaust Ser.). (Illus.). 128p. (YA). (gr. 9-12). 33.27 *(978-0-7660-3270-5(1))* Enslow Pubs., Inc.

—Hidden Teens, Hidden Lives: Primary Sources from the Holocaust. 2010. (True Stories of Teens in the Holocaust Ser.). (Illus.). 128p. (YA). (gr. 9-12). 33.27 *(978-0-7660-3271-2(X))* Enslow Pubs., Inc.

Byers, Ann. Courageous Teen Resisters: Primary Sources from the Holocaust. 2010. (True Stories of Teens in the Holocaust Ser.). (Illus.). 128p. (YA). (gr. 9-12). 33.27 *(978-0-7660-3269-9(8))* Enslow Pubs., Inc.

—Trapped-Youth in the Nazi Ghettos: Primary Sources from the Holocaust. 2010. (True Stories of Teens in the Holocaust Ser.). (Illus.). 128p. (YA). (gr. 9-12). 33.27 *(978-0-7660-3272-9(8))* Enslow Pubs., Inc.

—Youth Destroyed-The Nazi Camps: Primary Sources from the Holocaust. 2010. (True Stories of Teens in the Holocaust Ser.). (Illus.). 128p. (YA). (gr. 9-12). 33.27 *(978-0-7660-3273-6(6))* Enslow Pubs., Inc.

Chase, Odette. This Child's War: A World War II Memoir. unabr. ed. 2004. (ENG., Illus.). 122p. per. 15.00 *(978-0-9759421-0-9(7))* Red Bud Publishing.

DeSaix, Deborah Durland & Ruelle, Karen Gray. Peter's War. DeSaix, Deborah Durland, illus. Date not set. (Illus.). (J). *(978-0-8234-2416-0(2))* Holiday Hse., Inc.

Foreman, Michael. War Boy: A Wartime Childhood. 2006. (ENG., Illus.). 96p. (J). (gr. 4-7). pap. 16.99 *(978-1-84365-087-4(8))* Pavilion Bks. GBR. Dist: Independent Pubs. Group.

Garner, Eleanor Ramrath & Ramrath Garner, Eleanor. Eleanor's Story: An American Girl in Hitler's Germany, 1 vol. 2003. (ENG., Illus.). 288p. (YA). (gr. 7-18). pap. 9.95 *(978-1-56145-296-5(3))*, Q19196) Peachtree Pubs.

Innes, Stephanie & Endrulat, Harry. Bear on the Homefront, 1 vol. Deines, Brian, illus. 2014. (ENG.). 32p. (J). (gr. k-3). 17.95 *(978-1-927485-13-2(4))* Pajama Pr. CAN. Dist: Ingram Publisher Services.

Josephson, Judith Pinkerton. Growing up in World War II, 1941-1945. 2003. (Our America Ser.). (Illus.). 64p. (J). (gr. 4-7). lib. bdg. 26.60 *(978-0-8225-0660-7(2))* Lerner Publishing Group.

Oppenheim, Joanne F. Dear Miss Breed: True Stories of the Japanese American Incarceration During World War II & a Librarian Who Made a Difference. 2006. (ENG., Illus.). 288p. (J). (gr. 7-12). 22.99 *(978-0-439-56992-7(3))* Scholastic, Inc.

Owlkids Books Inc. Staff & Arato, Rona. The Last Train: A Holocaust Story. 2013. (ENG., Illus.). 144p. (J). (gr. 6). 16.95 *(978-1-926973-62-3(3))* Owlkids Bks. Inc. CAN. Dist: Publishers Group West (PGW).

Stones, A. J. Evacuation in World War II. 2016. (Stories of World War II Ser.). (ENG., Illus.). 32p. (J). (gr. 4-6). pap. 11.99 *(978-0-7502-8994-8(5))*, Wayland) Hachette Children's Group GBR. Dist: Hachette Bk. Group.

—Kindertransport. 2016. (Stories of World War II Ser.). (ENG., Illus.). 32p. (J). (gr. 4-6). pap. 11.99 *(978-0-7502-8989-4(9))*, Wayland) Hachette Children's Group GBR. Dist: Hachette Bk. Group.

Vander Zee, Ruth. Erika's Story. Innocenti, Roberto, illus. 2003. (ENG.). 24p. (J). (gr. 1-3). 19.99 *(978-1-56846-176-2(3))* Creative Co., The.

Welch, Catherine A. Children of the Relocation Camps. 2005. (Picture the American Past Ser.). (Illus.). 48p. (gr. 2-5). lib. bdg. 22.60 *(978-1-57505-350-9(0))* Lerner Publishing Group.

Whitman, Sylvia. Children of the World War II Home Front. 2005. (Picture the American Past Ser.). (Illus.). 48p. (J). (gr. 2-5). lib. bdg. 22.60 *(978-1-57505-484-1(1))* Lerner Publishing Group.

Wintrob, Kitty. I'm Not Going Back: Wartime Memoir of a Child Evacuee. 2009. *(978-0-9784435-1-9(0))* Now & Then Bks.

Ziemian, Joseph. The Cigarette Sellers of Three Crosses Square. 2005. (Library of Holocaust Testimonies Ser.). (Illus.). 168p. pap. 24.95 *(978-0-85303-686-9(1))* Vallentine Mitchell Pubs. GBR. Dist: ISBS Publisher Services.

WORLD WAR, 1939-1945—CHINA

Himsl, Sharon M. Events That Changed the World - 1940-1960. 2003. (EVENTS THAT CHANGED the WRLD Ser.). (ENG., Illus.). lib. bdg. 38.45 *(978-0-7377-1756-3(4))* Cengage Gale.

Otfinoski, Steven. Pilots in Peril! The Untold Story of U. S. Pilots Who Braved the Hump in World War II. 2016. (Encounter: Narrative Nonfiction Stories Ser.). (ENG.). 232p. (gr. 3-4). pap. 9.95 *(978-1-4914-5166-3(1))* Encounter Bks.

—Pilots in Peril! The Untold Story of U.S. Pilots Who Braved "The Hump" in World War II. 2015. (Encounter: Narrative Nonfiction Stories Ser.). (ENG., Illus.). 232p. (gr. 3-4). lib. bdg. 33.99 *(978-1-4914-5156-4(4))* Encounter Bks.

WORLD WAR, 1939-1945—EUROPE

Altman, Linda Jacobs. The Forgotten Victims of the Holocaust. 2003. (Holocaust in History Ser.). (Illus.). 104p. (J). (gr. 5-12). lib. bdg. 27.94 *(978-0-7660-1993-5(4))* Enslow Pubs., Inc.

Boas, Jacob. We Are Witnesses: Five Diaries of Teenagers Who Died in the Holocaust. 2009. (ENG.). 208p. (YA). (gr. 6-10). pap. 9.99 *(978-0-312-53567-4(8))*, 9780312535674) Square Fish.

Buckley, James, Jr. Adolf Hitler. 2017. (History's Worst Ser.). (ENG., Illus.). 208p. (J). (gr. 3-7). pap. 7.99 ***(978-1-4814-7942-4(3))***, Aladdin) Simon & Schuster Children's Publishing.

Byers, Ann. Rescuing the Danish Jews: A Heroic Story from the Holocaust. 2011. (Holocaust Through Primary Sources Ser.). (Illus.). 128p. (J). (gr. 9-12). lib. bdg. 33.27 *(978-0-7660-3321-4(X))* Enslow Pubs., Inc.

Chant, Christopher. The Defeat of the Nazis: The Allied Victory in Europe. 2017. (World War II Ser.: Vol. 5). (ENG.). (YA). (gr. 7-12). 24.95 ***(978-1-4222-3897-4(0))*** Mason Crest.

DeSaix, Deborah Durland & Ruelle, Karen Gray. Peter's War. DeSaix, Deborah Durland, illus. Date not set. (Illus.). (J). *(978-0-8234-2416-0(2))* Holiday Hse., Inc.

Havers, R. P. W. & O'Neill, Robert John. World War II: Europe, 1944-1945. 2010. (World War II: Essential Histories Ser.). (Illus.). 96p. (YA). (gr. 9-12). lib. bdg. 33.25 *(978-1-4358-9130-2(9))* Rosen Publishing Group, Inc., The.

Hoffman, Betty N. Liberation: Stories of Survival from the Holocaust. 2011. (Holocaust Through Primary Sources Ser.). (Illus.). 128p. (J). (gr. 6-18). pap. 10.95 *(978-1-59845-348-5(3))*; (gr. 9-12). lib. bdg. 33.27 *(978-0-7660-3319-1(8))* Enslow Pubs., Inc.

Jeffrey, Gary. The Western Front. 2012. (ENG., Illus.). 48p. (J). *(978-0-7787-4196-1(6))*; pap. *(978-0-7787-4203-6(2))* Crabtree Publishing Co.

Marshall Cavendish Corporation Staff. Global Chaos. 2010. (World War Ii Ser.). 128p. (gr. 6-9). lib. bdg. 35.64 *(978-0-7614-4948-5(5))* Marshall Cavendish Corp.

—Terror & Triumph. 2010. (World War Ii Ser.). 128p. (gr. 6-9). lib. bdg. 35.64 *(978-0-7614-4949-2(3))* Marshall Cavendish Corp.

Peyton, Katherine & George, Enzo. World War II in Europe & North Africa: Preserving Democracy. 2014. (Voices of War Ser.). 48p. (J). (gr. 4-6). lib. bdg. 31.36 *(978-1-62712-864-3(6))* Cavendish Square Publishing.

Rice, Earle, Jr. Blitzkrieg! Hitler's Lightning War. 2007. (Monumental Milestones Ser.). (Illus.). 48p. (YA). (gr. 4-7). lib. bdg. 29.95 *(978-1-58415-542-3(6))* Mitchell Lane Pubs., Inc.

Samuels, Charlie. Life under Occupation. 2012. (World War II Sourcebook Ser.). (Illus.). 48p. (gr. 5-12). lib. bdg. 37.10 *(978-1-936333-26-4(0))* Brown Bear Bks.

—World War II. 2011. (Americans at War: a Gareth Stevens Timeline Ser.). 48p. (J). (gr. 6-8). pap. 14.05 *(978-1-4339-5932-5(1))*; pap. 14.05 *(978-1-4339-5935-6(6))*; lib. bdg. 31.95 *(978-1-4339-5930-1(5))*; lib. bdg. 31.95 *(978-1-4339-5934-9(8))* Stevens, Gareth Publishing LLLP. (Gareth Stevens Secondary Library).

Stein, R. Conrad. World War II in Europe: From Normandy to Berlin. 2011. (United States at War Ser.). (Illus.). 128p. (J). (gr. 5-18). lib. bdg. 33.27 *(978-0-7660-3639-0(1))* Enslow Pubs., Inc.

Toll, Nelly S. Behind the Secret Window: A Memoir of a Hidden Childhood During World War II. 2003. (ENG.). 176p. (J). (gr. 3-7). 5.99 *(978-0-14-230241-5(4)*, Puffin Books) Penguin Young Readers Group.

World Book, Inc Staff, contrib. by. World War II in Europe. 2010. (J). *(978-0-7166-1509-5(6))* World Bk., Inc.

WORLD WAR, 1939-1945—FICTION

Adler, David A. Don't Talk to Me about the War. 2009. (ENG.). 224p. (J). (gr. 3-7). 7.99 *(978-0-14-241372-2(0)*, Puffin Books) Penguin Young Readers Group.

Alexander, Carol. When My Name Was Keoko. Friedland, Joyce & Kessler, Rikki, eds. 2008. (Novel-Ties Ser.). 29p. pap. 16.95 *(978-0-7675-1520-7(X))* Learning Links Inc.

Allen, Nancy. Amazing Grace: A Kentucky Girl with Gumption During World War II. 2014. Orig. Title: Amazing Grace: a Kentucky Girl with Gumption During World War II. (ENG., Illus.). 160p. (gr. 4-7). pap. 14.99 *(978-1-62619-405-2(X)*, History Pr., The) Arcadia Publishing.

Angus, Sam. A Horse Called Hero. 2014. (ENG.). 304p. (J). (gr. 4-7). 16.99 *(978-1-250-04508-9(8)*, 9781250045089) Feiwel & Friends.

Appelfeld, Aharon. Adam & Thomas. Green, Jeffrey M., tr. from HEB. Dumas, Philippe, illus. 2017. (ENG.). 160p. (J). (gr. 3-7). pap. 14.95 *(978-1-60980-744-3(8)*, Triangle Square) Seven Stories Pr.

Arrigan, Mary. Rabbit Girl. 2011. (ENG.). 224p. (J). (gr. 4-7). pap. 8.95 *(978-1-84780-156-2(0)*, Frances Lincoln) Quarto Publishing Group UK GBR. Dist: Hachette Bk. Group.

Arvidson, Douglas. Brothers of the Fire Star. Scarborough, Rob, illus. 2012. 207p. (YA). pap. 15.95 *(978-1-890109-91-2(6)*, Cross Time) Crossquarter Publishing Group.

Ashley, Bernard & Morgan, Andrew. Dead End Kids. 2015. (Cordelia Codd Ser.). (ENG.). 224p. (J). (gr. 4-6). pap. 10.99 *(978-1-4083-3895-7(5))* Hodder & Stoughton GBR. Dist: Hachette Bk. Group.

Avery, Al. A Yankee Flier in the Far East. Laune, Paul, illus. 2011. 224p. 44.95 *(978-1-258-06349-8(2))* Literary Licensing, LLC.

Avi. Don't You Know There's a War On? 2003. 208p. (J). (ENG.). (gr. 3-7). pap. 7.99 *(978-0-380-81544-9(3))*; 2nd ed. pap. *(978-0-439-53096-5(2)*, HarperCollins) HarperCollins Pubs.

—Don't You Know There's a War On? 2003. 193p. (gr. 3-7). 18.00 *(978-0-7569-1383-0(7))* Perfection Learning Corp.

—Who Was That Masked Man, Anyway? 2014. (ENG.). 176p. (J). (gr. 3-7). pap. 6.99 *(978-0-439-52355-4(9)*, Scholastic Paperbacks) Scholastic, Inc.

Ayres, Katherine. Voices at Whisper Bend. 2009. (Mysteries Through Time Ser.). 176p. (YA). (gr. 4-8). 31.95 *(978-1-60754-182-0(3))*; pap. 15.25 *(978-1-60754-183-7(1))* Windmill Bks.

Banks, Lynne Reid. Uprooted - a Canadian War Story. 2014. (ENG.). 336p. (J). 8.99 *(978-0-00-758943-2(3)*, HarperCollins Children's Bks.) HarperCollins Pubs. Ltd. GBR. Dist: HarperCollins Pubs.

—Uprooted - A Canadian War Story. 2015. (ENG.). 336p. (J). pap. 8.99 *(978-0-00-813235-4(6)*, HarperCollins Children's Bks.) HarperCollins Pubs. Ltd. GBR. Dist: HarperCollins Pubs.

Barker, Michelle. A Year of Borrowed Men. Benoit, Renne, illus. 2016. (ENG.). 40p. (J). (gr. 1-4). 18.95 *(978-1-927485-83-5(5))* Pajama Pr. CAN. Dist: Ingram Publisher Services.

Barrow, Randi. Saving Zasha. 2013. (ENG.). 256p. (J). (gr. 3-7). pap. 6.99 *(978-0-545-20633-4(2)*, Scholastic Paperbacks) Scholastic, Inc.

Barry, Rick. Gunner's Run: A World War II Novel. 2007. 215p. (YA). (gr. 8-12). per. 8.99 *(978-1-59166-761-2(5))* BJU Pr.

Bass, Karen. Graffiti Knight, 1 vol. 2014. (ENG., Illus.). 288p. (YA). (gr. 7-11). pap. 11.95 *(978-1-927485-53-8(3))* Pajama Pr. CAN. Dist: Ingram Publisher Services.

—Summer of Fire, 1 vol. 2009. (ENG.). 295p. (YA). (gr. 9-12). pap. 12.95 *(978-1-55050-415-6(0))* Coteau Bks. CAN. Dist: Orca Bk. Pubs. USA.

Bee, Harry. Printer Street's War. 2008. (ENG.). 140p. pap. 10.99 *(978-1-4196-5700-9(3))* CreateSpace Independent Publishing Platform.

Bell, Ted. Nick of Time. 2009. (Nick Mciver Adventures Through Time Ser.: 1). (ENG., Illus.). 464p. (J). (gr. 5-9). pap. 8.99 *(978-0-312-58143-5(2)*, 9780312581435) Square Fish.

—The Time Pirate. 2011. (Nick Mciver Adventures Through Time Ser.: 2). (ENG., Illus.). 480p. (J). (gr. 5-9). pap. 10.99 *(978-0-312-66549-4(0)*, 9780312665494) Square Fish.

Bishop, Claire Huchet. Twenty & Ten. 76p. (J). (gr. 3-5). pap. 4.99 *(978-0-8072-1418-3(3)*, Listening Library) Random Hse. Audio Publishing Group.

Blackford, Cheryl. Lizzie & the Lost Baby. (ENG.). 192p. (J). (gr. 5-7). 2017. pap. 6.99 *(978-0-544-93525-9(X))* 2016. 16.99 *(978-0-544-57099-3(5))* Houghton Mifflin Harcourt Publishing Co. (HMH Books For Young Readers).

Bloor, Edward. London Calling. 2008. (ENG., Illus.). 304p. (YA). (gr. 7-9). per. 8.99 *(978-0-375-84363-1(9)*, Ember) Random Hse. Children's Bks.

Boland, Shalini. A Shirtful of Frogs. 2012. 244p. pap. *(978-0-9569985-4-5(2))* Adrenalin Bks.

Booth, Martin. War Dog. 2012. (ENG.). 144p. (YA). (gr. 7). pap. 8.99 *(978-1-4424-7297-6(9)*, McElderry, Margaret K. Bks.) McElderry, Margaret K. Bks.

Borden, Louise. The Little Ships: The Heroic Rescue at Dunkirk in World War II. Foreman, Michael, illus. 2003. (ENG.). 32p. (J). (gr. 4-7). 7.99 *(978-0-689-85396-8(3)*, McElderry, Margaret K. Bks.) McElderry, Margaret K. Bks.

Borden, Louise & Borden, Louise W. Across the Blue Pacific: A World War II Story. Parker, Robert Andrew, illus. 2006. (ENG.). 48p. (J). (gr. -1-3). 17.00 *(978-0-618-33922-8(1))* Houghton Mifflin Harcourt Publishing Co.

Borden, Louise & Daly, Niki. The Greatest Skating Race: A World War II Story from the Netherlands. Daly, Niki, illus. 2004. (ENG., Illus.). 48p. (J). (gr. 4-7). 19.99 *(978-0-689-84502-4(2)*, McElderry, Margaret K. Bks.) McElderry, Margaret K. Bks.

Borden, Louise W. Across the Blue Pacific: A World War II Story. Parker, Robert Andrew, illus. 2015. (ENG.). 48p. (J). (gr. -1-3). 7.99 *(978-0-544-55552-5(X)*, HMH Books For Young Readers) Houghton Mifflin Harcourt Publishing Co.

Bowen, Robert Sidney. Dave Dawson at Guadalcanal. 2011. 242p. 46.95 *(978-1-258-01956-3(6))* Literary Licensing, LLC.

—Dave Dawson, Flight Lieutenant. 2011. 248p. 46.95 *(978-1-258-01820-7(9))* Literary Licensing, LLC.

Boyne, John. The Boy at the Top of the Mountain. 2017. (J). lib. bdg. 18.40 ***(978-0-606-39937-1(2))*** Turtleback Bks.

—The Boy in the Striped Pajamas. (ENG.). (YA). (gr. 7). 2006. 224p. 17.99 *(978-0-385-75106-3(0))* 2008. 240p. pap. 9.99 *(978-0-385-75189-6(3))* Fickling, David Bks. GBR. Dist: Penguin Random Hse. LLC.

—The Boy in the Striped Pajamas. 2011. 10.54 *(978-0-7848-3514-2(4)*, Everbind) Marco Bk. Co.

—The Boy in the Striped Pajamas. 2008. 215p. (gr. 7-12). 20.00 *(978-0-7569-8943-9(4))* Perfection Learning Corp.

—The Boy in the Striped Pajamas. 2007. (ENG.). 224p. (YA). (gr. 7-18). pap. 9.99 *(978-0-385-75153-7(2)*, Ember) Random Hse. Children's Bks.

—The Boy in the Striped Pajamas. rev. l.t. ed. 2007. (Thorndike Literacy Bridge Ser.). 247p. (YA). (gr. 7-12). 23.95 *(978-0-7862-9425-1(6))* Thorndike Pr.

—The Boy in the Striped Pajamas. 2007. 215p. (YA). (gr. 7-12). 20.85 *(978-1-4178-1823-5(9)*, Turtleback) Turtleback Bks.

—The Boy in the Striped Pajamas (Deluxe Illustrated Edition) Jeffers, Oliver, illus. 2016. (ENG.). 352p. (YA). (gr. 7). 18.99 *(978-0-399-55931-0(0)*, Knopf Bks. for Young Readers) Random Hse. Children's Bks.

Bradley, Kimberly Brubaker. For Freedom: The Story of a French Spy. 2005. 181p. 16.00 *(978-0-7569-5091-0(0))* Perfection Learning Corp.

—For Freedom: The Story of a French Spy. 2005. (ENG.). 192p. (YA). (gr. 7-9). mass mkt. 5.99 *(978-0-440-41831-3(3)*, Laurel Leaf) Random Hse. Children's Bks.

—The War That Saved My Life. (ENG.). (J). (gr. 4-7). 2016. 336p. 8.99 *(978-0-14-751048-8(1)*, Puffin Books) 2015. 320p. 17.99 *(978-0-8037-4081-5(6)*, Dial Bks) Penguin Young Readers Group.

—The War That Saved My Life. 2016. (J). lib. bdg. 19.65 *(978-0-606-38843-6(5))* Turtleback Bks.

Brigham, Anthea. Henrietta, World War II Hen: This Is a True Story. Brigham, Anthea, illus. 2008. (ENG., Illus.). 28p. (J). 7.00 *(978-0-9740778-2-6(8))* Whale's Jaw Publishing.

Bruchac, Joseph. Code Talker: A Novel about the Navajo Marines of World War Two. 2006. (ENG.). 240p. (YA). (gr. 7-18). 8.99 *(978-0-14-240596-3(5)*, Speak) Penguin Young Readers Group.

Buckey, Sarah Masters. The Light in the Cellar: A Molly Mystery. 2003. (American Girl Mysteries Ser.). (ENG., Illus.). 176p. (gr. 4-7). 10.95 *(978-1-59369-159-2(9))* American Girl Publishing, Inc.

Bunn, Bill. Kill Shot. 2015. (ENG.). 244p. pap. 16.99 *(978-1-938463-53-2(6))* Bitingduck Pr.

Burg, Ann. Rebekkah's Journey: A World War II Refugee Story. Iskowitz, Joel, illus. 2006. (Tales of Young Americans Ser.). (ENG.). 32p. (J). (gr. 3-7). 17.95 *(978-1-58536-275-2(1))* Sleeping Bear Pr.

Burkinshaw, Kathleen. The Last Cherry Blossom. 2016. (ENG.). 240p. (J). (gr. 5-8). 16.99 *(978-1-63450-693-9(6)*, Sky Pony Pr.) Skyhorse Publishing Co., Inc.

Burnford, Sheila. Bel Ria: Dog of War. 2006. (New York Review Children's Collection). (ENG.). 256p. (J). (gr. 4-7). 17.95 *(978-1-59017-211-7(6)*, NYR Children's Collection) New York Review of Bks., Inc., The.

Bylsma, Dan & Bylsma, Jay M. Slam Dunks Not Allowed! 2003. (Illus.). 238p. (YA). *(978-0-938682-72-1(5))*; pap. *(978-0-938682-77-6(6))* River Road Pubns., Inc.

Calkhoven, Laurie. Michael at the Invasion of France 1943. 3 vols. 2012. (Boys of Wartime Ser.: 3). (ENG.). 240p. (J). (gr. 4-7). 16.99 *(978-0-8037-3724-2(6)*, Dial Bks) Penguin Young Readers Group.

Campbell, Isaiah. AbrakaPOW. 2016. (ENG., Illus.). 400p. (J). (gr. 3-7). 16.99 *(978-1-4814-2634-3(6)*, Simon & Schuster Bks. For Young Readers) Simon & Schuster Bks. For Young Readers.

Carbone, Elisa & Wells, Rosemary. Diana's White House Garden. Hill, Jen, illus. 2016. (ENG.). 44p. (J). (gr. k-3). bds. 17.99 *(978-0-670-01649-5(7)*, Viking Books for Young Readers) Penguin Young Readers Group.

Carradice, Phil & Thomas, Frances. Hannah Goes to War. 2005. (ENG.). 144p. pap. 12.95 *(978-1-84323-461-6(0))* Beekman Bks., Inc.

Carter, Rachel. So Close to You. 2013. (ENG.). 336p. (YA). (gr. 9). pap. 9.99 *(978-0-06-208106-3(3)*, HarperTeen) HarperCollins Pubs.

Casanova, Mary. The Klipfish Code. 2012. (ENG.). 240p. (J). (gr. 5-7). pap. 6.99 *(978-0-547-74447-6(1))* Houghton Mifflin Harcourt Publishing Co.

Center for Learning Network Staff. Slaughterhouse-Five: Curriculum Unit. 2005. (Novel Ser.). 76p. (YA). tchr. ed., spiral bd. 19.95 *(978-1-56077-789-2(3))* Center for Learning, The.

Cerrito, Angela. The Safest Lie. 2015. (ENG.). 192p. (J). (gr. 3-7). 16.95 *(978-0-8234-3310-0(2))* Holiday Hse., Inc.

Chaconas, Dori. Pennies in a Jar. 1 vol. Lewin, Ted, illus. 2007. (ENG.). 32p. (J). (gr. 1-5). 16.95 *(978-1-56145-422-8(2))* Peachtree Pubs.

Chambers, Aidan. Postcards from No Man's Land. (ENG.). 320p. (YA). (gr. 9-18). 2007. 10.00 *(978-0-14-240788-2(7))* 2004. reprint ed. 8.99 *(978-0-14-240145-3(5))* Penguin Young Readers Group. (Speak).

Chang, Pei-Yu. Mr. Benjamin's Suitcase of Secrets. 2017. (ENG., Illus.). 48p. (J). (gr. -1-3). 18.95 ***(978-0-7358-4280-9(9))*** North-South Bks., Inc.

Chapman, Fern Schumer. Is It Night or Day? 2010. (ENG.). 224p. (J). (gr. 5-9). 17.99 *(978-0-374-17744-7(9)*, 9780374177447, Farrar, Straus & Giroux (BYR)) Farrar, Straus & Giroux.

Cheaney, J. B. My Friend the Enemy. 2007. 266p. (gr. 4-7). 16.50 *(978-0-7569-7946-1(3))* Perfection Learning Corp.

Clark, Kathy. Guardian Angel House, 1 vol. 2009. (Holocaust Remembrance Ser.). (ENG., Illus.). 180p. (J). (gr. 4-8). pap. 14.95 *(978-1-897187-58-6(0))* Second Story Pr. CAN. Dist: Orca Bk. Pubs. USA.

Coker, Rachel. Interrupted: A Life Beyond Words, 1 vol. 2013. (ENG.). 256p. (YA). pap. 9.99 *(978-0-310-72810-8(X))* Zondervan.

Cooper, Michelle. The FitzOsbornes at War. 2013. (Montmaray Journals). (ENG.). 560p. (YA). (gr. 7). pap. 10.99 *(978-0-307-93058-3(0)*, Ember) Random Hse. Children's Bks.

Cooper, Susan. Dawn of Fear. Gill, Margery, illus. 2007. (ENG.). 176p. (J). (gr. 5-7). pap. 7.99 *(978-0-15-206106-7(1))* Houghton Mifflin Harcourt Publishing Co.

Copeland, Cynthia L. Elin's Island. 2003. (Single Titles Ser.: up). (ENG.). 144p. (YA). (gr. 6-12). lib. bdg. 22.60 *(978-0-7613-2522-2(0)*, Millbrook Pr.) Lerner Publishing Group.

Cormier, Robert. Heroes. 2006. (York Notes Ser.). (ENG., Illus.). 112p. pap. *(978-1-4058-3559-6(1))* Pearson Education, Ltd.

Couloumbis, Audrey & Couloumbis, Akila. War Games. 2011. (ENG.). 240p. (J). (gr. 3-7). pap. 6.99 *(978-0-375-85629-7(3)*, Yearling) Random Hse. Children's Bks.

Cronin, Bernie. We're Coming Home. 2004. 56p. pap. *(978-1-84401-253-4(0))* Athena Pr.

Cummings, Mary. And the Baker's Boy Went to Sea. 2006. (Illus.). 195p. (YA). 16.95 *(978-0-9774855-0-5(1))* Sparkling Pr.

Cutler, Jane. My Wartime Summers. 2011. 160p. (gr. 4-6). pap. 12.95 *(978-1-4502-5419-9(5))* iUniverse, Inc.

Dalager, Stig. David's Story. 2010. (ENG., Illus.). 280p. (J). pap. 18.95 *(978-1-906582-04-3(1))* Aurora Metro Pubns. Ltd. GBR. Dist: Consortium Bk. Sales & Distribution.

Dallas, Sandra. Red Berries, White Clouds, Blue Sky. (ENG.). 216p. (J). (gr. 3-6). 2015. pap. 9.99 *(978-1-58536-907-2(1)*, 203820) 2014. 15.95 *(978-1-58536-906-5(3)*, 203673) Sleeping Bear Pr.

Davis, Tanita S. Mare's War. 2011. (ENG.). 352p. (YA). (gr. 7). pap. 9.99 *(978-0-375-85077-6(5)*, Knopf Bks. for Young Readers) Random Hse. Children's Bks.

Deborah Strandberg, Rebecca Reynolds and. Trammler Triplet Tales #2 - HIDDEN in TIME. 2007. 116p. pap. 8.94 *(978-1-4303-2097-5(4))* Lulu Pr., Inc.

Devries, Maggie. Hunger Journeys. 2012. (ENG.). 288p. (J). mass mkt. 7.99 *(978-1-55468-580-6(X)*, Harper Trophy) HarperCollins Pubs.

di Vries, Maggie. Hunger Journeys. 2014. 240p. (YA). (gr. 8). pap. 8.99 *(978-0-06-231351-5(7))* HarperCollins Pubs.

Dowswell, Paul. The Auslander. 2011. (ENG.). 304p. (YA). 17.99 *(978-1-59990-633-1(3)*, 9781599906331, Bloomsbury USA Childrens) Bloomsbury Publishing USA.

Doyle, Brian. Boy O'Boy, 1 vol. 2005. (ENG.). 162p. (YA). pap. 6.95 *(978-0-88899-654-1(3))* Groundwood Bks. CAN. Dist: Publishers Group West (PGW).

Dudley, David L. Caleb's Wars. 2011. (ENG.). 272p. (YA). (gr. 9). 17.99 *(978-0-547-23997-2(1))* Houghton Mifflin Harcourt Publishing Co.

Dunlop, Ed. The Incredible Rescues. Halverson, Tom, illus. 2003. 166p. (J). (gr. 4-7). 7.49 *(978-1-59166-012-5(2))* BJU Pr.

—The Search for the Silver Eagle. Halverson, Tom, illus. 2003. 159p. (J). (gr. 4-7). 7.49 *(978-1-59166-014-9(9))* BJU Pr.

Dunn, Joeming W. & Dunn, Ben. D-Day. Dunn, Joeming W. & Dunn, Ben, illus. 2016. (Graphic Warfare Ser.). (ENG., Illus.). 32p. (J). (gr. 3-8). 28.50 *(978-1-61641-979-0(2))* Magic Wagon.

Duras, Marguerite. Hiroshima Mon Amour, Level B.Tr. of Hiroshima My Love. (FRE.). (YA). (gr. 7-12). 9.95 *(978-0-88436-998-1(6)*, 40308) EMC/Paradigm Publishing.

Elliott, L. M. Under a War-Torn Sky. 2003. (ENG.). 288p. (J). (gr. 5-9). pap. 6.99 *(978-0-7868-1753-5(4))* Hyperion Pr.

—Under a War-Torn Sky. 2003. (J). (gr. 7-12). lib. bdg. 17.20 *(978-0-613-69092-8(3)*, Turtleback) Turtleback Bks.

Elvgren, Jennifer. The Whispering Town. Santomauro, Fabio, illus. 2014. (Holocaust Ser.). (ENG.). 32p. (J). (gr. 2-5). 17.95 *(978-1-4677-1194-4(2))*; 7.95 *(978-1-4677-1195-1(0))* Lerner Publishing Group.

Farrant, Natasha. What We Did for Love: Resistance, Heartbreak, Betrayal. 2014. (Illus.). 208p. (YA). (gr. 6-12). pap. 10.95 *(978-1-62324-029-5(8))* Enslow Pubs., Inc.

Faulkner, Matt. Gaijin: American Prisoner of War. 2014. (ENG., Illus.). 144p. (J). (gr. 3-7). 19.99 *(978-1-4231-3735-1(3))* Hyperion Bks. for Children.

Ferrari, Michael. Born to Fly. 2011. (ENG.). 224p. (J). (gr. 3-7). 6.99 *(978-0-375-84607-6(7)*, Yearling) Random Hse. Children's Bks.

Finn, K. C. The Mind's Eye. 2014. (Synsk Ser.: 1). (ENG.). 352p. (J). (gr. 10-12). pap. 12.99 *(978-1-940534-38-1(0))* Clean Teen Publishing.

Fisher, Rick. Unknown Heroes. 2007. (ENG., Illus.). 32p. (J). per. 14.95 *(978-1-59800-899-9(4))* Outskirts Pr., Inc.

Fleming, Candace. Boxes for Katje. Dressen-McQueen, Stacey, illus. 2003. (ENG.). 40p. (J). (gr. -1-3). 18.99 *(978-0-374-30922-0(1)*, 9780374309220, Farrar, Straus & Giroux (BYR)) Farrar, Straus & Giroux.

—Boxes for Katje. Dressen-McQueen, Stacey, illus. 2004. (YA). 27.95 incl. audio *(978-0-8045-6930-9(4)*, SAC6930) Spoken Arts, Inc.

Flood, Nancy Bo. Warriors in the Crossfire. 2013. (ENG.). 144p. (J). (gr. 6-9). pap. 7.95 *(978-1-62091-026-9(8))* Boyds Mills Pr.

Florida-James, Mark. Berlin Wolf. 2013. (ENG.). 336p. pap. *(978-1-78306-005-4(0))* Troubador Publishing Ltd.

Fox, Janet. The Charmed Children of Rookskill Castle. (ENG.). 400p. (J). (gr. 5). 2017. 8.99 *(978-0-14-751713-5(3)*, Puffin Books) 2016. (Illus.). 16.99 *(978-0-451-47633-3(6)*, Viking Books for Young Readers) Penguin Young Readers Group.

French, Jackie. Hitler's Daughter. 2003. (ENG.). 128p. (J). (gr. 3-7). 16.99 *(978-0-06-008652-7(1))* HarperCollins Pubs.

Friedman, D. Dina. Escaping into the Night. 2009. (ENG.). 208p. (J). (gr. 5-9). pap. 9.99 *(978-1-4169-8648-5(0)*, Simon & Schuster Bks. For Young Readers) Simon & Schuster Bks. For Young Readers.

Frische, Muffet. Moon Tears. 2014. (ENG.). 256p. (J). pap. 11.99 *(978-0-9916348-1-1(0))* Ten Story Bks., LLC.

Gadsby, Maggie. Owl Be Home for Christmas. 2012. (J). 14.95 *(978-1-62086-064-9(3))* Mascot Bks., Inc.

Gallaz, Christophe. ROSA BLANCA. 2nd ed. 2003. (Rosa y Manzana Ser.). (SPA., Illus.). 32p. *(978-84-85334-52-0(3)*, LG2811) Lóguez Ediciones ESP. Dist: Lectorum Pubns., Inc.

—Rose Blanche. Innocenti, Roberto, illus. 2011. (ENG.). 32p. (J). (gr. 5-17). pap. 10.99 *(978-0-89812-385-2(2))* Creative Co., The.

Giff, Patricia Reilly. Genevieve's War. Stadtlander, Becca, illus. 2017. (ENG.). 240p. (J). (gr. 3-7). 16.95 *(978-0-8234-3800-6(7))* Holiday Hse., Inc.

—Gingersnap. 2014. (ENG.). 160p. (J). (gr. 3-7). 6.99 *(978-0-440-42178-8(0)*, Yearling) Random Hse. Children's Bks.

—Willow Run. 2007. 149p. (J). 13.65 *(978-0-7569-7769-6(X))* Perfection Learning Corp.

—Willow Run. 2007. (ENG.). 160p. (J). (gr. 3-7). per. 5.99 *(978-0-440-23801-0(3)*, Yearling) Random Hse. Children's Bks.

Glatshteyn, Yankev. Emil & Karl. Shandler, Jeffrey, tr. 2008. (ENG.). 208p. (J). (gr. 4-9). per. 9.99 *(978-0-312-37387-0(2)*, 9780312373870) Square Fish.

Gleitzman, Morris. Once. 2005. 160p. (J). pap. *(978-0-14-330195-0(0)*, Puffin) Penguin Publishing Group.

—Then. 2013. (Once Ser.: 2). (ENG.). 224p. (YA). (gr. 7). pap. 9.99 *(978-1-250-00341-6(5)*, 9781250003416) Square Fish.

—Then. 2013. (YA). lib. bdg. 20.85 *(978-0-606-31904-1(2)*, Turtleback) Turtleback Bks.

Graber, Janet. Resistance. 2005. 144p. (YA). 15.95 *(978-0-7614-5214-0(1))* Marshall Cavendish Corp.

Grant, Michael. Silver Stars. 2017. (Front Lines Ser.: 2). (Illus.). 576p. (YA). (gr. 9). 18.99 *(978-0-06-234218-8(5)*, Tegen, Katherine Bks) HarperCollins Pubs.

Gratz, Alan. Projekt 1065: A Novel of World War II. 2016. (ENG.). 320p. (J). (gr. 4-7). 16.99 *(978-0-545-88016-9(5)*, Scholastic Pr.) Scholastic, Inc.

Graziani, E. War in My Town, 1 vol. 2015. (ENG., Illus.). 152p. (YA). (gr. 8-10). pap. 11.95 *(978-1-927583-71-5(3))* Second Story Pr. CAN. Dist: Orca Bk. Pubs. USA.

Green, Connie Jordan. The War at Home. 2nd ed. 2003. 144p. (J). pap. 15.00 *(978-0-916078-75-1(2))* Iris Publishing Group, Inc., The.

Greene, Bette. Summer of My German Soldier. 2006. (Puffin Modern Classics Ser.). (ENG.). 240p. (J). (gr. 5-18). 7.99 *(978-0-14-240651-9(1)*, Puffin Books) Penguin Young Readers Group.

Griffis, Molly Levite. The Rachel Resistance. 224p. 8.95 *(978-1-57168-553-7(7))* Eakin Pr.

—Simon Says. 2004. vi, 263p. (J). 22.95 *(978-1-57168-836-1(6))*; pap. *(978-1-57168-847-7(1))* Eakin Pr. (Eakin Pr.).

Grindley, Sally. Feather Wars. 2003. (ENG.). 1p. (J). pap. 12.99 *(978-0-7475-6338-9(1))* Bloomsbury Publishing Plc GBR. Dist: Independent Pubs. Group.

Gutman, Dan. Ted & Me. 2012. (Baseball Card Adventures Ser.). (Illus.). 208p. (J). (gr. 5-9). (ENG.). 15.99 *(978-0-06-123487-3(7))*; lib. bdg. 16.89 *(978-0-06-123488-0(5))* HarperCollins Pubs.

Gwaltney, Doris. Homefront. 2009. (ENG.). 320p. (J). (gr. 5-9). pap. 6.99 *(978-1-4169-9572-2(2)*, Simon & Schuster Bks. For Young Readers) Simon & Schuster Bks. For Young Readers.

Haar, Jaap Ter & Mearns, Martha. Boris. Poortvliet, Rien, illus. 2009. (J). pap. *(978-0-921100-72-0(8))* Inheritance Pubns.

Hahn, Mary Downing. Stepping on the Cracks. 2009. (ENG.). 224p. (J). (gr. 5-7). pap. 7.99 *(978-0-547-07660-7(6))* Houghton Mifflin Harcourt Publishing Co.

Hamley, Dennis. Divided Loyalties. 2010. (J). *(978-0-7636-3418-6(2))* Candlewick Pr.

Harlow, Joan Hiatt. Shadows on the Sea. (ENG., Illus.). (J). (gr. 3-7). 2005. 272p. pap. 7.99 *(978-0-689-84927-5(3))* 2003. 256p. 17.99 *(978-0-689-84926-8(5))* McElderry, Margaret K. Bks. (McElderry, Margaret K. Bks.).

—The Watcher. 2015. (ENG.). 304p. (J). (gr. 3-7). pap. 6.99 *(978-1-4424-2912-3(7)*, McElderry, Margaret K. Bks.) McElderry, Margaret K. Bks.

Hart, Derek. Secret of the Dragon's Eye. 2007. 264p. per. 16.95 *(978-0-595-42967-7(X))* iUniverse, Inc.

Hartnett, Sonya. The Children of the King. 2014. (ENG.). 272p. (J). (gr. 5). 16.99 *(978-0-7636-6735-1(8))* Candlewick Pr.

Hayes, Clair W. The Boy Allies in the Trenches: Midst Shot & Shell along the Aisne. 2007. (ENG.). 180p. pap. 19.99 *(978-1-4346-2323-2(8))*; 192p. pap. 21.99 *(978-1-4346-2381-2(5))* Creative Media Partners, LLC.

Haywood, Carolyn. Primrose Day. 2005. (ENG., Illus.). 176p. (J). (gr. 1-4). pap. 10.95 *(978-0-15-205229-4(1))* Houghton Mifflin Harcourt Publishing Co.

Helmer, Marilyn. One Splendid Tree. Eastman, Dianne, illus. 2007. (ENG.). 32p. (J). (gr. -1-3). 6.95 *(978-1-55453-166-0(7))* Kids Can Pr., Ltd. CAN. Dist: Hachette Bk. Group.

Herman, Charlotte. My Chocolate Year: A Novel with 12 Recipes. Pham, LeUyen, illus. 2008. (ENG.). 176p. (J). (gr. 3-7). 15.99 *(978-1-4169-3341-0(7)*, Simon & Schuster Bks. For Young Readers) Simon & Schuster Bks. For Young Readers.

Hesse, Karen. Aleutian Sparrow. McGillivray, Kim & Zerbetz, Evon, illus. 2005. (ENG.). 160p. (J). (gr. 4-9). reprint ed. pap. 7.99 *(978-1-4169-0327-7(5)*, McElderry, Margaret K. Bks.) McElderry, Margaret K. Bks.

—Aleutian Sparrow. Zerbetz, Evon, illus. 2005. 156p. (J). (gr. 5-9). 13.65 *(978-0-7569-5589-2(0))* Perfection Learning Corp.

—The Cats in Krasinski Square. Watson, Wendy, illus. 2004. (ENG.). 32p. (J). (gr. 2-5). 18.99 *(978-0-439-43540-6(4)*, Scholastic Pr.) Scholastic, Inc.

Hesse, Monica. Girl in the Blue Coat. (ENG.). 320p. (gr. 7-17). 2017. (YA). pap. 9.99 *(978-0-316-26063-3(0))* 2016. 17.99 *(978-0-316-26060-2(6))* 2016. (YA). E-Book *(978-0-316-26064-0(9))* Little, Brown Bks. for Young Readers.

—Girl in the Blue Coat. 2017. (YA). lib. bdg. 20.85 ***(978-0-606-39918-0(6))*** Turtleback Bks.

WXYZ

Heuvel, Eric & Miller, Lorraine T. A Family Secret. Miller, Lorraine T., tr. from DUT. Heuvel, Eric, illus. 2009. (ENG., Illus.). 64p. (J). (gr. 5-9). pap. 11.99 (978-0-374-42265-3(6), 9780374422653) Square Fish.

Hoffman, Emily Allen. A Friend of the Enemy. 2003. 108p. (J). pap. 7.95 (978-1-57249-312-4(7), White Mane Kids) White Mane Publishing Co., Inc.

Horvath, Polly. The Night Garden. 2017. (ENG.). 304p. (J). 16.99 **(978-0-374-30452-2(1)**, 9780374304522, Farrar, Straus & Giroux (BYR)) Farrar, Straus & Giroux.

Howard, Ellen. Different Kind of Courage. 2007. (ENG.). 184p. (J). (gr. 3-7). pap. 10.95 (978-1-4169-6730-9(3), Simon & Schuster/Paula Wiseman Bks.) Simon & Schuster/Paula Wiseman Bks.

Hughes, Dean. The Dean Hughes Collection: Soldier Boys; Search & Destroy; Missing in Action. 2015. (ENG., Illus.). 752p. (YA). (gr. 7). pap. 29.99 (978-1-4814-3997-8(9), Atheneum Bks. for Young Readers) Simon & Schuster Children's Publishing.

—Four-Four-Two. 2016. (ENG., Illus.). 272p. (YA). (gr. 7). 17.99 (978-1-4814-6252-5(0), Atheneum Bks. for Young Readers) Simon & Schuster Children's Publishing.

—Missing in Action. 2010. (ENG.). 240p. (J). (gr. 5-9). 16.99 (978-1-4169-1502-7(8), Atheneum Bks. for Young Readers) Simon & Schuster Children's Publishing.

—Soldier Boys. 2004. 230p. (gr. 7-12). 17.00 (978-0-7569-4566-4(6)) Perfection Learning Corp.

—Soldier Boys. 2003. (ENG.). 240p. (YA). (gr. 7-12). mass mkt. 7.99 (978-0-689-86021-8(8), Simon Pulse) Simon Pulse.

—Soldier Boys. 2015. (ENG., Illus.). 240p. (YA). (gr. 7). pap. 10.99 (978-1-4814-2704-3(0), Atheneum Bks. for Young Readers) Simon & Schuster Children's Publishing.

Hughes, Shirley. Hero on a Bicycle. 2013. (ENG., Illus.). 224p. (J). (gr. 5-9). 16.99 (978-0-7636-6037-6(X)) Candlewick Pr.

Hunter, Sara Hoagland. The Unbreakable Code. Miner, Julia, illus. 2007. (ENG.). 32p. (J). (gr. 1-3). per. 7.95 (978-0-87358-917-8(3)) Cooper Square Publishing Llc.

Ibbotson, Eva. The Dragonfly Pool. 2009. (ENG.). 384p. (J). (gr. 3-7). 7.99 (978-0-14-241486-6(7), Puffin Books) Penguin Young Readers Group.

—The Dragonfly Pool. 2008. (YA). 1.25 (978-1-4361-5202-0(X)); 122.75 (978-1-4361-5209-9(7)); 256.75 (978-1-4361-5206-8(2)); 90.75 (978-1-4361-5207-5(0)); 92.75 (978-1-4361-5205-1(4)); 120.75 (978-1-4361-5211-2(9)) Recorded Bks., Inc.

Jablonski, Carla. Defiance, Bk. 2. Purvis, Leland, illus. 2011. (Resistance Ser.: 2). (ENG.). 128p. (YA). (gr. 7-12). pap. 18.99 (978-1-59643-292-5(6), 9781596432925, First Second Bks.) Roaring Brook Pr.

—Resistance, Bk. 1. Purvis, Leland, illus. 2010. (Resistance Ser.: 1). (ENG.). 128p. (YA). (gr. 7-12). pap. 17.99 (978-1-59643-291-8(8), 9781596432918, First Second Bks.) Roaring Brook Pr.

—Victory: Resistance Book 3. Purvis, Leland, illus. 2012. (Resistance Ser.: 3). (ENG.). 128p. (YA). (gr. 7-3). pap. 17.99 (978-1-59643-293-2(4), 9781596432932, First Second Bks.) Roaring Brook Pr.

Joffo, Joseph. A Bag of Marbles: The Graphic Novel. 2013. 128p. pap. 29.27 (978-1-4677-1651-2(0)) Lerner Publishing Group.

—A Bag of Marbles: The Graphic Novel. Gauvin, Edward, tr. Bailly, Vincent, illus. 2013. (ENG.). 128p. (gr. 7-12). pap. 9.95 (978-1-4677-1516-4(6)); lib. bdg. 29.27 (978-1-4677-0700-8(7)) Lerner Publishing Group. (Graphic Universe™).

Johns, Eric. Home Front. 2012. 146p. pap. (978-1-4716-5390-2(0)) Lulu.com.

Johnston, Julie. Little Red Lies. 2015. (ENG., Illus.). 342p. (YA). (gr. 5). pap. 8.99 (978-1-77049-807-5(9), Tundra Bks.) Tundra Bks. CAN. Dist: Penguin Random Hse. LLC.

Jones, Marcia Thornton. Woodford Brave. Whipple, Kevin, illus. 2015. (ENG.). 200p. (J). (gr. 3-7). 16.95 (978-1-62979-305-4(1), Calkins Creek) Boyds Mills Pr.

Kacer, Kathy. Shanghai Escape, 1 vol. 2013. (Holocaust Remembrance Ser.). (ENG.). 204p. (J). (gr. 6-8). pap. 14.95 (978-1-927583-10-4(1)) Second Story Pr. CAN. Dist: Orca Bk. Pubs. USA.

Kadohata, Cynthia. Weedflower. (ENG.). 272p. (J). (gr. 5-9). 2009. pap. 7.99 (978-1-4169-7566-3(7)) 2006. (Illus.). 19.99 (978-0-689-86574-9(0)) Simon & Schuster Children's Publishing. (Atheneum Bks. for Young Readers).

Katz, Gwen C. Among the Red Stars. 2017. 384p. (YA). (gr. 8). 17.99 **(978-0-06-264274-5(X)**, HarperTeen) HarperCollins Pubs.

Katz, Jennifer A. The Era of Courting. 2006. 119p. pap. 19.95 (978-1-4241-3321-5(1)) PublishAmerica, Inc.

Keenan, Sheila. Dogs of War. Fox, Nathan, illus. 2013. (ENG.). 176p. (J). (gr. 3-7). pap. 12.99 (978-0-545-12888-9(9), Graphix) Scholastic, Inc.

Kemp, Kristin. The Boy in the Striped Pajamas: An Instructional Guide for Literature. 2015. (Great Works). (ENG., Illus.). 72p. (gr. 4-8). pap. 9.99 (978-1-4807-8507-6(5)) Shell Educational Publishing.

Kendall, Jane F. Maestoso Petra. Sanderson, Ruth, illus. 2010. (Horse Diaries: No. 4). (ENG.). 160p. (J). (gr. 3-7). pap. 7.99 (978-0-375-85842-0(3), Random Hse. Bks. for Young Readers) Random Hse. Children's Bks.

Kerkow, Larry. Angel Goes to Sea. 2010. 24p. 12.56 (978-1-4269-3490-2(4)) Trafford Publishing.

Kerr, Judith. En la Batalla de Inglaterra. (SPA.). 304p. (YA). (gr. 5-8). (978-84-204-3221-2(0), AF0691) Ediciones Alfaguara ESP. Dist: Lectorum Pubns., Inc.

—En la Batalla de Inglaterra. (SPA.). (YA). (gr. 5-8). pap. (978-84-345-8580-5(4), AF0691) Salvat Editores, S.A. ESP. Dist: Lectorum Pubns., Inc.

Kerr, M. E., pseud. Slap Your Sides. 2003. 198p. (YA). 13.65 (978-0-7569-4240-3(3)) Perfection Learning Corp.

Kezar, Wanda. It's a Scamp's Life! Derby, Sarah, illus. 2013. 186p. pap. 14.99 (978-1-62839-371-2(8)) Salem Author Services.

Kimpton, Paul & Kimpton, Ann Kaczkowski. Dog Tags: A Boy & His Bugle in America During WWII. 2012. (Adventures with Music Ser.: 2). (ENG.). 120p. (J). (gr. 4-7). pap. 8.95 (978-1-57999-882-0(8)) G I A Pubns., Inc.

—Starting Early: A Boy & His Bugle in America During WWII. 2011. (Adventures with Music Ser.: 1). (ENG., Illus.). 204p. (J). (gr. 4-7). pap. 8.95 (978-1-57999-805-9(4)) G I A Pubns., Inc.

Kindt, Matt. Super Spy. 2007. (Super Spy Ser.). (ENG., Illus.). 304p. pap. 19.95 (978-1-891830-96-9(1), 9781891830969) Top Shelf Productions.

King-smith, Dick. Spider Sparrow. unabr. ed. 2004. 176p. (J). (gr. 5-9). pap. 36.00 incl. audio (978-0-8072-8407-0(6), Listening Library) Random Hse. Audio Publishing Group.

Knight, Clayton & Royce, Ralph. We Were There at the Normandy Invasion. 2011. 192p. 42.95 (978-1-258-10198-5(X)) Literary Licensing, LLC.

Kositsky, Lynne. The Thought of High Windows. 2004. (ENG.). 176p. (J). (gr. 7-9). 6.95 (978-1-55337-622-4(6)) Kids Can Pr., Ltd. CAN. Dist: Hachette Bk. Group.

Landsberry, Belinda. Anzac Ted. 2016. (ENG., Illus.). 32p. (J). (gr. -1-5). 17.99 (978-1-921966-56-9(4), EK Bks.) Exisle Publishing Pty Ltd. AUS. Dist: Hachette Bk. Group.

Larson, Kirby. Dash. (Dogs of World War II Ser.). (ENG.). 256p. (J). (gr. 3-7). 2016. pap. 7.99 (978-0-545-41636-8(1), Scholastic Paperbacks) 2014. 17.99 (978-0-545-41635-1(3), Scholastic Pr.) Scholastic, Inc.

—Duke. (Dogs of World War II Ser.). (ENG.). 240p. (J). (gr. 3-7). 2015. pap. 7.99 (978-0-545-41638-2(8), Scholastic Paperbacks) 2013. 16.99 (978-0-545-41637-5(X), Scholastic Pr.) Scholastic, Inc.

—The Fences Between Us: The Diary of Piper Davis. 2010. (Dear America Ser.). (J). (ENG.). 320p. (gr. 3-7). 12.99 (978-0-545-22418-5(7)); (Illus.). 313p. pap. (978-0-545-27094-6(4)) Scholastic, Inc.

Lasky, Kathryn. Night Witches: A Novel of World War II. 2017. (ENG.). 224p. (J). (gr. 7). 17.99 (978-0-545-68298-5(3), Scholastic Pr.) Scholastic, Inc.

Lehman, Theodore H. Defying Odds. 2014. (YA). pap. (978-1-935604-63-1(5)) Gaon Bks.

LeSourd, Nancy. Attack at Pearl Harbor, 1 vol. 2008. (Liberty Letters Ser.). (ENG.). 224p. (J). pap. 7.99 (978-0-310-71389-0(7)) Zonderkidz.

Lewis, Floyd. The Foundered Mule. 2006. (YA). 9.95 (978-0-9788283-2-5(1)) Acacia Publishing, Inc.

Lieurance, Suzanne. The Lucky Baseball: My Story in a Japanese-American Internment Camp. 2009. (Historical Fiction Adventures (HFA) Ser.). (Illus.). 160p. (J). (gr. 3-6). lib. bdg. 29.27 (978-0-7660-3311-5(2)) Enslow Pubs., Inc.

Lois, Lowry. Compte les Etoiles. pap. 16.95 (978-2-211-03436-4(5)) Archimede Editions FRA. Dist: Distribooks, Inc.

—Number the Stars. (ENG.). 160p. (J). (gr. 5-7). 2011. pap. 7.99 (978-0-547-57709-8(5)) 25th anniv. ed. 2014. 17.99 (978-0-544-34000-8(0), HMH Books For Young Readers) Houghton Mifflin Harcourt Publishing Co.

—Number the Stars. 2004. 144p. (J). (gr. 5-9). pap. 29.00 incl. audio (978-1-4000-8637-5(X), Listening Library) Random Hse. Audio Publishing Group.

London, C. Alexander. Prisoners of War. 2014. (Dog Tags Ser.: 3). (ENG.). 192p. (J). (gr. 5-9). pap. 5.99 (978-0-545-47706-2(9), Scholastic Paperbacks) Scholastic, Inc.

Lynch, Chris. Alive & Kicking. 2015. 182p. (J). (978-0-545-78940-0(0), Scholastic Pr.) Scholastic, Inc.

—The Liberators. 2015. (World War II Ser.: 4). (ENG.). 192p. (J). (gr. 5-9). 18.99 (978-0-545-52304-2(4), Scholastic Pr.) Scholastic, Inc.

—The Right Fight. 2014. 189p. (YA). (978-0-545-63728-2(7), Scholastic Pr.) Scholastic, Inc.

—World War II Book 1: the Right Fight. 2014. (World War II Ser.). (ENG.). 192p. (J). (gr. 5-9). 18.99 (978-0-545-52294-6(3), Scholastic Pr.) Scholastic, Inc.

—World War II Book 2: Dead in the Water. 2014. (World War II Ser.: 2). (ENG.). 192p. (J). (gr. 5-9). 18.99 (978-0-545-52298-4(6), Scholastic Pr.) Scholastic, Inc.

MacDonald, Jerry. Red Eyes & Crazy Jake. 2009. 24p. pap. 15.95 (978-1-4389-2706-0(1)) AuthorHouse.

MacDonald, Maryann. Odette's Secrets. 2013. (ENG., Illus.). 240p. (YA). (gr. 5-8). 16.99 (978-1-59990-750-5(X), 9781599907505, Bloomsbury USA Childrens) Bloomsbury Publishing USA.

MacKay, Andrew. Young Lions Roar. 2012. 316p. pap. (978-1-909395-27-5(7)) Legend Pr.

MacPherson, M. j. The Magic Thread: Overcoming challenges during World War II, a young girl discovers secrets that change adversity into Adventure. 2009. 208p. pap. 17.95 (978-0-595-52812-7(0)) iUniverse, Inc.

Mah, Adeline Yen. Chinese Cinderella & the Secret Dragon Society. 2006. (ENG., Illus.). 256p. (J). (gr. 5-9). pap. 7.99 (978-0-06-056736-1(8)) HarperCollins Pubs.

Maruno, Jennifer. Kid Soldier. 2013. (ENG., Illus.). 208p. (YA). pap. 10.99 (978-1-4597-0677-4(3), 9781459706774) Dundurn CAN. Dist: Ingram Publisher Services.

Mason, Caroline. The Blacksmith's Cottage: A Pastoral War. 2009. 150p. pap. 13.95 (978-1-4327-4969-9(2)); 120p. pap. 33.95 (978-1-4327-2987-5(X)) Outskirts Pr., Inc.

Matas, Carol. Code Name Kris. 2007. (ENG.). 164p. (J). (gr. 3-7). pap. 12.95 (978-1-4169-6162-8(3), Aladdin) Simon & Schuster Children's Publishing.

—Lisa's War. 2007. (ENG.). 128p. (J). (gr. 3-7). pap. 11.95 (978-1-4169-6163-5(1), Aladdin) Simon & Schuster Children's Publishing.

—Turned Away: The World War II Diary of Devorah Bernstein. 2005. (Dear Canada Ser.). (ENG., Illus.). 208p. (J). (978-0-439-96946-8(8)) Scholastic Canada, Ltd.

Mazer, Harry. A Boy at War: A Novel of Pearl Harbor. 2004. (Illus.). 104p. (gr. 5-9). 16.00 (978-0-7569-4088-1(5)) Perfection Learning Corp.

—A Boy No More. 2007. 136p. (gr. 5-9). 16.00 (978-0-7569-8112-9(3)) Perfection Learning Corp.

—Heroes Don't Run. 2007. (Aladdin Historical Fiction Ser.). 113p. (gr. 3-7). 16.00 (978-0-7569-8111-2(5)) Perfection Learning Corp.

—The Last Mission. 192p. (YA). (gr. 7-18). pap. 4.99 (978-0-8072-1366-7(7), Listening Library) Random Hse. Audio Publishing Group.

McAllister, Cameron. The Tin Snail. Usher, Sam, illus. 2016. (ENG.). 288p. (J). (gr. 4-7). 16.99 (978-0-553-53638-6(9), Delacorte Bks. for Young Readers) Random Hse. Children's Bks.

McDonough, Yona Zeldis. The Bicycle Spy. 2016. (ENG.). 208p. (J). (gr. 3-7). 16.99 (978-0-545-85095-7(9), Scholastic Pr.) Scholastic, Inc.

McKay, Sharon E. End of the Line. 2014. (ENG., Illus.). 128p. (J). (gr. 4-6). pap. 12.95 (978-1-55451-658-2(7), 9781554516582) Annick Pr., Ltd. CAN. Dist: Publishers Group West (PGW).

McSwigan, Marie. Snow Treasure. Reardon, Mary, illus. 2006. (ENG.). 208p. (J). (gr. 3-7). 6.99 (978-0-14-240224-5(9), Puffin Books) Penguin Young Readers Group.

Mercer, Christa Blum. German War Child: Growing Up in World War II. 2004. (Illus.). 176p. pap. 14.95 (978-1-893597-07-5(5)) A. Borough Bks.

Merkel, Ruth Vitrano. Ann: 1833-1897. 2006. (Hannah's Girls Ser.). (Illus.). 112p. (J). (gr. 4-7). per. 9.99 (978-0-8280-1951-4(7)) Review & Herald Publishing Assn.

—Grace: 1890-1973, 6. 2006. (Hannah's Girls Ser.). (Illus.). 128p. (J). (gr. 4-7). per. 9.99 (978-0-8280-1953-8(3)) Review & Herald Publishing Assn.

—Marilla 1851-1916, 6 bks. 2006. (Hannah's Girls Ser.). (Illus.). 144p. (J). (gr. 4-7). per. 9.99 (978-0-8280-1952-1(5)) Review & Herald Publishing Assn.

—Ruthie: Born 1931. 2007. (Hannah's Girls Ser.). (Illus.). 144p. (J). (gr. 4-7). per. 9.99 (978-0-8280-1954-5(1)) Review & Herald Publishing Assn.

Metivier, Gary. Saluting Grandpa: Celebrating Veterans & Honor Flight, 1 vol. Rath, Robert, illus. 2012. (ENG.). 32p. (J). (gr. k-3). 16.99 (978-1-4556-1748-7(2)) Pelican Publishing Co., Inc.

Miller, Peggy Reiff. The Seagoing Cowboy. Ewart, Claire, illus. 2016. 39p. (J). (978-0-87178-212-0(X)) Brethren Pr.

Mochizuki, Ken. Baseball Saved Us. 97th rev. ed. 2014. (ENG.). 30p. (J). (gr. k-12). 15.65 (978-1-63245-249-8(9)) Lectorum Pubns., Inc.

—Baseball Saved Us. Lee, Dom, illus. (Picture Book Readalong Ser.). pap. 39.95 incl. audio compact disk (978-1-59112-917-2(6)); 2004. (J). (gr. -1-2). 25.95 incl. audio (978-1-59112-456-6(5)) Live Oak Media.

Morpurgo, Michael. An Elephant in the Garden. 2013. (ENG.). 224p. (J). (gr. 5-9). pap. 7.99 (978-1-250-03414-4(0), 9781250034144) Square Fish.

—Half a Man. O'Callaghan, Gemma, illus. 2015. (ENG.). 64p. (J). (gr. 5). 16.99 (978-0-7636-7747-3(7)) Candlewick Pr.

—A Medal for Leroy. 2014. (ENG.). 144p. (YA). (gr. 5-9). 16.99 (978-1-250-03980-4(0), 9781250039804) Feiwel & Friends.

Moulder, Holly. Crystal City Lights. 2013. (ENG.). 190p. (J). pap. 8.99 (978-0-9885295-0-2(5)) Blue Marlin Pubns.

Muchamore, Robert. Eagle Day. 2nd ed. 2009. (ENG., Illus.). 432p. (J). (gr. 7-17). 10.99 (978-0-340-95649-6(6)) Hodder & Stoughton GBR. Dist: Hachette Bk. Group.

—Secret Army. 2010. (ENG., Illus.). 384p. (YA). (gr. 7-17). pap. 10.99 (978-0-340-95650-2(X), Hodder Children's Books) Hachette Children's Group GBR. Dist: Hachette Bk. Group.

Myers, Walter Dean. Invasion. 2013. (YA). (978-0-545-57659-8(8), Scholastic Pr.) Scholastic, Inc.

Napoli, Donna Jo. Fire in the Hills. 2008. (ENG.). 240p. (YA). (gr. 7-18). 7.99 (978-0-14-241200-8(7), Speak) Penguin Young Readers Group.

Nielsen, Jennifer A. Behind Enemy Lines. (Infinity Ring Ser.: 6). (ENG.). 192p. (J). (gr. 3-7). 2016. pap. 6.99 (978-0-545-90121-5(9), Scholastic Pr.) 2013. 12.99 (978-0-545-38701-9(9)) Scholastic, Inc.

—Behind Enemy Lines. 2016. (Infinity Ring Ser.: 6). lib. bdg. 17.20 (978-0-606-38623-4(8)) Turtleback Bks.

Nobleman, Marc Tyler. Brave Like My Brother. 2016. (ENG.). 112p. (J). (gr. 2-5). 15.99 (978-0-545-88035-0(1), Scholastic Pr.) Scholastic, Inc.

Nosaka, Akiyuki. The Whale That Fell in Love with a Submarine. Takemori, Ginny Tapley, tr. from JPN. 2015. (ENG., Illus.). 192p. (YA). (gr. 3-7). pap. 14.95 (978-1-78269-027-6(1), Pushkin Press) Steerforth Pr.

Oelschlager, Vanita. Postcards from a War. Blanc, Mike & Bauknight, Wilfred, illus. 2009. (ENG.). 40p. (J). (gr. 1-4). 15.95 (978-0-9800162-9-1(0)); pap. 8.95 (978-0-9819714-0-7(7)) VanitaBooks.

Orlev, Uri. Lidia, Reina de Palestina. (SPA.). 158p. (YA). (gr. 5-8). (978-84-279-3237-1(5), NG8035) Noguer y Caralt Editores, S. A. ESP. Dist: Lectorum Pubns., Inc.

Orme, David. Blitz. 2007. (Sharp Shades Ser.). (ENG., Illus.). 64p. (J). (gr. 6-8). pap. 8.99 (978-0-237-53444-8(4)) Evans Brothers, Ltd. GBR. Dist: Independent Pubs. Group.

Osborne, Mary Pope. Danger in the Darkest Hour. Murdocca, Sal, illus. 2015. (Stepping Stone Book Ser.: No. 1). (ENG.). 192p. (J). (gr. 2-5). 14.99 (978-0-553-49772-4(3), Random Hse. Bks. for Young Readers) Random Hse. Children's Bks.

—My Secret War: The World War II Diary of Madeline Beck, Long Island, New York 1941. 2008. (Dear America Ser.). (J). (gr. 3-7). 39.95 incl. audio compact disk (978-1-4301-0359-2(0)) Live Oak Media.

Osborne, William. Hitler's Secret. 2013. (Illus.). 333p. (YA). (978-0-545-51533-7(5)); (ENG., 352p. (J). (gr. 7). 17.99 (978-0-545-49646-9(2)) Scholastic, Inc. (Chicken Hse., The).

—Winter's Bullet. 2016. (ENG.). 240p. (J). (gr. 7). 18.99 (978-0-545-85344-6(3), Chicken Hse., The) Scholastic, Inc.

Owen, James A. The Shadow Dragons. Owen, James A., illus. 2009. (Chronicles of the Imaginarium Geographica Ser.: 4). (ENG., Illus.). 432p. (YA). (gr. 7-18). 21.99 (978-1-4169-5879-6(7), Simon & Schuster Bks. For Young Readers) Simon & Schuster Bks. For Young Readers.

Park, Linda Sue. When My Name Was Keoko. 2004. 199p. (J). (gr. 5). 14.65 (978-0-7569-2928-2(8)) Perfection Learning Corp.

—When My Name Was Keoko. 2012. lib. bdg. 18.40 (978-0-606-24716-0(5), Turtleback) Turtleback Bks.

Parkhurst, Liz S. Under One Flag: A Year at Rohwer. Clifton, Tom, illus. 2006. (ENG.). 32p. (J). (gr. 3-7). 16.95 (978-0-87483-759-9(6), 1241971) August Hse. Pubs., Inc.

Parkinson, Curtis. Domenic's War: A Story of the Battle of Monte Cassino. 2006. (ENG.). 200p. (J). (gr. 5-9). per. 9.95 (978-0-88776-751-7(6), Tundra Bks.) Tundra Bks. CAN. Dist: Penguin Random Hse. LLC.

—Man Overboard! 2012. (ENG., Illus.). 152p. (J). (gr. 4-7). pap. 9.95 (978-1-77049-298-1(4), Tundra Bks.) Tundra Bks. CAN. Dist: Penguin Random Hse. LLC.

Patneaude, David. Thin Wood Walls. 2008. (ENG., Illus.). 240p. (J). (gr. 5-7). pap. 7.99 (978-0-618-80915-8(5)) Houghton Mifflin Harcourt Publishing Co.

Paulsen, Gary. The Quilt. 2005. 83p. (gr. 3-7). 16.00 (978-0-7569-4781-1(2)) Perfection Learning Corp.

—The Quilt. 2005. (ENG., Illus.). 96p. (J). (gr. 3-7). 6.99 (978-0-440-22936-0(7), Yearling) Random Hse. Children's Bks.

Pausewang, Gudrun. Traitor. (Carolrhoda YA Ser.). 2010. (ENG.). 224p. (YA). (gr. 7-12). pap. 9.95 (978-0-7613-6571-6(0), Carolrhoda Lab™) 2006. (Illus.). 220p. (J). (gr. -1-7). 16.95 (978-0-8225-6195-8(6), Carolrhoda Bks.) Lerner Publishing Group.

Pearsall, Shelley. Jump into the Sky. (ENG.). 352p. (J). 2013. (gr. 4-7). pap. 7.99 (978-0-440-42140-5(3), Yearling) 2012. (gr. 5). 16.99 (978-0-375-83699-2(3), Knopf Bks. for Young Readers) Random Hse. Children's Bks.

Peck, Richard. On the Wings of Heroes. 2008. (ENG.). 160p. (J). (gr. 3-7). 7.99 (978-0-14-241204-6(X), Puffin Books) Penguin Young Readers Group.

—On the Wings of Heroes. rev. l.t. ed. 2007. (Literacy Bridge Middle Reader Ser.). 171p. (J). (gr. 4-7). 23.95 (978-0-7862-9703-0(4)) Thorndike Pr.

Peet, Mal. Tamar: A Novel of Espionage, Passion, & Betrayal. (ENG., Illus.). 432p. (YA). (gr. 9). 2008. pap. 8.99 (978-0-7636-4063-7(8)) 2007. 17.99 (978-0-7636-3488-9(3)) Candlewick Pr.

Perl, Lila. Isabel's War. 2014. (ENG.). 224p. (J). (gr. 2-7). pap. 12.95 (978-1-939601-27-8(4)) Ig Publishing, Inc.

—Lilli's Quest. 2015. (ENG.). 224p. (J). (-9). pap. 12.95 (978-1-939601-53-7(3)) Ig Publishing, Inc.

Phillips, Dee. Over the Top. 2014. (Yesterday's Voices Ser.). (YA). lib. bdg. 19.60 (978-0-606-35582-7(0)) Turtleback Bks.

—Tail Gunner. 2014. (Yesterday's Voices Ser.). (YA). lib. bdg. 19.60 (978-0-606-35579-7(0)) Turtleback Bks.

Polacco, Patricia. The Butterfly. 2009. (ENG.). 48p. (J). (gr. 1-4). pap. 7.99 (978-0-14-241306-7(2), Puffin Books) Penguin Young Readers Group.

—Tucky Jo & Little Heart. Polacco, Patricia, illus. 2015. (ENG., Illus.). 48p. (J). (gr. -1-3). 17.99 (978-1-4814-1584-2(0), Simon & Schuster Bks. For Young Readers) Simon & Schuster Bks. For Young Readers.

Polak, Monique. What World Is Left, 1 vol. 2008. (ENG.). 232p. (YA). (gr. 7-12). pap. 12.95 (978-1-55143-847-4(X)) Orca Bk. Pubs. USA.

Preus, Margi. Shadow on the Mountain. 2014. (ENG., Illus.). 320p. (YA). (gr. 3-7). pap. 8.95 (978-1-4197-1159-6(8), Amulet Bks.) Abrams, Inc.

Prins, Piet. Hideout in the Swamp. 2006. (Illus.). 136p. (J). pap. (978-1-894666-73-2(9)) Inheritance Pubns.

—The Lonely Sentinel. 2006. (Illus.). 140p. (J). pap. (978-1-894666-72-5(0)) Inheritance Pubns.

Pryor, Bonnie. Simon's Escape: A Story of the Holocaust. 2010. (Historical Fiction Adventures (HFA) Ser.). (Illus.). 160p. (J). pap. 10.95 (978-1-59845-216-7(9)); (gr. 3-6). 29.27 (978-0-7660-3388-7(0)) Enslow Pubs., Inc.

Razzell, Mary. White Wave. (J). pap. 7.95 (978-0-88899-161-4(4)) Groundwood Bks. CAN. Dist: Publishers Group West (PGW).

Redmond, Shirley Raye. Pigeon Hero! Ettlinger, Doris, illus. 2005. (Ready-to-Read Ser.). 31p. (gr. k-2). 14.00 (978-0-7569-5560-1(2)) Perfection Learning Corp.

—Pigeon Hero! Ettlinger, Doris, illus. 2003. (Ready-To-Reads Ser.). (ENG.). 32p. (J). lib. bdg. 11.89 (978-0-689-85487-3(0), Aladdin Library) Simon & Schuster Children's Publishing.

—Pigeon Hero! Ettlinger, Doris, illus. 2003. (Ready-To-Reads Ser.). (ENG.). 32p. (J). (gr. k-2). pap. 3.99 (978-0-689-85486-6(2), Simon Spotlight) Simon Spotlight.

Reece, Colleen L. Last Page in the Diary. 2011. 94p. pap. 8.95 (978-1-61633-179-5(8)) Guardian Angel Publishing, Inc.

Reid, Charles. Ghost of Heroes Past. 2010. (ENG., Illus.). 170p. pap. 10.95 (978-1-55380-102-3(4)) Ronsdale Pr. CAN. Dist: SPD-Small Pr. Distribution.

—Hurricanes over London. 2005. (ENG., Illus.). 152p. (J). (gr. 3-9). pap., tchr. ed. 8.95 (978-0-921870-82-1(5)) Ronsdale Pr. CAN. Dist: Literary Pr. Group of Canada.

Rice, Dona Herwick & Sugarman, Dorothy. World War II: Battle of Normandy, 1 vol. 2009. (Building Fluency Through Reader's Theater Ser.). (ENG., Illus.). 32p. (J). (gr. 3-5). pap. 7.99 (978-1-4333-0553-5(4)) Teacher Created Materials, Inc.

Richmond, Caroline Tung. Darkest Hour. 2016. (ENG.). 320p. (J). (gr. 7). 17.99 (978-0-545-80127-0(3), Scholastic Pr.) Scholastic, Inc.

Rinaldi, Ann. Keep Smiling Through. 2005. (ENG.). 208p. (J). (gr. 2-5). pap. 13.95 (978-0-15-205399-4(9)) Houghton Mifflin Harcourt Publishing Co.

Rollason, Jane. Freddie's War Level 6 Advanced. 2010. (ENG.). 128p. pap. 14.50 (978-84-8323-909-4(4)) Cambridge Univ. Pr.

—Freddie's War Level 6 Advanced Book with CD-ROM & Audio CDs (3), 1 vol. 2010. (ENG.). 128p. cd-rom, audio compact disk 18.25 (978-84-8323-662-8(1)) Cambridge Univ. Pr.

Ross, Stewart. Dear Mum, I Miss You! Clark, Linda, illus. 54p. (J). (978-0-237-52318-3(3)) Evans Brothers, Ltd.

Rothstein, Evelyn. Evelyn & the Two Evas. Uhlig, Elizabeth, illus. 2013. 63p. (YA). pap. 12.95 (978-0-9834030-5-0(8)) Marble Hse. Editions.

Roy, James. Billy Mack's War. 2004. 245p. (J). pap. (978-0-7022-3479-8(6)) Univ. of Queensland Pr.

Ruby, Lois. Shanghai Shadows. 2006. (ENG.). 256p. (YA). 16.95 (978-0-8234-1960-9(6)) Holiday Hse., Inc.

Russo, Marisabina. I Will Come Back for You. 2014. (ENG.). 40p. (J). (gr. k-4). 7.99 (978-0-385-39149-8(8), Dragonfly Bks.) Random Hse. Children's Bks.

Rylant, Cynthia. I Had Seen Castles. 2004. (ENG.). 128p. (YA). (gr. 7-12). reprint ed. pap. 6.99 (978-0-15-205312-3(3)) Houghton Mifflin Harcourt Publishing Co.

—I Had Seen Castles. 2005. 97p. 15.95 (978-0-7569-5834-3(2)) Perfection Learning Corp.

Sales, Leila. Once Was a Time: An Alliteration Adventure. 2016. (ENG., Illus.). 272p. (J). (gr. 5-17). 16.99 (978-1-4521-4009-4(X)) Chronicle Bks. LLC.

Salisbury, Graham. House of the Red Fish. 2008. (Readers Circle Ser.). (ENG.). 320p. (YA). (gr. 7-9). mass mkt. 6.50 (978-0-440-23838-6(2), Laurel Leaf) Random Hse. Children's Bks.

—Hunt for the Bamboo Rat. 2014. (ENG., Illus.). 336p. (YA). (gr. 7). 16.99 (978-0-375-84266-5(7), Lamb, Wendy Bks.) Random Hse. Children's Bks.

—Under the Blood Red Sun. 246p. (YA). 22.00 (978-0-8446-7322-6(6)) Smith, Peter Pub., Inc.

Sands, Monty. King of Nine Mile Canyon. 2008. 124p. 11.99 (978-0-615-25788-4(7)) Sands, Monty.

Savit, Gavriel. Anna & the Swallow Man. 2016. (CHI.). 272p. (YA). (gr. 7). pap. **(978-957-33-3251-0(5))** Crown Publishing Co., Ltd.

—Anna & the Swallow Man. (ENG.). (YA). (gr. 7). 2017. 256p. pap. 9.99 **(978-0-553-52208-2(6)**, Ember) 2016. 240p. 17.99 (978-0-553-51334-9(6), Knopf Bks. for Young Readers) Random Hse. Children's Bks.

—Anna & the Swallow Man. 2017. lib. bdg. 20.85 **(978-0-606-39876-3(7))** Turtleback Bks.

Schott, Elizabeth, illus. Jake & Sam at the Empty Abbey. 2006. 96p. (J). per. 9.95 (978-0-9724421-1-4(1)) Fountain Square Publishing.

Schroder, Jack. Dugout. 2004. 190p. (YA). per. 12.95 (978-0-9745665-6-6(X)) Catalpa Pr.

Schröder, Monika. The Dog in the Wood. 2009. (ENG.). 168p. (J). (gr. 5-9). 17.95 (978-1-59078-701-4(3), Front Street) Boyds Mills Pr.

Schwartz, Ellen. Heart of a Champion. 2016. (ENG.). 272p. (J). (gr. 4-7). 16.99 (978-1-77049-880-8(X), Tundra Bks.) Tundra Bks. CAN. Dist: Penguin Random Hse. LLC.

Scorched Earth. 2013. (ENG., Illus.). 336p. (YA). (gr. 7-17). pap. 10.99 (978-1-4449-0233-4(4)) Hodder & Stoughton GBR. Dist: Hachette Bk. Group.

Sepahban, Lois. Paper Wishes. 2016. (ENG.). 192p. (J). 16.99 (978-0-374-30216-0(2), 9780374302160, Farrar, Straus & Giroux (BYR)) Farrar, Straus & Giroux.

—Paper Wishes. 2017. (J). lib. bdg. 18.40 **(978-0-606-39942-5(9))** Turtleback Bks.

Sepetys, Ruta. Salt to the Sea. l.t. ed. 2016. (ENG.). 500p. 24.99 (978-1-4104-9287-6(7)) Cengage Gale.

—Salt to the Sea, 9 vols. (ENG.). (YA). 2017. pap. 98.91 **(978-0-525-48681-7(X)**, Penguin Books) 2017. 448p. (gr. 7). pap. 10.99 **(978-0-14-242362-2(9)**, Penguin Books) 2016. (Illus.). 400p. (gr. 7-12). 18.99 (978-0-399-16030-1(2), Philomel Bks.) Penguin Young Readers Group.

—Salt to the Sea. 2017. lib. bdg. 22.10 **(978-0-606-40492-1(9))** Turtleback Bks.

Seredy, Kate. The Chestry Oak. 2015. (Illus.). 253p. (J). pap. 12.95 (978-1-930900-81-3(3)) Purple Hse. Pr.

Shepherd, Megan. The Secret Horses of Briar Hill. 2016. (ENG., Illus.). 240p. (J). (gr. 5). 16.99 (978-1-101-93975-8(3), Delacorte Bks. for Young Readers) Random Hse. Children's Bks.

Sherman, M. Zachary. A Time for War, 1 vol. Casas, Fritz, illus. 2011. (Bloodlines Ser.). (ENG.). 88p. (gr. 4-8). pap. 6.95 (978-1-4342-3097-3(X)); 26.65 (978-1-4342-2558-0(5)) Stone Arch Bks.

Sherman, M. Zachary & Lee, Raymund. Depth Charge, 1 vol. Bermudez, Raymund, illus. 2012. (Bloodlines Ser.). (ENG.). 88p. (gr. 4-8). pap. 6.95 (978-1-4342-3876-4(8)); lib. bdg. 26.65 (978-1-4342-3764-4(8)) Stone Arch Bks.

Simpson, Craig. Resistance. 2007. (ENG., Illus.). 368p. (YA). (gr. 7). pap. 15.99 (978-0-552-55571-5(1)) Transworld Publishers Ltd. GBR. Dist: Independent Pubs. Group.

Skrypuch, Marsha Forchuk. Making Bombs for Hitler. 2017. (ENG.). 240p. (J). (gr. 3-7). 17.99 (978-0-545-93191-5(6), Scholastic Pr.) Scholastic, Inc.

Smith, Annie Laura. The Legacy of Bletchley Park. 2004. (YA). mass mkt. 6.99 (978-0-9753367-1-7(1)) Onstage Publishing, LLC.

Smith, Daniel. My Friend the Enemy. 2014. (ENG.). 288p. (J). (gr. 3-7). 17.99 (978-0-545-66542-1(6), Chicken Hse., The) Scholastic, Inc.

Smith, Icy. Three Years & Eight Months. Kindert, Jennifer C., illus. 2013. (J). (978-0-9856237-8-4(0)) East West Discovery Pr.

Smith, Roland. Elephant Run. 2009. (ENG.). 336p. (J). (gr. 5-6). pap. 6.99 (978-1-4231-0401-8(3)) Hyperion Pr.

Smith, Sherri L. Flygirl. 2010. (ENG.). 304p. (YA). (gr. 7-18). 9.99 (978-0-14-241725-6(4), Speak) Penguin Young Readers Group.

—Flygirl. 2010. lib. bdg. 19.65 (978-0-606-14999-0(6), Turtleback) Turtleback Bks.

Smith, William D. Becoming a Superhero: Adventures of an American Superhero. 2008. 128p. per. 13.95 (978-1-4327-2071-1(6)) Outskirts Pr., Inc.

Snell, Roy Judson. Sparky Ames of the Ferry Command. Darwin, Erwin L., illus. 2012. 246p. 46.95 (978-1-258-25306-6(2)); pap. 31.95 (978-1-258-25572-5(3)) Literary Licensing, LLC.

Spinelli, Jerry. Milkweed. 2010. (ENG.). 240p. (YA). (gr. 7). pap. 9.99 (978-0-375-86147-5(5), Ember) Random Hse. Children's Bks.

Spradlin, Michael P. The Enemy Above. 2016. (ENG.). 240p. (J). (gr. 3-7). 16.99 (978-0-545-85782-6(1), Scholastic Pr.) Scholastic, Inc.

—Into the Killing Seas. 2015. (J). (ENG.). 224p. (gr. 3-7). 16.99 (978-0-545-72602-3(6), Scholastic Pr.); 185p. (978-0-545-83764-4(2)) Scholastic, Inc.

Spradlin, Michael P. Prisoner of War. 2017. (ENG.). 272p. (J). (gr. 7). 17.99 **(978-0-545-85783-3(X)**, Scholastic Pr.) Scholastic, Inc.

Spring, Debbie. The Righteous Smuggler, 1 vol. 2006. (Holocaust Remembrance Ser.). (ENG., Illus.). 160p. (J). (gr. 4-7). pap. 9.95 (978-1-896764-97-9(5)) Second Story Pr. CAN. Dist: Orca Bk. Pubs. USA.

Stein, R. Conrad. Someone Talked! 2011. (ENG.). 146p. (J). pap. 8.95 (978-1-935178-17-0(2), ChironBooks) Coleman/Perrin.

Stevenson, Sarah Jamila. The Truth Against the World. 2014. (ENG.). 360p. (YA). pap. 9.99 (978-0-7387-4058-4(6), Flux) North Star Editions.

Stier, Catherine. Welcome to America, Champ. Ettlinger, Doris, illus. 2013. (Tales of the World Ser.). (ENG.). 32p. (J). (gr. 1-4). 17.95 (978-1-58536-606-4(4), 202360) Sleeping Bear Pr.

Stone, Phoebe. The Romeo & Juliet Code. 2012. (ENG.). 320p. (J). (gr. 3-7). pap. 7.99 (978-0-545-21827-6(6), Levine, Arthur A. Bks.) Scholastic, Inc.

—Romeo Blue. (ENG.). 352p. (J). (gr. 3-7). 2015. pap. 7.99 (978-0-545-44361-6(X)) 2013. 16.99 (978-0-545-44360-9(1)) Scholastic, Inc. (Levine, Arthur A. Bks.).

Streatfeild, Noel. Party Shoes. 2008. (Oxford Children's Classics Ser.). (ENG., Illus.). 320p. (YA). 9.95 (978-0-19-272010-8(4)) Oxford Univ. Pr., Inc.

Stuchner, Joan Betty. A Time to Be Brave. Nugent, Cynthia, illus. 2014. (Stepping Stone Book(TM) Ser.). (ENG.). 112p. (J). (gr. 2-5). 4.99 (978-0-385-39205-1(2), Random Hse. Bks. for Young Readers) Random Hse. Children's Bks.

Sullivan, Jacqueline Levering. Annie's War. 2007. (Illus.). 183p. (J). (gr. 3-7). 15.00 (978-0-8028-5325-7(0), Eerdmans Bks For Young Readers) Eerdmans, William B. Publishing Co.

Sullivan, Laura L. Delusion. 2014. (ENG.). 352p. (YA). (gr. 7). pap. 18.99 (978-0-544-10478-5(1)) Houghton Mifflin Harcourt Publishing Co.

Sutherland, Robert. Survivor's Leave. 2010. (ENG., Illus.). 176p. pap. 10.95 (978-1-55380-097-2(4)) Ronsdale Pr. CAN. Dist: SPD-Small Pr. Distribution.

Swindells, Robert. Blackout. 2011. (ENG.). 224p. (J). (gr. 3-6). pap. 9.99 (978-0-552-56154-9(1)) Transworld Publishers Ltd. GBR. Dist: Independent Pubs. Group.

—Doodlebug Alley. (Illus.). 56p. (J). pap. 6.99 (978-0-7497-3860-0(X)) Egmont Bks., Ltd. GBR. Dist: Trafalgar Square Publishing.

—Shrapnel. 2009. (ENG., Illus.). 224p. (YA). (gr. 7-18). pap. 14.99 (978-0-552-55930-0(X)) Transworld Publishers Ltd. GBR. Dist: Independent Pubs. Group.

Tak, Bibi Dumon & Dumon Tak, Bibi. Soldier Bear. Hopman, Philip, illus. 2011. (ENG.). 158p. (J). 13.00 (978-0-8028-5375-2(7), Eerdmans Bks For Young Readers) Eerdmans, William B. Publishing Co.

Tamberg, Urve. The Darkest Corner of the World, 1 vol. 2016. (ENG.). 208p. (YA). (gr. 7-10). pap. 14.95 (978-1-77086-214-2(5), Dancing Cat Bks.) Cormorant Bks. Inc. CAN. Dist: Orca Bk. Pubs. USA.

Tarshis, Lauren. I Survived the Bombing of Pearl Harbor 1941. 2011. (I Survived Ser.: 4). (ENG.). 112p. (J). (gr. 2-5). pap. 4.99 (978-0-545-20698-3(7), Scholastic Paperbacks) Scholastic, Inc.

—I Survived the Bombing of Pearl Harbor 1941. 2011. (I Survived ... Ser.: No. 4). lib. bdg. 14.75 (978-0-606-23744-4(5), Turtleback) Turtleback Bks.

—I Survived the Nazi Invasion 1944. 2014. (I Survived Ser.: 9). (ENG.). 112p. (J). (gr. 2-5). pap. 4.99 (978-0-545-45938-9(9)) Scholastic, Inc.

—I Survived the Nazi Invasion 1944. 2014. (I Survived . Ser.: No. 9). lib. bdg. 14.75 (978-0-606-35397-7(6)) Turtleback Bks.

Taylor, Mary Ann. Traitors: A Gander's Cove Mystery. Casteel, Kay, illus. 2006. (J). mass mkt. 5.99 (978-0-9753367-9-3(7)) Onstage Publishing, LLC.

Ter Haar, Jaap. The Ice Road. Mearns, Martha, tr. from DUT. 2005. 157p. (J). (gr. k-9). pap. 5.95 (978-1-903015-38-4(3)) Barn Owl Bks, London GBR. Dist: Independent Pubs. Group.

Theobald, John Owen. What the Raven Brings. 2017. (Ravenmaster Trilogy Ser.: 2). (ENG., Illus.). 320p. (YA). (gr. 7-7). 9.99 **(978-1-78497-440-4(4))**; 22.99 (978-1-78497-438-1(2)) Head of Zeus GBR. Dist: Independent Pubs. Group.

Thor, Annika. A Faraway Island. Schenck, Linda, tr. 2011. (ENG.). 256p. (J). (gr. 3-7). 6.99 (978-0-375-84495-9(3), Yearling) Random Hse. Children's Bks.

—The Lily Pond. Schenck, Linda, tr. 2012. (ENG.). 224p. (J). (gr. 4-7). 7.99 (978-0-385-74040-1(9), Yearling) Random Hse. Children's Bks.

Thor, Annika & Schenck, Linda. Deep Sea. 2015. (ENG.). 240p. (YA). (gr. 9). 20.99 (978-0-375-99132-5(8), Delacorte Pr.) Random Hse. Children's Bks.

Travers, P. L. I Go by Sea, I Go by Land. Hermes, Gertrude, illus. 2016. (Vmc Ser.). (ENG.). 208p. (J). (gr. 4-17). 11.99 (978-0-349-00574-4(5), Virago Press) Little, Brown Book Group Ltd. GBR. Dist: Hachette Bk. Group.

Tripp, Valerie. Brave Emily. England, Tamara, ed. Backes, Nick, illus. 2006. (ENG.). 96p. (J). (gr. 4-7). pap. 6.95 (978-1-59369-210-0(2), American Girl) American Girl Publishing, Inc.

—Molly Story Collection. Backes, Nick, illus. 2004. (ENG.). 388p. 29.95 (978-1-59369-458-6(X)) American Girl Publishing, Inc.

Turnbull, Ann. Josie under Fire. 2009. (Historical House Ser.). 176p. (YA). (gr. 5-18). pap. 5.99 (978-0-7945-2335-0(8), Usborne) EDC Publishing.

Ungerer, Tomi. Otto: The Autobiography of a Teddy Bear. 2010. (ENG., Illus.). 36p. (gr. 7-17). 16.95 (978-0-7148-5766-4(1)) Phaidon Pr., Inc.

Upjohn, Rebecca. The Secret of the Village Fool, 1 vol. Benoit, Renné, illus. 2012. (ENG.). 32p. (J). (gr. 3-6). lib. bdg. 18.95 (978-1-926920-75-7(9)) Second Story Pr. CAN. Dist: Orca Bk. Pubs. USA.

Van Stockum, Hilda. The Borrowed House. 2016. 203p. (J). pap. (978-1-930900-89-9(9)) Purple Hse. Pr.

Venkatraman, Padma. Climbing the Stairs. 2010. (ENG., Illus.). 272p. (YA). (gr. 7-18). 9.99 (978-0-14-241490-3(5), Speak) Penguin Young Readers Group.

Voorhoeve, Anne C. My Family for the War. Reichel, Tammi, tr. from GER. 2015. (ENG.). 416p. (YA). (gr. 7). pap. 9.99 (978-0-14-751183-6(6), Speak) Penguin Young Readers Group.

Walters, Eric. Camp 30. 2005. (ENG.). 224p. (J). (gr. 3-7). 6.99 (978-0-14-301678-6(4), Penguin Canada) Penguin Canada CAN. Dist: Penguin Random Hse. LLC.

Waters, Zack C. Blood Moon Rider. 2006. (Florida Historical Fiction for Youth Ser.). (ENG.). 126p. (J). (gr. 4-9). 13.95 (978-1-56164-350-9(5)) Pineapple Pr., Inc.

Watkins, Steve. Awol in North Africa. 2016. (Ghosts of War Ser.: 3). (ENG.). 208p. (J). (gr. 3-7). pap. 5.99 (978-0-545-83706-4(5)) Scholastic, Inc.

Watkins, Yoko Kawashima & Watkins, Yoko K. So Far from the Bamboo Grove. 2008. (ENG., Illus.). 192p. (J). (gr. 3-7). reprint ed. pap. 5.99 (978-0-688-13115-9(8)) HarperCollins Pubs.

Watts, Irene. Seeking Refuge, 1 vol. Shoemaker, Kathryn, illus. 2017. (ENG.). 128p. (J). (gr. 3-6). pap. 15.95 (978-1-926890-02-9(7)) Tradewind Bks. CAN. Dist: Orca Bk. Pubs. USA.

Watts, Irene N. Escape from Berlin. 2013. (ENG., Illus.). 424p. (J). (gr. 3-7). pap. 17.95 (978-1-77049-611-8(4), Tundra Bks.) Tundra Bks. CAN. Dist: Penguin Random Hse. LLC.

Webb, Holly. Return to the Secret Garden. 2016. (ENG.). 224p. (J). (gr. 3-7). 16.99 (978-1-4926-3909-1(5), 9781492639091) Sourcebooks, Inc.

Weber, Judith Eichler. Seeking Safety. Martin, John F., illus. 2006. (Adventures in America Ser.). (J). (978-1-893110-46-5(X)) Silver Moon Pr.

Wein, Elizabeth. Code Name Verity. (ENG.). (YA). (gr. 9-17). 2013. 368p. pap. 9.99 (978-1-4231-5288-0(3)) 2012. 352p. 16.99 (978-1-4231-5219-4(0)) Hyperion Pr.

—Code Name Verity. 2013. (YA). lib. bdg. 20.85 (978-0-606-31760-3(0), Turtleback) Turtleback Bks.

—The Pearl Thief. 2017. (ENG.). 336p. (YA). (gr. 7-12). 18.99 (978-1-4847-1716-5(3)) Hyperion Bks. for Children.

—Rose under Fire. 2014. (ENG.). 384p. (YA). (gr. 9-17). pap. 9.99 (978-1-4231-8469-0(6)) Disney Pr.

Wells, Helen. Cherry Ames, Army Nurse. 2005. (Cherry Ames Nurse Stories Ser.: Bk. 3). 224p. (J). (gr. 4-7). 14.95 (978-0-9771597-2-7(8)) Springer Publishing Co., Inc.

—Cherry Ames, Chief Nurse. 2005. (Cherry Ames Nurse Stories Ser.: Bk. 4). 224p. (YA). (gr. 8-12). 14.95 (978-0-9771597-3-4(6)) Springer Publishing Co., Inc.

—Cherry Ames, Flight Nurse. 2006. (Cherry Ames Nurse Stories Ser.). 224p. (J). (gr. 3-7). 14.95 (978-0-8261-0397-0(9)) Springer Publishing Co., Inc.

—Cherry Ames, Senior Nurse. 2005. (Cherry Ames Nurse Stories Ser.: Bk. 2). 224p. (J). (gr. 4-7). 14.95 (978-0-9771597-1-0(X)) Springer Publishing Co., Inc.

West, Nancy. Chips - the War Dog: Based on the True-Life Adventures of the World War II K-9 Hero. 2nd ed. 2004. 183p. (J). per. 8.95 (978-0-9743659-1-6(2)) Hero Dog Pubns.

Westall, Robert. Blitzcat. 2015. (ENG.). 240p. (J). (gr. 4-6). pap. 8.99 (978-1-4472-8460-4(7)) Pan Macmillan GBR. Dist: Independent Pubs. Group.

Weston, Elise. The Coastwatcher, 1 vol. 2009. (ENG.). 160p. (J). (gr. 3-7). pap. 7.95 (978-1-56145-484-6(2)) Peachtree Pubs.

Whelan, Gloria. Burying the Sun. 2004. 224p. (J). (gr. 5-18). (ENG.). 15.99 (978-0-06-054112-5(1)); lib. bdg. 16.89 (978-0-06-054113-2(X)) HarperCollins Pubs.

—Summer of the War. 2006. 163p. (J). (gr. 5-9). lib. bdg. 16.89 (978-0-06-008073-0(6)); (978-1-4287-0030-7(7)) HarperCollins Pubs.

Wiebe, Kurtis J. Peter Panzerfaust Deluxe Edition Volume 1 HC. 2013. (Illus.). 364p. (YA). 39.99 (978-1-60706-778-8(1)) Image Comics.

Wilbur, Helen. Lily's Victory Garden. Steele, Robert, illus. 2010. (Tales of Young Americans Ser.). (ENG.). 32p. (J). (gr. 2-4). 16.95 (978-1-58536-450-3(9)) Sleeping Bear Pr.

Wilson, John. Flames of the Tiger. 2003. (ENG., Illus.). 176p. (J). (gr. 13-18). 6.95 (978-1-55337-619-4(6)) Kids Can Pr., Ltd. CAN. Dist: Hachette Bk. Group.

The Winter Horses. 2014. (ENG., Illus.). 288p. (YA). (gr. 7). 16.99 (978-0-385-75543-6(0), Knopf Bks. for Young Readers) Random Hse. Children's Bks.

Wishinsky, Frieda & Griffiths, Dean. Far from Home. Franson, Leanne & Owlkids Books Inc. Staff, illus. 2008. (Canadian Flyer Adventures Ser.: 11). (ENG.). 96p. (J). (gr. 1-4). pap. 7.95 (978-1-897349-43-4(2), Maple Tree Pr.) Owlkids Bks. Inc. CAN. Dist: Publishers Group West (PGW).

Wolf, Joan M. Someone Named Eva. 2009. (ENG., Illus.). 208p. (J). (gr. 5-7). pap. 7.99 (978-0-547-23766-4(9)) Houghton Mifflin Harcourt Publishing Co.

Wolfer, Dianne & Harrison-Lever, Brian. Photographs in the Mud. 2007. (Illus.). 32p. pap. 15.50 (978-1-921361-04-3(2)) Fremantle Pr. AUS. Dist: Independent Pubs. Group.

Wolff, Virginia Euwer. Bat 6. 256p. (J). (gr. 4-6). pap. 4.99 (978-0-8072-8223-6(5)); 2004. (gr. 5-9). pap. 36.00 incl. audio (978-0-8072-8222-9(7), YYA144SP) Random Hse. Audio Publishing Group. (Listening Library).

Woodbury, Mary. Flight of the Tiger Moth, 1 vol. 2007. (ENG.). 240p. (YA). (gr. 7-11). per. 8.95 (978-1-55050-364-7(2)) Coteau Bks. CAN. Dist: Orca Bk. Pubs. USA.

Woodson, Jacqueline. Coming on Home Soon. Lewis, Earl & Lewis, E. B., illus. 2004. (ENG.). 32p. (J). (gr. k-3). 17.99 (978-0-399-23748-5(8), G.P. Putnam's Sons Books for Young Readers) Penguin Young Readers Group.

Wulffson, Don L. & Wulffson, Don. Soldier X. 2003. (ENG.). 240p. (YA). (gr. 7-18). 6.99 (978-0-14-250073-6(9), Speak) Penguin Young Readers Group.

Wynne-Jones, Tim. The Emperor of Any Place. 2015. (ENG.). 336p. (YA). (gr. 9). 17.99 (978-0-7636-6973-7(3)) Candlewick Pr.

Zindel, Paul & Zindel, Paul. The Gadget. 2003. (ENG., Illus.). 192p. (YA). (gr. 7). mass mkt. 6.99 (978-0-440-22951-3(0), Laurel Leaf) Random Hse. Children's Bks.

Zusak, Markus. The Book Thief. 2014. (ENG.). 576p. (YA). 17.24 (978-1-63245-052-4(6)) Lectorum Pubns., Inc.

—The Book Thief. 2009. 12.64 (978-0-7848-1941-8(6), Everbind) Marco Bk. Co.

—The Book Thief. 2008. 552p. (gr. 7-12). 23.00 (978-0-7569-8440-3(8)) Perfection Learning Corp.

—The Book Thief. (ENG., Illus.). (YA). (gr. 7). 2016. 592p. lib. bdg. 22.99 (978-0-399-55652-4(4)) 2007. 592p. pap. 12.99 (978-0-375-84220-7(9)) 2013. 576p. pap. 12.99 (978-0-385-75472-9(8)) 2016. 592p. 19.99 (978-1-101-93418-0(2)) Random Hse. Children's Bks. (Knopf Bks. for Young Readers).

—The Book Thief. l.t. ed. 2006. (ENG.). 552p. 23.99 (978-1-4104-6806-2(2)); 757p. (YA). (gr. 7-12). 24.95 (978-0-7862-9021-5(8)) Thorndike Pr.

—The Book Thief. 2008. (ENG., Illus.). 560p. pap. (978-0-552-77389-8(1), Black Swan) Transworld Publishers Ltd.

—The Book Thief. 2007. 552p. lib. bdg. 24.50 (978-1-4177-9738-7(X)) 2013. lib. bdg. 24.50 (978-0-606-34656-6(2)) Turtleback Bks. (Turtleback).

—La Ladrona de Libros. 2010. (Vintage Espanol Ser.). Tr. of Book Thief. (SPA.). 544p. (YA). (gr. 7). pap. 12.99 (978-0-307-47573-2(5), Vintage Espanol) Knopf Doubleday Publishing Group.

WORLD WAR, 1939-1945—FRANCE

Bliven, Bruce, Jr. & Bliven, Bruce. Invasion: The Story of D-Day. 2007. (Sterling Point Books(r) Ser.). (ENG., Illus.). 176p. (J). (gr. 7). pap. 6.95 (978-1-4027-4141-8(3)) Sterling Publishing Co., Inc.

Cornioley, Pearl Witherington & Atwood, Kathryn J. Code Name Pauline: Memoirs of a World War II Special Agent. 2013. (Women of Action Ser.). (ENG., Illus.). 208p. (YA). (gr. 6). 19.95 (978-1-61374-487-1(0)) Chicago Review Pr., Inc.

D-Day & the Liberation of France. 2010. (Milestones in World History Ser.). (Illus.). 136p. (C). (gr. 9-18). 35.00 (978-1-60413-280-9(9), Chelsea Hse.) Facts On File, Inc.

Draper, Allison Stark. Pastor André Trocmé: Spiritual Leader of the French Village le Chambon. 2009. (Holocaust Biographies Ser.). 112p. (gr. 7-12). 63.90 (978-1-61513-390-1(9)) Rosen Publishing Group, Inc., The.

Drez, Ronald J. Remember D-Day: The Plan, the Invasion, Survivor Stories. (ENG., Illus.). 64p. (J). (gr. 5). 2015. pap. 7.99 (978-1-4263-2245-7(3)) 2004. 17.95 (978-0-7922-6666-2(8)) National Geographic Society. (National Geographic Children's Bks.).

Murray, Doug. D-Day. 2008. (Graphic Battles of World War II Ser.). (ENG., Illus.). 48p. (YA). (gr. 4-7). lib. bdg. 31.95 (978-1-4042-0786-8(4)) Rosen Publishing Group, Inc., The.

Ruelle, Karen Gray. The Grand Mosque of Paris: A Story of How Muslims Rescued Jews During the Holocaust. DeSaix, Deborah Durland, illus. 2010. (ENG.). 40p. (J). (gr. 3-18). pap. 8.95 (978-0-8234-2304-0(2)) Holiday Hse., Inc.

Wallace, Karen & Platt, Richard. D-Day Landings, Level 4: The Story of the Allied Invasion. 2004. (DK Readers Ser.). (ENG., Illus.). 32p. (J). (gr. 3-7). pap. 3.99 (978-0-7566-0275-8(0), DK Children) Dorling Kindersley Publishing, Inc.

Williams, Brian. The Normandy Beaches. 2011. (Place in History Ser.). 48p. (YA). (gr. 5-9). lib. bdg. 34.25 (978-1-84837-675-5(8)) Arcturus Publishing GBR. Dist: Black Rabbit Bks.

WORLD WAR, 1939-1945—GERMANY

Cain, Bill. Battle of the Bulge. 2008. (Graphic Battles of World War II Ser.). (ENG., Illus.). 48p. (YA). (gr. 4-7). lib. bdg. 31.95 (978-1-4042-0782-0(1)) Rosen Publishing Group, Inc., The.

Chant, Christopher. The Start of World War II: The Flood of the German Tide. 2017. (World War II Ser.: Vol. 5). (ENG.). (YA). (gr. 7-12). 24.95 **(978-1-4222-3894-3(6))** Mason Crest.

Davenport, John. The Nuremberg Trials. 2006. (World History Ser.). (ENG., Illus.). 96p. (YA). (gr. 7-10). lib. bdg. 34.95 (978-1-59018-634-3(6), Lucent Bks.) Cengage Gale.

Drez, Ronald J. Remember D-Day: The Plan, the Invasion, Survivor Stories. (ENG., Illus.). 64p. (J). (gr. 5). 2015. pap. 7.99 (978-1-4263-2245-7(3)) 2004. 27.90 (978-0-7922-6965-6(9)) 2004. 17.95 (978-0-7922-6666-2(8)) National Geographic Society. (National Geographic Children's Bks.).

McIlroy, Michelle. Sophie Scholl: Student Resister & Anti-Nazi Political Activist. 2017. (J). **(978-1-5383-8108-3(7))**; pap. **(978-1-5383-8107-6(9))** Rosen Publishing Group, Inc., The.

O'Reilly, Bill. Hitler's Last Days: The Death of the Nazi Regime & the World's Most Notorious Dictator. 2015. (Illus.). 320p. (J). pap. (978-1-62779-455-8(7)); (ENG., (gr. 5-9). 19.99 (978-1-62779-396-4(8), 9781627793964, Holt, Henry & Co. Bks. For Young Readers) Holt, Henry & Co.

—Hitler's Last Days: The Death of the Nazi Regime & the World's Most Notorious Dictator. Barcellona, Christine, ed. 2017. (ENG.). 336p. (J). pap. 12.99 (978-1-250-08859-8(3), 9781250088598) Square Fish.

Owlkids Books Inc. Staff & Arato, Rona. The Last Train: A Holocaust Story. 2013. (ENG., Illus.). 144p. (J). (gr. 6). 16.95 (978-1-926973-62-3(3)) Owlkids Bks. Inc. CAN. Dist: Publishers Group West (PGW).

Rice, Earle, Jr. Blitzrieg! Hitler's Lightning War. 2007. (Monumental Milestones Ser.). (Illus.). 48p. (YA). (gr. 4-7). lib. bdg. 29.95 (978-1-58415-542-3(6)) Mitchell Lane Pubs., Inc.

Saltzwedel, Hans H. Hans' Journal: A Young German's Memories of His Family's Survival During Germany's Darkest Days. 2003. (Illus.). 234p. per. 19.95 net. (978-1-931934-17-6(7)) Back Yard Pub.

Schloss, Eva & Powers, Barbara. The Promise: The Moving Story of a Family in the Holocaust. Yaron, Sophie, illus. 2006. (ENG.). 160p. (J). (gr. 13-18). 10.99 (978-0-14-132081-6(8)) Penguin Bks., Ltd. GBR. Dist: Independent Pubs. Group.

Sears, Stephen W. Air War Against Hitler's Germany. 2007. (ENG., Illus.). 176p. pap. 9.95 (978-1-59687-004-8(4)) IBks., Inc.

Welter, Anni. Child of War: How We Lived & Survived under the Third Reich. 2nd ed. 2003. Orig. Title: Child of the Third Reich: How We Lived & Survived. 160p. (YA). per. 14.95 (978-0-9741434-0-8(5)) A H W Publishing.

Zaugg, Sandra L. Escape. 2007. (Illus.). 95p. (J). (978-0-8163-2140-7(X)) Pacific Pr. Pubns.

WORLD WAR, 1939-1945—GREAT BRITAIN

Allport, Alan. The Battle of Britain. 2012. 128p. (J). 35.00 (978-1-60413-920-4(X), Chelsea Hse.) Facts On File, Inc.

Barber, Nicola. Churchill & the Battle of Britain: Days of Decision, 1 vol. 2013. (Days of Decision Ser.). (ENG.). 64p. (gr. 7-8). 35.99 (978-1-4329-7634-7(6)); pap. 10.95 (978-1-4329-7641-5(9)) Heinemann-Raintree.

Byers, Ann. Saving Children from the Holocaust: The Kindertransport. 2011. (Holocaust Through Primary Sources Ser.). (Illus.). 128p. (J). (gr. 6-18). pap. 10.95 (978-1-59845-344-7(0)); (gr. 9-12). lib. bdg. 33.27 (978-0-7660-3323-8(6)) Enslow Pubs., Inc.

Cornioley, Pearl Witherington & Atwood, Kathryn J. Code Name Pauline: Memoirs of a World War II Special Agent. 2013. (Women of Action Ser.). (ENG., Illus.). 208p. (YA). (gr. 6). 19.95 (978-1-61374-487-1(0)) Chicago Review Pr., Inc.

Gardner, Faye, et al. A Wartime Childhood: 2011. (When I Was Young Ser.). (ENG., Illus.). 32p. (J). pap. 10.99 (978-0-237-54384-6(2)) Evans Brothers, Ltd. GBR. Dist: Independent Pubs. Group.

Innes, Stephanie & Endrulat, Harry. Bear on the Homefront, 1 vol. Deines, Brian, illus. 2014. (ENG.). 32p. (J). (gr. k-3). 17.95 (978-1-927485-13-2(4)) Pajama Pr. CAN. Dist: Ingram Publisher Services.

Parsons, Martin. Evacuation in World War II. 2017. (History Detective Investigates Ser.). (ENG., Illus.). 32p. (J). (gr. 4-6). pap. 11.99 (978-0-7502-9639-7(9), Wayland) Hachette Children's Group GBR. Dist: Hachette Bk. Group.

—The History Detective Investigates: Air Raids in World War II. 2017. (History Detective Investigates Ser.). (ENG., Illus.). 32p. (J). (gr. 4-6). pap. 11.99 (978-0-7502-9651-9(8),

Wayland) Hachette Children's Group GBR. Dist: Hachette Bk. Group.
—Rationing World War II. 2017. (History Detective Investigates Ser.). (ENG., Illus.). 32p. (J). (gr. 4-6). pap. 11.99 *(978-0-7502-9631-1(3),* Wayland) Hachette Children's Group GBR. Dist: Hachette Bk. Group.
—Women in World War II. 2017. (History Detective Investigates Ser.). (ENG., Illus.). 32p. (J). (gr. 4-6). pap. 11.99 *(978-0-7502-9638-0(0),* Wayland) Hachette Children's Group GBR. Dist: Hachette Bk. Group.
Ridley, Sarah. Winston Churchill: ...And World War II. 2013. (History Makers Ser.). (Illus.). 24p. (J). (gr. 2-4). lib. bdg. 25.65 *(978-1-59771-393-1(7))* Sea-To-Sea Pubns.
Stephens, Chris S. A Wartime Scrapbook, Pack. 2004. (ENG., Illus.). 48p. pap. 42.95 *(978-1-84323-329-9(0))* Beekman Bks., Inc.
Vander Hook, Sue. Winston Churchill: British Prime Minister & Statesman, 1 vol. 2009. (Essential Lives Set 3 Ser.). (ENG., Illus.). 112p. (J). (gr. 6-12). lib. bdg. 35.64 *(978-1-60453-523-5(7))* ABDO Publishing Co.
Wintrob, Kitty. I'm Not Going Back: Wartime Memoir of a Child Evacuee. 2009. *(978-0-9784435-1-1(9))* Now & Then Bks.

WORLD WAR, 1939-1945—GUERRILLAS
see World War, 1939-1945—Underground Movements

WORLD WAR, 1939-1945—HOSPITALS
see World War, 1939-1945—Medical Care

WORLD WAR, 1939-1945—JAPAN
Chant, Christopher. The End of World War II: The Japanese Surrender. 2017. (World War II Ser.: Vol. 5). (ENG.). (YA). (gr. 7-12). 24.95 ***(978-1-4222-3898-1(9))*** Mason Crest.
—Japanese Aggression in the Pacific. 2017. (World War II Ser.: Vol. 5). (ENG.). (YA). (gr. 7-12). 24.95 ***(978-1-4222-3896-7(2))*** Mason Crest.
Grant, R. G. Why Did Hiroshima Happen? 2010. (Moments in History Ser.). (Illus.). 48p. (YA). (gr. 5-9). lib. bdg. 31.95 *(978-1-4339-4163-4(5));* (gr. 6-8). pap. 14.05 *(978-1-4339-4164-1(3),* Gareth Stevens Secondary Library) Stevens, Gareth Publishing LLLP.
Hyde, Natalie. Internment Camps. 2016. (Uncovering the Past: Analyzing Primary Sources Ser.). (ENG., Illus.). 48p. (J). (gr. 5-8). *(978-0-7787-2860-3(9))* Crabtree Publishing Co.
Kaelberer, Angie Peterson & Burgan, Michael. Japanese American Internment. 2017. (Eyewitness to World War II Ser.). (ENG.). 112p. (gr. 5-7). lib. bdg. 35.99 ***(978-0-7565-5581-8(7),*** CPB Grades 4-8) Compass Point Bks.
Literature Connections English: So Far from the Bamboo Grove. 2004. (gr. 6-12). *(978-0-395-77138-9(2),* 2-70216) Holt McDougal.
Ohlenroth, Patricia. Up from the Ashes: Rebuilding Japan after World War II. 2007. (Lucent Library of Historical Eras:Twentieth-Century Japan Ser.). (ENG., Illus.). 104p. (J). (gr. 3-7). lib. bdg. 34.80 *(978-1-4205-0028-8(7),* Lucent Bks.) Cengage Gale.
Peppas, Lynn. Hiroshima & Nagasaki. 2013. (ENG., Illus.). 48p. (J). *(978-0-7787-1171-1(4));* pap. *(978-0-7787-1179-7(X))* Crabtree Publishing Co.
Sandler, Martin W. Imprisoned: The Betrayal of Japanese Americans During World War II. 2013. (ENG., Illus.). 176p. (J). (gr. 5-8). 24.99 *(978-0-8027-2277-5(6),* 9780802722775, Bloomsbury USA Childrens) Walker & Co.
Smibert, Angie. 12 Incredible Facts about the Dropping of the Atomic Bombs. 2015. (Turning Points in US History Ser.). (ENG., Illus.). 32p. (J). (gr. 3-5). 19.95 *(978-1-63235-129-6(3),* 12-Story Library) Pr. Room Editions LLC.
Stein, R. Conrad. World War II in the Pacific: From Pearl Harbor to Nagasaki. 2011. (United States at War Ser.). (Illus.). 128p. (J). (gr. 5-18). lib. bdg. 33.27 *(978-0-7660-3640-6(5))* Enslow Pubs., Inc.
Stelson, Caren. Sachiko: A Nagasaki Bomb Survivor's Story. 2016. (ENG., Illus.). (gr. 5-12). 120p. 19.99 *(978-1-4677-8903-5(8));* 144p. 38.65 *(978-1-5124-1885-9(4));* 144p. 38.65 *(978-1-5124-0893-5(X));* (YA). 9.99 *(978-1-5124-1884-2(6))* Lerner Publishing Group. (Carolrhoda Bks.).
Whiting, Jim. The Story of the Attack on Pearl Harbor. 2005. (Monumental Milestones Ser.). (Illus.). 48p. (YA). (gr. 4-7). lib. bdg. 29.95 *(978-1-58415-397-9(0))* Mitchell Lane Pubs., Inc.

WORLD WAR, 1939-1945—JEWS
Alma, Ann. Brave Deeds: How One Family Saved Many from the Nazis. 2008. (ENG., Illus.). 96p. (J). (gr. 3-7). 17.95 *(978-0-88899-791-3(4))* Groundwood Bks. CAN. Dist: Publishers Group West (PGW).
Berne, Emma Carlson. Escaping the Nazis on the Kindertransport. 2017. (Encounter: Narrative Nonfiction Stories Ser.). (ENG., Illus.). 112p. (gr. 3-4). lib. bdg. 29.99 *(978-1-5157-4545-7(7))* Capstone Press of Coughlan Cos.
Blohm, Craig E. Holocaust Rescue & Liberation. 2015. (ENG., Illus.). 80p. (J). lib. bdg. *(978-1-60152-844-5(2))* ReferencePoint Pr., Inc.
Borden, Louise W. His Name Was Raoul Wallenberg. 2012. (ENG., Illus.). 144p. (YA). (gr. 7). 18.99 *(978-0-618-50755-9(8))* Houghton Mifflin Harcourt Publishing Co.
Brophy Down, Susan. Irena Sendler: Bringing Life to Children of the Holocaust. 2012. (ENG.). 112p. (J). pap. *(978-0-7787-2556-5(1));* (Illus.). *(978-0-7787-2553-4(7))* Crabtree Publishing Co.
Byers, Ann. Courageous Teen Resisters: Primary Sources from the Holocaust. 2010. (True Stories of Teens in the Holocaust Ser.). (Illus.). 128p. (YA). (gr. 9-12). 33.27 *(978-0-7660-3269-9(8))* Enslow Pubs., Inc.
—Oskar Schindler: Saving Jews from the Holocaust. 2005. (Holocaust Heroes & Nazi Criminals Ser.). (Illus.). 160p. (J). (gr. 6-12). lib. bdg. 27.93 *(978-0-7660-2534-9(9))* Enslow Pubs., Inc.
—Rescuing the Danish Jews: A Heroic Story from the Holocaust. 2011. (Holocaust Through Primary Sources Ser.). (Illus.). 128p. (J). (gr. 6-18). pap. 10.95 *(978-1-59845-343-0(2));* (gr. 9-12). lib. bdg. 33.27 *(978-0-7660-3321-4(X))* Enslow Pubs., Inc.
—Saving Children from the Holocaust: The Kindertransport. 2011. (Holocaust Through Primary Sources Ser.). (Illus.). 128p. (J). (gr. 6-18). pap. 10.95 *(978-1-59845-344-7(0));* (gr. 9-12). lib. bdg. 33.27 *(978-0-7660-3323-8(6))* Enslow Pubs., Inc.
Cohen, Robert Z. Jewish Resistance Against the Holocaust. 2014. (Documentary History of the Holocaust Ser.). (Illus.). 80p. (YA). (gr. 7-12). 34.25 *(978-1-4777-7601-8(X))* Rosen Publishing Group, Inc., The.
Darman, Peter, ed. The Holocaust & Life under Nazi Occupation. 2012. (World War II Ser.). (ENG., Illus.). 64p. (YA). (gr. 7-12). lib. bdg. 31.95 *(978-1-4488-9235-8(X))* Rosen Publishing Group, Inc., The.
Downing, David. Nazi Death Camps. 2005. (World Almanac Library of the Holocaust). (Illus.). 48p. (gr. 5-12). lib. bdg. 31.00 *(978-0-8368-5947-8(2),* Gareth Stevens Secondary Library) Stevens, Gareth Publishing LLLP.
Draper, Allison Stark. Pastor Andre Trocme: Spiritual Leader of the French Village, Le Chambon. 2005. (Holocaust Biographies Ser.). (Illus.). 112p. (YA). (gr. 7-12). lib. bdg. 34.60 *(978-0-8239-3378-5(4))* Rosen Publishing Group, Inc., The.
—Pastor André Trocmé: Spiritual Leader of the French Village le Chambon. 2009. (Holocaust Biographies Ser.). 112p. (gr. 7-12). 63.90 *(978-1-61513-390-1(9))* Rosen Publishing Group, Inc., The.
Finkelstein, Norman H. Remember Not to Forget: A Memory of the Holocaust. Hokanson, Lois & Hokanson, Lars, illus. 2004. (ENG.). 32p. pap. 12.95 *(978-0-8276-0770-5(9))* Jewish Pubn. Society.
Fishkin, Rebecca Love. Heroes of the Holocaust, 1 vol. 2011. (Holocaust Ser.). (ENG.). 64p. (gr. 6-7). pap. 9.10 *(978-0-7565-4443-0(2));* lib. bdg. 33.99 *(978-0-7565-4391-4(6))* Compass Point Bks. (CPB Grades 4-8).
Freedman, Jeri. The Warsaw Ghetto & Uprising. 2014. (Documentary History of the Holocaust Ser.). 80p. (YA). (gr. 7-12). 34.25 *(978-1-4777-7605-6(2))* Rosen Publishing Group, Inc., The.
Fremon, David K. Schindler, Wallenberg, Miep Gies: The Holocaust Heroes. 2014. (Remembering the Holocaust Ser.). 96p. (J). (gr. 6-12). 27.94 *(978-0-7660-6217-7(1))* Enslow Pubs., Inc.
Gottfried, Ted. Heroes of the Holocaust. Alcorn, Stephen, illus. (Holocaust History Ser.). 112p. (YA). (gr. 7-12). 22.95 *(978-1-58013-222-0(7),* Kar-Ben Publishing) Lerner Publishing Group.
Greek, Joe. Righteous Gentiles: Non-Jews Who Fought Against Genocide. 2014. (Documentary History of the Holocaust Ser.). 80p. (YA). (gr. 7-12). 34.25 *(978-1-4777-7611-7(7))* Rosen Publishing Group, Inc., The.
Hodge, Deborah. Rescuing the Children: The Story of the Kindertransport. 2012. (ENG., Illus.). 62p. (J). (gr. 5). 17.95 *(978-1-77049-256-1(9),* Tundra Bks.) Tundra Bks. CAN. Dist: Penguin Random Hse. LLC.
Idzikowski, Lisa. Raoul Wallenberg: Rescuer of Hungarian Jews During the Holocaust. 2017. (J). ***(978-1-5383-8118-2(4));*** pap. ***(978-1-5383-8117-5(6))*** Rosen Publishing Group, Inc., The.
Leyson, Leon. The Boy on the Wooden Box: How the Impossible Became Possible ... on Schindler's List. (ENG., Illus.). (J). (gr. 4-9). 2015. 256p. pap. 9.99 *(978-1-4424-9782-5(3))* 2013. 240p. 17.99 *(978-1-4424-9781-8(5))* Simon & Schuster Children's Publishing. (Atheneum Bks. for Young Readers).
—The Boy on the Wooden Box: How the Impossible Became Possible ... on Schindler's List. 2015. lib. bdg. 19.65 *(978-0-606-36097-5(2))* Turtleback Bks.
Lowery, Zoe & Roberts, Jeremy. Oscar Schindler, 01 vols., 1. 2016. (Holocaust Ser.). (ENG., Illus.). 112p. (J). 35.60 *(978-1-4994-6252-4(2),* Rosen Young Adult) Rosen Publishing Group, Inc., The.
Mazzeo, Tilar J. Irena's Children. 2016. (ENG., Illus.). 272p. (J). (gr. 5-7). 17.99 *(978-1-4814-4991-5(5),* McElderry, Margaret K. Bks.) McElderry, Margaret K. Bks.
McArthur, Debra. Raoul Wallenberg: Rescuing Thousands from the Nazis' Grasp. 2005. (Holocaust Heroes & Nazi Criminals Ser.). (Illus.). 160p. (J). (gr. 6-12). lib. bdg. 27.93 *(978-0-7660-2530-1(6))* Enslow Pubs., Inc.
Mochizuki, Ken. Pasajea la Libertad. 2004. (SPA., Illus.). (J). (gr. k-4). spiral bd. *(978-0-616-03091-2(6))* Canadian National Institute for the Blind/Institut National Canadien pour les Aveugles.
—Passage to Freedom: The Sugihara Story. 2005. 19.45 *(978-0-7569-4773-6(1))* Perfection Learning Corp.
Opdyke, Irene Gut. In My Hands: Memories of a Holocaust Rescuer. 2004. (ENG., Illus.). 304p. (YA). (gr. 9). mass mkt. 7.99 *(978-0-553-49411-2(2),* Laurel Leaf) Random Hse. Children's Bks.
—In My Hands: Memories of a Holocaust Rescuer. 2016. (ENG., Illus.). 288p. (YA). (gr. 9). pap. 10.99 *(978-0-553-53884-7(5),* Ember) Random Hse. Children's Bks.
Opdyke, Irene Gut & Armstrong, Jennifer. In My Hands: Memories of a Holocaust Rescuer. pap. *(978-0-385-72870-6(0))* Knopf Doubleday Publishing Group.
—In My Hands: Memories of a Holocaust Rescuer. 2009. 9.14 *(978-0-7848-2512-9(2));* 14.72 *(978-0-7848-2511-2(4))* Marco Bk. Co. (Everbind).
Rappaport, Doreen. Beyond Courage: The Untold Story of Jewish Resistance During the Holocaust. 2012. (ENG., Illus.). 240p. (J). (gr. 5). 22.99 *(978-0-7636-2976-2(6))* Candlewick Pr.
Rogow, Sally M. Faces of Courage: Young Heroes of World War II. 2008. (ENG., Illus.). 162p. pap. *(978-1-894694-67-4(8))* Granville Island Publishing.
Roy, Jennifer. Jars of Hope: How One Woman Helped Save 2,500 Children During the Holocaust. Owenson, Meg, illus. 2015. (Encounter: Narrative Nonfiction Picture Bks.). (ENG.). 32p. (gr. 3-5). lib. bdg. 27.32 *(978-1-4914-6072-6(5))* Encounter Bks.
Rubin, Susan Goldman. Irena Sendler & the Children of the Warsaw Ghetto. Farnsworth, Bill, illus. (ENG.). 40p. (J). 2016. (gr. 4-7). pap. 8.99 *(978-0-8234-2595-2(9))* 2011. (gr. 1-5). 18.95 *(978-0-8234-2251-7(8))* Holiday Hse., Inc.
Ruelle, Karen Gray. The Grand Mosque of Paris: A Story of How Muslims Rescued Jews During the Holocaust. DeSaix, Deborah Durland, illus. 2010. (ENG.). 40p. (J). (gr. 3-18). pap. 8.95 *(978-0-8234-2304-0(2))* Holiday Hse., Inc.
—Hidden on the Mountain: Stories of Children Sheltered from the Nazis in le Chambon. DeSaix, Deborah Durland, illus. 2007. (ENG.). 272p. (J). (gr. 5-18). 24.95 *(978-0-8234-1928-9(2))* Holiday Hse., Inc.
Simon, Emma & Streissguth, Thomas. Raoul Wallenberg, 01 vols., 1. 2016. (Holocaust Ser.). (ENG., Illus.). 112p. (J). 35.60 *(978-1-4994-6242-5(5),* Rosen Young Adult) Rosen Publishing Group, Inc., The.
Vaughan, Marcia. Irena's Jars of Secrets, 1 vol. Mazellan, Ron, illus. 2011. (ENG.). 40p. (J). 18.95 *(978-1-60060-439-3(0))* Lee & Low Bks., Inc.
Vaughan, Marcia & Mazellan, Ron. Irena's Jars of Secrets. 2015. (ENG.). (J). pap. 10.95 *(978-1-62014-252-3(X))* Lee & Low Bks., Inc.
Ziemian, Joseph. The Cigarette Sellers of Three Crosses Square. 2005. (Library of Holocaust Testimonies Ser.). (Illus.). 168p. pap. 24.95 *(978-0-85303-686-9(1))* Vallentine Mitchell Pubs. GBR. Dist: ISBS Publisher Services.
Zullo, Allan & Bovsun, Mara. Heroes of the Holocaust: True Stories of Rescues by Teens. 2005. (Illus.). 183p. (J). *(978-0-439-67608-3(8))* Scholastic, Inc.

WORLD WAR, 1939-1945—MEDICAL CARE
Farrell, Mary Cronk. Pure Grit: How American World War II Nurses Survived Battle & Prison Camp in the Pacific. 2014. (ENG., Illus.). 160p. (J). (gr. 3-7). 24.95 *(978-1-4197-1028-5(1),* Abrams Bks. for Young Readers) Abrams, Inc.
Lensky, Mordechai. A Physician Inside the Warswa Ghetto. 2009. 257p. (YA). pap. 27.50 *(978-0-9814686-3-1(2))* Yad Vashem Pubns. ISR. Dist: Coronet Bks.
Saxby, Claire. Meet Weary Dunlop. Lord, Jeremy, illus. 2016. (ENG.). 32p. (J). (gr. k-2). 14.99 *(978-0-85798-587-3(6))* Random Hse. Australia AUS. Dist: Independent Pubs. Group.

WORLD WAR, 1939-1945—NAVAL OPERATIONS
Grove, Philip D., et al. World War II: The War at Sea. 2010. (World War II: Essential Histories Ser.). (Illus.). 96p. (YA). (gr. 9-12). lib. bdg. 33.25 *(978-1-4358-9131-9(7))* Rosen Publishing Group, Inc., The.
Hopkinson, Deborah. Dive! World War II Stories of Sailors & Submarines in the Pacific. 2016. (ENG., Illus.). 384p. (J). (gr. 3-7). 17.99 *(978-0-545-42558-2(1),* Scholastic Pr.) Scholastic, Inc.
Kevin, McDonald. Tin Can Sailors Save the Day. 2015. (J). pap. 10.95 *(978-1-55571-786-5(1),* Paloma Bks.) L & R Publishing, LLC.
Mullenbach, Cheryl. Torpedoed! A World War II Story of a Sinking Passenger Ship & Two Children's Survival at Sea. 2017. (ENG.). 176p. (J). (gr. 5). 17.99 ***(978-1-61373-824-5(2))*** Chicago Review Pr., Inc.
Raum, Elizabeth. World War II Naval Forces, 1 vol. 2013. (You Choose: World War II Ser.). (ENG., Illus.). 112p. (gr. 3-4). pap. 6.95 *(978-1-62065-720-1(1),* You Choose Bks.) Capstone Press of Coughlan Cos.
—World War II Naval Forces: An Interactive History Adventure. 2013. (You Choose: World War II Ser.). (ENG.). 112p. (gr. 3-4). pap. 41.70 *(978-1-62065-721-8(X));* (Illus.). lib. bdg. 31.99 *(978-1-4296-4780-9(9))* Capstone Press of Coughlan Cos. (You Choose Bks.).
Sutcliffe, Jane & Kodera, Craig. Chester Nimitz & the Sea, 1 vol. 2013. (ENG., Illus.). 32p. (J). (gr. k-3). 16.99 *(978-1-4556-1796-8(2))* Pelican Publishing Co., Inc.
Townsend, John. Navy. 2016. (Action Force: World War II Ser.). 32p. (gr. 3-7). 31.35 *(978-1-59920-984-5(5),* Smart Apple Media) Black Rabbit Bks.
The U.S. Navy in World War II. 2014. (True Book(tm), a — World at War Ser.). (ENG.). 48p. (J). lib. bdg. 31.00 *(978-0-531-20497-9(9))* Scholastic Library Publishing.

WORLD WAR, 1939-1945—PACIFIC OCEAN
Beller, Susan Provost. Battling in the Pacific: Soldiering in World War II. 2007. (Soldiers on the Battlefront Ser.). (ENG., Illus.). 112p. (gr. 6-8). lib. bdg. 33.26 *(978-0-8225-6381-5(9))* Lerner Publishing Group.
Horner, D. M. & O'Neill, Robert John. World War II: The Pacific. 2010. (World War II: Essential Histories Ser.). (Illus.). 96p. (YA). (gr. 9-12). lib. bdg. 33.25 *(978-1-4358-9133-3(3))* Rosen Publishing Group, Inc., The.
Peyton, Katherine & George, Enzo. World War II in the Pacific: War with Japan. 2014. (Voices of War Ser.). (Illus.). 48p. (J). (gr. 4-6). lib. bdg. 31.36 *(978-1-62712-867-4(0))* Cavendish Square Publishing.
Samuels, Charlie. Life under Occupation. 2012. (World War II Sourcebook Ser.). (Illus.). 48p. (gr. 5-12). lib. bdg. 37.10 *(978-1-936333-26-4(0))* Brown Bear Bks.
World Book, Inc Staff, contrib. by. World War II in the Pacific. 2010. (J). *(978-0-7166-1510-1(X))* World Bk., Inc.

WORLD WAR, 1939-1945—PERSONAL NARRATIVES
Allen, Thomas B. Remember Pearl Harbor: American & Japanese Survivors Tell Their Stories. 2007. (Remember Ser.). (ENG., Illus.). 64p. (J). (gr. 5). 27.90 *(978-0-7922-3635-1(1),* National Geographic Children's Bks.) National Geographic Society.
—Remember Pearl Harbor: Japanese & American Survivors Tell Their Stories. 2015. (ENG., Illus.). 64p. (J). (gr. 5). pap. 7.99 *(978-1-4263-2248-8(8),* National Geographic Children's Bks.) National Geographic Society.
Altman, Linda Jacobs. Hidden Teens, Hidden Lives: Primary Sources from the Holocaust. 2010. (True Stories of Teens in the Holocaust Ser.). (Illus.). 128p. (YA). (gr. 9-12). 33.27 *(978-0-7660-3271-2(X))* Enslow Pubs., Inc.
Buchignani, Walter. Tell No One Who You Are: The Hidden Childhood of Régine Miller. 2008. (ENG., Illus.). 192p. (J). (gr. 4-7). pap. 12.95 *(978-0-88776-817-0(2),* Tundra Bks.) Tundra Bks. CAN. Dist: Penguin Random Hse. LLC.
Byers, Ann. Trapped-Youth in the Nazi Ghettos: Primary Sources from the Holocaust. 2010. (True Stories of Teens in the Holocaust Ser.). (Illus.). 128p. (YA). (gr. 9-12). 33.27 *(978-0-7660-3272-9(8))* Enslow Pubs., Inc.
McMullan, James. Leaving China: An Artist Paints His World War II Childhood. 2014. (ENG., Illus.). 128p. (YA). (gr. 7-12). 19.95 *(978-1-61620-255-2(6),* 73255) Algonquin Bks. of Chapel Hill.
Mihulka, Krystyna & Goddu, Krystyna Poray. Krysia: A Polish Girl's Stolen Childhood During World War II. 2017. (ENG., Illus.). 192p. (J). (gr. 5). 17.99 *(978-1-61373-441-4(7))* Chicago Review Pr., Inc.
Nicholson, Dorinda. Remember World War II: Kids Who Survived Tell Their Stories. 2015. (ENG., Illus.). 64p. (J). (gr. 5). pap. 7.99 *(978-1-4263-2251-8(8),* National Geographic Children's Bks.) National Geographic Society.
Opdyke, Irene Gut. In My Hands: Memories of a Holocaust Rescuer. 2004. (ENG., Illus.). 304p. (YA). (gr. 9). mass mkt. 7.99 *(978-0-553-49411-2(2),* Laurel Leaf) Random Hse. Children's Bks.
—In My Hands: Memories of a Holocaust Rescuer. 2016. (ENG., Illus.). 288p. (YA). (gr. 9). pap. 10.99 *(978-0-553-53884-7(5),* Ember) Random Hse. Children's Bks.
Opdyke, Irene Gut & Armstrong, Jennifer. In My Hands: Memories of a Holocaust Rescuer. pap. *(978-0-385-72870-6(0))* Knopf Doubleday Publishing Group.
—In My Hands: Memories of a Holocaust Rescuer. 2009. 9.14 *(978-0-7848-2512-9(2));* 14.72 *(978-0-7848-2511-2(4))* Marco Bk. Co. (Everbind).
Oppenheim, Joanne F. Dear Miss Breed: True Stories of the Japanese American Incarceration During World War II & a Librarian Who Made a Difference. 2006. (ENG., Illus.). 288p. (J). (gr. 7-12). 22.99 *(978-0-439-56992-7(3))* Scholastic, Inc.
Rauch, Georg. Unlikely Warrior: A Jewish Soldier in Hitler's Army. 2015. (ENG., Illus.). 352p. (YA). (gr. 7). 17.99 *(978-0-374-30142-2(5),* Farrar, Straus & Giroux (BYR)) Farrar, Straus & Giroux.

WORLD WAR, 1939-1945—PHILIPPINES
Otfinoski, Steven. World War II Infantrymen: An Interactive History Adventure. 2013. (You Choose: World War II Ser.). (ENG.). 112p. (gr. 3-4). pap. 41.70 *(978-1-62065-717-1(1),* You Choose Bks.) Capstone Press of Coughlan Cos.

WORLD WAR, 1939-1945—PICTORIAL WORKS
Bradley, James & Powers, Ron. Flags of Our Fathers: A Young People's Edition. 2005. (ENG., Illus.). 224p. (YA). (gr. 4-7). mass mkt. 7.99 *(978-0-440-22920-9(0),* Laurel Leaf) Random Hse. Children's Bks.
—Flags of Our Fathers: Heroes of Iwo Jima. 2003. (ENG., Illus.). 232p. (YA). (gr. 4-7). reprint ed. pap. 8.99 *(978-0-385-73064-8(0),* Delacorte Bks. for Young Readers) Random Hse. Children's Bks.
Callery, Sean. World War II. 2013. (Scholastic Discover More Ser.). (ENG.). 112p. (J). (gr. 5-9). 15.99 *(978-0-545-47975-2(4),* Scholastic Reference) Scholastic, Inc.

WORLD WAR, 1939-1945—POLAND
Brophy Down, Susan. Irena Sendler: Bringing Life to Children of the Holocaust. 2012. (ENG.). 112p. (J). pap. *(978-0-7787-2556-5(1));* (Illus.). *(978-0-7787-2553-4(7))* Crabtree Publishing Co.
Lensky, Mordechai. A Physician Inside the Warswa Ghetto. 2009. 257p. (YA). pap. 27.50 *(978-0-9814686-3-1(2))* Yad Vashem Pubns. ISR. Dist: Coronet Bks.
Mochizuki, Ken & Lee, Dom. Passage to Freedom: The Sugihara Story. 2010. (Rise & Shine Ser.). (ENG., Illus.). 32p. (C). pap. 14.95 *(978-1-58430-157-8(0))* National Geographic School Publishing, Inc.
Roy, Jennifer. Jars of Hope: How One Woman Helped Save 2,500 Children During the Holocaust. Owenson, Meg, illus. 2015. (Encounter: Narrative Nonfiction Picture Bks.). (ENG.). 32p. (gr. 3-5). lib. bdg. 27.32 *(978-1-4914-6072-6(5))* Encounter Bks.
Vaughan, Marcia. Irena's Jars of Secrets, 1 vol. Mazellan, Ron, illus. 2011. (ENG.). 40p. (J). 18.95 *(978-1-60060-439-3(0))* Lee & Low Bks., Inc.
Ziemian, Joseph. The Cigarette Sellers of Three Crosses Square. 2005. (Library of Holocaust Testimonies Ser.). (Illus.). 168p. pap. 24.95 *(978-0-85303-686-9(1))* Vallentine Mitchell Pubs. GBR. Dist: ISBS Publisher Services.

WORLD WAR, 1939-1945—PRISONERS AND PRISONS
Benge, Janet & Benge, Geoff. Jacob Deshazer: Forgive Your Enemies. 2009. (ENG.). 224p. (YA). pap. 9.99 *(978-1-57658-475-0(5))* YWAM Publishing.
—Louis Zamperini: Redemption. 2014. (ENG.). 218p. (YA). pap. 9.99 *(978-1-62486-049-2(4))* Emerald Bks.
Bryant, Jen. Music for the End of Time. Peck, Beth, illus. 2005. 32p. (J). (gr. 4-5). 17.00 *(978-0-8028-5229-8(7))* Eerdmans, William B. Publishing Co.
Deem, James M. The Prisoners of Breendonk: Personal Histories from a World War II Concentration Camp. 2015. (ENG., Illus.). 352p. (YA). (gr. 9). 18.99 *(978-0-544-09664-6(9),* HMH Books For Young Readers) Houghton Mifflin Harcourt Publishing Co.
Hickman, Pamela & Cavalluzzo, Jean Smith. Righting Canada's Wrongs: Italian Canadian Internment in the Second World War. 2012. (Righting Canada's Wrongs Ser.). (ENG., Illus.). 112p. (gr. 8-12). 34.95 *(978-1-4594-0095-5(X),* 9781459400955) Lorimer, James & Co., Ltd., Pubs. CAN. Dist: Casemate Pubs. & Bk. Distributors, LLC.
Hillenbrand, Laura. Unbroken: An Olympian's Journey from Airman to Castaway to Captive. 2014. (ENG., Illus.). 320p. (YA). (gr. 7). 19.99 *(978-0-385-74251-1(7));* lib. bdg. 22.99 *(978-0-375-99062-5(3))* Random Hse. Children's Bks. (Delacorte Pr.).
—Unbroken: An Olympian's Journey from Airman to Castaway to Captive (Young Readers Edition) 2017. lib. bdg. 22.10 ***(978-0-606-39867-1(8))*** Turtleback Bks.
—Unbroken (the Young Adult Adaptation) An Olympian's Journey from Airman to Castaway to Captive. 2017. (ENG.). 320p. (YA). (gr. 7). pap. 10.99 ***(978-0-385-74252-8(5),*** Ember) Random Hse. Children's Bks.
The Internment of Japanese Americans During World War II: Detention of American Citizens. 2010. (Milestones in American History Ser.). (Illus.). 128p. (gr. 6-12). 35.00 *(978-1-60413-681-4(2),* Chelsea Hse.) Facts On File, Inc.
Saxby, Claire. Meet Weary Dunlop. Lord, Jeremy, illus. (ENG.). 32p. (J). 2016. (gr. k-2). 14.99 *(978-0-85798-587-3(6))* 2015. (gr. -1-k). 21.99 *(978-0-85798-536-1(1))* Random Hse. Australia AUS. Dist: Independent Pubs. Group.
Schloss, Eva & Powers, Barbara. The Promise: The Moving Story of a Family in the Holocaust. Yaron, Sophie, illus. 2006. (ENG.). 160p. (J). (gr. 13-18). 10.99 *(978-0-14-132081-6(8))* Penguin Bks., Ltd. GBR. Dist: Independent Pubs. Group.
Viola, Herman J. & Layson, Annelex Hofstra. Lost Childhood: My Life in a Japanese Prison Camp During World War II. 2008. (ENG., Illus.). (J). (gr. 5). 112p. 15.95

(978-1-4263-0321-0(1)); 128p. lib. bdg. 23.90 *(978-1-4263-0322-7(X))* National Geographic Society. (National Geographic Children's Bks.).

Weintraub, Robert. No Better Friend: A Man, a Dog, & Their Incredible True Story of Friendship & Survival in World War II. 2016. (ENG., Illus.). 304p. (J). (gr. 5-17). 16.99 *(978-0-316-34467-8(2))* Little, Brown Bks. for Young Readers.

Yomtov, Nel. Tunnelling to Freedom: The Great Escape from Stalag Luft III. Valdrighi, Alessandro, illus. 2017. (Great Escapes of World War II Ser.). (ENG.). 32p. (gr. 3-4). pap. 7.95 *(978-1-5157-3536-6(2))*; lib. bdg. 30.65 *(978-1-5157-3531-1(1))* Capstone Press of Coughlan Cos. (Graphic Library).

WORLD WAR, 1939-1945—REFUGEES

Altman, Linda Jacobs. Escape-Teens on the Run: Primary Sources from the Holocaust. 2010. (True Stories of Teens in the Holocaust Ser.). (Illus.). 128p. (YA). (gr. 9-12). 33.27 *(978-0-7660-3270-5(1))* Enslow Pubs., Inc.

Hoffman, Betty N. Liberation: Stories of Survival from the Holocaust. 2011. (Holocaust Through Primary Sources Ser.). (Illus.). 128p. (J). (gr. 6-18). pap. 10.95 *(978-1-59845-348-5(3))*; (gr. 9-12). lib. bdg. 33.27 *(978-0-7660-3319-1(8))* Enslow Pubs., Inc.

Williams, Brenda & Williams, Brian. Saving the Persecuted. 2015. (Heroes of World War II Ser.). (ENG., Illus.). 48p. (gr. 4-6). 32.65 *(978-1-4109-8046-5(4))* Heinemann-Raintree.

Zaugg, Sandra L. Escape. 2007. (Illus.). 95p. (J). *(978-0-8163-2140-7(X))* Pacific Pr. Pubns.

WORLD WAR, 1939-1945—SECRET SERVICE

Burgan, Michael. World War II Spies, 1 vol. 2013. (You Choose: World War II Ser.). (ENG., Illus.). 112p. (gr. 3-4). pap. 6.95 *(978-1-62065-722-5(8)*, You Choose Bks.) Capstone Press of Coughlan Cos.

—World War II Spies: An Interactive History Adventure. 2013. (You Choose: World War II Ser.). (ENG.). 112p. (gr. 3-4). pap. 41.70 *(978-1-62065-723-2(6)*, You Choose Bks.) Capstone Press of Coughlan Cos.

—World War II Spies: An Interactive History Adventure, 1 vol. 2013. (You Choose: World War II Ser.). (ENG.). 112p. (gr. 3-4). lib. bdg. 31.99 *(978-1-4296-9898-6(5)*, You Choose Bks.) Capstone Press of Coughlan Cos.

Caravantes, Peggy. The Many Faces of Josephine Baker: Dancer, Singer, Activist, Spy. 2015. (Women of Action Ser.). (ENG., Illus.). 208p. (YA). (gr. 7). 19.95 *(978-1-61373-034-8(9))* Chicago Review Pr., Inc.

Cornioley, Pearl Witherington & Atwood, Kathryn J. Code Name Pauline: Memoirs of a World War II Special Agent. 2013. (Women of Action Ser.). (ENG., Illus.). 208p. (YA). (gr. 6). 19.95 *(978-1-61374-487-1(0))* Chicago Review Pr., Inc.

Goodman, Michael E. World War II Spies. 2015. (Illus.). 48p. (J). *(978-1-60818-603-7(2)*, Creative Education) Creative Co., The.

—World War II Spies: Wartime Spies. 2016. (Wartime Spies Ser.). (ENG.). 48p. (J). (gr. 5-9). pap. 12.00 *(978-1-62832-208-8(X)*, Creative Paperbacks) Creative Co., The.

Jeffrey, Gary. The Secret War. 2012. (ENG., Illus.). 48p. (J). *(978-0-7787-4195-4(8))*; pap. *(978-0-7787-4202-9(4))* Crabtree Publishing Co.

McCollum, Sean. Secrets of World War II. 2017. (Top Secret Files Ser.). (ENG., Illus.). 32p. (gr. 3-4). lib. bdg. 27.99 *(978-1-5157-4140-4(0)*, Edge Bks.) Capstone Press of Coughlan Cos.

Payment, Simone. American Women Spies of World War II. 2009. (American Women at War Ser.). 112p. (gr. 8-8). 63.90 *(978-1-61511-399-6(1))* Rosen Publishing Group, Inc., The.

Polette, Nancy. The Spy with the Wooden Leg: The Story of Virginia Hall. 2012. (ENG.). 160p. (J). pap. 12.95 *(978-1-934617-16-8(4))*; 16.95 *(978-1-934617-15-1(6))* Elva Resa Publishing, LLC. (Alma Little).

Price, Sean Stewart. World War II Spies, 1 vol. 2013. (Classified Ser.). (ENG.). 48p. (gr. 3-4). 31.99 *(978-1-4765-0122-2(X))* Capstone Press of Coughlan Cos.

Samuels, Charlie. Spying & Security. 2012. (World War II Sourcebook Ser.). 48p. (gr. 5-12). lib. bdg. 37.10 *(978-1-936333-25-7(2))* Brown Bear Bks.

—Spying & Security. 2017. (World War II Sourcebook Ser.). (ENG., Illus.). 48p. (J). (gr. 4-6). pap. 11.99 *(978-0-7502-8885-9(X)*, Wayland) Hachette Children's Group GBR. Dist: Hachette Bk. Group.

Sheinkin, Steve. Bomb: The Race to Build — & Steal — the World's Most Dangerous Weapon. 2012. (ENG., Illus.). 272p. (J). (gr. 5-9). 19.99 *(978-1-59643-487-5(2)*, 9781596434875) Roaring Brook Pr.

Throp, Claire. Spies & Codebreakers. 2015. (Heroes of World War II Ser.). (ENG., Illus.). 48p. (gr. 4-6). 32.65 *(978-1-4109-8047-2(2))* Heinemann-Raintree.

WORLD WAR, 1939-1945—SOVIET UNION

Dell, Pamela. The Soviet Night Witches: Brave Women Bomber Pilots of World War II. 2017. (Women & War Ser.). (ENG.). 32p. (gr. 3-4). lib. bdg. 27.99 ***(978-1-5157-7938-4(6)***, Snap Bks.) Capstone Press of Coughlan Cos.

Gottfried, Ted. The Great Fatherland War: The Soviet Union in World War II. Reim, Melanie K., illus. 2003. (Rise & Fall of the Soviet Union Ser.). 160p. (gr. 7-18). lib. bdg. 28.90 *(978-0-7613-2559-8(X)*, Twenty-First Century Bks.) Lerner Publishing Group.

Rauch, Georg. Unlikely Warrior: A Jewish Soldier in Hitler's Army. 2015. (ENG., Illus.). 352p. (YA). (gr. 7). 17.99 *(978-0-374-30142-2(5)*, Farrar, Straus & Giroux (BYR)) Farrar, Straus & Giroux.

WORLD WAR, 1939-1945—UNDERGROUND MOVEMENTS

Alma, Ann. Brave Deeds: How One Family Saved Many from the Nazis. 2008. (ENG., Illus.). 96p. (J). (gr. 3-7). 17.95 *(978-0-88899-791-3(4))* Groundwood Bks. CAN. Dist: Publishers Group West (PGW).

Atwood, Kathryn J. Women Heroes of World War II: 26 Stories of Espionage, Sabotage, Resistance, & Rescue. (Women of Action Ser.). (ENG.). 272p. (gr. 7). 2013. (YA). pap. 14.95 *(978-1-61374-523-6(0))* 2011. (Illus.). (J). 19.95 *(978-1-55652-961-0(9))* Chicago Review Pr., Inc.

Axelrod, Toby. Hans & Sophie Scholl: German Resisters of the White Rose. 2005. (Holocaust Biographies Ser.). (Illus.). 112p. (YA). (gr. 7-12). lib. bdg. 34.60 *(978-0-8239-3316-7(4)*, HBHOBI) Rosen Publishing Group, Inc., The.

Chaline, Eric. Secret Heroes of World War II: Tales of Courage from the Worlds of Espionage & Resistance. 2016. (Illus.). 224p. (YA). ***(978-1-4351-6251-8(X))*** Metro Bks.

Cornioley, Pearl Witherington & Atwood, Kathryn J. Code Name Pauline: Memoirs of a World War II Special Agent. 2013. (Women of Action Ser.). (ENG., Illus.). 208p. (YA). (gr. 6). 19.95 *(978-1-61374-487-1(0))* Chicago Review Pr., Inc.

Hoose, Phillip. The Boys Who Challenged Hitler: Knud Pedersen & the Churchill Club. 2015. (ENG., Illus.). 208p. (YA). (gr. 7-12). 19.99 *(978-0-374-30022-7(4)*, 9780374300227, Farrar, Straus & Giroux (BYR)) Farrar, Straus & Giroux.

Hopkinson, Deborah. Courage & Defiance: Stories of Spies, Saboteurs, & Survivors in World War II Denmark. 2016. (ENG.). 352p. (J). (gr. 3-7). pap. 6.99 *(978-0-545-59221-5(6))* 2015. (ENG., Illus.). 352p. (J). (gr. 3-7). 17.99 *(978-0-545-59220-8(8)*, Scholastic Pr.) 2015. *(978-0-545-91597-7(X))* Scholastic, Inc.

Levine, Ellen. Darkness over Denmark: The Danish Resistance & the Rescue of the Jews. 2005. (ENG., Illus.). 178p. (YA). (gr. 7-18). pap. 14.95 *(978-0-8234-1755-1(7))* Holiday Hse., Inc.

Polette, Nancy. The Spy with the Wooden Leg: The Story of Virginia Hall. 2012. (ENG.). 160p. (J). pap. 12.95 *(978-1-934617-16-8(4))*; 16.95 *(978-1-934617-15-1(6))* Elva Resa Publishing, LLC. (Alma Little).

Sahgal, Lara & Axelrod, Toby. Hans & Sophie Scholl, 01 vols., 1. 2016. (Holocaust Ser.). (ENG., Illus.). 112p. (J). 35.60 *(978-1-4994-6244-9(1)*, Rosen Young Adult) Rosen Publishing Group, Inc., The.

Walsh, Alison. Hugh O'Flaherty: His Wartime Adventures. 2011. (ENG., Illus.). 114p. (J). pap. 4.99 *(978-1-84889-058-9(3))* Collins Pr., The IRL. Dist: Vearsa.

WORLD WAR, 1939-1945—UNITED STATES

Bjorklund, Ruth. Internment: Japanese Americans in World War II. 2016. (Public Persecutions Ser.). 128p. (J). 45.64 *(978-1-5026-2323-2(4))* Cavendish Square Publishing.

Burgan, Michael. America in World War II. 2006. (Wars That Changed American History Ser.). 48p. (gr. 5-12). pap. 14.05 *(978-0-8368-7302-3(5))*; (Illus.). lib. bdg. 31.00 *(978-0-8368-7293-4(2))* Stevens, Gareth Publishing LLLP. (Gareth Stevens Secondary Library).

Center for Learning Staff. World War II: 1935-1945 — - Elementary U. S. History Series, 10 bks. 2003. (Social Studies Ser.). (Illus.). vi, 147p. (J). tchr. ed., spiral bd. 29.95 *(978-1-56077-737-3(0))* Center for Learning, The.

dePaola, Tomie. For the Duration: The War Years, 8 vols. dePaola, Tomie, illus. 2009. (26 Fairmount Avenue Book Ser.: 8). (ENG., Illus.). 80p. (J). (gr. 2-5). 17.99 *(978-0-399-25209-9(6)*, G.P. Putnam's Sons Books for Young Readers) Penguin Young Readers Group.

Donohue, Moira Rose. The Invasion of Normandy: Epic Battle of World War II. 2017. (Major Battles in US History (paperback) Ser.). (ENG., Illus.). 32p. (J). (gr. 4-7). pap. 9.95 ***(978-1-63517-080-1(X)***, Focus Readers) North Star Editions.

Dougherty, Steve. Pearl Harbor: The U. S. Enters World War II. 2009. (24/7 Goes to War Ser.). (ENG.). 64p. (J). (gr. 6-12). lib. bdg. 29.00 *(978-0-531-25525-4(5)*, Children's Pr.) Scholastic Library Publishing.

Dougherty, Steven. Pearl Harbor: The U. S. Enters World War II. 2009. (24/7: Goes to War-NEW Ser.). (ENG.). 64p. (J). (gr. 6-12). pap. 7.95 *(978-0-531-25450-9(X)*, Watts, Franklin) Scholastic Library Publishing.

Gitlin, Martin. The Great Depression & World War II: 1929-1945. 2007. (Presidents of the United States Ser.). (Illus.). 48p. (J). (gr. 4-7). lib. bdg. 29.05 *(978-1-59036-749-0(9))*; per. 10.95 *(978-1-59036-750-6(2))* Weigl Pubs., Inc.

—World War II on the Home Front: An Interactive History Adventure, 1 vol. 2012. (You Choose: History Ser.). (ENG.). 112p. (gr. 3-4). pap. 6.95 *(978-1-4296-7998-5(0))*; lib. bdg. 31.99 *(978-1-4296-6019-8(8))* Capstone Press of Coughlan Cos. (You Choose Bks.).

—World War II U. S. Homefront: A History Perspectives Book. 2014. (Perspectives Library). (ENG., Illus.). 32p. (J). (gr. 4-8). 28.50 *(978-1-63137-621-4(7)*, 205267) Cherry Lake Publishing.

Gitlin, Marty. World War II. 2016. (Illus.). 48p. (J). *(978-1-5105-1296-2(9))* SmartBook Media, Inc.

Grant, R. G. Why Did Hiroshima Happen? 2010. (Moments in History Ser.). (Illus.). 48p. (YA). (gr. 5-9). lib. bdg. 31.95 *(978-1-4339-4163-4(5))*; (gr. 6-8). pap. 14.05 *(978-1-4339-4164-1(3)*, Gareth Stevens Secondary Library) Stevens, Gareth Publishing LLLP.

Halpern, Monica & National Geographic Learning Staff. The Home Front During World War II. 2007. (Nonfiction Reading & Writing Workshops Ser.). (ENG., Illus.). 40p. pap. 19.95 *(978-0-7922-4558-2(X))* CENGAGE Learning.

Isserman, Maurice. World War II. 2nd rev. ed. 2010. (America at War Ser.). 272p. (gr. 6-12). 45.00 *(978-0-8160-8185-1(9)*, Chelsea Hse.) Facts On File, Inc.

Jones, Tina C. Mothballs, Mothballs All in the Hall: Memories of a Great World War II Hero. Jones, Tina C. & Balogh, Jared, illus. 2012. 48p. pap. 24.95 *(978-1-4560-7483-8(0))* America Star Bks.

Lassieur, Allison, et al. The World War II Experience: An Interactive History Adventure, 1 vol. 2014. (You Choose: History Ser.). (ENG.). 328p. (gr. 3-4). pap. 14.95 *(978-1-4765-2169-5(7)*, You Choose Bks.) Capstone Press of Coughlan Cos.

Marcovitz, Hal. Cause & Effect: World War II. 2017. (ENG.). 80p. (YA). (gr. 5-12). ***(978-1-68282-174-9(9))*** ReferencePoint Pr., Inc.

Marrin, Albert. FDR & the American Crisis. 2015. (ENG., Illus.). 336p. (YA). (gr. 7). 24.99 *(978-0-385-75359-3(4))*; lib. bdg. 27.99 *(978-0-385-75360-9(8))* Random Hse. Children's Bks. (Knopf Bks. for Young Readers).

McNeill, Allison & Hanes, Richard Clay. American Home Front in World War II Reference Library Cumulative Index. 2004. (American Homefront in World War II Reference Library). (ENG.). 32p. 5.00 *(978-0-7876-9125-7(9)*, UXL) Cengage Gale.

Oppenheim, Joanne F. Dear Miss Breed: True Stories of the Japanese American Incarceration During World War II & a Librarian Who Made a Difference. 2006. (ENG., Illus.). 288p. (J). (gr. 7-12). 22.99 *(978-0-439-56992-7(3))* Scholastic, Inc.

O'Reilly, Bill. The Day the World Went Nuclear: Dropping the Atom Bomb & the End of World War II in the Pacific. 2017. (ENG., Illus.). 320p. (J). 19.99 ***(978-1-250-12033-5(0)***, 9781250120335, Holt, Henry & Co. Bks. For Young Readers) Holt, Henry & Co.

Petersen, Christine. Rosie the Riveter. 2008. (Cornerstones of Freedom Ser.). (ENG.). 48p. (J). pap. 5.95 *(978-0-531-20840-3(0)*, Children's Pr.) Scholastic Library Publishing.

Peterson, Sheryl. The Great Depression & World War II. 2011. (Explorer Library: Language Arts Explorer Ser.). (ENG.). 32p. (gr. 4-8). pap. 14.21 *(978-1-61080-287-1(X)*, 201210); lib. bdg. 28.50 *(978-1-61080-199-7(7)*, 201174) Cherry Lake Publishing.

Rice, Earle, Jr. How Franklin D. Roosevelt Fought World War II. 2017. (Presidents at War Ser.). 128p. (J). (gr. 8-8). lib. bdg. 37.27 ***(978-0-7660-8527-5(9))*** Enslow Pubs., Inc.

Robertson, James. World War II: 1939-1945. Kunstler, Mort, illus. 2016. (See American History Ser.). (ENG.). 48p. (J). (gr. 2). 13.95 *(978-0-7892-1261-0(7)*, Abbeville Kids) Abbeville Pr., Inc.

Roppelt, Donna. Women Go to Work, 1941-1945. 2012. (J). pap. *(978-1-4222-2367-3(1))* Mason Crest.

—Women Go to Work, 1941-1945. Harrington, A. Page, ed. 2012. (Finding a Voice: Women's Fight for Equality in U. S. Society Ser.). 64p. (J). (gr. 5). 22.95 *(978-1-4222-2357-4(4))* Mason Crest.

Rose, Simon. World War II: 1939-1945. 2014. (Illus.). 48p. (J). *(978-1-62127-659-3(7))* Weigl Pubs., Inc.

Rubin, Susan Goldman. The Flag with Fifty-Six Stars: A Gift from the Survivors of Mauthausen. Farnsworth, Bill, illus. 2006. (ENG.). 40p. (J). (gr. 1-5). reprint ed. 6.95 *(978-0-8234-2019-3(1))* Holiday Hse., Inc.

Stein, R. Conrad. The Home Front During World War II in American History. 2003. (In American History Ser.). (Illus.). 112p. (J). (gr. 5-12). lib. bdg. 26.60 *(978-0-7660-1984-3(5))* Enslow Pubs., Inc.

—World War II in the Pacific: From Pearl Harbor to Nagasaki. 2011. (United States at War Ser.). (Illus.). 128p. (J). (gr. 5-18). lib. bdg. 33.27 *(978-0-7660-3640-6(5))* Enslow Pubs., Inc.

Stone, Tanya Lee. Courage Has No Color - The True Story of the Triple Nickles: America's First Black Paratroopers. 2013. (ENG., Illus.). 160p. (J). (gr. 5). pap. 17.99 *(978-0-7636-6548-7(7))*; 24.99 *(978-0-7636-5117-6(6))* Candlewick Pr.

Taylor, Charlotte & Kent, Deborah. The Internment of Japanese Americans. 2015. (Our Shared History Ser.). (ENG.). 128p. (J). (gr. 7-7). lib. bdg. 37.27 *(978-0-7660-7008-0(5))* Enslow Pubs., Inc.

The U.S. Army in World War II. 2014. (ENG.). 48p. (J). lib. bdg. 29.00 *(978-0-531-20496-2(0))* Scholastic Library Publishing.

Wallenfeldt, Jeff, ed. A New World Power: America from 1920 To 1945. 2012. (Documenting America: the Primary Source Documents of a Nation Ser.). (ENG., Illus.). 192p. (YA). (gr. 10-12). 82.20 *(978-1-61530-784-5(2))* Rosen Publishing Group, Inc., The.

Wallenfeldt, Jeffrey H. A New World Power: America from 1920 to 1945. 2012. (Documenting America: the Primary Source Documents of a Nation Ser.). (ENG., Illus.). 192p. (J). (gr. 10-12). lib. bdg. 41.10 *(978-1-61530-694-7(3))* Rosen Publishing Group, Inc., The.

Whiting, Jim. The Story of the Attack on Pearl Harbor. 2005. (Monumental Milestones Ser.). (Illus.). 48p. (YA). (gr. 4-7). lib. bdg. 29.95 *(978-1-58415-397-9(0))* Mitchell Lane Pubs., Inc.

Whitman Publishing, creator. Discover World War II: History Project Toolkit. 2011. pap. 19.95 *(978-0-7948-3588-0(0))* Whitman Publishing LLC.

World War II 1939-1945. 2010. (Discovering U. S. History Ser.). (Illus.). 136p. (gr. 5-8). 35.00 *(978-1-60413-358-5(9)*, Chelsea Hse.) Facts On File, Inc.

WORLD WIDE WEB

see also Internet

Colt, James P. & Rogers, Marcus K. Cyberpredators. 2011. (Cybersafety Ser.). (Illus.). 136p. (gr. 6-12). 39.95 *(978-1-60413-698-2(7))* Facts On File, Inc.

Green, Sara. Sergey Brin. 2014. (Tech Icons Ser.). (ENG., Illus.). 24p. (J). (gr. 3-8). lib. bdg. 25.95 *(978-1-60014-993-1(6)*, Pilot Bks.) Bellwether Media.

Hamilton, John. Internet, 1 vol. 2005. (Straight to the Source Ser.). (ENG., Illus.). 32p. (gr. k-6). 27.07 *(978-1-59197-544-1(1)*, Checkerboard Library) ABDO Publishing Co.

Hixson, Bryce. The Original World Wide Web. Hixson, Bryce, illus. 2003. (Illus.). (J). per. 12.95 *(978-1-931801-07-2(X))* Loose In The Lab.

McPherson, Stephanie Sammartino. Tim Berners-Lee: Inventor of the World Wide Web. 2009. (USA TODAY Lifeline Biographies Ser.). (ENG., Illus.). 112p. (J). (gr. 6-12). lib. bdg. 34.60 *(978-0-8225-7273-2(7))* Lerner Publishing Group.

Minton, Eric. Spam & Scams: Using Email Safely, 1 vol., 1. 2014. (Stay Safe Online Ser.). (ENG.). 32p. (J). (gr. 4-6). 26.25 *(978-1-4777-2934-2(8)*, PowerKids Pr.) Rosen Publishing Group, Inc., The.

Owings, Lisa. Stay Safe Online. 2013. (Library Smarts Ser.). (ENG., Illus.). 24p. (gr. -1-2). lib. bdg. 23.93 *(978-1-4677-1505-8(0)*, Lerner Pubns.) Lerner Publishing Group.

Popek, Emily. Understanding the World of User-Generated Content. 2010. (Digital & Information Literacy Ser.). (ENG.). 48p. (YA). pap. 11.75 *(978-1-4488-0598-3(8))*; lib. bdg. 29.25 *(978-1-4358-9431-0(6))* Rosen Publishing Group, Inc., The. (Rosen Reference).

Porterfield, Jason. Tim Berners-Lee, 01 vols., 1. 2016. (Tech Pioneers Ser.). (ENG.). 112p. (J). 35.60 *(978-1-4994-6290-6(5)*, Rosen Young Adult) Rosen Publishing Group, Inc., The.

Randolph, Ryan P. New Research Techniques: Getting the Most Out of Search Engine Tools. 2011. (Digital & Information Literacy Ser.). (ENG., Illus.). 48p. (J). pap. 11.75 *(978-1-4488-2292-8(0))*; lib. bdg. 29.25 *(978-1-4488-1321-6(2))* Rosen Publishing Group, Inc., The. (Rosen Reference).

Scientific American Staff. The Future of the Web. 2009. (Scientific American Cutting-Edge Science Ser.). 118p. (gr. 9-9). 63.90 *(978-1-60853-081-6(7))* Rosen Publishing Group, Inc., The.

Vanden-Heuvel, John C., Sr. & Ostrovsky, Andrey. ABCs of the Web. Holmes, Tom, illus. 2016. (ENG.). 28p. (J). (gr. -1-3). bds. 8.99 *(978-1-4998-0312-9(5))* Little Bee Books Inc.

Ward-Johnson, Chris. World Wide Web: A Magic Mouse Guide. Laughing Gravy Design Staff, illus. 2003. (Magic Mouse Guides). 32p. (J). lib. bdg. 23.94 *(978-0-7660-2262-1(5))* Enslow Pubs., Inc.

Web Wisdom. 2015. (Web Wisdom Ser.). (ENG.). 48p. (J). (gr. 5-5). 188.16 *(978-1-5026-0316-6(0))* Cavendish Square Publishing.

Yearling, Tricia. The Internet: What It Is & How to Use It. 2016. (Zoom in on Technology Ser.). (ENG., Illus.). 24p. (J). (gr. 2-2). lib. bdg. 22.60 *(978-0-7660-7382-1(3))* Enslow Pubs., Inc.

—The World Wide Web: What It Is & How to Use It. 2016. (Zoom in on Technology Ser.). (ENG., Illus.). 24p. (J). (gr. 2-2). pap. 9.35 *(978-0-7660-7386-9(6))* Enslow Pubs., Inc.

WORLD'S FAIRS

see Exhibitions; Fairs

WORMS

Alessi, Jolene. Zombie Fish. 2015. (Zombie Animals: Parasites Take Control! Ser.). (ENG., Illus.). 24p. (J). (gr. 2-3). pap. 8.15 *(978-1-4824-2840-7(7))* Stevens, Gareth Publishing LLLP.

Black, Nessa. Worms. 2017. (Spot Creepy Crawlies Ser.). (ENG.). 16p. (gr. k-3). 17.95 ***(978-1-68151-111-5(8))*** Amicus Publishing.

Bodden, Valerie. Creepy Creatures - Worms. 2011. (Creepy Creatures Ser.). (ENG.). 24p. (J). (gr. 1-3). pap. 7.99 *(978-0-89812-570-2(7)*, Creative Paperbacks) Creative Co., The.

—Worms. 2011. (Creepy Creatures Ser.). 24p. (J). (gr. 1-3). 24.25 *(978-1-58341-997-7(7)*, Creative Education) Creative Co., The.

—Worms. 2010. (ENG., Illus.). 24p. (J). 8.95 *(978-1-926853-77-2(6))* Saunders Bk. Co. CAN. Dist: Creative Co., The.

Cheek, Diane. Wiggly Workers. 2011. 28p. pap. 12.03 *(978-1-4634-0022-4(5))* AuthorHouse.

Ciletti, Barbara. Roundworms. 2017. (Awful, Disgusting Parasites Ser.). (ENG., Illus.). 32p. (J). (gr. 3-7). 31.35 ***(978-1-68072-009-9(0))*** Black Rabbit Bks.

—Tapeworms. 2017. (Awful, Disgusting Parasites Ser.). (ENG., Illus.). 32p. (J). (gr. 3-7). 31.35 ***(978-1-68072-010-5(4))*** Black Rabbit Bks.

Clark, Willow & Rockwood, Leigh. Worms Are Gross! 2010. (Creepy Crawlies Ser.). (Illus.). 24p. (gr. k-2). (YA). lib. bdg. 22.60 *(978-1-4488-0700-0(X))*; (J). pap. 8.25 *(978-1-4488-1361-2(1)*, PowerKids Pr.) Rosen Publishing Group, Inc., The.

Coleman, Miriam. Leeches Eat Blood!, 1 vol., 1. 2014. (Disgusting Animal Dinners Ser.). (ENG.). 24p. (J). (gr. k-5). 23.60 *(978-1-4777-2881-9(3)*, PowerKids Pr.) Rosen Publishing Group, Inc., The.

Evans, Arthur V. Grzimek's Student Animal Life Resource: Crustaceans, Mollusks & Segmented Worms. Harris, Madeline S. et al, eds. 2005. (Grzimek's Student Animal Life Resource Ser.). (ENG., Illus.). 384p. (J). (gr. 3-7). 106.00 *(978-0-7876-9411-1(8)*, UXL) Cengage Gale.

Gravel, Élise. The Worm. (Disgusting Critters Ser.). (ENG., Illus.). 32p. (J). (gr. 1-4). 2016. pap. 5.99 *(978-1-101-91841-8(1))* 2014. 10.99 *(978-1-77049-633-0(5))* Tundra Bks. CAN. (Tundra Bks.). Dist: Penguin Random Hse. LLC.

Gray, Susan H. Experiment with Bugs. 2010. (Explorer Junior Library: Science Explorer Junior Ser.). (ENG.). 32p. (gr. 3-6). lib. bdg. 28.50 *(978-1-60279-842-7(7)*, 200550) Cherry Lake Publishing.

Green, Jen. Worms. 2009. (Illus.). 52p. (J). *(978-0-7172-8078-0(0))* Grolier, Ltd.

Hanson, Lynne. Worm World: Clue Books. 2008. (Illus.). 32p. (J). pap. 4.00 *(978-1-58793-226-7(1))* Creekside Publishing.

Inserra, Rose. Worms. 2010. (Weird, Wild, & Wonderful Ser.). (Illus.). 24p. (J). (gr. 2-5). lib. bdg. 22.00 *(978-1-4339-3577-0(5)*, Gareth Stevens Learning Library) Stevens, Gareth Publishing LLLP.

Kalman, Bobbie. The Life Cycle of an Earthworm. 2003. (Life Cycle Ser.). (ENG., Illus.). 32p. (J). pap. *(978-0-7787-0696-0(6))* Crabtree Publishing Co.

—Les Vers de Terre. 2009. (Petit Monde Vivant Ser.). (FRE., Illus.). 32p. (J). pap. 9.95 *(978-2-89579-228-4(3))* Bayard Canada Livres CAN. Dist: Crabtree Publishing Co.

Kawa, Katie. Tapeworms. 2015. (Freaky Freeloaders: Bugs That Feed on People Ser.). (ENG.). 24p. (J). (gr. 2-3). 23.60 *(978-1-4994-0765-5(3)*, PowerKids Pr.) Rosen Publishing Group, Inc., The.

Kite, L. Patricia. Leeches. 2004. (Early Bird Nature Bks.). (ENG., Illus.). 48p. (gr. 2-5). 26.60 *(978-0-8225-3054-1(6)*, Lerner Pubns.) Lerner Publishing Group.

Lane, Bonnie. Bob the Inchworm & the Four Seasons. 2009. 20p. pap. 11.00 *(978-1-4389-9833-6(3))* AuthorHouse.

Lehman, Julie. Kyle in His Compost Pile: The Story of a Red Wiggler. 2010. 28p. pap. 14.99 *(978-1-4490-9112-5(1))* AuthorHouse.

Marsico, Katie. Leeches. 2015. (ENG., Illus.). 48p. (J). lib. bdg. *(978-0-531-21394-0(3)*, Orchard Bks.) Scholastic, Inc.

Mitchell, Susan K. Biggest vs. Smallest Creepy, Crawly Creatures. 2010. (Biggest vs. Smallest Animals Ser.). (Illus.). 24p. (J). 22.60 *(978-0-7660-3581-2(6)*, Enslow Elementary) Enslow Pubs., Inc.

Murray, Laura K. Worms. 2015. (Illus.). 32p. (J). *(978-1-60818-585-6(0)*, Creative Education) Creative Co., The.

—Worms: Seedlings. 2016. (Seedlings Ser.). (ENG.). 24p. (J). (gr. k-2). pap. 7.99 *(978-1-62832-190-6(3)*, Creative Paperbacks) Creative Co., The.

Nelson, Robin. Worms. 2009. pap. 34.95 *(978-0-7613-4111-6(0))*; (ENG.). 24p. 23.93 *(978-0-7613-4064-5(5)*, Lerner Pubns.) Lerner Publishing Group.

Neuman, Pearl. Bloodsucking Leeches. 2009. (No Backbone! Ser.). (Illus.). 24p. (J). (gr. k-3). lib. bdg. 21.28 *(978-1-59716-755-0(X))* Bearport Publishing Co., Inc.

Peters, Polly. The Wim Wom from the Mustard Mill. Angeletti, Roberta, illus. 2008. (Child's Play Library). (ENG.). 32p. (J). (gr. -1-3). pap. *(978-1-84643-253-8(7))* Child's Play International Ltd.

Schuetz, Kari. Mealworms. 2015. (Creepy Crawlies Ser.). (ENG., Illus.). 24p. (J). (gr. k-3). lib. bdg. 25.95 *(978-1-62617-224-1(2)*, Blastoff! Readers) Bellwether Media.

Smalley, Carol. A Project Guide to Sponges, Worms, & Mollusks. 2010. (Life Science Projects for Kids Ser.). (Illus.). 48p. (J). (gr. 4-8). lib. bdg. 29.95 *(978-1-58415-876-9(X))* Mitchell Lane Pubs., Inc.

Sobol, Richard. The Story of Silk: From Worm Spit to Woven Scarves. Sobol, Richard, illus. 2012. (Traveling Photographer Ser.). (ENG., Illus.). 40p. (J). (gr. 1-4). 17.99 *(978-0-7636-4165-8(0))* Candlewick Pr.

Somervill, Barbara A. Leeches: Waiting in the Water. 2009. (Bloodsuckers Ser.). 24p. (gr. 2-3). 42.50 *(978-1-61511-633-1(8)*, PowerKids Pr.) Rosen Publishing Group, Inc., The.

Sroda, George. Facts about Nightcrawlers: Redworms & Garden Worms. (Illus.). 157p. (J). reprint ed. 10.95 *(978-0-9604486-0-9(8))* Sroda, George.

Tilden, Thomasine E. Lewis. Worms! Parasites Plague a Village. 2011. (J). pap. *(978-0-545-32804-3(7))* Scholastic, Inc.

Trueit, Trudi Strain. Slugs, Snails, & Worms. 2013. 32p. (J). (gr. 6-9). 28.50 *(978-1-60870-247-3(2))* Cavendish Square Publishing.

—Slugs, Snails & Worms. 2013. (Backyard Safari 2 Ser.). 32p. (J). (gr. 6-9). pap. 10.58 *(978-1-62712-030-2(0))* Cavendish Square Publishing.

—Worms. 2009. (Benchmark Rebus Ser.). 24p. (gr. k-1). 15.95 *(978-0-7614-3966-0(8))* Marshall Cavendish Corp.

Veitch, Catherine. Bug Babies, 1 vol. 2013. (Animal Babies Ser.). (ENG.). 24p. (gr. -1-1). 22.65 *(978-1-4329-7495-4(5))*; pap. 35.94 *(978-1-4329-8427-4(6))*; pap. 6.95 *(978-1-4329-8420-5(9))* Heinemann-Raintree. (Acorn).

WORMS—FICTION

Amato, Mary. The Word Eater. Ryniak, Christopher, illus. 2005. (ENG.). 151p. (J). (gr. 3-7). reprint ed. pap. 7.99 *(978-0-8234-1940-1(1))* Holiday Hse., Inc.

Arnold, Caroline. Wiggle & Waggle. Peterson, Mary, illus. 2009. (ENG.). 48p. (J). (gr. k-3). pap. 5.95 *(978-1-58089-307-7(4))* Charlesbridge Publishing, Inc.

Austrian, J. J. Worm Loves Worm. Curato, Mike, illus. 2016. 32p. (J). (gr. -1-3). 17.99 *(978-0-06-238633-5(6))* HarperCollins Pubs.

Balash, Sue Beth. Mimi the Inchworm. 2009. (ENG.). 32p. pap. 10.95 *(978-1-933916-44-6(3)*, Ferne Pr.) Nelson Publishing & Marketing.

Barber, Alison. The Little Green Pea. Keiser, Paige, illus. 2009. (ENG.). 28p. (J). (gr. k-6). 15.95 *(978-1-58536-448-0(7))* Sleeping Bear Pr.

Barnes, Brenda J. Calvin Compost in Organic City: The Story of an Earthworm. Williams, Nancy E., ed. 2012. 28p. (J). (-18). pap. 10.98 *(978-1-938526-21-3(X))* Laurus Bks.

Bartolome, Teresita Africano. Where Is Warren D. Worm?, 1 vol. 2010. 28p. 24.95 *(978-1-4489-5869-6(5))* PublishAmerica, Inc.

Batten, Scott A. Johnny the Phoenix. 2008. 64p. pap. 23.95 *(978-1-4343-7297-0(9))* AuthorHouse.

Becton, Sarah Walker, et al. Wormy Worm. Becton, Daniel Walker, illus. 2007. 88p. (J). 19.95 *(978-1-878398-59-8(8)*, Blue Note Bks.) Blue Note Pubns.

Bedford, William. The Glowworm Who Lost Her Glow. Joyce, Sophie, illus. 2005. (Blue Go Bananas Ser.). (ENG.). 48p. (J). (gr. 1-2). *(978-0-7787-2652-4(5))* Crabtree Publishing Co.

Beitler, Stacey Ann. Willy Goes to School. 2011. 28p. pap. 14.50 *(978-1-61204-397-5(6)*, Strategic Bk. Publishing) Strategic Book Publishing & Rights Agency (SBPRA).

Bennett, Bonnie. Howard the Worm. 2011. 28p. pap. 16.95 *(978-1-4626-0004-5(2))* America Star Bks.

Bill, Poppa. The Adventures of Huggyman & Wiggly Worm: The Explorers meet Mr. Moley. 2011. (Illus.). 28p. pap. 14.09 *(978-1-4567-7295-6(3))* AuthorHouse.

Blackbird. Mr. Hookworm. Blackbird, illus. 2006. (Illus.). (J). per. 18.00 *(978-0-9789798-6-7(9)*, 978-0-9789798-6-7) Blackbird's World Publishing Co.

Brendler, Carol & Brendler, Carol H. Winnie Finn, Worm Farmer. Hoyt, Ard, illus. 2009. (ENG.). 32p. (J). (gr. -1-3). 17.99 *(978-0-374-38440-1(1)*, 9780374384401, Farrar, Straus & Giroux (BYR)) Farrar, Straus & Giroux.

Brody, Lazer. The Worry Worm. Shapiro, Rebecca, illus. 2007. 26p. (J). 26.95 *(978-0-9797530-1-5(5))* Nachum Publishing.

Brown, Adam. The Adventures of Wormie Wormington Book Three: Wormie & the Snowball. Smart, Andy, illus. 2013. 48p. pap. *(978-0-9919196-3-5(7))* Beckon Creative.

—The Adventures of Wormie Wormington Book Two: Wormie & the Kite. Smart, Andy, illus. 2013. 48p. pap. *(978-0-9919196-2-8(9))* Beckon Creative.

Brown, Adam & Smart, Andy. The Adventures of Wormie Wormington Book One: Wormie & the Fish. Smart, Andy, illus. 2013. (Illus.). 50p. pap. *(978-0-9919196-0-4(2))* Beckon Creative.

Bruel, Robert O. Bob & Otto. Bruel, Nick, illus. 2007. (ENG.). 32p. (J). (gr. -1-3). 17.99 *(978-1-59643-203-1(9)*, 9781596432031) Roaring Brook Pr.

Carpenter, Cindy. The Little Inchworm. 2008. 16p. per. 24.95 *(978-1-4241-9681-4(7))* America Star Bks.

Carr, Heather. The Jiggleworm. Carr, Greg, illus. 2005. 18p. (J). 21.95 incl. audio compact disk *(978-0-9768450-0-3(8)*, Giggletins) Le Bk. Moderne, LLC.

Clinton, Ann M. Stevie Inchworm. Canavan, Jean, illus. 2009. 24p. (J). 31.99 *(978-1-4363-9471-0(6))* Xlibris Corp.

Coccia, Mina. Mother Nature & Mz Bee. 2012. 36p. pap. 14.95 *(978-1-4575-0709-0(9))* Dog Ear Publishing, LLC.

Coldwell, Lamar. The Worm Hunt. 2016. (Rosen REAL Readers: STEM & STEAM Collection). 8p. (gr. 1-k). pap. 5.46 *(978-1-5081-2628-7(3)*, Rosen Classroom) Rosen Publishing Group, Inc., The.

Cook, Sherry & Johnson, Terri. Watery William, 26. Kuhn, Jesse, illus. l.t. ed. 2006. (Quirkles — Exploring Phonics through Science Ser.: 23). 32p. (J). 7.99 *(978-1-933815-22-0(1)*, Quirkles, The) Creative 3, LLC.

Coulton, Mia. Danny & the Little Worm. Coulton, Mia, photos by. 2004. (ENG., Illus.). pap. 5.35 *(978-0-9746475-6-2(X))* Maryruth Bks., Inc.

Cronin, Doreen. Diary of a Worm. 2003. (Illus.). (J). 127.92 *(978-0-06-056900-6(X))*; 127.92 *(978-0-06-056901-3(8))* HarperCollins Pubs.

—Diary of a Worm. Bliss, Harry, illus. 2003. 40p. (J). (gr. -1-3). (ENG.). 16.99 *(978-0-06-000150-6(X))*; lib. bdg. 18.89 *(978-0-06-000151-3(8))* HarperCollins Pubs.

—Diary of a Worm. Bliss, Harry, illus. pap. incl. audio compact disk *(978-1-59112-873-1(0))*; pap. incl. audio *(978-1-59112-869-4(2))*; pap. 16.95 incl. audio *(978-1-59112-867-0(6))*; pap. 18.95 incl. audio compact disk *(978-1-59112-871-7(4))* Live Oak Media.

—Diary of a Worm. 2004. (Illus.). (J). 28.95 incl. audio compact disk *(978-1-59112-872-4(2))* Live Oak Media.

—Diary of a Worm. 2013. (Diary of a Worm: I Can Read Level 1 Ser.). (J). lib. bdg. 13.55 *(978-0-606-31819-8(4)*, Turtleback) Turtleback Bks.

—Diary of a Worm: Nat the Gnat. Bliss, Harry, illus. 2014. (I Can Read Level 1 Ser.). (ENG.). 32p. (J). (gr. -1-3). pap. 3.99 *(978-0-06-208707-2(X))* HarperCollins Pubs.

—Diary of a Worm: Teacher's Pet. Bliss, Harry & Nez, John, illus. 2013. (I Can Read Level 1 Ser.). (ENG.). 32p. (J). (gr. -1-3). 16.99 *(978-0-06-208705-8(3))*; pap. 3.99 *(978-0-06-208704-1(5))* HarperCollins Pubs.

—Nat the Gnat. 2014. (Diary of a Worm: I Can Read Level 1 Ser.). (J). lib. bdg. 13.55 *(978-0-606-35494-3(8))* Turtleback Bks.

Cueva, Susana & Shibaja, Calixto. Lita the Hardworking Worm/Lita la Trabajadora. 2012. (ENG & SPA.). 26p. pap. 9.99 *(978-0-9883927-1-7(2))* Carsume.

Cummings, Troy. Day of the Night Crawlers. 2013. (Notebook of Doom Ser.: 2). (ENG.). 96p. (J). (gr. 1-3). 15.99 *(978-0-545-49324-6(2))*; pap. 4.99 *(978-0-545-49325-3(0))*; E-Book *(978-0-545-49327-7(7))* Scholastic, Inc.

—Day of the Night Crawlers. 2013. (Notebook of Doom Ser.: 2). lib. bdg. 14.75 *(978-0-606-32368-0(6)*, Turtleback) Turtleback Bks.

Defreitas, Henrietta. Henratty Mortimer Presents: Poppy the Most Beautiful Worm. 2012. (Illus.). 28p. pap. 21.35 *(978-1-4772-3890-5(5))* AuthorHouse.

Dinardo, Jeff. Worm & Farmer Maguire: Teamwork/Working Together. Joven, John, illus. 2014. (Funny Bone Readers: Being a Friend Ser.). 24p. (gr. -1-1). pap. 4.99 *(978-1-939656-07-0(9))* Red Chair Pr.

Donaldson, Julia. Superworm. Scheffler, Axel, illus. 2014. (ENG.). 32p. (J). (gr. -1-3). 16.99 *(978-0-545-59176-8(7)*, Levine, Arthur A. Bks.) Scholastic, Inc.

Dozier, Mike. The Little Inchworm with the Big Dream. 2009. (J). pap. 12.50 *(978-1-61623-365-5(6))* Independent Pub.

Duncan-Goetz, Betty. Squiggle the Wiggle Worm. 2011. (Illus.). 20p. (gr. -1). pap. 13.77 *(978-1-4269-5585-3(5))* Trafford Publishing.

Eastabrooks, Linda. Willie's New Home. 2008. 24p. per. 24.95 *(978-1-4241-8931-1(4))* America Star Bks.

Eldridge, VonDa. Wiggles the Worm, 1 vol. 2010. 26p. pap. 24.95 *(978-1-4489-2547-6(9))* PublishAmerica, Inc.

Ellefson, D. R. Willie Woolly Wiggle Worm. 2011. 20p. pap. 24.95 *(978-1-4626-2624-3(6))* America Star Bks.

Fettig, Pamela. Leelah at the Lake. Strecker, Darren, illus. 2010. 28p. pap. 9.99 *(978-1-60844-697-1(2))* Dog Ear Publishing, LLC.

Freeman, Marcia S. Catfish & Spaghetti. Stock, Rose, illus. 2013. (Maupin House Ser.). (ENG.). 48p. (gr. 3-5). pap. 4.50 *(978-0-929895-21-5(5))* Maupin Hse. Publishing.

French, Vivian. Yucky Worms. Ahlberg, Jessica, illus. 2012. (Read & Wonder Ser.). (ENG.). 32p. (J). (gr. -1-3). pap. 6.99 *(978-0-7636-5817-5(0))* Candlewick Pr.

—Yucky Worms. 2012. (Read & Wonder Ser.). lib. bdg. 17.20 *(978-0-606-23803-8(4)*, Turtleback) Turtleback Bks.

Friedman, Joe. Boobela & the Belching Giant. Childs, Sam, illus. 2010. (ENG.). 128p. 12.99 *(978-1-4440-0046-7(2))* Orion Publishing Group, Ltd. GBR. Dist: Hachette Bk. Group.

—Boobela, Worm & Potion Power. Childs, Sam, illus. 2010. (ENG.). 128p. 12.99 *(978-1-4440-0045-0(4))* Orion Publishing Group, Ltd. GBR. Dist: Hachette Bk. Group.

A Friend with No Name. 2006. (ENG., Illus.). 28p. per. 11.95 *(978-1-59800-476-2(X))* Outskirts Pr., Inc.

Gentry, J. B. Lily the Worm. 2011. 32p. pap. 15.99 *(978-1-4568-2926-1(2))* Xlibris Corp.

Georgieva, Zoia. Herman the Earth Worm: Illustrated by Emma C. Van Dyke. 2008. pap. 18.00 *(978-0-8059-8630-3(8))* Dorrance Publishing Co., Inc.

Gibson, James E. Rico, the Mysterious Worm, 1 vol. 2009. 17p. pap. 24.95 *(978-1-60749-148-4(6))* America Star Bks.

Gibson, Sylvia Scott. Ricky the Skating Worm & Friends, 1 vol. Gibson, Gregory V., illus. 2009. 21p. pap. 24.95 *(978-1-60836-473-2(9))* America Star Bks.

Gilbert, Scott W. The Adventures of Willie the Worm: Willie's Big Adventure. 2012. 28p. pap. 19.99 *(978-1-4772-5407-3(2))* AuthorHouse.

Gleitzman, Morris. Worm Story. 2016. (ENG.). 160p. (J). (gr. 1-3). 14.99 *(978-0-14-330893-5(9))* Random Hse. Australia AUS. Dist: Independent Pubs. Group.

Green, Brandon. This Wriggler Is a Giggler a Review of Diary of a Worm. 2017. (Text Connections Guided Close Reading Ser.). (J). (gr. 2). *(978-1-4900-1836-2(0))* Benchmark Education Co.

Hart, Janice. Henry & the Oranges: Henry's Wild Adventures. McDonald, Suzi, illus. 2010. 32p. pap. 13.00 *(978-1-60860-911-6(1)*, Eloquent Bks.) Strategic Book Publishing & Rights Agency (SBPRA).

Hemingway, Edward. Bad Apple: A Tale of Friendship. Hemingway, Edward, illus. 2012. (ENG., Illus.). 32p. (J). (gr. -1-k). 16.99 *(978-0-399-25191-7(X)*, G.P. Putnam's Sons Books for Young Readers) Penguin Young Readers Group.

—Bad Apple's Perfect Day. Hemingway, Edward, illus. 2014. (ENG., Illus.). 32p. (J). (gr. -1-k). 16.99 *(978-0-399-16036-3(1)*, G.P. Putnam's Sons Books for Young Readers) Penguin Young Readers Group.

Hicks, Betty. The Worm Whisperer. Hatke, Ben, illus. 2013. (ENG.). 192p. (J). (gr. 3-7). 17.99 *(978-1-59643-490-5(2)*, 9781596434905) Roaring Brook Pr.

How to Eat Fried Worms. 116p. (J). (gr. 3-5). pap. 5.50 *(978-0-8072-1382-7(9)*, Listening Library) Random Hse. Audio Publishing Group.

How to Eat Fried Worms. 2005. (J). *(978-1-59564-950-8(6))* Steps To Literacy, LLC.

Huber, Mike. Bree Finds a Friend. Cowman, Joseph, illus. 2014. (ENG.). 32p. (J). (gr. -1). 15.95 *(978-1-60554-211-9(3))* Redleaf Pr.

Hunter, Lee Hargus. Welby the Worm Who Lost His Wiggle. Thompson, Lydia, illus. 2004. 32p. (J). (gr. -1-1). *(978-1-930093-04-1(7))* Brookfield Reader, Inc., The.

Huston, Donna. Inch by Inch. 2006. (J). spiral bd. 19.95 *(978-0-9771192-3-3(8))* Shayne Publishing.

Ingle, L. G. Little Willy Wiggle & Johnny Amigo. 2012. 40p. pap. *(978-1-77097-479-1(2))* FriesenPress.

Karen, Frantz. Children's Parables: Earthly Stories with Heavenly Lessons for Children. 2013. 162p. pap. 13.95 *(978-1-4908-1675-3(5)*, WestBow Pr.) Author Solutions, Inc.

Kayaalp, Suzan. Inch Worm Inch Worm. Merrifield, Monarca, illus. 2013. 20p. pap. 12.95 *(978-1-62838-072-9(1))* Page Publishing Inc.

Knudsen, Michelle. A Slimy Story. Billin-Frye, Paige, illus. 2004. 32p. (J). lib. bdg. 20.00 *(978-1-4242-1150-0(6))* Fitzgerald Bks.

—A Slimy Story. Billin-Frye, Paige, illus. 2004. (Science Solves It! Ser.). 32p. (J). (gr. -1-3). pap. 5.95 *(978-1-57565-144-6(0))* Kane Press, Inc.

Krulik, Nancy & dePaola, Tomie. Revenge of the Killer Worms #16. Blecha, Aaron, illus. 2015. (George Brown, Class Clown Ser.: 16). (ENG.). 128p. (J). (gr. 1-3). bds. 4.99 *(978-0-448-48284-2(3)*, Grosset & Dunlap) Penguin Young Readers Group.

Kugler, Tina. Snail & Worm Again. 2017. (ENG., Illus.). 32p. (J). (gr. 1-4). 16.99 *(978-0-544-79249-4(1)*, HMH Books For Young Readers) Houghton Mifflin Harcourt Publishing Co.

Kügler, Tina & Kügler, Carson, illus. Snail & Worm: Meet My Friend. 2016. (ENG.). 32p. (J). (gr. 1-4). 16.99 *(978-0-544-49412-1(1)*, HMH Books For Young Readers) Houghton Mifflin Harcourt Publishing Co.

Lansky, Bruce. Early Birdy Gets the Worm. Wummer, Amy, illus. 2010. 10p. (J). bds. 6.99 *(978-1-4169-9316-2(9))* Meadowbrook Pr.

Macdonald, Alan. Dirty Bertie: Worms! Roberts, David, illus. 2008. 96p. (J). (gr. 4-7). 3.99 *(978-1-56148-645-8(0)*, Good Bks.) Skyhorse Publishing Co., Inc.

MacDonald, Alan. Worms!, 1 vol. Roberts, David, illus. 2013. (Dirty Bertie Ser.). (ENG.). 112p. (gr. 1-3). pap. 4.95 *(978-1-4342-4823-7(2))*; lib. bdg. 25.32 *(978-1-4342-4619-6(1))* Stone Arch Bks.

Martin, Jayme. Skinny Little Tree. 2013. (ENG.). 28p. (J). 18.95 *(978-1-4787-0813-1(1))*; pap. 13.95 *(978-1-4787-0870-4(0))* Outskirts Pr., Inc.

Masterson, Josephine. Worm's World. 2015. (Rosen REAL Readers: STEM & STEAM Collection). (ENG.). 8p. pap. 5.46 *(978-1-4994-9564-5(1)*, Rosen Classroom) Rosen Publishing Group, Inc., The.

Mathews, Leslie. Edgar Wants to Be Alone. Dumont, Jean-françois, illus. 2015. (ENG.). 26p. (J). 16.00 *(978-0-8028-5457-5(5)*, Eerdmans Bks For Young Readers) Eerdmans, William B. Publishing Co.

Matt & Dave. Yuck's Pet Worm. Baines, Nigel, illus. 2013. (Yuck Ser.). (ENG.). 112p. (J). (gr. 2-5). 15.99 *(978-1-4424-8150-3(1))*; pap. 6.99 *(978-1-4424-8149-7(8))* Simon & Schuster/Paula Wiseman Bks. (Simon & Schuster/Paula Wiseman Bks.).

McBrier, Page. The Chicken & the Worm. Peterson, Rick, illus. 2008. 36p. (J). *(978-0-9798439-2-1(8))* Heifer Project International.

Messner, Kate. Marty McGuire Digs Worms! Floca, Brian, illus. 2012. (ENG.). 176p. (J). (gr. -1-3). pap. 5.99 *(978-0-545-14247-2(4)*, Scholastic Pr.) Scholastic, Inc.

Mickiewicz, Ricky. The Adventure of Wormee the Worm. 2011. 36p. (gr. 4-6). pap. 16.86 *(978-1-4634-0007-1(1))* AuthorHouse.

Miller, H. James. Willy the Worm Gets Lost. 2011. 24p. pap. 15.99 *(978-1-4568-9801-4(9))* Xlibris Corp.

Morris, Ann. Surprise in Auntie's Garden! Varkarotas, Heather, illus. 2013. (ENG.). (J). (gr. -1-3). 14.95 *(978-1-62086-224-7(7))* Mascot Bks., Inc.

Mr. Worm. 2008. (ENG & SPA., Illus.). 64p. (J). 14.95 *(978-0-9787462-6-1(0))* Heritage Publishing Co.

Myrl, Melanie. Why Some Birds Don't Eat Worms. 2011. 16p. 8.99 *(978-1-4490-4092-5(6))* AuthorHouse.

Nelsen, Sissy. Wiggly & Giggly. 2012. 24p. pap. 17.99 *(978-1-4772-6721-9(2))* AuthorHouse.

Newman, Jeff. The Greedy Worm. 2014. (J). *(978-1-4424-7195-5(6)*, Simon & Schuster Bks. For Young Readers) Simon & Schuster Bks. For Young Readers.

Oberlin, Linda. Eco in the Garden. Oberlin, Linda, illus. 2013. (Illus.). 26p. pap. 10.00 *(978-0-9911382-0-3(1))* Little Worm Publishing.

O'Callahan, Jay. Herman & Marguerite: An Earth Story, 1 vol. O'Callahan, Laura, illus. 2003. (ENG.). 36p. (J). (gr. k-3). pap. 7.95 *(978-1-56145-283-5(1))* Peachtree Pubs.

Oliver, Charlene. The Life & Tails of Herman the Worm. 2010. 20p. pap. 10.49 *(978-1-4490-9357-0(4))* AuthorHouse.

Park, Linda Sue. Project Mulberry. 2007. 225p. (gr. 4-7). 17.00 *(978-0-7569-7921-8(8))* Perfection Learning Corp.

Pauli, Gunter. Shiitake Love Caffeine. 2007. (Zeri Fables Ser.). (ENG & SPA., Illus.). 32p. (J). (gr. k-3). pap. 9.95 *(978-958-692-833-5(0))* Fondo Editorial Grania, Fundacion Hogares Juveniles Campesinos COL. Dist: Chelsea Green Publishing.

Pilkey, Dav. Mighty Robot vs. the Naughty Nightcrawlers from Neptune. Santat, Dan, illus. 2016. (Ricky Ricotta Ser.: 8). (ENG.). 128p. (J). (gr. -1-3). 15.99 *(978-0-439-37708-9(0))* Scholastic, Inc.

—Ricky Ricotta's Mighty Robot vs. the Naughty Nightcrawlers from Neptune. Santat, Dan, illus. 2016. (Ricky Ricotta Ser.: 8). (ENG.). 128p. (J). (gr. -1-3). pap. 5.99 *(978-0-439-37709-6(9))* Scholastic, Inc.

Pinczes, Elinor J. Inchworm & a Half. Enos, Randall, illus. 2003. (ENG.). 32p. (J). pap. 6.99 *(978-0-618-31101-9(7))* Houghton Mifflin Harcourt Publishing Co.

Pisella, Donna. The Blue Goblin. 2013. (ENG.). 30p. (J). 22.95 *(978-1-4787-1269-5(4))* Outskirts Pr., Inc.

Ray, Angela M. Herbie the Worm's Journey for Apples. 2008. 23p. pap. 24.95 *(978-1-60672-698-3(6))* America Star Bks.

Rinaldo, Jim. Wally the Worm's Adventures on the Farm. 2011. 28p. pap. 15.99 *(978-1-4568-9102-2(2))* Xlibris Corp.

Rockwell, Thomas. How to Eat Fried Worms. (J). (gr. 3-5). 179p. pap. 4.99 *(978-0-8072-1395-7(0))*; 2004. 116p. pap. 29.00 incl. audio *(978-0-8072-8797-2(0))* Random Hse. Audio Publishing Group. (Listening Library).

Rodriguez, Raul. Mamma's Worm House. 2011. 28p. pap. 15.99 *(978-1-4568-8498-7(0))* Xlibris Corp.

Rogers, Martha. Bernie's Journey. 2012. 24p. pap. 13.99 *(978-1-4497-5185-2(7)*, WestBow Pr.) Author Solutions, Inc.

Rosno, Connie. This Is My Lucky Day. 2011. 16p. pap. 9.49 *(978-1-4567-5534-8(X))* AuthorHouse.

Runton, Andy. Owly & Wormy, Bright Lights & Starry Nights. Runton, Andy, illus. 2012. (ENG., Illus.). 40p. (J). (gr. -1-3). 17.99 *(978-1-4169-5775-1(8)*, Atheneum Bks. for Young Readers) Simon & Schuster Children's Publishing.

—Owly & Wormy, Friends All Aflutter! Runton, Andy, illus. 2011. (ENG., Illus.). 40p. (J). (gr. -1-2). 16.99 *(978-1-4169-5774-4(X)*, Atheneum Bks. for Young Readers) Simon & Schuster Children's Publishing.

Ryan, Nancy. The Bookworm & His New Book. 2012. 32p. pap. 24.95 *(978-1-4626-6492-4(X))* America Star Bks.

Saveley, Barb. Curse of Moonstone Island. 2009. (Illus.). 36p. pap. 16.99 *(978-1-4389-4938-3(3))* AuthorHouse.

Scanlon, Liz Garton. Noodle & Lou. Howard, Arthur, illus. 2011. (ENG.). 32p. (J). (gr. -1-1). 15.99 *(978-1-4424-0288-1(1)*, Beach Lane Bks.) Beach Lane Bks.

Scarry, Richard. Best Lowly Worm Book Ever! 2014. (ENG., Illus.). 32p. (J). (gr. -1-2). 15.99 *(978-0-385-38782-8(2)*, Random Hse. Bks. for Young Readers) Random Hse. Children's Bks.

—Richard Scarry's Let's Count with Lowly. 2013. (Richard Scarry's Concept Bks.). (ENG.). 18p. (J). (gr. -1 — 1). bds. 7.99 *(978-0-7641-6600-6(X))* Barron's Educational Series, Inc.

—Richard Scarry's the Adventures of Lowly Worm. 2010. (ENG., Illus.). 44p. (J). (gr. -1-2). 12.95 *(978-1-4027-7214-6(9))* Sterling Publishing Co., Inc.

Schlunke, Eva & Fitzgerald, Paul. Little Worm's Big Question, 1 vol. 2016. (ENG., Illus.). 36p. (J). (gr. -1-3). pap. 9.95 *(978-1-78026-261-1(2))* New Internationalist Pubns., Ltd. GBR. Dist: Consortium Bk. Sales & Distribution.

Sheppard, Hazel A. The Inchy Books: Inch Worm Goes a Mile; Inchy Goes the Extra Mile; Inchy Goes the Distance, 3bks. 2005. (Illus.). (J). 28.85 *(978-0-9725286-3-4(6))* Sheppard Publishing.

—Inchy Goes the Distance. 2005. (Illus.). (J). 9.95 *(978-0-9725286-2-7(8))* Sheppard Publishing.

Sprouse, Jackie. Orry & Izzy's Perfect Worm. 2010. 32p. pap. 15.95 *(978-0-557-39078-6(8))* Lulu Pr., Inc.

Sroda, George. The Life Story of TV Star Herman the Worm. Hughes, Janet, illus. 199p. (Orig.). (J). (gr. 3-18). 10.95 *(978-0-9604486-2-3(4))* Sroda, George.

Taft, Jean & dePaola, Tomie. Worm Weather. Hunt, Matt, illus. 2015. (ENG.). 32p. (J). (-k). bds. 3.99 *(978-0-448-48740-3(3)*, Grosset & Dunlap) Penguin Young Readers Group.

Terry, Jill. Jack & a Worm, 1 vol. 2010. 42p. pap. 24.95 *(978-1-4489-7069-8(5))* PublishAmerica, Inc.

Tomos, Angharad. Jam Poeth. 2005. (WEL., Illus.). 48p. pap. *(978-0-86243-145-7(X))* Y Lolfa.

Vento, Anthony. Holes Are Us: A Worm's Tale about Friendship & Trust. 2009. 40p. pap. 21.99 *(978-1-4415-3446-0(6))* Xlibris Corp.

Wiley, Melissa. Inch & Roly & the Sunny Day Scare. Jatkowska, Ag, illus. 2014. (Inch & Roly Ser.). (ENG.). 24p. (J). (gr. -1-1). 16.99 *(978-1-4424-9072-7(1)*, Simon Spotlight) Simon Spotlight.

—Inch & Roly & the Very Small Hiding Place. Jatkowska, Ag, illus. 2013. (Inch & Roly Ser.). (ENG.). 24p. (J). (gr. -1-1). 16.99 *(978-1-4424-5281-7(1))*; pap. 3.99 *(978-1-4424-5279-4(X))* Simon Spotlight. (Simon Spotlight).

—Inch & Roly Make a Wish. Jatkowska, Ag, illus. 2012. (Inch & Roly Ser.). (ENG.). 24p. (J). (gr. -1-1). 15.99 *(978-1-4424-5277-0(3))*; pap. 3.99 *(978-1-4424-5276-3(5))* Simon Spotlight. (Simon Spotlight).

Williams, Dawn. Winston J. Worm Hunts for a New Name. Chou, Joey, illus. 2010. 52p. (J). 15.00 *(978-0-9770783-5-6(3))* SunriseHouse Pubs.

Williams, Greg. Wilberton the Worm. 2011. 34p. pap. 19.00 *(978-1-60746-344-3(X))* FastPrncil, Inc.

Ziefert, Harriet & Kreloff, Elliot. Found an Apple. 2007. (I'm Going to Read(r) Ser.). (ENG., Illus.). 28p. (J). (gr. -1-k). pap. 3.95 *(978-1-4027-4295-8(9))* Sterling Publishing Co., Inc.

WORSHIP

see also Prayer

Barnhill, Carla. The One Year Devotions for Preschoolers 2. Kucharik, Elena, illus. 2010. (Little Blessings Ser.). (ENG.). 384p. (J). 14.99 *(978-1-4143-3445-5(1)*, Tyndale Kids) Tyndale Hse. Pubs.

Bernard, M. My First Mass Book. Date not set. (J). (gr. -1-3). pap. 1.95 *(978-0-88271-165-2(2))* Regina Pr., Malhame & Co.

Bissell, Sybil A. God & Me: A Journey of Divine Encounters. 2004. (ENG.). 118p. pap. 13.95 *(978-0-9747516-4-1(2)*, 1005) Heart Communications.

Brown, Barbara J. The Many Different Ways to Worship: Is apart of everyday Life. 2009. 48p. pap. 11.99 *(978-1-4490-3275-3(3))* AuthorHouse.

Brown, Carolyn A. My Worship Book Student Book. 2nd ed. 2004. (J). spiral bd. 14.99 *(978-0-9752605-3-1(7))* LOGOS System Assocs.

Bytheway, John. The Sacrament. Pinnock, Nathan, illus. 2013. 18.99 *(978-1-60907-790-7(3))* Deseret Bk. Co.

Children's Worship Activities, Year 3. 2003. 96p. 15.99 *(978-0-687-02818-4(3))* Abingdon Pr.

Cook, David C. Quiet Moment with God Devotional Journal for Teens. 2003. (Quiet Moments with God Ser.). (ENG.). 384p. (YA). pap. 19.99 *(978-1-56292-983-1(6)*, 1562929836) Cook, David C.

Elkins, Stephen. Tell Me about Praise & Worship. 2014. (Train 'Em Up Ser.). (ENG.). 24p. (J). pap. 4.99 *(978-1-4143-9676-7(7))* Tyndale Hse. Pubs.

Fears, Melissa. Thank God It's Sunday. 2004. (J). per. 6.95 *(978-0-89315-413-4(X))* Lambert Bk. Hse., Inc.

Fields, Doug & Eastman, Brett. Surrendering Your Life to Honor God, 1 vol. 2076. (Life Together Ser.). (ENG.). 144p. pap., stu. ed. 9.99 *(978-0-310-25338-9(1))* Zondervan.
God & Me! Devotions for Girls. 2004. (Illus.). 248p. (J). (gr. 5-7). spiral bd. 12.99 *(978-1-885358-85-1(7))*, Legacy Pr.) Rainbow Pubs. & Legacy Pr.
God Is a Promise Keeper. 2.99 *(978-0-7847-0857-6(6))* Standard Publishing.
Guest, John. Collective Worship Unwrapped: 33 Tried & Tested Story-Based Assemblies for Primary Schools. 2nd ed. 2013. 132p. pap. *(978-1-84101-618-4(7)*, Barnabas in Schools) Bible Reading Fellowship.
Jeanne Grieser & Pearson, Mary Rose. Worship Bulletins for Kids: Fall & Winter. 2004. (Illus.). 128p. (J). (gr. -1-7). pap. 13.95 *(978-1-58411-014-9(7))* Rainbow Pubs. & Legacy Pr.
—Worship Bulletins for Kids: Spring & Summer. 2004. 128p. (J). (gr. -1-7). pap. 13.95 *(978-1-58411-015-6(5))* Rainbow Pubs. & Legacy Pr.
Kinnaman, Scott A. Worshiping with Angels & Archangels: An Introduction to the Divine Service. Kirchhoff, Arthur, illus. 2005. 48p. 7.99 *(978-0-7586-1206-9(0))* Concordia Publishing Hse.
Lee, Witness. The Holy Word for Morning Revival: Ephesians 4:1-6:24, Vol. 2. (J). (gr. 6). *(978-0-7363-1593-7(4))* Living Stream Ministry.
Let's Go to Mass. 2003. (Illus.). *(978-2-89507-087-0(3))* Novalis Publishing.
Lutz, A. Fowler. Stories of the Child Jesus from Many Lands. 2003. (Illus.). viii, 175p. (J). pap. 10.95 *(978-1-928832-96-6(2))* Sophia Institute Pr.
Mortimer, F. L. Lines Left Out. 176p. (J). pap. 7.99 *(978-1-85792-593-7(9))* Christian Focus Pubns. GBR. Dist: Riverside.
My Precious Moments with God: Quiet Time Devotionals for Girls & Boys, White. (Precious Moments Ser.). (J). 19.95 *(978-1-55976-449-0(X))* CEF Pr.
Owens, L. L. Go Worship, 1 vol. Davidson, Chris, illus. 2010. (Let's Be Social Ser.). (ENG.). 32p. 28.50 *(978-1-60270-800-6(2)*, Looking Glass Library- Nonfiction) Magic Wagon.
Perkins, Nicole. I Believe God Will: Book of Devotion & Prayer for Children. Perkins, Nicole & Frisk, Maria, illus. 2008. 32p. (J). 7.00 *(978-0-9755566-1-0(4))* Azreal Publishing Co.
Richmond, Marianne. Bedtime Blessings. 2016. (ENG.). 32p. (J). (-2). 16.99 *(978-1-4926-4181-0(2)*, 9781492641810, Sourcebooks Jabberwocky) Sourcebooks, Inc.
Savary, Louis M. Rosary for Children. Date not set. (J). (gr. -1-3). pap. 1.25 *(978-0-88271-158-4(X))* Regina Pr., Malhame & Co.
—Way of the Cross. Date not set. (J). (gr. -1-3). pap. 1.95 *(978-0-88271-160-7(1))* Regina Pr., Malhame & Co.
SPCK. I Can Join in Common Worship: A Children's Communion Book. 2003. (Illus.). 24p. 5.00 *(978-0-281-05568-5(8))* SPCK Publishing GBR. Dist: Pilgrim Pr., The/United Church Pr.
St. James, Rebecca. 40 Days with God: A Devotional Journey. rev. ed. 2006. 112p. pap. 12.99 *(978-0-7847-1274-0(3)*, 23338) Standard Publishing.
Stiegemeyer, Julie. Things I Hear in Church. Mitter, Kathy, illus. 2003. 20p. (J). bds. 5.49 *(978-0-7586-0125-4(5))* Concordia Publishing Hse.
Stohs, Anita. Here Is the Church. Mitter, Kathy, illus. 2009. 32p. (J). (gr. -1). 8.99 *(978-0-7586-1633-3(3))* Concordia Publishing Hse.
Waller, Steven H. My Child: Boy. Fincher, Kathy, illus. 2008. 37p. (J). 11.95 *(978-0-88271-172-0(5))* Regina Pr., Malhame & Co.
—My Child: Girl. Fincher, Kathy, illus. 2009. 37p. (J). 11.95 *(978-0-88271-173-7(3))* Regina Pr., Malhame & Co.
We Worship. 2004. (gr. 5). suppl. ed. 1.75 *(978-0-8294-0853-9(3))* Loyola Pr.
Wood, Alix. Human Sacrifice. Wood, Alix, illus. 2013. (Why'd They Do That? Strange Customs of the Past Ser.). (Illus.). 32p. (J). (gr. 4-6). pap. 10.50 *(978-1-4339-9585-9(9))*; pap. 63.00 *(978-1-4339-9586-6(7))* Stevens, Gareth Publishing LLLP.
—Human Sacrifice. 2013. (Why'd They Do That? Strange Customs of the Past Ser.). (ENG., Illus.). 32p. (J). (gr. 4-6). lib. bdg. 26.60 *(978-1-4339-9584-2(0))* Stevens, Gareth Publishing LLLP.
5 Minute Interactive Worship Devotions for Kids Vol. 1: Names & Games. 2003. (J). per. 12.95 *(978-0-9746161-0-0(9))* Vision Pubns.

WOUNDED, FIRST AID TO
see First Aid

WRECKS
see Shipwrecks

WRENS—FICTION
Crew, Gary. The Cat on the Island. Warden, Gillian, illus. 2008. 32p. *(978-0-207-20070-0(X))* HarperCollins Pubs. Australia.
Lloyd-Jones, Sally. Baby Wren & the Great Gift, 1 vol. Corace, Jen, illus. 2016. (ENG.). 32p. (J). 16.99 *(978-0-310-73389-8(8))* Zonderkidz.

WRESTLING
see also Judo
ABDO Publishing Company Staff. Pro Wrestling Superstars. 2014. (Pro Wrestling Superstars Ser.: 8). (ENG.). 32p. (gr. 3-9). lib. bdg. 216.56 *(978-1-62403-133-5(1)*, SportsZone) ABDO Publishing Co.
Armstrong, Jesse. Big Show. 2015. (Wrestling Superstars Ser.). (ENG., Illus.). 24p. (J). (gr. 3-7). lib. bdg. 25.95 *(978-1-62617-178-7(5)*, Epic Bks.) Bellwether Media.
—Dolph Ziggler. 2015. (Wrestling Superstars Ser.). (ENG., Illus.). 24p. (J). (gr. 3-7). lib. bdg. 25.95 *(978-1-62617-179-4(3)*, Epic Bks.) Bellwether Media.
—Mark Henry. 2015. (Wrestling Superstars Ser.). (ENG., Illus.). 24p. (J). (gr. 3-7). lib. bdg. 25.95 *(978-1-62617-181-7(5)*, Epic Bks.) Bellwether Media.
Brady Games & BradyGames Staff. Slam City. 2014. (Ultimate Sticker Bks.). (ENG.). 18p. (J). (gr. k-4). pap. 6.99 *(978-1-4654-2509-6(8)*, DK) DK Games.
BradyGames Staff. WWE Superstars. 2015. (ENG.). 96p. (J). (gr. 1-4). pap. 12.99 *(978-1-4654-3946-8(3)*, DK) DK Games.
BradyGames Staff, et al. The Rock. 2014. (ENG., Illus.). 32p. (J). (gr. 1-3). pap. 3.99 *(978-1-4654-2295-8(1)*, DK) DK Games.
—Sheamus. 2014. (ENG., Illus.). 32p. (J). (gr. 1-3). pap. 3.99 *(978-1-4654-2297-2(8)*, DK) DK Games.
Brickweg, Jason. Santino Marella. 2013. (Illus.). 24p. (J). *(978-0-531-26807-0(1))* Bellwether Media.
Brownell, Richard. Wrestling. 2014. (Science Behind Sports Ser.). (ENG., Illus.). 128p. (gr. 7-10). lib. bdg. 39.40 *(978-1-4205-1022-5(3)*, Lucent Bks.) Cengage Gale.
Chandler, Matt. Outrageous Pro Wrestling Rivalries. 2015. (Sports Rivalries Ser.). (ENG.). 32p. (gr. 3-4). lib. bdg. 27.99 *(978-1-4914-2028-7(6))* Capstone Press of Coughlan Cos.
Chapman, Mike. The Sport of Lincoln 2003. (Illus.). 48p. (YA). pap. 5.95 *(978-0-9676080-6-8(6))* Culture Hse.
Chiu, David & Regis, Natalie. An Insider's Guide to Wrestling, 1 vol. 2015. (Sports Tips, Techniques, & Strategies Ser.). (ENG.). 48p. (YA). pap. 11.75 *(978-1-4777-8090-9(4)*, Rosen Central) Rosen Publishing Group, Inc., The.
Crabtree Staff & Johnson, Robin. Takedown Wrestling. 2012. (ENG., Illus.). 32p. (J). pap. *(978-0-7787-3182-5(0))* Crabtree Publishing Co.
Crossingham, John & Rouse, Bonna. Wrestling in Action. 2003. (Sports in Action Ser.). (ENG., Illus.). 32p. (J). (gr. 1-4). pap. *(978-0-7787-0356-3(8))*; lib. bdg. *(978-0-7787-0336-5(3))* Crabtree Publishing Co.
Davids, Tom & Davids, Veronica. Wrestling the ABCs: Creating Character & Fostering Fitness. 2009. (ENG.). 32p. (J). 17.95 *(978-1-933916-33-0(8))*; pap. 11.95 *(978-1-933916-34-7(6))* Nelson Publishing & Marketing.
Davies, Ross. Andre the Giant. 2009. (Wrestling Greats Ser.). 112p. (gr. 5-5). 63.90 *(978-1-60854-861-3(9))* Rosen Publishing Group, Inc., The.
—Bobo Brazil. 2005. (Wrestling Greats Ser.). (Illus.). 112p. (YA). (gr. 7-12). lib. bdg. 34.60 *(978-0-8239-3431-7(4))* Rosen Publishing Group, Inc., The.
—Wrestling Greats, 8 bks. Incl. Andre the Giant. lib. bdg. 34.60 *(978-0-8239-3430-0(6))*; Bobo Brazil. lib. bdg. 34.60 *(978-0-8239-3431-7(4))*; 112p. (YA). (gr. 7-12). (Illus.). 2005. Set lib. bdg. 202.00 *(978-0-8239-9446-5(5))* Rosen Publishing Group, Inc., The.
Dell, Pamela. Undertaker: Life of the Dead Man, 1 vol. 2012. (Pro Wrestling Stars Ser.). (ENG.). 48p. (gr. 3-4). lib. bdg. 31.99 *(978-1-4296-8679-2(0))* Capstone Press of Coughlan Cos.
Doeden, Matt. Combat Sports. 2015. (Summer Olympic Sports Ser.). (ENG., Illus.). 32p. (J). (gr. 2-4). 19.95 *(978-1-60753-807-3(5))* Amicus Publishing.
—The Miz: Pro Wrestling Superstar, 1 vol. 2014. (Pro Wrestling Superstars Ser.). (ENG.). 24p. (gr. 1-2). lib. bdg. 25.32 *(978-1-4765-4208-9(2)*, First Facts) Capstone Press of Coughlan Cos.
Dorling Kindersley Publishing Staff. How to Be a WWE Superstar. 2017. (DK Readers Ser.). (ENG.). 48p. (J). (gr. k-2). pap. 3.99 ***(978-1-4654-6287-9(2)***, DK Children) Dorling Kindersley Publishing, Inc.
Dorling Kindersley Publishing Staff, et al. WWE Ultimate Superstar Guide. 2015. (ENG., Illus.). 208p. (J). (gr. 3-7). 16.99 *(978-1-4654-3124-0(1)*, DK) DK Games.
Douglas, Peter. Wrestling: Contending on the Mat. 2017. (Preparing for Game Day Ser.: Vol. 10). (ENG.). (YA). (gr. 7-12). 24.95 ***(978-1-4222-3922-3(5))*** Mason Crest.
Ellis, Carol. Wrestling. 2010. (Martial Arts in Action Ser.). 48p. (gr. 6-7). lib. bdg. 29.93 *(978-0-7614-4941-6(8))* Marshall Cavendish Corp.
Fandel, Jennifer, et al. Pro Wrestling Stars. 2013. (Pro Wrestling Stars Ser.). (ENG.). 48p. (gr. 3-4). lib. bdg. 255.92 *(978-1-4296-9975-4(2))*; lib. bdg. 63.98 *(978-1-4296-9974-7(4))* Capstone Press of Coughlan Cos.
Frazel, Ellen. Wrestling. 2011. (Illus.). 24p. (J). *(978-0-531-20637-9(8))*; (ENG., (gr. 2-5). lib. bdg. 25.95 *(978-1-60014-571-1(X)*, Blastoff! Readers) Bellwether Media.
Freedman, Jeri. Professional Wrestling: Steroids in & Out of the Ring. 2009. (Disgraced! the Dirty History of Performance-Enhancing Drugs in Sports Ser.). (Illus.). 48p. (YA). (gr. 5-9). 29.25 *(978-1-4358-5305-8(9))* Rosen Publishing Group, Inc., The.
Gifford, Clive. Wrestling. 2010. (Combat Sports Ser.). 32p. (J). (gr. 2-5). lib. bdg. 28.50 *(978-1-59771-278-1(7))* Sea-To-Sea Pubns.
Gordon, Nick. Alberto Del Rio. 2012. (Pro Wrestling Champions Ser.). (ENG., Illus.). 24p. (J). (gr. 3-7). lib. bdg. 25.95 *(978-1-60014-782-1(8)*, Torque Bks.) Bellwether Media.
—Kofi Kingston. 2012. (Pro Wrestling Champions Ser.). (ENG., Illus.). 24p. (J). (gr. 3-7). lib. bdg. 25.95 *(978-1-60014-784-5(4)*, Torque Bks.) Bellwether Media.
—Mark Henry. 2012. (Pro Wrestling Champions Ser.). (ENG., Illus.). 24p. (J). (gr. 3-7). lib. bdg. 25.95 *(978-1-60014-785-2(2)*, Torque Bks.) Bellwether Media.
Greenberg, Keith Elliot. Pro Wrestling: From Carnivals to Cable TV. (Sports Legacy Ser.). (Illus.). (J). (gr. 7-12). 2005. 144p. 26.63 *(978-0-8225-3332-0(4))* 2003. 128p. pap. 9.95 *(978-0-8225-9864-0(7))* Lerner Publishing Group.
Hamilton, John. Steer Wrestling. 2013. (Xtreme Rodeo Ser.). (Illus.). 32p. (J). (gr. 3-9). lib. bdg. 27.07 *(978-1-61783-981-8(7)*, Abdo & Daughters) ABDO Publishing Co.
Johnson, Robin. Takedown Wrestling. 2012. (ENG., Illus.). 32p. (J). lib. bdg. *(978-0-7787-3155-9(3))* Crabtree Publishing Co.
Jones, Jen. Dwayne Johnson. 2016. (Hollywood Action Heroes Ser.). (ENG., Illus.). 32p. (gr. 3-4). lib. bdg. 27.99 *(978-1-5157-1096-7(3)*, Edge Bks.) Capstone Press of Coughlan Cos.
Kaelberer, Angie Peterson. The Big Show. 2015. (Pro Wrestling Superstars Ser.). (ENG.). 24p. (gr. 1-2). lib. bdg. 25.32 *(978-1-4914-2058-4(8))* Capstone Press of Coughlan Cos.
—Cool Pro Wrestling Facts. (Cool Sports Facts Ser.). (ENG.). 24p. (gr. k-1). 2011. pap. 41.70 *(978-1-4296-6373-1(1))* 2010. lib. bdg. 26.65 *(978-1-4296-5305-3(1))* Capstone Press of Coughlan Cos. (Pebble Plus).
Kaelberer, Angie Peterson & Raij, Emily. Pro Wrestling Superstars. 2015. (Pro Wrestling Superstars Ser.). (ENG.). 24p. (gr. 1-2). lib. bdg. 50.64 *(978-1-4914-2555-8(5)*, First Facts) Capstone Press of Coughlan Cos.
Kortemeier, Todd. Superstars of WWE. 2017. (Pro Sports Superstars Ser.). (ENG., Illus.). 24p. (J). (gr. k-2). pap. 8.99 *(978-1-68152-108-4(3))* Amicus.
—WWE Superstars. 2016. (Pro Sports Superstars Ser.). (ENG., Illus.). 24p. (J). (gr. 1-4). 20.95 *(978-1-60753-943-8(8))* Amicus Publishing.
Lebell, Gene. The Toughest Man Alive. 2003. (Illus.). 256p. 24.95 *(978-0-9531766-7-0(3))* New Awareness Network, Inc.
Linde, Barbara. Olympic Wrestling. 2009. (Great Moments in Olympic History Ser.). 48p. (gr. 5-6). 53.00 *(978-1-61513-166-2(3)*, Rosen Reference) Rosen Publishing Group, Inc., The.
Linde, Barbara M. Olympic Wrestling. 2007. (Great Moments in Olympic History Ser.). (Illus.). 48p. (YA). (gr. 5-9). lib. bdg. 29.25 *(978-1-4042-0972-5(7))* Rosen Publishing Group, Inc., The.
Luke, Andrew. Wrestling, Vol. 13. 2016. (Inside the World of Sports Ser.: Vol. 13). (ENG., Illus.). 80p. (J). (gr. 7-12). 24.95 *(978-1-4222-3468-6(1))* Mason Crest.
Markegard, Blake. Alberto Del Rio. 2014. (Wrestling Superstars Ser.). (ENG., Illus.). 24p. (J). (gr. 3-7). 25.95 *(978-1-62617-139-8(4)*, Epic Bks.) Bellwether Media.
—John Cena. 2014. (Wrestling Superstars Ser.). (ENG.). 24p. (J). (gr. 3-7). 25.95 *(978-1-62617-141-1(6)*, Epic Bks.) Bellwether Media.
—The Miz. 2014. (Wrestling Superstars Ser.). (ENG., Illus.). 24p. (J). (gr. 3-7). 25.95 *(978-1-62617-146-6(7)*, Epic Bks.) Bellwether Media.
—Rey Mysterio. 2014. (Wrestling Superstars Ser.). (ENG., Illus.). 24p. (J). (gr. 3-7). 25.95 *(978-1-62617-143-5(2)*, Epic Bks.) Bellwether Media.
—Santino Marella. 2014. (Wrestling Superstars Ser.). (ENG., Illus.). 24p. (J). (gr. 3-7). 25.95 *(978-1-62617-144-2(0)*, Epic Bks.) Bellwether Media.
—Sheamus. 2014. (Wrestling Superstars Ser.). (ENG., Illus.). 24p. (J). (gr. 3-7). 25.95 *(978-1-62617-145-9(9)*, Epic Bks.) Bellwether Media.
—Zack Ryder. 2014. (Wrestling Superstars Ser.). (ENG., Illus.). 24p. (J). (gr. 3-7). 25.95 *(978-1-62617-148-0(3)*, Epic Bks.) Bellwether Media.
Marx, Mandy R. Stars of Pro Wrestling, 1 vol. 2014. (Sports Stars Ser.). (ENG.). 24p. (gr. k-1). 26.65 *(978-1-4914-0594-9(5)*, Pebble Plus) Capstone Press of Coughlan Cos.
Mattern, Joanne. Wrestling. 2008. (Illus.). 24p. (J). (gr. 3-8). lib. bdg. *(978-1-60472-399-1(8))* Rourke Educational Media.
McClellan, Ray. Chris Jericho. 2014. (Wrestling Superstars Ser.). (ENG., Illus.). 24p. (J). (gr. 3-7). 25.95 *(978-1-62617-140-4(8)*, Epic Bks.) Bellwether Media.
—Undertaker. 2014. (Wrestling Superstars Ser.). (ENG., Illus.). 24p. (J). (gr. 3-7). 25.95 *(978-1-62617-147-3(5)*, Epic Bks.) Bellwether Media.
McIntosh, J. S. Wrestling. 2010. (Getting the Edge Ser.). 96p. (YA). lib. bdg. 24.95 *(978-1-4222-1743-6(4))* Mason Crest.
McNab, Chris. Wrestling. 2005. (Sports Injuries Ser.). (Illus.). 64p. (YA). lib. bdg. 19.95 *(978-1-59084-642-1(7))* Mason Crest.
Orr, Tamra. Day by Day with Dwayne the Rock Johnson. 2011. (Day by Day with... Ser.). (Illus.). 32p. (J). (gr. -1-2). lib. bdg. 25.70 *(978-1-58415-982-7(0))* Mitchell Lane Pubs., Inc.
Polydoros, Lori, et al. The Best of the Best. 2012. (Best of the Best Ser.). (ENG.). 32p. (gr. 1-2). lib. bdg. 53.30 *(978-1-4296-9135-2(2)*, Blazers) Capstone Press of Coughlan Cos.
Price, Roger & Stern, Leonard, creators. WWE Mad Libs. 2011. (Wwe Ser.). (ENG.). 48p. (J). (gr. 3-7). bds. 3.99 *(978-0-8431-9882-9(6)*, Mad Libs) Penguin Young Readers Group.
Price, Sean Stewart. The Kids' Guide to Pro Wrestling, 1 vol. 2011. (Kids' Guides). (ENG.). 32p. (gr. 3-4). lib. bdg. 27.99 *(978-1-4296-6008-2(2)*, Edge Bks.) Capstone Press of Coughlan Cos.
Raatma, Lucia. Rey Mysterio: High-Flying Luchador, 1 vol. 2013. (Pro Wrestling Stars Ser.). (ENG.). 48p. (gr. 3-4). 31.99 *(978-1-4296-9973-0(6))* Capstone Press of Coughlan Cos.
Regis, Natalie & Chiu, David. An Insider's Guide to Wrestling, 1 vol. 2015. (ENG.). 48p. (YA). 30.25 *(978-1-4777-8089-3(0)*, Rosen Reference) Rosen Publishing Group, Inc., The.
Sandler, Michael. The Rock. 2012. (Wrestling's Tough Guys Ser.). 24p. (J). (gr. 1-6). lib. bdg. 23.93 *(978-1-61772-574-6(9))* Bearport Publishing Co., Inc.
Skog, Jason, et al. Pro Wrestling Stars. 2012. (Pro Wrestling Stars Ser.). (ENG.). 48p. (gr. 3-4). lib. bdg. 191.94 *(978-1-4296-9182-6(4))* Capstone Press of Coughlan Cos.
St. John, Chris. Wrestling. 2012. (Master This! Ser.). (Illus.). 32p. (J). lib. bdg. 25.25 *(978-1-4488-5286-4(2)*, PowerKids Pr.) Rosen Publishing Group, Inc., The.
St John, Chris. Wrestling. 2016. (Master This Ser.). (ENG., Illus.). 32p. (J). (gr. 4-6). pap. 11.99 *(978-0-7502-9704-2(2)*, Wayland) Hachette Children's Group GBR. Dist: Hachette Bk. Group.
Stars of Pro Wrestling [Capstone Sole Source]. 2010. (Stars of Pro Wrestling Ser.). 32p. lib. bdg. 266.50 *(978-1-4296-5884-3(3)*, Edge Bks.) Capstone Press of Coughlan Cos.
Stone, Adam. Edge. 2011. (Pro Wrestling Champions Ser.). (ENG., Illus.). 24p. (J). (gr. 3-7). lib. bdg. 25.95 *(978-1-60014-635-0(X)*, Torque Bks.) Bellwether Media.
—Randy Orton. 2011. (Pro Wrestling Champions Ser.). (ENG., Illus.). 24p. (J). (gr. 3-7). lib. bdg. 25.95 *(978-1-60014-638-1(4)*, Torque Bks.) Bellwether Media.
—Triple H. 2011. (Pro Wrestling Champions Ser.). (ENG., Illus.). 24p. (J). (gr. 3-7). lib. bdg. 25.95 *(978-1-60014-641-1(4)*, Torque Bks.) Bellwether Media.
—The Undertaker. 2011. (Pro Wrestling Champions Ser.). (ENG., Illus.). 24p. (J). (gr. 3-7). lib. bdg. 25.95 *(978-1-60014-640-4(6)*, Torque Bks.) Bellwether Media.
Weil, Ann. Pro Wrestling Greats, 1 vol. 2011. (Best of the Best Ser.). (ENG.). 32p. (gr. 1-2). pap. 8.10 *(978-1-4296-7251-1(X))*; 26.65 *(978-1-4296-6497-4(5))*; pap. 47.70 *(978-1-4296-7252-8(8))* Capstone Press of Coughlan Cos. (Blazers).
Wells, Garrison. Amateur Wrestling: Combat on the Mat. 2012. (Martial Arts Sports Zone Ser.). (ENG., Illus.). 32p. (gr. 4-8). lib. bdg. 26.60 *(978-0-7613-8460-1(X)*, Lerner Pubns.) Lerner Publishing Group.
Wrestling Greats. 2005. (Illus.). 112p. (gr. 7-12). lib. bdg. 265.30 *(978-0-8239-3911-4(1))* Rosen Publishing Group, Inc., The.
Wyborny, Sheila. Dwayne Johnson. 2009. (People in the News Ser.). (ENG., Illus.). 128p. (YA). (gr. 7-12). lib. bdg. 33.95 *(978-1-4205-0125-4(9)*, LML02109-245439) Cengage Gale.

WRESTLING—FICTION
Davis, Terry. Vision Quest. 2015. (ENG., Illus.). 240p. (YA). (gr. 7). 19.99 *(978-1-4814-5636-4(9)*, Simon & Schuster Bks. For Young Readers) Simon & Schuster Bks. For Young Readers.
Eldridge, Jim. The Final Showdown: Match Six. 2016. (Wrestling Trolls Ser.: 6). (ENG., Illus.). 176p. (J). (gr. k-3). pap. 9.99 *(978-1-4714-0269-2(X))* Bonnier Publishing GBR. Dist: Independent Pubs. Group.
Garza, Xavier. Lucha Libre: The Man in the Silver Mask - A Bilingual Cuento. Garza, Xavier, illus. 2007. (SPA & ENG., Illus.). 40p. (J). (gr. 4-6). pap. 8.95 *(978-1-933693-10-1(X))* Cinco Puntos Pr.
—Lucha Libre: The Man in the Silver Mask - A Bilingual Cuento. Crosthwaite, Luis Humberto, tr. Garza, Xavier, illus. 2005. (ENG & SPA., Illus.). 40p. (J). (gr. 4-6). 17.95 *(978-0-938317-92-0(X))* Cinco Puntos Pr.
—Maximilian & the Bingo Rematch: A Lucha Libre Sequel. 2013. (Max's Lucha Libre Adventures Ser.). (ENG., Illus.). 208p. (J). (gr. 2-7). pap. 12.95 *(978-1-935955-46-7(2))* Cinco Puntos Pr.
Garza, Xavier, illus. The Great & Mighty Nikko. 2015. (ENG.). 32p. (J). pap. 7.95 *(978-1-935955-83-2(7))*; (gr. -1-4). 16.95 *(978-1-935955-82-5(9))* Cinco Puntos Pr.
—Maximilian & the Bingo Rematch: A Lucha Libre Sequel. 2013. (Max's Lucha Libre Adventures Ser.). (ENG.). 208p. (J). 19.95 *(978-1-935955-59-7(4))* Cinco Puntos Pr.
—Maximilian & the Mystery of the Guardian Angel. 2011. (Max's Lucha Libre Adventures Ser.). (SPA & ENG.). 160p. (J). (gr. 5-8). pap. 12.95 *(978-1-933693-98-9(3))* Cinco Puntos Pr.
Kowitt, H. N. Take Me to Your Loser. 2013. (Loser List Ser.: 4). (ENG.). 240p. (J). (gr. 3-7). 9.99 *(978-0-545-50795-0(2)*, Scholastic Pr.) Scholastic, Inc.
Lemke, Donald B. Chameleon Cage Match! Eliopoulos, Chris, illus. 2013. (Lucha Lizards Ser.). (ENG.). 48p. (gr. 1-3). pap. 5.95 *(978-1-4342-3874-0(1))*; lib. bdg. 23.99 *(978-1-4342-3285-4(9))* Stone Arch Bks.
Lubar, David. Dead Guy Spy. 2010. (Nathan Abercrombie, Accidental Zombie Ser.: 2). (ENG.). 176p. (J). (gr. 3-7). pap. 8.99 *(978-0-7653-2507-5(1)*, 9780765325075, Starscape) Doherty, Tom Assocs., LLC.
Lynch, Janet Nichols. Addicted to Her. 2010. (ENG.). 256p. (YA). (gr. 7-18). pap. 17.95 *(978-0-8234-2186-2(4))* Holiday Hse., Inc.
Maddox, Jake. Heavyweight Takedown. 2015. (Jake Maddox JV Ser.). (ENG.). 96p. (gr. 3-4). lib. bdg. 25.99 *(978-1-4342-9638-2(5))* Stone Arch Bks.
—Takedown. Tiffany, Sean, illus. 2008. (Jake Maddox Sports Stories Ser.). (ENG.). 72p. (gr. 2-3). 25.32 *(978-1-4342-0774-6(9))*; pap. 5.95 *(978-1-4342-0870-5(2))* Stone Arch Bks.
Martino, Alfred C. Pinned: There Can Be Only One Winner... 2006. (ENG., Illus.). 320p. (YA). (gr. 7-12). reprint ed. pap. 8.99 *(978-0-15-205631-5(9))* Houghton Mifflin Harcourt Publishing Co.
Morales, Yuyi. Niño: Wrestles the World. Morales, Yuyi, illus. 2013. (ENG., Illus.). 40p. (J). (gr. -1-3). 17.99 *(978-1-59643-604-6(2)*, 9781596436046) Roaring Brook Pr.
—Rudas: Niño's Horrendous Hermanitas. 2016. (ENG., Illus.). 40p. (J). 17.99 *(978-1-62672-240-8(4)*, 9781626722408) Roaring Brook Pr.
Mulhall, MB. Heavyweight. 2016. (ENG., Illus.). (J). 24.99 ***(978-1-63533-026-7(2))*** 2014. 230p. pap. 14.99 *(978-1-62798-712-7(6))* Dreamspinner Pr. (Harmony Ink Pr.).
Nickel, Scott. It's a Wrestling Mat, Not a Dance Floor, 1 vol. Santillan, Jorge H., illus. 2011. (Sports Illustrated Kids Victory School Superstars Ser.). (ENG.). 56p. (gr. 1-3). lib. bdg. 26.65 *(978-1-4342-2227-5(6))* Stone Arch Bks.
Richardson, William K. The Grappler. 2011. 184p. (J). (gr. 10-12). pap. 14.50 *(978-1-4269-6035-2(2))* Trafford Publishing.
Schaffter, Ehren. Through the Curtain. 2009. 239p. pap. 20.00 *(978-0-557-20001-6(6))* Lulu Pr., Inc.
Scieszka, Jon. See You Later, Gladiator. McCauley, Adam, illus. 2004. (Time Warp Trio Ser.: 9). (ENG.). 96p. (J). (gr. 2-4). pap. 5.99 *(978-0-14-240117-0(X)*, Puffin Books) Penguin Young Readers Group.
—See You Later, Gladiator. McCauley, Adam, illus. 2004. (Time Warp Trio Ser.: No. 9). 87p. (J). (gr. 4-7). 12.65 *(978-0-7569-5986-9(1))* Perfection Learning Corp.
Souhami, Jessica & Quarto Generic Staff. The Strongest Boy in the World. 2016. (ENG., Illus.). 32p. (J). (gr. k-3). pap. 12.99 *(978-1-84780-603-1(1)*, Frances Lincoln) Quarto Publishing Group UK GBR. Dist: Littlehampton Bk Services, Ltd.
Spinelli, Jerry. There's a Girl in My Hammerlock. 2008. 199p. (gr. 4-8). 16.00 *(978-0-7569-8465-6(3))* Perfection Learning Corp.
—There's a Girl in My Hammerlock. 2007. (ENG.). 208p. (J). (gr. 4-8). pap. 7.99 *(978-1-4169-3937-5(7)*, Aladdin) Simon & Schuster Children's Publishing.
Sterner, Nathan. Onami: The Great Wave. Dutchak, Shelly, illus. 2007. (J). per. *(978-0-9795529-0-8(7))* 716 Productions.
Villareal, Ray. Body Slammed! 2012. (YA). pap. 11.95 *(978-1-55885-749-0(4)*, Piñata Books) Arte Publico Pr.
Wallace, Rich. Takedown, No. 8. 2007. (Winning Season Ser.: Bk. 8). (ENG.). 128p. (J). (gr. 3-7). 5.99 *(978-0-14-240919-0(7)*, Puffin Books) Penguin Young Readers Group.
Weis, Lyle Percy. Let's Wrestle. (J). 5.95 *(978-0-9686899-4-3(9))* Hodgepog Bks. CAN. Dist: Coteau Bks.
Wheeler, Lisa. Dino-Wrestling. Gott, Barry, illus. 2013. (ENG.). 32p. (J). (gr. k-3). 16.95 *(978-1-4677-0212-6(9)*, Carolrhoda Bks.) Lerner Publishing Group.

W
X
Y
Z

WRIGHT, FRANK LLOYD, 1869-1959

Adkins, Jan. Frank Lloyd Wright. 2008. (Up Close Ser.). (ENG.). 304p. (YA). (gr. 7-18). 8.99 *(978-0-14-241244-2(9)*, Puffin Books) Penguin Young Readers Group.

Atlantic Publishing Group. People That Changed the Course of History: The Story of Frank Lloyd Wright 150 Years after His Birth. 2017. (ENG.). 180p. (YA). lib. bdg. 34.95 ***(978-1-62023-225-5(1)***, 54d8c914-cc51-4c1b-b9f9-19d84d64a41d) Atlantic Publishing Group, Inc.

Bennett, Doraine. Frank Lloyd Wright: Little World Biographies. 2013. (ENG.). 24p. (gr. k-3). pap. 8.95 *(978-1-61810-290-4(7))* Rourke Educational Media.

Fandel, Jennifer. Frank Lloyd Wright. (Illus.). (J). 2016. 80p. *(978-1-60818-718-8(7))* 2005. 48p. (gr. 5-9). lib. bdg. 21.95 *(978-1-58341-378-4(2))* Creative Co., The. (Creative Education).

Going, K. L. The Shape of the World: A Portrait of Frank Lloyd Wright. Stringer, Lauren, illus. 2017. (ENG.). 40p. (J). (gr. k-5). 17.99 ***(978-1-4424-7821-3(7))*** Beach Lane Bks.

Huxtable, Ada Louise. Frank Lloyd Wright: A Life. 2008. (Penguin Lives Ser.). (ENG., Illus.). 272p. (gr. 12-18). 15.00 *(978-0-14-311429-1(8)*, Penguin Books) Penguin Publishing Group.

Labrecque, Ellen. Who Was Frank Lloyd Wright? 2015. (Who Was... ? Ser.). lib. bdg. 16.00 *(978-0-606-37558-0(9))* Turtleback Bks.

Labrecque, Ellen & dePaola, Tomie. Who Was Frank Lloyd Wright? Copeland, Gregory & Harrison, Nancy, illus. 2015. (Who Was? Ser.). (ENG.). 112p. (J). (gr. 3-7). 5.99 *(978-0-448-48313-9(0)*, Grosset & Dunlap) Penguin Young Readers Group.

Levy, Janey. The Architecture of Frank Lloyd Wright: Understanding the Concepts of Parallel & Perpendicular. (PowerMath Ser.). 32p. 2009. (ENG., Illus.). (gr. 5-6). pap. 10.00 *(978-1-4042-5144-1(8)*, PowerKids Pr.) 2009. (gr. 4-5). 47.90 *(978-1-60851-418-2(8)*, PowerKids Pr.) 2005. (Illus.). (YA). (gr. 5-9). lib. bdg. 25.25 *(978-1-4042-2940-2(X))* Rosen Publishing Group, Inc., The.

Mayo, Gretchen Will. Frank Lloyd Wright. 2004. (Trailblazers of the Modern World Ser.). (Illus.). 48p. (gr. 5-12). pap. 14.05 *(978-0-8368-5261-5(3))*; lib. bdg. 31.00 *(978-0-8368-5101-4(3))* Stevens, Gareth Publishing LLLP. (Gareth Stevens Secondary Library).

Nardo, Don, ed. Frank Lloyd Wright. 2012. (Eye on Art Ser.). (ENG., Illus.). 128p. (J). (gr. 7-10). lib. bdg. 34.80 *(978-1-4205-0813-0(X)*, Lucent Bks.) Cengage Gale.

Simply Wright: A Journey into the Ideas of Frank Lloyd Wright's Architecture. 2004. (J). spiral bd. 17.95 *(978-0-9677348-3-5(5))* Castleconal Pr.

Thorne-Thomsen, Kathleen. Frank Lloyd Wright for Kids: His Life & Ideas. 2nd ed. 2014. (For Kids Ser.). (ENG., Illus.). 144p. (J). (gr. 4). pap. 16.95 *(978-1-61374-474-1(9))* Chicago Review Pr., Inc.

WRIGHT, ORVILLE, 1871-1948

Arrathoon, Leigh A. Men Who Changed the World Vol. II: The First Birdmen: Wilbur & Orville Wright. Davio, John, ed. Hajdyla, Ken, illus. 56p. (J). (gr. 5-6). pap. 5.95 *(978-0-9648564-6-2(8))* Archus Pr., LLC.

Berger, Melvin & Berger, Gilda. Can You Fly High, Wright Brothers? Dorman, Brandon, illus. 2007. (Scholastic Science Supergiants Ser.: Vol. 1). (ENG.). 48p. (J). (gr. 2-5). pap. 4.99 *(978-0-439-83378-3(7))* Scholastic, Inc.

Bingham, Jane. The Wright Brothers: First Flight. 2017. (Fact Cat: History Ser.). (ENG., Illus.). 24p. (J). (gr. k-2). pap. 9.99 ***(978-0-7502-9039-5(0)***, Wayland) Hachette Children's Group GBR. Dist: Hachette Bk. Group.

Borden, Louise, et al. Touching the Sky: The Flying Adventures of Wilbur & Orville Wright. Fiore, Peter M., illus. 2003. (ENG.). 64p. (J). (gr. k-3). 19.99 *(978-0-689-84876-6(5)*, McElderry, Margaret K. Bks.) McElderry, Margaret K. Bks.

Brown, Jonatha A. Los Hermanos Wright. Acosta, Tatiana & Gutierrez, Guillermo, trs. from ENG. 2004. (Gente Que Hay Que Conocer Ser.). (SPA., Illus.). 24p. (gr. 1-4). lib. bdg. 22.00 *(978-0-8368-4356-9(8)*, Weekly Reader Leveled Readers) Stevens, Gareth Publishing LLLP.

—Los Hermanos Wright. 2004. (People We Should Know Ser.).Tr. of Wright Brothers. (SPA.). 24p. (gr. 1-4). pap. 8.15 *(978-0-8368-4363-7(0)*, GHS33824, Weekly Reader Leveled Readers) Stevens, Gareth Publishing LLLP.

—The Wright Brothers. 2004. (People We Should Know Ser.). (Illus.). 24p. (gr. 1-4). lib. bdg. 22.00 *(978-0-8368-4314-9(2)*, Weekly Reader Leveled Readers) Stevens, Gareth Publishing LLLP.

Buckley, James, Jr. Who Were the Wright Brothers? Foley, Tim & Harrison, Nancy, illus. 2014. (Who Was? Ser.). (ENG.). 112p. (J). (gr. 3-7). 5.99 *(978-0-448-47951-4(6)*, Grosset & Dunlap) Penguin Young Readers Group.

Buckley, James. Who Were the Wright Brothers? Foley, Tim, illus. 2014. 106p. (J). *(978-1-101-99527-3(0))* Penguin Publishing Group.

Burke, Michelle Prater. The Story of the Wright Brothers. Johnson, Meredith, illus. 2016. (J). *(978-0-8249-1986-3(6)*, Ideal Pubns.) Worthy Publishing.

Carson, Mary Kay. The Wright Brothers for Kid: How They Invented the Airplane, 21 Activities Exploring the Science & History of Flight. D'Argo, Laura, illus. 2003. (For Kids Ser.). (ENG.). 160p. (J). (gr. 4). pap. 18.95 *(978-1-55652-477-6(3))* Chicago Review Pr., Inc.

Collins, Mary. Airborne: A Photobiography of Wilbur & Orville Wright. (Photobiographies Ser.). (ENG., Illus.). 64p. (J). (gr. 5). 2015. pap. 7.99 *(978-1-4263-2221-1(6))* 2003. 18.95 *(978-0-7922-6957-1(8)*, 53238483) National Geographic Society. (National Geographic Children's Bks.).

Crompton, Samuel Willard. The Wright Brothers: First in Flight. 2007. (Milestones in American History Ser.). (Illus.). 128p. (YA). (gr. 7-12). lib. bdg. 35.00 *(978-0-7910-9356-6(5))* Facts On File, Inc.

Cudeyro, Erica M. American History for Young Minds - Volume 1, Looking Towards the Sky, Book 1, the First Airplane. Butler, Lindsay L., illus. 2008. 20p. pap. 11.95 *(978-1-934925-34-8(9)*, Eloquent Bks.) Strategic Book Publishing & Rights Agency (SBPRA).

Dakers, Diane. Orville & Wilbur Wright: Pioneers of the Age of Flight. 2016. (Crabtree Groundbreaker Biographies Ser.). (ENG.). 112p. (J). (gr. 5-8). *(978-0-7787-2609-8(6))* Crabtree Publishing Co.

Davis, Lynn. The Wright Brothers, 1 vol. 2016. (ENG., Illus.). 24p. (J). *(978-1-62403-726-9(7))* ABDO Publishing Co.

Deines, Ann, ed. Wilbur & Orville Wright: A Handbook of Facts. 2007. (Illus.). 64p. per. 5.95 *(978-1-888213-75-1(2))* Eastern National.

Dorfman, Janet. The Wright Brothers. 2011. (Early Connections Ser.). (J). *(978-1-61672-564-8(8))* Benchmark Education Co.

Dunn, Joe. The Wright Brothers, 1 vol. Dunn, Ben, illus. 2007. (Bio-Graphics Ser.). (ENG.). 32p. (gr. 3-6). 28.50 *(978-1-60270-071-0(0)*, Graphic Planet- Nonfiction) ABDO Publishing Co.

Ford, Carin T. The Wright Brothers: Heroes of Flight. 2003. (Famous Inventors Ser.). (Illus.). 32p. (J). (gr. 1-4). lib. bdg. 23.94 *(978-0-7660-2002-3(9))* Enslow Pubs., Inc.

Graham, Ian. You Wouldn't Want to Be on the First Flying Machine! A High-Soaring Ride You'd Rather Not Take. Antram, David, illus. 2013. (You Wouldn't Want to... Ser.). (ENG.). 32p. (J). 29.00 *(978-0-531-25945-0(5))*; pap. 9.95 *(978-0-531-23042-8(2))* Scholastic Library Publishing. (Watts, Franklin).

—You Wouldn't Want to Be on the First Flying Machine! A High-Soaring Ride You'd Rather Not Take. 2013. (You Wouldn't Want To... Ser.). lib. bdg. 20.80 *(978-0-606-31631-6(0)*, Turtleback) Turtleback Bks.

Hamen, Susan E. The Wright Brothers, 1 vol. 2007. (Essential Lives Set 1 Ser.). (ENG., Illus.). 112p. (J). (gr. 6-12). lib. bdg. 35.64 *(978-1-59928-846-8(X))* ABDO Publishing Co.

Helfand, Lewis. The Wright Brothers. Banerjee, Sankha, illus. 2011. (Campfire Graphic Novels Ser.). (ENG.). 72p. (YA). (gr. 5-9). pap. 9.99 *(978-93-80028-46-0(6)*, Campfire) Steerforth Pr.

Hill, Lee Sullivan. The Flyer Flew! The Invention of the Airplane. Orback, Craig, illus. 2006. (On My Own Science Ser.). 48p. (J). (gr. 3-7). per. 6.95 *(978-1-57505-855-9(3))*; (gr. k-3). lib. bdg. 25.26 *(978-1-57505-758-3(1)*, Millbrook Pr.) Lerner Publishing Group.

James, Emily. The Wright Brothers. 2017. (Great Scientists & Inventors Ser.). (ENG.). 24p. (gr. k-1). lib. bdg. 26.65 *(978-1-5157-3885-5(X))* Capstone Press of Coughlan Cos.

Jenner, Caryn. First Flight Vol. 4: The Story of the Wright Brothers. 2004. (DK Readers Ser.). (Illus.). 48p. (gr. -1-3). 14.00 *(978-0-7569-3361-6(7))* Perfection Learning Corp.

Jenner, Caryn & Garrett, Leslie. First Flight, Level 4: The Story of the Wright Brothers. 2003. (DK Readers Ser.). (ENG., Illus.). 48p. (J). (gr. 3-7). pap. 3.99 *(978-0-7894-9291-3(1)*, DK Children) Dorling Kindersley Publishing, Inc.

Kuskowski, Alex & Craig, Diane. Super Simple Aircraft Projects: Inspiring & Educational Science Activities, 1 vol. 2016. (ENG., Illus.). 32p. (J). *(978-1-62403-728-3(3))* ABDO Publishing Co.

LaFontaine, Bruce. BOOST the Story of the Wright Brothers Coloring Book. 2013. (BOOST Educational Ser.). (ENG.). 32p. (J). (gr. 3-5). pap. 4.99 *(978-0-486-49440-1(3))* Dover Pubns., Inc.

Lefèvre-Garros, J. P. The Wright Brothers, Vol. 3. Uderzo, M., illus. 2012. (Cinebook Recounts Ser.: 3). (ENG.). 48p. (YA). (gr. 6-17). pap. 11.95 *(978-1-84918-100-6(4))* CineBook GBR. Dist: National Bk. Network.

MacLeod, Elizabeth. The Wright Brothers. Krystoforski, Andrej, illus. 2008. (Kids Can Read Ser.). (ENG.). 32p. (J). (gr. 1-3). 14.95 *(978-1-55453-053-3(9))*; pap. 3.95 *(978-1-55453-054-0(7))* Kids Can Pr., Ltd. CAN. Dist: Hachette Bk. Group.

Mayo, Gretchen Will & O'Hern, Kerri. Los Hermanos Wright. Isaacs, Rebekah & Timmons, Jonathan, illus. 2007. (Biografias Graficas (Graphic Biographies) Ser.). (SPA.). 32p. (gr. 5-8). lib. bdg. 27.00 *(978-0-8368-7883-7(3))* Stevens, Gareth Publishing LLLP.

—The Wright Brothers. Isaacs, Rebekah & Timmons, Jonathan, illus. 2006. (Graphic Biographies Ser.). 32p. (gr. 5-8). lib. bdg. 27.00 *(978-0-8368-6199-0(X))* Stevens, Gareth Publishing LLLP.

Mayo, Gretchen Will, et al. The Wright Brothers. 2006. (Graphic Biographies Ser.). (Illus.). 32p. (gr. 5-8). pap. 10.50 *(978-0-8368-6251-5(1))* Stevens, Gareth Publishing LLLP.

McCormick, Lisa Wade. Wright Brothers. 2005. (Scholastic News Nonfiction Readers Ser.). (Illus.). 24p. (J). pap. *(978-0-516-24786-1(7))* Children's Pr., Ltd.

McLaughlin, Kari Massie. My Adventure with the Wright Brothers. 2007. 44p. (J). 8.99 *(978-1-59092-471-6(1))* Blue Forge Pr.

McPherson, Stephanie Sammartino & Gardner, Joseph Sammartino. Wilbur & Orville Wright: Taking Flight. 2004. (Trailblazer Biography Ser.). (Illus.). 120p. (J). 30.60 *(978-1-57505-443-8(4)*, Carolrhoda Bks.) Lerner Publishing Group.

Mills, Nathan & Weir, William. The Wright Brothers: The First to Fly. 2012. (Rosen Readers Ser.). (ENG., Illus.). 24p. (J). (gr. 1-2). pap. 8.25 *(978-1-4488-8863-4(8)*, Rosen Classroom) Rosen Publishing Group, Inc., The.

Niz, Xavier, et al. The Wright Brothers & the Airplane, 1 vol. Erwin, Steve et al, illus. 2007. (Inventions & Discovery Ser.). (ENG.). 32p. (gr. 3-4). 30.65 *(978-0-7368-6845-7(3)*, Graphic Library) Capstone Press of Coughlan Cos.

Niz, Xavier W., et al. The Wright Brothers & the Airplane, 1 vol. Erwin, Steve, illus. 2007. (Inventions & Discovery Ser.). (ENG.). 32p. (gr. 3-4). per. 8.10 *(978-0-7368-7897-5(1)*, Graphic Library) Capstone Press of Coughlan Cos.

O'Hern, Kerri & Will Mayo, Gretchen. Los Hermanos Wright. 2007. (Biografias Graficas (Graphic Biographies) Ser.). (SPA.). 32p. (gr. 5-8). pap. 10.50 *(978-0-8368-7890-5(6))* Stevens, Gareth Publishing LLLP.

Old, Wendie C. The Wright Brothers: Aviation Pioneers & Inventors. 2015. (Legendary American Biographies Ser.). 96p. (J). (gr. 6-12). 27.94 *(978-0-7660-6505-5(7))*; pap. 10.95 *(978-0-7660-6506-2(5))* Enslow Pubs., Inc.

Orr, Tamra B. The Dawn of Aviation: The Story of the Wright Brothers. 2005. (Monumental Milestones Ser.). (Illus.). 48p. (YA). (gr. 4-7). lib. bdg. 29.95 *(978-1-58415-396-2(2)*, 1244922) Mitchell Lane Pubs., Inc.

O'Sullivan, Robyn. The Wright Brothers Fly. 2007. (History Chapters Ser.). (ENG., Illus.). 48p. (J). (gr. 1-4). lib. bdg. 17.90 *(978-1-4263-0188-9(X)*, National Geographic Children's Bks.) National Geographic Society.

Perkis, Andrea. The Wright Brothers Make History! 2012. (InfoMax Readers Ser.). (ENG., Illus.). 24p. (J). (gr. 1-2). pap. 8.25 *(978-1-4488-9076-7(4)*, Rosen Classroom) Rosen Publishing Group, Inc., The.

Rausch, Monica L. Los Hermanos Wright y el Avion. 2007. (Inventores y sus descubrimientos (Inventors & Their Discoveries) Ser.). (SPA., Illus.). 24p. (gr. 1-4). pap. 8.15 *(978-0-8368-8001-4(3))*; lib. bdg. 22.00 *(978-0-8368-7996-4(1))* Stevens, Gareth Publishing LLLP. (Weekly Reader Leveled Readers).

—The Wright Brothers & the Airplane. 2007. (Inventors & Their Discoveries Ser.). (Illus.). 24p. (gr. 1-4). pap. 8.15 *(978-0-8368-7733-5(0))*; lib. bdg. 22.00 *(978-0-8368-7502-7(8))* Stevens, Gareth Publishing LLLP. (Weekly Reader Leveled Readers).

Reed, Jennifer. Wilbur & Orville Wright: Trailblazers of the Sky. 2007. (Inventors Who Changed the World Ser.). (Illus.). 128p. (J). (gr. 5). lib. bdg. 34.60 *(978-1-59845-054-5(9)*, MyReportLinks.com Bks.) Enslow Pubs., Inc.

Roop, Peter & Roop, Connie. Let's Fly Wilbur & Orville! 2003. (Before I Made History Ser.). (Illus.). 60p. (J). *(978-0-439-55441-1(1))* Scholastic, Inc.

Schulz, Walter A. Johnny Moore & the Wright Brothers' Flying Machine. Bowles, Doug, illus. 2011. (History Speaks: Picture Books Plus Reader's Theater Ser.). 48p. pap. 56.72 *(978-0-7613-7633-0(X))*; (ENG.). (gr. 2-4). lib. bdg. 27.93 *(978-0-7613-5876-3(5)*, Millbrook Pr.) Lerner Publishing Group.

—Will y Orv. Translations.com Staff, tr. from ENG. Schulz, Janet, illus. 2006. (Yo Solo - Historia (on My Own - History) Ser.). (SPA.). 48p. (gr. 2-4). lib. bdg. 25.26 *(978-0-8225-6263-4(4))* Lerner Publishing Group.

Schulz, Walter A. & Schultz, Walter A. Johnny Moore & the Wright Brothers' Flying Machine. Bowles, Doug, illus. 2011. (History Speaks: Picture Books Plus Reader's Theater Ser.). (ENG.). 48p. (gr. 2-4). pap. 9.95 *(978-0-7613-7117-5(6))* Lerner Publishing Group.

Spilsbury, Louise. The Wright Brothers & the Airplane, 01 vols., 1. 2016. (Inventions That Changed the World Ser.). (ENG.). 32p. (J). pap. 10.00 *(978-1-5081-4643-8(8)*, PowerKids Pr.) Rosen Publishing Group, Inc., The.

Sproule, Anna. The Wright Brothers. 2005. (Giants of Science Bilingual Ser.). (J). 9.95 *(978-1-4103-0507-7(4)*, Blackbirch Pr., Inc.) Cengage Gale.

Stevenson, Augusta. Wilbur & Orville Wright: Boys with Wings. Laune, Paul, illus. 2011. 192p. (gr. 2-5). 42.95 *(978-1-258-07857-7(0))* Literary Licensing, LLC.

Stolfo, Paul. The Wright Brothers. 2009. (Real Life Readers Ser.). 12p. (gr. 2-3). pap. 5.90 *(978-1-4042-7955-1(5)*, Rosen Classroom) Rosen Publishing Group, Inc., The.

Tate, Suzanne. Flyer: A Tale of the Wright Dog. Melvin, James, illus. 2003. (Suzanne Tate's History Ser.). (J). pap. 4.95 *(978-1-878405-42-5(X))* Nags Head Art, Inc.

Tieck, Sarah. Wright Brothers, 1 vol. 2006. (First Biographies Ser.). (ENG., Illus.). 32p. (gr. -1-3). 27.07 *(978-1-59679-790-1(8)*, Buddy Bks.) ABDO Publishing Co.

Troupe, Thomas Kingsley. The Wright Brothers' First Flight: a Fly on the Wall History. Tejido, Jomike, illus. 2017. (Fly on the Wall History Ser.). (ENG.). 32p. (gr. 1-3). pap. 7.95 *(978-1-4795-9791-8(0))*; lib. bdg. 27.32 *(978-1-4795-9787-1(2))* Picture Window Bks.

Van Steenwyk, Elizabeth. One Fine Day: A Radio Play. Farnsworth, Bill, illus. 2004. 32p. (J). (gr. 3-5). 16.00 *(978-0-8028-5234-2(3))* Eerdmans, William B. Publishing Co.

Venezia, Mike. The Wright Brothers: Inventors Whose Ideas Really Took Flight. 2010. (Getting to Know the World's Greatest Inventors & Scientists Ser.). 32p. (J). (gr. 3-4). pap. 6.95 *(978-0-531-22353-6(1)*, Children's Pr.) Scholastic Library Publishing.

—The Wright Brothers: Inventors Whose Ideas Really Took Flight. Venezia, Mike, illus. 2010. (Getting to Know the World's Greatest Inventors & Scientists Ser.). (ENG., Illus.). 32p. (J). (gr. 3-4). 28.00 *(978-0-531-23732-8(X))* Scholastic Library Publishing.

Wadsworth, Ginger. The Wright Brothers. 2004. (History Maker Bios Ser.). (Illus.). 47p. (J). 26.60 *(978-0-8225-0199-2(6)*, Lerner Pubns.) Lerner Publishing Group.

Weir, William. The Wright Brothers: The First to Fly. 2012. (Beginning Biographies Ser.). (ENG., Illus.). 24p. (J). (gr. 1-3). 22.60 *(978-1-4488-8597-8(3)*, PowerKids Pr.) Rosen Publishing Group, Inc., The.

Will y Orv (Will & Orv) 2006. (J). pap. 6.95 *(978-0-8225-6615-1(X)*, Ediciones Lerner) Lerner Publishing Group.

WRIGHT, RICHARD, 1908-1960

Bloom, Harold, ed. Richard Wright's Black Boy. 2006. (Bloom's Modern Critical Interpretations Ser.). 150p. (C). (gr. 9). lib. bdg. 45.00 *(978-0-7910-8585-1(6)*, Chelsea Hse.) Facts On File, Inc.

Levy, Debbie. Richard Wright: A Biography. 2007. (Literary Greats Ser.). (ENG., Illus.). 160p. (gr. 7-12). lib. bdg. 33.26 *(978-0-8225-6793-6(8)*, Twenty-First Century Bks.) Lerner Publishing Group.

WRIGHT, WILBUR, 1867-1912

Arrathoon, Leigh A. Men Who Changed the World Vol. II: The First Birdmen: Wilbur & Orville Wright. Davio, John, ed. Hajdyla, Ken, illus. 56p. (J). (gr. 5-6). pap. 5.95 *(978-0-9648564-6-2(8))* Archus Pr., LLC.

Berger, Melvin & Berger, Gilda. Can You Fly High, Wright Brothers? Dorman, Brandon, illus. 2007. (Scholastic Science Supergiants Ser.: Vol. 1). (ENG.). 48p. (J). (gr. 2-5). pap. 4.99 *(978-0-439-83378-3(7))* Scholastic, Inc.

Bingham, Jane. The Wright Brothers: First Flight. 2017. (Fact Cat: History Ser.). (ENG., Illus.). 24p. (J). (gr. k-2). pap. 9.99 ***(978-0-7502-9039-5(0)***, Wayland) Hachette Children's Group GBR. Dist: Hachette Bk. Group.

Borden, Louise, et al. Touching the Sky: The Flying Adventures of Wilbur & Orville Wright. Fiore, Peter M., illus. 2003. (ENG.). 64p. (J). (gr. k-3). 19.99 *(978-0-689-84876-6(5)*, McElderry, Margaret K. Bks.) McElderry, Margaret K. Bks.

Brown, Jonatha A. Los Hermanos Wright. Acosta, Tatiana & Gutierrez, Guillermo, trs. from ENG. 2004. (Gente Que Hay Que Conocer Ser.). (SPA., Illus.). 24p. (gr. 1-4). lib. bdg. 22.00 *(978-0-8368-4356-9(8)*, Weekly Reader Leveled Readers) Stevens, Gareth Publishing LLLP.

—Los Hermanos Wright. 2004. (People We Should Know Ser.).Tr. of Wright Brothers. (SPA.). 24p. (gr. 1-4). pap. 8.15 *(978-0-8368-4363-7(0)*, GHS33824, Weekly Reader Leveled Readers) Stevens, Gareth Publishing LLLP.

—The Wright Brothers. 2004. (People We Should Know Ser.). (Illus.). 24p. (gr. 1-4). lib. bdg. 22.00 *(978-0-8368-4314-9(2)*, Weekly Reader Leveled Readers) Stevens, Gareth Publishing LLLP.

Buckley, James, Jr. Who Were the Wright Brothers? Foley, Tim & Harrison, Nancy, illus. 2014. (Who Was? Ser.). (ENG.). 112p. (J). (gr. 3-7). 5.99 *(978-0-448-47951-4(6)*, Grosset & Dunlap) Penguin Young Readers Group.

Buckley, James. Who Were the Wright Brothers? Foley, Tim, illus. 2014. 106p. (J). *(978-1-101-99527-3(0))* Penguin Publishing Group.

Burke, Michelle Prater. The Story of the Wright Brothers. Johnson, Meredith, illus. 2016. (J). *(978-0-8249-1986-3(6)*, Ideal Pubns.) Worthy Publishing.

Carson, Mary Kay. The Wright Brothers for Kid: How They Invented the Airplane, 21 Activities Exploring the Science & History of Flight. D'Argo, Laura, illus. 2003. (For Kids Ser.). (ENG.). 160p. (J). (gr. 4). pap. 18.95 *(978-1-55652-477-6(3))* Chicago Review Pr., Inc.

Collins, Mary. Airborne: A Photobiography of Wilbur & Orville Wright. (Photobiographies Ser.). (ENG., Illus.). 64p. (J). (gr. 5). 2015. pap. 7.99 *(978-1-4263-2221-1(6))* 2003. 18.95 *(978-0-7922-6957-1(8)*, 53238483) National Geographic Society. (National Geographic Children's Bks.).

Crompton, Samuel Willard. The Wright Brothers: First in Flight. 2007. (Milestones in American History Ser.). (Illus.). 128p. (YA). (gr. 7-12). lib. bdg. 35.00 *(978-0-7910-9356-6(5))* Facts On File, Inc.

Cudeyro, Erica M. American History for Young Minds - Volume 1, Looking Towards the Sky, Book 1, the First Airplane. Butler, Lindsay L., illus. 2008. 20p. pap. 11.95 *(978-1-934925-34-8(9)*, Eloquent Bks.) Strategic Book Publishing & Rights Agency (SBPRA).

Dakers, Diane. Orville & Wilbur Wright: Pioneers of the Age of Flight. 2016. (Crabtree Groundbreaker Biographies Ser.). (ENG.). 112p. (J). (gr. 5-8). *(978-0-7787-2609-8(6))* Crabtree Publishing Co.

Davis, Lynn. The Wright Brothers, 1 vol. 2016. (ENG., Illus.). 24p. (J). *(978-1-62403-726-9(7))* ABDO Publishing Co.

Deines, Ann, ed. Wilbur & Orville Wright: A Handbook of Facts. 2007. (Illus.). 64p. per. 5.95 *(978-1-888213-75-1(2))* Eastern National.

Dorfman, Janet. The Wright Brothers. 2011. (Early Connections Ser.). (J). *(978-1-61672-564-8(8))* Benchmark Education Co.

Dunn, Joe. The Wright Brothers, 1 vol. Dunn, Ben, illus. 2007. (Bio-Graphics Ser.). (ENG.). 32p. (gr. 3-6). 28.50 *(978-1-60270-071-0(0)*, Graphic Planet- Nonfiction) ABDO Publishing Co.

Ford, Carin T. The Wright Brothers: Heroes of Flight. 2003. (Famous Inventors Ser.). (Illus.). 32p. (J). (gr. 1-4). lib. bdg. 23.94 *(978-0-7660-2002-3(9))* Enslow Pubs., Inc.

Graham, Ian. You Wouldn't Want to Be on the First Flying Machine! A High-Soaring Ride You'd Rather Not Take. Antram, David, illus. 2013. (You Wouldn't Want to... Ser.). (ENG.). 32p. (J). 29.00 *(978-0-531-25945-0(5))*; pap. 9.95 *(978-0-531-23042-8(2))* Scholastic Library Publishing. (Watts, Franklin).

—You Wouldn't Want to Be on the First Flying Machine! A High-Soaring Ride You'd Rather Not Take. 2013. (You Wouldn't Want To... Ser.). lib. bdg. 20.80 *(978-0-606-31631-6(0)*, Turtleback) Turtleback Bks.

Hamen, Susan E. The Wright Brothers, 1 vol. 2007. (Essential Lives Set 1 Ser.). (ENG., Illus.). 112p. (J). (gr. 6-12). lib. bdg. 35.64 *(978-1-59928-846-8(X))* ABDO Publishing Co.

Helfand, Lewis. The Wright Brothers. Banerjee, Sankha, illus. 2011. (Campfire Graphic Novels Ser.). (ENG.). 72p. (YA). (gr. 5-9). pap. 9.99 *(978-93-80028-46-0(6)*, Campfire) Steerforth Pr.

Hill, Lee Sullivan. The Flyer Flew! The Invention of the Airplane. Orback, Craig, illus. 2006. (On My Own Science Ser.). 48p. (J). (gr. 3-7). per. 6.95 *(978-1-57505-855-9(3))*; (gr. k-3). lib. bdg. 25.26 *(978-1-57505-758-3(1)*, Millbrook Pr.) Lerner Publishing Group.

James, Emily. The Wright Brothers. 2017. (Great Scientists & Inventors Ser.). (ENG.). 24p. (gr. k-1). lib. bdg. 26.65 *(978-1-5157-3885-5(X))* Capstone Press of Coughlan Cos.

Jenner, Caryn. First Flight Vol. 4: The Story of the Wright Brothers. 2004. (DK Readers Ser.). (Illus.). 48p. (gr. -1-3). 14.00 *(978-0-7569-3361-6(7))* Perfection Learning Corp.

Jenner, Caryn & Garrett, Leslie. First Flight, Level 4: The Story of the Wright Brothers. 2003. (DK Readers Ser.). (ENG., Illus.). 48p. (J). (gr. 3-7). pap. 3.99 *(978-0-7894-9291-3(1)*, DK Children) Dorling Kindersley Publishing, Inc.

LaFontaine, Bruce. BOOST the Story of the Wright Brothers Coloring Book. 2013. (BOOST Educational Ser.). (ENG.). 32p. (J). (gr. 3-5). pap. 4.99 *(978-0-486-49440-1(3))* Dover Pubns., Inc.

Lefèvre-Garros, J. P. The Wright Brothers, Vol. 3. Uderzo, M., illus. 2012. (Cinebook Recounts Ser.: 3). (ENG.). 48p. (YA). (gr. 6-17). pap. 11.95 *(978-1-84918-100-6(4))* CineBook GBR. Dist: National Bk. Network.

MacLeod, Elizabeth. The Wright Brothers. Krystoforski, Andrej, illus. 2008. (Kids Can Read Ser.). (ENG.). 32p. (J). (gr. 1-3). 14.95 *(978-1-55453-053-3(9))*; pap. 3.95 *(978-1-55453-054-0(7))* Kids Can Pr., Ltd. CAN. Dist: Hachette Bk. Group.

Mayo, Gretchen Will & O'Hern, Kerri. Los Hermanos Wright. Isaacs, Rebekah & Timmons, Jonathan, illus. 2007. (Biografias Graficas (Graphic Biographies) Ser.). (SPA.). 32p. (gr. 5-8). lib. bdg. 27.00 *(978-0-8368-7883-7(3))* Stevens, Gareth Publishing LLLP.

—The Wright Brothers. Isaacs, Rebekah & Timmons, Jonathan, illus. 2006. (Graphic Biographies Ser.). 32p. (gr. 5-8). lib. bdg. 27.00 *(978-0-8368-6199-0(X))* Stevens, Gareth Publishing LLLP.

Mayo, Gretchen Will, et al. The Wright Brothers. 2006. (Graphic Biographies Ser.). (Illus.). 32p. (gr. 5-8). pap. 10.50 *(978-0-8368-6251-5(1))* Stevens, Gareth Publishing LLLP.

McCormick, Lisa Wade. Wright Brothers. 2005. (Scholastic News Nonfiction Readers Ser.). (Illus.). 24p. (J). pap. *(978-0-516-24786-1(7))* Children's Pr., Ltd.

McLaughlin, Kari Massie. My Adventure with the Wright Brothers. 2007. 44p. (J). 8.99 *(978-1-59092-471-6(1))* Blue Forge Pr.

McPherson, Stephanie Sammartino & Gardner, Joseph Sammartino. Wilbur & Orville Wright: Taking Flight. 2004. (Trailblazer Biography Ser.). (Illus.). 120p. (J). 30.60 *(978-1-57505-443-8(4)*, Carolrhoda Bks.) Lerner Publishing Group.

Mills, Nathan & Weir, William. The Wright Brothers: The First to Fly. 2012. (Rosen Readers Ser.). (ENG., Illus.). 24p. (J). (gr. 1-2). pap. 8.25 *(978-1-4488-8863-4(8)*, Rosen Classroom) Rosen Publishing Group, Inc., The.

Niz, Xavier, et al. The Wright Brothers & the Airplane, 1 vol. Erwin, Steve et al, illus. 2007. (Inventions & Discovery Ser.). (ENG.). 32p. (gr. 3-4). 30.65 *(978-0-7368-6845-7(3)*, Graphic Library) Capstone Press of Coughlan Cos.

Niz, Xavier W., et al. The Wright Brothers & the Airplane, 1 vol. Erwin, Steve, illus. 2007. (Inventions & Discovery Ser.). (ENG.). 32p. (gr. 3-4). per. 8.10 *(978-0-7368-7897-5(1)*, Graphic Library) Capstone Press of Coughlan Cos.

O'Hern, Kerri & Will Mayo, Gretchen. Los Hermanos Wright. 2007. (Biografías Gráficas (Graphic Biographies) Ser.). (SPA.). 32p. (gr. 5-8). pap. 10.50 *(978-0-8368-7890-5(6))* Stevens, Gareth Publishing LLLP.

Old, Wendie C. The Wright Brothers: Aviation Pioneers & Inventors. 2015. (Legendary American Biographies Ser.). 96p. (J). (gr. 6-12). 27.94 *(978-0-7660-6505-5(7))*; pap. 10.95 *(978-0-7660-6506-2(5))* Enslow Pubs., Inc.

Orr, Tamra B. The Dawn of Aviation: The Story of the Wright Brothers. 2005. (Monumental Milestones Ser.). (Illus.). 48p. (YA). (gr. 4-7). lib. bdg. 29.95 *(978-1-58415-396-2(2)*, 1244922) Mitchell Lane Pubs., Inc.

O'Sullivan, Robyn. The Wright Brothers Fly. 2007. (History Chapters Ser.). (ENG., Illus.). 48p. (J). (gr. 1-4). lib. bdg. 17.90 *(978-1-4263-0188-9(X)*, National Geographic Children's Bks.) National Geographic Society.

Perkis, Andrea. The Wright Brothers Make History! 2012. (InfoMax Readers Ser.). (ENG., Illus.). 24p. (J). (gr. 1-2). pap. 8.25 *(978-1-4488-9076-7(4)*, Rosen Classroom) Rosen Publishing Group, Inc., The.

Rausch, Monica L. Los Hermanos Wright y el Avion. 2007. (Inventores y sus descubrimientos (Inventors & Their Discoveries) Ser.). (SPA., Illus.). 24p. (gr. 1-4). pap. 8.15 *(978-0-8368-8001-4(3))*; lib. bdg. 22.00 *(978-0-8368-7996-4(1))* Stevens, Gareth Publishing LLLP. (Weekly Reader Leveled Readers).

—The Wright Brothers & the Airplane. 2007. (Inventors & Their Discoveries Ser.). (Illus.). 24p. (gr. 1-4). pap. 8.15 *(978-0-8368-7733-5(0))*; lib. bdg. 22.00 *(978-0-8368-7502-7(8))* Stevens, Gareth Publishing LLLP. (Weekly Reader Leveled Readers).

Reed, Jennifer. Wilbur & Orville Wright: Trailblazers of the Sky. 2007. (Inventors Who Changed the World Ser.). (Illus.). 128p. (J). (gr. 5). lib. bdg. 34.60 *(978-1-59845-054-5(9)*, MyReportLinks.com Bks.) Enslow Pubs., Inc.

Roop, Peter & Roop, Connie. Let's Fly Wilbur & Orville! 2003. (Before I Made History Ser.). (Illus.). 60p. (J). *(978-0-439-55441-1(1))* Scholastic, Inc.

Schulz, Walter A. Johnny Moore & the Wright Brothers' Flying Machine. Bowles, Doug, illus. 2011. (History Speaks: Picture Books Plus Reader's Theater Ser.). 48p. pap. 56.72 *(978-0-7613-7633-0(X))*; (ENG.). (gr. 2-4). lib. bdg. 27.93 *(978-0-7613-5876-3(5)*, Millbrook Pr.) Lerner Publishing Group.

—Will y Orv. Translations.com Staff, tr. from ENG. Schulz, Janet, illus. 2006. (Yo Solo - Historia (on My Own - History) Ser.). (SPA.). 48p. (gr. 2-4). lib. bdg. 25.26 *(978-0-8225-6263-4(4))* Lerner Publishing Group.

Schulz, Walter A. & Schultz, Walter A. Johnny Moore & the Wright Brothers' Flying Machine. Bowles, Doug, illus. 2011. (History Speaks: Picture Books Plus Reader's Theater Ser.). (ENG.). 48p. (gr. 2-4). pap. 9.95 *(978-0-7613-7117-5(6))* Lerner Publishing Group.

Spilsbury, Louise. The Wright Brothers & the Airplane, 01 vols., 1. 2016. (Inventions That Changed the World Ser.). (ENG.). 32p. (J). pap. 10.00 *(978-1-5081-4643-8(8)*, PowerKids Pr.) Rosen Publishing Group, Inc., The.

Sproule, Anna. The Wright Brothers. 2005. (Giants of Science Bilingual Ser.). (J). 9.95 *(978-1-4103-0507-7(4)*, Blackbirch Pr., Inc.) Cengage Gale.

Stevenson, Augusta. Wilbur & Orville Wright: Boys with Wings. Laune, Paul, illus. 2011. 192p. (gr. 2-5). 42.95 *(978-1-258-07857-7(0))* Literary Licensing, LLC.

Stolfo, Paul. The Wright Brothers. 2009. (Real Life Readers Ser.). 12p. (gr. 2-3). pap. 5.90 *(978-1-4042-7955-1(5)*, Rosen Classroom) Rosen Publishing Group, Inc., The.

Tate, Suzanne. Flyer: A Tale of the Wright Dog. Melvin, James, illus. 2003. (Suzanne Tate's History Ser.). (J). pap. 4.95 *(978-1-878405-42-5(X))* Nags Head Art, Inc.

Tieck, Sarah. Wright Brothers, 1 vol. 2006. (First Biographies Ser.). (ENG., Illus.). 32p. (gr. -1-3). 27.07 *(978-1-59679-790-1(8)*, Buddy Bks.) ABDO Publishing Co.

Troupe, Thomas Kingsley. The Wright Brothers' First Flight: a Fly on the Wall History. Tejido, Jomike, illus. 2017. (Fly on the Wall History Ser.). (ENG.). 32p. (gr. 1-3). pap. 7.95 *(978-1-4795-9791-8(0))*; lib. bdg. 27.32 *(978-1-4795-9787-1(2))* Picture Window Bks.

Van Steenwyk, Elizabeth. One Fine Day: A Radio Play. Farnsworth, Bill, illus. 2004. 32p. (J). (gr. 3-5). 16.00 *(978-0-8028-5234-2(3))* Eerdmans, William B. Publishing Co.

Venezia, Mike. The Wright Brothers: Inventors Whose Ideas Really Took Flight. 2010. (Getting to Know the World's Greatest Inventors & Scientists Ser.). 32p. (J). (gr. 3-4). pap. 6.95 *(978-0-531-22353-6(1)*, Children's Pr.) Scholastic Library Publishing.

—The Wright Brothers: Inventors Whose Ideas Really Took Flight. Venezia, Mike, illus. 2010. (Getting to Know the World's Greatest Inventors & Scientists Ser.). (ENG., Illus.). 32p. (J). (gr. 3-4). 28.00 *(978-0-531-23732-8(X))* Scholastic Library Publishing.

Weir, William. The Wright Brothers: The First to Fly. 2012. (Beginning Biographies Ser.). (ENG., Illus.). 24p. (J). (gr. 1-3). 22.60 *(978-1-4488-8597-8(3)*, PowerKids Pr.) Rosen Publishing Group, Inc., The.

Wilgus, Alison. Science Comics: Flying Machines: How the Wright Brothers Soared. Brooks, Molly, illus. 2017. (Science Comics Ser.). (ENG.). 128p. (J). pap. 12.99 *(978-1-62672-139-5(4)*, 9781626721395, First Second Bks.) Roaring Brook Pr.

Will y Orv (Will & Orv) 2006. (J). pap. 6.95 *(978-0-8225-6615-1(X)*, Ediciones Lerner) Lerner Publishing Group.

WRIGHT, WILBUR, 1867-1912—FICTION

Bailey, Gerry & Foster, Karen. The Wright Brothers' Glider. Radford, Karen & Noyes, Leighton, illus. 2008. (Stories of Great People Ser.). (ENG.). 40p. (J). (gr. 3-8). pap. *(978-0-7787-3715-5(2))*; lib. bdg. *(978-0-7787-3693-6(8))* Crabtree Publishing Co.

Glass, Andrew. The Wondrous Whirligig: The Wright Brothers¿ First Flying Machine. Glass, Andrew, illus. 2007. (Illus.). 30p. (J). reprint ed. 17.00 *(978-1-4223-6765-0(7))* DIANE Publishing Co.

Gutman, Dan. Race for the Sky: The Kitty Hawk Diaries of Johnny Moore. 2003. (ENG., Illus.). 192p. (J). (gr. 5-9). 19.99 *(978-0-689-84554-3(5)*, Simon & Schuster Bks. For Young Readers) Simon & Schuster Bks. For Young Readers.

Herodotus. The Wright Brothers Adventure. 2005. (Illus.). (J). *(978-0-9762509-1-3(8))* Society For The Understanding Of Early Child Development.

Rigsby, Annelle & Raffa, Edwina. Race to Kitty Hawk. 2003. (Adventures in America Ser.). (Illus.). 84p. (gr. 4). 14.95 *(978-1-893110-33-5(8))* Silver Moon Pr.

Sutton, Felix. We Were There at the First Airplane Flight. Matulay, Laszlo, illus. 2013. (ENG.). 192p. (J). (gr. 3-8). pap. 6.99 *(978-0-486-49258-2(3))* Dover Pubns., Inc.

Sutton, Felix & Loening, Grover. We Were There at the First Airplane Flight. Matulay, Laszlo, illus. 2011. 194p. 42.95 *(978-1-258-09600-7(5))* Literary Licensing, LLC.

WRITERS

see Authors

WRITING

see also Alphabet; Calligraphy; Ciphers; Cryptography; Hieroglyphics; Picture-Writing; Typewriting

Activity Worksheets. 2004. (J). spiral bd. 29.95 *(978-1-886441-64-4(2))* Zoo-phonics, Inc.

Amaze Us!, 6 vols. (Wildcats Ser.). 32p. (gr. 2-8). *(978-0-322-02442-7(0))* Wright Group/McGraw-Hill.

Amazing Maps: Level Q, 6 vols. (Wonder Worldtm Ser.). 48p. 39.95 *(978-0-7802-2945-7(2))* Wright Group/McGraw-Hill.

Analogies 1: Grade 7-8. 2004. (Analogies Ser.). pap. 7.25 *(978-0-8388-2225-8(8))* Educators Publishing Service, Inc.

Analogies 2: Grade 9-10. 2004. (Analogies Ser.). pap. 7.25 *(978-0-8388-2227-2(4))* Educators Publishing Service, Inc.

Analogies 3: Grade 11-12. 2004. (Analogies Ser.). pap. 7.25 *(978-0-8388-2229-6(0))* Educators Publishing Service, Inc.

Analogies 3: Grade11-12 Quiz Book. 2004. (Analogies Ser.). pap. 8.20 *(978-0-8388-2230-2(4))* Educators Publishing Service, Inc.

Anorak Press Staff. Anorak: Writing. 2013. (ENG., Illus.). 68p. (J). pap. 9.99 *(978-1-4236-3390-7(3)*, Anorak Pr.) Gibbs Smith, Publisher.

Aprende a Escribir. 2003. (SPA.). 22p. (J). (gr. -1-1). *(978-968-5308-89-2(6)*, Silver Dolphin en Español) Advanced Marketing, S. de R. L. de C. V.

Arnold, Clareen. Handwriting - Modern Manuscript. 2003. (Skill Builders Ser.). 80p. 2.95 *(978-1-932210-26-2(1))* Rainbow Bridge Publishing.

The Art of Calligraphy. 2004. (Classic Craft Cases Ser.). (ENG., Illus.). 64p. *(978-1-84229-800-8(3))* Top That! Publishing PLC.

Ashton, Christine. The Genie of the Bike Lamp: Level P, 6 vols. (Mountain Peaks Ser.). 128p. (gr. 6-18). 36.95 *(978-0-322-05892-7(9))* Wright Group/McGraw-Hill.

Beck, Esther. Cool Written Records: The Proof Is in the Paper, 1 vol. 2009. (Cool CSI Ser.). (ENG., Illus.). 32p. (YA). (gr. 3-6). 28.50 *(978-1-60453-488-7(5))* ABDO Publishing Co.

Beyond the Beyond, 6 vols. (Wildcats Ser.). 32p. (gr. 2-8). *(978-0-322-02444-1(7))* Wright Group/McGraw-Hill.

BJU Staff. Handwriting Worktext Grd 2. 2004. pap. 11.50 *(978-1-57924-103-2(4))* BJU Pr.

—Handwriting Worktext Grd 3. 2004. pap. 11.50 *(978-1-57924-215-2(4))* BJU Pr.

—Handwriting Worktext Grd 4. 2004. pap. 11.50 *(978-1-57924-263-3(4))* BJU Pr.

—Handwriting Worktext Grd 5. 2004. pap. 11.50 *(978-1-57924-298-5(7))* BJU Pr.

—Handwriting Worktext Grd 6. 2004. pap. 11.50 *(978-1-57924-352-4(5))* BJU Pr.

Bradshaw, Georgine & Wrighton, Charlene. Basic Kit - Kindergarten. Clark, Irene, illus. 2005. Orig. Title: Basic Kit II. (J). 249.95 *(978-1-886441-31-6(6))* Zoo-phonics, Inc.

—Kindergarten Zoo-per Kit. Clark, Irene, illus. 2005. (J). 499.95 *(978-1-886441-34-7(0)*, ZOP4219) Zoo-phonics, Inc.

—Preschool Zoo-per Kit. Clark, Irene, illus. 2005. (J). 449.95 *(978-1-886441-32-3(4)*, ZOP4218) Zoo-phonics, Inc.

Bright & Beyond - Writing. 2004. (J). *(978-0-9726170-9-3(4))* Pal Toys, LLC.

Brown Conroy, Erin. Writing Skillbuilders Bk. 1: A Fun-Filled Book of Prewriting Skills for Beginning Writers. 2004. (J). spiral bd. 14.95 *(978-0-9740981-6-6(7))* Celtic Cross Communications.

—Writing Skillbuilders Bk. 2: A Fun-Filled Activity Book to Build Strong Handwriting Skills. 2004. (J). spiral bd. 14.95 *(978-0-9740981-7-3(5))* Celtic Cross Communications.

—Writing Skillbuilders Bk. 3: A Fun-Filled Activity Book for Beautiful Cursive Handwriting. 2004. (J). spiral bd. 14.95 *(978-0-9740981-8-0(3))* Celtic Cross Communications.

Budgell, Gill & Ruttle, Kate. Cambridge Handwriting at Home: Forming Cursive Letters. 2015. (Penpals for Handwriting Ser.). (ENG.). 28p. pap. 5.95 *(978-1-84565-297-5(5))* Cambridge Univ. Pr.

—Cambridge Handwriting at Home: Forming Manuscript Letters. 2015. (Penpals for Handwriting Ser.). (ENG.). 28p. pap. 5.95 *(978-1-84565-295-1(9))* Cambridge Univ. Pr.

—Cambridge Handwriting at Home: Forming Uppercase Letters. 2015. (Penpals for Handwriting Ser.). (ENG.). 28p. pap. 5.95 *(978-1-84565-296-8(7))* Cambridge Univ. Pr.

—Cambridge Handwriting at Home: Getting Ready for Handwriting. 2015. (Penpals for Handwriting Ser.). (ENG.). 22p. pap. 5.95 *(978-1-84565-294-4(0))* Cambridge Univ. Pr.

—Penpals for Handwriting Year 2 Practice Book. 2nd rev. ed. 2015. (Penpals for Handwriting Ser.). (ENG.). 32p. pap. 12.44 *(978-1-316-50137-5(X))* Cambridge Univ. Pr.

—Penpals for Handwriting Year 3 Practice Book. 2nd rev. ed. 2015. (Penpals for Handwriting Ser.). (ENG.). 32p. pap. 12.44 *(978-1-316-50141-2(8))* Cambridge Univ. Pr.

Bukiet, Suzanne. Scripts of the World. 2nd ed. (Illus.). 91p. (YA). reprint ed. 19.95 *(978-0-9656274-1-2(1))* Another Language Pr.

Burke, Mary F. Four Square: The Personal Writing Coach, Grades 1-3. Radtke, Becky, illus. 2005. 112p. (J). pap. 12.95 *(978-1-57310-446-3(9))* Teaching & Learning Co.

Callella, Trisha. Daily Writing Warm-Ups: Grades 3-4. 2006. (Illus.). 128p. (J). (gr. 5-6). per. 13.99 *(978-1-59198-306-4(1))* Creative Teaching Pr., Inc.

—Daily Writing Warm-Ups: Grades 5-6. 2006. (SAM., Illus.). 128p. (J). (gr. 5-6). per. 13.99 *(978-1-59198-307-1(X))* Creative Teaching Pr., Inc.

Canavan, Roger. You Wouldn't Want to Live Without Writing! 2015. (You Wouldn't Want to Live Without Ser.). lib. bdg. 20.80 *(978-0-606-37474-3(4))* Turtleback Bks.

Carson-Dellosa Publishing Staff. Cursive Practice, Grade 2-3. 2010. (Home Workbooks Ser.). (ENG.). 64p. (gr. 2-3). pap. 4.49 *(978-1-60418-801-1(4))* Carson-Dellosa Publishing, LLC.

—Spelling & Writing for Beginners, Grade 1. 2010. (Home Workbooks Ser.). (ENG.). 64p. (gr. 1-1). pap. 4.49 *(978-1-60418-788-5(3))* Carson-Dellosa Publishing, LLC.

Cheaney, Janie B. Wordsmith Craftsman Grd 10 + 2004. pap. 16.00 *(978-1-929683-20-8(0))* Colbert Hse., LLC, The.

—Wordsmith Grd 7-9. 2004. pap. 16.00 *(978-1-929683-18-5(9))* Colbert Hse., LLC, The.

Citylit Kids. Write On! 2012. 68p. pap. 10.00 *(978-1-936328-10-9(0))* CityLit Pr.

Claire, Elizabeth. Hi! (Illus.). (J). wbk. ed. *(978-0-8056-0122-0(8))* Minerva Bks., Ltd.

Collins Easy Learning, Collins Easy. Pen Control - Wipe-Clean. 2017. (Collins Easy Learning Preschool Ser.). (ENG.). 24p. (J). (gr. -1-k). 7.99 ***(978-0-00-821290-2(2))*** HarperCollins Pubs. Ltd. GBR. Dist: Independent Pubs. Group.

Collins Easy Learning Staff & HarperCollins UK Staff. Writing Practice. 2012. (Collins Easy Learning Age 5-7 Ser.). (ENG., Illus.). 96p. (J). pap. 6.99 *(978-0-00-746726-6(5))* HarperCollins Pubs. Ltd. GBR. Dist: Independent Pubs. Group.

Coon, Nora. Teen Dream Jobs: How to Find the Job You Really Want Now! 2004. (Illus.). 132p. (YA). (gr. 8-12). per. 9.95 *(978-1-58270-093-9(1))* Beyond Words Publishing, Inc.

Corporate Contributor, ed. Diary of a Texas Kid. 2011. (State Journal Ser.). (ENG.). 128p. (J). (gr. 4-8). pap. 9.95 *(978-1-58536-608-8(0)*, 202225) Sleeping Bear Pr.

Culham, Ruth. Daily Trait Warm-Ups: 180 Revision & Editing Activities to Kick off Writing Time. 2009. (ENG.). 208p. 27.99 *(978-0-545-09599-0(9)*, Teaching Resources) Scholastic, Inc.

Cyberspace, 6 vols. (Wildcats Ser.). 32p. (gr. 2-8). *(978-0-322-00600-3(7))* Wright Group/McGraw-Hill.

David, Juliet. Learn & Play: Chalkboard Activities. Prole, Helen, illus. 2007. (Candle Bible for Toddlers Ser.). 12p. (J). (gr. -1-k). bds. 11.99 *(978-0-8254-7331-9(4)*, Candle Bks.) Lion Hudson PLC GBR. Dist: Kregel Pubns.

Davidson, Kay. Writing the Simple 6: A Writing Rubic for Kids. 2004. pap. 28.95 *(978-1-931334-38-9(2))* Pieces of Learning.

de Diaz, Rosario Ahumada. Juguemos con Letras: Ejercicios de Iniciacion a la Escritura. (SPA.). (J). pap. 9.95 *(978-968-24-0919-6(5)*, TRM40) Trillas Editorial, S. A. MEX. Dist: Continental Bk. Co., Inc.

Dinosaur Detective: 6 Each of 1 Anthology, 6 vols. (Wildcats Ser.). 32p. (gr. 2-8). *(978-0-322-00586-0(8))* Wright Group/McGraw-Hill.

Duke, Nell K. & Bennett-Armistead, V. Susan. Reading & Writing Informational Text in the Primary Grades: Research-Based Practices. 2003. (ENG., Illus.). 272p. (gr. k-3). pap. 27.99 *(978-0-439-53123-8(3))* Scholastic, Inc.

Dwyer, Carol. Cursive Writing 3-4. 2005. (ENG.). 64p. (Orig.). (J). (gr. 3-4). pap. 3.99 *(978-1-58947-398-0(1))* School Zone Publishing Co.

Early Stage 2 Models for Writing. 2003. 135.95 *(978-0-673-77820-8(7))* Celebration Pr.

Early Stage 2 Shared Writing Templates. 2003. 135.95 *(978-0-673-77821-5(5))* Celebration Pr.

Emergent Stage 1 Models for Writing. 2003. 135.95 *(978-0-673-77818-5(5))* Celebration Pr.

Emergent Stage 1 Shared Writing Templates. 2003. 135.95 *(978-0-673-77819-2(3))* Celebration Pr.

English I: Language Skills, Chapter 3 Activities. 2005. (Illus.). 54p. (YA). pap. 5.00 *(978-1-59476-139-3(6))* Paradigm Accelerated Curriculum.

Erickson, Karen. MEville to WEville Unit 1: Unit 1 ME, 2 Bks., manual and children's Bk. 2004. 292p. 75.00 *(978-0-9666667-5-5(5))* AbleNet, Inc.

Evan-Moor Educational Publishers, creator. Text-Based Writing Nonfiction, Grade 2: Common Core Mastery. 2014. (Text-Based Writing: Nonfiction: Common Core Mastery Ser.). (ENG., Illus.). 132p. (J). (gr. 2). pap. 9.99 *(978-1-61368-995-0(0))* Evan-Moor Educational Pubs.

Everett, Reese. Reciting the Pledge, Yes or No. 2016. (Seeing Both Sides Ser.). (ENG.). 32p. (gr. 3-6). 32.79 *(978-1-68191-381-0(X))* Rourke Educational Media.

Facts on File, Inc. Staff. Writing. 2012. (Discovering Careers Ser.). (Illus.). 122p. (gr. 4-9). 24.95 *(978-0-8160-8060-1(7)*, Ferguson Publishing Co.) Facts On File, Inc.

Fandel, Jennifer. You Can Write. 2012. (You Can Write Ser.). (ENG.). 24p. (gr. 1-2). pap. 41.70 *(978-1-4296-9320-2(7))*; pap. 250.20 *(978-1-4296-9321-9(5))*; pap. 13.90 *(978-1-4296-9493-3(9))* Capstone Press of Coughlan Cos. (First Facts).

Fandel, Jennifer & Fields, Jan. You Can Write. 2012. (You Can Write Ser.). (ENG.). 24p. (gr. 1-2). lib. bdg. 50.64 *(978-1-4296-9156-7(5)*, First Facts) Capstone Press of Coughlan Cos.

Feldgus, Eileen G. & Cardonick, Isabell. Kid Writing: A Systematic Approach to Phonics, Journals, & Writing Workshop. 2nd rev. ed. 192p. (J). (gr. k-2). pap. 26.50 *(978-0-322-06435-5(X))* Wright Group/McGraw-Hill.

Festival Fun: 6 Each of 1 Anthology, 6 vols. (Wildcats Ser.). 32p. (gr. 2-8). *(978-0-322-02424-3(2))* Wright Group/McGraw-Hill.

Findley, Violet. Cursive Writing Practice: Wacky Facts. 2016. (ENG., Illus.). 48p. (J). (gr. 2-5). pap. 10.99 *(978-0-545-94317-8(5))* Scholastic, Inc.

—Handwriting Practice: Wacky Facts. 2016. (ENG., Illus.). 48p. (J). (gr. k-3). pap. 10.99 *(978-1-338-03061-7(2))* Scholastic, Inc.

Fine, Jil. Writing in Ancient India. 2003. (Writing in the Ancient World Ser.). (Illus.). 24p. (J). lib. bdg. 22.60 *(978-0-8239-6508-3(2)*, PowerKids Pr.) Rosen Publishing Group, Inc., The.

Fire! Fire! 6 Each of 1 Anthology, 6 vols. (Wildcats Ser.). 32p. (gr. 2-8). *(978-0-322-00581-5(7))* Wright Group/McGraw-Hill.

FitzGerald, Elizabeth. Cursive First: An Introduction to Cursive Penmanship. 2nd ed. 2003. (Illus.). pap. 14.95 *(978-0-9744920-1-8(9))* LITHBTH Educational Services.

Flash Kids Editors, ed. Cursive Writing: Around the World in 26 Letters. Christoph, Jamey, illus. 2012. (ENG.). 112p. (J). (gr. 2-4). pap. 5.95 *(978-1-4114-6345-5(5)*, Spark Publishing Group) Sterling Publishing Co., Inc.

—Print Writing: A Creepy-Crawly Alphabet. Reese, Brandon, illus. 2012. (ENG.). 112p. (J). (gr. k-2). pap. 5.95 *(978-1-4114-6344-8(7)*, Spark Publishing Group) Sterling Publishing Co., Inc.

Flash Kids Editors, Flash Kids, ed. Write-On Wipe-off Cursive Writing. 2016. (Write-On Wipe-off Handwriting Cards Ser.). (ENG., Illus.). 80p. (J). (gr. 1-3). 10.95 *(978-1-4114-7890-9(8)*, Spark Publishing Group) Sterling Publishing Co., Inc.

Flath, Camden. Freelance & Technical Writers: Words for Sale. 2010. (New Careers for the 21st Century Ser.). (Illus.). 64p. (YA). (gr. 7-18). lib. bdg. 22.95 *(978-1-4222-1814-3(7))* Mason Crest.

Fluency Stage 3 Shared Writing Templates. 2003. 125.50 *(978-0-673-77822-2(3))* Celebration Pr.

Fredericks, Anthony D. & Lynott, Vicky. Write to Comprehend: Using Writing as a Tool to Build Reading Comprehension. 2007. (Illus.). 138p. per. 19.95 *(978-1-59647-120-7(4))* Good Year Bks.

Fredrich, Volker, illus. Rechtschreibtraining fuer die 1. Klasse. (Duden-Lernminuten Ser.). (GER.). 32p. (J). wbk. ed. *(978-3-411-70831-4(X))* Bibliographisches Institut & F. A. Brockhaus AG DEU. Dist: International Bk. Import Service, Inc.

—Rechtschreibtraining fuer die 1. und 2. Klasse. (Duden-Lernminuten Ser.). (GER.). 32p. (J). wbk. ed. *(978-3-411-70841-3(7))* Bibliographisches Institut & F. A. Brockhaus AG DEU. Dist: International Bk. Import Service, Inc.

Get Smart Skills Staff. PSSA Writing; Pennsylvania System of School Assessment. 2004. 192p. (gr. 11-18). pap. 14.95 *(978-1-932635-29-4(7))* Webster House Publishing LLC.

Gibbons, Casey Hartley. A Girl's Life with God. 2006. 160p. pap. 8.99 *(978-1-56309-757-7(5)*, N034115) New Hope Pubs.

Gould, Judith S. & Burke, Mary F. Four Square: The Personal Writing Coach, Grades 4-6. Ginger Illustration, illus. 2005. 112p. (J). pap. 12.95 *(978-1-57310-447-0(7))* Teaching & Learning Co.

—Four Square: The Personal Writing Coach, Grades 7-9. Wheeler, Ron, illus. 2005. 112p. (J). pap. 12.95 *(978-1-57310-448-7(5))* Teaching & Learning Co.

Gould, Judith S. & Gould, Evan Jay. Four Square: A Companion to the Four Square Writing Method: Writing in the Content Areas for Grades 1-4. Mitchell, Judy, ed. Radtke, Becky J., illus. 2004. 112p. (J). pap. 11.95 *(978-1-57310-421-0(3))* Teaching & Learning Co.

—Four Square: A Companion to the Four Square Writing Method: Writing in the Content Areas for Grades 5-9. Mitchell, Judy, ed. Wheeler, Ron, illus. 2004. 112p. (J). pap. 11.95 *(978-1-57310-422-7(1))* Teaching & Learning Co.

Greeley, August. Mayan Writing in Mesoamerica. 2009. (Writing in the Ancient World Ser.). 24p. (gr. 3-3). 42.50 *(978-1-60854-903-0(8)*, PowerKids Pr.) Rosen Publishing Group, Inc., The.

Green, Lyric & Meachen Rau, Dana. Future Ready Creative Writing Projects. 2017. (Future Ready Project Skills Ser.). 48p. (J). (gr. 3-4). pap. 11.70 ***(978-0-7660-8767-5(0))*** Enslow Pubs., Inc.

Group/McGraw-Hill, Wright. Babies: Collection 1. (Storyteller Interactive Writing Cards Ser.). (gr. k-3). *(978-0-322-09361-4(9))* Wright Group/McGraw-Hill.

—Bad News Good News: Level N, 6 vols. (Autumn Leaves Ser.). 128p. (gr. 3-6). 36.95 *(978-0-322-06733-2(2))* Wright Group/McGraw-Hill.

—The Butterfly: Collection 2. (Storyteller Interactive Writing Cards Ser.). (gr. k-3). *(978-0-322-09335-5(X))* Wright Group/McGraw-Hill.

—Cats: Collection 4. (Storyteller Interactive Writing Cards Ser.). (gr. k-3). *(978-0-322-09323-2(6))* Wright Group/McGraw-Hill.

—Early Fluency-Fluency Writing Kit. 2004. (Wright Group Literacy Ser.). (gr. k-3). 132.50 *(978-0-322-07021-9(X))* Wright Group/McGraw-Hill.

—Emergent Writing Kit. 2004. (Wright Group Literacy Ser.). (gr. k-3). 79.50 *(978-0-322-06615-1(8))* Wright Group/McGraw-Hill.

—Five Little Frogs: Collection 1. (Storyteller Interactive Writing Cards Ser.). (J). (gr. k-3). *(978-0-322-09363-8(5))* Wright Group/McGraw-Hill.

—In the Rain Forest, 6 vols. (Wildcats Ser.). 32p. (gr. 2-8). *(978-0-322-00599-0(X))* Wright Group/McGraw-Hill.

—Mischief & Mayhem: Level O, 6 vols. (Autumn Leaves Ser.). 128p. (gr. 3-6). 36.95 *(978-0-322-06727-1(8))* Wright Group/McGraw-Hill.

—Move it & Shake It! 6 Each of 1 Anthology, 6 vols. (Wildcats Ser.). 32p. (gr. 2-8). *(978-0-322-05621-3(7))* Wright Group/McGraw-Hill.

—Movie Magic, 6 vols. (Wildcats Ser.). 32p. (gr. 2-8). *(978-0-322-05630-5(6))* Wright Group/McGraw-Hill.

—The Music Scene, 6 vols. (Wildcats Ser.). 32p. (gr. 2-8). *(978-0-322-05631-2(4))* Wright Group/McGraw-Hill.

—On the Prowl: 6 Each of 1 Anthology, 6 vols. (Wildcats Ser.). 32p. (gr. 2-8). *(978-0-322-05852-1(X))* Wright Group/McGraw-Hill.

W
X
Y
Z

—The Party: Collection 1. (Storyteller Interactive Writing Cards Ser.). (gr. k-3). *(978-0-322-09364-5(3))* Wright Group/McGraw-Hill.
—Pigeon Princess: Level O, 6 vols. (Autumn Leaves Ser.). 128p. (gr. 3-6). 36.95 *(978-0-322-06729-5(4))* Wright Group/McGraw-Hill.
—Pixels & Paint, 6 vols. (Wildcats Ser.). 32p. (gr. 2-8). *(978-0-322-05625-1(X))* Wright Group/McGraw-Hill.
—Ready, Set, Pop! Collection 3. (Storyteller Interactive Writing Cards Ser.). (gr. k-3). *(978-0-322-09348-5(1))* Wright Group/McGraw-Hill.
—River Wild: 6 Each of 1 Anthology, 6 vols. (Wildcats Ser.). 32p. (gr. 2-8). *(978-0-322-05857-6(0))* Wright Group/McGraw-Hill.
—Sand: Collection 3. (Storyteller Interactive Writing Cards Ser.). (gr. k-3). *(978-0-322-09349-2(X))* Wright Group/McGraw-Hill.
—Slimed! 6 Each of 1 Anthology, 6 vols. (Wildcats Ser.). 32p. (gr. 2-8). *(978-0-322-05853-8(8))* Wright Group/McGraw-Hill.
—Tiger Level: Adventure Journal Set. (Wildcats Ser.). (gr. 2-8). 31.95 *(978-0-322-05790-6(6))* Wright Group/McGraw-Hill.
—Tiger Level: Lesson Plan Set. (Wildcats Ser.). (gr. 2-8). 96.50 *(978-0-322-06677-9(8))* Wright Group/McGraw-Hill.
—Tiger Level: Wildcats Tiger Complete Kit. (Wildcats Ser.). (gr. 2-8). 599.95 *(978-0-322-06483-6(X))* Wright Group/McGraw-Hill.
—What Sport Is It? Collection 3. (Storyteller Interactive Writing Cards Ser.). (gr. k-3). *(978-0-322-09352-2(X))* Wright Group/McGraw-Hill.
—Working Like a Dog: 6 Each of 1 Anthology, 6 vols. (Wildcats Ser.). 32p. (gr. 2-8). *(978-0-322-05854-5(6))* Wright Group/McGraw-Hill.
—Young & Wild: 6 Each of 1 Anthology, 6 vols. (Wildcats Ser.). 32p. (gr. 2-8). *(978-0-322-05851-4(1))* Wright Group/McGraw-Hill.
—Zoo Tales: 6 Each of 1 Anthology, 6 vols. (Wildcats Ser.). 32p. (gr. 2-8). *(978-0-322-05856-9(2))* Wright Group/McGraw-Hill.
—The 13th Floor: Level O, 6 vols. (Autumn Leaves Ser.). 128p. (gr. 3-6). 36.95 *(978-0-322-06731-8(6))* Wright Group/McGraw-Hill.
Hazan, Maurice, creator. Escrivons: Introduction to Writing in French. (FRE.). (J). 199.95 *(978-1-932770-66-7(6)*, FG11) Symtalk, Inc.
Headley, Shannon. Writing Organizers. 2004. 120p. (J). per. 14.95 *(978-0-9760534-1-5(1))* MK Publishing.
Healy, Nick. Image & Imagination: Ideas & Inspiration for Teen Writers. 2016. (ENG., Illus.). 256p. pap. 16.95 *(978-1-63079-044-8(3))* Switch Pr.
Hoffman, Joan. Tracing Trails Pre-Writing Skills. 2008. (ENG.). 32p. (J). pap. 3.99 *(978-1-60159-117-3(9))* School Zone Publishing Co.
Hohenthal, K. D., creator. The Reading & Writing Connection Journal with Herman the Crab No. 1: What Is the Story About? 2003. 70p. (J). spiral bd. 15.95 *(978-0-9716907-5-2(8)*, Ridgewood Publishing) Ridgewood Group, The.
HOP, LLC. Hooked on Handwriting Learn to Print. 2006. 24.99 *(978-1-933863-15-3(3))* HOP, LLC.
—Hooked on Learning Handwriting. 2006. 64p. 3.79 *(978-1-933863-91-7(9))* HOP, LLC.
Howard, Ian T. One Love, Two Worlds. Bishop, Tracey, illus. 2010. 36p. pap. 14.75 *(978-1-60911-771-9(9)*, Eloquent Bks.) Strategic Book Publishing & Rights Agency (SBPRA).
I Can Write Streetland. 2003. (J). Bk. 1. mass mkt., wbk. ed. 6.95 *(978-0-9743971-0-8(5))*Bk. 2. mass mkt., wbk. ed. 9.95 *(978-0-9743971-1-5(3))*Bk. 3. mass mkt., wbk. ed. 9.95 *(978-0-9743971-2-2(1))* Deziner Media International.
I Can Write Waterworld, Bk. 1. 2003. (J). mass mkt., wbk. ed. 6.95 *(978-0-9743971-4-6(8))* Deziner Media International.
Improving Student Writing: Paragraphs. 2004. (J). per. 12.95 *(978-1-56911-528-2(1))* Learning Resources, Inc.
Improving Student Writing: Sentences. 2004. (J). per. 12.95 *(978-1-56911-526-8(5))* Learning Resources, Inc.
In the News, 6 vols. (Wildcats Ser.). 32p. (gr. 2-8). *(978-0-322-02437-3(4))* Wright Group/McGraw-Hill.
In the News, 6 vols., Set 2. Incl. Climate Change. Brezina, Corona. (YA). lib. bdg. 31.95 *(978-1-4042-1913-7(7))*; Darfur: African Genocide. Xavier, John. (YA). lib. bdg. 31.95 *(978-1-4042-1912-0(9))*; Doping: Athletes & Drugs. Porterfield, Jason. (J). lib. bdg. 29.25 *(978-1-4042-1917-5(X))*; Green Technology: Earth-Friendly Innovations. Sobha, Geeta. (YA). lib. bdg. 31.95 *(978-1-4042-1914-4(5))*; Nukes: The Spread of Nuclear Weapons. Minneus, Steve. (YA). lib. bdg. 31.95 *(978-1-4042-1916-8(1))*; Oil: The Economics of Fuel. Jovinelly, Joann. (YA). lib. bdg. 31.95 *(978-1-4042-1915-1(3))*; (Illus.). 64p. (gr. 7-12). 2007. 2007. Set lib. bdg. 175.50 *(978-1-4042-1112-4(8))* Rosen Publishing Group, Inc., The.
Incredible Places: 6 Each of 1 Anthology, 6 vols. (Wildcats Ser.). 32p. (gr. 2-8). *(978-0-322-00587-7(6))* Wright Group/McGraw-Hill.
Jennison, Nancy. Integrating Test Prep into Reading & Writing Workshops: Classroom-Tested Lessons & Activities That Teach Students the Skills They Need to Become Successful Readers & Writers-And Excel on the Tests. 2011. (ENG.). 240p. pap. 25.99 *(978-0-545-14711-8(5)*, Teaching Resources) Scholastic, Inc.
Keats, Felicity. Dancing Pencils. 2007. (Illus.). 168p. pap. *(978-1-86900-163-6(X))* UmSinsi Pr. ZAF. Dist: Michigan State Univ. Pr.
Kids Can Learn Franklin Staff, ed. Printing. 2004. (Kids Can Learn with Franklin Ser.). (ENG., Illus.). 32p. (J). (gr. k-2). 3.95 *(978-1-55337-602-6(1))* Kids Can Pr., Ltd. CAN. Dist: Hachette Bk. Group.
—Ready for Printing. 2004. (Kids Can Learn with Franklin Ser.). (ENG., Illus.). 32p. (J). (gr. -1-1). 3.95 *(978-1-55337-603-3(X))* Kids Can Pr., Ltd. CAN. Dist: Hachette Bk. Group.
Kids Can Press Staff. Printing Practice. 2003. (Kids Can Learn with Franklin Ser.). (ENG., Illus.). 32p. (J). (gr. k-1). 3.95 *(978-1-55337-590-6(4))* Kids Can Pr., Ltd. CAN. Dist: Hachette Bk. Group.
Kovecses, Anna. One Hundred Words: A First Handwriting Book. 2016. (Learn with Little Mouse Ser.). (ENG., Illus.). 56p. (J). pap. 9.99 *(978-1-84780-801-1(8)*, Wide Eyed Editions) Quarto Publishing Group UK GBR. Dist: Littlehampton Bk Services, Ltd.
—One Hundred Words: Learn to Write Your First Letters with Little Mouse. 2016. (Learn with Little Mouse Ser.). (ENG.). 56p. (J). (gr. -1-k). pap. 9.99 *(978-1-84780-837-0(9)*, Wide Eyed Editions) Quarto Publishing Group UK GBR. Dist: Hachette Bk. Group.
Lamb, Stacey, illus. Wipe Clean Ready for Writing. 2011. (Wipe-Clean Bks). 20p. (J). pap. 7.99 *(978-0-7945-3076-1(1)*, Usborne) EDC Publishing.
Language Arts Explorer Junior. 2011. 24p. lib. bdg. 107.70 *(978-1-60279-997-4(0)*, 200938) Cherry Lake Publishing.
Laufer, Liora. Callirobics: Advanced Handwriting Exercises with Music from Around the World. (J). (gr. 2-9). pap. 19.95 incl. audio *(978-0-9630478-3-0(3)*, CL550) Callirobics.
Learning Company Books Staff, ed. Reader Rabbit: Writing Mechanics. 2003. (Illus.). 32p. (J). pap., wbk. ed. *(978-0-7630-7642-9(2))* Magma.
Learning to Write: 1-Year Personal Use Version. 2003. E-Book incl. cd-rom *(978-0-9726808-5-1(3))* MEIER Enterprises Inc.
Learning to Write: 12-Month Academic Access Version. 2003. (C). E-Book incl. cd-rom *(978-0-9726808-0-6(2))* MEIER Enterprises Inc.
Learning to Write (Gr. K-1) 2003. (J). *(978-1-58232-034-2(9))* ECS Learning Systems, Inc.
Libby, Kathryn. Cursive Connections: Modern Style. 2003. 84p. (J). (gr. 2-6). 10.99 *(978-0-9666572-2-7(5))* Acacia Publishing, Inc.
Licker, Lori. Writing-Right with Professor Pendleton Pencil. 2006. spiral bd. 21.95 *(978-0-9772196-0-5(7))* Writing-Right.
Loewen, Nancy. Writer's Toolbox, 4 vols., Set. Lyles, Christopher, illus. Incl. Once upon a Time: Writing Your Own Fairy Tale. lib. bdg. 27.32 *(978-1-4048-5335-5(9))*; Show Me a Story: Writing Your Own Picture Book. lib. bdg. 27.32 *(978-1-4048-5341-6(3))*; (Illus.). (gr. 2-4). (Writer's Toolbox Ser.). (ENG.). 32p. 2009. Set lib. bdg. 81.96 *(978-1-4048-5402-4(9))* Picture Window Bks.
Longman Publishing Staff. My Second Handwriting. Date not set. (ENG., Illus.). 32p. (J). pap. 61.25 *(978-0-582-51113-2(5))* Addison-Wesley Longman, Ltd. GBR. Dist: Trans-Atlantic Pubns., Inc.
Longman Publishing Staff & Dallas, Donald. My First Handwriting. Date not set. (ENG., Illus.). 32p. (J). pap. 61.25 *(978-0-582-51112-5(7))* Addison-Wesley Longman, Ltd. GBR. Dist: Trans-Atlantic Pubns., Inc.
Lynette, Rachel. Pencils Before the Store. McGeehan, Dan, illus. 2012. (Before the Store Ser.). (ENG.). 32p. (J). (gr. 2-5). lib. bdg. 29.93 *(978-1-60973-680-4(X)*, 201255) Child's World, Inc., The.
Ma, Karin & Taylor, Nicole. Differentiating Assessment in the Writing Workshop: Templates, Checklists, How-To'S, & Student Samples to Streamline Ongoing Assessments So You Can Plan & Teach More Effectively. 2009. (ENG.). 144p. pap. 24.99 *(978-0-545-05398-3(6)*, Teaching Resources) Scholastic, Inc.
Maps & Codes: 6 Each of 1 Anthology, 6 vols. (Wildcats Ser.). 32p. (gr. 2-8). *(978-0-322-00588-4(4))* Wright Group/McGraw-Hill.
Mayer, Mercer. Scholastic Success with Writing. 2003. (Success with Workbooks Ser.). (ENG.). 48p. (J). pap. 5.95 *(978-0-439-44496-5(9))* Scholastic, Inc.
McCain, Murray. Writing! Alcorn, John, illus. 2016. (ENG.). 48p. 17.95 *(978-1-62326-075-0(2))* AMMO Bks., LLC.
McOmber, Rachel B., ed. McOmber Phonics Storybooks Vol. 1: Writing Book. rev. ed. (Illus.). (J). *(978-0-944991-93-0(9))* Swift Learning Resources.
—McOmber Phonics Storybooks Vol. 2: Writing Book. rev. ed. (Illus.). (J). *(978-0-944991-94-7(7))* Swift Learning Resources.
Medcalf, Carol & Hempstock, Becky. Letts Monster Skills Practice e Writing Age 3-5. 2014. (Letts Monster Practice Ser.). (ENG.). 32p. (J). (gr. -1-k). pap. 6.99 *(978-1-84419-769-9(7))* HarperCollins Pubs. Ltd. GBR. Dist: Independent Pubs. Group.
Meyer-Hullmann, Kerstin, illus. Rechtschreibtraining fuer die 3. Klasse. (Duden-Lemminuten Ser.). (GER.). 44p. (J). wbk. ed. *(978-3-411-70801-7(8))* Bibliographisches Institut & F. A. Brockhaus AG DEU. Dist: International Bk. Import Service, Inc.
—Rechtschreibtraining fuer die 3. und 4. Klasse. (Duden-Lemminuten Ser.). (GER.). 44p. (J). wbk. ed. *(978-3-411-70811-6(5))* Bibliographisches Institut & F. A. Brockhaus AG DEU. Dist: International Bk. Import Service, Inc.
Meyer, Stephanie H., et al. Teen Ink: What Matters. 2003. (Teen Ink Ser.). (ENG., Illus.). 400p. (YA). pap. 17.95 *(978-0-7573-0063-9(4)*, HCI Teens) Health Communications, Inc.
Miller, Carol Rawlings. Powerful Paragraphs: Standards-Based Mini-Lessons - Overheads - Reproducibles. 2005. (Overhead Writing Lessons Ser.). (ENG., Illus.). 48p. (gr. 4-18). pap. 13.99 *(978-0-439-23193-0(0)*, Teaching Resources) Scholastic, Inc.
Minden, Cecilia & Roth, Kate. Language Arts Explorer Junior, 10 vols., Set. Incl. How to Write a Journal. lib. bdg. 25.64 *(978-1-60279-994-3(6)*, 200988); How to Write a Letter. lib. bdg. 25.64 *(978-1-60279-991-2(1)*, 200982); How to Write a Poem. lib. bdg. 25.64 *(978-1-60279-995-0(4)*, 200990); How to Write a Report. lib. bdg. 25.64 *(978-1-61080-105-8(9)*, 201112); How to Write about Your Adventure. lib. bdg. 25.64 *(978-1-61080-106-5(7)*, 201114); How to Write an Ad. lib. bdg. 25.64 *(978-1-61080-107-2(5)*, 201116); How to Write an E-Mail. lib. bdg. 25.64 *(978-1-60279-993-6(8)*, 200986); How to Write an Interview. lib. bdg. 25.64 *(978-1-60279-996-7(2)*, 200992); How to Write & Give a Speech. lib. bdg. 25.64 *(978-1-61080-108-9(3)*, 201118); 24p. (gr. 1-4). 2011. Set lib. bdg. 256.40 *(978-1-61080-153-9(9))* Cherry Lake Publishing.
Miss Conner'S Class. Look How We've Grown! A Collection of First Grade Writing. 2009. 52p. pap. 21.27 *(978-1-4389-6438-6(2))* AuthorHouse.
Mitchell, George. My handwriting & colouring Book. 2009. 64p. pap. 13.95 *(978-1-4452-3485-4(8))* Lulu Pr., Inc.
Moshel, Eluzer. Learn to Write. 2004. pap. 12.00 *(978-0-9728849-2-1(0))*; Vol. 1. pap. 8.50 *(978-0-9728849-0-7(4))*; Vol. 2. pap. 8.50 *(978-0-9728849-4-5(7))*; Vol. 3. pap. 8.50 *(978-0-9728849-7-6(1))* Cong Bais Tziporah.
Olien, Rebecca. Kids Write: Fantasy & Sci Fi, Mystery, Autobiography, Adventure & More! Kline, Michael, illus. 2005. (Kids Can Ser.). (ENG.). 128p. (YA). (gr. 7-14). 14.95 *(978-0-8249-6775-8(5)*, Ideal Pubns.) Worthy Publishing.
On & off the Road: 6 Each of 1 Anthology, 6 vols. (Wildcats Ser.). 32p. (gr. 2-8). *(978-0-322-02421-2(8))* Wright Group/McGraw-Hill.
Ottaway, Jacqueline. Riddle of the Seaplanes (Level S), 6 vols. (Mountain Peaks Ser.). 128p. (gr. 6-18). 36.95 *(978-0-322-05891-0(0))* Wright Group/McGraw-Hill.
Paradis, Anne. Caillou, Fun Tracing & Pen Control: Preschool Writing Activities. Sévigny, Eric, illus. 2016. (Write & Wipe Ser.). (ENG.). 24p. (J). (gr. -1-k). bds. 9.99 *(978-2-89718-260-1(1))* Caillouet, Gerry.
Penmanship 1, 2 vols., Set. 2004. (gr. 1). 25.50 *(978-0-7403-0207-7(8)*, JSP115); (Illus.). tchr. ed., stu. ed. 34.95 *(978-0-7403-0215-2(9)*, JSC100) Alpha Omega Pubns., Inc. (Horizons).
Penmanship 2, 2 vols., Set. 2004. (Illus.). (J). (gr. 2-3). tchr. ed., stu. ed. 25.50 *(978-0-7403-0211-4(6)*, JSP215) Alpha Omega Pubns., Inc.
Penpals for Handwriting Pen Licence Certificate. 2nd rev. ed. 2016. (Penpals for Handwriting Ser.). (ENG.). 300p. 15.63 *(978-1-84565-585-3(0))* Cambridge-Hitachi GBR. Dist: Cambridge Univ. Pr.
Peter Pauper Press, Inc., creator. Handwriting: Learn to Print! 2015. (ENG., Illus.). 96p. (J). pap. 5.99 *(978-1-4413-1816-9(X)*, 9781441318169) Peter Pauper Pr. Inc.
Priddy, Roger. Cursive Handwriting. 2017. (Wipe Clean Learning Bks.). (ENG., Illus.). 48p. (J). spiral bd. 8.99 *(978-0-312-52202-5(9)*, 9780312522025, Priddy Bks.) St. Martin's Pr.
Priestley, Michael. Writing: 25 Reproducible Mini-Tests That Help Students Prepare for & Succeed on Standardized Tests. 2008. (Standardized Test Practice Ser.). (ENG.). 64p. pap. 11.99 *(978-0-545-06402-6(3)*, Teaching Resources) Scholastic, Inc.
Pulse- Fun with Reading & Writing. 2006. cd-rom 4.99 *(978-1-60245-040-0(4))* GDL Multimedia, LLC.
Rau, Dana Meachen. Ace Your Creative Writing Project. 2009. (Ace It! Information Literacy Ser.). (Illus.). 48p. (J). (gr. 2-5). lib. bdg. 25.27 *(978-0-7660-3395-5(3))* Enslow Pubs., Inc.
Read, Write & Publish. (J). (gr. 5). 125.25 *(978-0-669-17767-1(9))* Houghton Mifflin Harcourt School Pubs.
Reading & Writing. 2004. (Help with Homework Ser.). 32p. (J). (gr. k-2). wbk. ed. 3.99 *(978-1-904586-24-1(4))*; (gr. 1-4). wbk. ed. 3.99 *(978-1-904586-20-3(1))* Byeway Bks.
Rechtschreibung 1. (Duden-Schuelerhilfen Ser.). (GER.). 80p. (J). (gr. 2-3). *(978-3-411-06312-3(2))* Bibliographisches Institut & F. A. Brockhaus AG DEU. Dist: International Bk. Import Service, Inc.
Rechtschreibung 2. (Duden-Schuelerhilfen Ser.). (GER.). 96p. (J). (gr. 3-4). *(978-3-411-06322-2(X))* Bibliographisches Institut & F. A. Brockhaus AG DEU. Dist: International Bk. Import Service, Inc.
Rechtschreibung 3. (Duden-Schuelerhilfen Ser.). (GER.). 96p. (J). (gr. 4-5). *(978-3-411-06332-1(7))* Bibliographisches Institut & F. A. Brockhaus AG DEU. Dist: International Bk. Import Service, Inc.
Rechtschreibung 4. (Duden-Schuelerhilfen Ser.). (GER.). 112p. (J). (gr. 5-6). *(978-3-411-05681-1(9))* Bibliographisches Institut & F. A. Brockhaus AG DEU. Dist: International Bk. Import Service, Inc.
Rechtschreibung 5. (Duden-Schuelerhilfen Ser.). (GER.). 112p. (YA). (gr. 7-8). *(978-3-411-05691-0(6))* Bibliographisches Institut & F. A. Brockhaus AG DEU. Dist: International Bk. Import Service, Inc.
Rechtschreibung und Wortkunde. (Duden-Schuelerduden Ser.). (GER.). 384p. (YA). (gr. 4-18). *(978-3-411-04215-9(X))* Bibliographisches Institut & F. A. Brockhaus AG DEU. Dist: International Bk. Import Service, Inc.
Rhodes, Immacula A. Write-N-Seek: Sight Words: Motivating Practice Pages to Help Kids Master Sight Words. 2017. (Write-N-Seek: Ser.). (ENG.). 64p. (gr. -1-2). pap. 10.99 ***(978-1-338-18022-0(3))*** Scholastic, Inc.
—Write-N-Seek: Word Families: Motivating Practice Pages to Help Kids Master Word Families. 2017. (Write-N-Seek: Ser.). (ENG.). 64p. (gr. -1-2). pap. 10.99 ***(978-1-338-18023-7(1))*** Scholastic, Inc.
Ridgewood Analogies. 2004. Bk. 1. pap., tchr. ed. 2.65 *(978-0-8388-2292-0(4))*Bk. 3. pap., tchr. ed. 2.65 *(978-0-8388-2294-4(0))* Educators Publishing Service, Inc.
Ridgewood Analogies Grade 4, Bk. 1. 2004. (Ridgewood Analogies Ser.). pap. 6.65 *(978-0-8388-2289-0(4))* Educators Publishing Service, Inc.
Ridgewood Analogies Grade 5, Bk. 2 2004. (Ridgewood Analogies Ser.). pap. 6.65 *(978-0-8388-2290-6(8))* Educators Publishing Service, Inc.
Ridgewood Analogies Grade 6, Bk. 3. 2004. (Ridgewood Analogies Ser.). 6.65 *(978-0-8388-2291-3(6))* Educators Publishing Service, Inc.
Right or Wrong? 6 Each of 1 Anthology, 6 vols. (Wildcats Ser.). 32p. (gr. 2-8). *(978-0-322-00598-3(1))* Wright Group/McGraw-Hill.
Rossi, Renzo. The Age of the Book. Baldanzi, Alessandro, illus. 2008. (Reading & Writing Ser.). 32p. (gr. 4-7). 28.50 *(978-0-7614-4321-6(5))* Marshall Cavendish Corp.
—A Gift from the Gods. Baldanzi, Alessandro, illus. 2008. (Reading & Writing Ser.). 32p. (gr. 4-7). 28.50 *(978-0-7614-4318-6(5))* Marshall Cavendish Corp.
—How Writing Began. Baldanzi, Alessandro, illus. 2008. (Reading & Writing Ser.). 32p. (gr. 4-7). 28.50 *(978-0-7614-4317-9(7)*, Benchmark Bks.) Marshall Cavendish Corp.
—The Revolution of the Alphabet. Baldanzi, Alessandro, illus. 2008. (Reading & Writing Ser.). 32p. (gr. 4-7). 28.50 *(978-0-7614-4320-9(7)*, Benchmark Bks.) Marshall Cavendish Corp.
Ruff, Karen S. Cooney. The Sensory Pen: Unique Writing Prompts for Journalism Students & Other Writers. 2004. (Illus.). 94p. (J). spiral bd. *(978-0-9761186-0-2(2))* Scribbler's Sword.
Ruffenach, Jessie E., et al. Learn along with Ashkii: First Grade Level 2. Whitethorne, Bahe, Jr., illus. 2003. (NAV & ENG.). 16p. (J). (gr. -1-3). pap. 7.95 *(978-1-893354-42-5(3))* Salina Bookshelf Inc.
—Learn along with Ashkii: Second Grade Level 1. Whitethorne, Bahe, Jr., illus. 2003. (ENG & NAV.). 16p. (J). (gr. -1-3). pap. 7.95 *(978-1-893354-43-2(1))* Salina Bookshelf Inc.
—Learn along with Ashkii: Second Grade Level 2. Whitethorne, Bahe, Jr., illus. 2003. (NAV & ENG.). 16p. (J). (gr. -1-3). pap. 7.95 *(978-1-893354-44-9(X))* Salina Bookshelf Inc.
—Learn along with Ashkii: Third Grade Level 1. Whitethorne, Bahe, Jr., illus. 2003. (NAV & ENG.). 16p. (J). (gr. 4-7). pap. 7.95 *(978-1-893354-45-6(8))* Salina Bookshelf Inc.
Sansen, Wanda. SWR Chart Pack. 2003. (J). pap. 9.95 *(978-1-880045-30-5(3))* Back Home Industries.
School Zone Publishing Company Staff. Bilingual Cursive Writing 3-4. 2007. (ENG.). 64p. (J). pap., wbk. ed. 3.99 *(978-1-58947-962-3(9))* School Zone Publishing Co.
—Bilingual Manuscript Writing K-2. 2007. (ENG.). 64p. (J). (gr. k-1). pap. 3.99 *(978-1-58947-961-6(0))* School Zone Publishing Co.
Service, Regina. The Ginger Family. 2006. 24p. per. 12.00 *(978-1-58961-391-1(0))* PageFree Publishing, Inc.
Shulte, Sharon. Sandy's Aunt. Shulte, Sara, illus. 2004. (J). per. 12.00 *(978-0-9747147-5-2(5))* MK Publishing.
Sicinski-Skeans, Sharon & Baron, Lindamichelle. Skills for Super Writers Softcover: Grade 3. 2003. (Writing Program Ser.). (J). tchr.'s training gde. ed. 19.95 *(978-0-7652-0759-3(1))* Modern Curriculum Pr.
—Transparencies. 2003. (J). (gr. 3). 23.50 *(978-0-7652-1045-6(2))*; (gr. 5). 23.50 *(978-0-7652-1047-0(9))* Modern Curriculum Pr.
—The Write Direction: Hardcover Student Book. 2003. (Illus.). (J). (gr. 4). stu. ed. 18.95 *(978-0-7652-0751-7(6))*; (gr. 5). stu. ed. 18.95 *(978-0-7652-0752-4(4))* Modern Curriculum Pr.
Silva, Patricia. Reading & Writing Today. Baldanzi, Alessandro, illus. 2008. (Reading & Writing Ser.). 32p. (gr. 4-7). 28.50 *(978-0-7614-4324-7(X)*, Benchmark Bks.) Marshall Cavendish Corp.
Sleeping Bear Press. Diary of a Pennsylvania Kid. 2011. (State Journal Ser.). (ENG.). 128p. (J). (gr. 4-8). pap. 9.95 *(978-1-58536-610-1(2)*, 202226) Sleeping Bear Pr.
Soper, Sandra. Reading & Writing, Bk. 3. rev. ed. (ENG., Illus.). 32p. (J). pap. 5.99 *(978-0-330-32075-7(0)*, Pan) Pan Macmillan GBR. Dist: Trafalgar Square Publishing.
Squiggles & Strokes, 6 vols., Pack. (Bookweb Ser.). 32p. (gr. 5-18). 34.00 *(978-0-7635-3795-1(0))* Rigby Education.
The Standard Pocket Chart. (Professional Resources Ser.). 29.95 *(978-0-7802-4243-2(2))* Wright Group/McGraw-Hill.
Steck-Vaughn Staff. Head for Home: Handwriting - Cursive. 2004. (Illus.). pap. 5.99 *(978-0-7398-8556-7(1))* Steck-Vaughn.
—Head for Home: Handwriting - Manuscript. 2004. (Illus.). pap. *(978-0-7398-8555-0(3))* Steck-Vaughn.
Stella, Heather. Get Ready for School Cursive. 2017. (Get Ready for School Ser.). (ENG., Illus.). 128p. (J). (gr. 3-7). spiral bd. 12.99 *(978-0-316-50251-1(0)*, Black Dog & Leventhal Pubs. Inc.) Hachette Bks.
—Get Ready for School Handwriting. 2017. (Get Ready for School Ser.). (ENG., Illus.). 128p. (J). (gr. -1-3). spiral bd. 12.99 *(978-0-316-50254-2(5)*, Black Dog & Leventhal Pubs. Inc.) Hachette Bks.
Stella, Heather & Lima, Athena Anna. Get Ready for First Grade: Spelling, Writing & Reading. 2012. (Get Ready for School Ser.). (ENG., Illus.). 320p. (J). (gr. -1-17). 17.95 *(978-1-57912-896-8(3)*, 81896, Black Dog & Leventhal Pubs. Inc.) Hachette Bks.
Stott, Jon C. Gerald McDermott & You, 1 vol. McDermott, Gerald, illus. 2004. (Author & YOU Ser.). 128p. (C). pap. 35.00 *(978-1-59158-175-8(3)*, LU1753, Greenwood) ABC-CLIO, LLC.
Sullivan, Mary. Lessons for Guided Writing: Whole-Class Lessons & Dozens of Student Samples with Teacher Comments to Effectively Scaffold the Writing Process. 2008. (ENG.). 128p. pap. 18.99 *(978-0-545-05401-0(X)*, Teaching Resources) Scholastic, Inc.
Tai, Elise See. Write & Draw Dinosaurs. 2014. (Wipe-Clean Stencil Bks.). (ENG., Illus.). 24p. (J). (gr. -1-1). bds. 9.99 *(978-0-7641-6710-2(3))* Barron's Educational Series, Inc.
Tell Me No Lies, 6 vols. (Ragged Island Mysteriestm Ser.). 161p. (gr. 5-7). 42.50 *(978-0-322-01654-5(1))* Wright Group/McGraw-Hill.
Thomas, Vernada. Pre-Handwriting Book. 2008. 200p. 29.99 *(978-1-4363-8001-0(4))*; pap. 19.99 *(978-1-4363-8000-3(6))* Xlibris Corp.
Trimmer, Joseph F. Writing Without a Purpose: AP Version. 14th ed. 2003. (YA). (gr. 6-12). 86.76 *(978-0-618-31848-3(8)*, 356312) CENGAGE Learning.
Tuszynski, Kathy Cromwell & Yarber, Angela. The Write Answer. 2003. (Illus.). 96p. (J). pap. 11.95 *(978-1-57310-407-4(8))* Teaching & Learning Co.
Vaughan, Marcia. Story Teller Quilts: Level S, 6 vols. (Raging Rivers Ser.). 128p. (gr. 3-6). 36.95 *(978-0-322-05899-6(6))* Wright Group/McGraw-Hill.
Veinje, Marie. Manuscript Writing K-2. Boyer, Robin, illus. 2005. (ENG.). 64p. (J). (gr. k-2). pap. 3.99 *(978-1-58947-397-3(3))* School Zone Publishing Co.
Voyages in English: Writing & Grammar. 2004. (gr. 4-18). *(978-0-8294-1305-2(7))*; (gr. 5-18). *(978-0-8294-1307-6(3))*; (gr. 5-18). tchr. ed. *(978-0-8294-0989-5(0))*; (gr. 5-18). tchr. ed., wbk. ed. *(978-0-8294-1323-6(5))*; (gr. 5-18). stu. ed. *(978-0-8294-0990-1(4))*; (gr. 5-18). stu. ed., wbk. ed. *(978-0-8294-1322-9(7))*; (gr. 6-18). *(978-0-8294-1310-6(3))*; (gr. 6-18). tchr. ed. *(978-0-8294-0991-8(2))*; (gr. 6-18). tchr. ed., wbk. ed. *(978-0-8294-1325-0(1))*; (gr. 6-18). stu. ed. *(978-0-8294-0992-5(0))*; (gr. 6-18). stu. ed., wbk. ed. *(978-0-8294-1324-3(3))*; (gr. 7-18). *(978-0-8294-1313-7(8))*; (gr. 7-18). tchr. ed. *(978-0-8294-0993-2(9))*; (gr. 7-18). tchr. ed., wbk. ed. *(978-0-8294-1328-1(6))*; (gr. 7-18). stu. ed. *(978-0-8294-0994-9(7))*; (gr. 7-18). stu. ed., wbk. ed. *(978-0-8294-1327-4(8))*; (gr. 8-18). *(978-0-8294-1315-1(4))*; (gr. 8-18). tchr. ed. *(978-0-8294-0995-6(5))*; (gr. 8-18). tchr. ed., wbk. ed. *(978-0-8294-1330-4(8))*; (gr. 8-18). stu. ed. *(978-0-8294-0996-3(3))*; (gr. 8-18). stu. ed., wbk. ed. *(978-0-8294-1329-8(4))* Loyola Pr.

Walton, Ruth. Let's Read a Book: Find Out about Books & How They Are Made. 2013. (Let's Find Out Ser.). (Illus.). 32p. (J). (gr. k-5). 28.50 *(978-1-59771-387-0(2))* Sea-To-Sea Pubns.

Watson, Joy. The Birthday Flood: Level O, 6 vols. (Raging Rivers Ser.). 128p. (gr. 3-6). 36.95 *(978-0-322-05896-5(1))* Wright Group/McGraw-Hill.

Webber, Diane. Do You Read Me? Famous Cases Solved by Handwriting Analysis! 2007. (24/7: Science Behind the Scenes Ser.). (ENG., Illus.). 64p. (YA). (gr. 9-12). 29.00 *(978-0-531-12066-8(X)*, Watts, Franklin) Scholastic Library Publishing.

What Is That Smell? S-Family Blends: Level B, 6 vols. (Wright Skills Ser.). 16p. (gr. k-3). 17.95 *(978-0-322-01461-9(1))* Wright Group/McGraw-Hill.

What's in the Woods? Consonant digraph review: Level C, 6 vols. (Wright Skills Ser.). 16p. (gr. k-3). 26.50 *(978-0-322-01497-8(2))* Wright Group/McGraw-Hill.

Willever, Lisa. Exciting Writing. 2004. 64p. pap., instr.'s hndbk. ed. 5.95 *(978-0-9760469-1-2(1)*, 329-003) Franklin Mason Pr.

Williams, Adrian & Sassoon, Rosemary. Penpals for Handwriting Font CD-ROM. 2nd rev. ed. 2015. (Penpals for Handwriting Ser.). (ENG.). cd-rom 203.69 *(978-1-84565-718-5(7))* Cambridge-Hitachi GBR. Dist: Cambridge Univ. Pr.

Williams, James D., et al. Writing & Language Arts: Writer's Workbook. (Writing & Language Arts Ser.). (gr. k-18). pap. 12.60 *(978-0-07-579635-0(X))*; (gr. 2-18). pap. 12.60 *(978-0-07-579637-4(6))* SRA/McGraw-Hill.

Williams, Lynette Gain. Handwriting Begins with Art: The Partner Book to ArbeZ ZebrA Teaches A to Z. 2007. 165p. (J). spiral bd. 19.99 *(978-0-9779063-1-4(0))* Gain Literacy Skills / Lynette Gain Williams.

Williams, Rozanne Lanczak & Faulkner, Stacey. Learn to Write Resource Guide: Grades K-2. 2006. (Illus.). 104p. (J). (gr. k-2). per. 13.99 *(978-1-59198-314-9(2))* Creative Teaching Pr., Inc.

Wise Owl Printing Plus Inc, creator. I Can Write Streetland, PreK-2: Integrated learning Workbook. 2006. (I Can Write Ser.). (Illus.). 78p. (J). (gr. -1-3). pap. 9.99 incl. audio compact disk *(978-0-9743971-3-9(X))* Deziner Media International.

Woods, Irons, & Greens: 6 Each of 1 Anthology, 6 vols. (Wildcats Ser.). 32p. (gr. 2-8). *(978-0-322-00589-1(2))* Wright Group/McGraw-Hill.

World Book, Inc. Staff, contrib. by. Hieroglyphics to Hypertext: A Timeline of the Written Word. 2016. (J). *(978-0-7166-3546-8(1))* World Bk.-Childcraft International.

Wrighton, Charlene & Bradshaw, Georgine. Basic Kit - Preschool. Clark, Irene, illus. 2005. Orig. Title: Basis Kit I. (J). 249.95 *(978-1-886441-30-9(8))* Zoo-phonics, Inc.

Write Right! Set 2. 2014. (Write Right! Ser.). 24p. (J). (gr. 2-5). 135.60 *(978-1-4824-1140-9(7))* Stevens, Gareth Publishing LLLP.

Write Right! Sets 1-2. 2014. (Write Right! Ser.). 24p. (J). (gr. 2-5). 271.20 *(978-1-4824-1179-9(2))* Stevens, Gareth Publishing LLLP.

Writer's Solution. Bronze Level. (YA). (gr. 7). stu. ed. 23.47 *(978-0-13-828781-8(3))*Copper Level. (J). (gr. 6). stu. ed. 23.47 *(978-0-13-828773-3(2))*Copper Level. (J). (gr. 6). pap. 1.97 *(978-0-13-434758-5(7))*Diamond Level. (YA). (gr. 12). stu. ed. 25.47 *(978-0-13-828831-0(3))*Gold Level. (YA). (gr. 9). stu. ed. 25.47 *(978-0-13-828807-5(0))*Platinum Level. (YA). (gr. 10). stu. ed. 25.47 *(978-0-13-828815-0(1))*Ruby Level. (YA). (gr. 11). stu. ed. 25.47 *(978-0-13-828823-5(2))*Silver Level. (YA). (gr. 8). stu. ed. 23.47 *(978-0-13-828799-3(6))* Prentice Hall PTR.

Writing Skills 3. 2004. (Writing Skills Ser.). pap. 12.00 *(978-0-8388-2052-0(2))* Educators Publishing Service, Inc.

Writing with Grace. 2nd ed. 2003. (Academy Handwriting Program Ser.: Vol. 4). (J). pap. 5.50 *(978-1-930367-88-3(0))* Christian Liberty Pr.

Zeros & Ones, 6 vols. (Wildcats Ser.). 32p. (gr. 2-8). *(978-0-322-02438-0(2))* Wright Group/McGraw-Hill.

Zoo-phonics Quick Tests for the Classroom. 2004. cd-rom *(978-1-886441-41-5(3))* Zoo-phonics, Inc.

WRITING—MATERIALS AND INSTRUMENTS

Blaxland, Wendy. Pencils. 2008. (How Are They Made? Ser.). 32p. (gr. 4-18). lib. bdg. 18.56 *(978-0-7614-3807-6(6)*, Benchmark Bks.) Marshall Cavendish Corp.

Fejtö, Raphaël. Pen. 2016. (Little Inventions Ser.). (ENG., Illus.). 32p. (J). (gr. 3-5). 9.95 *(978-1-77085-748-3(6)*, 9781770857483) Firefly Bks., Ltd.

Hayward, Linda. I Am a Pencil. Nicklaus, Carol, illus. 2003. (Silly Millies Ser.). 32p. lib. bdg. 17.90 *(978-0-7613-2904-6(8)*, Millbrook Pr.) Lerner Publishing Group.

Lynette, Rachel. Pencils. 2016. (J). *(978-1-4896-4539-5(X))* Weigl Pubs., Inc.

Silva, Patricia. Modern Times. Baldanzi, Alessandro, illus. 2008. (Reading & Writing Ser.). 32p. (gr. 4-7). 28.50 *(978-0-7614-4322-3(3)*, Benchmark Bks.) Marshall Cavendish Corp.

WRITING (AUTHORSHIP)

see Authorship; Journalism

WYOMING

Baldwin, Guy & Hart, Joyce. Wyoming. 2nd rev. ed. 2007. (Celebrate the States Ser.). 144p. (gr. 6). lib. bdg. 42.79 *(978-0-7614-2563-2(2)*, Benchmark Bks.) Marshall Cavendish Corp.

Brown, Vanessa. Wyoming. 2009. (Bilingual Library of the United States of America Ser.). (ENG & SPA.). 32p. (gr. 2-2). 47.90 *(978-1-60853-394-7(8)*, Editorial Buenas Letras) Rosen Publishing Group, Inc., The.

Feinstein, Stephen. Wyoming: A MyReportLinks.com Book. 2003. (States Ser.). (Illus.). 48p. (J). (gr. 4-10). lib. bdg. 25.26 *(978-0-7660-5030-3(0)*, MyReportLinks.com Bks.) Enslow Pubs., Inc.

Fontes, Justine & Fontes, Ron. Wyoming. 2003. (World Almanac Library of the States). (Illus.). 48p. (gr. 4-9). lib. bdg. 31.00 *(978-0-8368-5164-9(1)*, Gareth Stevens Learning Library) Stevens, Gareth Publishing LLLP.

—Wyoming: The Equality State. 2003. (World Almanac Library of the States). (Illus.). 48p. (gr. 4-9). pap. 14.05 *(978-0-8368-5335-3(0)*, Gareth Stevens Learning Library) Stevens, Gareth Publishing LLLP.

Frisch, Carlienne. Wyoming. 2012. (J). lib. bdg. 25.26 *(978-0-7613-4519-0(1)*, Lerner Pubns.) Lerner Publishing Group.

Gagliano, Eugene. C Is for Cowboy: A Wyoming Alphabet. Guy, Susan, illus. 2003. (Discover America State by State Ser.). (ENG.). 40p. (J). 17.95 *(978-1-58536-097-0(X))* Sleeping Bear Pr.

Galiano, Dean. Wyoming. Brusca, Maria Cristina, tr. from ENG. 2006. (Bilingual Library of the United States of America Ser.: Set 2). (ENG & SPA., Illus.). 32p. (J). (gr. 3-6). lib. bdg. 25.25 *(978-1-4042-3116-0(1))* Rosen Publishing Group, Inc., The.

Hanson-Harding, Alexandra. Wyoming. 2008. (ENG.). 80p. (J). pap. 7.95 *(978-0-531-20819-9(2)*, Children's Pr.) Scholastic Library Publishing.

Hanson-Harding, Alexandra L. Wyoming. 2003. (From Sea to Shining Sea Ser.: 2). (ENG., Illus.). 80p. (J). 30.50 *(978-0-516-22490-9(5)*, Children's Pr.) Scholastic Library Publishing.

Harasymiw, Roman. Devils Tower. 2014. (Scariest Places on Earth Ser.). (Illus.). 24p. (J). (gr. 2-5). 22.60 *(978-1-4824-1151-5(2))* Stevens, Gareth Publishing LLLP.

Lusted, Marcia Amidon. Wyoming: The Equality State. 2010. (Our Amazing States Ser.). (ENG.). 24p. (J). pap. 8.25 *(978-1-4488-0762-8(X))*; lib. bdg. 22.60 *(978-1-4488-0663-8(1))* Rosen Publishing Group, Inc., The. (PowerKids Pr.).

Marsh, Carole. Wyoming Current Events Projects: 30 Cool, Activities, Crafts, Experiments & More for Kids to Do to Learn about Your State! 2003. (Wyoming Experience Ser.). 32p. (gr. k-5). pap. 5.95 *(978-0-635-02069-7(6)*, Marsh, Carole Bks.) Gallopade International.

—Wyoming Geography Projects: 30 Cool, Activities, Crafts, Experiments & More for Kids to Do to Learn about Your State! 2003. (Wyoming Experience Ser.). 32p. (gr. k-5). pap. 5.95 *(978-0-635-01868-7(3)*, Marsh, Carole Bks.) Gallopade International.

—Wyoming Government Projects: 30 Cool, Activities, Crafts, Experiments & More for Kids to Do to Learn about Your State! 2003. (Wyoming Experience Ser.). 32p. (gr. k-5). pap. 5.95 *(978-0-635-01969-1(8)*, Marsh, Carole Bks.) Gallopade International.

—Wyoming People Projects: 30 Cool, Activities, Crafts, Experiments & More for Kids to Do to Learn about Your State! 2003. (Wyoming Experience Ser.). 32p. (gr. k-5). pap. 5.95 *(978-0-635-02019-2(X)*, Marsh, Carole Bks.) Gallopade International.

—Wyoming Symbols & Facts Projects: 30 Cool, Activities, Crafts, Experiments & More for Kids to Do to Learn about Your State! 2003. (Wyoming Experience Ser.). 32p. (gr. k-5). pap. 5.95 *(978-0-635-01919-6(1)*, Marsh, Carole Bks.) Gallopade International.

Mis, M. S. How to Draw Wyoming's Sights & Symbols. 2009. (Kid's Guide to Drawing America Ser.). 32p. (gr. k-k). 50.50 *(978-1-61511-106-0(9)*, PowerKids Pr.) Rosen Publishing Group, Inc., The.

Murray, Julie. Wyoming, 1 vol. 2006. (Buddy Book Ser.). (ENG., Illus.). 32p. (gr. 2-4). 27.07 *(978-1-59197-709-4(6)*, Buddy Bks.) ABDO Publishing Co.

Parker, Bridget. Wyoming. 2016. (States Ser.). (ENG., Illus.). 32p. (gr. 3-4). lib. bdg. 27.32 *(978-1-5157-0439-3(4))* Next Page Pr., The.

Petreycik, Rick. Wyoming. 2006. (It's My State! Ser.). (Illus.). 80p. (J). (gr. 4-7). lib. bdg. 29.93 *(978-0-7614-1930-3(6)*, Benchmark Bks.) Marshall Cavendish Corp.

Thomas, William David. Wyoming. 2006. (Portraits of the States Ser.). 32p. (gr. 2-6). pap. 10.50 *(978-0-8368-4729-1(6)*, Gareth Stevens Learning Library) Stevens, Gareth Publishing LLLP.

—Wyoming. 2006. (Portraits of the States Ser.). (Illus.). 32p. (gr. 2-6). lib. bdg. 26.00 *(978-0-8368-4712-3(1)*, Gareth Stevens Learning Library) Stevens, Gareth Publishing LLLP.

2006-2007 Tongue River Elementary 3rd Graders, text. Sheridan County History ABC Coloring & Activity Book - 2007. 2006-2007 Tongue River Elementary 3rd Graders, . 2007. (Illus.). 32p. (J). 3.95 *(978-0-9792871-1-4(1))* Sheridan County Historical Society Pr.

WYOMING—FICTION

Ahlman, Larry. Terror in the Tetons. Larsen, Chuck, ed. Hanson, Dana, illus. 2005. (YA). (gr. 9-12). pap. 9.95 *(978-0-9712906-2-4(8))* Ahlman Publishing.

Alphin, Elaine Marie. Dinosaur Hunter. Bolognese, Don, illus. 2004. (I Can Read Bks.). 48p. (gr. 2-4). 14.00 *(978-0-7569-3241-1(6))* Perfection Learning Corp.

Banks, Radine. Nochi Come Back. 2006. 112p. per. 12.20 *(978-1-4120-8803-9(8))* Trafford Publishing.

Bell, Cathleen Davitt. Little Blog on the Prairie. 2011. (ENG.). 288p. (YA). (gr. 7). pap. 9.99 *(978-1-59990-677-5(5)*, 9781599906775, Bloomsbury USA Childrens) Bloomsbury Publishing USA.

Bjornson, Nancy. Llamas, Ponies & Pyrite. 2007. (J). *(978-1-930596-82-5(0))* Amherst Pr.

Black Hills Summer. 2003. (YA). per. *(978-0-9740718-0-0(3))* Strathmoor Pr.

Brezenoff, Steve. The Yellowstone Kidnapping That Wasn't, 1 vol. Calo, Marcos, illus. 2012. (Field Trip Mysteries Ser.). (ENG.). 88p. (gr. 2-3). pap. 6.10 *(978-1-4342-4200-6(5))*; lib. bdg. 25.32 *(978-1-4342-3789-7(3))* Stone Arch Bks.

Burkhart, Jessica. Wild Hearts. 2015. (If Only... Ser.). (ENG.). 368p. (YA). (gr. 7). 17.99 *(978-1-61963-258-5(6)*, 9781619632585, Bloomsbury USA Childrens) Bloomsbury Publishing USA.

Clark, Joan. Ann Drew Jackson. Clark, Nathan, illus. 2007. 122p. per. 17.95 *(978-1-931282-45-1(5))* Autism Asperger Publishing Co.

—Jackson Whole Wyoming. 2005. 16.00 *(978-1-931282-72-7(2)*, 9945) Autism Asperger Publishing Co.

Curtin, Ann. Dreamcatcher. 2015. 201p. (YA). *(978-1-61271-246-8(0))* Zumaya Pubns. LLC.

Ellis, Edward Sylvester. Two Boys in Wyoming: A Tale of Adventure (Northwest Series No. 3) 2007. (ENG.). 204p. (J). pap. 20.99 *(978-1-4346-3792-5(1))*; 228p. pap. 22.99 *(978-1-4346-3793-2(X))* Creative Media Partners, LLC.

Farnsworth, Frances Joyce. Tike & Tiny in the Tetons. 2007. (Illus.). 172p. (J). pap. 14.95 *(978-0-943972-79-4(5))* Homestead Publishing.

Gebhart, Ryan. There Will Be Bears. 2016. (ENG.). 224p. (J). (gr. 5). pap. 8.99 *(978-0-7636-8765-6(0))* Candlewick Pr.

George, Jean Craighead. Snowboard Twist. Minor, Wendell, illus. 2004. (Outdoor Adventures Ser.). (ENG.). 32p. (J). 15.99 *(978-0-06-050595-0(8))* HarperCollins Pubs.

Hand, Cynthia. Boundless. 2013. (Unearthly Ser.: 3). (ENG.). 448p. (YA). (gr. 8). pap. 9.99 *(978-0-06-199621-4(1))*; 17.99 *(978-0-06-199620-7(3))* HarperCollins Pubs. (HarperTeen).

—Hallowed. 2012. (Unearthly Ser.: 2). (ENG.). (YA). (gr. 8). 432p. pap. 9.99 *(978-0-06-199619-1(X))*; 416p. 17.99 *(978-0-06-199618-4(1))* HarperCollins Pubs. (HarperTeen).

—Unearthly. 2011. (Unearthly Ser.: 1). (ENG.). 464p. (YA). (gr. 8). pap. 9.99 *(978-0-06-199617-7(3)*, HarperTeen) HarperCollins Pubs.

Hawley, Jim. Homer & Friends. 2012. 50p. pap. *(978-1-77097-709-9(0))* FriesenPress.

Hays, Sharon. The Tumbleweed Family. 2011. 28p. pap. 15.99 *(978-1-4568-6825-3(X))* Xlibris Corp.

Jacobs, Lily. The Littlest Bunny in Wyoming: An Easter Adventure. 2015. (ENG.). 32p. (J). (-3). 9.99 *(978-1-4926-1243-8(X)*, Sourcebooks Jabberwocky) Sourcebooks, Inc.

James, Eric. A Halloween Scare in Wyoming. Le Ray, Marina, illus. 2015. (ENG.). 32p. (J). (-5). 9.99 *(978-1-4926-2410-3(1)*, 9781492624103, Sourcebooks Jabberwocky) Sourcebooks, Inc.

—Santa's Sleigh Is on Its Way to Wyoming: A Christmas Adventure. Dunn, Robert, illus. 2016. (ENG.). 32p. (J). (-2). 12.99 *(978-1-4926-4365-4(3)*, 9781492643654, Sourcebooks Jabberwocky) Sourcebooks, Inc.

Jensen, Brandi Ann & Courtright, Jordan K. The Hilarious & Brave Adventures of Hog & Dog. 2011. 40p. pap. 16.95 *(978-1-4560-3955-4(5))* America Star Bks.

Kares, P. S. Hole-in-the-Wall with the Prairie Orphans. 2009. 32p. pap. 24.95 *(978-1-60813-521-9(7))* America Star Bks.

Law, Ingrid. Scumble. (ENG.). (J). (gr. 3-7). 2011. 432p. 8.99 *(978-0-14-241962-5(1)*, Puffin Books) 2010. 416p. 17.99 *(978-0-8037-3307-7(0)*, Dial Bks) Penguin Young Readers Group.

—Scumble. l.t. ed. 2011. (Companion to the Newberry Honor Winner Savvy Ser.). (ENG.). 575p. 23.99 *(978-1-4104-3531-6(8))* Thorndike Pr.

London, Jonathan. Desolation Canyon. London, Sean, illus. 2015. (Aaron's Wilderness Ser.: 1). (ENG.). 168p. (YA). pap. 12.99 *(978-1-941821-29-9(4)*, West Winds Pr.) Graphic Arts Ctr. Publishing Co.

Markle, Sandra. Family Pack. Marks, Alan, illus. 2011. (ENG.). 32p. (J). (gr. -1-3). 15.95 *(978-1-58089-217-9(5))* Charlesbridge Publishing, Inc.

Marsh, Carole. The Case of the Crybaby Cowboy. 2006. (3 Amigos Ser.). (Illus.). 54p. (J). (gr. 4-7). 14.95 *(978-0-635-06199-7(6))* Gallopade International.

—The Mystery at Grizzly Graveyard. 2014. (Real Kids, Real Places Ser.: Vol. 3). (ENG., Illus.). 158p. (J). (gr. 3-5). pap. 7.99 *(978-0-635-11187-6(X)*, Marsh, Carole Mysteries) Gallopade International.

—The Riddle of the Oogli Boogli. 2006. (Illus.). 54p. (J). (gr. 4-7). 14.95 *(978-0-635-06200-0(3))* Gallopade International.

Minich, Eric. Digger & the Search for Home. 2006. 48p. pap. 16.95 *(978-1-4241-0321-8(5))* PublishAmerica, Inc.

Neil, Deanna. Lost in Yellowstone: The Land of Curiosities, 1872-1873, vol. 2. 2nd rev. ed. 2015. (J). reprint ed. 19.99 *(978-0-9798800-9-4(2))* EcoSeekers, The.

Oneill, Elizabeth. Alfred Visits Wyoming. 2008. 24p. (J). pap. 12.00 *(978-0-9822288-1-4(3))* Global Business Information Strategies, Inc.

Sargent, Dave & Sargent, Pat. Hondo: (Silver Dun) Look for Good in Others, 30 vols., Vol. 34. Lenoir, Jane, illus. 2003. (Saddle up Ser.: Vol. 34). 42p. (J). pap. 10.95 *(978-1-56763-802-8(3))*; lib. bdg. 23.60 *(978-1-56763-801-1(5))* Ozark Publishing.

Silvano, Wendi. Love Is All Around Wyoming. Czernichowska, Joanna, illus. 2016. (ENG.). 32p. (J). (-6). 12.99 *(978-1-4926-2976-4(6)*, Sourcebooks Jabberwocky) Sourcebooks, Inc.

Smallman, Steve. Santa Is Coming to Wyoming. Dunn, Robert, illus. 2014. (ENG.). 32p. (J). (-3). 9.99 *(978-1-4926-0679-6(0)*, Sourcebooks Jabberwocky) Sourcebooks, Inc.

Sutherland, Tui T. & Sutherland, Kari H. The Menagerie. 2013. (Menagerie Ser.: 1). (ENG., Illus.). 288p. (J). (gr. 3-7). 16.99 *(978-0-06-078064-7(9))* HarperCollins Pubs.

Worthen, Johnny. Celeste. 2015. (Unseen Ser.). (ENG.). 376p. (YA). (gr. 7-12). pap. 14.99 *(978-1-63163-022-4(9)*, Jolly Fish Pr.) North Star Editions.

Yep, Laurence. The Traitor. 2004. (Golden Mountain Chronicles). 310p. (J). (gr. 5). 14.65 *(978-0-7569-3457-6(5))* Perfection Learning Corp.

WYOMING—HISTORY

Byers, Ann. Wyoming: Past & Present. 2010. (United States: Past & Present Ser.). (ENG.). 48p. (YA). pap. 11.75 *(978-1-4358-9527-0(4))*; lib. bdg. 29.25 *(978-1-4358-9500-3(2))* Rosen Publishing Group, Inc., The. (Rosen Reference).

Carole Marsh. Wyoming Indians. 2004. (Wyoming Experience Ser.). 36p. (gr. 3-8). pap. 7.95 *(978-0-635-02344-5(X))* Gallopade International.

Felix, Rebecca. What's Great about Wyoming? 2015. (ENG., Illus.). 32p. (J). (gr. 2-5). 26.65 *(978-1-4677-3882-8(4))* Lerner Publishing Group.

Gagliano, Eugene M. Four Wheels West: A Wyoming Number Book. Guy, Sue, illus. 2006. (Count Your Way Across the U. S. A. Ser.). (ENG.). 40p. (J). (gr. -1-3). 17.95 *(978-1-58536-210-3(7))* Sleeping Bear Pr.

—Little Wyoming. Urban, Helle, illus. 2010. (My Little State Ser.). (ENG.). 22p. (J). 9.95 *(978-1-58536-544-9(0))* Sleeping Bear Pr.

Hanel, Rachael. Wyoming. 2009. (This Land Called America Ser.). 32p. (YA). (gr. 3-6). 19.95 *(978-1-58341-803-1(2))* Creative Co., The.

Harvey, Dan. Rocky Mountain: Colorado, Utah, Wyoming, Vol. 19. 2015. (Let's Explore the States Ser.). (Illus.). 64p. (J). (gr. 5). 23.95 *(978-1-4222-3332-0(4))* Mason Crest.

Marsh, Carole. Exploring Wyoming Through Project-Based Learning: Geography, History, Government, Economics & More. 2016. (Wyoming Experience Ser.). (ENG.). (J). pap. 9.99 *(978-0-635-12374-9(6))* Gallopade International.

—I'm Reading about Wyoming. 2014. (Wyoming Experience Ser.). (ENG., Illus.). (J). pap., pap. 8.99 *(978-0-635-11325-2(2))* Gallopade International.

—Wyoming History Projects: 30 Cool, Activities, Crafts, Experiments & More for Kids to Do to Learn about Your State! 2003. (Wyoming Experience Ser.). 32p. (gr. k-5). pap. 5.95 *(978-0-635-01819-9(5)*, Marsh, Carole Bks.) Gallopade International.

—Wyoming Native Americans: A Kid's Look at Our State's Chiefs, Tribes, Reservations, Powwows, Lore & More from the Past to the Present. 2004. (Wyoming Experience Ser.). (Illus.). 36p. (J). (gr. 3-8). 29.95 *(978-0-635-02345-2(8))* Gallopade International.

Maynard, Charles W. Fort Laramie. 2009. (Famous Forts Throughout American History Ser.). 24p. (gr. 3-4). 42.50 *(978-1-61512-516-6(7)*, PowerKids Pr.) Rosen Publishing Group, Inc., The.

Ollhoff, Jim. Wyoming, 1 vol. 2009. (United States Ser.). (ENG., Illus.). 48p. (YA). (gr. 2-5). 27.07 *(978-1-60453-687-4(X))* ABDO Publishing Co.

Parker, Janice. Wyoming. 2011. (Guide to American States Ser.). (Illus.). 48p. (YA). (gr. 3-6). 29.99 *(978-1-61690-824-9(6))*; (J). *(978-1-61690-499-9(2))* Weigl Pubs., Inc.

—Wyoming: The Equality State. 2016. *(978-1-4896-4968-3(9))* Weigl Pubs., Inc.

Petreycik, Rick. Wyoming. 2014. (J). pap. *(978-1-62712-489-8(6))* Cavendish Square Publishing.

—Wyoming. 2014. (Illus.). 80p. (J). *(978-1-62712-225-2(7))* Musa Publishing.

Petreycik, Rick & Klepeis, Alicia. Wyoming. 2016. (ENG., Illus.). 80p. (J). 34.21 *(978-1-62713-259-6(7))* Cavendish Square Publishing.

Pratt, Laura. Wyoming: The Cowboy State. 2012. (J). *(978-1-61913-421-8(7))* Weigl Pubs., Inc.

Prentzas, G. S. Wyoming (Revised Edition) 2014. (America the Beautiful, Third Ser. (Revised Edition) Ser.). (ENG.). 144p. (J). lib. bdg. 40.00 *(978-0-531-28300-4(3))* Scholastic Library Publishing.

Sniffin, Bill. High Altitudes, Low Multitudes: More Stories about Wyoming, the Best Part of America, 1. 2003. (Illus.). 252p. per. 14.95 *(978-0-9639350-2-1(X)*, 2000) WCS Corp.

Tieck, Sarah. Wyoming, 1 vol. 2012. (Explore the United States Ser.). (ENG., Illus.). 32p. (J). (gr. 2-5). lib. bdg. 28.50 *(978-1-61783-390-8(8)*, Big Buddy Bks.) ABDO Publishing Co.

X

X, MALCOLM, 1925-1965

Archer, Jules. They Had a Dream: The Struggles of Four of the Most Influential Leaders of the Civil Rights Movement, from Frederick Douglass to Marcus Garvey to Martin Luther King Jr. & Malcolm X. 2016. (Jules Archer History for Young Readers Ser.). (ENG., Illus.). 272p. (J). (gr. 6). 16.99 *(978-1-63450-194-1(2)*, Sky Pony Pr.) Skyhorse Publishing Co., Inc.

Aretha, David. A Time for Martyrs: The Life of Malcolm X. 2012. (YA). 28.95 *(978-1-59935-328-9(8))* Reynolds, Morgan Inc.

Benson, Michael. Malcolm X. 2005. (Just the Facts Biographies Ser.). (ENG., Illus.). 112p. (gr. 5-12). 27.93 *(978-0-8225-2444-1(9))* Lerner Publishing Group.

Bourcier, Cammy S. Carlos Mencia. 2007. (Sharing the American Dream Ser.). 64p. (YA). (gr. 7-18). pap. 9.95 *(978-1-4222-0756-7(0))* Mason Crest.

—Malcolm X. 2009. (Sharing the American Dream Ser.). (Illus.). 64p. (YA). (gr. 7-12). 22.95 *(978-1-4222-0577-8(0))* Mason Crest.

Burlingame, Jeff. Malcolm X: Fighting for Human Rights. 2017. (Rebels with a Cause Ser.). 128p. (J). (gr. 8-8). lib. bdg. 37.27 ***(978-0-7660-8519-0(8))*** Enslow Pubs., Inc.

Burlingame, Jeff. Malcolm X: "I Believe in the Brotherhood of Man, All Men" 2010. (American Rebels Ser.). 160p. (YA). (gr. 7-12). 35.94 *(978-0-7660-3384-9(8))* Enslow Pubs., Inc.

Doeden, Matt. A Marked Man: The Assassination of Malcolm X. 2013. (ENG., Illus.). 88p. (J). (gr. 6-12). lib. bdg. 33.27 *(978-0-7613-5484-0(0)*, Twenty-First Century Bks.) Lerner Publishing Group.

Draper, Allison Stark. The Assassination of Malcolm X. 2009. (Library of Political Assassinations Ser.). 64p. (gr. 5-5). 58.50 *(978-1-60853-827-0(3))* Rosen Publishing Group, Inc., The.

Fay, Gail. Malcolm X, 1 vol. 2012. (American Biographies Ser.). (ENG.). 48p. (gr. 4-6). pap. 9.95 *(978-1-4329-6467-2(4)*, NA-h) Heinemann-Raintree.

—Malcolm X, 1 vol. Oxford Bible Staff, illus. 2012. (American Biographies Ser.). (ENG.). 48p. (gr. 4-6). lib. bdg. 32.65 *(978-1-4329-6456-6(9)*, NA-h) Heinemann-Raintree.

Graves, Renee. Malcolm X. 2003. (Cornerstones of Freedom Ser.). (ENG., Illus.). 48p. (J). 26.00 *(978-0-516-24224-8(5)*, Children's Pr.) Scholastic Library Publishing.

Gunderson, Jessica. A Biography of Malcolm X. Hayden, Seitu, illus. 2010. (American Graphic Ser.). (ENG.). 32p. (gr. 3-4). lib. bdg. 30.65 *(978-1-4296-5471-5(6)*, Graphic Library) Capstone Press of Coughlan Cos.

—X: A Biography of Malcolm X. Hayden, Seitu, illus. 2011. (American Graphic Ser.). (ENG.). 32p. (gr. 3-4). pap. 8.10 *(978-1-4296-6267-3(0))*; pap. 47.70 *(978-1-4296-6438-7(X))* Capstone Press of Coughlan Cos. (Graphic Library).

Haley, Alex. The Autobiography of Malcolm X. Bloom, Harold, ed. annot. ed. 2008. (Bloom's Guides). 168p. (C). (gr. 9). 30.00 *(978-0-7910-9832-5(X)*, Chelsea Hse.) Facts On File, Inc.

Jeffrey, Gary. Malcolm X & the Fight for African American Unity. 2012. (Graphic History of the Civil Rights Movement Ser.). (Illus.). 24p. (J). (gr. 3-8). pap. 8.15 *(978-1-4339-7488-5(6))*;

WXYZ

lib. bdg. 23.95 (978-1-4339-7487-8(8)) Stevens, Gareth Publishing LLLP.

Linde, Barbara M. Malcolm X. 2011. (Civil Rights Crusaders Ser.). 24p. (J). (gr. 2-5). pap. 8.15 (978-1-4339-5688-1(8), Gareth Stevens Learning Library); lib. bdg. 22.60 (978-1-4339-5686-7(1)) Stevens, Gareth Publishing LLLP.

Machajewski, Sarah. Malcolm X in His Own Words. 2014. (Eyewitness to History Ser.). 32p. (J). (gr. 4-6). pap. 63.00 (978-1-4824-1220-8(9)) Stevens, Gareth Publishing LLLP.

Malcolm X & the Black Pride Movement. 2009. (Lucent Library of Black History Ser.). 128p. (gr. 7-10). 34.80 (978-1-4205-0123-0(2), Lucent Bks.) Cengage Gale.

Mancini, Candice. Racism in the Autobiography of Malcolm X. 2008. (Social Issues in Literature Ser.). (ENG., Illus.). 175p. (YA). (gr. 10-12). 28.45 (978-0-7377-4261-9(5), LML02109-243175); pap. 40.95 (978-0-7377-4260-2(7), LML02109-243171) Cengage Gale. (Greenhaven Pr., Inc.).

Mis, Melody S. Meet Malcolm X. (Civil Rights Leaders Ser.). 24p. (gr. 2-3). 2009. 42.50 (978-1-61511-853-3(5), PowerKids Pr.) 2008. (Illus.). (YA). lib. bdg. 22.60 (978-1-4042-4214-2(7)) Rosen Publishing Group, Inc., The.

Myers, Walter Dean. Malcolm X: A Fire Burning Brightly. Jenkins, Leonard, illus. 2003. (ENG.). 40p. (J). (gr. k-3). pap. 6.99 (978-0-06-056201-4(3), Amistad) HarperCollins Pubs.

—Malcolm X: A Fire Burning Brightly. 2004. (J). 14.65 (978-0-7569-3199-5(1)) Perfection Learning Corp.

Robinson, Tom. Malcolm X: Rights Activist & Nation of Islam Leader, 1 vol. 2013. (Essential Lives Set 8 Ser.). (ENG.). 112p. (J). (gr. 6-12). lib. bdg. 35.64 (978-1-61783-893-4(4), Essential Library) ABDO Publishing Co.

Shabazz, Ilyasah. Malcolm Little: The Boy Who Grew up to Become Malcolm X. Ford, A. G., illus. 2014. (ENG.). 48p. (J). (gr. 1-5). 17.99 (978-1-4424-1216-3(X)) Simon & Schuster Children's Publishing.

Shabazz, Ilyasah & Magoon, Kekla. X. 2016. (ENG.). 384p. (YA). (gr. 9). 19.65 (978-0-606-39098-9(7)) Turtleback Bks.

Vietze, Andrew. The Life & Death of Malcolm X. 2017. (J). **(978-1-5383-8032-1(3))**; pap. **(978-1-5383-8031-4(5))** Rosen Publishing Group, Inc., The. (Rosen Young Adult).

X-MEN (FICTITIOUS CHARACTERS)—FICTION

Aaron, Jason. Wolverine & the X-Men by Jason Aaron - Volume 3. 2013. (ENG., Illus.). 112p. (J). (gr. 4-17). pap. 16.99 (978-0-7851-6000-7(0), Marvel Pr.) Disney Publishing Worldwide.

Bachalo, Chris, illus. Ultimate War, 6 vols., Vol. 5. 2006. (ENG.). 112p. (YA). (gr. 8-17). pap. 10.99 (978-0-7851-1129-0(8)) Marvel Worldwide, Inc.

Bradshaw, Nick & Bachalo, Chris, illus. Wolverine & the X-Men by Jason Aaron - Volume 2. 2013. (ENG.). 104p. (J). (gr. 4-17). pap. 16.99 (978-0-7851-5682-6(8), Marvel Pr.) Disney Publishing Worldwide.

Cassaday, John, illus. Astonishing X-Men - Gifted, Vol. 1. gif. ed. 2006. (ENG.). 152p. (YA). (gr. 8-17). pap. 14.99 (978-0-7851-1531-1(5)) Marvel Worldwide, Inc.

Claremont, Chris. X-Men Forever. 2011. (ENG., Illus.). 120p. (J). (gr. 4-17). pap. 16.99 (978-0-7851-4665-0(2)) Marvel Worldwide, Inc.

Davis, Alan, et al. The Road to Onslaught. Cruz, Roger et al, illus. 2014. (ENG.). 440p. (J). (gr. 4-17). pap. 39.99 (978-0-7851-8830-8(4)) Marvel Worldwide, Inc.

Disney Book Group Staff & Macri, Thomas. These Are the X-Men Level 1. Disney Storybook Artists Staff & Bachs, Ramon, illus. 2013. (World of Reading Ser.). (ENG.). 32p. (J). (gr. -1-k). pap. 3.99 (978-1-4231-7083-9(0)) Marvel Worldwide, Inc.

Dorling Kindersley Publishing Staff & Manning, Matthew K. Wolverine. 2009. (ENG., Illus.). 200p. (J). (gr. 8-12). 24.99 (978-0-7566-4547-2(6), DK Children) Dorling Kindersley Publishing, Inc.

Ferry, Pasqual, illus. Ultimate X-Men Fantastic Four. 2006. (ENG.). 152p. (J). (gr. 4-17). pap. 12.99 (978-0-7851-2292-0(3)) Marvel Worldwide, Inc.

Gallagher, Michael. X-Men, Magneto's Master Plan. Severin, Marie, illus. 24p. (YA). (gr. k-18). 12.95 (978-0-9627001-6-3(9)) Futech Educational Products, Inc.

—X-Men, Scourge of the Savage Land. Severin, Marie, illus. 24p. (YA). (gr. k-18). 12.95 (978-0-9627001-7-0(7)) Futech Educational Products, Inc.

Immonen, Stuart, illus. Magnetic North. 2006. (ENG.). 128p. (YA). (gr. 8-17). pap. 12.99 (978-0-7851-1906-7(X)) Marvel Worldwide, Inc.

Jensen, Jeff. X-Factor. Ranson, Arthur, illus. 2003. (X-Men Ser.: Vol. 1). 96p. (YA). pap. 9.99 (978-0-7851-1016-3(X)) Marvel Worldwide, Inc.

Kubert, Adam, et al, illus. Hellfire & Brimstone, 4 vols. 2006. (ENG.). 144p. (J). (gr. -1-17). pap. 12.99 (978-0-7851-1089-7(5)) Marvel Worldwide, Inc.

Kubert, Adam & Finch, David, illus. Return of the King, 7 vols. 2006. (ENG.). 192p. (YA). (gr. 8-17). pap. 16.99 (978-0-7851-1091-0(7)) Marvel Worldwide, Inc.

Kubert, Andy. Cry Wolf, Vol. 10. 2007. (ENG., Illus.). 96p. (YA). (gr. 8-17). pap. 8.99 (978-0-7851-1405-5(X)) Marvel Worldwide, Inc.

Lobdell, Scott, et al. X-Force: Phalanx Covenant. Cruz, Roger et al, illus. 2013. (ENG.). 256p. (J). (gr. 4-17). 39.99 (978-0-7851-6271-1(2)) Marvel Worldwide, Inc.

Mackie, Howard & Kavanagh, Terry. Gambit Classic - Volume 2. Janson, Klaus, illus. 2013. (ENG.). 208p. (J). (gr. 4-17). pap. 29.99 (978-0-7851-6790-7(0)) Marvel Worldwide, Inc.

Mackie, Howard, et al. X-Men - Age of Apocalypse Omnibus Companion. Dodson, Terry et al, illus. 2014. (ENG.). 992p. (J). (gr. 4-17). 99.99 (978-0-7851-8514-7(3)) Marvel Worldwide, Inc.

Macri, Thomas. The Story of the X-Men. 2013. (Marvel World of Reading Level 2 Ser.). (J). lib. bdg. 13.55 (978-0-606-32300-0(7), Turtleback) Turtleback Bks.

Marvel Comics Staff, creator. Ultimate X-Men, Bk. 1. 2006. (ENG., Illus.). 336p. (J). (gr. -1-17). pap. 24.99 (978-0-7851-2187-9(0)) Marvel Worldwide, Inc.

Marvel Press Group Staff, et al. The X-Men. Oliffe, Pat et al, illus. 2nd ed. 2014. (Origin Story Ser.). (ENG.). 48p. (J). (gr. 1-3). 8.99 (978-1-4231-7226-0(4)) Marvel Worldwide, Inc.

Marvel, Saga, et al. Marvel Saga. 2009. (Astonishing X-Men Ser.). (Illus.). 152p. pap. 14.99 (978-0-7851-3846-4(3)) Marvel Worldwide, Inc.

McDonnell, David, ed. Spiderman & Other Amazing Heroes. 2004. (Starlog Movie Magic Ser.). (YA). pap. (978-0-88013-065-3(2)) Profile Entertainment, Inc.

McGuinness, Ed & Stewart, Cameron, illus. Amazing X-Men, Vol. 1. 2014. (ENG.). 136p. (YA). (gr. 8-17). pap. 17.99 (978-0-7851-8821-6(5)) Marvel Worldwide, Inc.

Millar, Mark. Ultimate X-Men, 3 vols., Vol. 3. 2003. (Ultimate X-Men Ser.). (Illus.). 312p. 29.99 (978-0-7851-1131-3(X)) Marvel Worldwide, Inc.

Millar, Mark & Austen, Chuck. Ultimate X-Men, 2 vols., Vol. 2. Kubert, Adam et al, illus. 2003. (Ultimate X-Men Ser.). 336p. (YA). 29.99 (978-0-7851-1130-6(1)) Marvel Worldwide, Inc.

Milligan, Peter. Good Omens, Vol. 1. Allred, Mike, illus. 2003. (X-Statix Ser.). 128p. (YA). pap. 11.99 (978-0-7851-1059-0(3)) Marvel Worldwide, Inc.

—X-Force: Famous, Mutant & Mortal. Allred, Mike, illus. 2003. (X-Statix Ser.). 352p. (YA). 29.99 (978-0-7851-1023-1(2)) Marvel Worldwide, Inc.

Nicieza, Fabián. X-Force: Big Guns. Liefeld, Rob, illus. 2004. (X-Force Ser.). 136p. pap. 15.99 (978-0-7851-1483-3(1)) Marvel Worldwide, Inc.

Pak, Greg, et al. X-Men - X-Termination. Buffagni, Matteo et al, illus. 2013. (ENG.). 184p. (YA). (gr. 8-17). pap. 24.99 (978-0-7851-8443-0(0)) Marvel Worldwide, Inc.

Parker, Jeff, ed. Perfect World, Vol. 3. Molina, Jorge et al, illus. 2011. (ENG.). 144p. (J). (gr. 4-17). pap. 16.99 (978-0-7851-4666-7(0)) Marvel Worldwide, Inc.

Peterson, Brandon, illus. Ultimate X-Men - The Tempest, Vol. 9. 2006. (ENG.). 112p. (J). (gr. -1-17). pap. 10.99 (978-0-7851-1404-8(1)) Marvel Worldwide, Inc.

Publications International Ltd. Staff, ed. Look & Find Wolverine & X Men. 2009. 24p. (J). 7.98 (978-1-4127-3592-6(0), PIL Kids) Publications International, Ltd.

Rodi, Robert & Richards, Cliff. Rogue: Going Rogue. 2005. (X-Men Ser.). (Illus.). 144p. pap. 14.99 (978-0-7851-1336-2(3)) Marvel Worldwide, Inc.

Romita, John & Ditko, Steve, illus. X-Men - The Hidden Year, Vol. 2. 2012. (ENG.). 304p. (J). (gr. 4-17). pap. 34.99 (978-0-7851-6055-7(8)) Marvel Worldwide, Inc.

Sumerak, Marc. Big Trouble at the Big Top! Gurihiru Staff, illus. 2006. (X-Men Power Pack - 4 Titles Ser.). 24p. lib. bdg. 22.78 (978-1-59961-219-5(4)) Spotlight.

—Costumes On! Gurihiru Staff, illus. 2006. (X-Men Power Pack - 4 Titles Ser.). 24p. lib. bdg. 22.78 (978-1-59961-220-1(8)) Spotlight.

—Mind over Matter. Gurihiru Staff, illus. 2006. (X-Men Power Pack - 4 Titles Ser.). 24p. lib. bdg. 22.78 (978-1-59961-222-5(4)) Spotlight.

Thomas, Rich. The Uncanny X-Men: An Origin Story, 1 vol. The Storybook Art Group, illus. 2012. (Marvel Origins Ser.). (ENG.). 48p. (J). (gr. -1-4). lib. bdg. 24.21 (978-1-61479-012-9(4)) Spotlight.

Van Lente, Fred. Substitute. 2013. (Wolverine First Class Set 2 Ser.). (Illus.). 24p. (J). (gr. 2-6). lib. bdg. 24.21 (978-1-61479-181-2(3)) Spotlight.

X-Men. 2003. (J). (978-1-57657-859-9(3)) Paradise Pr., Inc.

X-Men Power Pack. 2006. (X-Men Power Pack Ser.). (ENG.). (J). 45.56 (978-1-59961-218-8(6)) Spotlight.

X-RAYS

Mattern, Joanne. X-Ray Machines. 2015. (Rookie Read-About(tm) Science: How Things Work Ser.). (ENG., Illus.). 32p. (J). lib. bdg. 25.00 (978-0-531-21371-1(4), Children's Pr.) Scholastic Library Publishing.

Olson, Karen. Cooper Gets a Cast. Pritchett and Hull Associates, Inc., illus. 2003. (J). 4.50 (978-0-939838-86-8(9)) Pritchett & Hull Assocs., Inc.

Sarver, Amy. Science at the Airport. 2007. (Reading Expeditions Ser.). (ENG., Illus.). 24p. (J). pap. 14.95 (978-0-7922-4568-1(7)) CENGAGE Learning.

Thiel, Kristin. Dorothy Hodgkin: Biochemist & Developer of Protein Crystallography. 2016. (Women in Science Ser.). 128p. (J). lib. bdg. 45.64 (978-1-5026-2313-3(7)) Cavendish Square Publishing.

Veasey, Nick. X-Treme X-Ray: See the World Inside Out! 2010. (ENG., Illus.). 48p. (J). (gr. 2-5). pap. 9.99 (978-0-545-21847-4(0), Scholastic Paperbacks) Scholastic, Inc.

Zonta, Pat. Jessica's X-Ray. Dobson, Clive, illus. 2006. (ENG.). 28p. (J). (gr. 1-3). pap. 9.95 (978-1-55297-577-0(0), 9781552975770) Firefly Bks., Ltd.

Y

YACHTS AND YACHTING

see also Sailing

Hamilton, S. L. America's Cup. 2013. (Xtreme Races Ser.). 32p. (J). (gr. 3-9). lib. bdg. 27.07 (978-1-61783-692-3(3), Abdo & Daughters) ABDO Publishing Co.

Hopping, Lorraine Jean. Crossing the Atlantic: One Family's Story. 2004. (ENG., Illus.). 16p. (J). (gr. 2-2). pap. 10.92 (978-0-7652-5186-2(8), Celebration Pr.) Pearson Schl.

YANGTZE RIVER AND VALLEY

Manning, Paul. The Yangtze. (River Adventures Ser.). 2014. (J). lib. bdg. 31.35 (978-1-59920-919-7(5)) 2013. 48p. (gr. 5-11). lib. bdg. 37.10 (978-1-59920-925-8(X)) Black Rabbit Bks.

Rice Jr., Earle. The Yangtze River. 2012. (J). lib. bdg. 29.95 (978-1-61228-299-2(7)) Mitchell Lane Pubs., Inc.

Simon, Charnan. The Noble Yangtze. 2004. (Geography of the World Ser.). (ENG., Illus.). 32p. (J). (gr. 3-6). 28.50 (978-1-59296-341-6(2), 200272) Child's World, Inc., The.

The Yangtzee. 2011. (River Journey Ser.). (ENG.). 48p. (YA). (gr. 5-8). 27.95 (978-1-4488-6014-2(8), Rosen Reference) Rosen Publishing Group, Inc., The.

YEARBOOKS

see also Almanacs; Calendars

Cohn, Scotti. One Wolf Howls, 1 vol. Detwiler, Susan, illus. 2009. (ENG.). 32p. (J). (gr. -1-3). 16.95 (978-1-934359-92-1(0)) Arbordale Publishing.

YELLOW FEVER

Cefrey, Holly. Yellow Fever. 2009. (Epidemics Ser.). 64p. (gr. 5-5). 58.50 (978-1-61512-309-4(1)) Rosen Publishing Group, Inc., The.

Jurmain, Suzanne. The Secret of the Yellow Death: A True Story of Medical Sleuthing. 2009. (ENG., Illus.). 112p. (J). (gr. 5-7). 19.00 (978-0-618-96581-6(5)) Houghton Mifflin Harcourt Publishing Co.

—Secret of the Yellow Death: A True Story of Medical Sleuthing. 2013. (ENG., Illus.). 112p. (J). (gr. 5-7). pap. 9.99 (978-0-547-74624-1(5)) Houghton Mifflin Harcourt Publishing Co.

Murphy, Jim. An American Plague: The True & Terrifying Story of the Yellow Fever Epidemic Of 1793. 2003. (ENG., Illus.). 176p. (J). (gr. 5-7). tchr. ed. 21.99 (978-0-395-77608-7(2)) Houghton Mifflin Harcourt Publishing Co.

YELLOWSTONE NATIONAL PARK

Apel, Melanie Ann. The Yellowstone Park Fire Of 1988. 2009. (Tragic Fires Throughout History Ser.). 48p. (gr. 5-8). 53.00 (978-1-60854-585-8(7), Rosen Reference) Rosen Publishing Group, Inc., The.

Aretha, David. Yellowstone National Park: Adventure, Explore, Discover. 2008. (America's National Parks Ser.). (Illus.). 128p. (J). (gr. 5-9). lib. bdg. 34.60 (978-1-59845-087-3(5)) Enslow Pubs., Inc.

Bauer, Marion Dane. Yellowstone. Wallace, John, illus. 2008. (Wonders of America Ser.). (ENG.). 32p. (J). (gr. -1-1). pap. 3.99 (978-1-4169-5404-0(X), Simon Spotlight) Simon Spotlight.

Craighead, Shirley A. Bugling Elk & Sleeping Grizzlies: The Who, What, & When of Yellowstone & Grand Teton National Parks. 2004. (ENG., Illus.). 48p. pap. 9.95 (978-0-7627-2864-0(7), Falcon Guides) Globe Pequot Pr., The.

Francis, Michael H. Yellowstone Memories: 30 Years of Photographs & Stories. 2005. (Illus.). 95p. 22.95 (978-1-931832-59-5(5), 8667872363) Riverbend Publishing.

Frisch, Nate. Preserving America: Yellowstone National Park. 2014. (Preserving America Ser.). (ENG., Illus.). 48p. (J). (gr. 4-7). pap. 12.00 (978-0-89812-881-9(1), Creative Paperbacks) Creative Co., The.

—Yellowstone National Park. 2013. (Illus.). 48p. (J). 35.65 (978-1-60818-198-8(7), Creative Education) Creative Co., The.

Gamble, Adam & Jasper, Mark. Good Night Yellowstone. Kelly, Cooper, illus. 2013. (Good Night Our World Ser.). (ENG.). 20p. (J). (— 1). bds. 9.95 (978-1-60219-079-5(8)) Good Night Bks.

George, Jean Craighead. The Wolves Are Back. Minor, Wendell, illus. 2008. (ENG.). 32p. (J). (gr. -1-3). 16.99 (978-0-525-47947-5(3), Dutton Books for Young Readers) Penguin Young Readers Group.

Gilbert, Sara. Yellowstone. 2016. (Illus.). 22p. (J). (978-1-60818-634-1(2), Creative Education) Creative Co., The.

Glastetter, KC & Hollman, Jeremie, photos by. Yellowstone Natl Park Abc Adv. 2010. (Illus.). 64p. (J). pap. 12.00 (978-0-87842-572-3(1)) Mountain Pr. Publishing Co., Inc.

Godkin, Celia. The Wolves Return. Godkin, Celia, illus. 2017. (ENG., Illus.). 32p. (J). (gr. 1-3). 17.95 (978-1-77278-011-6(1)) Pajama Pr. CAN. Dist: Ingram Publisher Services.

Goldish, Meish. Gray Wolves: Return to Yellowstone. 2016. (America's Animal Comebacks Ser.). (ENG.). 32p. (J). (gr. 2-7). pap. 8.95 **(978-1-944998-72-1(1))** Bearport Publishing Co., Inc.

Halfpenny, James C. Yellowstone Wolves in the Wild. 2003. (Illus.). 104p. per. 19.95 (978-1-931832-26-7(9), 8667872363) Riverbend Publishing.

Johanek, Durrae. What I Saw in Yellowstone: A Kid's Guide to Wonderland. Cauble, Christopher, photos by. 2012. (Illus.). (J). pap. 12.95 (978-1-60639-035-1(X)) Riverbend Publishing.

Kalman, Bobbie. Yellowstone National Park. 2009. (Introducing Habitats Ser.). (ENG., Illus.). 32p. (J). (gr. k-3). pap. (978-0-7787-2989-1(3)) Crabtree Publishing Co.

Marsh, Carole. I'm Reading about Yellowstone. 2016. (I'm Reading about Mount Rushmore Ser.). (ENG., Illus.). (J). pap. 7.99 (978-0-635-12184-4(0)) Gallopade International.

National Geographic Kids Staff & Holland, Ilona E. Buddy Bison Yellowstone. 2016. (ENG., Illus.). 32p. (J). (gr. -1-3). pap. 9.99 (978-1-4263-2297-6(6), National Geographic Children's Bks.) National Geographic Society.

Patent, Dorothy Hinshaw. When the Wolves Returned: Restoring Nature's Balance in Yellowstone. Hartman, Dan, illus. Hartman, Cassie & Hartman, Dan, photos by. 2008. (ENG.). 40p. (J). (gr. 1-4). 19.99 (978-0-8027-9686-8(9), 9780802796868, Bloomsbury USA Childrens) Bloomsbury Publishing USA.

Pecorella, Jane. Yellowstone: Our First National Park. 2009. (Reading Room Collection 2 Ser.). 24p. (gr. 3-4). 42.50 (978-1-60852-004-6(8), PowerKids Pr.) Rosen Publishing Group, Inc., The.

—Yellowstone, Our First National Park. 2003. (Reading Room Collection 2 Ser.). (Illus.). 24p. (J). lib. bdg. 22.60 (978-0-8239-3712-7(7)) Rosen Publishing Group, Inc., The.

Piehl, Janet. Yellowstone National Park. 2010. (Lightning Bolt Books (tm) — Famous Places Ser.). (ENG.). 32p. (gr. k-2). pap. 7.95 (978-0-7613-5588-5(X)); lib. bdg. 26.60 (978-0-7613-4455-1(1), Lerner Pubns.) Lerner Publishing Group.

Robson, Gary D. Who Pooped in the Park? Yellowstone. 2004. (Illus.). 48p. (J). pap. 11.95 (978-1-56037-273-8(7)) Farcountry Pr.

Swimow, Linda. Take on Yellowstone! 2011. 32p. pap. 12.99 (978-1-4490-2219-8(7)) AuthorHouse.

Wade, Linda R. & Hamilton, John. Yellowstone National Park, 1 vol. 2005. (National Parks Ser.). (ENG., Illus.). 32p. (gr. 3-8). 27.07 (978-1-59197-427-7(5), Abdo & Daughters) ABDO Publishing Co.

Wallace, Audra. Yellowstone. 2017. (Rookie National Parks Ser.). (ENG.). 32p. (J). lib. bdg. 25.00 **(978-0-531-23335-1(9)**, Children's Pr.) Scholastic Library Publishing.

—Yellowstone National Park. 2017. (True Book — National Parks Ser.). (ENG.). 48p. (J). lib. bdg. 31.00 **(978-0-531-23396-2(0)**, Children's Pr.) Scholastic Library Publishing.

Webster, Dawn & Yost, Emily. Yellowstone for Kids: A Kid's Guide to Yellowstone National Park. 2016. (Illus.). (J). (978-0-934948-40-1(2)) Yellowstone Forever.

Zschock, Martha Day. Hello, Yellowstone! 2012. (Hello! Ser.). (ENG., Illus.). 16p. (J). (gr. -1-k). bds. 9.95 (978-1-933212-61-6(6), Commonwealth Editions) Applewood Bks.

YETI

Colson, Mary. Bigfoot & the Yeti, 1 vol. King, Chris, illus. 2013. (Solving Mysteries with Science Ser.). (ENG.). 48p. (gr. 3-6). pap. 9.95 (978-1-4109-5505-0(2)) Heinemann-Raintree.

—Bigfoot & the Yeti, 1 vol. 2013. (Solving Mysteries with Science Ser.). (ENG., Illus.). 48p. (gr. 3-6). 29.99 (978-1-4109-5499-2(4)) Heinemann-Raintree.

Guiley, Rosemary Ellen & Dennett, Preston E. Bigfoot, Yeti, & Other Ape-Men. 2008. (Mysteries, Legends, & Unexplained Phenomena Ser.). (Illus.). 152p. (YA). (gr. 7-12). 29.95 (978-0-7910-9386-3(7)) Facts On File, Inc.

Hunter, Nick. Does the Yeti Exist? 2016. (Top Secret! Ser.). (ENG., Illus.). 48p. (gr. 4-6). lib. bdg. 33.32 (978-1-4109-8161-5(4)) Heinemann-Raintree.

Joline Anderson, Jennifer. Bigfoot & Yeti, 1 vol. 2014. (Creatures of Legend Ser.). (ENG., Illus.). 48p. (gr. 3-6). lib. bdg. 32.79 (978-1-62403-150-2(1)) ABDO Publishing Co.

McClellan, Ray. Bigfoot. 2014. (Unexplained Mysteries Ser.). (ENG., Illus.). 24p. (J). (gr. 3-7). lib. bdg. 25.95 (978-1-62617-103-9(3), Epic Bks.) Bellwether Media.

Nagle, Jeanne. Investigating the Abominable Snowman & Other Legendary Beasts, 1 vol. 2015. (ENG.). 48p. (J). 25.85 (978-1-62275-853-1(6), Britannica Educational Publishing) Rosen Publishing Group, Inc., The.

Rivkin, Jennifer. Searching for the Yeti. 2014. (Mysterious Monsters Ser.). (Illus.). 32p. (J). (gr. 3-6). 26.25 (978-1-4777-7097-9(6), PowerKids Pr.) Rosen Publishing Group, Inc., The.

Roberts, Steven. The Yeti! 2012. (Jr. Graphic Monster Stories Ser.). (ENG., Illus.). 24p. (J). (gr. 3-6). 25.25 (978-1-4488-7905-2(1)); pap. 10.60 (978-1-4488-8005-8(X)) Rosen Publishing Group, Inc., The. (PowerKids Pr.).

Shone, Rob. Bigfoot & Other Strange Beasts. 2009. (Graphic Mysteries Ser.). (ENG.). 48p. (YA). (gr. 5-5). 58.50 (978-1-61512-961-4(8), Rosen Reference) Rosen Publishing Group, Inc., The.

—Bigfoot & Other Strange Beasts. Spender, Nick, illus. 2006. (Graphic Mysteries Ser.). (ENG.). 48p. (YA). (gr. k-3). lib. bdg. 31.95 (978-1-4042-0793-6(7)) Rosen Publishing Group, Inc., The.

—Bigfoot & Other Strange Beasts. Spender, Nik, illus. 2006. (Graphic Mysteries Ser.). (ENG.). 48p. (gr. 5-8). pap. 14.05 (978-1-4042-0804-9(6)) Rosen Publishing Group, Inc., The.

Teitelbaum, Michael. Bigfoot Caught on Film: And Other Monster Sightings! 2008. (24/7: Science Behind the Scenes Ser.). (ENG., Illus.). 64p. (J). (gr. 9-12). 29.00 (978-0-531-12078-1(3), Watts, Franklin) Scholastic Library Publishing.

Truet, Turin & Gilman, Laura Anne. Searching for Yeti: The Abominable Snowman. 2011. (Mystery Explorers Ser.). (Illus.). 64p. (J). 31.95 (978-1-4488-4764-8(8)); 77.70 (978-1-4488-4781-5(8)); pap. 12.95 (978-1-4488-4773-0(7)) Rosen Publishing Group, Inc., The.

Walker, Kathryn. Mysteries of Giant Humanlike Creatures. 2008. (ENG., Illus.). 32p. (J). (gr. 3-7). pap. (978-0-7787-4156-5(7)); lib. bdg. (978-0-7787-4143-5(5)) Crabtree Publishing Co.

YOGA

Baptiste, Baron. My Daddy Is a Pretzel: Yoga for Parents & Kids. Fatus, Sophie, illus. (ENG.). 48p. (J). 2012. (gr. k-3). pap. 9.99 (978-1-84686-899-3(8)) 2004. (gr. -1-2). 16.99 (978-1-84148-151-7(3)) Barefoot Bks., Inc.

Beliveau, Kathy. The Yoga Game. Zaman, Farida, illus. 2012. (ENG.). 42p. (J). (gr. -1-2). pap. 9.95 (978-1-897476-72-7(8)) Simply Read Bks. CAN. Dist: Ingram Publisher Services.

—The Yoga Game by the Sea. Holmes, Denise, illus. 2015. (Yoga Game Ser.: 1). (ENG.). 32p. (J). 16.95 (978-1-927018-49-1(8)) Simply Read Bks. CAN. Dist: Ingram Publisher Services.

Bersma, Danielle & Visscher, Marjoke. Yoga Games for Children: Fun & Fitness with Postures, Movements & Breath. Evans, Amina Marix, tr. from DUT. Kooistra, Alex, illus. 2003. (SmartFun Activity Bks.). (ENG.). 160p. (J). pap. 14.95 (978-0-89793-389-6(3), Hunter Hse.) Turner Publishing Co.

Birkemoe, Karen. Strike a Pose: The Planet Girl Guide to Yoga. Collett, Heather, illus. 2007. (Planet Girl Ser.). (ENG.). 96p. (J). (gr. 5-9). 12.95 (978-1-55337-004-8(X)) Kids Can Pr., Ltd. CAN. Dist: Hachette Bk. Group.

Brukner, Lauren. The Keep-Calm Guru's Guide to Staying Awesome & in Control. Phillips-Smith, Anthony & Apsley House, London Staff, illus. 2016. (ENG.). 136p. 19.95 (978-1-78592-714-0(0), 8410) Kingsley, Jessica Pubs. GBR. Dist: Macmillan Distribution Ltd.

Buckley, Annie. The Breathing Bridge. (Illus.). 2012. (978-1-927004-14-2(4)) 2011. pap. (978-1-927004-13-5(6)) Brighter Bks. Publishing Hse.

—The Kids' Yoga Deck: 50 Poses & Games. Buckley, Annie, illus. 2003. (ENG., Illus.). 50p. (gr. 8-17). 14.95 (978-0-8118-3698-2(3)) Chronicle Bks. LLC.

Capucilli, Alyssa Satin. My First Yoga Class. Wachter, Jill, photos by. 2017. (My First Ser.). (ENG., Illus.). 32p. (J). (gr. -1-k). 16.99 **(978-1-5344-0485-4(6))**; pap. 3.99 **(978-1-5344-0484-7(8))** Simon Spotlight. (Simon Spotlight).

Chissick, Michael. Ladybird's Remarkable Relaxation: How Children (And Frogs, Dogs, Flamingos & Dragons) Can Use Yoga Relaxation to Help Deal with Stress, Grief, Bullying & Lack of Confidence. Peacock, Sarah, illus. 2013. (ENG.). 48p. (J). 19.95 (978-1-84819-146-4(4), 2259, Singing Dragon) Kingsley, Jessica Pubs. GBR. Dist: Macmillan Distribution Ltd.

—Sitting on a Chicken: The Best (Ever) 52 Yoga Games to Teach in Schools. Peacock, Sarah, illus. 2016. (ENG.). 112p. (J). pap. 24.95 (978-1-84819-325-3(4), 8674, Singing Dragon) Kingsley, Jessica Pubs. GBR. Dist: Macmillan Distribution Ltd.

Crabtree Editors & Wilson, Kyla. Stretch It Yoga. 2012. (Sports Starters Ser.). (ENG., Illus.). 32p. (J). (gr. 1-4). lib. bdg. (978-0-7787-3153-5(7)) Crabtree Publishing Co.

de Brunhoff, Laurent. Babar's Yoga for Elephants. 2006. (ENG., Illus.). 48p. (gr. -1-3). 10.95 *(978-0-8109-3076-6(5),* Abrams Image) Abrams, Inc.
Engel, Christiane. Yoga. 2016. (ABC for Me Ser.). (ENG.). 36p. (J). (gr. -1-1). 16.95 *(978-1-63322-146-8(6),* Walter Foster Jr) Quarto Publishing Group USA.
Fatus, Sophie, et al. Yoga Pretzels: 50 Fun Yoga Activities for Kids & Grownups. Fatus, Sophie, illus. 2005. (ENG., Illus.). 50p. (J). (gr. k-5). 14.99 *(978-1-905236-04-6(2))* Barefoot Bks., Inc.
Fulcher, Roz & Activity Books. Be Good to Your Body — Learning Yoga. 2013. (Dover Children's Activity Bks.). (ENG., Illus.). 64p. (J). (gr. 3-5). pap. 6.99 *(978-0-486-48830-1(6))* Dover Pubns., Inc.
Gates, Mariam. Good Morning Yoga: A Pose-By-Pose Wake up Story, 1 vol. Hinder, Sarah Jane, illus. 2016. (ENG.). 36p. (J). 17.95 *(978-1-62203-602-8(6),* 9781622036028) Sounds True, Inc.
—Good Night Yoga: A Pose-By-Pose Bedtime Story, 1 vol. Hinder, Sara Jane, illus. 2015. (ENG.). 36p. (J). 17.95 *(978-1-62203-466-6(X),* 162203466X) Sounds True, Inc.
Gillen, Jim & Gillen, Lynea. Yoga Calm for Children: Educating Heart, Mind, & Body. 2008. (ENG., Illus.). 181p. (J). per. 29.95 *(978-0-9799289-0-1(7))* Three Pebble Pr., LLC.
Humphrey, Mary. The Kids' Yoga Book of Feelings, 1 vol. Hamlin, Janet, illus. Frost, Michael, photos by. 2008. (ENG.). 40p. (J). (gr. 3-7). 15.99 *(978-0-7614-5424-3(1))* Marshall Cavendish Corp.
James, Sara. Yoga & Pilates. Hart, Diane H., ed. 2014. (Integrated Life of Fitness Ser.). (Illus.). 64p. (J). (gr. 7-18). pap. 11.95 *(978-1-4222-3204-0(2));* 23.95 *(978-1-4222-3166-1(6))* Mason Crest.
Kacev, Glenda. Bal Yoga for Kids. 2012. (ENG.). (J). spiral bd. *(978-1-4675-4826-7(X))* Independent Pub.
Kalish, Leah & Fatus, Sophie. Yoga Planet: 50 Fun Activities for a Greener World. 2008. (ENG., Illus.). (J). 14.99 *(978-1-84686-181-9(0))* Barefoot Bks., Inc.
Kramer, Susan. Yoga for all Kids, Preschoolers to Teens. 2010. 96p. pap. 14.95 *(978-0-557-42836-6(X))* Lulu Pr., Inc.
Lark, Liz. Yoga for Kids. Park, Clare, photos by. 2005. (Illus.). 127p. (J). reprint ed. pap. 20.00 *(978-0-7567-9410-1(2))* DIANE Publishing Co.
Leavitt, Amy. Yoga Fitness. 2014. (ENG.). 48p. (gr. 4-8). 29.95 *(978-1-61228-551-1(1))* Mitchell Lane Pubs., Inc.
MacAulay, Kelley. Yoga in Action. 2008. (FRE.). 32p. (J). pap. 9.95 *(978-2-89579-205-5(4))* Bayard Canada Livres CAN. Dist: Crabtree Publishing Co.
MacAulay, Kelley & Kalman, Bobbie. Yoga in Action. Crabtree, Marc, photos by. 2005. (Sports in Action Ser.). (ENG., Illus.). 32p. (J). (gr. 2-3). pap. *(978-0-7787-0364-8(9))* Crabtree Publishing Co.
MacLean, Kerry Lee. Peaceful Piggy Yoga. MacLean, Kerry Lee, illus. (ENG., Illus.). 32p. (J). 2016. (gr. -1-3). 12.99 *(978-0-8075-6388-5(9))* 2014. (gr. 1-3). 6.99 *(978-0-8075-6383-0(8))* Whitman, Albert & Co.
Marek, Susan. A Children's Guide to Chakras. 2009. 32p. pap. 14.95 *(978-0-578-00741-0(X))* Angelworks Pr.
Oostendorp, Leila Kadri. Animal Asanas: Yoga for Children. Bahia, Elsa, illus. 2017. (ENG.). 64p. (J). (gr. k-4). 16.95 ***(978-3-7913-7275-4(0))*** Prestel Verlag GmbH & Co KG. DEU. Dist: Penguin Random Hse. LLC.
Pajalunga, Lorena V. Yoga for Kids: Simple Animal Poses for Any Age. Forlati, Anna, illus. 2015. (ENG.). 32p. (J). (gr. -1-3). 16.99 *(978-0-8075-9172-7(6))* Whitman, Albert & Co.
Pegrum, Juliet. Yoga Fun for Toddlers, Children & You. 2010. (ENG., Illus.). 128p. pap. *(978-1-907030-14-7(X))* www.clickok.co.uk.
Pierce, Karen F. Yoga Bear: Yoga for Youngsters. Brinkman, Paula, illus. 2004. (ENG.). 48p. (J). (gr. -1-1). 15.95 *(978-1-55971-897-4(8))* Cooper Square Publishing Llc.
Power, Teresa. The ABCs of Yoga for Kids. Rietz, Kathleen, illus. 2009. (ENG.). 32p. (J). (gr. -1-3). 19.95 *(978-0-9822587-0-5(4),* 4e17cd6f-1cd3-4995-a291-23f8e9041df7) Stafford House.
Power, Teresa Anne. The ABCs of Yoga for Kids 56 Learning Cards. Rietz, Kathleen, illus. 2011. (ENG.). 57p. (J). 19.95 *(978-0-9822587-3-6(9))* Stafford House.
—ABECE de Yoga para Ninos. Rietz, Kathleen, illus. 2011. (ENG.). 32p. (J). pap. 8.95 *(978-0-9822587-4-3(7))* Stafford House.
Purperhart, Helen. The Yoga Adventure for Children: Playing, Dancing, Moving, Breathing, Relaxing. Evans, Amina Marix, tr. from DUT. Von Amelsfort, Barbra, illus. 2007. (ENG.). 144p. (gr. -1-6). per. 14.95 *(978-0-89793-470-1(9),* Hunter Hse.) Turner Publishing Co.
—Yoga Exercises for Teens: Developing a Calmer Mind & a Stronger Body. Evans, Amina Marix, tr. from DUT. van Amelsfort, Barbara, illus. 2008. (SmartFun Activity Bks.). (ENG.). 160p. (gr. 4). spiral bd. 19.95 *(978-0-89793-504-3(7));* pap. 14.95 *(978-0-89793-503-6(9))* Turner Publishing Co. (Hunter Hse.).
Randall, Kat. Yoga for Youngsters: Playful Poses for Little People. 2004. (Illus.). 24p. pap. 8.95 *(978-0-9749516-0-7(9))* Kat's Kids Kreation, A.
Rissman, Rebecca. Calm Girl: Yoga for Stress Relief. 2015. (Yoga for You Ser.). (ENG.). 64p. (gr. 4-5). lib. bdg. 34.65 *(978-1-4914-2121-5(5))* Capstone Press of Coughlan Cos.
—Fit Girl: Yoga for Fitness & Flexibility. 2015. (Yoga for You Ser.). (ENG.). 64p. (gr. 4-5). lib. bdg. 34.65 *(978-1-4914-2120-8(7))* Capstone Press of Coughlan Cos.
—Smart Girl: Yoga for Brain Power. 2015. (Yoga for You Ser.). (ENG.). 64p. (gr. 4-5). lib. bdg. 34.65 *(978-1-4914-2119-2(3))* Capstone Press of Coughlan Cos.
—Strong Girl: Yoga for Building Strength. 2015. (Yoga for You Ser.). (ENG.). 64p. (gr. 4-5). lib. bdg. 34.65 *(978-1-4914-2122-2(3))* Capstone Press of Coughlan Cos.
—Yoga for You. 2015. (Yoga for You Ser.). (ENG.). 64p. (gr. 4-5). lib. bdg. 138.60 *(978-1-4914-2558-9(X))* Capstone Press of Coughlan Cos.
—Yoga for You: Feel Calmer, Stronger, & Happier! 2017. (Good for You Ser.). (ENG., Illus.). 64p. (J). (gr. 3-7). 14.95 *(978-1-63322-319-6(1),* Walter Foster Jr) Quarto Publishing Group USA.
—Yoga for Your Mind & Body: A Teenage Practice for a Healthy, Balanced Life. 2015. (ENG., Illus.). 208p. (gr. 4-5). pap. 14.95 *(978-1-63079-013-4(3))* Switch Pr.
Ryzewski, Deborah. The Yoga ABC's with Alvin, Beatrice & Conner. 2005. (Illus.). (J). ring bd. 12.95 net. *(978-0-9765302-0-6(1))* Ryzewski, Deborah.
Schwartz, Ellen. I Love Yoga: A Source Book for Teens. Hodson, Ben, illus. 2003. (ENG.). 128p. (J). (gr. 5-18). pap. 9.95 *(978-0-88776-598-8(X),* Tundra Bks.) Tundra Bks. CAN. Dist: Penguin Random Hse. LLC.
Sheen, Barbara. Yoga. 2014. (Science Behind Sports Ser.). (ENG.). 128p. 39.40 *(978-1-4205-1229-8(3))* Cengage Gale.
Silas, Elizabeth & Goodney, Diane. Yoga. (Life Balance Ser.). (ENG.). 80p. (gr. 5-8). 2004. (YA). pap. 6.95 *(978-0-531-15577-6(3))* 2003. (Illus.). (J). 20.50 *(978-0-531-12258-7(1))* Scholastic Library Publishing. (Watts, Franklin).
Sumner, Christine. I Can Be: A Child's Whimsical Introduction to Yoga. Salopek, Kirk, illus. 2008. 32p. (J). 8.95 *(978-0-615-16566-0(4))* Q & J Bird Pr., LLC.
Tieck, Sarah. Yoga, 1 vol. 2013. (Move Your Body Ser.). (ENG.). 32p. (J). (gr. 2-5). 27.07 *(978-1-61783-565-0(X))* ABDO Publishing Co.
Whitford, Rebecca. Little Yoga: A Toddler's First Book of Yoga. Selway, Martina, illus. 2005. (ENG.). 32p. (J). (gr. -1 — 1). 11.99 *(978-0-8050-7879-4(7),* 9780805078794, Holt, Henry & Co. Bks. For Young Readers) Holt, Henry & Co.
Wilson, Kyla. Stretch It Yoga. 2012. (ENG., Illus.). 32p. (J). pap. *(978-0-7787-3164-1(2))* Crabtree Publishing Co.
Winters, Jaime. Get into Yoga. 2017. (Illus.). 32p. (J). ***(978-0-7787-3644-8(X))*** Crabtree Publishing Co.

YOM KIPPUR

Hashanah, Rosh & Kippur, Yom. Rosh Hashanah & Yom Kippur Coloring Book. 2.99 *(978-1-58330-168-5(2))* Feldheim Pubs.
Head, Honor. Celebrating Yom Kippur: The Jewish New Year. 2009. (We Love Holidays Ser.). 24p. (J). (gr. k-5). (ENG., Illus.). pap. 8.25 *(978-1-4358-2906-0(9));* lib. bdg. 22.60 *(978-1-4358-2846-9(1))* Rosen Publishing Group, Inc., The.
Zimmerman, Noam. Yom Kippur Children's Machzor. 2006. 64p. 15.95 *(978-965-229-362-6(8))* Gefen Publishing Hse., Ltd ISR. Dist: Gefen Bks.

YOM KIPPUR—FICTION

Adler, David A. Yom Kippur Shortstop. Ceolin, Andre, illus. 2017. (J). ***(978-1-68115-521-0(4))*** Behrman Hse., Inc.
Rouss, Sylvia A. Sammy Spider's First Yom Kippur. 2013. (Illus.). 32p. (J). pap. 16.95 *(978-1-4677-1639-0(1))* Lerner Publishing Group.
—Sammy Spider's First Yom Kippur. Kahn, Katherine Janus, illus. 2013. (High Holidays Ser.). (ENG.). 32p. (J). (gr. -1-3). 7.95 *(978-0-7613-9196-8(7),* Kar-Ben Publishing) Lerner Publishing Group.

YORKTOWN (VA.)

Rudolph, Ellen K. Willi Gets a History Lesson: In Virginia's Historic Triangle. Rudolph, Ellen K., photos by. 2007. (ENG., Illus.). 80p. pap. 24.00 *(978-0-9791348-0-7(3))* EKR Pubns.

YORKTOWN (VA.)—HISTORY—SIEGE, 1781

Anderson, Dale. The Battle of Yorktown. 2004. (Landmark Events in American History Ser.). (Illus.). 48p. (gr. 5-12). lib. bdg. 31.00 *(978-0-8368-5393-3(8),* Gareth Stevens Secondary Library) Stevens, Gareth Publishing LLLP.
Crewe, Sabrina & Anderson, Dale. The Battle of Yorktown. 2005. (Events That Shaped America Ser.). 32p. (gr. 3-6). lib. bdg. 26.00 *(978-0-8368-3412-3(7),* Gareth Stevens Learning Library) Stevens, Gareth Publishing LLLP.
Fradin, Dennis Brindell. The Battle of Yorktown. 2008. (Turning Points in U. S. History Ser.). 48p. (gr. 3-18). lib. bdg. 31.36 *(978-0-7614-3008-7(3),* Benchmark Bks.) Marshall Cavendish Corp.
Randolph, Joanne. The Call of Liberty: Marquis de Lafayette & the American Revolution. 2009. (Great Moments in American History Ser.). 32p. (gr. 3-3). 47.90 *(978-1-61513-152-5(3))* Rosen Publishing Group, Inc., The.
Roberts, Russell. Battle of Yorktown. 2011. (Technologies & Strategies in Battle Ser.). (Illus.). 48p. (J). (gr. 4-7). lib. bdg. 29.95 *(978-1-61228-074-5(9))* Mitchell Lane Pubs., Inc.
Vierow, Wendy. The Battle of Yorktown. 2009. (Atlas of Famous Battles of the American Revolution Ser.). 24p. (gr. 3-3). 42.50 *(978-1-60853-332-9(8),* PowerKids Pr.) Rosen Publishing Group, Inc., The.
Waldman, Scott P. The Battle of Yorktown. 2003. (Atlas of Famous Battles of the American Revolution Ser.). (Illus.). 24p. (J). lib. bdg. 22.60 *(978-0-8239-6331-7(4))* Rosen Publishing Group, Inc., The.

YOSEMITE NATIONAL PARK (CALIF.)

Ellis, Paula. Yosemite Activity Book, 1 vol. Nitzsche, Shane, illus. 2013. (Color & Learn Ser.). (ENG.). 64p. (J). (gr. 2-3). pap. 5.95 *(978-1-59193-299-4(8))* Adventure Pubns.
Frisch, Nate. Preserving America: Yosemite National Park. 2014. (Preserving America Ser.). (ENG.). 48p. (J). (gr. 4-7). pap. 12.00 *(978-0-89812-882-6(X),* Creative Paperbacks) Creative Co., The.
—Yosemite National Park. 2013. (Illus.). 48p. (J). 35.65 *(978-1-60818-199-5(5),* Creative Education) Creative Co., The.
Gilbert, Sara. Yosemite. 2016. 22p. (J). *(978-1-60818-635-8(0),* Creative Education) Creative Co., The.
Graf, Mike. My Yosemite: A Guide for Young Adventurers. Filice, Annette, illus. 2012. (J). *(978-1-59714-170-3(4))* Heyday.
—My Yosemite: A Guide for Young Adventurers. Filice, Annette, illus. 2012. (ENG.). 176p. (gr. 4). pap. 12.95 *(978-1-930238-30-5(4))* Yosemite Assn.
Herweck Rice, Dona. Travel Adventures: Yosemite: Perimeter & Area (Grade 4) 2017. (Mathematics Readers Ser.). (Illus.). 32p. (J). (gr. 4-4). pap. 8.99 ***(978-1-4258-5560-4(1))*** Teacher Created Materials, Inc.
Rosenstock, Barb. The Camping Trip That Changed America: Theodore Roosevelt, John Muir, & Our National Parks. Gerstein, Mordecai, illus. 2012. (ENG.). 32p. (J). (gr. 1-3). 17.99 *(978-0-8037-3710-5(6),* Dial Bks) Penguin Young Readers Group.
Wade, Linda R. Yosemite National Park, 1 vol. 2005. (National Park Ser.). (ENG., Illus.). 32p. (gr. 3-8). 27.07 *(978-1-59197-428-4(3),* Abdo & Daughters) ABDO Publishing Co.
Wadsworth, Ginger. Camping with the President. Dugan, Karen, illus. 2009. (ENG.). 32p. (J). (gr. 4-18). 16.95 *(978-1-59078-497-6(9),* Calkins Creek) Boyds Mills Pr.
Wallace, Audra. Yosemite. 2017. (True Book — National Parks Ser.). (ENG.). (J). 48p. pap. 7.95 ***(978-0-531-24022-9(3));*** 32p. lib. bdg. 25.00 ***(978-0-531-23334-4(0));*** 48p. lib. bdg. 31.00 ***(978-0-531-23395-5(2))*** Scholastic Library Publishing. (Children's Pr.).

YOSEMITE NATIONAL PARK (CALIF.)—FICTION

Bethune, Helen. A Road Trip to Yosemite, 1 vol. 2013. (Fiction Readers Ser.). (ENG., Illus.). 28p. (J). (gr. 2-2). pap. 6.99 *(978-1-4333-5569-1(8))* Shell Educational Publishing.
Wadsworth, Ginger. Yosemite's Songster: One Coyote's Story. San Souci, Daniel, illus. 2013. (ENG.). 32p. (J). (gr. -1-2). 15.95 *(978-1-930238-34-3(7))* Yosemite Assn.

YOSEMITE VALLEY (CALIF.)

Danneberg, Julie. John Muir Wrestles a Waterfall. Hogan, Jamie, illus. 2015. (ENG.). 32p. (J). (gr. -1-3). lib. bdg. 16.95 *(978-1-58089-586-6(7))* Charlesbridge Publishing, Inc.
Gamble, Adam & Jasper, Mark. Good Night Yosemite. McDonnell, Janet & Chan, Suwin, illus. 2016. (Good Night Our World Ser.). (ENG.). 20p. (J). (— 1). bds. 9.95 *(978-1-60219-389-5(4))* Good Night Bks.

YOUNG, BRIGHAM, 1801-1877

Encyclopaedia Britannica, Inc. Staff, compiled by. Brigham Young. 2008. 49.95 *(978-1-59339-525-4(6))* Encyclopaedia Britannica, Inc.
Sanford, William R. & Green, Carl R. Brigham Young: Courageous Mormon Leader. 2012. (Courageous Heroes of the American West Ser.). (Illus.). 48p. (J). pap. 8.95 *(978-1-4644-0089-6(X));* (gr. 5-18). 22.60 *(978-0-7660-4004-5(6))* Enslow Pubs., Inc.

YOUNG ADULTS

Here are entered works on people in the general age range of eighteen through twenty-five years.
see also Youth

Boersma, Heather. Dream Big: 30 Days to Life Beyond All You Could Ask or Imagine. 2012. ix, 119p. *(978-1-77069-453-8(6))* Word Alive Pr.
Dunagan, Cindy. Journaling Toward Moral Excellence Volume Four for Young Adults: A Character Building Workbook of 100 Thought-Provoking Questions to Help the Young Discover the Value of Moral Strength. 2004. (Journaling Toward Moral Excellence Ser.: Vol. 4). 107p. (YA). (gr. 11-18). 11.95 *(978-0-9759871-3-1(5))* Straight Paths Pr.
Epstein, Alex. The Circle Cast, 1 vol. 2011. (ENG., Illus.). 304p. (YA). (gr. 2-4). pap. 12.95 *(978-1-896580-63-0(7))* Tradewind Bks. CAN. Dist: Orca Bk. Pubs. USA.
Lee, Darrien. 16 Going on 21. 2008. (ENG., Illus.). 288p. (YA). (gr. 9). 9.95 *(978-1-933967-71-4(4),* Urban Renaissance) Kensington Publishing Corp.
McGuinness, Denis E. & Thomson, Sarah L. Gary Paulsen, 01 vols., 1. 2016. (All about the Author Ser.). (ENG., Illus.). 112p. (J). 35.60 *(978-1-4994-6268-5(9),* Rosen Young Adult) Rosen Publishing Group, Inc., The.
Meyer, Susan. Gayle Forman, 01 vols., 1. 2016. (All about the Author Ser.). (ENG., Illus.). 112p. (J). 35.60 *(978-1-4994-6272-2(7),* Rosen Young Adult) Rosen Publishing Group, Inc., The.
Peterson, Judy Monroe. First Budget Smarts. 2009. (J). 77.70 *(978-1-4358-5553-3(1));* pap. 12.95 *(978-1-4358-5552-6(3));* (Illus.). 64p. (gr. 7-12). lib. bdg. 31.95 *(978-1-4358-5273-0(7))* Rosen Publishing Group, Inc., The.
Popkin, Michael H. & Hendrickson, Peggy. Teens in Action: A Teen's Guide for Surviving & Thriving in the 21st Century. 2013. (ENG., Illus.). 216p. (J). (gr. 7-12). pap. 14.95 *(978-1-59723-273-9(4))* Active Parenting Pubs.

YOUTH

Here are entered works on the time of life between thirteen and twenty-five years, as well as on people in this general age range, including teenagers and young adults.
see also Adolescence; Boys; Dropouts; Girls

Allen, John. Growing up in China. 2017. (Growing up Around the World Ser.). (ENG.). 80p. (YA). (gr. 5-12). ***(978-1-68282-209-8(5))*** ReferencePoint Pr., Inc.
Anderson, Judith. Know the Facts about Personal Safety. 2009. (Illus.). 48p. (J). 70.50 *(978-1-4358-5465-9(9),* 1300674); (ENG., (J). lib. bdg. 29.25 *(978-1-4358-5340-9(7),* 1300674); (ENG., (YA). pap. 11.75 *(978-1-4358-5464-2(0),* 1300674) Rosen Publishing Group, Inc., The. (Rosen Reference).
Anniss, Matt. Music, Fashion, & Style. 2015. (Music Scene Ser.). (J). lib. bdg. 37.10 *(978-1-59920-912-8(8))* Black Rabbit Bks.
Aretha, David. On the Rocks: Teens & Alcohol. 2006. (ENG., Illus.). 144p. (YA). (gr. 9-13). 30.50 *(978-0-531-16792-2(5),* Watts, Franklin) Scholastic Library Publishing.
Ashabranner, Brent. Gavriel & Jemal: Two Boys of Jerusalem. Conklin, Paul, photos by. 2005. (Illus.). 94p. (J). (gr. 4-10). reprint ed. 12.00 *(978-0-7567-9758-4(6))* DIANE Publishing Co.
Baden-Powell, Robert. Scouting for Boys. 2013. pap. 16.99 *(978-1-4621-1233-3(1),* Horizon Pubs.) Cedar Fort, Inc./CFI Distribution.
Bailey, Diane. Cyber Ethics. (Cyber Citizenship & Cyber Safety Ser.). 48p. (gr. 5-5). 2009. 53.00 *(978-1-61512-102-1(1),* Rosen Reference) 2008. (Illus.). (YA). lib. bdg. 29.25 *(978-1-4042-1349-4(X),* 1276926) Rosen Publishing Group, Inc., The.
Bailey, Diane. Our Teenage Life in the Navajo Nation. 2017. (Illus.). 128p. (J). ***(978-1-4222-3908-7(X))*** Mason Crest.
Bailey, Lorilyn. The Original Dating Questionnaire for Teens: A Great Way to Get to Know Each Other. (Illus.). 128p. (Orig.). (YA). (gr. 7-12). pap. *(978-0-9641239-7-7(5))* Lormax Communications.
Bankston, John. Inhalants = Busted! 2006. (Busted! Ser.). (Illus.). 104p. (J). (gr. 6-12). lib. bdg. 33.27 *(978-0-7660-2472-4(5),* 1250497) Enslow Pubs., Inc.
Barrett, John E. Some Assembly Required: The Not-So-Secret Life of a Transgender Teen. 2014. (ENG., Illus.). 256p. (YA). (gr. 8). 17.99 *(978-1-4814-1675-7(8),* Simon & Schuster Bks. For Young Readers) Simon & Schuster Bks. For Young Readers.
Baruch-Feldman, Caren. The Grit Guide for Teens: A Workbook to Help You Build Perseverance, Self-Control, & a Growth Mindset. 2017. (ENG.). 152p. (YA). (gr. 6-12). pap. 16.95 *(978-1-62625-856-3(2))* New Harbinger Pubns.
Bauchner, Elizabeth. Teen Minorities in Rural North America: Growing up Different. 2009. (Youth in Rural North America Ser.). (Illus.). 96p. (YA). (gr. 3-7). lib. bdg. 22.95 *(978-1-4222-0014-8(0))* Mason Crest.
BeaverSimon. YOUNG AND AMAZING: TEENS AT THE TOP HIGH BEGINNING BOOK WITH ONLINE ACCESS. 2014. (ENG., Illus.). 24p. pap. 9.50 *(978-1-107-62252-4(2))* Cambridge Univ. Pr.
Bender, Alexandra Sabina. Alana's Advice... When There's a Clique, You've Got to Think Quick. 2007. (Illus.). 152p. (J). (gr. 4-10). per. 14.95 *(978-1-84590-075-5(8))* Crown Hse. Publishing.
Berman, Ron. Who's Got Next? Future Leaders of America. 2013. (Av2 Audio Chapter Bks.). (ENG., Illus.). 92p. (J). (gr. 4-7). lib. bdg. 27.13 *(978-1-62127-998-3(7),* AV2 by Weigl) Weigl Pubs., Inc.
Bernstein, Ben. Stressed Out! - For Teens: How to Be Calm, Confident, & Focused. 2014. (ENG., Illus.). 274p. (J). (gr. 8-12). pap. 18.95 *(978-1-939629-38-8(1),* 9781939629388) Familius LLC.
Bireda, Martha R. & Cummings, Jaha F. Omowali: The Child Returns Home - Reconnecting Our Children with Their True Culture. 2008. 232p. pap. *(978-4-902837-10-0(2))* Aoishima Kenkyusha.
Boersma, Heather. Dream Big: 30 Days to Life Beyond All You Could Ask or Imagine. 2012. ix, 119p. *(978-1-77069-453-8(6))* Word Alive Pr.
Bow, James. Binge Drinking. 2015. (ENG., Illus.). 48p. (J). *(978-0-7787-2200-7(7))* Crabtree Publishing Co.
Bradley, Michael J. Yes, Your Parents Are Crazy! A Teen Survival Handbook. Glasbergen, Randy, illus. 2004. (ENG.). 432p. pap. 14.95 *(978-0-936197-48-7(X))* Harbor Pr., Inc.
Brancato, Robin F. Food Choices: The Ultimate Teen Guide. 2010. (It Happened to Me Ser.: 28). (ENG.). 240p. (gr. 7-10). 50.00 *(978-0-8108-6109-1(7))* Scarecrow Pr., Inc.
Braner, Andy. Duplicate This! Showing Your Friends How to Live Like Jesus, 1 vol. 2008. (Invert Ser.). (ENG.). 272p. (YA). (gr. 13). pap. 12.99 *(978-0-310-27754-5(X))* Zondervan.
Braun, Eric. Taking Action to Improve People's Health. 2016. (Who's Changing the World? Ser.). (ENG., Illus.). 48p. (J). (gr. 4-6). 33.32 *(978-1-4677-9395-7(7));* 50.65 *(978-1-4677-9668-2(9),* Lerner Pubns.) Lerner Publishing Group.
Bryfonski, Dedria. Street Teens. 2011. (Opposing Viewpoints Ser.). (ENG., Illus.). 224p. (gr. 10-12). 48.80 *(978-0-7377-5761-3(2));* pap. 33.80 *(978-0-7377-5762-0(0),* Greenhaven Pr., Inc.) Cengage Gale.
Buckley, James. My Teenage Life in Greece. 2017. (Custom & Cultures of the World Ser.). (ENG.). (YA). (gr. 7-12). 23.95 ***(978-1-4222-3904-9(7))*** Mason Crest.
Cairney, Gemma. Open: a Toolkit for How Magic & Messed up Life Can Be. 2017. (ENG., Illus.). 320p. (YA). (gr. 9). 18.99 ***(978-1-5098-3611-6(X))*** Pan Macmillan GBR. Dist: Independent Pubs. Group.
Campbell, Carol P. & Orr, Tamra. Frequently Asked Questions about Teen Pregnancy. 2011. (FAQ: Teen Life Ser.). (J). lib. bdg. 31.95 *(978-1-4488-4627-6(7))* Rosen Publishing Group, Inc., The.
Campolo, Tony. You Can Make a Difference, 1 vol. 2008. (ENG.). 144p. (gr. 8-12). per. 10.98 *(978-0-8499-1885-8(5))* Nelson, Thomas Inc.
Canwell, Nancy. He's Got Your Back: A Daily Devotional for Juniors. 2014. (J). *(978-0-8280-2804-2(4))* Review & Herald Publishing Assn.
Carlson, Dale, et al. Out of Order: Young Adult Manual of Mental Illness & Recovery. 2014. (ENG., Illus.). 256p. (YA). pap. 14.95 *(978-1-884158-37-7(4))* Team Kreskin Productions, LLC.
Cartlidge, Cherese. Homeless Youth. 2016. (ENG., Illus.). 80p. (J). (gr. 5-12). *(978-1-60152-978-7(3))* ReferencePoint Pr., Inc.
Cartlidge, Cherese. Teens & Suicide. 2017. (Teen Mental Health Ser.). (ENG.). 80p. (J). (gr. 5-12). ***(978-1-68282-131-2(5))*** ReferencePoint Pr., Inc.
Cassriel, Betsy. My Teenage Life in Mexico. 2017. (Custom & Cultures of the World Ser.). (ENG.). (YA). (gr. 7-12). 23.95 ***(978-1-4222-3907-0(1))*** Mason Crest.
Centore, Michael. My Teenage Life in India. 2017. (Custom & Cultures of the World Ser.). (ENG.). (YA). (gr. 7-12). 23.95 ***(978-1-4222-3905-6(5))*** Mason Crest.
Centore, Michael & Lebeko, Tshwarelo. My Teenage Life in South Africa. 2017. (Illus.). 128p. (J). ***(978-1-4222-3911-7(X))*** Mason Crest.
Chopra, Deepak. Fire in the Heart: A Spiritual Guide for Teens. 2006. (ENG., Illus.). 208p. (YA). (gr. 7-12). pap. 14.99 *(978-0-689-86217-5(2),* Simon & Schuster Bks. For Young Readers) Simon & Schuster Bks. For Young Readers.
Cosmic Debris Etc., Inc. Staff, et al. Middle School. 2009. (Worst Case Scenario Ser.). (ENG., Illus.). 128p. (J). (gr. 6-8). pap. 10.99 *(978-0-8118-6864-8(8))* Chronicle Bks. LLC.
Crooks, Claire V. Engagement et Responsabilisation des Jeunes Autochtones: Trousse D'Outils DestinéE Aux Fournisseurs des Services. 2010. (FRE.). 168p. pap. 45.99 *(978-1-4269-1299-3(4))* Trafford Publishing.
Culp, Jennifer. I Have Been Sexually Abused. Now What?, 1 vol. 2015. (ENG.). 112p. (J). 35.60 *(978-1-4777-7976-7(0),* Rosen Young Adult) Rosen Publishing Group, Inc., The.
currie-mcghee, leanne. Teenage Alcoholism. 2011. (Compact Research Ser.). 96p. (YA). (gr. 7-12). lib. bdg. 27.95 *(978-1-60152-164-4(2))* ReferencePoint Pr., Inc.
Currie-McGhee, Leanne. Teenage Drug Abuse. 2011. (Compact Research Ser.). 96p. (YA). (gr. 7-12). lib. bdg. 27.95 *(978-1-60152-165-1(0))* ReferencePoint Pr., Inc.
De la Bédoyère, Camilla. Balancing Work & Play. 2010. (Healthy Lifestyles Ser.). 48p. (J). 35.65 *(978-1-60753-083-1(X))* Amicus Publishing.
—Personal Hygiene & Sexual Health. 2010. (Healthy Lifestyles Ser.). 48p. (J). 35.65 *(978-1-60753-087-9(2))* Amicus Publishing.
Dennis, Rainey. Passport 2 Purity. 2004. 29.99 *(978-1-57229-656-5(9))* FamilyLife.
Devon, Natasha, et al. The Self-Esteem Team's Guide to Sex, Drugs & WTFs?!! 2016. (ENG., Illus.). 288p. (YA). (gr. 7). pap. 15.95 *(978-1-78418-642-5(2))* Blake, John Publishing, Ltd. GBR. Dist: Independent Pubs. Group.

W X Y Z

Dobosz, Ann Marie. The Perfectionism Workbook for Teens: Activities to Help You Reduce Anxiety & Get Things Done. 2016. (ENG.). 200p. (YA). (gr. 6-12). pap. 16.95 *(978-1-62625-454-1(0))* New Harbinger Pubns.

Dru Tecco, Betsy. Food for Fuel: The Connection Between Food & Physical Activity. 2008. (Library of Nutrition Ser.). (Illus.). 48p. (YA). (gr. 8-12). lib. bdg. 29.25 *(978-1-4042-1871-0(8),* Rosen Reference) Rosen Publishing Group, Inc., The.

Dunagan, Cindy. Journaling Toward Moral Excellence Volume Three for Teenagers: A Character Building Workbook of 100 Thought-Provoking Questions to Help the Young Discover the Value of Moral Strength. 2004. (Journaling Toward Moral Excellence Ser.: Vol. 3). 107p. (YA). (gr. 8-10). 11.95 *(978-0-9759871-2-4(7))* Straight Paths Pr.

Eagen, Rachel. Suicide. 2010. (ENG.). 48p. (J). pap. *(978-0-7787-2138-3(8));* lib. bdg. *(978-0-7787-2131-4(0))* Crabtree Publishing Co.

Edelfield, Bruce & Moosa, Tracey J. Drug Abuse. 2011. (Teen Mental Health Ser.). (Illus.). 48p. (YA). (gr. 7-12). lib. bdg. 29.25 *(978-1-4488-4590-3(4))* Rosen Publishing Group, Inc., The.

Edge, Laura B. & Edge, Laura Bufano. From Jazz Babies to Generation Next: The History of the American Teenager. 2011. (People's History Ser.). (ENG.). 112p. (gr. 5-12). 33.26 *(978-0-7613-5868-8(4))* Lerner Publishing Group.

Emanuele, Patricia. Coping with Aggression. 2009. (Coping Ser.). 192p. (gr. 7-12). 63.90 *(978-1-61511-989-9(2))* Rosen Publishing Group, Inc., The.

Englandar, Anrenee. Dear Diary, I'm Pregnant: Ten Real Life Stories. 2nd rev. ed. 2010. (ENG., Illus.). 160p. (YA). (gr. 7-18). 21.95 *(978-1-55451-237-9(9),* 9781554512379); pap. 11.95 *(978-1-55451-236-2(0),* 9781554512362) Annick Pr., Ltd. CAN. Dist: Publishers Group West (PGW).

Esherick, Joan. Dying for Acceptance: A Teen's Guide to Drug- & Alcohol-Related Health Issues. 2006. (Science of Health Ser.). (Illus.). 128p. (YA). lib. bdg. 24.95 *(978-1-59084-847-0(0))* Mason Crest.

—The Laws That Protect Youth with Special Needs. Albers, Lisa et al, eds. 2014. (Living with a Special Need Ser.: 16). 128p. (J). (gr. 7-18). 25.95 *(978-1-4222-3039-8(2))* Mason Crest.

—Physical Challenges. Albers, Lisa et al, eds. 2014. (Living with a Special Need Ser.: 16). 128p. (J). (gr. 7-18). 25.95 *(978-1-4222-3041-1(4))* Mason Crest.

—Smoking-Related Health Issues. 2014. (Illus.). 128p. (J). *(978-1-4222-2803-6(7))* Mason Crest.

—Suicide & Self-Destructive Behaviors. McDonnell, Mary Ann & Forman, Sara, eds. 2013. (Young Adult's Guide to the Science of Health Ser.: 15). 128p. (J). (gr. 7-18). 24.95 *(978-1-4222-2817-3(7))* Mason Crest.

Espejo, Roman. Custody & Divorce. 2013. (Teen Rights & Freedoms Ser.). (ENG., Illus.). 176p. (gr. 10-12). lib. bdg. 42.00 *(978-0-7377-6400-0(7),* Greenhaven Pr., Inc.) Cengage Gale.

—How Does Advertising Impact Teen Behavior? 2011. (At Issue Ser.). (ENG.). 128p. (gr. 10-12). 39.40 *(978-0-7377-5578-7(4))* Cengage Gale.

—Sexting. 2015. (At Issue Ser.). (ENG.). 128p. (J). (gr. 10-12). pap. 27.80 *(978-0-7377-7186-2(0),* Greenhaven Pr., Inc.) Cengage Gale.

Espejo, Roman, ed. How Does Advertising Impact Teen Behavior. 2011. (At Issue Ser.). 128p. pap. 24.45 *(978-0-7377-5579-4(2),* Greenhaven Pr., Inc.) Cengage Gale.

Etler, Cyndy. We Can't Be Friends. 2017. (ENG.). 304p. (YA). (gr. 8-12). 17.99 ***(978-1-4926-3576-5(6))*** Sourcebooks, Inc.

Evans, Tony. Kingdom Quest - A Strategy Guide for Teens & Their Parents/Mentors: Taking Faith & Character to the Next Level, Ages 14+ 2015. (ENG., Illus.). 144p. pap. 10.99 *(978-1-58997-809-6(9))* Focus on the Family Publishing.

FAQ: Teen Life, 8 vols., Set. Incl. Frequently Asked Questions about Antidepressants. Peterson, Judy Monroe. lib. bdg. 31.95 *(978-1-4358-3547-4(6));* Frequently Asked Questions about Concussions. Bickerstaff, Linda. lib. bdg. 31.95 *(978-1-4358-3513-9(1));* Frequently Asked Questions about Driving & the Law. Roza, Greg. lib. bdg. 31.95 *(978-1-4358-3544-3(1));* Frequently Asked Questions about Foster Care. Sommers, Annie Leah. lib. bdg. 31.95 *(978-1-4358-3546-7(8));* Frequently Asked Questions about Online Gaming Addiction. Cefrey, Holly. lib. bdg. 31.95 *(978-1-4358-3548-1(4));* Frequently Asked Questions about Overscheduling & Stress. Harmon, Daniel E. lib. bdg. 31.95 *(978-1-4358-3514-6(X));* Frequently Asked Questions about Sleep & Sleep Deprivation. Peterson, Judy Monroe. lib. bdg. 31.95 *(978-1-4358-3512-2(3));* Frequently Asked Questions about Tanning & Skin Care. Brezina, Corona. lib. bdg. 31.95 *(978-1-4358-3545-0(X));* (YA). (gr. 7-12). 2010. (Illus.). 64p. 2010. Set lib. bdg. 234.00 *(978-1-4358-3608-2(1))* Rosen Publishing Group, Inc., The.

Fields, Doug. Creative Times with God: Discovering New Ways to Connect with the SAVIOR. 2009. (ENG.). 121p. pap. 9.99 *(978-0-7644-6298-6(9))* Group Publishing, Inc.

Fighting the Monster. 2004. (YA). ring bd. 59.95 *(978-0-9661256-2-7(2))* Youth Communication - New York Center.

Financial Security & Life Success for Teens. 2014. (Financial Security & Life Success for Teens Ser.). 80p. (YA). (gr. 7-12). pap. 84.90 *(978-1-4777-8110-4(2))* Rosen Publishing Group, Inc., The.

Frohnapfel-Krueger, Lisa. Teen Pregnancy & Parenting. Gale Editors, ed. 2010. (Current Controversies Ser.). (ENG.). 176-240p. pap. 28.45 *(978-0-7377-4924-3(5));* 176240p. (gr. 10-12). 44.10 *(978-0-7377-4923-6(7))* Cengage Gale. (Greenhaven Pr., Inc.).

Gaskins, Pearl Fuyo. I Believe In... Christian, Jewish, & Muslim Young People Speak about Their Faiths. 2004. (ENG., Illus.). 160p. (J). 18.95 *(978-0-8126-2713-8(X))* Cricket Bks.

Gay, Kathlyn. Activism: The Ultimate Teen Guide. 2016. (It Happened to Me Ser.: 47). (ENG., Illus.). 234p. (J). 45.00 *(978-1-4422-4293-7(0))* Rowman & Littlefield Publishers, Inc.

—Are You Fat? The Obesity Issue for Teens. 2014. (Got Issues? Ser.). (Illus.). 112p. (J). (gr. 6-12). lib. bdg. 33.27 *(978-0-7660-4322-0(3))* Enslow Pubs., Inc.

Gilbert, Laura. Everything You Need to Know about Compulsive Sexual Behavior. 2009. (Need to Know Library). 64p. (gr. 5-5). 58.50 *(978-1-60854-059-4(6))* Rosen Publishing Group, Inc., The.

Gillard, Arthur. Drug Abuse. 2013. (Issues That Concern You Ser.). (ENG., Illus.). 144p. (gr. 7-10). lib. bdg. 42.00 *(978-0-7377-6290-7(X),* Greenhaven Pr., Inc.) Cengage Gale.

Gitlin, Marty. Helping a Friend in an Abusive Relationship. 2016. (How Can I Help? Friends Helping Friends Ser.). 00064p. (J). (gr. 6-6). pap. 12.95 *(978-1-4994-6436-8(3))* Rosen Publishing Group, Inc., The.

Gordon, Sherri Mabry. Beyond Bruises: The Truth about Teens & Abuse. 2009. (Issues in Focus Today Ser.). (Illus.). 128p. (J). (gr. 6-12). lib. bdg. 33.27 *(978-0-7660-3064-0(4))* Enslow Pubs., Inc.

Grayson, Robert. Managing Your Digital Footprint. 2011. (Digital & Information Literacy Ser.). (Illus.). 48p. (YA). pap. 11.75 *(978-1-4488-2290-4(4));* lib. bdg. 29.25 *(978-1-4488-1319-3(0))* Rosen Publishing Group, Inc., The. (Rosen Reference).

Guillain, Charlotte. 101 Ways to Be a Great Role Model, 1 vol. 2011. (101 Ser.). (ENG., Illus.). 56p. (gr. 5-9). 34.65 *(978-1-4109-3900-5(6),* NA-r) Heinemann-Raintree.

Gutowski, Eva. My Life As Eva: Advice from Me to You. 2017. (Illus.). 199p. (J). pap. ***(978-1-5011-4672-5(6),*** Gallery Bks.) Gallery Bks.

Hagler, Gina. Money-Making Opportunities for Teens Who Are Artistic. 2013. (Make Money Now! Ser.). (Illus.). 80p. (YA). (gr. 7-12). lib. bdg. 33.25 *(978-1-4488-9387-4(9))* Rosen Publishing Group, Inc., The.

Hall, LaMarcus J. I Refuse to Let You Give Up: To My Teens Who Feel All Hope Is Gone... 2009. 52p. pap. 15.95 *(978-1-4327-3417-6(2))* Outskirts Pr., Inc.

Hamilton, Jill. Activism. 2009. (Issues That Concern You Ser.). (ENG., Illus.). 144p. (gr. 10-12). 42.00 *(978-0-7377-4493-4(6))* Cengage Gale.

Hansen, Mark & Ferber, Kevin S. Success 101 for Teens: Dollars & Sense for a Winning Financial Life. 2012. (ENG.). 176p. pap. 12.95 *(978-1-55778-901-3(0),* 4580c8ac-14b2-4d64-ae8a-be308d9302c6) Paragon Hse. Pubs.

Hare, Eric B. Skyscrapers: 365 Stories That Build You up: Daily Devotions for Juniors. 2009. (J). *(978-0-8280-2466-2(9))* Review & Herald Publishing Assn.

Harmon, Daniel E. First Job Smarts. 2009. (J). 77.70 *(978-1-4358-5543-4(4));* pap. 12.95 *(978-1-4358-5542-7(6));* (Illus.). 64p. (gr. 7-12). lib. bdg. 31.95 *(978-1-4358-5268-6(0))* Rosen Publishing Group, Inc., The.

Haugen, David M., ed. The Millennial Generation. 2012. (Opposing Viewpoints Ser.). (ENG., Illus.). 240p. (J). (gr. 10-12). pap. 29.45 *(978-0-7377-6327-0(2));* lib. bdg. 42.95 *(978-0-7377-6326-3(4))* Cengage Gale. (Greenhaven Pr., Inc.).

—Sex. 2013. (Teen Rights & Freedoms Ser.). (ENG., Illus.). 176p. (gr. 10-12). lib. bdg. 37.45 *(978-0-7377-6404-8(X),* Greenhaven Pr., Inc.) Cengage Gale.

Hawke, Rosanne. The Truth about Peacock Blue: A Powerful Story about One Girl's Fight for Justice in Pakistan. 2016. (ENG.). 272p. (YA). (gr. 8-11). pap. 11.99 *(978-1-74331-994-9(0))* Allen & Unwin AUS. Dist: Independent Pubs. Group.

Heiman, Diane & Suneby, Liz. See What You Can Be: Explore Careers That Could Be for You! Wood, Tracey, illus. 2009. (ENG.). 108p. (gr. 4-7). spiral bd. 9.95 *(978-1-59369-277-3(3))* American Girl Publishing, Inc.

Heing, Bridget. Critical Perspectives on Millennials. 2017. (Analyzing the Issues Ser.). 208p. (J). (gr. 8-8). lib. bdg. 47.93 ***(978-0-7660-8485-8(X))*** Enslow Pubs., Inc.

Henneberg, Susan. Money-Making Opportunities for Teens Who Like Working with Kids. 2013. (Make Money Now! Ser.). (Illus.). 80p. (YA). (gr. 7-12). lib. bdg. 33.25 *(978-1-4488-9385-0(2))* Rosen Publishing Group, Inc., The.

Hill, Katie Rain. Rethinking Normal: A Memoir in Transition. 2014. (ENG., Illus.). 272p. (YA). (gr. 8). 17.99 *(978-1-4814-1823-2(8),* Simon & Schuster Bks. For Young Readers) Simon & Schuster Bks. For Young Readers.

Hilton, John & Sweat, Anthony. How? Essential Skills for Living the Gospel. 2010. (Illus.). xii, 251p. (YA). 34.99 *(978-1-60641-789-8(4))* Deseret Bk. Co.

Hinds, Maurene J. Do You Know Your Rights? 2016. (Got Issues? Ser.). (ENG., Illus.). 112p. (J). (gr. 7-8). 37.27 *(978-0-7660-7193-3(6))* Enslow Pubs., Inc.

Hood, Korey K. Type 1 Teens: A Guide to Managing Your Diabetes. Ishe, Bryan, illus. 2010. 112p. (YA). (gr. 7-18). pap. 14.95 *(978-1-4338-0788-6(2),* Magination Pr.) American Psychological Assn.

Huddle, Lorena & Schleifer, Jay. Teen Suicide. 2011. (Illus.). 48p. (J). 167.70 *(978-1-4488-4873-7(3));* (YA). (gr. 7-12). lib. bdg. 29.25 *(978-1-4488-4586-6(6))* Rosen Publishing Group, Inc., The.

Hugel, Bob. I Did It Without Thinking: True Stories about Impulsive Decisions That Changed Lives. 2008. (Scholastic Choices Ser.). (ENG.). 112p. (J). pap. 8.95 *(978-0-531-20526-6(6),* Watts, Franklin) Scholastic Library Publishing.

Hunter, David. Teen Life among the Amish & Other Alternative Communities: Choosing a Lifestyle. 2009. (Youth in Rural North America Ser.). 96p. (J). (gr. 7-18). lib. bdg. 22.95 *(978-1-4222-0017-9(5))* Mason Crest.

Hunter, Miranda & Hunter, William. Sexually Transmitted Infections. McDonnell, Mary Ann & Forman, Sara, eds. 2013. (Young Adult's Guide to the Science of Health Ser.: 15). 128p. (J). (gr. 7-18). 24.95 *(978-1-4222-2814-2(2))* Mason Crest.

—Sexually Transmitted Infections. Forman, Sara & McDonnell, Mary Ann, eds. 2013. (Young Adult's Guide to the Science of Health Ser.). (Illus.). 128p. (J). (gr. 7-18). pap. 14.95 *(978-1-4222-3007-7(4))* Mason Crest.

Hurt, Avery Elizabeth. I Am a Teen Caregiver. Now What? 2016. (Teen Life 411 Ser.). 00112p. (J). (gr. 7-7). 37.10 *(978-1-5081-7204-8(8),* Rosen Young Adult) Rosen Publishing Group, Inc., The.

Jackson, J. S. Bye-Bye, Bully: A Kid's Guide for Dealing with Bullies. Alley, R. W., tr. Alley, R. W., illus. 2003. (J). per. 6.95 *(978-0-87029-369-6(9))* Abbey Pr.

Jacobs, Thomas A. What Are My Rights? Q&A about Teens & the Law. 3rd rev. ed. 2011. (ENG.). 224p. (YA). (gr. 6). pap. 15.99 *(978-1-57542-380-7(4))* Free Spirit Publishing, Inc.

Jacques, Michele Siuda. Teen Driving. 2012. (At Issue Ser.). (ENG.). 128p. (gr. 10-12). pap. 27.80 *(978-0-7377-6419-2(8),* Greenhaven Pr., Inc.) Cengage Gale.

Jaime, Everett. Baby Don't Smoke. Brown, Eliot R., illus. 2012. (ENG.). 40p. (J). pap. 9.95 *(978-1-935826-20-0(4))* Kalindi Pr.

Jamiolkowski, Raymond M. A Baby Doesn't Make the Man: Alternative Sources of Power & Manhood for Young Men. 2009. (Teen Pregnancy Prevention Library). 64p. (gr. 5-5). 58.50 *(978-1-60854-244-4(0))* Rosen Publishing Group, Inc., The.

Johanson, Paula. Money-Making Opportunities for Teens Who Like Pets & Animals. 2013. 80p. (YA). (gr. 7-12). 33.25 *(978-1-4488-9384-3(4))* Rosen Publishing Group, Inc., The.

Johnson, Greg. If I Could Ask God Just One Question: 80 Answers to Teens' Most-Asked Questions. 2016. (ENG.). 192p. pap. 7.99 *(978-1-63058-351-4(0),* Barbour Bks.) Barbour Publishing, Inc.

Johnson, Jason. How We See Things. 2012. 20p. pap. 17.99 *(978-1-4685-5832-6(3))* AuthorHouse.

Johnson, Nerissa & Parra, Angelo. Teen Reflections, Then & Now. 2011. (Readers' & Writers' Genre Workshop Ser.). (YA). pap. *(978-1-4509-3025-3(5))* Benchmark Education Co.

Jovinelly, Joann. Coping with Bipolar Disorder & Manic-Depressive Illness. 2009. (Coping Ser.). 192p. (gr. 7-12). 63.90 *(978-1-61511-992-9(2))* Rosen Publishing Group, Inc., The.

Kahaner, Ellen. Everything You Need to Know about Growing up Female. 2009. (Need to Know Library). 64p. (gr. 5-5). 58.50 *(978-1-60854-070-9(7))* Rosen Publishing Group, Inc., The.

Kaplan, Arie. Dating & Relationships: Navigating the Social Scene. 2011. (Young Man's Guide to Contemporary Issues Ser.). (ENG.). 104p. (YA). (gr. 9-12). lib. bdg. 34.60 *(978-1-4488-5523-0(3))* Rosen Publishing Group, Inc., The.

Katz, Naomi. Beautiful-Being an Empowered Young Woman. 2016. (ENG., Illus.). 154p. (J). pap. 16.95 *(978-1-59687-441-1(4),* ipicturebooks) ibooks, Inc.

Keen, Lisa. Out Law: What LGBT Youth Should Know about Their Legal Rights. 2007. (Queer Ideas/Queer Action Ser.: 2). (ENG.). 176p. (gr. 3-7). per. 13.00 *(978-0-8070-7966-9(9),* Beacon Pr.) Beacon Pr.

Kempster, Rachel & Leder, Meg. The Book of Me. 2016. (ENG.). 208p. (J). (gr. 6-12). pap. 14.99 *(978-1-4926-4194-0(4),* 9781492641940) Sourcebooks, Inc.

Keyishan, Elizabeth. Todo lo que necesitas saber sobre el cigarillo (Everything You Need to Know about Smoking) 2009. (Todo lo que necesitas (the Need to Know Library) Ser.). (SPA.). 64p. (gr. 6-6). 58.50 *(978-1-60854-407-3(9),* Editorial Buenas Letras) Rosen Publishing Group, Inc., The.

Keyishian, Elizabeth. Everything You Need to Know about Smoking. 2009. (Need to Know Library). 64p. (gr. 5-5). 58.50 *(978-1-60854-086-0(3))* Rosen Publishing Group, Inc., The.

—Smoking. rev. ed. 2005. (Need to Know Library). (Illus.). 64p. (J). (gr. 7-12). lib. bdg. 31.95 *(978-0-8239-4092-9(6))* Rosen Publishing Group, Inc., The.

Kiesbye, Stefan. Can Busy Teens Succeed Academically? 2009. (At Issue Ser.). (ENG.). 128p. (J). (gr. 10-12). 34.45 *(978-0-7377-4286-2(0),* Greenhaven Pr., Inc.) Cengage Gale.

Kimlan, Lanie & Alvergue, Anne. The Truth about Ecstasy. 2011. (Drugs & Consequences Ser.). (YA). (gr. 7-12). lib. bdg. 31.95 *(978-1-4488-4643-6(9))* Rosen Publishing Group, Inc., The.

Lambillion, Paul. Staying Cool. 2004. (Illus.). 196p. pap. 13.95 *(978-0-7171-3598-1(5))* M.H. Gill & Co. U. C. IRL. Dist: Hushion Hse. Publishing, Ltd.

Landau, Jennifer. Bipolar Disorder. 2013. (Teen Mental Health Ser.). (Illus.). 48p. (J). (gr. 7-12). 29.95 *(978-1-4777-1747-9(1))* Rosen Publishing Group, Inc., The.

—Helping a Friend with an Alcohol Problem. 2016. (How Can I Help? Friends Helping Friends Ser.). 00064p. (J). (gr. 6-6). pap. 12.95 *(978-1-4994-6448-1(7))* Rosen Publishing Group, Inc., The.

Landau, Jennifer. Teens Talk about Self-Esteem & Self-Confidence. 2017. ***(978-1-5081-7637-4(X))*** Rosen Publishing Group, Inc., The.

Latchana Kenney, Karen. The Hidden Story of Drugs, 1 vol., 1. 2014. (Undercover Story Ser.). (ENG.). 48p. (J). (gr. 5-8). 30.25 *(978-1-4777-2803-1(1),* Rosen Reference) Rosen Publishing Group, Inc., The.

Lee, Helen. Where in the World? Stories from Everywhere: Daily Devotions for Juniors. 2006. 373p. (J). *(978-0-8280-1874-6(X))* Review & Herald Publishing Assn.

Libal, Autumn. Fats, Sugars, & Empty Calories: The Fast Food Habit. 2007. (Obesity Ser.). (Illus.). 104p. (YA). (gr. 4-7). lib. bdg. 23.95 *(978-1-59084-943-9(4))* Mason Crest.

—Health Implications of Cosmetic Surgery, Makeovers, & Body Alterations. McDonnell, Mary Ann & Forman, Sara, eds. 2013. (Young Adult's Guide to the Science of Health Ser.: 15). 128p. (J). (gr. 7-18). 24.95 *(978-1-4222-2811-1(8))* Mason Crest.

—Runaway Train: Youth with Emotional Disturbance. 2003. (Youth with Special Needs Ser.). (Illus.). 127p. (YA). (gr. 7). pap. 14.95 *(978-1-4222-0429-0(4))* Mason Crest.

Lily, Henrietta M. & Harmon, Daniel E. Frequently Asked Questions about Alcohol Abuse & Binge Drinking. 2011. (FAQ: Teen Life Ser.). (J). lib. bdg. 31.95 *(978-1-4488-4629-0(3))* Rosen Publishing Group, Inc., The.

Lindsey, Brooklyn. Confessions of a Not-So-Supermodel: Faith, Friends, & Festival Queens, 1 vol. 2008. (Invert Ser.). (ENG., Illus.). 176p. (YA). (gr. 7-14). pap. 9.99 *(978-0-310-27753-8(1))* Zondervan.

Lindsey Reeves, Diane. Career Ideas for Teens in Education & Training. 2nd rev. ed. 2011. (Career Ideas for Teens Ser.). (Illus.). 182p. (gr. 6-12). 45.00 *(978-0-8160-8274-2(X))* Facts On File, Inc.

Lishak, Antony. Drugs. 2007. (What's That Got to Do with Me?/Watts Ser.). (Illus.). 32p. (YA). (gr. 4-7). lib. bdg. 28.50 *(978-1-59920-035-4(X))* Black Rabbit Bks.

Lublin, Nancy, et al. Do Something! A Handbook for Young Activists. 2010. (ENG., Illus.). 280p. (J). (gr. 4-7). pap. 13.95 *(978-0-7611-5747-2(6),* 15747) Workman Publishing Co., Inc.

Lucado, Max. Every Day Deserves a Chance: Wake up & Live!, 1 vol. 2007. (ENG., Illus.). 164p. (gr. 7-12). pap. 12.99 *(978-1-4003-1077-7(6))* Nelson, Thomas Inc.

Mack, Cassandra. Cool, Confident & Strong: 52 Power Moves for Girls. 2007. 100p. per. 11.95 *(978-0-595-47560-5(4),* Authors Choice Pr.) iUniverse, Inc.

Madsen, Susan Arrington. I Walked to Zion: True Stories of Young Pioneers on the Mormon Trail. 2008. 192p. pap. 9.95 *(978-1-59038-930-0(1))* Deseret Bk. Co.

Marcovitz, Hal. Teens & Career Choices. Developed in Association with the Gallup Organization Staff, ed. 2013. (Gallup Youth Survey: Major Issues & Trends Ser.: 14). 112p. (J). (gr. 7-18). 24.95 *(978-1-4222-2950-7(5))* Mason Crest.

—Teens & Family Issues. Developed in Association with the Gallup Organization Staff, ed. 2013. (Gallup Youth Survey: Major Issues & Trends Ser.: 14). 112p. (J). (gr. 7-18). 24.95 *(978-1-4222-2952-1(1))* Mason Crest.

—Teens & Race. Developed in Association with the Gallup Organization Staff, ed. 2013. (Gallup Youth Survey: Major Issues & Trends Ser.: 14). 112p. (J). (gr. 7-18). 24.95 *(978-1-4222-2955-2(6))* Mason Crest.

—Teens & Sex. Developed in Association with the Gallup Organization Staff, ed. 2013. (Gallup Youth Survey: Major Issues & Trends Ser.: 14). 112p. (J). (gr. 7-18). 24.95 *(978-1-4222-2957-6(2))* Mason Crest.

—Teens & Suicide. Developed in Association with the Gallup Organization Staff, ed. 2013. (Gallup Youth Survey: Major Issues & Trends Ser.: 14). 112p. (J). (gr. 7-18). 24.95 *(978-1-4222-2958-3(0))* Mason Crest.

—Teens & the Supernatural & Paranormal. Developed in Association with the Gallup Organization Staff, ed. 2013. (Gallup Youth Survey: Major Issues & Trends Ser.: 14). (Illus.). 112p. (J). (gr. 7-18). 24.95 *(978-1-4222-2959-0(9))* Mason Crest.

—Teens & the Supernatural & Paranormal. 2008. (Gallup Youth Survey, Major Issues & Trends Ser.). (Illus.). 112,128p. (J). (gr. 7-9). lib. bdg. 22.95 *(978-1-59084-876-0(4))* Mason Crest.

—Teens, Religion & Values. Developed in Association with the Gallup Organization Staff, ed. 2013. (Gallup Youth Survey: Major Issues & Trends Ser.: 14). 112p. (J). (gr. 7-18). 24.95 *(978-1-4222-2962-0(9))* Mason Crest.

Marsico, Katie. Alcohol Abuse. 2013. 80p. (YA). (gr. 7-12). 34.21 *(978-1-60870-848-2(9));* pap. 17.64 *(978-1-62712-125-5(0))* Cavendish Square Publishing.

—Drug Abuse. 2013. 80p. (YA). (gr. 7-12). 34.21 *(978-1-60870-852-9(7))* Cavendish Square Publishing.

Mason, Paul. Know the Facts about Drinking & Smoking. 2009. (J). 70.50 *(978-1-4358-5463-5(2),* Rosen Reference); (ENG.). 48p. (YA). pap. 11.75 *(978-1-4358-5462-8(4),* Rosen Reference); (ENG., Illus.). 48p. (YA). (gr. 5-9). lib. bdg. 29.25 *(978-1-4358-5339-3(3))* Rosen Publishing Group, Inc., The.

Mastromarino, Diane. Being a Teen: Words of Advice from Someone Who's Been There. (Illus.). 80p. pap. 8.95 *(978-0-88396-626-6(3),* Blue Mountain Pr.) Blue Mountain Arts Inc.

Matlock, Mark. Wisdom On... Making Good Decisions, 1 vol. 2008. (Invert Ser.). (ENG.). 144p. (YA). (gr. 7-14). pap. 9.99 *(978-0-310-27926-6(7))* Zondervan.

McClellan, Marilyn. The Big Deal about Alcohol: What Teens Need to Know about Drinking. 2004. (Issues in Focus Ser.). (Illus.). 128p. (J). lib. bdg. 27.94 *(978-0-7660-2163-1(7))* Enslow Pubs., Inc.

McDowell, Pamela. Teen Pregnancy. 2010. (ENG.). 48p. (J). pap. *(978-0-7787-2139-0(6));* lib. bdg. *(978-0-7787-2132-1(9))* Crabtree Publishing Co.

McGuire, Kara. All about the Green: The Teens' Guide to Finding Work & Making Money, 1 vol. 2014. (Financial Literacy for Teens Ser.). (ENG.). 64p. (gr. 6-7). lib. bdg. 33.99 *(978-0-7565-4372-3(X),* CPB Grades 4-8) Compass Point Bks.

—Cover Your Assets: The Teens' Guide to Protecting Their Money, Their Stuff, & Themselves, 1 vol. 2014. (Financial Literacy for Teens Ser.). (ENG.). 64p. (gr. 6-7). lib. bdg. 33.99 *(978-0-7565-4921-3(3))* Compass Point Bks.

—Making Money Work: A Teen's Guide to Saving, Investing, & Building Wealth, 1 vol. 2014. (Financial Literacy for Teens Ser.). (ENG.). 64p. (gr. 6-7). lib. bdg. 33.99 *(978-0-7565-4922-0(1),* CPB Grades 4-8) Compass Point Bks.

—Smart Spending: The Teens' Guide to Cash, Credit, & Life's Costs, 1 vol. 2014. (Financial Literacy for Teens Ser.). (ENG.). 64p. (gr. 6-7). lib. bdg. 33.99 *(978-0-7565-4923-7(X),* CPB Grades 4-8) Compass Point Bks.

—The Teen Money Manual: A Guide to Cash, Credit, Spending, Saving, Work, Wealth, & More, 1 vol. 2014. (ENG., Illus.). 208p. (gr. 6-7). pap. 9.95 *(978-1-62370-135-2(X))* Capstone Young Readers of Coughlan Cos.

McIntosh, Kenneth & Livingston, Phyllis. Youth with Alcohol & Drug Addiction: Escape from Bondage. 2009. (Helping Youth with Mental, Physical, & Social Challenges Ser.). (Illus.). 128p. (YA). (gr. 7-18). lib. bdg. 24.95 *(978-1-4222-0143-5(0))* Mason Crest.

McIntosh, Kenneth & Walker, Ida. Youth with Cultural/Language Differences: Interpreting an Alien World. 2009. (Helping Youth with Mental, Physical, & Social Challenges Ser.). (Illus.). 128p. (YA). (gr. 7-18). lib. bdg. 24.95 *(978-1-4222-0141-1(4))* Mason Crest.

McKay, Jenny. Children of the Holocaust. 2015. (ENG., Illus.). 80p. (J). (gr. 5-12). lib. bdg. *(978-1-60152-838-4(8))* ReferencePoint Pr., Inc.

Medina, Sarah. Know the Facts about Drugs. 2009. 48p. (J). 70.50 *(978-1-4358-5459-8(4));* (ENG.). (YA). pap. 11.75 *(978-1-4358-5458-1(6))* Rosen Publishing Group, Inc., The. (Rosen Reference).

Mercadante, Frank. Positively Dangerous: Live Loud, Be Real, Change the World. 2003. 117p. (YA). pap. 11.50 *(978-0-88489-790-3(7))* St. Mary's Pr. of MN.

Merino, Noel. Emancipation. Greenhaven Press Staff, ed. 2014. (Teen Rights & Freedoms Ser.). (ENG., Illus.). 176p. (gr. 10-12). lib. bdg. 42.00 *(978-0-7377-6999-9(8),* Greenhaven Pr., Inc.) Cengage Gale.

Meyers Jugendlexikon. (GER., Illus.). 672p. *(978-3-411-07804-2(9))* Bibliographisches Institut & F. A. Brockhaus AG DEU. Dist: i. b. d., Ltd.

Miles, Lisa & Chown, Xanna Eve. How to Survive Being Dumped. 2013. (Girl Talk Ser.). (Illus.). 48p. (J). (ENG.). (gr. 5-8). pap. 11.75 (978-1-4777-0716-6(6), Rosen Classroom); (gr. 5-8). pap. 70.50 (978-1-4777-0717-3(4), Rosen Reference); (ENG., (gr. 8-12). lib. bdg. 29.25 (978-1-4777-0704-3(2), Rosen Reference) Rosen Publishing Group, Inc., The.

Mintzer, Rich. Steroids = Busted! 2006. (Busted! Ser.). (Illus.). 112p. (J). (gr. 6). lib. bdg. 33.27 (978-0-7660-2471-7(7)) Enslow Pubs., Inc.

Monckeberg, Paulina. Artilugia 2007 English. 2006. (Pascualina Family of Products Ser.). 274p. (J). spiral bd. 14.99 (978-956-8222-49-9(9)) Pascualina Producciones S.A.

Moore, Andrew. Meditation. 2008. (Teen Mental Health Ser.). (Illus.). 48p. (YA). (gr. 7-12). lib. bdg. 29.25 (978-1-4042-1799-7(1)) Rosen Publishing Group, Inc., The.

Morgan, Nicola. Blame My Brain. 2007. (Illus.). 192p. (YA). pap. (978-1-4063-1116-7(2)) Walker Bks., Ltd.

Nagle, Jeanne. Great Lifelong Learning Skills. 2009. (Work Readiness Ser.). 64p. (gr. 6-6). 58.50 (978-1-60854-825-5(2)) Rosen Publishing Group, Inc., The.

Nagle, Jeanne M. Great Lifelong Learning Skills. 2008. (Work Readiness Ser.). (Illus.). 64p. (YA). (gr. 8-12). lib. bdg. 31.95 (978-1-4042-1424-8(0), 1277025) Rosen Publishing Group, Inc., The.

Nelson, David. Teen Drug Abuse. 2010. (Opposing Viewpoints Ser.). (ENG.). 240p. pap. 29.45 (978-0-7377-4993-9(8)); 224p. (gr. 10-12). 48.80 (978-0-7377-4992-2(X)) Cengage Gale. (Greenhaven Pr., Inc.).

Netzley, Patricia D. Teens & Sexting. 2015. (Illus.). 80p. (J). 28.95 (978-1-60152-916-9(3)) ReferencePoint Pr., Inc.

Noble, Alan R. Foundations of the Christian Faith. 2008. 160p. pap. 13.99 (978-1-60477-694-2(3)) Salem Author Services.

Oaks, Robert C. Believe! Helping Youth Learn to Trust in the Lord. 2003. (Illus.). xiii, 126p. (J). pap. 14.95 (978-1-59038-203-5(X)) Deseret Bk. Co.

Obesity: Modern-Day Epidemic, 10 vols., Set. Incl. Diet & Your Emotions: The Comfort Food Falsehood. Esherick, Joan. (J). 2004. lib. bdg. 23.95 (978-1-59084-950-7(7)); Fats, Sugars, & Empty Calories: The Fast Food Habit. Libal, Autumn. (YA). 2007. lib. bdg. 23.95 (978-1-59084-943-9(4)); Medications & Surgeries for Weight Loss: When Dieting Isn't Enough. Hunter, William. (YA). 2007. lib. bdg. 23.95 (978-1-59084-947-7(7)); (gr. 4-7). (Illus.). 104p. 2005. Set lib. bdg. 239.50 (978-1-59084-941-5(8)) Mason Crest.

Omnigraphics, Inc. Staff, contrib. by. Abuse & Violence Information for Teens: Health Tips about the Causes & Consequences of Abusive & Violent Behavior Including Facts about the Types of Abuse & Violence, the Warning Signs of Abusive & Violent Behavior, Health Concerns of Victims, & Getting Help & Staying Safe. 2nd ed. 2017. (Teen Health Ser.). 440p. (J). 69.00 **(978-0-7808-1456-1(8))** Omnigraphics, Inc.

Orr, Tamra. Coping with Racial Inequality. 2017. (Coping Ser.). 112p. (gr. 12-12). 37.10 **(978-1-5081-7396-0(6)**, Rosen Young Adult) Rosen Publishing Group, Inc., The.

Orr, Tamra. Home & Family Relationships. 2010. (Teens: Being Gay, Lesbian, Bisexual, or Transgender Ser.). (Illus.). 80p. (YA). (gr. 7-12). lib. bdg. 33.25 (978-1-4358-3579-5(4)) Rosen Publishing Group, Inc., The.

Orr, Tamra B. Money-Making Opportunities for Teens Who Like Working Outside. 2013. (Make Money Now! Ser.). (Illus.). 80p. (YA). (gr. 7-12). lib. bdg. 33.25 (978-1-4488-9383-6(6)) Rosen Publishing Group, Inc., The.

Owens, Peter. Teens, Health & Obesity. Developed in Association with the Gallup Organization Staff, ed. 2013. (Gallup Youth Survey: Major Issues & Trends Ser.: 14). 112p. (J). (gr. 7-18). 24.95 (978-1-4222-2961-3(0)) Mason Crest.

Pagels, Douglas. What Every Teen Needs to Know. 2010. (ENG.). 60p. 13.95 (978-1-59842-494-2(7)) Blue Mountain Arts Inc.

Paonessa, Mary. Growth & Development: Understanding Yourself, 8 vols. 3rd ed. 2003. (Human Growth & Development Ser.). (Illus.). 82p. (J). (gr. 8-18). pap. 11.00 (978-0-9711721-6-6(1), 394) Paon Pubns.

Pardes, Bronwen. Doing It Right: Making Smart, Safe, & Satisfying Choices about Sex. 2013. (ENG., Illus.). (YA). (gr. 9). 160p. 18.99 (978-1-4424-8370-5(9)); 146p. pap. 12.99 (978-1-4424-8371-2(7)) Simon Pulse. (Simon Pulse).

Parks, Peggy J. The Dangers of E-Cigarettes. 2016. (ENG.). 80p. (J). (gr. 5-12). (978-1-68282-014-8(9)) ReferencePoint Pr., Inc.

parks, peggy j. Teenage Sex & Pregnancy. 2011. (Compact Research Ser.). 96p. (YA). (gr. 7-12). lib. bdg. 27.95 (978-1-60152-168-2(5)) ReferencePoint Pr., Inc.

Parks, Peggy J. Teenage Suicide. 2011. (Compact Research Ser.). 96p. (YA). (gr. 7-12). lib. bdg. 27.95 (978-1-60152-156-9(1)) ReferencePoint Pr., Inc.

—Teens & Stress. 2015. (ENG., Illus.). 96p. (J). lib. bdg. (978-1-60152-768-4(3)) ReferencePoint Pr., Inc.

—Teens & Substance Abuse. 2015. (ENG., Illus.). 80p. (J). lib. bdg. (978-1-60152-832-2(9)) ReferencePoint Pr., Inc.

Payment, Simone. Friendship, Dating, & Relationships. 2010. (Teens: Being Gay, Lesbian, Bisexual, or Transgender Ser.). (Illus.). 80p. (YA). (gr. 7-12). lib. bdg. 33.25 (978-1-4358-3578-8(6)) Rosen Publishing Group, Inc., The.

Peal, Robert. Norman England. 2016. (Knowing History Ser.). (ENG.). 16p. (J). (gr. 6-9). 3.99 **(978-0-00-819527-4(7))** HarperCollins Pubs. Ltd. GBR. Dist: Independent Pubs. Group.

Penne, Barbra & Renehan, Patrick. Your Rights As an LGBTQ+ Teen. 2017. (LGBTQ+ Guide to Beating Bullying Ser.). 64p. (J). (gr. 12-11). 34.45 **(978-1-5081-7439-4(3)**, Rosen Young Adult) Rosen Publishing Group, Inc., The.

Peter, Val J. & Dowd, Tom. Boundaries: A Guide for Teens. 2004. 113p. (gr. 8-12). pap. 8.95 (978-1-889322-37-7(7), 25-014) Boys Town Pr.

Petrikowski, Nicki Peter. Teen Life 411: Set 3. 2015. (Teen Life 411 Ser.). (ENG.). 112p. (J). (gr. 6-7). 213.60 (978-1-4994-6190-9(9), Rosen Young Adult) Rosen Publishing Group, Inc., The.

Pfeifer, Kate Gruenwald & American Medical Association Staff. American Medical Association Boy's Guide to Becoming a Teen. Middleman, Amy B., ed. 2006. (ENG., Illus.). 128p. (gr. 4-7). per. 14.95 (978-0-7879-8343-7(8), Jossey-Bass) Wiley, John & Sons, Inc.

Phillips, Sherre Florence. The Teen Brain. 2007. (Gray Matter Ser.). (Illus.). 130p. (YA). (gr. 9-12). lib. bdg. 35.00 (978-0-7910-9415-0(4)) Facts On File, Inc.

Picklesimer, Olivia. Teen Sex. 2010. (At Issue Ser.). (ENG.). 128p. (gr. 10-12). 39.40 (978-0-7377-5095-9(2)); pap. 27.80 (978-0-7377-5096-6(0), Greenhaven Pr., Inc.) Cengage Gale.

Piehl, Norah. Underage Drinking. 2010. (Social Issues Firsthand Ser.). (Illus.). 192p. (J). 33.75 (978-0-7377-4799-7(4), Greenhaven Pr., Inc.) Cengage Gale.

Poole, H. W. Teen Parents, Vol. 12. 2016. (Families Today Ser.). (Illus.). 48p. (J). (gr. 5). 20.95 (978-1-4222-3624-6(2)) Mason Crest.

Rauf, Don. Social Network-Powered Investing & Saving Opportunities. 2013. (Teen's Guide to the Power of Social Networking Ser.). 80p. (YA). (gr. 7-12). 33.25 (978-1-4777-1684-7(X)); pap. 14.15 (978-1-4777-1917-6(2)) Rosen Publishing Group, Inc., The.

Regan Gregson, Susan. Cyber Literacy: Evaluating the Reliability of Data. 2009. (Cyber Citizenship & Cyber Safety Ser.). 48p. (gr. 5-5). 53.00 (978-1-61512-103-8(X), Rosen Reference) Rosen Publishing Group, Inc., The.

Reino, Jessica. Food Allergies: The Ultimate Teen Guide. 2015. (It Happened to Me Ser.: 45). (ENG., Illus.). 182p. (J). 45.00 (978-1-4422-3573-1(X)) Rowman & Littlefield Publishers, Inc.

Reynolds, Luke, ed. Break These Rules: 35 YA Authors on Speaking up, Standing Out, & Being Yourself. 2013. (ENG.). 224p. (YA). (gr. 7). pap. 12.95 (978-1-61374-784-1(5)) Chicago Review Pr., Inc.

Rich, Mari. My Teenage Life in Japan. 2017. (Custom & Cultures of the World Ser.). (ENG.). (YA). (gr. 7-12). 23.95 **(978-1-4222-3906-3(3))** Mason Crest.

Rodger, Ellen. Jazz Jennings: Voice for LGBTQ Youth. 2017. (Illus.). 32p. (J). **(978-0-7787-3419-2(6))** Crabtree Publishing Co.

Rosen Publishing Staff. Teen Life 411: Set 2, 1 vol. 2015. (Teen Life 411 Ser.). (ENG.). 112p. (YA). 284.80 (978-1-4777-7988-0(4), Rosen Young Adult) Rosen Publishing Group, Inc., The.

Rosenberg, Carol & Rosenberg, Gary. Jon & Jayne's Guide to Throwing, Going To, & Surviving Parties: Advice & More from Your Average but Xtraordinary Friends. 2008. (Jon & Jayne Doe Ser.). (ENG., Illus.). 128p. (YA). (gr. 7-11). pap. 9.95 (978-0-7573-0726-3(4)) Health Communications, Inc.

Saul, Laya. Ways to Help Disadvantaged Youth: A Guide to Giving Back. 2010. (How to Help Ser.). (Illus.). 48p. (J). (gr. 4-8). lib. bdg. 29.95 (978-1-58415-918-6(9)) Mitchell Lane Pubs., Inc.

Scherer, Lauri S. Dating. Gale, ed. 2014. (Issues That Concern You Ser.). (ENG., Illus.). 144p. (gr. 7-10). lib. bdg. 42.00 (978-0-7377-6288-4(8), Greenhaven Pr., Inc.) Cengage Gale.

Scott, Jerry & Borgman, Jim. Extra Cheesy Zits: A Zits Treasury. 2016. (Zits Ser.: 33). (ENG., Illus.). 208p. pap. 18.99 (978-1-4494-7982-4(0)) Andrews McMeel Publishing.

Seguin, Marilyn. No Ordinary Lives: Four 19th Century Teenage Diaries. 2009. (J). pap. (978-0-8283-2158-7(2)) Branden Bks.

Shames, Stephen. Transforming Lives: Turning Uganda's Forgotten Children into Leaders. Shames, Stephen, photos by. 2009. (Illus.). 40p. (YA). pap. 12.95 (978-1-59572-213-3(0)) Star Bright Bks., Inc.

Shea, John M. Self-Injury & Cutting: Stopping the Pain. 2013. (Helpline: Teen Issues & Answers Ser.). (ENG., Illus.). 80p. (YA). (gr. 7-12). lib. bdg. 33.25 (978-1-4488-9448-2(4), Rosen Classroom) Rosen Publishing Group, Inc., The.

Sheen, Barbara. Growing up in Mexico. 2017. (Growing up Around the World Ser.). (ENG.). 80p. (YA). (gr. 5-12). **(978-1-68282-221-0(4))** ReferencePoint Pr., Inc.

Simons, Rae. A Guide to Teaching Young Adults about Money. 2010. (Junior Library of Money). 64p. (YA). (gr. 7-18). pap. 9.95 (978-1-4222-1884-6(8)); lib. bdg. 22.95 (978-1-4222-1765-8(5)) Mason Crest.

Snyder, Gail. Growing up in Canada. 2017. (Growing up Around the World Ser.). (ENG.). 80p. (YA). (gr. 5-12). **(978-1-68282-207-4(9))** ReferencePoint Pr., Inc.

Snyder, Gail. Teens & Alcohol. Developed in Association with the Gallup Organization Staff, ed. 2013. (Gallup Youth Survey: Major Issues & Trends Ser.: 14). 112p. (J). (gr. 7-18). 24.95 (978-1-4222-2949-1(1)) Mason Crest.

Social Network-Powered Investing & Saving Opportunities. 2013. (Teen's Guide to the Power of Social Networking Ser.). 80p. (YA). (gr. 7-12). pap. 84.90 (978-1-4777-1918-3(0)) Rosen Publishing Group, Inc., The.

Sokol, Leslie & Fox, Marci G. The Think Confident, Be Confident Workbook for Teens: Activities to Create Unshakable Self-Confidence & Reach Your Goals. 2016. (ENG.). 224p. (YA). (gr. 6-12). pap. 16.95 (978-1-62625-483-1(4)) New Harbinger Pubns.

Spangenburg, Ray & Moser, Kit. Teen Fads: Fun, Foolish, or Fatal? 2003. (Teen Issues Ser.). (Illus.). 64p. (J). (gr. 6-12). lib. bdg. 22.60 (978-0-7660-1665-1(X)) Enslow Pubs., Inc.

Spencer, Lauren. Everything You Need to Know about Falling in Love. 2009. (Need to Know Library). 64p. (gr. 5-5). 58.50 (978-1-60854-067-9(7)) Rosen Publishing Group, Inc., The.

St. Stephen's Community House Staff. It's Not All Black & White: Multiracial Youth Speak Out. 2012. (ENG., Illus.). 120p. (YA). (gr. 7-12). pap. 12.95 (978-1-55451-380-2(4), 9781554513802) Annick Pr., Ltd. CAN. Dist: Publishers Group West (PGW).

Staley, Erin. I'm an Undocumented Immigrant, Now What? 2016. (Teen Life 411 Ser.). 00112p. (J). (gr. 7-7). 37.10 (978-1-5081-7193-5(9)) Rosen Publishing Group, Inc., The.

Stanley, Debbie. Everything You Need to Know about Student-on-Student Sexual Harassment. 2005. (Need to Know Library). (Illus.). 64p. (YA). (gr. 7-12). lib. bdg. 31.95 (978-0-8239-3281-8(8), NTSTHA) Rosen Publishing Group, Inc., The.

Stephens, Aarti, ed. Teenage Sexuality. 2012. (Opposing Viewpoints Ser.). (ENG., Illus.). 240p. (YA). (gr. 9-12). 42.95 (978-0-7377-5763-7(9)); 224p. (gr. 10-12). pap. 33.80 (978-0-7377-5764-4(7), Greenhaven Pr., Inc.) Cengage Gale.

Sterling Children's, Sterling. M. A. S. H. What Does Your Future Hold? 2017. (ENG., Illus.). 96p. (J). (gr. 2-6). pap. 6.95 **(978-1-4549-2278-0(8))** Sterling Publishing Co., Inc.

Stewart, Faith. Teens & Rural Education: Opportunities & Challenges. 2009. (Youth in Rural North America Ser.). (Illus.). 96p. (YA). (gr. 3-7). lib. bdg. 22.95 (978-1-4222-0015-5(9)) Mason Crest.

Stollers, Veronica & Keyishian, Elizabeth. Frequently Asked Questions about Smoking. 2011. (FAQ: Teen Life Ser.). (J). lib. bdg. 31.95 (978-1-4488-4631-3(5)) Rosen Publishing Group, Inc., The.

Synder, Gail. Teens & Smoking. 2015. (Illus.). 80p. (J). (978-1-60152-918-3(X)) ReferencePoint Pr., Inc.

Taylor, Julia V. The Body Image Workbook for Teens: Activities to Help Girls Develop a Healthy Body Image in an Image-Obsessed World. 2014. (ENG.). 200p. (YA). (gr. 6-12). pap. 16.95 (978-1-62625-018-5(9)) New Harbinger Pubns.

Tecco, Betsy Dru. Food for Fuel: The Connection Between Food & Physical Activity. (Library of Nutrition Ser.). (Illus.). 48p. 2008. (ENG.). (gr. 5-8). per. 11.75 (978-1-4042-1635-8(9)) 2004. (J). lib. bdg. 26.50 (978-1-4042-0303-7(6)) Rosen Publishing Group, Inc., The.

Teen Issues, 26 bks., Set. (Illus.). (YA). (gr. 6-12). lib. bdg. 344.10 (978-0-89490-887-3(1)) Enslow Pubs., Inc.

Teen Life 411: Set 4. 2016. (Teen Life 411 Ser.). 00112p. (J). (gr. 7-7). 296.80 (978-1-5081-7354-0(0), Rosen Young Adult) Rosen Publishing Group, Inc., The.

Teen Mental Health, 6 vols., Set. Incl. Addictive Personality. Juzwiak, Richard. lib. bdg. 29.25 (978-1-4042-1802-4(5)); Anxiety & Panic Attacks. Levin, Judith. lib. bdg. 29.25 (978-1-4042-1797-3(5)); Depression & Mood Disorders. Levin, Judith. lib. bdg. 29.25 (978-1-4042-1798-0(3)); Meditation. Moore, Andrew. lib. bdg. 29.25 (978-1-4042-1799-7(1)); (Illus.). 48p. (YA). (gr. 7-12). 2008. 2009. Set lib. bdg. 159.00 (978-1-4042-1888-8(2)) Rosen Publishing Group, Inc., The.

Teen Mental Health: Set 4. 2013. (Teen Mental Health Ser.). 48p. (YA). (gr. 7-12). 179.70 (978-1-4777-1761-5(7)) Rosen Publishing Group, Inc., The.

Teenage Refugees Speak Out. 2005. (Illus.). (gr. 7-12). lib. bdg. 344.50 (978-0-8239-9331-4(0)) Rosen Publishing Group, Inc., The.

A Teen's Guide to the Power of Social Networking. 2013. (Teen's Guide to the Power of Social Networking Ser.). 80p. (YA). (gr. 7-12). 133.00 (978-1-4777-1689-2(0)); pap. 339.60 (978-1-4777-7808-1(X)); pap. 56.60 (978-1-4777-7809-8(8)) Rosen Publishing Group, Inc., The.

Telgemeier, Raina. Smile. 2010. 21.00 (978-1-60686-896-6(9)) Perfection Learning Corp.

—Smile. 2010. (ENG.). 224p. (J). (gr. 3-7). 24.99 (978-0-545-13205-3(3)); (Illus.). pap. 10.99 (978-0-545-13206-0(1)) Scholastic, Inc. (Graphix).

—Smile. 2010. lib. bdg. 22.10 (978-0-606-14082-9(4), Turtleback) Turtleback Bks.

Townsend, John. 101 Things You Didn't Know about Your Body, 1 vol. 2011. (101 Ser.). (ENG., Illus.). 56p. (gr. 5-9). 34.65 (978-1-4109-3896-1(4), NA-r) Heinemann-Raintree.

The Truth about Violence. 2nd rev. ed. 2010. (Truth about Ser.). (Illus.). 224p. (C). (gr. 9). 35.00 (978-0-8160-7644-4(8)) Facts On File, Inc.

Turck, Mary C. Freedom Song: Young Voices & the Struggle for Civil Rights. 2008. (ENG., Illus.). 160p. (J). (gr. 4). pap. 18.95 (978-1-55652-773-9(X)) Chicago Review Pr., Inc.

Turnbull, Stephanie. Fun with Friends: Style Secrets for Girls. 2014. (Girl Talk Ser.). (ENG., Illus.). 32p. (J). (gr. 4-8). pap. 9.95 (978-1-77092-203-7(2)) Saunders Bk. Co. CAN. Dist: RiverStream Publishing.

Vizzini, Ned. Teen Angst? Naaah... A Quasi-Autobiography. 2010. (ENG.). 272p. (YA). (gr. 7). pap. 9.99 (978-0-385-73945-0(1), Ember) Random Hse. Children's Bks.

von Holleben, Jan & Helms, Antje. Does This Happen to Everyone? A Budding Adult's Guide to Puberty. 2014. (ENG.). 160p. (J). (gr. 5-12). 24.95 (978-3-89955-521-9(X)) Die Gestalten Verlag DEU. Dist: Penguin Random Hse. LLC.

Walsch, Neale Donald. Conversations with God for Teens. unabr. ed. 2004. 244p. (J). (gr. 7-18). pap. 38.00 incl. audio (978-0-8072-0856-4(6), LYA 368 SP, Listening Library) Random Hse. Audio Publishing Group.

Watkins, Christine. Age of Consent. Greenhaven Press Editors, ed. 2013. (At Issue Ser.). (ENG.). 128p. (gr. 10-12). pap. 27.80 (978-0-7377-6817-6(7)); lib. bdg. 39.40 (978-0-7377-6816-9(9)) Cengage Gale. (Greenhaven Pr., Inc.).

Watkins, Heidi. Social Networking. Friedman, Lauri S., ed. 2011. (Issues That Concern You Ser.). (ENG.). 144p. (gr. 10). lib. bdg. 36.95 (978-0-7377-5135-2(5)) Cengage Gale.

—Teens & Employment. 2011. (Issues That Concern You Ser.). (ENG.). 144p. (gr. 10-10). lib. bdg. 39.95 (978-0-7377-5208-3(4)) Cengage Gale.

Watson, Stephanie. Binge Drinking, 1 vol. 2011. (Essential Issues Set 3 Ser.). (ENG., Illus.). 112p. (J). (gr. 6-12). lib. bdg. 35.64 (978-1-61783-131-7(X)) ABDO Publishing Co.

Webber, Diane. The Skin You're In: Staying Healthy Inside & Out. 2008. (Scholastic Choices Ser.). (ENG.). 112p. (J). (gr. 7-18). pap. 8.95 (978-0-531-20527-3(4), Watts, Franklin) Scholastic Library Publishing.

Weierbach, Jane & Phillips-Hershey, Elizabeth. Mind over Basketball: Coach Yourself to Handle Stress. Beyl, Charles, illus. 2007. (Coach Yourself to Handle Stress Ser.). 48p. (J). (gr. 3-7). 14.95 (978-1-4338-0135-8(3), 4418006); per. 9.95 (978-1-4338-0136-5(1), 4418007) American Psychological Assn. (Magination Pr.).

Whiting, Jim & Li, Shi Yu. My Teenage Life in China. 2017. (Illus.). 128p. (J). **(978-1-4222-3902-5(0))** Mason Crest.

Whiting, Jim & Nabil, Muhammad. My Teenage Life in Egypt. 2017. (J). **(978-1-4222-3899-8(7))** Mason Crest.

Whitney, Brooks. How to Master the School Universe: Homework, Teachers, Tests, Bullies, & Other Ways to Survive the Classroom. Kennedy, Kelly, illus. 2004. 80p. (J). pap. (978-0-439-57902-5(3)) Scholastic, Inc.

Whittaker, Helen. How Toys Roll. 2012. (Toys & Forces Ser.). 32p. (gr. 1-4). lib. bdg. 27.10 (978-1-59920-468-0(1)) Black Rabbit Bks.

Wilcox, Christine. Teens & Body Image. 2015. (ENG., Illus.). 80p. (J). lib. bdg. (978-1-60152-828-5(0)) ReferencePoint Pr., Inc.

—Teens, Nutrition, & Dieting. 2015. (ENG., Illus.). 80p. (J). lib. bdg. (978-1-60152-834-6(5)) ReferencePoint Pr., Inc.

The Winners. 2005. (YA). 14.95 (978-0-9661256-4-1(9)) Youth Communication - New York Center.

Wohlenhaus, Kim, ed. Suicide Information for Teens. 2nd rev. ed. 2010. (Teen Health Ser.). 376p. lib. bdg. 69.00 (978-0-7808-1088-4(0)) Omnigraphics, Inc.

Wolny, Philip. Abusing Prescription Drugs. 2007. (Incredibly Disgusting Drugs Ser.). (Illus.). 48p. (YA). (gr. 5-9). lib. bdg. 29.25 (978-1-4042-1955-7(2)) Rosen Publishing Group, Inc., The.

Wroble, Lisa A. Dealing with Stress. 2011. (Life—a How-To Guide Ser.). (Illus.). 128p. (J). (gr. 6-18). pap. 10.95 (978-1-59845-309-6(2)) Enslow Pubs., Inc.

Zarate, Gustavo Azgad. Youth Law: A Practical Guide to Legal Issues That Affect Young Adults. 2nd ed. 2005. (YA). per. 25.00 (978-0-9763167-9-4(X)) Living Ministry, Inc.

YOUTH—FICTION

ABDO Publishing Company Staff. Jughead with Archie - 6 Titles, 6 vols., Set. 2007. (Jughead with Archie Ser.). (ENG., Illus.). 80p. 145.26 (978-1-59961-271-3(2)) Spotlight.

Abrahams, Peter, et al. Up All Night: A Short Story Collection. 2008. (Illus.). 240p. (J). (gr. 7). lib. bdg. 17.89 (978-0-06-137077-9(0)); 16.99 (978-0-06-137076-2(2)) HarperCollins Pubs. (Geringer, Laura Book).

Adkins, Jan. A Storm Without Rain. 2004. (ENG., Illus.). 179p. (YA). (gr. 7). 14.95 (978-0-937822-80-7(9)) WoodenBoat Pubns.

Aker, Don. The First Stone. 2004. (ENG.). 304p. (J). mass mkt. 6.99 (978-0-00-639286-6(5), Harper Trophy) HarperCollins Pubs.

Alcott, Louisa May. A Garland for Girls. l.t. ed. 2005. 376p. pap. (978-1-84637-049-6(3)) Echo Library.

Alsaid, Adi. Let's Get Lost. 2015. (ENG.). 384p. (YA). pap. 9.99 (978-0-373-21149-4(X), Harlequin Teen) Harlequin Enterprises, Ltd. CAN. Dist: HarperCollins Pubs.

Ando, Yuma. Sherlock Bones, Vol. 1. Sato, Yuki, illus. 2013. (Sherlock Bones Ser.). (ENG.). 200p. pap. 10.99 (978-1-61262-444-0(8)) Kodansha America, Inc.

Angel, Ann. Things I'll Never Say: Stories about Our Secret Selves. 2015. (ENG.). 320p. (YA). (gr. 9). 16.99 (978-0-7636-7307-9(2)) Candlewick Pr.

Anonymous. Lucy in the Sky. 2012. (ENG.). 288p. (YA). (gr. 9). 19.99 (978-1-4424-5187-2(4)); pap. 10.99 (978-1-4424-5185-8(8)) Simon Pulse. (Simon Pulse).

Attema, Martha. A Time to Choose. braille ed. 2003. (J). (gr. 2). spiral bd. (978-0-616-15262-1(0)) Canadian National Institute for the Blind/Institut National Canadien pour les Aveugles.

Baker, Samuel White. Cast up by the Sea by Sir Samuel W Baker Complete with Ten Illustrations by Huard. 2006. 408p. per. 26.99 (978-1-4255-4629-8(3)) Michigan Publishing.

Banting, Celia. I only said I couldn't Cope. 2006. (Illus.). 240p. (YA). per. 14.99 (978-0-9786648-2-4(5)) Wighita Pr.

—I Only Said I Didn't Want You Because I Was Terrified. 2006. (I Only Said Ser.: 4). 240p. (YA). pap. 14.99 (978-0-9786648-3-1(3)) Wighita Pr.

—I Only Said I Had No Choice. 2006. (I Only Said Ser.). (Illus.). 202p. (YA). pap. 14.99 (978-0-9786648-0-0(9)) Wighita Pr.

—I only said I was telling the Truth. 2006. 240p. (YA). per. 14.99 (978-0-9786648-4-8(1)) Wighita Pr.

—I Only Said Yes So That They'd Like Me. 2006. (Illus.). 224p. (YA). per. 14.99 (978-0-9786648-1-7(7)) Wighita Pr.

Baratz-Logsted, Lauren. Secrets of My Suburban Life. 2008. (ENG.). 240p. (YA). (gr. 9-18). pap. 7.99 (978-1-4169-2525-5(2), Simon Pulse) Simon Pulse.

Barnum, P. T. Dick Broadhead: A Story of Perilous Adve. 2006. pap. 30.95 (978-1-4286-1959-3(3)) Kessinger Publishing, LLC.

Bass, Karen. Summer of Fire, 1 vol. 2009. (ENG.). 295p. (YA). (gr. 9-12). pap. 12.95 (978-1-55050-415-6(0)) Coteau Bks. CAN. Dist: Orca Bk. Pubs. USA.

Batchelor, Rhonda. She Loves You. 2008. (ENG.). 136p. (YA). (gr. 7-8). pap. 11.99 (978-1-55002-789-1(1), Sandcastle Bks.) Dundurn CAN. Dist: Ingram Publisher Services.

Batista, Joaquin. Westward Eden. 2003. 196p. (YA). 28.95 (978-1-59113-371-1(8)); pap. 15.95 (978-1-59113-316-2(5)) Booklocker.com, Inc.

Beechwood, Beth, adapted by. Hannah Montana - Keeping Secrets. 2006. (Hannah Montana Ser.). (Illus.). 124p. (J). (gr. 3-7). 12.65 (978-0-7569-8317-8(7)) Perfection Learning Corp.

Beede, John R. Climb On! Dynamic Strategies for Teen Success. 2005. (YA). per. 12.95 (978-0-9765697-0-1(1)) Sierra Nevada Publishing Hse.

Belasen, Amy & Osborn, Jacob. Jenny Green's Killer Junior Year. 2008. (ENG.). 304p. (YA). (gr. 9-18). pap. 14.99 (978-1-4169-6792-7(3), Simon Pulse) Simon Pulse.

Birle, Pete. Locals Only. 2013. (Av2 Audio Chapter Bks.). (ENG.). 121p. (J). 27.13 (978-1-62127-985-3(5), AV2 by Weigl) Weigl Pubs., Inc.

Black, Jenna. Replica. 2013. (Replica Ser.: 1). (ENG.). 368p. (YA). (gr. 8-12). pap. 19.99 (978-0-7653-3371-1(6), 9780765333711, Tor Teen) Doherty, Tom Assocs., LLC.

Blume, Judy. Are You There God? It's Me, Margaret. 149p. (J). (gr. 4-6). pap. 3.50 (978-0-8072-1421-3(3)); (YA). (gr. 5-18). pap. 4.99 (978-0-8072-1508-1(2)) Random Hse. Audio Publishing Group. (Listening Library).

Boggess, Eileen. Mia the Meek. 2006. (ENG.). 155p. (gr. 6-9). per. 14.95 (978-1-890862-47-3(9)) Bancroft Pr.

—MIA the Meek. 2006. (Mia Fullerton Ser.: Bk. 1). 155p. (J). (gr. 6-11). 16.95 (978-1-890862-46-6(0)) Bancroft Pr.

Bolden-Thompson, Angela. When Company Comes. 2007. 254p. pap. 19.99 (978-0-615-14774-1(7)) Thompson, Angela Bolden.

Bone, Ian. Fat Boy Saves World. 2011. (ENG.). 240p. (YA). (gr. 7). pap. 11.99 (978-1-4424-3105-8(9), Simon Pulse) Simon Pulse.

Booth, Coe. Bronxwood. 2013. (ENG.). 336p. (J). (gr. 9). pap. 10.99 (978-0-439-92535-8(5), PUSH) Scholastic, Inc.

Bossley, Michele Martin. Tampered, 1 vol. 2013. (Orca Currents Ser.). (ENG.). 136p. (J). (gr. 5-9). pap. 9.95 (978-1-4598-0356-5(6)); lib. bdg. 16.95 (978-1-4598-0357-2(4)) Orca Bk. Pubs. USA.

Boudreau, Bobby A. Inspirational Stories for Spiritual Youth. 2010. 124p. 29.99 *(978-1-4490-8105-8(3))*; pap. 18.99 *(978-1-4490-8106-5(1))* AuthorHouse.

Bremer, Terry. Dandylion: The Most Misunderstood Flower. Pierce, M. Deborah, illus. 2003. 32p. (J). lib. bdg. 15.00 *(978-1-931646-90-1(2))* Beaver's Pond Pr., Inc.

Brenna, Beverley. Something to Hang on To. 2009. (ENG.). 176p. (J). pap. 12.95 *(978-1-897235-57-7(7))* Thistledown Pr., Ltd. CAN. Dist: Univ. of Toronto Pr.

Brian, Kate, pseud. Invitation Only. 2009. (Private Ser.: No. 2). (ENG.). 272p. (YA). pap. 9.99 *(978-1-4169-9947-8(7)*, Simon & Schuster Bks. For Young Readers) Simon & Schuster Bks. For Young Readers.

Brody, Jessica. Boys of Summer. 2016. (ENG., Illus.). 352p. (YA). (gr. 9). 17.99 *(978-1-4814-6349-2(7)*, Simon Pulse) Simon Pulse.

Bryant, Annie. Crush Alert. 2008. (Beacon Street Girls Ser.: 14). (ENG.). 288p. (J). (gr. 4-8). pap. 8.99 *(978-1-4169-6437-7(1)*, Aladdin) Simon & Schuster Children's Publishing.

—Lake Rescue. 2008. (Beacon Street Girls Ser.: 6). (ENG.). 256p. (J). (gr. 4-8). pap. 7.99 *(978-1-4169-6431-5(2)*, Aladdin) Simon & Schuster Children's Publishing.

—Worst Enemies/Best Friends. 2008. (Beacon Street Girls Ser.: 1). (ENG.). 240p. (J). (gr. 4-8). pap. 8.99 *(978-1-4169-6424-7(X)*, Aladdin) Simon & Schuster Children's Publishing.

Burk, Josh. The Summer of Saint Nick. 2007. (ENG.). 152p. (YA). per. 12.95 *(978-0-9768042-2-2(0))* Maven Of Memory Publishing.

Burkhart, Jessica. Jealousy. 2013. (Canterwood Crest Ser.: 17). (ENG.). 208p. (J). (gr. 4-7). pap. 7.99 *(978-1-4424-3657-2(3)*, Aladdin) Simon & Schuster Children's Publishing.

Burns, T. R. The Bad Apple. 2013. (Merits of Mischief Ser.: 1). (ENG.). 368p. (J). (gr. 3-7). pap. 7.99 *(978-1-4424-4030-2(9)*, Aladdin) Simon & Schuster Children's Publishing.

Carey, Anna. Deadfall. 2015. 256p. (J). pap. *(978-0-06-242788-5(1))* HarperCollins Pubs.

Carlson, Melody. Bad Connection. 2006. (Secret Life of Samantha Mcgregor Ser.: No. 1). (ENG.). 256p. (J). (gr. 7-12). per. 12.99 *(978-1-59052-692-7(9)*, Multnomah) Doubleday Religious Publishing Group, The.

—Meant to Be. 2005. (Diary of a Teenage Girl Ser.: Bk. 11). (ENG.). 272p. (J). (gr. 7-7). pap. 15.99 *(978-1-59052-322-3(9)*, Multnomah) Doubleday Religious Publishing Group, The.

Carroll, Jenny, pseud & Cabot, Meg. Code Name Cassandra. 2007. (1-800-Where-R-You Ser.: No. 2). (ENG., Illus.). 272p. (YA). (gr. 9-12). mass mkt. 6.99 *(978-1-4169-2704-4(2)*, Simon Pulse) Simon Pulse.

Carter, Ally. All Fall Down. 2015. (Embassy Row Ser.: 1). (ENG.). 320p. (J). (gr. 7). 17.99 *(978-0-545-65474-6(2)*, Scholastic Pr.) Scholastic, Inc.

Cartwheel: A Sequel to Double Eagle. 2013. (ENG.). 252p. (YA). 17.00 *(978-0-9844460-3-2(6))* Bucking Horse Bks.

Castlemon, Harry. No Moss; or, the Career of a Rolling Stone, by Harry Castlemon [Pseud.]. 2006. 328p. per. 23.99 *(978-1-4255-3290-1(X))* Michigan Publishing.

Chan, Queenie. The Dreaming Collection. 2010. (ENG., Illus.). 576p. pap. 19.99 *(978-1-4278-1871-3(1))* TOKYOPOP, Inc.

Chandler, Elizabeth. No Time to Die - The Deep End of Fear No. 2. 2010. (Dark Secrets Ser.: 2). (ENG.). 624p. (YA). (gr. 7). pap. 9.99 *(978-1-4169-9462-6(9)*, Simon Pulse) Simon Pulse.

Chapman, Patricia. Beth. 2011. 20p. pap. 16.95 *(978-1-4626-1060-0(9))* America Star Bks.

Chbosky, Stephen & Perez-Sauquillo, Vanesa. Las Ventajas de Ser Invisible. 2013. (SPA.). 272p. pap. 14.99 *(978-1-4767-3245-9(0)*, MTV Bks.) MTV Books.

Child, Lauren. Take Your Last Breath. Child, Lauren, illus. 2014. (Ruby Redfort Ser.: 2). (ENG., Illus.). 432p. (J). (gr. 5-9). pap. 7.99 *(978-0-7636-6932-4(6))* Candlewick Pr.

Clark, K. M. Beautiful Disaster. 2013. 106p. 24.99 *(978-1-4797-6506-5(6))*; pap. 15.99 *(978-1-4797-6505-8(8))* Xlibris Corp.

Clark, Terri A. Sleepless. 2008. (ENG.). 288p. (YA). (gr. 9-18). pap. 5.99 *(978-0-06-137596-5(9)*, HarperTeen) HarperCollins Pubs.

Coates-Smith, Renee. Bobby's Secret Is Out. 2007. (Illus.). 43p. (J). 12.95 *(978-0-615-14325-5(3))* Imani Productions.

Condon, Bill. No Worries. 2005. 216p. (YA). pap. *(978-0-7022-3491-0(5))* Univ. of Queensland Pr.

Connor, Naomi. I Am. 2011. 52p. pap. 22.49 *(978-1-4634-3673-5(4))* AuthorHouse.

Cormier, Robert. The Chocolate War. 191p. (YA). (gr. 7-18). pap. 4.99 *(978-0-8072-1428-2(0)*, Listening Library) Random Hse. Audio Publishing Group.

—The Chocolate War. 30th ed. 2004. (Readers Circle Ser.). (ENG.). 272p. (YA). (gr. 7-12). pap. 9.99 *(978-0-375-82987-1(3)*, Ember) Random Hse. Children's Bks.

Cotugno, Katie. 99 Days. (YA). (gr. 8). 2016. 400p. pap. 9.99 *(978-0-06-221639-7(2))* 2015. (ENG.). 384p. 17.99 *(978-0-06-221638-0(4))* HarperCollins Pubs.

Crane, Cheri J. Moment of Truth: A Novel. 2005. 238p. (YA). *(978-1-59156-727-1(0))* Covenant Communications.

Crouch, Katie. The White Glove War. 2013. (Magnolia League Ser.: 2). (ENG.). 320p. (YA). (gr. 10-17). pap. 9.00 *(978-0-316-18749-7(6)*, Poppy) Little, Brown Bks. for Young Readers.

Dakers, Diane. Bad Business, 1 vol. 2015. (Orca Currents Ser.). (ENG.). 128p. (J). (gr. 5-9). pap. 9.95 *(978-1-4598-0969-7(6))* Orca Bk. Pubs. USA.

Dance, Jennifer. Hawk. 2016. (ENG.). 248p. (YA). pap. 12.99 *(978-1-4597-3184-4(0))* Dundurn CAN. Dist: Ingram Publisher Services.

Darling, Angela. Lauren Likes Charlie: Does He Like Her Too? 2013. (Crush Ser.: 1). (ENG., Illus.). 176p. (J). (gr. 3-7). 15.99 *(978-1-4424-8038-4(6)*, Simon Spotlight) Simon Spotlight.

—Lauren's Beach Crush. 2013. (Crush Ser.: 1). (ENG., Illus.). 176p. (J). (gr. 3-7). pap. 5.99 *(978-1-4424-8036-0(X)*, Simon Spotlight) Simon Spotlight.

DC Comics. Teen Titans Go! - Team Up! 2017. (Passport to Reading Level 2 Ser.). (ENG., Illus.). 192p. (J). (gr. -1-3). 9.99 ***(978-0-316-54857-1(X))***; pap. 8.99 ***(978-0-316-54847-2(2))*** Little, Brown Bks. for Young Readers.

De Los Santos, Elizabeth G. The Secret House. 2011. 18p. pap. 16.95 *(978-1-4626-4409-4(0))* America Star Bks.

De Palma, Toni. The Devil's Triangle. 2013. 216p. pap. 14.99 *(978-1-939173-03-4(5))* Crescent Moon Pr.

Defilippis, Nunzio & Weir, Christina. The Avalon Chronicles, Vol. 2. 2013. (ENG., Illus.). 152p. (YA). 19.99 *(978-1-934964-90-3(5)*, 9781934964903) Oni Pr., Inc.

Delaney, Joseph. Slither, Bk. 11. 2014. (Last Apprentice Ser.). (ENG.). 432p. (YA). (gr. 8). pap. 9.99 *(978-0-06-219235-6(3)*, Greenwillow Bks.) HarperCollins Pubs.

Denis, Erik & LeBlanc, Natalie. The Bubble. 2005. 16p. 10.10 *(978-1-4116-6424-1(8))* Lulu Pr., Inc.

Devine, Eric. Look Past. 2016. (ENG.). 288p. (YA). (gr. 2-17). 16.95 *(978-0-7624-5921-6(2)*, Running Pr. Kids) Running Pr. Bk. Pubs.

DeVita, James. The Silenced. 2007. 512p. (J). (gr. 8-12). lib. bdg. 18.89 *(978-0-06-078464-5(4)*, HarperTeen) HarperCollins Pubs.

DeVita, James & Devita, James. The Silenced. 2007. (ENG.). 368p. (J). (gr. 8-12). 17.99 *(978-0-06-078462-1(8)*, HarperTeen) HarperCollins Pubs.

Divine, L. Frenemies. 2008. (ENG., Illus.). 304p. (YA). (gr. 9-12). 15.00 *(978-0-7582-2532-0(6)*, K-Teen/Dafina) Kensington Publishing Corp.

Doller, Trish. The Devil You Know. 2016. (ENG.). 256p. (YA). pap. 9.99 *(978-1-68119-022-8(2)*, 9781681190228, Bloomsbury USA Childrens) Bloomsbury Publishing USA.

Dower, Laura. On the Case. 2004. 170p. (J). lib. bdg. 16.92 *(978-1-4242-0648-3(0))* Fitzgerald Bks.

Doyle, Brian. Angel Square, 1 vol. 2nd ed. 2004. (ENG.). 144p. (J). pap. 9.95 *(978-0-88899-609-1(8))* Groundwood Bks. CAN. Dist: Publishers Group West (PGW).

—Covered Bridge. Date not set. (J). (gr. 4-6). pap. *(978-0-88899-190-4(8))* 2004. (ENG., Illus.). 120p. (YA). pap. 6.95 *(978-0-88899-603-9(9))* Groundwood Bks. CAN. Dist: Publishers Group West (PGW).

—Up to Low, 1 vol. 3rd ed. 2004. (ENG.). 115p. (J). pap. 6.95 *(978-0-88899-622-0(5))* Groundwood Bks. CAN. Dist: Publishers Group West (PGW).

—You Can Pick Me up at Peggy's Cove. Date not set. (J). (gr. 4-6). reprint ed. pap. 5.95 *(978-0-88899-231-4(9))* Groundwood Bks. CAN. Dist: Publishers Group West (PGW).

Drown, Merle. Lighting the World. 2015. (ENG.). 278p. pap. 18.00 *(978-0-9898971-4-3(1))* Whitepoint Pr.

Duval, Alex. Vampire Beach 2 - Ritual - Legacy. 2011. (Vampire Beach Ser.: 2). (ENG.). 448p. (YA). (gr. 9). pap. 9.99 *(978-1-4424-0694-0(1)*, Simon Pulse) Simon Pulse.

Eaton, Anthony. Fireshadow. 2004. 320p. (YA). *(978-0-7022-3381-4(1))* Univ. of Queensland Pr.

Echo of Hooves. 2005. (J). *(978-1-933343-10-5(9)*, PONY) Stabenfeldt Inc.

Edwards, Hazel. Stalker. 2003. 176p. pap. *(978-0-7344-0103-8(5)*, Lothian Children's Bks.) Hachette Australia.

Edwards, Mark. The Gang Book 1 the Saint's Bones. 2004. (YA). per. 10.95 *(978-0-9755704-0-1(4))* New Classics Pr.

Ellis, Deborah. No Safe Place. 2013. 224p. pap. *(978-1-4596-6447-0(7))* ReadHowYouWant.com, Ltd.

Elwell, Sharon. Caught in the Middle: Reflections of a Middle School Teacher. 2007. 112p. per. 10.95 *(978-1-4327-0621-0(7))* Outskirts Pr., Inc.

Emery, Airin. Dance Divas: The Dance Series (Book #2) 2013. 128p. pap. *(978-1-927794-01-2(3))* Lechner Syndications.

—Tap In: The Dance Series (Book #3) 2013. 118p. pap. *(978-1-927794-02-9(1))* Lechner Syndications.

Evangelista, Kate. No Second Chances. 2017. (Dodge Cove Trilogy Ser.). (ENG.). 224p. (YA). pap. 10.99 *(978-1-250-10067-2(4)*, 9781250100672) Feiwel & Friends.

Evans, Mari. I'm Late: The Story of Laneese & Moonlight & Alisha Who Didn't Have Anyone of Her Own. 2006. (Illus.). 86p. (J). (gr. 7-18). 14.95 *(978-1-933491-00-4(0))* Just Us Bks., Inc.

Evans, Richard. Michael Vey Books One & Two: The Prisoner of Cell 25; Rise of the Elgen. 2014. (Michael Vey Ser.). (ENG., Illus.). 720p. (YA). (gr. 7). pap. 13.99 *(978-1-4814-2034-1(8)*, Simon Pulse/Mercury Ink) Simon Pulse/Mercury Ink.

—The Prisoner of Cell 25. (Michael Vey Ser.: 1). (ENG., Illus.). (YA). (gr. 7). 2012. 352p. pap. 11.99 *(978-1-4424-6812-2(2))* 2011. 336p. 19.99 *(978-1-4516-5650-3(5))* Simon Pulse/Mercury Ink. (Simon Pulse/Mercury Ink).

Finn, K. C. Leighton's Summer. 2014. (Synsk Ser.: 2). (ENG.). 308p. (J). (gr. 10-12). pap. 11.99 *(978-1-940534-66-4(6))* Clean Teen Publishing.

—The Mind's Eye. 2014. (Synsk Ser.: 1). (ENG.). 352p. (J). (gr. 10-12). pap. 12.99 *(978-1-940534-38-1(0))* Clean Teen Publishing.

Fischer, Rusty. Vamplayers. 2011. (Living Dead Love Story Ser.). (ENG.). 384p. (YA). (gr. 6). pap. 9.95 *(978-1-60542-449-1(8)*, Gold Medallion) Medallion Pr., Inc.

Forney, Lane. The Super Power Teens 2: A Blast from the Past. 2010. 137p. pap. 14.99 *(978-0-557-09707-4(X))* Lulu Pr., Inc.

Francis, Brian. Fruit: A Novel about a Boy & His Nipples. 2004. (ENG., Illus.). 278p. pap. *(978-1-55022-620-1(7))* Rough Guides, Ltd.

Freeman, Lisa. Honey Girl. 2015. (ENG.). 288p. (J). (gr. 6). 16.99 *(978-1-63220-425-7(8)*, Sky Pony Pr.) Skyhorse Publishing Co., Inc.

Gaetz, Dayle Campbell. No Problem. 2004. (Orca Soundings Ser.). 87p. 19.95 *(978-0-7569-4317-2(5))* Perfection Learning Corp.

Gardam, Jane. Bilgewater. 2016. (ENG.). 208p. pap. 17.00 *(978-1-60945-331-2(X))* Europa Editions, Inc.

Garsch, Dawn. Babyshoes. 2004. (ENG.). 288p. (J). pap. 9.99 *(978-0-689-83778-4(X))* Simon & Schuster, Ltd. GBR. Dist: Simon & Schuster, Inc.

Garner, Paula. Phantom Limbs. 2016. (ENG.). 368p. (YA). (gr. 9). 16.99 *(978-0-7636-8205-7(5))* Candlewick Pr.

Ghent, Natale. Book of Living & Dying. 2006. (ENG.). 288p. (J). mass mkt. 6.99 *(978-0-00-639350-4(0)*, Harper Trophy) HarperCollins Pubs.

Gleitzman, Morris. Other Facts of Life. 2016. (ENG.). 144p. (J). (gr. 4-6). 14.99 ***(978-0-14-330878-2(5))*** Random Hse. Australia AUS. Dist: Independent Pubs. Group.

Gliori, Debi. No Matter What. 2017. (ENG., Illus.). 24p. (J). (—1). bds. 8.99 *(978-0-544-91584-8(4)*, HMH Books For Young Readers) Houghton Mifflin Harcourt Publishing Co.

Godbersen, Anna. Rumors. 2008. (Luxe Ser.: No. 2). (YA). (gr. 9-12). (ENG.). 304p. 17.99 *(978-0-06-134569-2(5))*; 423p. lib. bdg. 18.89 *(978-0-06-134570-8(9))* HarperCollins Pubs. (HarperTeen).

Goobie, Beth. Who Owns Kelly Paddik? 2004. (Orca Soundings Ser.). 89p. 19.95 *(978-0-7569-4358-5(2))* Perfection Learning Corp.

Gottesfeld, Jeff. Xo Ronette. 2013. (Campus Confessions Ser.). (ENG.). 160p. (YA). (gr. 9-12). pap. 9.95 *(978-1-62250-701-6(0))* Saddleback Educational Publishing, Inc.

Gough, Erin. Get It Together, Delilah! 2017. (ENG., Illus.). 336p. (YA). 16.99 *(978-1-4521-5187-8(3))* Chronicle Bks. LLC.

Graves, Judith. Second Skin. 2011. 280p. (J). pap. 16.99 *(978-1-61603-006-3(2))* Leap Bks.

—Under My Skin. Cox, Val, illus. 2010. 328p. (YA). (gr. 8-18). pap. 16.99 *(978-1-61603-000-1(3))* Leap Bks.

Gray, Amy. How to Be a Vampire: A Fangs-On Guide for the Newly Undead. Erwert, Scott, illus. 2009. (ENG.). 144p. (YA). (gr. 7-18). 14.99 *(978-0-7636-4915-9(5))* Candlewick Pr.

Gray, Keith. The Chain. 2013. (ENG.). 80p. (YA). (gr. 6-12). pap. 6.95 *(978-1-78112-173-3(7))*; lib. bdg. 22.60 *(978-1-78112-172-6(9))* Lerner Publishing Group.

Gray, P. J. Trippin' Book 1, 1 vol. 2015. (Trippin' Ser.). (ENG.). 64p. (YA). (gr. 9-12). 8.95 *(978-1-62250-931-7(5))* Saddleback Educational Publishing, Inc.

Griffin, Paul. Adrift. 2015. (ENG.). 240p. (J). (gr. 7). 17.99 *(978-0-545-70939-2(3)*, Scholastic Pr.) Scholastic, Inc.

Griffiths, Emma. After I Wake. 2016. (ENG., Illus.). (J). 24.99 ***(978-1-63477-931-9(2)***, Harmony Ink Pr.) Dreamspinner Pr.

Groth, Darren. Are You Seeing Me?, 1 vol. 2015. (ENG., Illus.). 288p. (YA). (gr. 8-12). 19.95 *(978-1-4598-1079-2(1))* Orca Bk. Pubs. USA.

Hall, S.C. Turns of Fortune & Other Tales. 2007. (ENG.). 116p. per. *(978-1-4065-1586-2(8))* Dodo Pr.

Hand, Cynthia. Unearthly. 2011. (Unearthly Ser.: 1). (ENG.). 464p. (YA). (gr. 8). pap. 9.99 *(978-0-06-199617-7(3)*, HarperTeen) HarperCollins Pubs.

Hapka, Catherine, pseud & Echols, Jennifer. Winter's Kiss: The Ex Games - The Twelve Dates of Christmas. 2012. (ENG.). 496p. (YA). (gr. 7). pap. 9.99 *(978-1-4424-5040-0(1)*, Simon Pulse) Simon Pulse.

Hardy, Melissa. The Geomancer's Compass. 2012. (ENG.). 272p. (YA). (gr. 7). 17.95 *(978-1-77049-292-9(5)*, Tundra Bks.) Tundra Bks. CAN. Dist: Penguin Random Hse. LLC.

Harley, Rex. Baby, Now That I've Found You. 2003. (ENG.). 200p. pap. 12.95 *(978-1-84323-107-3(7))* Beekman Bks., Inc.

Harris, Patrick. Where the Day Takes You volume One. 2010. 172p. pap. 10.00 *(978-0-557-04401-6(4))* Lulu Pr., Inc.

Harrop, Isobel. The Isobel Journal, 1 vol. 2014. (ENG.). 208p. (gr. 10-12). 16.95 *(978-1-63079-003-5(6))* Switch Pr.

Hasiuk, Brenda. Where the Rocks Say Your Name. 2006. (ENG.). 296p. per. 19.95 *(978-1-897235-11-9(9))* Thistledown Pr., Ltd. CAN. Dist: Univ. of Toronto Pr.

Hawley, Richard. Paul & Juliana: A Novel. 2003. 188p. (YA). 19.95 *(978-1-890862-33-6(9))* Bancroft Pr.

Heneghan, James & Charles, Norma M. Bank Job, 1 vol. 2009. (ENG.). 176p. (J). (gr. 4-8). pap. 14.95 *(978-1-55143-855-9(0))* Orca Bk. Pubs. USA.

Herron, Edward A. The Return of the Alaskan: Mailboat in the Outpost. Langley, Gene, illus. 2011. 190p. 42.95 *(978-1-258-09093-7(7))* Literary Licensing, LLC.

Highley, Kendra C. Defying Gravity. 2016. (ENG., Illus.). 210p. (J). pap. 14.99 *(978-1-68281-253-2(7))* Entangled Publishing, LLC.

Hill, David. Coming Back. 2007. (ENG.). 200p. per. 18.95 *(978-0-9542330-2-0(6))* Aurora Metro Pubns. Ltd. GBR. Dist: Consortium Bk. Sales & Distribution.

Hinton, Susan E. LA LEY DE LA CALLE. 2nd ed. 2003. (SPA., Illus.). 128p. (YA). (gr. 8-12). pap. 13.95 *(978-84-204-4858-9(3))* Santillana USA Publishing Co., Inc.

Hodgson, Miriam. Love from Dad: Stories about Fathers & Daughters. (ENG.). 160p. (J). pap. 8.99 *(978-0-7497-4330-7(1))* Egmont Bks., Ltd. GBR. Dist: Trafalgar Square Publishing.

Hogan, Edward. The Messengers. 2015. (ENG.). 224p. (YA). (gr. 9). 16.99 *(978-0-7636-7112-9(6))* Candlewick Pr.

Holubitsky, Katherine. Tweaked, 1 vol. 2008. (ENG.). 192p. (YA). (gr. 8-12). pap. 12.95 *(978-1-55143-851-1(8))* Orca Bk. Pubs. USA.

Hook. Wrinkled Crinkled Grapes: A Purple Monster. 2007. 52p. per. 8.95 *(978-0-595-42310-1(8))* iUniverse, Inc.

Hope, Laura Lee. Outdoor Girls in Florida. 2006. 26.95 *(978-1-4218-2982-1(7))*; pap. 11.95 *(978-1-4218-3082-7(5))* 1st World Publishing, Inc.

—Outdoor Girls in the Saddle. 2006. 26.95 *(978-1-4218-2983-8(5))*; pap. 11.95 *(978-1-4218-3083-4(3))* 1st World Publishing, Inc.

Hopkins, Cathy. Mates, Dates, & Diamond Destiny. 2011. (Mates, Dates Ser.). (ENG.). 272p. (YA). (gr. 7). pap. 12.99 *(978-1-4424-3082-2(6)*, Simon Pulse) Simon Pulse.

Hopkins, Ellen. Crank. 2013. lib. bdg. 24.50 *(978-0-606-35118-8(3))* Turtleback Bks.

Howe, Tina Field. Alysa of the Fields: Book One in the Tellings of Xunar-kun. 2006. (Illus.). 320p. (YA). pap. 16.95 *(978-0-9768585-1-5(7)*, 002) Howe, Tina Field.

Ice Water Press Staff. Secrets of the Deep. 2010. (J). pap. *(978-1-921639-95-1(4))* Ripley Entertainment, Inc.

Jacobs, Evan. Varsity 170, 1 vol., Bk. 10. 2015. (Gravel Road Ser.). (ENG.). (YA). (gr. 9-12). pap. 9.95 *(978-1-62250-889-1(0))* Saddleback Educational Publishing, Inc.

Johnson, Alaya Dawn. Love Is the Drug. 2014. (YA). pap. *(978-0-545-41782-2(1))*; (ENG.). 352p. (J). (gr. 9). 17.99 *(978-0-545-41781-5(3)*, Levine, Arthur A. Bks.) Scholastic, Inc.

Johnson, Angela. All This & Heaven Too: Heaven; the First Part Last; Sweet, Hereafter. 2013. (ENG., Illus.). 400p. (YA). (gr. 7). pap. 10.99 *(978-1-4424-8719-2(4)*, Simon & Schuster Bks. For Young Readers) Simon & Schuster Bks. For Young Readers.

Johnston, Jeffry W. Fragments. 2007. (ENG.). 208p. (YA). (gr. 7). per. 6.99 *(978-1-4169-2486-9(8)*, Simon Pulse) Simon Pulse.

Jones, Don. When the Firewood Comes. 2009. 86p. pap. 19.95 *(978-1-4489-9667-4(8))* America Star Bks.

Jones, Frewin. The Seventh Daughter. 2009. (Faerie Path Ser.: 3). (ENG.). 352p. (YA). (gr. 8). pap. 9.99 *(978-0-06-087110-9(5)*, HarperTeen) HarperCollins Pubs.

Jones, Kari. Shimmy, 1 vol. 2015. (Orca Limelights Ser.). (ENG.). 144p. (J). (gr. 6-9). pap. 9.95 *(978-1-4598-0764-8(2))* Orca Bk. Pubs. USA.

Judge, Emma. Ink Stained Hands. 2010. (ENG.). 96p. pap. *(978-1-907629-12-9(2))* ShieldCrest.

Karasyov, Carrie & Kargman, Jill. Jet Set. 2008. 256p. (J). (gr. 7-18). 16.99 *(978-0-06-143177-7(X))* HarperCollins Pubs.

Keane, Danni. No Big Deal. (ENG., Illus.). (J). 2016. 24.99 ***(978-1-63533-051-9(3))*** 2015. 186p. pap. 14.99 *(978-1-63216-723-1(9))* Dreamspinner Pr. (Harmony Ink Pr.).

Kearns, Ann. Dell's Discovery. 2006. 108p. (YA). per. 9.95 *(978-0-9710696-6-4(2))* Jordan Publishing, Inc.

Kellogg, Elijah. The Young Shipbuilders of Elm Island by Rev Elijah Kellogg. 2006. 316p. per. 23.99 *(978-1-4255-3063-1(X))* Michigan Publishing.

Kendall, Grace, ed. I See Reality: Twelve Short Stories about Real Life. 2016. (ENG.). 304p. (YA). 17.99 *(978-0-374-30258-0(8)*, 9780374302580, Farrar, Straus & Giroux (BYR)) Farrar, Straus & Giroux.

Keswick, Kitty. Freaksville. Cox, Val, illus. 2010. 328p. (YA). (gr. 8-12). pap. 16.99 *(978-1-61603-001-8(1))* Leap Bks.

Kijinski, Paul. Camp Limestone. 2006. (Illus.). 104p. (YA). per. 7.99 *(978-1-59958-016-6(0))* Journey Stone Creations, LLC.

King, Katina. Ride Wit' Me: A Young Adult Urban Tale. 2006. 144p. (J). per. 12.00 *(978-0-9724003-8-1(9))* Power Play Media.

Komorn, Julie, adapted by. Out of the Dark. 2004. (W. I. T. C. H. Ser.: Bk. 8). (Illus.). 128p. (J). lib. bdg. 16.92 *(978-1-4242-0789-3(4))* Fitzgerald Bks.

Komorn, Julie & Lenhard, Elizabeth, adapted by. The Light of Meridian. 2004. (W. I. T. C. H. Ser.: Bk. 7). (Illus.). 144p. (J). lib. bdg. 16.92 *(978-1-4242-0794-7(0))* Fitzgerald Bks.

Kopple, Deborah, ed. Heads in the Ground: Short Stories by Norwalk High School Honor's English Students. 2008. 188p. pap. 13.95 *(978-0-595-50775-7(1))* iUniverse, Inc.

Kravetz, Stacy. The Fosters: Keep Your Frenemies Close. 2015. (ENG.). 224p. (YA). (gr. 7-12). pap. 9.99 *(978-1-4847-1620-5(5))* Hyperion Bks. for Children.

Laidlaw, S. J. Fifteen Lanes. 2016. (ENG., Illus.). 302p. (YA). (gr. 9). 17.99 *(978-1-101-91780-0(6)*, Tundra Bks.) Tundra Bks. CAN. Dist: Penguin Random Hse. LLC.

Lancett, Peter. Seeing Red, 1 vol. unabr. ed. 2012. (Cutting Edge Ser.). (ENG.). 221p. (YA). (gr. 9-12). pap. 9.95 *(978-1-61651-759-5(X))* Saddleback Educational Publishing, Inc.

Lange, Erin Jade. Rebel, Bully, Geek, Pariah. 2016. (ENG.). 320p. (YA). 17.99 *(978-1-61963-498-5(8)*, 9781619634985, Bloomsbury USA Childrens) Bloomsbury Publishing USA.

Langston, Laura. Hot New Thing, 1 vol. 2014. (Orca Limelights Ser.). (ENG.). 136p. (J). (gr. 6-9). pap. 9.95 *(978-1-4598-0431-9(7))* Orca Bk. Pubs. USA.

Laughton, Geoff. Under the Stars. 2016. (ENG., Illus.). (J). 24.99 ***(978-1-63477-986-9(X)***, Harmony Ink Pr.) Dreamspinner Pr.

Layboume, Emmy. Monument 14. 2012. (Monument 14 Ser.: 1). (ENG.). 304p. (YA). (gr. 8-13). 17.99 *(978-0-312-56903-7(3)*, 9780312569037) Feiwel & Friends.

—Monument 14. 2013. (Monument 14 Ser.: 1). (ENG.). 352p. (YA). (gr. 8-13). pap. 10.99 *(978-1-250-02738-2(1)*, 9781250027382) Square Fish.

—Sky on Fire. 2013. (Monument 14 Ser.: 2). (YA). (ENG.). 224p. (gr. 8-13). 18.99 *(978-0-312-56904-4(1)*, 9780312569044); vi, 217p. *(978-1-4449-1765-9(X))* Feiwel & Friends.

Lee, J. A. The Trials of Edward Finlay. 2010. 223p. pap. 15.99 *(978-0-557-36757-3(3))* Lulu Pr., Inc.

Lenhard, Elizabeth. A Bridge Between Worlds. 2004. (W. I. T. C. H. Ser.: Bk. 10). 158p. (J). lib. bdg. 16.92 *(978-1-4242-0796-1(7))* Fitzgerald Bks.

—The Disappearance. 2004. (W. I. T. C. H. Ser.: Bk. 2). 158p. (J). lib. bdg. 16.92 *(978-1-4242-0799-2(1))* Fitzgerald Bks.

—Finding Meridian. 2004. (W. I. T. C. H. Ser.: Bk. 3). 158p. (J). lib. bdg. 16.92 *(978-1-4242-0801-2(7))* Fitzgerald Bks.

—Power of Five. 2004. 158p. (J). lib. bdg. 16.92 *(978-1-4242-0795-4(9))* Fitzgerald Bks.

Lenhard, Elizabeth, adapted by. The Disappearance. 2004. (W. I. T. C. H. Ser.). (Illus.). 144p. (J). 12.65 *(978-0-7569-4620-3(4))* Perfection Learning Corp.

—The Return of a Queen. 2004. (W. I. T. C. H. Ser.: Bk. 12). 152p. (J). lib. bdg. 16.92 *(978-1-4242-0797-8(5))* Fitzgerald Bks.

Leno, Katrina. Everything All at Once. 2017. 368p. (YA). (gr. 8). 17.99 *(978-0-06-249309-5(4)*, HarperTeen) HarperCollins Pubs.

Levithan, David. Boy Meets Boy. 2005. (ENG.). 224p. (YA). (gr. 7-12). reprint ed. per. 9.99 *(978-0-375-83299-4(8)*, Ember) Random Hse. Children's Bks.

Lewis, Linda. All for the Love of That Boy. 2007. (ENG.). 224p. (YA). (gr. 7). pap. 12.95 *(978-1-4169-6142-0(9)*, Simon Pulse) Simon Pulse.

Leznoff, Glenda. Heartache & Other Natural Shocks. 2015. (ENG., Illus.). 382p. (YA). (gr. 9). 19.99 *(978-1-77049-836-5(2)*, Tundra Bks.) Tundra Bks. CAN. Dist: Penguin Random Hse. LLC.

Lindquist, N. J. A Friend in Need. 2016. (Circle of Friends Ser.: Vol. 3). (ENG., Illus.). (YA). pap. ***(978-1-927692-06-6(7))*** That's Life! Communications.

—More Than a Friend. 2016. (Circle of Friends Ser.: Vol. 4). (ENG., Illus.). (YA). pap. ***(978-1-927692-07-3(5))*** That's Life! Communications.

—With Friends Like These. 2016. (Circle of Friends Ser.: Vol. 2). (ENG., Illus.). (YA). pap. ***(978-1-927692-05-9(9))*** That's Life! Communications.

Litrel, Suzanne M. Jackie Tempo & the Emperor's Seal. 2007. 172p. (YA). per. 13.95 *(978-0-595-46822-5(5))* iUniverse, Inc.

Lobdell, Scott. The Opposite Numbers. Rendon, Daniel et al, illus. 2006. 111p. (J). *(978-1-4156-9815-0(5))* Papercutz.
Lohans, Alison. Laws of Emotion. 2006. (ENG.). 207p. mass mkt. 9.95 *(978-1-895449-07-5(3))* Thistledown Pr., Ltd. CAN. Dist: Univ. of Toronto Pr.
Lovelace, Eloise. I Was a Boy Just Like You. 2011. 36p. pap. 15.14 *(978-1-4634-4378-8(1))* AuthorHouse.
Lynch, Chris. I Pledge Allegiance. 2011. (Vietnam Ser.: 1). (ENG.). 192p. (J). (gr. 3-7). 16.99 *(978-0-545-27029-8(4)*, Scholastic Pr.) Scholastic, Inc.
MacKay, Andrew. Young Lions Roar. 2012. 316p. pap. *(978-1-909395-27-5(7))* Legend Pr.
Maracle, Lee. Will's Garden. 2nd rev. ed. 2008. (ENG.). 194p. pap. 16.95 *(978-1-894778-59-6(6))* Theytus Bks., Ltd. CAN. Dist: Univ. of Toronto Pr.
Marchetta, Melina. Jellicoe Road. 2008. (ENG.). 432p. (YA). (gr. 9-18). 17.99 *(978-0-06-143183-8(4)*, HarperTeen) HarperCollins Pubs.
Margaret Penrose. Dorothy Dale's Queer Holidays. l.t. ed. 2007. (ENG.). 174p. pap. 21.99 *(978-1-4264-8931-0(5))* Creative Media Partners, LLC.
Marriott, Zoë. The Name of the Blade. 2014. (ENG.). 368p. (YA). (gr. 7). 16.99 *(978-0-7636-6957-7(1))* Candlewick Pr.
Maskame, Estelle. Did I Mention I Miss You? 2016. (Did I Mention I Love You (DIMILY) Ser.: 3). (ENG.). 352p. (YA). (gr. 8-12). pap. 10.99 *(978-1-4926-3221-4(X)*, 9781492632214) Sourcebooks, Inc.
Mason, Jane B. Without Annette. 2016. (ENG.). 336p. (YA). (gr. 7). 18.99 *(978-0-545-81995-4(4)*, Scholastic Pr.) Scholastic, Inc.
Mass, Wendy. 13 Gifts. 2013. (ENG.). 352p. (J). (gr. 3-7). pap. 6.99 *(978-0-545-31004-8(0))* Scholastic, Inc.
Matagrano, Joseph F. Forever Brothers. 2007. 396p. 26.95 *(978-1-4327-0963-1(1))*; per. 16.95 *(978-1-4327-1524-3(0))* Outskirts Pr., Inc.
Mattel Inc. Staff & Finn, Perdita. Ever after High. 2016. (ENG., Illus.). 32p. (J). (gr. -1-3). pap. 3.99 *(978-0-316-35677-0(8))* Little, Brown Bks. for Young Readers.
Mbuyazi, Phiwayinkosi G. The Wiby Kids - How It All Began. 2011. 204p. pap. 12.99 *(978-1-61667-337-6(0))* Raider Publishing International.
McCaffrey, Kate. Destroying Avalon. 2006. (ENG.). 240p. (J). pap. 13.00 *(978-1-921064-57-9(9))* Fremantle Pr. AUS. Dist: Independent Pubs. Group.
McCorkle, Mark & Schooley, Bob. Grudge Match. 2005. (Illus.). 80p. (J). *(978-1-4155-9100-0(8))* Disney Pr.
McCormick, Patricia. Sold. 2008. (ENG.). 272p. (J). (gr. 7-17). pap. 8.99 *(978-0-7868-5172-0(4))* Hyperion Pr.
McCormick, Wilfred. Quick Kick: A Bronc Burnett Story. 2011. 192p. 42.95 *(978-1-258-10149-7(1))* Literary Licensing, LLC.
—The Three-Two Pitch: A Bronc Burnett Story. 2011. 192p. 42.95 *(978-1-258-10008-7(8))* Literary Licensing, LLC.
McCreight, Kimberly. The Outliers. (Outliers Ser.: 1). (YA). (gr. 9). 2017. 368p. pap. 9.99 *(978-0-06-235910-0(X))* 2016. (ENG.). 352p. 18.99 *(978-0-06-235909-4(6))* HarperCollins Pubs.
McDonald, Abby. Sophomore Switch. 2010. (ENG., Illus.). 304p. (YA). (gr. 9). pap. 8.99 *(978-0-7636-4774-2(8))* Candlewick Pr.
Mcgill, Leslie. Gearhead. 2015. (Cap Central Ser.: 4). (YA). lib. bdg. 20.80 *(978-0-606-36839-1(6))* Turtleback Bks.
McPhee, Peter. Every Move, 1 vol. 2004. (Lorimer SideStreets Ser.). (ENG.). 184p. (YA). (gr. 9-12). 9.95 *(978-1-55028-850-6(4)*, 9781550288506) Lorimer, James & Co., Ltd., Pubs. CAN. Dist: Casemate Pubs. & Bk. Distributors, LLC.
Mechling, Lauren & Moser, Laura. Foreign Exposure: The Social Climber Abroad. 2007. (ENG.). 320p. (YA). (gr. 7-18). pap. 18.95 *(978-0-618-66379-8(7))* Houghton Mifflin Harcourt Publishing Co.
Meyer, Marissa. Cress. 2014. 552p. (YA). *(978-1-250-05632-0(2))* Feiwel & Friends.
Meyer, Stephanie H. & Meyer, John. Teen Ink: Written in the Dirt: A Collection of Short Stories, Poetry, Art & Photography. 2004. (ENG., Illus.). 360p. (YA). pap. 12.95 *(978-0-7573-0050-9(2)*, HCI Teens) Health Communications, Inc.
Mitchell, Randall. Teenership: Leadership for Teens. 2013. 112p. 29.99 *(978-1-4797-7767-9(6))*; pap. 19.99 *(978-1-4797-7766-2(8))* Xlibris Corp.
Morgan, Marlo. Making the Message Mine. Grimme, Jeannette, ed. Garrison, Carri, illus. Date not set. 115p. (Orig.). (YA). pap. *(978-1-883473-01-3(2))* MM Co.
Myers, Sharon A. Slumber Party. 2009. 73p. 24.99 *(978-1-4415-9854-7(5))*; pap. 15.99 *(978-1-4415-9853-0(7))* Xlibris Corp.
Nayeri, Daniel and Dina. Another Faust. 2010. (ENG., Illus.). 400p. (YA). (gr. 9). pap. 8.99 *(978-0-7636-4834-3(5))* Candlewick Pr.
Nazemian, Abdi. The Authentics. 2017. 288p. (YA). (gr. 8). 17.99 *(978-0-06-248646-2(2))* HarperCollins Pubs.
Nelson, Blake. Girl. 2007. (ENG.). 256p. (YA). (gr. 9-12). pap. 10.99 *(978-1-4169-4803-2(1)*, Simon Pulse) Simon Pulse.
Ness, Patrick. The Rest of Us Just Live Here. (YA). 2016. 336p. (gr. 9). pap. 9.99 *(978-0-06-240317-9(6)*, HarperTeen) 2015. (ENG.). 336p. (gr. 9-12). 17.99 *(978-0-06-240316-2(8)*, HarperTeen) 2015. 352p. *(978-1-4063-3116-5(3))* HarperCollins Pubs.
Nichols, Michael. Beating the Air. 2007. 176p. per. 24.95 *(978-1-4241-7795-0(2))* America Star Bks.
Nyman, Mary. High School Stories: Short Takes from the Writers' Club. 2010. 64p. pap. 8.95 *(978-1-4502-1585-5(8))* iUniverse, Inc.
Odentz, Howard. Wicked Dead. 2016. (ENG., Illus.). (YA). pap. 15.95 ***(978-1-61194-712-0(X))*** BelleBks., Inc.
On Thin Ice. 2005. per. *(978-0-9772505-2-3(0))* Adibooks.com.
Optic, Oliver, pseud. Outward Bound. 2007. 180p. (gr. 4-7). per. *(978-1-4068-4343-9(1))* Echo Library.
—Outward Bound: Or Young America Afloat. l.t. ed. 2007. (ENG.). 274p. pap. 23.99 *(978-1-4264-9153-5(0))* Creative Media Partners, LLC.
O'Shea, M.J. Blood Moon. 2016. (ENG., Illus.). (J). 24.99 ***(978-1-63477-941-8(X)**, Harmony Ink Pr.)* Dreamspinner Pr.
Parker, Mike. Break-In. 208p. pap. 6.95 *(978-0-86327-898-3(1))* Wolfhound Pr. IRL. Dist: Interlink Publishing Group, Inc.
Pastor, A. The Pearl Box: Containing One Hundred Beautiful Stories for Young People. 2007. (ENG.). 142p. pap. 18.99 *(978-1-4346-2865-7(5))*; 150p. pap. 19.99 *(978-1-4346-2873-2(6))* Creative Media Partners, LLC.
Pearson, Ridley. Kingdom Keepers the Return. 2017. (Kingdom Keepers Ser.). (ENG.). 480p. (J). (gr. 5-9). 17.99 *(978-1-4231-8433-1(5))* Hyperion Bks. for Children.
Penn, Astor. All the Devils Here. 2016. (ENG., Illus.). (YA). (gr. 8-12). 24.99 ***(978-1-63477-933-3(9)**,* Harmony Ink Pr.) Dreamspinner Pr.
Peymani, Christine. Super Starz Masquerade. 2007. (Illus.). 94p. (J). pap. *(978-0-439-91952-4(5))* Scholastic, Inc.
Pfitzenmaier, Audrey. Cheating Fate, 1 vol. 2008. (ENG.). 240p. (J). (gr. 8-18). pap. 12.95 *(978-1-897235-41-6(0))* Thistledown Pr., Ltd. CAN. Dist: Univ. of Toronto Pr.
Phelan, James. The Last Thirteen Book Six: 8. 2014. (ENG., Illus.). 192p. (J). pap. *(978-1-4431-3352-4(3))* Kane Miller.
Philips, A. If You Believe in Mermaids Don't Tell. 2007. 160p. per. 12.95 *(978-1-59858-359-5(X))* Dog Ear Publishing, LLC.
Pipkin, Bonnie. Aftercare Instructions. 2017. (ENG.). 368p. (YA). 17.99 *(978-1-250-11484-6(5)*, 9781250114846) Flatiron Bks.
Plotkin, Andy. The Black Block Legend. 2007. 64p. per. 19.95 *(978-1-4241-9190-1(4))* America Star Bks.
Plum, Amy. Dreamfall. 2017. (Dreamfall Ser.: 1). 288p. (YA). (gr. 9). 17.99 *(978-0-06-242987-2(6)*, HarperTeen) HarperCollins Pubs.
Polak, Monique. 121 Express, 1 vol. 2008. (Orca Currents Ser.). (ENG.). (J). (gr. 5-9). 144p. pap. 9.95 *(978-1-55143-976-1(X))*; 112p. lib. bdg. 16.95 *(978-1-55143-978-5(6))* Orca Bk. Pubs. USA.
Polikoff, Barbara Garland. Her Mother's Secret. 2012. (ENG.). 184p. (YA). pap. 14.99 *(978-0-9831938-7-6(8))* Allium Pr. of Chicago.
Poole-Carter, Rosemary. Juliette Ascending. 2007. (YA). pap. 14.00 *(978-1-929976-41-6(0)*, TOP) Top Pubns., Ltd.
Poulsen, David A. Last Sam's Cage. rev. ed. 2008. (ENG.). 222p. (YA). (gr. 9-18). per. *(978-1-55263-953-5(3))* Me to We.
Quince, Lia. Abby & Jules. 2009. *(978-1-933791-14-2(4))* Finial Publishing.
Rabb, Margo. Kissing in America. 2015. (ENG.). 400p. (YA). (gr. 9). 17.99 *(978-0-06-232237-1(0))* HarperCollins Pubs.
Raiku, Makoto. Animal Land 8. 2013. (Animal Land Ser.). (ENG., Illus.). 208p. (gr. 8-12). pap. 10.99 *(978-1-61262-250-7(X))* Kodansha America, Inc.
Ramsey, Jo. Blue Jeans & Sweatshirts. 2016. (ENG., Illus.). (J). 24.99 ***(978-1-63477-942-5(8)**,* Harmony Ink Pr.) Dreamspinner Pr.
Raymond, Jeanpaul. The Kids That Could. 2009. 40p. pap. 17.99 *(978-1-4389-5585-8(5))* AuthorHouse.
Reisfeld, Randi. Everyone Who's Anyone. 2007. (ENG.). 304p. (gr. 7-12). pap. 8.99 *(978-1-4231-0502-2(8))* Hyperion Pr.
Reyes, M. G. Emancipated. 2015. (Emancipated Ser.: 1). (ENG.). 400p. (YA). (gr. 9). 17.99 *(978-0-06-228895-0(4)*, Tegen, Katherine Bks) HarperCollins Pubs.
Ricci, Caitlin. Weathering the Storm. 2016. (ENG., Illus.). (J). 24.99 ***(978-1-63477-992-0(4))*** Dreamspinner Pr.
Rich, Juliann. Taking the Stand. 2015. (ENG.). 264p. (J). (gr. 7). pap. 11.95 *(978-1-62639-408-7(3))* Bold Strokes Bks.
Richards, Elizabeth. Wings. 2015. (Black City Novel Ser.: 3). (ENG.). 416p. (YA). (gr. 9). pap. 9.99 *(978-0-14-751140-9(2)*, Speak) Penguin Young Readers Group.
Riffe, Ruth. Survival Guide for the Teenage Life. Smith, Geoff & Aretha, David, eds. 2016. (ENG., Illus.). 124p. (J). pap. 12.49 *(978-1-61984-511-4(3))* Price World Publishing.
Ripley's Believe It or Not Editors & Ripley's Believe It Or Not! Staff. The Dragon's Triangle. 2010. (Rbi Ser.: 2). (ENG.). 128p. (J). pap. 4.99 *(978-1-893951-53-2(7))* Ripley Entertainment, Inc.
Ripley's Believe It Or Not! Staff. Running Wild. 2010. (Rbi Ser.: 3). (ENG.). 128p. (J). pap. 4.99 *(978-1-893951-55-6(3))* Ripley Entertainment, Inc.
—Secrets of the Deep. 2010. (Rbi Ser.: 4). (ENG.). 128p. (J). pap. 4.99 *(978-1-893951-54-9(5))* Ripley Entertainment, Inc.
Robins, Eleanor. Boy of Their Dreams, 1 vol. unabr. ed. 2011. (Carter High Chronicles Ser.). (ENG.). 51p. (YA). (gr. 9-12). pap. 7.95 *(978-1-61651-305-4(5))* Saddleback Educational Publishing, Inc.
—Double-Cross, 1 vol. unabr. ed. 2011. (Choices Ser.). (ENG.). 51p. (YA). (gr. 9-12). 7.95 *(978-1-61651-595-9(3))* Saddleback Educational Publishing, Inc.
—Friend or Foe?, 1 vol. unabr. ed. 2011. (Choices Ser.). (ENG.). 52p. (YA). (gr. 9-12). 7.95 *(978-1-61651-593-5(7))* Saddleback Educational Publishing, Inc.
—It Does Matter, 1 vol. unabr. ed. 2011. (Carter High Senior Year Ser.). (ENG.). 49p. (YA). (gr. 9-12). pap. 7.95 *(978-1-61651-324-5(1))* Saddleback Educational Publishing, Inc.
—It Is Not a Date, 1 vol. unabr. ed. 2011. (Carter High Chronicles Ser.). (ENG.). 51p. (YA). (gr. 9-12). pap. 7.95 *(978-1-61651-309-2(8))* Saddleback Educational Publishing, Inc.
—Just Be Yourself, 1 vol. unabr. ed. 2011. (Carter High Senior Year Ser.). (ENG.). 50p. (YA). (gr. 9-12). pap. 7.95 *(978-1-61651-325-2(X))* Saddleback Educational Publishing, Inc.
—The Last Time, 1 vol. unabr. ed. 2011. (Carter High Senior Year Ser.). (ENG.). 49p. (YA). (gr. 9-12). pap. 7.95 *(978-1-61651-326-9(8))* Saddleback Educational Publishing, Inc.
—No Exceptions, 1 vol. unabr. ed. 2011. (Choices Ser.). (ENG.). 52p. (YA). (gr. 9-12). 7.95 *(978-1-61651-597-3(X))* Saddleback Educational Publishing, Inc.
—No Limits, 1 vol. unabr. ed. 2011. (Choices Ser.). (ENG.). 52p. (YA). (gr. 9-12). 7.95 *(978-1-61651-598-0(8))* Saddleback Educational Publishing, Inc.
—One Date Too Many, 1 vol. unabr. ed. 2011. (Carter High Chronicles Ser.). (ENG.). 50p. (YA). (gr. 9-12). pap. 7.95 *(978-1-61651-310-8(1))* Saddleback Educational Publishing, Inc.
—One More Chance, 1 vol. unabr. ed. 2011. (Carter High Senior Year Ser.). (ENG.). 51p. (YA). (gr. 9-12). pap. 7.95 *(978-1-61651-327-6(6))* Saddleback Educational Publishing, Inc.
—The Secret Admirer Mystery, 1 vol. unabr. ed. 2011. (Carter High Mysteries Ser.). (ENG.). 48p. (YA). (gr. 9-12). 7.95 *(978-1-61651-567-6(8))* Saddleback Educational Publishing, Inc.
—Someone to Count, 1 vol. unabr. ed. 2011. (Carter High Senior Year Ser.). (ENG.). 50p. (YA). (gr. 9-12). pap. 7.95 *(978-1-61651-328-3(4))* Saddleback Educational Publishing, Inc.
—Time to Move On, 1 vol. unabr. ed. 2011. (Carter High Senior Year Ser.). (ENG.). 50p. (YA). (gr. 9-12). pap. 7.95 *(978-1-61651-329-0(2))* Saddleback Educational Publishing, Inc.
—Too Late, 1 vol. unabr. ed. 2011. (Carter High Chronicles Ser.). (ENG.). 52p. (YA). (gr. 9-12). pap. 7.95 *(978-1-61651-312-2(8))* Saddleback Educational Publishing, Inc.
—The Worst Year Ever, 1 vol. unabr. ed. 2011. (Carter High Senior Year Ser.). (ENG.). 50p. (YA). (gr. 9-12). pap. 7.95 *(978-1-61651-330-6(6))* Saddleback Educational Publishing, Inc.
—The Wrong Way, 1 vol. unabr. ed. 2011. (Carter High Senior Year Ser.). (ENG.). 52p. (YA). (gr. 9-12). pap. 7.95 *(978-1-61651-331-3(4))* Saddleback Educational Publishing, Inc.
Robinson, Gwen G. The Jensen Case. 2010. (Illus.). 228p. pap. *(978-0-7552-0496-0(4))* Authors OnLine, Ltd.
Roecker, Lisa & Roecker, Laura. The Liar Society. 2011. (Liar Society Ser.: 1). (ENG.). 368p. (YA). (gr. 7-12). pap. 9.99 *(978-1-4022-5633-2(7))* Sourcebooks, Inc.
Roman, Annette. 1 World Manga, Vol. 5. Ng, Leandro, illus. 2007. (1 World Manga Ser.). (ENG.). 240p. pap. 3.99 *(978-1-4215-1169-6(X))* Viz Media.
Ryan, Ann. The Little Wannabee. Ryan, Ann, illus. 2006. (ENG., Illus.). 24p. (J). 16.95 *(978-1-933660-31-8(7)*, Tadpole Pr. 4 Kids) Smooth Sailing Pr., LLC.
Ryan, Darlene. Five Minutes More, 1 vol. 2009. (ENG.). 224p. (YA). (gr. 7-12). pap. 12.95 *(978-1-55469-006-0(4))* Orca Bk. Pubs. USA.
Ryan, Darlene & Fernández, Queta. De Nadie Mas, 1 vol. 2008. (Spanish Soundings Ser.). (SPA.). 112p. (YA). (gr. 8-12). pap. 9.95 *(978-1-55143-969-3(7))* Orca Bk. Pubs. USA.
Ryan, Patrick. Gemini Bites. 2011. (ENG.). 240p. (J). (gr. 7-8). 17.99 *(978-0-545-22128-3(5)*, Scholastic Pr.) Scholastic, Inc.
Ryan, Tom. Totally Unrelated, 1 vol. 2013. (Orca Limelights Ser.). (J). (ENG.). 128p. (gr. 6-9). pap. 9.95 *(978-1-4598-0458-6(9))*; 120p. *(978-1-4598-0648-1(4))* Orca Bk. Pubs. USA.
—Way to Go, 1 vol. 2012. (ENG.). 224p. (YA). (gr. 8-12). pap. 12.95 *(978-1-4598-0077-9(X))* Orca Bk. Pubs. USA.
Sadd, Kenn. Crazy Cracked Pots. 2009. 144p. pap. 24.95 *(978-1-61546-673-3(8))* America Star Bks.
Saddleback Educational Publishing Staff, ed. Boy of Their Dreams. 2011. (Carter High Chronicles Ser.). (ENG.). 16p. (YA). (gr. 9-12). tchr. ed. 7.95 incl. cd-rom *(978-1-61651-315-3(2))* Saddleback Educational Publishing, Inc.
—Don't Blame Me. 2011. (Carter High Chronicles Ser.). (ENG.). 16p. (YA). (gr. 9-12). tchr. ed. 7.95 incl. cd-rom *(978-1-61651-317-7(9))* Saddleback Educational Publishing, Inc.
—The Easy Way. 2011. (Carter High Chronicles Ser.). (ENG.). 16p. (YA). (gr. 9-12). tchr. ed. 7.95 incl. cd-rom *(978-1-61651-316-0(0))* Saddleback Educational Publishing, Inc.
—One Date Too Many. 2011. (Carter High Chronicles Ser.). (ENG.). 16p. (YA). (gr. 9-12). tchr. ed. 7.95 incl. cd-rom *(978-1-61651-320-7(9))* Saddleback Educational Publishing, Inc.
—Right Kind of Win. 2011. (Carter High Chronicles Ser.). (ENG.). 16p. (YA). (gr. 9-12). cd-rom 7.95 *(978-1-61651-321-4(7))* Saddleback Educational Publishing, Inc.
—Twister, 1 vol. unabr. ed. 2011. (Heights Ser.). (ENG.). 49p. (gr. 5-8). 7.95 *(978-1-61651-626-0(7))* Saddleback Educational Publishing, Inc.
Saunders, Harry M. Teenagers on an Adventure: Journey of Two Boys & a Girl. 2013. 168p. pap. 19.95 *(978-1-62709-466-5(0))* America Star Bks.
Sawyer, Kim Vogel. Katy's Debate, 1 vol. 2015. (Katy Lambright Ser.). (ENG.). 208p. (YA). pap. 9.99 *(978-0-310-74755-0(4))* Zondervan.
—Katy's Decision, 1 vol. 2015. (Katy Lambright Ser.). (ENG.). 208p. (YA). pap. 9.99 *(978-0-310-74850-2(X))* Zondervan.
—Katy's Homecoming, 1 vol. 2015. (Katy Lambright Ser.). (ENG.). 208p. (YA). pap. 9.99 *(978-0-310-74835-9(6))* Zondervan.
—Katy's New World, 1 vol. 2015. (Katy Lambright Ser.). (ENG.). 208p. (YA). pap. 9.99 *(978-0-310-74782-6(1))* Zondervan.
Schaeffer, Teresa. The Questions Within, 1 vol. unabr. ed. 2012. (Cutting Edge Ser.). (ENG.). 143p. (YA). (gr. 9-12). pap. 9.95 *(978-1-61651-760-1(3))* Saddleback Educational Publishing, Inc.
Scheidies, Carolyn R. My Summer Journel: the Rescue. 2007. 96p. pap. 14.99 *(978-0-615-16029-0(8))* C R Pubns.
Schmatz, Pat. Lizard Radio. 2015. (ENG.). 288p. (YA). (gr. 9). 16.99 *(978-0-7636-7635-3(7))* Candlewick Pr.
Schraff, Anne. Leap of Faith, 1 vol. unabr. ed. 2011. (Urban Underground Ser.). (ENG.). 201p. (YA). (gr. 9-12). pap. 9.95 *(978-1-61651-588-1(0))* Saddleback Educational Publishing, Inc.
—The Lost, 1 vol. unabr. ed. 2011. (Urban Underground Ser.). (ENG.). 198p. (YA). (gr. 9-12). pap. 9.95 *(978-1-61651-585-0(6))* Saddleback Educational Publishing, Inc.
—The Quality of Mercy, 1 vol. unabr. ed. 2011. (Urban Underground Ser.). (ENG.). 183p. (YA). (gr. 9-12). pap. 9.95 *(978-1-61651-006-0(4))* Saddleback Educational Publishing, Inc.
—The Unforgiven, 1 vol. unabr. ed. 2011. (Urban Underground Ser.). (ENG.). 198p. (YA). (gr. 9-12). pap. 9.95 *(978-1-61651-586-7(4))* Saddleback Educational Publishing, Inc.
—Urban Underground Class Set. 2010. (J). pap. 119.50 *(978-1-61651-012-1(9))* Saddleback Educational Publishing, Inc.
—Urban Underground Complete Set. 2010. (J). pap. 190.20 *(978-1-61651-011-4(0))* Saddleback Educational Publishing, Inc.
—Waters Edge, 1 vol. unabr. ed. 2011. (Urban Underground Ser.). (ENG.). 197p. (YA). (gr. 9-12). pap. 9.95 *(978-1-61651-589-8(9))* Saddleback Educational Publishing, Inc.
—Wildflower, 1 vol. unabr. ed. 2011. (Urban Underground Ser.). (ENG.). 183p. (YA). (gr. 9-12). pap. 9.95 *(978-1-61651-009-1(9))* Saddleback Educational Publishing, Inc.
Scott, Jerry. Shredded. Borgman, Jim, illus. 2014. (Zits Ser.: 2). (ENG.). 224p. (YA). (gr. 8). pap. 9.99 *(978-0-06-222853-6(6)*, HarperTeen) HarperCollins Pubs.
Seib, Anke & Cameron, Emma. Out of This Place. 2013. (ENG.). 416p. (YA). (gr. 9). 17.99 *(978-0-7636-6404-6(9))* Candlewick Pr.
Self, Jeffery. Drag Teen. 2016. (ENG.). 272p. (YA). (gr. 9). 17.99 *(978-0-545-82993-9(3)*, PUSH) Scholastic, Inc.
Shaw, Esther. The Winter Mare. 2005. (ENG., Illus.). 198p. pap. *(978-1-84401-447-7(9))* Athena Pr.
Shepard, Sara. Ali's Pretty Little Lies. 2013. (Pretty Little Liars Companion Novel Ser.). (ENG.). 320p. (YA). (gr. 9). pap. 9.99 *(978-0-06-223337-0(8)*, HarperTeen) HarperCollins Pubs.
Sherrard, Valerie. Sam's Light. 2004. (ENG.). 200p. (YA). pap. 8.99 *(978-1-55002-535-4(X))* Dundurn CAN. Dist: Ingram Publisher Services.
Siegert, Mia. Jerkbait. 2016. (ENG.). 350p. (YA). (gr. 8). pap. 14.99 *(978-1-63163-066-8(0)*, Jolly Fish Pr.) North Star Editions.
Simone, Ni-Ni. Dear Yvette. 2016. (Throwback Diaries). (ENG., Illus.). 288p. (YA). (gr. 9). pap. 9.95 *(978-0-7582-8776-2(3)*, Dafina) Kensington Publishing Corp.
Sividious Stark & the Stadium Between Worlds. 2013. (ENG.). 236p. (YA). pap. 12.99 *(978-1-62108-273-6(3))* Covenant Communications, Inc.
Skogen, Jennifer. Sinews of Thy Heart #4. 2015. (Haunting of Grey Hills Ser.). (ENG.). 200-216p. (J). (gr. 9-12). lib. bdg. 27.13 *(978-1-68076-032-3(7)*, 1391657, Epic Pr.) ABDO Publishing Co.
Smith, Mary P. Wells. The Young Puritans in King Philip's War. Bridgman, L. J., illus. 2011. 396p. 54.95 *(978-1-258-05550-9(3))* Literary Licensing, LLC.
Smith, Naiya. Pinky Swear: The Heart Wants What the Heart Wants. 2012. 120p. (gr. 10-12). 23.99 *(978-1-4772-6552-9(X))*; pap. 14.95 *(978-1-4772-6554-3(6))* AuthorHouse.
Soto, Gary. Hey 13! 2011. (ENG.). 256p. (J). 16.95 *(978-0-8234-2395-8(6))* Holiday Hse., Inc.
Squires, Megan. The Rules of Regret, 0 vols. 2014. (ENG.). 290p. (YA). (gr. 9-12). pap. 9.99 *(978-1-4778-2488-7(X)*, 9781477824887, Skyscape) Amazon Publishing.
Stevenson, Robert Louis. Kidnapped & Catriona. 2007. (ENG.). 496p. per. *(978-1-84697-033-7(4))* Birlinn, Ltd.
Stevenson, Robin. The World Without Us. 2014. 240p. pap. *(978-1-4598-0681-8(6))* Orca Bk. Pubs.
Stinson, Kathy. 101 Ways to Dance, 1 vol. 2007. (ENG.). 176p. (YA). (gr. 8-12). pap. 10.95 *(978-1-897187-10-4(6))* Second Story Pr. CAN. Dist: Orca Bk. Pubs. USA.
Stone, Vicki L. Why Should I Stay A Virgin? 2004. 74p. (YA). per. *(978-1-59196-850-4(X))* Instant Pub.
The Strange & Beautiful Sorrows of Ava Lavender. 2014. 320p. (J). (gr. 9). E-Book 8.99 *(978-0-7636-7034-4(0))* Candlewick Pr.
Strasser, Todd & Thacker, Nola. The Shore: Shirt & Shoes Not Required; LB (Laguna Beach) 2011. (ENG.). 480p. (YA). (gr. 9). pap. 9.99 *(978-1-4424-1970-4(9)*, Simon Pulse) Simon Pulse.
Suarez, Maria. Mr Giggles. 2011. 20p. pap. 24.95 *(978-1-4626-3617-4(9))* America Star Bks.
Sullivan, Jenny. Nowhere Again. 2004. (ENG.). 230p. pap. 13.95 *(978-1-84323-297-1(9))* Beekman Bks., Inc.
Summer, Mary Elizabeth. Trust Me, I'm Lying. 2015. (ENG.). 352p. (YA). (gr. 7). pap. 9.99 *(978-0-385-74413-3(7)*, Ember) Random Hse. Children's Bks.
Swindells, Pat. Junk Food Hero. 2010. (ENG., Illus.). 280p. (J). (gr. 6). pap. 18.95 *(978-1-906582-02-9(5))* Aurora Metro Pubns. Ltd. GBR. Dist: Consortium Bk. Sales & Distribution.
Taylor, Drew Hayden. The Night Wanderer: A Native Gothic Novel. Wyatt, Michael, illus. 2007. (ENG.). 228p. (YA). (gr. 7-12). 21.95 *(978-1-55451-100-6(3)*, 9781554511006); 5th ed. pap. 12.95 *(978-1-55451-099-3(6)*, 9781554510993) Annick Pr., Ltd. CAN. Dist: Publishers Group West (PGW).
Terrell, Brandon. Second Chance Delivery. 2016. (Tartan House Ser.). (ENG., Illus.). 96p. (J). (gr. 5-12). pap. 9.95 *(978-1-63235-205-7(2)*, 12-Story Library) Pr. Room Editions LLC.
Terry, Chris L. Zero Fade. Knabb, Jacob & Vance, Leonard, eds. 2013. (ENG., Illus.). 294p. (gr. 6). pap. 12.00 *(978-0-9884804-3-8(3)*, 1362831) Curbside Splendor Publishing.
Thomley, Rebecca Gundersen. I Know He Is There: A Lift-A-Flap Book about Faith. Dorman, Brandon, illus. 2006. (J). *(978-1-59038-550-0(0))* Deseret Bk. Co.
Tibbets, Albert B. Youth, Youth, Youth: Stories of Challenge, Confidence & Comradeship. Tibbets, Albert B., ed. 2011. 256p. 47.95 *(978-1-258-05880-7(4))* Literary Licensing, LLC.
Tiernan, Cate. Awakening. 2007. (Sweep Ser.: 5). (ENG.). 192p. (YA). (gr. 7-18). pap. 7.99 *(978-0-14-241020-2(9)*, Speak) Penguin Young Readers Group.
—Book of Shadows - The Coven - Blood Witch. 2010. (Sweep Ser.: 1). (ENG.). 592p. (YA). (gr. 7-18). 8.99 *(978-0-14-241717-1(3)*, Speak) Penguin Young Readers Group.
Torres, J. Degrassi the Next Generation Extra Credit Suddenly, Last Summer. Northcott, Ed, illus. 2nd ed. 2006. (Degrassi the Next Generation Ser.). (ENG.). 128p. (J). pap. *(978-1-55168-320-1(2))* Fenn, H. B. & Co., Ltd.
—In My House. Rolston, Steve, illus. 4th ed. 2007. (Degrassi the Next Generation Ser.). (ENG.). 120p. (J). pap. *(978-1-55168-303-4(2))* Fenn, H. B. & Co., Ltd.
—Titans Together. 2014. (ENG., Illus.). 144p. (J). (gr. 2-5). pap. 12.99 *(978-1-4012-5367-7(9))* DC Comics.
Torres, J. & Kim, Eric. Missing You. 3rd ed. 2007. (Degrassi the Next Generation Ser.). (ENG., Illus.). 120p. (J). pap. *(978-1-55168-301-0(6))* Fenn, H. B. & Co., Ltd.

Tracey, Rhian. Isla & Luke: Make or Break? 2004. (ENG.). 1p. (J). pap. 12.95 *(978-0-7475-6649-6(6))* Bloomsbury Publishing Plc GBR. Dist: Independent Pubs. Group.

Ure, Jean. Gone Missing. 2007. (ENG., Illus.). 192p. (J). (gr. 4-7). pap. 8.99 *(978-0-00-722459-3(1)*, HarperCollins Children's Bks.) HarperCollins Pubs. Ltd. GBR. Dist: HarperCollins Pubs.

Van Dyne, Edith. Mary Louise. 2007. (ENG.). 148p. pap. 18.99 *(978-1-4264-1952-2(X))*; 144p. pap. 19.99 *(978-1-4264-2063-4(3))* Creative Media Partners, LLC.

Van Syckle, A. & Schwartz, Josh. The OC: 'twas the Night Before Chrismukkah. 2005. 206p. (YA). *(978-1-4156-3915-3(9))* Scholastic, Inc.

Varrato, Tony. Outrage. Doherty, Catherine, illus. 2007. (HIP Edge Ser.). 112p. (YA). (gr. 7-18). pap. *(978-1-897039-28-1(X))* High Interest Publishing (HIP).

Waite, Judy. Game Girls. 2007. (ENG.). 352p. (YA). (gr. 7). pap. 13.95 *(978-1-84270-618-3(7))* Andersen Pr. GBR. Dist: Independent Pubs. Group.

Walmsley, Tom. Kid Stuff: A Novel. 2004. (ENG.). 288p. 17.95 *(978-1-55152-153-4(9)*, 187) Arsenal Pulp Pr. CAN. Dist: Consortium Bk. Sales & Distribution.

Walters, Eric. Alexandria of Africa. 2008. (ENG.). 208p. (J). (gr. 7). pap. 12.95 *(978-0-385-66639-8(X)*, Doubleday Canada) Penguin Random House Canada Young Readers CAN. Dist: Penguin Random Hse. LLC.

—Splat!, 1 vol. 2008. (Orca Currents Ser.). (ENG.). (J). (gr. 5-9). 128p. pap. 9.95 *(978-1-55143-986-0(7))*; 112p. lib. bdg. 16.95 *(978-1-55143-988-4(3))* Orca Bk. Pubs. USA.

Walters, Gregory. Fouling Out, 1 vol. 2008. (ENG.). 176p. (J). (gr. 5-10). pap. 8.95 *(978-1-55143-714-9(7))* Orca Bk. Pubs. USA.

Walton, Leslye. The Strange & Beautiful Sorrows of Ava Lavender. (ENG.). 320p. (YA). (gr. 9). 2015. pap. 8.99 *(978-0-7636-8027-5(3))* 2014. 17.99 *(978-0-7636-6566-1(5))* Candlewick Pr.

—The Strange & Beautiful Sorrows of Ava Lavender. 2015. lib. bdg. 19.65 *(978-0-606-36879-7(5))* Turtleback Bks.

Warren, Bertie. Sammie's Journey to Freedom. 2006. (ENG.). 52p. per. 16.95 *(978-1-4241-5142-4(2))* America Star Bks.

Welford, Sue. Nowhere to Run. l.t. ed. 2006. 180p. per. *(978-1-905665-15-0(6))* Pollinger In Print.

—Secret Love. l.t. ed. 2006. pap. *(978-1-905665-10-5(5))* Pollinger In Print.

Westerfeld, Scott. Bogus to Bubbly: An Insider's Guide to the World of Uglies. Phillips, Craig, illus. 2008. (Uglies Ser.). (ENG.). 224p. (YA). (gr. 7). pap. 8.99 *(978-1-4169-7436-9(9)*, Simon Pulse) Simon Pulse.

Westergard, Tim. A Penny for Your Thoughts. 2008. 28p. pap. 24.95 *(978-1-60441-417-2(0))* America Star Bks.

Whitaker, Alecia. The Queen of Kentucky. 2013. (ENG.). 384p. (YA). (gr. 7-17). pap. 8.99 *(978-0-316-12494-2(X)*, Poppy) Little, Brown Bks. for Young Readers.

White, Tracy. How I Made It to Eighteen: A Mostly True Story. White, Tracy, illus. 2010. (ENG., Illus.). 160p. (YA). (gr. 9-13). 23.99 *(978-1-59643-454-7(6)*, 9781596434547) Roaring Brook Pr.

Wilson, Jacqueline. Kiss. 2010. (ENG., Illus.). 256p. (YA). (gr. 7-12). 32.99 *(978-1-59643-242-0(X)*, 9781596432420) Roaring Brook Pr.

Yansky, Brian. Utopia, Iowa. 2015. (ENG.). 336p. (YA). (gr. 9). 17.99 *(978-0-7636-6533-3(9))* Candlewick Pr.

Yee, Paul. What Happened This Summer, 1 vol. 2006. (ENG., Illus.). 178p. (YA). (gr. 8-12). per. 10.95 *(978-1-896580-88-3(2))* Tradewind Bks. CAN. Dist: Orca Bk. Pubs. USA.

Zindel, Paul. The Pigman's Legacy. 2005. 168p. (YA). (gr. 7-12). 13.65 *(978-0-7569-4962-4(9))* Perfection Learning Corp.

YOUTH MOVEMENT

Cruden, Alex, ed. Student Movements of The 1960s. 2012. (Perspectives on Modern World History Ser.). (ENG., Illus.). 224p. (J). (gr. 10-12). lib. bdg. 42.45 *(978-0-7377-6372-0(8)*, Greenhaven Pr., Inc.) Cengage Gale.

Halpin, Mikki. It's Your World — If You Don't Like It, Change It. 2014. 19.00 *(978-1-63419-713-7(5))* Perfection Learning Corp.

YUCATAN PENINSULA

Hayes, Amy. Ancient Maya Geography. 2016. (Spotlight on the Maya, Aztec, & Inca Civilizations Ser.). 32p. (J). (gr. 6-4). pap. 11.75 *(978-1-4994-1971-9(6)*, PowerKids Pr.) Rosen Publishing Group, Inc., The.

Sauri, Trudy. Gift of Yucatan Nouns A-Z. 2008. (ENG & SPA., Illus.). 64p. (J). per. 18.00 *(978-0-9797637-3-1(8))* Your Culture Gifts.

YUCATAN PENINSULA—FICTION

Maartman, Ben. The Lost Treasures of Yucatan: A Belizean Saga. 2004. (Illus.). 106p. (YA). pap. 14.50 *(978-1-4120-1487-8(5))* Trafford Publishing.

Marsh, Carole. The Mystery at the Mayan Ruins: Mexico. 2014. (Around the World in 80 Mysteries Ser.: Vol. 16). (ENG., Illus.). 133p. (J). (gr. 3-5). pap. 7.99 *(978-0-635-11163-0(2)*, Marsh, Carole Bks.) Gallopade International.

Sauri, Trudy. Gift of Yucatan Pancho's Quest. 2007. (ENG & SPA., Illus.). 64p. (J). per. 18.00 *(978-0-9797637-0-0(3))* Your Culture Gifts.

YUGOSLAVIA

Hughes, Christopher. Yugoslavia. 2003. (Nations in Conflict Ser.). 48p. (YA). 26.19 *(978-1-56711-549-9(7)*, Blackbirch Pr., Inc.) Cengage Gale.

YUGOSLAVIA—FICTION

Marusic, Matko. Do Angels Cry? Tales of the War. 2008. (ENG.). 159p. pap. 11.95 *(978-1-932010-23-7(8))* Ooligan Pr.

YUGOSLAVIA—HISTORY

Behnke, Alison. Serbia & Montenegro in Pictures. 2006. (Visual Geography Ser.). (Illus.). 80p. (YA). (gr. 7-12). lib. bdg. 27.93 *(978-0-8225-2679-7(4))* Lerner Publishing Group.

Ching, Jacqueline. Genocide & the Bosnian War. 2009. (Genocide in Modern Times Ser.). 64p. (gr. 6-6). 58.50 *(978-1-61512-672-9(4))* Rosen Publishing Group, Inc., The.

Flotz, Katherine Haeger. A Pebble in My Shoe: A Memoir. 2004. (Illus.). 185p. lib. bdg. 29.95 *(978-0-9657793-2-6(7))* Pannonia Pr.

Honovich, Nancy. Immigration from the Former Yugoslavia. 2005. (Changing Face of North America Ser.). (Illus.). 112p. (YA). lib. bdg. 24.95 *(978-1-59084-690-2(7))* Mason Crest.

Sullivan, Kimberly L. Slobodan Milosevic's Yugoslavia. 2009. (Dictatorships Ser.). (ENG., Illus.). 144p. (J). (gr. 9-12). 38.60 *(978-0-8225-9098-9(0)*, 1299571) Lerner Publishing Group.

Transchel, Kate. The Breakup of Yugoslavia: Conflict in the Balkans. 2006. (Arbitrary Borders Ser.). (Illus.). 134p. (C). (gr. 9). lib. bdg. 35.00 *(978-0-7910-8651-3(8)*, Chelsea Hse.) Facts On File, Inc.

YUKON—FICTION

Appel, Benjamin & Clark, Henry W. We Were There in the Klondike Gold Rush. Docktor, Irv, illus. 2011. 188p. 42.95 *(978-1-258-05908-8(8))* Literary Licensing, LLC.

Bell, Joanne. Juggling Fire, 1 vol. 2009. (ENG.). 184p. (YA). (gr. 7-12). pap. 12.95 *(978-1-55469-094-7(3))* Orca Bk. Pubs. USA.

Hobbs, William. Jason's Gold. unabr. ed. 2004. 240p. (J). (gr. 5-9). pap. 38.00 incl. audio *(978-0-8072-8229-8(4)*, Listening Library) Random Hse. Audio Publishing Group.

London, Jack. The Call of the Wild. 2014. iv, 96p. (J). pap. *(978-1-4677-4602-1(9)*, First Avenue Editions) Lerner Publishing Group.

—The Call of the Wild, 1 vol. VanArsdale, Anthony, illus. 2011. (Calico Illustrated Classics Ser.). (ENG.). 112p. (YA). (gr. 3-6). 27.07 *(978-1-60270-742-9(1))* Magic Wagon.

—The Call of the Wild. Moser, Barry, illus. 2011. (ENG.). 144p. (J). (gr. 4-9). pap. 8.99 *(978-1-4424-3411-0(2)*, Simon & Schuster Bks. For Young Readers) Simon & Schuster Bks. For Young Readers.

—The Call of the Wild. 2003. (Aladdin Classics Ser.). (ENG.). 160p. (J). (gr. 4-7). mass mkt. 6.99 *(978-0-689-85674-7(1)*, Aladdin) Simon & Schuster Children's Publishing.

—The Call of the Wild. Clift, Eva, tr. Clift, Eva, illus. 2003. (Values in Action Illustrated Classics Ser.). (J). *(978-1-59203-047-7(5))* Learning Challenge, Inc.

—The Call of the Wild. Corvino, Lucy, illus. 2005. (Classic Starts(tm) Ser.). (ENG.). 160p. (J). (gr. 2-4). 6.95 *(978-1-4027-1274-6(X))* Sterling Publishing Co., Inc.

—La Llamada de la Naturaleza. 2003. (Historias de Siempre Ser.).Tr. of Call of the Wild. (SPA., Illus.). 92p. (J). (gr. 5-8). pap. 10.95 *(978-84-204-5731-4(0))* Santillana USA Publishing Co., Inc.

—White Fang, 1 vol. VanArsdale, Anthony, illus. 2011. (Calico Illustrated Classics Ser.: No. 3). (ENG.). 112p. (J). (gr. 3-6). 27.07 *(978-1-61641-112-1(0))* Magic Wagon.

McMullan, Kate. Knight for a Day, 1 vol. Basso, Bill, illus. 2007. (Dragon Slayers' Academy Ser.: No. 5). (ENG.). 109p. (gr. 2-5). 24.21 *(978-1-59961-377-2(8))* Spotlight.

Wallace, Ian. The True Story of Trapper Jack's Left Big Toe. (Illus.). 32p. (J). 18.95 *(978-0-88899-415-8(X))* Groundwood Bks. CAN. Dist: Publishers Group West (PGW).

Wishinsky, Frieda. Crazy for Gold. Griffiths, Dean & Owlkids Books Inc. Staff, illus. 2007. (Canadian Flyer Adventures Ser.: 3). (ENG.). 96p. (J). (gr. 1-4). per. 9.95 *(978-1-897066-93-5(7)*, Maple Tree Pr.) Owlkids Bks. Inc. CAN. Dist: Publishers Group West (PGW).

Z

ZACCHAEUS (BIBLICAL FIGURE)

Lashbrook, Marilyn. Out on a Limb. Britt, Stephanie McFetridge, illus. 2012. 32p. (J). pap. 8.00 *(978-1-935014-37-9(4))* Hutchings, John Pubs.

Mackall, Dandi Daley. Zacchaeus & Jesus. Manuzak, Lisa, illus. 2016. (Flipside Stories Ser.). (ENG.). 48p. (J). 14.99 *(978-1-4964-1119-8(6))* Tyndale Hse. Pubs.

Zacchaeus: Physically Small but Spiritually Tall! (Illus.). 16p. (J). pap. 1.50 *(978-0-87162-871-8(6)*, E6038) Warner Pr., Inc.

ZAHARIAS, BABE DIDRIKSON, 1911-1956

Brocker, Susan. Sports Legends & Leyendas del Deporte: 6 English, 6 Spanish Adaptations. 2011. (ENG & SPA.). (J). 89.00 net. *(978-1-4108-5678-4(X))* Benchmark Education Co.

Ferrara, Cos. Babe Didrikson Zaharias: Outcast & Hero. 2004. (Girls Explore, Reach for the Stars Ser.). (Illus.). 109p. (J). 20.00 *(978-0-9749456-2-0(5)*, Girls Explore) Girls Explore LLC.

Knudson, R. R. Babe Didrikson: Athlete of the Century. Lewin, Ted, illus. 2015. (Women of Our Time Ser.). (ENG.). 80p. (J). (gr. 3-7). 7.99 *(978-0-14-751465-3(7)*, Puffin Books) Penguin Young Readers Group.

Lobby, Mackenzie. Babe Didrikson Zaharias: Groundbreaking All-Around Athlete, 1 vol. 2011. (Legendary Athletes Ser.). (ENG., Illus.). 112p. (YA). (gr. 7-12). 34.22 *(978-1-61714-755-5(9))* ABDO Publishing Co.

ZAIRE

see Congo (Democratic Republic)

ZAMBIA

Holmes, Timothy & Wong, Winnie. Zambia. 2nd rev. ed. 2008. (Cultures of the World Ser.). 144p. (gr. 6-18). lib. bdg. 42.79 *(978-0-7614-3039-1(3)*, Benchmark Bks.) Marshall Cavendish Corp.

Kalz, Jill. Victoria Falls. 2004. (Natural Wonders of the World Ser.). (Illus.). 32p. (J). lib. bdg. 18.95 *(978-1-58341-327-2(8)*, Creative Education) Creative Co., The.

Pearce, Q. L. Given Kachepa: Advocate for Human Trafficking Victims. 2007. (Young Heroes Ser.). (ENG., Illus.). 64p. (J). (gr. 4-8). lib. bdg. 35.70 *(978-0-7377-3668-7(2)*, Kidhaven) Cengage Gale.

Torres, John Albert. Meet Our New Student from Zambia. 2010. (Meet Our New Student Ser.). 48p. (J). (gr. 2-5). 29.95 *(978-1-58415-735-9(6))* Mitchell Lane Pubs., Inc.

Waters, Bella. Zambia in Pictures. 2009. (J). lib. bdg. 31.93 *(978-1-57505-955-6(X))* Twenty First Century Bks.

ZEBRAS

Anderson, Jill. Zebras. 2005. (Wild Ones Ser.). (ENG., Illus.). 24p. (J). (gr. -1-1). 12.95 *(978-1-55971-926-1(5))*; pap. 6.95 *(978-1-55971-927-8(3))* Cooper Square Publishing Llc.

Borgert-Spaniol, Megan. Baby Zebras. 2017. (Super Cute! Ser.). (ENG., Illus.). 24p. (J). (gr. k-3). lib. bdg. 25.95 *(978-1-62617-548-8(9)*, Blastoff! Readers) Bellwether Media.

Carmichael, L. E. Zebra Migration. 2012. (Animal Migrations Ser.). (ENG., Illus.). 32p. (J). (gr. 2-5). lib. bdg. 29.93 *(978-1-60973-627-9(3)*, 201204) Child's World, Inc., The.

Cunningham, Kevin. Zebras & Ostriches. 2016. (21st Century Junior Library: Better Together Ser.). (ENG.). 24p. (J). (gr. 2-5). 27.07 *(978-1-63471-082-4(7)*, 208407) Cherry Lake Publishing.

Doudna, Kelly. It's a Baby Zebra!, 1 vol. 2009. (Baby African Animals Ser.). (ENG., Illus.). 24p. (J). (gr. k-3). lib. bdg. 24.21 *(978-1-60453-160-2(6)*, SandCastle) ABDO Publishing Co.

Feldman, Thea. Milia's Big Day. 2006. (Illus.). (J). *(978-0-696-23290-9(1))* Meredith Bks.

Gareth Stevens Publishing Staff, contrib. by. Zebras. 2004. (All about Wild Animals Ser.). (Illus.). 32p. (gr. k-4). lib. bdg. 26.00 *(978-0-8368-4190-9(5)*, Gareth Stevens Learning Library) Stevens, Gareth Publishing LLLP.

Gish, Melissa. Living Wild: Zebras. 2013. (Living Wild Ser.). (ENG., Illus.). 48p. (J). (gr. 4-7). pap. 12.00 *(978-0-89812-780-5(7)*, Creative Paperbacks) Creative Co., The.

—Zebras. 2012. (Living Wild Ser.). (Illus.). 48p. (J). (gr. 5-12). 23.95 *(978-1-60818-173-5(1)*, Creative Education) Creative Co., The.

Gray, Susan H. Zebras Have Stripes. 2015. (Tell Me Why Library). (ENG., Illus.). 24p. (J). (gr. 2-5). 27.07 *(978-1-63362-001-8(8)*, 205916) Cherry Lake Publishing.

Guidoux, Valerie. Little Zebras. 2005. (Born to Be Wild Ser.). (Illus.). 24p. (gr. k-3). lib. bdg. 23.00 *(978-0-8368-4741-3(5)*, Gareth Stevens Learning Library) Stevens, Gareth Publishing LLLP.

Ipcizade, Catherine. Zebras. 2010. (African Animals Ser.). (ENG.). 24p. (gr. k-1). pap. 41.70 *(978-1-4296-5085-4(0)*, Pebble Plus) Capstone Press of Coughlan Cos.

—Zebras [Scholastic]. 2010. (African Animals Ser.). 24p. pap. 0.49 *(978-1-4296-5789-1(8)*, Pebble Plus) Capstone Press of Coughlan Cos.

Kuskowski, Alex. Zebras, 1 vol. 2014. (Zoo Animals Ser.). (ENG.). 24p. (J). (gr. k-3). lib. bdg. 24.21 *(978-1-62403-276-9(1)*, SandCastle) ABDO Publishing Co.

MacAulay, Kelley. Les Zebres. 2008. (FRE.). 32p. (J). pap. 9.95 *(978-2-89579-203-1(8))* Bayard Canada Livres CAN. Dist: Crabtree Publishing Co.

MacAulay, Kelley & Kalman, Bobbie. Endangered Zebras. 2007. (Earth's Endangered Animals Ser.). (ENG., Illus.). 32p. (J). (gr. 1-5). lib. bdg. *(978-0-7787-1864-2(6))*; pap. *(978-0-7787-1910-6(3))* Crabtree Publishing Co.

Markle, Sandra. Zebras. (Animal Prey Ser.). 2008. (Illus.). 39p. (J). (gr. 3-7). per. 7.95 *(978-0-8225-6065-4(8)*, First Avenue Editions) 2008. pap. 46.95 *(978-0-8225-9325-6(4))* 2007. (ENG., Illus.). 40p. (J). (gr. 3-6). lib. bdg. 25.26 *(978-0-8225-6062-3(3))* Lerner Publishing Group.

Meister, Cari. Zebras. 2015. (J). lib. bdg. 25.65 *(978-1-62031-171-4(2)*, Bullfrog Bks.) Jump! Inc.

Moldovo, Eustacia. Baby Zebras at the Zoo. 2015. (J). *(978-0-7660-6617-5(7))*; (ENG., Illus.). 24p. (gr. -1-1). pap. 9.35 *(978-0-7660-7093-6(X))* Enslow Pubs., Inc.

Murray, Julie. Zebras, 1 vol. (ENG.). 2012. 32p. 28.50 *(978-1-61783-222-2(7)*, Big Buddy Bks.) 2003. 24p. 25.65 *(978-1-57765-702-6(0)*, Buddy Bks.) ABDO Publishing Co.

Noble-Goodman, Katherine. Zebras. 2005. (Animals Animals Ser.). (Illus.). 48p. (gr. 3-7). lib. bdg. 29.93 *(978-0-7614-1871-9(7)*, Benchmark Bks.) Marshall Cavendish Corp.

Owings, Lisa. Meet a Baby Zebra. 2015. (ENG., Illus.). 32p. (J). (gr. k-2). 26.65 *(978-1-4677-8114-5(2))* Lerner Publishing Group.

Pelusey, Michael. Giraffes & Zebras. 2008. (Zoo Animals Ser.). 32p. (gr. 2-3). lib. bdg. 18.56 *(978-0-7614-3149-7(7)*, Benchmark Bks.) Marshall Cavendish Corp.

Peterson, Megan Cooley & Rustad, Martha E. H. Zebras Are Awesome! 2015. (Awesome African Animals! Ser.). (ENG.). 32p. (gr. 1-2). lib. bdg. 27.32 *(978-1-4914-1764-5(1))* Capstone Press of Coughlan Cos.

Pingry, Patricia A. Baby Zebra. Sharp, Chris, illus. 2004. (San Diego Zoo Animal Library: Vol. 6). (ENG.). 26p. (J). bds. 6.95 *(978-0-8249-6556-3(6)*, Ideal Pubns.) Worthy Publishing.

Raatma, Lucia. Plains Zebras. 2014. (Nature's Children Ser.). (ENG.). 48p. (J). lib. bdg. 28.00 *(978-0-531-21226-4(2))* Scholastic Library Publishing.

Reade, Clara. Zebras. 2012. (PowerKids Readers: Safari Animals Ser.). (ENG., Illus.). 24p. (J). (gr. k-2). pap. 8.25 *(978-1-4488-7535-1(8))*; lib. bdg. 22.60 *(978-1-4488-7395-1(9))* Rosen Publishing Group, Inc., The. (PowerKids Pr.).

Riggs, Kate. Amazing Animals: Zebras. 2014. (Amazing Animals Ser.). (ENG.). 24p. (J). (gr. 1-3). pap. 8.99 *(978-0-89812-932-8(X)*, Creative Paperbacks) Creative Co., The.

—Seedlings: Zebras. 2015. (Seedlings Ser.). (ENG.). 24p. (J). (gr. -1-1). pap. 7.99 *(978-1-62832-118-0(0)*, Creative Paperbacks) Creative Co., The.

—Zebras. (J). 2015. *(978-1-60818-518-4(4))* 2014. (Illus.). 24p. 25.65 *(978-1-60818-353-1(X))* Creative Co., The. (Creative Education).

Rustad, Martha E. H. Zebras & Oxpeckers Work Together. 2011. (Animals Working Together Ser.). (ENG.). 24p. (gr. k-1). pap. 41.70 *(978-1-4296-6369-4(3)*, Pebble Plus) Capstone Press of Coughlan Cos.

Schuh, Mari. Zebras. 2017. (Black & White Animals Ser.). (ENG., Illus.). 24p. (gr. k-1). lib. bdg. 21.99 *(978-1-5157-3374-4(2)*, Pebble Bks.) Capstone Press of Coughlan Cos.

Stone, Lynn M. Zebras. 2008. (Nature Watch Ser.). (ENG., Illus.). 48p. (gr. 4-8). lib. bdg. 27.93 *(978-0-8225-7511-5(6)*, Lerner Pubns.) Lerner Publishing Group.

Taylor, Trace. You Think You Know Zebras. 2005. (1-3Y Wild Animals Ser.). (ENG.). 24p. (J). (gr. k-2). pap. 5.99 *(978-1-59301-062-1(1))* American Reading Co.

Ticktock Media, Ltd. Staff. What Do Zebras Do? 2008. (What Do Animals Do? Ser.). (ENG.). 10p. (J). (gr. k — 1). bds. 4.95 *(978-1-84696-795-5(3)*, TickTock Books) Octopus Publishing Group GBR. Dist: Independent Pubs. Group.

Von Zumbusch, Amelie. Zebras. 2007. (Safari Animals Ser.). (Illus.). 24p. (J). (gr. 3-7). lib. bdg. 22.60 *(978-1-4042-3613-4(9)*, 1266071, PowerKids Pr.) Rosen Publishing Group, Inc., The.

von Zumbusch, Amelie. Zebras. 2009. (Safari Animals Ser.). 24p. (gr. 1-1). 42.50 *(978-1-60852-969-8(X)*, PowerKids Pr.) Rosen Publishing Group, Inc., The.

Von Zumbusch, Amelie. Zebras/Cebras. 2007. (Safari Animals / Animales de Safari Ser.). (SPA & ENG., Illus.). 24p. (J). (gr. k-3). lib. bdg. 22.60 *(978-1-4042-7609-3(2)*, PowerKids Pr.) Rosen Publishing Group, Inc., The.

von Zumbusch, Amelie. Zebras/Cebras. 2009. (Safari Animals/Animales de safari Ser.). (ENG & SPA.). 24p. (gr. 1-1). 42.50 *(978-1-60852-979-7(7)*, Editorial Buenas Letras) Rosen Publishing Group, Inc., The.

Wilsdon, Christina. Zebras. 2006. (J). 7.99 *(978-1-59939-033-8(7))* Cornerstone Pr.

—Zebras. 2009. (Amazing Animals Ser.). 48p. (J). (gr. 2-6). pap. 10.50 *(978-1-4339-2030-1(1)*, Gareth Stevens Learning Library); (gr. 3-6). lib. bdg. 28.00 *(978-0-8368-9113-3(9))* Stevens, Gareth Publishing LLLP.

Zebras. 2006. (Zootles Ser.). (J). 4.95 *(978-1-932396-23-2(3))* Wildlife Education, Ltd.

Zebra's Stripes. Date not set. (Touch & Feel Ser.). (Illus.). (J). 4.98 *(978-0-7525-9571-9(7))* Parragon, Inc.

Zobel, Derek. Zebras. 2011. (Animal Safari Ser.). (ENG., Illus.). 24p. (J). (gr. k-3). lib. bdg. 25.95 *(978-1-60014-611-4(2)*, Blastoff! Readers) Bellwether Media.

ZEBRAS—FICTION

Arnold, Vickie. The Baby Zebra Adventure. 2009. 20p. pap. 12.49 *(978-1-4389-5818-7(8))* AuthorHouse.

Austin, Cassie Rita. Peppermint. Austin, Cassie Rita, illus. 2011. (Illus.). 53p. 15.95 *(978-0-9846151-1-7(3))* Paintbrush Tales Publishing, LLC.

Beeson, Paul & Beeson, Lady Jan. Zeela the Zebra of a Different Color. Beeson, Jan, illus. 2013. 38p. pap. 12.99 *(978-0-9890482-5-5(X))* Beeson, Jan.

Bingham, Kelly. Circle, Square, Moose. Zelinsky, Paul O., illus. 2014. (ENG.). 48p. (J). (gr. -1-3). 17.99 *(978-0-06-229003-8(7)*, Greenwillow Bks.) HarperCollins Pubs.

—Z Is for Moose. Zelinsky, Paul O., illus. 2012. 32p. (J). (gr. -1-2). (ENG.). 16.99 *(978-0-06-079984-7(6))*; lib. bdg. 17.89 *(978-0-06-079985-4(4))* HarperCollins Pubs. (Greenwillow Bks.).

Cabatingan, Erin. A Is for Musk Ox. Myers, Matthew, illus. 2012. (Musk Ox Ser.: 1). (ENG.). 40p. (J). (gr. k-2). 18.99 *(978-1-59643-676-3(X)*, 9781596436763) Roaring Brook Pr.

—Musk Ox Counts. Myers, Matthew, illus. 2013. (Musk Ox Ser.: 2). (ENG.). 36p. (J). (gr. k-2). 16.99 *(978-1-59643-798-2(7)*, 9781596437982) Roaring Brook Pr.

—The World According to Musk Ox. Myers, Matthew, illus. 2014. (Musk Ox Ser.: 3). (ENG.). 40p. (J). (gr. k-2). 17.99 *(978-1-59643-799-9(5)*, 9781596437999) Roaring Brook Pr.

Campbell, James & Mould, Chris. Boyface & the Uncertain Ponies. 2015. (Boyface Ser.). (ENG., Illus.). 144p. (J). (gr. 2-4). pap. 8.99 *(978-1-4449-1805-2(2))* Hodder & Stoughton GBR. Dist: Hachette Bk. Group.

Castleton, Chaffee. Runty's Adventure: A Story of Love. Queen, Dana, illus. 2010. 97p. (J). pap. 17.95 *(978-0-578-06109-2(0))* Castleton, Julia J.

Cook, Sherry & Johnson, Terri. Zany Science Zeke, 26. Kuhn, Jesse, illus. l.t. ed. 2006. (Quirkles — Exploring Phonics through Science Ser.: 26). 32p. (J). 7.99 *(978-1-933815-25-1(6)*, Quirkles, The) Creative 3, LLC.

Craig, Bobby & Manifold, Delwyn. The Learning Adventures of Spot. 2011. 28p. pap. 24.95 *(978-1-4560-3110-7(4))* America Star Bks.

Creek, Silent. All the Ice of Afric. 2009. 160p. 22.95 *(978-1-4401-2118-0(4))* iUniverse, Inc.

Dahl, Michael. Bye-Bye Bottles, Zebra. Vidal, Oriol, illus. 2015. (Hello Genius Ser.). (ENG.). 20p. (gr. 1-2). bds. 7.99 *(978-1-4795-5792-9(7))* Picture Window Bks.

Dale, Jay. Little Zebra, 1 vol. East, Jacqueline, illus. 2012. (Wonder Words Ser.). (ENG.). 32p. (gr. k-2). pap. 5.99 *(978-1-4296-8906-9(4)*, Engage Literacy) Capstone Press of Coughlan Cos.

Derubertis, Barbara. Zachary Zebra's Zippity Zooming. Alley, R. W., illus. 2011. (Animal Antics A to Z Set III Ser.). pap. 45.32 *(978-0-7613-8435-9(9))* Kane Press, Inc.

deRubertis, Barbara. Zachary Zebra's Zippity Zooming. Alley, R. W., illus. 2011. (Animal Antics A to Z Ser.). 32p. (J). pap. 7.95 *(978-1-57565-351-8(6))*; lib. bdg. 22.60 *(978-1-57565-359-4(1))* Kane Press, Inc.

deRubertis, Barbara & DeRubertis, Barbara. Zachary Zebra's Zippity Zooming. Alley, R. W. 2012. (Animal Antics A to Z Ser.). 32p. (J). (gr. 2 — 1). cd-rom 7.95 *(978-1-57565-419-5(9))* Kane Press, Inc.

Domer, V. K. The Little Lambs & the Rainbow Zebra. 2011. 36p. 13.95 *(978-1-4497-0889-4(7)*, WestBow Pr.) Author Solutions, Inc.

Douglas-Hobbs, Kathy. Kobe & the Rescue Adventure. 2012. 16p. pap. 15.99 *(978-1-4772-0326-2(5))* AuthorHouse.

Ebume, Tim. Zebra Stripes: A Tail of Personal Branding. 2012. (Illus.). 48p. pap. 31.99 *(978-1-4691-4536-5(7))* Xlibris Corp.

Ellis, Libby. Ziggy the Zebra. Yoon, Salina, illus. 2005. 14p. (J). (gr. k-3). 9.95 *(978-1-58117-104-4(8)*, Intervisual/Piggy Toes) Bendon, Inc.

Gangloff, Sylviane, illus. Zoom the Zebra. 2015. (Talking Back Ser.). (ENG.). 36p. (J). (gr. -1-2). 7.95 *(978-0-7892-1246-7(3)*, Abbeville Kids) Abbeville Pr., Inc.

Grey, Chelsea Gillian. Leperit the Zebra. Denman, Michael & Huiett, William, illus. 2005. (Internet Interactive Ser.). (ENG.). 36p. (J). (gr. -1-3). 8.95 *(978-1-59249-440-8(4)*, SD6505); (gr. 2-2). 14.95 *(978-1-59249-438-5(2)*, H6505); (gr. 2-2). pap. 6.95 *(978-1-59249-439-2(0)*, S6505) Soundprints.

—Leperit the Zebra: African Wildlife Foundation. Denman, Michael L. & Huiett, William J., illus. 2005. (Meet Africa's Animals Ser.). (ENG.). 36p. (J). (gr. -1-2). 2.95 *(978-1-59249-441-5(2)*, S6555) Soundprints.

Harrington, Jenna. Katie Mcginty Wants a Pet! Simpson, Finn, illus. 2015. (ENG.). 32p. (J). (gr. -1-3). 16.99 *(978-1-58925-192-2(X))* Tiger Tales.

Henkes, Kevin. The Zebra Wall. 2005. (ENG., Illus.). 160p. (J). (gr. 3-7). pap. 6.99 *(978-0-06-073303-2(9)*, Greenwillow Bks.) HarperCollins Pubs.

ImageBooks Staff. Little Zebra. Put, Klaartje van der, illus. 2013. (Little Finger Puppet Board Bks.). (ENG.). 12p. (J). (gr.

-1 — 1). bds. 6.99 *(978-1-4521-1252-7(5))* Chronicle Bks. LLC.

Jacobs, Nadine. Zefir, la Cebra en Peligro. Vicens, Paula, tr. Jacobs, Nadine, illus. 2004. (SPA., Illus.). 32p. (J). 15.99 *(978-84-8470-108-8(5))* Corimbo, Editorial S.L. ESP. Dist: Lectorum Pubns., Inc.

Kim, JiYu. Zippy the Runner. Seon, JeongHyeon, illus. rev. ed. 2014. (MySELF Bookshelf Ser.). (ENG.). 32p. (J). (gr. k-2). pap. 11.94 *(978-1-60357-656-7(8))*; lib. bdg. 25.27 *(978-1-59953-647-7(1))* Norwood Hse. Pr.

Kim, YeoongAh. Shooting Stars Soccer Team. Lee, Hyeongjin, illus. rev. ed. 2014. (MySELF Bookshelf Ser.). (ENG.). 32p. (J). (gr. k-2). pap. 11.94 *(978-1-60357-657-4(6))* Norwood Hse. Pr.

—The Shooting Stars Soccer Team. Lee, Hyeongjin, illus. rev. ed. 2014. (MySELF Bookshelf Ser.). (ENG.). 32p. (J). (gr. k-2). lib. bdg. 25.27 *(978-1-59953-648-4(X))* Norwood Hse. Pr.

Kompelien, Tracy. Zebra Stripes, 1 vol. Nobens, Cheryl A., illus. 2006. (Animal Tales Ser.). (ENG.). 24p. (J). (gr. k-3). lib. bdg. 24.21 *(978-1-59679-971-4(4)*, SandCastle) ABDO Publishing Co.

—Zebra Stripes. Nobens, C. A., illus. 2006. (Fact & Fiction Ser.). 24p. (J). pap. 48.42 *(978-1-59679-972-1(2))* ABDO Publishing Co.

Law, Felicia. Zanzibar the Zebra: A Tale of Individuality. Messina, Lilli, illus. 2010. (Animal Fair Values Ser.). 32p. (J). (gr. -1-3). pap. 10.55 *(978-1-60754-807-2(0))*; lib. bdg. 22.60 *(978-1-60754-803-4(8))* Windmill Bks.

Lodge, Jo. Cosy Cuddlers: Zebra. 2004. (Cosy Cuddlers Ser.). (ENG., Illus.). 8p. (J). (gr. -1-k). pap. 7.99 *(978-1-4050-3456-2(4)*, Campbell Bks.) Pan Macmillan GBR. Dist: Independent Pubs. Group.

Madden, Gloria. Grandmothers Bedtime Stories. 2008. 68p. (gr. -1-7). pap. 10.49 *(978-1-4343-9201-5(5))* AuthorHouse.

Mallory, Nicole. I Wish I Was an Alligator. 2013. (ENG.). 29p. (J). pap. 15.95 *(978-1-4787-1066-0(7))* Outskirts Pr., Inc.

Meadows, Daisy. Savannah the Zebra Fairy. 2015. (Baby Animal Rescue Fairies Ser.: 4). (ENG.). 80p. (J). (gr. 2-5). pap. 4.99 *(978-0-545-70853-1(2)*, Scholastic Paperbacks) Scholastic, Inc.

—Savannah the Zebra Fairy. 2015. (Rainbow Magic — Baby Animal Rescue Fairies Ser.: 4). lib. bdg. 14.75 *(978-0-606-37052-3(8))* Turtleback Bks.

Mello, Craig. Difference: the Rainbow Zebra: An African Tale of Diversity. 2007. 40p. per. 24.95 *(978-1-4241-8269-5(7))* PublishAmerica, Inc.

Miller, Kathryn L. Abc's with Sadie: Sadie Goes to the Zoo. 2011. 32p. pap. 17.25 *(978-1-4269-5940-0(0))* Trafford Publishing.

Neiman, Jahcolyn Russell. Kekula. 2011. 32p. pap. 13.99 *(978-1-4520-8086-4(0))* AuthorHouse.

Nelson, M. R. The Zebra Said Shhh. Sheldon, Tamia, illus. 2013. 44p. pap. 9.99 *(978-1-62395-440-6(1))* Xist Publishing.

Nogales, Jill. Zebra on the Go, 1 vol. Rocha, Lorraine, illus. 2017. (ENG.). 32p. (J). (gr. -1-3). 16.95 *(978-1-56145-911-7(9))* Peachtree Pubs.

Nunez, Marisa. Camilla the Zebra. Villan, Oscar, illus. 2003. 32p. (J). 14.95 *(978-84-95730-39-8(1))* Kalandraka Catalunya, Edicions, S.L. ESP. Dist: Independent Pubs. Group.

—La Cebra Camila. Villan, Oscar, illus. 2005. (SPA.). 216p. (J). (gr. k-2). 16.95 *(978-84-95123-60-2(6)*, KA8243) Kalandraka Editora, S.L. ESP. Dist: Iaconi, Mariuccia Bk. Imports, Lectorum Pubns., Inc.

Pastis, Stephan. Beginning Pearls. 2013. lib. bdg. 20.85 *(978-0-606-31764-1(3)*, Turtleback) Turtleback Bks.

Paterson, Brian. The Picnic: Board Book. 2006. (ENG., Illus.). 16p. (J). (gr. -1). bds. 6.99 *(978-0-00-717421-8(7)*, HarperCollins Children's Bks.) HarperCollins Pubs. Ltd. GBR. Dist: Trafalgar Square Publishing.

—Zigby Camps Out. 2003. (Zigby Ser.). (ENG., Illus.). 32p. (J). (gr. -1-2). pap. 8.99 *(978-0-00-713180-8(1)*, HarperCollins Children's Bks.) HarperCollins Pubs. Ltd. GBR. Dist: Independent Pubs. Group.

Plant, Marilyn. Trinka's Magic Bracelet. 2012. 40p. pap. *(978-1-77067-956-6(1))* FriesenPress.

Rizvi, Sobia. Zebra Stripes. 2011. 24p. pap. 15.99 *(978-1-4653-4618-6(X))* Xlibris Corp.

Robaard, Jedda. The Little Zebra Who Lost His Stripes. 2013. (Illus.). (J). *(978-1-4351-5392-9(8))* Barnes & Noble, Inc.

Rudolph, Shaina & Royer, Danielle. All My Stripes: A Story for Children with Autism. Zivoin, Jennifer, illus. 2014. (J). pap. *(978-1-4338-1917-9(1)*, Magination Pr.) American Psychological Assn.

Sims, Lesley. How Zebras Got Their Stripes. 2009. (Young Reading Ser.). 64p. (J). 6.99 *(978-0-7945-2525-5(3)*, Usborne) EDC Publishing.

Soli, Doris. Jango the Little Dragon: The Wondrous Adventures of Little Dragon. 2011. (Illus.). 36p. pap. 17.07 *(978-1-4567-8487-4(0))* AuthorHouse.

Sulkowski, Jennifer Suzanne. A Pony Named Napoleon. 2013. 74p. 30.95 *(978-1-59299-979-8(4))*; pap. 22.95 *(978-1-59299-978-1(6))* Inkwater Pr.

Sullivan, Candida. Zippy & the Stripes of Courage. 2011. (J). pap. 13.99 *(978-1-937331-08-5(3))* ShadeTree Publishing, LLC.

Uvezian, Verne. The Day Benny Stuck His Neck Out. 2011. 12p. (gr. 1-2). 9.95 *(978-1-4567-3119-9(X))* AuthorHouse.

Volker, Kerstin. Emma Goes Shopping. 2003. (Funny Friends Lift-and-Learn Bks.). 14p. (J). 5.99 *(978-1-59384-021-1(7))* Parklane Publishing.

—Suzie Goes to Sleep. 2003. (Funny Friends Lift-and-Learn Bks.). (Illus.). 14p. (J). 5.99 *(978-1-59384-024-2(1))* Parklane Publishing.

Vrombaut, An. Zed the Zebra. Vrombaut, An, illus. 2013. (ENG., Illus.). 32p. (J). (gr. -1-k). pap. 8.99 *(978-1-4449-1303-3(4))* Hodder & Stoughton GBR. Dist: Hachette Bk. Group.

Walker, Anna. I Love Christmas. Walker, Anna, illus. 2009. (ENG., Illus.). 32p. (J). (gr. -1-1). 9.99 *(978-1-4169-8317-0(1)*, Simon & Schuster Bks. For Young Readers) Simon & Schuster Bks. For Young Readers.

—I Love My Dad. Walker, Anna, illus. 2010. (ENG., Illus.). 32p. (J). (gr. -1-1). 9.99 *(978-1-4169-8319-4(8)*, Simon & Schuster Bks. For Young Readers) Simon & Schuster Bks. For Young Readers.

—I Love My Mom. Walker, Anna, illus. 2010. (ENG., Illus.). 32p. (J). (gr. -1-1). 9.99 *(978-1-4169-8318-7(X)*, Simon & Schuster Bks. For Young Readers) Simon & Schuster Bks. For Young Readers.

—I Love to Dance. Walker, Anna, illus. 2011. (ENG., Illus.). 32p. (J). (gr. -1-1). 9.99 *(978-1-4169-8323-1(6)*, Simon & Schuster Bks. For Young Readers) Simon & Schuster Bks. For Young Readers.

—I Love to Sing. Walker, Anna, illus. 2011. (ENG., Illus.). 32p. (J). (gr. -1-1). 9.99 *(978-1-4169-8322-4(8)*, Simon & Schuster Bks. For Young Readers) Simon & Schuster Bks. For Young Readers.

—I Love Vacations. Walker, Anna, illus. 2011. (ENG., Illus.). 32p. (J). (gr. -1-1). 9.99 *(978-1-4169-8321-7(X)*, Simon & Schuster Bks. For Young Readers) Simon & Schuster Bks. For Young Readers.

Waller, Alesha. The Spotted Zebr. 2011. 20p. pap. 13.99 *(978-1-4634-7456-0(3))* AuthorHouse.

Weaver, Amy Garrett. Zoe the Zebra. Schneider, Robin, illus. 2009. 33p. pap. 24.95 *(978-1-60749-552-9(X))* PublishAmerica, Inc.

Wojtowycz, David, illus. Elephant Joe, Brave Firefighter! 2015. (Step into Reading Ser.). (ENG.). 32p. (J). (gr. -1-1). 12.99 *(978-0-375-97203-4(X)*, Random Hse. Bks. for Young Readers) Random Hse. Children's Bks.

ZENGER, JOHN PETER, 1697-1746

Gibson, Karen Bush. John Peter Zenger. 2006. (Profiles in American History Ser.). (Illus.). 48p. (J). (gr. 3-7). lib. bdg. 29.95 *(978-1-58415-437-2(3))* Mitchell Lane Pubs., Inc.

ZEPPELINS

see Airships

ZIMBABWE

Baughan, Michael Gray. Zimbabwe. Rotberg, Robert I., ed. 2012. (Evolution of Africa's Major Nations Ser.). (Illus.). 80p. (J). (gr. 7). 22.95 *(978-1-4222-2188-4(1))* Mason Crest.

—Zimbabwe. 2011. (J). pap. *(978-1-4222-2216-4(0))* Mason Crest.

Brimson, Samuel. United Kingdom-Zimbabwe, 8 vols. 2003. (Nations of the World Ser.: Vol. 8). (Illus.). 64p. (gr. 5-12). lib. bdg. 31.00 *(978-0-8368-5492-3(6)*, Gareth Stevens Secondary Library) Stevens, Gareth Publishing LLLP.

Chifamba-Barnes, Sarudzayi Elizabeth. The Village Story-Teller: Zimbabwean Folktales. 2009. (Illus.). 100p. (gr. 3-7). pap. *(978-0-9558082-1-0(9))* Lion Pr. Ltd., The.

Di Piazza, Francesca. Zimbabwe in Pictures. 2005. (Visual Geography Series, Second Ser.). (ENG., Illus.). 80p. (gr. 5-12). 31.93 *(978-0-8225-2399-4(X))* Lerner Publishing Group.

Downing, David & Thorpe, Yvonne. Zimbabwe. 2009. (Global Hotspots Ser.). 32p. (gr. 5-18). lib. bdg. 18.56 *(978-0-7614-4763-4(6))* Marshall Cavendish Corp.

Glynne, Andy. Juliane's Story: A Real-Life Account of Her Journey from Zimbabwe. 2017. (Seeking Refuge Ser.). (ENG.). 32p. (gr. 3-4). 27.32 ***(978-1-5158-1414-6(9))*** Picture Window Bks.

Haskins, Jim & Benson, Kathleen. Count Your Way Through Zimbabwe. Park, Janie Jaehyun, illus. 2006. (Count Your Way Ser.). (ENG.). 24p. (gr. 2-5). lib. bdg. 19.93 *(978-1-57505-885-6(5)*, Millbrook Pr.) Lerner Publishing Group.

Hatkoff, Craig, et al. Cecil's Pride: The True Story of a Lion King. 2016. (ENG., Illus.). 40p. (J). (gr. -1-3). 17.99 *(978-1-338-03445-5(6))* Scholastic, Inc.

Kalz, Jill. Victoria Falls. 2004. (Natural Wonders of the World Ser.). (Illus.). 32p. (J). lib. bdg. 18.95 *(978-1-58341-327-2(8)*, Creative Education) Creative Co., The.

Klepeis, Alicia. Zimbabwe. 2017. (J). pap. 19.95 ***(978-1-5026-2496-3(6))*** Cavendish Square Publishing.

Korky Paul: Biography of an Illustrator: Individual Title Six-Packs. (Discovery World Ser.). 24p. (gr. 1-2). 33.00 *(978-0-7635-8471-9(1))* Rigby Education.

Sheehan, Sean & Spilling, Michael. Zimbabwe. 3rd ed. 2014. (Cultures of the World, Third Ser.). (ENG., Illus.). 144p. (YA). (gr. 7). lib. bdg. 47.07 *(978-0-7614-8017-4(X))* Cavendish Square Publishing.

Trent, Tererai. The Girl Who Buried Her Dreams in a Can. Gilchrist, Jan Spivey, illus. 2015. (ENG.). 34p. (J). (gr. 1-3). 17.99 *(978-0-670-01654-9(3)*, Viking Books for Young Readers) Penguin Young Readers Group.

ZIMBABWE—FICTION

Chikuhwa, Jacob. From the Cradle to the Bonfire. 2012. 78p. pap. 16.95 *(978-1-4626-9859-2(X))* America Star Bks.

Chinodya, Shimmer. Tale of Tamari. 2003. (Illus.). 76p. pap. *(978-1-77922-026-4(X))* Weaver Pr.

Cooper, Ross Gordon. Clarence the Catfish. 2010. 32p. pap. 21.95 *(978-0-557-30913-9(1))* Lulu Pr., Inc.

Deogratias Simba. The Mystery Door. 2005. (Illus.). 22p. pap. *(978-9987-417-21-6(3))* Mkuki na Nyoka Pubs. TZA. Dist: Michigan State Univ. Pr.

Farmer, Nancy. The Ear, the Eye & the Arm. 2012. (ENG.). 336p. (J). (gr. 3-7). pap. 7.99 *(978-0-545-35661-9(X)*, Scholastic Paperbacks) Scholastic, Inc.

—The Ear, the Eye & the Arm. 2012. lib. bdg. 18.40 *(978-0-606-23944-8(8)*, Turtleback) Turtleback Bks.

Kandimba, V. T. Folktales from Zimbabwe: Short Stores. 2009. (Illus.). 56p. 24.99 *(978-1-4415-4281-6(7))* Xlibris Corp.

Kandimba, Vt. Folk Tales from Zimbabwe. 2009. 58p. pap. 15.99 *(978-1-4415-4280-9(9))* Xlibris Corp.

Knight, Deborah Janet. A Puzzling Picnic. Hauvette, Marion, illus. 2010. 32p. pap. 13.00 *(978-1-60860-963-5(4)*, Eloquent Bks.) Strategic Book Publishing & Rights Agency (SBPRA).

Lide, Emily. Zimbabwe. 2006. per. 11.95 *(978-1-59094-120-1(9))* Jawbone Publishing Corp.

Literature Connections English: Nervous Conditions. 2004. (gr. 6-12). *(978-0-395-77560-8(4)*, 2-80129) Holt McDougal.

Robert, Na'ima B. & Quarto Generic Staff. Far from Home. 2012. (ENG.). 352p. (J). (gr. 8-11). pap. 8.99 *(978-1-84780-006-0(8)*, Frances Lincoln) Quarto Publishing Group UK GBR. Dist: Hachette Bk. Group.

Rundell, Katherine. Cartwheeling in Thunderstorms. Castrillón, Melissa, illus. 2014. (ENG.). 256p. (J). (gr. 3-7). 17.99 *(978-1-4424-9061-1(6)*, Simon & Schuster Bks. For Young Readers) Simon & Schuster Bks. For Young Readers.

St. John, Lauren. The Last Leopard. 2010. (ENG.). 224p. (J). (gr. 3-7). 6.99 *(978-0-14-241515-3(4)*, Puffin Books) Penguin Young Readers Group.

Wallace, Jason. Out of Shadows. (ENG., Illus.). 272p. (J). (gr. 10). 2012. pap. 8.95 *(978-0-8234-2436-8(7))* 2011. 17.95 *(978-0-8234-2342-2(5))* Holiday Hse., Inc.

Williams, Michael. Diamond Boy. 2014. (Illus.). 384p. (YA). *(978-0-316-32067-2(6))* Little Brown & Co.

—Diamond Boy. 2014. (ENG., Illus.). 400p. (YA). (gr. 7-17). 18.00 *(978-0-316-32069-6(2))* Little, Brown Bks. for Young Readers.

—Now Is the Time for Running. 2013. (ENG.). 240p. (YA). (gr. 7-17). pap. 10.99 *(978-0-316-07788-0(7))* Little, Brown Bks. for Young Readers.

Wolfson, Steve. Elephants at the Airport. Brulot, Heleen, illus. 2013. 32p. pap. 11.95 *(978-0-9798324-5-1(4))* Argami Productions, LLC.

ZIONISM

Hurt, Avery. Arab Nationalism & Zionism. 2017. (J). ***(978-1-5026-2720-9(5))*** Cavendish Square Publishing.

Slavicek, Louise Chipley. The Establishment of the State of Israel. 2011. (Milestones in Modern World History Ser.). (Illus.). 128p. (C). (gr. 9). 35.00 *(978-1-60413-917-4(X)*, Chelsea Hse.) Facts On File, Inc.

Whiting, Jim. The Creation of Isreal. 2007. (Monumental Milestones Ser.). (Illus.). 48p. (YA). (gr. 4-7). lib. bdg. 29.95 *(978-1-58415-538-6(8))* Mitchell Lane Pubs., Inc.

ZIONISM—FICTION

Shapiro, David L. Sara's Journey. 2005. (ENG.). 224p. (gr. 7-12). per. 16.95 *(978-0-8276-0776-7(8))* Jewish Pubn. Society.

ZODIAC

Peters, Stephanie. Gemini. 2003. (Library of Constellations Ser.). (Illus.). 24p. (J). lib. bdg. 21.25 *(978-0-8239-6167-2(2)*, PowerKids Pr.) Rosen Publishing Group, Inc., The.

—Pisces. 2003. (Library of Constellations Ser.). (Illus.). 24p. (J). lib. bdg. 21.25 *(978-0-8239-6166-5(4)*, PowerKids Pr.) Rosen Publishing Group, Inc., The.

Peters, Stephanie True. Gemini. 2009. (Library of Constellations Ser.). 24p. (gr. 3-4). 45.00 *(978-1-60853-574-3(6)*, PowerKids Pr.) Rosen Publishing Group, Inc., The.

—Pisces. 2009. (Library of Constellations Ser.). 24p. (gr. 3-4). 45.00 *(978-1-60853-576-7(2)*, PowerKids Pr.) Rosen Publishing Group, Inc., The.

Stewart, Pat. Learning about the Zodiac. 2003. (Dover Little Activity Bks.). (ENG., Illus.). 16p. (J). (gr. 3-5). pap. 1.50 *(978-0-486-43024-9(3))* Dover Pubns., Inc.

Tang, Sanmu. Chinese Zodiac Animals. Jingwen, Zhu, tr. 2011. (ENG., Illus.). 56p. (J). (gr. 4-6). pap. 8.95 *(978-1-60220-977-0(4))* BetterLink Pr., Inc.

Zodiac Fun [Capstone Sole Source]. 2010. (Zodiac Fun Ser.). 32p. lib. bdg. 106.60 *(978-1-4296-5895-9(9)*, Snap Bks.) Capstone Press of Coughlan Cos.

ZOMO, THE RABBIT (FICTITIOUS CHARACTER)—FICTION

Ralles, H. J. Keeper of the Empire, Vol. 3. 2004. (Illus.). 235p. (J). pap. 9.95 *(978-1-929976-25-6(9))* Top Pubns., Ltd.

ZOO ANIMALS

Abbott, Simon. Pop & Play: Zoo Animals. 2013. (ENG., Illus.). 10p. (J). (gr. -1-k). bds. 7.99 *(978-0-7534-7163-0(9)*, 9780753471630, Kingfisher) Roaring Brook Pr.

ABDO Publishing Company Staff. Zoo Animals, bks. 6. 2014. (Zoo Animals Ser.: 6). (ENG.). 24p. (J). (gr. k-3). lib. bdg. 145.26 *(978-1-62403-270-7(2)*, SandCastle) ABDO Publishing Co.

Accord Publishing Staff. Zoo Babies. 2010. (ENG., Illus.). 12p. (J). (gr. -1). 9.99 *(978-0-7407-9201-4(6))* Andrews McMeel Publishing.

All about Baby Zoo Animals. 2015. (All about Baby Zoo Animals Ser.). (ENG.). 24p. (J). (gr. -1-1). 135.60 *(978-0-7660-7131-5(6))*; pap., pap., pap. 336.60 *(978-0-7660-6690-8(8))* Enslow Pubs., Inc.

All about Baby Zoo Animals: Set 3. 2016. (All about Baby Zoo Animals Ser.). 24p. (gr. 1-k). pap. 56.10 *(978-0-7660-7961-8(9))*; lib. bdg. 135.60 *(978-0-7660-7489-7(7))* Enslow Pubs., Inc.

Amery, Heather. Zoo Talkabout Board Book. Cartwright, Stephen, illus. 2008. (Talkabout Board Bks). 12p. (J). bds. 8.99 *(978-0-7945-1793-9(5)*, Usborne) EDC Publishing.

Andrews McMeel Publishing, LLC Staff. Zoo Babies. 2015. (ENG.). 12p. (J). bds. 5.99 *(978-1-4494-6058-7(5))* Andrews McMeel Publishing.

Animales Del Zoológico / Zoo Animals. 2015. (Animales Del Zoológico / Zoo Animals Ser.). (ENG & SPA.). 24p. (J). (gr. k-k). 135.60 *(978-1-4824-2975-6(6))* Stevens, Gareth Publishing LLLP.

Appleby, Alex. Dinosaurs at the Zoo. 2013. (Dinosaur School Ser.). 24p. (J). (gr. k-1). pap. 48.90 *(978-1-4339-9047-2(4))*; pap. 8.15 *(978-1-4339-9046-5(6))*; (ENG., Illus.). lib. bdg. 22.60 *(978-1-4339-9045-8(8))* Stevens, Gareth Publishing LLLP.

At the Zoo. (Boxset Small Ser.). 32p. *(978-1-4054-7068-1(2))* Parragon, Inc.

Ayers, Chris. My Daily Zoo: A Drawing Activity Book for All Ages. 2011. (ENG., Illus.). 96p. pap. 9.95 *(978-1-933492-63-6(5))* Design Studio Pr.

AZ Books Staff. Noisy Zoo. Tulup, Natalia, ed. 2012. (How We Speak Ser.). (ENG.). 12p. (J). (gr. -1-k). bds. 10.95 *(978-1-61889-094-8(8))* AZ Bks. LLC.

Becker, Helaine. Worms for Breakfast: How to Feed a Zoo. Boake, Kathy, illus. 2016. (ENG.). 40p. (J). (gr. 2-5). 16.95 *(978-1-77147-105-3(0)*, Owlkids) Owlkids Bks. Inc. CAN. Dist: Publishers Group West (PGW).

Beylon, Cathy. At the Zoo/en el Zoologico: Bilingual Coloring Book. Gongora, Oscar, tr. 2011. (Dover Children's Bilingual Coloring Book Ser.). (ENG & SPA., Illus.). 32p. (J). (gr. k-6). pap. 3.99 *(978-0-486-47814-2(9))* Dover Pubns., Inc.

Bishop, Celeste. A Visit to the Zoo. 2016. (Places in My Community Ser.). 00024p. (J). (gr. 1-1). pap. 8.25 *(978-1-4994-2772-1(7)*, PowerKids Pr.) Rosen Publishing Group, Inc., The.

Bleiman, Andrew & Eastland, Chris. ABC ZooBorns! 2012. (ZooBorns Ser.). (ENG., Illus.). 40p. (J). (gr. -1-1). 12.99 *(978-1-4424-4371-6(5)*, Beach Lane Bks.) Beach Lane Bks.

—ABC ZooBorns! 2013. (ZooBorns Ser.). (ENG., Illus.). 40p. (J). (gr. -1 — 1). bds. 7.99 *(978-1-4424-7376-8(2)*, Little Simon) Little Simon.

—Hello, Mommy ZooBorns! 2013. (ZooBorns Ser.). (ENG., Illus.). 24p. (J). (gr. -1-1). 16.99 *(978-1-4424-4382-2(0))*; pap. 3.99 *(978-1-4424-4383-9(9))* Simon Spotlight. (Simon Spotlight).

—I Love You, ZooBorns! 2012. (ZooBorns Ser.). (ENG., Illus.). 24p. (J). (gr. -1-1). 15.99 *(978-1-4424-4379-2(0))*; pap. 3.99 *(978-1-4424-4380-8(4))* Simon Spotlight. (Simon Spotlight).

—Nighty Night, ZooBorns. 2013. (ZooBorns Ser.). (ENG., Illus.). 24p. (J). (gr. -1-1). 16.99 *(978-1-4424-4385-3(5))*; pap. 3.99 *(978-1-4424-4386-0(3))* Simon Spotlight. (Simon Spotlight).

—Snuggle up, ZooBorns! 2015. (ZooBorns Ser.). (J). (ENG., Illus.). 24p. (J). (gr. -1-1). pap. 3.99 *(978-1-4814-3100-2(5))*; *(978-1-4806-9333-3(2))* Simon Spotlight. (Simon Spotlight).

—Splish, Splash, ZooBorns! 2015. (ZooBorns Ser.). (ENG., Illus.). 24p. (J). (gr. -1-1). 16.99 *(978-1-4814-3098-2(X)*, Simon Spotlight) Simon Spotlight.

—Welcome to the World, Zooborns! 2012. (ZooBorns Ser.). (ENG., Illus.). 24p. (J). (gr. -1-1). 16.99 *(978-1-4424-4376-1(6))*; pap. 3.99 *(978-1-4424-4377-8(4))* Simon Spotlight. (Simon Spotlight).

—ZooBorns! Zoo Babies from Around the World. 2010. (ZooBorns Ser.). (ENG.). 40p. (J). (gr. -1-1). 12.99 *(978-1-4424-1272-9(0)*, Beach Lane Bks.) Beach Lane Bks.

—ZooBorns! Zoo Babies from Around the World. 2012. (ZooBorns Ser.). (ENG.). 40p. (J). (gr. -1 — 1). bds. 7.99 *(978-1-4424-4329-7(4)*, Little Simon) Little Simon.

—1-2-3 ZooBorns! 2015. (ZooBorns Ser.). (ENG., Illus.). 32p. (J). (gr. -1-3). 14.99 *(978-1-4814-3103-3(X)*, Beach Lane Bks.) Beach Lane Bks.

Bloomsbury USA. My Zoo Animals. 2014. (ENG., Illus.). 32p. (J). (gr. -1-1). pap., act. bk. ed. 4.99 *(978-1-61963-305-6(1)*, 9781619633056, Bloomsbury USA Childrens) Bloomsbury Publishing USA.

Bosch, Sammy. Super Simple Zoo Critter Crafts: Fun & Easy Animal Crafts. 2016. (ENG., Illus.). 32p. (J). *(978-1-68078-165-6(0))* ABDO Publishing Co.

Boughton, Samantha. Day at the Zoo Adventure Coloring Book. 2014. (ENG., Illus.). 48p. (J). (gr. k). pap. 4.99 *(978-0-486-49154-7(4))* Dover Pubns., Inc.

Brannon, Cecelia H. Baby Gorillas at the Zoo. 2016. (All about Baby Zoo Animals Ser.). (ENG.). 24p. (J). (gr. k-1). pap. 9.35 *(978-0-7660-7141-4(3))*; (Illus.). 22.60 *(978-0-7660-7143-8(X))* Enslow Pubs., Inc.

—Baby Hippos at the Zoo. 2016. (All about Baby Zoo Animals Ser.). (ENG.). 24p. (J). (gr. k-1). pap. 9.35 *(978-0-7660-7145-2(6))*; (Illus.). lib. bdg. 22.60 *(978-0-7660-7148-3(0))* Enslow Pubs., Inc.

—Baby Penguins at the Zoo. 2016. (All about Baby Zoo Animals Ser.). (ENG., Illus.). 24p. (J). (gr. k-1). lib. bdg. 22.60 *(978-0-7660-7152-0(9))* Enslow Pubs., Inc.

—Baby Polar Bears at the Zoo. 2016. (All about Baby Zoo Animals Ser.). (ENG.). 24p. (J). (gr. k-1). pap. 9.35 *(978-0-7660-7154-4(5))*; (Illus.). lib. bdg. 22.60 *(978-0-7660-7156-8(1))* Enslow Pubs., Inc.

—Baby Turtles at the Zoo. 2016. (All about Baby Zoo Animals Ser.). (ENG.). 24p. (J). (gr. k-1). pap. 9.35 *(978-0-7660-7158-2(8))*; (Illus.). lib. bdg. 22.60 *(978-0-7660-7160-5(X))* Enslow Pubs., Inc.

—Baby Whales at the Zoo. 2016. (All about Baby Zoo Animals Ser.). 24p. (J). (gr. 1-k). 22.60 *(978-0-7660-7563-4(X))* Enslow Pubs., Inc.

Brown, Heather. Chomp! Zoo: A Pull-Tab Book. 2012. (ENG.). 12p. (J). (gr. -1-k). bds. 7.99 *(978-1-4494-2312-4(4))* Andrews McMeel Publishing.

Capstone Press. Zoo Animal Mysteries. 2010. (Zoo Animal Mysteries Ser.). (ENG.). 32p. lib. bdg. 143.94 *(978-1-4296-5901-7(7)*, Pebble Plus) Capstone Press of Coughlan Cos.

Carle, Eric & Chronicle Books Staff. 1, 2, 3, to the Zoo Train Flash Cards. 2013. (ENG., Illus.). 21p. (J). (gr. -1 — 1). 14.99 *(978-1-4521-1341-8(6))* Chronicle Bks. LLC.

Chilek, Laurie. Counting at the Zoo: Learning to Add 1 to One-Digit Numbers. (Math for the Real World Ser.). (ENG., Illus.). 8p. (gr. k-1). 2009. pap. 5.15 *(978-0-8239-8909-6(7))* 2004. 29.95 *(978-0-8239-7628-7(9))* Rosen Publishing Group, Inc., The.

Clark, Rosalyn. A Visit to the Zoo. 2017. (Bumba Books (tm) — Places We Go Ser.). (ENG.). 24p. (J). (gr. -1-1). 25.32 ***(978-1-5124-3373-9(X))*** Lerner Publishing Group.

Clarke, Phillip, ed. 100 Animals to Spot at the Zoo. McGregor, Malcolm, illus. 2009. (Spotter's Cards Ser.). 52p. (J). 9.99 *(978-0-7945-2254-4(8)*, Usborne) EDC Publishing.

Clemson, Wendy & Clemson, David. Zookeeper for a Day. 2007. (Math Adventures Ser.). (Illus.). 32p. (gr. 1-4). pap. 10.50 *(978-0-8368-8142-4(7))*; lib. bdg. 26.00 *(978-0-8368-7843-1(4))* Stevens, Gareth Publishing LLLP. (Gareth Stevens Learning Library).

Cryan, Mary Beth. Easy-to-Make Zoo Animals Finger Puppets. 2012. (Dover Children's Activity Bks.). (ENG., Illus.). 16p. (J). (gr. 2-5). 9.99 *(978-0-486-48844-8(6))* Dover Pubns., Inc.

Curtis, Jennifer Keats. La Camada con Suerte: Cachorros de Lobo Rescatados de un Incendio Forestal, 1 vol. Gomes, John, illus. 2015. (ENG & SPA.). 32p. (J). (gr. 2-5). pap. 9.95 *(978-1-62855-720-6(6))* Arbordale Publishing.

—La Historia de Kali: El Rescate de un Oso Polar Huérfano. Gomes, John, illus. 2014.Tr. of Kali's Story: an Orphaned Polar Bear Rescue. (SPA.). 32p. (J). (gr. 1-4). pap. 9.95 *(978-1-62855-226-3(3))* Arbordale Publishing.

—Kali's Story: An Orphaned Polar Bear Rescue, 1 vol. Gomes, John, photos by. 2014. (ENG., Illus.). 32p. (J). (gr. 1-4). 17.95 *(978-1-62855-208-9(5))* Arbordale Publishing.

—The Lucky Litter: Wolf Pups Rescued from Wildfire, 1 vol. Gomes, John, illus. 2015. (ENG.). 32p. (J). (gr. 2-5). 17.95 *(978-1-62855-718-3(4))* Arbordale Publishing.

—Primate School, 1 vol. 2015. (ENG & SPA., Illus.). 32p. (J). (gr. 2-5). 17.95 *(978-1-62855-555-4(6))* Arbordale Publishing.

Dawson, Emily C. The Zoo. 2010. (My Community Ser.). 24p. (J). 25.65 *(978-1-60753-024-4(4))* Amicus Publishing.

Dee, Nora. Spanish Words at the Zoo, Vol. 1. 2014. (Learn My Language! Spanish Ser.). 24p. (J). (gr. 1-2). (ENG.). pap. 8.15 *(978-1-4824-0358-9(7))*; 22.60 *(978-1-4824-0355-8(2))* Stevens, Gareth Publishing LLLP.

W X Y Z

DiCicco, Sue. 1, 2 at the Zoo. DiCicco, Sue, illus. 2012. (ENG., Illus.). 10p. (J). (— 1). bds. 6.99 *(978-0-545-43239-9(1))* Scholastic, Inc.

Dorling Kindersley Publishing Staff. Follow the Trail at the Zoo. 2017. (Follow the Trail Ser.). (ENG., Illus.). 14p. (J). (— 1). bds. 9.99 ***(978-1-4654-6140-7(X)***, DK Children) Dorling Kindersley Publishing, Inc.

—Petting Zoo. 2013. (DK Readers Ser.). (ENG., Illus.). 32p. (J). (gr. -1-1). pap. 3.99 *(978-1-4654-0944-7(0)*, DK Children) Dorling Kindersley Publishing, Inc.

—Tabbed Board Books: My First Zoo: Let's Meet the Animals! 2016. (Tab Board Bks.). (ENG., Illus.). 28p. (J). (— 1). bds. 9.99 *(978-1-4654-4883-5(7)*, DK Children) Dorling Kindersley Publishing, Inc.

Drews, Judith. The Zoo's Grand Opening: An ABC & Counting Book. 2014. (ENG., Illus.). 64p. 16.95 *(978-3-89955-714-5(X))* Die Gestalten Verlag DEU. Dist: Penguin Random Hse. LLC.

Earhart, Kristin, ed. Life-Size Zoo: From Tiny Rodents to Gigantic Elephants, an Actual Size Animal Encyclopedia. Fukuda, Toyofumi, photos by. 2009. (ENG., Illus.). 48p. (gr. -1). 17.95 *(978-1-934734-20-9(9))* Seven Footer Pr.

Encyclopaedia Britannica, Inc. Staff, compiled by. Discover English with Ben & Bella: Series 4: at the Zoo. 2010. 180.00 *(978-1-61535-351-4(8))* Encyclopaedia Britannica, Inc.

Feeding time at the Zoo: Individual Title Six-Packs. (gr. 1-2). 22.00 *(978-0-7635-9178-6(5))* Rigby Education.

Felix, Rebecca. Patterns at the Zoo. 2015. (21st Century Basic Skills Library: Patterns All Around Ser.). (ENG., Illus.). 24p. (J). (gr. k-3). pap. 12.79 *(978-1-63188-935-6(4)*, 206001) Cherry Lake Publishing.

Fisher, Diana, illus. Watch Me Draw the Zoo. 2013. (Watch Me Draw Ser.). 24p. (J). (gr. -1-2). 25.65 *(978-1-936309-90-0(4))* Quarto Publishing Group USA.

Franks, Katie. Elephants. 2014. (Zoo's Who's Who Ser.). 24p. (J). (gr. k-2). pap. 8.25 *(978-1-4777-6568-5(9)*, PowerKids Pr.) Rosen Publishing Group, Inc., The.

—Lions. 2014. (Zoo's Who's Who Ser.). (Illus.). 24p. (J). (gr. k-2). 23.60 *(978-1-4777-6475-6(5)*, PowerKids Pr.) Rosen Publishing Group, Inc., The.

—Sea Lions. 2014. (Zoo's Who's Who Ser.). (Illus.). 24p. (J). (gr. k-2). pap. 8.25 *(978-1-4777-6585-2(9)*, PowerKids Pr.) Rosen Publishing Group, Inc., The.

Fuerst, Jeffrey B. Feeding Time at the Zoo: Lap Book. 2009. (My First Reader's Theater Set B Ser.). (J). 28.00 *(978-1-4108-8541-8(0))* Benchmark Education Co.

Gallagher, Debbie. Penguins. 2009. (Zoo Animals 2 Ser.). 32p. (gr. 2). lib. bdg. 18.56 *(978-0-7614-4747-4(4))* Marshall Cavendish Corp.

—Seals & Sea Lions. 2009. (Zoo Animals 2 Ser.). 32p. (gr. 2). lib. bdg. 18.56 *(978-0-7614-4748-1(2))* Marshall Cavendish GBR. Dist: Marshall Cavendish Corp.

—Snakes. 2009. (Zoo Animals 2 Ser.). 32p. (gr. 2). lib. bdg. 18.56 *(978-0-7614-4749-8(0))* Marshall Cavendish Corp.

Galvin, Laura Gates. First Look at Zoo Animals. Fulcher, Roz, illus. 2009. (ENG.). 16p. (J). bds. 6.95 *(978-1-59249-998-4(8))* Studio Mouse LLC.

Gardner, Robert. How Heavy Is Heavy? Science Projects with Weight. 2015. (Hot Science Experiments Ser.). 48p. (J). (gr. 3-4). pap. 8.95 *(978-0-7660-6601-4(0)*, Enslow Elementary) Enslow Pubs., Inc.

Gregory, Josh. Elephants. 2012. (21st Century Basic Skills Library: Baby Zoo Animals Ser.). (ENG.). 24p. (gr. k-3). 22.79 *(978-1-61080-452-3(X)*, 202062); pap. 12.79 *(978-1-61080-626-8(3)*, 202236) Cherry Lake Publishing.

—Giraffes. 2012. (21st Century Basic Skills Library: Baby Zoo Animals Ser.). (ENG.). 24p. (gr. k-3). 22.79 *(978-1-61080-456-1(2)*, 202066); pap. 12.79 *(978-1-61080-630-5(1)*, 202240) Cherry Lake Publishing.

—Polar Bears. 2012. (21st Century Basic Skills Library: Baby Zoo Animals Ser.). (ENG.). 24p. (gr. k-3). (J). 22.79 *(978-1-61080-459-2(7)*, 202069); pap. 12.79 *(978-1-61080-633-6(6)*, 202243) Cherry Lake Publishing.

Gunzi, Christiane. Zoo. Zwemmer, Dominic, ed. 2015. (ENG., Illus.). 34p. (J). 7.95 *(978-1-906572-30-3(5))* Award Pubns. Ltd. GBR. Dist: Parkwest Pubns., Inc.

Halls, Kelly Milner & Sumner, William. Saving the Baghdad Zoo: A True Story of Hope & Heroes. Sumner, William, illus. 2010. (ENG., Illus.). 64p. (J). (gr. 3-18). 17.99 *(978-0-06-177202-3(X)*, Greenwillow Bks.) HarperCollins Pubs.

Harrison, Sarah. A Day at a Zoo. 2008. (Time Goes By Ser.). (ENG.). (gr. k-3). pap. 39.62 *(978-0-7613-4710-1(0))*; (Illus.). 24p. (J). lib. bdg. 22.60 *(978-1-58013-554-2(4))* Lerner Publishing Group.

Hatkoff, Craig. Knut: How One Little Polar Bear Captivated the World. 2007. (J). pap. 16.99 *(978-0-545-04717-3(X)*, Scholastic Pr.) Scholastic, Inc.

Hewett, Richard, illus. & photos by. A Monkey Baby Grows Up. Hewett, Richard, photos by. Hewett, Joan, photos by. 2004. (Baby Animals Ser.). 32p. (J). (gr. k-3). lib. bdg. 21.27 *(978-1-57505-199-4(0))* Lerner Publishing Group.

Holden, Pam. King of the Zoo, 6 pack. Cammell, Sandra, illus. 2009. (Red Rocket Readers Ser.). (ENG.). 16p. (gr. -1-1). pap. *(978-1-877363-13-9(8)*, Red Rocket Readers) Flying Start Bks.

Holtz, Monica Stauber. Behind the Zoo: Find Out What the Animals Eat & Do at Irvine Park Zoo, Chippewa Falls, Wisconsin. Opatz, Shane, illus. Opatz, Shane, photos by. 2011. (J). *(978-0-9837617-1-6(X))* Holtz Creative Enterprises.

Hullabaloo at the Zoo, 3 vols., Pack. (Sails Literacy Ser.). 24p. (gr. 1-18). 57.00 *(978-0-7578-3208-6(3))* Rigby Education.

Johnson, Bruce & McKay, Sindy. We Both Read-Zoo Day. Johnson, Meredith, illus. 2015. (We Both Read - Level 1 (Quality) Ser.). (ENG.). 44p. (J). (gr. k-2). pap. 4.99 *(978-1-60115-274-9(4))* Treasure Bay, Inc.

—Zoo Day/Dia Del Zoologico: Spanish/English Bilingual Edition (We Both Read - Level 1) Johnson, Meredith, illus. 2016. (We Both Read - Level 1 Ser.). (ENG & SPA.). (J). pap. 4.99 *(978-1-60115-078-3(4))* Treasure Bay, Inc.

Jones, Kimberly & Jones, Laura. Morning Zoo. 2009. 24p. pap. 11.99 *(978-1-4389-4086-1(6))* AuthorHouse.

Kalz, Jill. Zoo Adventure. Cerato, Mattia, illus. 2010. (A-MAZE-Ing Adventures Ser.). (ENG.). 32p. (gr. 1-2). lib. bdg. 26.65 *(978-1-4048-6024-7(X))* Picture Window Bks.

Katirgis, Jane. Baby Zoo Animals. 2010. (All about Baby Animals Ser.). (Illus.). 24p. (J). 22.60 *(978-0-7660-3796-0(7))*; pap. 7.95 *(978-1-59845-159-7(6))* Enslow Pubs., Inc. (Enslow Elementary).

Komiya, Teruyuki. More Life-Size Zoo: An All-New Actual-Size Animal Encyclopedia. Miyakoshi, Junko, tr. Matsuhashi, Toshimitsu, photos by. 2010. (ENG., Illus.). 48p. (gr. -1). 18.95 *(978-1-934734-19-3(5))* Seven Footer Pr.

Krych, Elizabeth. Magnetic Learning - Safari. 2015. (Magnetic Learning Ser.). (ENG., Illus.). 56p. (J). (gr. -1). 19.95 *(978-1-62686-333-0(4)*, Silver Dolphin Bks.) Readerlink Distribution Services, LLC.

Lazoo Publishing Staff. Colors! 2010. (ENG., Illus.). 10p. (J). bds. 6.99 *(978-1-934734-56-8(X))* Seven Footer Pr.

Levy, Barbara Soloff. Little Zoo Animal Mazes. 2006. (Dover Little Activity Bks.). (ENG., Illus.). 64p. (J). (gr. k-3). per. 1.99 *(978-0-486-44440-6(6))* Dover Pubns., Inc.

Lluch, Alex A. I Like to Learn Alphabet: Zoo Clues. 2011. (ENG.). 32p. (J). (gr. -1-k). bds. 4.95 *(978-1-934386-00-2(6))* WS Publishing.

Macken, JoAnn Early. Monkeys: Los Monos. 2004. (Animals I See at the Zoo/ Animales que veo en el zoologico (bilingual) Ser.). (SPA., Illus.). 24p. (gr. k-3). pap. 8.15 *(978-0-8368-4388-0(6)*, Weekly Reader Leveled Readers) Stevens, Gareth Publishing LLLP.

—Monkeys (Los Monos) 2004. (Animals I See at the Zoo/Animales que Veo en el Zoológico Ser.). (SPA., Illus.). 24p. (gr. k-3). lib. bdg. 22.00 *(978-0-8368-4383-5(5)*, Weekly Reader Leveled Readers) Stevens, Gareth Publishing LLLP.

—Penguins/Los Pingüinos. 2003. (Weekly Reader Early Learning Library). (ENG & SPA., Illus.). 24p. (J). (gr. k-3). pap. 8.15 *(978-0-8368-4006-3(2)*, Weekly Reader Leveled Readers) Stevens, Gareth Publishing LLLP.

Markarian, Margie. Who Scoops Elephant Poo? Working at a Zoo. 2010. (Wild Work Ser.). (ENG., Illus.). 32p. (gr. 1-2). 29.99 *(978-1-4109-3848-0(4)*, Read Me!) Heinemann-Raintree.

Markovics, Joyce. Mi Cuerpo Es Duro y Gris (Armadillo) 2016. (Pistas de Animales 2 Ser.). (SPA.). 24p. (J). (gr. -1-3). 17.95 *(978-1-944102-81-4(7))* Bearport Publishing Co., Inc.

—MIS Patas Son Palmeadas y Anaranjadas (Puffin) 2016. (Pistas de Animales 2 Ser.). (SPA.). 24p. (J). (gr. -1-3). 17.95 *(978-1-944102-80-7(9))* Bearport Publishing Co., Inc.

Markovics, Joyce L. My Body Is Tough & Gray. 2016. (Zoo Clues 2 Ser.). (ENG.). 24p. (J). (gr. -1-3). lib. bdg. 17.95 *(978-1-944102-63-0(9))* Bearport Publishing Co., Inc.

—My Feet Are Webbed & Orange. 2016. (Zoo Clues 2 Ser.). (ENG.). 24p. (J). (gr. -1-3). lib. bdg. 17.95 *(978-1-944102-62-3(0))* Bearport Publishing Co., Inc.

Marsico, Katie. Cheetahs. 2012. (21st Century Basic Skills Library: Baby Zoo Animals Ser.). (ENG.). 24p. (gr. k-3). 22.79 *(978-1-61080-453-0(8)*, 202063); pap. 12.79 *(978-1-61080-627-5(1)*, 202237) Cherry Lake Publishing.

—Chimpanzees. 2012. (21st Century Basic Skills Library: Baby Zoo Animals Ser.). (ENG.). 24p. (gr. k-3). 22.79 *(978-1-61080-455-4(4)*, 202065); pap. 12.79 *(978-1-61080-629-9(8)*, 202239) Cherry Lake Publishing.

—Hippopotamuses. 2012. (21st Century Basic Skills Library: Baby Zoo Animals Ser.). (ENG.). 24p. (gr. k-3). 22.79 *(978-1-61080-458-5(9)*, 202068); pap. 12.79 *(978-1-61080-632-9(8)*, 202242) Cherry Lake Publishing.

—Jaguars. 2012. (21st Century Basic Skills Library: Baby Zoo Animals Ser.). (ENG.). 24p. (gr. k-3). 22.79 *(978-1-61080-454-7(6)*, 202064); pap. 12.79 *(978-1-61080-628-2(X)*, 202238) Cherry Lake Publishing.

—Koala Bears. 2012. (21st Century Basic Skills Library: Baby Zoo Animals Ser.). (ENG.). 24p. (gr. k-3). 22.79 *(978-1-61080-457-8(0)*, 202067); pap. 12.79 *(978-1-61080-631-2(X)*, 202241) Cherry Lake Publishing.

Martin, Isabel. A Zoo Field Trip. 2015. (Let's Take a Field Trip Ser.). (ENG.). 24p. (gr. k-1). pap. 6.95 *(978-1-4914-2316-5(1)*, Pebble Plus) Capstone Press of Coughlan Cos.

Marx, David F. Doc Block. Phillips, Matt, illus. 2006. (Reader's Clubhouse Level 1 Reader Ser.). (ENG.). 24p. (J). (gr. 1-4). pap. 3.99 *(978-0-7641-3288-9(1))* Barron's Educational Series, Inc.

Mellark, Kat. Our Zoo Adventure: Compare Numbers. 2013. (Rosen Math Readers Ser.). (ENG.). 16p. (J). (gr. k-1). pap. 42.00 *(978-1-4777-1600-7(9))*; (Illus.). pap. 7.00 *(978-1-4777-1599-4(1))* Rosen Publishing Group, Inc., The. (Rosen Classroom).

Moldovo, Eustacia. Baby Elephants at the Zoo. 2015. (J). *(978-0-7660-6613-7(4))*; (ENG., Illus.). 24p. (gr. -1-1). pap. 9.35 *(978-0-7660-7089-9(1))* Enslow Pubs., Inc.

—Baby Lions at the Zoo. 2015. (J). *(978-0-7660-6609-0(6))*; (ENG., Illus.). 24p. (gr. -1-1). pap. 9.35 *(978-0-7660-7085-1(9))* Enslow Pubs., Inc.

—Baby Monkeys at the Zoo. 2015. (J). *(978-0-7660-6597-0(9))*; (ENG., Illus.). 24p. (gr. -1-1). pap. 9.35 *(978-0-7660-7073-8(5))* Enslow Pubs., Inc.

—Baby Pandas at the Zoo. 2015. (All about Baby Zoo Animals Ser.). (ENG., Illus.). 24p. (J). (gr. -1-1). 22.60 *(978-0-7660-7079-0(4))*; pap. 9.35 *(978-0-7660-7077-6(8))* Enslow Pubs., Inc.

—Baby Zebras at the Zoo. 2015. (J). *(978-0-7660-6617-5(7))*; (ENG., Illus.). 24p. (gr. -1-1). pap. 9.35 *(978-0-7660-7093-6(X))* Enslow Pubs., Inc.

Moore, Katharine & Sonne, Lisa T. E., texts. Zoo Animals. 2010. (Illus.). (J). *(978-1-4351-2492-9(8))* Barnes & Noble, Inc.

Morecroft, Richard, et al. Zoo Album. Lloyd-Diviny, Karen, illus. 2004. (ENG.). 48p. (J). (gr. 3). 17.95 *(978-1-59270-032-5(2))* Enchanted Lion Bks., LLC.

Mumme, Sarah. Guess Who's at the Zoo. Samuel, Janet, illus. 2015. (Guess Who's... Bks.). (ENG.). 10p. (J). (gr. -1 — 1). 5.99 *(978-0-7641-6801-7(0))* Barron's Educational Series, Inc.

Nault, Jennifer. Project Polar Bear. Kissock, Heather & Marshall, Diana, eds. 2003. (Zoo Life Ser.). (Illus.). 24p. (J). pap. 8.95 *(978-1-59036-060-6(5))* Weigl Pubs., Inc.

Newman, Patricia. Zoo Scientists to the Rescue. Crawley, Annie, photos by. 2017. (ENG., Illus.). (J). (gr. 4-8). lib. bdg. 33.32 ***(978-1-5124-1571-1(5)***, Millbrook Pr.) Lerner Publishing Group.

Novick, Mary & Hale, Jenny. Farm & Zoo. 2006. (Illus.). 32p. *(978-1-921049-26-2(X))* Little Hare Bks. AUS. Dist: HarperCollins Pubs. Australia.

Oehler, David A. The Cincinnati Zoo & Botanical Garden. 2003. (Great Zoos of the United States Ser.). (Illus.). 24p. (J). lib. bdg. 22.60 *(978-0-8239-6320-1(9)*, PowerKids Pr.) Rosen Publishing Group, Inc., The.

Olmedillas, Cathy, compiled by. Anorak. 2013. (ENG., Illus.). 64p. (J). pap. 9.99 *(978-1-4236-3340-2(7)*, Anorak Pr.) Gibbs Smith, Publisher.

Orr, Tamra. Working at the Zoo. 2011. (21st Century Junior Library: Careers Ser.). (ENG.). 24p. (gr. 2-5). lib. bdg. 25.64 *(978-1-60279-978-3(4)*, 200946) Cherry Lake Publishing.

Owen, Ruth. The Wild World of a Zoo Vet. 2015. (Get to Work with Science & Technology Ser.). (ENG.). 32p. (J). (gr. 2-7). lib. bdg. 26.60 *(978-1-910549-34-6(7))* Bearport Publishing Co., Inc.

Paiva, Johannah Gilman, ed. Zoo Friends. 2013. (Illus.). 20p. (J). bds. 8.99 *(978-1-77093-629-4(7))* Flowerpot Children's Pr. Inc. CAN. Dist: Cardinal Pubs. Group.

Pajalunga, Lorena V. Yoga for Kids: Simple Animal Poses for Any Age. Forlati, Anna, illus. 2015. (ENG.). 32p. (J). (gr. -1-3). 16.99 *(978-0-8075-9172-7(6))* Whitman, Albert & Co.

Parker, Gary & Parker, Mary. The Complete Zoo Adventure: A Field Trip in a Book. 2008. (Illus.). 160p. (J). (gr. -1). 18.99 *(978-0-89051-500-6(X))* Master Bks.

Pelusey, Michael. Giraffes & Zebras. 2008. (Zoo Animals Ser.). 32p. (gr. 2-3). lib. bdg. 18.56 *(978-0-7614-3149-7(7)*, Benchmark Bks.) Marshall Cavendish Corp.

—Zoo Animals, 6 bks., Set. Incl. Apes & Monkeys. Pelusey, Jane. lib. bdg. 18.56 *(978-0-7614-3144-2(6))*; Bears. Pelusey, Jane. lib. bdg. 18.56 *(978-0-7614-3147-3(0))*; Elephants. Pelusey, Jane. lib. bdg. 18.56 *(978-0-7614-3148-0(9))*; Giraffes & Zebras. lib. bdg. 18.56 *(978-0-7614-3149-7(7))*; Rhinoceroses & Hippopotamuses. Pelusey, Jane. lib. bdg. 18.56 *(978-0-7614-3150-3(0))*; Tigers & Lions. Pelusey, Jane. lib. bdg. 18.56 *(978-0-7614-3151-0(9))*; 32p. (gr. 2-3). (Zoo Animals Ser.). 2008. Set lib. bdg. 111.36 *(978-0-7614-3143-5(8)*, Benchmark Bks.) Marshall Cavendish Corp.

Pelusey, Michael & Pelusey, Jane. Bears. 2008. (Zoo Animals Ser.). 32p. (gr. 2-3). lib. bdg. 18.56 *(978-0-7614-3147-3(0)*, Benchmark Bks.) Marshall Cavendish Corp.

—Elephants. 2008. (Zoo Animals Ser.). 32p. (gr. 2-3). lib. bdg. 18.56 *(978-0-7614-3148-0(9)*, Benchmark Bks.) Marshall Cavendish Corp.

—Rhinoceroses & Hippopotamuses. 2008. (Zoo Animals Ser.). 32p. (gr. 2-3). lib. bdg. 18.56 *(978-0-7614-3150-3(0)*, Benchmark Bks.) Marshall Cavendish Corp.

—Tigers & Lions. 2008. (Zoo Animals Ser.). 32p. (gr. 2-3). lib. bdg. 18.56 *(978-0-7614-3151-0(9)*, Benchmark Bks.) Marshall Cavendish Corp.

Pettiford, Rebecca. Zoo. Fretland VanVoorst, Jenny, ed. 2016. (First Field Trips). 24p. (J). (gr. k-2). lib. bdg. 25.65 *(978-1-62031-299-5(9)*, Bullfrog Bks.) Jump! Inc.

—El Zoológico. 2016. (Los Primeros Viajes Escolares (First Field Trips)).Tr. of Zoo. (SPA.). 24p. (J). (gr. k-2). lib. bdg. 25.65 *(978-1-62031-333-6(2)*, Bullfrog Bks.) Jump! Inc.

Picthall, Chez. Flip Flaps Zoo. 2015. (ENG., Illus.). 18p. (J). 9.99 *(978-1-907604-53-9(7))* Award Pubns. Ltd. GBR. Dist: Parkwest Pubns., Inc.

—Zoo Animals. 2015. (ENG., Illus.). 10p. (J). 7.99 *(978-1-906572-06-8(2))* Award Pubns. Ltd. GBR. Dist: Parkwest Pubns., Inc.

Powell, Janet. Saint Louis Zoo. 2003. (Great Zoos of the United States Ser.). (Illus.). 24p. (J). lib. bdg. 22.60 *(978-0-8239-6318-8(7)*, PowerKids Pr.) Rosen Publishing Group, Inc., The.

—St. Louis Zoo. 2009. (Great Zoos of the United States Ser.). 24p. (gr. 3-4). 42.50 *(978-1-61513-226-3(0)*, PowerKids Pr.) Rosen Publishing Group, Inc., The.

Priddy, Roger. Busy Babies Zoo Animals. 2010. 8p. (J). bds. 4.99 *(978-0-312-50856-2(5)*, Priddy Bks.) St. Martin's Pr.

—Zoo: A Noisy Animal Book. 2017. (Baby's First Ser.). (ENG., Illus.). 8p. (J). bds. 8.99 *(978-0-312-52165-3(0)*, 9780312521653, Priddy Bks.) St. Martin's Pr.

Purperhart, Helen. The Yoga Zoo Adventure: Animal Poses & Games for Little Kids. van Amelsfort, Barbara, illus. 2008. (SmartFun Activity Bks.). (ENG.). 160p. (gr. k). spiral bd. 19.95 *(978-0-89793-506-7(3))*; pap. 14.95 *(978-0-89793-505-0(5))* Turner Publishing Co. (Hunter Hse.).

Reilly, Pamela. My Day at the Zoo. 2011. 24p. pap. 12.95 *(978-1-935268-72-7(4))* Halo Publishing International.

Ring, Susan. Elok. 2009. (J). *(978-1-60596-659-5(2))*; *(978-1-60596-660-1(6))* Weigl Pubs., Inc.

—Herbie. 2009. (J). *(978-1-60596-662-5(2))*; *(978-1-60596-661-8(4))* Weigl Pubs., Inc.

—Project Elephant. Kissock, Heather & Marshall, Diana, eds. 2003. (Zoo Life Ser.). 24p. (J). pap. 8.95 *(978-1-59036-056-9(7))* Weigl Pubs., Inc.

—Project Hippopotamus. Kissock, Heather & Marshall, Diana, eds. 2003. (Zoo Life Ser.). (Illus.). 24p. (J). pap. 8.95 *(978-1-59036-057-6(5))* Weigl Pubs., Inc.

—Project Hippopotamus. 2003. (Zoo Babies Ser.). (Illus.). 24p. (J). (gr. 2-4). lib. bdg. 24.45 *(978-1-59036-013-2(3))* Weigl Pubs., Inc.

—Project Orangutan. Marshall, Diana & Nault, Jennifer, eds. 2003. (Zoo Life Ser.). (Illus.). 24p. (J). pap. 8.95 *(978-1-59036-058-3(3))* Weigl Pubs., Inc.

—Project Otter. Kissock, Heather & Marshall, Diana, eds. 2003. (Zoo Life Ser.). (Illus.). 24p. (J). pap. 8.95 *(978-1-59036-059-0(1))* Weigl Pubs., Inc.

—Project Tiger. Marshall, Diana & Nault, Jennifer, eds. 2003. (Zoo Life Ser.). (Illus.). 24p. (J). pap. 8.95 *(978-1-59036-061-3(3))* Weigl Pubs., Inc.

Rivers-Moore, Debbie. In the Zoo. 2017. (My First Noisy Bath Bks.). (ENG.). 8p. (J). (gr. -1 — 1). 4.99 *(978-1-4380-7829-8(3))* Barron's Educational Series, Inc.

Robinson, Joanna Jarc. Andrew & Allen Learn about Adverbs. Boyer, Robin, illus. 2014. (Language Builders Ser.). (ENG.). 32p. (J). (gr. 2-4). pap. 11.94 *(978-1-60357-704-5(1))*; lib. bdg. 25.27 *(978-1-59953-669-9(2))* Norwood Hse. Pr.

Rudolph, Jessica. MIS Orejas Son Enormes y Peludas (Fennec Fox) 2016. (Pistas de Animales 2 Ser.). (SPA.). 24p. (J). (gr. -1-3). 17.95 *(978-1-944102-75-3(2))* Bearport Publishing Co., Inc.

—My Ears Are Huge & Fuzzy. 2016. (Zoo Clues 2 Ser.). (ENG.). 24p. (J). (gr. -1-3). lib. bdg. 17.95 *(978-1-944102-57-9(4))* Bearport Publishing Co., Inc.

Ruggieri, Linda. Amazing Animals: Critter Camp: Division (Grade 3) 2017. (Mathematics Readers Ser.). (Illus.). 32p. (gr. 3-3). 8.99 ***(978-1-4807-5800-1(0))*** Teacher Created Materials, Inc.

San Diego Zoo Staff. Count to 10 & Back Again: San Diego Zoo. 2004. (ENG., Illus.). 24p. (J). 7.95 *(978-0-8249-6552-5(3)*, Ideal Pubns.) Worthy Publishing.

Santa Maria, Christa, des. Zoo Animal Crafts, 01 vols., 1. 2016. (Creating Creature Crafts Ser.). (ENG., Illus.). 24p. (J). pap. 10.60 *(978-1-5081-9121-6(2)*, 1397694, Windmill Bks.) Rosen Publishing Group, Inc., The.

Scholastic, Inc. Staff, contrib. by. Baby Animals at the Zoo. 2013. (ENG.). 12p. (J). bds. 6.95 *(978-0-531-27251-0(6))* Scholastic Library Publishing.

Shahan, Sherry. Feeding Time at the Zoo. Shahan, Sherry, illus. 2014. (Step into Reading Ser.). (ENG., Illus.). 32p. (J). (gr. -1-1). lib. bdg. 12.99 *(978-0-375-97190-7(4)*, Random Hse. Bks. for Young Readers) Random Hse. Children's Bks.

Slade, Suzanne & Waites, Joan. What's New at the Zoo? An Animal Adding Adventure, 1 vol. 2009. (Basic Math Operations Ser.). (ENG., Illus.). 32p. (J). (gr. -1-3). 16.95 *(978-1-934359-93-8(9))*; pap. 8.95 *(978-1-60718-038-8(3)*, 9781607180388) Arbordale Publishing.

Sohn, Emily & Townsend, Laura. Animal Needs: Who's New at the Zoo? 2011. (iScience Readers Ser.). 24p. (J). (gr. k-2). lib. bdg. 21.27 *(978-1-59953-404-6(5))* Norwood Hse. Pr.

Stead, Tony. Should There Be Zoos? A Persuasive Text. 2011. (ENG., Illus.). 32p. (J). (gr. 3-7). pap. 29.99 *(978-1-57255-817-5(2))* Mondo Publishing.

Stillerman, Robbie. Color Your Own Zoo Animals Stickers. 2006. (Dover Sticker Bks.). (ENG., Illus.). 2p. (J). (gr. k-3). 2.95 *(978-0-486-44887-9(8))* Dover Pubns., Inc.

Swanson, Maggie. Zany Zoo Stained Glass Jr. Coloring Book. 2012. (Dover Stained Glass Coloring Book Ser.). (ENG.). 32p. (J). (gr. -1-5). pap. 3.99 *(978-0-486-49869-0(7))* Dover Pubns., Inc.

Taylor, Trace & Sanchez, Lucia M. En el zoológico (at the Zoo) 2011. (Animales Ser.). (SPA.). 16p. pap. 39.62 *(978-1-61541-419-2(3))* American Reading Co.

Wallace, Karen. A Trip to the Zoo. 2003. (DK Readers Ser.). (ENG., Illus.). 32p. (J). (gr. k-2). pap. 3.99 *(978-0-7894-9219-7(9)*, DK Children) Dorling Kindersley Publishing, Inc.

Walter Foster Creative Team. Learn to Draw Zoo Animals: Step-By-Step Instructions for More Than 25 Popular Animals. Cuddy, Robbin, illus. 2016. (Learn to Draw: Expanded Edition Ser.). (ENG.). 64p. (J). (gr. 3-5). lib. bdg. 33.32 *(978-1-939581-99-0(0)*, Walter Foster Jr) Quarto Publishing Group USA.

Ward, Finn. Elephants at the Zoo. 2015. (Zoo Animals Ser.). (ENG., Illus.). 24p. (J). (gr. k-k). pap. 8.15 *(978-1-4824-2589-5(0))* Stevens, Gareth Publishing LLLP.

—Giraffes at the Zoo. 2015. (Zoo Animals Ser.). (ENG., Illus.). 24p. (J). (gr. k-k). pap. 8.15 *(978-1-4824-2593-2(9))* Stevens, Gareth Publishing LLLP.

—Gorillas at the Zoo. 2015. (Zoo Animals Ser.). (ENG., Illus.). 24p. (J). (gr. k-k). pap. 8.15 *(978-1-4824-2597-0(1))* Stevens, Gareth Publishing LLLP.

—Ostriches at the Zoo. 2015. (Zoo Animals Ser.). (ENG., Illus.). 24p. (J). (gr. k-k). pap. 8.15 *(978-1-4824-2601-4(3))* Stevens, Gareth Publishing LLLP.

—Penguins at the Zoo. 2015. (Zoo Animals Ser.). (ENG., Illus.). 24p. (J). (gr. k-k). pap. 8.15 *(978-1-4824-2605-2(6))* Stevens, Gareth Publishing LLLP.

—Polar Bears at the Zoo. 2015. (Zoo Animals Ser.). (ENG., Illus.). 24p. (J). (gr. k-k). pap. 8.15 *(978-1-4824-2609-0(9))* Stevens, Gareth Publishing LLLP.

Wexo, John Bonnett. Focas y Leones Marinos. Rountree, Monica, tr. 2003. (Zoobooks Ser.). Orig. Title: Seals & Sea Lions. (SPA., Illus.). 24p. (J). (gr. k-6). lib. bdg. 15.95 *(978-1-888153-79-8(2))* Wildlife Education, Ltd.

Wilson, Phyllis M. My Two Friends. 2010. 24p. pap. 12.99 *(978-1-4520-7959-2(5))* AuthorHouse.

Wong, Angi Ma, illus. My Story: Reggie: The L.A. Gator. 2007. 25p. *(978-1-928753-12-4(4))* Pacific Heritage Bks.

Working with Animals: Individual Title Six-Packs. (gr. k-1). 23.00 *(978-0-7635-9035-2(5))* Rigby Education.

Yanofsky, Tsivia. Take Me to the Zoo: Lions, elephants & snakes in the Midrash & Nature. 2003. (ArtScroll Youth Ser.). 19.99 *(978-1-57819-099-7(1)*, ZOOH) Mesorah Pubns., Ltd.

A Zoo, 6 Packs. (Literatura 2000 Ser.). (gr. -1-1). 28.00 *(978-0-7635-0044-3(5))* Rigby Education.

Zoo Animal Mysteries, 1 vol. 2010. (Zoo Animal Mysteries Ser.). (ENG.). 24p. (gr. k-1). lib. bdg. 159.90 *(978-1-4296-4502-7(4)*, Pebble Plus) Capstone Press of Coughlan Cos.

Zoo Animals. 2015. (Zoo Animals Ser.). (ENG.). 24p. (J). (gr. k-k). 135.60 *(978-1-4824-2539-0(4))*; pap., pap., pap. 293.40 *(978-1-4824-3502-3(0))*; pap., pap., pap. 48.90 *(978-1-4824-3503-0(9))* Stevens, Gareth Publishing LLLP.

Zoo Animals for Kids: Amazing Pictures & Fun Fact Children Book. 2013. 32p. pap. 9.97 *(978-1-63022-042-6(6))* Speedy Publishing LLC.

The Zoo's Who's Who. 2014. (Zoo's Who's Who Ser.). 24p. (J). (gr. k-2). 141.60 *(978-1-4777-6899-0(8))*; pap. 49.50 *(978-1-4777-7254-6(5))* Rosen Publishing Group, Inc., The. (PowerKids Pr.).

ZOO ANIMALS—FICTION

Adam, Adam, et al. Who Is It? Two Yellow Eyes Shining in the Dark... 2012. (ENG., Illus.). 16p. (J). (gr. -1). bds. 9.95 *(978-2-7338-2146-6(6))* Auzou, Philippe Editions FRA. Dist: Consortium Bk. Sales & Distribution.

Anderson, Amanda. The Story of Larry the Hamster. 2008. 24p. pap. 24.95 *(978-1-60703-125-3(6))* America Star Bks.

AZ Books Staff. My Zoo. Yaroshevich, Angelica, ed. 2012. (Open the Book-I Am Alive Ser.). (ENG.). 8p. (J). (— 1). bds. 5.95 *(978-1-61889-044-3(1))* AZ Bks. LLC.

Babb, Gina. Zain & Zoe's Zoo Adventures: Numbers & Colors. 2011. 16p. 9.36 *(978-1-4520-5578-7(5))* AuthorHouse.

Bardhan-Quallen, Sudipta. Quackenstein Hatches a Family. Jones, Brian T., illus. 2010. (ENG.). 32p. (J). (gr. k-2). 15.95 *(978-0-8109-8973-3(5)*, Abrams Bks. for Young Readers) Abrams, Inc.

Barretta, Gene. Dear Deer: A Book of Homophones. 2007. (J). (gr. k-3). 29.95 incl. audio compact disk *(978-0-8045-4181-7(7))*; 27.95 incl. audio *(978-0-8045-6958-3(4))* Spoken Arts, Inc.

—Dear Deer: A Book of Homophones. Barretta, Gene, illus. 2010. (ENG., Illus.). 40p. (J). (gr. -1-2). pap. 7.99 *(978-0-312-62899-4(4)*, 9780312628994) Square Fish.

Beaumont, Karen. Wild about Us! Stevens, Janet, illus. 2015. (ENG.). 40p. (J). (gr. -1-3). 17.99 *(978-0-15-206294-1(7)*, HMH Books For Young Readers) Houghton Mifflin Harcourt Publishing Co.

Beilenson, Evelyn. The Zoo Is Closed Today! Kennedy, Anne, illus. 2014. (ENG.). 32p. (J). 16.99 *(978-1-4413-1526-7(8)*, 9781441315267) Peter Pauper Pr. Inc.

Berthiaume, Donna M. Our Cool School Zoo Revue. Jirak, Tracey, illus. 2008. 36p. pap. 24.95 *(978-1-60672-672-3(2))* America Star Bks.

Bianchi, John. Is the Spaghetti Ready?, 1 vol. Edwards, Frank, illus. 2008. (New Reader Ser.). (ENG.). 32p. (J). *(978-1-894323-35-2(1))* Bungalo Bks.

Bird, Benjamin. Scooby-Doo! Little Mysteries. 2015. (Scooby-Doo! Little Mysteries Ser.). (ENG.). 20p. (gr. -1 — 1). bds. 31.96 *(978-1-62370-449-0(9))* Capstone Press of Coughlan Cos.

—Scooby-Doo's ABC Mystery. 2015. (Scooby-Doo! Little Mysteries Ser.). (ENG., Illus.). 20p. (gr. -1 — 1). bds. 7.99 *(978-1-62370-175-8(9))* Capstone Press of Coughlan Cos.

Boland, Gerry. Marco Moves In. McGuinness, Áine, illus. 2012. (Rather Remarkable Grizzly Be Ser.). (ENG.). 64p. (J). 12.95 *(978-1-84717-229-7(6))* O'Brien Pr., Ltd., The IRL. Dist: Dufour Editions, Inc.

Bolden-Fournier, Laura. An Orangutan's Night Before Christmas, 1 vol. Jaskiel, Stan, illus. 2016. (ENG.). 32p. (J). (gr. k-3). 16.99 *(978-1-4556-2154-5(4))* Pelican Publishing Co., Inc.

Bostrom, Kathleen Long. The View at the Zoo. Francis, Guy, illus. 2011. 32p. (J). (gr. -1-3). 14.99 *(978-0-8249-5629-5(X)*, Ideal Pubns.) Worthy Publishing.

—A View at the Zoo. Francis, Guy, illus. 2015. (J). pap. *(978-0-8249-5669-1(9)*, Ideal Pubns.) Worthy Publishing.

Brannon, Pat. Quirky Kids Zoo. Jimena Pinto-Krowjiline, illus. 2011. 32p. pap. 11.99 *(978-1-933300-83-2(3))* Wandering Sage Pubns., LLC.

Bratcher, Shirley Kay. Tudy Goes to the Zoo. 2013. 24p. pap. 24.95 *(978-1-4626-9560-7(4))* America Star Bks.

Brennah-Nelson, Denise. Maestro Stu Saves the Zoo. 2012. (ENG., Illus.). 32p. (J). 15.95 *(978-1-58536-802-0(4))* Sleeping Bear Pr.

Brown, Joe. Race to the Rescue. Marchesi, Stephen, illus. 2009. (J). *(978-0-545-13473-6(0))* Scholastic, Inc.

Bryant, Jen. Call Me Marianne. Johnson, David, illus. 2006. 32p. (J). (gr. 1-4). 16.00 *(978-0-8028-5242-7(4)*, Eerdmans Bks For Young Readers) Eerdmans, William B. Publishing Co.

Çaglar, Atife. Sayabiliyorum. 2011. 16p. pap. *(978-1-4269-9408-1(7))* Trafford Publishing (UK) Ltd.

Campbell, Rod. Dear Zoo. Campbell, Rod, illus. 2005. (Dear Zoo & Friends Ser.). (ENG., Illus.). 20p. (J). (gr. -1-k). 14.99 *(978-0-689-87751-3(X)*, Little Simon) Little Simon.

—Dear Zoo. Campbell, Rod, illus. 2004. (Illus.). 16p. (J). (VIE & ENG.). bds. *(978-1-84444-183-9(0))*; (RUS & ENG., bds. *(978-1-84444-178-5(4))*; (CHI & ENG., bds. *(978-1-84444-171-6(7))* Mantra Lingua.

—Dear Zoo. 2004. (BEN & ENG., Illus.). 16p. (J). bds. *(978-1-84444-169-3(5))* Mantra Lingua.

—Dear Zoo. Campbell, Rod, illus. 2004. (Illus.). 16p. (J). (ENG & PER.). bds. *(978-1-84444-172-3(5))*; (ENG & FRE., bds. *(978-1-84444-173-0(3))*; (ENG & GUJ., bds. *(978-1-84444-174-7(1))*; (ENG & HIN., bds. *(978-1-84444-175-4(X))*; (ENG & PAN., bds. *(978-1-84444-176-1(8))*; (ENG & POR., bds. *(978-1-84444-177-8(6))*; (ENG & SPA., bds. *(978-1-84444-179-2(2))*; (ENG & SOM., bds. *(978-1-84444-180-8(6))*; (ENG & TUR., bds. *(978-1-84444-181-5(4))*; (URD & ENG., bds. *(978-1-84444-182-2(2))*; (CHI & ENG., bds. *(978-1-84444-170-9(9))*; (ENG & ALB., bds. *(978-1-84444-167-9(9))*; (ENG & ARA., bds. *(978-1-84444-168-6(7))* Mantra Lingua.

—Dear Zoo: From the Zoo. Campbell, Rod, illus. 25th ed. 2007. (ENG., Illus.). 18p. (J). (gr. -1 — 1). bds. 6.99 *(978-1-4169-4737-0(X)*, Little Simon) Little Simon.

Caple, Kathy. A Night at the Zoo. Caple, Kathy, illus. 2014. (I Like to Read(r) Ser.). (ENG., Illus.). 24p. (J). (gr. -1-3). 14.95 *(978-0-8234-3044-4(8))* Holiday Hse., Inc.

Carter, Stephanie. The Great Zoo Breakout That Never Happened. 2012. 24p. pap. 11.50 *(978-1-62212-043-7(4)*, Strategic Bk. Publishing) Strategic Book Publishing & Rights Agency (SBPRA).

A Change for Zoe: Individual Title Six-Packs. (gr. k-1). 23.00 *(978-0-7635-8840-3(7))* Rigby Education.

Chick, Bryan. Riddles & Danger. 2011. (Secret Zoo Ser.: 3). (ENG.). 288p. (J). (gr. 3-7). 16.99 *(978-0-06-198927-8(4)*, Greenwillow Bks.) HarperCollins Pubs.

—The Secret Zoo: Raids & Rescues. (Secret Zoo Ser.: 5). (ENG.). 272p. (J). (gr. 3-7). 2014. pap. 6.99 *(978-0-06-219229-5(9))* 2013. 16.99 *(978-0-06-219228-8(0))* HarperCollins Pubs. (Greenwillow Bks.).

—Secrets & Shadows. 2011. (Secret Zoo Ser.: 2). (ENG.). 272p. (J). (gr. 3-7). pap. 6.99 *(978-0-06-198926-1(6))*; 16.99 *(978-0-06-198925-4(8))* HarperCollins Pubs. (Greenwillow Bks.).

—Traps & Specters. 2013. (Secret Zoo Ser.: 4). (ENG.). 320p. (J). (gr. 3-7). pap. 6.99 *(978-0-06-219223-3(X)*, Greenwillow Bks.) HarperCollins Pubs.

Christian, Focus & Tnt Ministries Staff. God's Zoo. Chamick, Tim, illus. 2005. (King of Clubs Ser.). (ENG.). 96p. (J). per. 17.99 *(978-1-84550-069-6(5)*, 9781845500696) Christian Focus Pubns. GBR. Dist: Bookmasters Distribution.

Cochran, Jean M. If a Monkey Jumps onto Your School Bus. Morris, Jennifer & Morris, Jennifer E., illus. 2008. (ENG.). 32p. (J). (gr. -1-k). 16.95 *(978-0-9792035-2-7(X))* Pleasant St. Pr.

Cohn, Ariel. The Zoo Box. Steinke, Aron Nels, illus. 2014. (ENG.). 48p. (J). (gr. k-2). 17.99 *(978-1-62672-052-7(5)*, 9781626720527, First Second Bks.) Roaring Brook Pr.

Cole, Babette. Tarzana. 2nd ed. 2003. (Babette Cole Ser.).Tr. of Tarzanna!. (SPA., Illus.). 34p. (J). 12.95 *(978-84-233-2274-9(2))* Ediciones Destino ESP. Dist: Planeta Publishing Corp.

Craig, Sherryn. Locura de Medianoche en el Zoológico, 1 vol. Jones, Karen, illus. 2016. (SPA.). 32p. (J). (gr. k-3). pap. 9.95 *(978-1-62855-744-2(3))* Arbordale Publishing.

—Midnight Madness at the Zoo, 1 vol. Jones, Karen, illus. 2016. (ENG & SPA.). 32p. (J). (gr. k-3). 17.95 *(978-1-62855-730-5(3))* Arbordale Publishing.

Crispin, Barbara. City Zoo Blizzard Revue. Houghton, Roswitha, illus. 2003. 40p. 14.95 *(978-0-9716346-1-9(0))* Dancing Words Pr., Inc.

Crubel, Thomas K. Kyanna's Trip to the Zoo, 1 vol. 2010. 24p. pap. 24.95 *(978-1-4489-2926-9(1))* PublishAmerica, Inc.

Cuartas, Jennifer M. So Many Things. 2012. 28p. 24.95 *(978-1-4626-6328-6(1))* America Star Bks.

Curry, Peter, illus. Zoo Animals. 2016. (ENG.). 12p. (J). (gr. -1 — 1). bds. 4.99 *(978-1-4998-0261-0(7))* Little Bee Books Inc.

DeAngelo, Jeremy. The Out Crowd. 2006. (J). pap. *(978-0-88092-613-3(9))*; lib. bdg. *(978-0-88092-612-6(0))* Royal Fireworks Publishing Co.

Degman, Lori. 1 Zany Zoo. Jack, Colin, illus. 2010. (ENG.). 32p. (J). (gr. -1-2). 17.99 *(978-1-4169-8990-5(0)*, Simon & Schuster Bks. For Young Readers) Simon & Schuster Bks. For Young Readers.

Deich, Cheri Bivin. The Messy Monkey Tea Party. Genth, Christina, illus. 2007. 32p. (J). (gr. -1-3). 15.95 *(978-1-60108-006-6(9))* Red Cygnet Pr.

Dods, Emma. The Zoo. Daubney, Kate, illus. 2015. (I Explore Ser.). (ENG.). 12p. (J). (gr. -1-k). bds. 6.95 *(978-1-4549-1503-4(X))* Sterling Publishing Co., Inc.

Donnelly, Liza. A Hippo in Our Yard. Donnelly, Liza, illus. 2016. (ENG., Illus.). 32p. (J). 16.95 *(978-0-8234-3564-7(4))* Holiday Hse., Inc.

Doodler, Todd H. The Zoo I Drew. 2009. (ENG., Illus.). 56p. (J). (gr. -1-k). 14.99 *(978-0-375-85201-5(8)*, Random Hse. Bks. for Young Readers) Random Hse. Children's Bks.

Dyer, Heather. Tina & the Penguin. Levert, Mireille, illus. 2004. (ENG.). 32p. (J). (gr. k-3). pap. 5.95 *(978-1-55337-767-2(2))* Kids Can Pr., Ltd. CAN. Dist: Hachette Bk. Group.

Ebie, Mora. Going to the Zoo in Hawaii. 2006. (Illus.). 28p. (J). 10.95 *(978-1-56647-790-1(5))* Mutual Publishing LLC.

Elliott, Rebecca. Zoo Girl. Elliott, Rebecca, illus. 2013. (ENG., Illus.). 32p. (J). (gr. k-2). pap. 8.99 *(978-0-7459-6270-2(X))* Lion Hudson PLC GBR. Dist: Independent Pubs. Group.

Ellis, Andy. When Lulu Went to the Zoo. Ellis, Andy, illus. 2010. (ENG., Illus.). 32p. (J). (gr. -1-3). 16.95 *(978-0-7613-5499-4(9))* Lerner Publishing Group.

Ferron, Joanne. Luis Saves the Llama. 2012. (ENG.). 35p. (J). pap. 17.95 *(978-1-4327-7623-7(1))* Outskirts Pr., Inc.

Fischer, Kristen. Zoo Zen: A Yoga Story for Kids. Schaefer, Susi, illus. 2017. (ENG.). 32p. (J). (gr. -1-2). 17.95 *(978-1-62203-891-6(6))* Sounds True, Inc.

Fisher-Price. Fisher-Price Little People Let's Imagine at the Zoo. 2014. (Lift-The-Flap Ser.: 27). (ENG.). 10p. (J). (gr. -1-k). bds. 9.99 *(978-0-7944-3115-0(1)*, Reader's Digest Children's Bks.) Studio Fun International.

Fletcher, Donna. Sweet Baby Heather: Day at the Zoo. 2010. 24p. pap. 14.99 *(978-1-4520-2444-8(8))* AuthorHouse.

Frolick, Billy. Madagascar. Golden Books, illus. 2017. (Little Golden Book Ser.). (ENG.). 24p. (J). (-k). 4.99 ***(978-1-5247-6768-6(9)***, Golden Bks.) Random Hse. Children's Bks.

Gabretti, Tisa. The Number Zoo, 1 vol. 2009. (ENG.). 15p. 24.95 *(978-1-60813-941-5(7))* America Star Bks.

Geer-Drummond, Vanessa T. Olivia's Trip to the Zoo. 2011. 32p. (gr. -1). pap. 12.77 *(978-1-4567-4558-5(1))* AuthorHouse.

Gibbs, Stuart. Belly Up. (FunJungle Ser.). (ENG.). (J). (gr. 3-7). 2011. 320p. pap. 7.99 *(978-1-4169-8732-1(0))* 2010. (Illus.). 304p. 17.99 *(978-1-4169-8731-4(2))* Simon & Schuster Bks. For Young Readers. (Simon & Schuster Bks. For Young Readers).

—Panda-Monium. 2017. (FunJungle Ser.). (ENG., Illus.). 352p. (J). (gr. 3-7). 16.99 *(978-1-4814-4567-2(7)*, Simon & Schuster Bks. For Young Readers) Simon & Schuster Bks. For Young Readers.

—Poached. 2014. (FunJungle Ser.). (ENG., Illus.). 352p. (J). (gr. 3-7). 17.99 *(978-1-4424-6777-4(0)*, Simon & Schuster Bks. For Young Readers) Simon & Schuster Bks. For Young Readers.

Glassman, Bruce. Zoolidays. Kiaulevicius, Rolandas, illus. 2006. 32p. (J). (gr. -1-3). 15.95 *(978-1-60108-011-0(5))* Red Cygnet Pr.

Haber, Shel & dePaola, Tomie. The Animals' Vacation. Haber, Jan, illus. 2015. (G&d Vintage Ser.). (ENG.). 24p. (J). (gr. -1-k). bds. 7.99 *(978-0-448-48399-3(8)*, Grosset & Dunlap) Penguin Young Readers Group.

Hall, Michael. My Heart Is Like a Zoo. Hall, Michael, illus. (Illus.). (J). (gr. -1-k). 2013. (ENG.). 34p. bds. 7.99 *(978-0-06-191512-3(2))* 2009. (ENG., 32p. 16.99 *(978-0-06-191510-9(6))* 2009. 32p. lib. bdg. 17.89 *(978-0-06-191511-6(4))* HarperCollins Pubs. (Greenwillow Bks.).

Hamburg, Jennifer. A Moose That Says Moo. Truesdell, Sue, illus. 2013. (ENG.). 32p. (J). (gr. -1 — 1). 16.99 *(978-0-374-35058-1(2)*, 9780374350581, Farrar, Straus & Giroux (BYR)) Farrar, Straus & Giroux.

Heap, Sue. Danny's Drawing Book. Heap, Sue, illus. 2008. (ENG., Illus.). 32p. (J). (gr. -1-3). 9.99 *(978-0-7636-3654-8(1))* Candlewick Pr.

Heder, Thyra. Fraidyzoo. 2013. (ENG., Illus.). 48p. (J). (gr. k-2). 16.95 *(978-1-4197-0776-6(0)*, Abrams Bks. for Young Readers) Abrams, Inc.

Hensel, Boots. The Zoopendous Surprise! Gabriel, Andrea, illus. 2009. (ENG.). 32p. (J). (gr. -1-k). 16.95 *(978-0-9792035-5-8(4))* Pleasant St. Pr.

Hinchcliffe, L. T. For the Love of Prudence Possum. 2008. 76p. pap. 15.50 *(978-1-60693-136-3(9)*, Eloquent Bks.) Strategic Book Publishing & Rights Agency (SBPRA).

Ho, Jannie, illus. Muddle Zoo. 2013. (Muddle Bks.). (ENG.). 8p. (J). (gr. -1 — 1). 10.99 *(978-0-7641-6623-5(9))* Barron's Educational Series, Inc.

Hogg, Gary. Beautiful Buehla & the Zany Zoo Makeover. Chess, Victoria, illus. 2006. 32p. (J). (gr. -1-2). 15.99 *(978-0-06-009420-1(6)*, Tegen, Katherine Bks) HarperCollins Pubs.

Hopgood, Sally. See You Later, Alligator. Levey, Emma, illus. 2016. (ENG.). 32p. (J). (gr. -1-k). 16.99 *(978-1-5107-0484-8(1)*, Sky Pony Pr.) Skyhorse Publishing Co., Inc.

Ide, Laurie Shimizu. Okazu at the Zoo. Kanekuni, Daniel, illus. 2006. (J). *(978-1-56647-776-5(X))* Mutual Publishing LLC.

Ipcizade, Catherine. 'Twas the Day Before Zoo Day, 1 vol. Hodson, Ben, illus. 2008. (Basic Math Operations Ser.). (ENG.). 32p. (J). (gr. -1-2). 17.95 *(978-1-60718-585-7(7))* Arbordale Publishing.

Irwin, Bindi & Kunz, Chris. Trouble at the Zoo. 2011. (Bindi's Wildlife Adventures Ser.: 1). (ENG.). 112p. (gr. 3-6). pap. 5.99 *(978-1-4022-5514-4(4)*, Sourcebooks Jabberwocky) Sourcebooks, Inc.

Jones, Gareth P. The Clan of the Scorpion. Finlayson, Luke, illus. 2013. (Ninja Meerkats Ser.: 1). (ENG.). 128p. (J). (gr. 2-4). pap. 5.99 *(978-1-250-01664-5(9)*, 9781250016645) Square Fish.

Jones, Julie. The Problem at Pepperpine Zoo. Jones, Julie, illus. l.t. ed. 2004. (Illus.). 24p. (J). pap. 7.95 *(978-0-9745553-0-0(4))* Greenwood Street Publishing. GSP.

Katz, Karen. Roar, Roar, Baby! Katz, Karen, illus. 2015. (ENG., Illus.). 14p. (J). (gr. -1 — 1). bds. 6.99 *(978-1-4814-1788-4(6)*, Little Simon) Little Simon.

Kaufman, Seufert. Wee Wilhelmina & Her Magic Marbles. 2012. (ENG.). pap. *(978-1-4675-4364-4(0))* Independent Pub.

Ketteman, Helen. If Beaver Had a Fever, 0 vols. O'Malley, Kevin, illus. 2011. (ENG.). 32p. (J). (gr. -1-3). 16.99 *(978-0-7614-5951-4(0)*, 9780761459514, Amazon Children's Publishing) Amazon Publishing.

Klein, Adria F. Max Goes to the Zoo, 1 vol. Gallagher-Cole, Mernie, illus. 2007. (Read-It! Readers: the Life of Max Ser.). (ENG.). 24p. (gr. -1-2). lib. bdg. 21.32 *(978-1-4048-3677-8(2))*; per. 3.95 *(978-1-4048-3683-9(7))* Picture Window Bks. (Easy Readers).

Kline, Trish & Donev, Mary. A Day at the Zoo: KA Reader 3. 2007. (Illus.). 32p. (J). per. 20.00 *(978-0-9717234-5-0(1))* Ghost Hunter Productions.

Kurtz, Jane. Do Kangaroos Wear Seatbelts? Rossi, Ino, ed. Manning, Jane, illus. 2005. (ENG.). 32p. (J). (gr. -1-k). 16.99 *(978-0-525-47358-9(0)*, Dutton Books for Young Readers) Penguin Young Readers Group.

Landry, Barbara. A Day at the Zoo. 2012. 28p. pap. 24.95 *(978-1-4626-6684-3(1))* America Star Bks.

Latham, Irene. Don't Feed the Boy. Graegin, Stephanie, illus. 2012. (ENG.). 288p. (J). (gr. 3-7). 17.99 *(978-1-59643-755-5(3)*, 9781596437555) Roaring Brook Pr.

—Don't Feed the Boy. Graegin, Stephanie, illus. 2014. (ENG.). 304p. (J). (gr. 3-7). pap. 9.99 *(978-1-250-04428-0(6)*, 9781250044280) Square Fish.

Lendler, Ian. The Stratford Zoo Midnight Revue Presents Macbeth. Giallongo, Zack, illus. 2014. (Stratford Zoo Ser.). (ENG.). 80p. (J). (gr. 2-5). pap. 12.99 *(978-1-59643-915-3(7)*, 9781596439153, First Second Bks.) Roaring Brook Pr.

—The Stratford Zoo Midnight Revue Presents Romeo & Juliet. 2015. (Stratford Zoo Midnight Revue Presents Ser.). (J). lib. bdg. 25.75 *(978-0-606-38215-1(1))* Turtleback Bks.

Lunablau, Jani. Little Snowflake. 2006. (ENG., Illus.). 32p. (J). (gr. -1-k). *(978-1-59692-139-9(0))* MacAdam/Cage Publishing, Inc.

Malone, D. L. 52 Purple Monkeys. 2009. 24p. pap. 24.95 *(978-1-60749-085-2(4))* America Star Bks.

Mamma Macs. Mick Mac Adoo's Australian Zoo. 2013. 30p. pap. *(978-0-9923379-9-5(2))* Serenity Press.

Mandel, Peter. Zoo Ah-Chooo. Smith, Elwood H., illus. 2012. (ENG.). 32p. (J). 16.95 *(978-0-8234-2317-0(4))* Holiday Hse., Inc.

Marie, Jill Jana. Zoo Rendezvous. Zamboni, David, illus. 2008. 24p. pap. 12.95 *(978-0-9817572-9-2(4))* Peppertree Pr., The.

Marsh, Carole. The Zany Zoo Mystery. 2007. 128p. (J). pap. 5.99 *(978-0-635-06332-8(8))* Gallopade International.

Martin, Bill, Jr. Polar Bear, Polar Bear, What Do You Hear? Carle, Eric, illus. (Brown Bear & Friends Ser.). (J). 2012. (ENG.). 28p. (gr. -1-k). bds. 12.99 *(978-0-8050-9095-6(9)*, 9780805090956) 2010. (ENG.). 40p. (gr. -1-2). 8.99 *(978-0-8050-9245-5(5)*, 9780805092455) 2007. 32p. 7.95 *(978-0-8050-8798-7(2))* 20th anniv. ed. 2011. (ENG.). 32p. (gr. -1-k). 19.99 *(978-0-8050-9066-6(5)*, 9780805090666) Holt, Henry & Co. (Holt, Henry & Co. Bks. For Young Readers).

Martin, Bill, Jr. & Priddy, Roger. Polar Bear, Polar Bear, What Do You Hear? Carle, Eric, illus. 2011. (ENG.). 14p. (J). (gr. -1-k). bds. 14.95 *(978-0-312-51346-7(1)*, 9780312513467, Priddy Bks.) St. Martin's Pr.

Martin-Duttmann, Robin. Zoo on the Moon. 2013. 24p. pap. 12.97 *(978-1-62212-735-1(8)*, Strategic Bk. Publishing) Strategic Book Publishing & Rights Agency (SBPRA).

Massie, Diane Redfield. The Baby Beebee Bird. Kellogg, Steven, illus. 2003. (ENG.). 32p. (J). (gr. -1-1). pap. 6.99 *(978-0-06-051784-7(0))* HarperCollins Pubs.

Matthias, Catherine. Too Many Balloons. Sharp, Gene, illus. 2011. (Rookie Ready to Learn Ser.). 40p. (J). (gr. -1-k). pap. 5.95 *(978-0-531-26749-3(0))*; lib. bdg. 23.00 *(978-0-531-26449-2(1))* Scholastic Library Publishing. (Children's Pr.).

Matthias, Catherine & Sharp, Gene. Demasiados Globos. Sharp, Gene, illus. 2011. (Rookie Ready to Learn Español Ser.). (SPA., Illus.). 40p. (J). pap. 5.95 *(978-0-531-26792-9(X))*; lib. bdg. 23.00 *(978-0-531-26124-8(7))* Scholastic Library Publishing. (Children's Pr.).

McDonald, Regina. Friday Night at the Zoo, 1 vol. McDonald, Amanda, illus. 2010. 16p. 24.95 *(978-1-4489-4090-5(7))* PublishAmerica, Inc.

McMahon, Michael. The Zoo & You: A Guidebook, 1 vol. rev. ed. 2013. (Fiction Readers Ser.). (ENG., Illus.). 28p. (J). (gr. 3-3). pap. 8.99 *(978-1-4333-5606-3(6))* Shell Educational Publishing.

—The Zoo & You: A Guidebook. rev. ed. 2013. (Fiction Readers Ser.). (ENG., Illus.). 28p. (gr. 3-3). pap. 19.96 *(978-1-4807-1728-2(2))* Teacher Created Materials, Inc.

Meachen Rau, Dana. At the Zoo. 2007. (Fun Time Ser.). (Illus.). 24p. (gr. k-1). lib. bdg. 15.95 *(978-0-7614-2610-3(8)*, Benchmark Bks.) Marshall Cavendish Corp.

—En el Zoologico. 2007. (¡A Divertimos! Ser.). (SPA., Illus.). 24p. (gr. k-1). lib. bdg. 15.95 *(978-0-7614-2777-3(5)*, Benchmark Bks.) Marshall Cavendish Corp.

Meldrum, Margaret. Peter Panda & His Friends. 2009. (Illus.). 24p. pap. 11.49 *(978-1-4343-7826-2(8))* AuthorHouse.

Metzger, Steve. Dancing Clock. Nez, John Abbott, illus. 2011. (ENG.). 32p. 12.95 *(978-1-58925-100-7(8))*; (J). pap. 7.95 *(978-1-58925-429-9(5))* Tiger Tales.

Mitter, Matt. Fisher-Price Little People Let's Imagine at the Zoo / Imaginemos el Zoologico. Pixel Mouse House, Pixel Mouse, illus. 2015. (Lift-The-Flap Ser.: 31). (ENG.). 10p. (J). (gr. -1-k). bds. 9.99 *(978-0-7944-3559-2(9))* Reader's Digest Assn., Inc., The.

Munari, Bruno. Bruno Munari's Zoo. 2005. (ENG., Illus.). 48p. (J). (gr. -1-1). reprint ed. 19.99 *(978-0-8118-4830-5(2))* Chronicle Bks. LLC.

Nelson, M. R. The Zebra Said Shhh. Sheldon, Tamia, illus. 2013. 44p. pap. 9.99 *(978-1-62395-440-6(1))* Xist Publishing.

Norman, Kim. Still a Gorilla! Geran, Chad, illus. 2016. (ENG.). 32p. (J). (gr. -1-k). 16.99 *(978-0-545-75791-1(6))* Scholastic, Inc.

Normand, James G. My Funny Little Zoo. 2008. 48p. pap. 17.49 *(978-1-4389-2322-2(8))* AuthorHouse.

Oddo, Jennifer M. Asim the Awesome Possum: Asim Gets His Awesome. Lamb, T. S., illus. 2012. 36p. 16.95 *(978-0-9855906-2-8(9))* Pie Plate Publishing Co.

OHora, Zachariah. Stop Snoring, Bernard! OHora, Zachariah, illus. 2012. (ENG., Illus.). 32p. (J). (gr. -1-2). pap. 7.99 *(978-1-250-00717-9(8)*, 9781250007179) Square Fish.

Oud, Pauline. Going to the Zoo with Lily & Milo. Oud, Pauline, illus. 2011. (Lily & Milo Ser.). (ENG., Illus.). 28p. (J). (gr. k — 1). 12.95 *(978-1-60537-093-4(2))* Cobblestone Publishing Co.

Park, Linda Sue. Xander's Panda Party. Phelan, Matt, illus. 2013. (ENG.). 40p. (J). (gr. -1-3). 16.99 *(978-0-547-55865-3(1))* Houghton Mifflin Harcourt Publishing Co.

Parker, Emma. What a Hullabaloo. 2010. 20p. pap. *(978-1-877561-32-0(0))* First Edition Ltd.

Pauline, Christi. Hullabaloo at the Zoo. 2008. 28p. pap. 14.95 *(978-1-4389-1204-2(8))* AuthorHouse.

Pitt, Sarah. Peek a Boo! Zoo. 2009. (Little Peek a Boo Bks.). (Illus.). (J). bds. 9.99 *(978-1-934650-57-8(9))* Just For Kids Pr., LLC.

Priddy, Roger. Toddler Town - Zoo. 2014. (Toddler Town Ser.). (ENG.). 10p. (J). (gr. -1 — 1). bds. 7.99 *(978-0-312-51672-7(X)*, 9780312516727, Priddy Bks.) St. Martin's Pr.

Prince, Daniel. Zoe the Zookeeper. 2007. (Illus.). 48p. per. *(978-1-84748-047-7(0))* Athena Pr.

Purton, Marie. Josh's Day at the Zoo. 2006. (Illus.). 48p. pap. *(978-1-84401-606-8(4))* Athena Pr.

Ramoutar, Tagore. Brownie the Monkey Visits the Zoo. Cline, Ian, photos by. 2012. (Illus.). 38p. pap. *(978-1-907837-48-7(5))* Longshot Ventures, Ltd.

Random House. Farm Alarm! (Team Umizoomi) Fruchter, Jason, illus. 2014. (Step into Reading Ser.). (ENG.). 24p. (J). (gr. -1-1). pap. 3.99 *(978-0-385-38508-4(0)*, Random Hse. Bks. for Young Readers) Random Hse. Children's Bks.

Rathmann, Peggy. Good Night, Gorilla. Rathmann, Peggy, illus. 2004. (ENG., Illus.). 34p. (J). (gr. -1 — 1). bds. 15.99 *(978-0-399-24260-1(0)*, G.P. Putnam's Sons Books for Young Readers) Penguin Young Readers Group.

Ray, Keri. Dancing in the Rain: At the Zoo. 2009. 32p. pap. 12.99 *(978-1-4490-0673-0(6))* AuthorHouse.

Ray, Sandra. Grandma & Me Oh What Do We See When We Go to the Zoo? Bailey, Sidney, illus. 2011. 32p. 14.99 *(978-1-4520-8133-5(6))* AuthorHouse.

Redmond, E. S. Felicity Floo Visits the Zoo. Redmond, E. S., illus. 2009. (ENG., Illus.). 32p. (J). (gr. -1-k). 15.99 *(978-0-7636-3444-5(1))* Candlewick Pr.

Reid, A. Elaine Holt. Who Did Mr. Stork Bring to the Zoo? 2010. 28p. 15.00 *(978-1-4520-0419-8(6))* AuthorHouse.

Rey, H. A. & Rey, Margret. At the Zoo. 2007. (Curious George Ser.). (ENG., Illus.). 10p. (J). (gr. k — 1). bds. 6.99 *(978-0-618-80042-1(5))* Houghton Mifflin Harcourt Publishing Co.

Richard, Laurent. Wild Animals! Gauvin, Edward, tr. from FRE. Ryser, Nicolas, illus. 2014. (Tao, the Little Samurai Ser.: 5). (ENG.). 64p. (J). (gr. 2-5). lib. bdg. 29.27 *(978-1-4677-2098-4(4)*, Graphic Universe™) Lerner Publishing Group.

Richards, Dan. Can One Balloon Make an Elephant Fly? Newman, Jeff, illus. 2016. (ENG.). 40p. (J). (gr. -1-3). 17.99 *(978-1-4424-5215-2(3))* Simon & Schuster Bks. For Young Readers.

Richardson, Justin & Parnell, Peter. And Tango Makes Three. Cole, Henry, illus. 2005. (ENG.). 32p. (J). (gr. -1-3). 17.99 *(978-0-689-87845-9(1)*, Simon & Schuster Bks. For Young Readers) Simon & Schuster Bks. For Young Readers.

—And Tango Makes Three: 10th Anniversary Edition. Cole, Henry, illus. 10th ed. 2015. (ENG.). 40p. (J). (gr. -1-3). 17.99 *(978-1-4814-4884-0(6)*, Simon & Schuster Bks. For Young Readers) Simon & Schuster Bks. For Young Readers.

Roskifte, Kristin. Animal Beauty. 2015. (ENG., Illus.). 50p. (J). 17.00 *(978-0-8028-5454-4(0)*, Eerdmans Bks For Young Readers) Eerdmans, William B. Publishing Co.

Ruiz-Flores, Lupe. The Woodcutter's Gift/el Regalo del Lenador. Ventura, Gabriela Baeza, tr. from ENG. Jerome, Elaine, illus. 2007. (SPA & ENG.). 32p. (J). (gr. -1-2). 16.95 *(978-1-55885-489-5(4)*, Piñata Books) Arte Publico Pr.

Russell, David. Who'z Who at the Zoo. 2012. (Illus.). 26p. pap. 12.95 *(978-1-4575-1395-4(1))* Dog Ear Publishing, LLC.

Ryan, Candace. Zoo Zoom! Pamintuan, Macky, illus. 2015. (ENG.). 32p. (J). (gr. -1-1). 16.99 *(978-1-61963-357-5(4)*, 9781619633575, Bloomsbury USA Childrens) Bloomsbury Publishing USA.

Sansone, V. K. A Strange Day at the Zoo. 2009. 32p. pap. 14.98 *(978-0-557-06519-6(4))* Lulu Pr., Inc.

Scanlon, Jack. Rainbow Zoo. 2006. (Neighborhood Readers Ser.). (ENG., Illus.). 8p. (gr. -1-3). pap. 5.15 *(978-1-4042-6686-5(0)*, Rosen Classroom) Rosen Publishing Group, Inc., The.

Schultz, Lucy & Shultz, Lucy. Zoo Faces. Larranaga, Ana, illus. 2007. (ENG.). 12p. (J). (gr. -1 — 1). bds. 6.99 *(978-1-58476-556-1(9)*, IKIDS) Innovative Kids.

Scollon, Bill, adapted by. Zootopia. 2016. (Illus.). 60p. (J). ***(978-1-4806-9793-5(1)***, Golden Bks.) Random Hse. Children's Bks.

Scotton, Rob. Splat & the Cool School Trip. Scotton, Rob, illus. 2013. (Splat the Cat Ser.). (ENG., Illus.). 40p. (J). (gr. -1-3). 17.99 *(978-0-06-213386-1(1))* HarperCollins Pubs.

Shannon, Carol. Dusky Langurs at the Zoo. 2013. 40p. pap. 16.95 *(978-1-4525-1014-9(8)*, Balboa Pr.) Author Solutions, Inc.

Sierra, Judy. Wild about Books. Brown, Marc, tr. Brown, Marc, illus. 2004. (ENG.). 40p. (J). (gr. -1-2). 16.95 *(978-0-375-82538-5(X)*, Knopf Bks. for Young Readers) Random Hse. Children's Bks.

—Wild about You! Brown, Marc, illus. 2012. (ENG.). 40p. (J). (gr. -1-3). 17.99 *(978-0-307-93178-8(1)*, Knopf Bks. for Young Readers) Random Hse. Children's Bks.

—ZooZical. Brown, Marc, illus. 2011. (ENG.). 40p. (J). (gr. -1-2). 17.99 *(978-0-375-86847-4(X)*, Knopf Bks. for Young Readers) Random Hse. Children's Bks.

Sklar, David. A Day at the Zoo with My Daddy. 2013. 24p. pap. 17.99 *(978-1-4817-0152-5(5))* AuthorHouse.

Smallman, Steve. Poo in the Zoo. Grey, Ada, illus. 2015. (ENG.). 32p. (J). (gr. -1-3). 16.99 *(978-1-58925-197-7(0))* Tiger Tales.

—Spot a Lot Animal Escape. Slater, Nicola, illus. 2014. (ENG.). (J). (gr. -1-3). *(978-1-4723-5096-1(0))* Parragon Bk. Service Ltd.

Smith, Danna. Dos en el Zoológico: Un Libro para Contar. Petrone, Valeria, illus. 2011.Tr. of Two at the Zoo - A Counting Book. (ENG & SPA.). 30p. (J). (gr. k — 1). bds. 4.99 *(978-0-547-58137-8(8))* Houghton Mifflin Harcourt Publishing Co.

Snyder, Marilyn. A Second Chance for Tina. Shiffman, Lena, illus. 2003. (Hello Reader! Ser.). (J). *(978-0-439-44154-4(4))* Scholastic, Inc.

Stead, Philip C. A Sick Day for Amos McGee. Stead, Erin E., illus. 2010. (ENG.). 32p. (J). (gr. -1-1). 17.99 *(978-1-59643-402-8(3)*, 9781596434028) Roaring Brook Pr.

—A Sick Day for Amos Mcgee: Book & CD Storytime Set. Stead, Erin E., illus. 2017. (ENG.). 32p. (J). 12.99 *(978-1-4272-8722-9(8)*, 9781427287229) Macmillan Audio.

Swain, Cynthia. Wishing with Pennies. 2006. (Early Explorers Ser.). (J). pap. *(978-1-4108-6041-5(8))* Benchmark Education Co.

Tait, Barbara. Timothy Toot... Goes to the Zoo. 2011. (Illus.). 28p. (J). 24.95 *(978-1-58909-961-6(3))* Bookstand Publishing.

Taplin, Sam. Noisy Zoo. Wildish, Lee, illus. 2009. (Busy Sounds Board Book Ser.). 10p. (J). (gr. -1). bds. 18.99 *(978-0-7945-2517-0(2)*, Usborne) EDC Publishing.

Taylor, Qiana. Jordyen & Lionnel the Seal. 2013. 24p. pap. 24.95 *(978-1-62709-057-5(6))* America Star Bks.

Thompson, Kay & McClatchy, Lisa. Eloise Visits the Zoo. Lyon, Tammie, illus. 2009. (Eloise Ser.). (ENG.). 32p. (J). (gr. -1-1). pap. 3.99 *(978-1-4169-8642-3(1)*, Simon Spotlight) Simon Spotlight.

Tillworth, Mary. A Friend at the Zoo/un Amigo en el Zoologico (Bubble Guppies) Gomez, Yuliana, tr. Random House Editors, illus. 2014. (Pictureback(R) Ser.). (ENG.). 24p. (J). (gr. -1-2). 3.99 *(978-0-385-37928-1(5)*, Random Hse. Bks. for Young Readers) Random Hse. Children's Bks.

Tinsley, Jillian. Wally the Warthog. Wood, Douglas, illus. 2012. 24p. (J). pap. 10.99 *(978-1-61254-782-4(6))* Small Pr., The.

Trapani, Iza. Old Macdonald Had a... Zoo? Trapani, Iza, illus. 2017. (ENG., Illus.). 32p. (J). (-k). lib. bdg. 16.99 ***(978-1-58089-729-7(0))*** Charlesbridge Publishing, Inc.

Valentine, Sophie. Zoo Hullabaloo, 1 vol. rev. ed. 2013. (Fiction Readers Ser.). (ENG., Illus.). 12p. (J). (gr. 1-1). pap. 12.96 *(978-1-4807-1137-2(3))*; pap. 4.99 *(978-1-4333-5458-8(6))* Shell Educational Publishing.

Vassallo, Theresa. Day at the Zoo Sing-along. 2011. 20p. pap. 24.95 *(978-1-4560-6832-5(6))* America Star Bks.

Vrombaut, An. Georgina the Giraffe. 2013. (ENG., Illus.). 32p. (J). (gr. -1-k). pap. 9.99 *(978-1-4449-1298-2(4))* Hodder & Stoughton GBR. Dist: Hachette Bk. Group.

—Henrietta the Hairy Hippo. Vrombaut, An, illus. 2013. (ENG., Illus.). 32p. (J). (gr. -1-k). pap. 8.99 *(978-1-4449-1299-9(2))* Hodder & Stoughton GBR. Dist: Hachette Bk. Group.

—Kevin the Crocodile. 2013. (ENG., Illus.). 32p. (J). (gr. -1-k). pap. 9.99 *(978-1-4449-1301-9(8))* Hodder & Stoughton GBR. Dist: Hachette Bk. Group.

—Zed the Zebra. Vrombaut, An, illus. 2013. (ENG., Illus.). 32p. (J). (gr. -1-k). pap. 8.99 *(978-1-4449-1303-3(4))* Hodder & Stoughton GBR. Dist: Hachette Bk. Group.

Wan, Joyce. Peek-A-Boo Zoo. 2015. (ENG., Illus.). 14p. (J). (— 1). bds. 6.99 *(978-0-545-75042-4(3)*, Cartwheel Bks.) Scholastic, Inc.

Weston Woods Staff, creator. Wild about Books. 2011. 29.95 *(978-0-439-80485-1(X))* Weston Woods Studios, Inc.

Weston Woods Studios Inc. Staff, creator. Good Night, Gorilla. 2004. (J). 18.95 *(978-1-55592-419-5(0))*; 38.75 *(978-1-55592-421-8(2))* Weston Woods Studios, Inc.

White, George. Halloween at the Zoo: A Pop-up Trick of Treat Experience. 2007. (Illus.). 16p. (J). 16.99 *(978-0-9795441-0-1(6))* Jumping Jack Pr.

Wilson, Karma. Animal Strike at the Zoo - It's True! Spengler, Margaret, illus. 2006. (ENG.). 32p. (J). (gr. -1-1). 16.99 *(978-0-06-057502-1(6))* HarperCollins Pubs.

—Never, Ever Shout in a Zoo. Cushman, Douglas, illus. 2004. (ENG.). 32p. (J). (gr. -1-3). 16.99 *(978-0-316-98564-2(3))* Little, Brown Bks. for Young Readers.

Winthrop, Elizabeth & Winthrop. Dancing Granny, 1 vol. Murdocca, Sal, illus. 2003. (ENG.). 32p. (J). 16.95 *(978-0-7614-5141-9(2))* Marshall Cavendish Corp.

Wu, Mike. Ellie. Wu, Mike, illus. 2015. (ENG., Illus.). 40p. (J). (gr. -1-k). 16.99 *(978-1-4847-1239-9(0))* Disney Publishing Worldwide.

—Ellie in Concert. Wu, Mike, illus. 2017. (ENG., Illus.). 40p. (J). (gr. -1-k). 16.99 *(978-1-4847-1238-2(2))* Hyperion Bks. for Children.

Young, Judy. Digger & Daisy Go to the Zoo. 2013. (ENG.). (J). *(978-1-58536-841-9(5))* Sleeping Bear Pr.

—Digger y Daisy Van Al Zoológico (Digger & Daisy Go to the Zoo) Sullivan, Dana, illus. 2016. (I AM a READER: Digger & Daisy Ser.). (SPA & ENG.). 32p. (J). (gr. k-2). 9.99 *(978-1-62753-951-7(4)*, 204174) Sleeping Bear Pr.

The Zany Zanimal Zoo. 2005. (Illus.). 40p. (J). 14.95 *(978-0-9769738-0-5(4))* Redel, Nicole.

ZOOGEOGRAPHY

see Animal Distribution

ZOOLOGICAL GARDENS

see Zoos

ZOOLOGICAL SPECIMENS—COLLECTION AND PRESERVATION

see also Taxidermy

Markarian, Margie. Who Cleans Dinosaur Bones? Working at a Museum. 2010. (Wild Work Ser.). (ENG.). 32p. (gr. 1-2). pap. 8.29 *(978-1-4109-3857-2(3)*, Read Me!) Heinemann-Raintree.

ZOOLOGY

see also Anatomy, Comparative; Animals; Embryology; Evolution; Fossils; Natural History; Physiology, Comparative; Psychology, Comparative

also names of divisions, classes, etc. of the animal kingdom (e.g. Invertebrates; Vertebrates; birds; Mammals; etc.)

Abbott, Henry. Hormigueros (Inside Anthills) 2015. (Las Casas de Los Animales (Inside Animal Homes) Ser.). (ENG & SPA.). 24p. (J). (gr. 2-3). 23.60 *(978-1-4994-0593-4(6)*, PowerKids Pr.) Rosen Publishing Group, Inc., The.

ABDO Publishing Company Staff. Creature Features. 2007. (Creature Features Ser.). 307.80 *(978-1-59928-877-2(X)*, Super SandCastle) ABDO Publishing Co.

Anderson, Holly Lynn. Unexplained Monsters & Cryptids. 2015. (J). *(978-1-61900-071-1(7))* Eldorado Ink.

Arnosky, Jim. Following the Coast. Arnosky, Jim, illus. 2004. (ENG., Illus.). 32p. (J). (gr. 3-18). 15.99 *(978-0-688-17117-9(6))* HarperCollins Pubs.

Artell, Mike. Pee-Yew! The Stinkiest, Smelliest Animals, Insects, & Plants on Earth! 2006. (Illus.). 96p. (YA). per. 14.95 *(978-1-59647-054-5(2))* Good Year Bks.

AZ Books, creator. Walk Around Africa. 2012. (Put Together Ser.). (ENG., Illus.). 16p. (J). (gr. -1-k). spiral bd. 6.95 *(978-1-61889-191-4(X))* AZ Bks. LLC.

Beaumont, Holly. Animal Body Coverings. 2015. (Animal Body Coverings Ser.). (ENG.). 24p. (gr. 1-3). lib. bdg. 93.28 *(978-1-4846-2537-8(4)*, Heinemann Read & Learn) Heinemann-Raintree.

Belton, Blair. Be a Zoologist. 2014. (Be a Scientist! Ser.). 32p. (J). (gr. 3-6). pap. 10.50 *(978-1-4824-1286-4(1))* Stevens, Gareth Publishing LLLP.

Berne, Emma Carlson. Coyotes. 2014. (Scavengers: Eating Nature's Trash Ser.). (Illus.). 24p. (J). (gr. k-5). lib. bdg. 23.60 *(978-1-4777-6607-1(3)*, PowerKids Pr.) Rosen Publishing Group, Inc., The.

—Flesh Flies. 2014. (Scavengers: Eating Nature's Trash Ser.). (Illus.). 24p. (J). (gr. k-5). lib. bdg. 23.60 *(978-1-4777-6588-3(3)*, PowerKids Pr.) Rosen Publishing Group, Inc., The.

Blough, Glenn O. After the Sun Goes Down: The Story of Animals at Night. Bendick, Jeanne, illus. 2011. 50p. (gr. 1). 35.95 *(978-1-258-09913-8(6))* Literary Licensing, LLC.

Broderip, W. J. Zoological Recreations. 2006. pap. 36.95 *(978-1-4286-3565-4(3))* Kessinger Publishing, LLC.

Brown, Jonatha A. Las Cabezas y los Cuellos de los Animales. 2006. (En que se diferencian los animales (Why Animals Look Different) Ser.). (SPA., Illus.). 24p. (J). (gr. 1-4). lib. bdg. 22.00 *(978-0-8368-7412-9(9)*, Weekly Reader Leveled Readers) Stevens, Gareth Publishing LLLP.

—Las Colas de los Animales. 2006. (En que se diferencian los animales (Why Animals Look Different) Ser.). (SPA., Illus.). 24p. (J). (gr. 1-4). lib. bdg. 22.00 *(978-0-8368-7413-6(7)*, Weekly Reader Leveled Readers) Stevens, Gareth Publishing LLLP.

Brown, Martin. Lesser Spotted Animals. 2016. (ENG.). 56p. (J). (gr. 2-5). 18.99 *(978-1-338-08934-9(X))* Scholastic, Inc.

Buckland, Francis Trevelyan. Log-Book of a Fisherman & Zoologist. 2011. 422p. pap. 32.95 *(978-1-4460-5845-9(X)*, Kent Pr.) Kent Communications, Ltd.

Burgan, Michael. Bat Researcher. 2010. (Benchmark Rockets: Dirty & Dangerous Jobs Ser.). 32p. (J). (gr. 3-6). 28.50 *(978-1-60870-170-4(0))* Marshall Cavendish Corp.

Burgess, Thornton W. The Burgess Animal Book for Children. 2005. 29.95 *(978-1-4218-0996-0(6))*; 304p. pap. 14.95 *(978-1-59540-696-5(4))* 1st World Publishing, Inc. (1st World Library - Literary Society).

—The Burgess Animal Book for Children. 2009. 248p. 26.99 *(978-1-60512-323-3(4))*; (Illus.). pap. 13.99 *(978-1-60512-423-0(0))* Akasha Publishing, LLC. (Akasha Classics).

—The Burgess Animal Book for Children. (J). 28.95 *(978-0-8488-0716-0(2))* Amereon Ltd.

—The Burgess Animal Book for Children. Fuertes, Louis Agassiz, illus. 2008. 284p. (gr. 4-7). pap. *(978-1-4099-2052-6(6))* Dodo Pr.

—The Burgess Animal Book for Children. 2004. (Dover Children's Classics Ser.). (ENG., Illus.). 288p. (gr. 1-5). pap. 9.99 *(978-0-486-43745-3(0))* Dover Pubns., Inc.

—The Burgess Animal Book for Children. 2010. (Illus.). 130p. (gr. 4-7). pap. 19.99 *(978-1-153-69658-6(4))*; 146p. pap. 21.89 *(978-1-152-50810-1(5))* General Bks. LLC.

—The Burgess Animal Book for Children. Fuertes, Louis Agassiz, illus. 2011. 478p. 52.95 *(978-1-169-84273-1(9))* 2010. 478p. 42.36 *(978-1-163-21392-6(6))* 2010. 478p. pap. 30.36 *(978-1-162-64734-0(5))* 2004. 476p. (gr. 4-7). 52.95 *(978-1-4326-2165-0(3))* Kessinger Publishing, LLC.

—The Burgess Animal Book for Children. 2004. reprint ed. pap. 1.99 *(978-1-4192-5555-7(X))* Kessinger Publishing, LLC.

—The Burgess Animal Book for Children. Fuertes, Louis Agassiz, illus. 2004. reprint ed. pap. 37.95 *(978-1-4179-2978-8(2))* Kessinger Publishing, LLC.

—The Burgess Animal Book for Children (Yesterday's Classics) Fuertes, Louis Agassiz, illus. 2006. (J). per. 13.95 *(978-1-59915-171-7(5))* Yesterday's Classics.

Burgess, Thornton W. & Fuertes, Louis Agassiz. The Burgess Animal Book for Children. 2010. (ENG.). 484p. pap. 38.75 *(978-1-171-73852-7(8))*; 486p. pap. 38.75 *(978-1-176-23716-2(0))* Creative Media Partners, LLC.

Canetti, Yanitzia. Adivina, Adivinador: ¿Quién está Escondido? 2010. (SPA.). 24p. (J). pap. *(978-1-59835-126-2(5)*, BrickHouse Education) Cambridge BrickHouse, Inc.

—Guess Who? Who Crosses Here? 2010. (ENG.). 24p. (J). pap. 8.99 *(978-1-59835-136-1(2)*, BrickHouse Education) Cambridge BrickHouse, Inc.

—Guess Who? Who's Hiding? 2010. (ENG.). 24p. (J). pap. 8.99 *(978-1-59835-137-8(0)*, BrickHouse Education) Cambridge BrickHouse, Inc.

—Guess Who? Who's Looking at Me? 2010. (ENG.). (J). pap. 8.99 *(978-1-59835-138-5(9)*, BrickHouse Education) Cambridge BrickHouse, Inc.

—Guess Who? Who's Shadow Is This? 2010. (ENG.). 24p. (J). pap. 8.99 *(978-1-59835-140-8(0))* Cambridge BrickHouse, Inc.

—Guess Who? Whose Skin Is This? 2010. (ENG.). (J). pap. 8.99 *(978-1-59835-142-2(7)*, BrickHouse Education) Cambridge BrickHouse, Inc.

—Guess Who? Whose Tracks Are These? 2010. (ENG.). 24p. (J). pap. 8.99 *(978-1-59835-141-5(9)*, BrickHouse Education) Cambridge BrickHouse, Inc.

—Quien cruza por Aqui? Adivina, Adivinador. 2010. (SPA.). 24p. (J). pap. 8.99 *(978-1-59835-125-5(7)*, BrickHouse Education) Cambridge BrickHouse, Inc.

—Quien deja esta Huella? Adivina, Adivinador. 2010. (SPA.). 24p. (J). pap. 8.99 *(978-1-59835-130-9(3)*, BrickHouse Education) Cambridge BrickHouse, Inc.

—¿Quién se oculta tras la Luz? 2010. (SPA.). 24p. (J). pap. 8.99 *(978-1-59835-128-6(1)*, BrickHouse Education) Cambridge BrickHouse, Inc.

—¿Quién tiene esta Piel? 2010. (SPA.). 24p. (J). pap. 8.99 *(978-1-59835-131-6(1)*, BrickHouse Education) Cambridge BrickHouse, Inc.

—Rhyming Tongue Twisters Animals. 2010. 32p. (J). 6.99 *(978-1-59835-269-6(5)*, BrickHouse Education) Cambridge BrickHouse, Inc.

—Trabalenguas Zoológicos. 2010. (SPA.). 32p. (J). pap. 6.99 *(978-1-59835-159-0(1)*, BrickHouse Education) Cambridge BrickHouse, Inc.

Casper, Julie Kerr. Animals: Creatures That Roam the Planet. 2007. (Natural Resources Ser.). (Illus.). 179p. (J). (gr. 7-12). lib. bdg. 39.50 *(978-0-8160-6353-6(2))* Facts On File, Inc.

Catala, Ellen. Snakes & Lizards, 6 vols. 2003. (Yellow Umbrella Early Level Ser.). (ENG.). 16p. (gr. k-1). pap. 35.70 *(978-0-7368-3017-1(0)*, Yellow Umbrella Bks.) Capstone Press of Coughlan Cos.

Clarke, Ginjer L. Maxed Out! Gigantic Creatures from the Past. Mueller, Pete, illus. 2010. (Penguin Young Readers, Level 3 Ser.). (ENG.). 48p. (J). (gr. 1-3). mass mkt. 3.99 *(978-0-448-44827-5(0)*, Penguin Young Readers) Penguin Young Readers Group.

Clarke, Nadine. Get Bushwise: on Safari Desert, River, Bushveld: A Young Explorer's Guide. 2013. 192p. pap. 23.00 *(978-1-4317-0206-0(4))* Penguin Random House Grupo Editorial ESP. Dist: Casemate Pubs. & Bk. Distributors, LLC.

Cook, Gladys Emerson. Zoo Animals. 2011. 54p. 36.95 *(978-1-258-10530-3(6))* Literary Licensing, LLC.

Dale, Kim. What Am I? (Illus.). 32p. pap. *(978-0-7344-0125-0(6)*, Lothian Children's Bks.) Hachette Australia.

Davies, Nicola. Tiny Creatures: The World of Microbes. Sutton, Emily, illus. 2014. (ENG.). 40p. (J). (gr. k-3). 15.99 *(978-0-7636-7315-4(3))* Candlewick Pr.

De la Bédoyère, Camilla. Fastest & Slowest. 2010. (Animal Opposites Ser.). (ENG., Illus.). 32p. (J). (gr. -1-3). pap. 5.95 *(978-1-55407-809-7(1)*, 9781554078097) Firefly Bks., Ltd.

Dorling Kindersley Publishing Staff & Ring, Susan. Mammals, 6 vols., Set. 2003. (Yellow Umbrella Early Level Ser.). (ENG.). 16p. (gr. k-1). pap. 35.70 *(978-0-7368-2996-0(2)*, Yellow Umbrella Bks.) Capstone Press of Coughlan Cos.

Evans, Hubert R. Forest Friends: Stories of Animals, Fish, & Birds, West of the Rockies. 2012. 260p. 47.95 *(978-1-258-23041-8(0))*; pap. 32.95 *(978-1-258-24397-5(0))* Literary Licensing, LLC.

Facts on File, Inc. Staff. Animals. 2010. (New Discovering Careers for Your Future Ser.). (Illus.). 128p. (gr. 4-9). 24.95 *(978-0-8160-8044-1(5)*, Ferguson Publishing Co.) Facts On File, Inc.

Fulbright, Jeannie. Exploring Creation with Zoology 1: The Flying Creatures of Day Five. Wile, Jay L., ed. 2005. (Illus.). xvi, 240p. (J). 35.00 *(978-1-932012-61-3(3))* Apologia Educational Ministries, Inc.

Gaarder-Juntti, Oona. What Lives in Antarctica?, 1 vol. 2008. (Animal Habitats Ser.). (ENG., Illus.). 24p. (J). (gr. k-3). 25.65 *(978-1-60453-169-5(X))* ABDO Publishing Co.

—What Lives in the Arctic?, 1 vol. 2008. (Animal Habitats Ser.). (ENG., Illus.). 24p. (J). (gr. k-3). 25.65 *(978-1-60453-172-5(X))* ABDO Publishing Co.

Gardner, Jane. Animal Science, Vol. 11. Lewin, Russ, ed. 2015. (Science 24/7 Ser.). (Illus.). 48p. (J). (gr. 5). lib. bdg. 20.95 *(978-1-4222-3405-1(3))* Mason Crest.

Green, Ivah E. Animals under Your Feet. Reece, Maynard, illus. 2011. 140p. 40.95 *(978-1-258-06244-6(5))* Literary Licensing, LLC.

Helman, Andrea. Northwest Animal Babies. Wolfe, Art, photos by. 2006. (ENG., Illus.). 32p. (J). (gr. -1-2). pap. 10.99 *(978-1-57061-462-0(8)*, Little Bigfoot) Sasquatch Bks.

Hestermann, Josh & Hestermann, Bethanie. Zoology for Kids: Understanding & Working with Animals, with 21 Activities. 2015. (For Kids Ser.). (ENG., Illus.). 144p. (J). (gr. 4). pap. 18.95 *(978-1-61374-961-6(9))* Chicago Review Pr., Inc.

Holden, Pam. Hoppity Hop, 6 pack. Morris, Sandra, illus. 2009. (Red Rocket Readers Ser.). (ENG.). 16p. (gr. -1-1). pap. *(978-1-877363-19-1(7)*, Red Rocket Readers) Flying Start Bks.

Holland, Mary. Animal Mouths, 1 vol. 2015. (Animal Adaptations Ser.). (ENG.). 32p. (J). (gr. 1-4). 17.95 *(978-1-62855-552-3(1))* Arbordale Publishing.

Jackie, Glassman. Amazing Arctic Animals, Vol. 2. 2014. (Penguin Young Readers, L3 Ser.). (ENG.). 48p. (J). (gr. 2-12). 8.24 *(978-1-63245-253-5(7))* Lectorum Pubns., Inc.

Jolivet, Joëlle. Zoo - Ology. Jolivet, Joëlle, illus. rev. ed. 2003. (ENG., Illus.). 40p. (J). (gr. -1-3). 29.99 *(978-0-7613-1894-1(1)*, 9780761318941) Roaring Brook Pr.

Kalman, Bobbie. Big Science Ideas. 2008. (J). pap. *(978-0-7787-3292-1(4))* Crabtree Publishing Co.

—How Does It Move? 2008. (Looking at Nature Ser.). (ENG., Illus.). 24p. (J). (gr. -1-2). pap. *(978-0-7787-3342-3(4))*; lib. bdg. *(978-0-7787-3322-5(X))* Crabtree Publishing Co.

—Nature's Cleaners. 2008. (Big Science Ideas Ser.). (ENG., Illus.). 32p. (J). (gr. 1-4). pap. *(978-0-7787-3300-3(9))*; lib. bdg. *(978-0-7787-3280-8(0))* Crabtree Publishing Co.

—Le Regne Animal. 2004. (Petit Monde Vivant Ser.). (FRE., Illus.). 32p. (J). pap. 10.95 *(978-2-89579-025-9(6))* Bayard Canada Livres CAN. Dist: Crabtree Publishing Co.

Kessel, Quinta Cattell. Mama Is A Mammal. Kessel, Margaret May, illus. 2005. 80p. (J). 16.95 *(978-0-9725027-3-3(4))* Vernissage Pr., LLC.

Kite, Lorien. Anteaters. 2009. (Illus.). 52p. (J). ***(978-0-7172-8058-2(6))*** Grolier, Ltd.

Kratt, Chris & Kratt, Martin. Wild Animal Babies! Random House, illus. 2016. (Step into Reading Ser.). (ENG.). 24p. (J). (gr. -1-1). 4.99 *(978-1-101-93171-4(X)*, Random Hse. Bks. for Young Readers) Random Hse. Children's Bks.

Kravetz, Jonathan. Locusts. 2006. (Gross Bugs Ser.). (Illus.). 24p. (J). (gr. -1-3). lib. bdg. 22.60 *(978-1-4042-3042-2(4)*, PowerKids Pr.) Rosen Publishing Group, Inc., The.

—Ticks. 2009. (Gross Bugs Ser.). 24p. (gr. 3-4). 42.50 *(978-1-61513-233-1(3)*, PowerKids Pr.) Rosen Publishing Group, Inc., The.

Lee, Justin. How to Draw African Animals. 2009. (Kid's Guide to Drawing Ser.). 24p. (gr. 3-3). 47.90 *(978-1-61511-008-7(9)*, PowerKids Pr.) Rosen Publishing Group, Inc., The.

Lewin, Betsy & Lewin, Ted. Elephant Quest Elephant Quest, 1 vol. 2014. (ENG., Illus.). 48p. (J). pap. 11.95 *(978-1-62014-183-0(3))* Lee & Low Bks., Inc.

El Libro de los Acertijos Zoologicos. (Coleccion Acertijos). (SPA.). (YA). (gr. 5-8). pap. *(978-950-724-261-8(9)*, LMA8236) Lumen ARG. Dist: Lectorum Pubns., Inc.

The Life Cycles Library. (Illus.). (J). (gr. k-5). 112.50 *(978-0-8239-7185-5(6))* Rosen Publishing Group, Inc., The.

Long, William. Secrets of the Woods. 2007. 148p. 19.99 *(978-1-59986-710-6(9))* Filiquarian Publishing, LLC.

Martin, Ruth. Little Explorers: the Animal World. Sanders, Allan, illus. 2016. (Little Explorers Ser.). (ENG.). 18p. (J). (gr. -1-3). 9.99 *(978-1-4998-0249-8(8))* Little Bee Books Inc.

Mattern, Joanne. Animals of the Savannah. 2009. (Reading Room Collection 2 Ser.). 24p. (gr. 3-4). 42.50 *(978-1-60851-957-6(0)*, PowerKids Pr.) Rosen Publishing Group, Inc., The.

McDonnell, Julia . Being a Sloth. 2013. (Can You Imagine Ser.). 32p. (gr. 2-5). pap. 10.50 *(978-1-4824-3274-9(9))* Rosen Publishing Group, Inc., The.

Miller, Debbie S. Arctic Lights, Arctic Nights. Van Zyle, Jon, illus. 2007. (ENG.). 32p. (J). (gr. k-4). pap. 8.99 *(978-0-8027-9636-3(2)*, 9780802796363, Bloomsbury USA Childrens) Bloomsbury Publishing USA.

Miller, Janet. Cut, Color & Paste: God's Creatures. 2004. (Illus.). 96p. (J). (gr. -1-2). 11.95 *(978-1-885358-81-3(4))* Rainbow Pubs. & Legacy Pr.

Morgan, Sally. Insect Eaters. 2004. (J). lib. bdg. 27.10 *(978-1-59389-174-9(1))* Chrysalis Education.

Myers, Jack. The Puzzle of the Platypus: And Other Explorations of Science in Action. Rice, John, illus. 2008. (ENG.). 64p. (J). (gr. 4-7). 17.95 *(978-1-59078-556-0(8))* Boyds Mills Pr.

Nagelhout, Ryan. Clownfish. 2013. (Underwater World Ser.). (Illus.). 24p. (J). (gr. k-2). pap. 8.15 *(978-1-4339-8564-5(0))*; lib. bdg. 22.60 *(978-1-4339-8563-8(2))* Stevens, Gareth Publishing LLLP.

Nsrc. Science & Technology for Children BOOKS: Plant Growth & Development. 2007. (Illus.). 64p. (J). *(978-1-933008-39-4(3)*, Science and Technology Concepts (STC)) Smithsonian Science Education Ctr. (SSEC).

Orr, Tamra. Camouflage & Mimicry in the Wild. 2003. (Extreme Animals Ser.). (J). pap. *(978-1-58417-257-4(6))* Lake Street Pubs.

Owen, Ruth. Zoologists & Ecologists. 2013. (Out of the Lab: Extreme Jobs in Science Ser.). 32p. (J). (gr. 3-6). 25.25 *(978-1-4777-1293-1(3))*; pap. 10.00 *(978-1-4777-1384-6(0))* Rosen Publishing Group, Inc., The. (PowerKids Pr.).

Page, Robin & Jenkins, Steve. What Do You Do with a Tail Like This? 2008. (ENG., Illus.). 32p. (J). (gr. -1-3). pap. 7.95 *(978-0-618-99713-8(X))* Houghton Mifflin Harcourt Publishing Co.

Petrie, Kristin. Ticks, 1 vol. 2009. (Bugs! Ser.). (ENG.). 32p. (gr. 3-6). 27.07 *(978-1-60453-072-8(3)*, Checkerboard Library) ABDO Publishing Co.

Pierson, Clara Dillingham. Among the Forest People (Yesterday's Classics) 2005. (Illus.). 148p. (J). per. 8.95 *(978-1-59915-018-5(2))* Yesterday's Classics.

—Among the Pond People (Yesterday's Classics) 2005. (Illus.). 160p. (J). per. 8.95 *(978-1-59915-021-5(2))* Yesterday's Classics.

Pipe, Jim. Swarms. 2009. (Scary Creatures Ser.). (ENG., Illus.). 32p. (J). (gr. 3-5). 27.00 *(978-0-531-21674-3(8)*, Children's Pr.); pap. 8.95 *(978-0-531-21045-1(6)*, Watts, Franklin) Scholastic Library Publishing.

Rake, Jody Sullivan. Carcass Chewers of the Animal World. 2015. (Disgusting Creature Diets Ser.). (ENG.). 32p. (gr. 1-2). 26.65 *(978-1-4914-1998-4(9))* Capstone Press of Coughlan Cos.

—Spines, Horns, & Armor: Animal Weapons & Defenses. 2012. (Animal Weapons & Defenses Ser.). (ENG.). 32p. (gr. 1-2). pap. 47.70 *(978-1-4296-8502-3(6)*, Blazers) Capstone Press of Coughlan Cos.

Redfern, Nick. True Stories of Real-Life Monsters. 2014. (Off the Record! Ser.). (Illus.). 288p. (J). (gr. 7-12). 38.25 *(978-1-4777-7835-7(7))* Rosen Publishing Group, Inc., The.

Reeves, Diane Lindsey. Career Ideas for Kids Who Like Animals & Nature. Bond, Nancy, illus. 2nd rev. ed. 2007. (Career Ideas for Kids Ser.). 208p. (gr. 4-9). 32.95 *(978-0-8160-6539-4(X)*, Ferguson Publishing Co.) Facts On File, Inc.

Riggs, Kate. Vultures. 2015. (Illus.). 24p. (J). *(978-1-60818-492-7(7)*, Creative Education) Creative Co., The.

Rissman, Rebecca. Animal Spikes & Spines, 1 vol. 2011. (ENG.). 24p. (gr. -1-1). pap. 9.95 *(978-1-4329-5500-7(4))*; 25.99 *(978-1-4329-5355-3(9))* Heinemann-Raintree. (Acorn Read-Aloud).

—Antlers, 1 vol. 2011. (Animal Spikes & Spines Ser.). (ENG.). 24p. (gr. -1-1). pap. 6.29 *(978-1-4329-5044-6(4))*; 22.65 *(978-1-4329-5037-8(1))* Heinemann-Raintree. (Acorn).
—Spines, 1 vol. 2011. (Animal Spikes & Spines Ser.). (ENG.). 24p. (gr. -1-1). pap. 6.29 *(978-1-4329-5048-4(7))*; 22.65 *(978-1-4329-5041-5(X))* Heinemann-Raintree. (Acorn).
Rodriguez, Ana Maria. The Secret of the Deceiving Striped Lizard... & More! 2017. (Animal Secrets Revealed! Ser.). 48p. (J). (gr. 4-4). pap. 11.70 ***(978-0-7660-8853-5(7))***; lib. bdg. 27.93 ***(978-0-7660-8625-8(9))*** Enslow Pubs., Inc.
Rooney, Anne. A Math Journey Through the Animal Kingdom. 2014. (ENG.). 32p. (J). *(978-0-7787-0732-5(6))* Crabtree Publishing Co.
Rose, Simon. Taxidermist. 2014. (J). *(978-1-4896-1006-5(5))* Weigl Pubs., Inc.
Rushworth, Gary. What Makes an Animal an Animal? Set Of 6. 2011. (Navigators Ser.). (J). pap. 48.00 net. *(978-1-4108-6230-3(5))* Benchmark Education Co.
Salariya, David, creator. Scary Creatures, 6 vols., Set. Incl. Arctic. Clarke, Penny. 27.00 *(978-0-531-20449-8(9)*, Children's Pr.); Jellyfish - Scary Creatures. Cheshire, Gerard. 27.00 *(978-0-531-20446-7(4)*, Children's Pr.); Killer Whales. Malam, John. 27.00 *(978-0-531-20447-4(2))*; Lizards - Scary Creatures. Cheshire, Gerard. 27.00 *(978-0-531-20448-1(0)*, Children's Pr.); Of the Night. Malam, John. 27.00 *(978-0-531-20424-5(3)*, Children's Pr.); Scary Creatures of the Rain Forest. Clarke, Penny. 27.00 *(978-0-531-20544-0(4)*, Children's Pr.); (Illus.). 32p. (J). (gr. 2-7). 2008. Set lib. bdg. 156.00 o.p. *(978-0-531-20416-0(2)*, Watts, Franklin) Scholastic Library Publishing.
Schulte, Mary. Dover Demon. 2009. (Mysterious Encounters Ser.). (ENG., Illus.). 48p. (J). 29.00 *(978-0-7377-4570-2(3)*, Greenhaven Pr., Inc.) Cengage Gale.
Shields, Mary & Grace, Susan. What's a Shrew to You? Van Zyle, Jon, illus. 2008. (J). *(978-0-9618348-7-6(0))* Pyrola Publishing.
Silvey, Anita & National Geographic Kids Staff. Untamed: The Wild Life of Jane Goodall. 2015. (ENG., Illus.). 96p. (J). (gr. 3-7). 18.99 *(978-1-4263-1518-3(X)*, National Geographic Children's Bks.) National Geographic Society.
Somervill, Barbara A. Ticks: Digging for Blood. 2009. (Bloodsuckers Ser.). 24p. (gr. 2-3). 42.50 *(978-1-61511-636-2(2)*, PowerKids Pr.) Rosen Publishing Group, Inc., The.
Spilsbury, Louise. Sea Otters, 1 vol. 2013. (Living in the Wild: Sea Mammals Ser.). (ENG., Illus.). 48p. (gr. 4-6). pap. 9.95 *(978-1-4329-7072-7(0))*; lib. bdg. 33.32 *(978-1-4329-7065-9(8))* Heinemann-Raintree. (Heinemann InfoSearch).
—Zoologists in the Field. 2010. (Big Picture: People & Culture Ser.). (ENG.). 24p. (gr. 1-2). pap. 41.70 *(978-1-4296-5822-5(3)*, First Facts) Capstone Press of Coughlan Cos.
Tagliaferro, Linda. Galapagos Islands: Nature's Delicate Balance at Risk. 2005. (Discovery! Ser.). (Illus.). 120p. (gr. 5-12). lib. bdg. 27.93 *(978-0-8225-0648-5(3))* Lerner Publishing Group.
Taylor, Barbara. Arctic & Antarctic. 2012. (DK Eyewitness Bks.). (ENG.). 72p. (J). (gr. 3-7). 16.99 *(978-0-7566-9071-7(4)*, DK Children) Dorling Kindersley Publishing, Inc.
Time Living Wonders: The Marvels & Mysteries of Life on Earth. 2009. (Time Inc. Home Entertainment Library-Bound Titles Ser.). (ENG.). 128p. (gr. 5-12). 39.93 *(978-0-7613-4229-8(X)*, Twenty-First Century Bks.) Lerner Publishing Group.
Uncover a T. Rex. 2004. (J). bds. 22.95 *(978-1-932855-10-4(6))* becker&mayer! books.
Vaughn, Marcia. I Howl, I Growl: Southwest Animal Antics. Powell, Polly, illus. 2003. (ENG.). 26p. (J). (gr. -1-k). bds. 7.95 *(978-0-87358-835-5(5))* Cooper Square Publishing Llc.
Wadsworth, Pamela. Golwg Gyntaf Ar Bethau Byw. Owen, Ken & Owen, Siân, illus. 2005. (WEL.). 24p. pap. *(978-1-85596-250-7(0))* Dref Wen.
Wood, J. G. Illustrated Natural History: Arranged Fo. 2006. pap. 27.95 *(978-1-4286-0489-6(8))* Kessinger Publishing, LLC.
World Book, Inc Staff, contrib. by. Encyclopedia of Animals. 2013. (Illus.). (J). *(978-0-7166-7518-1(8))* World Bk., Inc.
El Zoologico, 2 Packs. (Chiquilibros Ser.). (SPA.). (gr. -1-1). 12.00 *(978-0-7635-8556-3(4))* Rigby Education.
Zoologists & Ecologists. 2013. (Out of the Lab: Extreme Jobs in Science Ser.). 32p. (J). (gr. 3-6). pap. 60.00 *(978-1-4777-1385-3(9)*, PowerKids Pr.) Rosen Publishing Group, Inc., The.

ZOOLOGY—ANATOMY
see Anatomy, Comparative

ZOOLOGY, ECONOMIC
see also Domestic Animals; Insect Pests
Ridley, Sarah. In the Home. 2010. (J). 28.50 *(978-1-59920-328-7(6))* Black Rabbit Bks.
Sherman, Jill. Animals & Fish. 2017. (J). ***(978-0-7660-9238-9(0))*** Enslow Pubs., Inc.

ZOOLOGY OF THE BIBLE
see Bible—Natural History

ZOOS
Appleby, Alex. Dinosaurs at the Zoo. 2013. (Dinosaur School Ser.). 24p. (J). (gr. k-1). pap. 48.90 *(978-1-4339-9047-2(4))*; pap. 8.15 *(978-1-4339-9046-5(6))*; (ENG., Illus.). lib. bdg. 22.60 *(978-1-4339-9045-8(8))* Stevens, Gareth Publishing LLLP.
Avery, Sherrie. Miami Metrozoo. (Great Zoos of the United States Ser.). 24p. 2009. (gr. 3-4). 42.50 *(978-1-61513-222-5(8))* 2003. (Illus.). (J). lib. bdg. 22.60 *(978-0-8239-6316-4(0))* Rosen Publishing Group, Inc., The. (PowerKids Pr.).
Ayers, Amy. Contando en el Zoologico. 2007. (Las matimaticas en nuestro mundo (Spanish- Math in Our World) Ser.). (SPA.). 24p. (gr. 1-2). pap. 8.15 *(978-0-8368-8496-8(5)*, Weekly Reader Leveled Readers) Stevens, Gareth Publishing LLLP.
—Counting at the Zoo. 2007. (Math in Our World Ser.). (Illus.). 24p. (gr. 1-2). lib. bdg. 22.00 *(978-0-8368-8469-2(8)*, Weekly Reader Leveled Readers) Stevens, Gareth Publishing LLLP.
AZ Books Staff & Evans, Olivia. Making the Zoo. Sisoj, Natalja, ed. 2012. (Modeling Clay Bk Ser.). (ENG., Illus.). 12p. (J). (gr. -1-2). bds. 10.95 *(978-1-61889-196-9(0))* AZ Bks. LLC.
Baby's Very First Slide & See Zoo. 2017. (Baby's Very First Slide & See BDs Ser.). (ENG.). (J). bds. 14.99 ***(978-0-7945-3878-1(9)***, Usborne) EDC Publishing.
Battistoni, I. At the Zoo: Learning the Z Sound. 2009. (PowerPhonics Ser.). 24p. (gr. 1-1). 39.90 *(978-1-60851-433-5(1)*, PowerKids Pr.) Rosen Publishing Group, Inc., The.
Becker, Helaine. Worms for Breakfast: How to Feed a Zoo. Boake, Kathy, illus. 2016. (ENG.). 40p. (J). (gr. 2-5). 16.95 *(978-1-77147-105-3(0)*, Owlkids) Owlkids Bks. Inc. CAN. Dist: Publishers Group West (PGW).
Bishop, Celeste. A Visit to the Zoo. 2016. (Places in My Community Ser.). 00024p. (J). (gr. 1-1). pap. 8.25 *(978-1-4994-2772-1(7)*, PowerKids Pr.) Rosen Publishing Group, Inc., The.
Chilek, Deborah. A Trip to the Zoo. 2008. (Real Readers - Upper Emergent Ser.). (ENG., Illus.). 12p. (gr. 1-2). pap. 5.90 *(978-0-8239-8202-8(5))* Rosen Publishing Group, Inc., The.
Clark, Rosalyn. A Visit to the Zoo. 2017. (Bumba Books (tm) — Places We Go Ser.). (ENG.). 24p. (J). (gr. -1-1). 25.32 ***(978-1-5124-3373-9(X))*** Lerner Publishing Group.
Colby, Jennifer. Zoo. 2016. (21st Century Junior Library: Explore a Workplace Ser.). (ENG., Illus.). 24p. (J). (gr. 2-5). 27.07 *(978-1-63471-080-0(0)*, 208399) Cherry Lake Publishing.
Color All About: The Zoo: A Coloring Book about Going to the Zoo. 2004. (Illus.). (J). *(978-0-9763307-2-1(5))* Food Marketing Consultants, Inc.
Curtis, Jennifer Keats. Animal Helpers: Zoos, 1 vol. 2013. (Animal Helpers Ser.). (ENG.). 32p. (J). (gr. 2-5). pap. 9.95 *(978-1-60718-850-6(3))* Arbordale Publishing.
Dale, Jay. The Zookeeper, 1 vol. 2012. (Engage Literacy Magenta Ser.). (ENG.). 32p. (gr. k-2). pap. 5.99 *(978-1-4296-8864-2(5)*, Engage Literacy) Capstone Press of Coughlan Cos.
Dawson, Emily C. The Zoo. 2010. (My Community Ser.). 24p. (J). 25.65 *(978-1-60753-024-4(4))* Amicus Publishing.
Dee, Nora. Spanish Words at the Zoo, Vol. 1. 2014. (Learn My Language! Spanish Ser.). (ENG.). 24p. (J). (gr. 1-2). pap. 8.15 *(978-1-4824-0358-9(7))* Stevens, Gareth Publishing LLLP.
Dorling Kindersley Publishing Staff & Baker, Nick. Bug Zoo. 2010. (ENG., Illus.). 64p. (J). (gr. k-3). 12.99 *(978-0-7566-6166-3(8))* Dorling Kindersley Publishing, Inc.
Estigarribia, Diana. Smithsonian National Zoological Park. (Great Zoos of the United States Ser.). 24p. 2009. (gr. 3-4). 42.50 *(978-1-61513-225-6(2)*, PowerKids Pr.) 2003. (Illus.). (J). lib. bdg. 22.60 *(978-0-8239-6317-1(9))* Rosen Publishing Group, Inc., The.
Friedman, Sharon. Grin & Bear It: Zoo Jokes to Make You Roar. Gable, Brian, illus. 2005. (Make Me Laugh! Ser.). 32p. (J). (gr. k-3). lib. bdg. 19.93 *(978-1-57505-660-9(7))* Lerner Publishing Group.
Galvin, Laura Gates. Tamarin's Mealtime. Cohen, Jessie, illus. 2005. (Let's Go to the Zoo! Ser.). (ENG.). 16p. (J). (gr. -1-k). 5.95 *(978-1-56899-858-9(9))* Soundprints.
Gangelhoff, Jeanne M. & Belk, Bradford. A Walk Through the Minnesota Zoo. Gangelhoff, Gene, illus. 32p. (J). 9.95 *(978-0-9635006-1-8(9))* G J & B Publishing.
Gorman, Jacqueline Laks. The Zoo. 2005. (I Like to Visit Ser.). (Illus.). 24p. (gr. k-3). pap. 8.15 *(978-0-8368-4463-4(7))*; lib. bdg. 22.00 *(978-0-8368-4456-6(4))* Stevens, Gareth Publishing LLLP. (Weekly Reader Leveled Readers).
—The Zoo (El Zoologico) 2005. (I Like to Visit/ Me gusta visitar Ser.). (ENG & SPA., Illus.). 24p. (gr. k-3). pap. 8.15 *(978-0-8368-4607-2(9)*, Weekly Reader Leveled Readers) Stevens, Gareth Publishing LLLP.
Gorman, Jacqueline Laks & Laks Gorman, Jacqueline. The Zoo/El Zoológico. Acosta, Tatiana & Gutiérrez, Guillermo, trs. 2005. (I Like to Visit/Me Gusta Visitar Ser.). (ENG & SPA., Illus.). 24p. (gr. k-3). lib. bdg. 22.00 *(978-0-8368-4600-3(1)*, Weekly Reader Leveled Readers) Stevens, Gareth Publishing LLLP.
Great Zoos of the United States. (Illus.). (J). (gr. k-5). 112.50 *(978-0-8239-7267-8(4))* Rosen Publishing Group, Inc., The.
Guidone, Lisa M. What Happens at a Zoo? 2008. (Where People Work Ser.). 24p. (J). (gr. -1-3). lib. bdg. 22.00 *(978-0-8368-9272-7(0)*, Weekly Reader Leveled Readers) Stevens, Gareth Publishing LLLP.
—What Happens at a Zoo?/¿Qué pasa en un Zoológico? 2008. (Where People Work Ser.). 24p. (gr. -1-3). pap. 8.15 *(978-0-8368-9371-7(9)*, Weekly Reader Leveled Readers) Stevens, Gareth Publishing LLLP.
Guidone, Lisa M. & Nations, Susan. What Happens at a Zoo?/¿Qué pasa en un Zoológico? 2008. (Where People Work/Dónde Trabaja la Gente? Ser.). (SPA & ENG.). 24p. (gr. -1-3). pap. 8.15 *(978-0-8368-9377-9(8)*, Weekly Reader Leveled Readers) Stevens, Gareth Publishing LLLP.
—What Happens at a Zoo?/¿Qué pasa en un Zoológico? 2008. (Where People Work/Dónde Trabaja la Gente? Ser.). (SPA & ENG.). 24p. (J). (gr. -1-3). lib. bdg. 22.00 *(978-0-8368-9278-9(X)*, Weekly Reader Leveled Readers) Stevens, Gareth Publishing LLLP.
Halls, Kelly Milner & Sumner, William. Saving the Baghdad Zoo: A True Story of Hope & Heroes. Sumner, William, illus. 2010. (ENG., Illus.). 64p. (J). (gr. 3-18). 17.99 *(978-0-06-177202-3(X)*, Greenwillow Bks.) HarperCollins Pubs.
Harrison, Sarah. A Day at a Zoo. 2008. (Time Goes By Ser.). (ENG.). (gr. k-3). pap. 39.62 *(978-0-7613-4710-1(0))* Lerner Publishing Group.
Hogan, Martina, illus. Rainbow Zoo. 2016. (Early Birds Ser.). (ENG.). 12p. (J). (gr. -1 — 1). bds. 6.99 *(978-1-4998-0209-2(9))* Little Bee Books Inc.
Johnson, Bruce. We Read Phonics-A Day at the Zoo. Johnson, Meredith, illus. 2012. 32p. (J). 9.95 *(978-1-60115-349-4(X))*; pap. 4.99 *(978-1-60115-350-0(3))* Treasure Bay, Inc.
Johnson, Bruce & Johnson, Meredith, illus. A Day at the Zoo. 2012. 27p. (J). *(978-1-60115-595-5(6))* Treasure Bay, Inc.
Johnson, Bruce & McKay, Sindy. We Both Read-Zoo Day. Johnson, Meredith, illus. 2015. (We Both Read - Level 1 (Quality) Ser.). (ENG.). 44p. (J). (gr. k-2). pap. 4.99 *(978-1-60115-274-9(4))* Treasure Bay, Inc.
Kalz, Jill. Zoo Adventure. Cerato, Mattia, illus. 2010. (A-MAZE-Ing Adventures Ser.). (ENG.). 32p. (gr. 1-2). lib. bdg. 26.65 *(978-1-4048-6024-7(X))* Picture Window Bks.
Kawa, Katie. My First Trip to the Zoo. Livingston, Jessica, illus. 2012. (My First Adventures Ser.). (ENG.). 24p. (J). (gr. k-2). pap. 8.15 *(978-1-4339-6259-2(4))*; lib. bdg. 22.60 *(978-1-4339-6257-8(8))* Stevens, Gareth Publishing LLLP.
—My First Trip to the Zoo: Mi Primera Visita Al Zoológico. Livingston, Jessica, illus. 2012. (My First Adventures / Mis primeras aventuras Ser.). (ENG & SPA.). 24p. (J). (gr. k-2). lib. bdg. 22.60 *(978-1-4339-6635-4(2))* Stevens, Gareth Publishing LLLP.
Kent, Lorna, illus. At the Zoo. 2004. 8p. (J). bds. 3.99 *(978-1-85854-084-9(4))* Brimax Books Ltd. GBR. Dist: Byeway Bks.
King, Corinne & Fenton, Corinne. Queenie: One Elephant's Story. Gouldthorpe, Peter, illus. 2013. (ENG.). 24p. (J). (gr. k-3). 16.99 *(978-0-7636-6375-9(1))* Candlewick Pr.
Kirsten, A. We Bring the Zoo to You. 2005. 32p. pap. 9.95 *(978-0-9704876-5-0(7))* First Mom's Club, The.
Kumon Publishing, creator. My Book of Coloring at the Zoo: Ages 3, 4, 5. 2007. (Kumon Workbooks Ser.). (Illus.). 80p. per. 7.95 *(978-1-933241-39-5(X))* Kumon Publishing North America, Inc.
Larousse Mexico Staff, ed. Mi Pequena Encicopedia Larousse el Zoologico. 2006. (SPA., Illus.). 38p. (gr. -1 — 1). pap. 3.95 *(978-970-22-1193-8(X))* Larousse, Ediciones, S. A. de C. V. MEX. Dist: Houghton Mifflin Harcourt Publishing Co.
Liebman, Daniel & Liebman, Dan. Guardian de Zoologico. 2003. (Quiero Ser). (SPA., Illus.). 24p. (J). (gr. -1-2). pap. 5.99 *(978-1-55297-730-9(7)*, 9781552977309) Firefly Bks., Ltd.
—I Want to Be a Zookeeper. 2003. (I Want to Be Ser.). (ENG., Illus.). 24p. (J). (gr. -1-2). 14.95 *(978-1-55297-699-9(8)*, 9781552976999); pap. 3.99 *(978-1-55297-697-5(1)*, 9781552976975) Firefly Bks., Ltd.
Lyon, George Ella & Catalanotto, Peter. Mother to Tigers. 2003. (ENG., Illus.). 32p. (J). (gr. k-3). 18.99 *(978-0-689-84221-4(X)*, Atheneum/Richard Jackson Bks.) Simon & Schuster Children's Publishing.
Macaulay, David. How Machines Work: Zoo Break! 2015. (ENG., Illus.). 32p. (J). (gr. 2-5). 19.99 *(978-1-4654-4012-9(7)*, DK Children) Dorling Kindersley Publishing, Inc.
Macken, JoAnn Early. Animals I See at the Zoo/Animales Que Veo en el Zoológico, 4 bks. Coffey, Colleen & Carrillo, Consuelo, trs. Incl. Giraffes/Las Jirafas. (SPA & ENG., Illus.). 24p. (gr. k-3). 2002. lib. bdg. 22.00 *(978-0-8368-4000-1(3)*, Weekly Reader Leveled Readers); (SPA & ENG.). Illus.). 2003. Set lib. bdg. 74.40 o.p. *(978-0-8368-3997-5(8)*, Weekly Reader) Stevens, Gareth Publishing LLLP.
—Animals I See at the Zoo/Animales Que Veo en el Zoológico, 4 bks. Incl. Bears/Los Osos. 2002. pap. 8.15 *(978-0-8368-4003-2(8))*; Elephants/Los Elefantes. 2002. pap. 8.15 *(978-0-8368-4004-9(6))*; Penguins/Los Pingüinos. (J). 2003. pap. 8.15 *(978-0-8368-4006-3(2))*; 24p. (gr. k-3)., Weekly Reader Leveled Readers (SPA & ENG., Illus.). 2003. pap. o.p. *(978-0-8368-4002-5(X)*, Weekly Reader) Stevens, Gareth Publishing LLLP.
Martin, Isabel. A Zoo Field Trip. 2015. (Let's Take a Field Trip Ser.). (ENG.). 24p. (gr. k-1). pap. 6.95 *(978-1-4914-2316-5(1)*, Pebble Plus) Capstone Press of Coughlan Cos.
Maxwell, Cassandre. Fur, Fins, & Feathers: Abraham Dee Bartlett & the Invention of the Modern Zoo. 2015. (ENG., Illus.). 34p. (J). 17.00 *(978-0-8028-5432-2(X)*, Eerdmans Bks For Young Readers) Eerdmans, William B. Publishing Co.
McCullough, Ana L. The Zoo at the End of My Book. 2009. 32p. pap. 16.49 *(978-1-4389-0535-8(1))* AuthorHouse.
McReynolds, Stacy. San Antonio Zoo. (Great Zoos of the United States Ser.). 24p. 2009. (gr. 3-4). 42.50 *(978-1-61513-223-2(6))* 2003. (Illus.). (J). lib. bdg. 22.60 *(978-0-8239-6319-5(5))* Rosen Publishing Group, Inc., The. (PowerKids Pr.).
Newman, Patricia. Zoo Scientists to the Rescue. Crawley, Annie, photos by. 2017. (ENG., Illus.). (J). (gr. 4-8). lib. bdg. 33.32 ***(978-1-5124-1571-1(5)***, Millbrook Pr.) Lerner Publishing Group.
Nunn, Daniel. Eddie & Ellie's Opposites at the Zoo, 1 vol. 2013. (Eddie & Ellie's Opposites Ser.). (ENG., Illus.). 24p. (gr. -1-k). 22.65 *(978-1-4109-5340-7(8))*; pap. 7.95 *(978-1-4109-5345-2(9))* Heinemann-Raintree. (NA-r).
O'Connell, Caitlin. Bridge to the Wild: Behind the Scenes at the Zoo. Rodwell, Timothy, photos by. 2016. (ENG., Illus.). 208p. (J). (gr. 5-7). 18.99 *(978-0-544-27739-7(2)*, HMH Books For Young Readers) Houghton Mifflin Harcourt Publishing Co.
Oehler, David A. The Cincinnati Zoo & Botanical Garden. 2003. (Great Zoos of the United States Ser.). (Illus.). 24p. (J). lib. bdg. 22.60 *(978-0-8239-6320-1(9)*, PowerKids Pr.) Rosen Publishing Group, Inc., The.
Olmedillas, Cathy, compiled by. Anorak. 2013. (ENG., Illus.). 64p. (J). pap. 9.99 *(978-1-4236-3340-2(7)*, Anorak Pr.) Gibbs Smith, Publisher.
Orr, Tamra. How Did They Build That? Zoo. 2011. (Community Connections: How Did They Build That? Ser.). (ENG.). 24p. (gr. 2-5). lib. bdg. 25.64 *(978-1-61080-113-3(X)*, 201120) Cherry Lake Publishing.
—Working at the Zoo. 2011. (21st Century Junior Library: Careers Ser.). (ENG.). 24p. (gr. 2-5). lib. bdg. 25.64 *(978-1-60279-978-3(4)*, 200946) Cherry Lake Publishing.
Pearce, Claudia. San Diego Zoo. 2009. (Great Zoos of the United States Ser.). 24p. (gr. 3-4). 42.50 *(978-1-61513-224-9(4)*, PowerKids Pr.) Rosen Publishing Group, Inc., The.
Pearce, Claudia & Worley, Karen E. San Diego Zoo. Bohn, Ken & Garrison, Ron, illus. Bohn, Ken & Garrison, Ron, photos by. 2003. (Great Zoos of the United States Ser.). 24p. (J). lib. bdg. 22.60 *(978-0-8239-6321-8(7)*, PowerKids Pr.) Rosen Publishing Group, Inc., The.
Pettiford, Rebecca. Zoo. Fretland VanVoorst, Jenny, ed. 2016. (First Field Trips). 24p. (J). (gr. k-2). lib. bdg. 25.65 *(978-1-62031-299-5(9)*, Bullfrog Bks.) Jump! Inc.
—El Zoológico. 2016. (Los Primeros Viajes Escolares (First Field Trips)).Tr. of Zoo. (SPA.). 24p. (J). (gr. k-2). lib. bdg. 25.65 *(978-1-62031-333-6(2)*, Bullfrog Bks.) Jump! Inc.
Powell, Elizabeth. Math at the Zoo. 2016. (Math Is Everywhere! Ser.). 00024p. (J). pap. 8.15 *(978-1-4824-5500-7(5))* Stevens, Gareth Publishing LLLP.
Powell, Janet. Saint Louis Zoo. 2003. (Great Zoos of the United States Ser.). (Illus.). 24p. (J). lib. bdg. 22.60 *(978-0-8239-6318-8(7)*, PowerKids Pr.) Rosen Publishing Group, Inc., The.
—St. Louis Zoo. 2009. (Great Zoos of the United States Ser.). 24p. (gr. 3-4). 42.50 *(978-1-61513-226-3(0)*, PowerKids Pr.) Rosen Publishing Group, Inc., The.
Priddy, Roger. At the Zoo. 2006. (Bright Baby Touch & Feel Ser.). (ENG., Illus.). 10p. (J). (gr. -1 — 1). bds. 4.95 *(978-0-312-49857-3(8)*, 9780312498573, Priddy Bks.) St. Martin's Pr.
Rauen, Amy & Ayers, Amy. Counting at the Zoo. Andersen, Gregg, photos by. 2007. (Math in Our World Ser.). (Illus.). 24p. (gr. 1-2). pap. 8.15 *(978-0-8368-8478-4(7)*, Weekly Reader Leveled Readers) Stevens, Gareth Publishing LLLP.
Ring, Susan. Project Otter. Kissock, Heather & Marshall, Diana, eds. 2003. (Zoo Life Ser.). (Illus.). 24p. (J). pap. 8.95 *(978-1-59036-059-0(1))* Weigl Pubs., Inc.
Rissman, Rebecca. Going to a Zoo, 1 vol. 2012. (World of Field Trips Ser.). (ENG.). 24p. (gr. -1-1). lib. bdg. 22.65 *(978-1-4329-6070-4(9)*, Acorn) Heinemann-Raintree.
Ritchey, Kate & Bader, Bonnie. Lion, Tiger, & Bear, Level 4. 2015. (Penguin Young Readers, Level 4 Ser.). (ENG., Illus.). 48p. (J). (gr. 3-4). pap. 3.99 *(978-0-448-48336-8(X)*, Penguin Young Readers) Penguin Young Readers Group.
Roe-Pimm, Nancy. Colo's Story. 2011. (ENG.). 80p. (gr. 4-8). 18.95 *(978-0-9841554-4-6(9))*; pap. 8.95 *(978-0-9841554-5-3(7))* Columbus Zoo & Aquarium, The.
Rolle, Elvy P. Five Little Children at the Zoo. Stasuyk, Max, illus. 2016. (ENG.). 26p. (J). pap. 13.95 *(978-1-4796-0534-7(4)*, Aspect) Grand Central Publishing.
Rosa-Mendoza, Gladys. Let's Go to the Zoo!/Vamos Al Zoologico! Elkerton, Andy, illus. 2007. (English Spanish Foundations Ser.). (ENG & SPA.). 20p. (J). (gr. -1-k). bds. 6.95 *(978-1-931398-20-6(8))* Me+Mi Publishing.
Ruggieri, Linda. Amazing Animals: Critter Camp: Division (Grade 3) 2017. (Mathematics Readers Ser.). (Illus.). 32p. (gr. 3-3). 8.99 ***(978-1-4807-5800-1(0))*** Teacher Created Materials, Inc.
Salas, Laura Purdie. Y Is for Yak: A Zoo Alphabet, 1 vol. 2010. (Alphabet Fun Ser.). (ENG.). 32p. (gr. 1-2). lib. bdg. 27.32 *(978-1-4296-4465-5(6)*, A+plus Bks.) Capstone Press of Coughlan Cos.
Shaw, Gina. Curious about Zoo Vets. 2015. (Illus.). (J). *(978-1-4844-6359-8(5)*, Grosset & Dunlap) Penguin Publishing Group.
Shea, Therese. Discovering STEM at the Zoo. 2015. (STEM in the Real World Ser.). (ENG., Illus.). 24p. (J). (gr. 2-3). pap. 8.25 *(978-1-4994-0928-4(1)*, PowerKids Pr.) Rosen Publishing Group, Inc., The.
Smith, Roland & Smith, Marie. Z Is for Zookeeper: A Zoo Alphabet. Cole, Henry, illus. (ENG.). 40p. (J). (gr. k-6). 2005. 16.95 *(978-1-58536-158-8(5))* 2007. pap. 7.95 *(978-1-58536-329-2(4))* Sleeping Bear Pr.
Soundprints, creator. Tiger Cub See-and-Do. 2011. (Let's Go to the Zoo! Ser.). (ENG., Illus.). 16p. (gr. -1). 5.95 *(978-1-60727-460-5(4))* Soundprints.
Stead, Tony. Should There Be Zoos? A Persuasive Text. 2011. (ENG., Illus.). 32p. (J). (gr. 3-7). pap. 29.99 *(978-1-57255-817-5(2))* Mondo Publishing.
Tieck, Sarah. Zookeepers, 1 vol. 2011. (Extreme Jobs Ser.). (ENG., Illus.). 32p. (J). (gr. 2-5). 28.50 *(978-1-61783-029-7(1))* ABDO Publishing Co.
Toufexis, George. At the Zoo Stickers. 2011. (Dover Little Activity Books Stickers Ser.). (ENG.). 8p. (J). (gr. k-3). pap. 1.99 *(978-0-486-48181-4(6))* Dover Pubns., Inc.
Wagner, Jeff. My Day... at the Zoo. Alvarado, Paulo, illus. 2004. 20p. (J). bds. *(978-0-9754515-0-2(2))* Wagner Entertainment.
Who Lives at the Zoo? 2004. (Who Lives... Ser.). 12p. (J). bds. 4.99 *(978-1-85854-645-2(1))* Brimax Books Ltd. GBR. Dist: Byeway Bks.
Winterberg, Jenna. The Zoo: A Step-by-Step Drawing & Story Book. Fisher, Diana, illus. 2006. (Watch Me Draw Ser.). (ENG.). 24p. (J). (gr. -1-3). pap. 4.95 *(978-1-56010-798-9(7)*, 1560107987) Quarto Publishing Group USA.
The Zoo, 2 Packs. (Chiquilibros Ser.). (gr. -1-1). 12.00 *(978-0-7635-8536-5(X))* Rigby Education.
Zoo (Gr. PreK-5) 2003. (J). *(978-1-58232-027-4(6))* ECS Learning Systems, Inc.

ZOOS—FICTION
Adams, William J. Goin' to the Zoo / Vamos Al Zoologico. Stiglich, Tom, illus. 2007. (ENG & SPA.). 58p. (J). pap. 10.95 *(978-0-9772757-2-4(8))* Mandy & Andy Bks., Inc.
—Goin' to the Zoo Coloring Book: Vamos Al Zoologico. Stiglich, Tom, illus. 2007. (ENG & SPA.). (J). pap. 3.95 *(978-0-9772757-3-1(6))* Mandy & Andy Bks., Inc.
Adler, David A. Young Cam Jansen & the Lions' Lunch Mystery. Natti, Susanna, illus. 2007. (Young Cam Jansen Ser.: 13). (ENG.). 32p. (J). (gr. 1-3). 13.99 *(978-0-670-06171-6(9)*, Viking Books for Young Readers) Penguin Young Readers Group.
—Young Cam Jansen & the Lions' Lunch Mystery, No. 13. Natti, Susanna, illus. 2008. (Young Cam Jansen Ser.: 13). (ENG.). 32p. (J). (gr. 1-3). mass mkt. 3.99 *(978-0-14-241176-6(0)*, Penguin Young Readers) Penguin Young Readers Group.
Alexander, Carmen. Zoo 1000 Miles. Henderson, Cecil, illus. 2005. 42p. (J). (gr. -1-5). pap. 9.99 *(978-1-886383-57-9(X))* Blue Forge Pr.
Alien at the Zoo, 6 vols. (Sunshinetm Ser.). 16p. (gr. k-18). 29.50 *(978-0-7802-5429-9(5))* Wright Group/McGraw-Hill.
Anderson, Amanda. The Story of Larry the Hamster. 2008. 24p. pap. 24.95 *(978-1-60703-125-3(6))* America Star Bks.
Anderson, Dawn. Chimpance, Como Yo ! 2006. (Illus.). (J). 15.95 *(978-0-9786570-1-7(2))* Opposable Thumb Pr.
—Chimpanzee, Like Me! 2006. (Illus.). (J). 15.95 *(978-0-9786570-0-0(4))* Opposable Thumb Pr.
Arnold, Vickie. The Baby Zebra Adventure. 2009. 20p. pap. 12.49 *(978-1-4389-5818-7(8))* AuthorHouse.
Asch, Frank. The Lending Zoo. Asch, Frank, illus. 2016. (ENG., Illus.). 32p. (J). (gr. -1-3). 16.99 *(978-1-4424-6678-4(2)*, Aladdin) Simon & Schuster Children's Publishing.

W X Y Z

Avila, Nelson Moreno. The Boy & the Zoo. 2012. 32p. pap. 16.95 *(978-1-4497-7474-5(1)*, WestBow Pr.) Author Solutions, Inc.

AZ Books. Big Zoo Book. 2013. (Smart Pad Ser.). (ENG.). 14p. (J). (gr. -1-k). bds. 19.95 *(978-1-61889-418-2(8))* AZ Bks. LLC.

AZ Books, creator. Magic Zoo. 2012. (Baby Book Ser.). (ENG., Illus.). 10p. (J). (gr. -1 — 1). bds. 4.95 *(978-1-61889-284-3(3))* AZ Bks. LLC.

Bamboo Zoo Set: Meet Lester Panda & his Friends. 2006. (J). 17.95 *(978-0-9774493-1-6(9))* Bamboo Zoo, LLC.

Battle, Cleaton D. A Saturday Surprise. Cooper, Emmanuel, illus. 2006. 68p. (J). pap. 11.95 *(978-1-59663-504-3(5)*, Castle Keep Pr.) Rock, James A. & Co. Pubs.

Bercowetz, Cynthia. Grandpa Herman's Petting Zoo. 2007. (Illus.). 48p. (J). per. 14.95 *(978-0-9708430-9-8(7))* Uitti, Daniel.

Bhadresa, G. N. Tymrose a Fantasy. 2012. 120p. *(978-1-4602-0561-7(8))*; pap. *(978-1-4602-0560-0(X))* FriesenPress.

Bhakta, Sanjini. The Chocolate Pony. 2010. 28p. pap. 12.99 *(978-1-4490-9761-5(8))* AuthorHouse.

Blance, Ellen & Cook, Tony. Monster Goes to the Zoo. Date not set. (Illus.). 24p. pap. 129.15 *(978-0-582-18599-9(8))* Addison-Wesley Longman, Ltd. GBR. Dist: Trans-Atlantic Pubns., Inc.

BookSource Staff, compiled by. Petting Zoo. 2013. (DK Reader Pre Level Ser.). lib. bdg. 13.55 *(978-0-606-32439-7(9)*, Turtleback) Turtleback Bks.

Bratcher, Shirley Kay. Tudy Goes to the Zoo. 2013. 24p. pap. 24.95 *(978-1-4626-9560-7(4))* America Star Bks.

Brennah-Nelson, Denise. Maestro Stu Saves the Zoo. 2012. (ENG., Illus.). 32p. (J). 15.95 *(978-1-58536-802-0(4))* Sleeping Bear Pr.

Brezenoff, Steven. The Missing Bully: An Interactive Mystery Adventure. Calo, Marcos, illus. 2017. (You Choose Stories: Field Trip Mysteries Ser.). (ENG.). 112p. (gr. 3-7). lib. bdg. 32.65 *(978-1-4965-2642-7(2))* Stone Arch Bks.

Bridwell, Norman. Clifford Visits the Zoo. Bridwell, Norman, illus. 2014. (ENG., Illus.). 40p. (J). (— 1). 12.99 *(978-0-545-66896-5(4))* Scholastic, Inc.

Britner, Scott & Britner, Melissa. Tyler & Destiny Tales: Lunch at the Zoo. 2004. 17p. (J). pap. 8.33 *(978-1-4116-0919-8(0))* Lulu Pr., Inc.

Broach, Elise. The Wolf Keepers. Ratterree, Alice, illus. 2016. (ENG.). 352p. (J). 16.99 *(978-0-8050-9899-0(2)*, 9780805098990, Holt, Henry & Co. Bks. For Young Readers) Holt, Henry & Co.

Brooks, Heather. Hercules: A Matter of Trust. 2009. (Running Horse Ridge Ser.: 2). (ENG.). 224p. (J). (gr. 5-18). pap. 6.99 *(978-0-06-142981-1(3))* HarperCollins Pubs.

Brown, Joe. Race to the Rescue. Marchesi, Stephen, illus. 2009. (J). *(978-0-545-13473-6(0))* Scholastic, Inc.

Browne, Anthony. Little Beauty. Browne, Anthony, illus. 2010. (ENG., Illus.). 32p. (J). (gr. -1-2). pap. 6.99 *(978-0-7636-4967-8(8))* Candlewick Pr.

—Little Beauty. 2010. lib. bdg. 17.20 *(978-0-606-14714-9(4)*, Turtleback) Turtleback Bks.

Bryant, Jen. Call Me Marianne. Johnson, David, illus. 2006. 32p. (J). (gr. 1-4). 16.00 *(978-0-8028-5242-7(4)*, Eerdmans Bks For Young Readers) Eerdmans, William B. Publishing Co.

Burkhart, Lorene. Raccoon Tales: Hip, Flip, Skip & Boo go to the Zoo. 2007. (Illus.). (J). 8.95 *(978-0-9790975-2-2(5))* Burkhart Bks.

Burson, Ronda Pfohl. Monk-Monk the Monkey. 2010. 20p. 10.49 *(978-1-4520-0351-1(3))* AuthorHouse.

Caletti, Deb. The Nature of Jade. 2008. (ENG.). 320p. (YA). (gr. 7-12). pap. 10.99 *(978-1-4169-1006-0(9)*, Simon Pulse) Simon Pulse.

Campbell, Susan. Little Jimmy: The Itty Bitty Fifty Foot Tall Giraffe. 2011. 24p. pap. 24.95 *(978-1-4626-2929-9(6))* America Star Bks.

Caple, Kathy. A Night at the Zoo. Caple, Kathy, illus. 2014. (I Like to Read(r) Ser.). (ENG., Illus.). 24p. (J). (gr. -1-3). 14.95 *(978-0-8234-3044-4(8))* Holiday Hse., Inc.

Carney, Larry, adapted by. Silly Book/CD - Silly Zoo. 2010. (Illus.). 24p. (J). pap. 6.95 incl. cd-rom *(978-1-60072-155-7(9))* PC Treasures, Inc.

Carolan, Dr. Where Are My Slippers? A Book of Colors. Carolan, Joanna F., illus. 2007. 32p. 17.95 *(978-0-9715333-7-0(7))* Banana Patch Pr.

Castellucci, Cecil. The Queen of Cool. 2007. (ENG., Illus.). 176p. (YA). (gr. 9-18). pap. 7.99 *(978-0-7636-3413-1(1))* Candlewick Pr.

Chambers, Whittaker, tr. from GER. The City Jungle. 2014. (Bambi's Classic Animal Tales Ser.). (ENG., Illus.). 288p. (J). (gr. 3-7). pap. 7.99 *(978-1-4424-8751-2(8)*, Aladdin) Simon & Schuster Children's Publishing.

Chartier, Doris E. Ben's Desert Journey. 2009. 32p. pap. 14.49 *(978-1-4389-7756-0(5))* AuthorHouse.

Chick, Bryan. Riddles & Danger. 2011. (Secret Zoo Ser.: 3). (ENG.). 288p. (J). (gr. 3-7). 16.99 *(978-0-06-198927-8(4)*, Greenwillow Bks.) HarperCollins Pubs.

—The Secret Zoo. 2010. (Secret Zoo Ser.: 1). (ENG.). 304p. (J). (gr. 3-7). 16.99 *(978-0-06-198750-2(6)*, Greenwillow Bks.) HarperCollins Pubs.

—The Secret Zoo: Traps & Specters. 2012. (Secret Zoo Ser.: 4). (ENG.). 320p. (J). (gr. 3-7). 16.99 *(978-0-06-219222-6(1)*, Greenwillow Bks.) HarperCollins Pubs.

—The Secret Zoo: Raids & Rescues. (Secret Zoo Ser.: 5). (ENG.). 272p. (J). (gr. 3-7). 2014. pap. 6.99 *(978-0-06-219229-5(9))* 2013. 16.99 *(978-0-06-219228-8(0))* HarperCollins Pubs. (Greenwillow Bks.).

—Secrets & Shadows. 2011. (Secret Zoo Ser.: 2). (ENG.). 272p. (J). (gr. 3-7). pap. 6.99 *(978-0-06-198926-1(6))*; 16.99 *(978-0-06-198925-4(8))* HarperCollins Pubs. (Greenwillow Bks.).

—Traps & Specters. 2013. (Secret Zoo Ser.: 4). (ENG.). 320p. (J). (gr. 3-7). pap. 6.99 *(978-0-06-219223-3(X)*, Greenwillow Bks.) HarperCollins Pubs.

Choldenko, Gennifer. Notes from a Liar & Her Dog. 2003. (ENG.). 240p. (J). (gr. 3-7). pap. 7.99 *(978-0-14-250068-2(2)*, Puffin Books) Penguin Young Readers Group.

—Notes from a Liar & Her Dog. 2004. 224p. (J). (gr. 4-7). pap. 38.00 incl. audio *(978-0-8072-2097-9(3)*, Listening Library) Random Hse. Audio Publishing Group.

Clark, Seneca & Giardi, Sandy. Lily & the Imaginary Zoo, 1. Decedue, Julie, illus. 2005. (ENG.). 30p. (J). 15.95 *(978-0-9767276-1-3(7))* Three Bean Pr.

Clarkson, Kelly. River Rose & the Magical Lullaby. Hughes, Laura, illus. 2016. 32p. (J). (gr. -1-3). 18.99 *(978-0-06-242756-4(3))* HarperCollins Pubs.

Cobb, Amelia. The Lonely Lion Cub. 2016. (Zoe's Rescue Zoo Ser.: 1). (ENG., Illus.). 128p. (J). (gr. 2-5). pap. 4.99 *(978-0-545-84220-4(4)*, Scholastic Paperbacks) Scholastic, Inc.

—The Lucky Snow Leopard. 2016. (Zoe's Rescue Zoo Ser.: 4). (ENG.). 128p. (J). (gr. 2-5). pap. 4.99 *(978-0-545-84226-6(3)*, Scholastic Paperbacks) Scholastic, Inc.

—Silky Seal Pup. 2016. (Zoe's Rescue Zoo Ser.: 3). (ENG.). 128p. (J). (gr. 2-5). pap. 4.99 *(978-0-545-84224-2(7)*, Scholastic Paperbacks) Scholastic, Inc.

Cole, Babette. Tarzana. 2nd ed. 2003. (Babette Cole Ser.).Tr. of Tarzanna! (SPA., Illus.). 34p. (J). 12.95 *(978-84-233-2274-9(2))* Ediciones Destino ESP. Dist: Planeta Publishing Corp.

Colhoun, Sheelah. Elric's Florida Holiday. Cotton, Sue Lynn, illus. 2012. 20p. pap. 13.95 *(978-1-61493-110-2(0))* Peppertree Pr., The.

Cook, Melissa. Anna & the Garden Fairy: Anna's Little Black Bear. 2009. (ENG., Illus.). 20p. (J). 14.95 *(978-1-57197-501-0(2)*, Ivy House Publishing Group) Pentland Pr., Inc.

Cottrell, Kim. Jimmy Has the Bugaloo Zoo Flu. 2009. 32p. pap. 12.99 *(978-1-4389-5209-3(0))* AuthorHouse.

Craig, Sherryn. Locura de Medianoche en el Zoológico, 1 vol. Jones, Karen, illus. 2016. (SPA.). 32p. (J). (gr. k-3). pap. 9.95 *(978-1-62855-744-2(3))* Arbordale Publishing.

—Midnight Madness at the Zoo, 1 vol. Jones, Karen, illus. 2016. (ENG & SPA.). 32p. (J). (gr. k-3). 17.95 *(978-1-62855-730-5(3))* Arbordale Publishing.

Cressey, Roger. The Talking Giraffe. Cressey, Roger, illus. 2013. (Illus.). 118p. pap. *(978-1-78222-143-2(3))* Paragon Publishing, Rothersthorpe.

Crispin, Barbara. City Zoo Blizzard Revue. Houghton, Roswitha, illus. 2003. 40p. 14.95 *(978-0-9716346-1-9(0))* Dancing Words Pr., Inc.

Crofoot, Nancy. Sandy & Mitzi: Off to the Zoo. Rawal, Ishita, illus. 2013. 48p. pap. 24.95 *(978-1-62709-868-7(2))* America Star Bks.

Cunningham, Sheila S. Willow's Walkabout: A Children's Guide to Boston. Kelleher, Kathie, illus. 2012. (ENG.). 32p. (J). (gr. 1-3). 17.95 *(978-1-59373-096-3(9))* Bunker Hill Publishing, Inc.

Curry, Don, ed. The Crate Escape No. 2. 2008. (I Can Find It Ser.). 22p. (J). 7.99 *(978-0-696-23490-3(4))* Meredith Bks.

—Esape Africa. 2008. 22p. (J). 15.95 *(978-0-696-23488-0(2))* Meredith Bks.

Dakota, Heather. Emma's Very Busy Week. Panaccione, Nancy, illus. 2009. 31p. (J). *(978-0-545-17227-1(6))* Scholastic, Inc.

Danneberg, Julie. Field-Trip Fiasco. Love, Judy, illus. 2015. (Mrs. Hartwells Classroom Adventures Ser.). (ENG.). 32p. (J). (gr. k-3). 16.95 *(978-1-58089-671-9(5))* Charlesbridge Publishing, Inc.

DiGuardo, Maggie & Leventis, Kelly. Celly. 2012. (J). 14.95 *(978-1-937406-17-2(2))* Mascot Bks., Inc.

Dill, Mark. Maddie & Me: Go to the Zoo. 2012. 40p. pap. 20.99 *(978-1-4685-7481-4(7))* AuthorHouse.

Dods, Emma. The Zoo. Daubney, Kate, illus. 2015. (I Explore Ser.). (ENG.). 12p. (J). (gr. -1-k). bds. 6.95 *(978-1-4549-1503-4(X))* Sterling Publishing Co., Inc.

Douglas-Hobbs, Kathy. Kobe & the Rescue Adventure. 2012. 16p. pap. 15.99 *(978-1-4772-0326-2(5))* AuthorHouse.

Eberhart, Nancy. The Adventures of Granny: Granny Goes to the Zoo. Pyers, Kelsey, illus. 2007. (J). 24p. per. 10.99 *(978-1-59879-372-7(1))*; (gr. -1-3). 13.99 *(978-1-59879-373-4(X))* Lifevest Publishing, Inc.

Ebie, Mora. Going to the Zoo in Hawaii. 2006. (Illus.). 28p. (J). 10.95 *(978-1-56647-790-1(5))* Mutual Publishing LLC.

Elliott, George. The Boy Who Loved Bananas. Krystoforski, Andrej, illus. 2005. 32p. (J). (gr. -1-2). 15.95 *(978-1-55337-744-3(3))* Kids Can Pr., Ltd. CAN. Dist: Hachette Bk. Group.

Elliott, Rebecca. Zoo Girl. Elliott, Rebecca, illus. 2012. (ENG., Illus.). 32p. (J). (gr. k-2). 14.99 *(978-0-7459-6323-5(4))* Lion Hudson PLC GBR. Dist: Independent Pubs. Group.

Emerson, Carl. Monster Boy's Field Trip, 1 vol. Levin, Lon, illus. 2008. (Monster Boy Ser.). (ENG.). 32p. (gr. -1-4). 28.50 *(978-1-60270-236-3(5)*, Looking Glass Library) ABDO Publishing Co.

Everyday Signs of Zoo Animals. 2007. (J). bds. *(978-0-9791059-1-3(9))* Dakitab, Inc.

Faulconer, Maria. A Mom for Umande. Hartung, Susan Kathleen, illus. 2014. (ENG.). 32p. (J). (gr. -1-3). 16.99 *(978-0-8037-3762-4(9)*, Dial Bks) Penguin Young Readers Group.

Feiffer, Jules. A Room with a Zoo. Feiffer, Jules, illus. 2005. (ENG., Illus.). 192p. (gr. 2-17). 16.95 *(978-0-7868-3702-1(0)*, di Capua, Michael Bks.) Hyperion Bks. for Children.

Finn, Rebecca, illus. Busy Zoo. 2016. (Busy Bks.). (ENG.). 10p. (J). (gr. -1). bds. 8.95 *(978-1-4549-1944-5(2))* Sterling Publishing Co., Inc.

Finnegan, Evelyn M. My Little Friend Goes to the Zoo. Bruno, Margaret Farrell, illus. 2006. 32p. (J). (gr. -1-3). reprint ed. pap. 7.00 *(978-1-4223-5402-5(4))* DIANE Publishing Co.

Fisher-Price. Fisher-Price Little People Let's Imagine at the Zoo. 2014. (Lift-The-Flap Ser.: 27). (ENG.). 10p. (J). (gr. -1-k). bds. 9.99 *(978-0-7944-3115-0(1)*, Reader's Digest Children's Bks.) Studio Fun International.

Foster, Evelyn. Alan & the Animals. 2011. (Tadpoles Ser.). (ENG., Illus.). 24p. (J). (gr. k-2). *(978-0-7787-0573-4(0))*; pap. *(978-0-7787-0584-0(6))* Crabtree Publishing Co.

French, Jackie. My Pa the Polar Bear. 2015. (Wacky Families Ser.: 08). 128p. 5.99 *(978-0-207-20078-6(5))* HarperCollins Pubs. Australia AUS. Dist: HarperCollins Pubs.

Friedlander, Tim. The I Like Me Dance! Edwards, W M, illus. 2007. (Playdate Kids Musical Ser.). 27p. (J). (gr. -1-3). 14.95 incl. audio compact disk *(978-1-933721-07-1(3))* Playdate Kids Publishing.

Gabretti, Tisa. The Number Zoo, 1 vol. 2009. (ENG.). 15p. 24.95 *(978-1-60813-941-5(7))* America Star Bks.

Gale, Eric Kahn. The Zoo at the Edge of the World. Nielson, Sam, illus. (ENG.). 240p. (J). (gr. 3-7). 2015. pap. 6.99 *(978-0-06-212517-0(6))* 2014. 16.99 *(978-0-06-212516-3(8))* HarperCollins Pubs.

Gamble, Adam. Good Night Zoo. Kelly, Cooper, illus. 2007. (Good Night Our World Ser.). (ENG.). 26p. (J). (gr. k — 1). bds. 9.95 *(978-1-60219-018-4(6))* Good Night Bks.

Gamble, Adam & Jasper, Mark. Good Night Central Park. Palmer, Ruth, illus. 2013. (Good Night Our World Ser.). (ENG.). 20p. (J). (— 1). bds. 9.95 *(978-1-60219-082-5(8))* Good Night Bks.

Garland, Michael. Last Night at the Zoo. Garland, Michael, illus. 2003. (ENG., Illus.). 32p. (J). (gr. k-2). pap. 10.95 *(978-1-59078-167-8(8))* Boyds Mills Pr.

Gibbs, Stuart. Belly Up. (FunJungle Ser.). (ENG.). (J). (gr. 3-7). 2011. 320p. pap. 7.99 *(978-1-4169-8732-1(0))* 2010. (Illus.). 304p. 17.99 *(978-1-4169-8731-4(2))* Simon & Schuster Bks. For Young Readers. (Simon & Schuster Bks. For Young Readers).

—Big Game. 2015. (FunJungle Ser.). (ENG.). 352p. (J). (gr. 3-7). 17.99 *(978-1-4814-2333-5(9)*, Simon & Schuster Bks. For Young Readers) Simon & Schuster Bks. For Young Readers.

—Panda-Monium. 2017. (FunJungle Ser.). (ENG., Illus.). 352p. (J). (gr. 3-7). 16.99 *(978-1-4814-4567-2(7)*, Simon & Schuster Bks. For Young Readers) Simon & Schuster Bks. For Young Readers.

—Poached. 2014. (FunJungle Ser.). (ENG., Illus.). 352p. (J). (gr. 3-7). 17.99 *(978-1-4424-6777-4(0)*, Simon & Schuster Bks. For Young Readers) Simon & Schuster Bks. For Young Readers.

Go to the Zoo, Level 1. 2016. (Ladybird Readers Ser.). (ENG., Illus.). 48p. (J). (gr. 2-4). pap. 9.99 *(978-0-241-25414-1(0))* Penguin Bks., Ltd. GBR. Dist: Independent Pubs. Group.

Goode, Teresa. Jayhawk Adventures, a Day at the Zoo. Kotrous, Chad, illus. 2006. 29p. (J). (gr. 1-3). pap. 5.95 *(978-0-9646898-5-5(5))* Leathers Publishing.

Goulbourne, Nathaniel. The Aliens Zoo. 2013. (Illus.). 28p. pap. 21.35 *(978-1-4817-8198-5(7))* AuthorHouse.

Grieser, Jeanne K. Touch & Feel Petting Zoo. Pedler, Caroline, illus. 2010. (ENG.). 20p. (J). (gr. k — 1). bds. 9.95 *(978-1-4027-6524-7(X))* Sterling Publishing Co., Inc.

Gulliver, Amanda, illus. Zoo. 2011. (Baby Rattle Bks.). 12p. (J). (gr. -1-k). 6.99 *(978-0-7641-6394-4(9))* Barron's Educational Series, Inc.

Gutman, Dan. Miss Child Has Gone Wild! Paillot, Jim, illus. 2011. (My Weirder School Ser.: 1). 112p. (J). (gr. 1-5). (ENG.). pap. 4.99 *(978-0-06-196916-4(8))*; lib. bdg. 15.89 *(978-0-06-196917-1(6))* HarperCollins Pubs.

Hamburg, Jennifer. A Moose That Says Moo. Truesdell, Sue, illus. 2013. (ENG.). 32p. (J). (gr. -1 — 1). 16.99 *(978-0-374-35058-1(2)*, 9780374350581, Farrar, Straus & Giroux (BYR)) Farrar, Straus & Giroux.

Hamilton, Kersten. Tyger Tyger. 2011. (ENG.). 336p. (YA). (gr. 7). pap. 18.99 *(978-0-547-57732-6(X))* Houghton Mifflin Harcourt Publishing Co.

—When the Stars Threw down Their Spears. (ENG.). 400p. (YA). (gr. 7). 2014. pap. 8.99 *(978-0-544-22771-2(9)*, HMH Books For Young Readers) 2013. 16.99 *(978-0-547-73964-9(8))* Houghton Mifflin Harcourt Publishing Co.

Hand, Renne. What Would You Do If You Were Left at the Zoo? Mathieu, Middy, illus. 2012. 24p. pap. 8.99 *(978-1-938768-06-4(X))* Gypsy Pubns.

Harkrader, Lisa. Snoozy Zoo. 2016. (Spring Forward Ser.). (J). (gr. 2). *(978-1-4900-9424-3(5))* Benchmark Education Co.

Harris, Robie H. Who's in My Family? All about Our Families. Westcott, Nadine Bernard, illus. 2012. (Let's Talk about You & Me Ser.). (ENG.). 40p. (J). (gr. -1-2). 15.99 *(978-0-7636-3631-9(2))* Candlewick Pr.

Harrison, Sarah. A Day at a Zoo. 2009. (Time Goes By Ser.). (ENG.). 24p. (gr. k-3). pap. 6.95 *(978-1-58013-800-0(4)*, First Avenue Editions) Lerner Publishing Group.

Hasany, Syed M. Stop the Train, Monkey! 2013. 28p. pap. 16.09 *(978-1-4669-7792-1(2))* Trafford Publishing.

Heder, Thyra. Fraidyzoo. 2013. (ENG., Illus.). 48p. (J). (gr. k-2). 16.95 *(978-1-4197-0776-6(0)*, Abrams Bks. for Young Readers) Abrams, Inc.

Higgins, Jim. The Enchanted Nursery: Heather & Hamish, Fun in Florida, Reggie Rabbit at the Seaside, Percy Penguin's Friends. 2009. (Illus.). 36p. pap. 15.49 *(978-1-4389-9904-3(6))* AuthorHouse.

Hillert, Margaret. Dear Dragon Goes to the Zoo. Schimmell, David, illus. 2010. (BeginningtoRead Ser.). 32p. (J). (gr. k-2). lib. bdg. 22.60 *(978-1-59953-348-3(0))* Norwood Hse. Pr.

—Little Puff. Dammer, Mike, illus. 2016. (BeginningtoRead Ser.). (ENG.). 32p. (J). (gr. -1-2). pap. 11.94 *(978-1-60357-941-4(9))*; (gr. k-2). 22.60 *(978-1-59953-800-6(8))* Norwood Hse. Pr.

Hilliard, Michael. Butter Bee Grows up Too Fast! 2010. 20p. pap. 12.49 *(978-1-4490-7300-8(X))* AuthorHouse.

Ho, Jannie, illus. Muddle Zoo. 2013. (Muddle Bks.). (ENG.). 8p. (J). (gr. -1 — 1). 10.99 *(978-0-7641-6623-5(9))* Barron's Educational Series, Inc.

Howell, Heather. Emanuele Goes to the Zoo. 2010. 20p. 10.49 *(978-1-4490-4816-7(1))* AuthorHouse.

Hudson, Marilyn A. Elephant Hips Are Expensive! A Tale of the Sooner State. Fulco, Haley, illus. 2007. 50p. (J). per. *(978-0-9778850-2-2(X)*, WhorlBooks Thumbprints) Whorl Bks.

Ide, Laurie Shimizu. Okazu at the Zoo. Kanekuni, Daniel, illus. 2006. (J). *(978-1-56647-776-5(X))* Mutual Publishing LLC.

The Imaginary Zoo. 2007. (J). 16.95 *(978-0-9789880-0-5(0))* Wild About Learning, Inc.

Ipcizade, Catherine. 'Twas the Day Before Zoo Day, 1 vol. Hodson, Ben, illus. 2008. (Basic Math Operations Ser.). (ENG.). 32p. (J). (gr. -1-2). 17.95 *(978-1-60718-585-7(7))* Arbordale Publishing.

It's a Zoo! Individual Title, 6 Packs. (gr. -1-2). 27.00 *(978-0-7635-9454-1(7))* Rigby Education.

Jantzen, Doug. Henry Hyena, Why Won't You Laugh? Claude, Jean, illus. 2015. (ENG.). 32p. (J). (gr. -1-2). 17.99 *(978-1-4814-2822-4(5)*, Aladdin) Simon & Schuster Children's Publishing.

Jarman, Julia. Class Two at the Zoo. Chapman, Lynne, illus. 2007. (Carolrhoda Picture Bks.). (ENG.). 32p. (J). (gr. k-2). 16.95 *(978-0-8225-7132-2(3)*, Carolrhoda Bks.) Lerner Publishing Group.

Jerome, Kate Boehm. The Chef down at the Zoo. 2005. (J). 15.95 *(978-0-9769087-2-2(7)*, Grand Kidz, The) Vertical Connect Pr.

Jobling, Curtis. Old MacDonald Had a Zoo. McLaughlin, Tom, illus. 2014. (ENG.). 32p. (J). (gr. -1-k). pap. 10.99 *(978-1-4052-6712-0(7))* Egmont Bks., Ltd. GBR. Dist: Independent Pubs. Group.

Judybee. The Zoo Crew Play Ball. LittlePinkPebble, illus. 2011. 40p. pap. *(978-1-78092-000-9(8))* MX Publishing, Ltd.

Kangaroo at the Zoo IR. 2017. (Phonics Readers Ser.). (ENG.). (J). pap. 6.99 ***(978-0-7945-3716-6(2)**, Usborne)* EDC Publishing.

Kann, Victoria. Pinkalicious & the Pinkatastic Zoo Day. Kann, Victoria, illus. 2012. (I Can Read Level 1 Ser.). (ENG., Illus.). 32p. (J). (gr. -1-3). 16.99 *(978-0-06-218780-2(5))*; pap. 3.99 *(978-0-06-218779-6(1))* HarperCollins Pubs.

—Pinkalicious & the Pinkatastic Zoo Day. 2012. (Pinkalicious I Can Read Ser.). (J). lib. bdg. 13.55 *(978-0-606-26527-0(9)*, Turtleback) Turtleback Bks.

Katz, Karen. Roar, Roar, Baby! Katz, Karen, illus. 2015. (ENG., Illus.). 14p. (J). (gr. -1 — 1). bds. 6.99 *(978-1-4814-1788-4(6)*, Little Simon) Little Simon.

Keating, Jess. How to Outfox Your Friends When You Don't Have a Clue. 2015. (My Life Is a Zoo Ser.: 3). (ENG.). 304p. (J). (gr. 4-7). pap. 7.99 *(978-1-4926-1794-5(6)*, 9781492617945, Sourcebooks Jabberwocky) Sourcebooks, Inc.

—How to Outrun a Crocodile When Your Shoes Are Untied. 2014. (My Life Is a Zoo Ser.: 1). (ENG.). 288p. (J). (gr. 4-7). pap. 7.99 *(978-1-4022-9755-7(6)*, 9781402297557, Sourcebooks Jabberwocky) Sourcebooks, Inc.

—How to Outswim a Shark Without a Snorkel. 2015. (My Life Is a Zoo Ser.: 2). (ENG.). 304p. (J). (gr. 4-7). pap. 7.99 *(978-1-4022-9758-8(0)*, 9781402297588, Sourcebooks Jabberwocky) Sourcebooks, Inc.

Keene, Carolyn. The Zoo Crew. Pamintuan, Macky, illus. 14th ed. 2008. (Nancy Drew & the Clue Crew Ser.: 14). (ENG.). 96p. (J). (gr. 1-4). pap. 4.99 *(978-1-4169-5899-4(1)*, Aladdin) Simon & Schuster Children's Publishing.

Ken Lindstrom To Ken Lindstrom. Ollie & Grampa Go to the Zoo: How the Polar Bear Got to the Zoo. Jones., Amber, illus. 2011. 28p. pap. 12.49 *(978-1-4520-1529-3(5))* AuthorHouse.

Kertell, Lynn Maslen. My School Trip. 2012. (BOB Books: Scholastic Readers Level 1 Ser.: 3). lib. bdg. 13.55 *(978-0-606-26232-3(6)*, Turtleback) Turtleback Bks.

Kirby, Stan. Captain Awesome & the Missing Elephants. O'Connor, George, illus. 2014. (Captain Awesome Ser.: 10). (ENG.). 128p. (J). (gr. k-4). 16.99 *(978-1-4424-8995-0(2))*; pap. 5.99 *(978-1-4424-8994-3(4))* Little Simon. (Little Simon).

Klein, Adria F. Max Goes to the Zoo, 1 vol. Gallagher-Cole, Mernie, illus. 2007. (Read-It! Readers: the Life of Max Ser.). (ENG.). 24p. (gr. -1-2). lib. bdg. 21.32 *(978-1-4048-3677-8(2))*; per. 3.95 *(978-1-4048-3683-9(7))* Picture Window Bks. (Easy Readers).

Kline, Trish & Donev, Mary. A Day at the Zoo: KA Reader 3. 2007. (Illus.). 32p. (J). per. 20.00 *(978-0-9717234-5-0(1))* Ghost Hunter Productions.

Kloes, Carol. En el Zoologico. 2007.Tr. of At the Zoo. (SPA., Illus.). 16p. (gr. k-1). pap. 7.95 *(978-1-61181-395-1(6)*, Kaeden Bks.) Kaeden Corp.

Korman, Gordon. Zoobreak. (J). 2010. (ENG.). 240p. (gr. 3-7). pap. 6.99 *(978-0-545-12500-0(6)*, Scholastic Paperbacks) 2009. 230p. *(978-0-545-20027-1(X)*, Scholastic Pr.) Scholastic, Inc.

Krulik, Nancy. Going Batty. John and Wendy Staff, illus. 2009. (Katie Kazoo, Switcheroo Ser.: 32). (ENG.). 80p. (J). (gr. 2-4). pap. 4.99 *(978-0-448-45042-1(9)*, Grosset & Dunlap) Penguin Young Readers Group.

Larson, Angela. Anthony Smoochiano: First Loves. 2012. pap. *(978-1-4507-7998-2(0))* Independent Pub.

—Harry Hiccers: Friends of A Feether. 2012. pap. *(978-1-4507-7996-8(4))* Independent Pub.

Latham, Irene. Don't Feed the Boy. Graegin, Stephanie, illus. 2012. (ENG.). 288p. (J). (gr. 3-7). 17.99 *(978-1-59643-755-5(3)*, 9781596437555) Roaring Brook Pr.

—Don't Feed the Boy. Graegin, Stephanie, illus. 2014. (ENG.). 304p. (J). (gr. 3-7). pap. 9.99 *(978-1-250-04428-0(6)*, 9781250044280) Square Fish.

Lawson, Jennifer. The Secret Tea Party at the Zoo. 2010. (Illus.). 34p. pap. 19.95 *(978-0-557-13707-7(1))* Lulu Pr., Inc.

Lee, Howard. A Day at the Zoo. Reasoner, Charles, illus. 2009. (Inside Outside Board Bks.). 10p. (J). bds. 10.99 *(978-1-934650-55-4(2))* Just For Kids Pr., LLC.

Lee, Steven. TruthQuest: In the Beginning. 2009. 72p. (J). pap. 6.95 *(978-1-4327-3473-2(3))* Outskirts Pr., Inc.

LeMae, Katie. The Color Bunch Goes to the Zoo. 2010. 48p. pap. 17.89 *(978-1-4520-1223-0(7))* AuthorHouse.

Lilienstein, Jennel. Trip to the Zoo. 2003. (J). 8.99 *(978-0-9741215-3-6(3))* Stories of My Life, The.

Lubratt, Mark. Buffy Meets the Zoonicorns. Weingartner, Sara, illus. 2015. 32p. (J). 16.95 *(978-1-59298-893-8(8))* Beaver's Pond Pr., Inc.

Mack, Paulette. Cookout at Grandma's House: The Adventures of Mielle & Cheeky. 2006. (ENG., Illus.). 24p. per. 10.95 *(978-1-59800-998-9(2))* Outskirts Pr., Inc.

MacPherson, Dwight L. Lil' Hellions. O'Reilly, Sean Patrick, ed. 2011. (Illus.). 82p. (YA). pap., pap. 14.95 *(978-1-926914-37-4(6))* Arcana Studio, Inc.

Mademann Vaughan, Kathryn. My Day at the Zoo. Martin, Don, illus. 2004. (J). per. 19.95 *(978-0-9747447-1-1(9))* Chaser Media LLC.

Mae, Darcie. Sammy & Robert. 2008. 24p. pap. 24.95 *(978-1-60474-811-6(7))* America Star Bks.

Mandel, Peter. Zoo Ah-Choooo. Smith, Elwood H., illus. 2012. (ENG.). 32p. (J). 16.95 *(978-0-8234-2317-0(4))* Holiday Hse., Inc.

Marciano, John Bemelmans. Madeline Loves Animals. 2005. (Madeline Ser.). (ENG., Illus.). 16p. (J). (gr. -1 — 1). bds.

8.99 *(978-0-670-06021-4(6),* Viking Books for Young Readers) Penguin Young Readers Group.
Marinaro, Stacy. Treasure Monkey. 2008. 32p. pap. 15.95 *(978-1-4357-2840-0(8))* Lulu Pr., Inc.
Marlow, Herb. The Tiger's Den. Head, Pat, illus. 2003. 22p. (J). 19.95 *(978-1-893595-37-8(4))* Four Seasons Bks., Inc.
Marsalis, Dustin S. The Alligator Astronauts Go to the Zipper Zoo. 2013. 36p. pap. 15.99 *(978-1-4624-0678-4(5),* Inspiring Voices) Author Solutions, Inc.
Marsh, Carole. The Zany Zoo Mystery. 2007. 128p. (J). pap. 5.99 *(978-0-635-06332-8(8))* Gallopade International.
Marsoli, Lisa Ann. Let's Go to the Zoo. Smitherton, Jeb, illus. 2005. (J). bds. 14.99 *(978-0-9767325-4-9(8))* Toy Quest.
—Let's Go to the Zoo & Leaping Lilly. Smitherton, Jeb, illus. 2005. (J). bds. 19.99 *(978-0-9767325-6-3(4))* Toy Quest.
Martin, Kentrell. Shelly Goes to the Zoo. Rodriguez, Marc, illus. 2013. 32p. pap. 8.50 *(978-0-9851845-1-3(5))* Shelly's Adventures LLC.
Mason, Albert. Ooshu the Monkey Escapes from the Zoo. 2009. 40p. pap. 16.99 *(978-1-4389-0974-5(8))* AuthorHouse.
Massie, Diane Redfield. The Baby Beebee Bird. Kellogg, Steven, illus. 2003. (ENG.). 32p. (J). (gr. -1-1). pap. 6.99 *(978-0-06-051784-7(0))* HarperCollins Pubs.
Mayer, Mercer. Professor Wormbog in Search for the Zipperump-a-Zoo. 2011. (Classic Collectible Ser.: 1). (ENG.). 42p. (J). (gr. -1-3). pap. 12.95 *(978-1-60746-765-6(8),* Premiere) FastPrncil, Inc.
McAdams, Susan. Shubert. McAdams, Caleb, illus. 2008. 16p. per. 24.95 *(978-1-4241-9756-9(2))* America Star Bks.
McNeal, Cari. What Would I Do If I Had a Zoo? Balogh, Jared, illus. 2012. 36p. 24.95 *(978-1-4560-4006-2(5))* America Star Bks.
Meachen Rau, Dana. En el Zoologico. 2007. (¡A Divertirnos! Ser.). (SPA., Illus.). 24p. (gr. k-1). lib. bdg. 15.95 *(978-0-7614-2777-3(5),* Benchmark Bks.) Marshall Cavendish Corp.
Meldrum, Margaret. Peter Panda & His Friends. 2009. (Illus.). 24p. pap. 11.49 *(978-1-4343-7826-2(8))* AuthorHouse.
Merrick, Gabriel. It's Time for a Field Trip. 2017. (Let's Tell Time Ser.). 24p. (J). (gr. 4-6). 23.60 ***(978-1-5081-5724-3(3),*** PowerKids Pr.) Rosen Publishing Group, Inc., The.
Merveille, David. Hello Mr. Hulot. 2013. (ENG., Illus.). 32p. (J). (gr. -1-3). 17.95 *(978-0-7358-4135-2(7))* North-South Bks., Inc.
Metzger, Steve. Dancing Clock. Nez, John Abbott, illus. 2011. (ENG.). 32p. 12.95 *(978-1-58925-100-7(8));* (J). pap. 7.95 *(978-1-58925-429-9(5))* Tiger Tales.
Meyers, Haily & Meyers, Kevin. At the Zoo, 1 vol. 2016. (ENG., Illus.). 22p. (J). bds. 9.99 *(978-1-4236-4245-9(7))* Gibbs Smith, Publisher.
Michaels, Evan. Tressa & Dan's Picnic at the Zoo. 2010. (Illus.). 34p. (J). pap. 19.95 *(978-0-9826865-0-8(1))* Win Publishing, LLC.
Michaels, Rune. Fix Me. 2011. (ENG., Illus.). 160p. (YA). (gr. 9). 16.99 *(978-1-4169-5772-0(3),* Atheneum Bks. for Young Readers) Simon & Schuster Children's Publishing.
Michalak, Jamie. Joe & Sparky Get New Wheels. Remkiewicz, Frank, illus. 2013. (Candlewick Sparks Ser.). (ENG.). 48p. (J). (gr. k-4). pap. 3.99 *(978-0-7636-6641-5(6))* Candlewick Pr.
Middleton, Nancy. The Zookeeper's Christmas Eve. 2009. 36p. pap. 16.50 *(978-1-60693-302-2(7),* Eloquent Bks.) Strategic Book Publishing & Rights Agency (SBPRA).
Miller, Kathryn L. Abc's with Sadie: Sadie Goes to the Zoo. 2011. 32p. pap. 17.25 *(978-1-4269-5940-0(0))* Trafford Publishing.
Mitchell, Rae. Anna's Wish. 2009. 24p. pap. 13.50 *(978-1-60860-441-8(1),* Eloquent Bks.) Strategic Book Publishing & Rights Agency (SBPRA).
Moncure, Jane Belk. Hop-Skip-Jump-a-Roo Zoo: A Book about Imitating. Girouard, Patrick, illus. 2013. (Magic Castle Readers Ser.). (ENG.). 32p. (J). (gr. -1-2). 25.64 *(978-1-62323-566-6(9),* 206300) Child's World, Inc., The.
Morrison, Cathy. I Want a Pet. 2012. (ENG.). 32p. (J). *(978-1-58925-113-7(X))* Tiger Tales.
Mothergoose-Zany Zoo. 2003. (J). per. *(978-1-57657-167-5(X))* Paradise Pr., Inc.
Mucklow, Hope. Rojo the Baby Red Panda at the Zoo: An Allegory about Self-Worth Through a Red Panda & Giant Panda Comparison. 2014. (ENG., Illus.). 32p. (J). (gr. -1-3). 14.95 *(978-1-62086-593-4(9))* Mascot Bks., Inc.
Munari, Bruno. Bruno Munari's Zoo. 2005. (ENG., Illus.). 48p. (J). (gr. -1-1). reprint ed. 19.99 *(978-0-8118-4830-5(2))* Chronicle Bks. LLC.
Munns, Skye. Who's at the Zoo. 2011. 24p. pap. 28.03 *(978-1-4568-5447-8(X))* Xlibris Corp.
Murray, Laura. The Gingerbread Man Loose at the Zoo. Lowery, Mike, illus. 2016. (ENG.). 32p. (J). (gr. k-3). 16.99 *(978-0-399-16867-3(2),* G.P. Putnam's Sons Books for Young Readers) Penguin Young Readers Group.
My Big Book of Beginner Books about Me. 2011. (Beginner Books(R) Ser.). (ENG., Illus.). 208p. (J). (gr. -1-2). 16.99 *(978-0-307-93183-2(8),* Random Hse. Bks. for Young Readers) Random Hse. Children's Bks.
My Uncle Has Wheels. 2005. (J). 8.00 *(978-0-9767077-1-4(3))* Carson, Tracy.
Na, Il Sung, illus. The Opposite Zoo. 2016. (ENG.). 24p. (J). (-k). 16.99 *(978-0-553-51127-7(0),* Knopf Bks. for Young Readers) Random Hse. Children's Bks.
Neely, M. W. Saving the Kilda Street Zoo. 2012. 218p. 29.99 *(978-1-4771-0179-7(9));* pap. 19.99 *(978-1-4771-0178-0(0))* Xlibris Corp.
Nguyen, Taohuu. Mighty Mite 2: Zoo Gone Wild. Nguyen, Taohuu, illus. 2007. (Illus.). (J). 14.95 *(978-0-9788469-2-3(3))* Amazing Factory, The.
Noble, Kate. Pamela's Plan. Bass, Rachel, illus. (Zoo Stories Ser.). 32p. (J). (gr. -1-4). 15.95 *(978-0-9631798-4-5(5))* Salmon Run Pr.
Nosy Crow Staff. Bizzy Bear: Zookeeper. Davies, Benji, illus. 2015. (Bizzy Bear Ser.). (ENG.). 8p. (J). (— 1). bds. 6.99 *(978-0-7636-7603-2(9),* Nosy Crow) Candlewick Pr.
O'Hely, Eileen. Penny on Safari. Phelan, Nicky, illus. 2010. (ENG.). 192p. (J). pap. 15.95 *(978-1-85635-572-8(1))* Mercier Pr., Ltd., The IRL. Dist: Dufour Editions, Inc.
OHora, Zachariah. Stop Snoring, Bernard! OHora, Zachariah, illus. 2012. (ENG., Illus.). 32p. (J). (gr. -1-2). pap. 7.99 *(978-1-250-00717-9(8),* 9781250007179) Square Fish.
Olson, Kevin Noel. Eerey Tocsin in the Cryptoid Zoo. Hammack, Debi, illus. 2006. (ENG.). 176p. (YA). per. 15.95 *(978-1-887560-17-7(3),* Cornerstone Bk. Publishers) Poll, Michael Publishing.
One for Me, Zoo for You. 2003. (J). per. *(978-1-57657-855-1(0))* Paradise Pr., Inc.
The Opposite Zoo. 2017. (ENG.). 24p. (J). (-k). bds. 6.99 *(978-0-399-55412-4(2),* Knopf Bks. for Young Readers) Random Hse. Children's Bks.
Oud, Pauline. Going to the Zoo with Lily & Milo. Oud, Pauline, illus. 2011. (Lily & Milo Ser.). (ENG., Illus.). 28p. (J). (gr. k — 1). 12.95 *(978-1-60537-093-4(2))* Cobblestone Publishing Co.
Oxford-White, Bly. Mr. Woo's Zoo. l.t. ed. 2003. (Illus.). 16p. (J). *(978-0-9740833-2-2(1))* Port Town Publishing.
Paling, Chris. The Adventures of Rumble, Tumble, & Titch: Uncertain Times. 2010. 62p. pap. 9.99 *(978-1-60911-263-9(6),* Eloquent Bks.) Strategic Book Publishing & Rights Agency (SBPRA).
Papp, Robert, illus. Monkey Trouble. 2011. (Boxcar Children Mysteries Ser.: 127). (ENG.). 128p. (J). (gr. 1-5). pap. 5.99 *(978-0-8075-5240-7(2))* Whitman, Albert & Co.
—Monkey Trouble. 2011. (Boxcar Children Mysteries Ser.: 127). (ENG.). 128p. (J). (gr. 1-5). lib. bdg. 14.99 *(978-0-8075-5239-1(9))* Whitman, Albert & Co.
Parish, Herman. Amelia Bedelia Chapter Book #4: Amelia Bedelia Goes Wild! (Special Edition) 2014. (ENG.). 160p. (J). *(978-0-06-227058-0(3),* Collins Design) HarperCollins Pubs.
—Amelia Bedelia Goes Wild! Avril, Lynne, illus. 2014. (Amelia Bedelia Ser.: No. 4). (ENG.). 160p. (J). (gr. 1-5). 15.99 *(978-0-06-209507-7(2),* Greenwillow Bks.) HarperCollins Pubs.
—Goes Wild! Avril, Lynne, illus. 2014. (Amelia Bedelia Ser.: No. 4). (ENG.). 160p. (J). (gr. 1-5). pap. 5.99 *(978-0-06-209506-0(4),* Greenwillow Bks.) HarperCollins Pubs.
Pauline, Christi. Hullabaloo at the Zoo. 2008. 28p. pap. 14.95 *(978-1-4389-1204-2(8))* AuthorHouse.
Peck, J. L. Mr Crabby Pants & the Zoo. 2012. 24p. pap. 17.99 *(978-1-4685-7953-6(3))* AuthorHouse.
Peeler, Penny. The Adventures of Spike & Sally. 2011. 52p. pap. 15.99 *(978-1-4568-9981-3(3))* Xlibris Corp.
Peterka, Edward S. Zoe Isabella Goes to the Zoo. 2011. 32p. pap. 12.77 *(978-1-4520-0305-4(X))* AuthorHouse.
Phillips, Dee. Baby's Day. 2009. (Flip Flap Fun Bks.). (ENG.). 5p. (J). (gr. -1-k). bds. 5.95 *(978-1-84696-087-1(8),* TickTock Books) Octopus Publishing Group GBR. Dist: Independent Pubs. Group.
Piano, Maureen. When Flamingos Fly: Discovering the Wonders of the World. 2006. (Illus.). 44p. (J). (gr. -1-3). pap. 12.99 incl. audio compact disk *(978-1-59092-362-7(6))* Blue Forge Pr.
Pichon, Liz. Penguins. 2008. (J). *(978-0-545-08292-1(7),* Orchard Bks.) Scholastic, Inc.
Pilkey, Dav. The Dumb Bunnies Go to the Zoo. (Dumb Bunnies Ser.). (ENG.). 32p. 2009. (J). (gr. -1-3). 16.99 *(978-0-545-03937-6(1))* 2007. pap. 5.99 *(978-0-439-93049-9(9))* Scholastic, Inc.
Plant, David J. Hungry Roscoe. 2015. (ENG., Illus.). 40p. (J). (gr. -1-2). 17.95 *(978-1-909263-53-6(2))* Flying Eye Bks. GBR. Dist: Consortium Bk. Sales & Distribution.
Potter, Tracy. Charlie the Chimp's Day Out. 2013. 24p. pap. 24.95 *(978-1-63000-036-3(1))* America Star Bks.
Power, Michael. The Zoo. 2009. 201p. pap. 13.75 *(978-1-60695-075-3(4))* EchoRoad, Inc.
Priddy, Roger. Noisy Peekaboo: Zoo. 2016. (Noisy Peekaboo Ser.). (ENG.). 8p. (J). bds. 9.99 *(978-0-312-52061-8(1),* 9780312520618, Priddy Bks.) St. Martin's Pr.
—Toddler Town - Zoo. 2014. (Toddler Town Ser.). (ENG.). 10p. (J). (gr. -1 — 1). bds. 7.99 *(978-0-312-51672-7(X),* 9780312516727, Priddy Bks.) St. Martin's Pr.
Prince, Daniel. Zoe the Zookeeper. 2007. (Illus.). 48p. per. *(978-1-84748-047-7(0))* Athena Pr.
Random House Staff. A Friend at the Zoo (Bubble Guppies) Random House Staff & Nunn, Paul, illus. 2013. (Pictureback(R) Ser.). (ENG.). 16p. (J). (gr. -1-2). pap. 3.99 *(978-0-449-81389-8(4),* Random Hse. Bks. for Young Readers) Random Hse. Children's Bks.
—I Can Be... A Zoo Vet/I Can Be... A Cheerleader. Riley, Kellee, illus. 2011. (Pictureback(R) Ser.). (ENG.). 32p. (J). (gr. -1-2). pap. 4.99 *(978-0-375-87265-5(5),* Random Hse. Bks. for Young Readers) Random Hse. Children's Bks.
Rathmann, Peggy. Good Night, Gorilla. Rathmann, Peggy, illus. 2004. (ENG., Illus.). 34p. (J). (gr. -1 — 1). bds. 15.99 *(978-0-399-24260-1(0),* G.P. Putnam's Sons Books for Young Readers) Penguin Young Readers Group.
Ready Reader Staff. Good-Bye Zoo: Consonant Z, Level K. 2003. (J). (gr. -1-3). 24.50 *(978-0-8136-1451-9(1))* Modern Curriculum Pr.
Redmond, E. S. Felicity Floo Visits the Zoo. Redmond, E. S., illus. (ENG., Illus.). 32p. (J). 2010. (-k). pap. 6.99 *(978-0-7636-4975-3(9))* 2009. (gr. -1-k). 15.99 *(978-0-7636-3444-5(1))* Candlewick Pr.
Reilly, Carmel & Young, Karen. Anna Goes to the Zoo. 2008. (Rigby Focus Forward: Level D Ser.). (Illus.). 24p. (J). (gr. 4-7). pap. *(978-1-4190-3663-7(7),* Rigby) Pearson Education Australia.
Rey, H. A. Curious George Goes to the Zoo. 2014. (Curious George 8x8 Ser.). lib. bdg. 14.75 *(978-0-606-23335-4(0),* Turtleback) Turtleback Bks.
Rey, H. A. & Rey, Margret. Curious George Goes to the Zoo. 2014. (Curious George Ser.). (ENG., Illus.). 24p. (J). (gr. -1-3). 4.99 *(978-0-544-11000-7(5))* Houghton Mifflin Harcourt Publishing Co.
—My First Words at the Zoo, Set. gif. ed. 2010. (Curious Baby Curious George Ser.). (ENG., Illus.). 12p. (J). (gr. -1 — 1). 14.99 *(978-0-618-99953-8(1))* Houghton Mifflin Harcourt Publishing Co.
Rey, Margret & Rey, H. A. Feeds the Animals, 1 vol. Vipah Interactive Staff, illus. 2005. (Read along Book & CD Ser.). (ENG.). 24p. (J). (gr. -1-3). audio compact disk 10.99 *(978-0-618-60387-9(5))* Houghton Mifflin Harcourt Publishing Co.
Rippin, Sally. The Extra-Special Helper. Fukuoka, Aki, illus. 2014. (ENG.). 48p. (J). pap. 4.99 *(978-1-61067-099-9(X))* Kane Miller.
Rissi, Anica Mrose. Anna, Banana, & the Monkey in the Middle. Park, Meg, illus. 2015. (Anna, Banana Ser.: 2). (ENG.). 128p. (J). (gr. 1-5). 15.99 *(978-1-4814-1608-5(1),* Simon & Schuster Bks. For Young Readers) Simon & Schuster Bks. For Young Readers.
Robinson, Tom. Fibonacci Zoo, 1 vol. Wald, Christina, illus. 2015. (ENG.). 32p. (J). (gr. 1-4). 17.95 *(978-1-62855-553-0(X))* Arbordale Publishing.
Rochfort, Barry. The Adventures of Mortimer the Marmot. 2015. (ENG.). 107p. (J). (gr. 2-3). mass mkt. 11.95 *(978-1-78554-739-3(9),* dd7dabfb-8041-475e-8062-7133d7abcf1d) Austin, Stan AUS. Dist: Bookmasters Distribution.
Rosen, Kymberlee S. Do You Have Better Manners Than the Monkeys at the Zoo? 2010. (Illus.). 32p. pap. 13.00 *(978-1-60911-179-3(6),* Eloquent Bks.) Strategic Book Publishing & Rights Agency (SBPRA).
Rosenthal, Pamela. My Trip to the Zoo. 2005. (Illus.). 48p. (J). lib. bdg. 24.95 *(978-1-932762-28-0(0))* Elderberry Press, Inc.
Rosoff, Meg. There Is No Dog. (ENG.). 288p. (YA). (gr. 7). 2013. pap. 8.99 *(978-0-14-242384-4(X),* Speak) 2012. 17.99 *(978-0-399-25764-3(0),* G.P. Putnam's Sons Books for Young Readers) Penguin Young Readers Group.
Roy, Ron. A Thief at the National Zoo. Bush, Timothy, illus. 2008. (Capital Mysteries Ser.: No. 9). 87p. (gr. k-3). 15.00 *(978-0-7569-8329-1(0))* Perfection Learning Corp.
—A Thief at the National Zoo. Bush, Timothy, illus. 2007. (Capital Mysteries Ser.: No. 9). (ENG.). 96p. (J). (gr. 1-4). per. 4.99 *(978-0-375-84804-9(5),* Random Hse. Bks. for Young Readers) Random Hse. Children's Bks.
Russell, David. Who'z Who at the Zoo. 2012. (Illus.). 26p. pap. 12.95 *(978-1-4575-1395-4(1))* Dog Ear Publishing, LLC.
Rutley, Erika L. Adventures in Pup-A-Dupping. 2012. 36p. pap. 24.95 *(978-1-62709-710-9(4))* America Star Bks.
Sampson, Brent. One Wacky Wasp: The Perfect Children's Book for Kids Ages 3-6 Who Are Learning to Read. 2010. 24p. (J). 14.95 *(978-1-4327-6217-9(6));* pap. 9.95 *(978-1-4327-0465-0(6))* Outskirts Pr., Inc.
Sansone, V. K. A Strange Day at the Zoo. 2009. 32p. pap. 14.98 *(978-0-557-06519-6(4))* Lulu Pr., Inc.
Saudo, Coralie. My Dad at the Zoo. Di Giacomo, Kris, illus. 2016. (ENG.). 32p. (J). (gr. -1-2). 17.95 *(978-1-59270-190-2(6))* Enchanted Lion Bks., LLC.
Sauer, Tammi. Oh, Nuts! Krall, Dan, illus. 2012. (ENG.). 32p. (J). 17.89 *(978-1-59990-467-2(5),* 9781599904672); (gr. -1-6). 16.99 *(978-1-59990-466-5(7),* 9781599904665) Bloomsbury Publishing USA. (Bloomsbury USA Childrens).
Sava, Scott Christian. Animal Crackers. 2011. (Illus.). 152p. pap. 11.99 *(978-1-60010-619-4(6))* Idea & Design Works, LLC.
Sax, Anita. Oscar & the Zoo. Jasuna, Aija, illus. 2013. 32p. (J). 14.95 *(978-1-60131-174-0(5))* Big Tent Bks.
Scanlon, Jack. Rainbow Zoo. 2006. (Neighborhood Readers Ser.). (ENG., Illus.). 8p. (gr. -1-3). pap. 5.15 *(978-1-4042-6686-5(0),* Rosen Classroom) Rosen Publishing Group, Inc., The.
Seuss, Dr. If I Ran the Zoo. 2014. (Classic Seuss Ser.). (ENG., Illus.). 64p. (J). (gr. k-4). 17.99 *(978-0-385-37905-2(6),* Random Hse. Bks. for Young Readers) Random Hse. Children's Bks.
Shalev, Michal. How to Be Famous. Shalev, Michal, illus. 2016. (ENG., Illus.). 32p. (J). (gr. -1-1). 16.99 *(978-1-77657-029-4(4));* 9.99 *(978-1-77657-045-4(6));* 33.32 *(978-1-77657-047-8(2));* 33.32 *(978-1-77657-057-7(X))* Gecko Pr. NZL. Dist: Lerner Publishing Group.
Shannon, Carol. Dusky Langurs at the Zoo. 2013. 40p. pap. 16.95 *(978-1-4525-1014-9(8),* Balboa Pr.) Author Solutions, Inc.
Shirley, Alice. The Gentle Lion & the Little Owlet. Shirley, Alice, illus. 2013. Orig. Title: Owlet & Pussycat. (ENG., Illus.). 32p. (J). (gr. -1-k). pap. 8.99 *(978-1-84365-199-4(8),* Pavilion) Pavilion Bks. GBR. Dist: Independent Pubs. Group.
Shoopman, Jim. Cowboy Zack & the Monkey from the Muggletown Zoo. 2013. 50p. pap. 13.98 *(978-0-9887836-2-1(2))* Taylor and Seale Publishing, LLC.
Shrode, Donna. Fun with Nan: A Trip to the Zoo. 2012. 28p. pap. 19.99 *(978-1-4685-4598-2(1))* AuthorHouse.
Sklar, David. A Day at the Zoo with My Daddy. 2013. 24p. pap. 17.99 *(978-1-4817-0152-5(5))* AuthorHouse.
Smith, Danna. Dos en el Zoológico: Un Libro para Contar. Petrone, Valeria, illus. 2011.Tr. of Two at the Zoo - A Counting Book. (ENG & SPA.). 30p. (J). (gr. k — 1). bds. 4.99 *(978-0-547-58137-8(8))* Houghton Mifflin Harcourt Publishing Co.
Smith, Kristie Lyn. Dottie & Dots See Animal Spots: Learning Braille with Dots & Dottie. 2007. 52p. per. 8.95 *(978-0-595-47130-0(7))* iUniverse, Inc.
Snow, Peggy. My Favorite Places from a to Z. Barber, Brian, illus. 2007. (My Favorites Ser.). (ENG.). 32p. (J). (gr. -1). lib. bdg. 15.99 *(978-1-934277-03-4(7))* Mam Green Publishing, Inc.
Snyder, Marilyn. A Second Chance for Tina. Shiffman, Lena, illus. 2003. (Hello Reader! Ser.). (J). *(978-0-439-44154-4(4))* Scholastic, Inc.
Sobel, Deane. Philip the Sea Lion. 2012. (ENG.). (J). pap. *(978-1-4675-2347-9(X))* Independent Pub.
Soderberg, Erin. Monkey See, Monkey Zoo. Francis, Guy, illus. 2010. (ENG.). 160p. (YA). (gr. 2-4). pap. 5.99 *(978-1-59990-558-7(2),* 9781599905587, Bloomsbury USA Childrens) Bloomsbury Publishing USA.
Sparkes, Ali. Anaconda Adventure. Collins, Ross, illus. 2014. (S. W. I. T. C. H. Ser.: 13). (ENG.). 104p. (J). (gr. 2-5). lib. bdg. 27.93 *(978-1-4677-2116-5(6),* Darby Creek) Lerner Publishing Group.
Sparks, David. Flat-Top Sam & the Junkyard Elephant. Sparks, David, illus. 2008. (Illus.). 36p. pap. 12.95 *(978-1-59858-587-2(8))* Dog Ear Publishing, LLC.
Spooner, Joe. The Elephant Walk. McCann, Michelle, ed. Spooner, Joe, illus. 2005. (ENG., Illus.). 36p. (J). (gr. -1-3). 15.00 *(978-0-9745686-3-8(5))* ACS, LLC Amica Creative Services.
Stead, Philip C. A Sick Day for Amos McGee. Stead, Erin E., illus. 2010. (ENG.). 32p. (J). (gr. -1-1). 17.99 *(978-1-59643-402-8(3),* 9781596434028) Roaring Brook Pr.
Steele, Michael Anthony. Vampire Zoo Hullabaloo. Jeralds, Scott, illus. 2017. (Scooby-Doo! Beginner Mysteries Ser.). (ENG.). 112p. (J). (gr. 2-3). lib. bdg. 22.65 ***(978-1-4965-4770-5(5))*** Capstone Press of Coughlan Cos.
Stofko, Michael D. A Visit from the Zoo. 2011. 32p. pap. 12.77 *(978-1-4567-2968-4(3))* AuthorHouse.
Stone, Jessica J. Picnic at the Zoo. 2011. 24p. 11.32 *(978-1-4567-4386-4(4))* AuthorHouse.
Stossel, Sage. On the Loose in Washington, D. C. 2013. (ENG., Illus.). 28p. (J). (gr. -1-3). 14.95 *(978-1-938700-14-9(7),* Commonwealth Editions) Applewood Bks.
Sutherland, Tui T. & Sutherland, Kari. Dragon on Trial. 2015. (Menagerie Ser.: 2). (ENG.). 320p. (J). (gr. 3-7). pap. 6.99 *(978-0-06-085145-3(7))* HarperCollins Pubs.
Sutherland, Tui T. & Sutherland, Kari H. The Menagerie. (Menagerie Ser.: 3). (J). (gr. 3-7). 2016. 368p. pap. 6.99 *(978-0-06-078069-2(X))* 2015. (ENG.). 368p. 16.99 *(978-0-06-078067-8(3))* 2013. (ENG., Illus.). 288p. 16.99 *(978-0-06-078064-7(9))* HarperCollins Pubs.
Sutton, Laurie S. Going Ape. Gordon, Eric A. & Gordon, Steven E., illus. 2012. (I Can Read Level 2 Ser.). (ENG.). 32p. (J). (gr. -1-3). pap. 3.99 *(978-0-06-188522-8(3))* HarperCollins Pubs.
—Going Ape. 2012. (Justice League Classic: I Can Read! Ser.). (J). lib. bdg. 13.55 *(978-0-606-26260-6(1),* Turtleback) Turtleback Bks.
Swartz, Patricia. Pig-A-Poo Moves to the Zoo. 2009. (Illus.). 28p. pap. 14.99 *(978-1-4490-4616-3(9))* AuthorHouse.
Taber-Montgomery, Kathy. We Live in a Zoo. 2012. 24p. pap. *(978-1-4602-0028-5(4))* FriesenPress.
Thompson, Berine. Tedi the Bear & His Pals Adventure at the Zoo! 2005. 44p. per. 21.99 *(978-1-4208-1007-3(3))* AuthorHouse.
Thompson, Kay. Eloise at the Wedding. Pack. 2012. (Eloise Ser.). (ENG.). 192p. (J). (gr. -1-1). pap. 15.96 *(978-1-4424-4949-7(7),* Simon Spotlight) Simon Spotlight.
Thompson, Kay & McClatchy, Lisa. Eloise Visits the Zoo. Lyon, Tammie, illus. 2009. (Eloise Ser.). (ENG.). 32p. (J). (gr. -1-1). pap. 3.99 *(978-1-4169-8642-3(1),* Simon Spotlight) Simon Spotlight.
Tinsley, Jillian. Wally the Warthog. Wood, Douglas, illus. 2012. 24p. (J). pap. 10.99 *(978-1-61254-782-4(6))* Small Pr., The.
Toral, Miguel A. Babu Goes Back to the Zoo. 2009. 32p. pap. 15.70 *(978-1-4389-6330-3(0))* AuthorHouse.
Tsong, Jing Jing & BeachHouse Publishing. Aloha Zoo. 2010. (ENG.). 16p. (J). (gr. -1-1). bds. 7.95 *(978-1-933067-32-2(2))* Beachhouse Publishing, LLC.
Vicuna, Claudio Orrego. The Surprising Adventures of Balthazar. 2011. (Peace, Justice, Human Rights, & Freedom in Latin America Ser.). (SPA & ENG.). 160p. 15.00 *(978-1-58966-218-6(0))* Univ. of Scranton Pr.
Waldron, Kevin. Mr. Peek & the Misunderstanding at the Zoo. Waldron, Kevin, illus. 2010. (ENG., Illus.). 48p. (J). (gr. k-12). 15.99 *(978-0-7636-4549-6(4),* Templar) Candlewick Pr.
—Panda-Monium at Peek Zoo. Waldron, Kevin, illus. 2014. (ENG., Illus.). 40p. (J). (gr. -1-2). 16.99 *(978-0-7636-6658-3(0),* Templar) Candlewick Pr.
Wall, Laura. Goose Goes to the Zoo. Wall, Laura, illus. 2016. (Illus.). 48p. (J). (gr. -1-3). 12.99 *(978-0-06-232441-2(1))* HarperCollins Pubs.
Weatherstone, Hollie. When the Pandas Came to Scotland. 2012. (Illus.). 20p. pap. 19.82 *(978-1-4772-3528-7(0))* AuthorHouse.
Weston Woods Studios Inc. Staff, creator. Good Night, Gorilla. 2004. (J). 38.75 *(978-1-55592-421-8(2));* 18.95 *(978-1-55592-419-5(0))* Weston Woods Studios, Inc.
What Would I Do If I Lived at the Zoo? 2004. (Illus.). 12p. (J). 5.95 *(978-0-9759321-2-4(8))* Rascal Treehouse Publishing.
Williams, Emma. The Story of Hurry. Quraishi, Ibrahim, illus. 2014. (ENG.). 38p. (J). (gr. -1-2). 16.95 *(978-1-60980-589-0(5),* Triangle Square) Seven Stories Pr.
Willis, Jeanne. Penguin Pandemonium: the Rescue. 2013. (Awesome Animals Ser.). (ENG., Illus.). 176p. (J). (gr. 2-6). pap. 6.99 *(978-1-4380-0306-1(4))* Barron's Educational Series, Inc.
Wilson, Karma. Never, Ever Shout in a Zoo. Cushman, Douglas, illus. 2004. (ENG.). 32p. (J). (gr. -1-3). 16.99 *(978-0-316-98564-2(3))* Little, Brown Bks. for Young Readers.
Winkler, Henry, et al. How to Hug an Elephant #6. Garrett, Scott, illus. 2015. (Here's Hank Ser.: 6). (ENG.). 128p. (J). (gr. 1-3). bds. 14.99 *(978-0-448-48657-4(1));* bds. 5.99 *(978-0-448-48656-7(3))* Penguin Young Readers Group. (Grosset & Dunlap).
Winnard, Rebecca Victoria & Winnard, Linda. Giraffe Liberation: An Act of Freedom. 2006. 53p. pap. 16.95 *(978-1-4241-0552-6(8))* PublishAmerica, Inc.
Winthrop, Elizabeth & Winthrop. Dancing Granny, 1 vol. Murdocca, Sal, illus. 2003. (ENG.). 32p. (J). 16.95 *(978-0-7614-5141-9(2))* Marshall Cavendish Corp.
Wu, Mike. Ellie. Wu, Mike, illus. 2015. (ENG., Illus.). 40p. (J). (gr. -1-k). 16.99 *(978-1-4847-1239-9(0))* Disney Publishing Worldwide.
Zaring, Laurie. Who Could You Be at the Zoo? Barlup, Jessica, illus. 2013. 24p. pap. 12.95 *(978-1-61244-175-7(0))* Halo Publishing International.
Zschock, Martha Day. Hello, Rhode Island! 2011. (Hello! Ser.). (ENG., Illus.). 16p. (J). (gr. -1-k). bds. 9.95 *(978-1-933212-62-3(4),* Commonwealth Editions) Applewood Bks.

ZULU (AFRICAN PEOPLE)

Gleimius, Nita, et al. The Zulu of Africa. 2005. (First Peoples Ser.). (Illus.). 48p. (gr. 4-8). 23.95 *(978-0-8225-0661-4(0))* Lerner Publishing Group.
Spilsbury, Richard. Shaka Zulu, 1 vol. 2013. (Hero Journals). (ENG., Illus.). 48p. (gr. 4-6). 33.32 *(978-1-4109-5361-2(0));* pap. 9.95 *(978-1-4109-5368-1(8))* Heinemann-Raintree. (NA-r).

ZULU (AFRICAN PEOPLE)—FICTION

Powers, J. L. This Thing Called the Future. 2011. (FRS & ENG.). 208p. (J). (gr. 7-11). 16.95 *(978-1-933693-95-8(9))* Cinco Puntos Pr.

ZULUS

see Zulu (African People)

W X Y Z

PUBLISHER NAME INDEX

10 Finger Pr., (*978-0-9728131; 978-1-933174*) 8435 Belize Pl., Wellington, FL 33414 USA Tel 561-434-9044; Toll Free: 866-7-author
E-mail: mahesh@10fingerspress.com
Web site: http://www.10fingerspress.com
Dist(s): **Midpoint Trade Bks., Inc.**

10 To 2 Children's Bks., (*978-0-9849487; 978-0-615-74608-1; 978-0-615-74627-2; 978-0-615-79610-9; 978-0-615-79632-1; 978-0-615-84753-5; 978-0-615-87923-9*) P.O. Box 5173, Clinton, NJ 08809 USA Tel 610-570-4196
E-mail: darylkcobb@yahoo.com
Web site: http://www.darylcobb.com
Dist(s): **CreateSpace Independent Publishing Platform.**

100 Book Challenge *See* **American Reading Co.**

101 Bk. *Imprint of* **Michaelson Entertainment**

1105 West House, (*978-0-9976172*) P.O. Box 1835, McKinney, TX 75070 USA Tel 214-606-7735
E-mail: hello@knookerdoodle.com.

114th Aviation Co. Assn., (*978-0-9742465*) 15151 Berry Trail, Suite 403, Dallas, TX 75248-6319 USA
E-mail: steve@stibbens.com.

11th Hour Productions *See* **Twilight Tales, Inc.**

121 Pubns., (*978-0-9841931; 978-0-692-58320-3*) 13200 Shadow Mountain Dr., Saratoga, CA 95070 USA (SAN 858-690X)
E-mail: mattweber11@yahoo.com
Web site: http://www.121publications.com
Dist(s): **CreateSpace Independent Publishing Platform**
Independent Pubs. Group.

1212 Pr., (*978-0-9764985*) 1212 Beverley Rd., Brooklyn, NY 11218 USA Tel 718-462-4004
E-mail: rgistudio@earthlink.net.

12-Story Library *Imprint of* **Pr. Room Editions LLC**

13 Hands Pubns., (*978-0-9767260*) Div. Crooked Roads Productions, LLC, Orders Addr.: 914 Westwood Blvd., #518, Los Angeles, CA 90024 USA Fax: 310-388-6012
E-mail: mnaughton@earthlink.net
Web site: http://www.13handsonline.com; http://www.gildedhearse.com.

13th & Joan, (*978-0-9916015; 978-0-9985210; 978-0-9989702*) 500 N. Michigan Ave. Suite No. 600, Chicago, IL 60611 USA Tel 770-609-9833
E-mail: info@13thandjoan.com
Web site: www.13thandjoan.com.

153 Fish Publishing, (*978-0-9747918*) 230 SW Railroad St., Sheridan, OR 97378-1745 USA.

1610 Media, LLC *See* **Appointed Media Group, LLC**

16th Avenue Pr., (*978-0-9742854*) P.O. Box 166, Portage, MI 49081 USA Fax: 269-372-6970
E-mail: theawrites@sbcglobal.net
Web site: http://www.fearnoflame.com.

16th Place Publishing, (*978-0-9745152*) 171 S. 16th Pl., Pocatello, ID 83201 USA
E-mail: brobergbook@yahoo.com
Web site: http://www.stoleninnocencebook.com.

1776 Pr., (*978-0-9825243*) 19 Coleman Rd., Wethersfield, CT 06109 USA.

1-800 ProColor, Incorporated *See* **Robertson Publishing**

1948, (*978-0-692-73934-1; 978-0-692-74533-5; 978-0-692-75287-6; 978-0-692-77028-3*) 333 jones Lester Rd., ROXBORO, NC 27574 USA Tel 336-599-8006.

1Ellipsis Press *See* **Ellipsis Pr.**

1st Impression Publishing, (*978-0-9763365*) P.O. Box 10339, Burbank, CA 91510-0339 USA Tel 818-843-1300; Fax: 818-846-5657
E-mail: sahysen@earthlink.net
Web site: http://www.1stimpressionpublishing.com.

1st World Library *See* **Groundbreaking Pr.**

1st World Library - Literary Society *Imprint of* **1st World Publishing, Inc.**

1st World Publishing *Imprint of* **1st World Publishing, Inc.**

1st World Publishing, Inc., (*978-0-9638502; 978-1-887472; 978-1-59540; 978-1-4218*) Orders Addr.: 1100 N. 4th St., Suite 9, Fairfield, IA 52556-2169 USA Toll Free: 877-209-5004; *Imprints*: 1st World Publishing (Frst Wrld Pub); 1st World Library - Literary Society (1st Wrld); Sunstar Publishing (SunstarPub)
E-mail: ed@1stworldpublishing.com; order@1stworldpublishing.com; info@1stworldpublishing.com; rodney@1stworldlibrary.org
Web site: http://www.1stworldpublishing.com
Dist(s): **Follett School Solutions**
Lightning Source, Inc.
New Leaf Distributing Co., Inc.

1stBooks Library *See* **AuthorHouse**

1stWorld Library, Limited *See* **1st World Publishing, Inc.**

2 Donn Bks., (*978-0-9770893*) 11354 Links Dr., Reston, VA 20190-4807 USA (SAN 256-7407)
Web site: http://www.2donnbooks.com.

20/20 Publishing, (*978-0-9668718*) Orders Addr.: 3941 S. Bristol Suite D520, Santa Ana, CA 92704 USA Tel 800-991-3296
E-mail: dawn@dawnmartin.com
Web site: http://www.dawnmartin.com
Dist(s): **Distributors, The.**

2020 Vision Pr., (*978-0-9710675*) 2744 Crown Point, Las Cruces, NM 88011 USA Tel 505-532-9693; Fax: 505-532-9694
E-mail: josh@joshhunt.com
Web site: http://www.joshhunt.com.

20th Maine, Inc., (*978-0-9704408*) 859 Lawrence Rd., Pownal, ME 04069-6118 USA
E-mail: pat@20thmaine.com
Web site: http://www.20thmaine.com.

21st Century Pr., (*978-0-9660906; 978-0-9700639; 978-0-9717009; 978-0-9725719; 978-0-9728899; 978-0-9749811; 978-0-9766243; 978-0-9771964; 978-0-9779535; 978-0-9817769; 978-0-9824428; 978-0-9827616; 978-0-9838359; 978-0-9894317; 978-0-9911004; 978-0-9863864; 978-0-9981392) 3308 S. Meadowlark Ave., Springfield, MO 65807 USA Tel 417-889-4803; Fax: 417-889-2210; Toll Free: 800-658-0284; Imprints:* Sonship Press (Sonship Pr) Do not confuse with 21st Century Press in Southlake, TX
E-mail: lee@21stcenturypress.com
Web site: https://www.21stcenturypress.com
Dist(s): **Anchor Distributors**
Bookmasters Distribution
CreateSpace Independent Publishing Platform
Send The Light Distribution LLC
Two Rivers Distribution.

21st Century Pubs., (*978-0-9607298*) 1320 Curt Gowdy Dr., Cheyenne, WY 82009 USA (SAN 239-1740) Tel 307-638-2254
E-mail: chismaturi@prodigy.net
Web site: http://www.triplecrownwinnerearlsande.com
Dist(s): **Emery-Pratt Co.**
Blackwell.

21st Century Publishing, (*978-0-9722624*) 16 W. Pacific Ave. No. 3, Henderson, NV 89015 USA Tel 702-564-1665; Fax: 702-564-4190
E-mail: brouff55@anv.net.

21st Century Publishing Hse. (CHN) (*978-7-5391; 978-7-88861; 978-7-900386*) *Dist. by* **Chinasprout.**

22 West Bks., (*978-0-9767788*) Orders Addr.: P.O. Box 155, Sheldonville, MA 02070-0155 USA
E-mail: chris@22wb.com
Web site: http://www.22wb.com.

23rd St. Publishing, (*978-0-9800821*) Orders Addr.: P.O. Box 863734, Plano, TX 75086-3734 USA (SAN 855-1421) Tel 214-717-7244
E-mail: stacy@23rdstpublishing.com
Web site: http://23rdStPublishing.com
Dist(s): **Follett School Solutions.**

25 Dreams Educational Media, (*978-0-9768019*) 8622 Bellanca Ave., Suite J, Los Angeles, CA 90045 USA.

2B Pr., (*978-0-9765430*) 206 Clear Springs, Peachtree City, GA 30269 USA Tel 770-487-1348
E-mail: tami@2bpress.com
Web site: http://www.2bpress.com.

2D Cloud, (*978-0-615-25380-0; 978-0-578-01983-3; 978-1-937541*) Orders Addr.: P.O. Box 6281, Minneapolis, MN 55406 USA Tel 612-568-8459
Web site: http://www.2dcloud.com
Dist(s): **Consortium Bk. Sales & Distribution.**

2DHse. Publishing, (*978-0-615-75181-8; 978-0-615-76647-8; 978-0-9895256*) 2075 Clover Dr., Monterey Park, CA 91735 USA Tel 818-793-9252
E-mail: 2dhouse@earthlink.net.

2Giggles, (*978-0-9801020*) 25811 Mill Pond Ln., Spring, TX 77373 USA
E-mail: vineandfig@gmail.com.

2Lakes Publishing, (*978-0-9722400*) Orders Addr.: 3661 Natalie Way, Bandon, OR 97411 USA
E-mail: heidi2lakes@2lakespublishing.com
Web site: http://www.2lakespublishing.com
Dist(s): **Independent Pubs. Group.**

2MPower, (*978-0-9767046*) 25231 Grissom Rd., Laguna Hills, CA 92653-5237 USA Tel 949-837-1268; Fax: 949-470-0659
E-mail: amovigen@yahoo.com
Web site: http://www.2mpwr.com.

3 Fates Pr., (*978-1-940938*) 2025 Bell Rd., Morgantown, IN 46160 USA Tel 269-235-4737; *Imprints*: Line By Lion Publications (LineByLion)
E-mail: admin@3fatespress.com
Web site: www.3fatespress.com.

3 Pals Media, LLC, (*978-0-9770960*) 424 Greenleaf Ave., Burlington, WA 98233 USA Tel 360-755-2299; Fax: 360-755-8010
Web site: http://www.pumpkinpatchpals.com.

3,000 Letters, (*978-0-9983577*) 240 e. Connecticut Ave., southern pines, NC 28387 USA Tel 910-690-3190
E-mail: gayvinpowers07@gmail.com
Web site: www.gayvinpowers.com.

302 Publishing, (*978-0-9790165*) 9139 SW Excalibur Pl., Portland, OR 97219-9721 USA Tel 503-246-2499 (phone/fax).

353rd Regimental History Project, (*978-0-9748916*) 2650 N. 64th, Wavnatusa, WI 53213-1407 USA Tel 414-444-7120
E-mail: suzannb@wyoming.com.

360 Degrees *Imprint of* **Tiger Tales**

360 Marketing, LLC, (*978-0-9702654*) 6 Trumbull St., Saintnington, CT 06378 USA Tel 860-535-2240; Fax: 860-535-3243 (call first)
E-mail: three60mrk@aol.com; claudia@chasem2.com.

3-C Institute for Social Development, (*978-0-9779290; 978-0-9789871; 978-1-934409*) 1903 N. Harrison Ave., Suite 101, Cary, NC 27513 USA Tel 919-677-0101; Fax: 919-677-0112
E-mail: info@3cisd.com
Web site: http://www.3cisd.com.

3cs Publishing, The, (*978-0-9773341*) P.O. Box 8096, Silver Spring, MD 20907 USA
Web site: http://www.the3cs.com.

3D Alley, Inc., (*978-0-9776845*) 4525 Harding Rd., Suite 317, Nashville, TN 37205 USA.

3G Publishing, Inc., (*978-0-9833544; 978-0-9854968; 978-1-941247*) 3508 Pk. Lake Ln., Norcross, GA 30092 USA Tel 404-553-1566; Fax: 770-676-0626 Do not confuse with 3G Publishing, Inc in New Berlin, WI
E-mail: myrna.gale@gmail.com
Web site: 3gpublishinginc.com.

3H Dowsing International LLC, (*978-0-9656653; 978-1-932229*) W10160 Cty. Rd. C, Wautoma, WI 54982 USA Tel 920-787-4747; Fax: 920-787-2006
E-mail: ilovedowsing@hotmail.com
Web site: http://store.yahoo.com/dowsing.

3N Media Group, (*978-0-9741686*) P.O. Box 705, Morris Plains, NJ 07950 USA Fax: 240-220-0500
E-mail: 3nmediagrp@optonline.net.

3perfections, (*978-0-9759909*) 833 Great Oaks Trail, Eagan, MN 55123 USA Tel 651-905-1098
E-mail: perfections3@aol.com
Web site: http://www.3perfections.com.

4 Childrens Sake Pubns., (*978-0-9752982*) Orders Addr.: P.O. Box 594, Moosup, CT 06354 USA; Edit Addr.: 357 N. Main St., Moosup, CT 06354 USA.

4 Sonkist Angels *See* **Four Sonkist Angels**

4000 Years of Writing History, (*978-0-9748786*) P.O. Box 484, Redondo Beach, CA 90277-0484 USA
Web site: http://www.lmlk.com.

405 Pubns., (*978-0-9790832; 978-0-692-91923-1*) Orders Addr.: 10026 S. Linn Ave, Oklahoma City, OK 73159 USA (SAN 852-3754); *Imprints*: Three Ring Circus Publishing House, Inc. (MYID_I_THREE R)
E-mail: quimbysneet@gmail.com
Web site: http://www.quimbysneet.com
Dist(s): **Lightning Source, Inc.**

43 Degrees North LLC, (*978-0-9744444*) P.O. Box 781, Wilson, NY 14172 USA Tel 716-751-3604; Fax: 716-751-0105
E-mail: jeff@tailgatetrivia.com
Web site: http://www.tailgatetrivia.com.

44 Enterprises, (*978-0-615-22510-4; 978-0-615-24951-3*) 820A W. 47th St., Savannah, GA 31405 USA.

45th Parallel Concepts Ltd., (*978-0-9747615*) Orders Addr.: 106 Main St. PMB 152, Houlton, ME 04730 USA
E-mail: postmaster@americanschoolhousereader.com
Web site: http://www.americanschoolhousereader.com
Dist(s): **Unique Bks., Inc.**

45th Parallel Press *Imprint of* **Cherry Lake Publishing**

47North *Imprint of* **Amazon Publishing**

4All Ages LLC, (*978-0-9787986*) 5 Murdock Rd., Suite 100, East Rockaway, NY 11518 USA (SAN 851-643X) Tel 516-561-3146
E-mail: laws123@aol.com
Web site: http://www.colorpets.com.

4Elliott Publishing, Inc., (*978-0-9846963*) 6829 NW 15th Ave., Miami, FL 33142 USA Tel 786-277-2693
E-mail: sxye320@yahoo.comtees.

4mPr., (*978-0-9896681*) 2639 Sherrie Ln., Thompsons Stn, TN 37179 USA Tel 615-815-7447; Fax: 615-790-6119
E-mail: jpmarrs@gmail.com.

4N Publishing LLC, (*978-0-9741319; 978-0-9798841*) Orders Addr.: 44-73 21st St., D-6, Long Island City, NY 11101 USA Tel 718-482-1135
E-mail: brendan@4npublishing.com; erin@4npublishing.com; lj@4npublishing.com
Web site: http://www.4npublishing.com.

4RV Publishing, LLC, (*978-0-9797513; 978-0-9818685; 978-0-9840708; 978-0-9825886; 978-0-9826423; 978-0-9826594; 978-0-9828346; 978-0-9832740; 978-0-9838018; 978-0-9852661; 978-0-9889617; 978-1-940310*) P.O. Box 6482, Edmond, OK 73083-6482 USA
E-mail: president@4rvpublishingllc.com
Web site: http://www.4rvpublishingllc.com
Dist(s): **Follett School Solutions.**

4th Dimension Enterprises, Inc., (*978-0-9819088*) 40 Memorial Hwy. Apt. 27N, New Rochelle, NY 10801-8340 USA
E-mail: info@4thdimensionpublishing.com
Web site: http://www.4thdimensionpublishing.com.

4th Division Pr. *Imprint of* **Kurdyla, E L Publishing LLC**

5 Continents (ITA) (*978-88-7439*) *Dist. by* **HachBkGrp.**

5 Fold Media LLC, (*978-0-9825775; 978-0-9827980; 978-1-936578; 978-1-942056*) 5701 East Cir. Dr. No. 338, Cicero, NY 13039 USA
E-mail: cathy@5foldmedia.com
Web site: http://www.5foldmedia-store.com; http://www.5foldmedia.com.

5 Muses Publishing, (*978-0-9786180*) 100 Andover Pk. Ste 150-108, TUKWILA, WA 98188 USA
E-mail: rlpolhill@5musespublishing.com
Web site: http://www.5MusesPublishing.com.

5 Prince Publishing, (*978-0-615-46134-2; 978-0-615-52891-5; 978-0-9848529; 978-0-9853345;*

978-0-615-64941-2; 978-0-615-65268-9; 978-0-615-65747-9; 978-0-615-66869-7; 978-0-615-68734-6; 978-0-615-68919-7; 978-1-939217; 978-1-63112) Orders Addr.: P.O. Box 16507, Denver, CO 80216 USA Tel 303-257-0389
E-mail: books@5princebooks.com
Web site: www.5princebooks.com
Dist(s): **CreateSpace Independent Publishing Platform**
Lightning Source, Inc.
Smashwords.

5 Spot *Imprint of* **Grand Central Publishing**

5 Star Pubns., LLC, *(978-0-9843881; 978-0-9832473; 978-0-9854386)* c/o Tlj Bookstore, Llc, 9134 Piscataway Rd. No. 805, Clinton, MD 20735 USA
E-mail: shawn5star@yahoo.com; shawncvalentine@yahoo.com
Web site: http://www.5starpublications.net
Dist(s): **Icon Distribution.**

5 Star Stories, Inc., *(978-0-9659470)* Orders Addr.: 14625 Greenville St., Houston, TX 77015-4711 USA Tel 713-455-1073; Fax: 713-583-7017
E-mail: isellfantasy@hotmail.com
Web site: http://www.TexasSecedes.com.

50/50 Publishing *See* **Soulo Communications**

5,6 Pickup Sticks Publishing, *(978-0-9762145)* 2493 Sunridge Ave., SE, Atlanta, GA 30315 USA Tel 404-627-9132
E-mail: tcmac1@bellsouth.net.

671 Press *See* **Octane Pr.**

6-mile Roots, *(978-0-9771255)* 1469 260th, Marion, KS 66861 USA Tel 620-924-5254
E-mail: joel@hillsborofreepress.com.

7 Robots, Inc., *(978-0-9778454)* 714 Washington Ave., Suite No. 9, New York, NY 11238 USA
Web site: http://www.7robots.com
Dist(s): **Diamond Comic Distributors, Inc.**

711Press *Imprint of* **Vendera Publishing**

716 Productions, *(978-0-9795529)* 3200 Airport Ave., Suite 16, Santa Monica, CA 90405 USA
Web site: http://learningwhoweare.com.

7th Generation *Imprint of* **Book Publishing Co.**

80 West Publishing, Inc., *(978-0-9763417)* 2222 Ponce de Leon Blvd., 6th Flr., Coral Gables, FL 33134 USA Tel 305-448-8117; Fax: 305-448-8453
E-mail: joellen@adkinsadv.com.

826 Valencia, *(978-0-9768467; 978-0-9770844; 978-0-9779289; 978-0-9790073; 978-1-934750)* 826 Valencia St., San Francisco, CA 94110 USA
E-mail: alvaro@826valencia.com
Web site: http://www.826valencia.org
Dist(s): **Publishers Group West (PGW).**

826michigan, *(978-0-9779289; 978-0-9827293; 978-0-9966315)* 115 E. Liberty St., Ann Arbor, MI 48104-2109 USA
Web site: http://www.826michigan.org.

8-Ball Express, Inc., *(978-0-9747273)* 316 California, Suite 529, Reno, NV 89509-1650 USA Tel 415-776-1596 (for wholesale orders); Toll Free: 877-368-2255 (for retail sales only)
E-mail: rgivens@toast.net
Web site: http://www.8-ballbible.com.

978-0-8283Branden Books *See* **Branden Bks.**

A & B Books *See* **A & B Distributors & Pubs. Group**

A & B Distributors & Pubs. Group, *(978-1-881316; 978-1-886433)* Div. of A&B Distributors, 1000 Atlantic Ave., Brooklyn, NY 11238 USA (SAN 630-9216) Tel 718-783-7808; Fax: 718-783-7267; Toll Free: 877-542-6657; 146 Lawrence St., Brooklyn, NY 11201 (SAN 631-385X)
E-mail: maxtay@webspan.net
Dist(s): **D & J Bk. Distributors**
Red Sea Pr.

A & D Bks., *(978-0-9743294)* 3708 E. 45th St., Tulsa, OK 74135 USA Tel 918-748-4348 (phone/fax)
E-mail: a_dbooks@live.com.

A & E Children's Pr., *(978-0-9728134)* 6107 S. Jericho Way, Centennial, CO 80016 USA
E-mail: maked4@aol.com.

A & E Sivells Pubns. *Imprint of* **Word For Word Publishing Co.**

A & L Communications, Inc., *(978-0-9714320)* 1946 Magnolia Crest Ln., Sugar Land, TX 77478 USA
E-mail: allysoncward@yahoo.com
Web site: http://www.algiershistory.com
Dist(s): **Forest Sales & Distributing Co.**

A & M Writing and Publishing,, *(978-0-9764824; 978-0-9861841)* 3127 Allen Way, Santa Clara, CA 95051 USA Tel 408-244-8053; Fax: 408-244-8098
E-mail: ctillson@amwriting.com
Web site: http://www.amwriting.com
Dist(s): **Partners Bk. Distributing, Inc.**

A & W Enterprises, *(978-0-9617896)* P.O. Box 8133, Roanoke, VA 24014 USA (SAN 665-603X) Tel 540-427-1154; Toll Free: 800-484-1492 (ext. 4267)
E-mail: gwalker@interlink.com.

A B C-123 Publishing, *(978-0-9711474; 978-0-578-16435-9)* Orders Addr.: P.O. Box 100145, Staten Island, NY 10310 USA Fax: 718-980-4416; 718-351-4863; Toll Free: 866-339-3936; Edit Addr.: 159 New Dorp Plaza, 2nd Flr., Staten Island, NY 10306 USA; P.O. Box 30096, Staten Island, NY 30096
E-mail: thomas@deweydoes.com; contact@deweydoes.com
Web site: http://www.deweydoes.com.

A B C-Clio Information Services *See* **ABC-CLIO, LLC**

A B Publishing, *(978-1-881545; 978-1-59765)* P.O. Box 83, North Star, MI 48862-0083 USA Toll Free: 800-882-6443
E-mail: abpub@abpub.com
Web site: http://www.abpub.com
Dist(s): **Send The Light Distribution LLC**
Spring Arbor Distributors, Inc.

A+ Bilingue/Bilingual *Imprint of* **Capstone Press of Coughlan Cos.**

A Blessed Heritage Educational Resources, *(978-0-9759320; 978-0-9767866)* 10602 Redwood Dr., Baytown, TX 77520 USA
E-mail: belinda.bullard@blessedheritage.com
Web site: http://www.blessedheritage.com.

A. Borough Bks., *(978-0-9640606; 978-1-893597)* Orders Addr.: 3901 Silver Bell Dr., Charlotte, NC 28211 USA Tel 704-364-1788; Fax: 704-366-9079; Toll Free: 800-843-8490
E-mail: humorbooks@aol.com
Dist(s): **Parnassus Bk. Distributors.**

A Buen Paso S.C.P. (ESP) *(978-84-937211; 978-84-938036; 978-84-939414; 978-84-940533; 978-84-941579; 978-84-942854) Dist. by* **Lectorum Pubns.**

A Cappela Publishing, *(978-0-9656309; 978-0-9724979; 978-0-9779139; 978-0-9818933; 978-0-9846177; 978-0-9850202)* P.O. Box 3691, Sarasota, FL 34230-3691 USA (SAN 253-567X) Tel 941-351-2050; Fax: 941-351-4735; *Imprints:* Advocate House (Advoca Hse) Do not confuse with A Cappella Publishing, Los Angeles, CA
E-mail: acappub@aol.com
Web site: http://www.acappela.com; http://www.lillythelash.com.

A Cappella Bks., *(978-1-55652)* 814 N. Franklin, Chicago, IL 60610 USA Tel 312-337-0747; Fax: 312-640-0542; Toll Free: 800-888-4741
E-mail: publish@ipgbook.com; orders@ipgbook.com
Web site: http://www.ipgbook.com
Dist(s): **Independent Pubs. Group.**

A Different Kind of Safari LLC, *(978-0-9890134)* 39 Skunk Hollow Rd., Jericho, VT 05495 USA Tel 802-238-0822
E-mail: hchipp@comcast.net
Web site: www.adifferentkindofsafari.com.

AEVAC, Inc., *(978-0-913356)* 7 Silver Lake Dr., Summit, NJ 07901-3233 USA (SAN 204-5567).

A H W Publishing, *(978-0-9741434)* 1124 W. 19th Ave., Spokane, WA 99203 USA (SAN 255-4070)
E-mail: annifrommainz@dc4pc.net.

A I G A / Art With Heart *See* **Art With Heart Press**

AIMS International Bks., Inc., *(978-0-922852)* 7709 Hamilton Ave., Cincinnati, OH 45231-3103 USA (SAN 630-270X) Tel 513-521-5590; Fax: 513-521-5592; Toll Free: 800-733-2067
E-mail: aimsbooks@fuse.net
Web site: http://www.aimsbooks.com
Dist(s): **Shen's Bks.**

A I T/Planet Lar, *(978-0-9676847; 978-0-9709360; 978-1-932051)* 2034 47th Ave., San Francisco, CA 94116 USA Tel 415-504-7516 (phone/fax)
E-mail: larry@ait-planetlar.com
Web site: http://www.ait-planetlar.com
Dist(s): **Diamond Comic Distributors, Inc.**
Diamond Bk. Distributors
L P C Group.

A JuneOne Production *Imprint of* **JuneOne Publishing Hub**

AK Peters, Ltd., *(978-1-56881; 978-1-138-05124-9)* 5 Commonwealth Rd. Suite 2c, Natick, MA 01760 USA (SAN 299-1810) Tel 508-651-0887 All inquiries; Fax: 508-651-0889; 7625 Empire Dr., Florence, KY 41042
E-mail: service@akpeters.com
Web site: http://www.akpeters.com
Dist(s): **Follett School Solutions**
MyiLibrary
Taylor & Francis Group.

A Kidz World *Imprint of* **ABUAA, Inc.**

ALPI International, Ltd., *(978-1-886647)* 1685 34th St., Oakland, CA 94608 USA Tel 510-655-6456; Fax: 510-655-2093; Toll Free: 800-678-2574
E-mail: becky@alpi.net.

AMG Pubs., *(978-0-89957; 978-1-61715; 978-1-63070)* Subs. of AMG Publishing Inc., Orders Addr.: P.O. Box 22000, Chattanooga, TN 37422 USA Tel 423-894-6060; Fax: 423-894-9511; Toll Free Fax: 800-265-6690; Toll Free: 800-266-4977; Edit Addr.: 6815 Shallowford Rd., Chattanooga, TN 37421 USA (SAN 211-3074) Toll Free Fax: 800-266-4577; 800-265-6690; *Imprints:* Living Ink Books (Liv Ink Bks)
E-mail: trevor@amgpublishers.com; sales@AMGpublishers.com
Web site: http://www.amgpublishers.com; http://www.livinginkbooks.com
Dist(s): **Anchor Distributors**
Spring Arbor Distributors, Inc.

AMICA Publishing Hse., *(978-1-884187)* Div. of AMICA International, 844 Industry Dr., No. 20, Seattle, WA 98188-3410 USA Tel 206-467-1035; Fax: 206-467-1522
E-mail: amica@ix.netcom.com
Web site: http://www.amicaint.com.

AMSC, Adventures in Math & Social Studies for Children, *(978-1-889639)* Orders Addr.: 818 W. Grover St., Lynden, WA 98264 USA Tel 360-354-4412; Toll Free: 800-306-1772
E-mail: math1@earthlink.net.

A N A D E M, Incorporated *See* **Anadem Publishing, Inc.**

A New Day..A New Way!, *(978-0-9749177)* 5525B Via La Mesa, Laguna Woods, CA 92637 USA Tel 949-340-0615; Fax: 949-723-0030
E-mail: kathleenscott@anewday-anewway.com; kathleen_scott@sbcglobal.net
Web site: http://www.anewday-anewway.com
Dist(s): **New Leaf Distributing Co., Inc.**

APTE, Inc., *(978-1-889651; 978-1-931872; 978-1-932736; 978-1-933229)* 820 Church St., Suite 300, Evanston, IL 60201 USA Toll Free: 800-494-1112
E-mail: pierred@apte.com; sally@apte.com
Web site: http://www.apte.com
Dist(s): **Brodart Co.**
Educational Resources
Follett School Solutions
Learning Services.

A PAR Educational, LLC, *(978-0-578-12712-5; 978-0-9973365)* 300 Adams Dr. Apt 301, McKees Rocks , PA 15136 USA.

ARO Publishing Co., *(978-0-89868)* Box 193, 398 S. 1100 W., Provo, UT 84601 USA (SAN 212-6370) Tel 801-377-8218; Fax: 801-818-0616
E-mail: arobook@yahoo.com
Dist(s): **Forest Hse. Publishing Co., Inc.**

A Road to Discovery Series Guide *Imprint of* **Perry Heights Pr.**

ASDA Publishing, Inc., *(978-0-9632319)* 904 Forest Lake Dr., Lakeland, FL 33809 USA Tel 841-859-2194.

A S Q C Quality Press *See* **ASQ Quality Pr.**

A Story Plus Children Bks., *(978-0-9778477)* Div. of Top Award, Inc., P.O. Box 1174, Pine Lake, GA 30072-1174 USA (SAN 850-3907) Tel 404-667-2619
E-mail: astoryplu@comcast.net
Web site: http://www.astoryplus.com.

A StoryPlus *See* **A Story Plus Children Bks.**

A. V. P., Incorporated *See* **IBE, Inc.**

A. W. Ink, Inc., *(978-0-9820932)* P.O. Box 1184, Kamas, UT 84036-1184 USA
E-mail: lesliesaunders@kw.com.

A4J Publishing, *(978-0-9831372)* P.O. Box 1101, Orlando, FL 32802 USA Tel 678-358-9820; Fax: 407-237-0135
E-mail: vikki@a4jpublishing.com
Web site: www.a4jpublishing.com.

AAA POP, *(978-0-9762282)* 4147 S. Tenmile Lake, Lakeside, OR 97449 USA
Web site: http://www.aaapop.com.

AAA Reality Games LLC, *(978-0-9837264)* 11693 San Vicente Blvd. Suite 380, Los Angeles, CA 90049 USA Tel 310-696-1045
E-mail: hartgetzen@hotmail.com
Dist(s): **Smashwords.**

Aaduna, *(978-0-9768626)* 2021 Del Norte Ave., Saint Louis, MO 63117 USA Tel 314-647-3437
E-mail: mroach@thecollegeschool.org
Web site: http://www.senecorps.com.

Aakenbaaken & Kent, *(978-1-938436)* 2206 White Oak Dr., Valdosta, GA 31602 USA Tel 917-607-8263
E-mail: akeditor@inbox.com.

Açedrex Publishing *See* **Acedrex Publishing**

A&D Xtreme *Imprint of* **ABDO Publishing Co.**

A&M Moonlight Creations, *(978-1-938783)* 5848 Birchwood Dr, Mentor, OH 44060 USA Tel 440-257-5008
E-mail: comboj2@yahoo.com
Web site: www.mortalrealmwitch.com.

AAO Publishing, *(978-0-9786431)* a/o Melody Farloe, P.O. Box 6208, Beverly Hills, CA 90212 USA
E-mail: puffybuffy1@yahoo.com
Web site: http://www.puffybuffy.com.

Aardvark Global Publishing, *(978-0-9770328; 978-1-933570; 978-1-59971; 978-1-4276)* 9587 S. Grandview Dr., Sandy, UT 84092 USA Do not confuse with Aardvark Global Publishing, Atlanta, GA
E-mail: info@eckohousepublishing.com
Web site: http://eckohousepublishing.com/; http://aardvarkglobalpublishing.com/; http://eckobooks.com
Dist(s): **AK Pr. Distribution**
Follett School Solutions
Lulu Pr., Inc.
SPD-Small Pr. Distribution.

Aardvark Pubs., *(978-0-615-13532-8; 978-0-615-13673-8; 978-0-615-14219-7; 978-0-615-17808-0)* 1615 Shannon Rd., Girard, OH 44420 USA
E-mail: info@aardvarkpublishers.com
Web site: http://www.aardvarkpublishers.com
Dist(s): **Lulu Pr., Inc.**

Aardvark's Weedpatch Pr., *(978-0-9755567)* P.O. Box 1841, Rogue River, OR 97537-1841 USA
Web site: http://www.aardvarksweedpatch.com.

AARO Publishing, *(978-1-893563)* Orders Addr.: P.O. Box 1281, Palisade, CO 81526 USA; Edit Addr.: PO Box 1281 Palisade, Co 81526, Palisade, CO 81526 USA (SAN 255-7185) Tel 970-314-7690 (phone/fax)970 985 4018
E-mail: carwe@earthlink.net
Web site: http://www.snowff.com
Dist(s): **Follett School Solutions.**

Aaron Bk. Publishing, *(978-0-9819195)* 1093 Bristol Caverns Hwy., Bristol, TN 37620 USA (SAN 856-924X) Tel 423-212-1208
E-mail: info@aaronbookpublishing.com
Web site: http://www.aaronbookpublishing.com.

Aaron C Ministries, *(978-1-933519)* 1005 Pine Oak Dr., Edmond, OK 73034-5139 USA Tel 405-348-3410
E-mail: bible@jpdawson.com
Web site: http://www.jpdawson.com.

Aaron Levy Pubns., LLC, *(978-1-931463)* 1760 Stumpf Blvd., Gretna, LA 70056 USA Tel 504-258-4332
E-mail: aaronlevy1@aol.com; kelleylevy12@gmail.com
Web site: http://www.goodlifemediallc.com.

Aaron Press *See* **Publishing Assocs., Inc.**

Aaron-Barrada, Inc., *(978-0-9768671; 978-0-615-12767-5)* 79 Valley High, Ruffs Dale, PA 15679 USA Tel 724-696-4332; Fax: 612-545-3210
E-mail: aaronbarradainc@aol.com
Web site: http://www.pottiestickers.com.

Aarow Pr., *(978-0-9749046)* 3215 Buckingham Ave., Lakeland, FL 33803 USA (SAN 255-8653) Tel 863-709-8882 (phone/fax)
E-mail: aarowpress@yahoo.com.

AB Rolle Publications *See* **ABR Pubns.**

A-BA-BA-HA-LA-MA-HA Pubs. *Imprint of* **Windy Press International Publishing Hse., LLC**

Abacus Bks., Inc., *(978-0-9716292)* Div. of Abacus Bks.com, 1420 58th Ave. N, Saint Petersburg, FL 33703 USA Tel 727-742-3889; Fax: 727-522-0606
E-mail: necole@abacusbooks.com; info@abacusbooks.com
Web site: http://www.abacusbooks.com.

Abadaba Reading LLC, *(978-0-9789473)* P.O. Box 80, Charlottesville, VA 22902-5335 USA (SAN 852-0240)
Web site: http://www.adabadaalphabet.com.

aBASK Publishing, *(978-0-9843855; 978-0-9962399)* 320 National Pl., Apt 5, Longmont, CO 80501-3326 USA
E-mail: Publisher@AbaskPublishing.com; kathygode@yahoo.com
Web site: http://abaskpublishing.com.

Abba's Hse. International Publishing, *(978-0-692-37641-6; 978-0-692-39156-3; 978-0-9971037)* 3015 W. Maplewood Ave, Bellingham, WA 98225 USA Tel 360-201-5574
E-mail: gatheringtheharvest@yahoo.com
Web site: www.anthonyecclesiastes.com.

†ABBE Pubs. Assn. of Washington, D.C., *(978-0-7883; 978-0-88164; 978-0-941864; 978-1-55914)* Orders Addr.: 4111 Gallows Rd., Virginia Div., Annandale, VA 22003 USA (SAN 239-1430)
E-mail: abbe.publishers@verizon.net; vze3hcqz@verizon.net; *CIP.*

Abbeville Kids *Imprint of* **Abbeville Pr., Inc.**

†Abbeville Pr., Inc., *(978-0-7892; 978-0-89659; 978-1-55859)* 137 Varick St., 5th Flr., New York, NY 10013 USA (SAN 211-4755) Tel 212-366-5585; Fax: 212-366-6966; Toll Free: 800-278-2665; 1094 Flex Dr., Jackson, TN 38301; *Imprints:* Abbeville Kids (Abbeville Kids)
E-mail: abbeville@abbeville.com
Web site: http://www.abbeville.com
Dist(s): **Follett School Solutions**
Ingram Publisher Services
MyiLibrary
ebrary, Inc.; *CIP.*

Abbey Pr., *(978-0-87029)* 1 Hill Dr., Saint Meinrad, IN 47577-0128 USA (SAN 201-2057) Tel 812-357-8215; Fax: 812-357-8388; Toll Free: 800-325-2511
E-mail: customerservice@abbeypress.com
Web site: http://www.abbeypress.com/
Dist(s): **Open Road Integrated Media, Inc.**
Open Road Distribution.

Abbott Avenue Pr., *(978-0-9767514)* 859 Hollywood Way, Suite 258, Burbank, CA 91505 USA
E-mail: info@abbottavenuepress.com
Web site: http://www.abbottavenuepress.com.

Abbott Pr. *Imprint of* **Author Solutions, Inc.**

ABC *Imprint of* **DC Comics**

ABC Bk. *Imprint of* **Michaelson Entertainment**

ABC Bks. (AUS) *(978-0-7333; 978-1-74086; 978-0-646-51687-5) Dist. by* **HarperCollins Pubs.**

ABC Bks., *(978-0-9785108)* P.O. Box 2246, Sunnyvale, CA 94087-2246 USA Do not confuse with ABC Books in Plano, TX.

ABC Children's Bks. (AUS) *(978-0-9577218) Dist. by* **HarperCollins Pubs.**

ABC Development, Inc., *(978-0-9767179)* 6869 Stapoint Ct., Suite 107, Winter Park, FL 32792 USA Tel 407-671-6000; Fax: 407-671-6602; Toll Free: 800-222-3053
E-mail: sales@abc-development.com
Web site: http://www.abc-development.com.

ABC Pr., *(978-0-9758622)* 550 Iron Mountain Rd., El Dorado, AR 71730 USA Tel 870-863-5779 Do not confuse with ABC Pr. in Walnut Creek, CA
E-mail: srwood@suddenlink.net
Web site: http://RamonaWoodBooks.com.

ABC Pubs., *(978-0-9772685)* 32 Meadowlark Ln., Willingboro, NJ 08046-2108 USA Tel 609-880-0897
E-mail: fg@abc-advantage.com
Web site: http://www.abc-advantage.com.

ABC Schermerhorn Walters Company *See* **Schermerhorn, Walters Co.**

†ABC-CLIO, LLC, *(978-0-275; 978-0-313; 978-0-8371; 978-0-86569; 978-0-87287; 978-0-87436; 978-0-89789; 978-0-89930; 978-0-903450; 978-0-938865; 978-1-56308; 978-1-56720; 978-1-57607; 978-1-85109; 978-1-58683; 978-1-59158; 978-0-9742537; 978-1-59884; 978-1-4408; 978-1-61069) 130 Cremona Dr., Santa Barbara, CA 93117 USA (SAN 301-5467) Tel 805-968-1911; Fax: 805-685-9685; Toll Free: 800-368-6868; P.O. Box 93116, Goleta, CA 93116 (SAN 857-7099); Imprints:* Greenwood (GreenWABC); Libraries Unlimited (LibdUnltd); Linworth Publishing, Incorporated (Linworth)
E-mail: customerservice@abc-clio.com; service@abc-clio.com; salesuk@abc-clio.com
Web site: http://www.abc-clio.com
Dist(s): **Bookhouse, The**
Casemate Academic
Ebsco Publishing
Follett School Solutions
MyiLibrary
ebrary, Inc.; *CIP.*

Abccurate Business Ventures, *(978-0-9755341)* P.O. Box 2236, Smyrna, TN 37167 USA Tel 615-831-7100
E-mail: editor@abccurate.com
Web site: http://www.abccurate.com.

ABCDE Academic Bks. for Children's Development Through Education, *(978-0-9754008)* P.O. Box 374, Shrub Oak, NY 10588 USA.

ABCDMoon *See* **ABCDMoon Publishing**

ABCDMoon Publishing, *(978-0-9729216)* P.O. Box 910732, Lexington, KY 40591-0732 USA Tel 859-873-5031
E-mail: tex@charliethemonkey.com; amy@charliethemonkey.com
Web site: http://www.charliethemonkey.com.

ABCs Connection, Inc., *(978-0-9755475)* 1209 Caribou Crossing, Suite 101, Durham, NC 27713 USA Tel 919-451-4991; Fax: 919-484-1980
E-mail: casey_wallace@yahoo.com
Web site: http://www.abcsconnection.com.

ABC's Unlimited *See* **See abc's LC**

Abdelsalam Corp., *(978-0-9755975)* 2499 Trewigtown Rd., Colmar, PA 18915 USA.

Abdiel Productions, *(978-0-9768088)* 4802 Nassau Ave., NE, No. 31, Tacoma, WA 98422-4632 USA.

Abdo & Daughter *Imprint of* **ABDO Publishing Co.**

Abdo & Daughters *Imprint of* **ABDO Publishing Co.**

Abdo & Daughters Publishing *See* **ABDO Publishing Co.**

Abdo Kids *Imprint of* **ABDO Publishing Co.**

†ABDO Publishing Co., *(978-0-939179; 978-1-56239; 978-1-57765; 978-1-59197; 978-1-59679; 978-1-59928; 978-1-59961; 978-1-60270; 978-1-60453; 978-1-61613; 978-1-61714; 978-1-61758; 978-1-61783; 978-1-61784; 978-1-61785; 978-1-61786; 978-1-61787; 978-1-61478; 978-1-61479; 978-1-61480; 978-1-62401; 978-1-62402; 978-1-62403; 978-1-62968; 978-1-62969; 978-1-62970; 978-1-68076; 978-1-68077; 978-1-68078; 978-1-68079; 978-1-68080; 978-1-5321) Div. of ABDO Publishing Group, Orders Addr.: 8000 W. 78th St. Suite 310, Edina, MN 55439 USA (SAN 662-9172) Tel 952-831-2120; Fax: 952-831-1632; Toll Free Fax: 800-862-3480; Toll Free: 800-800-1312; Imprints:* Abdo & Daughters (Abdo & Dghtrs); Checkerboard Library (Checkerboard Library); SandCastle (SndCastle); Buddy Books (Buddy Bks); Super SandCastle (SuperSandcastle); Essential Library (EssentialLibrary); A&D Xtreme (A&DXtreme); SportsZone (SportsZone); Big Buddy Books (BigBuddy); Graphic Planet- Nonfiction (GRAPHIC PLANE); Graphic Planet- Fiction (GRAPHIC FICTI); Looking Glass Library (LOOKING LIBRA); Abdo & Daughter (ABDO & DAUGHTE); Spotlight (Spotlight); Core Library (CoreLibrary); Calico Chapter Books (CalicoChapter); Abdo Kids (AbdoKids); EPIC Press (EPICPress)
E-mail: info@abdopublishing.com
Web site: http://www.abdopublishing.com
Dist(s): **Capstone Pub.**
Ebsco Publishing
Follett School Solutions
MyiLibrary; *CIP.*

Abecedarian Bks., *(978-0-9763106; 978-0-9791401; 978-0-9822985; 978-0-9915275)* 2817 Forest Glen Dr., Baldwin, MD 21013-9574 USA Tel 410-692-6777; 877-782-2221; Fax: 410-692-9125 Do not confuse with Abecedarian Books in Portland, OR
E-mail: books@abeced.com
Web site: http://www.abeced.com
Dist(s): **Book Clearing Hse.**

Abedus Pr., *(978-0-9763091)* P.O. Box 8018, La Crescenta, CA 91224-0018 USA (SAN 256-2936)
E-mail: jadams@usc.edu.

Abegg Press *See* **Milner Crest Publishing, LLC**

Abelard Bks. (GBR) *(978-0-9558483) Dist. by* **LuluCom.**

Abelson Pr., *(978-0-9830421)* Orders Addr.: 8334 E. 133rd St., GRANDVIEW, MO 64030 USA Tel 816-398-5859
E-mail: jabelson27@gmail.com.

Abernathy Hse. Publishing, *(978-0-9741940)* Orders Addr.: P.O. Box 1109, Yarmouth, ME 04096-1109 USA (SAN 255-4380) Tel 207-838-6170
E-mail: info@abernathyhousepub.com; abernathyhp@aol.com
Web site: http://www.abernathyhousepub.com
Dist(s): **Brodart Co.**
Follett School Solutions.

Abidenme Bks., *(978-0-9714515)* P.O. Box 144, Island Heights, NJ 08732-0144 USA (SAN 254-1203) Fax: 732-573-0551; Toll Free: 888-540-8022
E-mail: angela@booksformilitarykids.com
Web site: http://booksformilitarykids.com.

Abiding Life Ministries International, *(978-0-9670843; 978-0-9819546)* Orders Addr.: P.O. Box 620998, Littleton, CO 80162-0998 USA (SAN 299-8629) Tel 303-972-0859; 719-485-5558; Fax: 303-973-2682; Edit Addr.: 8191 Southpark Ln. Unit 102, Littleton, CO 80120-4639 USA; 3525 Canyon Heights Rd., Pueblo, CO 81005; *Imprints:* Abiding Life Press (Abiding Life Pr)
E-mail: AbideLife@aol.com
Web site: http://www.abidinglife.com.

Abiding Life Pr. *Imprint of* **Abiding Life Ministries International**

Abiding Life Press *See* **Abiding Life Ministries International**

Abilene Christian Univ. Pr., *(978-0-89112; 978-0-915547; 978-1-68426)* ACU Box 29138, Abilene, TX 79699-9138 USA (SAN 207-1681) Tel 325-674-2720; Fax: 325-674-6471; Toll Free: 800-444-4228; *Imprints:* Leafwood Publishers (LeafwoodPubs)
E-mail: lettie.morrow@acu.edu
Web site: http://www.acupressbooks.com/; http://www.leafwoodpublishers.com
Dist(s): **Anchor Distributors**
INscribe Digital
Send The Light Distribution LLC
ebrary, Inc.

†Abingdon Pr., *(978-0-687; 978-1-4267; 978-1-63088; 978-1-5018)* Div. of United Methodist Publishing House, Orders Addr.: P.O. Box 801, Nashville, TN 37202-3919 USA (SAN 201-0054) Tel 615-749-6409; Fax: 615-749-6056; Toll Free: 800-627-1789; Edit Addr.: 201 Eighth Ave., S., Nashville, TN 37202 USA (SAN 699-9956) Tel 615-749-6000; Toll Free Fax: 800-445-8189; Toll Free: 800-672-1789; *Imprints:* Cokesbury (Cokebury)
E-mail: cokes_serv@cokesbury.com
Web site: http://www.abingdonpress.com/; http://www.umph.org
Dist(s): **Church Publishing, Inc.**
Follett School Solutions
Ingram Publisher Services
Simon & Schuster, Inc.
United Methodist Publishing Hse.
ebrary, Inc.; *CIP.*

Abique, Incorporated *See* **Abique Pub**

Abique Pub, *(978-1-892298)* Orders Addr.: 50 Haystack Pl., Pagosa Springs, CO 81147 USA Tel 970-731-2513 during spring and summer; 214-466-1074 during winter; Edit Addr.: 1512 Country Ln., Allen, TX 75002 USA Tel 972-359-0136 Fall and winter
E-mail: abique@gmail.com.

AbleNet, Inc., *(978-0-9666667; 978-0-9764246; 978-0-9819934; 978-0-9825180; 978-1-935696; 978-1-62744)* 2625 Patton Rd., Roseville, MN 55113 USA Tel 651-294-2200; Toll Free: 800-322-0956; 1081 Tenth Ave./Southeast, Minneapolis, MN 55414
E-mail: kbrown@ablenetinc.com; customerservice@ablenetinc.com
Web site: http://www.ablenetinc.com
Dist(s): **Follett School Solutions.**

Abligio Bks., *(978-1-934437)* 4226 S. Rock St., Gilbert, AZ 85297-4536 USA (SAN 853-2362) Tel 480-272-6063
E-mail: publisher@abligio.com
Web site: http://abligio.com.

ABM Enterprises, Inc., *(978-0-9656688)* Orders Addr.: P.O. Box 123, Amelia Court House, VA 23002-0123 USA Tel 804-561-3655; Fax: 804-561-2065; Edit Addr.: 16311 Goodesbridge Rd., Amelia Court House, VA 23002 USA
E-mail: LarryDavies@SowingSeedsofFaith.com
Web site: http://www.SowingSeedsofFaith.com.

Abolet Publishing, *(978-0-9774555; 978-0-9818984)* 1348 East Capitol St., NE, Washington, DC 20003 USA (SAN 856-8618)
Web site: http://www.ronkoshes.com.

Aboriginal Studies Pr. (AUS) *(978-0-85575; 978-0-908097; 978-0-646-33600-8; 978-1-922059; 978-1-925302) Dist. by* **IPG Chicago.**

Abounding Love Ministries, Inc., *(978-0-9678519)* Orders Addr.: P.O. Box 425, Jackson, CA 95642 USA Tel 209-296-7264 (phone/fax); Edit Addr.: 225 Endicott Ave., Jackson, CA 95642-2512 USA
E-mail: alms@aboundinglove.org
Web site: http://www.aboundinglove.org.

About Comics, *(978-0-9716338; 978-0-9753958; 978-0-9790750; 978-0-9819563; 978-1-936404)* 1569 Edgemont Dr., Camarillo, CA 93010-3130 USA
E-mail: rights@aboutcomics.com
Web site: http://www.aboutcomics.com
Dist(s): **Diamond Comic Distributors, Inc.**
Diamond Bk. Distributors.

About Time Publishing, *(978-0-9791550; 978-0-9821214; 978-0-9847928; 978-0-9983133)* 29792 Harper Rd., Junction City, OR 97448 USA Tel 541-954-6724
E-mail: michael@judeco.net; mfaris1950@gmail.com
Web site: http://www.abouttimepublishing.com; http://www.judeco.net.

About Your Time LLC, *(978-0-9744768; 978-0-9799737; 978-0-9844266)* P.O. Box 582, S. Orange, NJ 07079 USA Tel 646-232-3212; Fax: 973-766-1019
E-mail: ayt1@busybodybook.com
Web site: http://www.busybodybook.com
Dist(s): **Publishers Storage & Shipping.**

Above the Clouds Publishing, *(978-1-60227)* P.O. Box 313, Stanhope, NJ 07874 USA (SAN 852-1328) Fax: 973-448-7789; Toll Free: 800-936-2319
E-mail: publisher@abovethecloudspublishing.com
Web site: http://abovethecloudspublishing.com
Dist(s): **Follett School Solutions.**

Abovo Publishing, *(978-0-9762007)* P.O. Box 1231, Bonita, CA 91908 USA
E-mail: abovo@cox.net
Dist(s): **Bookmasters Distribution**
Quality Bks., Inc.

ABR Pubns., *(978-0-9742367)* Orders Addr.: 1945 Cliff Valley Way, Ste. 250b, Atlanta, GA 30329 USA Tel 404-510-3131; Fax: 404-371-1838
E-mail: roll6128@bellsouth.net
Web site: http://www.drboydpublications.com
Dist(s): **Follett School Solutions.**

Abrams & Co. Pubs., Inc.,
Dist(s): **Abrams Learning Trends.**

Abrams Appleseed *Imprint of* **Abrams, Inc.**

Abrams Bks. for Young Readers *Imprint of* **Abrams, Inc.**

Abrams ComicArts *Imprint of* **Abrams, Inc.**

Abrams, Harry N. Incorporated *See* **Abrams, Inc.**

Abrams Image *Imprint of* **Abrams, Inc.**

Abrams, Inc., *(978-0-8109; 978-1-4197; 978-1-61769; 978-1-61312; 978-1-68335)* Orders Addr.: The Market Building Third Floor, 72-82 Rosebery Ave., London, EC1R 4RW GBR Tel 020 7713 2060; Fax: 020 7713 2061; Edit Addr.: 115 West 18th St., New York, NY 10011 USA (SAN 200-2434) Tel 212-206-7715; Fax: 212-519-1210; *Imprints:* Amulet Books (Amulet Bks); Abrams Books for Young Readers (ABYR); Abrams Image (Abrams Image); Abrams ComicArts (Abram ComicArts); Abrams Appleseed (AbramsAppleseed); Abrams Noterie (Abrams Noterie)
E-mail: webmaster@abramsbooks.com
Web site: http://www.abramsbooks.com
Dist(s): **Ediciones Universal**
Follett School Solutions
Hachette Bk. Group.

Abrams Noterie *Imprint of* **Abrams, Inc.**

ABREN (A Bk. to Read Empowers Nicaraguans), *(978-1-937314)* 1310 Mercy St., Mountain View, CA 94041 USA Tel 415-637-4243
E-mail: kmundera@yahoo.com.

Abril BookStore & Publishing, *(978-0-9704131; 978-0-9772265; 978-0-9796842)* 415 E. Broadway, Suite 102, Glendale, CA 91205 USA Tel 818-243-4112; Fax: 818-243-4158
E-mail: noor@abrilbooks.com; abrilbooks@earthlink.net
Web site: http://www.abrilbooks.com
Dist(s): **Follett School Solutions.**

Absalon Pr., *(978-0-9846687)* 34192 Capistrano by the Sea, Dana Point, CA 92629 USA (SAN 920-1335) Tel 949-493-6953 (phone/fax)
E-mail: jody.payne@cox.net
Web site: www.absalonpress.com.

Absecon Lighthouse, *(978-0-9779988)* 31 S. Rhode Island Ave., Atlantic City, NJ 08401 USA Tel 609-441-1360; Fax: 609-449-1919
E-mail: abseconlighthouse@verizon.net
Web site: http://www.abseconlighthouse.org.

Absey & Co., *(978-1-888842)* 23011 Northcrest, Spring, TX 77389 USA Tel 281-257-2340; Fax: 281-251-4676; Toll Free: 888-412-2739
E-mail: Abseyandco@aol.com
Web site: http://www.absey.biz
Dist(s): **Bibliotech, Inc.**
Brodart Co.
Follett School Solutions.

ABTA Pubns. & Products, *(978-0-9761517; 978-0-9844660)* P.O. Box 492123, Redding, CA 96049 USA Fax: 530-221-0917
E-mail: info@abtaproducts.com
Web site: http://www.autismandbehavior.com.

ABUAA, Inc., *(978-0-9760406)* Orders Addr.: P.O. Box 1542, Whitefish, MT 59937 USA Fax: 406-362-3407; Edit Addr.: 7347 Farm to Market Rd., Whitefish, MT 59937 USA; *Imprints:* A Kidz World (Kidz Wrld)
E-mail: info@akidzworld.com
Web site: http://www.akidzworld.com.

Abuzz Bks., *(978-0-9715865)* P.O. Box 15753, Scottsdale, AZ 85267 USA
E-mail: author@20umbrellas.com
Dist(s): **Quality Bks., Inc.**

Abysso Bks., *(978-0-9747228)* 817 E. Mackinac Ave., Oak Creek, WI 53154 USA
E-mail: asala@mac.com
Web site: http://www.pottersfield.posthaven.com; pottersfield.posthaven.com.

AC Pubns. Group LLC, *(978-1-933302)* P.O. Box 260543, Lakewood, CO 80226 USA
E-mail: dksimoneau@acpublicationsgroup.com
Web site: http://www.acpublicationsgroup.com.

AC Writings, *(978-0-9796780)* 322 PUNTA BAJA Dr., Solana Beach, CA 92075 USA (SAN 854-0896).

Acacia Publishing, Inc., *(978-0-9666572; 978-0-9671187; 978-0-9762224; 978-0-9774306; 978-0-9788283; 978-0-9790826; 978-0-9792531; 978-0-9793273; 978-0-9814629; 978-1-935089)* 770 N. Monterey St. Ste. C, Gilbert, AZ 85233-3821 USA Toll Free: 866-265-4553
E-mail: jason@hiredpen.com; editor@acaiapublishing.com; kgray@acaciapublishing.com
Web site: http://www.acaciapublishing.com
Dist(s): **Book Clearing Hse.**
Follett School Solutions.

Academic Edge, Inc., *(978-0-9754754; 978-0-9814537)* Orders Addr.: P.O. Box 23605, Lexington, KY 40523-3605 USA Tel 859-224-3000; Fax: 812-331-8021; Edit Addr.: 216 E. Allen St., Suite 143, Bloomington, IN 47402 USA
E-mail: george@academicedge.com
Web site: http://www.academicedge.com.

Academic Internet Publishers Incorporated *See* **Cram101 Inc.**

Academic Solutions, Inc., *(978-0-9635364; 978-0-9740200)* Orders Addr.: P.O. Box 102, Harvard, MA 01451 USA Tel 978-456-6829; Fax: 978-456-3053; Toll Free: 877-222-3765 (877-ACADSOL)
E-mail: asibooks@acadsol.com
Web site: http://www.acadsol.com.

Academic Systems Corp., *(978-1-928962)* 2933 Bunker Hill Ln. Ste. 107, Santa Clara, CA 95054-1124 USA Toll Free: 800-694-6830
E-mail: info@academic.com
Web site: http://www.academic.com.

Academic Therapy Pubns., Inc., *(978-0-87879; 978-1-57128; 978-1-63402)* 20 Commercial Blvd., Novato, CA 94949-6191 USA (SAN 201-2111) Tel 415-883-3314; Fax: 415-883-3720; Toll Free: 800-422-7249
E-mail: sales@academictherapy.com; customerservice@academictherapy.com
Web site: http://www.academictherapy.com; http://www.highnoonbooks.com
Dist(s): **Cambium Education, Inc.**
Follett School Solutions
P C I Education
PRO-ED, Inc.

Academy Chicago Pubs., Ltd. *Imprint of* **Chicago Review Pr., Inc.**

†Academy of American Franciscan History, *(978-0-88382)* 1712 Euclid Ave., Berkeley, CA 94709 USA (SAN 201-1964) Tel 510-548-1755; Fax: 510-549-9466
E-mail: acadafh@fst.edu
Web site: http://www.aafh.org
Dist(s): **Univ. Pr. of Florida**; *CIP.*

Academy Park Pr. *Imprint of* **Williamson County Public Library**

Accelarated Christian Education, Inc., *(978-1-56265)* P.O. Box 1438, Lewisville, TX 75067-1438 USA Tel 972-315-1776; Fax: 972-315-8681.

Accelerator Bks., *(978-0-9815245; 978-0-9841399; 978-0-9838940; 978-0-9848966; 978-0-692-79234-6)* P.O. Box 1241, Princeton, NJ 08542 USA Tel 732-642-9721
E-mail: gemma@acceleratorbooks.com
Web site: http://www.acceleratorbooks.com.

Accent On Success, *(978-0-9743700)* 29 Benton Pl., Saint Louis, MO 63104 USA Tel 314-664-6110; Fax: 314-664-6577
E-mail: jbishop@accentonsuccess.com
Web site: http://www.TeachingMoments.com.

Accent Pubns. *Imprint of* **Ajoyin Publishing, Inc.**

Access for Disabled Americans, *(978-1-928616)* 301 Village Sq., Orinda, CA 94563-2505 USA
E-mail: PSmither@aol.com
Web site: http://maxpages.com/disabledaccess; http://www.accessfordisabled.com.

Access-4-All, Inc., *(978-0-9744908)* P.O. Box 220751, Sain Louis, MO 63122-0751 USA Tel 314-821-7011; Fax: 314-909-8086
E-mail: steve@access-4-all.com
Web site: http://www.access-4-all.com.

Accessibilities, *(978-0-9774546)* 1131 E. Spruce St., Sault Ste. Marie, MI 49783 USA
E-mail: geri.taeckens@isahealthfund.org
Web site: http://www.isahealthfund.org.

Acclaim Pr., Inc., *(978-0-9773198; 978-0-9790025; 978-0-9798802; 978-1-935001; 978-1-938905; 978-1-942613)* Orders Addr.: P.O. Box 238, Morley, MO 63767 USA Tel 573-472-9800; Fax: 573-472-1608; Toll Free: 877-427-2665; Edit Addr.: 171 Co. Hwy. 430, Oran, MO 63771 USA
Web site: http://www.acclaimpress.com
Dist(s): **Follett School Solutions**
Partners Bk. Distributing, Inc.

Acclimated Spooks, Light, & Power, *(978-0-615-25755-6)* 1106 W. 2nd, Tahlequah, OK 74464 USA
E-mail: gracelandwest@gmail.com
Web site: http://www.acclimatedspooks.com
Dist(s): **Lulu Pr., Inc.**

Accordian Bks., *(978-0-9754098)* Orders Addr.: P.O. Box 69912, West Hollywood, CA 90069 USA (SAN 256-0046); Edit Addr.: 69912 W. Hollywood, Hollywood, CA 90069 USA
E-mail: crystalilluminations@msn.com.

Ace Academics, Inc., *(978-1-57633; 978-1-881374)* 69 Tulip St., Bergenfield, NJ 07621 USA Tel 201-784-0001; Fax: 201-784-7704; *Imprints:* Exambusters (Exambusters)
E-mail: highself@aol.com; info@exambusters.com; exambusters@gmail.com
Web site: http://www.exambusters.com
Dist(s): **INscribe Digital**
eBookit.com

Ace Bks. *Imprint of* **Penguin Publishing Group**

Ace Reid Enterprises *See* **Cowpokes Cartoon Bks.**

Acedrex Publishing, *(978-1-937291)* 550 N. Harrison Rd. No. 5101, Tucson, AZ 85748 USA Tel 401-743-0052
E-mail: acedrexpublishing@yahoo.com
Web site: acedrex.com.

Acen Press *See* **DNA Pr.**

ACER Pr. (AUS) *(978-0-85563; 978-0-86431; 978-1-74286) Dist. by* **Intl Spec Bk.**

Acey, Mary J., *(978-0-9771920)* 178-39 147th Ave., Springfield Gardens, NY 11434 USA Tel 718-949-2670; Fax: 718-949-7464
E-mail: jestac1@aol.com.

Aceybee Publishing, *(978-0-9763958)* 285 W. Kootenai, No. 7, Richfield, ID 23349-5344 USA.

Achiev *See* **Achieve Pubns.**

Achieve Pubns., *(978-0-9727762; 978-0-615-12053-9)* Orders Addr.: 1216 Scobee Dr., Lansdale, PA 19446 USA Fax: 215-368-1431 (fax orders)
E-mail: achievepub@verizon.net
Web site: http://www.achievepublications.com
Dist(s): **Book Clearing Hse.**
Follett School Solutions.

Achieve3000, *(978-1-932166; 978-0-615-12027-0; 978-1-935675; 978-1-938916; 978-1-63256)* 1091 River Ave., Lakewood, NJ 08701 USA Tel 732-367-5505; Fax: 732-367-2313; Toll Free: 877-803-6505
E-mail: kelly.tanko@achieve3000.com
Web site: http://www.achieve3000.com.

Achievers Technology Resource, Inc., *(978-0-9716113)* PMB No. 455, 442 Rte. 202-206 N., Bedminster, NJ 07921-1522 USA (SAN 254-2811)
Web site: http://www.achieversrus.com.

Achieving Corporate Excellence, Inc., *(978-0-9746262)* Orders Addr.: P.O. Box 651119, Vero Beach, FL 32965-1119 USA Toll Free: 877-656-8313; Edit Addr.: 8003 Kenwood Rd., Fort Pierce, FL 34951 USA
Web site: http://www.acespeaks.com.

ACME Pr., *(978-0-9629880)* Orders Addr.: P.O. Box 1702, Westminster, MD 21158 USA Tel 410-848-7577; Edit Addr.: 1116 E. Deep Run Rd., Westminster, MD 21158 USA
Dist(s): **Follett School Solutions.**

Acmon Blue Publishing, *(978-0-9744792)* P.O. Box 475, Tujunga, CA 91043-0475 USA (SAN 255-5638) Tel 818-352-2551 (phone/fax)
E-mail: info@acmonblue.com
Web site: http://www.acmonblue.com.

Acorn *Imprint of* **Heinemann-Raintree**

Acorn *Imprint of* **Oak Tree Publishing**

Acorn Bks., *(978-0-9648957; 978-0-9837299)* P.O. Box 7348, Springfield, IL 62791-7348 USA Tel 217-525-8202; Fax: 217-525-8212 Do not confuse with companies iwth the same or similar name in Kansas, MO, Bloomington, IN, St. Albans, VT
E-mail: amy@afterabortion.org; elliotinstitute@gmail.com
Web site: http://www.afterabortion.org
Dist(s): **Lightning Source, Inc.**
MyiLibrary.

Acorn Bks., *(978-0-9664470; 978-1-930472)* 7337 Terrace, Kansas City, MO 64114-1256 USA Tel 816-523-8321; Fax: 816-333-3843; Toll Free: 888-422-0320 Do not confuse with companies with the same or similar name in Springfield, IL, Bloomington, IN, St. Albans, VT
E-mail: jami.parkison@micro.com
Web site: http://www.acornbks.com.

Acorn Guild Press, LLC *See* **Marion Street Pr., LLC**

Acorn Hill Pr., *(978-0-9788889)* 155 Parkhurst Dr., Jackson, MS 39202 USA Tel 601-668-3533.

Acorn Pr., The (CAN) *(978-0-9698606; 978-1-894838) Dist. by* **Orca Bk Pub.**

Acorn Publishing, *(978-0-937921)* Div. of Vitesse Pr., PMB 367, 45 State St., Montpelier, VT 05601 USA (SAN 659-4840) Tel 802-229-4243; Fax: 802-229-6939 Do not confuse with companies with the same or similar name in Midvale, UT, Broomfield, CO, Battle Creek, MI, Sisters, OR, Suffern, NY,Saltlake City, UT, Portland, OR, Sping Lake, MI
E-mail: dick@vitessepress.com
Web site: http://www.vitessepress.com
Dist(s): **Hood, Alan C. & Co., Inc.**

Acorn Publishing, *(978-0-9678801; 978-0-9710988; 978-0-9728969; 978-0-9774449)* Div. of Development

Initiatives, 186 N. 23rd St., Battle Creek, MI 49015-1711 USA (SAN 854-6258) Tel 269-962-8184 (phone\fax); Toll Free: 877-700-2219 (phone\fax) Do not confuse with companies with the same or similar name in Broomfield, CO, Midvale, UT, Montpelier, VT, Sisters, OR, Suffern, NY, Salt Lake City, UT, Portland, OR, Sping Lake, MI
E-mail: editor@acornpublishing.com
Web site: http://www.acornpublishing.com.

Acorn Read-Aloud *Imprint of* **Heinemann-Raintree**

Acoustic Learning Inc., *(978-0-9761435; 978-0-9800581; 978-1-936412)* 215 Prospect Ave., Highland Park, IL 60035-3357 USA
E-mail: eartraining@aruffo.com
Web site: http://www.acousticlearning.com.

Acres Publishing, *(978-0-9741081)* 311 Prospect St., Alton, IL 62002 USA.

Acrobatic Cats Publishing *See* **MJ Brooks Co.**

ACS, LLC Amica Creative Services, *(978-0-9726535; 978-0-9794686; 978-0-9794771; 978-0-9801942; 978-0-9816822; 978-0-9822482; 978-0-9826401)* 13970 SW 72nd Ave., Portland, OR 97223 USA (SAN 255-0091) Tel (503)886-8900; Fax: (503)746-5224
E-mail: ross@ideasbyacs.com
Web site: http://www.ideasbyacs.com
Dist(s): **American West Bks.**

ACTA Pubns., *(978-0-87946; 978-0-914070; 978-0-915388)* 5559 Howard St., Skokie, IL 60077-2621 USA (SAN 204-7489) Toll Free Fax: 800-397-0079; Toll Free: 800-397-2282; 4848 N. Clark St., Chicago, IL 60640
E-mail: actapublications@aol.com
Web site: http://www.actapublications.com
Dist(s): **BookMobile**
INscribe Digital
Spring Arbor Distributors, Inc.

Actar D, *(978-0-9893317; 978-1-940291; 978-1-945150)* 355 Lexington Ave. 8th FL, New York, NY 10017 USA Tel 212-966-2207; Fax: 212-966-2214
E-mail: brian@actar-d.com
Web site: www.actar-d.com
Dist(s): **Ingram Publisher Services.**

Action Bks., *(978-0-900575; 978-0-9765692; 978-0-9799755; 978-0-9831480; 978-0-9898048)* Dept Of English, U. Of Notre Dame 356 O'shaughnessy Hall, Notre Dame, IN 46556 USA
Web site: http://www.actionbooks.org
Dist(s): **SPD-Small Pr. Distribution.**

Action Factor, Inc., *(978-0-9720763; 978-0-9754618)* PMB 218, 3195 Dayton-Xenia Rd., Suite 900, Beavercreek, OH 45434-6390 USA Tel 937-426-4364 (phone/fax)
E-mail: cgifford@actionfactor.com
Web site: http://www.actionfactor.com.

Action Lab Entertainment, *(978-0-9854952; 978-0-9859652; 978-1-939352; 978-1-63229)* 306 Bridlewood Ct., Canonsburg, PA 15317 USA Tel 513-313-7612
E-mail: spryor@actionlabcomics.com
Web site: http://www.actionlabcomics.com
Dist(s): **Diamond Comic Distributors, Inc.**
Diamond Bk. Distributors
MyiLibrary.

Action Organizing, *(978-0-9721964)* Div. of Successful Organizing Solutions, Orders Addr.: 406 Shato Ln., Madison, WI 53716 USA Tel 608-441-6767; Edit Addr.: P.O. Box 202, Milton, WI 53563 USA Tel 608-868-4079; Toll Free: 888-577-6655
E-mail: info@SOSorganize.net; sales@SOSorganize.net
Web site: http://www.actionorganizing.com.

Action Publishing, Inc., *(978-1-882210)* Div. of Action Products International, Inc., 344 Cypress Rd., Ocala, FL 34472-3108 USA Tel 352-687-2202; Fax: 352-687-4961; Toll Free: 800-772-2846 Do not confuse with companies with the same or similar name in Newport Beach, CA, Burlingame, CA, West Los Angeles, CA, Houstin, TX, Chicago, IL, Glendale, CA, Austin, TX.

Actionopolis *Imprint of* **Komikwerks, LLC**

Active Images, *(978-0-9740567; 978-0-9766761)* Orders Addr.: 8910 Rayford Dr., Los Angeles, CA 90045 USA Tel 310-215-0362; Fax: 775-890-5787 do not confuse with Active Images, Incorporated in Sterling, VA
E-mail: richard@comicraft.com
Web site: http://www.activeimages.com
Dist(s): **Lightning Source, Inc.**
Partners Pubs. Group, Inc.

Active Learning Corp., *(978-0-912813)* P.O. Box 254, New Paltz, NY 12561 USA (SAN 282-7794) Tel 845-255-0844; Fax: 845-255-8796
E-mail: panmans@newpaltz.edu; info@activelearning.com
Web site: http://www.activelearningcorp.com.

Active Learning Systems, LLC, *(978-1-57652)* P.O. Box 254, Epping, NH 03042 USA Tel 603-679-3332; Fax: 603-679-2611; Toll Free: 800-644-5059
E-mail: info@iimresearch.com
Web site: http://www.iimresearch.com.

Active Media Publishing, LLC, *(978-0-9745645; 978-0-9848808; 978-1-940367)* Orders Addr.: 614 E. Hwy 50 No. 235, Clermont, FL 34711 USA (SAN 255-6545); 614 E. Hwy 50 No. 235, Clermont, FL 34711 (SAN 255-6545); *Imprints:* Red Giant Entertainment (RedGiant)
E-mail: wizbenny@aol.com
Web site: http://redgiantentertainment.com
Dist(s): **Diamond Comic Distributors, Inc.**
Diamond Bk. Distributors
Elsevier.

Active Parenting Pubs., *(978-0-9618020; 978-1-880283; 978-1-59723)* 1955 Vaughn Rd. NW, Suite 108, Kennesaw, GA 30144-7808 USA (SAN 666-301X) Tel 770-429-0565; Fax: 770-429-0334; Toll Free: 800-825-0060
E-mail: cservice@activeparenting.com; ckeller@activeparenting.com
Web site: http://www.activeparenting.com
Dist(s): **Follett School Solutions**
National Bk. Network.

Active Spud Pr., *(978-0-9845388)* 324 E. 13th St., No. 3, New York, NY 10003 USA Tel 818-518-7381
E-mail: steve@activespudpress.com
Web site: http://www.activespudpress.com.

Active Synapse, *(978-0-9677255)* Orders Addr.: 5336 Park Lane Dr., Columbus, OH 43231-4072 USA
E-mail: Daryn@ActiveSynapse.com
Web site: http://www.activesynapse.com
Dist(s): **Brodart Co.**
Cold Cut Comics Distribution
Diamond Distributors, Inc.
Emery-Pratt Co.
Follett School Solutions
Midwest Library Service.

Activity Resources Co., Inc., *(978-0-918932; 978-1-882293)* Orders Addr.: P.O. Box 4875, Hayward, CA 94540 USA (SAN 209-0201) Tel 510-782-1300; Fax: 510-782-8172; Edit Addr.: 20655 Hathaway Ave., Hayward, CA 94541 USA
E-mail: info@activityresources.com
Web site: http://www.activityresources.com
Dist(s): **Delta Education, LLC**
Follett School Solutions
Seymour, Dale Pubns.

ACTNew Bks., *(978-0-9762326)* 12687 Blue Star Memorial Hwy., South Haven, MI 49090 USA
E-mail: actnewbooks@yahoo.com
Web site: http://www.actnewbooks.com.

Actual Magic Enterprises, LLC, *(978-0-9891807)* 17606 N. 17th Pl., Unit 1106, Phoenix, AZ 85022 USA Tel 602-992-5552
E-mail: debmctiernan@centurylink.net
Web site: www.deborahmctiernan.com.

Ad Center, The *See* **Leathers Publishing**

Ad Stellae Bks., *(978-0-615-31487-7; 978-0-615-31488-4; 978-0-615-34834-6; 978-0-615-62523-2; 978-0-615-64517-9; 978-0-615-80434-7; 978-0-692-29376-8)* 3088 Delta Pines Dr., Eugene, OR 97408 USA Fax: 866-302-3827
Web site: http://www.adstellaebooks.com
Dist(s): **CreateSpace Independent Publishing Platform**
Smashwords.

Adam Enterprises *See* **Amberwood Pr.**

Adam Hill Pubns., *(978-0-9769360)* Orders Addr.: 9001 SW 55 Ct., Fort Lauderdale, FL 33328 USA Tel 954-983-5005
Web site: http://www.adamhilldesign.com
Dist(s): **Follett School Solutions.**

Adams, Anne Marie Rea, *(978-0-9742782)* 9 Terraza Dr., Newport Coast, CA 92657-1510 USA.

Adams, Carl M, *(978-0-9899710)* 1207 Honu Loop, Aiea, HI 96701 USA Tel 309-696-7636
E-mail: cmadams6@yahoo.com.

Adams, Clint *See* **Credo Italia**

Adam's Creations Publishing, LLC, *(978-0-9785695)* Div. of JAH Innovations, Inc., 550 Fossett Rd., Zebulon, GA 30295 USA (SAN 851-0091) Tel 404-909-1025
E-mail: info@adamscreationspublishing.com
Web site: http://www.adamscreationspublishing.com
Dist(s): **BCH Fulfillment & Distribution.**

Adams, Evelyn, *(978-0-9761102)* 727 Virginia Ave., Midland, PA 15059-1429 USA Tel 724-643-9968; Fax: 724-775-8648
E-mail: rjb@timesnet.net
Web site: http://www.storiesfromvic.com.

Adams, Jeanette *See* **Camelot Tales**

†Adams Media Corp., *(978-0-937860; 978-1-55850; 978-1-58062; 978-1-59337; 978-1-59869; 978-1-60550; 978-1-4405; 978-1-5072)* Div.of Simon & Schuster, Inc., Orders Addr.: Simon and Schuster, Inc. Ordering Processing Dept. 100 Front St., Riverside, NJ 08075-1197 USA (SAN 215-2886) Toll Free Fax: 800-943-9831; Toll Free: 800-223-2336; Edit Addr.: Adams Media 57 Littlefield St., Avon, MA 02322 USA Tel 508-427-7100
E-mail: Khelsea.Purvis@simonandschuster.com; Purchaseorders@simonandschuster.com
Web site: http://www.simonandschuster.com
Dist(s): **Cranbury International**
CreateSpace Independent Publishing Platform
Ebsco Publishing
Follett School Solutions
Curreri, Michelle Morrow
MyiLibrary
Simon & Schuster, Inc.
ebrary, Inc.; *CIP.*

Adams Printing Pr. (IRL) *(978-1-906818) Dist. by* **Midpt Trade.**

Adams Publishing *See* **Adams Media Corp.**

Adams Publishing, *(978-0-9729189)* 320 Lincoln Rd., Branchland, WV 25506 USA Tel 304-824-2504 (phone/fax) Do not confuse with companies with the same or similar name in Topanga, CA, Rainier, WA, Boston, MA
E-mail: Adamspublisher@zoominternet.net
Web site: http://www.geocities.com/daycarebook/index.html.

Adamson, Mac, *(978-0-9779369)* P.O. Box 690, Midway, UT 84049 USA Tel 801-318-8544
E-mail: madamson@kids4fitkids.org
Web site: http://kids4fitkids.org.

Adams-Pomeroy Pr., *(978-0-9661009; 978-0-9967921)* Orders Addr.: P.O. Box 189, Albany, WI 53502 USA Tel 608-862-3645; Fax: 608-862-3647; Toll Free: 877-862-3645; Edit Addr.: 103 N. Jackson St., Albany, WI 53502 USA
E-mail: adamspomeroy@ckhnet.com
Dist(s): **Follett School Solutions.**

Adaptive Studios, *(978-0-9960666; 978-0-9864484; 978-0-9964887; 978-1-945293)* 3623 Hayden Ave., Culver City, CA 90232 USA Tel 310-876-1675
E-mail: tj@adaptivestudios.com
Web site: adaptivestudios.com
Dist(s): **Ingram Publisher Services**
MyiLibrary.

Added Upon, Inc., *(978-0-9740319)* Orders Addr.: P.O. Box 65327, Vancouver, WA 98665 USA
E-mail: dunnjessel@msn.com.

Addi-Boo Bks., *(978-0-9911410)* 78 Ryerson St., Brooklyn, NY 11205 USA Tel 347-512-7882
E-mail: stephen.epps@eppsscholars.org.

Addison Wesley, *(978-0-06; 978-0-13; 978-0-201; 978-0-321; 978-0-582; 978-0-673; 978-0-8053)* 75 Arlington St., Suite 300, Boston, MA 02116 USA Tel 617-848-7500
Web site: http://www.aw-bc.com
Dist(s): **Pearson Education**
Pearson Technology Group.

Addison Wesley Schl., Orders Addr.: a/o Order Dept., 200 Old Tappan Rd., Old Tappan, NJ 07675 USA Toll Free Fax: 800-445-6991; Toll Free: 800-922-0579; Edit Addr.: 75 Arlington St., Boston, MA 02116 USA Tel 617-848-7500; *Imprints:* Scott Foresman (S-Foresman)
Web site: http://www.aw-bc.com.

Addison-Wesley Educational Pubs., Inc., *(978-0-321; 978-0-328; 978-0-673)* Div. of Addison Wesley Longman, Inc., 75 Arlington St., Boston, MA 02116 USA Tel 617-848-7500; Toll Free: 800-447-2226; *Imprints:* Scott Foresman (Scott Frsmn); Scott Foresman (S-Foresman)
Web site: http://www.awl.com.

†Addison-Wesley Longman, Inc., *(978-0-201; 978-0-321; 978-0-582; 978-0-673; 978-0-8013; 978-0-8053; 978-0-9654123)* Orders Addr.: 200 Old Tappan Rd., Old Tappan, NJ 07675 USA (SAN 299-4739) Toll Free: 800-922-0579; Edit Addr.: 75 Arlington St., Suite 300, Boston, MA 02116 USA (SAN 200-2000) Tel 617-848-7500; Toll Free: 800-447-2226
E-mail: pearsoned@eds.com; orderdeptnj@pearsoned.com
Web site: http://www.awl.com
Dist(s): **Continental Bk. Co., Inc.**
MyiLibrary
Pearson Education
Trans-Atlantic Pubns., Inc.; *CIP.*

Addison-Wesley Longman, Ltd. (GBR) *(978-0-582) Dist. by* **Trans-Atl Phila.**

Addison-Wesley Publishing Company, Incorporated *See* **Addison-Wesley Longman, Inc.**

Addy's Rescue Fund, *(978-0-692-75867-0; 978-0-692-87784-5; 978-0-692-90384-1)* 642 Tamarack Ln, LEMOORE, CA 93245 USA Tel 559-904-1705.

Adelante Productions, Inc., *(978-0-9748017)* 600 Columbus Ave., 8G, New York, NY 10024 USA
E-mail: info@adelantepro.com
Web site: http://www.adelantepro.com.

Adhemar Pr. USA, *(978-0-578-06275-4)* 7440 S. Black Hawk, No. 15-102, Englewood, CO 80112 USA
E-mail: jtbeiser@gmail.com.

AdHouse Bks., *(978-0-9721794; 978-0-9770304; 978-1-935233)* 3905 Brook Road., Richmond, VA 23227 USA
Dist(s): **Diamond Comic Distributors, Inc.**
Diamond Bk. Distributors.

Adibooks.com, *(978-0-9728909; 978-0-9743872; 978-0-9748753; 978-0-9758993; 978-0-9760575; 978-0-9763465; 978-0-9764322; 978-0-9767424; 978-0-9772505; 978-0-9776044; 978-0-9778606; 978-0-9779682; 978-0-9787515; 978-0-9789741; 978-0-9791289; 978-0-9794769; 978-0-9797885; 978-0-9801635; 978-0-9815594; 978-0-9817447; 978-0-9821073; 978-0-9823972; 978-0-9841294; 978-0-9843390; 978-0-9845852; 978-0-9846346; 978-0-9852824; 978-0-9887395; 978-0-9899978; 978-0-9914043; 978-0-9960318; 978-0-9904151; 978-0-9908554;) 181 Industrial Ave., Lowell, MA 01852 USA Fax: 978-458-3026*
E-mail: tcampbell@kingprinting.com
Web site: http://www.adibooks.com
Dist(s): **Cardinal Pubs. Group.**

Adirondack Kids Pr., *(978-0-9707044; 978-0-9826250)* 39 Second St., Camden, NY 13316 USA Tel 315-245-2437
E-mail: info@adirondackkids.com
Web site: http://www.adirondackkids.com.

†Adirondack Mountain Club, Inc., *(978-0-935272; 978-1-931951; 978-0-9896073; 978-0-9961168; 978-0-9986371)* 814 Goggins Rd., Lake George, NY 12845-4117 USA (SAN 204-7691) Tel 518-668-4447 (customer service); Fax: 518-668-3746; Toll Free: 800-395-8080 (orders only)
E-mail: pubs@adk.org; adkinfo@adk.org
Web site: http://www.adk.org
Dist(s): **Alpenbooks Pr. LLC**
Equinox, Ltd.
North Country Bks., Inc.
Peregrine Outfitters; *CIP.*

Adisoft, Inc., *(978-0-9674897)* Orders Addr.: P.O. Box 2094, San Leandro, CA 94577-2094 USA Tel 510-483-3556; Fax: 510-483-3885; Edit Addr.: 664 Joaquin Ave., San Leandro, CA 94577 USA; *Imprints:* Wawa Press (Wawa)
E-mail: information@adisoft-inc.com
Web site: http://www.adisoft-inc.com.

Adiva, Incorporated *See* **TEG Publishing**

Adjust Communications, *(978-0-9765973)* 905 Hwy. 321 NW, Suite No. 364, Hickory, NC 28601 USA Tel 828-850-3237; Fax: 866-334-4360
Web site: http://www.victoryafterhighschool.com.

Adler, Karen, *(978-0-9679772)* 34738 McDaniel Dr., Northfork, CA 93643 USA Tel 559-877-2033.

Admirable Publishing LLC, *(978-0-9986891)* P.O. Box 881821, Port St. Lucie, FL 34988 USA Tel 772-332-5822
E-mail: debrasweeting@icloud.com.

Adonoke Inc., *(978-0-9773180)* 8354 Craine Dr., Manlius, NY 13104-9421 USA
E-mail: info@adonokebooks.com
Web site: http://www.adonokebooks.com.

Adoption Tribe Publishing *See* **MMB Enterprises, LLC**

ADR BookPrint *See* **ADR Inc.**

ADR Inc., *(978-0-9742743; 978-0-9761513; 978-0-9795033; 978-0-9802452; 978-0-9819864; 978-0-9908488)* 2012 Northern Ave., Wichita, KS 67216 USA Tel 316-522-5599; Fax: 316-522-5445; Toll Free: 800-767-6066
E-mail: bcatron@adr.biz
Web site: http://www.adr.biz.

Adrema Pr., *(978-0-9717290; 978-1-59611)* Orders Addr.: P.O. Box 14592, North Palm Beach, FL 33408 USA; Edit Addr.: P.O. Box 14157, North Palm Beach, FL 33408-2368 USA
E-mail: media@melissaa.com
Web site: http://adremapress.com
Dist(s): **CreateSpace Independent Publishing Platform**
Lightning Source, Inc.

ADV Manga, *(978-1-57813)* Div. of A. D. Vision, Inc., 5750 Bintliff, Suite 200, Houston, TX 77036 USA
Web site: http://www.ADVFilms.com
Dist(s): **Diamond Comic Distributors, Inc.**
Diamond Bk. Distributors.

Advance Cal Tech, Inc., *(978-0-943759)* 210 Clary Ave., San Gabriel, CA 91776-1375 USA (SAN 242-2603).

Advance Materials Ltd. (GBR) *(978-0-9532440) Dist. by* **Cambridge U Pr.**

Advance Publishers, Incorporated *See* **Advance Pubs. LLC**

Advance Pubs. LLC, *(978-0-9619525; 978-1-57973; 978-1-885222)* 1060 Maitland Center Cmns Blvd. Ste. 365, Maitland, FL 32751-7499 USA (SAN 244-9226) Toll Free: 800-777-2041
E-mail: advpublish@aol.com; questions@adv-pub.com
Web site: http://www.advancepublishers.com.

Advance Publishing, Inc., *(978-0-9610810; 978-1-57537)* 6950 Fulton St., Houston, TX 77022 USA (SAN 263-9572) Tel 713-695-0600; Fax: 713-695-8585; Toll Free: 800-917-9630; *Imprints:* Another Sommer-Time Story (Another Sommer) Do not confuse with Advance Publishing, Brownburg, IN
E-mail: info@advancepublishing.com
Web site: http://www.advancepublishing.com
Dist(s): **Follett School Solutions.**

Advanced Marketing, S. de R. L. de C. V. (MEX) *(978-970-718) Dist. by* **Bilingual Pubns.**

Advanced Publishing LLC, *(978-0-9857367; 978-1-63132)* 3200 A Danville Blvd. Suite 204, Alamo, CA 94507 USA Tel 925-837-7303
E-mail: eric@aliveeastbay.com
Web site: www.alivebookpublishing.com.

Advantage BibleStudy *Imprint of* **Advantage Bks.**

Advantage Books *See* **Advantage Bks., LLC**

Advantage Bks., *(978-0-9754332; 978-1-59755)* Div. of Advantage Pr., Inc., Orders Addr.: P.O. Box 160847, Altamonte Springs, FL 32716 USA; *Imprints:* Advantage Childrens (Advan Childrens); Advantage BibleStudy (Adv BibleStudy) Do not confuse with companies with the same or similar name in Newport Beach, CA, Silver Spring, MD
E-mail: mike@advbooks.com
Web site: http://advbookstore.com.

Advantage Bks., LLC, *(978-0-9660366; 978-0-9714609; 978-0-9823326)* 3268 Arcadia Pl.NW, Washington, DC 20015-2330 USA (SAN 253-8237) Tel 202-966-4044; Fax: 2002-966-1561; Toll Free: 888-238-8588 Do not confuse with companies with the same or similar name in New Port Beach, CA, Longwood, FL
E-mail: advantagebooksdc@aol.com
Web site: http://www.addvance.com
Dist(s): **National Bk. Network.**

Advantage Childrens *Imprint of* **Advantage Bks.**

Advantage World Pr., *(978-1-932450)* Div. of TheMoneyCoach.net, LLC, P.O. Box 1307, Mountainside, NJ 07092 USA (SAN 255-7452) Fax: 866-494-2461; Toll Free: 866-494-2461
Web site: http://www.themoneycoach.net
Dist(s): **Lightning Source, Inc.**
Smashwords.

Advent Truth Ministries, *(978-0-9749490)* P.O. Box 307, Forsyth, GA 31029 USA Tel 404-322-5683
E-mail: adventtruth@yahoo.com
Web site: www.adventtruth.org; www.thesabbathtruth.org.

Adventure & Discovery Pr., *(978-0-9744672)* P.O. Box 11631, Syracuse, NY 13218 USA Toll Free: 800-682-2662.

Adventure Beyond The Horizon *See* **Omega Pr.**

Adventure Bks. of Seattle, *(978-0-9823271; 978-0-692-32193-5)* 2415 I St. NE, No. D, Auburn, WA 98002 USA (SAN 857-8664) Tel 253-929-6259
Web site: http://www.adventurebooksofseattle.com
Dist(s): **Lightning Source, Inc.**

Adventure Boys Inc., *(978-0-9791922; 978-0-9791952; 978-0-9796392)* 11005 35th Ave. NE, Seattle, WA 98119-6809 USA (SAN 852-727X) 11/20/06: Do not be confused with Madison Park Greetings & Front Porch Classics, Inc.
Web site: http://www.adventureboys.com.

Adventure Hse., *(978-1-886937; 978-1-59798)* 914 Laredo Rd., Silver Spring, MD 20901-1867 USA Tel 301-754-1589; Fax: 978-215-7412
E-mail: sales@adventurehouse.com
Web site: http://www.adventurehouse.com
Dist(s): **Diamond Comic Distributors, Inc.**
Diamond Bk. Distributors.

Adventure in Discovery, *(978-0-9743414)* 18011 N. Hwy. A1A, Jupiter, FL 33477 USA Tel 561-746-8410
E-mail: info@adventureindiscovery.com
Web site: http://adventureindiscovery.com/
Dist(s): **Follett School Solutions**
Southern Bk. Service

Sunburst Bks., Inc., Distributor of Florida Bks.
Adventure Pr., *(978-0-9758654)* Orders Addr.: P.O. Box 1778, Canon City, CO 81215 USA Tel 208-880-7899; P.O. Box 1778, Canon City, CO 81215 Tel 208-880-7899
E-mail: antelope85@hotmail.com
Web site: http://www.kingsventures.com.
Adventure Productions, Inc., *(978-0-9614904)* 3404 Terry Lake Rd., Fort Collins, CO 80524 USA (SAN 693-3955) Tel 970-493-8776; Fax: 970-484-5825 Do not confuse with Adventure Productions, Reno, NV.
E-mail: cjansen@wild-west.com.
Adventure Pubns., *(978-0-934860; 978-1-885061; 978-1-59193)* Div. of Keen Communications, Orders Addr.: 820 Cleveland St., S., Cambridge, MN 55008 USA (SAN 212-7199) Tel 763-689-9800; Fax: 763-689-9039; Toll Free Fax: 877-374-9016; Toll Free: 800-678-7006
E-mail: orders@adventurepublications.net; custservice@adventurepublications.net
Web site: http://www.adventurepublications.net
Dist(s): **MyiLibrary**
Publishers Group West (PGW)
TNT Media Group, Inc.
Two Rivers Distribution.
Adventures at Hound Hotel *Imprint of* **Picture Window Bks.**
Adventures Galore, *(978-0-9759542)* Orders Addr.: P.O. Box 748, Lake George, CO 80827 USA Tel 719-748-8458; Fax: 719-748-8459; Edit Addr.: 35100 Hwy. 24, Lake George, CO 80827 USA
Web site: http://www.adventuresgalore.com.
Adventures in Print, *(978-0-615-37286-0; 978-0-9908487; 978-0-9972665; 978-0-9974036)* 55 Greenview Dr. Apt 6, Manchester, NH 03102 USA Tel 603-728-7701
E-mail: i.message99@live.com.
Adventures of Everyday Geniuses, The *Imprint of* **Mainstream Connections Publishing**
Adventures of Henry, LLC, *(978-1-936813)* 627 Evans St., Oshkosh, WI 54901 USA Tel 920-252-3578
E-mail: Darrin.Anderson@gmail.com
Web site: Www.adventuresofhenry.com.
Adventures of Hillary, The *Imprint of* **Nelson Publishing, LLC**
Adventures of Lady LLC, The, *(978-0-9789984)* 4907 White Bud Ct., Windermere, FL 34786 USA (SAN 852-1360).
Adventures Unlimited Pr., *(978-0-932813; 978-1-931882; 978-1-935487; 978-1-939149)* Orders Addr.: P.O. Box 74, Kempton, IL 60946 USA (SAN 630-1126) Tel 815-253-6390; Fax: 815-253-6300; Edit Addr.: 303 Main St., Kempton, IL 60946 USA (SAN 250-3484)
E-mail: auphq@frontiernet.net
Web site: http://www.adventuresunlimitedpress.com
Dist(s): **New Leaf Distributing Co., Inc.**
SCB Distributors.
Advocate Hse. *Imprint of* **A Cappela Publishing**
AE Pubns. (GBR) *(978-1-906672; 978-1-907708) Dist. by* **IPG Chicago.**
Aea Media, LLC, *(978-0-9862908)* 500 Umstead Dr., Chapel Hill, NC 27516 USA Tel 919-357-6948
E-mail: atkinsae@gmail.com
Web site: terrowintrilogy.com.
Aegaeon Publishing, *(978-1-934810)* Div. of Aegaeon Group International, One Penn Plaza 250 W. 34th St., 36th Flr., New York, NY 10119 USA Tel 212-835-1629
Web site: http://www.aegaeonpublishing.com.
Aegean Design, *(978-0-9758803)* 5009 20th Ave., NW, Seattle, WA 98107 USA Tel 206-612-9698
E-mail: bdarling@handofzeus.com
Web site: http://www.aegeandesign.net.
Aegypan, *(978-1-59818; 978-1-60312)* Div. of Alan Rodgers Bks., 4750 Lincoln Blvd., No. 360, Marina del Rey, CA 90292-9303 USA.
Aenor Trust, The, *(978-0-9724251; 978-0-9766401; 978-0-9768128)* Orders Addr.: P.O. Box 1410, Silverton, OR 97381 USA; Edit Addr.: 1286 Pressler Court S., Salem, OR 97306 USA
Web site: http://www.aenortrust.org; http://www.stellarlane.org.
Aeon Publishing Inc., *(978-0-9713099; 978-0-9718509; 978-1-932047; 978-1-932303; 978-1-932560; 978-1-59526; 978-1-933626; 978-1-60594)* Orders Addr.: 7580 NW 5th St. #16535, Fort Lauderdale, FL 33318 USA Tel 954-726-0902; Fax: 954-726-0903; Toll Free: 866-229-9244; *Imprints*: Llumina Christian Books (LluminaChrist); Llumina Press (Llumina Pr); Llumina Kids (Llumina Kids)
E-mail: diane@llumina.com
Web site: http://www.llumina.com.
Aeon Publishing, Incorporated *See* **Breezeway Books**
AequiLibris Publishing LLC, *(978-0-9816446)* Orders Addr.: P.O. Box 1542, New London, NH 03257 USA
Web site: http://www.AequiLibrisPublishing.com.
Aerial Photography Services, Inc., *(978-0-936672; 978-1-880970; 978-0-9789603; 978-0-9815804; 978-0-9836193; 978-0-9916287)* 2511 S. Tryon St., Charlotte, NC 28203 USA (SAN 214-2791) Tel 704-333-5143; Fax: 704-333-4911
E-mail: aps@aps-1.com; gregg@aps-1.com
Web site: http://www.aps-1.com.
Aerospace 1 Pubns., *(978-0-9705150)* 8 Brookstone Ct., Streamwood, IL 60107 USA
E-mail: aerospace1@aol.com.
Aesop Pubs., LLC, *(978-0-9725218)* 11153 Powder Horn Dr., Potomac, MD 20854 USA
E-mail: plastcfgs@aol.com
Dist(s): **Bookmasters Distribution.**
AFCHRON, *(978-1-892824; 978-1-938976)* Orders Addr.: 701 Givens Ln., Minneapolis, MN 55411 USA; *Imprints*: afchron.com (afchroncom)
E-mail: afchron5@aol.com
Web site: http://www.afchron.com
Dist(s): **Copyright Clearance Ctr., Inc.**
EBSCO Media.
afchron.com *Imprint of* **AFCHRON**
Affirming Faith, *(978-0-9798627; 978-0-9897373)* 1181 Whispering Knoll Ln., Rochester Hills, MI 48306 USA (SAN 854-591X) Tel 248-909-5735; Fax: 248-608-1756
E-mail: loriwagner@affirmingfaith.com
Web site: http://www.affirmingfaith.com
Dist(s): **Pentecostal Publishing Hse.**
Africa World Pr., *(978-0-86543; 978-1-59221)* 541 W. Ingham Ave., Suite B, Trenton, NJ 08638 USA (SAN 692-3925) Tel 609-695-3200; Fax: 609-695-6466
E-mail: customerservice@africaworldpressbooks.com
Web site: http://www.africaworldpressbooks.com.
African American Chronicle Software Publishing Corporation *See* **AFCHRON**
African American Images, *(978-0-913543; 978-0-9749000; 978-1-934155)* P.O. Box 1799, Chicago Hts, IL 60412-1799 USA Toll Free: 800-552-1991
E-mail: aai@africanamericanimages.com; customer@africanamericanimages.com
Web site: http://AfricanAmericanImages.com
Dist(s): **Ebsco Publishing**
Follett School Solutions
Independent Pubs. Group
MyiLibrary
ebrary, Inc.
African Christian Pr. (GHA) *(978-9964-87) Dist. by* **Mich St U Pr.**
Africana Homestead Legacy Pubs., Inc., *(978-0-9653308; 978-0-9770904; 978-0-9799537; 978-0-9818939; 978-0-9825842; 978-0-9831151; 978-1-937622)* Orders Addr.: 926 Haddonfield Rd., Suite E. #329, Cherry Hill, NJ 08002 USA (SAN 914-4811) Tel 856-673-0363; *Imprints*: Nefu Books (Nefu Bks)
E-mail: sales@ahlpub.com; customer-service@ahlpub.com
Web site: http://www.ahlpub.com.
Afrolez Productions, LLC, *(978-0-615-16123-5)* P.O. Box 58085, Philadelphia, PA 19102-8085 USA Tel 215-701-6150
E-mail: contact@notherapedocumentary.org
Web site: http://www.notherapedocumentary.org.
After Happily Ever After *Imprint of* **Stone Arch Bks.**
AfterShock Comics, *(978-0-9795939; 978-0-9801479; 978-1-935002; 978-0-692-94590-2)* 15300 Ventura Blvd Suite 507, Sherman Oaks, CA 91403 USA
E-mail: stephannilson@aftershock.ninja
Web site: www.aftershockcomics.com
Dist(s): **Diamond Comic Distributors, Inc.**
Afton Historical Society Pr., *(978-0-9639338; 978-1-890434; 978-0-9976296)* Orders Addr.: 165 Western Ave. N., Suite 15, St. Paul, MN 55102 USA Tel 651-436-8443; Toll Free: 800-436-8443
E-mail: aftonpress@gmail.com
Web site: http://www.aftonpress.com
Dist(s): **Bookmen, Inc.**
Brodart Co.
Coutts Information Services
Eastern Bk. Co.
Follett School Solutions
Galda Library Services, Inc.
Afton Publishing, *(978-0-89359)* Orders Addr.: P.O. Box 1399, Andover, NJ 07821-1399 USA (SAN 692-2570) Tel 973-579-2442; Fax: 973-579-2842; Toll Free: 888-238-6665
E-mail: info3@aftonpublishing.com
Web site: http://www.aftonpublishing.com.
Agapy LLC, *(978-0-9721328; 978-1-938522)* 13700 Wood Flower Ct., Granger, IN 46530 USA
E-mail: info@agapy.com; president@agapy.com
Web site: http://www.agapy.com
Dist(s): **Lightning Source, Inc.**
Agapy Publishing *See* **Agapy LLC**
Agate Publishing, Inc., *(978-0-940625; 978-0-9609516; 978-1-57284; 978-0-9724562; 978-1-932841)* 1501 Madison St., Evanston, IL 60202 USA
Web site: http://www.agatepublishing.com
Dist(s): **MyiLibrary**
Publishers Group West (PGW)
ebrary, Inc.
A-Gator Publishing,
AGB Publishing, *(978-1-930908)* Div. of Mini Enterprises - M.E., 19425 Bankers House Dr., Katy, TX 77449-0243 USA; *Imprints*: AGB/me (AGB-me)
E-mail: minienterprises@msn.com; minitaylr@msn.com.
AGB/me *Imprint of* **AGB Publishing**
AGC Outreach Ministry, *(978-0-9774115)* 528 Starrett Ln., Ligonier, PA 15658 USA Tel 724-238-0341
E-mail: stevenjsmith799@adelphia.net
Web site: www.agcoutreach.com.
Ageless Treasures, *(978-0-9705726)* Orders Addr.: 3536 Saint Andrews Village Cir., Louisville, KY 40241-2664 USA (SAN 253-794X) Tel 502-412-5940; Fax: 502-327-6233
E-mail: dcw0810@insightbb.com; carlawebb@agelesstreasures.net.
Agent of Danger *Imprint of* **Komikwerks, LLC**
Agents of Change, *(978-1-928992)* Div. of Granite Publishing, LLC, P.O. Box 1429, Columbus, NC 28722-1429 USA Tel 828-894-3088; Fax: 828-894-8454; Toll Free: 800-366-0264
E-mail: brian@5thworld.com
Web site: http://5thworld.com
Dist(s): **New Leaf Distributing Co., Inc.**
Age-Trotters Press *See* **Cameltrotters Publishing**
Agile Pr., *(978-0-9718239)* P.O. Box 1939, Chicago, IL 60690-1939 USA
E-mail: agilepress@agileresearch.com.
AGL Editions, *(978-0-9745629)* 1000 Bay Dr., No. 524, Niceville, FL 32578 USA.
Aglob Publishing, *(978-0-9708560; 978-1-59427)* P.O. Box 4036, Hallandale, FL 33008 USA Tel 954-456-1476; Fax: 954-456-3903
E-mail: info@aglobpublishing.com; info@aglob.com
Web site: http://www.aglobpublishing.com.
Agora Pubns., Inc., *(978-1-887250; 978-0-9904599)* 17 Dean St., Millis, MA 02054 USA (SAN 851-8521) Tel 508-376-1073 (phone/fax)
E-mail: agorapub@verizon.net; info@agorapublication.com
Web site: http://www.agorapublications.com
Dist(s): **Philosophy Documentation Ctr.**
Agreka Bks., LLC, *(978-1-888106; 978-0-9777072; 978-1-934243)* P.O. Box 14405, Scottsdale, AZ 85267-14405 USA Tel 480-767-1774; Toll Free Fax: 888-771-7758; Toll Free: 800-360-5284
E-mail: info@agreka.com
Web site: http://www.agreka.com; http://www.utahbooks.com; http://www.historypreserved.com
Dist(s): **Lightning Source, Inc.**
Quality Bks., Inc.
Agua Caliente Pr., *(978-0-9768275)* 4352 Riley Rd., Gladwin, MI 48624 USA Tel 989-426-8400
E-mail: maryhansen4@hotmail.com.
Aguilar, Altea, Taurus, Alfaguara, S.A. de C.V (MEX) *(978-968-19) Dist. by* **Santillana.**
Aguilar, Altea, Taurus, Alfaguara, S.A. de C.V (MEX) *(978-968-19) Dist. by* **TwoRivers.**
Aguilar Chilena de Ediciones, Ltd. (CHL) *(978-956-239; 978-956-347) Dist. by* **Ediciones.**
Aguilar Chilena de Ediciones, Ltd. (CHL) *(978-956-239; 978-956-347) Dist. by* **Santillana.**
Aguilar Editorial (MEX) *Dist. by* **Santillana.**
Aguirre Cox, Vicki & Ernest, *(978-0-9767994)* 10810 Lake Path Dr., San Antonio, TX 78217 USA Tel 210-364-8590; Fax: 210-653-3089
E-mail: vacemas@aol.com.
Aha! Elora Danan Productions, *(978-0-9786729)* P.O. Box 428, Estero, FL 33928 USA
Dist(s): **Follett School Solutions.**
aha! Process, Inc., *(978-0-9647437; 978-1-929229; 978-1-934583; 978-1-938248)* P.O. Box 727, Highlands, TX 77562-0727 USA Tel 281-426-5300; Fax: 281-426-5600; Toll Free: 800-424-9484
Web site: http://www.ahaprocess.com
Dist(s): **Follett School Solutions**
Greenleaf Book Group.
A-Head Publishing, *(978-0-9816283)* 41 Via Del Sol, Nicasio, CA 94946 USA (SAN 856-0862)
E-mail: aheadpublishing@gmail.com
Web site: http://www.a-headpublishing.com.
Ahlman Publishing, *(978-0-9712906)* Div. of KODIAK Publishing, 9525 W. 230 St., Morristown, MN 55052 USA Tel 507-685-4247; Fax: 507-685-4280
E-mail: larryahlman@hotmail.com
Web site: http://www.ahlmans.com/mittens.html
Dist(s): **Partners Bk. Distributing, Inc.**
Ahzar's Bk. Co. Publishing, *(978-0-9746130)* 3675 So. Rainbow Blvd No. 107, Las Vegas, NV 89103 USA Tel 702-391-1914; Fax: 702-871-8777
E-mail: croesus@joimail.com.
Aidan's Butterfly Pubns., *(978-0-9787341)* 4946 W. Laurie Ln., Glendale, AZ 85302 USA Fax: 623-776-9921
E-mail: eetagt@aol.com.
Ailam Publishing LLC, *(978-0-9837759)* 12900 S. May, Calumet Park, IL 60827 USA (SAN 860-2859)
E-mail: ailampublishing@aol.com.
A.I.M. Enterprises, *(978-0-9772303)* 507 Grace - Stockham, Aurora, NE 68818-7019 USA
Web site: http://www.aim4theheart.com.
Aim Higher Bks., *(978-0-9713292)* 10556 Combie Rd., Suite 6242, Auburn, CA 95602 USA
E-mail: sales@aimhigherbooks.com
Web site: http://www.AimHigherBooks.com.
Aim Higher Publishing *See* **Aim Higher Bks.**
AIMS Education Foundation, *(978-1-881431; 978-1-932093; 978-1-60519)* Orders Addr.: 1595 S. Chestnut Ave., Fresno, CA 93702-4706 USA Tel 559-255-4094; Fax: 559-255-6396; Toll Free: 888-733-2467
E-mail: aimsed@aimsedu.org
Web site: http://www.aimsedu.org.
AIMS Multimedia, *(978-0-8068)* 1 Discovery Pl., Silver Spring, MD 20910-3354 USA (SAN 687-3464) Toll Free: 800-367-2467
Web site: http://www.aimsmultimedia.com/
Dist(s): **Follett School Solutions**
Weston Woods Studios, Inc.
Air & Nothingness Pr., *(978-0-9679429; 978-0-9991953)* 2224 Delaware Ave., Pittsburgh, PA 15218 USA
E-mail: info@aanpress.com
Web site: http://www.aanpress.com.
airjam.com, *(978-0-9786478)* 3379 C1/2 Road, Palisade, CO 81526 USA.
Airplane Reader Publishing, *(978-0-9702405; 978-0-9765485)* Div. of Pro Leisure Tour, Inc., 9260 E. Lake Pl., Greenwood Village, CO 80111 USA (SAN 253-6935) Fax: 303-221-2766 24-hour dedicated fax line; Toll Free: 877-611-6222 voice mail, 24 hours
E-mail: theo@12milestoparadise.com; tedsimendinger@comcast.net; ted@funnyted.com
Web site: http://www.proleisuretour.com; http://www.piggychurch.com; http://www.12milestoparadise.com; http://www.richwithoutmoney.org; http://www.jurassictrout.com; http://www.tukibanjo.com.
Airways International, Inc., *(978-0-9653993)* Orders Addr.: P.O. Box 1109, Sandpoint, ID 83864 USA Tel 208-263-2098; Fax: 208-263-5906; Edit Addr.: P.O. Box 1109, Sandpoint, ID 83864 USA
E-mail: airways@airwaysmag.com
Web site: http://www.airwaysmag.com.
AJM Bks., *(978-0-9896211)* 11121 W. Amelia Ave, Avondale, AZ 85392 USA Tel 623-877-9114
E-mail: ajohnsonmccurdy@yahoo.com.
Ajoyin Publishing, Inc., *(978-0-9787472; 978-0-9792739; 978-0-9818488; 978-1-60920)* Orders Addr.: P.O. Box 342, Three Rivers, MI 49093 USA; Edit Addr.: 55919 Buckhorn Rd., Three Rivers, MI 49093 USA (SAN 852-9817) Toll Free: 888-273-4569; *Imprints*: Accent Publications (Acent)
E-mail: pam@ajoyin.com
Web site: http://www.ajoyin.com.
AJS Pubns., Inc., *(978-0-931298; 978-1-892291; 978-0-9904772)* 229 Brier Ct., Island Lake, IL 60042 USA (SAN 223-5846) Tel 847-526-5027; Fax: 847-487-5229 Do not confuse with AJS Publishing, Inc., Los Angeles, CA
Web site: http://www.ajspublications.com.
AK Classics, LLC, *(978-0-9814945; 978-0-692-92223-1)* P.O. Box 77023, Charlotte, NC 28271-7003 USA
E-mail: marcuskimbrough@aol.com
Web site: www.akclassicstories.com.
AKA Wendy Wonder, *(978-0-9967904)* 3020 SW 15th Ct, Gresham, OR 97080 USA Tel 541-771-3711
E-mail: mssveen@aol.com.
Akasha Classics *Imprint of* **Akasha Publishing, LLC**
Akasha Publishing, LLC, *(978-1-60512)* Orders Addr.: 2050 Emerald Ln., Fairfield, IA 52556 USA Fax: 866-485-5727; Toll Free: 877-745-7317; *Imprints*: Akasha Classics (Akasha Classics)
E-mail: registrar@akashapublishing.com
Web site: http://www.akashapublishing.com
Dist(s): **Follett School Solutions**
Lightning Source, Inc.
Akashic Bks., *(978-1-888451; 978-0-9719206; 978-1-933354; 978-1-936070; 978-1-61775)* 232 Third St., No. B404, Brooklyn, NY 11215 USA Tel 718-643-9193; Fax: 718-643-9195; *Imprints*: Black Sheep (BlckSheep)
E-mail: info@akashicbooks.com
Web site: http://www.akashicbooks.com
Dist(s): **Consortium Bk. Sales & Distribution**
Follett School Solutions
MyiLibrary
Open Road Integrated Media, Inc.
SPD-Small Pr. Distribution
ebrary, Inc.
AKA:yoLa, *(978-0-9842288; 978-1-936688; 978-1-942168)* 315 Bernadette Dr. Ste 3, Columbia, MO 65203 USA Tel 573-864-1479; *Imprints*: Compass Flower Press (CompassFlower)
Web site: http://www.akayola.com; www.compassflowerpress.com; www.aka-publishing.com
Dist(s): **eBookit.com.**
AKB Design, *(978-0-9748702)* Orders Addr.: 17640 Corkill Rd., #27, Desert Hot Springs, CA 92241 USA Tel 760-329-3233; 760-895-5646
Web site: www.akbdesign.com.
Akinleye, Titilope, *(978-0-9983312)* 3410 whispering hills Pl., Laurel, MD 20724 USA Tel 301-317-3924
E-mail: Titiakinleye@yahoo.com.
Akmaeon Publishing, LLC, *(978-0-9850410; 978-0-9988827)* 309 Pirkle Ferry Rd. Suite C200, Cumming, GA 30040 USA Tel 404-402-3793
E-mail: free3055@bellsouth.net.
AKMO Pubs., *(978-0-9745952)* P.O. Box 669, Odessa, FL 33556-9998 USA.
Akom Publishing Hse., *(978-0-9799134)* 244 Madison Ave., No. 745, New York, NY 10016 USA
E-mail: Akom2000@aol.com
Web site: http://www.akompublishinghouse.com.
Alaafia Kids Co., *(978-0-9788737)* 1020 Stonebrook Rd. Unit B, Sykesville, MD 21784-6173 USA.
Alabama Folklife Assn., *(978-0-9672672; 978-0-9772132)* Orders Addr.: c/o Alabama Center for Traditional Culture, 410 N. Hull St, Montgomery, AL 36104 USA Tel 334-242-3601; Fax: 334-269-9098
E-mail: joycecauthen@bellsouth.net
Web site: http://www.alabamafolklife.org.
Alabaster Bk. Pub., *(978-0-9725031; 978-0-9768108; 978-0-9790949; 978-0-9796866; 978-0-9815763; 978-0-9823005; 978-0-9846137; 978-0-9846320; 978-0-9840004; 978-0-9860300; 978-0-9912660; 978-0-9861790; 978-0-9982352)* Orders Addr.: P.O. Box 401, Kernersville, NC 27285 USA Tel 336-295-4322; Fax: 336-996-2011; P.O. Box 401, Kernersville, NC 27285 Fax: 336-996-2011; Edit Addr.: 324 Lakeside Dr., Kernersville, NC 27284 USA
E-mail: pblshralabaster@aol.com; ljdixie@aol.com
Web site: http://www.publisheralabaster.org; http://www.PublisherAlabaster.biz.
Alabaster Books *See* **Alabaster Bk. Pub.**
Aladdin *Imprint of* **Simon & Schuster Children's Publishing**
Aladdin Library *Imprint of* **Simon & Schuster Children's Publishing**
Aladdin Paperbacks *Imprint of* **Simon & Schuster Children's Publishing**
Aladdin/Beyond Words,
Dist(s): **Simon & Schuster, Inc.**
Alarie, Shirley, *(978-0-9968087)* 10423 Hallmark Blvd, Riverview, FL 33578 USA Tel 413-441-9769
E-mail: shirleyalarie@gmail.com
Web site: http://shirleyalarie.com/.
Alaska Avenue Pr., *(978-0-9748091)* 5770 Alaska Ave., Alto, MI 49302-9714 USA Tel 616-868-0308
E-mail: stonehillis47657@aol.com.
Alaska Geographic Assn., *(978-0-930931; 978-0-9602876; 978-0-9825765; 978-1-938494)* 241 N. C St., Anchorage, AK 99501 USA (SAN 223-5269) Tel 907-274-8440; Fax: 907-274-8343
E-mail: dwhitecar@alaskageographic.org
Web site: http://www.alaskageographic.org.
Alaska Independent Pubs., *(978-0-9743369; 978-0-9797442; 978-0-9883390)* Orders Addr.: P.O. Box 1125, Homer, AK 99603 USA Toll Free: 877-210-2665
E-mail: wizard@cosmichamlet.net
Dist(s): **Wizard Works.**
Alaska Native Language Ctr., *(978-0-933769; 978-1-55500)* Univ. of Alaska, P.O. Box 757680, Fairbanks, AK

99775-7680 USA (SAN 692-9796) Tel 907-474-7874; Fax: 907-474-6586
E-mail: fntla@uaf.edu
Web site: http://www.uaf.edu/anlc
Dist(s): **Chicago Distribution Ctr.**
Todd Communications
Wizard Works.

Alaska Natural History Association *See* **Alaska Geographic Assn.**

Alaska Northwest Bks. *Imprint of* **Graphic Arts Ctr. Publishing Co.**

Alaska Zoo, The, (*978-0-9673915*) 4731 O'Malley Rd., Anchorage, AK 99516 USA.

Alazar Pr. *Imprint of* **Royal Swan Enterprises, Inc.**

Alba House *See* **St Pauls/Alba Hse. Pubs.**

Albatros (ARG) (*978-950-24*) *Dist. by* **Lectorum Pubns.**

Albatross Pubs., (*978-0-615-45506-8; 978-1-946963*) Orders Addr.: Corso Europa 382, Villaricca Napoli , 80010 ITA Tel 406-219-4006; Edit Addr.: 54-3853 Akoni Pule Hwy, Kapaau, HI 96755 USA
E-mail: albatrosspublishers@gmail.com.

Albee, Michael, (*978-0-9745405*) 1575 W. Mable, Anaheim, CA 92802 USA Tel 714-863-2149
E-mail: malbee@fairmontschools.net.

Albers, Christine, (*978-0-615-19666-4*) 6924 Brookview Dr., Urbandale, IA 50322 USA Tel 515-270-4606
E-mail: albears5@msn.com.

Albin-Michel, Editions (FRA) (*978-2-226*) *Dist. by* **Distribks Inc.**

Album Publishing Company, Incorporated *See* **RJI Publishing**

ALCAPS, LLC, (*978-0-9769769*) 4004 Cibola Village Dr., NE, Albuquerque, NM 87111 USA
Web site: http://www.heartstohearts.net.

Alchemist's Almanac *See* **Pseudepigrapha Publishing**

Alchemy Bks., (*978-0-931290*) 1029 Solano Ave., No. E, Albany, CA 94706-1680 USA (SAN 111-3119).

Alchemy Creative, Inc., (*978-0-9675901*) 4650 Cardinal Dr., Beaumont, TX 77705 USA Tel 409-842-5240 ext 18
Web site: http://www.ecpadventures.com; http://www.adventuresoftheelements.com/.

Alchemy Ranch Books *See* **BRYN WILLIAMS LLC**

ALCJR Enterprises, (*978-0-9752760; 978-0-692-60956-9*) P.O. Box 4067, Midlothian, VA 23112-0001 USA Tel 804-677-4557; Fax: 804-744-0100
E-mail: alcjr@verizon.net
Web site: http://www.alcjr.com.

Aldelo Systems Inc., (*978-0-9765992*) 4641 Spyres Way Ste. 4, Modesto, CA 95356-9802 USA
E-mail: sales@aldelo.com
Web site: http://www.aldelo.com.

Alderac Entertainment Group, (*978-1-887953; 978-1-59472*) 4045 Guasti Rd., No. 210, Ontario, CA 91761 USA
E-mail: kcarpenter@alderac.com; dlepore@alderac.com
Web site: http://www.alderac.com
Dist(s): **PSI (Publisher Services, Inc.).**

Aldine de Gruyter *See* **Aldine Transaction**

Aldine Transaction, (*978-0-202*) Div. of Transaction Publishers, 390 Campus Dr., Somerset, NJ 08873 USA (SAN 212-4726) Fax: 732 748 9801; Toll Free: 888 999 6778; c/o Rutgers — The State University of New Jersey, 35 Berrue Cir., Piscataway, NJ 08854
E-mail: orders@transactionpub.com
Web site: http://www.transactionpub.com
Dist(s): **MyiLibrary**
Transaction Pubs.
ebrary, Inc.

Alef Design Group, (*978-1-881283*) 4423 Fruitland Ave., Los Angeles, CA 90058 USA Tel 323-582-1200; Fax: 323-585-0327; Toll Free: 800-845-0662
E-mail: jane@torahaura.com
Web site: http://www.torahaura.com
Dist(s): **Follett School Solutions.**

Alegria Hispana Pubns., (*978-0-944356*) Orders Addr.: P.O. Box 3765, Ventura, CA 93003 USA (SAN 243-4695) Tel 805-642-3969; Edit Addr.: 958 Scenic Way Dr., Ventura, CA 93003-1435 USA (SAN 243-4709).

Alethea In Heart, (*978-0-9719805; 978-1-932370*) 10183 N. Aero Dr. Ste. 2, Hayden, ID 83835-5058 USA
E-mail: truthinheart@hotmail.com
Web site: http://www.truthinheart.com.

Alex Joseph Publishing, (*978-0-9988744*) 2120 N Pass Ave, Burbank, CA 91505 USA
E-mail: leadintoink@gmail.com.

Alexander Art L.P., (*978-1-883576*) P.O. Box 1417, Beaverton, OR 97075-1417 USA Tel 503-362-7939; Fax: 503-361-7401; Toll Free: 800-896-4630
E-mail: sales@alexanderart.com
Web site: http://www.alexanderart.com.

Alexander, Lorraine *See* **Alexander, Raine**

Alexander Pubns., (*978-0-9623078*) Orders Addr.: P.O. Box 518, Forney, TX 75126 USA Tel 972-552-9519; Edit Addr.: 806 E. Buffalo St., Forney, TX 75126 USA.

Alexander, Raine, (*978-0-9816301*) 2356 Peeler Rd., Dunwoody, GA 30338 USA
E-mail: 2raine@gmail.com
Web site: www.EdoSchool.org.

Alexander-Marcus Publishing, (*978-0-9760944*) 1115 Tunnel Rd., Santa Barbara, CA 93105 USA
E-mail: andreamarcuslaw@cox.net.

Alexie Bks., (*978-0-9679416*) Div. of Alexie Enterprises, Inc., P.O. Box 3843, Carmel, IN 46082 USA Tel 317-844-5638; Fax: 317-846-0788
E-mail: BusJobs@aol.com; alexie8@aol.com; sales@alexiebooks.com
Web site: http://www.alexieenterprises.com
Dist(s): **Distributors, The.**

AlexMax Publishing Inc., (*978-0-9796643*) Orders Addr.: 4919 Flat Shoals Pkwy Suite 107B-137, Decatur, GA 30034 USA Tel 404-981-4442
E-mail: isbninfo@alexmaxpublishing.com
Web site: http://www.alexmaxpublishing.com.

ALEXZUS Bks., (*978-0-9724733*) 244 Fifth Ave., Suite B260, New York, NY 10001 USA
E-mail: jenbvic@aol.com.

Alfaguara *Imprint of* **Santillana USA Publishing Co., Inc.**

Alfaguara Juvenil *Imprint of* **Santillana USA Publishing Co., Inc.**

Alfaguara S.A. de Ediciones (ARG) (*978-950-511; 978-987-04*) *Dist. by* **Santillana.**

Alfranpedoc, (*978-1-930502*) 4100 W. Coyote Ridge Tr., Tucson, AZ 85746 USA Tel 213-926-0762
E-mail: Waylandhi@aol.com
Web site: http://www.books-by-doc.com.

Alfred Publishing Co., Inc., (*978-0-7390; 978-0-87487; 978-0-88284; 978-1-58951; 978-1-4574; 978-1-4706*) Orders Addr.: P.O. Box 10003, Van Nuys, CA 91410-0003 USA; Edit Addr.: 123 Dry Rd., Oriskany, NY 13424 USA Tel 315-736-1572; Fax: 315-736-7281; *Imprints*: Warner Bros. Publications (Warner Bro); Suzuki (Szuki)
E-mail: customerservice@alfred.com; permissions@alfred.com; submissions@alfred.com
Web site: http://www.alfred.com
Dist(s): **Follett School Solutions**
Leonard, Hal Corp.

†Algonquin Bks. of Chapel Hill, (*978-0-7611; 978-0-912697; 978-0-945575; 978-1-56512; 978-1-61620*) Div. of Workman Publishing Co., Inc., Orders Addr.: 225 Varick St. Flr. 9, New York, NY 10014-4381 USA Toll Free Fax: 800-521-1832 (fax orders, customer sevice); Toll Free: 800-722-7202 (orders, customer service); Edit Addr.: P.O. Box 2225, Chapel Hill, NC 27515-2225 USA (SAN 282-7506) Tel 919-967-0108 (editorial, publicity, marketing); Fax: 919-933-0272 (editorial, publicity, marketing)
E-mail: dialogue@algonquin.com; inquiring@algonquin.com; brunson@algonquin.com
Web site: http://www.algonquin.com; http://www.booksellerscorner.com
Dist(s): **Workman Publishing Co., Inc.**; *CIP.*

ALHsiccesslines, (*978-0-615-62527-0*) 13737 Dunbar Terr., Germantown, MD 20874 USA Tel 301-540-2928
E-mail: ALHpromo@aol.com.

Alianza Editorial, S. A. (ESP) (*978-84-206*) *Dist. by* **Continental Bk.**

Alianza Editorial, S. A. (ESP) (*978-84-206*) *Dist. by* **Lectorum Pubns.**

Alianza Editorial, S. A. (ESP) (*978-84-206*) *Dist. by* **AIMS Intl.**

Alianza Editorial, S. A. (ESP) (*978-84-206*) *Dist. by* **Distribks Inc.**

Alianza Editorial, S. A. (ESP) (*978-84-206*) *Dist. by* **Libros in Spanish, LLC.**

Alias Enterprises LLC *See* **Lamp Post Inc.**

Alien Time Treasure, (*978-0-9727309*) P.O. Box 2665, Newport, RI 02840 USA
E-mail: webmaster@alientimetreasure.com
Web site: http://alientimetreasure.com.

Aliso Street Productions, (*978-0-9840120*) P.O. Box 36422, Albuquerque, NM 87176 USA Tel 505-414-6366
E-mail: AlisoStreet@aol.com.

All About Kids Publishing, (*978-0-9700863; 978-0-9710278; 978-0-9744446; 978-0-9801468; 978-0-615-11427-9; 978-0-9963756*) Orders Addr.: P.O. Box 159, Gilroy, CA 95021 USA (SAN 253-8601) Tel 408-337-1152
E-mail: lguevara@allaboutkidspub.com
Web site: www.oliverbrightside.com; www.allaboutkidspub.com
Dist(s): **Lightning Source, Inc.**
Pathway Bk. Service.

All Around Our World Publishing Co., Inc., (*978-0-9799050*) 629 Park Ave., Beloit, WI 53511 USA Tel 608-207-9777; Fax: 608-207-9888
E-mail: brendaaaow@charter.net.

All For One Pr., (*978-0-9745951*) 29193 Northwestern Hwy, No. 658, Southfield, MI 48034 USA (SAN 255-6804) Tel 313-617-4012
E-mail: allforonepress@hotmail.com.

All Gold Publishing Co., (*978-0-9701519*) Orders Addr.: P.O. Box 13504, Dayton, OH 45413-0504 USA Tel 937-586-9804; Edit Addr.: 907 Reist, Dayton, OH 45408-1350 USA
E-mail: allgoldceo@netzero.net
Web site: http://www.allgoldpublishing.com.

All Hallows Eve Pr., (*978-0-9853082*) 20 Robert Dr., Hyde Park, NY 12538 USA Tel 914-489-9529
E-mail: ddavies@artisticwitchery.com
Web site: www.artisticwitchery.com.

All Health Chiropractic Ctrs. Inc., (*978-0-9770527*) 567 Church St., Royersford, PA 19468 USA (SAN 256-6443) Tel 610-948-4161
E-mail: susiequsie6@aol.com
Web site: http://www.drsnappy.com.

All Kidding Aside, (*978-0-9794317*) 2829 S. Cypress, Sioux City, IA 51106 USA Tel 712-276-4315
E-mail: bestma34@cableone.net
Web site: http://www.allkiddingaside.biz.

All Nations Pr., (*978-0-9725110; 978-0-9777954; 978-0-9912721*) P.O. Box 10821, Tallahassee, FL 32302 USA Do not confuse with companies with the same or similar name in Colorado Springs, CO, Southlake, TX
E-mail: rcamp427@gmail.com; allnationseditors@gmail.com
Web site: http://http:/allnationseditors.wix.com/books-seller
Dist(s): **Follett School Solutions**
Itasca Bks.

All Over Creation, (*978-0-9788950*) P.O. Box 382, Madera, CA 93639 USA
E-mail: astorybytory@yahoo.com.

All Star Pr., (*978-0-9767816; 978-1-937376*) 944 Oakview Rd., Tarpon Springs, FL 34689 USA Tel 502-713-3149
E-mail: allstarpress@verizon.net
Web site: www.allstarpress.com
Dist(s): **Smashwords.**

All That Productions, Inc., (*978-0-9679441; 978-0-9903422*) Orders Addr.: P.O. Box 1594, Humble, TX 77347 USA Tel 281-878-2062
E-mail: allthat3@peoplepc.com.

Allaf, Mashhad Al, (*978-0-9722722*) P.O. Box 2063, Chester, VA 23831-8440 USA.

Allecram Publishing, (*978-0-9764198*) P.O. Box 6003, Dayton, OH 45405 USA Tel 937-278-6630
E-mail: marcellaashe@sbcglobal.net
Web site: http://www.allecrampublishing.com.

Allegheny Pr., (*978-0-910042*) 19323 Elgin Rd., Corry, PA 16407 USA (SAN 201-2456) Tel 814-664-8504
E-mail: hjohn@tbscc.com
Dist(s): **Follett School Solutions.**

Allegiant Publishing Group, (*978-1-945737*) 171 Durham Rd., Dover, NH 03820 USA Tel 603-343-8107
E-mail: info@allegiantpublishing.com
Web site: www.allegiantpublishing.com.

Allen & Unwin (AUS) (*978-0-04; 978-0-86861; 978-1-86373; 978-1-86448; 978-1-875680; 978-0-7299; 978-1-86508; 978-1-74114; 978-1-74115; 978-1-74175; 978-1-74176; 978-1-74237; 978-1-74269; 978-1-877505; 978-0-7316-7153-3; 978-0-646-24696-3; 978-1-74331; 978-1-74343;-1-76011; 978-1-925266; 978-1-925267; 978-1-925268; 978-1-76029; 978-1-925393; 978-1-925394; 978-1-925395; 978-1-76052; 978-1-925575; 978-1-925576; 978-1-925577; 978-1-76063*) *Dist. by* **IPG Chicago.**

Allen, Edward Publishing, LLC, (*978-0-9853123; 978-0-9967663; 978-0-9983730*) 73 Terri Sue Ct., Hampton, VA 23666 USA Tel 757-768-5544
E-mail: jprice@edwardallenpublishing.com
Web site: http://www.edwardallenpublishing.com
Dist(s): **BookBaby.**

Allen, Jeffrey S. & Roger J. Klein *See* **Inner Coaching**

Allen Publishing, USA *See* **ALEXZUS Bks.**

Allen, Toi Operations, (*978-0-9753787*) 11300 E. 85th Terr., Raytown, MO 64138 USA Tel 816-737-5293; Fax: 816-923-2634
E-mail: itasca2001@aol.com.

Allen-Ayers Bks., (*978-0-9658702*) 4621 S. Atlantic Ave., No. 7603, Ponce Inlet, PA 32127 USA Tel 386-761-3956
E-mail: allen-ayers@cfl.rr.com.

AllensRusk Pr., (*978-0-9672246*) P.O. Box 100213, Nashville, TN 38134 USA Tel 615-365-0993
E-mail: allensrusk@aol.com.

Allergic Child Publishing Group, (*978-1-58628*) 6660 Delmonico Dr., Suite D249, Colorado Springs, CO 80919 USA Tel 719-338-0202; Fax: 719-633-0375
E-mail: nicole@allergicchild.com
Web site: http://www.allergicchild.com
Dist(s): **Follett School Solutions.**

Alli Kat Publishing, (*978-0-9788725*) 2353 Alexandria Dr., Suite 201, Lexington, KY 40504 USA Tel 859-264-7700; Fax: 859-264-7744
E-mail: eyemanjlh@aol.com.

Allied Publishing *See* **Flying Frog Publishing, Inc.**

Alligator Boogaloo, (*978-0-9721416*) 2531 San Jose Ave, Alameda, CA 94501 USA
E-mail: jerroldconnors@gmail.com; business@alligatorboogaloo.com
Web site: http://www.alligatorboogaloo.com.

Alligator Pr., (*978-0-9675658; 978-0-9884057; 978-0-9914334*) Orders Addr.: P.O. Box 526368, Salt Lake City, UT 84152 USA Tel 512-762-5427 Do not confuse with Alligator Press, Carson City, NV
E-mail: k.kimball333@gmail.com
Web site: http://www.alligatorpress.com
Dist(s): **BookBaby.**

Allium Pr. of Chicago, (*978-0-9840676; 978-0-9831938; 978-0-9890535; 978-0-9967558*) 1530 Elgin Ave., Forest Park, IL 60130 USA (SAN 858-3331)
Web site: http://www.alliumpress.com/
Dist(s): **Follett School Solutions**
INscribe Digital
Lightning Source, Inc.
Smashwords.

Allocca Biotechnology, LLC, (*978-0-9659987; 978-0-9769213*) 19 Lorraine Ct., Northport, NY 11768 USA Tel 631-757-3919; Fax: 631-757-3918
E-mail: john@allocca.com
Web site: http://www.allocca.com.

Allocca, Christine A., (*978-0-615-21480-1*) 3940 Laurel Canyon Blvd., No. 399, Studio City, CA 91604 USA Tel 818-486-2730
Web site: http://www.little-green-giants.com.

Allocca Technology & Healthcare Research *See* **Allocca Biotechnology, LLC**

Allosaurus Pubs., (*978-0-9620900; 978-1-888325*) Div. of North Carolina Learning Institute for Fitness & Education, Orders Addr.: P.O. Box 10245, Greensboro, NC 27404 USA (SAN 250-0906) Tel 336-292-6999
E-mail: ally@infionline.net
Web site: http://www.allosauruspublishers.com
Dist(s): **Follett School Solutions.**

Allured Business Media, (*978-0-931710; 978-1-932633*) 336 Gundersen Dr. Ste. A, Carol Stream, IL 60188-2403 USA (SAN 222-4933)
Web site: http://www.alluredbooks.com/
Dist(s): **ebrary, Inc.**

Allured Publishing Corporation *See* **Allured Business Media**

Allworth Pr. *Imprint of* **Skyhorse Publishing Co., Inc.**

AllWrite Advertising & Publishing, (*978-0-9744935; 978-0-9844931; 978-0-9887332; 978-1-941716*) Orders Addr.: 241 Pechtree St. NE Suite 400, Atlanta, GA 30303 USA Tel 770-284-8983; Fax: 770-284-8986; Edit Addr.: P.O. Box 1071, Atlanta, GA 30301 USA Tel 404-221-0703
E-mail: info@allwritepublishing.com; annette@allwritepublishing.com
Web site: http://www.allwritepublishing.com; http://www.e-allwrite.com
Dist(s): **Lightning Source, Inc.**

†Allyn & Bacon, Inc., (*978-0-205; 978-0-321*) Div. of Pearson Higher Education & Professional Group, Orders Addr.: c/o Prentice Hall/Allyn & Bacon, 200 Old Tappan Rd., Old Tappan, NJ 07675 USA Toll Free Fax: 800-445-6991; Toll Free: 800-922-0579 (customer service); 800-666-9433 (ordering); 111 Tenth St., Des Moines, IA 50309 Tel 515-284-6751; Fax: 515-284-2607; Toll Free: 800-278-3525; Edit Addr.: 75 Arlington St., Suite 300, Boston, MA 02116 USA (SAN 201-2510)
E-mail: ab_webmaster@abacon.com
Web site: http://www.abacon.com
Dist(s): **MyiLibrary**
Pearson Education
Pearson Technology Group; *CIP.*

Alma Bks. (GBR) (*978-0-9517497; 978-1-84688*) *Dist. by* **Macmillan.**

Alma Classics *Imprint of* **Bloomsbury Publishing USA**

Alma Little *Imprint of* **Elva Resa Publishing, LLC**

Alma Pr., (*978-0-9746333*) 1204 Abbot Kinney Blvd., Venice, CA 90291 USA (SAN 255-6723) Fax: 310-314-3883
E-mail: info@almapress.com
Web site: http://www.almapress.com.

Almadraba Infantil y Juvenil (ESP) (*978-84-92702*) *Dist. by* **Lectorum Pubns.**

Almanac Publishing Co., (*978-1-928720*) Mt. Hope Ave., Lewiston, ME 04240 USA Tel 207-755-2246; Fax: 207-755-2422
Web site: http://www.farmersalmanac.com
Dist(s): **Sterling Publishing Co., Inc.**

Almond Publishing, (*978-0-9777314*) P.O. Box 573, Petaluma, CA 94953 USA (SAN 850-0673)
E-mail: contact@almondpublishing.com
Web site: http://www.almondpublishing.com.

Aloha Publications *See* **catBOX Entertainment, Inc.**

Aloha Wellness Pubs., (*978-0-9727548*) 2333 Kapiolani Blvd., Suite 2108, Honolulu, HI 96826 USA (SAN 255-0539) Tel 808-941-8253; Fax: 808-925-4233; Toll Free: 866-233-6941
E-mail: crites@hawaii.rr.com
Web site: http://www.alohawellnesstravel.com
Dist(s): **Booklines Hawaii, Ltd.**

Alouette Enterprises, Inc., (*978-0-9797577; 978-0-9799922*) 7307 E. Solano Dr., Scottsdale, AZ 85250 USA
E-mail: DonnaFridrych@aol.com.

Alpen Bks, 4602 Chennault Beach Rd. Ste. B1, Mukilteo, WA 98275-5016 USA.

Alpenrose Pr., (*978-0-9603624; 978-1-889385*) Orders Addr.: P.O. Box 4245, Frisco, CO 80443 USA (SAN 222-2612) Tel 970-409-1479
E-mail: alpenrosepress@msn.com
Web site: http://www.alpenrosepress.com
Dist(s): **Alpenbooks Pr. LLC.**

Alpha *Imprint of* **Dorling Kindersley Publishing, Inc.**

Alpha & Omega Publishing, (*978-0-9767778*) 3409 Daniel Place Dr., Charlotte, NC 28213 USA Tel 704-724-1683; Fax: 270-721-6019 Do not confuse iwth companies with the same name in Fremont, NE, Springfield, OR
E-mail: alphaomega@carolina.rr.com.

Alpha Behavior Consultants, (*978-0-9758755*) 12740 NW 11th St., Miami, FL 33172 USA
E-mail: info@alphbehc.com
Web site: http://www.alphabehc.com.

Alpha Bible Pubns., (*978-1-877917*) P.O. Box 155, Hood River, OR 97031 USA; P.O. Box 157, Morton, WA 98356 Tel 541-386-6634
Dist(s): **Pentecostal Publishing Hse.**
eBookit.com.

Alpha Connections, (*978-0-9715779; 978-0-9747610; 978-1-936933*) 530 W. Idaho Blvd., Emmett, ID 83617 USA
E-mail: contact@dragonsfuryseries.com
Web site: http://www.dragonsfuryseries.com
Dist(s): **Lightning Source, Inc.**
Smashwords.

Alpha Heartland Press *See* **Heartland Foundation, Inc.**

Alpha Learning World, Inc., (*978-0-9791680*) 1064 Mohegan Rd., Venice, FL 34293 USA (SAN 852-6362)
E-mail: trisley1@verizon.net
Web site: http://alphalearningworld.com.

Alpha Omega Pubns., Inc., (*978-0-7403; 978-0-86717; 978-1-58095*) 300 N. McKemy Ave., Chandler, AZ 85226-2618 USA Tel 602-438-2717; Fax: 480-785-8034; Toll Free: 800-682-7391; 804 N. 2nd Ave. E., Rock Rapids, IA 51246 (SAN 853-2826) Tel 800-622-3070; Fax: 712-472-4856; *Imprints*: Lifepac (Lifepac); Horizons (Hrnzns AZ); Weaver (Weaver)
E-mail: cpatterson@aop.com
Web site: http://www.aop.com
Dist(s): **Follett School Solutions**
Send The Light Distribution LLC
Spring Arbor Distributors, Inc.

Alpha OmeGa Publishing, (*978-0-9658073*) 1217 Cape Coral Pkwy., Cape Coral, FL 33904 USA Tel 941-542-3666; Fax: 941-945-7963; Toll Free: 800-542-3666; 4219 SE First Ct., Cape Coral, FL 33904
E-mail: GPMueller@aol.com
Web site: http://www.Floridawest.com/Liestorm.

Alpha Run Pr., LLC, (*978-0-9761182; 978-1-933289*) Orders Addr.: P.O. Box 15079, Silver Spring, MD 20914-5079 USA Tel 202-508-3392; Edit Addr.: 1717 K St. NW, Suite 600, Washington, DC 20036 USA
E-mail: alpharp@aol.com
Web site: http://www.alpharunpress.com.

Alpha Shade, Inc., (*978-0-9768705*) 11850 85th Pl., N., Maple Grove, MN 55369 USA Tel 763-424-9316
E-mail: alphashade1@aol.com
Web site: http://www.alpha-shade.com.

Alpha Writers Ltd., (*978-0-9772018*) Orders Addr.: P.O. Box 561262, The Colony, TX 75056 USA (SAN 256-9256) Fax: 425-955-0859; Toll Free: 866-751-4340 Outside of Dallas
E-mail: source@alphawritersltd.com
Web site: http://www.alphawritersltd.com.

Alpha-kidZ, (*978-0-9749220; 978-0-9823534*) P.O. Box 1552, West Monroe, LA 71294-1552 USA Tel 318-651-0833; Fax: 318-396-4073
Web site: http://www.alphakidz.com.

AlphaLove Publishing, (*978-0-9764307*) P.O. Box 248, South Orange, NJ 07079 USA Fax: 973-275-3973.

For full information on wholesalers and distributors, refer to the Wholesaler and Distributor Name Index

Alpine Archaeological Consultants, Inc., *(978-0-9743137)* P.O. Box 2075, Montrose, CO 81402-2075 USA Tel 970-249-6761; Fax: 970-249-8482
E-mail: susan_chandler@alpinearchaeology.com
Web site: http://www.alpinearchaeology.com.

†Alpine Pubns., Inc., *(978-0-931866; 978-1-57779)* Orders Addr.: 38262 Linman Rd., Crawford, CO 81415 USA (SAN 255-2094) Tel 970-921-5005; Fax: 970-921-5081; Toll Free: 800-777-7257
E-mail: customerservice@alpinepub.com; alpine@paonia.com; alpinepubl@aol.com
Web site: http://www.alpinepub.com
Dist(s): **Follett School Solutions**
Partners/West Book Distributors; *CIP.*

Alpine River Pr., *(978-0-9891471)* 660 Haley LN, Red Bluff, CA 96080 USA Tel 530-200-2745
E-mail: alpineriverpress@gmail.com.

Alta Omnimedia, *(978-0-9726360)* 2 Valley View Ave., Ste. 116, San Jose, CA 95127 USA
Web site: http://www.altaomnimedia.com.

Alta Publishing LLC, *(978-0-9767120)* P.O. Box 108, Bellvue, CO 80512 USA (SAN 256-4874) Do not confuse with companies with the same name in Sandy, UT, Midvale, UT.

Alta Retreat Ctr., *(978-0-9746151)* 20 Alta School Rd., Alta, WY 83414 USA Tel 307-353-8200; Fax: 208-354-4002
E-mail: altacp@ida.net.

Altea, Ediciones, S.A. - Grupo Santillana (ESP) *(978-84-372) Dist. by* **Lectorum Pubns.**

Altea, Ediciones, S.A. - Grupo Santillana (ESP) *(978-84-372) Dist. by* **Santillana.**

Altea, Ediciones, S.A. - Grupo Santillana (ESP) *(978-84-372) Dist. by* **TwoRivers.**

Alterna Comics, *(978-0-9797874; 978-1-934985; 978-1-945762)* Div. of Alterna Comics, Inc., Orders Addr.: 23 Trumpet Ln., Levittown, NY 11756 USA Tel 516-304-6733; Fax: 516-644-2386
E-mail: publisher@alternacomics.com
Web site: http://www.alternacomics.com
Dist(s): **Diamond Comic Distributors, Inc.**
Independent Pubs. Group
MyiLibrary.

Alternative Comics, *(978-1-891867; 978-1-934460; 978-1-68148)* 21607B Stevens Creek Blvd., Cupertino, CA 95014 USA Do not confuse with companies with the same or similar name in Goleta, GA, Billerica, MA
E-mail: marc@wowcool.com
Web site: http://www.indyworld.com
Dist(s): **Consortium Bk. Sales & Distribution**
Diamond Comic Distributors, Inc.
Diamond Bk. Distributors
Last Gasp of San Francisco.

Alternative Press, Incorporated *See* **Alternative Comics**

AlterNet Bks., *(978-0-9633687; 978-0-9752724)* 77 Federal St., 2nd Flr., San Francisco, CA 94107 USA Tel 415-284-1420; Fax: 415-284-1414
E-mail: valrie@alternet.org
Web site: http://www.alternet.org.

Althos *See* **DiscoverNet**

A-Lu Publishing, *(978-0-9817092)* 4257 Holiday Rd., Traverse City, MI 49686 USA
Dist(s): **BookBaby.**

Alvarado, Rudolph *See* **Caballo Pr. of Ann Arbor**

ALVARADOPLUS, *(978-0-9791782)* 315 Luna St., Apt 1B, San Juan, PR 00901-1488 USA (SAN 852-6710)
E-mail: ALVARADOPlus@aol.com.

Alvarez, Jesus, *(978-0-9792507)* 254 San Diego Ave., Brownsville, TX 78526 USA Tel 956-542-2722
E-mail: alvarcorp@msn.com.

A.M. Green Publishing, *(978-1-935479)* P.O. Box 1085, Amston, CT 06231 USA Tel 617-391-7350
E-mail: JSmith@amgreenpublishing.com
Web site: http://www.amgreenpublishing.com.

AM Ink Publishing, *(978-0-9845801; 978-0-9852146; 978-0-9884468; 978-0-9910330; 978-1-943201)* 76 Pheasant Dr., Springfield, MA 01119-0111 USA (SAN 859-8142) Tel 413-222-1143
E-mail: Mike@AuthorMike.com
Web site: http://www.AMInkPublishing.com; http://darkinkbooks.com/Dark_Ink/Welcome.html.

Ama Deus Energy Pr., *(978-0-9962780; 978-0-9987414)* 1065 Alden Nash, Lowell, MI 49331 USA Tel 616-340-7892
E-mail: bcomos@sbcglobal.net
Web site: www.ama-deus-international.com.

AMA Verlag GmbH (DEU) *(978-3-89922; 978-3-927190; 978-3-932587) Dist. by* **Mel Bay.**

†Amacom, *(978-0-7612; 978-0-8144)* Div. of American Management Association, Orders Addr.: 600 AMA Way, Saranac Lake, NY 12983 USA (SAN 227-3578) Tel 518-891-5510; Fax: 518-891-2372; Toll Free: 800-250-5308 (orders & customer service); Edit Addr.: 1601 Broadway, New York, NY 10019-7420 USA (SAN 201-1670) Tel 212-586-8100; Fax: 212-903-8168; 1 Ingram Blvd., La Vergne, TN 37086
E-mail: pubservice@amanet.org
Web site: http://www.amacombooks.org
Dist(s): **Ebsco Publishing**
Follett School Solutions
MyiLibrary
Productivity Pr.
Wybel Marketing Group
ebrary, Inc.; *CIP.*

Amadeus Press *Imprint of* **Leonard, Hal Corp.**

Amalgamated Widgets Unlimited, *(978-0-615-54280-5; 978-0-692-74884-8; 978-0-692-76379-7)* 2995 Woodside Rd., Suite 400-166, Woodside, CA 94062 USA Tel 650-780-9288; 425-298-6552
E-mail: ng@awun.net
Web site: dandelorn.com
Dist(s): **CreateSpace Independent Publishing Platform**
Dummy Record Do Not USE!!!!.

amana pubns., *(978-0-915957; 978-1-59008)* Div. of amana corp., 10710 Tucker St., Beltsville, MD 20705-2223 USA (SAN 630-9798) Tel 301-595-5999; Fax: 301-595-5888; Toll Free: 800-660-1777
E-mail: amana@igprinting.com
Web site: http://www.amana-publications.com.

Amani Publishing, LLC, *(978-0-9752851; 978-0-9788937; 978-0-9815847; 978-0-9833666)* P.O. Box 12045, Tallahassee, FL 32317 USA Tel 850-264-3341 Do not confuse with Amani Publishing in Pineville, LA
E-mail: amanipublishing@aol.com
Web site: http://www.barbarajoewilliams.com
Dist(s): **Lightning Source, Inc.**

Amaquemecan, Editorial (MEX) *(978-968-7205) Dist. by* **Continental Bk.**

Amaquemecan, Editorial (MEX) *(978-968-7205) Dist. by* **AIMS Intl.**

AMARA Entertainment, *(978-0-9760745)* 1024 Frans Rd., Westfield, NC 27053 USA Tel 336-351-3437 (phone/fax)
E-mail: rpitt@charlesthechef.com
Web site: http://www.charlesthechef.com.

Amato, G. J., *(978-0-615-38545-7; 978-0-9829962; 978-0-9894561)* 5 Westview Ct., Avon, CT 06001-4540 USA Tel 860-675-6712
E-mail: gaetanoja@aol.com
Web site: getkidsmovingnow.com.

AmazeBk. Pr., *(978-0-9986360)* 5729 SE 50th Ave, Portland, OR 97206 USA Tel 503-961-2656
E-mail: clubchris@gmail.com.

Amazement Square, *(978-0-9815308)* 27 Ninth St., Lynchburg, VA 24504 USA
Web site: http://www.amazementsquare.org.

Amazing Drama Anointed Voices Original Music, *(978-0-9725827)* 1256 Cranwood Square N., Columbus, OH 43229-1341 USA Tel 614-431-5311
E-mail: kfd43229@aol.com
Web site: http://www.keys.decisivenet.com.

Amazing Dreams Publishing, *(978-0-9719628)* P.O. Box 1811, Asheville, NC 28802 USA
E-mail: contact@amazingdreamspublishing.com
Web site: http://www.amazingdreamspublishing.com
Dist(s): **ASP Wholesale**
CreateSpace Independent Publishing Platform.

Amazing Factory, The, *(978-0-9776282; 978-0-9788469; 978-0-9790302)* 5527 San Gabriel Way, Orlando, FL 32837 USA
E-mail: theamazingfactory@hotmail.com
Web site: http://www.theamazingfactory.com.

Amazing Herbs Pr., *(978-0-9742962)* 545 8th Ave., Suite 401, New York, NY 10018 USA Tel 770-982-0107; Fax: 770-982-0273; Toll Free: 800-241-9138 (orders)
E-mail: tnc100@bellsouth.net
Web site: http://www.amazingherbspress.com.

AMazing Pubns., *(978-0-9763434)* 337 W. Napa St., Sonoma, CA 95476 USA.

Amazing Publishing Company, A *See* **Rhymeglow LLC**

Amazon Children's Publishing *Imprint of* **Amazon Publishing**

Amazon Publishing, *(978-0-8034; 978-1-61109; 978-1-4778; 978-1-5039; 978-1-5420)* 2021 7th Ave., Seattle, WA 98121 USA; *Imprints:* Amazon Children's Publishing (AmazonChldns); Thomas & Mercer (Thomas&MercerA); Montlake Romance (Montlake); 47North (FortySevN); Jet City Comics (JetCityComics); Two Lions (TwoLions); Skyscape (Skyscape)
E-mail: apub-metadata@amazon.com; Customerservice@brilliancepublishing.com
Web site: http://www.amazon.com/amazoncrossing; http://www.apub.com/; http://www.amazon.com/amazonpublishing
Dist(s): **Brilliance Publishing, Inc.**
CreateSpace Independent Publishing Platform
MyiLibrary.

AmazonCrossing *See* **Amazon Publishing**

Ambassador Bks. *Imprint of* **Paulist Pr.**

Ambassador Bks., Inc., *(978-0-9646439; 978-1-929039)* 446 Main St. Ste. 19, Worcester, MA 01608-2368 USA Toll Free: 800-577-0909
E-mail: info@ambassadorbooks.com
Web site: http://www.ambassadorbooks.com
Dist(s): **Christian Bk. Distributors**
Spring Arbor Distributors, Inc.

Ambassador International *Imprint of* **Emerald Hse. Group, Inc.**

Ambassador Pubns., *(978-1-58572)* 3110 E. Medicine Lake Blvd., Plymouth, MN 55441 USA Tel 763-545-5631; Fax: 763-545-0079
E-mail: parished@aflc.org
Web site: http://www.aflc.org.

Ambassador-Emerald, International *Imprint of* **Emerald Hse. Group, Inc.**

Amber Bks., *(978-0-9655064; 978-0-9702224; 978-0-9727519; 978-0-9749779; 978-0-9767735; 978-0-9790976; 978-0-9824922; 978-1-937269)* Div. of Amber Communications Group, Inc., Orders Addr.: 1334 E. Chandler Blvd., Suite 5-D67, Phoenix, AZ 85048 USA Tel 602-743-7211; 602-743-7426; Fax: 480-283-0991; *Imprints:* Colossus Books (Colossus)
E-mail: amberbks@aol.com
Web site: http://www.amberbooks.com
Dist(s): **A & B Distributors & Pubs. Group**
African World Bks.
Book Wholesalers, Inc.
Brodart Co.
D & J Bk. Distributors
Follett School Solutions
Independent Pubs. Group
Midwest Library Service
Quality Bks., Inc.
Unique Bks., Inc.

Amber Lotus *See* **Amber Lotus Publishing**

Amber Lotus Publishing, *(978-0-945798; 978-1-56937; 978-1-885394; 978-1-60237; 978-1-63136)* P.O. Box 11329, Portland, OR 97211-0329 USA Toll Free: 800-326-2375
E-mail: info@amberlotus.com
Web site: http://www.amberlotus.com
Dist(s): **Banyan Tree Bks.**
Follett School Solutions.

Amber Marie Publishing, *(978-0-9771981)* 10413 Coffee Grinder Ct., Las Vegas, NV 89129 USA (SAN 256-9744) Tel 702-238-3846.

Amber Skye Publishing LLC, *(978-0-9819860; 978-0-9831839; 978-0-9894003; 978-0-692-47081-7; 978-0-9977266)* 1935 Berkshire Dr., Eagan, MN 55122 USA
E-mail: publisher@amberskyepublishing.com
Web site: http://www.amberskyepublishing.com; www.itascabooks.com
Dist(s): **CreateSpace Independent Publishing Platform**
Itasca Bks.

Amber Trust, The *See* **Aenor Trust, The**

Amber Woods Publishing, *(978-0-9743717)* P.O. Box 280, Excelsior, MN 55331 USA Tel 952-476-1670
Web site: http://www.amberwoodspublishing.com.

Amberjack Publishing Co., *(978-0-692-30068-8; 978-0-692-30154-8; 978-0-692-33339-6; 978-0-692-33341-9; 978-0-692-39045-0; 978-0-692-40203-0; 978-0-692-42948-8; 978-0-692-42951-8; 978-0-692-44642-3; 978-0-692-44646-1; 978-0-692-46743-5; 978-0-692-48712-9; 978-0-692-50148-1; 978-0-692-51719-2; 978-0-692-51720-8; 978-0-692-53639-1; 978-0-692-53640-7; 978-0-692-58289-3; 978-0-692-58297-8; 978-0-692-58721-8; 978-0-9972377; 978-1-944995)* P.O. Box PO Box 4668 #89611, New York, NY 10163 USA; *Imprints:* Little Adventures (Little Advent)
Dist(s): **Midpoint Trade Bks., Inc.**

Amberley Publishing (GBR) *(978-1-84868; 978-1-4456) Dist. by* **IPG Chicago.**

Amberock Pubns., *(978-0-9754636)* P.O. Box 491, Dallas, NC 28034 USA
Web site: http://www.meandmybassguitar.com.

Amberwaves, *(978-0-9708913)* P.O. Box 487, Becket, MA 01223 USA (SAN 256-4254) Tel 413-623-0012; 413-623-6042 (phone/fax); 305 Brooker Hill Rd., Becket, MA 01223 Tel 413-623-0012; Fax: 413-623-6042
E-mail: shenwa@bcn.net
Web site: http://www.amberwaves.org.

Amberwood Pr., *(978-0-9630243; 978-0-9776445; 978-0-615-95885-9)* 509 Albany Post Rd., New Paltz, NY 12561-3629 USA Do not confuse with Amberwood Pr., in Ventura, CA
E-mail: nava@vegkitchen.com
Web site: http://www.vegkitchen.com
Dist(s): **CreateSpace Independent Publishing Platform**
Independent Pubs. Group.

Ambrosia Press LLC, *(978-0-9729346; 978-0-9778656; 978-0-9525344; 978-0-9862590)* 2 Waban Rd., Timberlake, OH 44095 USA Tel 440-951-7780; Fax: 440-951-0565
E-mail: willowhse@yahoo.com; ambrosia03@att.net
Web site: http://www.ruthfawcettbooks.com.

Ameeramac Bks. *Imprint of* **Ameeramac Bks. Inc.**

Ameeramac Bks. Inc., *(978-0-9762911)* Div. of Ameeramac Reporting, Inc., 168 Putnam Ave., Brooklyn, NY 11216-1606 USA Tel 917-353-1644; Fax: 718-636-8210; *Imprints:* Ameeramac Books (AmeeraBks)
E-mail: ameeramac@optonline.com.

Ameeramac Reporting, Incorporated *See* **Ameeramac Bks. Inc.**

Amelia Street Press *See* **Prytania Pr.**

Amereon Ltd., *(978-0-8488; 978-0-88411; 978-0-89190; 978-1-59683)* Orders Addr.: P.O. Box 1200, Mattituck, NY 11952 USA (SAN 201-2413) Tel 631-298-5100; Fax: 631-298-5631; *Imprints:* Rivercity Press (Rivercity Pr); American Reprint Company (Am Repr)
E-mail: info@amereon.net
Dist(s): **Follett School Solutions**
Ingram Publisher Services.

America Hispanic Consulting Group Inc., *(978-0-9978819)* P.O. Box 1709, Fresno, CA 93717 USA Tel 559-392-3710
E-mail: susan@cottoncandybooks.com
Web site: www.cottoncandybooks.com.

America Sports Publishing, *(978-0-9721199)* Orders Addr.: P.O. Box 132, Brookfield, OH 44403 USA Tel 330-448-0866; Toll Free: 866-255-2267; Edit Addr.: 6881 Stewart Rd., Brookfield, OH 44403 USA Fax: 330-448-0936
E-mail: Info@AthleticScholarshipBook.com
Web site: http://www.AthleticScholarshipBook.com
Dist(s): **Cardinal Pubs. Group**
Quality Bks., Inc.
Unique Bks., Inc.

America Star Bks., *(978-1-61102; 978-1-63249; 978-1-63382; 978-1-63448; 978-1-68090; 978-1-68122; 978-1-68176; 978-1-68229; 978-1-63508; 978-1-68290; 978-1-68394)* 550 Highland St. Ste 105, Frederick, MD 21701 USA Tel 301-228-2595; Fax: 301-228-2596; P.O. Box 151, Frederick, MD 21705
Web site: www.americastarbooks.pub
Dist(s): **Independent Pubs. Group.**

American Animal Hospital Assn. Pr., *(978-0-941451; 978-0-9616498; 978-1-58326)* Orders Addr.: 12575 W. Bayaud Ave., Lakewood, CO 80228 USA (SAN 224-4799) Tel 303-986-2800; Fax: 303-986-1700; Toll Free: 800-252-2242
E-mail: msc@aahanet.org
Web site: http://press.aahanet.org
Dist(s): **Matthews Medical Bk. Co.**

American Antiquarian Society, *(978-0-912296; 978-0-944026; 978-1-929545)* 185 Salisbury St., Worcester, MA 01609 USA (SAN 206-474X) Tel 508-752-5221; Fax: 508-754-9069
E-mail: library@mwa.org
Web site: http://www.americanantiquarian.org
Dist(s): **Oak Knoll Pr.**

American Assn. of Veterinary Parasitologists, *(978-0-9770942)* 3915 S. 48th St. Terr., Saint Joseph, MO 64503 USA
Web site: http://www.aavp.org.

American Atheist Pr., *(978-0-910309; 978-0-911826; 978-1-57884; 978-0-9981819)* Subs. of Charles E. Stevens, P.O. Box 5733, Parsippany, NJ 07054-6733 USA (SAN 206-7188) Tel 908-276-7300; Fax: 908-276-7402
E-mail: editor@atheists.org; info@atheists.org
Web site: http://www.atheists.org.

American Bar Assn., *(978-0-89707; 978-1-57073; 978-1-59031; 978-1-60442; 978-1-61632; 978-0-615-36849-8; 978-0-615-36850-4; 978-1-61438; 978-1-62722; 978-1-63425)* 321 N Clark St, 20th FL, Chicago, IL 60654 USA (SAN 211-4798) Tel 312-988-6011 Toll Free: 800-285-2221
E-mail: natalie.cirar@americanbar.org
Web site: http://www.americanbar.org
Dist(s): **MyiLibrary**
National Bk. Network.

American Bible Society, *(978-0-8267; 978-1-58516; 978-1-937628; 978-1-941448; 978-1-941449)* Orders Addr.: 6201 E. 43rd St., Tulsa, OK 74135-6562 USA (SAN 662-7129) Toll Free Fax: 866-570-2877; Edit Addr.: 1865 Broadway, New York, NY 10023-9980 USA (SAN 203-5189) Tel 212-408-1200; Fax: 212-408-1305; 700 Plaza Dr., 2nd Flr., Secaucus, NJ 07094
E-mail: info@americanbible.org
Web site: http://www.bibles.org; http://www.americanbible.org
Dist(s): **Anchor Distributors.**

American Bk. Co., *(978-1-932410; 978-1-59807; 978-1-62800; 978-1-64117)* 103 Executive Dr., Woodstock, GA 30188 USA Tel 770-928-2834 Toll Free: 888-254-5877 Do not confuse with companies with the same name in Chesterfield, VA, Knoxville, TN, Florence, AL
E-mail: dpintozzi@americanbookcompany.com
Web site: http://www.americanbookcompany.com.

American Book Publishing *See* **American Bk. Publishing Group**

American Bk. Publishing Group, *(978-1-930586; 978-1-58982; 978-0-615-54716-9)* P.O. Box 65624, Salt Lake City, UT 84165 USA (SAN 254-4725) Fax: 801-382-0881; Toll Free: 888-288-7413; *Imprints:* Bedside Books (Bedside Bks); Millennial Mind Publishing (Millennial Mind)
E-mail: orders@american-book.com; info@american-book.com; operations@american-book.com
Web site: http://www.american-book.com
Dist(s): **Seven Locks Pr.**

American Bookworks Corp., *(978-0-9622813; 978-1-884965)* 309 Florida Hill Rd., Ridgefield, CT 06877 USA Tel 203-438-0345; Fax: 203-438-0379
E-mail: info@abwcorporation.com
Web site: http://www.abwcorporation.com.

†American Camping Assn., *(978-0-87603)* 5000 State Rd. 67, N., Martinsville, IN 46151-7902 USA (SAN 201-2596) Tel 765-342-8456 (General Info.); Fax: 765-349-6357 (orders); Toll Free: 800-428-2267 (orders)
E-mail: bookstore@aca-camps.org
Web site: http://www.acacamps.org
Dist(s): **Independent Pubs. Group**; *CIP.*

American Cancer Society, Inc., *(978-0-944235; 978-1-60443)* 250 Williams St., Atlanta, GA 30303-1002 USA (SAN 227-6941) Tel 404-320-3333; Fax: 404-325-9341; Toll Free: 800-ACS-2345
Web site: http://www.cancer.org
Dist(s): **Independent Pubs. Group**
McGraw-Hill Cos., The
McGraw-Hill Professional Publishing
MyiLibrary
Wiley-Blackwell.

American Carriage Hse. Publishing, *(978-0-9705734; 978-1-935176)* P.O. Box 1778, Penn Valley, CA 95946 USA Tel 530-432-8860; Fax: 530-265-9650 Do not confuse with Carraige House Publishing in Middleton, CA
E-mail: info@americancarriagehousepublishing.com; editor@americancarriagehousepublishing.com; research@americancarriagehousepublishing.com; assistant@americancarriagehousepublishing.com
Web site: http://www.americancarriagehousepublishing.com
Dist(s): **Send The Light Distribution LLC**
Smashwords.

†American Chemical Society, *(978-0-8412)* 1155 16th St., NW, Washington, DC 20036 USA (SAN 201-2626) Tel 202-872-4600; Toll Free: 800-227-5558; 2001 Evans Rd., Cary, NC 27513
E-mail: service@acs.org; help@acs.org
Web site: http://www.acs.org; http://www.ChemCenter.org
Dist(s): **Follett School Solutions**
Oxford Univ. Pr., Inc.; *CIP.*

American Classical League, The, *(978-0-939507)* Orders Addr.: 860 NW Washington Blvd. Suite A, Hamilton, OH 45013 USA (SAN 225-8358) Tel 513-529-7741; Fax: 513-529-7742
E-mail: info@aclclassics.org
Web site: http://www.aclclassics.org.

American Correctional Assn., *(978-0-929310; 978-0-942974; 978-1-56991)* 206 N. Washington St. Ste. 200, Alexandria, VA 22314-2528 USA (SAN 204-8051) Toll Free: 800-222-5646 (ext. 1860)
Web site: http://www.aca.org.

American Dental Assn., *(978-0-910074; 978-1-932305; 978-1-60122; 978-1-935201; 978-0-9860279; 978-1-941807; 978-1-68447)* 211 E. Chicago Ave.,

Publisher Name Index

Chicago, IL 60611 USA (SAN 202-4519) Tel 312-440-2568; 312-440-2500; Fax: 312-440-7461
E-mail: survey@ada.org
Web site: http://www.ada.org.

American Diabetes Assn., *(978-0-945448; 978-1-58040)* Orders Addr.: 1701 N. Beauregard St., Alexandria, VA 22311 USA Toll Free Fax: 800-998-3103 (orders); Toll Free: 800-323-4900 (orders)
E-mail: lboswell@diabetes.org
Web site: http://www.diabetes.org
Dist(s): **McGraw-Hill Cos., The**
McGraw-Hill Professional Publishing
McGraw-Hill Trade
MyiLibrary
Publishers Group West (PGW).

American Dog *Imprint of* **Ideate Prairie**

American Driving Society, *(978-0-9727292)* P.O. Box 278, Cross Plains, WI 53528-0278 USA Do not confuse with American Driving Society in Lakeville, CT
E-mail: ann@americandrivingsociety.org
Web site: http://www.americandrivingsociety.org.

American Fisheries Society, *(978-0-913235; 978-1-888569; 978-1-934874)* 5410 Grosvenor Ln., Suite 110, Bethesda, MD 20814-2199 USA (SAN 284-964X) Tel 301-897-8616; Fax: 301-897-5080
E-mail: main@fisheries.org; afspubs@pbd.com
Web site: http://www.fisheries.org
Dist(s): **PBD, Inc.**

American French Genealogical Society, *(978-1-929920; 978-1-932749; 978-1-60305)* Orders Addr.: P.O. Box 830, Woonsocket, RI 02895 USA; Edit Addr.: 78 Earle St., Woonsocket, RI 02895 USA
E-mail: RDBeaudry@afgs.org
Web site: http://www.afgs.org.

American Girl *Imprint of* **American Girl Publishing, Inc.**

†**American Girl Publishing, Inc.,** *(978-0-937295; 978-1-56247; 978-1-58485; 978-1-59369; 978-1-60958; 978-1-68337)* Subs. of Mattel, Inc., Orders Addr.: P.O. Box 620991, Middleton, WI 53562-0991 USA Tel 608-836-4848; Toll Free Fax: 800-257-3865; Toll Free: 800-233-0264; Edit Addr.: 8400 Fairway Pl., Middleton, WI 53562 USA (SAN 298-6337) Tel 608-836-4848; Fax: 608-831-7089; *Imprints:* American Girl (Amer Girl); Pleasant Company (Pleasnt Co)
Web site: http://www.americangirlpublishing.com
Dist(s): **Follett School Solutions;** *CIP.*

American Gramaphone LLC *See* **Mannheim Steamroller L.L.C.**

American Ground Water Trust, *(978-0-9641186)* Orders Addr.: 16 Centre St., Concord, NH 03301 USA Tel 603-228-5444; Fax: 603-228-6557
E-mail: trustinfo@agwt.org
Web site: http://www.agwt.org.

American Health Publishing, *(978-0-9754443)* Orders Addr.: P.O. Box 282, Clarence, NY 14031 USA Tel 716-741-0177 Do not confuse with Americanhealth Publishing Company in Dallas, TX
E-mail: americahealthpub@aol.com
Web site: http://www.growingahealthyfamily.com.

American Heritage Publishing, *(978-0-9754859; 978-0-578-12953-2)* 5710 Mt. Repose Ln., NW, Norcross, GA 30092-1428 USA Tel 404-495-3720 (phone/fax)
E-mail: trjc@mindspring.com
Web site: http://www.privilegesofwar.com
Dist(s): **BookBaby.**

American Historical Pr., *(978-0-9654754; 978-1-892724)* 10755 Sherman Way, Suite 2, Sun Valley, CA 91352 USA Tel 818-503-0133; Fax: 818-503-9081; Toll Free: 800-550-5750
E-mail: ahp@amhistpress.com
Web site: http://www.amhistpress.com/
Dist(s): **Chicago Distribution Ctr.**

American Home-School Publishing, LLC, *(978-0-9667067; 978-0-9779000)* Orders Addr.: 6102 SE. State Rte. C, Cameron, MO 64429 USA (SAN 254-7244) Tel 816-632-1503; Fax: 816-632-1448; Toll Free Fax: 800-557-0234; Toll Free: 800-684-2121
E-mail: booklovers@ahsp.com
Web site: http://www.ahsp.com.

American Humanist Assn., *(978-0-931779)* 1777 T St., NW, Washington, DC 20009-7125 USA (SAN 266-9412) Tel 202-238-9088; Fax: 202-238-9047; Toll Free: 800-837-3792; *Imprints:* Humanist Press (Humanist Press)
E-mail: bmagee@americanhumanist.org; jmelchior@americanhumanist.org; jxiao@americanhumanist.org
Web site: http://www.thehumanist.org; http://www.americanhumanist.org; http://humanistpress.com
Dist(s): **Lightning Source, Inc.**

American Institute For CPCU, *(978-0-89462; 978-0-89463)* 720 Providence Rd., Malvern, PA 19355 USA (SAN 210-1629) Tel 610-644-2100; Fax: 610-640-9576; Toll Free: 800-644-2101
E-mail: cserv@cpcuiia.org
Web site: http://www.aicpcu.org.

American Institute for Property & Liability Underwriters, Incorporated *See* **American Institute For CPCU**

American International Distribution Corp., Orders Addr.: P.O. Box 574, Williston, VT 05495-0020 USA Tel 800-390-3149; Fax: 802-864-7626; Toll Free: 888-822-9942; Edit Addr.: 50 Winter Sport Ln., Williston, VT 05495 USA (SAN 630-2238) Toll Free: 800-488-2665
E-mail: jmacon@aidcvt.com
Web site: http://www.aidcvt.com/Specialty/Home.asp.

American International Printing & Marketing *See* **Graphix Network**

American LaserTechnic, *(978-0-9741805)* 1300 NE Miami Gardens Dr. Apt. 407, Miami, FL 33179-4731 USA
E-mail: dan-gregory@attbi.com
Web site: http://www.americanlasertechnic.com.

American Law Institute, *(978-0-8318)* 4025 Chestnut St., Philadelphia, PA 19104-3099 USA (SAN 204-756X) Tel 215-243-1656 Director of Books; 215-245-1654 (Library); 215-243-1700 (Customer Service); Fax: 215-243-0319; Toll Free: 800-253-6397
E-mail: mcarroll@ali-cle.org; namster@ali.org
Web site: http://www.ali-cle.org; http://www.ali.org.

†**American Library Assn.,** *(978-0-8389; 978-1-937589)* 50 E. Huron St., Chicago, IL 60611 USA (SAN 201-0062) Tel 312-280-2425; 312-944-8085; Fax: 770-280-4155 (Orders); Toll Free: 800-545-2433; 866-746-7252 (Orders); P.O. Box 932501, Atlanta, GA 31193-2501; *Imprints:* Huron Street Press (HuronStPr)
E-mail: EditionsMarketing@ala.org
Web site: http://www.ala.org; http://www.alastore.ala.org
Dist(s): **Ebsco Publishing**
Follett School Solutions
Independent Pubs. Group
MyiLibrary
ebrary, Inc.; *CIP.*

American Literary Pr., *(978-1-56167; 978-1-934696)* Orders Addr.: 8019 Belair Rd., Suite 10, Baltimore, MD 21236 USA Tel 410-882-7700; Fax: 410-882-7703; Toll Free: 800-873-2003; *Imprints:* Shooting Star Edition (SSE)
E-mail: americanliterarypress@comcast.net
Web site: http://www.my-new-publisher.com
Dist(s): **MyiLibrary.**

American Literary Publishing *Imprint of* **LifeReloaded Specialty Publishing LLC**

American Map Corp., *(978-0-8416)* Div. of Langenscheidt Pubs., Inc., P.O. Box 780010, Maspeth, NY 11378-0010 USA (SAN 202-4624) Toll Free: 800-432-6277
E-mail: customerservice@americanmap.com
Web site: http://www.americanmap.com
Dist(s): **Fujii Assocs.**
Langenscheidt Publishing Group.

†**American Mathematical Society,** *(978-0-8218; 978-0-8284; 978-1-4704)* Orders Addr.: 201 Charles St., Providence, RI 02904 USA (SAN 250-3263) Tel 401-455-4000; Fax: 401-331-3842; Toll Free: 800-321-4267; *Imprints:* Chelsea Publishing Company, Incorporated (Chelsea Pub Co)
E-mail: las@ams.org
Web site: http://www.ams.org
Dist(s): **Ebsco Publishing**
ProQuest LLC; *CIP.*

American Meteorological Society, *(978-0-933876; 978-1-878220; 978-1-935704; 978-1-940033; 978-1-944970)* 45 Beacon St, Boston, MA 02108-3693 USA (SAN 225-2139) Tel 617-227-2425; Fax: 617-742-8718
Web site: http://www.ametsoc.org/ams
Dist(s): **Chicago Distribution Ctr.**
MyiLibrary
Springer
ebrary, Inc.

American Mythology Productions, *(978-1-945205)* P.O. Box 325, Bel Air, MD 21014 USA Tel 410-652-7008
E-mail: james@americanmythologyproductions.com
Web site: www.americanmythology.net
Dist(s): **Diamond Comic Distributors, Inc.**
Diamond Bk. Distributors.

American Poets Society *Imprint of* **Gem Printing**

†**American Psychological Assn.,** *(978-0-912704; 978-0-945354; 978-1-55798; 978-1-59147; 978-0-9792125; 978-1-4338)* Orders Addr.: P.O. Box 92984, Washington, DC 20090-2984 USA (SAN 685-3137) Tel 202-336-6123; 202-336-5510 202-336-5502 (orders); Toll Free: 800-374-2721; Edit Addr.: 750 First St., NE, Washington, DC 20002-4242 USA (SAN 255-5921) Tel 202-336-5500; P.O. Box 77318, Washington, DC 20013-8318 Toll Free: 800-374-2721; *Imprints:* Magination Press (Magination Press)
E-mail: ghughes@spa.org; jmacomber@apa.org; books@apa.org
Web site: http://www.apa.org
Dist(s): **Follett School Solutions**
Oxford Univ. Pr., Inc.; *CIP.*

American Quilter's Society *Imprint of* **Collector Bks.**

American Reading Co., *(978-1-59301; 978-1-61541; 978-1-61406; 978-1-63437; 978-1-64053)* 201 S. Gulph Rd., King Of Prussia, PA 19406 USA (SAN 930-3553) Tel 610-992-4150; Toll Free: 866-810-2665
E-mail: robbie.byerly@americanreading.com
Web site: http://www.americanreading.com
Dist(s): **Follett School Solutions.**

American Reprint Co. *Imprint of* **Amereon Ltd.**

American Retrospects, LLC, *(978-0-9747666)* Orders Addr.: P.O. Box 352576, Toledo, OH 43635-2576 USA Tel 419-824-4500; Fax: 419-885-4255
E-mail: jkw@americanretro.net; jkw@bex.net; mds@bex.net; mds@americanretro.net
Web site: http://www.americanretro.net.

American Revolution Publishing, *(978-0-9760948)* 12514 Mustang Dr., Poway, CA 92064 USA Tel 858-842-1812 (phone/fax)
E-mail: amrevpub@cox.net
Web site: http://www.gwuh.com; http://www.amrevpub.com; http://www.americanrevolutionpublishing.com
Dist(s): **Book Clearing Hse.**
Quality Bks., Inc.

American Schl. of Classical Studies at Athens, *(978-0-87661; 978-1-62139)* 6-8 Charlton St., Princeton, NJ 08540-5232 USA (SAN 201-1697) Tel 609-683-0800; Fax: 609-924-0578
E-mail: castein@ascsa.org
Web site: http://www.ascsa.edu.gr/publications
Dist(s): **Casemate Pubs. & Bk. Distributors, LLC**
Casemate Academic
Firebrand Technologies
MyiLibrary
ebrary, Inc.

American Society for Microbiology *See* **ASM Pr.**

American Society of Mechanical Engineers, The, *(978-0-7918)* 22 Law Dr.,, Fairfield, NJ 07007-2300 USA (SAN 201-1379) Tel 973-882-1176; Fax: 973-882-1717; Toll Free: 800-843-2763
E-mail: pruskil@asme.org
Web site: http://www.asme.org.

American Society of Plant BIOLOGISTS, *(978-0-943088)* 15501 Monona Dr., Rockville, MD 20855-2768 USA (SAN 240-3366) Tel 301-251-0560; Fax: 301-279-2996
E-mail: aspp@aspp.org
Web site: http://aspp.org.

American Society of Plant Physiologists *See* **American Society of Plant BIOLOGISTS**

American Success Institute, Inc., *(978-1-884864)* 31 Central St. #5, Wellesley, MA 02482 USA Tel 781-237-7368
E-mail: info@Success.org
Web site: http://www.success.org
Dist(s): **BookBaby.**

American Swedish Historical Museum, *(978-0-9800761)* 1900 Pattison Ave., Philadelphia, PA 19145-5901 USA Tel 215-389-1776; Fax: 215-389-9901
E-mail: info@americanswedish.org
Web site: http://www.americanswedish.org.

American Technical Pubs., Inc., *(978-0-8269)* 10100 Orland Pkwy., Orland Park, IL 60467-5756 USA (SAN 206-8141) Toll Free: 800-323-3471
E-mail: service@americantech.net
Web site: http://www.americantech.net
Dist(s): **Follett School Solutions.**

American Traveler Pr., *(978-0-914846; 978-0-935810; 978-0-939650; 978-1-55838; 978-1-885590; 978-1-58581)* Orders Addr.: 5738 N. Central Ave., Phoenix, AZ 85012 USA (SAN 220-0864) Tel 602-234-1574; Fax: 602-234-3062; Toll Free: 800-521-9221; *Imprints:* Golden West Publishers (GoldenWest)
E-mail: info@AmericanTravelerPress.com
Web site: http://www.PrimerPublishers.com; http://www.RenaissanceHousePublishers.com; http://www.AmericanTravelerPress.com; http://www.ClayThompsonBooks.com; http://www.GoldenWestPublishers.com; www.GoldenWestCookbooks.com
Dist(s): **Chicago Distribution Ctr.**
Follett School Solutions
INscribe Digital.

American Trek Bks., *(978-0-9815221; 978-0-9821178)* 1371 Morley Ave., Rochester Hills, MI 48307 USA (SAN 855-7748).

American Trust Pubns., *(978-0-89259)* 745 Mcclintock Dr., Suite 314, Burr Ridge, IL 60527 USA (SAN 664-6158)
Dist(s): **Halalco Bks.**
Meta Co., LLC.

American Univ. in Cairo Pr., *(978-977-424; 978-1-936190; 978-977-416; 978-1-936481; 978-1-61797)* 113 Kasr el Aini St., Cairo, AE 11511 EGY Tel 3542964; Fax: 3557565; 420 Fifth Ave., New York, NY 10018-2729 Tel 212-730-8800; Fax: 212-730-1600
E-mail: aucpress@aucegypt.edu
Web site: http://www.aucegypt.edu
Dist(s): **Books International, Inc.**
Casemate Academic
MyiLibrary
Oxford Univ. Pr., Inc.
ebrary, Inc.

American Water Works Assn., *(978-0-89867; 978-1-58321; 978-1-61300; 978-1-62576)* 6666 W. Quincy Ave., Denver, CO 80235-3098 USA (SAN 212-8241) Tel 303-347-6266; Fax: 303-794-7310; Toll Free: 800-926-7337 (customer service/orders)
E-mail: mramey@awwa.org
Web site: http://www.awwa.org
Dist(s): **Follett School Solutions**
ebrary, Inc.

American Wind Power Ctr., *(978-0-9679480)* Div. of National Windmill Project, Inc., 1501 Canyon Lake Dr., Lubbock, TX 79403 USA Tel 806-747-8734; Fax: 806-740-0668
E-mail: charris@windmill.com
Web site: http://www.windmill.com.

American World Publishing, *(978-0-615-16443-4; 978-0-615-16444-1; 978-0-615-16701-5)* P.O. Box 534, Union City, GA 30291 USA
E-mail: andrewhitmore@yahoo.com
Dist(s): **Lulu Pr., Inc.**

Americana Souvenirs & Gifts, *(978-1-890541)* 206 Hanover St., Gettysburg, PA 17325-1911 USA (SAN 169-7366) Toll Free: 800-692-7436.

America's Great Stories, *(978-0-615-34265-8)* 10100 Yankee Hill Rd., Lincoln, NE 68526 USA Tel 402-486-1776
E-mail: terrificteam@aol.com.

Americas Group, The, *(978-0-935047)* Subs. of Harris/Ragan Management Group, 654 N. Sepulveda Blvd. Ste. 1, Los Angeles, CA 90049-2170 USA (SAN 694-4698) Toll Free: 800-966-7716
E-mail: hrmg@aol.com
Web site: http://www.americasgroup.com
Dist(s): **Penton Overseas, Inc.**

Amerisearch, Inc., *(978-0-9653557; 978-0-9753455; 978-0-9778085; 978-0-9827101; 978-0-9896491)* Orders Addr.: P.O. Box 20163, Saint Louis, MO 63123 USA (SAN 254-6426) Tel 314-487-4395; Fax: 314-487-4489; Toll Free: 888-872-9673 (888-USA-WORD); Edit Addr.: 4346 Southview Way Dr., Saint Louis, MO 63129 USA
E-mail: wjfederer@gmail.com
Web site: http://www.amerisearch.net.

AmeriTales Entertainment, LLC, *(978-0-9798739)* 3525 Del Mar Heights Rd., Suite 623, San Diego, CA 92130 USA Tel 858-449-6900; Fax: 425-795-6026
E-mail: tcarter@ameritales.com
Dist(s): **Follett School Solutions.**

Amerotica *Imprint of* **NBM Publishing Co.**

Amethyst Moon *See* **Amethyst Moon Publishing and Services**

Amethyst Moon Publishing and Services, *(978-0-9792426; 978-1-935354; 978-1-935714)* Orders Addr.: P.O. Box 87885, Tucson, AZ 85754 USA
Web site: http://www.ampubbooks.com.

Amharic Kids, *(978-0-9797481)* 7201 88th Ave., Brooklyn Park, MN 55445 USA Tel 612-636-7878
E-mail: hamish@bellward.com
Web site: http://www.amharickids.com
Dist(s): **Follett School Solutions.**

Amherst Pr., *(978-0-910122; 978-0-942495; 978-1-930596)* Div. of The Guest Cottage, Inc., Orders Addr.: P.O. Box 774, Saint Germain, WI 54558 USA (SAN 213-9820) Tel 715-477-0424; Fax: 715-477-0405; Toll Free: 800-333-8122; Edit Addr.: P.O. Box 774, Saint Germain, WI 54558 USA (SAN 666-6450) Do not confuse with companies with the same name in Amherst, NY, North Hampton, NH
E-mail: sales@theguestcottage.com
Web site: http://www.theguestcottage.com
Dist(s): **Partners Bk. Distributing, Inc.**

Amiaya Entertainment, *(978-0-9745075; 978-0-9777544)* 1154 E. 229 St., Apt. 12C, Bronx, NY 10466 USA.

Amichai Charnoff, *(978-0-692-81729-2; 978-0-692-82098-8)* 11812 Smoketree Rd., POTOMAC, MD 20854 USA Tel 301-706-7385
E-mail: amicharnoff@gmail.com; amicharnoff@gmail.com
Dist(s): **CreateSpace Independent Publishing Platform.**

Amicus, *(978-1-68152)* P.O. Box 1329, Mankato, MN 56002 USA Tel 507-388-5164
E-mail: dbrown@amicuspublishing.us; info@amicuspublishing.us
Web site: www.amicuspublishing.us
Dist(s): **Chronicle Bks. LLC**
Hachette Bk. Group.

Amicus Educational *See* **Amicus Publishing**

Amicus High Interest *Imprint of* **Amicus Publishing**

Amicus Illustrated *Imprint of* **Amicus Publishing**

Amicus Pr., *(978-0-914861)* 4201 Underwood Rd., Baltimore, MD 21218 USA (SAN 289-0518) Tel 301-889-5056.

Amicus Publishing, *(978-1-60753; 978-1-68151)* P.O. Box 1329, Mankato, MN 56002 USA Tel 507-388-5164; Fax: 507-388-4797; *Imprints:* Amicus High Interest (High Interest); Amicus Illustrated (Illustrate); Amicus Readers (Readers)
E-mail: info@amicuspublishing.us
Web site: http://www.amicuspublishing.us
Dist(s): **Follett School Solutions**
MyiLibrary.

Amicus Readers *Imprint of* **Amicus Publishing**

AMIDEAST, *(978-0-913957)* 1730 M. St. NW, Suite 1100, Washington, DC 20036-4505 USA (SAN 286-7184) Tel 202-776-9600; Fax: 202-776-7000
E-mail: inquiries@amideast.org
Web site: http://www.amideast.org.

Amigo Pubns., Inc., *(978-0-9658533)* Orders Addr.: P.O. Box 666, Los Olivos, CA 93441-0666 USA Tel 805-686-4616; Fax: 805-688-3427; Toll Free: 888-502-6446; Edit Addr.: 3029 W. Hwy. 154, Los Olivos, CA 93441-0666 USA
E-mail: Amigo@Conquistador.com
Web site: http://www.conquistador.com; http://www.equibooks.com.

Amira Rock Publishing, *(978-0-9821075; 978-0-9828007; 978-0-9833354)* 31 High St., Felton, PA 17322 USA (SAN 857-2844).

Amistad *Imprint of* **HarperCollins Pubs.**

AMMO Bks., LLC, *(978-0-9786076; 978-1-934429; 978-1-62326; 978-0-9976536)* 300 S Raymond Ave Suite 3, Pasadena, CA 91105 USA (SAN 851-1128) Tel 323-223-2666; Fax: 323-978-4200; 1 Ingram Blvd., La Vergne, TN 37086
E-mail: contact@ammobooks.com; paul@ammobooks.com
Web site: http://www.ammobooks.com
Dist(s): **Follett School Solutions**
Ingram Publisher Services.

Ammons Communications, Ltd., *(978-0-9651232; 978-0-9753023; 978-0-9815702; 978-0-9824099; 978-0-9827611; 978-0-9837382; 978-0-9853728; 978-0-9892169; 978-0-9895694; 978-0-9913803; 978-0-9908766; 978-0-9965199; 978-0-9971647; 978-0-9987359)* 29 Regal Ave., Sylva, NC 28779 USA (SAN 851-0881) Tel 828-631-4587 (phone/fax); *Imprints:* Catch the Spirit of Appalachia (CSA)
E-mail: amyammons1@frontier.com
Web site: http://www.spiritofappalachia.org; http://www.catchthespiritofappalachia.com; http://www.storiesofmountainfolk.com; http://www.csabooks.com.

AMN Publishing, *(978-0-9728129)* P.O. Box 352, Massapequa, NY 11758 USA
E-mail: AMNPub@aol.com
Web site: http://amnpub.tripod.com.

Amoeba Bks., *(978-0-9786473)* 5260 Rogers Rd., G-6, Hamburg, NY 14075 USA
E-mail: marketing@amoebabooks.com
Web site: http://www.amoebabooks.com
Dist(s): **Follett School Solutions.**

Amped Media, *(978-0-9742287)* 22 Shaw Pl., Walla Walla, WA 99362 USA.

Ampelon Publishing, LLC, *(978-0-9748825; 978-0-9786394; 978-0-9798104; 978-0-9817705; 978-0-9823286; 978-0-9840095; 978-0-9893419; 978-0-9982617; 978-0-9990527)* P.O. Box 140675, Boise, ID 83714 USA
E-mail: info@ampelonpublishing.com
Web site: http://www.ampelonpublishing.com
Dist(s): **Smashwords.**

Ampersand, Inc., *(978-0-9745932; 978-0-9761235; 978-0-9818126; 978-0-9905603; 978-0-9962525; 978-0-9974493; 978-0-9985222; 978-0-9994775)* Orders Addr.: 515 Madison St., New Orleans, LA 70116 USA
Web site: http://www.ampersandworks.com
Dist(s): **Follett School Solutions.**

Amsco Music *Imprint of* **Music Sales Corp.**

AMSCO Schl. Pubns., Inc., *(978-0-87720; 978-1-56765)* 315 Hudson St., Suite 501, New York, NY 10013-1085 USA (SAN 201-1751) Toll Free: 866-902-6726 all orders
Web site: http://www.amscopub.com
Dist(s): **Bolchazy-Carducci Pubs.**

AMSI Venture, Incorporated *See* **Sleep Garden, Inc.**

Amulet Bks. *Imprint of* **Abrams, Inc.**

Anachel Communications, *(978-0-615-62081-7)* 2008 Waterstone Dr., Franklin, TN 37069 USA Tel 615-370-8450
E-mail: carrie@anachel.com
Web site: www.carriegerlachcecil.com.

Anadem Publishing, Inc., *(978-0-9646891; 978-1-890018)* 3620 N. High St., Suite 201, Columbus, OH 43214 USA Tel 614-262-2539; Fax: 614-262-6630; Toll Free: 800-633-0055
E-mail: anadem@erinet.com
Web site: http://www.anadem.com.

Anaiah, Ruth, *(978-0-9769675)* P.O. Box 2142, Brandon, FL 33509-2142 USA
E-mail: dozministry2001@yahoo.com.

Anamchara Bks. *Imprint of* **Harding Hse. Publishing Sebice Inc.**

Anancy Bks. LLC, *(978-0-9753297; 978-1-941553)* Div. of Anancy Enterprise LLC, P.O. Box 28677, San Jose, CA 95159-8677 USA Tel 408-286-0726 Call Anytime; Fax: 408-947-0668 Fax Anytime
Web site: http://www.Anancybooks.com.

Anancybooks.com *See* **Anancy Bks. LLC**

Ananda Publications *See* **Crystal Clarity Pubs.**

Ananse Pr., *(978-0-9605670; 978-0-9749437)* Orders Addr.: P.O. Box 22565, Seattle, WA 98122-0565 USA (SAN 216-3292) Tel 206-325-8205; Fax: 206-328-4371; 1504 32nd Ave. S., Seattle, WA 98144-3918 (SAN 241-6123)
E-mail: gumbomedia@earthlink.net; gumbomedia@yahoo.com
Web site: http://home.usaa.net/~gumbomedia/ananse/index.htm.

Anar Bks. LLC, *(978-0-9748285)* 10266 Virginia Swan Pl., Cupertino, CA 95014-2025 USA
E-mail: anoopbusiness@yahoo.com
Web site: http://www.anarbooks.com.

Anat Tour, *(978-0-9978432)* 6340 Raydel Ct., San Diego, CA 92120 USA Tel 619-920-1213
Dist(s): **CreateSpace Independent Publishing Platform.**

Anaya Multimedia, S.A. (ESP) *(978-84-415; 978-84-7614)* *Dist. by* **Continental Bk.**

Anbeyond Pr., *(978-0-9744014)* 10420 NE 190th St., Bothell, WA 98011 USA (SAN 255-7886) Tel 425-483-9943; 22833 Bothell Everett Hwy. No. 102, PMB 1227, Bothell, WA 98021
E-mail: rm@anbeyond.com
Web site: http://www.anbeyond.com.

Ancestral Light Publishing, *(978-0-9718530)* 1969 S. Alafaya Trail, No. 322, Orlando, FL 32828 USA Tel 407-382-1707; Fax: 509-356-6971
E-mail: gigante@uaia.org.

Ancestral Tracks, *(978-0-9701266; 978-0-9754161)* P.O. Box 1064, Hillsboro, OR 97123-1064 USA
E-mail: books@ancestraltracks.com; cbeattie@ancestraltracks.com; ginger@ancestraltracks.com
Web site: http://www.ancestraltracks.com.

Anchor *Imprint of* **Knopf Doubleday Publishing Group**

Anchor Group, *(978-0-9852663; 978-0-9855385; 978-0-9882707; 978-0-615-71893-4; 978-0-9886334; 978-0-9888476; 978-0-9891753; 978-0-9897073; 978-0-615-91474-9; 978-0-9915174)* 225 Brookside Dr., FLUSHING, MI 48433 USA Tel 810-964-3767 (Tel/Fax)
E-mail: rourkewrites@gmail.com
Dist(s): **CreateSpace Independent Publishing Platform.**

Anchorage Foundation Pr., *(978-0-9795266)* 1518 Mohle Dr., Austin, TX 78703 USA
Dist(s): **Greenleaf Book Group.**

Ancient Days Pubs., *(978-0-9741405)* P.O. Box 356, Landisville, PA 17538 USA
E-mail: abrdl@ptd.net.

Ancient Faith Publishing, *(978-0-9622713; 978-1-888212; 978-0-9822770; 978-1-936270; 978-1-944967)* Orders Addr.: P.O. Box 748, Chesterton, IN 46304 USA Tel 831-336-5118; Fax: 831-336-8882; Toll Free: 800-967-7377; Edit Addr.: 1550 Birdie Way, Chesterton, IN 46304 USA (SAN 175-8624) Tel 831-336-5118; Fax: 831-336-8682; Toll Free: 800-967-7377
Web site: http://www.conciliarpress.com
Dist(s): **Midpoint Trade Bks., Inc.**
Spring Arbor Distributors, Inc.

Ancient Golf Publishing *See* **LuckySports**

Ancient Studios, *(978-0-9744216; 978-0-692-95854-4)* 13 Pine St. 0, Winooski, VT 05404 USA Tel 8023389293
E-mail: janivescampbell@aol.com
Dist(s): **CreateSpace Independent Publishing Platform.**

Ancient Wisdom Pubns., *(978-0-9753093; 978-0-9792665; 978-0-9815971; 978-0-692-00084-7; 978-0-9824994; 978-1-936690; 978-0-615-58775-2; 978-1-940849)* Div. of Murine Communications, 1804 Miekle Ave, Woodland, CA 95776 USA
Web site: https://www.facebook.com/andras.nagy1
Dist(s): **CreateSpace Independent Publishing Platform**
Lightning Source, Inc.
Lulu Pr., Inc.

Andersen Pr. (GBR) *(978-0-86264; 978-0-905478; 978-1-84270; 978-1-84939; 978-1-78344)* *Dist. by* **Trafalgar.**

Andersen Pr. (GBR) *(978-0-86264; 978-0-905478; 978-1-84270; 978-1-84939; 978-1-78344)* *Dist. by* **Lerner Pub.**

Andersen Pr. (GBR) *(978-0-86264; 978-0-905478; 978-1-84270; 978-1-84939; 978-1-78344)* *Dist. by* **IPG Chicago.**

Anderson, George, *(978-0-9743682; 978-0-9819004)* 12301 Wilshire Blvd., Suite 418, Los Angeles, CA 90025 USA Tel 310-207-3591; Fax: 310-207-6234
E-mail: georgeandereson@aol.com
Web site: http://www.andersonservices.com.

Anderson House Foundation *See* **Windy Press International Publishing Hse., LLC**

Anderson Law Group, *(978-0-9728128; 978-0-9797860)* 3225 Mcleod Dr., Las Vegas, NV 89121 USA; 3225 Mcleod Dr., Las Vegas, NV 89121
E-mail: tmathis@bossoffice.com
Web site: http://www.BossOffice.com.

Anderson Pr., *(978-0-942479)* 706 W. Davis, Ann Arbor, MI 48103-4855 USA (SAN 667-3600) Tel 734-994-6182; Fax: 734-994-5207 Do not confuse with Anderson Pr., Laguna Niguel, CA.

Anderson Publishing, *(978-0-9718249)* Orders Addr.: P.O. Box 5544, Douglasville, GA 30154 USA Toll Free: 866-942-0790 (phone/fax); Edit Addr.: 5178 Holly Springs Dr., Douglasville, GA 30135 USA Do not confuse with companies with the same or similar name in Navato, CA, Saginawi, MI, Burley, ID, Cincinnati, MO, Anacortes, WA, Indio, CA
E-mail: canderson@andersonpub.com
Web site: http://www.andersonpub.com
Dist(s): **ACW Pr.**

Anderson, Sara *See* **Sara Anderson Children's Bks.**

ANDInternational, *(978-0-9762291)* 74 Woodcleft Ave., Freeport, NY 11520 USA Tel 516-546-2025; Fax: 516-546-6010; Toll Free: 800-229-2634
E-mail: orders@andihq.com; andihq@aol.com
Web site: http://www.andihq.com.

Andre Deutsch (GBR) *(978-0-233)* *Dist. by* **Trafalgar.**

Andre Deutsch (GBR) *(978-0-233)* *Dist. by* **IPG Chicago.**

Andre Deutsch (GBR) *(978-0-233)* *Dist. by* **Trans-Atl Phila.**

Andres & Blanton, *(978-0-9830318; 978-0-9966721)* 42 Corey Ln., Niantic, CT 06357 USA Tel 860-941-9258
E-mail: sscheyder@sbcglobal.net.

†Andrews McMeel Publishing, *(978-0-8362; 978-0-939251; 978-1-57939; 978-0-7407; 978-1-4494; 978-1-5248)* Orders Addr.: c/o Simon & Schuster, Inc., 100 Front St., Riverside, NJ 08075 USA Toll Free Fax: 800-943-9831; Toll Free: 800-943-9839 (Customer Service); 800-897-7650 (Credit Dept.); Edit Addr.: 1130 Walnut St., Kansas City, MO 64106-2109 USA (SAN 202-540X) Toll Free: 800-851-8923
Web site: http://www.AndrewsMcMeel.com
Dist(s): **Follett School Solutions**
Simon & Schuster, Inc.; *CIP.*

Andromeda Pr., Inc., *(978-0-9820649; 978-1-938503)* 2600 Birdie Thompson Dr., Pocatello, ID 83201 USA Tel 208-406-1220
E-mail: Andromedapress@gmail.com; strialbe@gmail.com.

Andrus, Ashley, *(978-0-9772000)* 104 Kempton Dr., Lafayette, LA 70508-6547 USA
E-mail: aia@andrus.com.

Anela Publishing *See* **Abidenme Bks.**

Anemone Publishing, *(978-0-9759264)* 16 Rope Ferry Rd, Hanover, NH 03755 USA Tel 603-643-0922
E-mail: carolynne.krusi.99@alum.dartmouth.org.

AnEx Pubns., *(978-0-9711774)* 9 Bartlet St., Suite 131, Andover, MA 01810 USA Toll Free: 866-616-4400
E-mail: rich_hewett@yahoo.com
Web site: http://www.anexx.com.

Angel Applications, *(978-0-615-18904-8)* 1624 Yorktown Dr., Charlottesville, VA 22901 USA Tel 434-293-2819 (phone/fax)
E-mail: kgarstang@cstone.net
Dist(s): **R J Communications, LLC.**

Angel City Pr., *(978-1-883318; 978-1-62640)* 2118 Wilshire Blvd., PMB 880, Santa Monica, CA 90403-5784 USA (SAN 298-3370) Tel 310-395-9982; Fax: 310-395-3353; Toll Free: 800-949-8039 (orders)
E-mail: smcauley@angelcitypress.com
Web site: http://www.angelcitypress.com.

Angel Eyes Publishing, *(978-0-9755346)* 1914 Hollywood Rd., Atlanta, GA 30318 USA (SAN 256-0542) Tel 404-566-0598
E-mail: dawnettelounds@yahoo.com
Web site: http://www.angeleyespublishing.com.

Angel Fingers Foundation *See* **Mullins Pubns. & Apparel, LLC**

Angel Heart Children's Pr., *(978-0-9712124)* Orders Addr.: P.O. Box 63, East Enterprise, IN 47019 USA Tel 812-594-2438; Fax: 812-594-2438
E-mail: dianemccarty@hotmail.com
Web site: http://www.geocities.com/hs_mom2000.

Angel Insights Press *See* **Stop N Go Fitness**

Angel Island Assoc., *(978-0-9667352)* P.O. Box 866, Tiburon, CA 94920 USA Tel 415-435-3522; Fax: 415-435-2950
E-mail: valaia@att.net
Web site: http://www.angelisland.org
Dist(s): **Follett School Solutions.**

Angel Mind, *(978-0-9729866)* 5776-D Lindero Canyon Dr. #123, Westlake Village, CA 91362 USA Tel 818-424-2619; Fax: 818-780-8880
E-mail: bill@angelmind.net
Web site: http://www.angelmind.net.

Angel Pr., *(978-0-9716590)* Div. of The Angelic Light Research Institute, Orders Addr.: P.O. Box 1375, Sedona, AZ 86339 USA Tel 928-451-1222; 928-853-5753 Do not confuse with companies with the same or similar names in Tiburon, CA, Pell City, AL, Concord, NC, Rancho Santa Margarita, CA, St. Thomas, VI, TraversAFB, CA. Monterey, CA
E-mail: angelpress@angelsangelsangels.org; angels@angelsangelsangels.org
Web site: http://www.angelsangelsangels.org; http://www.angelsangelsangels.com; http://www.angelsangelsangels.net; http://www.angellightfeather.com.

Angela's Bookshelf *See* **A B Publishing**

AngelBooks, *(978-0-9771749)* 4340 Janesville, Bel Aire, KS 67220 USA
Web site: http://www.thesecretofpink.com.

Angelic Encounter,

Angel's BBQ, *(978-0-578-16633-9)* 21 W. Oglethorpe Ln, Savannah, GA 314019 USA.

Angel's Boy Enterprises, *(978-0-9755352)* 8306 Wilshire Blvd., No. 3004, Beverly Hills, CA 90211 USA
Web site: http://www.angelboi.com.

Angel's Diary, *(978-0-615-31217-0; 978-0-9860041)* 6321 Thunder Blitz Ave., Las Vegas, NV 89131 USA.

Angels Landing, *(978-0-9899141)* 347 Butterfly Ln., Hermitage, PA 16148 USA Tel 724-977-0847
E-mail: trpags@roadrunner.com
Web site: https://sites.google.com/site/littlelambs20/.

Angels of Agape, *(978-0-615-25466-1)* 211 Shawnee Valley, East Stroudsburg, PA 18302 USA Tel 973-460-3882
E-mail: angelsofagape@yahoo.com
Web site: http://www.angelsofagape.com.

Angelus Pr., *(978-0-935952; 978-1-892331; 978-1-937843)* Div. of Society of Saint Pius X, 2915 Forest Ave., Kansas City, MO 64109 USA (SAN 222-769X) Tel 816-753-3150; Fax: 816-753-3557; Toll Free Fax: 888-855-9022; Toll Free: 800-966-7337 (orders)
E-mail: info@angeluspress.org; stownshend@angeluspress.org; bklaske@angeluspress.org
Web site: http://www.angeluspress.org.

Angelworks Pr., *(978-0-578-00741-0; 978-0-578-12854-2)* 901 Brutscher St., No.D144, Newberg, OR 97132 USA Tel 503-830-0741; 17884 Kelok Rd., Lake Oswego, OR 97034
E-mail: susan@susanmarek.com
Dist(s): **Lulu Pr., Inc.**

Angie Blue Bks., LLC, *(978-0-9677547)* 376 County Road 2740., Mico, TX 78056-5353 USA
E-mail: info@AngieBlue.com
Web site: http://www.AngieBlue.com.

AngiesInk, *(978-0-615-17415-0)* P.O. Box 323, Tuskegee Institute, AL 36087 USA
E-mail: angiesink@bellsouth.net
Dist(s): **Lulu Pr., Inc.**

Angle Press *See* **Angle Valley Pr.**

Angle Valley Pr., *(978-0-9711950)* P.O. Box 4098, Winchester, VA 22604 USA (SAN 255-8629) Tel 540-539-1260
E-mail: anglevalleypress@yahoo.com
Web site: http://www.AngleValleyPress.com
Dist(s): **Bookmasters Distribution**
Lightning Source, Inc.

Anglican Bk. Ctr. (CAN) *(978-0-919030; 978-0-919891; 978-0-921846; 978-1-55126)* *Dist. by* **Forward Movement.**

Anglo-American Book Company, Limited (UK) *See* **Crown Hse. Publishing**

Angry Bicycle *Imprint of* **Walter, Wendy D.**

Animal Band Productions, Inc., The, *(978-0-9752619)* P.O. Box 392, Mount Juliet, TN 37121 USA Tel 615-754-8701
E-mail: info@theanimalband.com
Web site: http://www.theanimalband.com.

Animal Crackers Publishing, LLC, *(978-0-9798343)* 1143 Auraria Pkwy. No. A-201, Denver, CO 80204 USA (SAN 854-5170)
Web site: www.animalcrackerspublishing.com.

Animal Hero Kids, *(978-0-615-99522-9)* 13782 151 Ln. N., Jupiter, FL 33478 USA Tel 561-236-8843
E-mail: Susanh@animalherokids.org
Web site: AnimalHeroKids.org.

Animal Media Group LLC, *(978-0-578-11078-3; 978-0-578-11129-2; 978-0-578-11217-6; 978-0-578-11218-3; 978-0-9912550; 978-0-9861489; 978-0-9974315; 978-1-947895)* 100 First Ave. Suite 1100, Pittsburgh, PA 15222 USA
Dist(s): **Consortium Bk. Sales & Distribution**
Follett School Solutions
INscribe Digital.

Animal Teachers Enterprises, *(978-0-9788858)* 5902G Queenston St., Springfield, VA 22152 USA
E-mail: snork5902g@yahoo.com
Web site: http://funkman.org/animal/services/catalog.html.

Animal Tracks Pr., *(978-0-9760342)* P.O. Box 432, Cotah, CA 94931 USA (SAN 256-1808) Tel 707-776-8019; Fax: 707-795-2919
Web site: http://www.animaltrackspress.com.

Animalations, *(978-0-9776628; 978-1-933818)* 4186 Melodia Songo Ct., Las Vegas, NV 89135 USA (SAN 257-9111) Fax: 702-804-4220; Toll Free Fax: 866-670-8337; Toll Free: 866-670-8337
E-mail: info@animalations.com
Web site: http://Animalations.com.

AnimeVillage.com *See* **Bandai Entertainment, Inc.**

Anjana Publishing (HKG) *(978-988-12394; 978-988-12395; 978-988-15028)* *Dist. by* **Bookmasters.**

ANKA, *(978-0-615-73378-4)* 3165 Nostrand Ave., 6B, Brooklyn, NY 11229 USA Tel 917-294-2939
E-mail: anna.kaplun@gmail.com.

Ankh Bks. (CAN) *(978-0-9738036)* *Dist. by* **Mtn Bk Co.**

Ann Arbor Editions LLC, *(978-1-58726)* 2500 S. State St., Ann Arbor, MI 48104 USA Tel 734-913-1302; Fax: 734-913-1249; 1094 Flex Dr., Jackson, TN 38301; *Imprints:* Mitten Press (Mitten Pr)
E-mail: ljohnson@aaeditions.com
Web site: http://www.annarbormediagroup.com; http://www.mittenpress.com; http://www.aaeditions.com
Dist(s): **Follett School Solutions**
Two Rivers Distribution.

Ann Arbor Media Group, LLC *See* **Ann Arbor Editions LLC**

Annadale Comics, *(978-0-9972562; 978-1-945582)* 72 Lorrain Avenu, Staten Island, NY 10312 USA Tel 718-967-1470
E-mail: johnrap316@gmail.com.

Annade Publishing, *(978-0-9761740)* 18964 Lauder, Detroit, MI 48235 USA
Web site: www.annade.com.

Annapolis Publishing Co., *(978-1-884878)* Orders Addr.: 3430 2nd St. # 400, Brooklyn, MD 21225-1603 USA (SAN 631-4414) Toll Free: 800-536-1414
E-mail: Katherine@AnnapolisPublishing.com
Web site: http://www.AnnapolisPublishing.com; http://www.mewarren.com; http://www.AnnapolisBooks.com.

AnnArt Pr., *(978-0-9769719)* R R 1, Box 621, Richards, MO 64778 USA.

Annedawn Publishing, *(978-0-9632793; 978-0-9755153)*
E-mail: annedawn@aol.com.

Anness Publishing (GBR) *(978-1-85967; 978-1-86147; 978-1-901289; 978-1-901688; 978-1-84038; 978-0-7548; 978-1-84090; 978-1-903141; 978-1-84215; 978-1-84309; 978-1-84322; 978-1-84476; 978-1-84477; 978-1-84681; 978-0-85723; 978-1-78019)* *Dist. by* **Natl Bk Netwk.**

Anness Publishing, Inc., *(978-1-886890)* 39 Sandy Ln., Eatontown, NJ 07724-2445 USA (SAN 299-0563) Toll Free: 800-354-9657
E-mail: AFioravanti@anness.com
Dist(s): **National Bk. Network.**

Annick Pr., Ltd. (CAN) *(978-0-920236; 978-0-920303; 978-1-55037; 978-1-55451)* *Dist. by* **PerseuPGW.**

Annie Mouse Bks., *(978-0-9793379; 978-0-9914094)* P.O. Box 142, Harrisville, PA 16038 USA (SAN 853-1676)
E-mail: anniemousebooks@gmail.com; anniemousebooks@yahoo.com
Web site: http://www.anniemousebooks.com.

Annie's *Imprint of* **Annie's Publishing, LLC**

Annie's Media, LLC *See* **Annie's Publishing, LLC**

Annie's Publishing, LLC, *(978-0-88195; 978-0-9638031; 978-0-9655269; 978-1-57367; 978-1-882138; 978-1-931171; 978-1-59012; 978-1-59217; 978-0-9748217; 978-1-59635; 978-1-933602; 978-1-64025)* 111 Corporate Dr., Big Sandy, TX 75755 USA Fax: 260-589-8093 (Clothilde); *Imprints:* Annie's (Annies)
Web site: http://www.drgnetwork.com
Dist(s): **Follett School Solutions**
Independent Pubs. Group
MyiLibrary
ebrary, Inc.

Annika Pubns., *(978-0-9670516)* Orders Addr.: P.O. Box 264, Fergus Falls, MN 56537 USA Tel 218-736-7735; Edit Addr.: R.R. 4, Box 50, Fergus Falls, MN 56537 USA.

Anno Domini, *(978-0-9792145; 978-1-939689)* 584 Ironwood Terr., Woodburn, OR 97071 USA (SAN 852-7946) Tel 971-226-4356.

†Annual Reviews, Inc., *(978-0-8243)* 4139 El Camino Way, P.O. Box 10139, Palo Alto, CA 94303-0139 USA (SAN 201-1816) Tel 650-493-4400; Fax: 650-424-0910; Toll Free: 800-523-8635 (including California, Alaska, Hawaii & Canada)
E-mail: service@annualreviews.org
Web site: http://www.AnnualReviews.org; *CIP.*

Anointed Pubs., *(978-0-9763841)* Orders Addr.: 1227-40 Seaton Rd., Durham, NC 27713 USA Tel 919-806-0651; Edit Addr.: 1227-40 seaton Rd., Durham, NC 27713 USA
E-mail: jainjie@msn.com
Web site: http://www.joanjai.com
Dist(s): **Brown Enterprises, Inc.**

Anointed Publishing Co., *(978-0-615-19205-5; 978-0-615-25069-4; 978-0-615-36490-2; 978-0-615-37865-7; 978-0-615-78457-1)* 8123 Winter Blue Ct., Springfield, VA 22153 USA Tel 321-947-0706
Web site: http://www.cheniselytrelle.com.

Anointed Word Pubns., *(978-0-9744024)* 611 N. Pennsylvania Ave., Lansing, MI 48912 USA Tel 517-372-3407.

Anomaly Publishing, *(978-0-9800123)* 3700 Ceres Dr., Salt Lake City, UT 84124 USA Tel 801-278-3245
Dist(s): **Smashwords.**

Anorak Pr. *Imprint of* **Gibbs Smith, Publisher**

Another Ep Publishing, *(978-0-9740685; 978-0-615-11795-9)* Div. of Episodes By Wroe, P.O. Box 300, Walnut, CA 91788-0300 USA (SAN 253-2530) Tel 909-448-5356.

Another Language Pr., *(978-0-922852)* 7709 Hamilton Ave., Cincinnati, OH 45231-3103 USA Tel 513-521-5590; Fax: 513-521-5592; Toll Free: 800-733-2067
E-mail: aimsbooks@juno.com
Dist(s): **AIMS International Bks., Inc.**

Another Sommer-Time Story *Imprint of* **Advance Publishing, Inc.**

AnotherThinkComing Pr., *(978-0-692-82443-6; 978-0-9987767)* 19830 WALLFLOWER LN, APPLE VALLEY, CA 92308-3643 USA Tel 760-553-1644
E-mail: d_thompson@hotmail.com; d_thompson@hotmail.com; d_thompson@hotmail.com
Dist(s): **CreateSpace Independent Publishing Platform.**

Answers in Genesis *See* **Answers in Genesis Ministries**

Answers in Genesis Ministries, *(978-1-893345; 978-1-60092; 978-1-62691)* Orders Addr.: P.O. Box 510, Hebron, KY 41048 USA Fax: 859-727-2299; Toll Free: 800-778-3390
E-mail: dzordel@answersingenesis.org
Web site: http://www.answersingenesis.org
Dist(s): **Master Bks.**
New Leaf Pub. Group
Send The Light Distribution LLC.

ANT Bank$ *See* **VIP INK Publishing Group, Inc.**

Antarctic Pr., Inc., *(978-0-930655; 978-0-9663588; 978-0-9728978; 978-1-932453; 978-0-9768043; 978-0-9776424; 978-0-9787725; 978-0-9792723; 978-0-9797719; 978-0-9801255; 978-0-9816647; 978-0-9822253; 978-0-9823742; 978-0-9841107; 978-0-9843375; 978-0-9844879; 978-0-9831823; 978-0-9837934; 978-0-9850925; 978-1-939364)* *Div. of Ben Dunn Corp., 7272 Wurzbach Rd., Suite 204, San Antonio, TX 78240 USA Tel 210-614-0396; Fax:*

Publisher Name Index

210-614-5029 *Do not confuse with Antarctic Pr., Bellevue, WA*
E-mail: apcog1@gmail.com
Web site: http://www.antarctic-press.com
Dist(s): **Diamond Comic Distributors, Inc.**
Diamond Bk. Distributors
MyiLibrary.

Anthem Pr. (GBR) *(978-1-898855; 978-1-84331; 978-0-85728; 978-1-78308) Dist. by* **Bolchazy-Carducci.**

Anthem Pr. (GBR) *(978-1-898855; 978-1-84331; 978-0-85728; 978-1-78308) Dist. by* **Bks Intl VA.**

AntHill Publishing, *(978-0-9718544)* 5315 Clarendon Rd., Brooklyn, NY 11203 USA Tel 718-629-0294 (phone/fax) Do not confuse with Ant Hill Publishing in Gorman, TX
E-mail: anthillpublishing@hotmail.com

Anthology of Poetry, Inc., *(978-1-883931)* Orders Addr.: P.O. Box 698, Asheboro, NC 27204-0698 USA Tel 336-626-7762; Fax: 336-626-2622; Edit Addr.: 307 E. Salisbury St., Asheboro, NC 27203 USA
E-mail: poetry@anthologyofpoetry.com
Web site: http://www.anthologyofpoetry.com.

Anthro Co., The, *(978-1-878464)* 200 Carroll St., No. 21, Susanville, CA 96130 USA Tel 530-251-5712
E-mail: devajan@earthlink.net
Web site: http://www.ishifacts.com
Dist(s): **Social Studies Schl. Service.**

Anthroposophic Press, Incorporated *See* **SteinerBooks, Inc.**

Anticipation Pr., *(978-0-9754046)* 3563 Sueldo St. Ste. Q, Sn Luis Obisp, CA 93401-7332 USA Do not confuse with Anticipation Press in Cheyenne, WY
E-mail: doingbigbiz@aol.com
Web site: http://www.anticipationpress.com; http://www.zacacreekdevelopment.com.

Antioch Publishing Co., *(978-0-7824; 978-0-89954; 978-1-4017)* Div. of Trends International, 5188 W. 74th St., Indianapolis, IN 46268 USA Tel 317-388-4060; 317-388-1414; Toll Free: 800-315-2110 Do not confuse with Antioch Publishing Co., Torrance, CA
Web site: http://www.antioch.com.

Antipodes Bks. & Beyond, 9707 Fairway Ave., Silver Spring, MD 20901-3001 USA Tel 301-602-9519; Fax: 301-565-0160
E-mail: Antipode@antipodesbooks.com
Web site: http://www.antipodesbooks.com.

Antique Collectors' Club (GBR) *(978-0-902028; 978-0-907462; 978-1-85149; 978-1-905377; 978-0-9504269) Dist. by* **Natl Bk Netwk.**

Antique Collectors' Club, *(978-0-902028; 978-0-907462; 978-1-85149)* Orders Addr.: Eastworks, 116 Pleasant St., Easthampton, MA 01027 USA (SAN 630-7787) Tel 413-529-0861; Fax: 413-529-0862; Toll Free: 800-252-5231 (orders)
E-mail: info@antiquecc.com; sales@antiquecc.com
Web site: http://www.antiquecollectorsclub.com
Dist(s): **National Bk. Network.**

Antiques, Incorporated *See* **Kovels Antiques, Inc.**

Antiquity Publishing, *(978-0-9793284)* 4127 McLaughlin Ave., No. 15, Los Angeles, CA 90066-5445 USA Tel 310-390-9093 (phone/fax)
E-mail: Randwulf@humnet.ucla.edu
Dist(s): **Bookmasters Distribution.**

Antlers & Fins LLC, *(978-0-9800643)* P.O. Box 82, Henefer, UT 84033 USA
E-mail: info@billygoeshunting.com
Web site: http://www.BillyGoesHunting.com.

Anton Berkshire Publishing, *(978-0-9746330)* Orders Addr.: P.O. Box 372, Markle, IN 46770 USA (SAN 255-6618); Edit Addr.: 9374 N. Marzane Rd., Markle, IN 46770 USA
Web site: http://www.antonberkshirepublishing.com.

Antoniades, Basil, *(978-0-615-24661-1)* 9 Belden Ct., Timonium, MD 21093 USA Tel 410-560-9911
E-mail: basilantoniades@earthlink.net
Web site: http://www.havingfunwithgreekmythology.com
Dist(s): **Lulu Pr., Inc.**

Antrim Hse., *(978-0-9662783; 978-0-9762091; 978-0-9770633; 978-0-9792226; 978-0-9798451; 978-0-9817883; 978-0-9823970; 978-0-9843418; 978-1-936482; 978-1-943826)* 21 Goodrich Rd., Simsbury, CT 06070-1804 USA; P.O. Box 111, Tariffville, CT 06081
Web site: http://www.antrimhousebooks.com
Dist(s): **BookBaby**
Distributors, The.

Antroll Publishing Co., *(978-1-877656)* 2616 Elmont St., Wheaton, MD 20902 USA Tel 301-942-0492.

Anvil Bks., Ltd. (IRL) *(978-0-900068; 978-0-947962; 978-1-901737) Dist. by* **Dufour.**

Anyone Can Write bks., *(978-0-9771470)* 2890 N. Hills Dr., NE, Atlanta, GA 30305-3210 USA Tel 404-261-1616
Web site: http://www.anyonecanwrite.com.

Anystar Publishing, *(978-0-9767047)* P.O. Box 182067, Arlington, TX 76096 USA
E-mail: anystarpublishing@yahoo.com
Web site: http://www.anystarpub.com.

Anythings Possible, Inc., *(978-1-892186)* Orders Addr.: 1863 N. Farwell Ave., Milwaukee, WI 53202 USA Fax: 414-226-4901; Toll Free: 800-543-7153
E-mail: info@special-kids.com
Web site: http://www.special-kids.com.

Anzalone, Frank, *(978-0-9770788)* P.O. Box 110422, Campbell, CA 95011 USA Tel 408-247-7572; Fax: 408-984-1519
E-mail: info@mckyfoto.com
Web site: http://www.mckyfoto.com.

AoPS Inc., *(978-0-9773045; 978-1-934124)* Orders Addr.: 10865 Rancho Bernardo Rd Ste 100, San Diego, CA 92127 USA Tel 858-675-4555; Fax: 855-430-9531; Toll Free Fax: 855-430-9531
E-mail: orders@artofproblemsolving.com
Web site: http://www.artofproblemsolving.com; http://www.beastacademy.com.

Aoyama Publishing *See* **Marble Hse. Editions**

AP Bks., *(978-0-9841927)* P.O. Box 799, Pennington, NJ 08534 USA Fax: 609-730-1286
Dist(s): **Cardinal Pubs. Group.**

AP Publishing, *(978-0-9722906)* Orders Addr.: P.O. Box 160, Merrimac, WI 53561 USA
Web site: http://www.wildlife-trails.com
Dist(s): **Lightning Source, Inc.**

APA Publications Services (SGP) *(978-9971-925; 978-9971-982; 978-981-234; 978-981-4120; 978-981-246; 978-981-4137; 978-981-258; 978-981-268; 978-981-282) Dist. by* **IngramPubServ.**

Apage4You Bk. Publishing, *(978-0-9723616)* 2025 Balla Way, Suite 200, Grand Prairie, TX 75051-3907 USA Tel 972-264-2892; Fax: 214-722-1254; Toll Free: 800-519-7323
E-mail: apage4you@starband.net
Web site: http://www.publishfast.com; http://www.apage4youpublishing.com.

Ape Entertainment, *(978-0-9741398; 978-0-9791050; 978-0-9801314; 978-1-934944; 978-1-936340; 978-1-937676; 978-1-62782)* P.O. Box 7100, San Diego, CA 92167 USA
Dist(s): **Diamond Comic Distributors, Inc.**
Diamond Bk. Distributors.

Ape Pen Publishing *See* **Ballard, Donald W.**

Aperturas Foundation, *(978-0-9745220)* P.O. Box 25163, Chicago, IL 60625 USA Tel 773-478-7973
E-mail: aperturas@yahoo.com
Web site: http://www.aperturas.info.

Aperture Pr., LLC, *(978-0-615-40395-3; 978-0-615-41313-6; 978-0-615-41888-9; 978-0-9833010; 978-0-9836878; 978-0-9850026; 978-0-9889351; 978-0-9910962; 978-0-9909302; 978-0-9973020)* 201 Washington St. Suite 533, Reading, PA 19601 USA Tel 484-525-0009
E-mail: steve@aperturepress.net
Web site: http://www.aperturepress.net
Dist(s): **Lulu Pr., Inc.**

Apex Performance Solutions, LLC, *(978-0-9824519)* 467 Springdale Rd., Westfield, MA 01085 USA Tel 413-562-2299; Fax: 413-562-2289; 113 Ne Carleston Oaks Dr., Port St.Lucie, FL 34983
E-mail: jwojcik@apexperformancesolutions.com
Web site: http://www.apexperformancesolutions.com
Dist(s): **Follett School Solutions**
Partners Pubs. Group, Inc.

APG Sales & Distribution Services, Div. of Warehousing and Fulfillment Specialists, LLC (WFS, LLC), 7344 Cockrill Bend Blvd., Nashville, TN 37209-1043 USA (SAN 630-818X) Toll Free: 800-327-5113
E-mail: sswift@agpbooks.com
Web site: http://www.apgbooks.com.

APG Sales & Fulfillment *See* **APG Sales & Distribution Services**

APILA Ediciones (ESP) *(978-84-937102; 978-84-937896; 978-84-939736) Dist. by* **Lectorum Pubns.**

Aplastic Anemia + MDS International Foundation, *(978-0-9755572)* Orders Addr.: P.O. Box 613, Annapolis, MD 21404-0613 USA Tel 410-867-0242; Fax: 410-867-0240; Toll Free: 800-747-2820; Edit Addr.: P.O. Box 310, Churchton, MD 20733-0310 USA
E-mail: help@aamds.org
Web site: http://www.aamds.org.

Aplus Bks. *Imprint of* **Capstone Press of Coughlan Cos.**

Apocalyptic Tangerine Pr., *(978-0-9821138; 978-0-9897496)* Orders Addr.: 1969 Laurel Ave., No. 5, Saint Paul, MN 55104-5820 USA Tel 304-942-4912.

Apodixis Press *See* **Read Well Publishing Inc.**

Apollo Computer Systems, Inc., *(978-0-9610582)* 616 14th St., Arcata, CA 95521 USA (SAN 264-651X) Tel 707-822-0318.

Apollo Pubs., *(978-0-9718532; 978-0-9721368; 978-1-932832; 978-1-946599)* P.O. Box 9, Santa Cruz, CA 95063 USA Tel 831 479 9626 (phone/fax); 800-881-0181
E-mail: michael@apollopub.com
Web site: http://www.apollopub.com
Dist(s): **TNT Media Group, Inc.**

Apollo Science Pubs., LLC, *(978-0-9814551)* P.O. Box 26671, San Diego, CA 92196 USA Tel 858-635-6558
E-mail: zhibo.zhang@ieee.org
Web site: http://www.aspublishers.com.

Apologetics Pr., Inc., *(978-0-932859; 978-1-60063)* 230 Landmark Dr., Montgomery, AL 36117-2752 USA (SAN 688-9190) Tel 334-272-8558; Fax: 334-270-2002; Toll Free: 800-234-8558 (orders only)
E-mail: mail@apologeticspress.org
Web site: http://www.apologeticspress.org
Dist(s): **Send The Light Distribution LLC.**

Apologia Educational Ministries, Inc., *(978-0-9656294; 978-1-932012; 978-1-935495; 978-1-940110; 978-1-946506)* 1106 Meridian Plaza Ste 220/340, Anderson, IN 46016 USA Tel 765-608-3280; Fax: 765-608-3290; Toll Free: 888-524-4724
E-mail: mailbag@apologia.com; patti@apologia.com
Web site: http://www.apologia.com.

Apologue Entertainment, LLC, *(978-0-9819825)* Orders Addr.: 1075 Meghan Ave., Algonquin, IL 60102 USA
E-mail: gary.mack@apologueentertainment.com
Web site: http://www.apologueentertainment.com.

Appalachian Hse., *(978-0-9662800)* Orders Addr.: P.O. Box 627, Boiling Springs, PA 17007 USA (SAN 299-5328) Tel 717-609-6234
E-mail: apphouse@pa.net.

Appalachian Log Publishing Co., The, *(978-1-885935)* Orders Addr.: P.O. Box 20297, Charleston, WV 25362-1297 USA Tel 304-342-5789; Edit Addr.: 878 Anaconda Ave., Charleston, WV 25302 USA
E-mail: gregory@newwave.net.

†Appalachian Mountain Club Bks., *(978-0-910146; 978-1-878239; 978-1-929173; 978-1-934028; 978-1-62842)* 5 Joy St., Boston, MA 02108 USA (SAN 203-4808) Tel 617-523-0655; Fax: 617-523-0722; Toll Free: 800-262-4455
E-mail: kbreunig@outdoors.org; alakri@outdoors.org
Web site: http://www.outdoors.org
Dist(s): **Globe Pequot Pr., The**
National Bk. Network; *CIP.*

Applause Theatre & Cinema *Imprint of* **Leonard, Hal Corp.**

Apple Corps Pubs., *(978-0-9619484; 978-1-934397)* 1600 Sunset Ln., Oklahoma City, OK 73127 USA (SAN 245-0461) Fax: 888-375-7017; Toll Free: 800-335-9208
E-mail: tom@tomquaid.com
Dist(s): **Univ. of Oklahoma Pr.**

Apple Cover Books *See* **New Monic Bks.**

Apple House Publishing, *(978-0-9966954)* 8 Orchard Blossom Rd, Windham, NH 03087 USA Tel 301-717-3034
E-mail: jennifersmithwriter@outlook.com
Web site: www.jenniferwsmith.com.

Apple Pie Pubs., *(978-0-9675123)* 5745 SW 75th St., PMB 325, Gainesville, FL 32608 USA Tel 352-472-2833 (phone/fax); Fax: 352-335-9080
E-mail: applepienow@aol.com
Web site: http://www.applepienow.com.

AppleNobb Books *See* **Happy Apple Bks.**

Apples & Honey Pr. *Imprint of* **Behrman Hse., Inc.**

Applesauce Pr. *Imprint of* **Cider Mill Pr. Bk. Pubs., LLC**

Appleseed Pr. Bk. Pub. LLC, *(978-1-60464)* Orders Addr.: 12 Port Farm Rd., Kennebunkport, ME 04046-0404 USA (SAN 854-5405) Tel 207-641-3489; Fax: 207-967-8233
E-mail: appleseedgiftbooks@mac.com
Web site: http://www.appleseedpress.com.

†Applewood Bks., *(978-0-918222; 978-1-55709; 978-1-889833; 978-1-933212; 978-1-4290; 978-0-9819430; 978-1-60889; 978-0-9844156; 978-0-9836416; 978-1-938700; 978-0-9882885; 978-1-941216; 978-1-5162; 978-1-944038; 978-1-945187)* 1 River Rd., Carlisle, MA 01741-1820 USA (SAN 210-3419) Toll Free: 800-277-5312; 1 Ingram Blvd., La Vergne, TN 37086; *Imprints:* Commonwealth Editions (CommonwealthEd)
E-mail: applewood@awb.com; svec@awb.com
Web site: http://www.awb.com
Dist(s): **Follett School Solutions**
Ingram Publisher Services; *CIP.*

Applied Database Technology, Inc., *(978-0-9742610)* 715 E. Sprague Ave. Suite 125, Spokane, WA 99202 USA
Web site: http://www.applieddatabase.com.

Appointed Media Group, LLC, *(978-0-9984148)* 1425 Battlefield Blvd. No. 1934, Chesapeake, VA 23327 USA Tel 757-935-7180
E-mail: roy@appointedpictures.org.

Apprentice Hse., *(978-1-934074; 978-1-62720)* Dept. Communication/Loyola College in MD, 4501 N. Charles St., Baltimore, MD 21210 USA.

Apprentice Shop Bks., LLC, *(978-0-9723410; 978-0-9842549; 978-0-9850144)* P.O. Box 375, Amherst, NH 03031 USA Fax: 603-472-2588
E-mail: apprenticeshpbks@aol.com
Web site: http://www.apprenticeshopbooks.com
Dist(s): **Follett School Solutions.**

Appropriate Solutions Press *See* **Echo Point Bks. and Media**

Apricot Pr., *(978-1-885027)* P.O. Box 98, Nephi, UT 84648 USA Toll Free: 800-731-6145
E-mail: books@apricotpress.com
Web site: http://www.apricotpress.com.

April Arts Press & Productions, *(978-0-9650918)* P.O. Box 64, Morgan Hill, CA 95038-0064 USA
E-mail: books@aprilartspress.com
Web site: http://www.aprilartspress.com
Dist(s): **Follett School Solutions.**

April Press *See* **April Arts Press & Productions**

APS Publishing, *(978-0-9906361; 978-1-945145)* 5739 S. Calumet Ave Unit 1s, Chicago, IL 60637 USA Tel 773-440-2004; 847-942-6135
E-mail: authorspromotingsuccess@gmail.com
Web site: www.weareaps.com.

AP's Travels *See* **Aunt Patty's Travels-London**

Apte, Stu, *(978-0-615-20409-3; 978-0-9821227)* 133 Plantation Dr., Tavernier, FL 33070 USA Tel 305-852-7440 (phone/fax)
E-mail: stuwho@bellsouth.net
Dist(s): **Emerald Bk. Co.**

Aquarian Age Publishing, Inc., *(978-0-9767530)* 250, 56th St., Fort Lauderdale, FL 33334 USA
E-mail: info@aquarianagepublishing.com
Web site: http://www.lawsofhealing.com; http://www.aquarianagepublishing.com.

Aquarius Pr., *(978-0-9718214; 978-0-9819208; 978-0-9846212; 978-0-9852877; 978-0-9897357; 978-0-9961390; 978-0-9971996; 978-0-9985278; 978-0-9992232)* Orders Addr.: P.O. Box 23096, Detroit, MI 48223 USA Tel 313-515-8122; Toll Free Fax: 877-979-3639 Do not confuse with companies with the same or similar names in Santa Fe, NM, Baltimore, MD, Watchung, NJ
E-mail: aquariuspress@sbcglobal.net; aquariuspress@gmail.com
Web site: http://www.AUXmedia.studio; http://www.AquariusPress.net; http://www.WillowLit.net
Dist(s): **Ingram Publisher Services**
SPD-Small Pr. Distribution.

Aqueduct Pr., *(978-0-9746559; 978-1-933500; 978-1-61976)* P.O. Box 95787, Seattle, WA 98145-2787 USA (SAN 256-131X); 4 White Brook Rd., Gilsum, NH 6448
Web site: http://www.aqueductpress.com
Dist(s): **Follett School Solutions**
Pathway Bk. Service.

Aquila Ink Publishing, *(978-0-9760789)* P.O. Box 160, Rio Nido, CA 95471 USA (SAN 850-9050) Tel 707-799-5981; 707-887-9090; Fax: 707-869-2973
E-mail: aquila@aquilaink.com
Web site: http://www.aquilaink.com.

Aquinas & Krone Publishing, LLC, *(978-0-9800448; 978-0-9843526; 978-0-9849505)* P.O. Box 1304, Merchantville, NJ 08109 USA (SAN 855-0751) Tel 856-665-3999.

A.R. Harding Publishing Co., *(978-0-936622)* 2878 E. Main St., Columbus, OH 43209 USA (SAN 206-4936) Tel 614-231-9585
E-mail: erics@furfishgame.com.

Aradiance Publishing, *(978-0-9715737)* P.O. Box 13855, Mill Creek, WA 98082 USA.

Arago Publishing, LLC, *(978-0-9742698; 978-0-9788457)* 90087 Cape Arago Hwy., Coos Bay, OR 97420 USA (SAN 255-4607)
E-mail: surfdance@iceinternet.com.

Arango-Duque, J. F. *See* **Arango's Publishing**

Arango's Publishing, *(978-0-9655750)* 1776 Polk St., No. 3K-032, Hollywood, FL 33020 USA (SAN 299-2078)
E-mail: arangoduke@aol.com
Dist(s): **Hispanic Bks. Distributors & Pubs., Inc.**
Lectorum Pubns., Inc.
Libros Sin Fronteras
Quality Bks., Inc.

Aranjo, Karl, *(978-0-9770667)* 16 Greenwood, Irvine, CA 92604 USA Tel 949-786-8765
E-mail: karlaranjo@yahoo.com
Web site: http://guitaru.com.

Arbiter Pr., *(978-0-9621385; 978-0-615-35216-9; 978-0-615-35859-8)* 1732 N. Lakemont Ave., Winter Park, FL 32792 USA (SAN 251-1282); 1732 Arbor Pk. Dr., Winter Park, FL 32789 Tel 407-647-2606
E-mail: chsblackwell@gmail.com
Dist(s): **Bookazine Co., Inc.**

Arbor Bks., *(978-0-9771870; 978-0-9777764; 978-0-9786107; 978-0-9790469; 978-0-9794118; 978-0-9800582; 978-0-9818658; 978-0-9841992)* 244 Madison Ave., No. 254, New York, NY 10016 USA; 19 Apero Rd., Suite 301, Ramsey, NJ 7446 Do not confuse with Arbor Books in Media, PA
Web site: http://www.arborbooks.com
Dist(s): **Follett School Solutions.**

Arbordale Publishing, *(978-0-9764943; 978-0-9768823; 978-0-9777423; 978-1-934359; 978-1-60718; 978-1-62855)* 612 Johnnie Dodds Blvd., Suite A2, Mount Pleasant, SC 29464 USA (SAN 256-6109) Tel 843-971-6722; Fax: 843-216-3804
E-mail: leegerman@arbordalepublishing.com
Web site: http://www.arbordalepublishing.com
Dist(s): **BWI**
Baker & Taylor Bks.
Brodart Co.
Ediciones Enlace de PR, Inc.
Follett School Solutions
Ingram Publisher Services.

Arborville Bks., *(978-0-9886988)* 2115 Nature Cove Ct. No. 203, Ann Arbor, MI 48104 USA Tel 734-663-8175
E-mail: arborvillebooks@gmail.com
Dist(s): **Lulu Pr., Inc.**

Arborwoodgen LLC, *(978-0-9973686)* 23500 Cristo Rey Dr. Unit 107D, Cupertino, CA 95014-6520 USA Tel 650-967-3008
E-mail: wualan@labmed2.ucsf.edu.

Arbutus Pr., *(978-0-9665316; 978-0-9766104; 978-1-933926)* Orders Addr.: 2364 Pinehurst Trail, Traverse City, MI 49686 USA Tel 231-946-7240
E-mail: editor@arbutuspress.com
Web site: http://www.arbutuspress.com
Dist(s): **Follett School Solutions.**

Arc Manor, *(978-0-9786536; 978-0-9794154; 978-1-60450; 978-1-61242)* P.O. Box 10339, Rockville, MD 20849 USA Tel 240-645-2214; Fax: 310-388-8449; *Imprints:* TARK Classic Fiction (TARK Classic Fiction); Serenity Publishers (Serenity Pubs)
E-mail: admin@arcmanor.com
Web site: http://www.HeartsKiss.com; http://www.ArcManor.com; http://www.PhoenixPick.com; http://www.PhoenixRider.com; http://http://www.ManorWodehouse.com; http://www.galaxysedge.com/
Dist(s): **Follett School Solutions**
Smashwords.

Arcade Publishing *Imprint of* **Skyhorse Publishing Co., Inc.**

Arcadia Bks. Ltd. (GBR) *(978-1-900850; 978-1-905147; 978-1-906413; 978-1-908129; 978-1-910050; 978-1-911350) Dist. by* **Bookmasters.**

Arcadia Publications *See* **Linden Hill Publishing**

Arcadia Publishing, *(978-0-7385; 978-1-58973; 978-1-59629; 978-1-4396; 978-0-60949; 978-1-61423; 978-1-4671; 978-1-62584; 978-1-62585; 978-1-62619; 978-0-9903765; 978-1-944313; 978-1-5316; 978-1-5402; 978-1-64111; 978-1-64112)* Orders Addr.: 420 Wando Park Blvd., Mount Pleasant, SC 29464 USA (SAN 255-268X) Tel 843-853-2070; Fax: 843-853-0044; Toll Free: 888-313-2665; *Imprints:* History Press, The (HistoryPress) Do not confuse with Arcadia Publishing in Greenwood Village, CO
E-mail: sales@arcadiapublishing.com
Web site: http://www.arcadiapublishing.com
Dist(s): **INscribe Digital**
MyiLibrary.

Arcadiam Games, *(978-0-9769951)* 3106 NE 83rd Ave., Portland, OR 97220 USA
E-mail: travisbrown@crossroads-rpg.com
Web site: http://www.crossroads-rpg.com.

Arcadian Hse., *(978-0-9766666)* 3040 Rightmire Blvd., Columbus, OH 43221 USA
E-mail: lyn@arcadianhouse.com
Web site: http://www.arcadianhouse.com.

Arcana Studio, Inc., *(978-0-9763095; 978-0-9809204; 978-1-926914; 978-1-927424; 978-1-927421)* 930 Winthrop Ln., Rockford, IL 61107 USA
Web site: http://www.arcanastudio.com
Dist(s): **Diamond Comic Distributors, Inc.**
Diamond Bk. Distributors.

Archaeopress (GBR) *(978-0-9539923; 978-1-905739; 978-1-78491) Dist. by* **CasemateAcad.**

Archaia Entertainment *Imprint of* **Boom! Studios**

Archangel Studios, LLC, *(978-0-9714714)* 507 S. Parish Pl., Burbank, CA 91506-2951 USA
E-mail: thredstar_hq@hotmail.com
Web site: http://www.theredstar.com
Dist(s): **Diamond Comic Distributors, Inc.**
Diamond Bk. Distributors.

ArcheBooks *Imprint of* **ArcheBooks Publishing, Inc.**

ArcheBooks Publishing, Inc., *(978-1-59507)* 6081 Silver King Blvd. Unit 903, Cape Coral, FL 33914 USA Tel 239-542-7595; 9101 W. Sahara Ave., Las Vegas, NV 89117; *Imprints:* ArcheBooks (ArchBks)
E-mail: publisher@archebooks.com
Web site: http://www.archebooks.com
Dist(s): **Follett School Solutions.**

Archeion Press, LLC *See* **Akasha Publishing, LLC**

Archeological Assessments, Inc., *(978-0-9638956; 978-0-9794044)* P.O. Box 1631, Nashville, AR 71852 USA
E-mail: aaimjb@aol.com
Web site: http://www.arkansasstories.com.

Archer Fields, Inc., *(978-0-9627767; 978-1-56466)* 155 Sixth Ave., New York, NY 10013 USA Tel 212-627-1999; Fax: 212-627-9484; Toll Free: 800-338-2665
Dist(s): **D.A.P./Distributed Art Pubs.**

Archer's Pr., *(978-0-615-68449-9; 978-0-615-70040-3; 978-0-615-70731-0; 978-0-9894749; 978-0-692-23029-9; 978-0-692-41131-5; 978-0-692-47473-0; 978-0-692-61477-8; 978-0-692-62625-2)* 2795 Parker Rd., Florissant, MO 63033 USA Tel 3146168101
Web site: www.archerspress.com
Dist(s): **CreateSpace Independent Publishing Platform.**

Archeworks, *(978-0-9753405)* 625 N. Kingsbury St., Chicago, IL 60610 USA Tel 312-867-7254; Fax: 312-867-7260
E-mail: info@archeworks.org
Web site: http://www.archeworks.org.

Archie Comic Pubns., Inc., *(978-1-879794; 978-1-936975; 978-1-61988; 978-1-62738; 978-1-68183; 978-1-68255)* 629 Fifth Ave, Suite 100, Pelham, NY 10803-1242 USA Tel 914-381-5155; Fax: 914-381-2335; *Imprints:* Archie Comics (Archie Comics); Dark Circle Comics (Dark Circle)
E-mail: haroldb@archiecomics.com
Web site: http://www.archiecomics.com
Dist(s): **Diamond Comic Distributors, Inc.**
Diamond Bk. Distributors
Follett School Solutions
Penguin Random Hse. LLC
Random Hse., Inc.

Archie Comics *Imprint of* **Archie Comic Pubns., Inc.**

Archie Publishing, *(978-0-9779064)* P.O. Box 521732, Salt Lake City, UT 84152-1732 USA (SAN 850-5616) Tel 801-232-3840
E-mail: mcf@archiepublishing.com
Web site: http://www.archiepublishing.com
Dist(s): **American West Bks.**

Archimede Editions (FRA) *(978-2-211) Dist. by* **Distribks Inc.**

Archipelago Pr., *(978-1-893335)* Orders Addr.: P.O. Box 1540, Los Gatos, CA 95031 USA (SAN 299-7541) Tel 408-354-5587 (phone/fax) Do not confuse with companies with the same name in Saint Thomas, VI, Friday Harbor, WA
E-mail: pelago2000@aol.com
Web site: http://www.rosswell.com.

Archival Services, Incorporated *See* **Red River Pr.**

Archives Pr. *Imprint of* **Media Assocs.**

Archives Press, The *See* **Media Assocs.**

Archus Pr., LLC, *(978-0-9648564; 978-1-893047; 978-0-9852248)* 620 Miller St., Rochester, MI 48307 USA Tel 248-218-0356; Toll Free: 888-275-5639
E-mail: leigharrathoon@gmail.com.

Archway Publishing, *(978-1-4808)* Div. of Author Solutions, Inc., 1663 Liberty Drive, Bloomington, IN 47403 USA Fax: 317-454-0544 Toll Free: 888-242-5904
Web site: http://www.archwaypublishing.com
Dist(s): **Author Solutions, Inc.**
Bookmasters Distribution.

Arco *Imprint of* **Peterson's**

Arcoiris Records, Inc., *(978-1-57417)* P.O. Box 7428, Berkeley, CA 94707 USA Tel 510-527-5539
Dist(s): **Follett School Solutions**
Lectorum Pubns., Inc.

Arctos Pr., *(978-0-9657015; 978-0-9725384; 978-0-9897847)* 116 Cloud View Rd., Sausalito, CA 94965 USA Tel 415 331 2503
Web site: http://www.members.aol.com/runes/index.html
Dist(s): **Quality Bks., Inc.**
SPD-Small Pr. Distribution.

Arcturus Pubs., Inc., *(978-0-916877)* P.O. Box 606, Cherry Hill, NJ 08003 USA (SAN 653-9718) Tel 609-428-3863.

Arcturus Publishing (GBR) *(978-1-900032; 978-1-84193; 978-1-84837; 978-1-84858; 978-1-78212; 978-1-78404; 978-1-78428; 978-1-78599; 978-1-78828) Dist. by* **Black Rab.**

Arcturus Publishing (GBR) *(978-1-900032; 978-1-84193; 978-1-84837; 978-1-84858; 978-1-78212; 978-1-78404; 978-1-78428; 978-1-78599; 978-1-78828) Dist. by* **Bookmasters.**

Ardden Entertainment (GBR) *(978-0-9561259) Dist. by* **Diamond Book Dists.**

Arden Pr., Inc., *(978-0-912869)* Orders Addr.: P.O. Box 418, Denver, CO 80201 USA (SAN 277-6553) Tel 303-697-6766; Fax: 303-697-3443; Edit Addr.: 20723 Seminole Rd., Indian Hills, CO 80454 USA Do not confuse with Arden Pr. Inc., Cleveland, OH
E-mail: ardenpress@msn.com
Dist(s): **Follett School Solutions.**

Ardent Writer Pr., LLC, The, *(978-1-938667; 978-1-64066)* 1014 Stone Dr., Brownsboro, AL 35741 USA Tel 256-694-6744
E-mail: gierhartsteve@att.net.

ARDI Research Pr., *(978-0-9640600)* 13571 Millpond Way, San Diego, CA 92129 USA (SAN 298-1866) Fax: 619-484-0377
E-mail: roger@rdooley.com.

Area Fifty One Productions *See* **Media Blasters, Inc.**

Argami Productions, LLC, *(978-0-9798324)* 774 Verona Lake Dr., Weston, FL 33326 USA; 4501 Forbes Blvd, Lanham, MD 20706
E-mail: ellenwv@aol.com
Dist(s): **Follett School Solutions.**

Argee Pubs., *(978-0-917961)* 4453 Manitou, Okemos, MI 48864 USA (SAN 247-7858) Tel 517-349-1254.

Argonaut Publishing Co., *(978-0-9635118)* 284 Clearview Rd., Chuluota, FL 32766 USA (SAN 297-8199) Tel 407-977-5207 (phone) Do not confuse with companies with the same or similar name in Los Angeles, CA, Santa Barbara, CA
E-mail: spottedtail@spottedtail.com
Web site: http://www.spottedtail.com.

Argonauts, The, *(978-0-615-23045-0; 978-0-615-33914-6; 978-0-9827842)* Orders Addr.: 929 Canterbury Ln., Waukesha, WI 53188 USA
E-mail: smkstoll@yahoo.com
Web site: http://www.theArgonauts.com.

Argos Gameware *See* **H&M Systems Software, Inc.**

Argus Enterprises International, Inc., *(978-0-9801555; 978-0-9819075; 978-0-9823050; 978-0-9841342; 978-0-9842596; 978-0-9845142; 978-0-9846195; 978-0-9846348; 978-0-9846439; 978-0-615-50768-2; 978-0-615-50816-0; 978-0-615-50820-7; 978-0-615-51728-5; 978-0-615-51733-9; 978-0-615-51734-6; 978-0-615-52229-6; 978-0-615-52387-3; 978-0-615-52392-7; 978-0-615-52688-1; 978-0-615-53228-8; 978-0-615-53320-9; 978-0-615-53503-6; 978-0-615-53629-3; 978-0-615-54552-3; 978-0-615-55032-9; 978-0-615-55098-5; 978-0-615-55127-2; 978-0-615-55238-5) Orders Addr.: P.O. Box 914, Kernersville, NC 27285 USA Tel 336-354-7173; Fax: 336-993-2497; Edit Addr.: 9001 Ridge Hill St., Kernersville, NC 27284 USA*
Web site: http://www.a-argusbooks.com; http://www.abetterbewrite.com; http://abook4you.com
Dist(s): **CreateSpace Independent Publishing Platform**
Follett School Solutions.

Arise Foundation, *(978-1-58614)* P.O. Box 2147, Jupiter, FL 33468-2147 USA (SAN 253-4835) Toll Free: 888-680-6100
E-mail: yisaacs@ariselife-skills.org
Web site: http://www.ariselife-skills.org
Dist(s): **Follett School Solutions.**

Aristata Publishing, *(978-0-9754912)* 16429 Lost Canyon Rd., Santa Clarita, CA 91387 USA (SAN 256-6508) Tel 661-299-9478 (phone/fax)
E-mail: aristata@craigelliottgallery.com; celliott@socal.rr.com
Web site: http://www.craigelliottgallery.com
Dist(s): **APG Sales & Distribution Services.**

ARIVA Publishing, *(978-0-9822952; 978-1-938056)* 244 Madison Ave, Suite 7100, New York, NY 10016-2817 USA Tel 646-706-7129
E-mail: info@arivapublishing.com
Dist(s): **Greenleaf Book Group.**

Arizona Blueberry Studios, *(978-0-9727894)* P.O. Box 5, Pasadena, CA 91102 USA Toll Free: 800-767-7186
E-mail: books@rossanthony.com
Web site: http://www.rossanthony.com/books.

Arizona Elk Society, *(978-0-9825181)* P.O. Box 190, Peoria, AZ 85380 USA.

Arizona Highways, *(978-0-916179; 978-1-893860; 978-1-932082; 978-0-9822788; 978-0-9845709; 978-0-9837132; 978-0-9887875; 978-0-9916228; 978-0-9971247; 978-0-9987893; 978-0-9989812; 978-0-9989813)* Div. of Arizona Dept. of Transportation, 2039 W. Lewis Ave., Phoenix, AZ 85009 USA (SAN 294-8974)
E-mail: mbianchi@azdot.gov; aphares@azdot.gov; kmero@azdot.gov
Web site: http://www.arizonahighways.com.

†**Arizona Historical Society**, *(978-0-910037)* 949 E. Second St., Tucson, AZ 85719 USA (SAN 201-6982) Tel 520-628-5774; Fax: 520-628-5695
Dist(s): **University of Arizona Pr.**
Univ. of New Mexico Pr.; *CIP.*

Arizona Sonora Desert Museum Pr., *(978-1-886679)* Arizona Sonora Desert Museum, 2021 N. Kinney Rd., Tucson, AZ 85743 USA Tel 520-883-3061; Fax: 520-883-3048
E-mail: asdmpress@desertmuseum.org; info@desertmuseum.org
Web site: http://www.desertmuseum.org
Dist(s): **Rio Nuevo Pubs.**

Arizona State Univ., Arizona Ctr. for Medieval & Renaissance Studies, *(978-0-922365)* c/o Arizona State Univ., Arizona Ctr. for Medieval & Renaissance Studies, Rms. 4426-4442, P.O. Box 874402, Tempe, AZ 85287-4402 USA (SAN 251-2424) Tel 602-727-6503; 480-965-5900; Fax: 602-727-6505; 480-965-1681
E-mail: mrts@asu.edu
Web site: http://www.asu.edu/clas/acmrs/mrts
Dist(s): **Chicago Distribution Ctr.**

Ark Hse. Pr. (AUS) *(978-0-9752044; 978-0-9757986; 978-0-9775671; 978-0-9803458; 978-0-9804523; 978-0-9805414; 978-1-921589; 978-0-9873888; 978-0-9875839; 978-0-9875932; 978-0-9922699; 978-0-9923452; 978-0-9925192; 978-0-9925726; 978-0-9941941; 978-0-9942832; 978-0-9943675; 978-0-9944299; 978-0-9945516; 978-0-9945968; 978-0-9953917; 978-0-9954215; 978-0-6480451; 978-0-6480508; 978-0-6480845; 978-0-6481016; 978-0-6481734) Dist. by* **STL Dist.**

Ark Watch Holdings LLC, *(978-0-9765358; 978-0-615-25019-9; 978-0-615-25020-5; 978-0-615-25021-2; 978-0-578-05938-9; 978-0-615-99015-6; 978-0-692-39260-7; 978-0-692-57098-2; 978-0-692-57589-5; 978-0-692-58048-6; 978-0-692-59038-6; 978-0-692-59199-4)* Div. of Serpentauria Media LLC, 4766 E. Eden Dr., Cave Creek, AZ 85331-3870 USA
E-mail: erikauthor@aol.com; arkwatchholdingsllc@hotmail.com
Web site: http://www.arkwatch.com
Dist(s): **CreateSpace Independent Publishing Platform.**

Arlene, Carmen Hibbs, *(978-0-9762567)* 584 Choctaw Dr., Madisonville, KY 42431 USA Tel 270-821-1968
E-mail: arlenehibbs@yahoo.com
Web site: http://www.heavenlyharborbooks.com.

Arlington Pubns., *(978-0-9753611)* 2205 Manera St., Odessa, TX 79763 USA Tel 432-582-0272; Fax: 432-332-2499 Do not confuse with Arlington Publications Incorporated in Arlington, TX
E-mail: tommwhite@cableone.net.

Armadillo Bks., *(978-0-9786132)* 4735 NE 24th Ave., Portland, OR 97211 USA (SAN 851-0865) Do not confuse with Armadillo Books in Houston, TX
E-mail: phtdoyle@yahoo.com
Web site: http://www.edgarfont.com; http://www.nextreststopearth.com
Dist(s): **Follett School Solutions.**

Armchair Pr., LLC, *(978-0-9744627)* P.O. Box 215, Ross, CA 94957-0215 USA Tel 415-460-9750; Fax: 415-460-0850
E-mail: ozzie@armchairpress.com.

Arment Biological Press *See* **Coachwhip Pubns.**

Armour of Light Publishing, *(978-0-9620604; 978-0-9788590; 978-0-9817120; 978-0-9825476; 978-0-9857539)* P.O. Box 778, Chapel Hill, NC 27514 USA (SAN 249-4337)
E-mail: publisher@armourofllight.org
Web site: http://www.armourofllight.org.

Armstrong, Greg, *(978-0-578-11703-4; 978-0-578-12191-8; 978-0-578-12368-4)* 27082 O Neill Dr., Unit 325, Ladera Ranch, CA 92694 USA Tel 949-701-7190.

Armstrong Valley Publishing Co., *(978-1-928798)* Orders Addr.: P.O. Box 1275, Murfreesboro, TN 37133-1275 USA Tel 615-895-5445; Fax: 615-893-2688; Edit Addr.: 2568 Armstrong Valley Rd., Murfreesboro, TN 37128 USA
E-mail: rsanders@raider.net.

Arnica Publishing, *(978-0-9728538)* Orders Addr.: P.O. Box 543, Choteau, MT 59422 USA; Edit Addr.: 3961 Hwy 89 S., Choteau, MT 59422 USA
E-mail: arnica@3rivers.net; pbechtold1@gmail.com.

Arnica Publishing, Incorporated *See* **ACS, LLC Arnica Creative Services**

Arnold, Patricia *See* **www.margaretmouse.com publishing co.**

Arnstein, Bennett, *(978-0-9620058)* 3049 W. Eighth St., No. 535, Los Angeles, CA 90005 USA (SAN 247-5162) Tel 213-388-3517
E-mail: b_arnstein@hotmail.com.

ARose Books Publishing, LLC, *(978-0-9723970; 978-0-9740636; 978-0-9819298; 978-0-9846081; 978-0-692-37550-1; 978-1-945986)* 23219 Stringtown Rd. #304, Clarksburg, MD 20871 USA Fax: 888-889-6945 (phone/fax)
Web site: http://www.arosebooks.com
Dist(s): **CreateSpace Independent Publishing Platform.**

Around The Globe Pr., *(978-0-9760573)* 11505 E. Calle Javelina, Tucson, AZ 85748-6339 USA Tel 520-290-8915
E-mail: aroundtheglobepress@earthlink.net
Web site: http://www.aroundtheglobepress.com.

Around the Way Book Publishers *See* **Around the Way Books**

Around the Way Books, *(978-0-9755342)* P.O. Box 1497, Waterbury, CT 06721 USA Toll Free: 888-610-5969
E-mail: htaylor@AroundTheWayBooks.com; info@aroundthewaybooks.com
Web site: http://www.AroundTheWayBooks.com
Dist(s): **Lushena Bks.**

Around The World Pubns., LLC, *(978-0-9772591)* P.O. Box 1024, Franktown, CO 80116-1024 USA Do not confuse with Around The World Publications in Seattle, WA
E-mail: bbrasier@etsgroup.com
Web site: http://www.worldthroughchildseyes.com.

Arrest Me Not Publishing *See* **As Seen on the Internet / Arrest Me Not**

Arrinton Pubns., *(978-0-9754540)* Orders Addr.: P.O. Box 2573, Chesapeake, VA 23327 USA Tel 757-450-6068; Fax: 757-410-4215; Edit Addr.: 1601 Orchard Grove Dr., Chesapeake, VA 23320-1411 USA
E-mail: gobooks@cox.net.

Arrow Pubns., *(978-0-9715514; 978-0-9765849)* Orders Addr.: 16653 E. Kingstree Blvd., Fountain Hills, AZ 85268-5439 USA Do not confuse with companies with the same or similar names in Cedar Rapids, IA, Kensington, MD
E-mail: arrowpublications@cox.net
Web site: http://www.arrowpublications.net.

Arrowhead Publishing, *(978-0-9640056)* 1238 Riva Rose Cir., Castle Rock, CO 80104-9650 USA Tel 303-663-9415 Do not confuse with companies with the same name in Lake Arrowhead, CA, Carlsbad, CA.

Arruzza, Richard *See* **Three Spots Productions**

Arsenal Pulp Pr. (CAN) *(978-0-88978; 978-1-55152) Dist. by* **Consort Bk Sales.**

Arseya, LLC, *(978-0-9745185; 978-1-935093)* 10 Pleasantville Rd., New Vernon, NJ 07976 USA (SAN 255-6588) Tel 973-993-1504; Fax: 973-993-9182; *Imprints:* Arseya Publishing (Arseya Pub)
E-mail: arseya@arseya.com
Web site: http://www.arseya.com.

Arseya Publishing *Imprint of* **Arseya, LLC**

Art & Creativity For Healing, Inc., *(978-0-9748462)* 26079 Getty Dr., Laguna Niguel, CA 92677 USA Tel 949-367-1902; Fax: 949-367-1904
E-mail: laurie@art4healing.org
Web site: http://www.art4healing.org.

Art & Soul Expressions, *(978-0-9729192)* P.O. Box 957, Mount Shasta, CA 96067 USA.

Art as Responsar *See* **Art as Responsa LLC**

Art as Responsa LLC, *(978-0-578-05270-0; 978-0-9845456)* 2550 Southshore Blvd., Lake Oswego, OR 97034 USA (SAN 859-631X) Tel 503-344-6065 (phone/fax); Fax: 503-344-6065; ART AS RESPONSA LLC 2550 Southshore Blvd., Lake Oswego, OR 97034
E-mail: marsha@art-responsa.com
Web site: http://www.artasresponsa.com; http://www.art-responsa.com; www.marshaplafkin.com.

A.R.T Bks. 4Kids, *(978-0-9968775)* 6256 Hillandale Dr. Apt 106, Lithonia, GA 30058 USA Tel 404-821-1726
E-mail: Reading_Is_Golden@yahoo.com.

Art In The Heartland, *(978-0-9725461; 978-0-9752839; 978-0-9762103; 978-0-9766587; 978-0-9778450)* P.O. Box 1785, Columbus, IN 47202-1785 USA
E-mail: sbreeding@artintheheartland.com
Web site: http://www.breedingbooks.com; http://www.artintheheartlandbooks.com.

Art Night Bks., *(978-0-9794004)* 3348 N. Dousman St., Milwaukee, WI 53212 USA Tel 414-213-7443
E-mail: devintrudell@mac.com; angievasquez13@sbcglobal.net
Web site: http://artnightbooks.com.

Art Of Essex Fine Art, The, *(978-0-615-31464-8)* 3007 Lakewood Ct., Jefferson City, MO 65109 USA
Web site: www.essexgarner.com.

Art of War Plus Bks. *Imprint of* **Clearbridge Publishing**

Art Official Media LLC, *(978-0-9768061; 978-0-9834874; 978-0-9883825)* Orders Addr.: P.O. Box 39323, Baltimore, MD 21212 USA Tel 443-693-7622; Edit Addr.: 1044 Radnor Ave., Baltimore, MD 21212 USA
Web site: http://www.artofficialmedia.com; http://www.UrbaniaMag.com
Dist(s): **Afrikan World Bk. Distributor.**

Art With Heart Press, *(978-0-9715240; 978-0-9841365)* Div. of Art with Heart, Orders Addr.: P.O. Box 94402, Seattle, WA 98124-6702 USA (SAN 850-2676)
E-mail: info@artwithheart.org
Web site: http://www.artwithheart.org
Dist(s): **Partners/West Book Distributors.**

ArtAnswer, *(978-0-9755413; 978-0-9771520)* P.O. Box 50387, Billings, MT 59105 USA Tel 406-672-8482
E-mail: artanswer@artanswer.com
Web site: http://www.artanswer.com.

†**Arte Publico Pr.**, *(978-0-934770; 978-1-55885; 978-1-61192; 978-1-5185)* Univ. of Houston 4902 Gulf Fwy, Bldg. 19, Rm. 100, Houston, TX 77204-2004 USA (SAN 213-4594) Tel 713-743-2998; 713-743-3080; Fax: 713-743-2847; Toll Free: 800-633-2783; Univ. of Houston 4902 Gulf Freeway, Rm. 100, Houston, TX 77023; *Imprints:* Piñata Books (Pinata Bks)
E-mail: bkorders@uh.edu; appinfo@uh.edu
Web site: http://www.artepublicopress.com
Dist(s): **Book Wholesalers, Inc.**
Booksource, The
Bound to Stay Bound Bks.
Brodart Co.
Children's Plus, Inc.
Follett School Solutions
Keystone Bks. & Media LLC
Lectorum Pubns., Inc.
Mackin Educational Resources
Midwest Library Service
Perfection Learning Corp.
Perma-Bound Bks.
Quality Bks., Inc.
Rainbow Bk. Co.
Unique Bks., Inc.
Yankee Bk. Peddler, Inc.
ebrary, Inc.; *CIP.*

Artemesia Publishing, LLC, *(978-1-932926)* Orders Addr.: 9 Mockingbird Hill Rd., Tijeras, NM 87059 USA Tel 505-286-0892; *Imprints:* Kinkajou Press (Kinkajou Pr)
E-mail: info@artemesiapublishing.com; g.habiger@artemesiapublishing.com
Web site: http://www.apbooks.net; http://www.artemesiapublishing.com; http://www.tangent-games.com; http://www.kinkajoupress.com/
Dist(s): **Bks. West**
Follett School Solutions
Hachette Bk. Group.

Artemisia Enterprises, *(978-0-9755416)* P.O. Box 3106 Mosshall Way, San Jose, CA 95135 USA
E-mail: sales@amazonheart.org
Web site: http://www.amazonheart.org.

Artesian Pr., *(978-1-58659)* 372 South 900 W., Provo, UT 84601 USA (SAN 253-1259) Tel 801-375-0800; Fax: 801-222-9199; Toll Free Fax: 888-326-3125; Toll Free: 888-734-9355; 20 Commercial Blvd., Novato, CA 94949
E-mail: info@artesianpress.com
Web site: http://www.artesianpress.com
Dist(s): **Follett School Solutions.**

Arthritis Foundation, *(978-0-912423; 978-0-692-63011-2)* 1330 W. Peachtree St., Atlanta, GA 30309 USA (SAN 267-677X) Tel 404-965-7622; Fax: 404-872-9559; Toll Free: 800-283-7800 Do not confuse with Arthritis Foundation, Southfield, MI
E-mail: sbernstein@arthritis.org
Web site: http://www.arthritis.org.

Article One *See* **Marsh Creek Pr.**

Artisan, *(978-1-57965; 978-1-885183)* Div. of Workman Publishing Co., Inc., 225 Varick St. Flr. 9, New York, NY 10014-4381 USA Toll Free: 800-967-5630 Do not confuse with Artisan, Wheaton, IL
E-mail: artisan@workman.com
Dist(s): **Workman Publishing Co., Inc.**

Artisan House *See* **Artisan**

Artisan Pubs., *(978-0-934666)* P.O. Box 1529, Muskogee, OK 74402 USA (SAN 211-8408) Tel 918-682-8341; Fax: 918-682-1263.

Artisan Sales *See* **Artisan Pubs.**

Artist Designs, *(978-0-9760409)* P.O. Box 548, Webster, WI 54893 USA Tel 715-222-2362.

Artist Studios, Ltd., *(978-1-931037; 978-1-59487; 978-1-61562)* 444 Spear St. Ste. 101, San Francisco, CA 94105-1693 USA.

Artistic Angels Corp., *(978-0-9890410)* 535 Valley View Rd. Apt. D301, Branson, MO 65616 USA Tel 417-544-1766; Fax: 417-544-1766
E-mail: artisticangels4you@yahoo.com.

Artistic Creations Bk. Publishing, *(978-0-9796843; 978-0-692-76837-2; 978-0-9982826)* 2215 6th Ave., Apt. D, Moline, IL 61265 USA
E-mail: bookwoman1110@hotmail.com
Web site: http://beserrashomebasedbiz.blogspot; http://artisticcreationsbookpublishing.books.officelive.com/default.aspx; http://site/discoveryourtalentshow/; http://site/fairytalekidssite/
Dist(s): **Partners Bk. Distributing, Inc.**

Artistic Ventures LLC, *(978-0-9771495)* Orders Addr.: 3 Glade Mallow Rd., Malta, NY 12020 USA; Edit Addr.: 3 Glade Mallow Rd., Malta, NY 12020-4326 USA; *Imprints:* Artistic Ventures Publishing (Artistic Ventures)
E-mail: dawn@artistic-ventures.com
Web site: http://www.artistic-ventures.com
Dist(s): **Follett School Solutions.**

Artistic Ventures Publishing *Imprint of* **Artistic Ventures LLC**

Artists On Video, LLC / (d/b/a) MN Productions, *(978-0-9799440; 978-1-937106)* 84 Chaumont Sq. NW, Atlanta, GA 30327 USA.

Artists' Orchard, LLC, The, *(978-0-9843166; 978-0-9857014; 978-0-9964592)* P.O. Box 113117, Pittsburgh, PA 15241 USA (SAN 859-0389) Tel 724-255-6408
E-mail: sales@theartistsorchard.com; publish@theartistsorchard.com
Web site: http://theartistsorchard.com.

Artist's Pr., *(978-0-924556)* P.O. Box 16087, Minneapolis, MN 55416-0087 USA Tel 952-486-8353
E-mail: artistspress@aim.com
Web site: http://www.artistspress.com.

ArtMar Productions, *(978-0-9799089)* 60 W. 71st St., No. 1B, New York, NY 10023 USA (SAN 854-7416)
E-mail: mlhorowitz@aol.com
Web site: http://www.marlynhorowitz.com
Dist(s): **Bookmasters Distribution.**

Art-Medium, *(978-0-9817971)* P.O. Box 390739, Mountain View, CA 94039-0739 USA (SAN 856-5848)
E-mail: tangobelly@yahoo.com
Web site: http://www.AKPhotography.net.

Artos Press Enterprises *See* **Creative Cranium Concept, The**

Artpacks, *(978-0-9790247; 978-0-9834637)* 535 22nd St., NE, Rochester, MN 55906 USA (SAN 852-2227) Tel 507-273-2529
E-mail: storymatters@charter.net.

Artrum Media, *(978-0-9840574; 978-0-9841957; 978-0-9845352; 978-0-9837050; 978-1-938107)* 627 Brickle Ridge Rd., Decatur, TN 37322 USA (SAN 858-3080)
E-mail: info@artrummedia.com
Web site: http://www.artrummedia.com
Dist(s): **New Tradition Bks.**

Arts and Minds Studio Inc., *(978-0-9767048)* Div. of Brian Alan Lane & Donna Cohen Lane, 19655 NW Stavis Bay Rd., Seabeck, WA 98380-9797 USA Tel 360-830-2614 (phonefax)
E-mail: bal@brianalanlane.com; dc@donnacohen.com
Web site: http://www.artsandminds.studio/; http://www.atinytale.com/; http://www.mindgameswithaserialkiller.com/.

Arts Pubns., *(978-0-9766590)* P.O. Box 3006, Evansdale, IA 50707-0006 USA (SAN 256-4963) Tel 319-287-5901 (phone/fax) Do not confuse with Arts Publications in Corte Madera, CA
E-mail: ceremonypress@mchsi.com; infoartspublications@mchsi.com
Web site: http://www.artspublicationsbooks.com.

ArtScroll Series *Imprint of* **Mesorah Pubns., Ltd.**

Artstreet LLC, *(978-0-9758971)* 10 Crestmont Rd. Apt. 7P, Montclair, NJ 07042-1936 USA Toll Free: 866-543-7878
E-mail: sjimenez@brandstreetllc.com
Web site: http://www.brandstreetllc.com.

Artsy Bee, LLC, *(978-0-615-75521-2; 978-0-692-48443-2; 978-0-692-58845-1)* 133 Naperville Dr., Cary, NC 27519-5409 USA Tel 919-274-6155
E-mail: rtbliss@gmail.com.

Artust Nasus Publishing, *(978-0-9763260)* 500 Rosita Ave., PO Box 1515, Westcliffe, CO 81252 USA
Web site: http://www.naturallybalancedhealth.com.

Artworks International, *(978-1-57938)* Orders Addr.: 3101 Clairmont Rd., Suite C, Atlanta, GA 30329 USA (SAN 255-6456) Tel 404-214-4331; Fax: 404-214-4390
E-mail: derek.adams@andersonpress.com
Web site: http://www.andersonpress.com.

Arundel Press *See* **Arundel Publishing**

Arundel Publishing, *(978-1-933608)* 36 Crystal Farm Rd., Warwick, NY 10990 USA Do not confuse with Arundel Press in Seattle, WA
E-mail: Sharon.Scott@ArundelPublishing.com
Dist(s): **Follett School Solutions**
Ingram Publisher Services.

Arutam Pr., *(978-0-9745477)* 62 Ave Maria, Monterey, CA 93940 USA Tel 831-375-6005
E-mail: emurray@sacredsite.com
Web site: http://www.elizabethmurray.com.

Arzana, Inc., *(978-0-9770475)* Orders Addr.: P.O. Box 60473, Potomac, MD 20859 USA Tel 301-437-0017
E-mail: balance@arzanaworld.com
Web site: http://www.arzanaworld.com.

As Sabr Pubns. *Imprint of* **Imago Pr.**

As Seen on the Internet / Arrest Me Not, *(978-0-9640336)* P.O. Box 608685, Cleveland, OH 44108-0685 USA Tel 440-487-8413; Fax: 425-963-3821
Web site: http://www.asseenontheinternet.tv.

As Simple As That Publishing, *(978-0-9728666)* Orders Addr.: P.O. Box 25 Fern Road, Southampton, NY 11968 USA
Web site: http://www.simpleasthat.com.

As Sparkle Speaks & Informs/ASSI, *(978-0-9706187)* Orders Addr.: P.O. Box 1313, Madison, TN 37116-1313 USA Tel 615-860-9762; Fax: 615-870-0959; Edit Addr.: 1672 Liberty Hill Dr., Madison, TN 37115 USA
E-mail: searlessparkle@aol.com.

ASA Publishing Company *See* **ASA Publishing Corp.**

ASA Publishing Corp., *(978-1-886528; 978-0-615-13671-4; 978-0-615-14056-8; 978-0-615-14611-9; 978-0-615-15185-4; 978-0-615-15682-8; 978-0-615-17383-2; 978-0-615-18613-9; 978-0-615-18894-2; 978-0-615-21769-7; 978-0-615-21856-4; 978-0-615-25705-1; 978-0-615-26064-8; 978-0-615-26127-0; 978-0-615-27139-2; 978-0-615-27323-5; 978-0-9819570; 978-0-9841442; 978-0-9826490; 978-0-9828135; 978-0-615-44821-3; 978-0-615-46081-9; 978-0-615-46083-3; 978-0-615-46622-4; 978-0-615-46780-1; 978-0-615-47496-0; 978-0-615-47775-6; 97) 105 E. Front St., Suite 101, Monroe, MI 48161 USA Tel 734-230-7174; Fax: 734-230-7176*
E-mail: asapublishingcorporation@gmail.com; asapublisher@gmail.com
Web site: http://www.asapublishingcorporation.com/
Dist(s): **CreateSpace Independent Publishing Platform**
Lightning Source, Inc.

ASA-CSSA-SSSA, *(978-0-89118)* 5585 Guilford Rd., Madison, WI 53711 USA (SAN 206-2879) Tel 608-268-4960; Fax: 608-273-2021
E-mail: books@agronomy.org; books@crops.org; books@soils.org
Web site: http://www.soils.org; http://www.crops.org; http://www.agronomy.org.

A.S.A.P., *(978-0-9797642)* 303 Indian Point Rd., Bar Harbor, ME 04609-9751 USA
Dist(s): **D.A.P./Distributed Art Pubs.**

Asbury Heritage Publishing, *(978-0-9859132)* 4601 Abercorne Terr., Louisville, KY 40241 USA Tel 502-897-3241; Fax: 502-897-3241
E-mail: bakerbutterfly@gmail.com.

Ascend Bks., LLC, *(978-0-9817166; 978-0-9841130; 978-0-9830619; 978-0-9836952; 978-0-9856314; 978-0-9889964; 978-0-9893095; 978-0-9912756; 978-0-9904375; 978-0-9961944; 978-0-9966742; 978-0-9989224)* 7221 W. 79th St. Suite 206, Overland Park, KS 66204 USA (SAN 856-3454) Tel 913-948-5500; Fax: 913-948-7770
E-mail: bsnodgrass@ascendbooks.com; cdrummond@ascendbooks.com
Web site: http://www.ascendbooks.com
Dist(s): **American West Bks.**
BookMasters, Inc.
Follett School Solutions
MyiLibrary
Partners Bk. Distributing, Inc.
News Group, The
ebrary, Inc.

Ascend Media, LLC *See* **Ascend Bks., LLC**

Ascended Ideas, *(978-0-9795103; 978-0-692-00063-2; 978-0-9823969)* P.O. Box 120, Coldiron, KY 40819-0120 USA
Web site: http://www.ascendedideas.com.

Ascending Realm Publishing, *(978-0-9762135)* P.O. Box 2223, Centennial, CO 80161-2223 USA
E-mail: brandon@ascendingrealm.com
Web site: http://www.ascendingrealm.com.

Ascension Education, *(978-0-9640837)* Orders Addr.: P.O. Box 504, Venice, CA 90294 USA Tel 310-254-4092; Edit Addr.: 1814 Pacific Ave., No. 17, Venice, CA 90291 USA
E-mail: ascension2020@comcast.net
Web site: http://www.ascension-education.com.

Ascension Lutheran Church, *(978-0-9715472)* 314 W. Main St., Danville, VA 24541 USA Tel 434-792-5795; Fax: 434-799-3900
E-mail: chrismonsministry@gmail.com
Web site: http://www.chrismon.org.

Ascension Pr., *(978-0-9659228; 978-0-9742238; 978-0-9744451; 978-1-932631; 978-1-932645; 978-1-932927; 978-1-934217; 978-1-935940; 978-1-945179)* Orders Addr.: W5180 Jefferson St., Necedah, WI 54646 USA (SAN 256-0224) Tel 608-565-2024; Fax: 608-565-2025; Toll Free: 800-376-0520; Edit Addr.: P.O. Box 1990, West Chester, PA 19341 USA Tel 610-696-7795; Fax: 610-696-7796; Toll Free: 800-376-0520; 20 Hagerty Blvd., Suite 3, West Chester, PA 19341
E-mail: mflickinger@ascensionpress.com
Web site: http://www.ascensionpress.com
Dist(s): **Follett School Solutions.**

Ascent Pubns., *(978-0-9815302)* P.O. Box 928, Warrenton, MO 63383 USA
E-mail: michael@ascentpublications.com; info@ascentpublications.com
Web site: http://www.ascentpublications.com.

Ascribed *Imprint of* **dg ink**

ASD Publishing, *(978-0-9836049; 978-0-9853441; 978-0-9961029)* 102 Arlington Ave., Hawthorne, NJ 07506 USA Tel 973-280-0145
E-mail: bbscout@hotmail.com
Dist(s): **BookBaby.**

ASE Media, *(978-0-9768890)* 5777 Crowntree Ln. Apt 208, ORLANDO, FL 32829 USA
E-mail: anne@easterlingfamily.com
Web site: http://www.asemedia.com.

Ashay by the Bay, *(978-0-9704048)* Orders Addr.: P.O. Box 2394, Union City, CA 94587 USA Tel 510-477-0967; Edit Addr.: P.O. Box 2394, Union City, CA 94587-7394 USA
E-mail: poetashay@aol.com
Web site: http://www.ashaybythebay.com.

Ashberry Lane, *(978-0-9893967; 978-1-941720)* P.O. Box 665, Gaston, OR 97119 USA Tel 503-860-5069
E-mail: christina@ashberrylane.net
Web site: www.ashberrylane.net.

Ashland Creek Pr. *Imprint of* **Byte Level Research**

Ashley & Taylor Publishing, Co., *(978-0-9745469)* P.O. Box 2793, Huntsville, AL 35804 USA Tel 256-430-1889
E-mail: AshleyTaylor4God@comcast.net.

AshleyAlan Enterprises, *(978-0-9702171; 978-0-9710145)* Orders Addr.: P.O. Box 1510, Kyle, TX 78640-1510 USA Tel 512-405-3065; Fax: 512-405-3066; Edit Addr.: 115 Hogan, Kyle, TX 78640 USA
E-mail: celestem@kyle-tx.com
Web site: http://www.ashleyanlan.com.

Ashlye V. Enterprises, LLC, *(978-0-9792934)* P.O. Box 3301, Columbia, SC 29230 USA Tel 803-361-1161; Fax: 803-772-2878; Toll Free: 866-382-3558
E-mail: ashlyev@gmail.com
Web site: http://www.ashlyev.com.

Ashmolean Museum (GBR) *(978-0-900090; 978-0-907849; 978-1-85444) Dist. by* **Natl Bk Netwk.**

Ashtabula County Genealogical Society, *(978-1-888851)* 860 Sherman St., Geneva, OH 44041-9101 USA Tel 440-466-4521; Fax: 440-466-0162
E-mail: acgs@ashtabulagen.org
Web site: http://www.ashtabulagen.org.

Ashway Pr., *(978-0-9754575)* Div. of Ashway, 5624 Double Tree Cir., Birmingham, AL 35242 USA Tel 205-995-8482
E-mail: janetpeine@aol.com
Web site: http://www.givingmeaway.com.

ASI, *(978-0-9759271)* 12 Brandywine Dr., Warwick, NY 10990 USA
Web site: www.asipublishing.com.

Asia for Kids *Imprint of* **Infini Pr., LLC**

Asiana Media, *(978-0-9778944)* Orders Addr.: P.O. Box 13693, Tempe, AZ 85284-0062 USA Tel 602-743-7155; *Imprints:* Juice & Berriesr, The (The Juice & Ber)
E-mail: info@asianamedia.com; info@thejuiceandberries.com
Web site: http://www.asianamedia.com; http://www.thejuiceandberries.com; http://www.faithittomakeit.com.

Asimow, Dyanne, *(978-0-9859522)* 8071 Willow Glen Rd., Los Angeles, CA 90046 USA Tel 323-654-3075
E-mail: dyanne8071@sbcglobal.net.

ASJA Pr. *Imprint of* **iUniverse, Inc.**

ASK Publishing, L.L.C., *(978-0-9742967)* 34046 Jefferson Ave., St Clr Shores, MI 48082-1162 USA (SAN 255-4976)
E-mail: admin@askpublishingllc.net
Web site: http://www.askpublishingllc.net
Dist(s): **Quality Bks., Inc.**

ASL Tales, *(978-0-9818139)* Orders Addr.: P.O. Box 80354, Portland, OR 97210 USA
E-mail: info@asltales.net
Web site: http://www.asltales.net
Dist(s): **Follett School Solutions.**

Aslan Publishing, *(978-0-944031)* Owned by Renaissance Book Services Corp., 2490 Black Rock Tpke., No. 342, Fairfield, CT 06432 USA (SAN 242-6129) Tel 203-374-4766; Toll Free: 800-786-5427
E-mail: information@AslanPublishing.com; harold@aslanpublishing.com; aslan@sevenlive.net
Web site: http://www.AslanPublishing.com
Dist(s): **APG Sales & Distribution Services.**

ASM Pr., *(978-0-914826; 978-1-55581; 978-1-68367; 978-0-578-19314-4)* Div. of American Society For Microbiology, 1752 N St., NW, Washington, DC 20036 USA (SAN 202-1153) Toll Free Fax: 1-800-546-1503; P.O. Box 605, Herndon, VA 20172
E-mail: books@asmusa.org
Web site: http://www.asmpress.org; www.asmscience.org
Dist(s): **Follett School Solutions**
MyiLibrary
Rittenhouse Bk. Distributors
Wiley, John & Sons, Inc.
ebrary, Inc.

ASMedia Publishing, *(978-0-9743407)* 299 Swanville Rd., Frankfort, ME 04438 USA Fax: 207-223-5241
E-mail: asmedia2002@aol.com.

ASP Corp. Entertainment Group, Inc., *(978-0-9754147)* 3695 F Cascade Rd., Suite 229, Atlanta, GA 30331 USA Tel 404-344-7700; Fax: 404-344-7700
Web site: http://www.hannibaltrilogy.com.

Aspect *Imprint of* **Grand Central Publishing**

Aspect Bk. *Imprint of* **TEACH Services, Inc.**

Aspen Bks., *(978-1-56236)* Div. of Worldwide Pubs., Inc., P.O. Box 1271, Bountiful, UT 84011-1271 USA Toll Free: 800-748-4850
E-mail: jasay@qwest.net; prawlins@aspenbook.com
Dist(s): **Cedar Fort, Inc./CFI Distribution**
Origin Bk. Sales, Inc.

Aspen Light Publishing, *(978-0-9743620; 978-0-9834896; 978-0-9913920)* Orders Addr.: 13506 Summerport Village Pkwy. Suite #155, Windermere, FL 34786 USA Fax: 407-910-2453; Toll Free: 800-437-1695
E-mail: orders@aspenlightpublishing.com
Dist(s): **DeVorss & Co.**

Aspen MLT, Inc., *(978-0-9774821; 978-0-9823628; 978-0-9854473; 978-1-941511; 978-1-944902; 978-1-946960)* 5855 Green Valley Cir. Suite 111, Culver City, CA 90230-9023 USA (SAN 257-6260) Fax: 310-348-9731
Web site: www.aspencomics.com
Dist(s): **Diamond Comic Distributors, Inc.**
Diamond Bk. Distributors.

Aspirations Media, Inc., *(978-0-9776043; 978-0-9800034)* 7755 Lakeview Ln., Spring Lake Park, MN 55432 USA (SAN 257-7305)
Web site: http://www.aspirationsmediainc.com.

Aspire Publishing, *(978-0-9799021)* 30081 Canyon Creek, Trabuco Canyon, CA 92679 USA
Web site: 4aspirebooks.com.

Aspiring Author's Ink., *(978-0-692-84269-0; 978-0-692-85975-9; 978-0-692-85976-6; 978-0-692-89859-8; 978-0-692-91465-6; 978-0-692-92876-9; 978-0-692-93998-7; 978-0-692-94523-0; 978-0-9994400)* 6400 NW 106th PL, Alachua, FL 32615 USA Tel 352-363-4944
E-mail: kandraalbury@gmail.com
Web site: kandraalbury.org.

Aspiring Families Press, *(978-0-9961941)* 12625 High Bluff Drive, Suite 104, Dan Diego, CA 92130 USA Tel 858-531-1122
E-mail: azmairamaker@gmail.com; j@monkeycmedia.com
Web site: www.aspiringfamiliespress.com.

ASQ Quality Pr., *(978-0-87389)* Div. of American Society for Quality, 600 N. Plankinton Ave., P.O. Box 3005, Milwaukee, WI 53203 USA (SAN 683-5244) Tel 414-272-8575; Fax: 414-270-8810; Toll Free: 800-248-1946
E-mail: qpress@asq.org
Web site: https://asq.org/quality-press
Dist(s): **American Technical Pubs., Inc.**
Follett School Solutions.

Associated Arts Pub., *(978-0-9840358)* 536 Tiara Dr., Grand Junction, CO 81507 USA Tel 970-241-8024
E-mail: suehughey@optimum.net
Web site: http://SCStrange.com; HerbysSecretFormula.com
Dist(s): **CreateSpace Independent Publishing Platform**
Follett School Solutions.

Assn. of Asthma Educators, *(978-0-9821228)* 1215 Anthony Ave., Columbia, SC 29201-1701 USA Tel 803-540-7530; Fax: 803-254-3773; Toll Free: 888-988-7747
E-mail: marie.queen@queencommunicationsllc.com
Web site: http://www.asthmaeducators.org.

Assn. of Christian Schls. International, *(978-1-58331)* Orders Addr.: P.O. Box 65130, Colorado Springs, CO 80962-5130 USA; Edit Addr.: 731 Chapel Hills Dr., Colorado Springs, CO 80920 USA (SAN 689-5751) Tel 719-528-6906; Fax: 719-531-0631; Toll Free: 800-367-0798 (orders only)
E-mail: webmaster@acsi.org; info@acsi.org
Web site: http://www.acsi.org.

Association of Jewish Libraries, *(978-0-929262)* P.O. Box 1118, Teaneck, NJ 07666 USA
E-mail: ajlibs@osu.edu; publications@jewishlibaries.org
Web site: http://www.jewishlibraries.org.

Assouline (FRA) *(978-2-84323; 978-2-908228; 978-2-7594) Dist. by* **TwoRivers.**

AS-Sunnah Foundation of America *See* **Islamic Supreme Council of America**

Asta Publications, LLC, *(978-0-9777060; 978-1-934947)* Orders Addr.: P.O. Box 1735, Stockbridge, GA 30281 USA Fax: 678-814-1370; Toll Free: 800-482-4190
E-mail: acollins@astapublications.com; ahoward@astapublications.com
Web site: http://www.astapublications.com; http://www.astapublication.com; http://www.astaskids.com
Dist(s): **A & B Distributors & Pubs. Group**
BookBaby.

Astakos Publishing, *(978-0-9792991)* P.O. Box 227, Roscoe, IL 61073-9330 USA Tel 815-623-6616
E-mail: astakospublishing@charter.net
Web site: http://www.astakospublishing.com
Dist(s): **Follett School Solutions**
Quality Bks., Inc.

A-Star*, *(978-0-9858935)* 13 W. St. Apt. 2, Greenfield, MA 01301 USA Tel 415-505-5873
E-mail: info@adriennenunez.net
Web site: www.adriennenunez.net.

Asteroid Publishing, *(978-0-9841187)* 251 Middle Rd., Boxborough, MA 01719 USA Tel 978-549-0464
Dist(s): **Smashwords.**

Aston & James Publications *See* **Aston & James Publishing, LLC**

Aston & James Publishing, LLC, *(978-1-946745)* 500 N. Michigan Ave., Chicago, IL 60611 USA Tel 773-412-6212
Dist(s): **CreateSpace Independent Publishing Platform.**

Astonish Comics, *(978-0-9721259)* 10061 Riverside Dr., Suite No. 785, Toluca Lake, CA 91602 USA
Web site: http://www.theastonishfactory.com
Dist(s): **Diamond Comic Distributors, Inc.**
Diamond Bk. Distributors.

Astor Pr., *(978-0-9764119; 978-0-615-14497-9; 978-0-615-18601-6; 978-0-615-21360-6; 978-0-615-26465-3; 978-0-578-00527-0; 978-0-578-01799-0; 978-0-578-02611-4; 978-0-578-02667-1; 978-0-9899257)* 12 Walcott St., Maynard, MA 01754 USA
E-mail: info@astorpress.com; mail@shanddaramon.com; ken@kenlanger.com
Web site: http://www.astorpress.com; http://brassbellbooks.com
Dist(s): **Lulu Pr., Inc.**
Smashwords.

Astor-Honor, Inc., *(978-0-8392)* 16 E. 40th St., Third Flr., New York, NY 10016 USA (SAN 203-5022) Tel 212-840-8800; Fax: 212-840-7246.

Astral Publishing Co., *(978-0-9645867)* Orders Addr.: P.O. Box 3955, Santa Barbara, CA 93130-3955 USA (SAN 298-5705) Tel 805-967-7667; Edit Addr.: 333 Old Mill Rd., No. 324, Santa Barbara, CA 93110 USA
E-mail: wveigele@aol.com
Web site: http://www.astralpublishing.com
Dist(s): **Quality Bks., Inc.**

Astri My Astri Publishing, *(978-0-9760541; 978-0-9859712)* 602 3rd Ave. SW, Waukon, IA 52172 USA Tel 563-568-6229; Fax: 563-568-5377
E-mail: gourleyd@mchsi.com; deb@astrimyastri.com; gourleydeb@gmail.com
Web site: http://www.astrimyastri.com.

Astronaut Ink, *(978-0-9772727)* Orders Addr.: 180 Newbury St. 4106, Danvers, MA 01923 USA
E-mail: joe@popartproperties.com
Web site: http://www.popartproperties.com.

ASunnyDay Publishing, *(978-0-9818366)* 17 Hillside Ave., Suite 102, Rockville Centre, NY 11570 USA Tel 516-884-7661
E-mail: dariarosebooks@gmail.com
Web site: http://www.dariarosebooks.com.

At Ease Pr., *(978-0-917921)* Div. of Be at Ease School of Etiquette, 1212 W. Ben White Blvd., #214, Austin, TX 78704-7197 USA (SAN 656-9900)
E-mail: haroldalmon@gmail.com; schoolofetiquette@ateasepress.com
Web site: http://ateasepress.com; http://baeschoolofetiquette.blogspot.com/; http://baesoe.com
Dist(s): **Lulu Pr., Inc.**

At Peace Media, LLC, *(978-0-9742002)* 1117 E. Putnam Ave., No. 345, Riverside, CT 06878 USA Tel 203-698-2688; Fax: 203-698-3441; Toll Free: 800-575-7715
E-mail: john@atpeacemedia.com
Web site: http://www.atpeacemedia.com.

Atelier Finwhale, *(978-0-9882561)* P.O. Box 60608, Palo Alto, CA 94306-9991 USA Tel 650-787-2198
E-mail: 3marjorie14@gmail.com.

Atelier Mythologie, *(978-0-9899905; 978-1-945308)* 3815 E Pike, Seattle, WA 98122 USA Tel 206-724-4144
E-mail: publisher@ateliermythologie.com.

Athanata Arts, Ltd., *(978-0-9727993)* P.O. Box 321, Garden City, NY 11530 USA (SAN 255-5018) Tel 516-742-8735
E-mail: info@athanata.com
Web site: http://www.athanata.com.

Athanatos Publishing Group, *(978-0-9791276; 978-0-9822776; 978-1-936830; 978-1-947844)* PO Box 57, Greenwood, WI 54437 USA (SAN 852-5234)
E-mail: publisher@suzeteo.com
Web site: http://www.suzeteo.com.

Athenaeum Music & Arts Library *Imprint of* **Library Assn. of La Jolla**

Atheneum Bks. for Young Readers *Imprint of* **Simon & Schuster Children's Publishing**

Atheneum/Anne Schwartz Bks. *Imprint of* **Simon & Schuster Children's Publishing**

Atheneum/Caitlyn Dlouhy Books *Imprint of* **Simon & Schuster Children's Publishing**

Atheneum/Richard Jackson Bks. *Imprint of* **Simon & Schuster Children's Publishing**

AthertonCustoms, *(978-0-578-00865-3; 978-0-615-33485-1; 978-0-9827167)* 6536 Aldergate Ln., Las Vegas, NV 89110 USA Tel 702-438-6596
E-mail: jim@athertoncustoms.com
Web site: http://www.athertoncustoms.com
Dist(s): **Lulu Pr., Inc.**

ATInternational Pubs., *(978-0-9773816)* 227 Sunflower Ln., West Windsor, NJ 08550-2439 USA
E-mail: atinetus@yahoo.com.

Atkinson, Janet Irene *See* **Irene, Jan Pubns.**

Atlantic Bks., Ltd. (GBR) *(978-1-903809; 978-1-84354; 978-1-84887; 978-0-85789; 978-0-85740; 978-1-78239) Dist. by* **IPG Chicago.**

Atlantic Bridge Publishing, *(978-0-9700930; 978-0-9706913; 978-1-931761; 978-1-59578; 978-1-62210)* 10509 Sedgegrass Dr., Indianapolis, IN 46235 USA Tel 317-826-8059 Do not confuse with Bridge Works Publishing Company, Inc. in Bridgehampton, NY
E-mail: linda@atlanticbridge.net
Web site: http://www.liquidsilverbooks.com; http://www.atlanticbridge.net
Dist(s): **INscribe Digital.**

Atlantic Publishing Company *See* **Atlantic Publishing Group, Inc.**

Atlantic Publishing Group, Inc., *(978-0-910627; 978-1-60138; 978-1-62023)* 1405 SW. 6th Ave., Ocala, FL 34471-0640 USA (SAN 268-1250) Toll Free: 800-814-1132 Do not confuse with companies with the same or similar name in Tabor City, NC , Aurora, IL , Lakeland, FL , Combs, KY , Neosho, MO
E-mail: info@atlantic-pub.com; sales@atlantic-pub.com
Web site: http://www.atlantic-pub.com
Dist(s): **MyiLibrary.**

Atlantida (ARG) *(978-950-08) Dist. by* **AIMS Intl.**

Atlas Games *Imprint of* **Trident, Inc.**

Atlas Publishing *Imprint of* **Atlas Publishing LLC**

Atlas Publishing LLC, *(978-0-9969679; 978-1-945033)* 42072 5th St Suite 103, Temecula, CA 92590 USA Tel 858-222-3747; *Imprints:* Atlas Publishing (AtlasP)
E-mail: permissions@atlaspublishing.biz; brent@atlaspublishing.biz
Web site: http://www.atlaspublishing.biz
Dist(s): **Ingram Publisher Services.**

AtlasBooks Distribution *See* **Bookmasters Distribution**

Atom Pr., 926 Flemington St., Pittsburgh, PA 15217 USA Tel 951-801-0391
E-mail: atomtitan@hotmail.com.

Atombank Bks., *(978-0-9905160)* 111 Pheasant Walk, Guilderland, NY 12303 USA Tel 518-421-5962
E-mail: atombankbooks@gmail.com
Web site: atombankbooks.com.

Atomic Basement, 1222 N. Commonwealth Ave. Apt. No. 4, Los Angeles, CA 90029-2058 USA Tel 386-679-9106
E-mail: oilerhggns@aol.com.

Atomic Fruit Pr., *(978-0-9753225)* 404 13th Ave., Huntington, WV 25701 USA
Web site: http://www.apocalyptictangerine.com.

Atria Bks. *Imprint of* **Simon & Schuster**

Atria Bks *Imprint of* **Atria Bks.**

Atria Bks., Div. of Simon & Schuster, 1230 Avenue of the Americas, New York, NY 10020 USA; *Imprints:* Beyond Words/Atria Books (AtriaBks); Atria Books (AtriBksimp); Keywords Press (Keywords Press)
Dist(s): **Follett School Solutions**
MyiLibrary
Simon & Schuster, Inc.

Atria/Emily Bestler Bks. *Imprint of* **Atria/Emily Bestler Bks.**

Atria/Emily Bestler Bks., 1230 Avenue of the Americas, New York, NY 10020 USA; *Imprints:* Atria/Emily Bestler Books (AEBB)
Dist(s): **Simon & Schuster, Inc.**

Atrium Publishing, Incorporated *See* **mTrellis Publishing, Inc.**

Attack The Text / Magedo Publishing *See* **Attack The Text Publishing**

Attack The Text Publishing, *(978-0-9755923; 978-0-9842882)* 905 N. Pacific St., No. C, Oceanside, CA 92831 USA
Web site: http://www.attackthetext.com; http://www.magedo.com.

Attainment Co., Inc., *(978-0-934731; 978-1-57861; 978-1-943148; 978-1-944315)* Orders Addr.: P.O. Box 930160, Verona, WI 53593 USA (SAN 694-1656) Tel 608-845-7880; Fax: 608-845-8040; Toll Free: 800-327-4269; Edit Addr.: 504 Commerce Pkwy., Verona, WI 53953 USA (SAN 631-6174); *Imprints:* IEP Resources (IEP Res)
E-mail: info@attainmentcompany.com; sue@attainmentcompany.com; ameyer@attainmentcompany.com
Web site: http://www.attainmentcompany.com/
Dist(s): **Bookmasters Distribution**
Follett School Solutions
Linx Educational Publishing, Inc.
Sunburst Communications, Inc.

Attic Studio Pr. *Imprint of* **Attic Studio Publishing Hse.**

Attic Studio Publishing Hse., *(978-1-883551)* Orders Addr.: P.O. Box 75, Clinton Corners, NY 12514 USA (SAN 298-2838) Tel 845-266-8100; Fax: 845-266-5515; Toll Free: 800-974-5533 (orders); Edit Addr.: 564 Schultzville Rd., Clinton Corners, NY 12514 USA (SAN 298-2846); *Imprints:* Attic Studio Press (Attic Studio); Maple Corners Press (Maple Corners Pr)
E-mail: collegeavepress@aol.com; atticstudiopress@aol.com
Dist(s): **BookBaby**
Emerald Bk. Co.
Spring Arbor Distributors, Inc.

Atticus, C. J., *(978-0-9887780)* 41 Radford Ct. Sw, Marietta, GA 30060 USA Tel 770-805-9422
E-mail: atticus@cjatticus.com.

Attitude Pie Publishing, *(978-0-692-01275-8; 978-0-692-90265-3)* 2100 NE 214th St., North Miami Beach, FL 33179 USA Tel 305-725-0446; 419-281-5100 X1151
E-mail: MPYANOWSKI@BOOKMASTERS.COM
Dist(s): **Bookmasters Distribution.**

Attitudes in Dressing, Inc., *(978-0-9766640)* 1350 Broadway, New York, NY 10018 USA Tel 212-279-3492; Fax: 212-564-3426; Toll Free: 800-899-0503
Web site: http://www.bodywrappers.com.

ATU Golden Pubns., *(978-0-9753119)* 8283 Main St., Bokeelia, FL 33922 USA
E-mail: chrissydl@aol.com
Web site: http://www.pgaa.com.

Auckland Univ. Pr. (NZL) *(978-1-86940; 978-1-77558) Dist. by* **IPG Chicago.**

Audible Studios on Brilliance Audio *Imprint of* **Brilliance Publishing, Inc.**

Audio Bookshelf, *(978-1-883332; 978-0-9741711; 978-0-9761932; 978-0-9814890; 978-1-935430)* Orders Addr.: 44 Ocean View Dr., Middletown, RI 02842 USA Tel 401-849-2333; Fax: 401-842-0440; Toll Free: 800-234-1713; Edit Addr.: P.O. Box 83, Belfast, ME 04915-0083 USA
E-mail: dd@audiobookshelf.com
Web site: http://www.audiobookshelf.com
Dist(s): **AudioGO**
Follett School Solutions
Landmark Audiobooks
Professional Media Service Corp.

Audio Craft Press *See* **AudioCraft Publishing, Inc.**

Audio Holdings, LLC, *(978-1-60136)* P.O. Box 119, Franklin Park, NJ 08823 USA (SAN 851-0776) Tel 732-940-4286; Fax: 732-940-0534
E-mail: mgladishev@gmail.com
Dist(s): **Ebsco Publishing.**

Audio Partners, Incorporated *See* **Audio Partners Publishing Corp.**

Audio Partners Publishing Corp., *(978-0-88690; 978-0-945353; 978-1-55504; 978-1-57270)* 42 Whitecap Dr., North Kingstown, RI 02852-7445 USA (SAN 253-4622) Toll Free Fax: 877-492-0873; Toll Free: 800-621-0182
E-mail: info@audiopartners.com
Dist(s): **Follett School Solutions**
Landmark Audiobooks
Two Rivers Distribution.

Audio Renaissance *See* **Macmillan Audio**

AudioCraft Publishing, Inc., *(978-1-893699; 978-1-942950)* Orders Addr.: P.O. Box 281, Topinabee, MI 49791 USA Tel 231-238-0338; Fax: 231-238-0339; Toll Free: 888-420-4244; Edit Addr.: P.O. Box 281, Topinabee, MI 49791 USA
E-mail: ck@americanchillers.com; store@americanchillers.com; shawn@americanchillers.com
Web site: http://www.audiocraftpublishing.com; http://www.michiganchillers.com; http://www.americanchillers.com
Dist(s): **Follett School Solutions**
Partners Bk. Distributing, Inc.

†AudioGO, *(978-0-563; 978-0-7540; 978-0-7927; 978-0-89340; 978-1-55504; 978-1-60283; 978-1-60998; 978-1-62064; 978-1-62460; 978-1-4815; 978-1-4821)* Orders Addr.: c/o Perseus, 1094 Flex Dr., Jackson, TN 38301 USA; Edit Addr.: 42 Whitecap Dr., North Kingstown, RI 02852-7445 USA (SAN 858-7701) Toll Free: 800-621-0182; *Imprints:* Sound Library (SoundLib)
E-mail: laura.almeida@audiogo.com
Web site: http://www.audiogo.com/us/
Dist(s): **Ebsco Publishing**
Findaway World, LLC
Follett School Solutions
INscribe Digital
Two Rivers Distribution; *CIP.*

Audioscope, *(978-1-57375)* Div. of K-tel International (USA), Inc., 2605 Fernbrook Ln., N., No. H-O, Plymouth, MN 55447 USA Tel 612-559-6888; Fax: 612-559-6848; Toll Free: 800-328-6640
Web site: http://www.ktel.com
Dist(s): **Follett School Solutions.**

Auditors of God, The (GBR) *(978-0-9561587; 978-0-9572919) Dist. by* **LuluCom.**

Audrey Pr., *(978-1-936426)* P.O. Box 6113, Maryville, TN 37802 USA Tel 865-254-4463
E-mail: valarie@audreypress.com
Web site: www.audreypress.com
Dist(s): **Bookmasters Distribution.**

Audrey Productions, *(978-0-9722673)* 7809 Paper Flower Ct., Las Vegas, NV 89128 USA Tel 702-228-4803 (phone/fax)
Dist(s): **Follett School Solutions.**

Audubon Pr. & Christian Bk. Service, *(978-0-9652883; 978-0-9742365; 978-0-9820731)* Orders Addr.: P.O. Box 8055, Laurel, MS 39441 USA Tel 601-649-8572; Fax: 601-649-8571; Toll Free: 800-405-3788; Edit Addr.: 2601 Audubon Dr., Laurel, MS 39440 USA
E-mail: buybooks@audubonpress.com
Web site: http://www.audubonpress.com.

Augsburg Bks. *Imprint of* **Augsburg Fortress, Pubs.**

†Augsburg Fortress, Pubs., *(978-0-8006; 978-0-8066; 978-1-4514; 978-1-5064)* Orders Addr.: P.O. Box 1209, Minneapolis, MN 55440-1209 USA (SAN 169-4081) Toll Free Fax: 800-722-7766; Toll Free: 800-328-4648 (orders only); Edit Addr.: 510 Marquette 8th Fl., Minneapolis, MN 55402 USA Tel 800-328-4648 800-722-7766; *Imprints:* Fortress Press (Fortress Pr); Augsburg Books (Augsburg Bks); Sparkhouse Family (Sparkhse)
E-mail: customerservice@augsburgfortress.org; info@augsburgfortress.org; subscriptions@augsburgfortress.org; copyright@augsburgfortress.org; international@augsburgfortress.org
Web site: http://www.augsburgfortress.org
Dist(s): **ebrary, Inc.**; *CIP.*

Augsburg Fortress Publishers, Publishing House of The Evangelical Lutheran Church in America *See* **Augsburg Fortress, Pubs.**

†August Hse. Pubs., Inc., *(978-0-87483; 978-0-935304; 978-1-939160; 978-1-941459; 978-1-941460; 978-1-947301)* 3500 Piedmont Rd. NE, Suite 310, Atlanta, GA 30305 USA (SAN 223-7288) Tel 404-442-4425; Fax: 404-442-4435; Toll Free: 800-284-8784; 3500 Piedmont Rd. Suite 310, Atlanta, GA 30305; *Imprints:* August House Story Cove (August Hse Story Cove)
E-mail: ahinfo@augusthouse.com; order@augusthouse.com
Web site: http://www.augusthouse.com
Dist(s): **Findaway World, LLC**
Follett School Solutions
National Bk. Network; *CIP.*

August House Story Cove *Imprint of* **August Hse. Pubs., Inc.**

August Too Publishing, *(978-0-9767103)* 1346 E. Poinsettia St., Long Beach, CA 90805-3128 USA
E-mail: writeme@paulcarhart.com.

Augusta Win Publishing, *(978-0-9766597)* Orders Addr.: P.O. Box 53, Turin, NY 13473 USA; Edit Addr.: 6159 W. Main, Turin, NY 13473 USA
E-mail: augustawinpub@yahoo.com
Web site: http://www.augustawinpublishing.com.

Augustana College Geology Dept. Pr., *(978-0-9797015)* 639 38th St., Rock Island, IL 61201-2296 USA Tel 309-794-7318; Fax: 309-794-7564
Web site: http://www.augustana.edu.

Augustine Pr., *(978-0-9626431)* 900 Old Koenig Ln., No. 135, Austin, TX 78756 USA Tel 512-459-5194; Fax: 512-451-0755
E-mail: morganp@flash.net.

Augustinians of the Assumption *See* **Ambassador Bks., Inc.**

Augustus Publishing, *(978-0-9759453; 978-0-9792816; 978-0-9825415; 978-1-935883)* Div. of Augustus Productions, 600 W. 218 St., Suite 3K, New York, NY 10034 USA Tel 646-526-7998
E-mail: jc@augustuspublishing.com; gfhood1@aol.com; aw@augustuspublishing.com
Web site: http://www.augustuspublishing.com
Dist(s): **A & B Distributors & Pubs. Group**
Follett School Solutions
Independent Pubs. Group
MyiLibrary
Publishers Group West (PGW).

Aunt Dee's Attic, Inc., *(978-0-9679437; 978-0-9829416)* 3361 N. Maple Rd., Ann Arbor, MI 48105 USA Tel 734-668-6738; Fax: 734-668-0182; Toll Free: 800-352-6797
E-mail: dianne@elansys.com; author@auntdeesattic.com
Web site: http://www.auntdeesattic.com.

Aunt Patty's Travels-London, *(978-0-9659668)* 4811 Wesleyan Woods Dr., Macon, GA 31210 USA.

Aunt Strawberry Bks., *(978-0-9669988)* Orders Addr.: P.O. Box 819, Boulder, CO 80306-0819 USA (SAN 299-9811) Tel 303-449-3574; Fax: 303-444-9221
E-mail: readasbs@hotmail.com
Dist(s): **Brodart Co.**
Follett School Solutions.

Auntie B Publishing *See* **BaHart Pubns. / Eight Legs Publishing**

Aunty Ems Boutique, *(978-0-9742122)* P.O. Box 1963, Havasu Lake Landing, CA 92363 USA.

Aura Printing, Inc., *(978-0-911643)* 88 Parkville Ave., Brooklyn, NY 11230 USA (SAN 237-9317) Tel 718-435-9103; Fax: 718-871-9488
Dist(s): **Bookazine Co., Inc.**

Aura Productions LLC *See* **Simple Ink, LLC**

Aurandt, Paul H II, *(978-0-9887774)* 1035 Pk. Ave., River Forest, IL 60305 USA Tel 708-366-5371; Fax: 708-366-9184
E-mail: paul@paulharvey.com
Web site: http://www.paulharvey.com.

Auricle Ink Pubs., *(978-0-9661826; 978-0-9825785)* P.O. Box 20607, Sedona, AZ 86341 USA Tel 928-284-0860
E-mail: rcarmen27@yahoo.com
Web site: http://www.hearingproblems.com
Dist(s): **Academic Bk. Ctr., Inc.**
Bk. Hse., Inc., The
Brodart Co.
Coutts Information Services
Emery-Pratt Co.
Follett School Solutions
Franklin Bk. Co., Inc.
Majors, J. A. Co.
Matthews Medical Bk. Co.
Midwest Library Service
Yankee Bk. Peddler, Inc.

Auriga, Ediciones S.A. (ESP) *(978-84-7281) Dist. by* **Continental Bk.**

Aurora Books *Imprint of* **Eco-Justice Pr., LLC**

Aurora Bks., *(978-0-9753508)* 512 Willow Branch Rd., Norman, OK 73072 USA
E-mail: aurorabooks@netzero.net.

Aurora Libris Corp., *(978-1-932233)* 40 E. 83rd St., Apt. 35, New York, NY 10028 USA Toll Free: 866-763-8411
E-mail: lavinia@laviniasworld.com
Web site: http://www.laviniasworld.com.

Aurora Metro Pubns. Ltd. (GBR) *(978-0-9515877; 978-0-9536757; 978-0-9542330; 978-0-9546912; 978-0-9551566; 978-1-906582; 978-0-9566329) Dist. by* **Consort Bk Sales.**

Aurora Pubs., Inc., *(978-0-9791758)* Orders Addr.: 5970 S.W. 18th St., No. 117, Boca Raton, FL 33433-7197 USA; Edit Addr.: 814 N. Franklin St., Chicago, IL 60610 USA
E-mail: aurorapublishers@aol.com
Web site: http://www.aurorapublishers.com
Dist(s): **Ebsco Publishing**
Follett School Solutions
Independent Pubs. Group
MyiLibrary.

Aurora Publishing, Incor[porated *See* **Aurora Publishing, Inc.**

Aurora Publishing, Inc., *(978-1-934496)* 3655 Torrance Blvd., Suite 430, Torrance, CA 90503 USA; *Imprints:* Deux (Deux); LuvLuv (LuvLuv) Do not confuse with companies with the same or similar name in Arljgton, VA, College Grove, TN., West Palm Beach, FL, Eagle River, AK, West Hartford, CT, Fort Lauderdale, FL
E-mail: info@aurora-publishing.com
Web site: http://www.aurora-publishing.com; http://www.deux-press.com; http://www.luvluv-press.com
Dist(s): **Diamond Comic Distributors, Inc.**
Diamond Bk. Distributors.

Austin & Charlie Adventures *Imprint of* **Paw Print Pubns.**

Austin & Company, Inc., *(978-0-9657153)* 104 S. Union St., Suite 202, Traverse City, MI 49684 USA (SAN 631-1466) Tel 231-933-4649; Fax: 231-933-4659
E-mail: aandn@aol.com
Web site: http://www.austinandcompanyinc.com.

Austin & Nelson Publishing *See* **Austin & Company, Inc.**

Austin Christopher Swift, *(978-0-9764208)* 154 Golden Autumn Pl., Woodlands, TX 77384 USA Tel 956-421-5750; Fax: 956-421-5721
E-mail: john@toppmarketing.com.

Austin Energy Green Building Program, *(978-0-9679069)* Orders Addr.: P.O. Box 1088, Austin, TX 78767 USA Tel 512-322-6172; Fax: 512-505-3711; Edit Addr.: 721 Barton Springs Rd., Austin, TX 78704 USA
E-mail: dick.peterson@austinenergy.com
Web site: http://www.austinenergy.com.

Austin, Laurie , *(978-0-578-18226-1)* 15627 158th Ave SE, Renton, WA 98058 USA.

Austin, Stan (AUS) *(978-0-646-35644-0) Dist. by* **Bookmasters.**

Austin, Stephen F. State Univ. Pr., *(978-1-936205; 978-1-62288)* Orders Addr.: P.O. Box 13002, Nacogdoches, TX 75962 USA Tel 936-468-1078; Fax: 936-468-2614; Edit Addr.: 1936 North St. Liberal Arts N., 203 English, Nacogdoches, TX 75962 USA
Dist(s): **MyiLibrary**
Texas A&M Univ. Pr.
ebrary, Inc.

Australian Academic Pr. (AUS) *(978-1-875378; 978-1-921513; 978-1-922117; 978-1-925644) Dist. by* **IngramPubServ.**

Australian Fishing Network (AUS) *(978-0-9587143; 978-1-86513; 978-1-86252-412-5; 978-0-646-00117-3; 978-0-646-15871-6; 978-0-646-19310-6; 978-0-646-20528-1; 978-0-646-20908-1; 978-0-646-21731-4; 978-0-646-24873-8; 978-0-646-25433-3; 978-0-646-25434-0; 978-0-646-30130-3; 978-0-646-31918-6) Dist. by* **Cardinal PubGr.**

Auteur Publishing (GBR) *(978-1-903663; 978-1-906733) Dist. by* **Col U Pr.**

Authentic Media (GBR) *(978-0-8499; 978-0-85009; 978-1-86024; 978-1-78078) Dist. by* **EMI CMG Dist.**

Author Academy Elite, *(978-0-692-31830-0; 978-1-943526; 978-1-946114; 978-0-692-85391-7; 978-1-64085; 978-0-692-88922-0; 978-1-61984-661-6)* P.O. Box 43, Powell, OH 43065 USA Tel 7402720093
Dist(s): **CreateSpace Independent Publishing Platform.**

Author at Work *Imprint of* **Owen, Richard C. Pubs., Inc.**

Author Solutions, Inc., Div. of Penguin Group (USA) Inc., 1663 Liberty Dr., Bloomington, IN 47403 USA Tel 812-334-5223; Toll Free: 877-655-1722; *Imprints:* WestBow Press (WestBowPr); Balboa Press (BalboaPr);

Inspiring Voices (InspVoices); Abbott Press (AbbottPr); PartridgeIndia (PARTRIDGEINDIA)
E-mail: sfurr@authorsolutions.com
Web site: http://www.authorsolutions.com
Dist(s): **Bookmasters Distribution**
CreateSpace Independent Publishing Platform
Xlibris Corp.
Zondervan.

AuthorHouse, *(978-1-58500; 978-0-9675669; 978-1-58721; 978-1-58820; 978-0-7596; 978-1-4033; 978-1-4107; 978-1-4140; 978-1-4184; 978-1-4208; 978-1-4259; 978-1-4343; 978-1-4389; 978-1-4490; 978-1-4520; 978-1-61764; 978-1-4567; 978-1-4582; 978-1-4624; 978-1-4633; 978-1-4634; 978-0-9846457; 978-1-4670; 978-1-4678; 978-1-4685; 978-1-4772; 978-1-4817; 978-1-4918; 978-1-4969; 978-1-5049; 978-1-5065; 978-1-5246; 978-1-5462) Div. of Author Solutions, Inc., 1663 Liberty Dr., Suite 200, Bloomington, IN 47403 USA (SAN 253-7605) Fax: 812-336-5449; Toll Free: 888-519-5121; Imprints*: Life Rich Publishing (Life Rich Pub)
E-mail: authorsupport@authorhouse.com; emilyguldin@yahoo.com; sfurr@authorsolutions.com; jburns@authorsolutions.com
Web site: http://www.facebook.com/daveywizzletooth1; http://www.authorhouse.com
Dist(s): **Author Solutions, Inc.**
BookBaby
Bookmasters Distribution
CreateSpace Independent Publishing Platform
Follett School Solutions
Ingram Publisher Services
Lulu Pr., Inc.
MyiLibrary
Smashwords.

AuthorMike Ink *See* **AM Ink Publishing**

Authors & Artists Publishers of New York, Inc., *(978-0-9708053; 978-0-9724922; 978-0-9740683; 978-0-9754298; 978-0-9763993; 978-0-9766716; 978-0-9771482; 978-0-9786211; 978-0-9787113; 978-0-9819746; 978-0-9825971; 978-0-9839121; 978-0-9850947)* 21 Sta. Rd. Suite 211, Wilton, CT 06897 USA; *Imprints*: Ithaca Press (IthacaPress)
Web site: http://www.ithacapress.com
Dist(s): **Follett School Solutions.**

Authors Choice Pr. *Imprint of* **iUniverse, Inc.**

Author's Connection Pr., *(978-0-927206)* 777 College Pk. Dr., SW No. 60, Albany, OR 97322-8430 USA
Web site: http://www.acpublish.com.

Authors' Discovery Cooperation, Inc., *(978-0-9794443; 978-0-9800854; 978-0-9844730)* 165 Cherry Ln., Robert Lee, TX 76945 USA (SAN 853-4276) Tel 325-453-4595
E-mail: ldudney@nwol.net
Web site: http://www.authorsdiscovery.com.

Authors' Press, The *See* **Quantum Manifestations Publishing**

Author's Publishing, LLC, *(978-0-9728902; 978-1-60415)* 104 Lake June Rd. NW, Lake Placid, FL 33852 USA
E-mail: debono@strato.net
Web site: http://www.fantasyreaders.com.

Autism & Behavior Training Associates *See* **ABTA Pubns. & Products**

Autism Asperger Publishing Co., *(978-0-9672514; 978-1-931282; 978-1-934575; 978-1-937473; 978-1-942197)* Orders Addr.: P.O. Box 23173, Overland Park, KS 66283-0173 USA Tel 913-599-3311; Fax: 913-492-2546; 11209 Strang Line Rd, Lenexa, KS 66215 (SAN 920-9220); Edit Addr.: 15490 Qunvira, Overland Park, KS 66221 USA
E-mail: kmcbr41457@aol.com
Web site: http://www.asperger.net
Dist(s): **Follett School Solutions.**

Autism Research Institute, *(978-0-9740360)* 4182 Adams Ave., San Diego, CA 92116 USA Fax: 619-563-6840
E-mail: sait97302@yahoo.com
Web site: http://www.autismresearchinstitute.com.

Automatic Pictures Publishing, *(978-0-9818737; 978-0-9892221; 978-0-9912729)* 5721 Valley Oak Dr., Los Angeles, CA 90068 USA Tel 323-935-1800; Fax: 323-935-8040
E-mail: automaticstudio@gmail.com
Web site: http://www.lookingglasswars.com
Dist(s): **Diamond Comic Distributors, Inc.**
Diamond Bk. Distributors
Publishers Group West (PGW).

Automatic Publishing *See* **Automatic Pictures Publishing**

Automobile Assn. (GBR) *(978-0-7495; 978-0-86145; 978-0-901088; 978-1-872163) Dist. by* **Trafalgar.**

Automobile Assn. (GBR) *(978-0-7495; 978-0-86145; 978-0-901088; 978-1-872163) Dist. by* **IPG Chicago.**

Automobiles-Memory Lane Publishing, *(978-0-9746667)* Orders Addr.: P.O. Box 228, Vicksburg, MI 49097 USA (SAN 255-7118) Tel 269-649-3614 (phone/fax); Edit Addr.: 2294 E. VW Ave., Vicksburg, MI 49097 USA.

Autonomedia, *(978-0-936756; 978-1-57027)* Orders Addr.: P.O. Box 568, Brooklyn, NY 11211-0568 USA; Edit Addr.: 55 S. Eleventh St., #4b, Brooklyn, NY 11211-0568 USA (SAN 221-3869) Tel 718-963-2603
E-mail: info@autonomedia.org
Web site: http://www.autonomedia.org
Dist(s): **AK Pr. Distribution**
Lulu Pr., Inc.
SPD-Small Pr. Distribution.

Autumn Hill Bks., Inc., *(978-0-9754444; 978-0-9843036; 978-0-9827466; 978-0-9987400)* P.O. Box 22, Iowa City, IA 52244 USA Tel 319-354-2456; 814 N. Franklin St., Chicago, IL 60610
E-mail: info@autumnhillbooks.com
Web site: http://www.autumnhillbooks.com
Dist(s): **Ebsco Publishing**
Follett School Solutions
Independent Pubs. Group
MyiLibrary.

Autumn Hse. Publishing, *(978-0-9637825)* Orders Addr.: P.O. Box 763833, Dallas, TX 75376 USA; Edit Addr.: 1535 Acapulco Dr., Dallas, TX 75232 USA Tel 214-376-8959 Do not confuse with the same or similar name in Lexington, KY, Hagerstown, MD
E-mail: millijp@earthlink.net.

Autumn Hse. Publishing Co., *(978-0-8127; 978-1-878951)* Div. of Review & Herald Publishing Assn., 55 W. Oakridge Dr., Hagerstown, MD 21740 USA Do not confuse with companies with the same name in Lexington, KY, Dallas, TX.

Autumn Publishing Group, LLC, *(978-1-890877)* Orders Addr.: P.O. Box 71604, Madison Heights, MI 48071 USA Tel 248-589-5249; Fax: 248-585-5715; Toll Free: 888-876-4114; Edit Addr.: 30755 Barrington Ave., Madison Heights, MI 48071 USA
Web site: http://www.wiredin.net/childcare
Dist(s): **Unique Bks., Inc.**

Auzou, Philippe Editions (FRA) *(978-2-7338) Dist. by* **Consort Bk Sales.**

AV2 by Weigl *Imprint of* **Weigl Pubs., Inc.**

Avalerion Bks., Inc., *(978-0-9834119)* 190 Beagle Rd., Bethel, PA 19507 USA Tel 717-933-9999
E-mail: avalerionbooks@yahoo.com.

Avalon Publishing Group, *(978-0-7867; 978-0-88184; 978-0-929654; 978-0-931188; 978-0-938410; 978-0-941423; 978-1-56025; 978-1-56201; 978-1-56858; 978-1-56924; 978-1-58005; 978-1-878067; 978-1-60094)* Div. of Perseus Books Group, 161 William St., 16th Flr., New York, NY 10038 USA Tel 646-375-2570; Fax: 646-375-2571
Web site: http://www.thundersmouth.com; http://www.avalonpub.com; http://www.sealpress.com; http://www.marlowepub.com
Dist(s): **Bilingual Pubns. Co., The**
CreateSpace Independent Publishing Platform
Ebsco Publishing
Follett School Solutions
Hachette Bk. Group
MyiLibrary.

Avant Garde Publishing *See* **The Publishing Place LLC**

Avant-garde Bks., *(978-0-9743676; 978-0-9908992; 978-0-9977566; 978-1-946753)* Orders Addr.: P.O. Box 566, Mableton, GA 30126 USA Tel 770-739-4039 Do not confuse with Avant garde Publishing in Norman, OK
E-mail: brightsmile.hardy@live.com
Web site: www.avantgardebooks.net.

Avant-garde Publishing Company *See* **Avant-garde Bks.**

Avari Pr., *(978-1-933770)* 2198 Old Philadelphia Pk., Lancaster, PA 17602 USA (SAN 257-9413)
E-mail: av42@antham.net.

Avatar Pr., Inc., *(978-0-9706784; 978-1-59291)* 9 Triumph Dr., Urbana, IL 61802 USA Tel 217-384-2211; Fax: 217-384-2216 Do not confuse with companies with the same or similar name in Sunnyside, NY, Atlanta, GA, Brick, NJ
E-mail: william@avatarpress.net
Web site: http://www.avatarpress.com
Dist(s): **Diamond Comic Distributors, Inc.**
Diamond Bk. Distributors
Simon & Schuster
Simon & Schuster, Inc.

Avatar Pubns., Inc. (CAN) *(978-0-9735379; 978-0-9738442; 978-0-9737401; 978-0-9738555; 978-1-897455) Dist. by* **indiCo.**

Ave Maria Pr., *(978-0-87061; 978-0-87793; 978-0-88347; 978-0-939516; 978-1-893732; 978-1-932057; 978-1-59471; 978-1-933495; 978-0-9972710)* P.O. Box 428, Notre Dame, IN 46556-0428 USA (SAN 201-1255) Tel 574-287-2831; Fax: 574-239-2904; Toll Free Fax: 800-282-5681; Toll Free: 800-282-1865
E-mail: avemariapress.1@nd.edu
Web site: http://www.forestofpeace.com; http://www.avemariapress.com; http://www.sorinbooks.com
Dist(s): **Fujii Assocs.**
MyiLibrary.

Aventine Pr, *(978-0-9719382; 978-0-9722932; 978-1-59330)* 750 State St. Unit 319, San Diego, CA 92101-6073 USA Toll Free: 866-246-6142
E-mail: info@aventinepress.com
Web site: http://www.aventinepress.com
Dist(s): **Ingram Publisher Services.**

AverHill Pr., *(978-0-9766107)* 2545 SW Terwilliger Blvd., No. 807, Portland, OR 97201 USA.

Avery *Imprint of* **Penguin Publishing Group**

Avery Color Studios, Inc., *(978-0-932212; 978-1-892384)* 511 D Ave., Gwinn, MI 49841 USA (SAN 211-1470) Tel 906-346-3908; Fax: 906-346-3015; Toll Free: 800-722-9925
E-mail: avery@portup.com
Dist(s): **Partners Bk. Distributing, Inc.**
Hale, Robert & Co., Inc.

Avery Goode-Reid Pubs., *(978-0-9766620)* P.O. Box 702, Ormond Beach, FL 32175-0702 USA Tel 386-615-0493
E-mail: marianstomblin@aol.com
Web site: http://www.mariantomblin.com.

Avery's, Tom Totally Tennis, *(978-0-9727444)* 5771 12th Ave., NW, Naples, FL 34119 USA
Web site: http://tomavery.com.

Avian Welfare Coalition, Inc., *(978-0-615-19395-3)* 1923 Ashland Ave., Saint Paul, MN 55104 USA
E-mail: info@avianwelfare.org
Web site: http://www.avianwelfare.org.

Aviation Supplies & Academics, Inc., *(978-0-940732; 978-1-56027; 978-1-61954; 978-1-63134)* 7005 132nd Pl., SE, Newcastle, WA 98059-3153 USA (SAN 219-709X) Tel 425-235-1500; Fax: 425-235-0128; Toll Free: 800-272-2359
E-mail: asa@asa2fly.com
Web site: http://www.asa2fly.com
Dist(s): **Aviation Bk. Co.**
Follett School Solutions
Independent Pubs. Group
Legato Pubs. Group
MyiLibrary
Wing Aero
ebrary, Inc.

Avid Readers Publishing Group, *(978-0-9797106; 978-0-9801438; 978-1-935105; 978-1-61286)* 2802 Belshire Ave., Lakewood, CA 90715 USA Tel 562-243-5918; Toll Free: 888-966-6835
E-mail: arpg@ericpatterson.name
Web site: http://www.avidreaderspg.com.

Avisson Pr., Inc., *(978-1-888105)* Orders Addr.: P.O. Box 38816, Greensboro, NC 27438-8816 USA (SAN 298-8127) Tel 336-288-6989; Fax: 336-288-6989; Edit Addr.: 3007 Taliaferro Rd., Greensboro, NC 27408 USA (SAN 298-8097)
Dist(s): **Follett School Solutions.**

Avista Products, *(978-0-9798741)* 2411 NE Loop 410. Ste. 108, San Antonio, TX 78217-6600 USA
E-mail: cbooker@avistaproducts.com
Web site: http://www.avistaproducts.com.

Avitable Publisher *See* **Avitable Pub.**

Aviva Gittle Publishing, *(978-0-692-35568-8; 978-1-942736)* 330 Rayford Rd. 177, Spring, TX 77386 USA Tel 619-577-0126
Web site: http://gotogittle.com/
Dist(s): **CreateSpace Independent Publishing Platform.**

Avocus Publishing, Inc., *(978-0-9627671; 978-1-890765)* 4 White Brook Rd., Gilsum, NH 03448 USA (SAN 248-2223) Tel 603-357-0236; Fax: 603-357-2073; Toll Free: 800-345-6665
E-mail: info@avocus.com
Web site: http://www.avocus.com
Dist(s): **Pathway Bk. Service.**

Avon Bks. *Imprint of* **HarperCollins Pubs.**

Avon Impulse *Imprint of* **HarperCollins Pubs.**

Avoomba Group Co., 6505 Manton Way, Lanham, MD 20706 USA Toll Free: 888-331-1074
E-mail: seb@avoomba.com.

AW2 Visions, *(978-0-615-41407-2; 978-0-692-29349-2; 978-0-692-50071-2)* 15323 Ensenada Dr., Houston, TX 77083 USA Tel 281-561-7714; Fax: 281-561-7070
E-mail: awashington88@comcast.net.

A.W.A. Gang *Imprint of* **Journey Stone Creations, LLC**

Awa Pr. (NZL) *(978-0-9582509; 978-0-9582538; 978-0-9582629; 978-0-9582750; 978-0-9582916; 978-1-877551; 978-1-927249; 978-1-927249-13-0; 978-1-927249-14-7) Dist. by* **IPG Chicago.**

Awaken Publishing *See* **Now Age Knowledge**

Awaken Specialty Pr., *(978-0-9794713)* P.O. Box 491, Centerton, AR 72719 USA (SAN 853-5248) Tel 479-586-2574
E-mail: celeste@awakenspecialtypress.com
Web site: http://www.awakenspecialtypress.com
Dist(s): **Follett School Solutions.**

Award Pubns. Ltd. (GBR) *(978-0-86163; 978-1-84135; 978-0-9537785; 978-1-904618; 978-1-905503; 978-1-907604; 978-1-906572; 978-1-78270; 978-1-909763) Dist. by* **Parkwest Pubns.**

Awareness Pubns., *(978-0-9744163)* 310-A S. Alu Rd., Wailuku, HI 96793 USA Tel 808-244-3782 Do not confuse with companies with the same name in Greenfield, WI, Santa Maria, CA, Houston, TX, Pocomoke City, MD
E-mail: awarep@mauigateway.com
Web site: http://www.awarenesspublications.org
Dist(s): **New Leaf Distributing Co., Inc.**

Awen Hse. Publishing, *(978-0-9826670)* 8949 Bellcove Cir., Colorado Springs, CO 80920 USA Tel 719-287-7074
E-mail: dunning.rebecca@gmail.com
Web site: http://www.rebeccadunning.com.

Awesome Bk. Publishing, *(978-0-9840538; 978-0-9895194)* P.O. Box 1157, Roseland, FL 32957 USA Tel 321-632-0177.

Awesome Guides, Inc., *(978-0-9703694; 978-0-9723218)* 127 W. Fairbanks Ave., Suite No. 421, Winter Park, FL 32789 USA Fax: 407-678-4337
E-mail: sales@awesomeguides.com; cl@awesomeguides.com
Web site: http://www.awesomeguides.com.

Awe-Struck E-Books, Incorporated *See* **Awe-Struck Publishing**

Awe-Struck Publishing, *(978-1-928670; 978-1-58749)* Div. of Mundania Pr., LLC, 6470a Glenway Ave. #109, Cincinnati, OH 45211 USA (SAN 854-4980); *Imprints*: Byte/Me Teen Book (Byte Me Teen); Earthling Press (Earthling Prss)
E-mail: dan@mundania.com
Web site: http://www.awe-struck.net.

Awkward Labs, *(978-0-615-79808-0)* P.O. Box 398, Felton, DE 19943 USA Tel 302-430-6077
E-mail: wjwalton@yahoo.com.

AWOC.COM, *(978-0-9707507; 978-1-62016)* P.O. Box 2819, Denton, TX 76202 USA
E-mail: editor@awoc.com
Web site: http://www.awoc.com.

A-Works New York, Incorporated *See* **One Peace Bks., Inc.**

Axiom Hse., *(978-0-9760237)* P.O. Box 2901, Fairfax, VA 22031 USA
E-mail: orders@axiomhouse.com
Web site: http://www.axiomhouse.com/index.htm
Dist(s): **Bookmasters Distribution**
Follett School Solutions.

Axiom Pr. *Imprint of* **Genesis Communications, Inc.**

Axios Pr., *(978-0-9661908; 978-0-9753662; 978-1-60419)* P.O. Box 118, Mount Jackson, VA 22842 USA Tel 540-984-3829; Fax: 540-984-3843; Toll Free: 888-542-9467 (orders only); 4501 Forbes Blvd., Lanham, MD 20706 Do not confuse with Axios Publishing Corporation, Seattle, WA
E-mail: info@axiosinstitute.org
Web site: http://www.axiosinstitute.org
Dist(s): **Follett School Solutions**
MyiLibrary
National Bk. Network.

Axle Publishing Co., Inc., *(978-0-9755895)* Orders Addr.: P.O. Box 269, Rockdale, TX 76567 USA (SAN 256-3746) Tel 800-866-2685 (Toll-Free); 512-446-0644 (Jody's Direct Line); Fax: 512-446-2686 Fax Line; Edit Addr.: 1506 O'Kelley Rd., Rockdale, TX 76567 USA Tel 512-446-0644; Toll Free: 800-866-2685
E-mail: jody@axlegalench.com; jody@laid-back.com; roosterrdz@aol.com
Web site: http://www.axlegalench.com; http://www.laid-back.com; http://www.roostermorris.com
Dist(s): **Follett School Solutions.**

Aylen Publishing, *(978-0-9708623; 978-0-9765040; 978-0-9857708; 978-0-9910084; 978-0-9862848)* Subs. of Master Planning Group International, 7830 E. Camelback Re No. 711, Scottsdale, AZ 85251 USA Toll Free: 800-443-1976
Web site: http://www.masterplanninggroup.com; http://www.Aylen.com.

AZ Bks. LLC, *(978-1-61889)* 9330 LBJ Freeway, Dallas, TX 74243 USA Tel 214-438-3922; Fax: 214-561-6795; 245 8Th Ave., #180, New York, NY 10011
E-mail: anastasia.lobynko@az-books.com; support@booksonix.com
Dist(s): **Follett School Solutions.**

AZ Group Publishing House *See* **AZ Bks. LLC**

Azaida Media, LLC, *(978-0-9864405)* 7726 Gunston Plaza No. 1648, Lorton, VA 22199 USA Tel 571-303-1800
E-mail: info@azaidamedia.com
Web site: http://www.azaidamedia.com.

Azalea Creek Publishing, *(978-0-9677934)* c/o Tom Kendrick, 308 Bloomfield Rd., Sebastopol, CA 95472 USA Tel 707-823-2911 (phone/fax)
E-mail: azalea@sonic.net
Web site: http://www.sonic.net/dragonfly/azaleaforth.html; http://www.sonic.net/dragonfly/adhtml.html; http://southwestdragonflies.net/Order_Form.html; http://southwestdragonflies.net/ColoringBook.html
Dist(s): **American West Bks.**
Bored Feet Pr.
Rio Nuevo Pubs.

AZIAM Bks., *(978-0-9884449; 978-0-9898077; 978-0-9862075)* P.O. Box 267, Santa Monica, CA 90406 USA Tel 310-913-1315
E-mail: info@aziam.com.

AZIAM Yoga *See* **AZIAM Bks.**

Azimuth Pr., *(978-0-9632074; 978-1-886218)* 4041 Bowman Blvd., Suite 211, Macon, GA 31210 USA Tel 770-994-9449; Fax: 770-996-6928 Do not confuse with companies with the same or similar name in Alexander, NC, Arnold, MD.

Azoka Co., The, *(978-0-9745560)* P.O. Box 323, Greenland, NH 03885 USA Tel 603-772-0181; Fax: 603-772-0550
Web site: http://www.seacoastcenter.com.

Azreal Publishing Co., *(978-0-9755566)* Orders Addr.: P.O. Box 21139, Tallahassee, FL 32312 USA; Edit Addr.: 1937 Saxon St., Tallahassee, FL 32310 USA
Web site: http://.

Azrec Book Publishing *See* **Aztec Bk. Publishing**

Azro Pr., Inc., *(978-0-9660239; 978-1-929115)* Orders Addr.: 1704 Llano St., Suite B, PMB 342, Santa Fe, NM 87505 USA Tel 505-989-3272; Fax: 505-989-3832
E-mail: books@azropress.com
Web site: http://www.azropress.com
Dist(s): **Follett School Solutions**
SCB Distributors.

Aztec 5 Publishing, *(978-0-9769478)* Orders Addr.: P.O. Box 11693, Glendale, AZ 85318 USA Tel 623-537-4567 (phone/fax)
E-mail: aztec5publishing@aol.com.

Aztec Bk. Publishing, *(978-0-9787674; 978-0-9801258; 978-0-9838916; 978-0-9905293)* 1606 Delaware Ave., Wilmington, DE 19806 USA Tel 302-575-1993; Fax: 302-575-1977
Web site: http://www.azteccopies.com.

Aztex Corp., *(978-0-89404)* P.O. Box 50046, Tucson, AZ 85703-1046 USA (SAN 210-0371) Tel 520-882-4656; Fax: 520-792-8501
E-mail: ac@aztexcorp.com
Web site: http://www.aztexcorp.com.

AZTexts Publishing, Inc., *(978-0-9677292)* P.O. Box 93487, Phoenix, AZ 85070-3487 USA Tel 480-283-0994 (phone/fax); 1043 E. Amberwood Dr., Phoenix, AZ 85048
E-mail: aztexts@cox.net
Web site: http://FrecklesFriends.org; http://www.aztexts.com
Dist(s): **Quality Bks., Inc.**

Azure Communications, *(978-0-9618741)* Orders Addr.: P.O. Box 23387, New Orleans, LA 70183 USA (SAN 668-7695); Edit Addr.: 37383 Overland Trail, Prairieville, LA 70769 USA (SAN 668-7709) Tel 225-744-4094
E-mail: gszczurek@eatel.net.

Azuria Bks., *(978-0-9796444)* P.O. Box 535, Clyde, NC 28721 USA Tel 828-627-9685
E-mail: timbramlett@charter.net.

B & B Educational Advancement & Pubns., Inc., *(978-1-937065)* 1407 Ford St., Golden, CO 80401 USA (SAN 860-1801) Tel 303-279-8659; Fax: 303-648-5135
E-mail: lmrpc@aol.com.

B&B Publishing, *(978-1-885813)* 63418 Everett Rd., Coos Bay, OR 97420 USA Tel 541-269-9277 Do not confuse with companies with the same or similar name in Fort Collins, CO, Westminster, CO, Walworth, WI, Greenfield, IN
Dist(s): **Partners/West Book Distributors.**

B & R Samizdat Express *See* **Samizdat Express**

B B Y Publications *See* **bby Publications at The University of West Alabama**

B de BLOK (Ediciones B) (ESP) *(978-84-15579; 978-84-939613; 978-84-16712; 978-84-16075; 978-84-939242; 978-84-939614; 978-84-939615) Dist. by* **Spanish.**

BF Publishing, *(978-0-9653327)* 17503 Brushy River Ct., Houston, TX 77095-6905 USA Tel 281-256-1213 Do not confuse with B.F. Publishing, Huntington Beach, CA
E-mail: BFPub1@aol.com
Dist(s): **Origin Bk. Sales, Inc.**

B F Q Press, Incorporated *See* **TotalRecall Pubns.**

B G R Publishing *See* **EMG Networks**

B.R. Publishing Co., *(978-0-9625593; 978-1-884538)* 1725 Pinebrook Dr., Knoxville, TN 37909 USA Tel 423-691-1990.

B Small Publishing (GBR) *(978-1-874735; 978-1-902915; 978-1-905710; 978-1-908164; 978-1-909767; 978-1-911509) Dist. by* **IPG Chicago.**

B. T. Brooks, *(978-0-9772282)* Orders Addr.: 7015 Crabapple Ln., Kansas City, MO 64129 USA Tel 816-810-1277; 7015 Crabapple Ln., Kansas City, MO 64129 Tel 816-810-1277
E-mail: btbrookspublish@aol.com.

B V Wespat, *(978-0-9713342; 978-0-9788934; 978-0-9819699)* 1641 N. Memorial Dr., Lancaster, OH 43130 USA
Dist(s): **Brodart Co.**
Partners Bk. Distributing, Inc.

B2Z Publishing, Inc., *(978-0-9712070)* Orders Addr.: P.O. Box 307, Severna Park, MD 21146 USA (SAN 254-1068) Tel 410-431-8890; Fax: 410-431-5236
E-mail: towardcure@aol.com
Web site: http://www.mabcie.com.

B3 Publishing, *(978-0-9767849)* Div. of Dream Believer Factory, Inc., Orders Addr.: P.O. Box 360170, Strongsville, OH 44136 USA; Edit Addr.: 19428 Bennington Dr., Strongsville, OH 44136 USA
E-mail: dbfiest@roadrunner.com.

Babbling Bks., *(978-0-9798609)* 3849 Prado Dr., Sarasota, FL 34235-3528 USA
E-mail: babblingbooks@yahoo.com.

Babel Books, Inc *See* **Pintos, Yoselem G.**

Babel Libros (COL) *(978-958-8445; 978-958-97602; 978-958-98273) Dist. by* **Lectorum Pubns.**

Babl Books, Incorporated, *(978-1-68304)* 1 E. Ctr. St Suite 209, Provo, UT 84606 USA Toll Free: 844-311-9649
E-mail: contact@bablbooks.com
Web site: http://www.bablbooks.com.

Baboosic Enterprises, LLC, *(978-0-9787660)* P.O. Box 6102, Bloomington, IN 47408-9990 USA
Web site: http://www.bunnyrabbitonthemoon.com.

Baby Abuelita Productions, Inc., *(978-0-9788379; 978-0-615-19145-4)* 6619 S. Dixie Hwy. No. 139, Miami, FL 33143 USA (SAN 851-7207) Toll Free: 877-722-8352
E-mail: cfenster@babyabuelita.com
Web site: http://www.babyabuelita.com.

Baby Einstein Co., LLC, The, *(978-1-892309; 978-1-931580)* Subs. of Walt Disney Productions, 1233 Flower St., Glendale, CA 91201 USA Tel 818-544-4842
E-mail: ellen.portantino@disney.com
Web site: http://www.babyeinstein.com
Dist(s): **Disney Publishing Worldwide**
Penton Overseas, Inc.
Right Start, Inc.
Rounder Kids Music Distribution.

Baby Faye Bks. *Imprint of* **Northstar Entertainment Group, LLC**

Baby Music Boom, Inc., *(978-0-9647786)* Orders Addr.: P.O. Box 62188, Minneapolis, MN 55426 USA Tel 612-470-1667; Fax: 612-474-1297; Toll Free: 888-470-1667; Edit Addr.: 19000 Maple Ln., Deephaven, MN 55331 USA
E-mail: babyboomms@aol.com
Web site: http://www.babymusicboom.com.

Baby Professor (Education Kids) *Imprint of* **Speedy Publishing LLC**

Baby Shadows, *(978-0-9744928)* 150 W. 56th St., Suite 4410, New York, NY 10019 USA (SAN 255-6367)
Web site: http://www.babyshadows.com.

Baby Shark Productions, *(978-0-9765125)* 15338 Roberts Ave., Jacksonville, FL 32218-1833 USA Tel 904-751-1564
E-mail: jackbradford90@aol.com
Web site: http://www.gregmoutafis.com.

Baby Tattoo Bks., *(978-0-9729388; 978-0-9778949; 978-0-9793307; 978-0-9845210; 978-1-61404)* 6045 Longridge Ave., Van Nuys, CA 91401 USA (SAN 255-2159) Tel 818-416-5314
E-mail: info@babytatto.com
Web site: http://www.babytattoo.com
Dist(s): **SCB Distributors.**

Bacchus Bks., *(978-0-9717952)* Div. of Petmida, Incorporated, P.O. Box 1801, Pacific Palisades, CA 90272 USA Fax: 310-459-4233; Toll Free: 877-604-6522
E-mail: customerservice@domdeluise.com
Web site: http://www.domdeluise.com.

Back Bay Bks. *Imprint of* **Little Brown & Co.**

Back Channel Pr., *(978-0-9767590; 978-0-9789546; 978-1-934582)* 170 Mechanic St., Portsmouth, NH 03801 USA Tel 603-436-9485
E-mail: ngstudio@comcast.net
Web site: http://www.nancygrossmanbooks.com
Dist(s): **Lightning Source, Inc.**

Back Home Industries, *(978-1-880045)* Orders Addr.: P.O. Box 22495, Milwaukie, OR 97269 USA Tel 503-654-2300; Fax: 503-659-9351; Edit Addr.: 8431 SE 36th Ave., Portland, OR 97222 USA
E-mail: backhome@integrity.com
Web site: http://webs.integrity.com/backhome.

Back In THE BRONX, *(978-0-9657221)* Orders Addr.: P.O. Box 141H, Scarsdale, NY 10583 USA Tel 914-592-1647; Fax: 914-592-4893; Toll Free: 800-727-6695; Edit Addr.: 40 Herkimer Rd., Scarsdale, NY 10583 USA
E-mail: info@backinthebronx.com
Web site: http://www.backinthebronx.com.

Back River Company, The, LLC, *(978-0-9672882)* 238 Robinson St. # 13, Wakefield, RI 02879-3549 USA.

Back Yard Pub., *(978-0-9707560; 978-1-931934)* Div. of Wensel Enterprises, 7720 N. Moonwind Terr., Dunnellon, FL 34433 USA Tel 352-795-0844; Fax: 352-795-0813
E-mail: wwensel@backyardpublisher.com; wwensel@hughes.net; wensel@hughes.net
Web site: http://www.backyardpublisher.com.

Back2Life, Inc., *(978-0-9760151)* 8608 N. Richmond Ave., 1st Flr., Kansas City, MO 64157 USA Tel 816-835-4477; Fax: 816-891-7789
E-mail: ckehoe@back2life.us
Web site: http://www.back2life.us.

Back2Life Ministries *See* **Back2Life, Inc.**

Backinprint.com *Imprint of* **iUniverse, Inc.**

Backintyme *Imprint of* **Backintyme Publishing**

Backintyme Publishing, *(978-0-939479)* 1341 Grapevine Rd., Crofton, KY 42217 USA (SAN 663-2726) Tel 270-985-8568; *Imprints:* Backintyme (Backintyme FL)
E-mail: backintyme@mehrapublishing.com
Web site: http://www.backintyme.biz.

Backpack Bowie *See* **Educational Expertise, LLC**

Backpack Pubs., *(978-0-9854439)* P.O. Box 1156, Hermitage, PA 16148 USA Tel 724-346-4636; Fax: 724-346-2007
E-mail: rbs@elink123.net
Web site: www.backpackpublishers.com.

Backroads Pr., *(978-0-9642371; 978-0-9724033)* Orders Addr.: P.O. Box 651, Mooresville, IN 46158 USA Tel 317-831-2815 (phone/fax); Edit Addr.: 452 Tulip Dr., Mooresville, IN 46158 USA
E-mail: wend@quest.net
Web site: http://www.publishershomepages.com/php/Backroads_Press.

Backwaters Pr., The, *(978-0-9677149; 978-0-9726187; 978-0-9765231; 978-0-9785782; 978-0-9793934; 978-0-9816936; 978-1-935218)* 3502 N. 52nd St., Omaha, NE 68104-3506 USA Tel 402-451-4052
E-mail: thebackwaterspress@gmail.com
Web site: http://www.thebackwaterspress.org
Dist(s): **SPD-Small Pr. Distribution.**

Backwoods Publishing Co., *(978-0-9722501)* Rte. 1, Box 270, Boswell, OK 74727 USA Do not confuse with Backwoods Publishing in Logan, OH.

Backyard Ambassador Reader Publishing Co., *(978-0-9793808)* 2 New Grant Ct., Columbia, SC 29209 USA
E-mail: caroline.bennett@att.com
Web site: http://www.bareader.com.

Backyard Scientist, Inc., *(978-0-9618663; 978-1-888427)* P.O. Box 16966, Irvine, CA 92623 USA (SAN 219-1725) Tel 714-551-2392; Fax: 714-552-5351
E-mail: backyrdsci@aol.com.

Bad Choices Media, *(978-0-9721327)* P.O. Box 827, Chincoteague Island, VA 23336 USA
E-mail: acanfld@gmail.com; andrea@studio4264.com; andrea@badchoicesmedia.com.

Bad Frog Art/SMG Bks, *(978-0-9795361)* Orders Addr.: 14931 251st Pl. SE, Issaquah, WA 98027 USA
E-mail: steve@stevegritton.info
Web site: www.stevegritton.info.

Bad Publishing, *(978-0-9765414)* 21522 5th Pl. S., DeMoines, WA 98198 USA Tel 206-824-6106
E-mail: edwardhl@hsd401.org.

Badalamenti, Andrew, *(978-0-615-25180-6)* 206 Franklin Rd., Denville, NJ 07834 USA
Dist(s): **Lulu Pr., Inc.**

badalato, *(978-0-692-80076-8)*
Dist(s): **CreateSpace Independent Publishing Platform.**

BadCoaches, Incorporated *See* **Tony Franklin Cos., The**

Badgerland Bks. LLC, *(978-0-9765510)* Orders Addr.: 5407 Marsh Woods Dr., McFarland, WI 53558 USA
E-mail: sales@badgerlandbooks.com; joe_martino@uwbucky.com
Web site: http://www.badgerlandbooks.com; http://www.uwbucky.com
Dist(s): **Follett School Solutions.**

Badi Publishing Corporation *See* **Changing-Times.net**

Badiru, Adedeji, *(978-0-9768100)* P.O. Box 341441, Beavercreek, OH 45434 USA
E-mail: deji@badiru.com
Web site: abicspublications.com.

Baen Bks., *(978-0-671; 978-1-55594; 978-0-7434)* Orders Addr.: c/o Simon & Schuster, 200 Old Tappan Rd., Old Tappan, NJ 07675 USA Fax: 800-445-6991; Toll Free: 800-223-2336; Edit Addr.: c/o Simon & Schuster, 1230 Ave. of the Americas, New York, NY 10020 USA (SAN 658-8417) Tel 212-698-7000; Toll Free: 800-223-2348 (customer service)
Web site: http://www.simonsays.com/
Dist(s): **Diamond Comic Distributors, Inc.**
Diamond Bk. Distributors
Simon & Schuster
Simon & Schuster, Inc.

Baha'i Publishing, *(978-1-931847; 978-1-61851)* Orders Addr.: 2427 Bond St., University Park, IL 60466-3101 USA Toll Free Fax: 800-705-4923; Toll Free: 800-705-4925; Edit Addr.: 415 Linden Ave., Wilmete, IL 60091-2886 USA Tel 847-425-7950; Fax: 847-425-7951
Web site: http://www.bahaibooksusa.com/
Dist(s): **Follett School Solutions.**

Baha'i Publishing Trust, U.S., *(978-0-87743)* 415 Linden Ave., Wilmette, IL 60091 USA
Dist(s): **Baha'i Distribution Service.**

BaHar Publishing, L.C., *(978-0-9718939; 978-0-9818219; 978-0-9837742)* 1429 Commercial St., Waterloo, IA 50702 USA Toll Free: 888-600-6033
E-mail: chaveevahdread@yahoo.com
Web site: http://www.baharpublishing.com.

BaHart Pubns. / Eight Legs Publishing, *(978-0-9760348)* PMB 70, PO Box 7000, Rolling Hills Estates, CA 90274 USA
E-mail: octopusrex@earthlink.net
Web site: http://www.octopusrex.com.

Bailey, Martha, *(978-0-9786448)* 6882 S. Peaceful Hills Rd., Morrison, CO 80465 USA Tel 303-697-4591 (phone/fax)
E-mail: nebjr@earthlink.net.

Bailiwick Pr., *(978-1-934649)* 3836 Tradition St., Fort Collins, CO 80526-3107 USA; 250 W. 57Th St. 15Th Flr., New York, NY 10016
Web site: http://bailiwickpress.com
Dist(s): **Follett School Solutions**
Independent Pubs. Group
Legato Pubs. Group
MyiLibrary
ebrary, Inc.

Baker Academic, *(978-0-8010)* Div. of Baker Publishing Group, Orders Addr.: P.O. Box 6287, Grand Rapids, MI 49516-6287 USA Toll Free Fax: 800-398-3111 (orders only); Toll Free: 800-877-2665 (orders only); Edit Addr.: 6030 Fulton Ave., Ada, MI 49301 USA Tel 616-676-9185; Fax: 616-676-9573
Web site: http://www.bakerpublishinggroup.com
Dist(s): **Baker Publishing Group**
ebrary, Inc.

Baker & Taylor Bks., *(978-0-8480; 978-1-222; 978-1-223)* Orders Addr.: Commerce Service Ctr., 251 Mt. Olive Church Rd., Commerce, GA 30599 USA (SAN 169-1503) Tel 404-335-5000; Toll Free: 800-775-1200 (customer service); 800-775-1800 (orders); Reno Service Ctr., 1160 Trademark Dr., Suite 111, Reno, NV 89511 (SAN 169-4464) Tel 775-850-3800; Fax: 775-850-3826 (customer service); Toll Free Fax: 800-775-1700 (orders); Edit Addr.: Bridgewater Service Ctr. 1120 US Hwy. 22, E., Bridgewater, NJ 08807 USA (SAN 169-4901) Toll Free: 800-775-1500 (customer service); Momence Service Ctr., 501W. Gladiolus St., Momence, IL 60954-1799 (SAN 169-2100) Tel 815-472-2444 (international customers); Fax: 815-472-9886 (international customers); Toll Free: 800-775-2300 (customer service, academic libraries)
E-mail: btinfo@btol.com
Web site: http://www.btol.com.

Baker & Taylor, CATS, *(978-1-4352; 978-1-4395; 978-1-4420; 978-1-4487; 978-1-4517; 978-1-4806; 978-1-5182)* 1120 Rte. 22 E., Bridgewater, NJ 08807 USA Toll Free: 800-775-1500; *Imprints:* Paw Prints (Paw Prints USA)
Web site: http://www.baker-taylor.com/pawprints
Dist(s): **Baker & Taylor Bks.**
Follett School Solutions.

Baker & Taylor Publishing Group *See* **Readerlink Distribution Services, LLC**

Baker Book House, Incorporated *See* **Baker Publishing Group**

Baker Bks., *(978-0-8010; 978-0-913686)* Div. of Baker Publishing Group, Orders Addr.: P.O. Box 6287, Grand Rapids, MI 49516-6287 USA (SAN 299-1500) Toll Free Fax: 800-398-3111 (orders only); Toll Free: 800-877-2665 (orders only); Edit Addr.: 6030 E. Fulton, Ada, MI 49301 USA (SAN 201-4041) Tel 616-676-9185; Fax: 616-676-9573
Web site: http://www.bakerpublishinggroup.com
Dist(s): **Baker Publishing Group**
Faith Alive Christian Resources
Follett School Solutions
Twentieth Century Christian Bks.
ebrary, Inc.

Baker College Publishing Co., *(978-1-885545)* Div. of Baker College, 1050 W. Bristol Rd., Flint, MI 48507 USA Toll Free: 800-339-9879
Dist(s): **Follett School Solutions.**

Baker, Helen Interiors, Inc., *(978-0-9743511)* Orders Addr.: P.O. Box 367, West Harwich, MA 02671 USA Tel 508-432-0287; Fax: 508-430-7744; Edit Addr.: 94 Main St., West Harwich, MA 02671 USA
E-mail: hbunce@attbi.com
Web site: http://www.shoppingthecape.com.

Baker Publishing Group, *(978-0-8007; 978-0-8010; 978-1-58743; 978-1-4412; 978-1-4934; 978-1-68196; 978-1-5409)* Orders Addr.: P.O. Box 6287, Grand Rapids, MI 49516-6287 USA Tel 616-676-9573; Toll Free Fax: 800-398-3111 (orders only); Toll Free: 800-877-2665 (orders only); Edit Addr.: 6030 E. Fulton, Ada, MI 49301 USA Tel 616-676-9185; Fax: 616-676-9573; Toll Free Fax: 800-398-3111; Toll Free: 800-877-2665
E-mail: webmaster@bakerpublishinggroup.com
Web site: http://www.bakerbooks.com; http://www.bakerpublishinggroup.com
Dist(s): **Follett School Solutions**
Twentieth Century Christian Bks.
christianaudio
ebrary, Inc.

Baker Trittin Concepts *See* **Baker Trittin Pr.**

Baker Trittin Pr., *(978-0-9729256; 978-0-9752880; 978-0-9787316; 978-0-9814893)* P.O. Box 277, Winona Lake, IN 46590-0277 USA Fax: 574-269-6100; Toll Free: 1-888-741-4386; *Imprints:* Innovative Christian Publications (Innov Chris Pubns); Tweener Press (Tweener Pr)
E-mail: paul@btconcepts.com
Web site: http://www.bakertrittinpress.com; http://www.gospelstoryteller.com.

Baker, Walter H. Company *See* **Baker's Plays**

Baker's Plays, *(978-0-87440)* Div. of Samuel French, Inc., 45 W. 25th St., New York, NY 10010 USA (SAN 202-3717) Tel 212-255-8085; Fax: 212-627-7754
E-mail: info@bakersplays.com
Web site: http://www.bakersplays.com.

Balaam Books LLC, *(978-0-9785585)* 1825 W. Ave., Unit 11, Miami Beach, FL 33139-1441 USA (SAN 850-9972) Tel 305-531-9351; Fax: 305-531-9348
E-mail: Info@BalaamBooks.com
Web site: http://www.BalaamBooks.com.

Balance Bks., Inc., *(978-0-9743908)* P.O. Box 86, Des Plaines, IL 60016-0086 USA
Web site: http://www.balance-books.com
Dist(s): **Distributors, The.**

Balanced Families, *(978-0-9759468)* 432 N. 750 E., Lindon, UT 84042 USA Tel 801-380-3247; Fax: 801-785-3938
E-mail: info@starsofthesky.com.

Balanced Systems, Inc., *(978-0-9760037)* 995 Artdale, White Lake, MI 48383 USA.

Balboa Pr. *Imprint of* **Author Solutions, Inc.**

Balboa Pr., Div. of Hay House, Inc., 1663 Liberty Dr., Bloomington, IN 47403 USA Tel 877-407-4847
E-mail: customersupport@balboapress.com
Web site: http://www.balboapress.com
Dist(s): **Author Solutions, Inc.**
Bookmasters Distribution
Zondervan.

Balcony Bks., *(978-0-615-46893-8; 978-0-9879732-4-5)* 1606 Willow Ln., McKinney, TX 75070 USA Tel 214-790-4686; 469-879-8696
Dist(s): **CreateSpace Independent Publishing Platform**
Dummy Record Do Not USE!!!!.

Bald Eagle Bks., *(978-0-9852032)* 25 Channel Ctr. St. No. 404, Boston, MA 02210 USA Tel 781-608-0626; Fax: 781-465-7999
E-mail: gpallotta@vzw.blackberry.net
Web site: www.jerrypallotta.com.

Baldner, Jean V., *(978-0-9615317)* 1618 Burnett Ave., Ames, IA 50010-5337 USA (SAN 694-6526).

Baldwin, Christopher John, *(978-1-938384)* P.O. Box 1141, Northhampton, MA 01061 USA Tel 360-705-2742
E-mail: chrisjohnbaldwin@gmail.com.

Balhund Entertainment, LLC, *(978-0-9743277)* 3018 Paulcrest Dr., Los Angeles, CA 90046 USA Tel 323-848-8778
Web site: http://www.magusgame.com.

Baliko, Janelle A., *(978-0-9799012)* 45486 Locust Grove Dr., Valley Lee, MD 20692-3217 USA
E-mail: itdoesnthavetobepink@yahoo.com
Web site: http://www.itdoesnthavetobepink.com.

Ball, Michael, *(978-0-9765750)* 2000 Bradley Ln., Russellville, AR 72801-4627 USA.

Ball Publishing, *(978-0-9626796; 978-1-883052)* Orders Addr.: P.O. Box 9, Batavia, IL 60510-0009 USA Tel 630-208-9080; Fax: 630-208-9350; Toll Free Fax: 888-888-0014; Toll Free: 888-888-0013 (U.S. & Canada only); Edit Addr.: P.O. Box 1660, West Chicago, IL 60186-1660 USA
E-mail: info@ballpublishing.com
Web site: http://www.ballbookshelf.com
Dist(s): **Independent Pubs. Group.**

Ball, Rulon Jay *See* **JBall Publishing**

Ballad Productions, *(978-0-9753663)* Orders Addr.: P.O. Box 4, North Miami Beach, FL 33164 USA Tel 786-285-3619; Edit Addr.: 163rd St., Suite No. 4, North Miami Beach, FL 33164 USA
E-mail: drlaz770@aol.com
Web site: http://www.drlaz.com.

Ballantine Bks. *Imprint of* **Random House Publishing Group**

Ballantine, Robert *See* **P.F.B. Publishing**

Ballard & Tighe Pubs., *(978-0-937270; 978-1-55501; 978-1-59989)* Div. of Educational Ideas, Inc., 471 Atlas St., Brea, CA 92821 USA (SAN 200-7991) Tel 714-990-4332; Fax: 714-255-9828; Toll Free: 800-321-4332
Web site: http://www.ballard-tighe.com.

Ballard, Donald W., *(978-0-9768779)* Orders Addr.: 37823 Menard Ct., Fremont, CA 94536 USA Toll Free: 800-506-7401
E-mail: donballard@comcast.net
Web site: http://www.magicalhotel.com.

BalletMet Dance Centre, *(978-0-692-01667-1)* 322 Mount Vernon Ave., Columbus, OH 43235 USA Tel 614-586-8635
E-mail: education@balletmet.org
Web site: http://www.balletmet.org
Dist(s): **BookMasters.**

Ballinger Printing & Graphics, *(978-0-9754957; 978-0-615-20730-8)* 906 Hutchings Ave., Ballinger, TX 76821 USA Tel 325-365-8206; Fax: 325-365-2209; Toll Free: 888-915-8206
E-mail: michael.o.white@att.net; ballingerprinting@verizon.net
Dist(s): **Publishers Services.**

Balloon Bks. *Imprint of* **Sterling Publishing Co., Inc.**

Balloon Magic, *(978-1-931084)* 928 W. 20 N., Orem, UT 84057-1918 USA; *Imprints:* Penny's Publishing (Pennys Pubng)
E-mail: mlh@balloonmagic.com
Web site: http://www.balloonmagic.com.

Ballybunnion Bks., *(978-0-9726340)* Orders Addr.: P.O. Box 6357, Virginia Beach, VA 23456 USA; Edit Addr.: 833 Maitland Dr., Virginia Beach, VA 23454 USA
E-mail: brian@wbrianmurphy.com
Web site: http://www.warrenmurphy.com.

Ballyhoo Books *See* **Ballyhoo BookWorks, Inc.**

Ballyhoo BookWorks, Inc., *(978-0-936335)* Orders Addr.: P.O. Box 534, Shoreham, NY 11786 USA (SAN 697-8487); Edit Addr.: 1 Sylvan Dr., Wading River, NY 11792 USA (SAN 698-2239) Tel 631-929-8148
E-mail: ballyhoo@optonline.net.

Ballyhoo Printing, *(978-0-9742792; 978-0-9800580; 978-0-9976224)* 187 W. Frontage Rd., Lewistown, MT 59457 USA Tel 406-538-7988
E-mail: ballyhoo@ballyhooprinting.com
Web site: http://www.ballyhooprinting.com.

Balona Bks., *(978-0-9765479; 978-1-934376)* P.O. Box 690106, Stockton, CA 95269-0106 USA
E-mail: author@balona.com; jonathan@balona.com
Web site: http://www.balona.com.

Balticbard Publishing *Imprint of* **Leyva, Barbara**

Balue Fox Publishing Company *See* **McWilliams Mediation Group Ltd.**

Balzer & Bray *Imprint of* **HarperCollins Pubs.**

Bamboo River Pr., *(978-0-9798173)* 12565 SE Callahan Rd., Portland, OR 97086-9708 USA (SAN 854-4484) Tel 503-761-4360
Web site: http://www.bambooriverpress.com.

Bamboo Zoo, LLC, *(978-0-9774493)* 1637 Dahlia St., Denver, CO 80220 USA (SAN 257-5965) Tel 720-323-4955
E-mail: kim@bamboo-zoo.com
Web site: http://www.bamboo-zoo.com.

Banana Bunch Publishing, *(978-0-9761763)* 2260 Banana St., Saint James City, FL 33956 USA Tel 239-283-9306.

Banana Oil Bks. *Imprint of* **Cyberwizard Productions**

Banana Patch Pr., *(978-0-9715333; 978-0-9800063)* Orders Addr.: P.O. Box 950, Hanapepe, HI 96716 USA (SAN 254-3087) Tel 808-335-5944; Fax: 808-335-3830; Toll Free: 800-914-5944
E-mail: carolan@aloha.net
Web site: http://www.bananapatchpress.com
Dist(s): **Booklines Hawaii, Ltd.**
Islander Group.

Banana Pr., *(978-0-9799065)* 2935 S. Fish Hatchery Rd., No. 3, Suite 254, Fitchburg, WI 53711 USA Tel 608-658-0023
E-mail: info@bananalady.com
Web site: http://www.bananalady.com.

Bancroft Pr., *(978-0-9631246; 978-0-9635376; 978-1-890862; 978-1-61088)* P.O. Box 65360, Baltimore, MD 21209-9945 USA Tel 410-358-0658; Fax: 410-764-1967; Toll Free: 800-637-7377 Do not confuse with Bancroft Pr., San Rafael, CA
E-mail: bruceb@bancroftpress.com
Web site: http://www.bancroftpress.com
Dist(s): **Academic Bk. Ctr., Inc.**
BookMasters, Inc.
Book Wholesalers, Inc.
Bk. Hse., Inc., The
Bookmasters Distribution
Brodart Co.
Coutts Information Services
Emery-Pratt Co.
Follett School Solutions
Mackin Library Media
Midwest Library Service
Smashwords
Yankee Bk. Peddler, Inc.

Banda Pr. International, Inc., *(978-0-9773175)* 6050 Stetson Hills Blvd., No. 313, Colorado Springs, CO 80922 USA
Web site: http://www.bandapress.com.

Bandai Entertainment, Inc., *(978-1-58354; 978-1-59409; 978-1-60496)* Div. of Bandai Entertainment, Inc., 5551 Katella Ave., Cypress, CA 90630 USA Tel 714-816-9760; Fax: 714-816-6708; Toll Free: 877-772-6463
Web site: http://www.bandai-ent.com
Dist(s): **Diamond Comic Distributors, Inc.**
Diamond Bk. Distributors
Follett School Solutions.

B&H Bks. *Imprint of* **B&H Publishing Group**

B&H Kids *Imprint of* **B&H Publishing Group**

†B&H Publishing Group, *(978-0-8054; 978-0-87981; 978-1-55819; 978-1-58640; 978-0-8400; 978-1-4336)* Div. of LifeWay Christian Resources of the Southern Baptist Convention, One LifeWay Plaza MSN 114, Nashville, TN 37234-0114 USA (SAN 201-937X) Tel 615-251-2520; Fax: 615-251-5026 (Books Only); 615-251-2036 (Bibles Only); 615-251-2413 (Gifts/Supplies Only); Toll Free: 800-725-5416; 800-251-3225 (retailers); 800-296-4036 (orders/returns); 800-448-8032 (consumers); 800-458-2772 (churches); *Imprints:* B&H Books (B&H Bks.); B&H Kids (B&H Kids)
E-mail: broadmanholman@lifeway.com; heather.counsellor@bhpublishinggroup.com; wes.banks@bhpublishinggroup.com; laurene.martin@lifeway.com
Web site: http://www.bhpublishinggroup.com; http://www.lifeway.com
Dist(s): **Follett School Solutions**
christianaudio; *CIP.*

B&J Marketing LLC, *(978-0-9774606)* 17 Robbins Wilks Rd., Bassfield, MS 39421 USA Tel 601-731-2447
E-mail: wastvedt@bellsouth.net.

Bangzoom Pubs., *(978-0-9728646; 978-0-9772927; 978-0-9779099)* Div. of Bangzoom Software, Inc., 14 Storrs Ave., Braintree, MA 02184 USA (SAN 256-6923) Toll Free: 800-589-7333
Web site: http://www.bangzoom.com
Dist(s): **Partners Pubs. Group, Inc.**

Bangzoom Software, Incorporated *See* **Bangzoom Pubs.**

Banis & Associates *See* **Science & Humanities Pr.**

Banks, A J & Associates, Incorporated *See* **BaHar Publishing, L.C.**

Banner of Truth, The, *(978-0-85151)* Orders Addr.: P.O. Box 621, Carlisle, PA 17013 USA Tel 717-249-5747; Fax: 717-249-0604; Toll Free: 800-263-8085; Edit Addr.: 63 E. Louther St., Carlisle, PA 17013 USA (SAN 112-1553)
E-mail: info@banneroftruth.org
Web site: http://www.banneroftruth.co.uk
Dist(s): **Spring Arbor Distributors, Inc.**

Banta, Sandra, *(978-0-9799729)* 16849A Willow Glen Rd., Brownsville, CA 95919 USA Tel 530-675-2010
E-mail: sfbanta@aol.com
Web site: http://www.lilonesbooks.com.

Bantam *Imprint of* **Random House Publishing Group**

Bantam Bks. for Young Readers *Imprint of* **Random Hse. Children's Bks.**

Bantam Doubleday Dell Large Print Group, Inc., *(978-0-385)* Orders Addr.: 2451 S. Wolf Rd., Des Plaines, IL 60018 USA Toll Free: 800-323-9872 (orders); 800-258-4233 (EDI ordering); Edit Addr.: 1540 Broadway, New York, NY 10036-4094 USA
Dist(s): **Beeler, Thomas T. Pub.**

Banyan Bks., *(978-0-615-63108-0)* 251 Bethany Farms Dr., *Ball Ground, GA 30107 USA Tel 770-315-1244* Do not confuse with Banyan Books in Miami, FL, Santa Barabara, CA
Web site: www.juliekorzenko.com
Dist(s): **CreateSpace Independent Publishing Platform.**

Banyan Hypnosis Center for Training & Services, Inc., *(978-0-9712290)* 1431 Warner Ave. Ste. E, Tustin, CA 92780-6444 USA (SAN 253-9381)
E-mail: Maureen@hypnosiscenter.com.

Banyan Publishing, Incorporated *See* **Banyan Hypnosis Center for Training & Services, Inc.**

Banyon Publishing, Inc., *(978-0-9747960)* 235 W Brandon Blvd., Suite 223, Brandon, FL 33511 USA Fax: 813-243-0701
E-mail: banyonpublishing@aol.com
Web site: http://www.banyonpublishing.com.

Baobab Publishing, *(978-0-692-52890-7; 978-0-692-52959-1; 978-0-692-52981-2; 978-0-692-52993-5; 978-0-692-54987-2; 978-0-692-55392-3; 978-0-692-59517-6; 978-0-692-59520-6; 978-0-692-63252-9; 978-0-692-66153-6; 978-0-692-68957-8; 978-0-692-72627-3; 978-0-9982231; 978-1-947045) 7421 Penland Dr., Riverdale, GA 30296 USA Tel 770-376-5243*
Dist(s): **CreateSpace Independent Publishing Platform.**

Baptist Publishing Hse., *(978-0-89114)* Div. of Baptist Missionary Assn. of America, P.O. Box 7270, Texarkana, TX 75505-7270 USA (SAN 183-6544) Tel 870-772-4550; Fax: 870-772-5451; Toll Free: 800-333-1442
E-mail: info@bph.org; pathway@bph.org
Web site: http://www.bph.org.

Baptist Spanish Publishing Hse./Casa Bavtista de Publicaciones: Mundo Hispano, *(978-0-311)* 7000 Alabama St., El Paso, TX 79914 USA (SAN 299-920X) Tel 916-566-9656; Fax: 916-562-6502; Toll Free: 800-755-5958
E-mail: cbpsales1@juno.com
Web site: http://casabautista.org.

Barabara Pr., *(978-0-9719097)* 5929 S. Kolmar Ave., Chicago, IL 60629 USA Tel 773-735-1176 (phone/fax)
E-mail: captsma@comcast.net
Web site: http://www.barabarapress.com.

Barach Publishing, *(978-0-9767453)* 900 N. Walnut Creek, Suite 100, No. 280, Mansfield, TX 76063 USA
E-mail: lgonzalez@barachpublishing.com
Web site: http://www.barachpublishing.com.

Baraka Bks. (CAN) *(978-0-9812405; 978-1-926824) Dist. by* **IPG Chicago.**

Barany Publishing, *(978-0-9832960; 978-0-9895004; 978-1-944841)* 771 Kingston Ave. No. 108, Oakland, CA 94611 USA Tel 510-333-7320
E-mail: BETH@BETHBARANY.COM
Web site: http://www.bethbarany.com
Dist(s): **Smashwords.**

Barbary Coast Books *See* **Gold Street Pr.**

Barbour & Company, Incorporated *See* **Barbour Publishing, Inc.**

Barbour Bks. *Imprint of* **Barbour Publishing, Inc.**

Barbour Publishing, Inc., *(978-0-916441; 978-1-55748; 978-1-57748; 978-1-58660; 978-1-59310; 978-1-59789; 978-1-60260; 978-1-60742; 978-1-61626; 978-1-62029; 978-1-62416; 978-1-62836; 978-1-63058; 978-1-63409; 978-1-944836; 978-1-68322)* Orders Addr.: P.O. Box 719, Uhrichsville, OH 44683 USA (SAN 295-7094) Tel 740-922-5948; Toll Free Fax: 800-220-5948; Toll Free: 800-852-8010; *Imprints:* Barbour Books (Barbour Bks); GoTandem (GoTandem)
E-mail: info@barbourbooks.com
Web site: http://www.barbourbooks.com
Dist(s): **Anchor Distributors**
Follett School Solutions
Spring Arbor Distributors, Inc.

Barcelona Pubs., *(978-0-9624080; 978-1-891278; 978-1-937440; 978-1-945411)* Orders Addr.: 10231 Plano Rd., Dallas, TX 78132 USA (SAN 298-6299) Tel 214-553-9795; Toll Free: 866-620-6943
E-mail: barcelonapublishers@gvtc.com; warehouse@barcelonapublishers.com
Web site: http://www.barcelonapublishers.com
Dist(s): **MyiLibrary**
Ware-Pak, Inc.
ebrary, Inc.

Barcharts, Inc., *(978-1-57222; 978-1-4232)* 6000 Park of Commerce, Blvd. D, Boca Raton, FL 33487-8230 USA (SAN 299-5026) Tel 561-989-3666 ext.3054; Fax: 561-989-3722; Toll Free: 800-226-7799
E-mail: jmijares@barcharts.com
Web site: http://www.quickstudycharts.com
Dist(s): **Follett School Solutions.**

Bard College Pubns. Office, *(978-0-941276; 978-1-931493; 978-1-936192)* P.O. Box 5000, Annandale-on-Hudson, NY 12504-5000 USA Tel 845-758-7872 (7418); Fax: 845-758-7554; *Imprints:* Center for Curatorial Studies (Ctr Curatorial Studies)
E-mail: admission@bard.edu; info@levy.org
Web site: http://www.levy.org; http://www.bard.edu
Dist(s): **D.A.P./Distributed Art Pubs.**

Bard, Frank, *(978-0-9767098)* Orders Addr.: 3801 Corbett Rd., North Lewisburg, OH 43060-9616 USA Tel 937-869-0235
E-mail: fbard@ctcn.net
Web site: http://www.ctcn.net/~febard.

Bardic Pr., *(978-0-9745667)* P.O. Box 761, Oregon House, CA 95962-0761 USA Tel 539-692-1180
E-mail: info@bardic-press.com; andrew@bardic-press.com
Web site: http://www.bardic-press.com.

Bardin & Marsee Publishing, *(978-0-9770169; 978-0-9792394; 978-0-9840857; 978-1-60969)* po box 190351, Birmingham, AL 35219 USA (SAN 854-6215) Toll Free: 866-846-4338
E-mail: bobby@bardinmarsee.com
Web site: http://www.bardinmarsee.com.

Bare Bones Training & Consulting Company *See* **Straus, Jane**

BareBones Publishing, *(978-0-9779601)* P.O. Box 8, McDonough, NY 13801 USA
Web site: http://www.dustinwarburton.com; http://www.bonfed.com; http://www.BareBonespublishing.com
Dist(s): **BCH Fulfillment & Distribution.**

Barefoot Bks., Inc., *(978-1-84148; 978-1-898000; 978-1-901223; 978-1-902283; 978-1-905236; 978-1-84686)* Orders Addr.: 2067 Mass Ave., 5th Fl., Cambridge, MA 02140 USA Tel 866-417-2369; Fax: 888-346-9138
E-mail: ussales@barefootbooks.com
Web site: http://www.barefootbooks.com
Dist(s): **Banta Packaging & Fulfillment.**

Barefoot Pr., *(978-1-882133)* Orders Addr.: P.O. Box 28514, Raleigh, NC 27611 USA (SAN 248-5656) Tel 919-834-1164; Edit Addr.: 700 W. Morgan St., Raleigh, NC 27603 USA (SAN 248-5664).

Barker, Lesley, *(978-0-9763211)* 1630 Rathford Dr., Saint Louis, MO 63146-3911 USA
E-mail: askiesley@teamlesley.com
Web site: http://www.teamlesley.com.

Barnarie Pubns., *(978-0-9619463)* 735 Nardo Rd., Encinitas, CA 92024 USA (SAN 245-0070) Tel 760-753-6950.

Barn Owl Bks, London (GBR) *(978-1-903015) Dist. by* **IPG Chicago.**

Barnaby & Co., *(978-0-9642836; 978-0-615-74648-7)* 30 W. Chester St., Nantucket, MA 02554 USA Tel 508-901-1793
E-mail: barnaby@nantucket.net.

Barnaby Bks., Inc., *(978-0-940350)* 3290 Pacific Heights Rd., Honolulu, HI 96813 USA (SAN 217-5010) Fax: 808-531-0089
E-mail: barnaby@lava.net; publisher@barnabybooks.com
Web site: http://www.barnabybooks.com
Dist(s): **Bess Pr., Inc.**

Barnes & Noble Bks.-Imports, *(978-0-389)* 4720 Boston Way, Lanham, MD 20706 USA (SAN 206-7803) Tel 301-459-3366; Toll Free: 800-462-6420
Dist(s): **Rowman & Littlefield Publishers, Inc.**

Barnes & Noble, Inc., *(978-0-7607; 978-0-88029; 978-1-4028; 978-1-4114; 978-1-4351; 978-1-61551; 978-1-61552; 978-1-61553; 978-1-61554; 978-1-61555; 978-1-61556; 978-1-61557; 978-1-61558; 978-1-61559; 978-1-61560; 978-1-61679; 978-1-61680; 978-1-61681; 978-1-61682; 978-1-61683; 978-1-61684; 978-1-61685; 978-1-61686; 978-1-61687; 978-1-61688; 978-1-970008) 76 Ninth Ave., 9th Flr., New York, NY 10011 USA (SAN 141-3651) Tel 212-414-6385; 122 Fifth Ave., New York, NY 10011; Imprints:* Blackbirch Press, Incorporated (Blackbirch Pr); SparkNotes (SparkNotes)
E-mail: smcculloch@bn.com
Dist(s): **Bookazine Co., Inc.**
Dover Pubns., Inc.
Sterling Publishing Co., Inc.

Barnes Printing, *(978-0-9658838; 978-0-9863483)* 1076 Klopman Mill Rd., Denton, NC 27239-7305 USA Tel 336-859-1964; Fax: 336-859-4923
E-mail: elizabeth@barnesprinting.com
Web site: www.barnesprinting.com.

Barnesyard Bks., *(978-0-9674681)* P.O. Box 254, Sergeantsville, NJ 08557 USA Tel 609-397-6600; Fax: 609-397-3262
E-mail: info@barnesyardbooks.com
Web site: http://www.barnesyardbooks.com
Dist(s): **Follett School Solutions.**

Barnette, Donald, *(978-0-9747816)* 591 Mira Vista Ave., Oakland, CA 94610-1928 USA.

Barnhardt & Ashe Publishing, Inc., *(978-0-9715402; 978-0-9801744)* 444 Brickell Ave., Suite 51, PMB 432, Miami, FL 33131 USA Toll Free: 800-283-6360
E-mail: barnhardtashe@aol.com
Web site: http://www.barnhardtashepublishing.com.

Barr, Tricia, *(978-0-9989777)* P.O. Box 1224, SAHUARITA, AZ 85629 USA Tel 520-954-4422
Dist(s): **Lightning Source, Inc.**

Barranca Pr., *(978-1-939604)* 1450 Couse St. (No. 10), Taos, NM 87571 USA Tel 575-613-1026
E-mail: lisa@barrancapress.com
Web site: www.barrancapress.com.

Barren Hill Bks., *(978-0-9769896)* 646 Highland Ave., South Portland, ME 04106 USA Tel 207-767-3268
E-mail: info@BarrenHillBooks.com
Web site: http://www.barrenhillbooks.com/.

Barrett's Bookshelf, *(978-0-9728731)* 16165 SW Inverurie Rd., Lake Oswego, OR 97035 USA Tel 503-697-4208.

Barricks, Jeri Ministry, *(978-0-9743512)* P.O. Box 347, Buffalo, NY 14225 USA Fax: 716-685-6839
E-mail: jeribar37@hotmail.com
Web site: http://www.jeribarricks.net.

Barringer Publishing, *(978-0-9825109; 978-0-9828425; 978-0-9831989; 978-0-9833088; 978-0-9839050; 978-0-9851184; 978-0-9882034; 978-0-9891694; 978-0-9896338; 978-0-9903935; 978-0-9908209; 978-0-9961973; 978-0-9989069)* 2317 Harrier Run, Naples, FL 34105 USA
Web site: barringerpublishing.com
Dist(s): **Follett School Solutions.**

†Barron's Educational Series, Inc., *(978-0-7641; 978-0-8120; 978-1-4380)* Orders Addr.: 250 Wireless Blvd., Hauppauge, NY 11788-3917 USA (SAN 201-453X) Fax: 631-434-3723; 631-434-8067 (Sales Dept. Orders); Toll Free: 800-645-3476 (ext. 204 or 214 for Orders); a/o Georgetown Book Warehouse, 34 Armstrong Ave., Georgetown, ON L7G 4R9 (SAN 115-2033) Tel 905-458-5506; Fax: 905-877-5575; Toll Free Fax: 800-887-1594 Do not confuse with BARRONS, Monroe, WA
E-mail: barrons@barronseduc.com; info@barronseduc.com; orders@barronseduc.com; clopez@barronseduc.com
Web site: http://www.barronseduc.com
Dist(s): **Ebsco Publishing**
Follett School Solutions; *CIP.*

Barrow, Shelley *See* **Mikenzi's Kardz & Bks. Llc.**

†Barrytown/Station Hill Pr., *(978-0-88268; 978-0-930794; 978-1-58177; 978-1-886449)* 120 Station Hill Rd., Barrytown, NY 12507 USA (SAN 214-1485) Tel 845-758-5293; Fax: 845-758-9838
E-mail: publishers@stationhill.org
Web site: http://www.stationhill.org/
Dist(s): **Midpoint Trade Bks., Inc.**
Redwing Bk. Co.
SPD-Small Pr. Distribution; *CIP.*

Barsotti Bks., *(978-0-9642112; 978-0-9818188)* 2239 Hidden Valley Ln., Camino, CA 95709-9722 USA Tel 530-642-8341; Fax: 530-642-9703
E-mail: jb@barsottibooks.com
Web site: http://www.barsottibooks.com.

Bartleby Pr., *(978-0-910155; 978-0-935437)* 8600 Foundry St. Savage Mill Box 2043, Savage, MD 20763 USA (SAN 241-2098) Tel 301-949-2443; Fax: 301-949-2205; Toll Free: 800-953-9929
E-mail: Inquiries@bartlebythepublisher.com
Web site: http://www.BartlebythePublisher.com
Dist(s): **Casemate Pubs. & Bk. Distributors, LLC**
MyiLibrary.

Bartlett Park, *(978-0-9823672)* 127 Myrtle St., Apt. 4, Boston, MA 02114 USA
E-mail: knoefel@bartlettpark.com.

Barton Bks., *(978-0-615-69695-9; 978-0-615-78343-7)* Orders Addr.: 4505 Sentinel Ct., Rocklin, CA 95677 USA Tel 916-787-0962; *Imprints:* Flickerfawn (Flickerfawn)
E-mail: dredsovm@me.com; dredsovm@wavecable.com
Web site: www.flickerfawn.com; www.FionaThornBook.com; www.jbartonbooks.com.

Barton, D.C. Publishing, *(978-0-9759426)* P.O. Box 3057, Lakeland, FL 33801-6602 USA Tel 863-665-5986
E-mail: dfcbible@aol.com.

Barton Publications, *(978-0-9778455)* Orders Addr.: 1613 Sunrise Ln., Eau Claire, WI 54703-2574 USA
E-mail: bartonpub@ymail.com
Web site: http://www.westmusic.com/1002410-print-music-books/m1090-music-therapy-books/m1090i-texts/biomedical-foundations-of-music-as-therapy-838708.htm
Dist(s): **West Music Co.**

Barton-Veerman Co., *(978-0-9724616; 978-0-9978516)* 205 N Washington St, Wheaton, IL 60187 USA Tel 630-871-1212
E-mail: accounting@livingstonecorp.com
Web site: http://www.livingstonecorp.com
Dist(s): **BookBaby.**

Bartram Team, The, *(978-0-615-31220-0)* 1251 Pine Valley Dr., New Bern , NC 28562 USA.

Bas Relief, LLC, *(978-0-9657472)* Orders Addr.: P.O. Box 645, Union, WV 24983 USA Tel 304-832-6647
E-mail: Barea@basrelief.org
Web site: http://www.basrelief.org
Dist(s): **Follett School Solutions.**

Bas Relief Publishing *See* **Bas Relief, LLC**

Bases Loaded Bks. *Imprint of* **ChildrenzBks.**

Basic Black Publishing, *(978-0-9801320)* Orders Addr.: 8584 W. Appleton Ave., Unit X, Milwaukee, WI 53225 USA.

Basic Distribution, Inc., 360 Hurst St., Linden, NJ 07036 USA Tel 908-523-0555; Fax: 908-523-0373
E-mail: ssullivan@basicdistributioninc.com
Web site: http://www.basicdistributioninc.com.

Basic Health Pubns., Inc., *(978-1-59120)* 28812 Top of the World Dr., Laguna Beach, CA 92651 USA (SAN 858-4893) Tel 949-715-7327; Fax: 949-415-7328; Toll Free: 800-575-8890 (orders only)
E-mail: ngoldfind@basicmediagroup.com
Web site: http://www.basichealthpub.com
Dist(s): **Follett School Solutions**
Ingram Publisher Services.

Basic Knowledge Publishing Co., *(978-1-885501)* 1024 Debbie Ln., Maryville, MO 64468 USA Tel 816-562-2665.

Basic Skills Assessment & Educational Services, *(978-1-888786)* 19146 S. Molalla Ave., Oregon City, OR 97045-8975 USA Tel 503-650-5282; Fax: 503-557-2953
E-mail: basicsk@MSN.COM
Web site: http://www.basicskills.net.

Basketball Fundamentals *See* **SportAmerica**

Bass Cove Bks., *(978-0-9630074)* 57 North St., Kennebunkport, ME 04046 USA Tel 207-967-4152
E-mail: amabee@adelphia.net.

Bass, Sheila, *(978-0-9766366)* 23 Conn. St., Woodsville, NH 03785 USA
E-mail: a_15bass@yahoo.com.

Bassan, Malca, *(978-0-9744039; 978-0-692-25535-3)* 9801 Collins Ave., Apt. 15Q, Bal Harbor, FL 33154 USA Tel 305-868-0365; Fax: 305-865-6992
E-mail: mabassan27@gmail.com.

Bastion Pr., Inc., *(978-0-9714392; 978-1-59263)* Orders Addr.: P.O. Box 46753, Seattle, WA 98146 USA; Edit Addr.: 8405 16th Ave., SW., Seattle, WA 98106-2365 USA Tel 206-763-3368; Fax: 206-763-3370 Do not confuse with Bastion Pr., Los Angeles, CA
E-mail: jim@bastionpress.com
Web site: http://www.bastionpress.com
Dist(s): **Studio 2 Publishing, Inc.**

Bat Wing Pr *Imprint of* **Harbor Hse.**

Bat-El Publishing, *(978-0-9832025)* 3400 Colville Pl., Encino, CA 91436 USA Tel 818-461-9294
E-mail: talyanai7@gmail.com.

Batelier Publishing, *(978-0-9789429)* 3140 Bourbon St. Cir., Rockwall, TX 75032 USA
E-mail: batelierpublishing@yahoo.com
Web site: http://www.batelier.bravehost.com.

Batfish Bks., *(978-0-9728653)* Div. of O'Neill, Michael P. Photography, Inc., P.O. Box 32909, Palm Beach Gardens, FL 33420-2909 USA (SAN 255-1780) Tel 305-333-7166; Fax: 561-840-1939
E-mail: mpo@msn.com
Web site: http://www.batfishbooks.com
Dist(s): **Follett School Solutions**
Southern Bk. Service.

†**Bathtub Row Pr.**, *(978-0-941232)* Orders Addr.: P.O. Box 43, Los Alamos, NM 87544 USA (SAN 276-9603) Tel 505-662-2660; Fax: 505-662-6312; Edit Addr.: 1050 Bathtub Row, Los Alamos, NM 87544 USA (SAN 241-9025)
E-mail: shar5992@gmail.com
Web site: http://losalamoshistory.org; *CIP.*

Battat, Inc., *(978-0-9794542; 978-0-9843722; 978-0-9844904; 978-0-9883165; 978-0-9891839; 978-0-9963272; 978-0-692-81454-3; 978-0-692-82334-7; 978-0-692-82578-5; 978-0-692-82579-2; 978-0-692-89111-7; 978-0-692-96027-1)* 1560 Military Tpke., Plattsburgh, NY 12901-7458 USA (SAN 853-4683).

Battle Creek Area Mathematics & Science Ctr., *(978-1-933281)* 765 Upton Ave., Battle Creek, MI 49015 USA Tel 269-965-9440
Web site: http://bcmsc.k12.mi.us.

Batyah & Assocs. Publishing, *(978-0-9749571)* 2013 Vernier, Grosse Pointe Woods, MI 48236 USA
E-mail: baroberts07@yahoo.com.

Batyah Productions, Inc., *(978-0-9649608)* 6434 Saxet St., Houston, TX 77055-5317 USA.

BAU Publishing Group, *(978-0-9766770)* Orders Addr.: 1808 STRAWBERRY Dr., RIO RANCHO, NM 87144 USA
E-mail: tize@tize.biz; admin@baupublishing.com
Web site: http://www.baupublishing.com.

Bauer, Linda, *(978-0-9798146)* Orders Addr.: P.O. Box 308, Eastford, CT 06242 USA
Dist(s): **CreateSpace Independent Publishing Platform.**

Bauer Media Bks. (AUS) *(978-0-949128; 978-0-949892; 978-1-86396; 978-1-74245; 978-0-646-36336-3; 978-1-906312) Dist. by* **HachBkGrp.**

Bauhan Publishing LLC, *(978-0-87233)* Orders Addr.: P.O. Box 117, Peterborough, NH 03458 USA (SAN 204-384X) Tel 603-567-4430
E-mail: sales@bauhanpublishing.com; sbauhan@bauhanpublishing.com
Web site: http://www.bauhanpublishing.com
Dist(s): **East-West Export Bks.**
Univ. Pr. of New England.

Bauhan, William L. Incorporated *See* **Bauhan Publishing LLC**

Baum & Baum, LLC, *(978-0-9839373)* 14196 Cranston St., Livonia, MI 48154-4251 USA Tel 734-422-0546
E-mail: lbaum@mi.rr.com
Dist(s): **Bookmasters Distribution.**

Baumbach, Laura *See* **MLR Pr., LLC**

Baxter Pr., *(978-1-888237; 978-0-9907879; 978-0-9973372; 978-1-947505)* 700 S. Friendswood Dr., Suite C, Friendswood, TX 77546 USA Tel 281-992-0628; Fax: 815-572-5115
E-mail: baxter2@flash.net
Web site: http://baxterpress.com
Dist(s): **Greenleaf Book Group**
Spirit Rising.

Bay Horse Creations LLC, *(978-0-9749320)* 508 W. Irvine Rd., Phoenix, AZ 85086 USA Tel 602-818-7879
Web site: http://www.bayhorsecreations.com.

Bay Light Publishing, *(978-0-9670280; 978-0-9741817)* P.O. Box 3032, Mooresville, NC 28117 USA (SAN 299-9196) Tel 704-664-7541; Fax: 704-664-2712; Toll Free: 866-541-3895
E-mail: baylightpub@compuserve.com
Web site: http://www.baylightpub.com.

Bay Media, Inc., *(978-0-9665239; 978-0-9717047; 978-0-9823354)* Orders Addr.: 550m Ritchie Hwy., #271 Severna Pk., Severna Park, MD 21146 USA Tel 410-647-8402; Fax: 410-544-4640
Web site: http://www.baymed.com.

Bay Mills Indian Community, *(978-0-9758801)* 12140 W. Lakeshore Dr., Brimley, MI 49715 USA
Web site: http://www.bmic.net.

Bay Oak Pubs., Ltd., *(978-0-9704692; 978-0-9741713; 978-0-9800874)* 34 Wimbledon Dr., Dover, DE 19904 USA
E-mail: bayoakpublishers@aol.com
Web site: http://www.bayoakpublishers.com
Dist(s): **Follett School Solutions**
Washington Bk. Distributors.

Bay Publishing, *(978-0-9822046)* P.O. Box 4569, Santa Rosa, CA 95402-4569 USA (SAN 857-5401)
E-mail: ron@bayyellow.com.

Bay Villager, The, *(978-0-9769742)* 4923 43rd. St., Dickinson, TX 77539 USA
E-mail: lindalou36@hotmail.com.

Bay, William Music, *(978-0-9859227; 978-0-9888327; 978-0-9983842)* 4 Denny Ln., St. Louis, MO 63131 USA Tel 314-707-7366
E-mail: bill@melbay.com
Dist(s): **Mel Bay Pubns., Inc.**

Bayard Editions (FRA) *(978-2-227; 978-2-7009; 978-2-7470; 978-2-915480; 978-2-9518356) Dist. by* **Distribks Inc.**

Bayberry Cottage Gallery, *(978-0-615-61021-4; 978-0-615-89363-1)* 9074 Highland St., Mauricetown, NJ 08329 USA Tel 856-785-9927
E-mail: nanptidy@yahoo.com
Web site: http://nancy-patterson.artistwebsites.com.

Bayeux Arts, Inc. (CAN) *(978-1-896209; 978-1-897411; 978-1-988440) Dist. by* **Chicago Distribution Ctr.**

Bayliss, Erin, *(978-0-9778471)* 320 Roan Dr., Grants Pass, OR 97526 USA
E-mail: rise4him@q.com.

Baylor College of Medicine, *(978-1-888997; 978-1-944035)* Div. of Center for Educational Outreach, Orders Addr.: Center For Educational Outreach Baylor College Of Medicine One Baylor Plaza, Bcm411, Houston, TX 77030 USA Tel 713-798-8200; Fax: 713-798-8201; Toll Free: 800-798-8244; *Imprints:* BioEd (BioEd)
E-mail: edoutreach@bcm.edu; nmoreno@bcm.edu; marthay@bcm.edu; mslopez@bcm.edu
Web site: http://www.bcm.edu/edoutreach; http://www.bioedonline.org; http://www.bcm.edu.

Baylor Univ. Pr., *(978-0-918954; 978-1-878804; 978-1-932792; 978-1-60258; 978-1-4813)* 1920 S. Fourth St., Waco, TX 76706 USA Tel 254-710-3164; Fax: 254-710-3440
E-mail: Diane_Smith@baylor.edu
Web site: http://www.baylorpress.com
Dist(s): **Hopkins Fulfillment Services**
MyiLibrary
ebrary, Inc.

Bayou Publishing, *(978-1-886298)* Div. of Bayou Publishing, LLC, Orders Addr.: 2524 Nottingham, Houston, TX 77005 USA (SAN 859-2810) Tel 713-526-4558; Fax: 713-526-4342; Toll Free: 800-340-2034 Do not confuse with Bayou Publishing, Longboat Key, FL
E-mail: info@bayoupublishing.com; orders@bayoupublishing.com; vloos@bayoupublishing.com
Web site: http://www.bayoupublishing.com
Dist(s): **BookMasters, Inc.**
Bookmasters Distribution
Quality Bks., Inc.
Unique Bks., Inc.

Bayport Pr. *Imprint of* **Wellness Pubn.**

Baysmore Bks., *(978-0-9857160; 978-0-692-78985-8)* P.O. Box 21402, Long Beach, CA 90801 USA Tel 562-208-3646
E-mail: baysmorebooks@gmail.com.

bazow, thomas, *(978-0-9777725)* 4845 Romaine Spring Dr., Fenton, MO 63026-5840 USA
Web site: http://www.inhistimepublishing.com.

Bazuji Publishing LLC, *(978-0-9761555)* 3843 53rd St., SE, Tappen, ND 58487 USA (SAN 256-2626) Toll Free: 800-615-7606
Web site: http://www.bazuji.com.

BB International Productions, Inc., *(978-0-9754329)* 1200 W. Ave., Suite 707, Miami Beach, FL 33139-4316 USA
Web site: http://www.bibiadventures.com.

BBC Audiobooks America *See* **AudioGO**

BBI Incorporated *See* **Bush Brothers & Co.**

BBM Bks., *(978-1-938504)* 21 Harbor Pointe Dr., Corona del Mar, CA 92625 USA Tel 949-302-5849
E-mail: inspiredcreationsca@gmail.com.

BBR *Imprint of* **BBR: Books for Brilliance & Resilience**

BBR: Books for Brilliance & Resilience, *(978-0-9753245)* P.O. Box 5236, Takoma Park, MD 20913-5236 USA Toll Free: 888-898-2322; *Imprints:* BBR (B B R)
Web site: http://www.letscommunicate.org.

BBRACK Productions, Inc., *(978-0-9728837)* 1345-B Triad Ctr. Dr., No. 181, Saint Peters, MO 63376 USA Tel 636-936-2311
E-mail: 1stB@bbrack.com
Web site: http://www.bbrack.com.

B-Bright publishing, *(978-1-943417)* 16210 tahoe dr, Jersey Village, TX 77040 USA Tel 281-606-5820
E-mail: gdbanks@gmail.com.

bby Publications at The University of West Alabama, *(978-1-885775)* Div. of College of Education, Orders Addr.: UWA Station 60, Livingston, AL 35470 USA Tel 205-652-5406; Fax: 205-652-5400
E-mail: tpartridge@uwa.edu; dknight@uwa.edu
Web site: http://www.bbypublications.com.

BC Publishing, *(978-0-9740511)* 633-1 Elk Ct., Fayetteville, NC 28301 USA Tel 910-578-2621; *Imprints:* Kids1st Books (Kids1st Bks) Do not confuse with BC Publishing in Tampa, FL
E-mail: dbradleyclarke@yahoo.com.

BCM International Inc., *(978-0-86508)* 201 Granite Run Dr., Suite 260, Lancaster, PA 17601 USA (SAN 211-7762) Tel 717-560-9601 Main Phone Number; Toll Free: 888-226-4685
E-mail: info@bcmintl.org
Web site: http://www.bcmintl.org
Dist(s): **CLC Pubns.**
Send The Light Distribution LLC.

BCM Publications, Incorporated *See* **BCM International Inc.**

BCP Pubns., *(978-0-615-20692-9; 978-0-615-21056-8; 978-0-578-02129-4)* 3215 E. 17th St., Vancouver, WA 98661 USA
E-mail: bcpwriter2000@yahoo.com
Web site: http://www.authortree.com/bcpwriter2000
Dist(s): **AuthorHouse.**

BDA Publishing, *(978-0-9794716)* P.O. Box 541715, Dallas, TX 75354-1715 USA Tel 972-532-8805; Fax: 214-350-9275; 3163 Citation Dr., Dallas, TX 75229-5840
E-mail: bbd@sbcglobal.net
Web site: http://www.evanbrain.com; http://barrybdoyle.com/.

Be Naturally Curious, *(978-1-942403)* 160 W 85th St., New York, NY 10024 USA Tel 347-229-5559
E-mail: valerie@benaturallycurious.com
Web site: www.benaturallycurious.com.

Be There Bedtime Stories LLC, *(978-0-692-74330-0)* 35 Giovanni Aisle, IRVINE, CA 92614 USA Tel 949-394-1714.

Beach Bks., *(978-0-9763052; 978-0-615-57831-6)* 430 Noe St., San Francisco, CA 94114 USA Tel 415-251-3845
E-mail: gyaltsen@yahoo.com
Web site: http://www.jefferybeach.com
Dist(s): **CreateSpace Independent Publishing Platform.**

Beach Front Bks., *(978-0-9651281)* P.O. Box 545, East Bridgewater, MA 02333 USA Tel 508-378-9319; Fax: 508-378-7621 Do not confuse with Beach Front Books in East Bridgewater, MA
E-mail: beachfrontbooks@aol.com.

Beach Lane Bks. *Imprint of* **Beach Lane Bks.**

Beach Lane Bks., Div. of Simon & Schuster Children's Publishing, 1230 Ave. of the Americas, New York, NY 10020 USA; *Imprints:* Beach Lane Books (BeachLane)
Dist(s): **Follett School Solutions**
Simon & Schuster, Inc.

Beach Lloyd Pubs., LLC, *(978-0-9743158; 978-0-9792778; 978-0-9819417)* Orders Addr.: P.O. Box 2183, Southeastern, PA 19399-2183 USA (SAN 255-4992) Tel 610-407-0130; Fax: 775-254-0633; Toll Free: 866-218-3253; Edit Addr.: 40 Cabot Dr., Wayne, PA 19087-5619 USA
E-mail: beachlloyd@erols.com
Web site: http://www.beachlloyd.com
Dist(s): **MBS Textbook Exchange, Inc.**

Beachcomber Press.com, *(978-0-9800630)* 33021 Adelante St., Temecula, CA 92592 USA Tel 951-699-2932
E-mail: ashleyludwig@verizon.net.

Beachfront Bks., *(978-0-9768816)* Orders Addr.: P.O. Box 16-287, Seattle, WA 98116 USA; Edit Addr.: 5641 Beach Dr. SW, Seattle, WA 98116 USA
Web site: http://www.beachfront books.org
Dist(s): **Follett School Solutions.**

Beachfront Publishing, *(978-1-892339)* Div. of Words, Words, Words, Inc., Orders Addr.: P.O. Box 811922, Boca Raton, FL 33481 USA; 4705 Brook Top Ct., Raleigh, NC 27606
E-mail: info@beachfrontentertainment.com
Web site: http://www.beachfrontentertainment.com
Dist(s): **Follett School Solutions.**

BeachHouse Bks. *Imprint of* **Science & Humanities Pr.**

Beachhouse Publishing, LLC, *(978-0-9729905; 978-1-933067)* P.O. Box 5464, Kaneohe, HI 96744 USA
E-mail: info@beachhousepublishing.com
Web site: www.beachhousepublishing.com
Dist(s): **Booklines Hawaii, Ltd.**
Islander Group.

BeachWalk Bks. Inc., *(978-0-9770158)* P.O. Box 446, Glenview, IL 60025 USA Tel 847-729-2222; Fax: 847-729-5215; Toll Free Fax: 866-720-3222; 2136 Fir St., Glenview, IL 60025
E-mail: amcdonald@beachwalkbooks.com
Web site: http://www.beachwalkbooks.com.

Beachwalker Pr., *(978-0-9727639)* 5557 SW Village Pl., Beaverton, OR 97007 USA Tel 503-799-6061; Fax: 503-644-9335
E-mail: beachwalkerpress@aol.com
Web site: http://www.beachwalkerpress.com.

Beacon Hill Pr. of Kansas City, *(978-0-8341)* Div. of Nazarene Publishing Hse., 2923 Troost, Kansas City, MO 64109 USA (SAN 241-6328) Tel 816-931-1900; Fax: 816-753-4071; Toll Free: 800-877-0700 (orders only)
E-mail: nphdirect@nph.com; orders@nph.com; inquiry@bhillkc.com
Web site: http://www.nph.com; http://www.bhillkc.com
Dist(s): **Nazarene Publishing Hse.**

Beacon Pr. *Imprint of* **Beacon Pr.**

Beacon Pr., *(978-0-8070)* Orders Addr.: 25 Beacon St., Boston, MA 02108-2892 USA (SAN 201-4483) Tel 617-742-2110; Fax: 617-723-3097; *Imprints:* Beacon Press (BeaconPress)
E-mail: marketing@beacon.org
Web site: http://www.beacon.org
Dist(s): **Ebsco Publishing**
Houghton Mifflin Harcourt Publishing Co.
Houghton Mifflin Harcourt Trade & Reference Pubs.
MyiLibrary
Penguin Random Hse. LLC
Random Hse., Inc.

Beacon Publishing, *(978-1-929266; 978-0-9841318; 978-1-937509; 978-1-942611; 978-1-63582)* 631 U.S. Hwy. 1, Suite 403, North Palm Beach, FL 33408 USA (SAN 858-5024) Tel 888-618-5253; 2330 Kemper Ln., Cincinnati, OH 45206 Do not confuse with Beacon Publishing in Theodore, AL, Brimfield, MA
E-mail: shawna@dynamiccatholic.com; nathan@beaconpublishinginc.com; kwhalen@beaconpublishinginc.com
Web site: http://www.matthewkelly.org; http://www.beaconpublishinginc.com/
Dist(s): **BookBaby**
Follett School Solutions
Smashwords.

Beacon Street Girls *Imprint of* **B*tween Productions, Inc.**

BeActive Publishing Co., *(978-0-9722714)* 29834 N. Cave Creek Rd., S118, PMB 142, Cave Creek, AZ 85331-7831 USA Tel 480-563-0315; Fax: 480-502-0664
Web site: http://www.beactivesportsmarketing.com.

Beagle Bay Bks., *(978-0-9679591; 978-0-9749610)* Div. of Beagle Bay, Inc., 2325 Homestead Pl., Reno, NV 89509-3657 USA
E-mail: info@beaglebay.com
Web site: http://www.beaglebay.com
Dist(s): **Brodart Co.**

Beagle Bks. Publishing, LLC, *(978-0-9841813)* 43 Highridge Rd., Westport, MA 02790 USA (SAN 858-6519).

Bean Bk. Publishing, *(978-0-9761990)* 9246 E. Havasupai Dr., Scottsdale, AZ 85255 USA Tel 480-502-1257 (phone/fax)
E-mail: dawn.crichton@dcranch.com; Juliecrichton@cox.net
Web site: http://www.stringbeansorjellybeans.com; http://www.bean-books.com.

Bean Sprouts *Imprint of* **Standard Publishing**

Beaner Bks., *(978-0-9849293)* 541 Redford Pl. Dr., Rolesville, NC 27571 USA Tel 855-286-9687
E-mail: alphabetownusa@gmail.com
Web site: http://www.alphabetownusa.com.

BeanPole Bks. *Imprint of* **Harren Communications, LLC**

Beanstalk Pubns, *(978-0-9785302)* 4762 Camino del Rey, Santa Barbara, CA 93110 USA Tel 805-448-0898
E-mail: mjmckechnie@beanstalkpublications.com
Web site: http://www.beanstalkpublications.com.

Bear & Company *See* **Boyds Collection Ltd., The**

†**Bear & Co.**, *(978-0-939680; 978-1-879181; 978-1-59143)* Orders Addr.: P.O. Box 388, Rochester, VT 05767-0388 USA; Edit Addr.: One Park St., Rochester, VT 05767 USA (SAN 216-7174) Tel 802-767-3174; Fax: 802-767-3726; Toll Free: 800-246-8648; *Imprints:* Bear Cub Books (Bear Cub Books)
E-mail: customerservice@innertraditions.com; info@innertraditions.com
Web site: http://www.innertraditions.com
Dist(s): **Book Wholesalers, Inc.**
Bookazine Co., Inc.
Brodart Co.
Inner Traditions International, Ltd.
Integral Yoga Pubns.
MyiLibrary
New Leaf Distributing Co., Inc.
Nutri-Bks. Corp.
Partners Bk. Distributing, Inc.
Partners/West Book Distributors
Phoenix Distributors
Quality Bks., Inc.
Simon & Schuster
Simon & Schuster, Inc.; *CIP.*

Bear Cub Bks. *Imprint of* **Bear & Co.**

Bear Star Pr., *(978-0-9657177; 978-0-9719607; 978-0-9793745; 978-0-9850584)* 185 Hollow Oak Dr., Cohasset, CA 95973 USA Tel 530-891-0360
E-mail: bethannspencer@gmail.com
Web site: http://www.bearstarpress.com
Dist(s): **BookMobile**
SPD-Small Pr. Distribution.

Bear State Bks., *(978-1-892622)* Orders Addr.: P.O. Box 96, Exeter, CA 93221 USA Tel 559-280-8547; Fax: 559-594-5383; Edit Addr.: 199 E. Pine St., Exeter, CA 93221 USA Tel 559-280-8547
E-mail: cdbrewer@gmx.com
Web site: bearstatebooks.com.

Bearhead Publishing, LLC, *(978-0-9776260; 978-0-9799153; 978-0-9824373; 978-0-9829307; 978-1-937508)* P.O. Box 16539, Louisville, KY 40256 USA (SAN 257-7798); 2217 Mary Catherine Dr., Louisville, KY 40216
E-mail: garyd@sissymarlyn.com; garydbhp@insightbb.com
Web site: http://www.sissymarlyn.com; http://www.bearheadpublishing.com.

Bearing Bks. *Imprint of* **Red Cygnet Pr.**

Bearly Cooking *Imprint of* **Mountain n' Air Bks.**

BearManor Media, *(978-0-9714570; 978-1-59393; 978-1-62933)* P.O. Box 1129, Duncan, OK 73534-1129 USA Tel 580-252-3547; Fax: 814-690-1559
E-mail: benohmart@gmail.com
Web site: http://www.bearmanormedia.com.

Bearport Publishing Co., Inc., *(978-1-59716; 978-1-936087; 978-1-936088; 978-1-936089; 978-1-936090; 978-0-9824758; 978-0-9824759; 978-0-9824760; 978-0-9824761; 978-0-9824762; 978-0-9824763; 978-0-9824764; 978-1-61772; 978-1-62724; 978-1-943074; 978-1-943553; 978-1-944102; 978-1-944997; 978-1-944998; 978-1-68402) 45 W. 21st St., Ste. 3B, New York, NY 10010 USA (SAN 256-2103) Toll Free: 877-337-8577 (and fax)*
E-mail: kenngoin@earthlink.net; info@bearportpublishing.com; vyaw@bearportpublishing.com
Web site: http://www.bearportpublishing.com
Dist(s): **Follett School Solutions**
MyiLibrary.

Bear's Designs Unlimited, *(978-0-9638473)* 7505 320th St., W., Northfield, MN 55057 USA Tel 507-645-9050; Toll Free: 800-497-8757.

Bearwallow Blessings Ministries, *(978-0-9768514)* HC 63 Box 77A-1 Rte. 637, Jewell Ridge, VA 24622 USA
Web site: http://www.bearwallowblessings.com.

Beascoa, Ediciones S.A. (ESP) *(978-84-488; 978-84-7546) Dist. by* **Lectorum Pubns.**

Beascoa, Ediciones S.A. (ESP) *(978-84-488; 978-84-7546) Dist. by* **Distribks Inc.**

Beascoa, Ediciones S.A. (ESP) *(978-84-488; 978-84-7546) Dist. by* **TwoRivers.**

Beast Stew, *(978-0-9821734)* 6244 Old Lagrange Rd. PO Box 617, Crestwood, TX 40014 USA
Dist(s): **Greenleaf Book Group.**

Beatin' Path Pubns., LLC, *(978-0-9795470; 978-0-9797522; 978-0-9825839; 978-0-9832648; 978-0-9882814; 978-0-9894773; 978-0-9861795; 978-0-9963591)* Orders Addr.: 302 E. College St., Bridgewater, VA 22812-1509 USA (SAN 853-7003) Tel 540-478-4833; Fax: 540-828-6903
E-mail: beatinpath@mac.com
Web site: http://www.beatinpathpublications.com
Dist(s): **Music in Motion**
Music is Elementary
Plank Road Publishing
West Music Co.

Beau Francis Pr., *(978-0-9792147)* 4100 Newport Pl., Suite 400, Newport Beach, CA 92660 USA Tel 949-499-0679.

Beaufort Bks., Inc., *(978-0-8253; 978-0-9852135)* 27 W. 20th St., Suite 1102, New York, NY 10011 USA (SAN 215-2304) Tel 212-727-0190; Fax: 212-727-0195
E-mail: midpointny@aol.com
Dist(s): **Follett School Solutions**
Midpoint Trade Bks., Inc.

Beautiful America Publishing Co., *(978-0-89802)* Orders Addr.: P.O. Box 244, Woodburn, OR 97071-0244 USA (SAN 251-2548) Tel 503-982-4616; Fax: 503-982-2825; Toll Free: 800-874-1233; Edit Addr.: 2600 Progress Way, Woodburn, OR 97071 USA (SAN 211-4623)
E-mail: bapco@beautifulamericapub.com
Web site: http://www.beautifulamericapub.com
Dist(s): **Follett School Solutions**
Koen Pacific
Partners/West Book Distributors.

Beautiful Feet Bks., *(978-0-9643803; 978-1-893103)* 1306 Mill St., San Luis Obispo, CA 93401-2817 USA Toll Free: 800-889-1978
E-mail: russell@bfbooks.com
Web site: http://www.bfbooks.com
Dist(s): **Follett School Solutions.**

Beautiful Zion Baptist Church *See* **A & L Communications, Inc.**

Beaver Island Arts, *(978-0-9708575)* P.O. Box 40, Bay City, MI 49708-0040 USA (SAN 253-8385) Tel 517-894-5925
E-mail: mblocksma@yahoo.com
Web site: http://beaverislandarts.com
Dist(s): **Follett School Solutions**
Indiana Univ. Pr.
Ingram Publisher Services
Partners Bk. Distributing, Inc.

Beaver Meadow Publishing, *(978-0-9742085)* 11 Clarence Russell Rd., Thurman, NY 12885 USA Tel 518-623-9305; 352-463-3089
E-mail: PerkinFL@aol.com
Web site: http://www.persisgranger.com.

Beaver's Pond Pr., Inc., *(978-1-890676; 978-1-931646; 978-1-59298)* 7104 Ohms Ln., Suite 101, Edina, MN 55439 USA Tel 952-829-8818
E-mail: heather@beaverspondpress.com
Web site: http://www.beaverspondpress.com
Dist(s): **Itasca Bks.**

Because Time Flies, Inc., *(978-0-9652652; 978-0-9754073)* 155 N. Harbor Dr., Concourse Suite 2, Chicago, IL 60601-7364 USA Tel 312-938-0938; Fax: 312-938-0029; Toll Free: 800-694-4786
E-mail: journals@covad.net
Web site: http://www.becausetimeflies.com.

Beck Global Publishing, *(978-0-9816942)* 10600 E. Rte. Y, Ashland, MO 65010 USA
Web site: http://www.beckpillowtalk.com.

Beck Publishing *See* **Beck Global Publishing**

Becker, Christie, *(978-0-9728116)* 7 Whispering Pines Ct., Hilton Head, SC 29926-2542 USA
E-mail: beachbeckers@msn.com
Web site: http://www.cbeckerbooks.com.

Becker Doyle & Associates *See* **BDA Publishing**

Becker, Frank *See* **Greenbush Pr.**

Becker, Savan C., *(978-0-615-23554-7)* 1521 Farlow Ave., Crofton, MD 21114 USA Tel 443-292-8098; Fax: 443-603-2998
E-mail: savan@psinerspace.net
Dist(s): **Lulu Pr., Inc.**

becker&mayer! books, *(978-0-9700346; 978-0-9748486; 978-1-932855; 978-1-60380)* 11120 NE 33rd Pl. No. 101, Bellevue, WA 98004-1448 USA (SAN 760-7792) Toll Free: 866-319-5900; *Imprints:* SmartLab (SmartLab)
E-mail: cindyd@beckermayer.com; info@beckermayer.com
Web site: http://www.beckermayer.com; http://www.everydaywisdom.net
Dist(s): **Bks. Are Fun, Ltd.**
Chronicle Bks. LLC
Hachette Bk. Group
INscribe Digital
Midpoint Trade Bks., Inc.

Becket, *(978-0-9898785; 978-1-941240)* 78665 Villeta Dr, La Quinta, CA 92253 USA Tel 760-413-0031
E-mail: ibecket7@gmail.com.

Beckham House Publishers, Incorporated *See* **Beckham Pubns. Group, Inc.**

Beckham Pubns. Group, Inc., *(978-0-931761; 978-0-9802380; 978-0-9816505; 978-0-9823876; 978-0-9841991; 978-0-9827943; 978-0-9833402; 978-0-9848243; 978-0-9905904; 978-0-9984870)* Orders Addr.: P.O. Box 4066, Silver Spring, MD 20914-4066 USA (SAN 683-2237) Tel 301-384-7995; Fax: 866-659-3306; Toll Free Fax: 866-659-3306; Edit Addr.: 13619 Cedar Creek Ln., Silver Spring, MD 20904-5308 USA
E-mail: barry@beckhamhouse.com
Web site: http://www.beckhamhouse.com
Dist(s): **Bookmasters Distribution.**

Becklyns, LLC, *(978-0-9860222)* 23 Bob White Way, Weatogue, CT 06089 USA.

Beckon Bks. *Imprint of* **Southwestern Publishing Group, Inc.**

Become a Millionaire *See* **Grampa Jones's Publishing Co.**

Bed Bks., *(978-1-933652)* 101 Westgate Dr., Trinidad, CA 95570 USA
Web site: http://www.readinginbed.com; http://www.bedbooks.NET.

Bedazzled Ink Publishing Co., *(978-0-9759555; 978-1-934452; 978-1-939562; 978-1-943837; 978-1-945805)* 2137 Pennsylvania Ave., Fairfield, CA 94533 USA; *Imprints:* Dragonfeather Books (Dragonfeather Bks)
E-mail: publisher@bedazzledink.com
Web site: http://www.bedazzledink.com
Dist(s): **Follett School Solutions**
Independent Pubs. Group.

Bedell, Barbara F., *(978-0-9743731)* 74 Hidden Bay Dr., S Dartmouth, MA 02748-3089 USA
E-mail: bb280z@yahoo.com.

Bedford Hse. Bks., *(978-0-9960916)* 93 hancock St., brooklyn, NY 11216 USA Tel 917-815-5969
E-mail: dave@bedfordhousebooks.com.

Bedford/Saint Martin's, *(978-0-312; 978-1-4576)* Div. of Holtzbrinck Publishers, Orders Addr.: 16365 James Madison Hwy., Gordonsville, VA 22942 USA Tel 540-672-7600; Toll Free Fax: 800-672-2054; Toll Free: 888-330-8477; Edit Addr.: 33 Irving Pl., New York, NY 10003 USA Tel 212-375-7000; Fax: 212-614-1885; Toll Free: 800-223-1715; 75 Arlington St., Boston, MA 02116 Tel 617-399-4000; Fax: 617-426-8582; Toll Free: 800-779-7440
E-mail: permissionsdept@bedfordstmartins.com; communication@bedfordstmartins.com
Web site: http://www.bfwpub.com
Dist(s): **Follett School Solutions**
Macmillan
Springer.

Bednark, Sara, *(978-0-615-18545-3)* 10013 SE Eastmont Dr., Damascus, OR 97089 USA
E-mail: rbednark@gmail.com
Web site: http://www.sara.bednark.com
Dist(s): **Lulu Pr., Inc.**

Bedrock Books, Incorporated *See* **Dry, Paul Bks., Inc.**

Bedside Bks. *Imprint of* **American Bk. Publishing Group**

Bee at Ease Press *See* **At Ease Pr.**

Bee Creative, LLC, *(978-0-615-75686-8; 978-0-615-94698-6; 978-0-615-98240-3; 978-0-9975745)* 2704 NW 119th, Oklahoma City, OK 73120 USA Tel 405-924-9265
E-mail: callie.belinda@gmail.com
Web site: www.beecreativeinc.com.

Beech, Michael, *(978-0-9817741)* 8603 W. 84th Cir., Arvada, CO 80005 USA Tel 303-456-5350
Web site: http://www.ebookselfpublishing.com; http://www.digital3dstereo.com.

Beech River Bks., *(978-1-930149; 978-0-9776514; 978-0-9793778; 978-0-9825214; 978-0-9839367; 978-0-9905814)* P.O. Box 62, Center Ossipee, NH 03814 USA Tel 603-539-3537; *Imprints:* Writer's Publishing Cooperative (Writ Pub Coop)
E-mail: banddmarion@roadrunner.com
Web site: http://www.beechriverbooks.com
Dist(s): **Enfield Publishing & Distribution Co., Inc.**

Beech Seal Press, Incorporated *See* **Images from the Past, Inc.**

Beecher Scott, *(978-0-9763077)* 1925 Westchester Rd. Apt. 214, Waterloo, IA 50701-4522 USA.

Beecroft Publishing (GBR) *(978-0-9546186) Dist. by* **LightSource CS.**

Beekman & Hathaway, *(978-0-9758970)* P.O. Box 2355, Amherst, MA 01004-2355 USA
E-mail: cdc@beekmanandhathaway.com
Web site: http://www.beekmanandhathaway.com
Dist(s): **Independent Pubs. Group.**

Beekman Bks., Inc., *(978-0-8464)* 300 Old All Angels Hill Rd., Wappingers Falls, NY 12590 USA (SAN 170-1622) Tel 845-297-2690; Fax: 845-297-1002
E-mail: manager@beekmanbooks.com
Web site: http://www.beekmanbooks.com
Dist(s): **Follett School Solutions.**

BeeLine Bks., *(978-0-9903368)* 2 Fallgreen Ct., Santa Rosa, CA 95409 USA Tel 414-686-4777
E-mail: bonjourdwd@comcast.net.

Beeman Jorgensen, Inc., *(978-0-929758)* 7510 Allisonville Rd., Indianapolis, IN 46250 USA (SAN 250-1279) Tel 317-841-7677; Fax: 317-849-2001; Toll Free: 800-553-5319
Dist(s): **Hachette Bk. Group**
MBI Distribution Services/Quayside Distribution
Practice Ring.

BeerBooks.com, *(978-0-9662084; 978-0-9819282; 978-0-9904513)* P.O. Box 771012, Cleveland, OH 44107 USA
E-mail: email@beerbooks.com
Web site: http://www.beerbooks.com.

Bee's Ink Publishing, *(978-0-615-57799-9; 978-0-615-63296-4)* 15800 Hwy. 3 No. 113, Webster, TX 77598 USA Tel 713-876-3222
E-mail: bwilsonent@aol.com.

Beeson, Jan, *(978-0-9890482)* 232 E. 52nd St., San Bernardino, CA 92404 USA Tel 714-936-1390
E-mail: rotcmpj@charter.net.

Beetle Bug Bks., *(978-0-9658365)* Orders Addr.: P.O. Box 4636, San Clemente, CA 92674 USA (SAN 299-3864) Tel 949-498-0162; Fax: 949-498-2531; Edit Addr.: 1504 Avenida Hacienda, San Clemente, CA 92672 USA (SAN 299-3872)
E-mail: BookOrders@BeetleBugBooks.com
Web site: http://www.BeetleBugBooks.com
Dist(s): **Follett School Solutions**
Unique Bks., Inc.

Beevinwood, Inc., *(978-0-9652902)* Orders Addr.: 5748 Clark Rd., West Manchester, OH 45382 USA Tel 937-678-9910; Fax: 937-678-7715
E-mail: C1C2C3@aol.com.

Beex Art Bks., *(978-0-9724358)* P.O. Box 9143, Fountain Valley, CA 92728-9143 USA.

Before Christmas Pr., *(978-0-9759902)* Orders Addr.: 15170 State Rte. 550, Athens, OH 45701 USA
Web site: http://www.beforechristmaspress.com.

Before Someday Publishing, *(978-0-9850659; 978-1-943598)* P.O. Box 371, Apex, NC 27502-9998 USA
E-mail: beforesomeday@gmail.com.

Begin Smart LLC, *(978-1-934618; 978-1-60906)* 515 Valley St., Suite 180, Maplewood, NJ 07040 USA (SAN 854-0497) Tel 973-763-8191; Fax: 973-763-5944
E-mail: info@beginsmartbooks.com
Dist(s): **Sterling Publishing Co., Inc.**

Begoo Bks., LLC, *(978-0-9884922)* 48 N. Clover Dr., Great Neck, NY 11021 USA Tel 516-314-4808
E-mail: culily@aol.com.

Behave'n Kids Pr., *(978-0-9714405)* 8922 Cuming St., Omaha, NE 68114 USA Tel 402-926-4373; Fax: 402-926-3898
E-mail: janiep@behavenkids.com
Web site: http://www.behavenkids.com/
Dist(s): **Book Clearing Hse.**

Behavenkids Press *See* **Behave'n Kids Pr.**

Behavioral Health & Human Development Ctr., *(978-0-9777672)* 4517 Lorino St., Suite 1, Metairie, LA 70006 USA Tel 504-454-3015
E-mail: carlos@littleduckyjr.com
Web site: http://littleduckyjr.com.

Behind the Scenes Bks., *(978-0-9770879)* 90 Windsor Dr., Pine Brook, NJ 07058 USA Tel 973-274-9472; Fax: 973-274-9272
E-mail: ma@behindthescenesmarketing.com.

Behrman Hse., Inc., *(978-0-87441; 978-1-68115)* 11 Edison Pl., Springfield, NJ 07081 USA (SAN 201-4459) Tel 973-379-7200; Fax: 973-379-7280; Toll Free: 800-221-2755; *Imprints:* Apples & Honey Press (ApplesandHoney)
E-mail: webmaster@behrmanhouse.com; orders@behrmanhouse.com; customersupport@behrmanhouse.com
Web site: http://www.behrmanhouse.com; http://www.arepublish.com
Dist(s): **Follett School Solutions.**

Beijing Language & Culture Univ. Pr., China (CHN) *(978-7-5619) Dist. by* **China Bks.**

Beil, Frederic C. Pub., Inc., *(978-0-913720; 978-1-929490)* Orders Addr.: 609 Whitaker St., Savannah, GA 31401 USA (SAN 240-9909) Tel 912-233-2446
Web site: http://www.beil.com.

Belgrave Hse., *(978-0-9660643; 978-0-9741068; 978-0-9801778; 978-0-9821717; 978-0-9844144; 978-1-61084; 978-1-947812)* 190 Belgrave Ave., San Francisco, CA 94117-4228 USA Tel 415-661-5025; Fax: 415-661-5703
E-mail: neff@belgravehouse.com
Web site: http://www.belgravehouse.com.

Believers Publishing, *(978-0-9795680)* 2245 N. Green Valley Pkwy., Suite 282, Henderson, NV 89014 USA
E-mail: believerspublishing@gmail.com
Web site: http://believerspublishing.com
Dist(s): **Send The Light Distribution LLC.**

Belisarian Bks., *(978-0-9658481)* Div. of Iconoclast, 6513 NW 30th Terr., Bethany, OK 73008 USA Tel 405-789-1030
E-mail: belisarianbooks@yahoo.com
Web site: http://www.belisarianbooks.tk/.

Belknap Digital Archives, *(978-0-9747471)* Orders Addr.: P.O. Box 1487, Meredith, NH 03253 USA Tel 603-279-8358; Edit Addr.: 20 True Rd., Unit No. 86, Meredith, NH 03253 USA
E-mail: apollock@worldpath.net
Web site: http://www.belknapdigital.com.

Belknap Pr. *Imprint of* **Harvard Univ. Pr.**

Belknap Publishing & Design, *(978-0-9723420; 978-0-9816403)* P.O. Box 22387, Honolulu, HI 96823-2387 USA; *Imprints:* Calabash Books (Calabash Bks)
Web site: http://belknappublishing.com
Dist(s): **Booklines Hawaii, Ltd.**
Follett School Solutions.

Bell, Albert, *(978-0-9979288)* 22 W. 12th St., Holland, MI 49423 USA Tel 616-395-7558
E-mail: bell@hope.edu
Web site: www.albertbell.com.

Bell Bridge Bks. *Imprint of* **BelleBks., Inc.**

Bell, Megan, *(978-0-9889775)* 5710 Fox Chase Trail, Galena, OH 43021 USA Tel 740-548-6550
E-mail: meganericbell@gmail.com.

Bell Pond Bks. *Imprint of* **SteinerBooks, Inc.**

Bella & Bruno Bks., *(978-0-9894402)* 34-08 30th St. Apt A22, Astoria, NY 11106 USA Tel 585-746-2696
E-mail: aneeck@rochester.rr.com
Web site: bellaandbrunobooks.com.

Bella & Harry, LLC, *(978-0-9837092; 978-1-937616; 978-1-946768)* 15057 Sweetgum St., Delray Beach, FL 33446 USA (SAN 920-3052) Tel 855-235-5211; Fax: 561-637-3235; 1 Ingram Rd., La Vergne, TN 37086
E-mail: BellaAndHarryGo@aol.com
Web site: www.BellaAndHarry.com
Dist(s): **Follett School Solutions**
Ingram Publisher Services.

Bella Bks., Inc., *(978-0-930044; 978-0-941483; 978-1-56280; 978-0-9677753; 978-1-931513; 978-1-59493)* Orders Addr.: P.O. Box 10543, Tallahassee, FL 32302 USA Tel 850-576-2370; Fax: 850-576-3498; Toll Free: 800-729-4992
E-mail: Linda@BellaBooks.com
Web site: http://www.bellabooks.com
Dist(s): **Bella Distribution**
Ingram Publisher Services
Two Rivers Distribution.

Bella Publishing *See* **Bellissima Publishing, LLC**

Bella Rosa Bks., *(978-0-9747685; 978-1-933523; 978-1-62268)* P.O. Box 4251, Rock Hill, SC 29732 USA
E-mail: info@bellarosabooks.com
Web site: http://www.bellarosabooks.com
Dist(s): **Follett School Solutions.**

Bellaboozle Books, Inc., *(978-0-9765398)* 104 Lariat Dr., Canonsburg, PA 15317-3284 USA
E-mail: lkravec@adelphia.net.

Bellagio Pr. *Imprint of* **Taj Bks. International LLC**

Bellamy, Christopher Daniel, *(978-0-9979039)* 1105 Huntsman Cir., Pensacola, FL 32514 USA Tel 254-498-1559
E-mail: danbellamy@yahoo.com
Web site: www.inflatedstory.com.

Bellastoria Pr., *(978-0-615-40644-2; 978-0-9910861; 978-1-942209)* 100 Hilltop Rd., Longmeadow, MA 01106 USA Tel 413-567-3278
E-mail: lcardilloplatzer@hotmail.com
Web site: http://www.lindacardillo.com/.

Belle Isle Bks. *Imprint of* **Brandylane Pubs., Inc.**

Belle Lumiere True News, 2525 Squaw Ct., Antioch, CA 94531-8003 USA Toll Free: 888-473-1555; *Imprints:* Holmes Bookshop (Holmes Bkshop).

Belle Media International, Incorporated *See* **Belle Media International, Inc. Div of True News**

Belle Media International, Inc. Div of True News, *(978-0-9703419; 978-1-60361)* Div. of Belle Lumiere True News, Orders Addr.: P.O. Box 191024, San Francisco, CA 94119 USA Tel 949-813-5343
E-mail: holmesbookshop@yahoo.com; BelleBusiness@yahoo.com; dr.miawhite@yahoo.com.

BelleAire Pr., *(978-0-9640138; 978-0-9765234)* 5707 NW 50th Pl., Gainesville, FL 32653-4079 USA Tel 352-377-1870
E-mail: belleairepress@earthlink.net
Dist(s): **Atlas Bks.**
Bookmasters Distribution
Follett School Solutions
MyiLibrary.

BelleBks., Inc., *(978-1-893896; 978-0-9673035; 978-0-9759653; 978-1-933417; 978-0-9768760; 978-0-9802453; 978-0-9821756; 978-0-9841258; 978-0-9843256; 978-1-935661; 978-1-61026; 978-1-61194)* 4513 Ernie Dr., Memphis, TN 38116 USA Tel 901-344-9024; Fax: 901-344-9068; *Imprints:* Bell Bridge Books (Bell Bridge); ImaJinn Books (ImaJinnBooks)
E-mail: bellebooks@bellebooks.com; debbsmith@aol.com; production@bellebooks.com
Web site: http://www.BelleBooks.com; http://www.BellBridgeBooks.com
Dist(s): **MyiLibrary.**

Bellerophon Bks., *(978-0-88388)* Orders Addr.: P.O. Box 21307, Santa Barbara, CA 93121-1307 USA (SAN 254-7856) Tel 805-965-7034; Fax: 805-965-8286; Toll Free: 800-253-9943
E-mail: bellerophonbooks@bellerophonbooks.com
Web site: http://www.bellerophonbooks.com
Dist(s): **Follett School Solutions.**

Bellissima Publishing, LLC, *(978-0-9768417; 978-0-9771916; 978-0-9776993; 978-0-9790449; 978-0-9793358; 978-0-9794006; 978-0-9794815; 978-1-935118; 978-1-935630; 978-1-61477)* Orders Addr.: P.O. Box 650, Jamul, CA 91935 USA
E-mail: pdweigandjd@aol.com; admin@bellissimapublishing.com
Web site: http://www.bellissimapublishing.com; http://www.surfergirlsummer.com; http://bellissimapublishing.viewwork.com/bellissima_publishing_llc/selfolio.html.

Bello, Andres (CHL) *(978-956-13) Dist. by* **Continental Bk.**

Bellota *Imprint of* **Heinemann-Raintree**

Bellreh Publishing, *(978-0-9966102)* 2501 Ohio Dr, No. 214, Plano, TX 75093 USA Tel 716-946-7308
E-mail: sheriabell@gmail.com
Web site: www.sheriabell.com.

Bellwether Media, *(978-1-60014; 978-1-61211; 978-1-61891; 978-1-62617; 978-1-68103)* Orders Addr.: 5357 Penn Ave. S., Minneapolis, MN 55347 USA (SAN 920-8135) Tel 612-825-2545; Fax: 612-825-2544; Toll Free Fax: 800-675-6679; Toll Free: 800-679-8068; *Imprints:* Blastoff! Readers (Blastoff Rdrs); Torque Books (Torque Bks); Pilot Books (PilotBks); Epic Books (EpicBks); Express Books (Express Bks); Black Sheep (BlackiSheepUSA); Blastoff! Discovery (MYID_O_BLASTOF)
E-mail: laura@bellwethermedia.com; jmartin@bellwethermedia.com; geena@bellwethermedia.com
Web site: http://www.bellwethermedia.com
Dist(s): **Follett Media Distribution**
Follett School Solutions.

Belmar Pubns., *(978-0-9746366)* 504 - 17th Ave., South Belmar, NJ 07719 USA Fax: 212-737-5211
E-mail: arthurpaone@aol.com.

Belshe, Judy *See* **Snuggle Up Bks.**

Beluga-Duga Pr., *(978-1-932176)* Orders Addr.: P.O. Box 923, Willits, CA 95490 USA; Edit Addr.: 700 E. Gobbi St., NO. 138, Ukiah, CA 95482 USA.

Ben Franklin Pr., *(978-0-9772447; 978-0-615-64586-5)* 910 S. Hohokam Dr., Suite 104, Tempe, AZ 85281 USA Tel 480-968-7959; Fax: 480-966-3694
E-mail: rickburress@benfranklinpress.net.

BenBella Bks., *(978-1-932100; 978-1-933771; 978-0-9792331; 978-1-935251; 978-1-935618; 978-1-936661; 978-1-937856; 978-1-939529; 978-1-940363; 978-1-941631; 978-1-942952; 978-1-944648; 978-1-946885)* 10300 N Central Expy Suite 400, Dallas, TX 75231 USA Tel 214-750-3600; Fax: 214-750-3645; 387 Park Ave. St., New York, NY 10016
E-mail: brittney@benbellabooks.com
Web site: http://www.benbellabooks.com
Dist(s): **Follett School Solutions**
Independent Pubs. Group
Ingram Publisher Services
MyiLibrary
ebrary, Inc.

Bench Press *See* **Gallant Hse. Publishing**

Benchmark Bks. *Imprint of* **Marshall Cavendish Corp.**

Benchmark Book Craft, *(978-0-9744015)* P.O. Box 19583, Colorado City, CO 81019 USA Tel 719-676-3009.

Benchmark Education Co., *(978-1-58344; 978-1-892393; 978-1-59000; 978-1-4108; 978-1-60437; 978-1-60634; 978-1-935440; 978-1-935441; 978-1-60859; 978-1-935469; 978-1-935470; 978-1-935471; 978-1-935472; 978-1-935473; 978-1-61672; 978-1-936254; 978-1-936255; 978-1-936256;-1-936257; 978-1-936258; 978-1-4509; 978-1-4900; 978-1-5021; 978-1-5125; 978-1-5322) 145 Huguenot St 8th Flr, New Rochelle, NY 10801 USA Tel 914-637-7200; Toll Free Fax: 877-732-8273; Toll Free: 877-236-2465*
E-mail: bhaggerty@benchmarkeducation.com
Web site: http://www.benchmarkeducation.com.

Bendon, Inc., *(978-1-57759; 978-1-58117; 978-1-888443; 978-1-888567; 978-1-4037; 978-1-932209; 978-1-59394; 978-1-60139; 978-1-61568; 978-1-4530; 978-1-61405; 978-1-62191; 978-1-62615; 978-1-63109; 978-1-63346; 978-1-5050)* 1840 Baney Rd. South, Ashland, OH 44805 USA (SAN 803-317X); *Imprints:* Spirit Press (SpiritPr); Intervisual/Piggy Toes (IntervisPiggy)
Web site: http://www.bendonpub.com.

Bendon Publishing International *See* **Bendon, Inc.**

Bendt Family Ministries *See* **Valerie Bendt**

Benedetti, Jef, *(978-0-9801372)* 4242 Johnstown Rd., Gahanna, OH 43230 USA (SAN 855-2991).

Benefactory, Inc., The, *(978-1-58021; 978-1-882728)* 3 Baneberry Ln., Riverwoods, IL 60015-3534 USA Toll Free: 800-729-7251
E-mail: benefactry@aol.com.

Benicia Literary Arts, *(978-0-9703737)* P.O. Box 763, Benicia, CA 94510 USA Tel 707-745-5540 (phone/fax)
E-mail: editor@carquinezreview.com
Web site: http://www.carquinezreview.com.

Benitez Productions, *(978-0-9966030)* P.O. Box 16101, Encino, CA 91416 USA Tel 818-343-5159
E-mail: art@joebenitez.com
Web site: joebenitez.com
Dist(s): **Diamond Comic Distributors, Inc.**

Benjamin Franklin Pr., *(978-0-9789827; 978-0-9795257; 978-0-9799941)* P.O. Box 51936, Pacific Grove, CA 93950 USA Fax: 831-626-3734
E-mail: loye@benjaminfranklinpress.com
Web site: http://www.benjaminfranklinpress.com
Dist(s): **BookBaby.**

Benjamin Pr., *(978-0-9663478; 978-0-9793431; 978-0-9836106)* Div. of Elmwood Inn Fine Teas, P.O. Box 100, Perryville, KY 40468 USA Tel 859-236-6641; Toll Free Fax: 888-879-0467; Toll Free: 800-765-2139 Do not confuse with Benjamin Pr., Northampton, MA
E-mail: BR@benjaminpress.com
Web site: http://www.benjaminpress.com
Dist(s): **Midpoint Trade Bks., Inc.**
Partners Pubs. Group, Inc.

Benjey Media *See* **Tuxedo Pr.**

Bennett, Robert *See* **Archeological Assessments, Inc.**

Bennett/Novak & Co., Inc., *(978-0-9713454)* 8500 Holloway Dr., Los Angeles, CA 90069 USA Tel 310-657-2975; Fax: 310-657-4006
Dist(s): **National Bk. Network.**

Bennovations Publishing Services, *(978-0-9721066)* P.O. Box 28906, San Diego, CA 92198 USA Tel 858-663-5302; Fax: 858-777-5779
E-mail: info@bennovations.com
Web site: http://www.bennovations.com.

Benoy Publishing, *(978-0-9720809; 978-1-932162)* 735 Bragg Dr., Unit H, Wilmington, NC 28412 USA Tel 910-796-0424 (phone/fax)
E-mail: bbppdodo@aol.com
Web site: http://www.benoypublishing.com.

Benson, Lyn, *(978-0-615-13524-3)* 7063 E. Briarwood Dr., Centennial, CO 80112 USA Fax: 303-736-4075
E-mail: lynbenson@msn.com.

Benson, Queen M., *(978-0-615-12716-3)* 106 James River Dr., Newport News, VA 23601 USA
E-mail: dbbenson@verizon.net
Web site: http://www.lactose-limited.com.

Bent Castle Workshops, *(978-0-9768848)* P.O. Box 10551, Rochester, NY 14610-0551 USA
E-mail: knot@enchantedglyph.com
Web site: http://www.bentcastle.com.

BentDaiSha, LLC, *(978-0-9749465)* 11020 E. Indigo Bush Pl., Tucson, AZ 85748-3558 USA
E-mail: bentdaisha@cox.net.

Bentivegna, Fred, *(978-0-9766228)* 445 W. 27th St., Chicago, IL 60616 USA Tel 312-225-5514 (phone/fax)
E-mail: fbentivegna@sbcglobal.net.

Bentle Bks., *(978-0-9746904)* Orders Addr.: P.O. Box 2274, Oakhurst, CA 93644 USA Fax: 559-683-6206; Edit Addr.: 42564 Buckeye Rd., Oakhurst, CA 93644 USA
E-mail: terrahulse@sierratel.com
Web site: http://www.bentlebooks.com
Dist(s): **Follett School Solutions.**

Bentley, Trish, *(978-0-9774752)* 347 E. 6th St., Apt. 2B, New York, NY 10002 USA.

Benton, John Bks., *(978-0-9635411)* 127 S. El Molino Ave., Pasadena, CA 91101-2510 USA Tel 626-405-0950; Fax: 818-564-0952
Dist(s): **Spring Arbor Distributors, Inc.**

Berbay Publishing (AUS) *(978-0-9806711; 978-0-9942895; 978-0-9943841) Dist. by* **IPG Chicago.**

Beres, Nancy, *(978-0-9752801)* 2025 Willow Glen Ln., Columbus, OH 43229-1550 USA.

Berg, Jeremy, *(978-0-9791700; 978-0-9837422; 978-1-939790)* 2204 E. Grand Ave., Everett, WA 98201-3339 USA
Web site: http://www.lorian.org.

Bergli Bks. (CHE) *(978-3-9520002; 978-3-905252; 978-2-88407; 978-3-03869) Dist. by* **ISD USA.**

Bergner, Bobby, *(978-0-615-21301-9; 978-0-615-22870-9)* 237 Sycamore Ln., Phoenixville, PA 19460 USA
Web site: http://www.moofax.com.

Bergstrom Bks., *(978-0-9787648)* 521 12th Ave. NE., Devils Lake, ND 58301 USA Tel 701-662-3320
E-mail: Candace@lakechevy.com.

Berkeley Major Publishing, *(978-0-9720691)* 8282 Skyline Cir., Oakland, CA 94605-4230 USA Fax: 419-791-7109
E-mail: dailon@progidy.net; BMP@berkeleymp.com
Web site: http://www.berkeleymp.com.

Berkeley Science Bks., *(978-0-9764138)* 529 Bonnie Dr., El Cerrito, CA 94530 USA Tel 510-524-8094
E-mail: wdflannery@aol.com.

Berkley *Imprint of* **Penguin Publishing Group**

Berkshire Publishing Group, *(978-0-9743091; 978-0-9770159; 978-1-933782; 978-1-61472)* 120 Castle St., Great Barrington, MA 01230 USA Tel 413-528-0206; Fax: 413-541-0076
E-mail: info@berkshirepublishing.com; cservice@berkshirepublishing.com
Web site: http://www.berkshirepublishing.com
Dist(s): **Follett School Solutions**
MyiLibrary.

Berlin, Stuart, *(978-0-615-22518-0; 978-0-615-48240-8; 978-0-9914128)* 1910 Larch St., Simi Valley, CA 93065 USA
E-mail: westwing1910@yahoo.com.

Berlin, Theodore *See* **Theodore Berlin Publishing**

Berlitz Publishing, 46-35 54th Rd., Maspeth, NY 11378 USA
E-mail: customerservice@langenscheidt.com
Web site: http://www.berlitzbooks.com
Dist(s): **Ingram Publisher Services**
Langenscheidt Publishing Group.

Bernard Design *See* **Elmdale Park Books**

Bernson Pr., *(978-0-9720509)* Orders Addr.: P.O. Box 55563, Sherman Oaks, CA 91413 USA Tel 818-785-5290; Fax: 818-785-0948; Edit Addr.: 5530 Allot Ave., Sherman Oaks, CA 91401 USA
E-mail: janet.bernson@gmail.com; thehealingartist@mac.com; bernsonpress@aol.com
Web site: http://www.thehealingartist.com; www.janetbernson.com.

Bernstein, Susan, *(978-0-9706596)* 31100 Northwestern Hwy., Farmington Hills, MI 48344-2519 USA Tel 248-737-8400; Fax: 248-737-4392; Toll Free: 800-225-5726
E-mail: les380414744@aol.com
Web site: http://www.epominonousepstein.com.

Berry, Joy Enterprises, *(978-1-60577)* 146 W. 29th St., Suite 11RW, New York, NY 10001 USA Tel 212-868-8282; Fax: 212-868-4110
Web site: http://www.joyberrymedia.com
Dist(s): **Two Rivers Distribution.**

Bertelsman, Verlagsgruppe C. GmbH (DEU) *(978-3-570) Dist. by* **Distribks Inc.**

Bertrand Brasil Editora SA (BRA) *(978-85-286) Dist. by* **Distribks Inc.**

Berwick Court Publishing, *(978-0-615-34122-4; 978-0-615-35191-9; 978-0-9838846; 978-0-9889540; 978-0-9909515; 978-1-944376)* Orders Addr.: 1562 Willow Rd., Northfield, IL 60093 USA Tel 312-772-3799
E-mail: matt@berwickcourt.com
Web site: http://berwickcourt.com.

Beshqoy, Nisreen, *(978-0-9759181)* P.O. Box 3846, Costa Mesa, CA 92628-3846 USA
E-mail: nisreenbeshqoy@hotmail.com
Web site: http://www.arabicandislamicbooksbynisreen.com.

Bess Pr., Inc., *(978-0-935848; 978-1-57306; 978-1-880188; 978-0-615-50460-5; 978-0-615-56510-1)* 3565 Harding Ave., Honolulu, HI 96816 USA (SAN 239-4111) Tel 808-734-7159; Fax: 808-732-3627
E-mail: kelly@besspress.com
Web site: http://www.besspress.com
Dist(s): **China Books & Periodicals, Inc.**
Follett School Solutions
Univ. of Hawaii Pr.

Best Books *See* **Library Reprints, Inc.**

Best Fairy Bks., *(978-0-9632524; 978-0-9786791)* 1241 Chateau Green Ct., Bel Air, MD 21015 USA (SAN 851-2930) Tel 410-879-7578; P.O. Box 455, Bel Air, MD 21014
E-mail: fairybooklady@aol.com
Dist(s): **Follett School Solutions**
Independent Pubs. Group
Midpoint Trade Bks., Inc.

Best Friends Books *See* **Children's Kindness Network**

Best Friends Productions, *(978-0-9765140)* 131 Bank St., New York, NY 10014-2177 USA
Web site: http://www.bestfriendsproductions.com.

Best of East Texas Pubs., *(978-1-878096)* Div. of Bob Bowman & Assocs., 515 S. First, Lufkin, TX 75901 USA Tel 409-634-7444; Fax: 409-634-7750.

Best Publishing Co., *(978-0-941332; 978-1-930536; 978-1-947239)* Div. of WCHMedia Group, Orders Addr.: 631 U.S. Hwy. 1, Ste 307, North Palm Beach, FL 33408 USA (SAN 238-9509) Tel 561-776-6066; Fax: 561-776-7476
E-mail: lorraine@bestpub.com
Web site: http://www.bestpub.com
Dist(s): **Rittenhouse Bk. Distributors.**

†**Bethany Hse. Pubs.,** *(978-0-7642; 978-0-87123; 978-1-55661; 978-1-56179; 978-1-57778; 978-1-880089; 978-1-59066)* Div. of Baker Publishing Group, Orders Addr.: P.O. Box 6287, Grand Rapids, MI 49516-6287 USA Toll Free Fax: 800-398-3111 (orders); Toll Free: 800-877-2665 (orders); Edit Addr.: 11400 Hampshire Ave., S., Bloomington, MN 55438-2455 USA (SAN 201-4416) Tel 952-829-2500; Fax: 952-996-1393
E-mail: orders@bakerbooks.com
Web site: http://www.bethanyhouse.com
Dist(s): **Anchor Distributors**
Appalachian Bible Co.
Baker Publishing Group
Brodart Co.
Cambridge Univ. Pr.
Faith Alive Christian Resources
Follett School Solutions
Send The Light Distribution LLC
Spring Arbor Distributors, Inc.
Beeler, Thomas T. Pub.; *CIP.*

Bethlehem Bks., *(978-1-883937; 978-1-932350)* Div. of Bethlehem Community, Orders Addr.: 10194 Garfield St. S., Bathgate, ND 58216-4031 USA Tel 701-265-3725; Fax: 701-265-3716; Toll Free: 800-757-6831 Do not confuse with bethlehem Books in Richmond, VA
E-mail: contact@bethlehembooks.com
Web site: http://www.bethlehembooks.com
Dist(s): **Follett School Solutions**
Ignatius Pr.
Spring Arbor Distributors, Inc.

Betrock Information Systems, Inc., *(978-0-9629761)* 7770 Davie Rd. Ext., Hollywood, FL 33024 USA Tel 954-981-2821; Fax: 954-981-2823
E-mail: Lori@betrock.com
Web site: http://www.hortworld.com.

Bettenhausen, Jo Anne *See* **CBM Publishing**

Better Be Write Pub., A, *(978-0-9767732; 978-0-9771971; 978-0-9788985)* Orders Addr.: P.O. Box 914, Kernersville, NC 27284 USA Tel 336-354-7173; 9001 Ridge Hill St., Kernersville, NC 27284
E-mail: argusenterprises@hotmail.com
Web site: http://www.abetterbewrite.com.

Better Chinese LLC, *(978-1-60603; 978-1-68194)* P.O. Box 695, Palo Alto, CA 94303 USA Tel 650-384-0902; 2479 E Bayshore Rd., Suite 110, Palo Alto, CA 94303 Tel 650-384-0902; Fax: 702-442-7968
E-mail: usa@betterchinese.com
Web site: http://www.BetterChinese.com.

Better Comics, *(978-0-9728070)* P.O. Box 541924, Dallas, TX 75354-1924 USA
E-mail: JESmith@bettercomics.com
Web site: http://www.bettercomics.com.

Better Day Publishing Company *See* **Better Day Publishing LLC**

Better Day Publishing LLC, *(978-0-9767189; 978-0-9796763)* Orders Addr.: 3695f Cascade Rd. #2161, Atlanta, GA 30331 USA Tel 770-885-7072
E-mail: contact@betterdaypublishing.com
Web site: http://www.betterdaypublishing.com
Dist(s): **Follett School Solutions.**

Better Homes & Gardens Books *See* **Meredith Bks.**

Better Karma, LLC, *(978-0-9824329; 978-0-9828426; 978-0-9847753; 978-0-9962897)* 6018 Goldenrod Ct., Alexandria, VA 22310 USA (SAN 858-1495) Tel 703-971-1072
E-mail: publisher@betterkarmapublishing.com
Web site: http://www.BetterKarmaPublishing.com
Dist(s): **Bookmasters Distribution**
Smashwords.

Better Me Bks., Inc., *(978-0-9770294)* P.O. Box 834, Marlton, NJ 08053 USA Tel 609-206-6318; Fax: 856-489-0234
E-mail: bettermebooks@aol.Com
Web site: http://www.bettermebooks.com.

Better Non Sequitur, *(978-0-9743235)* 11925 Via Zapata, El Cajon, CA 92019 USA Tel 619-246-5190
E-mail: steven@betternonsequitur.com
Web site: http://www.betternonsequitur.com.

Better Than One Publishing, *(978-0-9758958)* 27582 120th St., Staples, MN 56479 USA
Web site: http://www.creatingedumaterials.com.

Better Tomorrow Publishing, A, *(978-0-9795768)* P.O. Box 2975, Upper Marlboro, MD 20773-2975 USA Fax: 301-576-8070
E-mail: andy@abettertomorrowpublishing.net; sandy@abtpub.com
Web site: http://abettertomorrowpublishing.net.

BetterLink Pr., Inc., *(978-1-60220)* 99 Pk. Ave., R.R. Donnelley, New York, NY 10016 USA
Dist(s): **Penguin Publishing Group**
Simon & Schuster, Inc.
Tuttle Publishing
Univ. of Hawaii Pr.

Bettino, Teresa Adele, *(978-0-9742842)* 8403 Cosby Ln., Mechanicsville, VA 23116 USA Tel 804-779-2672
E-mail: tbettino@msn.com.

Betts, Linda, *(978-0-9767802)* Orders Addr.: 6050 Pagenkopf Rd., Maple Plain, MN 55359 USA Tel 763-479-2789; Fax: 763-476-6508
E-mail: lynrae@hotmail.com.

Betty Crocker *Imprint of* **Houghton Mifflin Harcourt Publishing Co.**

Between the Lakes Group, LLC, *(978-0-9727403; 978-0-9766342; 978-0-9791000; 978-0-9826073)* Orders Addr.: P.O. Box 13, Taconic, CT 06079-0013 USA Tel 860-824-0640
E-mail: geoff@betweenthelakes.com
Web site: http://www.betweenthelakes.com.

Beverly Hills Publishing, *(978-0-9758870; 978-0-9777074; 978-0-9791967)* 291 S. La Cienega Blvd., Suites 107/108, Beverly Hills, CA 90211-3325 USA (SAN 850-0029) Tel 310-854-0705; Fax: 310-854-1840; Toll Free: 800-521-5669
E-mail: silvers@bevhillspub.com
Web site: http://www.bevhillspub.com.

Beyond the Stars, Incorporated *See* **Beyond the Stars Pubns.**

Beyond the Stars Pubns., *(978-0-9763635)* 14902 Preston Rd., Suite 404-764, Dallas, TX 75254 USA
E-mail: rjohnson@beyondthestarsbooks.com
Web site: http://www.beyondthestarsbooks.com.

Beyond Words Publishing, Inc., *(978-0-941831; 978-1-58270; 978-1-885223)* 20827 NW Cornell Rd., Suite 500, Hillsboro, OR 97124-9808 USA (SAN 666-4210) Tel 503-531-8700; Fax: 503-531-8773; Toll Free: 800-284-9673
E-mail: info@beyondword.com; sales@beyondword.com
Web site: http://www.beyondword.com
Dist(s): **Follett School Solutions**
Simon & Schuster, Inc.

Beyond Words/Atria Bks. *Imprint of* **Atria Bks.**

Beyond Your Words, *(978-0-9788789)* P.O. Box 5842, Newport Beach, CA 92662-9266 USA
Web site: http://www.beyondyourwords.com.

Bezalel Bks., *(978-0-9792258; 978-0-9794976; 978-0-9800483; 978-0-9818854; 978-0-9821222; 978-0-9823388; 978-0-9844864; 978-1-936453)* P.O. Box 300427, Waterford, MI 48330 USA
E-mail: bezalelbooks@gmail.com
Web site: http://www.bezalelbooks.com.

BFG Pr., LLC, *(978-0-9820307)* Div. of The PIE Group, P.O. Box 2269, Ewa Beach, HI 96706 USA (SAN 857-0590) Tel 808-428-0733
Web site: http://www.bfgpress.com/.

BGA Stories, *(978-0-9724806)* 3414 Forest Hills Cir., Garland, TX 75044-2000 USA (SAN 254-878X) Tel 972-496-0416
E-mail: bga@bgastories.com
Web site: http://www.bgastories.com.

Bhakta Program Institute *See* **Rupanuga Vedic College**

BHB International, Incorporated *See* **Continental Enterprises Group, Inc. (CEG)**

BHF Publishing, *(978-0-9801913; 978-0-615-13143-6)* 7139 Hwy. 85, Suite 274, Riverdale, GA 30274 USA Tel 678-925-4175
E-mail: melissabowan@hotmail.com; stdennis@highly-favored.net
Web site: http://www.highly-favored.net.

Bianimale Foundation *See* **Flying Elephants Pr.**

Bibia, LLC, *(978-0-9826276; 978-0-615-74924-2; 978-1-940760)* PMB206 2880 Bicentennial Pkwy., Suite 100, Henderson, NV 89044 USA Tel 702-896-0967; *Imprints:* Bibia Publishing (Bibia)
E-mail: bibiapublishing@gmail.com
Web site: www.bibiapublishing.com.

Bibia Publishing *Imprint of* **Bibia, LLC**

Bible Based Studies, *(978-0-9797786)* 1134 SE 3rd St., Crystal River, FL 34429 USA Tel 352-795-5128
E-mail: info@biblebasedstudies.org
Web site: http://www.biblebasedstudies.org.

Bible Facts Pr., *(978-0-9762892; 978-0-9772942)* 631 Martin Ave. Suite 1, Rohnert Park, CA 94928 USA
Web site: http://www.biblefactspress.com.

Bible Game *Imprint of* **IMAGINEX, LLC**

Bible League, *(978-1-882536; 978-1-61825; 978-1-61870; 978-1-62826)*
E-mail: info@bibleleagueusa.com
Web site: http://www.bibleleagueusa.com.

Bible Pathway Ministries, *(978-1-879595)* Orders Addr.: P.O. Box 20123, Murfreesboro, TN 37133 USA Tel 615-896-4243; Fax: 615-893-1744; Toll Free: 800-598-7884; Edit Addr.: P.O. Box 20123, Murfreesboro, TN 37129-0123 USA
E-mail: mail@biblepathway.org
Web site: http://www.biblepathway.org
Dist(s): **Send The Light Distribution LLC.**

Bible Visuals International, Inc., *(978-1-932381; 978-1-933206; 978-1-64104)* Orders Addr.: P.O. Box 153, Akron, PA 17501-0153 USA
Web site: http://www.biblevisuals.org.

Bible-4-Life.com *See* **SundaySchoolNetwork.com**

Bibleco, Inc., *(978-0-9746058; 978-0-9754978)* 153 Pinehurst Dr., Easton, PA 18042 USA (SAN 256-0801) Fax: 610-438-3964; *Imprints:* Biblemania (Bibleman)
E-mail: biblemania@aol.com
Web site: http://www.biblemania.com.

Biblemania *Imprint of* **Bibleco, Inc.**

BibleRhymes *Imprint of* **BibleRhymes Publishing, L.L.C.**

BibleRhymes Publishing, L.L.C., *(978-0-9790605; 978-1-947049)* Orders Addr.: 54211 Horizon Dr., Shelby Township, MI 48316 USA (SAN 852-3207); *Imprints:* BibleRhymes (BibleRhymes USA)
E-mail: CustomerService@BibleRhymes.com
Web site: http://www.BibleRhymes.com.

Biblesoft, Inc., *(978-1-56514)* 22030 Seventh Ave., S., Suite 204, Seattle, WA 98198-6235 USA (SAN 298-7473) Tel 206-824-0547; Fax: 206-824-2729
Web site: http://www.biblesoft.com
Dist(s): **Anchor Distributors**
Spring Arbor Distributors, Inc.

BiblesPlus, *(978-0-9769109)* 13741 Annandale Dr., No. 20D, Seal Beach, CA 90740 USA Toll Free: 866-924-2537
E-mail: biblesplus7@yahoo.com
Web site: http://www.biblesplus.com.

Biblical Counseling Institute *See* **Skinner, Kerry L.**

Biblical Standards Pubns., *(978-0-9678798)* 287 Caldwell Dr., Maggie Valley, NC 28751 USA Tel 828-926-0606
E-mail: waltdot@primeline.com.

Biblio Bks. International, *(978-0-9729545; 978-0-9741190; 978-0-9748524; 978-0-9766681; 978-0-9785565; 978-0-9833352)* Kendall Tamiami Executive Airport 14005 SW 127th St., Miami, FL 33186 USA Tel 786 573 3999; Fax: 786 573 2090
E-mail: info@bibliobooks.com
Web site: http://www.bibliobooks.com.

Biblio Resource Pubns., Inc., *(978-1-934185)* 108 1/2 S. Moore St., Bessemer, MI 49911 USA Tel 906-364-2190
E-mail: info@BiblioResource.com
Web site: http://www.BiblioResource.com
Dist(s): **Follett School Solutions.**

Biblio Services, Inc., *(978-1-59608; 978-1-61887; 978-1-64131)* 205 Calle Federico Costa Ste 109, San Juan, PR 00918-1305 USA Tel 787-753-1231; Fax: 787-753-1222
E-mail: vale@biblioservices.com; anthony@biblioservices.com
Web site: http://www.biblioservices.com.

Biblioasis (CAN) *(978-0-9735881; 978-0-9735971; 978-1-897231; 978-0-9738184; 978-1-926845) Dist. by* **Consort Bk Sales.**

BiblioBazaar *See* **Creative Media Partners, LLC**

Bibliograf, S.A. (ESP) *(978-84-7153; 978-84-8332) Dist. by* **Continental Bk.**

Bibliograf, S.A. (ESP) *(978-84-7153; 978-84-8332) Dist. by* **Distribks Inc.**

Bibliographisches Institut & F. A. Brockhaus AG (DEU) *(978-3-411) Dist. by* **Continental Bk.**

Bibliographisches Institut & F. A. Brockhaus AG (DEU) *(978-3-411) Dist. by* **IBD Ltd.**

Bibliographisches Institut & F. A. Brockhaus AG (DEU) *(978-3-411) Dist. by* **Intl Bk Import.**

Bibliographisches Institut & F. A. Brockhaus AG (DEU) *(978-3-411) Dist. by* **Distribks Inc.**

BiblioLife *Imprint of* **Creative Media Partners, LLC**

Bibliotech Pr., *(978-1-61895)* 2502 Canada Blvd. No. 1, Glendale, CA 91208 USA Tel 818-546-1554
E-mail: BibliotechPress@gmail.com.

Biblo & Tannen Booksellers & Pubs., Inc., *(978-0-8196)* P.O. Box 302, Cheshire, CT 06410 USA (SAN 202-4071) Tel 203-250-1647 (phone/fax); Toll Free: 800-272-8778
E-mail: biblo.moser@gte.net.

BIC Alliance, *(978-0-9768310)* Orders Addr.: P.O. Box 40166, Baton Rouge, LA 70835 USA Fax: 225-751-9993; Toll Free: 800-460-4242; Edit Addr.: 6378 Quinn Dr., Baton Rouge, LA 70817 USA
E-mail: brady@bicalliance.com
Web site: http://www.bicpublishing.com.

Bicast, Inc., *(978-0-9638258; 978-0-9701008; 978-0-9766753)* Orders Addr.: P.O. Box 2676, Williamsburg, VA 23187 USA Tel 757-229-3276; Fax: 757-253-2273; Toll Free: 800-767-8273; Edit Addr.: 231 K Parkway Dr., Williamsburg, VA 23185 USA
E-mail: bicastpub@aol.com; jogaertner@hughes.net
Web site: http://www.lighthousesusa.com.

Bickico Enterprises, Inc., *(978-0-9746508; 978-0-9834081)* 19W042 Ave. Normandy E., Oak Brook, IL 60523 USA
E-mail: bickico@aol.com.

BICs Pr., *(978-0-9764253)* 1866 John F. Kennedy Blvd., No. B1, Jersey City, NJ 07305 USA.

Bicycle Bell Bks., *(978-0-9981468)* 10808 NW 75th St., KANSAS CITY, MO 64152 USA Tel 816-659-5268
E-mail: j.ballou@sbcglobal.net
Web site: BicycleBellBooks.com.

Bienna Bks., *(978-0-9815075)* 21310 Poplar Way, Brier, WA 98036 USA Tel 206-774-3649.

Big Bear Publishing U.S., *(978-0-9801215)* P.O. Box 191, Ronks, PA 17572-9611 USA (SAN 855-2517) Tel 717-768-4644
E-mail: lonniebrinkley@yahoo.com
Web site: http://www.ibelievesanta.com.

Big Belly Bks., *(978-0-9749554; 978-0-692-37003-2; 978-0-9961792)* Orders Addr.: 2778 W. Schuss Mtn. Dr., Bellaire, MI 49615 USA; Edit Addr.: 2778 W. Schuss Mtn. Dr., Bellaire, MI 49615 USA
E-mail: sc@bigbellybooks.com
Web site: http://www.bigbellybooks.com.

Big Bks. for Little People *Imprint of* **Friendly Planet**

Big Book Pr., LLC, *(978-0-9793219; 978-0-9848920)* Orders Addr.: 47774 Scots Borough Sq., Potomac Falls, VA 20165 USA Tel 240-355-3465
E-mail: frankchawkins@gmail.com; books@boysguidebooks.com; books@bigbookpress.com; books@girlsguidebooks.net; books@boysandgirlsguidebooks.com
Web site: http://www.boysguidebooks.blogspot.com; http://www.boysguidebooks.com; http://www.girlsguidebooks.net; http://www.bigbookpress.com; http://www.boysandgirlsguidebooks.com
Dist(s): **Independent Pubs. Group**
MyiLibrary
Small Pr. United.

Big Bk. Pubns., *(978-0-615-17074-9; 978-0-615-21065-0)* P.O. Box 7867, Largo, MD 20792 USA
E-mail: nicole@bigbookpublications.com
Web site: http://www.nigbookpublications.com.

Big Books, by George!, *(978-1-59246)* Orders Addr.: P.O. Box 1018, Keller, TX 76244 USA; Edit Addr.: 901 Briar Ridge Dr., Keller, TX 76244 USA
Dist(s): **Follett School Solutions.**

Big Brown Box, Inc., The, *(978-0-9764647)* 443 Hill Rd., Douglassville, PA 19518-9530 USA Tel 610-385-7587
Web site: http://www.thebigbrownbox.com
Dist(s): **Book Clearing Hse.**

Big Buddy Bks. *Imprint of* **ABDO Publishing Co.**

Big City Publishing, *(978-0-9762071; 978-0-9845873)* 230 Central St., Auburndale, MA 02492 USA Fax: 617-795-1650
E-mail: mellisa@bigcitypublishing.com
Web site: http://www.anglesfromtheattic.com.

Big Company, LLC, The, *(978-0-9800752)* 4790 Irvine Blvd., Suite 105-176, Irvine, CA 92620 USA (SAN 855-1383)
E-mail: info@thebigcompanyllc.com.

Big Country Publishing, LLC, *(978-0-9845088; 978-0-9847831; 978-1-938487)* 7691 Shaffer Pkwy., Suite C, Littleton, CO 80127 USA.

Big Creek Publishing, *(978-0-9742021)* Orders Addr.: P.O. Box 884, Sunberry, OH 43074 USA Tel 740-965-4127; Fax: 740-965-9541; Edit Addr.: 930 Joe Walker Rd., Sunbury, OH 43074 USA (SAN 255-4054) Tel 740-965-4127
E-mail: bigcreekpublishing@msn.com.

Big Dreams Publishing, *(978-0-9771868)* 8180 S. Allison Ct., Littleton, CO 80128 USA.

Big Earth Publishing *See* **Bower Hse.**

Big Entertainment, Inc., *(978-0-9645175; 978-1-57780)* 2255 Glades Rd., Suite 237W, Boca Raton, FL 33431-7395 USA Tel 407-998-8000; Fax: 407-998-2974
Dist(s): **Kable Media Services.**

Big Guy Bks., Inc., *(978-1-929945)* 1615 Orchard Wood Rd., Encinitas, CA 92024-5654 USA (SAN 253-0392) Toll Free: 800-536-3030; 814 N. Franklin, Chicago, IL 60610
E-mail: info@bigguybooks.com; bernadette@bigguybooks.com
Web site: http://www.timesoldiers.com; http://www.bigguybooks.com
Dist(s): **Follett School Solutions**
Independent Pubs. Group.

Big H Bks. *Imprint of* **Harvey, Alan**

Big Head Pr., *(978-0-9743814; 978-0-9853167)* P.O. Box 1853, Round Rock, TX 78680 USA
E-mail: contact@bigheadpress.com
Web site: http://www.bigheadpress.com
Dist(s): **Diamond Comic Distributors, Inc.**

Big Idea Productions, P.O. Box 189, Lombard, IL 60148 USA Tel 630-652-6000; Fax: 630-652-6001
Dist(s): **Vision Video**
Word Entertainment.

Big Ideas Learning, LLC, *(978-1-60840; 978-1-68033; 978-1-63598)* 1762 Norcross Rd., Erie, PA 16510 USA (SAN 857-751X) Tel 814-824-6365; 814-824-6370; Fax: 814-824-6377; Toll Free Fax: 888-432-9245; Toll Free: 877-552-7766
E-mail: wputnam@larsontexts.com
Web site: http://bigideaslearning.com
Dist(s): **Houghton Mifflin Harcourt Publishing Co.**
Macmillan.

Big Kid Bks., *(978-0-9771990)* 6671 Sunset Blvd., No. 1585-101, Los Angeles, CA 90028 USA.

Big Kid Science, *(978-0-9721819; 978-1-937548; 978-1-944161)* 680 Iris Ave., Boulder, CO 80304 USA; 814 N. Franklin St., Chicago, IL 60610
E-mail: jeff@bigkidscience.com
Web site: http://www.jeffreybennett.com
Dist(s): **Follett School Solutions**
Independent Pubs. Group
MyiLibrary
ebrary, Inc.

Big Kids Productions (Publishing), *(978-0-930249)* 15 Marco Ln., Rochester, NY 14622-3228 USA (SAN 670-8617)
E-mail: pattiup@rochester.rr.com
Web site: http://www.rochesternyeats.com
Dist(s): **North Country Bks., Inc.**

Big Kids Publishing, Incorporated *See* **Big Kids Productions (Publishing)**

Big Lil' Bks., *(978-0-9749041)* Div. of ShadeTree Publishing, 3625 Tallman SE, Grand Rapids, MI 49508 USA
E-mail: janiceintheshade@msn.com.

Big Mouth Hse. *Imprint of* **Small Beer Pr.**

Big Picture Press *Imprint of* **Candlewick Pr.**

Big Picture, The, *(978-0-9794304; 978-0-9882125)* 5976 Leland, Ann Arbor, MI 48105-9309 USA Tel 734-223-4933
E-mail: kmaclean@kjmaclean.com
Web site: http://www.kjmaclean.com/.

Big Ransom Studio, *(978-0-9754728; 978-1-933732)* P.O. Box 489, Georgetown, TX 78627-0489 USA
E-mail: sales@bigransom.com
Web site: http://www.mindtrippress.com
Dist(s): **Mind Trip Pr.**

Big River Distribution, *(978-0-9795944; 978-0-9823575; 978-0-9845519)* Orders Addr.: 8214 Exchange Way, Saint Louis, MO 63144 USA (SAN 631-9114) Tel 314-918-9800; Fax: 314-918-9804
E-mail: info@bigriverdist.com; randy@bigriverdist.com
Web site: http://www.bigriverdist.com
Dist(s): **Follett School Solutions.**

Big Secret, The, *(978-0-9724924)* P.O. Box 1994, Slidell, LA 70459 USA Tel 985-781-8704 (phone/fax)
Web site: http://www.thebigsecret.org.

Big Sil LLC., *(978-0-9967352; 978-0-9983357)* P.O. Box 1755, Hoboken, NJ 07030 USA Tel 201-615-9601
E-mail: bigsiladventures@gmail.com.

Big Sky Stories Publishing *See* **Arnica Publishing**

Big Smile, Inc., *(978-0-9761891)* P.O. Box 1042, Stroudsburg, PA 18360 USA Fax: 646-542-5319
E-mail: marcjohnjefferies@yahoo.com
Web site: http://www.marcjohnonline.com.

Big Smile Pr., LLC, *(978-0-9888462)* 180 Hollow Way, Ingleside, IL 60041 USA Tel 847-973-9084
E-mail: kellyp123@comcast.net.

Big Tent Bks., *(978-1-60131)* 115 Bluebill Dr., Savannah, GA 31419 USA (SAN 851-1136); *Imprints*: Parents Publishing Group (Parents Pub); Castlebridge Books (Castlebridge Bks)
E-mail: admin@dragonpencil.com; admin@bigtentbooks.com
Web site: http://www.bigtentbooks.com
Dist(s): **Castlebridge Distribution**
Music, Bks. & Business, Inc.

Big Tent Entertainment, Inc., *(978-1-59226)* 216 W. 18th St., New York, NY 10011 USA Tel 212-604-0064
Dist(s): **Midpoint Trade Bks., Inc.**

Big Tomato Pr., *(978-0-9791233)* Orders Addr.: 1480 Sutterville Rd., Sacramento, CA 95822 USA Tel 916-798-2125
E-mail: jocelyn@bigtomatopress.com
Web site: http://www.bigtomatopress.com
Dist(s): **Follett School Solutions.**

Big Valley Pr., *(978-0-9765372)* 401 E. Holum St, Deforest, WI 53532 USA Tel 608-513-0724
E-mail: stuart@stotts.com
Web site: http://www.bigvalleypress.com
Dist(s): **Follett School Solutions.**

Big Valley Publishing, *(978-0-9726004)* 516 N. Chinowth, Visalia, CA 93291 USA Do not confuse with company with similar name in Northridge, CA
E-mail: erkna@aol.com.

Big Wave Bks., *(978-0-9754979)* P.O. Box 108, Charlestown, RI 02813 USA Tel 401-322-8711
Web site: http://www.bigwavebooks.com.

Biggaloo Bks., *(978-0-9818145)* 660 Fairway Terr., Naples, FL 34103 USA (SAN 856-6267)
Dist(s): **Music, Bks. & Business, Inc.**

Big-head fish, *(978-0-9765007)* 311 W. 95st., Suite 1an, New York, NY 10025 USA Tel 212-316-0860
E-mail: info@bigheadfish.com/
Web site: http://www.bigheadfish.com/.

BigKids Bilingual Bks., *(978-0-9844310)* P.O. Box 537, Glendale, CA 91209 USA (SAN 859-385X) Tel 626-407-8886
E-mail: jalexan@alumni.usc.edu
Web site: http://www.bigkidsbilingualbooks.com.

Bilal, Nabeeh, *(978-0-615-95158-4; 978-0-692-57311-2; 978-0-692-62252-0; 978-0-692-75743-7; 978-0-692-81373-7; 978-0-692-91555-4)* Orders Addr.: 1888 Savannah Pl SE, washington, DC 20020 USA Tel 202-421-8241; 700 S. Berendo St. Apt. 403, Los Angeles, CA 90005
E-mail: mtcanady@gmail.com; nabeeh_bilal@hotmail.com
Web site: http://www.callaloothebook.com.

Bilbo Bks., *(978-0-9800108; 978-0-9981627)* 1384 W. Peachtree St., NW, No. C-4, Atlanta, GA 30309-2913 USA
E-mail: bilbobookspublishing@gmail.com.

Bilingual Dictionaries, Inc., *(978-0-933146; 978-1-946986)* Orders Addr.: P.O. Box 1154, Murrieta, CA 92564 USA (SAN 221-9697) Tel 951-296-2445; Fax: 951-296-9911; 42225 Remington Ave, A4, Temecula, CA 92590 (SAN 990-4972) Tel 951-296-2445; Fax: 951-296-9911
E-mail: support@bilingualdictionaries.com
Web site: http://www.bilingualdictionaries.com
Dist(s): **Booksource, The**
Follett School Solutions.

Bilingual Educational Services, Inc., *(978-0-86624; 978-0-89075)* 2514 S. Grand Ave., Los Angeles, CA 90007 USA (SAN 218-4680) Tel 213-749-6213; Fax: 213-749-1820; Toll Free: 800-448-6032
E-mail: sales@besbooks.com
Web site: http://www.besbooks.com
Dist(s): **Follett School Solutions.**

Bilingual Language Materials *See* **MAAT Resources, Inc.**

Bilingual Language Materials *Imprint of* **MAAT Resources, Inc.**

Bilingual Pr./Editorial Bilingue, *(978-0-916950; 978-0-927534; 978-1-931010; 978-1-939743)* Orders Addr.: Hispanic Research Ctr. Arizona State Univ. P.O. Box 875303, Tempe, AZ 85287-5303 USA (SAN 208-5526) Fax: 480-965-8309; Toll Free: 800-965-2280; Edit Addr.: Bilingual Review Pr. Administration Bldg. Rm. B-255 Arizona State Univ., Tempe, AZ 85281 USA
E-mail: brp@asu.edu
Web site: http://www.asu.edu/brp
Dist(s): **Libros Sin Fronteras**
SPD-Small Pr. Distribution.

Bilingual Pubns., *(978-0-9644678)* P.O. Box 12678, Denver, CO 80212 USA Tel 303-433-0979 Do not confuse with Bilingual Pubns. Co., New York, NY.

Bilingual Pubns. Co., The, 270 Lafayette St., New York, NY 10012 USA (SAN 164-8993) Tel 212-431-3500; Fax: 212-431-3567 Do not confuse with Bilingual Pubns., in Denver, CO
E-mail: lindagoodman@juno.com; spanishbks@aol.com.

Bilingual Stone Arch Readers *Imprint of* **Stone Arch Bks.**

Bill of Rights Institute, The, *(978-1-932785; 978-0-692-23022-0; 978-0-692-89225-1)* 200 N. Glebe Rd. Ste. 200, Arlington, VA 22203-3756 USA Toll Free: 800-838-7870
E-mail: sales@billofrightsinstitute.org; mwong@billofrightsinstitute.org; wneal@billofrightsinstitute.org
Web site: http://www.billofrightsinstitute.org
Dist(s): **CLEARVUE/eav, Inc.**
Social Studies Schl. Service
Teacher's Discovery.

Billiard Congress of America, *(978-1-878493)* 5 Piedmont Ctr NE Ste. 435, Atlanta, GA 30305-1509 USA
E-mail: amy@bca-pool.com; marketing@bca-pool.com
Web site: http://www.bca-pool.com.

Billings, David J., *(978-0-9789036)* 12441 SE Lusted Rd., Sandy, OR 97055-7556 USA
E-mail: david@davidjbillings.com; david@roadtripbook.com
Web site: http://www.roadtripbook.com.

Billings Worldwide Brain, *(978-0-9654169)* P.O. Box 701, Addison, TX 75001 USA (SAN 299-2426)
E-mail: dave@hamr.com
Web site: http://www.hamr.com
Dist(s): **Distributors, The.**

Billion $ Baby Pubns., *(978-0-9707945)* 22817 Ventura Blvd., Suite 408, Woodland Hills, CA 91364 USA (SAN 254-3265) Toll Free Fax: 888-232-9022; Toll Free: 800-499-2771
E-mail: Diedra@BabyPublications.com; dottie@babypublications.com
Web site: http://www.BabyPublication.com.

Billionaire Butterfly, LLC, *(978-0-9852262; 978-0-692-81697-4; 978-0-692-81764-3)* 109-15 Queens Blvd. Apt. 2C, Forest Hills, NY 11375 USA Tel 718-810-8700
E-mail: lenaure@gmail.com.

Billiot, Wendy Wilson, *(978-0-9762592)* 2715 Bayou DuLarge Rd., Theriot, LA 70397 USA
E-mail: wwbilliot@gmail.com
Web site: http://www.wetlandbooks.com.

Billy Jo Bks., *(978-0-9765088)* 9111 Oat Ave., Gerber, CA 96035-9723 USA Tel 530-385-1820
E-mail: biljoho@earthlink.net.

Billy the Bear & His Friends, Inc., *(978-0-9641338)* 1909 Munster Ave., Saint Paul, MN 55116 USA Tel 651-699-7636; Fax: 651-690-4815.

Bimini Bks., *(978-0-9753118)* 9553 SW 189 Terr., Suite 200, Miami, FL 33157 USA Tel 305-256-0638
E-mail: biminibooks@aol.com.

Bindlestick Bks., *(978-0-578-16673-5; 978-0-578-16732-9; 978-0-692-59737-8; 978-0-692-70921-4; 978-0-692-70929-0; 978-0-692-77061-0)* 616 1/2 Canyon Rd., Santa Fe, NM 87501 USA Tel 917-679-8080
E-mail: jeffreyschweitzer01@gmail.com
Web site: www.bindlestickbooks.com.

Bindu Bks. *Imprint of* **Inner Traditions International, Ltd.**

Binet International, *(978-0-942787)* P.O. Box 1429, Carlsbad, CA 92008 USA (SAN 667-7088) Tel 760-941-7929.

Bing Note, Inc., *(978-0-9794323)* 300 Caldecott Ln., No. 215, Oakland, CA 94618 USA
E-mail: lisa@bingnote.com
Web site: http://www.bingnote.com.

Bingham Putnam Publishing, *(978-0-9760504)* 326 Newport Dr., No. 1710, Naples, FL 34114 USA.

Bingo Bks., Inc., *(978-1-933530)* P.O. Box 3355, Austin, TX 78763-3355 USA Toll Free: 877-246-4644
Web site: http://www.bingobooks.com.

Binney & Smith, Inc., *(978-0-86696)* P.O. Box 431, Easton, PA 18042 USA (SAN 216-5899).

Binx Bks., *(978-0-9801796)* 33 W. Delaware Pl. Apt. 9F, Chicago, IL 60610-7361 USA.

Bio Rx, *(978-0-9772977)* 10828 Kenwood Rd., Cincinnati, OH 45242-2812 USA
E-mail: info@biorx.net
Web site: http://www.biorx.net.

Bio-Dynamic Farming & Gardening Assn., Inc., *(978-0-938250)* 25844 Butler Rd., Junction City, OR 97448 USA (SAN 224-9871) Tel 541-998-0105; Fax: 541-998-0406; Toll Free: 888-516-7797
E-mail: info@biodynamics.com
Web site: http://www.biodynamics.com
Dist(s): **New Leaf Distributing Co., Inc.**
Small Changes, Inc.
SteinerBooks, Inc.

BioEd *Imprint of* **Baylor College of Medicine**

Biographical Publishing Co., *(978-0-9637240; 978-1-929882; 978-0-9913521; 978-0-9976028)* 95 Sycamore Dr., Prospect, CT 06712-1493 USA (SAN 298-2692) Tel 203-758-3661; Fax: 253-793-2618
E-mail: biopub@aol.com
Web site: http://www.biopub.us
Dist(s): **Pathway Bk. Service.**

BIONIC Pr., *(978-0-9892448)* 8612 S. Terra Pointe Way, West Jordan, UT 84088 USA Tel 801-231-1969
E-mail: r.harkness@hsc.utah.edu
Web site: www.bionicpressbooks.com.

Bios for Kids *Imprint of* **Panda Publishing, L.L.C.**

Birch Brook Pr., *(978-0-913559; 978-0-9789974; 978-0-9842003; 978-0-9915777)* P.O. Box 81, Delhi, NY 13753 USA (SAN 631-5321) Fax: 607-746-7453 (phone/fax)
E-mail: birchbrook@copper.net
Web site: http://www.birchbrookpress.info.

Birch Island, *(978-0-9772692; 978-0-9818668; 978-0-615-96113-2)* P.O. Box 988 27 Dillingham Rd., Manchester, VT 05254 USA (SAN 257-1625) Tel 802-362-0074; 802-342-7844
E-mail: historicalpages@yahoo.com
Web site: http://www.historicalpages.com
Dist(s): **CreateSpace Independent Publishing Platform**
Independent Pubs. Group.

Birch Tree Publishing, *(978-0-615-60274-5; 978-0-9894487)* 3830 Valley Centre Dr. Suite 705-432, San Diego, CA 92130 USA Tel 858-212-6111 Do not confuse with Birch Tree Publishing in Miami, FL, Southbury, CT
E-mail: nimpentoad@gmail.com
Dist(s): **CreateSpace Independent Publishing Platform.**

Birchall Publishing, *(978-0-9857816)* P.O. Box 92054, Oceanside, CA 92054 USA Tel 720-347-0771
E-mail: lorrielbirchall@gmail.com.

Birdcage Books *See* **Birdcage Pr.**

Birdcage Pr., *(978-1-889613; 978-1-59960)* 853 Alma St., Palo Alto, CA 94301 USA Tel 650-462-6300; Fax: 650-462-6305; Toll Free: 800-247-6553
E-mail: info@birdcagepress.com
Web site: http://www.birdcagepress.com.

Birdsall, Bonnie Thomas, *(978-0-9762679)* 3421 Lacewood Rd., Tampa, FL 33618 USA
E-mail: swimtaichibon@juno.com.

Birdseed Bks., *(978-0-9774142)* 520 17th St., Dallas, WI 54733 USA; *Imprints*: Birdseed Books for Kids (Birdseed Books for Kids)
Web site: http://www.birdseedbooksforkids.com
Dist(s): **Independent Pubs. Group.**

Birdseed Books for Kids *Imprint of* **Birdseed Bks.**

Birdsong Bks., *(978-0-9662761; 978-0-9833406)* Orders Addr.: 1322 Bayview Rd., Middletown, DE 19709 USA Tel 302-378-7274; Fax: 302-378-0339; Edit Addr.: 814 N. Franklin St, Chicago, IL 60610 USA
E-mail: birdsongbooks@delaware.net
Web site: http://www.birdsongbooks.com
Dist(s): **Common Ground Distributors, Inc.**
Follett School Solutions
Independent Pubs. Group
MyiLibrary.

Birkhauser Boston, *(978-0-8176)* Div. of Springer-Verlag GmbH & Co. KG, Orders Addr.: P.O. Box 2485, Secaucus, NJ 07094 USA (SAN 241-6344) Tel 201-348-4033; Edit Addr.: 675 Massachusetts Ave., Cambridge, MA 02139 USA (SAN 213-2869) Tel 617-876-2333; Toll Free: 800-777-4643 (customer service)
Web site: http://www.birkhauser.com
Dist(s): **Follett School Solutions**
Metapress
MyiLibrary
Springer
ebrary, Inc.

Birlinn, Ltd. (GBR) *(978-1-874744; 978-1-84158; 978-1-84341; 978-1-84697; 978-0-85790; 978-1-78027)*
Dist. by **Casemate Pubs.**

Birt Hse. Publishing, *(978-0-578-11306-7; 978-0-578-11315-9)* 100 Bluebonnet St., Apt. 108, Stephenville, TX 76401 USA.

Bisham Hill Bks., *(978-0-9744281)* Orders Addr.: 25 Old Kings Hwy. N. Ste. 13, #192, Darien, CT 06820 USA
E-mail: sales@bishamhill.com
Web site: http://www.bishamhill.com.

Bishop Museum Pr., *(978-0-910240; 978-0-930897; 978-1-58178)* Orders Addr.: 1525 Bernice St., Honolulu, HI 96817-2704 USA (SAN 202-408X) Tel 808-847-8260; 808-848-4135; *Imprints*: Kamahoi Press (Kamahoi Pr)
E-mail: press@bishopmuseum.org
Web site: http://www.bishopmuseum.org
Dist(s): **Booklines Hawaii, Ltd.**
Islander Group.

Bishop, Susan Lynn, *(978-0-9772878)* Orders Addr.: P.O. Box 13, Onley, IL 62450 USA Tel 618-392-4011; Edit Addr.: P.O. Box 13, Olney, IL 62450-0013 USA
E-mail: suzyb@wabash.net.

Bisiar Music Publishing, *(978-0-9753091)* Orders Addr.: P.O. Box 424, Evergreen, CO 80437-0424 USA (SAN 256-0356) Tel 303-670-0752 (phone/fax); Edit Addr.: 3661 A Evergreen Pkwy., Evergreen, CO 80437-0424 USA
E-mail: bisiar@earthlink.net
Web site: http://www.eddiespaghettiusa.com.

Bison Bks. *Imprint of* **Univ. of Nebraska Pr.**

Bit of Boston Bks., A, *(978-0-9788637)* Orders Addr.: 208 Commonwealth Ave., Boston, MA 02116 USA; Edit Addr.: P.O. Box 990208, Boston, MA 02116 USA
E-mail: jamesrholland@mindspring.com.

Bitingduck Pr., *(978-1-938463)* 1262 Sunnyoaks Cir., Altadena, CA 91001 USA Tel 626-507-8033
E-mail: jay@bitingduckpress.com
Web site: http://www.bitingduckpress.com
Dist(s): **Follett School Solutions**
Midpoint Trade Bks., Inc.
SPD-Small Pr. Distribution.

Bitter Oleander Pr., The, *(978-0-9664358; 978-0-9786335; 978-0-9883525; 978-0-9862049; 978-0-9993279)* 4983 Tall Oaks Dr., Fayetteville, NY 13066-9776 USA (SAN 855-9686)
E-mail: info@bitteroleander.com
Web site: http://www.bitteroleander.com
Dist(s): **SPD-Small Pr. Distribution.**

Bitterroot Mountain Publishing, *(978-0-9817874; 978-0-9852784; 978-1-940025)* P.O. Box 3508, Hayden, ID 83835-3508 USA.

Bitty Book Pr., (*978-1-887270*) 851 Mt. Vernon Ct., Naperville, IL 60563 USA Tel 630-420-1887; Fax: 630-963-0341; Toll Free: 800-750-6649; 2736 Maple Ave., Downers Grove, IL 60515
E-mail: maryannako@aol.com
Web site: http://www.namepower101.com.

Bixie Gate Publishing, (*978-0-9773433*) 22694 SW Lincoln St., Sherwood, OR 97140 USA (SAN 257-3474)
E-mail: shannonk23@comcast.net
Web site: http://www.bixiegatepublishing.com; http://www.shannonkeegan.com.

Biz4Kids *Imprint of* **Round Cow Media Group**

Bizzy Girls Publishing, (*978-0-9833532*) 1508 Veteran Ave. No. 205, Los Angeles, CA 90024 USA Tel 310-467-7300
E-mail: dekanafani@yahoo.com
Web site: Www.bizzygirls.com.

Bjelkier Pr., (*978-0-9828217*) 1620 Louis Ln., Hastings, MN 55033 USA (SAN 859-9025) Tel 651-437-8244
E-mail: toysammy@embarqmail.com.

Bjelopetrovich, Beba Foundation, (*978-0-9745724*) 5555 W. Howard St., Skokie, IL 60077-2621 USA Tel 847-679-6710; Fax: 847-679-6717.

†BJU Pr., (*978-0-89084; 978-1-57924; 978-1-59166; 978-1-60682; 978-1-62856*) 1700 Wade Hampton Blvd., Greenville, SC 29614 USA (SAN 223-7512) Tel 864-242-5731; 864-370-1800 (ext. 4397; Fax: 864-298-0268; Toll Free Fax: 800-525-8398; Toll Free: 800-845-5731; *Imprints:* JourneyForth (JmyForth); Bloomsbury Visual Arts (BloomsVisual)
E-mail: bjup@bjup.com
Web site: http://www.bjupress.com
Dist(s): **Follett School Solutions**; *CIP.*

BKB Group, Inc., The, (*978-0-9747628*) Orders Addr.: 11146 Harbour Springs Cr., Boca Raton, FL 33428 USA Tel 561-218-1215; Fax: 561-218-1214; Toll Free: 888-321-7664; Edit Addr.: 11146 HARBOUR SPRINGS CR., 11146 HARBOUR SPRINGS CR., BOCA RATON, FL 33428 USA
E-mail: rfproductions@adelphia.net
Web site: http://www.billybutterfly.com.

Bk.ify by Sanitaryum *Imprint of* **Sanitaryum**

Bks. for Young Learners *Imprint of* **Owen, Richard C. Pubs., Inc.**

Black Academy Pr., Inc., (*978-0-87831*) Orders Addr.: 4011 Old Court Rd., Pikesville, MD 21208-2808 USA (SAN 218-6489)
E-mail: bapress@aol.com; info@blackacademypress.com
Web site: http://www.blackacademypress.com.

Black, Amy Jackson, (*978-0-615-16743-5*) 107 Southglen, Terre Haute, IN 47802 USA
E-mail: godzgrl4evr@msn.com
Dist(s): **Lulu Pr., Inc.**

Black and White Publishing Ltd. (GBR) (*978-1-873631; 978-0-9515151; 978-1-902927; 978-1-903265; 978-1-84502; 978-1-910230; 978-1-78530*) *Dist. by* **IPG Chicago.**

Black Bart Bks., (*978-0-615-20238-9; 978-0-615-23723-7; 978-0-578-01524-8; 978-0-578-02511-7; 978-0-578-08320-9*) 3447 Little Carpenter Creek Rd., Fernwood, ID 83830 USA
Web site: http://www.blackbaradventures.com
Dist(s): **Lulu Pr., Inc.**

Black Bed Sheet Bks., (*978-0-9822530; 978-0-9842136; 978-0-9833773; 978-0-9858829; 978-0-9886590; 978-0-615-88139-3; 978-0-615-90327-9; 978-0-615-90623-2; 978-0-615-90684-3; 978-0-615-94207-0; 978-0-615-94575-0; 978-0-615-94689-4; 978-0-615-94893-5; 978-0-615-99827-5; 978-0-692-21851-8; 978-0-692-23039-8; 978-0-692-23974-2; 978-0-692-24044-1; 978-0-692-24087-8; 978-0-692-25565-0; 978-0-692-25829-3; 978-0-692-26626-7; 978-0-692-26983-1; 978-0-692-27830-7; 978-0-692-31231-5; 978-0-692-31456-2; 978-0-692-31673-3; 9) 7865 Valley Quail Ct., Antelope, CA 95843-2031 USA (SAN 857-6785)*
E-mail: bbsadmin@downwarden.com
Web site: http://www.downwarden.com/blackbedsheet; https://www.downwarden.com/blackbedsheetdigital
Dist(s): **CreateSpace Independent Publishing Platform.**

Black Belt Training, (*978-0-9759744*) 9109 Cochran Heights, Dallas, TX 75220 USA Tel 214-351-2234 (phone/fax)
E-mail: drted@wwwin.com
Web site: http://www.wwwin.com.

Black Bird Bks., (*978-0-9763238*) Orders Addr.: P.O. Box 901, Ankeny, IA 50021 USA; Edit Addr.: P.O. Box 901, Ankeny, IA 50021-0901 USA
E-mail: lizzie3blackbird@hotmail.com.

Black Cat *Imprint of* **Grove/Atlantic, Inc.**

Black, Clinton L., (*978-0-9620180*) Orders Addr.: P.O. Box 9096, Fort Lauderdale, FL 33310 USA Tel 954-722-0415; Fax: 954-720-7674
E-mail: thepurposeofhumanlife@yahoo.com
Dist(s): **Southern Bk. Service.**

Black Coat Pr. *Imprint of* **HollywoodComics.com, LLC**

Black Coffee Publishing, (*978-0-9745238*) Orders Addr.: 5543 Edmondson Pike, No. 213, Nashville, TN 37211-5808 USA Tel 615-969-5516
E-mail: bcpubl@aol.com
Web site: http://www.blackcoffeepublishing.com.

Black Creek Publishing Group, (*978-0-9895323; 978-0-9904596; 978-0-9962919; 978-0-9978983*) 2102 Kimberton Rd. No. 266, Kimberton, PA 19460 USA Tel 832-350-3029
E-mail: jchenry@blackcreekpublishinggroup.com
Web site: www.blackcreekpublishinggroup.com.

Black Diamond Publishing, (*978-0-9715139*) 415 E. 32nd St., Indianapolis, IN 46205 USA Do not confuse with Black Diamond Publishing in Brooklyn,NY
E-mail: LWatk82805@aol.com; BDPub@aol.com; Linda@lindawatkins.org
Web site: http://www.lindawatkins.org.

Black Dog & Leventhal Pubs. Inc. *Imprint of* **Hachette Bks.**

Black Dog Books, (*978-1-884449; 978-1-928619*) 1115 Pine Meadows Ct., Normal, IL 61761 USA Tel 309-310-6984
E-mail: info@blackdogbooks.net; blackdogbooks_tomroberts@yahoo.com
Web site: http://www.blackdogbooks.net.

Black Dog Publishing Ltd. (GBR) (*978-0-9521773; 978-1-901033; 978-1-904772; 978-1-906155; 978-1-907317; 978-1-908966; 978-1-910433*) *Dist. by* **TwoRivers.**

Black Dolphin Diving, (*978-0-9646281*) 5022 Two Harbors, Avalon, CA 90704-5022 USA Tel 310-510-2109
E-mail: bkdolphin@aol.com
Web site: http://www.divecatalina.com.

Black Dome Pr. Corp., (*978-0-9628523; 978-1-883789*) 1011 Rte. 296, Hensonville, NY 12439 USA (SAN 257-6996) Tel 518-734-6357; Fax: 518-734-5802; Toll Free: 800-513-9013; 649 Delaware Ave., Delmar, NY 12054
E-mail: blackdomep@aol.com
Web site: http://www.blackdomepress.com
Dist(s): **Follett School Solutions**
North Country Bks., Inc.

Black Dot Pubns., (*978-0-9649740*) Orders Addr.: P.O. Box 1068, Ojai, CA 93024 USA Tel 805-640-8825; Edit Addr.: 1208 Gregory St., Ojai, CA 93023 USA
E-mail: blackdotpubs@yahoo.com
Web site: http://www.backdotpubs.com; http://www.chuckhillig.com
Dist(s): **New Leaf Distributing Co., Inc.**

Black Falcon Publications *See* **LMW Works**

Black Forest Pr., (*978-1-58275; 978-1-881116*) Div. of Black Forest Enterprises, Orders Addr.: P.O. Box 6342, Chula Vista, CA 91909-6342 USA Fax: 619-482-8704; Toll Free: 800-451-9404 (General Information, Submission Inquiries and Acquisitions); 888-808-5440 (Book Sales, Marketing and Promotion); Edit Addr.: 1075 Hayuco Plz., Chula Vista, CA 91910-7006 USA (SAN 298-8445); *Imprints:* Sonnenschein Books (Sonnenschein Bks)
E-mail: bfp@blackforestpress.com
Web site: http://www.blackforestpress.com.

Black Garnet Pr., (*978-0-9832383; 978-0-9911790*) 1313 St. Helena Ave., Santa Rosa, CA 95404 USA Tel 707-526-3331
E-mail: sandybaker131@gmail.com
Web site: sandybakerwriter.com.

Black Hat Pr., (*978-0-9614462; 978-1-887649*) Orders Addr.: P.O. Box 12, Goodhue, MN 55027-0012 USA (SAN 689-4259) Tel 651-923-4590; Edit Addr.: 508 Second Ave., Goodhue, MN 55027-0012 USA
E-mail: blackhatpress@yahoo.com.

Black Hawk Pr., Inc., The, (*978-0-9778731; 978-0-9817613*) 803 Charter Pl., Charlotte, NC 28211 USA Tel 704-364-1164
E-mail: info@blackhawkpress.com
Web site: http://www.blackhawkpress.com
Dist(s): **Blu Sky Media Group.**

Black Heron Pr., (*978-0-930773; 978-1-936364*) Orders Addr.: P.O. Box 13396, Mill Creek, WA 98145 USA (SAN 677-623X) Fax: 425-355-4929; Edit Addr.: 27 West 20Th St., New York, NY 10011 USA
E-mail: Jgoldberon@aol.com
Web site: http://www.blackheronpress.com
Dist(s): **Follett School Solutions**
Midpoint Trade Bks., Inc.
ebrary, Inc.

Black Jackal Bks. Ltd.,

Black Jasmine, (*978-0-9788802*) 46 Pleasant St., Sharon, MA 02067 USA
E-mail: deemajoan@yahoo.com
Web site: http://www.deemasglass.com.

Black, Judith Storyteller, (*978-0-9701073*) 33 Prospect St., Marblehead, MA 01941 USA Tel 781-631-4417
E-mail: jb@storiesalive.com
Web site: http://www.storiesalive.com.

Black Lab Publishing LLC, (*978-0-9742815*) Orders Addr.: P.O. Box 6244, Laconia, NH 03247 USA Tel 603-714-8023; 606-524-1114
E-mail: loni@bearandkatie.com
Web site: http://www.bearandkatie.com; http://www.blacklabpublishing.com.

Black Literary, Inc., (*978-0-615-22609-5; 978-0-615-30323-9; 978-0-615-37753-7*) P.O. Box 492, Catlett, VA 20119 USA Tel 540-788-4992
E-mail: CHancasky@aol.com.

Black Oak Media, Inc., (*978-0-9790401; 978-1-61876*) P.O. Box 122, Cherry Valley, IL 61016 USA Do not confuse with companies with a similar name in Lincoln, NE, Lambertville, NJ, Springfield, MO
E-mail: info@blackoakmedia.org
Web site: http://www.blackoakmedia.org
Dist(s): **Follett School Solutions.**

Black Oak Press, Illinois *See* **Black Oak Media, Inc.**

Black Orb *See* **Angie Blue Bks., LLC**

Black Pearl Bks., (*978-0-9728005; 978-0-9766007; 978-0-9773438*) Orders Addr.: 3653-F Flakes Mill Road, PMB 306, Atlanta, GA 30034 USA Do not
E-mail: hurst@blackpearlbooks.com
Web site: http://www.blackpearlbooks.com
Dist(s): **African World Bks.**
American Wholesale Bk. Co.
Bookazine Co., Inc.
Brodart Co.
Quality Bks., Inc.

Black Plum Bks., (*978-0-9785317*) Orders Addr.: 1302 Abby Ct., Juneau, AK 99801-9599 USA
Web site: http://www.blackplumebooks.com
Dist(s): **Follett School Solutions.**

Black Rabbit Bks., (*978-1-58340; 978-1-887068; 978-1-59920; 978-1-77092; 978-1-62310; 978-1-62588; 978-1-68071; 978-1-68072*) Orders Addr.: P.O. Box 3263, Mankato, MN 56002 USA (SAN 925-4862); Edit Addr.: 123 S. Broad St., Mankato, MN 56001 USA (SAN 858-902X); *Imprints:* Smart Apple Media (SmartAppleMed); Bolt (Bolt)
E-mail: info@blackrabbitbooks.com; production@blackrabbitbooks.com
Web site: http://www.blackrabbitbooks.com
Dist(s): **Follett School Solutions**
INscribe Digital
RiverStream Publishing
Scholastic, Inc.
myON.

Black River Trading Co., (*978-0-9649083; 978-0-9797492*) P.O. Box 7, Oxford, MI 48371 USA (SAN 854-2724) Tel 248-628-5150; Fax: 248-628-6422
E-mail: jane@whoopforjoy.com
Web site: http://www.whoopforjoy.com
Dist(s): **Bookmen, Inc.**

Black Rose Writing, (*978-0-615-20158-0; 978-0-615-20274-7; 978-0-615-20494-9; 978-0-615-20616-5; 978-0-9821012; 978-0-9819742; 978-0-9825542; 978-0-9825823; 978-1-935605; 978-1-61296; 978-1-944715; 978-1-68433*) P.O. Box 1540, Castroville, TX 78009 USA
E-mail: creator@blackrosewriting.com; sales@blackrosewriting.com
Web site: http://www.blackrosewritiing.com; http://www.blackrosewriting.com/books
Dist(s): **Lightning Source, Inc.**
Lulu Pr., Inc.

Black Sheep *Imprint of* **Akashic Bks.**

Black Sheep *Imprint of* **Bellwether Media**

Black Society Pages, Inc., (*978-0-9758611*) 228 S. Washington St., Alexandria, VA 22314 USA.

Black Squirrel Bks. *Imprint of* **Kent State Univ. Pr.**

Black Threads Pr., (*978-0-9824796*) 3037 S. Buchanan St., Arlington, VA 22206-1512 USA
Web site: http://www.BlackThreads.com
Dist(s): **CreateSpace Independent Publishing Platform**
Lightning Source, Inc.

Blackberry Hill Pr., (*978-0-9792947*) Orders Addr.: 2860 Mohawk St., Sauquoit, NY 13456-3322 USA Tel 315-737-5147
Web site: http://www.dorothystacy.com
Dist(s): **North Country Bks., Inc.**

Blackberry Maine, (*978-0-942396; 978-0-615-15951-5; 978-0-9824389*) 617 E. Neck Rd., Nobleboro, ME 04555 USA (SAN 207-7949) Tel 207-729-5083; Fax: 207-729-6783
E-mail: chimfarm@gwi.net
Web site: http://www.blackberrybooksme.com
Dist(s): **SPD-Small Pr. Distribution.**

Blackberry Pubns., (*978-0-9776987; 978-0-9972260*) 3915 11th Street, Ecorse, MI 48229 USA Tel 313-297-7809; 313-627-1520
E-mail: blackberrybooks@yahoo.com.

Blackberry Pubs., (*978-0-615-12702-6*) 2545 Hwy. 76, Portland, TN 37148 USA Tel 615-325-3970
E-mail: fussellb@comcast.net
Web site: http://www.blackberrypublishers.com
Dist(s): **Sadler, Dale.**

Blackberry: Salted in the Shell *See* **Blackberry Maine**

Blackbirch Pr., Inc. *Imprint of* **Barnes & Noble, Inc.**

Blackbirch Pr., Inc. *Imprint of* **Cengage Gale**

Blackbirch Pr., Inc. *Imprint of* **Lerner Publishing Group**

Blackbirch Pr., Inc. *Imprint of* **Sunstone Pr.**

Blackbirch Pr., Inc. *Imprint of* **Peel Productions, Inc.**

Blackbirch Pr., Inc. *Imprint of* **Soundprints**

Blackbirch Pr., Inc. *Imprint of* **Seacoast Publishing, Inc.**

Blackbirch Pr., Inc. *Imprint of* **Cherry Lake Publishing**

Blackbirch Pr., Inc. *Imprint of* **Mardick Pr.**

Blackbird Bks., (*978-1-61053*) 1012 3rd Street, Suite 301, Santa Monica, CA 90403 USA Tel 310-422-7098
E-mail: editor@bbirdbooks.com
Web site: http://www.bbirdbooks.com.

Blackbird's World Publishing Co., (*978-0-9789798*) Orders Addr.: P.O. Box 475, Clyde, TX 79510 USA Tel 325-201-2495; Edit Addr.: Box 475 212 Hunt St., Clyde, TX 79510 USA
E-mail: blackbird@blackbirdsworldpublishingcompany.net
Web site: http://blackbirdsworldpublishingcompany.net.

Blackfoot Burkino Cherokee Publishing, (*978-0-9722724*) Orders Addr.: P.O. Box 58074, Houston, TX 77258 USA Tel 832-504-1331; Edit Addr.: 1912 Trentwood Pl., Charlotte, NC 28216 USA
E-mail: bbcpublishin80@gmail.com.

Blackfairs Pr., (*978-0-9745206*) 2319 Branner Dr., Menlo Park, CA 94025 USA.

Blacklock Nature Photography, (*978-0-9634991; 978-1-892472*) P.O. Box 560, Moose Lake, MN 55767-0560 USA
E-mail: Blacklock@pinenat.com
Dist(s): **Adventure Pubns.**

BlacknBlue Pr. UK *Imprint of* **Blacknblue Pr.**

Blacknblue Pr., (*978-0-9677652; 978-0-9840718*) 108 Benarr Ave., Fort Walton Beach, FL 32548 USA Tel 850-862-2874 (phone/fax); 13 Dellands Overton, Basingstoke, RG25 3LD Tel 1256 770736 (phone/fax); *Imprints:* BlacknBlue Press UK (BlacknBlue Pr UK)
E-mail: edddwicke@hotmail.com
Web site: http://www.blacknbluepress.info
Dist(s): **Lightning Source, Inc.**

Blacksmith Bks. (HKG) (*978-962-86732; 978-988-17742; 978-988-99799; 978-988-19003; 978-988-16139; 978-988-13765*) *Dist. by* **Natl Bk Netwk.**

Blacksmith Bks., LLC, (*978-0-9772515*) P.O. Box 4228, Lisle, IL 60532-9228 USA; 6141 Dixon Dr., Lisle, IL 60532-4151
E-mail: maboone1@comcast.net.

Black-Smith Enterprises, (*978-0-9762720*) 31536 Avondale, Westland, MI 48186 USA
E-mail: janaya_black@yahoo.com
Web site: http://www.black-smithenterprises.com
Dist(s): **Lightning Source, Inc.**

Blackstaff Pr., Ltd. (GBR) (*978-0-85640*) *Dist. by* **Dufour.**

Blackstone Audio Books, Incorporated *See* **Blackstone Audio, Inc.**

Blackstone Audio, Inc., (*978-0-7861; 978-1-4332; 978-1-4417; 978-1-4551; 978-1-4708; 978-1-4829; 978-1-4830; 978-1-5046; 978-1-5047; 978-1-5384; 978-1-5385*) 31 Mistletoe Rd., Ashland, OR 97520 USA (SAN 173-2811) Fax: 800-482-9294; Toll Free Fax: 800-482-9294; Toll Free: 800-729-2665
E-mail: Orders@blackstoneaudio.com; megan.wahrenbrock@blackstoneaudio.com
Web site: http://www.blackstoneaudio.com
Dist(s): **Ebsco Publishing**
Findaway World, LLC
Follett School Solutions
Hachette Bk. Group
HarperCollins Pubs.
INscribe Digital
Listen & Live Audio, Inc.
MyiLibrary
OverDrive, Inc.
Penguin Publishing Group
Recorded Bks., Inc.
Simon & Schuster, Inc.
Zondervan.

Blackstone Editions, (*978-0-9725017; 978-0-9816402*) 312-24 Wellesley St. W., Toronto, ON M4Y 2X6 CAN Tel 647-344-2206
Web site: http://www.blackstoneeditions.com.

Blacktastic.net, (*978-0-9834275; 978-0-9961146*) 7945 Fincastle Ct., Sacramento, CA 95829 USA Tel 916-525-1703
E-mail: brotherhypnotic@hotmail.com.

Blacktypewriter Pr. *Imprint of* **Pittsburgh Literary Arts Network LLC**

BlackWords Press *See* **KA Productions, LLC**

Blade Publishing, (*978-1-929409*) 110 W. C St. Ste. 1300, San Diego, CA 92101-3978 USA (SAN 254-7678)
E-mail: bladeinternational@yahoo.com.

BladeRunner Publishing, (*978-0-9785477*) P.O. Box 4298, Greenville, SC 29608 USA Tel 864-313-6182
E-mail: bladerunnerpublishing@charter.net.

Bladestar Publishing, (*978-0-9787931*) Orders Addr.: 1499 N. 950 W., Orem, UT 84057 USA Fax: 484-414-1674
E-mail: Promotion@BladestarPublishing.com
Web site: http://www.bladestarpublishing.com
Dist(s): **Brodart Co.**

Blaft Pubns., ., ., CA 1 USA
Web site: http://www.blaft.com/
Dist(s): **SPD-Small Pr. Distribution**
Smashwords.

Blair, John F. Pub., (*978-0-89587; 978-0-910244*) Orders Addr.: 1406 Plaza Dr., Winston-Salem, NC 27103 USA (SAN 201-4319) Tel 336-768-1374; Fax: 336-768-9194; Toll Free: 800-222-9796
E-mail: sutton@blairpub.com
Web site: http://www.blairpub.com
Dist(s): **Smashwords.**

Blake, Edna, (*978-0-9668906*) 7 Babble Creek Ct., O Fallon, MO 63368-8321 USA.

Blake, John Publishing, Ltd. (GBR) (*978-0-905846; 978-1-85782; 978-1-903402; 978-1-904034; 978-1-84358; 978-1-84454; 978-1-78219; 978-1-78418; 978-1-78606*) *Dist. by* **IPG Chicago.**

Blake, Monica, (*978-0-9764155*) P.O. Box 475233, San Francisco, CA 94147 USA Tel 415-995-2515; Fax: 415-876-1002
E-mail: blakesfo@yahoo.com.

Blake-Virostko, Pamela, (*978-0-9801975*) 7546 S. Virostko Rd., Rockville, IN 47872 USA Tel 765-548-2635
E-mail: PVirostko@aol.com.

Blanchard, Graham, (*978-0-9854090; 978-0-9897949; 978-0-692-85033-6*) P.O. Box 300235, Austin, TX 78703 USA Tel 512-647-2099
E-mail: callie@grahamblanchard.com
Web site: http://www.grahamblanchard.com
Dist(s): **Ingram Publisher Services**
Send The Light Distribution LLC.

Blancmange Publishing LLC, (*978-0-9779488*) P.O. Box 17184, Memphis, TN 38187-7184 USA (SAN 850-7023).

Blanket Street Publishing, (*978-0-9760929*) 17278 Summit Hills Dr., Santa Clarita, CA 91387 USA
E-mail: kstrauss@socal.rr.com.

Blastoff! Discovery *Imprint of* **Bellwether Media**

Blastoff! Readers *Imprint of* **Bellwether Media**

Blatant Times, (*978-0-9744376*) 608 Patton Rd., Great Bend, KS 67530 USA
Web site: http://www.cpcis.net.

Blaumond Pr., (*978-0-9789031*) 740 SE. Greenville Blvd., Suite 400, Box 283, Greenville, NC 27858 USA (SAN 851-9021) Tel 252-754-4837; Fax: 252-353-0732
E-mail: info@blaumondpress.com
Web site: http://www.blaumondpress.com.

Blaze Publishing, LLC, (*978-0-9970104; 978-1-945519*) 64 Melvin Dr., Fredericksburg, VA 22406 USA Tel 703-470-8323
E-mail: kdehaba@blazepub.com; etilton@blazepub.com
Web site: www.blazepub.com
Dist(s): **Midpoint Trade Bks., Inc.**

Blaze, Ronan *See* **Medal Bks.**

Blazers *Imprint of* **Capstone Press of Coughlan Cos.**

Blazing Ideas Ltd., (*978-0-9801243; 978-0-9856029; 978-0-9992828*) 11141 Blackforest way, Gaithersburg, MD 20879 USA Tel 301-476-0778
E-mail: lotit2000@yahoo.com; ookubena@gmail.com; ololade@blazing-ideas.com; olayemi@blazing-ideas.com
Web site: www.blazing-ideas.com.

BLD Enterprises *See* **Innovo Publishing, LLC**

Blessed and Highly Favored *See* **BHF Publishing**

Blessed Beginnings Publishing, (*978-0-9727201*) P.O. Box 241282, Milwaukee, WI 53223 USA Tel 414-351-6467
E-mail: pinksolitaire97@yahoo.com.

Blessings Unlimited, LLC, (*978-0-9742796*) P.O. Box 186, Highland Springs, VA 23075 USA Tel 804-640-7137 Do not confuse with Blessings Unlimited in Bloomington, MN
Web site: http://www.blessingsunlimited.info.

Blind Ferret Entertainment (CAN) *(978-0-9736946) Dist. by* **Diamond Book Dists.**

Blind Wolf Studios, *(978-0-9749941)* P.O. Box 465, Cross River, NY 10518 USA
Web site: http://www.blindwolfstudios.com.

Blink,
Dist(s): **Zondervan.**

Bliss Group, *(978-0-9885359; 978-1-940021)* 725 River Rd. No. 32-215, Edgewater, NJ 07020 USA Tel 551-333-9409
E-mail: alansrbradshaw@gmail.com
Dist(s): **Lightning Source, Inc.**
MyiLibrary.

Bliss on Tap, *(978-0-9763768; 978-0-9825098; 978-0-9896143)* 28326 Wellfleet Ln., Saugus, CA 91350 USA
E-mail: pephillipson@aol.com
Web site: http://www.godthedyslexicdog.com
Dist(s): **MyiLibrary.**

Blister Books LLC *See* **Mother Lode Pr. LLC**

Bloated Toe Publishing, *(978-0-9795741; 978-0-9836925; 978-1-939216)* P.O. Box 324, Peru, NY 12972 USA Tel 518-563-9469 (phone/fax)
E-mail: sales@bloatedtoe.com
Web site: http://www.bloatedtoe.com.

Bloch Publishing Co., *(978-0-8197)* 5875 Mining Ter. Ste. 104, Jacksonville, FL 32257-3225 USA (SAN 214-204X)
E-mail: BlochPub@worldnet.att.net
Web site: http://www.blochpub.com/
Dist(s): **Follett School Solutions.**

Block Publishing, *(978-0-9761625)* 1120 Forest Ave., No. 306, Pacific Grove, CA 93950 USA Fax: 831-655-4830
E-mail: blockpub@sbcglobal.net
Web site: http://www.blockpublishing.com
Dist(s): **Bookmasters Distribution**
Follett School Solutions.

Block System, The, *(978-0-9665545; 978-0-9800875)* 4619 Ranch View Rd., Fort Worth, TX 76109 USA Tel 817-732-2633; Fax: 817-732-0836
E-mail: andblock@gmail.com
Web site: http://www.blockcenter.com.

BlogIntoBook.com *Imprint of* **Price World Publishing**

Blondvic Enterprises, *(978-0-692-81633-2)* 141 E. 4th St., # 420, Saint Paul, MN 55101 USA Tel 651-295-4033
E-mail: stacybecker@comcast.net; stacybecker@comcast.net.

Blood Moon Productions, Ltd., *(978-0-9748118; 978-0-9786465; 978-1-936003)* 75 St. Marks Pl., Staten Island, NY 10301 USA Tel 718-556-9410; Fax: 718-816-4092; 4501 Forbes Blvd., Lanham, MD 20706
E-mail: DanforthPrince@hotmail.com
Web site: http://www.bloodmoonproductions.com
Dist(s): **Alamo Square Distributors**
Bookazine Co., Inc.
Follett School Solutions
MyiLibrary
National Bk. Network
ebrary, Inc.

Blood-Horse, Inc., The, *(978-0-936032; 978-0-939049; 978-1-58150)* Div. of The Blood-Horse, Inc., 3101 Beaumont Centre Cir., Lexington, KY 40513 USA (SAN 203-5294) Tel 859-278-2361 (Retailers); Fax: 859-276-6868; Toll Free: 800-866-2361 (Retailers); *Imprints:* Eclipse Press (Eclip Press)
E-mail: info@eclipsepress.com
Web site: http://www.eclipsepress.com
Dist(s): **Smashwords**
Western International, Inc.

Bloodletting Pr., *(978-0-9720859; 978-0-9768531; 978-1-935006)* 25222 E Welches Rd Unit 29 USA, Welches, OR 97067 USA Tel 503-298-4811
Web site: http://www.miskatonicbooks.com.

Bloom & Grow Bks., *(978-1-931969)* Div. of Bloom & Grow, Inc., Orders Addr.: 149 S. Barrington Ave., #363, Los Angeles, CA 90049 USA Tel 310-472-0505
E-mail: stephanie@bloomandogrow.com; info@bloomandgrow.com
Web site: http://www.bloomandgrow.com; http://www.placetogrow.com
Dist(s): **Beyda for Bks., LLC.**

Bloom & Grow, Incorporated *See* **Bloom & Grow Bks.**

Bloom, Barbara, *(978-0-615-64962-5; 978-0-9883351)* 11907 Oakcroft Dr., Houston, TX 77070 USA Tel 832-717-7818
Web site: www.smartscarlet.com
Dist(s): **CreateSpace Independent Publishing Platform.**

Blooming Tree Pr., *(978-0-9718348; 978-0-9769417; 978-1-933831)* Div. of Hees Enterprises, LLC, Orders Addr.: P.O. Box 140934, Austin, TX 78714-0934 USA Tel 512-921-8846; Fax: 512-873-7710; Edit Addr.: 10703 Jonwood Way, Austin, TX 78753 USA Tel 512-921-8846; Fax: 512-873-7710; *Imprints:* Ready Blade (Ready Blade)
E-mail: email@bloomingtreepress.com; bloomingtree@gmail.com
Web site: http://www.bloomingtreepress.com.

Blooming Twig Books LLC, *(978-0-9777736; 978-1-933918; 978-1-61343; 978-1-937753)* Orders Addr.: 320 S. Boston Suite 1026, Tulsa, OK 74103 USA Tel 866-389-1482; Fax: 866-298-7260
Web site: http://www.bloomingtwig.com
Dist(s): **Cardinal Pubs. Group.**

BloomingFields, *(978-0-9645971)* 44 Voyagers Ln., Ashland, MA 01721 USA; *Imprints:* Wisdom Audio-Books (Wisdom Aud-Bks)
E-mail: markpoetry@hotmail.com.

Bloom's Literary Criticism *Imprint of* **Facts On File, Inc.**

Bloomsbury Academic & Professional *See* **Bloomsbury Academic & Professional**

Bloomsbury Academic & Professional, *(978-1-4411; 978-1-62892)* 175 Fifth Ave., New York, NY 10010 USA; *Imprints:* Fairchild Books (Fairchild Bks)
E-mail: AskAcademic@BloomsburyUSA.com
Web site: http://www.bloomsburyacademicusa.com/html/
Dist(s): **Bloomsbury Publishing USA**
Casemate Academic
Macmillan
MyiLibrary
National Bk. Network.

Bloomsbury Activity Bks. *Imprint of* **Bloomsbury Publishing USA**

Bloomsbury Pr., *(978-0-9667039)* 4340 Anza St., No. 6, San Francisco, CA 94121 USA Do not confuse with Bloomsberry Pr., New York, NY
Dist(s): **Macmillan.**

Bloomsbury Publishing Plc (GBR) *(978-0-225; 978-0-245; 978-0-264; 978-0-333; 978-0-485; 978-0-510; 978-0-540; 978-0-567; 978-0-7136; 978-0-7475; 978-0-7478; 978-0-85045; 978-0-85177; 978-0-85263; 978-0-85314; 978-0-85496; 978-0-86292; 978-0-906515; 978-0-907582; 978-0-948230;-1-85399; 978-1-85532; 978-1-85973; 978-1-899791; 978-1-901362; 978-0-212; 978-0-85146; 978-0-85147; 978-0-85317; 978-0-86019; 978-0-946716; 978-0-9507160; 978-1-902579; 978-1-84113; 978-1-85691; 978-1-897737; 978-0-9506785; 978-1-873590; 978-1-84) Dist. by* **Trafalgar.**

Bloomsbury Publishing Plc (GBR) *(978-0-225; 978-0-245; 978-0-264; 978-0-333; 978-0-485; 978-0-510; 978-0-540; 978-0-567; 978-0-7136; 978-0-7475; 978-0-7478; 978-0-85045; 978-0-85177; 978-0-85263; 978-0-85314; 978-0-85496; 978-0-86292; 978-0-906515; 978-0-907582; 978-0-948230;-1-85399; 978-1-85532; 978-1-85973; 978-1-899791; 978-1-901362; 978-0-212; 978-0-85146; 978-0-85147; 978-0-85317; 978-0-86019; 978-0-946716; 978-0-9507160; 978-1-902579; 978-1-84113; 978-1-85691; 978-1-897737; 978-0-9506785; 978-1-873590; 978-1-84) Dist. by* **Players Pr.**

Bloomsbury Publishing Plc (GBR) *(978-0-225; 978-0-245; 978-0-264; 978-0-333; 978-0-485; 978-0-510; 978-0-540; 978-0-567; 978-0-7136; 978-0-7475; 978-0-7478; 978-0-85045; 978-0-85177; 978-0-85263; 978-0-85314; 978-0-85496; 978-0-86292; 978-0-906515; 978-0-907582; 978-0-948230;-1-85399; 978-1-85532; 978-1-85973; 978-1-899791; 978-1-901362; 978-0-212; 978-0-85146; 978-0-85147; 978-0-85317; 978-0-86019; 978-0-946716; 978-0-9507160; 978-1-902579; 978-1-84113; 978-1-85691; 978-1-897737; 978-0-9506785; 978-1-873590; 978-1-84) Dist. by* **IPG Chicago.**

Bloomsbury Publishing Plc (GBR) *(978-0-225; 978-0-245; 978-0-264; 978-0-333; 978-0-485; 978-0-510; 978-0-540; 978-0-567; 978-0-7136; 978-0-7475; 978-0-7478; 978-0-85045; 978-0-85177; 978-0-85263; 978-0-85314; 978-0-85496; 978-0-86292; 978-0-906515; 978-0-907582; 978-0-948230;-1-85399; 978-1-85532; 978-1-85973; 978-1-899791; 978-1-901362; 978-0-212; 978-0-85146; 978-0-85147; 978-0-85317; 978-0-86019; 978-0-946716; 978-0-9507160; 978-1-902579; 978-1-84113; 978-1-85691; 978-1-897737; 978-0-9506785; 978-1-873590; 978-1-84) Dist. by* **Consort Bk Sales.**

Bloomsbury Publishing Plc (GBR) *(978-0-225; 978-0-245; 978-0-264; 978-0-333; 978-0-485; 978-0-510; 978-0-540; 978-0-567; 978-0-7136; 978-0-7475; 978-0-7478; 978-0-85045; 978-0-85177; 978-0-85263; 978-0-85314; 978-0-85496; 978-0-86292; 978-0-906515; 978-0-907582; 978-0-948230;-1-85399; 978-1-85532; 978-1-85973; 978-1-899791; 978-1-901362; 978-0-212; 978-0-85146; 978-0-85147; 978-0-85317; 978-0-86019; 978-0-946716; 978-0-9507160; 978-1-902579; 978-1-84113; 978-1-85691; 978-1-897737; 978-0-9506785; 978-1-873590; 978-1-84) Dist. by* **Natl Bk Netwk.**

Bloomsbury Publishing Plc (GBR) *(978-0-225; 978-0-245; 978-0-264; 978-0-333; 978-0-485; 978-0-510; 978-0-540; 978-0-567; 978-0-7136; 978-0-7475; 978-0-7478; 978-0-85045; 978-0-85177; 978-0-85263; 978-0-85314; 978-0-85496; 978-0-86292; 978-0-906515; 978-0-907582; 978-0-948230;-1-85399; 978-1-85532; 978-1-85973; 978-1-899791; 978-1-901362; 978-0-212; 978-0-85146; 978-0-85147; 978-0-85317; 978-0-86019; 978-0-946716; 978-0-9507160; 978-1-902579; 978-1-84113; 978-1-85691; 978-1-897737; 978-0-9506785; 978-1-873590; 978-1-84) Dist. by* **Macmillan.**

Bloomsbury Publishing USA, *(978-1-58234; 978-1-59691; 978-1-59990; 978-1-60819; 978-1-84706; 978-1-61963; 978-1-62040; 978-1-62356; 978-1-62892; 978-1-63286; 978-1-5013; 978-1-68119; 978-1-63557; 978-1-5476)* Orders Addr.: 16365 James Madison Hwy., Gordonsville, VA 22942-8501 USA Tel 888-330-8477; Toll Free: 888-330-8477; Edit Addr.: 175 Fifth Ave., Suite 300, New York, NY 10010 USA Toll Free: 888-330-8477; 1385 Broadway, New York, NY 10018 Tel 212-419-5300; *Imprints:* Bloomsbury USA Childrens (Bloom Child); Bloomsbury USA (BloomsburyUSA); Alma Classics (AlmaClassics); Osprey (OspreyUSA); Bloomsbury Sport (BloomSport); Bloomsbury Activity Books (BloomActivity)
E-mail: bloomsbury.kids@bloomsburyusa.com; nathaniel.knaebel@bloomsbury.com; mike.o'connor@bloomsbury.com
Web site: http://www.bloomsburyusa.com
Dist(s): **Casemate Academic**
INscribe Digital
Macmillan
MyiLibrary
Penguin Random Hse. LLC
St. Martin's Pr.

Bloomsbury Sport *Imprint of* **Bloomsbury Publishing USA**

Bloomsbury USA *Imprint of* **Bloomsbury Publishing USA**

Bloomsbury USA Childrens *Imprint of* **Walker & Co.**

Bloomsbury USA Childrens *Imprint of* **Bloomsbury Publishing USA**

Bloomsbury Visual Arts *Imprint of* **BJU Pr.**

Blow's Innovation to Art - (BIA), *(978-0-9820772)* 8090 Atlantic Blvd, E-160, Jacksonville, FL 32211 USA Tel 904-469-1169 business number
E-mail: biabizz@aol.com; blows.art@gmail.com
Web site: http://www.myspace.com/biabizz1
Dist(s): **Lightning Source, Inc.**

BLPH, Inc., *(978-0-9759158; 978-0-9772425; 978-0-9791099)* P.O. Box 764, Springfield, OR 97477-0132 USA
E-mail: printing@bestlittleprinthouse.com
Web site: http://www.bestlittleprinthouse.com.

BLR Bks., *(978-0-9721839)* 94 Circle Dr., Waltham, MA 02452 USA
Dist(s): **Pathway Bk. Service.**

Blu Phi'er Publishing, LLC, *(978-0-9772034; 978-0-9799884; 978-0-9823845; 978-0-9858378)* 2400 W. Grand Ave., Marshall, TX 75670 USA Tel 903-935-4223
E-mail: phierstarter@bluphier.com
Web site: http://www.bluphier.com.

Blue Apple Bks., *(978-1-934706; 978-1-60905)* 515 Valley St., Suite 180, Maplewood, NJ 07040 USA (SAN 854-4727) Fax: 973-763-5944
E-mail: info@blueapplebooks.com
Web site: http://www.blueapplebooks.com
Dist(s): **Chronicle Bks. LLC**
Consortium Bk. Sales & Distribution
Hachette Bk. Group
Learning Connection, The
Penguin Random Hse. LLC
Random Hse., Inc.

Blue Bark Pr., *(978-0-615-18110-3)* 7 View South Ave., Jamaica Plain, MA 02130 USA Tel 617-840-3418.

Blue Barn, Inc., *(978-0-692-84662-9; 978-0-692-84810-4; 978-0-692-84855-5)* 4313 Bluebell Ave., STUDIO CITY, CA 91604 USA Tel 310-625-2837
E-mail: jeffwcrawford5+LVP0003368@gmail.com; jeffwcrawford5+LVP0003368@gmail.com.

Blue Bear Publishing *See* **Beach Front Bks.**

Blue Begonia Pr., *(978-0-911287)* 311 Hillcrest Dr, Selah, WA 98942 USA (SAN 268-3652) Tel 509-452-9748
E-mail: adpeters@charter.net
Web site: http://bluebegoniapress.com
Dist(s): **Partners/West Book Distributors.**

Blue Bike Bks. (CAN) *(978-0-9739116; 978-1-897278; 978-1-926700) Dist. by* **Lone Pine.**

Blue Blanket Publishing, *(978-0-9903623)* 16 Poland Spring Rd., Auburn, ME 04210 USA Tel 207-402-0954
E-mail: cjiadonisi@gmail.com.

Blue Bk. Pubns., Inc., *(978-0-9625943; 978-1-886768; 978-1-936120; 978-1-947314)* 8009 34th Ave. S., Suite 250, Minneapolis, MN 55425 USA (SAN 860-4452) Tel 952-854-5229; Fax: 952-853-1486; Toll Free: 800-877-4867 Do not confuse with Blue Book Pubs., Inc. in La Jolla, CA
E-mail: bluebook@bluebookinc.com; support@bluebookinc.com
Web site: http://www.bluebookinc.com
Dist(s): **Alfred Publishing Co., Inc.**
Follett School Solutions
Music Sales Corp.
Omnibus Pr.

Blue Botte, *(978-0-9896257)* 14907 W. Autumn Ln., Nine Mile Falls, WA 99026 USA Tel 509-465-4534
E-mail: willarda2z@msn.com.

Blue Boy Publishing Co., *(978-0-9742632)* P.O. Box 691, Camillus, NY 13031-0691 USA.

Blue Brush Media, *(978-0-9777382)* 851 Monroe Ave., NE, Renton, WA 98056 USA (SAN 850-0878) Tel 425-818-8850 Do not confuse with Dolphin Media LLC in Huntsville, AL
E-mail: kunle@mamaAfricana.com
Web site: http://www.bluebrushmedia.com
Dist(s): **Follett School Solutions**
NewLife Bk. Distributors.

Blue Cat (GBR) *(978-0-9559851) Dist. by* **LuluCom.**

Blue Cat Bks, *(978-0-9779763)* P.O. Box 2818, Covina, CA 91722 USA Tel 626-339-1223
E-mail: info@bluecatpublishers.com
Web site: http://bluecatpublishers.com.

Blue Chip Publishing, *(978-0-9673970)* Orders Addr.: P.O. Box 26657, Austin, TX 78755 USA Tel 512-345-3021; Fax: 512-345-0181; Edit Addr.: 4119 Circletree Loop, Austin, TX 78731 USA Do not confuse with Blue Chip Publishing Corp., Keizer, OR
E-mail: MAMA19@aol.com.

Blue Cove Publishing, *(978-1-945595)* P.O. Box 1828, Dunnellon, FL 34430 USA Tel 352-489-0436
E-mail: mbatesd@aol.com
Web site: www.bluecovepublishing.com.

Blue Crown Pr., *(978-0-615-52468-9; 978-0-9839308; 978-0-9855874; 978-1-68366-510-6)* P.O. Box 871826, Canton, MI 48187 USA Tel 734-905-0068
E-mail: author@emlynchand.com
Web site: www.novelpublicity.com.

Blue Cubicle Pr., LLC, *(978-0-9745900; 978-0-9827136; 978-1-938583)* P.O. Box 250382, Plano, TX 75025-0382 USA Tel 972-824-0646; *Imprints:* Castle Builder Press (Castle Builder)
Web site: http://www.bluecubiclepress.com.

Blue Devil Games, *(978-0-9763795)* P.O. Box 19359, Plantation, FL 33318 USA Tel 954-315-0920
Web site: http://www.bluedevilgames.com.

Blue Dolphin Publishing, Inc., *(978-0-931892; 978-1-57733)* Orders Addr.: P.O. Box 8, Nevada City, CA 95959 USA (SAN 223-2480) Tel 530-477-1503; Fax: 530-477-8342; Toll Free: 800-643-0765; Edit Addr.: 13340-d Grass Valley Ave., Grass Valley, CA 95945 USA (SAN 696-009X); *Imprints:* Papillon Publishing (Papillon Pubng)
E-mail: bdolphin@bluedolphinpublishing.com; clemens@bluedolphinpublishing.com
Web site: http://www.bluedolphinpublishing.com
Dist(s): **Follett School Solutions**
New Leaf Distributing Co., Inc.

Blue Dragon Publishing, *(978-0-9832454; 978-1-939696)* P.O. Box 247, Lightfoot, VA 23090 USA Tel 757-941-5007
E-mail: BlueDragonPub@cox.net
Web site: http://www.blue-dragon-publishing.com.

Blue Dream Studios, *(978-0-9789168)* 1133 Cedarview Ln., Franklin, TN 37067-4075 USA
Web site: http://www.bluedreamstudios.com
Dist(s): **Diamond Comic Distributors, Inc.**
Diamond Bk. Distributors
Diamond Distributors, Inc.

Blue Eagle Bks., Inc., *(978-0-9794655)* 5773 Woodway, PMB 190, Houston, TX 77057 USA Tel 713-789-1516 (phone/fax)
E-mail: sjones@blueeaglebooks.com
Web site: http://blueeaglebooks.com
Dist(s): **Independent Pubs. Group.**

Blue Earth Bks. *Imprint of* **Capstone Press of Coughlan Cos.**

Blue Eyed Mayhem Publishing, *(978-0-9794545)* 6 Hopemont Dr., Mount Laurel, NJ 08054 USA Tel 609-781-0291
Dist(s): **Smashwords.**

Blue Forge Pr., *(978-1-883573; 978-1-886383; 978-1-59092)* Div. of Blue Forge Group, Orders Addr.: 7419 Ebbert Dr., SE, Port Orchard, WA 98367 USA (SAN 299-1330) Tel 360-769-7174 phone
E-mail: blueforgepress@gmail.com
Web site: http://www.blueforgepress.com.

Blue Fox Pr., *(978-0-9763119)* Pierce Arrow Bldg., 1685 Elmwood Ave., Suite 315, Buffalo, NY 14207-2407 USA Tel 716-447-1590; Fax: 716-837-7066
E-mail: bluefoxpress@yahoo.com
Web site: http://www.bluefoxpress.com.

Blue Gate Bks., *(978-0-9792612)* P.O. Box 2137, Nevada City, CA 95959 USA (SAN 852-923X) Tel 530-263-4501
E-mail: babette@babettedonaldson.com; info@emmaleabooks.com
Web site: http://www.bluegatebooks.com; http://www.sidecarscooter.com; http://www.emmaleabooks.com; http://www.Fun-With-Tea.com.

Blue Horizon Publishing Co., *(978-0-9658786; 978-0-9955738-0-2)* 25012 S. Harmony Rd., Cheney, WA 99004-9798 USA Tel 509-235-8547.

Blue Horse Books *Imprint of* **Great Lakes Literary, LLC**

Blue Ink Pr., *(978-0-9817234)* 1246 Heart Ave., Amherst, OH 44001 USA Tel 440-823-8320
E-mail: dougk@icehorseadventures.com
Web site: http://www.icehorseadventures.com
Dist(s): **Blu Sky Media Group.**

Blue Jay Bks. *Imprint of* **Crooked River Pr.**

Blue Kitty, The, *(978-0-9796814)* P.O. Box 254, Syracuse, NY 13214 USA
E-mail: info@thebluekitty.com.

Blue Lantern Books *See* **Laughing Elephant**

Blue Lion Productions, Ltd, *(978-0-9761132)* 302 Smith St., Freeport, NY 11520 USA Tel 516-546-4611
E-mail: info@bluelionproductions.com
Web site: http://www.bluelionproductions.com.

Blue Lobster Pr., *(978-0-9709569)* Orders Addr.: 3919 Union St., Levant, ME 04456-4358 USA
E-mail: books@bluelobsterpress.com; poet@robertpottle.com
Web site: http://www.bluelobsterpress.com.

Blue Logic Publishing, *(978-0-9860669)* P.O. Box 797492, Dallas, TX 75379 USA Tel 972-380-1467
E-mail: contact@bluelogicpublishing.com
Web site: www.bluelogicpublishing.com.

Blue Lotus Wave, *(978-0-9789624)* Orders Addr.: 15 Surrey Dr., Riverside, CT 06878-1516 USA (SAN 852-0631) Tel 203-344-1344 Do not confuse with Blue Lotus Press in Palmyra, MA.

blue manatee children's Bookstore *See* **Blue Manatee Press**

Blue Manatee Press, *(978-1-936669)* 3054 Madison Rd., Cincinnati, OH 45209 USA (SAN 920-4601) Tel 513-731-2665
E-mail: press@bluemanateebooks.com; johnsandy@bluemanateebooks.com
Web site: www.bluemanateepress.com
Dist(s): **Independent Pubs. Group.**

Blue Marble Bks. *Imprint of* **Sphinx Publishing**

Blue Marlin Pubns., *(978-0-9674602; 978-0-9792918; 978-0-9885295)* 823 Aberdeen Rd., West Bay Shore, NY 11706 USA Tel 631-666-0353 (phone/fax)
E-mail: jude@bluemarlinpubs.com
Web site: http://www.BlueMarlinPubs.com
Dist(s): **Follett School Solutions.**

Blue Mountain Arts Inc., *(978-0-88396; 978-1-58786; 978-1-59842; 978-1-68088)* Orders Addr.: P.O. Box 4549, Boulder, CO 80306 USA (SAN 299-9609) Tel 303-449-0536; Fax: 303-417-6434; 303-417-6496; Toll Free Fax: 800-943-6666; 800-545-8573; Toll Free: 800-525-0642; *Imprints:* Blue Mountain Press (Blue Mntn Pr); Rabbit's Foot Press (Rabb Ft Pr)
Web site: http://www.sps.com/.

Blue Mountain Arts (R) by SPS Studios, Incorporated *See* **Blue Mountain Arts Inc.**

Blue Mountain Pr. *Imprint of* **Blue Mountain Arts Inc.**

Blue Mustang Pr., *(978-0-9759737; 978-1-935199)* 175B Mansfield Ave., Suite 240, Norton, MA 02766 USA Tel 206-350-2823 (phone/fax)
E-mail: info@bluemustangpress.com
Web site: http://www.bluemustangpress.com.

Blue Note Bks. *Imprint of* **Blue Note Pubns.**

Blue Note Pubns., *(978-1-878398; 978-0-9830758; 978-0-9855562; 978-0-9895563; 978-0-9903068; 978-0-9963066; 978-0-9977638)* Orders Addr.: 721 N.

For full information on wholesalers and distributors, refer to the Wholesaler and Distributor Name Index

Dr. Ste. D, Melbourne, FL 32934 USA Toll Free: 800-624-0401 (order number); *Imprints:* Blue Note Books (Blue Note Bks)
E-mail: bluenotepress@gmail.com
Web site: http://www.bluenotebooks.com.

Blue Owl Editions, *(978-0-9672793)* 6254 Girvin Dr., Oakland, CA 94611 USA Tel 510-482-3038 (phone/fax)
E-mail: edanti@ispwest.com; enricoanti@yahoo.com
Dist(s): **Smashwords.**

Blue Peach Publishing, *(978-0-615-15922-5)* 2 Wyeth Cir., Southborough, MA 01772 USA
Dist(s): **Lulu Pr., Inc.**

Blue Pig Productions, *(978-1-932545)* P.O. Box 691779, Orlando, FL 32869-1779 USA (SAN 255-4763) Tel 407-854-5679 (phone/fax)
E-mail: bluepigprod@aol.com
Web site: http://www.repunzal.com.

Blue Planet Press *See* **Ninth Planet Pr.**

Blue Portal Pr. LLC, *(978-0-9893963)* 2400 Wilderness Way, Marietta, GA 30066 USA Tel 404-372-1530
E-mail: red170@yahoo.com
Web site: http://blueportalpressllc.weebly.com/.

Blue Rider Pr. *Imprint of* **Penguin Publishing Group**

Blue River Pr., *(978-0-9718959; 978-0-9763361; 978-0-9799240; 978-0-9819289; 978-1-935628; 978-1-68157; 978-0-9963247)* Orders Addr.: 2402 N. Shadeland Ave., Suite A, Indianapolis, IN 46219 USA Tel 317-352-8200; Fax: 317-352-8202; Toll Free: 800-296-0481 Do not confuse with Blue River Press in Bloomingdale, IL
E-mail: tdoherty@cardinalpub.com
Web site: http://www.cardinalpub.com; www.brpressbooks.com
Dist(s): **Cardinal Pubs. Group**
MyiLibrary.

Blue Scarab Pr., *(978-0-937179)* Orders Addr.: 811 Normandie Blvd., Bowling Green, OH 43402 USA (SAN 658-4640) Tel 419-819-4506
E-mail: haraldwyndham@gmail.com.

Blue Scribbles Publishing, *(978-0-615-24897-4)* P.O. Box 2054, Centreville, VA 20120 USA
E-mail: bluescribbles@gmail.com
Web site: http://www.bluescribbles.com.

Blue Shoe Publishing, *(978-0-9725552)* c/o Christine Merser, 38 W. 74th St., 3A, New York, NY 10023 USA Tel 212-579-0310
E-mail: inquiry@blueshoestrategy.com; inquiry@blueshoepublishing.com; LLim@BlueShoeStrategy.com
Web site: http://www.blueshoepublishing.com.

Blue Shutter Bks., *(978-0-9729379)* Orders Addr.: 5125 Schultz Bridge Rd., Zionsville, PA 18092-2543 USA Tel 215-541-3362; Fax: 425-491-4282
E-mail: rworthington@blueshutterbooks.com
Web site: http://www.blueshutterbooks.com.

Blue Skies Above Texas Co., *(978-0-9800019)* 14781 Memorial Dr., No. 399, Houston, TX 77079 USA Tel 281-920-0043
E-mail: BlueSkiesAboveTexas@yahoo.com.

Blue Sky at Night Publishing, *(978-0-9768623)* 25679 360th Ave., Hillman, MN 56338-2431 USA
E-mail: Jill@JournalBuddies.com
Web site: http://www.JournalBuddies.com.

Blue Sky Daisies, *(978-0-9905529; 978-1-944435)* 1907 N. Valleyview, Wichita, KS 67212 USA Tel 316-573-9733
E-mail: blueskydaisies@gmail.com
Web site: www.blueskydaisies.wordpress.com.

Blue Sky Ink, *(978-1-59475)* P.O. Box 1067, Brentwood, TN 37024-1067 USA (SAN 255-7401) Tel 805-677-6815
Dist(s): **Send The Light Distribution LLC.**

Blue Sky Pr., The *Imprint of* **Scholastic, Inc.**

Blue Sky Pr., *(978-0-9746896)* P.O. Box 6192, Malibu, CA 90264-6192 USA Tel 818-706-9814; 557 Broadway., New York, NY 10012 Do not confuse with Blue Sky Press in San Jose CA, Placerville CO, Silver Spring MD, Berkeley CA, Dallas TX
E-mail: laura@lauralarsen.com
Web site: http://www.lauralarsen.com
Dist(s): **Follett School Solutions.**

Blue Socks Media LLC, *(978-0-692-80162-8; 978-0-692-80714-9)* 2108 S. Boulevard, Suite 108, Charlotte, NC 28203 USA Tel 704-562-4502
E-mail: tsteedman@raggs.com
Web site: http://www.raggs.com.

Blue State Pr., *(978-0-9773674)* 17771 Plumtree Ln., Yorba Linda, CA 92886 USA.

Blue Suit Bks., *(978-0-9748563)* P.O. Box 840057, New Orleans, LA 70184 USA (SAN 255-8998) Tel 504-450-4334
E-mail: bluesuit@imaginationmovers.com
Web site: http://www.imaginationmovers.com.

Blue Thistle Pr., *(978-0-9760505; 978-0-9786302)* 6187 FM 314, Ben Wheeler, TX 75754-4030 USA Tel 903-539-2500
E-mail: lkayers@hotmail.com
Web site: http://www.lindaayersbooks.com.

Blue Thunder Bks., *(978-0-9673000; 978-0-9839454)* 16717 Van Owens St., Lake Balboa, CA 91406 USA //Do not confuse with Blue Thunder Bks in Grand Rapids, MI
E-mail: d@savage1.com
Web site: http://SAVAGE1.com; http://www.CoolCatLovesYou.com.

Blue Thunder One, Inc., *(978-0-9719284)* P.O. Box 2435, Riverview, MI 48192 USA.

Blue Tie Publishing, *(978-0-9777972)* 1 Hale Rd., East Hampton, CT 06424 USA Tel 860-267-0432
E-mail: tanner@sbcglobal.net.

Blue Tiger Publishing, *(978-0-9759903)* P.O. Box 3776, Glendale, CA 91221-0776 USA Tel 310-497-9291
E-mail: travis_english@charter.net.

Blue Tree LLC, *(978-0-9711321; 978-0-9792014; 978-0-9802245; 978-0-9893088)* Orders Addr.: P.O. Box 148, Portsmouth, NH 03802 USA Tel 603-436-0831; Fax: 603-686-5054
E-mail: contact@thebluetree.com
Web site: http://www.thebluetree.com.

Blue Unicorn Edition, LLC, *(978-1-891355; 978-1-58396)* 12300 NW 56th Ave., Gainesville, FL 32653 USA Toll Free Fax: 866-334-1497 (orders)
E-mail: tienda1@instabook.net
Web site: http://www.instabookpublisher.com.

Blue Vase Productions, *(978-0-9770125)* 2455 Otay Ctr. Dr. Apt 118 Ste 252, San Diego, CA 92154 USA (SAN 257-4454) Fax: 619-819-6311
E-mail: legal@eljarronazul.com; ventas@eljarronazul.com
Web site: http://www.eljarronazul.com.

Blue Water Pr., LLC, *(978-0-9796046)* 8814 Sir Barton Ln., Waxhaw, NC 28173 USA Tel 704-551-9051
E-mail: Tonibranner@aol.com; jmacgregor@cadencemarketinggroup.com.

Blue Water Publishing, *(978-0-9796160)* 805 N. Orange Ave., Fallbrook, CA 92028-1525 USA
E-mail: bluewaterpub@sbcglobal.net.

Blue Willow Pr., *(978-0-9767473)* 197 Lamplight Ln., Bozeman, MT 59718 USA Tel 406-388-0272; Fax: 423-318-2329
E-mail: bluewillowpress@yahoo.com; obachs@juno.com
Web site: http://www.bluewillowpress.com
Dist(s): **Canyonlands Pubns.**

Blue Wing Pubns., Workshops & Lectures, *(978-0-9795663; 978-0-692-73942-6)* 11985 N. Cayce Ln, Casa Grande, AZ 85194 USA Toll Free: 877-591-4156
E-mail: sdk@bluewingworkshops.com
Web site: http://www.bluewingworkshops.com
Dist(s): **CreateSpace Independent Publishing Platform.**

Blue Zebra Entertainment, Incorporated *See* **Murphey, Hiromi**

Blueberry Illustrations, *(978-0-692-75274-6)* 104 Overlook Bend, Kingsland, GA 31548 USA Tel 912-409-7343
E-mail: SLCarrollauthor@gmail.com.

Bluebonnets, Boots & Bks. Pr., *(978-0-9645493; 978-0-9800061)* 11010 Hanning Ln., Houston, TX 77041-5006 USA; P.O. Box 19632, Houston, TX 77224-9632
E-mail: rita@bookconnectiononline.com
Web site: http://www.ABCsPress.com
Dist(s): **Complete Book & Media Supply**
Follett School Solutions
News Group
Partners Pubs. Group, Inc.

Bluechip Publishers *See* **BlueChip Pubs.**

BlueChip Pubs., *(978-0-930251)* Orders Addr.: P.O. Box 4204, Jackson, WY 83001 USA
E-mail: info@bluechippublishers.com
Dist(s): **Lightning Source, Inc.**

BlueCougar Studios, *(978-0-615-16770-1; 978-0-615-17434-1)* 3805 Grandview Ave., NW No. 4, Roanoke, VA 24012 USA
E-mail: info@bluecougarsrufios.com
Dist(s): **Lulu Pr., Inc.**

Bluedoor, llc, *(978-1-59984; 978-1-68135)* 10949 Bren Rd., E., Minneapolis, MN 55343 USA Tel 952-934-1624; Fax: 952-934-4269; Toll Free: 800-979-1624
E-mail: mary@bluedoorpublishing.com
Web site: http://bluedoorpublishing.com.

Bluefire *Imprint of* **Random Hse. Children's Bks.**

Bluefish River Pr., *(978-0-9714701)* P.O. Box 1398, Duxbury, MA 02332 USA
E-mail: dpallai@bluefishriverpress.com
Web site: http://www.bluefishriverpress.com.

BlueLine Book Publishers *See* **Great American Pubs.**

Blueline Publishing, *(978-0-9776906)* P.O. Box 11569, Denver, CO 80211 USA (SAN 856-2539) Tel 303-477-5272; Fax: 866-876-2915
Web site: http://www.bluelinepub.com
Dist(s): **Follett School Solutions.**

BlueMoonGreenLake, *(978-0-9968237)* 700 N. Colorado Blvd, Denver, CO 80206 USA Tel 303-548-8507
E-mail: Kellymcondon66@gmail.com
Web site: www.BlueMoonGreenLake.com.

BlueSky Publishing, *(978-0-9724386)* Div. of BlueSky Medical Group, Inc., 6965 El Camino Real Suite 105-602, Carlsbad, CA 92009 USA Tel 760-603-8130; 760-603-8331 (phone/fax)
E-mail: publishingdivision@blueskymedical.com
Web site: http://www.boypresident.com.

Bluestocking Pr., *(978-0-942617)* Orders Addr.: P.O. Box 1014, Placerville, CA 95667 USA (SAN 667-2981) Tel 530-622-8586; Fax: 530-642-9222; Toll Free: 800-959-8586 (orders); Edit Addr.: 3333 Gold Country Dr., El Dorado, CA 95623 USA (SAN 667-299X)
E-mail: customerservice@bluestockingpress.com
Web site: http://www.bluestockingpress.com.

Bluestone Bks., *(978-0-9720046)* P.O. Box 761, Edmonds, WA 98020 USA
Web site: http://www.cmc.net/~jlwrig.

Bluewater Productions, Inc., *(978-0-9792751)* 2950 Newmarket Pl., Suite 101, Bellingham, WA 98226 USA Tel 360-778-1033
Web site: http://www.bluewaterprod.com/
Dist(s): **Diamond Comic Distributors, Inc.**
Diamond Bk. Distributors
MyiLibrary
SCB Distributors.

Bluewater Pubns., *(978-0-9719946; 978-1-934610)* 1812 CR 111, Killen, AL 35645 USA Tel 256-349-6087 Do not confuse with Heart Of Dixie Publishing Corporation in Foley, AL
E-mail: malcolm.broyles@gmail.com
Web site: www.bluewaterpublications.com
Dist(s): **Follett School Solutions.**

Bluewood Bks., *(978-0-912517)* Div. of The Siyeh Group, Inc., P.O. Box 689, San Mateo, CA 94010 USA (SAN 265-3214) Tel 650-548-0754; Fax: 650-548-0654
E-mail: Bluewoodb@aol.com
Dist(s): **Follett School Solutions**
L P C Group
SCB Distributors.

Bluffton Bks., *(978-0-89986; 978-0-9702635)* Orders Addr.: 714b Kodiak Trail, Cedar Park, TX 78613 USA
E-mail: ethno777@mac.com.

Blume (ESP) *(978-84-89396; 978-84-932442; 978-84-95939; 978-84-9801) Dist. by* **IPG Chicago.**

Blumont Company, The, *(978-0-9776024)* 161 Great Rd., Littleton, MA 01460 USA (SAN 257-702X) Tel 781-899-6468
E-mail: slblu@netway.com.

Blurb, Inc., *(978-1-4579; 978-1-320; 978-1-5184; 978-1-364; 978-1-366; 978-1-367; 978-1-388; 978-1-389)* Orders Addr.: 580 California St. #300, San Francisco, CA 94104 USA (SAN 860-0813)
E-mail: jcarlton@blurb.com; msiemers@blurb.com
Web site: http://www.blurb.com
Dist(s): **Lulu Pr., Inc.**

Blushing Rose Publishing, *(978-1-884807)* Orders Addr.: P.O. Box 2238, San Anselmo, CA 94979-2238 USA Tel 415-407-0170 Toll Free: 800-898-2263
E-mail: nancya555@yahoo.com
Web site: http://www.blushingrose.com.

BMC Advertising, Incorporated *See* **BMCFerrell**

BMCFerrell, *(978-0-9764460; 978-0-9788242)* 6450 S. Lewis Ave. Ste. 300, Tulsa, OK 74136-1068 USA
Web site: http://www.bmcferrell.com.

BMG, Incorporated *See* **RPM Publishing**

BMI Educational Services, *(978-0-922443; 978-1-60684; 978-1-60933; 978-1-63071; 978-1-5367)* Orders Addr.: 26 Haypress Rd., Cranbury, NJ 08512 USA (SAN 760-7032); Edit Addr.: P.O. Box 800, Dayton, NJ 08810-0800 USA (SAN 169-4669) Tel 732-329-6991; Fax: 732-329-6994; Toll Free Fax: 800-986-9393 (orders only); Toll Free: 800-222-8100 (orders only)
E-mail: info@bmionline.com
Web site: http://www.bmionline.com/.

BN Publishing, *(978-1-68411)* 3503 Jack Northrup Ave., Ste. # Z2741, Hawthorne, CA 90250 USA
E-mail: info@bnpublishing.com
Web site: http://www.bnpublishing.com.

Boarding House Publishing, *(978-0-9725365; 978-0-9774432)* 3896 Miramonte Ave., Loveland, CO 80538 USA
Web site: http://www.rdeducation.home.att.net.

Boathouse Press *See* **BoathouseBooks**

BoathouseBooks, *(978-0-9776469)* P.O. Box 244, Tiburon, CA 94920 USA
Web site: http://boathousebooks.com
Dist(s): **Follett School Solutions.**

Bob Thomas Bks., *(978-0-9717682)* Orders Addr.: P.O. Box 853, Black Mountain, NC 28711 USA; Edit Addr.: P.O. Box 815, Kure Beach, NC 28449 USA Toll Free Fax: 866-615-0417.

Bobcat Publishing, *(978-0-9776419)* 5105 Cascabel Rd., Atascadero, CA 93422 USA (SAN 852-9051)
E-mail: llyn@llynsplace.com; llyntroy@sbcglobal.net
Web site: http://www.llynsplace.com.

Bobrich Publishing *See* **Wollaston Pr.**

Boca Raton Museum of Art, *(978-0-936859)* 501 Plaza Real, Mizner Park, Boca Raton, FL 33432 USA (SAN 278-2251) Tel 561-392-2500; Fax: 561-391-6410
E-mail: jkaminski@bocamuseum.org; iford@bocamuseum.org
Web site: http://www.bocamuseum.org
Dist(s): **Antique Collectors' Club**
RAM Pubns. & Distribution.

BoCook Publishing, *(978-0-9848791)* 12702 SE 222nd Dr., Damascus, OR 97089 USA Tel 503-853-1362
E-mail: janet_l_carlson@yahoo.com
Dist(s): **Bookmasters Distribution.**

Bodkin Pointe Pr., *(978-0-9752684)* Orders Addr.: P.O. Box 654, Gibson Island, MD 21056 USA; 116 Tim Mara Dr., Jupiter, FL 33477 Tel 561-629-2528
E-mail: cathy@bodkinpointepress.com
Web site: http://www.bodkinpointepress.com.

Bodleian Library (GBR) *(978-1-85124; 978-0-900177) Dist. by* **Chicago Distribution Ctr.**

Body & Mind Productions, Inc., *(978-0-9742569; 978-0-9752648; 978-0-9771609; 978-0-9792177; 978-0-9820889; 978-0-9828370; 978-0-9830885; 978-0-9855550; 978-0-9904468)* 9429 Cedar Heights Ave., Las Vegas, NV 89134-0194 USA Tel 949-263-4676
E-mail: bodymindheal@aol.com
Web site: http://www.healingreiki.com
Dist(s): **Follett School Solutions**
New Leaf Distributing Co., Inc.
Quality Bks., Inc.

Body Tone Multimedia, *(978-0-9760650)* P.O. Box 580691, Elk Grove, CA 95758-0012 USA
E-mail: body_tone_multimedia@mac.com
Web site: http://www.bodytonemultimedia.com.

Bodycrafting Systems, Inc., *(978-0-9745265)* Orders Addr.: P.O. Box 1512, Nokomis, FL 34274 USA Fax: 941-484-9650
Web site: http://www.kidpowerfitness.com.

BodyLife Publishers *See* **Windblown Media**

Boettcher, Ashley L., *(978-0-9768123)* Orders Addr.: P.O. Box 997, Southwick, MA 01077-0997 USA (SAN 256-5811) Tel 413-569-9492 available from 10am to 5pm m-f and 11am to 4pm sat; Edit Addr.: 45 Powder Mill Rd., Southwick, MA 01077 USA
E-mail: ljabphil413@juno.com
Web site: http://www.ALBbooks.com.

Bohemian Trash Studios, *(978-0-9767540)* 3322 Clearview, San Angelo, TX 76904 USA Tel 325-944-3282; *Imprints:* Star Cross'd Destiny (Star Cross)
Web site: http://www.bohemiantrash.com.

Bohobza Music, *(978-0-9744943)* P.O. Box 745, Teaneck, NJ 07666-0745 USA Tel 201-862-1692 (phone/fax)
E-mail: wetalkjazz@aol.com
Web site: http://www.ronibenhur.com.

Bois Pubns., *(978-0-9727967; 978-0-9971403)* 5411 Colfax Pl., Oklahoma City, OK 73112 USA Tel 405-947-7988 Evening; 405-713-4757 Daytime
E-mail: au444@cox.net; athomas14@cox.net
Web site: http://au4444.blogspot.com/.

Boland, Janie M., *(978-0-692-78147-0; 978-0-692-83475-6; 978-0-692-86491-3; 978-0-692-93936-9)* 4128 Abbott Dr., BAKERSFIELD, CA 93312 USA Tel 559-936-9838.

†**Bolchazy-Carducci Pubs.,** *(978-0-86516; 978-1-61041)* 1570 Baskin Rd., Mundelein, IL 60060-4474 USA (SAN 219-7685) Toll Free: 800-392-6453
E-mail: jcull@bolchazy.com
Web site: http://www.bolchazy.com
Dist(s): **Follett School Solutions**
MyiLibrary; *CIP.*

Bold Strokes Bks., *(978-1-933110; 978-1-60282; 978-1-62639; 978-1-63555)* Orders Addr.: 430 Herrington Rd., Johnsonville, NY 12094 USA Tel 518-753-6642; Fax: 518-753-6648
E-mail: bsb@boldstrokesbooks.com; publisher@boldstrokesbooks.com
Web site: http://www.boldstrokesbooks.com
Dist(s): **Abraham Assocs. Inc.**
Bella Distribution
Bookazine Co., Inc.
Two Rivers Distribution.

Bold Venture Pr., *(978-0-9712246)* 2726 NW 104th Avenue, No. 105, Sunrise, FL 33322 USA Tel 609-346-4184
E-mail: boldventurepress@aol.com
Web site: http://www.boldventurepress.com.

Bollix Bks., *(978-1-932188)* 1609 W. Callender Ave., Peoria, IL 61606 USA
E-mail: staley.krause@insightbb.com
Web site: http://www.bollixbooks.com
Dist(s): **Follett School Solutions**
PSI (Publisher Services, Inc.).

Bollywood Groove, *(978-1-945792)* 1304 N Wood St., Unit 1, Chicago, IL 60622 USA Tel 312-772-6559
E-mail: info@bollygroove.com.

Bolt *Imprint of* **Black Rabbit Bks.**

Bolton Publishing LLC, *(978-0-9855312)* Orders Addr.: 7255 N. US Hwy. 377, Rochelle, TX 76872-3019 USA
E-mail: ghbolton51@gmail.com.

Bon Tiki Bks., *(978-0-9747072)* 8100 Thomas Dr., Panama City Beach, FL 32408 USA
E-mail: bontiki@knology.net
Web site: http://www.sparkythorne.com.

Bondcliff Bks., *(978-0-9657475; 978-1-931271)* Orders Addr.: P.O. Box 385, Littleton, NH 03561 USA Toll Free: 800-859-7581; Edit Addr.: 8 Bluejay Ln., Littleton, NH 03561 USA
E-mail: bondclif@ncia.net
Dist(s): **Peregrine Outfitters.**

Bongiorno Bks., *(978-0-9715819)* P.O. Box 83-2345, Richardson, TX 75083 USA Tel 972-671-6117; Fax: 972-671-0601
E-mail: info@bongiornobooks.com
Web site: http://www.tangledhearts.com; http://www.bongiornobooks.com
Dist(s): **Nonetheless Pr.**

Bongo Comics Group *Imprint of* **Bongo Entertainment, Inc.**

Bongo Entertainment, Inc., *(978-0-9642999; 978-1-892849; 978-1-940293)* 1440 S. Sepulveda, 3rd Flr., Los Angeles, CA 90025 USA Tel 310-966-6168; Fax: 310-966-6181; *Imprints:* Bongo Comics Group (Bongo Comics Grp).

Bonita and Hodge Publishing Group, *(978-0-9838935)* 2701 Waterford Cir., Nashville, TN 37221 USA; *Imprints:* Seraphina (Seraphina)
E-mail: bandhpublishing@gmail.com; booknerd436@gmail.com; sheliawritesbooks@yahoo.com.

Bonita & Hodge Publishing Group *See* **Bonita and Hodge Publishing Group**

Bonne Amie Publishing *See* **Chantilly Books**

Bonner, Larry, *(978-0-9747855)* 305 Chapwith Rd., Garner, NC 27529-4882 USA
Web site: http://www.bigrawhidebutte.com.

Bonneville Bks. *Imprint of* **Cedar Fort, Inc./CFI Distribution**

Bonneville B.V. (NLD) *(978-90-73304) Dist. by* **CFI Dist.**

Bonnier Publishing (GBR) *(978-1-78576) Dist. by* **IPG Chicago.**

Bonus Bks., Inc., *(978-0-929387; 978-0-931028; 978-0-933893; 978-1-56625)* 875 N. Michigan Ave., Suite 1416, Chicago, IL 60611 USA (SAN 630-0804) Tel 312-467-0580; Fax: 312-467-9271
E-mail: amanda@bonusbooks.com
Web site: http://www.bonusbooks.com
Dist(s): **National Bk. Network**
Send The Light Distribution LLC.

Boo Bks., Inc., *(978-1-887864)* 7628 S. Paulina, Chicago, IL 60620 USA Tel 312-873-1584; Toll Free: 800-205-1140.

Booger Red's Bks., Inc., *(978-0-9650751)* P.O. Drawer G, Clifton, CO 81520 USA Tel 970-434-4140
E-mail: booger-gj@att.net.

Bk. Bench, The, *(978-1-891142)* 617 Herschler Ave., Evanston, WY 82930 USA Tel 307-789-3642
E-mail: atterol@allwest.net.

Bk. Club of America, *(978-1-59384)* 1812 Front St., Scotch Plains, NJ 07076-1103 USA (SAN 255-3279) Do not confuse with Book Club of America in Mechanicsburg, PA
E-mail: dcarey@bookclubusa.com.

Bk. Club of California, The, *(978-0-9819597)* 312 Sutter St., Suite 500, San Francisco, CA 94108 USA.

Book Co. Publishing Pty, Ltd., The (AUS) *(978-1-74047; 978-1-86309; 978-1-74202) Dist. by* **Penton Overseas.**

Book Couple LLC, The, *(978-0-9908458)* 21161 Via Ventura, BOCA RATON, FL 33433 USA Tel 561-218-4237
E-mail: gary@thebookcouple.com
Web site: www.thebookcouple.com.

Bk. Ends, *(978-0-9677817)* 2001 N. Halsted St. Ste. 201, Chicago, IL 60614-4365 USA
E-mail: sacredflight@yahoo.com
Web site: http://www.sacredflight.com
Dist(s): **Independent Pubs. Group.**

Bk. Garden Publishing, *(978-0-9818614)* Orders Addr.: 147 Roesch Ave., Oreland, PA 19075 USA
E-mail: JDHoliday51@gmail.com; JDHoliday51@outlook.com; jangen51@verizon.net
Web site: http://jdholiday.blogspot.com; https://www.barnesandnoble.com/s/%22J.D.+Holiday%22?_requestid=793356; http://jdswritersblog.blogspot.com.

Book Guild, Ltd. (GBR) *(978-1-85776; 978-0-86332; 978-1-84624; 978-1-909716)* *Dist. by* **Trans-Atl Phila.**

Book Her Publications *Imprint of* **Lyrically Korrect Publishing**

Book Hse. (GBR) *(978-1-904194; 978-1-904642; 978-1-905087; 978-1-906714; 978-1-907184; 978-1-910184; 978-1-911242)* *Dist. by* **Sterling.**

Book Hse. (GBR) *(978-1-904194; 978-1-904642; 978-1-905087; 978-1-906714; 978-1-907184; 978-1-910184; 978-1-911242)* *Dist. by* **Black Rab.**

Book Jungle *Imprint of* **Standard Pubns., Inc.**

Bk. Nook Productions, *(978-0-9748990)* P.O. Box 101, Richmond, TX 77406 USA Tel 832-721-7655
E-mail: stephiemara@aol.com
Dist(s): **Follett School Solutions.**

Book of Hope International *See* **OneHope**

Bk. of Signs Foundation, *(978-0-9773009)* 444 E. Roosevelt Rd., Suite 173, Lombard, IL 60148 USA Tel 630-914-5015.

Book Peddlers, *(978-0-916773; 978-1-931863)* 2828 Hedberg Dr., Hopkins, MN 55305-3403 USA (SAN 653-9548) Toll Free: 800-255-3379
E-mail: vlansky@bookpeddlers.com
Web site: http://www.practicalparenting.com; http://www.bookpeddlers.com
Dist(s): **Gryphon Hse., Inc.**
MyiLibrary
Publishers Group West (PGW)
Skandisk, Inc.

Book Pubs. Network, *(978-1-887542; 978-0-9755407; 978-1-935359; 978-1-937454; 978-1-940598; 978-1-945271)* P.O. Box 2256, Bothell, WA 98041 USA Tel 425-483-3040; Fax: 425-483-3098; 27 W. 20th St., New York, NY 10011
E-mail: sherynhara@earthlink.net
Web site: http://www.bookpublishersnetwork.com
Dist(s): **BookBaby**
Danforth Bk. Distribution
Epicenter Pr., Inc.
Follett School Solutions
Greenleaf Book Group
Midpoint Trade Bks., Inc.
MyiLibrary
Partners Bk. Distributing, Inc.
Smashwords.

Bk. Pubs. of El Paso, *(978-0-944551; 978-0-9836455; 978-0-9916296; 978-0-9979247; 978-0-9992117)* a/o Book Publishers of El Paso, 2200 San Jose Ave., El Paso, TX 79930 USA Tel 915-778-6670 (phone/fax) Do not confuse with Sundance Pr., Glen Carbon, IL
E-mail: bpep2@sbcglobal.net
Web site: bookpublishersofelpaso.com.

†Book Publishing Co., *(978-0-913990; 978-1-57067; 978-0-9669317; 978-0-9673108; 978-0-9779183; 978-1-939053)* P.O. Box 99, Summertown, TN 38483 USA (SAN 202-439X) Tel 931-964-3571; Fax: 931-964-3518; Toll Free: 888-260-8458; *Imprints:* Native Voices (Native Voices); 7th Generation (SeventhGen)
E-mail: info@bookpubco.com
Web site: http://www.bookpubco.com
Dist(s): **CreateSpace Independent Publishing Platform**
Follett School Solutions
Four Winds Trading Co.
Integral Yoga Pubns.
New Leaf Distributing Co., Inc.
Nutri-Bks. Corp.
Orca Bk. Pubs. USA
Partners Bk. Distributing, Inc.
Rio Nuevo Pubs.
Smashwords; *CIP.*

Book Sales, Inc., *(978-0-7628; 978-0-7858; 978-0-89009; 978-1-55521; 978-1-57715; 978-1-4161)* Orders Addr.: 400 1st Ave N. Ste. 300, Minneapolis, MN 55401-1721 USA (SAN 169-488X) Toll Free: 800-526-7257; Edit Addr.: 276 Fifth Ave., Suite 206, New York, NY 10001 USA (SAN 299-4062) Tel 212-779-4972; Fax: 212-779-6058; *Imprints:* Chartwell (Chrtwell); Wellfleet (Wellfleet); Knickerbocker Press (Knickerbock)
E-mail: sales@booksalesusa.com
Web site: http://www.booksalesusa.com/
Dist(s): **Continental Bk. Co., Inc.**
Hachette Bk. Group
MyiLibrary.

Bk. Shelf, *(978-0-9714160; 978-0-9913845)* Orders Addr.: P.O. Box 320804, Fairfield, CT 06825 USA Tel 203-257-0158
E-mail: service@bookshelf123.com; michellespraybooks@gmail.com
Web site: http://www.bookshelf123.com; http://www.myabcsbook.com/; http://www.havingscoliosis.com/.

Book Shop, Ltd., The, *(978-1-936199)* 35 E. 9th St., No. 74, New York, NY 10003 USA Tel 917-388-2493; Fax: 917-534-1304
E-mail: nancy@thebookshopltd.com
Web site: http://thebookshopltd.com.

Bk. Stops Here, *(978-0-9631612)* 1108 Rocky Point Ct., NE, Albuquerque, NM 87123 USA Tel 505-296-9047 (phone/fax)
E-mail: gldjvb@home.com
Web site: http://www.bookstopshere.com.

Book Web Publishing, Limited, *(978-0-9716567; 978-0-9795733)* P.O. Box 81, Bellmore, NY 11710 USA
E-mail: jeri@jerifink.com; donna@bookwebpublishing.com
Web site: http://www.bookwebpublishing.com.

Book Wholesalers, Inc., *(978-0-7587; 978-1-4046; 978-1-4131; 978-1-4155; 978-1-4156; 978-1-4287)* 1847 Mercer Rd., Lexington, KY 40511-1001 USA (SAN 135-5449) Toll Free: 800-888-4478
E-mail: jcamco@bwibooks.com; lison@bwibooks.com
Web site: http://www.bwibooks.com
Dist(s): **Follett School Solutions.**

Bookaroos Publishing, Inc., *(978-0-9678167)* Orders Addr.: P.O. Box 8518, Fayetteville, AR 72703 USA Tel 479-443-0339; Fax: 479-443-0339; Edit Addr.: 484 E. Pharris Dr., Fayetteville, AR 72703 USA
E-mail: books@bookaroos.com; tammybronson@bookaroos.com
Web site: http://www.bookaroos.com; http://www.seahorserun.com; http://www.tammybronson.com; http://www.tinysnail.com
Dist(s): **Follett School Solutions.**

Bookateer Publishing, *(978-0-9819368; 978-1-936476)* 4 Park Ave., Uncasville, CT 06382 USA
E-mail: mj@denicalisdragonchronicles.com; grizlegirl@sbcglobal.net
Web site: www.grizlegirlproductions.com; www.bookateerpublishing.com; www.denicalisdragonchronicles.com
Dist(s): **Smashwords.**

Bk.Baby Print, *(978-1-61927; 978-1-63192; 978-1-943612; 978-1-68222)* 7905 N. Rt. 130, Pennsauken, NJ 08034 USA Toll Free: 877-961-6878
E-mail: jfoley1@discmakers.com; support@print.bookbaby.com
Web site: bookbaby.com; http://www.print.bookbaby.com
Dist(s): **BookBaby**
Independent Pubs. Group.

Bookblast Marketing *See* **BookBlastPRO Inc.**

BookBlastPRO Inc., *(978-1-946854; 978-1-947352; 978-1-64133)* 25220 Hancock Ave. No. 300, Murrieta, CA 92592 USA Tel 951-365-5313
E-mail: postprod@bookblastpro.com
Web site: http://bookblastpro.com/.

BookBound Publishing, *(978-1-932367)* Orders Addr.: 26500 W. Agoura Rd., Suite 102-593, Calabasas, CA 91302 USA (SAN 256-3177) Toll Free: 866-985-2665
E-mail: stacyquest@bookbound.net
Web site: http://www.bookbound.net; http://bookboundpublishing.com.

BookChamp LLC., *(978-0-9760111)* c/o Winter & Company P.C, 605 King Georges Post Rd., Fords, NJ 08863 USA
E-mail: info@bookchamp.net
Web site: http://www.bookchamp.net
Dist(s): **Chicago Review Pr., Inc.**
Independent Pubs. Group.

Bookcraft, Inc. *Imprint of* **Deseret Bk. Co.**

BookCrafters, *(978-0-9845194; 978-0-9832819; 978-0-9837470; 978-1-937862; 978-1-943650)* Orders Addr.: 12056 Ridgeview Ln., Parker, CO 80138-7141 USA (SAN 859-6352) Tel 720-851-0397
E-mail: bookcrafterscolorado@gmail.com
Web site: http://bookcrafters.net
Dist(s): **Advocate Distribution Solutions**
BookPartners, Inc.
Lightning Source, Inc.
Send The Light Distribution LLC
Smashwords.

Bookends Pr., *(978-0-9724926; 978-0-9740922; 978-1-932667; 978-1-938315)* Orders Addr.: 4130 NW 16th Blvd., Gainesville, FL 32604 USA Fax: 352-373-6905; Toll Free: 800-881-3208; P.O. Box 14513, Gainsville, FL 32604
E-mail: copyright@renaissance-printing.com
Web site: http://www.bookendspress.com
Dist(s): **Freeman Family Ministries**
Rosewood Foundation, The
StarCrossed Productions
Truth Pubns.

Booker Lane Press *See* **Punta Gorda Pr.**

BOOKGEMSFORKIDS, *(978-0-9763596)* 111 Primrose Ln., Wyomissing, PA 19610 USA
E-mail: sukumar@idreampublications.com
Web site: http://www.idreampublications.com.

BookLight Pr., *(978-0-9841307; 978-0-615-73688-4)* Orders Addr.: 5994 S. Holly St. #118, Greenwood Village, CO 80111 USA (SAN 858-5164) Tel 303-916-8124; Edit Addr.: P.O. Box 380161, Cambridge, MA 02139-0161 USA
E-mail: jmarsh@booklightpress.com
Web site: www.booklightpress.com
Dist(s): **Follett School Solutions.**

Booklines Hawaii, Ltd., *(978-1-929844; 978-1-58849; 978-1-60274)* Div. of Islander Group, 269 Pali'i St., Mililani, HI 96789 USA (SAN 630-6624) Tel 808-676-0116; Fax: 808-676-0634
E-mail: customerservice@booklines.com
Web site: http://www.booklineshawaii.com
Dist(s): **Follett School Solutions**
Islander Group.

Booklocker.com, Inc., *(978-1-929072; 978-1-931391; 978-1-59113; 978-1-60145; 978-1-60910; 978-1-61434; 978-1-62141; 978-1-62646; 978-1-63263; 978-1-63490; 978-1-63491; 978-1-63492)* 200 2nd Ave. S. #526, Saint Petersburg, FL 33701 USA (SAN 254-363X) Fax: 305-768-0261
E-mail: booklocker@booklocker.com; angela@writersweekly.com
Web site: http://www.booklocker.com; http://www.writersweekly.com.

BookLogix, *(978-0-615-18278-0; 978-0-615-18390-9; 978-0-615-25890-4; 978-1-61005; 978-1-63183; 978-0-9978038)* 1264 Old Alpharetta Rd., Alpharetta, GA 30005 USA (SAN 860-0376) Tel 770-346-9979; Fax: 888-564-7890
E-mail: Angela@booklogix.com; Ahmad@booklogix.com
Web site: http://www.booklogix.com.

Booklogix Publishing Services *See* **BookLogix**

BookMann Pr. *Imprint of* **Mann Publishing Group**

Bookmark Bks., LLC, *(978-0-9764163)* P.O. Box 2996, Chester, VA 23831 USA Tel 804-706-6399 (phone/fax)
E-mail: bookmarkbooks@verizon.net.

Bookmark, The, *(978-0-930227)* Orders Addr.: 29021 Ave. Sherman, Unit 109, Santa Clarita, CA 91355 USA (SAN 694-6410) Tel 661-294-8022; Fax: 661-294-8027; Toll Free: 800-220-7767 Do not confuse with other companies with the same name in Marietta, GA, Knightstown, IN
E-mail: thebookmark@earthlink.net
Web site: http://www.thebookmark.com.

Bookmasters Distribution, Div. of BookMasters, Inc., Orders Addr.: 30 Amberwood Pkwy., Ashland, OH 44805 USA (SAN 631-936X) Fax: 419-281-6883; Toll Free: 800-247-6553; 800-537-6727; 800-266-5564
E-mail: orders@atlasbooks.com
Web site: http://www.bookmasters.com/.

Bookmates *Imprint of* **Penny Laine Papers, Inc.**

BookMobile *See* **Syren Bk. Co.**

BookPartners, LLC, *(978-1-936495)* 725 3rd St. P.O. Box 790, Cedar Key, FL 32625-0790 USA Tel 352-543-9307; Fax: 603-375-5373
E-mail: jpdwyer@dwyerogrady.com
Web site: www.bookpartners.org.

BookPatch LLC, The, *(978-1-62030; 978-1-63318; 978-1-68273; 978-1-946447; 978-1-946634; 978-1-946812; 978-1-946982; 978-1-947136; 978-1-947289; 978-1-947519; 978-1-947778; 978-1-947962)* 4400 N. Scottsdale Rd., Scottsdale, AZ 85251 USA Tel 602-403-5600
E-mail: victor@thebookpatch.com
Web site: http://www.thebookpatch.com
Dist(s): **BookBaby**
Lightning Source, Inc.
Lulu Pr., Inc.

BookPatch.com, The *See* **BookPatch LLC, The**

Bookpublisher.com *See* **Wheatmark, Inc.**

Bks. Are Fun, Ltd., *(978-0-9649777; 978-1-58209; 978-1-890409; 978-1-59795; 978-1-60626)* 1 Readers Digest Rd., Pleasantville, NY 10570-7000 USA
E-mail: msmall@booksarefun.com
Web site: http://www.booksarefun.com
Dist(s): **Sandvik Publishing.**

Books by Bookends *See* **Long Dash Publishing**

Books by Kids LLC, *(978-0-615-19963-4; 978-0-9830954)* 1021 Oak St., Jacksonville, FL 32204 USA Tel 904-376-7029; Fax: 904-355-1832
Web site: http://www.booksbykids.com
Dist(s): **Chicago Distribution Ctr.**

Bks. by Matt, *(978-0-9727660)* 33 Stoddard Way, Berkeley, CA 94708 USA Tel 510-849-2986; Fax: 510-849-1012
E-mail: mylamby@hotmail.com.

Books for Brats *Imprint of* **Little Redhaired Girl Publishing, Inc.**

Bks. for Children of the World, *(978-0-9661186; 978-0-9762078)* 6701 N. Bryant Ave., Oklahoma City, OK 73121 USA Tel 405-721-7417; Fax: 405-478-4352; Toll Free: 888-838-0003.

Bks. for Children Publishing, *(978-0-9830172)* Orders Addr.: P.O. Box 202, Inlet, NY 13360 USA; Edit Addr.: 578 Oyster Rake Rd., Kiawah Island, SC 29455 USA Tel 843-573-7429; 315-357-3422; 843-513-7023
E-mail: wguiffre@frontiernet.net.

Books International, Inc., *(978-1-891078)* Orders Addr.: P.O. Box 605, Herndon, VA 20172-0605 USA (SAN 131-761X) Tel 703-661-1500; Fax: 703-661-1501
E-mail: bimail@presswarehouse.com.

Bks. on Demand, *(978-0-608; 978-0-7837; 978-0-8357; 978-0-598)* Div. of UMI, 300 N. Zeeb Rd., Ann Arbor, MI 48106-1346 USA Tel 734-761-4700; Fax: 734-665-5022; Toll Free: 800-521-0600
E-mail: info@umi.com
Web site: http://www.umi.com.

Bks. on the Path, *(978-0-9743390)* P.O. Box 436, Barker, TX 77413-0436 USA Tel 281-492-6050; Fax: 832-201-7620; Toll Free: 866-875-7284
E-mail: info@patriarchspath.org
Web site: http://www.booksonthepath.com.

Bks. That Will Enhance Your Life, *(978-0-615-20297-6; 978-0-615-38405-4; 978-0-9831419; 978-0-9838457; 978-0-9848980; 978-0-692-68079-7)* Div. of Andrews Leadership International, 8816 Ave. M New St., Brooklyn, NY 11236 USA Tel 917-327-1029; *Imprints:* BTWEYL (BTWEYL)
E-mail: risingtideentertainment@yahoo.com; vision@booksthatwillenhanceyourlife.com
Web site: http://www.booksthatwillenhanceyourlife.com.

Books To Believe In *Imprint of* **Thornton Publishing, Inc.**

Books To Remember *Imprint of* **Flyleaf Publishing**

Bks. Unbound E-Publishing Co., *(978-1-59201)* 1110 Kerwin St., Piscataway, NJ 08854-3323 USA
Web site: http://www.booksunbound.com.

Books2Go, *(978-1-59590)* 780 Reservoir Ave., Suite 243, Cranston, RI 02910 USA Tel 401-537-9175
E-mail: books2go@writerscollective.net
Web site: http://www.mybooks2go.com.

Books-A-Million, Inc., *(978-1-63111; 978-1-5325)* 402 Industrial Dr., Birmingham, AL 35211 USA Tel 205-942-3737
E-mail: Publishing@BooksAMillion.com
Web site: www.booksamillion.com.

BooksbyDave Inc., *(978-0-9768867)* Orders Addr.: 5010 James loop, Killeen, TX 76542 USA Tel 254-628-1961
E-mail: project17us@yahoo.com
Web site: http://www.geocities.com/oilsbydave.

Booksforboys, *(978-0-9761440)* 8 Marigold Ct., Holtsville, NY 11742 USA
Web site: http://booksforboys.com.

Bookshelf Global Publishing, *(978-0-9755395; 978-0-9766954; 978-0-9779012; 978-0-9800430; 978-0-9850656)* 503 Second Ave., Destin, FL 32541 USA (SAN 850-4652) Tel 770-560-8016
E-mail: office@bookshelfglobal.com
Web site: http://www.bookshelfglobal.com.

Bookshelf, The *See* **Open Door Publishers, Inc.**

Booksmart Pubns., *(978-0-9790896)* Orders Addr.: P.O. Box 4774, Mission Viejo, CA 92690 USA (SAN 852-4211) Tel 949-462-0076; Edit Addr.: 19 Bolero, Mission Viejo, CA 92692 USA
E-mail: b_smart@cox.net
Web site: http://www.booksmartpublications.com.

booksonnet.com, *(978-1-888562; 978-0-9675540)* Div. of Shoestring Productions, P.O. Box 36-5540, Saint Augustine, FL 32085 USA Tel 904-829-3812 Do not confuse with companies with the same name in Prather CA, Santa Barbara CA, Aptos CA, Belvedere CA, Albion CA, Pensacola, FL
E-mail: billbooks@bellsouth.net
Dist(s): **Lightning Source, Inc.**

Booksource, The, *(978-0-7383; 978-0-8335; 978-0-911891; 978-0-9641084; 978-1-886379; 978-1-890760; 978-0-7568; 978-1-4117; 978-1-4178; 978-1-60446; 978-1-4364)* Div. of GL group, Inc., Orders Addr.: 1230 Macklind Ave., Saint Louis, MO 63110-1432 USA (SAN 169-4324) Tel 314-647-0600 Toll Free Fax: 800-647-1923; Toll Free: 800-444-0435
E-mail: shankins@booksource.com
Web site: http://www.booksource.com.

Bookstand Publishing, *(978-1-58909; 978-1-61863; 978-1-63498)* 305 Vineyard Town Ctr., Suite 302, Morgan Hill, CA 95037 USA Tel 408-852-1832; Fax: 408-852-1812
E-mail: orders@bookstandpublishing.com
Web site: http://www.BookstandPublishing.com.

Bookstrand-Siren Publishing, Incorporated *See* **Siren-BookStrand, Inc.**

Booksville, U.S.A., *(978-0-9630887; 978-0-9720041)* P.O. Box 710352, Houston, TX 77271-0352 USA Tel 713-726-8115 (phone/fax); *Imprints:* Circle of Friends (CirFriends)
E-mail: elkewat@aol.com; lindawatersbooks@aol.com; ethnicbooks@aol.com
Web site: http://lindawaters.com.

BooktiMookti Pr., *(978-0-9800952)* P.O. Box 17520, Seattle, WA 98127 USA
E-mail: helen@booktimookti.com
Web site: http://www.BooktiMookti.com; http://www.RuntFarm.com
Dist(s): **Itasca Bks.**

Booktrope, *(978-0-9841786; 978-1-935961; 978-1-62015; 978-1-5137)* Div. of Libertary Co., 1219 Sixteenth Ave East, Seattle, WA 98112 USA (SAN 858-639X) Tel 206-235-3384; *Imprints:* Booktrope Editions (Booktrope Edtns); Vox Dei (VoxDei)
E-mail: publisher@booktrope.com; production@booktrope.com; info@booktrope.com; accounting@booktrope.com
Web site: http://www.booktrope.com.

Booktrope Editions *Imprint of* **Booktrope**

Bookworm Bks., *(978-0-9749423)* P.O. Box 77277, Washington, DC 20013 USA (SAN 255-8874) Fax: 202-387-5127; Toll Free: 877-302-0067
E-mail: info@bookwormbooks.biz
Web site: http://www.bookwormbooks.biz
Dist(s): **Independent Pubs. Group.**

Boom Entertainment, Inc., 5670 Wilshire Blvd., Ste 450, Los Angeles, CA 90036 USA
Dist(s): **Diamond Comic Distributors, Inc.**
Diamond Bk. Distributors
Follett School Solutions
Simon & Schuster, Inc.

Boom! Studios, *(978-1-932386; 978-1-934506; 978-1-60886; 978-1-936393; 978-1-61398; 978-1-939867; 978-1-68159; 978-1-68415; 978-1-64144)* 1800 Century Pk. E., Suite 200, Los Angeles, CA 90067 USA Tel 310-895-7746; 5670 Wilshire Blvd., Suite No. 450, Los Angeles, CA 90036; *Imprints:* Archaia Entertainment (ArchaiaEnt)
Web site: http://www.boom-studios.com
Dist(s): **MyiLibrary**
Simon & Schuster, Inc.
Simon & Schuster Children's Publishing.

Boone Bks., *(978-0-9765294)* P.O. Box 262147, Plano, TX 75026-2147 USA Toll Free: 800-755-6628
E-mail: cadprof@boonebooks.com
Web site: http://www.boonebooks.com.

Boosey & Hawkes, Inc., 229 W. 28th St. Flr. 11, New York, NY 10001-5915 USA
E-mail: bhsales@ny.boosey.com
Web site: http://www.boosey.com
Dist(s): **Leonard, Hal Corp.**

Boot in the Door Pubns., *(978-0-9788183)* P.O. Box 2435, Anahuac, TX 77514-2435 USA
E-mail: lesaboutin@gmail.com; dlkboutin@windstream.net.

Booth, John Harvey, *(978-0-9754291)* 246 Schilling St., West Lafayette, IN 47906 USA Tel 765-743-8728
E-mail: jhbooth2003@yahoo.com.

Boothroyd & Allnut, *(978-0-578-11204-6; 978-0-9904207)* 5115 68th Ave. NE, Marysville, WA 98270 USA.

Borah Pr., *(978-0-9657879)* 1100 Rd. M, Redwood Valley, CA 95470 USA Tel 707-485-0922; Fax: 707-485-7071
E-mail: JPack@pacific.net.

Border Pr., *(978-0-9650977; 978-0-9843150; 978-0-9848915; 978-0-9898641; 978-0-9862801; 978-0-9968737)* Orders Addr.: P.O. Box 3124, Sewanee, TN 37375 USA Tel 337-577-1762; Toll Free Fax: 866-669-3207
E-mail: borderpress@gmail.com
Web site: http://borderpressbooks.com.

Borders Group, Inc., *(978-0-681)* 100 Phoenix Dr., Ann Arbor, MI 48108 USA Tel 734-477-1100
Web site: http://www.borders.com.

Borders Personal Publishing, *(978-1-4134)* a/o Pam Durant, 2 International Plaza, Suite 340, Philadelphia, PA 19113 USA Tel 610-915-5214; Fax: 610-915-0294; Toll Free: 888-795-4274
E-mail: dave@xlibris.com
Dist(s): **Xlibris Corp.**

Borders Pr., *(978-0-681)* Div. of Borders Group, Inc., 100 Phoenix Dr., Ann Arbor, MI 48108 USA; *Imprints:* State Street Press (State St Pr)
Web site: http://www.bordersstores.com; http://www.bordersgroupinc.com; http://www.borders.com.

BorderStone Pr., LLC, *(978-0-9842284; 978-1-936670)* Orders Addr.: P.O. Box 1383, Mountain Home, AR 72653 USA Tel 870-405-1146; 436 Olympic Dr., MOUNTAIN HOME, 72654 Tel 870-405-1146
E-mail: borderstonepress@gmail.com
Web site: http://www.borderstonepress.com; http://www.facebook.com/pages/BorderStone-Press-LLC/137970880138?ref=ts.

Bordighera Incorporated, *(978-1-884419; 978-1-59954)* Orders Addr.: P.O. Box 1374, Lafayette, IN 47902-1374 USA; Edit Addr.: John D. Calandra Italian American Institute 25 W. 43rd St., 17th Flr., New York, NY 10036 USA Tel 212-642-2005
E-mail: dstarewich@verizon.net; anthony.tamburri@qc.cuny.edu
Dist(s): **SPD-Small Pr. Distribution.**

Borealis Bk. *Imprint of* **Minnesota Historical Society Pr.**

Borealis Pr., *(978-0-9632651; 978-0-9819950)* P.O. Box 230, Surry, ME 04684 USA Tel 207-667-3700; Fax: 207-667-9649; Toll Free: 800-669-6845.

Borgo Press *See* **Borgo Publishing**

Borgo Publishing, *(978-0-9843979; 978-0-9883893; 978-0-9905431; 978-0-9968783; 978-0-9984606; 978-0-9993830)* 3811 Derby Downs Dr., Tuscaloosa, AL 35405 USA Tel 205-454-4256
E-mail: borgogirl@bellsouth.net.

Born to Blaze Ministries, *(978-0-9762910)* 2131 20th St SE, Buffalo, MN 55313-4813 USA Tel 612-207-5682
E-mail: info@borntoblaze.com
Web site: http://www.borntoblaze.com.

borntalking.com, *(978-0-9720892)* 34116 Blue Heron Dr., Solon, OH 44139-5641 USA
E-mail: david@borntalking.com
Web site: http://www.borntalking.com.

Borromeo Bks., *(978-0-9763098)* Orders Addr.: P.O. Box 7273, Saint Paul, MN 55107 USA.

Boshu Pr., *(978-0-9755624)* 3 Dogwood Ct., Greenville, NC 27858 USA
E-mail: boshucelli@earthlink.net.

BOSS Business Services *See* **Anderson Law Group**

Boss Paws Publishing, *(978-0-9769058)* 2536 Ridgewood Ave., Louisville, KY 40217 USA Tel 502-649-6864
E-mail: ag@animalgambill.org.

Bosse, Andre Ctr., *(978-0-9786128)* 302 Hanson St., Hart, MI 49420-1385 USA Tel 231-873-1707; Fax: 231-873-1456
E-mail: maltbie7@charter.net
Web site: http://www.andrebossecenter.org.

BOT Publishing, LLC, *(978-0-9759493)* P.O. Box 62, Mount Pleasant, SC 29465 USA
Web site: http://thebeautyoftruth.com.

Botero de Borrero, Beatriz & Martha Olga Botero de Gomez (COL) *(978-958-33) Dist. by* **Lectorum Pubns.**

Bothwell Pr., *(978-0-9855353)* 664 H St., Salt Lake City, UT 84103 USA (SAN 920-3397) Tel 801-532-2204 Do not confuse with Bothwell Pr. in Athens, GA
E-mail: Bothwellpress@gmail.com.

Bo-Tree Hse., *(978-0-9832227; 978-0-9968516)* 1749 Del Mar Dr., Idaho Falls, ID 83404 USA Tel 208-524-2491 650-701-4645 (Cell); 650-701-4645 (cell)
E-mail: Debu.majumdar@botreehouse.com
Web site: http://www. botreehouse.com
Dist(s): **CreateSpace Independent Publishing Platform**
Follett School Solutions
Lightning Source, Inc.
Smashwords.

Bottom of the Hill Publishing, *(978-1-935785; 978-1-61203; 978-1-4837)* 200 Terry Rd., Somerville, TN 38068 USA Tel 901-465-8497
E-mail: info@bottomofthehillpublishing.com
Web site: bottomofthehillpublishing.com
Dist(s): **MyiLibrary.**

Bouje Publishing, LLC, *(978-0-9779265)* Orders Addr.: 17659 Montebello Rd, Cupertino, CA 95014 USA.

Boulden Publishing, *(978-1-878076; 978-1-892421)* Div. of Turtle Pine, Inc., Orders Addr.: P.O. Box 1186, Weaverville, CA 96093-1186 USA Tel 530-623-5399; Fax: 530-623-5525; Toll Free: 800-238-8433
E-mail: ken@bouldenpublishing.com
Web site: http://www.bouldenpublishing.com
Dist(s): **Follett School Solutions**
MAR*CO Products, Inc.
Social Studies Schl. Service
Sunburst Communications, Inc.

Boulder Street Bks. LLC, *(978-0-578-06778-0)* P.O. Box 380, Green Mountain Falls, CO 80819 USA
E-mail: editor@boulderstreetbooks.com
Web site: http://www.boulderstreetbooks.com
Dist(s): **Outskirts Pr., Inc.**

Bouncing Ball Bks., Inc., *(978-1-934138)* P.O. Box 6509, Spring Hill, FL 34611-6509 USA (SAN 851-6073)
E-mail: bouncingballbooks@yahoo.com
Web site: http://www.bouncingballbooks.com.

Bound & Determined Pubs., *(978-0-9704006)* Orders Addr.: 18116 Woodrow Rd., Brainerd, MN 56401 USA
E-mail: adamrmarcotte@yahoo.com
Web site: http://www.sover.net/~niliacus/a&h/; http://www.adamandheidi.net.

Bound by Grace Pr., LLC, *(978-0-9787087)* Orders Addr.: 924 Campbell Ct., Batavia, IL 60510 USA Tel 630-772-7172
E-mail: denise@boundbygracepress.com
Web site: http://www.boundbygracepress.com
Dist(s): **Theological Bk. Service.**

Bound Publishing *See* **Spellbound River Pr.**

Bounty Project, The, *(978-0-9665861)* 6310 Georgetown Pike, McLean, VA 22101 USA Tel 703-442-7557
E-mail: kjackson@1771.org.

Bourgeois Media & Consulting, *(978-0-9796288; 978-0-9827877; 978-0-9830355; 978-0-9831971; 978-0-9834868; 978-0-9840281; 978-0-9854244; 978-0-9967348)* 1712 E. Riverside Dr. 124, Austin, TX 78741 USA; *Imprints:* Creative House Kids Press (CreatHseKids)
E-mail: chpress@live.com
Web site: http://bourgeoismedia.com.

Boutin, Lesa *See* **Boot in the Door Pubns.**

Boutique Natural Health Solutions, LLC, *(978-0-9982234)* 4410 Wood Creek Dr, Marietta, GA 30062 USA Tel 404-200-6851; Fax: 404-200-6851
E-mail: birgit@birgitscoaching.com.

Boutique of Quality Books Publishing Co., Inc., *(978-1-60808; 978-0-9828689; 978-0-9831699; 978-1-937084; 978-1-939371; 978-1-945448)* 960 Oaktree Blvd., Christiansburg, VA 24073 USA Tel 678-316-4150; Fax: 678-999-3738; *Imprints:* BQB Publishing (BQBPubng); WriteLife Publishing (WriteLifePub)
E-mail: writelife@boutiqueofqualitybooks.com
Web site: http://www.bqbpublishing.com
Dist(s): **INscribe Digital**
Independent Pubs. Group
New Leaf Distributing Co., Inc.

Bow Historical Bks.,
Dist(s): **Oxford Univ. Pr., Inc.**

Bowden Music Co., *(978-0-9702219)* 1511 Grand Ave., Fort Worth, TX 76106 USA Tel 817-624-1547 (phone/fax)
E-mail: essieb@mindspring.com.

Bower Bks. *Imprint of* **Storybook Meadow Publishing**

†Bower Hse., *(978-0-915024; 978-0-917895; 978-0-929969; 978-0-933472; 978-0-942394; 978-0-9634607; 978-0-9643161; 978-0-9653751; 978-0-9657159; 978-1-55566; 978-1-56579; 978-1-879483; 978-1-889593; 978-1-890768; 978-0-9704098; 978-1-931599; 978-0-9713678; 978-0-9718378; 978-1-932557; 978-1-934553; 978-1-60648; 978-1-942280; 978-1-917895) P.O. Box 7459, Denver, CO 80207 USA (SAN 209-2425) Toll Free Fax: 800-217-7104; Toll Free: 800-217-7104; Imprints:* Trails Books (Trails Bks); Johnson Books (JohnsonBks); Westcliffe Publishers (WestcliffePubs)
E-mail: books@bowerhousebooks.com; margaret@bowerhousebooks.com
Web site: http://www.bowerhousebooks.com; *CIP.*

Bowers, Renata *See* **Frieda B.**

Bowles, Sharon, *(978-0-692-67659-2)* 9 Wellington Ct., Little Rock, AR 72227 USA Tel 501-517-6084
E-mail: sharon@aristotle.net.

Bowman's Pr., LLC, *(978-1-933142)* 9321 226th St. SE, Woodinville, WA 98077 USA
E-mail: info@bowmanspress.com
Web site: http://www.bowmanspress.com.

Bowmar/Noble Pubs., *(978-0-8107; 978-0-8372)* 220 E. Danieldale Dr., De Soto, TX 75115-2490 USA (SAN 201-4157).

Bowrider Pr., *(978-0-9825663)* 1451 Fairbanks Pl., Los Angeles, CA 90026 USA Tel 310-497-1789
Dist(s): **Follett School Solutions.**

Box Girls, The, *(978-0-9769908)* 149 S. Barrington Ave, No. 126, Los Angeles, CA 90049 USA Fax: 310-440-0145
Web site: http://www.theboxgirls.com.

Boxer Bks., Ltd. (GBR) *(978-0-9547373; 978-1-905417; 978-1-910126) Dist. by* **Sterling.**

Boxes & Arrows, Incorporated *See* **Backintyme Publishing**

Boyars, Marion Pubs., Inc., *(978-0-7145; 978-0-905223)* 237 E. 39th St., No. 1A, New York, NY 10016-2110 USA (SAN 284-981X) Tel 212-697-1599; Fax: 212-808-0664; Toll Free: 800-283-3572 (orders only)
Dist(s): **Consortium Bk. Sales & Distribution**
MyiLibrary.

Boyars, Marion Pubs., Ltd. (GBR) *(978-0-7145; 978-1-84230) Dist. by* **Consort Bk Sales.**

Boyce, S. M., *(978-1-939997)* Orders Addr.: PO BOX 777, Blaine, WA 98231 USA
E-mail: boyce@smboyce.com
Web site: http://smboyce.com.

Boydell & Brewer, Inc., *(978-0-85115; 978-0-85991; 978-0-907239; 978-0-938100; 978-1-57113; 978-1-58046; 978-1-85566; 978-1-870252; 978-1-878822; 978-1-879751; 978-1-900639; 978-1-84384; 978-1-84383; 978-1-64014)* Div. of Boydell & Brewer Group, Ltd., Orders Addr.: 668 Mount Hope Ave., Rochester, NY 14620-2731 USA (SAN 013-8479) Tel 585-275-0419; Fax: 585-271-8778
E-mail: boydell@boydellusa.net; boydell@boydell.co.uk
Web site: http://www.boydellandbrewer.com
Dist(s): **Casemate Academic**
MyiLibrary
ebrary, Inc.

Boyds Collection Ltd., The, *(978-0-9712840; 978-0-9713174)* 75 Cunningham Rd., Gettysburg, PA 17325-7142 USA
E-mail: alana@boydsstuff.com
Web site: http://www.boydsstuff.com.

Boyds Mills Pr., *(978-1-56397; 978-1-878093; 978-1-886910; 978-1-59078; 978-1-932425; 978-1-62091; 978-1-62979; 978-0-9961172; 978-0-9961173; 978-1-943283; 978-1-68238; 978-1-68329; 978-1-68437)* Div. of Highlights For Children, Inc., 815 Church St., Honesdale, PA 18431 USA (SAN 852-3177) Tel 570-251-4513 Toll Free: 800-490-5111 Admin line; 877-512-8366; 800-874-8817 Cust Svc Columbus, OH; *Imprints:* Wordsong (Wordsong); Calkins Creek (Calkins Creek); Front Street (FrtSt); Lemniscaat (Lemnisca); Highlights (Highlights)
E-mail: admin@boydsmillspress.com; honesdale-cs@boydsmillspress.com; marketing@boydsmillspress.com
Web site: http://www.boydsmillspress.com; http://www.wordsongpoetry.com; http://www.calkinscreekbooks.com; http://www.frontstreetbooks.com
Dist(s): **Follett School Solutions**
INscribe Digital
Lectorum Pubns., Inc.
Penguin Random Hse. LLC
Perfection Learning Corp.
Ingram Academic
Two Rivers Distribution.

Boynton, Colin (GBR) *(978-0-9559931) Dist. by* **LuluCom.**

Boys Read Bks., *(978-0-9801224)* 3211 NW 75th St., Seattle, WA 98117 USA Tel 206-321-5500
E-mail: john@boysread.org.

Boys Town, Nebraska Center, Public Service Division *See* **Boys Town Pr.**

Boys Town Pr., *(978-0-938510; 978-1-889322; 978-1-934490; 978-1-936734; 978-1-944882)* Div. of Father Flanagan's Boys' Home, Orders Addr.: 14100 Crawford St., Omaha, NE 68010 USA (SAN 215-8477) Tel 402-498-1320; Fax: 402-498-1310; Toll Free: 800-282-6657
E-mail: btpress@boystown.org
Web site: http://www.boystownpress.org
Dist(s): **Brodart Co.**
Quality Bks., Inc.

bPlus Bks. *Imprint of* **Bumble Bee Publishing**

BPM Research LLC, *(978-0-9829224)* 939 Bloomfield St., Hoboken, NJ 07030 USA Tel 551-226-9372
E-mail: michael@bpm-research.com
Web site: http://www.bpm-research.com.

BPT Media, *(978-0-9772126)* P.O. Box 28663, Philadelphia, PA 19151-0663 USA
E-mail: vharris52@gmail.com.

BQB Publishing *Imprint of* **Boutique of Quality Books Publishing Co., Inc.**

Bradbury, Heidi, *(978-0-692-90149-6)* 2244 E. Ojai Ave., OJAI, CA 93023 USA Tel 805-701-4945
E-mail: heidi@heidibradburyfineart.com
Dist(s): **Lightning Source, Inc.**

Bradford Pr., Inc., *(978-0-9705618; 978-0-9801563)* Orders Addr.: P.O. Box 6802, South Bend, IN 46660-6802 USA Tel 574-876-3601; Fax: 574-255-9358 Do not confuse with companies with same name in Bradford, MA, Palm Beach, FL, Chicago, IL
E-mail: BradfordPress@comcast.net; Info@Bradford-Press.com
Web site: http://www.Bradford-Press.com.

Bradford-Franklin, *(978-0-9767676)* P.O. Box 495, Hartsville, TN 37074 USA Tel 615-374-3712; Fax: 615-374-4649
E-mail: bradfordfranklin@bellsouth.net
Web site: http://www.jackmccall.com.

Bradley, Judy & Assocs., LLC, *(978-0-615-57032-7)* 230 E. 45th St., Savannah, GA 31405 USA Tel 912-232-7636
E-mail: judybee58@gmail.com.

BradyBooks *See* **Nature Works Press**

Bradybooks.biz, *(978-0-9754169)* 1888 County Road 72., Bailey, CO 80421-2175 USA
E-mail: readbradybooks@aol.com
Web site: http://bradybooks.biz.

Braided Image, *(978-0-9725170)* 3064 Old New Cut Rd., Springfield, TN 37172 USA
E-mail: masterbraider@mindspring.com
Web site: http://www.braidedimage.com.

Braided Way Media, *(978-0-9835428)* 585 Sleepy Hollow Dr., Uniontown, OH 44685 USA Tel 330-495-6450
E-mail: olinhimr@mountunion.edu.

Brailleink, *(978-0-9769313)* 1704 Holly St., Austin, TX 78702-5424 USA Toll Free: 800-324-2919
E-mail: info@brailleink.org
Web site: http://www.brailleink.org.

Brainbow Pr., *(978-0-9796715; 978-0-9825867)* 7914 N. Roundstone Dr., Tucson, AZ 85741 USA (SAN 854-0594) Tel 520-481-1919
E-mail: 19@19.org; edipyuksel@gmail.com; brainbowpress@gmail.com
Web site: http://www.brainbowpress.com; http://www.islamicreform.org; http://www.yuksel.org; http://www.19.org
Dist(s): **Lightning Source, Inc.**

BrainBox, Limited *See* **Gray Jay Bks.**

Brainchild Publishing *See* **Mindfull Publishing**

Brainerd Enterprises, *(978-0-9747441)* 419 Old Clyde Pk. Rd., Livingston, MT 59047 USA Tel 406-222-8273; Fax: 406-222-3769
E-mail: sally@heirofkingmeldh.com
Web site: http://www.heirofkingmeldh.com.

BrainFriendly Learning, *(978-0-9759226)* 6801 6th St., NW, Washington, DC 20012-1911 USA Tel 202-723-7337; Fax: 202-726-6117
E-mail: stevecarroll@speakeasy.net
Web site: http://www.kathleencarroll.com.

Brainstorm Co., The, *(978-0-9728354)* Orders Addr.: 11684 Ventura Blvd., No. 970, Studio City, CA 91604 USA (SAN 255-5174) Tel 818-763-2674
E-mail: weddinggames@hotmail.com
Web site: http://www.TheBrainstormCompany.com
Dist(s): **Independent Pubs. Group.**

Brainstorm Pubns., Inc., *(978-0-9723429)* 24 NE 24th Ave., Pompano Beach, FL 33062 USA Tel 954-941-3329; Fax: 954-943-7708 Do not confuse with Brainstorm Publications in Lake Oswego, OR
E-mail: tditocco@brainstormpublications.com
Web site: http://www.brainstormpublications.com.

BrainStorm 3000, *(978-0-9651174)* P.O. Box 80513, Goleta, CA 93118 USA Tel 805-448-7149; 805-448-7149
Dist(s): **Educational Bk. Distributors.**

BrainStream, *(978-0-9785892)* 21307 Park Valley Dr., Katy, TX 77450-4811 USA
E-mail: bvogt@brainstream.com.

Braintext, Inc., *(978-0-9816270)* 3660 Wilshire Blvd. Ste. 400, Los Angeles, CA 90010-2753 USA
E-mail: info@braintext.com
Web site: http://www.braintext.com.

BrainX, Inc., *(978-0-9741604)* 45 Rincon Dr. Unit 1033B, Camarillo, CA 93012-8424 USA
E-mail: info@brainx.com
Web site: http://www.brainx.com
Dist(s): **Majors, J. A. Co.**
Rittenhouse Bk. Distributors.

Braley & Thompson, Inc., *(978-1-883239)* P.O. Box 1396, Saint Albans, WV 25177-1396 USA Tel 304-722-1704; Fax: 304-722-1709; Toll Free: 800-258-5453.

Bran Nue Productions, *(978-0-615-44662-2; 978-0-9851574)* 7878 LaSalle Ave. No. 231, Baton Rouge, LA 70806 USA Tel 225-200-4451
E-mail: brannuepro@gmail.com.

Branch Springs Publishing, *(978-0-9727622)* Orders Addr.: 500 Watts Dr., Huntsville, AL 35801 USA Tel 256 539 1064; Edit Addr.: 500 Watts Dr., Huntsville, AL 35801 USA
E-mail: fchap10220@aol.com.

Branching Plot Bks., *(978-0-9860166; 978-0-9891840)* 5815 Lacey Blvd SE Unit 8027, Lacey, WA 98503 USA
E-mail: arthurmills@branchingplotbooks.com
Web site: http://www.branchingplotbooks.com.

Brand Nu Words *Imprint of* **Nunes Productions, LLC**

Brand, Shoshana, *(978-0-9978213)* 44633 31st St. W, Lancaster, CA 93536 USA Tel 818-217-6060; Fax: 818-217-6060
E-mail: creativerosh@gmail.com.

Branded Black Publishing, *(978-0-9746913)* P.O. Box 950781, Oklahoma City, OK 73195 USA
Web site: http://www.ebonymarshal.com; http://www.brandedblackpublishing.com; http://www.gospelofthegun.com; http://www.seanchandler.com.

Brandeis Univ., Rose Art Museum, *(978-0-9726641; 978-0-9761593)* 415 South St., Waltham, MA 02254 USA (SAN 278-243X) Tel 781-736-3434; Fax: 781-736-3439
E-mail: tjking@brandeis.edu
Web site: http://www.brandeis.edu/rose
Dist(s): **D.A.P./Distributed Art Pubs.**

Branden Bks., *(978-0-8283)* Div. of Branden Publishing Co., P.O. Box 812094, Wellesley, MA 02482 USA (SAN 201-4106) Tel 781-235-3634; Fax: 781-790-1056
E-mail: branden@brandenbooks.com; danteu@danteuniversity.org
Web site: http://www.brandenbooks.com; http://www.danteuniversity.org; http://www.adolphcaso.com
Dist(s): **Brodart Co.**
Follett School Solutions
eBookit.com.

Brandylane Pubs., Inc., *(978-0-9627635; 978-1-883911; 978-0-9838264; 978-0-9849588; 978-0-9859358; 978-1-939930; 978-1-947860)* Orders Addr.: 5 S. 1st St., Richmond, VA 23219-3716 USA; *Imprints:* Belle Isle Books (Belleisle)
E-mail: rhpruett@brandylanepublishers.com
Web site: http://www.brandylanepublishers.com
Dist(s): **Baker & Taylor International**
Follett School Solutions
Lightning Source, Inc.
Smashwords.

Brass Frog Bookworks, *(978-0-9847096; 978-0-9857191; 978-0-9899412)* 2764 Compass Dr. Suite 201-2, Grand Junction, CO 81506 USA Tel 909-239-0344; Fax: 970-434-9361
E-mail: phoff@outlook.com
Web site: www.BrassFrogBookworks.com
Dist(s): **BookMasters.**

Brass, Robin Studio, Inc. (CAN) *(978-1-896941) Dist. by* **Midpt Trade.**

BrassHeart Music, *(978-0-9673762; 978-0-9721478; 978-0-9826278)* 256 S. Robertson Blvd., Suite 2288, Beverly Hills, CA 90211 USA Tel 323-932-0534; Fax: 323-937-6884; 323-933-4209; *Imprints:* Kid's Creative Classics (Kids Creative Classics); Dream A World (Dream A World)
E-mail: bunny@dreamaworld.com; brassheartmusic@aol.com
Web site: http://www.brassheartmusic.com; http://www.dreamaworld.com
Dist(s): **DeVorss & Co.**
Music Design, Inc.
New Leaf Distributing Co., Inc.

Braun Pubns., *(978-0-9774302)* 150 Clinton Ln., Spring Valley, NY 10977 USA.

Brave Ulysses Bks., *(978-0-9700125; 978-0-615-16272-0; 978-0-615-18969-7; 978-0-615-22032-1; 978-0-615-26030-3)* P.O. Box 1877, Asheville, NC 28802 USA
E-mail: cecil@braveulysses.com; info@braveulysses.com
Dist(s): **Lulu Pr., Inc.**
Parnassus Bk. Distributors.

Braveheart Pr., LLC, *(978-0-9763935)* 23852 Pacific Coast Hwy., Suite 572, Malibu, CA 90265 USA Tel 310-770-7831; Fax: 310-456-5109 do not confuse with BraveHeart Press in Woodland Park, CO
E-mail: showrunnerbrv@aol.com
Web site: http://www.braveheartpressllc.com.

Braziller, George Inc., *(978-0-8076)* 171 Madison Ave., Suite 1103, New York, NY 10016 USA (SAN 201-9310) Tel 212-889-0909; Fax: 212-689-5405
Dist(s): **Norton, W. W. & Co., Inc.**
Penguin Random Hse. LLC.

Brazos Valley Pr., *(978-0-9726822)* Orders Addr.: P.O. Box 215, Calvert, TX 77837-0215 USA Tel 979-364-2439;

Fax: 800-881-2032; Edit Addr.: 508 E. Texas, Calvert, TX 77837 USA (SAN 858-2947)
E-mail: jkennedy@brazosvalleypress.com
Web site: http://www.brazosvalleypress.com

Brda, Tracy, *(978-0-9742355)* P.O. Box 510065, Saint Louis, MO 63129 USA Tel 314-293-0015; Fax: 636-343-0564
E-mail: info@power-twins.com.

Bread & Butter Bks., *(978-0-9800816)* 229 E. Ct. St., Cincinnati, OH 45202 USA Tel 513-884-0468
E-mail: jkiddielit@cinci.rr.com.

Break-A-Leg Bks., *(978-0-9668522)* 12332 Laurel Terr., Studio City, CA 91604 USA Tel 818-508-5585; Fax: 818-752-0682.

Breakaway Bks., *(978-1-55821; 978-1-891369; 978-1-62124)* P.O. Box 24, Halcottsville, NY 12438 USA Tel 607-326-4805; Fax: 212-898-0408; Toll Free: 800-548-4348 (voicemail) Do not confuse with Breakaway Bks., Albany, TX
E-mail: breakawaybooks@gmail.com
Web site: http://www.breakawaybooks.com
Dist(s): **Consortium Bk. Sales & Distribution.**

Breaking Cycles Bks., *(978-0-9741202)* Orders Addr.: P.O. Box 402, Severn, MD 21144-0402 USA Tel 410-519-6787
E-mail: BrCyBks@msn.com
Web site: http://www.breaking-cycles-visions-of-hope.com.

Breaking the Barrier, Inc., *(978-0-9712817; 978-0-9728570; 978-0-9758573; 978-0-9777987; 978-0-9817961; 978-0-9846477; 978-0-9846490; 978-0-9903122; 978-0-9963192; 978-0-9976527)* 63 Shirley Rd., Groton, MA 01450 USA Fax: 978-448-1237; Toll Free: 866-862-7325 Do not confuse with Breaking the Barrier Ministry, Inc. in Pennsauken, NJ
E-mail: info@tobreak.com; john@tobreak.com
Web site: http://www.tobreak.com.

Breakneck Bks. *Imprint of* **Variance Publishing, LLC**

Breakneck Books *See* **Breakneck Media**

Breakneck Media, *(978-0-9786551; 978-0-9796929; 978-0-9836017; 978-0-9840423; 978-0-9886725; 978-1-941539)* 20 Sampson Rd., Rochester, NH 03867 USA
E-mail: info@jeremyrobinsononline.com
Web site: http://www.jeremyrobinsononline.com.

Brealey, Nicholas Publishing, *(978-0-9839558; 978-1-941176)* 20 Park Plaza, Suite 1115A, Boston, MA 02116 USA
Dist(s): **Consortium Bk. Sales & Distribution**
Hachette Bk. Group
MyiLibrary.

Breath & Shadows Productions, *(978-0-9720176; 978-0-9821029)* P.O. Box 10557, Tampa, FL 33679 USA Tel 813-251-8187
Web site: http://www.breathandshadows.com.

Breathless Vintage Enterprises, *(978-0-9842053)* Orders Addr.: PO Box 28168, Portland, OR 97228 USA (SAN 858-7221)
E-mail: morgan@breathlessvintage.com.

Breckling Pr., *(978-0-9721218; 978-1-933308)* 283 Michigan Ave., Elmhurst, IL 60126 USA
Web site: http://www.brecklingpress.com
Dist(s): **Independent Pubs. Group.**

Bree's Gift Publishing, *(978-0-9748512)* 3840 Listerman Rd., Howell, MI 48855 USA Tel 517-552-9184
E-mail: kimmie67@sbcglobal.net.

Breezeway Books, *(978-1-62550)* 7101 W. Commercial Blvd. No. 4E, Tamarac, FL 33319 USA Tel 954-726-0902; Fax: 954-726-0903
E-mail: dgreenspan@llumina.com
Web site: www.llumina.com.

Breezy Reads, *(978-0-9759784; 978-1-938327)* Orders Addr.: 2800 N Bogus Basin Rd APT C103, Boise, ID 83702 USA (SAN 256-3762)
E-mail: breezyreads@gmail.com
Web site: http://www.breezyreads.com.

Bremer Press *See* **Zachmeyer, Mary L.**

BrenMar Communications, *(978-0-9903034)* 17313 Hialeah Dr., Odessa, FL 33556 USA Tel 813-920-9761
E-mail: authorbrendamartin@gmail.com
Web site: http://www.brendamartin.net.

Brenneman, Lynette, *(978-0-9859737)* 260 Brenneman Rd., Lancaster, PA 17603 USA Tel 717-872-4815
E-mail: lleaman@verizon.net.

Brenner Publishing, LLC, *(978-0-9777203)* P.O. Box 584, Hicksville, NY 11802-0584 USA Tel 516-433-0804.

Brentwood Christian Pr. *Imprint of* **Brentwood Communications Group**

Brentwood Communications Group, *(978-0-916573; 978-1-55630; 978-1-59581)* 4000 Beallwood Ave., Columbus, GA 31904 USA (SAN 297-1895) Tel 706-576-5787 Toll Free: 800-334-8861; *Imprints:* Brentwood Christian Press (BrtwdChrist Pr) Do not confuse with Brentwood Communications Group in Vista, CA
E-mail: brentwood@knology.net
Web site: http://www.brentwoodbooks.com; http://www.brentwoodreview.com; http://www.newchristianbooks.com
Dist(s): **Ingram Publisher Services.**

Brentwood Home Video, *(978-0-7378; 978-0-924739; 978-1-57119; 978-1-879902)* Div. of Brentwood Communications, Inc., 810 Lawrence Dr., Suite 100, Newbury Park, CA 91320 USA Toll Free: 888-335-0528
E-mail: brentcom@earthlink.net
Web site: http://www.ssetsites.com/e-bci/default.htm
Dist(s): **Follett School Solutions.**

Brentwood Kids Co. *Imprint of* **Brentwood Music, Inc.**

Brentwood Music, Inc., *(978-0-7601; 978-1-55897)* 2555 Meridian Blvd. Ste. 100, Franklin, TN 37067-6364 USA Toll Free: 800-333-9000 (audio & video orders); 800-846-7664 (book orders); *Imprints:* Brentwood Kids Company (Brentwood Kids)
Web site: http://www.providentmusic.com
Dist(s): **Appalachian Bible Co.**
Central South Christian Distribution
Leonard, Hal Corp.
New Day Christian Distributors Gifts, Inc.
Provident Music Distribution
Spring Arbor Distributors, Inc.

Brentwood Publishing Group *See* **Writing for the Lord Ministries**

Brentwood-Benson Music Publishing, *(978-1-59802; 978-0-9830602)* Orders Addr.: 101 Winners Cir., Brentwood, TN 37027 USA (SAN 256-9574) Toll Free: 800-846-7664
E-mail: sales@brentwoodbenson.com; jroher@brentwoodbenson.net
Web site: http://www.brentwoodbenson.com
Dist(s): **Leonard, Hal Corp.**

†**Brethren Pr.,** *(978-0-87178)* Div. of Church of the Brethren, 1451 Dundee Ave., Elgin, IL 60120-1694 USA (SAN 201-9329) Tel 847-742-5100; 800-441-3712; Fax: 847-742-1407; Toll Free: 800-441-3712
E-mail: brethren_press_gb@brethren.org
Web site: http://www.brethrenpress.com
Dist(s): **Follett School Solutions**; *CIP.*

Brethren Revival Fellowship, *(978-0-9745027; 978-0-9777766; 978-0-9828895; 978-1-946688)* 26 United Zion Cir., Lititz, PA 17543-7956 USA Fax: 717-625-0511
E-mail: harpri@dejazzd.com; brf@brfwitness.org
Web site: http://www.brfwitness.org.

Brewer, Neil, *(978-0-9771807)* 5290 Cedar Way Dr., NE, Corydon, IN 47112 USA Tel 812-952-3482
E-mail: 8oclock@aye.net
Web site: http://www.booksbybrewer.com
Dist(s): **BookBaby.**

Brewer Technologies, *(978-0-9774748)* P.O. Box 141, Cornwall, PA 17016 USA Tel 717-228-1708; Fax: 717-228-1709; Toll Free: 877-449-2556
E-mail: nicholelmoore@comcast.net
Web site: http://www.tonybrewer.com.

Brewer's Historical Publications *See* **Bear State Bks.**

Brewster Moon, *(978-0-9854423)* 13940 Cedar Rd. Suite 386, University Heights, OH 44118 USA Tel 216-408-1616
E-mail: tbrown@brewstermoon.com.

Brewster, Robert, *(978-0-615-37153-5)* 185 NE 4th Ave. Apt 317, Delray Beach, FL 33483 USA Tel 561-400-7799
Dist(s): **Outskirts Pr., Inc.**

Brian J. Publishing, Incorporated *See* **Holography Sells**

Briarcliffe Press *See* **Sunny Palms Pr.**

Brickey E-Publishing, *(978-0-9758964)* 1029E Salisbury St., Kernersville, NC 27284-3063 USA
E-mail: mainoffice@brickey-epublishing.com
Web site: http://www.brickey-epublishing.com.

BrickHouse Bks., Inc., *(978-0-932616; 978-1-935916; 978-1-938144)* 306 Suffolk Rd., Baltimore, MD 21218 USA (SAN 209-4622) Tel 410-235 7690
E-mail: charriss@towson.edu
Web site: http://www.towsonu.edu
Dist(s): **INscribe Digital**
Itasca Bks.

BrickHouse Education *Imprint of* **Cambridge BrickHouse, Inc.**

Bridge Ink, *(978-0-9641963)* 32580 SW Arbor Lake Dr., Wilsonville, OR 97070-8471 USA
E-mail: bob@bridgeink.com
Web site: http://www.bridgeink.com
Dist(s): **Far West Bk. Service**
Follett School Solutions
Partners/West Book Distributors.

Bridge Pubns., Inc., *(978-0-88404; 978-1-57318; 978-1-4031; 978-1-61177; 978-1-4572)* Orders Addr.: 5600 E. Olympic Blvd., Commerce, CA 90022 USA (SAN 208-3884) Tel 323-888-6200; Fax: 323-888-6210; Toll Free: 800-722-1733; Edit Addr.: 4751_Fountain Ave., Los Angeles, CA 90029 USA
E-mail: annamow@bridgepub.com; daniellem@bridgepub.com; donamow@bridgepub.com
Web site: http://www.bridgepub.com; http://www.clearbodyclearmind.com; http://www.scientology.org; http://www.dianetics.org
Dist(s): **Bookazine Co., Inc.**
Brodart Co.
Follett School Solutions
Landmark Audiobooks.

Bridge Publishing Group, *(978-0-9728439)* P.O. Box 1673, Walnut, CA 91788-1673 USA Tel 909-444-9088; Fax: 909-595-9526
E-mail: dafangzeng@yahoo.com.

Bridge To Life Ministries, Incorporated *See* **Advent Truth Ministries**

Bridge-Logos Foundation *See* **Bridge-Logos, Inc.**

Bridge-Logos, Inc., *(978-0-88270; 978-0-912106; 978-0-9841034; 978-1-61036)* Orders Addr.: 14260 W. Newberry Rd, Newberry, FL 32669 USA (SAN 253-5254) Tel 352-727-9324; Toll Free: 800-935-6467 (orders only); 800-631-5802 (orders only)
E-mail: SWooldridge@bridgelogos.com
Web site: http://www.bridgelogos.com
Dist(s): **Anchor Distributors**
Send The Light Distribution LLC
Spring Arbor Distributors, Inc.

Bridges to Better Learning, *(978-0-9970558)* 3201 NE 183 St. Apt. 508, Aventura, FL 33160 USA Tel 954-849-1157; Fax: 305-682-0032
E-mail: dwander6@gmail.com.

Bridgestone Bks. *Imprint of* **Capstone Press of Coughlan Cos.**

Bridgeway Bks., *(978-1-933538; 978-1-934454)* Div. of BookPros, LLC, 2100 Kramer Ln., Suite 300, Austin, TX 78758 USA Tel 512-478-2028
Web site: http://www.bridgewaybooks.net.

BR:IEFing Assocs. of New England, *(978-0-9706105)* Orders Addr.: P.O. Box 3159, Kingston, NY 12402-3159 USA Tel 845-339-0998; Edit Addr.: 289 Fair St., Suite 2A, Kingston, NY 12401-3844 USA.

Briggs, Sharon, *(978-0-615-13051-4)* 109 Hope Way, Auburn, KY 42206 USA
E-mail: sharondeneice109@yahoo.com.

Brigham Young Univ., *(978-0-8425)* 205 UPB, Provo, UT 84602 USA (SAN 201-9337) Tel 801-422-2809; Fax: 801-422-0591; *Imprints:* BYU Creative Works (BYUCreative)
E-mail: diane_foerster@byu.edu
Web site: http://www.upb.byu.edu
Dist(s): **Brigham Young Univ. Print Services**
Chicago Distribution Ctr.
Follett School Solutions
Indiana Univ. Pr.
Univ. of Chicago Pr.

Bright & Morning Star Bks., *(978-0-9986879)* 19506 Whitewood Dr., Spring, TX 77373 USA
E-mail: sharon47@embarqmail.com.

Bright Cloud Publishing, *(978-0-9770727)*
E-mail: brightcloud@verizon.net
Web site: http://www.brightcloudpublishing.com.

Bright Connections Media, *(978-1-62267)* 233 N. Michigan Ave. Suite 2000, Chicago, IL 60601 USA Tel 312-729-5800
E-mail: orders@innlog.net
Web site: www.brightconnectionsmedia.com
Dist(s): **Continental Sales**
Independent Pubs. Group.

Bright Eyes Pr., *(978-0-9728019)* 862 Congressional Rd., Simi Valley, CA 93065 USA Tel 805-579-0027
E-mail: kassie@kgraves.com
Web site: http://www.brighteyespress.com.

Bright Hse. Publishing, LLC, *(978-0-9981891)* 1303 Clover Valley Way, Edgewood, MD 21040 USA Tel 443-819-8919
E-mail: yvannabright@gmail.com.

Bright Ideas! Educational Resources, *(978-1-892427)* P.O. Box 333, Cheswold, DE 19936 USA Toll Free: 877-492-8081
E-mail: hogan@inet.net.

BRIGHT IDEAS GRAPHICS, *(978-0-692-79823-2; 978-0-692-83463-3; 978-0-692-87847-7; 978-0-692-93004-5; 978-0-692-93084-7)* 1105 S. OLMSTED PARKWAY, MIDDLETOWN, DE 19709 USA Tel 609-481-7089.

Bright of America, *(978-1-930355)* 300 Greenbrier Rd., Summersville, WV 26651 USA Tel 304-872-3000; Fax: 304-872-3033; Toll Free: 800-917-2368.

Bright Ring Publishing, Inc., *(978-0-935607)* P.O. Box 31338, Bellingham, WA 98228-3338 USA (SAN 696-0537) Tel 360-592-9201; Fax: 360-592-4503; Toll Free: 800-480-4278; 250 W. 57th St. 15th Flr., New York, NY 10107
E-mail: maryann@brightring.com
Web site: http://www.brightring.com/books
Dist(s): **Ebsco Publishing**
Follett School Solutions
Gryphon Hse., Inc.
Independent Pubs. Group
Legato Pubs. Group
MyiLibrary.

Bright Sky Pr., *(978-0-9704729; 978-0-9709987; 978-1-931721; 978-1-933979; 978-1-936474; 978-1-939055; 978-1-942945)* Orders Addr.: 2365 Rice Blvd., Suite 202, Houston, TX 77005 USA Tel 713-533-9300; Fax: 713-528-2432 Do not confuse with Breakaway Bks., Halcottsville, NY
Web site: http://www.brightskypress.com
Dist(s): **BookMasters, Inc.**
Bookmasters Distribution
Follett School Solutions
Independent Pubs. Group
MyiLibrary
Sterling Publishing Co., Inc.
ebrary, Inc.

Bright Solutions for Dyslexia, LLC, *(978-0-9744343; 978-0-9755871)* 2059 Camden Ave., Suite 186, San Jose, CA 95124-2024 USA Tel 408-559-3652; Fax: 408-377-0503
E-mail: susan@brightsolutions.us
Web site: http://www.brightsolutions.us.

Bright Sparks *Imprint of* **Parragon, Inc.**

Bright Spots, *(978-0-9769150)* P.O. Box 3868, Rancho Santa Fe, CA 92067 USA Toll Free: 888-301-8880
E-mail: lmameson@msn.com
Web site: http://www.brightspotsgames.com.

Bright Tyke Creations LLC, *(978-0-615-33119-5; 978-0-615-63721-1)* 217 Sassafras St., New Florence, PA 15944 USA
Web site: http://www.brighttykecreations.info.

BrightBerry Pr., *(978-0-9720924)* 4262 Kennebec Rd., Dixmont, ME 04932 USA Tel 207-234-4225
E-mail: jeanhay@brightberrypress.com; dbright@brightberrypress.com
Web site: http://www.brightberrypress.com
Dist(s): **CreateSpace Independent Publishing Platform.**

Bright-Brights Media Co., The, *(978-0-9752553)* 1059 Briar Ave., Provo, UT 84604 USA Tel 801-375-3455.

Brighter Child *Imprint of* **Carson-Dellosa Publishing, LLC**

Brighter Day Publishing, *(978-0-615-26080-8; 978-0-9841855)* P.O. Box 505, Washington Township, MI 48094 USA
Web site: http://www.publishinganswers.com.

Brighter Horizons Publishing, *(978-1-929662)* P.O. Box 448, Littleton, CO 80160 USA Tel 303-347-2904; Fax: 303-795-5951
E-mail: brighterhorizons@earthlink.net
Web site: http://home.earthlink.net/~brighterhorizons
Dist(s): **Book Wholesalers, Inc.**

Brighter Minds Children's Publishing, *(978-1-57791)* Div. of Brighter Child Interactive, LLC, 600 D Lakeview Plaza Blvd., Worthington, OH 43085 USA Tel 614-430-3021; Fax: 614-430-3152; *Imprints:* Little Melody Press (Little Melody Pr); Penny Candy Press (Penny Candy Pr)
E-mail: ranf@brightermindsmedia.com; books@Brightermindspublishing.com
Web site: http://www.brightermindspublishing.com
Dist(s): **Two Rivers Distribution.**

Brightline Publishing *See* **Rainbow Reach**

Brighton Publishing LLC, *(978-1-936587; 978-1-62183)* 501 W. Ray Rd. Suite No. 4, Chandler, AZ 85225 USA Tel 602-487-2964
E-mail: donald@brightonpublishing.com
Web site: brightonpublishing.com.

Brightside Co., *(978-0-9743720)* 5040 S. Elmira St., Greenwood Village, CO 80111-3608 USA (SAN 255-5573) Tel 303-694-6065; Fax: 303-694-1009
E-mail: cynthiadormer@msn.com
Dist(s): **Independent Pubs. Group.**

Brightwell Publishing, LLC, *(978-0-9776033)* 7151 Delmar Blvd., Saint Louis, MO 63130-4304 USA (SAN 257-7046) Tel 314-662-2736
E-mail: publisher@brightwellpublishing.net
Web site: http://www.brightwellpublishing.net; http://maryedwardswertsch.net.

Brilliance Publishing *See* **Brilliance Publishing, Inc.**

Brilliance Publishing, Inc., *(978-0-930435; 978-1-56100; 978-1-56740; 978-1-58788; 978-1-59086; 978-1-59355; 978-1-59600; 978-1-59710; 978-1-59737; 978-1-4233; 978-1-4418; 978-1-61106; 978-1-4558; 978-1-4692; 978-1-4805; 978-1-4915; 978-1-5012; 978-1-5113; 978-1-5226; 978-1-5318; 978-1-5366; 978-1-5436; 978-1-9786) Orders Addr.: P.O. Box 887, Grand Haven, MI 49417 USA (SAN 690-1395) Tel 616-846-5256; Fax: 616-846-0630; Toll Free: 800-648-2312 (phone/fax, retail & library orders); Edit Addr.: 1704 Eaton Dr., Grand Haven, MI 49417 USA (SAN 858-138X) Toll Free: 800-648-2312 x330; Imprints:* Audible Studios on Brilliance Audio (AudibleStudios)
E-mail: sales@brillianceaudio.com; customerservice@brillianceaudio.com; jcraig@brilliancepublishing.com
Web site: http://www.brilliancepublishing.com
Dist(s): **Bolinda Publishing, Inc.**
Bookazine Co., Inc.
Diamond Bk. Distributors
Findaway World, LLC
Follett School Solutions
Readerlink Distribution Services, LLC.

Brimax Books Ltd. (GBR) *(978-0-86112; 978-0-900195; 978-0-904494; 978-1-85854; 978-1-904952; 978-1-905279; 978-1-84656) Dist. by* **Byeway Bks.**

BrimWood Pr., *(978-0-9770704)* 1941 Larsen Dr., Camino, CA 95709 USA Tel 530-644-7538; Fax: 530-647-9208; *Imprints:* Tools For Young Historians (Tools YngHist)
E-mail: marcia@brimwoodpress.com
Web site: http://www.brimwoodpress.com.

Brindle Pr., *(978-0-9749080)* 14121 Cardinal Ln., Houston, TX 77079 USA
Web site: http://www.brindlepress.com.

Brinkley Bks., Inc., *(978-0-9793288)* P.O. Box 1753, Healdsburg, CA 95448 USA
E-mail: laura@brinkleybooks.com
Web site: http://www.brinkleybooks.com
Dist(s): **BCH Fulfillment & Distribution.**

Brinsights, LLC, *(978-0-9799454; 978-0-615-31228-6; 978-0-615-36380-6)* 141 E. 88th St., New York, NY 10128-2248 USA (SAN 854-848X)
E-mail: geri@brinsights.net; linaperl@gmail.com
Web site: http://www.mygreensanta.com
Dist(s): **Independent Pubs. Group.**

BRIO Pr., *(978-0-9817830; 978-0-9819290; 978-0-9826687; 978-1-937061)* 12 S. Sixth St., No.1250, Minneapolis, MN 55402 USA (SAN 856-5376) Tel 612-746-8800; Fax: 612-746-8811; Toll Free: 888-333-7979
E-mail: tmiller@briobooks.com
Web site: http://www.briobooks.com.

BRIO Publishing *See* **BRIO Pr.**

Briona Glen Publishing, LLC *See* **Grey Gate Media, LLC**

Briscoe, Nicole , *(978-0-578-17838-7)* 8302 Widgeon Place, Laurel, MD 20724 USA.

Brisk Pr., *(978-0-9770885; 978-0-9799254; 978-0-9832758; 978-0-9899895; 978-0-9966774; 978-0-9987907)* 13 Chestnut Ct. Unit D, Brielle, NJ 08730-1371 USA
E-mail: brisk.press@gmail.com
Web site: http://www.briskpress.com
Dist(s): **Bella Distribution**
Two Rivers Distribution.

Bristol Hse., Ltd., *(978-0-917851; 978-1-885224)* P.O. Box 4020, Anderson, IN 46013 USA (SAN 225-4638) Tel 765-644-0856; Fax: 765-622-1045; Toll Free: 800-451-7323.

Bristol Park Bks., *(978-0-88486)* 252 W. 38th St. Suite 206, New York, NY 10018-5806 USA (SAN 859-533X)
Dist(s): **National Bk. Network**
Sterling Publishing Co., Inc.

Bristol Publishing Co., *(978-0-9755667)* P.O. Box 3103, San Angelo, TX 76902-3103 USA Do not confuse with Bristal Publishing Company in San Jacinto, CA
E-mail: bristolpublishing@sbcglobal.net
Dist(s): **Alliance Bk. Co.**

Briston Hse. (CAN) *(978-1-894921) Dist. by* **IPG Chicago.**

Britannica Educational Publishing *Imprint of* **Rosen Publishing Group, Inc., The**

Brite Bks., *(978-0-9726363)* Orders Addr.: P.O. Box 801, Ortonville, MI 48462 USA; Edit Addr.: 1580 Duck Creek Ln., Ortonville, MI 48462 USA
E-mail: twebb@britebooks.org; twebb@tawglobal.com
Web site: http://www.britebooks.org; http://www.tawglobal.com; http://www.promises-for-life.com.

Brite International *See* **Brite Music, Inc.**

Brite Music, Inc., *(978-0-944803)* Orders Addr.: P.O. Box 65688-0688, Salt Lake City, UT 84165 USA (SAN 244-948X) Tel 801-263-9191; Fax: 801-263-9198; Edit

Addr.: P.O. Box 171076, Salt Lake Cty, UT 84117-1076 USA (SAN 244-9498)
Web site: http://www.britemusic.com.

Brite Pr., *(978-0-9743185)* 3447 Countyline Rd., Chalfont, PA 18914-3625 USA Tel 215-822-1659; Fax: 305-402-8163
E-mail: tntdns@aol.com.

British Library, Historical Print Editions *Imprint of* **Creative Media Partners, LLC**

British Library, The (GBR) *(978-0-7123) Dist. by* **IPG Chicago.**

Britt Allcroft Productions, *(978-0-9743690; 978-0-9767139; 978-0-9793343)* 133 Wadsworth Ave., Santa Monica, CA 90405 USA Tel 310-428-4033; Fax: 310 392 9769
E-mail: holly_wright@verizon.net
Web site: http://www.brittallcroftproductions.com.

Brittany's Bks, *(978-0-9778796)* 1736 Crest Pl., Colorado Spgs, CO 80911-1110 USA
E-mail: admin@brittanysbooks.com
Web site: http://www.brittanysbooks.com.

Britton & Case Prs., *(978-0-9980066)* 10871 S. Durand Rd, Durand, MI 48429 USA.

Broad Creek Pr., *(978-0-9837148; 978-0-9904662)* P.O. Box 43, Mount Airy, NC 27030 USA Tel 336-473-7256
Dist(s): **BookBaby.**

Broad View Publishing, *(978-0-9815384)* P.O. Box 2726, Bristol, CT 06011-2726 USA Tel 860-793-7618
E-mail: info@broadviewpublishing.com; pubicity@painisnotadisease.com
Web site: http://www.broadviewpublishing.com; http://www.painisnotadisease.com.

Broadcast Quality Productions, Inc., *(978-0-9716136)* 3199 Nottaway Ct., Atlanta, GA 30341 USA Tel 404-292-7777 (phone/fax)
Web site: http://www.bqproductions.com.

Broader Horizon Books *See* **Littletonhouse Publishing**

Broadman & Holman Publishers *See* **B&H Publishing Group**

Broadnax, Cassandra A.L., *(978-0-9771608)* 295 Pannel Rd., Reidsville, NC 27320 USA.

BroadStreet Publishing, *(978-1-4245)* Orders Addr.: 2745 Chicory Rd., Racine, WI 53403 USA (SAN 990-2635); Edit Addr.: 8646 Eagle Creek Cir. Suite 210, Savage, MN 55378 USA (SAN 256-8535) Tel 952-300-6250; Fax: 612-437-4726
E-mail: michelle.winger@broadstreetpublishing.com
Web site: http://www.BROADSTREETPUBLISHING.COM.

BroadSword Comics/ Jim Balent Studios, *(978-0-9745367)* P.O. Box 596, Brodheadsville, PA 18322 USA
E-mail: tarot@jimbalent.com
Web site: http://www.jimbalent.com.

Broadway Bks. *Imprint of* **Crown/Archetype**

Broadway Cares, *(978-0-9754840)* 165 W. 46th St., 13th Flr., New York, NY 10036 USA Tel 212-840-0770; Fax: 212-840-0551
E-mail: viola@bcefa.org.

Broadway Play Publishing, Inc., *(978-0-88145)* P.O. Box 1901, New York, NY 10021-0049 USA (SAN 260-1699)
E-mail: BroadwayPl@aol.com; bppi@broadwayplaypubl.com
Web site: http://www.BroadwayPlayPubl.com
Dist(s): **Follett School Solutions**
MyiLibrary.

Broccoli Bks. *Imprint of* **Broccoli International USA, Inc.**

Broccoli International USA, Inc., *(978-1-932480; 978-1-59741)* Orders Addr.: P.O. Box 66078, Los Angeles, CA 90066 USA Tel 310-815-0600; Fax: 310-815-0660; Edit Addr.: 11806 Gorham Ave. Apt. 4, Los Angeles, CA 90049-5446 USA; *Imprints:* Broccoli Books (Broccoli Bks)
E-mail: info@broccolibooks.com; ardith@bro-usa.com; wholesale@broccolibooks.com; books@animegamers.com; wholesale@bro-usa.com
Web site: http://www.bro-usa.com; http://www.broccolibooks.com; http://www.synch-point.com; http://www.boysenberrybooks.com
Dist(s): **Diamond Bk. Distributors**
Simon & Schuster, Inc.

Brockhaus, F. A., GmbH (DEU) *(978-3-325; 978-3-7653) Dist. by* **Intl Bk Import.**

Brodie, Richard *See* **Firebreak Publishing Co.**

Broken Bread Publishing, *(978-0-9769464)* 6417 S. Iris Way, Littleton, CO 80123-3135 USA
E-mail: books@brokenbreadpublishing.com
Web site: http://www.brokenbreadpublishing.com
Dist(s): **Spring Arbor Distributors, Inc.**

Broken Oak Publishing, *(978-0-9795020)* P.O. Box 255, Ridgetop, TN 37152 USA.

Broken Shackle Publishing, International, *(978-0-9759908)* P.O. Box 20312, Piedmont, CA 94620 USA
E-mail: jstickmon@msn.com.

Bromwell Bks., *(978-0-9753345)* 2500 E. Fourth Ave., Denver, CO 80206 USA Tel 303-388-5969; Fax: 303-764-7544
E-mail: steven_replogle@dpsk12.org
Web site: http://bromwell.dpsk12.org.

Bronwen Publishing, *(978-0-9779267)* 4 Colchester Pl., Suite 4A, Newtown, PA 18940 USA (SAN 850-6426) Tel 215-968-2204
Web site: http://www.bronwenpublishing.com
Dist(s): **Follett School Solutions.**

Bronwynn Pr., LLC, *(978-0-9821404; 978-0-9848487)* P.O. Box 297, Troy, NY 12182 USA Tel 518-328-7891
E-mail: bell@bronwynnpress.com
Web site: http://www.bronwynnpress.com; http://www.gappy.tv.

Bronx Originals Books *See* **Daylight Bks.**

Brook Farm Bks., *(978-0-919761)* 479 U.S. Hwy. 1, P.O. Box 246, Bridgewater, ME 04735 USA (SAN 133-9095) Tel 506-375-4680 (phone/fax); Toll Free: 877-375-4680
E-mail: jean@brookfarmbook.com; jean@brookfarmbooks.com
Dist(s): **Brodart Co.**
Independent Pubs. Group
ebrary, Inc.

Brookehaven Publishing, *(978-0-9844867; 978-1-940905)* P.O. Box 352, Rocklin, CA 95677 USA
E-mail: info@brookehavenpublishing.com
Web site: http://www.brookehavenpublishing.com
Dist(s): **Lulu Pr., Inc.**
Smashwords.

Brookes, Paul H. Publishing Company Incorporated *See* **Brookes Publishing**

Brookes Publishing, *(978-0-933716; 978-1-55766; 978-1-59857; 978-1-68125)* Orders Addr.: P.O. Box 10624, Baltimore, MD 21285-0624 USA (SAN 212-730X) Tel 410-337-9580; Fax: 410-337-8539; Toll Free: 800-638-3775 (customer service/ordering/billing/fulfillment); Edit Addr.: 409 Washington Ave., Suite 500, Baltimore, MD 21204 USA (SAN 666-6485)
E-mail: custserv@brookespublishing.com
Web site: http://www.brookespublishing.com
Dist(s): **Follett School Solutions.**

Brookfield Reader, Inc., The, *(978-0-9660172; 978-1-930093)* 137 Peyton Rd., Sterling, VA 20165-5605 USA (SAN 299-4445)
Dist(s): **Book Wholesalers, Inc.**
Brodart Co.
Quality Bks., Inc.

Brooklyn Botanic Garden, *(978-0-945352; 978-1-889538)* 1000 Washington Ave., Brooklyn, NY 11225-1099 USA (SAN 203-1094) Tel 718-623-7200; 718-625-5838; Fax: 718-622-7839; 718-857-2430
E-mail: rlpodell@bbg.org
Web site: http://www.bbg.org
Dist(s): **Sterling Publishing Co., Inc.**

Brooklyn Pubs., *(978-1-930961; 978-1-931000; 978-1-931805; 978-1-932404; 978-1-60003)* Orders Addr.: P.O. Box 248, Cedar Rapids, IA 52406 USA
E-mail: orders@brookpub.com; customerservice@brookpub.com; steven@brookpub.com
Web site: http://www.brookpub.com
Dist(s): **Follett School Solutions.**

Brooklyn Publishing Company *See* **Brooklyn Pubs.**

Brooks & Brooks, *(978-0-9682530)* 5510 Owensmouth Ave. Apt. 102, Woodland Hls, CA 91367-7011 USA
E-mail: runningbrooks@hotmail.com.

Brooks, Andree Aelion, *(978-0-9702700)* 15 Hitchcock Rd., Westport, CT 06880 USA Tel 203-226-9834; Fax: 203-226-0814
E-mail: andreebrooks@hotmail.com.

†Brooks/Cole, *(978-0-12; 978-0-15; 978-0-314; 978-0-534; 978-0-8185; 978-1-56527; 978-0-495)* Div. of Thomson Learning, Orders Addr.: 7625 Empire Dr., Florence, KY 41042-2978 USA Tel 606-525-2230; Toll Free: 800-354-9706 (orders); Edit Addr.: 511 Forest Lodge Rd., Pacific Grove, CA 93950 USA (SAN 202-3369) Tel 831-373-0728; Fax: 831-375-6414; 10 Davis Dr., Belmont, CA 94002 Tel 650-595-2350
E-mail: info@brookscole.com
Web site: http://www.brookscole.com; http://www.duxbury.com
Dist(s): **CENGAGE Learning**
Houghton Mifflin Harcourt Trade & Reference Pubs.; *CIP.*

Brooks/Cole Publishing Company *See* **Brooks/Cole**

Brookshire Pubns., Inc., *(978-1-880976)* 200 Hazel St., Lancaster, PA 17603 USA Tel 717-392-1321; Fax: 717-392-2078
E-mail: carla@brookshireprinting.com.

Brookteam Corp., *(978-0-9745864)* P.O. Box 276225, Boca Raton, FL 33427 USA Fax: 561-367-9976; Toll Free: 866-571-7878; *Imprints:* Shirt Tales (Shirt Tales)
E-mail: brookteam@worldnet.att.net
Web site: http://www.brookteam.com.

Brophy, Doris Anne, *(978-0-9745232)* 90 Bingham Ave., Rumson, NJ 07760 USA Tel 732-345-7276
E-mail: dambrophy@yahoo.com.

Broqueville Publishing, Inc., *(978-0-9669024; 978-0-9719413)* 1260 Logan Ave., Suite B3, Costa Mesa, CA 92626 USA (SAN 255-0083) Tel 714-624-6441; Fax: 714-668-9972
E-mail: bookorders@broqueville.com
Web site: http://www.broqueville.com.

Brosen Bks., *(978-0-9830359)* 124 Wave, Laguna Beach, CA 92651 USA Tel 949-374-4127
E-mail: bryan@brosencreative.com
Web site: www.brosenbooks.com
Dist(s): **Follett School Solutions.**

Brosquil Edicions, S.L. (ESP) *(978-84-95620; 978-84-96154; 978-84-9795) Dist. by* **Lectorum Pubns.**

Bross Publishing, *(978-0-9763561)* 168 Island Pond Rd., No. 1, Manchester, NH 03109 USA (SAN 256-355X) Tel 603-623-2503 (phone/fax)
E-mail: brosspublishing@sunnyfla.us.

BrotherBiz Publishing, *(978-0-615-47658-2)* 96 School St., Lexington, MA 02421 USA Tel 781-862-3962
E-mail: BrotherBiz@earthlink.net.

Brothers N Publishing Corp., *(978-0-9886272)* 565 S. Mason Rd. No. 204, Katy, TX 77450 USA Tel 832-472-8200
E-mail: brothersnbooks@gmail.com.

Brotman-Marshfield Curriculums, *(978-0-9762568)* 22 Howard St., Newton, MA 02458 USA Tel 617-332-5616; Fax: 617-332-9679
E-mail: brotmanco@aol.com.

Broviak Publishing, *(978-0-9897522)* 10203 holly berry Cir., fishers, IN 46038 USA Tel 317-776-0421
E-mail: broviak@evilteacher.com.

Brown Barn Bks., *(978-0-9746481; 978-0-9768126; 978-0-9798824)* Div. of Pictures of Record, Inc., Orders Addr.: Editorial@brownbarnbooks.com 119 Kettle Creek Rd., Weston, CT 06883 USA Tel 203-227-3387; Fax: 203-222-9673
E-mail: editorial@brownbarnbooks.com
Web site: http://www.brownbarnbooks.com
Dist(s): **BookBaby**
Follett School Solutions.

Brown Bear Books, *(978-0-9670861)* 325 High St., Santa Cruz, CA 95060 USA Tel 831-457-1135
E-mail: brwnbear@sasquatch.com.

Brown Bear Bks., *(978-1-933834; 978-1-936333)* PMB 20, 6890 E. Sunrise Dr., Suite 120, Tucson, AZ 85750-0739 USA
E-mail: info@brownreference.com
Dist(s): **Black Rabbit Bks.**

Brown Bks. *Imprint of* **Olivo, Andy**

Brown, Bonnie M., *(978-0-9624705)* 548 Saint Johns Pl., Franklin, TN 37064-8901 USA
E-mail: bonnibear@aol.com.

Brown Books Publishing Group, *(978-0-9713265; 978-0-9744597; 978-0-9753907; 978-1-933285; 978-1-934812; 978-1-61254)* 16250 Knoll Trail Dr. Ste 205, Dallas, TX 75248 USA Tel 972-381-0009; Fax: 972-248-4336
E-mail: auburn.layman@brownbooks.com
Web site: http://www.brownbooks.com; http://www.thep3press.com
Dist(s): **BookBaby**
Follett School Solutions.

Brown Books Small Press *See* **Small Pr., The**

Brown County Historical Society, *(978-0-9641499)* Orders Addr.: P.O. Box 1411, Green Bay, WI 54305-1411 USA Tel 920-437-1840; Fax: 920-455-4518; Edit Addr.: 1008 S. Monroe Ave., Green Bay, WI 54301-3206 USA Do not confuse with Brown County Historical Society, Nashville, IN, New Ulm, MN
E-mail: bchs@netnet.net
Web site: http://www.browncohistoricalsoc.org.

Brown County Historical Society, *(978-0-9765095; 978-0-9964029)* 2 N. Broadway, New Ulm, MN 56073 USA Fax: 507-354-1068 Do not confuse with Brown County Historical Society in Green Bay, WI
E-mail: officemanager@browncountyhistorymnusa.org.

Brown, David Book Company, The *See* **Casemate Academic**

Brown Dog Bks., *(978-0-9721967)* P.O. Box 2196, Flemington, NJ 08822 USA
E-mail: darhosta@mac.com
Web site: http://www.browndogbooks.com
Dist(s): **Book Wholesalers, Inc.**
Brodart Co.
Follett Media Distribution
Follett School Solutions.

Brown Girls Publishing *Imprint of* **INscribe Digital**

Brown, Harold *See* **Brown&Matthews**

Brown, Kathleen, *(978-0-9796063)* P.O. Box 1920, Clemmons, NC 27012 USA (SAN 853-8719) Tel 336-778-0699
E-mail: rbrown20221@bellsouth.net.

Brown, Kawani, *(978-0-9971763)* 1017 Chestnut ave., Long Beach, CA 90813 USA Tel 909-913-0260
E-mail: nahbexpo@gmail.com.

Brown, Nielsen, *(978-0-9725581)* Orders Addr.: P.O. Box 4174 , Estes Park, CO 80517 USA
E-mail: kristinnielsen@msn.com.

Brown, Samuel E., *(978-0-9770372)* P.O. Box 7009, Jackson, MS 39282 USA Tel 601-540-5470
E-mail: pcsandc@hotmail.com.

Brown&Matthews, *(978-0-9759370)* 2923 E. Michigan St., Orlando, FL 32806 USA (SAN 256-2030)
E-mail: jkmatthews@cfl.rr.com
Web site: http://www.cafepress.com/sitm; http://www.janetmatthews.com.

Brownell, F. & Son, Pubs., *(978-0-9767409; 978-0-9789127)* P.O. Box 76, Montezuma, IA 50171 USA
Web site: http://www.brownells.com.

Brownian Bee Pr., *(978-0-9789688)* 37574 Dew Drop Rd., Lanesboro, MN 55949 USA
E-mail: info@brownianbee.com
Web site: http://www.brownianbee.com
Dist(s): **Unique Bks., Inc.**

Brownstone Monkey Productions, Inc., *(978-0-9785773)* 55 W. 84th St., No. 9, New York, NY 10024-1002 USA Tel 212-933-4168; Fax: 212-228-6149
E-mail: nicole@brownstonemonkey.com; kfiore@nyc.rr.com
Web site: http://brownstonemonkey.com; http://lenithepug.com.

BRP Publishing Group, *(978-0-9801506; 978-1-935460; 978-1-941295)* P.O. Box 822674, Vancouver, WA 98682 USA
E-mail: publisher@nitisbooks.com; publisher@barkingrainpress.org
Web site: http://www.nitisbooks.com; http://www.barkingrainpress.org
Dist(s): **CreateSpace Independent Publishing Platform**
Lightning Source, Inc.
Mackin Educational Resources
OverDrive, Inc.

Brujo Film Production *See* **Pascualina Producciones S.A.**

Bruno, Elizabeth *See* **Uitti, Daniel**

Brunson Publishing, *(978-0-9758614)* Orders Addr.: P.O. Box 1133, Alamogordo, NM 88310 USA Tel 706-367-1334
E-mail: oldmaid4jesus@yahoo.com; tim@teenpact.com
Web site: http://www.oldmaidministries.com; http://www.teenpact.com.

Brunswick Publishing Corp., *(978-0-931494; 978-1-55618)* 593 Southlake Blvd., Richmond, VA 23236-3092 USA (SAN 211-6332)
E-mail: brunswickbooks@verizon.net; info@brunswickbooks.com
Web site: http://www.brunswickbooks.com/.

Bruño, Editorial (ESP) *(978-84-216) Dist. by* **Lectorum Pubns.**

Bruño, Editorial (ESP) *(978-84-216) Dist. by* **Dist Plaza Mayor.**

Brush Creek Publishing, *(978-0-692-75888-5)* 6690 Little Galilee Rd., CLINTON, IL 61727 USA Tel 217-219-0323.

Bryan House Publishers, Incorporated *See* **ECS Learning Systems, Inc.**

Bryan, Tracy Publishing, *(978-0-692-70088-4; 978-0-692-70091-4; 978-0-692-71069-2; 978-0-692-81614-1; 978-0-692-83014-7; 978-0-692-83153-3)* 2886 rickenbacker trail, PORT ORANGE, FL 32128 USA Tel 386-299-5310.

Bryan-Kennedy Entertainment, LLC, *(978-0-615-34098-2; 978-0-615-34699-1; 978-0-9885358)* 177 village blvd, Santa Rosa Beach, FL 32459 USA Tel 615-376-9939
E-mail: mackennedy@mac.com
Web site: http://www.Bryan-Kennedy.com.

Bryars, Bart, *(978-0-692-82963-9)* 2521 Piedmont Rd. NE #2432, ATLANTA, GA 30324 USA Tel 917-251-0463
E-mail: jeffwcrawford5+LVP0003234@gmail.com; jeffwcrawford5+LVP0003234@gmail.com.

Bryce Cullen Publishing, *(978-1-935752)* P.O. Box 731, Alpine, NJ 07620 USA Tel 201-888-8570
E-mail: publish@brycecullen.com
Web site: http://www.brycecullen.com
Dist(s): **Lightning Source, Inc.**

BRYN WILLIAMS LLC, *(978-0-9881814; 978-0-9909461)* Orders Addr.: 655 Orville Rd. E., Eatonville, WA 98328 USA
E-mail: cb@cbwilliams.us
Web site: www.cbwilliams.us.

Bryson Taylor Press *See* **Bryson Taylor Publishing**

Bryson Taylor Publishing, *(978-0-9773738; 978-0-9841934; 978-0-9882940; 978-0-9983867)* Div. of Bryson Taylor Inc., 199 New County Rd., Saco, ME 04072 USA (SAN 257-4403) Tel 207-838-2146
E-mail: deb@brysontaylor.com
Web site: http://www.brysontaylorpublishing.com.

Brzamo Publishing, *(978-0-9743580)* 887 Richart Ln., Greenwood, IN 46142 USA.

B'Squeak Productions, *(978-0-9746782)* P.O. Box 151, Menlo Park, CA 94026-0151 USA
E-mail: rights@bsqueak.com
Web site: http://www.bsqueak.com.

BTSena Pubns., *(978-0-692-20521-1; 978-0-692-78537-9; 978-0-692-79943-7; 978-0-692-90381-0; 978-0-692-91765-7)* 2703 N Northacres Dr., Hobbs, NM 88240 USA Tel 5754411649
Dist(s): **CreateSpace Independent Publishing Platform.**

B*tween Productions, Inc., *(978-0-9746587; 978-0-9758511; 978-1-933566)* 1666 Massachusetts Ave., Suite 17, Lexington, MA 02420 USA Tel 781-863-8228; Fax: 781-863-8338; *Imprints:* Beacon Street Girls (B Street Girls)
E-mail: kblais@btweenproductions.com
Web site: http://www.beaconstreetgirls.com.

BTWEYL *Imprint of* **Bks. That Will Enhance Your Life**

Bubble Gum Pr., *(978-0-9729833; 978-0-9839907)* 1420 N. State St., Aberdeen, SD 57401-2167 USA
E-mail: bmehrmantraut@msn.com
Web site: http://www.bubblegumpress.com
Dist(s): **Follett School Solutions.**

Bubblegum Bks., *(978-0-9754621)* P.O. Box 94106, Cleveland, OH 44101-6106 USA
E-mail: info@bubblegumbooks.com
Web site: http://www.bubblegumbooks.com
Dist(s): **Mariposa Pr.**
SCB Distributors.

Buchbinder, Leonardo, *(978-0-9774044; 978-0-615-34717-2)* 8001 NW 84 Terr., Tamarac, FL 33321 USA Tel 954-261-9488
E-mail: mstenn5031@aol.com.

Buck Engineering Company, Incorporated, Lab-Volt Systems Division *See* **Lab-Volt Systems, Inc.**

Buck Publishing, *(978-0-9725912)* Orders Addr.: P.O. Box 12231, Roanoke, VA 24023-2231 USA Tel 540-985-0618 (phone/fax); Edit Addr.: 710 Ferdinand Ave., No. 9, Roanoke, VA 24016 USA Do not confuse with companies with the same or similar name in Birmingham, AL, Fairbanks, AK.

Buckbeech Studios, *(978-0-9771494)* Orders Addr.: P.O. Box 430, Stanford, IN 47463-0430 USA Tel 812-369-6061; Edit Addr.: 30 Amberwood Pkwy., Ashland, OH 44805 USA
E-mail: publisher@buckbeech.com
Web site: http://www.buckbeech.com
Dist(s): **Follett School Solutions.**

Bucket Fillers, Inc., *(978-0-9960999; 978-0-9974864; 978-1-945369)* P.O. Box 255, Brighton, MI 48116 USA Tel 810-229-5468; Fax: 810-588-6782
E-mail: info@bucketfillers101.com
Web site: http://www.bucketfillers101.com
Dist(s): **Independent Pubs. Group.**

Bucket Fillosophy *See* **Bucket Fillers, Inc.**

Bucket of Books *See* **Bimini Bks.**

Bucking Horse Bks., *(978-0-9844460)* P.O. Box 8507, Missoula, MT 59807 USA
E-mail: collard@bigsky.net
Web site: http://www.buckinghorsebooks.com
Dist(s): **Mountain Pr. Publishing Co., Inc.**

Bucknell Univ. Pr., *(978-0-8387)* Taylor Hall, Lewisburg, PA 17837 USA
E-mail: naf006@bucknell.edu
Web site: http://www.departments.bucknell.edu/univ_press/
Dist(s): **Associated Univ. Presses**
Baker & Taylor International

MyiLibrary
Rowman & Littlefield Publishers, Inc.
TextStream
ebrary, Inc.

Buddha's Light Publications USA Corp, *(978-0-9715612; 978-0-9717495; 978-1-932293; 978-1-939596)* 3456 S. Glenmark Dr., Hacienda Heights, CA 91745 USA Tel 626-961-9697; 84 Margaret St., London, w1w 8td Tel 020-7636-8394; Fax: 020-7580-6220
E-mail: blpusacorp@gmail.com
Web site: http://www.blpusa.com
Dist(s): **Follett School Solutions.**

Buddha's Light Publishing *See* **Buddha's Light Publications USA Corp**

Buddhi Pubns., *(978-0-9644226)* Orders Addr.: P.O. Box 208, Canyon, CA 94516 USA Tel 510-376-7796; Fax: 510-376-3503; Edit Addr.: 35 Pinehurst Rd., Canyon, CA 94516 USA.

Buddhist Text Translation Society, *(978-0-88139; 978-0-917512; 978-1-60103; 978-0-88139-767-3)* Affil. of Dharma Realm Buddhist Assoc., Orders Addr.: 4951 Bodhi Way, Ukiah, CA 95482 USA Tel 707-462-0939; Fax: 707-462-0949; Edit Addr.: 4951 Bodhi Way,, Ukiah, CA 95482 USA (SAN 281-3556) Tel 707-468-9112 (phone/fax)
E-mail: hchih@netzero.net; hengdzu@drba.org; bttsonline@snetworking.com
Web site: http://www.bttsonline.org
Dist(s): **Follett School Solutions.**

Buddies Publishing, LLC, *(978-1-946719)* 37263 Charter Oaks Blvd., Clinton Township, MI 48036 USA Tel 586-855-6400
E-mail: philpirkola@gmail.com
Web site: http://www.buddiespublishing.com.

Budding Artists, Inc., *(978-1-888108)* 222 Palisades Ave., Santa Monica, CA 90402-2734 USA.

Budding Biologist, *(978-0-9855481)* 2939 NE 11TH Terr., Gainesville, FL 32609 USA Tel 919-621-5725
E-mail: kcallis@ufl.edu
Dist(s): **Independent Pubs. Group.**

Budding Family Publishing, *(978-0-9741882)* P.O. Box 2078, Manhattan Beach, CA 90267-2078 USA Fax: 310-374-1030
E-mail: renee@buddingfamily.com
Web site: http://www.buddingfamily.com.

Buddy Bks. *Imprint of* **ABDO Publishing Co.**

Buddy Bks. Publishing, *(978-0-9799980; 978-1-934887)* P.O. Box 3354, Pinehurst, NC 28374 USA Tel 910-295-2876
E-mail: admin@buddybookspublishing.com
Web site: http://www.buddybookspublishing.com.

Buenaventura Pr., *(978-0-9766848; 978-0-9800039; 978-1-935443)* P.O. Box 23661, Oakland, CA 94623 USA
Web site: http://www.buenaventurapress.com
Dist(s): **D.A.P./Distributed Art Pubs.**

Buffalo Fine Arts Academy *See* **Buffalo Fine Arts/Albright-Knox Art Gallery**

†Buffalo Fine Arts/Albright-Knox Art Gallery, *(978-0-914782; 978-1-887457)* Albright-Knox Art Gallery, 1285 Elmwood Ave., Buffalo, NY 14222 USA (SAN 202-4845) Tel 716-882-8700; Fax: 716-882-1958; *CIP.*

Bug Boy Bks., *(978-0-615-19036-5)* 2085 Kenneth St., Burton, MI 48529 USA
E-mail: nativeamericanandrew@yahoo.com; andrew@bugboyandy.com
Dist(s): **Lulu Pr., Inc.**

Bug Boy Publishing *See* **Bug Boy Bks.**

BugaBk. llc, *(978-0-9888974)* 7667 Cahill Rd. Suite 100, Edina, MN 55439 USA Tel 952-943-1441
E-mail: dustinh@bugabook.com
Web site: www.bugabook.com.

Bugeye Bks., *(978-0-9722249)* 10645 N. Tatum Blvd., Suite 200-246, Phoenix, AZ 85028 USA Tel 602-980-7101; Fax: 480-483-3460
E-mail: insightstudios@cox.net
Web site: http://www.bugeyebooks.com.

Buggs Books *See* **Mogul Comics**

Buhman, Ron, *(978-0-9747961)* Orders Addr.: ., Aransas Pass, TX 78335 USA; Edit Addr.: P.O. Box P O Box 634, Aransas Pass, TX 78335 USA Tel 361-944-0671; Fax: 361-944-0671
E-mail: rkb919@juno.com
Web site: http://jam-packed-action.com.

Build Your Story, *(978-0-9748416)* Orders Addr.: P.O. Box 6003, Midlothian, VA 23112 USA Fax: 810-592-2479; Toll Free: 866-807-8679; Edit Addr.: 2212 Water Horse Ct., Midlothian, VA 23112 USA
E-mail: oscar@buildyourstory.com
Web site: http://www.buildyourstory.com.

Builders' Stone Publishing, LLC, *(978-0-9791504)* 6932 Sylvan Woods Dr., Sanford, FL 32771 USA (SAN 852-5994) Tel 407-549-5066
E-mail: pschoemann@broadandcassel.com
Web site: http://www.buildersstonepublishing.com.

Building Blocks, LLC, *(978-0-943452)* 38 W. 567 Brindlewood Ln., Elgin, IL 60123 USA (SAN 240-6063) Tel 847-742-1013; Fax: 847-742-1054 (orders); Toll Free: 800-233-2448 Do not confuse with companies with similar and same name in Madison,NJ, Westbury NY
E-mail: dick@bblocksonline.com
Web site: http://www.bblocksonline.com
Dist(s): **Gryphon Hse., Inc.**

†Bulfinch, *(978-0-8212)* Div. of Little Brown & Co., Orders Addr.: 3 Center Plaza, Boston, MA 02108-2084 USA Tel 617-227-0730; Fax: 617-263-2857; Toll Free Fax: 800-286-9471; Toll Free: 800-759-0190; Edit Addr.: Time & Life Bldg. 1271 Ave. of the Americas, New York, NY 10020 USA Toll Free: 800-343-9204 Do not confuse with Bullfinch Pr., Minnetonka, MN
E-mail: cust.service@twbg.com
Web site: http://www.twbookmark.com/arts/index.html
Dist(s): **Follett School Solutions**
Leonard, Hal Corp.
Hachette Bk. Group
MyiLibrary; *CIP.*

Bull, David Publishing, Inc., *(978-0-9649722; 978-1-893618; 978-1-935007)* 4250 E. Camelback Rd., Suite K150, Phoenix, AZ 85018 USA Tel 602-852-9500; Fax: 602-852-9503; Toll Free: 800-831-1758
E-mail: dbull@bullpublishing.com; info@bullpublishing.com; tmoore@bullpublishing.com
Web site: http://www.bullpublishing.com.

Bullard, Belinda *See* **A Blessed Heritage Educational Resources**

Bulldog Pr., *(978-0-9672710)* P.O. Box 620358, Woodside, CA 94062-0358 USA Tel 650-851-8218; Fax: 650-851-1753 Do not confuse with companies with the same name in Frankfort, IN, Whittier, CA
E-mail: dputnam555@aol.com
Web site: http://www.americanbulldogger.com.

Bullfrog Bks. *Imprint of* **Jump! Inc.**

BullsEye, LLC *See* **Hargrave Pr.**

Bumble Bee Bks., *(978-0-9914701)* 1804 Benodot St., Champaign, IL 61822 USA Tel 217-898-7835
E-mail: storytym@comcast.net.

Bumble Bee Publishing, *(978-0-9754342; 978-1-933982)* Div. of Bumble Bee Productions, Inc., Orders Addr.: 725 Watch Island Reach, Chesapeake, VA 23320 USA (SAN 256-1611) Tel 757-410-9409 (phone/fax); Toll Free: 866-782-9533 (phone/fax); Edit Addr.: P.O. Box 1757, Chesapeake, VA 23327-1757 USA (SAN 256-162X) Tel 747-410-9409; 5721 M St., Lincoln, NE 68510 (SAN 256-1638); *Imprints:* bPlus Books (bPlus Bks)
E-mail: buzz707@bbpmail.com
Web site: http://www.yesterdaywehadahurricane.com; http://www.bumblebeepublishing.com; http://www.rubyleethebumblebee.com; http://www.bumblebeeproductions.com; http://www.bplusbooks.com.

Bumples, *(978-0-9700952)* 676 Post Rd., Darien, CT 06820-4717 USA
E-mail: bumples@aol.com; Bumples@aol.com.

Bumpy Pumpkin, *(978-0-9754696)* 3405 Heather Dr., Augusta, GA 30909 USA
Web site: http://www.bumpypumpkin.com.

Bundoran Pr. (CAN) *(978-0-9782052; 978-0-9877352; 978-1-927881; 978-0-9880674) Dist. by* **D C D.**

Bunim and Bannigan Ltd., *(978-1-933480)* PMB 157, 111 E. 14th St., New York, NY 10003-4103 USA
Web site: http://www.bunim&bannigan.com; http://www.bunimbannigan.com
Dist(s): **Itasca Bks.**

Bunker Hill Publishing, Inc., *(978-1-59373)* 285 River Rd., Piermont, NH 03779-3009 USA; 27 W. 20th St., New York, NY 10011
E-mail: mail@bunkerhillpublishing.com
Web site: http://www.bunkerhillpublishing.com
Dist(s): **Follett School Solutions**
Midpoint Trade Bks., Inc.
National Bk. Network.

Bunny & The Crocodile Pr., The, *(978-0-938572)* 1821 Glade Ct., Annapolis, MD 21403-1945 USA Tel 410-267-7432 (phone/fax); *Imprints:* Forest Woods Media Productions (Forest Woods Media)
E-mail: gracecav@comcast.net
Web site: http://www.members.aol.com/grace7623/grace.htm.

Bunster, Alejandra, *(978-0-692-40506-2; 978-0-692-73515-2)* 254 San Sebastian Ave., Coral Gables, FL 33134 USA Tel 305-446-5673
E-mail: abunster@carrollton.org.

Burden-Evans, Patricia, *(978-0-615-15120-5)* 1814 Palmyra Dr., Greenville, MS 38701 USA
E-mail: pevan6@aol.com
Dist(s): **Lulu Pr., Inc.**

BurgYoung Publishing, *(978-0-9716511)* 4105 E. Florida Ave., No. 300, Denver, CO 80222 USA Tel 303-757-5406
E-mail: tmcco@msn.com; infoby@burgyoungpublishing.com
Web site: http://www.burgyoungpublishing.com; http://www.gettingtoknowgod.com.

Buried Treasure Publishing, *(978-0-9800993; 978-0-615-14018-6)* 2813 NW Westbrooke Cir., Blue Springs, MO 64015 USA
E-mail: sales@buriedtreasurepublishing.com; duaneporter@yahoo.com
Web site: http://buriedtreasurepublishing.com
Dist(s): **Lulu Pr., Inc.**

Burkhardt The Artist, *(978-0-9762996)* P.O. Box 35, Alexandria, KY 41001 USA Tel 859-694-6000
E-mail: rockyburk@hotmail.com
Web site: http://www.rockyburkhardt.com.

Burkhart Bks., *(978-0-9790975)* 4000 N. Meridian St., Suite 17G, Indianapolis, IN 46208 USA (SAN 852-4270)
E-mail: l.burkhart@sbcglobal.net
Web site: http://www.burkhartnetwork.com
Dist(s): **Distributors, The**
Partners Bk. Distributing, Inc.

Burley Creek Studio *See* **White Dog Studio**

Burlington, David, *(978-0-9772136)* 16723 Basin Oak., San Antonio, TX 78247-6220 USA
E-mail: dave@bassfishingaskdave.com
Web site: http://www.bassfishingaskdave.com.

Burlington National, Inc., *(978-1-57706)* Orders Addr.: P.O. Box 841, Mandeville, LA 70470 USA Tel 504-250-7228; Edit Addr.: 6301 Perrier, New Orleans, LA 70118 USA
E-mail: books@burlingtonnational.com.

Burman Books, Inc. (CAN) *(978-0-9736632; 978-0-9737166; 978-0-9739097; 978-1-897404; 978-0-9781380; 978-1-927005) Dist. by* **InnovativeLog.**

Burney Enterprises Unlimited, *(978-0-9745360)* P.O. Box 401402, Redford, MI 48240-9402 USA.

BurnhillWolf, *(978-0-9645655)* 321 Prospect St., NW, Lenoir, NC 28645 USA Tel 704-754-0287
E-mail: Burnwolf@charter.net
Web site: http://www.burnhillwolf.com
Dist(s): **CreateSpace Independent Publishing Platform.**

Burning Bush Creation, *(978-0-9768680; 978-1-60390)* 2114 Queen Ave. N., Minneapolis, MN 55411-2435 USA Tel 612-529-0198; Fax: 612-529-0199
E-mail: ron@mcconico.com
Web site: http://www.burningbushcreation.com.

Burns, Phillys, *(978-0-9620065)* 7450 Olivetas Ave., No. 230, La Jolla, CA 92037 USA (SAN 247-526X).

BurnsBooks, *(978-0-9726099)* 50 Joe's Hill Rd., Danbury, CT 06811 USA Tel 203-744-0232
E-mail: burnsbookspub@aol.com
Web site: http://www.burnsbookspublishing.com.

Burt Creations *See* **Burt, Steven E.**

Burt, Steven E., *(978-0-9649283; 978-0-9741407; 978-0-9856188)* Orders Addr.: 17101 SE. 94th Berrien Ct., The Villages, FL 32162 USA (SAN 253-925X) Tel 352-391-8292
E-mail: passtev@aol.com
Web site: http://www.SteveBurtBooks.com.

Burton, Kenneth Hugh, *(978-0-9747043)* Orders Addr.: P.O. Box 38142, Atlanta, GA 30334 USA Tel 404-799-1908; Edit Addr.: 406 Collier Ridge Dr. NW, Atlanta, GA 30318-7312 USA
E-mail: notrub18@bellsouth.net.

Buscher, Julie W., *(978-0-9786352)* Orders Addr.: P.O. Box 627, Brighton, CO 80601-0627 USA (SAN 851-1802) Tel 303-659-7354
E-mail: julobush2@q.com
Web site: http://www.homerthehelicopter.com.

Bush, Bill *See* **Bush Publishing Inc.**

Bush Brothers & Co., *(978-0-9779308)* 1016 E. Weisgarber Rd., Knoxville, TN 37909-2683 USA.

Bush Publishing Inc., *(978-0-9723102; 978-0-9778728; 978-0-9798113; 978-0-9824391; 978-0-9836109)* 5427 S. 94th E. Ave., Tulsa, OK 74104 USA
Web site: http://www.bushpublishing.com.

Bushweller, Ellie, *(978-0-615-24478-5)* 9 Worth St., South Burlington, VT 05403 USA
Dist(s): **Lulu Pr., Inc.**

Business Angel Pr., *(978-0-9798909)* 174 W. Foothill Blvd., No. 327, Monrovia, CA 91016 USA (SAN 854-6738) Tel 626-357-1922; Fax: 818-475-1474; Toll Free: 800-705-6545
E-mail: contact@businessangelpress.com
Web site: http://www.businessangelpress.com.

Business Bks. International, *(978-0-916673)* P.O. Box 1587, New Canaan, CT 06840 USA (SAN 297-1860) Tel 203-966-9645; Fax: 203-966-6018
E-mail: lesdv@businessbooksusa.com
Web site: http://www.businessbooksusa.com.

Business Bks., LLC, *(978-0-9723714)* 2709 Washington Ave., 21A, Evansville, IN 47714 USA
E-mail: mbussingbu@aol.com
Web site: http://www.bussinessbooksllc.com.

Business Jobs *See* **Alexie Bks.**

Business Plus *Imprint of* **Grand Central Publishing**

Business Word, The *See* **Sterling Investments I, LLC DBA Twins Magazine**

Buster B.B. Publishing, *(978-0-9726691)* 1530 Indian Springs Rd., Pine Beach, NY 12566 USA
E-mail: mirror38@aol.com
Web site: http://www.reflectionsseminars.com.

Busy Bee Bks., *(978-0-9759281)* 2160 110th St., SE, Delano, MN 55328 USA Tel 952-237-7218
E-mail: debbyanderson@juno.com.

Butler Bk. Publishing, *(978-0-9627459; 978-1-884532; 978-1-935497; 978-1-941953)* Orders Addr.: 608 Briar Hill Rd., Louisville, KY 40206 USA (SAN 990-0667) Tel 502-897-9393; Fax: 502-897-9797
E-mail: ckbutler@aol.com; eric@butlerbooks.com; billy@butlerbooks.com
Web site: http://www.butlerbooks.com
Dist(s): **Follett School Solutions.**

Butler Book Publishing Services, Incorporated *See* **Butler Bk. Publishing**

Butler Ctr. for Arkansas Studies, *(978-0-9708574; 978-0-9800897; 978-1-935106; 978-1-945624)* c/o Central Arkansas Library System, 100 Rock St., Little Rock, AR 72201 USA
Web site: http://www.cals.org; http://www.butlercenter.org
Dist(s): **Chicago Distribution Ctr.**
MyiLibrary
Univ. of Arkansas Pr.

BuTo, Ltd. Co., *(978-0-9729569)* P.O. Box 9018, Austin, TX 78766 USA (SAN 255-4321) Fax: 512-450-0372
E-mail: butoltdco@aol.com
Web site: http://www.buto.biz.

Buttar, Deborah *See* **GMEC Publishing**

Buttercup Media, *(978-0-9768152)* Orders Addr.: P.O. Box 222003, Dallas, TX 75222 USA Tel 214-890-6833
E-mail: michael.p.collins1@gmail.com
Dist(s): **BookBaby.**

Butterfly Bk. Makers, *(978-0-9754117)* 1450 W. 800 N., Orem, UT 84057 USA
E-mail: hatfiron@aol.com.

Butterfly Books *See* **Black Garnet Pr.**

Butterfly Ink Publishing, *(978-0-9745423)* 20637 Skouras Dr., Winnetka, CA 91306 USA
E-mail: butterflyinkpub@aol.com; kim@butterflyinkpublishing.com
Web site: http://www.butterflyinkpublishing.com.

Butterfly Park Educational Materials, Inc., *(978-0-9744575)* 3126 Elmira Ct., Denver, CO 80238-2929 USA
E-mail: butterflypark@comcast.net
Web site: http://www.butterflyparkphonics.com.

Butterfly Pavilion, *(978-0-9729000)* 6252 W. 104th Ave., Westminster, CO 80020 USA Tel 303-469-5441; Fax: 303-657-5944
E-mail: plennyson@butterflies.org
Web site: http://www.butterflies.org.

Butterfly Press *See* **Butterfly Productions, LLC**

Butterfly Productions, LLC, *(978-0-9752936)* 165 Shadow Rock Dr., Sedona, AZ 86336 USA Tel 928-204-2811; Fax: 928-204-9118 Do not confuse with companies with the same or similar name in New York, NY, Worcester, MA, Houston, TX, Old Town, ME, Dayton, OH, Cochranville, PA, Princeton, NJ , Amherst, MA, Charston, WV, Pheonix, AZ
E-mail: butterfly@sedona.net
Web site: http://www.butterflyproductions.info.

Butterfly Typeface, The, *(978-1-942022; 978-0-9909919; 978-0-692-48438-8; 978-1-947656)* 8509 W MARKHAM, LITTLE ROCK, AR 72215 USA Tel 501-681-0080
E-mail: butterflytypeface.imw@gmail.com
Web site: www.butterflytypeface.com.

Butterhouse Publishing, *(978-0-9763971)* 12251 N. 32nd St., Suite 4, Phoenix, AZ 85032 USA
E-mail: financialstories@juno.com.

Buttermilk Bks., *(978-0-9978909)* 1482 Highland Cir., Myrtle Beach, SC 29575 USA Tel 843-655-5377
E-mail: tomwinn@sc.rr.com.

Buttermoth Pr. (AUS) *(978-0-9803367) Dist. by* **LuluCom.**

Butters Pr., *(978-0-9754960)* 2047 Gale Rd., Eaton Rapids, MI 48827 USA
Web site: http://www.throughtheears.com.

Butterworth-Heinemann *Imprint of* **Elsevier Science & Technology Bks.**

Button Bks. (GBR) *(978-1-908985) Dist. by* **PerseuPGW.**

Button Flower Pr., *(978-0-9747836)* 7422 Westview Dr., Boardman, OH 44512 USA.

Buttonberry Bks., *(978-0-9768227)* 29 Sawmill Rd., Lebanon, NJ 08833 USA
Web site: http://www.buttonberrybooks.com
Dist(s): **Follett School Solutions.**

Buttonweed Pr., L.L.C., *(978-0-9755675)* 204 7th St W. # 125, Northfield, MN 55057-2419 USA (SAN 256-1700)
E-mail: info@buttonweedpress.com
Web site: http://www.buttonweedpress.com
Dist(s): **Follett School Solutions**
Partners Bk. Distributing, Inc.

Buttonwood Pr., *(978-0-9660685; 978-0-9742920; 978-0-9823351; 978-0-9891462; 978-0-9965562; 978-0-9972464)* Orders Addr.: P.O. Box 716, Haslett, MI 48840 USA Tel 517-339-9871; Fax: 517-339-5908; Edit Addr.: 5951 Buttonwood Dr., Haslett, MI 48840 USA Do not confuse with companies with the same name Champaign, IL, Potomac, MD, New York, NY, Solvang, CA
E-mail: rlbald@aol.com
Web site: http://www.buttonwoodpress.com
Dist(s): **Partners Bk. Distributing, Inc.**

Buy Books on the Web.Com *See* **Infinity Publishing**

Buy Rite, *(978-0-9723744; 978-1-60421)* 88 Vanderveer Rd., Freehold, NJ 07728 USA Tel 732-294-9000; Fax: 732-294-9363; Toll Free: 888-777-7952
Web site: http://www.buyriteinc.com.

Buz-Land Presentations, Inc., *(978-0-9766990)* 73 Harding Rd., Wyckoff, NJ 07481 USA Tel 201-848-0595; 73 Harding Rd., Wyckoff, NJ 07481-2730 (SAN 256-5692)
E-mail: buzi.bee@verizon.net
Web site: http://www.buz-land.com; www.WWRT.org.

Buzzard Pr. International, *(978-0-9648488)* 506 W. Donna Dr., Merced, CA 95348 USA Tel 209-723-6738; Fax: 209-723-6253
E-mail: buzzard@buzzardpress.com
Dist(s): **Sunbelt Pubns., Inc.**

Buzzy's Bks., *(978-0-9719054)* P.O. Box 566, Grafton, MA 01519 USA Tel 508-839-2442; Fax: 508-839-7396
E-mail: buzzy@buzzysbooks.org
Web site: http://www.buzzysbooks.org.

By Grace Enterprises, *(978-0-9663629; 978-1-940591)* 9515 Twin Oaks Dr., Manvel, TX 77578-5307 USA
E-mail: huletteppl@aol.com; pamlv@aol.com
Web site: http://www.bygraceent.com
Dist(s): **Follett School Solutions.**

by shayne, *(978-0-9725593)* P.O. Box 221474, Santa Clarita, CA 91322 USA
Web site: http://www.byshayne.com.

By The Creek Pubns., *(978-0-9974810)* 238 Shore Brook Ln., Commerce Twp., MI 48390 USA Tel 248-390-3906
E-mail: lindakmclean@yahoo.com.

ByD Pr., *(978-0-9721035)* 1424 33rd St., NW, Washington, DC 20007 USA Tel 202-342-9189 (phone/fax)
E-mail: bydpress@erols.com.

BYE Publishing Services, *(978-0-9656739)* Orders Addr.: 915 L St., Suite 144, Sacramento, CA 95814 USA Tel 916-529-3119 Corporate Hq; Fax: 916-683-1476; Edit Addr.: 5245 College Ave., Suite 333, Oakland, CA 94618 USA Tel 510-272-0101
E-mail: byepublishing@comcast.net
Web site: http://www.byepublishing.com.

Byeway *Imprint of* **Byeway Bks.**

Byeway Bks., *(978-1-85997; 978-1-904586; 978-1-933581; 978-1-934004; 978-1-60176)* 15941 W. 65th St., Shawnee, KS 66217-9342 USA Toll Free Fax: 866-426-3929; Toll Free: 866-429-3929; *Imprints:* Byeway (Byeway)
E-mail: customerservice@byewaybooks.com
Web site: http://www.byewaybooks.com/how_to_order.html.

Byrd, Fay T., *(978-0-9776805)* 9325 Pan Ridge Rd., Baltimore, MD 21234 USA (SAN 257-9898) Tel 410-661-0295
E-mail: faysangelharp@aol.com
Web site: www.faysangelharp.com.

Byte Level Research, *(978-0-9796475; 978-1-61822)* 2305 Ashland St. No. C417, Ashland, OR 97520 USA (SAN 853-9847); *Imprints:* Ashland Creek Press (AshlandCreek)
Web site: http://www.bytelevelbooks.com; http://www.ashlandcreekpress.com
Dist(s): **Follett School Solutions**
INscribe Digital.

Byte Me! Inc., *(978-0-9798611; 978-0-615-14953-0)* P.O. Box 60705, Reno, NV 89506 USA (SAN 854-5863) Tel 775-772-6378; 775-972-3322; Fax: 775-972-3323 Never after 5p.m. pst
E-mail: saraw1@clearwire.net; alma_corazon12@yahoo.com
Web site: http://www.cdebooksbyteme.org; http://www.stores.lulu.com/georgiahedrick;

http://www.stores.lulu.com/georgiahedrick;
http://www.stores.lulu.com/georgiahedrick
Dist(s): **Lulu Pr., Inc.**
Byte/Me Teen Bk. *Imprint of* **Awe-Struck Publishing**
BYU Creative Works *Imprint of* **Brigham Young Univ.**
C A Filius *See* **Charwood Pubns.**
C & C Educational Materials, LLC, *(978-0-9640524; 978-0-9747205; 978-0-9963509)* 12514 Dermott Dr., Houston, TX 77065 USA
E-mail: barbara.cobaugh@att.net
Web site: www.strategiesforstaar.com.
C & C Productions, *(978-0-9753273)* PMB 254, 330 SW 43rd St., No. K, Renton, WA 98055 USA.
C&D Enterprises, *(978-0-9633231; 978-0-9765938)* P.O. Box 7201, Arlington, VA 22207-7201 USA Fax: 703-276-3033
E-mail: harryfp@comcast.net.
C&D International, *(978-0-937347)* 111 Ferguson Ct., Suite 105, Irving, TX 75062-7014 USA (SAN 659-1523) Toll Free: 800-231-0442.
C & H Pubns., *(978-0-9740882)* 31201 S. 596 Ln., Grove, OK 74344 USA.
†C & T Publishing, *(978-0-914881; 978-1-57120; 978-1-60705; 978-1-61745)* Orders Addr.: 1651 Challenge Dr., Concord, CA 94520 USA (SAN 289-0720) Tel 925-677-0377; Fax: 925-617-0374; Toll Free: 800-284-1114; *Imprints:* Stash Books (StashBks); FunStitch Studio (FunStitch Stu)
E-mail: ctinfo@ctpub.com
Web site: http://www.ctpub.com
Dist(s): **Follett School Solutions**
MyiLibrary
National Bk. Network
ebrary, Inc.; *CIP.*
CBI Pr., *(978-0-9705812)* 6 Jeffrey Cir., Bedford, MA 01730 USA Do not confuse with C B I Press, Arlington, VA
E-mail: nancy_nugent@comcast.net
Web site: http://www.cbipress.com.
C. B. Publishing House, Incorporated *See* **Cubbie Blue Publishing**
C C L S Publishing Hse., *(978-1-928882; 978-0-7428)* 3191 Coral Way, Suite 114, Miami, FL 33145-3209 USA (SAN 254-4695) Tel 305-529-2257; Fax: 305-443-8538; Toll Free: 800-704-8181
E-mail: info@cclscorp.com
Web site: http://www.cclscorp.com
Dist(s): **Continental Bk. Co., Inc.**
CEF Pr., *(978-1-55976)* Div.of Child Evangelism Fellowship, Orders Addr.: P.O. Box 348, Warrenton, MO 63383 USA Tel 636-456-4321; Fax: 636-456-2078; Toll Free: 800-748-7710; Edit Addr.: 2300 E. Hwy. M, Warrenton, MO 63383 USA (SAN 211-7789)
E-mail: custserv@cefonline.com
Web site: http://www.cefonline.com;
http://www.cefpress.com.
CES Industries, Inc., *(978-0-86711)* 2023 New Hwy., Farmingdale, NY 11735-1103 USA (SAN 237-9864)
E-mail: m.nesenoff@cesindustries.com
Web site: http://www.cesindustries.com.
CFKR Career Materials, Inc., *(978-0-934783; 978-1-887481)* P.O. Box 99, Meadow Vista, CA 95722-0099 USA (SAN 694-2547) Toll Free Fax: 800-770-0433; Toll Free: 800-525-5626
E-mail: requestinfo@cfkr.com; cfkr@cfkr.com;
order@cfkr.com
Web site: http://www.cfkr.com.
C I S Communications, Inc., *(978-0-935063; 978-1-56062)* 180 Park Ave., Lakewood, NJ 08701 USA (SAN 694-5953) Tel 732-905-3000; Fax: 732-367-6666.
CMSP Projects, *(978-0-942851)* School of Engineering, 51 Astor Pl., New York, NY 10003 USA (SAN 667-6731) Tel 212-228-0950.
CPI Pubs., *(978-0-9648363)* Div. of Christopher Productions, Inc., 1115 David Ave., Pacific Grove, CA 93950 USA Tel 818-831-9268; Fax: 818-845-2128
Dist(s): **Austin & Company, Inc.**
CPI Publishing, Inc., 311 E. 51st St., New York, NY 10022 USA (SAN 218-6896) Tel 212-753-3800
Dist(s): **Modern Curriculum Pr.**
CPM Educational Program, *(978-1-885145; 978-1-931287; 978-1-60328)* 1233 Noonan Dr., Sacramento, CA 95822 USA Tel 916-446-9936; Fax: 916-444-5263
E-mail: cpm@cpm.org; bradley@cpm.org
Web site: http://www.cpm.org.
C R C Publications *See* **Faith Alive Christian Resources**
C R C World Literature Ministries *See* **C R C World Literature Ministries/Libros Desafio**
C R C World Literature Ministries/Libros Desafio, *(978-0-939125; 978-1-55883; 978-1-55955)* Subs. of CRC Pubns., 2850 Kalamazoo Ave., SE, Grand Rapids, MI 49560 USA (SAN 251-3269) Tel 616-224-0785 (customer service); Fax: 616-224-0834; Toll Free: 800-333-8300
E-mail: info@worldliterature.org
Web site: http://www.worldliterature.org/
Dist(s): **Faith Alive Christian Resources.**
CRM, *(978-0-9713534; 978-1-933341)* Orders Addr.: P.O. Box 2124, Hendersonville, NC 28793 USA Tel 828-877-3356; Fax: 828-890-1511; Edit Addr.: 1916 Reasonover Rd., Cedar Mountain, NC 28218 USA
E-mail: crm@ciridmus.com
Web site: http://www.ciridmus.com
Dist(s): **Send The Light Distribution LLC.**
C R Pubns., *(978-0-615-15964-5; 978-0-615-15981-2; 978-0-615-16029-0; 978-0-615-16673-5)* 415 E. 15th, Kearny, NE 68847-6959 USA
Web site: http://www.IDealinHope.com/author
Dist(s): **Lulu Pr., Inc.**
†CSS Publishing Co., *(978-0-7880; 978-0-89536; 978-1-55673; 978-0-615-84860-0)* Orders Addr.: 5450 N. Dixie Hwy., Lima, OH 45807-9559 USA Tel 800-241-4056; 419-227-1818; Fax: 419-228-9184; Toll Free: 800-241-4056 Customer Service; 800-537-1030 Orders; Edit Addr.: P.O. Box 4503, Lima, OH 45802-4503 USA (SAN 207-0707) Tel 419-227-1818; Fax: 419-228-9184; Toll Free: 800-537-1030 (Orders); 800-241-4056 (Customer Service); *Imprints:* Fairway Press (Fairway Pr) Do not confuse with CSS Publishing in Tularosa, NM
E-mail: editor@csspub.com; csr@csspub.com;
info@csspub.com; orders@csspub.com
Web site: http://www.csspub.com
Dist(s): **Spring Arbor Distributors, Inc.**; *CIP.*
C T A, Inc., *(978-0-9712618; 978-0-9718985; 978-0-9728816; 978-0-9744640; 978-0-9747923; 978-0-9754499; 978-0-9759330; 978-1-933234; 978-1-935404; 978-1-943216; 978-1-947699)* P.O. Box 1205, Fenton, MO 63026-1205 USA Tel 636-305-3100; Toll Free: 800-999-1874
Web site: http://www.ctainc.com.
C Turtle Publishing, *(978-0-9979656)* 30 N. Gould St. Suite 5467, Sheridan, WY 82801 USA Tel 812-786-5594
E-mail: kylelbmorey@gmail.com
Web site: www.cturtlepublishing.com.
C. W. Historicals, LLC, *(978-0-9637745)* Orders Addr.: P.O. Box 113, Collingswood, NJ 08108 USA Tel 856-854-1290; Fax: 856-854-1290 (*69); Edit Addr.: 901 Lakeshore Dr., Westmont, NJ 08108 USA
E-mail: cwhist@erols.com.
C Z M Press *See* **Touchstones Discussion Project**
C2 (C squared) Publishing, *(978-0-9773115)* P.O. Box 5269, Vienna, WV 26105 USA
E-mail: noelclntn@yahoo.com;
princeofwarwood@gmail.com.
Caballito Children's Bks. *Imprint of* **Caballo Pr. of Ann Arbor**
Caballo Pr. of Ann Arbor, *(978-0-615-18757-0; 978-0-9824766; 978-0-615-44366-9; 978-0-9840418; 978-0-692-39908-8; 978-0-692-50604-2; 978-0-692-82464-1)* Orders Addr.: 24 Frank Lloyd Wright Dr. P.O. Box 415, Ann Arbor, MI 48106-0445 USA Tel 734-972-5790; *Imprints:* Caballito Children's Books (Caballito)
E-mail: admin@caballopress.com
Web site: http://www.caballopress.com
Dist(s): **CreateSpace Independent Publishing Platform**
Lightning Source, Inc.
Cabat Studio Pubns., *(978-0-913521)* 627 N. Fourth Ave., Tucson, AZ 85705 USA (SAN 285-1539) Tel 520-622-6362
E-mail: junecabat@hotmail.com.
Cabbage Patch Pr., *(978-0-9729044)* 841 Washington St., Suite 111, Franklin Square, NY 11010 USA Tel 516-437-8460; Fax: 516-483-7701
E-mail: cabbagepatchpress@hotmail.com
Web site: http://www.cabbagepatchpress.com.
CABI (GBR) *(978-0-85198; 978-0-85199) Dist. by* **Stylus Pub VA.**
Cable Publishing, *(978-0-9799494; 978-1-934980)* 14090 E. Keinenen Rd., Brule, WI 54820 USA Tel 715-372-8497; Fax: 715-372-8448
Web site: http://www.cablepublishing.com
Dist(s): **Follett School Solutions.**
Caboandcoral.com, *(978-0-615-17598-0; 978-0-692-00269-8; 978-0-692-01170-6; 978-0-9833841)* 1227 Stratford Ct., Del Mar, CA 92014 USA
E-mail: udo@caboandcoral.com
Web site: http://www.caboandcoral.com.
Cactus Publishing, LLC, *(978-0-9766674)* 1235 S. Gilbert Rd., Suite 3-62, Mesa, AZ 85204 USA Do not confuse with companies iwht the same or similar name in East Perth, WA, Atlanta, GA, Peoria, AZ
E-mail: glsweetaz@msn.com.
Cadcim Technologies, *(978-0-9663537; 978-1-932709; 978-1-936646; 978-1-942689; 978-1-64057)* 525 St. Andrews Dr., Schererville, IN 46375 USA Tel 219-614-7235; 219-228-4908; Fax: 270-717-0185
E-mail: cadcim@yahoo.com; sales@cadcim.com
Web site: http://www.cadcim.com.
Cadence Group, The *See* **New Shelves Bks.**
Cadmos Verlag GmbH (DEU) *(978-3-86127; 978-3-925760) Dist. by* **IPG Chicago.**
Cadogan Guides (GBR) *(978-0-946313; 978-0-947754; 978-1-85744; 978-1-86011; 978-1-78194) Dist. by* **Globe Pequot.**
Cafe Lango *See* **Pavilion Pubs.**
Cahill Publishing, *(978-0-9744027)* 1016-F Brentwood Way, Atlanta, GA 30350 USA
E-mail: e-diane@hotmail.com.
Cahill Publishing Company *See* **Advance Publishing, Inc.**
Cahokia Mounds Museum Society, *(978-1-881563)* 30 Ramey St., Collinsville, IL 62234 USA Tel 618-344-7316; Fax: 618-346-5162
E-mail: cmms@ezl.com; giftshop@ezl.com
Web site: http://www.cahokiamounds.com.
CAI Publishing, *(978-0-9787766; 978-0-9971381)* Orders Addr.: 807 Black Duck Dr., Port Orange, FL 32127-4726 USA (SAN 851-6006) Tel 386-383-5198
E-mail: wacummins@clearwire.net
Web site: http://www.caipublishing.net
Dist(s): **Lightning Source, Inc.**
Caillouet, Gerry, *(978-0-578-05418-6; 978-2-89718)* 8193 Emerick Rd., West Milton, OH 45383 USA Tel 937-698-3656
E-mail: ggoutdoors@aol.com
Web site: http://www.godsgreatoutdoors.org
Dist(s): **Publishers Group West (PGW)**
Perseus Bks. Group.
Caitboo LLC, *(978-0-9818717)* 2474 Walnut St., No. 260, Cary, NC 27518-9212 USA (SAN 856-7948) Tel 919-851-8646
E-mail: caitboo@gmail.com
Web site: http://www.caitboo.com.
Caitlin Pr., Inc. (CAN) *(978-0-920576; 978-1-894759; 978-1-927575; 978-1-987915) Dist. by* **Midpt Trade.**
Calabash Bks. *Imprint of* **Belknap Publishing & Design**
Calaca Pr., *(978-0-9660773; 978-0-9717035; 978-0-9843359)* Orders Addr.: P.O. Box 2309, National City, CA 91951 USA Tel 619-434-9036 (phone/fax); Edit Addr.: 502 Rose Dr., National City, CA 91950 USA; *Imprints:* Red CalacArts Publications (Red CalacArts)
E-mail: calacapress@cox.net
Web site: http://calacapress.com;
http://redcalacartscollective.org;
http://www.myspace.com/calacalandia
Dist(s): **BookMobile**
SPD-Small Pr. Distribution.
Calaroga Publishing, *(978-0-9815793)* 619 Madison St., Suite 110, Oregon City, OR 97045 USA
Web site: www.slimsaneandsexy.com.
Caldwell, Judy, *(978-0-9774463)* 11216 Windy Peak Rdg., Sandy, UT 84094 USA Fax: 801-571-1422
E-mail: jlynncaldwell@msn.com.
Caleb's Pr., *(978-0-9729568)* 421 Seminole Ct., High Point, NC 27265-8631 USA Tel 336-887-6846; Fax: 888-726-9304
E-mail: calebspress@aol.com
Web site: http://www.calebspress.com.
Caledonia Pr., LLC, *(978-0-9890975)* P.O. Box 436166, Louisville, KY 40253 USA Tel 502-773-5874
E-mail: gbgodby@insightbb.com
Web site: http://giovannagodby.com.
Calfee, Susan S. *See* **Wordwhittler Bks.**
Cali Publishing, *(978-0-9793004)* 2875 NE 191st St., Suite 511, Aventua, FL 33180 USA Tel 786-200-9374; Fax: 305-937-4161
E-mail: lallouz@glmace.com
Web site: http://www.calipublishing.com.
Caliber Comics, *(978-0-941613; 978-0-9826549; 978-0-9836307; 978-0-9857493; 978-0-9960306; 978-1-942351; 978-1-63529)* P.O. Box 44114 Parkside, Canton, MI 48187 USA (SAN 666-1777) Tel 734-453-8346; 734-812-8733
E-mail: calcomic@aol.com
Web site: http://www.calibercomics.com
Dist(s): **Diamond Comic Distributors, Inc.**
MyiLibrary.
Caliber Pubns., *(978-0-9673696)* 1295 Lincoln Dr., Marion, IA 52302 USA Tel 319-294-9468; Fax: 319-373-1370; Toll Free: 877-480-5790
E-mail: larson1965@aol.com
Web site: http://www.calpubs.com.
Caliburn Bks. *Imprint of* **MQuills Publishing**
Calico Chapter Bks. *Imprint of* **ABDO Publishing Co.**
Calico Chapter Bks *Imprint of* **Magic Wagon**
Calico Chapter Bks. *Imprint of* **Magic Wagon**
Calico Connection, Inc., The, *(978-0-9767658)* 300 N. David Ln., Muskogee, OK 74403 USA Tel 918-687-6577 Do not confuse with Calico Publishing in Seabrook, TX
E-mail: calicoasay@cox.net.
Calico Publishing *See* **Calico Connection, Inc., The**
California Foundation for Agriculture in the Classroom, *(978-0-615-26927-6; 978-0-615-34893-3; 978-0-615-44052-1; 978-0-9850855)* 2300 River Plaza Dr., Sacramento, CA 95833 USA.
California Is Me, *(978-0-9742010)* P.O. Box 23841, Alexandria, VA 22304 USA Tel 202-321-1425
E-mail: QueenC@caliisme.com
Web site: http://www.caliisme.com.
California Street *Imprint of* **Firefall Editions**
Calkins Creek *Imprint of* **Boyds Mills Pr.**
Callanish Pr, *(978-0-9786186)* Div. of Linn Literary Group, LLC, 165 ForestBrook Dr., #134, Lewisville, TX 75067 USA
E-mail: paul@linnliterarygroup.com
Web site: www.linnliterarygroup.com.
Callaway Editions, Inc., *(978-0-935112)* Div. of Callaway Arts & Entertainment, 19 Fulton St., 5th Fl., New York, NY 10038-2100 USA (SAN 213-2931) Fax: 212-929-8087
E-mail: info@callaway.com
Web site: http://www.callaway.com
Dist(s): **Abrams, Inc.**
Holt, Henry & Co.
Hachette Bk. Group
National Bk. Network
Penguin Random Hse. LLC
Penguin Publishing Group
Simon & Schuster Children's Publishing.
Calliope Publications *See* **Sounds Devine**
Callirobics, *(978-0-9630478)* Orders Addr.: P.O. Box 6634, Charlottesville, VA 22906 USA Tel 804-293-7055; Fax: 804-293-9008; Toll Free: 800-769-2891; Edit Addr.: 1616 King Mountain Rd., Charlottesville, VA 22901 USA
E-mail: cal-avir@cfw.com
Web site: http://www.callirobics.com.
Callis Editora Ltda (BRA) *(978-85-7416; 978-85-85642) Dist. by* **IPG Chicago.**
Callout Pr., *(978-0-9971911)* PO Box 250, Olalla, WA 98359 USA Tel 512-250-8546
E-mail: robertcalkins@adminismith.com.
Cally Pr., *(978-0-9766199)* 3964 Loftlands Dr., Earlysville, VA 22936 USA
E-mail: callypress@aol.com.
Calm Flame Publishing Co., *(978-0-9745263)* 10745 Gilespie St., Las Vegas, NV 89123 USA.
Calm Unity Books *See* **Calm Unity Pr.**
Calm Unity Pr., *(978-1-882260)* 3922 23rd St., San Francisco, CA 94114-3303 USA Fax: 415-821-5389 (Call before faxing); *Imprints:* Pelagia Press (Pelagia Pr)
E-mail: rabar@mindspring.com.
Calvary Chapel Church, Inc., *(978-0-9708600; 978-1-932283)* 2401 W. Cypress Creek Rd., Fort Lauderdale, FL 33309 USA
E-mail: snt@thecalebgroup.com; kirk@calvaryftl.org
Dist(s): **Send The Light Distribution LLC.**
Calvin Partnership, LLC, *(978-1-891533)* 40 Ardmore Rd., Ho-Ho-Kus, NJ 07443-1008 USA Tel 201-670-8412; Fax: 201-670-0464
E-mail: jahelka@attglobal.net.
Calychio Publishing, *(978-0-9649156; 978-0-9964126)* 4138 Kildare St., Eugene, OR 97404 USA Tel 501-653-8990
E-mail: tshionyim@yahoo.com.
Camas Pr., *(978-0-9856698)* 2219 240th Ave. SE, Sammamish, WA 98075 USA Tel 425-922-5064
E-mail: info@camaspress.com.
Camber Pr., *(978-0-9727455)* 807 Central Ave. # 2, Peekskill, NY 10566-2039 USA
Web site: http://www.camberpress.com.
Cambium Education, Inc., *(978-0-944584; 978-1-57035; 978-1-59318; 978-1-932282; 978-1-4168; 978-1-60218; 978-1-60697)* 4093 Specialty Pl., Longmont, CO 80504 USA (SAN 243-945X) Tel 303-651-2829; Fax: 303-907-8694; Toll Free: 800-547-6747 (orders only)
E-mail: publishing@sopriswest.com;
customerservice@cambiumlearning.com
Web site: http://www.sopriswest.com.
Cambria Creations, LLC, *(978-0-9770916)* 515 Main St., Johnston, PA 15901 USA Tel 814-535-5571; Fax: 814-535-1079
E-mail: djwlaw@wvdsl.net.
Cambridge Bks. *Imprint of* **Write Words, Inc.**
Cambridge Bk. Co., *(978-0-8428)* Div. of Simon & Schuster, Inc., 4350 Equity Dr., Box 249, Columbus, OH 43216 USA (SAN 169-5703) Toll Free: 800-238-5833
Web site: http://www.simonsays.com/.
Cambridge BrickHouse, Inc., *(978-1-58018; 978-1-59835)* 60 Island St. Suite 102 E., Lawrence, MA 01844 USA; *Imprints:* CBH Books (CBH Bks); BrickHouse Education (BrickHse)
E-mail: edelgado@cambridgebh.com;
ycanetti@cambridgebh.com;
mkamelle@cambridgebh.com
Web site: http://www.cambridgebh.com;
http://www.brickhouseeducation.com
Dist(s): **Ediciones Universal**
Follett School Solutions
Lectorum Pubns., Inc.
Cambridge Educational Services, Inc., *(978-1-58894)* 2860 S River Rd, Des Plaines, IL 60018 USA Tel 847-299-2930; Fax: 847-299-2933 Do not confuse with Cambridge Educational in Charleston, WV
Web site: http://www.cambridgeed.com.
Cambridge House Pr. *Imprint of* **Sterling & Ross Pubs.**
Cambridge Hse. Publishing Co., LLC, *(978-0-9711359)* P.O. Box 383, Saddle River, NJ 07458 USA Fax: 973-777-8075
E-mail: cambridgehouse@verizon.net
Web site: http://www.cezanneismissing.com;
http://www.cambridgehousepublishing.com
Dist(s): **Independent Pubs. Group.**
Cambridge Univ. Pr. (GBR) *(978-0-521; 978-1-108; 978-1-107; 978-1-139; 978-1-316) Dist. by* **Cambridge U Pr.**
†Cambridge Univ. Pr., *(978-0-521; 978-0-511)* Orders Addr.: 100 Brook Hill Dr., West Nyack, NY 10994-2133 USA (SAN 281-3769) Tel 845-353-7500; Fax: 845-353-4141; Toll Free: 800-872-7423 (orders, returns, credit & accounting); 800-937-9600; Edit Addr.: 32 Avenue of the Americas, New York, NY 10013-2473 USA (SAN 200-206X) Tel 212-924-3900; Fax: 212-691-3239
E-mail: customer_service@cup.org; orders@cup.org;
information@cup.org
Web site: http://www.cambridge.org/
Dist(s): **Baker Bks.**
Boydell & Brewer, Inc.
Casemate Academic
CreateSpace Independent Publishing Platform
Ebsco Publishing
Cengage Gale
ISD
Ingram Publisher Services
Lightning Source, Inc.
Rittenhouse Bk. Distributors
ebrary, Inc.; *CIP.*
Cambridge Way Publishing, *(978-0-9746976)* 149 Cambridge Way, Macon, GA 31220-8736 USA (SAN 255-8041) Tel 478-475-1763
E-mail: whwatson2@cox.net.
Cambridge-Hitachi (GBR) *(978-1-84565) Dist. by* **Cambridge U Pr.**
Camelot Publishing, *(978-0-9754063)* Orders Addr.: P.O. Box 500057, Lake Los Angeles, CA 93535 USA (SAN 256-0666)
E-mail: camelotpublishing@hotmail.com
Web site: http://www.camelotpublishing.com.
Camelot Tales, *(978-0-9672375)*
E-mail: jeanette.adams@hotmail.com
Web site: http://www.bellowinghills.com.
Cameltrotters Publishing, *(978-0-9666110; 978-0-9764475)* Orders Addr.: P.O. Box 3026, Pinedale, CA 93650-3526 USA Tel 559-447-9393 (phone/fax)
E-mail: ted@atborgeas.com
Web site: http://www.atborgeas.com.
Cameo Pubns., LLC, *(978-0-9715739; 978-0-9744149; 978-0-9744966; 978-0-9774659)* Orders Addr.: 2175 Deer Run Trl., Jacksonville, FL 32246-1068 USA
E-mail: info@cameopublications.com;
publisher@cameopublications.com
Web site: http://www.cameopublications.com
Dist(s): **Bookazine Co., Inc.**
CreateSpace Independent Publishing Platform
Distributors, The
New Leaf Pub. Group
Scholastic, Inc.
Shenanigan Bks.
Cameron & Co., Inc., *(978-0-918684; 978-1-937359; 978-1-944903)* 3, Petaluma, CA 94952 USA; 1094 Flex Drive., Jackson, TN 38301
Dist(s): **Follett School Solutions**
MyiLibrary
Publishers Group West (PGW).
Camino Bks., Inc., *(978-0-940159; 978-1-933822; 978-1-68098)* P.O. Box 59026, Philadelphia, PA 19102

USA (SAN 664-225X) Tel 215-413-1917; Fax: 215-413-3255
E-mail: camino@caminobooks.com
Web site: http://www.caminobooks.com
Dist(s): **Follett School Solutions**
INscribe Digital
Partners Pubs. Group, Inc.

Camino E.E. & Bk. Co., *(978-0-940808; 978-1-55893)* Orders Addr.: a/o Jan Linzy, P.O. Box 6400, Incline Village, NV 89450 USA (SAN 219-841X) Tel 775-831-3078 (phone/fax); Fax: 775-831-3078 (phone/fax)
E-mail: info@camino-books.com
Web site: http://www.camino-books.com.

Camino Real Calendar LLC, *(978-0-9743501)* P.O. Box 17667, Anaheim, CA 92817 USA Toll Free: 800-200-6331
E-mail: support@caminosports.com
Web site: http://www.caminosports.com

Camino Real Sports Marketing *See* **Camino Real Calendar LLC**

Cammilleri Productions, *(978-0-615-25933-8)* 2565 San Clemente Dr., Unit 206, Corta Mesa, CA 92626 USA (SAN 857-507X) Tel 714-486-1318
E-mail: jcammilleri@ca.rr.com.

Camozzi, Victor, *(978-0-692-58132-2; 978-0-692-75176-3)* 7220 Lapin Cove, AUSTIN, TX 78739 USA Tel 512-468-7188.

Camp Pope Publishing, *(978-0-9628936; 978-1-929919)* Orders Addr.: P.O. Box 2232, Iowa City, IA 52244 USA Tel 319-351-2407; Fax: 319-339-5964; Toll Free: 800-204-2407; Edit Addr.: 1117 E. Davenport, Iowa City, IA 52245 USA
E-mail: mail@camppope.com
Web site: http://www.camppope.com
Dist(s): **Lightning Source, Inc.**

Campabadal Gili, Mónica (ESP) *(978-84-92636) Dist. by* **IPG Chicago.**

Campanita Bks. *Imprint of* **Editorial Campana**

CampCrest Publishing, *(978-0-9763257)* 385 Hidden Hollow Ln., Chickamauga, GA 30707 USA
E-mail: sallyworland@mindspring.com.

Campfire *Imprint of* **Steerforth Pr.**

Camping Guideposts *See* **Wordshed**

Campus Crusade for Christ, *(978-1-56399)* Affil. of Campus Crusade for Christ International, Orders Addr.: 375 Hwy. 74 S., Suite A, Peachtree City, GA 30269 USA Tel 770-631-9940; Fax: 770-631-9916; Toll Free: 800-827-2788
E-mail: customerservice@campuscrusade.org
Web site: http://www.campuscrusade.com.

Can Do Duck Publishing, *(978-0-9768384)* P.O. Box 1045, Voorhees, NJ 08043 USA Tel 856-816-5255; Fax: 856-429-0094
E-mail: ducktormorty@thecandoduck.com
Web site: http://www.thecandoduck.com.

Can of Worms Pr. (GBR) *(978-1-904104) Dist. by* **IPG Chicago.**

Canal History & Technology Pr. *Imprint of* **Moore, Hugh Historical Park & Museums, Inc.**

Canal History & Technology Press *See* **Moore, Hugh Historical Park & Museums, Inc.**

Canary Connect Pubns., *(978-0-9643462)* Div. of SOBOLE, Inc., 605 Holiday Rd., Coralville, IA 52241-1016 USA Tel 319-338-3827; Fax: 612-435-3340; *Imprints:* Just Think Books (Just Think Bks)
E-mail: sondrak@canaryconnect.com
Web site: http://www.canaryconnect.com; http://www.justthinkbooks.com; http://www.simplechoicesforhealthiereating.com; http://www.transitionstobetterliving.com
Dist(s): **Follett School Solutions**
Integral Yoga Pubns.
Nutri-Bks. Corp.

Candalyse Publishing, *(978-0-9798217; 978-0-9802275; 978-0-9817112)* Orders Addr.: P.O. Box 783, Smallwood, NY 12778 USA; Edit Addr.: 57 Karl Ave., Smallwood, NY 12778-0783 USA; *Imprints:* Chaklet Coffee Books (ChakletCoffee)
E-mail: candalysepublishing@gmail.com; chakletcoffee@gmail.com
Web site: http://www.candalysepublishing.com; http://www.chakletbooks.com
Dist(s): **Lightning Source, Inc.**

C&C Educational Materials, LLC *See* **C & C Educational Materials, LLC**

C&K Publishing Co., *(978-0-9844342)* Orders Addr.: P.O. Box 291162, Columbia, SC 29229 USA Tel 803-414-0180; Fax: 803-462-1188; Edit Addr.: 320 Whitehurst Way, Columbia, SC 29229 USA
E-mail: candkpub@bellsouth.net.

Candle Light Pr., *(978-0-9743147; 978-0-9766053; 978-0-9895371; 978-0-9966176)* 1470 Walker Way, Coralville, IA 52242 USA Do not confuse with Candle Light Press in Martinez, CA.
E-mail: ding@candlelightpress.com
Web site: http://www.candlelightpress.com
Dist(s): **Follett School Solutions.**

Candlelight Stories, Inc., *(978-0-615-14024-7)* 9909 Topanga Canyon Blvd., Chatsworth, CA 91311 USA
E-mail: orders@candlelightstories.com
Web site: http://www.candlelightstories.com
Dist(s): **Lulu Pr., Inc.**

Candleshoe Bks., *(978-0-9825089)* 3122 N. California Ave., Suite 3L, Chicago, IL 60618 USA
E-mail: info@candleshoebooks.com
Web site: http://www.candleshoebooks.com
Dist(s): **Music, Bks. & Business, Inc.**

Candleshoe Press, Inc. *See* **Candleshoe Bks.**

Candlewick Entertainment *Imprint of* **Candlewick Pr.**

†Candlewick Pr., *(978-0-7636; 978-1-56402; 978-1-5362)* Div. of Walker Bks., London, England, 99 Dover St., Somerville, MA 02144 USA Tel 617-661-3330; Fax: 617-661-0565; *Imprints:* Templar (Templar); Nosy Crow (NosyCrow); Big Picture Press (Big Picture Pr); Candlewick Entertainment (Candlewick Entmt) Do not confuse with Candlewick Pr., Crystal Lake, IL
E-mail: bigbear@candlewick.com; salesinfo@candlewick.com
Web site: http://www.candlewick.com/
Dist(s): **Follett School Solutions**
Penguin Random Hse. LLC
Perfection Learning Corp.
Random Hse., Inc.; *CIP.*

Candlewood Pr. *Imprint of* **Harding Hse. Publishing Sebice Inc.**

C&V 4 Seasons Publishing, *(978-0-692-26548-2; 978-0-9864036)* P.O. Box 683, Mayflower, AR 72106 USA Tel 501-336-4726
E-mail: mariahoskins50@yahoo.com
Web site: in process.

Candy Cane Bks. *Imprint of* **Sunlight Publishing**

Candy Wrapper Inc., *(978-1-940556)* 2885 Sanford Ave SW No. 26878, Grandville, MI 49418 USA Tel 703-867-1489
E-mail: winintl@gmail.com.

Candy's Creations *See* **Fruitbearer Publishing, LLC**

Cane River Trading Co., Inc., *(978-0-9744189)* 1473 Cty. Rte. 26, Climax, NY 12042-2211 USA Tel 518-731-8598
E-mail: ny5kmagi@aol.com
Web site: http://members.aol.com/CaneR71456/.

Canh Nam Pubs., *(978-0-9749097; 978-0-9772129; 978-0-9799345; 978-0-9883504)* 2607 Military Rd., Arlington, VA 22207 USA
E-mail: canhnam@dc.net.

Canis Lupus Productions, *(978-0-9661789)* Orders Addr.: P.O. Box 128262, San Diego, CA 92102-8262 USA; Edit Addr.: 1940 Third Ave., Unit 406, San Diego, CA 92101-2622 USA Tel 310-873-3232 (phone/fax)
E-mail: jlbrooks@email.com.

Canmore Pr., *(978-1-887774)* Orders Addr.: P.O. Box 510794, Melbourne Beach, FL 32951-0794 USA Tel 321-729-0078; Fax: 321-724-1162; *Imprints:* Wynden (Wynden)
E-mail: publish@canmorepress.com
Web site: http://www.canmorepress.com.

Cannady, John, *(978-0-9754345)* 6126 Dunwoody Ct., Montgomery, AL 36117-5012 USA
E-mail: katphishe@starband.net
Web site: http://www.hopetkd.com.

Cannoli Cultural Art Ctr., Inc., *(978-0-9754919)* P.O. Box 750458, Dayton, OH 45475 USA Toll Free: 866-995-8472
E-mail: luisa@cannoli.org
Web site: http://www.cannoli.org.

Cannon, K. L., *(978-0-9675594)* 9412 Meadow Vale, Austin, TX 78758 USA Tel 512-837-6281; Fax: 512-837-7205
E-mail: cankl@msn.com.

Cannon Publishing Group, *(978-0-9766291)* 230 Merrill Rd., Walla Walla, WA 99362 USA
Web site: http://www.cannonpublishinggroup.com.

Canoed Sun Publishing, LLC, *(978-0-9836081)* 902 Franklin Ave., Council Bluffs, IA 51503 USA Tel 402-541-6452.

Canon Pr., *(978-1-885767; 978-1-930443; 978-1-59128; 978-1-935000; 978-1-944503; 978-1-947644)* Div. of Credenda Agenda, Orders Addr.: P.O. Box 8729, Moscow, ID 83843 USA (SAN 257-3792); 207 N Main St, Moscow, ID 83843 (SAN 990-1671) Tel 208-596-3867 Do not confuse with companies with the same or similar names in Grand Rapids, MI, Centerville, UT
E-mail: sandy@canonpress.com; brian@canonpress.org
Web site: http://www.canonpress.com
Dist(s): **Follett School Solutions.**

Canon Pubs., *(978-0-9889696)* 10 Canon Cir., Greenwood Village, CO 80111 USA Tel 303-721-8266; Fax: 303-721-8266
E-mail: Debra@DebraFine.com
Dist(s): **Midpoint Trade Bks., Inc.**
ebrary, Inc.

Canongate Bks. (GBR) *(978-0-86241; 978-0-903937; 978-1-84195; 978-1-84767; 978-0-85786; 978-1-78211) Dist. by* **PerseuPGW.**

Cantab Publishing, *(978-0-9745150)* P.O. Box 381591, Cambridge, MA 02238-1591 USA.

Cantata Learning, *(978-1-63290; 978-1-68410)* 1710 Roe Crest Dr., North Mankato, MN 56003 USA Tel 952-224-0518
E-mail: info@cantatalearning.com
Web site: cantatalearning.com
Dist(s): **Capstone Press of Coughlan Cos.**
Capstone Pub.

Cantemos-bilingual bks. and music, *(978-0-9623930; 978-1-892306)* Orders Addr.: 15696 Altamira Dr., Chino Hills, CA 91709 USA Tel 909-393-8372
E-mail: jarjetb@writeme.com; bakergeorgette@yahoo.com
Web site: http://www.cantemosco.com; http://www.simplespanishsongs.com
Dist(s): **Continental Bk. Co., Inc.**
Follett School Solutions
Midwest Library Service.

Canterbury Hse. Publishing, Ltd., *(978-0-9825396; 978-0-9829054; 978-0-9881897; 978-0-9908416; 978-0-9970119; 978-1-945401)* 6928 W Country Club Dr N, Sarasota, FL 34243 USA Tel 941-312-6912
Web site: www.canterburyhousepublishing.com
Dist(s): **Ingram Content Group Inc.**
Smashwords.

Canterwine Pr., *(978-0-9764184)* 608 Longview Ave., Anacortes, WA 98221 USA Tel 360-941-4692
E-mail: canterwinepress@hotmail.com
Web site: http://www.canterwinepress.com.

Cantu, Ricardo, *(978-0-615-14898-4; 978-0-615-15149-6; 978-0-615-18600-9)* 2389 Tobello Blvd., Indianapolis, IN 46234 USA
E-mail: ricardocantu6908@sbcglobal.net
Dist(s): **Lulu Pr., Inc.**

Canyon Beach Visual Communications, *(978-0-9754221)* PMB 108, 10 St. Francis Way, Unit 9, Cranberry Township, PA 16066 USA Tel 724-612-5784
E-mail: info@canyonbeach.com
Web site: http://www.canyonbeach.com.

Cap & Compass, LLC, *(978-0-9717366)* 132 Chestnut St., Branford, CT 06405 USA Tel 203-483-7005
E-mail: jesse@capandcompass.com
Web site: http://www.capandcompass.com
Dist(s): **Bookmasters Distribution.**

Capercaillie Bks., Ltd (GBR) *(978-0-9542905; 978-0-9545206; 978-0-9549625; 978-0-9551246; 978-1-909305) Dist. by* **Wlsn Assocs.**

Capital Apple Pr., *(978-0-9830686)* 742 Front St. No. 1, Catasauqua, PA 18032 USA Tel 610-596-0266.

Capital City Bks. LLC, *(978-0-9842881; 978-0-9835788)* c/o Hartwood Publishing, 1 N. 5th St., Suite 511, Richmond, VA 23219 USA Tel 804-836-6870; Fax: 804-644-3092
E-mail: capitalcitybooks@gmail.com
Web site: http://www.capitalcitybooks.com.

Capital Communications, Inc., *(978-0-9647700)* P.O. Box 10338, Sarasota, FL 34278-0338 USA Tel 941-342-9088; Fax: 941-377-3120; Toll Free: 800-546-8378
E-mail: capital@investors.org
Web site: http://www.investors.org.

Capital Publishing, *(978-0-9773016)* 6311 10th Ave., Brooklyn, NY 11219 USA Tel 718-921-6400; Fax: 718-921-0160
E-mail: pommedia@pommedia.com.

Capitol Advantage Publishing *See* **Congress At Your Fingertips**

Cappella Publishing, A, *(978-0-9760271)* 20505 Yorba Linda Blvd., Suite 505, Yorba Linda, CA 92886 USA Tel 714-336-2350; Fax: 714-685-7773
E-mail: cgriffiths@acappellapublishing.com
Web site: http://www.acappellapublishing.com.

Capri Publishing, *(978-0-9769132; 978-0-9788612)* 4401 NW 39th St., #518, Midwest City, OK 73112 USA Tel 405-623-7619
E-mail: capripub@aol.com
Web site: http://www.capripublishing.net.

Capriccio Publishing, *(978-0-9770076)* 11100 SW 93rd Ct. Rd., Suite 10-405, Ocala, FL 34481 USA Tel 352-873-1403.

Capricorn Hse. Publishing, *(978-0-9791702; 978-1-60466)* 5122 Annesway Dr., Nashville, TN 37205 USA
E-mail: pclif@comcast.net.

Capricorn Publishing, *(978-0-9753970; 978-0-9774757)* 706 E. Brewster St., Appleton, WI 54911 USA Tel 920-475-0674; Fax: 920-954-9533
E-mail: getovd@yahoo.com
Web site: http://www.CapricornPublishing.com.

Capricorn Publishing, Incorporated *See* **Capricorn Publishing**

CAPS, LLC *See* **ALCAPS, LLC**

Capstone *Imprint of* **Wiley, John & Sons, Inc.**

Capstone Academics LLC, *(978-1-933557)* 3815 N. Brookfield Rd., Suite No. 104-122, Brookfield, WI 53045 USA (SAN 256-6761) Tel 262-754-4699; Toll Free: 888-922-7786
E-mail: contact@capstoneacademics.com
Web site: http://www.capstoneacademics.com.

Capstone Bks. *Imprint of* **Capstone Press of Coughlan Cos.**

Capstone Bks., *(978-0-9752843)* P.O. Box 7025, Greenwood, IN 46142 USA Tel 317-414-4770; 1710 Roe Crest Drive, N. Mankato, MN 56003
Web site: http://www.capstonebooks.com
Dist(s): **Follett School Solutions.**

Capstone Classroom, *(978-1-62521; 978-1-4966)* Div. of Capstone Publishers, Orders Addr.: 1710 Roe Crest Dr., North Mankato, MN 56003 USA Toll Free Fax: 888-262-0705; Toll Free: 800-747-4992; Edit Addr.: 5050 Lincoln Dr, Edina, MN 55436 USA; *Imprints:* Legends in Their Own Lunchbox (LegendsIn)
E-mail: k.monyhan@coughlancompanies.com; customerservice@capstonepub.com
Web site: http://www.capstoneclassroom.com
Dist(s): **Capstone Pub.**
Casemate Pubs. & Bk. Distributors, LLC
Follett School Solutions.

Capstone Digital, Div. of Capstone Pubs., Orders Addr.: 151 Good Counsel Dr., Mankato, MN 56002 USA Toll Free Fax: 888-262-0705; Toll Free: 800-747-4992; Edit Addr.: 7825 Telegraph Rd., Bloomington, MN 55438 USA; *Imprints:* Capstone Interactive Library (CapstoneInter)
Web site: http://www.capstonepub.com
Dist(s): **Capstone Press of Coughlan Cos.**
Follett School Solutions.

Capstone Interactive Library *Imprint of* **Capstone Digital**

Capstone Press, Incorporated *See* **Capstone Press of Coughlan Cos.**

Capstone Pr., Inc., *(978-0-9667204)* 172 Dipper Ln., No. 6, Decatur, IL 62522 USA Tel 217-422-6033 Do not confuse with Capstone Pr., Inc., Mankato, MN
E-mail: jsjcj@fgi.net.

Capstone Press of Coughlan Cos., *(978-0-7368; 978-1-56065; 978-1-4296; 978-1-62065; 978-1-4765; 978-1-4914; 978-1-5157; 978-1-5435)* Div. of Coughlan Publishing, 1905 Lookout Dr., North Mankato, MN 55033 USA Tel 507-385-8215; Fax: 507-388-3752; Orders Addr.: 1710 Roe Crest Dr., North Mankato, MN 56003 USA (SAN 254-1815) Toll Free Fax: 888-262-0705; Toll Free: 800-747-4992; Edit Addr.: 5050 Lincoln Dr Suite 200, Edina, MN 55436 USA Fax: 952-933-2410; Toll Free: 888-517-8977; *Imprints:* Pebble Books (Pebble Bks); Bridgestone Books (Bridgestone Bks); Blue Earth Books (Blue Earth Bks); A+ Books (Aplus Bks); Capstone Books (Capstone Bks); Yellow Umbrella Books (Yell Umbrella); Edge Books (EdgeBks); Fact Finders (FactFind); First Facts (FirsFacts); Blazers (Blazers); A+ Bilingue/Bilingual (ABiling); Graphic Library (GraphLib); Graphic Library en espanol (GraLibespanol); High Five Reading (RBL) (HiFiveRBL); Let Freedom Ring (LetFreeRing); Letter Books (Letter Bks); NA (CAP) (NC CAP); Pebble Plus (PebPlus); Pebble Plus Bilingue/Bilingual (PebbPlusBil); Phonics Readers (PhonicReads); Snap Books (Snap Bks); Social Studies Collections (SSC); Yellow Umbrella en espanol (Yellowen espan); You Choose Books (Yu Choose); Wonder Readers (WONDER READERS); Engage Literacy (ENGAGE LITERAC) Do not confuse with Capstone Pr., Inc. in Decatur, IL
E-mail: customerservice@capstonepub.com
Web site: http://www.capstone-press.com; http://www.capstonepub.com; http://www.capstoneclassroom.com
Dist(s): **Capstone Pub.**
Continental Bk. Co., Inc.
Follett School Solutions
Lectorum Pubns., Inc.
MyiLibrary
SPD-Small Pr. Distribution.

Capstone Pub.,

Capstone Publishing Group LLC *See* **OakTara Publishing Group LLC**

Capstone Young Readers *See* **Capstone Young Readers of Coughlan Cos.**

Capstone Young Readers of Coughlan Cos., *(978-1-62370; 978-1-68436)* Div. of Capstone Publishers, Orders Addr.: 1710 Roe Crest Dr., North Mankato, MN 56003 USA Tel 507-345-8100; Toll Free Fax: 888-262-0705; Toll Free: 800-747-4992; Edit Addr.: 5050 Lincoln Dr, Edina, MN 55436 USA Tel 952-224-0558; *Imprints:* Wear-A-Book (WearaBook)
E-mail: k.monyhan@coughlancompanies.com
Web site: http://www.capstonepub.com
Dist(s): **Capstone Pub.**

Captain & Harry LLC, The, *(978-0-9724777)* 8875 Section Line Rd., Harbor Beach, MI 48441-9616 USA
E-mail: janlangley5@gmail.com
Web site: http://www.michiganghoststories.net; http://www.thecaptainandharry.com.

Captain Caleb Communications, *(978-0-9703021)* 1250 Cynder Ct., Annapolis, MD 21401-7504 USA Tel 410 626 8904; 410-626-8904
E-mail: jcurtis@toad.net
Web site: http://www.oysterbook.com.

Captain Fiddle Pubns., *(978-0-931877)* 4 Elm Ct., Newmarket, NH 03857 USA (SAN 686-0508) Tel 603-659-2658
E-mail: cFiddle@tiac.net
Web site: http://www.captainfiddle.com.

Captain, Tamira R. *See* **Stories From Four Publishing Co.**

Captio Corp., *(978-0-9766614)* 2230 Tioga Dr., Menlo Park, CA 94025-6640 USA
Web site: http://www.captio.com.

Capture Bks., *(978-0-9798664)* 12331 Checkerboard Cir., Norman, OK 73026 USA (SAN 854-6207) Tel 405-485-8131
Web site: http://capturebooks.com.

Captured Light Distribution, LLC, *(978-0-9761074)* PMB 112 1201 Yelm Ave., Yelm, WA 98597 USA Tel 360-400-2537
E-mail: missbfc@msn.com
Web site: http://www.whatthebleep.com.

Capturing Memories, *(978-0-9727759)* 9228 SW 209th St, Vashon, WA 98070 USA Tel 206-463-5652
E-mail: roger@capturingmemories.com; stories@capturingmemories.com
Web site: http://www.capturingmemories.com.

Captus, LLC, *(978-0-9776627)* 32725 Ledge Hill Dr., Solon, OH 44139 USA Tel 440-498-9178; Fax: 440-238-2967
E-mail: cziance@yahoo.com
Web site: http://www.babyalmamater.com.

Capybara Madness, *(978-0-9899847)* 700 Jerrys Ln., Buda, TX 78610 USA Tel 512-751-6667
E-mail: typaldos@gmail.com
Web site: www.capybaramadness.com.

Caravan of Dreams Productions, *(978-0-929856)* Div. of Caravan of Dreams, 512 Main St. Ste. 1500, Fort Worth, TX 76102-3922 USA (SAN 250-4855).

Carazona Creations LLC, *(978-0-9753724)* PO Box 635, Clarkdale, AZ 86324 USA Toll Free: 888-328-3300
E-mail: carazona@carazonacreations.com
Web site: http://www.carazonacreations.com.

Carden Jennings Publishing Co., Ltd., *(978-1-891524)* 375 Greenbrier Dr., Suite 100, Charlottesvle, VA 22901-1618 USA
Web site: http://www.cjp.com.

Cardigras.com *See* **airjam.com**

Cardinal Brands, Inc., *(978-1-932435)* 1251 SW Arrowhead Rd. Ste. A, Topeka, KS 66604-4061 USA Toll Free: 800-444-0038
Web site: http://www.witty-one.com; http://www.cardinalbrands.com.

Cardinal Pr., *(978-0-9779518)* 19 W. 76th St. Suite 1be, New York, NY 10023 USA
Web site: http://www.cardinal-press.com.

Cardinal Pubs. Group, 2402 N. Shadeland Ave. Ste. A, Indianapolis, IN 46219-1746 USA (SAN 631-7936)
E-mail: tdoherty@in.net.

Cardlings, *(978-0-9760108)* Orders Addr.: P.O. Box 931, Pueblo, CO 81002 USA; Edit Addr.: 815 W. 14th St., Pueblo, CO 81003 USA
E-mail: gnome@cardlings.com
Web site: http://www.cardlings.com.

Career Pr., Inc., *(978-1-56414; 978-1-60163; 978-1-63265)* Orders Addr.: 12 Parish Dr., Wayne, NJ 07470 USA (SAN 694-3640) Toll Free: 1-800-227-3371 (outside New Jersey); *Imprints:* New Page Books (New Page Bks)
E-mail: sales@careerpress.com
Web site: http://www.careerpress.com; http://www.newpagebooks.com
Dist(s): **Follett School Solutions**
Lightning Source, Inc.
MyiLibrary
Penguin Random Hse. LLC
ebrary, Inc.

Carefree Publishing *Imprint of* **Milano, Jacque & Assocs.**

Carey III, John, (978-0-9799876) 5510 NE. Antioch Suite 133, Gladstone, MO 64118 USA (SAN 854-9222)
E-mail: ecarey1222@yahoo.com.
Carey, Rebecca, (978-0-9791331) 1035 S. 43rd St., Wilmington, NC 28403-4369 USA
E-mail: because@aol.com
Web site: http://www.bigarthouse.com.
Carey, William Library Pubs., (978-0-87808) Orders Addr.: 129 Mobilization Dr., Waynesboro, GA 30830 USA (SAN 208-2101) Tel 706-554-1594; Fax: 706-554-7444; Toll Free: 866-732-6657; Edit Addr.: P.O. Box 40129, Pasadena, CA 91114 USA
E-mail: inquiry@wclbooks.com
Web site: http://www.wclbooks.com
Dist(s): **Gabriel Resources**
Send The Light Distribution LLC.
Cargill Consulting, Inc., (978-0-9743780) 19836 Linda Ln., Harrah, OK 73045-9351 USA
Web site: http://www.cargillconsulting.com.
Caribbean Publishing *See* **Coconut Pr., LLC**
Caribbean Scene, (978-0-9678030) 5 Walnut Ave., East Norwich, NY 11732 USA.
CaribbeanReads, (978-0-615-22865-5; 978-0-9832978; 978-0-9899305; 978-0-9908659; 978-0-9964358; 978-0-9978900; 978-0-9992372) 10314 Collingham Dr., Fairfax, VA 22032 USA Tel 202-683-0611
E-mail: carol.mitchell@caribbeanreads.com
Web site: www.caribbeanreads.com.
Caritas Communications, (978-0-9668228; 978-0-9753259; 978-0-9799390; 978-0-615-76666-9; 978-0-615-87196-7) 216 N. Green Bay Road, No. 208, Thiensville, WI 53092-2010 USA Tel 414-531-0503; Fax: 262-238-9039 Do not confuse with Caritas Communications Incorporated in New York, NY, Rhinebeck, NY
E-mail: dgawlik@wi.rr.com
Dist(s): **CreateSpace Independent Publishing Platform.**
Carleton Bks., (978-0-9759738) 335 N. Main Ave., Tucson, AZ 85701 USA.
Carlisle Pr.- Walnut Creek, (978-0-9642548; 978-1-890050; 978-1-933753) 2673 Township Rd., No. 421, Sugarcreek, OH 44681 USA Tel 330-852-1900; Fax: 330-852-3285; Toll Free: 800-852-4482 Do not confuse with companies with the same name in Mechanicsburg, PA, Sedona, AZ, Benbrook, TX.
CarLou Interactive Media & Publishing, (978-0-9759325) 12439 Magnolia Blvd., No. 170, Valley Village, CA 91607 USA
E-mail: tess@worldtrust.org
Web site: http://www.carloumedia.com.
Carlsbad Caverns Guadalupe Mountains Assn., (978-0-916907) P.O. Box 1417, Carlsbad, NM 88221-1417 USA (SAN 268-6627) Tel 505-785-2485.
Carlsbad Caverns Natural History Association *See* **Carlsbad Caverns Guadalupe Mountains Assn.**
Carlsen Verlag (DEU) (978-3-551) *Dist. by* **Distribks Inc.**
Carlson, Debra R., (978-0-9765950) 1705 N. 160th St., Omaha, NE 68118-2408 USA
Web site: http://www.cozykidspress.com.
Carlson Pr., (978-0-9972220) 614 BRADBURY RD, MONROVIA, CA 91016 USA Tel 951-541-7944
E-mail: carlsonlighthouse@hotmail.com.
Carlton Bks., Ltd. (GBR) (978-1-85868; 978-1-84222; 978-1-84442; 978-1-84732; 978-1-78097) *Dist. by* **Sterling.**
Carlton Bks., Ltd. (GBR) (978-1-85868; 978-1-84222; 978-1-84442; 978-1-84732; 978-1-78097) *Dist. by* **IPG Chicago.**
Carlton Kids (GBR) (978-1-78312) *Dist. by* **Sterling.**
Carmean Productions LLC, (978-0-9839799) 1905 NW 37th Blvd., Gainesville, FL 32605 USA Tel 352-514-5625
E-mail: John@johncarmean.com
Web site: www.carmeanproductions.com.
Carmel Concepts, Ltd., (978-0-9646285) 50 Mt. Tiburon Rd., Tiburon, CA 94920 USA Tel 415-435-8066; Fax: 415-435-3750.
Caregie Learning Inc., (978-1-930804; 978-1-932409; 978-1-934239; 978-1-934800; 978-1-935162; 978-1-936152; 978-1-60972) 437 Grant St., Frick Bldg., 20th Flr., Pittsburgh, PA 15219 USA Tel 412-690-2442 Toll Free: 888-851-7094
Web site: http://carnegielearning.com.
Carney Educational Services, (978-1-930288) 1150 Foothill Blvd., Ste B, La Canada, CA 91011 USA Toll Free: 888-511-7737
E-mail: michellecarroll67@gmail.com
Web site: http://www.thebrightmind.com
Dist(s): **Sunbelt Pubns., Inc.**
Carnifex Pr., (978-0-9759727; 978-0-9789583) P.O. Box 1686, Ormond Beach, FL 32175 USA Tel 386-677-2980
E-mail: carnifexpress@hotmail.com
Web site: http://www.carnifexpress.net.
Carnivore Games, (978-0-9749150) Orders Addr.: P.O. Box 846, Londonderry, NH 03053-0846 USA; Edit Addr.: 12 Emerald Dr., Derry, NH 03038 USA
E-mail: brad@carnivoregames.com
Web site: http://www.carnivoregames.com/.
Carol Kalhagen-Tamanaha, (978-0-9799493) 36020 Big Trout Rd., Hebo, OR 97122 USA
E-mail: beartotem@earthlink.net
Web site: http://www.CarolKalhagenWildlifeart.com.
Carolina Academic Pr., (978-0-89089; 978-1-59460; 978-1-61163; 978-1-5310) 700 Kent St., Durham, NC 27701 USA (SAN 210-7848) Tel 919-489-7486; Fax: 919-493-5668
E-mail: tim@cap-press.com; css@cap-press.com
Dist(s): **Follett School Solutions.**
Carolina Biological Supply Co., (978-0-89278; 978-1-4350) 2700 York Rd., Burlington, NC 27215-3398 USA (SAN 249-2784) Tel 336-584-0381; Fax: 910-584-3399; Toll Free Fax: 800-222-7112; Toll Free: 800-334-5551
E-mail: carolina@carolina.com
Web site: http://www.carolina.com
Dist(s): **Follett School Solutions.**
Carolina Canines for Service Inc., (978-0-9800070) P.O. Box 12643, Wilmington, NC 28405-1823 USA Tel 910-362-8181; Fax: 910-362-8184; Toll Free: 866-910-3647
Web site: http://www.carolinacanines.org.
Carolina Children, (978-0-9794580) P.O. Box 862, Mauldin, SC 29662 USA
Web site: http://carolinachildren.net.
†**Carolina Wren Pr.,** (978-0-932112) 120 Morris St., Durham, NC 27701 USA (SAN 213-0327) Tel 919-560-2738; Fax: 919-560-2759
E-mail: carolinawrenpress@gmail.com
Web site: http://www.carolinawrenpress.org
Dist(s): **Follett School Solutions**
MyiLibrary; *CIP.*
Carolrhoda Bks. *Imprint of* **Lerner Publishing Group**
Carolrhoda Lab™ *Imprint of* **Lerner Publishing Group**
Carolyn & Kristina's Bookshelf, (978-0-615-18357-2) 550 Brittany Ct., North Huntingdon, PA 15642 USA
E-mail: prin66@aol.com; cnkbkshelf@aim.com
Dist(s): **Lulu Pr., Inc.**
Carolyn Clare Givens Writing & Editing, (978-0-9988454; 978-978-099-884-4) 7412 Shadowstone Dr., Charlotte, NC 28270 USA Tel 734-837-3436; Fax: 734-837-3436
E-mail: carolynclaregivens@gmail.com
Web site: http://carolyncgivens.com.
Carousel Pubns., Inc., (978-0-9759382) P.O. Box 225, Springfield, NJ 07081 USA
Web site: http://www.net2infinity/aplaceinthesky.
Carp Cove Pr., (978-0-9703752) Orders Addr.: 9099 Oneida River Pk. Dr., Clay, NY 13041 USA Tel 315-652-4964
E-mail: carpcovepress@holisticanimal.com; Colleen@holisticanimal.com
Web site: http://www.holisticanimal.com/.
Carp Hse. Pr., (978-0-9860663; 978-0-9860663-0-6) 4403-B Catlin Cir., Carp interim, CA 93013 USA Tel 805-684-0691
E-mail: Gold2@cox.com.
Carpe Viam Productions, LLC, (978-0-9892949) Orders Addr.: 3217 E. Shea Blvd. No. 305, Phoenix, AZ 85028 USA (SAN 920-8356) Tel 602-762-1473
E-mail: dwight@theLittleRedRacingCar.com
Web site: www.theLittleRedRacingCar.com.
Carpenter's Son Publishing, (978-0-9832846; 978-0-9835571; 978-0-9839876; 978-0-9849771; 978-0-9849772; 978-0-9851085; 978-0-9883043; 978-0-9883962; 978-0-9885931; 978-0-9889403; 978-0-9893722; 978-1-940262; 978-1-942557; 978-1-942587; 978-1-945507; 978-1-946889) 307 Verde Meadow Dr., Franklin, TN 37067 USA Tel 615-472-1128
E-mail: larry@christianbookservices.com
Dist(s): **Ingram Publisher Services**
MyiLibrary
Send The Light Distribution LLC
Smashwords.
Carriage House Publishing *See* **American Carriage Hse. Publishing**
Carrier, Therese, (978-0-9797648) 2020 Fieldstone Pkwy., Suite 900 PMB 121, Franklin, TN 37069 USA
Web site: http://hwbdproductions.com.
Carrington Bks., (978-0-9787143; 978-0-9820003; 978-0-9819656) P.O. Box 451399, Los Angeles, CA 90045 USA Tel 310-628-5557; 12975 Agustin Pl., No. A-109, Playa Vista, CA 90094
Web site: http://www.StudentSafetyTips.com.
Carroll, Sherry, (978-0-9752994) P.O. Box 34603, Washington, DC 20774 USA
E-mail: carrollcom01@aol.com.
Carson, Tracy, (978-0-9767077) 1998 66th St., SE, Bismarck, ND 58504-3835 USA
Web site: http://www.grandmaisnowabutterfly.com.
Carson-Dellosa Publishing Company, Incorporated *See* **Carson-Dellosa Publishing, LLC**
Carson-Dellosa Publishing, LLC, (978-0-88724; 978-1-57156; 978-1-57332; 978-1-59441; 978-1-60022; 978-1-60418; 978-1-936022; 978-1-936023; 978-1-936024; 978-0-9823625; 978-0-9823626; 978-0-9823627; 978-0-692-00200-1; 978-1-60996; 978-1-62057; 978-1-62223; 978-1-62399; 978-1-62442; 978-1-62648; 978-1-4838) *Orders Addr.: P.O. Box 35665, Greensboro, NC 27425 USA Tel 336-632-0084; Fax: 336-808-3249; Toll Free: 800-321-0943; Imprints:* DJ Inkers (DJInk); HighReach Learning, Incorporated (HghRchLrn); Brighter Child (BrighterChild); Spectrum (Spectrum Dell); Frank Schaffer Publications (FS Pubns); Instructional Fair (InstFair); Key Education Publishing Company, LLC (KeyEduc); Thinking Kids (ThinkKids)
Web site: http://www.carsondellosa.com
Dist(s): **Follett School Solutions.**
Carsume, (978-0-9883927) 16509 Old Forest Rd., Hacienda Heights, CA 91745 USA Tel 626-968-2192
E-mail: sumeta@verizon.net.
Cartoon Connections Pr., (978-0-9657136) P.O. Box 10889, White Bear Lake, MN 55110 USA (SAN 299-352X) Tel 651-429-1244; 651-429-7660; 24145 435Th Ave., Aitkin, MN 56431
E-mail: CartoonC@aol.com
Web site: http://www.cartooningbasics.com; http://www.cartoonconnections.com
Dist(s): **Follett School Solutions**
F&W Media, Inc.
Cartoon Network Books *Imprint of* **Penguin Young Readers Group**
Cartoonmario.com, (978-0-9766755) 5084 S. 65th St., Greenfield, WI 53220-4504 USA Tel 414-541-9221 (phone/fax)
E-mail: mdm@cartoonmario.com
Web site: http://www.cartoonmario.com.
Cartwheel Bks. *Imprint of* **Scholastic, Inc.**
Caruso, Kevin M. *See* **Aerospace 1 Pubns.**
Caryn Solutions, LLC, (978-0-9791046) Orders Addr.: P.O. Box 635, Naples, FL 34106 USA (SAN 852-4726) Tel 239-404-5820
E-mail: caryn@carynsolutions.com
Web site: http://www.carynsolutions.com.
Casa Bautista de Publicaciones, (978-0-311) Div. of Southern Baptist Convention, Orders Addr.: P.O. Box 4255, El Paso, TX 79914 USA (SAN 220-0139) Tel 915-566-9656; Fax: 915-562-6502; Toll Free: 800-755-5958; *Imprints:* Editorial Mundo Hispano (Edit Mundo)
E-mail: epena@casabautista.org
Web site: http://www.casabautista.org
Dist(s): **Smashwords.**
Casa Creacion *Imprint of* **Charisma Media**
Casa de Estudios de Literatura y Talleres Artisticos Amaquemecan A.C. (MEX) (978-968-6465) *Dist. by* **Lectorum Pubns.**
Casa de Periodistas Editorial, (978-0-9743102) Orders Addr.: P.O. Box 9021787, San Juan, PR 00902-1787 USA; Edit Addr.: Calle de la Luna, Esq. Calle de San José, San Juan, PR 00902-1787 USA
E-mail: multiser@coqui.net
Web site: http://www.asppro.org.
Casa de Snapdragon LLC, (978-0-9793075; 978-0-9840530; 978-0-9845681; 978-1-937240) Orders Addr.: 12901 Bryce Ave., NE, Albuquerque, NM 87112 USA Tel 505-508-5513
E-mail: sales@casadesnapdragon.com; managingeditor@casadesnapdragon.com
Web site: http://www.casadesnapdragon.com
Dist(s): **Smashwords.**
Casa Nazarena de Publicacions, (978-1-56344) 6401 The Paseo, Kansas City, MO 64131 USA Tel 816-333-7000; Fax: 816-333-1748; Toll Free: 800-462-8711
E-mail: donnie@nph.com
Dist(s): **Nazarene Publishing Hse.**
Cascade Design Publishing *See* **Cascade, Inc.**
Cascade, Inc., (978-0-9726173) 1085 Commonwealth Ave., PMB 253, Boston, MA 02215 USA Tel 617-558-1038; *Imprints:* Philograph (Philograph)
E-mail: info@philograph.com
Web site: http://www.philograph.com.
Cascade Pass, Inc., (978-1-880599; 978-0-615-39461-9; 978-1-935999) Orders Addr.: 4223 Glencoe Ave., Suite C-105, Marina del Rey, CA 90292 USA Tel 310-305-0210; Fax: 310-305-7850; Toll Free: 888-837-0704
E-mail: jlc@cascadepass.com
Web site: http://www.cascadepass.com
Dist(s): **Follett School Solutions.**
Cascade Writing, (978-0-9767519) 1808 Lake Dr., Camano Island, WA 98282 USA Tel 360-387-8023
E-mail: dennisc@whidbey.net.
Cascadia Publishing Hse., LLC, (978-0-9665021; 978-1-931038; 978-1-68027) Orders Addr.: 126 Klingerman Rd., Telford, PA 18969 USA Tel 215-723-9125; Fax: 215-721-2312
E-mail: editor@cascadiapublishinghouse; mking@cascadiapublishinghouse.com; contact@cascadiapublishinghouse.com
Web site: http://www.pandorapressus.com; http://www.cascadiapublishinghouse.com
Dist(s): **Follett School Solutions**
Herald Pr.
Cascarano, John *See* **Lock & Mane**
Casemate Academic, (978-0-9774094; 978-1-935488) Orders Addr.: P.O. Box 511, Oakville, CT 06779 USA (SAN 630-9461) Tel 860-945-9329; Fax: 860-945-9468; Toll Free: 800-791-9354; Edit Addr.: 20 Main St., Oakville, CT 06779 USA
E-mail: queries@dbbconline.com
Web site: http://www.oxbowbooks.com
Dist(s): **Casemate Pubs. & Bk. Distributors, LLC.**
Casemate Pubs. & Bk. Distributors, LLC, (978-0-9711709; 978-1-932033; 978-1-935149; 978-1-61200) Orders Addr.: 1950 Lawrence Rd., Havertown, PA 19083 USA; 22883 Quicksilver Dr., Herndon, VA 20166 (SAN 631-9386) Tel 703-661-1500; Edit Addr.: 180 Varick St. Suite 816, New York, NY 10014 USA
E-mail: casemate@casematepublishing.com
Web site: http://www.casematepublishing.com
Dist(s): **Follett School Solutions**
MBI Distribution Services/Quayside Distribution
MyiLibrary
Open Road Integrated Media, Inc.
ebrary, Inc.
Caseys World Bks., (978-0-9765872) Orders Addr.: 1998 Skyline Dr., Saintughton, WI 53589 USA Tel 608-335-0401 Please call with any questions. Leave a voice message if no answer.
E-mail: kate@caseysworld.net
Web site: http://www.caseysworld.net.
Caslon Books *See* **Slangman Publishing**
Caslon Pr., (978-0-9728144) 315 Richards Ave., Portsmouth, NH 03801-5239 USA Tel 603-431-6823
E-mail: jbf@fergus.com
Web site: http://www.jbf.fergus.com.
Caso, George R., (978-0-9719290) 2445 Babylon Tpke., Merrick, NY 11566 USA Tel 516-379-9397.
Cassandra Armstrong *See* **Storm Moon Pr., LLC**
Cassette & Video Learning Systems *See* **Watch & Learn, Inc.**
Castadream LLC, (978-0-692-47520-1) 69 Shaker CT, GUILFORD, CT 06437 USA Tel 203-361-6300.
Castellated Pr., (978-0-9746416) 21325 NE 130th Ave., Fort McCoy, FL 32134 USA
E-mail: shzarnek@gmail.com
Web site: http://www.castellatedpress.com.
Casterman, Editions (FRA) (978-2-203; 978-2-542) *Dist. by* **Distribks Inc.**
Castillo, Ediciones, S. A. de C. V. (MEX) (978-968-6635; 978-968-7415; 978-970-20) *Dist. by* **Mariuccia Iaconi Bk Imports.**
Castillo, Ediciones, S. A. de C. V. (MEX) (978-968-6635; 978-968-7415; 978-970-20) *Dist. by* **Lectorum Pubns.**
Castillo, Ediciones, S. A. de C. V. (MEX) (978-968-6635; 978-968-7415; 978-970-20) *Dist. by* **Macmillan.**
Castle Builder Pr. *Imprint of* **Blue Cubicle Pr., LLC**
Castle Keep Pr. *Imprint of* **Rock, James A. & Co. Pubs.**
Castle Pacific Publishing, (978-0-9653869; 978-0-9749305; 978-0-9774168) P.O. Box 77089, Seattle, WA 98177 USA Tel 206-839-0984; Toll Free: 888-756-2665 (888-756-BOOK)
Web site: http://www.castlepacific.com.
Castle Pr., (978-0-9669263; 978-0-9835012) 1222 N. Fair Oaks Ave., Pasadena, CA 91103 USA Fax: 626-789-7385
E-mail: george@castlepress.com.
Castle Rock Creative, Inc., (978-0-9820544; 978-1-939445; 978-1-943754; 978-0-9982107) 212 Grey Ave., Evanston, IL 60202 USA (SAN 857-1023) Tel 847-328-2561 (phone/fax)
Web site: http://www.daveneta.com; www.Trailblazerbooks.com.
Castlebay, Inc., (978-0-9748145) P.O. Box 168, Round Pond, ME 04564-0168 USA Tel 207-529-5438
E-mail: castlebay@castlebay.net.
Castleberry Farms Pr., (978-1-891907) Orders Addr.: P.O. Box 337, Poplar, WI 54864 USA Tel 715-364-8404
E-mail: cbfarmpr@centurytel.net
Web site: http://www.castleberryfarmspress.com; http://www.cbfarmpr.com.
Castlebridge Bks. *Imprint of* **Big Tent Bks.**
Castlebrook Pubns., (978-0-9641697; 978-0-9798242; 978-0-615-99230-3; 978-0-692-53831-9; 978-0-692-61641-3) Orders Addr.: P.O. Box 132, Camp Meeker, CA 95419 USA; 1535 Farmers Ln., Pmb #237, Santa Rosa, CA 95405
E-mail: castlebrookpublications@aol.com
Web site: http://www.youdrawitbooks.com; http://www.printanddraw.com
Dist(s): **CreateSpace Independent Publishing Platform**
Follett School Solutions.
Castleconal Pr., (978-0-9677348) 1517 National Ave., Madison, WI 53716 USA Tel 608-222-6051; Fax: 608-221-5264
E-mail: dfleming@madison.k12.wi.us.
Castlegate Pr., (978-0-9743588) 457 Terraces Ct., Mesquite, NV 89027 USA Tel 303-550-3360; Fax: 702-346-2058.
Castleton, Julia J, (978-0-578-06109-2) P.O. Box 880371, Pukalani, HI 96788 USA.
Castro, Shirley, (978-0-9790307) 10110 Oldham Ln., Bakersfield, CA 93306 USA Tel 661-374-8436
Web site: http://www.pelicanfamily.com.
Cat Marcs Publishing, (978-0-9843899; 978-1-943786) P.O. Box 54, Silverdale, WA 98383 USA Tel 360-271-4448
E-mail: crysmm307@aol.com; info@catmarcs.com
Web site: http://crystalmarcos.com/; http://catmarcs.com/.
Catalpa Pr., (978-0-9745665; 978-0-9763810; 978-0-615-56579-8) P.O. Box 27303, Oakland, CA 94602-0303 USA (SAN 256-4068)
E-mail: jack@jackschroder.com; staff@catalpapress.com
Web site: http://www.jackschroder.com; http://www.malpracticebooks.com.
Catalyst Game Labs *Imprint of* **InMediaRes Productions**
Catamount Publishing LLC, (978-0-9752922) P.O. Box 30015, Denver, CO 80218 USA Tel 303-839-1687 Do not confuse with Catamount Publishing LLC in Allenstown, NH.
Catapulta Pr., (978-0-9762986) 2242 Hemingway Dr., Suite H, Fort Myers, FL 33912 USA.
Catawba Publishing Co., (978-1-59712) 5945 Orr Rd. Ste. F, Charlotte, NC 28213-7314 USA
E-mail: info@catawbapublishing.com
Web site: http://www.catawbapublishing.com.
catBOX Entertainment, Inc., (978-0-9706062) Orders Addr.: P.O. Box 1077, Oklahoma City, OK 73101 USA Tel 405-232-1400; Edit Addr.: P.O. Box 1077, Oklahoma City, OK 73101 USA
E-mail: alohapublishing@aol.com
Web site: http://www.catdetectives.com; http://www.catboxentertainment.com.
Catch 22 Publishing Inc., (978-0-9759691) 1511M Sycamore Ave #198, Hercules, CA 94547 USA Tel 510-691-6695
E-mail: info@catch22publishing.com
Web site: http://www.catch22publishing.com.
Catch the Spirit of Appalachia *Imprint of* **Ammons Communications, Ltd.**
Catch-A-Winner Publishing, (978-0-9845630; 978-0-9985254) P.O. Box 160125, San Antonio, TX 78280 USA Tel 210-387-8189
E-mail: jamestaylor22@live.com.
Catechesis of the Good Shepherd *Imprint of* **Liturgy Training Pubns.**
Cathedral of the Holy Spirit, (978-0-917595) Div. of Chapel Hill Harvester Church, 4650 Flat Shoals Rd., Decatur, GA 30034 USA (SAN 657-1484) Tel 404-243-5020; Fax: 404-243-5927; Toll Free: 800-241-4702.
Cathedral Pr./Encycloware, (978-0-9626554) 2703 Townes Dr., Greenville, NC 27858 USA Tel 252-341-8906
E-mail: encycloware@suddenlink.net
Web site: http://www.KabalyonKey.com.
Cathie, Kyle Ltd. (GBR) (978-1-85626) *Dist. by* **IPG Chicago.**
Cathier Pr., (978-0-9720445) 156 Gates Rd., Lizella, GA 31052 USA.
Catholic Answers, Inc., (978-1-888992; 978-1-933919; 978-1-938983; 978-1-941663; 978-1-68357) 2020 Gillespie Way, El Cajon, CA 92020-0908 USA Tel 619-387-7200; Fax: 619-387-0042; Toll Free: 888-291-8000 (orders)
E-mail: mobrien@catholic.com
Web site: http://www.catholic.com.
Catholic Authors Pr., (978-0-9776168; 978-0-9789432) 203 Fairfield Ave., Hartford, CT 06114 USA
E-mail: books@catholicauthors.org
Web site: http://www.catholicauthors.org.
Catholic Bk. Publishing Corp., (978-0-89942; 978-0-9623410; 978-1-878718; 978-1-933066; 978-1-937913; 978-1-941243; 978-1-947070) 77 West End Rd., Totowa, NJ 07512-1405 USA (SAN 204-3432) Tel 973-890-2400; Fax: 973-890-2410; Toll Free:

800-892-6657; *Imprints:* Resurrection Press (Resurrection Pr)
E-mail: resurpress@aol.com
Web.site: http://www.catholicbkpub.com
Dist(s): **ACTA Pubns.**
Moshy Brothers, Inc.
Spring Arbor Distributors, Inc.

Catholic Heritage Curricula *See* **Little Way Pr.**

Catholic Heritage Curricula, (*978-0-9788376; 978-0-9824585; 978-0-9836832; 978-0-9851642; 978-0-9858343; 978-0-9883797; 978-0-9913264; 978-1-946207*) 2505 Texas Drive, Suite 102, Irving, TX 75062 USA
Web site: https://www.chcweb.com.

Catholic World Mission, (*978-0-9747571; 978-0-9765180; 978-1-933643*) 33 Rossotto Dr., Hamden, CT 06514 USA Tel 203-848-3323; Fax: 203-407-4823
E-mail: george.sirois@catholicworldmission.org
Web site: http://www.catholicworldmission.org.

Cats Ink, (*978-0-9763441*) P.O. Box 387, Chagrin Falls, OH 44022 USA Tel 440-247-6486
Web site: http://www.lillieandrose.com.

CatsCurious Pr., (*978-0-9790889*) 5312 Dillon Cir., Haltom City, TX 76137 USA (SAN 852-4084) Tel 210-326-8239; Toll Free Fax: 866-372-2490
E-mail: sonyamshannon@charter.net
Web site: http://www.catscratchbooks.com; http://www.catscuriouspress.com
Dist(s): **Follett School Solutions.**

Catskill Ctr. for Conservation & Development, Inc., (*978-0-9616712*) General Delivery, Arkville, NY 12406 USA (SAN 660-9953) Tel 914-586-2611; Fax: 914-586-3044; Rte. 28, Arkville, NY 12406 (SAN 660-9961)
E-mail: cccd@catskill.net
Web site: http://catshillcenter.org.

Catslip Arts, LLC, (*978-0-9729414*) 668 Cook St., Suite 200, Denver, CO 80206 USA Tel 303-322-9483; Fax: 303-758-6388
E-mail: books@catsliparts.com
Web site: http://www.catsliparts.com.

Catterfly Pr., (*978-0-9741074*) 122 Eagle Ridge Rd., Lake Orion, MI 48360-2612 USA Tel 248-789-2227; Fax: 248-393-2535
E-mail: frejen111@aol.com
Web site: http://www.catterflypress.com.

CattLeLogos Brand Management Systems, (*978-0-9745612*) 2522 Lombard St., Suite 300, Philadelphia, PA 19146-1025 USA Fax: 215-827-5578
E-mail: info@cattlelogos.com
Web site: http://www.cattlelogos.com.

Catto Creations, LLC, (*978-0-9702633; 978-1-938078*) 3125 Crusade Ln., Green Bay, WI 54313 USA Tel 920-494-4237; 920 494 4237
E-mail: cattocreations@gmail.com
Web site: http://www.cattocreations.com.

Caution Bks., (*978-0-9754148*) P.O. Box 2235, Newport Beach, CA 92659 USA
Web site: http://www.cautionbooks.com.

Cave Hollow Pr., (*978-0-9713497*) 304 Grover St., Warrensburg, MO 64093-2439 USA
E-mail: rmkinder@sprintmail.com
Web site: http://www.cavehollowpress.com.

Caveat Press, Incorporated *See* **White Cloud Pr.**

Cavendish Children's Bks. *Imprint of* **Marshall Cavendish Corp.**

Cavendish Square *See* **Cavendish Square Publishing**

Cavendish Square Publishing, (*978-0-7614; 978-1-60870; 978-1-62712; 978-1-5026*) 303 Pk. Ave. S. Suite 1247, New York, NY 10010 USA (SAN 760-9639) Tel 646-205-7426; *Imprints:* Exhibit A (Exhibit A)
E-mail: hollyc@rosenpub.com; csq_cs@csqpub.com
Web site: http://www.cavendishsq.com
Dist(s): **Follett School Solutions**
MyiLibrary.

Cavizzana Press *See* **21st Century Pubs.**

†**Caxton Pr.,** (*978-0-87004*) Div. of Caxton Printers. Ltd., 312 Main St., Caldwell, ID 83605-3299 USA (SAN 201-9698) Tel 208-459-7421; Fax: 208-459-7450; Toll Free: 800-657-6465
E-mail: publish@caxtonprinters.com; wcornell@caxtonpress.com; sgipson@caxtonpress.com
Web site: http://www.caxtonpress.com
Dist(s): **MyiLibrary**
Univ. of Nebraska Pr.; *CIP.*

Caxton Printers, Limited *See* **Caxton Pr.**

Caxton, Wm Ltd., (*978-0-940473*) P.O. Box 220, Ellison Bay, WI 54210-0220 USA (SAN 135-1303) Tel 920-854-2955.

CB Publishing & Design *Imprint of* **UBUS Communications Systems**

CBAY Bks., 4501 Forbes Blvd., Lanham, MD 20706 USA
Dist(s): **Follett School Solutions**
Independent Pubs. Group
National Bk. Network.

CBH Bks. *Imprint of* **Cambridge BrickHouse, Inc.**

CBM Publishing, (*978-0-9743988*) P.O. Box 6938, Lincoln, NE 68506 USA
E-mail: mvbettenhausen@alltel.net.

CCA & B, LLC, (*978-0-9769907; 978-0-9843651; 978-0-9887032; 978-0-9970920; 978-0-9988109*) Orders Addr.: 3350 Riverwood Pkwy. Suite 300, Atlanta, GA 30339 USA Fax: 678-990-1182; Toll Free: 877-919-4105
E-mail: sales@elfontheshelf.com; christa@elfontheshelf.com
Web site: http://elfontheshelf.com; http://www.ccaandb.com; http://alightinthenight.com.

CCC of America, (*978-1-56814*) P.O. Box 166349, Irving, TX 75016-6349 USA (SAN 298-7546) Toll Free: 800-935-2222
E-mail: customerservice@cccofamerica.com
Web site: http://www.cccofamerica.com
Dist(s): **Liguori Pubns.**

CCH Services, Inc., (*978-0-9768383*) 8862 Earhart Ave., Los Angeles, CA 90045 USA Tel 562-895-0682
Web site: http://www.realworldrecovery.com.

CCP Publishing & Entertainment, (*978-0-9677385; 978-0-9800655; 978-0-9801265*) 9602 Glenwood Rd. No. 362, Brooklyn, NY 11236 USA
E-mail: info@cccowan.com
Web site: http://www.cccowan.com; http://www.isaiahbooksworldwide.com; http://www.acuriousmindbooks.com; http://www.ccppublishing.com; http://www.amandaadventures.com.

CCRiddles, (*978-0-9785118; 978-0-9819833; 978-1-941747*) 878 Laramie Ct., Newbury Park, CA 91320 USA Tel 805-338-4170; Fax: 805-498-2901
E-mail: ccriddles@gmail.com
Web site: http://www.ccriddles.com.

CD Publishing, (*978-0-9859042*) 38041 Manzanita St., Newark, CA 94560 USA Tel 510-709-7459
E-mail: caseydevargas@yahoo.com.

CDS Books *See* **Vanguard Pr.**

CE Bilingual Bks. LLC, (*978-0-9801305*) P.O. Box 31848, Philadelphia, PA 19104-1848 USA (SAN 855-2819) Fax: 215-352-0409; 28 Eight St., Hicksville, NY 11801
E-mail: cebilingualbooks@gmail.com
Web site: http://www.cebilingualbooks.com
Dist(s): **Follett School Solutions.**

Ce Code Efficiency, Inc., (*978-0-9769931*) Orders Addr.: P.O. Box 1184, State College, PA 16804-1184 USA; Edit Addr.: 120 E. Beaver Ave., #208, State College, PA 16801 USA
E-mail: rlp188@psu.edu
Web site: http://www.personal.psu.edu/rlp188.

Cebrano Publishing, (*978-0-9761366*) P.O. Box 27236, Barrigada, GU 96921 USA
E-mail: billyb1937@yahoo.com.

Cedar Bay Pr., L.L.C., (*978-1-57555*) P.O. Box 230084, Portland, OR 97281-0084 USA (SAN 298-6361)
E-mail: cedarbay@hotmail.com.

Cedar Creek Publishing, (*978-0-9790205; 978-0-9842449; 978-0-9839192; 978-0-9891465; 978-1-942882*) P.O. Box 115, Bremo Bluff, VA 23022 USA (SAN 857-1368) Tel 434-842-6203
E-mail: cedarcreekbooks@aol.com
Web site: http://www.cedarcreekauthors.com
Dist(s): **BCH Fulfillment & Distribution.**

Cedar Creek Publishing Service, (*978-0-9659419*) P.O. Box 115, Bremo Bluff, VA 23022 USA Tel 434-842-6203 Do not confuse with companies with same or similar names in Hayward, CA, Anderson, IN, Indianapolis, IN
E-mail: cedarcreekbooks@aol.com.

Cedar Crest Bks., (*978-0-910291*) 17 Lookout Ave., Natick, MA 01760 USA (SAN 241-2837) Tel 508-653-8839
E-mail: davidrottenberg@yahoo.com; publisher@cedarcrestbooks.com
Web site: http://www.cedarcrestbooks.com
Dist(s): **Follett School Solutions.**

Cedar Fort, Inc. *Imprint of* **Cedar Fort, Inc./CFI Distribution**

Cedar Fort, Inc./CFI Distribution, (*978-0-88290; 978-0-934126; 978-1-55517; 978-1-59955; 978-1-4621*) 2373 West 700 South, Springville, UT 84663 USA (SAN 170-2858) Tel 801-489-4084; Fax: 801-489-1097; Toll Free: 800-759-2665; *Imprints:* Bonneville Books (Bonneville Bks); Horizon Publishers (HorPubs); Cedar Fort, Incorporated (Cedar Fort); Sweetwater Books (Sweetwater Bks)
E-mail: skybook@cedarfort.com
Web site: http://www.cedarfort.com
Dist(s): **Follett School Solutions**
Todd Communications.

Cedar Grove Bks., (*978-0-9740212; 978-0-9835077; 978-1-941958*) 2215 High Point Dirve, Carrolton, TX 75007 USA (SAN 255-3732) Tel 415-364-8292; Fax: 415-276-9858
E-mail: rperry@cedargrovebooks.com
Web site: http://www.cedargrovebooks.com
Dist(s): **Independent Pubs. Group**
Small Pr. United.

Cedar Hse. Pubs., (*978-0-9676289*) Orders Addr.: P.O. Box 399, Monroe, VA 24574 USA Tel 434-929-8002 (phone/fax); Fax: 434-929-1059; Edit Addr.: 407 Eastview Dr., Madison Heights, VA 24572 USA
E-mail: info@cedarhousepublishers.com
Web site: http://www.cedarhousepublishers.com
Dist(s): **Send The Light Distribution LLC.**

Cedar Loft Productions *See* **Cedar Loft Publishing**

Cedar Loft Publishing, (*978-0-615-95768-5; 978-0-692-22011-5; 978-0-9907449; 978-0-692-31333-6; 978-0-692-43060-6; 978-0-692-44612-6; 978-0-692-54041-1; 978-0-692-62473-9; 978-0-692-65781-2; 978-0-692-66121-5; 978-0-692-68130-5; 978-0-692-70082-2; 978-0-692-73427-8; 978-0-9979156) P.O. Box 1125, Petersburg, WV 26847 USA Tel 304-470-0189*
E-mail: jennymckinney23@gmail.com
Web site: http://clpublishing.net
Dist(s): **CreateSpace Independent Publishing Platform.**

Cedar Shamrock Publishing, (*978-0-9760680*) P.O. Box 70775, Madison, WI 53707 USA
Web site: http://www.wyattwalker.com
Dist(s): **Partners Bk. Distributing, Inc.**

Cedar Tree Bks., (*978-0-9657328; 978-1-892142*) P.O. Box 4256, Wilmington, DE 19807-0256 USA
E-mail: books@ctpress.com
Web site: http://www.cedartreebooks.com.

Cedar Tree Publishing, (*978-0-9658075*) 201 Matilda St NE Ste. B, Grand Rapids, MI 49503-1593 USA Do not confuse with Cedar Tree Publishing, Cedaredge, CO
E-mail: georan@tapshoe,com
Web site: http://www.cedartreepublishing.com; www.johnnietuitel.com
Dist(s): **Austin & Company, Inc.**

Cedar Valley Publishing, (*978-0-615-12024-9*) P.O. Box 621, Jesup, IA 50648 USA Do not confuse with Cedar Valley Publishing in Cascade, WI.

Cedar Valley Publishing, (*978-1-933476*) N6854 Cedar Valley Rd., Fredonia, WI 53021 USA Tel 920-994-9906; Fax: 262-376-2991 Attn: Tracey Jackson Do not confuse with Cedar Valley Publishing in Cascade, WI, Jesup, IA
E-mail: stacey@cedarvalleypublishing.com
Web site: http://www.cedarvalleypublishing.com
Dist(s): **Follett School Solutions.**

Cedartip Co., The, (*978-0-9771844*) Orders Addr.: P.O. Box 231, Manhattan, KS 66505-0231 USA; Edit Addr.: 3004 Pawnee Cir., Manhattan, KS 66502-1973 USA
E-mail: orders@cedartip.com
Web site: http://www.cedartip.com.

Celebra Young Readers *Imprint of* **Penguin Publishing Group**

Celebration Pr. *Imprint of* **Pearson Schl.**

Celebration Pr., Orders Addr.: 135 South Mount Zion Rd. P.O. Box 2500, Lebanon, IN 46052 USA Toll Free Fax: 800-393-3156; Toll Free: 800-526-9907; *Imprints:* Good Year Books (GYB) Do not confuse with Celebration Press in Onalaska WI, Denver CO
Web site: http://www.aw-bc.com; http://www.pearsonlearning.com/rightsPerm.rtf.

Celeste Ediciones, S.A. (ESP) (*978-84-8211; 978-84-87553*) *Dist. by* **Lectorum Pubns.**

Celestial Arts *Imprint of* **Potter/TenSpeed/Harmony**

Celestine Pr., (*978-0-9749382; 978-0-578-08538-8*) 25 Ashland St., Rochester, NY 14620 USA (SAN 255-9927)
E-mail: hellerest@earthlink.net
Web site: http://www.celestinepress.com
Dist(s): **Lulu Pr., Inc.**

Cellar Door Publishing, (*978-0-9766831*) 3439 NE Sandy Blvd, Suite 309, Portland, OR 97232 USA
Web site: http://www.cellardoorpublishing.com.

Celltrition, (*978-0-9746378*) 13472 Vidalia Rd., Pass Christian, MS 39571 USA Tel 228-586-2455.

Cellular Publishing, (*978-1-886358*) Div. of Lakeshore Business Services, P.O. Box 119, Sedona, AZ 86339-0119 USA Tel 520-300-7711; Fax: 413-825-8356.

Celo Valley Bks., (*978-0-923687*) 160 Ohle Rd., Burnsville, NC 28714 USA (SAN 251-7973) Tel 828-675-5918
E-mail: diatoday@msn.com.

Celstumo Publishing, (*978-0-9761041*) A Subs. of Celebration Studios of Missouri, Orders Addr.: P.O. Box 201, Glencoe, MO 63038 USA Tel 636-458-1819 (phone/fax)
E-mail: celstumo@celstumo.com
Web site: http://www.celstumo.com.

Celtic Cat Publishing, (*978-0-9658950; 978-0-9819238; 978-0-9847836; 978-0-9891380; 978-0-9905945; 978-1-947020*) Orders Addr.: 5111 Green Valley Dr, Knoxville, TN 37914 USA Tel 865-541-7130; Edit Addr.: 5111 Green Valley Dr, Knoxville, TN 37901 USA Tel 865-248-3133
E-mail: info@celticcatpublishing.com
Web site: http://www.celticcatpublishing.com.

Celtic Cross Communications, (*978-0-9740981; 978-0-9887271*) 5114 Canyon Oaks Dr., Brighton, MI 48114 USA
Web site: http://www.celticcrosscommunications.com
Dist(s): **Send The Light Distribution LLC.**

Celtic Marketing Inc., (*978-0-9777135*) 6311 W. Gross Point Rd., Niles, IL 60714-3919 USA (SAN 853-0688)
E-mail: info@projectplaybooks.com
Web site: www.projectplaybooks.com.

Celtic Sunrise, (*978-0-9840893*) P.O. Box 174, New Ringgold, PA 17960 USA (SAN 858-3900) Fax: 570-943-2102
Web site: http://www.celticsunrise.com
Dist(s): **Bookmasters Distribution.**

CEM Ventures, Ltd., (*978-0-9760072*) P.O. Box 1713, Harwich, MA 02645 USA Tel 508-896-4988; Fax: 508-896-2586; Toll Free: 866-246 — 7800; 112 Griffith's Pond Rd., Brewster, MA 02631
E-mail: cemventures@yahoo.com
Web site: http://www.jaysonthebluejay.com.

†**Cengage Gale,** (*978-0-13; 978-0-7876; 978-0-8103; 978-0-936474; 978-1-57302; 978-1-878623; 978-1-59413; 978-1-59414; 978-1-59415; 978-1-4144; 978-1-4205; 978-1-59722; 978-1-4328; 978-1-5358*) Subs. of Cengage Learning, Orders Addr.: P.O. Box 9187, Farmington Hills, MI 48333-9187 USA Toll Free Fax: 800 414 5043; Toll Free: 800 877 4253; Edit Addr.: 27500 Drake Rd., Farmington Hills, MI 48331 USA (SAN 213-4373) Tel 248-699-8495 Toll Free: 800-877-4253; a/o Wheeler Publishing, 295 Kennedy Memorial Dr., Waterville, ME 04901 Toll Free: 800 223 1244; *Imprints:* UXL (UXL); Macmillan Reference USA (Macmillan Ref); Charles Scribner's Sons (C Scribners Sons); Kidhaven (Kidhaven); Blackbirch Press, Incorporated (Blackbirch Pr); Lucent Books (Lucent Books); Greenhaven Press, Incorporated (Greenhaven Pr); Five Star (Five Star ME); Wheeler Publishing, Incorporated (Wheel); Walker Large Print (Walker Large Pt); Five Star Trade (Five Star Trade); Kennebec Large Print (Kennebec Lrg); KidHaven Publishing (KidHaven Publ)
E-mail: gale.salesassistance@thomson.com
Web site: http://www.gale.com
Dist(s): **Follett School Solutions**
Send The Light Distribution LLC
Smashwords
Thorndike Pr.; *CIP.*

†**Cengage Heinle,** (*978-0-8384; 978-0-88377; 978-0-912066; 978-1-4130*) Div. of Cengage Learning, Orders Addr.: 10650 Toebben Dr., Independence, KY 41051 USA Toll Free Fax: 800 487 8488
E-mail: reply@heinle.com
Web site: http://www.heinle.com
Dist(s): **CENGAGE Learning**; *CIP.*

Cengage Learning *Imprint of* **CENGAGE Learning**

CENGAGE Learning, Orders Addr.: 10650 Toebben Dr., Independence, KY 41051 USA (SAN 200-2213) Tel 859-525-6620; Fax: 859-525-0978; Toll Free Fax: 800-487-8488; Toll Free: 800-354-9706; *Imprints:* Cengage Learning (CengLearning)
Web site: http://www.cengage.com/
Dist(s): **Delmar Cengage Learning**
Follett School Solutions
OptumInsight, Inc.

Cengage Learning Australia (AUS) (*978-0-17; 978-0-646-20862-6; 978-0-646-20863-3; 978-0-646-22565-4; 978-0-646-22598-2; 978-0-646-24330-6; 978-0-646-26850-7; 978-0-646-26853-8; 978-0-646-26854-5; 978-0-646-26855-2; 978-0-646-47716-9*) *Dist. by* **Cheng Tsui.**

CENGAGE Learning Custom Publishing, (*978-0-87393; 978-0-931920; 978-0-7593; 978-1-4266; 978-0-357; 978-1-4390; 978-1-111; 978-1-133; 978-1-285; 978-1-305; 978-1-337*) 5191 Natrop Blvd., Mason, OH 45240 USA Toll Free: 800-543-0487
E-mail: debbie.stowell@cengage.com
Web site: http://www.thomsoncustom.com
Dist(s): **CENGAGE Learning**
Follett School Solutions.

†**Cengage South-Western,** (*978-0-03; 978-0-324; 978-0-538*) Div. of Cengage Learning, 5191 Natorp Blvd., Mason, OH 45040 USA (SAN 202-7518) Tel 513 229 1000; Toll Free Fax: 800-437-8488; Toll Free: 800-354-9706 (orders only); 800-543-0487
Web site: http://www.thomsonedu.com/
Dist(s): **CENGAGE Learning**
International Thomson Computer Pr.; *CIP.*

Cenozoic Pr., (*978-0-615-38180-0; 978-0-615-52278-4*) 354 Via La Canada No. 7, Orange, CA 92869 USA Tel 714-928-6648
E-mail: arajic@gmail.com.

Ctr. for American Places, Inc., (*978-1-930066; 978-1-935195*) 600 S. Michigan Ave., Chicago, IL 60605 USA Tel 312-344-6943; Fax: 312-344-8070
E-mail: CAPwest@att.net
Web site: http://www.americanplaces.org
Dist(s): **Chicago Distribution Ctr.**
Univ. of Chicago Pr.
Univ. Pr. of Mississippi
Univ. of Georgia Pr.

Ctr. for Appalachian Trail Studies, (*978-0-9636342; 978-0-9707916*) Orders Addr.: 17 S. Meadow Dr., Sudbury, MA 01776 USA Tel 781-752-6100 (phone/fax)
E-mail: orders@trailplace.com
Web site: http://trailplace.com/orders.html.

Center for Applications of Psychological Type, Inc., (*978-0-935652*) 2815 NW 13th St., Suite 401, Gainesville, FL 32609 USA (SAN 213-9162) Tel 352-375-0160; Fax: 352-378-0503; Toll Free: 800-777-2278
E-mail: naima@capt.org
Web site: http://www.capt.org.

Center for Applied Psychology, Incorporated *See* **Childswork/Childsplay**

Ctr. for Basque Studies, (*978-1-877802; 978-1-935709*) 1664 N. Virginia St., MS 2322, Reno, NV 89557-2322 USA Tel 775-784-4854; Fax: 775-784-1355
E-mail: basque@unr.edu
Web site: http://basquebooks.myshopify.com/
Dist(s): **University of Nevada Pr.**

Ctr. For Cultural Leadership, (*978-0-9745948*) P.O. Box 70, La Grange, CA 95239 USA
Web site: http://www.christianculture.com.

Center for Economic Research & Social Change *See* **Haymarket Bks.**

Ctr. for Educational Policy Research, (*978-0-9729538*) 720 E. 13th Ave., Suite 201, Eugene, OR 97401 USA Tel 541-346-6153; Fax: 541-346-6154; Toll Free: 877-766-2279
E-mail: Terri_Heath@s4s.org
Web site: http://www.s4s.org.

Center for Learning, The, (*978-1-56077*) Orders Addr.: 590 E. Western Reserve Rd. Unit 10-h, Youngstown, OH 44514 USA Tel 800-767-9090; Toll Free Fax: 888-767-8080; Toll Free: 800-767-9090 (ordering); Edit Addr.: 29313 Clemens Rd. Ste. 2E, Westlake, OH 44145-1052 USA (SAN 248-2029)
E-mail: ahollis@centerforlearning.org
Web site: http://www.centerforlearning.org.

Center for Loss & Life Transition *See* **Companion Pr.**

Center for Self-Actualization, Incorporated, The, (*978-0-9758799; 978-0-9788389; 978-0-9823847; 978-0-615-38102-2; 978-0-9846266; 978-0-9851608*) P.O. Box 98466, Atlanta, GA 30359-2166 USA Tel 770-623-4133; Fax: 770-623-3853
E-mail: centerforself@yahoo.com
Web site: http://www.selfactualized.org.

†**Ctr. for Strategic & International Studies,** (*978-0-89206; 978-0-615-19961-0*) 1800 K St., NW, Washington, DC 20006 USA (SAN 281-4021) Tel 202-887-0200; Fax: 202-775-3199; 4501 Forbes Blvd., Lanhan, MD 20706
E-mail: books@csis.org
Web site: http://www.csis.org; http://www.csisbookstore.org
Dist(s): **Books International, Inc.**
Follett School Solutions
MyiLibrary
Rowman & Littlefield Publishers, Inc.; *CIP.*

Ctr. for the Affirmation of Responsible Education, (*978-0-9740071*) 496 Gold Ct., San Andreas, CA 95249 USA Tel 209-754-9218
E-mail: jnorton2@earthlink.net.

Center for the Collaborative Classroom, (*978-1-57621; 978-1-885603; 978-1-59892; 978-1-61003; 978-1-68246*) 1250 53 rd St., Ste. 3, Emeryville, CA 94608 USA Tel 510-533-0213; Fax: 510-464-3670; Toll Free: 800-666-7270
E-mail: pubs@devstu.org; brandon_holroyd@devstu.org; bholroyd@collaborativeclassroom.org
Web site: http://www.devstu.org; http://www.collaborativeclassroom.org
Dist(s): **Booksource, The.**

Ctr. for Victims of Torture, The, *(978-0-9759789)* 717 E. River Rd., Minneapolis, MN 55455 USA Tel 612-436-4800.

Ctr. for Western Studies, *(978-0-931170)* Div. of Augustana University, Orders Addr.: Augustana Univ. 2001 S. Summit Ave., Sioux Falls, SD 57197 USA (SAN 211-4844) Tel 605-274-4007; Fax: 605-274-4999
E-mail: harry.thompson@augie.edu; cws@augie.edu
Web site: http://augie.edu/cws
Dist(s): **Dakota West Bks.**

Center For Youth Issues, Incorporated *See* **National Ctr. For Youth Issues**

Ctr. of SW Studies, Fort Lewis College, *(978-0-9727664)* 1000 Rim Dr., Durango, CO 81301 USA
E-mail: gulliford_a@fortlewis.edu
Web site: http://www.swcenter.fortlewis.edu.

Ctr. Stage Puppets, *(978-0-9795087)* P.O. Box 8279, Bend, OR 97708 USA Tel 541-420-7943
E-mail: info@centerstagepuppets.com
Web site: http://www.centerstagepuppets.com.

Centering Corp., *(978-1-56123)* P.O. Box 4600, Omaha, NE 68104-0600 USA (SAN 298-1815) Tel 402-553-1200; Fax: 402-553-0507
E-mail: j1200@aol.com
Web site: http://www.centering.org
Dist(s): **Follett School Solutions.**

CenterLine Media, *(978-0-9754212; 978-0-9814896)* 115 Greenwood Ave., Ambler, PA 19002-5709 USA Tel 215-646-4591; Fax: 215-933-6819
E-mail: info@centerlinemedia.com
Web site: http://www.centerlinemedia.com.

Centerpunch Pr., *(978-0-9724882)* P.O. Box 43151, Cincinnati, OH 45243 USA Tel 513-561-3392 (phone/fax)
E-mail: info@centerpunchpress.com
Web site: http://www.centerpunchpress.com.

Centerstream Publishing, *(978-0-931759; 978-1-57424)* Orders Addr.: P.O. Box 17878, Anaheim Hills, CA 92817 USA (SAN 683-8022) Tel 714-779-9390 (phone/fax)
E-mail: centerstrm@aol.com
Web site: http://www.pma-online.org
Dist(s): **Booklines Hawaii, Ltd.**
Leonard, Hal Corp.
MyiLibrary.

Centipede Dragon A Benevolent Creature, *(978-0-692-23349-8; 978-0-692-33306-8; 978-0-692-84099-3; 978-0-692-88976-3)* 7002 Memorial Heights Dr., Alexandria, VA 22306 USA Tel 703-975-0993
Dist(s): **CreateSpace Independent Publishing Platform.**

Central Ave. Pr, *(978-0-9715344; 978-0-9798452)* 8400 Menaul Blvd. NE, Suite A No. 211, Albuquerque, NM 87112 USA
E-mail: oelfkej@aol.com
Web site: http://www.centralavepress.com
Dist(s): **Bookmasters Distribution**
Quality Bks., Inc.

Central Avenue Publishing (CAN) *(978-1-926760; 978-0-9812737; 978-1-77168) Dist. by* **IPG Chicago.**

Central Coast Bks./Pr., *(978-0-9658776; 978-1-930401)* Orders Addr.: P.O. Box 3654, San Luis Obispo, CA 93403 USA (SAN 631-1547) Tel 805-534-0307 (phone/fax); Edit Addr.: 831 a Via Esteban, Samn Luis, Obispo, CA 94301 USA (SAN 631-1539)
E-mail: ccbooks@surfari.net.

Central Coast Press *See* **Central Coast Bks./Pr.**

Central Conference of American Rabbis/CCAR Pr., *(978-0-88123; 978-0-916694)* 355 Lexington Ave., 18th Flr., New York, NY 10017-6603 USA (SAN 204-3262) Tel 212-972-3636; Fax: 212-692-0819; Toll Free: 800-935-2227
E-mail: ccarpress@ccarnet.org; info@ccarnet.org
Web site: http://ccarpress.org.

Central Orb Publishing, *(978-0-9818818)* P.O. Box 830, Orem, UT 84059-0830 USA
E-mail: Thesoulalliance@Hotmail.com
Web site: http://www.createspace.com/3347335; http://www.lulu.com/thesoulalliance; http://www.createspace.com/3351702.

Central Park Media Corp., *(978-1-56219; 978-1-57800; 978-1-887692; 978-1-58664)* 250 W. 57th St. Ste. 1723, New York, NY 10107-1708 USA (SAN 631-3191) Toll Free: 800-833-7456; *Imprints:* CPM Manga (CPM Manga); CPM Comics (CPM Comics); Manga 18 (Manga Eighteen); CPM Manhwa (CPM Manhwa)
E-mail: info@teamcpm.com
Web site: http://www.centralparkmedia.com/; http://www.cpmpress.com/
Dist(s): **Hobbies Hawaii Distributors.**

Central Park Tutors Bks., *(978-0-692-76743-6; 978-0-9988340)* 244 Fifth Avenue, Suite 2231, New York, NY 10001 USA Tel 917-502-9108; Fax: 917-502-9108
E-mail: michaelawallach@yahoo.com
Web site: http://centralparktutors.com/subject/books/
Dist(s): **Midpoint Trade Bks., Inc.**

Central Recovery Pr., *(978-0-9799869; 978-0-9818482; 978-1-936290; 978-1-937612; 978-1-942094)* 3321 N. Buffalo Dr. Suite 275, Las Vegas, NV 89129 USA (SAN 854-9532) Tel 702-868-5830; Fax: 702-868-5831; 387 Pk. Ave. S., New York, NY 10016
E-mail: nschenck@centralrecovery.com; vkilleen@centralrecovery.com
Web site: http://www.centralrecoverypress.com
Dist(s): **Consortium Bk. Sales & Distribution**
Follett School Solutions
Health Communications, Inc.
MyiLibrary.

Centro Bks., LLC, *(978-1-933572)* 3636 Fieldston Rd. Apt. 6P, Bronx, NY 10463-2041 USA (SAN 256-7229)
Web site: http://www.centrobooks.com.

Centro de Informacion y Desarrollo de la Comunicacion y la Literatura (MEX) *(978-968-494) Dist. by* **Continental Bk.**

Centro de Informacion y Desarrollo de la Comunicacion y la Literatura (MEX) *(978-968-494) Dist. by* **Mariuccia Iaconi Bk Imports.**

Centro de Informacion y Desarrollo de la Comunicacion y la Literatura (MEX) *(978-968-494) Dist. by* **Lectorum Pubns.**

Centro de Informacion y Desarrollo de la Comunicacion y la Literatura (MEX) *(978-968-494) Dist. by* **AIMS Intl.**

Centurion Pr., *(978-0-9800805)* 740 Breeze Hill Rd., #171, Vista, CA 92081 USA Fax: 760-631-3607
E-mail: fedthought@gmail.com
Web site: http://www.centurionpress.com.

Cepia LLC., *(978-0-9777241)* 121 Hunter Ave., Suite 103, Saint Louis, MO 63124 USA Tel 314-725-4900; Fax: 314-725-4919
E-mail: support@cepiallc.com
Web site: http://www.cepiallc.com.

Cerebellum Corp., *(978-1-58198; 978-1-886156; 978-1-59626; 978-1-61867)* 145 Corte Madera Town Ctr, Ste 406, rte Madera, CA 94925 USA (SAN 299-240X) Tel 415-541-9901; Fax: 805-426-8136; Toll Free: 800-238-9669
E-mail: customerservice@cerebellum.com; cerebell@mindspring.com; admin@cerebellum.com
Web site: www.cerebellum.com; http://www.standarddeviants.com
Dist(s): **Follett School Solutions.**

Cerebral Press International, *(978-0-916309)* HC-71 Box 121-1, Thornfield, MO 65762 USA (SAN 295-9461) Tel 417-679-4748
E-mail: lagunapress@braintypes.com
Web site: http://www.braintypes.com.

Ceres Pr., *(978-0-9606138; 978-1-886101)* P.O. Box 87, Woodstock, NY 12498 USA (SAN 217-0949) Tel 845-679-5573; Toll Free: 888-804-8848 Do not confuse with Ceres Pr., Stamford, CT
E-mail: cem620@aol.com
Web site: http://www.heathyhighways.com
Dist(s): **Integral Yoga Pubns.**
New Leaf Distributing Co., Inc.
Nutri-Bks. Corp.
Partners Bk. Distributing, Inc.

Ceres Software, Incorporated *See* **Inspiration Software, Inc.**

Certified Firearms Instructors, LLC, *(978-0-9741480)* P.O. Box 131254, Saint Paul, MN 55113-1254 USA Tel 952-935-2414; Fax: 952-935-4122
E-mail: jolson@gw.hamline.edu
Web site: http://www.aacfi.com.

CET *Imprint of* **Greater Cincinnati TV Educational Foundation**

C E V Multimedia, Ltd., *(978-1-57078; 978-1-59535; 978-1-60333; 978-1-61459)* Orders Addr.: P.O. Box 65265, Lubbock, TX 79464 USA Tel 806-745-8820; Fax: 806-745-5300; Toll Free Fax: 800-243-6398; Toll Free: 800-922-9965; Edit Addr.: 1020 SE Loop 289, Lubbock, TX 79404 USA
E-mail: cev@cevmultimedia.com
Web site: http://www.cevmultimedia.com
Dist(s): **Follett School Solutions.**

CFM, *(978-0-9728620; 978-0-9769071; 978-0-9908661)* 112 Greene St., New York City, NY 10012 USA Tel 212-966-3864; Fax: 212-226-1041
E-mail: info@cfmgallery.com
Web site: http://www.cfmgallery.com.

CG Star, L.L.C. *See* **C-It Entertainment Group, LLC**

C.G.S. Pr., *(978-0-9660726)* P.O. Box 1394, Mountainside, NJ 07092 USA Tel 908-233-8293 (phone/fax)
E-mail: Gwynnic2000@aol.com.

Chacmool Pr., *(978-0-9789391)* 849 W. University Pkwy., Baltimore, MD 21210 USA
E-mail: publisher@chacmoolpress.com
Web site: http://www.chacmoolpress.com.

Chafie Pr., LLC, *(978-0-9833190; 978-0-9903532)* 7557 Rambler Rd. Suite 626, Dallas, TX 75231 USA Tel 214-628-8600
E-mail: trish.jones@chafiehds.com
Web site: http://www.chafiepress.com
Dist(s): **Follett School Solutions**
Pathway Bk. Service.

Chagrin River Publishing Co., *(978-1-929821; 978-0-615-32246-9)* Orders Addr.: P.O. Box 173, Chagrin Falls, OH 44022 USA Tel 440-893-9250; Edit Addr.: 21 E. Summit St., Chagrin Falls, OH 44022 USA
Dist(s): **Follett School Solutions.**

Chai Yo Maui Pr., *(978-0-615-31840-0; 978-0-9855804)* P.O. Box 331, Kihei, HI 96753 USA.

Chaklet Coffee Bks *Imprint of* **Candalyse Publishing**

Chamberlain Hart Enterprises, Inc., *(978-0-9749756)* P.O. Box 1600, Fairfield, IA 52556 USA Tel 641-469-3717; Fax: 641-469-6647
E-mail: che@iowatelecom.net
Web site: http://www.chamberlainhart.com.

Chambers Kingfisher Graham Publishers, Incorporated *See* **Larousse Kingfisher Chambers, Inc.**

Chameleon Designs, *(978-0-9701573)* P.O. Box 61855, North Charleston, SC 29419 USA Tel 843-761-7426
E-mail: yeleth@aol.com.

Chamike Pubs., *(978-1-884876)* 9000 Doris Dr., Fort Washington, MD 20744 USA Tel 301-248-4034.

Champion Athlete Publishing Company *See* **National Assn. of Speed & Explosion**

Championship Chess, *(978-0-9729456; 978-0-9772489)* Div. of Teachable Tech, Inc., Orders Addr.: 3565 Evans Rd., Atlanta, GA 30340 USA Toll Free: 888-328-7373
E-mail: dj@championshipchess.net
Web site: http://www.championshipchess.net.

Champlain Avenue Bks., Inc., *(978-0-9855008; 978-0-9896347; 978-0-9908256; 978-1-943063)* 2360 Corporate Cir. Suite 400, Henderson, NV 89074-7722 USA Tel 760-684-5861
E-mail: champlainavenuebooks@hotmail.com
Web site: champlainavenuebooks@hotmail.com
Dist(s): **Smashwords.**

Chan, David, *(978-0-9754302)* 12511 Fox Trace Ln., Houston, TX 77066-4029 USA Tel 281-580-7042
E-mail: david@chancomputerhelp.com.

Chandler Hse. Pr., *(978-0-9636277; 978-1-886284)* P.O. Box 20126, Worcester, MA 01602 USA Fax: 508-753-7419
E-mail: chandlerhousepress@yahoo.com
Web site: http://www.chandlerhousebooks.com
Dist(s): **Follett School Solutions.**

Chandler/White Publishing Co., *(978-1-877804)* 517 W. Midvale Ave., Philadelphia, PA 19144-4617 USA
Dist(s): **Alliance Hse., Inc.**

Change Is Strange, Inc., *(978-0-9755902)* 3630 21st St., Boulder, CO 80304-1608 USA
E-mail: info@changeisstrange.com
Web site: http://www.changeisstrange.com
Dist(s): **Follett School Solutions.**

Change the Universe Pr., *(978-0-615-21144-2)* 9607 Bolton Rd., Los Angeles, CA 90034 USA Tel 310-963-8644
E-mail: yasgur@jclla.org; jlipner@irell.com
Web site: http://www.maxsaidyes.com.

Changing Lives Changing The World, Incorporated *See* **Changing Lives Publishing**

Changing Lives Publishing, *(978-0-9653700; 978-0-9774513; 978-0-9798553)* Div. of Changing Lives Changing The World, Inc., P.O. Box 132, Sharpes, FL 32959 USA Tel 321-637-1128; Toll Free: 866-578-1900
E-mail: print2publish@gmail.com
Web site: http://www.print2publish.com.

Changing-Times.net, *(978-0-9741930)* Orders Addr.: P.O. Box 39651, Phoenix, AZ 85069-9651 USA
Web site: http://www.changing-times.net.

Channel Kids *Imprint of* **Channel Photographics**

Channel Photographics, *(978-0-9744029; 978-0-9766708; 978-0-9773399; 978-0-9819942; 978-0-9826137; 978-0-9832983)* 980 Lincoln Ave Ste 200B, San Rafael, CA 94901 USA; *Imprints:* Channel Kids (ChannKids)
E-mail: adrianne@globalpsd.com; steven@globalpsd.com
Web site: http://www.channelphotographics.com
Dist(s): **Publishers Group West (PGW)**
SCB Distributors.

Channel Publishing, Ltd., *(978-0-945501; 978-1-933053; 978-1-946729)* 4750 Longley Ln., Suite 209, Reno, NV 89502 USA (SAN 247-1256) Tel 775-825-0880; Fax: 775-825-5633; Toll Free: 800-248-2882
E-mail: info@channelpublishing.com
Web site: http://www.channelpublishing.com.

Chantilly Books, *(978-0-9841960)* Div. of Boone Amie Publishing, Orders Addr.: 14240-A Sullyfield Cir., Chantilly, VA 20151 USA (SAN 858-6853) Fax: 703-830-7100
E-mail: sue@a-childs-book.com
Web site: http://www.a-childs-book.com.

Chapel Hill Press, Inc., *(978-1-880849; 978-1-59715)* 1829 E. Franklin St., Bldg. 700a, Chapel Hill, NC 27514-5863 USA Tel 919-942-8389; Fax: 919-869-2066
E-mail: publisher@chapelhillpress.com; dennis.mcgill@chapelhillpress.com; luz@chapelhillpress.com; edwina.woodbury@chapelhillpress.com
Web site: http://www.chapelhillpress.com
Dist(s): **Blair, John F. Pub.**
Follett School Solutions.

Chapelle *Imprint of* **Sterling Publishing Co., Inc.**

Chapin Hse. Bks. *Imprint of* **Florida Historical Society**

Chapman, Chris & Eric P. Hvolboll, *(978-0-9765061)* 2741 Cuerta Rd., Santa Barbara, CA 93105 USA Fax: 805-882-9897.

Chapman Pr., LLC, *(978-0-9725420)* 949 S. Josephine St., Denver, CO 80209 USA
E-mail: taylor@babsonfarms.com; taylor@babsonfarms.com
Web site: http://www.chapmanpress.com.

Chapter & Verse Pr., *(978-0-9724549)* 7350 Detrick Jordan Pike, Springfield, OH 45502-9660 USA Tel 937-964-0294
E-mail: nashvila@bright.net.

Chapter Bks. *Imprint of* **Spotlight**

Chapter Readers *Imprint of* **Picture Window Bks.**

Character Arts, *(978-0-9772259)* 37 Pond Rd., Bldg. 2, Wilton, CT 06897 USA Tel 203-834-0323.

Character Development Group, Inc., *(978-0-9653163; 978-1-892056)* Div. of Character Development Group, Inc., Orders Addr.: P.O. Box 35136, Greensboro, NC 27425-5136 USA Tel 336-668-9373; Fax: 336-668-9375; Edit Addr.: 8646 W. Market St. Suite 102, Greensboro, NC 27409 USA
E-mail: info@charactereducation.com
Web site: http://www.charactereducation.com
Dist(s): **Follett School Solutions.**

Character Development Publishing *See* **Character Development Group, Inc.**

Character-in-Action *Imprint of* **Quiet Impact, Inc.**

CharFaye Publishing, Incorporated *See* **FayeHouse. Pr. International**

Charisma Hse. *Imprint of* **Charisma Media**

Charisma Kids *Imprint of* **Charisma Media**

Charisma Media, *(978-0-88419; 978-0-930525; 978-1-59185; 978-1-59979; 978-1-61638; 978-1-62136; 978-1-62998; 978-1-62999)* Div. of Creation House Pr., 600 Rinehart Rd., Lake Mary, FL 32746 USA (SAN 677-5640) Tel 407-333-0600; Fax: 407-333-7100; Toll Free: 800-283-8494; *Imprints:* Charisma House (Charisma Hse); Casa Creacion (Casa Cre); Creation House (CreatHse); Siloam Press (Siloam Pr); Charisma Kids (Charisma Kids); Realms (Realms); Frontline (Frontline FLA)
Web site: http://www.charismamedia.com/
Dist(s): **Dake Publishing**
Follett School Solutions
INscribe Digital
Lulu Pr., Inc.
Pura Vida Bks., Inc.
SPD-Small Pr. Distribution
Send The Light Distribution LLC.

Charles Reasoners Little Cuddles *Imprint of* **Picture Window Bks.**

Charles River Media, *(978-1-886801; 978-1-58450)* Orders Addr.: P.O. Box 960, Herndon, VA 20172 USA (SAN 254-1564) Fax: 703-996-1010; Toll Free: 800-382-8505; Edit Addr.: 25 Thomson Pl., Boston, MA 02210-1202 USA
E-mail: info@charlesriver.com
Web site: http://www.charlesriver.com
Dist(s): **CENGAGE Learning**
Delmar Cengage Learning
ebrary, Inc.

Charles River Pr., *(978-0-9754913; 978-0-9791304; 978-0-9793844; 978-0-9820946; 978-1-936185; 978-1-940676)* 37 Evergreen Rd., Norton, MA 02766 USA Fax: 508-297-3628; P.O. Box 1122, Mansfield, MA 02048 (SAN 256-2251); *Imprints:* Gap Tooth Publishing (Gap Tooth Pubng) Do not confuse with Charles River Pr. in Alexandria, VA
E-mail: jwomack@charlesriverpress.com; customerservice@charlesriverpress.com
Web site: http://www.charlesriverpress.com.

Charles Scribner's Sons *Imprint of* **Cengage Gale**

Charlesbridge Publishing, Inc., *(978-0-88106; 978-0-935508; 978-1-57091; 978-1-58089; 978-1-879085; 978-1-60734; 978-0-9822939; 978-0-9823064; 978-1-936140; 978-1-63289)* Orders Addr.: c/o Penguin Random House, 400 Hahn Rd., Westminster, MD 21157 USA Toll Free Fax: 800-669-1536; Toll Free: 800-733-3000; Edit Addr.: 85 Main St., Watertown, MA 02472 USA (SAN 240-5474) Tel 617-926-0329; Fax: 617-926-5720; Toll Free Fax: 800-926-5775; Toll Free: 800-225-3214; *Imprints:* Mackinac Island Press, Incorporated (Mackinac); Imagine Publishing (ImaginePub); Charlesbridge Teen (CharlesbridgeT)
E-mail: orders@charlesbridge.com
Web site: http://www.charlesbridge.com
Dist(s): **Continental Bk. Co., Inc.**
Follett School Solutions
Lectorum Pubns., Inc.
MyiLibrary
Penguin Random Hse. LLC
Random Hse., Inc.

Charlesbridge Teen *Imprint of* **Charlesbridge Publishing, Inc.**

Charlie & Albert, *(978-0-9801329)* 2920 Applewood Ct., Suite 192, Atlanta, GA 30345-1401 USA Tel 770-938-8863.

Charlie's Gift, *(978-0-9786795)* 920 York Rd., Suite 350, Hinsdale, IL 60521 USA Tel 630-399-8164.

Charming Pubns., *(978-0-9773531)* Orders Addr.: P.O. Box 90792, Austin, TX 78709-0792 USA Tel 512-288-4803
E-mail: minia.lopez@gmail.com
Web site: http://www.happychildrenbooks.com.

Chartwell *Imprint of* **Book Sales, Inc.**

Charwood Pubns., *(978-0-615-58076-0; 978-0-615-66672-3; 978-0-9910347; 978-0-692-79990-1; 978-0-692-80308-0; 978-0-9986914)* Orders Addr.: P.O. Box 14881, Long Beach, CA 90853 USA Tel 562-810-7176
E-mail: charlesfilius@gmail.com
Web site: www.charlesfilius.com; www.charwoodpublications.com.

Chaser Media LLC, *(978-0-9747447)* P.O. Box 99, Dorset, VT 05251 USA
Web site: http://www.chasermedia.com.

Chateau Thierry Pr., *(978-0-935046)* Div. of Joan Thiry Enterprises, Ltd., 2100 W. Estes, Chicago, IL 60645 USA (SAN 281-4056) Tel 773-262-2234; Fax: 773-262-2235
E-mail: percival6390@sbcglobal.net.

Chatoyant, *(978-0-9661452)* P.O. Box 832, Aptos, CA 95001 USA (SAN 253-9454) Tel 831-662-2723
E-mail: books@chatoyant.com
Web site: http://www.chatoyant.com.

Chauncey Park Pr., *(978-0-9667808)* Div. of Charles Chauncey Wells, Inc., 735 N. Grove Ave., Oak Park, IL 60302-1551 USA Tel 708-524-0695; Fax: 708-524-0742
E-mail: chauncey@wells1.com
Web site: http://www.wells1.com.

CHB Media, *(978-0-9822819; 978-0-9851507; 978-0-9886315; 978-0-9911189; 978-0-9863842)* Div. of Christian Heartbeat, Inc., 3039 Needle Palm Dr., Edgewater, FL 32141 USA Tel 386-690-9295
E-mail: christianheartbeat@gmail.com
Web site: http://www.chbmediaonline.com.

Checker Book Publishing Group *See* **Devil's Due Digital, Inc. - A Checker Digital Co.**

Checkerboard Library *Imprint of* **ABDO Publishing Co.**

†Checkerboard Pr., Inc., *(978-1-56288)* 1560 Revere Rd., Yardley, PA 19067-4351 USA; *CIP.*

Checkmark Bks. *Imprint of* **Facts On File, Inc.**

Cheerful Cherub, *(978-0-9753417)* Orders Addr.: 10071 S. Maples Ln., Highlands Ranch, CO 80129 USA Tel 303-471-8472; Edit Addr.: 10071 S. Maples Ln., Highlands Ranch, CO 80129 USA
E-mail: coloradodonna@q.com
Web site: http://www.cheerfulcherub.com.

Chelsea Clubhouse *Imprint of* **Facts On File, Inc.**

Chelsea Green Publishing, *(978-0-930031; 978-1-890132; 978-1-931498; 978-1-933392; 978-1-60358)* Orders Addr.: P.O. Box 428, White River Junction, VT 05001 USA (SAN 669-7631) Tel 802-295-6300; Fax: 802-295-6444; Toll Free: 800-639-4099; Edit Addr.: 85 N. Main St., Suite 120, White River Junction, VT 05001 USA
E-mail: info@chelseagreen.com
Web site: http://www.chelseagreen.com
Dist(s): **Follett School Solutions.**

Chelsea Hse. *Imprint of* **Facts On File, Inc.**

Chelsea Media *See* **Chelsea Multimedia**

Chelsea Multimedia, *(978-0-9822348)* P.O. Box 4668 19830, New York, NY 10163-4668 USA Tel 203-853-0540; *Imprints:* Chelsea Press (Chelsea Press)
Web site: http://www.chelseapress.com
Dist(s): **CreateSpace Independent Publishing Platform.**

Chelsea Pr. *Imprint of* **Chelsea Multimedia**

Chelsea Publishing Co., Inc. *Imprint of* **American Mathematical Society**

Chemical Heritage Foundation, *(978-0-941901)* 315 Chestnut St., Philadelphia, PA 19106-2702 USA (SAN

666-0193) Tel 215-925-2222; Fax: 215-925-1954; Toll Free: 888-224-6006
E-mail: booksales@chemheritage.org
Web site: http://www.chemheritage.org.

Cheng & Tsui Co., *(978-0-88727; 978-0-917056; 978-1-62291)* 25 West St., Boston, MA 02111-1213 USA (SAN 169-3387) Tel 617-988-2401; Fax: 617-426-3669
E-mail: service@cheng-tsui.com
Web site: http://www.cheng-tsui.com
Dist(s): **Chinasprout, Inc.**
Follett School Solutions.

Cheng Chung Bk. Co., Ltd. (TWN) *(978-957-09) Dist. by* **Cheng Tsui.**

Cheniere Pr., *(978-0-9725146; 978-0-9786260)* 151 La Jolla Dr., Santa Barbara, CA 93109 USA
E-mail: webmaster@cheniere.org.

Cherakota Books *See* **Cherakota Publishing**

Cherakota Publishing, *(978-0-9795678)* Orders Addr.: P.O. Box 603, Two Harbors, MN 55616 USA
E-mail: info@cherakotapublishing.com
Web site: http://www.cherakotapublishing.com.

Cherish the Children *See* **Chris A. Zeigler Dendy Consulting LLC**

Cherokee Bks., *(978-0-9640458; 978-1-930052)* Orders Addr.: 24 Meadow Ridge Pkwy. Dover, De 19904, Dover, DE 19904-5800 USA Tel 302-734-8782; Fax: 302-734-3198 Do not confuse with Cherokee Bks., Ponca City, OK
E-mail: mithanna@aol.com
Web site: http://www.cherokeebooks.com
Dist(s): **Washington Bk. Distributors.**

Cherokee Publishing Company *See* **Cherokee Bks.**

Cherry Lake Publishing, *(978-1-60279; 978-1-61080; 978-1-62431; 978-1-62753; 978-1-63137; 978-1-63188; 978-1-63362; 978-1-63470; 978-1-63471; 978-1-63472; 978-1-5341)* 1215 Overidgeview Ct., Ann Arbor, MI 48103 USA Tel 248-705-2045; 1750 Northway Dr., Suite 101, North Mankato, MN 56003 (SAN 858-9275) Tel 866-918-3956; Toll Free Fax: 866-489-6490; *Imprints:* Blackbirch Press, Incorporated (Blackbirch Pr); 45th Parallel Press (45 Parallel)
E-mail: customerservice@cherrylakepublishing.com; benmondloch@me.com; lois.hume@sleepingbearpress.com
Web site: http://cherrylakepublishing.com; www.sleepingbearpress.com
Dist(s): **Follett School Solutions**
MyiLibrary.

Cherry Lane Books *See* **Cherry Lane Music Co.**

†Cherry Lane Music Co., *(978-0-89524; 978-1-57560; 978-1-60378)* 6 E. 32nd St., 11th Flr., New York, NY 10016 USA (SAN 219-0788) Tel 212-561-3000; Fax: 212-251-0822
E-mail: print@cherrylane.com
Web site: http://www.cherrylane.com
Dist(s): **Leonard, Hal Corp.**
MyiLibrary; *CIP.*

Cherry Street Pr., *(978-0-9764921)* 139A N. 22nd St., Philadelphia, PA 19103 USA Fax: 215-568-4329
Dist(s): **Follett School Solutions.**

Cherry, Tasha *See* **Pop Academy of Music**

Cherry Tree Bks., *(978-0-9666832; 978-0-9774665)* 433 Perkins Rd., Weybridge, VT 05753 USA Tel 802-545-2474
E-mail: idahw@pshift.com; lmwash@together.net
Web site: http://www.cherrytreebooks.net.

Cherry Tree Lane Publishing, *(978-0-9771858)* 125 Cobblestone Ct., Berea, OH 44017-1079 USA
E-mail: sharesom@wowway.com.

Cherry Tree Pr. LLC, *(978-0-9772771)* Orders Addr.: 525 W. 14th St., #185, Traverse City, MI 49684-4968 USA Tel 231-421-1012; Edit Addr.: 526 W. 14th St., No. 185, Traverse City, MI 49684-4968 USA Do not confuse with Cherry Tree Press in Palo Alto, CA
E-mail: info@cherrytreepress.com
Web site: http://www.CherryTreePress.com; http://www.AmlaColorToo.com
Dist(s): **Partners Bk. Distributing, Inc.**

Cherrytree Pubns., Inc., *(978-0-9677757)* 881 Ocean Dr., No. 18B, Biscayne, FL 33149 USA Tel 305-361-1828.

Chesapeake & Ohio Historical Society, Inc., *(978-0-939487)* P.O. Box 79, Clifton Forge, VA 24422 USA (SAN 225-3798)
E-mail: cohs@cohs.org
Dist(s): **Hachette Bk. Group.**

Chesed Avraham Temple, *(978-0-9801799)* Orders Addr.: P.O. Box 35456, Los Angeles, CA 90035 USA (SAN 855-4137) Tel 310-654-0303
E-mail: meissany@ca.rr.com
Web site: http://www.EbrahimNeissany.com.

Cheshire House Bks., *(978-0-9675073)* P.O. Box 2484, New York, NY 10021 USA Tel 212-861-5404 (phone/fax)
E-mail: Chershirehouse@webtv.net
Web site: http://www.samthecat.com
Dist(s): **Brodart Co.**
Follet Higher Education Grp
Follett School Solutions.

Chess Library, The, *(978-0-9661889)* 12615 SW 297th Way, Vashon, WA 98070 USA
E-mail: pkmccready@netscape.net; admin@thechesslibrary.com
Web site: http://www.thechesslibrary.com.

Chester Comix, LLC, *(978-0-9729616; 978-1-933122; 978-0-692-95704-2)* P.O. Box 5653, Williamsburg, VA 23188 USA
E-mail: chestercomix@yahoo.com
Web site: http://www.chestercomix.com
Dist(s): **Follett School Solutions.**

Chester Music (GBR) *(978-0-7119) Dist. by* **H Leonard.**

Chester Music *Imprint of* **Music Sales Corp.**

Cheval International, *(978-0-9640610; 978-1-885351)* P.O. Box 706, Black Hawk, SD 57718-0706 USA
E-mail: cheval@rapidnet.com
Web site: http://www.chevalinternational.com
Dist(s): **Barnes & Noble Bks.-Imports.**

Chi Chi Rodriguez Bks., *(978-0-9797641)* P.O. Box 1155, Avondale, PA 19311 USA Tel 610-806-2013 Alternate #610-806-2013
Web site: http://www.marisadejesus.com.

Chiappini, Lydia , *(978-0-9669355)* 60 Gaisler Rd., Blairstown, NJ 07825 USA Tel 908-362-5604
E-mail: lydiachiappini@yahoo.com.

Chiaramonti, Gregory, *(978-0-615-13848-0)* 825 Cherry St., Trenton, NJ 08638-3322 USA
E-mail: gcmonti@yahoo.com
Web site: http://www.probie-thespaceprobe.com
Dist(s): **Lulu Pr., Inc.**

Chicago Children's Museum, *(978-0-9759580)* Navy Pier, 700 E. Grand Ave., Chicago, IL 60611 USA Tel 312-527-1000; Fax: 312-527-9082
Web site: http://www.chichildrensmuseum.org
Dist(s): **Follett School Solutions**
Independent Pubs. Group
ebrary, Inc.

Chicago Distribution Ctr., Orders Addr.: 11030 S. Langley Ave., Chicago, IL 60628 USA (SAN 630-6047) Tel 773-702-7000 (International); Fax: 773-702-7212 (International); Toll Free Fax: 800-621-8476 (USA/Canada); Toll Free: 800-621-2736 (USA/Canada); 800-621-8471 (credit & collections)
E-mail: custserv@press.uchicago.edu; orders@press.uchicago.edu
Web site: http://www.press.uchicago.edu; http://www.press.uchicago.edu/presswide/cdc/.

†Chicago Review Pr., Inc., *(978-0-89733; 978-0-912777; 978-0-913705; 978-0-914090; 978-0-914091; 978-0-915864; 978-1-55652; 978-1-56976; 978-1-61373; 978-1-61374; 978-1-64160)* 814 N. Franklin St., Chicago, IL 60610 USA (SAN 213-5744) Tel 312-337-0747; Toll Free: 800-888-4741 (orders only); *Imprints:* Hill, Lawrence Books (Lawrence Hill); Zephyr Press (ZephPr); Academy Chicago Publishers, Limited (AcadChicagoPubs)
E-mail: frontdesk@chicagoreviewpress.com; orders@ipgbook.com
Web site: http://www.ipgbook.com; http://www.chicagoreviewpress.com
Dist(s): **AK Pr. Distribution**
Cobblestone Publishing Co.
Ebsco Publishing
Follett School Solutions
Gryphon Hse., Inc.
Independent Pubs. Group
Lulu Pr., Inc.
MyiLibrary
SAGE Pubns., Inc.
ebrary, Inc.; *CIP.*

Chicago Spectrum Pr., *(978-1-58374; 978-1-886094)* Div. of Evanston Publishing Inc., Orders Addr.: 6611 Foxcroft Rd., Prospect, KY 40059 USA Tel 502-899-1919; Toll Free: 800-594-5190; 888-266-5780 (888-BOOKS-80)
E-mail: dorothykavka@twc.com
Web site: www.fineartbykavka.com.

Chicago Unzipped, *(978-0-9771699; 978-0-9817538)* 633 Clark St., No. 2-634, Evanston, IL 60208 USA (SAN 856-4558) Tel 847-491-8757
Web site: http://www.chicagounzipped.com.

Chick Light Publishing, *(978-0-9769198)* 845 Monticello Ct., Cape Coral, FL 33904 USA Tel 239-945-1939 (phone/fax)
E-mail: vince@chicklight.com
Web site: http://chicklight.com.

Chick Pubns., Inc., *(978-0-937958; 978-0-7589)* P.O. Box 3500, Ontario, CA 91761-1019 USA (SAN 211-7770) Tel 909-987-0771; Fax: 909-941-8128; Toll Free: 800-932-3050
E-mail: orderdesk@chick.com
Web site: http://www.chick.com.

Chickaloon Village Publishing, *(978-0-9767217)* Orders Addr.: P.O. Box 1105, Chickaloon, AK 99674 USA Tel 907-745-0707; Fax: 907-745-0709
E-mail: cvadmin@chickaloon.org
Web site: http://www.chickaloon.org.

Chicken Hse., The *Imprint of* **Scholastic, Inc.**

Chicken Socks *Imprint of* **Klutz**

Chicken Soup for the Soul Publishing, LLC, *(978-1-935096; 978-1-61159)* 132 E. Putnam Ave., Cos Cob, CT 06807 USA; 180 Varick St. Suite 816, New York, NY 10014; *Imprints:* CSS Backlist (CSSBacklist)
E-mail: evergreenstables@hotmail.com
Dist(s): **Follett School Solutions**
Leonard, Hal Corp.
MyiLibrary
Open Road Integrated Media, Inc.
Simon & Schuster
Simon & Schuster, Inc.

Chickering-Moller Project, *(978-0-9860799)* 414 W. 16th Street, Traverse City, MI 49684 USA.

Chicory Pr., *(978-0-9785886)* 49 Maple Ave., Morgantown, WV 26501 USA Tel 304-292-1115
E-mail: efaulkes@mail.wvu.edu.

Chien, Paris *See* **La Librairie Parisienne**

Chihuly Workshop, Inc., *(978-0-9608382; 978-1-57684)* Orders Addr.: P.O. Box 70856, Seattle, WA 98127 USA (SAN 240-3579) Tel 206-297-1304; Fax: 206-297-6207; Toll Free: 800-574-7272 (trade orders) Do not confuse with Portland Pr., Inc., Chapel Hill, NC
E-mail: jacobb@portlandpress.net
Web site: http://www.chihuly.com; http://www.portlandpress.net; http://www.chihulyworkshop.com
Dist(s): **Follett School Solutions.**

ChikChatr Ink, *(978-0-9766634)* P.O. Box 3302, Brentwood, TN 37024-3302 USA Tel 615-731-7422.

Child Advocates, Inc., *(978-0-9754953)* 2401 Portsmouth, Suite 210, Houston, TX 77098 USA Tel 713-529-1396; Fax: 713-529-1390
Web site: http://www.childadvocates.org
Dist(s): **Follett School Solutions.**

Child & Family Pr. *Imprint of* **Child Welfare League of America, Inc.**

Child Life Bks., LLC, *(978-0-9771143; 978-0-9791687)* 22303 Charlotte Dr., Torrance, CA 90505-2118 USA
E-mail: liana@mannersicare.com.

Child Scope Productions, *(978-0-9678778)* Div. of Moschea Promotions, 5016 N. Lydell Ave., White Fish Bay, WI 53217 USA Tel 414-332-1897; Fax: 414-332-1609
E-mail: mosch@execpc.com.

Child Sensitive Communication, LLC, *(978-0-9743197; 978-1-933803; 978-0-9979174; 978-0-9986292)* P.O. Box 150806, Nashville, TN 37215-0806 USA; *Imprints:* Karyn Henley Resources (Krayn Henley)
Web site: http://www.karynhenley.com; http://throatofthenight.com
Dist(s): **Brown Bks.**

†Child Welfare League of America, Inc., *(978-0-87868; 978-1-58760)* Orders Addr.: P.O. Box 932831, Atlanta, GA 31193-2831 USA Tel 770-280-4164; Toll Free: 800-407-6273; Edit Addr.: 2345 Crystal Dr., Suite 250, Arlington, VA 22202 USA (SAN 201-9876) Tel 703-412-2400; Fax: 703-412-2401 (orders only); PBD 420 Eagleview Blvd., Exton, PA 19341 (SAN 851-2558) Tel 202-638-2952; Fax: 202-638-4004; *Imprints:* C W L A Press (CWLA Pr); Child & Family Press (Child-Family Pr)
E-mail: order@cwla.org
Web site: http://www.cwla.org/pubs
Dist(s): **Lectorum Pubns., Inc.;** *CIP.*

Child1st Pubns., LLC, *(978-0-9844972; 978-0-9829873; 978-1-936981; 978-1-947484)* Orders Addr.: PO Box 150226, Grand Rapids, MI 49515 USA
Web site: http://www.child1st.com
Dist(s): **Follett School Solutions.**

Childcraft Education Corp., *(978-1-890275; 978-1-58669)* Div. of School Specialty, 2920 Old Tree Dr., Lancaster, PA 17603 USA Tel 717-391-4027; Fax: 717-397-7436; Toll Free: 800-631-5652
E-mail: kmyers@childcrafteducation.com
Web site: http://www.childcrafteducation.com/.

Childhood Anxiety Network *See* **Selective Mutism Anxiety Research & Treatment Ctr.**

Children *Imprint of* **Star Light Pr.**

Children Concept Publishing, *(978-0-9745219)* Orders Addr.: P.O. Box 1179, Highland, MI 48357 USA; Edit Addr.: 1651 S. Milford Rd., Highland, MI 48357 USA.

Children Learning Awareness, Safety & Self-Defense, *(978-0-9768273)* Orders Addr.: 16815 Gault St., Lake Balboa, CA 91406 USA Tel 818-990-9909 (phone/fax); *Imprints:* CLASS Publications (CLASS Pubns)
E-mail: janet@classeducation.org; janet@classpublications.com
Web site: http://www.classeducation.org; http://www.classpublications.com
Dist(s): **Class Pubns., Inc.**

Children Left Behind, *(978-0-9829203)* P.O. Box 129, Berryville, AR 72616 USA Tel 870-654-3207
E-mail: LKHudd@yahoo.com
Web site: http://childrenleftbehind.org.

Children of Color/The Indra Collection, *(978-0-9746779)* P.O. Box 992, Great Falls, VA 22066 USA
Web site: http://www.childrenofcolor.com.

Children's Better Health Institute, *(978-1-885453)* Div. of Benjamin Franklin Literary & Medical Society, Inc., 1100 Waterway Blvd., Indianapolis, IN 46202 USA Tel 317-636-8881; Fax: 317-684-8094; Toll Free: 800-558-2376.

Childrens Bible Society, *(978-0-9777446)* Orders Addr.: P.O. Box 96, Hemet, CA 92546 USA Tel 951-652-9456; Edit Addr.: 1123 W. Acacia Ave., Hemet, CA 92543 USA
E-mail: kristy@actstracts.com
Web site: http://www.childrensbiblesociety.org/.

Children's Book Press *Imprint of* **Lee & Low Bks., Inc.**

Children's Bookshoppe Stop, The, *(978-0-9728393)* P.O. Box 62261, Virginia Beach, VA 23466 USA Tel 757-671-7779 (phone/fax)
E-mail: seetcbs@exis.net
Web site: http://www.surftcbs.com.

Children's Classic Book Pubs., *(978-0-9794753)* Orders Addr.: 103 Josh Ln., Poolville, TX 76487 USA (SAN 853-5280)
E-mail: orders@snerfycat.com; misterfish@snerfycat.com; ccbp@snerfycat.com
Web site: www.SnerfyCat.com.

Children's Express Foundation, Inc., *(978-0-9621641)* 1331 H St. NW, Suite 900, Washington, DC 20005 USA (SAN 251-6993) Tel 202-737-7377; Fax: 202-737-0193
E-mail: s1@dc.ce.org
Web site: http://www.ce.org.

Children's Illustrated Classics,

Children's Insight *Imprint of* **Insight Services, Inc**

Children's Kindness Network, *(978-0-9662268; 978-0-9745184)* Orders Addr.: 1323 Barkleigh Ln., Franklin, TN 37064 USA Tel 970-453-0410; Fax: 970-453-7375; Toll Free: 800-699-4541
E-mail: ted@moozie.com
Dist(s): **Bibliotech, Inc.**

Children's Legacy, *(978-0-9629365)* Orders Addr.: P.O. Box 300305, Denver, CO 80203 USA; Edit Addr.: 2553 Dexter St., Denver, CO 80207 USA Tel 303-830-7595.

Children's Literacy Pubns., *(978-0-9710432)* P.O. Box 5581, Sun City Center, FL 33571 USA Toll Free Fax: 1-866-350-4502; Toll Free: 1-800-585-1893
E-mail: janet@makereadingfirst.com
Web site: http://www.makereadingfirst.com.

Children's Pr. *Imprint of* **Scholastic Library Publishing**

Children's Psychological Health Ctr., Inc., The, *(978-0-9790846)* 2105 Divisadero St., San Francisco, CA 94115 USA Tel 415-292-7119; Fax: 415-749-2802
E-mail: gil.kliman@cphc-sf.org
Web site: http://www.cphc-sf.org.

Children's Publishing, *(978-0-9725803; 978-0-9789347)* Orders Addr.: 101 Crepe Myrtle Ln., Georgetown, TX 78633-4724 USA (SAN 254-9328) Toll Free: 877-864-7364
E-mail: carlson@childrenspublishing.com
Web site: http://www.childrenspublishing.com
Dist(s): **Quality Bks., Inc.**
Speech Bin, Inc., The.

Children's Success Unlimited LLC, *(978-0-9829613)* 160 Greentree Dr., Suite 101, Dover, DE 19904 USA Tel 917-208-7785
E-mail: bolbrys@ion-partners.com
Dist(s): **Emerald Bk. Co.**
Greenleaf Book Group.

Children's Village Foundation, Inc., *(978-0-9740481)* 1350 W. Hanley Ave., Coeur d'Alene, ID 83815 USA Tel 208-667-1189; Fax: 208-664-5735
E-mail: tinka@thechildrensvillage.org
Web site: http://www.thechildrensvillage.org.

ChildrenzBks., *(978-0-9748989)* P.O. Box 1431, Tucson, AZ 85702-1431 USA; *Imprints:* Bases Loaded Books (Bases Loaded Bks)
E-mail: sales@childrenzbooks.com
Web site: http://www.childrenzbooks.com.

†Child's World, Inc., The, *(978-0-89565; 978-0-913778; 978-1-56766; 978-1-59296; 978-1-60253; 978-1-60954; 978-1-60973; 978-1-61473; 978-1-62323; 978-1-62687; 978-1-63143; 978-1-63407; 978-1-5038)* 1980 Lookout Dr., Mankato, MN 56003 USA (SAN 858-5385) Tel 507-385-1044; Fax: 888-320-2329; Toll Free Fax: 800-599-7323; *Imprints:* Spirit of Americar (Spirit of Am)
E-mail: info@childsworld.com; mary.berendes@childsworld.com; mike.peterson@childsworld.com
Web site: http://www.childsworld.com
Dist(s): **Peterson Publishing Co., Inc.;** *CIP.*

Childswork/Childsplay, *(978-1-882732; 978-1-58815; 978-1-931704)* Div. of The Guidance Channel, Orders Addr.: P.O. Box 760, Plainview, NY 11803-0760 USA Tel 516-349-5520; Fax: 516-349-5521; Toll Free Fax: 800-262-1886; Toll Free: 800-962-1141; 45 Executive Dr. Ste. 201, Plainview, NY 11803-1738
E-mail: karens@at-risk.com; info@childswork.com
Web site: http://www.childswork.com.

Chiliric Pubns., *(978-0-9755253)* 1423 6th St., Eureka, CA 95501 USA Tel 707-443-4046
Web site: http://www.geocities.com/harleysgreatadventures/; http://www.Geocities.com/harleys_great_adventures.

Chimera Pubns. (GBR) *(978-1-901388; 978-1-903931) Dist. by* **PerseuPGW.**

Chimeric Pr., *(978-0-9847122)* 5299 Rau Rd., West Branch, MI 48661 USA Tel 989-343-9953
E-mail: info@chimericpress.com
Web site: www.chimericpress.com.

Chin & A Pr., *(978-0-9746341)* 2809 79th Ave., Brooklyn Park, MN 55444 USA Tel 763-549-8821
E-mail: jlodien@earthlink.net; ChinAndAPress@earthlink.net
Web site: http://www.allbeethere.com.

Chin Music Pr., *(978-0-9741995; 978-0-9844576; 978-0-9850416; 978-0-9887693; 978-1-63405)* 2621 24th Ave. W., Seattle, WA 98199 USA Tel 206-380-1947 (phone/fax)
E-mail: bruce@chinmusicpress.com
Web site: http://www.chinmusicpress.com
Dist(s): **Consortium Bk. Sales & Distribution**
Follett School Solutions
MyiLibrary.

†China Books & Periodicals, Inc., *(978-0-8351)* 360 Swift Ave., Suite 48, South San Francisco, CA 94080 USA (SAN 145-0557) Tel 650-872-7718; 650-872-7076; Fax: 650-872-7808
E-mail: chris@chinabooks.com
Web site: http://www.chinabooks.com
Dist(s): **Follett School Solutions**
SPD-Small Pr. Distribution; *CIP.*

China House Gallery, China Institute in America *See* **China Institute Gallery, China Institute in America**

China Institute Gallery, China Institute in America, *(978-0-9654270; 978-0-9774054; 978-0-9893776; 978-0-692-93086-1)* Div. of China Institute in America, 100 Washington St., New York, NY 10006 USA (SAN 110-8743) Tel 212-744-8181; Fax: 212-628-4159
E-mail: gallery@chinainstitute.org
Web site: http://www.chinainstitute.org
Dist(s): **Art Media Resources, Inc.**
Simon & Schuster, Inc.
Tuttle Publishing.

China Language University Pr. (CHN) *(978-7-88703) Dist. by* **China Bks.**

Chinasoft (AUS) *(978-1-876739; 978-0-646-06656-1; 978-0-646-06657-8; 978-0-646-06658-5; 978-0-646-13326-3; 978-0-646-13327-0; 978-0-646-13328-7; 978-0-646-22328-5; 978-0-646-22329-2; 978-0-646-22330-8; 978-0-646-25096-0; 978-0-646-25097-7) Dist. by* **Cheng Tsui.**

Chinasprout, Inc., *(978-0-9707332; 978-0-9747302; 978-0-9820227; 978-1-945947)* 110 W. 32nd St., Flr. 6, New York, NY 10001-3205 USA Toll Free: 800-644-2611
E-mail: info@chinasprout.com
Web site: http://www.chinasprout.com
Dist(s): **China Books & Periodicals, Inc.**
Follett School Solutions.

Ching Ying Center *See* **Manning, Laurie**

Chipman, Marilyn, *(978-0-9745857)* P.O. Box 441233, Aurora, CO 80044-1233 USA
E-mail: chipman@mscd.edu
Web site: http://www.marilynchipman.com.

Chipotle Publishing, LLC, *(978-0-9823918; 978-0-9965218)* 631 N. Stephanie St., Suite 282, Henderson, NV 89014 USA Tel 702-565-0746
E-mail: megan@chipotlepublishing.com
Web site: http://www.chipotlepublishing.com.

Chippewa Valley Museum, *(978-0-9636191)* Orders Addr.: P.O. Box 1204, Eau Claire, WI 54702 USA Tel

715-834-7871; Fax: 715-834-6624; Edit Addr.: Carson Park Dr., Eau Claire, WI 54702 USA
E-mail: info@cvmuseum.com
Web site: http://www.cvmuseum.com
Dist(s): **Chicago Distribution Ctr.**
Univ. of Wisconsin Pr.

Chiron Pubns., *(978-0-933029; 978-1-888602; 978-1-63051)* 932 Hendersonville Rd.; STE 104, Asheville, NC 28803 USA (SAN 689-1659) Tel 828-333-5245; Fax: 828-333-4787; Toll Free: 800-397-8109
E-mail: stevebuser@gmail.com
Web site: http://www.chironpublications.com.

ChironBooks *Imprint of* **Coleman/Perrin**

Chisholm, Juan Phillip *See* **Green Light Bks. and Publishing, LLC**

ChiZine Pubns. (CAN) *(978-0-9809410; 978-0-9812978; 978-1-926851; 978-0-9813746; 978-1-77148) Dist. by* **Consort Bk Sales.**

Choc Lit Limited (GBR) *(978-1-906931; 978-1-78189) Dist. by* **Casemate Pubs.**

Chock-Lit Pubns., *(978-0-9742344)* 26 Douvaine Ct., The Woodlands, TX 77382 USA
E-mail: publisher@chocklitpublications.com
Web site: http://www.chocklitpublications.com.

Chocolate Sauce, *(978-0-9740268; 978-0-9911314)* 211 E. 60th street, sweet C3, New York, NY 10022 USA
Web site: http://www.chocolatesaucebooks.com
Dist(s): **SPI Bks.**

Choice PH, *(978-0-9841910; 978-0-9887595; 978-0-9991517)* 412 Olive Ave., Suite 305, Huntington Beach, CA 92648 USA (SAN 858-6829)
E-mail: choiceph@aol.com
Dist(s): **eBookIt.com.**

Choice Point Editions, *(978-0-9778774)* 7883 N. Pershing AVE., Stockton, CA 95207 USA Tel 209-952-7108; Fax: 209-951-3216
E-mail: choicepointeditions@inreach.com
Web site: http://www.choicepointeditions.com.

Choice Publishing House *See* **Choice PH**

ChoiceMaker Pty. Ltd., The (AUS) *(978-0-9805673; 978-1-921790; 978-1-925186; 978-1-925233; 978-1-925234; 978-1-925235; 978-1-925246; 978-1-925247; 978-1-925248; 978-1-925249; 978-1-925250; 978-1-925251; 978-1-925252) Dist. by* **Lerner Pub.**

Choices Education Program, Watson Institute, Brown University *See* **Choices Program, Watson Institute, Brown Univ.**

Choices For Tomorrow, *(978-0-9748689)* 43H Meadow Pond Dr., Leominster, MA 01453 USA
E-mail: moniquehoude@yahoo.com.

Choices International, *(978-0-9768530)* Orders Addr.: P.O. Box 408, Berries Springs, MI 49103 USA Tel 269-471-9718 (phone/fax); Edit Addr.: P.O. Box 408, Berrien Sprgs, MI 49103-0408 USA
E-mail: pennyturner@sbcglobal.net; yourchoices@choicesinternational.info.

Choices Program, Watson Institute, Brown Univ., *(978-1-891306; 978-1-60123)* The Choices Program-Brown Univ. Box 1948, Providence, RI 02912 USA Tel 401-863-3155; Fax: 401-863-1247
E-mail: choices@brown.edu
Web site: http://www.choices.edu.

Cholita Prints & Pub. Co., *(978-0-9742956)* Orders Addr.: P.O. Box 8018, Sante Fe, NM 87504 USA; Edit Addr.: 655 W. San Francisco St., Sante Fe, NM 87501 USA
E-mail: cholitaprints@comcast.net
Dist(s): **Follett School Solutions.**

Choo Choo Clan, *(978-0-9788670)* 1616 Brockton Ave., Apt. 104, Los Angeles, CA 90025 USA Tel 626-715-3342
E-mail: joey0724@hotmail.com
Web site: http://www.choochooclan.com.

Chooseco LLC, *(978-0-9745356; 978-1-933390; 978-1-937133)* Orders Addr.: P.O. Box 46, Waitsfield, VT 05673 USA (SAN 852-1131); Edit Addr.: 49 Fiddler's Green, Waitsfield, VT 05673 USA (SAN 852-1158) Tel 802-496-2595
E-mail: mbounty@chooseco.com; liz@chooseco.com
Web site: http://www.cyoa.com; http://www.chooseco.com
Dist(s): **Follett School Solutions.**

Choosing The Best Publishing, *(978-0-9724890; 978-0-9819748; 978-0-9819759; 978-0-9974442)* 2625 Cumberland Pkwy., Suite 200, Atlanta, GA 30339 USA Tel 770-803-3100; Fax: 770-803-3110; Toll Free: 800-774-2378
E-mail: bcook@ctbpublishing.com; book@ctbpublishing.com
Web site: http://www.choosingthebest.org
Dist(s): **Independent Pubs. Group.**

Choristers Guild, *(978-1-929187)* 2834 W. Kingsley Rd., Garland, TX 75041-2498 USA (SAN 689-9188) Tel 972-271-1521; Fax: 972-840-3113
E-mail: choristers@choristersguild.org
Web site: http://www.choristersguild.org
Dist(s): **Faith Alive Christian Resources**
Lorenz Corp., The.

Chosen Bks., *(978-0-8007)* Div. of Baker Publishing Group, Orders Addr.: P.O. Box 6287, Grand Rapids, MI 49516-6287 USA Toll Free Fax: 800-398-3111 (orders only); Toll Free: 800-877-2665 (orders only); Edit Addr.: 6030 E. Fulton, Ada, MI 49301 USA Tel 616-676-9185; Fax: 616-676-9573
Web site: http://www.bakerpublishinggroup.com
Dist(s): **Baker Publishing Group**
Faith Alive Christian Resources.

Chosen Word Publishing, *(978-0-9707536; 978-0-9748056; 978-0-9754779)* P.O. Box 481886, Charlotte, NC 28269 USA Tel 704-527-2177; Fax: 704-527-1677
E-mail: jeannette@chosenwordpublishing.com
Web site: http://www.chosenwordpublishing.com.

ChosenButterfly Publishing, *(978-0-9831637; 978-0-9915202; 978-1-945377)* P.O. Box 515, Millville, NJ 08332 USA Tel 856-357-3801
Web site: http://www.cb-publishing.com
Dist(s): **Smashwords.**

Chou Chou Pr., *(978-0-9606140; 978-0-9716605; 978-0-9789152)* 4 Whimbrel Ct., Okatie, SC 29909 USA (SAN 220-2379) Tel 631-744-5784
E-mail: chouchou@hargray.com; info@bilingualkids.com
Web site: http://www.bilingualkids.com
Dist(s): **Follett School Solutions.**

Chowder Bay Bks., *(978-0-9795364)* P.O. Box 5542, Lake Worth, FL 33466-5542 USA (SAN 853-7119)
Web site: http://www.chowderbaybooks.com.

CHPublishing, Incorporated *See* **Triumphant Living Enterprises, Inc.**

Chris A. Zeigler Dendy Consulting LLC, *(978-0-9679911)* P.O. Box 189, Cedar Bluff, AL 35959 USA Fax: 256-779-5203
E-mail: chrisdendy@mindspring.com
Web site: http://www.chrisdendy.com
Dist(s): **Follett School Solutions.**

Chris Six Group, The, *(978-0-9899182)* P.O. Box 1829, New York, NY 10159-1829 USA Tel 718-514-0452
E-mail: thechrissixgroup@msn.com.

Christ Inspired, Inc., *(978-1-4183)* 2263 Dicey Rd., Weatherford, TX 76085-3619 USA
Web site: http://www.christinspired.com.

Christian Aid Ministries, *(978-1-885270)* Orders Addr.: P.O. Box 360, Berlin, OH 44610 USA Tel 330-893-2428; Fax: 330-893-2305; Edit Addr.: 4464 S.R. 39 E., Berlin, OH 44610 USA Tel 216-893-2428.

Christian Bible Studies, *(978-0-9763357)* P.O. Box 11155, Lansing, MI 48911 USA Tel 517-272-9076
E-mail: verseyawilliams@sbcglobal.net
Web site: http://www.christianstudies7.com.

Christian Courier Pubns., *(978-0-9678044; 978-1-932723)* P.O. Box 55265, Stockton, CA 95205 USA Tel 209-472-2475
E-mail: david@christiancourier.com
Web site: http://www.christiancourier.com.

Christian Education Resources, *(978-1-933479)* P.O. Box 320099, Cocoa Beach, FL 32932 USA.

Christian Faith Publishing, *(978-1-68197; 978-1-63525; 978-1-63575; 978-1-64028; 978-1-64079; 978-1-64114; 978-1-64140)* 296 Chestnut St., Meadville, PA 16335 USA Tel 646-503-4906
E-mail: dustin@christianfaithpublishing.com
Web site: ChristianFaithPublishing.com.

Christian Focus Pubns. (GBR) *(978-0-906731; 978-1-85792; 978-1-871676; 978-1-84550; 978-1-78191) Dist. by* **Spring Arbor Dist.**

Christian Focus Pubns. (GBR) *(978-0-906731; 978-1-85792; 978-1-871676; 978-1-84550; 978-1-78191) Dist. by* **Bookmasters.**

Christian Focus Pubns. (GBR) *(978-0-906731; 978-1-85792; 978-1-871676; 978-1-84550; 978-1-78191) Dist. by* **STL Dist.**

Christian, Harvey Pubs. Inc., *(978-1-932774)* 3107 Hwy. 321, Hampton, TN 37658 USA Tel 423-768-2297
E-mail: books@harveycp.com
Web site: http://www.harveycp.com.

Christian Heartbeat Incorporated *See* **CHB Media**

Christian Liberty Pr., *(978-1-930092; 978-1-930367; 978-1-932971; 978-1-935796; 978-1-62982)* Div. of Church of Christian Liberty, 502 W. Euclid Ave., Arlington Heights, IL 60004 USA
E-mail: e.shewan@christianlibertypress.com; linak@christianlibertypress.com; larsj@christianlibertypress.com
Web site: http://www.christianlibertypress.com.

Christian Life Bks., *(978-0-9646289; 978-1-931393)* Subs. of River Revival Ministries, Inc., Orders Addr.: P.O. Box 36355, Pensacola, FL 32516-6355 USA Tel 850-457-7057; Fax: 850-458-9339
E-mail: mail@drlarrymartin.org
Web site: http://www.rrmi.org.

Christian Life Workshops *See* **Noble Publishing Assocs.**

Christian Light Pubns., Inc., *(978-0-87813)* 1066 Chicago Ave., Harrisonburg, VA 22802 USA (SAN 206-7315) Tel 540-434-0768; Fax: 540-433-8896
E-mail: johnh@clp.org.

Christian Living Books, Inc. *Imprint of* **Pneuma Life Publishing, Inc.**

Christian Logic, *(978-0-9745315)* PMB 168, 429 Lake Park Blvd., Muscatine, IA 52761 USA Tel 309-537-3641
E-mail: hans@christianlogic.com
Web site: http://www.christianlogic.com.

Christian Novel Studies, *(978-0-9707712)* 5208 E. Lake Rd., Saginaw, MN 55779 USA Tel 218-729-9733; Fax: 509-271-8614
E-mail: cnsroe@aol.com; chsroe@aol.com
Web site: http://www.christiannovelstudies.homestead.com.

Christian Science Publishing Society, The *See* **Eddy, The Writings of Mary Baker**

Christian Services Publishing, *(978-1-879854)* Div. of Christian Services Network, 1975 Janich Ranch Ct., El Cajon, CA 92019 USA Tel 619-334-0706; Fax: 619-579-0685; Toll Free: 800-484-6184 Do not confuse with Christian Services, Damascus, MD
E-mail: tim@csnbooks.com
Web site: http://csnbooks.com.

Christian Visionary Communications, *(978-0-9746867)* P.O. Box 63, Sharon Center, OH 44274-0063 USA
E-mail: lorshir3@verizon.net
Web site: http://www.christianary.org.

Christian Visual Arts of California, *(978-0-9766584)* 64969 Pine St., Hume, CA 93628-9619 USA Tel 559-335-2797; Fax: 559-335-2107
E-mail: dajohnson@spiralcomm.net.

Christian Voice Publishing, A, *(978-0-9776747; 978-0-9786580; 978-1-934327)* 2031 W. Superior St. Ste. 1, Duluth, MN 55806-2036 USA.

Christiangela Productions, *(978-0-9720773)* 3340 SE. Federal Hwy., #310, Saintart, FL 34997 USA.

Christine, Yates, *(978-0-9741210)* 13165 Oak Farm Dr., Woodbridge, VA 22192 USA
Web site: http://www.freekidcrafts.com.

Christine's Closet, *(978-0-9713405)* 10300 Grand Oak Dr., Austin, TX 78750 USA Tel 512-918-9255; Fax: 512-873-9818; Toll Free: 800-591-1165
E-mail: chrissy@chrissy.com
Web site: http://www.chrissy.com.

Christopher Winkle Products *See* **First Stage Concepts**

†Chronicle Bks. LLC, *(978-0-8118; 978-0-87701; 978-0-938491; 978-1-4521)* Div. of The McEvoy Group, Orders Addr.: 680 Second St., San Francisco, CA 94107 USA (SAN 202-165X) Tel 415-537-4200; Fax: 415-537-4460; Toll Free Fax: 800-286-9471; Toll Free: 800-759-0190 (orders only); Edit Addr.: 3 Center Plaza, Boston, MA 2108 USA; *Imprints:* SeaStar Books (SeaStar Chronic); Handprint Books (HandprintBks)
E-mail: order.desk@hbgusa.com; customer.service@hbgusa.com
Web site: http://www.chroniclebooks.com
Dist(s): **Diamond Bk. Distributors**
Follett School Solutions
Leonard, Hal Corp.
Hachette Bk. Group
Ingram Publisher Services
Music Sales Corp.; *CIP.*

Chronicle Guidance Pubns., Inc., *(978-0-912578; 978-1-55631)* Orders Addr.: 66 Aurora St., Moravia, NY 13118-3569 USA Tel 315-497-0330; 315-497-3359; Toll Free: 800-622-7284
E-mail: CustomerService@ChronicleGuidance.com
Web site: http://www.chronicleguidance.com
Dist(s): **Follett School Solutions.**

Chronos Press *See* **WingSpan Publishing**

Chrysalis Education, *(978-1-929298; 978-1-930643; 978-1-931983; 978-1-932333; 978-1-59389)* Div. of The Creative Company, 1980 Lookout Dr., North Mankato, MN 56003 USA Tel 507-388-6273; Fax: 507-388-2746; Toll Free: 800-445-6209
E-mail: schlichted@aol.com; info@thecreativecompany.us
Dist(s): **Creative Co., The.**

Chrysalis Pr., *(978-0-9795933)* Orders Addr.: P.O. Box 13129, Newport Beach, CA 92658 USA (SAN 853-8514)
E-mail: amber@chrysalispress.com
Web site: http://www.Chrysalispress.com
Dist(s): **Follett School Solutions.**

Chubasco Publishing Company *See* **Perelandra Publishing Co.**

Chucklebks. Publishing, *(978-0-9702730)* 27 Brown St., Andover, MA 01810 USA Tel 978-749-0674
E-mail: jeff@chucklebooks.com
Web site: http://www.chucklebooks.com; http://www.incredibleassemblies.com
Dist(s): **Partners Bk. Distributing, Inc.**

Chung, Jo Anne *See* **Vision Unlimited Pr.**

Church at Cane Creek *See* **No Greater Joy Ministries, Inc.**

Church Hse. Publishing (GBR) *(978-0-7151; 978-0-9562821; 978-1-78140) Dist. by* **Westminster John Knox.**

Church Hymnal Corporation *See* **Church Publishing, Inc.**

Church Publishing, Inc., *(978-0-89869; 978-1-59627; 978-1-59628; 978-1-64065)* Orders Addr.: 19 E. 34th St., New York, NY 10016 USA (SAN 857-0140) Tel 212-592-1800; Fax: 212-779-3392; Toll Free: 800-242-1918; Edit Addr.: 19 East 34th st, New York, NY 10016 USA; *Imprints:* Living the Good News (LTGN)
E-mail: rmasteller@cpg.org; lsimonello@cpg.org
Web site: http://www.churchpublishing.org
Dist(s): **Abingdon Pr.**
Macmillan
MyiLibrary
Open Road Integrated Media, Inc.

Church Without Walls Publications, USA *See* **Masha, Segun Inc.**

Chuttani, Kabir, *(978-0-9749364)* 8 Nameloc Rd., Plymouth, MA 02360-1418 USA.

CicadaSun, *(978-0-9779808)* P.O. Box 90834, Austin, TX 78709-0834 USA
E-mail: service@cicadasun.com
Web site: http://www.cicadasun.com.

CIFC Pr., *(978-0-615-18435-7)* 65 Bayard St., New York, NY 10013 USA
E-mail: christinaseid@chinatownicecreamfactory.com
Web site: http://www.chinatownicecreamfactory.com
Dist(s): **Lulu Pr., Inc.**

Cideb (ITA) *(978-88-7754; 978-88-530) Dist. by* **Distribks Inc.**

Cider Mill Pr. Bk. Pubs., LLC, *(978-1-933662; 978-1-60433; 978-1-941868)* 12 Port Farm Rd., Kennebunkport, ME 04046 USA (SAN 257-1927) Tel 207-967-8232; Fax: 207-967-8233; *Imprints:* Applesauce Press (Applesauce Pr)
E-mail: johnwhalen@cidermillpress.com
Web site: http://www.cidermillpress.com
Dist(s): **Simon & Schuster**
Simon & Schuster, Inc.
Sterling Publishing Co., Inc.

Cidermill Bks., *(978-0-9748483)* P.O. Box 32250, San Jose, CA 95152-2250 USA
E-mail: info@cidermillbooks.com
Web site: http://www.cidermillbooks.com.

CiDuMos, *(978-0-692-77143-3; 978-0-692-77666-7; 978-0-692-80223-6; 978-0-692-80597-8)* 405 Woodway Ln., Longview, TX 75605 USA Tel 903-240-6959
Web site: www.cimowrites.com
Dist(s): **CreateSpace Independent Publishing Platform.**

Ciletti Publishing Group, Inc., The, *(978-0-917665; 978-0-9768655)* 2421 Redwood Ct., Longmont, CO 80503 USA Tel 720-494-1473; Fax: 720-494-1471
E-mail: barbaraj@odysseybooks.net
Dist(s): **Follett School Solutions.**

Cinco Puntos Pr., *(978-0-938317; 978-1-933693; 978-1-935955; 978-1-941026; 978-1-947627)* 701 Texas Ave., El Paso, TX 79901 USA (SAN 661-0080) Tel 915-838-1625; Fax: 915-838-1635; Toll Free: 800-566-9072
E-mail: leebyrd@cincopuntos.com
Web site: http://www.cincopuntos.com
Dist(s): **Consortium Bk. Sales & Distribution**
Follett School Solutions
Lectorum Pubns., Inc.
MyiLibrary.

Cinealta Pr., *(978-0-9821065)* 2060 W. Mulberry Dr., Chandler, AZ 85286-6771 USA
Web site: http://www.cinealtapress.com.

CineBook (GBR) *(978-1-905460; 978-1-84918) Dist. by* **Natl Bk Netwk.**

Cinnamon Bay Entertainment Group, *(978-0-9727116)* 1300 W. Menlo Ave No. 113, Hemet, CA 92543 USA
E-mail: rsdan4043@yahoo.com.

Cinnamon Ridge Publishing, *(978-0-9800762)* 7121 W. Craig Rd., Suite 113, No. 284, Las Vegas, NV 89129 USA.

Circelli, Kristina, *(978-0-9763728; 978-0-615-40270-3)* 9655 Crotty Ave., Hastings, FL 32145 USA Tel 386-290-7294
E-mail: kristinacircelli@gmail.com
Web site: www.kristinacircelli.com.

Circle Journey, Ltd., *(978-0-9741104)* 22 East Gay St., Suite 801, Columbus, OH 43215 USA Fax: 614-564-7795; Toll Free: 877-247-2534
E-mail: connections@circlejourney.com
Web site: http://www.circlejourney.com.

Circle of Friends *Imprint of* **Booksville, U.S.A.**

Circle Pr., *(978-0-9651601; 978-0-9743661; 978-1-933271)* Div. of Circle Media, Inc., Orders Addr.: 33 Rossotto Dr., Hamden, CT 06514 USA Tel 203-230-3805; Fax: 203-230-3838; Toll Free: 888-881-0729; Edit Addr.: 432 Washington Ave., North Haven, CT 06473 USA Do not confuse with companies with the same name in Huntington Beach, CA, New York, NY, Itasca, IL
E-mail: victor@catholicformation.com.

Circle Studios, *(978-0-9768022)* 200 Medicine Way, Eureka Springs, AR 72632 USA Tel 479-253-5826
Dist(s): **Follett School Solutions.**

Circumpolar Pr., *(978-1-878051)* Subs. of Wizard Works, P.O. Box 1125, Homer, AK 99603 USA Tel 907-235-8757 (phone/fax); Toll Free: 877-210-2665
E-mail: wizard@xyz.net
Web site: http://www.xyz.net/~wizard.

Ciro's Bks., *(978-0-9676643; 978-1-934499)* 4152 Meridian St., No. 6, Bellingham, WA 98226 USA
E-mail: info@cirosbooks.com
Web site: http://www.cirosbooks.com; http://www.howwouldyouvote.us; http://www.onepersononevoteonline.com
Dist(s): **BCH Fulfillment & Distribution**
Smashwords.

Cirrus Publishing, LLC, *(978-0-9755678)* Orders Addr.: P.O. Box 291724, Davie, FL 33329-1724 USA Fax: 954-965-2643
E-mail: cirruspublish@aol.com
Web site: http://www.yessy.com/wildimages.

Cisco Pr., *(978-0-7357; 978-1-57870; 978-1-58705; 978-1-58713)* Div. of Pearson Technology Group, 800 E. 96th St., Indianapolis, IN 46240-3770 USA Toll Free: 800-545-5914 Do not confuse with Cisco Pr., Torrance, CA
E-mail: bulkorders@ciscopress.com
Web site: http://www.ciscopress.com
Dist(s): **Alpha Bks.**
MyiLibrary
Pearson Education
Pearson Technology Group.

C-It Entertainment Group, LLC, *(978-0-9718151)* 230 S. Hamilton Dr. Unit 204, Beverly Hills, CA 90211 USA Tel 213-925-1535; Fax: 213-291-1473
E-mail: dennischristen@hotmail.com
Web site: http://www.booksnflicks.com.

Citified Pubns., *(978-0-9832174)* 1310 Valley Lake Dr., Schaumburg, IL 60195 USA Tel 708-308-2854
E-mail: djsbchi@gmail.com.

Citizen Pr, *(978-0-9779100)* P.O. Box 1369, Glendale, CA 91209-1369 USA Tel 310-497-7419; Fax: 818-450-0518
E-mail: citizen@citizenpress.net
Web site: http://www.citizenpress.net.

Citizens Publishing, *(978-0-9755597)* 17636 W. Neuberry Ridge Dr., Lockport, IL 60441 USA
Web site: http://www.citizenspublishing.com.

Citrus Roots - Preserving Citrus Heritage Foundation, *(978-0-9669508)* Orders Addr.: P.O. Box 4038, BALBOA, CA 92661 USA Tel 949-673-7877
Web site: http://www.citrusroots.com.

City Castles Publishing, *(978-0-615-22213-4; 978-0-615-26743-2; 978-0-615-56258-2)* 12160 E. Iowa Dr., Aurora, CO 80012 USA
Web site: http://www.citycastles.com.

City Creek Pr., Inc., *(978-1-883841)* P.O. Box 8415, Minneapolis, MN 55408-0415 USA
E-mail: orders@citycreek.com
Web site: http://www.citycreek.com
Dist(s): **Follett School Solutions.**

†City Lights Bks., *(978-0-87286)* 261 Columbus Ave., San Francisco, CA 94133 USA (SAN 202-1684) Tel 415-362-1901; Fax: 415-362-4921
E-mail: staff@citylights.com
Web site: http://www.citylights.com
Dist(s): **Consortium Bk. Sales & Distribution**
MyiLibrary
SPD-Small Pr. Distribution; *CIP.*

City Monsters Bks. (CAN) *(978-2-924734) Dist. by* **PerseuPGW.**

City of Elmhurst, *(978-0-9708003)* 209 N. York St., Elmhurst, IL 60126 USA Tel 630-530-3000; Fax: 630-530-3014
E-mail: nancy.wilson@elmhurst.org
Web site: http://www.elmhurst.org.

City of God, St. Joseph's Hill of Hope, *(978-1-892957)* Orders Addr.: P.O. Box 1055, Brea, CA 92822 USA Tel 714-528-6962; Fax: 714-528-0707; Edit Addr.: 7351 Carbon Canyon Rd., Brea, CA 92823 USA
E-mail: mail@themiracleofstjoseph.org
Web site: http://www.themiraicleofstjoseph.org.

City of Manassas Department of Social Services, *(978-0-9747385)* 9324 West St. Ste. 201, Manassas, VA 20110-5198 USA.

City of Oaks Publishing, *(978-0-9967304; 978-1-944260)* 1816 Hilton St., Raleigh, NC 27608 USA Tel 984-255-5049
E-mail: cityofoakspublishing@gmail.com.

City on a Hill, Inc., *(978-0-9779521)* 4085 Hancock Bridge Pkwy., Suite 111-269, North Fort Myers, FL 33903 USA Tel 614-488-6953
E-mail: info@cityonahillinc.org
Web site: http://www.cityonahillinc.org.

City Salvage Records, *(978-0-9713865)* 195 St. Marks Ave., No. 4, Brooklyn, NY 11238 USA Tel 718-857-6822
E-mail: andy@citysalvagerecords.com
Web site: http://citysalvagerecords.com.

CityLit Pr., *(978-1-936328)* c/o CityLit Project, 120 S. Curley St., Baltimore, MD 21224-2235 USA Tel 410-274-5691
E-mail: info@citylitproject.org
Web site: http://www.citylitprojet.org.

CityWeb Corp., *(978-0-9719803)* P.O. Box 702216, Tulsa, OK 74170-2216 USA Tel 918-369-0544
E-mail: citywebcorporation@acken.com
Web site: http://www.citywebbooks.com.

Civitas:Institute for the Study of Civil Society (GBR) *(978-1-903386) Dist. by* **Coronet Bks.**

CJ Publishing Co., *(978-0-9655777)* Div. of McPhaul, Inc, 4027 18th St., Ecorse, MI 48229 USA
E-mail: cjpublishingcompany@gmail.com.

CJR, *(978-0-9796411; 978-1-941607; 978-1-943764)* 8079 Barcarole Ct., Springfield, VA 22153-2945 USA Tel 571-481-5396
E-mail: books.kiteb@gmail.com
Web site: http://www.go2melik.org/NewBridgesTextbooks.lsp.

CJT Publishing, *(978-0-692-83362-9)* 500 Veterans Memorial Pkwy., East Providence, RI 02914 USA Tel 843-469-4417
E-mail: cjtalbert@pga.com.

CK Bks., *(978-0-9797580)* 395A S. Hwy. 65, No. 324, Lincoln, CA 95648 USA.

CKE Pubns., *(978-0-935133; 978-1-932327)* Div. of Carolyn Kyle Enterprises, Orders Addr.: P.O. Box 12869, Olympia, WA 98508-2869 USA (SAN 695-197X) Toll Free: 800-428-7402; Edit Addr.: P.O. Box 12869, Olympia, WA 98508-2869 USA
E-mail: ckepubs@aol.com
Web site: http://www.ckepublications.com.

CKK Educational, LLC., *(978-0-9743499; 978-0-9963087)* 17 W. 8th St., Ocean City, NJ 08226-3430 USA Tel 609-398-1949; Toll Free: 866-543-5463
Web site: http://www.tannersmanners.com.

cky *See* **Congregation Kehilas Yaakov (CKY)**

CLADACH Publishing, *(978-0-9670386; 978-0-9759619; 978-0-9818929; 978-0-9891014; 978-1-945099)* P.O. Box 336144, Greeley, CO 80633 USA Tel 970-371-9530
E-mail: office@cladach.com
Web site: http://www.cladach.com.

Claim Stake Productions *See* **Claim Stake Publishing, LLC**

Claim Stake Publishing, LLC, *(978-1-936284)* P.O. Box 1586, Aspen, CO 81612 USA
E-mail: pfioravante@tmwent.com
Web site: http://www.travelswithgannonandwyatt.com
Dist(s): **Bookmasters Distribution.**

Claire Pubns. (GBR) *(978-1-871098; 978-1-904572) Dist. by* **Parkwest Pubns.**

Clairmont Pr., Inc., *(978-0-9623319; 978-1-56733)* Orders Addr.: P.O. Box 11743, Montgomery, AL 36111 USA Tel 334-874-8638; Edit Addr.: Rte. 2, Box 191, Selma, AL 36701 USA.

Clandestine Pr., The, *(978-0-9766261)* 314 Taylor Pl., Ithaca, NY 14850-3135 USA Tel 607-273-8036
E-mail: dohertyprint@juno.com.

Clapper Publishing Co., *(978-0-930184)* Div. of Clapper Publishing Co., Inc., 2400 E. Devon, Suite 375, Des Plaines, IL 60018 USA (SAN 210-7104) Tel 847-635-5800; Fax: 847-635-6311.

Clara Publishing, *(978-0-9706347; 978-0-692-45828-0)* Orders Addr.: 680 Napa Ct., Claremont, CA 91711-1553 USA (SAN 254-7236)
E-mail: clarapub@ca.rr.com
Web site: http://www.magicunion.com.

Clarence-Henry Bks., *(978-0-615-19572-8; 978-0-578-05235-9; 978-0-615-42297-8; 978-0-9882909)* 4135 Teton Pl., Alexandria, VA 22312 USA
Web site: http://www.c-hbooks.com.

Claretian Pubns., *(978-0-89570)* 205 W. Monroe St., 9th Flr., Chicago, IL 60606 USA (SAN 207-5598) Tel 312-236-7782
E-mail: taylorm@claretians.org.

Clarion Bks. *Imprint of* **Houghton Mifflin Harcourt Publishing Co.**

Clarion Bks. *Imprint of* **Houghton Mifflin Harcourt Trade & Reference Pubs.**

Clarionton Press *See* **Twelve Star Pr.**

Clark Bks., *(978-0-9741677; 978-0-615-11591-7; 978-0-615-11769-0)* 599 Shapleigh Corner Rd., Shapleigh, ME 04076 USA (SAN 630-2017) Tel 207-636-1769 Do not confuse with Clark Books in Baton Rouge, LA
E-mail: clarkbooks@metrocast.net
Web site: http://www.clarkbooksmaine.com.

Clark, I. E. Publications *See* **Family Plays**

Clark, N. Laurie *See* **Clark Pubs.**

Clark Productions Ltd. Inc., *(978-0-9777289)* P.O. Box 583, Little Rock, AR 72203 USA Tel 501-280-9424
E-mail: ouida-clark56@yahoo.com.

Clark Pubs., *(978-0-9641197)* 133 Chestnut St., Amherst, MA 01002 USA Tel 413-549-0575; 941-255-0431
E-mail: ellusmith@aol.com
Dist(s): **Brodart Co.**
North Country Bks., Inc.
Quality Bks., Inc.

Clark Publishing, Inc., *(978-1-883589; 978-0-9822201; 978-0-9825057; 978-0-9827453; 978-0-9832639)* Orders Addr.: P.O. Box 34102, Lexington, KY 40588 USA Toll Free: 800-944-3995; Edit Addr.: 250 E. Short St., Lexington, KY 40507 USA Toll Free: 859-944-3995 Do not confuse with companies with same or similar names in Tacoma, WA, Topeka, KS, Annapolis, MD
E-mail: bclark@theclarkgroupinfo.com
Web site: http://www.theclarkgroupinfo.com; http://www.kyalmanac.com; http://www.clarkpublishing.com; http://www.clarklegacies.com
Dist(s): **Follett School Solutions.**

Clarkson Potter *Imprint of* **Potter/TenSpeed/Harmony**

CLASS Publications *Imprint of* **Children Learning Awareness, Safety & Self-Defense**

Classic Bks., *(978-1-58201; 978-0-7426)* Orders Addr.: P.O. Box 130, Murrieta, CA 92564-0130 USA Tel 951-767-1803; Fax: 951-767-0133
Dist(s): **Reprint Services Corp.**

Classic Bookwrights *Imprint of* **Lindaloo Enterprises**

Classic Comic Store, Ltd. (GBR) *(978-1-906814; 978-1-910619) Dist. by* **Casemate Pubs.**

Classic Textbooks, *(978-1-4047)* Div of Classic Books, Orders Addr.: P.O. Box 130, Murrieta, CA 92564-0130 USA
E-mail: newbookorders@gmail.com.

Classical Academic Pr., *(978-1-60051)* 3920 Market St., Camp Hill, PA 17011-4202 USA
Web site: http://www.classicalacademicpress.com.

Classical Comics (GBR) *(978-1-906332; 978-1-907127) Dist. by* **PerseuPGW.**

Classical Home Education *See* **Pandia Pr.**

Classical Learning Universe, LLC, *(978-0-9721733; 978-0-9763376; 978-0-9793021)* 305 W. Broadway, Suite 184, New York, NY 10013 USA Tel 718-357-2431; Fax: 718-357-2432; Toll Free: 888-684-5922
E-mail: lindsay@classicallearning.com
Web site: http://www.classicallearning.com.

Classical Magic, Inc., *(978-0-9675997; 978-0-9794947)* P.O. Box 1809, Banner Elk, NC 28604 USA Tel 828-898-7764 (phone/fax); 828-898-9571
E-mail: comapers@skybest.com
Web site: http://www.classicalmagic.net
Dist(s): **Book Clearing Hse.**

Classics International Entertainment, Inc., *(978-1-57209)* 324 Main Ave., Suite 183, Norwalk, CT 06851 USA Tel 203-849-8977; Fax: 203-847-5746.

Classroom Complete Pr. *Imprint of* **Rainbow Horizons Publishing, Inc.**

Claudia & Monica: Freshman Girls *Imprint of* **Stone Arch Bks.**

Claudia Cristina Cortez *Imprint of* **Stone Arch Bks.**

Clavis (ROM) *(978-973-97411) Dist. by* **PerseuPGW.**

Clavis Publishing, *(978-1-60537)* 814 N. Franklin St., Chicago, IL 60610 USA; 250 West 57Th St. 15Th Flr., New York, NY 10016
E-mail: info@clavis.be
Web site: http://www.clavis.be
Dist(s): **Follett School Solutions**
Independent Pubs. Group
Legato Pubs. Group.

Clawfoot Publishing, *(978-0-9747881)* 1236 S. Pekin Rd., Woodland, WA 98674 USA Tel 360-901-9932; Fax: 360-225-1311
E-mail: bobsbooks@zerfing.com
Web site: http://www.zerfing.com/bobsbooks.

Claybar Publishing, *(978-0-9787918)* 4007 Greenbriar Dr., Suite E, Stafford, TX 77477-3923 USA (SAN 851-5778) Tel 281-491-4009; Fax: 281-491-4024; Toll Free: 888-491-9533
E-mail: cbarclay@qdiinc.com
Web site: http://www.qdiinc.com
Dist(s): **Bookmasters Distribution.**

Clayro Corp., *(978-0-9709523)* P.O. Box 270605, Oklahoma City, OK 73137-0605 USA Tel 405-373-2347; Fax: 405-373-0923
E-mail: waderoddy@yahoo.com
Web site: http://tcpublishers.com.

Clayton, Mike, *(978-0-9772622)* 639 Howard Rd., West Point, NY 10996-1510 USA
Web site: http://www.session6wrestling.com.

Clean Teen Publishing, *(978-0-9894701; 978-1-940534; 978-1-63422)* P.O. Box 561326, The Colony, TX 75056 USA Tel 469-583-8737
E-mail: submissions@cleanteenpublishing.com
Web site: http://www.cleanteenpublishing.com; www.crimsontreepublishing.com
Dist(s): **Lightning Source, Inc.**
Midpoint Trade Bks., Inc.

Clear Braces L.L.C., *(978-0-9790682)* 1530 Palisade Ave., Fort Lee, NJ 07024 USA Tel 201-947-6453
E-mail: drjfortlee@aol.com
Web site: http://www.pediatric-dentistry.com.

Clear Creek Pubs., *(978-0-9653543; 978-0-9975839)* Orders Addr.: 115 Clear Creek Ct., Fayetteville, GA 30215 USA Tel 770-461-9460
E-mail: patcruzan@aol.com.

Clear Fork Publishing, *(978-0-9899568; 978-0-9974370; 978-1-946101)* 102 S. Swenson, Stamford, TX 79553 USA Tel 325-773-5550; *Imprints:* Spork (Spork)
E-mail: callie@clearforkmediagroup.com
Web site: clearforkpublishing.com.

Clear Horizon, *(978-0-9773569; 978-1-936187)* 605 Silverthorn Rd., Gulf Breeze, FL 32561 USA Tel 850-934-0819; Fax: 850-934-9981
E-mail: info@maxpress.com; ginac@maxpress.com
Web site: http://www.maxpress.com.

Clear Light Pubs., *(978-0-940666; 978-1-57416)* 823 Don Diego, Santa Fe, NM 87501 USA (SAN 219-7758) Tel 505-989-9590; Fax: 505-989-9519; Toll Free: 800-253-2747; 823 Don Diego, Santa Fe, CA 87501 Do not confuse with Clear Light Pub., Seattle, WA
E-mail: service@clearlightbooks.com; janet@clearlightbooks.com
Web site: http://www.clearlightbooks.com
Dist(s): **Follett School Solutions.**

Clear Water Pr., *(978-0-9742972; 978-0-9828995)* 1909 S. Stagecoach Dr., Olathe, KS 66062 USA Do not confuse with Clear Water Press in Reno, NV
E-mail: editor@clearwaterpress.com
Web site: http://www.clearwaterpress.com
Dist(s): **Send The Light Distribution LLC.**

Clearbridge Publishing, *(978-1-929194)* Orders Addr.: P.O. Box 33772, Seattle, WA 98133 USA (SAN 857-8524) Tel 206-533-9357; Fax: 206-546-9756; *Imprints:* Art of War Plus Books (Art War Plus)
E-mail: garyg@clearbridge.com
Web site: http://www.clearbridge.com; http://www.booksonstrategy.com.

Clearwater Publishing, *(978-0-9769465)* 4300 NW 23rd Ave. Ate. 233, Gainesville, FL 32605 USA Toll Free: 866-766-5103.

ClearWaters Publishing, *(978-0-9841439)* 7539 Parkview Dr., Columbia, SC 29223 USA Tel 803-404-8893
E-mail: clearwatersllc@yahoo.com; thomashuntersjr@yahoo.com
Web site: http://www.tjhunteronline.com.

Cleis Pr., *(978-0-939416; 978-1-57344; 978-1-936740; 978-1-62778; 978-1-940550; 978-1-63228)* 2246 Sixth St, Berkeley, CA 94710-2219 USA (SAN 284-9976) Tel 510-845-8000; Fax: 510-845-8001; Toll Free: 800-780-2279; 387 Pk. Ave. S., New York, NY 10016
E-mail: kwuest@cleispress.com
Web site: http://www.cleispress.com
Dist(s): **Follett School Solutions**
MyiLibrary
National Bk. Network
Red Wheel/Weiser
Simon & Schuster, Inc.

Clem Publishing, *(978-0-9772225)* P.O. Box 246, Danvers, IL 61732 USA Tel 309-530-0710; 116 W. North St., Danvers, IL 61732
E-mail: josephclem@hotmail.com.

Clements, J. S. Corporation *See* **Clements, Jehan**

Clements, Jehan, *(978-0-9622500)* Orders Addr.: P.O. Box 543, Tarrytown, NY 10591 USA Tel 914-293-7884
E-mail: storyteller1@optonline.net
Web site: http://www.flipoverpicturebooks.com.

Clendenin Fine Art Concepts, *(978-0-9897662)* 8160 Manitoba St., No. 104, Playa del Rey, CA 90293 USA Tel 310-821-3941; Fax: 310-821-2282
E-mail: aclendenin@verizon.net
Web site: www.clendeninfineart.com.

Cleo and Olive, *(978-0-692-75647-8)* 44 Buckelew Bridge Rd., ANNISTON, AL 36207 USA Tel 256-239-3135.

Clerisy Pr., *(978-0-9617367; 978-1-57860; 978-1-878208; 978-0-9777651)* Div. of Keen Communications, Orders Addr.: 2204 First Ave. South Suite 102, Birmingham, AL 35233 USA (SAN 255-478X) Tel 513-861-4045; Fax: 512-861-4430; Toll Free: 800-913-9563; Edit Addr.: 387 Pk. Ave. S., New York, NY 10016 USA
E-mail: info@emmisbooks.com; info@guildpress.com
Web site: http://www.clerisypress.com
Dist(s): **Follett School Solutions**
MyiLibrary
Publishers Group West (PGW)
ebrary, Inc.

Cleveland Clinic Pr., *(978-1-59624)* c/o Lawrence D. Chilnick, 9500 Euclid Ave., NA32, Cleveland, OH 44195 USA Tel 216-444-1158; Fax: 216-444-9385
E-mail: chilnil@ccf.org
Web site: http://www.clevelandclinicpress.org
Dist(s): **Ingram Publisher Services.**

†Cleveland Museum of Art, *(978-0-910386; 978-0-940717; 978-1-935294)* 11150 East Blvd., Cleveland, OH 44106-1797 USA (SAN 278-4572) Tel 216-421-7340; Fax: 216-421-9409; Toll Free: 1-877-262-4748
E-mail: bbradley@clevelnadart.org
Web site: http://www.clevelandart.org
Dist(s): **Art Media Resources, Inc.**
Chicago Distribution Ctr.
D.A.P./Distributed Art Pubs.
Hopkins Fulfillment Services
Hudson Hills Pr. LLC
Ohio Univ. Pr.
Univ. of Washington Pr.; *CIP.*

Cleveland Stock Images, *(978-0-9617637; 978-0-692-86770-9)* 7124 Baker Ln., Chagrin Falls, OH 44023 USA (SAN 664-8533) Tel 216-548-4484; Fax: 216-249-5828
E-mail: jsjido@aol.com.

Clever Factory, The, *(978-1-59277; 978-1-64038)* 545 Mainstream Dr., Suite 406, Nashville, TN 37228 USA.

CleverKits,LLC, *(978-0-9778771)* 12 Brinckerhoff Ave, Stamford, CT 06905-3201 USA Fax: 267-821-7523
E-mail: cleverkits@yahoo.com
Web site: http://www.cleverkits.com.

CLF Publishing, *(978-0-9857372; 978-0-9884237; 978-0-9892358; 978-0-9899408; 978-0-9960815; 978-0-9961971; 978-1-945102)* 10063 Maple Ave., Hesperia, CA 92345 USA Tel 760-669-8149
E-mail: DRCWE@YAHOO.COM
Dist(s): **Lulu Pr., Inc.**

Cliff House, *(978-1-68320)* 1600 Cliff Rd E, Burnsville, MN 55337 USA
Dist(s): **RiverStream Publishing.**

Cliff Road Bks., *(978-1-60261)* 3437 Cliff Rd., Birmingham, AL 35222 USA (SAN 857-409X)
E-mail: holly@cliffroadbooks.com.

Clifton Carriage House Pr., *(978-0-9825713)* 12 S. Sixth St., No. 1250, Minneapolis, MN 55402 USA Fax: 612-746-8811
E-mail: wreynolds@briobooks.com
Web site: http://www.briobooks.com.

Clinch, David *See* **Clinch Media**

Clinch Media, *(978-0-9800835)* 1339 Mill Glen Dr., Atlanta, GA 30338 USA (SAN 855-1588) Tel 770-730-1721
E-mail: clinch@bellsouth.net
Web site: http://www.theleprechauntrap.com.

Clocktower Hill Research & Publishing Group, LLC, *(978-0-9832130)* 23 Oakfield Dr., Rome, GA 30161 USA Tel 706-936-0254; Fax: 973-201-1755; *Imprints:* Lucas Violet (LucasViolet)
E-mail: davidehrler@clocktowerhill.com
Web site: http://www.clocktowerhill.com.

ClockTower Pubns., *(978-0-9704280)* 203 Skyland Dr., Dept. I, Staunton, VA 24401-2358 USA Tel 540-885-6614
E-mail: trgww@ntelos.net.

CLOJ Publishing, *(978-0-9767711)* 544 Rialto Ave., Venice, CA 90291-4248 USA (SAN 256-5129) Tel 310-399-6126
E-mail: publisher@clojpublishing.com
Web site: http://www.clojpublishing.com.

Cloonfad Pr., *(978-0-9744744; 978-0-9769404; 978-0-9797772)* Orders Addr.: P.O. Box 106, Cassville, NJ 08527 USA Tel 732-833-9800 (phone/fax)
E-mail: cloonfad@optonline.net
Web site: http://www.cloonfadpress.com
Dist(s): **Wilson & Assocs.**

Cloquet River Pr., *(978-0-9720050; 978-0-9792175)* 5353 Knudsen Rd, Duluth, MN 55803 USA Tel 218-721-3213; Fax: 218-725-5074
E-mail: cloquetriverpress@yahoo.com
Web site: http://www.cloquetriverpress.com
Dist(s): **Partners Bk. Distributing, Inc.**

Closer Looks Bks., *(978-0-9763593)* 864 Horns Corners Rd., Cedarburg, WI 53012 USA
E-mail: sggk@wi.rr.com
Web site: http://home.wi.rr.com/acloserlookbooks.

Clotho Pr., *(978-0-9821271)* 13205 Bluhill Rd., Silver Spring, MD 20910 USA Tel 301-962-8984
E-mail: polka.dot@verizon.net
Web site: http://www.womenmakingamerica.com
Dist(s): **Midpoint Trade Bks., Inc.**

Cloud 9 Ranch, *(978-0-9767690)* 231 Jung Blvd., E, Naples, FL 34120 USA Tel 239-353-6877; Fax: 239-353-7579
E-mail: nsfcloud9@aol.com
Web site: http://www.cloud9ranch.info.

Cloud, Kat Creations, *(978-0-692-88310-5; 978-0-692-88311-2)* 903 E Constitution Dr., Chandler, AZ 85225 USA Tel 480-748-0826
Dist(s): **Lightning Source, Inc.**

Cloud Lake Publications *See* **Cloud Lake Publishing**

Cloud Lake Publishing, *(978-0-9787054)* Orders Addr.: 1083 Vine St., No. 185, Healdsburg, CA 95448-9544 USA
E-mail: marylynn@winecountrywriter.com; mlarchibald@mac.com
Web site: http://www.winecountrywriter.com.

Cloud Mountain Publishing *See* **Easter Island Foundation**

Cloudless Sky, *(978-0-9978443)* P.O. Box 32992, Santa Fe, NM 87594 USA Tel 505-670-3177
E-mail: derekfis@yahoo.com.

Cloudmaker Entertainment, *(978-0-9743989)* 7654 195th Ave. Ct. E., Bonney Lake, WA 98390 USA Tel 253-862-1490 (phone/fax)
E-mail: trox@cloudmakerentertainment.com
Web site: http://www.cloudmakerentertainment.com.

Cloudstone, *(978-1-879846)* 10 Patchin Pl., New York, NY 10011 USA Tel 212-929-6871.

Cloudwalker Publications *See* **Working Title Publishing**

Clouser, Lisa M., *(978-0-692-53171-6; 978-0-692-63828-6; 978-0-9977202)* 11 Countryside Ct., Camp Hill, PA 17011 USA Tel 717-737-3334
Dist(s): **CreateSpace Independent Publishing Platform.**

Club Pro Products, *(978-0-9725721)* 153 Raquet Club Dr., Rancho Mirage, CA 92270 USA
E-mail: info@robstanger.com
Web site: http://www.robstanger.com.

Club4Girls *Imprint of* **Club4Girls Publishing Co.**

Club4Girls Publishing Co., *(978-0-9712297)* 4017 Dutch Harbor Ct., Raleigh, NC 27606-8604 USA Tel 919-387-9939; *Imprints:* Club4Girls (ClubFourGirls)
E-mail: bob@sas.com.

ClueSearchPuzzles.com, *(978-0-9753879)* 7645 N. Union Blvd. #175, Colorado Springs, CO 80920-3863 USA Tel 719-659-9034
E-mail: books@cluesearchpuzzles.com
Web site: http://www.cluesearchpuzzles.com.

Cluster Storm Publishing, *(978-1-56998)* Orders Addr.: 507 E. 3750 N., Provo, UT 84604 USA Tel 801-623-9101
E-mail: cjmartell@gmail.com.

CMB Publishing Co., *(978-0-9722969)* 24 Appleton St., Suite 1, Boston, MA 02116 USA Tel 617-306-5581; Fax: 617-451-0168
E-mail: info@cmbpublishing.com
Web site: http://www.cmbpublishing.com/.

CMC Publishing, *(978-0-9787336)* 1 Heritage Pl., Nesconset, NY 11767 USA
E-mail: colleenssite@yahoo.com.

CMS Enterprises, *(978-0-9768170)* Orders Addr.: P.O. Box 8039, Van Nuys, CA 91409 USA (SAN 256-5226); Edit Addr.: 6429 Whitman Ave., Van Nuys, CA 91406 USA
E-mail: cms55@hotmail.com.

CNL Publishing, *(978-0-9766921)* 105 Wedgewood Dr., Fairfield, AL 35064 USA Tel 205-835-5444; Fax: 205-923-3218.

CNPIECSB, 332 W Cermak Rd., Apt. 2D, Chicago, IL 60616 USA.

Coach Enterprises, *(978-0-9636706)* 616 Munntown Rd., Finleyville, PA 15332 USA Tel 724-348-4843; Fax: 724-348-5549.

Coach Hse. Bks. (CAN) *(978-1-55245; 978-1-77056) Dist. by* **Consort Bk Sales.**

Coachwhip Pubns., *(978-1-930585; 978-1-61646)* 1505 English Brook Dr., Landisville, PA 17538 USA
E-mail: chadarment@verizon.net
Web site: http://www.coachwhipbooks.com.

Coal City Stories, *(978-0-9849028)* 1101 Cole Dr., Lilburn, GA 30047 USA Tel 678-896-9493 (Tel/Fax)
E-mail: emilie.bush@gmail.com; machineseat@hotmail.com
Web site: CoalCitySteam.com.

Coal Hole Productions, *(978-0-9709630)* 207 Hemlock Ln., Bloomsburg, PA 17815 USA Tel 570-784-4561
E-mail: ceo@coalhole.com
Web site: http://www.coalhole.com
Dist(s): **Partners Bk. Distributing, Inc.**

Coal Under Pressure Pubns., *(978-0-9763400; 978-0-9913704)* Div. of Coal Under Pressure, LLC, Orders Addr.: 42625 Hwy. 27 N. #156, Davenport, FL 33837 USA Tel 347-829-7487
E-mail: coalunderpressurepubs@gmail.com
Web site: http://www.coalunderpressure.com.

Coast View Publishing, *(978-0-9849732)* 638 Camino De Los Mares Suite H130-157, San Clemente, CA 92673 USA Tel 949-388-7996
E-mail: coastviewpublishing@yahoo.com.

Coastal Carolina Pr., *(978-1-928556)* Orders Addr.: P.O. Box 9111, Chapel Hill, NC 27515-9111 USA
E-mail: books@coastalcarolinapress.org
Web site: http://www.coastalcarolinapress.org
Dist(s): **Blair, John F. Pub.**
Parnassus Bk. Distributors.

Coastal Publishing Carolina, Inc., *(978-0-9705727; 978-1-931650)* 504 Amberjack Way, Summerville, SC 29485 USA Tel 843-821-6168; Fax: 843-851-6949
E-mail: coastalpublishing@earthlink.net
Web site: http://coastalpublishing.net/.

Coastal Publishing, LLC, *(978-0-9755573)* No. 226, 1133 Bal Harbor Blvd., Suite 1139, Punta Gorda, FL 33950-6574 USA Tel 941-505-5547.

Cobalt Pr., *(978-0-9747805)* P.O. Box 5393, Hauppauge, NY 11788 USA Do not confuse with Cobalt Pr. in Minneapolis, MN
Web site: http://www.geocities.com/corrinedzwil/index.html.

Cobblestone Publishing Co., *(978-0-382; 978-0-942389; 978-0-9607638)* Div. of Cricket Magazine Group, 30 Grove St., Suite C, Peterborough, NH 03458 USA (SAN 237-9937) Tel 603-924-7209; Fax: 603-924-7380; Toll Free: 800-821-0115; P.O. Box 487, Effingham, IL 62401
E-mail: custsvc@cobblestone.mv.com
Web site: http://www.cobblestonepub.com
Dist(s): **Americana Publishing, Inc.**
Follett School Solutions.

Cochise County Juvenile Detention Ctr., *(978-0-9771011)* P.O. Box 208, Bisbee, AZ 85603 USA Fax: 520-432-7136
Web site: http://www.co.cochise.az.us/schools.

Cochran, Russ Co., The, *(978-0-939947; 978-0-9816923)* P.O. Box 469, West Plains, MO 65775 USA (SAN 663-8236) Fax: 417-256-6666
E-mail: russcochran333@gmail.com
Web site: http://www.russcochran.com.

Cockburn Publishing, *(978-1-887461)* 1504 Mithra St., New Orleans, LA 70122-2018 USA.

Cockey, EJ & Company *See* **ThePaintedWord, Ltd.**

Coconut Info, *(978-1-929317)* Orders Addr.: P.O. Box 75460, Honolulu, HI 96836 USA Tel 808-947-6543; Fax: 808-923-6544
E-mail: sales@coconutinfo.com; info@coconutinfo.com
Web site: http://www.coconutinfo.com
Dist(s): **Booklines Hawaii, Ltd.**

Coconut Pr., LLC, *(978-0-9702168; 978-0-9778913)* Div. of Puerto Rico Postcard Co., Inc, Orders Addr.: P.O. Box 309540, Saint Thomas, VI 00803 USA Tel 787-248-3774; Fax: 787-253-8449; Edit Addr.: P.O. Box 79710, Carolina, PR 00984 USA Do not confuse with companies with same or similar names in Coral Gables, FL, Missouri City, TX
E-mail: Angelaspenceley1@msn.com
Dist(s): **Puerto Rico Postcard.**

Coda Grove Publishing, *(978-0-9889113)* P.O. Box 275, Fairfax, VT 05454 USA Tel 802-849-2777
E-mail: codagrovepub@gmail.com.

Codra Enterprises, Incorporated *See* **Green Egg Media, Inc.**

Cody's Guide, *(978-0-9755305)* 3855 Humbug Creek Rd., Applegate, OR 97530 USA
Web site: http://www.codysguide.com.

Coffee Hse. Ink, *(978-0-9663176)* 32370 SE Judd Rd., Eagle Creek, OR 97022 USA Tel 503-637-3277; Fax: 503-423-7980
E-mail: donmillll@aol.com
Web site: http://www.coffeehouseink.com.

Coffee Hse. Pr., *(978-0-918273; 978-1-56689)* 79 13th Ave NE Ste. 110, Minneapolis, MN 55413-1073 USA (SAN 206-3883); 387 Pk. Ave. S., New York, NY 10016
Web site: http://www.coffeehousepress.org
Dist(s): **BookMobile**
Consortium Bk. Sales & Distribution
Follett School Solutions
MyiLibrary
SPD-Small Pr. Distribution.

Coffragants (CAN) *(978-2-921997; 978-2-89517; 978-2-89558) Dist. by* **Penton Overseas.**

Coghlan Group, The *See* **Phoenix International, Inc.**

Cogi Garden Bks., *(978-0-692-83770-2; 978-0-692-85083-1)* 811 Lyon St NE, Grand Rapids, MI 49503 USA Tel 301-367-2830
E-mail: dirmeyer@gmail.com
Dist(s): **CreateSpace Independent Publishing Platform.**

Cognella Academic Publishing *Imprint of* **Cognella, Inc.**

Cognella, Inc., *(978-0-9763162; 978-1-934269; 978-1-935551; 978-1-60927; 978-1-62131; 978-1-62661; 978-1-63189; 978-1-63487; 978-1-5165)* 3970 Sorrento Valley Blvd. Suite 500, San Diego, CA 92121 USA (SAN 990-1701) Toll Free: 800-200-3908; *Imprints:* Cognella Academic Publishing (CognellaAcad)
E-mail: accounting@universityreaders.com; ap@cognella.com
Web site: http://www.universityreaders.com; http://www.cognella.com.

Cohen, Deanna Moreau, *(978-0-9747081)* 1626a Garden St., Santa Barbara, CA 93101-1110 USA
E-mail: liftveil2@cs.com.

Cohen, Sonia *See* **Gigi Enterprises**

Cohn, Tricia, *(978-0-9743847)* 16158 Highgate Dr., Riverside, CA 92503-8718 USA Tel 714-272-6972
E-mail: triciacohn@beobi.com
Web site: http://www.beobi.com.

Coho Press *See* **Dot Dot Bks.**

Cokesbury *Imprint of* **Abingdon Pr.**

Cola, Arthur, *(978-0-9789423)* 425 Robins Run, Papa Adventures, Burlington, WI 53105 USA
E-mail: arthurcola@yahoo.com
Dist(s): **Partners Bk. Distributing, Inc.**

Colbert Hse., LLC, The, *(978-1-887399)* Orders Addr.: P.O. Box 786, Mustang, OK 73064-0786 USA Tel 405-204-0043
E-mail: customerservice@colberthouse.com
Web site: http://www.colberthouse.com.

Colbert House, The *See* **Colbert Hse., LLC, The**

Colby Studio, *(978-0-9978198)* P.O. Box 681, Castine, ME 04421 USA Tel 207-322-0432
E-mail: kasey@eternav.com
Web site: ivystories.com.

Cold River Pubns., *(978-0-9712867; 978-0-692-52577-7)* P.O. Box 606, Long Lake, NY 12847-0606 USA Tel 518-624-3581
E-mail: criver@telenet.net; criver@telenent.net
Web site: http://www.coldriverwoodworks.com
Dist(s): **Smashwords.**

Cole Publishing, *(978-0-9678779; 978-0-9773973; 978-0-9787317)* 13428 Maxella Ave., Suite 701, Marina Del Rey, CA 90292 USA (SAN 256-856X) Fax: 310-209-2448
E-mail: candace@candacecole.com; ccpprod@aol.com
Web site: http://candacecole.com/.

Cole, Reginald, *(978-0-692-81245-7)* 1705 Inverness Ave., Dundalk, MD 21222 USA Tel 301-502-2964
E-mail: reggie.cole@outlook.com.

Cole-Dai, Phyllis, *(978-0-615-24350-4)* 712 6th St., Brookings, SD 57006 USA Tel 605-692-7001
E-mail: phyllis@phylliscoledai.com; coledai@brookings.net
Web site: http://www.phylliscoledai.com.

Coleman, CJ, *(978-0-9773651)* 2191 Craig Springs Rd., Sturgis, MS 39769 USA Tel 662-312-4383
E-mail: cillycreations@hotmail.com
Web site: http://www.cillycreations.com.

Coleman Ranch Pr., *(978-0-9677069)* Orders Addr.: P.O. Box 1496, Sacramento, CA 95812 USA Tel 916-393-9032; Toll Free Fax: 888-532-4190; Toll Free: 877-765-3225
E-mail: colemanranch@comcast.net
Web site: http://www.CRPRESS.com.

Coleman, Wim *See* **Coleman/Perrin**

Coleman/Perrin, *(978-1-935178)* 405 Walnut St., Chapel Hill, NC 27517 USA Tel 919-338-8119; *Imprints:* ChironBooks (ChironBooks)
E-mail: wim-pat@gmail.com; info@chironbooks.com
Web site: http://www.playsonideas.com; http://www.chironbooks.com; http://www.madeirapress.com
Dist(s): **BookBaby**
Pathway Bk. Service.

Colihue (ARG) *(978-950-581) Dist. by* **AIMS Intl.**

Collector Bks., *(978-0-89145; 978-1-57432; 978-1-60460)* Div. of Schroeder Publishing Co., Inc., Orders Addr.: P.O. Box 3009, Paducah, KY 42003 USA (SAN 157-5368) Tel 270-898-6211; 270-898-7903; Fax: 270-898-8890; 270-898-1173; Toll Free: 800-626-5420 (orders only); Edit Addr.: 5801 Kentucky Dam Rd., Paducah, KY 42003 USA (SAN 200-7479); *Imprints:* American Quilter's Society (Am Quilters Soc)
E-mail: Info@collectorbooks.com; info@AQSquilt.com
Web site: http://www.collectorbooks.com; http://www.americanquilter.com/.

Collectors Pr., Inc., *(978-0-9635202; 978-1-888054; 978-1-933112)* Orders Addr.: P.O. Box 230986, Portland, OR 97281 USA Tel 503-684-3030; Fax: 503-684-3777; Toll Free: 800-423-1848; Edit Addr.: P.O. Box 230986, Portland, OR 97281-0986 USA
E-mail: lperry@collectorspress.com; rperry@collectorspress.com
Web site: http://www.collectorspress.com
Dist(s): **Universe Publishing**
Worldwide Media Service, Inc.

College & Career Pr., LLC, *(978-0-9745251; 978-0-9829210)* P.O. Box 300484, Chicago, IL 60630 USA Tel 773-282-4671; Fax: 773-282-4671; P.O. Box 300484, Chicago, IL 60630
E-mail: andymorkes@gmail.com
Web site: http://www.collegeandcareerpress.com; http://www.ccpnewsletters.com
Dist(s): **Brodart Co.**
Follett School Solutions.

College Assistance & Scholarship Help, Incorporated *See* **College Assistance, Inc.**

College Assistance, Inc., *(978-0-9760251)* Orders Addr.: 7235 Promenade Dr. Apt. J401, Boca Raton, FL 33433-6982 USA Toll Free: 866-346-7890
E-mail: librodereecy@aol.com; thecollegebook@aol.com
Web site: http://www.librodelauniversidad.com; http://www.thecollegebook.com; http://www.reecysbook.com.

College Hse. Enterprises, LLC, *(978-0-9655911; 978-0-9700675; 978-0-9723567; 978-0-9762413; 978-0-9792581; 978-1-935673)* 5713 Glen Cove Dr., Knoxville, TN 37919-8611 USA (SAN 253-5831) Tel 865-558-6111 (phone/fax)
Web site: http://www.collegehousebooks.com.

College of DuPage Pr., *(978-1-932514)* Orders Addr.: 425 Fawell Blvd., Glen Ellyn, IL 60137 USA Fax: 630-942-3333; Toll Free: 800-290-4474
E-mail: software@cod.edu
Web site: http://www.dupagepress.com.

College Planning Network, *(978-1-880344)* 914 E. Jefferson, Campion Tower, Seattle, WA 98122 USA Tel 206-323-0624; Fax: 206-323-0623
E-mail: seaspn@collegeplan.org
Web site: http://www.collegeplan.org.

College Prowler, Inc., *(978-1-932215; 978-1-59658; 978-1-4274)* 5001 Baum Blvd. Ste. 750, Pittsburgh, PA 15213-1856 USA Toll Free Fax: 800-772-4972; Toll Free: 800-290-2682; *Imprints:* Off The Record (Off The Rcd)
E-mail: joey@collegeprowler.com; luke@collegeprowler.com
Web site: http://www.collegeprowler.com.

Collegiate Kids Bks., LLC, *(978-0-9836211; 978-0-692-01848-4; 978-0-9886542)* 3956 2nd St. Dr. NW, Hickory, NC 28601 USA Tel 828-773-5398
E-mail: bryan@collegiatekidsbooks.com
Web site: http://www.collegiatekidsbooks.com.

Collins *Imprint of* **HarperCollins Pubs.**

Collins Design *Imprint of* **HarperCollins Pubs.**

Collins Pr., The (IRL) *(978-0-9516306; 978-1-898256; 978-1-903464; 978-1-905172; 978-1-84889) Dist. by* **Dufour.**

Collins, Robert, *(978-0-9766426)* 865 Helke Rd., Vandalia, OH 45377 USA; *Imprints:* Peregrine Communications (Peregrine Comm)
E-mail: adaglo@gemair.com
Web site: http://www.ufoconspiracy.com/.

Colonel Davenport Historical Foundation, *(978-0-9755934)* P.O. Box 4703, Rock Island, IL 61204 USA
Web site: http://www.davenporthouse.org.

†**Colonial Williamsburg Foundation**, *(978-0-87935; 978-0-910412)* P.O. Box 3532, Williamsburg, VA 23187-3532 USA (SAN 128-4630) Fax: 757-565-8999 (orders only); Toll Free: 800-446-9240 (orders only)
Web site: http://www.colonialwilliamsburg.com
Dist(s): **Antique Collectors' Club**
National Bk. Network
University of Virginia Pr.; *CIP.*

Color & Learn, *(978-0-9795190)* P.O. Box 1592, Saint Augustine, FL 32085-1592 USA (SAN 853-6023)
Web site: http://www.colorandlearn.com.

Color & Light Editions, *(978-0-9671527; 978-0-9835239)* 371 Drakes View Dr., Inverness, CA 94937 USA Tel 415-663-1616
E-mail: kathleenpgoodwin@gmail.com
Web site: http://BlairGoodwin.com
Dist(s): **Partners Bk. Distributing, Inc.**

Color Loco *See* **Color Loco, LLC**

Color Loco, LLC, *(978-0-9770652; 978-0-9788778)* 213 Woodland Dr., Downingtown, PA 19335-9335 USA
Web site: http://www.ColorLoco.com.

Colorado Associated University Press *See* **Univ. Pr. of Colorado**

Colorful Bks. Pr., *(978-0-9746152)* 935 Ottawa Ave., Ypsilanti, MI 48198 USA.

Colorful Crayons For Kids Publishing, LLC *See* **Jeb Cool Kids Entertainment, Inc**

Colossus Bks. *Imprint of* **Amber Bks.**

Columba Pr. (IRL) *(978-0-948183; 978-1-85607; 978-1-78218) Dist. by* **Dufour.**

†**Columbia Univ. Pr.**, *(978-0-231)* Orders Addr.: 61 W. 62nd St., New York, NY 10023-7015 USA (SAN 212-2480) Toll Free Fax: 800-944-1844; Toll Free: 800-944-8648 x 6240 (orders); Edit Addr.: 61 W. 62nd St., New York, NY 10023 USA (SAN 212-2472) Tel 212-459-0600; Fax: 212-459-3678; 387 Pk. Ave., S., New York, NY 10016
E-mail: cupbooks@columbia.edu
Web site: http://www.columbia.edu/cu/cup
Dist(s): **Cambridge Univ. Pr.**
Casemate Academic
CreateSpace Independent Publishing Platform
De Gruyter, Inc.
Ebsco Publishing
Follett School Solutions
ISD
MyiLibrary
Ingram Academic
Wiley, John & Sons, Inc.
ebrary, Inc.; *CIP.*

Columbine Pr., *(978-0-9651272; 978-0-9768570; 978-0-9965407)* Orders Addr.: P.O. Box 1950, Cripple Creek, CO 80813 USA Tel 719-689-2141; Edit Addr.: 340 Colorado Ave., Cripple Creek, CO 80813 USA Do not confuse with companies with the same name in Bainbridge Island, WA, East Hampton, NY
E-mail: pkmacv@earthlink.net.

Columbus Zoo & Aquarium, The, *(978-0-9841554)* 4850 W. Powell Rd., P.O. Box 400, Powell, OH 43065 USA (SAN 858-589X) Tel 614-645-3400; Fax: 614-645-3465
E-mail: fran.baby@columbuszoo.org
Web site: http://www.columbuszoo.org.

Column Hall Concepts, LLC, *(978-0-9786584)* 217 - 82nd St., Brooklyn, NY 11209 USA Tel 718-836-1072
Web site: http://www.heydadthebook.com
Dist(s): **Follett School Solutions.**

Combel Editorial, S.A. (ESP) *(978-84-7864; 978-84-9825) Dist. by* **IPG Chicago.**

Combs-Hulme Publishing, *(978-0-9769854)* 1720 Eldridge Ave. W., Saint Paul, MN 55113 USA Tel 651-631-2173 Do not confuse with Combs Publishing in Winston-Salem, NC
E-mail: lvhulme@aol.com.

Come & Get It Publishing, *(978-0-9653042; 978-0-9753883; 978-0-692-64839-1)* Orders Addr.: P.O. Box 1562, Madison, VA 22727 USA Tel 540-829-0516 Toll Free: 800-825-9008; Edit Addr.: 214 E. Spencer St., No. 1, Culpeper, VA 22701 USA
E-mail: comeandgetproducts@gmail.com
Dist(s): **Publishers Group West (PGW).**

Comfort Tales, LLC, *(978-0-9741586)* Orders Addr.: 47 Watsons Way, Medford, NJ 08055 USA (SAN 255-464X) Tel 856-988-0884; Fax: 856-988-8499
E-mail: comforttales@aol.com.

Comic Library International, *(978-1-929515)* 2049 Alfred St., Pittsburgh, PA 15212-1426 USA; *Imprints:* Solovisions (Solovisions)
E-mail: gbstudios@comcast.net
Web site: http://www.geocities.com/SoHo/Cafe/9669/clipage.html
Dist(s): **Diamond Comic Distributors, Inc.**

Comics Lit *Imprint of* **NBM Publishing Co.**

ComicsOne Corp./Dr. Masters, *(978-1-58899)* P.O. Box 14232, Fremont, CA 94539-1532 USA
Dist(s): **Diamond Comic Distributors, Inc.**
Diamond Bk. Distributors
L P C Group.

Command Performance Language Institute, *(978-0-929724)* 25 Hopkins Ct., Berkeley, CA 94706 USA (SAN 250-1694) Tel 510-524-1191; Fax: 510-527-9880
E-mail: consee@aol.com
Web site: http://www.hometown.aol.com/commandperform1/myhomepage/business.html
Dist(s): **Alta English Publishers**
Applause Learning Resources
Athelstan Pubns.
Betty Segal, Inc.
BookLink
Calliope Bks.
Carlex
Continental Bk. Co., Inc.
Delta Systems Company, Inc.
Educational Showcase
Edumate-Educational Materials, Inc.
European Bk. Co., Inc.
Follett School Solutions
Gessler Publishing Co., Inc.
International Bk. Ctr., Inc.
Midwest European Pubns.
Miller Educational Materials
Multi-Cultural Bks. & Videos, Inc.
Sky Oaks Productions, Inc.
SpeakWare
Teacher's Discovery
Tempo Bookstore
2Learn-English
World of Reading, Ltd.

Command Publishing, LLC, *(978-0-9778356)* 43311 Joy Rd. Suite 201, Canton, MI 48187-2075 USA (SAN 850-2706).

Commercial Communications Incorporated *See* **Great Lakes Design**

Commission on Culture and Tourism, *(978-0-9759389)* 1 Constitution Plz., Hartford, CT 06103-1803 USA
E-mail: kazkozlowski@snet.net.

Committee for Children, *(978-0-9741388)* 568 First Ave. S., Suite 600, Seattle, WA 98104-2804 USA Toll Free: 800-634-4449
Web site: http://www.cfchildren.org.

Common Courtesy, *(978-0-9746148)* 709 Uwharrie St., Asheboro, NC 27203 USA Tel 336-629-5274
E-mail: jdortch@earthlink.net.

Commonwealth Books, LLC *See* **Commonwealth Books of Virginia, LLC**

Commonwealth Books of Virginia, LLC, *(978-0-9825922; 978-0-9854863; 978-0-9904018; 978-0-9909592; 978-0-9961368; 978-1-943642)* 59 McFarland Point Dr, No. 12, Boothbay Harbor , ME 04538 USA Tel 703-307-7715; 434-242-4128
E-mail: jct@commonwealthbooks.org; info@commonwealthbooks.org
Web site: http://www.commonwealthbooks.org; http://www.commonwealthbooks.org; www.thomasjeffersonsenlightenment.org; www.bayardtberndt.org
Dist(s): **Independent Pubs. Group**
MyiLibrary
Small Pr. United
ebrary, Inc.

Commonwealth Editions *Imprint of* **Applewood Bks.**

Communication Service Corporation *See* **Gryphon Hse., Inc.**

Community Voice Media, LLC, *(978-0-9776613; 978-0-9885741)* P.O. Box 564, Round Hill, VA 20142-5640 USA Tel 540-751-2214; Fax: 540-751-2215
E-mail: bobbicarducci@communityvoicemedia.com
Web site: http://www.communityvoicemedia.com.

Community Works!, *(978-0-9742213)* 13313 Country Way Cir., Fredericksburg, VA 22404 USA
E-mail: arayu1@comcast.net; carol@carolynnfitzpatrick.com
Web site: http://www.carolynnfitzpatrick.com
Dist(s): **New Leaf Distributing Co., Inc.**

Companhia das Letras (BRA) *(978-85-7164; 978-85-85095; 978-85-85466; 978-85-359) Dist. by* **Distribks Inc.**

Companhia Melhoramentos de Sao Paulo Industrias de Papel (BRA) *(978-85-06) Dist. by* **Lectorum Pubns.**

Companion Pr., *(978-1-879651; 978-1-61722)* Div. of Ctr. for Loss & Life Transition, 3735 Broken Bow Rd., Fort Collins, CO 80526 USA Tel 970-226-6050; Fax: 970-226-6051; Toll Free Fax: 800-922-6051 (orders only) Do not confuse with companies with the same name in Santa Barbara, CA, Aliso Viejo, CA
E-mail: wolfelt@centerforloss.com
Web site: http://www.centerforloss.com
Dist(s): **Ebsco Publishing**
Independent Pubs. Group
MyiLibrary
ebrary, Inc.

Company's Coming Publishing, Ltd. (CAN) *(978-0-9690695; 978-0-9693322; 978-1-895455; 978-1-896891; 978-1-897069; 978-1-897477; 978-1-927126; 978-1-77207) Dist. by* **Lone Pine.**

Compass *Imprint of* **Raphel Marketing, Inc.**

Compass Books *See* **Lake Street Pubs.**

Compass Flower Pr. *Imprint of* **AKA:yoLa**

Compass Point Bks., *(978-0-7565)* Div. of Coughlan Publishing, Orders Addr.: 1710 Roe Crest Dr., North Mankato, MN 56003 USA (SAN 254-2013) Toll Free Fax: 877-371-1539; Toll Free: 877-371-1536; 1710 Roe Crest Dr., North Mankato, MN 56003; *Imprints:* CPB Grades 4-8 (CPBFour); CPB Grades K-3 (CPBK); For Fun! (For Fun); Profiles of the Presidents (ProPres); Signature Lives (SigLives); We the People (WethePeople); Headline Science (HEADLINE SCIEN)
E-mail: custserv@compasspointbooks.com; k.monyhan@coughlancompanies.com
Web site: http://www.compasspointbooks.com; http://www.capstonepub.com
Dist(s): **Capstone Press of Coughlan Cos.**
Capstone Pub.
Chinasprout, Inc.
Ebsco Publishing
Follett School Solutions.

Compass Publishing *See* **Sunesis Publishing Co.**

Compass Publishing, *(978-0-9753102)* Orders Addr.: P.O. Box 280188, Lakewood, CO 80228-0188 USA (SAN 256-0186) Tel 818-264-9606 (phone/fax); Fax: 818-433-7445; Edit Addr.: 1912 Rivera Rd., Santa Fe Spring, CA 90670 USA
E-mail: billhowey@actorsmenu.com
Web site: http://www.actorsmenu.com
Dist(s): **Follett School Solutions**
Independent Pubs. Group.

Compassion Outreach Ministry *See* **Stott, Darrel Ministry**

Compassion Pets Publishing, *(978-0-615-13428-4; 978-0-615-30968-2)* 34672 Hardtack Ln., Shingletown, CA 96088 USA (SAN 858-5954) Tel 530-474-1038
E-mail: compassionpet.pub@frontiernet.net
Web site: http://www.compassionpets.com.

Compendium, Inc., Publishing & Communications, *(978-0-9640178; 978-1-888387; 978-1-932319; 978-1-935414; 978-1-938298; 978-1-943200; 978-1-946873)* Orders Addr.: P.O. Box 5308, Lynnwood, WA 98046-5308 USA (SAN 253-7109) Tel 425-673-2238; Fax: 425-673-6949; Toll Free: 800-914-3327; Edit Addr.: 600 N. 36th St. Ste. 400, Seattle, WA 98103-8699 USA
E-mail: kobi@compendiuminc.com; connie@compendiuminc.com; carolanne@compendiuminc.com
Web site: http://www.compendiuminc.com; http://www.live-inspired.com
Dist(s): **APG Sales & Distribution Services.**

Complete in Christ Ministries, Inc., *(978-0-9795007)* P.O. Box 42027, Baton Rouge, LA 70835 USA
E-mail: completeinchrist@cox.net
Web site: http://www.cicmblog.com.

Comprecom, *(978-0-9772809)* 411 Hess Ave., Golden, CO 80401 USA.

Comprehensive Health Education Foundation, *(978-0-935529; 978-1-57021)* 159 S. Jackson St. Ste. 510, Seattle, WA 98104-4416 USA (SAN 696-3668) Toll Free: 800-323-2433
E-mail: chefstaff@chef.org
Web site: http://www.chef.org/.

Compsych Systems, Inc., Pubns. Div., *(978-0-929948)* Div. of Compsych Systems, Inc., P.O. Box 1568, Pacific Palisades, CA 90272 USA (SAN 250-8281) Tel 310-454-6426 (phone/fax)
Web site: http://www.jeanettegriver.com
Dist(s): **Follett School Solutions.**

Computer Age Education *See* **Learning Net, The**

Computer Athlete Media, *(978-0-9820447)* P.O. Box 687, Princeton Junction, NJ 08550 USA
E-mail: support@computerathlete.net
Web site: http://www.computerathlete.net.

Computer Classics (R), *(978-0-9721216; 978-0-9748870; 978-0-9836019; 978-0-9899265)* 5036 Suter Dr., Nashville, TN 37211-5155 USA
E-mail: computerclassics@mindspring.com
Web site: http://www.computer-classics.com.

ComQwest, LLC, *(978-0-9753454)* 1350 E. Flamingo Rd., Suite No. 265, Las Vegas, NV 89119 USA
Web site: http://www.comqwest.com.

ComteQ Publishing, *(978-0-9674074; 978-0-9766889; 978-0-9793771; 978-1-935232; 978-1-941501)* Div. of ComteQ Communications, LLC, Orders Addr.: 101 N. Washington Ave. Suite 1b, Margate, NJ 08402 USA Tel 609-487-9000; Fax: 609-487-9099
E-mail: publisher@comteqpublishing.com
Web site: http://www.comteqpublishing.com
Dist(s): **BookBaby.**

Comunicadora Koine, Inc., *(978-0-9794682; 978-0-9834966)* Orders Addr.: P.O. Box RR3 Box 3801, San Juan, PR 00926 USA Tel 787-642-2053; Fax: 787-753-7077; Edit Addr.: 1118 Calle Padres Capuchinos, Rio Piedras, PR 00925 USA
E-mail: comunicadorakoine@gmail.com
Web site: http://www.comunicadorakoine.com.

ConArtistE Pubng., *(978-0-9755386)* 6084 Churn Creek Rd., Redding, CA 96002 USA Tel 530-209-4338
E-mail: conartiste@msn.com
Web site: www.conartiste.com.

Concepcion, Jorge, *(978-0-9761779)* 9125 SW 56th Ter., Miami, FL 33173-1605 USA
E-mail: jconcepcion1@msn.com.

Concept Media Group, LLC, The, *(978-0-9864191)* P.O. Box 211801, Dallas, TX 75211-1801 USA Tel 214-854-2150
E-mail: sherilyn@theconceptmediagroup.com
Web site: www.TheConceptMediaGroup.com.

Concepts *See* **Developmental Vision Concepts**

Concepts 'N' Publishing, *(978-1-879940)* Orders Addr.: P.O. Box 10413, College Station, TX 77842 USA
Web site: http://www.ethaernm.homestead.com.

Concepts Redefined, *(978-0-692-83922-5; 978-0-692-83939-3; 978-0-9986630)* 11739 Mango cross ct., Seffner, FL 33584 USA Tel 813-598-9481
E-mail: creynolds70@verizon.net; creynolds70@verizon.net; creynolds70@verizon.net
Web site: www.jaycethebee.com
Dist(s): **CreateSpace Independent Publishing Platform.**

Concerned Christians, *(978-0-9768352)* P.O. Box 18, Mesa, AZ 85211 USA Tel 480-833-2537; Fax: 480-833-4116
E-mail: jim@concernedchristians.org
Web site: http://www.concernedchristians.org.

Concerned Communications, *(978-0-936785; 978-1-58938)* Orders Addr.: P.O. Box 1000, Siloam Springs, AR 72761-1000 USA (SAN 699-8623) Tel 501-594-9000; Fax: 501-549-4002; Toll Free: 800-447-4332; Edit Addr.: 700 E. Granite St., Siloam Springs, AR 72761 USA (SAN 699-8631)
E-mail: lustwrt@areasonfor.com
Web site: http://www.areasonfor.com
Dist(s): **Project Patch.**

Conciliar Press *See* **Ancient Faith Publishing**

Concinnity Initiatives, *(978-0-9842146; 978-0-615-49009-0; 978-0-615-53946-1)* 2733 Meade St., Denver, CO 80211-4076 USA
E-mail: kevin.mccaffrey@firstpersonpublishing.com; jeffrey.fugate@navy.mil
Web site: http://www.firstpersonpublishing.com.

Concordia Publishing Hse., *(978-0-570; 978-0-7586)* Subs. of Lutheran Church Missouri Synod, 3558 S. Jefferson Ave., Saint Louis, MO 63118-3968 USA (SAN 202-1781) Tel 314-268-1000; Fax: 314-268-1360; Toll Free Fax: 800-490-9889 (orders only); Toll Free: 800-325-3040 (orders only); 800-325-0191
E-mail: cphorder@cph.org
Web site: http://www.cph.org.

Concourse Pr., *(978-0-911323)* Subs. of East-West Fine Arts Corp., Orders Addr.: 14 Ridgeview Rd., Newtown Sq, PA 19073-3002 USA (SAN 269-249X); Edit Addr.: P.O. Box 8265, Philadelphia, PA 19101 USA
E-mail: site.concoursepress@gmail.com
Web site: http://www.ConcoursePress.com
Dist(s): **Brodart Co.**

Concrete Jungle Pr., *(978-0-9749048; 978-1-945610)* 47-04 168th St., Flushing, NY 11358 USA
E-mail: dw@dwaynedworsky.com
Web site: http://www.dwaynedworsky.com; www.alphacentauriandbeyond.com.

Condor Designs, *(978-0-692-80859-7; 978-0-692-80933-4)* P.O. Box 155, FISH CAMP, CA 93623 USA Tel 559-341-8854
E-mail: mscondor@gmail.com; mscondor@gmail.com.

Conerly, Lawrence, *(978-0-9765669)* 85 Mt. Canaan Rd., Tylertown, MS 39667 USA
E-mail: augsept@bellsouth.net.

Conexion Educativa, *(978-0-9702021)* 900 Alameda St., Villa Granada, San Juan, PR 00923 USA Tel 787-766-4448; Fax: 787-250-8709
E-mail: conexion@coqui.net
Web site: http://home.coqui.net/conexion.

Conflict Games, LLC, *(978-0-9824507)* Orders Addr.: 15 Green Hill Ct., Nanuet, NY 10954 USA Tel 845-689-9014
E-mail: mscott@conflictroleplaying.com
Web site: http://www.conflictbooks.com/.

Cong Bais Tziporah, *(978-0-9728849; 978-0-9767166; 978-1-934098)* 3 Harrison Ave., Spring Valley, NY 10977 USA.

Congregation Agudat Achim, *(978-0-9770172)* 2117 Union St., Schenectady, NY 12309 USA
Web site: http://www.divinekosher.com.

Congregation Kehilas Yaakov (CKY), *(978-0-9770352; 978-0-9847019)* 2 Omni Ct., Lakewood, NJ 08701 USA Tel 732-942-8374.

Congress At Your Fingertips, *(978-1-879617; 978-0-9969346; 978-0-9994368)* Div. of Capitol Advantage, LLC, Orders Addr.: P.O. Box 309, Newington, VA 22122 USA Tel 703-550-9500; Fax: 703-550-0406; Toll Free: 877-827-3321
Web site: http://congressatyourfingertips.com.

Congressional Publishing, Inc., *(978-0-9762916)* P.O. Box 1318, Leesburg, VA 20177 USA Tel 703-777-6737; Fax: 703-777-6272
E-mail: congressionalpub@verizon.net
Web site: http://www.congressionalpublishing.com.

Coniston Designs (AUS) *(978-0-86435)* *Dist. by* **IPG Chicago.**

Conley, Bill, *(978-0-9773991; 978-0-9801317)* 3435 Heritage Oaks Dr., Hilliard, OH 43026 USA Fax: 614-529-8865
E-mail: coachconley@coachbillconley.com
Web site: http://www.coachbillconley.com.

Conley, Connie, *(978-0-9800898)* 4555 SW Willow St., Seattle, WA 98136 USA (SAN 855-1731)
E-mail: puppyluck@comcast.net.

Connect *Imprint of* **Stone Arch Bks.**

Connect With Your Kid Bks., *(978-0-9746094)* 106 Central Park Sq., No.150, Los Alamos, NV 87544 USA Toll Free: 888-388-5437
E-mail: DrSillyScience@comcast.net
Web site: http://www.DrSillyScience.com.

Connected 2 The Father Publishing *See* **Urban Advocacy**

Connecticut Pr., The, *(978-0-9825468; 978-0-9977907)* 36 Wildlife Ct., Cheshire, CT 06410 USA Tel 203-257-6020
E-mail: pjmalia@connecticutpress.com; celestemalia@connecticutpress.com
Web site: http://www.connecticutpress.com
Dist(s): **Lightning Source, Inc.**

Connection, *(978-0-9743687)* 601 Daniel Ct., Nashville, TN 37221-6512 USA.

Connections Bk. Publishing, Ltd. (GBR) *(978-1-85906)* *Dist. by* **Red Wheel Weiser.**

Connelly Pr., The, *(978-0-9797415)* 243 Abrahams Ln., Villanova, PA 19085 USA Tel 610-316-1997
Dist(s): **eBookit.com.**

Connexions Unlimited, *(978-1-929785)* 1021 Silver Lake Blvd., Frankfort, KY 40601 USA Tel 502-695-5181.

Connors, E. W. Publishing Co., *(978-0-9635587)* P.O. Box 691, Buffalo, NY 14205-0691 USA Tel 716-851-1343.

Conscience Studio, *(978-0-9828492)* 90 W. Univ. St., Alfred, NY 14802-1134 USA (SAN 859-9203) Tel 607-587-9111
E-mail: ConscienceStudio@gmail.com
Web site: http://www.consciencestudio.com.

Conscious Living Pubns., *(978-1-890580)* 15 Linden Ln., York, ME 03909 USA Tel 207-351-3316; Fax: 207-351-3369
E-mail: info@leonardjacobson.com
Dist(s): **New Leaf Distributing Co., Inc.**

Consciousness-Based Education Association, *(978-0-9727877)* 1100 Univ. Manor Dr., B-24, Fairfield, IA 52556 USA Tel 641-472-1663; Fax: 641-472-3116; Toll Free: 888-472-1677
E-mail: info@cbeprograms.org
Web site: http://www.cbeprograms.org.

Consejo Estatal Electoral (MEX) *(978-970-58)* *Dist. by* **Santillana.**

Consilient Pubns., *(978-0-9746242)* 8176 S. Centaur Dr., Evergreen, CO 80439 USA Tel 303-679-1538
E-mail: stephanie@cost-benefit-jr.com
Web site: http://www.cost-benefit-jr.com.

Consortium Bk. Sales & Distribution, Div. of Ingram Content Group, Orders Addr.: 1094 Flex Dr., Jackson, TN 38301-5070 USA; Edit Addr.: 34 13th Ave NE, Suite 100, Minneapolis, MN 55413-1007 USA (SAN 200-6049) Toll Free: 800-283-3572 (orders)
E-mail: info@cbsd.com
Web site: http://www.cbsd.com/
Dist(s): **Follett School Solutions.**

Consortium Publishing Co., *(978-0-9644681; 978-0-9707173; 978-0-9748830)* Div. of Creative Ideas, Inc., Orders Addr.: P.O. Box 998, Jacksonville, IL 62651 USA; Edit Addr.: P.O. Box 1535, Jacksonville, IL 62651-1535 USA Tel 217-243-7628 (phone/fax); Toll Free: 800-419-8698; 888-456-7235; 4 Sunnydale Ave., Jacksonville, IL 62650
E-mail: consortm@aol.com
Web site: http://www.creativeideas.com.

Consortium, The *See* **Consortium Publishing Co.**

Constitutional Rights Foundation, *(978-1-886253)* 601 S. Kingsley Dr., Los Angeles, CA 90005 USA (SAN 225-6401) Tel 213-487-5590; Fax: 213-386-0459; Toll Free: 800-488-4273 Do not confuse with Constitutional Rights Foundation Chicago in Chicago, IL
E-mail: crf@crf.usa
Web site: http://www.crf-usa.org.

Consultant's Unlimited *See* **Schwarz Pauper Pr.**

Consumer Pr., The, *(978-0-9717119)* 6 Berkley Rd., Glenville, NY 12302 USA (SAN 254-5446)
E-mail: richesq@mindspring.com
Web site: http://www.theconsumerpress.com.

†Consumer Reports Bks., *(978-0-89043)* Div. of Consumers Union of U. S., Inc., 101 Truman Ave., Yonkers, NY 10703 USA (SAN 224-1048) Tel 914-378-2000; Fax: 914-378-2925; Toll Free: 800-500-9760 (book dept.)
Web site: http://www.consumerreports.org/
Dist(s): **Ingram Publisher Services**; *CIP.*

Consumers Union of U. S., Inc., *(978-0-89043; 978-0-9755388; 978-1-933524)* Orders Addr.: 540 Barnum Ave., Bridgeport, CT 06608 USA (SAN 661-9800); Edit Addr.: 101 Truman Ave., Yonkers, NY 10703 USA (SAN 269-3518) Tel 914-378-2000; Fax: 914-378-2925
Web site: http://ConsumersReports.org
Dist(s): **Ingram Publisher Services**
Macmillan.

Contemplation Corner Pr., *(978-0-9707979; 978-0-9758748)* 1229 Randy Rd., Ashland City, TN 37015 USA Tel 615-746-8220; Fax: 615-746-3697
E-mail: ccpress1@bellsouth.net
Web site: http://www.contemplationcornerpress.com.

Contemporary Fiction *Imprint of* **Noel, Jaren**

Contender Entertainment Group (GBR) *(978-1-84357)* *Dist. by* **IPG Chicago.**

Continental Bk. Co., Inc., *(978-0-9626800)* Eastern Div., 80-00 Cooper Ave., Bldg. No. 29, Glendale, NY 11385 USA (SAN 169-5436) Tel 718-326-0560; Fax: 718-326-4276; Toll Free: 800-364-0350; Western Div., 625 E. 70th Ave., No. 5, Denver, CO 80229 (SAN 630-2882) Tel 303-289-1761; Fax: 303-289-1764
E-mail: hola@continentalbook.com; esl@continentalbook.com; bonjour@continentalbook.com; tag@continentalbook.com
Web site: http://www.continentalbook.com
Dist(s): **Follett School Solutions.**

Continental Enterprises Group, Inc. (CEG), Orders Addr.: 108 Red Row St., Easley, SC 29640-2820 USA (SAN 631-0915)
E-mail: ContactUs@centerprisesgrp.com.

Continental Pr., Inc., *(978-0-8454; 978-1-5240)* Orders Addr.: 520 E. Bainbridge St., Elizabethtown, PA 17022 USA (SAN 202-182X) Tel 717-367-1836; Fax: 717-367-5660; Toll Free: 800-233-0759; *Imprints:* Seedling Publications (Seedlg Pubns)
E-mail: educationsales@continentalpress.com
Web site: http://www.continentalpress.com.

Continental Sales, 213 W. Main St., Barrington, IL 60010-0010 USA Tel 847-381-6530.

Continental Sales, Inc.,; *Imprints:* New in Chess (New Chess); Raven Tree Press (Raven Tree Pr); Raven Tree Press,Csi (RAVEN TREE PRE); New In Chess,Csi (NEW IN CHESS,C)
Dist(s): **National Bk. Network.**

Contmedia Inc,

Conundrum Pr. (CAN) *(978-0-9685161; 978-0-9680364; 978-0-9689496; 978-1-894994; 978-1-77262)* *Dist. by* **Consort Bk Sales.**

CONVERPAGE, *(978-0-9728155; 978-0-9815720; 978-0-9820733; 978-0-9825854; 978-0-9835784; 978-0-9851721; 978-0-9858282; 978-0-615-84393-3; 978-0-9910923)* 23 Acorn St., Scituate, MA 02066-3324 USA
E-mail: pmccallum@comcast.net
Web site: www.converpage.com.

Conversations for Action and Listening Pubn., *(978-0-692-43550-2; 978-0-9977110)* 95 Westminster Dr., Oakland , CA 94618 USA Tel 5102203334
Dist(s): **CreateSpace Independent Publishing Platform.**

Conway, Kathleen R., *(978-0-9897763; 978-0-9973737)* 5 Camelot Ln., Bourne, MA 02532 USA Tel 508-415-1295
E-mail: capecodscribe@yahoo.com
Web site: http://www.capecodscribe.com; https://wickedwhalepublishing.wordpress.com
Dist(s): **BookBaby**
Cape Cod Scribe.

Cook, Cheryl *See* **Heavenly C. Publishing**

Cook Communication, *(978-0-9726996)* Orders Addr.: 6086 Dunes Dr., Sanford, NC 27332 USA Tel 312-859-8090; 919-498-6421; Fax: 866-652-8493
E-mail: cookcomm@gte.net; cookcomm@ameritech.net
Web site: http://www.author-me.com; http://www.reservebooks.com.

Cook, David, *(978-0-9741629)* P.O. Box 657, Albemarle, NC 28001 USA Do not confuse with companies with the same name in Chapel Hill, NC, Boerne, TX
E-mail: info@dac-and.com
Web site: http://www.dac-and.com.

Cook, David C., *(978-0-7814; 978-0-88207; 978-0-89191; 978-0-89693; 978-0-912692; 978-1-55513; 978-1-56476; 978-1-4347)* 4050 Lee Vance View, Colorado Springs, CO 80918 USA (SAN 206-0981) Tel 719-536-0100; Fax: 719-536-3244; Toll Free: 800-708-5550; 800-323-7543 (Customer Service)
E-mail: wendi.lord@davidccook.com
Web site: http://www.davidccook.com
Dist(s): **Follett School Solutions.**

Cook, David C. Publishing Company *See* **Cook, David C.**

Cook, Ken Co., *(978-0-9652491)* 9929 W. Silver Spring Dr., Milwaukee, WI 53225 USA Tel 414-466-6060; Fax: 414-466-0840
E-mail: nics@kencook.com
Web site: http://www.kencook.com.

Cookbook Resources, LLC, *(978-0-9677932; 978-1-931294; 978-1-59769)* 541 Doubletree Dr., Highland Village, TX 75077 USA (SAN 253-5262) Tel 972-317-0245; Fax: 972-317-6404; Toll Free: 866-229-2665
E-mail: lauren@cookbookresources.com
Web site: http://www.cookbookresourses.com
Dist(s): **Bk. Marketing Plus.**

Cookie Bear Pr., Inc., *(978-0-9701155)* Orders Addr.: P.O. Box 5074, Buffalo Grove, IL 60089 USA (SAN 253-6579) Tel 847-955-0001; 847-478-9202; Fax: 847-955-0002; Edit Addr.: 205 Thompson Blvd., Buffalo Grove, IL 60089 USA
E-mail: info@cookiebearpress.com
Web site: http://www.cookiebearpress.com
Dist(s): **Distributors, The**
Independent Pubs. Group.

Cookie Jar, *(978-1-933799; 978-1-60095)* Cookie Jar Entertainment, Inc., P.O. Box 35665, Greensboro, NC 27425 USA Fax: 336-808-3249; Toll Free: 800-321-0903; *Imprints:* Doodlebops (Doodlebops)
Web site: http://www.cinar.com/EN/
Dist(s): **Carson-Dellosa Publishing, LLC.**

Cookie O'Gorman, *(978-0-9978174)* 105 Carver Ct., Warner Robins, GA 31088 USA Tel 478-218-0166
E-mail: aireeahna@cox.net.

Cool Kids Create, *(978-0-9797297)* 48 Beach 217 St., Breezy Point, NY 11697 USA
Web site: http://www.coolkidscreate.com
Dist(s): **BCH Fulfillment & Distribution.**

Cool, Kim @ Historic Venice Pr., *(978-0-9721655)* 312 Shore Rd., Venice, FL 34285 USA
Web site: http://www.historicvenicepress.com
Dist(s): **American Wholesale Bk. Co.**
Bk. Warehouse
Southern Bk. Service.

Cool Things Pr., *(978-0-615-20795-7; 978-0-615-20796-4; 978-0-615-78176-1; 978-0-692-45762-7)* P.O. Box 3852, Concord, NH 03302-3952 USA Tel 6037157852
Dist(s): **CreateSpace Independent Publishing Platform**
Lulu Pr., Inc.

Coolbular Inc, *(978-0-578-15459-6; 978-0-9980946)* PO Box 1764, Evergreen, CO 80439 USA
E-mail: author.adir.rondack@gmail.com
Web site: http://to-kill-a-predator.com/.

Coolmath.com, Inc., *(978-0-9791628)* P.O. Box 4386, Costa Mesa, CA 92628-4386 USA
Web site: http://Coolmath.com.

Coon, Kathy, *(978-0-9741300)* P.O. Box 14267, Baton Rouge, LA 70898 USA
Web site: http://www.dogintelligencetest.com.

Cooper, Gene, *(978-0-615-85312-3)* 6 Peter Cooper Rd. Apt. 3C, New York, NY 10010 USA Tel 212-228-5083
E-mail: cooper.gene82@gmail.com.

Cooper Publishing, *(978-1-59655)* Orders Addr.: P.O. Box 1974, Englewood, FL 34295 USA Tel 941-587-0396
E-mail: cooper.publishing@yahoo.com.

Cooper, Robbi, *(978-0-9749643)* 9 Scott Crescent, Austin, TX 78703 USA
Web site: http://www.everythingfromthegarden.com.

Cooper Square Publishing Llc,
Dist(s): **National Bk. Network.**

Cooperative Kids, *(978-0-9821121)* P.O. Box 432, Enfield, CT 06083-0432 USA (SAN 857-2917) Tel 860-265-2272
E-mail: info@cooperativekids.com
Web site: http://www.cooperativekids.com.

Cooperfly Books *See* **Cooperfly Creative Arts, Inc.**

Cooperfly Creative Arts, Inc., *(978-0-9669504; 978-0-9970476)* 3184 Plainfield NE PMB 248, Grand Rapids, MI 49525 USA Tel 616-364-5870
E-mail: kevin@tomatocollection.com
Web site: http://www.tomatocollection.com
Dist(s): **Indig, Stanley M. Specialty Pubn.**

Cooper's Pack, *(978-0-9794882)* Div. of Cooper's Pack Publishing, Orders Addr.: 1900 W. Nickerson St., Suite 116-130, Seattle, WA 98119 USA (SAN 853-5825) Tel 206-235-1886 Toll Free: 877-278-3278
E-mail: brandon@cooperspack.com
Web site: http://www.CoopersPack.com.

Copeland, Kenneth Pubns., *(978-0-88114; 978-0-938458; 978-1-57562; 978-1-60463)* Subs. of Eagle Mountain International Church, Kenneth Copeland Ministries, Fort Worth, TX 76192 USA Tel 817-252-2700; Toll Free: 800-600-7395
E-mail: mjohnson@kcm.org
Web site: http://www.kcm.org.contact.html
Dist(s): **Anchor Distributors**
Appalachian Bible Co.
Central South Christian Distribution
Harrison House Pubs.
New Day Christian Distributors Gifts, Inc.
Spring Arbor Distributors, Inc.

Copernicus Pr., *(978-0-9741638)* 933 Dwyer Ave., Saint Louis, MO 63122 USA Tel 314-822-8597 Do not confuse with Copernicus Pr. in Atlanta, GA
E-mail: nikolom@slu.edu
Web site: http://www.Copernicuspress.com
Dist(s): **Unique Bks., Inc.**

Copley Custom Textbooks, *(978-0-87411; 978-1-58152; 978-1-58390)* Div. of XanEdu Publishing Inc., 530 Great Rd., Acton, MA 01720 USA (SAN 687-4959) Tel 978-263-9090; Fax: 978-263-9190; Toll Free: 800-562-2147; *Imprints:* Copley Publishing Group (Copley Pub Grp)
E-mail: textbook@copleypublishing.com; publish@copleycustom.com
Web site: http://www.xanedu.com.

Copley Publishing Group *See* **Copley Custom Textbooks**

Copley Publishing Group *Imprint of* **Copley Custom Textbooks**

Coppenrath, F. Verlag KG (DEU) *(978-3-88547; 978-3-920192; 978-3-8157) Dist. by* **Distribks Inc.**

Copper Moon Press *See* **TangleTown Media Inc.**

Coptic Orthodox Church - Diocese of Los Angeles Saint Paul Brotherhood *See* **Saint Paul Brotherhood**

Coram Deo Pr., *(978-0-9769054)* One Nelson Pkwy., 2400 FM 407, Highland Village, TX 75077 USA Tel 972-318-5222; Fax: 972-692-5140
E-mail: press@coramdeoacademy.org
Web site: http://www.coramdeopress.com.

Corbett Features, *(978-0-9762294)* Div. of Corbett Features, 100 Cummings Ctr. Suite 432-a, Beverly, MA 01915 USA Tel 978-232-1124; Fax: 978-232-1124; *Imprints:* Griffin Comics (Griffin Comics)
E-mail: cdesign.ma.ultranet@rcn.com
Web site: http://www.corbettfeatures.com.

Corbus Systems, *(978-0-9742347)* 20368 Forestwood, Southfield, MI 48706 USA Tel 248-356-9427
E-mail: info@corbus-systems.com
Web site: http://www.corbus-systems.com.

Corby Books, *(978-0-9776458; 978-0-9819605; 978-0-9827846; 978-0-9833586; 978-0-9859377; 978-0-9890731; 978-0-9912451; 978-0-9961362)* 51679 Stoneham Way, Granger, IN 46530 USA
E-mail: prestonward1@aol.com; jimtach@aol.com.

CORD Communications, *(978-1-55502; 978-1-57837)* Subs. of Ctr. for Occupational Research & Development, Orders Addr.: P.O. Box 21206, Waco, TX 76702-1206 USA Tel 254-776-1822; Fax: 254-776-3906; Toll Free: 800-231-3015; Edit Addr.: 324 Kelly Dr., Waco, TX 76710 USA
E-mail: webmaster@cord.org
Web site: http://www.cord.org/index.cfm.

Cordon Pubns., *(978-0-9822083; 978-0-9826984; 978-0-615-39009-3; 978-0-9829049; 978-0-9834908; 978-0-9839858; 978-1-937912)* 5161 Great Lakes Dr. So., Evansville, IN 47715 USA (SAN 857-5460) Tel 812-303-9070
E-mail: coraseaman@hotmail.com
Web site: http://www.Cordon Publications.com.

Cordoves, Barbara & Gladys M., *(978-0-9637252)* 2800 SW 106th Ave., Miami, FL 33165-2748 USA.

Core Knowledge Foundation, *(978-1-890517; 978-1-933486; 978-1-68380)* Orders Addr.: 801 E. High St., Charlottesville, VA 22902 USA Tel 434-977-7550; Fax: 434-977-0021; Toll Free: 800-238-3233
E-mail: mjones@coreknowledge.org; coreknow@coreknowledge.org
Web site: http://www.coreknowledge.org.

Core Library *Imprint of* **ABDO Publishing Co.**

Core Publishing & Consulting, Inc., *(978-1-933079)* 13016 Bee St., Suite 208, Dallas, TX 75234 USA (SAN 256-1514) Tel 214-926-4742; Fax: 972-243-5854
E-mail: stan.peterson@sbcglobal.net
Web site: www.core-publishing.com.

CoreyJF Publishing, *(978-0-9895101)* 12299 Greenleaf Ave., Potomac, MD 20854 USA Tel 301-564-3058
E-mail: corey@coreyjf.com
Web site: www.coreyjf.com; www.egrettheelephant.com.

Corgi Tales Publishing, *(978-0-615-26492-9)* 57715 Hwy. 58, McKittrick, CA 93251 USA
Dist(s): **Lulu Pr., Inc.**

Corimbo, Editorial S.L. (ESP) *(978-84-8470; 978-84-95150) Dist. by* **Mariuccia Iaconi Bk Imports.**

Corimbo, Editorial S.L. (ESP) *(978-84-8470; 978-84-95150) Dist. by* **Lectorum Pubns.**

Corimbo, Editorial S.L. (ESP) *(978-84-8470; 978-84-95150) Dist. by* **Distribks Inc.**

Cork Hill Pr., *(978-1-59408)* P.O. Box 117, Carmel, IN 46082-0117 USA
Web site: http://www.corkhillpress.com
Dist(s): **CreateSpace Independent Publishing Platform.**

Corman Productions, *(978-0-9655749)* 6729 Dume Dr., Malibu, CA 90265 USA Tel 310-457-7524; Fax: 310-457-5941
E-mail: Dikkybird@aol.com.

Cormier, Shawn *See* **Pine View Pr.**

Cormorant Bks. Inc. (CAN) *(978-0-920953; 978-1-896951; 978-1-897151; 978-1-77086) Dist. by* **Orca Bk Pub.**

Corn Tassel Pr., *(978-0-9752597)* 9655 Corn Tassel Ct., Columbia, MD 21046 USA Fax: 301-776-6538.

Cornell, A.J. Pubns., *(978-0-9727439; 978-0-9850501)* 18-74 Corporal Kennedy St., Bayside, NY 11360 USA Tel 718-423-4082
Dist(s): **Bookmasters Distribution.**

Cornell Maritime Pr./Tidewater Pubs. *Imprint of* **Schiffer Publishing, Ltd.**

†**Cornell Univ. Pr.,** *(978-0-8014; 978-0-87546; 978-1-5017)* Orders Addr.: P.O. Box 6525, Ithaca, NY 14851 USA (SAN 281-5680) Tel 607-277-2211; Toll Free Fax: 800-688-2877; Toll Free: 800-666-2211; Edit Addr.: Sage House, 512 E. State St., Ithaca, NY 14851 USA (SAN 202-1862) Tel 607-277-2338
E-mail: cupressinfo@cornell.edu; orders@nbninternational.com; cupress-sales@cornell.edu
Web site: http://www.cornellpress.cornell.edu
Dist(s): **CUP Services**
Casemate Academic
De Gruyter, Inc.
Follett School Solutions
Hachette Bk. Group
Longleaf Services
MyiLibrary
ebrary, Inc.; *CIP.*

Cornerstone Bk. Publishers *Imprint of* **Poll, Michael Publishing**

Cornerstone Family Ministries/Lamplighter Publishing, *(978-1-58474)* Orders Addr.: P.O. Box 777, Waverly, PA 18471 USA Tel 717-585-1314; Fax: 717-587-4246; Toll Free: 888-246-7735; Edit Addr.: Waverly Community Ctr., Main St., S. Wing, 2nd Flr., Waverly, PA 18471 USA
E-mail: cfm@epix.net
Web site: http://www.agospel.com
Dist(s): **Follett School Solutions.**

Cornerstone Pr., *(978-0-918476)* 1825 Bender Ln., Arnold, MO 63010-0388 USA (SAN 210-0584) Tel 636-296-9662 Do not confuse with companies with the same name in Edison, NJ, Kents Hill, ME, Pearland, TX, Stevens Point, WI
E-mail: anthsum@sbcglobal.net.

Cornerstone Pr., *(978-0-9668488; 978-0-9774802; 978-0-9846739)* c/o Univ. of Wisconsin, Dept. of English, TLC @ LRC, University of Wisconsin — Stevens Point, Stevens Point, WI 54481-3897 USA Tel 715-346-2849; Fax: 715-346-2849 Do not confuse with companies with the same name in Kents Hill, ME, Arnold, MO
E-mail: dan.dieterich@uwsp.edu.

Cornerstone Pr. Chicago, *(978-0-940895)* 939 W. Wilson, Chicago, IL 60640 USA (SAN 664-7200) Tel 773-561-2450; 773-989-4920; Fax: 773-989-2076; Toll Free: 888-407-7377
E-mail: cspress@jpusa.org
Web site: http://www.cornerstonepress.com.

Cornerstone Press, Incorporated *See* **Patria Pr., Inc.**

Cornerstone Publishing, Inc., *(978-1-882185)* Orders Addr.: P.O. Box 23015, Evansville, IN 47724 USA (SAN 298-735X) Tel 812-470-3971 Do not confuse with companies with the same name in Decatur, GA, Altamonte Springs, FL, Wichita, KS
E-mail: cornerstonepublishinghouse@gmail.com
Web site: http://www.cornerstonepublishinghouse.com
Dist(s): **Book Clearing Hse.**
Lightning Source, Inc.

Cornerstonia, *(978-0-9828588)* 9457 Venezia Plantation Dr., Orlando, FL 32829 USA Tel 407-222-4287
E-mail: author@cornerstonia.com
Web site: http://www.cornerstonia.com.

CornerWind Media, L.L.C., *(978-0-9741072)* Orders Addr.: 2635 Whitehall Ct., Rock Hill, SC 29732 USA Tel 803-329-7140; Fax: 803-329-7145
Web site: http://www.twiggyleaf.com; http://www.cornerwind.com.

Corning Museum of Glass, *(978-0-87290)* One Museum Way, Corning, NY 14830 USA (SAN 202-1897) Fax: 607-974-7365; Toll Free: 800-732-6845
E-mail: cmg@cmog.org; pr@cmog.org
Web site: http://www.cmog.org
Dist(s): **Associated Univ. Presses**
Casemate Academic
Hudson Hills Pr. LLC
National Bk. Network.

Corona Pr., *(978-1-891619)* 4535 Palmer Ct., Niwot, CO 80503 USA Tel 303-247-1455; Fax: 303-417-0355; Toll Free: 888-648-3877 Do not confuse with Corona Pr., Brooklandville, MD
E-mail: coronapress@aol.com.

Coronet Bks., *(978-0-89563)* 311 Bainbridge St., Philadelphia, PA 19147 USA (SAN 210-6043) Tel 215-925-2762; Fax: 215-925-1912 Do not confuse with Coronet Bks. & Pubns., Eagle Point, OR
E-mail: ronsmolin@earthlink.net; order@coronetbooks.com
Web site: http://www.coronetbooks.com
Dist(s): **MyiLibrary.**

Corpus Communications *See* **Caritas Communications**

Corraini (ITA) *(978-88-86250; 978-88-87942; 978-88-7570) Dist. by* **Dist Art Pubs.**

Corroluna Pr., *(978-0-9986661)* 904 Queenstown Rd., Lancaster, VA 22503 USA Tel 804-387-3653; Fax: 804-387-3653
E-mail: mjbeswickart@gmail.com
Web site: maryjobeswick.com.

Cortright Fellowship Pr., *(978-0-9706684)* P.O. Box 434, Allegan, MI 49010 USA
E-mail: ekklesia@accn.org
Web site: http://www.redbay.com/ekklesia.

Corunda, Ediciones, S.A. de C.V. (MEX) *(978-968-6044; 978-968-7444) Dist. by* **AIMS Intl.**

Corwin Pr., *(978-0-7619; 978-0-8039; 978-1-57517; 978-1-879179; 978-1-4129)* Affil. of Sage Pubns., Inc., 2455 Teller Rd., Thousand Oaks, CA 91320-2218 USA Tel 805-499-9734; 805-499-9774 (customer service); Fax: 805-499-0871; 805-499-5323
E-mail: info@sagepub.com
Web site: http://www.corwinpress.com
Dist(s): **Follett School Solutions**
MyiLibrary
SAGE Pubns., Inc.
ebrary, Inc.

Corwin Press, Incorporated *See* **Corwin Pr.**

Coryell, Skip *See* **White Feather Press, LLC**

Cosimo Classics *Imprint of* **Cosimo, Inc.**

Cosimo, Inc., *(978-1-59605; 978-1-60206; 978-1-60520; 978-1-61640; 978-1-944529; 978-1-945934)* 116 W. 23rd Street, 5th Fl, New York, NY 10011-1818 USA Tel 212-989-3616; Fax: 212-989-3662; *Imprints:* Cosimo Classics (CosClassics)
E-mail: adake@cosimobooks.com; info@cosimobooks.com
Web site: http://www.cosimobooks.com
Dist(s): **Follett School Solutions**
INscribe Digital.

Cosmic Gargoyle Creative Solutions, *(978-0-9835843)* 3883 Turtle Creek Blvd. No. 1202, Dallas, TX 75219 USA Tel 214-679-4725; *Imprints:* Lonely Swan Books (Lonely Swan)
E-mail: cosmicgargoyle@gmail.com
Dist(s): **Smashwords.**

COSMIC VORTEX, *(978-0-9719580)* Div. of TETRA XII Inc., Orders Addr.: P.O. Box 322, Paia, HI 96779 USA
E-mail: atlantis@archaeologist.com; aloha@mauivortex.com
Web site: http://www.atlantistoday.com; http://atlantis-motherland.com.

Cosmographia Pubns., *(978-0-615-60710-8)* 6 1/2 W. 3rd St., Spencer, IA 51301 USA Tel 712-580-3271
E-mail: hnewgard@gmail.com.

Cosmos Books *See* **Prime**

Cosmos Publishing, *(978-0-9660449; 978-1-932455)* 262 River Vale Rd., River Vale, NJ 07675 USA (SAN 631-0486) Tel 201-664-3494; Fax: 201-664-3402 Do not confuse with companies with the same in Bellevue, WA, Saint Louis, MO
E-mail: info@greeceinprint.com
Web site: http://www.greeceinprint.com.

Cosmos Publishing Company, Incorporated *See* **Cosmos Publishing**

Costume & Fashion Pr. *Imprint of* **Quite Specific Media Group, Ltd.**

Cote Literary Group, The, *(978-1-929175)* 483 Old Carolina Ct., Mount Pleasant, SC 29464 USA (SAN 850-4881) Tel 843-881-6080; Fax: 843-278-8456
E-mail: editor@corinthianbooks.com; dickcote@earthlink.net
Web site: http://www.corinthianbooks.com
Dist(s): **Brodart Co.**
Follett School Solutions
Quality Bks., Inc.
eBookit.com.

Coteau Bks. (CAN) *(978-0-919926; 978-1-55050; 978-0-9780316) Dist. by* **Orca Bk Pub.**

Cotler, Joanna Books *Imprint of* **HarperCollins Pubs.**

Cotsen Occasional Pr., *(978-0-9666084; 978-0-9745168; 978-0-9971510)* Div. of Cotsen Family Foundation, 12100 Wilshire Blvd. Suite 905, Los Angeles, CA 90025 USA Tel 310-826-9113
E-mail: jolie@cotsenfamilyoffice.com
Web site: http://www.hesdegraaf.com/hes/.

Cottage Door Pr., *(978-1-68052)* 218 James St., Barrington, IL 60010 USA (SAN 990-1051) Tel 224-228-6000
E-mail: kfinnamore@cottagedoorpress.com; contactus@cottagedoorpress.com; ksholly@cottagedoorpress.com
Web site: http://www.cottagedoorpress.com.

cottage in the woods Pr., *(978-0-9971552)* 3917 Lyman Rd, oakland, CA 94602 USA Tel 510-316-7182
E-mail: yosgurl@yahoo.com.

Cotton Candy Pr. *Imprint of* **Unveiled Media, LLC**

Cotton, Karen O., *(978-0-692-25813-2; 978-0-692-27344-9; 978-0-692-85154-8)* 5006 Foxen Ct., Cheyenne, WY 82001 USA Tel 307-214-0277
E-mail: cotton.karen@gmail.com
Web site: karencotton.net.

Cottonwood Graphics, Incorporated *See* **Cottonwood Publishing, Inc.**

Cottonwood Pr., Inc., *(978-1-877673; 978-1-936162)* 109-B Cameron Dr., Fort Collins, CO 80525 USA Tel 970-204-0715; Fax: 970-204-0761; Toll Free: 800-864-4297 Do not confuse with companies with same name in Novato, CA, Lawrence, KS, Wilsonville, OR
E-mail: cottonwood@cottonwoodpress.com
Web site: http://www.cottonwoodpress.com
Dist(s): **Independent Pubs. Group**
ebrary, Inc.

CottonWood Publishing Co., *(978-0-9766804)* 840 W. Washington St., Ann Arbor, MI 48103 USA Do not confuse with Cottonwood Publishing Company in Saint George, UT Helena MT.

Cottonwood Publishing, Inc., *(978-0-9626999; 978-1-886370)* 296 Willowbrook Dr., Helena, MT 59602-7764 USA Toll Free: 800-937-6343 Do not confuse with Cottonwood Publishing in Saint George, UT Ann Arbor MI
E-mail: oldmt@mt.net
Web site: http://www.oldmontana.com
Dist(s): **CreateSpace Independent Publishing Platform**
Mountain Pr. Publishing Co., Inc.

Coulee Region Pubns., Inc., *(978-0-9650629)* 307 Twin Oak Dr., Altoona, WI 54720-1383 USA.

Counce, Paula, *(978-0-9762776)* 1628 Bob O Link Dr., Venice, FL 34293 USA
Web site: http://www.ajourneyremembered.com.

†**Council for Agricultural Science & Technology (CAST),** *(978-1-887383)* 4420 W. Lincoln Way, Ames, IA 50014-3347 USA (SAN 225-7416) Tel 515-292-2125; Fax: 515-292-4512; Toll Free Fax: 800-375-2278; Toll Free: 800-762-4232
E-mail: cast@cast-science.org
Web site: http://www.cast-science.org; *CIP.*

Council for Indian Education, *(978-0-89992)* Orders Addr.: 1240 Burlington Ave., Billings, MT 59102-4224 USA Tel 406-248-3465; Fax: 406-248-1297
E-mail: cie@cie-mt.org
Web site: http://www.cie-mt.org
Dist(s): **Follett School Solutions.**

Council Oak Bks., *(978-0-933031; 978-1-57178)* Orders Addr.: 2822 Van Ness Ave., San Francisco, CA 94109 USA (SAN 689-5522) Tel 415-931-7700; Fax: 415-931-9911; Toll Free: 800-247-8850 (orders only)
E-mail: order@counciloakbooks.com; publicity@counciloakbooks.com
Web site: http://www.counciloakbooks.com
Dist(s): **Independent Pubs. Group**
New Leaf Distributing Co., Inc.
Univ. of Oklahoma Pr.

Count On Learning, *(978-0-9771472)* 1406 Arlington Ave., Baton Rouge, LA 70808 USA
E-mail: admin@countonlearning.com
Web site: http://www.countonlearning.com.

Counterbalance Bks., *(978-0-9774906; 978-0-9799592; 978-0-9989923)* P.O. Box 876, Duvall, WA 98019-0876 USA
E-mail: admin@counterbalancebooks.com; publisher@counterbalancebooks.com
Web site: http://www.counterbalancebooks.com.

Counterpath Pr., *(978-1-933996)* P.O. Box 18351, Denver, CO 80218 USA
E-mail: tr@counterpathpress.org
Web site: http://www.counterpathpress.org
Dist(s): **SPD-Small Pr. Distribution.**

Counterpoint LLC *See* **Counterpoint Pr.**

Counterpoint Pr., *(978-1-58243; 978-1-887178; 978-1-59376; 978-1-61902; 978-1-944869; 978-1-64009)* 2560 Ninth St., Suite 318, Berkeley, CA 94710-2205 USA Fax: 510-704-0268
E-mail: info@counterpointpress.com
Web site: http://www.counterpointpress.com
Dist(s): **Lulu Pr., Inc.**
MyiLibrary.

Countinghouse Pr., Inc., *(978-0-9664732; 978-0-9786191; 978-0-9911102)* 6632 Telegraph Rd., Suite 311, Bloomfield Hills, MI 48301 USA Tel 248-642-7191; Fax: 248-642-7192
E-mail: lcharla@comcast.net
Web site: http://www.countinghousepress.com.

Country Boy Publishing Co., *(978-0-9795574)* Orders Addr.: 300 Collier Dr., Winter Haven, FL 33884 USA
E-mail: dgreen12@tampabay.rr.com
Web site: http://www.countryboypublishing.com.

Country Bumpkin Pubns. USA, *(978-0-9677938)* 212 California Ave., Watertown, NY 13601 USA Tel 315-782-0941
E-mail: bsteve3@twcny.rr.com.

Country Girl Publishing, *(978-0-615-26902-3)* 5537 Shallowriver Rd., Clinton, MD 20735 USA.

Country Kid Publishing LLC, *(978-0-9754624; 978-0-9963649)* 951 Canyon Tr Ct., Yorkville, IL 60560 USA
E-mail: michaelwaguespack@gmail.com
Web site: http://www.countrykidpublishing.com
Dist(s): **Angler's Bk. Supply**
Follett School Solutions.

Country Messenger Pr. Publishing Group, LLC, *(978-0-9619407; 978-0-9801554; 978-1-937162)* 27657 Hwy. 97, Okanogan, WA 98840 USA (SAN 244-5638) Tel 253-216-6364
E-mail: kfreel@cmppg.org; edna@cmppg.org
Web site: http://www.cmppg.com.

Country Side Pr., The, *(978-0-9746360)* Orders Addr.: 49850 Miller Rd., North Powder, OR 97867 USA Tel 541-856-3239
E-mail: debbys@rconnects.com
Web site: http://www.thecountrysidepress.com.

Courage to Change *See* **CTC Publishing**

Courier Publications *See* **Christian Courier Pubns.**

Course Technology, *(978-0-534; 978-0-619; 978-0-7600; 978-0-7895; 978-0-87709; 978-0-87835; 978-0-89426; 978-0-928763; 978-1-56527; 978-1-878748; 978-1-4188; 978-1-59863; 978-1-4239; 978-1-60334)* Div. of Cengage Learning, Orders Addr.: 20 Channel Ctr St., Boston, MA 02210-3402 USA Toll Free Fax: 800-881-8922
E-mail: Esales@thomsonlearning.com; stacy.hiquet@thomson.com; cheryl.mondillo@thomson.com
Web site: http://www.course.com/
Dist(s): **CENGAGE Learning**
Delmar Cengage Learning
Ebsco Publishing
Leonard, Hal Corp.
ebrary, Inc.

Courtyard Publishing, LLC, *(978-0-9795260)* Div. of Alchemical Courtyard, LLC, 1688 Meridian Ave., 10th Flr., Miami Beach, FL 33139 USA Tel 305-695-9380
E-mail: info@courtyardpublishing.com
Web site: http://www.courtyardpublishing.com.

†**Covenant Communications,** *(978-0-9649122)* 1009 Jones St., Old Hickory, TN 37138 USA Tel 615-847-2066; Fax: 615-860-3601; Toll Free: 800-979-3882 Do nt oconfuse with Covenant Communications in Old Hickory, TN
Dist(s): **Quality Bks., Inc.**; *CIP.*

Covenant Communications, Inc., *(978-1-55503; 978-1-57734; 978-1-59156; 978-1-59811; 978-1-60861; 978-1-62108; 978-1-68047; 978-1-5244)* Orders Addr.: 920 E State Rd Ste F, American Fork, UT 84003-0416 USA (SAN 169-8540) Tel 801-756-9966; 801-756-1041; Fax: 801-756-1049; Toll Free: 800-662-9545; Edit Addr.: 920 E. State Rd., Suite F, American Fork, UT 84003 USA Toll Free: 800-662-9545 Do not confuse with Covenant Communications in American Fork, UT
E-mail: verls@covenant-lds.com
Web site: http://www.covenant-lds.com
Dist(s): **Follett School Solutions.**

Covenant of Light Publishing *See* **Sorcerer's Pr., The**

Covenant Support Network *See* **The 101 Group, Inc.**

Coventry Pool & Garden Houses *See* **Manor Hse. Publishing Co., Inc.**

Covercraft *Imprint of* **Perfection Learning Corp.**

Covered Bridge Bks., *(978-0-9722027)* 336 Covered Bridge Rd., Cherry Hill, NJ 08034-2949 USA.

Covered Bridge Children's Books *See* **Covered Bridge Bks.**

Covered Wagon Publishing LLC, *(978-0-9723259)* P.O. Box 473038, Aurora, CO 80047 USA (SAN 254-7813) Tel 303-751-0992; Fax: 303-632-6794
E-mail: CoveredWagon@comcast.net
Web site: http://www.RockyMountainMysteries.com.

Cow Heard Records, *(978-0-9763012)* 3622 Altura Ave., La Crescenta, CA 91214 USA
Web site: http://www.thesunflowers.com.

Cowan, Pricilla J., *(978-0-9822542; 978-0-9841194; 978-0-9840083; 978-0-9891159; 978-0-9896988)* 11594 SW 135th Ave., Tigard, OR 97223 USA
Web site: http://www.storiesbypj.com.

Cowboy Collector Pubns., *(978-0-9628078)* Orders Addr.: P.O. Box 7486, Long Beach, CA 90807 USA Tel 714-840-3942; Edit Addr.: 4677 Rio Ave., Long Beach, CA 90805 USA Tel 213-428-6972
Dist(s): **Hervey's Booklink & Cookbook Warehouse.**

Cowboy Magazine, *(978-0-9765969)* Orders Addr.: P.O. Box 126, La Veta, CO 81055 USA Tel 719-742-5250; Fax: 719-742-3034; Edit Addr.: 124 N. Main St., La Veta, CO 81055 USA
E-mail: workincowboy@amigo.net
Web site: http://www.cowboymagazine.com.

Cowgirl Peg Bks. *Imprint of* **Cowgirl Peg Enterprises**

Cowgirl Peg Enterprises, *(978-0-9721057; 978-0-615-59075-2; 978-0-692-95998-5)* Orders Addr.: P.O. Box 293055, Kerrville, TX 78029 USA; *Imprints:* Cowgirl Peg Books (Cowgirl Peg Books)
E-mail: cowgirlpeg2@gmail.com
Web site: http://www.cowgirlpeg.com
Dist(s): **Bks. West**
Follett School Solutions.

†**Cowley Pubns.,** *(978-0-936384; 978-1-56101)* Div. of Society of St. John the Evangelist, 4 Brattle St., Cambridge, MA 02138 USA (SAN 213-9987) Fax: 617-441-0300; Toll Free: 800-225-1534; 4501 Forbes Blvd., Lanhan, MD 20706
E-mail: cowley@cowley.org
Web site: http://www.cowley.org
Dist(s): **Follett School Solutions**
Forward Movement Pubns.
Ingram Publisher Services
MyiLibrary
National Bk. Network
Rowman & Littlefield Publishers, Inc.
ebrary, Inc.; *CIP.*

Cowpokes Cartoon Bks., *(978-0-917207)* P.O. Box 290868, Kerrville, TX 78029-0868 USA (SAN 656-089X) Tel 830-257-7446 (phone/fax); Toll Free: 800-257-7441 (phone/fax)
E-mail: cartoons@cowpokes.com
Web site: http://www.cowpokes.com.

Cox, Dee, *(978-0-9669672)* 2309 Limerick Dr., Tallahassee, FL 32308 USA Tel 850-893-1789
E-mail: gccox@mail.istal.com.

Cox, Julie, *(978-0-9742118)* P.O. Box 77966, Fort Worth, TX 76177 USA
E-mail: info@facereadingacademy.com
Web site: http://www.facereadingacademy.com.

Coyote Canyon Pr., *(978-0-9796607; 978-0-9821298; 978-0-9890080)* 693 Black Hills Dr., Claremont, CA 91711-2928 USA Toll Free Fax: 800-319-4707
E-mail: tom@coyotecanyonpress.com
Web site: http://www.coyotecanyonpress.com.

Coyote Cowboy Co., *(978-0-939343)* Orders Addr.: P.O. Box 2190, Benson, AZ 85602 USA (SAN 663-0820) Tel 520-586-1077; Toll Free: 800-654-2550; Edit Addr.: 1251 S. Red Chile Rd., Benson, AZ 85602 USA
E-mail: cindylou@baxterblack.com
Web site: http://www.baxterblack.com
Dist(s): **Follett School Solutions.**

Coyote Moon Publishing *See* **Cowgirl Peg Enterprises**

CoZi Publishing LLC, *(978-0-9749151)* P.O. Box 211, Rutland, VT 05702-0211 USA
E-mail: publish@cozi.com
Web site: http://www.cozi.com.

Cozy Graphics Corp., *(978-1-932002; 978-1-59343)* 61-20 G.C.P., Apt. B1204, Forest Hills, NY 11375 USA Tel 718-592-9782 (phone/fax); *Imprints:* Cozy Publishing House (Cozy Pub Hse)
E-mail: publisher@cozygraphics.com
Web site: http://www.cozygraphics.com.

Cozy Publishing Hse. *Imprint of* **Cozy Graphics Corp.**

CPB Grades 4-8 *Imprint of* **Compass Point Bks.**

CPB Grades K-3 *Imprint of* **Compass Point Bks.**

CPCC Pr., *(978-1-59494)* P.O. Box 35009, Charlotte, NC 28235-5009 USA Tel 704-330-6789
E-mail: cpccpress@cpcc.edu; melissa.wilson@cpcc.edu; amy.rogers@cpcc.edu; emma.reynolds@cpcc.edu
Web site: http://www.cpccservicescorp.com; http://https://cpccpress.com/.

CPM Comics *Imprint of* **Central Park Media Corp.**

CPM Manga *Imprint of* **Central Park Media Corp.**

CPM Manhwa *Imprint of* **Central Park Media Corp.**

CPR Pubng, *(978-0-9778597)* 740 13th St., Fennimore, WI 53809 USA.

CQ Pr. Library Reference *Imprint of* **CQ Pr.**

†**CQ Pr.,** *(978-0-7401; 978-0-87187; 978-0-9625531; 978-1-56692; 978-1-56802; 978-1-933116; 978-1-60426; 978-0-9823537; 978-1-60871)* Div. of SAGE Pubns., Inc., Orders Addr.: a/o Order Dept., 2300 N. St. NW, Suite 800, Washington, DC 20037 USA (SAN 256-470X) Toll Free: 866-427-7737 (customer service - orders); *Imprints:* C Q Press Library Reference (CQ Pr Lib Ref)
E-mail: customerservice@cqpress.com
Web site: http://www.cqpress.com
Dist(s): **MyiLibrary**
SAGE Pubns., Inc.
ebrary, Inc.; *CIP.*

CR Publishing, *(978-0-9982115)* 947 W. 5950 S., Spanish Fork, UT 84660 USA Tel 801-376-5982; Fax: 801-376-5982
E-mail: christina.utah@gmail.com.

CrackBoom! Bks. (CAN) *(978-2-9815807) Dist. by* **PerseuPGW.**

Cracker the Crab LLC, *(978-0-9725560)* P.O. Box 80475, Simpsonville, SC 29680-0475 USA Do not confuse with Two Bear Publishing Company in Alpine, CA
E-mail: jillkcogdill@twobearproducts.com; jcogdill@crackerthecrab.com; jkcogdill@msn.com
Web site: http://www.crackerthecrab.com.

Craig, Frankye, *(978-0-9794904)* 1735 Caughlin Creek Rd., Reno, NV 89519 USA Tel 775-747-1138; Fax: 775-747-1138
E-mail: FrankyeEBD@aol.com.

Craigmore Creations, *(978-0-9844422; 978-1-940052)* Orders Addr.: 4110 SE Hawthorne Blvd PMB 114, Portland, OR 97214-5246 USA (SAN 860-2786)
E-mail: info@craigmorecreations.com
Web site: http://www.craigmorecreations.com
Dist(s): **Independent Pubs. Group**
Partners/West Book Distributors.

Crain, Suzanne, *(978-0-9763254)* 10423 Brickey Rd., Red Bud, IL 62278-3519 USA
E-mail: slcrain@hcis.net.

Cram101 Inc., *(978-1-4288; 978-1-61654; 978-1-61698; 978-1-61744; 978-1-61461; 978-1-61490; 978-1-61812; 978-1-61830; 978-1-61905; 978-1-61906; 978-1-4672; 978-1-4784; 978-1-4902; 978-1-4970; 978-1-5388)* 40 W. Easy St., Suite 1, Simi Valley, CA 93021 USA (SAN 851-2175); 6593 Collins Dr., Ste. D18, Moorpark, CA 93021
E-mail: www.palitt.com
Web site: http://www.cram101.com.

Cranberry Quill Publishing Co., *(978-0-9741406; 978-0-9884899; 978-0-9914246; 978-0-9965986)* P.O. Box 26227, Fayetteville, NC 28301-4901 USA Tel 910-257-5109
E-mail: rgibbsquill@gmail.com; info@cranberryquill.com
Web site: http://www.cranberryquill.com.

Crane Bks., *(978-0-9647924)* Div. of Math in Motion, 668 Stony Hill Rd., No. 233, Yardley, PA 19067 USA Tel 215-321-5556; Fax: 215-310-9412
E-mail: info@mathinmotion.com
Web site: http://www.mathinmotion.com.

†**Crane Hill Pubs.,** *(978-0-9621455; 978-1-57587; 978-1-881548)* 3608 Clairmont Ave., Birmingham, AL 35222-3508 USA Tel 205-714-3007; Fax: 205-714-3008
E-mail: cranemail@cranehill.com
Web site: http://www.cranehill.com
Dist(s): **Independent Pubs. Group**; *CIP.*

Crane Institute of America, Inc., *(978-0-9744279; 978-0-9855502; 978-1-946269)* 3880 Saint Johns Pkwy., Sanford, FL 32771 USA Tel 407-322-6800; Fax: 407-330-0660; Toll Free: 800-832-2726
E-mail: annc@craneinstitute.com; info@craneinstitute.com
Web site: http://www.craneinstitute.com.

Crane Publishing, *(978-0-9753608)* 308 Trinity Rd., Venice, FL 34293 USA Do not confuse with companies with the same name in Paramus, New Jersey.
E-mail: jborza@josephborza.com; jborza@cranepublishing.net
Web site: http://www.cranepublishing.net.

Cranky Pants Publishing, LLC, *(978-0-9759627)* 2 Upland Rd., W., Arlington, MA 02474 USA
E-mail: ssanzo@yahoo.com
Dist(s): **Bookmasters Distribution.**

Crary Pubns., *(978-0-9743436; 978-0-9980887)* 5233 Painted Pebble St., North Las Vegas, NV 89081 USA
E-mail: tabrown@crarypublications.com
Web site: http://www.CraryPublications.com
Dist(s): **Lightning Source, Inc.**

Crawford, Dana, *(978-0-9742362)* 921 N. Chaparral, Suite 208, Corpus Christi, TX 78401-0208 USA
E-mail: wt.loss@ccinternet.net
Web site: http://www.naturalweight.net.

Crawford, Quinton Douglass, *(978-0-615-14879-3)* 225 Santa Ana Ct., Fairfield, CA 94533 USA
Web site: http://www.knowledgefortomorrow.com
Dist(s): **Lulu Pr., Inc.**

Crazy Man Press, LLC, *(978-0-9743553)* 33 University Sq., Suite 254, Madison, WI 53715-1042 USA Tel 608-215-0532
E-mail: info@crazymanpress.com
Web site: http://www.crazymanpress.com.

Crazy Pet Pr., The, *(978-0-9744749)* 655 N. Azusa Ave., No. 104, Azusa, CA 91708 USA Tel 831-438-2730; Fax: 831-438-2764; Toll Free: 877-860-2100
E-mail: kpbooks@calcentral.com
Web site: http://www.crazydog.com; http://www.crazypetpress.com; http://www.kidoodlepetpress.com.

†**CRC Pr. LLC,** *(978-0-8493; 978-0-87762; 978-0-87819; 978-0-935184; 978-1-56676; 978-1-57491; 978-1-58488; 978-1-58716; 978-1-4200; 978-1-4398; 978-1-4665; 978-1-4822; 978-1-4987; 978-1-351)* Subs. of Taylor & Francis, Inc., Orders Addr.: 6000 Broken Sound Pkwy., NW, Ste. 300, Boca Raton, FL 33487 USA Tel 800-272-7737 Toll Free Fax: 800-374-3401; Edit Addr.: 270 Madison Ave., New York, NY 10016 USA
E-mail: orders@crcpress.com; Theresa.Gutierrez@taylorandfrancis.com
Web site: http://www.crcpress.com; http://www.taylorandfrancis.com
Dist(s): **Ebsco Publishing**
Follett School Solutions
MyiLibrary
Oxford Univ. Pr., Inc.
Rittenhouse Bk. Distributors
Taylor & Francis Group
ebrary, Inc.; *CIP.*

CRE Lease Talk, Incorporated, *(978-0-9820726)* Orders Addr.: P.O. Box 341594, Memphis, TN 38134-1084 USA Tel 901-399-0967
E-mail: valencia.mackie@comcast.net; valencia@creleasetalk.com
Web site: http://www.CRELeaseTalk.com.

Create Loving Kindness, *(978-0-9977115)* 1313 N. Ritchie Ct., Chicago, IL 60610 USA Tel 310-220-7733
E-mail: debsmazor@gmail.com.

Created For You, *(978-0-615-17773-1; 978-0-615-17775-5; 978-0-9819968)* Orders Addr.: P.O. Box 4448, Horseshoe Bay, TX 78657 USA; Edit Addr.: 305 Sunspot, Horseshoe Bay, TX 78657-4448 USA Tel 830-596-2726
Dist(s): **Publishers Services.**

CreateSpace *See* **CreateSpace Independent Publishing Platform**

CreateSpace Independent Publishing Platform, *(978-1-58898; 978-1-5423; 978-1-59109; 978-1-59456; 978-1-59457; 978-1-4196; 978-1-4348; 978-1-4382; 978-1-4392; 978-1-4404; 978-1-4414; 978-1-4421; 978-1-61550; 978-1-4486; 978-1-4495; 978-1-4499; 978-1-4505; 978-1-4515; 978-1-4528; 978-1-4536; 978-1-4537; 978-1-4538; 978-1-4563; 978-1-4564; 978-1-4565; 978-1-61789; 978-1-4609; 978-1-4610; 978-1-4611; 978-1-61396; 978-1-61397; 978-1-4635; 978-1-4636; 978-1-4637; 978-1-4662; 978-1-4663; 978-1-4664; 978-1-61914; 978-1-61915; 978-1-61916; 978) Orders Addr.: 4900 LaCross Rd., North Charleston, SC 29406 USA (SAN 255-2132) Tel 843-225-4700 (Ask for ordering department); Fax: 843-577-7506; Toll Free: 866-308-6235; 4900 LaCross Rd., North Charleston, SC 29406*
E-mail: info@createspace.com
Web site: http://www.createspace.com.

Creation By Design, *(978-0-9828077; 978-1-936532)* 95 Bennett Rd., Teaneck, NJ 07666 USA Tel 914-714-3300
E-mail: CrtnByDsgn@aol.com
Dist(s): **Send The Light Distribution LLC.**

Creation Hse. *Imprint of* **Charisma Media**

Creation Instruction Publishing, *(978-1-928765)* Orders Addr.: P.O. Box 304, Plentywood, MT 59254 USA Tel 406-895-2689; Edit Addr.: 1770 S. Overland, Juniata, NE 68955 USA
E-mail: creation1@juno.com
Web site: http://www.creationinstruction.org/.

Creation Resource Foundation, *(978-0-9672713)* P.O. Box 570, El Dorado, CA 95667 USA Tel 530-626-4447; Fax: 530-626-5215; Toll Free: 800-497-1454
E-mail: info@creationresource.org
Web site: http://www.awesomeworks.com; http://www.creationresource.org/
Dist(s): **Send The Light Distribution LLC.**

Creative 3, LLC, *(978-1-933815)* 2236 E Spring Hill Rd., Springfield, MO 65804 USA Tel 417-882-2145; Fax: 417-882-2145; Toll Free Fax: 800-866-1360; Toll Free: 800-866-1360; *Imprints:* Quirkles, The (The Quirkles)
E-mail: info@quirkles.com; thequirkles@aol.com
Web site: http://www.quirkles.com.

Creative Attic, Inc., The, *(978-0-9653955)* P.O. Box 187, Canterbury, NH 03224 USA Tel 603-783-9103; Fax: 603-783-0118; Toll Free: 888-566-6539
E-mail: the5kids@aol.com.

Creative Bk. Publishing (CAN) *(978-0-920021; 978-0-920884; 978-1-895387; 978-1-894294; 978-1-897174; 978-1-77103) Dist. by* **Orca Bk Pub.**

Creative Bk. Pubs., *(978-0-9754818; 978-0-9763093; 978-0-9765467; 978-0-9779662; 978-0-9795460)* 1912 Falcon Dr., Ridgefield, WA 98642 USA
Web site: http://www.creativebookpublishers.com.

Creative Communication, *(978-1-60050)* Orders Addr.: P.O. Box 303, Smithfield, UT 84335 USA Tel 435-713-4411; Fax: 435-713-4422; Edit Addr.: 1488 . 200 W., Logan, UT 84341 USA Do not confuse with companies with the same or similar name in Forest Grove, OR, Seattle, WA, Trabuco Canyon, CA, NIxa, MO, Chelan, WA, La Mesa, CA, Kalamazoo, MI
E-mail: drtom@poeticpower.com
Web site: http://www.poeticpower.com.

Creative Co., The, *(978-0-87191; 978-0-88682; 978-0-89812; 978-1-56660; 978-1-56846; 978-1-58341; 978-1-60818; 978-1-62832; 978-1-68277; 978-1-64000; 978-1-64026)* 123 S. Broad St., Mankato, MN 56001 USA Tel 507-388-6273; Fax: 507-388-4797; Toll Free: 800-445-6209; *Imprints:* Creative Editions (Creative Eds); Creative Education (Creat Educ); Creative Paperbacks (Creative Paperbks) Do not confuse with The Creative Co., Lawrenceburg, IN
E-mail: info@thecreativecompany.us; kate.riggs@thecreativecompany.us
Web site: http://www.thecreativecompany.us
Dist(s): **Abraham Assocs. Inc.**
Hachette Bk. Group
RiverStream Publishing.

Creative Continuum, Inc., *(978-0-9713804; 978-1-932252; 978-1-62192)* 2910 E. La Palma Ave. Ste. C, Anaheim, CA 92806-2618 USA
E-mail: info@creativecontinuum.com
Web site: http://www.creativecontinuum.com.

Creative Conversations, *(978-0-9768235)* 11767 W. Coal Mine Dr., Littleton, CO 80127 USA Tel 303-437-8533.

Creative Cranium Concept, The, *(978-0-9741009)* Orders Addr.: 2560 Reed Ave, Marshalltown, IA 50158 USA Tel 303-875-8742; Edit Addr.: 2560 Reed Ave, Marshalltown, IA 50158 USA Tel 303-875-8742
E-mail: Rhonda@RhondaSpellman.com
Web site: http://www.rhondaspellman.com; http://AutismWithRhonda.com.

Creative Creature Publishing, *(978-0-9964983)* 22 Hampton Rd, Montgomery, IL 60538 USA Tel 630-440-3249
E-mail: creativecreaturepublishing@gmail.com
Web site: http://www.creativecreaturepublishing.com/.

Creative Curriculum Initiatives, *(978-0-9786500; 978-1-60409)* 80 Fifth Ave., Suite 1503, New York, NY 10011 USA Tel 212-242-7827; Fax: 212-242-3523.

Creative Dragon Pr., *(978-0-9831996)* 208A Oxhead Rd., Centereach, NY 11720 USA Tel 631-738-9082
E-mail: cheryl_orlassino@hotmail.com.

Creative Dreaming Ltd., *(978-0-615-14010-0; 978-0-615-14725-3; 978-0-615-15431-2; 978-0-615-15487-9; 978-0-615-15521-0; 978-0-615-16439-7; 978-0-615-17664-2; 978-0-615-18006-9; 978-0-615-18260-5; 978-0-615-18340-4; 978-0-615-18424-1; 978-0-615-18654-2; 978-0-615-18886-7; 978-0-615-23631-5) 6433 Topanga Canyon Blvd., No. 120, Woodland Hills, CA 91303 USA*
Dist(s): **Lulu Pr., Inc.**

Creative Editions *Imprint of* **Creative Co., The**

Creative Education *Imprint of* **Creative Co., The**

Creative Education & Publishing, *(978-0-9824964; 978-0-9825969; 978-0-9835315; 978-0-9859066; 978-0-9903851)* 3339 Ardley Ct., Falls Church, VA 22041 USA Tel 703-856-7005
E-mail: alameddine_kaddoura@yahoo.com; info@creativeeducationandpublishing.com
Web site: http://www.creativeeducationandpublishing.com.

Creative Educational Video *See* **C E V Multimedia, Ltd.**

Creative Energy, LLC, *(978-0-9821062; 978-0-9829825; 978-1-945372)* 20322 Sequoia Trace, Spring, TX 77379 USA (SAN 857-2771)
E-mail: drkmcleod@yahoo.com.

Creative Enterprises, *(978-1-880675)* 1040 Harvard Blvd., Dayton, OH 45406-5047 USA (SAN 253-5491) Tel 937-278-7159; Toll Free: 888-266-5777 Do not confuse with companies with the same or similar name in Mattapoisett, MA, Cordova, TN, Brooklyn, NY, Kittery, ME, Montgomery Village, MD
E-mail: allen45406@aol.com
Web site: http://creative-enterprises.org.

Creative Home & Family Endeavors, *(978-0-9747306)* 1555 Main St., Suite A-3-287, Windsor, CO 80550 USA Tel 970-221-0737
E-mail: endeavors4@aol.com.

†**Creative Homeowner,** *(978-0-932944; 978-1-58011; 978-1-880029)* Div. of Courier Corporation, 24 Park Way, Upper Saddle River, NJ 07458-9960 USA (SAN 213-6627) Tel 201-934-7100; Fax: 201-934-8971; Toll Free: 800-631-7795
E-mail: info@creativehomeowner.com
Web site: http://www.creativehomeowner.com
Dist(s): **Dover Pubns., Inc.**
Follett School Solutions
MyiLibrary; *CIP.*

Creative House Press *See* **Bourgeois Media & Consulting**

Creative Hse. Kids Pr. *Imprint of* **Bourgeois Media & Consulting**

Creative Image Pubs., *(978-0-9742667)* 102 E. Main, Georgetown, KY 40324 USA
E-mail: Kathy@creativeimagepublishers.com
Web site: http://www.creativeimagepublishers.com.

Creative Learning Books *See* **Aradiance Publishing**

Creative Learning Consultants, Incorporated *See* **Pieces of Learning**

Creative Learning Exchange, *(978-0-9753169; 978-0-9960128)* 27 Central St., Acton, MA 01720-3522 USA (SAN 850-8836) Tel 978-287-0070; Fax: 978-287-0080
E-mail: stuntzln@clexchange.org
Web site: http://www.clexchange.org.

Creative Life Publishing, *(978-0-9779072)* 210 Indian Oak Dr., No. 1163, Waleska, GA 30183 USA Tel 770-720-1975
E-mail: affiliate@caroleoconnell.com
Web site: http://www.caroleoconnell.com.

Creative Marketing Concepts, Inc., *(978-0-9761408)* 2775 Jade St., Mora, MN 55051 USA Tel 320-679-4105; Fax: 320-679-3349; Toll Free: 800-605-4280 Do not confuse with companies with the same name in Saint Louis, MO, Los Angeles, CA
E-mail: cmc@creativemk.com
Web site: http://www.creativemk.com.

Creative Media Partners, LLC, *(978-1-115; 978-1-4264; 978-1-4346; 978-1-4375; 978-0-554; 978-0-559; 978-0-526; 978-0-341; 978-0-469; 978-0-699; 978-1-103; 978-1-110; 978-1-113; 978-1-116; 978-1-117; 978-1-140; 978-1-141; 978-1-142; 978-1-143; 978-1-144; 978-1-145; 978-1-146; 978-1-147; 978-1-148; 978-1-149; 978-1-170; 978-1-171; 978-1-172; 978-1-173; 978-1-174; 978-1-175; 978-1-176; 978-1-177; 978-1-178; 978-1-179; 978-1-240;*

978-1-241; 978-1-242; 978-1-243; 978-1-244; 978-1-245; 978-1-246; 978-1-247; 978-1-248; 978-1-2) P.O. Box 21206, Charleston, SC 29413 USA Tel 843-696-0416; Fax: 843-853-9251; 33 Cannon St., Charleston, SC 29403 Tel 843-408-2303; Imprints: BiblioLife (Bibliolife); Nabu Press (Nabu Pr); British Library, Historical Print Editions (BritLibrary); Wentworth Press (Wentworth Pr) 11/15/05 Owner also owns Indigo, Inc. of Charleston, SC but the two companies are not connected. LT
E-mail: jason@creativmedia.io; info@bibliolife.com; info@bibliolabs.com
Web site: support.creativemedia.io; http://www.bibliobazaar.com; www.bibliolabs.com
Dist(s): **MyiLibrary.**

Creative Media Publishing, *(978-0-9826435; 978-0-9835393; 978-1-938438)* P.O. Box 6270, Whittier, CA 90609-6270 USA Tel 714-542-1212
E-mail: info@creativemedia.net
Web site: http://www.CreativeMedia.net
Dist(s): **Lulu Pr., Inc.**

Creative Medicine: Healing Through Words, LLC, *(978-0-9965324; 978-0-9986011; 978-978-099)* P.O. Box 2749, Tappahannock, VA 22560 USA Tel 804-833-4171
E-mail: Ronnie@creative-medicine.com
Web site: www.creative-medicine.com.

Creative Minds Pubns., *(978-0-9769737)* Orders Addr.: 2325 Crowncrest Dr., Richmond, VA 23233 USA Tel 804-740-6010; Fax: 804-798-1531
E-mail: kcstarke@aol.com
Dist(s): **Follett School Solutions.**

Creative Noggin, *(978-0-9899450)* 29610 Double Eagle Cir., Boerne, TX 78015 USA Tel 830-981-8222
E-mail: tracy@creativenoggin.com
Dist(s): **Independent Pubs. Group.**

Creative Nutrition & Wellness, *(978-0-615-12437-7)* P.O. Box 7000-233, Redondo Beach, CA 90277 USA Fax: 310-792-0428
Web site: http://www.creativenutrition.com.

Creative Paperbacks *Imprint of* **Creative Co., The**

Creative Publishing, *(978-0-9744833)* 2221 Justin Rd., No. 119-123, Flower Mound, TX 75028 USA Tel 281-251-1751 (phone/fax) Do not confuse with companies with the same or similar name in Roseboro, NC, Greenville, SC, Lawrenceville, GA, Shrevport, LA, College Station, TX, Tustin, CA
E-mail: support@creativekidsonthemove.com
Web site: http://www.creativekidsonthemove.com.

Creative Publishing Consultants, *(978-0-9824730)* 19 Hilltopper Ct., Blythewood, SC 29016-8745 USA.

Creative Publishing International *Imprint of* **Quarto Publishing Group USA**

Creative Publishing International *Imprint of* **Quarto Publishing Group USA**

Creative Quill Publishing, Inc., *(978-0-9709906)* Orders Addr.: P.O. Box 4028, Salem, OR 97302 USA; Edit Addr.: 460 Myers S., Salem, OR 97302 USA Tel 503-363-2843
E-mail: mavist@aol.com; Creativequill@aol.com
Web site: http://www.creativequill.us.

Creative Sharp Presentations, Incorporated *See* **SHARP Literacy, Inc.**

Creative Sources, *(978-0-9759613)* 105 N. Harvest Crest Ct., Highland, IL 62249 USA
E-mail: LLS@empowering.com
Web site: http://www.KidsDoRead.com; http://www.creativesourcespublishing.com.

Creative Styles *See* **JFW, Ltd.**

Creative Success Works, *(978-0-9759551)* 752 E. Lake Lndg., Marietta, GA 30062-3876 USA
E-mail: creativesuccess@comcast.net
Web site: http://www.creativesuccessworks.com.

Creative Teaching Assocs., *(978-1-878669; 978-1-930818; 978-1-931474; 978-1-932918)* Orders Addr.: P.O. Box 7766, Fresno, CA 93747 USA (SAN 297-6803) Tel 559-294-2141 Toll Free: 800-767-4282 (800-767-4CTA); Edit Addr.: P.O. Box 7766, Fresno, CA 93747-7766 USA
Web site: http://www.mastercta.com
Dist(s): **Follett School Solutions.**

Creative Teaching Pr., Inc., *(978-0-88160; 978-0-916119; 978-1-57471; 978-1-59198; 978-1-60689; 978-1-61601; 978-1-62186; 978-1-63445; 978-1-68310)* Orders Addr.: P.O. Box 2723, Huntington Beach, CA 92647-0723 USA Tel 714-895-5047; Fax: 714-895-6547; Toll Free Fax: 800-444-4287; Edit Addr.: 6262 Katella Ave., Cypress, CA 90630 USA (SAN 294-9180) Tel 714-895-5047; Toll Free Fax: 800-229-9929; Toll Free: 800-444-4287; *Imprints:* Learning Works, The (The Lrning Works)
E-mail: webmaster@creativeteaching.com; we.listen@creativeteaching.com
Web site: http://www.creativeteaching.com; http://www.thelearningworks.com; http://www.learntoreadkidsclub.com
Dist(s): **Follett School Solutions**
Pacific Learning, Inc.

Creative Thinkers, Incorporated *See* **Let's Think-kids Foundation, Inc.**

Creative Well, The, *(978-0-9700108)* P.O. Box 2121, Ashtabula, OH 44005 USA Tel 440-964-0338.

Creative with Words Pubns., *(978-0-936945)* P.O. Box 223226, Carmel, CA 93922 USA (SAN 658-6961) Fax: 408-655-8627
E-mail: cwwpub@usa.net.

Creative Works, *(978-0-9727499)* 3747 Redwood Cir., Palo Alto, CA 94306 USA Tel 650-493-3747.

Creative Writing & Publishing Co., *(978-1-887636)* P.O. Box 511848, Milwaukee, WI 53203-0311 USA
E-mail: Cbritt1@wi.rr.com.

Creative Writing Pr., Inc., *(978-0-9708382)* 1830 Stephenson Hwy., Troy, MI 48083-2173 USA Toll Free: 800-760-6397
E-mail: rodgers@mich.com
Web site: http://thepoetrylady.com.

CreativeMedia, Incorporated *See* **Creative Media Publishing**

Creativity Pr., *(978-1-934396; 978-0-9952290-2-0)* P.O. Box 1313, Anacortes, WA 98221 USA Do not confuse with Creativity Press in Cleveland, OH
E-mail: anne@Aanneolwin.com
Web site: http://www.creativitypress.com.

Creatopia Productions - Lamy, New Mexico, *(978-0-9637467; 978-0-9854527)* 31 Cerro Cir. # B, Lamy, NM 87540-9682 USA
E-mail: wrayl@hotmail.com
Web site: http://www.members.tripod.com/~lyne4lyne/
Dist(s): **Adventures Unlimited Pr.**
Barnes & Noble Bks.-Imports
CreateSpace Independent Publishing Platform.

Credo Hse. Pubs., *(978-0-9787620; 978-1-935391; 978-1-62586)* 3148 Plainfield Ave. NE., Suite 111, Grand Rapids, MI 49525-3285 USA
E-mail: connect@credocommunications.net
Web site: http://www.credocommunications.net.

Credo Italia, *(978-0-9768375)* Orders Addr.: 350 Bay St., Suite 100-124, San Francisco, CA 94123 USA
E-mail: info@ClintAdams.com
Web site: http://www.ClintAdams.com.

Creed, Julie, *(978-0-9728181)* 17 Los Abitos, Rancho Santa Margarita, CA 92688 USA
E-mail: julie@qabranding.com
Web site: http://www.qabranding.com.

Creek Sound Bks., *(978-0-9743840)* 120 Misty Way, Cosby, TN 37722 USA Tel 606-523-5324
E-mail: rapowell7@msn.com.

Creekside Publishing, *(978-0-9972349)* 14 Mill St., Morris, NY 13808 USA Tel 607-263-5531
E-mail: LesDieh60@aol.com
Web site: www.lesleyadiehl.com.

Creekside Publishing, *(978-0-692-69750-4)* 2310 Homestead Rd. Suite C1-155, Los Altos, CA 94024-7302 USA Tel 408-730-1511
E-mail: hansonreading@gmail.com
Web site: www.hansonreading.com.

Creepy Little Productions, *(978-0-9704159)* 3726 W. Augusta Ave., Phoenix, AZ 85051 USA Tel 602-625-6596; Fax: 602-242-3046
E-mail: christy@atgproductions.com; madamem@creepylittlestories.com
Web site: http://www.creepylittlestories.com
Dist(s): **PSI (Publisher Services, Inc.).**

Creevy, Anne *See* **ABC Bks.**

Creflo Dollar Ministries Pubns., *(978-1-931172; 978-1-59089)* Orders Addr.: P.O. Box 490124, College Park, GA 30349 USA Tel 770-210-5700; Fax: 770-210-5701; Edit Addr.: 2500 Burdett Rd., College Park, GA 30349 USA
E-mail: mfleming@worldchangers.org; mocarter@worldchangers.org; dfidler@worldchangers.org; tdavis@worldchangers.org
Web site: http://www.creflodollarministries.org
Dist(s): **Send The Light Distribution LLC.**

CreoXimius Publishing Company, *(978-0-9776617)* 970 E. Smith Rd., Medina, OH 44256 USA
Web site: http://www.debrae.com.

Crescent Moon Pr., *(978-0-9816011; 978-0-9818484; 978-0-9823065; 978-0-9841805; 978-0-9828200; 978-0-9846394; 978-1-937254; 978-1-939173; 978-0-9906274; 978-0-9908827; 978-0-9862871)* 1385 Hwy. 35, Box 269, Middletown, NJ 07748 USA
E-mail: publisher@crescentmoonpress.com
Web site: http://www.crescentmoonpress.com.

Crescent Moon Publishing (GBR) *(978-1-86171; 978-1-871846) Dist. by* **IndiCo.**

Crescent Renewal Resource *See* **Who Chains You**

CREST Pubns., *(978-0-9725546; 978-0-9912995)* P.O. Box 481022, Charlotte, NC 28269 USA Do not confuse with Crest Publications, Richardson, TX
Web site: http://www.crestpub.com.

Creston Bks., *(978-1-939547)* 965 Creston Rd., Berkeley, CA 94708 USA Tel 510-928-1765
E-mail: solsetimo@yahoo.com
Dist(s): **Publishers Group West (PGW)**
Two Rivers Distribution.

Crews Pubns., LLC, *(978-0-9795236)* 7483 Garnet Dr., Jonesboro, GA 30236 USA Tel 770-617-9688
E-mail: crewspublications@yahoo.com
Web site: http://www.gscrews.com.

Cribsheet Publishing *See* **Blue Shoe Publishing**

Cricket Bks., *(978-0-8126)* Div. of Carus Publishing Co., 70 E. Lake St. Ste. 300, Chicago, IL 60601-5945 USA Tel 312-701-1720
Web site: http://www.cricketmag.com/home.asp
Dist(s): **Cobblestone Publishing Co.**
Ebsco Publishing
Follett School Solutions.

Cricket Productions, Incorporated *See* **Scrumps Entertainment, Inc.**

Cricket XPress of Minnesota, *(978-0-9822534)* 504 Bluebird Ct., Sartell, MN 56377 USA Tel 320-267-8978
E-mail: CricketXPressMN@charter.net.

Crickhollow Bks. *Imprint of* **Great Lakes Literary, LLC**

CrimethInc. Workers' Collective, *(978-0-9709101; 978-0-9989822)* P.O. Box 13998, Salem, OR 97309 USA Tel 928-222-9129
E-mail: house@crimethinc.com
Web site: http://www.crimethinc.com
Dist(s): **AK Pr. Distribution.**

Crimson Cloak Publishing, *(978-0-692-30069-5; 978-0-692-31345-9; 978-0-692-32698-5; 978-0-692-33222-1; 978-0-692-36488-8; 978-1-68160)* P.O. Box 36, Pilot Knob, MO 63663 USA Tel 573-639-7591
E-mail: carly@crimsoncloakpublishing; rhianna_al_mere@yahoo.com
Web site: www.crimsoncloakpubliishing.com
Dist(s): **Ingram Publisher Services.**

Crimson Oak Publishing LLC, *(978-0-9822725; 978-0-9829505)* P.O. Box 1389, Pullman, WA 99163 USA
E-mail: info@crimsonoakpublishing.com
Web site: http://www.crimsonoakpublishing.com
Dist(s): **Smashwords.**

Crippen & Landru Pubs., *(978-1-885941; 978-1-932009; 978-1-936363)* Orders Addr.: P.O. Box 9315, Norfolk, VA 23505-9315 USA Tel 757-622-6656 (phone/fax); Toll Free: 877-622-6656 (phone/fax); Edit Addr.: 627 New Hampshire Ave., Norfolk, VA 23508 USA Tel 757-622-6656 (phone/fax)
E-mail: info@crippenlandru.com
Web site: http://www.crippenlandru.com
Dist(s): **Follett School Solutions.**

Criqueville Pr., *(978-0-9705404)* Orders Addr.: P.O. Box 1227, Princeton, NJ 08542-1227 USA Tel 908-359-7834; Edit Addr.: 2 Dogwood Ln., Princeton, NJ 08542-1227 USA (SAN 255-982X)
E-mail: criquevillepress@hotmail.com.

Crises Research Pr., *(978-0-86627)* 301 W. 45th St., New York, NY 10036 USA (SAN 238-9274).

Crispin Bks. *Imprint of* **Great Lakes Literary, LLC**

Crispus Medical Pr., *(978-0-9640389)* 7923 Leschi Rd., SW, Lakewood, WA 98498 USA Toll Free: 877-464-6469.

Cristal Publishing Co., *(978-0-9779124)* P.O. Box 14-4828, Coral Gables, FL 33114-4828 USA
E-mail: cristal228@bellsouth.net
Dist(s): **Ediciones Universal**
Follett School Solutions.

Critical Path Publishing, *(978-0-9740605)* P.O. Box 1073, Clayton, CA 94517-9073 USA Do not confuse with Critical Path Publishing Company in Denville, NJ
E-mail: cpp@silcon.com
Dist(s): **Book Publishing Co.**

Critical Thinking Books & Software *See* **Critical Thinking Co., The**

Critical Thinking Co., The, *(978-0-89455; 978-0-910974; 978-1-60144)* Orders Addr.: 1991 Sherman Ave Ste 200, North Bend, OR 97459 USA (SAN 207-0510) Tel 800-458-4849 Toll Free: 800-458-4849
E-mail: GaleO@criticalthinking.com; AbbeyH@criticalthinking.com; service@criticalthinking.com
Web site: http://www.criticalthinking.com
Dist(s): **Follett School Solutions.**

Critter Camp Inc., *(978-0-9772825)* 1190 Scenic Ave., Lummi Island, WA 98262 USA Tel 360-758-4269 (phone/fax)
E-mail: midiana@clearwire.net.

Critter Pubns., *(978-1-928972)* P.O. Box 413, Leicester, MA 01524-0413 USA
E-mail: del@critterp.com
Web site: http://www.critterp.com.

Critter Publishing, *(978-0-9754615)* Orders Addr.: P.O. Box 585, Readfield, ME 04355 USA Tel 207-685-5527 (phone/fax); Edit Addr.: 70 Walker Rd., Readfield, ME 04355 USA
E-mail: soniccomics@gwi.net
Web site: http://www.sonicpublishing.com.

Critters Up Close *Imprint of* **Wildlife Education, Ltd.**

CrittersInc, *(978-0-9745997)* 19611 Longview Terr., Salinas, CA 93908 USA
Web site: http://www.crittersinc.com.

CRM Enterprises, *(978-0-615-13155-9; 978-0-615-13278-5; 978-0-615-33279-6; 978-0-615-96051-7; 978-0-692-80739-2)* 411 Coram Avenue, Shelton, CT 06484 USA.

Croce, Pat & Co., *(978-0-9897533)* P.O. Box 520A, Villanova, PA 19085 USA Tel 610-520-1890; Fax: 610-525-5279
E-mail: sbarbacane@piratesoul.com.

Crocodile Bks. *Imprint of* **Interlink Publishing Group, Inc.**

Crocodiles Not Waterlilies Entertainment, *(978-0-9798297)* 58 Maiden Ln., Fifth Flr., San Francisco, CA 94108 USA (SAN 854-4921) Fax: 801-892-2230
E-mail: jodeen@crocpond.com.

Crofton Creek Pr., *(978-0-9700917; 978-0-9767268)* 2303 Gregg Rd., SW, South Boardman, MI 49680 USA Tel 231-369-2325; Fax: 231-369-4382; Toll Free: 877-255-3117
E-mail: publisher@croftoncreek.com
Web site: http://www.croftoncreek.com
Dist(s): **Partners Bk. Distributing, Inc.**
Wayne State Univ. Pr.

Cronies, *(978-1-929566)* Div. of Reproductive Images, 22738 Roscoe Blvd., No. 225, Canoga Park, CA 91304-3350 USA Tel 818-773-4888; Fax: 818-773-8808; Toll Free: 800-232-8099
E-mail: SethJ@CRONIES.com.

Cronus College, *(978-0-9760045; 978-0-9779897)* Div. of e-Pluribus Unum Publishing Co., P.O. Box 941, Lafayette, CA 94549 USA; *Imprints:* Reluctant Reader Books (ReluctRead)
Web site: http://www.cronuscollege.com.

Crooked Creek Publishing, LLC, *(978-0-9786084)* Orders Addr.: P.O. Box 479, Iola, WI 54945 USA Tel 715-445-5359; Edit Addr.: 460 E State St., Iola, WI 54945 USA
E-mail: crookedcreekpublishing@gmail.com
Dist(s): **Stevens International.**

Crooked River Pr., *(978-0-9778586)* P.O. Box 21, Cuyahoga Falls, OH 44221 USA Tel 330-701-3375; *Imprints:* Blue Jay Books (Blue Jay Bks)
E-mail: Books@CrookedRiverPress.com
Web site: http://www.CrookedRiverPress.com.

Crosam Pr., *(978-0-9774822; 978-0-9790337; 978-0-9798351; 978-0-9818903)* Orders Addr.: 681 Beverly Dr., Lake Wales, FL 33853 USA Tel 863-676-5737; Fax: 863-676-2285; Toll Free: 877-676-2285
E-mail: winksampson22@aol.com
Web site: http://www.feathersandfur.com; http://www.crosampress.com.

Crosby Advanced Medical Systems Inc., *(978-0-9846293)* 13556 Dornoch Dr., Ste. 1, Orlando, FL 32828 USA Tel 407-823-9502.

Cross & Crown Publishing, *(978-0-9785523; 978-0-9817728; 978-0-9886778)* 342 Meadow Green Dr., Ringgold, GA 30736 USA Tel 706-937-3798
E-mail: eddunlop@juno.com
Web site: http://www.dunlopministries.com
Dist(s): **Follett School Solutions.**

Cross Dove Publishing, LLC, *(978-0-9656513)* 1704 Esplanade, Front, Redondo Beach, CA 90277-8710 USA Tel 310-375-8400; Fax: 310-373-5912; 27 West 20Th St., New York, NY 10011
Web site: http://www.marysson.com; http://www.crossdove.com
Dist(s): **Follett School Solutions**
MyiLibrary.

Cross Pointe Printing, *(978-0-9742154)* 14417 N. 42nd St., Phoenix, AZ 85032-5437 USA
E-mail: dan@crosspointeprinting.com.

Cross Product Pubns., *(978-0-9793087; 978-0-9826837)* 3222 Cascade Hills Dr., NW, Cleveland, TN 37312 USA.

Cross Pubns., *(978-0-9771926; 978-0-9850996)* Orders Addr.: 502 E. Liberty Ave., Stillwater, OK 74075 USA Tel 405-564-5641 Do not confuse with Cross Publications in Safford, AZ, Savannah, GA
Web site: www.lulu.com/greenpheon7
Dist(s): **Lulu Pr., Inc.**

Cross Reference Imprints, *(978-0-9725139)* 3607 Hycliffe Ave., Louisville, KY 40207 USA Tel 502-897-2719
E-mail: Pneuma@eclipsetel.com.

Cross Time *Imprint of* **Crossquarter Publishing Group**

Cross Training Publishing, *(978-1-887002; 978-1-929478; 978-0-9821652; 978-0-9845750; 978-1-938254)* P.O. Box 1874, Keary, NE 68848 USA (SAN 298-7406) Tel 308-293-3891; Fax: 308-338-2058; Toll Free: 800-430-8588
E-mail: gordon@crosstrainingpublishing.com; gthiessen@mac.com
Web site: http://www.crosstrainingpublishing.com
Dist(s): **Follett School Solutions.**

CrossBearers Publishing, *(978-0-9716365)* Div. of Reconciliation Ministries, Inc., Orders Addr.: 3101 Troost Ave., Kansas City, MO 64109 USA Tel 816-931-4751; Fax: 816-931-0142; P.O. Box 45642, Kansas City, MO 64171 Tel 816-449-2825; Fax: 816-449-5231; *Imprints:* St. Nicholas Press (St Nich Pr)
E-mail: frpaisius@hotmail.com; stnicholaspress@gmail.com
Web site: http://www.stmaryofegypt.net/.

CrossGeneration Comics, Inc., *(978-1-931484; 978-1-59314)* 9030 Lake Chase Island Way, Tampa, FL 33626-1942 USA
E-mail: jbreitbeil@crossgen.com
Web site: http://www.crossgen.com
Dist(s): **Diamond Comic Distributors, Inc.**

Crossing Guard Bks. *Imprint of* **Crossing Guard Bks., LLC**

Crossing Guard Bks., LLC, *(978-0-9770141)* Orders Addr.: P.O. Box 1792, Loveland, CO 80538 USA Tel 970-672-8078; *Imprints:* Crossing Guard Books (CrossGrdBks)
E-mail: Sarah@CrossingGuardBooks.com
Web site: http://www.CrossingGuardBooks.com.

Crossing Pr *Imprint of* **Potter/TenSpeed/Harmony**

Crossing Trails Pubns., *(978-0-9726095)* 4804 Kentwood Ln., Woodbridge, VA 22193 USA Tel 703-590-4449; Fax: 703-878-2119
E-mail: whnesbitt@compuserve.com
Web site: http://www.crossingtrails.com.

Cross-Lengua Productions *See* **KALEXT Productions, LLC**

Cross-Over, *(978-0-9749455; 978-0-9882835; 978-0-9987894)* 190 Vista Linda Ave., Durango, CO 81303 USA Tel 970-385-1809 (phone/fax); Toll Free: 866-385-1809
E-mail: info@homeschoolhowtos.com
Web site: http://fastphonics.weebly.com/; http://homeschoolhowtos.com/.

Crossover Comics *See* **Gavila Publishing**

Crossquarter Publishing Group, *(978-1-890109)* Div. of Earth Healers Inc., Orders Addr.: P.O. Box 23749, Santa Fe, NM 87502 USA Tel 505-690-3923 (phone); Fax: 214-975-9715 (fax); Edit Addr.: P.O. Box 23749, Santa Fe, NM 87502-3749 USA; *Imprints:* Cross Time (Crosstime)
E-mail: info@crossquarter.com
Web site: http://www.crossquarter.com
Dist(s): **Follett School Solutions**
New Leaf Distributing Co., Inc.

Crossroad Pr., *(978-0-9834348; 978-1-937530; 978-1-941408; 978-1-946025)* 141 Brayden Dr., HERTFORD, NC 27944 USA Tel 252-340-3952
E-mail: publisher@crossroadpress.com
Web site: http://store.crossroadpress.com
Dist(s): **Follett School Solutions.**

†Crossroad Publishing Co., The, *(978-0-8245)* 831 Chestnut Ridge Rd., Spring Valley, NY 10977-6356 USA (SAN 287-0118); 814 N. Franklin St., Chicago, IL 60610
E-mail: office@crossroadpublishing.com; publisher@crossroadpublishing.com
Web site: http://www.crossroadpublishing.com
Dist(s): **Independent Pubs. Group**; *CIP.*

CrossStaff Publishing, *(978-0-9743876; 978-0-9800755)* P.O. Box 288, Broken Arrow, OK 74013 USA Tel 918-369-9293; Fax: 413-723-4384; Toll Free: 866-862-2278
E-mail: info@crossstaff.com
Web site: http://www.crossstaff.com.

Crosswalk Bks., *(978-0-9746269)* P.O. Box 176, American Fork, UT 84003 USA (SAN 255-7657)
Web site: http://www.crosswalkbooks.com.

†Crossway, *(978-0-89107; 978-1-58134; 978-1-4335; 978-1-68216)* Div. of Good News Pubs., 1300 Crescent St., Wheaton, IL 60187 USA (SAN 211-7991) Tel 708-682-4300; Fax: 630-682-4785; Toll Free:

Publisher Name Index

800-323-3890 (sales only); *Imprints:* Crossway Bibles (Crossway Bibles)
E-mail: permissions@gnpcb.org
Web site: http://www.crossway.org
Dist(s): **L I M Productions, LLC**
Vision Video; *CIP.*
Crossway Bibles *Imprint of* **Crossway**
Crossway Books *See* **Crossway**
Crossways International, *(978-1-891245)* 7930 Computer Ave., S., Minneapolis, MN 55435-5415 USA Tel 952-832-5454; Fax: 952-832-5553; Toll Free: 800-257-7308
E-mail: info@crossways.org
Web site: http://www.crossways.org.
Crosswinds Bks., *(978-0-9726573)* P.O. Box 143, Keller, TX 76244 USA
E-mail: jroach35@earthlink.net.
Crosswinds Pr., Inc., *(978-0-9825559; 978-0-9838155)* 126 Crosswinds Dr., Groton, CT 06340 USA
Web site: http://www.crosswindspress.com.
Crouch, Valeria *See* **Zig the Pig**
Crouse, Donna J., *(978-0-9765339)* P.O. Box 250, Jersey, VA 22481 USA Tel 540-775-7787; Fax: 540-775-1682
E-mail: df_crouse@msn.com.
Crow Dog Pr., *(978-0-9727656)* 541 Hunter Ave., Modesto, CA 95350 USA
E-mail: jackrandom@earthlink.net
Web site: http://www.jackrandom.com.
Crow Flies Pr., *(978-0-9814910; 978-0-9983139)* P.O. Box 614, South Egremont, MA 01258 USA (SAN 855-7144)
E-mail: publisher@crowfliespress.com
Web site: http://www.crowfliespress.com
Dist(s): **BookBaby**
Follett School Solutions
SCB Distributors.
Crow, R.L. Pubns., *(978-0-9722958; 978-0-9971780)* P.O. Box 262, Penn Valley, CA 95946 USA
E-mail: wsgainer@comcast.net
Dist(s): **SPD-Small Pr. Distribution.**
Crowder, Jack L., *(978-0-9616589)* Orders Addr.: P.O. Box 250, Bernalillo, NM 87004 USA (SAN 659-8064) Tel 505-867-5812 (phone/fax); Edit Addr.: 500 Beehive Ln., Bernalillo, NM 87004 USA (SAN 659-8072)
E-mail: crowdercon@aol.com.
Crowell, Peter T. Pubns., *(978-0-9740290)* 1323 Marlborough St., Philadelphia, PA 19125 USA
E-mail: petertcrowell@gmail.com
Web site: http://www.petertcrowell.com
Dist(s): **Partners Bk. Distributing, Inc.**
Crown *Imprint of* **Crown/Archetype**
Crown Books For Young Readers *Imprint of* **Random Hse. Children's Bks.**
Crown Hse. Publishing, *(978-1-899836; 978-1-904424; 978-1-84590; 978-0-9823573; 978-1-935810; 978-1-78135; 978-1-78583)* Orders Addr.: P.O. Box 2223, Williston, VT 05495 USA Fax: 802-864-7626; Toll Free: 877-925-1213; Edit Addr.: Crown Bldg., Bancyfelin, Carmarthen, Dyfed SA33 5ND GBR Tel 01267 211345; 01267 211880; Fax: 01267 211882; 01267 211593; 6 Trowbridge Dr., Suite 5, Bethel, CT 06801 Tel 203-778-1300; Fax: 203-778-9100; Toll Free: 866-272-8497
E-mail: books@crownhouse.co.uk; info@CHPUS.com
Web site: http://www.crownhouse.co.uk/; http://www.CHPUS.com; http://www.crownhousepublishing.com
Dist(s): **MyiLibrary.**
Crown Media Publishing *See* **Crown Media Publishing**
Crown Media Publishing, *(978-0-692-60979-8; 978-0-692-61041-1; 978-0-692-61106-7; 978-0-692-61190-6; 978-0-692-63234-5; 978-0-692-63291-8; 978-0-692-63333-5; 978-0-9990279)* P.O. Box 4838, Omaha, NE 68104 USA Tel 4025782578
Dist(s): **CreateSpace Independent Publishing Platform.**
Crown Peak Publishing, *(978-0-9645663)* Orders Addr.: P.O. Box 317, New Castle, CO 81647 USA Tel 970-618-1748
E-mail: ann@crownpeakpublishing.com
Web site: http://www.methetree.com; http://www.annlouiseramsey.com; http://www.crownpeakpublishing.com; http://www.justbeyoubook.com; http://www.tamingthedragon.net; http://www.icannotsleep.net.
†Crown Publishing Group, Div. of Random Hse., Inc., Orders Addr.: 400 Hahn Rd., Westminster, MD 21157 USA Tel 410-848-1900; Toll Free Fax: 800-659-2436; Toll Free: 800-733-3000; 800-726-0600; Edit Addr.: 1745 Broadway, New York, NY 10019 USA (SAN 200-2639) Tel 212-751-2600; Toll Free Fax: 800-659-2436; *Imprints:* Multnomah Books (Multnom Bks); WaterBrook Press (WaterBrook)
E-mail: customerservice@randomhouse.com; crownpublicity@randomhouse.com
Web site: http://www.randomhouse.com/
Dist(s): **Follett School Solutions**
MyiLibrary
Penguin Random Hse. LLC
Random Hse., Inc.; *CIP.*
Crown/Archetype, 1745 Broadway, New York, NY 10019 USA; *Imprints:* Broadway Books (BwayBks); Crown (CrowA)
Dist(s): **Penguin Random Hse. LLC.**
Crowne Pointe *See* **White Phoenix**
Crowned Warrior Publishing *Imprint of* **Walters, Steve Ministries**
Crowood Pr., Ltd. (GBR) *(978-0-946284; 978-1-85223; 978-1-86126; 978-1-84797; 978-1-78500) Dist. by* **IPG Chicago.**
Crowood Pr., Ltd. (GBR) *(978-0-946284; 978-1-85223; 978-1-86126; 978-1-84797; 978-1-78500) Dist. by* **HachBkGrp.**
CrowsNest Publishing, *(978-0-9710225)* 11513 Crows Nest Rd., Clarksville, MD 21029-1601 USA Tel 410-531-3110
E-mail: hannon@erols.com.
Crowther, Debra, *(978-0-9741295)* P.O. Box 1870, Three Rivers, TX 78071 USA Tel 361-786-4703; Fax: 361-786-2579
Web site: http://www.jackthewestie.com.
Cruce de Caminos, *(978-0-9885392)* 10 Akron St., Suite 100, Cambridge, MA 02138-1281 USA Tel 617-384-9499
E-mail: crucedecaminos.org@gmail.com.
Crucifiction Games, *(978-0-9778263)* P.O. Box 654, Selah, WA 98942 USA Tel 509-697-7393; 509-952-6270
E-mail: cweedin@crucifictiongames.com
Web site: http://www.crucifictiongames.com
Dist(s): **Lightning Source, Inc.**
Crumb Elbow Publishing, *(978-0-89904)* P.O. Box 294, Rhododendron, OR 97049 USA (SAN 679-128X) Tel 503-622-4798.
CrumbGobbler Pr. *Imprint of* **Downtown Wetmore Pr.**
Crumly, Billie, *(978-0-9760577)* P.O. Box 281, Geraldine, AL 35974 USA.
Crumm, David Media, LLC, *(978-1-934879; 978-1-939880; 978-1-942011)* 42015 Ford Rd., Suite 234, Canton, MI 48187 USA (SAN 855-3637) Tel 734-786-3813
E-mail: admin@DavidCrummMedia.com
Web site: http://www.ReadTheSpirit.com.
Crunchpeep Media, *(978-0-9749469)* a/o Steven Merahn, 1700 Market St., 6th Flr., Philadelphia, PA 19103 USA Tel 215-832-0181
E-mail: smerahn@crunchpeep.com.
Crush Publishing, *(978-0-9798869; 978-0-9853434; 978-0-9910756)* Orders Addr.: 8209 Foothill Blvd No. A124, Sunland, CA 91040 USA Do not confuse with Crush Publishing in Brooklyn, NY
E-mail: wink@crushpublishing.com
Web site: http://www.crushpublishing.com.
Crushing Hearts and Black Butterfly Publishing, *(978-0-615-60362-9; 978-0-615-60460-2; 978-0-615-60592-0; 978-0-615-60593-7; 978-0-615-60597-5; 978-0-615-61380-2; 978-0-615-61435-9; 978-0-615-62403-7; 978-0-615-63475-3; 978-0-615-66682-2; 978-0-615-66683-9; 978-0-615-66684-6; 978-0-615-66760-7; 978-0-615-67525-1; 978-0-615-68166-5; 978-0-615-68247-1; 978-0-615-69025-4; 978-0-615-70249-0; 978-0-615-70607-8; 978-0-615-70608-5; 978-0-615-70656-6; 978-0-615-71144-7; 978-0-615-72063-0; 978-0-615-72064-7; 978-0-615-72065-4; 978-0-615-72906-0;) 710 Saratoga Cir., Algonquin, IL 60102 USA Tel 224-234-9677*
Web site: www.crushingheartsandblackbutterfly.com
Dist(s): **CreateSpace Independent Publishing Platform.**
Crying Cougar Pr., *(978-0-615-31150-0; 978-0-615-33106-5; 978-0-615-34888-9; 978-0-615-40439-4; 978-0-615-53634-7; 978-0-9859802)* 3559 Ruffin Rd. Suite 155, San Diego, CA 92123 USA
Dist(s): **Smashwords.**
Crysalis Publishing, Inc., *(978-0-9745190)* 10 Main St., Suite 4A, PMB 227, Woodbridge, NJ 07095 USA
Web site: http://www.chrysalispublishinc.com.
crysta luna studios, *(978-0-615-43657-9; 978-0-9887006)* 14995 SW Onyx Ct., Beaverton, OR 97007 USA Tel 503-933-1817
E-mail: smirlsmirl@gmail.com.
Crystal Ball Publishing, LLC., *(978-1-932277)* 107 Skiff Ave., Frankfort, NY 13340 USA
E-mail: Nerbo@msn.com; Sales@CrystalBallPublishing.com; Insight@CrystalBallPublishing.com
Web site: http://www.crystalballpublishing.com; http://www.gypsykids.com.
Crystal Clarity Pubs., *(978-0-916124; 978-1-56589; 978-1-878265)* 14618 Tyler-Foote Rd., Nevada City, CA 95959 USA (SAN 201-1778) Tel 530-478-7600 (intl. orders, cust. serv.); Fax: 530-478-7610 (orders); Toll Free: 800-424-1055
E-mail: sales@crystalclarity.com
Web site: http://www.crystalclarity.com
Dist(s): **Instructional Video**
Koen Pacific
MyiLibrary
National Bk. Network
New Leaf Distributing Co., Inc.
Nutri-Bks. Corp.
Princeton Bk. Co. Pubs.
ebrary, Inc.
Crystal Journeys Publishing, *(978-1-880737)* 130 Cochise Dr., Sedona, AZ 86351-7927 USA Tel 520-284-5730
Dist(s): **Light Technology Publishing, LLC.**
Crystal Mosaic Bks., *(978-0-9836303; 978-0-9911061; 978-0-9981136)* PO Box 1276, Hillsboro, OR 97123 USA Tel 971-645-3204
E-mail: liome45@hotmail.com.
Crystal Pr., *(978-0-9632123; 978-0-9670886; 978-0-9746109)* 1750 Orr Ave., Simi Valley, CA 93065 USA Tel 805-527-4369; Fax: 805-582-3949 Do not confuse with Crystal Pr. in Houston, TX
E-mail: crystalpress@aol.com
Web site: http://www.Crystalpress.org.
Crystal Productions, *(978-0-924509; 978-1-56290)* Orders Addr.: 1812 Johns Dr., Glenview, IL 60025 USA (SAN 920-8224); Edit Addr.: 1812 Johns Dr., Glenview, IL 60025 USA (SAN 653-2489) Tel 847-657-8144; Fax: 847-657-8149; Toll Free Fax: 800-657-8149; Toll Free: 800-255-8629
E-mail: custserv@crystalproductions.com
Web site: http://www.crystalproductions.com
Dist(s): **Baker & Taylor Fulfillment, Inc.**
Follett School Solutions.
Crystal Springs Bks. *Imprint of* **Staff Development for Educators**
CS Media Resources, *(978-0-9764992)* Orders Addr.: 12 W. Willow Grove Ave. Suite 121, Philadelphia, PA 19118-3952 USA Toll Free: 877-866-8309
E-mail: csmr@csmediaresources.com
Web site: http://www.csmediaresources.com.
CSE Publishing, *(978-0-9743567)* 706 Radcliffe Ave., Lynn Haven, FL 32444-3039 USA (SAN 255-5581) Fax: 850-271-9874; Toll Free: 866-262-8776
E-mail: tchardy@bellsouth.net.
CSI Publishing *See* **Decere Publishing**
CSIRO Publishing (AUS) *(978-1-922173; 978-1-4863) Dist. by* **Stylus Pub VA.**
CSS Backlist *Imprint of* **Chicken Soup for the Soul Publishing, LLC**
CSS Publishing, *(978-0-9721679)* 108A Gallegos Ln., Tularosa, NM 88352 USA (SAN 254-6477) Fax: 505-585-4908 Do not confuse with C S S Publishing Company in Lima, OH
E-mail: rblanks@netmdc.com; csspublishing@hotmail.com.
CT Bookshelf, *(978-0-9837301; 978-0-9972140; 978-0-9974963)* 309 4th St. SE No. 5, Washington, DC 20003 USA Tel 202-546-7126
E-mail: author.travis@gmail.com
Web site: www.travisbooks.com.
CTC Publishing, *(978-0-9747789; 978-1-934073)* 10431 Lawyers Rd., Vienna, VA 22181-2822 USA (SAN 851-7908) Toll Free: 800-942-0962
E-mail: pitts@ndmc.com
Web site: http://www.couragetochange.com/
Dist(s): **Follett School Solutions.**
Ctr. for Curatorial Studies *Imprint of* **Bard College Pubns. Office**
Ctrl+Alt+Del Prodns., *(978-0-9764678)* P.O. Box 206392, New Haven, CT 06520 USA Tel 508-274-5804
E-mail: absath@ctrlaltdel-online.com
Web site: http://www.ctrlaltdel-online.com.
Cub Bks. *Imprint of* **Global Business Information Strategies, Inc.**
Cubbie Blue Publishing, *(978-0-9706341; 978-1-932824)* 546 Flanders Dr., Saint Louis, MO 63122-1618 USA
E-mail: rahandler@earthlink.net
Web site: ravencrestpublishing.com
Dist(s): **BookBaby.**
Cubby Hole Tales, *(978-0-9754591)* 524 Moores Mill Rd., Pelzer, SC 29669 USA Tel 864-947-6426
E-mail: telvajo@bellsouth.net
Web site: http://www.talesfromtwocousins.com.
Cube Marketing, *(978-0-9893091)* 51 9th Ave., Newark, NJ 07107 USA Tel 973-482-4101
E-mail: deidre.knight@gmail.com.
Cuccia, Louis, *(978-0-9727415)* 603 Winthrop, Smyrna, TN 37167 USA Tel 615-355-6821; Fax: 615-355-0171
E-mail: Lcuccia@aol.com.
Cuddehe Services *See* **Found Link**
Cullor Bks. (CAN) *(978-0-9684576) Dist. by* **Lone Pine.**
Cully, Amanda, *(978-0-9971120)* 5303 e village rd, Long beach, CA 90808 USA Tel 562-494-6179
E-mail: Blebow75@aol.com.
Culpepper, Felix International, Inc., *(978-0-9740435)* Orders Addr.: P.O. Box 70, Jefferson City, TN 37760-0070 USA (SAN 255-2752) Tel 865-475-4993; Fax: 914-470-1091; Edit Addr.: 2476 Tarr Rd., Talbott, TN 37877 USA
E-mail: gfac@cshore.com; peteculpepper@helpkidswhohavecancer.org; pete@felixculpepper.com
Web site: http://www.bigboxhead.com; http://www.felixculpepper.com
Dist(s): **American Wholesale Bk. Co.**
Cult Classics Pub., *(978-0-692-54687-1; 978-0-9981068)* 1613 A Black Duck Terr., Carrollton, TX 75010 USA Tel 214-731-8767
Web site: www.Cultclassicspublisher.com
Dist(s): **CreateSpace Independent Publishing Platform.**
Cultural Connections, *(978-0-9636629; 978-1-57371)* 23499 Shakeridge Rd., Volcano, CA 95689 USA Toll Free: 888-234-5412
E-mail: culture123@volcano.net.
Culturatti Ink, *(978-0-9712383; 978-0-692-42185-7; 978-0-692-42186-4; 978-0-692-92033-6)* 9465 Counselors Row Suite 200, Indianapolis, IN, IN 46240 USA
E-mail: erika@culturattikids.net
Web site: http://www.culturattiink.com.
Culture Connection, The *See* **Culturatti Ink**
Culture Hse., *(978-0-9676080; 978-0-9819484)* Orders Addr.: P.O. Box 293, Newton, IA 50208 USA Tel 641-792-0920; Edit Addr.: 3830 Harbor Ave., Newton, IA 50208-9040 USA
E-mail: museum@pcpartner.net
Web site: http://www.mike-chapman.com.
Culture of Life, Inc., *(978-0-9761457)* 1054 Windy Knoll Rd., West Chester, PA 19382-7433 USA.
CultureGrams World Edition *Imprint of* **ProQuest LLC**
Culturelink Pr., *(978-0-9759276)* Orders Addr.: P.O. Box 3538, San Diego, CA 92163 USA (SAN 256-1174); Edit Addr.: 1435 Essex St., No.3, San Diego, CA 92103 USA
Web site: http://www.culturelinkpress.com.
Cumberland Hse. *Imprint of* **Sourcebooks, Inc.**
Cummings Pr., *(978-0-9767063)* 1939 Mt. Vernon Pl., Dunwoody, GA 30338-4417 USA Tel 770-512-8115 (phone/fax).
Cummins Associates International *See* **CAI Publishing**
Cummins, Judi, *(978-0-9760377)* Orders Addr.: P.O. Box 10 Chosen Spot Apartments, Canandaigua, NY 14424 USA
E-mail: jcummins1@rochester.rr.com.
Cumquat Publishing Company *See* **Floppinfish Publishing Co., Ltd.**
Cumuli, *(978-0-9709730)* Div. of Cumuli, Inc., P.O. Box 1174, Port Orchard, WA 98366 USA Tel 360-871-9493 (phone/fax)
E-mail: fletcher@cumuli.com; susan@cumuli.com
Web site: http://www.cumuli.com; http://www.cumulipress.com.
Cune *See* **Cune Pr., LLC**
Cune Pr., LLC, *(978-1-885942; 978-1-61457)* Div. of Scott Davis Co., P.O. Box 31024, Seattle, WA 98103 USA (SAN 298-3648) Tel 206-789-7055; Fax: 206-774-0592
E-mail: bowker@cunepress.com
Web site: http://www.cunepress.com; http://www.cunepress.net
Dist(s): **Bolchazy-Carducci Pubs.**
Smashwords.
Cupola Pr., *(978-0-9793345; 978-0-9834046; 978-0-9857932)* 3280 Withers Ave., Lafayette, CA 94549-2128 USA Tel 925-285-7754
E-mail: info@cupolapress.com
Web site: http://www.cupolapress.com
Dist(s): **Independent Pubs. Group**
MyiLibrary.
Curbside Splendor Publishing, *(978-0-615-40443-1; 978-0-9834228; 978-0-9884804; 978-0-9888258; 978-1-940430; 978-1-945883)* 2816 N. Kedzie No. 2, Chicago, IL 60618 USA Tel 312-342-5935
E-mail: victor@curbsidesplendor.com
Web site: www.curbsidesplendor.com
Dist(s): **Consortium Bk. Sales & Distribution**
MyiLibrary.
†Curbstone Pr., *(978-0-915306; 978-1-880684; 978-1-931896)* P.O. Box 45, Willimantic, CT 06226-0045 USA (SAN 209-4282)
E-mail: info@curbstone.org
Web site: http://www.curbstone.org
Dist(s): **Chicago Distribution Ctr.**
Lectorum Pubns., Inc.
SPD-Small Pr. Distribution; *CIP.*
Curcumin Bks. *Imprint of* **Davlaw Press**
Curiosity Quills Pr., *(978-1-62007)* Orders Addr.: P.O. Box 2160, Reston, VA 20195 USA (SAN 920-9700) Tel 800-998-2509
E-mail: editor@curiosityquills.com
Web site: http://curiosityquills.com.
Curiosmith, *(978-0-9817505; 978-1-935626; 978-1-941281; 978-1-946145)* P.O. Box 390293, Minneapolis, MN 55439-0293 USA (SAN 856-4450)
E-mail: shopkeeper@curiosmith.com
Web site: http://www.curiosmith.com.
Curious Kids Guides, *(978-0-9789140)* 2561 Bunker Hill, Ann Arbor, MI 48105-3432 USA Tel 734-665-0533
E-mail: eisbruchs@aol.com
Web site: http://www.CuriousKidsGuides.com
Dist(s): **Partners Bk. Distributing, Inc.**
CuriousDots, *(978-0-9893751)* 81 Prospect St., Acton, MA 01720 USA Tel 978-263-1713; Fax: 978-263-1713
E-mail: curiousdots@gmail.com.
Currach Pr. (IRL) *(978-1-85607) Dist. by* **Dufour.**
Curran, M.J., *(978-0-9768984)* 640 Gooseberry Dr., No. 1207, Longmont, CO 80503 USA Tel 720-206-9099
E-mail: mjcurran@hotmail.com.
Curran Pr. and Editorial Consulting, LLC, *(978-1-970002)* 20 Smith Rd., Rockport, MA 01966 USA
E-mail: damaris@curraneditorial.com
Web site: www.curranpress.curraneditorial.com.
Currency Pr. (AUS) *(978-0-86819; 978-0-9596937; 978-1-921428; 978-1-921429; 978-1-925004; 978-1-925005; 978-1-925210; 978-1-925359; 978-1-76062) Dist. by* **Antipodes Bks.**
Current Clinical Strategies Publishing, *(978-0-9626030; 978-1-881528; 978-1-929622; 978-1-934323)* P.O. Box 1753, Blue Jay, CA 92317 USA (SAN 298-4490) Tel 949-348-8404; Fax: 949-348-8405; Toll Free Fax: 800-965-9420; Toll Free: 800-331-8227
E-mail: info@ccspublishing.com
Web site: http://www.ccspublishing.com/ccs
Dist(s): **Majors, J. A. Co.**
Matthews Medical Bk. Co.
Rittenhouse Bk. Distributors.
Current Publishing Corp., *(978-1-878663)* 30151 Tomas St., Rancho Santa Margarita, CA 92688 USA Toll Free: 800-729-7234.
Curriculum Associates, Incorporated *See* **Curriculum Assocs., LLC**
Curriculum Assocs., LLC, *(978-0-7609; 978-0-89187; 978-1-55915; 978-1-4957)* Orders Addr.: P.O. Box 2001, North Billerica, MA 01862-0901 USA (SAN 659-6304) Toll Free: 800-225-0248; Edit Addr.: 153 Rangeway Rd., North Billerica, MA 01862 USA Tel 978-667-8000; Toll Free Fax: 800-366-1158; Toll Free: 800-225-0248
E-mail: DAndreoli@CAinc.com; info@curriculumassociates.com; info@cainc.com
Web site: http://www.curriculumassociates.com.
Curriculum Publishing, Presbyterian Church (U. S. A.), *(978-1-57153)* 100 Witherspoon St., Louisville, KY 40202-1396 USA Tel 502-569-5090; Fax: 502-569-8329; Toll Free: 800-524-2612; *Imprints:* Witherspoon Press (Witherspoon Pr)
Web site: http://www.pcusa.org/pcusa/currpub; http://www.bridgeresources.org
Dist(s): **Westminster John Knox Pr.**
Currie & Smith Publishing *See* **T.Y.M. Publishing**
Currier Davis Publishing *See* **GRAND Media, LLC**
Curry Brothers Publishing Group, *(978-0-9798364; 978-0-9818956)* 608 Sandy Spring Trail, Madison, TN 37115 USA
E-mail: cbmpg@yahoo.com
Web site: http://currybrotherspublishing.com.
Curry, Dean Bks., *(978-0-9835022)* 1717 S. Union Ave., Tacoma, WA 98405 USA Tel 253-756-5310
E-mail: hschmick@life-center.org.
Cursack Bks., *(978-1-933439)* 31 Hubbard Rd., Dover, NH 03820 USA
E-mail: info@cursackbooks.com
Web site: http://www.cursackbooks.com
Dist(s): **Ediciones Universal.**
Curtis Elliott Designs, Ltd., *(978-0-9742438)* 5250 Franklin St., Unit C-1, Hilliard, OH 43026 USA Tel 614-771-7978
E-mail: info@creativecoloringbooks.com
Web site: http://www.creativecoloringbooks.com.

Curtis Publishing Company *See* **Cedar Creek Publishing Service**

Customer Centered Consulting Group, Inc., *(978-0-9762493)* 5729 Lebanon Dr., Suite 144-222, Frisco, TX 75034 USA Tel 469-633-9833; Fax: 469-633-9843
E-mail: dreed@cccginc.com
Web site: http://www.cccginc.com.

Cute & Cuddly Productions, Inc., *(978-0-9761318)* 4401 Shallowford Rd., Suite 162-161, Roswell, GA 30075 USA Tel 678-478-6071 (phone/fax)
E-mail: cuteandcuddlyproductions@msn.com
Web site: http://www.bigbillandbuddies.com.

CVD Publishing, *(978-0-9743520)* 1254 Grizzly Flat Ct., Auburn, CA 95603 USA Tel 530-885-4988
E-mail: grizlyflat@jps.net
Web site: http://www.CVDbooks.com.

CVTrahan Publishing, LLC *Imprint of* **Trahan, Virginia A. - Author**

CWG Pr., *(978-0-9788186; 978-0-9906714)* 1517 NE. 5th Ter Apt 1, Fort Lauderdale, FL 33304 USA Tel 954-524-5953
E-mail: editor@cwgpress.com
Web site: http://www.cwgpress.com.

CWLA Pr. *Imprint of* **Child Welfare League of America, Inc.**

CWS Studios, Inc., *(978-0-9785827; 978-0-615-92291-1)* 5414 W. Barry Ave., Chicago, IL 60641 USA
Web site: http://www.cws-studios.com.

Cyan Communications (GBR) *(978-0-9542829; 978-1-904879; 978-1-905736) Dist. by* **IPG Chicago.**

Cyber Haus, *(978-1-931373)* 159 Delaware Ave., #145, Delmar, NY 12054 USA Tel 518-478-9798
E-mail: cyhaus@msn.com
Web site: http://www.revolutionaryday.com/; http://www.cyhaus.com/.

Cyber Publishing Co., *(978-0-9637419; 978-0-9747870)* 421 Ave. De Teresa, Grants Pass, OR 97526 USA (SAN 255-691X) Tel 541-474-1077; Fax: 541-474-2829
E-mail: intrchild@aol.com.

Cyber Tiger Pr., *(978-0-615-18259-9)* Planetarium Station, New York, NY 10024 USA
E-mail: bill@billweberstudios.com
Dist(s): **Lulu Pr., Inc.**

Cybereditions (TM) *Imprint of* **Lisa Loucks Christenson Publishing, LLC**

Cyberlab Publishing, *(978-0-9746501)* P.O. Box 618, Dimondale, MI 48821-0618 USA Tel 517-974-8068; Fax: 517-887-9029
E-mail: ministerjd@yahoo.com
Web site: http://www.cyberlabpublishing.com.

Cyberosia Publishing, *(978-0-9709474; 978-0-9742713)* 3864 Shelley Dr., Mobile, AL 36693-3933 USA
E-mail: scottobrown@gmail.com
Dist(s): **Diamond Distributors, Inc.**

Cyberwizard Productions, *(978-0-9795788; 978-0-9815669; 978-0-9821352; 978-1-936021)* 1403 Iron Springs Rd. No. 36, Prescott, AZ 86305 USA; *Imprints:* Banana Oil Books (Banana Oil)
Web site: http://cyberwizardproductions.com; http://www.cyberwizardproductions.com/Chaco_Canyon_Books/; http://wildplainspress.webs.com; http://www.cyberwizardproductions.com/Ancient_Tomes_Press; http://www.cyberwizardproductions.com/Altered_Dimensions_Press; http://www.cyberwizardproductions.com/Banana_Oil_Books/; http://www.cyberwizardproductions.com/Diminuendo_Poetry/; http://firesidemysteries.webs.com; http://www.cyberwizardproductions.com/Toy_Box_Books/
Dist(s): **Send The Light Distribution LLC**

Cyclops Pr., *(978-0-9740269)* 1342 Van Buren Ave., Saint Paul, MN 55104-1926 USA.

Cyclotour Guide Bks., *(978-1-889602)* Orders Addr.: P.O. Box 10585, Rochester, NY 14610-0585 USA; Edit Addr.: 160 Harvard St., Rochester, NY 14607 USA
E-mail: cyclotour@cyclotour.com; cyclotour@frontiernet.net
Web site: http://www.cyclotour.com.

Cygnet Publishing Group, Inc./Coolreading.com (CAN) *(978-1-55305) Dist. by* **Orca Bk Pub.**

Cymbal Technique 101, *(978-0-9762593)* 440 Ross Rd., Fort Walton Beach, FL 32547 USA
E-mail: edward_capps@cymbaltechnique101.com
Web site: http://www.cymbaltechnique101.com.

Cynthia Eden *See* **Hocus Pocus Publishing, Inc.**

Cypress Bay Publishing, *(978-0-9746747)* 910 W. Harney Ln., Lodi, CA 95242 USA (SAN 255-6928) Tel 209-365-6114
E-mail: nclaus@clearwire.net.

Cypress Communications, *(978-0-9636412; 978-0-9896043)* 35 E. Rosemont Ave., Alexandria, VA 22301 USA Tel 703-548-0532 (phone/fax) Do not confuse with companies with similar names in Leawood, KS, Saint Paul, MN, Cypress, TX
E-mail: jcclifford@earthlink.net
Web site: http://www.lighthousehistory.info; http://www.CivilWarDrummerBoy.com
Dist(s): **Partners Bk. Distributing, Inc.**

Cypress Knees Publishing, *(978-0-9745863; 978-0-9763757)* Div. of Top Brass Outdoors, Orders Addr.: P.O. Box 209, Starkville, MS 39760 USA Tel 662-323-1559; Fax: 662-323-7466; Edit Addr.: 312 Industrial Pk., Rd., Starkville, MS 39759 USA
E-mail: eric@topbrasstackle.com
Web site: http://www.topbrasstackle.com; http://www.outdooryouthadventures.com.

CyPress Pubns., *(978-0-9672585; 978-0-9776958; 978-1-935083)* P.O. Box 2636, Tallahassee, FL 32316-2636 USA Fax: 850-254-7112
E-mail: lraymond@nettally.com
Web site: http://cypresspublications.com
Dist(s): **Smashwords.**

Cypress Publishing *See* **Cypress Communications**

Cyr Design Publishing, *(978-0-9774543)* P.O. Box 1662, Nashua, NH 03061-1662 USA
Web site: http://cyrdesign.com.

Cyrano Bks., *(978-0-615-55618-5)* 3348 kaunaoa St., Honolulu, HI 96815 USA Tel 808-381-5205
E-mail: cindykm@hawaii.rr.com.

Cyrano Bks., *(978-0-9990993)* 918 12th avenue, 1000, honolulu, HI 96816 USA Tel 808-492-4553; Fax: 808-492-4553
E-mail: cmackey11@icloud.com
Web site: www.cyranobooks.com.

Czechoslovak Genealogical Society International, *(978-0-9651932)* Orders Addr.: P.O. Box 16225, Saint Paul, MN 55116-0225 USA Tel 763-595-7799; Edit Addr.: 8582 Timberwood Rd., Woodbury, MN 55125-7620 USA Tel 651-739-7543
E-mail: cgsi@comcast.net
Web site: http://www.cgsi.org.

D. A. W. Enterprise, *(978-0-9628081)* 1314 Bainbridge St., Philadelphia, PA 19147 USA Tel 215-424-2016.

D & S Marketing Systems, Inc., *(978-1-878621; 978-0-9787199; 978-1-934780)* 1205 38th St., Brooklyn, NY 11218-3705 USA Tel 718-633-8383; Fax: 718-633-8385; Toll Free: 800-633-8383
E-mail: dsmarketing@aol.com; info@dsmarketing.com
Web site: http://www.dsmarketing.com.

D B W, Incorporated *See* **Just Like Me, Inc.**

DDDD Pubns., *(978-0-9635341; 978-1-885519)* 3407 Brown Rd., Saint Louis, MO 63114-4329 USA (SAN 631-2675).

D H Publishing LLC, *(978-0-9800263)* 515 E. Carefree Hwy., No. 652, Phoenix, AZ 85085-8839 USA
E-mail: deserthillspublishing@hotmail.com.

D K Publishing, Incorporated *See* **Dorling Kindersley Publishing, Inc.**

D. W. Ink, *(978-1-892313)* P.O. Box 5470, Huntsville, AL 35814 USA Fax: 205-721-1269.

D. W. Publishing, *(978-0-9741774)* 226 McFarland St., Grand Blanc, MI 48439 USA Tel 810-695-8985
E-mail: dan@dwpublishing.com
Web site: http://www.dwpublishing.com.

Da Capo Lifelong *Imprint of* **Da Capo Pr., Inc.**

†Da Capo Pr., Inc., *(978-0-201; 978-0-306; 978-0-7382; 978-0-938289; 978-0-946771; 978-0-9627613; 978-1-55561; 978-1-58097; 978-1-873376; 978-1-882810; 978-1-885119)* A Member of Perseus Books Group, Orders Addr.: 5500 Central Ave., Boulder, CO 80301 USA Fax: 303-449-3356 (customer service); Toll Free: 800-371-1669 (customer service); Edit Addr.: 11 Cambridge Ctr., Cambridge, MA 02142 USA Tel 617-252-5200; Fax: 617-252-5285; *Imprints:* Da Capo Lifelong (DaCapoLife)
E-mail: westview.orders@perseusbooks.com
Web site: http://www.perseusbooksgroup.com
Dist(s): **Blackstone Audio, Inc.**
CreateSpace Independent Publishing Platform
Ebsco Publishing
Follett School Solutions
Hachette Bk. Group
MyiLibrary
ebrary, Inc.; *CIP.*

Da Wong Bks., *(978-0-9744360; 978-0-615-73234-3)* 4070 Cactus Rd., Shingle Springs, CA 95682 USA Tel 530-676-6060 (phone/fax)
E-mail: eslhotel@yahoo.com.

DAAB Media Gmbh (DEU) *(978-3-942597) Dist. by* **InnovativeLog.**

Dabel Brothers Production LLC., *(978-0-9764011; 978-0-9779333)* 6070 Autumn View Trail, Acworth, GA 30101 USA
E-mail: ldabel@dabelbrothers.com
Web site: http://www.dabelbrothers.com/
Dist(s): **Diamond Comic Distributors, Inc.**
Diamond Bk. Distributors.

Dabrishus, Mara, *(978-0-9961872)* 16 Pepper Creek Dr., Pepper Pike, OH 44124 USA Tel 412-818-2116
E-mail: mdabris@gmail.com
Web site: www.maradabrishus.com.

DAC Educational Pubns., *(978-1-930731)* 4325 Carlton Pl., Yorba Linda, CA 92886 USA
E-mail: DACpublis@aol.com.

DaChosen Publishing, *(978-0-9762627)* Orders Addr.: P.O. Box PO BOX 831253, Stone Mountain, GA 30083 USA Toll Free: 800-442-7170
E-mail: traewing@gmail.com
Web site: http://www.dachosen.com.

Daddy Bean Bks., *(978-0-9842929)* 42 W. 38th St., Suite 1001, New York, NY 10018 USA Tel 212-840-2326
E-mail: Pwalsh@walshfamilymedia.com
Web site: http://www.walshfamilymedia.com.

Daddy's Heroes, Inc., *(978-0-9792111)* 4799 Baxter St., Santa Barbara, CA 93110 USA
E-mail: karun@daddysheroes.com
Web site: http://www.daddysheroes.com.

Dadielte Production, *(978-0-9799273; 978-0-9981419)* Orders Addr.: 12910 Fontainebleau Dr., Moreno Valley, CA 92556-1266 USA (SAN 854-7645)
E-mail: gema118@hotmail.com.

Dafina *Imprint of* **Kensington Publishing Corp.**

Dahomey Publishing Co., *(978-0-9723570)* Orders Addr.: 50 Hall Rd., Winchendon, MA 01475 USA (SAN 255-4542) Tel 978-297-1820; Fax: 978-297-2519
Web site: http://www.DahomeyPublishing.com.

Dailey International Pubs., *(978-0-9666251)* 500 Laurel Oaks Ln., Alpharetta, GA 30004-4508 USA
E-mail: franklyn@daileyint.com
Web site: http://www.daileyint.com.

Daily Racing Form,
Dist(s): **National Bk. Network.**

Daimon Verlag (CHE) *(978-3-85630) Dist. by* **Bookmasters.**

Daisy Publishing, *(978-0-9740641)* P.O. Box 681171, Franklin, TN 37068 USA Do not confuse with Daisy Publishing in Massapequa Park, NY, Altoona, PA.

Dakitab, Inc., *(978-0-9791059)* Orders Addr.: 2906 W. Grand Blvd., Detroit, MI 48202 USA (SAN 852-4408) Fax: 248-360-6148
E-mail: aid@awaytoread.com
Web site: http://www.awaytoread.com.

Dakota Assocs., Inc., *(978-0-615-14589-1; 978-0-615-18375-6)* P.O. Box 321, W. Bloomfield, NY 14585 USA
Web site: http://www.dakotaassociates.com
Dist(s): **Lulu Pr., Inc.**

Dakota Bks., *(978-0-9632861)* Orders Addr.: 2801 Daubenbiss, No. 1, Soquel, CA 95073 USA (SAN 630-9445) Tel 831-477-7174
E-mail: llogan@cruzio.com.

Dakota Rose, *(978-0-9727056)* 23725 260th Ave., Okaton, SD 57562 USA Tel 605-669-2529
E-mail: dakotarose746@goldenwest.net.

Dakota Skies Photography *See* **Johnny Sundby Photography**

Dale Seymour Publications *Imprint of* **Pearson Schl.**

Dale, Shelley *See* **Norman Bks.**

Dales Large Print Bks. (GBR) *(978-1-85389; 978-1-84262) Dist. by* **Ulverscroft US.**

Daley, Robert, *(978-0-9800839)* P.O. Box 5518, Keaau, HI 96749-5518 USA Tel 808-982-6688; Fax: 808-982-7824
E-mail: thedaleys@bythebookministries.org.

Dally, James W. Associates *See* **College Hse. Enterprises, LLC**

Dalton Publishing (GBR) *(978-0-9541886) Dist. by* **Midpt Trade.**

Dalton, William, *(978-0-9764395)* 1338 N. Laurel Ave., West Hollywood, CA 90046 USA Tel 310-800-0811
E-mail: urban_mystic@yahoo.com.

Damamli Publishing Co., *(978-0-9753584)* 25A Crescent Dr., No.171, Pleasant Hill, CA 94523-3501 USA (SAN 256-100X) Fax: 923-674-9461
E-mail: tookie@tookie.com; president@damamli.com
Web site: http://www.damamli.com.

Damiano Sara, Janeen, *(978-0-9786404)* 108 W. Village Dr., Saint Augustine, FL 32095 USA
Web site: http://www.wheresilly.com.

Damnation Bks., *(978-1-61572; 978-1-62929)* P.O. Box 3931, Santa Rosa, CA 95402-9998 USA
Web site: http://www.damnationbooks.com; http://www.eternalpress.biz.

Dan Dan Fantasy, *(978-0-9834315)* 18483 Five Points, Redford, MI 48240 USA Tel 734-776-5478
E-mail: paintballman@sbcglobal.net.

Dance & Movement Pr. *Imprint of* **Rosen Publishing Group, Inc., The**

Dance Horizons *Imprint of* **Princeton Bk. Co. Pubs.**

Dancer's Publishing, *(978-0-9749848)* 2103 Harrison NW, Suite 2-336, Olympia, WA 98502 USA.

Dances With Horses, Inc., *(978-0-9763489)* P.O. Box 819, Rexburg, ID 83440 USA Tel 800-871-7635; Fax: 208-356-7817; Toll Free: 800-871-7635
E-mail: frankbell@horsewhisperer.com
Web site: http://www.horsewhisperer.com.

Dancing Dakini Pr., *(978-0-9836333)* 77 Morning Sun Dr., Sedona, AZ 86336 USA Tel 505-466-1887
E-mail: editor@dancingdakinipress.com
Web site: www.dancingdakinipress.com.

Dancing Force, The, *(978-0-9726119)* 2249 Reeves Creek Rd., Suite B, Selma, OR 97538 USA (SAN 255-156X) Tel 541-597-2093 (phone/fax)
E-mail: dancingforce@ureach.com
Dist(s): **DeVorss & Co.**

Dancing Journey Pr., *(978-0-9847662)* 434 Ulman Rd., Thetford Center, VT 05075 USA Tel 802-785-4717
E-mail: Ginger.Wallis@valley.net.

Dancing Magic Heart Bk., *(978-0-9790041)* Div. of Douglas/Steinman Productions, 1841 Broadway, Suite 1103, New York, NY 10023 USA Tel 212-765-9848; Fax: 212-765-9848
E-mail: faithdouglas@earthlink.net
Web site: http://www.douglas-steinman.com
Dist(s): **New Leaf Resources.**

Dancing Mommy Pr., *(978-0-9971084)* 242 St. Paul Dr., Alamo, CA 94507 USA Tel 925-876-4546
E-mail: jeryl@ronjer.com.

Dancing Moon Pr., *(978-1-892076; 978-1-937493; 978-1-945587)* P.O. Box 832, Newport, OR 97365-0062 USA Tel 541-574-7708 (work)
E-mail: carla@dancingmoonpress.com
Web site: http://www.dancingmoonpress.com
Dist(s): **Partners/West Book Distributors.**

Dancing With Bear Publishing, *(978-0-9988339)* P.O. Box 281, San Marcos, TX 78667 USA Tel 512-665-6188 Do not confuse with Dancing With Bear Publishing in Antlers, OK
E-mail: debbieroppolo@gmail.com
Web site: dancingwithbearpublishing.com.

Dancing Words Pr., Inc., *(978-0-9716346)* Orders Addr.: P.O. Box 1575, Severna Park, MD 21146 USA; Edit Addr.: 12 Sonneborn Ln., Severna Park, MD 21146 USA Tel 410-647-1441 (phone/fax)
E-mail: dwpinc@aol.com
Web site: http://www.dancingwordspress.com
Dist(s): **Quality Bks., Inc.**

D&C Publishing, *(978-0-692-77041-2; 978-0-692-78854-7)* 2062 S. Taylor, cleveland heights, OH 44118 USA Tel 216-321-1101
E-mail: ladoshaw@yahoo.com
Web site: www.rdthairsalon.com.

Dandelion Publishing, *(978-0-9793930)* 6234 Eliza Ln., North Las Vegas, NV 89031 USA (SAN 853-330X)
E-mail: sand.d@cox.net
Web site: http://DandelionPublishing.com.

Dandy Lion Pubns., *(978-0-931724; 978-1-883055)* P.O. Box 190, Sn Luis Obisp, CA 93406-0190 USA (SAN 211-5565) Toll Free: 800-776-8032
E-mail: dandy@dandylionbooks.come
Web site: http://www.dandylionbooks.com.

Dangberg, Grace Foundation, Incorporated *See* **Sage Hill Pubs., LLC**

DAngelo, Gus, *(978-0-615-45567-9; 978-0-615-70443-2)* 752 Clayton St., San Francisco, CA 94117 USA Tel 415-550-0514
E-mail: gus@sanfranciscoabc.com
Dist(s): **Independent Pubs. Group.**

Daniel & Daniel, Pubs., Inc., *(978-0-931832; 978-0-936784; 978-1-56474; 978-1-880284)* P.O. Box 2790, McKinleyville, CA 95519 USA (SAN 215-1995) Tel 707-839-3495; Fax: 707-839-3242; Toll Free: 800-662-8351; *Imprints:* Fithian Press (Fithian Press)
E-mail: dandd@danielpublishing.com
Web site: http://www.danielpublishing.com
Dist(s): **SCB Distributors.**

Dankworth Publishing, *(978-0-9855676; 978-0-9987888)* 309 Reamer Pl., Oberlin, OH 44074 USA Tel 612-309-5126
E-mail: mindybrueggemann@yahoo.com.

DanMar Publishing, *(978-0-9749407)* 112 E. Pennsylvania Blvd., Feasterville, PA 19053 USA Tel 215-364-1112; Fax: 215-364-3231
E-mail: drlavanga@aol.com
Web site: http://www.drlavanga.com.

Danny & Ester's Fortunate Adventures, *(978-0-9833667)* 1979 Willow Ave., Worthington, MN 56187 USA Tel 507-376-5889
E-mail: mccuen@mchsi.com
Dist(s): **Adventure Pubns.**

Dante's Publishing *See* **Solomon's Bks.**

Dantone, Desni, *(978-0-9895090)* 114 Alderwood Dr., Greensburg, PA 15601 USA Tel 724-261-0096
Dist(s): **CreateSpace Independent Publishing Platform.**

Danza Pubns., *(978-0-9774552)* P.O. Box 252053, West Bloomfield, MI 48325 USA Toll Free: 800-457-2157
Web site: http://www.elaineserling.com.

D.A.P./Distributed Art Pubs., *(978-1-881616; 978-1-891024; 978-1-933045; 978-1-935202; 978-1-938922; 978-1-942884)* Orders Addr.: 75 Broad St., Suite 630, New York, NY 10004 USA (SAN 630-6446) Tel 212-627-1999; Fax: 212-627-9484; Toll Free Fax: 800-478-3128; Toll Free: 800-338-2665
E-mail: dap@dapinc.com
Web site: http://www.artbook.com/.

Dar Asadeeq Publishing & Distribution, Inc., *(978-0-615-52712-3; 978-0-9853772)* 646 Oaklawn Ave., Chula Vista, CA 91910 USA Tel 619-761-5329
E-mail: alsadeeq.usa@gmail.com
Web site: www.daralsadeeq.com.

Dara Publishing LLC, *(978-0-9975059)* 1649 Nostrand Ave., Brooklyn, NY 11226 USA Tel 347-962-8363
E-mail: denifa@yahoo.com.

Darby Creek *Imprint of* **Lerner Publishing Group**

Dare to Dream Scholarship, Incorporated *See* **Cole Publishing**

Dargaud Publishing Co. (FRA) *(978-0-917201; 978-2-205) Dist. by* **Distribks Inc.**

Dark Circle Comics *Imprint of* **Archie Comic Pubns., Inc.**

Dark Continents Publishing, *(978-0-9831603; 978-0-9836245; 978-0-9848931; 978-0-615-68082-8; 978-0-615-69182-4; 978-0-615-71013-6; 978-0-615-71015-0; 978-0-615-71017-4; 978-0-615-71018-1; 978-0-615-71019-8; 978-0-615-71840-8; 978-0-615-83145-9; 978-0-615-84491-6; 978-0-615-88140-9; 978-0-615-91582-1; 978-0-615-96489-8; 978-0-615-97495-8; 978-0-692-24951-2) P.O. Box 276, Tiskilwa, IL 61368 USA Tel 815-646-4748*
E-mail: DMYoungquist@darkcontinents.com
Web site: www.darkcontinents.com
Dist(s): **CreateSpace Independent Publishing Platform.**

Dark Forest Pr., *(978-0-9764226)* 1310 N. Oak St., Apt. 408, Arlington, VA 22209 USA Tel 202-368-4341; P.O. Box 9133, Arlington, VA 22210 (SAN 256-4475) Tel 202-368-4341 Do not confuse with Dark Forest Press in Denver, CO.

Dark Horse Comics, *(978-1-56971; 978-1-878574; 978-1-59307; 978-1-59582; 978-1-59617; 978-1-61655; 978-1-61659; 978-1-62115; 978-1-63008; 978-1-5067)* 10956 SE Main St., Milwaukie, OR 97222 USA Tel 503-652-8815; Fax: 503-654-9440
E-mail: dhcomics@darkhorse.com
Web site: http://www.darkhorse.com
Dist(s): **Diamond Comic Distributors, Inc.**
Diamond Bk. Distributors
Penguin Random Hse. LLC
Random Hse., Inc.

Dark Overlord Media *See* **Empty Set Entertainment**

Dark Passages *Imprint of* **Whorl Bks.**

Dark Skull Studios, *(978-0-9797080)* 17711 Barker Bluff Ln., Cypress, TX 77433 USA (SAN 854-1922) Tel 832-220-6734
E-mail: richardleon@darkskullstudios.com
Web site: http://www.darkskullstudios.com.

Darker Intentions Pr., *(978-0-9769612; 978-0-9827597)* P.O. Box 569, Freehold Twp., NJ 07728-0569 USA Tel 732-299-6212
E-mail: jzdakota@hotmail.com.

Darkerwood Publishing Group, *(978-0-9669788; 978-0-9788975; 978-1-938839)* P.O. Box 2011, Arvada, CO 80001 USA
E-mail: swordarkeereon@gmail.com; ofs.admin@gmail.com; darkerwoodpublishing@gmail.com
Web site: http://www.demonolatry.org/dbpub.htm.

Darling & Co. *Imprint of* **Laughing Elephant**

Darling Pr. LLC, *(978-0-9765761)* Orders Addr.: 19740 SW 49th Ave., Tualatin, OR 97062 USA
Web site: http://www.darlingpress.com
Dist(s): **Bottman Design, Inc.**

Darnell Publishing, *(978-0-9755616)* P.O. Box 341825, Tampa, FL 33694 USA
Web site: http://www.abrink.com.

Dart Publishing, *(978-0-692-80432-2; 978-0-692-84334-5)* 1198 Spruance St., San Jose, CA 95128 USA Tel 408-280-7611
E-mail: juliedart@comcast.ney.

DASANBOOKS, *(978-0-9819542; 978-0-9828016; 978-0-9839594)* 120 Sylvan Ave., Englewood Cliffs, NJ 07632 USA
Dist(s): **Midpoint Trade Bks., Inc.**

Dash & Doodles Productions, *(978-0-615-22279-0; 978-0-578-08121-2)* 4810 Kellywood Dr., Glen Allen, VA 23060 USA Tel 804-527-1033
E-mail: dashanddoodles@aol.com
Web site: http://www.askdash.com
Dist(s): **Lulu Pr., Inc.**

Data Trace Legal Publishers, Incorporated *See* **Data Trace Publishing, Co.**

Data Trace Publishing, Co., *(978-0-9637468; 978-1-57400)* Orders Addr.: P.O. Box 1239, Brooklandville, MD 21022 USA Tel 410-494-4994; Fax: 410-494-0515; Toll Free: 800-342-0454; Edit Addr.: 110 West Rd., Suite 227, Towson, MD 21204 USA
E-mail: info@datatrace.com
Web site: http://www.datatrace.com/legal.

Databooks *See* **Chandler Hse. Pr.**

Daughter Culture Pubns., *(978-0-935281)* P.O. Box 127924, San Diego, CA 92112 USA (SAN 695-7447) Tel 619-432-5491.

Daughters Arise, LLC, *(978-0-9744178)* 2648 E. Workman Ave., Suite 314, West Covina, CA 91791 USA Tel 770-808-1199; Fax: 770-216-1626
E-mail: fhenley@daughtersarise.com
Web site: http://www.daughtersarise.com.

Daven, Christian Publishing, *(978-0-578-00257-6)* 6504 Mendius Ave., NE, Albuquerque, NM 87109 USA Tel 505-315-2984
Dist(s): **Lulu Pr., Inc.**

Davenport, May Pubs., *(978-0-943864; 978-0-9603118; 978-0-9794140)* 26313 Purissima Rd., Los Altos Hills, CA 94022-4539 USA (SAN 212-467X) Tel 650-947-1325; Fax: 650-947-1373
E-mail: mdbooks@earthlink.net
Dist(s): **Todd Communications.**

Davenport Pr. (CAN) *(978-0-9736803; 978-0-9782552) Dist. by* **IPG Chicago.**

Davenport, Sheena, *(978-0-9747625)* 3535 Riverview Approach, Ellenwood, GA 30294 USA Tel 404-241-3106
E-mail: szdavenport@yahoo.com.

David & Charles Pubs. (GBR) *(978-0-7153; 978-1-4463) Dist. by* **FplusW Media.**

David, Elizabeth A., *(978-0-9740170)* P.O. Box 766, Fairhaven, MA 02719-0700 USA Tel 508-979-5593
E-mail: yasny@comcast.net
Web site: http://www.zorena.com.

†David, Jonathan Pubs., Inc., *(978-0-8246)* 68-22 Eliot Ave., Middle Village, NY 11379 USA (SAN 169-5274) Tel 718-456-8611; Fax: 718-894-2818
E-mail: jondavpub@aol.com
Web site: http://www.jdbooks.com; *CIP.*

David Mortimore Baxter *Imprint of* **Stone Arch Bks.**

†Davidson, Harlan Inc., *(978-0-88295)* 773 Glenn Ave., Wheeling, IL 60090-6000 USA (SAN 201-2375) Tel 847-541-9720; Fax: 847-541-9830
E-mail: harlandavidson@harlandavidson.com
Web site: http://www.harlandavidson.com; *CIP.*

Davis, A. S. Media Group, *(978-0-9666352; 978-0-9729150; 978-0-9759022; 978-0-9766013; 978-0-9776245; 978-0-9787719; 978-1-934724)* Orders Addr.: P.O. Box 590780, San Francisco, CA 94159 USA
E-mail: info@greenlinepub.com
Web site: http://www.greenlinepub.com.

Davis Bks. LLC, *(978-0-9770142)* Orders Addr.: P.O. Box 6291, Cincinnati, OH 45206 USA Tel 513-687-1943
E-mail: georgedisselkamp@yahoo.com
Web site: http://www.davisbooks.cjb.net
Dist(s): **Docustar.**

Davis, James (Jim), *(978-0-9760960)* 1700 W. Washington St. Apt. A507, Springfield, IL 62702-6447 USA.

Davis, Paul *See* **Royal Hse. Publishing**

Davis Pubns., Inc., *(978-0-87192; 978-1-61528; 978-1-64164)* 50 Portland St., Worcester, MA 01608 USA (SAN 201-3002) Tel 508-754-7201; Fax: 508-791-0779; Toll Free: 800-533-2847
E-mail: rfrederics@davisart.com; mnicholson@davisart.com
Web site: http://www.davisart.com
Dist(s): **Sterling Publishing Co., Inc.**

Davis, Tamela, *(978-0-9772923; 978-0-9821196; 978-0-9826608; 978-0-9836089)* P.O. Box 502, Carmel, IN 46082 USA
E-mail: sales@growingwithgrammer.com; tinydee64@sbcglobal.net
Web site: http://www.growingwithgrammer.com.

Davlaw Press, *(978-0-9776917)* Orders Addr.: P.O. Box 4317, Harrisburg, PA 17111 USA (SAN 257-9863) Tel 717-441-5451; Fax: 717-441-4925; *Imprints:* Curcumin Books (Curcumin Bks)
E-mail: larry@davlawpress.com
Web site: http://www.davlawpress.com.

Davus Publishing, *(978-0-915317)* P.O. Box 292, Buffalo, NY 14213-7101 USA (SAN 289-9787) Tel 519-426-2077
E-mail: davus@kwic.com; davuspub@sympatico.ca
Web site: http://www.kwic.com/~davus; http://www3.sympatico.ca/drbeasley; http://www.davuspublishing.com
Dist(s): **Coutts Information Services.**

DAW *Imprint of* **DAW**

DAW, 375 Hudson St., 3rd Flr., New York, NY 10014 USA; *Imprints:* DAW (DAW)
Dist(s): **Penguin Random Hse. LLC.**

Dawasoft, *(978-0-9764218)* 150-35 119th Rd., Jamaica, NY 11434 USA Tel 347-954-6479
E-mail: dawasoft@yahoo.com.

Dawn Chorus Pr. *Imprint of* **Perennis, Sophia**

Dawn of a New Day Pubns., The *Imprint of* **Konkori International**

Dawn of Day Childrens Publishing Co., Inc., *(978-0-9666857)* 73 Ireland Pl., PMB 201, Amityville, NY 11757 USA (SAN 253-0198) Tel 631-225-5513; Fax: 631-225-5431; Toll Free: 800-575-7040
E-mail: information@dawnofday.com
Web site: http://www.dawnofday.com.

Dawn Pubns., *(978-0-916124; 978-1-878265; 978-1-883220; 978-1-58469)* 12402 Bitney Springs Rd., Nevada City, CA 95959 USA (SAN 856-8294) Tel 530-478-0111; Fax: 530-274-7778; Toll Free: 800-545-7475 Do not confuse with Dawn Pubns. in Pasadena, TX
E-mail: nature@dawnpub.com; info@dawnpub.com
Web site: http://www.dawnpub.com
Dist(s): **Brodart Co.**
Common Ground Distributors, Inc.
Follett School Solutions
Ingram Bk. Co.
Territory Titles.

DawQuin LLC, *(978-0-9842787)* P.O. Box 1800, Troy, MI 48099 USA (SAN 858-9461) Tel 248-765-7276
E-mail: publisher@dawquin.com
Web site: www.dawquin.com.

Day By Day *See* **Day By Day Recovery Resources, LLC**

Day By Day Recovery Resources, LLC, *(978-0-9674915; 978-1-934569)* Orders Addr.: 2186 N. Clack Canyon Rd., Kingman, AZ 86409 USA Tel 887-447-1683
E-mail: business@pocketsponsor.com
Web site: http://www.day-by-day.org
Dist(s): **Mentor Bks.**

Day I Hit a Home Run Enterprise, The, *(978-0-9831950)* 7389 Brookville Rd., Oxford, OH 45056 USA Tel 513-290-2189
E-mail: mullenmike122@yahoo.com
Web site: www.thedayihitahomerun.com
Dist(s): **Independent Pubs. Group.**

Day to Day Enterprises, *(978-1-890905)* Orders Addr.: 8396 Maryland Rd., Pasadena, MD 21122-4655 USA (SAN 299-7118) Tel 443-817-2129; Fax: 443-817-2129; *Imprints:* Eco Fiction Books (Eco Fiction Bks); Writers Collective, The (Writers Coll)
E-mail: books@daytodayenterprises.com
Web site: http://www.daytodayenterprises.com
Dist(s): **Book Clearing Hse.**
Midpoint Trade Bks., Inc.

Day3 Productions, Inc., *(978-0-9777361)* 215 Tower Rd, McKenzie, TN 38201 USA (SAN 850-0770) Tel 731-352-6081
E-mail: jeff@day3productions.com
Web site: http://www.day3productions.com.

Daylight Bks., *(978-0-9632177; 978-0-9840220)* 671 W. 193rd St. #4j New York, NY 10040 USA Tel 646-265-3294
E-mail: smartin34@earthlink.net
Dist(s): **ebrary, Inc.**

Daylight Pubs., *(978-0-9764103; 978-0-9792755)* 8255 S Wright Pl., Broken Arrow, OK 74014 USA Tel 918-357-1266
E-mail: kathy@daylightpublishers.com
Web site: http://www.daylightpublishers.com.

DayOne Pubns. (GBR) *(978-0-902548; 978-1-903087; 978-1-84625) Dist. by* **STL Dist.**

Days of Glory Publishing, *(978-0-9770206)* 28 Branden Way, Tolland, CT 06084 USA.

Daystar Press *See* **TopNotch Pr.**

Dayton International Peace Museum *See* **Peace Power Pr.**

Dazzling Inc., *(978-0-9749170)* P.O. Box 236, Allston, MA 02134 USA
Web site: http://www.rootfriends.com.

DC Comics, *(978-0-930289; 978-1-56389; 978-1-4012)* Div. of Warner Bros.- A Time Warner Entertainment Co., 1700 Broadway, New York, NY 10019 USA Tel 212-636-5400; Fax: 212-636-5979; *Imprints:* Vertigo (Vertigo); Paradox (Paradox); A B C (A B C); Wildstorm (Wildstorm); DC Kids (DCKids); Minx (Minx); MAD (MAD DC)
E-mail: booksales@dccomics.com
Web site: http://www.dccomics.com
Dist(s): **Eastern News Distributors**
MyiLibrary
Penguin Random Hse. LLC
Random Hse., Inc.

DC Kids *Imprint of* **DC Comics**

DC Super Heroes *Imprint of* **Stone Arch Bks.**

DC Super-Pets *Imprint of* **Picture Window Bks.**

DC Super-villains *Imprint of* **Stone Arch Bks.**

DCTS Publishing, *(978-0-9653904)* Div. of Hamilton Ministry, P.O. Box 40216, Santa Barbara, CA 93140 USA Tel 805-570-3168; Toll Free: 800-965-8150
E-mail: dennis@dctspub.com
Web site: http://www.dctspub.com.

de Fosseway, Marquis (GBR) *(978-0-9561561) Dist. by* **LuluCom.**

De La Flor (ARG) *(978-950-515) Dist. by* **LD Bks Inc.**

De La Luz Pubns., *(978-0-9748326)* 121 W. Hickory St., Denton, TX 76201 USA Tel 940-367-1651; Fax: 940-323-0488
E-mail: ccarrasco1@chater.net.

De Loach, George P., *(978-0-9768362)* 475 W. Fallen Leaf Cir., Wasilla, AK 99654 USA Tel 907-376-2680
E-mail: gdeloach@juno.com.

De Portola Pr., *(978-0-692-47363-4)* 33780 Linda Rosea Rd., Temecula, CA 92592 USA Tel 951-551-5338
Dist(s): **CreateSpace Independent Publishing Platform.**

Deaf Missions, *(978-1-59799)* Orders Addr.: 21199 Greenview Rd., Council Bluffs, IA 51503-4190 USA
Web site: http://www.deafmissions.com.

Deal, Darlene, *(978-0-9747299)* P.O. Box 521, North Hollywood, CA 91603-0521 USA Tel 818-752-7065 (phone/fax).

DeAngelis, Anthony, *(978-0-9754853)* 101 Cypress Ave., San Bruno, CA 94066-5420 USA
E-mail: a.deangelis@worldnet.att.net.

Dean's Bks., Inc., *(978-0-9728607)* 1426 S. Kansas Ave., Topeka, KS 66612 USA Tel 785-357-4708
E-mail: contact@oilcanbook.com
Web site: http://www.oilcanbook.com.

Dearborn Publishing, *(978-1-891685)* Div. of The Mae Group LLC, Orders Addr.: 7389 N. 150 W., Lake Village, IN 46349 USA Tel 219-689-1286; Fax: 219-992-9356
E-mail: chermytalent@yahoo.com; johngraham@att.net.

Dearborn Real Estate Education *Imprint of* **Kaplan Publishing**

Dearborn Trade, A Kaplan Professional Company *See* **Kaplan Publishing**

Deb on Air Bks., *(978-0-9727615)* Orders Addr.: P.O. Box 580055, Elk Grove, CA 95758 USA Tel 916-684-3551.

Debate, Editorial (ESP) *(978-84-7444; 978-84-8306) Dist. by* **AIMS Intl.**

Debi, Kennedy *See* **nJoy Bks.**

DeCa Communications, LLC, *(978-0-9762262)* 300 Williamsburg Dr., Mandeville, LA 70471 USA
Web site: http://www.decacom.info.

Decere Publishing, *(978-0-9717013; 978-0-9816572)* 5590 Bunky Way, Atlanta, GA 30338 USA Tel 404-474-2830; Fax: 770-399-5883 Do not confuse with CSI Publishing in Monterey Park, CA
E-mail: mark@decere.com
Web site: http://www.decere.com.

Dedalus Bks. Ltd. (GBR) *(978-0-946626; 978-1-873982; 978-1-903517; 978-1-904556; 978-1-907650; 978-1-909232; 978-1-910213) Dist. by* **SCB Distributo.**

Deep Dish Design, *(978-0-9755033)* 15012 Cherry Ln., Burnsville, MN 55306 USA
E-mail: jb@deepdishdesign.com
Web site: http://www.deepdishdesign.com.

Deep Roots Pubns., *(978-0-9671713; 978-0-9819528)* Orders Addr.: P.O. Box 114, Saratoga, NY 12866 USA Tel 518-583-8920; Fax: 518-584-3919; Edit Addr.: 229 Lake Ave., Saratoga, NY 12866 USA
E-mail: drpalmer2002@yahoo.com
Web site: http://www.deeprootspublications.com
Dist(s): **North Country Bks., Inc.**

Deep Waters Pr., *(978-0-9748171)* Suite 100, 77 Court St., Laconia, NH 03246 USA (SAN 255-8777) Tel 603-520-1214; P.O. Box 452, Meredith, NH 03253 Tel 603-524-2585
E-mail: halclyon@yahoo.com; deepwaterspress@yahoo.com
Web site: http://www.DeepWaterspress.com.

Deeper Roots Pubns. & Media, *(978-1-930547)* Orders Addr.: 13 W. Lakeshore Dr., Cherokee Village, AR 72529 USA
E-mail: deeperroots@aol.com
Web site: http://www.DeeperRoots.com.

Deeper Waters, *(978-0-615-36602-9; 978-0-615-43255-7; 978-0-615-58840-7)* 11520 Grandview Rd., Kansas City,, MO 64137 USA Tel 816-765-9900
E-mail: blake.cadwell@gmail.com.

Deepercalling Media, Inc., *(978-0-9726135; 978-1-59601)* 1200 Mt. Diablo Blvd., Suite 108, Walnut Creek, CA 94596 USA (SAN 254-9360) Fax: 925-939-4010
E-mail: info@deepercalling.com
Web site: http://www.deepercalling.com
Dist(s): **Whitaker Hse.**

Deer Creek Publishing, *(978-0-9651452)* Orders Addr.: P.O. Box 2594, Nevada City, CA 95959 USA Fax: 530-478-1759 Do not confuse with Deer Creek Publishing, Provo, UT.

Deer Oaks, Inc., *(978-0-9764700)* P.O. Box 429, Barrington, IL 60011-0429 USA.

Deerbrook Editions, *(978-0-9712488; 978-0-9828100; 978-0-9904287; 978-0-9975051; 978-0-9991062)* P.O. Box 542, Cumberland, ME 04021-0542 USA
E-mail: jewillh@gmail.com; info@deerbrookeditions.com
Web site: http://www.deerbrookeditions.com; http://www.idesignbooks.com; http://deerbrookeditions.wordpress.com
Dist(s): **SPD-Small Pr. Distribution.**

Defense Dept. *Imprint of* **United States Government Printing Office**

Defense Research LLC, *(978-0-9749873)* 211 Kirkland Ave. Apt. 216, Kirkland, WA 98033-6578 USA
E-mail: sales@defenseresearch.org
Web site: http://www.defenseresearch.org.

Defiance In Print, *(978-0-9771641)* Orders Addr.: 9412 S Belfort Cr, Tamarac, FL 33321 USA (SAN 256-9663) Tel 561-235-1828
E-mail: miller2554@gmail.com.

Defiant Pr. *Imprint of* **Passkey Pubns.**

Defined Mind, Inc., *(978-0-9763767)* 580 Broadway, Suite 912, New York, NY 10012 USA Tel 212-925-5138 (Hours: M-F 9:30 am-5:30 pm)
E-mail: info@defmind.com
Web site: http://www.defmind.com.

DeForest Pr., *(978-0-9649922; 978-1-930374; 978-0-615-99631-8)* Orders Addr.: P.O. Box 383, Rogers, MN 55374 USA Tel 763-428-2997; Fax: 877-747-3123; Toll Free: 877-747-3123; Edit Addr.: P.O. Box 383, Rogers, MN 55374 USA
E-mail: shane@deforestpress.com
Web site: http://www.deforestpress.com.

DeFranco Entertainment, *(978-1-929845)* P.O. Box 1425, Thousand Oaks, CA 91358-1425 USA Fax: 805-376-2953
E-mail: tdefranco@vcnet.com.

Degenhardt, Scott, *(978-0-9765671)* P.O. Box 11182, Murfreesboro, TN 37129 USA Tel 615-890-9484
E-mail: anything@thedegshop.com
Web site: http://www.thedegshop.com.

DeGraaf Publishing, *(978-0-9678385)* 903 W. Morse St., Plant City, FL 33563 USA Tel 813-752-2348; 813-967-7489 (Cell phone)
E-mail: robdegraaf@verizon.net
Web site: http://www.degraafpublishing.com.

Degree Network, LLC *See* **Marilux Pr.**

Dehghanpisheh, Corine, *(978-0-9851930; 978-0-692-41280-0; 978-0-9978985)* P.O. Box 30302, New York, NY 10011 USA Tel 646-580-8655
E-mail: cmardi2@gmail.com.

Deitch, Jeffrey Inc., *(978-0-9633037; 978-0-9648530; 978-0-9753243; 978-0-9778686; 978-0-9815771)* 76 Grand St., New York, NY 10013 USA Tel 212-343-7300
E-mail: info@deitch.com
Web site: http://www.deitch.com
Dist(s): **D.A.P./Distributed Art Pubs.**

Dejohn Enterprises, *(978-0-9754528)* 1121 Elm St., Peekskill, NY 10566 USA
E-mail: dejohnenterprise@aol.com
Web site: http://www.thereturnofsf.com.

Deka Pr., *(978-0-9645045)* P.O. Box 812, Christmas Valley, OR 97641 USA Tel 541-576-3900; Fax: 541-576-3909
E-mail: katym@teleport.com.

DEKpress *See* **Parent Positive Pr.**

DeKruyff, Ruth, *(978-0-9797549)* Orders Addr.: P.O. Box 380604, San Antonio, TX 78268 USA; Edit Addr.: 5911 Forest Rim, San Antonio, TX 78240 USA.

Del Alma Pubns., LLC, *(978-0-9822422)* 3615 Stop 36 A, Zapata, TX 78076 USA.

Del Gatto, Maria, *(978-0-9747509)* 2227 South 3rd St., Philadelphia, PA 19148 USA Tel 215-271-7165
Web site: http://www.shapettes.com.

Del George, Dana, *(978-0-578-00730-4)* 1025 1/2 Magnolia St., South Pasadena, CA 91030 USA
Dist(s): **Lulu Pr., Inc.**

Del Rey *Imprint of* **Random House Publishing Group**

Del Sol Pubns., *(978-0-9722936)* P.O. Box 1112, Ventura, CA 93002 USA Do not confuse with Del Sol Publications in Two River, WI
E-mail: info@delsolpublications.com
Web site: http://www.delsolpublications.com.

Del Sol Publishing, *(978-1-58186)* 29257 Bassett Rd., Westlake, OH 44145 USA (SAN 299-4178) Tel 440-892-5524; Fax: 440-892-5546; Toll Free: 888-335-7651
E-mail: delsolbooks@telocity.com
Dist(s): **Lectorum Pubns., Inc.**

Delabarre Publishing, *(978-0-9829247; 978-0-9836125; 978-1-61941)* P.O. Box 714, Conway, MA 01341 USA Tel 413-475-0087
E-mail: jeff@jeffrutherford.com.

Delacorte Bks. for Young Readers *Imprint of* **Random Hse. Children's Bks.**

Delacorte Pr. *Imprint of* **Random Hse. Children's Bks.**

Delacorte Pr. *Imprint of* **Random House Publishing Group**

Delacorte Pr *Imprint of* **Random House Publishing Group**

Delatorre, Maria *See* **Father's Hse. Publishing**

DeLaVega, T., *(978-0-9754328)* Orders Addr.: P.O. Box 760, Hanapepe, HI 96716 USA Tel 808-335-2704; Fax: 808-335-5469; Edit Addr.: 3691 Uwao St., Hanapepe, HI 96716 USA
E-mail: tim.delavega@verizon.net
Web site: http://www.napaliphoto.com.

Delittle Storyteller Co., *(978-1-892633)* Orders Addr.: 1562 Pinehurst Dr., Casselberry, FL 32707 USA Tel 407-699-7769
E-mail: delittlestoryteller@yahoo.com
Web site: http://www.delittlestoryteller.com.

Dell, Jacob J., *(978-0-9744544)* 6518 Chasethorn Dr., San Antonio, TX 78249-4825 USA
E-mail: books@jacobjdell.com
Web site: http://www.jacobjdell.com/books.

Dellas, Melanie, *(978-0-9830163)* 4405 Pescadero Ave., San Diego, CA 92107 USA Tel 858-442-7916
E-mail: mdellas@hotmail.com
Web site: http://www.Mythological-Creatures.com.

Dellinger, Hampton, *(978-0-615-24971-1)* 4306 Peachway Dr., Durham, NC 27705 USA
Dist(s): **Lulu Pr., Inc.**

Dellwin Publishing Co., Inc., *(978-0-9765267)* P.O. Box 23391, Brooklyn, NY 11202-3391 USA
E-mail: dellwin5@aol.com
Web site: http://www.therockmastersystem.com.

†Delmar Cengage Learning, *(978-0-314; 978-0-7668; 978-0-7693; 978-0-8273; 978-0-87350; 978-0-916032; 978-0-944132; 978-0-9653629; 978-1-56253; 978-1-56593; 978-1-56930; 978-1-4018; 978-1-4180; 978-1-4283; 978-1-4354)* Div. of Cengage Learning, Orders Addr.: c/o Thomson Learning Order Fulfilment, P.O. Box 6904, Florence, KY 41022 USA Toll Free Fax: 800 487 8488; Toll Free: 800 347 7707; c/o Thomson Delmar Learning Clinical Health Care Series, P.O. Box 3419, Scranton, PA 18505-0419 Fax: 570-347-9072; Toll Free: 888-427-5800; Edit Addr.: P.O. Box 15015, Albany, NY 12212-5015 USA (SAN 206-7544) Tel 518-348-2300; Fax: 518-373-6345; Toll Free: 800-998-7498; 5 Maxwell Dr., Clifton Park, NY 12065- (SAN 658-0440) Tel 518-348-2300; Fax 518-881-1256; Toll Free: 800-998-7498
E-mail: matthew.grover@thomson.com; clinicalmanuals@thomson.com
Web site: http://www.delmarlearning.com; http://www.clinicalmanuals.com/
Dist(s): **CENGAGE Learning**
Follett School Solutions
Gryphon Hse., Inc.
OptumInsight, Inc.
Pearson Education
Rittenhouse Bk. Distributors
ebrary, Inc.; *CIP.*

DeLorme, *(978-0-89933)* P.O. Box 298, Yarmouth, ME 04096 USA (SAN 220-1208) Tel 207-846-7000; Fax: 207-846-7051; Toll Free Fax: 800-575-2244 (orders); Toll Free: 800-335-6763 (orders only)
E-mail: reseller@delorme.com
Web site: http://www.delorme.com
Dist(s): **Benchmark LLC**
Hammond World Atlas Corp.
Langenscheidt Publishing Group
Many Feathers Bks. & Maps
Rand McNally.

DeLorme Mapping Company *See* **DeLorme**
Delphi Bks., *(978-0-9663397; 978-0-9765185; 978-0-9846015)* Orders Addr.: P.O. Box 6435, Lee's Summit, MO 64064 USA Toll Free: 800-431-1579 (orders)
E-mail: DelphiBks@yahoo.com
Web site: http://www.DelphiBooks.us; http://www.FranBaker.com
Dist(s): **Brodart Co.**
Emery-Pratt Co.
Midwest Library Service.
Delphinium *Imprint of* **HarperCollins Pubs.**
Delta Education, Incorporated *See* **Delta Education, LLC**
Delta Education, LLC, *(978-0-87504; 978-1-58356; 978-1-59242; 978-1-59821; 978-1-60395; 978-1-60902; 978-1-62571; 978-1-64011)* 80 Northwest Blvd., Nashua, NH 03063 USA (SAN 630-1711) Toll Free: 800-442-5444
E-mail: ngosselin@delta-edu.com
Web site: http://www.delta-education.com.
Delta Gamma Ctr., *(978-0-9748523)* 1750 S. Big Bend Blvd., Saint Louis, MO 63117-2402 USA Toll Free: 800-341-4310
E-mail: info@dgckids.org
Web site: http://www.dgckids.org.
Delta Stream Media, *(978-0-9776939; 978-1-945899)* Div. of Natural Math, 309 Silvercliff, Cary, NC 27513 USA (SAN 257-9987) Tel 919-388-1721
E-mail: maria@naturalmath.com
Web site: http://www.naturalmath.com
Dist(s): **American Mathematical Society.**
Delta Systems Company, Inc., *(978-0-937354; 978-1-887744; 978-1-932748; 978-1-934960; 978-1-936299; 978-1-936402; 978-1-62167)* Orders Addr.: 1400 Miller Pkwy., McHenry, IL 60050-7030 USA (SAN 220-0457) Tel 815-363-3582; Fax: 815-363-2948; Toll Free Fax: 800-909-9901; Toll Free: 800-323-8270; *Imprints:* Raven Tree Press (Raven Tree Pr)
E-mail: d.patchin@DeltaPublishing.com; L.Bruell@DeltaPublishing.com; j.patchin@deltapublishing.com
Web site: http://www.deltapublishing.com; http://www.raventreepress.com
Dist(s): **Follett Media Distribution**
National Bk. Network.
DEMDACO, *(978-1-932139)* Div. of DD Traders, Inc., 5000 W. 134th St., Leawood, KS 66209-7806 USA Toll Free: 888-336-3226
Web site: http://www.demdaco.com.
Demeter Books *See* **Lake Street Pr.**
DeMosi *See* **DeMosi Publishing**
DeMosi Publishing, *(978-0-9708523)* Orders Addr.: P.O. Box 60606, Chicago, IL 60660 USA
E-mail: demosipublishing@email.com.
Den Publishing Co., *(978-0-9742195)* P.O. Box 93336, Albuquerque, NM 87199-3336 USA Fax: 505-822-8035.
DeNicest Concepts, *(978-0-9763973)* P.O. Box 1831, Buffalo, NY 14240 USA.
Denim Design Lab LLC, *(978-0-9773012)* P.O. Box 5853, San Clemente, CA 92674-9998 USA Tel 949-366-3307; Fax: 949-366-3304
E-mail: denimdesignlab@aol.com
Web site: http://www.denimdesignlab.com.
Denison, T. S. & Co., Inc., *(978-0-513)* Orders Addr.: P.O. Box 1650, Grand Rapids, MI 49501-5431 USA (SAN 201-3142) Tel 616-802-3000; Fax: 616-802-3009; Toll Free Fax: 800-543-2690; Toll Free: 800-253-5469
Dist(s): **Lectorum Pubns., Inc.**
Denlinger, Dennis, *(978-0-9742567)* Orders Addr.: 46 Purdy St., Harrison, NY 95821 USA; Edit Addr.: P.O. Box 60431, Sacramento, CA 95860-0431 USA Tel 916-488-9643 Phone/fax); Toll Free: 800-431-1579 fulfillment
E-mail: dennis@footarch.com
Web site: http://www.footarch.com
Dist(s): **Book Clearing Hse.**
Denney Literary Services, *(978-0-9654698; 978-0-9707469)* 2907 Noah St., Chattanooga, TN 37406-1928 USA Tel 423-622-0419; *Imprints:* DLS Books (DLS Bks)
E-mail: denney2907@earthlink.net.
Dennis West, *(978-0-9978774)* 8212 Sleeping Bear Dr NW, Albuquerque, NM 87120 USA Tel 214-505-0179
E-mail: cwickwire@att.net.
Dennison, Donna, *(978-0-9760484)* 121 Tuxedo, San Antonio, TX 78209-3712 USA.
Densmore-Reid Pubns., *(978-0-9700827)* 67 S. 24th St., Richmond, IN 47374 USA Tel 765-939-2984 (phone/fax)
E-mail: ddgreens@netscape.net
Web site: http://www.densmorereid.com/.
Dental Wellness Institute, *(978-0-9815630)* 321 S. Main St., No. 503, Sebastopol, CA 95472 USA (SAN 855-8795) Tel 707-829-7220; Toll Free: 800-335-7755
E-mail: dentwell@pacbell.net
Web site: http://www.dentalwellness4u.com
Dist(s): **Cardinal Pubs. Group.**
Denver Broncos, *(978-0-9759579)* INVESCO Field at Mile High, 1701 Bryant St., Suite 900, Denver, CO 80204 USA
Web site: http://www.denverbroncos.com.
Denwit Publishing, *(978-0-9960973)* 822 Cotton Grove Rd., Jackson, TN 38305 USA Tel 731-616-5099
E-mail: gcdenwiddie@gmail.com
Web site: gcdenwiddie.com.
DEO Consulting, Inc., *(978-0-9728793)* 16334 Boardwalk Terr., Orland Hills, IL 60477 USA
E-mail: dale@mbd2.com
Web site: http://www.mbd2.com.
DePalma, Vanessa, *(978-0-9728135)* 49 Tropez Point, Rochester, NY 14626 USA Tel 585-723-9699
E-mail: vdepalma@frontiernet.net.
Dept. of Chamorro Affairs, *(978-1-883488)* P.O. Box 2950, Hagatna, GU 96932 USA Tel 671-477-6447
E-mail: lbaguon@yahoo.com
Web site: http://www.dca.guam.gov.
Depot Bks., *(978-0-9717611)* Orders Addr.: 87 Throckmorton Ave., Mill Valley, CA 94941 USA; Edit Addr.: 8 Madrona St., Mill Valley, CA 94941 USA.
Dept. of the Army *Imprint of* **United States Government Printing Office**
Dercum Audio, *(978-1-55656)* 1501 County Hospital Rd., Nashville, TN 37218 USA (SAN 658-7607) Tel 615-254-2408
E-mail: DawsonC@locc.com
Web site: http://www.bookcase.com/Dercum
Dist(s): **APG Sales & Distribution Services.**
Dercum Press/Dercum Audio *See* **Dercum Audio**
Derke, Connie, *(978-0-9747063)* 6418 W. 13100 S., Herriman, UT 84065 USA Tel 801-254-8711
E-mail: derke1904@msn.com.
Derrick, Paul, *(978-0-9744875)* Orders Addr.: 918 N. 30th St., Waco, TX 76707-2502 USA Tel 254-753-6920 (phone/fax)
E-mail: pjderrick@aol.com
Web site: http://stargazerpaul.com.
Derry Lane Publishing, *(978-0-692-82325-5; 978-0-692-83659-0)* 1225 Derry Ln., WEST CHESTER, PA 19380 USA Tel 314-800-7731
E-mail: priyaponnapula@gmail.com; priyaponnapula@gmail.com.
Derrydale Pr., The, *(978-1-56416; 978-1-58667)* Div. of Rowman & Littlefield Publishing Group, Orders Addr.: 15200 NBN Way, Blue Ridge Summit, PA 17214 USA Tel 717-794-3800 (Sales, Customer Service, MIS, Royalties, Inventory Mgmt., Dist., Credit & Collections); Fax: 717-794-3803 (Customer Service &/or orders only); 717-794-3857 (Sales & MIS); 717-794-3856 (Royalties, Inventory Mgmt., & Dist.); Toll Free Fax: 800-338-4550 (Customer Service &/or orders); Toll Free: 800-462-6420 (Customer Service &/or orders); Edit Addr.: 4501 Forbes Blvd., Lanham, MD 20706 USA Tel 301-459-3366; Fax: 301-459-5748
E-mail: sdriver@derrydalepress.com
Web site: http://www.derrydalepress.com
Dist(s): **MyiLibrary**
National Bk. Network
Rowman & Littlefield Publishers, Inc.
ebrary, Inc.
Desdemona's Dreams LLC, *(978-0-9968874)* 4229 N. Derbigny, New Orleans, LA 70117 USA Tel 818-645-7390
E-mail: zachmohr77@gmail.com
Web site: https://desdemonasdreams.com/.
†**Deseret Bk. Co.**, *(978-0-87579; 978-0-87747; 978-1-57345; 978-1-59038; 978-1-60641; 978-1-60907; 978-1-60908; 978-1-62972; 978-1-62973)* Div. of Deseret Management Corp., P.O. Box 30178, Salt Lake City, UT 84130 USA (SAN 150-763X) Tel 801-517-3165 (Wholesale Dept.); 801-534-1515; Fax: 801-517-3338; Toll Free: 800-453-3876; *Imprints:* Bookcraft, Incorporated (Bkcraft Inc); Shadow Mountain (ShadMtn); Ensign Peak (EnsignPeak)
E-mail: wholesale@deseretbook.com; dbwhsale@deseretbook.com
Web site: http://www.deseretbook.com; http://www.shadowmountain.com
Dist(s): **Blackstone Audio, Inc.**; *CIP.*
Desert Badger Pr., *(978-0-9767555)* 4147 E. Megan Dr., Tucson, AZ 85712 USA
Web site: http://www.elderlawtucson.com.
Desert Bear Publishing, *(978-0-9765389)* P.O. Box 72313, Phoenix, AZ 85050 USA Tel 480-538-0842; Fax: 602-926-2429.
Desert Hills Publishing *See* **D H Publishing LLC**
Desert Sage Pr., *(978-0-615-72020-3; 978-0-9897133)* P.O. Box 357, Eagle, ID 83616 USA Tel 208-860-2464; Fax: 208-938-1554
Web site: www.desertsagepress.com
Dist(s): **CreateSpace Independent Publishing Platform.**
Desert Song Productions, *(978-0-9743402)* P.O. Box 35052, Tucson, AZ 85740 USA
E-mail: brian@brianjharris.com
Web site: http://www.brianjharris.com.
Desert Well Network, LLC, *(978-1-59236)* P.O. Box 1026 Florin Rd, #303, Sacramento, CA 95831 USA
E-mail: admin04@desertwellnetwork.com
Web site: http://www.DesertWellNetwork.com
Dist(s): **Lightning Source, Inc.**
Desert West Publishing, *(978-0-578-03542-0)* P.O. Box 35, Fairview, UT 84629 USA
Dist(s): **Lulu Pr., Inc.**
DesertStar Communications, LLC, *(978-0-9769815)* Orders Addr.: P.O. Box 243988, Boynton Beach, FL 33424-3988 USA
Web site: http://www.desertstarcommunications.com.
Desideramus Publishing, *(978-0-9975883)* 802 Peachwood Bend Dr., Houston, TX 77077 USA Tel 281-597-8867
E-mail: Barbarabdenson@gmail.com
Web site: Desideramus.com.
Design Media Publishing Ltd. (HKG) *(978-988-19738-4-9; 978-988-12967)* *Dist. by* **Bookmasters.**
Design Originals *Imprint of* **Fox Chapel Publishing Co., Inc.**
Design Pr. Bks. *Imprint of* **Savannah College of Art & Design Exhibitions**
Design Studio Pr., *(978-0-9726676; 978-1-933492; 978-1-62465)* Orders Addr.: 5022 Eagle Rock Blvd., Los Angeles, CA 90041 USA
Web site: http://www.designstudiopress.com
Dist(s): **Diamond Bk. Distributors**
Ingram Publisher Services.
Design Vault, LLC *See* **Design Vault Pr., LLC**
Design Vault Pr., LLC, *(978-0-9768974; 978-0-615-93708-3; 978-0-692-68465-8)* 11813 E 105th St N, Owasso, OK 74055 USA Tel 918.625.1483
Web site: www.designvault.net
Dist(s): **CreateSpace Independent Publishing Platform.**
DesignAbility, *(978-0-9786425)* P.O. Box 9988, Salt Lake City, UT 84109 USA
Web site: http://www.design-ability.com.
Designed World Learning, LLC, *(978-0-9763351)* Suite 105-124, 1933 Hwy. 35, Wall, NJ 07719 USA
Web site: http://www.designedworldlearning.com.
Designs For Progress, Inc., *(978-0-9793902)* 24601 Milfay Rd., No. 5, Depew, OK 74028 USA
E-mail: dmccalment@aol.com.
Desktop Prepress Services, *(978-0-615-15679-8; 978-0-615-15817-4; 978-0-615-19039-6; 978-0-615-19643-5; 978-0-615-19723-4; 978-0-615-25624-5; 978-0-578-00420-4; 978-0-578-01448-7; 978-0-578-02385-4; 978-0-578-02469-1; 978-0-578-03167-5; 978-0-578-04693-8; 978-0-578-08235-6; 978-0-578-15292-9)* 808 S. New Bethel Blvd., Ada, OK 74820 USA
Web site: http://www.desktopprepress.com
Dist(s): **Lulu Pr., Inc.**
Deste Foundation (GRC) *Dist. by* **Dist Art Pubs.**
Destination Pubs. *Imprint of* **Pulte, Therese Marie**
Destined For Greatness Publisher *See* **Empowering People Pub.**
Destinee Media, *(978-0-9759082; 978-0-9832768; 978-1-938367)* c/o McCall, 301 Iberian Way, Apt. 253, Sandpoint, ID 83864 USA
Web site: http://www.destineemedia.com.
Destiny Image Europe (ITA) *(978-88-900588; 978-88-89127; 978-88-96727)* *Dist. by* **STL Dist.**
Destiny Image Pubs., *(978-0-7684; 978-0-914903; 978-1-56043; 978-0-9716036)* 167 Walnut Bottom Rd., Shippensburg, PA 17257 USA (SAN 253-4339) Tel 717-532-3040; Fax: 717-532-9291; Toll Free: 800-722-6774
E-mail: dnj@destinyimage.com
Web site: http://www.destinyimage.com
Dist(s): **Anchor Distributors**
Appalachian Bible Co.
Send The Light Distribution LLC
Spring Arbor Distributors, Inc.
Detail Press *See* **Blue Tree LLC**
Determined Productions, Inc., *(978-0-915696)* P.O. Box 2150, San Francisco, CA 94126-2150 USA (SAN 212-7385) Tel 415-433-0660; Fax: 415-421-0929.
Detroit International Pr., *(978-0-9766622)* 900 Wilshire Dr. Ste. 202, Troy, MI 48084-1600 USA
E-mail: vince@detroitip.com.
Dettman Design Services, *(978-0-615-38527-3)* 718 Logan Ave., Elgin, IL 60120 USA Tel 847-888-2178
E-mail: t.dettman@sbcglobal.net.
Deutscher Taschenbuch Verlag GmbH & Co KG (DEU) *(978-3-423)* *Dist. by* **Distribks Inc.**
Deux *Imprint of* **Aurora Publishing, Inc.**
DeuxRay Productions, *(978-0-615-52915-8)* 2401 Capitan Ave., San Diego, CA 92104 USA Tel 619-987-5505; Fax: 619-291-4404
E-mail: deuxray@cox.net
Web site: www.inmyownbackyard.org.
Developmental Studies Center *See* **Center for the Collaborative Classroom**
Developmental Vision Concepts, *(978-0-9635507; 978-0-9747810)* Orders Addr.: P.O. Box 400, Tehachapi, CA 93581 USA Tel 661-822-3106; Edit Addr.: 316 S. Green, Tehachapi, CA 93581 USA
E-mail: stoebner@lightspeed.net.
Devenny, Jenny, *(978-0-692-78650-5)* 257 Gold St. Apt. 1002, Brooklyn, NY 10009 USA Tel 917-232-7377
E-mail: jennydevenny@gmail.com.
Devere Publishng, Inc., *(978-0-9787988)* P.O. Box 970965, Orem, UT 84097-0965 USA (SAN 851-6456) Tel 801-434-7558 (phone/fax)
E-mail: boblamx@gmail.com
Web site: http://winningorlosing.com.
Devil's Due Digital, Inc. - A Checker Digital Co., *(978-0-9710249; 978-0-9741664; 978-0-9753808; 978-1-933160; 978-1-61799)* 217 Byers Rd., Miamisburg, OH 45342 USA
E-mail: info@checkerbpg.com
Web site: http://www.checkerbpg.com
Dist(s): **Brodart Co.**
Haven Distributors
Tales of Wonder.com.
Devil's Due Publishing, Inc., *(978-1-932796; 978-1-934692)* 2217 W. Roscoe St., Chicago, IL 60618-6209 USA
E-mail: swells@devilsdue.net; d.davis@devilsdue.net
Web site: http://www.devilsdue.net
Dist(s): **Diamond Comic Distributors, Inc.**
Diamond Bk. Distributors
Publishers Group West (PGW).
†**Devin-Adair Pubs., Inc.**, *(978-0-8159)* P.O. Box A, Old Greenwich, CT 06870 USA (SAN 112-062X) Tel 203-531-7755; Fax: 718-359-8568; *CIP.*
Devonshire Bks., *(978-0-615-33660-2)* 918 W. Browning St., Appleton, WI 54914 USA Tel 920-954-5733
E-mail: fiwrgirl3@hotmail.com.
Devora Publishing *Imprint of* **Simcha Media Group**
DeVore & Sons, Incorporated *See* **Fireside Catholic Bibles**
DeVorss & Co., *(978-0-87516)* Orders Addr.: P.O. Box 1389, Camarillo, CA 93011-1389 USA (SAN 168-9886) Tel 805-322-9010; Fax: 805-322-9011; Toll Free: 800-843-5743; Edit Addr.: 553 Constitution Ave., Camarillo, CA 93012-8510 USA; *Imprints:* Devorss Publications (Devorss Pubns)
E-mail: service@devorss.com
Web site: http://www.devorss.com
Dist(s): **Health and Growth Assocs.**
New Leaf Distributing Co., Inc.
Devorss Pubns. *Imprint of* **DeVorss & Co.**
DeWard Publishing Co., Ltd., *(978-0-9798893; 978-0-9819703; 978-1-936341; 978-1-947929)* P.O. Box 6259, Chillicothe, OH 45601 USA Toll Free: 800-300-9778
E-mail: nathan_ward@hotmail.com
Web site: http://www.dewardpublishing.com.
Dewberry Pr., *(978-0-9854076; 978-0-9910340)* P.O. Box 604, Pflugerville, TX 78660 USA Tel 512-522-0596
E-mail: dewberrypress@yahoo.com
Web site: www.dewberrypress.com
Dist(s): **Lightning Source, Inc.**
Dewey Does *See* **A B C-123 Publishing**
Dewey Pubns., Inc., *(978-0-9615053; 978-1-878810; 978-1-932612; 978-1-934651; 978-1-941825)* 1840 Wilson Blvd Suite 203, Arlington, VA 22201 USA (SAN 694-1451) Tel 703-524-1355
E-mail: deweypublications@gmail.com
Web site: http://www.deweypub.com.
Dewey's Good News Balloons, *(978-1-880215)* 1202 Wildwood Dr., Deer Park, TX 77536 USA Tel 281-479-2759; Fax: 281-476-9997; Toll Free: 888-894-6597
E-mail: balloonz@flash.net.
Dey Street Bks. *Imprint of* **HarperCollins Pubs.**
Dezaim Productions and Management, LLC, *(978-0-9770111)* 1385 Chancellor Cir., Bensalem, PA 19020 USA.
Deziner Media International, *(978-0-9743971; 978-0-615-23060-3; 978-0-615-28400-2; 978-0-9819912)* P.O. Box 239, Marrero, LA 70073 USA Tel 504-292-9101; 1472 Ames Blvd., Marrero, LA 70072
E-mail: dezinermedia@aol.com
Web site: http://www.writeabc123.com.
DFC Pubs., *(978-0-9793987)* 31 W. Smith St., Amityville, NY 11701 USA (SAN 853-3695)
E-mail: contactus@urbanclubbooks.com
Web site: http://www.urbanclubbooks.com.
dg ink, *(978-0-9772577)* Orders Addr.: P.O. Box 1182, Daly City, CA 94017-1182 USA Tel 650-994-2662; Fax: 650-991-3050; *Imprints:* Ascribed (Ascribed)
E-mail: dg@dg-ink.net; info@dg-ink.net
Web site: http://www.dg-ink.net
Dist(s): **Follett School Solutions.**
†**Dharma Publishing**, *(978-0-89800; 978-0-913546)* Orders Addr.: 35788 Hauser Bridge Rd., Cazadero, CA 95421 USA (SAN 201-2723) Tel 707-847-3717; Fax: 707-847-3380; Toll Free: 800-873-4276
E-mail: contact@dharmapublishing.com; order@dharmapublishing.com
Web site: http://www.dharmapublishing.com/
Dist(s): **National Bk. Network**
Wisdom Pubns.; *CIP.*
Di Angelo Pubns., *(978-0-9850853; 978-1-942549)* 4265 San Felipe No. 1100, Houston, TX 77027 USA Tel 713-960-6636.
Di Bella, Brenda, *(978-0-615-38253-1)* 6643 Haskell Ave. No. 205, Van Nuys, CA 91406 USA Tel 818-235-3040
E-mail: comiab@yahoo.com
Web site: http://www.imuptobigthings.com.
Di Capua, Michael *Imprint of* **Scholastic, Inc.**
di Capua, Michael Bks. *Imprint of* **Hyperion Bks. for Children**
Di Maggio, Richard *See* **Consumer Pr., The**
Diakonia Publishing, *(978-0-9676528; 978-0-9725609; 978-0-9747278; 978-0-9772483; 978-0-9800877)* P.O. Box 9512, Greensboro, NC 27429-0512 USA Tel 336-707-2610
E-mail: diakoniapublishing@hotmail.com
Web site: http://www.ephesians412.com.
Dial *Imprint of* **Penguin Publishing Group**
Dial Bks *Imprint of* **Penguin Publishing Group**
Dial Bks *Imprint of* **Penguin Young Readers Group**
Dialogue Systems, Incorporated *See* **Metropolitan Teaching & Learning Co.**
Dialogues in Self Discovery LLC, *(978-1-934450)* P.O. Box 43161, Montclair, NJ 07043 USA (SAN 853-2745) Tel 973-714-2800; Fax: 973-746-2853
E-mail: discoveroption@aol.com.
Diamond Bk. Distributors, *(978-1-64031)* Div. of Diamond Comic Distributors, Inc., Orders Addr.: 1966 Greenspring Dr., Suite 300, Timonium, MD 21093 USA (SAN 110-9502) Tel 410-560-7100; Fax: 410-560-2583; Toll Free: 800-452-6642; *Imprints:* William M. Gaines Agent, INC. (WILLIAM M. GAI)
E-mail: books@diamondbookdistributors.com
Web site: http://www.diamondcomics.com; http://www.diamondbookdistributors.com/
Dist(s): **Elsevier**
MyiLibrary
SCB Distributors
SPD-Small Pr. Distribution.
Diamond Book Distributors Inc. *See* **Diamond Comic Distributors, Inc.**
Diamond Clear Vision *Imprint of* **Illumination Arts LLC**
Diamond Comic Distributors, Inc., *(978-1-59396; 978-1-60584)* 1966 Greenspring Dr., Suite 300, Timonium, MD 21093 USA Tel 410-560-7100; Fax: 410-560-2583; Toll Free: 800-452-6642
E-mail: books@diamondbookdistributors.com
Web site: http://www.diamondbookdistributors.com/
Dist(s): **Diamond Bk. Distributors.**
Diamond Creek Publishing, *(978-0-9713811)* P.O. Box 2068, Flagstaff, AZ 86003-2068 USA
Web site: http://www.apathways.com.
Diamond Event Planning, Inc., *(978-0-9766901)* 50-44 193rd St., Fresh Meadows, NY 11365 USA Tel 718-357-6144; Fax: 718-357-6685
E-mail: bridepro@aol.com
Web site: http://www.awedwitharedhead.com.
Diamond Farm Bk. Pubs., Div. of Yesteryear Toys & Books, Inc., Orders Addr.: P.O. Box 537, Alexandria Bay, NY 13607 USA (SAN 674-9054) Tel 613-475-1771; Fax: 613-475-3748; Toll Free Fax: 800-305-5138 (Order Line); Toll Free: 800-481-1353 (Order Line)
E-mail: info@diamondfarm.com
Web site: http://www.diamondfarm.com.
Diamond Fly Publishing, Inc., *(978-0-9817938)* 5224 Kings Mills Rd. Suite 264, Mason, OH 45040-2319 USA (SAN 856-566X)
Web site: http://www.diamondflypublishing.com.

Diamond Select Toys & Collectibles, (978-1-931724) Div. of Diamond Comics Distributors, 1966 Greenspring Dr., Suite 300, Timonium, MD 21093 USA Tel 410-560-7100; Fax: 410-560-7589; Toll Free: 800-452-6642
E-mail: wjason@diamondcomics.com
Web site: http://www.diamondselecttoys.com
Dist(s): **Diamond Comic Distributors, Inc.**
Diamond Bk. Distributors
Simon & Schuster, Inc.

Diamond Spine Publishing, (978-0-9765119; 978-0-9906238) 42 Lake Ave., Ext., Suite 188, Danbury, CT 06811 USA Fax: 203-775-3311
E-mail: steeling@sinfulnyms.com.

Diamond Springs Pr., (978-0-9729940) 8085 Diamond Springs Dr., Helena, MT 59602 USA Tel 406-458-9220
E-mail: sagewood@qwest.net.

Diamond Star Pr., (978-0-9774335) P.O. Box 490817, Los Angeles, CA 90049-0817 USA (SAN 257-6457)
E-mail: info@diamondstarpress.com.

Diamond Triple C Ranch, (978-0-9790652) 801 Floral Vale Blvd., Yardley, PA 19067 USA (SAN 852-324X) Tel 215-497-3188; Fax: 215-497-3190
Web site: http://www.diamondtriplecranch.com.

DIANE Publishing Co., (978-0-7881; 978-0-941375; 978-1-56806; 978-0-7567; 978-1-4223; 978-1-4289; 978-1-4379; 978-1-4578) Orders Addr.: P.O. Box 617, Darby, PA 19023-0617 USA (SAN 667-1217) Tel 610-461-6200; Fax: 610-461-6130; Toll Free: 800-782-3833; Edit Addr.: 330 Pusey Ave., No. 3 rear, Collingdale, PA 19023 USA Tel 610-461-6200; Fax: 610-461-6130; Toll Free: 800-782-3833
E-mail: cfisher@dianepublishing.net
Web site: http://www.dianepublishing.net.

Diarmuid Inc., (978-1-59347) Orders Addr.: P.O. Box 357580, Gainesville, FL 32635 USA Toll Free: 877-475-3277; Edit Addr.: 2630 N.W. 41st St., Suite D-1, Gainesville, FL 32606 USA
E-mail: kuo49@aol.com; dalia@greatleaps.com
Web site: http://www.greatleaps.com.

DiaShah Pr., LLC, (978-0-9761207) Orders Addr.: P.O. Box 43804, Nottingham, MD 21236 USA
E-mail: diashahpress@yahoo.com
Web site: http://www.debrasawyer.com; http://www.diashahpress.com.

DIASOT Pubns., (978-0-9844649) P.O. Box 705, Pittsburg, KS 66762 USA (SAN 859-4759)
E-mail: DIASOTPublications@gmail.com.

Diaz, Bethany, (978-0-692-76474-9; 978-0-692-76476-3; 978-0-692-79593-4; 978-0-692-79666-5) 895 Riverside Dr Apt E157, WENATCHEE, WA 98801 USA Tel 253-820-3953.

Dibble Institute for Marriage Education, The, (978-0-9652427; 978-0-9761349; 978-0-9828395; 978-1-940815) Orders Addr.: P.O. Box 7881, Berkeley, CA 94707-0881 USA Tel 510-528-7975 (Main Office); Fax: 972-226-2824 (Customer Service Fax); Toll Free: 800-695-7975 (Customer Service); Edit Addr.: 728 Coventry Rd., Kensington, CA 94707 USA
E-mail: relationshipskills@DibbleInstitute.org
Web site: http://www.buildingrelationshipskills.org; http://www.DibbleInstitute.org.

Dickerman, David, (978-0-692-76993-5; 978-0-692-76994-2) 317 Hale St., PENNINGTON, NJ 08534 USA Tel 347-834-7819.

Dickow, Gregory Ministries, (978-1-932833) Orders Addr.: P.O. Box 7000, Chicago, IL 60680 USA Tel 847-645-9100; Fax: 847-842-9200; Edit Addr.: 2500 Beverly Rd., Hoffman Estates, IL 60192 USA
E-mail: gdmpartnerrelations@changinglives.org
Web site: http://www.changinglives.org.

Dickson Keanaghan, LLC, (978-0-9749146; 978-1-933230) 265 Jerusalem Ave., Hicksville, Long Island,, NY 11801-4931 USA Tel 516-578-5874 cell phone; Fax: 516-433-5734 office fax
E-mail: jckunzjr@dicksonkeanaghan.com
Web site: DicksonKeanaghan.com
Dist(s): **Lightning Source, Inc.**

Dickson-Keanaghan Publishing Group, LLC *See* **Dickson Keanaghan, LLC**

Dictionary Project, Inc., The, (978-0-9745292; 978-0-9771777; 978-1-934669) P.O. Box 566, Sullivan's Island, SC 29482 USA (SAN 255-5999)
E-mail: wordpower2@aol.com.

Didax Educational Resources, Inc., (978-1-58324; 978-1-885111) 395 Main St., Rowley, MA 01969 USA Tel 978-948-2340 (ext. 350); Fax: 978-948-2813; Toll Free: 800-458-0024
Web site: http://www.didax.com.

Die Gestalten Verlag (DEU) (978-3-931126; 978-3-89955) *Dist. by* **Prestel Pub NY.**

Die Gestalten Verlag (DEU) (978-3-931126; 978-3-89955) *Dist. by* **Peng Rand Hse.**

Diettribe Enterprises *See* **Steve Diet Goedde**

Dietz Pr., (978-0-87517; 978-0-692-55454-8; 978-0-692-55455-5) Orders Addr.: 930 Winfield Rd., Petersburg, VA 23803-4748 USA Tel 804-733-0123; Fax: 804-733-3514; Toll Free: 800-391-6833
E-mail: wsmith@owenprinting.com; customerservice@dietzpress.com
Web site: http://www.dietzpress.com
Dist(s): **American Wholesale Bk. Co.**
Barnes&Noble.com
Emery-Pratt Co.
Follett School Solutions.

Different Friends, (978-1-892750) Orders Addr.: P.O. Box 40208, Cincinnati, OH 45240 USA Tel 513-825-1514; Edit Addr.: 703 Yorkhaven Rd., Cincinnati, OH 45246 USA.

Different Worlds Pubns., (978-0-9753999) 1600 Portola Dr., San Francisco, CA 94127-1402 USA (SAN 256-0577)
E-mail: info@diffworlds.com
Web site: http://www.diffworlds.com.

DiFrancesco, Joe, (978-0-9712682) 35 Meadow Creek Ln., Glenmoore, PA 19343-2017 USA
E-mail: josephdifran@comcast.net.

Digging Clams n Oregon, (978-0-9767508) P.O. Box 746, Newport, OR 97365 USA (SAN 850-9700) Tel 541-265-5847
E-mail: williamlackner001@msn.com.

Digibots Corp., (978-0-9755725) Orders Addr.: P.O. Box 6803, Katy, TX 77491 USA Tel 281-599-1095; Fax: 281-599-0391; Toll Free: 877-375-8794; Edit Addr.: 3710 Havenmoor Pl., Katy, TX 77449 USA
E-mail: drew3710@msn.com
Web site: http://www.digibots.us.

Digireads.com *See* **Digireads.com Publishing**

Digireads.com Publishing, (978-0-9753222; 978-1-59625; 978-1-59674; 978-1-4209) 3921 Harvard Rd., Lawrence, KS 66049 USA
E-mail: digireads@yahoo.com
Web site: http://www.digireads.com
Dist(s): **Ingram Publisher Services**
Lightning Source, Inc.
Neeland Media, LLC.

Digital Antiquaria, Inc., (978-1-58057) 2 Sand Hill Rd., Morristown, NJ 07960-5928 USA
E-mail: info@DigitalAntiquaria.com
Web site: http://digitalantiquaria.com.

Digital Manga Distribution *See* **Digital Manga Publishing**

Digital Manga Publishing, (978-1-56970) Div. of Digital Manga, Inc., 1487 W. 178th St. Ste. 300, Gardena, CA 90248-3253 USA (SAN 111-817X) Toll Free: 866-897-7300
E-mail: contact@emanga.com
Web site: http://www.dmpbooks.com/
Dist(s): **Diamond Comic Distributors, Inc.**
Diamond Bk. Distributors
Random Hse., Inc.

Digital Quest Inc., (978-1-934873; 978-1-947262) 525 Thomastown Ln., Ridgeland, MS 39157 USA Tel 601-856-2237; Fax: 601-856-2576
Web site: http://www.digitalquest.com.

Digital Scanning, Inc., (978-1-58218) 344 Gannett Rd., Scituate, MA 02066 USA (SAN 299-8734) Tel 781-545-2100
E-mail: info@digitalscanning.com
Web site: http://www.digitalscanning.com
Dist(s): **Lightning Source, Inc.**
TextStream
ebrary, Inc.

Digital Vista, Inc., (978-0-9817625; 978-0-9976807; 978-0-9983375) 24 Amity Pl., Massapequa, NY 11758 USA (SAN 856-4825); *Imprints:* DV Books (MYID_W_DV BKS)
E-mail: info@digitalvista.net.

digital@batesjackson llc, (978-1-932583; 978-0-9831157; 978-0-9885895) 17-21 Elm St., Buffalo, NY 14203 USA Tel 716-854-3000; Fax: 716-847-1965
E-mail: mybook@batesjackson.com
Web site: http://www.batesjackson.com.

DigitalKu, (978-0-9763168) 7913 N. Highview Dr., Milwaukee, WI 53223 USA
Web site: http://www.digitalku.com/.

Digi-Tall Media, (978-0-9785728; 978-0-9793944; 978-0-9802093; 978-0-9840655; 978-0-9828950; 978-0-9837334; 978-0-9850007; 978-0-9894024; 978-0-9913654; 978-0-9863958; 978-0-9972356; 978-0-9982406; 978-0-9989286) 6205 Oregon Ct., Plano, TX 75023 USA Tel 972-352-0324 Digi Tall Media Distributor
E-mail: editorshepherd@gmail.com
Web site: https://www.instagram.com/digi.tall.media.ig/; https://twitter.com/DigiTallMedia1; https://www.facebook.com/groups/207015945987971/; https://www.facebook.com/Digi.Tall.Media.books/; http://www.digi-tall-media.com; http://www.story-e-books.com.

Digitex-U Pubns., (978-0-615-15579-1) 6655 Malvern Ave., Philadelphia, PA 19151 USA Tel 215-738-4678
E-mail: raincloud1@gmail.com
Web site: http://www.myspace.com/raincoud1
Dist(s): **Lulu Pr., Inc.**

DiGuiseppi, Joseph, (978-0-9768348) Orders Addr.: 4 Richmond Rd., Newtown, CT 06470-1214 USA
E-mail: joedigspi@hotmail.com
Web site: http://www.joedigspi.com.

Dillies, Lyn, (978-0-615-66530-6; 978-0-615-67484-1) 15 Laurel Ln., Westport, MA 02790 USA Tel 508-636-2484
E-mail: lyn@magicoflyn.com.

Dilligaf Publishing, (978-0-9639070; 978-0-9701020; 978-1-931207) Orders Addr.: 98 Main St., Ellsworth, ME 04605 USA Tel 207-667-5351
E-mail: studio3marty@acadia.net; vze277g4@verizon.net.

Dillon, Elena, (978-0-9886353; 978-0-9908804) 15035 Live Oak Springs, Canyon Country, CA 91387 USA Tel 661-406-2369
E-mail: info@elenadillon.com.

Dilly Green Bean Games, (978-0-9744698; 978-0-9801898) 33 Hillview Rd., Gorham, ME 04038 USA
E-mail: dillygreenbeangames@dillygreenbeangames.com; jay@indirpg.com; jay@dillygreenbeangames.com
Web site: http://www.dillygreenbeangames.com.

Dimensions, (978-0-9882694; 978-0-9703270-6-2) 1595 Parliament Ct., Fairfield, OH 45014 USA Tel 513-829-4196; Fax: 513-829-4545
E-mail: hw2000@zoomtown.com
Web site: http://www.henryhwilliamson.com.

Dimensions in Media, Inc., (978-0-9762273) 24191 N. Forest Dr., Lake Zurich, IL 60047 USA Tel 847-726-2093
E-mail: debbie@dimensionsinmedia.com
Web site: http://www.be-still.com
Dist(s): **Independent Pubs. Group.**

Dingles & Co., (978-1-891997; 978-1-59646) P.O. Box 508, Sea Girt, NJ 08750 USA
E-mail: dinglesco@aol.com
Dist(s): **Central Programs**
Gumdrop Bks.

Dingobi Publishing, (978-0-9772819) P.O. Box 4533, Rock Island, IL 61204-4533 USA.

Dings Bks., (978-0-9748890) 411 Schoolhouse Ln., Shippensburg, PA 17257 USA
E-mail: dingscenter@yahoo.com.

Dino Entertainment AG (DEU) (978-3-89748; 978-3-932268) *Dist. by* **Distribks Inc.**

Dino-Mike! *Imprint of* **Stone Arch Bks.**

Dinosaur Fund, (978-0-9748618) 711 E. St. SE, No. 104, Washington, DC 20003-2879 USA Tel 202-547-3326
E-mail: dinosaurfund@juno.com; shill@laser-image.com
Web site: http://www.dinosaurfund.org.

Dinoship, Inc., (978-0-9728585; 978-1-933384) 105 W. 73rd St., No. 1B, New York, NY 10023 USA Tel 212-721-5056; Fax: 212-595-0247; 299 Broadway, No. 1016, New York, NY 10007
E-mail: bob@dinoship.com
Web site: http://www.dinoship.com.

DinRo, (978-0-9744412) 7545 Gladstone Dr., No. 205, Naperville, IL 60565 USA Fax: 630-305-3695.

Diogenes Verlag AG (CHE) (978-3-257) *Dist. by* **Intl Bk Import.**

Diogenes Verlag AG (CHE) (978-3-257) *Dist. by* **Distribks Inc.**

Diomo Square Bks., (978-0-9765948) 4911 SW 43rd Ave., Portland, OR 97206-5011 USA
E-mail: diomo@earthlink.net.

Dion's Pubn., (978-0-9795739; 978-0-9836893) 3002 Royston Rd., Charlotte, NC 28208 USA Tel 574-307-2496
E-mail: tokereke@gmail.com.

Direct Access Publishing, (978-0-9796473) 1402 Auburn Wy No. No. 232, Auburn, WA 98002 USA (SAN 853-9952) Tel 206-725-3001; Toll Free: 877-725-3009
E-mail: directt_access@yahoo.com.

Direct World Publishing, (978-0-9787591; 978-0-9987832) 11712 Jefferson Ave STE C194, Newport News, VA 23606 USA Tel 949-302-7738
E-mail: jenniferyu28@gmail.com; directworldusa@gmail.com
Web site: http://www.JenniferYu.com; www.directworldapp.com.

Directions in Education, Training & Consultation, (978-0-9664681) Orders Addr.: P.O. Box 2478, Gig Harbor, WA 98335 USA Tel 253-858-7261; Edit Addr.: 4720 Birchtree Ln., NW, Gig Harbor, WA 98335 USA
E-mail: lbaker@HarborNet.com
Web site: http://www.pebblesinthepond.com.

DirkDesigns, LLC, (978-0-9790923) P.O. Box 3754, West Lafayette, IN 47996 USA.

Dirks Publishing *See* **Dirks Publishing, LLC**

Dirks Publishing, LLC, (978-0-9823145) P.O. Box 348, Rantoul, IL 61866-0348 USA Fax: 206-339-8510
E-mail: julie@dirkspublishing.com
Web site: http://www.dirkspublishing.com.

Disciple One Publishing, (978-0-9791883) Div. of Disciple Group Production, 10153 1/2 Riverside Dr., No. 467, Toluca Lake, CA 91602 USA Tel 323-654-8579
E-mail: baronjay@yourlittleblackbook.net
Web site: http://www.yourlittleblackbook.net
Dist(s): **Lushena Bks.**

Disciple Publishing Co., (978-0-615-23763-3) P.O. Box 554, Beaufort, SC 29901 USA Tel 843-379-9955; Fax: 843-379-9956; Toll Free: 866-245-8182
E-mail: dpc@hargray.com
Web site: http://www.dpchope.com.

Discipleship Pubns. International, (978-1-57782; 978-1-884553) 300 5th Ave. Ste. 5, Waltham, MA 02451-8749 USA Toll Free: 888-374-2665
E-mail: spjones@icoc.org; dpibooks@icoc.org
Web site: http://www.dpibooks.org
Dist(s): **Independent Pubs. Group**
ebrary, Inc.

Discipleship Resources *Imprint of* **Upper Room Bks.**

Discover Writing Company *See* **Discover Writing Pr.**

Discover Writing Pr., (978-0-9656574; 978-1-931492) Orders Addr.: P.O. Box 264, Shoreham, VT 05770 USA Tel 802-897-7022; Fax: 802-897-2084; Toll Free: 800-613-8055
E-mail: registrar@discoverwriting.com; ann@discoverwriting.com; administrator@discoverwriting.com; barry@discoverwriting.com
Web site: http://www.discoverwriting.com.

DiscoverNet, (978-0-9728053; 978-0-9742787; 978-0-9746943; 978-1-932813) 2474 Walnut St., Suite 105, Cary, NC 27518 USA Tel 919-301-0109; Fax: 919-557-2261
E-mail: lharte@discovernet.com
Web site: http://www.qicbooks.com.

Discovery Communications *See* **Discovery Education**

Discovery Education, (978-1-56331; 978-1-58738; 978-1-59527; 978-1-60288; 978-1-60711; 978-0-9824299; 978-1-61629; 978-1-61708; 978-1-61828; 978-1-68220) One Discovery Pl., Silver Spring, MD 20910 USA Tel 240-662-2000; Toll Free: 888-892-3484
E-mail: megan.faller@discovery.com; sara_fisher@discovery.com
Web site: http://www.discoveryeducation.com
Dist(s): **Explorations**
Follett School Solutions
Insight Guides
Langenscheidt Publishing Group.

Discovery Enterprises, Limited *See* **History Compass, LLC**

Discovery Hse. Pubns., (978-0-929239; 978-1-57293; 978-1-62707; 978-1-64070) Div. of R B C Ministries, Orders Addr.: P.O. Box 3566, Grand Rapids, MI 49501 USA (SAN 248-8949) Tel 616-942-9218; Fax: 616-957-5741; Toll Free: 800-653-8333; Edit Addr.: 3000 Kraft Ave., SE, Grand Rapids, MI 49512 USA (SAN 248-8957) Tel 616-942-6770; Fax: 616-974-2224
E-mail: dhp@rbc.org; rwatson@dhp.org
Web site: http://www.dhp.org
Dist(s): **CLC Pubns.**

Discovery Pr. Pubns., Inc., (978-0-9645159) 400 E. 3rd Ave., No. 901, Denver, CO 80203 USA (SAN 298-5691) Tel 303-355-9689; Fax: 303-733-3474
E-mail: discoverypresspub@comcast.net
Web site: http://www.discoverypresspub.com
Dist(s): **Brodart Co.**
Quality Bks., Inc.

Discovery Pubns. (GBR) (978-0-9538222; 978-0-9550458) *Dist. by* **Irish Bks Media.**

Disenos del Arte, Inc., (978-0-9820784) P.O. Box 11441, San Juan, PR 00910 USA Tel 787-722-1060; Fax: 787-728-3092
E-mail: dasant@delartepr.com
Web site: http://www.delartepr.com.

Disinformation Co. Ltd., The, (978-0-9713942; 978-0-9729529; 978-1-932857; 978-1-934708; 978-1-939517) 220 E. 23rd St., Suite 500, New York, NY 10010 USA
E-mail: books@disinfo.com
Dist(s): **Follett School Solutions**
Red Wheel/Weiser
ebrary, Inc.

Dismondy, Maria Inc., (978-0-615-47393-2; 978-0-615-51620-2; 978-0-9848558; 978-0-9976085) Orders Addr.: 5449 Sylvia, Dearborn, MI 48124 USA Tel 248-302-1800
E-mail: mariadismondy@mac.com
Web site: http://www.cardinalrulepress.com
Dist(s): **Independent Pubs. Group**
Partners Bk. Distributing, Inc.

Disney Editions *Imprint of* **Disney Pr.**

Disney Lucasfilm Press *Imprint of* **Disney Publishing Worldwide**

†Disney Pr., (978-0-7868; 978-1-56282; 978-1-4231) Div. of Disney Bk. Publishing, Inc., A Walt Disney Co., 44 S. Broadway. Flr. 16, White Plains, NY 10601-4411 USA Toll Free: 800-759-0190; *Imprints:* Disney Editions (Disney Ed)
Web site: http://www.disney.com/disneybooks/index.html
Dist(s): **Hachette Bk. Group**
Libros Sin Fronteras
Little Brown & Co.
Perfection Learning Corp.; *CIP.*

Disney Publishing Worldwide, (978-1-892309; 978-1-931580; 978-1-4231; 978-1-4847; 978-1-368; 978-1-368-01377-2) Subs. of Walt Disney Productions, 44 S. Broadway, 10th Flr., White Plains, NY 10601 USA Tel 914-288-4316; 1101 Flower St., Glendale, CA 91201; *Imprints:* Marvel Press (Marvel Pr); Disney Lucasfilm Press (Lucasfilm Pr)
Web site: http://www.disney.go.com; http://www.hyperionbooksforchildren.com; books.disney.com
Dist(s): **Blackstone Audio, Inc.**
Follett School Solutions
Hachette Bk. Group.

Disneyland/Vista Records & Tapes *See* **Walt Disney Records**

Disposition Sketch Bks. *Imprint of* **MacBride, E. J. Pubn., Inc.**

Disruptive Publishing, (978-1-59654; 978-1-60872; 978-1-62657) 735 Ivy League Ln., Rockville, MD 20850 USA
E-mail: service.blackmask@gmail.com
Web site: http://www.dispub.com
Dist(s): **Diamond Bk. Distributors.**

Distinct Pr., (978-0-9916089; 978-1-943103) 6822 22nd Ave. N., St. Petersburg, FL 33710-3918 USA Tel 727-238-7884
E-mail: theageofattraction@gmail.com; waldorfinspired@yahoo.com
Web site: www.DistinctPress.com
Dist(s): **Lightning Source, Inc.**

Distribooks, Inc., Div. of MED, Inc., 8124 N. Ridgeway, Skokie, IL 60076 USA (SAN 630-9763) Tel 847-676-1596; Fax: 847-676-1195
E-mail: info@distribooks.com.

Distribuidora Norma, Inc., (978-1-881700; 978-1-935164) Div. of Carvajal International, Orders Addr.: P.O. Box 195040, San Juan, PR 00919-5040 USA Tel 787-788-5050; Fax: 787-788-7161; Edit Addr.: Carretera 869 Km 1.5 Barrio Palmas Royal Industrial, Catano, PR 00962 USA
Web site: http://www.norma.com.

Distribuidora Plaza Mayor, 1500 Ave. Ponce de Leon Local 2 El Cinco, San Juan, PR 1 USA.

Éditions Chouette (CAN) (978-2-89450; 978-2-921198; 978-2-9800909; 978-2-89718) *Dist. by* **Distribks Inc.**

Éditions Tourbillon (FRA) (978-2-84801; 979-10-276) *Dist. by* **HachBkGrp.**

Ditto Enterprises, (978-0-9967559) 119 Grove Clover Ln., Montgomery, TX 77316 USA Tel 713-824-3105
E-mail: denfield97@aol.com.

Diversified A+ Pubns., (978-0-9773526) P.O. Box 13, Winchendon, MA 01475 USA
E-mail: Dpipub@aol.com
Web site: http://www.dpublications.com.

Diversified Publishing, 1745 Broadway, New York, NY 10019 USA; *Imprints:* Living Language (LiviLang)
Dist(s): **Penguin Random Hse. LLC.**

Diversion Books *See* **Diversion Publishing Corp.**

Diversion Pr., (978-1-935290) P.O. Box 30277, Clarksville, TN 37040 USA (SAN 857-0264)
E-mail: diversionpress@yahoo.com
Web site: http://www.diversionpress.com.

Diversion Publishing Corp., (978-0-9845151; 978-0-9829050; 978-0-9833371; 978-0-9838395; 978-0-9839885; 978-1-938120; 978-1-62681; 978-1-68230; 978-1-63576) 443 Park Avenue S., Ste. 1008, New York, NY 10016 USA (SAN 990-6304) Tel

212-675-5556; 212-961-6390; *Imprints:* EverAfter Romance (EverAfterRoman)
E-mail: info@diversionbooks.com; charles@efit.com
Web site: http://www.diversionbooks.com
Dist(s): **Ingram Publisher Services**
MyiLibrary
Smashwords
Two Rivers Distribution.

Diversity Foundation, The, *(978-0-9797193)* 505 W., 10200 S., South Jordan, UT 84095 USA Tel 801-553-4556; Fax: 801-553-4600; Toll Free: 888-216-2122
Web site: http://www.thediversityfoundation.org
Dist(s): **Partners Pubs. Group, Inc.**

Diversity Ink Publishing, *(978-0-9767258)* P.O. Box 2414, Santa Maria, CA 93457 USA.

Diversity Matters Pr., *(978-0-578-06591-5; 978-0-9839020)* 5555 DTC Pkwy., Suite C3200, Greenwood Village, CO 80111 USA.

Dividion Group, LLC, The, *(978-0-9769366)* Orders Addr.: P.O. Box 2678, North Canton, OH 44720 USA
E-mail: turnekash22@aol.com; bigheds@bigheds.com
Web site: http://www.bigheds.com.

Divine House Ministries *See* **Kingdom Sound Pubs.**

Divine Inspiration Publishing, LLC, *(978-0-9820490)* P.O. Box 210414, Auburn Hills, MI 48326 USA (SAN 857-1090) Fax: 248-927-0357
E-mail: stevecogswell@comcast.net; scogswell@divineinspirationpublishing.com
Web site: http://www.divineinsirationpublishing.com.

Divine Intertwine Publishing, *(978-0-9754489)* P.O. Box 4088, Ocean City, MD 21843 USA.

Divine Mercy Pr., *(978-0-9755471)* 3216 Mission Ave. Apt. 138, Oceanside, CA 92058-1348 USA
E-mail: divinemercy@hypersurf.com.

Divine Ministry of North Florida, Inc., *(978-0-9773356)* P.O. Box 5668, Gainesville, FL 32627-5668 USA (SAN 257-3652)
E-mail: ade0201@yahoo.com
Web site: http://www.divineministry.net.

Divine Physiology International Ministries, *(978-0-9983379)* P.O. Box 159175, Nashville, TN 37215 USA Tel 615-509-5557
E-mail: bnalnc@aol.com.

DJ Blues Publishing, *(978-0-9743985)* 403 Dula Cir., Duncanville, TX 75116 USA
E-mail: hipdjblues@earthlink.net
Web site: http://www.djblues.com.

DJ Inkers *Imprint of* **Carson-Dellosa Publishing, LLC**

DK *Imprint of* **Dorling Kindersley Publishing, Inc.**

DK *Imprint of* **DK Games**

DK Children *Imprint of* **Dorling Kindersley Publishing, Inc.**

DK Eyewitness Travel *Imprint of* **Dorling Kindersley Publishing, Inc.**

DK Games, 1745 Broadway, New York, NY 10019 USA; *Imprints:* DK (DK)
Dist(s): **Penguin Random Hse. LLC.**

Dksmo-Press, Izdatel'skaja firma (RUS) *(978-5-04) Dist. by* **Distribks Inc.**

DL Grant, LLC, *(978-0-9853713; 978-0-9882084; 978-0-9889947; 978-0-9914542; 978-1-942017)* 3621 Huntwick Dr., Orange, TX 77632 USA Tel 409-779-6807
E-mail: dgauthor@gmail.com.

DLG, LLC *See* **DL Grant, LLC**

dLife - For Your Diabetes Life, *(978-0-9777463)* Div. of LifeMed Media, 101 Franklin St., Westport, CT 06880-0688 USA (SAN 850-1254) Tel 203-454-6985; Fax: 203-454-6986
E-mail: info@dlife.com
Web site: http://www.dlife.com.

DLS Bks. *Imprint of* **Denney Literary Services**

DM Creative, *(978-0-9798445)* 16032 Samoa Ct., Tega Cay, SC 29708-2970 USA
Web site: http://www.hamstersam.com; http://davemcdonald.com/.

Dm Productions, *(978-0-615-14860-1; 978-0-615-15990-4)* 10596 N. Washington Blvd., Indianapolis, IN 46280 USA
Web site: http://dmprod.blogspot.com/
Dist(s): **Lulu Pr., Inc.**

DMH Pr., Inc., *(978-0-9746153)* 10 Beachside Dr., No. 302, Vero Beach, FL 32963 USA (SAN 256-0127) Fax: 631-325-1340
Web site: http://www.dollyadventures.com.

DMT Publishing, *(978-0-9726189; 978-0-9749144; 978-0-9785553; 978-0-9800813; 978-0-9824259; 978-1-935821)* 900 N. 400 W. , Bldg. 12, North Salt Lake, UT 84054 USA
Web site: http://www.dmtpublishing.com.

DNA Pr., *(978-0-9664027; 978-0-9748765; 978-1-933255)* P.O. Box 572, Eagleville, PA 19408-0572 USA (SAN 256-5005) Fax: 501-694-5495
E-mail: editors@dnapress.com
Web site: http://www.dnapress.com
Dist(s): **Independent Pubs. Group.**

do be you, *(978-0-9794262)* 229 Vincent Ave. N., Minneapolis, MN 55405 USA
E-mail: info@i-get-around.com
Web site: http://www.i-get-around.com.

Do Good Pr., *(978-0-9974263)* 9950 Scripps Lake Blvd. No. 104, San Diego, CA 92131 USA Tel 858-800-5080
E-mail: info@dogoodpress.com
Web site: www.dogoodpress.com.

Do Life Right, Inc., *(978-0-9824829; 978-1-937848)* P.O. Box 61, Sahuarita, AZ 85629 USA
E-mail: lisa@wrightontimebooks.com
Web site: http://www.doliferight.com
Dist(s): **CreateSpace Independent Publishing Platform.**

Do The Write Thing Foundation of DC, *(978-1-930357; 978-0-692-86055-7)* 56 T. St. , NW, Washington, DC 20001-1009 USA Tel 202-758-0397; Fax: 202-758-0397
E-mail: chilshil@netscape.net; dothewritething1@gmail.com
Web site: www.dothewritethingdc.com.

Do Well Studio, *(978-0-692-86200-1)* 68 Tupper Rd. No. 7, Sandwich, MA 02563 USA Tel 617-966-4636
E-mail: donna@dowellstudio.com
Web site: dowellstudio.com.

Dobie Book Publishing *See* **Mowery, Julia**

Dockter, Toni, *(978-0-9712201)* P.O. Box 1532, Soquel, CA 95073-1532 USA
E-mail: tonette101@aol.com
Web site: http://percyveerance.com.

Doctor Dolittle's Library *Imprint of* **PhotoGraphics Publishing**

DocUmeant Publishing, *(978-0-9788831; 978-0-9825608; 978-0-9826005; 978-0-9832122; 978-1-937801; 978-0-692-30306-1)* Orders Addr.: 1730 Rainbow Dr., Clearwater, FL 33755 USA Tel 727-565-2130; Fax: 727-446-2217; Edit Addr.: 244 5th Avenue, Suite G-200, New York, NY 10001 USA
E-mail: info@documeant.net; publisher@documeantpublishing.com
Web site: http://www.DocUmeantPublishing.com
Dist(s): **CreateSpace Independent Publishing Platform**
Lightning Source, Inc.
Lulu Pr., Inc.

Dodi Pr., *(978-0-9767273; 978-0-9851067)* Orders Addr.: 10 Brookstone Dr., Sicklerville, NJ 08081 USA (SAN 860-3200)
E-mail: cherilnc@cherilnclarke.com; monica.r.bey@gmail.com
Web site: www.myfamilyproducts.com; www.dodipress.com.

Dog Ear Publishing, LLC, *(978-0-9762173; 978-0-9766603; 978-1-59858; 978-1-60844; 978-1-4575)* 4010 W. 86th St., Suite H, Indianapolis, IN 46268 USA Tel 317-228-3656; Fax: 317-489-3506; Toll Free: 866-823-9613
E-mail: rayr@dogearpublishing.net
Web site: http://www.dogearpublishing.net
Dist(s): **Ingram Publisher Services**
Lightning Source, Inc.
Lulu Pr., Inc.
Smashwords.

Dog Soldier Pr., *(978-0-9718658)* P.O. Box 1782, Ranchos de Taos, NM 87557-1782 USA (SAN 254-4733) Tel 505-751-3781; Fax: 505-758-4071
E-mail: dogsoldier@newmexico.com
Web site: http://www.dogsoldierpress.com.

Dog-Eared Pubns., *(978-0-941042)* Orders Addr.: P.O. Box 620863, Middleton, WI 53562-0863 USA (SAN 281-6059) Tel 608-831-1410 (phone/fax); Toll Free: 888-364-3277; Edit Addr.: 4642 Toepfer Rd., Middleton, WI 53562 USA
E-mail: field@dog-eared.com
Web site: http://www.dog-eared.com
Dist(s): **Common Ground Distributors, Inc.**
Paradise Cay Pubns.
Partners/West Book Distributors.

Doggerel Daze, *(978-0-9722820)* 10144 Riedel Pl., Cupertino, CA 95014 USA.

DogHouse Pr., *(978-0-9761497)* 150 Chestnut St., Park Forest, IL 60466 USA Toll Free: 877-413-8997
E-mail: kimberly@rjsystems.us
Web site: http://www.doghousepress.com.

Doghouse Publishing, Incorporated *See* **Mess Hall Writers**

Dogs in Hats Children's Publishing Co., *(978-1-59445)* P.O. Box 182, Grand Haven, MI 49417 USA Tel 616-844-2220; Fax: 616-844-2922
E-mail: customerservice@dogsinhats.com
Web site: http://www.dogsinhats.com
Dist(s): **Follett School Solutions.**

Dogs4dogs, *(978-0-9771265)* P.O. Box 675432, Rancho Santa Fe, CA 92067-5432 USA
Web site: http://www.dogs4dogs.com.

Dogtown Artworks, *(978-0-9777126)* 704 N. Main St. Suite 102, Tuscola, IL 61953 USA Tel 217-689-4575
E-mail: dogtownartworks@mac.com; dogtownartworks@gmail.com; pringle.photography@gmail.com
Web site: http://www.dogtownartworks.com
Dist(s): **Independent Pubs. Group.**

Dogwalk Pr., *(978-0-9766846)* Div. of Dan Gersten & Assocs., LLC, 29636 Quail Run Dr., Agoura Hills, CA 91301 USA Tel 818-735-0280; Fax: 818-991-1838
Web site: http://www.askcurtisthedog.com.

Dogwise *See* **Dogwise Publishing**

Dogwise Publishing, *(978-1-929242; 978-1-61781)* Orders Addr.: 403 S. Mission, Wentachee, WA 98801 USA (SAN 631-1415) Tel 509-663-9115; Fax: 509-662-7233; Toll Free: 800-776-2665
E-mail: mail@dogwise.com; charlenew@dogwise.com; nate.woodward@dogwise.com
Web site: http://www.dogwise.com.

Dohate Pr., *(978-0-9767003)* Orders Addr.: 1809 Brookhaven Dr., Austin, TX 78704 USA Tel 512-442-0576
E-mail: donbutlerbooks@earthlink.net.

Doherty, Tom Assocs., LLC, *(978-0-312; 978-0-7653; 978-0-8125)* Div. of Holtzbrinck Publishers, Orders Addr.: 16365 James Madison Hwy., Gordonsville, VA 22942-8501 USA Toll Free Fax: 800-672-2054; Toll Free: 888-330-8477; Edit Addr.: 175 Fifth Ave., New York, NY 10010 USA Tel 212-674-5151; Fax: 540-672-7540 (customer service); *Imprints:* Forge Books (Forge Bks); Orb Books (Orb Bks); Tor Books (Tor Books); Starscape (Starscape); Tor Fantasy (Tor Fan); Tor Science Fiction (TorSciFic); Tor Teen (Tor Teen); Tor Romance (Tor Romance)
E-mail: inquiries@tor.com
Web site: http://www.tor.com/
Dist(s): **Cambridge Univ. Pr.**
CreateSpace Independent Publishing Platform
Libros Sin Fronteras
Macmillan
MyiLibrary
Perfection Learning Corp.

Doing Good Ministries, *(978-0-9667054)* 217 Bayview Way, Chula Vista, CA 91910 USA Tel 619-476-7230
E-mail: moehlenpah@aol.com
Web site: http://www.doinggood.org.

Dokument forlag, Fotograf Malcolm Jacobsson (SWE) *(978-91-973981; 978-91-85639) Dist. by* **SCB Distributo.**

Dollison Road Bks., *(978-0-9855540)* 247 E. 4700 N., Provo, UT 84604 USA Tel 417-883-0601
E-mail: JeanStringam@gmail.com
Web site: jeanstringam.com; DollisonRoadBooks.com.

Dollworks, *(978-0-9760064; 978-1-60304)* 6693 Lake Shore Dr., Newport, MI 48166-9716 USA; P.O. Box 66075, Newport, MI 48166
E-mail: nanciejack@aol.com.

Dolly Dimple Ink Children's Bks., *(978-0-9773506)* 5484 Atlantic View, Saint Augustine, FL 32080 USA Tel 904-460-0997
E-mail: effiemaeshearin@aol.com
Web site: http://www.dollydimpleink.com.

Dolphin Media *See* **Blue Brush Media**

Dolphin Publishing, *(978-1-878400)* P.O. Box 16656, West Palm Beach, FL 33416-6656 USA Tel 561-585-8901; Toll Free: 800-547-7867 Do not confuse with companies with the same name in Richardson, TX, Mattawan, MI
E-mail: nicotinefree@bellsouth.net
Web site: http://www.davidcjones.com.

Dolphins Publishing, *(978-0-9892565)* 1931 SW 17th Pl., Cape Coral, FL 33991 USA
E-mail: coach4u13@yahoo.com.

Dominick Pictures, *(978-0-9726092)* P.O. Box 1925, New York, NY 10013 USA.

Dominie Elementary *Imprint of* **Pearson Schl.**

Dominie Pr., Inc., *(978-0-7685; 978-1-56270)* Div. of Pearson Learning, 145 S. Mount Zion Rd., Lebanon, IN 46052-8186 USA (SAN 630-947X) Toll Free: 800-232-4570
E-mail: info@dominie.com
Web site: http://www.dominie.com.

DOMINIONHOUSE Publishing & Design, *(978-0-9755234; 978-0-9815463; 978-0-9828366; 978-0-9839869; 978-0-9888718; 978-0-9905031; 978-0-9971980)* Orders Addr.: P.O. Box 681938, Orlando, FL 32868 USA Tel 407-880-5790 (phone/fax)
Web site: http://www.mydominionhouse.com.

Don Cohen-The Mathman, *(978-0-9621674; 978-0-9779493)* Orders Addr.: 809 Stratford Dr., Champaign, IL 61821-4140 USA (SAN 251-866X) Tel 217-356-4555; Fax: 217-356-4593; Toll Free: 800-356-4559
E-mail: mathman@shout.net
Web site: http://www.shout.net/~mathman
Dist(s): **Rainbow Re-Source Ctr.**

Don Paul Publishing, LLC, *(978-0-9655792; 978-0-9816477; 978-1-941818)* P.O. Box 17062, Portland, OR 97217 USA Tel 503-764-9100
E-mail: jenna7jennifer@gmail.com; jennifer@donpaulpublishing.com
Web site: http://www.donpaulpublishing.com.

Don Quixote Publishing Co. Inc., *(978-0-9749196; 978-0-578-06784-1)* 905 Brickell Bay Dr., Unit 230, Miami, FL 33131 USA (SAN 255-884X) Tel 305-379-6151; Fax: 305-379-5156
E-mail: panza1209@aol.com; camote@manuelmartinezdreamer.com
Web site: http://www.manuelmartinezdreamer.com.

Don Rand's Classy Collectibles, *(978-0-9773775)* 26585 Fawn., Lake Forest, CA 92630-6728 USA.

DoNascimento.com/Bks., *(978-0-9835120)* 520 Ashford Dr., Coppell, TX 75019 USA Tel 214-810-2443; Fax: 501-423-3868
E-mail: douglas@donascimento.com; nicoledonascimento@gmail.com
Web site: http://www.donascimento.com/Books.

Donegal Publishing Co., *(978-0-9788128)* Orders Addr.: 1850 Industrial St., #307, Los Angeles, CA 90021 USA (SAN 851-6782) Tel 310-598-6340; Fax: 310-349-3441; Toll Free: 866-964-4919
E-mail: editor@donegalpublishing.com; richie-d@comcast.net; donegalpublishing@mac.com
Web site: http://www.donegalpublishing.com; http://www.jerryland.net.

Dong, Jianming, *(978-0-692-80729-3)* 3181 Louis Rd., PALO ALTO, CA 94303 USA Tel 408-685-1089
E-mail: dongjianming@gmail.com; dongjianming@gmail.com.

Donkey Publishing, *(978-0-9887454)* 16582 Hutchison Rd., Odessa, FL 33556 USA Tel 813-781-7143
E-mail: TOM@BRAYFIELDS.COM.

Donkey Quest Books *See* **Donkey's Quest Pr.**

Donkey's Quest Pr., *(978-0-9961139)* 40 Sherwood Rd., Medford, MA 02155 USA
E-mail: ccbaha1@gmail.com
Web site: http://donkeysquestpress.com.

Donnellan, Martha *See* **Pine Cone Pr.**

Donovan, Kevin M. *See* **Billy the Bear & His Friends, Inc.**

Don't Eat Any Bugs Prodns., *(978-0-9728177; 978-0-9802314; 978-0-9887329)* P.O. Box 291, Tehachapi, CA 93581 USA
E-mail: Ray@rayfriesen.com
Web site: http://www.donteatanybugs.com
Dist(s): **National Bk. Network.**

Don't Eat Any Bugs Productions,
Dist(s): **National Bk. Network.**

Don't Look Publishing, *(978-0-9728234)* P.O. Box 486, Moose Lake, MN 55767 USA.

Don't Run With Knives Publications *See* **Academic Solutions, Inc.**

Don't Sweat It, Inc., *(978-0-9888712; 978-0-692-63804-0; 978-0-692-63805-7)* 547 N. Las Palmas Ave., Los Angeles, CA 90004 USA Tel 310-435-7713
E-mail: ivana@princessivana.com
Web site: www.dontsweatitmedia.com.

Dontstickdontstuff, *(978-0-9888861)* 5426 E. Via Los Caballos, Paradise Valley, AZ 85253 USA Tel 480-600-4690
E-mail: dontstickdontstuff@gmail.com
Dist(s): **BookBaby**
New Shelves Distribution.

Doodle Publishing, *(978-0-9719518)* 2219 Tam-O-Shanter Ct., Carmel, IN 46032 USA Tel 317-538-6995
E-mail: adam10spro@aol.com.

Doodlebops *Imprint of* **Cookie Jar**

DoodleCake *Imprint of* **Irresistible Pr., LLC**

Dooley Bks., Ltd, *(978-0-9786605)* 53 W. Jackson No. 1240, CHICAGO, IL 60604 USA
Web site: http://www.Dooleybooks.com.

Doorlight Pubns., *(978-0-9778372; 978-0-9838653; 978-0-9982233)* 4 Central Ave., South Hadley, MA 01075 USA.

Doorposts, *(978-1-891206)* 5905 SW Lookingglass Dr., Gaston, OR 97119-9241 USA Tel 503-357-4749; Fax: 503-357-4909 Do not confuse with Doorposts, Lansdale, PA
E-mail: orders@doorposts.com
Web site: http://www.doorposts.com.

Dora, Liza, *(978-0-692-43392-8; 978-0-692-43393-5; 978-0-692-53087-0; 978-0-692-59885-6; 978-0-692-88259-7)* 5015 60th St., Lubbock, TX 79414 USA Tel 713-534-7538
E-mail: lizabrightdora@gmail.com.

Dorcas Pubns., LLC, *(978-0-9769829)* 890 Woodland Ave., Corydon, IN 47112 USA Tel 812-738-4361; Fax: 812-738-2259
E-mail: wfwilson@aol.com
Web site: http://www.dorcaspublications.com.

Dorcas Publishing, *(978-0-9762375)* Div. of Heavenly Patchwork Charity Bks., Orders Addr.: 12101 N. MacArthur, Suite 137, Oklahoma City, OK 73162-1800 USA Tel 405-751-3885 (phone/fax)
E-mail: buckboardquilts@cox.net
Web site: http://www.heavenlypatchwork.com.

Dorchester Publishing Co., Inc., *(978-0-505; 978-0-8439; 978-1-4285)* Orders Addr.: 200 Madison Ave., Suite 2000, New York, NY 10016 USA (SAN 264-0090); P.O. Box 6640, Wayne, PA 19087 Toll Free: 800-481-9191
Dist(s): **MyiLibrary.**

Dork Storm Pr., *(978-1-930964; 978-1-933288)* P.O. Box 45063, Madison, WI 53744 USA Fax: 608-225-1352
Web site: http://www.dorkstorm.com
Dist(s): **PSI (Publisher Services, Inc.).**

†Dorling Kindersley Publishing, Inc., *(978-0-7894; 978-1-56458; 978-1-879431; 978-0-7566; 978-1-4654)* Div. of Penguin Publishing Group, 375 Hudson St., 2nd Flr., New York, NY 10014 USA (SAN 253-0791) Tel 212-213-4800; Fax: 212-213-5240; Toll Free: 877-342-5357 (orders only); *Imprints:* Alpha (AlphaUSA); DK (DKUSA); DK Children (DKChildren); DK Eyewitness Travel (DKEyewitness)
E-mail: Annemarie.Cancienne@dk.com; customer.service@dk.com
Web site: http://www.dk.com
Dist(s): **Continental Bk. Co., Inc.**
Ebsco Publishing
Follett School Solutions
Penguin Random Hse. LLC
Penguin Publishing Group
Hale, Robert & Co., Inc.
Sunburst Communications, Inc.; *CIP.*

Dormouse Productions, Inc., *(978-1-889300)* 25 NE 99th St., Miami, FL 33138-2338 USA Tel 305-379-4990; Fax: 305-379-7990
E-mail: dmouse@juno.com.

Dorn Enterprises *See* **Susy Dorn Productions, LLC**

Dorothy, a publishing project, *(978-0-9844693; 978-0-9897607; 978-0-9973666)* P.O. Box 300433, Saint Louis, MO 63130 USA
E-mail: editors@dorothyproject.com
Web site: http://www.dorothyproject.com
Dist(s): **SPD-Small Pr. Distribution.**

Dorothy Payne & Virginia Letourneau, *(978-0-9747823)* 300 E. 33rd St., Apt. 7C, New York, NY 10016 USA
Web site: http://www.cityislandclamdigger.com.

Dorrance Publishing Co., Inc., *(978-0-8059; 978-0-4349; 978-1-4809)* 701 Smithfield St. Third Flr., Pittsburgh, PA 15222 USA (SAN 201-3363) Tel 412-288-4543; Fax: 412-288-1786; Toll Free: 800-788-7654; 800-695-7599; *Imprints:* RoseDog Books (RoseDog Bks)
E-mail: rpiotrowski@dorrancepublishing.com; dorrordr@dorrancepublishing.com
Web site: http://www.dorrancepublishing.com; www.dorrancebookstore.com.

†Dorset Hse. Publishing, *(978-0-932633)* 3143 Broadway Suite 2b, New York, NY 10027 USA (SAN 687-794X) Tel 212-620-4053; Fax: 212-727-1044; Toll Free: 800-342-6657
E-mail: info@dorsethouse.com; littlewest@dorsethouse.com
Web site: http://www.dorsethouse.com; http://www.littlewestpress.com; *CIP.*

Dory Pr., *(978-0-9633240)* 13396 Wakefield Rd., Sedley, VA 23878 USA Tel 757-220-9206.

Doses of Reality, Inc., *(978-0-9754024)* 634 Ceape Ave, Oshkosh, WI 54901 USA Tel 920-573-9884
E-mail: dosesofreality@yahoo.com.

Dot Dot Bks., *(978-0-9670750)* 420 16th St., Bellingham, WA 98225 USA Tel 360-220-1686
E-mail: dana.rozier@gmail.com
Dist(s): **Independent Pubs. Group**
Small Pr. United.

Dothan Publishing *See* **Moriah Ministries**

Double B Pubns., *(978-0-929526)* 4123 N. Longview, Phoenix, AZ 85014 USA (SAN 249-6615) Tel 602-996-7129; Fax: 602-996-6928
E-mail: bfischerppg@aol.com.

Publisher Name Index

Double Dagger Pr., (*978-0-9729293*) 256 Ridge Ave., Gettysburg, PA 17325-2404 USA (SAN 255-7517) Tel 717-334-5392
E-mail: mplank@doubledaggerpress.com
Web site: http://www.doubledaggerpress.com.

Double Dap Bks., (*978-0-615-29693-7*) 3700 Mansell Rd., Suite 220, Alpharetta, GA 30022 USA.

Double Edge Pr., (*978-0-9774452; 978-0-9819514; 978-1-938002*) Orders Addr.: 72 Ellview Rd., Scenery Hill, PA 15360 USA (SAN 257-5019) Tel 724-518-6737; *Imprints:* Hummingbird World Media (HummbirdWrld)
E-mail: cuttingedge@atlanticbb.net
Web site: http://www.doubleedgepress.com
Dist(s): **ebrary, Inc.**

DOUBLE R Bks. *Imprint of* **Rodrigue & Sons Co./Double R Books Publishing**

Double R Publishing, LLC, (*978-0-9713381; 978-0-9718696; 978-0-9770534*) 7301 W. Flagler St., Miami, FL 33144 USA Tel 305-262-4240; Fax: 305-262-4115; Toll Free: 877-262-4240
E-mail: abcsbook@abcsbook.com
Web site: http://www.abcsbook.com
Dist(s): **ABC'S Bk. Supply, Inc.**

Double Roads *See* **Karenzo Media**

Doubleday *Imprint of* **Knopf Doubleday Publishing Group**

Doubleday Bks. for Young Readers *Imprint of* **Random Hse. Children's Bks.**

Doubleday Canada, Ltd. (CAN) (*978-0-385; 978-0-7704*) *Dist. by* **Random.**

Doubleday Publishing *See* **Knopf Doubleday Publishing Group**

Doubleday Religious Publishing Group, The, Div. of Random Hse., Inc., Orders Addr.: 400 Hahn Rd., Westminster, MD 21157 USA Tel 410-848-1900; Toll Free: 800-726-0600 (customer service); 800-733-3000; Edit Addr.: 12265 Oracle Blvd., Suite 200, Colorado Springs, CO 80921 USA (SAN 299-4682) Tel 719-590-4999; Fax: 719-590-8977; Toll Free Fax: 800-294-5686; Toll Free: 800-603-7051; *Imprints:* Multnomah (Mltnmah) Do not confuse with WaterBrook Pr., Great Falls, VA
Web site: http://www.randomhouse.com/waterbrook
Dist(s): **Anchor Distributors**
MyiLibrary
Penguin Random Hse. LLC
Random Hse., Inc.

DOUBLE-R BKS. *Imprint of* **Rodrigue & Sons Co./Double R Books Publishing**

DoubleStar, LLC, (*978-0-9742558*) 9672 Litzsinger Rd., Saint Louis, MO 63124-1494 USA
E-mail: doublestarllc@sbcglobal.net
Web site: http://www.cogno.com.

Douglas, Bettye Forum, Inc., The, (*978-0-9703183*) 6608 N. Western Ave., No. 327, Oklahoma City, OK 73116 USA Tel 405-528-1773; Fax: 405-842-7541; Toll Free: 800-354-0680
E-mail: bettye_douglas@excite.com
Web site: http://www.bettyedouglas.com.

Dougy Ctr., (*978-1-890534*) Orders Addr.: P.O. Box 86852, Portland, OR 97286 USA Tel 503-542-4833; Fax: 503-777-3097; Edit Addr.: 3909 SE 52nd Ave., Portland, OR 97206 USA
E-mail: kathleenr@dougy.org
Web site: http://www.dougy.org.

Doulos Christou Pr., (*978-0-9744796; 978-1-934406*) 57 N. Ruial St. Englewood Christian Church, Indianapolis, IN 46201-3330 USA
E-mail: douloschristoupress@yahoo.com
Web site: http://www.douloschristou.com.

Dove Books and Audio *Imprint of* **Phoenix Bks., Inc.**

Dove Publishing, Inc., (*978-0-9766578*) P.O. Box 310326, Atlanta, GA 31131 USA Do not confuse with companies with the same or similar name in Houston, TX, Decatur, GA, Forest heights, MD, Lake Konkonkma, NY
Web site: http://www.dovepub.com.

†**Dover Pubns., Inc.**, (*978-0-486; 978-1-60660*) Div. of Courier Corporation, 31 E. Second St., Mineola, NY 11501 USA (SAN 201-338X) Tel 516-294-7000; Fax: 516-873-1401 (orders only); Toll Free: 800-223-3130 (orders only)
E-mail: rights@doverpublications.com
Web site: http://www.doverdirect.com; http://www.doverpublications.com
Dist(s): **Continental Bk. Co., Inc.**
INscribe Digital
MyiLibrary
Beeler, Thomas T. Pub.; *CIP.*

DoveTail Hse., Inc., (*978-0-9706244; 978-0-9772935; 978-0-9800099; 978-0-9862832; 978-1-943181*) P.O. Box 501995, San Diego, CA 92150 USA Tel 858-581-5954; Fax: 858-668-1771
E-mail: dovepub@san.rr.com.

Dovetail Publishing, (*978-0-9651284*) P.O. Box 19945, Kalamazoo, MI 49019 USA Tel 616-342-2900; Fax: 616-342-1012; Toll Free: 800-222-0070
E-mail: dovetail@mich.com
Web site: http://www.mich.com/~dovetail
Dist(s): **Independent Pubs. Group**
Quality Bks., Inc.

Down County Media *See* **Bad Choices Media**

Down East Bks., (*978-0-89272; 978-0-924357*) Div. of Rowman & Littlefield Publishing Group, Inc., P.O. Box 679, Camden, ME 04843 USA (SAN 208-6301) Tel 207-594-9544; Fax: 207-594-0147; Toll Free: 800-766-1670 Wholesale orders; 800-685-7962 Retail orders
E-mail: pblanchard@downeast.com; tbregy@downeast.com
Web site: http://www.countrysportpress.com; http://www.downeastbooks.com
Dist(s): **Follett School Solutions**
MyiLibrary
National Bk. Network
TNT Media Group, Inc.
ebrary, Inc.

Down The Road Publishing, (*978-0-9754427*) 172 White Oak Dr., Batesville, IN 47006 USA (SAN 256-2227)
E-mail: timt@downtheroad.org
Web site: http://www.downtheroad.org.

Down The Shore Publishing Corp., (*978-0-945582; 978-0-9615208; 978-1-59322*) Orders Addr.: P.O. Box 100, West Creek, NJ 08092 USA Tel 609-812-5076; Fax: 609-812-5098; Edit Addr.: P.O. Box 100, West Creek, NJ 08092 USA (SAN 661-082X)
E-mail: info@down-the-shore.com; orders@down-the-shore.com; downshore@comcast.net
Web site: http://www.down-the-shore.com
Dist(s): **Partners Bk. Distributing, Inc.**
Sourcebooks, Inc.

Down-To-Earth-Bks., (*978-1-878115*) P.O. Box 488, Ashfield, MA 01330 USA Tel 413-628-0227
E-mail: maryskole@aol.com
Web site: http://www.spinninglobe.net.

Downtown Bookworks, (*978-1-935703; 978-1-941367*) 285 W. Broadway, Suite 600, New York, NY 10013 USA Tel 646-613-0707
Dist(s): **Simon & Schuster, Inc.**

Downtown Wetmore Pr., (*978-0-9795302*) Orders Addr.: 13451 Wetmore Rd., San Antonio, TX 78247 USA (SAN 853-7070) Tel 210-490-7222; Fax: 210-490-8222; Toll Free Fax: 877-490-8222; Toll Free: 877-490-7222; *Imprints:* CrumbGobbler Press (CrumbGobbler)
E-mail: downtownwetmore@earthlink.net; info@crumbgobbler.com
Web site: http://www.downtownwetmore.com.

Dr. Gazebo Publishing *See* **Snow In Sarasota Publishing**

Dr. Jay, LLC, (*978-0-9860063*) P.O. Box 422, Green Farms, CT 06838 USA
E-mail: yroehler@bookpublishing.com.

Dr. Joyce STARR Publishing, (*978-0-9792333; 978-0-9882394*) Orders Addr.: 20533 Biscayne Blvd., No. 509, Aventura, FL 33180 USA Tel 786-693-4223
E-mail: joyce.starr@gmail.com
Web site: http://drjoycestarr.com; http://starrpublications.com; http://starrpublishing.com.

Dr. Mark Stuart Berlin *See* **Berlin, Stuart**

Dr. Mary's Bks., (*978-0-9765453*) 180 90th Ave. SE, Kensal, ND 58455 USA Tel 701-435-2388
E-mail: dwayneerickson@agristar.net
Web site: http://www.shopnd.com.

Dr. Patricia Garfield's Ctr. for Creative Dreami, (*978-0-692-79633-7; 978-0-692-79635-1*) 130 Rancho Dr., TIBURON, CA 94920 USA Tel 415-383-7770.

Draft2Digital, (*978-1-4977; 978-1-4989; 978-1-5014; 978-1-5022; 978-1-5070; 978-1-5130; 978-1-5163; 978-1-5199; 978-1-5242; 978-1-5337; 978-1-5365; 978-1-5401; 978-1-386*) 5629 SE 67th St., Oklahoma City, OK 73135 USA Fax: 866-358-6413; Toll Free Fax: 866-358-6413; Toll Free: 866-336-5099
E-mail: support@draft2digital.com
Web site: www.draft2digital.com.

Drago, Vincent, (*978-0-692-00630-6; 978-0-9846189*) 218 Heather Glen Way, Madison, MS 39110 USA Tel 342-487-0904
Dist(s): **Bookmasters Distribution.**

Dragon Dog Pr., Inc., (*978-0-9770121*) P.O. Box 5399, Godfrey, IL 62035 USA Tel 618-467-0738
E-mail: ryucope@sbcglobal.net
Web site: http://www.dragondogpress.com.

Dragon Hill Publishing (CAN) (*978-1-896124*) *Dist. by* **Lone Pine.**

Dragon Scale Publishing, (*978-1-943183*) 8466 N Stonebridge LN, Eagle Mountain, UT 84005 USA Tel 801-471-0502
E-mail: Dragonscalebooks@outlook.com
Web site: www.Dragonscalepublishing.com.

Dragon Tree Bks., (*978-0-9884024; 978-0-9916200; 978-0-9862641; 978-0-9963081; 978-0-9974513; 978-0-9977478*) 1620 SW 5th Ave., Pompano Beach, FL 33060 USA Tel 954-788-4775
E-mail: editors@editingforauthors.com
Web site: http://editingforauthors.com.

Dragonbrush Arts, (*978-0-9960374*) 34242 Vauxhill Dr. Apt. No. 7, Paw Paw, MI 49079 USA Tel 269-254-0663
E-mail: d.monroe@dragonbrusher.com
Web site: dragonbrusher.com.

Dragoneagle Pr., (*978-0-9787465*) Orders Addr.: P.O. Box Box 30856, Bethesda, MD 20824 USA Tel 732-861-0449; Fax: 301-897-2786
E-mail: info@dragoneagle.com
Web site: http://www.dragoneagle.com.

Dragonetti, (*978-0-9763161*) 2211 Aspenwood Dr., Holt, MI 48842 USA Fax: 517-699-4340
E-mail: vince@vincedragonetti.com
Web site: http://www.vincedragonetti.com.

DragonEye Publishing, (*978-0-9767832; 978-1-61500*) Orders Addr.: c/o ISOTUT Publisher, 511 W. Water St. Apt E, Elmira, NY 14905 USA (SAN 857-7110) Tel 607-333-5256 For questions about ordering
E-mail: Michael.Kiser@DragonEyePublishers.com
Web site: http://www.DragonEyePublishers.com.

Dragonfeather Bks. *Imprint of* **Bedazzled Ink Publishing Co.**

Dragonfly Bks. *Imprint of* **Random Hse. Children's Bks.**

Dragonfly Entertainment, (*978-0-9745213*) 97 Chartwell Ct., Rochester, NY 14618-5376 USA; *Imprints:* Dragonfly Flipz (Dragonfly Flipz)
E-mail: dfly@earthlink.net
Web site: http://www.dragonflyent.net.

Dragonfly Flipz *Imprint of* **Dragonfly Entertainment**

Dragonfly Group Ltd. (GBR) (*978-0-9935293*) *Dist. by* **IPG Chicago.**

Dragonfly Ministries, (*978-0-9788289*) 295 Noble Cir., Vernon Hills, IL 60061-2927 USA
E-mail: info@dragonflyministries.com
Web site: http://www.dragonflyministries.com.

Dragonfly Publishing, Inc., (*978-0-9710473; 978-0-9755888; 978-0-9765786; 978-0-9778651; 978-0-9787421; 978-0-9794660; 978-0-9797574; 978-0-9801376; 978-0-9817049; 978-0-9819080; 978-0-9840980; 978-1-936381; 978-1-941278*) 2440 Twin Ridge Dr., Edmond, OK 73034-1943 USA Do not confuse with companies with the same or similar name in Mount Enterprise, TX , Whethersfield, CT , San Antonio, TX ,
Web site: http://www.dragonflypubs.com
Dist(s): **Smashwords.**

Dragonflyer Pr., (*978-0-944933*) Div. of American Water Gardens, Inc., 2460 N. Euclid Ave., Upland, CA 91784-1184 USA (SAN 245-7660) Toll Free: 800-558-0676
E-mail: info@dragonflyerpress.com; cuber@uberadv.com
Web site: http://www.vnwg.com; http://www.dragonflyerpress.com
Dist(s): **Midpoint Trade Bks., Inc.**

Dragonhawk Publishing, (*978-1-888767*) Div. of Life Magic Enterprises, Inc., P.O. Box 1316, Jackson, TN 38302 USA Tel 901-987-3334; Fax: 901-987-2484
Dist(s): **Austin & Company, Inc.**
New Leaf Distributing Co., Inc.

Dragonon, Inc., (*978-0-9763398*) 9378 Mason Montgomery Rd., Suite 108, Mason, OH 45040 USA (SAN 256-3398) Tel 513-227-9224
E-mail: dmeyer@dragonon.com.

Dragonseed Pr., (*978-0-9678115*) Orders Addr.: 19020 Brookfield Dr., Chagrin Falls, OH 44023 USA
E-mail: dragonseedpress@aol.com
Web site: http://www.m-c-ryan.com.

DragonWing Bks., (*978-0-9761444*) 9107 Brunners Run Ct., Columbia, MD 21045 USA Tel 301-509-5451
E-mail: liz@dragonwingbooks.com
Web site: http://www.dragonwingbooks.com.

Drake, Edwin, (*978-0-9743405*) R.R. 5, Box 5417, Saylorsburg, PA 18353 USA Tel 570-992-2914
E-mail: edrakee@enter.net.

Drake Feltham Publishing, (*978-0-578-10548-2*) 22113 Palos Verdes Blvd., Torrance, CA 90503 USA
Dist(s): **Outskirts Pr., Inc.**

Drake Univ., Anderson Gallery, (*978-0-9749296*) 25th St. & Carpenter Ave., Des Moines, IA 50311 USA Tel 515-271-1994; Fax: 515-271-2558
E-mail: cira.pascual-marquina@drake.edu
Web site: http://www.drake.edu/andersongallery.

Drama Publishers *See* **Quite Specific Media Group, Ltd.**

Drama Tree Pr., (*978-0-9741670; 978-0-9821852; 978-0-9985676*) 150 Iota Ct., Madison, WI 53706 USA
E-mail: dramatree@mail.com
Web site: http://www.dramatree.com.

Dramaline Pubns., (*978-0-940669; 978-0-9611792*) 36851 Palm View Rd., Rancho Mirage, CA 92270-2417 USA (SAN 285-239X) Tel 760-770-6076; Fax: 760-770-4507
E-mail: drama.line@verizon.net
Web site: http://www.dramaline.com
Dist(s): **Distributors, The.**

DramaQueen, L.L.C., (*978-0-9766045; 978-1-933809; 978-1-60331*) Orders Addr.: P.O. Box 2626, Stafford, TX 77497 USA Fax: 281-498-4723; Toll Free: 800-883-1518 (ext. 2)
E-mail: orders@onedramaqueen.com; info@onedramaqueen.com
Web site: http://www.onedramaqueen.com
Dist(s): **AAA Anime Distribution.**

Dramatic Improvements Publishing, (*978-0-9768251*) 226 Perrine Ave., Auburn, NY 13021-1715 USA
E-mail: twoods@dramaimp.com
Web site: http://www.dramaimp.com.

Dramatic Publishing Co., (*978-0-87129; 978-1-58342; 978-1-61959*) Orders Addr.: 311 Washington St., Woodstock, IL 60098 USA (SAN 201-5676) Tel 815-338-7170; Fax: 815-338-8981; Toll Free Fax: 800-334-5302; Toll Free: 800-448-7469
E-mail: plays@dramaticpublishing.com
Web site: http://www.dramaticpublishing.com.

Dramatists Play Service, Inc., (*978-0-8222*) 440 Park Ave., S., New York, NY 10016 USA (SAN 207-5717) Tel 212-683-8960; Fax: 212-213-1539
E-mail: postmaster@dramatists.com
Web site: http://www.dramatists.com.

Drane, John Wanzer, (*978-0-578-10633-5*) 5 Derry Dr., Horse Shoe, NC 28742 USA.

Draper Publishing, (*978-0-9913342*) 1701 Willow Oak Ln., Dalton, GA 30721 USA Tel 706-260-5496
E-mail: duraniemaria39@yahoo.com
Web site: mariarochelle.com.

Draw Three Lines Publishing, (*978-0-9749418; 978-0-9826202*) P.O. Box 1522, Hillsboro, OR 97123 USA Tel 503-648-9905
E-mail: hastings@draw3lines.com
Web site: http://www.draw3lines.com.

Drawn & Quarterly Pubns. (CAN) (*978-0-9696701; 978-1-896597; 978-1-894937; 978-1-897299; 978-1-77046*) *Dist. by* **Macmillan.**

DrDryland.Com, LLC, (*978-0-9766490*) P.O. Box 1281, Ashland, OR 97520 USA
Web site: http://www.DrDryland.Com.

Dream A World *Imprint of* **BrassHeart Music**

Dream Bee Pubns., (*978-0-9661572*) 3325 C 1/2 Rd., Palisade, CO 81526 USA Tel 970-434-7501
E-mail: bee@dreambee.com
Web site: http://www.dreambee.com
Dist(s): **Bks. West**
Partners/West Book Distributors.

Dream Big Toy Co., (*978-1-940731*) 249 Merton Ave., Alen Ellyn, IL 60137 USA Tel 877-351-1031
E-mail: jnorgaard@dreambigtoycompany.com
Dist(s): **Independent Pubs. Group**
MyiLibrary.

Dream Character, Inc., (*978-0-9765543; 978-0-9785418*) Orders Addr.: 21143 Hawthorne Blvd. # 453, Torrance, CA 90503 USA; Edit Addr.: 2049 Pacific Coast Hwy. #453, Torrance, CA 90503 USA (SAN 256-4793) Tel 310-530-8015
E-mail: info@dreamcharacter.com
Web site: http://www.dreamcharacter.com
Dist(s): **Independent Pubs. Group.**

Dream Creek Pr., (*978-0-9771515*) 401 Taylor St., Ashland, OR 97520 USA
E-mail: bethart@mind.net
Web site: http://www.bbcreativecards.com.

Dream Dance Pubns., (*978-0-9769192*) P.O. Box 902, Redmond, WA 98073 USA Tel 425-898-9240
E-mail: briggs870@msn.com.

Dream Factory Bks., (*978-0-9701195*) Orders Addr.: P.O. Box 874, Enumclaw, WA 98022 USA (SAN 253-2611) Tel 360-663-0508; Fax: 360-825-7952; Toll Free Fax: 877-377-7030; Edit Addr.: 58402 114th St., E., Enumclaw, WA 98022-7305 USA
E-mail: sensel@earthlink.net
Web site: http://dreamfactorybooks.com
Dist(s): **Independent Pubs. Group.**

Dream, Feral LLC, (*978-0-9835970*) 774 Mays Blvd. Ste 10-473, Incline Village, NV 89451 USA Tel 415-555-1212
E-mail: susan@feraldream.com.

Dream House Pr., (*978-0-9671555*) 2714 Ophelia Ct., San Jose, CA 95122 USA Tel 408-274-4574; Fax: 408-274-0786; Toll Free: 877-274-4574
E-mail: mr_art@prodigy.net; dreamhousepress@yahoo.com
Dist(s): **Brodart Co.**
Midwest Library Service
Milligan News Co., Inc.
Partners/West Book Distributors
Yankee Bk. Peddler, Inc.

Dream Image Pr., LLC, (*978-0-9744812*) P.O. Box 454, Northbrook, IL 60065-0454 USA Tel 847-480-8998
E-mail: drashley@dreamimagepress.com
Dist(s): **Follett School Solutions.**

Dream On Pubns., (*978-0-9761151*) Orders Addr.: P.O. Box 190265, Fort Lauderdale, FL 33319 USA (SAN 256-2057)
E-mail: books@dreamonpublications.com.

Dream Publications, I, Incorporated *See* **BOOKGEMSFORKIDS**

Dream Ridge Pr., (*978-0-9792084*) P.O. Box 625, Aurelia, IA 51005 USA Tel 712-660-8409
E-mail: rainbowfarm2006@yahoo.com; tpeiffer67@yahoo.com
Web site: http://www.lulu.com/trishacp; http://www.rainbowfarmbooks.com; http://www.authorsden.com/trishacp
Dist(s): **Lulu Pr., Inc.**

Dream Scape Publishing, LLC, (*978-0-9795519; 978-0-615-13650-9*) 805 Dunwood Ct., Chesapeake, VA 23322 USA Tel 757-717-2734
E-mail: dreamscape2@cox.net.

Dream Secret Inc., The, (*978-0-615-18103-5*) P.O. Box 2012, Sandy, UT 84091 USA Tel 801-518-7770
E-mail: lscread@yahoo.com.

Dream Ship Publishing Co., (*978-0-9729155*) 1512 River Rock Trace, Woodstock, GA 30188 USA
E-mail: info@dreamshipbooks.com.

Dream Star Productions, (*978-0-9772027*) Orbisson Sq. 4306 S. Peoria Ave., Ste 705, Tulsa, OK 74105-3922 USA Tel 918-630-7580; Fax: 918-749-1717
Web site: http://www.kbaustin.com.

Dream Weaver Ministries, Inc., (*978-0-9800259*) Pmb#123 1631 Rock Springs Rd., Apopka, FL 32712-2229 USA (SAN 855-0239) Toll Free: 888-397-7772.

Dream Workshop Publishing Co., LLC, The, (*978-0-9786940*) Orders Addr.: 4421 Bachelor Creek Rd., Asheboro, NC 27205 USA (SAN 851-3635) Tel 336-879-8108
E-mail: info@dreamworkshoppub.com; publisher@dreamworkshoppub.com
Web site: http://www.dreamworkshoppub.com; http://www.spenceraliens,com.

Dream Yard Pr., (*978-0-615-72969-5*) 1085 Washington Ave., Bronx, NY 10456 USA Tel 718-588-8007; Fax: 718-588-8310
E-mail: neilwald@aol.com
Web site: dreamyard.com; neilwaldman.com.

Dream&Achieve Bks., (*978-0-9859298*) 2609 W. 84th Pl., Merrillville, IN 46410 USA Tel 219-218-5145
Web site: www.weenzcat.com.

Dreamcatcher Bks., (*978-0-9848484*) 892 Jensen Ln., Windsor, CA 95492 USA Tel 707-292-0272 Do not confuse with Dreamcatcher Books in Las Vegas, NM
E-mail: alvarezgang@yahoo.com
Web site: http://www.jenniferlynnalvarez.com/.

Dream-Catcher Pubns., (*978-0-9752878*) 22265 Petersburg, Eastpointe, MI 48021 USA.

DreamDog Pr., (*978-0-9666199*) 2308 Mount Vernon Ave., Alexandria, VA 22301-1328 USA
E-mail: rainey@dreamdog.com
Web site: http://www.dreamdog.com.

DreamerLand, (*978-0-9763250*) Orders Addr.: 1018 3rd St., Hermosa Beach, CA 90254 USA Tel 310-406-9371
E-mail: christo@dreamerland.com; info@dreamerland.com
Web site: http://www.Dreamerland.com
Dist(s): **Diamond Bk. Distributors.**

DreamHse. Publishing Inc.,

DreamLand Mediaworks LLC, (*978-0-9884657*) 3712 Lake Catherine Dr., Harvey, LA 70058 USA Tel 504-756-5589; Fax: 504-366-2606
E-mail: MavrikLdy@aol.com.

Dreams 2 Wings LLC, (*978-0-9797781*) 100 N. 72nd Ave., Wausau, WI 54401 USA Tel 715-842-1133; Fax: 715-842-1155
E-mail: fred@lanepatents.com.

Dreams Due Media Group, Inc., (*978-0-9789202*) P.O. Box 1018, Firestone, CO 80520 USA Tel 303-241-3155 Toll Free: 877-462-1710
Web site: http://www.dreamsdue.com.

Dreams of Dragons, (*978-0-578-12149-9; 978-0-615-97831-4*) P.O. Box 312, Malden, MO 63863 USA Tel 573-576-7435
E-mail: drwilliamembry@yahoo.com
Web site: http://www.drakoandrawr.com.

Dreamscape, LLC *See* **Dreamscape Media, LLC**

Dreamscape Media, LLC, *(978-0-9745563; 978-0-9747118; 978-0-9760996; 978-0-9761981; 978-0-9771510; 978-0-9772338; 978-0-9774680; 978-0-9776262; 978-0-9777098; 978-1-933938; 978-1-61120; 978-1-62406; 978-1-62923; 978-1-63379; 978-1-68141; 978-1-68262; 978-1-5200; 978-1-9749) Orders Addr.: 1417 Timberwolf Dr., Holland, OH 43538 USA Tel 419-867-6965*
E-mail: molah@dreamscapeab.com
Web site: http://www.dreamscapeab.com
Dist(s): **Findaway World, LLC**
Follett School Solutions
Ingram Publisher Services.

Dreamschooner Pr., *(978-0-9899128)* 15 Beacon St., Natick, MA 01760 USA Tel 773-368-4386
E-mail: rfelty@gmail.com
Web site: dreamschoonerpress.com.

Dreamspinner Pr., *(978-0-9795048; 978-0-9801018; 978-0-9815084; 978-0-9817372; 978-1-935192; 978-1-61581; 978-1-61372; 978-1-62380; 978-1-62798; 978-1-63216; 978-1-63476; 978-1-63477; 978-1-63533; 978-1-64080; 978-1-64108)* 5032 Capital Cir. SW Suite 2, PMB #279, Tallahassee, FL 32305-7886 USA (SAN 915-5562); *Imprints:* Harmony Ink Press (HarmonyInk); DSP Publications (DSPPubns)
E-mail: contact@dreamspinnerpress.com
Web site: http://www.dreamspinnerpress.com
Dist(s): **INscribe Digital**
Independent Pubs. Group.

Dreamstreet Studios, Inc. (A Div. of DSMV Industries, Inc.), *(978-0-9892295)* 1800 Grand Ave., Nashville, TN 37212 USA Tel 615-321-9029
E-mail: songmerch@aol.com.

Dreamtime Publishing, *(978-0-9741726)* P.O. Box 834, Tahlequah, OK 74465 USA Tel 918-456-8639.

Dreamwand, *(978-0-615-32313-8; 978-0-9913715)* 715 N. Croft Ave., Los Angeles, CA 90069-5303 USA Tel 323-424-4095
E-mail: dreamwandbooks@yahoo.com; theafflictedgirls@dreamwand.net
Web site: http://www.theafflictedgirls.com.

Dreistadt, Jessica R., *(978-0-578-02239-0)* 1700 Sullivan Trail, No. 311, Easton, PA 18040 USA
Dist(s): **Lulu Pr., Inc.**

Drenttel, William Editions *See* **Winterhouse Editions**

Dressler, Avi, *(978-0-9744309)* 35 Old Brick Rd., East Hills, NY 11577-1816 USA.

Dressler, Craig, *(978-0-9778247)* 5341 NE Webster Ct., Portland, OR 97218 USA Tel 503-281-4214.

Driftwood Pr., *(978-0-9638803)* Orders Addr.: P.O. Box 284, Yachats, OR 97498 USA; Edit Addr.: 62 Gender Dr., Yachats, OR 97498 USA Tel 541-547-3484
E-mail: njguni@clubinernet.fr.

Drinian Pr., LLC, *(978-0-9785165; 978-0-9820609; 978-0-9833069; 978-1-941929)* Orders Addr.: P.O. Box 63, Huron, OH 44839 USA
E-mail: drinianpress@frontier.com
Web site: http://drinianpress.com; http://smithwrite.net.

Drinking Gourd Pr., *(978-0-578-13425-3; 978-0-578-13426-0)* 414 Jefferson Ave., Apt. 1, Brooklyn, NY 11221 USA.

Driving Vision, Inc., *(978-0-9766329)* 2117 S. Ventura Dr., Tempe, AZ 85282 USA
Web site: http://www.drivingvision.com.

DrMaster Pubns. Inc., *(978-1-59796)* 48531 Warm Springs Blvd., Suite 408, Fremont, CA 94539 USA Tel 510-687-1388 (phone/fax)
Web site: http://www.drmasterpublications.com
Dist(s): **Diamond Comic Distributors, Inc.**
Diamond Bk. Distributors.

Droemersche Verlagsanstalt Th. Knaur Nachf. - GmbH & Co. (DEU) *(978-3-426) Dist. by* **Distribks Inc.**

Drollery Pr., *(978-0-940920)* 1524 Benton St., Alameda, CA 94501-2420 USA (SAN 223-1808) Tel 510-521-4087.

DRT Pr., *(978-1-933084)* Orders Addr.: P.O. Box 427, Pittsboro, NC 27312 USA Tel 919-360-7073; Fax: 866-562-5040; Edit Addr.: 395 Bill Thomas Rd., Moncure, NC 27559 USA
E-mail: editorial@drtpress.com
Web site: http://www.drtpress.com
Dist(s): **BWI**
Bk. Hse., The
Brodart Co.
Follett School Solutions
Quality Bks., Inc.

Drummond Publishing Group, The, *(978-0-9755080; 978-1-59763)* 4 Collins Ave., Plymouth, MA 02360-4809 USA Do not confuse with Rec#s 786442, 791375, 1194043
E-mail: f_allen@drummondpub.com
Web site: http://www.drummondpub.com.

Drumstick Media, *(978-0-9764791)* Div. of Old Goats, Inc., 5805 Hwy. 93 S., Whitefish, MT 59937 USA Tel 406-862-8938; Fax: 406-862-8936; Toll Free: 800-404-8279
E-mail: robert@drumstickmedia.com; james@drumstickmedia.com
Web site: http://www.baxterowengraham.com; http://www.drumstickmedia.com.

Drunk Duck Comics, *(978-0-9748960)* P.O. Box 869, Pittston, PA 18640 USA
E-mail: rubbermallet@verizon.net; arrkelaan@hotmail.com
Web site: http://www.drunkduck.com.

Dry, Paul Bks., Inc., *(978-0-9664913; 978-0-9679675; 978-1-58988)* 1616 Walnut St. Ste. 808, Philadelphia, PA 19103-5308 USA
E-mail: pdb@pauldrybooks.com
Web site: http://www.pauldrybooks.com
Dist(s): **Consortium Bk. Sales & Distribution**
Independent Pubs. Group.

Dryad Pr., *(978-0-931848; 978-1-928755)* P.O. Box 11233, Takoma Park, MD 20913 USA (SAN 206-197X) Tel 301-891-3729
E-mail: dryadpress@yahoo.com
Web site: http://www.dryadpress.com
Dist(s): **SPD-Small Pr. Distribution.**

Dryden Publishing, *(978-0-9644370; 978-1-929204)* P.O. Box 482, Dryden, WA 98821-0482 USA
E-mail: dryden@csiconnect.com.

Dryland, David *See* **DrDryland.Com, LLC**

DSA Publishing & Design, Inc., *(978-0-9774451; 978-0-9818229; 978-0-9848057)* 6900 Edgewater Dr., Mckinney, TX 75070 USA
Web site: http://www.dsapubs.com
Dist(s): **Chicago Distribution Ctr.**

DSP Pubns. *Imprint of* **Dreamspinner Pr.**

DTaylor Bks., *(978-0-615-36081-2)* 415 Armour Dr., Apt. 12204, Atlanta, GA 30324 USA Tel 404-838-9678.

DTJ, LLC, *(978-0-9765731)* P.O. Box 635, Sequim, WA 98382 USA.

D-Tower Pubns., *(978-0-9770386)* 8028 Pine St., Ethel, LA 70730-3853 USA Tel 225-335-0802
E-mail: swbloopers@yahoo.com.

Dube, Tory, *(978-0-9886193)* 3168 41st St. No. 1f, Astoria, NY 11103 USA Tel 603-781-1440
E-mail: torydube@gmail.com
Web site: www.lovelythankyou.com.

Dubois, Ricardo S., *(978-0-615-15411-4; 978-0-615-15412-1; 978-0-615-15413-8; 978-0-615-16958-3; 978-0-615-17232-3; 978-0-615-18220-9; 978-0-615-19724-1)* 16015 Creekround Dr., Praireville, LA 70769 USA Tel 225-802-6001
E-mail: craftycajun@yahoo.com
Dist(s): **Lulu Pr., Inc.**

Duckett, Brenda, *(978-0-615-17289-7)* 27 Millswood Dr., Clarkville, TN 37042 USA Tel 931-906-8649
E-mail: bduckett1@bellsouth.net
Dist(s): **Lulu Pr., Inc.**

Duckpond Publishing, Inc., *(978-0-9720350)* 130 Hillside Ln., Roswell, GA 30076 USA Tel 770-649-9947; Fax: 770-594-8058
E-mail: theducks@duckpondpublishing.com
Web site: http://www.duckpondpublishing.com.

Dude Publishing *Imprint of* **National Professional Resources, Inc.**

Dudek, Mike, *(978-0-9740380; 978-0-9968182)* 505 Duwell St., Johnston, PA 15906 USA Tel 814-536-1500; Fax: 814-536-8952
E-mail: mike@dudekins.com; jetset15906@yahoo.com
Web site: www.rascaljokes.com.

Dudley, Joshua Patrick, *(978-0-615-16396-3; 978-0-615-18871-3)* 4 Heritage Village Dr., Unit 102, Nashua, NH 03062 USA Tel 603-459-9687
E-mail: admin@joshuapatrickdudley.com; lostinozbook@yahoo.com
Web site: http://www.ostinozbook.com; http://www.lostinozbook.com
Dist(s): **Lulu Pr., Inc.**

DUENDE Bks., *(978-0-9777973; 978-0-615-14984-4; 978-0-615-15099-4)* Div. of DeCo Communications, 13900 Fiji Way, Apt. 306, Marina del Rey, CA 90292 USA Tel 310-486-0983
E-mail: denizr@verizon.net
Web site: http://www.duendebooks.blogspot.com
Dist(s): **Lulu Pr., Inc.**

†Dufour Editions, Inc., *(978-0-8023)* Orders Addr.: P.O. Box 7, Chester Springs, PA 19425-0007 USA (SAN 201-341X) Tel 610-458-5005; Fax: 610-458-7103; Toll Free: 800-869-5677
E-mail: info@dufoureditions.com
Web site: http://www.dufoureditions.com; *CIP.*

Duke Publishing & Software Corp., *(978-0-9745406)* P.O. Box 3429, Los Altos, CA 94024 USA Tel 408-245-3853; Fax: 408-245-9289
E-mail: info@aboutthekids.org
Web site: http://www.aboutthekids.org.

†Duke Univ. Pr., *(978-0-8223; 978-1-4780)* P.O. Box 90660, Durham, NC 27708-0660 USA (SAN 201-3436) Tel 919-687-3600; Fax: 919-688-4574; 905 W. Main S., Ste.18B, Durham, NC 27701 Tel 919-687-3600; Fax: 919-688-4574; Toll Free: 888-651-0122
E-mail: orders@dukepress.edu; subscriptions@dukepress.edu; hlw@dukepress.edu
Web site: http://www.dukeupress.edu
Dist(s): **MyiLibrary**
ebrary, Inc.; *CIP.*

Dukes World, Inc., *(978-0-9664506)* P.O. Box 85, Yonkers, NY 10704 USA Tel 917-403-7661
E-mail: dukesworldinc@aol.com
Web site: http://www.chillstreetgang.com.

Dulany, Joseph P., *(978-0-9708830)* 6200 Oregon Ave NW Apt. 236, Washington, DC 20015-1529 USA
E-mail: josephdulany@msn.com
Web site: http://www.onceasoldier.com.

Duling Designs, *(978-0-9743445)* P.O. Box 1996, Marco Island, FL 34146-1996 USA
E-mail: jsduling87@aol.com.

Dume Publishing *See* **Corman Productions**

Dunamis Development, *(978-0-9767066)* 3972-J Barranca Pkwy., Suite 115, Irvine, CA 92606 USA Tel 949-263-0063.

Dundurn (CAN) *(978-0-88762; 978-0-88882; 978-0-88924; 978-0-919028; 978-0-919670; 978-0-9690454; 978-1-55002; 978-1-55488; 978-1-4597; 978-1-77070) Dist. by* **IngramPubServ.**

Dunemere Bks., *(978-0-9972701; 978-0-692-74279-2; 978-0-9984997; 978-0-9988851; 978-1-947936)* 430 E. 86th St., New York, NY 10028 USA Tel 212-472-9012
E-mail: ecarey@dunemerebooks.com
Web site: dunemerebooks.com
Dist(s): **Independent Pubs. Group.**

Dunlop, Edward *See* **Cross & Crown Publishing**

Dunn, Hunter, *(978-0-9761732)* 410 Old Spring Rd., Danville, VA 24540-5206 USA.

Dunn, Michael *See* **Big Secret, The**

Dunne, Thomas Bks. *Imprint of* **St. Martin's Pr.**

Duo Pr. Llc (US) *Imprint of* **Duo Pr. LLC**

Duo Pr. LLC, *(978-0-9796213; 978-0-9825295; 978-0-9838121; 978-1-938093; 978-1-946064; 978-1-947458)* 265 Stanmore Rd., Baltimore, MD 21212 USA; *Imprints:* Duo Press Llc (US) (DUO PRESS LLC)
E-mail: info@duopressbooks.com
Web site: http://www.duopressbooks.com
Dist(s): **MyiLibrary**
Workman Publishing Co., Inc.
ebrary, Inc.

Duplicates Printing, *(978-0-9749953)* Orders Addr.: P.O. Box 2398, Pawleys Island, SC 29585 USA Tel 843-237-3998; Edit Addr.: 14329 Ocean Hwy. Unit 115, Pawleys Isl, SC 29585-4816 USA
E-mail: slingshot@sc.rr.com.

Dupuis North Publishing, *(978-0-9749199)* 76 N. Church St., Clayton, GA 30525 USA Tel 828-524-9520; Fax: 828-349-1945.

Duracell & the National Ctr. for Missing & Exploited Children (NCMEC), *(978-0-9795307)* 415 Nadison Ave., New York, NY 10018 USA Tel 212-613-4904.

duran, oscar, *(978-0-615-72225-2; 978-0-9886109)* 6204 sw 18th St, Miramar, FL 33023 USA Tel 954-986-4082; Fax: 954-986-4082
Dist(s): **CreateSpace Independent Publishing Platform.**

Durban House Press, Incorporated *See* **Fireside Pr., Inc.**

Durland Alternatives Library, *(978-0-9740184)* 127 Anabel Taylor Hall, Ithaca, NY 14853-1001 USA Tel 607-255-6486; Fax: 607-255-9985
E-mail: alt-lib@cornell.edu
Web site: http://www.alternativeslibrary.org.

Durst, Sanford J., *(978-0-915262; 978-0-942666; 978-1-886720)* 106 Woodcleft Ave., Freeport, NY 11520 USA (SAN 211-6987) Tel 516-867-3333; Fax: 516-867-3397
E-mail: sjdbooks@verizon.net.

Dust Bunny Games LLC, *(978-0-9747833)* Orders Addr.: 3744 Mistflower Ln., Naperville, IL 60564-5921 USA Tel 630-244-0335; Fax: 630-922-6995; Edit Addr.: 3744 Mistflower Ln., Naperville, IL 60564-5921 USA
E-mail: info@dustbunnygames.com
Web site: http://www.dustbunnygames.com.

Duthaluru, Vidhya, *(978-0-9797657)* 247 Levinberg Ln., Wayne, NJ 07470 USA.

Dutton Adult *Imprint of* **Penguin Publishing Group**

Dutton Books for Young Readers *Imprint of* **Penguin Young Readers Group**

Dutton Caliber *Imprint of* **Penguin Publishing Group**

Dutton Juvenile *Imprint of* **Penguin Publishing Group**

Dutton, Mary, *(978-0-692-90204-2)* 1408 Adams St., PORT TOWNSEND, WA 98368 USA Tel 360-344-2498
E-mail: mhdcashew@juno.com
Dist(s): **Lightning Source, Inc.**

Duval Publishing, *(978-0-9745637)* Orders Addr.: P.O. Box 4255, Key West, FL 33041 USA Toll Free: 800-355-8562; Edit Addr.: 3717 Eagle Ave., Key West, FL 33040 USA
Web site: http://www.southerncoastaldesigns.com.

DV Bks. *Imprint of* **Digital Vista, Inc.**

DVTVFilm, *(978-0-9678094)* 3 Temi Rd., Framingham, MA 01701 USA
E-mail: todd@dvtvfilm.com; info@themonkeykingsdaughter.com; todd@themonkeykingsdaughter.com
Web site: http://www.dvtvfilm.com; http://www.themonkeykingsdaughter.com.

Dwitt Publishing, *(978-0-9741352)* 9249 17th St SE, Saint Cloud, MN 56304-9709 USA
E-mail: dickawit@aol.com
Web site: http://www.dwittpublishing.com.

Dykema Engineering, Incorporated *See* **Dykema Publishing Co.**

Dykema, Marjorie *See* **One Coin Publishing, LLC**

Dykema Publishing Co., *(978-0-9660705; 978-0-9701538)* Div. of Dykema Engineering, Inc., 3264 W. Normandy Ave., Roseburg, OR 97470 USA Tel 541-957-0259; Fax: 541-677-7146
E-mail: odykema@mcsi.net
Web site: http://www.oregonwriters.com.

Dykes, William R. III, *(978-0-9740987)* 317 Luchase Rd., Linden, VA 22642 USA.

Dynagraphix *Imprint of* **Elliott, Jane**

Dynamic Forces, Incorporated *See* **Dynamic Forces, Inc.**

Dynamic Forces, Inc., *(978-0-9749638; 978-1-933305; 978-1-60690; 978-1-5241)* 113 Gaither Dr., Ste. 205 Suite B, Mt. Laurel, NJ 08054 USA; *Imprints:* Dynamite Entertainment (Dyna Enter)
E-mail: marketing@dynamite.com
Web site: http://www.dynamicforces.com; http://www.dynamite.com
Dist(s): **Diamond Comic Distributors, Inc.**
Diamond Bk. Distributors.

Dynamic Publishing Co., Inc., *(978-0-9656808)* Orders Addr.: P.O. Box 120, Calumet City, IL 60409 USA Tel 708-868-0512; Fax: 708-868-0549; Toll Free: 800-884-1840 Do not confuse with Dynamic Publishing, Sugar Land, TX,
E-mail: dpc123@ymail.com
Web site: http://www.DynamicPublishingCompany.com.

Dynamite Entertainment *Imprint of* **Dynamic Forces, Inc.**

DynaStudy, Inc., *(978-0-9776270; 978-0-9777909; 978-1-933854; 978-1-935005)* 1401 Broadway St. Suite 100, Marble Falls, TX 78654 USA
E-mail: info@dynastudy.com
Web site: http://dynanotes.com.

Dynasty Publishing, Inc., *(978-0-9790444; 978-0-9793490)* P.O. Box 11997, Kansas City, MO 64138-0997 USA Do not confuse with Dynasty Publishing in Honolulu, HI
E-mail: info@dynastypublishinginc.com
Web site: http://www.dynastypublishinginc.com.

DZ Publishing, LLC, *(978-0-9753660; 978-0-9889975)* 7360 Lincoln Dr., #2, Scottsdale, AZ 85258 USA Tel 949-922-7042
E-mail: szipp22@gmail.com
Web site: http://www.mycollegesuccess.com.

E & D Bks., Ltd., *(978-0-9794413)* P.O. Box 211, Ruby, NY 12475 USA (SAN 853-4314)
E-mail: info@buddyboobysbirthmark.com
Web site: http://www.buddyboobysbirthmark.com
Dist(s): **Beekman Bks., Inc.**

E & E Publishing, *(978-0-9719898; 978-0-9748933; 978-0-9791606; 978-0-9831499)* P.O. Box 3346, Omaha, NE 68103 USA Tel 402-578-2563 Do not confuse with E & E Publishing, Junction City, OR
E-mail: EveHeidiWrites@gmail.com.

E & H Publishing Co., Inc., *(978-0-9717295)* P.O. Box 4, Burkeville, VA 23922 USA
E-mail: greanes@earthlink.net.

EBP Latin America Group, Inc., *(978-1-56409)* 175 E. Delaware Pl. Apt. 8806, Chicago, IL 60611-7753 USA.

E B S C O Industries, Inc., *(978-0-913956; 978-1-888751)* Orders Addr.: P.O. Box 1943, Birmingham, AL 35201-1943 USA (SAN 201-3584) Tel 205-991-6600; Fax: 205-995-1636; Toll Free: 800-826-3024; Edit Addr.: 5724 Hwy. 280 E., Birmingham, AL 35242 USA
Web site: http://www.ebsco.com.

ECO Herpetological Pub. & Dist., *(978-0-9713197; 978-0-9767334; 978-0-9788979; 978-0-9832789; 978-0-9852936; 978-1-938850)* 4 Rattlesnake Canyon Rd., Rodeo, NM 88056 USA Tel 575-557-5757; Fax: 575-557-7575
E-mail: ecoorders@hotmail.com
Web site: http://www.reptileshirts.com
Dist(s): **BookBaby**
Serpent's Tale Natural History Bk. Distributors, Inc.
T-Rex Products.

EECI, Inc., *(978-0-9649379; 978-0-9722686; 978-1-933193)* 8055 W. Manchester Ave., 1st Flr., Playa Del Rey, CA 90293 USA
E-mail: rwoo@eecinternational.com.

E. F. S. Online Publishing, *(978-0-9701344)* Div. of E. F. S. Enterprises, Inc., 2844 Eighth Ave., Suite 6-E, New York, NY 10039 USA Tel 212-283-8899; Fax: 212-283-6280
E-mail: efsenterprises@hotmail.com
Web site: http://www.efs-enterprises.com.

E Innovative Ideas, *(978-0-9799540)* 800 SE 4th St., Suite 501, Fort Lauderdale, FL 33301 USA Tel 954-527-1070
E-mail: einnovate@aol.com.

E. J. Publishing, *(978-0-9764444; 978-0-9770303)* 4529 Hillcrest Rd., Birmingham, AL 35224-2818 USA Toll Free Fax: 866-864-6087; Toll Free: 866-864-6085
E-mail: elysia@ejpub.com
Web site: http://www.ejpub.com
Dist(s): **Baker & Taylor International**
CreateSpace Independent Publishing Platform.

EKS Publishing Co., *(978-0-939144)* 322 Castro St., Oakland, CA 94607-3028 USA (SAN 216-1281) Tel 510-251-9100; Fax: 510-251-9102; Toll Free: 877-743-2739
E-mail: orders@EKSpublishing.com
Web site: http://www.ekspublishing.com.

E M C Publishing *See* **EMC/Paradigm Publishing**

EMG Networks, *(978-1-56843)* Div. of Educational Management Group, 1 Lake St., No. 3B-47, Upper Saddle River, NJ 07458-1813 USA Tel 602-970-3250; Fax: 602-970-3460; Toll Free: 800-842-6791.

E M McIntyre, *(978-0-9988993)* 2125 S. 108th St., Omaha, NE 68144 USA Tel 402-393-3971; *Imprints:* Little Hound Publishing (MYD_M_LITTLE)
E-mail: redkingtrilogy@gmail.com.

E M Pubns., *(978-0-9749739; 978-0-9794331; 978-0-9893569; 978-0-9905099)* Orders Addr.: P.O. Box 780900, Wichita, KS 67278-0900 USA
Web site: http://www.enloeministries.org.

ERIC Clearinghouse on Rural Education & Small Schls., *(978-1-880785)* Div. of Appalachia Educational Laboratory, Inc., Orders Addr.: P.O. Box 1348, Charleston, WV 25325-1348 USA Tel 304-347-0437; Fax: 304-347-0467; Toll Free: 800-624-9120; Edit Addr.: 1031 Quarrier St., Suite 610, Charleston, WV 25301 USA
E-mail: ericrc@ael.org
Web site: http://www.ael.org/eric.

ESP, Inc., *(978-0-8209)* Orders Addr.: P.O. Box 839, Tampa, FL 33601-0839 USA; Edit Addr.: 1212 N. 39th St., Suite 444, Tampa, FL 33605-5890 USA (SAN 241-497X) Do not confuse with E S P Inc., Woodlands, TX
E-mail: epublish@tampabay.rr.com
Web site: http://www.espbooks.com.

†ETC Pubns., *(978-0-88280)* 700 E. Vereda del Sur, Palm Springs, CA 92262 USA (SAN 124-8766) Tel 760-325-5352; Fax: 760-325-8841; Toll Free: 800-382-7869
E-mail: etcbooks@earthlink.net; *CIP.*

E T Nedder *Imprint of* **Paulist Pr.**

E3 Concepts LLC, *(978-0-9797375)* 3311 Mulberry Dr., Bloomington, IN 47401 USA Tel 812-360-7488; Fax: 888-876-5152
E-mail: chris.berry@linkedblocks.com
Web site: http://www.linkedblocks.com.

E3 Resources, *(978-1-933383)* 317 Main St., Suite 207, Franklin, TN 37064 USA (SAN 631-9076) Toll Free: 888-354-9411
Web site: http://www.e3resources.org.

Eager Minds Pr. *Imprint of* **Warehousing & Fulfillment Specialists, LLC (WFS, LLC)**

Eagle Bk. Bindery, *(978-0-9772304; 978-1-934333)* 2704 Camelot Ave., NW, Cedar Rapids, IA 52405 USA Tel 319-265-8210
E-mail: sales@eaglebookbindery.com
Web site: http://www.eaglebookbindery.com.

Eagle Creek Pubns., LLC, *(978-0-9769093)* P.O. Box 781166, Indianapolis, IN 46278 USA (SAN 257-3490) Tel 317-870-9902; Fax: 317-870-9904; Toll Free:

Publisher Name Index

866-870-9903 Do not Confuse with Eagle Creek Publications in Prior Lake, MN
E-mail: ben@eaglecreekpubs.com
Web site: http://www.eaglecreekpubs.com.

Eagle Editions, Ltd., *(978-0-914144; 978-0-9660706; 978-0-9721060; 978-0-9761034; 978-0-9794035)* Orders Addr.: P.O. Box 580, Hamilton, MT 59840 USA Tel 406-363-5415; Fax: 406-375-9270; Toll Free: 800-255-1830; Edit Addr.: 752 Bobcat Ln., Hamilton, MT 59840 USA
E-mail: eagle@eagle-editions.com
Web site: http://www.eagle-editions.com
Dist(s): **MBI Distribution Services/Quayside Distribution.**

Eagle Publishing *See* **Majestic Eagle Publishing**

Eagle River Type & Graphics *See* **Northbooks**

Eagle Trail Pr., *(978-0-9851876; 978-0-9892807; 978-0-9974267)* P.O. Box 3671, Parker, CO 80134 USA Tel 720-295-2208
E-mail: info@EagleTrailPress.com.

Eagle Tree Pr., *(978-0-9792499)* Div. of M. Kay Howell, P.O. Box 1060, Rainier, OR 97048-1060 USA (SAN 852-8950)
Web site: http://fairyempire.biz.

Eaglebrook Press *See* **Oldcastle Publishing**

Eaglehouse, Carolyn, *(978-0-9773263)* 521 E. Uwchlan Ave., Chester Springs, PA 19425 USA
Web site: http://www.chesterspringscreamery.com.

Eaglemont Pr., *(978-0-9662257; 978-0-9748411; 978-1-60040)* 13228 NE 20th St. Ste. 300, Bellevue, WA 98005-2049 USA (SAN 254-2102) Toll Free: 877-590-9744
E-mail: info@eaglemontpress.com
Web site: http://www.eaglemontpress.com.

Eagle's Wings Educational Materials, *(978-1-931292)* P.O. Box 502, Duncan, OK 73534 USA Tel 580-252-1555 (phone/fax)
E-mail: info@EaglesWingsEd.com
Web site: http://www.EaglesWingsEd.com.

Eaglesquest Publishing, *(978-0-9745860)* LTN Enterprises, 11852 Shady Acres Ct., Riverton, UT 84065 USA
E-mail: lestern@earthlink.net
Web site: http://www.thepaddedgirdle.com;
http://www.findingyour new normal.com.

Eakin Pr. *Imprint of* **Eakin Pr.**

†Eakin Pr., *(978-0-89015; 978-1-57168; 978-0-9789150; 978-1-934645; 978-1-935632)* Div. of Sunbelt Media, P.O. Box 90159, Austin, TX 78709-0159 USA (SAN 207-3633) Tel 254-235-6161; Fax: 254-235-6230; Toll Free: 800-880-8642; *Imprints:* Eakin Press (Eakin Pr); Nortex Press (Nortex Pr)
E-mail: sales@eakinpress.com; kris@eakinpress.com
Web site: http://www.eakinpress.com
Dist(s): **Follett School Solutions**
Hervey's Booklink & Cookbook Warehouse
Twentieth Century Christian Bks.
Wolverine Distributing, Inc.; *CIP.*

Eardley Pubns., *(978-0-937630)* Div. of Elizabeth Claire, Inc., Orders Addr.: 2100 Mccomas Way Suite 607, Virginia Beach, VA 23456 USA (SAN 215-6377) Tel 757-430-4308; Fax: 757-430-4309; Toll Free: 888-296-1090
E-mail: eceardley@aol.com
Web site: http://www.elizabethclaire.com
Dist(s): **BookLink, Inc.**
Delta Systems Company, Inc.

Early Foundations Pubs., *(978-0-9670728; 978-0-9742131; 978-1-936215)* P.O. Box 442, Jenison, MI 49429 USA
E-mail: orders@efpublishers.org
Web site: http://www.efpublishers.org.

Early Learning Assessment 2000, *(978-0-9667830; 978-0-9746447)* P.O. Box 21003, Roanoke, VA 24018 USA
E-mail: eanaatwork@aol.com.

Early Learning Foundation, LLC, *(978-0-9755415)* 5184 Milroy, Brighton, MI 48116 USA
E-mail: bob@earlylearningfoundation.com
Web site: http://www.earlylearningfoundation.com
Dist(s): **Midpoint Trade Bks., Inc.**

Early Lighr Pr., LLC, *(978-0-9799179)* P.O. Box 317, Boyds, MD 20841-0317 USA
E-mail: lee@earlylightpress.com
Web site: http://www.earlylightpress.com
Dist(s): **MyiLibrary.**

Early Rise Pubns., *(978-0-9741082)* Orders Addr.: 350 S. Cty. Rd., Suite 102-134, Palm Beach, FL 33480 USA Tel 877-419-3648 (phone/fax)
E-mail: info@earlyrisepublications.com
Web site: http://www.earlyrisepublications.com
Dist(s): **CreateSpace Independent Publishing Platform.**

EarlyLight Bks., Inc., *(978-0-9797455; 978-0-9832014; 978-0-9853037)* P.O. Box 984, Clyde, NC 28721 USA
Web site: http://www.earlylightbooks.com
Dist(s): **Charlesbridge Publishing, Inc.**
Penguin Random Hse. LLC
Random Hse., Inc.

Earnshaw Bks. (HKG) *(978-988-17149) Dist. by* **IPG Chicago.**

Earth Arts NW, *(978-0-9792207)* P.O. Box 25183, Portland, OR 97298-0183 USA
E-mail: tribal@spiritone.com
Web site: http://www.earthandspirit.org.

Earth Aware Editions *Imprint of* **Mandala Publishing**

Earth Star Pubns., *(978-0-944851)* P.O. Box 117, Pagosa Springs, CO 81147-1800 USA (SAN 244-9315) Tel 970-731-0694; Fax: 970-731-0694 call first
E-mail: starbeacon@gmail.com
Web site: http://earthstar.tripod.com.

EarthBound Bks., *(978-0-9771818)* P.O. Box 549, North Egremont, MA 01252 USA (SAN 256-9183) Tel 413-528-9042
E-mail: info@earthboundbooks.com
Web site: www.earthboundbooks.com.

Earthen Vessel Production, Inc., *(978-1-887400)* 3620 Greenwood Dr., Kelseyville, CA 95451 USA Tel 707-279-9621; Fax: 707-279-8769
E-mail: books@earthen.com; request@earthen.com
Web site: http://www.earthen.com.

Earthlight *See* **Light24**

Earthling Pr. *Imprint of* **Awe-Struck Publishing**

Earthshaker Bks., *(978-0-9790357)* 400 Melville Ave., Saint Louis, MO 63130 USA (SAN 852-2545) Tel 314-862-8177
E-mail: albonnie@mindspring.com
Dist(s): **Bookmasters Distribution**
MyiLibrary
ebrary, Inc.

EarthTime Pubns., *(978-0-9663286)* Orders Addr.: 5662 Calle Real, #169, Santa Barbara, CA 93117 USA (SAN 299-5727) Tel 805-898-2263; Fax: 805-898-9460
E-mail: donna@seemamoon.com
Web site: http://www.seemamoon.com.

Earthwalk Pr., *(978-0-915749)* 5432 La Jolla Hermosa Ave., La Jolla, CA 92037-7613 USA (SAN 293-9258)
Dist(s): **Booklines Hawaii, Ltd.**
Langenscheidt Publishing Group.

Earthways *See* **Earthways Guided Canoe Trips and School of Wilderness Living**

Earthways Guided Canoe Trips and School of Wilderness Living, *(978-0-9761714)* 159 Earthways Rd., Canaan, ME 04924 USA Tel 207-426-8138
E-mail: info@earthways.net
Web site: http://www.earthways.net.

Ear Twiggles Productions, Inc., *(978-0-9762573)* 14610 Luna Media, San Diego, CA 92127 USA Tel 858-756-8644; Fax: 858-756-8235
E-mail: contactus@eartwiggles.com
Web site: http://www.eartwiggles.com.

Eas'l Pubns., *(978-1-57377)* Div. of The Idea Shop, Inc., Orders Addr.: P.O. Box 22088, Saint Louis, MO 63126 USA Tel 314-892-9222; Fax: 314-892-9607; Edit Addr.: 11150 Lindbergh Business Ct., Suite 107, Saint Louis, MO 63123 USA
E-mail: easlpub@l1.net
Web site: http://www.easlpublications.com.

East End Hospice, Inc., *(978-0-9754932)* Orders Addr.: P.O. Box 1048, Westhampton Beach, NY 11978 USA Tel 631-288-8400; Fax: 631-288-8492; Edit Addr.: 481 Westhampton River Head Rd., Westhampton Beach, NY 11978 USA
E-mail: info@eeh.org
Web site: http://www.eeh.org.

East River Pr., *(978-0-9791283)* 455 FDR Dr., No. B1205, New York, NY 10002-5915 USA Do not confuse with companies with the same or similar name in Largo, MD, NEw YOrk, NY, Chester, NY.

East Stream Group, LLC, *(978-0-9910342)* 46 Bonnie Brae Dr., Weaverville, NC 28787 USA Tel 828-775-4812
E-mail: robin@eaststreamgroup.com.

East West Discovery Pr., *(978-0-9669437; 978-0-9701654; 978-0-9799339; 978-0-9821675; 978-0-9832278; 978-0-9856237; 978-0-9913454; 978-0-9973947)* P.O. Box 3585, Manhattan Beach, CA 90266 USA Tel 310-545-3730; Fax: 310-545-3731
E-mail: info@eastwestdiscovery.com;
icy@eastwestdiscovery.com
Web site: http://www.eastwestdiscovery.com
Dist(s): **Follett School Solutions.**

East West Hse, *(978-0-9778403)* 899 S. Plymouth Ct. Apt 2106, Chicago, IL 60605 USA.

Easter Island Foundation, *(978-1-880636)* Orders Addr.: P.O. Box 6774, Los Osos, CA 93412-6774 USA Tel 805-528-8558; Fax: 805-534-9301
E-mail: eif@att.net
Web site: http://www.islandheritage.org.

Eastern Digital Resources, *(978-0-9815953)* P.O. Box 1451, Clearwater, SC 29822 USA Tel 803-439-2938
E-mail: jrigdon@researchonline.net;
sales@researchonline.net
Web site: http://www.researchonline.net.

†Eastern National, *(978-0-915992; 978-1-888213; 978-1-59091)* 470 Maryland Dr., Suite 1, Fort Washington, PA 19034 USA (SAN 630-4044)
E-mail: erich@Easternnational.org
Web site: http://www.easternnational.org; *CIP.*

Eastern National Park & Monument Association *See* **Eastern National**

Eastern Slope Publisher, *(978-0-9746996; 978-0-9839956)* Orders Addr.: P.O. Box 20357, Reno, NV 89515-0357 USA; Edit Addr.: 205 Urban Rd., Reno, NV 89509-3662 USA
E-mail: pdcafferata@sbcglobal.net.

Eastland Pr., *(978-0-939616)* Orders Addr.: 1240 Activity Dr., No. D, Vista, CA 92081 USA (SAN 665-6900) Tel 760-598-9695 sales office; Fax: 760-598-6083 sales office; Toll Free Fax: 800-241-3329 sales office; Toll Free: 800-453-3278 sales office; Edit Addr.: P.O. Box 99749, Seattle, WA 98139 USA (SAN 216-6216) Tel 206-217-0204 editorial office; Fax: 206-217-0205 editorial office
E-mail: orders@eastlandpress.com;
info@eastlandpress.com
Web site: http://www.eastlandpress.com
Dist(s): **Matthews Medical Bk. Co.**
New Leaf Distributing Co., Inc.
Redwing Bk. Co.
Rittenhouse Bk. Distributors.

Eastland Studios *See* **Eastwind Studios**

Eastlight Pr., *(978-0-9743121)* 1976 Savanna, Fairfield, IA 52556 USA
E-mail: gadef@mac.com.

Easton Studio Pr., LLC, *(978-0-9743806; 978-0-9798248; 978-1-935212; 978-1-63226)* P.O. Box 3131, Westport, CT 06880-3131 USA; *Imprints:* Prospecta Press (ProspectaPr)
Web site: http://www.eastonsp.com/live/
Dist(s): **Ingram Publisher Services**
MyiLibrary
ebrary, Inc.

Eastwaterfront Pr., *(978-0-9769771)* P.O. Box 220-554, Brooklyn, NY 11222 USA
E-mail: pdolack@gis.net.

Eastwind Studios, *(978-0-9755635; 978-0-615-36383-7; 978-0-615-36384-4; 978-0-615-36385-1)* P.O. Box 750, San Bernardino, CA 92402 USA Tel 909-725-7337
E-mail: lindaadams35@yahoo.com; philyeh@mac.com
Web site: http://www.ideaship.com;
http://www.wingedtiger.com
Dist(s): **Booklines Hawaii, Ltd.**

Eastword Publications Development, Incorporated *See* **Lincoln Library Pr., Inc., The**

Easy Reach Corp., *(978-0-615-50973-0; 978-0-615-59362-3; 978-0-9883620)* HC 76 Box 121, Daisy, OK 74540 USA Tel 918-569-4803
E-mail: npyle@kiamichiwb.org.

Easy Readers *Imprint of* **Picture Window Bks.**

Eat Your Peas Publishing, *(978-0-9743210)* 330 Conestoga Rd., Wayne, PA 19087 USA Tel 610-995-0495; Fax: 610-995-0496
E-mail: lisa@richeyassociates.com
Web site: http://www.mannerstogo.com.

EB Benjamin, LLC, *(978-0-615-38727-7; 978-0-615-43887-0)* 413 Mosby Dr, Leesburg, VA 20175 USA Tel 219-669-8474
E-mail: solalife@gmail.com
Dist(s): **CreateSpace Independent Publishing Platform.**

Ebed Pr., *(978-0-9741927; 978-1-933484; 978-0-9774825; 978-1-934050)* 3103 Villa Ave., Bronx, NY 11468-1356 USA Tel 718-788-2484; Fax: 718-788-7760; Toll Free: 800-224-7808
E-mail: info@ebedpress.com
Web site: http://www.ebedpress.com.

Ebeling, Vicki, *(978-0-9779768; 978-0-9981925)* 1250 6th St., Hermosa beach, CA 90254 USA Tel 310-530-0770
E-mail: books@pieravenuepublishing.com
Web site: http://www.educatingamerica.us
Dist(s): **Bookmasters Distribution.**

Ebenezer A.M.E. Church, *(978-0-9748834)* 7707 Allentown Rd., Fort Washington, MD 20744 USA Tel 301-248-8833; Fax: 301-248-6894
Web site: http://www.ebenezerame.org.

Ebks. On The Net *Imprint of* **Write Words, Inc.**

EBL Coaching, *(978-0-9772110; 978-0-9778391)* 167 E. 82nd St., Suite 1A, New York, NY 10023 USA Tel 646-342-9380; Fax: 212-937-2305
E-mail: elevy@eblcoaching.com
Web site: http://www.eblcoaching.com.

Ebon Research Systems *See* **Ebon Research Systems Publishing, LLC**

Ebon Research Systems Publishing, LLC, *(978-0-915960; 978-0-9648313)* 812 Sweetwater Club Blvd., Longwood, FL 32779 USA (SAN 254-6698) Tel 407-786-9200; Fax: 407-682-2384
E-mail: femillionaire@embarqmail.com
Web site: http://www.daretobebooks.com;
http://www.ebonresearchsystems.com.

EbonyEnergy Publishing, Inc., *(978-0-9722795; 978-0-9755092; 978-1-59825)* Div. of Highest Good Pubns., Orders Addr.: P.O. Box 43476, Chicago, IL 60643 USA (SAN 255-3953) Tel 773-445-4946; Fax: 773-233-5178; Toll Free: 877-447-1266; *Imprints:* Highest Good Publications (Highest Good Pubns)
E-mail: info@ebonyenergypublishing.com;
cherylwash@yahoo.com
Web site: http://www.ebonyenergy.com;
http://gemliteraryfoundation.org;
http://ebonyenergybooks.com;
http://ebonyenergykids.com;
http://www.ebonyenergypublishing.com;
http://highestgoodpublications.com;
http://pocketbooksforyoursoul.com
Dist(s): **Biblio Distribution**
ebrary, Inc.

eBookit.com, *(978-1-4566)* Div. of Archieboy Holdings, LLC, 365 Boston Post Rd., No. 311, Sudbury, MA 01776 USA
Web site: http://www.ebookit.com.

eBooks2go *See* **eBooks2go Inc**

eBooks2go Inc, *(978-1-61813; 978-1-5457)* 1111 N. Plaza Dr., Ste. 300, Schaumburg, IL 60173 USA Tel 847-598-1150
E-mail: ram@ebooks2go.net
Web site: www.gantecpublishing.com;
http://www.ebooks2go.com/.

E-Booksgen, *(978-1-893767)* 40 Sandy Pond South, East Wakefield, NH 03830 USA Tel 603-522-9951
E-mail: e-booksgen@e-booksgen.com
Web site: http://www.e-booksgen.com;
http://www.e-booksgen.com/E-WW2DOC.html.

eBooksOnDisk.com, *(978-0-9719101; 978-1-932157)* Orders Addr.: P.O. Box 30432, Gulf Breeze, FL 32503 USA Tel 850-261-1981
E-mail: thomas@ebooksondisk.com
Web site: http://www.ebooksondisk.com;
http://www.confederatemilitaryhistory.com
Dist(s): **CreateSpace Independent Publishing Platform**
Lightning Source, Inc.

ebooksonthe.net *See* **Dilligaf Publishing**

ebooksonthe.net *See* **Write Words, Inc.**

eBookstand Books *See* **Bookstand Publishing**

E-BookTime LLC, *(978-0-9717625; 978-1-932701; 978-1-59824; 978-1-60862)* 6598 Pumpkin Rd., Montgomery, AL 36108 USA Toll Free: 877-613-2665
E-mail: publishing@e-booktime.com
Web site: http://www.e-booktime.com.

Ebury Publishing (GBR) *(978-0-09; 978-0-426; 978-0-7126; 978-0-7535; 978-0-85223; 978-0-86369; 978-1-85227; 978-0-907080; 978-0-903446; 978-1-905042; 978-1-904978; 978-0-427; 978-1-84670; 978-1-905264; 978-1-4735) Dist. by* **IPG Chicago.**

Ecco *Imprint of* **HarperCollins Pubs.**

Echelon Press Publishing, *(978-1-59080)* Orders Addr.: 9055 Thamesmeade Rd. Apt. G, Laurel, MD 20723-5807 USA; *Imprints:* Quake (Quake)
E-mail: admin@echelonpress.com;
echelonpress@gmail.com
Web site: http://www.echelonpress.com;
http://quakeme.com
Dist(s): **Brodart Co.**
Lightning Source, Inc.
Partners Bk. Distributing, Inc.
Smashwords.

Echo & the Bat Pack *Imprint of* **Stone Arch Bks.**

Echo Point Bks. and Media, *(978-0-9638784; 978-0-615-56118-9; 978-1-62654; 978-1-63561)* Orders Addr.: 22 Browne Court, No. 100, Brattleboro, VT 05301 USA
E-mail: editorial@echopointbooks.com;
fred@epbm.mygbiz.com
Web site: www.echopointbooks.com
Dist(s): **Rodale Institute Bookstore.**

Echo Valley Pr, *(978-0-9860734)* P.O. Box 449, Glen Arbor, MI 49636 USA.

Echoes Joint Venture, *(978-0-9759995)* Intensive English Program, UD, 1845 E. Northgate Dr., Irving, TX 75062 USA.

EchoRoad, Inc., *(978-0-9770886)* P.O. Box 900324, Sandy, UT 84090 USA Tel 801-942-7144
E-mail: besteditor@aol.com; Laura@EchoRoad.com
Web site: http://www.EchoRoad.com.

ECity Publishing *Imprint of* **ECity Publishing**

E-City Publishing, *(978-0-615-16430-4)* 150 Rustic Ridge Rd., Fredericksburg, VA 22405 USA
Dist(s): **Publishers Services.**

ECity Publishing, *(978-0-9716006; 978-0-9830425)* Orders Addr.: P.O. Box 5033, Everglades City, FL 34139 USA Tel 239-695-2905; 102 E. Broadway, Everglades City, FL 34139; *Imprints:* ECity Publishing (ECity Pubng)
E-mail: ecitypublishing@earthlink.net
Web site: http://www.ecity-publishing.com.

Eckankar, *(978-1-57043)* Orders Addr.: P.O. Box 27300, Minneapolis, MN 55427 USA (SAN 253-7192) Fax: 952-380-2295; Toll Free: 800-568-3463
E-mail: eckbooks@eckankar.org
Web site: http://www.eckankar.org
Dist(s): **BookMobile.**

Eckerd College Leadership Development Institute, *(978-0-9764173)* 4200 54th Ave. S., St. Petersburg, FL 33711 USA Tel 727-864-8213; Fax: 727-864-7575; Toll Free: 800-753-0444
E-mail: ldi@eckerd.edu
Web site: http://www.eckerd.edu/ldi.

Eckl, Joseph J., *(978-0-9746686)* 346 Country Brook Ln., Harvard, IL 60033-7807 USA
E-mail: ecklindpil@aol.com.

Ecky Thump Bks., Inc., *(978-0-9815883)* 1411 N. California St., Burbank, CA 91505-1902 USA
Web site: http://www.achristmasbox.com
Dist(s): **Partners Pubs. Group, Inc.**

Eclectic Dragon Pr., *(978-0-9746016)* P.O. Box 91, Laie, HI 96762-1294 USA.

Eclipse Pr. *Imprint of* **Blood-Horse, Inc., The**

Eclipse Solutions (UK) Ltd. (GBR) *(978-0-9556910) Dist. by* **LuluCom.**

Eco Fiction Bks. *Imprint of* **Day to Day Enterprises**

Eco Images, *(978-0-938423)* Orders Addr.: P.O. Box 61413, Virginia Beach, VA 23466-1413 USA (SAN 661-230X); Edit Addr.: 4132 Blackwater Rd., Virginia Beach, VA 23457 USA (SAN 661-2318) Tel 757-421-3929
E-mail: wildfood@cox.net
Web site: http://www.ecoimages-us.com.

Eco-Busters, *(978-1-885091)* 1198 Old Castleberry Rd, Brewton, AL 36426 USA.

Eco-Justice Pr., LLC, *(978-0-9660370; 978-0-9891296; 978-1-945432)* P.O. Box 5409, Eugene, OR 97405 USA; *Imprints:* Aurora Books (AuroraBks)
E-mail: info@ecojusticepress.com;
orders@ecojusticepress.com
Web site: ecojusticepress.com.

Ecology Comics, *(978-0-9643421)* 465 B. Kawailoa Rd., Kailua, HI 96734 USA Tel 808-261-1018; Fax: 808-531-3177.

EcoSeekers, The, *(978-0-9798800)* P.O. Box 637, Nyack, NY 10960 USA (SAN 854-6339)
E-mail: info@theecoseekers.com
Web site: http://www.theecoseekers.com
Dist(s): **Midpoint Trade Bks., Inc.**

Eco-thumb Publishing Co., *(978-0-9778536)* 1212 S. Naper Blvd., Suite 119-337, Naperville, IL 60540 USA (SAN 850-4113) Tel 630-853-9758
Web site: http://www.ecothumb.com;
http://www.sendmethesoap.com.

Ecotrust, *(978-0-9676364; 978-0-9779332)* 721 NW 9th Ave. Ste. 200, Portland, OR 97209-3448 USA
Web site: http://www.ecotrust.org
Dist(s): **Oregon State Univ. Pr.**
University of Arizona Pr.

ECS Learning Systems, Inc., *(978-0-944459; 978-1-57022; 978-1-58232; 978-1-60539)* P.O. Box 440, Bulverde, TX 78163 USA (SAN 243-6167) Toll Free Fax: 877-688-3226; Toll Free: 800-688-3224
Web site: http://www.ecslearningsystems.com.

Ecstatic Exchange, The, *(978-0-615-13570-0; 978-0-615-13599-1; 978-0-615-14273-9; 978-0-615-14505-1; 978-0-615-15116-8; 978-0-615-16308-6; 978-0-615-18394-7; 978-0-615-18412-8; 978-0-615-20490-1; 978-0-615-22182-3; 978-0-615-23628-5; 978-0-578-00773-1; 978-0-578-01004-5; 978-0-578-01084-7; 978-0-578-01690-0; 978-0-578-02569-8; 978-0-578-02765-4; 978-0-578-04677-8; 978-0-578-04905-2;*

978-0-578-06116-0; 978-0-578-07145-9; 978-0-578-07482-5; 978-0-578-07608-9; 978-0-578-08293-6; 978-0-578-08512-8; 978-0-578-08891-4;) 670 Morris Pk. Rd., Philadelphia, PA 19151 USA Tel 215-477-8927
E-mail: abdalhayy@danielmoorepoetry.com
Web site: http://www.danielmoorepoetry.com; www.ecstaticxchange.wordpress.com
Dist(s): **Lulu Pr., Inc.**

Ectopic Publishing, *(978-0-9759695)* 3638 Lovejoy Ct. NE, Olympia, WA 98506 USA
E-mail: bryanrandall@ectopicpublishing.com
Web site: http://www.ectopicpublishing.com.

Ed. Acespanish S.A.C.- Lima, Peru, *(978-0-9762361)* 4806 Alta Loma Dr., Austin, TX 78749 USA Tel 512-784-6333
Web site: http://www.acespanish.com.

E.D. Insight Bks., *(978-0-9761552)* P.O. Box 514, Beverly Hills, CA 90213-0514 USA
E-mail: brady@edinsight.com
Web site: http://www.edinsight.com.

Ed Musica, *(978-1-932637)* 1219 La Casa Dr., San Marcos, CA 92078 USA
E-mail: alfredo@edmusica.com
Web site: www.edmusica.com.

Edamex, Editores Asociados Mexicanos, S. A. de C. V. (MEX) *(978-968-409; 978-970-661) Dist. by* **Giron Bks.**

EDC Publishing, *(978-0-7460; 978-0-86020; 978-0-88110; 978-1-58086; 978-0-7945; 978-1-60130)* Orders Addr.: P.O. Box 470663, Tulsa, OK 74147-0663 USA (SAN 658-0505); Edit Addr.: 10302 E. 55th Pl., Tulsa, OK 74146-6515 USA (SAN 107-5322) Tel 918-622-4522; Fax: 918-665-7919; Toll Free Fax: 800-747-4509; Toll Free: 800-475-4522; *Imprints:* Usborne (UsborneU)
E-mail: edc@edcpub.com
Web site: http://www.edcpub.com
Dist(s): **Continental Bk. Co., Inc.**
Lectorum Pubns., Inc.
Libros Sin Fronteras.

EDCO Publishing, Inc., *(978-0-9712692; 978-0-9749412; 978-0-9798088)* 2648 Lapeer Rd., Auburn Hills, MI 48326 USA (SAN 254-4261) Fax: 248-475-9122; Toll Free: 888-510-3326
E-mail: lynette@edcopublishing.com; martha@edcopublishing.com
Web site: http://www.edcopublishing.com
Dist(s): **Partners Bk. Distributing, Inc.**

EDCON Publishing Group, *(978-0-8481; 978-1-56872)* 30 Montauk Blvd., Oakdale, NY 11769 USA Tel 631-567-7227; Fax: 631-567-8745; Toll Free Fax: 888-518-1564; Toll Free: 888-553-3266
E-mail: dale@edconpublishing.com
Web site: http://www.edconpublishing.com
Dist(s): **Findaway World, LLC**
Follett School Solutions.

Eddie Crabtree Ministries, *(978-0-9765830)* Orders Addr.: P.O. Box 846, Salem, VA 24153 USA Tel 540-562-1500; Fax: 540-562-2695; Edit Addr.: 1928 Loch Haven Dr., Roanoke, VA 24019 USA
E-mail: eddiecrabtreeministries@valleywordministries.org.

Eddy, The Writings of Mary Baker, *(978-0-87510; 978-0-87952)* Orders Addr.: 210 Massachusetts Ave P03-25, Boston, MA 02115 USA (SAN 203-6541) Tel 617-450-2517
E-mail: gilibertos@csps.com
Web site: http://www.spirituality.com.

Edebé (ESP) *(978-84-236) Dist. by* **Ediciones.**

Edebé (ESP) *(978-84-236) Dist. by* **Lectorum Pubns.**

Edelsa Grupo Didascalia, S.A. (ESP) *(978-84-389; 978-84-7711; 978-84-85786) Dist. by* **Continental Bk.**

Edelsa Grupo Didascalia, S.A. (ESP) *(978-84-389; 978-84-7711; 978-84-85786) Dist. by* **Distribks Inc.**

Edelson, Madelyn, *(978-0-9770131)* 69 Bay Ave., H, Huntington, NY 11743 USA
E-mail: mbedelson@optonline.net
Web site: http://www.beechwindpress.com.

Eden Entertainment Ltd., Inc., *(978-0-9672819; 978-0-9835380)* 1277 1st St. Suite 1, Key West, FL 33040 USA Tel 305-294-7928
E-mail: MarcusVarner@Hotmail.com; DanielJReynen@Hotmail.com
Web site: http://www.truesecretof.com; http://www.dietisdead.com; http://www.webefit.com.

Eden Studios, Inc., *(978-1-891153; 978-1-933105)* 6 Dogwood Ln., Londonville, NY 12211 USA Tel 518-331-2063; Fax: 425-962-2593
E-mail: edenprod@aol.com
Web site: http://www.edenstudios.net
Dist(s): **PSI (Publisher Services, Inc.).**

EdenTree Publishing, *(978-0-692-78131-9; 978-0-9982113)* P.O. Box 1174, PORTSMOUTH, OH 45662 USA Tel 740-285-3954
E-mail: frwarnock@yahoo.com.

Edes Publishing Co., *(978-0-9788010; 978-1-943472)* 1224 E. Hadley, Las Cruces, NM 88001 USA (SAN 851-6561)
E-mail: publisher@edes.net
Web site: http://www.edes.net.

Edgar Road Publishing, *(978-0-615-20414-7)* 938 Tuxedo Blvd., Webster Groves, MO 63119 USA Tel 314-541-9235; Fax: 314-961-9044
E-mail: edgarroadpublishing@gmail.com
Dist(s): **R J Communications, LLC.**

Edge Bks. *Imprint of* **Capstone Press of Coughlan Cos.**

Edgecliff Pr. LLC., *(978-0-9798659; 978-0-9819271; 978-0-9844622; 978-0-9839486)* Mid-century Modern Bldg. 9066 Long Ln., Cincinnati, OH 45231 USA (SAN 854-6150) Tel 513-348-9120 Hours 9 to 5 EST
E-mail: Info@edgecliffpress.com
Web site: http://www.edgecliffpress.com; http://www.edgecliffkids.com.

EDGEucation Publishing, *(978-1-932689)* Orders Addr.: P.O. Box 852013, Yukon, OK 73085-2013 USA; Edit Addr.: 1441 NW 47th St., Oklahoma City, OK 73085-2013 USA
E-mail: edgeucation@sbcglobal.net.

Edgewood Publishing, LLC, *(978-0-9792645)* P.O. Box 153, Adell, WI 53001 USA Tel 920-994-2483.

Ediciones Alas, Inc., *(978-0-9753799)* Orders Addr.: P.O. Box 327495, Fort Lauderdale, FL 33332 USA; Edit Addr.: 6061 SW 195th Ave., Pembroke Pines, FL 33332 USA
E-mail: mm@miliymolo.com
Web site: http://www.miliymolo.com.

Ediciones Alfaguara (ESP) *(978-84-204) Dist. by* **Lectorum Pubns.**

Ediciones Alfaguara (ESP) *(978-84-204) Dist. by* **Santillana.**

Ediciones Alfaguara (ESP) *(978-84-204) Dist. by* **TwoRivers.**

Ediciones B (ESP) *(978-84-406; 978-84-7735; 978-84-666; 978-84-9872; 978-84-15420) Dist. by* **IPG Chicago.**

Ediciones B (ESP) *(978-84-406; 978-84-7735; 978-84-666; 978-84-9872; 978-84-15420) Dist. by* **Spanish.**

Ediciones B Mexico (MEX) *(978-84-406; 978-84-7735; 978-607-480) Dist. by* **Spanish.**

Ediciones Cátedra (ESP) *(978-84-376) Dist. by* **Continental Bk.**

Ediciones de la Torre (ESP) *(978-84-7960; 978-84-85277; 978-84-85866; 978-84-86587) Dist. by* **AIMS Intl.**

Ediciones de la Torre (ESP) *(978-84-7960; 978-84-85277; 978-84-85866; 978-84-86587) Dist. by* **Libros Fronteras.**

Ediciones del Bronce (ESP) *(978-84-8453; 978-84-89854) Dist. by* **Planeta.**

Ediciones del Laberinto (ESP) *(978-84-8483; 978-84-87482) Dist. by* **Ediciones.**

Ediciones Destino (ESP) *(978-84-233; 978-84-9710) Dist. by* **Continental Bk.**

Ediciones Destino (ESP) *(978-84-233; 978-84-9710) Dist. by* **Lectorum Pubns.**

Ediciones Destino (ESP) *(978-84-233; 978-84-9710) Dist. by* **AIMS Intl.**

Ediciones Destino (ESP) *(978-84-233; 978-84-9710) Dist. by* **Planeta.**

Ediciones El Salvaje Refinado *See* **Refined Savage Editions / Ediciones El Salvaje Refinado, The**

Ediciones La Fragatina (ESP) *(978-84-16226) Dist. by* **IPG Chicago.**

Ediciones la Gota de Agua, *(978-0-9771987; 978-0-9819303; 978-0-9964627)* 1937 Pemberton St., Philadelphia, PA 19146-1825 USA Tel 215-546-9421
E-mail: info@edicioneslagotadeagua.com
Web site: http://edicioneslagotadeagua.com
Dist(s): **Ediciones Universal**
GOBI Library Solutionis from EBSCO.

Ediciones Lea S.A. (ARG) *(978-987-1257; 978-987-21776; 978-987-22032; 978-987-22079; 978-987-634; 978-987-718) Dist. by* **IPG Chicago.**

Ediciones Lerner *Imprint of* **Lerner Publishing Group**

Ediciones Norte, Inc., *(978-1-931928)* P.O. Box 29461, San Juan, PR 00929-0461 USA Tel 787-701-0909; Fax: 787-701-0922
Web site: http://www.edicionesnorte.com
Dist(s): **Independent Pubs. Group.**

Ediciones Nuevo Espacio *See* **Ediciones Nuevo Espacio-AcademicPressENE**

Ediciones Nuevo Espacio-AcademicPressENE, *(978-1-930879)* Orders Addr.: 39 Redfern Rd., Eatontown, NJ 07724 USA
E-mail: AcademicPressENE@gmail.com
Web site: http://www.editorialene.com; http://www.editorial-ene.com
Dist(s): **Book Wholesalers, Inc.**
Brodart Co.

Ediciones Obelisco (ESP) *(978-84-7720; 978-84-86000; 978-84-9777; 978-84-940745; 978-84-941549; 978-84-16117) Dist. by* **Spanish.**

Ediciones Oniro S.A. (ESP) *(978-84-89920; 978-84-922523; 978-84-9754; 978-84-95456) Dist. by* **Bilingual Pubns.**

Ediciones Oniro S.A. (ESP) *(978-84-89920; 978-84-922523; 978-84-9754; 978-84-95456) Dist. by* **Lectorum Pubns.**

Ediciones Rodeno (ESP) *(978-84-938364; 978-84-942689) Dist. by* **IPG Chicago.**

Ediciones Santillana, Inc., *(978-1-57581; 978-1-60484; 978-1-61875)* Div. of Santillana-S. A. (SP), P.O. Box 195462, San Juan, PR 00919-5462 USA Tel 787-781-9800; Fax: 787-782-6149; Toll Free: 800-981-9822
E-mail: molivero@santillanapr.net; areynoso@santillanapr.net; cvazquez@santillanapr.net
Web site: http://www.gruposantillana.com
Dist(s): **Santillana USA Publishing Co., Inc.**

Ediciones Situm, Incorporated *See* **Biblio Services, Inc.**

Ediciones SM, *(978-1-933279; 978-1-934801; 978-1-935556; 978-1-936534; 978-1-939075; 978-1-940343; 978-1-63014)* Barrio Palmas, 776 Calle 7 Suite 2, Catano, PR 00962-6335 USA Tel 787-625-9800; Fax: 787-625-9799
Web site: http://www.ediciones-smpr.com.

Ediciones Universal, *(978-0-89729; 978-1-59388)* Orders Addr.: P.O. Box 450353, Miami, FL 33245-0353 USA (SAN 658-0548); Edit Addr.: 3090 SW Eighth St., Miami, FL 33135 USA (SAN 207-2203) Tel 305-642-3355; Fax: 305-642-7978
E-mail: marta@ediciones.com; ediciones@ediciones.com
Web site: http://www.ediciones.com
Dist(s): **Lectorum Pubns., Inc.**

Ediciones Urano de México (MEX) *(978-607-95139; 978-607-7835; 978-607-9344) Dist. by* **Spanish.**

Ediciones Urano S. A. (ESP) *(978-84-7953; 978-84-95618; 978-84-95752; 978-84-86344; 978-84-95787; 978-84-96711; 978-84-96886; 978-84-92916; 978-84-9944) Dist. by* **Spanish.**

Ediciones y Distribuciones Codice, S.A. (ESP) *(978-84-357) Dist. by* **Continental Bk.**

Edifytainment Bks., *(978-0-9753427)* 213 Regent Cir., Inglewood, CA 90301 USA Tel 310-677-9744
E-mail: edifytainmentbooks@prodigy.net
Web site: http://www.bobettejamison-harrison.com/edifytainmentbooks.html.

Edilupa Ediciones, S.L. (ESP) *(978-84-932571; 978-84-932843; 978-84-96252; 978-84-96609) Dist. by* **Lectorum Pubns.**

eDimples, Inc., *(978-0-9787759)* 9249 S. Broadway, 200-161, Highlands Ranch, CO 80129 USA Tel 303-284-1331 (phone/fax)
E-mail: greg@edimples.com
Web site: http://www.edimples.com.

Edinboro Bk. Arts Collective, *(978-0-9747001)* Orders Addr.: P.O. Box 77, Edinboro, PA 16412 USA; Edit Addr.: 103 Tarbell Ln., Edinboro, PA 16412 USA
E-mail: winterberger@edinboro.edu.

Edinborough Pr., *(978-1-889020)* P.O. Box 13790, Roseville, MN 55113-2293 USA (SAN 299-2825) Tel 651-415-1034; Toll Free Fax: 800-566-6145; Toll Free: 888-251-6336 (Orders Only)
E-mail: books@edinborough.com
Web site: http://www.edinborough.com
Dist(s): **Independent Pubs. Group ebrary, Inc.**

Edinburgh Univ. Pr. (GBR) *(978-0-7486; 978-0-85224) Dist. by* **OUP.**

Edinumen, Editorial (ESP) *(978-84-89756; 978-84-85789; 978-84-95986; 978-84-9848) Dist. by* **Cambridge U Pr.**

Edit et Cetera *See* **Edit et Cetera Ltd.**

Edit et Cetera Ltd., *(978-0-9746122; 978-0-9769989; 978-0-9832270)* P.O. Box 551, Canon City, CO 81215 USA
E-mail: familybookhouse@aol.com
Web site: http://www.familybookhouse.com.

EDITER'S Publishing Hse., *(978-0-9706814; 978-0-9743743)* 654 Schafer Pl., Escondido, CA 92025 USA Tel 619-339-7030; Fax: 760-294-2685
E-mail: books@editers.com
Web site: http://www.editers.com.

EDITER'S Publishing Hse. (MEX) *(978-968-6966; 978-968-5432) Dist. by* **EDITERS Pub Hse.**

Editex, Editorial S.A. (ESP) *(978-84-7131) Dist. by* **Lectorum Pubns.**

Edition Axel Menges GmbH (DEU) *(978-3-930698; 978-3-932565; 978-3-936681) Dist. by* **Natl Bk Netwk.**

Edition Chimaira (DEU) *(978-3-930612; 978-3-89973) Dist. by* **Serpents Tale.**

Edition Q, Inc., *(978-0-86715; 978-1-883695)* 551 N. Kimberly Dr., Carol Stream, IL 60188-1881 USA Tel 630-682-3223; Fax: 630-682-3907; Toll Free: 800-421-0387
E-mail: quintpub@aol.com; service@quintbook.com
Web site: http://www.quintpub.com.

Editions Alexandre Stanke (CAN) *(978-2-89558) Dist. by* **Bookmasters.**

Editions de la Montagne Verte, Inc. (CAN) *(978-0-9737681; 978-1-897277) Dist. by* **Lone Pine.**

Editions de la Paix (CAN) *(978-2-921255; 978-2-922565; 978-2-9800785; 978-2-89599) Dist. by* **World of Reading.**

Editions du Petit Music (FRA) *(978-2-84607) Dist. by* **Distribks Inc.**

Editions du Seuil (FRA) *(978-2-02) Dist. by* **Distribks Inc.**

Editions Fleurus (FRA) *(978-2-215; 978-2-250; 978-2-7289) Dist. by* **Distribks Inc.**

Editions Milan (FRA) *(978-2-7459; 978-2-84113; 978-2-86726) Dist. by* **Distribks Inc.**

Editora Campamocha, *(978-1-934802)* 1609 Chicago Av., McAllen, TX 78501 USA.

Editores Mexicanos Unidos (MEX) *(978-968-15) Dist. by* **Ediciones.**

Editorial Betania *See* **Grupo Nelson**

Editorial Brief (ESP) *(978-84-931888) Dist. by* **IPG Chicago.**

Editorial Buenas Letras *Imprint of* **Rosen Publishing Group, Inc., The**

Editorial Busqueda, *(978-0-9744408; 978-0-9760652; 978-0-9798461; 978-0-9843607)* Calle Pinero, No. 113, San Juan, PR 00925-3612 USA.

Editorial Campana, *(978-0-9725611; 978-1-934370)* 19 W. 85th St., New York, NY 10024 USA (SAN 854-2791) Tel 212-721-4062 (phone/fax); *Imprints:* Campanita Books (Campanita Bks)
E-mail: gycultura@aol.com
Web site: http://www.editorialcampana.com
Dist(s): **Downtown Bk. Ctr., Inc.**

Editorial Cultural, Inc., *(978-1-56758; 978-84-399)* Orders Addr.: P.O. Box 21056, San Juan, PR 00928 USA; Edit Addr.: Calle Robles, No. 51, San Juan, PR 00928 USA
E-mail: angiev@editorialculturalpr.com; alamo48@gmail.com
Web site: http://www.editorialculturalpr.com.

Editorial de Nuevo Extremo S.A. (ARG) *(978-950-9681; 978-987-1068; 978-987-1427; 978-987-609) Dist. by* **IPG Chicago.**

Editorial Diana, S.A. (MEX) *(978-968-13) Dist. by* **Continental Bk.**

Editorial Diana, S.A. (MEX) *(978-968-13) Dist. by* **Lectorum Pubns.**

Editorial Diana, S.A. (MEX) *(978-968-13) Dist. by* **Giron Bks.**

Editorial Edaf, S.L. (ESP) *(978-84-7640; 978-84-7166; 978-84-414) Dist. by* **Spanish.**

Editorial El Antillano, Inc., *(978-0-9755661; 978-0-9793026)* 104 Jefferson St., Suite 5-B, Santurce, PR 00911 USA Tel 787-982-4060
E-mail: olga_otero@mspr.net
Web site: http://www.elantillano.com.

Editorial Everest, S.A (ESP) *(978-84-441) Dist. by* **Lectorum Pubns.**

Editorial Flamboyant (ESP) *Dist. by* **Lectorum Pubns.**

Editorial Homagno, *(978-0-9727467)* Div. of Homagno Group, Inc., P.O. Box 960227, Miami, FL 33296 USA
Web site: http://www.homagno.com.

Editorial Humanitas, *(978-0-9650104)* Orders Addr.: 2006 23rd Ave., E., Seattle, WA 98112-2936 USA Tel 206-616-9394
E-mail: oberle@mindspring.com
Web site: http://www.mindspring.com/~oberle/PRbirds.htm
Dist(s): **Representaciones Borinquenas, Inc.**

Editorial Imagen, *(978-1-64081; 978-1-5419-9001-2)* calmayo 2982, Dallas, TX 75224 USA Tel 351-464-8532
E-mail: negociandres2@gmail.com.

Editorial John Louis von Neumann, Inc., *(978-0-9748297; 978-0-9779982)* Urb. Villa Fontana, 3NS-15 Via Lourdes, Carolina, PR 00983-4650 USA Tel 787-630-6330; Fax: 787-257-4979
E-mail: josejuandiaz@gmail.com
Web site: http://josejuandiaz.com
Dist(s): **Representaciones Borinquenas, Inc.**

Editorial Leetra (MEX) *Dist. by* **Lectorum Pubns.**

Editorial Libros en Red, *(978-1-59754; 978-1-62915)* 5018 57th Ave., Apt. B8, Bladensburg, MD 20710 USA
E-mail: administracion@librosenred.com
Web site: http://www.librosenred.com
Dist(s): **Ediciones Universal.**

Editorial Libsa, S.A. (ESP) *(978-84-7630; 978-84-662) Dist. by* **Continental Bk.**

Editorial Libsa, S.A. (ESP) *(978-84-7630; 978-84-662) Dist. by* **Lectorum Pubns.**

Editorial Lumen (ESP) *(978-84-264) Dist. by* **Lectorum Pubns.**

Editorial Lumen (ESP) *(978-84-264) Dist. by* **Distribks Inc.**

Editorial Miglo Inc., *(978-0-9671705)* 1560 Grand Concourse, Apt. 504, Bronx, NY 10457 USA
E-mail: jcmalone01@aol.com
Web site: http://www.edimiglo.com.

Editorial Mundo Hispano *Imprint of* **Casa Bautista de Publicaciones**

Editorial Oceano de Mexico (MEX) *(978-607-400) Dist. by* **IPG Chicago.**

Editorial Oceano De Mexico, S.A. DE C.V. (MEX) *(978-970-651; 978-968-6321) Dist. by* **Lectorum Pubns.**

Editorial Panamericana, Inc., *(978-1-881744; 978-1-934139; 978-1-61725)* Orders Addr.: Urb. Puerto Nuevo 1336 F.d. Roosevelt Ave., San Juan, PR 00920 USA Tel 787-277-7988; Fax: 787-277-7240; Edit Addr.: P.O. Box 25189, San Juan, PR 00928-5189 USA Tel 787-277-7988; Fax: 787-277-7240
E-mail: info@editorialpanamericana.com; cbaez@editorialpanamericana.com
Web site: http://www.editorialpanamericana.com.

Editorial Pax (MEX) *(978-968-860; 978-968-461) Dist. by* **IPG Chicago.**

Editorial Planeta, S. A. (ESP) *(978-84-08; 978-84-320; 978-84-395; 978-84-8460; 978-970-37) Dist. by* **TwoRivers.**

Editorial Plaza Mayor, Inc., *(978-1-56328)* Avenida Ponce De Leon 1527, Barrio El Cinco, Rio Piedras, PR 00926 USA Tel 787-764-0455; Fax: 787-764-0465
E-mail: patrigut@prtc.net
Dist(s): **Continental Bk. Co., Inc.**
Ediciones Universal
Lectorum Pubns., Inc.
Libros Sin Fronteras.

Editorial Porrua (MEX) *(978-968-432; 978-968-452; 978-970-07) Dist. by* **Continental Bk.**

Editorial Portavoz *Imprint of* **Kregel Pubns.**

Editorial Resources, Inc., *(978-0-9745923)* 4510 Seneca St., Pasadena, TX 77504-3568 USA
E-mail: anng@editorial-resources.com
Web site: http://www.editorial-resources.com.

Editorial Sendas Antiguas, LLC, *(978-1-932789)* 1730 Leffingwell Ave., Grand Rapids, MI 49525-4532 USA Tel 616-365-9073 (phone/fax); 616-365-0699; Fax: 616-365-1990
E-mail: info@sendasantiguas.com; sales@sendasantiguas.com; greendykbill@aol.com
Web site: http://www.sendasantiguas.com
Dist(s): **Send The Light Distribution LLC.**

Editorial Sudamericana S.A. (ARG) *(978-950-07; 978-950-37) Dist. by* **Lectorum Pubns.**

Editorial Sudamericana S.A. (ARG) *(978-950-07; 978-950-37) Dist. by* **Distribks Inc.**

Editorial Unilit, *(978-0-7899; 978-0-945792; 978-1-56063)* Div. of Spanish Hse., Inc., 1360 NW 88th Ave., Miami, FL 33172-3093 USA (SAN 247-5979) Tel 305-592-6136; Fax: 305-592-0087; Toll Free: 800-767-7726
E-mail: sales1@unidial.com
Web site: http://www.editorialunilit.com/
Dist(s): **Bethany Hse. Pubs.**
Lectorum Pubns., Inc.
Pura Vida Bks., Inc.

Editorial Vida Abundante, *(978-0-9765828)* P.O. Box 1073, Fajardo, PR 00738 USA Tel 787-860-3555
Web site: http://www.vidaabundante.org.

Editorial Voluntad S.A. (COL) *(978-958-02) Dist. by* **Continental Bk.**

Editorial Voluntad S.A. (COL) *(978-958-02) Dist. by* **Distr Norma.**

Editorium, The, *(978-1-60096; 978-1-4341)* 3907 Marsha Dr., West Jordan, UT 84081 USA Tel 801-750-2498 Cell
E-mail: lyon.jack@gmail.com
Web site: http://www.editorium.com; http://www.wakinglionpress.com; http://www.templehillbooks.com.

Edivision Compania Editorial, S.A. de C.V. (MEX) *(978-968-890) Dist. by* **Continental Bk.**

Edizioni PIEMME spa (ITA) *(978-88-384; 978-88-566; 978-88-585) Dist. by* **Distribks Inc.**

EDR, *(978-0-9794615)* P.O. Box 22, Waterport, NY 14571 USA
E-mail: sakina@edrsinc.com
Web site: http://www.edrsinc.com; http://www.omariworld.com.

EdTechLens, *(978-0-9912337)* 1834 Lenox Rd., SCHENECTADY, NY 12308 USA Tel 518-393-9460
E-mail: ellen@ellensenisi.com
Web site: https://www.edtechlens.com
Dist(s): **Follett School Solutions.**

Edu Designs, *(978-0-9795017)* Orders Addr.: 16 Atwood St. Apt B, Hartford, CT 06105 USA Tel 626-940-4768; Edit Addr.: P.O. Box 660518, Arcadia, CA 91066 USA Tel 626-940-4768
E-mail: edudesigns.org@gmail.com.

Educa Vision Inc., *(978-1-881839; 978-1-58432; 978-1-62632)* 7550 NW 47th Ave., Coconut Creek, FL 33073 USA (SAN 760-873X) Tel 954-968-7433; Fax: 954-970-0330
E-mail: educa@aol.com
Web site: http://www.educavision.com; http://www.educabrazil.org; http://www.caribbeanstudiespress.com; www.educalanguage.com
Dist(s): **Follett School Solutions.**

Educare Pr., *(978-0-944638)* P.O. Box 17222, Seattle, WA 98107 USA Tel 206-782-4797; Fax: 206-782-4802 Do not confuse with EduCare, Colorado Springs, CO
E-mail: educarepress@hotmail.com
Web site: http://www.educarepress.com.

Education and More, Inc., *(978-0-9755809)* 1760 Clayton Cir., Cumming, GA 30040-7860 USA Tel 678-455-7667
E-mail: education@educationandmore.com
Web site: http://www.educationandmore.com.

Education Ctr., Inc., *(978-1-56234)* Orders Addr.: P.O. Box 9753, Greensboro, NC 27429 USA Tel 336-854-0309; Fax: 336-547-1590; Toll Free: 800-334-0298; Edit Addr.: 3515 W. Market St., Greensboro, NC 27403 USA (SAN 256-6311) Fax: 336-851-8218; 4224 Tudor Ln. Ste. 101, Greensboro, NC 27410-8145 (SAN 256-632X); *Imprints:* Mailbox Books, The (The Mailbox Bks)
E-mail: jmartin@theeducationcenter.com; mjones@themailbox.com
Web site: http://theeducationcenter.com; http://www.themailbox.com
Dist(s): **Sharpe, M.E. Inc.**

Education Services Australia Ltd. (AUS) *(978-1-86366; 978-0-9758070; 978-1-74200; 978-0-646-19608-4; 978-0-646-21423-8; 978-0-646-24402-0; 978-0-646-24701-4; 978-0-646-25530-9) Dist. by* **Cheng Tsui.**

Education That, LLC, *(978-0-692-73656-2; 978-0-692-77912-5; 978-0-9984254)* 5850 Waterloo Rd. Suite 140, Columbia, MD 21045 USA Tel 443-324-7388; 5850 Waterloo Rd. Suite 140, Columbia, MD 21045
E-mail: mbooker@educationthat.com
Web site: www.educationthat.com.

Educational Activities, Inc., *(978-0-7925; 978-0-89525; 978-0-914296; 978-1-55737)* Orders Addr.: P.O. Box 87, Baldwin, NY 11510 USA; Edit Addr.: 1947 Grand Ave., Baldwin, NY 11510 USA (SAN 207-4400) Tel 516-223-4666; Fax: 516-623-9282; Toll Free: 800-797-3223
E-mail: learn@edact.com
Web site: http://www.edact.com
Dist(s): **Follett School Solutions.**

Educational Adventures *See* **Mighty Kids Media**

Educational Consulting by Design, LLC, *(978-0-692-59277-9)* 216 Anderson Rd, Glenoma, WA 98336 USA Tel 360-280-8841
E-mail: jcollierllc@gmail.com.

Educational Development Corporation *See* **EDC Publishing**

Educational Expertise, LLC, *(978-0-9713450)* 427 E. Belvedere Ave., Baltimore, MD 21212 USA
Web site: http://www.educationalexpertise.com.

Educational Impressions, *(978-0-910857; 978-1-56644)* Orders Addr.: P.O. Box 77, Hawthorne, NJ 07507 USA (SAN 274-4899) Tel 973-423-4666; Fax: 973-423-5569; Toll Free: 800-451-7450; Edit Addr.: 210 Sixth Ave., Hawthorne, NJ 07507 USA
E-mail: awpeller@word.net.att.net
Web site: http://www.awpeller.com
Dist(s): **Continental Bk. Co., Inc.**

Educational Media Corp., *(978-0-932796; 978-1-930572)* Orders Addr.: 1443 Old York Rd., Warminster, PA 18974 USA Fax: 215-956-9041; Toll Free: 800-448-2197; Edit Addr.: 4256 Central Ave. NE, Minneapolis, MN 55421-2920 USA (SAN 212-4203) Tel 763-781-0088; Fax: 763-781-7753; Toll Free: 800-966-3382
E-mail: emedia@educationalmedia.com
Web site: http://www.educationalmedia.com.

Educational Publishing Concepts, Inc., *(978-1-892354)* P.O. Box 665, Wheaton, IL 60189 USA Tel 630-653-5336; Fax: 630-653-5368 Do not confuse with Educational Publishing Concepts, Inc., Walla Walla, WA
E-mail: Jerryw@newkidsmedia.com
Web site: http://www.newkidsmedia.com.

Educational Publishing LLC, *(978-1-60436)* Orders Addr.: 51 Saw Mill Pond Rd., Edison, NJ 08817-6025 USA Toll Free: 800-554-2296; Edit Addr.: 10 W. 33rd St. Rm. 910, New York, NY 10001-3306 USA (SAN 854-2422)
Web site: http://www.earlystartchild.com.

Educational Research & Applications, LLC, *(978-0-9762724)* P.O. Box 1242, Danville, CA 94526 USA.

Educational Resources, Inc., *(978-1-931574)* 1691 Highland Pkwy., Saint Paul, MN 55116 USA Tel 651-592-3688; Fax: 651-690-2188 Do not confuse with companies with same name in Shawnee Mission, KS, Columbia, SC, Elgin, IL
E-mail: Edres1691@aol.com
Web site: http://www.eduresources.org.

Educational Solutions, Inc., *(978-0-87825)* 99 University Pl., 6th Flr., New York, NY 10003-4555 USA (SAN 205-6186) Tel 212-674-2988 Do not confuse with Educational Solutions, Stafford, TX.

Educational Testing Service, *(978-0-88685)* P.O. Box 6108, Princeton, NJ 08541-6108 USA (SAN 238-034X) Tel 609-771-7243; Fax: 609-771-7385 Do not confuse with Educational Testing Service in Washington, DC
E-mail: lsavadge@ets.org; j.womack@ets.org; cbrodsky@ets.org
Web site: http://www.ets.org
Dist(s): **Independent Pubs. Group.**

Educational Tools, Inc., *(978-0-9766802; 978-0-9774310; 978-1-933797)* 3500 Beachwood Ct., Suite 102, Jacksonville, FL 32224 USA Fax: 904-998-1941; Toll Free: 800-586-9940
E-mail: rpettus@educationaltools.org
Web site: http://www.educationaltools.org.

Educational Video Resources *See* **Summit Interactive**

Educators for the Environment *See* **Energy Education Group**

Educators Publishing Service, Inc., *(978-0-8388; 978-1-4293)* P.O. Box 9031, Cambridge, MA 02139-9031 USA (SAN 201-8225) Toll Free: 800-435-7728; 625 Mount Auburn St., Cambridge, MA 02138
E-mail: epsbooks@epsbooks.com
Web site: http://www.epsbooks.com.

Educ-Easy Bks., *(978-0-9664217; 978-0-9912724; 978-0-9864034; 978-0-9963893; 978-0-9968972)* POB 6366, Greenville, SC 29606 USA Tel 910-798-5042
E-mail: gisela.hausmann@yahoo.com
Web site: http://www.NakedDetermination.com.

EDUKIT, L.L.C., *(978-0-9765917)* P.O. Box 821, Suffern, NY 10901 USA
E-mail: edukitco@aol.com
Web site: http://www.edukit.biz.

Edupress, Inc., *(978-1-56472)* P.O. Box 800, Fort Atkinson, WI 53538-0800 USA Toll Free: 800-835-7978 Do not confuse with EduPress, Pittsburgh, PA
E-mail: info@edupressinc.com
Web site: http://www.edupressinc.com.

Edu-Steps, Inc., *(978-0-9771101; 978-0-9863690)* Orders Addr.: 4644 N. 22nd St. Suite 1161, Phoenix, AZ 85016-4699 USA Tel 480-570-3888; Fax: 602-795-6837
E-mail: patdoran@edu-steps.com
Web site: http://www.edu-steps.com.

Edutech Learning Resource Ctr., *(978-0-9768208)* 1361 NE 158 St., North Miami Beach, FL 33162 USA Tel 305-947-6393
E-mail: edutech_learning@yahoo.com.

Edutunes, *(978-1-930979)* 2067 Rurline Dr., Saint Louis, MO 63146 USA Tel 808-728-8863
E-mail: missjenny@edutunes.com
Web site: http://www.edutunes.com.

Edward, Isaac Adams, *(978-0-692-80001-0)* 2527 S. Meridian St., Puyallup, WA 98373 USA Tel 206-886-5453
E-mail: menatiworld@hotmail.com.

Edwards, Idella, *(978-0-615-56814-0; 978-0-615-65355-6; 978-0-9896802; 978-0-9986662)* 602 Lake Harbor Dr., Marion, IL 62959 USA Tel 618-997-5237
E-mail: idellapearl@frontier.com.

Edwards, Michael, *(978-0-9720952)* 310 N. Front St., Suite No. 4, Box 248, Wilmington, NC 28401 USA
E-mail: neversanever@hotmail.com.

Edwards, R. G. Publishing, *(978-0-615-13336-2; 978-0-615-16739-8; 978-0-615-17785-4)* P.O. Box 978, Goodlettsville, TN 37070 USA
Dist(s): **Lulu Pr., Inc.**

Edwards, R.G. Publishing *See* **Edwards, R. G. Publishing**

ee publishing & productions, inc., *(978-0-9753843; 978-0-9798466)* P.O. Box 7006, Fairfax Station, VA 22039 USA Tel 703-256-1721 (phone/fax)
E-mail: info@eeppinc.com; lsaker@eeppinc.com
Web site: http://www.eeppinc.com.

eeBoo Corp., *(978-1-59461; 978-1-68227)* 170 West 74th St., Ste. 102, New York, NY 10023 USA (SAN 860-4371) Fax: 212-678-1922
E-mail: christine@eeboo.com
Web site: http://www.eeboo.com.

Eelman's Pr., *(978-0-9747053)* Orders Addr.: P.O. Box Box 359, South Orleans, MA 02662 USA Tel 607-277-0612; Edit Addr.: Davis Rd., South Orleans, MA 02662 USA.

Eepie Pr., *(978-0-9755606)* 1412 Greenbrier Pkwy., Suite 145-B, Norfolk, VA 23320 USA Tel 757-424-5868; Fax: 757-424-5845
E-mail: info@eepiepress.com
Web site: http://www.eepiepress.com
Dist(s): **Print & Ship.**

Eerdmans Bks For Young Readers *Imprint of* **Eerdmans, William B. Publishing Co.**

†Eerdmans, William B. Publishing Co., *(978-0-8028; 978-1-4674)* 2140 Oak Industrial Dr NE, Grand Rapids, MI 49505 USA (SAN 220-0058) Tel 616-459-4591; Fax: 616-459-6540; Toll Free: 800-253-7521 (orders); *Imprints:* Eerdmans Books For Young Readers (Eerdmans Bks)
E-mail: info@eerdmans.com; customerservice@eerdmans.com
Web site: http://www.eerdmans.com
Dist(s): **Faith Alive Christian Resources**
Forward Movement Pubns.
Lightning Source, Inc.
Send The Light Distribution LLC; *CIP*

EFFE Bks., *(978-0-9773583)* P.O. Box 3448, Winter Park, FL 32790-23448 USA (SAN 257-3784) Tel 407-645-2326
E-mail: tfunaro@summittech.us
Web site: http://www.effebooks.com
Dist(s): **Midpoint Trade Bks., Inc.**

Effective Literacy Methods, *(978-0-9706094)* 57 Knollwood Dr., Rochester, NY 14618-3512 USA
E-mail: info@newphonics.com; rkb@newphonics.com
Web site: http://www.newphonics.com.

Efforts Unified, *(978-0-9763523)* 244 Fifth Ave., No. N259, New York, NY 10001 USA.

EG Bks., *(978-0-615-54589-9; 978-0-615-55920-9)* 360 Oak St., Oakfield, WI 53065 USA Tel 920-583-3329
E-mail: e.garner3@gmail.com.

Egap Gifa Bks. *Imprint of* **Leafcollecting.com Publishing Co.**

Egbert, Bill, *(978-0-9979779)* 3507 N Cole Rd No. 101, Boise, ID 83704-0770 USA
E-mail: begbert2@yahoo.com.

Egg Hill Pubns., *(978-0-9652351; 978-0-692-56474-5)* Orders Addr.: 113 Cottontail Ln., Centre Hall, PA 16828-8508 USA Tel 814-360-4401
E-mail: jandhfra2@yahoo.com
Dist(s): **Partners Bk. Distributing, Inc.**

Egger Publishing, Inc., *(978-1-886050; 978-1-934262)* P.O. Box 12248, Scottsdale, AZ 85267 USA Tel 480-596-5100; Fax: 480-951-2276; Toll Free: 888-937-7355
E-mail: regger@sittonspelling.com
Web site: http://www.sittonspelling.com
Dist(s): **Northwest Textbook Depository.**

Egmont Bks., Ltd. (GBR) *(978-0-416; 978-0-603; 978-0-7497; 978-0-7498; 978-1-4052) Dist. by* **Trafalgar.**

Egmont Bks., Ltd. (GBR) *(978-0-416; 978-0-603; 978-0-7497; 978-0-7498; 978-1-4052) Dist. by* **IPG Chicago.**

Eifrig Publishing, *(978-0-9795518; 978-1-936172; 978-1-63233)* P.O. Box 66, Lemont, PA 16851-0066 USA (SAN 858-6462) Fax: 888-340-6543; Toll Free: 888-340-6543
E-mail: contact@eifrigpublishing.com
Web site: http://www.eifrigpublishing.com
Dist(s): **BookBaby**
Follett School Solutions.

EJMP, *(978-0-615-77563-0)* 2421 SW Candletree Dr Apt 6, Topeka, KS 66614 USA Tel 785-338-0625
Dist(s): **CreateSpace Independent Publishing Platform.**

EK Success Ltd., *(978-1-930232)* P.O. Box 1141, Clifton, NJ 07014-1141 USA Tel 973-458-0092; Fax: 973-594-0545; Toll Free: 800-524-1349
E-mail: success@eksuccess.com
Web site: http://www.eksuccess.com.

EKADOO Publishing Group, *(978-0-9747387)* Orders Addr.: P.O. Box 2286, North Redondo Beach, CA 90278 USA Toll Free: 877-252-3404; Edit Addr.: 123 West First St., Suite 675, Casper, WY 82601 USA
E-mail: info@ekadoo.com
Web site: http://www.ekadoo.com.

Ekaré,
Dist(s): **Lectorum Pubns., Inc.**

Ekaré Europa S.L. (ESP) *(978-84-933060; 978-84-934863; 978-84-936504) Dist. by* **Lectorum Pubns.**

Ekare, Ediciones (VEN) *(978-980-257; 978-84-8351; 978-84-937212; 978-84-937767) Dist. by* **Mariuccia Iaconi Bk Imports.**

Ekare, Ediciones (VEN) *(978-980-257; 978-84-8351; 978-84-937212; 978-84-937767) Dist. by* **Lectorum Pubns.**

Eklektika Pr., Inc., *(978-0-9651672; 978-0-9765465; 978-0-9823250)* Orders Addr.: P.O. Box 157, Chelsea, MI 48118 USA Tel 734-730-5161; Edit Addr.: 6401 Conway Rd., Chelsea, MI 48118 USA
Web site: http://www.theseniorsguide.com; http://www.meandmycaregivers.com
Dist(s): **Alliance Bk. Co.**
Distributors, The.

EKR Pubns., *(978-0-9791348)* 257 N. Calderwood St., #356, Alcoa, TN 37701-2111 USA (SAN 852-5293) Tel 727-517-2767 (publisher contact); Toll Free Fax: 866-790-0417 (orders/publisher); Toll Free: 800-266-5564 (orders/AtlasBooks)
Web site: http://www.willigetsahistorylesson.com; http://www.ekrpublications.com.

Ekwike Bks. & Publishing, *(978-0-9661598; 978-0-9789972)* Orders Addr.: P.O. Box 470, New York, NY 10034 USA Tel 718-798-5788 (phone/fax); Edit Addr.: 4417 Edson Ave., Bronx, NY 10466 USA Tel 917-306-7244 (cell)
E-mail: ikebezi@juno.com.

Ekwike Publications *See* **Ekwike Bks. & Publishing**

El Aleph Editores, S.A. (ESP) *(978-84-7669; 978-84-85501) Dist. by* **Ediciones.**

El Assali, Amira, *(978-0-9777650)* 23842 Alicia Pkwy Apt. 248, Mission Viejo, CA 92691 USA Tel 714-478-2114
E-mail: amiraalassaly@hotmail.com.

El Brown Training Solutions, *(978-0-9909512)* 2987 District Ave, Fairfax, VA 22031 USA Tel 571-422-3636
E-mail: elbrown@kinderjam.com
Web site: www.elbrowntrainings.com.

El Cid Editor Incorporated, *(978-0-9669968; 978-1-4135; 978-1-4492; 978-1-5129)* Div. of E-Libro Corp., 17555 Atlantic Blvd. # 4, Sunny Isl Bch, FL 33160-2996 USA; 16699 Collins Ave., No. 1003, Miami, FL 33160 Tel 305-466-0155
E-mail: editor@e-libro.com
Web site: http://www.e-libro.net; http://www.e-libro.com
Dist(s): **MyiLibrary**
ProQuest LLC
ebrary, Inc.

El Hogar y La Moda, S.A. (ESP) *(978-84-7183) Dist. by* **AIMS Intl.**

El Jefe, *(978-0-9742840)* P.O. Box 7871, Pueblo West, CO 81007 USA
E-mail: rearch145@aol.com.

El Publications *See* **Jesus Estanislado**

El Zarape Pr., *(978-0-9789954; 978-0-692-69574-6; 978-0-692-72032-5)* 1413 Jay Ave., McAllen, TX 78504-3327 USA (SAN 852-1514)
E-mail: wegotwords@hotmail.com
Dist(s): **CreateSpace Independent Publishing Platform.**

Elan Systems, Incorporated *See* **Aunt Dee's Attic, Inc.**

Elderberry Press, Inc., *(978-0-9658407; 978-1-930859; 978-1-932762; 978-1-934956)* 1393 Old Homestead Rd., Oakland, OR 97462 USA (SAN 254-6604) Tel 541-459-6043 Do not confuse with Elderberry Pr., Encinitas, CA
E-mail: editor@elderberrypress.com
Web site: http://www.elderberrypress.com
Dist(s): **Smashwords.**

Eldergivers, *(978-0-9742262)* 1755 Clay St., San Francisco, CA 94109 USA
E-mail: info@eldergivers.org
Web site: http://www.eldergivers.org.

Eldorado Ink, *(978-1-932904; 978-1-61900)* P.O. Box 100097, Pittsburgh, PA 15233-4842 USA Tel 412-688-0444; Fax: 412-688-8545; Toll Free: 800-783-6767
E-mail: info@eldoradoink.com
Web site: http://www.eldoradoink.com.

Elea Pr., *(978-0-615-34357-0; 978-0-615-67531-2; 978-0-615-75642-4; 978-0-692-21410-7)* Orders Addr.: P.O. Box 2351, Livermore, CA 94551 USA
Web site: http://www.nursiesbook.com; http://www.nightweaning.com
Dist(s): **Lightning Source, Inc.**

Electa Architecture (GBR) *(978-1-904313) Dist. by* **HachBkGrp.**

eLectio Publishing, *(978-0-615-77551-7; 978-0-615-79001-5; 978-0-615-79469-3; 978-0-615-79864-6; 978-0-615-80543-6; 978-0-615-81846-7; 978-0-615-82555-7; 978-0-615-82645-5; 978-0-615-83096-4; 978-0-615-83772-7; 978-0-615-83878-6; 978-0-615-84548-7; 978-0-615-85867-8; 978-0-615-87769-3; 978-0-615-88179-9; 978-0-615-88473-8; 978-0-615-90365-1; 978-0-615-90866-3; 978-0-615-91122-9; 978-0-615-91680-4; 978-0-615-92441-0; 978-0-615-93116-6; 978-0-615-93337-5; 978-0-615-93550-8; 978-0-615-93822-6; 978-0-615-94869-0;) 1361 Bristol Ln., Aubrey, TX 76227 USA Tel 2149988361*
Web site: http://www.eLectioPublishing.com
Dist(s): **CreateSpace Independent Publishing Platform**
Ingram Publisher Services.

Electret Scientific Co., *(978-0-917406)* P.O. Box 4132, Star City, WV 26504 USA (SAN 206-4715) Tel 304-594-1639 (phone/fax)
E-mail: U1a00439@wvnet.edu.

Electric Theatre Radio Hour, *(978-0-9848486)* 2200 Market St. Suite 735, Galveston, TX 77550 USA Tel 409-750-8915
E-mail: brendadonaloio@sbcglobal.net.

Eleftheria Publishing, *(978-0-9826040)* 6041 N. Fifth Pl., Phoenix, AZ 85012 USA Tel 602-214-5695
E-mail: michael@michaelenewton.com
Web site: http://www.eleftheriapublishing.com
Dist(s): **Lightning Source, Inc.**

Elemental Pubs., *(978-0-9765403)* 4404 Whistling Way, Raleigh, NC 27616 USA Tel 919-217-2092.

Elemental Publishing LLC *See* **Elemental Science Inc.**

Elemental Science Inc., *(978-1-935614)* 1800 Kraft DR Suite 207, Blacksburg, VA 24060 USA
E-mail: info@elementalscience.com
Web site: http://www.elementalscience.com.

Elena Marcus Negoita, *(978-0-615-57545-2)* 2240 Blake St. No. 315, Berkeley, CA 94704 USA
Web site: www.doghappiness.net
Dist(s): **CreateSpace Independent Publishing Platform.**

ElephantSide Pr., *(978-0-9716873)* 33 Bedford St., Suite 10, Lexington, MA 02420 USA (SAN 255-4062).

Eleuthera Press *See* **Windsong Publishing Co.**

Elevé Arts Publishing *See* **Eleve Publishing**

Elevator Group, The, *(978-0-9786854; 978-0-9820384; 978-0-9819719; 978-0-9824945; 978-0-9825282)* P.O. Box 207, Paoli, PA 19301 USA (SAN 851-3104) Tel 610-296-4966; Fax: 610-644-4436; P.O. Box 207, Paoli, PA 19301 Tel 610-296-4966; Fax: 610-644-4436
E-mail: TheElevatorGroup@comcast.net
Web site: http://www.TheElevatorGroup.com; http://www.TEGFaith.com
Dist(s): **MyiLibrary**
ebrary, Inc.

Eleve Publishing, *(978-0-9827304)* 3001 S. Jay St., Denver, CO 80227 USA Tel 720-560-2448
E-mail: larryelwood@gmail.com.

Elf Garb, *(978-0-615-64129-4; 978-0-9881822)* 96 Idlewell Bld, Weymouth, MA 02188 USA Tel 781-331-7949
E-mail: kelley@elfgarb.com
Web site: www.elfgarb.com.

Elfa Bks., *(978-0-578-10974-9; 978-0-578-10978-7; 978-0-578-11908-3; 978-0-578-12216-8; 978-0-578-12227-4; 978-0-578-12965-5; 978-0-578-12975-4; 978-0-578-13661-5; 978-0-578-13735-3)* 14967 Merlot Dr., Sterling Heights, MI 48312 USA Tel 586-634-4321
E-mail: elfabooks@yahoo.com
Web site: http://www.elfabooks.com.

Elgar, Edward Publishing, Inc., *(978-1-84064; 978-1-85278; 978-1-85898; 978-1-84376; 978-1-84542; 978-1-84720)* Orders Addr.: P.O. Box 960, Herndon, VA 20172-0960 USA Tel 800-390-3149; Fax: 802-864-7626; Edit Addr.: 9 Dewey Ct., Northampton, MA 01060-3815 USA (SAN 299-4615)
E-mail: elgarinfo@e-elgar.com; kwight@e-elgar.com; asturmer@e-elgar.com
Web site: http://www.e-elgar.com
Dist(s): **Books International, Inc.**
MyiLibrary.

Elgea Publishing, *(978-0-9972884)* 11960 Tivoli Pk. Row, San Diego, CA 92128 USA Tel 858-649-6311
E-mail: chomermd108@aol.com
Web site: www.drchristinehorner.com.

Elias Pubns., LLC, *(978-0-9726247)* P.O. Box 49704, Sarasota, FL 34230 USA Tel 941-556-5656; Fax: 720-920-7262
E-mail: eliaspublications@hotmail.com
Web site: http://www.eliaspublications.com.

Eliassen Creative, *(978-1-937160; 978-0-9892097)* 10328 Horseback Ridge Ave., las Vegas, NV 89144 USA Tel 702-328-2637
E-mail: sunshinenelson@hotmail.com.

eLiberty Pr., *(978-0-9755608)* 2250 N. University Pkwy. No. 4888, Provo, UT 84604 USA Tel 801-427-6630; Fax: 801-373-5999
E-mail: info@elibertypress.com; sales@elibertypress.com
Web site: http://www.elibertypress.com
Dist(s): **Alibris**
Powells.com.

Elim Publishing, *(978-0-9713711; 978-1-59919)* Div. of Elim Gospel Church, 1679 Dalton Rd., Lima, NY 14485 USA Tel 716-624-5560; Fax: 716-624-9677
E-mail: randy@elimpublishing.com
Web site: http://www.elimpublishing.com
Dist(s): **Lightning Source, Inc.**

Elissian Publishing Co., *(978-0-615-47664-3)* 9715 FM 620 N No. 11203, Austin, TX 78726 USA Tel 512-913-5553; Fax: 512-436-9796
E-mail: derniolesen@hotmail.com.

Elizabooks, *(978-0-9762839)* 5515 Catfish Ct., Waunakee, WI 53597 USA Tel 608-849-1984; Fax: 608-849-1985; Toll Free: 888-603-1984
E-mail: liz@elizabookspublishing.com
Web site: http://www.elizabooks.com.

Elk River Pr., *(978-0-9710389)* 1125 Central Ave., Charleston, WV 25302 USA Tel 304-342-1848; Fax: 304-343-0594 Do not confuse with companies with the same or similar name in Altamont, KS, Athens, AL.
E-mail: wvbooks@verizon.net
Web site: http://www.wvbookco.com
Dist(s): **West Virginia Book Co., The.**

Elkarez Publishing Co., *(978-0-9819100)* 327 Sheldon Ave., Staten Island, NY 10312 USA Tel 718-966-5205
E-mail: info@elkarezpublishing.com
Web site: http://www.elkarezpublishing.com.

Eller Books *See* **Brethren Pr.**

Elliott, Jane, *(978-0-9741254)* 707 Country Club Rd., Schofield, WI 54476 USA; *Imprints:* Dynagraphix (Dynagraphix).

Ellipsis Pr., *(978-0-9637536; 978-1-940400)* 3555 78th St., #41, New York, NY 11372 USA Tel 718-840-9373 Do not confuse with Ellipsis Pr. in Campbell, CA
E-mail: info@ellipsispress.com
Web site: http://www.ellipsispress.com
Dist(s): **SPD-Small Pr. Distribution.**

Ellis Pr., The, *(978-0-933180; 978-0-944024)* Div. of Spoon River Poetry Pr., P.O. Box 6, Granite Falls, MN 56241 USA (SAN 214-008X) Tel 507-537-6463 Do not confuse with Ellis Pr., in Charlottesville, VA
E-mail: pichaske@southwest.msus.edu
Web site: http://www.southwest.msus.edu/faculty/pichaske/plains.htm.

Ellison, Penny, *(978-0-9771121)* Orders Addr.: P.O. Box 510082, Miami, FL 33151 USA Tel 786-222-1443; Edit Addr.: 4877 Registry Ln NW, Kennesaw, GA 30152-2891 USA.

Elly Blue Publishing *Imprint of* **Microcosm Publishing**

Elma Colletes & Sons, *(978-0-9719337)* 5895 Gardens Reach Cove, Memphis, TN 38120-2523 USA Fax: 901-747-0040
E-mail: mschnap1@midsouth.rr.com.

Elmdale Park Books, *(978-0-9860593)* PO BOX 26553, OVERLAND PARK, KS 66225 USA Tel 913-908-0129; Fax: 913-945-1426
E-mail: tekobernard@yahoo.com
Web site: www.tekobernard.com.

Elohim Bks., *(978-0-9768831)* Orders Addr.: P.O. Box 1027, Howell, MI 48844 USA.

Eloquence Pr., *(978-0-9753300; 978-0-9824954; 978-0-9913283; 978-0-692-89832-1)* Orders Addr.: 51689 Via Bendita, La Quinta, CA 92253 USA (SAN 255-9676) Tel 760-698-8482
E-mail: jeadon@cox.net; jeadon2@gmail.com
Web site: http://www.eadonbooks.com; http://www.theamericandramaseries.com; http://.

Eloquent Bks. *Imprint of* **Strategic Book Publishing & Rights Agency (SBPRA)**

Eloquent Rascals, *(978-0-9907094; 978-0-9989949)* 30 Lorden Ln., Weare, NH 03281 USA Tel 845-787-3832
E-mail: eloquentrascals@gmail.com.

Elora Media, LLC, *(978-0-9786813)* PMB 112, 1201 Yelm Ave., Yelm, WA 98597-9859 USA Tel 360-894-6369
E-mail: betsy@eloramedia.com.

Elora Pr., *(978-0-9786813)* Div. of Elora Media, LLC, PMB 112, 1201 Yelm Ave., Yelm, WA 98597-9859 USA (SAN 851-3228) Toll Free: 888-440-8972
E-mail: betsy@eloramedia.com
Web site: http://www.eloramedia.com.

Elotos Pr., LLC, *(978-0-9821737)* 1220 N. Market St., Suite 808, Wilmington, DE 19808 USA
E-mail: info@elotos.com
Web site: http://www.ELOTOS.com.

ELP Bks., *(978-0-9841650)* P.O. Box 1506, Gardena, CA 90249 USA (SAN 858-6098) Tel 213-928-6724
E-mail: emmja_p@sbcglobal.net
Web site: http://www.elpbooks.net.

Elsevier *Imprint of* **Elsevier - Health Sciences Div.**

Elsevier - Health Sciences Div., *(978-0-323; 978-0-443; 978-0-444; 978-0-7020; 978-0-7216; 978-0-7234; 978-0-7236; 978-0-7506; 978-0-8016; 978-0-8151; 978-0-920513; 978-0-932883; 978-1-55664; 978-1-56053; 978-1-898507; 978-1-932141; 978-1-4160; 978-1-4377; 978-1-4557)* Subs. of Elsevier Science, Orders Addr.: a/o Customer Service, 3251 Riverport Ln., Maryland Heights, MO 63043 USA Tel 314-453-7010; Fax: 314-447-8030; Toll Free Fax: 800-535-9935; Toll Free: 800-545-2522; 800-460-3110 (Customers Outside US); 1799 Highway 50, Linn, MO 65051 (SAN 200-2280); Edit Addr.: 1600 John F. Kennedy Blvd., Suite 1800, Philadelphia, PA 19103-2899 USA Tel 215-239-3900; Fax: 215-239-3990; Toll Free: 800-523-4069; *Imprints:* Mosby (MosElsHlth); Elsevier (ElsevHlth)
E-mail: usbkinfo@elsevier.com
Web site: http://www.elsevier.com; http://www.us.elsevierhealth.com/
Dist(s): **Elsevier**
MyiLibrary
TNT Media Group, Inc.
ebrary, Inc.

Elsevier Science - Health Sciences Division *See* **Elsevier - Health Sciences Div.**

Elsevier Science & Technology Bks., Orders Addr.: P.O. Box 28430, Saint Louis, MO 63146-0930 USA Toll Free Fax: 800-535-9935; Toll Free: 800-545-2522; 800-460-3110 (Customers Outside US); Edit Addr.: 525 B St., Suite 1900, San Diego, CA 92101 USA Toll Free: 1-800-894-3434; 200 Wheeler Rd., 6th Flr., Burlington, MA 01803 Tel 781-313-4700; *Imprints:* Butterworth-Heinemann (Butter Sci Hein)
E-mail: bookstore.orders@elsevier.com
Web site: http://www.elsevier.com/; http://www.syngress.com
Dist(s): **CreateSpace Independent Publishing Platform**
Ebsco Publishing
Elsevier - Health Sciences Div.
Elsevier
Follett School Solutions
Leonard, Hal Corp.
LEXIS Publishing
MyiLibrary
Oxford Univ. Pr., Inc.
Rittenhouse Bk. Distributors
Vital Source Technologies, Inc.
ebrary, Inc.

Elsewhere Editiions *Imprint of* **Steerforth Pr.**

Eltsar Pr., *(978-0-9769275; 978-0-9833990; 978-0-9850892)* 40453 Cherokee Oaks Dr., Three Rivers, CA 93271-9617 USA Tel 559-561-3270
Dist(s): **Lulu Pr., Inc.**

Elv Enterprises, *(978-0-9829669)* P.O. Box 2225, La Jolla, CA 92038 USA Tel 858-336-6499
E-mail: rainierpage@ymail.com.

Elva Resa *Imprint of* **Elva Resa Publishing, LLC**

Elva Resa Publishing, LLC, *(978-0-9657483; 978-1-934617)* 8362 Tamarack Village, Suite 119-106, Saint Paul, MN 55125 USA Tel 651-357-8770 orders & general info; Fax: 501-641-0777 orders accepted by fax; *Imprints:* Elva Resa (Elva Resa); Alma Little (Alma Little)
E-mail: orders@elvaresa.com
Web site: http://www.elvaresa.com
Dist(s): **Follett School Solutions.**

ELW Pubns., *(978-0-9766233)* 1831 Secretary's Rd., Scottsville, VA 24590 USA Tel 434-295-1678; *Imprints:* His Grace Is Sufficient (HGIS)
E-mail: bridgeministry@aol.com.

Elysian Editions *Imprint of* **Princeton Bk. Co. Pubs.**

Elysian Hills, *(978-0-9635589)* Orders Addr.: P.O. Box 40693, Albuquerque, NM 87196 USA Tel 505-897-2734; Fax: 505-897-4614; Edit Addr.: 919 Western Meadows, Albuquerque, NM 87114 USA
E-mail: EdDziczek@aol.com.

Elytra & Antenna, *(978-0-9719129; 978-0-9802401)* 4663 Ruby Ln., Brunswick Hills, OH 44212 USA Tel 330-273-1918
E-mail: elytraandantenna@lycos.com
Web site: http://www.elytraandantenna.com.

ELZ Publishing, *(978-0-9772717)* 33 Sheridan Rd., Wellesley, MA 02481 USA Tel 781-237-7417; Fax: 781-237-7429
E-mail: elzahniser@mindspring.com
Web site: http://elzpublishing.com.

EM Greenberg Pr., Inc., *(978-0-9634561; 978-0-615-40288-8)* 1245 Sixteenth St., Suite 210, Santa Monica, CA 90402 USA Tel 310-454-0502 (phone/fax)
E-mail: elainergordonphd@gmail.com
Web site: http://elainegordon.com.

Emaculate Publishing, *(978-1-931855)* P.O. Box 1804, Woodbridge, VA 22195-1074 USA (SAN 254-2005)
E-mail: emaculatepublishing@yahoo.com; info@emaculatepublishing.com
Web site: http://www.emaculatepublishing.com.

eMaginationFlow, Incorporated *See* **CuriousDots**

Emarketing Of Michigan, LLC, *(978-0-615-38985-1; 978-0-615-88247-5)* Orders Addr.: 11127 Kings Ct., Sterling Heights, MI 48312 USA Tel 586-838-0099; Fax: 586-275-2295
Web site: http://www.readwithmax.com; http://www.emarketingofmichigan.com.

Ember *Imprint of* **Random Hse. Children's Bks.**

Embrace Communications, *(978-0-9668878)* 6887 Red Mountain Rd., Livermore, CO 80536 USA Tel 970-416-9076; Fax: 970-407-0083
E-mail: suengayReynolds@aol.com
Dist(s): **Spring Arbor Distributors, Inc.**

Embracing Life, *(978-0-9985540)* 709 Phar Lap Ln., Bahama, NC 27503 USA Tel 919-308-8889
E-mail: lfovercash@gmail.com.

EMC Publishing, *(978-0-9884707; 978-0-692-36034-7)* 11718 S.E. Federal Hwy. #245, Hobe Sound, FL 33455 USA Tel 504-669-9099.

†EMC/Paradigm Publishing, *(978-0-7638; 978-0-8219; 978-0-88436; 978-0-912022; 978-1-56118; 978-1-5338)* Div. of EMC Corp., 875 Montreal Way, Saint Paul, MN 55102 USA (SAN 201-3800) Toll Free Fax: 800-328-4564; Toll Free: 800-328-1452
E-mail: publish@emcp.com; educate@emcp.com
Web site: http://www.emcp.com
Dist(s): **Continental Bk. Co., Inc.**; *CIP.*

Emecé Editores S.A. (ARG) *(978-950-04; 978-950-519) Dist. by* **Lectorum Pubns.**

Emecé Editores S.A. (ARG) *(978-950-04; 978-950-519) Dist. by* **Planeta.**

Emece Editores (ESP) *(978-84-95908) Dist. by* **Ediciones.**

Emece Editores (ESP) *(978-84-95908) Dist. by* **Lectorum Pubns.**

EMedia Corp., *(978-1-891155)* 664 NE Northlake Way, Seattle, WA 98105-6428 USA Toll Free: 888-363-3424
E-mail: custserv@emediamusic.com
Web site: http://www.emediamusic.com.

Emerald Bk. Co., *(978-1-934572; 978-1-937110)* Div. of Greenleaf Bk. Group, 4425 Mo Pac Expy., Suite 600, Austin, TX 78735 USA
Dist(s): **Greenleaf Book Group**
MyiLibrary.

Emerald Bks., *(978-1-883002; 978-1-932096; 978-1-62486)* Orders Addr.: P.O. Box 635, Lynnwood, WA 98046 USA (SAN 298-7538) Tel 425-771-1153; Fax: 425-775-2383; Toll Free: 800-922-2143; Edit Addr.: 7825 230th St. SW, Edmonds, WA 98026 USA Do not confuse with Emerald Bks. in Westfield, NJ
E-mail: wlwalsh@seanet.com
Web site: http://www.ywampublishing.com
Dist(s): **YWAM Publishing.**

Emerald City Publishing, *(978-0-9675082)* Do not confuse with A Class Act, Sierra Madre, CA
E-mail: eagle3.fox1@gmail.com.

Emerald Funding Corp, *(978-0-692-52542-5; 978-0-692-80620-3)* 7029 Caviro Ln., BOYNTON BEACH, FL 33437 USA Tel 954-961-3352.

Emerald Hse. Group, Inc., *(978-1-889893; 978-1-932307; 978-1-935507; 978-1-62020)* 411 Univ. Ridge, Suite B14, Greenville, SC 29601 USA Tel 864-235-2434; Fax: 864-235-2491; Toll Free: 800-209-8570; *Imprints:* Ambassador-Emerald, International (Ambassador-Emerald); Ambassador International (Ambassador Intl)
E-mail: info@emeraldhouse.com
Web site: http://www.emeraldhouse.com; www.ambassador-international.com
Dist(s): **Christian Bk. Distributors**
Follett School Solutions
Spring Arbor Distributors, Inc.

Emerald Shamrock Pr. LLC, *(978-0-9841880)* 1031 Parkland Rd., Lake Orion, MI 48360 USA (SAN 858-6675) Tel 248-393-6082
E-mail: bridget.mary@comcast.net
Web site: http://www.onechildoneplanet.com.

Emerald Star Pr., *(978-0-615-29908-2; 978-0-615-36644-9; 978-0-615-39280-6; 978-0-9831993)* P.O. Box 2621, Atlanta, GA 30331 USA.

EMI CMG Distribution,
E-mail: distribution@emicmg.com
Web site: http://www.emicmgdistribution.com.

Emidra Publishing, *(978-0-9723569)* P.O. Box 770, Fair Oaks, CA 95628 USA (SAN 255-0369) Tel 916-961-2540 (phone/fax); 10416 Fair Oaks Blvd., Fair Oaks, CA 95628
E-mail: emidra@msn.com
Web site: http://www.emidrapublishing.com.

EMK Pr., *(978-0-9726244; 978-1-942571)* Div. of EMK Group, LLC, 16 Mt. Bethel Rd., No. 219, Warren, NJ 07059 USA (SAN 255-0318) Tel 732-469-7544; Fax: 732-469-7861
E-mail: carriekitze@emkpress.com
Web site: http://www.emkpress.com
Dist(s): **Quality Bks., Inc.**

EMMA Pubns., *(978-0-9800074)* P.O. Box 654, Northville, MI 48168 USA (SAN 854-977X)
E-mail: info@emmapublications.com
Web site: http://www.emmapublications.com
Dist(s): **Partners Bk. Distributing, Inc.**

Emma's Pantry, *(978-0-9648437)* 0373 Sopris Creek Rd., #7, Basalt, CO 81621 USA Tel 970-927-4661
E-mail: eewalling@yahoo.com
Web site: http://www.pages.prodigy.com/legends/.

Emmaus Road, International, *(978-1-880185)* 7150 Tanner Ct., San Diego, CA 92111 USA Tel 619-292-7020
E-mail: emmaus_road@eri.com
Web site: http://www.eri.org.

Emmaus Road Publishing, *(978-0-9663223; 978-1-931018; 978-1-937155; 978-1-940329; 978-1-941447; 978-1-63446; 978-1-945125; 978-1-947792)* 1468 Parkview Cir., Steubenville, OH 43952 USA Tel 740-264-9535; Fax: 740-283-4011; Toll Free: 800-398-5470
E-mail: cerickson@emmausroad.org
Web site: http://www.emmausroad.org.

Emmis Books *See* **Clerisy Pr.**

Emnes Systems, *(978-0-9661636)* 7212 Antares Dr., Suite 100, Gaithersburg, MD 20879 USA Tel 240-683-8502
E-mail: ecfchang@msn.com
Web site: http://www.emnes.com.

Emnin Books *Imprint of* **Hay Hse., Inc.**

Emotional Content, LLC, *(978-0-9817543)* 1445 S. Carmelina Ave., Los Angeles, CA 90025 USA
E-mail: info@biographicnovel.com; eiji@wadirum.com; latinsamurai@gmail.com
Web site: http://www.biographicnovel.com; http://www.emotionalcontent.net.

Empak Publishing Co., *(978-0-922162; 978-0-9616156)* Subs. of Empak Enterprises, Inc., P.O. Box 8596, Chicago, IL 60680-8596 USA (SAN 699-9182) Tel 312-642-3434; Fax: 312-642-9657; Toll Free: 800-477-4554
E-mail: empak@email.msn.com
Web site: http://www.empakpub.com.

Empire Holdings *Imprint of* **Kodel Group, LLC, The**

Empire Holdins - Literary Division for Young Readers *Imprint of* **Kodel Group, LLC, The**

Empire Publishing, *(978-0-9766246)* 1117 Desert Ln., Suite 1362, Las Vegas, NV 89102 USA Fax: 413-714-5213.

Empire Publishing Service, *(978-1-58690)* P.O. Box 1344, Studio City, CA 91614-0344 USA (SAN 630-5687) Tel 818-784-8918
E-mail: empirepubsvc@att.net.

Empowered Entertainment, *(978-0-9767076)* 5853 Liberty Creek Dr. N., Indianapolis, IN 46254 USA
E-mail: andrew@chameleonchronicles.com
Web site: http://www.chameleonchronicles.com.

Empowered Faith International, *(978-0-9768416)* P.O. Box 156, Marietta, GA 30061 USA Tel 770-218-6215
E-mail: pbbell@ecclive.org
Web site: http://www.empoweredfaith.org.

Empowered Flower Girl, *(978-0-9978800)* 4921 Crooks, M-11, Royal Oak, MI 48073 USA Tel 313-492-3879
E-mail: rkamaria@gmail.com
Web site: www.empoweredflowergirl.com.

Empowering People Pub., *(978-0-9762639; 978-0-578-16865-4)* Orders Addr.: P.O. Box 329, Rex, GA 30273 USA Tel 850-328-1698
E-mail: altrell@tinapipkin.com; info@tinapipkin.com; altrellpipkin@yahoo.com
Web site: http://www.tinapipkin.com; http://www.empoweringpeopleinc.com; http://www.altrellpipkin.com.

Emprise Publishing *See* **Emprise Publishing & Media**

Emprise Publishing & Media, *(978-0-9717581; 978-0-9725121)* 3643 South Ave., Springfield, MO 65807 USA
E-mail: martyb@powermarkcomics.com.

Empty Harbor Productions, LLC, *(978-0-9790699)* 4 Sarah Lynn Ln., Suite 127, Conroe, TX 77303 USA Toll Free: 866-419-2921
E-mail: emptyharbor@msn.com
Web site: http://www.sticman.net.

Empty Set Entertainment, *(978-0-615-28744-7; 978-0-615-36542-8; 978-0-9831963; 978-1-939366)* Orders Addr.: PO Box 122710, San Diego, CA 92112-2710 USA (SAN 920-7694)
Dist(s): **BookBaby**
Bookmasters Distribution.

Empty Sky *Imprint of* **Zeromayo Studios, LLP**

Empyrion Publishing, *(978-0-692-21367-4; 978-0-692-22501-1; 978-0-692-23065-7; 978-0-692-25133-1; 978-0-692-26300-6; 978-0-692-29670-7; 978-0-692-32818-7; 978-0-692-34586-3; 978-0-692-35427-8; 978-0-692-35803-0; 978-0-692-37463-4; 978-0-692-39027-6; 978-0-692-39961-3; 978-0-692-50806-0; 978-0-692-53646-9; 978-0-692-56921-4; 978-0-692-57186-6; 978-0-692-57448-5; 978-0-692-58459-0; 978-0-692-59421-6; 978-0-692-60449-6; 978-0-692-61946-9; 978-0-692-62947-5; 978-0-692-71074-6; 978-0-692-71963-3; 978-0-9981013) PO Box 140914, Broken Arrow, OK 74014 USA Tel 9184512676 Do not confuse with Empyrion Publishing in Winter Garden, FL*
E-mail: rickmanis@hotmail.com
Dist(s): **CreateSpace Independent Publishing Platform.**

Enchanted Forest Publishing, *(978-0-9910700)* P.O. Box 453, Volcano, HI 96785-0453 USA Tel 808-333-8052
E-mail: enchantedforestpublishing@gmail.com.

Enchanted Lion Bks., LLC, *(978-1-59270)* 201 Richards St. Ste. 4, Brooklyn, NY 11231-1537 USA
E-mail: zoeclaud@earthlink.com; enchantedlionbooks@yahoo.com
Dist(s): **Consortium Bk. Sales & Distribution**
Farrar, Straus & Giroux
Two Rivers Distribution.

Enchanted Quill Publications *See* **Stuart & Weitz Publishing Group**

Enchanted Self Pr., *(978-0-9798952)* 603 S. Edgemere Dr., West Allenhurst, NJ 07711 USA.

Enchantment Pr., *(978-0-9832074)* 14 Valle Escondido, Placitas, NM 87043 USA Tel 505-350-0227
E-mail: lisa.goldman@comcast.net.

Enclave *Imprint of* **Gilead Publishing, LLC**

Encore Performance Publishing, *(978-1-57514)* Orders Addr.: P.O. Box 692, Orem, UT 84059 USA Tel 801-785-9343; Fax: 801-785-9394
E-mail: encoreplay@aol.com
Web site: http://www.encoreplay.com.

Encore Pubns., *(978-0-9798718)* P.O. Box 117, Stoughton, WI 53589 USA Tel 608-877-9692; Fax: 608-877-9693
E-mail: masonfinancial@charter.net; bonita.mason@peachbandana.com
Web site: http://PeachBandana.com.

Encounter Bks., *(978-1-893554; 978-1-59403; 978-1-64177)* Div. of Encounter for Culture & Education, Inc., 900 Broadway., Suite 601, New York, NY 10003-1237 USA (SAN 253-1585) Toll Free Fax: 877-811-1461 (orders); Toll Free: 800-786-3839 (inquiries, MS proposals)
E-mail: kwong@encounterbooks.com
Web site: http://www.encounterbooks.com
Dist(s): **Capstone Pub.**
Ebsco Publishing
Ingram Publisher Services
MyiLibrary
ebrary, Inc.

Encyclopaedia Britannica, Inc., *(978-0-7826; 978-0-8347; 978-0-85229; 978-0-87827; 978-1-59339; 978-1-60835; 978-1-61535; 978-0-9823819; 978-0-9823820; 978-0-9823821; 978-0-9823822; 978-0-9823823; 978-0-9823824; 978-1-62513; 978-1-68382)* 325 N. La Salle St., Chicago, IL 60654 USA (SAN 204-1464) Toll Free Fax: 800-344-9624 (fax orders); Toll Free: 800-323-1229; 800-621-3900 (orders); 2nd Flr., Unity Wharf Mill St., London, SE1 2BH Tel 020 7500 7800; Fax: 020 7500 7878
E-mail: enquiries@britannica.co.uk; contact@eb.com
Web site: http://www.eb.com; http://www.britannica.co.uk
Dist(s): **Continental Bk. Co., Inc.**
Ebsco Publishing
Follett School Solutions
MyiLibrary
Pearson Education
Pearson Technology Group
ebrary, Inc.

Endeavor Press *See* **Endeavor Publishing**

Endeavor Pr., *(978-0-9728656)* P.O. Box 4307, Chicago, IL 60680 USA Tel 312-420-6675 Do not confuse with Endeavor Press in Gilbert, AZ
E-mail: rogerrange@endeavorpress.net
Web site: http://www.endeavorpress.com.

Endeavor Publishing, *(978-0-9743843)* 4204 E. Marshall Ave., Gilbert, AZ 85297 USA Tel 480-632-1306 (phone/fax) Do not confuse with Endeavor Press in Annapolis, MD
E-mail: endeavorpublishing@yahoo.com
Web site: http://www.dowkump.com.

Energetic Press, LLC *See* **Four Dolphins Pr., LLC**
Energion Pubns., *(978-1-893729; 978-1-938434; 978-1-63199)* P.O. Box 841, Gonzalez, FL 32560 USA Tel 850-525-3916
E-mail: pubs@energion.com
Web site: http://www.energion.com; https://energiondirect.com.
Energy Education Group, *(978-0-9744765)* Div. of The California Study, Inc., Orders Addr.: 664 Hilary Dr., Tiburon, CA 94920 USA Tel 415-435-4574; Fax: 415-435-7737
E-mail: energyforkeeps@aol.com
Web site: http://www.energyforkeeps.org
Dist(s): **PixyJack Pr., Inc.**
Engage Literacy *Imprint of* **Capstone Press of Coughlan Cos.**
EngGoGIC, LLC, *(978-0-9882142)* P.O. Box 364, PLAINSBORO, NJ 08536 USA Tel 609-716-6165
E-mail: contact@enggogic.com
Dist(s): **BookBaby.**
Engine Hse. Bks., *(978-0-615-19130-0; 978-0-615-19495-0; 978-0-615-20663-9; 978-0-615-21565-5; 978-0-578-00775-5; 978-0-578-01960-4; 978-1-936211)* 330 WCR 16½, Longmont, CO 80504 USA
Web site: http://www.enginehousebooks.com
Dist(s): **Lulu Pr., Inc.**
Smashwords.
Engineering is Elementary, *(978-0-918866; 978-0-9774084; 978-1-933758; 978-1-936789; 978-1-940314)* 1 Science Pk., Boston, MA 02114 USA (SAN 210-4687) Tel 617-589-0230
E-mail: mhiggins@mos.org
Web site: www.mos.org/eie.
Enginuity, LLC, *(978-1-929645)* Orders Addr.: P.O. Box 20607, San Jose, CA 95160 USA Tel 408-268-9740; Toll Free Fax: 888-268-9740; Toll Free: 888-618-4263; Edit Addr.: 3629 Bryant St., Palo Alto, CA 94306-4209 USA
E-mail: sales@enginuity.com; support@enginuity.com
Web site: http://www.enginuity.com.
Englefield & Arnold, Incorporated *See* **Englefield & Assocs., Inc.**
Englefield & Assocs., Inc., *(978-1-884183; 978-1-59230)* Div. of Show What You Know Publishing, Orders Addr.: P.O. Box 341348, Columbus, OH 43234-1348 USA Tel 614-764-1211; Fax: 614-764-1311; Toll Free: 877-727-7464 (877-PASSING); Edit Addr.: 6344 Nicholas Dr., Columbus, OH 43235 USA
E-mail: eapub@eapublishing.com; marketing@eapublishing.com
Web site: http://www.showwhatyouknowpublishing.com/.
English Garden Talk Pr., *(978-0-9763572; 978-0-9779257; 978-0-9858431; 978-0-9915290; 978-0-9971342)* 536 W. Hoptree Ct., Louisville, CO 80027 USA
E-mail: sanddollar5643@aol.com
Dist(s): **Lulu Pr., Inc.**
Enhancing Health, Inc., *(978-0-9744479)* P.O. Box 1882, Duluth, GA 30096 USA
E-mail: info@thefitgolfer.com.
ENHEART Publishing, *(978-0-9654899; 978-0-9838882)* Orders Addr.: P.O. Box 620086, Charlotte, NC 28262 USA Tel 980-272-1410 (phone/fax)
E-mail: info@enheartpublishing.com
Web site: http://www.enheartpublishing.com
Dist(s): **BookBaby**
Parnassus Bk. Distributors.
Enigma Productions, *(978-0-9794321)* Orders Addr.: 2444 Crooks Rd. Apt. 41, Troy, MI 48084-5335 USA
Web site: http://www.enigmaw.com.
Enisen Publishing, *(978-0-9702908; 978-0-9763070)* 2118 Wilshire Blvd., # 351, Santa Monica, CA 90403-5784 USA (SAN 253-3308) Tel 310-989-4069; Fax: 310-576-7278 Do not confuse with companies with the same name in Clermont, FL, Hollywood, CA, Otis Orchards, WA
E-mail: publishing@enisen.com
Web site: http://www.enisen.com.
Enlighten Learning, *(978-0-9755865)* 269 S. Beverly Dr., No. 139, Beverly Hills, CA 90212 USA Tel 310-358-2995.
Enlighten Pubns., *(978-0-9706226)* Orders Addr.: P.O. Box 525, Vauxhall, NJ 07088 USA Toll Free: 866-862-8626
E-mail: books@enlightenpublications.com
Web site: http://www.authorsden.com/jackiehardrick; www.enlightenpublications.com.
Enlightened Bks., *(978-0-9769541; 978-0-692-02980-0)* Orders Addr.: P.O. Box 7423, NewPort Beach, CA 92658 USA Tel 949-644-1376; Edit Addr.: 1 Belcourt Dr., Newport Beach, CA 92660 USA
E-mail: enlightenedbooks13@gmail.com
Web site: http://www.enlightenedbooks.com.
Enlightened Learners Publishing, *(978-0-692-86351-0; 978-0-692-86392-3; 978-0-692-87855-2)* 1935 Sabra Dr, Tallahassee, FL 32303 USA Tel 631-949-6886
E-mail: quashierf@yahoo.com.
†**Enna, Inc.**, *(978-0-9737509; 978-0-9780970; 978-0-9781460; 978-1-897363; 978-1-926537)* 1602 Carolina St., Unit B3, Bellingham, WA 98229 USA Tel 360-306-5369; Fax: 360-547-6504
E-mail: collin@enna.com; tsepley@enna.com
Web site: http://www.enna.com; *CIP.*
Ennis, Scott, *(978-0-692-71256-6; 978-0-692-82285-2)* 3751 Sommers St., Jacksonville, FL 32205 USA Tel 904-673-5994
Dist(s): **CreateSpace Independent Publishing Platform.**
Enricharamics, Inc., *(978-1-889654)* 8416-905 O'Connor Ct., Richmond, VA 23228 USA Tel 804-747-5826.
Ensign Peak *Imprint of* **Deseret Bk. Co.**
Ensign Peak *Imprint of* **Shadow Mountain Publishing**
Enslow Elementary *Imprint of* **Enslow Pubs., Inc.**
†**Enslow Pubs., Inc.**, *(978-0-7660; 978-0-89490; 978-1-59845; 978-1-4644; 978-1-4645; 978-1-4646; 978-1-62285; 978-1-62293; 978-1-62324; 978-1-62400)* Orders Addr.: P.O. Box 398, Berkeley Heights, NJ 07922-0398 USA (SAN 213-7518) Tel 908-771-9400; Fax: 908-771-0925; Toll Free: 800-398-2504; Edit Addr.: 40 Industrial Rd., Berkeley Heights, NJ 07922-0398 USA; *Imprints*: MyReportLinks.com Books (MyRptLnks); Enslow Elementary (Enslow Elmntry)
E-mail: customerservice@enslow.com; hollyc@rosenpub.com
Web site: http://www.enslow.com; http://www.chasingroses.com; http://www.jasminehealth.com; http://www.enslowclassroom.com; http://www.myreportlinks.com; www.speedingstar.com; www.bluewaveclassroom.com; www.scarletvoyage.com
Dist(s): **Follett School Solutions**
MyiLibrary; *CIP.*
Entangled Publishing, LLC, *(978-1-937044; 978-1-62061; 978-1-62266; 978-1-63375; 978-1-943113; 978-1-943114; 978-1-943336; 978-1-943892; 978-1-68281; 978-1-64063)* 2614 S. Timberline Rd Ste No. 109, Fort Collins, CO 80525 USA Fax: 970-797-9107; *Imprints*: Entangled Teen (EntangledTeen)
E-mail: publisher@entangledpublishing.com
Web site: http://www.entangledpublishing.com
Dist(s): **Lightning Source, Inc.**
Macmillan
MyiLibrary
Two Rivers Distribution.
Entangled Teen *Imprint of* **Entangled Publishing, LLC**
Entelechy Education, LLC, *(978-0-9887813)* 10810 Symphony Way, Columbia, MD 21044 USA Tel 410-730-5570
E-mail: Gary@EntelechyEd.com
Web site: www.EntelechyEd.com.
Enterprise Incorporated *See* **TLK Pubns.**
Enterprize Publishing Co., Inc., *(978-1-893490)* 1036 Parkway Blvd., Brookings, SD 57006 USA Tel 605-692-7778; Fax: 605-997-3194
E-mail: cfcecil@home.com.
Entertainment Ministry, The, *(978-0-9707798; 978-0-9717316; 978-0-9728003; 978-0-9765142; 978-0-9791259; 978-0-9817549; 978-0-9827891)* 5584 Monument Rd., Antioch, TN 37013-2311 USA Toll Free: 800-999-0101
Web site: http://www.entmin.com
Dist(s): **Send The Light Distribution LLC.**
Entertainment Pubns., Inc., *(978-1-880248; 978-1-58553; 978-1-59878; 978-1-60967)* Maple Corporate Ctr. 1414 E. Maple Rd., Troy, MI 48083 USA Tel 248-404-1000
E-mail: NationalRetail@entertainment.com
Web site: http://www.entertainment.com
Dist(s): **Waldenbooks, Inc.**
Entertainment Publications Operating Company, Incorporated *See* **Entertainment Pubns., Inc.**
Enthusi Adams, Inc., *(978-0-9670245)* 2792 W. Pekin Rd., Spring Boro, OH 45066 USA Tel 937-743-6381; Fax: 513-743-3292
E-mail: enthusiadams@earthlink.net
Web site: http://www.enthusiadams.com.
Entomological Society of America, *(978-0-938522; 978-0-9776209; 978-0-9966674)* 10001 Derekwood Ln., Suite 100, Lanham, MD 20706-4876 USA (SAN 200-9307) Tel 301-731-4535; Fax: 301-731-4538
E-mail: esa@entsoc.org
Web site: http://www.entsoc.org.
Entry Way Publishing *See* **Digi-Tall Media**
EniCare Consulting, Inc., *(978-0-9710925)* Orders Addr.: 2809 Blairmont Dr., Midland, MI 48642 USA Tel 989-839-9177
E-mail: bstrawter@chartermi.net
Web site: http://www.envicareinc.com.
Environmental Protection Agency *Imprint of* **United States Government Printing Office**
Environmental Systems Research Institute *See* **ESRI, Inc.**
Environments, Inc., *(978-1-59794)* P.O. Box 1348, Beaufort, SC 29901-1348 USA Tel 843-846-8155; Fax: 843-846-2999; Toll Free Fax: 800-343-2987; Toll Free: 800-342-4453
E-mail: environments@eichild.com
Web site: http://www.eichild.com.
Envisage Publishing, *(978-0-9729042)* Orders Addr.: P.O. Box 557, Queens Village, NY 11428 USA; Edit Addr.: 89-52 208th St., Queens Village, NY 11427 USA
E-mail: drndavoren@hotmail.com
Web site: http://www.envisagepublishing.com
Dist(s): **Lulu Pr., Inc.**
Evision Editions, Ltd., *(978-0-9762814)* Orders Addr.: P.O. Box 442, Gaylord, MI 49734 USA; Edit Addr.: 2020 Brink Trail, Gaylord, MI 49735 USA.
Envision EMI, Inc., *(978-0-9745760)* 1919 Gallows Rd. Ste. 700, Vienna, VA 22182-4007 USA.
EoH Publishing, *(978-0-9761322)* P.O. Box 120804, Nashville, TN 37212 USA (SAN 256-257X) Tel 615-584-2071; Toll Free: 866-352-9263
E-mail: wanda.scott@live.com.
E-O-L Publishing Corp., *(978-0-9753705)* P.O. Box 110 Keely Circle, New Smyrna Beach, FL 32168 USA
E-mail: jvoss2@cfl.rr.com
Web site: http://www.eolpublishing.com.
Eos *Imprint of* **HarperCollins Pubs.**
EPEI Pr., *(978-0-9729065)* Orders Addr.: 1450 S. New Wilke Rd., Suite 102, Arlington Heights, IL 60005 USA Tel 847-670-6992; Fax: 847-670-7466; Toll Free: 877-670-7444; Edit Addr.: 1749 Golf Rd., No. 204, Mount Prospect, IL 60056 USA
E-mail: sara@getprepared.org
Web site: http://www.getprepared.org.
Ephemeron Pr., *(978-0-912290)* 1510 Perdidio Ct., Melbourne, FL 32940 USA Tel 321-752-0167
E-mail: johnknapp2@gmail.com
Web site: http://www.ephemeronpress.com.
EPI Bks., *(978-0-9726075; 978-0-9796536; 978-0-9843655; 978-0-9826006)* 2364 Roll Dr., San Diego, CA 92154 USA Fax: 619-869-8501; *Imprints*: EPI Kid Books (EPI Kid Bks)
Web site: http://www.EPIBooks.com
Dist(s): **Anderson Merchandisers.**
EPI Kid Bks. *Imprint of* **EPI Bks.**
Epic Bks. *Imprint of* **Bellwether Media**
Epic Pr. *Imprint of* **ABDO Publishing Co.**
Epic Pr., *(978-0-9801061; 978-1-941185)* P.O. Box 141624, Austin, TX 78714-1624 USA
E-mail: sh@epic-press.com
Web site: http://www.epic-press.com.
EPIC Publishing Co., *(978-0-9674025; 978-0-9763870)* 1405 Ten Palms Ct., Las Vegas, NV 89117-1404 USA (SAN 253-2840) Do not confuse with companies with the same or similar name in Erie, PA, Canon City, CO, Greeley, CO
E-mail: rxl@epicpublishing.com
Web site: http://www.epicpublishing.com.
Epicality Bks., LLC, *(978-0-9838594)* 4501 Pk. Glen Rd., No. 216, St. Louis Park, MN 55416 USA Tel 612-751-7947
E-mail: matthewjamesbeier@gmail.com.
Epicenter Literary Software, *(978-0-9760222; 978-1-938609)* 6514 Seventh St., NW, Washington, DC 20012-2622 USA Tel 202-829-2427
E-mail: carolivia@carolivia.org
Web site: http://www.carolivia.org.
Epicenter Pr., Inc., *(978-0-945397; 978-0-9708493; 978-0-9724944; 978-0-9745014; 978-0-9790470; 978-0-9800825; 978-1-935347; 978-1-941890)* Orders Addr.: 6524 NE 181st ST No. 2, Kenmore, WA 98028 USA; Edit Addr.: 6524 NE 181st ST No. 2, Kenmore, WA 98028 USA (SAN 246-9405) Do not confuse with companies with similar names in Kanehoe, HI, Long Beach, CA, Oakland, CA
E-mail: info@epicenterpress.com; phil@epicenterpress.com; aubrey@epicenterpress.com
Web site: http://www.epicenterpress.com
Dist(s): **Smashwords.**
Epigraph Bks. *Imprint of* **Monkfish Bk. Publishing Co.**
e-Pluribus Unum Publishing Company *See* **Cronus College**
Epoca, Editorial, S.A. de C.V. (MEX) *(978-968-6769; 978-970-627) Dist. by* **Giron Bks.**
Eppy's Creations, *(978-0-615-16983-5)* P.O. Box 1103, Swansboro, NC 28584 USA
Dist(s): **Lulu Pr., Inc.**
eProduction Services *See* **Kepler Pr.**
EPS Digital, *(978-0-9772315)* P.O. Box 5185, De Pere, WI 54115-5185 USA.
ePub Bud, *(978-1-61061; 978-1-61979; 978-1-62154; 978-1-62314; 978-1-62590; 978-1-62776; 978-1-62840)* 427 California Ave., Santa Monica, CA 90403 USA Tel 310-980-4668
E-mail: josh@epubbud.com
Web site: http://www.epubbud.com
Dist(s): **BookBaby**
INscribe Digital
Lulu Pr., Inc.
EQ Recordings, *(978-0-578-01991-8)* 3750 Brayton Ave., Long Beach, CA 90807 USA.
EQUALS *Imprint of* **Univ. of California, Berkeley, Lawrence Hall of Science**
Equidata Publishing, *(978-0-9714185)* Orders Addr.: P.O. Box 8116, Surprise, AZ 85374 USA Tel 623-476-7503; Edit Addr.: 13781 W. Crocus Dr. Surprise, Az 85379, Surprise, AZ 85379 USA
E-mail: jobrien6@cox.net
Web site: http://www.equidatapublishing.com.
Equimax USA, Inc., *(978-0-9668082)* HC65 Box 271, Alpine, TX 79830 USA Tel 432-371-2610; Fax: 432-371-2612; Toll Free: 800-759-9494
E-mail: employment@equimax.com
Web site: http://www.equixmax.com.
Equine Graphics Publishing Group, *(978-1-887932; 978-0-9855309; 978-0-9962336)* Orders Addr.: 58 Indian Hill Rd., Uncasville, CT 06382 USA Tel 860-892-8891; *Imprints*: SmallHorse Press (SmallHorse Pr)
E-mail: editor@newconcordpress.com; toniweeone@smallhorse.com; info@equinegraphicspublishing.com; sales@romancingthehorse.com
Web site: http://www.smallhorse.com; http://www.newconcordpress.com; http://www.equinegraphicspublishing.com; http://www.tonileland.com
Dist(s): **Smashwords.**
Equitel Publishing Co., *(978-0-9789131)* 53 Mount Ida Rd., Suite 2, Dorchester, MA 02122-1735 USA
Web site: http://www.equitelpublishing.com.
Erazo, Carlos, *(978-0-9759757; 978-0-9796253)* P.O. Box 2111, Bayamon, PR 00960-2111 USA
E-mail: erazo2001@prtc.net
Web site: http://www.erazolabor.com
Dist(s): **Representaciones Borinquenas, Inc.**
Erickson Pr., *(978-1-60217)* Orders Addr.: P.O. Box 33, Yankton, SD 57078 USA (SAN 852-0402); Edit Addr.: 329 Broadway, Yankton, SD 57078 USA
Web site: http://www.ericksonpress.com.
Erickson, Rakel L., *(978-0-9744422)* P.O. Box 86, Fertile, MN 56540-0086 USA
E-mail: thomas_robinson@unl.nodak.edu.
Erickson, Tim, *(978-1-59492)* 8801 Fremont Ave S., Minneapolis, MN 55420-2642 USA
E-mail: terickson21@mn.rr.com
Web site: http://www.deathswhisper.com.
Erie Harbor Productions, *(978-0-9717828)* Orders Addr.: 223 W. Cornell Ave., Suite B, Pontiac, MI 48340 USA
E-mail: harbormaster@erieharbor.com
Web site: http://www.erieharbor.com.
ErieKIDS, Inc., *(978-0-9779822)* 4544 W. Ridge Rd., Suite One, Erie, PA 16506 USA (SAN 850-668X) Tel 814-835-3430
Web site: http://www.eriekids.com.
Eriginal Bks. LLC, *(978-0-9829213; 978-1-61370)* 13868 SW 151 Ct., Miami, FL 33196 USA Tel 305-763-2706; 10854 SW 88 St Suite 220, Miami, FL 33176
E-mail: marlene.moleon@gmail.com.
Erin Go Bragh Publishing, *(978-0-9882745; 978-1-941345)* 1885 FM 2673 No. 3, Canyon Lake, TX 78133 USA Tel 830-515-8187; Fax: 866-652-5165
E-mail: kjs@hamiltontroll.com; kjs@kathleensbooks.com; kjs@eringobraghpublishing.com
Web site: www.HamiltonTroll.com; www.ErinGoBraghPublishing.com; www.KathleensBooks.com.
Eringer Travel Guides *See* **Writer's Cramp, Inc.**
Erinsillart, *(978-0-9779155)* 739 31 ave, san francisco, CA 94121 USA Tel 415-816-0766
E-mail: erin@erinsillart.com
Web site: http://www.erinsillart.com.
ERPublishing, LLC, *(978-0-9766568)* P.O. Box 152, Old Greenwich, CT 06870 USA
Web site: http://www.erpublishing.com.
Ervin, Imogene *See* **Finer Moments**
Ervin, Randy, *(978-0-578-05732-3; 978-0-578-09147-1; 978-0-578-16686-5; 978-0-578-18433-3)* 1113 Stinson Ave., Mattoon, IL 61938 USA.
Ervin, Robert E., *(978-0-9746189)* 552 Keystone Station Rd., Jackson, OH 45640 USA Tel 740-286-2693; Fax: 740-286-0756
E-mail: multicominc@adelphia.net
Web site: http://johnhuntmorgan.com.
Eryn Lace, *(978-0-615-38779-6)* 223 Pacific St. Unit B, Santa Monica, CA 90405 USA Tel 323-620-7434
E-mail: jwkobernick@hotmail.com.
Eschia Bks. (CAN) *(978-0-9810942; 978-1-926696) Dist. by* **Lone Pine.**
Escuela de Musica *See* **Ed Musica**
Eslinger Hse. Publishing, *(978-0-9763033)* 17762 Neff Ranch Rd., Yorba Linda, CA 92886-9013 USA
E-mail: gilberstadt@earthlink.net.
Esmaili, Inc., *(978-0-9656185)* P.O. Box 421382, Dallas, TX 75342 USA Tel 214-521-9600; Fax: 214-526-9617.
ESOL Publishing, *(978-0-9793761)* 10305 Colony View Dr., Fairfax, VA 22032 USA (SAN 853-2796) Tel 703-250-7097
E-mail: ESOLPublishing@aol.com; mcpuginrodas@aol.com
Web site: http://www.Createspace.com/3382900
Dist(s): **CreateSpace Independent Publishing Platform**
Reading Matters, Inc.
Espasa Calpe, S.A. (ESP) *(978-84-239; 978-84-339; 978-84-8326; 978-84-670) Dist. by* **Continental Bk.**
Espasa Calpe, S.A. (ESP) *(978-84-239; 978-84-339; 978-84-8326; 978-84-670) Dist. by* **Ediciones.**
Espasa Calpe, S.A. (ESP) *(978-84-239; 978-84-339; 978-84-8326; 978-84-670) Dist. by* **Lectorum Pubns.**
Espasa Calpe, S.A. (ESP) *(978-84-239; 978-84-339; 978-84-8326; 978-84-670) Dist. by* **Distribks Inc.**
Espasa Calpe, S.A. (ESP) *(978-84-239; 978-84-339; 978-84-8326; 978-84-670) Dist. by* **Libros Fronteras.**
Espasa Calpe, S.A. (ESP) *(978-84-239; 978-84-339; 978-84-8326; 978-84-670) Dist. by* **Planeta.**
Esquire Publishing, Inc., *(978-0-9745045; 978-0-9816554)* 5900 Harper Rd., Suite 107, Solon, OH 44139 USA (SAN 856-146X) Tel 440-528-0156; Fax: 440-528-0157
E-mail: esq@pollock-law.com
Web site: http://www.monsterbooks.net
Dist(s): **Partners Pubs. Group, Inc.**
ESRI, Inc., *(978-1-879102; 978-1-58948)* 380 New York St., Redlands, CA 92373-8100 USA Fax: 909-307-3082; Toll Free: 800-447-9778; *Imprints*: ESRI Press (ESRI Pr)
E-mail: esripress@esri.com
Web site: http://www.esri.com/esripress
Dist(s): **Cengage Gale**
Independent Pubs. Group
Ingram Publisher Services
MyiLibrary
Trans-Atlantic Pubns., Inc.
ESRI Pr. *Imprint of* **ESRI, Inc.**
Essential Library *Imprint of* **ABDO Publishing Co.**
Estreno Plays, *(978-0-9631212; 978-1-888463)* 18 Van Hise Dr., Perrineville, NJ 08535 USA Tel 609-443-4787; Fax: 212-346-1435
E-mail: iridelens@aol.com; sberardini@aol.com
Web site: http://www.rci.rutgers.edu/~estrplay/webpage.html.
†**ETA hand2mind**, *(978-0-7406; 978-0-914040; 978-0-923832; 978-0-938587; 978-1-57162; 978-1-57452; 978-1-63406)* Div. of A. Daigger & Company, 500 Greenview Ct., Vernon Hills, IL 60061 USA (SAN 285-7553) Tel 847-816-5050; Fax: 847-816-5066; Toll Free: 800-445-5985; *Imprints*: SunSprouts (SUNSPROUTS); Super Source The (SUPER SOURCE)
E-mail: info@hand2mind.com
Web site: http://www.hand2mind.com; *CIP.*
ETAhand2mind *See* **ETA hand2mind**
Etcetera Pr. LLC, *(978-0-9785160; 978-0-9826781; 978-1-936824)* 146 Hills W. Way, Richland, WA 99352 USA (SAN 850-864X)
E-mail: mreilly@etcpress.net
Web site: http://etcpress.net
Dist(s): **CreateSpace Independent Publishing Platform**
Lightning Source, Inc.
Eternal Foundations Curriculum, *(978-1-932505)* P.O. Box 1213, Atascadero, CA 93423 USA Tel 805-466-1910
E-mail: tsgaddis@tcsn.net.
Eternal Studios, *(978-1-887814)* 15235 Rainhollow, Houston, TX 77070 USA Tel 713-370-8384
Dist(s): **Diamond Comic Distributors, Inc.**
Eternity Pr., *(978-0-9758989)* 2828 Brannon Ave., Saint Louis, MO 63139-1438 USA Toll Free: 800-886-7587; 1 Brounger Rd., Constantia, 7806 Tel 447521578414
Web site: http://www.cenveo.com
Dist(s): **Smashwords.**
Ethics Trading (GBR) *(978-0-9556887) Dist. by* **LuluCom.**

Ethos Of Commerce Pubs., Ltd., (978-0-9741412) 3535 E. Coast Hwy. No. 216, Corona del Mar, CA 92625 USA Tel 949-862-5826
E-mail: ethosofcommerce@yahoo.com
Web site: http://www.geocities.com/EthosOfCommerce.

Etiquette, Etc., LLC *See* **CKK Educational, LLC.**

ETN, Inc., (978-0-9759629; 978-0-9855450) 3540 W. Sahara Ave., No. 25, Las Vegas, NV 89102 USA
E-mail: eworth@etnbooks.com.

Etopia Pr., (978-1-936751; 978-1-937976; 978-1-939194; 978-1-940223; 978-1-941692; 978-1-944138; 978-1-947135) 117 Bellevue Ave. Ste. 202B, Newport, RI 02840 USA Tel 401-846-0010
E-mail: apmelton@gmail.com
Web site: www.etopia-press.net.

eTreasures Publishing, (978-0-9740537) Orders Addr.: P.O. Box 71813, Newnan, GA 30271 USA Tel 770-683-8032; Edit Addr.: 4442 Lafayette St., Marianna, FL 32446 USA Tel 850-209-0329
E-mail: publisher@etreasurespublishing.com
Web site: http://www.etreasurespublishing.com
Dist(s): **Smashwords.**

Etruscan Pr., (978-0-9718228; 978-0-9745995; 978-0-9797450; 978-0-9819687; 978-0-9832944; 978-0-9839346; 978-0-9886922; 978-0-9897532; 978-0-9903221; 978-0-9977455; 978-0-9987508) 84 West South St., Wilkes-Barre, PA 18766 USA Tel 570-408-4546; Fax: 570-408-3333
E-mail: bill@etruscanpress.org
Web site: http://www.etruscanpress.org
Dist(s): **Consortium Bk. Sales & Distribution**
MyiLibrary
SPD-Small Pr. Distribution.

ETS Publishing, (978-0-9816642) Orders Addr.: 9341 Clovercroft Rd., Franklin, TN 37067 USA (SAN 856-1583)
E-mail: info@etspublishinghouse.com
Web site: http://www.thisbespromise.com; http://www.etspublishing.com.

Ettelloc Publishing, (978-0-615-78622-3; 978-0-615-83429-0; 978-0-9898304) 734 Franklin Avenue, Suite 235, Garden City, NY 11530 USA Tel 5169244411
Dist(s): **CreateSpace Independent Publishing Platform.**

Ettrick Bks., (978-0-9963451) P.O. Box 340488, New York, NY 11234 USA Tel 602-743-7426
E-mail: ettrickbooks2015@gmail.com.

Eudon Publishing, (978-0-9765423) P.O. Box 9, Goddard, KS 67052 USA Tel 316-210-4649; Fax: 316-233-1075
E-mail: gsmith@EudonPublishing.com
Web site: http://www.EudonPublishing.com
Dist(s): **BWI**
Brodart Co.
Follett School Solutions.

eugenus STUDIOS, (978-0-578-09572-1) 445 Lakeview Rd., Craryville, NY 12521 USA
E-mail: victor@eugenus.com
Web site: http://www.captaincrossbones.com; http://www.eugenus.com.

Eupanapue-Auntella's Rooster Pubns., (978-0-615-32789-1) P.O. Box 5803, Denver, CO 80217-5803 USA Tel 720-272-5570; *Imprints:* RoosterBugglePue Books (RoosBugglePue)
E-mail: Eupanapue_AuntellasRoosterPub@q.com
Web site: http://www.roosterbugglepue.com.

Euphema Press, (978-0-9779600) P.O. Box 2314, Bowie, MD 20718 USA
Web site: http://www.euphema.com.

Eureka Productions, (978-0-9712464; 978-0-9746648; 978-0-9787919; 978-0-9825630; 978-0-9963888) 8778 Oak Grove Rd., Mount Horeb, WI 53572 USA
Web site: http://www.graphicclassics.com
Dist(s): **Diamond Comic Distributors, Inc.**
Diamond Bk. Distributors.

Europa Editions, Inc., (978-1-933372; 978-1-60945; 978-0-9968778) Div. of Edizioni E/O (Rome, Italy), 214 W. 29th St Suite 1003, New York, NY 10001 USA; Italian Office, Via Gabriela Camozzi 1, Roma, 00195
E-mail: Christian@europaeditions.com
Web site: http://www.europaeditions.com/
Dist(s): **MyiLibrary**
Penguin Random Hse. LLC
Penguin Publishing Group
Random Hse., Inc.

European Language Institute (ITA) (978-88-8148; 978-88-85148; 978-88-536) *Dist. by* **Distribks Inc.**

EV Publishing Corp., (978-0-9727787) 1628 E. Southern Ave., Suite 9, PMB 237, Tempe, AZ 85282 USA Fax: 480-966-8627
E-mail: info@evpub.com
Web site: http://www.evpub.com.

Eva Publishing, LLC, (978-0-9786799) 345 W. Broadway, Shelbyville, IN 46176 USA (SAN 851-321X) Tel 317-398-0231 (phone/fax)
E-mail: jmesser@lightbound.com.

EvangeCube International *See* **E3 Resources**

Evangel Author Services, (978-1-933858; 978-0-9823957) Div. of Brethren in Christ Media Ministries, 2000 Evangel Way, P.O. Box 189, Nappanee, IN 46550 USA Tel 574-773-3164; Fax: 574-773-5934; Toll Free: 800-253-9315
E-mail: info@evangelpublishing.com; sales@evangelpublishing.com
Web site: http://www.evangelpress.com; http://www.evangelpublishing.com.

Evangel Press *See* **Evangel Publishing Hse.**

Evangel Publishing Hse., (978-0-916035; 978-1-928915; 978-1-934233; 978-0-692-00906-2) Div. of Brethren in Christ Media Ministries, Orders Addr.: P.O. Box 189, Nappanee, IN 46550 USA (SAN 211-7940) Tel 574-773-3164; Fax: 574-773-5934; Toll Free: 800-253-9315 (order); Edit Addr.: 2000 Evangel Way, Nappanee, IN 46550 USA Fax: 574-773-5934; Toll Free: 800-253-9315
E-mail: sales@evangelpublishing.com
Web site: http://www.evangelpublishing.com
Dist(s): **Anchor Distributors**
Partners Bk. Distributing, Inc.
Spring Arbor Distributors, Inc.

Evangelista, Susan, (978-0-9769602) 1261 W. Fulton Ave., Grand Rapids,, MI 49504 USA
Web site: http://micart.net.

Evan-Moor Educational Pubs., (978-1-55799; 978-1-59673; 978-1-4409; 978-1-60792; 978-1-60793; 978-1-935353; 978-1-60823; 978-1-60963; 978-1-61365; 978-1-61366; 978-1-61367; 978-1-61368; 978-1-62938) Sub. of Evan-Moor Corporation, 18 Lower Ragsdale Dr., Monterey, CA 93940 USA (SAN 242-5394) Tel 800-976-1915; 831-649-5901; Fax: 831-649-6256; Toll Free Fax: 800-777-4332; Toll Free: 800-777-4362
E-mail: customerservice@evan-moor.com; sterling@evan-moor.com
Web site: http://www.evan-moor.com
Dist(s): **Follett School Solutions**
Spring Arbor Distributors, Inc.

Evans Brothers, Ltd. (GBR) (978-0-237) *Dist. by* **IPG Chicago.**

†Evans, M. & Co., Inc., (978-0-87131; 978-1-59077) 216 E. 49th St., New York, NY 10017 USA (SAN 203-4050) Tel 212-688-2810
E-mail: editorial@mevans.com
Dist(s): **MyiLibrary**
National Bk. Network
Rowman & Littlefield Publishers, Inc.
ebrary, Inc.; *CIP.*

Evans, Robert, (978-0-9766468; 978-0-9884466) 1065 Saint Helena Way, Sebastopol, CA 95472 USA
E-mail: rgevans@sonic.net.

Evening Star Enterprise, Inc., (978-0-9790210; 978-0-9841611) Orders Addr.: P.O. Box 254, Wilmore, KY 40390-1072 USA (SAN 852-2111) Tel 859-421-0243; Edit Addr.: 408 Kinlaw Dr., Wilmore, KY 40390-1072 USA
E-mail: Rgray@Eveningstarenterprise.com
Web site: http://www.eveningstarenterprise.com/Home.html.

Evening Sun Pr., (978-0-9726781) 8332 Melrose Ave., West Hollywood, CA 90069 USA Tel 310-657-9092
E-mail: lc@pictureentertainment.com.

Evenson, Laurel, (978-0-9666834) 675 Moon Lake Dr., Cambridge, MN 55008 USA Tel 612-689-4093.

Event-Based Science Institute, Inc., (978-0-9747576) 6609 Paxton Rd., Rockville, MD 20852-3659 USA
Web site: http://www.eventbasedscience.com.

EverAfter Romance *Imprint of* **Diversion Publishing Corp.**

Everbind *Imprint of* **Marco Bk. Co.**

Everbind/Marco Book Company *See* **Marco Bk. Co.**

Eveready Letter & Advertising Inc., (978-0-9758714; 978-0-9777623; 978-0-9814694; 978-0-9820757; 978-0-9826118; 978-0-9837256; 978-0-9858365; 978-0-9897161; 978-0-9963917; 978-0-9981522) 1817 Broadway, Nashville, TN 37203 USA
Web site: http://eveready-usa.com
Dist(s): **Ingram Publisher Services.**

Everest Bks., (978-0-9754146) 16026 N. 54th St., Scottsdale, AZ 85254 USA Tel 602-684-5644; Fax: 602-595-7152
E-mail: grahamhfoster@msn.com
Web site: http://www.pacificseminars.com.

Everest Editora (ESP) (978-84-241; 978-972-750) *Dist. by* **Continental Bk.**

Everest Editora (ESP) (978-84-241; 978-972-750) *Dist. by* **Lectorum Pubns.**

Everett Pr. *Imprint of* **Rosen Publishing Group, Inc., The**

Everett Pr. *Imprint of* **State Standards Publishing, LLC**

Everette Publishing (EP), LLC, (978-0-9672539) 106 Tillerson Dr., Newport News, VA 23602 USA Tel 757-344-9092; 757-877-6943; Fax: 757-988-0909
E-mail: EverettePublish@cox.net
Web site: http://www.Webunlimted.com.

Evergreen House Publishing LLC *Imprint of* **WaveCloud Corp.**

Evergreen Pr. *Imprint of* **Genesis Communications, Inc.**

Evergreen Press *See* **Genesis Communications, Inc.**

Evergreen Pr. of Brainerd, LLC, (978-0-9661599; 978-0-9755252; 978-0-9819766) P.O. Box 465, Brainerd, MN 56401 USA Tel 218-851-4843; 201 W. Laurel St., Brainerd, MN 56401
E-mail: tenlee@evergreenpress.net
Web site: http://www.evergreenpress.net.

Everlasting Publishing, (978-0-9778083; 978-0-9824844; 978-0-9852739; 978-0-9983858) P.O. Box 1061, Yakima, WA 98907 USA (SAN 850-2919) Tel 509-225-9829; P.O. Box 1061, Yakima, WA 98907 Tel 509-225-9829
E-mail: dpride42@gmail.com
Web site: http://everlastingpublishing.org.

Everwas Publishing, (978-0-9777735) 200 Broken Arrow Way S., Sedona, AZ 86351-8743 USA Tel 928-284-0457; Fax: 928-284-9225
E-mail: kroyce88@esedona.net.

Everybody Run Music, (978-0-578-04648-8) 186-A W. Lemon Ave., Monrovia, CA 91016 USA
E-mail: eshouse@hotmail.com.

Everyday Learning Corp., (978-0-9630009; 978-1-57039; 978-1-877817) 2 Prudential Plaza, Suite 1200, Chicago, IL 60601 USA Tel 312-233-7820; Fax: 312-540-5848; Toll Free: 800-382-7670
Web site: http://www.everydaylearning.com.

Everyday Mathtools Publishing Company *See* **Everyday Learning Corp.**

Everydaysanctuary Pubns., (978-0-9761900) 12514 Maria Cir., Broomfield, CO 80020-5324 USA
Web site: http://www.everydaysanctuary.net.

Everyman Chess (GBR) (978-1-85744) *Dist. by* **Natl Bk Netwk.**

Everyman's Library *Imprint of* **Knopf Doubleday Publishing Group**

Everything Journals, (978-0-9980714) 4544 Cielo Ln., Las Vegas, NV 89130 USA Tel 702-458-2201
E-mail: mignard2201@gmail.com.

Evil Hat Productions LLC, (978-0-9771534; 978-1-61317) Orders Addr.: 1905 Blackbriar St, Silver Spring, MD 20903 USA Tel 240-EHP-BLUE (240-347-2583)
E-mail: feedback@evilhat.com
Web site: http://www.evilhat.com/
Dist(s): **Diamond Comic Distributors, Inc.**
Diamond Bk. Distributors.

Evil Twin Pubns., (978-0-9712972; 978-0-9763355) P.O. Box 2, Livingston Manor, NY 12758 USA Tel 917-971-2450
E-mail: info@eviltwinpublications.com
Web site: http://www.eviltwinpublications.com
Dist(s): **AK Pr. Distribution**
D.A.P./Distributed Art Pubs.

eVision, LLC, (978-0-9768579) Orders Addr.: 334 Sixth Ave. S., Birmingham, AL 35205 USA Tel 205-283-7690; Fax: 205-252-3090
Web site: http://www.eVisionLLC.net
Dist(s): **Parnassus Bk. Distributors.**

Evolved Publishing, (978-0-615-60885-3; 978-0-615-61939-2; 978-1-62253) Orders Addr.: 4985 N 125th St, Butler, WI 53007 USA
E-mail: Admin@EvolvedPub.com
Web site: http://www.evolvedpub.com/press/
Dist(s): **CreateSpace Independent Publishing Platform**
Draft2Digital
Lightning Source, Inc.
Smashwords.

Evolved Self Publishing, (978-0-9779470) 723 Springtown Rd., Tillson, NY 12486 USA Tel 845-658-8270; Fax: 845-658-3718
E-mail: publisher@evolvedself.com
Web site: http://www.evolvedself.com
Dist(s): **Smashwords.**

EvoraBooks, LLC, (978-0-9725071) P.O. Box 397, Canton, CT 06019 USA
E-mail: evorabooks@snet.net
Web site: http://www.booksbyevora.com.

Ewers Family Partnership, (978-0-9987475) 404 Ridge Rd., Boulder City, NV 89005 USA Tel 702-294-7718; Fax: 702-294-7718
E-mail: lifelake@embarqmail.com.

Ewuramma, (978-0-9849805) 1850 Lafayette Ave. Apt. 3A, Bronx, NY 10473 USA Tel 646-220-6432
E-mail: ehboah@aol.com.

Exact Change, (978-1-878972) 5 Brewster St., Cambridge, MA 02138 USA Tel 617-492-5405; Fax: 617-492-5669
E-mail: info@exactchange.com; mailinglist@exactchange.com
Web site: http://www.exactchange.com
Dist(s): **D.A.P./Distributed Art Pubs.**

Exambusters *Imprint of* **Ace Academics, Inc.**

Examined Solutions PTE. Ltd., (978-1-68374) 9450 SW Gemini Dr., No. 21372, Beaverton, OR 97008 USA (SAN 990-1426) Tel 888-248-4521
E-mail: admin@speedypublishing.com; examinedsolutions@gmail.com.

ExamWise *Imprint of* **Total Recall Learning, Inc.**

Exceed, LLC, (978-0-9771722) 715 E. 100 N., Lindon, UT 84042 USA (SAN 256-8519) Tel 801-785-7931
E-mail: kcooper@exceed.bz
Web site: http://www.exceed.bz.

Excel Digital Pr., (978-0-9712249; 978-0-9718254; 978-0-9749202; 978-0-9786376) Orders Addr.: P.O. Box 703978, Dallas, TX 75370-3978 USA Tel 972-307-3075; Fax: 469-619-2292; Edit Addr.: 2515 Daybreak Dr., Dallas, TX 75287 USA
E-mail: bookeagle@hotmail.com
Web site: http://www.exceldigitalpress.com.

Excel Heritage Group, Inc., (978-0-692-88807-0) 2007 Remington Oaks Cir, CARY, NC 27519 USA Tel 678-549-6517
Dist(s): **Lightning Source, Inc.**

Excellence Enterprises, (978-0-9627735) 3040 Aspen Ln., Palmdale, CA 93550-7985 USA Tel 661-267-2220; Fax: 661-267-2946
E-mail: lavonne.taylor@sbcglobal.net
Web site: http://vonnieshealthspot.com.

Excellence Student Incentives, (978-0-9789612) 18942 Muirland, Detroit, MI 48221 USA (SAN 852-1107) Tel 313-646-6079; Fax: 313-449-0396
E-mail: beatthemeap@yahoo.com
Web site: http://www.beatthemeap.com.

Excellent Bks., (978-0-9628014; 978-1-880780)
E-mail: books@excellentbooks.com
Web site: http://www.excellentbooks.com.

Excite Kids Pr. *Imprint of* **Publishing Services @ Thomson-Shore**

Exclusive Editions *Imprint of* **Parragon, Inc.**

Executive Books *See* **Tremendous Life Bks.**

Executive Performances, Inc., (978-0-9748220) P.O. Box 93, Palos Park, IL 60464 USA; *Imprints:* Executive Performances Publishing (Exec Perform Pubng)
E-mail: magicriz@aol.com.

Executive Performances Publishing *Imprint of* **Executive Performances, Inc.**

Exeter Pr., (978-0-9700612; 978-0-9797407) Orders Addr.: 223 Commonwealth Ave., Boston, MA 02116 USA Tel 617-267-7720; Fax: 617-262-6948; Edit Addr.: 223 Commonwealth Ave., Boston, MA 02116 USA (SAN 854-2554)
E-mail: davidburke@commonwealthfilms.com
Web site: http://www.exeterpress.com.

Exhibit A *Imprint of* **Scholastic, Inc.**

Exhibit A *Imprint of* **TR Bks.**

Exhibit A *Imprint of* **Cavendish Square Publishing**

Exhibit A Pr., (978-0-9633954; 978-0-9815519) 4657 Cajon Way, San Diego, CA 92115 USA Tel 619-286-6350; Fax: 619-286-1591
E-mail: mail@exhibitapress.com
Web site: http://www.exhibitapress.com
Dist(s): **Bookmasters Distribution**
MyiLibrary.

Exisle Publishing Pty Ltd. (AUS) (978-1-921497; 978-1-921966; 978-1-925335; 978-0-646-95875-0) *Dist. by* **HachBkGrp.**

Exit Studio, (978-0-9640868; 978-0-9831891) 1466 N. Quinn St., Arlington, VA 22209 USA Tel 703-312-7121; Fax: 703-894-2741
E-mail: efontanez@exitstudio.com
Web site: http://www.exitstudio.com
Dist(s): **Follett School Solutions**
Independent Pubs. Group.

Exley, Helen Giftbooks (GBR) (978-0-905521; 978-1-85015; 978-1-86187; 978-1-905130; 978-1-84634; 978-1-78485) *Dist. by* **Natl Bk Netwk.**

ExpandingBooks.com, (978-0-9721764; 978-1-934443) 200 W. 34th, Suite 953, Anchorage, AK 99503 USA Tel 907-278-9800; Fax: 877-552-7200
E-mail: cherylkirk@gmail.com; expandingbooks@gmail.com
Web site: http://www.expandingpress.com; http://www.expandingbooks
Dist(s): **Taku Graphics.**

Experiment LLC, The, (978-1-61519) 260 Fifth Ave., Suite 3 S., New York, NY 10001-6425 USA (SAN 857-961X)
E-mail: info@theexperimentpublishing.com
Web site: http://www.theexperimentpublishing.com
Dist(s): **Workman Publishing Co., Inc.**

Expert Systems for Teachers *Imprint of* **Teaching Point, Inc.**

Explorations Early Learning, (978-0-615-15718-4; 978-0-615-15719-1) 1524 Summit St., Sioux City, IA 51103 USA Tel 712-202-1627
E-mail: jeffajohnson@cableone.net
Web site: http://www.explorationsearlylearning.com
Dist(s): **Lulu Pr., Inc.**

Explorer Media *Imprint of* **Simon & Barklee, Inc./ExplorerMedia**

Explorer's Bible Study, (978-1-889015; 978-0-9787993; 978-1-935424) 2652 Hwy. 46 S., Dickson, TN 37055 USA Tel 615-446-7316; Fax: 615-446-7951; Toll Free: 800-657-2874; P.O. Box 425, Dickson, TN 37056 Toll Free: 800-657-2874
Web site: http://www.explorerbiblestudy.org.

Exploring California Insects *Imprint of* **Insect Sciences Museum of California**

Express Bks. *Imprint of* **Bellwether Media**

Expressions Woven, (978-0-9668179) P.O. Box 1004, Waterford, CT 06385 USA Tel 860-442-1332; Fax: 860-447-9916
E-mail: dreaminthelight@alum.rpi.edu
Web site: http://www.poetryin.com
Dist(s): **Lightning Source, Inc.**

Expressive Design Group, Inc., (978-0-9845278; 978-1-936676) 49 Garfield St., Holyoke, MA 01040 USA (SAN 859-6654) Tel 413-315-6296; Fax: 413-315-6271; Toll Free: 800-848-6685
E-mail: richard.marks@theedg.net
Web site: http://www.theedg.net.

Expressive Ink, (978-0-9759362) Orders Addr.: P.O. Box 74, Foreston, MN 56330 USA; Edit Addr.: 305 Pheasant Ln., Foreston, MN 56330-5540 USA Tel 320-294-4022
E-mail: express@bctelco.net
Web site: http://www.natknows.com.

Exquisite Thoughts, Incorporated *See* **CCP Publishing & Entertainment**

Extejt, Gabriele *See* **McGab Publishing**

Exterminating Angel Pr., (978-1-935259) 1892 Colestin Rd., Ashland, OR 97520 USA
Dist(s): **Consortium Bk. Sales & Distribution**
MyiLibrary.

Extra Point Pubs., (978-0-9801749; 978-0-9840847; 978-0-9846377; 978-0-9882595; 978-0-9904882; 978-0-9973309) Orders Addr.: P.O. Box 871, Perry, GA 31069 USA; Edit Addr.: 315 Hampton Ct., Perry, GA 31069 USA (SAN 855-4129) Tel 478-224-3267; Fax: 478-218-0306
Web site: http://www.die-hardfans.com.

Eye Bks. (GBR) (978-1-903070; 978-1-908646; 978-1-78563) *Dist. by* **IPG Chicago.**

Eye of Newt, The, (978-0-9762565) 5203 Cedar Springs Rd, Dallas, TX 75235-8537 USA Tel 214-520-1739
Web site: http://www.theyeofnewt.com.

Eyres, John, (978-0-9769762) 12713 Willowyck Dr., Saint Louis, MO 63146 USA.

EZ Comics, (978-0-9795887) 12, Pine Top Rd., Barrington, RI 02806-1706 USA
E-mail: vshah.ezcomics@gmail.com; vshah@ezcomics.com
Web site: http://ezcomics.com.

EZ Muzik Publishing, (978-0-615-24181-4; 978-0-9822805; 978-0-692-01686-2) P.O. Box 50826, Santa barbara, CA 93108 USA Tel 805-886-0799
E-mail: patrikpiano@aol.com.

Ezra's Earth Publishing, (978-0-9727855) P.O. Box 3036, South Pasadena, CA 91031 USA (SAN 255-0555)
E-mail: information@ezrasearth.com
Web site: http://www.ezrasearth.com
Dist(s): **Quality Bks., Inc.**

Ezra's Engine Publishing *See* **Ezra's Earth Publishing**

F & S Music KS Publishing Co., (978-0-9745630; 978-0-9765787) Orders Addr.: P.O. Box 11805, Jackson, MS 39283 USA; Edit Addr.: 1902 Queens Road Ave., Jackson, MS 39213 USA
E-mail: lanniespann@yahoo.com
Web site: lanniespannmcbride.com.

FC&A Publishing, (978-0-915099; 978-1-890957; 978-1-932470; 978-1-935574) 103 Clover Green, Peachtree City, GA 30269-1695 USA (SAN 289-7946)

Publisher Name Index

Tel 770-487-6307; Fax: 770-631-4357; Toll Free: 800-537-1275
E-mail: charlotte_carpenter@fca.com; anne_kaufmann@fca.com
Web site: http://www.fca.com.

F E A Publishing *See* **FEA Ministries**

FA LLC, *(978-0-692-74187-0; 978-0-692-79747-1)* 7582 Cresthill Dr., Longmont, CO 80504 USA Tel 303-859-0121; Toll Free: 303-859-0121
Dist(s): **CreateSpace Independent Publishing Platform.**

Fabbri Editori - RCS Libri (ITA) *(978-88-450; 978-88-451; 978-88-452; 978-88-454) Dist. by* **Distribks Inc.**

†Faber & Faber, Inc., *(978-0-571)* Affil. of Farrar, Straus & Giroux, LLC, Orders Addr.: c/o Van Holtzbrinck Publishing Services, 16365 James Madison Hwy., Gordonsville, VA 22942 USA Fax: 540-572-7540; Toll Free: 888-330-8477; Edit Addr.: 19 Union Sq., W, New York, NY 10003-3304 USA (SAN 218-7256) Tel 212-741-6900; Fax: 212-633-9385
E-mail: sales@fsgbooks.com
Web site: http://www.fsgbooks.com
Dist(s): **Continental Bk. Co., Inc.**
ISD
Macmillan
MyiLibrary
Penguin Random Hse. LLC
Publishers Group West (PGW); *CIP.*

Faber & Faber, Ltd. (GBR) *(978-0-571; 978-1-78335) Dist. by* **Alfred Pub.**

Faber, David *See* **Faber Pr.**

Faber Music, Ltd. (GBR) *(978-0-571) Dist. by* **Alfred Pub.**

Faber Piano Adventuresr, *(978-1-61677)* 3042 Creek Dr., Ann Arbor, MI 48108 USA Tel 734-975-1995; Fax: 734-332-7823
Dist(s): **Leonard, Hal Corp.**

Faber Pr., *(978-0-9768763)* Orders Addr.: 5638 Lake Murray Blvd., No.206, La Mesa, CA 91942 USA (SAN 256-8071) Tel 619-517-2662; Fax: 619-255-2354
E-mail: annavennis@yahoo.com
Web site: http://www.becauseofromek.com.

Fabled Films LLC, *(978-1-944020)* 200 Park Ave. S., New York, NY 10003 USA Tel 212-220-5804; *Imprints:* Fabled Films Press LLC (Fabled Film)
E-mail: StaceyAshton@fabledfilms.com
Web site: www.fabledfilms.com
Dist(s): **Consortium Bk. Sales & Distribution.**

Fabled Films Pr. LLC *Imprint of* **Fabled Films LLC**

Fablefy LLC, *(978-0-578-18496-8)* 2515 Plaza Dr., Woodbridge, NJ 07095 USA.

FableVision Pr., *(978-1-891405)* 308 Congress St. # 6, Boston, MA 02210-1027 USA Toll Free: 888-240-3734
E-mail: info@fablevision.com; shoppe@fablevision.com
Web site: http://www.fablevision.com; http://www.fablevision.com/shoppe.

Fabula, *(978-0-9915194; 978-0-9915195)* P.O. Box 2709, Redmond, WA 98073 USA Tel 314-495-6939
E-mail: kkennedy0929@gmail.com

Face 2 Face Games Publishing, *(978-0-9728197; 978-0-9761156)* 36 The Arcade, 65 Weybosset St., Providence, RI 02903 USA Tel 401-351-0362 (phone/fax)
E-mail: lwhalen@face2facegames.com
Web site: http://www.face2facegames.com
Dist(s): **PSI (Publisher Services, Inc.).**

Fact Finders *Imprint of* **Capstone Press of Coughlan Cos.**

Factors Pr., *(978-0-9700582)* Orders Addr.: 14718 Ellison Ave., Omaha, NE 68116-4336 USA
E-mail: Info@FactorsPress.com.

†Facts On File, Inc., *(978-0-8160; 978-0-87196; 978-1-60413; 978-1-4381; 978-1-61753)* Orders Addr.: 132 W. 31st St., 17th Flr., New York, NY 10001-2006 USA (SAN 201-4696) Tel 212-967-8800; 212-896-4296 (customer service); Fax: 917-339-0325; 917-339-0323; Toll Free Fax: 800-678-3633; Toll Free: 800-322-8755; *Imprints:* Checkmark Books (Checkmark); Ferguson Publishing Company (Ferg Pub Co); Chelsea House (ChelsHse); Chelsea Clubhouse (ChelseaClub); Bloom's Literary Criticism (Bloom's Lit); World Almanac Books (WrldAlmanac)
E-mail: custserv@factsonfile.com; Sales@ChelseaHouse.com
Web site: http://www.factsonfile.com; http://www.fergpubco.com; http://www.chelseahouse.com
Dist(s): **Casemate Academic**
CreateSpace Independent Publishing Platform
Ebsco Publishing
Follett School Solutions
Infobase Learning
MyiLibrary
Simon & Schuster, Inc.
ebrary, Inc.; *CIP.*

Faden, Ellen, *(978-0-9821231)* 145 Plaza Dr., Suite 207-224, Vallejo, CA 94590 USA (SAN 857-3166) Tel 415-342-1552
E-mail: efaden1@gmail.com
Web site: http://www.kabbalah-dating.com.

Faerieground *Imprint of* **Stone Arch Bks.**

Fahnestock Pr., *(978-0-9747981)* 310 Dennytown Rd., Putman Valley, NY 10579-1423 USA (SAN 255-8564) Tel 212-894-1219
E-mail: weigman676@aol.com.

Fair, Barbara A., *(978-0-9621174)* Orders Addr.: P.O. Box 241155, Detroit, MI 48224 USA (SAN 250-7447); Edit Addr.: P.O. Box 26101, Fraser, MI 48026-6101 USA (SAN 250-7455).

Fair Havens Pubns., *(978-0-9664803)* P.O. Box 1238, Gainsville, TX 76241 USA Tel 940-668-6044; Fax: 940-668-6984; Toll Free: 800-771-4861
E-mail: fairhavens@fairhavenspub.com
Web site: http://www.fairhavenspub.com; http://www.ageofgrace.com
Dist(s): **Anchor Distributors**
Spring Arbor Distributors, Inc.

Fair Winds Pr. *Imprint of* **Quarto Publishing Group USA**

Fairchild Bks. *Imprint of* **Bloomsbury Academic & Professional**

Fairchild Bks., *(978-0-87005; 978-1-56367; 978-1-60901)* Div. of Bloomsbury Publishing, c/o Sandra Washington, 750 Third Ave., 8th Floor, New York, NY 10017 USA (SAN 201-470X) Tel 212-630-3875; Fax: 212-630-3868; Toll Free: 800-932-4724
Web site: http://www.fairchildbooks.com
Dist(s): **MyiLibrary.**

Fairfax Lectern, Inc., The, *(978-0-9701756)* 4280-Redwood Hwy., No. 11, San Rafael, CA 94903 USA Tel 415-479-1128; Fax: 415-479-9024
E-mail: scalised@aol.com
Web site: http://www.fairfax-lectern.com; http://www.professordave.com
Dist(s): .

Fairfield Language Technologies *See* **Rosetta Stone Ltd.**

Fairhaven Bk. Pubs., *(978-1-929649)* Orders Addr.: 35425 Mojave St., Lucerne Vly, CA 92356 USA; Edit Addr.: P.O. Box 105, Lucerne Valley, CA 92356 USA Tel 760-248-6446; Fax: 206-337-5431; Toll Free: 877-342-6657
E-mail: values@charactervalues.com
Web site: http://www.charactervalues.com; http://www.charactervalues.org; http://www.world-peace.org; http://www.charactervalues.net; http://www.charactervalues.net
Dist(s): **Quality Bks., Inc.**

Fairland Bks., *(978-0-9818154)* P.O. Box 63, West Friendship, MD 21794 USA
Web site: http://fairlandbooks.com
Dist(s): **Emerald Bk. Co.**

†Fairmont Pr., Inc., *(978-0-88173; 978-0-915586)* 700 Indian Trail, Lilburn, GA 30047 USA (SAN 207-5946) Tel 770-925-9388; Fax: 770-381-9865
Web site: http://www.fairmontpress.com
Dist(s): **Assn. of Energy Engineers**
Ebsco Publishing
Lulu Pr., Inc.
Taylor & Francis Group; *CIP.*

Fairway Pr. *Imprint of* **CSS Publishing Co.**

Fairwood Pr., *(978-0-9668184; 978-0-9746573; 978-1-933846; 978-0-9789078; 978-0-9820730)* 21528 104th St. Ct. E., Bonney Lake, WA 98391 USA Tel 253-269-2640; *Imprints:* Media Man! Productions (MeidaMan)
E-mail: patrick@fairwoodpress.com
Web site: http://www.fairwoodpress.com.

†Faith Alive Christian Resources, *(978-0-930265; 978-0-933140; 978-1-56212; 978-1-59255; 978-1-62025)* 2850 Kalamazoo Ave., SE, Grand Rapids, MI 49560 USA (SAN 212-727X) Tel 616-224-0784; Fax: 616-224-0834; Toll Free Fax: 888-642-8606; Toll Free: 800-333-8300; P.O. Box 5070, Burlington, ON L7R 3Y8 Toll Free Fax: 888-642-8606; Toll Free: 800-333-8300
E-mail: sales@faithaliveresources.org
Web site: http://www.faithaliveresources.org
Dist(s): **Lulu Pr., Inc.**; *CIP.*

Faith & Action Team, *(978-1-931984; 978-1-60382)* 429 Us Hwy. 65, Walnut Shade, MO 65771 USA
E-mail: elizabeth@faithandactionseries.org
Web site: http://www.faithandactionseries.org; http://www.seriefeyaccion.org
Dist(s): **MyiLibrary.**

Faith & Action/RD *See* **Faith & Action Team**

Faith & Life Pr., *(978-0-87303)* Orders Addr.: P.O. Box 347, Newton, KS 67114-0347 USA (SAN 658-0637) Tel 316-283-5100; Fax: 316-283-0454; Toll Free: 800-245-7894 (orders only); Edit Addr.: 718 Main St., Newton, KS 67114-0347 USA (SAN 201-4726)
E-mail: flp@gcmc.org
Web site: http://www.2southwind.net/~gcmc/flp.html
Dist(s): **Herald Pr.**
Spring Arbor Distributors, Inc.

Faith Baptist Church Publications *See* **FBC Pubns. & Printing**

Faith Bks. & MORE, *(978-0-9820197; 978-0-9841729; 978-0-9842378; 978-0-9845779; 978-0-9846507; 978-0-9852729; 978-0-9860159; 978-0-9860247; 978-1-939761)* 3255 Lawrenceville-Suwanee Rd., Suite P250, Suwanee, GA 30024 USA (SAN 857-0337) Tel 678-232-6156; Fax: 888-479-4540
E-mail: publishing@faithbooksandmore.com
Web site: http://www.faithbooksandmore.com; http://www.facebook.com/corpconnoisseur; http://www.facebook.com/faithbooksandmorepublishing.

Faith Communications *Imprint of* **Health Communications, Inc.**

F.A.I.T.H. Ministries Publishing House *See* **FM Publishing Co.**

Faith Pubns., *(978-0-9743167)* 5301 Edgewood Rd., College Park, MD 20740 USA Tel 301-982-2061 Do not confuse with companies with the same name in Milton, FL, Haviland, KS
E-mail: faith@alhuda.org.

Faithful Life Pubs., *(978-0-9749836; 978-0-9821408; 978-0-9824931; 978-0-9845208; 978-0-9829105; 978-0-9832039; 978-1-937129; 978-1-63073)* Div. of With Integrity Ministries, 3335 Galaxy Way, North Fort Myers, FL 33903-1419 USA Tel 239-652-0135; Toll Free: 800-699-2623
E-mail: editor@FLPublishers.com
Web site: http://www.faithfullife.com; http://www.FLPublishers.com.

Faithful Publishing, *(978-0-9759941; 978-0-9779889; 978-1-940911)* P.O. Box 345, Buford, GA 30515-0345 USA Tel 770-932-7335; Fax: 678-482-4446; *Imprints:* Pixelated Publishing (Pixel Pubng)
E-mail: faithfulpublishing@yahoo.com; alwzapr@bellsouth.net
Web site: http://www.eighttwelvepublishing.com.

FaithWalker Publishing *Imprint of* **Markowitz, Darryl**

Faithwords *Imprint of* **Hachette Nashville**

Falcon Guides *Imprint of* **Globe Pequot Pr., The**

Falcon Pr. International, *(978-1-884459)* 2150 Almaden Rd., No. 141, San Jose, CA 95125 USA Tel 408-677-4875
E-mail: getty@gettyambau.com.

Falcon Publishing LTD, *(978-0-9746959)* P.O. Box 6099, Kingwood, TX 77325 USA
E-mail: gwen@falconpublishing.com
Web site: http://www.falconpublishing.com.

Falcor Bks., *(978-0-9723530)* P.O. Box 1055, Yorktown, VA 23692-1055 USA Tel 757-872-6649; Toll Free: 866-872-6649
E-mail: info@falcorbooks.com
Web site: http://www.falcorbooks.com.

†Falk Art Reference, *(978-0-932087)* Div. of artprice.com, Orders Addr.: P.O. Box 833, Madison, CT 06443 USA (SAN 686-5240) Tel 203-245-2246; Fax: 203-245-5116; Toll Free: 800-278-4274; Edit Addr.: 61 Beekman Pl., Madison, CT 06443-2400 USA Do not confuse with companies with the same name in Tacoma, WA
E-mail: info@falkart.com
Web site: http://www.falkart.com; http://www.artprice.com; *CIP.*

Fall River *Imprint of* **Sterling Publishing Co., Inc.**

Fall Rose Bks., *(978-0-9742185)* P.O. Box 39, Kittery Point, ME 03905 USA Tel 207-439-2878
Web site: http://www.fallrosebooks.com.

Falls Media *See* **Seven Footer Pr.**

Falter, Laury, *(978-0-615-29498-8; 978-0-615-53342-1; 978-0-615-58386-0; 978-0-9855110; 978-0-9890362; 978-0-9969259)* 8245 Cupertino Heights Way, Las Vegas, NV 89178 USA.

Fame's Eternal Bks., LLC, *(978-0-9753721)* 15740 Rockford Rd. #312, Plymouth, MN 55446 USA Tel 512-468-8873
E-mail: tammymate@aol.com
Web site: http://www.fameseternalbooks.com.

Familius LLC, *(978-1-938301; 978-1-939629; 978-1-942672; 978-1-942934; 978-1-944822; 978-1-945547; 978-1-64170)* 1254 Commerce Way, Sanger, CA 93657 USA (SAN 990-1515) Tel 801-552-7298; 559-876-2170
E-mail: christopher@familius.com
Web site: www.familius.com
Dist(s): **MyiLibrary.**

Family Bks., *(978-0-9728460)* Orders Addr.: P.O. Box 730, Petaluma, CA 94953-0730 USA Do not confuse with companies with the same name in Glendale, CA, Dana Point, CA
E-mail: familybooks2003@yahoo.com.

Family Bks. at Home, *(978-0-9753127; 978-1-933200)* 375 Hudson St., 2nd Fl., New York, NY 10014-3657 USA.

Family Enterprises, *(978-0-9773858)* 2678 Challis Creek Rd., Box 981, Challis, ID 83226-0981 USA Do not confuse with Family Enterprises in Milwaukee, WI.

Family Guidance & Outreach Ctr. of Lubbock, *(978-0-9767215)* 5 Briercroft Office Pk., Lubbock, TX 79412-3007 USA Tel 806-747-5577; Fax: 806-747-5119
E-mail: wedwards23@cox.net.

Family Harvest Church, *(978-1-889723)* 18500 92nd Ave., Tinley Park, IL 60477 USA (SAN 801-4817) Tel 708-614-6000; Fax: 708-614-8288; Toll Free: 800-622-0017
E-mail: winner@winninginlife.org
Web site: http://www.winninginlife.org
Dist(s): **Smashwords.**

Family Learning Assn., Inc., *(978-0-9719874)* 3925 Hagan St. Ste. 103, Bloomington, IN 47401-8649 USA
Web site: http://www.kidscanlearn.com.

Family Legacy Ministries, *(978-0-9797879)* Orders Addr.: P.O. Box 811, Rocky Point, NC 28457 USA Tel 910-675-1825
E-mail: publishing@familylegacyministries.org
Web site: http://www.familylegacyministries.org.

Family Life Productions, *(978-1-883761)* 2460 Hobbit Ln., Fallbrook, CA 92028-3679 USA (SAN 239-1090) Tel 760-728-6437; Fax: 760-728-5309; Toll Free: 800-886-2767.

Family Nutrition Ctr. P.C., *(978-0-9770756)* 98 Harding Rd., Glen Rock, NJ 07452-1317 USA
E-mail: everyday7foods@earthlink.net.

Family Of Man Pr., The *Imprint of* **Hutchison, G.F. Pr.**

Family Plays, *(978-0-87602; 978-0-88680)* Div. of Dramatic Publishing, Orders Addr.: 311 Washington St., Woodstock, IL 60098-3308 USA (SAN 282-7433) Tel 815-338-7170
E-mail: msergel@dpcplays.com
Web site: http://www.familyplays.com; http://www.dramaticpublishing.com.

Family Rocks, The, *(978-0-9747466)* 256 S. Robertson Blvd., Beverly Hills, CA 90211-2898 USA Tel 310-358-5106; Fax: 310-734-1594
E-mail: sales@coupon-directory.com
Web site: http://www.coupon-directory.com.

Family Value Publishing, *(978-0-9645180)* R.R. 2, Box 110A, Nevis, MN 56467 USA Tel 218-732-1349.

FamilyLife, *(978-1-57229; 978-1-60200)* Div. of Campus Crusade for Christ, 5800 Ranch Dr., Little Rock, AR 72223 USA Tel 501-223-8663; Fax: 501-224-2529; Toll Free: 800-404-5052
Web site: http://www.familylife.com.

FancyCrazy Publishing, *(978-0-9745386)* 254 Harrison St., 1st Fl., Nutley, NJ 07110 USA Tel 917-279-5920
E-mail: fch3000@yahoo.com; baltazarray@gmail.com
Web site: http://www.FancyCrazyHydrants.TV.

F&W Media, Inc., *(978-0-89134; 978-0-89879; 978-0-932620; 978-1-55870; 978-1-58180; 978-1-58297; 978-1-884910; 978-1-892127; 978-1-59963; 978-1-60061; 978-1-4402; 978-1-4403; 978-0-578-03300-6; 978-1-940038)* Orders Addr.: 10151 Carver Rd., Ste 200, Blue Ash, OH 45242 USA Tel 513-531-2690; Fax: 513-531-1843; Toll Free Fax: 888-590-4082; Toll Free: 800-289-0963; Edit Addr.: Brunel House Forde Close, Newton Abbot, TQ12 4PU GBR Tel 01626 323200; Fax: 01626 323319; *Imprints:* North Light Books (North Lght Bks); Impact (Impct); Simon Pulse (SimonPulse)
E-mail: amber.ziegler@fwmedia.com; mark.griffin@fwmedia.com
Web site: http://www.artistsmagazine.com; http://www.artistsnetwork.com; http://www.davidandcharles.co.uk; http://www.krause.com; http://www.familytreemagazine.com; http://www.howdesign.com; http://www.idonline.com; http://www.memorymakersmagazine.com; http://www.popularwoodworking.com; http://www.writersdigest.com; http://www.writersmarket.com; http://www.writersonlineworkshops.com; http://www.fwpublications.com; http://www.fwmedia.co.uk
Dist(s): **Consortium Bk. Sales & Distribution**
Ebsco Publishing
Follett School Solutions
Leonard, Hal Corp.
MBI Distribution Services/Quayside Distribution
MyiLibrary
Simon & Schuster, Inc.
ebrary, Inc.

Fantagraphics Bks., *(978-0-930193; 978-1-56097; 978-1-60699; 978-1-68396)* 7563 Lake City Way, NE, Seattle, WA 98115 USA (SAN 251-5571) Tel 206-524-1967; Fax: 206-524-2104; Toll Free: 800-657-1100
E-mail: zura@fantagraphics.com; diva@eroscomix.com; fbicomix@fantagraphics.com
Web site: http://www.fantagraphics.com; http://eroscomix.com
Dist(s): **Diamond Comic Distributors, Inc.**
Diamond Bk. Distributors
Norton, W. W. & Co., Inc.

Fantasías Puertorriqueñas, *(978-0-9785676)* calle Mendez Vigo No. 275, Dorado, PR 00646 USA Tel 787-796-6154
E-mail: dreifrenrios@prtc.net.

Fantasy Flight Games, *(978-1-887911; 978-1-58994; 978-1-61661; 978-1-63344)* 1975 County Road B2 W. Ste. 1, Saint Paul, MN 55113-2725 USA
Web site: http://www.fantasyflightgames.com
Dist(s): **Diamond Comic Distributors, Inc.**
Diamond Bk. Distributors.

Fantasy Flight Publishing, Incorporated *See* **Fantasy Flight Games**

Fantasy Island Bk. Publishing, *(978-0-615-51504-5; 978-0-615-51588-5; 978-0-615-51700-1; 978-0-615-52006-3; 978-0-615-53089-5; 978-0-615-53298-1; 978-0-615-53335-3; 978-0-615-53343-8; 978-0-615-53573-9; 978-0-615-53921-8; 978-0-615-53931-7; 978-0-615-54265-2; 978-0-615-54266-9; 978-0-615-54356-7; 978-0-615-54612-4; 978-0-615-55011-4; 978-0-615-56148-6; 978-0-615-56200-1; 978-0-615-56208-7; 978-0-615-56231-5; 978-0-615-56302-2; 978-0-615-56762-4; 978-0-615-57170-6; 978-0-615-57732-6; 978-0-615-57819-4; 978-0-615-58605-2;) 1244 N. Linwood Ave., Indianapolis, IN 46201 USA Tel 317-966-9814*
Web site: htpp://www.fantasyislandbookpublishing.com; htpp://www.flbpub.com
Dist(s): **Lightning Source, Inc.**

Fantasy Island Pr., *(978-0-9766628)* 320 W. 7th St., Beach Heaven, NJ 08008 USA Tel 609-492-4000; Fax: 609-492-3512
E-mail: webmaster@fantasyislandpark.com
Web site: http://www.fantasyislandpark.com.

Fantasy Prone Comics, *(978-0-9762842; 978-0-615-32076-2; 978-0-615-36782-8; 978-0-615-39550-0)* 3625 Fredonia Dr., Suite 2, Hollywood, CA 90068 USA (SAN 631-8606) Tel 310-270-6612
E-mail: blakeleibel1@hotmail.com
Web site: http://www.fantasyprone.com
Dist(s): **Diamond Bk. Distributors.**

Far Out Fairy Tales *Imprint of* **Stone Arch Bks.**

Farah, Barbara, *(978-0-9769346)* P.O. Box 350, Center Harbor, NH 03226 USA Tel 603-253-7142
E-mail: bbfarah@yahoo.com.

Faraway Publishing, *(978-0-9710130)* Orders Addr.: P.O. Box 765, Highlands, NC 28741-0765 USA Fax: 828-526-5622
E-mail: faraway@nctv.com.

FarBeyond Publishing LLC, *(978-1-936872)* 8185 SW Birchwood Rd., Portland, OR 97225 USA (SAN 920-5276) Tel 503-683-3013
E-mail: publish@farbeyond.com
Web site: http://farbeyond.com
Dist(s): **CreateSpace Independent Publishing Platform**
Quality Bks., Inc.

Farcountry Pr., *(978-0-938314; 978-1-56037; 978-1-59152)* Orders Addr.: P.O. Box 5630, Helena, MT 59604 USA (SAN 220-0732) Tel 406-422-1263; Fax: 406-443-5480; Toll Free: 800-821-3874; 2750 Broadwater, Helena, MT 59602; *Imprints:* Sweetgrass Books (SweetgrassBks)
E-mail: books@farcountrypress.com
Web site: http://www.farcountrypress.com
Dist(s): **INscribe Digital**
Partners Bk. Distributing, Inc.
TNT Media Group, Inc.

Farmer's Daughter Pr., *(978-0-615-66088-2; 978-0-692-37657-7; 978-0-9979274)* P.O. Box 772, Hebron, CT 06248 USA Tel 860-384-3049
Dist(s): **CreateSpace Independent Publishing Platform.**

†Farrar, Straus & Giroux, (978-0-374) Div. of Holtzbrinck Publishers, Orders Addr.: c/o Holtzbrinck Publishers, 16365 James Madison Hwy., Gordonsville, VA 22942 USA Toll Free Fax: 800-672-2054; Toll Free: 888-330-8477; Edit Addr.: 18 W. 18th St., New York, NY

10011-4607 USA (SAN 206-782X); *Imprints:* Hill & Wang (Hil-Wang); Farrar, Straus & Giroux (BYR) (FSGBYR); Sunburst (SunbFSG)
E-mail: sales@fsgee.com; fsg.editorial@fsgee.com
Web site: http://www.fsgbooks.com/
Dist(s): **Continental Bk. Co., Inc.**
Lectorum Pubns., Inc.
Macmillan
MyiLibrary
Perfection Learning Corp.
SPD-Small Pr. Distribution; *CIP.*

Farrar, Straus & Giroux (BYR) *Imprint of* **Farrar, Straus & Giroux**

F.A.S.T. Learning LLC, *(978-1-59792)* 3447 S Birch St, Denver, CO 80222 USA Tel 720-537-7599
E-mail: becky@crsuccesslearning.com
Web site: http://www.fastlearningllc.com.

FastPrncil, Inc., *(978-1-60746; 978-1-61933; 978-1-63364; 978-1-4999; 978-1-68133)* 1608 W. Campbell Ave. Suite 239, Campbell, CA 95008 USA Tel 408-540-7571; Fax: 408-540-7572; *Imprints:* Premiere (PremierPenc)
E-mail: operations@fastpencil.com; author_services@fastpencil.com
Web site: http://www.fastpencil.com.

FastPublishing.com *See* **ExpandingBooks.com**

Fasttrack Teaching Materials, *(978-1-893742)* 6215 Lavell Court, Springfield, VA 22152 USA Tel 703-644-4612
E-mail: davburns@fasttrackteaching.com.

Father & Son Publishing, *(978-0-942407; 978-1-935802)* 4909 N. Monroe St., Tallahassee, FL 32303 USA (SAN 667-0229) Tel 850-562-3927; 850-562-0907; Fax: 850-562-0916; Toll Free: 800-741-2712 (orders only)
E-mail: lance@fatherson.com; jean@fatherson.com
Web site: http://www.fatherson.com
Dist(s): **Dot Gibson Distribution.**

Father's Hse. Publishing, *(978-0-9785308)* Orders Addr.: P.O. Box 161597, Miami, FL 33116 USA Fax: 305-235-0352
E-mail: mariadelatorre9@bellsouth.net.

Father's Pr., LLC, *(978-0-9779407; 978-0-9795394; 978-0-9824982; 978-0-9825321; 978-0-9833739)* 2424 SE 6th. St., Lee's Summit, MO 64063 USA Tel 816-600-6288 (phone/fax)
E-mail: fatherspress@yahoo.com
Web site: http://www.fatherspress.com.

Fauna Nirvana LLC, *(978-0-9982242)* 21015 Sylvanwood Ave., Lakewood, CA 90715 USA Tel 626-278-9845
E-mail: steverbarrett7@gmail.com
Web site: www.averyandmasa.com.

Faux Paw Media Group, *(978-0-9777340; 978-0-9779539; 978-0-9825387; 978-1-935824)* 178 Cliff Dr., Laguna Beach, CA 92651 USA (SAN 850-637X)
Web site: http://www.fauxpawproductions.com.

FAVA Pr., *(978-0-9801396)* 1401 Sherman St., Geneva, OH 44041 USA (SAN 855-3173).

Favonian Books *See* **Arts and Minds Studio Inc.**

Favorable Impressions, *(978-0-7808; 978-0-9674698; 978-1-931360)* Div. of Elm Park Pr., Orders Addr.: P.O. Box 69018, Pleasant Ridge, MI 48069 USA Tel 248-544-2421 (phone/fax); Toll Free: 866-246-2341; Edit Addr.: 9 Elm Park Blvd., Pleasant Ridge, MI 48069 USA
E-mail: danoptt@tir.com; danoepp@tir.com.

Favored Publishing, Inc., *(978-0-9791374)* P.O. Box 734, Jackson, MS 39205-0734 USA Tel 601-316-2193
E-mail: jriley_collins@yahoo.com.

Favorite Recipes Press *See* **Southwestern Publishing Group, Inc.**

Favorite Uncle Bks., LLC, *(978-0-9711665)* 23228 Lawrence, Dearborn, MI 48128 USA Tel 313-406-2040
E-mail: john@johntocco.com.

Favortwou Publishing, *(978-0-9774107; 978-0-9799006; 978-0-615-12362-2; 978-0-9823883)* 6339 Harbin Woods Dr., Morrow, GA 30260-1835 USA
E-mail: favortwou@hotmail.com
Web site: http://www.favortwov.net.

Faye Bks., *(978-0-615-16371-0; 978-0-615-16610-0; 978-0-615-16737-4; 978-0-578-02146-1)* 305 Halls Ln., Shepherdsville, KY 40165 USA; P.O. Box 387, Shepherdsville, KY 40165
Web site: http://www.fayebooks.zoomshare.com
Dist(s): **Lulu Pr., Inc.**

FayeHouse. Pr. International, *(978-0-9655222)* 1568 St. Margaret's Rd., Annapolis, MD 21401 USA Tel 443-822-9144; Fax: 410-349-9413 (Call before faxing)
E-mail: Charletfaye@aol.com.

FayRe Pr., *(978-0-9771301)* 513 Mount Evans Rd., Golden, CO 80401 USA (SAN 257-9340) Tel 303-526-7726 (phone/fax)
E-mail: theblueumbrella@earthlink.net.

FBC Pubns. & Printing, *(978-1-933594; 978-1-60208)* 3794 Oleander Ave., Fort Pierce, FL 34982 USA Tel 772-461-6460; Fax: 772-461-6474
E-mail: printing@fbcpublications.com
Web site: http://www.fbcpublications.com.

FBS Publishing Co., *(978-0-615-18629-0; 978-0-615-18633-7; 978-0-615-21316-3)* 5520 Grandview Ln., Doylestown, PA 18902 USA Tel 877-853-2267
Dist(s): **Publishers Services.**

F.C.E. Publishing, *(978-0-615-46463-3; 978-0-692-63419-6; 978-0-692-83736-8; 978-0-692-94214-7)* 1020 Amber Falls Ln., North Las Vegas, NV 89081 USA Tel 702-900-8434; Fax: 702-459-7805
E-mail: jazzwlv@gmail.com.

FEA Ministries, *(978-0-9618730; 978-0-9749168; 978-1-933716)* Orders Addr.: P.O. Box 1065, Hobe Sound, FL 33475 USA (SAN 668-6877) Tel 772-546-8426; Fax: 772-546-9379; Edit Addr.: 11305 SE Gomez Ave., Hobe Sound, FL 33455 USA
E-mail: orders@gospelpublishingmission.org
Web site: http://www.gospelpublishingmission.org.

Fear2love Pr., *(978-1-937861)* P.O. Box 1824, Point Roberts, WA 98281 USA Tel 814-409-8083
E-mail: lisa@fear2love.com.

FEARON *Imprint of* **Pearson Schl.**

Feather Insight Pr., *(978-0-9982769)* 6710 94th St. Ct NW, Gig Harbor, WA 98332-8455 USA Tel 906-361-1047
E-mail: alexandrafolz@gmail.com.

Feather River Publishing, *(978-0-615-16630-8)* 28 S. Garfield Ave., North Platte, NE 69101 USA Tel 308-532-4025
Dist(s): **Publishers Services.**

Feather Rock Bks., Inc., *(978-1-934066)* Orders Addr.: 4245 Chippewa Ln., Maple Plain, MN 55359 USA; Edit Addr.: P.O. Box 99, Maple Plain, MN 55359 USA (SAN 851-1829) Tel 952-473-9091
E-mail: jadams@featherrockbooks.com
Web site: http://www.featherrockbooks.com.

Featherproof Bks., *(978-0-9771992; 978-0-9825808; 978-0-9831863)* 2201 W. Crystal St., No. 3, Chicago, IL 60622 USA
E-mail: mail@featherproof.com
Web site: http://www.featherproof.com
Dist(s): **MyiLibrary**
Publishers Group West (PGW).

Federal Emergency Management Agency *Imprint of* **United States Government Printing Office**

Federal Street Pr., *(978-1-892859; 978-1-59695)* Div. of Merriam Webster, Inc., P.O. Box 281, Springfield, MA 01102 USA (SAN 859-4678) Fax: 413-731-5979; 47 Federal St., Springfield, MA 01105
E-mail: info@federalstreetpress.com; lbrodeur@m-w.com
Web site: http://www.federalstreetpress.com.

Federation Pr. (AUS) *(978-1-86287; 978-1-876067; 978-0-646-17924-7; 978-1-76002) Dist. by* **Gaunt.**

Feed My Sheep, *(978-0-9768958)* P.O. Box 16438, Rural Hall, NC 27045 USA Do not confuse with Feed My Sheep in Brunswick, GA, Detroit, MI.

Feed My Sheep Bks., *(978-0-9769152)* P.O. Box 05340, Detroit, MI 48205 USA Do not confuse with companies with the same name in Rural Hall, NC, Brunswick, GA.

Feeley, Lisa & Craig, *(978-0-9743159)* 19229 Lupine Ct., Noblesville, IN 46060 USA.

Fegley, Elizabeth *See* **Healing Hands Pr.**

Feil, *(978-0-9741588)* 15 Fox Meadow Ln., Merrimack, NH 03054 USA
Web site: http://www.theservingart.com/creativewriting.

Fein, Bruce, *(978-0-9745049)* 5400 Lochmor Ave., Las Vegas, NV 89130 USA
Web site: http://www.oxymoronbooks.com.

Feiwel & Friends, *(978-0-312)* 175 Fifth Ave., New York, NY 10010 USA Tel 646-307-5151
Web site: http://www.holtzbrinckus.com
Dist(s): **Macmillan**
Perfection Learning Corp.

Feldheim, Philipp Incorporated *See* **Feldheim Pubs.**

†**Feldheim Pubs.**, *(978-0-87306; 978-1-58330; 978-1-59826; 978-1-68025)* 208 Airport Executive Park., Nanuet, NY 10954-5262 USA (SAN 106-6307) Toll Free: 800-237-7149
E-mail: sales@feldheim.com; eli@feldheim.com
Web site: http://www.feldheim.com
Dist(s): **David, Jonathan Pubs., Inc.**
Libros Sin Fronteras; *CIP.*

Feldick, Les Ministries, *(978-1-885344)* 30706 W. Lona Valley Rd., Kinta, OK 74552 USA Tel 918-768-3218; Fax: 918-768-3219; Toll Free: 800-369-7856
Web site: http://www.lesfeldick.org.

Feldman, Enrique C, *(978-0-9974877)* 4927 N. Sabino Gulch Ct., Tucson, AZ 85750 USA Tel 520-861-3001
E-mail: enriquehankfeldman@gmail.com
Web site: www.globallearning.foundation.

Felix Comics, Inc., *(978-0-615-12660-9)* 123 Rt. 23 S., Hamburg, NJ 07419 USA Toll Free: 800-343-3549 (800-34-FELIX)
Web site: http://www.felixthecat.com.

Fell Pr., The, *(978-0-9759430)* 8926 N. Greenwood, No. 289, Niles, IL 60714 USA
Web site: http://www.thefellpress.com
Dist(s): **SCB Distributors.**

Fellowship Pr., *(978-0-914390; 978-1-943388)* 5820 Overbrook Ave., Philadelphia, PA 19131 USA (SAN 201-6117) Tel 215-879-8929; Fax: 215-879-6307; Toll Free: 888-786-1786
E-mail: info@bmf.org
Web site: http://www.bmf.org
Dist(s): **Ilmhouse Inc.**
New Leaf Distributing Co., Inc.
Omega Pubns., Inc.

Felony & Mayhem, LLC, *(978-1-933397; 978-1-934609; 978-1-937384; 978-1-63194)* 156 Waverly Pl., New York, NY 10014 USA Tel 212-731-2440; Fax: 212-656-1227
E-mail: jmusha@felonyandmayhem.com
Web site: http://www.felonyandmayhem.com
Dist(s): **MyiLibrary**
National Bk. Network.

Felsen Ink, *(978-1-62272)* 1599 NW 101st St., Clive, IA 50325 USA Tel 515-226-9372
E-mail: holly.welch@gmail.com
Web site: www.felsenink.com.

†**Feminist Pr. at The City Univ. of New York**, *(978-0-912670; 978-0-935312; 978-1-55861; 978-1-936932)* 365 Fifth Ave., New York, NY 10016 USA (SAN 213-6813) Tel 212-817-7915; Fax: 212-817-2988
E-mail: lglazer@gc.cuny.edu; info@feministpress.org
Web site: http://www.feministpress.org
Dist(s): **Consortium Bk. Sales & Distribution**
Continental Bk. Co., Inc.
CreateSpace Independent Publishing Platform
MyiLibrary
SPD-Small Pr. Distribution
Women Ink; *CIP.*

Fence Bks. *Imprint of* **Fence Magazine, Inc.**

Fence Magazine, Inc., *(978-0-9663324; 978-0-9713189; 978-0-9740909; 978-0-9771064; 978-1-934200; 978-0-9864373; 978-1-944380)* Div. of Fence Bks., New Library 320 Univ. At Albany 1400 Washington Ave., Albany, NY 12222 USA Tel 518-591-8162 (phone/fax); *Imprints:* Fence Books (Fence Bks)
E-mail: fence@albany.edu
Web site: http://www.fencemag.com; http://www.fencebooks.com
Dist(s): **DeBoer, Bernhard Inc.**
Consortium Bk. Sales & Distribution
SPD-Small Pr. Distribution
Univ. Pr. of New England.

Fencepost Communications Inc., *(978-0-9776487)* Orders Addr.: P.O. Box Fencepost Communications, Inc., P O Box 398, Hinsdale, IL 60522-0398 USA Tel 630-850-9755; Toll Free: 888-648-0008; Edit Addr.: 49 1/2 S. Washington St., Hinsdale, IL 60521 USA.

Feng Liu Productions, *(978-0-9727089)* P.O. Box 248, Mill Valley, CA 94942 USA
Dist(s): **Independent Pubs. Group.**

Fen's Rim, *(978-0-9713603)* Orders Addr.: P.O. Box 885, Elk Rapids, MI 49629 USA Tel 231-264-6800; Edit Addr.: 104 Dexter St., Elk Rapids, MI 49629 USA
E-mail: mail@fensrim.com
Web site: http://www.fensrim.com.

Fenton Publishing Company *See* **Octopus Publishing Co.**

Fenwyn Pr., *(978-0-913062)* Orders Addr.: P.O. Box 245, Rapid City, SD 57709 USA Tel 605-343-6070; Fax: 605-348-2108; Toll Free: 800-821-6343; Edit Addr.: 3635 Homestead St., Rapid City, SD 57703 USA.

Feral Hse., *(978-0-922915; 978-1-932595; 978-1-936239; 978-1-62731)* 1240 W. Sims Way, No. 124, Port Townsend, WA 98368 USA (SAN 251-5423) Tel 323-666-3311; Fax: 323-297-4331
E-mail: info@feralhouse.com
Web site: http://www.feralhouse.com
Dist(s): **Consortium Bk. Sales & Distribution**
MyiLibrary
ebrary, Inc.

Feral Pr., Inc., *(978-0-9649349; 978-1-930094)* 304 Strawberry Field Rd., Flat Rock, NC 28731 USA Tel 828-694-0438; Fax: 828-694-0438; *Imprints:* Rivet Books (Rivet Bks)
E-mail: gchet@feralpressinc.com
Web site: http://www.feralpressinc.com.

Fergus & Lady Publishing, *(978-0-9786975)* 2310 Del Mar Rd., No. 10, Montrose, CA 91020 USA.

Ferguson, Linda, *(978-0-9755288)* 383 Alewine Dr., Boaz, AL 35957-5034 USA
E-mail: lkinspire@yahoo.com
Web site: http://www.l-n-kinspirationalbooks.com/.

Ferguson Publishing Co. *Imprint of* **Facts On File, Inc.**

Ferguson, Suzanie Pamela, *(978-0-9658745)* 4609 Maplewood Dr., Suffolk, VA 23435 USA Tel 757-483-5721
E-mail: lferg72184@aol.com.

Fern Creek Pr., *(978-0-9625737; 978-1-893651)* P.O. Box 1322, Clayton, GA 30525 USA Tel 706-782-5379; Fax: 706-782-5379
E-mail: brian@ferncreekpress.com
Web site: http://rabun.net/boyd.

Fern Creek Publishing *See* **Fern Creek Pr.**

Fern Rock Falls Pr., *(978-0-9762409)* 22105 Fisk Rd., Noti, OR 97461-9718 USA Tel 541-935-3920
E-mail: dandq@rio.com.

Fernandez USA Publishing, 203 Argonne Ave., Suite B, PMB 151, Long Beach, CA 90803-1777 USA Tel 562-901-2370; Fax: 562-901-2372; Toll Free: 800-814-8080
Web site: http://www.fernandezusa.com
Dist(s): **Continental Bk. Co., Inc.**

Ferne Pr. *Imprint of* **Nelson Publishing & Marketing**

Fernhouse Pr., *(978-0-9759363)* P.O. Box 73, Woodstock, VT 05067 USA
Web site: http://www.fernhouse.com.

Fernhurst Bks. (GBR) *(978-0-906754; 978-1-898660; 978-1-904475; 978-1-909911) Dist. by* **Casemate Pubs.**

Fernwood & Hedges Bks., *(978-0-615-72092-0; 978-0-9890698; 978-0-615-80386-9; 978-0-615-81583-1)* 7612 Fountain Ave., West Hollywood, CA 90046 USA Tel 213-910-2887
Dist(s): **CreateSpace Independent Publishing Platform.**

ferrocement.com, *(978-0-9748016)* P.O. Box 31 S. St., Bernardston, MA 01337-0133 USA Fax: 413-648-9098
E-mail: garrett@ferrocement.com.

Fertig, Howard Incorporated *See* **Fertig, Howard Publisher**

†**Fertig, Howard Publisher**, *(978-0-86527)* Orders Addr.: 80 E. 11th St., New York, NY 10003 USA (SAN 201-4777) Tel 212-982-7922; Fax: 212-982-1099
E-mail: orders@hfertigbooks.com
Web site: http://www.hfertigbooks.com; *CIP.*

Fetch! Publishing, *(978-0-9746324)* 27881 La Paz Rd., Suite G-124, Laguna Niguel, CA 92677 USA Fax: 877-426-3809; Toll Free Fax: 877-426-3809; Toll Free: 877-899-9454
Web site: http://fetchpublishing.com.

Fey, Sid Designs, Inc., *(978-0-9753530)* Box 184, 335 E. Geneva Rd., Carol Stream, IL 60188 USA Tel 630-668-6607; Fax: 630-668-6282
E-mail: zpdduda@earthlink.net
Web site: http://www.thebeinggame.com.

Fickling, David Bks. (GBR) *(978-1-910200; 978-1-910989) Dist. by* **Peng Rand Hse.**

Fiction Focus *See* **Story Direction**

Fiction Picture Bks. *Imprint of* **Picture Window Bks.**

Fiction Publishing, Inc., *(978-0-9796752; 978-0-9814956; 978-0-9819727; 978-0-9825086; 978-0-9826168; 978-0-9827442; 978-0-9830007; 978-0-9837803)* 5626 Travelers Way, Fort Pierce, FL 34982 USA Tel 772-489-5811
E-mail: fictionpub@bellsouth.net
Web site: http://www.fictionpublishinginc.com.

Fiction Works, The, *(978-1-58124)* Orders Addr.: 3328 SW Cascade Ave., Corvallis, OR 97333 USA Tel 541-730-2044; Fax: 541-738-2648
E-mail: fictionworks@me.com
Web site: http://www.fictionworks.com
Dist(s): **Brodart Co.**
Untreed Reads Publishing, LLC.

FictionSpin, *(978-0-9724007; 978-0-9817897)* P.O. Box 885, Pacific Palisades, CA 90272 USA (SAN 255-0431) Tel 310-456-0677
E-mail: ASCBooks@aol.com; FictionSpin@aol.com
Web site: http://ASCBooks@aol.com; http://www.fictionspin.com.

Fiddlehead Pr., *(978-0-615-88594-0; 978-0-615-90572-3; 978-0-692-02414-0; 978-1-68013)* 2129 Bethel St. NE, Olympia, WA 98506 USA Tel 360-357-7800
Dist(s): **CreateSpace Independent Publishing Platform.**

Fideli Publishing, Inc., *(978-1-60414)* 119 W. Morgan St., Martinsville, IN 46151 USA (SAN 854-0772) Toll Free: 888-343-3542
E-mail: info@fidelipublishing.com
Web site: http://www.fidelipublishing.com
Dist(s): **BookBaby**
MyiLibrary
Smashwords.

Fidelity Heart Publishing, *(978-0-9748522)* Orders Addr.: P.O. Box 1758, Houston, TX 77251 USA; Edit Addr.: 3923 Teal Run Pl., Ct, Fresno, TX 77545-7049 USA
E-mail: slmccraw@fidelityheart.com
Web site: http://www.fidelityheart.com.

Field Mouse Productions, *(978-0-9647586; 978-0-9888021)* Div. of Associated Design Services, Inc., Orders Addr.: P.O. Box 392, Grand Island, NE 68802 USA Tel 308-380-3315; 308-380-3215; Edit Addr.: 454 8th Ave., Palmer, NE 68864 USA
E-mail: skidi@aol.com; rtstron@aol.com; JeanLukesh@aol.com
Web site: http://www.fieldmousebooks.com; http://www.fieldmouseproductions.com
Dist(s): **Lightning Source, Inc.**

Field Stone Pubs., *(978-0-9645272)* 331 Fields Hill Rd., Conway, MA 01341 USA Tel 413-369-4091
E-mail: author@johnrdixonbooks.com
Web site: http://www.JohnRDixonBooks.com.

Fielder Group, *(978-0-9639986; 978-0-9789058)* Orders Addr.: P.O. Box 510, Benton, KY 42025 USA Tel 888-255-9248; Fax: 270-362-7130; Toll Free: 888-255-9248
E-mail: barbara@thefieldergroupusa.com
Web site: http://www.thefieldergroupusa.com.

Fielder, John Publishing, *(978-0-9832769; 978-0-9860004; 978-0-9914990; 978-0-9985080)* P.O. Box 26890, Silverthorne, CO 80497 USA Tel 303-907-2179
E-mail: john@johnfielder.com.

Fieldhouse LLC, *(978-0-9768353)* P.O. Box 541, Lawrence, KS 66044 USA
Dist(s): **Midpoint Trade Bks., Inc.**

Fields Communications & Publishing *See* **Fields Publishing, Inc.**

Fields of Gold Publishing, Inc., *(978-0-9746296; 978-0-9848034; 978-1-940894)* P.O. Box 128438, Nashville, TN 37212-3304 USA Tel 615-335-2014; 615-567-3371; *Imprints:* Fog Ink (FogInk)
E-mail: tneftzger@comcast.net; amy@fogink.com
Web site: http://www.fogink.com
Dist(s): **Brodart Co.**
Lightning Source, Inc.

Fields Publishing, Inc., *(978-1-57843)* 8120 Sawyer Brown Rd. Ste. 108, Nashville, TN 37221-1410 USA
E-mail: Fieldsco@mindspring.com
Web site: http://www.fieldspublishing.com.

Fieldstone Hill Pr., *(978-0-9767762)* 321 Old Saluda Dam Rd., Easley, SC 29640 USA
Web site: http://www.fieldstone-hill.net.

Fiery Studios, *(978-0-9743110)* P.O. Box 51595, Kalamazoo, MI 49005-1595 USA
Web site: http://www.vogelein.com
Dist(s): **Diamond Comic Distributors, Inc.**
Diamond Bk. Distributors.

Fifth Ave Pr., *(978-0-9755390)* 413 Salt Pond Rd., Bethany Beach, DE 19930 USA Tel 302-537-9633; Fax: 302-537-0210; Toll Free: 800-862-6443 Do not confuse with Fifth Avenue Press in Fargo, ND and New York, NY.
E-mail: bethanybil@aol.com
Web site: http://www.e-studio8.com/fifthstreetpress.

Fifth Paw Pr., *(978-0-9816188)* 40 Adelphi St., No. 3, Brooklyn, NY 11205 USA Tel 718-288-6141
E-mail: demo-dog@earthlink.net; fifthpawpress@earthlink.net
Web site: http://www.fifthpawpress.com
Dist(s): **Ebsco Publishing**
Independent Pubs. Group.

Fig & The Vine, LLC, The, *(978-0-9841087; 978-0-615-49661-0; 978-0-615-62717-5; 978-0-9883370; 978-0-692-48233-9)* Orders Addr.: 753 Winthrop St., Mount Pleasant, SC 29464-2946 USA Fax: 843-881-8425; Toll Free Fax: 843-881-8425
E-mail: figandvine@mail.com; carolinahomeandgarden@mail.com; publisher@thefigandthevine.com
Web site: http://thefigandthevine.com.

Fighting Words Publishing, *(978-0-9755279)* P.O. Box 7, Highwood, IL 60040 USA Tel 847-266-1965; Fax: 847-266-0840
E-mail: magmem@aol.com; rmk@robertmkatzmanwriter.com
Web site: http://www.fightingwordsbook.com; http://www.robertmkatzmanwriter.com.

Figment, *(978-0-9837232)* 118 E. 64th St., New York, NY 10065 USA Tel 212-893-8790
E-mail: jlewis@figment.com
Web site: http://www.figment.com
Dist(s): **MyiLibrary.**

Figure 8 Pr., (*978-0-9630376*) Orders Addr.: P.O. Box 248, Rolling Ground, WI 54631 USA
E-mail: figure8press@gmail.com
Web site: http://figure8press.com.

Figures In Motion, (*978-0-9818566; 978-1-944481*) 2150 Cabernet Way, Livermore, CA 94550 USA (SAN 856-7336) Tel 925-583-5670; 510-482-8500; Fax: 925-583-5670
E-mail: cathy@figuresinmotion.com; info@figuresinmotion.com
Web site: http://www.figuresinmotion.com.

Filaretos, William, (*978-0-9724520*) 220 W. Canton St. # 3, Boston, MA 02116-5814 USA
E-mail: william_filaretos@thepotionoftime.com
Web site: http://www.ThePotionofTime.com.

Filion, Rita-Anneliese, (*978-0-9749142*) 26 Elizabeth Ln., Saratoga Springs, NY 12866-2804 USA
E-mail: sirdino@noblebones.com
Web site: http://www.noblebones.com.

Filiquarian Publishing, LLC, (*978-0-9770505; 978-1-59986*) Orders Addr.: 110 W. Grant St. Unit 2c, Minneapolis, MN 55403 USA Tel 612-207-2335; *Imprints:* FQ Classics (FQ Classics).

Fillet Of Horn Publishing, (*978-0-9753077*) 35000 Muskrat Rd., Barnesville, OH 43713 USA Tel 740-758-5050; Fax: 740-758-5114
Web site: http://www.filletofhorn.com
Dist(s): **Bookmasters Distribution**
ebrary, Inc.

Film Ideas, Inc., (*978-1-57557; 978-1-60572*) 308 N. Wolf Rd., Wheeling, IL 60090 USA Tel 847-419-0255; Fax: 847-419-8933; Toll Free: 800-475-3456
E-mail: info@filmideas.com
Web site: http://www.filmideas.com
Dist(s): **Follett School Solutions.**

Filsinger & Co., Ltd., (*978-0-916754*) 288 W. 12th St., New York, NY 10014 USA (SAN 208-3574) Tel 212-243-7421.

Filter Pr., LLC, (*978-0-86541; 978-0-910584*) P.O. Box 95, Palmer Lake, CO 80133 USA (SAN 201-484X) Tel 719-481-2420 (phone/fax); Toll Free: 888-570-2663
E-mail: info@filterpressbooks.com; doris@filterpressbooks.com
Web site: http://www.filterpressbooks.com.

Financial Safari Pr., (*978-0-9777993*) 1135 Kildaire Farm Rd., Suite 200, Cary, NC 27512 USA Tel 919-657-4201
E-mail: capitaltax@gmail.com.

Finch Bks. Co., (*978-0-9661457*) Orders Addr.: P.O. Box 545, Tularosa, NM 88352 USA; Edit Addr.: 1418 Apple Ave., Tularosa, NM 88352 USA Tel 505-585-8037; Fax: 505-585-8039
Dist(s): **MBI Distribution Services/Quayside Distribution.**

Find Your Way Publishing, Inc., (*978-0-9824692; 978-0-9849322; 978-1-945290*) P.O. Box 667, Norway, ME 04268 USA
E-mail: melissa@findyourwaypublishing.com
Web site: http://www.findyourwaypublishing.com.

Findaway World, LLC, (*978-1-59895; 978-1-60252; 978-1-60514; 978-1-60640; 978-1-60775; 978-1-60812; 978-1-60847; 978-1-61545; 978-1-61574; 978-1-61587; 978-1-61637; 978-1-61657; 978-1-61707; 978-1-4676; 978-1-5094*) 31999 Aurora Rd., Solon, OH 44139 USA (SAN 853-8778)
Web site: http://www.findawayworld.com; http://www.playawaydigital.com
Dist(s): **Follett School Solutions**
MyiLibrary.

Finding the Cause, LLC, 39738 Calle Azucar, Murrieta, CA 92562 USA Tel 760-724-8104
E-mail: Dr.king@findingthecause.com
Web site: Www.FindingTheCause.com.

Fine Art Editions *Imprint of* **North American International**

Fine Print Pr., The, (*978-0-9644365; 978-1-888960*) 350 Ward Ave., Suite 106, Honolulu, HI 96814-4091 USA Fax: 425-955-1909
E-mail: info@fineprintpress.com
Web site: http://www.fineprintpress.com
Dist(s): **Midpoint Trade Bks., Inc.**
Partners Pubs. Group, Inc.

Fine Print Publishing Co., (*978-0-9640713; 978-1-892951*) Orders Addr.: P.O. Box 916401, Longwood, FL 32791-6401 USA Tel 407-814-7777; Fax: 407-814-7677; Edit Addr.: 1350 Sheeler Rd., Apopka, FL 32703 USA
E-mail: books@fprint.net.

Finer Moments, (*978-0-9771549*) P.O. Box 22102, Robbinsdale, MN 55422 USA Tel 612-302-7830
E-mail: finermoments@earthlink.net
Web site: http://www.finermoments.net.

Finest Bks., (*978-1-935679*) 959 W. Jericho Tpke., Smithtown, NY 11787 USA Tel 615-479-0877; Fax: 631-864-1565
E-mail: michaelsheahan@msn.com
Web site: http://www.finestbks.com.

Fingerprint Bks., (*978-0-9709861*) P.O. Box 534, Redlands, CA 92373 USA (SAN 253-7923) Tel 909-307-9993 (phone/fax)
E-mail: mglis2t@earthlink.net.

Finial Publishing, (*978-1-933791*) P.O. Box 346, Mercer Island, WA 98040 USA
Web site: http://www.finialpublishing.com.

Finkelstein, Ruth, (*978-0-9628157*) 27 Saddle River Rd., Airmont, NY 10952-3034 USA.

Finlay Prints, Inc., (*978-0-9766998*) Orders Addr.: 74 Fifth Ave., 6D, New York, NY 10011 USA Tel 212-463-7173
E-mail: finlayprints@earthlink.net.

Finley Flowers *Imprint of* **Picture Window Bks.**

Finneran, Lisa, (*978-0-9777744*) 9709 River Rd., Newport News, VA 23601-2360 USA
E-mail: arkangels@cox.net.

Finney Co., Inc., (*978-0-89317; 978-0-912486; 978-0-933855; 978-0-9617767; 978-0-9639705; 978-1-880654; 978-1-893272*) Orders Addr.: 8075 215th St. W., Lakeville, MN 55044 USA (SAN 206-412X) Tel 952-469-6699; Fax: 952-469-1968; Toll Free Fax: 800-330-6232; Toll Free: 800-846-7027; *Imprints:* Windward Publishing (Windward Publng); Lone Oak Press, Limited (LoneOak)
E-mail: feedback@finneyco.com
Web site: http://www.finneyco.com; http://www.ecopress.com; http://www.pogopress.com; http://www.astragalpress.com
Dist(s): **Book Wholesalers, Inc.**
Brodart Co.
Follett School Solutions
Southern Bk. Service.

Fiore, (*978-0-9661235*) Orders Addr.: P.O. Box 50663, Phoenix, AZ 85076 USA Tel 602-759-0048; Toll Free: 888-443-4677; Edit Addr.: 4030 E. Lavender Ln., Phoenix, AZ 85044 USA.

Fire Flies Entertainment, LLC, (*978-0-9787302*) 1077 North Ave., Suite 114, Elizabeth, NJ 07208 USA Tel 212-561-1654; Fax: 908-351-1888
Dist(s): **INscribe Digital.**

Fire Mountain Pr., (*978-1-929374*) Orders Addr.: P.O. Box 3851, Hillsboro, OR 97123 USA Tel 503-846-9057 (phone/fax); 503-219-5643 (phone/fax)
Web site: http://www.firemountainpress.com.

Firebird *Imprint of* **Penguin Young Readers Group**

Firebreak Publishing Co., (*978-0-9761448*) Orders Addr.: P.O. Box 995, Pacific Palisades, CA 90272-0995 USA Tel 310-454-3105
E-mail: r.brodie@verizon.net
Web site: http://www.firebreakpublishing.com.

Firebug Fairy Tales, (*978-0-615-58954-1; 978-0-615-58955-8*) P.O. Box 680396, Charlotte, NC 28216 USA Tel 704-398-9923
E-mail: ejkisinger@yahoo.com.

Firefall *See* **Firefall Editions**

Firefall Editions, (*978-0-915090; 978-1-939434*) Div. of Firefallmedia, 4905 Tunlaw St., Alexandria, VA 22312 USA Tel 510-549-2461; *Imprints:* California Street (Calif St)
E-mail: firefallmedia@att.net; literary@att.net
Web site: http://www.firefallmedia.com; http://www.firefallfilms.com; http://www.blotbooks.com; http://www.lostshoerecords.com; http://www.sim-book.com; http://www.lovinglicks.com; http://www.blue-loves.com; http://www.metech.us; http://www.shift-alt-delete.com; http://www.spacespa.net; http://www.1across.com; http://mz.firefallmedia.com; http://www.scifun.us
Dist(s): **Audible.com**
Brodart Co.
Follett School Solutions.

Firefly Bks., Ltd., (*978-0-920668; 978-1-55209; 978-1-895565; 978-1-896284; 978-1-55297; 978-1-55407*) Orders Addr.: c/o Frontier Distributing, 1000 Young St., Suite 160, Tonawanda, NY 14150 USA (SAN 630-611X) Tel 203-222-9700; Toll Free Fax: 800-565-6034; Toll Free: 800-387-5085; Edit Addr.: 8514 Long Canyon Dr., Austin, TX 78730-2813 USA
E-mail: service@fireflybooks.com
Web site: http://www.fireflybooks.com/
Dist(s): **Lectorum Pubns., Inc.**

Firefly Games, (*978-0-9747671*) 7525 Garden Gate Dr., Citrus Hts, CA 95621-1909 USA
E-mail: patrick@firefly-games.com
Web site: http://www.firefly-games.com.

FireFly Lights, (*978-0-9856863*) 1403 Delano St. No. 7, Houston, TX 77003 USA Tel 281-536-3915
E-mail: lacycarneywrites@gmail.com.

FireFly Publishings & Entertainment *See* **FireFly Publishings & Entertainment LLC**

FireFly Publishings & Entertainment LLC, (*978-0-9774126; 978-0-9846428*) Orders Addr.: P.O. Box 1346, Snellville, GA 30078 USA; Edit Addr.: 845 Common Oak Pl., Lawrenceville, GA 30045 USA (SAN 257-6597)
E-mail: fireflypublishingent@yahoo.com; dorced58@yahoo.com
Web site: http://www.fireflypublishingent.com
Dist(s): **Follett School Solutions.**

Fireglass Publishing, (*978-0-9857523*) P.O. Box 98370, Poulsbo, WA 98370 USA
E-mail: info@fireglasspublishing.com.

FireHydrant Creative Studios, Inc., (*978-0-9826066; 978-1-937176*) 52 Huntleigh Woods, Saint Louis, MO 63132 USA Tel 314-822-0833
E-mail: administrator@FireHydrantCS.com
Web site: http://www.FireHydrantCS.com.

Firelight Press, Inc., (*978-0-9786555; 978-1-934517*) 550 Larchmont Dr., Cincinnati, OH 45215 USA (SAN 851-2353); P.O. Box 15758, Cincinnati, OH 45215 Tel 513-646-6803; Fax: 513-821-2830 Do not confuse with companies with the same name in Independence, MO, Solvang, CA
E-mail: books@firelightpress.com
Web site: http://firelightpress.com.

Firelight Publishing, Inc., (*978-0-9707206*) Orders Addr.: P.O. Box 444, Sublimity, OR 97385-0444 USA Toll Free: 866-347-3544; Edit Addr.: 226 Division St., SW, Sublimity, OR 97385-9637 USA Tel 503-767-0444; Fax: 503-769-8980; Toll Free: 866-347-3544
E-mail: info@firelightpublishing.com; editor@firelightpublishing.com; webmaster@firelightpublishing.com; orders@firelightpublishing.com
Web site: http://www.firelightpublishing.com
Dist(s): **Partners/West Book Distributors.**

Firenze Pr., (*978-0-9711236*) Orders Addr.: P.O. Box 6892, Wyomissing, PA 19610-0892 USA (SAN 254-315X); Edit Addr.: 612 Museum Rd., Reading, PA 19610-0892 USA Tel 610-374-7048; Fax: 610-478-7992 Do not confuse with Leonardo Pr., Camden, ME
E-mail: hailejohnjr@msn.com; HaileJohnJr@msn.com; InkPenCJH@msn.com
Web site: http://caroljhaile.com.

Fireproof Ministries, (*978-0-9741849*) P.O. Box 150169, Grand Rapids, MI 49515 USA
E-mail: info@fireproofministries.com
Web site: http://www.fireproofministries.com.

Fireship Pr., (*978-1-934757; 978-1-935585; 978-1-61179*) P.O. Box 68412, Tucson, AZ 85737 USA Tel 520-360-6228
E-mail: tmg@en.com
Web site: http://www.FireshipPress.com.

Fireside Catholic Bibles, (*978-1-55665*) Div. of Fireside Catholic Bibles, Orders Addr.: P.O. Box 780189, Wichita, KS 67278-0189 USA Tel 316-267-3211; Fax: 316-267-1850; Toll Free: 888-676-2040; Edit Addr.: 9020 E. 35th St., N., Wichita, KS 67226 USA (SAN 854-0780)
E-mail: info@firesidebibles.com; llear@devore.cc
Web site: http://www.firesidebibles.com
Dist(s): **Spring Arbor Distributors, Inc.**

Fireside Critters, (*978-0-9753248*) Orders Addr.: P.O. Box 283, Vermilion, OH 44089 USA; Edit Addr.: P.O. Box 283, Vermillion, OH 44089 USA
E-mail: FiresideCritters@AOL.com.

Fireside Pr., Inc., (*978-1-930754; 978-0-9779863; 978-0-9800067; 978-0-9818486; 978-1-935451; 978-0-9825292; 978-1-935764*) 10000 N. Central Exp, Suite 400, Dallas, TX 75231 USA
E-mail: info@durbanhouse.com; john7@durbanhouse.com
Web site: http://www.durbanhouse.com
Dist(s): **BookMasters**
MyiLibrary
National Bk. Network
ebrary, Inc.

Firesidenook, (*978-0-9887214*) 10072 Forestedge Ln, Miamisburg, OH 45342 USA Tel 937-776-0019
E-mail: strangedad1@yahoo.com.

Firestorm Editions, (*978-0-9855541*) 14314 Rockdale Rd., Clear Spring, MD 21722 USA Tel 815-642-0700
E-mail: cashives@gmail.com.

Fireweed Pr., (*978-1-878660*) Orders Addr.: P.O. Box 482, Madison, WI 53701-0482 USA; Edit Addr.: 638 Gately Terr., Madison, WI 53711 USA Tel 608-233-0300 Do not confuse with companies with same name in Falls Church, VA, Fairbanks, AK, Evergreen, CO Seattle, WA
E-mail: tmccormi@wisc.edu.

Fireweed Pr., (*978-0-9772528*) Orders Addr.: P.O. Box 31037, Seattle, WA 98103 USA; Edit Addr.: 1807 N. 36th St., Seattle, WA 98103 USA Do not confuse with Fireweed Press in Falls Church, VA Fairbanks, AK, Madison, WI, Evergreen, CO AJ
E-mail: fireweedpress@comcast.net.

First Assist Pubns., (*978-0-9724865*) P.O. Box 608, Woodland Hills, CA 91365 USA Fax: 818-346-8988
E-mail: e21sherr@aol.com.

First Associates Publishing, (*978-0-9618835*) P.O. Box 1281, Richmond, VA 23218-1281 USA (SAN 242-5289) Tel 804-254-0662; Fax: 804-524-5138; Toll Free: 877-247-8343
E-mail: earl@fapbooks.com.

First Avenue Editions *Imprint of* **Lerner Publishing Group**

First Biographies *Imprint of* **Reynolds, Morgan Inc.**

First Bks., (*978-0-912301; 978-0-9823476; 978-1-61007; 978-1-937090*) 6750 SW Franklin St., Suite A, Portland, OR 97223 USA (SAN 297-9063) Tel 503-968-6777; Fax: 503-968-6779
E-mail: customerservice@firstbooks.com
Web site: http://www.firstbooks.com
Dist(s): **Bookazine Co., Inc.**
Partners Bk. Distributing, Inc.

First Century Publishing, (*978-1-885273*) Div. of First Century Church Ministries, P.O. Box 130, Delmar, NY 12054 USA Tel 518-439-3544; Fax: 518-439-0105; Toll Free: 800-570-6060
E-mail: dnbubar1@nycap.rr.com; 1century@nycap.rr.com
Web site: http://www.firstcenturypublishing.com
Dist(s): **Send The Light Distribution LLC.**

First Choice Entertainment *See* **Papilion Pr.**

First Christmas Project, (*978-0-9769828*) 333 Brooks Bend, Brownsburg, IN 46112 USA
Web site: http://www.firstchristmaspresent.com
Dist(s): **Send The Light Distribution LLC.**

First Class Fitness Systems, Inc., (*978-0-9747008*) 23901 Civic Ctr. Way, Suite 342, Malibu, CA 90265 USA Tel 310-456-3043
E-mail: Mario@myfitfamily.com
Web site: http://myfitfamily.com.

First Edition Design eBook Publishing, (*978-0-9837342; 978-1-937520; 978-1-62287; 978-1-5069*) 5202 Old Ashwood Dr., Sarasota, FL 34233 USA (SAN 860-2719) Tel 941-921-2607; Fax: 617-249-1694; P.O. Box 20217, Sarasota, FL 34276 Tel 941-921-2607; Fax: 941-866-7510
E-mail: dgordon@firsteditiondesign.com
Web site: http://www.firsteditiondesignpublishing.com.

First Facts *Imprint of* **Capstone Press of Coughlan Cos.**

First Flight Bks., (*978-0-9763675; 978-0-9836035; 978-0-9860666; 978-0-9974973*) Div. of The Copy Workshop, 2144 N. Hudson, RB, Chicago, IL 60614 USA Tel 773-871-1179; Fax: 773-281-4643
E-mail: firstflightbooks@aol.com
Web site: http://www.firstflightbooks.com.

First Light Publishing, (*978-0-9754411; 978-0-692-51651-5; 978-0-692-51652-2*) 14402 Twickenham Pl., Chesterfield, VA 23832 USA Do not confuse with First Light Publishing in Chagrin Falls, OH
E-mail: briantherock@cs.com
Dist(s): **Parklane Publishing.**

First Mom's Club, The, (*978-0-9704876; 978-0-9728180; 978-0-9764557; 978-1-935822*) 367 Eric Way, Grants Pass, OR 97526-8820 USA
E-mail: dianne@thefirstmomsclub.com
Web site: http://www.thefirstmomsclub.com
Dist(s): **Alliance Bk. Co.**

First Person Publishing *See* **Concinnity Initiatives**

First Second Bks. *Imprint of* **Roaring Brook Pr.**

First Stage Concepts, (*978-0-9667719; 978-1-931430*) Orders Addr.: P.O. Box 3390, Redondo Beach, CA 90277-1390 USA Tel 310-371-6834; Fax: 310-370-3392; Edit Addr.: 5410 W. 190th St., No. 98, Torrance, CA 90503-1045 USA
E-mail: quickstartguitar@msn.com
Web site: http://www.QuickStartGuitar.com.

First Steps Pr., (*978-0-9659944*) Orders Addr.: P.O. Box 380122, Clinton Township, MI 48038-0060 USA Tel 810-463-5670; Edit Addr.: 38453 Gail, Clinton Township, MI 48036 USA.

First Steps Publishing, (*978-1-937333; 978-1-944072*) 105 Westwind St., Gleneden Beach, OR 97388 USA Tel 541-961-7641
E-mail: susan@firststepspublishing.com
Web site: http://www.FirstStepsPublishing.com.

First Word Publishing, The, (*978-0-9708590*) 305 Lind Ave., SW, No. 9, Renton, WA 98055 USA Tel 425-254-8575
E-mail: dejonfw@ayhoo.com.

Firsthand *Imprint of* **Heinemann**

First-Sight Publishing, (*978-0-9770363*) 9636 Nevada Ave., Chatsworth, CA 91311 USA Tel 818-207-6334
E-mail: sabrinawright1961@yahoo.com.

Fischer, Carl LLC, (*978-0-8258*) Orders Addr.: 588 N. Gulph Rd. Ste. B, Kng Of Prussa, PA 19406-2831 USA Toll Free: 800-762-2328; Edit Addr.: 65 Bleeker St., New York, NY 10012-2420 USA (SAN 107-4245) Tel 212-772-0900; Fax: 212-477-6996; Toll Free: 800-762-2328
E-mail: cf-info@carlfischer.com
Web site: http://www.carlfischer.com
Dist(s): **Follett School Solutions**
Leonard, Hal Corp.

Fish Creek Productions, LLC, (*978-0-9973651*) P.O. Box 131401, Spring, TX 77393 USA Tel 832-341-2372
E-mail: contact@fishcreekproductions.com.

Fish Decoy.com, Ltd., (*978-0-9748721; 978-0-9759386*) Orders Addr.: P.O. Box 321, Cross River, NY 10518 USA (SAN 256-1093) Tel 914-533-5181; Edit Addr.: 71 Conant Valley Rd., Pound Ridge, NY 10576 USA; 218 Honey Hallow Rd., Pound Ridge, NY 10576
Web site: http://www.fishdecoystore.com
Dist(s): **Antique Collectors' Club.**

Fish Head Pubns., LLC, (*978-1-934627*) 5013 W. Buckskin Tr., Glendale, AZ 85310 USA
Web site: http://www.fishheadpublications.com.

Fish Tales Publishing, (*978-0-9795860*) Orders Addr.: 65 Glen Rd., PMB 128, Garner, NC 27529 USA (SAN 853-8344) Tel 919-320-7428
E-mail: Books@fishtales.org
Web site: http://www.fishtales.org.

Fishbowl International, Inc., (*978-0-9745188; 978-0-9765619*) Orders Addr.: P.O. Box 362, Roxie, MS 39661 USA Tel 601-384-0219; Fax: 601-384-1667
E-mail: fishbowlinternational@yahoo.com
Web site: http://www.fishbowlinternational.com.

Fishcake Publishing, Incorporated *See* **Benicia Literary Arts**

Fisher Amelie, (*978-0-615-48662-8; 978-0-615-58205-4; 978-0-9888125; 978-0-9978769*) 905 Dee Ln., Bedford, TX 76022 USA Tel 817-657-0252
E-mail: mediastem@hotmail.com.

Fisher & Hale Publishing, (*978-0-9742037*) Div. of Horizon Bks., Orders Addr.: 6525 Gunpark Dr. 370, #250, Boulder, CO 80301 USA; Edit Addr.: 18841 E. Cornell Ave., Aurora, CO 80013 USA
E-mail: slmclean@hotmail.com
Web site: http://www.fisherhale.com.

Fisher Enterprises, (*978-0-9767265*) P.O. Box 1342, Eagle, ID 83616 USA Tel 208-939-6650; Fax: 208-939-7480 Do not confuse with Fisher Enterprises, Inc. In Edmonds, WA
E-mail: ggfisher@earthlink.net.

Fisher Hill, (*978-1-878253*) 5267 Warner Ave., No. 166, Huntington Beach, CA 92649 USA (SAN 254-1289) Tel 714-377-9353; Fax: 714-377-9495; Toll Free: 800-214-8110
E-mail: fisher.k@mac.com
Web site: http://www.Fisher-Hill.com
Dist(s): **Delta Systems Company, Inc.**

Fisher, John Wilfred, (*978-0-9771093*) 25216 Arrow Highline Rd., Juliaetta, ID 83535 USA Tel 208-843-7159
E-mail: jwfisher@starband.net.

Fisher King Enterprises, (*978-0-9776076; 978-0-9810344; 978-1-926715; 978-1-77169*) Orders Addr.: 109 E 17th St, Ste 80, Cheyenne, WY 82001 USA (SAN 257-7410) Tel 307-222-9575; 831-238-7799; Fax: 831-621-4667; *Imprints:* il piccolo editions (il piccolo)
E-mail: orders@fisherkingpress.com; fisherkingpress@gmail.com
Web site: http://www.fisherkingpress.com
Dist(s): **Fisher King Bks.**

Fisher King Press *See* **Fisher King Enterprises**

Fisher Wilcoxon *See* **Fisher Hill**

Fisher-Paner Publishing, (*978-0-615-19778-4; 978-0-615-23931-6*) 1919 Sorrento Pl., Richmond, VA 23238 USA
Dist(s): **Lulu Pr., Inc.**

Fishman, Greg *See* **Fishman, Greg Jazz Studios**

Fishman, Greg Jazz Studios, (*978-0-9766153; 978-0-9843492; 978-0-9914078*) 824 Custer Ave., Evanston, IL 60202 USA
E-mail: greg1111@aol.com
Web site: http://www.gregfishmanjazzstudios.com.

Fishnet Pubns./Ministries, (*978-0-9667517*) 8440 Fairwind Ct., Indianapolis, IN 46256 USA
E-mail: canddjohnson@comcast.net.

Fisticuff Publishing, 2529 Whetstone ln, Myrtle Beach, SC 29579 USA Tel 607-759-5075
Dist(s): **CreateSpace Independent Publishing Platform.**

Fit Kids, (*978-0-9709301*) 175 W. 200 S., Suite 2012, Salt Lake City, UT 84101-1459 USA Tel 801-521-0109; Fax: 801-521-8360; Toll Free: 888-234-8543
E-mail: brucebellco@earthlink.net
Web site: http://www.fitkids.org.

Fit Kids Publishing, (978-0-9895095) P.O. Box 4149, Auburn, CA 95604 USA Tel 650-339-2727
E-mail: katherine@fitkidspublishing.com
Web site: http://www.fitkidspublishing.com
Dist(s): **Partners Pubs. Group, Inc.**

Fitch, Michele Marko, (978-0-615-14996-7) 2103 Wilkerson St., South Boston, MA 24592 USA
E-mail: familyfitch@myembarg.com
Dist(s): **Lulu Pr., Inc.**

Fithian Pr *Imprint of* **Daniel & Daniel, Pubs., Inc.**

Fitness Information Technology, Inc., (978-0-9627926; 978-1-885693; 978-1-935412; 978-1-940067) Orders Addr.: P.O. Box 6116, Morgantown, WV 26506 USA; Edit Addr.: 375 Birch St., Morgantown, WV 26506-6116 USA Tel 304-293-6888; Fax: 304-293-6658; Toll Free: 800-477-4348
E-mail: ICPE@mail.wvu.edu; matthew.brann@mail.wvu.edu
Web site: http://www.fitinfotech.com
Dist(s): **Cardinal Pubs. Group**
National Bk. Network
Unifacmanu International Trading Co., Inc.
ebrary, Inc.

Fitzgerald Bks., (978-1-887238; 978-1-59054; 978-1-4242) Div. of Central Programs, Inc., Orders Addr.: P.O. Box 505, Bethany, MO 64424 USA Tel 660-425-7777; Fax: 660-425-3929; Toll Free: 800-821-7199; Edit Addr.: 802 N. 41st St., Bethany, MO 64424 USA
E-mail: wecare@gumdropbooks.com
Web site: http://www.gumdropbooks.com
Dist(s): **Gumdrop Bks.**

Fitzgerald, Caryn, (978-0-615-17982-7; 978-0-615-21500-6) P.O. Box 1343, Mansfield, TX 76063 USA
Web site: http://www.samfitzgerald.com
Dist(s): **Lulu Pr., Inc.**

Five Degrees of Frannie, (978-0-9679115) P.O. Box 178, North Greece, NY 14515 USA Tel 716-467-9136
E-mail: ohfrannie@aol.com.

Five Oaks Pr., (978-0-9779325) P.O. Box 251, Lake Lure, NC 28746-0251 USA
E-mail: davidklett@bellsouth.net
Web site: http://www.lakelurechronicles.com.

Five O'clock Dog, (978-0-9767887) Orchid # 1170, Corona del Mar, CA 92625 USA Tel 949-422-5909
Web site: http://www.fiveodog.com.

Five Ponds Pr., (978-0-9727156; 978-0-9824133; 978-0-9824583; 978-1-935813) 30 Hidden Spring Dr., Weston, CT 06883-1144 USA
E-mail: lou@fivepondspress.com
Web site: http://www.fivepondspress.com.

Five Star *Imprint of* **Cengage Gale**

Five Star Christian Pubns., (978-0-9740142; 978-0-9777291) 312 SE 24th Ave., Cape Coral, FL 33990 USA Tel 239-574-1000
E-mail: info@5scp.com
Web site: http://www.gulfcoastbaptistchurch.com; www.fivestarchristianministries.com.

Five Star Pr., (978-0-9673102) Orders Addr.: P.O. Box 8454, Richmond, VA 23226 USA Tel 804-282-6069; Edit Addr.: 1910 Byrd Ave., Suite 12, Richmond, VA 23230 USA.

Five Star Trade *Imprint of* **Cengage Gale**

Five Valleys Publishing (GBR) (978-0-9566042) *Dist. by* **LightSource CS.**

FizzBang Science, (978-0-9718480) 807 Murlay Dr., Plain City, OH 43064 USA Tel 614-873-8860 (phone/fax)
E-mail: blrohrig@worldnet.att.net
Web site: http://www.fizzbangscience.com.

Flaghouse, Inc., (978-0-9713648; 978-1-932032) 601 Rte. 46 W., Hasbrouck Heights, NJ 07604-3116 USA (SAN 631-3086) Tel 201-288-7600; Fax: 201-288-7887; Toll Free Fax: 800-793-7900
Web site: http://www.flaghouse.com.

Flagship Church Resources *Imprint of* **Group Publishing, Inc.**

Flamburis, Georgia, (978-0-615-47908-8) 5 Griggs Pl., Allston, MA 02134 USA Tel 617-783-9425
E-mail: gf_mae@yahoo.com.

Flame Tree Publishing (GBR) (978-1-874634; 978-1-903817; 978-1-904041; 978-1-84451; 978-1-84786; 978-1-78361) *Dist. by* **Bookmasters.**

Flaming Pen Pr., (978-0-615-27115-6; 978-0-615-28423-1; 978-0-615-34476-8; 978-0-615-36650-0; 978-0-615-41089-0; 978-0-615-93500-3) 130 N. Society Rd., Canterbury, CT 06331 USA
Dist(s): **CreateSpace Independent Publishing Platform.**

Flammarion et Cie (FRA) (978-2-08) *Dist. by* **Distribks Inc.**

Flammer, Josephine, (978-0-615-16197-6; 978-0-615-25550-7) P.O. Box 225, Adirondack, NY 128008 USA
E-mail: joannflammer@aol.com
Web site: http://joannflammer.com
Dist(s): **Lulu Pr., Inc.**

Flash Blasters, Incorporated *See* **Ace Academics, Inc.**

Flashlight Pr., (978-0-9729225; 978-0-9799746; 978-1-936261; 978-1-947277) 527 Empire Blvd., Brooklyn, NY 11225-3121 USA
E-mail: ed.assist@flashlightpress.com
Web site: http://www.flashlightpress.com
Dist(s): **Independent Pubs. Group**
MyiLibrary
ebrary, Inc.

FlashPaws Productions, (978-0-9674929) 7714 Rolling Fork Ln., Houston, TX 77040-3432 USA Tel 713-896-8484 (phone/fax)
E-mail: info@flashpaws.com
Web site: http://www.flashpaws.com
Dist(s): **Greenleaf Book Group.**

Flat Hammock Pr., (978-0-9718303; 978-0-9758699; 978-0-9773725; 978-0-9795949; 978-0-9818960) 5 Church St., Mystic, CT 06355 USA Tel 860-572-2722; Fax: 860-572-2755
E-mail: info@flathammockpress.com
Web site: http://www.flathammockpress.com.

Flat Kids *Imprint of* **Smart Smiles Co., The**

Flatiron Bks., (978-1-250-08290-9) Div. of Macmillan, 175 Fifth Ave., New York, NY 10010 USA Tel 646-307-5151
Web site: www.flatironbooks.com.

Flaxenfluff Pr., LLC, (978-0-9743890) P.O. Box 2287, Broken Arrow, OK 74013 USA
Web site: http://www.flaxenfluff.com.

Fleming, G. Faye *See* **Faye Bks.**

Fleming, Randall, (978-0-9841616) P.O. Box 252, Point Reyes Station, CA 94956 USA.

Flesk Pubns., (978-0-9723758; 978-1-933865; 978-1-64041) 2871 Mission St., Santa Cruz, CA 95060 USA
E-mail: info@fleskpublications.com
Web site: http://www.fleskpublications.com
Dist(s): **Publishers Group West (PGW)**
SCB Distributors.

Fletcher, C J Publishing LLC, (978-0-9755255) Orders Addr.: P.O. Box 784, Independence, KS 67301 USA (SAN 256-1050) Tel 620-331-5182; Fax: 620-331-5183; Toll Free: 800-814-8513; Edit Addr.: 212- 214 E. Myrtle, Independence, KS 67301 USA
E-mail: cjdcpa@cableone.net.

Fletcher, Kerstin, (978-0-9891660) 3529 San Sonita Pl., Santa Rosa, CA 95403 USA Tel 707-523-2174
E-mail: rb1993@sbcglobal.net.

Fletcher, Robert *See* **Iron Mountain Pr.**

Fleur Art Productions, (978-0-9741277) 32 N. Goodwin Ave., Elmsford, NY 10523 USA Fax: 914-206-3558; Toll Free: 866-353-8727; *Imprints:* Fleur Publishing (Fleur Pubng)
E-mail: agents@fleur.ws
Web site: http://www.fleur.ws
Dist(s): **E-Pros DG.**

Fleur De Lis Publishing, LLC, (978-0-9821956) P.O. Box 2521, South Portland, ME 04116-252121 USA
E-mail: cmunson667@aol.com.

Fleur Publishing *Imprint of* **Fleur Art Productions**

Fleuve Noir (FRA) (978-2-265) *Dist. by* **Distribks Inc.**

Flickerfawn *Imprint of* **Barton Bks.**

Flight Time LLC, (978-0-9858024; 978-0-9943153-4-2) 12182 Deer Chase Dr., Cincinnati, OH 45240 USA Tel 513-702-3126
E-mail: lalakerns@aol.com.

Flinders Pr., (978-0-9843955) P.O. Box 3975, Burbank, CA 91508-3975 USA (SAN 859-2829) Tel 818-714-0455
E-mail: flinderspress@gmail.com
Web site: http://www.flinderspress.com
Dist(s): **Independent Pubs. Group.**

Flinn Scientific, Inc., (978-1-877991; 978-1-933709) Orders Addr.: P.O. Box 219, Batavia, IL 60510 USA (SAN 630-1800) Fax: 866-452-1436; Toll Free: 800-452-1261; Edit Addr.: 770 N. Raddant Rd., Batavia, IL 60510 USA
E-mail: flinn@flinnsci.com.

Flip n Flop Learning, LLC, (978-0-9801772; 978-0-9853372) 6752 Castenson Rd., Bryan, TX 77808 USA
E-mail: senoragose@verizon.net
Web site: http://www.flipfloplearning.com.

Flip Publishing, (978-0-9769342) P.O. Box 1072, Hawthorne, CA 90251 USA
E-mail: flippublishing@yahoo.com
Web site: www.flippublishing.net
Dist(s): **Independent Pubs. Group.**

Flipp Sports, (978-0-9744443) 960 Turnpike St., Canton, MA 02021 USA Tel 781-821-8788; Fax: 781-821-4088
E-mail: jmarnikovic@flippsports.com
Web site: http://www.flippsports.com.

Flippin' Bks. LLC, (978-0-9742500) 25450 Williams Ridge, Warrenton, MO 63383 USA Tel 636-456-6224
E-mail: thw@flippinbooks.com
Web site: http://www.flippinbooks.com.

FloBound Poems Publications, (978-0-9705819) Orders Addr.: P.O. Box 3101, Fredericksburg, VA 22402-3101 USA
E-mail: floboundpoems@aol.com; morningpoemsflog@aol.com
Web site: http://www.floboundpoems.com.

Flood Crest Pr., (978-1-934130) 604 E. Spring St., New Albany, IN 47150 USA Tel 812-944-5116; Fax: 812-944-5277
E-mail: ops@destinationsbooksellers.com
Web site: http://www.destinationsbooksellers.com.

Flood, Tim, (978-0-9797159) 1349 E. Ellis Dr., Tucson, AZ 85719 USA
Web site: http://www.dreamsofaballinflight.com.

Floodgate Publishing, (978-0-9761355) P.O. Box 1475, Castle Rock, WA 98611 USA.

Floppinfish Publishing Co., Ltd., (978-0-9629124; 978-0-615-70203-2; 978-0-692-34807-9; 978-0-692-87027-3) P.O. Box 4932, Saint Louis, MO 63108 USA Tel 314-567-8697
E-mail: wm4932@yahoo.com
Web site: http://www.JoeKeylon.com; http://www.pixofpeople.com
Dist(s): **Big River Distribution**
Partners Bk. Distributing, Inc.

Floppy Cat Co., (978-0-9823818) 2315 Devon Ave., Tea, SD 57064 USA
E-mail: jenn@greenleafbookgroup.com.

Flora Delaterre Productions, (978-0-9792302) P.O. Box 8474, Missoula, MT 59807 USA Tel 406-728-2977
Web site: http://www.floradelaterre.com.

Flores, Angie, (978-0-9979738) 3650 Newton St. No. 31, Torrance, CA 90505 USA Tel 310-408-3764
E-mail: crafty125@hotmail.com.

Flores, Travis, (978-0-9759077) P.O. Box 143, Newport, OH 45768 USA Tel 740-473-2999 (phone/fax)
E-mail: sparkeythespider@aol.com
Web site: http://www.sparkeythespider.com.

Floricanto Pr., (978-0-915745; 978-0-9796457) Div. of Inter American Development, 650 Castro St., Suite 120, No. 331, Mountain View, CA 94041-2055 USA (SAN 293-9169) Tel 415-552-1879; Fax: 702-995-1410
E-mail: info@floricantopress.com; rcabello@floricantopress.com
Web site: http://www.floricantopress.com.

Florida Div. of Historical Resources, (978-0-9642289; 978-1-889030) Div. of Florida Dept. of State, c/o Bureau of Historic Preservation, 500 S. Bronough St., Tallahassee, FL 32399-0250 USA Tel 850-487-2333; Fax: 850-922-0496; Toll Free: 800-847-7278
Web site: http://www.flheritage.com.

Florida Historical Society, (978-1-886104; 978-0-9771079; 978-0-9817337) 435 Brevard Ave., Cocoa, FL 32922 USA Tel 321-690-1971; *Imprints:* Chapin House Books (Chapin Hse)
E-mail: FHSPress@myfloridahistory.org; chris.brotemarkle@myfloridahistory.org
Web site: www.floridabooks.net; www.myfloridahistory.org.

Florida Kids Pr., Inc., (978-0-9792304; 978-0-9863325) 11802 Magnolia Falls Dr., Jacksonville, FL 32258-2587 USA
Web site: http://www.janewoodbooks.com
Dist(s): **Partners Bk. Distributing, Inc.**

Florida Science Source, Inc., (978-0-944961) Orders Addr.: P.O. Box 8217, Longboat Key, FL 34228-8217 USA (SAN 245-6974); Edit Addr.: 28 Eagle Ridge Rd., Sapphire, NC 28774-9681 USA (SAN 245-6982)
E-mail: fssource@aol.com
Web site: http://www.ultimacitrus.com/fssource.

Floris Bks. (GBR) (978-0-86315; 978-0-903540; 978-1-78250) *Dist. by* **SteinerBooks Inc.**

Floris Bks. (GBR) (978-0-86315; 978-0-903540; 978-1-78250) *Dist. by* **Gryphon Hse.**

Flourish Publishing Hse., (978-0-9851659) P.O. Box 1661, Frisco, CO 80443 USA Tel 405-760-1118
E-mail: garystallings@yahoo.com.

Flower Press *See* **Flowerfield Enterprises**

Flower Publishing, (978-0-9852608) 1003 Deer Creek Church Rd., Forest Hill, MD 21050 USA Tel 443-528-3033
E-mail: gfdbuilders@yahoo.com.

Flower Sprouts, (978-0-615-21179-4; 978-0-615-21180-0; 978-0-615-21683-6) P.O. Box 1843, Morro Bay, CA 93443 USA Tel 805-772-5808 (phone/fax); 245 Morro Bay Blvd., Morro Bay, CA 1111
Web site: http://www.seawindgallery.com
Dist(s): **Lulu Pr., Inc.**

Flowerfield Enterprises, (978-0-942256) 10332 Shaver Rd., Kalamazoo, MI 49024-6744 USA (SAN 217-7358) Tel 269-327-0108; Fax: 269-327-7009
E-mail: nancy@wormwoman.com
Web site: http://www.wormwoman.com.

Flowerpot Children's Pr. Inc. (CAN) (978-1-77093; 978-1-897533; 978-0-9784200; 978-1-926988; 978-1-4867) *Dist. by* **Cardinal PubGr.**

Flowerpot Pr., Div. of MitSo Media Inc., 142 Second Ave., Franklin, TN 37064 USA
E-mail: anne@flowerpotpress.com
Web site: http://www.flowerpotpress.com.

Fluckiger, Jay D. *See* **Harmony Hse. Publishing Co.**

Fluckiger, Kory, (978-0-615-15654-5) 3640 Gramercy Ave., Ogden, UT 84403 USA Tel 801-791-3461
E-mail: kory@koryfluckiger.com
Web site: http://www.koryfluckiger.com
Dist(s): **Lulu Pr., Inc.**

Fluency Fast Language Classes, Inc., (978-0-9824687) Orders Addr.: P.O. Box 165, Manitou Springs, CO 80829 USA Tel 719-633-6000; Toll Free: 866-999-3583; Edit Addr.: 707 Manitou Blvd., Colorado Springs, CO 80904 USA
E-mail: karen@fluencyfast.com
Web site: http://www.fluencyfast.com.

Flugul Pubng, (978-0-9779390) P.O. Box 6090, Cincinnati, OH 45206 USA
E-mail: VLI@flugulpublishing.com
Web site: http://www.Flugulpublishing.com
Dist(s): **Lulu Pr., Inc.**

Fluharty, Linda Cunningham, (978-0-9759097) 833 Carnforth Dr., Baton Rouge, LA 70810 USA
E-mail: LCFlu@aol.com
Web site: http://www.lindapages.com.

Flutter-By Productions, (978-0-9714734) 1415 Panther Ln. # 214, Naples, FL 34109-7874 USA
Web site: http://www.flutter-byproductions.com
Dist(s): **APG Sales & Distribution Services.**

Flux *Imprint of* **Llewellyn Pubns.**

Flux *Imprint of* **North Star Editions**

Flux: Image Theory Group, (978-0-9790786) 101 N. 7th St., No. 226, Phoenix, AZ 85034 USA.

Flying Cloud Bks., (978-0-615-13477-2) 123 Moore Rd., Sudbury, MA 01776 USA
E-mail: mail@paulgreenspan.com
Web site: http://www.paulgreenspan.com
Dist(s): **Lulu Pr., Inc.**

Flying Dolphin Pr. *Imprint of* **Knopf Doubleday Publishing Group**

Flying Elephants Pr., (978-0-9746981; 978-0-9766715; 978-1-933632) Flying Elephants Productions 210 East 5th St., 3rd Flr., New York, NY 10003 USA
Web site: http://www.gregorycolbert.com
Dist(s): **Two Rivers Distribution.**

Flying Eye Bks. (GBR) (978-1-909263) *Dist. by* **Consort Bk Sales.**

Flying Frog Pubs.,
Dist(s): **Ideals Pubns.**

Flying Frog Publishing, (978-0-9666647) 567 Westcove Dr., Wasilla, AK 99654-7161 USA Tel 907-373-6994 (phone/fax); Toll Free: 888-673-6994 Do not confuse with Flying Frog Publishing, Reisterstown, MD
E-mail: jobshlh@corecom.net
Web site: http://www.galaxymall.com/children/alaskariddles
Dist(s): **Todd Communications**
Wizard Works.

Flying Frog Publishing, Inc., (978-1-57755; 978-1-884628; 978-1-934967; 978-1-60745; 978-1-63560) 2219 York Rd., Suite 300, Lutherville, MD 21093 USA Tel 443-901-2100; Fax: 443-901-2104
Web site: http://www.flyingfrogpub.com
Dist(s): **Ideals Pubns.**

Flying Owl Pubns, (978-0-9820769) 2268 Brighton, Holland, MI 49424 USA Tel 616-399-3857
E-mail: denuyl@chartermi.net.

Flying Pig Publishing, (978-0-9746110) P.O. Box 304, Harvard, MA 01451 USA
E-mail: douglee41@yahoo.com
Web site: http://deelee.net.

Flying Point Pr., (978-0-9904604) The Pilot House, Boston, MA 02110 USA Tel 617-734-7560
E-mail: peggy@flyingpointpress.com.

Flying Rhino Productions, Incorporated *See* **Flying Rhinoceros, Inc.**

Flying Rhinoceros, Inc., (978-1-883772; 978-1-59168; 978-0-9822773) 1440 NW Overton St., Portland, OR 97209 USA (SAN 857-7501) Tel 503-552-8777; Fax: 503-445-8375; Toll Free: 800-537-4466
E-mail: flyingrhino@flyingrhino.com; melson@flyingrhino.com
Web site: http://www.flyingrhino.com.

Flying Scroll Publishing, LLC, (978-0-9742432; 978-0-9848099) P.O. Box 246, Fort Atkinson, WI 53538 USA Tel 920-723-3454
E-mail: info@flyingscrollpublishing.com
Web site: http://www.flyingscrollpublishing.com.

Flying Solo Pr., LLC, (978-1-940137) 1116 Cherokee St, Denver, CO 80204 USA Tel 303-733-3751
E-mail: paulaertker@gmail.com
Web site: www.crimetravelers.com.

Flying Squirrel Press *See* **Heritage Heart Farm**

Flying Turtle Publishing, (978-0-615-31741-0; 978-0-9851492; 978-0-9911378; 978-0-9907104; 978-0-9989979) 7216 Birch Ave., Hammond, IN 46324 USA
Web site: http://flyingturtlepublishing.com
Dist(s): **Smashwords.**

Flyleaf Publishing, (978-0-9658246; 978-1-929262; 978-1-60541) Orders Addr.: P.O. Box 287, Lyme, NH 03768-0185 USA Tel 800-449-7006; Fax: 888-619-6419; P.O. Box 287, Lyme, NH 03768-0287 Toll Free: 800-449-7006; *Imprints:* Books To Remember (Bks To Remember)
E-mail: laura@flyleafpublishing.com
Web site: http://www.flyleafpublishing.com.

Flywheel Publishing Co., (978-1-930826) Orders Addr.: 1375 Sunnyhills Rd., Oakland, CA 94610 USA (SAN 253-2441) Tel 510-407-7577; Fax: 510-373-6060
E-mail: admin@flywheel.us
Web site: http://www.flywheel.us.

FM Publishing Co., (978-1-931671) Div. of F.A.I.T.H. Ministries, Inc., Orders Addr.: P.O. Box 10618, Casa Grande, AZ 85130 USA Tel 520-280-0223; Toll Free Fax: 800-518-1219
E-mail: fmpublishing2011@gmail.com; fasthelpministries@gmail.com
Dist(s): **CreateSpace Independent Publishing Platform**
Lulu Pr., Inc.

FM Rocks Kids, LLC *See* **Playdate Kids Publishing**

FMA Publishing, (978-0-9774411) 1920 Pacific Ave. No. 16152, Long Beach, CA 90806 USA (SAN 257-4977) Tel 310-438-3483; Fax: 310-438-3486
E-mail: info@fmapublishing.com
Web site: http://www.fmapublishing.com.

Fo Guang Shan International Translation Ctr., (978-1-943211) 3456 Glenmark Dr., Hacienda Heights, CA 91745 USA Tel 626-330-8361
E-mail: fgsitc@gmail.com
Web site: fgsitc.org.

Focus *Imprint of* **Hackett Publishing Co., Inc.**

Focus Group, Inc., (978-0-9766968) 2201 SW 152nd St. Ste. 3, Burien, WA 98166-2080 USA
E-mail: pubs@focusgroupseattle.com.

†Focus on the Family Publishing, (978-0-929608; 978-1-56179; 978-1-58997; 978-1-60482; 978-1-62405; 978-1-62471; 978-1-68332; 978-1-68424; 978-1-68428) 8605 Explorer Dr., Colorado Springs, CO 80920 USA (SAN 250-0949) Fax: 719-531-3356; Toll Free: 800-232-6459
E-mail: robert.huntrods@fotf.org; permissions@fotf.org
Web site: http://www.focusonthefamily.com
Dist(s): **Follett School Solutions**
Gospel Light Pubns.
Nelson, Tommy
Tyndale Hse. Pubs.
Zondervan; *CIP.*

Focus Publishing, (978-1-885904; 978-1-936141) Orders Addr.: P.O. Box 665, Bemidji, MN 56619 USA Tel 218-759-9816 Toll Free: 800-913-6287; Edit Addr.: 502 Third St., NW, Bemidji, MN 56601 USA
E-mail: jan@focuspublishing.com
Web site: http://focuspublishing.com
Dist(s): **Spring Arbor Distributors, Inc.**

Focus Readers *Imprint of* **North Star Editions**

Fodor's Travel Guides *See* **Fodor's Travel Pubns.**

Fodor's Travel Pubns., Div. of Random Hse., Information Group, Orders Addr.: 400 Hahn Rd., Westminster, MD 21157 USA Tel 410-848-1900; Toll Free: 800-726-0600; Edit Addr.: 1745 Broadway, New York, NY 10019 USA Tel 212-782-9000
Web site: http://www.fodors.com
Dist(s): **Ingram Publisher Services**
Libros Sin Fronteras
MyiLibrary
Penguin Random Hse. LLC
Random Hse., Inc.

Fog City Pr., (978-1-875137; 978-1-887451; 978-1-892374; 978-1-929156; 978-1-74089) Subs. of Weldon Owen, Inc., 2215-R Market St., No. 123, San Francisco, CA 94114 USA Tel 415-626-9636
E-mail: gilblock@sirius.com
Dist(s): **INscribe Digital**
Ingram Publisher Services.

Fog Ink *Imprint of* **Fields of Gold Publishing, Inc.**

Publisher Name Index

Foglight Pr., *(978-0-9755848)* Orders Addr.: P.O. Box 160322, Sacramento, CA 95816 USA
E-mail: info@foglightpress.com
Web site: http://www.foglightpress.com
Dist(s): **Bookazine Co., Inc.**

folder leaf *Imprint of* **Story Time Stories That Rhyme**

Foley, Mark, *(978-0-615-19609-1)* 4 3rd Ave., Annville, PA 17003 USA
Dist(s): **Lulu Pr., Inc.**

Folk Prophet Bks., *(978-0-578-00160-9)* 140 S. 200 E., Lindon, UT 84042 USA
E-mail: books@folkprophet.com
Dist(s): **Lulu Pr., Inc.**

Folklore Publishing (CAN) *(978-1-894864; 978-1-897206; 978-1-926677) Dist. by* **Lone Pine.**

Follett Library Resources *See* **Follett School Solutions**

Follett School Solutions, *(978-0-329; 978-0-88153; 978-0-924917; 978-1-4898; 978-1-5160; 978-1-5181; 978-1-5379; 978-1-5444; 978-1-5490)* Div. of the Follett Corp., Orders Addr.: a/o McHenry Warehouse, 1340 Ridgeview Dr., McHenry, IL 60050 USA (SAN 169-1902) Toll Free: 888-511-5114; a/o Patti Hall: R & R Bindery Services, 499 Rachel Rd., Girard, IL 62640 (SAN 155-8412) Tel 815-759-1700; *Imprints:* Follettbound (Follettbnd)
Web site: http://www.follett.com
Dist(s): **Baker & Taylor Bks.**

Follettbound *Imprint of* **Follett School Solutions**

Follmer Group, The, *(978-0-925065; 978-1-933478; 978-1-935871; 978-1-943137)* 5758 S. Blackstone Ave., Chicago, IL 60637 USA Tel 773-643-1902; Fax: 773-643-1903
E-mail: david@thedavidfollmergroup.com
Web site: http://www.thedavidfollmergroup.com.

Folsom Fallies Pr., *(978-0-9760790)* Orders Addr.: P.O. Box 348, Folsom, NM 88419 USA Tel 505-278-2520
E-mail: kristene@folsomfallies.com
Web site: http://www.folsomfallies.com.

Fond du Lac Head Start, *(978-0-615-69899-1)* 1720 Big Lake Rd., Cloquet, MN 55720 USA Tel 218-878-8130; Fax: 218-878-8115
E-mail: barbaraforcier@fdlrez.com
Web site: fdlrez.com.

Fondo de Cultura Económcia,
Dist(s): **Fondo de Cultura Economica USA.**

Fondo de Cultura Economica USA, 2293 Verus St., San Diego, CA 92154 USA (SAN 860-1380) Tel 619-429-0455; Fax: 619-651-9684; Toll Free: 800-532-3872
E-mail: orders@fceusa.com; drazo@fceusa.com; fondosales@fceusa.com
Web site: http://www.fceusa.com
Dist(s): **Giron Bks.**
Latin American Book Source, Inc.
Lectorum Pubns., Inc.

Fondo Editorial Grania, Fundacion Hogares Juveniles Campesinos (COL) *(978-958-8233; 978-958-9321) Dist. by* **Chelsea Green Pub.**

Fons Vitae *See* **Fons Vitae of Kentucky, Inc.**

Fons Vitae of Kentucky, Inc., *(978-1-887752; 978-1-941610)* 49 Mockingbird Valley Dr., Louisville, KY 40207-1366 USA Tel 502-897-3641
E-mail: fonsvitaeky@aol.com
Web site: http://www.fonsvitae.com
Dist(s): **Independent Pubs. Group.**

Food Allergy & Anaphylaxis Network, *(978-1-882541)* 11781 Lee Jackson Hwy. Suite 160, Fairfax, VA 22033 USA Tel 703-691-3179; Fax: 703-691-2713; Toll Free: 800-929-4040
E-mail: faan@foodallergy.org
Web site: http://www.foodallergy.org.

Food Allergy Network *See* **Food Allergy & Anaphylaxis Network**

Food & Agriculture Organization of the United Nations (ITA) *(978-92-5) Dist. by* **Rowman.**

Food Enhancement Enterprises, *(978-0-9747247)* Orders Addr.: P.O. Box 60581, Sacramento, CA 95680 USA; Edit Addr.: 2148 Bluebird Ln., Sacramento, CA 95821 USA
E-mail: hsdell@lanset.com
Web site: http://www.pizzareconsidered.com.

Food Marketing Consultants, Inc., *(978-0-9763307; 978-1-59949)* 2805 N. Commerce Pkwy., Miramar, FL 33025 USA Tel 954-322-2668 Toll Free: 877-493-2633
Web site: http://www.colorallabout.com.

Food Network Kitchens *Imprint of* **Meredith Bks.**

Food Safety & Inspection Service *Imprint of* **United States Government Printing Office**

FoodPlay Productions, *(978-0-9642858)* 1 Sunset Ave., Hatfield, MA 01038 USA Tel 413-247-5400; Fax: 413-247-5405; Toll Free: 800-366-3752 (Orders)
E-mail: store@foodplay.com
Web site: http://www.foodplay.com
Dist(s): **Partners Pubs. Group, Inc.**

Foolosophy Media, *(978-0-9779928)* 1528 Primrose Ln., Panama City, FL 32404 USA (SAN 850-8186) Tel 850-871-2304; 850-899-1972; Fax: 850-871-2304
E-mail: wisemullet@gmail.com.

Foothill-Hydroponics, *(978-0-9669557)* 10705 Burbank Blvd., N., North Hollywood, CA 91601 USA Tel 818-760-0688; Fax: 818-760-4025
E-mail: mohsen@foothillhydroponics.com
Web site: http://www.foothill-hydroponic.com.

Footprints Pr., *(978-0-9679813)* 71 Hudson St., New York, NY 10013 USA Tel 212-267-9300; Fax: 212-267-9400.

For Children With Love Pubns., *(978-0-578-00980-3; 978-0-9831221; 978-0-9994002)* 99 Peacedale St., Bristol, CT 06010 USA
E-mail: Cathy.forchildren@gmail.com
Web site: http://www.forchildrenwithlove.com.

For Dummies *Imprint of* **Wiley, John & Sons, Inc.**

For Fun! *Imprint of* **Compass Point Bks.**

For Him Pr., *(978-0-9858899)* P.O. Box 2207, Morristown, TN 37816 USA Tel 423-307-8137
E-mail: claudia-scribe@live.com
Web site: claudia-clues.com.

For Little Folks, *(978-0-9771236)* P.O. Box 571, Dresden, OH 43821 USA.

For Such A Time As This Ministries, *(978-0-9725890)* 510 Swank Rd., Hollsopple, PA 15935-8116 USA Tel 814-479-7710; Fax: 814-479-4874; Toll Free: 877-378-4374
E-mail: jpstobaugh@aol.com
Web site: http://www.forsuchatimeasthis.com.

For The Love of Dog Bks., *(978-0-9761124)* 635 NE Buffalo, Portland, OR 97211 USA Tel 503-286-5351
E-mail: stelljes@aol.com
Web site: http://www.silvertonbobbie.com
Dist(s): **Far West Bk. Service**
Partners/West Book Distributors.

Forbes Literary Ltd. Inc., *(978-0-9776284)* P.O. Box 494, Grover, MO 63040-1621 USA Tel 314-753-6142; Fax: 636-405-1963
E-mail: forbeslit@sbcgobal.net
Web site: http://www.forbesliterary.com.

Fore Angels Pr., *(978-0-9658920; 978-0-9799947)* 267 Woodbury Rd., Huntington, NY 11743 USA Tel 631-385-0336
E-mail: annaarts@verizon.net.

Foreign Policy Assn., *(978-0-87124)* 470 Park Ave. S., 2nd Flr., New York, NY 10016-6819 USA (SAN 212-9426) Tel 212-481-8100; Fax: 212-481-9275; Toll Free: 800-628-5754; 800-477-5836 (orders)
Web site: http://www.fpa.org.

Forelle Graphics, *(978-0-9770918)* 1015 Atlantic Blvd., Suite 89, Atlantic Beach, FL 32233 USA
E-mail: forelle-graphics@yahoo.com.

Forest Hill Publishing, LLC, *(978-0-9759251; 978-0-9771113)* 13200 Forest Hill Ave., East Cleveland, OH 44112 USA Tel 216-761-8316 (phone/fax); Fax: 253-799-8316; *Imprints:* PlayGround (PlayGrnd OH); SpringTree (SpringTree); FortuneChild (FortuneChild) Do not confuse with Forest Hill Publishing in Downers Grove, IL
E-mail: email@foresthillpublishing.com
Web site: http://www.foresthillpublishing.com.

Forest Hse. Publishing Co., Inc., *(978-1-56674; 978-1-878363)* P.O. Box 738, Lake Forest, IL 60045 USA Tel 847-295-8287; Fax: 847-295-8201; Toll Free: 800-394-7323.

Forest Service *Imprint of* **United States Government Printing Office**

Forest Woods Media Productions *Imprint of* **Bunny & The Crocodile Pr., The**

Forever *Imprint of* **Grand Central Publishing**

Forever Young Pubs., *(978-0-9774422)* Orders Addr.: P.O. Box 216, Niles, MI 49120 USA Fax: 269-683-7153
E-mail: cheri@foreveryoungpublishers.com
Web site: http://www.foreveryoungpublishers.com
Dist(s): **Midpoint Trade Bks., Inc.**
Partners Bk. Distributing, Inc.

Forge Bks. *Imprint of* **Doherty, Tom Assocs., LLC**

Forgotten Bks., *(978-1-60506; 978-1-60620; 978-1-60680; 978-1-4400; 978-1-4510)* 8345 NW 66th St., Miami, FL 33166 USA (SAN 854-9354)
E-mail: director@forgottenbooks.org
Web site: http://www.forgottenbooks.org/
Dist(s): **CreateSpace Independent Publishing Platform.**

Fork in the Road Pubs., *(978-0-9740825)* 1883 145th Pl. SE, Bellevue, WA 98007-6019 USA Tel 425-644-4285
Web site: http://www.raincitycookingschool.com.

Forks Pr., *(978-0-9816641)* 4-02 Summit Ave., Fair Lawn, NJ 07410 USA (SAN 856-1575) Tel 201-310-3297; 646-208-2161
E-mail: info@forkspress.com
Web site: http://www.forkspress.com.

Formac Publishing Co., Ltd. (CAN) *(978-0-88780; 978-0-921921; 978-1-55277; 978-1-4595) Dist. by* **Casemate Pubs.**

Forsberg, Michael Photography, *(978-0-9754964)* 100 N. 8th St., Suite 150, Lincoln, NE 68508-1369 USA Toll Free: 888-812-3790 Do not confuse with Platte Publishing Company in Denver, CO
E-mail: patty@michaelforsberg.com
Web site: http://www.michaelforsberg.com
Dist(s): **Univ. of Nebraska Pr.**

Fortitude Graphic Design & Printing, *(978-0-9741611; 978-0-578-06241-9; 978-0-9863173; 978-0-9977136; 978-0-692-88090-6; 978-0-9991334)* 841 Gibson St., Kalamazoo, MI 49001-2540 USA
E-mail: fortitude2@sbcglobal.net
Web site: www.comvoicesonline.com; www.fortitudegdp.com.

Fortner, Ray, *(978-0-9726365)* Orders Addr.: 3501 Baisden Rd., Pensacola, FL 32503-3458 USA.

Fortress Pr. *Imprint of* **Augsburg Fortress, Pubs.**

FortuneChild *Imprint of* **Forest Hill Publishing, LLC**

Forum Gallery, *(978-0-9675826; 978-0-9744129)* 745 Fifth Ave., New York, NY 10051 USA Tel 212-355-4547; 212-355-4545; Fax: 212-355-4547
E-mail: gallery@forumgallery.com
Dist(s): **D.A.P./Distributed Art Pubs.**

Forward Communications *See* **NetNia Publishing Co.**

Forward Movement Pubns., *(978-0-88028)* 300 West Fourth St., Cincinnati, OH 45202 USA (SAN 208-3841) Tel 513-721-6659; Fax: 513-721-0729; Toll Free: 800-543-1813 (orders only)
E-mail: Orders@forwarddaybyday.com
Web site: http://www.forwardmovement.org
Dist(s): **Bookmasters Distribution.**

Forword, *(978-0-9623937)* 16526 W. 78th St., Suite 335, Eden Prairie, MN 55346 USA Tel 612-944-7761; Fax: 612-944-8674.

Foster Branch Publishing, 20 Poplar St., No. 2, Jersey City, NJ 07307 USA
E-mail: dolphinupatree@hotmail.com.

Foster, Dennis, *(978-0-9771956)* P.O. Box 363, Millwood, VA 22646 USA.

Foster, Hicks & Assocs., *(978-0-9790709)* Orders Addr.: 4053 Harlan St., loft 201, Emeryville, CA 94608-9460 USA Tel 510-540-1241
E-mail: info@fosterhicks.com
Dist(s): **Bookmasters Distribution.**

Foster, Walter Publishing, Incorporated *See* **Quarto Publishing Group USA**

Foston Adolescent Workshop, Inc., *(978-0-9641709; 978-1-930362)* P.O. Box 726, Clarksville, TN 37041 USA Tel 931-906-4623; Fax: 931-645-3500; Toll Free: 800-418-0374
E-mail: minfoston@aol.com
Web site: http://www.drfoston.com.

Foulsham, W. Co., Ltd. (GBR) *(978-0-572) Dist. by* **APG.**

Found Link, *(978-0-615-43601-2; 978-0-9836659)* 13125 Ladybank Ln., Herndon, VA 20171 USA Tel 703-966-2175
E-mail: jlcuddehe@verizon.net
Web site: www.CuddeheServices.com.

Foundation For Cosmetic Surgery, The, *(978-0-9799438)* 400 Newport Center Dr. Ste. 800, Newport Beach, CA 92660-7607 USA
E-mail: bryan@griffinpublishing.com; ffps2007@yahoo.com
Web site: http://www.beautybybrennan.com.

Foundation, Pr. The, *(978-0-9765987)* P.O. Box 182, Westport, CT 06881 USA Do not confuse with companies with the same name in New York, NY, Anaheim, CA
Web site: http://www.thefoundationpress.com.

Foundation Pr., *(978-0-9767272)* 13832 Gimbert Ln., Santa Ana, CA 92705-2849 USA Do not confuse with companies with the same name in New York, NY, Westport, CT.

Foundations for Learning, LLC, *(978-0-9726479; 978-1-933546)* 246 W. Manson Hwy., PMB 144, Chelan, WA 98816 USA Toll Free: 800-553-5950
E-mail: info@gophonics.com
Web site: http://www.gophonics.com.

Foundations in Brass *See* **Cymbal Technique 101**

Foundation, Inc., *(978-0-9797125; 978-0-9859251)* 701 E. Gate Dr. Suite 300, Mt. Laurel, NJ 08054 USA Tel 856-533-1600; Fax: 856-533-1601; Toll Free: 888-977-5437
E-mail: rmclaughlin@foundationsinc.org
Web site: http://www.foundationsinc.org.

Foundry Bks. (GBR) *(978-1-901543) Dist. by* **Casemate Pubs.**

Fountain Blue Publishing, *(978-0-615-81358-5; 978-1-62868)* P.O. Box 657, Squaw Valley, CA 93675 USA Tel 213-986-6835
E-mail: fountainbluepublishing@gmail.com
Web site: www.fountainbluepublishing.com.

Fountain Publishing, *(978-0-9659164; 978-0-9748423; 978-0-9822172; 978-1-936665)* Orders Addr.: P.O. Box 80011, Rochester, MI 48308 USA (SAN 253-8571) Tel 248-651-2934; Toll Free: 877-736-8598; Edit Addr.: 375 Olivewood Ct., Rochester, MI 48306 USA Tel 810-651-1153 Do not confuse with Fountain Publishing in Pittsburgh, PA
E-mail: fnpublish@aol.com; jk@fountainpublishing.com
Web site: http://www.fountainpublishing.com.

Fountain Square Publishing, *(978-0-9724421)* 786 Old Ludlow, Cincinnati, OH 45220 USA.

Four Blocks, Div. of Carson-Dellosa Publishing Company, Inc., Orders Addr.: P.O. Box 35665, Greensboro, NC 27425 USA Tel 336-632-0084; Fax: 336-808-3249; Toll Free: 800-321-0943
Dist(s): **Carson-Dellosa Publishing, LLC.**

Four Dolphins Pr. *Imprint of* **Four Dolphins Pr., LLC**

Four Dolphins Pr., *(978-0-9745746)* Orders Addr.: P.O. Box 93601, Los Angeles, CA 90093 USA (SAN 255-626X) Tel 323-304-2053; Edit Addr.: 2700 N. Cahuenga Blvd., E., Suite 1403, Los Angeles, CA 90068-2139 USA.

Four Dolphins Pr., LLC, *(978-0-9799315)* P.O. Box 833, Scott Depot, WV 25560 USA Tel 304-757-8125; *Imprints:* Four Dolphins Press (Four Dolphin)
Web site: http://www.SadMadGladBooks.com.

Four Dolphins Press/Smart Communications, Incorporated *See* **Four Dolphins Pr.**

Four Elephants Pr., *(978-1-940051)* 11828 La Grange Ave., Los Angeles, CA 90025 USA Tel 310-477-4564
E-mail: annaka.harris@gmail.com
Dist(s): **MyiLibrary**
Publishers Group West (PGW).

Four Foot Pr. LLC, *(978-0-9820817)* 12647 Galveston Ct., Suite 114, Manassas, VA 20112 USA
E-mail: dcgenesis@hotmail.com; fourfootpress@yahoo.com
Web site: http://fourfootpress.com.

Four Menards, The, *(978-0-9887969; 978-0-9891734; 978-0-9903872; 978-0-9904521)* P.O. Box 17265, Asheville, NC 28816 USA Tel 828-335-0284; Fax: 828-484-9873
E-mail: thefourmenards@gmail.com
Web site: N/A.

Four Panel Pr., *(978-0-9674102; 978-0-9971090)* P.O. Box 50032, Eugene, OR 97405 USA Tel 541-343-6436; Fax: 541-684-0787
E-mail: tedlay@comcast.net
Web site: http://www.stonesoupcartoons.com
Dist(s): **Bookmasters Distribution.**

Four Phoenixes Publishing, *(978-0-9976205)* 6407 N. Post Oak Rd., Peoria, IL 61603 USA Tel 309-256-6406
E-mail: joechianakas@gmail.com.

Four Pine Farms *See* **Four Pines Farms**

Four Pines Farms, *(978-0-9860701)* 683 Feldhauser Rd, Frederic, MI 49733 USA
E-mail: yroehler@bookpublishing.com.

Four Seasons Bks., Inc., *(978-0-9666858; 978-1-893595)* P.O. Box 395, Ben Wheeler, TX 75754 USA Tel 903-963-1442; Fax: 903-963-1525; Toll Free: 800-852-7484
E-mail: hcmarlow@yahoo.com; editor@fourseasonsbookstore.com
Web site: http://www.herbmarlow.com; http://www.fourseasonsbookstore.com.

Four Seasons Pubs., *(978-0-9656811; 978-1-891929; 978-1-932497)* Orders Addr.: P.O. Box 51, Titusville, FL 32781 USA Tel 321-632-2932; Fax: 321-632-2935; Edit Addr.: 4350 N. U.S. Hwy. 1, Cocoa, FL 32927 USA
E-mail: fseasons@bellsouth.net
Dist(s): **Follett School Solutions.**

Four Seasons Publishing, *(978-0-578-05005-8)* 105 Ansley Pl., Harlem, GA 30814 USA
E-mail: tedhoodjr@arkansas.net
Web site: http://www.thecardinalnest.com.

Four Sonkist Angels, *(978-0-9753117)* 4985 Wiltshire Ln., Suwanee, GA 30024 USA
E-mail: Michelle@FourSonkistAngels.com
Web site: http://www.FourSonkistAngels.com.

Four Star Publishing, *(978-0-9815894)* P.O. Box 871784, Canton, MI 48187 USA
E-mail: fourstarpublishing@comcast.net.

FourFront Media & Music, *(978-0-9743420)* Orders Addr.: 1245 S. 128th St., Seattle, WA 98168 USA Tel 206-282-6116
E-mail: chris@chrisknab.net
Web site: http://www.fourfrontmusic.com.

Foursquare Media, ICFG, *(978-0-9635581; 978-0-9802392)* 1910 W. Sunset Blvd., Suite 200, Los Angeles, CA 90026 USA Tel 213-989-4493; Fax: 213-413-3824
E-mail: rwulfestieg@foursquare.org
Web site: http://www.foursquare.org.

Fourth Generation Pubs., *(978-0-9706186)* PMB 146,14625 Baltimore Ave., Laurel, MD 20707-4902 USA (SAN 253-5513) Tel 301-497-9948.

Fox Chapel Publishing Co., Inc., *(978-0-932944; 978-1-56523; 978-1-57421; 978-1-58011; 978-1-880029; 978-1-85974; 978-0-9777004; 978-1-60765; 978-1-4971; 978-1-4972; 978-1-5048; 978-1-64124)* Orders Addr.: 1970 Broad St., East Petersburg, PA 17520 USA (SAN 920-8887) Tel 717-560-4703; Fax: 717-560-4702; Toll Free Fax: 888-369-2885; Toll Free: 800-457-9112 (orders); *Imprints:* Design Originals (Design Orig)
E-mail: sales@carvingworld.com; alan@foxchapelpublishing.com; Younger@foxchapelpublishing.com
Web site: http://www.foxchapelpublishing.com/; http://www.scrollsawer.com/; http://www.carvingworld.com; http://www.foxchapelpublishing.com; www.d-originals.com
Dist(s): **Independent Pubs. Group.**

Fox Print Bks., *(978-0-9729587)* 200 Seashore Ave., Peaks Island, ME 04108 USA Tel 207-899-0781
E-mail: eleanor.morse@gmail.com.

Fox Ridge Pubns., *(978-0-9856215; 978-0-9904281; 978-0-9967683)* 8805 State Rd 144, Kewaskum, WI 53040 USA Tel 715-630-2433
E-mail: lisalickel@gmail.com.

Fox Run Pr., LLC, *(978-0-9819607; 978-0-9825930)* 7840 Bullet Rd., Peyton, CO 80831 USA
Web site: http://www.FoxRunPress.com; http://www.ShadowFoxBook.com.

Fox Song Bks., *(978-0-9744989; 978-0-9837310)* Orders Addr.: P.O. Box 548, Ferndale, WA 98248 USA
E-mail: fox@foxsongbooks.com; orders@foxsongbooks.com; amy.foxsongbooks@gmail.com; foxsongbooks@gmail.com
Web site: http://foxsongbooks.com
Dist(s): **Lightning Source, Inc.**

Fox Valley Habitat for Humanity, *(978-0-9914127)* 1300 S. Broadway, Montgomery, IL 60538 USA Tel 630-859-3333
E-mail: R.Kelso@foxvalleyhabitat.org
Web site: www.foxvalleyhabitat.org.

FoxAcre Pr., *(978-0-9671783; 978-0-9709711; 978-0-9818487; 978-1-936771)* 401 Ethan Allen Ave., Takoma Park, MD 20912 USA Fax: 301-560-2482
E-mail: info@foxacre.com
Web site: http://www.foxacre.com
Dist(s): **Smashwords.**

Foxcroft, Jennifer, *(978-0-9909895)* 1020 15th St., Denver, CO 80202 USA Tel 615-839-4698
E-mail: jenfoxy@me.com
Web site: jenniferfoxcroft.com.

Foxglove Pr., *(978-1-882959)* P.O. Box 210602, Nashville, TN 37221-0602 USA Fax: 615-646-8188; 2606 Eugenia Ave., Nashville, TN 37211 Do not confuse with companies with the same name in Corte Mandera, CA, Bryn Mawr, PA
Dist(s): **Midpoint Trade Bks., Inc.**

FoxRock, Inc., *(978-0-9643740; 978-0-9714705)* 61 Fourth Ave., No. 4, New York, NY 10003 USA Tel 212-505-6880; Fax: 212-673-1039
E-mail: evergreen@nyc.rr.com
Web site: http://www.evergreenreview.com.

Fox's Den Publishing, *(978-0-9816107)* P.O. Box 6156, Sevierville, TN 37864-6156 USA
E-mail: foxsdenpublishing@hotmail.com.

FPI Publishing, *(978-0-9768215)* P.O. Box 247, Havre de Grace, MD 21078 USA Tel 410-459-9087
E-mail: gyleen@colourfulstitches.com
Web site: http://www.colourfulstitches.com.

FQ Classics *Imprint of* **Filiquarian Publishing, LLC**

Fragile X Assn. of Georgia, *(978-0-9727865)* 3161 W. Somerset Ct., Marietta, GA 30067-5045 USA Tel 770-988-9275; Fax: 770-988-8255; Rood End Hse., 6 Stortford Rd., Great Dunmow, CM6 1DA Tel 01371 875100
E-mail: info@fragilex.k-web.co.uk; frax@bellsouth.net
Web site: www.fragilex.org.uk; http://www.myextraspecialbrother.com.

978-0-692-74504-5; 978-1-946232) 110 Evergreen St., Glade Spring, VA 24340 USA Tel 276-451-0331
E-mail: rondacaudill@yahoo.com
Dist(s): **CreateSpace Independent Publishing Platform.**

Full Moon Publishing LLC, *(978-0-9666021; 978-0-9785402; 978-0-9820352; 978-0-9846357; 978-0-9888683; 978-0-9976707)* Orders Addr.: 433 Mystic Point Dr., Bluffton, SC 29909 USA Tel 219-688-3093 Do not confuse with Full Moon Publishing, Norton, MA
E-mail: fullmoonpub@sc.rr.com
Web site: http://www.fullmoonpub.com
Dist(s): **Smashwords.**

Full Quart Pr. *Imprint of* **Holly Hall Pubns., Inc.**

Full Satchel Pr. (CAN) *(978-0-9731960) Dist. by* **Wlsn Assocs.**

Fullerton Bks., Inc., *(978-0-9652918)* Orders Addr.: P.O. Box 1, Waveland, MS 39576 USA Tel 972-412-3131; 228-457-5323; Fax: 509-278-0766
E-mail: info@vincevance.com
Web site: http://www.vincevance.com.

FullofPep Pubns., *(978-0-9760684)* P.O. Box 367, Columbia, SC 29202 USA
E-mail: fullofpeppublications@yahoo.com.

Fulton Bks., *(978-1-63338)* 296 Chestnut St., Meadville, PA 16335 USA Tel 646-503-4822
E-mail: dusty@fultonbooks.com
Web site: fultonbooks.com.

Fulton, David Pubs. (GBR) *(978-1-85346; 978-1-84312) Dist. by* **Taylor and Fran.**

Fultus *See* **Fultus Corp.**

Fultus Corp., *(978-0-9744339; 978-1-59682)* P.O. Box 50095, Palo Alto, CA 94303 USA Fax: 650-745-0873; *Imprints:* Fultus Publishing (Ful Pubng)
E-mail: production@fultus.com
Web site: http://www.fultus.com; http://elibrary.fultus.com; http://store.fultus.com; http://writers.fultus.com
Dist(s): **Lightning Source, Inc.**

Fultus Publishing *Imprint of* **Fultus Corp.**

Fun 4 Kids Publishing *Imprint of* **Stray Dog Pr., LLC**

Fun Fitness Publishing, *(978-0-9762483; 978-0-615-35686-0)* 16 Paulsboro Rd., Woolwich, NJ 08055 USA Tel 609-410-3717 (phone/fax); Fax: 609-257-4079
E-mail: jeyre2@comcast.net; funfitness@comcast.net
Web site: http://www.janeeyre-art.com; http://www.funfitnesstraining.weebly.com.

Fun Places Publishing, *(978-0-9646737; 978-0-9833832)* 6124 Capetown St., Lakewood, CA 90713 USA Tel 562-867-5223
E-mail: orders@funplaces.com
Web site: http://www.funplaces.com
Dist(s): **American West Bks.**
Sunbelt Pubns., Inc.

Fun Publishing Co., *(978-0-938293)* 2121 Alpine Pl., No. 402, Cincinnati, OH 45206 USA (SAN 661-1761) Tel 513-533-3636; Fax: 513-421-7269 Do not confuse with companies with the same or similar names in Scottsdale, AZ, Fort Lauderdale, FL, Indianapolis, IN
E-mail: funpublish@aol.com
Web site: http://www.funpublishing.com.

Fun Time Flowers *See* **Flower Sprouts**

Fun to Read Bks. with Royally Good Morals *Imprint of* **MKADesigns**

Funcastle Pubns., *(978-0-9645771)* Orders Addr.: P.O. Box 51217, Riverside, CA 92517 USA Tel 951-653-5200; Fax: 951-653-4300; Edit Addr.: 20833 Millbrook St., Riverside, CA 92508 USA.

Fundacion Intermon (ESP) *(978-84-604; 978-84-8452; 978-84-89970; 978-84-921977) Dist. by* **Mariuccia Iaconi Bk Imports.**

Fundacion Intermon (ESP) *(978-84-604; 978-84-8452; 978-84-89970; 978-84-921977) Dist. by* **Lectorum Pubns.**

Fundamental Christian Endeavors, *(978-1-931787)* 49191 Cherokee Rd., Newberry Springs, CA 92365 USA Tel 760-257-3503; Fax: 760-652-4808
Web site: http://www.ironwood.org.

Fundamental Wesleyan Pubs., *(978-0-9629383; 978-0-9761003; 978-0-9914251)* 2120 Culverson Ave., Evansville, IN 47714 USA Tel 812-476-2996
E-mail: victorpau@aol.com
Web site: http://www.fwponline.cc.

FUNdamentals/Leap In Faith, *(978-0-9834645)* P.O. Box 491, Abingdon, MD 21009 USA Tel 443-484-2512
E-mail: Fundamentals123@aol.com
Web site: Fundamentals123.com
Dist(s): **Partners Pubs. Group, Inc.**

Fundcraft Publishing, *(978-1-931413; 978-1-935397)* Orders Addr.: P.O. Box 340, Collerville, TN 38027 USA Tel 901-853-7070; Fax: 901-853-6196; Edit Addr.: 410 Hwy. 72 W., Collierville, TN 38017 USA Tel 901-853-7070
E-mail: info@fundcraft.com
Web site: http://www.fundcraft.com.

FungChung, Nikko M, *(978-0-9981497)* 505 Benton Drive, Apt. 4312, Allen, TX 75013 USA Tel 347-724-0000; Fax: 347-724-0000
E-mail: nikko.fungchung@gmail.com
Web site: www.awabookseries.com.

Funk, Sherree *See* **Serving One Lord Resources**

Funnel Cloud 9, Inc., *(978-0-9767297)* 545 Tom Treece Rd., Morristown, TN 37814 USA
Web site: http://www.fc9.net.

Funny Bone Bks., *(978-0-9771836; 978-0-9790240; 978-0-9799121; 978-0-9822288; 978-0-9841507)* 3435 Golden Ave., No. 302, Apt. 302, Cincinnati, OH 45226 USA
E-mail: dpendery@newforms.com
Web site: http://www.bookmasters.com/funnybones.

FunnyGuy.Comedy, *(978-0-9747398)* 123 N. Kings Rd., Los Angeles, CA 90048 USA
E-mail: dave@funnyguy.com
Web site: http://www.funnyguy.com.

FunStitch Studio *Imprint of* **C & T Publishing**

Fur, George, *(978-0-9752985)* 165 Laurel Ave., Menlo Park, CA 94025 USA
E-mail: yfur@msn.com.

Fury Publishing & Distributing, *(978-0-9747049)* 325 Washington Ave. No. 214, Kent, WA 98032 USA Tel 253-520-3111
E-mail: furypublishing@msn.com
Web site: http://www.fury2000.com.

Futech Educational Products, Inc., *(978-0-9627001; 978-1-889192)* 2999 N. 44th St., Suite 225, Phoenix, AZ 85018-7248 USA Tel 602-808-8765; Fax: 602-278-5667; Toll Free: 800-597-6278.

Future Comics, *(978-0-9744225)* 220 W. Brandon Blvd., Brandon, FL 33511 USA Tel 813-655-1900; Fax: 813-662-3250; Toll Free: 877-226-6427
E-mail: info@futurecomicsonline.com
Web site: http://www.futurecomicsonline.com.

Future Education, Incorporated *See* **Future Horizons, Inc.**

Future Horizons, Inc., *(978-1-885477; 978-1-932565; 978-1-935274; 978-1-935567; 978-0-9860673; 978-1-941765)* 721 W. Abram St., Arlington, TX 76013 USA Tel 817-277-0727; Fax: 817-277-2270; Toll Free: 800-489-0727
E-mail: kelly@fhautism.com
Web site: http://www.FHautism.com
Dist(s): **BookBaby**
Follett School Solutions
Ingram Publisher Services
MyiLibrary.

Fuze Publishing, LLC, *(978-0-9841412; 978-0-9849908; 978-0-9897306; 978-0-9965553; 978-0-9974956)* 2305-C Ashland Street, No. 312, Ashland, OR 97520 USA.

F+W Media, Incorporated *See* **F&W Media, Inc.**

FWB Pubns., *(978-0-9829070; 978-0-9847974; 978-0-9887437; 978-0-615-85868-5; 978-1-940609; 978-0-615-87554-5; 978-0-615-87589-7; 978-0-615-89973-2; 978-0-615-91387-2; 978-0-615-94095-3; 978-0-692-21431-2; 978-0-692-30634-5; 978-0-692-30835-6; 978-0-692-34282-4)* 1006 Rayme Dr., COLUMBUS, OH 43207-8738 USA Tel 573-330-7728
E-mail: alton.loveless@prodigy.net
Dist(s): **CreateSpace Independent Publishing Platform.**

FWOMP Publishing, *(978-0-9760096)* 935 Lighthouse Ave. No. 21, Pacific Grove, CA 93950 USA
Web site: http://www.fwomp.com
Dist(s): **Sunbelt Pubns., Inc.**

FX Digital Photo, *(978-0-9769009)* 9 Maison Way, Toms River, NJ 08757-6413 USA
Web site: http://www.fxdigitalphoto.com.

Fyhrie, Stephanie, *(978-0-9989821; 978-0-9989821-0-6)* 13316 E 7th Ave, Spokane Valley, WA 99216 USA Tel 509-499-1445
E-mail: tc@taylorchristianmarketing.com.

G & K Publishing, *(978-0-615-15770-2)* P.O. Box 445, Johnstown, OH 43031 USA
E-mail: eking@byroncarmichael.com
Web site: http://www.byroncarmichael.com; http://GandKPublishing.com.

G & R Publishing, *(978-1-56383)* 507 Industrial St., Waverly, IA 50677 USA Toll Free Fax: 800-866-7496; Toll Free: 800-383-1679; 800-887-4445
E-mail: gandr@gandrpublishing.com; gifts@cqbookstore.com
Web site: http://www.cookbookprinting.com; http://www.cqbookstore.com
Dist(s): **CQ Products.**

G. B. Enterprises *See* **Kent Communications, Ltd.**

G C B Publishing *See* **Holly Hall Pubns., Inc.**

G F W C of South Dakota/Daughters of Dakota *See* **Sky Carrier Pr.**

G I A Pubns., Inc., *(978-0-941050; 978-1-57999; 978-1-62277)* 7404 S. Mason Ave., Chicago, IL 60638 USA (SAN 205-3217) Tel 708-496-3800; Fax: 708-496-3828; Toll Free: 800-442-1358
E-mail: custserv@giamusic.com
Web site: http://www.giamusic.com
Dist(s): **Faith Alive Christian Resources**
Independent Pubs. Group
MyiLibrary.

G J & B Publishing, *(978-0-9635006)* 22442 University Ave., N., Cedar, MN 55011 USA Tel 612-434-0786.

G Publishing *See* **G Publishing LLC**

G Publishing LLC, *(978-0-9727582; 978-0-9773267; 978-0-9776780; 978-0-9788536; 978-0-9790691; 978-0-9796978; 978-0-9801297; 978-0-9814650; 978-0-9820002; 978-0-9823533; 978-0-9843426; 978-0-9834307; 978-0-9849360; 978-0-9883374; 978-0-9862379; 978-0-9971579; 978-0-9985990)* P.O. Box 24374, Detroit, MI 48224-2348 USA Toll Free: 866-882-1159; 4826 Harvard Rd., Detroit, MI 48224 Do not confuse with G Publishing in Sebastopol, CA
E-mail: jhun@gpublishingsuccess.com; juthegen@sbcglobal.net
Web site: http://www.gpublishingsuccess.com.

G R M Assocs., *(978-0-933813; 978-0-929093)* 290 W. End Ave., 16A, New York, NY 11111 USA Tel 212-874-5964; Fax: 212-874-6425; *Imprints:* Taylor Productions (Taylor Prods)
Dist(s): **Independent Pubs. Group.**

G R Publishing, *(978-0-9668530)* 460 Brookside Way, Felton, CA 95018 USA
E-mail: pub@grandmarose.com
Web site: http://www.grandmarose.com.

G R T Pubns., *(978-0-9678420; 978-0-9716906)* P.O. Box 1845, Provo, UT 84603 USA Tel 801-374-2587 (phone/fax)
E-mail: grtpublications@juno.com
Web site: http://www.rogerpminert.

G Schirmer, Inc. *Imprint of* **Leonard, Hal Corp.**

G T Labs, *(978-0-9660106; 978-0-9788037)* P.O. Box 8145, Ann Arbor, MI 48107 USA Tel 734-994-0474; Fax: 734-764-4487
E-mail: info@gt-labs.com
Web site: http://www.gt-labs.com
Dist(s): **Diamond Comic Distributors, Inc.**
Diamond Bk. Distributors.

G340 Publishing, *(978-0-9843837)* 7115 N. Division St. Suite B #132, Spokane, WA 99207-2242 USA (SAN 859-2462) Tel 509-850-0340
E-mail: service @g340.com; grealy@gmail.com
Web site: http://g340.com.

Gabriel Pr., *(978-0-9721888)* 255 Calle San Sebastian, San Juan, PR 00901 USA Do not confuse with companies with the same name in Phoenix, AZ, Ventura, CA, Fort Lauderdale, FL, Saratoga, CA, Sacramento, CA, San Juan, PR, Littleton, CO
E-mail: paolanogueras@gmail.com
Web site: http://www.paolanogueras.net
Dist(s): **Lectorum Pubns., Inc.**

Gabriel Resources, Orders Addr.: P.O. Box 1047, Waynesboro, GA 30830 USA Tel 706-554-1594; Fax: 706-554-7444; Toll Free: 800-732-6657 (8MORE-BOOKS); Edit Addr.: 129 Mobilization Dr., Waynesboro, GA 30830 USA.

Gabriele Capelli Editore Sagl (CHE) *(978-88-87469) Dist. by* **SPD-Small Pr Dist.**

Gaff Pr., *(978-0-9619629)* Orders Addr.: P.O. Box 1024, Astoria, OR 97103 USA (SAN 245-8403); Edit Addr.: P.O. Box 1024, Astoria, OR 97103-1024 USA (SAN 245-8411)
E-mail: gaffpres@pacifier.com
Web site: http://www.gaffpress.com.

Gaffney, Linda, *(978-0-9787501)* Orders Addr.: PMB 2682 2103 Harrison Ave., NW, Olympia, WA 98502 USA Tel 360-584-8566
Web site: http://www.HomeplacePress.com.

Gago, Noel, *(978-0-692-44889-2; 978-0-692-72531-3; 978-0-692-72538-2)* 14261 nw 22nd st, PEMBROKE PINES, FL 33028 USA Tel 7182165431.

Gail's Guides, *(978-1-881005)* Orders Addr.: 134 West Canyonview Dr., Longview, WA 98632 USA
E-mail: guides@oz.net; info@gailsguides.com
Web site: http://www.gailsguides.com
Dist(s): **Anderson News - Tacoma**
Aramark
News Group, The
Partners/West Book Distributors.

Gain Literacy Skills / Lynette Gain Williams, *(978-0-9779063)* 10659 Rookwood Dr., San Diego, CA 92131-1619 USA (SAN 850-5608)
E-mail: gainliteracy@sbcglobal.net.

Gakushu Kenkyu-Sha (JPN) *(978-4-05) Dist. by* **IngramPubServ.**

Galactic Bks., *(978-0-9769400)* 9827 Endora Ct., Owings Mills, MD 21117 USA
Web site: http://www.galacticbooks.usafreespace.com.

Galahad Publishing, *(978-0-918483)* 6035 Vantage Ave., Suite 100, North Hollywood, CA 91606-4637 USA (SAN 657-680X) Tel 818-761-5198; Fax: 818-766-8645; Toll Free: 888-349-4878
Web site: http://www.GalahadPublishing.com.

Galaxia Publishing Group, LLC, *(978-0-9741657)* P.O. Box 61054, Phoenix, AZ 85082-1054 USA Tel 480-279-0836; Fax: 480-279-0863
E-mail: info@galaxiapg.com; LatonyaJordanSmith@yahoo.com
Web site: http://www.galaxiapg.com.

Galaxias Productions, *(978-0-9835631; 978-0-9850529)* 200 W. 90th St. No. 9B, New York, NY 10024 USA Tel 212-712-1540
E-mail: alwooten411@yahoo.com
Web site: www.arthurwooten.com
Dist(s): **Smashwords.**

Galaxy Bks., *(978-0-9671358; 978-0-9935428-2-4)* 244 Madison Ave., PMB 231, New York, NY 10016-2817 USA Fax: 212-428-6747; Toll Free: 877-425-2992
E-mail: Galaxybooks@yahoo.com.

Galaxy Pr., LLC, *(978-1-59212; 978-1-61986)* Orders Addr.: 7051 Hollywood Blvd., Suite 200, Hollywood, CA 90028 USA (SAN 254-6906) Tel 323-466-7815; Fax: 323-466-7817; Edit Addr.: 6121 Malburg Way, vernon, CA 90058 USA
E-mail: jwills@galaxypress.com; kcatalano@galaxypress.com; jgoodwin@galaxypress.com; sarahc@galaxypress.com
Web site: http://www.galaxypress.com/; http://www.battlefieldearth.com; http://www.writersofthefuture.com; http://www.goldenagestories.com
Dist(s): **Follett School Solutions**
Gumdrop Bks.

Galen Pr., Ltd., *(978-1-883620)* Orders Addr.: P.O. Box 64400, Tucson, AZ 85728-4400 USA (SAN 254-1823) Tel 520-577-8363; Fax: 520-529-6459; Toll Free: 800-442-5369 (orders only) Do not confuse with Galen Pr. in Madison, NJ
E-mail: ml@galenpress.com; sales@galenpress.com
Web site: http://www.galenpress.com
Dist(s): **Majors, J. A. Co.**
Matthews Medical Bk. Co.
Rittenhouse Bk. Distributors.

Gali Girls, Inc., *(978-0-9773673)* 48 Cranford Pl., Teaneck, NJ 07666 USA Tel 201-862-1989
Web site: http://www.galigirls.com.

Galileo Pr., *(978-0-913123; 978-0-9817519)* 3637 Blackrock Rd., Upperco, MD 21155-9322 USA (SAN 240-6543) Do not confuse with companies with the same or similar name in Edmonds, WA, Brooklyn, NY
E-mail: jawendell@aol.com
Dist(s): **Pathway Bk. Service.**

Galison, *(978-0-7353; 978-0-929648; 978-0-939456; 978-1-56155)* Div. of The McEvoy Group, 28 W. 44th St., Suite 1411-12, New York, NY 10036 USA Tel 212-354-8840; Fax: 212-944-8682; Toll Free: 800-322-6663
E-mail: sales@galison.com
Web site: http://www.galison.com
Dist(s): **Hachette Bk. Group**
McEvoy Group, The.

Gallagher, Carole M., *(978-0-9702197)* 431 S. Main St., Williamstown, NJ 08094 USA Tel 856-875-1575; Fax: 856-875-1998.

Gallant Hse. Publishing, *(978-0-9660373)* 1329 Hwy. 395n, Ste 10 Pmb 114, Gardnerville, NV 89410 USA Toll Free: 877-577-2244
E-mail: gallanthouse@hotmail.com.

†Gallaudet Univ. Pr., *(978-0-913580; 978-0-930323; 978-1-56368; 978-1-944838)* 800 Florida Ave., NE, Washington, DC 20002-3695 USA (SAN 205-261X) Tel 202-651-5488; Fax: 202-651-5489; Toll Free Fax: 800-621-8476; Toll Free: 888-630-9347 (TTY)
E-mail: valencia.simmons@gallaudet.edu
Web site: http://gupress.gallaudet.edu
Dist(s): **Chicago Distribution Ctr.**
Ebsco Publishing
Follett School Solutions; *CIP.*

Gallery Bks. *Imprint of* **Gallery Bks.**

Gallery Bks., 1230 Ave. of the Americas, New York, NY 10020 USA; *Imprints:* Gallery Books (Gallery Imp)
Dist(s): **Simon & Schuster, Inc.**

Galletti, Barbara, *(978-0-9748737)* 2509 Lawnside Rd., Timonium, MD 21093-2605 USA Tel 410-252-6568
E-mail: gallettinotes@hotmail.com.

Gallimard, Editions (FRA) *(978-2-07) Dist. by* **Distribks Inc.**

Gallopade International, *(978-0-635; 978-0-7933; 978-0-935326; 978-1-55609)* Orders Addr.: 6000 Shakerag Hl. # 314, Peachtree Cty, GA 30269-6523 USA (SAN 213-8441) Toll Free Fax: 800-871-2979; Toll Free: 800-536-2438; *Imprints:* Marsh, Carole Family CD-Rom (C Marsh); Marsh, Carole Books (C Mrsh Bks); Marsh, Carole Mysteries (CarolMarshMyst)
E-mail: michael@gallopade.com
Web site: http://www.gallopade.com
Dist(s): **Follett School Solutions.**

Gallopade: Publishing Group *See* **Gallopade International**

Gallup Pr., *(978-1-59562)* 1251 Avenue of the Americas, 23rd Fl., New York, NY 10020 USA Tel 212-899-4709; Fax: 212-899-4899; Toll Free: 877-242-5587
Web site: http://www.gallup.com
Dist(s): **MyiLibrary**
Simon & Schuster
Simon & Schuster, Inc.

Gambit Pubns., Ltd. (GBR) *(978-1-901983; 978-1-904600; 978-1-906454; 978-1-910093) Dist. by* **TwoRivers.**

Game Day Press *See* **Timberwood Pr.**

Game Designers' Workshop, *(978-0-943580; 978-1-55878)* 1418 N. Clinton Blvd., Bloomington, IL 61701 USA (SAN 240-656X) Tel 309-531-4076
E-mail: farfuture@gmail.com
Dist(s): **PSI (Publisher Services, Inc.).**

Gametasia, *(978-0-692-32164-5; 978-0-9862942)* 14252 Morning Glory Rd., Tustin, CA 92680 USA Tel 714-838-9408
E-mail: pamela@freedomwithinfoundation.org.

Gam-Jam Publishing Company *See* **Pendleton Publishing, Inc.**

Gamlin, Stephen, *(978-0-9767993)* P.O. Box 5, Goffstown, NH 03045 USA Tel 603-560-3360; Fax: 603-774-8698; Toll Free: 877-560-3360
E-mail: Steve@InspiredBySteve.com
Web site: http://www.InspiredBySteve.com.

Gamoke, John, *(978-0-9771290)* 6645 Humboldt Ave. S., Richfield, MN 55423 USA; *Imprints:* JoZanephine Originals (MYID_Z_JOZANEP).

GanDale Associates Houston *See* **Holocaust Museum Houston**

Gant, Linda G. Gifted Creations *See* **Readers Are Leaders**

Gantt Smith Publishing Hse., *(978-0-9847885)* 875 Victor Ave. Apt., 235, Inglewood, CA 90302 USA Tel 310-673-5114
E-mail: migs13@sbcglobal.net.

Gaon Bks., *(978-0-9820657; 978-0-9825439; 978-1-935604)* Div. of Gaon Institute for Tolerance Studies, P.O. Box 23924, Santa Fe, NM 87502-3924 USA Tel 505-920-7771
E-mail: gaonbooks@gmail.com
Web site: http://www.gaonbooks.com.

Gap Tooth Publishing *Imprint of* **Charles River Pr.**

Garcia, Cezanne, *(978-0-9728041)* 30405 Cupeno Ln., Temecula, CA 92592-2540 USA Tel 951-506-6407 (phone\fax)
E-mail: stgarcia@fda.net.

Garcia, Jeffrey, *(978-0-9840942)* 3000 Avenida Ciruela, Carlsbad, CA 92009 USA Tel 760-822-0222.

Garden Fleetfoot Pr., *(978-0-9762544)* Orders Addr.: P.O. Box 1188, Okemos, MI 48805 USA
E-mail: info@gardenfleetfoot.com
Web site: http://gardenfleetfoot.com
Dist(s): **Partners Pubs. Group, Inc.**

Garden, Randa, *(978-0-615-12322-6)* 3503 Portia Pl., Norfolk, NE 68701 USA Tel 402-371-0544
E-mail: jrgarden@cableone.net
Web site: www.pennythepenguin.com.

Gardner, Colin, *(978-0-9720348; 978-0-615-11851-2)* 1677 S. 75 E., Bountiful, UT 84010-5218 USA Tel 801-296-2109 (phone/fax)
E-mail: colingardner@juno.com.

Gardner, Dianne Lynn, *(978-0-692-47613-0; 978-0-692-89976-2; 978-0-692-90949-2; 978-0-692-91279-9; 978-0-692-92044-2; 978-0-692-92048-0; 978-0-692-92874-5)* 9385 Olalla Valley Rd. SE, Port Orchard, WA 98367 USA Tel 253-851-0339
Web site: http://gardnersart.com
Dist(s): **CreateSpace Independent Publishing Platform.**

Gardner Pubns., *(978-0-9659163)* 235 E. Main St., No. 119, Hendersonville, TN 37075 USA Tel 615-824-5100; Fax: 615-824-3400; Toll Free: 800-297-8179
E-mail: harveylgardner@bbsco.com
Web site: http://www.bbsco.com.

Gareth Stevens Hi-Lo Must Reads *Imprint of* **Stevens, Gareth Publishing LLLP**

Gareth Stevens Learning Library *Imprint of* **Stevens, Gareth Publishing LLLP**

Gareth Stevens Secondary Library *Imprint of* **Stevens, Gareth Publishing LLLP**

Garfein, Stanley, *(978-0-9787422)* 1110 Lasswade Dr., Tallahassee, FL 32312-2845 USA Tel 850-385-1538; Fax: 850-531-0276
E-mail: StaGarfein@aol.com.

Garing, Bernard, *(978-0-9765809)* 6304 Caleigh Dr., Charlestown, IN 47111-7713 USA.

Garland City Bks. of Watertown, *(978-0-9890509)* P.O. Box 604, Black River, NY 13612 USA Tel 315-783-0728
E-mail: rothensu@yahoo.com.

Garland, Daniel, *(978-0-9768414)* 6247 Cascade Hwy., NE, Silverton, OR 97381 USA
E-mail: danielggarland@msn.com.

Garlic Pr., *(978-0-931993; 978-1-930820)* Orders Addr.: 899 S. College Mall, Suite 381, Bloomington, IN 47401 USA (SAN 686-1105) Tel 800-789-0554; Toll Free Fax: 800-789-5576 Do not confuse with companies with the same name in Kirkwood, MO, New London, NH, Abingdon MD, Lenox MA, Kansas City, MO
E-mail: garlic.press@att.net
Web site: http://www.garlicpress.com
Dist(s): **Independent Pubs. Group.**

Garr, Sherry B., *(978-0-9759866)* 3456 S. Mulberry Dr., Saint George, UT 84790 USA
Web site: http://www.gumfounded.com.

Garrelts, Christopher *See* **Squarey Head, Inc.**

Garrett, Debbie Behan, *(978-0-615-24202-6; 978-0-615-42184-1)* P.O. Box 210571, Dallas, TX 75211-0571 USA Tel 214-337-5928; Fax: 214-337-8127
E-mail: blackdolls@sbcglobal.net
Web site: http://blackdollcollecting.com.

Garrigues Hse. Pubs., *(978-0-9620844; 978-1-931014)* 2746 Stein Ln., Lewisburg, PA 17837 USA (SAN 249-969X) Tel 570-204-2906; 2746 Stein Ln., Lewisburg, PA 17837 (SAN 249-9703)
E-mail: jim@garrigueshouse.com
Web site: http://www.garrigueshouse.com.

Garry & Donna, LLC, *(978-0-9815617)* P.O. Box 30021, Las Vegas, NV 89173 USA.

Gasior, Julie, *(978-0-615-18824-9; 978-0-615-18884-3)* 6404 Shadow Oaks Ct., Monmouth Jct, NJ 08852-2297 USA
E-mail: juliespotions@gmail.com
Web site: http://juliespotions.com
Dist(s): **Lulu Pr., Inc.**

Gask Castle Pr., *(978-0-9843717)* 1725 Starmont Trail, Knoxville, TN 37909 USA Tel 865-310-8947
E-mail: phillip@gaskcastlepress.com.

Gaslight Pubns., *(978-0-934468)* P.O. Box 1344, Studio City, CA 91614-0344 USA Tel 818-784-8918
Dist(s): **Empire Publishing Service**
Players Pr., Inc.

GASLight Publishing, *(978-0-9754796; 978-1-933869)* P.O. Box 1025, Leander, TX 78646 USA Tel 512-528-1727; Fax: 512-259-8671
E-mail: ken@gaslightpublishing.com; kenschaefer@totalaccess.net
Web site: http://www.gsalightpublishing.com
Dist(s): **Smashwords.**

GateKeepers International, Incorporated, *(978-0-9745483)* 15245 Jessie Dr., Colorado Springs, CO 80921 USA
E-mail: Femritegki@gmail.com
Web site: http://www.gatekeepersintl.org.

GateKeepers Ministries International, *(978-0-9754535)* 3600 Earl Ave., Pennsauken, NJ 08110 USA Toll Free: 866-910-2810
Web site: http://www.gkmi.org.

Gateway Learning Corporation *See* **HOP, LLC**

Gateways Bks. & Tapes, *(978-0-89556)* Div. of I.D.H.H.B., Inc., P.O. Box 370, Nevada City, CA 95959 USA (SAN 211-3635) Tel 530-477-8101; Fax: 530-272-0184; Toll Free: 800-869-0658
E-mail: orders@gatewaysbooksandtapes.com; info@gatewaysbooksandtapes.com
Web site: http://www.gatewaysbooksandtapes.com
Dist(s): **Independent Pubs. Group**
MyiLibrary
ebrary, Inc.

Gathering Place Pubs., Inc., *(978-0-9754622; 978-0-615-38236-4; 978-0-9828311)* P.O. Box 341, Kaysville, UT 84037-8403 USA (SAN 256-0658) Fax: 801-451-6008
E-mail: sales@stonesquest.com
Web site: http://www.rebuildshattereddreams.com; http://www.stonesquest.com.

Gatorbytes *Imprint of* **Univ. Pr. of Florida**

†Gaunt, Inc., *(978-0-912004; 978-1-56169; 978-1-60449)* 3011 Gulf Dr., Holmes Beach, FL 34217-2199 USA (SAN 202-9413) Tel 941-778-5211; Fax: 941-778-5252
E-mail: info@gaunt.com; sales@gaunt.com
Web site: http://www.gaunt.com; *CIP.*

Gaunt, William W. & Sons, Incorporated *See* **Gaunt, Inc.**

Gauntlet, Inc., *(978-0-9629659; 978-1-887368; 978-1-934267)* 5307 Arroyo St., Colorado Springs, CO 80922 USA Tel 719-591-5566; Fax: 719-591-6676
E-mail: gauntlet66@aol.com; info@gauntletpress.com
Web site: http://www.gauntletpress.com.

Gauthier Pubns. Inc., *(978-0-9820812; 978-0-9833593; 978-0-615-71779-1; 978-1-942314)* P.O. Box 806241, Saint Clair Shores, MI 48080 USA (SAN 857-2119) Tel 313-458-7141; Fax: 586-279-1515; *Imprints:* Frog Legs Ink (Frog Legs Ink); Hungry Goat Press (Hungry Goat)
E-mail: info@gauthierpublications.com
Web site: http://www.FrogLegsInk.com; http://www.EATaBOOK.com
Dist(s): **BWI**
Brodart Co.
CreateSpace Independent Publishing Platform
Diamond Bk. Distributors
Follett School Solutions
OverDrive, Inc.

Gavila Publishing, *(978-0-9748466)* 20-23 43 St., Astoria, NY 11105 USA
Web site: http://www.gavila.com.

Gavin, Fred Enterprises, *(978-0-935668)* 96 Byron St., East Boston, MA 02128 USA (SAN 221-1629).

Gaviota Ediciones (ESP) *(978-84-392) Dist. by* **Lectorum Pubns.**

Gavlak, L.J. Publishing, *(978-0-9740357)* Orders Addr.: P.O. Box 72, Kylertown, PA 16847 USA Tel 814-345-6391; Edit Addr.: Rollingston Rd., Kylertown, PA 16847 USA
E-mail: largav@juno.com.

Gazarik, Rebecca, *(978-0-9802258)* 637 Pine Run Rd., Apollo, PA 15613-9313 USA
Web site: http://www.rebeccagazarik.com/.

Gazelle Pr. *Imprint of* **Genesis Communications, Inc.**

Gazing In Publishing, *(978-0-9839318)* P.O. Box 197, Columbia, SC 29147 USA Tel 803-743-8810
E-mail: winmilawe@gmail.com.

Gazoobi Tales, *(978-0-9679364)* P.O. Box 19614, Seattle, WA 98109-6614 USA
E-mail: info@gazoobitales.com
Web site: http://www.gazoobitales.com.

GDG Publishing, *(978-0-9787549; 978-0-9796625; 978-0-9797952; 978-0-9855335)* Orders Addr.: 2063 Continental Dr. NE, Atlanta, GA 30345 USA (SAN 851-5182) Tel 404-248-0012; Fax: 404-248-1487 Do not confuse with GDG Publishing in Oxnard, CA
E-mail: glennondesign@comcast.net
Web site: http://www.gdgpublishing.com.

GDL Multimedia, LLC, *(978-1-60245)* 2513 179th Ave E., Lake Tapps, WA 98391-6453 USA
E-mail: greg@gdlmultimedia.com
Web site: http://www.gdlmultimedia.com
Dist(s): **KSG Distributing.**

GDM Consulting Services LLC, *(978-0-9763738)* 5 Alluvium Lakes Dr., Voorhees, NJ 08043 USA
Web site: http://www.gdmcs.com.

G.E. Bks., *(978-0-9886402)* 14 Edith Ln., Douglasville, GA 30134 USA
E-mail: kimg@visionbookcompany.com
Web site: www.visionbookcompany.com.

Gecko Pr. (NZL) *(978-0-9582598; 978-0-9582787; 978-0-9582720; 978-1-877467; 978-1-877579; 978-1-927271; 978-1-77657) Dist. by* **Lerner Pub.**

Geckostufs, Incorporated *See* **Words & Pictures Publishing, Inc.**

Geddes, Anne Publishing (AUS) *(978-1-921652; 978-1-922024) Dist. by* **TwoRivers.**

Geez Pr., *(978-0-9816574)* P.O. Box 711, Elmore, OH 43416-0711 USA
Web site: http://home.woh.rr.com/geezpress.

Gefen Bks., *(978-0-86343)* 11 Edison Pl., Springfield, NJ 07081 USA (SAN 856-8065)
E-mail: gefenny@gefenpublishing.com
Web site: http://www.gefenpublishing.com.

Gefen Publishing Hse., Ltd (ISR) *(978-965-229) Dist. by* **Gefen Bks.**

Gefen Publishing Hse., Ltd (ISR) *(978-965-229) Dist. by* **Strauss Cnslts.**

Gem Bk. Pubs., *(978-0-9633723; 978-1-887651)* Div. of Fred Ward Productions, Inc., Orders Addr.: 2575 Barrymore Dr., Malibu, CA 90265-2955 USA Tel 310-456-9949; Fax: 310-456-9799
E-mail: fred@fredwardgems.com; charlotte@fredwardgems.com
Web site: http://www.fredwardgems.com/.

Gem Printing, *(978-0-9743429)* Orders Addr.: 600 Reisterstown Rd., Suite 200G, Baltimore, MD 21208 USA Tel 410-764-1617; Fax: 410-764-7471; *Imprints:* American Poets Society (Amer Poets)
E-mail: poetryamericaorders@yahoo.com
Web site: http://www.poetryamerica.com.

Gem Pubns., *(978-0-9742354)* 3520 McNally Ave., Altadena, CA 91001 USA
E-mail: gregmiddleton@earthlink.net
Web site: http://www.gempublications.com.

GemmaMedia, *(978-1-934848; 978-1-936846)* 230 Commercial St., Boston, MA 02109 USA (SAN 855-2037)
E-mail: info@gemmamedia.com; trish@gemmamedia.com
Web site: http://www.gemmamedia.com
Dist(s): **Ingram Publisher Services**
MyiLibrary.

GEMS *Imprint of* **Univ. of California, Berkeley, Lawrence Hall of Science**

Gems International Incorporated *See* **Gems International, LLC**

Gems International, LLC, *(978-0-9728626)* 119 Fern St., Darby, PA 19023 USA
E-mail: polishmeprofessional@gmail.com
Web site: www.rayfieldsrules.com.

Gemstone Literary, *(978-0-9801692)* 27943 Seco Canyon Rd., No. 212, Los Angeles, CA 91350 USA
Web site: http://www.GemTal.com.

Gemstone Publishing, Inc., *(978-0-911903; 978-1-888472; 978-1-60360)* Div. of Diamond Comic Distributors, Inc., 1966 Greenspring Dr., Suite 405, Timonium, MD 21093 USA Tel 410-427-9432; Fax: 410-252-4582 Do not confuse with companies with same or similar names in Thornville, OH, Lebanon, OR, Lauderdale Lakes, FL, Sugarland, TX
Web site: http://www.gemstonepub.com
Dist(s): **Diamond Comic Distributors, Inc.**
Diamond Bk. Distributors
SPD-Small Pr. Distribution.

Gen Manga Entertainment, Inc., *(978-0-9836134; 978-0-9850644; 978-1-939012)* 250 Pk. Ave., Suite 7002, New York, NY 10177 USA Tel 646-535-0090
E-mail: editor@genmanga.com
Web site: www.genmanga.com
Dist(s): **Diamond Comic Distributors, Inc.**
Diamond Bk. Distributors.

Gene Caven, *(978-0-578-09100-6; 978-0-9987416)* 61 Hidden Hill Rd, Tryon, NC 28782 USA Tel 828-817-9160.

Genealogical Publishing Company, Incorporated *See* **Genealogical.com**

†Genealogical.com, *(978-0-8063)* 3600 Clipper Mill Rd. Suite 260, Baltimore, MD 21211-1953 USA (SAN 206-8370) Toll Free: 800-296-6687 (orders & customer service); 3600 Clipper Mill Rd. Suite 260, Baltimore, MD 21211 (SAN 920-8755) Tel 410-837-8271; Fax: 410-752-8492
E-mail: hoffman@genealogical.com
Web site: http://www.Genealogical.com; *CIP.*

General Board of Global Ministries, The United Methodist Church, *(978-1-890569; 978-1-933663)* 475 Riverside Dr. Rm. 1473, New York, NY 10115 USA Tel 212-870-3731; Fax: 212-870-3654; *Imprints:* WD/GBGM Books (WD GBGM)
E-mail: cscott@gbgm-umc.org; KDonato@gbgm-umc.org
Web site: http://www.gbgm-umc.org
Dist(s): **Cokesbury**
Mission Resource Ctr.

General Bks. LLC, *(978-1-234; 978-1-77045; 978-1-150; 978-1-151; 978-1-152; 978-1-153; 978-1-154; 978-1-155; 978-1-156; 978-1-157; 978-1-158; 978-1-159; 978-1-230; 978-1-231; 978-1-232; 978-1-233; 978-1-235; 978-1-236; 978-1-238; 978-1-239; 978-1-130)* Orders Addr.: Box 29000, NAS485, Miami, FL 33102 USA
E-mail: support@general-books.net
Web site: www.general-books.net.

Generosity Philosophy, *(978-0-9961703)* 9848 Bobcat St., Aumsville, OR 97325 USA Tel 503-507-7069
E-mail: kim.trumbo@gmail.com.

Genesis Communications, Inc., *(978-0-9637311; 978-1-58169)* P.O. Box 191540, Mobile, AL 36619 USA Tel 251-443-7900; Fax: 251-443-7090; Toll Free: 800-367-8203; *Imprints:* Evergreen Press (Evergm Pr AL); Gazelle Press (Gazelle Pr); Axiom Press (Axiom Press)
E-mail: Jeff@evergreen777.com
Web site: http://www.evergreenpress.com
Dist(s): **BookBaby**
Spring Arbor Distributors, Inc.

Genesis Group *See* **Genesis Publishing**

Genesis Publishing, *(978-0-9770668)* Div. of Brad Worthley International, 12819 SE 38th St., No. 375, Bellevue, WA 98006 USA
E-mail: bradworthley@msn.com
Web site: http://www.bradworthley.com
Dist(s): **Midpoint Trade Bks., Inc.**

Genet Pr. LLC, *(978-0-9846663)* 9907 Cranapple Ct., Springdale, MD 20774 USA Tel 301-636-6353
E-mail: mayimona_ngwala@hotmail.com
Web site: www.genetpress.com.

Genius In A Bottle Technology Corp, *(978-0-9768429)* Orders Addr.: 910 NW 42nd St., Miami, FL 33127-2755 USA
E-mail: geniusinfo@geniusinabottle.net
Web site: http://www.geniusinabottle.net; http://www.cafepress.com/forevergirl; http://www.cafepress.com/geniusbooks; http://www.cafepress.com/gumo; http://www.cafepress.com/gkid; http://www.cafepress.com/cleversunburst; http://www.cafepress.com/tou; http://www.cafepress.com/foreverman; http://www.cafepress.com/forever4; http://www.cafepress.com/whateverr; http://www.cafepress.com/robospace; http://www.cafepress.com/battlegirlgear; http://www.cafepress.com/geniusinabottle; http://www.ca

Gentle Giraffe Pr., *(978-0-9747921; 978-0-9777394; 978-0-9801746)* 7405 Barra Dr., Bethesda, MD 20817 USA Tel 202-423-4205; Fax: 334-460-0724; Toll Free: 888-424-4723
E-mail: info@gentlegiraffe.com
Web site: http://www.gentlegiraffe.com.

Gentle Thoughts for Hard Spots, *(978-0-9988274)* 401 RIVER ROCK Rd., CHALLIS, ID 83226 USA Tel 298-833-4681
E-mail: karenw@custertel.net.

Gently Spoken Communications, *(978-0-9711794; 978-0-9746491; 978-0-9776096; 978-0-615-11369-2; 978-0-615-11845-1; 978-0-692-55642-9)* P.O. Box 365, St. Francis, MN 55070 USA Tel 763-506-9933; Fax: 763-506-9934; Toll Free: 877-224-7886
E-mail: info@gentlyspoken.com
Web site: http://www.gentlyspoken.com.

Genuine Prints, LLC, *(978-0-615-23040-5)* P.O. Box 328, Carpentersville, IL 60110 USA Fax: 847-844-9073; Toll Free: 888-853-0001
E-mail: info@nicoandlola.com
Web site: http://www.nicoandlola.com.

Geography Matters, Inc., *(978-0-9702403; 978-1-931397; 978-1-62863)* P.O. Box 92, Nancy, KY 42544 USA Tel 606-636-4678; Fax: 606-636-4697; Toll Free: 800-426-4650
E-mail: geomatters@geomatters.com
Web site: http://www.geomatters.com.

George, H. Publishing, *(978-0-9728183)* Orders Addr.: 14513 Bayes Ave., Lakewood, OH 44107 USA Tel 216-319-4575
E-mail: ninthohio@sbcglobal.net.

Geoscience Information Services, *(978-0-9777100)* Orders Addr.: P.O. Box 911, West Falmouth, MA 02574-0911 USA Tel 508-540-6490
E-mail: geoinfo@comcast.net.

Gequalsa, *(978-0-9792518)* 2710 Walnut St., Orlando, FL 32806 USA.

Gerardian Inkspot & Paint Society, *(978-0-9786675)* St. Gerard's Church, 240 W. Robb Ave., Lima, OH 45801 USA.

Gerber, Judie *See* **Seachild**

Gere Publishing, *(978-0-9743995; 978-0-9981987)* 113 Leonard Rd., Shutesbury, MA 01072-9783 USA (SAN 257-4594) Tel 413-259-1741
E-mail: claudia@claudiagereco.com
Web site: http://www.gerepublishing.com.

Gerhardt, Paul L., *(978-0-615-13556-4; 978-0-615-16208-9; 978-0-615-16270-6; 978-0-615-23707-7; 978-0-615-23721-3)* P.O. Box 111141, Tacoma, WA 98411 USA
Web site: http://www.paulgerhardt.com
Dist(s): **Lulu Pr., Inc.**

Geringer, Laura Book *Imprint of* **HarperCollins Pubs.**

Gernand, Linda, *(978-0-9755025)* 523 Oyster Creek Dr., Richwood, TX 77531 USA.

Gersten, Dan & Associates LLC *See* **Dogwalk Pr.**

Gerstenblatt, Judith Furedi *See* **Lucky & Me Productions, Inc.**

Gestalt Pubns., *(978-0-9764065)* 3828 Clinton Ave. S., Minneapolis, MN 55409-1314 USA Tel 612-822-4419.

Gestalt Publishing Pty, Ltd. (AUS) *(978-0-9775628; 978-0-9807823; 978-1-922023) Dist. by* **D C D.**

Get Happy Tips, LLC, *(978-0-9860272)* 515 SW 18th Ave. No. 19, Fort Lauderdale, FL 33312 USA Tel 786-314-8199
E-mail: gethappytips@gmail.com
Web site: http://www.gethappytips.com.

Get Life Right Foundation, The *See* **Life Force Bks.**

Get Published, *(978-1-4501; 978-1-4525)* 1663 Liberty Dr., Bloomington, IN 47403 USA Tel 812-650-0913; Fax: 812-339-6554; Toll Free: 877-217-3420 Do not confuse with Get Published in Valparaiso, IN
E-mail: customersupport@dellartepress.com
Dist(s): **Author Solutions, Inc.**
CreateSpace Independent Publishing Platform.

Getchu Bks. *Imprint of* **Lake 7 Creative, LLC**

Getting There, *(978-0-9707274)* P.O. Box 1412, Asheville, NC 28802-1412 USA Tel 828-645-5908
E-mail: bmayers@charter.net
Web site: http://www.paddlingasheville.com
Dist(s): **Common Ground Distributors, Inc.**

Getty, J. Paul Trust Publications *See* **Getty Pubns.**

†Getty Pubns., *(978-0-89236; 978-0-941103; 978-1-60606; 978-1-947440)* Orders Addr.: P.O. Box 49659, Los Angeles, CA 90049-0659 USA Tel 310-440-7333; Fax: 818-779-0051; Edit Addr.: 1200 Getty Ctr. Dr., Suite 500, Los Angeles, CA 90049-1682 USA (SAN 208-2276) Tel 310-440-7365; Fax: 310-440-7758; Toll Free: 800-223-3431; *Imprints:* J. Paul Getty Museum (J P Getty)
E-mail: pubsinfo@getty.edu; pubsinfo@getting.edu; mwinter@getty.edu
Web site: http://www.getty.edu/publications
Dist(s): **Casemate Academic**
Chicago Distribution Ctr.
Hachette Bk. Group
Lectorum Pubns., Inc.
Libros Sin Fronteras
Oxford Univ. Pr., Inc.; *CIP.*

GGMI Incorporated *See* **God's Glory Media**

Ghim, John Yun, *(978-0-9656864)* 1139 Queen Anne Pl. Apt. 106, Los Angeles, CA 90019-7105 USA
E-mail: coolghim@yahoo.com.

GHL Publishing LLC, *(978-0-9726419)* P.O. Box 26462, Collegeville, PA 19426 USA (SAN 254-9875) Tel 610-831-1442; Fax: 610-831-1443
E-mail: c.lagunilla@att.net
Web site: http://www.GHLPublishing.com.

Gholson, C. D., *(978-0-9725974)* 2341 W. Pierce, Harrison, MI 48625 USA Tel 898-539-5312
E-mail: goatlocker@msn.com.

Ghost Hse. Bks. *Imprint of* **Lone Pine Publishing USA**

Ghost Hunter Productions, *(978-0-9717234; 978-1-934307)* P.O. Box 1199, Helena, MT 59624 USA
E-mail: info@ibw-books.com
Web site: http://www.ibw-books.com.

G-Host Publishing, *(978-0-9649088)* Orders Addr.: 8701 Lava Pl., West Hills, CA 91304-2126 USA Tel 818-340-6676 (phone/fax)
E-mail: robanne@ix.netcom.com.

Giant in the Playground, *(978-0-9766580; 978-0-9854139)* 2417 Welsh Rd., Suite 21 No. 328, Philadelphia, PA 19114 USA
E-mail: rich@giantitp.com
Web site: http://www.giantitp.com
Dist(s): **Diamond Comic Distributors, Inc.**
Diamond Bk. Distributors.

Giant in the Playground Games *See* **Giant in the Playground**

Giant Robot Bks., *(978-0-9749492)* P.O. Box 641639, Los Angeles, CA 90064 USA Tel 310-479-7311
E-mail: books@giantrobot.com
Web site: http://www.giantrobot.com
Dist(s): **Trucatriche.**

†Gibbs Smith, Publisher, *(978-0-87905; 978-0-941711; 978-1-58685; 978-1-4236)* Orders Addr.: P.O. Box 667, Layton, UT 84041 USA (SAN 201-9906) Tel 801-544-9800; Fax: 801-544-5582; Toll Free Fax: 800-213-3023 (orders); Toll Free: 800-748-5439 (orders); 800-835-4993 (Customer Service order only); Edit Addr.: 1877 E. Gentile St., Layton, UT 84040 USA Tel

801-544-9800; Fax: 801-546-8853; *Imprints:* Anorak Press (Anorak Pr)
E-mail: info@gibbs-smith.com; tradeorders@gibbs-smith.com
Web site: http://www.gibbs-smith.com
Dist(s): **Publishers Group West (PGW)**
Publishers Group International, Inc.; *CIP.*

Gibson Bks. *Imprint of* **Glory Days Group Publishing**

Gibson, C. R. Co., *(978-0-7667; 978-0-8378; 978-0-937970)* 401 BNA Dr., Bldg 200, Suite 600, Nashville, TN 37217 USA Toll Free: 800-243-6004 (ext. 2895)
E-mail: customerservice@crgibson.com
Web site: http://www.andersonpress.com.

Gibson, Cita, *(978-0-9727964)* P.O. Box 411236, Melbourne, FL 32941 USA Tel 316-210-6422; Fax: 321-757-7385
E-mail: maloon57@aol.com
Web site: http://www.citagibson.com.

Gibson Tech Ed, Incorporated *See* **GSS Tech Ed**

Giddy Up, LLC, *(978-0-932125; 978-1-59524)* 3630 Plaza Dr., Ann Arbor, MI 48108 USA (SAN 255-6847)
E-mail: stiehl@giddyup.com
Web site: http://www.giddyup.com.

Gifted Education Pr., *(978-0-910609)* Orders Addr.: P.O. Box 1586, Manassas, VA 20108 USA; Edit Addr.: 10201 Yuma Ct., Manassas, VA 20109 USA (SAN 694-132X) Tel 703-369-5017; Toll Free: 800-484-1406 (code 6857)
E-mail: mfisher345@home.com
Web site: http://GIFTEDEDPRESS.COM.

Gifted Psychology Press, Incorporated *See* **Great Potential Pr., Inc.**

Gigarjian, Ani & Linda Avedikian, *(978-0-9717799)* 169 S. Main St., Sherborn, MA 01770 USA
E-mail: gigarjian@comcast.net
Web site: http://www.armeniankids.com.

Giggletins *Imprint of* **Le Bk. Moderne, LLC**

Giggling Gorilla Productions, LLC, *(978-0-9770700)* 3444 Laredo Ln., Escondido, CA 92025-7807 USA
E-mail: zoomanmike@earthlink.net
Web site: http://www.gigglinggorillaproductions.com.

GiGi Bks., *(978-0-9740847)* 17480 Old Waterford Rd., Leesburg, VA 20176 USA Tel 703-669-9781; Fax: 703-669-9782
E-mail: ganderson@gigiaudiobooks.com
Web site: http://www.gigiaudiobooks.com.

Gigi Enterprises, *(978-0-615-12926-6)* P.O. Box 133, Irvington, NY 10533-0133 USA Fax: 914-591-9249
E-mail: sonia0904@aol.com.

GIL Pubns., *(978-0-9626035; 978-0-9802185; 978-0-615-75814-5)* P.O. Box 80275, Brooklyn, NY 11208 USA Fax: 718-386-6434
E-mail: kumasi@gilpublications.com
Web site: http://www.gilpublications.com
Dist(s): **A & B Distributors & Pubs. Group**
Bk. Hse., Inc., The.

Gilbert, Drexel Enterprises, Inc., *(978-0-9818464)* Orders Addr.: P.O. Box 364, Daphne, AL 36526 USA
E-mail: drexelgilbert@drexelgilbert.com
Web site: http://www.drexelgilbert.com.

Gilbert Square Bks., *(978-0-9745308)* 2115 Plymouth SE, Grand Rapids, MI 49506 USA Tel 616-245-1050
E-mail: kvidro2003@yahoo.com
Web site: http://www.squarepears.com.

Gilboy Publishing, *(978-0-9774696)* 3521 River Narrows Rd., Hilliard, OH 43026-7833 USA.

Gilchrist & Guy Publishing, *(978-0-9747990)* 2112 Colina Vista Way, Costa Mesa, CA 92627 USA
E-mail: rguy2112@comcast.net.

Gilded Dog Enterprises LLC, *(978-0-9793483)* 106 High Point Dr., Churchville, PA 18966 USA (SAN 853-1943) Tel 215-322-5592; Fax: 215-396-6832
Web site: http://gildeddog.com.

Gilder Lehrman Institute of American History, The, *(978-0-9663843; 978-1-932821; 978-0-9970330)* Orders Addr.: 49 W. 45th St., 6th Flr., New York, NY 10036 USA Tel 646-366-9666; Fax: 646-366-9669
E-mail: ahlstrom@gilderlehrman.org
Web site: http://www.gilderlehrman.org.

Gile, John Communications *See* **JGC/United Publishing Corps**

Gilead Publishing, LLC, *(978-1-68370)* 304 E. Forest Ave., Wheaton, IL 60187 USA; *Imprints:* Enclave (EnclaveUSA)
Web site: www.gileadpublishing.com
Dist(s): **Kregel Pubns.**

Giles, D. Ltd. (GBR) *(978-1-904832; 978-1-907804; 978-1-911282) Dist. by* **Consort Bk Sales.**

Giles, W. Marie *See* **Giles, Willie M.**

Giles, Willie M., *(978-0-9728944)* Orders Addr.: P.O. Box 3757, Pensacola, FL 32516-3757 USA
Web site: http://www.wix.com/booksbywmariegiles
Dist(s): **CreateSpace Independent Publishing Platform.**

Gilgamesh Publishing (GBR) *(978-1-908531) Dist. by* **Consort Bk Sales.**

Gilgit Pr., LLC, *(978-0-9746283)* P.O. Box 4881, Richmond, VA 23220 USA
Web site: http://www.gilgitpress.com.

Gill, Jim Music, *(978-0-9679038; 978-0-9815721)* Subs. of Jim Gill, Inc., Orders Addr.: P.O. Box 2263, Oak Park, IL 60303 USA Tel 708-763-9864; Fax: 708-763-9888; Edit Addr.: 835 N. Kenilworth Ave., Oak Park, IL 60303-9888 USA
E-mail: jimgill@jimgill.com
Web site: http://www.jimgill.com.

Gillette, Frances A., *(978-0-9636066)* P.O. Box 351, Yacolt, WA 98675 USA
E-mail: copia@copia.com; ward@infinitecolor.com; lithoinusa@centurytel.net
Web site: http://www.copia.com
Dist(s): **Adventure Pubns.**

Gilliam, T. & Associates, LLC, *(978-0-9762703)* 1696 Georgetown Rd., Unit B, Hudson, OH 44236 USA Tel 330-342-5940; Fax: 330-463-5730; Toll Free: 877-316-5097
E-mail: tgilliam@healthybodyweight.com
Web site: http://www.healthybodyweight.com.

Gilpatrick, Gil, *(978-0-9650507)* Orders Addr.: P.O. Box 461, Skowhegan, ME 04976 USA Tel 207-453-6959; Edit Addr.: 369 Middle Rd., Fairfield, ME 04937 USA
E-mail: gil@gilgilpatrick.com
Web site: http://www.gilgilpatrick.com.

Gimme Gimme Toys & Games, Inc., *(978-0-9762524)* 1418 N. Clinton Blvd., Bloomington, IL 61701 USA
Web site: http://www.gimmegimme.ca
Dist(s): **PSI (Publisher Services, Inc.).**

Gina Art Books *See* **Pipton Pr.**

Gina's Ink, *(978-0-9740454)* P.O. Box 11650, Denver, CO 80211 USA
Web site: http://www.cassandrasangel.com.

Ginebra, Fidel, *(978-0-615-15410-7)* Urb. La Plata, M-19 Calle Rubi, Cayey, PR 00736 USA
E-mail: fbloodguard@gmail.com
Dist(s): **Lulu Pr., Inc.**

Ginger Nielson - Children's Bk. Illustration, *(978-0-615-92252-2; 978-0-9913093; 978-0-692-78023-7)* 278 Sand Hill Rd., Peterborough, NH 03458 USA Tel 603-924-3775; *Imprints:* HallaVision Publishing (MYID_X_HALLAVI)
E-mail: gingernielson@gmail.com.

Ginger Pr., The, *(978-0-9785151)* P.O. Box 45753, Omaha, NE 68145-0753 USA
Dist(s): **Greenleaf Book Group**
Independent Pubs. Group.

Gingerbread Hse., *(978-0-940112)* 602 Montauk Hwy., Westhampton Beach, NY 11978 USA (SAN 217-0760) Tel 631-288-5119; Fax: 631-288-5179 Do not confuse with Gingerbread House, The, Savannah GA
Web site: http://www.gingerbreadbooks.com
Dist(s): **Independent Pubs. Group.**

Gingko Pr., Inc., *(978-1-58423; 978-1-934471)* Orders Addr.: 1321 Fifth St., Berkeley, CA 94710 USA (SAN 860-4436) Tel 510-898-1195; Fax: 510-898-1196 Do not confuse with Gingko Pr. in New York, NY
E-mail: account@gingkopress.com
Web site: http://www.gingkopress.com
Dist(s): **MyiLibrary**
Publishers Group West (PGW).

Ginn, Don & Co., *(978-0-9755438)* 11228 Vista Sorrento Pkwy, Suite I-303, San Diego, CA 92130 USA Tel 858-720-8433; Fax: 858-720-8733; Toll Free: 888-357-7313
E-mail: donginn@sbcglobal.net.

GIP House *See* **Summit Hse. Pubs.**

Girasol Collectables Inc., *(978-0-9797639; 978-0-9820890; 978-0-9820891; 978-0-9854755)* P.O. Box 5289, Mansfield, OH 44901-5289 USA
Web site: http://www.girasolcollectables.com.

Girl Named Pants, Inc., A, *(978-0-9755959)* 8954 Stonebriar Dr., Clarence Ctr., NY 14032-9373 USA
Web site: http://www.agirlnamedpants.com.

Girl Pr., Inc., *(978-0-9659754)* P.O. Box 480389, Los Angeles, CA 90048-1389 USA
E-mail: gp@girlpress.com
Web site: http://www.girlpress.com.

Girl Scouts of the USA, *(978-0-88441)* 420 Fifth Ave., New York, NY 10018 USA (SAN 203-4611) Tel 212-852-8000; Fax: 212-852-6511
E-mail: bnelson@girlscouts.org
Web site: http://www.girlscouts.org/.

Girl Twirl Comics, *(978-0-9742450; 978-0-9766707; 978-0-9794207)* Orders Addr.: P.O. Box 88, Sebastopol, CA 95473 USA Tel 707-546-7121 Do not confuse with Jane's World in Seattle, WA
Web site: http://www.janecomics.com
Dist(s): **Diamond Comic Distributors, Inc.**
Diamond Bk. Distributors.

Girls Explore *Imprint of* **Girls Explore LLC**

Girls Explore LLC, *(978-0-9749456)* Orders Addr.: P.O. Box 54, Basking Ridge, NJ 07920 USA (SAN 256-2677) Fax: 908-842-9166; *Imprints:* Girls Explore (GilExplore)
Web site: http://www.girls-explore.com
Dist(s): **Brodart Co.**

Girls In Da Game Publishing, *(978-0-9674454)* Orders Addr.: 5916 Las Virgenes Rd. No. 596, Calabasas, CA 91302 USA
E-mail: corneliagailgroundup@gmail.com
Web site: http://www.facebookthenewlook.com
Dist(s): **Lightning Source, Inc.**

GIRLS KNOW HOW *Imprint of* **NouSoma Communications, Inc.**

Girls of Faith, *(978-0-9764304)* P.O. Box 535, Rogersville, MO 65742 USA
E-mail: orders@girlsoffaith.com
Web site: http://www.girlsoffaith.com.

Girls-Connect *See* **Bizzy Girls Publishing**

Giro Pr., *(978-1-878857)* Orders Addr.: P.O. Box 203, Croton-on-Hudson, NY 10520 USA Tel 914-271-8924; Fax: 914-271-6552; Edit Addr.: 44 Morningside Dr., Croton-on-Hudson, NY 10520 USA
E-mail: info@giropress.com
Web site: http://www.giropress.com.

Giron Bks., *(978-0-9741393; 978-0-9915442)* 2141 W. 21st St., Chicago, IL 60608-2608 USA Tel 773-847-3000; Fax: 773-847-9197; Toll Free: 800-405-4276
E-mail: juanmanuel@gironbooks.com
Web site: http://www.gironbooks.com.

Girouard, John E., *(978-0-9791579)* c/o Capital AMG, 4800 Montgomery Sq. No. M-25, Bethesda, MD 20814 USA Tel 215-500-1989; Fax: 866-289-4613
E-mail: rfwinans@verizon.net
Web site: http://www.johngirouard.com.

Gish Creative, *(978-0-9728507; 978-0-615-74202-1)* 1940-A Fountainview, PMB 116, Houston, TX 77057 USA Tel 713-532-1173 (phone/fax)
Web site: http://www.gishcreative.com; http://www.thesummerbook.com.

Giunti Gruppo Editoriale (ITA) *(978-88-09; 978-88-507; 978-88-440) Dist. by* **Distribks Inc.**

Giusti-Gambini, J.M. Publishing, LLC, *(978-0-615-36873-3; 978-0-9829496)* 7259 Creeks Bend Ct., West Bloomfield, MI 48322 USA Tel 248-855-0869
E-mail: jogambini@comcast.net
Web site: http://www.poetino.com; http://www.jmgiusti-gambinipublishing.com.

Gival Pr., LLC, *(978-1-928589; 978-1-940724)* P.O. Box PO Box 3812, Arlington, VA 22203 USA (SAN 852-9787) Tel 703-351-0079 (phone)
E-mail: givalpress@yahoo.com
Web site: http://www.givalpress.com; http://www.givalpressstore.com
Dist(s): **CreateSpace Independent Publishing Platform**
Ediciones Universal
Follett School Solutions.

Givens, Florence Rosie *See* **FloBound Poems Publications**

Givinity Pr., *(978-0-9728654; 978-1-943803)* 3374 Maplewood Ct., Fargo, ND 58104-6224 USA (SAN 255-1527) Tel 701-235-4241; Fax: 701-280-2016; Toll Free: 866-221-5860
E-mail: ellen@givinity.com
Web site: http://www.givinity.com
Dist(s): **Brodart Co.**
Follett School Solutions.

Gizicki-Lipson, Coryn *See* **In the Sky Publishing**

Gizmo Enterprises, Inc., *(978-0-9759638)* Orders Addr.: 6511 Nova Driver No. 108, Davie, FL 33317 USA
E-mail: perry@colorcutter.com
Web site: http://www.colorcutter.com; http://www.gizmoLine.com.

Gizmo Pr., *(978-0-9749911)* 6990 Poco Bueno Cir., Sparks, NV 89436 USA Tel 775-626-4533; Fax: 775-425-5290
E-mail: mjarcher@aol.com; greg.nielsen@charter.net.

GL Design, *(978-0-9745882; 978-1-933983)* 1930 Central Ave. Unit E., Boulder, CO 80301 USA
E-mail: distrib@gldesignpub.com
Web site: http://www.gldesignpub.com
Dist(s): **Lightning Source, Inc.**

Gladstone Publishing, *(978-1-928681)* Do not confuse with Gladstone Publishing, Prescott, AZ
E-mail: dmsmart@onesmartladyproductions.com
Web site: http://www.gladstonepublishing.com; http://www.onesmartladyproductions.org
Dist(s): **BookBaby.**

Glass, Michael B. & Assocs., Inc., *(978-0-940429)* 735 Calebs Path/Glaro Bldg., Hauppauge, NY 11788 USA (SAN 664-3574).

†Glastonbury Pr., *(978-0-944963)* Orders Addr.: 454 Las Gallinas Ave., No. 108, San Rafael, CA 94903 USA Tel 415-492-2140; 415-686-4150 Do not confuse with Glastonbury Pr., Whittier, CA
E-mail: starstone@comcast.net; misty@glastonburypress.com
Web site: http://www.glastonburypress.com
Dist(s): **CreateSpace Independent Publishing Platform**; *CIP.*

Glavin, Kevin, *(978-0-9825466)* 23 Vassar Aisle, Irvine, CA 92612 USA
E-mail: admin@kevinglavinpublishing.com
Web site: http://www.rockstarsrainbow.com; http://www.kevinglavinpublishing.com.

Gleasner, Bill & Diana Inc., *(978-0-9651185)* 7994 Holly Ct., Denver, NC 28037 USA Tel 704-483-9301; Fax: 704-483-6309
E-mail: dgleasner@aol.com
Dist(s): **Booklines Hawaii, Ltd.**

Glenbridge Publishing, Ltd., *(978-0-944435)* 19923 E. Long Ave., Centennial, CO 80016 USA (SAN 243-5403) Tel 720-870-8381; Fax: 720-230-1209; Toll Free: 800-986-4135 (orders only)
E-mail: glenbridge@qwestoffice.net
Web site: http://www.glenbridgepublishing.com.

Glencannon Pr., *(978-0-9637586; 978-1-889901)* Orders Addr.: P.O. Box 1428, El Cerrito, CA 94530 USA; *Imprints:* Palo Alto Books (Palo Alto)
E-mail: merships@yahoo.com
Web site: http://www.glencannon.com.

†Glencoe/McGraw-Hill, *(978-0-02; 978-0-07)* Div. of The McGraw-Hill Education Group, 8787 Orion Pl., Columbus, OH 43240-4027 USA Toll Free: 800-334-7344
E-mail: customer.service@mcgraw-hill.com
Web site: http://www.glencoe.com
Dist(s): **Follett School Solutions**
Libros Sin Fronteras
McGraw-Hill Cos., The; *CIP.*

Glenhaven Pr., *(978-0-9637265; 978-0-9741279)* 24871 Pylos Way, Mission Viejo, CA 92691 USA Tel 949-770-1486
E-mail: glenhavn@thevision.net; jacki@hydrasystems.com
Dist(s): **J & J Bk. Sales.**

Glenmere Pr., *(978-0-9852948; 978-0-9903139)* Orders Addr.: 26 Kings Ridge Rd., Warwick, NY 10990 USA
E-mail: lois@glenmerepress.com; lois@wingedbooks.com
Web site: http://www.glenmerepress.com; http://www.wingedbooks.com
Dist(s): **CreateSpace Independent Publishing Platform**
INscribe Digital
Independent Pubs. Group
Lightning Source, Inc.

Glenn, Lauren, *(978-0-9772459)* 2436 Oakdale St., Tallahassee, FL 32308 USA.

Glenn, Peter Pubns., *(978-0-87314)* 824 E. Atlantic Ave. Ste. 7, Delray Beach, FL 33483-5300 USA (SAN 201-9930)
E-mail: gjames@pgdirect.com
Web site: http://www.pgdirect.com.

Glenneyre Pr. LLC, *(978-0-9768040; 978-1-934602)* 20555 Devonshire St., Box 203, Chatsworth, CA 91311-9133 USA
E-mail: myn@wordsushi.com
Web site: http://www.glenneyrepress.com.

Glens Falls Printing LLC, *(978-1-933575)* 51 Hudson Ave., Glens Falls, NY 12801 USA (SAN 256-7148) Tel 518-793-0555; Fax: 518-793-8624; Toll Free: 866-793-0555
E-mail: bob@gfprinting.com
Web site: http://www.gfprinting.com; http://www.spiritoftheadirondacksbook.com; http://www.commonmanbooks.com.

Glitter Creek, Inc., *(978-0-9744520)* 2919 Westridge Ave., Cincinnati, OH 45238 USA Toll Free: 888-982-7335
Web site: http://www.glittercreek.com.

Glitterati, Inc., *(978-0-9721152; 978-0-9765851; 978-0-9777531; 978-0-9793384; 978-0-9801557; 978-0-9822669; 978-0-9823412; 978-0-9823799; 978-0-9832702; 978-0-9851696; 978-0-9881745; 978-0-9891704; 978-0-9913419; 978-0-9903808; 978-0-9905320; 978-0-9862500; 978-0-9962930; 978-1-943876) 322 W. 57th St. No. 19T, New York, NY 10019 USA Tel 212-362-9119; Fax: 646-607-4433*
E-mail: jguerrero@glitteratiincorporated.com
Web site: http://www.glitteratiincorporated.com
Dist(s): **National Bk. Network.**

Global Academic Publishing, *(978-0-9633277; 978-1-883058; 978-1-58684)* Global Academic Publishing, Binghamton Univ., Binghamton, NY 13902-6000 USA Tel 607-777-4495; 607-777-2745 (contact Barnes & Noble for orders); Fax: 607-777-6132
E-mail: gporders@binghamton.edu
Web site: http://www.academicpublishing.binghamton.edu
Dist(s): **Hesteria Records & Publishing Co.**
State Univ. of New York Pr.

Global Age Publishing/Global Academy Pr., *(978-1-887176)* 16057 Tampa Palms Blvd., W., No. 219, Tampa, FL 33647 USA Tel 813-991-4982; Fax: 813-973-8166.

Global Alliances, *(978-0-9759126)* 82-09 166th St., Hillcrest, NY 11432 USA.

Global Authors Pubns., *(978-0-9728513; 978-0-9742161; 978-0-9766449; 978-0-9779680; 978-0-9798087; 978-0-9821223; 978-0-9845926; 978-0-9846536; 978-0-9861109)* P.O. Box 954, Green Cove Springs, FL 32043 USA; 730 Donnelly St., Eustis, FL 32726 Tel 904-425-1608
E-mail: gapbook@yahoo.com
Web site: http://www.globalauthorspublications.com.

Global Awareness Publishing Co., *(978-1-885888)* 1102 Hickory St., Madison, WI 53715-1726 USA.

Global Business Information Strategies, Inc., *(978-1-60231)* Orders Addr.: P.O. Box 610135, Newton, MA 02461 USA (SAN 852-1980) Tel 617-795-0519; Fax: 617-795-0211; Edit Addr.: 965 Walnut St., Suite 100, Newton, MA 02461 USA; *Imprints:* Cub Books (Cub Bks)
E-mail: publishing@gbisi.com
Web site: http://gbisi.com.

Global Commitment Publishing, *(978-1-884931)* Div. of Alpert & Assocs., 3544 Winfield Ln., NW, Washington, DC 20007 USA Tel 202-338-4975; Fax: 202-835-0668; 5505 Connecticut Ave., Washington, DC 20015.

Global Communications *See* **Inner Light - Global Communications**

Global Community Communications Publishing, *(978-0-9647357; 978-0-9822423; 978-1-937919)* P.O. Box 1613, Tubac, AZ 85646-1613 USA Tel 520-603-9932
E-mail: info@GlobalCommunityCommunicationsPublishing.org
Web site: http://www.GlobalCommunityCommunicationsPublishing.org.

Global Content Ventures, *(978-0-9799901)* P.O. Box 6370, Lancaster, PA 17607 USA.

Global Education Advance, *(978-0-9796019; 978-0-9801674; 978-1-935434)* 345 Barton Rd. at Lone Mountain, Dayton, TN 37321-7635 USA Tel 423-775-2949
E-mail: GlobalEdAdvance@aol.com
Web site: http://www.globaledadvance.org.

Global Education Resources, LLC, *(978-1-934046)* 37 Station Rd., Madison, NJ 07940 USA (SAN 851-1012) Tel 973-410-0840; Fax: 973-410-1603
E-mail: myoshida@globaledresources.com
Web site: http://www.globaledresources.com.

Global Goddess Pr., *(978-0-692-71437-9)* 20212 Village 20, Camarillo, CA 93012 USA Tel 805-504-5050
E-mail: endangeredabcs@yahoo.com.

Global Institute for Maximizing Potential, Incorporated, *(978-0-9772020; 978-0-9825776; 978-0-9830337)* 92 Mt. Zion Way, Ocean Grove, NJ 07756 USA Tel 732-776-7360
E-mail: richert@globalinst.com
Web site: http://www.globalinst.com.

Global Learning, Inc., *(978-1-59867)* 1001 SE Water Ave., Suite 310, Portland, OR 97214 USA Toll Free: 888-548-2787 Do not confuse with Global Learning Inc. in Brielle, NJ
Web site: http://www.litart.com.

Global Partnership, LLC, *(978-0-9644706)* Orders Addr.: P.O. Box 894, Murray, KY 42071 USA (SAN 255-4186) Tel 562-884-0062; Edit Addr.: 100 N. 6th St., Murray, KY 42071 USA
E-mail: steveneschmitt@cs.com; erin@wakeuplive.com
Web site: http://www.businessolympians.com
Dist(s): **Seven Locks Pr.**

Global Pr., *(978-0-9792151)* 2083 Ridge Point Dr., Los Angeles, CA 90049 USA Tel 310-476-8336.

Global Publications (S S I P S) *See* **Global Academic Publishing**

Global Publishing, *(978-0-911649)* 51 Bell Rock Plaza, Suite A, PMB 511, Sedona, AZ 86351 USA (SAN 299-3627)

For full information on wholesalers and distributors, refer to the Wholesaler and Distributor Name Index

Tel 928-284-5544; Fax: 928-284-5545 Do not confuse with companies with the same name in Meimingham, MI, Costa Mesa, CA, Las Angeles, CA, Florence, MA, Memphis, TN, Sauk Rapids, MN, Fort Lauderdale, FL, Fort Worth, TX, Salt Lake City, UT
E-mail: minorwood@earthlink.net
Web site: http://www.wealthysoul.com
Dist(s): **New Leaf Distributing Co., Inc.**

Global Truth Publishing, *(978-0-9740465)* Orders Addr.: 1001 Bridgeway, Suite 474, Sausalito, CA 94965 USA Tel 415-331-1102; Fax: 415-331-2265
E-mail: sales@globaltruthpublishing.com
Web site: http://www.globaltruthpublishing.com.

Global Village Kids, LLC, *(978-0-9760472)* 4111 Calavo Dr., La Mesa, CA 91941-7051 USA Tel 619-303-0929; Fax: 925-888-8471
E-mail: seth.burns@globalvillagekids.com
Web site: http://www.globalvillagekids.com
Dist(s): **AV Cafe, Inc., The**
BWI
Iaconi, Mariuccia Bk. Imports
Wayland Audio-Visual.

GlobalVision Travel Resources, Inc., *(978-0-9800147)* 4831 Las Virgenes Rd., No. 115, Calabasas, CA 91302-1911 USA
E-mail: LCohen@getglobalvision.com
Web site: http://getglobalvision.com.

GLOBE *Imprint of* **Pearson Schl.**

Globe Fearon Educational Publishing, *(978-0-13; 978-0-8224; 978-0-8359; 978-0-87065; 978-0-88102; 978-0-912925; 978-0-915510; 978-1-55555; 978-1-55675)* Div. of Pearson Education Corporate Communications, Orders Addr.: 4350 Equity Dr., P.O. Box 2649, Columbus, OH 43216-2649 USA Toll Free Fax: 800-393-3156; Toll Free: 800-848-9500; 800-321-3106 (customer service); Edit Addr.: One Lake St., Upper Saddle River, NJ 07458 USA
Web site: http://www.pearsonschool.com
Dist(s): **Cambridge Bk. Co.**
Follett School Solutions
IFSTA.

†Globe Pequot Pr., The, *(978-0-7627; 978-0-87106; 978-0-88742; 978-0-914788; 978-0-933469; 978-0-934802; 978-0-941130; 978-1-56440; 978-1-57034; 978-1-58574; 978-1-59228; 978-1-59921; 978-1-4779; 978-1-4930)* Orders Addr.: P.O. Box 480, Guilford, CT 06437-0480 USA (SAN 201-9892) Tel 888-249-7586; Toll Free Fax: 800-820-2329 (in Connecticut); Toll Free: 800-243-0495 (24 hours); 800-336-8334; Edit Addr.: 246 Goose Ln., Guilford, CT 06437 USA Tel 203-458-4500; Fax: 203-458-4600; Toll Free Fax: 800-336-8334; *Imprints:* Lyons Press (Lyons); Falcon Guides (Fal-Guides); TwoDot (Two-D)
E-mail: info@globepequot.com
Web site: http://www.globepequot.com
Dist(s): **Chelsea Green Publishing**
MyiLibrary
National Bk. Network
Rowman & Littlefield Publishers, Inc.; *CIP.*

Globe Pubs., *(978-0-9623663; 978-1-882614)* 724 Fair Meadows Dr., Saginaw, TX 76179-1017 USA.

Globe Publishing, *(978-0-9765168)* Orders Addr.: P.O. Box 3040, Pensacola, FL 32516-3040 USA Tel 850-453-3453; Fax: 850-456-6001; Edit Addr.: 8590 Hwy 98 W., Pensacola, FL 32506 USA Do not confuse with Globe Publishing in Salt Lake City, UT
Web site: http://www.gme.org.

Globo, Editora SA (BRA) *(978-85-217; 978-85-250) Dist. by* **Distribks Inc.**

Globo Libros, *(978-0-9706953)* Orders Addr.: P.O. Box 4025, Sunnyside, NY 11104 USA; Edit Addr.: 402 E. 64th St. Apt. 6C, New York, NY 10021-7826 USA
E-mail: dstockwell@globolibros.com
Web site: http://www.globolibros.com.

Glolar Multimedia Productions, *(978-0-9707746)* P.O. Box 721452, San Diego, CA 92172-1452 USA
E-mail: info@Glolar.com; info@glolar.com
Web site: http://www.glolar.com.

Glory Be Collectibles, *(978-0-9795127; 978-0-578-06528-1; 978-0-578-07491-7)* 2169 Green Canyon Rd., Fallbrook, CA 92028 USA (SAN 853-6627) Tel 760-723-5222; Fax: 760-723-4433
E-mail: sales@glorybe.com
Web site: http://www.glorybe.com.

Glory Bound Books Las Vegas *See* **Glorybound Publishing**

Glory Days Group Publishing, *(978-0-9755145)* P.O. Box 1869, Glen Burnie, MD 21060-1869 USA Tel 410-766-0005 (phone/fax); *Imprints:* Gibson Books (Gibson Bks)
E-mail: drgibson123@yahoo.com
Web site: http://www.glorydayspublishing2day4u.com.

Glorybound Publishing, *(978-0-9766718; 978-0-979654; 978-0-9802481; 978-1-60789)* 6401 E. 2nd St. #f, Prescott Valley, AZ 86314 USA (SAN 256-4564) Do not confuse with Glory Bound Books in Marlette, MI
E-mail: sherihauser@yahoo.com; gloryboundpublishing@yahoo.com
Web site: http://www.gloryboundpublishing.com.

Glover Publishing and Community Outsourcing, *(978-0-692-81946-3; 978-0-9986222)* 16306 Thornridge Dr., Grand Blanc, MI 48501 USA Tel 810-423-5118
E-mail: gg.writer.glove@gmail.com; gg.writer.glove@gmail.com; gg.writer.glove@gmail.com
Web site: www.GloverPCO.com
Dist(s): **CreateSpace Independent Publishing Platform.**

Glow Word Bks., *(978-0-9859834; 978-1-942514)* P.O. Box 705, Willernie, MN 55090 USA Tel 720-443-3320
E-mail: glowwordbooks@gmail.com
Web site: http://www.glowwordbooks.com
Dist(s): **CreateSpace Independent Publishing Platform**
Lightning Source, Inc.

Glowacki, Helen, *(978-0-9847211; 978-0-9890214; 978-0-9893807; 978-0-9913916)* 2319 Saratoga Bay Dr., West Palm Beach, FL 33409 USA Tel 561-845-8493
E-mail: wally_helen@yahoo.com
Web site: www.helenglowacki.com.

Glynworks Publishing, *(978-0-9795912)* 2630 International Dr. #929b, Ypsilanti, MI 48197 USA
Web site: http://www.glynworkspublishing.com
Dist(s): **Lightning Source, Inc.**

GMC Distribution (GBR) *(978-0-946819; 978-1-86108; 978-1-78494) Dist. by* **IngramPubServ.**

GMEC Publishing, *(978-0-9794302)* P.O. Box 4470, Lake Tahoe, NV 89449-4470 USA Tel 704-992-2272; Fax: 704-992-2271
E-mail: MrsButtar@aol.com; StoriesThatTeach@aol.com
Web site: http://www.DebbieButtar.com; http://www.ChildrensStoriesThatTeach.com.

GMI Bks., *(978-0-9841809)* 7250 Franklin Ave., No.1407, Hollywood, CA 90046 USA
E-mail: richard@thegirlfromatlantis.com; doubleosix@aol.com
Web site: http://www.thegirlfromatlantis.com.

Gnatcatcher Children'S Bks., *(978-0-9778005)* 1451 E. Armando Dr., Long Beach, CA 90807 USA Tel 562-427-1200
E-mail: maryhoch@excite.com.

GND Publishing *See* **Y-IREAD Publishing**

Gnomon Pr., *(978-0-917788)* P.O. Box 475, Frankfort, KY 40602-0475 USA (SAN 209-0104) Tel 502-223-1858 (phone/fax)
E-mail: jgnomon@aol.com
Dist(s): **SPD-Small Pr. Distribution.**

Gnosophia Pubs., *(978-0-9773391)* 3800 New Hampshire Ave. NW Apt 507, Washington, DC 20011-7932 USA (SAN 257-3210) Tel 202-709-7580; Toll Free Fax: 866-525-0247
E-mail: admin@wisdomforthesoul.org; info@wisdomforthesoul.org; admin@gnosophia.com
Web site: http://www.wisdomforthesoul.org; http://www.gnosophia.com.

Go Ask Anyone, Inc., *(978-0-9742866)* 38 Irwin St., No.3, Winthrop, MA 02152 USA
Web site: http://www.goaskanyone.com.

Go Daddy Productions, Inc., *(978-0-9753938)* 2010 Ripley Point Ct., Odenton, MD 21113 USA Tel 443-226-4747
E-mail: mejagan@yahoo.com
Web site: http://www.go-daddyproductions.com.

Go Flag Football, *(978-0-9772203)* 1978 Shiloh Valley Trail, Kennesaw, GA 30144 USA
Web site: http://www.goflagfootball.com.

Go Jolly Bks., *(978-0-9822824; 978-1-942937)*
Web site: http://www.gojollybooks.com.

Go Team, LLC, *(978-0-9797040)* 1427 Heatherwood Rd., Columbia, SC 29205 USA (SAN 854-1566)
E-mail: deliacorrigan@mindspring.com
Web site: http://www.goteambooks.com.

Goals Unlimited Pr., *(978-0-9632562)* Div. of Equestrian Education Systems, P.O. Box 460125, Huson, MT 59846 USA Tel 406-626-5764; Fax: 406-626-5774
E-mail: jhascoop@aol.com
Web site: http://www.equestrianeducation.org
Dist(s): **Mountain Pr. Publishing Co., Inc.**
Western International, Inc.

Goatee Graphics, *(978-0-9657257)* P.O. Box 591840, San Francisco, CA 94159-1840 USA (SAN 256-8985) Tel 415-272-6117
E-mail: goatee848@yahoo.com
Web site: http://www.undertherimbook.com.

Goblin Fern Pr. *Imprint of* **HenschelHAUS Publishing**

†Godine, David R. Pub., *(978-0-87923; 978-1-56792; 978-1-57423)* Orders Addr.: P.O. Box 450, Jaffrey, NH 03452 USA Tel 603-532-4100; Fax: 603-532-5940; Toll Free Fax: 800-226-0934; Toll Free: 800-344-4771; Edit Addr.: Fifteen Court Sq., Suite 320, Boston, MA 02108 USA (SAN 213-4381) Tel 617-451-9600; Fax: 617-350-0250
E-mail: info@godine.com; order@godine.com
Web site: http://www.godine.com
Dist(s): **Baker & Taylor International**
INscribe Digital
MyiLibrary
eBookit.com; *CIP.*

Godinez-Hammermaster Design, *(978-0-9773205)* 122 Eugenia Dr., Ventura, CA 93003 USA (SAN 257-7127)
E-mail: artposter@sbcglobal.net.

Godiva Girl Records & Publishing, Incorporated *See* **Girls In Da Game Publishing**

God's Bible School & College *See* **Revivalist Pr., The**

God's Glory Media, *(978-0-9772647)* Div. of God'sGloy Ministries International Inc., P.O. Box 1430, Dacula, GA 30019 USA (SAN 257-1528)
E-mail: office@godsglory.org
Web site: http://www.GodsGlory.org.

God's Greatest Gift, LLC, *(978-0-9796477)* Orders Addr.: P.O. Box 185, Manchester, MI 48158-8513 USA (SAN 853-9855) Tel 734-320-5111; Edit Addr.: 520 City Rd., Manchester, MI 48158-8513 USA Fax: 734-428-0084
E-mail: godsgreatestgift@comcast.net
Web site: http://www.godsgreatestgift.net
Dist(s): **Partners Pubs. Group, Inc.**

God's World Publications *See* **God's World Pubns. Inc.**

God's World Pubns. Inc., *(978-1-882440; 978-0-9844605; 978-0-9855957)* 12 All Souls Crescent, Asheville, NC 28803 USA (SAN 254-1696) Tel 828-253-8063; Fax: 828-253-1556
E-mail: edufeedback@ gwpub.com; pub@gwnews.com
Web site: http://www.learnwithworld.com/writewithworld/.

Godspeed Pr., *(978-0-9798250)* 430 Davis Dr., Suite 270, Morrisville, NC 27560 USA Tel 404-457-4097
E-mail: deanthewriter@gmail.com.

Goin' Native, Inc., *(978-0-9891323; 978-0-692-83288-2)* P.O. Box 617153, Orlando, FL 32861 USA Tel 407-897-3522; Fax: 407-896-4614
E-mail: info@goinnative.com.

GoKnow, Incorporated *See* **GoKnow Learning**

GoKnow Learning, *(978-0-9762083; 978-0-9767504; 978-0-9786499)* 2084 S. State St., Ann Arbor, MI 48104-4608 USA Toll Free: 877-482-3439
Web site: http://www.goknow.com.

Golan, Hanna, *(978-0-9779723)* 17340 Hamlin St., Lake Balboa, CA 91406 USA (SAN 850-7732) Tel 818-342-4969
E-mail: hannagolan2000@yahoo.com
Web site: http://blessthechildren.com.

GO-LA-NV Pr., *(978-0-9741826)* P.O. Box 1897, Huntsville, TX 77342-1897 USA Tel 936-291-2906
E-mail: rhvann@sbcglobal.net.

Gold 5 Publishing, *(978-0-9904017)* 5599 Sherwood Ct., Newburgh, IN 47630 USA Tel 334-614-6103
E-mail: gold5publishing@gmail.com.

Gold Angel Press *See* **ONLY1EARTH, LLC**

Gold Boy Music & Pubn., *(978-0-9761992)* 108 Highland Tr., Chapel Hill, NC 27516 USA (SAN 256-2499) Tel 919-500-3023
E-mail: rob@musicgoldboy.com
Web site: thechristmasauntie.com; http://www.musicgoldboy.com
Dist(s): **BCH Fulfillment & Distribution.**

Gold Boy Music & Publishing *See* **Gold Boy Music & Pubn.**

Gold Charm Publishing, LLC, *(978-0-9744855)* Orders Addr.: P.O. Box 161, Nottingham, NH 03290 USA Tel 603-942-7925 (phone/fax); Edit Addr.: 82 Priest Rd., Nottingham, NH 03290 USA.

Gold Design, LLC *See* **Toy Rocket Studios, LLC**

Gold Leaf Pr., *(978-1-886769)* Orders Addr.: 2229 Alter Rd., Detroit, MI 48215 USA Tel 313-331-3571; 262-342-0018 Oleand Publications; Fax: 313-308-3063; 262-342-0018 Oleand Publications; Toll Free: 800-838-8854 Do not confuse with companies with the same name in Seattle, WA, Starke FL
E-mail: rebecca@goldleafpress.com; wings@oleand.com
Web site: http://www.goldleafpress.com; http://www.oleand.com
Dist(s): **Oleand Pubns.**

Gold Medallion *Imprint of* **Medallion Pr., Inc.**

Gold Street Pr., *(978-1-934533)* 814 Montgomery St., San Francisco, CA 94133 USA Tel 415-291-0100; Fax: 415-291-8841
E-mail: michelled!@weldonowen.com
Web site: http://www.weldonowen.com; http://www.goldstreetpress.com.

Golden Anchor Pr., *(978-1-886864)* 625 Elrod Rd., Bowling Green, KY 42104 USA Tel 270-780-9334
E-mail: smithdale2@aol.com; goldnanchr@aol.com
Web site: http://www.Everykidawinner.com
Dist(s): **Partners/West Book Distributors**
Quality Bks., Inc.
Unique Bks., Inc.

Golden Bks. *Imprint of* **Random Hse. Children's Bks.**

Golden Bks. Adult Publishing Group *Imprint of* **St. Martin's Pr.**

Golden, Brian *See* **PastWays Inc.**

Golden Eagle Publishing Hse., Inc., *(978-0-9744205; 978-0-9753533; 978-0-9759122; 978-0-9769364)* 9201 Wilshire Blvd., Suite 205, Beverly Hills, CA 90210 USA Tel 310-273-9176; Fax: 310-273-0954
E-mail: info@goldeneaglepublishing.com
Web site: http://www.goldeneaglepublishing.com
Dist(s): **Greenleaf Book Group.**

Golden Gate National Parks Conservancy, *(978-0-9625206; 978-1-883869; 978-1-932519)* 201 Fort Mason, 3rd Flr., San Francisco, CA 94123 USA Tel 415-561-3000; Fax: 415-561-3033
Web site: http://www.parksconservancy.org/
Dist(s): **Yosemite Assn.**

Golden Gate Publishing, *(978-0-9856631)* P.O. Box 27478, San Francisco, CA 94127 USA Tel 415-753-2930
E-mail: GoldenGatePublishing@gmail.com
Web site: GoldenGatePublish.com.

Golden Gryphon Pr., *(978-0-9655901; 978-1-930846)* 3002 Perkins Rd., Urbana, IL 61802 USA (SAN 299-1829) Tel 217-384-4205 (phone/fax); Fax: 217-352-9748
E-mail: Gryphon@goldengryphon.com
Web site: http://www.goldengryphon.com
Dist(s): **Independent Pubs. Group**
MyiLibrary
ebrary, Inc.

Golden Guides from Saint Martin's Pr. *Imprint of* **St. Martin's Pr.**

Golden Harvest Publishing Co., *(978-0-9747904)* 4849 Valley Rd., Rosedale, VA 24280 USA Tel 276-880-9862; Fax: 276-880-1146
E-mail: adda@mounet.com.

Golden Inspirational *Imprint of* **Random Hse. Children's Bks.**

Golden Mastermind Seminars, Inc., *(978-0-9740924; 978-1-934919; 978-0-692-03130-8)* Orders Addr.: 6507 Pacific Ave., Suite 329, Stockton, CA 95207 USA (SAN 255-2639) Fax: 209-467-3260; Toll Free: 800-595-6632
E-mail: erica@goldenmastermind.com
Web site: http://www.goldenmastermind.com
Dist(s): **Bookmasters Distribution.**

Golden Monkey Publishing, LLC, *(978-0-9719632)* 24 Meadowood Ln., Old Saybrook, CT 06475 USA (SAN 254-5322)
Web site: http://www.goldenmonkeypublishing.com.

Golden Oak Publishers *See* **Golden Oak Pubs. L.P.**

Golden Oak Pubs. L.P., *(978-1-929248; 978-1-936346)* Orders Addr.: P.O. Box 136967, Fort Worth, TX 76163 USA Tel 800-479-3545; Toll Free Fax: 800-479-3545
E-mail: MattS@goldenoakpublishers.com
Web site: http://www.HaroldBullock.com.

Golden Palace Publishing, *(978-0-9851472)* 215 W. 95th St., PH-D, New York, NY 10025 USA Tel 917-882-5185; Fax: 718-862-8044
E-mail: jay.friedenberg@gmail.com.

Golden Peach Publishing, *(978-1-930655)* 1223 Wilshire Blvd., #1510, Santa Monica, CA 90403 USA Tel 310-623-0835; 310-272-6809
E-mail: marketing@goldenpeachbooks.com; info@goldenpeachbooks.com; goldenpeachbooks@gmail.com
Web site: http://goldenpeachbooks.com.

Golden Perils Pr., *(978-0-615-15007-9; 978-0-615-19452-3; 978-0-578-00320-7; 978-0-578-00360-3; 978-0-578-00361-0)* 2 McKee Dr., Old Orchard Beach, ME 04064 USA Tel 207-934-3074
E-mail: goldenperils@aol.com
Web site: http://www.howardhopkins.com
Dist(s): **Lulu Pr., Inc.**

Golden Rain Tree Pr., *(978-0-9744107)* Div. of Leland Foerster Photography, 307 Fowles St., Oceanside, CA 92054 USA Tel 760-433-2554 (phone/fax)
E-mail: lelandfoerster@sbcglobal.net
Web site: http://www.lelandfoerster.com
Dist(s): **Sunbelt Pubns., Inc.**

Golden Valley Pr., *(978-0-9718053)* 24905 Mica Ridge Rd., Custer, SD 57730 USA
E-mail: horsted@dakotaphoto.com
Web site: http://www.goldenvalleypress.com.

Golden Voice Enterprises, *(978-0-9643301)* 8503 Summerdale Rd., No. 371, San Diego, CA 92126 USA.

Golden West Publishers *Imprint of* **American Traveler Pr.**

Golden Wings Enterprises, *(978-0-9700103; 978-0-9749241; 978-0-9794340)* P.O. Box 468, Orem, UT 84059-0468 USA
E-mail: BJ@bjrowley.com
Web site: http://www.bjrowley.com.

Golden/Disney *Imprint of* **Random Hse. Children's Bks.**

Goldenrod Pr., *(978-0-9748333)* Orders Addr.: P.O. Box 71, Algona, IA 50511 USA Tel 515-295-7090; Edit Addr.: 2509 S. State St., Algona, IA 50511-7296 USA
E-mail: slotjm@yahoo.com.

Goldleaf Games, LLC, *(978-0-9748757)* P.O. Box 804, Lawrence, KS 66044 USA
E-mail: gary@goldleafgames.com
Web site: http://www.goldleafgames.com.

Goldmann, Wilhelm Verlag GmbH (DEU) *(978-3-442) Dist. by* **Distribks Inc.**

Goldner, Harriet LLC, *(978-0-9779676)* P.O. Box 480003, Delray Beach, FL 33448 USA
E-mail: hgoldnerbooks@bellsouth.net
Web site: http://www.JewishFamilyFun.com.

Goldsberry, Booty, *(978-0-9792875)* 10 Windsor Pl., Poland, ME 04274 USA Tel 207-998-5710
E-mail: elattanzi@bookmasters.com.

Goldwrite Publishing, *(978-0-9767933; 978-0-615-13858-9)* 1224 Gallatin Ct., Hampton, GA 30228 USA Tel 678 510-6941
E-mail: asheagold@yahoo.com
Dist(s): **BookBaby**
Lulu Pr., Inc.

Golfing Bee, LLC, *(978-0-692-78420-4; 978-0-9983495)* 8815 First Bloom Rd., Charlotte, NC 28277 USA Tel 503-507-2712
E-mail: golfingbee45@gmail.com.

Golly Gee-pers, *(978-0-9964175)* 923 Mountain View Dr., Lafayette, CA 94549 USA Tel 925-324-4418
E-mail: gollygee_pers@yahoo.com
Web site: www.gollygee-pers.com.

Gom Foxtail *Imprint of* **Gom Publishing, LLC**

Gom Publishing, LLC, *(978-0-9729197; 978-1-932966)* P.O. Box 211110, Columbus, OH 43221 USA (SAN 255-3988) Tel 614-876-7097; Toll Free Fax: 866-422-8292; Toll Free: 866-466-2608; *Imprints:* Gom Foxtail (Gom Foxtail)
E-mail: sfox@gompublishing.com
Web site: http://www.gompublishing.com.

Gonzalez, David J. Ministries, *(978-0-9741561)* P.O. Box 847, Lake Delton, WI 53940 USA Tel 608-254-5150
E-mail: dgm@mountainfaith.org
Web site: http://www.mountainfaith.org.

Good Bks. *Imprint of* **Skyhorse Publishing Co., Inc.**

Good Catch Publishing, *(978-0-9772383; 978-0-9785152; 978-0-9792475; 978-1-934635; 978-1-938478; 978-1-68085)* Orders Addr.: P.O. Box 6551, Aloha, OR 97007 USA (SAN 257-0289) Tel 503-475-2005; Fax: 503-356-9685; Toll Free: 877-967-3224; Edit Addr.: 4074 NW 169th Ave., Beaverton, OR 97006 USA Fax: 503-356-9685; Toll Free: 877-967-3224
E-mail: nathanlindley@goodcatchpublishing.com; admingcp@gmail.com
Web site: http://www.goodcatchpublishing.com; http://www.testimonybooks.com.

Good Harbor Pr., *(978-0-9799638; 978-0-615-32057-1)* 80 Walsh St., Medford, MA 02155 USA Tel 781-396-1733.

Good News Connections, *(978-0-9728900)* Orders Addr.: P.O. Box 66573, Austin, TX 78766 USA Toll Free: 888-899-3207 Do not confuse with The Good News Connections, Inc. in Orlando, FL
E-mail: stayton@xc.org
Web site: http://www.GoodNewsConnections.com.

Good News Fellowship Ministries, *(978-0-9629559; 978-1-888081)* Div. of Funtasy Pubns., 220 Sleepy Creek Rd., Macon, GA 31210-5720 USA Tel 478-757-8071; Fax: 478-757-0136; Toll Free: 800-300-9630
E-mail: goodnews@reynoldscable.net
Web site: http://www.goodnews.netministries.org; http://kathiewaltersministry.com
Dist(s): **Anchor Distributors.**

Good News Productions, International, *(978-1-59305)* Orders Addr.: P.O. Box 222, Joplin, MO 64802-0222 USA Tel 417-782-0060; Fax: 417-782-3999; Edit Addr.: 2111 N. Main, Joplin, MO 64802-0222 USA
E-mail: gnpi@gnpi.org
Web site: http://www.gnpi.org.

Good Night Bks., *(978-0-9777979; 978-1-60219)* 36 Route 6A, Sandwich, MA 02563 USA
E-mail: adam@goodnightourworld.com
Web site: http://goodnightbooks.com
Dist(s): **Islander Group**
MyiLibrary

Penguin Random Hse. LLC
ebrary, Inc.

Good Reading Bks., *(978-1-888042; 978-0-578-17942-1)* Div. of Southern Printing, Imaging & Typography, Inc., 153 Shady Oaks Dr., Lafayette, LA 70506 USA.

Good Roots Publishing, *(978-0-9745187)* Orders Addr.: P.O. Box 3493, Homer, AK 99603-3493 USA Tel 907-235-5283; Edit Addr.: 62315 Fireweed Ave., Homer, AK 99603-3493 USA
Dist(s): **Wizard Works.**

Good Sound Publishing, *(978-0-9821563; 978-1-935743)* 295 Olive Ave., Palo Alto, CA 94306 USA Fax: 650-227-2320; Toll Free: 888-686-2669
E-mail: info@goodsoundpublishing.com
Web site: http://www.goodsoundpublishing.com.

Good Success Publishing, *(978-0-9837895; 978-0-9978332)* P.O. Box 134, Oxon Hill, MD 20750 USA Tel 301-467-8885
E-mail: info@drcelesteowens.com
Web site: www.drcelesteowens.com
Dist(s): **BookBaby.**

Good Thoughts Publishing *See* **Cardinal Pr.**

Good Times at Home LLC, *(978-0-9840338)* 1933 Hwy. 35 Suite 105-335, Belmar, NJ 07719 USA Tel 732-803-1902
E-mail: vinnie@vinniecurto.com.

Good Turn Publishing, *(978-0-9794393)* 1 Bancroft Rd., Wellesley, MA 02481 USA
Web site: http://www.goodturnpublishing.com.

Good vs Evil *Imprint of* **Stone Arch Bks.**

Good Works Pr., *(978-0-9634472; 978-1-888572)* 4121 Whitfield Ave., Fort Worth, TX 76109 USA Tel 817-927-8808.

Good Works Publishing Hse., *(978-0-9744733)* P.O. Box 52217, Houston, TX 77052-2217 USA Tel 713-708-8852
E-mail: wonderlandhudson@yahoo.com.

Good Year Bks. *Imprint of* **Celebration Pr.**

Good Year Bks., *(978-1-59647)* P.O. Box 91858, Tucson, AZ 85752-1858 USA (SAN 854-4050) Toll Free Fax: 888-511-1501; Toll Free: 888-511-1530
E-mail: publisher@goodyearbooks.com; sales@goodyearbooks.com; marketing@goodyearbooks.com; orders@goodyearbooks.com
Web site: http://www.goodyearbooks.com.

Goodall, Barry, *(978-0-9763932)* 218 Tucker Sta. Rd, Louisville, KY 40243 USA Tel 502-817-8530
E-mail: bgoodal1@jefferson.k12.ky.us.

Goode, Ty *See* **Tytam Publishing**

Goodheart-Willcox Pub., *(978-0-87006; 978-1-56637; 978-1-59070; 978-1-60525; 978-1-61960; 978-1-63126; 978-1-68311; 978-1-63563)* Orders Addr.: 18604 West Creek Dr., Tinley Park, IL 60477-6243 USA (SAN 203-4387) Tel 708-687-5000; Fax: 708-687-5068; Toll Free Fax: 888-409-3900; Toll Free: 800-323-0440
E-mail: custserv@g-w.com; jff@g-w.com
Web site: http://www.g-w.com.

Goodmedia Communications, LLC, *(978-0-615-60107-6; 978-0-9883237; 978-0-9911148)* 25 Highland Pk. Village, No. 100-810, Dallas, TX 75205 USA Tel 214-240-4503
E-mail: info@GoodMediaCommunications.com
Web site: www.GoodMediaCommunications.com.

Goodtimes Software *See* **GT Interactive Software**

Goodwin, Brian, *(978-0-615-16104-4)* 53-823 Kamehameha Hwy., Hauula, HI 96717-9658 USA
Dist(s): **Lulu Pr., Inc.**

Goodwin, Evelyn, *(978-0-615-16145-7; 978-0-615-16344-4)* 2345 Ala Wai Blvd. Apt. 917, Honolulu, HI 96815-5017 USA
Dist(s): **Lulu Pr., Inc.**

goodworksebooks.com, *(978-0-9773192)* 3084 CR 310, Brazoria, TX 77422 USA
Web site: http://goodworksebooks.com.

GoodyGoody Bks., *(978-0-9702546)* P.O. Box 1073, Sun City, AZ 85372-1073 USA
E-mail: charlie-the-cat@cox.net
Web site: http://www.charliethecat.com.

Goofy Guru Publishing, *(978-0-9726130)* 405 Kiowa Pl., Boulder, CO 80303 USA.

Goon Dog Publishing, *(978-0-9791612)* 309 W. 14th, Suite 32, New York, NY 10014-0014 USA (SAN 852-6206) Tel 212-645-2096
E-mail: monk@ispwest.com
Web site: http://owenopolis.com.

Goops Unlimited, *(978-0-9712368; 978-0-9834865)* P.O. Box 1809, Battle Ground, WA 98604-1809 USA Tel 360-687-1891; Fax: 360-687-2097; Toll Free: 800-861-1891
E-mail: barbara@thegoops.com
Web site: http://www.thegoops.com.

Goose Creek Pubs., Inc., *(978-1-59633)* 4227 Vermont Ave., Louisville, KY 40211 USA Tel 502-714-9985
E-mail: wanda@goosecreekpublishers.com
Web site: http://www.goosecreekpublishers.com.

Goose River Pr., *(978-1-930648; 978-1-59713)* 3400 Friendship Rd., Waldoboro, ME 04572 USA Tel 207-832-6665
E-mail: gooseriverpress@roadrunner.com
Web site: http://www.gooseriverpress.com
Dist(s): **Lightning Source, Inc.**

Gooseberry Patch *Imprint of* **Rowman & Littlefield Publishers, Inc.**

Goosebottom Bks. LLC, *(978-0-9845098; 978-0-9834256; 978-1-937463)* 543 Trinidad Ln., Foster City, CA 94404-6061 USA (SAN 859-8029) Tel 650-204-4076
E-mail: info@goosebottombooks.com; shirin.bridges@goosebottombooks.com
Web site: http://www.goosebottombooks.com
Dist(s): **Independent Pubs. Group**
Publishers Group West (PGW).

Gordon Rocket, *(978-1-941037)* P.O. Box 120023, Chula, CA 91912 USA Tel 619-272-8235
E-mail: mxreynoso@gmail.com
Web site: gordonrocket.com.

Gordon, Scott, *(978-0-9963574)* 30 Serenity Ln., Laguna Niguel, CA 92677 USA Tel 949-280-2799
E-mail: repioneer32@gmail.com.

Goretti Publishing, *(978-0-9778451)* Orders Addr.: 1150 N. Loop 1604 W., Ste. 108-410, San Antonio, TX 78248 USA (SAN 850-3176) Tel 210-274-2769; Fax: 210-493-6080 attn: 410
E-mail: publishedworks@aol.com
Web site: http://www.thetexasmermaid.com
Dist(s): **Bk. Marketing Plus.**

Gorgias Pr., LLC, *(978-0-9713097; 978-0-9715986; 978-1-931956; 978-1-59333; 978-1-60724; 978-1-61719; 978-1-61143; 978-1-4632)* 954 River Rd., Piscataway, NJ 08854-5504 USA (SAN 853-0629)
E-mail: info@gorgiaspress.com; sales@gorgiaspress.com
Web site: http://www.gorgiaspress.com
Dist(s): **ebrary, Inc.**

Gormley Publishing, *(978-0-9794500; 978-0-9827503; 978-0-692-61920-9)* Orders Addr.: 1520 Courtney Dr., Washington Court House, OH 43160-8920 USA
Web site: http://www.gormleypublishing.com.

Gorp Group Pr., The, *(978-0-9724249)* 7450 OLIVETAS Ave. No. 386, LA JOLLA, CA 92037 USA Tel 858-412-4424; 208-720-7980; Toll Free: 888-729-4677
E-mail: gorp2@earthlink.net
Web site: http://www.thegorp.com.

†**Gospel Advocate Co., Inc.,** *(978-0-89225)* Orders Addr.: P.O. Box 150, Nashville, TN 37202 USA (SAN 205-2792) Tel 615-254-8781; Fax: 615-254-7411; Toll Free: 800-251-8446; Edit Addr.: 1006 Elm Hill Pike, Nashville, TN 37210 USA (SAN 662-0213)
E-mail: kerry@gospeladvocate.com; keaton@gospeladvocate.com; haimericus@juno.com
Web site: http://www.gospeladvocate.com; *CIP.*

Gospel Light *Imprint of* **Gospel Light Pubns.**

Gospel Light Pubns., *(978-0-8307)* Orders Addr.: 1957 Eastman Ave., Ventura, CA 93003 USA (SAN 299-0873) Tel 805-644-9721; Fax: 805-289-0200; Toll Free: 800-446-7735 (orders only); *Imprints:* Gospel Light (Gospel Light); Regal Books (Regal Bks) Do not confuse with companies with similar names in Brooklyn, NY, Delight, AR
E-mail: info@gospellight.com; kyleloffelmacher@gospellight.com
Web site: http://www.gospellight.com
Dist(s): **Christian Bk. Distributors**
Cook, David C.
Faith Alive Christian Resources.

Gospel Missionary Union, *(978-0-9617490; 978-1-890940)* 10000 N. Oak Trafficway, Kansas City, MO 64155 USA (SAN 664-1830) Tel 816-734-8500; Fax: 816-734-4601
E-mail: info@gmu.org
Web site: http://www.gmu.org.

†**Gospel Publishing Hse.,** *(978-0-88243; 978-1-60731)* Div. of General Council of the Assemblies of God, 1445 N. Boonville Ave., Springfield, MO 65802-1894 USA (SAN 206-8826) Tel 417-862-2781; Fax: 417-862-5881; Toll Free Fax: 800-328-0294; Toll Free: 800-641-4310 (orders only)
E-mail: webmaster@gph.com
Web site: http://www.gospelpublishing.com
Dist(s): **Appalachian Bible Co.**
BookMasters, Inc.
Bookmasters Distribution
Ingram Publisher Services
Lulu Pr., Inc.
MyiLibrary
Spring Arbor Distributors, Inc.; *CIP.*

Gospel Puzzles *See* **Cluster Storm Publishing**

Gossamer Bks., *(978-0-9729016)* 444 Eastwood Dr., Petaluma, CA 94954 USA (SAN 255-2671) Tel 707-765-1992; Fax: 707-765-6507 Do not confuse with Gossamer Books LLC in Belmont, CA
E-mail: dcr530@cs.com.

Gossamer Bks., LLC, *(978-0-9742502)* P.O. Box 455, Belmont, CA 94002 USA Fax: 650-257-4058 Do not confuse with Gossamer Books in Petaluma, CA
E-mail: info@gossamerbooks.com
Web site: http://www.gossamerbooks.com.

GoTandem *Imprint of* **Barbour Publishing, Inc.**

Gothic Image Pubns. (GBR) *(978-0-906362) Dist. by* **SCB Distributo.**

Gottlieb, Rachel E, *(978-0-692-60407-6)* 62 Old Orchard Ln., Scarsdale, NY 10583 USA Tel 917-494-7236
E-mail: raycraz1@gmail.com.

GOTTSEGEN, JOSH, *(978-0-9909270)* 11924 Mayfield Ave 4, Los Angeles, CA 90049 USA Tel 310-804-5077
E-mail: JOSHGOTTSEGEN@ME.COM
Web site: http://www.jooshsjuicebar.com.

Goulart-Johnston, Michelle, *(978-0-9980932)* 1375 E Grand Ave. No. 318, Arroyo Grande, CA 93420 USA Tel 805-539-9214
E-mail: michgoulart@gmail.com.

Goulasche Pr., *(978-0-9771466)* 1352 Ithilien, Excelsior, MN 55331 USA.

Gourley, Deb Nelson *See* **Astri My Astri Publishing**

Gozo Bks. *Imprint of* **Premio Publishing & Gozo Bks., LLC**

Gozo Books, LLC *See* **Premio Publishing & Gozo Bks., LLC**

G.P. Hoffman Publishing, *(978-0-9798230)* 2224 Heather Ln., Lincoln, NE 68512 USA.

G.P. Putnam's Sons *Imprint of* **Penguin Publishing Group**

G.P. Putnam's Sons Books for Young Readers *Imprint of* **Penguin Publishing Group**

G.P. Putnam's Sons Books for Young Readers *Imprint of* **Penguin Young Readers Group**

Grace Acres Pr., *(978-1-60265)* P.O. Box 22, Larkspur, CO 80118 USA (SAN 852-5978) Tel 303-681-9995; Fax: 303-681-2716
E-mail: Anne@GraceAcresPress.com
Web site: http://www.graceacrespress.com.

Grace & Mercy Publishing, *(978-0-9672049; 978-0-9764763)* Orders Addr.: P.O. Box 11531, Fort Wayne, IN 46857 USA; Edit Addr.: 7408 Mill Run, Suite B, Fort Wayne, IN 46819 USA.

Grace Communications Publishing *See* **Grace Publishing**

Grace Contrino Abrams Peace Education Foundation *See* **Peace Education Foundation**

Grace Hse. Publishing, *(978-0-9633633)* Div. of R. Allan McCauley Law Office, 6237 N. 15th St., Phoenix, AZ 85014 USA Tel 602-265-9151 Do not confuse with Grace House Publishing in Mahomet, IL.

Grace Publishing, *(978-1-893555)* Div. of Abundant Grace Fellowship, 11118 Robious Rd., Richmond, VA 23235-3724 USA Toll Free: 877-884-7223 Do not confuse with companies with the same name in Seattle, WA, Farmington Hills, MI, Broken Arrow, OK, Waldorf, MD, Elma, NY, Woodinville, WA & New Prague, MN
E-mail: drmhunt@bellsouth.net; carylives@atthi.com; dremlenehunt@earthlink.net
Web site: http://www.abundantgrace.org; http://www.drmarlenehunt.com.

Grace Publishing, *(978-0-9769985)* P.O. Box 17980, Seattle, WA 98123 USA (SAN 256-6257) Tel 206-818-9769 Do not confuse with companies with the same name in Farmington Hills, MI, Broken Arrow, OK, Waldorf, MD, Richmond, VA, Elma, NY, Woodinville, WA & New Prague, MN
E-mail: vonukk@comcast.net
Web site: http://www.rcberg.com.

Grace Walk Ministries *See* **Grace Walk Resources, LLC**

Grace Walk Resources, LLC, *(978-0-9664736)* Orders Addr.: P.O. Box 6537, Douglasville, GA 30135 USA Tel 800-472-2311; Toll Free: 800-472-2311
E-mail: info@gracewalk.org
Web site: http://www.gracewalk.org.

GraceWorks Interactive, *(978-0-9760548; 978-1-935915)* P.O. Box 2613, Corvallis, OR 97339-2613 USA Toll Free: 877-785-3496 (phone/fax)
E-mail: tim@graceworksinteractive.com
Web site: http://www.graceworksinteractive.com.

Graffeg Limited (GBR) *(978-0-9544334; 978-1-905582; 978-1-909823) Dist. by* **IPG Chicago.**

grafixCORP, *(978-0-9778374)* Orders Addr.: P.O. Box 1441, Mount Vernon, WA 98273-9827 USA
Web site: http://www.grafixCORP.com.

Grafton and Scratch Pubs. (CAN) *(978-0-9879023; 978-0-9881216; 978-1-927979; 978-1-926495) Dist. by* **Bookmasters.**

Graham Bay, Jeanette, *(978-0-9771210)* 770 Victor Rd., Macedon, NY 14502 USA.

Graham Cracker Kids, *(978-0-9716475; 978-0-615-11409-5)* 1661 Hunt Rd., El Cajon, CA 92019 USA Tel 619-258-7571; Fax: 619-258-5412
E-mail: grncrkrkds@aol.com
Web site: http://www.grahamcrackerkids.com.

Graham, Rita, *(978-0-578-13165-8)*.

Grampa Jones's Publishing Co., *(978-0-9748266; 978-0-615-11169-8; 978-0-9893868)* P.O. Box 93, Heron, MT 59844-0093 USA (SAN 214-4700)
Web site: http://www.become-a-millionaire.com.

Gran Gran Series, *(978-0-9840237)* 8549 Hartham Pk. Ave., Raleigh, NC 27616 USA Tel 919-295-4750
E-mail: mhopkins25@nc.rr.com.

Grand Bks., Inc., *(978-0-930809)* P.O. Box 212, Crystal, MI 48818 USA (SAN 677-6361) Tel 517-875-4674; 517-235-4427
E-mail: jwrites@yahoo.com.

Grand Canyon Assn., *(978-0-938216; 978-1-934656)* Orders Addr.: P.O. Box 399, Grand Canyon, AZ 86023-0399 USA (SAN 215-7675) Tel 928-638-7141; 928-638-7030; Fax: 928-638-2494; Toll Free: 800-858-2808
E-mail: lsantamaria@grandcanyon.org; clittleboy@grandcanyon.org
Web site: http://www.grandcanyon.org.

Grand Canyon Natural History Association *See* **Grand Canyon Assn.**

Grand Canyon Orphan, *(978-0-9764260)* P.O. Box 438, Mina, NV 89422 USA
E-mail: info@grandcanyonorphan.com
Web site: http://www.grandcanyonorphan.com.

Grand Central Pr., *(978-0-9771696; 978-0-9817987)* 125 N. Broadway, Santa Ana, CA 92701 USA (SAN 256-8284) Tel 714-567-7238
E-mail: tgayer@fullerton.edu
Web site: http://www.grandcentralartcenter.com
Dist(s): **SCB Distributors.**

†**Grand Central Publishing,** *(978-0-446; 978-0-7595; 978-1-4555; 978-1-5387; 978-1-5460)* Orders Addr.: c/o Little Brown & Co., 3 Center Plaza, Boston, MA 02108-2084 USA Toll Free Fax: 800-286-9471; Toll Free: 800-759-0190; Edit Addr.: 237 Park Ave., New York, NY 10017 USA (SAN 281-8892) Fax: 800-331-1664; Toll Free Fax: 800-759-0190; 1290 Avenue of the Americas, New York, NY 10104; *Imprints:* Vision (VisionC); Business Plus (Busn Plus); Forever (Forever); Sixth Avenue Books (SixthAveBks); 5 Spot (FiveSpot); Aspect (Aspect); Jimmy Patterson (JimmyPat)
E-mail: renee.supriano@twbg.com; customer.service@hbgusa.com
Web site: http://www.hbgusa.com
Dist(s): **Blackstone Audio, Inc.**
Findaway World, LLC
Follett School Solutions
Hachette Bk. Group
Lectorum Pubns., Inc.
Libros Sin Fronteras
Little Brown & Co.
MyiLibrary
Perelandra, Ltd.
Beeler, Thomas T. Pub.
TextStream
Thorndike Pr.
iPublish.com; *CIP.*

Grand Daisy Pr., *(978-0-9848608; 978-0-9962843)* 625 Stetson Rd., Elkins Park, PA 19027-2524 USA Tel 215-380-6710
E-mail: karenptoz@gmail.com
Web site: www.granddaisypress.com; www.karentoz.com.

Grand Hank Productions, Inc., *(978-0-9767236)* P.O. Box 23488, Philadelphia, PA 19143 USA Tel 215-724-5260
Web site: http://www.grandhank.com.

Grand Kidz, The *Imprint of* **Vertical Connect Pr.**

Grand Marais Publishing, *(978-0-615-34796-7)* 1441 Huntington Dr., No. 234, South Pasadena, CA 91030 USA Tel 626-441-1154
E-mail: grandmaraispublishing@gmail.com.

GRAND Media, LLC, *(978-0-930507; 978-0-615-51541-0)* 4791 Baywood Point Dr. S., Gulfport, FL 33711 USA (SAN 670-963X) Tel 727-327-9039; Fax: 727-323-9587
E-mail: jonmicocci@att.net
Web site: http://www.deathfromchildabuse.com.

Grand Productions, *(978-0-9795386)* 1914 Karly Ct., Panama City, FL 32405 USA (SAN 853-7194).

Grand Teton Assn., *(978-0-931895; 978-1-940093)* P.O. Box 170, Moose, WY 83012 USA (SAN 686-0303) Tel 307-739-3606; Fax: 307-739-3423
E-mail: grte_assoc@partner.nps.gov
Web site: http://www.grandtetonpark.org.

Grand Teton Natural History Association *See* **Grand Teton Assn.**

Grand Valley State Univ., *(978-0-9709811)* 1 Campus Dr., 107 Lake Superior Hall, Allendale, MI 49401 USA Tel 616-895-3488
E-mail: royer@river.it.gvsu.edu
Dist(s): **Michigan State Univ. Pr.**

Grandfeather Pr., *(978-0-9832355)* 1221 S. 7th St., Renton, WA 98057 USA Tel 425-902-1852
E-mail: publishing@grandfeather.com
Web site: www.grandfeather.com
Dist(s): **Lightning Source, Inc.**

Grandin Bk. Co., *(978-0-910523)* P.O. Box 2206, Provo, UT 84603-2206 USA (SAN 260-1931) Tel 801-225-2020; Fax: 801-222-0176; Toll Free: 800-292-2003.

Grandkidsandme, Inc., *(978-0-9741710)* 1764 Hampshire Ave., Saint Paul, MN 55116 USA (SAN 255-3902) Tel 651-695-1988; Fax: 651-699-5966
E-mail: don@grandkidsandme.com
Web site: http://www.grandkidsandme.com
Dist(s): **Independent Pubs. Group.**

Grandma Chubby's Bks., *(978-0-9728535)* P.O. Box 902308, Sandy, UT 84090-2308 USA Tel 801-571-6617; Fax: 801-571-2285
E-mail: lsashby@juno.com
Dist(s): **Granite Publishing & Distribution.**

"Grandma's Hope Notes", *(978-0-9677477)* P.O. Box 868, Anchor Point, AK 99556 USA Tel 907-235-0502 (phone/fax).

Grandoc Publishing, *(978-0-9761739)* 3923 Hidden Way NE, Rochester, MN 55906-5590 USA Tel 507-287-9121
E-mail: grandoc@mac.com; drjohngraner@mac.com.

Grandreams Bks., Inc., *(978-1-59340)* Div. of Robert Frederick, 360 Hurst St., Linden, NJ 07036 USA (SAN 254-9832) Fax: 908-523-0373
E-mail: ssullivan@grandreamsbooks.com.

Granite Publishing & Distribution, *(978-1-890558; 978-1-930980; 978-1-932280; 978-1-59936)* 868 N. 1430 W., Orem, UT 84057 USA (SAN 631-0605) Tel 801-229-9023; Fax: 801-229-1924; Toll Free: 800-574-5779 Do not confuse with companies with same or similar names in Madison, WI, Columbus, NC
E-mail: granite@granitepublishing.biz; gregg@granitepublishing.biz
Web site: http://granitepublishing.biz.

Granite Publishing, LLC, *(978-0-926524; 978-0-9632310; 978-1-893183)* P.O. Box 1429, Columbus, NC 28722 USA Tel 828-894-3088; Fax: 828-894-8454; Toll Free: 800-366-0264 Do not confuse with companies with same or similar names in Madison, WI, Orem, UT, Siloam Springs, AR
E-mail: brian@5thworld.com
Web site: http://www.5thworld.com
Dist(s): **New Leaf Distributing Co., Inc.**
Smashwords.

Grannie Annie Family Story Celebration, The, *(978-0-9677685; 978-0-9793296; 978-0-9969394)* P.O. Box 11343, Saint Louis, MO 63105 USA Tel 314-550-6396; Fax: 636-527-2822
E-mail: familystories@thegrannieannie.org
Web site: http://www.TheGrannieAnnie.org.

Granny's Pub Co., *(978-0-9749950)* P.O. Box 1701, Granbury, TX 76048 USA Tel 817-605-9004; Fax: 817-605-1180
E-mail: granny@loralie.com
Web site: http://www.loralie.com.

Grape Elephant MarketPr., *(978-0-9760646)* 13025 Ct. Pl., Burnsville, MN 55337 USA Tel 612-281-2566
E-mail: jill@grapeelephant.com
Web site: http://www.grapeelephant.com.

Graphic Arts Bks., *(978-0-944197; 978-1-941821; 978-1-943328; 978-1-5131; 978-1-5132; 978-1-5133)* P.O. Box 56118, Portland, OR 97238 USA Tel 503-254-5591; Fax: 503-254-5609
Dist(s): **Independent Pubs. Group**
Ingram Publisher Services
MyiLibrary.

Graphic Arts Ctr. Publishing Co., Orders Addr.: P.O. Box 10306, Portland, OR 97296-0306 USA (SAN 201-6338) Tel 503-226-2402; Fax: 503-223-1410 (executive & editorial); Toll Free Fax: 800-355-9685 (sales office); Toll Free: 800-452-3032; *Imprints:* Alaska Northwest Books (Alaska NW Bks); West Winds Press (West Winds Pr)
E-mail: sales@gacpc.com
Web site: http://www.gacpc.com
Dist(s): **Ingram Publisher Services**
Univ. of Oklahoma Pr.

Graphic Expressions *See* **Graphics North**

Graphic Flash *Imprint of* **Stone Arch Bks.**

Graphic Library *Imprint of* **Capstone Press of Coughlan Cos.**
Graphic Library en espanol *Imprint of* **Capstone Press of Coughlan Cos.**
Graphic Novels *Imprint of* **Spotlight**
Graphic Planet *Imprint of* **Magic Wagon**
Graphic Planet- Fiction *Imprint of* **ABDO Publishing Co.**
Graphic Planet- Nonfiction *Imprint of* **ABDO Publishing Co.**
Graphic Quest *Imprint of* **Stone Arch Bks.**
Graphic Revolve *Imprint of* **Stone Arch Bks.**
Graphic Revolve en Español *Imprint of* **Stone Arch Bks.**
Graphic Sparks *Imprint of* **Stone Arch Bks.**
Graphic Spin en Español *Imprint of* **Stone Arch Bks.**
Graphic Universe™ *Imprint of* **Lerner Publishing Group**
Graphically Speaking, Inc., *(978-0-9729975)* 15509 Lloyd St., Omaha, NE 68144 USA Tel 402-330-1144; Fax: 402-334-3311
E-mail: fontstudios@cox.net
Web site: http://www.fontstudios.com.
Graphics North, *(978-0-9643452; 978-0-615-29759-0; 978-0-9829503)* P.O. Box 218, Jay, NY 12941 USA Tel 518-946-7741
E-mail: graphicsnorth@yahoo.com
Web site: graphicsnorth.com.
Graphics North, *(978-0-692-79724-2)* 42 Mela Ln., Rancho Palos Verdes, CA 90275 USA Tel 310-780-0643
E-mail: brengreen@gmail.com.
Graphic-Sha (JPN) *(978-4-7661) Dist. by* **Diamond Book Dists.**
Graphic-Sha (JPN) *(978-4-7661) Dist. by* **D C D.**
Graphic International, Inc., *(978-0-916189)* 8780 19th St., No. 199, Alto Loma, CA 91701 USA (SAN 294-9342) Tel 909-987-1921; Fax: 435-514-5975
E-mail: lmartres@phototripusa.com
Web site: http://www.phototripusa.com
Dist(s): **Bks. West**
Canyonlands Pubns.
Mountain n' Air Bks.
Graphis, U.S., Inc., *(978-1-888001; 978-1-931241; 978-1-932026)* Orders Addr.: c/o ABDI, Inc., Buncher Commerce Pk. Ave. A, Bldg. 16, Leetsdale, PA 15056-1304 USA Tel 412-741-3679; Fax: 412-741-0934; Toll Free: 800-209-4234 (for Canada & USA); Edit Addr.: 307 Fifth Ave., 10th Flr., New York, NY 10016 USA Tel 212-532-9387 (ext. 226); Fax: 212-213-3229; Toll Free: 800-209-4234
Web site: http://www.graphis.com
Dist(s): **Innovative Logistics**
Watson-Guptill Pubns., Inc.
Graphite Pr., *(978-0-9755810; 978-1-938313)* 2025 Lexington Parkway, Niskayuna, NY 12309-4205 USA (SAN 256-0712) Tel 206-222-2400; Fax: 206-222-2002
E-mail: publish@graphitepress.com
Web site: http://www.graphitepress.com.
Graphix *Imprint of* **Scholastic, Inc.**
Graphix Network, *(978-0-9740673; 978-0-9752832; 978-0-9762301; 978-0-9777043)* Orders Addr.: P.O. Box 2745, Evans, GA 30809 USA Tel 706-210-1000; Fax: 706-210-1111; Edit Addr.: 4104 Colben Blvd., Suite C, Evans, GA 30809 USA Tel 706-210-1000; Fax: 706-210-1111
E-mail: graphixnetwork@hotmail.com; sales@graphixnetwork.com
Web site: http://www.graphixnetwork.com.
Grappling Arts Pubns., LLC, *(978-0-9721097)* 1282 Watson Ave., Costa Mesa, CA 92626 USA
E-mail: info@grapplingarts.net
Web site: http://www.grapplingarts.net
Dist(s): **BookMasters, Inc.**
Cardinal Pubs. Group.
Grass Root Enterprises, *(978-1-886075)* 16315 Forest Way Dr., Houston, TX 77090-4716 USA Tel 281-444-4103; Fax: 281-444-5804.
Grassdale Publishers, Incorporated *See* **Saxon Pubs., Inc.**
Grasshopper Dream Productions, *(978-0-615-12337-0; 978-0-615-12724-8; 978-0-615-35616-7)* Orders Addr.: P.O. Box 1831, Saint Petersburg, FL 33731-1831 USA Tel 813-382-4230; Edit Addr.: 121 E. Davis Blvd., No. 104, Tampa, FL 33731 USA
E-mail: kokopelli911@hotmail.com
Web site: http://www.kokopelli-butterfly.com.
Grassroots Educational Service *See* **Right On Programs, Inc.**
Grassroots Publishing Group, *(978-0-9794805; 978-0-9975677)* 9404 Southwick Dr., Bakersfield, CA 93312 USA (SAN 853-5493) Tel 661-368-2624; Fax: 661-368-2624
E-mail: nesta@sbcglobal.net.
Grateful Day Pr., *(978-0-9882804)* 24 Dewey Mt Rd., Saranac Lake, NY 12983 USA Tel 518-891-2278; Fax: 518-891-1645
E-mail: gratefuldaypress@gmail.com.
Grateful Steps, *(978-0-9789548; 978-1-935130; 978-0-9962490; 978-1-945714)* 1091 Hendersonville Rd., Asheville, NC 28801 USA (SAN 856-471X) Tel 828-277-0998; Fax: 828-277-8027
Web site: http://www.gratefulsteps.com.
Gratia et Veritas Press *See* **Papillon Publishing**
Gratitude Works, *(978-0-578-13447-5)* 6255 Whitsett Ave, North Hollywood, CA 91606 USA.
Grau, Ryon, *(978-0-9772559)* 6824 Falstone Dr., Frederick, MD 21702 USA
E-mail: ryon@landmarkletters.com
Web site: http://www.spankledelia.com.
Gravitas Pubns., Inc., *(978-0-9749149; 978-0-9765097; 978-0-9799459; 978-0-9817731; 978-0-9823163; 978-1-936114; 978-1-941181)* PO Box 90338, Albuquerque, NM 97199 USA Tel 505-266-2761; Fax: 505-266-2762; Toll Free: 888-466-2761
E-mail: office@gravitaspublications.com
Web site: http://www.gravitaspublications.com.
Gravley, Debbie Bybee, *(978-0-9771793)* Orders Addr.: P.O. Box 268, Gaston, OR 97119 USA; Edit Addr.: 12320 S.W. Springhill Rd., Gaston, OR 97119 USA.
Graw, Victoria, *(978-0-9787901)* P.O. Box 458, Orange, MA 01364 USA (SAN 851-6138)
E-mail: Vgraw@aol.com.
Gray and Company, Publishers, *(978-0-9631738; 978-1-886228; 978-1-59851; 978-1-938441)* Orders Addr.: 1588 E. 40th St., 3A, Cleveland, OH 44103 USA Tel 216-431-2665; Fax: 216-431-7933; Toll Free: 800-915-3609
E-mail: sales@grayco.com
Web site: http://www.grayco.com.
Gray Jay Bks., *(978-0-9754539)*
E-mail: Contact@GrayJaybooks.com
Web site: http://www.grayjaybooks.com.
Gray, Susan *See* **Two's Company**
Grayer Publishing, *(978-0-9785536)* P.O. Box 788, Flossmoor, IL 60422 USA
E-mail: ac@grayerpublishing.com
Web site: http://www.grayerpublishing.com.
Graymalkin Media, *(978-1-935169; 978-1-63168; 978-1-63507)* Orders Addr.: 1413 Greenfield Ave., Suite 103, Los Angeles, CA 90025 USA Tel 310-231-8202 (phone/fax)
Web site: http://www.graymalkin.com
Dist(s): **Follett School Solutions**
Midwest Tape.
Grayson, Kate, *(978-0-9774357)* 2307 58th Ave. E., Bradenton, FL 34203 USA (SAN 257-5000)
E-mail: kgrayson1@aol.com.
Graziano, Claudia *See* **Meerkat's Adventures Bks.**
GRC Bks., *(978-0-578-06866-4; 978-0-578-08611-8; 978-0-578-12011-9)* 704 Robinson Rd., Sebastopol, CA 95472 USA Tel 707-829-9191
E-mail: martyr@sonic.net
Dist(s): **Lulu Pr., Inc.**
Great AD-Ventures, *(978-0-9665053)* P.O. Box 8011, Boise, ID 83707 USA Fax: 208-336-5797; Toll Free: 800-390-5687
E-mail: theplace@lesbois.com; book@freeread.com
Web site: http://www.freeread.com/.
Great Adventures Publishing, *(978-0-9747972)* 465 Hill St., Laguna Beach, CA 92651 USA Tel 949-494-5797
E-mail: paigeturner5@hotmail.com.
Great American Pr., The, *(978-0-9777996; 978-0-9798776; 978-0-9814627)* 551 League City Pkwy., League City, TX 77573 USA (SAN 850-2773) Tel 281-557-4300 (phone/fax)
Web site: http://www.thegreatamericanpress.com.
Great American Pubs., *(978-0-9779053; 978-1-934817)* 171 Lone Pine Church Rd., Lena, MS 39094 USA Tel 601-854-5954; Fax: 601-854-5958
E-mail: info@gapublishers.com; ssimmons@gapublishers.com
Web site: http://www.greatamericanpublishers.com
Dist(s): **Appalachian Bk. Distributors**
Bk. Marketing Plus
Bks. West
Dot Gibson Distribution
Forest Sales & Distributing Co.
Rumpf, Raymond & Son
Southwest Cookbook Distributors.
Great Authors Online, *(978-0-9773869)* 16440 Monterey St., Lake Elsinore, CA 92530 USA Tel 951-674-3246; Fax: 951-245-3608
E-mail: rodgerolsen@yahoo.com
Web site: http://greatauthorsonline.com.
Great Big Comics *See* **Great Big Comics, Big Tex Films**
Great Big Comics, Big Tex Films, *(978-0-9746784; 978-0-9844728; 978-0-615-49875-1)* Div. of The Big Tex Movin' Picture Company, LLC, 31 E. Bonneymead Cir., The Woodlands, TX 77381 USA
E-mail: bh@wondervista.com; avast@shebuccaneer.com
Web site: http://www.wondervista.com; http://www.greatbigcomics.com
Dist(s): **Diamond Distributors, Inc.**
Great Bks. Foundation, *(978-0-945159; 978-1-880323; 978-1-933147; 978-1-939014)* 35 E. Wacker Dr. Ste. 400, Chicago, IL 60601-2105 USA (SAN 205-3292) Toll Free: 800-222-5870
E-mail: hurleyp@greatbooks.org
Web site: http://www.greatbooks.org.
Great Character Development Workbook, The, *(978-0-9728417)* P.O. Box 1852, Kingston, WA 98346 USA
Web site: http://www.thegreatcharacterdevelopmentworkbook.com.
Great Expectations Bk. Co., *(978-1-883943)* P.O. Box 2067, Eugene, OR 07402 USA Tel 541-343-2647; Fax: 541-343-0568
E-mail: fred@pinehillgraphics.com.
Great I-AM Publishing Co., The, *(978-0-9762788)* Orders Addr.: P.O. Box 30412, Wilmington, DE 19805 USA Tel 302-888-2477; Fax: 302-416-5085; Edit Addr.: 25 Roselane Rosegate, New Castle, DE 19720 USA
E-mail: watkinstyree2@aol.com.
Great Ideas for Teaching, Inc., *(978-1-886143)* Orders Addr.: P.O. Box 444, Wrightsville Beach, NC 28480-0444 USA Tel 910-256-4494; Fax: 910-256-4493; Toll Free Fax: 800-839-8498; Toll Free: 800-839-8339; Edit Addr.: 6800 Wrightsville Ave., No. 16, Wilmington, NC 28403 USA
E-mail: gift@wilmington.net
Web site: http://www.gift-inc.com.
Great Ideas Pr., Ltd., *(978-1-884949)* 4130 166th Pl. SW, Lynnwood, WA 98037 USA Tel 425-774-6611
E-mail: JamesRobert@jamesrobertdeal.com
Web site: http://www.whattoserveagoddess.com.
Great Kids Helping Great Kids, Incorporated *See* **America's Great Stories**
Great Lakes Bks. *Imprint of* **Wayne State Univ. Pr.**
Great Lakes Design, *(978-0-9761274)* P.O. Box 511534, Milwaukee, WI 53203 USA
Web site: http://www.vikingadventure.net.
Great Lakes Literary, LLC, *(978-1-883953; 978-1-933987)* 3147 S. Pennsylvania Ave., Milwaukee, WI 53207 USA; *Imprints:* Crickhollow Books (Crickhollow); Crispin Books (CrispinBks); Blue Horse Books (BlueHorse)
E-mail: info@CrickhollowBooks.com
Web site: http://www.CrickhollowBooks.com; http://www.CrispinBooks.com
Dist(s): **BookBaby**
BookMobile
Itasca Bks.
Great Lakes Literary, LLCorp. *See* **Great Lakes Literary, LLC**
Great Lakes Press, Inc., *(978-0-9614760; 978-1-881018; 978-1-939085)* Orders Addr.: P.O. Box 374, Cottleville, MO 63338 USA Fax: 636-273-6086
E-mail: service@glpbooks.com
Web site: http://www.glpbooks.com; http://www.greatlakespress.com.
Great Mastiff Corp., *(978-0-9759166)* 9945 E. Whitebirch Rd., Port wing, WI 54865 USA Tel 715-774-3247
E-mail: greatmastiff@hotmail.com
Web site: http://www.greatmastiff.com.
Great Nation Publishing, *(978-0-578-05549-7; 978-0-578-06529-8; 978-0-615-44374-4; 978-0-615-60214-1; 978-0-9891056)* Orders Addr.: 3828 Salem Rd., No. 56, Covington, GA 30016 USA
E-mail: brian@authorbrianthompson.com
Web site: http://www.authorbrianthompson.com
Dist(s): **Smashwords.**
Great Ocean Publishers *See* **Great River Bks.**
Great Persuader Publishing, The, *(978-0-9712581)*
E-mail: greatpersuader@hotmail.com; Info@Poetryisalive.com.
Great Plains Pr., *(978-0-9632459; 978-0-9861616)* 1103 Canyon Rd., Santa Fe, NM 87501 USA
E-mail: dirk@rainbowplace.com
Web site: http://www.greatplainspress.com/.
†**Great Potential Pr., Inc.,** *(978-0-910707; 978-1-935067)* 1650 N. Kolb, Suite 200, Tucson, AZ 85715 USA (SAN 260-2385) Tel 520-777-6161; Fax: 520-777-6217
E-mail: info@greatpotentialpress.com
Web site: http://www.facebook.com/GreatPotentialPress; http://www.greatpotentialpress.com
Dist(s): **Bookmen, Inc.**; *CIP.*
Great Reads Bks., *(978-0-9718694)* P.O. Box 2112, Bellaire, TX 77402-2112 USA (SAN 254-5462)
E-mail: greatreadsbooks@earthlink.net; publish@novelpro.com
Web site: http://www.novelpro.com.
†**Great River Bks.,** *(978-0-915556)* 161 M St., Salt Lake City, UT 84103 USA (SAN 207-527X) Tel 801-532-4833
E-mail: info@greatriverbooks.com
Web site: http://www.greatriverbooks.com
Dist(s): **Crown Hse. Publishing**
Midpoint Trade Bks., Inc.; *CIP.*
Great Smoky Mountains Assn., *(978-0-937207)* 115 Park Headquarters Rd., Gatlinburg, TN 37738 USA (SAN 658-7267) Tel 865-436-7318; Fax: 865-436-6884
E-mail: Curt@gsmassoc.org
Web site: http://www.smokiesinformation.org.
Great Smoky Mountains Natural History Association *See* **Great Smoky Mountains Assn.**
Great Source Education Group, Inc., *(978-0-669; 978-0-9638133; 978-1-57185)* Subs. of Houghton Mifflin Harcourt Supplemental Pubs., 181 Ballardvale St., Wilmington, MA 01887 USA Tel 978-661-1500; Fax: 978-661-1331; Toll Free Fax: 800-289-3994; Toll Free: 800-289-4490
Web site: http://www.greatsource.com
Dist(s): **Houghton Mifflin Harcourt Publishing Co.**
Great Texas Line Pr., *(978-1-892588)* Orders Addr.: P.O. Box 11105, Fort Worth, TX 76110 USA Tel 817-922-8929; Fax: 817-926-0420
E-mail: greattexas@hotmail.com
Web site: http://www.greattexasline.com
Dist(s): **Baker & Taylor Bks.**
Bk. Marketing Plus
Bks. West
Forest Sales & Distributing Co.
Great Valley Bks. *Imprint of* **Heyday**
Great West Publishing, *(978-0-9796199; 978-0-9974553)* Orders Addr.: P.O. Box 31631, Tucson, AZ 85751-1631 USA (SAN 853-9146); *Imprints:* Sentry Books (Sentry Bks)
Web site: http://www.sentrybooks.com.
Great White Bird Publishing, *(978-0-9792474)* Orders Addr.: P.O. Box 667, Hiram, GA 30141-0667 USA Tel 770-947-6817; *Imprints:* GWB (GWB)
E-mail: davidthackston@bellsouth.net
Web site: http://www.myspace.com/thackston.
Great White Dog Picture Company *See* **Light-Beams Publishing**
Greater Cincinnati TV Educational Foundation, *(978-0-9744419)* 1223 Central Pkwy., Cincinnati, OH 45214-2812 USA Tel 513-381-4033; Fax: 513-381-7520; *Imprints:* CET (Cet)
E-mail: edtech@wcet.pbs.org
Web site: http://www.wcet.org.
Greater Truth Pubs., *(978-0-9653078; 978-1-937151)* P.O. Box 4332, Lafayette, IN 47903 USA Do not confuse with Griffin Publishing, Glendale, CA
E-mail: gtp@ao-soft.com
Web site: http://www.ao-soft.com/gtpub/.
Greatest Books Pub., *(978-1-937775; 978-1-62236; 978-81-8423-059-8)* 2764 N. Green Valley Pkwy., Henderson, NV 89014 USA Tel 951-760-8499
E-mail: lbbooks1234@gmail.com.
GreatWineFinds.com *See* **GWF Publishing & Henry's Helpers**
GreeHee Publishing, *(978-0-9779590)* Orders Addr.: 125 Susan St., Myrtle Creek, OR 97457-9741 USA Tel 541-863-6631
E-mail: astrologyandmore@gmail.com
Web site: http://www.greehee.com; http://www.talesoftamoor.com
Dist(s): **Quality Bks., Inc.**
Smashwords.
†**Green Dragon Bks.,** *(978-0-89334; 978-1-62386)* 2875 S. Ocean Blvd. Ste 200, Palm Beach, FL 33480 USA (SAN 658-0882) Toll Free Fax: 888-874-8844; Toll Free: 800-874-8844; *Imprints:* Humanics Learning (Humanics Lrng) Do not confuse with Humanics ErgoSystems, Inc., Reseda, CA
E-mail: info@greendragonbooks.com
Web site: http://www.greendragonbooks.com; http://www.humanicslearning.com; http://www.humanicsdealer.com
Dist(s): **Borders, Inc.**
Midpoint Trade Bks., Inc.
New Leaf Distributing Co., Inc.
Two Rivers Distribution; *CIP.*
Green E-Bks., *(978-1-938848; 978-0-9990528; 978-0-9994577)* 6145 N. Tapestry Way, Boise, ID 83714 USA Tel 208-608-8325; Fax: 208-441-6024
E-mail: jason@greene-books.com.
Green Egg Media, Inc., *(978-1-937212)* 17821 Mitchell N, Irvine, CA 92614 USA Tel 949-756-8400; Fax: 949-756-8484
E-mail: garyk@codra.com
Web site: www.codra.com.
Green Ghost Pr., *(978-0-615-24430-3; 978-0-615-24648-2; 978-0-615-33363-2; 978-0-615-38560-0)* P.O. Box 691882, West Hollywood, CA 90069 USA
E-mail: waideriddle@hotmail.com; greenghostpress@hotmail.com
Web site: http://www.waideriddle.com
Dist(s): **Left Bank Bks.**
Tattered Cover Bookstore.
Green Goat Bks., *(978-0-615-15585-2)* P.O. Box 11256, Bainbridge Island, WA 98110 USA Tel 206-842-3412; Fax: 206-842-0570; Toll Free: 866-776-4543
E-mail: contact@greengoatbooks.com
Web site: http://www.greengoatbooks.com
Dist(s): **Greenleaf Book Group.**
Green Hill Publishers *See* **Jameson Bks., Inc.**
Green Igric Pr., *(978-0-9776170)* P.O. Box 82454, Columbus, OH 43202 USA Tel 614-267-9426.
Green Irene, *(978-0-9742280)* P.O. Box 5, Huron, OH 44839 USA
E-mail: chager@buckeye-express.com
Web site: http://www.redandgreenchoices.com.
Green Key Books *See* **Practical Christianity Foundation**
Green Kids Club, Inc., *(978-0-9836602; 978-1-939871)* 1425 Higham St., Idaho Falls, ID 83402 USA Tel 208-528-8718
E-mail: peggy_hinman@yahoo.com.
Green Kids Pr., LLC, *(978-1-939377)* 23 T St. NW, Washington, DC 20001-1008 USA (SAN 920-458X) Tel 202-518-7070; Fax: 202-588-0931
E-mail: jucles@hotmail.com
Web site: www.Green-KidsPress.com
Dist(s): **Midpoint Trade Bks., Inc.**
Partners Pubs. Group, Inc.
Green Lady Pr., The *Imprint of* **RealityIsBooks.com, Inc.**
Green Light Bks. and Publishing, LLC, *(978-0-9755110)* Orders Addr.: 4509 Lake Lawne Ave., Orlando, FL 32808 USA
E-mail: juan_chisholm@yahoo.com
Web site: http://www.greenlightbooks.org.
Green Mansion Pr. LLC, *(978-0-9714612; 978-0-9746457)* 501 E. 79th St., Suite 16A, New York, NY 10021-0773 USA (SAN 254-2684) Tel 212-396-2667; Fax: 212-937-4685
E-mail: info@greenmansionpress.com
Web site: http://www.greenmansionpress.com.
Green, Mary, *(978-0-9764639)* 737 Buffalo Valley Rd., Cookeville, TN 38501-3862 USA
E-mail: greenmajt@frontiernet.net
Web site: http://www.bigfootlady.net.
Green Nest LLC, *(978-0-9772392)* 18662 Macarthur Blvd. Suite 200, Irvine, CA 92612 USA Fax: 949-387-3806
Web site: http://www.greennest.com
Dist(s): **Pathway Bk. Service.**
Green Owl, Inc., *(978-0-9727273)* 23834 SE 248th St., Maple Valley, WA 98038 USA (SAN 255-0679)
E-mail: owl@greenowl.org
Web site: http://www.greenowl.org.
Green Pastures Pr., *(978-0-9627643; 978-1-884377)* HC 67, Box 91-A, Mifflin, PA 17058 USA Tel 717-436-9115.
Green Pastures Publishing, Inc., *(978-0-9664276; 978-0-9720580)* Orders Addr.: P.O. Box 804, Windsor, CO 80550 USA Tel 970-686-7242
Dist(s): **Independent Pubs. Group.**
Green Sheet Inc., The, *(978-0-9670947)* P.O. Box 6008, Petaluma, CA 94955-6008 USA Fax: 707-586-1738; Toll Free: 800-757-4441
E-mail: grnsht@aol.com
Web site: http://www.greensheet.com.
Green Tiger Pr. *Imprint of* **Laughing Elephant**
Green Writers Pr., *(978-0-9893104; 978-0-9899838; 978-0-9960872; 978-0-9909733; 978-0-9961357; 978-0-9962676; 978-0-9968973; 978-0-9974526; 978-0-9982604; 978-0-9987012; 978-0-9990766)* 34 Miller Rd., Brattleboro, VT 05301 USA Tel 802-380-1121
E-mail: dcdesignteamvt@gmail.com
Web site: www.greenwriterspress.com
Dist(s): **Midpoint Trade Bks., Inc.**
Greenberg, Carmel *See* **Kicks and Giggles Today**
Greenberg, Scott *See* **Jump Start Performance Programs**
Greenblatt, Kim, *(978-0-9777282; 978-1-60622)* 6600 Melba Ave., West Hills, CA 91307 USA (SAN 850-0649).
Greenbrier/Scentex *See* **Bright of America**
Greenbush Pr., *(978-0-9766720; 978-0-9836460; 978-0-615-95792-0)* Orders Addr.: 21518 Karpathos Ln., Spring, TX 77388-3262 USA (SAN 256-5048) Tel 281-210-7017 Office phone
E-mail: frankbecker@depressionproofchurch.com; frankbecker@frankbecker.com; frank@greenbushpress.com
Web site: http://www.cross-trainer.org; http://www.greenbushpress.com; http://www.frankbecker.com.

Publisher Name Index

Greene & Sandell, *(978-0-9834681)* 45 Church St. Apt. 1, Boston, MA 02116 USA Tel 617-426-7278
E-mail: greenesandell@gmail.com.

Greene, A.S. & Co., *(978-0-9761723)* 1828 Kings Hwy., Lincoln Park, MI 48146 USA Fax: 313-388-0447
E-mail: anitazoya@yahoo.com.

Greene Bark Pr., Inc., *(978-1-880851)* P.O. Box 1108, Bridgeport, CT 06601-1108 USA Tel 203-372-4861; Fax: 203-371-5856
E-mail: Greenebark@aol.com
Web site: http://www.greenebarkpress.com.

Greene, Brenda H. *See* **Three Willows Pr.**

Greene, Marjorie A., *(978-0-9741764)* 124 Caughman Park Dr., Columbia, SC 29209 USA Tel 803-783-5430; Fax: 803-783-5430
E-mail: remaininme@msn.com.

Greenfield Enterprises, Ltd. (HKG) *(978-962-563) Dist. by* **Cheng Tsui.**

Greenhaven Pr., Inc. *Imprint of* **Cengage Gale**

Greenhaven Publishing *Imprint of* **Greenhaven Publishing LLC**

Greenhaven Publishing LLC, *(978-1-5345)* 353 3rd Ave., Suite 255, New York, NY 10010 USA (SAN 990-171X) Tel 212-420-1205; Fax: 212-614-7385; Toll Free Fax: 844-317-7405; Toll Free: 844-317-7404; *Imprints:* KidHaven Publishing (KidHaven Publ); Lucent Press (Lucent Pr); Greenhaven Publishing (GreenHav)
E-mail: gh_custserv@greenhaven.com; hollyc@rosenpub.com.

Greenhill Bks./Lionel Leventhal, Ltd. (GBR) *(978-0-947898; 978-1-85367) Dist. by* **HachBkGrp.**

Greenleaf Book Group, *(978-0-9665319; 978-1-929774; 978-0-9790842; 978-1-60832; 978-1-61486; 978-1-62634)* Orders Addr.: 4005-B Banister Ln., Austin, TX 78704 USA Tel 512-891-6100; Fax: 512-891-6150; Toll Free: 800-932-5420; Edit Addr.: P.O. Box 91869, Austin, TX 78709 USA; *Imprints:* Greenleaf Book Group Press (GBGP)
E-mail: tanya@greenleafbookgroup.com
Web site: http://www.greenleafbookgroup.com.

Greenleaf Book Group Pr. *Imprint of* **Greenleaf Book Group**

Greenleaf Pr., *(978-1-882514)* 1570 Old Laguardo Rd E., Lebanon, TN 37087-8958 USA (SAN 297-8555) Toll Free Fax: 866-725-0785 Do not confuse with Greenleaf Pr., Breckenridge, CO
E-mail: info@greenleafpress.com
Web site: http://www.greenleafpress.com.

Greenline Publications *See* **Davis, A. S. Media Group**

GreenPoint Computer Services *See* **GIL Pubns.**

Greenroom Bks., *(978-0-9712163)* 12 N. Juniper St., Hampton, VA 23669-2416 USA (SAN 254-2501) Tel 757-726-2651 (phone/fax)
E-mail: brad@greenroombooks.com; publisher@greenroombooks.com
Web site: http://www.greenroombooks.com
Dist(s): **Brodart Co.**

Greensboro Historical Museum, Inc., *(978-0-9747456)* 130 Summit Ave., Greensboro, NC 27401-3016 USA Tel 336-373-2043; Fax: 336-373-2204
Web site: http://www.greensborohistory.org.

Greentown Glass Co., *(978-0-9723958)* Orders Addr.: P.O. Box 771, Westfield, IN 46074-0771 USA Tel 765-455-0595; Edit Addr.: 3703 Robin Dr., Kokomo, IN 46902 USA
Web site: http://www.greentownglasscompany.com.

Greenville Family Partnership, *(978-0-9759699)* P.O. Box 10203, Greenville, SC 29603-0203 USA Tel 864-467-4099; Fax: 864-467-4102
Web site: http://www.redribbonworks.org.

Greenwillow Bks. *Imprint of* **HarperCollins Pubs.**

Greenwood *Imprint of* **ABC-CLIO, LLC**

Greenwood Hill Pr., *(978-0-9797868; 978-0-9836382; 978-0-9846912; 978-0-9881748; 978-0-9915961; 978-0-9989643)* W 7048 Savannah Ln., Delavan, WI 53115 USA; *Imprints:* OddInt Media (OddIntMedia)
E-mail: mjohnson@fullpo.com.

Greenwood, Lori Ministries, Inc., *(978-0-9747956)* Orders Addr.: 17622 32nd Pl W., Lynnwood, WA 98037-7714 USA (SAN 255-8297)
E-mail: lgministries@cs.com
Web site: http://www.thevisionlink.com.

Greenwood Street Publishing. GSP, *(978-0-9745553)* 1539 W. Townley Ave., Phoenix, AZ 85021 USA Tel 602-997-4444; Fax: 602-997-5959 Do not confuse with Greenwood Publishing in Wixom, MI
E-mail: julie@gg-az.com; info@greenwoodstreet.com
Web site: http://www.greenwoodstreet.com.

Gregory, Charles, *(978-0-9745432)* 17697 Palmer St., Melvindale, MI 48122 USA (SAN 255-7991) Tel 313-389-2836
E-mail: charles_gregory@ameritech.net
Web site: http://www.charles_gregory/index.html
Dist(s): **Lulu Pr., Inc.**

Gregory, Charles Matthew, *(978-0-9766442)* 5101 Boarshead Rd. No. 102, Minnetonka, MN 55345 USA Tel 612-845-7134
Web site: www.mikascomic.com.

Grendel Roleplaying, *(978-1-929928)* 1420 S. Ave. F, Portales, NM 88130 USA
E-mail: author@paulbspence.com
Web site: http://www.paulbspence.com.

Grenevitch, Betsy Coffman, *(978-0-9747113)* 1450 Hewatt Rd., Lilburn, GA 30047 USA Tel 678-344-6100 (phone/fax)
E-mail: blindangel@joimail.com.

Grenwood Publishing *See* **Greenwood Street Publishing. GSP**

Gresham, Joel, *(978-0-9708446)* 2201 Morgan Pl., Atlanta, GA 30324 USA Tel 404-512-0445
E-mail: undercolorjg@yahoo.com.

Grey Gate Media, LLC, *(978-0-9787318; 978-0-9801004; 978-1-61807)* 20 Fisherville Rd., #173, Concord, NH 03303 USA Tel 603-801-2208; Fax: 603-676-7882; *Imprints:* Little Blue Flower Press (Little Blue Flow).

Grey Gecko Pr., *(978-0-9836185; 978-0-9854400; 978-1-938821; 978-1-945760)* 565 S Mason Rd Ste 154, Katy, TX 77450 USA Tel 713-489-5731
E-mail: jason@greygeckopress.com
Web site: http://www.greygeckopress.com
Dist(s): **Lightning Source, Inc.**

†Grey Hse. Publishing, *(978-0-939300; 978-1-891482; 978-1-930956; 978-1-59237; 978-1-61925; 978-1-68217)* 4919 Rte. 22, Amenia, NY 12501 USA Tel 518-789-8700; Fax: 518-789-0556; Toll Free: 800-562-2139; 4919 Rte. 22, Amenia, NY 12501 Tel 518-789-8700; Fax: 518-789-0556; Toll Free: 800-562-2139; *Imprints:* Universal Reference Publications (Universal Ref Pubns)
E-mail: books@greyhouse.com
Web site: http://www.greyhouse.com
Dist(s): **Ebsco Publishing**
MyiLibrary
ebrary, Inc.; *CIP.*

Grey Stone Bks. (GBR) *(978-0-9515996; 978-1-902017) Dist. by* **PerseuPGW.**

GreyCore Pr., *(978-0-9671851; 978-0-9742074)* 3833 Hilton Ave NE, Albuquerque, NM 87110-1059 USA
E-mail: joan123@frontiernet.net.

Greyhound Bks., *(978-0-9724136; 978-1-59677)* 2000 Stock Creek Rd., Knoxville, TN 37920 USA Tel 865-405-3002
E-mail: cynmob@aol.com; editor@bushidopress.com
Web site: http://www.dogbooks.org.

Greystone Books Ltd. (CAN) *(978-1-55365; 978-1-77100) Dist. by* **PerseuPGW.**

Grid Pr. *Imprint of* **L & R Publishing, LLC**

Grief Watch, *(978-0-9615197; 978-0-9724241; 978-0-9916312; 978-0-692-37070-4)* Div. of Metanoia Peace Community United Methodist Church, 2116 NE 18th Ave., Portland, OR 97212 USA (SAN 694-2911) Tel 503-284-7426; Fax: 503-282-8985
E-mail: webmaster@griefwatch.com
Web site: http://www.griefwatch.com
Dist(s): **ACTA Pubns.**
CreateSpace Independent Publishing Platform.

GRIFFIN *See* **Griffin**

Griffin, *(978-0-312-60750-0)* 915 Electric Ave., Venice, CA 90291 USA.

Griffin Comics *Imprint of* **Corbett Features**

Griffin, Curtis Monroe, *(978-0-9749583)* 3250 Oneal Cir., Boulder, CO 80301-1424 USA.

Griffin Group Publishing LLC, *(978-0-692-01920-7)* 3419 Westminister Suite 320, Dallas, TX 75205 USA.

Griffin Publishing *See* **Greater Truth Pubs.**

Griffin Publishing Group, *(978-1-58000; 978-1-882180)* P.O. Box 28627, Santa Ana, CA 92799-8627 USA Toll Free: 800-472-9741 Do not confuse with Griffin Publishing, Ogden, UT
E-mail: griffinbooks@earthlink.net; mvonarx@griffinpublishing.com
Web site: http://www.griffinpublishing.com
Dist(s): **BHB Fulfillment**
Sundaykool Bulletins.

Griffin, Sandi Zambarano, *(978-1-883838)* 10840 Kimberfyld Ln., Port Saint Lucie, FL 34986 USA Tel 561-461-6830
Dist(s): **Bookazine Co., Inc.**

Griffith, John *See* **Rosetta Stone Communications**

Griffith, Tara, *(978-0-692-83481-7)* 1330 Worley Ave NW, CANTON, OH 44703 USA Tel 330-617-3594
E-mail: jeffwcrawford5+LVP0003269@gmail.com; jeffwcrawford5+LVP0003269@gmail.com.

Griggs Music Co., *(978-0-9753385)* 228 Pope Bend Rd., Cedar Creek, TX 78612 USA Tel 512-303-2744
Web site: http://www.griggsmusic.net.

Grigsby, Cynthia, *(978-0-9786840)* 4304 Hillyer St., Fairfax, VA 22032-1418 USA
E-mail: cgrigsby6@yahoo.com.

Griha, *(978-0-9748503)* 23 Iron Bark Ln., Aliso Viejo, CA 92656 USA
Web site: http://www.griha.com.

Grijalbo, Editorial (MEX) *(978-968-419; 978-970-05) Dist. by* **Continental Bk.**

Grijalbo, Editorial (MEX) *(978-968-419; 978-970-05) Dist. by* **AIMS Intl.**

Grijalbo Mondadori, S.A.-Junior (ESP) *(978-84-253; 978-84-397; 978-84-7419; 978-84-478; 978-84-7423) Dist. by* **Continental Bk.**

Grijalbo Mondadori, S.A.-Montena (ESP) *(978-84-7515; 978-84-85297; 978-84-8441) Dist. by* **Lectorum Pubns.**

Grijalbo-Dargaud, S.A. Editores (ESP) *(978-84-7510) Dist. by* **Distribks Inc.**

Grimes, Richard, *(978-0-9770594)* 111 Lankford Dr., Georgetown, KY 40324 USA.

Gripper Products, *(978-0-916176)* 787 N. 24th St., Philadelphia, PA 19130-2540 USA (SAN 206-3816) Tel 215-765-9362
E-mail: reluctantspy@gmail.com
Dist(s): **CreateSpace Independent Publishing Platform**
Lightning Source, Inc.
Smashwords.

Grizlegirl Productions *See* **Bookateer Publishing**

Grizzly Adams Productions, Inc., *(978-0-9667985; 978-1-929296; 978-1-931602; 978-1-933424; 978-1-934646)* Orders Addr.: P.O. Box 298, Baker City, OR 97814 USA; Edit Addr.: 2850 Myrtle St., Baker City, OR 97814 USA
Dist(s): **Send The Light Distribution LLC.**

Grizzly Bks Publishing, *(978-0-9747951; 978-0-9749634)* Orders Addr.: PMB Box 136, Dahlonega, GA 30533 USA Tel 706-864-2349 (phone/fax); Edit Addr.: 240 Wal-Mart Way, Dahlonega, GA 30533 USA
E-mail: ancient12@linkamerica.net
Web site: http://www.grizzlybookz.com.

Grizzly Ridge Publishing, *(978-0-9793963)* P.O. Box 268, West Glacier, MT 59936 USA
Web site: http://www.grizzlyridgepublishing.com.

Grolier *Imprint of* **Scholastic Library Publishing**

Grolier Online *Imprint of* **Scholastic Library Publishing**

Grolier Publishing *See* **Scholastic Library Publishing**

Grolier Publishing, *(978-0-516; 978-0-531)* 90 Old Sherman Tpke., Danbury, CT 06816E USA Tel 203-797-3500; Fax: 203-797-3657
E-mail: agraham@grolier.com
Web site: www.scholasticlibrary.com.

Grosinger, Crain Publishing, *(978-0-9720054)* Orders Addr.: P.O. Box 55, Mandan, ND 58554 USA Tel 701-202-1293; Edit Addr.: 210 Collins Ave., Mandan, ND 58554 USA
Web site: http://www.johnsbook.net; http://www.crainbooks.com
Dist(s): **Partners Bk. Distributing, Inc.**

Gross, H. H., *(978-0-9754699)* P.O. Box 122606, San Diego, CA 92112 USA
E-mail: hhgross@lycos.com
Web site: http://www.hhgross.net.

Gross, Roxanna, *(978-0-615-16398-7)* 3 S. Cedarwood Ct., Alexandria, KY 41001 USA
E-mail: roxie@zoomtown.com
Dist(s): **Lulu Pr., Inc.**

Grosset & Dunlap *Imprint of* **Penguin Publishing Group**

Grosset & Dunlap *Imprint of* **Penguin Young Readers Group**

Grossman, Dina *See* **Tzipora Pubns., Inc.**

Groundbreaking Pr., *(978-0-9718562; 978-0-9745624; 978-0-9765821; 978-0-9773535; 978-0-9777795; 978-0-9793542; 978-0-9831030; 978-0-9850651)* Orders Addr.: 8305 Arboles Cir., Austin, TX 78737 USA Tel 512-657-8780
E-mail: brad@groundbreaking.com
Web site: http://www.groundbreaking.com.

Groundwood Bks. (CAN) *(978-0-88899; 978-1-55498) Dist. by* **PerseuPGW.**

Group Books *See* **Group Publishing, Inc.**

†Group Publishing, Inc., *(978-0-7644; 978-0-931529; 978-0-936664; 978-1-55945; 978-1-4707)* Orders Addr.: 1515 Cascade Ave., Loveland, CO 80538-8681 USA (SAN 214-4689) Tel 970-669-3836; Fax: 970-679-4373; Toll Free: 800-635-0404; 800-447-1070 (consumer orders only); 800-541-5200 (trade orders only); *Imprints:* Flagship Church Resources (Flagship Church)
E-mail: cbuxman@grouppublishing.com
Web site: http://www.grouppublishing.com
Dist(s): **Appalachian Bible Co.**
Faith Alive Christian Resources
Spring Arbor Distributors, Inc.
Twentieth Century Christian Bks.; *CIP.*

Grove Creek Publishing, LLC, *(978-1-933963)* 1159 N. 950 E., Pleasant Grove, UT 84062 USA Tel 801-471-5652
E-mail: noonws@yahoo.com
Web site: http://www.grovecreekpublishing.com.

Grove Educational Technologies, *(978-0-936735)* 6435 Yamhill St., SE, Portland, OR 97215-2027 USA (SAN 699-9840); 27 Hy Pl., Lake Grove, NY 11755 (SAN 699-9859)
E-mail: geta@juno.com.

†Grove/Atlantic, Inc., *(978-0-8021; 978-0-87113; 978-1-55584; 978-1-61185)* 841 Broadway, 4th Flr., New York, NY 10003-4793 USA (SAN 201-4890) Tel 212-614-7850; Fax: 212-614-7886; Toll Free: 800-521-0178; *Imprints:* Black Cat (BlackCat)
Web site: http://www.groveatlantic.com/
Dist(s): **MyiLibrary**
Publishers Group West (PGW)
Two Rivers Distribution; *CIP.*

Growing & Learning Pr., *(978-0-9795773)* 228 Woodward Ave, Buffalo, NY 14214 USA (SAN 853-8093).

Growing Art Pr., *(978-1-934367)* 419 NW 16th St., Corvallis, OR 97330 USA (SAN 852-9612)
E-mail: stickmaker@comcast.net.

Growing Field *Imprint of* **Growing Field Bks.**

Growing Field Bks., *(978-0-9770391; 978-0-9857057; 978-0-9891881)* 2012 Pacific Ct., Fort Collins, CO 80528 USA (SAN 851-7193); *Imprints:* Growing Field (Growing Field) Do not confuse with companies with the same or similar name in Lawrence, KSThomaston, CT, Los Angeles, CA, Huntsville, AL, New YOrk, NY, Glen Head, NY
E-mail: Mhoog@growingfield.com
Web site: http://www.Growingfield.com
Dist(s): **Brodart Co.**
Follett School Solutions
Hertzberg-New Method Inc.

Growing Little Readers, *(978-0-9777150)* 1105 Kyle Ct., Chesapeake, VA 23322 USA
Web site: http://growinglittlereaders.com.

Growing Senses Pubns., *(978-0-9973189)* 5842 Cranbrook Trail, Traverse City, MI 49685 USA Tel 231-881-4138
E-mail: growingsensespublications@gmail.com.

Growing with the Saints, Inc., *(978-0-9798889)* 2812 Longwood Ct., Fort Wayne, IN 46845 USA Tel 260-489-8493
E-mail: melissa@growingwiththesaints.com
Web site: http://www.growingwiththesaints.com.

Growing Years *Imprint of* **Port Town Publishing**

Growth Publishing, *(978-1-893505)* Div. of Growth Central LLC, Orders Addr.: 6545 N. Via Divina, Tucson, AZ 85750-0971 USA Tel 520-299-2550; Fax: 520-577-6998
E-mail: growthcentral@gmail.com
Web site: http://www.growthcentral.com/.

Growth-Ink, *(978-0-9799636)* 4025 State St., No. 9, Santa Barbara, CA 93110 USA (SAN 854-9303)
E-mail: Growthink1@aol.com.

Gruber Enterprises, *(978-0-9770413)* 21521 Finlan, Saint Clair Shores, MI 48080 USA
Web site: http://www.thelegendofthebrog.com.

Grubish, Donald, *(978-0-9771179)* 1326 Goodwin Ave N., Saint Paul, MN 55128-6164 USA.

Grubnedor Pr., *(978-0-9795407; 978-0-9989368)* 8121 Allison Pl., Arvada, CO 80005 USA (SAN 853-7186)
E-mail: dmrodenburg@comcast.net
Web site: grubnedorpress.com.

Grupo Anaya, S.A. (ESP) *(978-84-207; 978-84-667) Dist. by* **Continental Bk.**

Grupo Anaya, S.A. (ESP) *(978-84-207; 978-84-667) Dist. by* **Lectorum Pubns.**

Grupo Anaya, S.A. (ESP) *(978-84-207; 978-84-667) Dist. by* **AIMS Intl.**

Grupo Anaya, S.A. (ESP) *(978-84-207; 978-84-667) Dist. by* **Distribks Inc.**

Grupo Nelson, *(978-0-8499; 978-0-88113; 978-0-89922; 978-1-60255)* Div. of Thomas Nelson, Inc., 501 Nelson Pl., Nashville, TN 37217 USA (SAN 240-6349) Tel 615-889-9000; Fax: 615-883-9376; Toll Free: 800-251-4000
Web site: http://www.editorialcaribe.com
Dist(s): **Ediciones Universal**
Libros Sin Fronteras
Luciano Bks.
Nelson, Thomas Inc.
Pan De Vida Distributors
Peniel Productions
Twentieth Century Christian Bks.
Zondervan.

Gryphon House Inc *Imprint of* **Gryphon Hse., Inc.**

Gryphon Hse., Inc., *(978-0-87659; 978-0-917505; 978-1-58904)* Orders Addr.: 6848 Leon's Way, Lewisville, NC 27023 USA (SAN 169-3190) Tel 800-638-0928; Fax: 800-638-7576; Toll Free: 800-638-0928; *Imprints:* Robins Lane Press (Robins Ln Pr); School Age Notes (School-Age); Gryphon House Inc (GHI)
E-mail: info@ghbooks.com
Web site: http://www.gryphonhouse.com
Dist(s): **CENGAGE Learning**
INscribe Digital
Independent Pubs. Group
MyiLibrary
ebrary, Inc.

Gryphon Pr., The, *(978-0-940719)* 6808 Margarets Ln., Edina, MN 55439 USA Tel 952-941-5993; Fax: 952-941-6593
E-mail: eb6@earthlink.net
Dist(s): **Consortium Bk. Sales & Distribution.**

G.S. Enterprises of America Inc., *(978-0-9763141)* P.O. Box 776, Frankfort, KY 40602-0776 USA Tel 502-227-8226; Fax: 502-227-8223
E-mail: lstafford173@gmail.com
Web site: http://www.bedtimeboomer.com.

GS Publishers *See* **GSVQ Publishing**

GSP Players, LLC, *(978-0-9792640)* 8033 Sunset Blvd., No. 1024, Los Angeles, CA 90046 USA.

GSR Communications, *(978-0-9717507)* 6090 SW Elm Ave., Beaverton, OR 97005 USA
E-mail: gsr@teleport.com.

GSS Tech Ed, *(978-0-9712340; 978-0-9895576)* 31500 Grape St. Bldg. 3-364, Lake Elsinore, CA 92532 USA Tel 951-471-4932; Fax: 951-471-4981; Toll Free Fax: 866-367-6180; Toll Free: 800-422-1100
Web site: http://www.GSSTechEd.com
Dist(s): **All Electronics Corp.**
Pitsco Education.

GSVQ Publishing, *(978-1-933156)* 1350 E. Flamingo Rd., Suite 50, Las Vegas, NV 89119-5263 USA Tel 866-347-9244; *Imprints:* VisionQuest Kids (VisionQuest Kids); Visikid Books (Visikid Bks)
E-mail: contactus@gsvisionquest.com
Web site: http://www.gsvisionquest.com; http://www.visikidbooks.com.

GT Bks. LLC, *(978-0-9765845)* 19 Housman Ct., Maplewood, NJ 07040-3006 USA
Web site: http://www.gtbooks.net.

GT Interactive Software, *(978-1-56893; 978-1-58869)* 417 Fifth Ave., New York, NY 10016 USA Tel 212-726-4243; Fax: 212-726-4204
E-mail: efierro@gtinteractive.com
Web site: http://gtinteractive.com.

Guadeloupe, Emmanuel & Augustine 'Gus' Logie *See* **Plain Vision Publishing**

Guangdong New Era Publishing Hse. (CHN) *(978-7-5405) Dist. by* **Chinasprout.**

Guardian Angel Publishing, *(978-0-9763990)* 415 Meadow View Dr., Lavon, TX 75166-1245 USA Do not confuse with companies with the same or similar name in Carby, OR, Saint Louis, MO
E-mail: admin@tommytellbooks.com
Web site: http://www.tommytellbooks.com.

Guardian Angel Publishing, Inc., *(978-1-933090; 978-1-935137; 978-1-61633)* 12430 Tesson Ferry Rd., No. 186, Saint Louis, MO 63128 USA (SAN 858-7833) Do not confuse with companies with same name in Canby, OR and Hubbard, OR., The Colony, TX
E-mail: publisher@guardianangelpublishing.com
Web site: http://www.guardianangelpublishing.com.

Guardian of Truth Foundation, *(978-0-9620615; 978-1-58427)* Orders Addr.: P.O. Box 9670, Bowling Green, KY 42102 USA Tel 317-745-4708; Edit Addr.: 420 Old Morgantown Rd., Bowling Green, KY 42102 USA (SAN 249-4221)
E-mail: mikewillis1@compuserve.com.

Guardians of Order (CAN) *(978-0-9682431; 978-1-894525) Dist. by* **PSI Ga.**

Guardsman Press *See* **Moondance Publishing**

Guerra, Justin A., *(978-0-692-87963-4)* 14685 Eagle River Rd, EASTVALE, CA 92880 USA Tel 760-912-3560
E-mail: jeffwcrawford5+LVP0003671@gmail.com; jeffwcrawford5+LVP0003671@gmail.com.

Guest Cottage, Incorporated, The, 8821 Hwy 47, Woodruff, WI 54568 USA Tel 715-358-5195; Fax: 715-358-9456
E-mail: amherst@networth.net
Web site: http://www.amherstpress.com
Dist(s): **Chicago Distribution Ctr.**

Guevara, Alexis S., *(978-0-9765663)* 1625 Palo Alto St., No. 208, Los Angeles, CA 90026 USA
E-mail: sa_guevara@msn.com
Web site: http://www.selectaUSA.com; http://www.alexisguevara.com.

Guia, Elizabeth, *(978-0-9764280)* 2956 Bird Ave. # 8, Miami, FL 33133-4542 USA
E-mail: eguiam@msn.com.

Guide to South Florida Off-Road Bicycling *See* **DeGraaf Publishing**

Guideline Pubns. Co., (978-1-882951) Div. of Marketing Support Services, Orders Addr.: P.O. Box 801094, Atlanta, GA 30101 USA Fax: 770-424-0778; Toll Free: 800-552-1076
E-mail: sales@guidelinepub.com
Web site: http://www.guidelinepub.com.

Guiding Horizons, (978-0-9749763) 2201 Heritage Crest Dr., Valrico, FL 33594-5120 USA
Web site: http://www.guidinghorizons.com.

Guidry Assocs., Inc., (978-0-9724667) P.O. Box 2280, Winchester, VA 22604 USA Tel 540-545-8800; *Imprints:* Who's Who In Sports (Who's Who In Sp)
E-mail: info@whoswhoinsports.com
Web site: http://www.whoswhoinsports.com.

Guilford Pubns., (978-0-89862; 978-1-57230; 978-1-59385; 978-1-60623; 978-1-60918; 978-1-4625) Orders Addr.: 370 Seventh Avenue, Suite 1200, New York, NY 10001-1020 USA (SAN 212-9442) Tel 212-431-9800; Fax: 212-966-6708; Toll Free: 800-365-7006
E-mail: info@guilford.com
Web site: http://www.guilford.com
Dist(s): **Ebsco Publishing**
MyiLibrary
Rittenhouse Bk. Distributors
ebrary, Inc.

Guilin City Publishing, (978-0-9818622) P.O. Box 9621, Pittsburgh, PA 15226 USA
E-mail: info@guilincitypublishing.com
Web site: http://www.guilincitypublishing.com.

Guilty Mom Pr., (978-0-9708415) 172 Dolphin Cir., Marina, CA 93933 USA Tel 831-384-8459
E-mail: plumtckrd@aol.com
Dist(s): **One Small Voice Foundation.**

Guinness World Records Ltd. (GBR) (978-0-85112; 978-1-892051; 978-0-900424; 978-1-904994; 978-1-908843; 978-1-910561) *Dist. by* **Macmillan.**

GuitarVoyager Inc., (978-0-9785992) 3616 Calvend Ln., Kensington, MD 20895 USA Tel 240-486-3849; Fax: 301-949-1647
E-mail: guitarvoyager@gmail.com
Web site: http://www.guitarvoyager.com.

Gullah Girl Publishing, (978-0-9967540)
E-mail: bftafwife1@yahoo.com.

Gulley Institute of Creative Learning, Inc., (978-1-928561) Orders Addr.: P.O. Box 652, Meridian, MS 39302 USA Tel 601-483-0963; Fax: 601-483-0962; Edit Addr.: P.O. Box 1266, Inglewood, CA 90308-1266 USA
E-mail: Gulstem7@aol.com.

Gulley, Wayne, (978-0-9843505; 978-0-9886117; 978-0-9981252) P.O. Box 8807, Spring Valley Lake (Victorville), CA 92395 USA
E-mail: wagpublishing@me.com
Web site: www.michelangelotangelo.com.

Gulliver Bks. *Imprint of* **Harcourt Children's Bks.**

Gumbo Multimedia Entertainment, (978-0-9762838; 978-0-9832329) P.O. Box 371641, Miami, FL 32821 USA
E-mail: srodriguez@lushenabks.com; Jeff@JeffRivera.com
Web site: http://www.JeffRivera.com; http://www.GumboWriters.com
Dist(s): **NetSource Distribution**
Smashwords.

GumShoe Press, (978-0-9777538) Orders Addr.: 411 Chartley Pk. Rd., Reisterstown, MD 21136 USA (SAN 850-1769) Tel 410-971-8229
E-mail: tjmysteryauthor@aol.com
Web site: http://www.authorsden.com/tjperkins.

Guppy Publishing LLC, (978-0-9788553) PMB 221, 6749 S. Westnedge, Suite K, Portage, MI 49002 USA Fax: 269-327-3168
E-mail: dkennis@charter.net
Web site: http://www.guppypublishing.com.

Gurevich, Leonid, (978-0-9753458) 4 Remington Ln., Plymouth, MA 02360-1424 USA
E-mail: lgurev3007@aol.com.

Guru Graphics, (978-0-9729759) 500 Creekside Ct., Golden, CO 80403-1903 USA Tel 303-278-0177
E-mail: levropes@attbi.com.

Gurze Bks., (978-0-936077) Orders Addr.: P.O. Box 2238, Carlsbad, CA 92018 USA (SAN 697-0818) Tel 760-434-7533; Fax: 760-434-5476; Toll Free: 800-756-7533; Edit Addr.: 5145-B Avenida Encinas, Carlsbad, CA 92018 USA (SAN 697-0826)
E-mail: gurze@aol.com; qzcati@aol.com
Web site: http://www.gurze.com
Dist(s): **MyiLibrary**
Publishers Group West (PGW)
Quality Bks., Inc.

Gustav's Library, (978-0-9758914) 1011 E. High St., Davenport, IA 52803 USA Tel 563-323-2283
E-mail: gustav@gustavslibrary.com
Web site: http://www.gustavslibrary.com.

Gutenberg Publishers *See* **Albatross Pubs.**

Guzman, Maria del C., (978-0-9855639) 39 Arenas St., Aguirre, PR 00794 USA Tel 787-853-2542
E-mail: mguzman_aguirre@yahoo.com.

GW Publishing (GBR) (978-0-9535397; 978-0-9546701; 978-0-9551564; 978-0-9554145; 978-0-9561211; 978-0-9570844) *Dist. by* **Wlsn Assocs.**

Gwasg Prifysgol Cymru / Univ. of Wales Pr. (GBR) (978-0-7083; 978-0-900768; 978-1-900477; 978-1-78316) *Dist. by* **Chicago Distribution Ctr.**

GWB *Imprint of* **Great White Bird Publishing**

Gwenwst Bks., (978-0-9914423) P.O. Box 457, Willernie, MN 55090 USA Tel 651-280-7232
E-mail: John.digley@gmail.com
Web site: Pending.

GWF Publishing & Henry's Helpers, (978-0-9768442)
E-mail: henryshelpers@yahoo.com
Web site: http://www.henryshelpers.com.

Gye Nyame Hse., (978-1-886098) Orders Addr.: P.O. Box 42248, Philadelphia, PA 19101 USA (SAN 299-0415) Tel 215 229 1751; Edit Addr.: 6810 Old York Rd., Philadelphia, PA 19126 USA Tel 215-548-2175
E-mail: gyenyamehouse@aol.com.

Gye Nyame Press *See* **Love II Learn Bks.**

Gypsy Heart Pr., (978-0-9832514; 978-0-9969984) 127 RAINBOW Dr. No. 2756, Livingston, TX 77399 USA Tel 979-446-8563
E-mail: erin@erin-casey.com
Dist(s): **Ingram Publisher Services.**

Gypsy Hill Publishing,

Gypsy Pubns., (978-0-9842375; 978-1-938768) 325 Green Oak Dr., Troy, OH 45373-4396 USA
E-mail: fishermh@juno.com; meg.fisher@yahoo.com
Web site: http://www.gypsypublications.com.

H & R Magic Bks., (978-0-9727938) 3839 Liles Ln., Humble, TX 77396 USA Tel 281-540-7229
Web site: http://www.magicbookshop.com.

H Bar Pr., (978-0-9794104; 978-0-9893092) 729 Westview St., Philadelphia, PA 19119-3533 USA (SAN 853-3644) Tel 215-844-8054; Fax: 215-844-1399
E-mail: kwford@verizon.net; hbar.press@verizon.net
Dist(s): **Smashwords.**

H E C Software, Inc., (978-0-928424; 978-1-62382) 60 N. Cutler Dr., No. 101, North Salt Lake, UT 84054 USA (SAN 669-6201) Tel 801-295-7054; Fax: 801-295-7088; Toll Free: 800-333-0054
E-mail: info@readinghorizons.com
Web site: http://www.readinghorizons.com.

H H Krsna Balaram Swami, (978-0-9631403) Orders Addr.: P.O. Box 27127, Baltimore, MD 21230 USA; Edit Addr.: 1613 Webster St., Baltimore, MD 21230 USA Tel 301-752-7531.

H M Bricker, (978-0-615-42163-6; 978-0-9838738) Orders Addr.: 2279 Grass Lake Rd., Lindenhurst, IL 60046 USA
E-mail: santanobeard@comcast.net; birdman1211@comcast.net
Web site: http://www.grandpabrickerbooks.com.

H M S Pubns., Inc., (978-1-888732) P.O. Box 524, Niantic, CT 06357 USA Tel 860-739-3187; Toll Free: 888-739-3187
E-mail: hmspublications@earthlink.net
Dist(s): **Follett School Solutions**
Quality Bks., Inc.
ebrary, Inc.

H. O. M. E. (Holding Onto Memorable Experiences) *See* **Do The Write Thing Foundation of DC**

H R M Software *See* **Human Relations Media**

Haag Environmental Press *See* **Haag Pr.**

Haag Pr., (978-0-9665497; 978-0-9710260; 978-0-9797511) Div. of Haag Environmental Co., Inc., Orders Addr.: 315 E. Market St., Sandusky, OH 44870 USA (SAN 852-6583) Tel 419-621-9329; Fax: 419-621-8669
E-mail: haagpress@aol.com; help@haagpress.com
Web site: http://www.haagpress.com.

Haan Graphic Publishing Services, Limited *See* **Southfarm Pr.**

Haas, Melissa, (978-0-578-06935-7; 978-0-9897689) 711 Bellaire Ave., Pittsburgh, PA 15226 USA
E-mail: catulathebook@gmail.com
Web site: http://www.catulathebook.com.

Haber-Schaim & Associates *See* **Science Curriculum, Inc.**

Hability Solution Services, Inc., (978-1-932062) P.O. Box 2595, Kearney, NE 68848 USA Tel 308-338-9238; Fax: 308-338-9208; Toll Free: 888-814-3238
E-mail: info@habsol.com; info@ideamagicbooks.com
Web site: http://www.habsol.com; http://www.ideamagicbooks.com.

Habit House *See* **Roedway Pr.**

Hachai Publications, Incorporated *See* **Hachai Publishing**

Hachai Publishing, (978-0-922613; 978-1-929628; 978-1-945560) 527 Empire Blvd., Brooklyn, NY 11225 USA (SAN 251-3749) Tel 718-633-0100; Fax: 718-633-0103
E-mail: info@hachai.com
Web site: http://www.hachai.com
Dist(s): **Kerem Publishing.**

Hachette Audio, (978-1-57042; 978-1-58621; 978-1-59483; 978-1-60024; 978-1-60788; 978-1-5491) Div. of Hachette Book Group, 1290 Ave. of the Americas, New York, NY 10104 USA Tel 212-364-1100; Fax: 212-364-1923; Toll Free: 800-759-0190
E-mail: audiobooks.publicity@hbgusa.com
Web site: http://www.hachettebookgroupusa.com/publishing_hachette-audio.aspx
Dist(s): **Blackstone Audio, Inc.**
Findaway World, LLC
Follett School Solutions
Grand Central Publishing
Hachette Bk. Group
Libros Sin Fronteras
Landmark Audiobooks.

Hachette AudioBooks *See* **Hachette Audio**

Hachette Bks. *Imprint of* **Hachette Bks.**

Hachette Bk. Group, (978-0-446; 978-1-60941; 978-1-61113; 978-1-61969; 978-1-4789) Div. of Hachette Group Livre, Orders Addr.: 3 Center Plaza, Boston, MA 02108 USA (SAN 852-5463) Tel 617-263-1828; Toll Free Fax: 800-286-9471; Toll Free: 800-759-0190; Edit Addr.: P.O. Box 2146, Johannesburg, 2196 ZAF Tel 2711 783-7565; Fax: 2711 883-6866; *Imprints:* L,B Kids (LB Kids)
Web site: http://www.hachettebookgroup.com
Dist(s): **Blackstone Audio, Inc.**
Findaway World, LLC
Follett School Solutions
MyiLibrary
Perfection Learning Corp.
Time Inc. Bks.

Hachette Bks., Div. of Hachette Book Group, Orders Addr.: 3 Center Plaza, Boston, MA 02108-2084 USA Tel 617-227-0730; Toll Free Fax: 800-286-9471; Toll Free: 800-759-0730; Edit Addr.: 237 Park Ave., New York, NY 10017 USA Tel 212-364-0600; Fax: 212-364-0952; *Imprints:* Hachette Books (HachetteBks); Black Dog & Leventhal Publishers, Inc. (BlackDog Lev)
Dist(s): **Blackstone Audio, Inc.**
Hachette Bk. Group
MyiLibrary
Open Road Integrated Media, Inc.

Hachette Children's Group (GBR) (978-0-7502; 978-1-85881; 978-1-84255; 978-1-4440; 978-1-4449) *Dist. by* **IPG Chicago.**

Hachette Children's Group (GBR) (978-0-7502; 978-1-85881; 978-1-84255; 978-1-4440; 978-1-4449) *Dist. by* **HachBkGrp.**

Hachette Groupe Livre (FRA) (978-2-01) *Dist. by* **Distribks Inc.**

Hachette Ireland (IRL) (978-0-340; 978-1-4447; 978-1-4736) *Dist. by* **HachBkGrp.**

Hachette Nashville, (978-0-446) Div. of Hachette Book Group, 10 Cadillac Dr., Brentwood, TN 37027 USA Tel 615-221-0996; *Imprints:* Faithwords (Faithwrds)
Dist(s): **Blackstone Audio, Inc.**
Hachette Bk. Group
MyiLibrary.

†**Hackett Publishing Co., Inc.**, (978-0-87220; 978-0-915144; 978-0-915145; 978-0-941051; 978-1-58510; 978-1-60384; 978-1-62466) Orders Addr.: P.O. Box 44937, Indianapolis, IN 46244-0937 USA (SAN 201-6044) Tel 317-635-9250; Fax: 317-635-9292; Toll Free Fax: 800-783-9213; *Imprints:* Focus (FocusUSA)
E-mail: customer@hackettpublishing.com
Web site: http://www.hackettpublishing.com
Dist(s): **ebrary, Inc.**; *CIP.*

Hadassah's Crown LLC, (978-0-9981230) 750 September Chase, Wellford, SC 29385 USA Tel 864-708-1214
E-mail: soncunnlev@gmail.com.

Hadrosaur Pr., (978-1-885093) P.O. Box 2194, Mesilla Park, NM 88047-2194 USA Tel 505-527-4163; *Imprints:* LBF/Hadrosaur (LBF Hadrs)
E-mail: hadrosaur@zianet.com
Web site: http://www.hadrosaur.com.

Hafabanana Press *See* **KB Bks. & More**

Hagan, Theda *See* **Hagan, Theda Bks.**

Hagan, Theda Bks., (978-0-9678032; 978-0-9827155) 47 Corner Dr., Madisonville, KY 42431 USA Tel 270-821-6968
E-mail: thedahagan@yahoo.com
Web site: http://www.heavenlyharborbooks.com/default.htm.

Hager, Robert, (978-0-9727676) 101 Crawford, Suite 2C, Houston, TX 77002 USA
Web site: http://www.saurcana.com/pages/about_author.html.

Hahn, Beverly, (978-0-9722494) Orders Addr.: P.O. Box 66, Hilmak, CA 95324 USA; Edit Addr.: 9613 Ailanthus Ave., Delhi, CA 95315 USA (SAN 254-7376).

Hairball Pr., (978-0-9646781) 2318 2nd Ave., Suite 591, Seattle, WA 98121 USA Tel 206-932-8173.

Hairston Enterprises, LLC, (978-0-9762958) 582 Bristol Ln., Birmingham, AL 35226 USA Tel 205-369-4022
E-mail: kchairston@yahoo.com
Web site: http://www.forgottenrules.com; http://www.forgottenrules.org; http://www.theforgottenrules.com; http://www.theforgottenrules.org.

Hairston, Rodney, (978-0-9760689) 75 Fern Oak Cir. Apt. 201, Stafford, VA 22554-8459 USA
E-mail: rhairston@jbmanagement.com.

Haislip, Allen, (978-0-9767640) Orders Addr.: 32 Marquette Dr., Florissant, MO 63031-3839 USA.

Haiti World, (978-0-9793039) P.O. Box 5663, Vernon Hills, IL 60061 USA Tel 847-514-9967
E-mail: haitiworld@yahoo.com.

Halbur Publishing, (978-0-9603520) 142 Angela Dr., Santa Rosa, CA 95403-1702 USA (SAN 212-9469)
E-mail: dhalbur@sonic.net.

Halcyon Pr., (978-0-941970) 18-05 215 St., Flushing, NY 11360 USA (SAN 238-244X) Tel 212-631-9640 Do not confuse with companies with same or similar name in Hendersonville, NC, Dallas, TX, Houston, TX.

Halcyon Pr., Ltd., (978-0-9706054; 978-1-931823; 978-0-9830676) P.O. Box 260, Pearland, TX 77588-0260 USA (SAN 253-9934) Toll Free: 866-774-5786 Do not confuse with companies with same or similar name in Hendersonville, NC, Flushing, NY, Dallas, TX
E-mail: david.raley@gmail.com
Web site: http://www.halcyonpress.com
Dist(s): **Bk. Marketing Plus.**

Haldane Mason, Ltd. (GBR) (978-1-902463; 978-1-905339; 978-1-909720) *Dist. by* **Trans-Atl Phila.**

Hale Kuamo'o Hawaiian Language Ctr. at UHH, (978-0-9665331; 978-1-930339; 978-0-9741580) Div. of Ka Haka 'Ula o Ke'elikolani/College of Hawaiian Language at UH Hilo, 200 W. Kawili St., Hilo, HI 96720-4091 USA Tel 808-974-7339; Fax: 808-974-7686
E-mail: contact@ahapunanaleo.org
Web site: http://www.olelo.hawaii.edu; http://www.ahapunanaleo.org.

Hale Publishing, (978-0-9636219; 978-0-9729583; 978-0-9772268; 978-0-9815257; 978-0-9823379; 978-0-9845039; 978-0-9833075; 978-0-9847746; 978-0-9858893; 978-1-939847) 1712 N. Forest St., Amarillo, TX 79106 USA Tel 806-376-9900 Toll Free: 800-378-1317
E-mail: books@ibreastfeeding.com; alicia.ingram@halepublishing.com
Web site: http://www.ibreastfeeding.com.

Haley's, (978-0-9626308; 978-1-884540; 978-0-9897667; 978-0-9916102; 978-0-9967730; 978-0-9982735) Orders Addr.: 488 S. Main St., Athol, MA 01331 USA Tel 978-249-9400 (phone/fax); Toll Free: 800-215-8805 (phone/fax); Edit Addr.: 488 S. Main St., Athol, MA 01331 USA
E-mail: haley.antique@verizon.net
Web site: http://www.mattawasongcycle.com; http://www.haleysantiques.com
Dist(s): **Follett School Solutions.**

Half-Pint Kids, Inc., (978-1-59256) Orders Addr.: 646 Crabapple Ln., Ellwood City, PA 16117 USA Tel 724-809-8023
Web site: http://halfpintkids.com.

Hall & Humphries Publishing Hse., (978-0-9758521) Orders Addr.: P.O. Box 371021, Decatur, GA 30037-1021 USA; Edit Addr.: 2652 Rainbow Pkwy., Decatur, GA 30034 USA Tel 404-625-4486.

Hall, Annalisa, (978-0-615-22113-7) 14271 Anabelle Dr., Poway, CA 92064 USA
Dist(s): **Lulu Pr., Inc.**

Hall, Kenneth, (978-0-615-19649-7) 1857 Morris Ave., Lincoln Park, MI 48146-1328 USA
E-mail: kenhall321@yahoo.com
Dist(s): **Lulu Pr., Inc.**

Hall, Monique P. Productions, (978-0-9772634) 167 Wyatt Earp Loop, Nolanville, TX 76559 USA (SAN 851-6391) Tel 254-462-2990
E-mail: nickiepop777@gmail.com; moniquephallproductions@gmail.com
Web site: http://nickiepopart.com.

Hall, Nancy Inc., (978-1-884270) 7 W. 18th St., 6th Flr., New York, NY 10011 USA Tel 212-674-3408; Fax: 212-353-1521
E-mail: Nhallinc@aol.com.

Hall Press *See* **Hallcienda**

Hall, Stephen & Denise, (978-0-9753305) 1237 Prairie Dell Rd., Union, MO 63084-4310 USA
E-mail: wordsofahunter@cs.com.

HallaVision Publishing *Imprint of* **Ginger Nielson - Children's Bk. Illustration**

Hallcienda, (978-0-932218) Orders Addr.: P.O. Box 9066, San Bernardino, CA 92427 USA (SAN 211-7061) Tel 909-887-3466; P.O. Box 9066, San Bernardino, CA 92427 (SAN 665-7060) Tel 909-887-3466.

Hallelujah Acres Publishing, (978-0-929619) P.O. Box 2388, Shelby, NC 28151 USA (SAN 249-7891) Tel 704-481-1700; Fax: 704-481-0345
E-mail: chet@hacres.com
Web site: http://www.hacres.com
Dist(s): **Send The Light Distribution LLC.**

Haller Company, The, (978-0-9743961) Orders Addr.: P.O. Box 207, Burlingame, CA 94010 USA Tel 650-348-3900; Fax: 650-558-9012; Edit Addr.: 1325 Howard Ave., Burlingame, CA 94010 USA
Web site: http://www.hallercompany.com.

Hallmark Card, Inc., (978-0-87529; 978-1-59530; 978-1-63059) 2501 McGee, Kansas City, MO 64141-6580 USA (SAN 202-2672) Tel 816-274-5111
Dist(s): **Independent Pubs. Group**
Univ. of New Mexico Pr.

Hallmark Emporium, (978-0-9665055) 9201 Russell Ave., S., Bloomington, MN 55431 USA Tel 612-884-2601; Fax: 612-703-0218
E-mail: dead541@aol.com
Web site: http://members.aol.com/dead 541/index.html.

Halo Publishing International, (978-0-9718350; 978-0-9797429; 978-1-935268; 978-1-61244; 978-1-78280) 5549 Canal Rd., Cleveland, OH 44125 USA
Web site: http://www.halopublishing.com.

Hameray Publishing Group, Inc., (978-1-60559; 978-1-62817; 978-1-64039) 11545 Sorrento Valley Rd., Suite 310, San Diego, CA 92121 USA Tel 858-369-5200; Fax: 858-369-5201; Toll Free Fax: 858-369-5209; Toll Free: 866-918-6173
E-mail: christine@hameraypublishing.com
Web site: http://www.hameraypublishing.com.

Hamilton Bks., (978-0-7618) Div. of Rowman & Littlefield Publishing Group, Orders Addr.: 15200 NBN Way, Blue Ridge Summit, PA 17214 USA Tel 717-794-3800 (Sales, Customer Service, MIS, Royalties, Inventory Mgmt., Dist., Credit & Collections); Fax: 717-794-3803 (Customer Service &/or orders only); 717-794-3857 (Sales & MIS); 717-794-3856 Royalties, Inventory Mgmt. & Dist.); Toll Free Fax: 800-338-4550 (Customer Service &/ or orders); Toll Free: 800-462-6420 (Customer Service &/ or orders); Edit Addr.: 4501 Forbes Blvd., Suite 200, Lanham, MD 20706 USA Tel 301-459-3366; Fax: 301-459-5748 Short Discount, please contact rlpgsales@rowman.com
Web site: http://www.rlpgbooks.com
Dist(s): **Follett School Solutions**
MyiLibrary
National Bk. Network
Rowman & Littlefield Publishers, Inc.
ebrary, Inc.

Hamilton Ministries *See* **DCTS Publishing**

Hamline Univ. Pr., (978-0-9633686; 978-0-9723721; 978-1-934458) 1536 Hewitt Ave., MS-C1916, Saint Paul, MN 55104-2490 USA
E-mail: bhansonhegg01@hamline.edu
Web site: http://www.hamline.edu.

Hammad, Salma *See* **Lucent Interpretations, LLC**

Hammersmark Books *See* **Kluis Publishing, LLC**

Hammond, Incorporated *See* **Hammond World Atlas Corp.**

Hammond, Roger, (978-0-9763822) 4915 Avon Ln., Sarasota, FL 34238 USA
Web site: http://www.pelithepelican.com.

†**Hammond World Atlas Corp.**, (978-0-7230; 978-0-8437) Subs. of Langenscheidt Pubs., Inc., 193 Morris Ave., Springfield, NJ 07081-1211 USA (SAN 202-2702)
E-mail: rstrung@americanmap.com
Web site: http://www.Hammondmap.com
Dist(s): **Langenscheidt Publishing Group**; *CIP.*

Hampton Roads Publishing Co., Inc., (978-0-9624375; 978-1-57174; 978-1-878901) Orders Addr.: P.O. Box 8107, Charlottesvle, VA 22906-8107 USA (SAN 299-8874) Toll Free Fax: 800-766-9042; Toll Free: 800-766-8009
E-mail: hrpc@hrpub.com
Web site: http://www.hamptonroadspub.com
Dist(s): **Hay Hse., Inc.**
Red Wheel/Weiser.

Hampton-Brown Books *See* **National Geographic School Publishing, Inc.**

Hamster Huey Pr., (978-0-9749090) 7627 84th Ave., Ct., NW, Gig Harbor, WA 98335-6237 USA Tel 253-851-7839; Fax: 253-853-3493
E-mail: phs@oz.net
Web site: http://www.hamsterhueypress.com.

Hamster Pr., *(978-0-9645669; 978-0-9724630)* Orders Addr.: P.O. Box 27471, Seattle, WA 98125 USA Fax: 206-363-2878
E-mail: hamstrpres@aol.com
Web site: http://www.billschelly.com
Dist(s): **Diamond Comic Distributors, Inc. FM International Syco Distribution.**

†Hancock Hse. Pubs., *(978-0-88839; 978-0-919654; 978-1-55205)* 1431 Harrison Ave., Blaine, WA 98230-5005 USA (SAN 665-7079) Tel 604-538-1114; Fax: 604-538-2262; Toll Free Fax: 800-983-2262; Toll Free: 800-938-1114; 19313 Zero Ave., Surrey, BC V3S 9R9 (SAN 115-3730)
E-mail: sales@hancockhouse.com
Web site: http://www.hancockhouse.com; *CIP.*

Hand Print Pr., *(978-0-9679846; 978-0-615-74893-1; 978-0-9914762)* Orders Addr.: P.O. Box 576, Blodgett, OR 97326 USA Tel 541-438-4300; Edit Addr.: 395 Grant Creek Rd., Eddyville, OR 97343 USA
E-mail: kiko@handprintpress.com; potlatch@cmug.com
Web site: http://www.handprintpress.com
Dist(s): **Chelsea Green Publishing CreateSpace Independent Publishing Platform.**

Handersen Publishing, *(978-1-941429; 978-1-947854)* PO Box 21843, Lincoln, NE 68542 USA
E-mail: editors@handersenpublishing.com; stinkwavesmagazine@hotmail.com
Web site: http://handersenpublishing.com/; www.stinkwavesmagazine.com.

Handfinger Pr., *(978-0-9838294)* 833 Eastview Ave., Delray Beach, FL 33483 USA Tel 561-654-8680; Fax: 561-684-1508
E-mail: wendyg52@hotmail.com
Dist(s): **Independent Pubs. Group.**

H&H Publishing, *(978-0-9975411)* 2403 Craig Rd Se, Olympia, WA 98501 USA Tel 360-918-6976
E-mail: puzzlebabe2002@yahoo.com.

H&M Systems Software, Inc., *(978-1-885936)* 600 E. Crescent Ave., Suite 203, U Saddle Riv, NJ 07458-1846 USA Toll Free: 800-327-3713; *Imprints*: StudioLine Photo (StudioLine)
E-mail: Info@HM-Software.com
Web site: http://www.Gameware.com; http://www.HM-Software.com; http://www.StudioLine.biz
Dist(s): **Victory Multimedia.**

Handprint Bks. *Imprint of* **Chronicle Bks. LLC**

Handprint Bks., *(978-1-929766; 978-1-59354)* 413 Sixth Ave., Brooklyn, NY 11215-3310 USA
E-mail: publisher@handprintbooks.com
Web site: http://www.handprintbooks.com
Dist(s): **Chronicle Bks. LLC Hachette Bk. Group Learning Connection, The Penton Overseas, Inc. Random Hse., Inc.**

Hands to the Plow, Inc., *(978-1-930914)* P.O. Box 567, Webster, WI 54893 USA Tel 715-349-7185
E-mail: tomkelby@handstotheplow.org
Web site: http://www.handstotheplow.org.

Handstand Kids, *(978-0-9792107; 978-0-9847476)* 23346 Pk. Colombo, Calabasas, CA 91302 USA (SAN 852-7822) Tel 818-917-7200
E-mail: yvette@handstandkids.com
Web site: http://www.handstandkids.com.

H&W Publishing Inc., *(978-0-9800934)* P.O. Box 53515, Cincinnati, OH 45253 USA Tel 513-687-3968; Fax: 513-761-4221
E-mail: kwatkins1@fuse.net
Web site: http://www.handwpublishing.com.

Handwriting Without Tears, *(978-1-891627; 978-1-934825; 978-1-939814)* Div. of No Tears Learning Inc., 8001 MacArthur Blvd., Cabin John, MD 20818-1607 USA Tel 301-263-2700; Fax: 301-263-2707; Toll Free: 888-983-8409
Web site: http://www.hwtears.com; http://www.getsetforschool.com.

Hanford Mead Pubs., Inc., *(978-0-9643158; 978-1-59275)* P.O. Box 8051, Santa Cruz, CA 95061 USA (SAN 253-9195) Tel 831-459-6855; Fax: 831-426-4474
E-mail: info@hanfordmead.com
Web site: http://www.hanfordmead.com; http://www.soulcollage.com; http://www.ethicsofcaring.com
Dist(s): **New Leaf Distributing Co., Inc.**

†Hanging Loose Pr., *(978-0-914610; 978-1-882413; 978-1-931236; 978-1-934909)* 231 Wyckoff St., Brooklyn, NY 11217 USA (SAN 206-4960) Fax: 212-243-7499
E-mail: print225@aol.com
Web site: http://www.hangingloosepress.com
Dist(s): **Partners/West Book Distributors SPD-Small Pr. Distribution**; *CIP.*

Hanks, Scott, *(978-0-9794157; 978-0-9799518; 978-0-9815083)* 1781 E. 800th Rd., Lawrence, KS 66049 USA (SAN 853-4098) Tel 785-887-2203; Fax: 785-887-2204
E-mail: mt@heritagebaptistchurch.cc
Web site: http://www.heritagebaptistchurch.cc.

Hannacroix Creek Bks., Inc., *(978-1-889262; 978-1-938998)* 1127 High Ridge Rd., No. 110, Stamford, CT 06905-1203 USA (SAN 299-9560) Tel 203-968-8098; Fax: 203-968-0193
E-mail: Hannacroix@aol.com
Web site: http://www.hannacroixcreekbooks.com
Dist(s): **Brodart Co.** *Emery-Pratt Co.* **Follett School Solutions Midwest Library Service Quality Bks., Inc. TextStream Unique Bks., Inc.**

Hannel Educational Consulting, *(978-0-9764776)* 1131 W. Palm Ln., Phoenix, AZ 85007-1536 USA Tel 602-524-7647; Fax: 602-253-2693
Web site: http://www.hannel.com.

Hannibal Bks., *(978-0-929292; 978-1-934749; 978-1-61315)* Div. of KLMK Communications, Inc., Orders Addr.: 313 S. 11th St. Suite A, Garland, TX 75040 USA Tel 800-747-0738; Fax: 888-252-3022; Toll Free Fax: 888-252-3022; Toll Free: 800-747-0738; Edit Addr.: 313 S. 11th St., Garland, TX 75040 USA Fax: 888-252-3022
E-mail: hannibalbooks@earthlink.net; orders@hannibalbooks.com; louismoore@hannibalbooks.com
Web site: http://www.hannibalbooks.com
Dist(s): **Lightning Source, Inc. Spring Arbor Distributors, Inc.**

Hannover Hse. *Imprint of* **Truman Pr., Inc.**

Hansen, Charles Educational Music & Bks., Inc., *(978-0-8494)* 1820 West Ave., Miami Beach, FL 33139 USA (SAN 205-0609) Tel 305-532-5461; Fax: 305-672-8729
E-mail: khansen507@aol.com
Web site: http://www.hansenpublications.com/
Dist(s): **Hansen Hse.**

Hansen, Diane, *(978-0-9761988)* P.O. Box 1051, Redondo Beach, CA 90278 USA Tel 310-379-8006
Web site: http://thosearemyprivateparts.com.

Hansen House Publishing, Inc., *(978-0-9819709)* 711 W. 17th St., Suite D-2, Costa Mesa, CA 92627 USA Do not confuse with Mark Victor Hansen & Associates in Newport Beach, CA
Dist(s): **Hay Hse., Inc.**

Hansen, Marc Stuff!, *(978-0-9794643)* P.O. Box 621, Greenville, MI 48838 USA
E-mail: marchansenstuff@gmail.com
Web site: http://www.marchansenstuff.com.

Hanson, Tracie, *(978-0-9799185)* Orders Addr.: 94 Pletcher Dr., Yorkville, IL 60560 USA Tel 815-440-5681
E-mail: tracie777@sbcglobal.net
Web site: http://www.newworldbaby.net.

Happy About, *(978-0-9633302; 978-1-60005; 978-1-60773)* 21265 Stevens Creek Blvd., Suite 205, Cupertino, CA 95014 USA Tel 408-257-3000
E-mail: info@happyabout.info
Web site: http://www.happyabout.info
Dist(s): **Ebsco Publishing MyiLibrary OverDrive, Inc.**

Happy Apple Bks., *(978-0-9890903)* 852 Riven Oak Dr., Murrells Inlet, SC 29576 USA Tel 843-458-8740
E-mail: wickedisbetter@yahoo.com; mattellerin@yahoo.com
Web site: http://www.happyapplebooks.com.

Happy Bks. Pr., *(978-0-9787826)* 29877 Westhaven Dr., Agoura, CA 91301 USA Tel 818-879-1268
E-mail: ghuyette@charter.net; happybookspress@vrillustration.com
Web site: http://www.vrillustration.com.

Happy Cat Bks. (GBR) *(978-1-899248; 978-1-903285; 978-1-905117)* *Dist. by* **Star Brght Bks.**

Happy Day *Imprint of* **Tyndale Hse. Pubs.**

Happy Dolphin Pr., *(978-0-9986381; 978-1-947678)* 16685 Lake Circle Dr., No. 1020, Fort Myers, FL 33908 USA Tel 239-910-1355
E-mail: editor@happydolphinpress.com
Web site: www.HappyDolphinPress.com.

Happy Hamster Press, The *See* **Imagination Workshop, The**

Happy Heart Kids Publishing, *(978-0-9763143)* Orders Addr.: 2912 Beane Rd., Lenoir, NC 28645-8653 USA (SAN 256-3029) Tel 828-302-9500; 828-754-4126 (phone/fax); Fax: 828-758-8409
E-mail: mshelen@charter.net
Web site: http://www.happyheartkids.com.

Happy Hearts Family, The, *(978-0-615-34485-0; 978-0-9899470)* 2044 Loggia, Newport Beach, CA 92660 USA Tel 949-701-8296
E-mail: marlanal@cox.net
Web site: http://thehappyheartsfamily.com.

Happy Horse Publishing, Ltd., *(978-0-9727849)* Orders Addr.: P.O. Box 15767, Chevy Chase, MD 20825 USA Tel 301-589-8888; Edit Addr.: 5910 Connecticut Ave., Chevy Chase, MD 70875 USA
E-mail: eashe@happyhorse.us
Web site: http://www.happyhorsekids.com.

HAPPY HOUSE PR., *(978-0-615-87080-9; 978-0-615-88154-6)* 1301 Birdsall St., Old Hickory, TN 37138 USA Tel 6155547064 Do not confuse with Happy House Press in Tillamook, OR
Web site: www.happyhousepress.com
Dist(s): **CreateSpace Independent Publishing Platform.**

Happy Kappy Karacters, *(978-0-615-45522-8; 978-0-615-65651-9)* 20 Secora Rd., Suite 312, Monsey, NY 10952 USA
E-mail: georgegisser@aol.com; marshall@nydesign.com
Web site: www.nydesign.com; www.kappythekangaroo.com.

Happy Viking Crafts, *(978-0-9740175)* Orders Addr.: P.O. Box 35, Mahomet, IL 61853 USA; Edit Addr.: 1001 Sunrise Cir., Mahomet, IL 61853-3536 USA Tel 217-586-2497.

Happy Women Publishing Co., *(978-0-9745627)* 11487 57th St E., Parrish, FL 34219-5818 USA
E-mail: hwp@toerrific.com
Web site: http://toerrific.com
Dist(s): **Continental Enterprises Group, Inc. (CEG).**

Happyland Media, *(978-0-9726418)* Orders Addr.: P.O. Box 20398, Castro Valley, CA 94546 USA; Edit Addr.: 20283 Santa Marie Ave., Castro Valley, CA 94546 USA
E-mail: info@happylandmedia.com
Web site: http://www.happylandmedia.com.

Harambee Pr., *(978-0-9769846)* P.O. Box 353, Macatawa, MI 49434 USA
Web site: http://www.harambeepress.com.

Harbinger Pr., *(978-0-9674736; 978-0-9723998)* 2711 Buford Rd. PMB 383, Richmond, VA 23235-2423 USA (SAN 299-9994) Do not confuse with companies with the same or similar names in Woodland Hills, CA, Corte Madera, CA
E-mail: keith@harbpress.com
Web site: http://www.harbpress.com.

Harbor Hse., *(978-1-891799)* 629 Stevens Xing., Augusta, GA 30907-9566 USA; *Imprints*: Bat Wing Press (Bat Wing Pr)
E-mail: peggycheney@harborhousebooks.com; harborhouse@harborhousebooks.com
Web site: http://www.harborhousebooks.com.

Harbor Hse. Pubs., Inc., *(978-0-937360)* 221 Water St., Boyne City, MI 49712 USA (SAN 200-5751) Tel 616-582-2814; Fax: 616-582-3392; Toll Free: 800-491-1760
E-mail: harbor@harborhouse.com
Web site: http://www.harborhouse.com.

Harbor Island Bks., *(978-0-9741787)* 1214 W. Boston Post Rd., No. 245, Mamaroneck, NY 10543 USA (SAN 255-9137) Tel 914-420-9782; Fax: 914-835-7897
E-mail: publisher@lyingawake.net; hfurbush@earthlink.net
Web site: http://www.lyingawake.net/
Dist(s): **Partners/West Book Distributors.**

Harbor Mountain Pr., *(978-0-9786009; 978-0-9815560; 978-0-9882755)* P.O. Box 519, Brownsville, VT 05037 USA
Web site: http://www.harbormountainpress.org; www.spdbooks.org; petermoney.com
Dist(s): **GenPop Bks. SPD-Small Pr. Distribution.**

Harbor Pr., Inc., *(978-0-936197)* Orders Addr.: P.O. Box 1656, Gig Harbor, WA 98335 USA (SAN 696-8953) Tel 253-851-5190; Fax: 253-851-5191; Edit Addr.: P.O. Box 1656, Gig Harbor, WA 98335-3656 USA (SAN 696-8961) Do not confuse with companies with the same name in Friday Harbor, WA, Austin, TX, Ardmore, PA
E-mail: young2327@mindspring.com
Web site: http://www.harborpress.com
Dist(s): **National Bk. Network.**

Harborseal Publishing Co., *(978-0-9652963; 978-0-9787308)* Orders Addr.: P.O. Box 126, Seal Cove, ME 04674-0126 USA Tel 207-244-7753; Edit Addr.: Rte. 102, Captain's Quarters Rd., Seal Cove, ME 04674 USA
Dist(s): **Magazines, Inc.**

HarborTown Histories, *(978-0-9710984)* 6 Harbor Way, Santa Barbara, CA 93109 USA
E-mail: baker@sbcc.net.

Harbour Arts, LLC, *(978-0-9778196)* 1790 Philippe Pkwy., Safety Harbor, FL 34695 USA
Web site: http://www.harbourarts.com.

Harbour Publishing Co., Ltd. (CAN) *(978-0-920080; 978-1-55017)* *Dist. by* **Midpt Trade.**

Harbourside Pr., *(978-0-9740552)* 7892 Sailboat Key Blvd., Suite 506, South Pasadena, FL 33707 USA Tel 727-543-5855
E-mail: harbours@harboursidepress.com
Web site: http://www.harboursidepress.com
Dist(s): **Greenleaf Book Group.**

Harcourt Achieve *See* **Houghton Mifflin Harcourt Supplemental Pubs.**

Harcourt Brace & Company *See* **Harcourt Trade Pubs.**

Harcourt Brace School Publishers *See* **Harcourt Schl. Pubs.**

Harcourt Children's Bks *Imprint of* **Harcourt Children's Bks.**

Harcourt Children's Bks., *(978-0-15)* Div. of Houghton Mifflin Harcourt Trade & Reference Pubs., Orders Addr.: 6277 Sea Harbor Dr., Orlando, FL 32887 USA Toll Free Fax: 800-235-0256; Toll Free: 800-543-1918; 465 S. Lincoln Dr., Troy, MO 63379 Toll Free Fax: 800-235-0266; Toll Free: 800-543-1918; Edit Addr.: 15 E. 26th St., 15th Flr., New York, NY 10010 USA Tel 212-592-1000; Fax: 212-592-1011; 525 B St., Suite 1900, San Diego, CA 92101 Tel 619-231-6616; *Imprints*: Gulliver Books (Gulliver Bks); Red Wagon Books (Red Wagon Bks); Harcourt Children's Books (HCB)
E-mail: Andrew.porter@harcourt.com
Web site: http://www.HarcourtBooks.com
Dist(s): **Houghton Mifflin Harcourt Publishing Co. Harcourt Trade Pubs.**

Harcourt Schl. Pubs., *(978-0-15)* Div. of Houghton Mifflin Harcouty School Publishers, 9205 Southpark Ctr. Loop, Orlando, FL 32819 USA (SAN 299-4585) Tel 407-345-2000; Fax: 407-352-3445; Toll Free Fax: 800-874-6418 (orders); Toll Free: 800-225-5425 (orders)
E-mail: hbspcs@harcourt.com
Web site: http://www.harcourtschool.com/
Dist(s): **Houghton Mifflin Harcourt Trade & Reference Pubs. Lectorum Pubns., Inc.**

†Harcourt Trade Pubs., *(978-0-15)* Div. of Houghton Mifflin Harcourt Trade & Reference Pubs., Orders Addr.: 6277 Sea Harbor Dr., Orlando, FL 32887 USA (SAN 200-285X) Tel 619-699-6707; Toll Free Fax: 800-235-0256; Toll Free: 800-543-1918 (trade orders, inquiries, claims); Edit Addr.: 15 E. 26th St., New York, NY 10010 USA Tel 212-592-1000; Fax: 212-592-1011; 525 B St., Suite 1900, San Diego, CA 92101-4495 (SAN 200-2736) Tel 619-231-6616; *Imprints*: Silver Whistle (Silver Whistle)
E-mail: andrewporter@harcourt.com
Web site: http://www.HarcourtBooks.com
Dist(s): **MyiLibrary**; *CIP.*

hard girl bk. club, *(978-0-9748712)* 4143 S. Adelle, Mesa, AZ 85212 USA Tel 480-241-1351; Fax: 480-354-4727; Toll Free: 800-307-5261
E-mail: tkempton@cox.net
Web site: http://hardgirlbookclub.com.

Hard Made Books *See* **HM Bks.**

Hard Shell Word Factory, *(978-1-58200; 978-0-7599)* Orders Addr.: 6470a Glenway Ave. #109, Cincinnati, OH 45211 USA (SAN 631-4899) Toll Free Fax: 888-460-4752; Toll Free: 888-232-0808; Edit Addr.: 6470a Glenway Ave. #109, Cincinnati, OH 45211 USA Toll Free: 888-232-0808
E-mail: books@hardshell.com; books@mundania.com
Web site: http://www.hardshell.com
Dist(s): **CreateSpace Independent Publishing Platform News Group, The.**

Harder, Polly *See* **R. H. Publishing**

Hardie Grant Bks. (AUS) *(978-1-86498; 978-1-876719; 978-1-74066; 978-1-74270; 978-1-74273; 978-0-9807835; 978-0-646-49937-6; 978-1-74358; 978-1-74379)* *Dist. by* **IPG Chicago.**

Hardie Grant Egmont Pty, Ltd. (AUS) *(978-1-920878; 978-1-921098; 978-1-921288; 978-1-921417; 978-1-921502; 978-1-921564; 978-1-921690; 978-1-921759; 978-1-921848; 978-1-74297; 978-1-76012; 978-1-76050)* *Dist. by* **IPG Chicago.**

Hardin Publishing, LLC, *(978-0-9742704)* 1380 W. Paces Ferry Rd., Suite 180, Atlanta, GA 30327 USA Tel 404-504-6619; Fax: 404-264-3583 Do not confuse with Hardin Publishing Company in Avera, GA
E-mail: proper@piedmont-atl.com; yntema@hardinpublishing.net
Web site: http://www.hardinpublishing.net.

Harding Hse. Publishing Sebice Inc., *(978-1-933630; 978-1-937211; 978-1-62524)* 220 Front St., Vestal, NY 13850-1514 USA; *Imprints*: Anamchara Books (Anamchara Bks); Village Earth Press (Village Earth); Candlewood Press (Candlewood Pr.)
E-mail: info@anamcharabooks.com
Web site: http://www.hardinghousepages.com; http://www.villageearthpress.com; http://www.anamcharabooks.com
Dist(s): **Follett School Solutions Smashwords.**

Hardnett Publishing, *(978-0-9789310; 978-0-692-21182-3)* 2114 Keithshire Ct., Conyers, GA 30013 USA
E-mail: info@hardnettpublishing.com
Web site: http://www.hardnettpublishing.com.

Hardtke Publishing Co., *(978-0-9718166)* 2217 Second Ave. E., No. 1, Hibbing, MN 55746-1966 USA (SAN 254-4601) Tel 218-262-6510
Web site: http://www.libertyandlove.com/.

Hardway Pr., *(978-0-9717148; 978-0-9840221; 978-0-9974422; 978-0-692-94359-5)* 16 W. Pacific Ave. No.3, Hendersen, NV 89015-7383 USA Tel 702-564-1665; Fax: 702-564-4190
Web site: http://www.brianrouff.com.

Hardy, John M. Publishing Co., *(978-0-87244; 978-0-9717667; 978-0-9798391; 978-0-9903714; 978-1-946182)* Orders Addr.: 11152 Westheimer Rd., #667, Houston, TX 77042 USA Tel 281-438-7500; Fax: 281-438-7501
E-mail: publisher@johnhardypublishing.com; sales@johnhardypublishing.com
Web site: http://www.johnmhardy.com; www.texasbookpublishers.org; www.texianpress.com; www.ironmtnpress.com; http://www.johnhardypublishing.com; http://www.calientexpress.com.

Hargrave Pr., *(978-0-9744885; 978-0-9817195)* P.O. Box 524, Nantucket, MA 02554 USA (SAN 856-3519)
E-mail: sales@hargravepress.com
Web site: http://www.hargravepress.com
Dist(s): **BookMasters.**

Hargroves, Ann *See* **Hargroves Publishing Co.**

Hargroves Publishing Co., *(978-0-9742277)* P.O. Box 985, Virginia Beach, VA 23451-0985 USA
Web site: http://www.annhhargroves.com.

Harlan Publishing Company *See* **Diakonia Publishing**

Harlan Rose Publishing, *(978-0-9853466)* 920 Fall Creek, Grapevine, TX 76051 USA Tel 469-951-8499
E-mail: Flyingunicom99@yahoo.com.

Harlequin Enterprises, Ltd. (CAN) *(978-0-373; 978-1-55166; 978-1-58314; 978-1-55254; 978-0-7783; 978-1-55373; 978-1-4268; 978-1-4592; 978-1-4603; 978-84-687-2370-9; 978-0-919622; 978-1-335; 978-1-4880; 978-1-4882)* *Dist. by* **HarperCollins Pubs.**

Harlin Jacque Pubns., *(978-0-940938)* Orders Addr.: P.O. Box 336, Garden City, NY 11530 USA (SAN 281-7667) Tel 516-489-0120; Fax: 516-292-9120; Edit Addr.: 89 Surrey Ln., Hempstead, NY 11550-3521 USA (SAN 281-7659) Tel 516-489-8564; *Imprints*: Pen & Rose Press (Pen&Rose Pr)
E-mail: harlinjacquepub@aol.com
Web site: http://www.lindamichellebaron.com.

Harmon Creek Pr., *(978-0-9820852)* 1763 Diamond Head Dr., Tiki Island, TX 77554 USA
E-mail: lnicholson@bookpublishing.com.

Harmony Healing Hse., *(978-0-9787179; 978-0-9854037)* 530 Miramonte Ave., Lakeport, CA 95453 USA (SAN 851-3570).

Harmony Hse. Publishing Co., *(978-0-9725289)* P.O. Box 868, Rexburg, ID 83440 USA Tel 208-359-1595 (phone/fax)
E-mail: jaydef@cableone.net
Web site: http://www.debtfreestepbystep.com.

Harmony Ink Pr. *Imprint of* **Dreamspinner Pr.**

Harmony Pubns., LLC, *(978-0-9787586)* 100 W. Sta. Sq. Dr. Suite 230, Pittsburgh, PA 15219 USA (SAN 851-5468) Tel 412-670-3901; Fax: 724-934-4275
E-mail: harmonypublications@hotmail.com
Web site: http://www.colormyworld.info/.

Harmony Spirit Publishing Co., Inc., *(978-0-9762392)* 148 Westgate Dr., Saint Peters, MO 63376 USA
E-mail: lynowak@mail.win.org.

Harold, Elsie L., *(978-0-9764644)* 1701 Eleni Ct., Virginia Bch, VA 23453-2886 USA
E-mail: turtlesie@aol.com.

Harper Entertainment *Imprint of* **HarperCollins Pubs.**

Harper, Joel D., *(978-0-9714254)* 310 n. indian hill blvd No. 442, Claremont, CA 91711 USA Tel 909-447-5320
E-mail: info@freedomthree.com
Web site: http://www.freedomthree.com; www.joelharper.net; www.allthewaytotheocean.com.

Harper Kids Hse., *(978-0-9747218)* 10061 Riverside Dr., Suite 438, Toluca Lake, CA 91602 USA Tel 818-955-5301; *Imprints:* Young Women Programming (YWProgram)
E-mail: hannah@hannahsway.com
Web site: http://www.hannasway.com
Dist(s): **HarperCollins Pubs.**

Harper Paperbacks *Imprint of* **HarperCollins Pubs.**

Harper Perennial *Imprint of* **HarperCollins Pubs.**

Harper Trophy *Imprint of* **HarperCollins Pubs.**

Harper, Vicky *See* **Little Bookstore Who Could, The**

Harper Voyager *Imprint of* **HarperCollins Pubs.**

Harper-Arrington Publishing, *(978-0-9764161)* 18701 Grand River Ave., 105, Detroit, MI 48223 USA Tel 313-283-4494; Fax: 248-281-0373; Toll Free: 888-435-9234
E-mail: info@harperarringtonmedia.com
Web site: http://www.hapub.com/.

HarperChildren's Audio *Imprint of* **HarperCollins Pubs.**

HarperCollins *Imprint of* **HarperCollins Pubs.**

HarperCollins *Imprint of* **HarperCollins Pubs.**

HarperCollins Canada, Ltd. (CAN) *(978-0-00; 978-0-06; 978-0-690; 978-1-84887; 978-1-4434) Dist. by* **HarperCollins Pubs.**

†**HarperCollins Pubs.**, *(978-0-00; 978-0-06; 978-0-380; 978-0-688; 978-0-690; 978-0-694; 978-0-87795; 978-1-55710)* Div. of News Corp., Orders Addr.: 1000 Keystone Industrial Pk., Scranton, PA 18512-4621 USA (SAN 215-3742) Tel 570-941-1500; Toll Free Fax: 800-822-4090; Toll Free: 800-242-7737 (orders only); Edit Addr.: 10 E. 53rd St., New York, NY 10022-5299 USA (SAN 200-2086) Tel 212-207-7000; *Imprints:* Julie Andrews Collection (Julie Andrews); Harper Trophy (HarperTrophy); HarperFestival (HarperFestival); Cotler, Joanna Books (JoCotler); Geringer, Laura Book (LauraGeringer); Greenwillow Books (GreenwillowBks); HarperCollins (HarperCollCh); HarperChildren's Audio (HarperChildAud); Tegen, Katherine Books (KTegenBooks); Morrow, William & Company (WmMorrow); Avon Books (AvonBooks); Eos (Eos Harper); Harper Entertainment (HarperEntert); HarperCollins (HarperCollinsT); Harper Perennial (HarperPerenl); Harper Paperbacks (HarperPaper); Amistad (AmistadHarper); Rayo (Rayo Harper); Ecco (Ecco Harper); ReganBooks (ReganBooks); Collins (Collins); Morrow, Willam Cookbooks (MorrowCookbks); Collins Design (CollinsDesign); HarperTeen (HarperTeen); HarperLuxe (HarperLuxe); HarperOne (HarperOne); William Morrow Paperbacks (WILLIAM MORROW); Balzer & Bray (Balzer & Bray); Walden Pond Press (Walden Pond); Avon Impulse (AVON IMPULSE); Newmarket for It Books (NewmarkforItBks); Witness Impulse (WitnessImp); Harper Voyager (HarperVoyager); Dey Street Books (DeyStBks); Delphinium (Delphinium HC)
Web site: http://www.harpercollins.com; http://www.harpercollinschildrens.com
Dist(s): **Casemate Academic**
Ebsco Publishing
Findaway World, LLC
Follett School Solutions
F&W Media, Inc.
Lectorum Pubns., Inc.
MyiLibrary
Zondervan; *CIP.*

HarperCollins Pubs. Australia (AUS) *(978-0-207; 978-0-7322; 978-0-85835; 978-1-86256; 978-1-86371; 978-1-86378; 978-1-876288; 978-0-7304; 978-1-74050; 978-1-921504; 978-1-4607; 978-1-74309; 978-0-7316-3320-3; 978-0-646-10869-8; 978-0-646-39434-3; 978-1-922033) Dist. by* **HarperCollins Pubs.**

HarperCollins Pubs. Ltd. (GBR) *(978-0-00; 978-0-01; 978-0-06; 978-0-246; 978-0-261; 978-0-586; 978-0-85152; 978-0-411; 978-1-55468) Dist. by* **Trafalgar.**

HarperCollins Pubs. Ltd. (GBR) *(978-0-00; 978-0-01; 978-0-06; 978-0-246; 978-0-261; 978-0-586; 978-0-85152; 978-0-411; 978-1-55468) Dist. by* **HarperCollins Pubs.**

HarperCollins Pubs. Ltd. (GBR) *(978-0-00; 978-0-01; 978-0-06; 978-0-246; 978-0-261; 978-0-586; 978-0-85152; 978-0-411; 978-1-55468) Dist. by* **IPG Chicago.**

HarperFestival *Imprint of* **HarperCollins Pubs.**

HarperLuxe *Imprint of* **HarperCollins Pubs.**

HarperOne *Imprint of* **HarperCollins Pubs.**

HarperTeen *Imprint of* **HarperCollins Pubs.**

Harpeth Ridge Pr., *(978-0-9974449)* 304 Harpeth Ridge Dr., Nashville, TN 37221 USA Tel 615-352-1672
E-mail: judithwolfmandell@gmail.com.

Harptoons Publishing, *(978-0-615-35469-9; 978-0-615-41337-2; 978-0-615-45321-7; 978-0-615-59572-6; 978-0-615-68599-1; 978-0-9960197)* P.O. Box 428847, Blue Ash, OH 45242 USA (SAN 859-6921) Tel 330-259-7088
E-mail: steve@studioharpster.com
Web site: www.harptoons.com.

Harrassowitz (DEU) *(978-3-447) Dist. by* **ISD USA.**

Harren Communications, LLC, *(978-0-9667359; 978-0-9831032)* Southern Belle Books, P.O. Box 242, Midway, FL 32343 USA Tel 850-294-8923; Fax: 850-539-9731; *Imprints:* BeanPole Books (BeanPole Bks)
E-mail: publisher@beanpolebooks.com
Web site: http://www.beanpolebooks.net
Dist(s): **Two Rivers Distribution.**

Harren Press/Harren Professional Press *See* **Harren Communications, LLC**

Harrington Artwerkes Booksellers, *(978-0-9778042)* P.O. Box 10648, Burke, VA 22009-0648 USA
E-mail: sjph@cox.net
Web site: http://www.amazingartbros.com.

Harrington Park Pr. *Imprint of* **Haworth Pr., Inc., The**

Harriot Publishing, *(978-0-578-17487-7; 978-0-578-19268-0; 978-0-578-19269-7)* 1504 Filmore Rd, Fort Washington, MD 20744 USA.

Harris, Candice *See* **Harris, K Publishing, Inc.**

Harris Communications, Inc., *(978-0-9727520)* 15155 Technology Dr., Eden Prairie, MN 55344-2277 USA (SAN 255-0512) Tel 952-906-1180; Fax: 952-906-1099; Toll Free: 800-825-6758
E-mail: mail@harriscomm.com
Web site: http://www.harriscomm.com.

Harris, H. E. & Company *See* **Whitman Publishing LLC**

Harris, Jennifer, *(978-0-9989251)* 1821 Barker Rd., Thompsons Station, TN 37179 USA Tel 615-299-6268
E-mail: jeffandjenniferharris@gmail.com.

Harris, K Publishing, Inc., *(978-0-9770331)* P.O. Box 3091, Brandon, FL 33509-3091 USA
Web site: http://www.khpinc.com.

Harris, Monica *See* **Keep Empowering Yourself Successfully**

Harris, Pleshette Communications Inc. Publishing, *(978-0-9754380)* P.O. Box 491282, Lawrenceville, GA 30049 USA Tel 678-910-6128; Fax: 770-237-9358
E-mail: contact@phc1.org
Web site: http://phc1.org.

Harris, Polly, *(978-0-9749375)* 6041 E Akron St., Mesa, AZ 85205 USA Tel 480-654-1213
E-mail: pollyharris@sbcglobal.net.

Harris, Samuel, *(978-0-9759253)* 21660 Boschome Dr., Kildeer, IL 60047-8616 USA
E-mail: sf864@aol.com; eharris864@aol.com
Dist(s): **Partners Bk. Distributing, Inc.**

Harrison, Bobby, *(978-0-9771752)* 444 Shooting Star Tr., Gurley, AL 35748 USA Tel 256-776-2003; Fax: 256-776-2003
E-mail: bnharri@aol.com; ivorybillwp@aol.com
Web site: http://www.bobbyharrison.com
Dist(s): **Impact Photographics.**

Harrison House, Incorporated *See* **Harrison House Pubs.**

†**Harrison House Pubs.**, *(978-0-89274; 978-1-57794; 978-1-60683; 978-1-68031)* Orders Addr.: P.O. Box 35035, Tulsa, OK 74153 USA (SAN 208-676X) Tel 918-523-5700; Toll Free Fax: 800-830-5688; Toll Free: 800-888-4126; Edit Addr.: 7498 E. 46th Pl., Tulsa, OK 74145 USA Tel 918-523-5700; Toll Free Fax: 800-830-5688; Toll Free: 800-888-4126
E-mail: lisad@harrisonhouse.com; juliew@harrisonhouse.com
Web site: http://www.harrisonhouse.com
Dist(s): **Anchor Distributors**
Appalachian Bible Co.
Distributors, The
Spring Arbor Distributors, Inc.; *CIP.*

Harry & Stephanie Bks., *(978-0-9760875)* P.O. Box 172, Bronxville, NY 10708 USA Tel 914-961-6601
E-mail: harryandstephanie@yahoo.com
Web site: http://www.harryandstephanie.com.

Harseal Publications *See* **Harborseal Publishing Co.**

Hart, Chris Bks. *Imprint of* **Sixth&Spring Bks.**

hart Hse. publishing's, *(978-0-692-68612-6; 978-0-692-88008-1; 978-0-692-92066-4)* 406 E. walton, warrenton, MO 63383 USA Tel 636-359-3073
E-mail: cshart45@gmail.com
Web site: harthousepublishings.com
Dist(s): **CreateSpace Independent Publishing Platform.**

Hart Street Pubs., *(978-0-9793637)* 12157 Antibes St., Jacksonville, FL 32224 USA.

Hart-Burn Pr., *(978-0-9740318)* P.O. Box 99, Newton Junction, NH 03859-0099 USA
E-mail: stevehart7@yahoo.com
Web site: http://www.facebook.com/stevehart7
Dist(s): **Smashwords.**

Hartland Pubns., *(978-0-923309; 978-1-60564)* Div. of Hartland Institute of Health & Education, P.O. Box 1, Rapidan, VA 22733 USA (SAN 252-0834) Tel 540-672-3566; Fax: 540-672-3568; Toll Free: 800-774-3566
E-mail: jcarmouche@hartland.edu
Web site: http://www.hartlandpublications.com; http://www.hartlandbooks.com.

Hartlyn Kids Media, LLC, *(978-0-615-48984-1; 978-0-615-50182-6; 978-0-615-50503-9; 978-0-615-54948-4)* 45 Cowles St., Hartford, CT 06114 USA Tel 866-962-9993
E-mail: info@hartlynkids.com
Web site: http://www.hartlynkids.com.

Hartsuyker, Alice, *(978-0-9770441)* 1258 Fordham Dr. Apt. 204, Glendale Hts, IL 60139-4869 USA
E-mail: info@insidedharma.org; info@alicememoir.com
Web site: http://www.insidedharma.org; http://www.alicememoir.com.

Hart-Whitlow Pubs., *(978-0-9637951)* 1845 Brandywine Dr., Lenoir City, TN 37772 USA Tel 865-986-8553
E-mail: dickins@utk.edu.

Harvard Business Review Pr., *(978-0-87584; 978-1-57851; 978-1-59139; 978-1-4221; 978-1-62527; 978-1-63369)* 60 Harvard Way, Boston, MA 02163 USA (SAN 202-277X) Tel 617-783-7400; 617 495 6181; Fax: 617-783-7492; Toll Free: 888-500-1016 6-19-01 faxed 2nd prefix app, charge, KC
E-mail: corpcustserv@hbsp.harvard.edu
Web site: http://www.hbsp.harvard.edu; http://www.harvardbusinessonline.com
Dist(s): **Ingram Publisher Services**
McGraw-Hill Professional Publishing
MyiLibrary.

Harvard Business School Press *See* **Harvard Business Review Pr.**

†**Harvard Common Pr.**, *(978-0-87645; 978-0-916782)* 535 Albany St., Boston, MA 02118 USA (SAN 208-6778) Tel 617-423-5803; Fax: 617-695-9794; Toll Free: 888-657-3755
E-mail: orders@harvardcommonpress.com
Web site: http://www.harvardcommonpress.com
Dist(s): **Houghton Mifflin Harcourt Publishing Co.**
Houghton Mifflin Harcourt Trade & Reference Pubs.
Hachette Bk. Group
Independent Pubs. Group
MyiLibrary
ebrary, Inc.; *CIP.*

Harvard Education Publishing Group (HEPG), *(978-0-916690; 978-1-891792; 978-1-934742; 978-1-61250; 978-1-68253)* Orders Addr.: c/o Pssc, Harvard Education Press 46 Development Rd., Fitchburg, MA 01420 USA Fax: 978-348-1233 (book order); Toll Free: 888-437-1437 Book Order Line; Edit Addr.: 8 Story St., First Flr., Cambridge, MA 02138 USA (SAN 913-9753) Tel 617-495-3432 editorial office phone; Fax: 617-496-3584 (orders); *Imprints:* Harvard Educational Review Reprint Series (Harv Ed Review)
E-mail: laura_clos@harvard.edu; sumita_mukherji@gse.harvard.edu; christina_deyoung@gse.harvard.edu
Web site: hepg.org.

Harvard Educational Review Reprint Series *Imprint of* **Harvard Education Publishing Group (HEPG)**

Harvard Perspectives in American Sports *Imprint of* **Harvard Perspectives Pr.**

Harvard Perspectives Pr., *(978-0-9715778)* P.O. Box 400827, Cambridge, MA 02140-0009 USA; *Imprints:* Harvard Perspectives in American Sports (Harvard Pers Amer Sp)
E-mail: harvardperspecpr@aol.com; indieKindle@gmail.com
Web site: http://indieKindle.blogspot.com.

†**Harvard Univ. Pr.**, *(978-0-674; 978-0-916724; 978-0-935617)* Orders Addr.: c/o Triliteral LLC, 100 Maple Ridge Dr., Cumberland, RI 02864 USA Tel 401-531-2800; Fax: 401-531-2801; Toll Free Fax: 800-406-9145; Toll Free: 800-405-1619; 800-448-2242; Edit Addr.: 79 Garden St., Cambridge, MA 02138 USA (SAN 200-2043) Tel 617-495-2600; Fax: 617-495-5898; *Imprints:* Belknap Press (Belknap)
E-mail: contact_hup@harvard.edu
Web site: http://www.hup.harvard.edu
Dist(s): **Casemate Academic**
De Gruyter, Inc.
Ebsco Publishing
Wiley, John & Sons, Inc.
ebrary, Inc.; *CIP.*

Harvest Hse. Pubs., *(978-0-7369; 978-0-89081; 978-1-56507)* 990 Owen Loop, N., Eugene, OR 97402-9173 USA (SAN 207-4745) Tel 541-302-0729; Fax: 541-302-0731; Toll Free: 888-501-6991
E-mail: pat.mathis@harvesthousepublishers.com; onix@harvesthousepublishers.com
Web site: http://www.harvesthousepublishers.com
Dist(s): **Faith Alive Christian Resources**
INscribe Digital
Lulu Pr., Inc.
MyiLibrary
Twentieth Century Christian Bks.

Harvest Pubns., *(978-0-9654272)* 1928 Oxbow Rd., Minneapolis, KS 67467 USA Tel 913-392-2750 Do not confuse with companies with same name in Berkeley, CA, Arlington Heights, IL, Fort Worth, TX, Jacksonville, TX
E-mail: Adharvest@juno.com
Web site: http://www.pma-online.org/list/7345.html.

Harvest Sun Pr., LLC, *(978-0-9743668)* Orders Addr.: P.O. Box 826, Fairacres, NM 88033 USA Tel 479-283-4000; Fax: 505-526-6930; Edit Addr.: 4109 Broken Arrow Cv., Springdale, AR 72764-7503 USA
E-mail: info@harvestsunpress.com
Web site: http://www.harvestsunpress.com.

Harvey, Alan, *(978-0-9766354)* P.O. Box 235, Chapel Hill, NC 27514 USA; *Imprints:* Big H Books (Big H Bks)
Web site: http://www.lomeharvey.com.

Harwell, William, *(978-0-9728274)* HC 63 Box 1, Hanna, UT 84031 USA.

Haskell & Judy Rosenthal, *(978-0-9966802)* 2215 Briar Branch Dr., Houston, TX 77042 USA Tel 713-785-4278
E-mail: brosenthal@fb.com.

Haskell, Rachael A., *(978-0-615-21356-9; 978-0-615-25625-2)* 6177 Sun Blvd., No. 404, Staint Petersburg, FL 33715 USA Tel 727-698-2543; Fax: 727-865-6507
E-mail: hangingwithib@yahoo.com
Dist(s): **Lulu Pr., Inc.**

Hassan, Aref, *(978-0-9823812)* 301 S. Main St., Winters, TX 79567 USA Tel 325-754-4424.

Hassan, Marian, *(978-0-9766616)* 430 Mendota Rd. W., Suite 219, West Saint Paul, MN 55118 USA
E-mail: mhassan1@yahoo.com.

Hat Trick Publishing, *(978-0-9860405)* 8169 Outer Dr., S., Traverse City, MI 49685 USA.

Hatch Ideas, Inc., *(978-0-9792558)* P.O. Box 14, Pine Plains, NY 12567 USA.

Hatherleigh Co., Ltd., The, *(978-1-57826; 978-1-886330)* 5-22 46th Ave., Suite 200, Long Island City, NY 11101-5215 USA (SAN 298-878X) Tel 212-832-1584; Fax: 212-832-1502; Toll Free Fax: 800-621-8892; Toll Free: 800-367-2550; *Imprints:* Hatherleigh Press (Hath Pr)
E-mail: info@hatherleigh.com
Web site: http://www.hatherleigh.com; http://www.getfitnow.com
Dist(s): **MyiLibrary**
Penguin Random Hse. LLC
Random Hse., Inc.

Hatherleigh Pr. *Imprint of* **Hatherleigh Co., Ltd., The**

Hathi Chiti Bks. for Kids, *(978-0-615-37071-2; 978-0-615-37072-9; 978-0-9829362)* 203 Rivington St. Suite 2L, New York, NY 10002 USA Tel 212-920-1844
Web site: http://www.hathichiti.com
Dist(s): **National Bk. Network.**

Hatje Cantz Verlag GmbH & Co KG (DEU) *(978-3-7757) Dist. by* **Dist Art Pubs.**

Hatpin Press *See* **MusiKinesis**

Hatton, Robert, *(978-0-692-79740-2)* 12010 Teeside Dr., Fredericksburg, VA 22407 USA Tel 804-310-8246
E-mail: roberthattonsr@gmail.com.

Have Hope Publishing, *(978-0-9762044)* Orders Addr.: P.O. Box 20892, Baltimore, MD 21209 USA Tel 410-367-6179 (phone/fax); Edit Addr.: 5033 Yellowwood Ave., Baltimore, MD 21209 USA
E-mail: teachertalk@jhu.edu.

Haven Bks., *(978-0-9659480; 978-1-58436)* 10153 1/2 Riverside Dr., Suite 629, North Hollywood, CA 91602 USA Tel 818-503-2518; Fax: 818-508-0299
E-mail: Havenbks@aol.com; reya@havenbooks.net; info@havenbooks.net
Web site: http://www.havenbooks.net
Dist(s): **National Bk. Network**
ebrary, Inc.

Haven Harbor, *(978-0-9729863)* P.O. Box 2197, Huntington Beach, CA 92647-0197 USA
Web site: http://www.havenharbor.com.

HavenBound Publishing, *(978-0-9761733)* Orders Addr.: 1076 Pinnacle Dr., Waynesville, NC 28786 USA; Edit Addr.: 1305 Old Balsam Rd., Waynesville, NC 28786 USA; *Imprints:* HBHavenBound Publishing (HBHavenBnd)
E-mail: joseph@introductiontojesus.com; carolyn@havenbound.net; havenbound@havenbound.net.

Haver, Nancy, *(978-0-9795696)* 19 Moorland St., Amherst, MA 01002 USA Tel 413-549-1337
E-mail: nhaver@crocker.com.

Hawaii Fine Art Studio, *(978-0-615-21549-5)* 1028 Tirol Ln., Lake Arrowhead, CA 92352 USA.

Hawaii Fishing News, *(978-0-944462; 978-0-9884939)* 6650 Hawaii Kai Dr., No. 201, Honolulu, HI 96825 USA (SAN 243-6612) Tel 808-395-4499; Fax: 808-396-3474
E-mail: fishnews@pixi.com
Web site: http://www.hawaiifishingnews.com/hfn
Dist(s): **Booklines Hawaii, Ltd.**

Hawaiian Service, Inc., *(978-0-930492)* 94-527 Puahi St., Waipahu, HI 96797-4208 USA (SAN 205-0463) Tel 808-676-5026; Fax: 808-676-5156
Dist(s): **Booklines Hawaii, Ltd.**

Hawaya, Inc., *(978-0-9644149)* Orders Addr.: P.O. Box 300, Kailua, HI 96734 USA Tel 808-261-0589; Fax: 808-531-0957; Edit Addr.: 1564 Ulupii St., Kailua, HI 96734 USA
E-mail: ksullivan@pixi.com
Dist(s): **Booklines Hawaii, Ltd.**

Hawk Mountaintop Publishing, *(978-0-9672162)* P.O. Box 88, Piercy, CA 95587 USA Tel 707-247-3409
E-mail: hawk@saber.net.

Hawk Planners, *(978-0-9759702; 978-0-9776843)* 916 Silver Spur Rd. Suite 203, Rolling Hills Estates, CA 90274 USA
Toll Free: 888-442-9575
E-mail: matthawkphd@msn.com
Web site: http://www.hawkplanners.com; http://www.satorsports.com
Dist(s): **Cardinal Pubs. Group.**

HAWK Publishing Group, *(978-0-9673131; 978-1-930709)* 7107 S. Yale, No. 345, Tulsa, OK 74136 USA (SAN 299-9293) Tel 918-492-3677; Fax: 918-492-2120
E-mail: wb@hawkpub.com
Web site: http://www.hawkpub.com
Dist(s): **Bookmasters Distribution.**

Hawkeye Enterprises, *(978-0-9743061)* P.O. Box 252, Seal Rock, OR 97376-0252 USA Tel 541-563-4577
E-mail: hawkeye@oregonfast.net.

Hawkibinkler Pr., *(978-0-9721069)* 7725 N. Fowler, Portland, OR 97217 USA Tel 503-286-0945
E-mail: ruskin@streetfoodsecrets.com
Web site: http://www.streetfoodsecrets.com.

Hawks, Lyn, *(978-0-9888837)* 310 Ferguson Rd., Chapel Hill, NC 27516 USA Tel 919-929-5344
E-mail: lynhawks@gmail.com
Web site: www.lynhawks.com.

Haworth, Margaret, *(978-0-9740313)* 1625 W. May St. Apt. 3, Wichita, KS 67213-3578 USA.

†**Haworth Pr., Inc., The**, *(978-0-7890; 978-0-86656; 978-0-917724; 978-1-56022; 978-1-56023; 978-1-56024)* Div. of Taylor & Francis Group, 325 Chestnut St., Philadelphia, PA 19106-2614 USA (SAN 211-0156) Toll Free Fax: 800-895-0582; Toll Free: 800-429-6784; *Imprints:* Harrington Park Press (Harrington Park)
E-mail: orders@haworthpress.com; getinfo@haworthpress.com; barnold@haworthpress.com; docdelivery@haworthpress.com; tbronstein@haworthpress.com
Web site: http://www.haworthpress.com
Dist(s): **Barnes & Noble, Inc.**
Bookazine Co., Inc.
Borders, Inc.
Columbia Univ. Pr.
Distributors, The
Matthews Medical Bk. Co.
New Leaf Distributing Co., Inc.
Quality Bks., Inc.
Rittenhouse Bk. Distributors
SPD-Small Pr. Distribution
Unique Bks., Inc.
Waldenbooks, Inc.; *CIP.*

Hawthorn Pr. (GBR) *(978-0-9507062; 978-1-869890; 978-1-903458; 978-1-907359) Dist. by* **SteinerBooks Inc.**

Hawthorne Bks. & Literary Arts, Inc., *(978-0-9716915; 978-0-9766311; 978-0-9790188; 978-0-9833049; 978-0-9834775; 978-0-9838504; 978-0-9860007;*

Publisher Name Index

978-0-9893604; 978-0-9904370; 978-0-9970683; 978-0-9988257) 2201 NE 23rd Ave. 3rd Flr., Portland, OR 97212 USA
E-mail: rhughes@hawthornebooks.com
Web site: Http://hawthornebooks.com
Dist(s): **Publishers Group West (PGW).**

†**Hay Hse., Inc.,** *(978-0-937611; 978-0-945923; 978-1-56170; 978-1-891751; 978-1-58825; 978-1-4019)* Orders Addr.: P.O. Box 5100, Carlsbad, CA 92018-5100 USA (SAN 630-477X) Tel 760-431-7695 ext 112; Fax: 760-431-6948; Toll Free Fax: 800-650-5115 (orders only); Toll Free: 800-654-5126 (orders only); 2776 Loker Ave. W, Carlsbad, CA 92010 (SAN 257-3024) Tel 800-654-5126; Fax: 800-650-5115; *Imprints:* Hay House Lifestyles (Hay Hse Lifestyles); Emnin Books (Emnin Bks)
E-mail: kjohnson@hayhouse.com; pcrowe@hayhouse.com
Web site: http://www.hayhouse.com
Dist(s): **Follett School Solutions**
Lectorum Pubns., Inc.; *CIP.*

Hay Hse. Lifestyles *Imprint of* **Hay Hse., Inc.**

Haydenburri Lane, *(978-0-9758785; 978-0-9801849; 978-0-9822149)* 6114 LaSalle Ave., No. 285, Oakland, CA 94611-2802 USA Toll Free: 888-425-2636
Web site: http://www.haydenburrilane.com.

Haymarket Bks., *(978-1-931859; 978-1-60846)* 4015 N. Rockwell, Chicago, IL 60618 USA Tel 773-583-7884
E-mail: orders@haymarketbooks.org
Web site: http://www.haymarketbooks.org
Dist(s): **Consortium Bk. Sales & Distribution**
MyiLibrary
ebrary, Inc.

Haynes Manuals, Inc., *(978-1-56392; 978-1-85010; 978-1-85960; 978-1-62092)* Div. of Haynes Publishing Group, 861 Lawrence Dr., Newbury Park, CA 91320 USA (SAN 200-9838) Tel 805-498-6703; Fax: 805-498-2867; Toll Free: 800-442-9637; 1299 Bridgestone Pkwy., LaVergne, TN 37086 Fax: 615-793-5325; Toll Free: 800-242-4637
Web site: http://www.haynes.com/
Dist(s): **Delmar Cengage Learning**
Hachette Bk. Group
MBI Distribution Services/Quayside Distribution.

Haynes Publications, Incorporated *See* **Haynes Manuals, Inc.**

Haynes Publishing PLC (GBR) *(978-0-85696; 978-0-900550; 978-1-56392; 978-1-85010; 978-1-85260; 978-1-85960; 978-1-84425; 978-0-85733; 978-1-78521)* *Dist. by* **HachBkGrp.**

Haynes,Chilton,

HazardousWeather Preparedness Institute, *(978-0-9742794)* 5203 N. Oaks Dr., Greensboro, NC 27455-1229 USA
E-mail: rjackson@weatherpreparedness.com
Web site: http://www.weatherpreparedness.com.

Hazel Street Productions, *(978-0-9786988)* P.O. Box 5936, Sherman Oaks, CA 91413-5936 USA
Web site: http://www.hazelst.com.

†**Hazelden,** *(978-0-89486; 978-0-89638; 978-0-935908; 978-0-942421; 978-1-56246; 978-1-56838; 978-1-59285; 978-1-61649)* 15251 Pleasant Valley Rd., P.o. Box 176, Center City, MN 55012-0176 USA (SAN 209-4010) Fax: 651-213-4044; Toll Free: 800-328-9000; P.O. Box 176, RW4, Center City, MN 55012 Tel 651-213-4000; Toll Free: 800-328-9000
E-mail: bosterbauer@hazelden.org
Web site: http://www.hazelden.org
Dist(s): **BookMobile**
Follett School Solutions
Health Communications, Inc.
MyiLibrary
Simon & Schuster, Inc.
ebrary, Inc.; *CIP.*

Hazelden Publishing & Educational Services *See* **Hazelden**

HB Publishing, LLC, *(978-0-9711776; 978-0-615-19967-2)* Orders Addr.: P. O. Box 1703, Dewey, AZ 86327 USA Tel 714-625-6337; Fax: 714-625-6337
E-mail: nadinelalich@yahoo.com
Web site: http://hugbandit.com.

HBHavenBound Publishing *Imprint of* **HavenBound Publishing**

H.B.P., Inc., *(978-0-9753285; 978-0-9789617; 978-0-9853898; 978-0-9971299)* 952 Frederick St., Hagerstown, MD 21740 USA
E-mail: jdaniels@hbp.com
Web site: http://www.hbp.com.

HCI Teens *Imprint of* **Health Communications, Inc.**

Head of Zeus (GBR) *(978-1-908800; 978-1-78185; 978-1-78408; 978-1-78669; 978-1-78497)* *Dist. by* **IPG Chicago.**

Head On Dialogue Publishing, *(978-0-9770550)* Orders Addr.: P.O. Box 11400, Oakland, CA 94611 USA; Edit Addr.: 509 El Dorado No. 309, Piedmont, CA 94611 USA Tel 510-677-3267
E-mail: headondialogue@yahoo.com.

Head Pr. Publishing, *(978-0-9758924; 978-0-9832837)* 3804 Pk. Bend Dr., Flower Mound, TX 75022 USA Tel 817-410-9490
E-mail: headpresspublish@aol.com
Web site: http://www.headpress.info
Dist(s): **Send The Light Distribution LLC.**

Headline Bks., Inc., *(978-0-929915; 978-0-938467; 978-1-882658; 978-1-946664)* Orders Addr.: P.O. Box 52, Terra Alta, WV 26764 USA (SAN 250-8559) Tel 304-789-3001; Fax: 304-789-6427; Toll Free: 800-570-5951; *Imprints:* Publisher Page (Pub Page); Headline Kids (HeadlineKids)
E-mail: cathy@headlinebooks.com
Web site: http://www.headlinebooks.com
Dist(s): **American Wholesale Bk. Co.**
American West Bks.
Brodart Co.
Coutts Information Services
Follett School Solutions
Midwest Library Service
News Group, The.

Headline Kids *Imprint of* **Headline Bks., Inc.**

Headline Publishing Group (GBR) *(978-0-7472; 978-0-7553; 978-1-4722)* *Dist. by* **Trafalgar.**

Headline Publishing Group (GBR) *(978-0-7472; 978-0-7553; 978-1-4722)* *Dist. by* **HachBkGrp.**

Headline Science *Imprint of* **Compass Point Bks.**

Headrick, Gordon, *(978-0-9771385)* M. F. W. High School 1775 W. Lowell Ave., Tracy, CA 95376 USA.

Heads First (1st), *(978-0-9761969)* 4207 Magnolia Ln., Sugar Land, TX 77478 USA Tel 281-844-3719
E-mail: heads1st@aol.com
Web site: http://www.headsfirst.com.

Healing Arts Pr. *Imprint of* **Inner Traditions International, Ltd.**

Healing Flood Bks., Inc., *(978-0-9746497)* Orders Addr.: 3108 N. Longmore St., Chandler, AZ 85224 USA
E-mail: freebook@healingflood.com; prb@healingflood.com; sales@hospitalbooks.net; jerry@hospitalbooks.net; marketing@healingflood.com
Web site: http://www.healingflood.com; http://www.hospitalbooks.net.

Healing Hands Pr., *(978-0-9747686)* Div. of Holistic Home Health Care, 1329 N. Wembley Cir., Port Orange, FL 32128 USA Tel 386-322-4888
Web site: http://www.love-heals.com.

Healing Society, Inc., *(978-0-9720282; 978-1-932843)* Orders Addr.: P.O. Box 4503, Sedona, AZ 86340-9978 USA; Edit Addr.: 6560 Hwy. 179, Suite 114, Sedona, AZ 86351 USA Tel 877-504-1106
E-mail: dcrenshaw@hspub.com; moh@hspub.com
Web site: http://www.healingsociety.com; http://www.bodynbrain.com
Dist(s): **New Leaf Distributing Co., Inc.**

Healing Tree Arts, *(978-0-9779643)* P.O. Box 3398, Laguna Hills, CA 92654 USA (SAN 850-7775)
Web site: http://www.healingtreearts.com.

Health & Beauty Ctr., LLC, *(978-0-9747253)* P.O. Box 363, Oregon City, OR 97045 USA Toll Free: 888-648-7771
E-mail: support@healthnbeauty.com; support@perfect-prescription.com
Web site: http://www.healthnbeauty.com; http://www.perfect-prescription.com.

†**Health Communications, Inc.,** *(978-0-932194; 978-1-55874; 978-0-7573; 978-0-9910732)* Orders Addr.: 3201 SW 15th St., Deerfield Beach, FL 33442-8190 USA (SAN 212-100X) Tel 954-360-0909; Fax: 954-360-0034; Toll Free: 800-441-5569; *Imprints:* HCI Teens (HCI Teens); Faith Communications (Faith Comns) Do not confuse with Health Communications, Inc., Edison, NJ
E-mail: terip@hcibooks.com; lorig@hcibooks.com
Web site: http://www.hcibooks.com
Dist(s): **Bookazine Co., Inc.**
Islander Group
Partners/West Book Distributors
Southern Bk. Service
Western Pubns. Service; *CIP.*

Health New England, *(978-0-9777159)* One Monarch Pl., Springfield, MA 01144-1500 USA (SAN 850-0436) Tel 413-787-4000; Toll Free: 800-842-4464
Web site: http://www.hne.com; http://www.hnestore.com; http://www.hnewhizkidz.com.

Health Press *See* **Health Press NA Incorporated**

Health Press NA Incorporated, *(978-0-929173)* P.O. Box 37470, Albuquerque, NM 87176 USA (SAN 248-5036) Tel 505-888-1394; Fax: 505-212-0612
E-mail: goodbooks@healthpress.com
Web site: http://www.healthpress.com.

Health Success Media, LLC, *(978-0-9820121)* P.O. Box 21092, Bradenton, FL 34204 USA (SAN 857-0043)
E-mail: elana.devorah@gmail.com; Elana@ConquerProstateCancer.com
Web site: http://www.ConquerProstateCancer.com.

Healthful Living Bks. *Imprint of* **Unique Executive Pubs.**

HealthMark Multimedia, *(978-0-9717399)* 1828 L St., NW, Suite 250, Washington, DC 20036 USA
E-mail: hm@healthmarkmultimedia.com; amcfarren@healthmarkmultimedia.com
Web site: http://www.HealthMarkMultimedia.com.

Healthnets, *(978-0-615-20972-2)* 2921 Emmorton Rd., Abingdon, MD 21009 USA Tel 410-515-7858
E-mail: milleniumdiet@gmail.com
Web site: http://www.Milleniumdiet.com/.

Healthoot, Inc., *(978-0-9968393)* P.O. Box 2782, Running Springs, CA 92382 USA Tel 909-261-5205
E-mail: jaimestiansen@gmail.com.

HealthSprings, LLC, *(978-0-9718120; 978-0-9740697; 978-0-9748263)* 1759 Grandstand, San Antonio, TX 78238 USA Tel 210-521-7650; Fax: 210-521-7141
E-mail: sabra@zoeyzones.com
Web site: http://www.zoeyzones.com.

HealthTeacher, *(978-0-9785578; 978-0-9817969)* 5200 Maryland Way Ste. 100, Brentwood, TN 37027-5072 USA Toll Free: 800-514-1362
E-mail: tod@relegent.com
Web site: http://www.healthteacher.com.

Healthy Life Pr., Inc., *(978-0-9727328)* Orders Addr.: 1574 Gulf Rd., PMB 72, Point Roberts, WA 98281-9602 USA; Edit Addr.: 2667 Stellar Ct., Coquitlam, BC V3E 1H1 CAN Tel 604-682-5838; Fax: 604-468-1217
E-mail: rszefler@shaw.ca; info@starthealthylife.com
Web site: http://www.starthealthylife.com.

Hear My Heart Publishing, *(978-0-9862331; 978-1-945620)* 313 E. Oak St., Skiatook, OK 74070 USA Tel 918-510-1483
E-mail: hearmyheart02@yahoo.com
Web site: hearmyheart.net.

Heard Word Publishing, LLC, *(978-0-9801060)* 3051 W. 105th Ave. No. 350253, Westminster, CO 80031 USA
E-mail: hispublishingllc@yahoo.com; Beatrice@TheGetOverItGal.com
Web site: www.TheGetOverItGal.com.

Hearst Communications, Inc., *(978-0-87851; 978-1-58816)* 250 W. 55th St., New York, NY 10019-5288 USA
E-mail: jdeval@hearst.com
Web site: http://www.hearst.com
Dist(s): **Hearst Bks.**
Sterling Publishing Co., Inc.

Heart 4 Clowning Pr., A, *(978-0-9799093)* 905 Hwy 321 NW., No. 215, Hickory, NC 28601 USA Tel 828-326-0662
E-mail: aheart4clowning@gmail.com
Web site: http://www.AHeart4Clowning.com.

Heart & Harp LLC, *(978-0-9742174)* Orders Addr.: P.O. Box 818, Walled Lake, MI 48390-0818 USA Tel 313-938-9847
E-mail: HeartandHarp@comcast.net
Web site: http://www.heartandharp.net.

Heart Arbor Bks., *(978-1-891452)* Orders Addr.: P.O. Box 542, Grand River, OH 44045 USA (SAN 299-6073) Tel 440-257-0722; Toll Free: 877-977-4422.

Heart Bound Pr., *(978-0-615-25721-1)* Orders Addr.: 2141 Via Pacheco, Palos Verdes, CA 90274 USA Tel 310-375-3716; Fax: 310-373-2702
E-mail: heartboundpublishing@yahoo.com.

Heart Communications, *(978-0-9694176; 978-0-9747516)* P.O. Box 710791, Oak Hill, VA 20171 USA (SAN 116-404X) Tel 641-715-3900 (ext. 20889)
E-mail: info@heartcommunications.com
Web site: http://www.HeartCommunications.com.

Heart Flame Publishing, *(978-0-9726618)* P.O. Box 790038, Virgin, UT 84779-0038 USA (SAN 853-2532) Fax: 435-635-2613
Web site: http://www.heartflamepublishing.com
Dist(s): **Bookmasters Distribution.**

Heart Of Dixie Publishing *See* **Bluewater Pubns.**

Heart Path Publishing, *(978-0-9712305)* P.O. Box 44, Keene, TX 76059 USA Tel 817-681-3877 Do not confuse with Heart Path Publishing, Atlanta, GA
Web site: http://www.guidemagazine.org.

Heart Seed Pr., *(978-0-615-37628-8; 978-0-9831945)* 4440 N. Canyon Rd, Camino, CA 95709 USA Tel 530-644-4812
E-mail: acircleisdrawn@gmail.com
Web site: http://acircleisdrawn.org.

Heart to Heart Publishing, Inc., *(978-0-9742806; 978-0-9802486; 978-1-937008)* Orders Addr.: 528 Mud Creek Rd., Morgantown, KY 42261 USA Tel 270-526-5589; Fax: 270-526-7489; Toll Free: 888-526-5589
E-mail: hawkinslindaj@yahoo.com
Web site: http://www.lindajhawkins.com; http://www.hearttoheartpublishinginc.com
Dist(s): **BookBaby.**

Heartfelt Bks., *(978-0-9763933)* 149 Thunderbird Trail, Carol Stream, IL 60188-1982 USA.

HeartFelt Stories LLC, *(978-0-9778113)* 5767 Kempton Run Ct., Columbus, OH 43235 USA (SAN 850-3036)
E-mail: heartfeltstories@hotmail.com
Web site: http://www.heartfeltstoriesllc.com
Dist(s): **Blu Sky Media Group.**

Heartful Loving Pr., *(978-0-9723639)* Div. of Illui International, 1450 Orange Grove Ave., Santa Barbara, CA 93105 USA Tel 805-687-7442; Fax: 805-687-3042
E-mail: howard@heartfullovingpress.com
Web site: http://www.heartfullovingpress.com; http://www.howtobeafamily.com; http://www.firstloverememberances.com; http://www.howtobethebestlover.com
Dist(s): **Partners Bk. Distributing, Inc.**

Hearthstone Rose, *(978-0-9836682)* 1156 Valleyview Dr., Lawrence, PA 15055 USA Tel 724-746-0662
E-mail: conniedonaldson@comcast.net.

Heartland Foundation, Inc., *(978-0-943177)* Orders Addr.: P.O. Box 887, Ames, IA 50010 USA Toll Free: 866-385-2027; Edit Addr.: 413 Northwestern Ave., Ames, IA 50010 USA (SAN 668-3010) Tel 515-232-1054
E-mail: lssn@att.net
Web site: http://mcmillenbooks.com
Dist(s): **McMillen Bk. Distributors.**

Heartlight Girls, *(978-0-9787689)* P.O. Box 370546, Denver, CO 80237 USA Tel 303-690-5603
E-mail: debra @heartlightgirls.com; debragano@aol.com
Web site: http://www.heartlightgirls.com.

Heartohopia Pr., *(978-0-9725184)* 2007 NE 59 Pl., Suite 105, Fort Lauderdale, FL 33308 USA
Web site: http://www.heartohopia.com.

HeartQuake Publishing *See* **Hunt Thompson Media**

Heartrock Pr., *(978-0-9817668)* P.O. Box 135, Langley, WA 98260 USA Tel 360-321-5603
Web site: http://NWDragons.com.

Heartsome Press *See* **Heartsome Publishing**

Heartsome Publishing, *(978-0-9726408)* 220 Norfolk St., Walpole, MA 02081 USA Tel 508-553-3858; Fax: 508-668-1998
E-mail: rrhearts@comcast.net
Web site: http://www.nolobsterplease.com/.

Heartstrings Publishing, *(978-0-9760733)* Orders Addr.: P.O. Box 8255, Fernando Beach, FL 32035 USA; Edit Addr.: Marchette Burette Market, Amelia Island Plantation, Fernandina Beach, FL 32034 USA
E-mail: mledlen@aol.com.

Heart-to-Heart Pubns., *(978-0-9744565)* 18237 N. 51st Pl., Scottsdale, AZ 85254 USA Tel 602-485-0793
E-mail: cpruett1@cox.net.

Heath, Jonathan Publishing, *(978-0-9715837)* 10 Willowstream Dr., Vernon, CT 06066 USA Tel 860-875-8373
E-mail: lenpam@snet.net.

Heather & Highlands Publishing, *(978-1-58478)* Div. of Heather & Highlands Publishing, Orders Addr.: 2384 Tokay Ct., Paradise, CA 95969 USA (SAN 254-0932) Tel 530-876-8986; Fax: 530-876-8989; Toll Free: 888-999-2358; *Imprints:* Highland Children's Press (Hghlnd Child)
E-mail: pawprintsorders@pawprintspress.com; pawprints@pawprintspress.com; tew@tewatsononline.com; heatherandhighlands@heatherandhighlandspublishing.com
Web site: http://www.pawprintspress.com; http://www.tewatsononline.com; http://heatherandhighlandspublishing.com
Dist(s): **Book Wholesalers, Inc.**
Brodart Co.

Heavenly C. Publishing, *(978-0-9746361)* P.O. Box 335, West Chester, OH 45071 USA
Web site: http://www.heavenlyCPublishing.com.

Heavenly Realm Publishing, *(978-0-9714874; 978-0-9825589; 978-0-9828802; 978-0-9833418; 978-0-9835202; 978-0-9839969; 978-1-937911; 978-1-944383)* Orders Addr.: P.O. Box 682532, Houston, TX 77268 USA Tel 866-216-0696; Toll Free: 877-599-3237
E-mail: heavenlyrealm@heavenlyrealmpublishing.com
Web site: http://www.heavenlyrealmpublishing.com
Dist(s): **Lightning Source, Inc.**

Hebler, Dave, *(978-0-9765392)* 5891 S. Military Trail, 5A-PMB, Lake Worth, FL 33463-6920 USA Tel 561-642-6696
E-mail: daveahebler@aol.com
Web site: http://www.protectingwomen.com.

Hebler, Michael, *(978-0-615-39525-8; 978-0-9833884; 978-0-692-67408-6; 978-0-692-70134-8)* 1344 Kingswood Ct., Fort Myers, FL 33919 USA Tel 562-857-1524; *Imprints:* Night After Night Publications, Incorporated (NightAfterNight)
E-mail: michaelhebler@gmail.com
Web site: http://www.michaelhebler.com
Dist(s): **CreateSpace Independent Publishing Platform.**

Hedgebury (AUS) *(978-0-9873437)* *Dist. by* **NewShelves.**

Hedger, Ralph, *(978-0-9753880)* 208 Chaucer Rd., Charlottesville, VA 22901-2215 USA
E-mail: rehedger@aol.com.

Heel Verlag GmbH (DEU) *(978-3-89365; 978-3-922858; 978-3-89880; 978-3-95843)* *Dist. by* **Natl Bk Netwk.**

Heersink, Roland, *(978-0-9770473)* 18303 Starboard Dr., Houston, TX 77058-4362 USA
Web site: http://www.fairytunes.com.

Heflin & Thrall Language Pubns., Inc., *(978-0-9723341)* 2109 Stanford, Jacksonville, TX 75766 USA Toll Free: 888-313-3310
E-mail: jheflin@language-publications.com.

Hegemony Pr., *(978-0-9754114)* 5205 Pacific Ave., Tacoma, WA 98405 USA Tel 253-671-2665; Fax: 253-475-2665; Toll Free: 888-671-2665.

Heiderer, Conrad, *(978-0-9746699)* P.O. Box 405, Glen Arbor, MI 49636 USA Tel 231-334-6680 Toll Free: 888-877-0994
E-mail: cehj1200@hotmail.com
Web site: http://www.twigma.com.

Heifer Project International, *(978-0-9755996; 978-0-9798439; 978-0-9819788)* Orders Addr.: 1 World Ave., Little Rock, AR 72203-8058 USA Tel 800-422-1311; Fax: 501-907-2802
E-mail: info@heifer.org
Web site: http://www.heifer.org.

†**Heinemann,** *(978-0-325; 978-0-434; 978-0-435; 978-1-59469)* Orders Addr.: P.O. Box 6926, Portsmouth, NH 03802 USA Toll Free: 800-225-5800; Edit Addr.: 361 Hanover St., Portsmouth, NH 03801 USA (SAN 210-5829) Tel 603-431-7894; Fax: 603-431-7840; *Imprints:* Firsthand (Firsthnd)
E-mail: info@heinemann.com
Web site: http://www.heinemann.com
Dist(s): **ABC-CLIO, LLC**
Follett School Solutions
Leonard, Hal Corp.
Pearson Education
Trans-Atlantic Pubns., Inc.; *CIP.*

Heinemann Educational Books, Incorporated *See* **Heinemann**

Heinemann First Library *Imprint of* **Heinemann-Raintree**

Heinemann InfoSearch *Imprint of* **Heinemann-Raintree**

Heinemann Read & Learn *Imprint of* **Heinemann-Raintree**

Heinemann State Studies *Imprint of* **Heinemann-Raintree**

.Heinemann-Raintree *See* **Heinemann-Raintree**

Heinemann-Raintree, *(978-0-431; 978-1-57572; 978-1-58810; 978-1-4034; 978-1-4109; 978-1-4329; 978-1-4846)* Div. of Capstone, Orders Addr.: 1710 Roe Crest Dr., North Mankato, MN 56003 USA Toll Free Fax: 888-844-5329; Toll Free: 800-747-4992; Halley Court Freepost PO Box 1125, Oxford, OX2 8YY; *Imprints:* Acorn (AcornHR); Acorn Read-Aloud (Acorn Read); Bellota (Bellota); Heinemann First Library (HeineFirst Lib); Heinemann InfoSearch (HeineInfoSearc); Heinemann Read & Learn (HeinReadnLearn); Heinemann State Studies (HeinemanStStud); NA-h (NA-h); NA-r (NA-r); Raintree Freestyle (RaintrFreestyl); Raintree Freestyle Express (RantFreExp); Raintree Fusion (RaintreeFusion); Raintree Perspectives (RainPerspect); Sci-Hi (Sci-Hi); Read Me! (Read Me)
E-mail: k.monyhan@coughlancompanies.com; customerservice@capstonepub.com
Web site: http://www.heinemannlibrary.com/; http://www.capstonepub.com; http://www.capstoneclassroom.com
Dist(s): **Capstone Pub.**
Follett School Solutions
Lectorum Pubns., Inc.

Heinle & Heinle Publishers, Inc. *See* **Cengage Heinle**

Heinrich, Tyson Chul, *(978-0-615-23894-4; 978-0-578-00492-1; 978-0-578-01337-4; 978-0-578-01343-5; 978-0-9962209)* 4295 Hitch Blvd., Moorpark, CA 93021 USA
Web site: http://www.tysonheinrich.com.

Heins Pubns., *(978-0-9671762; 978-0-9748680)* 2016 Leonard Ct., Eau Claire, WI 54703 USA Toll Free: 800-554-3467
E-mail: revheins@wwt.net.

Heinz, Derek *See* **Heinz, Derek**

Heinz, Derek, *(978-0-578-19115-7)* 1124 NE Lilac St. 107, Issaquah, WA 98029 USA.
Helen Bolton Ministries *See* **Bolton Publishing LLC**
Helen Darling *See* **My Darling-Tots Pubns.**
Heliand Publishing Corp., *(978-0-9770712)* P.O. Box 477, Pleasant Grove, UT 84062 USA
E-mail: submissions@heliandpublishing.com
Web site: http://www.heliandpublishing.com.
Heliograph, Inc., *(978-0-9668926; 978-1-930658)* 26 Porter St., Somerville, MA 02143-2215 USA
E-mail: info@heliograph.com
Web site: http://www.heliograph.com.
Heliotrope Bks., LLC, *(978-0-9816198; 978-0-9832940; 978-0-9904012; 978-1-942762)* 125 E. 4th St., New York, NY 10003 USA Tel 212-477-1783
E-mail: publishers@heliotropebooks.com; nonirose@earthlink.net
Web site: http://www.heliotropebooks.com
Dist(s): **Ingram Publisher Services.**
Hellgate Pr. *Imprint of* **L & R Publishing, LLC**
Helm Literary Publishing *See* **Helm Publishing**
Helm Publishing, *(978-0-9723011; 978-0-9760919; 978-0-9769193; 978-0-9778205; 978-0-9792328; 978-0-9801780; 978-0-9820605; 978-0-9841397; 978-0-9830109; 978-0-9850488)* Orders Addr.: P.O. Box 9691, Treasure Island, FL 33740 USA (SAN 254-7562) Tel 815-621-3336; Edit Addr.: P.O. Box 9691, Treasure Island, FL 33740 USA Tel 815-621-3336
E-mail: dianne@publishersdrive.com
Web site: http://www.publishersdrive.com.
Helms, Jo Publishing, *(978-0-9745319)* 824 S. Schaefer St., Appleton, WI 54915 USA
E-mail: cheesedawg@earthlink.net; ilovegrizz@earthlink.net
Web site: http://www.grizz.20megsfree.com.
HELORO Publishing Group, *(978-0-9785435; 978-0-615-15932-4; 978-0-615-15933-1; 978-0-615-16034-4)* 860 Appletree Ct., Northbrook, IL 60062-3402 USA (SAN 850-9549) Tel 847-207-1087 mobile phone Do not confuse with companies with the same or similar name in Minneapolis, MN, Great Neck, NY
Web site: http://www.HELORO.com
Dist(s): **Lulu Pr., Inc.**
H.E.L.P. for Self-Education, *(978-0-9766991)* 960 Perth Rd., Troutman, NC 28166 USA Tel 704-528-5866; Fax: 704-585-9397
E-mail: swedship@bellsouth.net
Web site: http://www.home.bellsouth.net/p/pwp-helpeducate.
Helping Hands Children's Bks., *(978-0-9762274)* 421 26th St., Marion, IA 52302 USA Tel 319-373-4169
E-mail: mary@mysak.com.
Helping Hands Therapeutic Services, *(978-0-9855978)* P.O. Box 1452, Columbus, GA 31902 USA Tel 770-310-0510
E-mail: mirrorbuzz99@gmail.com.
Helpingwords, *(978-0-615-16066-5; 978-0-615-23505-9; 978-0-578-03620-5; 978-0-578-05059-1; 978-0-578-06008-8; 978-0-9828529; 978-0-9977922)* 66 Prospect St., Manchester, NH 03104 USA Tel 603-668-1975
E-mail: kathy@kathybrodsky.com
Web site: http://www.kathybrodsky.com
Dist(s): **Enfield Publishing & Distribution Co., Inc.**
Helps4Teachers, *(978-0-9778548)* 145 Gardenside Ct., Fallbrook, CA 92028 USA (SAN 850-4180) Tel 760-723-0504
E-mail: rstur@roadrunner.com
Web site: http://www.helps4teachers.com.
Hemed Books, Incorporated *See* **Lambda Pubs., Inc.**
Henderson Publishing, *(978-1-891029)* Orders Addr.: 811 Eva's Walk, Pounding Mill, VA 24637 USA Tel 276-964-2291.
Hendley, Jeff *See* **L'Edge Pr.**
Hendrickson Publishers, Incorporated *See* **Hendrickson Pubs. Marketing, LLC**
†**Hendrickson Pubs. Marketing, LLC,** *(978-0-913573; 978-0-917006; 978-0-943575; 978-1-56563; 978-1-84306; 978-1-59856; 978-1-61970; 978-1-68307)* Orders Addr.: P.O. Box 3473, Peabody, MA 01961-3473 USA (SAN 285-2772) Fax: 978-531-8146; Toll Free: 800-358-3111; Edit Addr.: 140 Summit St., Peabody, MA 01960 USA (SAN 663-6594) Fax: 978-573-8414 Do not confuse with Hendrickson Group, Sandy Hook, CT
E-mail: editorial@hendrickson.com
Web site: http://www.hendrickson.com; *CIP.*
Henisz, Jerzy E., *(978-0-615-13851-0)* Orders Addr.: P.O. Box 1089, Sharon, CT 06069 USA; Edit Addr.: 33 Hospital Hill Rd., Sharon, CT 06069 USA
Dist(s): **Lulu Pr., Inc.**
Henry Helps *Imprint of* **Picture Window Bks.**
Henry, Ian Pubns. (GBR) *(978-0-86025) Dist. by* **Players Pr.**
Henry, Ian Pubns. (GBR) *(978-0-86025) Dist. by* **Empire Pub Srvs.**
Henry, Patti, *(978-0-9817155)* 9114 Tepee Trail, Houston, TX 77064 USA (SAN 856-3268) Tel 281-894-4131
E-mail: patti@patti-henry.com
Web site: http://www.patti-henry.com.
Henry Quill Pr., *(978-1-883960)* 7340 Lake Dr., Fremont, MI 49412-9146 USA Tel 231-924-3026; Fax: 231-928-2802.
HenschelHAUS Publishing, *(978-0-9647663; 978-0-9722099; 978-1-59598)* 2625 S. Greeley St., Suite 201, Milwaukee, WI 53207 USA Tel 414-486-0653; Fax: 262-565-2058; *Imprints:* Goblin Fern Press (Goblin Fern)
E-mail: kira@henschelHAUSbooks.com
Web site: http://www.goblinfernpress.com; http://www.mavenmarkbooks.com; http://www.henschelHAUSbooks.com; http://www.threetowerspress.com
Dist(s): **Smashwords.**
Hensley, Michael, *(978-0-9747389)* P.O. Box 2952, Ranchos de Taos, NM 87557 USA
Web site: http://www.michaelmhensley.com.
Henzel, Richard, *(978-0-9747237; 978-0-9826688; 978-0-9846715)* 1106 N. Taylor, Oak Park, IL 60302 USA Tel 312-296-8396
E-mail: richard@richardhenzel.com
Web site: http://www.richardhenzel.com; http://www.richardhenzel.com/marktwain
Dist(s): **Audible.com**
Midwest Tape.
†**Herald Pr.,** *(978-0-8361; 978-1-5138)* Div. of MennoMedia, Inc., Orders Addr.: 1251 Virginia Ave., Harrisonburg, VA 22802 USA (SAN 202-2915) Fax: 1-316-283-0454; Toll Free: 1-800-245-7894; 800-631-6535 (Canada only) Do not confuse with Herald Pr., Charlotte, NC
E-mail: info@mennomedia.org
Web site: http://www.mennomedia.org
Dist(s): **Ebsco Publishing**
Faith Alive Christian Resources
Send The Light Distribution LLC
Spring Arbor Distributors, Inc.; *CIP.*
†**Herald Publishing Hse.,** *(978-0-8309)* Orders Addr.: P.O. Box 390, Independence, MO 64051-0390 USA Tel 816-521-3015; Fax: 816-521-3066 (customer services); Toll Free: 800-767-8181; Edit Addr.: 1001W. Walnut St., Independence, MO 64051-0390 USA (SAN 111-7556) Tel 816-257-0200
E-mail: sales@HeraldHouse.org
Web site: http://www.heraldhouse.org; *CIP.*
Herdman, Susan E., *(978-0-578-01491-3)* 4639 Sunset Ridge, Santa Fe, NM 87507 USA
E-mail: susan@susanheerdman.com
Web site: http://americanadolescents.com
Dist(s): **Lulu Pr., Inc.**
Heritage Bks., *(978-0-7884; 978-0-917890; 978-0-940907; 978-1-55613; 978-1-888265; 978-1-58549; 978-1-68034)* 5810 Ruatan St, Berwyn Heights, MD 20740 USA (SAN 209-3367) Tel 800-876-6103; Fax: 800-876-6103; Toll Free: 800-876-6103
E-mail: Info@HeritageBooks.com
Web site: http://www.HeritageBooks.com; http://www.WillowBendBooks.com
Dist(s): **CreateSpace Independent Publishing Platform.**
Heritage Builders, LLC, *(978-0-615-30423-6; 978-0-615-30734-3; 978-0-615-30735-0; 978-0-615-31024-4; 978-0-692-00827-0; 978-1-939011; 978-1-940242; 978-1-941437; 978-1-942603; 978-1-945549)* 3105 Locan Ave., Clovis, CA 93619 USA
Dist(s): **Bookmasters Distribution**
MyiLibrary
Publishers Group West (PGW).
Heritage Heart Farm, *(978-0-9706348)* Orders Addr.: 21387 Rd. 128, Oakwood, OH 45873 USA Tel 419-594-2258
E-mail: heritageheartfarm@roadrunner.com; kohart@tds.net
Web site: http://www.heritageheartfarm.com.
Heritage Hse. (CAN) *(978-0-919214; 978-1-895811; 978-1-894384; 978-0-9690546; 978-1-894974; 978-1-926613; 978-1-926936; 978-1-927051; 978-1-927527; 978-1-77203) Dist. by* **Orca Bk Pub.**
Heritage Music Pr., *(978-0-89328)* Div. of The Lorenz Corp., Orders Addr.: 501 E. Third St., Dayton, OH 45401-0802 USA Tel 937-228-6118; Toll Free: 800-444-1144
E-mail: order@lorenz.com
Web site: http://www.lorenz.com.
Heritage National Publishing, *(978-0-9983202)* 412 S. White St. No. 129, Athens, TN 37303 USA Tel 423-920-0776
E-mail: mountmaaziah@aol.com.
Heritage Publishing, *(978-0-9672363)* 23507 E. State Rte. P, Pleasant Hill, MO 64080 USA Tel 816-540-4768; 913-338-3893 Do not confuse with companies with the same or similar names in Dallas, TX, Enumclaw, WA, Chicago, IL, Beverly Hills, CA, Loveland, CO, Valley Center, KS, Peabody, MA, Whitesboro, TX, Pleasant Hill, MO, Springdale, AR, Charlotte, NC, Thomasville, GA, North Little Rock, AR, Baton Rouge, LA, Stockton, CA, carthage, MO
E-mail: peggytucker@juno.com.
Heritage Publishing, *(978-0-692-39278-2; 978-0-692-57340-2; 978-0-692-62722-8; 978-0-9974318; 978-0-692-72236-7; 978-0-692-81935-7; 978-0-9987766)* 1261 Andrew Donelson, Hermitage, TN 37076 USA Tel 615-440-6228
E-mail: jsteph1135@gmail.com.
Heritage Publishing Co., *(978-0-9787462)* 4393 Mission Inn Ave., Riverside, CA 92501 USA (SAN 851-5247) Tel 951-788-7878; Fax: 951-788-1206
E-mail: rich1rodriguez@sbcglobal.net; isabel@isabelelias.com
Web site: http://IsabelElias.com.
Heritage Youth, Inc., *(978-0-9740753)* 6245 Esplanade Ave., Baton Rouge, LA 70806-6144 USA.
Hermes Pr., *(978-0-9710311; 978-1-932563; 978-1-61345)* 2100 Wilmington Rd., New Castle, PA 16105-1931 USA Tel 724-652-0511; Fax: 724-652-5597 Do not confuse with companies with same or similar names in Brooks, ME, Vista, CA. Ferndale, MI
Web site: http://www.hermespress.com
Dist(s): **Diamond Comic Distributors, Inc.**
Diamond Bk. Distributors.
Hermes Pubs., Inc., *(978-0-9766543)* P.O. Box 186, Roselle Park, NJ 07207 USA (SAN 256-453X) Toll Free: 888-557-5527
E-mail: dollarnet@aol.com.
Hermit Chum Publishing, *(978-0-9760317)* 6901 S. McClintock, No. 245, Tempe, AZ 89283 USA.
Hermit's Grove, The, *(978-0-9655687; 978-0-9863639)* P.O. Box 0691, Kirkland, WA 98083-0691 USA Tel 425-828-4124; Fax: 425-803-2025
E-mail: paul@thehermitsgrove.org
Web site: http://www.thehermitsgrove.org
Dist(s): **New Leaf Distributing Co., Inc.**
Hern, Nick Bks., Ltd. (GBR) *(978-1-85459; 978-1-84842; 978-1-78001) Dist. by* **Consort Bk Sales.**
Hero Builder Comics, *(978-0-615-31157-9)* 1713 Golden Ct., Bellingham, WA 98226 USA.
Hero Dog Pubns., *(978-0-9743659)* 14 Eastview Ave., Pleasantville, NY 10570 USA (SAN 255-545X) Tel 914-525-6483
E-mail: herodogpubl@msn.com
Web site: www.herodogpublications.com
Dist(s): **BCH Fulfillment & Distribution.**
Herobrine Publishing, *(978-0-615-94047-2; 978-0-692-36105-4; 978-0-692-36106-1; 978-0-692-36369-0; 978-0-692-36679-0; 978-0-692-36690-5; 978-0-9864441; 978-1-943330)* 18340 Yorba Linda Blvd Suite 107-119, Yorba Linda, CA 92886 USA Tel 7147439845; *Imprints:* Zack Zombie Publishing (MYID_C_ZACK ZO)
E-mail: info@herobrinepublishing.com; info@zackzombiepublishing.com
Web site: http://sapientbizsolutions.com
Dist(s): **CreateSpace Independent Publishing Platform.**
Heroes & Leaders, *(978-0-9801408)* 616 Kaufman St., Forney, TX 75126 USA (SAN 855-3165)
Web site: http://www.zertelo.com.
Heroic Publishing, Inc., *(978-0-929729)* 6433 California Ave., Long Beach, CA 90805 USA (SAN 250-0582) Tel 562-428-4124 (phone/fax)
E-mail: heroicpub@aol.com
Web site: http://www.heroicpub.com
Dist(s): **Diamond Comic Distributors, Inc.**
Herrington Teddy Bears, *(978-0-9722343)* 8945 Research Dr., Irvine, CA 92618-4237 USA Toll Free: 866-482-2327
E-mail: chris@herringtonco.com
Web site: http://www.herringtonteddybears.com.
Herrod, Ron L. Evangelism Ministries Association (R.H.E.M.A), *(978-0-9763789)* P.O. Box 6447, Sevierville, TN 37864 USA
E-mail: emily@ronherrod.org; ron@ronherrod.org
Web site: http://ronherrod.org.
hersh, patrice, *(978-0-692-76668-2; 978-0-692-84974-3)* 1865 jacob st, cortlandt manor, NY 10567 USA Tel 914-737-6095
E-mail: pattihersh@aol.com.
Hershberger, Ivan & Fannie, *(978-0-9725806)* 8219 CR 192, Holmesville, OH 44633 USA.
Hershenson, Bruce, *(978-1-887893)* Orders Addr.: P.O. Box 874, West Plains, MO 65775 USA Tel 417-256-9616; Fax: 417-257-6948
E-mail: mail@emovieposter.com
Web site: http://www.emovieposter.com
Dist(s): **Austin & Company, Inc.**
Partners Pubs. Group, Inc.
Heryin Publishing Corp., *(978-0-9762056; 978-0-9787550; 978-0-9845523)* 1033 E. Main St., No. 202, Alhambra, CA 91801 USA Tel 626-289-2238; Fax: 626-289-3865
E-mail: info@heryin.com
Dist(s): **Independent Pubs. Group.**
Herzog, Joyce, *(978-1-887225)* 900 Airport Rd., #21, Chattanooga, TN 37421 USA Tel 423-553-6387
E-mail: joyceoffice@aol.com
Web site: http://JoyceHerzog.com; http://JoyceHerzog.info; http://ScaredyCatReadingSystem.com.
Hesperus Pr. (GBR) *(978-1-84391; 978-1-78094) Dist. by* **IPG Chicago.**
Hester Publishing, *(978-0-9789388)* 219 Blackberry Cir., Colchester, VT 05446 USA
E-mail: sales@hesterpublishing.com
Web site: http://hesterpublishing.com.
Hetherington Hall, *(978-0-9839963)* 888 Logan St. Suite 9A, Denver, CO 80203 USA Tel 720-883-4848
E-mail: lisa@hetheringtonhall.com
Web site: www.hetheringtonhall.com.
Hetman Publishing (GBR) *(978-0-9561592) Dist. by* **LuluCom.**
Hewell Publishing, *(978-1-56870)* 2722 N. Josey Ln. Suite 100, Carrollton, TX 75007 USA
E-mail: sally.hewell@alphagraphics.com
Web site: http://www.hewellpublishing.com.
Hewett, Katherine J.E., *(978-0-578-03065-4; 978-0-578-09202-7)* 625 Gregory Dr. Apt. 85, Crp Christi, TX 78412-3061 USA
E-mail: kathewett@aol.com
Dist(s): **Lulu Pr., Inc.**
Hewitt Research Foundation, Inc., *(978-0-913717; 978-1-57896)* Orders Addr.: P.O. Box 9, Washougal, WA 98671 USA (SAN 286-1852) Tel 360-835-8708; Fax: 360-835-8697; Toll Free: 800-348-1750; Edit Addr.: 2103 B St., Washougal, WA 98671 USA
E-mail: hewitths@aol.com
Web site: http://www.homeeducation.org.
Hewitt Research, Incorporated *See* **Hewitt Research Foundation, Inc.**
Hexagon Blue, *(978-0-9729958)* P.O. Box 1790, Issaquah, WA 98027-0073 USA (SAN 255-3406)
E-mail: maryjesse@gmail.com
Web site: http://www.hexagonblue.com
Dist(s): **Quality Bks., Inc.**
Hey U.G.L.Y., Inc., *(978-0-9759004)* 8057 N. 300 E., Rolling Prairie, IN 46371 USA
Web site: http://www.heyugly.org.
Heyday, *(978-0-930588; 978-0-9666691; 978-1-890771; 978-1-59714)* Orders Addr.: P.O. Box 9145, Berkeley, CA 94709 USA (SAN 207-2351) Tel 510-549-3564; Fax: 510-549-1889; 1633 University Ave., Berkeley, CA 94703-1424; *Imprints:* Great Valley Books (Grt Valley Bks)
E-mail: orders@heydaybooks.com; david@heydaybooks.com; christopher@heydaybooks.com
Web site: http://www.heydaybooks.com.
Heyday Books *See* **Heyday**
Heyokah Publishing Co., *(978-0-9656124; 978-1-930910)* 7244 Lattigo Dr., Nampa, ID 83687 USA Tel 208-465-5809
E-mail: hiheyokah@aol.com
Dist(s): **New Leaf Distributing Co., Inc.**
Heywood, Joseph, *(978-0-692-82719-2; 978-0-692-82723-9)*
Hez-N-Tales, *(978-0-9745349)* 11037 Hopewell Rd., Boaz, KY 42027 USA
Web site: http://www.feedinghislambs.org.
Hi Willow Research & Publishing, *(978-0-931510; 978-1-933170)* Orders Addr.: P.O. Box 720400, San Jose, CA 95172-0400 USA (SAN 211-3945) Toll Free: 800-873-3043
E-mail: sales@lmcsource.com
Web site: http://www.lmcsource.com
Dist(s): **Follett School Solutions**
L M C Source.
Hibiscus Publishing, *(978-0-9792963; 978-0-9842831)* 1499 Gormican Ln., Naples, FL 34110 USA Fax: 239-514-0238
E-mail: hibiscus311@comcast.net
Web site: http://www.hibiscuspublishing.com.
Hiccup Cottage Pubns., *(978-0-9718724)* 316 10th St., NE, Charlottesville, VA 22902 USA Tel 434-980-5347
E-mail: hiccupcottage@yahoo.com.
Hickle Pickle Publishing, *(978-1-881958)* 4450 Allison Dr., Michigan Center, MI 49254 USA Tel 517-764-1117
E-mail: hicklepickle@modempool.com
Web site: www.hicklepickle.com.
Hickory Bark Productions, *(978-0-9748047)* 3355 N. Five Mile Rd., Suite 332, Boise, ID 83713 USA Tel 208-322-7239.
Hickory Grove Pr., *(978-0-9679915; 978-0-9854725)* Orders Addr.: 3151 Treeco Ln., Bellevue, IA 52031 USA Tel 563-583-4767 (phone/fax) Do not confuse with Hickory Grove Pr., Canton, OH
E-mail: challengemath@aol.com
Web site: http://www.challengemath.com.
Hickory Tales Publishing, *(978-0-9709104; 978-0-9787555)* Orders Addr.: 841 Newberry St., Bowling Green, KY 42103 USA Tel 270-791-3242
E-mail: jadonel@aol.com
Web site: http://www.hickorytales.com.
Hickory Tree Publishing, *(978-0-9893157; 978-0-9985754)* 123 High St., Ashland, OR 97520 USA Tel 541-864-0541
E-mail: finley.ra@gmail.com
Web site: http://www.hickorytreebooks.blogspot.com
Dist(s): **eBookit.com.**
Hidden Curriculum Education, *(978-0-9755103)* Orders Addr.: P.O. Box 222041, Hollywood, FL 33022 USA Tel 954-457-8098; Fax: 954-457-3331
Web site: http://www.collegefaqbook.com.
Hidden Forest Pubs., *(978-0-9755117)* 269 Co. Hwy. 250, Guin, AL 35563-2700 USA.
Hidden Manna Pubns., *(978-0-9891683; 978-0-9915261; 978-0-9864066)* 249 Larch St., Priest River, ID 83856 USA Tel 208-412-3087
E-mail: artnbooks@gmail.com
Web site: www.gentleshepherd.com.
Hidden Path Pubn., Inc., *(978-0-9711534)* 304 Briarwood Rd., Statesville, NC 28677 USA Tel 704-878-0716; 704-224-4832
E-mail: dkellysteele@aol.com.
Hidden Pictures, *(978-0-9678159; 978-0-9843088)* Orders Addr.: P.O. Box 63, Tipp City, OH 45371-9103 USA (SAN 253-6862) Tel 937-667-6288; Fax: 937-669-4178
E-mail: liz@hiddenpictures.com
Web site: http://www.hiddenpicturepuzzle.com.
Hidden Talent Pr., *(978-0-9776114)* Orders Addr.: P.O. Box 9052, Missoula, MT 59807 USA
Web site: http://www.iysofwar.com.
Hidden Valley Farm Pub., *(978-0-615-17173-9)* P.O. Box 172, Perry, NY 14530 USA
E-mail: theotherherald@yahoo.com
Web site: http://www.tfrice.etsy.com
Dist(s): **Lulu Pr., Inc.**
Hidden Wolf Bks., *(978-0-9911045; 978-0-9968922; 978-0-9994345)* 155 W. Genung St., St. Augustine, FL 32086 USA Tel 904-797-5964
E-mail: nsinatsch@hotmail.com.
HiddenSpring *Imprint of* **Paulist Pr.**
Hieble, Helen, *(978-0-615-77684-2; 978-0-692-79708-2)* 685 Knox Rd., Wayne, PA 19087 USA Tel 610-688-4961; Fax: 610-688-0869
Dist(s): **CreateSpace Independent Publishing Platform.**
Hierophant Publishing Services *See* **Hieropub LLC**
Hierophantasm, *(978-0-9837905)* 190 W. Fifth Ave. P. O. Box 792, Clifton, IL 60927 USA Tel 815-694-0010
E-mail: Andy@hierophantasm.com
Web site: hierophantasm.com.
Hieropub LLC, *(978-0-9727940)* P.O. Box 895, Pottstown, PA 19464 USA Tel 610-705-0282
E-mail: patholl@hieropub.com; pholl@comcast.net
Web site: http://www.hieropub.com; http://www.hatheadbooks.com
Dist(s): **Quality Bks., Inc.**
Higgins, Christine, *(978-0-9975649)* 571 Woodbine Ave., Towson, MD 21204 USA Tel 410-825-6404
E-mail: chriswrite73@comcast.net.
Higgins Publishing, *(978-0-9815202; 978-1-941580)* P.O. Box 99396, Emeryville, CA 94662-9396 USA Fax: 888-481-1738
E-mail: contact@higginspublishing.com
Web site: http://www.higginspublishing.com.
Higginson Bk. Co., *(978-0-7404; 978-0-8328)* 148 Washington St., Salem, MA 01970 USA (SAN 247-9400) Tel 978-745-7170; Fax: 978-745-8025
E-mail: higginsn@cove.com
Web site: http://higginsonbooks.com.
High Desert Productions, *(978-0-9652920)* Orders Addr.: P.O. Box 5506, Bisbee, AZ 85603 USA Tel 520-432-5288; Edit Addr.: 511 Mance St., Bisbee, AZ 85603 USA
Dist(s): **Rio Nuevo Pubs.**
High Five *Imprint of* **Red Brick Learning**
High Five Reading (RBL) *Imprint of* **Capstone Press of Coughlan Cos.**
High Ground Productions, Incorporated *See* **High Ground Pubns.**

Publisher Name Index

High Ground Pubns., *(978-0-9720153)* 80 Supai Dr., Sedona, AZ 86351 USA (SAN 254-5748) Tel 360-945-2485
E-mail: Karen@amatteroftime.org
Web site: http://www.amatteroftime.org.

High Hill Pr., *(978-1-60653)* 2731 Cumberland Landing, Saint Charles, MO 63303 USA (SAN 856-2806) Tel 636-928-2212
E-mail: HighHillPress@aol.com
Web site: http://www.highhillpress.com.

High Hopes Publishing, *(978-0-9708417; 978-0-9905129)* Subs. of Communication Arts Multimedia, Inc., 1618 Williams Dr., Suite No. 5, Georgetown, TX 78628 USA Tel 512-868-0548 (phone/fax); Toll Free: 888-742-0074
E-mail: mail@commartsmultimedia.com
Web site: http://www.highhopespublishing.com.

High Mountain Publishing, *(978-0-9718609)* Bookmasters (high Mountain Pub) 30 Amberwood Pkwy. P.o. Box 388, Ashland, OH 44805 USA Tel 818-645-8621
E-mail: uescher@hotmail.com
Web site: http://www.howtotrick.com.

High Noon Bks., *(978-0-87879; 978-1-57128)* Div. of Academic Therapy Publications, Inc., 20 Leveroni Ct., Novato, CA 94949-5746 USA Tel 415-883-3314; Toll Free: 800-422-7249
E-mail: customerservice@academictheapy.com
Web site: http://www.highnoonbooks.com.

High Standards Publishing, Incorporated *See* **True Exposures Publishing, Inc.**

High Star Pr., *(978-0-9981808)* 217 Teaberry Ln., South Abington Township, PA 18411 USA Tel 570-479-6491
E-mail: cindynoonan49@gmail.com
Web site: cindynoonan.com.

High Tide Pr., *(978-0-9653744; 978-1-892696)* 2081 Calistoga Dr. Ste. 2N, New Lenox, IL 60451-4833 USA Do not confuse with The Trinity Foundation, Hobbs, NM
E-mail: alex@hightidepress.com; mregan@hightidepress.com
Web site: http://www.hightidepress.com.

High Tide Pubns., *(978-0-9884637; 978-0-615-72863-6; 978-0-692-34939-7; 978-0-692-37913-4; 978-0-692-38423-7; 978-0-692-45585-2; 978-0-692-45595-1; 978-0-692-50369-0; 978-0-692-54851-6; 978-0-692-56405-9; 978-0-692-57700-4; 978-0-692-57708-0; 978-0-692-57961-9; 978-0-692-60854-8; 978-0-692-62932-1; 978-0-692-67079-8; 978-0-692-70597-1; 978-0-692-74482-6; 978-1-945990)* *Orders Addr.: 1000 Bland Point Rd, Deltaville, VA 23043 USA Tel 804-776-8478*
E-mail: hightidepublications@yahoo.com
Web site: hightidepublications.com
Dist(s): **CreateSpace Independent Publishing Platform**
Ingram Publisher Services.

Higher Age Pr., *(978-0-9979034)* 5222 Univ. Ave NE, No. 304A, Seattle, WA 98105 USA Tel 425-891-9129
E-mail: hansenjake@hotmail.com
Web site: jakehansennovels.com.

Higher Balance Institute, *(978-0-9759080; 978-1-939410)* 515 NW Saltzman Rd., No.726, Portland, OR 97229 USA Tel 503-646-4000; Toll Free: 800-935-4007
E-mail: publishing@higherbalance.com
Web site: http://www.higherbalance.com.

Higher Ground Pr., *(978-0-9766062; 978-0-9838321)* Orders Addr.: P.O. Box PO 1381, Allen, TX 75013 USA Tel 214-680-9779
E-mail: info@highergroundpress.com
Web site: http://www.highergroundpress.com
Dist(s): **Brigham Distribution.**

Higher Power Publishing, *(978-0-9787631)* 702 Twilight Dr., Garland, TX 75040 USA Tel 214-298-9563
E-mail: higherpowerpublishing@hotmail.com
Web site: http://www.higherpowerpublishing.biz
Dist(s): **Lightning Source, Inc.**

Highest Good Pubns. *Imprint of* **EbonyEnergy Publishing, Inc.**

Highland Children's Pr. *Imprint of* **Heather & Highlands Publishing**

Highland Press *See* **Highland Pr. Publishing**

Highland Pr., *(978-0-910722)* 10108 Johns Rd., Boerne, TX 78006 USA (SAN 204-0522) Do not confuse with companies of the same name or similar in Birmingham, AL, Wilsonville, OR, Tonasket, WA, Bryson City, NC, San Rafael, CA, High Springs, FL.

Highland Pr., *(978-0-9630273)* Div. of The Alabama Booksmith, 5512 Crestwood Blvd., Birmingham, AL 35212-4131 USA (SAN 297-8628) Do not confuse with companies with the same name in Boerne, TX, Wilsonville, OR, Tonasket, WA, Bryson City, NC, San Rafael, CA, High Springs, FL
E-mail: booksmith@mindspring.com.

Highland Pr. Publishing, *(978-0-9746249; 978-0-9787139; 978-0-9800356; 978-0-9815573; 978-0-9818550; 978-0-9823615; 978-0-9842499; 978-0-9833960; 978-0-9846541; 978-0-9850690; 978-0-9895262; 978-0-9916439; 978-1-942606)* Orders Addr.: P.O. Box 2292, High Springs, FL 32655 USA (SAN 851-4275); *Imprints*: Pandora (Pandora) Do not confuse with companies with the same or similar name in Sacramento, CA, Birmingham, AL, Wilsonville, ORBoerne, TX, San Rafael, CA, Bryson City, NC, Tonasket, WA
E-mail: The.Highland.Press@gmail.com; Mickeytl@aol.com
Web site: http://www.highlandpress.org.

Highlight Publishing, *(978-0-9741734)* P.O. Box 27, Little Falls, MN 56345 USA Tel 320-630-1463; Toll Free: 866-336-6681
E-mail: books@highlightpublishing.com
Web site: http://www.highlightpublishing.com.

Highlights *Imprint of* **Boyds Mills Pr.**

Highlights for Children, *(978-0-87534)* Orders Addr.: P.O. Box 269, Columbus, OH 43216-0269 USA (SAN 281-7810) Tel 614-486-0631; Fax: 614-876-8564; Toll Free: 800-255-9517; Edit Addr.: 803 Church St., Honesdale, PA 18431 USA (SAN 281-7802) Tel 570-253-1080; Fax: 570-253-1179
E-mail: eds@highlights.com
Web site: http://www.highlights.com
Dist(s): **Boyds Mills Pr.**
INscribe Digital
Ingram Publisher Services.

Highlights of Chicago Pr., *(978-0-9710487; 978-0-9907771)* 4325 N. Central Park Ave., Chicago, IL 60618 USA Tel 773-509-0008 (phone/fax)
E-mail: bturner@highlightsofchicago.com
Web site: http://www.highlightsofchicago.com.

High-Lonesome Bks., *(978-0-944383)* Orders Addr.: P.O. Box 878, Silver City, NM 88062 USA (SAN 243-3079) Tel 505-388-3763; Fax: 505-388-5705; Toll Free: 800-380-7323 (orders only)
E-mail: Cherie@High-LonesomeBooks.com
Web site: http://www.high-lonesomebooks.com
Dist(s): **Univ. of New Mexico Pr.**

High-Pitched Hum Inc., *(978-0-9759818; 978-0-9777290; 978-0-9787995; 978-0-9792780; 978-1-934666; 978-0-9885818; 978-0-9914847)* 321 15th St., N., Jacksonville Beach, FL 32250 USA
E-mail: breynolds@jettyman.com
Web site: http://www.highpitchedhum.net.

HighPoint Publishing, Inc., *(978-1-933190)* Orders Addr.: 3975 E. Highway 290., Dripping Spgs, TX 78620-4287 USA (SAN 256-2952)
E-mail: kenc@highpointpublishing.com; milena@highpointpublishing.com
Web site: http://www.HighPointPublishing.com.

HighReach Learning, Incorporated *Imprint of* **Carson-Dellosa Publishing, LLC**

†High/Scope Pr., *(978-0-929816; 978-0-931114; 978-1-57379)* Div. of High/Scope Educational Research Foundation, 600 N. River St., Ypsilanti, MI 48198-2898 USA (SAN 211-9617) Tel 734-485-2000; Fax: 734-485-0704; Toll Free Fax: 800-442-4329 (orders); Toll Free: 800-407-7377 (orders only)
E-mail: info@highscope.org
Web site: http://www.highscope.org
Dist(s): **CENGAGE Learning**
Delmar Cengage Learning
Follett School Solutions; *CIP*.

Highsmith Inc., *(978-0-913853; 978-0-917846; 978-1-57950; 978-1-932146; 978-1-59847; 978-1-60213)* P.O. Box 5210, Janesville, WI 53547-5210 USA (SAN 159-8740) Toll Free: 800-448-4887; 401 S. Wright Rd., Janesville, WI 53547 (SAN 858-9674) Toll Free Fax: 800-835-2329; Toll Free: 800-554-4661; *Imprints*: Upstart Books (Upstart Bks)
Web site: http://www.highsmith.com
Dist(s): **Mackin Bk. Co.**

Highsmith Press, LLC *See* **Highsmith Inc.**

Hignites, Tom Miracle Studio, *(978-1-934017)* Orders Addr.: 1977 Mayfield Rd., Richfield, WI 53076-5307 USA (SAN 850-9611) Tel 262-628-5577; Fax: 262-628-5580; Edit Addr.: 3070 Hwy. 145, Richfield, WI 53076-5307 USA
E-mail: jbrown@miracle-homes.com
Web site: http://tomhignitesmiraclestudios.com.

Hilarity Waters Pr., *(978-0-615-49668-9)* 1117 SW 126th St., Oklahoma City, OK 73170 USA Tel 405-990-9891
E-mail: andrews.africabound@gmail.com
Web site: www.hilaritywaterspress.com.

Hildebrand, Betty, *(978-0-9753729)* 116 Rosetta Ct., Springdale, OH 45246 USA
E-mail: deona@bethart.com
Web site: http://www.bethart.com.

Hill & Wang *Imprint of* **Farrar, Straus & Giroux**

Hill, Lawrence Bks. *Imprint of* **Chicago Review Pr., Inc.**

Hill, Napoleon Foundation, *(978-1-880369)* Friends of Napoleon Hill, 19458 S. La Grange Rd., Mokena, IL 60448 USA Tel 847-998-0408; Fax: 847-998-6890; Toll Free Fax: 800-957-9124; Toll Free: 800-957-9114
E-mail: 70543.3377@compuserve.com
Web site: http://www.naphill.org.

Hill Publishing *See* **SunHill Pubs.**

Hill Song Pr., *(978-0-9745159; 978-0-692-29132-0; 978-0-692-41911-3; 978-0-692-68393-4; 978-0-692-82104-6; 978-0-692-88303-7)* Orders Addr.: P.O. Box 486, Lawrence, KS 66044 USA Tel 785-330-3779; Toll Free: 800-266-5564; Edit Addr.: 3807 Hunters Hill Dr., Lawrence, KS 66049 USA
E-mail: tom.mach@yahoo.com
Web site: http://www.hillsongpress.com
Dist(s): **CreateSpace Independent Publishing Platform.**

Hill, Stephanie & Clarissa, *(978-0-9785539)* P.O. Box 13212, Baltimore, MD 21203-3212 USA (SAN 850-9816) Tel 443-838-9426
E-mail: sachedesignsinc@yahoo.com
Web site: http://www.sachedesigns.com.

Hill Street Pr., LLC, *(978-1-892514; 978-1-58818)* P.O. Box 49468, Athens, GA 30604-9468 USA Toll Free: 800-295-0365
E-mail: info@hillstreetpress.com
Web site: http://www.hillstreetpress.com
Dist(s): **Gibbs Smith, Publisher**
Beeler, Thomas T. Pub.

Hillegass, Anette, *(978-0-692-80034-8; 978-0-692-81058-3)*.

Hillrow Editions, *(978-0-9897958)* 150 Spreading Oak Dr., Scotts Valley, CA 95066 USA Tel 831-439-9888
E-mail: chriz9@yahoo.com.

Hillside Education, *(978-0-9766386; 978-0-9798469; 978-0-9831800; 978-0-9885106; 978-0-9906720; 978-0-9969986; 978-0-9976647; 978-0-9991706)* 475 Bidwell Hill Rd., Lake Ariel, PA 18436 USA (SAN 257-4446)
E-mail: info@hillsideeducation.com; sales@hillsideeducation.com
Web site: http://www.hillsideeducation.com.

Hillside Pr., *(978-0-9627530)* Affil. of Ridgetop Pr., 280 E. Birch Hill Rd., Fairbanks, AK 99712 USA Tel 907-457-7834; Fax: 907-457-7835; Toll Free: 800-390-8999 Do not confuse with companies with the same name in Los Angeles, CA, Carversville, PA, Vista, CA, Collegeville, PA, Wolcott, CT
E-mail: jhaigh@polarnet.com
Web site: http://www2.polarnet.com/~jhaigh/
Dist(s): **News Group, The**
Partners/West Book Distributors
Todd Communications.

Hillside Pr., *(978-0-9815895)* P.O. Box 241, Midway, FL 32343 USA
E-mail: ljhill@hillsidepress.net
Web site: http://www.hillsidepress.net
Dist(s): **Two Rivers Distribution.**

Hilton Publishing *See* **Hilton Publishing Co.**

Hilton Publishing Co., *(978-0-9654553; 978-0-9675258; 978-0-9716067; 978-0-9743144; 978-0-9764443; 978-0-9773160; 978-0-9777779; 978-0-9800649; 978-0-9815381; 978-0-9841447; 978-0-9847566; 978-0-9904283; 978-0-9983282)* Orders Addr.: 1630 45th Ave. Ste. 103, Munster, IN 46321-3959 USA Toll Free: 866-455-1070
E-mail: info@hiltonpub.com
Web site: http://www.hiltonpub.com
Dist(s): **Independent Pubs. Group**
SCB Distributors.

Himminbjorg Publishing, Inc., *(978-0-9749416)* P.O. Box 6493, Napa, CA 94581 USA Tel 707-251-9526 (phone/fax)
E-mail: himminbjorg@aol.com
Web site: http://www.wyrdsway.com.

Hines, Jerry, *(978-0-615-17723-6)* 2660 Suzanne Cir., White Bear Lake, MN 55110 USA
E-mail: jerryhines@comcast.net
Dist(s): **Lulu Pr., Inc.**

Hinman, Bobbie E. Incorporated *See* **Best Fairy Bks.**

Hinman Publishing, *(978-0-9723525)* 2943 Breakwater Way, Longmont, CO 80503 USA
E-mail: jshinman@earthlink.net.

Hinson, Rebecca Publishing, *(978-1-938360; 978-1-942765; 978-1-947623)* Orders Addr.: 818 N. Palmway, Lake Worth, FL 33460 USA Tel 561-267-5756
E-mail: rebeccahinson@bellsouth.net
Dist(s): **Follett School Solutions.**

Hinterland Sky Pr., *(978-0-9818880)* 37 W. Black Oak Dr., Asheville, NC 28804-1809 USA
E-mail: frances.ruiz@gmail.com
Web site: http://www.hinterlandsky.com.

HinterWelt Enterprises, LLC, *(978-0-9740096)* 7504 W. Hickory Creek Dr., Frankfort, IL 60423-9094 USA
E-mail: winna@hinterwelt.com
Web site: http://www.hinterwelt.com.

Hip Hop Schl. Hse., *(978-0-9768674)* 8618 S. Constance, Chicago, IL 60617 USA Tel 793-218-4204.

Hippocratic Pr., The, *(978-0-9753516)* 281A Fairhaven Hill Rd., Concord, MA 01742 USA Tel 978-369-0739
E-mail: ccowanmd@hippocraticpress.com
Web site: http://www.hippocraticpress.com.

†Hippocrene Bks., Inc., *(978-0-7818; 978-0-87052; 978-0-88254)* 171 Madison Ave., New York, NY 10016-1002 USA (SAN 213-2060) Tel 718-454-2366 (sales); 212-685-4371 (editorial); Fax: 718-454-1391 (sales/order inquiry); 212-779-9338 (editorial)
E-mail: hippocre@ix.netcom.com
Web site: http://www.hippocrenebooks.com
Dist(s): **Continental Bk. Co., Inc.**
Ingram Publisher Services
Two Rivers Distribution; *CIP*.

Hired Pen, Inc., The *See* **Acacia Publishing, Inc.**

His Feast Publishing, *(978-0-9677722)* Div. of Feast of Tabernacles Ministries, P.O. Box 444, Forest Lake, MN 55025 USA
E-mail: Hisfeast@aol.com.

His Grace Is Sufficient *Imprint of* **ELW Pubns.**

His Hands, Inc., *(978-0-9720881)* Orders Addr.: P.O. Box 7063, Oak Ridge, TN 37831 USA Tel 865-482-9562; Edit Addr.: 82 E. Tennesse Ave., Apt. 117, Oak Ridge, TN 37830 USA (SAN 255-2930) Tel 865-482-9562
E-mail: hishandstn@netzero.com
Web site: http://www.hishands.org.

His Kids Publishing, Inc., *(978-0-9720417)* Orders Addr.: P.O. Box 72172, Marietta, GA 30007 USA Tel 770-998-3240; Fax: 770-998-4943; Edit Addr.: 1544 Sandpoint Dr., Roswell, GA 30075 USA
E-mail: management@intrag-publishing.com
Web site: http://www.intrag-publishing.com.

H.I.S. Publishing LLC *See* **Heard Word Publishing, LLC**

His Sonshine, Inc., *(978-0-9758880)* 13214 Barwick Rd., Del Ray Beach, FL 33445 USA.

His Story, *(978-0-9766951)* 1409 Coolhurst, Sherwood, AR 72120 USA
Web site: http://www.hisstory.org.

His Work Christian Publishing, *(978-0-9778328; 978-0-9798290; 978-0-9799189; 978-0-615-43443-8; 978-0-9854469)* Div. of His Work Christian Ministries, Orders Addr.: P.O. Box 563, Ward Cove, AK 99928 USA Tel 206-274-8474; Fax: 614-388-0664
E-mail: hiswork@hisworkpub.com; editor@hisworkpub.com
Web site: http://www.hisworkpub.com
Dist(s): **Lightning Source, Inc.**

Hispanic Institute of Social Issues, *(978-0-9771167; 978-0-9797814; 978-1-936885)* P.O. Box 50553, Mesa, AZ 85208-0028 USA
Web site: http://www.hisi.org.

Historic Mint Co., The, *(978-0-9753767)* 36 Sandwedge Dr., Henderson, NV 89074-1714 USA Toll Free: 877-264-6266
Web site: http://www.historicmint.com.

Historic Philadelphia, Inc., *(978-0-9855319)* 150 S. Independence Mall, W. Suite 550, Philadelphia, PA 19106 USA Tel 215-629-5801
E-mail: debiflora@about-books.com; msdarlaf@gmail.com
Web site: http://www.historicphiladelphia.org.

Historic Pr.-South, *(978-0-9645990)* Orders Addr.: P.O. Box 407, Gatlinburg, TN 37738 USA Tel 423-436-4163; Toll Free: 800-279-2603; Edit Addr.: 367 Buckhorn Rd., Gatlinburg, TN 37738 USA.

Historic Tours of America, Inc., *(978-0-9752698)* 201 Front St., Suite 224, Key West, FL 33040 USA Tel 305-292-8920; Fax: 305-295-4999
E-mail: psmith@historictours.com
Web site: http://www.historictours.com.

Historical Pages Company *See* **Birch Island**

Historical Society of Western Pennsylvania, *(978-0-936340)* 1212 Smallman St., Pittsburgh, PA 15222-4208 USA (SAN 214-0276)
E-mail: babutko@heinzhistorycenter.org
Web site: http://www.einzhistorycenter.org.

History Compass, LLC, *(978-1-57960; 978-1-878668; 978-1-932663)* 25 Leslie Rd., Auburndale, MA 02466 USA (SAN 297-2611) Tel 617-332-2202; Fax: 617-332-2210
E-mail: info@historycompass.com; lisa@historycompass.com
Web site: http://www.historycompass.com
Dist(s): **Follett School Solutions**
Ingram Publisher Services
Social Studies Schl. Service.

History Factory, *(978-1-882771)* 14140 Parke Long Ct., Suite G, Chantilly, VA 20151 USA Tel 703-631-0500; Fax: 703-631-1124
E-mail: jburkitt@historyfactory.com; info@historyfactory.com; mgaffney@historyfactory.com.

History Jukebox, LLC, *(978-0-9791118)* P.O. Box 467, Marshall, MI 49068 USA Tel 269-781-8357; Fax: 269-781-8760; Toll Free: 866-977-7664
E-mail: info@historyjukebox.org
Web site: http://www.historyjukebox.org.

History Pr. Ltd., The (GBR) *(978-0-7509; 978-0-7524; 978-0-86299; 978-0-904387; 978-1-84015)* *Dist. by* **IPG Chicago.**

History Pr., The *Imprint of* **Arcadia Publishing**

Hit Records, LLC, *(978-0-9816719)* P.O. Box 8702, Canton, OH 44711 USA
E-mail: svitale@hitrecordsusa.com
Web site: http://www.hitrecordsusa.com.

Hi-Tech Software, *(978-1-928618; 978-1-936735)* 10 Little Tarn Ct., Hamburg, NJ 07419-1262 USA
E-mail: harry@htsoftware.com
Web site: http://www.htsoftware.com.

Hither Creek Pr., *(978-0-9700555)* 14 Holman St., Laconia, NH 03246-3016 USA Do not confuse with Hither Creek Press in Nantucket, MA
E-mail: hithercreekpress@aol.com.

Hi-Time Pflaum *See* **Pflaum Publishing Group**

Hive Collective, *(978-0-9884774)* 30 Shelburne Rd., Merrimack, NH 03054 USA Tel 603-423-1071
E-mail: stan@findtheaxis.com
Web site: http://hiveauthors.wordpress.com.

HK Comics Ltd. (HKG) *(978-962-85278; 978-988-98437; 978-988-97972)* *Dist. by* **Diamond Book Dists.**

HM Bks., *(978-0-9796476; 978-0-9820126)* Div. of HM Entertainment Inc.,
E-mail: meja_mwangi@yahoo.com; mejamwangi@yahoo.com
Web site: http://www.mejamwangi.com; http://www.skylineafrica.com.

HMH Books For Young Readers *Imprint of* **Houghton Mifflin Harcourt Publishing Co.**

HMSI, Inc., *(978-0-615-29442-1; 978-0-9842662; 978-0-9826945; 978-0-9851996)* 50768 Van Buren Dr., Plymouth, MI 48170 USA
Web site: http://www.PublishHMSI.com.

HNB Publishing, *(978-0-9664286; 978-0-9728061; 978-0-9828874)* Orders Addr.: 250 W. 78th St., No. 3FF, New York, NY 10024 USA Tel 212-873-5382; 347-260-1376
E-mail: sales@hnbpub.com
Web site: http://www.hnbpub.com.

Hoard, W.D. & Sons Co., *(978-0-932147; 978-0-9960753)* P.O. Box 801, Fort Atkinson, WI 53538-0801 USA (SAN 686-4341) Tel 920-563-5551; Fax: 920-563-7298; *Imprints*: Hoard's Dairyman (Hoards Dairyman)
Web site: http://www.hoards.com.

Hoard's Dairyman *Imprint of* **Hoard, W.D. & Sons Co.**

Hobar Pubns., *(978-0-89317; 978-0-913163; 978-0-933855; 978-0-9616847; 978-1-55797)* Div. of Finney Co., Orders Addr.: 8075 215th St. W., Lakeville, MN 55044 USA (SAN 283-1120) Tel 952-469-6699; Fax: 952-469-1968; Toll Free Fax: 800-330-6232; Toll Free: 800-846-7027
E-mail: feedback@finneyco.com
Web site: http://www.finney-hobar.com
Dist(s): **Book Wholesalers, Inc.**
Brodart Co.
Follett School Solutions
Midpoint Trade Bks., Inc.
Southern Bk. Service.

Hobbes End Publishing, LLC, *(978-0-9763510; 978-0-9859110)* Div. of Hobbes End Entertainment, P.O. Box 193, Aubrey, TX 76227 USA
Web site: http://www.hobbesendpublishing.com
Dist(s): **Smashwords.**

Hobblebush Bks., *(978-0-9636413; 978-0-9760896; 978-0-9801672; 978-0-9845921; 978-1-939449)* 17-a Old Milford Rd., Brookline, NH 03033 USA
E-mail: hobblebush@charter.net; amy.hobblebush@charter.net
Web site: http://www.Hobblebush.com; www.poorrichardslament.com
Dist(s): **Distributors, The**
SPD-Small Pr. Distribution.

Hobbs, Brenda F., *(978-0-9772970)* 14303 Greenview Rd., Detroit, MI 48223 USA
E-mail: bhobbs101@aol.com.

Hobbs, Constance (GBR) *(978-0-9556783)* *Dist. by* **LuluCom.**

Hobby Horse Publishing, LLC, *(978-0-615-89154-5)* P.O. Box 22, Peterborough, NH 03458 USA Tel 555-555-5555
E-mail: info@hobbyhorsepublishing.com
Web site: www.HobbyHorsePublishing.com.

Hobby Hse. Publishing Group, *(978-0-9727179)* Orders Addr.: 48 Hickory Hill Rd., Box 1527, Jackson, NJ 08527 USA
Web site: http://www.hobbyhousepublishinggroup.com.

Hocus Pocus Publishing, Inc., *(978-0-9855544; 978-0-9910276; 978-1-942840)* 32730 Whimbret Way, Spanish Fort, AL 36527 USA Tel 251-454-8117
E-mail: nicholasroussos@gmail.com; cynthia@cynthiaeden.com
Web site: www.hocuspocuspublishing.com; www.cynthiaeden.com.

Hodder & Stoughton (GBR) *(978-0-245; 978-0-340; 978-0-550; 978-0-7131; 978-0-7195; 978-1-85998; 978-1-84032; 978-1-84456; 978-1-84854; 978-1-4447; 978-1-4736)* *Dist. by* **Trafalgar.**

Hodder & Stoughton (GBR) *(978-0-245; 978-0-340; 978-0-550; 978-0-7131; 978-0-7195; 978-1-85998; 978-1-84032; 978-1-84456; 978-1-84854; 978-1-4447; 978-1-4736)* *Dist. by* **HachBkGrp.**

Hodder Education Group (GBR) *(978-0-340; 978-0-412; 978-0-450; 978-0-7122; 978-0-7131; 978-0-7506; 978-0-85264; 978-0-947054; 978-0-86003; 978-1-874958; 978-1-902984; 978-1-4441; 978-1-905735; 978-1-4718)* *Dist. by* **OUP.**

Hodder Education Group (GBR) *(978-0-340; 978-0-412; 978-0-450; 978-0-7122; 978-0-7131; 978-0-7506; 978-0-85264; 978-0-947054; 978-0-86003; 978-1-874958; 978-1-902984; 978-1-4441; 978-1-905735; 978-1-4718)* *Dist. by* **Trans-Atl Phila.**

Hodder Education Group (GBR) *(978-0-340; 978-0-412; 978-0-450; 978-0-7122; 978-0-7131; 978-0-7506; 978-0-85264; 978-0-947054; 978-0-86003; 978-1-874958; 978-1-902984; 978-1-4441; 978-1-905735; 978-1-4718)* *Dist. by* **IngramPubServ.**

Hoffman, Mark *See* **Hramiec Hoffman Publishing**

Hoffmann Partnership, The, *(978-0-9753106)* 349 Martin Ln., Bloomingdale, IL 60108-1326 USA
E-mail: Catherine@WriteHappy.com; info@writehappy.com
Web site: http://www.writehappy.com
Dist(s): **Publishers' Graphics, L.L.C.**

Hogan Publishing LLC, *(978-0-9779504)* 2708 E. Edison, Tucson, AZ 85716 USA
E-mail: benjamin@madseadog.com
Web site: http://www.madseadog.com.

Hogs Back Bks. (GBR) *(978-1-907432)* *Dist. by* **IPG Chicago.**

Hohm Pr., *(978-0-934252; 978-1-890772; 978-1-935387)* Div. of Hohm, Inc., P.O. Box 2501, Prescott, AZ 86302 USA (SAN 221-0924) Tel 520-778-9189; Fax: 520-717-1779; Toll Free: 800-381-2700 (orders only)
E-mail: staff@hohmpress.com; pinedr@goodnet.com; hpproduction@cableone.net
Web site: http://www.hohmpress.com
Dist(s): **SCB Distributors.**

Holberton, Paul Publishing (GBR) *(978-1-903470; 978-1-907372)* *Dist. by* **Casemate Pubs.**

Holbrook Studios, *(978-0-9762440)* Orders Addr.: P.O. Box 3064, Beverly Hills, CA 90212 USA; Edit Addr.: 754 E. S. Temple, Salt Lake city, UT 84102 USA.

Hole's Greenhouses & Gardens, Ltd. (CAN) *(978-0-9682791; 978-1-894728)* *Dist. by* **Lone Pine.**

Holes In My Socks Publishing, *(978-0-9771891)* P.O. Box 266, Paola, KS 66071 USA Tel 913-557-4508
E-mail: stephgun2@aol.com; christydreiling@att.net.

†Holiday Hse., Inc., *(978-0-8234)* Orders Addr.: 425 Madison Ave., New York, NY 10017 USA (SAN 202-3008) Tel 212-688-0085; Fax: 212-688-0395
E-mail: holiday@holidayhouse.com
Web site: http://www.holidayhouse.com
Dist(s): **MyiLibrary**
Open Road Integrated Media, Inc.; *CIP.*

Holiness.com, *(978-0-9743831)* 1271 Washington Ave., PMB 165, San Leandro, CA 94577 USA Tel 510-384-8082
E-mail: suppliers@holiness.com
Web site: http://www.holiness.com.

Holism Publishing, *(978-0-9818297)* Orders Addr.: P.O. Box 3385, Palm Beach, FL 33480-1585 USA Tel 561-533-7704 (phone/fax)
E-mail: curecare@bellsouth.net; info@holismpublishing.com
Web site: http://www.HolismPublishing.com; http://www.HolismMovement.com
Dist(s): **New Leaf Distributing Co., Inc.**

Holland Brown, *(978-0-9797006; 978-0-9897544)* 2509 Portland Ave The Anchor Bldg., Louisville, KY 40202-1008 USA
E-mail: stephanie@thegreenbuilding.com
Web site: http://www.hollandbrownbooks.com.

Holland, Gretchen, *(978-0-9768340)* 4437 Craig Dr., Fort Collins, CO 80526 USA Tel 970-282-1338.

Hollandays Publishing Corp., *(978-0-9708224; 978-0-9728844; 978-0-9753239; 978-0-9769459; 978-0-9799003)* 8459 N. Main St. Ste. 118, Dayton, OH 45415-1324 USA Toll Free: 800-792-3537
E-mail: zhensler@hollandays.net
Web site: http://www.hollandays.net
Dist(s): **Partners Bk. Distributing, Inc.**

Hollar, Cheryl Public Relations, *(978-0-9763826)* Orders Addr.: 218 S. Cheatham St., Franklinton, NC 27525 USA Tel 919-494-2150
E-mail: cherylfhollar@yahoo.com; billythebunnybooks@yahoo.com.

Hollingale Bks. LLC, *(978-0-9907895)* 55 N. Merchant St. No. 1481, American Fork, UT 84003 USA Tel 801-855-6448
E-mail: paige@hollingale.com
Web site: www.hollingale.com.

Hollingsworth, Kenneth, *(978-0-9771572)* 2215 Janet Ct., Cedar Hill, TX 75104-1021 USA (SAN 256-8926)
Web site: http://www.hollingsworthtexas.com/plantingtheseeds.

Hollow Mountain Publishing LLC, *(978-0-9981676)* 2266 Possum Hollow Dr, Camdenton, MO 65020 USA Tel 573-207-0699
E-mail: diannakilpack@outlook.com.

Holly Hall Pubns., Inc., *(978-0-9645396; 978-1-888306)* P.O. Box 254, Elkton, MD 21922-0254 USA Tel 410-392-2300; Fax: 410-620-9877; Toll Free: 800-211-0719; *Imprints:* Full Quart Press (Full Quart Pr)
Dist(s): **Spring Arbor Distributors, Inc.**

HollyBear Pr., *(978-0-9651067)* Orders Addr.: P.O. Box 4257, Prescott, AZ 86302-4257 USA Tel 928-776-4689; Edit Addr.: 910 Stevens Dr., Prescott, AZ 86305 USA
E-mail: monamc2@msn.com.

Hollygrove Publishing, Inc., *(978-0-9777939; 978-0-9840904)* 4100 W. Eldorado Pkwy., Suite 100-182, McKinney, TX 75070 USA (SAN 850-170X) Tel 972-837-6191
E-mail: bsmith@hollygrovepublishing.com
Web site: http://www.hollygrovepublishing.com.

Hollym International Corp., *(978-0-930878; 978-1-56591)* Orders Addr.: 2647 Gateway Rd. No. 105-223, Carlsbad, CA 92009 USA Tel 760-539-9880; Edit Addr.: 2647 Gateway Rd. No. 105-223, Carlbad, CA 92009 USA (SAN 211-0172) Tel 760-814-9880; Fax: 908-353-0255 Do not confuse with Hollym Corporation Pubs., New York, NY
E-mail: gracepresa@gmail.com; contact@hollym.com
Web site: http://www.hollym.com.

Hollywood Jesus Bks., *(978-0-9759577; 978-0-9787554)* P.O. Box 48282, Burien, WA 98166 USA Tel 206-241-6149
E-mail: editor@hjbooks.com
Web site: http://www.hjbooks.com.

Hollywood Operating System, *(978-1-893899)* 3108 W. Magnolia Blvd., Burbank, CA 91505-3045 USA
E-mail: hollywoodos@aol.com
Web site: http://www.HollywoodOS.com.

HollywoodComics.com, LLC, *(978-0-9740711; 978-1-932983; 978-1-934543; 978-1-935558; 978-1-61227)* P.O. Box 17270, Encino, CA 91416 USA (SAN 255-366X) Tel 818-995-7733; *Imprints:* Black Coat Press (Black Coat Pr)
E-mail: info@hollywoodcomics.com; info@riviereblanche.com; jean-marc@hollywoodcomics.com; info@blackcoatpress.com
Web site: http://www.hexagoncomics.com; http://www.blackcoatpress.com; http://www.riviereblanche.com.

Holman, Doris Anne, *(978-0-9667192; 978-0-9758630)* 5 Oak Ledge Rd., Harpswell, ME 04079 USA.

Holmes Bookshop *Imprint of* **Belle Lumiere True News**

Holmes Investments & Holdings LLC, *(978-0-9962102; 978-0-9992369)* P.O. Box 1021, Lakewood, CA 90714 USA Tel 562-472-8202
E-mail: quentinholmes@hotmail.com
Web site: www.quentinholmes.com
Dist(s): **Lightning Source, Inc.**

Holocaust Museum Houston, *(978-0-9659781; 978-0-9773988)* 5401 Caroline St., Houston, TX 77004-6804 USA Tel 713-942-8000; Fax: 713-942-7953
E-mail: info@hmh.org
Web site: http://www.hmh.org
Dist(s): **Hervey's Booklink & Cookbook Warehouse.**

Holocaust Survivors' Memoirs Project, *(978-0-9760739; 978-0-9814686)* c/o World Jewish Congress, 633 Third Ave., Flr. 21, New York, NY 10017 USA Fax: 212-318-6176
E-mail: survivorsmemoirs@aol.com.

Holofcener, Mark, *(978-0-9718626)* 7323 Island Cir., Boulder, CO 80301-3905 USA
E-mail: mark@evansadventure.com
Web site: http://www.evansadventure.com.

Holography Sells, *(978-0-9741087)* 1305 Kirks Ln., Dresher, PA 19025 USA (SAN 255-3627)
E-mail: sales@snookybook.com
Web site: http://www.snookybook.com.

Holt Enterprise, LLC, *(978-0-9740016)* Orders Addr.: P.O. Box 414, Riverside, NJ 08075 USA (SAN 255-2760) Tel 856-764-7043; Fax: 856-764-0851; Toll Free: 888-944-4658; Edit Addr.: 147 N. Fairview St., Riverside, NJ 08075 USA
E-mail: HoltEnterprise@comcast.net; holt109@comcast.net
Dist(s): **Quality Bks., Inc.**

Holt, Henry & Co. Bks. For Young Readers *Imprint of* **Holt, Henry & Co.**

†Holt, Henry & Co., *(978-0-03; 978-0-8050)* Div. of Holtzbrinck Publishers, Orders Addr.: 16365 James Madison Hwy., Gordonsville, VA 22942-8501 USA Toll Free Fax: 800-672-2054; Toll Free: 888-330-8477; Edit Addr.: 115 W. 18th St., 5th Flr., New York, NY 10011 USA (SAN 200-6472) Tel 212-886-9200; Fax: 540-672-7540 (customer service); *Imprints:* Metropolitan Books (Metropol Bks); Times Books (Times Bks); Holt, Henry & Company Books For Young Readers (HH Bks Yng Read); Holt Paperback (Holt Paperbck)
E-mail: info@hholt.com
Web site: http://www.henryholt.com
Dist(s): **Giron Bks.**
Lectorum Pubns., Inc.
Macmillan
Perfection Learning Corp.
Weston Woods Studios, Inc.; *CIP.*

Holt, Max Media., *(978-0-9966104; 978-1-944537)* 303 Casacabel Pl, Mt Juliet, TN 37122 USA Tel 731-819-4241
E-mail: sandymaxholt@yahoo.com
Web site: www.maxholtmedia.com.

Holt McDougal, *(978-0-395; 978-0-8123; 978-0-86609; 978-0-88343; 978-0-618)* Subs. of Houghton Mifflin Harcourt Publishing Co., Orders Addr.: 1900 S. Batavia Ave., Geneva, IL 60134 USA Toll Free: 888-872-8380; Edit Addr.: P.O. Box 1667, Evanston, IL 60204 USA (SAN 202-2532) Toll Free: 800-323-5435; 800-462-6595 (customer service); 909 Davis St., Evanston, IL 60201 Tel 847-869-2300; Fax: 847-869-0841
Web site: http://www.mcdougallittell.com.

Holt Paperback *Imprint of* **Holt, Henry & Co.**

Holtz Creative Enterprises, *(978-0-9817247; 978-0-9837617)* 3103 Terry Ln., Eau Claire, WI 54703 USA Tel 715-835-2705
E-mail: holtzenterprises@sbcglobal.net.

Holtzbrinck Publishers *See* **Macmillan**

Holy Heroes LLC, *(978-0-9801121; 978-1-936330)* 728 Hanna Woods, Cramerton, NC 28032 USA (SAN 855-2401)
E-mail: kandkdavison@bellsouth.net
Web site: http://www.holyheroes.com.

Holy Macro! Bks. *Imprint of* **Tickling Keys, Inc.**

Holzwarth Pubns. (DEU) *(978-3-935567; 978-3-00)* *Dist. by* **Dist Art Pubs.**

Homa & Sekey Bks., *(978-0-9665421; 978-1-931907; 978-1-62246)* 3rd Floor, North Tower Mack-Cali Center III 140 East Ridgewood Ave, Paramus, NJ 07652 USA Tel 800-870-HOMA (4662) (Orders only); 201-261-8810; Fax: 201-261-8890
E-mail: info@homabooks.com
Web site: http://www.homabooks.com.

Homagno Group, Incorporated *See* **Editorial Homagno**

Home Box Office, Inc., *(978-0-910765; 978-0-9828167)* 1100 Sixth Ave., New York, NY 10036 USA (SAN 260-2032) Tel 212-512-1000.

Home Discipleship Pr., *(978-0-9753133; 978-0-9785678)* 6645 W. Steger Rd., Monee, IL 60449 USA Tel 708-235-1901; Fax: 708-235-1904
E-mail: leaders@homediscipleship.orf
Web site: http://www.homediscipleshippress.org.

Home Planet Bks., *(978-0-9743712; 978-0-9887978)* 2300 8th St., Olivenhain, CA 92024-6565 USA Tel 760-634-4947
E-mail: sales@homeplanetbooks.com.

Home Sales Enhancements *See* **Castlebrook Pubns.**

Home Schl. in the Woods, *(978-0-9720265; 978-0-9815523; 978-0-9842041; 978-0-9913678)* 3997 Roosevelt Hwy., Holley, NY 14470 USA Tel 585-964-8188
E-mail: eduardoopak@yahoo.com
Web site: http://www.homeschoolinthewoods.com.

Homebound Pubns., *(978-1-938846; 978-1-947003)* P.O. Box 1442, Pawcatuck, CT 06379 USA Tel 860-599-8761
E-mail: lmbrowning@homeboundpublications.com; orders@homeboundpublications.com; info@homeboundpublications.com
Web site: http://homeboundpublications.com
Dist(s): **Midpoint Trade Bks., Inc.**

Homegrown Pubns.,LLC, *(978-0-9799635)* P.O. Box 173, Red Wing, MN 55066 USA
Web site: http://www.homegrownpublications.com.

Homelight Pr., *(978-0-9749936)* P.O. Box 1901, Huntersville, NC 28070-1901 USA Toll Free: 877-438-6657
E-mail: homeligh@bellsouth.net.

Homer Historical Society, *(978-0-9770022)* 107 N. Main St., Homer, IL 61849 USA Tel 217-896-2549.

Homes for the Homeless Institute, Inc., *(978-0-9641784; 978-0-9724425; 978-0-9825533)* 50 Cooper Sq. Flr. 4, New York, NY 10003-7144 USA; *Imprints:* White Tiger Press (Wht Tiger Pr)
E-mail: info@icphusa.org
Web site: www.icphusa.org; www.whitetigerpress.org.

HomeScholar Bks., *(978-0-9754934)* 2311 Harrison Rd., Nashville, NC 27856 USA Tel 252-459-9279; *Imprints:* Literary Lessons (LitLessons)
Web site: http://www.homescholarbooks.com.

Homeschool Journey, *(978-0-9762918; 978-0-9825006)* 4625 Devon, Lisle, IL 60532 USA Tel 630-277-6200
E-mail: homeschooljourney@gmail.com
Web site: http://www.homeschooljourney.com.

Homespun Video, P.O. Box 340, Woodstock, NY 12498 USA Tel 914-246-2550; Fax: 914-246-5282; Toll Free: 800-338-2737
E-mail: hmspn@aol.com
Web site: http://www.homespuntapes.com
Dist(s): **Follett Media Distribution**
Leonard, Hal Corp.

Homestead Publishing, *(978-0-943972)* 4388 17th St., San Francisco, CA 94114 USA (SAN 241-029X) Tel 415-621-5039
E-mail: info@homesteadpublishing.net
Web site: http://homesteadpublishing.net; http://www.homesteadpublishing.net.

Honey Locust Pr. *Imprint of* **Wolfmont, LLC**

Honeycomb Adventures Pr., LLC, *(978-0-9820886; 978-0-9836808)* P.O. Box 1215, Hemingway, SC 29554 USA Tel 843-558-0133
E-mail: queenbjan@sc.rr.com
Web site: http://honeycombadventures.com
Dist(s): **Lightning Source, Inc.**

Honeysuckle Acres, *(978-0-9963033)* 146 Rockfish Run Rd., Scottsville, VA 24590 USA Tel 434-566-6675
E-mail: kayepearse@gmail.com.

Honno Welsh Women's Pr. (GBR) *(978-1-870206; 978-1-906784; 978-1-909983)* *Dist. by* **IPG Chicago.**

Honorable Pr., *(978-0-9719727)* 2432 Wilshire Ct., Decatur, GA 30035 USA.

HonorNet, *(978-0-9753036; 978-0-9788726; 978-0-9820590; 978-1-938021)* P.O. Box 910, Sapulpa, OK 74067 USA
E-mail: mail@honornet.net
Web site: http://honornet.net
Dist(s): **Destiny Image Pubs.**

Hood, Alan C. & Co., Inc., *(978-0-911469)* P.O. Box 775, Chambersburg, PA 17201 USA (SAN 270-8221) Tel 717-267-0867; Fax: 717-267-0572; Toll Free Fax: 888-844-9433; 4501 Forbes Blvd., Lanham, MD 20706
E-mail: hoodbooks@pa.net
Web site: http://www.hoodbooks.com
Dist(s): **Follett School Solutions.**

Hood, Ted *See* **Four Seasons Publishing**

Hooker, Lou, *(978-0-9755106)* 6900 Chamberlain, Fremont, MI 49412 USA Tel 231-924-3555
E-mail: lvhook@ncats.net.

Hoopoe Bks. *Imprint of* **I S H K**

Hoot N' Cackle Pr., *(978-0-9659381)* 1928 S. Mayfair, Springfield, MO 65804 USA Tel 417-887-0837; Fax: 417-886-3994
E-mail: rlipe@usipp.net
Web site: http://www.mowrites4kids.drury.edu/authors/lipe/.

Hoots, Dani, *(978-1-942023)* P.O. Box 329, Jefferson, OR 97352 USA Tel 503-689-0100
E-mail: danimariehoots@yahoo.com.

Hoover, Linda, *(978-0-9981806)* 3050 Craig Rd, Springfield, OH 45502 USA Tel 397-631-1566
E-mail: lhoover2@Hotmail.com.

HOP, LLC, *(978-1-887942; 978-1-931020; 978-1-933863; 978-1-60143; 978-1-60242; 978-1-60498; 978-1-60499)* Educate, Inc., 1407 Fleet St. Flr. 1, Baltimore, MD 21231-2859 USA
Web site: http://www.hookedonphonics.com
Dist(s): **Simon & Schuster, Inc.**

Hope Chest Legacy, Inc., *(978-1-59565)* P.O. Box 1398, Littlerock, CA 93543 USA Toll Free: 888-554-7292
E-mail: hopechestlegacy@gmail.com
Web site: http://hopechestlegacy.com.

Hope Farm Pr. & Bookshop, *(978-0-910746)* 15 Jane St., Saugerties, NY 12477-1511 USA (SAN 204-0697) Toll Free: 800-883-5778 (orders)
E-mail: hopefarm@hopefarm.com
Web site: http://www.hopefarm.com; http://www.hopefarmbooks.com
Dist(s): **North Country Bks., Inc.**

Hope for Families, Inc., *(978-0-9676489)* P.O. Box 238, Hatfield, PA 19440 USA Tel 215-280-5369
E-mail: ibmbam@fast.net.

Hope Harvest Ministries *See* **Hope Harvest Publishing**

Hope Harvest Publishing, *(978-0-9716523; 978-0-9763695; 978-0-9771318; 978-0-9779898)* Div. of H&H Bindery & Distribution Centre, P.O. Box 8353, Kentwood, MI 49518 USA Tel 616-307-3080; Fax: 616-458-8991
E-mail: hopeharvest@comcast.net
Web site: http://www.hopeharvest.com; http://www.blessly.com
Dist(s): **Anchor Distributors**
Anderson Merchandisers
H & H Distribution
Spirit Filled Pr., Inc.
Spring Arbor Distributors, Inc.

Hope International Printshop, *(978-0-9748096)* Orders Addr.: P.O. Box 1182, Hobe Sound, FL 33475 USA; Edit Addr.: 8436 SE Bayberry Terr., Hobe Sound, FL 33475 USA.

Hope of Vision Publishing, *(978-0-9753795; 978-0-9818253; 978-0-9831371; 978-0-9837082; 978-0-9852746; 978-0-9884773; 978-0-9912483; 978-1-942871)* 43 Yale St., Bridgeport, CT 06605 USA (SAN 856-6410) Tel 203-338-1301; Fax: 203-413-1593
Web site: http://www.hopeofvisionpublishing.com.

Hope Pr., *(978-1-878267)* Orders Addr.: P.O. Box 188, Duarte, CA 91009-0188 USA (SAN 200-3244) Tel 626-303-0644; Fax: 626-358-3520; Toll Free: 800-321-4039; Edit Addr.: 1110 Mill Run, Monvaia, CA 91016 USA Tel 626-303-0644 Do not confuse with Hope Pr., Pittsville, WI
E-mail: hoepress@earthink.net; dcomings@earthlink.net
Web site: http://www.hopepress.com; http://www.didmancreategod.com.

Hope Rekindled Pr. *See* **Risen Heart Pr.**

Hopecopious Productions, *(978-0-9982922)* 1720 SW 346th Pl, Federal Way, WA 98023 USA Tel 253-927-9279; Fax: 253-927-9279
E-mail: Connect@Hopecopious.com
Web site: Hopecopious.com.

HopeRoad Publishing Ltd (GBR) *(978-1-908446)* *Dist. by* **Consort Bk Sales.**

Hopewell Pubns., LLC, *(978-0-9726906; 978-1-933435)* P.O. Box 11, Titusville, NJ 08560-0011 USA Tel 609-818-1049; Fax: 609-964-1718 Do not confuse with companies with the same or similar name in Longmont, CO, Austin, TX, Springdale, AZ
E-mail: publisher@hopepubs.com
Web site: http://www.hopepubs.com
Dist(s): **Univ. Pr. of New England.**

Hopkins, KC, *(978-0-615-23929-3)* 409 Orchid Trail, Franklin, TN 37174 USA Tel 615-618-4997
E-mail: kchopkins1276@yahoo.com
Dist(s): **Lulu Pr., Inc.**

Hopkins Publishing, *(978-0-9839326; 978-1-62080)* 201 Faircrest Dr. No. 3687, Cleburne, TX 76033 USA Tel 210-595-9313
E-mail: leah@hopkinspublishing.com; justin@hopkinspublishing.com
Web site: http://www.facebook.com/churchofchristbooks; http://hopkinspublishing.com/; http://twitter.com/#!/cofcbooks; https://www.smashwords.com/profile/view/hopkinspublishing
Dist(s): **Lightning Source, Inc.**
Send The Light Distribution LLC.

Hoppenbrouwers, Toke *See* **Monte Nido Pr.**

HOPS Pr., LLC, *(978-1-892784)* Orders Addr.: 12 Quartz St., Pony, MT 59747-0697 USA Tel 406-685-3222
E-mail: orders@hollowtop.com
Web site: http://www.hopspress.com
Dist(s): **Chelsea Green Publishing**
Mountain Pr. Publishing Co., Inc.

Horan Publishing, *(978-0-9769980)* P.O. Box 740485, Orange City, FL 32774-0485 USA
E-mail: horanpublishing@wmconnect.com.

Horizon Bks., *(978-0-9787987)* Orders Addr.: 768 Hardtimes Rd., Farmville, VA 23901 USA (SAN 851-6243) Tel 434-223-3235 (phone/fax)
E-mail: eicherjs@kinex.net
Web site: http://www.readingwithhorizon.com.

Horizon Line Pr., *(978-0-9749426)* 77 N. River Dr., Roseburg, OR 97470 USA
E-mail: dj@knights-of-avalon.com
Web site: http://www.knights-of-avalon.net/.

Horizon Pubs. *Imprint of* **Cedar Fort, Inc./CFI Distribution**

Horizons *Imprint of* **Alpha Omega Pubns., Inc.**

Horowitz Creative Media, Incorporated *See* **ArtMar Productions**

Horse & Dragon Publishing, *(978-0-9759488)* 241 Coast Hill Dr., Suite A, Indian Harbour Beach, FL 32937 USA Tel 321-821-2220; Fax: 321-821-2226; Toll Free: 877-374-6815
E-mail: bob@robertclark.us
Web site: http://www.robertclark.us.

Horse Creek Pubns., *(978-0-9722217)* 945 Mockingbird Ln., Norman, OK 73071-4802 USA
E-mail: sue.schrems@horsecreekpublications.com
Web site: http://www.horsecreekpublications.com.

Horton, David *See* **Negro Publishing, LLC**

Horvath, Janet, *(978-0-9713735)* 122 Virginia St., Saint Paul, MN 55102 USA (SAN 255-5441) Tel 612-870-4200; Fax: 612-454-2554
E-mail: jhorvathcello@hotmail.com
Web site: http://www.playinglesshurt.com.

Ho's, Jane Children Bks., *(978-0-9619126)* 700 Kipling Ct., El Sobrante, CA 94803 USA (SAN 243-4954) Tel 510-222-2621.

Hosannah Pubns., *(978-0-9786031)* 507 W. Manheim St., Bldg.18 , Apt.D, Philadelphia, PA 19144-4859 USA Tel 215-991-6154; Fax: 215-991-0609
E-mail: fourhosannah@verizon.net.

Hospice & Community Care Pubns., *(978-0-9774691)* Orders Addr.: P.O. Box 993, Rock Hill, SC 29731 USA (SAN 257-6309) Tel 803-329-4663; Fax: 803-329-5935; Toll Free: 800-895-2273; Edit Addr.: P.O. Box 993, Rock Hill, SC 29731-6993 USA
Web site: http://www.hospicecommunitycare.org.

Hospice of Saint John, The, *(978-0-9742849)* 1320 Everett Ct., Lakewood, CO 80215 USA.

Hot off the Pr., *(978-0-933491; 978-0-9605904; 978-1-56231; 978-1-59776)* 1250 NW 3rd Ave., Canby, OR 97013 USA (SAN 216-3977) Toll Free: 800-227-9595
E-mail: info@hotp.com
Web site: http://www.craftpizazz.com.

Hot Page Pr. *Imprint of* **Potter Assocs.**

HotComb Pr., *(978-0-9787940)* 6230 Wilshire Blvd., Suite 805, Los Angeles, CA 90048-5104 USA
E-mail: info@hotcombpress.com
Web site: http://hotcombpress.com.

HotDiggetyDog Pr., *(978-0-9741417; 978-0-9844645)* P.O. Box 747, Shepherdsville, KY 40165 USA Tel 502-376-5966; Fax: 208-474-1227
E-mail: leighanne@thewoodybooks.com
Web site: http://www.thewoodybooks.com.

Houghton Mifflin Bks. for Children *Imprint of* **Houghton Mifflin Harcourt Trade & Reference Pubs.**

Houghton Mifflin Company *See* **Houghton Mifflin Harcourt Publishing Co.**

Houghton Mifflin Company (School Division) *See* **Houghton Mifflin Harcourt School Pubs.**

Houghton Mifflin Company Trade & Reference Division *See* **Houghton Mifflin Harcourt Trade & Reference Pubs.**

Houghton Mifflin Harcourt Learning Technology, *(978-0-7630; 978-1-930106)* Div. of Houghton Mifflin Harcourt Publishing Co., 100 Pine St. Ste. 1900, San Francisco, CA 94111-5205 USA Toll Free: 800-223-6925; 125 Cambridgepark Dr., Cambridge, MA 02140-2329
E-mail: info@riverdeep.net; international@riverdeep.net
Web site: http://www.riverdeep.com
Dist(s): **Follett School Solutions.**

†**Houghton Mifflin Harcourt Publishing Co.,** *(978-0-395; 978-0-87466; 978-0-9631591; 978-1-57630; 978-1-881527; 978-0-618; 978-0-544; 978-0-547; 978-1-328; 978-0-358)* Orders Addr.: 9205 Southpark Ctr. Loop, Orlando, FL 32819 USA Toll Free: 800-225-3362; Edit Addr.: 222 Berkeley St., Boston, MA 02116 USA (SAN 215-3793) Tel 617-351-5000; 125 High St., Boston, MA 02110; *Imprints:* Clarion Books (Clarion Bk); Betty Crocker (Betty Crocker); HMH Books For Young Readers (HMH Bks FYR)
Web site: http://www.hmco.com
Dist(s): **CENGAGE Learning**
Cheng & Tsui Co.
Continental Bk. Co., Inc.
ETA hand2mind
Ebsco Publishing
Follett School Solutions
Houghton Mifflin Harcourt Trade & Reference Pubs.
Houghton Mifflin Harcourt Supplemental Pubs.
Larousse Kingfisher Chambers, Inc.
Lectorum Pubns., Inc.
MyiLibrary
Perelandra, Ltd.
TextStream
ebrary, Inc.; *CIP.*

Houghton Mifflin Harcourt School Pubs., *(978-0-395; 978-0-669)* Orders Addr.: 1900 Batavia Ave., Geneva, IL 60134-3399 USA Toll Free Fax: 800-733-2098; Toll Free: 800-733-2828; 1175 N. Stemmons Fwy., Lewisville, TX 75067-2516 Toll Free: 800-733-2828; Edit Addr.: 222 Berkeley St., Boston, MA 02116 USA Tel 617-351-5000; Fax: 617-227-5409
E-mail: eduwebmaster@hmco.com
Web site: http://www.eduplace.com
Dist(s): **Follett School Solutions.**

Houghton Mifflin Harcourt Supplemental Pubs., *(978-1-60032; 978-1-60277)* 10801 N. Mopac Expressway, Bldg. 3, Austin, TX 78759 USA
Web site: www.harcourtachieve.com.

Houghton Mifflin Harcourt Trade & Reference Pubs., *(978-0-395; 978-0-89919; 978-0-618)* Orders Addr.: 9205 Southpark Ctr. Loop, Orlando, FL 32819 USA Tel 978-661-1300; Toll Free: 800-225-3362; Edit Addr.: 222 Berkeley St., Boston, MA 02116 USA (SAN 200-2388) Tel 617-351-5000; Fax: 617-227-5409; 215 Park Ave S., 12th Flr., New York, NY 10003-1621; *Imprints:* Clarion Books (Clarion Bk); Sandpiper (Sandpiper); Houghton Mifflin Books for Children (HMBC)
E-mail: trade_sub_rights@hmco.com
Web site: http://www.hmco.com/; http://www.houghtonmifflinbooks.com
Dist(s): **CENGAGE Learning**
CreateSpace Independent Publishing Platform
Ebsco Publishing
Follett School Solutions
Houghton Mifflin Harcourt Publishing Co.
Harcourt Trade Pubs.
Lectorum Pubns., Inc.
MyiLibrary.

Houkura (AUS) *(978-0-9805090) Dist. by* **Bookmasters.**

Ho'ulu Hou Project: Stories Told by Us *Imprint of* **Na Kamalei Koolauloa Early Education Program**

HourGlass Publishing, *(978-0-9860205; 978-1-946223)* 2095 Hwy. 211 NW Suite 2F-152, Braselton, GA 30517 USA Tel 678-439-9229; Fax: 866-855-1971
E-mail: info@hourglasspublishing.com
Web site: www.HourGlassPublishing.com.

Hourglass Unlimited, *(978-0-9829673; 978-0-615-52585-3; 978-0-615-65278-8; 978-0-692-63352-6)* 7111 N, 72nd Ave, Glendale, AZ 85303 USA Tel 815-210-0695
E-mail: deatrikingbey@yahoo.com
Dist(s): **CreateSpace Independent Publishing Platform.**

House, David, *(978-0-9777086)* 1488 Madelyn Ave SE, Salem, OR 97306-3552 USA
Web site: http://www.space-worthy.com.

House of Anansi Pr. (CAN) *(978-0-88784; 978-1-77089; 978-1-4870) Dist. by* **PerseuPGW.**

House of David *See* **Key of David Publishing**

House of Prayer Ministries, Inc., *(978-1-882825)* 2428 Florian Ct., Decatur, IL 62526 USA Tel 217-428-7077 (phone/fax)
E-mail: vikischerer@comcast.net
Web site: www.houseofprayerministries.com.

House of the Guilded Scribe, *(978-0-615-28905-2; 978-0-615-55608-6; 978-0-9914351)* P.O. Box 432, Mount Pocono, PA 18344 USA
E-mail: sales@prissyandmissy.com; theguildedscribe@gmail.com
Web site: http://www.wonderfulwondersart.com; http://www.prissyandmissy.com/; http://www.prissyandmissy.com.

House of The Lord Fellowship, *(978-0-9673530)* Orders Addr.: P.O. Box 235, Lock Haven, PA 17745 USA Tel 570-748-6455; Fax: 570-748-6858; Edit Addr.: 201 W. Main St., Lock Haven, PA 17745 USA
E-mail: ssnyder@houseofthelordfellowship.org
Web site: http://www.houseofthelordfellowship.org.

House of Usher *See* **Abysso Bks.**

House Upon A Hill Bks., *(978-0-9795826)* Orders Addr.: P.O. Box 140322, Broken Arrow, OK 74014 USA; Edit Addr.: 19546 E. 42nd St. S., Broken Arrow, OK 74014 USA.

Houston Enterprises, *(978-0-9712861; 978-0-9907800; 978-0-9862339; 978-0-9862349)* Orders Addr.: 6320 Rucker Rd. Suite E, Indianapolis, IN 46220 USA Tel 317-726-1901; Fax: 317-726-1902; Toll Free: 888-826-8082
E-mail: info@scotthouston.com
Web site: http://www.scotthouston.com.

Houston Zoo, Inc., *(978-0-9762385)* 1513 N. MAcGregor, Houston, TX 77030 USA Tel 713-533-6500; Fax: 713-533-6755
E-mail: gwarfield@houstonzoo.org
Web site: http://www.houstonzoo.org.

"How Do You Know", *(978-0-9675574)* Orders Addr.: P.O. Box 831172, Stone Mountain, GA 30083 USA
E-mail: pjgastonbooks@yahoo.com.

How Great Thou ART Pubns., *(978-0-9700405; 978-0-9717874; 978-0-9859000)* Orders Addr.: P.O. Box 48, Mcfarlan, NC 28102-0048 USA Tel 704-851-3117; Fax: 704-851-3111; Toll Free: 800-982-3729; Edit Addr.: 357 McFarlin Rd, Morven, NC 28119 USA
E-mail: matthew@howgreatthouart.com
Web site: http://www.howgreatthouart.com/.

How to Make & Keep Friends, LLC, *(978-0-692-53121-1; 978-0-9972808)* 60 Willow Rd., Ayer, MA 01432 USA Tel 978-392-9865
Web site: http://www.howtomakeandkeepfriends.com
Dist(s): **CreateSpace Independent Publishing Platform.**

Howard Bks. *Imprint of* **Howard Books**

Howard Books, Div. of SIMON & SCHUSTER, 1230 Ave. of the Americas, New York, NY 10020 USA; *Imprints:* Howard Books (Howard Imp)
Dist(s): **Simon & Schuster, Inc.**

Howard, Emma Bks., *(978-1-886551)* P.O. Box 385, New York, NY 10024-0385 USA Tel 212-996-2590 (phone/fax)
E-mail: emmahowardbooks@verizon.net
Web site: http://www.EellGrassGirls.com.

Howard, Marissa, *(978-0-9985935)* 104 Hampton Loop Unit 1, Minot AFB, ND 58704 USA Tel 719-439-5500
E-mail: marissahowardbooks@gmail.com.

Howard Printing, Inc., *(978-0-9793790)* 14 Noahs Ln., Brattleboro, VT 05301 USA Tel 802-254-3550; Fax: 802-257-1453
E-mail: info@howardprintinginc.com
Web site: http://www.howardprintinginc.com.

Howe, Tina Field, *(978-0-9768585)* P.O. Box 581, Waverly, NY 14892 USA (SAN 256-8276) Tel 607-329-2458
Web site: http://www.tinafieldhowe.com.

Howell Bk. Hse. *Imprint of* **Wiley, John & Sons, Inc.**

Howell Canyon Pr., *(978-1-931210)* 1475 N Bundy Dr., Los Angeles, CA 90049 USA (SAN 255-3015) Toll Free: 888-252-0411 (Orders)
E-mail: info@HowellCanyonPress.com
Web site: http://www.AddisonTheDog.com; http://www.howellcanyonpress.com/; http://www.drdeanhowell.com/; http://www.TrishaHowell.com
Dist(s): **Ingram Publisher Services.**

Howell, M Kay *See* **Eagle Tree Pr.**

Howell, Steven, *(978-0-615-15346-9; 978-0-615-19997-9)* 697 Superior Ln., Clarksville, TN 37043 USA Tel 931-358-6022
E-mail: mrmrshowell2@yahoo.com
Dist(s): **Lulu Pr., Inc.**

Howie, C.J. Co., *(978-1-885275)* 1695 Quigley Rd., Columbus, OH 43227-3433 USA Tel 614-237-5474.

HP Trade *Imprint of* **Penguin Publishing Group**

HPN Publishing, *(978-0-9768451)* 22902 Sonriente Trail, Trabuco Canyon, CA 92679 USA.

HR Dowling, *(978-0-692-83760-3)* 5006 51st Ave SW, Seattle, WA 98136 USA Tel 206-747-2055
E-mail: hrdowling@hotmail.com.

H.R. Wallace Publishing, *(978-0-692-31112-7; 978-0-692-31125-7; 978-0-692-31138-7; 978-0-692-31621-4; 978-0-692-31624-5; 978-0-692-31627-6; 978-0-692-31634-4; 978-0-692-31635-1; 978-0-692-31637-5; 978-0-692-31639-9; 978-0-692-31644-3; 978-0-692-31646-7; 978-0-692-31648-1; 978-0-692-31649-8; 978-0-692-31651-1; 978-0-692-31660-3; 978-0-692-31667-2; 978-0-692-31668-9; 978-0-692-32363-2; 978-0-692-32368-7; 978-0-692-32370-0; 978-0-692-32374-8; 978-0-692-32377-9; 978-0-692-32378-6; 978-0-692-32501-8; 978-0-692-32502-5;) 909 Mayfield Rd., Sharpsville, PA 16150 USA*
Dist(s): **CreateSpace Independent Publishing Platform.**

Hramiec Hoffman Publishing, *(978-0-9746901)* 6911 M-119 Hwy., Harbor Springs, MI 49740 USA Tel 231-526-1011
Dist(s): **Partners Bk. Distributing, Inc.**

Hub City Pr., *(978-0-9638731; 978-1-891885; 978-1-938235)* Orders Addr.: 186 West Main St., Spartanburg, SC 29306 USA Tel 864-577-9349; Fax: 864-577-0188
E-mail: bteter@bellsouth.net
Web site: http://www.hubcity.org
Dist(s): **Blair, John F. Pub.**
Publishers Group West (PGW).

Hub City Writers Project *See* **Hub City Pr.**

Hubbard Scientific, Inc., *(978-0-8331)* Orders Addr.: P.O. Box 760, Chippewa Falls, WI 54729-1468 USA (SAN 202-3121) Tel 715-723-4427; Fax: 715-723-8021; Toll Free: 800-323-8368; Edit Addr.: P.O. Box 760, Chippewa Fls, WI 54729-0760 USA
Web site: http://www.hubbardscientific.com.

Hubbell, Gerald, *(978-0-9762042)* 4127 Roanoke Rd., Kansas City, MO 64111 USA Tel 816-531-4427
Web site: http://www.malverack.com.

Huckleberry Pr., *(978-0-9653035; 978-1-890570; 978-1-58584)* Orders Addr.: P.O. Box 51772, Durham, NC 27707 USA Tel 646-205-8057 (phone/fax) Do not confuse with Huckleberry Pr., Gig Harbor, WA
E-mail: HucksPress@yahoo.com
Web site: http://www.huckleberrypress.com.

Hudson Bks., *(978-0-9749860; 978-0-9762502; 978-0-9764459; 978-0-9767789; 978-0-9786296; 978-0-9822553)* 244 Madison Ave., No. 254, New York, NY 10016 USA Fax: 718-225-5556; Toll Free: 877-822-2500
Web site: http://www.thefloatingallery.com.

Hudson Hills Press, Incorporated *See* **Hudson Hills Pr. LLC**

†**Hudson Hills Pr. LLC,** *(978-0-933920; 978-0-9646042; 978-1-55595)* Orders Addr.: P.O. Box 205, Manchester, VT 05254 USA; Edit Addr.: 74-2 Union St., Manchester, VT 05254 USA (SAN 213-0815) Tel 802-362-6450; Fax: 802-362-6459
E-mail: artbooks@hudsonhills.com
Web site: http://www.hudsonhills.com/
Dist(s): **Art Institute of Chicago**
National Bk. Network; *CIP.*

Hudson House Publishing & Productions *See* **Whorl Bks.**

Hudson, Jessie, *(978-0-9778922)* 14814 Forward Pass, San Antonio, TX 78248 USA
Web site: http://www.OLLIEANDFRIENDS.com.

Hudson, Mary C., *(978-0-9627745; 978-0-9722937)* 1125 Karen Way, Mountainview, CA 94040 USA Tel 650-948-1270.

Hudson Publishing Group, The, *(978-1-60349)* 356 Glenwood Ave., East Orange, NJ 07017 USA Tel 973-672-7701; Fax: 973-677-7570; *Imprints:* Marimba Books (MarimbaBks)
E-mail: justusbook@aol.com
Dist(s): **Just Us Bks., Inc.**

Hufnagel Software, *(978-0-9743881)* P.O. Box 747, Clarion, PA 16214-0747 USA Tel 814-226-5600; Fax: 814-226-5551
Web site: http://www.hufsoft.com/books.

Hug Bandit Publishing *See* **HB Publishing, LLC**

Hughes, Betty Barber *See* **Puwaii International, LLC**

Huginn & Muninn, *(978-1-937571)* 1240 W. Sims Way No. 93, Port Townsend, WA 98368 USA Tel 206-202-0998
E-mail: wyrddesign@unseen.is; huginnandmuninn@gmx.com; heathenmama@gmx.com; carrie@carrieoverton.com
Web site: huginnandmuninn.net.

Huia Pubs. (NZL) *(978-0-908975; 978-1-877266; 978-1-877241; 978-1-877283; 978-1-86969; 978-0-9582517; 978-1-77550; 978-1-77550-255-5; 978-1-77550-297-5; 978-1-77550-244-9; 978-1-77550-295-1; 978-1-77550-238-8; 978-1-77550-294-4; 978-1-77550-239-5; 978-1-77550-257-9; 978-1-77550-241-8; 978-1-77550-243-2; 978-1-77550-252-4; 978-1-77550-296-8; 978-1-77550-250-0; 978-1-77550-242-5; 978-1-77550-247-0; 978-1-77550-253-1; 978-1-77550-240-1; 978-1-77550-245-6; 978-1-77550-254-8; 978-1-77550-248-7; 978-1-77550-256-2) Dist. by* **UH Pr.**

Hula Moon Pr., *(978-0-9794649)* P.O. Box 11173, Honolulu, HI 96828 USA Tel 808-947-6470
Dist(s): **BookBaby.**

Human Factor LLC, *(978-0-9816472)* P.O. Box 3742, Washington, DC 20027 USA (SAN 856-1109)
E-mail: info@humanfactor.net
Web site: http://www.humanfactor.net.

†**Human Kinetics Pubs.,** *(978-0-7360; 978-0-87322; 978-0-88011; 978-0-918438; 978-0-931250; 978-1-4504; 978-1-4925)* Orders Addr.: P.O. Box 5076, Champaign, IL 61825-5076 USA (SAN 211-7088) Tel 217-351-5076; Toll Free: 800-747-4457; Edit Addr.: 1607 N. Market St., Champaign, IL 61820 USA (SAN 658-0866) Tel 217-351-5076; Fax: 217-351-2674; Toll Free: 800-747-4457
E-mail: humank@hkusa.com; info@hkusa.com
Web site: http://www.humankinetics.com; http://www.hkusa.com
Dist(s): **Follett School Solutions**
MyiLibrary
ebrary, Inc.; *CIP.*

Human Relations Media, *(978-1-55548; 978-1-62706)* 41 Kensico Dr., Mount Kisco, NY 10549 USA (SAN 287-4873) Tel 914-244-0486; Fax: 914-244-0485; Toll Free: 800-431-2050
Web site: http://www.hrmvideo.com.

Human Values 4 Kids Foundation, The, *(978-0-9798986)* Orders Addr.: 11498 Pyrites Way, Gold River, CA 95670-6226 USA; Edit Addr.: 11498 Pyrites Way, Gold River, CA 95670-6226 USA
E-mail: vvnambiar@sbcglobal.net
Web site: http://www.thehumanvalues4kidsfoundation.org.

†**Humana Pr.,** *(978-0-89603; 978-1-58829; 978-1-59259; 978-1-59745; 978-1-934115; 978-1-60327; 978-1-60761; 978-1-61737; 978-1-61779; 978-1-62703)* 233 Spring St., New York, NY 10013 USA (SAN 212-3606) Fax: 212-460-1575; Toll Free: 800-SPRINGER
E-mail: service-ny@springer.com
Web site: http://humanapress.com; http://www.springer.com
Dist(s): **American Assn. for Clinical Chemistry, Inc.**
CreateSpace Independent Publishing Platform
Ebsco Publishing
Metapress
MyiLibrary
Rittenhouse Bk. Distributors
Springer
ebrary, Inc.; *CIP.*

Humane Society Pr. *Imprint of* **National Assn. for Humane & Environmental Education**

Humanics Learning *Imprint of* **Green Dragon Bks.**

Humanics Publishing Group *See* **Green Dragon Bks.**

Humanist Pr. *Imprint of* **American Humanist Assn.**

Humanoids, Inc., *(978-0-9672401; 978-1-930652; 978-1-59465)* Orders Addr.: 8033 Sunset Blvd. #628, Los Angeles, CA 90046 USA Tel 323-522-5466; Fax: 323-892-2848
E-mail: alex.donoghue@humanoids.com
Web site: http://www.humanoids.com/
Dist(s): **Diamond Comic Distributors, Inc.**
DKE Toys
Ingram Publisher Services.

Humming Meadow Ranch, *(978-0-9766431)* 47265 Twin Pines Rd., Banning, CA 92220-9656 USA Tel 951-849-1803; Fax: 951-849-9091
E-mail: elaine@hummingmeadowranch.com
Web site: http://www.hummingmeadowranch.com.

Hummingbird Mountain Pr., *(978-0-9746792)* P.O. Box 127, Midpines, CA 95345-0127 USA
Web site: http://www.sierratel.com/hummingbirdmountain.

Hummingbird World Media *Imprint of* **Double Edge Pr.**

Humor & Communication, *(978-0-9677844; 978-0-9820466)* 709 Doe Trail, Edmond, OK 73012 USA
E-mail: hduncan2@cox.net
Web site: http://www.hallduncan.com.

Humphreys, Kevin, *(978-0-9745727)* P.O. Box 10731, Spokane, WA 99220 USA; 1312 N. Brook Terrace St., Spokane, WA 99224-5678.

Hundred Ways LLC, A, *(978-0-9789544)* 18034 Ventura Blvd., No. 491, Encino, CA 91316 USA Tel 818-708-0558
E-mail: admin@ahundredways.com
Web site: http://www.whenwordsdream.com.

Hungry Bear Publishing, *(978-0-9754007; 978-0-9857607)* Orders Addr.: 40 McClelland St., Saranac Lake, NY 12983 USA Tel 518-891-5559
Web site: http://www.hungrybearpublishing.com
Dist(s): **North Country Bks., Inc.**

Hungry Goat Pr. *Imprint of* **Gauthier Pubns. Inc.**

Hungry Tiger Pr., *(978-0-9644988; 978-1-929527)* 5995 Dandridge Ln., Suite 121, San Diego, CA 92115-6575 USA
E-mail: books@hungrytigerpress.com
Web site: http://www.hungrytigerpress.com.

Hungry Tomato r *Imprint of* **Lerner Publishing Group**

Hunt, J. L. Publishing, *(978-0-9769401)* Orders Addr.: 27881 La Paz Rd., Suite G-124, Laguna Niguel, CA 92677 USA Tel 949-751-7511; Fax: 949-363-8559
E-mail: james@chewnomore.com.

Hunt, J.L. Publishing *See* **Hunt, J. L. Publishing**

Hunt, John Publishing Ltd. (GBR) *(978-1-85608; 978-1-903019; 978-1-84298; 978-1-903816; 978-1-905047; 978-1-84694; 978-1-78099) Dist. by* **Natl Bk Netwk.**

Hunt, John Publishing Ltd. (GBR) *(978-1-85608; 978-1-903019; 978-1-84298; 978-1-903816; 978-1-905047; 978-1-84694; 978-1-78099) Dist. by* **STL Dist.**

Hunt Thompson Media, *(978-0-9630377)* P.O. Box 8927, Santa Fe, NM 87504 USA Tel 415-794-0667 (cell)
E-mail: cjhunt@huntthompsonmedia.com; cjhunt3@gmail.com
Web site: http://www.PerfectHumanDiet.com; http://www.HuntThompsonMedia.com; www.CJHuntReports.com.

Hunter Hse. *Imprint of* **Turner Publishing Co.**

Hunter, J. H. Publishing, *(978-0-9718274)* 8100 Schmuck Rd., Evansville, IN 47712 USA Tel 812-985-5013.
Hunter, Julius K. *See* **J.K.H. Enterprises**
Hunter, Karen Media, *(978-0-9820221; 978-0-9845060)* P.O. Box 632, South Orange, NJ 07079 USA (SAN 857-0167)
Web site: http://www.karenhuntermedia.com; http://www.karenhuntermedia.com; www.readourbooks.com.
Hunter Pubns., *(978-0-9654185)* P.O. Box 433, Vallejo, CA 94589 USA Tel 707-645-8714; Fax: 707-644-7880.
Hunter Publishing, Inc., *(978-1-55650; 978-1-58843)* Orders Addr.: 222 Clematis St., West Palm Beach, FL 33401 USA Do not confuse with Hunter Publishing, Inc., Hobe Sound, FL
E-mail: comments@hunterpublishing.com
Web site: http://www.hunterpublishing.com
Dist(s): **Ebsco Publishing**
MyiLibrary
ebrary, Inc.
HuntForMo Creations, *(978-0-9740182)* 3718 Brentford Rd., Randallstown, MD 21133 USA Toll Free: 800-327-9779
E-mail: monique@huntformo.com
Web site: http://www.huntformo.com.
Huntington Library Pr., *(978-0-87328)* Div. of Huntington Library, Art Collections & Botanical Gardens, 1151 Oxford Rd., San Marino, CA 91108 USA (SAN 202-313X) Tel 626-405-2172; Fax: 626-585-0794
E-mail: booksales@huntington.org
Web site: http://www.Huntington.org/HEHPubs.html
Dist(s): **California Princeton Fulfillment Services**
D.A.P./Distributed Art Pubs.
Univ. of California Pr.
Huntington Library Publications *See* **Huntington Library Pr.**
Huntington Ludlow Media Group, *(978-0-9789057)* 5320 Maverick Dr., Grand Prairie, TX 75052-2617 USA (SAN 851-9080)
Web site: http://www.huntingtonludlow.com.
Huntly Hse., *(978-0-9885349; 978-0-615-73405-7)* 1965 Murcer Ln., Elgin, IL 60123 USA Tel 847-312-5904
E-mail: cfurtick@huntlyhouse.com
Web site: www.huntlyhouse.com.
Hunton, Carroll & Wenonah, *(978-0-9758873)* P.O. Box 1048, Albuquerque, NM 87103-1048 USA
E-mail: alan@excelstaff.com.
Huqua Pr., *(978-0-615-43791-0; 978-0-9838120; 978-0-9906966; 978-0-692-41669-3)* 8730 Sunset Blvd., Los Angeles, CA 90069 USA Tel 818-981-5262
E-mail: judy@magpyemedia.com
Dist(s): **MyiLibrary**
Open Road Integrated Media, Inc.
Huron River Pr., *(978-1-932399)* Orders Addr.: P.O. Box 310, Chelsea, MI 48118 USA Tel 734-913-9447; Fax: 734-332-4733; Edit Addr.: 320 N. Main St., Suite 100, Chelsea, MI 48118 USA
E-mail: info@huronriverpress.com
Web site: http://www.huronriverpress.com
Dist(s): **Partners Bk. Distributing, Inc.**
Huron Street Pr. *Imprint of* **American Library Assn.**
Hurst, Carol Consultants, *(978-0-9748509)* 41 Colony Dr., Westfield, MA 01085 USA Tel 413-562-3412
E-mail: carol@carolhurst.com
Web site: http://www.carolhurst.com
Dist(s): **Follett School Solutions.**
Huseby, Kirby, *(978-0-9778494)* P.O. Box 8034, Kentwood, MI 49518 USA
E-mail: staytoond@aol.com.
Husky Trail Pr. LLC, *(978-0-9722918; 978-1-935258)* Orders Addr.: P.O. Box 705, East Lyme, CT 06333-0705 USA Tel 860-739-7644; Fax: 860-739-3702
Web site: http://www.huskytrailpress.com.
Hussl, Gloria, *(978-0-9791468)* 5818 Trinity Rd., Needville, TX 77461 USA Tel 832-595-5678
E-mail: gloriasunrisefarms@yahoo.com.
Hutchings, John Pubs., *(978-1-935014)* 621 Dogleg Ln., Bartlett, IL 60103 USA Tel 630-736-6088; *Imprints:* Lessons From The Vine (LFTV)
E-mail: kaththompson@att.net.
Hutchison, G.F. Pr., *(978-1-885631; 978-0-9796279)* 319 S. Block, Suite 17, Fayetteville, AR 72701-6484 USA Tel 479-587-1726; *Imprints:* Family Of Man Press, The (Family Of Man Pr)
E-mail: drwriterguy@netscape.net
Web site: http://www.thehappinessplace.com.
Hutman Productions, *(978-0-9702386; 978-0-9833573; 978-0-9854486)* P.O. Box 268, Linthicum, MD 21090 USA Tel 410-789-0930
E-mail: cbladey@mail.bcpl.net
Web site: http://www.bcpl.net/~cbladey/hutmanA.html.
Hutt, Sarah, *(978-0-9743417)* 1140 Washington St., No. 7, Boston, MA 02118 USA Tel 617-482-4722
Web site: http://www.mymotherslegacy.com.
Hutton Electronic Publishing, *(978-0-9742894; 978-0-9785171; 978-0-9888775)* 160 N. Compo Rd., Westport, CT 06880 USA
E-mail: huttonbooks@hotmail.com
Web site: http://www.huttonelectronicpublishing.com.
Hydra Pubns., *(978-0-615-43242-7; 978-0-615-49378-7; 978-0-615-49820-1; 978-0-615-49950-5; 978-0-615-50445-2; 978-0-615-56017-5; 978-0-615-56345-9; 978-0-615-56584-2; 978-0-615-59650-1; 978-0-615-59651-8; 978-0-615-59822-2; 978-0-615-60737-5; 978-0-615-63328-2; 978-0-615-63783-9; 978-0-615-63858-4; 978-0-615-63863-8; 978-0-615-63882-9; 978-0-615-65016-6; 978-0-615-67766-8; 978-0-615-67970-9; 978-0-615-67972-3; 978-0-615-67974-7; 978-0-615-68018-7; 978-0-615-68422-2; 978-0-615-68969-2; 978-0-615-69010-0;)* *337 Clifty Dr., Madison, IN 47250 USA Tel 812-574-4113*
Web site: http://www.hydrapublications.com
Dist(s): **CreateSpace Independent Publishing Platform**
Dummy Record Do Not USE!!!!.
Hydra Publishing *See* **Hylas Publishing**
Hydrangea Pr., *(978-0-9768418)* 22 Plumer Rd., Epping, NH 03042 USA Tel 603-679-9544
E-mail: mswegles@comcast.net
Web site: http://www.plumercrest.com.
Hylas Publishing, *(978-1-59258)* 129 Main St., Irvington, NY 10533 USA Fax: 914-591-3220
E-mail: hydrapublishing@mac.com
Dist(s): **St. Martin's Pr.**
Hyles Pubns., *(978-0-9709488; 978-0-9745499; 978-0-9764247; 978-0-9778936; 978-0-9800594; 978-0-9819603; 978-1-62289)* Div. of Prepare Now Resources, Orders Addr.: 507 State St., Hammond, IN 46320 USA Tel 219-932-0711
E-mail: arrowcomp@sbcglobal.net; stubblefieldl@fbchammond.com; dillon@pulse18.com
Web site: http://www.pulse18.com.
Hymns Ancient & Modern Ltd (GBR) *(978-0-334; 978-1-85311; 978-0-907547; 978-1-84825) Dist. by* **Westminster John Knox.**
†Hyperion Bks. for Children, *(978-0-7868; 978-1-56282)* Div. of Disney Bk. Publishing, Inc., A Walt Disney Co., Orders Addr.: 3 Center Plaza, Boston, MA 02108 USA Toll Free: 800-759-0190; Edit Addr.: 114 Fifth Ave., New York, NY 10011 USA Tel 212-633-4400; Fax: 212-633-4833; *Imprints:* Jump at the Sun (Jump at the Sun); Volo (Volo); di Capua, Michael Books (diCapua Bks)
Web site: http://www.disney.com; http://www.hyperionbooksforchildren.com
Dist(s): **Disney Publishing Worldwide**
Hachette Bk. Group
Little Brown & Co.; *CIP.*
†Hyperion Paperbacks for Children, *(978-0-7868; 978-1-56282)* Div. of Disney Bk. Publishing, Inc., A Walt Disney Co., 114 Fifth Ave., New York, NY 10011 USA Tel 212-633-4400; Fax: 212-633-4833
Web site: http://www.disney.com
Dist(s): **Hachette Bk. Group**
Little Brown & Co.; *CIP.*
†Hyperion Pr., *(978-0-7868; 978-1-56282; 978-1-4013)* Div. of Disney Bk. Publishing, Inc., A Walt Disney Co., Orders Addr.: c/o HarperCollins Publishers, 1000 Keystone Industrial Park, Scranton, PA 18512-4621 USA Toll Free: 800-242-7737; Edit Addr.: 114 Fifth Ave., New York, NY 110011 USA Tel 917-661-2000
Web site: http://www.hyperionbooks.com
Dist(s): **Blackstone Audio, Inc.**
Follett School Solutions
Hachette Bk. Group
MyiLibrary; *CIP.*
hyperwerks *See* **Hyperwerks Entertainment**
Hyperwerks Entertainment, *(978-0-9770213)* 1830 Stoner Ave. Apt. 6, Los Angeles, CA 90025-7319 USA
Web site: http://www.hyperwerks.com.
i ZGOOL Media, *(978-0-9885898)* 100 Andover Pk. W Suite 150-237, Tukwila, WA 98188 USA Tel 206-851-1065
E-mail: fredbc11@gmail.com.
I AM Foundation, The, *(978-0-9645224; 978-0-9831780; 978-0-615-70944-4)* 7825 Fay Ave., Suite 200, La Jolla, CA 92037 USA Tel 619-297-7010
E-mail: iam@iamfoundation.org
Web site: http://www.iamfoundation.org
Dist(s): **CreateSpace Independent Publishing Platform**
DeVorss & Co.
New Leaf Distributing Co., Inc.
I AM Publishing, *(978-0-9905276)* 2370 Hwy 89A No. 11, Sedona, AZ 86336 USA Tel 805-729-0515
E-mail: danielposney@gmail.com
Web site: www.OneWhiteStone.com.
I Am Your Playground LLC, *(978-0-9769580)* P.O. Box 301, Fanwood, NJ 07023-0301 USA Fax: 908-301-0777; Toll Free: 888-759-4736 (888-PLY-GRND)
E-mail: john@iamyourplayground.com
Web site: http://www.iamyourplayground.com.
I & L Publishing, *(978-0-9661244; 978-1-930002)* 174 Oak Dr. Pkwy., Oroville, CA 95966 USA Tel 530-589-5048; Fax: 530-589-3551; Toll Free: 888-443-4722
E-mail: iolamoore@juno.com
Dist(s): **Morris Publishing.**
I. b. d., Ltd., *(978-0-88431)* 24 Hudson St., Kinderhook, NY 12106 USA (SAN 630-7779) Tel 518-758-1755; Fax: 518-758-6702
E-mail: lankhof@ibdltd.com
Web site: http://www.ibdltd.com.
IBE, Inc., *(978-0-916547; 978-0-9785848)* Div. of Inspiration Bks. East, Inc., Orders Addr.: P.O. Box 352, Jemison, AL 35085 USA (SAN 295-4672) Tel 205-646-2941; Edit Addr.: 170 Cty. Rd. 749, Jemison, AL 35085 USA
E-mail: communications@inbookseast.org
Web site: http://www.inbookseast.org.
I. B. Hoofinit Co., *(978-1-928890)* Orders Addr.: 94 Rte. 130, Forestdale, MA 02644 USA
E-mail: ibhoofinit@yahoo.com
Web site: http://ibhoofinit.com.
I. B. Tauris & Co., Ltd. (GBR) *(978-0-302; 978-0-85667; 978-1-85043; 978-1-86064; 978-1-84511; 978-1-84885; 978-1-78076; 978-0-85773; 978-1-78453; 978-0-85772; 978-0-85771; 978-1-78130; 978-1-78672; 978-1-78673) Dist. by* **Macmillan.**
I. B. Tauris & Co., Ltd. (GBR) *(978-0-302; 978-0-85667; 978-1-85043; 978-1-86064; 978-1-84511; 978-1-84885; 978-1-78076; 978-0-85773; 978-1-78453; 978-0-85772; 978-0-85771; 978-1-78130; 978-1-78672; 978-1-78673) Dist. by* **Bookmasters.**
I C A, *(978-0-9747506)* P.O. Box 910, Wayne, MI 48184-9998 USA Fax: 734-595-1869
E-mail: codemanray@aol.com
Web site: http://www.thefemalecode.com.
I Can Do All Things Productions, *(978-0-9745787)* 8 Loveland St., Madison, NJ 07940 USA Tel 973-377-5970; Fax: 973-377-5970
E-mail: seucony@optonline.net
Web site: http://www.perfectpraisebooks.com.
I E E E * Standards *See* **IEEE**
I F V, Inc., *(978-1-931861)* 1045 Coddington Rd., Ithaca, NY 14850 USA
E-mail: ifv@lightlink.com
Web site: http://www.classicalfencing.com.
I Have A Voice Enterprises, *(978-0-9746192)* P.O. Box 83, Peshtigo, WI 54157 USA
Web site: http://www.thehidersstory.com.
I Play Math Games *See* **IPMG Publishing**
I S H K, *(978-0-86304; 978-0-900860; 978-1-883536; 978-1-933779; 978-1-942698; 978-1-944493; 978-1-946270; 978-1-948013)* Div. of Institute for the Study of Human Knowledge, Orders Addr.: P.O. Box 400541, Cambridge, MA 02140 USA (SAN 226-4536) Tel 617-497-4124; Fax: 617-500-0268; Toll Free Fax: 800-223-4200; Toll Free: 800-222-4745; Edit Addr.: Ishk-hoopoe 171 Main St. #140, Los Altos, CA 94022 USA Tel 650-948-9428; *Imprints:* Malor Books (Malor Bks); Hoopoe Books (Hoopoe Books)
E-mail: ishkbooks@aol.com; ishkadm@aol.com
Web site: http://www.ishkbooks.com; http://www.hoopoekids.com
Dist(s): **Borders, Inc.**
New Leaf Distributing Co., Inc.
I S M Teaching Systems, Inc., *(978-1-56775)* 14132 Desert Willow, El Paso, TX 79938 USA Tel 915-856-6365; Fax: 915-856-6367; Toll Free: 800-453-4476
E-mail: Email4ism@aol.com
Web site: http://www16.inetba.com/ismteachingsystemsinc.
I S R P Press *See* **Sound Reading Solutions**
I Save A Tree, *(978-0-9714299; 978-0-9744670; 978-0-9745659; 978-1-61015)* Orders Addr.: P.O. Box 3006, Arcadia, FL 34265 USA
Web site: http://www.garrettbooks.com; http://www.isaveatree.com.
I See *Imprint of* **Picture Window Bks.**
I See Puppy, LLP, *(978-0-9774277)* Orders Addr.: 107 Richard Mine Rd., Dover, NJ 07801 USA (SAN 257-554X) Tel 973-361-8637; Fax: 973-361-8035
E-mail: info@iseepuppy.com
Web site: http://www.iseepuppy.com.
I WANNA BEE DESIGNS, *(978-0-9986664)* 2117 Markland Dr., Chesapeake, VA 23325 USA Tel 757-424-1357
E-mail: maadukes@yahoo.com.
i wantz Publishing, *(978-0-9727998)* P.O. Box 9305, Grand Rapids, MI 49509-0305 USA
E-mail: elizabeth@iwantz.com
Web site: http://www.iwantz.com.
i-5 Publishing LLC, *(978-0-87714; 978-0-944875; 978-0-9629525; 978-1-882770; 978-1-889540; 978-1-931993; 978-1-59378; 978-0-9745407; 978-1-933342; 978-1-933958; 978-1-935484; 978-1-937049; 978-1-62008; 978-1-62187)* 10 Bridge St., Bldg. C, Metuchen, NJ 08840 USA Tel 949-855-8822 (ext. 1003); Fax: 732-960-3107
Dist(s): **MyiLibrary**
Two Rivers Distribution.
IAC Publishing, *(978-0-9748383)* 3432 Denny St., No. 3, Pittsburgh, PA 15201 USA Toll Free: 877-592-0237
Web site: http://www.irishamericancatholic.com.
Iaconi, Mariuccia Bk. Imports, *(978-0-9628720)* P.O. Box 77023, San Francisco, CA 94107-0023 USA (SAN 161-1364) Toll Free: 800-955-9577
E-mail: mibibook@ixnetcom.com
Web site: http://www.mibibook.com
Dist(s): **Lectorum Pubns., Inc.**
IAD Pr. (AUS) *(978-0-949659; 978-1-86465; 978-0-9596206; 978-0-7316-3607-5; 978-0-7316-7458-9; 978-0-7316-7915-7; 978-0-646-04154-4; 978-0-646-20261-7) Dist. by* **IPG Chicago.**
IAHunt, *(978-0-9986851)* 7102 Capitol View Dr., McLean, VA 22101 USA Tel 703-893-0809
E-mail: iah2nd@aol.com.
IamCoach.com Publishing, *(978-0-9754761)* P.O. Box 60088, King of Prussia, PA 19406 USA
E-mail: publishing@iamcoach.com
Web site: http://www.IamCoach.com/chess/publishing/
Dist(s): **SCB Distributors.**
IAMPress, *(978-0-9768782; 978-0-9794839)* 3053 Dumbarton Rd., Memphis, TN 38128 USA Tel 901-358-2226; Fax: 901-358-8102
E-mail: renford@iam-cor.org
Web site: http://www.iam-cor.org
Dist(s): **Lulu Pr., Inc.**
IAMSA Creations, LLC *See* **Unlimited Possibilities Publishing, LLC**
Iberian Press *See* **7 Robots, Inc.**
Ibex Pubs., Inc., *(978-0-936347; 978-1-58814)* Orders Addr.: P.O. Box 30087, Bethesda, MD 20824 USA (SAN 696-866X) Tel 301-718-8188; Fax: 301-907-8707; Toll Free: 888-718-8188
E-mail: info@ibexpub.com
Web site: http://www.ibexpublishers.com.
IBJ Custom Publishing, *(978-0-9745673; 978-0-9776675; 978-0-9798830; 978-1-934922; 978-1-939550)* 41 E. Washington St., Suite 200, Indianapolis, IN 46204 USA
Dist(s): **Cardinal Pubs. Group.**
IBJ Media Custom Publishing *See* **IBJ Custom Publishing**
IBks., Inc.,
Dist(s): **National Bk. Network.**
ibooks, Inc., *(978-0-671; 978-0-7434; 978-1-58824; 978-1-59176; 978-1-59687; 978-1-59687-543-2)* 100 Jericho Quadrangle, Ste. 300, Jericho, NY 11753-2702 USA; *Imprints:* Milk & Cookies (Milk-Cookie); ipicturebooks (Ipicbks)
Web site: http://www.ibooksinc.com.
ibooks, Incorporated/ipictures.com *See* **ibooks, Inc.**
I C Creative, Inc., *(978-0-9742714)* 2300 Michigan Ct., Suite B, Arlington, TX 76016 USA Tel 817-459-8079; Fax: 817-460-0430
E-mail: joi@stayintouchmail.com
Web site: http://www.stayintouchmail.com.
ICAN Press *See* **Black Forest Pr.**
ICanPublish, *(978-0-9711480)* Div. of Heckman Bindery, Inc., P.O. Box 89, North Manchester, IN 46962 USA (SAN 253-9500) Tel 260-982-2107; Fax: 260-982-1130; Toll Free: 800-334-3628
E-mail: dave_mcintyre@heckmanbindery.com.
Ice Age Park and Trail Foundation, Inc., *(978-0-9627079)* 2453 Atwood Ave. STOP 4, Madison, WI 53704-5682 USA
E-mail: iat@iceagetrail.org
Web site: http://www.iceagetrail.org.
Ice Cube Pr., LLC, *(978-1-888160)* 205 N. Front St., North Liberty, IA 52317 USA (SAN 298-9085) Tel 319-626-2055; 319-594-6022
E-mail: steve@icecubepress.com; steve@southslope.net
Web site: http://www.icecubepress.com
Dist(s): **Quality Bks., Inc.**
Ice Mountain Publishing, *(978-0-9748814)* P.O. Box 1418, Salida, CO 81201 USA
E-mail: nathanward@amigo.net.
Icecat Bks., *(978-0-9764308; 978-0-9768670)* 1243 Old Canyon Dr., Hacienda Heights, CA 91745 USA Tel 626-333-2430
E-mail: contact@icecatbooks.com
Web site: http://www.icecatbooks.com.
Ichabod Ink, *(978-0-9766641)* 418 Lake George Cir., West Chester, PA 19382 USA.
iCharacter.org, *(978-1-62387; 978-1-63474)* Orders Addr.: 6-9 Trinity St., Dublin, 2 IRL; *Imprints:* Kidible (Kidible)
E-mail: info@icharacter.org
Web site: www.icharacter.org.
Icicle Falls Publishing Co., *(978-0-9749360)* Orders Addr.: HC 31, Box 5118A, Wasilla, AK 99654 USA; Edit Addr.: Hc31 B0x 5118a, Wasilla, AK 99654 USA
Web site: www.alaskanstoires.com
Dist(s): **News Group, The.**
Icon Group International, Inc., *(978-0-7576; 978-0-7418; 978-0-597; 978-0-497; 978-0-546; 978-1-114)* Div. of Icon Group, Ltd., P.O. Box 27740, Las Vegas, NV 89126-7440 USA (SAN 299-8122) Tel 858-635-9410; Fax: 858-635-9414
E-mail: ula@icongroupbooks.com; meta@icongroupbooks.com; orders@icongroupbooks.com
Web site: http://www.icongrouponline.com
Dist(s): **CreateSpace Independent Publishing Platform**
Ebsco Publishing
MyiLibrary.
Icon Language Systems, Inc. *See* **Ampersand, Inc.**
Idaho State Journal, *(978-0-9749865; 978-0-615-47497-7)* Orders Addr.: P.O. Box 431, Pocatello, ID 83204 USA; Edit Addr.: P.O. Box 431, Pocatello, ID 83204-0431 USA
Web site: http://www.journalnet.com.
Idea & Design Works, LLC, *(978-0-9712282; 978-0-9719775; 978-1-932382; 978-1-933239; 978-1-60010; 978-1-61377; 978-1-62302; 978-1-63140; 978-1-68405; 978-1-68406)* 2765 Truxtun Rd., San Diego, CA 92106 USA (SAN 255-1926) Tel 858-270-1315; Fax: 858-270-1308; 5080 Santa Fe St., San Diego, CA 92109-1609; *Imprints:* Worthwhile Books (Worthwhile Bks)
E-mail: chris@idwpublishing.com
Web site: http://www.idwpublishing.com/
Dist(s): **Diamond Comic Distributors, Inc.**
Diamond Bk. Distributors
L P C Group
MyiLibrary
Open Road Integrated Media, Inc.
Penguin Random Hse. LLC.
Idea, Inc., *(978-0-9701566)* 403 5th Pl NW, Austin, MN 55912-3051 USA Toll Free: 800-828-1231 (phone/fax)
E-mail: Idea_inc@smig.net
Web site: http://www.ccjournal.com.
Idea Network LA Inc., *(978-0-9773301)* 201 S. Santa Fe Ave. No. 105, Los Angeles, CA 90012 USA Tel 213-613-1252; Fax: 213-613-1440.
Ideal Pubns. *Imprint of* **Worthy Publishing**
IdeaList Enterprises, Inc., *(978-0-9758794)* P.O. Box 101187, Chicago, IL 60610 USA.
Ideate Prairie, *(978-0-9762564)* P.O. Box 65, Genoa, IL 60135 USA Tel 815-986-6577; *Imprints:* American Dog (Am Dog)
E-mail: cpierce@ideate-prairie.com
Web site: http://www.americandogtales.com; http://www.ideate-prairie.com.
Identity Pr., *(978-0-9753482)* P.O. Box 46224, Cincinnati, OH 45246-0224 USA Tel 513-313-5907 Do not confuse with companies with the same or similar name in Fountain Valley, CA, Cambridge, MA
E-mail: discovteenesteem@aol.com.
Idle Winter Pr., *(978-0-615-75103-0; 978-0-615-75329-4; 978-0-615-75375-1; 978-0-615-75790-2; 978-0-615-89153-8; 978-0-692-36927-2; 978-0-692-37191-6; 978-0-692-37441-2; 978-0-692-37871-7; 978-0-692-37934-9; 978-0-692-37993-6; 978-0-692-38122-9; 978-0-692-38502-9; 978-0-692-41873-4; 978-0-692-41874-1; 978-0-692-45244-8; 978-0-692-55074-8; 978-0-692-68244-9; 978-1-945687)* *4525 SE 61st Ave., Portland, OR 97206 USA Tel 503-772-1214*
Web site: http://IdleWinter.com
Dist(s): **CreateSpace Independent Publishing Platform.**
Idlehour Entertainment, *(978-0-9778063)* P.O. Box 12048, Glendale, AZ 85318 USA (SAN 850-3001) Tel 623-780-1434; Fax: 623-780-1438
Web site: http://www.idlehourentertainment.com.
Idyllworks, LLC, *(978-0-9794647)* 2904 Rippling Brook Ln., Dickinson, TX 77539-6199 USA
Web site: http://www.JamboNation.com.
†IEEE, *(978-0-7803; 978-0-87942; 978-1-55937; 978-0-7381; 978-1-4244; 978-1-61284; 978-1-4577; 978-1-4673; 978-1-62195; 978-1-4799; 978-1-5044; 978-1-5090; 978-1-5386)* Orders Addr.: P.O. Box 1331, Piscataway, NJ 08855-1331 USA (SAN 250-6130) Tel 732-981-0060; Fax: 732-981-0027; Toll Free: 800-701-4333; Edit Addr.:

445 Hoes Ln., Piscataway, NJ 08855-1331 USA Tel 732-981-0060; 732-981-5300; 732-562-3828; 800-678-4333; 732-562-3966; Fax: 732-981-1769; 732-562-1746; 732-562-1971
E-mail: confpubs@ieee.org; customer-service@ieee.org
Web site: http://www.ieee.org
Dist(s): **Curran Assocs., Inc.**
MyiLibrary
Oxford Univ. Pr., Inc.
Wiley, John & Sons, Inc.; *CIP.*

IEP Resources *Imprint of* **Attainment Co., Inc.**

IFLY Bks., *(978-0-9758888)* P.O. Box 894134, Temecula, CA 92589 USA.

I.Form Ink, Publishing, *(978-0-9763274)* Div. of Insu-Form, Inc., 41921 Beacon Hill, Suite A, Palm Desert, CA 92211 USA Tel 760-779-0657; Fax: 760-779-5143
E-mail: john@hackergroup.org.

IFWG Publishing Inc., *(978-0-9843298; 978-0-615-50936-5; 978-0-615-51846-6; 978-0-615-52105-3; 978-0-615-55249-1; 978-0-615-55424-2; 978-0-615-55642-0; 978-0-615-56093-9; 978-0-615-56121-9)* 302 Horseshoe Ln., Rockaway Beach, MO 65740 USA (SAN 859-0842) Toll Free: 800-337-3038
E-mail: ifwg-publishing@live.com; r.a.knowlton@ifwgpublishing.com
Web site: http://ifwgpublishing.weebly.com/index.html
Dist(s): **CreateSpace Independent Publishing Platform.**

Ig Publishing *See* **Ig Publishing, Inc.**

Ig Publishing, Inc., *(978-0-9703125; 978-0-9752517; 978-0-9771972; 978-0-9788431; 978-0-9815040; 978-1-935439; 978-1-939601; 978-1-63246)* 392 Clinton Ave. Apt. 1S, Brooklyn, NY 11238-1187 USA (SAN 254-0444)
Web site: http://www.igpub.com; www.lizzieskurnickbooks.com
Dist(s): **Consortium Bk. Sales & Distribution**
SPD-Small Pr. Distribution
ebrary, Inc.

IGI Pr., *(978-0-9709443; 978-0-9777121; 978-0-9799963; 978-0-9820870; 978-0-9825503; 978-0-9829273)* 241 First Ave. N., Minneapolis, MN 55401 USA (SAN 854-1876) Tel 612-338-8973 Toll Free: 888-805-8973
E-mail: igi@igipublishing.com
Web site: http://www.igipublishing.com.

IGlobal Educational Services, *(978-0-9882271; 978-1-944346)* 1000 Heritage Ctr. Cir., Round Rock, TX 78664 USA Tel 800-427-8422
E-mail: iglobal.educational@gmail.com.

IGMI Publishing, *(978-0-9655933)* Div. of PrissyH, P.O. Box 1735, Las Vegas, NM 87745-9602 USA Tel 505-425-9292
E-mail: favplagget@aol.com.

Ignatius Pr., *(978-0-89870; 978-1-58617; 978-1-62164; 978-1-68149)* Orders Addr.: P.O. Box 1339, Fort Collins, CO 80522-1339 USA (SAN 855-3556) Tel 970-221-3920; Fax: 970-221-3964; Toll Free Fax: 800-278-3566; Toll Free: 877-320-9276 (bookstore orders); 800-651-1531 (credit card orders, no minimum, individual orders); Edit Addr.: 1348 10th Ave., San Francisco, CA 94122 USA (SAN 214-3887) Toll Free: 800-651-1531
E-mail: info@ignatius.com
Web site: http://www.ignatius.com
Dist(s): **Follett School Solutions**
Midpoint Trade Bks., Inc.
Spring Arbor Distributors, Inc.

Ignite! Learning, *(978-0-9791935; 978-0-9798418; 978-1-934763; 978-1-937822)* 2905 San Gabriel Suite 212, Austin, TX 78705 USA Tel 512-697-7000; Fax: 512-697-7001; Toll Free: 866-464-4648
E-mail: support@ignitelearning.com; jbohls@ignitelearning.com
Web site: http://www.ignitelearning.com

Ignite Reality, *(978-0-9776771; 978-0-9816258)* P.O. Box 1804, Burlingame, CA 94011-1804 USA (SAN 856-0781)
E-mail: drjenniferleigh@gmail.com
Web site: http://www.drjenniferaustinleigh.com.

Ignition Pr. *Imprint of* **Publishing Services @ Thomson-Shore**

igou, asia, *(978-0-692-67491-8; 978-0-692-75292-0)* 317 Riblett Ln., Wilmington, DE 19808 USA Tel 302-332-7564.

IGR Limited *See* **EKADOO Publishing Group**

Iguana Adventures Publishing *See* **Publish To Go Pubns.**

I.H.S. Pubs., *(978-0-9847656)* 3920 S. Old Hwy. 94 Suite 33, St. Charles, MO 63304 USA Tel 636-447-6000.

IIEI Pr., *(978-0-9773098; 978-0-9797244; 978-0-615-52608-9)* 11225 N. 28th Dr., Suite B-201, Phoenix, AZ 85029 USA Tel 602-648-5750; Fax: 602-648-5755; Toll Free: 800-474-8013
E-mail: info@expandglobal.com
Web site: http://www.expandglobal.com/iiei-press/.

Ijiwola Pr., Gregory *Imprint of* **Summit Hse. Pubs.**

IJN Publishing, Inc., *(978-1-933894)* 724 NE. 4th St. #9, Hallandale, FL 33009 USA (SAN 850-4474) Fax: 954-457-2277; P.O. Box 630577, Miami, FL 33163
E-mail: gerald@ijnpublishing.com
Web site: http://www.whatliesbeneaththebed.com; http://www.ijnpublishing.com.

IJustWantToSleep, Inc., *(978-0-9744357)* 18 Timothy Ln., Candler, NC 28715 USA
E-mail: store@ijustwanttosleep.com; author@ijustwanttosleep.com
Web site: http://www.ijustwanttosleep.com.

IKIDS *Imprint of* **Innovative Kids**

il piccolo editions *Imprint of* **Fisher King Enterprises**

Ile Orunmila Communications, *(978-0-9644247; 978-0-9714949; 978-0-9825100)* Orders Addr.: P.O. Box 2326, San Bernardino, CA 92405 USA Tel 909-475-5851; Fax: 909-475-5850; Toll Free: 888-678-6645; Edit Addr.: 515 W. 21st St., San Bernardino, CA 92405 USA
E-mail: fsorunmila@aol.com
Web site: http://www.IleOrunmila.com
Dist(s): **Original Pubns.**

Illui International *See* **Heartful Loving Pr.**

Illumina Publishing, *(978-0-9718600; 978-0-9818092)* P.O. Box 2643, Friday Harbor, WA 98250-2643 USA Tel 360-378-6047
E-mail: illumina@rockisland.com
Web site: http://www.illuminapublishing.com; http://www.illuminabookdesign.com.

Illumination Arts *See* **Inspire Every Child dba Illumination Arts**

Illumination Arts LLC, *(978-0-9829225; 978-0-9846874)* 6788 Lakeview Dr, FRAZIER PARK, CA 93225 USA Tel 617-472-1443; 661-289-5007; *Imprints:* Diamond Clear Vision (DiamondClear)
E-mail: thpjr52@aol.com
Web site: http://www.illuminationarts.us; http://www.diamondclearvision.com.

Illumination Arts Publishing Co., Inc., *(978-0-935699; 978-0-9701907; 978-0-9740190)* Orders Addr.: P.O. Box 1865, Bellevue, WA 98009 USA (SAN 696-2599) Tel 425-644-7185; Fax: 425-644-9274; Toll Free: 888-210-8216; Edit Addr.: 808 6th St S. Ste. 200, Kirkland, WA 98033-6768 USA
E-mail: liteinfo@illumin.com
Web site: http://www.illumin.com
Dist(s): **DeVorss & Co.**
Follett School Solutions
Koen Pacific
New Leaf Distributing Co., Inc.
Partners/West Book Distributors
Quality Bks., Inc.

Illumination Pubns., *(978-0-9789511)* 2802 Floore Ct., Louisville, KY 40299-1610 USA (SAN 852-0313) Tel 502-491-5664 Do not confuse with Illumination Publications in West Toluca lake, CA.

Illumination Studios, *(978-0-9741381)* 5924 Woodoak Dr., Dallas, TX 75249 USA
E-mail: contact@illuminationstudios.com
Web site: http://www.illuminationstudios.com.

Illusion Factory, The, *(978-0-9747331; 978-1-932949)* 21800 Burbank Blvd., Suite 225, Woodland Hills, CA 91367 USA (SAN 255-7096) Tel 818-598-8400; Fax: 818-598-8494
E-mail: ewong@illusionfactory.com
Web site: http://www.illusionfactory.com.

Illusionary Magic LLC, *(978-0-9834201)* 104 Donato Cir., Scotch Plains, NJ 07076 USA Tel 877-322-2723; Fax: 908-322-0421
E-mail: info@bradross.com
Web site: http://www.BradRoss.com.

Illustrate to Educate, *(978-0-9892732)* 2313 Quincy St. Apt. No. 2, Durham, NC 27703 USA Tel 919-908-1254
E-mail: everettar@hotmail.com.

Illustrated Bks. *Imprint of* **Jorge Pinto Bks.**

ILMHOUSE LLC, *(978-0-9726607)* P.O. Box 535, Unionville, PA 19375-0535 USA
Web site: http://www.thetruemarriage.com.

ILT Publishing, *(978-0-9774409)* Div. of Integrated Learning Technology, Inc., 1410 Steeplechase Rd., Downingtown, PA 19335 USA (SAN 257-4950) Tel 484-883-7107 (phone/fax)
E-mail: info@iltpublishing.com; rebejames@smartmail.com; presetco@iltpublishing.com
Web site: http://www.iltpublishing.com; http://www.tommilance.com; http://rebejames.com.

I.M. Enterprises, *(978-0-9777882)* P.O. Box 111, Rochester, MA 02770 USA (SAN 850-1645); *Imprints:* Light Works Publishing (Light Works)
E-mail: imenterprises@hotmail.com
Web site: http://www.imenterprises.org.

IM Pr., *(978-0-9654651; 978-0-9716911; 978-0-615-43634-0; 978-0-9857952)* Orders Addr.: P.O. Box 5346, Takoma Park, MD 20913-5346 USA Tel 301-587-1202; Edit Addr.: 7214 Cedar Ave., Takoma Park, MD 20912 USA Do not confuse with companies with the same name in Cincinnati, OH, Fairfax Station, VA
E-mail: efaine@yahoo.com
Web site: http://www.takoma.com/ned/home.htm
Dist(s): **Book Clearing Hse.**

Imaajinn This, *(978-0-9767342)* P.O. Box 294, West Haven, CT 06516 USA (SAN 256-484X) Tel 203-710-4906
Web site: http://www.robleyblake.com.

Image Cascade Publishing, *(978-0-9639607; 978-1-930009; 978-1-59511)* 420 Lexington Ave., Suite 300, New York, NY 10170 USA (SAN 253-2972) Tel 212-297-6240; Toll Free: 800-691-7779
E-mail: jc@imagecascade.com
Web site: http://www.imagecascade.com
Dist(s): **BookMasters, Inc.**

Image Comics, *(978-1-58240; 978-1-887279; 978-1-60706; 978-1-63215; 978-1-5343)* 2001 Center St., Berkeley, CA 94704 USA
E-mail: info@imagecomics.com
Web site: http://www.imagecomics.com/
Dist(s): **Diamond Comic Distributors, Inc.**
Diamond Bk. Distributors
L P C Group
Trucatriche.

Image Express Inc., *(978-0-9664634; 978-0-615-50572-5)* P.O. Box 66536, Austin, TX 78766 USA Tel 512-401-4900; Toll Free: 888-794-4300
Web site: http://greatday.com
Dist(s): **CreateSpace Independent Publishing Platform.**

Image Formation, *(978-0-9763440)* 23233 N. Pima, No. 113-102, Scottsdale, AZ 85255 USA
E-mail: lance@themummymountainstory.com
Web site: http://www.themummymountainstory.com.

Image Pr., Inc., *(978-1-891548)* Orders Addr.: P.O. Box 2407, Edmond, OK 73083-2407 USA Tel 405-844-6007; Fax: 405-348-5577; Edit Addr.: 247 N. Broadway, Suite 101, Edmond, OK 73034 USA.

Image Publishing, Ltd., *(978-0-911897)* Subs. of Roger Miller Photo, Ltd., 1411 Hollins St., Baltimore, MD 21223 USA (SAN 264-6781) Tel 410-566-1222; 410-233-1234; Fax: 410-233-1241 Do not confuse with companies with the same or similar names in Encino, CA, Wilton, CT
E-mail: rmpl.ipl@verizon.net
Web site: http://www.rogermillerphoto.com.

IMAGECRAFTERS, *(978-0-9773478)* Orders Addr.: 1644 Masters Ct., Naperville, IL 60563 USA (SAN 257-3709) Tel 630-355-1449
E-mail: imgcft@mc.net.

Imagery Pr., *(978-0-9754287)* P.O. Box 337, Carpinteria, CA 93014-0337 USA
E-mail: books@imagerypress.com.

Images & Pages, *(978-0-9788332)* P.O. Box 118120, Carrolton, TX 75007 USA
E-mail: deguzman@imagesandpages.com
Web site: http://imagesandpages.com.

Images Co., *(978-0-9677017; 978-1-62385)* 109 Woods of Arden Rd., Staten Island, NY 10312 USA
E-mail: j.iovine@verizon.net; imagesco@bellatlantic.net; imagesco@verizon.net
Web site: http://www.imagesco.com.

Images For Presentation, *(978-0-9749531)* 176 Second St., Saint James, NY 11780 USA Tel 631-361-7908
E-mail: imagesforpres@aol.com.

Images from the Past, Inc., *(978-1-884592)* 155 W. Main St., P.O. Box 137, Bennington, VT 05201-0137 USA Tel 802-442-3204 (phone/fax); Toll Free: 888-442-3204
E-mail: info@ImagesfromthePast.com
Web site: http://www.ImagesfromthePast.com
Dist(s): **Ingram Publisher Services.**

Images Pr., *(978-1-891577)* 27920 Roble Alto St., Los Altos Hills, CA 94022 USA (SAN 299-4844) Tel 650-948-9251; 650-948-8251; Fax: 650-941-6114 Do not confuse with companies with the same name in San Leandro, CA, New York, NY
E-mail: bugsmom2@aol.com
Web site: http://www.images-press.com
Dist(s): **Quality Bks., Inc.**

Images Unlimited Publishing, *(978-0-930643)* P.O. Box 305, Maryville, MO 64468 USA (SAN 242-0163) Tel 660-582-4279; *Imprints:* Snaptail Press (Snaptail Pr)
E-mail: images@cebridge.net; info@imagesunlimitedpub.com; Lee@imagesunlimitedpub.com
Web site: http://www.imagesunlimitedpub.com; http://www.snaptail.com; http://www.snaptailpress.com; http://www.imagesunlimitedpublishing.com; http://www.cookingandkids.com/blog; http://www.healthykidseatingtips.com; http://www.caringmomshealthykids.com
Dist(s): **Brodart Co.**
Follett School Solutions.

Imaginarium Pr., *(978-0-615-45112-1; 978-0-9978066)* 254 W. 98th St. Apt.1E, New York, NY 10025 USA Tel 410-963-1854
E-mail: josephrbecker@gmail.com.

Imaginary Lines, Incorporated *See* **Sally Ride Science**

Imagination Arts Pubns., *(978-0-9746119)* P.O. Box 103, Mahwah, NJ 07430 USA Tel 201-529-5105; Fax: 201-529-5105
E-mail: imaginationarts@optonline.net
Web site: http://www.iapbooks.com.

Imagination Publishing-Orlando, *(978-0-9817123; 978-0-615-38566-2)* P.O. Box 802, Loughman, FL 33858 USA (SAN 856-3152)
E-mail: paul@HubbleRevealsCreation.com
Web site: http://www.TheSecretDoorway.com; http://www.HubbleRevealsCreation.com/
Dist(s): **BookBaby.**

Imagination Stage, Inc., *(978-0-9723729)* 4908 Auburn Ave., Bethesda, MD 20814 USA Tel 301-961-6060; Fax: 301-718-9526
E-mail: lagogliati@aol.com
Web site: http://www.imaginationstage.org.

Imagination Station Pr., *(978-0-9742575)* 4560 N. 25th Rd., Arlington, VA 22207-4147 USA Tel 703-528-5828
E-mail: epyatt1@comcast.net.

Imagination Workshop, The, *(978-0-9744437)* 4150 Abbott Ave., N., Minneapolis, MN 55422 USA
E-mail: imaginationworkshop@yahoo.com.

Imaginative Publishing, Ltd., *(978-0-9743335; 978-0-9767948)* P.O. Box 150008, Fort Worth, TX 76108 USA Tel 817-246-6436 (phone/fax); Toll Free: 877-246-6436 (phone/fax)
E-mail: publisher@imaginativepublishing.com
Web site: http://www.imaginativepublishing.com.

Imaginator Pr., *(978-0-9745603; 978-1-936917)* 6400 Baltimore National Pike Suite 170A-194, Baltimore, MD 21228-3915 USA
E-mail: sruth@ImaginatorPress.com
Web site: http://www.ImaginatorPress.com
Dist(s): **Beagle Bay Bks.**
Lightning Source, Inc.

Imagine Books *See* **Imagine! Studios**

Imagine Publishing *Imprint of* **Charlesbridge Publishing, Inc.**

Imagine Publishing, *(978-0-9758899)* 7620 Dogleg Rd., Dayton, OH 45414 USA Fax: 937-890-7949
E-mail: skyblu40@earthlink.net.

Imagine! Studios, *(978-0-9761317; 978-0-9764353; 978-0-9767913; 978-1-937944)* PO Box 16298, High Point, NC 27261 USA Tel 941-999-1278
E-mail: contact@artsimage.com
Web site: http://www.artsimagine.com
Dist(s): **BookBaby.**

Imagine That Enterprises, *(978-0-9723067)* P.O. Box 29315, Saint Louis, MO 63126 USA
E-mail: underthedove@hotmail.com
Web site: http://www.underthedove.com.

Imagine the Possibilities, LLC *See* **Imagining Possibilities**

Imagineland, Ltd., *(978-0-9765038)* P.O. Box 10134, College Station, TX 77842-0134 USA
Web site: http://www.imagineland.com
Dist(s): **Smashwords.**

IMAGINEX, LLC, *(978-0-9753620)* P.O. Box 1375, Frisco, TX 75034 USA; *Imprints:* Bible Game (BibleGame)
Web site: http://www.imnex.net.

Imagining Possibilities, *(978-0-9747426)* P.O. Box 266, Gwynedd Valley, PA 19437-0266 USA.

Imago, *(978-0-9765179)* 14220 Duckett Rd., Brandywine, MD 20613-9343 USA Tel 856-812-0400; Toll Free Fax: 866-268-9003; Toll Free: 866-413-6864.

Imago Pr., *(978-0-9725303; 978-0-9799341; 978-1-935437; 978-0-9981791)* 3710 E. Edison St., Tucson, AZ 85716-2912 USA; *Imprints:* As Sabr Publications (AsSabr)
Web site: http://www.imagobooks.com; http://www.oasisjournal.org.

ImaJinn Bks. *Imprint of* **BelleBks., Inc.**

Imani Productions, *(978-0-615-14325-5)* 2261 Bernwood Dr., Erie, PA 16510 USA Tel 814-897-0502
E-mail: umemesababu@aol.com
Web site: http://www.imaniproductions.org.

Imani-MCHS, *(978-0-9729586)* 3445 W. 66th Pl., Chicago, IL 60629 USA Tel 773-925-6473
E-mail: imanimchs@aol.com.

I-Mar, *(978-0-9741052)* 5150 Rancho Rd., Huntingtn Bch, CA 92647-2074 USA
Web site: http://www.i-mar.net.

ImaRa Publishing, *(978-0-9843111)* Orders Addr.: 3002 230th Ln., SE, Sammamish, WA 98075 USA
E-mail: vrpearce@msn.com
Web site: http://www.imarapublishing.com.

ImBost Inc., *(978-0-9848626)* 158 E. 100 St. Ste 6R, New York, NY 10029 USA Tel 917-482-5178
E-mail: taekwontales@gmail.com.

Imdalind Pr., *(978-0-9884837; 978-0-9914313; 978-0-9964632)* 7377 W. Jefferson Rd., Magna, UT 84044 USA Tel 801-259-4043
E-mail: me@rebeccaethington.com.

Immediex Publishing, *(978-1-932968)* 540 Evelyn Pl., Beverly Hills, CA 90210 USA Tel 310-273-1585
E-mail: rodney@immediex.com
Web site: www.immediex.com
Dist(s): **Smashwords.**

Immedium, *(978-1-59702)* P.O. Box 31846, San Francisco, CA 94131 USA
Web site: http://www.immedium.com
Dist(s): **Consortium Bk. Sales & Distribution**
MyiLibrary.

Immortal Works LLC, *(978-0-692-78113-5; 978-0-692-83650-7; 978-0-692-88092-0; 978-0-9990205)* 1505 Glenrose Dr., SALT LAKE CITY, UT 84104 USA Tel 801-651-4024.

Immortality Pr., *(978-0-9795753)* 1005 Winthrope Chase Dr., Alpharetta, GA 30004 USA
E-mail: publisher@immortalitypress.com; order@immortalitypress.com
Web site: http://www.immortalitypress.com.

Imogen Rose, *(978-0-615-34507-9; 978-0-615-37681-3; 978-0-9828002; 978-0-9850797; 978-0-9856766; 978-1-940015)* 18 Westwinds Dr., Princeton Junction, NJ 08550 USA
E-mail: portalchronicles@hotmail.com
Dist(s): **Lulu Pr., Inc.**
Smashwords.

Impact *Imprint of* **F&W Media, Inc.**

Impact Bks. *Imprint of* **Stone Arch Bks.**

Impact Pubns., *(978-0-942710; 978-1-57023)* Div. of Development Concepts, Inc., 9104 Manassas Dr., Suite N, Manassas Park, VA 20111-5211 USA (SAN 240-1142) Tel 703-361-7300; Fax: 703-335-9486 Do not confuse with companies with the same name in Evanston, IL, Mandeville, LA, Southfield, MI
E-mail: krannich@impactpublications.com
Web site: http://www.impactpublications.com
Dist(s): **Follett School Solutions**
MyiLibrary
National Bk. Network
ebrary, Inc.

Impact Publications, Incorporated *See* **Specialty Pr., Inc.**

Impact Pubs. *Imprint of* **New Harbinger Pubns.**

Impetus Pr., *(978-0-9776693)* P.O. Box 10025, Iowa City, IA 52240-0001 USA Tel 319-321-6282 Do not confuse with Impetus Press in Atlanta, GA
E-mail: jennifer@impetuspress.com
Web site: http://www.impetuspress.com
Dist(s): **SPD-Small Pr. Distribution.**

Impossible Dreams Publishing Co., *(978-0-9786422)* 4123 Rancho Grande Pl., NW., Albuquerque, NM 87120 USA (SAN 851-139X)
E-mail: Quixote1818@aol.com
Web site: http://www.impossibledreamspub.com
Dist(s): **Bookmasters Distribution.**

Impressions By Veronica, *(978-0-692-80171-0)* .

Impressions Ink, *(978-1-882626)* 3918 Peachtree Ln., Memphis, TN 38135-9115 USA Tel 901-388-5382; Fax: 901-385-0256; Toll Free: 800-388-5382.

Imprexions Publishing Co., *(978-0-9742922)* 4910 Benley Ct., Apt 1, Manitowoc, WI 54220 USA Tel 309-550-1243
E-mail: listinsky@hotmail.com.

Imprint (IND) *(978-81-902436) Dist. by* **Macmillan.**

Imprint Academic (GBR) *(978-0-907845; 978-1-84540) Dist. by* **IngramPubServ.**

Imprint.li, *(978-0-9894891; 978-0-9897418)* 11015 122nd Ave. Kp N., Gig Harbor, WA 98329 USA Tel 253-853-4199
E-mail: carolyn@imprint.li
Web site: www.imprint.li.

Imprints, *(978-1-883986)* Div. of Spectrum Bks., Orders Addr.: P.O. Box 4365, Thousand Oaks, CA 91359 USA Tel 808-707-3336; Fax: 808-707-4446; Edit Addr.: 32151 Sailview Ln., Westlake Village, CA 91359 USA
Dist(s): **Continental Bk. Co., Inc.**

Impulse Surf, *(978-0-9744247)* Orders Addr.: 1106 Second St., PMB 823, Encinitas, CA 92024 USA Tel

760-431-6883; Fax: 760-436-7158; Edit Addr.: 7200 Ponto Dr., Carlsbad, CA 92009 USA
E-mail: franklinlives@yahoo.com
Web site: http://www.impulsesurf.com.

In Ardua Tendit Pr., *(978-0-9749673)* 464 Leton Dr., Columbia, SC 29210 USA Tel 803-608-0804
E-mail: mail@jessmaccallum.com
Web site: http://www.jessmaccallum.com
Dist(s): **BookBaby.**

In Audio *Imprint of* **Sound Room Pubs., Inc.**

In Between Bks., *(978-0-935430; 978-0-9802007)* P.O. Box 790, Sausalito, CA 94966 USA (SAN 213-6236) Tel 415-383-8447; Fax: 415-381-1938; 415-381-3513
E-mail: inbetweenbooks@atthebutterflytree.com; karla@inbetweenbooks.com; juno@inbetweenbooks.com
Web site: http://www.atthebutterflytree.com.

In Cahoots, *(978-0-9745990)* 105 Los Padres Way, Unit 6, Buellton, CA 93427 USA Do not confuse with In Cahoots in Marietta, GA
Dist(s): **SPD-Small Pr. Distribution.**

In Cider Pr., *(978-0-9721716)* P.O. Box 228, Barton, VT 05822 USA Tel 802-754-8889.

In Motion Books Incorporated *See* **Dakitab, Inc.**

In Our Words Inc., *(978-1-938040)* 6104 City Pl., Edgewater, NJ 07020 USA Tel 201-280-7399
E-mail: ahn.jaesuk@gmail.com.

In Search Of The Universal Truth (ISOTUT) *See* **DragonEye Publishing**

In the Desert, *(978-0-9744005)* 7990 E. Snyder Rd., No. 5106, Tucson, AZ 85750-9009 USA
Web site: http://www.inthedesert.biz.

In the Hands of a Child, *(978-1-60308)* 3271 Kerlikowske Rd., Coloma, MI 49038-8913 USA Toll Free: 866-426-3701
E-mail: niki@handsofachild.com; sales@handsofachild.com; info@handsofachild.com
Web site: http://www.Handsofachild.com.

In The Hse. Publishing Co., *(978-0-9760441)* 1122 N. 84th St., Seattle, WA 98103 USA
E-mail: projectfile@hotmail.com
Web site: http://www.projectgirl.com.

In The Lead Publishing *See* **Lone Cypress Pubs.**

In the Sky Publishing, *(978-0-9740438)* Orders Addr.: 26300 Ford Rd., No. 407, Dearborn Heights, MI 48127 USA Tel 313-792-0694
E-mail: cmlipson@wideopenwest.com
Web site: http://www.intheskypublishing.com.

In the Think of Things *See* **Rainbow Resource Ctr., Inc.**

In the Think of Things *Imprint of* **Rainbow Resource Ctr., Inc.**

In This Together Media, *(978-0-9858956; 978-0-9898166)* 5 Evergreen Ln., Larchmont, NY 10538 USA Tel 914-833-1189
E-mail: calbertine@gmail.com
Web site: www.inthistogethermedia.com
Dist(s): **INscribe Digital.**

In Time Pubns. Inc., *(978-0-9762857)* P.O. Box 190537, Fort Lauderdale, FL 33319 USA
Web site: http://www.intimepublications.com.

Inane Blabbering Bks. (GBR) *(978-0-9559798) Dist. by* **LuluCom.**

Inanna Pubns. & Education, Inc. (CAN) *(978-0-9681290; 978-0-9736709; 978-0-9782233; 978-0-9808822; 978-1-926708; 978-1-77133) Dist. by* **SPD-Small Pr Dist.**

Incentive Pubns., Inc., *(978-0-86530; 978-0-913916; 978-1-62950)* 233 N. Michigan Ave., Suite 2000, Chicago, IL 60601 USA (SAN 203-8005) Toll Free: 800-421-2830
E-mail: info@incentivepublications.com
Web site: http://www.incentivepublications.com
Dist(s): **Independent Pubs. Group**
MyiLibrary
ebrary, Inc.

Inch By Inch Pubns., LLC, *(978-0-9670941)* P.O. Box 15, Okemos, MI 48805 USA Tel 716-688-1515; Fax: 716-636-4058; Toll Free: 877-462-4967
E-mail: chofher@aol.com
Web site: http://www.inchbyinchbooks.com
Dist(s): **Partners Pubs. Group, Inc.**

Inclement Pr., *(978-0-9819736; 978-0-9886669)* P.O. Box 120, Sidney, IA 51652 USA.

Inclusive Books LLC, *(978-0-9778143)* 3027 New Natchez Trace, Nashville, TN 37215 USA Tel 615-383-1065
E-mail: estelle@estellecondra.com
Web site: http://www.inclusivebooks.com.

Incorgnito Publishing Pr. *Imprint of* **Market Management Group**

Incorporated Trustees of the Gospel Worker Society, The, *(978-0-9617506; 978-1-59843; 978-1-934981; 978-1-935338; 978-1-936272; 978-1-936897; 978-1-936898)* Div. of Union Gospel Pr., 1980 Brookpark Rd., Cleveland, OH 44109 USA (SAN 664-2845) Toll Free: 800-638-9988
Web site: http://www.uniongospelpress.com.

Incredible Kid, LLC, *(978-0-9755836)* 7095 Hollywood Blvd., Suite 461, Hollywood, CA 90028 USA.

Independence Books *See* **America Star Bks.**

Independent Media Institute *See* **AlterNet Bks.**

Independent Pub., *(978-1-4243; 978-1-59975; 978-1-60402; 978-1-60461; 978-1-60530; 978-1-60585; 978-1-60643; 978-1-60702; 978-1-60725; 978-1-60743; 978-1-61539; 978-1-61584; 978-1-61623; 978-1-61658; 978-1-4507; 978-1-4675; 978-1-4951; 978-0-9927847; 978-1-5323;-1-5323-0640-2) Div. of Bar Code Graphics, 875 N. Michigan Ave., Suite 2650, Chicago, IL 60615 USA Fax: 312-595-0725; Toll Free: 800-662-0701; 65 E. Wacker Pl., 18th Flr., Chicago, IL 60601 Tel 312-595-0600; Toll Free: 800-662-0703 Do not confuse with Independent Publishers in Bountiful, UT*
E-mail: pubserv@barcode-us.com
Web site: http://www.publisherservices-us.com; http://www.isbn-us.com
Dist(s): **Consortium Bk. Sales & Distribution**
D.A.P./Distributed Art Pubs.
Ebsco Publishing
Epicenter Pr., Inc.
Follett School Solutions
Leonard, Hal Corp.
Hay Hse., Inc.
Independent Pubs. Group
Lulu Pr., Inc.
Midpoint Trade Bks., Inc.
Outskirts Pr., Inc.
SCB Distributors
SPD-Small Pr. Distribution
Smashwords
TNT Media Group, Inc.
Univ. of Arkansas Pr.
eBookit.com
ebrary, Inc.

Independent Pub., *(978-1-62951; 978-1-63041; 978-1-63102; 978-1-63415; 978-1-943438; 978-1-943579; 978-1-943730; 978-1-943932; 978-1-944169; 978-1-944170; 978-1-944171; 978-1-944541; 978-1-944819; 978-1-944820; 978-1-945239; 978-1-945563; 978-1-63535; 978-1-947099) 427 California Ave Unit 1, Santa Monica, CA 90403 USA Tel 310-980-4668 Do not confuse with Independent Publisher in Chicago, IL, Pasadena, CA*
E-mail: ahoohooahoo@yahoo.com
Dist(s): **Lulu Pr., Inc.**

Independent Publisher Services, *(978-1-4243; 978-0-692-73622-7)* Orders Addr.: 444 N. Michigan Ave., #3500, Chicago, IL 60611 USA Toll Free: 800-662-0701
E-mail: sales@barcode-us.com
Dist(s): **Follett School Solutions**
Islander Group
Miller Trade Bk. Marketing.

Independent Pubs. Group, *(978-1-4956; 978-1-5136-1835-7)* Subs. of Chicago Review Pr., 814 N. Franklin, Chicago, IL 60610 USA (SAN 201-2936) Tel 312-337-0747; Fax: 312-337-5985; Toll Free: 800-888-4741
E-mail: frontdesk@ipgbook.com
Web site: http://www.ipgbook.com; http://www.trafalgarsquarepublishing.com.

Independent Spirit Publishing, *(978-0-9666919; 978-0-578-09203-4; 978-0-615-86951-3; 978-0-615-93315-3; 978-0-615-95976-4)* 15994 325th St., Goodhue, MN 55027 USA
Web site: http://www.nataliebuskethomas.com
Dist(s): **Lulu Pr., Inc.**

INDI Best *Imprint of* **INDI, LLC**

INDI, LLC, *(978-0-9789247; 978-1-935636)* 15508 W. Bell Rd. Suite 101-315, Surprise, AZ 85374-3436 USA Tel 623-556-2751; Fax: 602-524-7550; *Imprints:* INDI Best (INDIBest)
E-mail: jerry@writersreaders.com
Web site: http://www.writersreaders.com
Dist(s): **BookBaby**
Smashwords.

INDI Publishing Group *See* **INDI, LLC**

India Research Pr. (IND) *(978-81-87943; 978-81-901098) Dist. by* **IPG Chicago.**

Indian Hill Gallery of Fine Photography, *(978-0-9669079)* 671 River Rd., Wells, VT 05774 USA Tel 802-325-2274; Fax: 802-325-2276
E-mail: info@stephenschaub.com
Web site: http://www.indianhillgallery.com
Dist(s): **RAM Pubns. & Distribution.**

Indian Territory Publishing, *(978-0-9727068)* P.O. Box 43, Bennington, OK 74723-0043 USA
E-mail: wes@wesparker-itp.com; wes.parker@us.army.mil
Web site: http://www.wesparker-itp.com.

†Indiana Historical Society, *(978-0-87195)* 450 W. Ohio St., Indianapolis, IN 46202-3269 USA (SAN 201-5234) Tel 317-233-9557; 317-232-1882; Fax: 317-233-0857; Toll Free: 800-447-1830
E-mail: rvaught@indianahistory.org; cbennett@indianahistory.org
Web site: http://www.indianahistory.org
Dist(s): **Distributors, The**
Indiana Univ. Pr.; *CIP.*

†Indiana Univ. Pr., *(978-0-253; 978-0-86196)* 601 N. Morton St., Bloomington, IN 47404-3797 USA (SAN 202-5647) Fax: 812-855-7931; Toll Free: 800-842-6796; *Imprints:* Quarry Books (Quarry Books)
E-mail: iuporder@indiana.edu
Web site: http://www.iupress.indiana.edu
Dist(s): **Ebsco Publishing**
Ingram Publisher Services
Lightning Source, Inc.
MyiLibrary
Transaction Pubs.
ebrary, Inc.; *CIP.*

., Orders Addr.: 528 E. Lorain St., Oberlin, OH 44074-1298 USA (SAN 134-2118) Tel 440-775-7777; Toll Free Fax: 800-344-5059; Toll Free: 800-321-3883 (orders only); 800-458-9303 (backorder status only); 800-334-9882 (support programs/technical support); Whitlow Campus Store-indiCo 1 1550 Clarke Dr., DUBUQUE, IA 52001-3198 (SAN 990-560X)
E-mail: service@goindico.com; orders@goindico.com
Web site: http://www.nacscorp.com.

Indie Artist Pr., *(978-1-62522)* Orders Addr.: 90 W 100 N No. 6, Price, UT 84501 USA
Web site: http://www.indieartistpress.com
Dist(s): **Suite 3 Productions.**

Indie Christian Book Group *Imprint of* **IndieGo Publishing LLC**

Indie Publishing Group, *(978-0-692-43389-8; 978-1-5307; 978-1-988656)* 242 W dilcrest, Florence, KY 41042 USA Tel (859)3718242
Web site: JacobCartlidge.com
Dist(s): **CreateSpace Independent Publishing Platform.**

IndieArtz, Inc., *(978-0-9753252)* 1650 Margaret St., Suite 302-131, Jacksonville, FL 32204-3869 USA
Web site: http://www.indieartz.com.

IndieGo ePublishing LLC *See* **IndieGo Publishing LLC**

IndieGo Publishing LLC, *(978-0-9846685; 978-0-9887048; 978-0-9916307; 978-0-9860953; 978-0-9976021; 978-1-946824)* Orders Addr.: 2341 Evenglow Ct., Deltona, FL 32725 USA; *Imprints:* Indie Christian Book Group (Indie Christ BG)
E-mail: indiegopublishing@gmail.com
Web site: http://www.indiegopublishing.com/.

Indigo Custom Publishing *See* **Sphinx Publishing**

Indigo Hse. Publishing, LLC, *(978-0-615-17978-0; 978-0-9820687)* 6938 Beverly Ln., Scottsdale, AZ 85254 USA
E-mail: MicaMoonBooks@gmail.com
Web site: http://www.micamoonbooks.com.

Indigo Impressions, *(978-0-9788339)* Orders Addr.: P.O. Box 501, Speonk, NY 11972-0501 USA
E-mail: meghanspd@yahoo.com
Dist(s): **BookBaby.**

Indigo, LLC, *(978-0-9758995)* 7486 North Shore Rd., Norfolk, VA 23505 USA Tel 757-622-3319
E-mail: lee@indigoart.net
Web site: http://www.indigoart.net
Dist(s): **Norfolk SPCA.**

Indigo Pubns., *(978-0-9646680)* Orders Addr.: 68-1030 Mauna Lani Point Dr., Kamuela, HI 96743 USA (SAN 298-9921) Tel 808-345-2001; 808-345-0805
E-mail: mel@malinowski.com; judy@malinowski.com
Web site: http://www.snorkelguides.com.

Indigo Sea Pr., LLC, *(978-1-935171; 978-1-938101; 978-1-63066)* 931-B S. Main St., Box 145, Kernersville, NC 27284 USA
E-mail: willhodam@yahoo.com; indigoseapress@gmail.com
Web site: http://secondwindpublishing.com/; http://indigoseapress.com
Dist(s): **Smashwords.**

Individualized Education Systems/Poppy Lane Publishing, *(978-0-938911)* Orders Addr.: P.O. Box 5136, Fresno, CA 93755 USA (SAN 661-8405) Tel 559-299-4639; Edit Addr.: 134 Poppy Ln., Clovis, CA 93612 USA (SAN 661-8413)
E-mail: Bette1234@aol.com
Web site: http://www.poppylane.com
Dist(s): **American West Bks.**

IndoEuropeanPublishing.com, *(978-1-60444)* 4215 Vineland Ave., No. 17, Studio City, CA 91602 USA
E-mail: Alfredagha@gmail.com
Web site: http://IndoEuropeanPublishing.com.

Indulgence Pr., *(978-0-9742191)* 250 N. 3rd Ave. #224, Minneapolis, MN 55401 USA Tel 612-379-4743
Web site: http://www.indulgencepress.com.

Industrial Gingerbread, *(978-0-9860691)* 61-33 ALDERTON ST, REGO PARK, NY 11374 USA Tel 718-478-8537
E-mail: richard.a.west@jpmchase.com.

IndyPublish.com, *(978-1-58827; 978-1-4043; 978-1-4142; 978-1-4219; 978-1-4280; 978-1-4353; 978-1-4378; 978-1-4491)* 170 Gore St. Suite 405, Cambridge, MA 02141 USA
E-mail: info@indypublish.com
Dist(s): **Lightning Source, Inc.**
TextStream.

Infant Learning Co., The, *(978-0-9657510; 978-1-931026)* 5009 Isle Royal Ct., Oceanside, CA 92057 USA Tel 760-630-6204; Fax: 760-630-3894; Toll Free: 888-463-2681
E-mail: brendan@infantlearning.com; lisa@infantlearning.com
Web site: http://www.infantlearning.com; http://www.yourbabycanread.com
Dist(s): **Penton Overseas, Inc.**

Infini Pr., LLC, *(978-1-932457)* Orders Addr.: P.O. Box 9096, Cincinnati, OH 45209-9096 USA Toll Free: 800-765-5885; Edit Addr.: 1120 Ave. of the Americas, Fourth Flr., New York, NY 10036 USA; *Imprints:* Asia for Kids (Asia for Kids)
E-mail: info@infinipress.com
Web site: http://www.infinipress.com
Dist(s): **Follett School Solutions**
Master Communications, Inc.

Infinite Adventure, *(978-0-9790720)* 6043 S. Danielson Way, Chandler, AZ 85249 USA
E-mail: amb0457@cox.net
Web site: http://www.members.cox.net/valuevolga.

Infinite Light Publishing, *(978-0-9884537; 978-0-9970467; 978-1-947925)* 5142 Hollister Ave. No. 115, Santa Barbara, CA 93111 USA Tel 805-350-3239
E-mail: ayn@infinitelightpublishing.com; info@infinitelightpublishing.com; aynsgold@yahoo.com
Web site: www.ayncatessullivan.com; www.astoryofbecoming.net; www.infinitelightpublishing.com.

Infinite Love Publishing, *(978-0-9794827)* 15127 NE 24th St., No. 341, Redmond, WA 98052 USA (SAN 853-5264) Toll Free: 888-733-7105
E-mail: sales@jackiechristie.com; dotti@dotdesign.net
Web site: http://www.jackiechristie.com.

Infinite Visions Forum, *(978-0-9770405)* Orders Addr.: P.O. Box 938, La Verne, CA 91750 USA Tel 909-593-7332 (phone/fax); Edit Addr.: 4095 Fruit St., SP 938, La Verne, CA 91750 USA
E-mail: ivforum@aol.com.

Infinity Oak Bks., *(978-0-9885066)* Orders Addr.: P.O. Box 195964, Dallas, TX 75219 USA Tel 972-803-4744
E-mail: jillksayre@me.com.

Infinity One Publishing, *(978-0-9772888)* P.O. Box 725394, Atlanta, GA 31139 USA Tel 678-760-6664; Fax: 617-507-8352
E-mail: thesleepysteve@yahoo.com.

Infinity Publishing *See* **Macro Publishing Group**

Infinity Publishing, *(978-0-9640184)* 8525 Evergreen Ln., Darien, IL 60561 USA Tel 708-985-2300; Fax: 708-985-2339 Do not confuse with companies with same name in Seattle WA, Lansing IL, West Palm Beach, FL.

Infinity Publishing, *(978-0-9665678; 978-1-892896; 978-0-7414; 978-1-4958)* Div. of Buy Books On The Web.Com, 1094 New Dehaven St., Suite 100, West Conshohocken, PA 19428 USA Tel 610-941-9999; Fax: 610-941-9959; Toll Free: 877-289-2665
E-mail: info@infinitypublishing.com
Web site: http://www.buybooksontheweb.com; http://www.infinitypublishing.com/
Dist(s): **Smashwords.**

Infinity Publishing Co., *(978-0-9799487)* 11111 N. Scottsdale Rd., Suite 205, Scottsdale, AZ 85260 USA Tel 480-703-0606
E-mail: pchambers8@cox.net
Web site: http://www.infinitypublishingcompany.com.

Infinity Studios LLC, *(978-1-59697)* 2601 Hilltop Dr. Apt. 815, San Pablo, CA 94806-5797 USA Do not confuse with companies with the same or similar name in Austin, TX
E-mail: info@infinitystudios.com
Web site: http://www.infinitystudios.com
Dist(s): **Diamond Comic Distributors, Inc.**
Diamond Bk. Distributors.

Influence, *(978-1-936699; 978-1-937830; 978-1-938309; 978-1-62912)* 1445 N. Boonville Ave., Springfield, MO 65802 USA Tel 417-831-8000; Fax: 417-862-5881
E-mail: apargo@ag.org; SUPPORT@INFLUENCERESOURCES.COM; tbledsoe@ag.org
Web site: http://store.influenceresources.com/
Dist(s): **BookMasters, Inc.**
Lulu Pr., Inc.
MyiLibrary
ebrary, Inc.

Infobus, Inc., *(978-0-9771184)* 19 Yellow Brook Rd., Holmdel, NJ 07733-1967 USA Tel 732-332-0232.

InfoHi Publishing, *(978-0-9678605; 978-0-9717849)* P.O. Box 1688, Fremont, CA 94538 USA Tel 831-685-1063
E-mail: linda@infohi.com
Web site: http://www.infohi.com
Dist(s): **Booklines Hawaii, Ltd.**

Information Age Publishing, Inc., *(978-1-930608; 978-1-931576; 978-1-59311; 978-1-60752; 978-1-61735; 978-1-62396; 978-1-68123; 978-1-64113)* P.O. Box 79049, Charlotte, NC 28271 USA (SAN 925-9228) Tel 704-752-9125; Fax: 704-752-9113 Do not confuse with Information Age Publishing in Exeter, NH
E-mail: iap@infoagepub.com; info@infoagepub.com
Web site: http://www.infoagepub.com
Dist(s): **ebrary, Inc.**

Infusionmedia Publishing, *(978-0-9704852; 978-0-9718677; 978-0-9796586; 978-0-9843101)* 140 N. 8th St., Suite 205, Lincoln, NE 68508-1358 USA (SAN 253-9136) Tel 402-477-2065 (phone/fax)
E-mail: info@infusionmediapublishing.com
Web site: http://www.infusionmediapublishing.com
Dist(s): **Smashwords.**

Ingenuity 31 Inc., *(978-0-578-05331-8)* 109 N. Church St., Waynesboro, PA 17268 USA
E-mail: ingenuity31@yahoo.com.

Ingle, Rosalie, *(978-0-578-09876-0)* P.O. Box 8636, St. Joseph, MO 64508 USA.

Ingleside Pr., *(978-1-929883)* P.O. Box 30029, Baltimore, MD 21215 USA
E-mail: inglesidepress@yahoo.com
Web site: http://www.behance.net/inglesidepress.

Ingram Publisher Services, Orders Addr.: Customer Services, Box 512 1 Ingram Blvd., LaVergne, TN 37086 USA Toll Free Fax: 800-838-1149; Edit Addr.: 1 Ingram Blvd., LaVergne, TN 37086 USA (SAN 631-8630) Tel 615-793-5000; Fax: 615-213-5811
E-mail: customer.service@ingrampublisherservices.com; Publisher@ingrampublisherservices.com; Retailer@ingrampublisherservices.com
Web site: http://www.ingrampublisherservices.com.

Ingram, Sean Inc., *(978-0-9749049; 978-0-615-11910-6)* 176 Lane Rd., Stantonsburg, NC 27883 USA Tel 919-517-7326; Fax: 919-870-7227
E-mail: sean@seaningram.com
Web site: http://www.seaningram.com.

Ingram's Nutrition Consultations, *(978-0-9769379)* 43889 Bayview Ave. Apt. 40107, Clinton Twp, MI 48038-7073 USA; 7701 Corporate Dr., No.212, Houston, TX 77036 (SAN 850-5179) Tel 281-513-4596; Fax: 713-771-2177
E-mail: admin@ingramsnutritionconsultations.com
Web site: http://www.ingram's nutrition.com.

INgrooves *See* **INscribe Digital**

Inhabit Media Inc. (CAN) *(978-0-9782186; 978-1-926569; 978-1-927095; 978-1-77227) Dist. by* **IPG Chicago.**

Inheritance Pr., Inc., *(978-0-9638086; 978-0-9749501)* Orders Addr.: P.O. Box 580, Trenton, NC 28585-0580 USA; Edit Addr.: 388 Henderson Ln., Trenton, NC 28585 USA.

Inherst, Marie, *(978-0-9749785)* 52670 TH 180, Beallsville, OH 43716-9226 USA.

Ink & Feathers Comics, *(978-0-9664974)* Div. of Ink & Feathers Calligraphy, Orders Addr.: 202 E. Grove St., Streator, IL 61364 USA Tel 815-672-1171
E-mail: nerwonduh@hotmail.com
Web site: http://www.ifcomics.com.

Ink & Quill Pubs. *Imprint of* **Mystic Pubs., Inc.**

Ink & Scribe, *(978-0-9679817; 978-1-931947)* Div. of Wise River Companies, Inc., 3101 Kintzley Ct. Unit J, Laporte, CO 80535-9393 USA Toll Free: 888-616-7720
E-mail: books@northfortynews.com
Web site: http://www.inkandscribe.com.

Ink Well, (978-0-9767578) P.O. Box 786, Winlock, WA 98596 USA; *Imprints:* Ink Well Publishing (I W P) Do not confuse with Ink Well in Hermosa Beach, CA.
Ink Well Publishing *Imprint of* **Ink Well**
Inkberry Pr., (978-0-9742148) 15521 Shell Point Blvd., Fort Myers, FL 33908 USA Tel 239-466-2757
E-mail: wallykain@comcast.net.
Inkberry Pr., (978-0-9838293) 4110 S. Highland Dr. Suite 340, Salt Lake City, UT 84124 USA Tel 801-949-1083
E-mail: editorial@leatherwoodpress.com.
Inkblot Bks., (978-1-932461) Orders Addr.: 1285 Stratford Ave STE-G No. 115, Dixon, CA 95620 USA; Edit Addr.: 415 Mast Ct, Dixon, CA 95620 USA
E-mail: kathompson@gmail.com
Web site: http://www.inkblotbooks.com
Dist(s): **Smashwords.**
Inkling Bks., (978-1-58742) 584 Homewood Dr., Auburn, AL 36830 USA Tel 334-369-9613
E-mail: editor@inklingbooks.com
Web site: http://www.inklingbooks.com/
Dist(s): **CreateSpace Independent Publishing Platform**
Smashwords.
Inklings Publishing, (978-0-9910211; 978-1-944428) 7222 Granvia Dr., Houston, TX 77083 USA Tel 281-736-7168
E-mail: fbrady.03@comcast.net
Web site: http://inklingspublishing.com.
Inknbeans Pr., (978-0-615-62429-7; 978-0-615-62896-7; 978-0-615-63408-1; 978-0-615-64400-4; 978-0-615-68085-9; 978-0-615-71952-8; 978-0-615-72837-7; 978-0-615-73222-0; 978-0-9886670; 978-0-615-73861-1; 978-0-615-74204-5; 978-0-615-74488-9; 978-0-615-74719-4; 978-0-615-74944-0; 978-0-615-74958-7; 978-0-615-74961-7; 978-0-615-75145-0; 978-0-615-75791-9; 978-0-615-75854-1; 978-0-615-76442-9; 978-0-615-76749-9; 978-0-615-77178-6; 978-0-615-77534-0; 978-0-615-78970-5; 978-0-615-80657-0; 978-0-615-81135-2; 978-) 25060 Hancock Ave. Bldg 103 Suite 458, Murrieta, CA 92560 USA Tel 951-471-8184
Web site: inknbeans.com
Dist(s): **CreateSpace Independent Publishing Platform.**
Inkshares, (978-1-941758; 978-1-942645; 978-1-947848) 415 Jackson St Suite B, San Francisco, CA 94111 USA Tel 919-418-0895
E-mail: thad@inkshares.com
Web site: inkshares.com
Dist(s): **Ingram Publisher Services.**
Inkspil Publishing, (978-0-9833877; 978-0-615-79874-5) 1676 W. Bryn Mawr, Chicago, IL 60660 USA Tel 708-824-8465
E-mail: inkspillbooks@gmail.com
Web site: www.inkspillbooks.com
Dist(s): **CreateSpace Independent Publishing Platform.**
Inkspill Publishing House *See* **Inkspil Publishing**
Inkwater Pr., (978-0-9719414; 978-1-59299; 978-1-62901) Div. of First Books, 6750 SW Franklin St., Suite A, Portland, OR 97223 USA Tel 503-968-6777; Fax: 503-968-6779
E-mail: orders@inkwaterpress.com
Web site: http://www.inkwaterpress.com; http://www.firstbooks.com.
Inkwell Books LLC, (978-0-9658158; 978-0-9718155; 978-0-9728118; 978-0-9740971; 978-0-9766340; 978-0-9786202; 978-0-9814648; 978-0-9829589; 978-0-9833247; 978-0-9848019; 978-0-9852501; 978-0-9883568; 978-1-939625; 978-0-9861743) Orders Addr.: 10632 N. Scottsdale Rd. Unit 695, Scottsdale, AZ 85254 USA Tel 480-315-3781
E-mail: info@inkwellbooksllc.com
Web site: http://inkwellbooksllc.com/.
Inkwell Productions, LLC *See* **Inkwell Books LLC**
InMediaRes Productions, (978-0-9792047; 978-1-934857; 978-1-936876; 978-1-941582; 978-1-942487; 978-1-947335) 303 91st Ave., PMB 202 E502, Lake Stevens, WA 98258 USA Fax: 425-948-1301; *Imprints:* Catalyst Game Labs (Catalyst Game)
Web site: http://www.imrpro.com; http://www.catalystgamelabs.com
Dist(s): **PSI (Publisher Services, Inc.).**
Innate Foundation Publishing, (978-0-9745866) 9682 Sherwood Dr., Blaine, WA 98230 USA Tel 360-441-9156
E-mail: rca@robertclydeaffolter.com
Web site: http://www.innatefoundation.com.
Inner Circle Publishing, (978-0-9770682) 1407 Crane St., Schenectady, NY 12303 USA Tel 518-377-0548.
Inner City Publications *See* **Citified Pubns.**
Inner Coaching, (978-0-9636027) 1108 Western Ave., Watertown, WI 53094 USA Tel 920-262-0439; Fax: 920-261-8801
E-mail: kids@readysetrelax.com
Web site: http://www.innercoaching.com
Dist(s): **Independent Pubs. Group**
New Leaf Distributing Co., Inc.
Quality Bks., Inc.
Inner Learning, (978-1-930640) 349 N. Detroit St., Los Angeles, CA 90036 USA Tel 323-549-0279; 923-549-0279; Fax: 323-549-0289
Dist(s): **Feldheim Pubs.**
Inner Light - Global Communications, (978-0-938294; 978-1-892062; 978-1-60611) Orders Addr.: P.O. Box 753, New Brunswick, NJ 08903 USA (SAN 662-0191) Tel 646-331-6777; Edit Addr.: 1231 Hamilton St., Somerset, NJ 08873 USA
E-mail: mrufo@hotmail.com
Dist(s): **Distributors, The**
Distributors International
New Leaf Distributing Co., Inc.
Quality Bks., Inc.
Red Wheel/Weiser
Unique Bks., Inc.
†**Inner Traditions International, Ltd.,** (978-0-89281; 978-1-59477; 978-1-62055) Orders Addr.: P.O. Box 388, Rochester, VT 05767-0388 USA Tel 802-767-3174; Fax: 802-767-3726; Toll Free Fax: 800-246-8648; Edit Addr.: One Park St., Rochester, VT 05767 USA (SAN 208-6948) Tel 802-767-3174; Fax: 802-767-3726; *Imprints:* Healing Arts Press (Heal Arts VT); Bindu Books (Bindu Bks)
E-mail: customerservice@innertraditions.com; info@innertraditions.com
Web site: http://www.innertraditions.com
Dist(s): **Beekman Bks., Inc.**
Book Wholesalers, Inc.
Bookazine Co., Inc.
Brodart Co.
Integral Yoga Pubns.
Library Sales of N.J.
Lotus Pr.
MyiLibrary
New Leaf Distributing Co., Inc.
Nutri-Bks. Corp.
Partners/West Book Distributors
Quality Bks., Inc.
Simon & Schuster
Simon & Schuster, Inc.
Unique Bks., Inc.; *CIP.*
Inner Wisdom Pubns., (978-0-9656741; 978-0-9774921) 22850 Summit Rd., Los Gatos, CA 95033 USA (SAN 299-2450) Tel 408-353-2050; Fax: 408-353-4663; Toll Free: 888-468-4335
E-mail: 15minutemiracle@verizon.net
Web site: http://www.15MinuteMiracle.com.
InnerChamp Bks., (978-0-9663949) P.O. Box 11362, Santa Rosa, CA 95406 USA Tel 707-571-8023; Fax: 707-546-3764
E-mail: inrchamp@aol.com
Web site: http://www.innerchamp.com.
Innerchild Publishing, Inc., (978-0-9768078) Orders Addr.: P.O. Box 142317, Fayetteville, GA 30214-2317 USA.
Innerchoice Publishing, (978-0-9625486; 978-1-56499) 24426 S. Main, Carson, CA 90745 USA Tel 310-816-3085; Fax: 310-816-3092
Dist(s): **Jalmar Pr.**
InnerCircle Publishing, (978-1-882918; 978-0-9723191; 978-0-9755214; 978-0-9762924) 522 Sadie St. Apt. 2, Laurens, IA 50554-1553 USA
Web site: http://www.innercirclepublishing.com; http://www.rev-press.com.
InnerRESOURCES Pubns., (978-0-9728389) 109 E. 73rd St., New York, NY 10021 USA
E-mail: jeff@jefflandau.com; jefflandau@innerresources.org
Web site: http://jeffs.smugmug.com/; http://www.jefflandau.com; http://www.innerresources.org; http://www.flickr.com/photos/8ideas/
Dist(s): **Lightning Source, Inc.**
innertuber, (978-0-9742742) 2124 NE 7th St., Gainesville, FL 32609 USA.
Innov8 Studios, (978-0-9754544) 16 Cedarwood Dr., Ballston Lake, NY 12019 USA
E-mail: innov8studios@nycap.rr.com.
Innovation Game, The, (978-0-9643819) 8509 Irvington Ave., Bethesda, MD 20817 USA Tel 301-530-4299.
Innovation Pr., The, (978-1-943147) 391 SE Crystal Creek Cir, Issaquah, WA 98027 USA Tel 360-870-9988
E-mail: acitro@theinnovationpress.com
Web site: www.theinnovationpress.com
Dist(s): **Legato Pubs. Group.**
Innovative Christian Pubns. *Imprint of* **Baker Trittin Pr.**
Innovative Kids, (978-1-58476; 978-1-60169) Div. of Innovative USA, Inc., 18 Ann St., Norwalk, CT 06854-2258 USA Tel 203-838-6400; Fax: 203-855-5582; *Imprints:* IKIDS (IKIDS)
E-mail: info@innovativekids.com
Web site: http://www.innovativekids.com
Dist(s): **Hachette Bk. Group.**
Innovative Language, LLC, (978-0-9765236) P.O. Box 1593, Eugene, OR 97440-1593 USA.
Innovative Logistics, Orders Addr.: 575 Prospect St., Lakewood, NJ 08701 USA (SAN 760-6532) Tel 732-534-7001; 732-363-5679; Fax: 732-363-0338
E-mail: innlogorders@innlog.net
Web site: http://www.innlog.net.
Innovo Pr. *Imprint of* **Innovo Publishing, LLC**
Innovo Publishing, LLC, (978-0-9815403; 978-1-936076; 978-1-61314) 159 College St., Collierville, TN 38017 USA Fax: 901-221-4055; Toll Free: 888-546-2111; *Imprints:* Innovo Press (Innovo Pr)
E-mail: info@innovopublishing.com
Web site: http://www.innovopublishing.com.
Inprint Bks., (978-0-9814510; 978-0-9973316) 1223 Wilshire Blvd., Suite 1413, Santa Monica, CA 90403 USA (SAN 855-5923).
INscribe Digital, (978-1-61750; 978-1-62517) Div. of IPG, 55 Francisco St. Suite 710, San Francisco, CA 94105 USA; *Imprints:* Brown Girls Publishing (BrownGirls)
E-mail: digitalpublishing@ingrooves.com
Web site: http://www.INscribeDigital.com
Dist(s): **Independent Pubs. Group**
Lulu Pr., Inc.
Insect Lore, (978-1-891541) Orders Addr.: P.O. Box 1535, Shafter, CA 93263 USA Tel 661-746-6047; Fax: 661-746-0334; Toll Free: 800-548-3284; Edit Addr.: 132 S. Beech St., Shafter, CA 93263 USA
E-mail: john@insectlore.com
Web site: http://www.insectlore.com.
Insect Sciences Museum of California, (978-0-9764454) 3644 Calafia Ave., Oakland, CA 94605 USA; *Imprints:* Exploring California Insects (Ex CA In)
E-mail: insectnet@aol.com
Web site: http://www.bugpeople.org.
Insight Editions, (978-1-933784; 978-1-60887; 978-0-615-39977-5; 978-0-615-50360-8; 978-0-615-50366-0; 978-1-68298; 978-1-68383) 800 A St., San Rafael, CA 94901 USA; P.O. Box 3088, San Rafael, CA 94912 Tel 415-526-1370; Fax: 866-509-0515 eFax
Web site: http://www.insighteditionscreative.com
Dist(s): **Simon & Schuster, Inc.**
Insight Editions LP/ IncrediBuilds *See* **Insight Editions**
Insight Publishing Group, (978-1-930027; 978-1-932503) Div. of Insight International, Inc., 8801 S. Yale, Suite 410, Tulsa, OK 74137 USA Tel 918-493-1718; Fax: 918-493-2219; Toll Free: 800-924-8264 Do not confuse with companies with similar names in Parker, CO, Yreka,CA, Jacksonville, FL, Woodbridge, VA, Salt Lake City, UT
E-mail: info@freshword.com
Web site: http://www.freshword.com
Dist(s): **Smashwords.**
Insight Services, Inc, (978-0-9786034) 1020 Hummingbird Ct., Springfield, TN 37172-5563 USA (SAN 851-092X); *Imprints:* Children's Insight (Children's Insight)
E-mail: childrensinsight@learnlivebetter.com
Web site: http://www.learnlivebetter.com.
Insight Studios, LLC *See* **Bugeye Bks.**
Insight Technical Education, (978-0-9722058; 978-0-9755280) 13410 NE 92nd St., Vancouver, WA 98682 USA Tel 360-852-6152
E-mail: webinfo@sixbranches.com
Web site: http://www.insightteched.com.
Inspirasian Pr. LLC, (978-0-9743882) P.O. Box 460256, San Francisco, CA 94146-0256 USA Tel 415-282-7925; Fax: 415-282-6427
Web site: http://www.inspirasian.com
Dist(s): **Bookmasters Distribution.**
Inspiration Pr. Inc., (978-0-9798395) 8598 N. W. St., Coral Springs, FL 33071 USA
Dist(s): **TNT Media Group, Inc.**
Inspiration Software, Inc., (978-0-928539; 978-1-932463; 978-1-933238; 978-1-934425) 9400 SW Beaverton Hillsdale Hwy., No. 300, Beaverton, OR 97005 USA (SAN 670-8234) Toll Free: 800-877-4292
E-mail: jbrooks@inspiration.com
Web site: http://www.inspiration.com
Dist(s): **Follett School Solutions.**
Inspirational Hse. of America, (978-0-9768598) 93 Jay Ln., Gasburg, VA 23857 USA.
Inspire Every Child dba Illumination Arts, (978-0-615-50779-8; 978-0-9855417) 808 6th St. S., Ste 200, Kirkland, WA 98033 USA Tel 425-968-5097; Fax: 425-968-5634
E-mail: jthompson@illumin.com
Web site: www.illumin.com.
Inspire Media, LLC *See* **Motivision Media**
Inspire Press, Inc., (978-0-9741800) P.O. Box 33241, Los Gatos, CA 95030 USA Tel 408-395-2003; Fax: 408-904-4662
E-mail: sharper@inspirepress.com
Web site: http://www.inspirepress.com.
Inspire Pubns., (978-0-9725292) 13229 Middle Canyon Rd., Carmel Valley, CA 93924 USA (SAN 255-1225) Tel 831-917-6059; Fax: 831-659-8460
E-mail: larryhayes@mynamestartswith.com; lhayes@mynamestartswith.com
Web site: http://www.mynamestartswith.com.
Inspire U., LLC, (978-0-9792361) 30520 Rancho California Rd., Suite 107-64, Temecula, CA 92591 USA (SAN 852-8535).
Inspired By Family, (978-0-9787074) 1332 Westmore Ct., Srevens Point, WI 54481 USA
Web site: http://www.inspiredbyfamily.com.
Inspired by the Beach Co., (978-0-9790415) Orders Addr.: P.O. Box 174, Simpsonville, MD 21150-0174 USA
E-mail: mjareaux@ureach.com
Web site: http://www.26thingstoteach.com.
Inspired By the Beach Publishing *See* **Inspired by the Beach Co.**
InspirEd Educators, (978-1-933558; 978-1-938275) 350 Waverly Hall Cir., Roswell, GA 30075 USA Tel 770-649-7571; Fax: 770-642-7568; Toll Free: 866-WE-INSPIRE (866-934-6774)
E-mail: sharon@inspirededucators.com; lainey@inspirededucators.com
Web site: http://www.inspirededucators.com.
Inspired Idea, (978-1-931203) 4105 Buckthorn Ct., Flower Mound, TX 75028 USA
E-mail: Eve@pharaohsofthebible.com; Eve@Engelbrite.com
Web site: http://www.kneelingmedia.org.
Inspiring Voices *Imprint of* **Author Solutions, Inc.**
Instant Help Books *Imprint of* **New Harbinger Pubns.**
Instant Pub., (978-1-59196; 978-1-59872; 978-1-60458; 978-1-61422) Orders Addr.: P.O. Box 985, Collierville, TN 38027 USA Tel 901-853-7070; Fax: 901-853-6196; Toll Free: 800-259-2592; Edit Addr.: 410 Hwy 72 W., Collierville, TN 38017 USA
Web site: http://www.instantpublisher.com
Dist(s): **BookBaby**
Lulu Pr., Inc.
Smashwords.
Instantpublisher.com *See* **Instant Pub.**
Institute For Behavior Change Incorporated The, (978-0-9770503) 9900 W. Sample Rd., Suite 300, Coral Springs, FL 33065 USA Tel 954-755-6639; Fax: 954-755-4100
E-mail: rhall3318@acn.net
Web site: http://www.afterthestormchildrensbook.com.
Institute for Conscious Change, The, (978-0-9743443) Div. of BioPlan Associates, Inc., Orders Addr.: 8987 E. Tanque Verde Rd. Ste. 309, Tucson, AZ 85749-9399 USA
E-mail: info@ConsciousChange.org
Web site: http://www.ConsciousChange.org.
Institute for Creation Research, (978-0-932766; 978-1-935587; 978-1-946246) 1806 Royal Ln., Dallas, TX 75229 USA Tel 214-615-8331.
Institute for Disabilities Research & Training, Inc., (978-0-9667589; 978-0-9752933; 978-0-9760818; 978-0-9789373) 11323 Amherst Ave., Wheaton, MD 20902 USA Tel 301-942-4326; Fax: 301-942-4439
E-mail: sales@idrt.com
Web site: http://www.idrt.com.
Institute for Economic Democracy Pr., Inc., (978-0-9624423; 978-0-9753555; 978-1-933567) 13851 N. 103rd Ave., Sun City, AZ 85351-4520 USA Tel 623-583-2518; Toll Free: 888-533-1020 (credit card orders)
E-mail: cc@ccus.info; ied@ied.info
Web site: http://www.ied.info.
Institute for Food & Development Policy/Food First Bks., (978-0-935028; 978-0-9970989) 398 60th St., Oakland, CA 94618-1212 USA (SAN 213-327X) Tel 510-654-4400; Fax: 510-654-4551
E-mail: marthak@foodfirst.org
Web site: http://www.foodfirst.org
Dist(s): **L P C Group**
Two Rivers Distribution.
Institute For Outdoor Awareness, Inc, (978-0-9835176; 978-0-9915227) 41 Linden Ave., Rutledge, PA 19070 USA Tel 610-544-8335
E-mail: phil@bartowassoc.com
Web site: phil@bartowassoc.com.
Institute for Preventative Sports Med., (978-0-9745655) P.O. Box 7032, Ann Arbor, MI 48107 USA Tel 734-434-3390; Fax: 734-572-4503
E-mail: admin@ipsm.org
Web site: http://www.ipsm.org.
Institute for Vaishnava Studies, (978-0-9981871) 1515 NW 7th Pl., Gainesville, FL 32603-1208 USA Tel 570-814-2150
E-mail: ivspublishing@gmail.com.
Institute of Cybernetics Research, Inc., (978-1-893375; 978-1-58578) Orders Addr.: 15 W. 139th St. Apt. 10G, New York, NY 10037-1516 USA
E-mail: icri@usa.net; journal_of_amateur_computing-subscribe@yahoogroups.com
Web site: http://groups.yahoo.com/groups/journal_of_amateur_computing/join
Dist(s): **American Heritage Magazine**
Analos Magazine
Theme Stream, Inc.
Wiley, John & Sons, Inc.
Institute of Physics Publishing, (978-0-7503; 978-0-85274; 978-0-85498) The Public Ledte Bldg., Suite 1035 150 S. Independence Mall, W., Philadelphia, PA 19106 USA (SAN 298-2315) Tel 215-627-0880; Fax: 215-627-0879; Toll Free: 800-632-0880; Dirac House Temple Back, Bristol, BS1 6BE Tel 44 (0) 117 929 7481; Fax: 44 (0) 117 930 1186
E-mail: book.enquiries@iop.org
Web site: http://bookmark.iop.org
Dist(s): **CRC Pr. LLC**
National Bk. Network.
Instream Flow Council, (978-0-9716743) c/o Wyoming Game & Fish, 5400 Bishop Blvd., Cheyenne, WY 82002 USA Tel 307-777-4600; Fax: 307-777-4611
E-mail: tannea@state.wy.us
Dist(s): **Bookmasters Distribution.**
Instructional Fair *Imprint of* **Carson-Dellosa Publishing, LLC**
Instructional Resources Co., (978-1-879478) P.O. Box 111704, Anchorage, AK 99511-1704 USA Tel 907-345-6689 (phone/fax)
E-mail: susan@susancanthony.com
Web site: http://www.susancanthony.com.
Instrument Society of America *See* **ISA**
Insu-Form, Incorporated *See* **I.Form Ink, Publishing**
Intaglio, Inc., (978-0-9748034) P.O. Box 211296, Montgomery, AL 36109 USA Tel 706-593-2749; Fax: 334-260-9373
E-mail: sperez@intaglioinc.com
Web site: http://www.intaglioinc.com.
Intaglio Pr., (978-0-944091) Orders Addr.: P.O. Box 9952, College Station, TX 77842 USA (SAN 242-7133) Tel 409-696-7800; Toll Free: 800-768-5565; Edit Addr.: 8709 Bent Tree, College Station, TX 77845 USA (SAN 242-7141)
E-mail: HDETHL9414@aol.com.
†**Integral Yoga Pubns.,** (978-0-932040; 978-1-938477) Satchidananda Ashram-Yogaville, 108 Yogaville Way, Buckingham, VA 23921 USA (SAN 285-0338) Tel 434-969-3121 ex 102; Fax: 434-969-1303; Toll Free: 800-262-1008 (orders)
Web site: http://www.yogaville.org
Dist(s): **BookMasters, Inc.**
Bookmasters Distribution
MyiLibrary
New Leaf Distributing Co., Inc.
ebrary, Inc.; *CIP.*
Intelligent Concepts, Inc., (978-0-9740612) 1889 N. Airport Dr., Lehi, UT 84043 USA Tel 801-766-0262
E-mail: joe@intelcon.biz
Web site: http://www.intelcon.biz.
Intellipop, LLC, (978-0-9743805) 2701 Troy Center Dr., Suite 275, Troy, MI 48084 USA Tel 248-269-6091; Fax: 248-269-6092
E-mail: info@intellipop.com
Web site: http://www.intellipop.com.
Interaction Point Games, LLC, (978-1-936326) 4544 Chowen Ave. N., Robbinsdale, MN 55422 USA
E-mail: brent@interactionpoint.com; info@interactionpoint.com
Web site: http://www.interactionpoint.com.
Interaction Pubs., Inc., (978-1-57336) Orders Addr.: P.O. Box 900, Fort Atkinson, WI 53538 USA; Edit Addr.: W5527 State Rd. 106, Fort Atkinson, WI 53538-0800 USA (SAN

631-2950) Tel 920-563-9571; Fax: 920-563-7395; Toll Free: 800-359-0961
E-mail: sales@interact-simulations.com; interact@highsmith.com
Web site: http://www.interact-simulations.com/; http://www.teachinteract.com.

Interactive Eye, L.L.C. *Imprint of* **Interactive Knowledge, Inc.**

Interactive Knowledge, Inc., (*978-0-9759464*) 142 High St., No. 618, Portland, ME 04101 USA Tel 207-775-2278; Fax: 413-778-6861; *Imprints:* Interactive Eye, L.L.C. (InterEye) Do not confuse with Interactive Knowledge, Inc., Charlotte, NC
E-mail: support@iknow.net
Web site: http://www.iknow.net.

Interactive Media Publishing, (*978-0-9744391; 978-1-934332*) Orders Addr.: P.O. Box 1407, Phoenix, OR 97535-1407 USA (SAN 256-095X) Tel 541-535-5552; Fax: 888-900-1598; *Imprints:* Once Upon A Time in a Classroom (OnceUponTime)
E-mail: orders@i-mediapub.com; linda@i-mediapub.com
Web site: http://www.i-mediapub.com; http://www.interactivemediapub.com
Dist(s): **New Leaf Distributing Co., Inc.**

Interactive Publishing Corporation (CAN) (*978-0-9918589*) *Dist. by* **Midpt Trade.**

Interactive Pubns. Pty, Ltd. (AUS) (*978-1-876819; 978-1-921479; 978-1-921869; 978-0-646-32685-6; 978-0-646-32746-4; 978-1-922120; 978-1-925231*) *Dist. by* **LightSource CS.**

Interactive Pubns. Pty, Ltd. (AUS) (*978-1-876819; 978-1-921479; 978-1-921869; 978-0-646-32685-6; 978-0-646-32746-4; 978-1-922120; 978-1-925231*) *Dist. by* **CreateSpace.**

Interactive Stories, (*978-0-692-23199-9; 978-0-692-36847-3; 978-0-692-37008-7; 978-1-945906*) 2001 Kingston Rd, Farmington, UT 84025 USA Tel 801-867-7493
Web site: http://minecraft-interactive.com
Dist(s): **CreateSpace Independent Publishing Platform.**

Intercollegiate Studies Institute, Incorporated *See* **ISI Bks.**

Intercultural Communication Services, Inc., (*978-0-9741881; 978-0-9773359*) 2580 SW 76th Ave., Portland, OR 97225-3305 USA Fax: 503-292-6817
E-mail: jolinda@jolindaosborne.com
Web site: http://www.jolindaosborne.com

Interdimensional Pr., (*978-0-9827753; 978-0-9911970*) 480 Lakeview Dr. Suite 107, Brentwood, CA 94513 USA Tel 925-513-1596 (phone/fax)
E-mail: pmcculley@comcast.net
Dist(s): **Lightning Source, Inc.**

Interface Publishing *See* **IGI Pr.**

Interior Dept. *Imprint of* **United States Government Printing Office**

Interlink Bks. *Imprint of* **Interlink Publishing Group, Inc.**

Interlink Publishing Group, Inc., (*978-0-940793; 978-1-56656; 978-1-62371*) 46 Crosby St., Northampton, MA 01060-1804 USA (SAN 664-8908) Tel 413-582-7054; Fax: 413-582-6731; Toll Free: 800-238-5465; *Imprints:* Crocodile Books (Crocodile Bks); Interlink Books (Interlink Bks)
E-mail: info@interlinkbooks.com; editor@interlinkbooks.com
Web site: http://www.interlinkbooks.com
Dist(s): **MyiLibrary**
Publishers Group West (PGW).

Interlink Resources International *See* **CJR**

Intermedia Publishing Group, (*978-0-9820458; 978-0-9819682; 978-1-935529; 978-1-935906; 978-1-937654; 978-0-615-56309-1*) Orders Addr.: P.O. Box 2825, Peoria, AZ 85380 USA Tel 623-337-8710; Fax: 623-867-9469
E-mail: halton@intermediapr.com; ldavis@intermediapr.com
Web site: http://www.intermediapub.com.

Intermedio Editores S.A. (COL) (*978-958-637*) *Dist. by* **Random.**

International Alliance Pro-Publishing, LLC, (*978-1-60942*) 7260 W. Azure Dr. 140-744, Las Vegas, NV 89130 USA Tel 206-339-9080
E-mail: therebox@yahoo.com
Web site: http://www.iappublishing.net.

International Arts & Artists, (*978-0-9662859; 978-0-9767102; 978-0-9883497; 978-0-9973099*) 9 Hillyer Ct., NW, Washington, DC 20008 USA Fax: 202-333-0758
E-mail: design@artsandartists.org; designstudio@artsandartists.org
Web site: http://www.artsandartists.org
Dist(s): **Tuttle Publishing**
Univ. of Washington Pr.

†**International Bk. Ctr., Inc.,** (*978-0-86685; 978-0-917062*) 2007 Laurel Dr., P.O. Box 295, Troy, MI 48099 USA (SAN 169-4014) Tel 248-879-7920; 586-254-7230; Fax: 586-254-7230
E-mail: ibc@ibcbooks.com
Web site: http://www.ibcbooks.com; *CIP.*

International Bk. Import Service, Inc., Orders Addr.: 161 Main St., P.O. Box 8188, Lynchburg, TN 37352-8188 USA (SAN 630-5679) Tel 931-759-7400; Fax: 931-759-7555; Toll Free: 800-277-4247
E-mail: IBIS@IBIService.com
Web site: http://www.IBIService.com.

International Business Pubns., USA, (*978-0-7397; 978-0-9646241; 978-1-57751; 978-1-4330; 978-1-4387; 978-1-5145*) P.O. Box 15343, Washington, DC 20003 USA Tel 202-546-2103; Fax: 202-546-3275; 6301 Stevenson Ave., # 1317, Alexandria, VA 22304 Tel 202-656-2103; Fax: 202-546-3275 Do not confuse with International Business Pubn., Inc. in Cincinnati, OH
E-mail: rusric@erols.com; ibpusa@comcast.net; ibpusa3@gmail.com
Web site: http://www.ibpus.com
Dist(s): **Lulu Pr., Inc.**

International Church of the Foursquare Gospel *See* **Foursquare Media, ICFG**

International Comics & Entertainment L.L.C., (*978-1-929090; 978-1-932575*) 1005 Mahone St., Fredericksburg, VA 22401 USA Tel 540-899-9186; Fax: 540-899-9196
E-mail: kblue@ic-ent.com
Web site: http://www.ic-ent.com
Dist(s): **Diamond Comic Distributors, Inc.**

International Council for Computers in Education *See* **International Society for Technology in Education**

International Council for Gender Studies, (*978-1-929656*) Orders Addr.: P.O. Box 702, Waxahachie, TX 75168 USA Fax: 972-937-9930; Toll Free: 800-317-6958
E-mail: rivilian@yahoo.com; icgsinfo@yahoo.com
Web site: http://www.fiveaspects.com; www.5aspects.org.

International Debate Education Assn., (*978-0-9702130; 978-0-9720541; 978-1-932716; 978-1-61770*) 224 W. 57th St., New York, NY 10019 USA Tel 212-547-6932; Fax: 646-557-2416; 105 E. 22nd St. Suite 915, New York, NY 10010 Tel 212-300-6076 x9
E-mail: martin.greenwald@opensocietyfoundations.org
Web site: http://www.idebate.org
Dist(s): **Books International, Inc.**

International Development Ctr., (*978-0-9774483; 978-0-9799873*) P.O. Box 25163, Arlington, VA 22202 USA Tel 703-766-0643
E-mail: mi.productions@yahoo.com; ouatiss@yahoo.com.

International Educational Improvement Ctr. Pr., (*978-1-884169*) Orders Addr.: c/o Dr. Archie W. Earl, Sr., Mathematics Dept. School of Science & Technology Norfolk State University, Norfolk, VA 23504 USA Tel 757-823-9564
E-mail: awearl@nsu.edu
Web site: http://www.webspawner.com/users/ieicpress/index.html.

International Graphic Group, (*978-0-9821692*) 838 Reedy St., Cincinnati, OH 45202 USA Tel 513-321-7884; Fax: 513-621-1619
E-mail: sales@iggbooks.com.

International Institute for Ecological Agriculture, (*978-0-9790437*) 309 Cedar St. No.127, Santa Cruz, CA 95060 USA (SAN 852-2847) Tel 831-471-9164; Toll Free: 888-737-6228
E-mail: ourstore@permaculture.com
Web site: http://www.permaculture.com.

International Language Centre, 1753 Connecticut Ave., NW, Washington, DC 20009 USA (SAN 209-1615) Tel 202-332-2894; Fax: 202-462-6657
E-mail: richard@newsinform.com; zisa@newsinform.com
Web site: http://www.newsinform.com.

International Learning Systems, Incorporated *See* **International Language Centre**

International Linguistics Corp., (*978-0-939990; 978-1-887371; 978-0-9814540*) 12220 Blue Ridge Blvd., Suite G, Grandview, MO 64030 USA (SAN 220-2573)
E-mail: jennifer@learnables.com
Web site: http://www.learnables.com.

International Localization Network, (*978-1-935018; 978-1-945423*) 109 Sunset Ct. No. 2., Hamburg, NY 14075 USA Tel 913-773-8323
E-mail: randy2905@gmail.com
Web site: www.ilncenter.com.

International Marine/Ragged Mountain Pr. *Imprint of* **McGraw-Hill Professional Publishing**

†**International Monetary Fund,** (*978-0-939934; 978-1-55775; 978-1-58906; 978-1-61635; 978-1-4518; 978-1-4519; 978-1-4527; 978-1-4552; 978-1-4623; 978-1-4639; 978-1-4755; 978-1-4843; 978-1-4983; 978-1-5135*) c/o Publications Department, 700 19th St., NW, Washington, DC 20431 USA (SAN 203-8188) Tel 202-623-7899
E-mail: tdelrosario@imf.org; salavi@imf.org; jbeardow@imf.org
Web site: http://www.imf.org; http://.www.cibrary.imf.org
Dist(s): **Bernan Assocs.**
MyiLibrary
Rowman & Littlefield Publishers, Inc.
ebrary, Inc.; *CIP.*

International Pacific Halibut Commission, (*978-0-9776931*) P.O. Box 95009, Seattle, WA 98145-2009 USA Tel 206-634-1838
E-mail: lauri@iphc.washington.edu
Web site: http://www.iphc.washington.edu.

International Scientific Ctr., (*978-0-9630594*) 2655 E. 21st St., Brooklyn, NY 11235 USA Tel 718-368-2918.

International Society for Technology in Education, (*978-0-924667; 978-1-56484*) 175 W. Broadway., Suite 300, Eugene, OR 97401-3003 USA (SAN 296-7693) Toll Free: 800-336-5191
E-mail: iste@iste.org
Web site: http://www.iste.org
Dist(s): **Follett School Solutions.**

International Society of Sephardic Leadership Council *See* **ISLC**

International Specialized Book Services *See* **ISBS Publisher Services**

International Standard Book Numbering (ISBN) Agency (interim numbering procedure) *See* **U. S. ISBN Agency**

International Step by Step Assn., (*978-1-931854; 978-1-60195*) 400 W. 59th St., New York, NY 10019 USA
E-mail: info@issa.nl
Web site: http://www.issa.nl.

International Tamil Language Foundation, (*978-0-9676212; 978-0-9793059*) 8417 Autumn Dr., Woodridge, IL 60517 USA Tel 630-985-3141; Fax: 630-985-3199
E-mail: Thiru@kural.org
Web site: http://www.kural.org.

International Training, Incorporated *See* **ITI Holdings, Inc.**

International Univ. Line, (*978-0-9636817; 978-0-9720774*) P.O. Box 2525, La Jolla, CA 92038 USA Tel 858-457-0595; Fax: 858-581-9073
E-mail: info@iul-press.com.

International Vaquero Productions, (*978-0-9761103*) 730 W. 8th St., Claremont, CA 91711 USA
E-mail: ivp1@me.com
Web site: http://www.kurtbeardsley.com.

International Wizard of Oz Club, The, (*978-1-930764*) P.O. Box 26249, San Francisco, CA 94126-6249 USA Fax: 510-642-7589 Do not confuse with International Wizard of OZ Club, Appleton, WI
E-mail: phanff@library.berkeley.edu
Web site: http://ozclub.org.

Interpact Press *See* **Schwartau, Winn LLC**

Interplay Productions, (*978-1-57629*) 16815 Von Karman Ave., Irvine, CA 92606-4920 USA Tel 714-553-6655; Fax: 714-252-2820.

InterPress, (*978-0-9744173*) 14056 Fort Valley Rd., Fort Valley, VA 22652 USA; *Imprints:* Fort Valley Geology Study Center (Ft Valley)
E-mail: wjmelson@shentel.net
Web site: http://interpressusa.com.

InterRelations Collaborative, Inc., (*978-0-9761753*) P.O. Box 6280, Hamden, CT 06517-3503 USA.

Interset Pr., (*978-1-57433*) Orders Addr.: 35 Burns Hill Rd., Wilton, NH 03086 USA Tel 603-654-2949
E-mail: artistafloat@earthlink.net; woad@earthlink.net
Dist(s): **Lulu Pr., Inc.**

Interstellar Publishing Co., (*978-0-9645957; 978-1-889599*) Orders Addr.: P.O. Box 7306, Beverly Hills, CA 90212 USA (SAN 298-5829) Tel 310-247-8154 (orders); Fax: 310-247-0622
E-mail: Interstlr@aol.com
Web site: http://www.interstellarpublishing.com.

Interstellar Trading & Publishing Company *See* **Interstellar Publishing Co.**

†**InterVarsity Pr.,** (*978-0-8308; 978-0-87784*) Div. of InterVarsity Christian Fellowship of the USA, Orders Addr.: P.O. Box 1400, Downers Grove, IL 60515 USA (SAN 202-7089) Tel 630-734-4000; Fax: 630-734-4200; Toll Free: 800-843-7225 (other depts.); 800-843-9487 (orders); 800-843-1019 (customer service); 800-873-0143 (electronic ordering)
E-mail: email@ivpress.com
Web site: http://www.ivpress.com
Dist(s): **Midpoint Trade Bks., Inc.**
christianaudio
ebrary, Inc.; *CIP.*

Intervisual/Piggy Toes *Imprint of* **Bendon, Inc.**

InterWeave Corp., (*978-0-9771936; 978-0-9841041*) Orders Addr.: 5364 Ehrlich Rd. No. 248, Tampa, FL 33624 USA Tel 813-933-4431; Fax: 813-933-4311
E-mail: kimberly@wheredoyoufindgod.com; kking@wheredoyoufindgod.com
Web site: http://www.wheredoyoufindgod.com.

Into Action Publications *Imprint of* **Microcosm Publishing**

IntoPrint Publishing LLC, (*978-1-62352*) 4322 Harding Pike, SUite 417, Nashville, TN 37205 USA Tel 615-210-8593
E-mail: jpcampbell3@mac.com; jonathanperry@comcast.net.

Intralife Systems Publishing, (*978-0-9703102*) P.O. Box 1555, Layton, UT 84041 USA Tel 801-544-2470; Fax: 801-544-2518
E-mail: admin@frogbuster.com
Web site: http://www.frogbuster.com.

Intrepid Films, LLC, (*978-1-929931*) Orders Addr.: P.O. Box 566, Boulder, CO 80306-0566 USA Tel 303-443-2426; Fax: 303-541-9737; Toll Free: 800-279-0802
E-mail: sportinc@msn.com; marya@intrepidfilms.com
Web site: http://www.intrepidfilms.com.

Intrepid Ink, LLC, (*978-0-9843857; 978-1-935774; 978-1-937022; 978-1-943403*) Orders Addr.: P.O. Box 302, McFarland, WI 53558 USA Tel 608-318-3636; *Imprints:* Resurrected Press (ResurrectedPr)
E-mail: publisher@intrepidink.com; irene@intrepidink.com
Web site: http://www.intrepidink.com.

Intrigue Publishing, (*978-0-9762181; 978-0-9794788; 978-0-9893696; 978-1-940758*) 10200 Twisted Stalk Ct., Upper Marlboro, MD 20772 USA
E-mail: dbcamacho@hotmail.com
Web site: http://www.intriguepublishing.com
Dist(s): **Independent Pubs. Group.**

Intuitive Arts Pr., (*978-0-9741334*) 15 E. Northwest Hwy., Suite 15 B, Palatine, IL 60067 USA
E-mail: katychance@juno.com
Web site: http://www.peakperformanceliving.info.

invenTEAM, LLC, (*978-0-9729599; 978-0-9833729*) 65064 Cline Falls Rd., Bend, OR 97701 USA (SAN 255-4593) Tel 541-948-0015
E-mail: e.wally@bendcable.com
Web site: http://www.e-wally.org.

Invisible College Pr., LLC, The, (*978-1-931468*) Orders Addr.: P.O. Box 209, Woodbridge, VA 22194 USA Tel 703-590-4005; Edit Addr.: 1206 N. Danville St., Arlington, VA 22201 USA; 3703 Del Mar Dr., Woodbridge, VA 22193
E-mail: manager@invispress.com
Web site: http://www.invispress.com/.

Invision Pubns., (*978-0-9767337*) 1136 Sherman Ave., Suite C4, Bronx, NY 10456 USA Tel 718-538-6102
E-mail: puzzles@puzzlesforus.com
Web site: http://www.puzzlesforus.com.

Invoke A Blessing Inc., (*978-0-9831902*) P.O. Box 163772, Fort Worth, TX 76161-3772 USA
E-mail: yuritereshchenko@hotmail.com; Yuritereshchenko@hotmail.com.

Invoke A Blessing Ministry *See* **Invoke A Blessing Inc.**

Inward Reflections, Inc., (*978-0-9746783*) P.O. Box 1747, Brockton, MA 02303-1747 USA
E-mail: inwardreflections@homestead.com.

Inyati Press, (*978-0-9777440*) P.O. Box 453, fulton, CA 95439 USA
E-mail: milton@webbellis.org
Web site: http://www.webbellis.org.

I.Om.Be Pr., (*978-1-882161*) Orders Addr.: P.O. Box 1387, New York, NY 10159 USA
Web site: http://about.me/josefinaBaezAyombeT.

IOS Pr., Inc., (*978-90-407; 978-90-5199; 978-90-6275; 978-0-9673355; 978-1-58603; 978-90-298; 978-1-60750; 978-1-61499*) 4502 Rachael Manor Dr., Fairfax, VA 22032 USA Tel 703-323-5600; Fax: 703-323-3668; Nieuwe Hemweg 6B, Amsterdam, 1013 BG (SAN 858-995X) Tel 31 (0)20 688 33 55; Fax: 31 (0)20 687 00 19
E-mail: iosbooks@iospress.com; orders@iospress.com
Web site: http://www.iospress.com
Dist(s): **Ebsco Publishing**
Metapress
MyiLibrary
ebrary, Inc.

Iowa Greyhound Association *See* **McKinnon, Robert Scott**

Ipaatti, (*978-0-9984282*) 12500 Flatwood circel, Fairfax, VA 22033 USA Tel 703-901-7904
E-mail: kumar.sivalingam@ipaatti.com
Web site: www.ipaatti.com.

ipicturebooks *Imprint of* **ibooks, Inc.**

iPlayMusic, Inc., (*978-0-9760487; 978-0-9797683*) P.O. Box 391775, Mountain View, CA 94039 USA Tel 650-969-3387; Fax: 650-969-3680; Toll Free: 866-594-3344
E-mail: quincy@iplaymusic.com
Web site: http://www.iplaymusic.com
Dist(s): **Leonard, Hal Corp.**
Music Sales Corp.

IPMG Publishing, (*978-1-934218*) 18362 Erin Bay, Eden Prairie, MN 55347 USA (SAN 852-2057)
E-mail: webmaster@iplaymathgames.com
Web site: http://www.iplaymathgames.com.

Ippolito, Eva Marie, (*978-0-9705350; 978-0-615-11326-5*) 10316 W. Oakmont Dr., Sun City, AZ 85351-3528 USA.

Iran Books *See* **Ibex Pubs., Inc.**

Irene, Jan Pubns., (*978-0-9653428*) Orders Addr.: P.O. Box 934, Sonora, CA 95370 USA Tel 209-532-2470; Fax: 209-532-0277; Edit Addr.: 19575 Roselyn Ln., Sonora, CA 95370 USA
E-mail: janirene@mlode.com.

Irene Press *See* **Quindaro Pr.**

Iris Pallas-Luke E-Writings/E-Literature, (*978-0-9765637*) 12472 Lake Underhill Rd., Suite 267, Orlando, FL 32828 USA
E-mail: irispallasluke@msn.com; noir@noirpallasluke.com
Web site: http://www.irispallas-luke.com; http://www.barbarapallas-luke.com; http://www.vernninapallas-luke.com; http://www.noirpallas-luke.com.

Iris Pr. *Imprint of* **Iris Publishing Group, Inc., The**

Iris Publishing Group, Inc., The, (*978-0-916078; 978-1-60454*) 969 Oak Ridge Turnpike, No. 328, Oak Ridge, TN 37830-8832 USA Tel 865-483-0837; Fax: 865-481-3793; Toll Free: 800-881-2119; *Imprints:* Iris Press (Iris)
E-mail: rcumming@irisbooks.com
Web site: htt://irisbooks.com.

Irish American Bk. Co., Subs. of Roberts Rinehart Pubs., Inc., P.O. Box 666, Niwot, CO 80544-0666 USA Tel 303-652-2710; Fax: 303-652-2689; Toll Free: 800-452-7115
E-mail: irishbooks@aol.com
Web site: http://www.irishvillage.com.

Irish Bks. & Media, Inc., (*978-0-937702*) Orders Addr.: 2904 41st Ave S., Minneapolis, MN 55406-1814 USA (SAN 111-8870) Toll Free: 800-229-3505 Do not confuse with Irish Bks. in New York, NY
E-mail: Irishbook@aol.com
Web site: http://www.irishbook.com.

Irish Genealogical Foundation, (*978-0-940134*) Div. of O'Laughlin Pr., P.O. Box 7575, Kansas City, MO 64116 USA (SAN 218-4834) Tel 816-454-2410
E-mail: mike@Irishroots.com
Web site: http://www.IrishRoots.com
Dist(s): **Irish Bks. & Media, Inc.**

Iron Arm International, (*978-0-9746989*) 1 Reid St., Amsterdam, NY 12010-3424 USA Tel 518-842-9299
E-mail: Ironarm1@aol.com
Web site: http://www.uechiryu-karate.com
Dist(s): **Tuttle Publishing.**

Iron Fire Publishng Co., (*978-0-9817791*) 3702 Manhattan Ave., Suite 101, Fort Collins, CO 80526 USA (SAN 856-5465)
E-mail: mike@iron-fire.com
Web site: http://www.destinationstationseries.com.

Iron Mountain Pr., (*978-0-9722961*) Orders Addr.: P.O. Box 7, New Milford, NY 10959 USA (SAN 256-0097)
E-mail: info@ironmountainpress.com
Web site: http://www.ironmountainpress.com.

Ironbound Pr., (*978-0-9763857*) P.O. Box 250, Winter Harbor, ME 04693-0250 USA Tel 207-963-2355; Fax: 320-323-2434 Do not confuse with Ironbound Pr. in Scotch Plains, NJ
E-mail: sales@ironboundpress.com
Web site: http://www.ironboundpress.com.

Ironcreek Pr., (*978-0-9766017*) 147 S. Randolph Ave., Asheboro, NC 27203 USA Tel 336-521-9105
E-mail: crottymartha@yahoo.com.

Ironcroft Publishing, (*978-0-9771688*) 11093 Alberta Dr., Brighton, MI 48114 USA
Web site: http://www.ironcroft.com
Dist(s): **BookBaby**
Partners Bk. Distributing, Inc.

Irongate Pr., (*978-0-9754746*) Orders Addr.: 1237 W. Seascape Dr., Gilbert, AZ 85233 USA Tel 480-813-2056
E-mail: jpascoe@irongatepress.com; j3pascoe@gmail.com
Web site: http://www.irongatepress.com
Dist(s): **Canyonlands Pubns.**
Forest Sales & Distributing Co.
Rio Nuevo Pubs.

Ironhorse Publishing Co., (*978-0-9747039*) 308 B W. Market St., Gratz, PA 17030 USA Fax: 717-365-7399 do not confuse with Ironhorse Publishing in Hayden Lake, ID
E-mail: pennvalleyprint@epix.net.

Publisher Name Index

Irresistible Pr., LLC, *(978-1-946047)* 150 Ogilvie Dr., John Day, OR 97845 USA Tel 541-575-4387; *Imprints:* DoodleCake (DoodleCake)
E-mail: ccnrs@craigemcmillan.com
Web site: www.irresistiblepress.com
Dist(s): **Ingram Publisher Services**
Lightning Source, Inc.

†Irvington Pubs., *(978-0-512; 978-0-8290; 978-0-8422; 978-0-89197)* Orders Addr.: P.O. Box 286, New York, NY 10276-0286 USA Fax: 212-861-0998; Toll Free Fax: 800-455-5520; Toll Free: 800-472-6037
Dist(s): **Addicus Bks.**
MyiLibrary; *CIP.*

Irwin, Christine, *(978-0-615-15008-6; 978-0-578-00787-8)* 4N 265 Avard Rd., West Chicago, IL 60185 USA
Dist(s): **Lulu Pr., Inc.**

Irwin, Esther L., *(978-0-9778462)* 3531 Grove Dr., Cheyenne, WY 82001 USA Tel 307-632-2060
E-mail: Elivroman@bresnan.net.

†ISA, *(978-0-87664; 978-1-55617; 978-0-9791330; 978-0-9792343; 978-1-934394; 978-1-936007; 978-1-937560; 978-1-939660; 978-1-941546; 978-1-945541)* 67 Alexander Dr., Research Triangle Park, NC 27709 USA (SAN 202-7054) Tel 919-549-8411; Fax: 919-549-8288
E-mail: info@isa.org; ebell@isa.org; lelrod@isa.org
Web site: http://www.isa.org
Dist(s): **INscribe Digital**; *CIP.*

Isaac Publishing *See* **Ajoyin Publishing, Inc.**

Isaac Publishing, *(978-0-9787141; 978-0-9825218; 978-0-9853109; 978-0-9885930; 978-0-9892905; 978-0-9916145; 978-0-9967245; 978-0-9977033)* 6731 Curran St., McLean, VA 22101 USA Tel 703-288-1681
E-mail: usa@barnabasaid.org
Web site: http://www.barnabasbooks.org
Dist(s): **BookBaby**
Midpoint Trade Bks., Inc.
Send The Light Distribution LLC.

Isaacs, John, *(978-0-9779676)* 643 N. Main St., Lawrenceburg, KY 40342 USA (SAN 850-6191) Tel 502-418-1521
E-mail: jisaacs@kheaa.com.

Isabella Products, Inc., *(978-1-936503; 978-1-62334; 978-1-63083; 978-1-68186)* 23 Bradford St. 2nd Flr., Concord, MA 01742 USA Tel 978-287-0007; Fax: 309-405-1865; *Imprints:* StarWalk Kids Media (StarWalkKids)
E-mail: liz.nealon@isabellaproducts.com; support@fablelearning.com; gabrielle.howard@fablelearning.com
Web site: http://www.fablelearning.com; http://www.isabellaproducts.com
Dist(s): **INscribe Digital**
StarWalk Kids.

ISBS Publisher Services, 920 NE 58th Ave., Suite 300, Portland, OR 97213-3786 USA (SAN 169-7129) Tel 503-287-3093; Fax: 503-280-8832; Toll Free: 800-944-6190
E-mail: info@isbs.com
Web site: http://www.isbs.com
Dist(s): **ebrary, Inc.**

iScribe Pubns. LLC, *(978-0-9883126)* 1006 Westbriar Dr., Henrico, VA 23238 USA Tel 804-441-3400; Fax: 804-741-7741
E-mail: info@iscribepublications.com.

ISD, 70 Enterprise Dr., Suite 2, Bristol, CT 06010 USA Tel 860-584-6546; Fax: 860-540-1001
E-mail: orders@isdistribution.com
Web site: https://www.isdistribution.com/.

Isha Enterprises, Inc., *(978-0-936981)* P.O. Box 25970, Scottsdale, AZ 85255 USA (SAN 658-7895) Tel 480-502-9454; Fax: 480-991-5635; Toll Free: 800-641-6015
E-mail: info@easygrammar.com
Web site: http://www.easygrammar.com.

Ishi Pr. International, *(978-0-923891)* Div. of The Ishi Pr. (Japan), 461 Peachstone Terr., San Rafael, CA 94903-1327 USA (SAN 249-0749) Tel 917-507-7226
E-mail: samhsloan@gmail.com
Web site: http://www.anusha.com/ordering.html.

ISI Bks., *(978-1-882926; 978-1-932236; 978-1-933859; 978-1-935191; 978-1-61017)* 3901 Centerville Rd., Wilmington, DE 19807-1938 USA Toll Free Fax: 800-621-8476 (orders in the US & CAN); Toll Free: 800-526-7022; 800-621-2736 (orders M-F in the US & CAN)
E-mail: bookpub@isi.org
Web site: http://www.isibooks.org
Dist(s): **Chicago Distribution Ctr.**
MyiLibrary
Open Road Integrated Media, Inc.
Open Road Distribution
Univ. of Chicago Pr.

ISIS Large Print Bks. (GBR) *(978-0-7531; 978-1-85089; 978-1-85695)* *Dist. by* **Transaction Pubs.**

Isis Publishing Hse., Inc., *(978-0-9662281)* 4620 Kings Hwy., Brooklyn, NY 11234 USA
E-mail: isispublishingco@aol.com.

Islamic Bk. Service, 1209 Cleburne, Hoston, TX 77004 USA (SAN 169-2453) Tel 713-528-1440; Fax: 713-528-1085.

Islamic Ctr. of Sacramento, The, *(978-0-9769245)* Div. of Sacramento Computers, c/o Sacramento Computers, 2022 4th St. #2, Sacramento, CA 95818 USA
E-mail: shamdani@mindspring.com
Web site: http://www.hineaf.net.

Islamic Supreme Council of America, *(978-1-930409; 978-1-938058)* Orders Addr.: 17195 Silver Pkwy. #401 Fenton, MI 48430, Fenton, MI 48430 USA Tel 810-593-1222; Fax: 810-815-0518; Toll Free: 800-278-6624; Edit Addr.: 17195 Silver Pkwy. #401 Fenton Michigan 48430, Fenton, MI 48430 USA
E-mail: staff@islamicsupremecouncil.org; aliyah@sunnah.org
Web site: http://www.worde.org.

Island Friends LLC, *(978-0-9729987)* 11 Promontory Ct., Hilton Head Island, SC 29928 USA
E-mail: benjo@adelphia.net
Web site: http://www.islandfriends.net
Dist(s): **Sandlapper Publishing Co., Inc.**

Island Heritage Publishing, *(978-0-89610; 978-0-931548; 978-1-59700)* Div. of The Madden Corp., 94-411 Koaki St., Waipahu, HI 96797 USA (SAN 211-1403) Tel 808-564-8800; Fax: 808-564-8888; Toll Free: 800-468-2800
E-mail: ihorders@welcometotheislands.com
Web site: http://www.welcometotheislands.com
Dist(s): **Madden Corp., The**
Midpoint Trade Bks., Inc.

Island In The Sky Publishing Co., *(978-0-9760328)* 60 Meadow Lakes, East Windsor, NJ 08520 USA
Web site: http://www.MemoriesOfWWII.com.

Island Ink, *(978-0-9657849)* Orders Addr.: P.O. Box 1818, Indiantown, FL 34956 USA Tel 561-597-3778; Fax: 561-597-4691.

Island Institute, *(978-0-942719; 978-0-9835613)* 386 Main St., Box 648, Rockland, ME 04841-3345 USA (SAN 667-7274) Tel 207-594-9209; Fax: 207-594-9314
E-mail: inquiry@islandinstitute.org; publications@islandinstitute.org
Web site: http://www.islandinstitute.org
Dist(s): **Magazines, Inc.**

Island Media Publishing, LLC, *(978-0-9829908)* 120 N. 15th St., Fernandina Beach, FL 32034 USA Tel 904-556-3002
E-mail: islandmediapublishing@gmail.com.

Island Moon Pr., *(978-0-9755605)* P.O. Box 956, Oaks, PA 19456-0956 USA Tel 610-935-2378; Toll Free: 877-252-8262
E-mail: islandquest@msn.com
Web site: http://www.IslandMoonPress.com.

Island Nation Pr., LLC, *(978-0-9657437; 978-1-892738)* Orders Addr.: 144 Rowayton Woods Dr., Norwalk, CT 06854 USA Tel 203-852-0028; Fax: 203-852-0528; Toll Free: 888-356-1450 [Direct Order Line]
E-mail: cvaleallen@earthlink.net
Web site: http://www.charlottevaleallen.com.

Island Paradise Publishing, *(978-0-9705889; 978-0-9855153)* Orders Addr.: P.O. Box 163, Haleiwa, HI 96712 USA Tel 808-638-9640; Edit Addr.: 59-465 KeWaena Rd., Haleiwa, HI 96712 USA
E-mail: CooperKool@Hawaii.rr.com
Dist(s): **Booklines Hawaii, Ltd.**

Islandport Pr., Inc., *(978-0-9671662; 978-0-9763231; 978-1-934031; 978-1-939017; 978-1-944762)* Orders Addr.: P.O. Box 10, Yarmouth, ME 04096 USA Tel 207-846-3344; Fax: 207-846-3955; Edit Addr.: 267 US Rte. 1, Suite B, Yarmouth, ME 04096 USA
E-mail: deanlunt@islandportpress.com
Web site: http://www.islandportpress.com
Dist(s): **Bookmasters Distribution**
Follett School Solutions
INscribe Digital
MyiLibrary
ebrary, Inc.

IslandWood, *(978-0-9821633)* Orders Addr.: 4450 Blakely Ave. NE, Bainbridge Island, WA 98110 USA Tel 206-855-4300; Fax: 206-855-4301
Web site: http://www.IslandWood.org.

ISLC, *(978-0-9763226)* c/o Alfassa, 15 W. 16th St., 6th Flr., New York, NY 10011 USA Tel 917-207-4344
E-mail: shelomo@alfassa.com.

Isle of Dogs Publishing, Co., *(978-0-9741321)* 4008 - 83rd Ave. SE, Snohomish, WA 98290 USA
E-mail: connieraestrain@msn.com; ConnieRaeStrain@IsleofDogsPublishing.com
Web site: http://www.isleofdogspublishing.com.

Isles of the Sea Pubs., *(978-0-9728126)* Orders Addr.: P.O. Box 51352, Provo, UT 84605-1352 USA Tel 801-427-5209; Edit Addr.: 2052 S. California Ave., No. 12, Provo, UT 84044 USA
E-mail: drrlesa@hotmail.com.

Islewest Publishing, *(978-0-9641919; 978-1-888461)* Div. of Carlisle Communications, Ltd., 4242 Chavenelle Dr., Dubuque, IA 52002-2650 USA (SAN 299-5018)
E-mail: mjgraham@carcomm.com
Web site: http://www.islewest.com.

Israel Book Shop *See* **Israel Bookshop Pubns.**

Israel Bookshop Pubns., *(978-0-9670705; 978-1-931681; 978-1-60091)* 501 Prospect St., No. 97, Lakewood, NJ 08701 USA Tel 732-901-3009; Fax: 732-901-4012; Toll Free: 888-536-7427
E-mail: sales@israelbookshoppublications.com
Web site: http://www.israelbookshoppublications.com.

ISS, *(978-1-934942)* 2 Shaker Rd. Ste. D103, Shirley, MA 01464-2535 USA (SAN 855-6164)
E-mail: print@issexpress.com
Web site: http://www.imagesoftware.com.

Istoria Hse., *(978-0-9816538)* Orders Addr.: P.O. Box 6342, Vernon Hills, IL 60061 USA (SAN 856-1370)
E-mail: info@istoriahouse.com
Web site: http://www.istoriahouse.com.

Italica Pr., *(978-0-934977; 978-1-59910)* 595 Main St., Suite 605, New York, NY 10044 USA (SAN 695-1805) Tel 917-371-0563
E-mail: inquiries@italicapress.com
Web site: http://www.italicapress.com.

Itasca Bks., *(978-0-9767054)* Orders Addr.: 5120 Cedar Lake Rd. S., Minneapolis, MN 55416 USA (SAN 855-3823) Tel 952-345-4488; Fax: 952-920-0541; Toll Free: 800-901-3480
E-mail: mjung@itascabooks.com
Web site: http://www.itascabooks.com
Dist(s): **BookMobile.**

iTeenBooks Inc., *(978-0-9798997; 978-0-9852925)* P.O. Box 171, Middletown, NJ 07748-0171 USA.

Ithaca Pr. *Imprint of* **Authors & Artists Publishers of New York, Inc.**

Ithuriel's Spear, *(978-0-9749502; 978-0-9793390; 978-0-9835791; 978-1-943209)* 939 Eddy St., Apt. 102, San Francisco, CA 94109 USA Tel 415-440-3204
plainfeather@gmail.com
E-mail: plainfeather@gmail.com
Web site: http://www.ithuriel.com
Dist(s): **BookMobile**
SPD-Small Pr. Distribution.

ITI Holdings, Inc., *(978-1-931451; 978-1-61011)* 1321 SE Decker Ave, Stuart, FL 34994 USA Tel 207-729-4201; Fax: 207-729-4453; Toll Free: 888-778-9073
E-mail: flemming.elleboe@tdisdi.com; brian.carney@tdisdi.com; worldhq@tdisdi.com
Web site: http://www.tdisdi.com.

Itiya Publishing, Inc., *(978-0-9770312)* 217 Ave. Unvi. Interanericana PMB 161, San German, PR 00683 USA
E-mail: gpita@itiyainc.com
Web site: http://www.itiyainc.com.

ITRON Publishing, *(978-0-9786863)* 6510 LBJ Freeway, Suite 200, Dallas, TX 75240 USA (SAN 851-2817) Tel 972-934-2811; Fax: 972-934-1705.

It's A Habit! Co., The, *(978-0-9713664)* 2238 Harwood St., Los Angeles, CA 90031-1238 USA Tel 323-254-7772
Web site: http://www.itsahabit.com.

It's a Lifestyle Fitness, *(978-0-9890227)* 1 Evergreen Pl., Morristown, NJ 07960 USA (SAN 920-783X) Tel 973-267-2121
E-mail: gregorycrawford@ymail.com.

It's About Time, Herff Jones Education Division *See* **It's About Time, Herff Jones Education Div.**

It's About Time, Herff Jones Education Div., *(978-1-891629; 978-1-58591; 978-1-60720; 978-1-68231)* Orders Addr.: 333 N. Bedford Rd. # 110, Mt. Kisco, NY 10549 USA Tel 914-273-2233; Fax: 914-273-2227; Toll Free: 888-698-8463 Do not confuse with companies with the same name in Los Gatos, CA, Santa Monica, CA
E-mail: generalinfo@herffjones.com
Web site: http://www.its-about-time.com.

It's Good 2B Good LLC,
Dist(s): **Bookmasters Distribution.**

It's Me Briana, LLC, *(978-0-9793904; 978-0-9838492)* P.O. Box 12386, Atlanta, GA 30355 USA
Web site: http://www.brianasneighborhood.com.

It's My Hair! Magazine, *(978-0-692-74966-1; 978-0-692-77197-6; 978-0-692-83141-0; 978-0-692-88297-9; 978-0-692-93394-7)* P.O. Box 18593, ATLANTA, GA 31126 USA Tel 470-755-2061.

ITSMEEE Industries, *(978-0-9677231)* 13918 E. Mississippi Ave., No 213, Aurora, CO 80012 USA Tel 303-229-7584
E-mail: itsmeeeindustries@outlook.com.

Itty Bitty Bks., *(978-0-9760691)* 1682 NW 785 Rd., Bates City, MO 64011 USA Tel 816-697-3617 (phone/fax)
E-mail: waynedyer@gmail.com.

Itty Bitty Kitty *Imprint of* **Singing Moon Pr.**

Itty Bitty Witch Works, *(978-0-9768573)* P.O. Box 532, Kernville, CA 93238 USA Tel 760-376-3973 (phone/fax)
E-mail: ittybittywitch@sierranet.us
Web site: http://ittybittywitch.com.

iUniverse, Inc. *Imprint of* **iUniverse, Inc.**

iUniverse, Inc., *(978-0-9665514; 978-1-58348; 978-0-9668591; 978-1-893652; 978-0-595; 978-0-9795279; 978-1-60528; 978-1-4401; 978-1-936236; 978-1-4502; 978-1-4620; 978-1-4697; 978-1-4759; 978-1-4917; 978-1-5320)* Orders Addr.: 1663 Liberty Dr., Suite 300, Bloomington, IN 47403 USA (SAN 254-9425) Toll Free: 800-288-4677; *Imprints:* Writers Club Press (Writers Club Pr); Writer's Showcase Press (Writers Showcase); Backinprint.com (Backinprint); ASJA Press (ASJA Pr); Authors Choice Press (Authors Choice Pr); Mystery Writers of America Presents (Myst Write Amer); Mystery & Suspense Press (Mystery & Suspense); Weekly Reader Teacher's Press (Weekly Rd Tch); Writers Advantage Press (Writers Adv Pr); iUniverse, Inc. (iUni Inc); iUniverse Star (iUniverse Star)
E-mail: post.production@iuniverse.com; book.orders@iuniverse.com; bethany.dirks@iuniverse.com
Web site: http://www.iUniverse.com; http://iuniverse.com
Dist(s): **Author Solutions, Inc.**
Bookmasters Distribution
CreateSpace Independent Publishing Platform
Smashwords
Zondervan.

iUniverse Star *Imprint of* **iUniverse, Inc.**

iUniverse.com, Incorporated *See* **iUniverse, Inc.**

Iverson, Theodore, *(978-0-9747378)* P.O. Box 3671, Grand Canyon, AZ 86023-3671 USA.

Ivey Leaf Publishing, *(978-0-9981801)* 8508 Jean Parrish Ct. NE, Albuquerque, NM 87122 USA Tel 505-400-1785
Dist(s): **CreateSpace Independent Publishing Platform.**

Ivoryton Pr., *(978-0-9814663)* P.O. Box 485, Ivoryton, CT 06442 USA Tel 860-581-8133
E-mail: Ivoryton.Press@gmail.com.

Ivy Advising LLC, *(978-0-9771568)* 50 Livingston St., Brooklyn, NY 11201 USA (SAN 256-8934).

Ivy Fund, The, *(978-0-9754003)* 33 Irving St., Waltham, MA 02451-0758 USA
E-mail: courtney@ivysplace.org
Web site: http://ivysplace.org.

Ivy Group, The (GBR) *Dist. by* **HachBkGrp.**

Ivy Hill Bunch, LLC, *(978-0-9743619)* P.O. Box 1053, La Quinta, CA 92253 USA Tel 760-771-0834; Fax: 760-771-1910; Toll Free: 866-892-5795
E-mail: lynn@ivyhillbunch.com
Web site: http://www.saddyandgladdy.com.

Ivy House Publishing Group *Imprint of* **Pentland Pr., Inc.**

IvyStone Pr., *(978-0-9755771)* P.O. Box 50, Emmalena, KY 41740 USA
E-mail: hodson@tgtel.com
Web site: http://www.mountainrainbow.com.

iwishyouicecreamandcake, *(978-0-9792019)* 3871 W. Millers Bridge Rd., Tallahassee, FL 32312 USA Fax: 850-893-9616
E-mail: carolhmoore@yahoo.com
Web site: http://iwishyouicecreamandcake.com.

Iyengar, Malathi, *(978-0-9753912)* 14748 Morrison St., Sherman Oaks, CA 91403 USA
E-mail: msiyengar@yahoo.com
Web site: http://www.rangoli.org.

iynx publishing (GBR) *(978-0-9535413; 978-0-9540583)* *Dist. by* **Dufour.**

IZA Publishing Co., *(978-0-9674241)* 253 Pvt. Rd. 2410, Uvalde County, TX 78801 USA Tel 361-946-3132; Fax: 361-946-2000
E-mail: smith-ma@swhell.net.

IZS, Inc., *(978-0-9764684)* 34 E. Franklin St., Bellbrook, OH 45305-1746 USA Tel 937-848-8896
E-mail: pantherbay@aol.com
Web site: http://www.pantherbay.com.

J A F S, Inc., *(978-0-9709533)* 8846 Worthington Cir., Indianapolis, IN 46278 USA Tel 317-802-9784; Fax: 317-870-8772
E-mail: jmcclaine3@home.com
Dist(s): **Austin & Company, Inc.**
Midpoint Trade Bks., Inc.
Partners Pubs. Group, Inc.

J A G Pubns., *(978-0-943327)* 11288 Ventura Blvd., No. 301, Studio City, CA 91604 USA (SAN 668-4157) Tel 818-505-9002 (phone/fax) Do not confuse with Jag Publications in Los Angeles, CA
E-mail: info@jagpublications-esl.com
Web site: http://www.jagpublications-esl.com.

J A Interests, Inc., *(978-0-9769648)* P.O. Box 1472, Versailles, KY 40383 USA.

J A S Pr., Inc., *(978-0-9666920; 978-0-9773316)* Orders Addr.: P.O. Box 1925, Bolingbrook, IL 60440 USA Tel 630-226-1635; Edit Addr.: 155 Ashcroft Dr., Bolingbrook, IL 60490 USA Tel 630-226-1635
E-mail: jaspress@mindspring.com.

J & J Publishing Co., *(978-0-9759831)* Box 305, 9728 US Hwy. 277, Elgin, OK 73538 USA Do not confuse with companies with same or similar name in Los Angeles, CA, Buffalo, NY, Englewood, CO, Darien, IL, Frankfurt, IL MD
E-mail: djw73@aol.com.

J & J Publishing Co., *(978-0-9705008; 978-0-615-73754-6; 978-0-9961018)* P.O. Box 291205, Columbia, SC 29229 USA Tel 803-968-5196
E-mail: jjpublisher@yahoo.com
Web site: http://www.jandjpublishingonline.com.

J & K Publishing, *(978-0-9790487)* 5221 Collins St., Suite 101, Panama City, FL 32404 USA
E-mail: jnbowen@netscape.com.

J&M Publishing, *(978-0-9646590)* 2417 Valley View Rd., Narvon, PA 17555 USA Tel 610-286-5489 Do not confuse with companies with the same name in Lebanon, TN, Fayetteville, NC, Phoenix, AZ.

J B Communications, Inc., *(978-1-55987)* 101 W. 55th St., No. 2D, New York, NY 10019-5346 USA Tel 212-246-0900; *Imprints:* Sunny Books (Sunny Bks).

J. B. J. Enterprises *See* **Morgan, E. A.**

J. Caro & Associates *See* **Cowboy Collector Pubns.**

J J Publishing, *(978-0-9604610)* 1312 Arthur St., Hollywood, FL 33019 USA (SAN 220-0090) Tel 954-929-3559 (phone/fax).

J L Publishing Co., *(978-0-9790774)* 2901 Ranch Rd, Apt. 511, Paragould, AR 72450 USA.

J M D's Business Services, *(978-0-9712641)* 52 Lee Ave., Wallingford, CT 06492-3610 USA
Web site: http://www.jmdsbusinessservices.com; http://www.liquidchariot.com.

J M Pubns., *(978-0-9638007)* Orders Addr.: P.O. Box 753427, Memphis, TN 38115 USA; Edit Addr.: 3830 Scottsdale Ave., Memphis, TN 38115 USA (SAN 255-0598) Tel 901-368-3414; Fax: 901-566-1978; Toll Free: 888-321-4747
E-mail: jmpub1@midsouth.rr.com
Web site: http://www.jmpublications.com.

J. Paul Getty Museum *Imprint of* **Getty Pubns.**

J. Taylor Publishing, *(978-0-9834058; 978-1-937744)* 5448 Apex Peakway No. 198, Apex, NC 27502 USA Tel 919-249-7318
E-mail: production@jtaylorpublishing.com
Web site: http://www.jtaylorpublishing.com.

J2B Publishing LLC, *(978-0-9911994; 978-1-941927)* 4251 Columbia Pk. Rd., Pomfret, MD 20675 USA Tel 202-557-8097
E-mail: GladToDoIt@gmail.com
Web site: www.GladToDoIt.net; www.J2BLLC.com.

Jacana Media (ZAF) *(978-1-874955; 978-1-919931; 978-1-919777; 978-1-4314)* *Dist. by* **IPG Chicago.**

Jacera Publishing, *(978-1-943992)* 14918 EL TESORO DR, HOUSTON, TX 77083 USA Tel 281-772-2549
E-mail: jen.m.gabler@gmail.com.

Jack Hook Publishing, *(978-0-9837863)* 1288 Columbus Ave., No. 279, San Francisco, CA 94133 USA Tel 310-889-4728
E-mail: susan.saville@jackhook.com
Web site: www.jackhook.com.

Jack Walker Pr., *(978-1-945378)* 945 Bay View Cir., Mukwonago, WI 53149 USA Tel 262-955-6675
E-mail: amyloujenkins@gmail.com
Web site: www.JackWalkerPress.com.

Jack's Bookshelf, Inc., *(978-1-928907)* 224 Woodland Dr., Vista, CA 92083 USA.

Jackson, Amber, *(978-0-692-84096-2)* 5390 Amber Cove Way, FLOWERY BRANCH, GA 30542 USA Tel 404-694-4387
E-mail: jeffwcrawford5+LVP0003324@gmail.com; jeffwcrawford5+LVP0003324@gmail.com.

Jackson Joy LLC, *(978-0-692-84728-2; 978-0-692-84760-2)* P.O. Box 922, GRAYSON, GA 30017 USA Tel 770-375-0635
E-mail: jeffwcrawford5+LVP0003332@gmail.com; jeffwcrawford5+LVP0003332@gmail.com.

Jackson, Linda *See* **Jackson Publishing**

Jackson Publishing, *(978-0-9716442)* 7661 Forstoria Cove, Southaven, MS 38672 USA Tel 901-413-5748 Do not confuse with companies with the same name in Jackson, MS; Clarkston, MI
E-mail: jackson35015@bellsouth.net.

Jackson, Robert, *(978-0-9761420)* 12807 Prospect Knolls Dr., Bowie, MD 20720 USA
E-mail: trebor_jackson@yahoo.com
Web site: http://www.amazinglibertteens.com.

Jacobob Pr., LLC, *(978-0-9705827; 978-0-9772817; 978-0-9820960; 978-0-9838072; 978-0-9852887; 978-0-9857477; 978-0-9860361; 978-0-9911151; 978-0-9914066; 978-0-9916416; 978-0-692-53701-5; 978-0-692-55660-3)* 11035 Ridge Forest Ct., Saint Louis, MO 63126-3429 USA (SAN 257-1862) Tel 314-843-4829
E-mail: jacobobsw@sbcglobal.net
Web site: http://jacobobpress.com
Dist(s): **Follett School Solutions**
Jacobob Pr. Distributing
Unique Bks., Inc.

Jacobs, Karen, *(978-0-9850440; 978-0-9982119)* 40 Indian Carry Rd., Moultonborough, NH 03254 USA Tel 617-838-1872
E-mail: kjacobs@bu.edu.

Jacqueline Beverly Hills, *(978-0-9664783)* 650 The Village, Unit 215, Redondo Beach, CA 90277-2734 USA
E-mail: jacquih3@yahoo.com
Web site: http://jbhbooks.com.

Jacquet-Acea, Russell, *(978-0-9771919)* 3645 Whitman Ave. N., Seattle, WA 98103 USA Tel 206-547-7026; Fax: 810-454-1721
E-mail: rjacquet2@msn.com
Web site: http://rjacquet.tripod.com.

JADA Pr., *(978-0-9747501; 978-0-9761110; 978-0-9764115; 978-0-9771343; 978-0-9788724; 978-0-9800629; 978-0-9843558; 978-0-9848365; 978-0-9907961)* 4375 Confederate Point Rd. #6-H, Jacksonville, FL 32210 USA Tel 904-226-8876 (leave a message)
Web site: http://www.jadapress.com.

JadaStar *See* **Star Publish LLC**

Jade Enterprises, *(978-0-9753410)* 11807 S. Fair Hollow Ln., Suite 106, Houston, TX 77043-1033 USA Tel 713-416-0109
Web site: http://www.authorsden.com/deborahkfrontiera.

Jade Publishing, *(978-0-9985390)* 700 Ciro St., Donna, TX 78537 USA Tel 956-570-1023
E-mail: rossylima@jadepublishing.org
Web site: www.jadepublishing.org.

Jade Ram Publishing, *(978-1-877721)* 3003 Wendy's Way, No. 9, Anchorage, AK 99517-1466 USA Tel 907-248-0979; Fax: 907-272-8432
E-mail: jaderam@alaska.net
Dist(s): **Publication Consultants**
Todd Communications
Wizard Works.

Jade Tree Bks., *(978-0-9888610)* P.O. Box 2132, Cherry Hill, NJ 08034 USA Tel 215-913-3456
E-mail: pangj@comcast.net.

Jadenaila Publishing, *(978-0-615-12544-2)* 7340 S. Union Creek Way 5G, Salt Lake City, UT 84047 USA Tel 801-916-1037
E-mail: kidsbooksbynaila@hotmail.com
Web site: http://www.kidsbooksbynaila.com.

Jades Publishing, *(978-0-9743352)* Orders Addr.: P.O. Box 485, Fayette, OH 43521 USA Tel 419-237-3128; Edit Addr.: 24022-T, Fayette, OH 43521 USA
E-mail: amadsj@bright.net; amadsj@bright.nett.

Jaffe Book Solutions, Div. of Booksource, 1230 Macklind Ave, Saint Louis, MO 63110-1432 USA
Dist(s): **Booksource, The.**

Jaffrey, Kamal, *(978-0-9753673)* 400 Technology Sq., Cambridge, MA 02139 USA.

Jahs Publishing Group, *(978-0-9701144; 978-0-9747550; 978-0-615-49893-5; 978-0-615-50005-8)* 6304 Somerset Rd., Riverdale, MD 20737 USA Tel 301-326-6468
Web site: http://www.jahspublishing.com
Dist(s): **CreateSpace Independent Publishing Platform.**

Jakobi Publishing, LLC, *(978-0-9972358)* 5820 Perry Rd., Elkton, FL 32033 USA Tel 904-377-3915
E-mail: heather.hamel@hotmail. om
Web site: heatherhamel.com.

Jalali, Yassaman *See* **Saman Publishing**

JA-M Pubs., LLC, *(978-0-9728975)* 2358 Pinewood Blvd., Bitely, MI 49309 USA Tel 231-745-8641; 269-363-2955 Do not confuse with companies with the same or similar name in Mount Pleasant, SC, Comstock Park, MI
E-mail: joycex4@msn.com; jandmck@gmail.com
Web site: http://ja-mpublishers.weebly.com.

Jama Kids, *(978-0-9772711)* 612 N. St., Beaufort, SC 29902 USA Tel 843-522-1577
E-mail: janspringle@earthlink.net.

Jamaldinian, Yousef, *(978-0-9766657)* 5207 Olley Ln., Burke, VA 22015 USA Tel 571-212-9471
E-mail: joedinian@yahoo.com.

James, JoAnn, *(978-0-9764406)* P.O. Box 11459, Eugene, OR 97440 USA
E-mail: joann_james@comcast.net.

James Stevenson Pub., *(978-1-885852)* 1500 Oliver Rd., Suite K-109, Fairfield, CA 94533 USA Tel 707-469-0237; Fax: 206-350-2954
E-mail: ceo@jspub.com
Web site: http://www.jspub.com
Dist(s): **Marangio, Charles F. Distribution.**

†**Jameson Bks., Inc.,** *(978-0-89803; 978-0-915463; 978-0-916054)* 722 Columbus St., P.O. Box 738, Ottawa, IL 61350 USA (SAN 281-7578) Tel 815-434-7905; Fax: 815-434-7907; Toll Free: 800-426-1357
E-mail: jamesonbooks@yahoo.com
Dist(s): **Midpoint Trade Bks., Inc.**; *CIP.*

Jamestown, *(978-0-07; 978-0-8092; 978-0-8442; 978-0-89061; 978-0-913327; 978-0-941263; 978-1-56943)* Div. of Glencoe/McGraw-Hill, Orders Addr.: P.O. Box 543, Blacklick, OH 43004-0543 USA Fax: 614-860-1877; Toll Free: 800-334-7344; Edit Addr.: P.O. Box 508, Columbus, OH 43216 USA Toll Free: 800-872-7323
Web site: http://www.jamestowneducation.com
Dist(s): **Libros Sin Fronteras**
McGraw-Hill Cos., The.

Jamiram Publishing, *(978-0-9790434)* 1760 Harbeck Rd., Grants Pass, OR 97527 USA
Web site: http://jamiram.com.

JamSum Limited, *(978-0-9770754)* 621 S. Main St., Bellefontaine, OH 43311-1725 USA Toll Free: 866-857-2061
E-mail: publish@jamsum.com
Web site: http://www.jamsum.com.

Jan & San *See* **Jerome, Janice**

Jan-Carol Publishing, INC., *(978-0-9767793; 978-0-9801504; 978-0-9822337; 978-0-9841870; 978-0-9843192; 978-0-9845470; 978-0-9846398; 978-0-9834885; 978-0-9848050; 978-0-9850272; 978-1-939289; 978-1-945619)* Orders Addr.: PO Box 701, Johnson City, TN 37605 USA Tel 423-926-9983; *Imprints:* Little Creek Books (LittleCreek)
Web site: www.voicemagazineforwomen.com; www.jancarolpublishing.com.

Jandie Jams Music LLC, *(978-0-9796150)* 1036 Katy Ln., Longmont, CO 80504 USA (SAN 853-8999)
E-mail: jandiejams@comcast.net
Web site: http://www.kidcleveronline.com.

Jane & Street Pubs. Ltd., *(978-0-9745077)* 302-A W. 12th St., No. 197, New York, NY 10014 USA
Web site: http://www.janeandstreet.com.

Janelle Pubns., Inc., *(978-0-9626739; 978-1-890265)* Orders Addr.: P.O. Box 811, De Kalb, IL 60115-0811 USA Tel 815-756-2300; Fax: 815-756-4799; Toll Free: 800-888-8834; Edit Addr.: 1189 Twombley Rd., De Kalb, IL 60115 USA
E-mail: info@janellepublications.com
Web site: http://www.janellepublications.com.

Jane's World *See* **Girl Twirl Comics**

Janik Pr., *(978-0-9883938)* P.O. Box 12034, Fort Wayne, IN 46862 USA Tel 260-804-8044
E-mail: nikbenedict@yahoo.com.

Janis, Tim Ensemble, Inc., *(978-0-9773335)* P.O. Box 315, Kennebunk, ME 04043 USA (SAN 257-280X) Tel 207-985-3463.

Jan's Bks., *(978-0-9797139)* Orders Addr.: 1780 Phillips, Berkley, MI 48072 USA Tel 248-545-5160.

Jan's Looks & Books *See* **Jan's Bks.**

Jansen, Marilyn, *(978-0-9761070)* P.O. Box 278, Makawao, HI 96768 USA Tel 808-572-0699 phone/fax
E-mail: jamarilyn2008@aol.com
Web site: http://amaryllisofhawaii.com
Dist(s): **Booklines Hawaii, Ltd.**

Janze Pubns., *(978-0-9629142; 978-0-9794955)* 930 Bargo St, London, KY 40741-2713 USA
E-mail: janzepub@windstream.net.

Japan Pubns. (U.S.A.), Inc., *(978-0-87040; 978-1-57883)* Subs. of Japan Pubns., Inc. (Tokyo, Japan), 160 Spruce Knob Rd., Middletown Springs, VT 05757-4432 USA (SAN 680-0513) Tel 802-235-2814
Dist(s): **Diamond Comic Distributors, Inc.**
Diamond Bk. Distributors
Oxford Univ. Pr., Inc.

Japanime Co., Ltd. (JPN) *(978-4-921205) Dist. by* **Diamond Book Dists.**

Japanime Co., Ltd. (JPN) *(978-4-921205) Dist. by* **D C D.**

Jappa Pubns., *(978-0-9720694)* 1808 N. 79th St., Kansas City, KS 66112 USA Tel 913-205-2361
E-mail: Ongi.entertainment@gmx.com
Web site: http://www.pandaoki.com.

Jappamation Studios *See* **Jappa Pubns.**

Jarndyce & Jarndyce Pr., *(978-0-9721916; 978-0-9772720; 978-0-9817269; 978-0-9836173; 978-0-9894271; 978-0-9910077; 978-0-9864238)* Div. of PSA Consulting, Inc., 305 Snow Shoe Dr., Southgate, KY 41071 USA (SAN 860-2433) Tel 513-382-4315; 513-304-3633; Fax: 855-361-8591
E-mail: info@cincybooks.com
Web site: http://www.cincybooks.com
Dist(s): **BookBaby.**

Jarrett Publishing Co., *(978-0-9624723; 978-1-882422; 978-0-9795493; 978-1-935022)* P.O. Box 1460, Ronkonkoma, NY 11779-0426 USA Toll Free: 800-859-7679
E-mail: info@jarrettpub.com
Web site: http://www.jarrettpub.com.

Jarvis Printing *See* **Mitchell, Damien Pardow**

Jasmine Pr., *(978-0-930069)* 2224 Ogden Ave., Bensalem, PA 19020 USA (SAN 669-9650) Tel 215-244-0525.

Jasnans Publishing Co., *(978-0-9761759)* P.O. Box 873633, Wasilla, AK 99687-3633 USA
E-mail: hallaifa@mtaonline.net
Web site: http://www.jasnanspublishing.com.

Jason & Nordic Pubs., *(978-0-944727)* P.O. Box 441, Hollidaysburg, PA 16648 USA (SAN 244-9374) Tel 814-696-2920; Fax: 814-696-4250; *Imprints:* Turtle Books (Turtle Books)
E-mail: turtlbks@jasonandnordic.com
Web site: http://www.jasonandnordic.com.

Jason Foundation for Education *See* **JASON Project, The**

Jason Jacques Gallery Pr. The, *(978-0-9788371; 978-0-615-55775-5)* 29 E. 73rd St., No. 1, New York, NY 10021-3501 USA (SAN 851-7568) Tel 212-535-7500; Fax: 212-535-5757
E-mail: jason@jasonjacques.com
Web site: http://www.jasonjacques.com.

JASON Project, The, *(978-0-9763809; 978-0-9787574; 978-1-935211; 978-1-945126)* Orders Addr.: 44983 Knoll Sq. Suite 150, Ashburn, VA 20147 USA Tel 703-822-7238; Fax: 703-673-1060; Toll Free: 888-527-6600
E-mail: info@jason.org
Web site: http://www.jason.org.

Jasper State Brand, Inc., *(978-0-9820228; 978-0-9833366)* 311 N. Robertson Blvd., Suite 363, Beverly Hills, CA 90211 USA (SAN 857-0213) Tel 310-801-7737
E-mail: judith@jasperstate.com.

Jatkar, Deven, *(978-0-692-59340-0; 978-0-9977181)* 2050 Jamison Pl., Santa Clara, CA 95051 USA Tel 408-506-0156
E-mail: jatkar.deven@gmail.com.

javariBook, *(978-0-9679161)* P.O. Box 230551, New York, NY 10023 USA
E-mail: javaribook@javari.com
Web site: http://www.javaribook.com; http://www.globalwidetrade.com.

Jawbone Publishing Corp., *(978-0-9702959; 978-1-59094)* 1540 Happy Valley Cir., Newnan, GA 30263-4035 USA (SAN 253-5335); *Imprints:* Top Shelf (Top); Jawbreakers for Kids (Jawbreakers)
E-mail: marketing@jawbonepublishing.com
Web site: http://www.jawbonepublishing.com.

Jawbreakers for Kids *Imprint of* **Jawbone Publishing Corp.**

JaxPublishing.net, *(978-0-9798316)* 11727 Invierno Dr., San Diego, CA 92124-2883 USA Tel 619-757-7016; Fax: 858-277-6418
E-mail: atom@atomart.net
Web site: http://www.atomart.net.

Jay, Ronald Publishing, *(978-0-9744383)* 301 33rd St., Fort Madison, IA 52627 USA (SAN 255-769X) Tel 319-372-4781
E-mail: racrooks@lisco.com.

Jay Street Pubs., *(978-0-9639999; 978-1-889534)* Div. of G-Communications, P.O. Box 230944, New York, NY 10023-0016 USA
E-mail: jaystpub@i-2000.com.

JayJo Bks., LLC, *(978-0-9639449; 978-1-891383)* Orders Addr.: P.O. Box 760, Plainview, NY 11803-0760 USA (SAN 178-5435) Tel 516-349-5520; Fax: 800-262-1886; Toll Free: 800-999-6884; Edit Addr.: 45 Executive Dr. Ste. 201, Plainview, NY 11803-1738 USA
E-mail: jayjobook@guidancechannel.com
Web site: http://www.jayjo.com
Dist(s): **Follett School Solutions**
Quality Bks., Inc.
Unique Bks., Inc.

Jaylil Publishing Co., *(978-0-9748165)* Orders Addr.: P.O. Box 656551, Flushing, NY 11365 USA
E-mail: jaylilpublishing@aol.com
Web site: http://www.jaylilpublishing.com
Dist(s): **Culture Plus Bk. Distributors**
Seaburn Bks.

Jazwares Distribution, Inc., *(978-0-9724983; 978-0-9765714; 978-1-933752)* 555 Sawgrass Corporate Pkwy., Sunrise, FL 33325-6211 USA
E-mail: julio@jazwares.com
Web site: http://www.projectkitsforkids.com.

Jazz Path Publishing, *(978-0-9760977)* P.O. Box 381810, Cambridge, MA 02238 USA
Web site: http://www.jazzpath.com.

Jazzy Kitty Greetings Marketing & Publishing Co., *(978-0-9768540; 978-0-9843255; 978-0-9830548; 978-0-9851453; 978-0-9892656; 978-0-9916648; 978-0-9970848; 978-0-9988433)* 19 Lukens Dr. Suite 200, G1, New Castle, DE 19720 USA Tel 877-782-5550; Fax: 800-376-2807; Toll Free: 877-782-5550
E-mail: publishing@jazzykitty.net
Web site: http://www.jazzykittypublishing.com.

JazzyKitty Greetings *See* **Jazzy Kitty Greetings Marketing & Publishing Co.**

JB Information Station, *(978-0-934334)* P.O. Box 19333, Saint Louis, MO 63125 USA (SAN 213-4128) Tel 314-638-3404; 3888 Via Miralesta Dr., Saint Louis, MO 63125
E-mail: empoweredparenting@earthlink.net
Web site: http://www.JoanBramsch.com.

JB Max Publishing (CAN) *(978-0-9736330) Dist. by* **IPG Chicago.**

J.B. Vample, *(978-0-9969817; 978-0-9969817-6-7)* 1013 E Ellet St., Philadelphia, PA 19150 USA Tel 267-334-8423
E-mail: jessycapritchett@yahoo.com.

JBall Publishing, *(978-0-9764179)* 393 W. 300 N., Smithfield, UT 84335 USA Tel 435-563-9437
Web site: http://pumpkinglow.com.

JBIRD INK, Ltd., *(978-0-9715253; 978-0-9850732)* 109 Knutson Dr., Madison, WI 53704 USA Tel 608-554-0803
E-mail: info@jbirdink.com
Web site: http://www.jbirdink.com.

JBT Publishing, *(978-0-9792059)* Orders Addr.: 1485 Christina Ln., Lake Forest, IL 60045 USA (SAN 852-7644) Tel 781-760-2357; Fax: 419-735-0603
E-mail: jtedesco@gis.net.

JCCJ Pr., *(978-0-9770207)* 81 River Rd., Norfolk, MA 02056 USA Tel 508-528-4767.

JCTT, LLC, *(978-0-9766926)* 412 Capote Peak Dr., Georgetown, TX 78633 USA
E-mail: linleyw@msn.com
Web site: http://www.mathemagicians.info.

JD Entertainment, *(978-0-9772240)* 1731 Cherry Rd., Memphis, TN 38117 USA
E-mail: directorrsp@yahoo.com
Web site: http://www.jkdenny.com
Dist(s): **Partners Bk. Distributing, Inc.**

JD Publishing, *(978-0-9793972)* Div. of Redpsych Production, P.O. Box 696, Fairfax, CA 94978 USA (SAN 853-3431) Tel 773-793-7622
E-mail: redpsychproductions@yahoo.com
Web site: http://www.redpsych.com; http://www.monkeyandtheengineer.com.

Jeb Cool Kids Entertainment, Inc, *(978-0-9744123; 978-0-9859430)* 8208 Norton Ave., Unit 2, Los Angeles, CA 90046 USA
E-mail: jebcoolkids@gmail.com
Web site: http://www.jebcoolkids.com
Dist(s): **BookBaby.**

JEC Publishing Company *See* **Recipe Pubs.**

Jeffers Pr., *(978-0-9745776; 978-0-9777618)* 2700 Neilson Way, Suite 1428, Santa Monica, CA 90405 USA Tel 310-450-4008; Toll Free: 877-450-4008
E-mail: mark@jefferspress.com
Web site: http://www.jefferspress.com
Dist(s): **National Bk. Network.**

Jefferson Pr., *(978-0-9718974; 978-0-9778086; 978-0-9800164; 978-0-615-27680-9)* P.O. Box 115, Lookout Mountain, TN 37350 USA
E-mail: dmagee@jeffersonpress.com; info@jeffersonpress.com
Web site: http://www.jeffersonpress.com
Dist(s): **Independent Pubs. Group.**

Jefferson, Thomas University Press *See* **Truman State Univ. Pr.**

Jellyroll Productions *See* **Osborne Enterprises Publishing**

JEM Bks., Inc., *(978-0-9754317)* 10466 E. Sheena Dr., Scottsdale, AZ 85255-1742 USA
E-mail: rmahoney@jem-books.com
Web site: http://www.jem-books.com.

Jenkins-Simmons, Glenda, *(978-0-9758586)* 692 Mulberry Dr., Biloxi, MS 39532 USA Tel 228-388-7540
E-mail: res55472@cs.com.

Jennie's Music Room Bks., *(978-0-9842392)* 4241 Filmore St., Chincoteague Island, VA 23336 USA (SAN 858-8236)
Web site: http://www.ginasfamilystore.com; http://www.jmrbooks.com
Dist(s): **Smashwords.**

Jennings, J. Publishing Company *See* **Jennings Publishing**

Jennings Publishing, *(978-0-9700038)* 5012 Kahn St., Carmichael, CA 95608 USA Tel 916-863-1638; Fax: 916-863-5807
E-mail: jane@jenningspub.com
Web site: http://www.jenningspub.com
Dist(s): **Omnibus Pr.**

Jenpet Publishing, *(978-0-9726794)* P.O. Box 2542, Alameda, CA 94501 USA Tel 510-521-3582
E-mail: jj@jenpet.com
Web site: http://www.jenpet.com.

JenPrint Pubns., LLC, *(978-0-9653791)* 12195 Hwy. 92 Suite 114-162, Woodstock, GA 30188 USA
E-mail: margarette@jenprint.com
Web site: http://www.jenprint.com
Dist(s): **Book Clearing Hse.**
Follett School Solutions
Quality Bks., Inc.

Jensen, Lissa, *(978-0-9666973)* 958 Summer Holly Ln., Encinitas, CA 92024 USA Tel 760-944-6345.

Jensen, Travis, *(978-0-9754439)* 23 Los Palmos Dr., San Francisco, CA 94127-2309 USA
E-mail: thesfmasher@yahoo.com
Web site: http://www.sfmasher.cjb.net.

Jensonbooks, *(978-0-9794414)* P.O. Box 416, Greenfield, MA 01302-0416 USA (SAN 853-4322).

Jentmedia, *(978-0-578-03676-2)* P.O. Box 1304, Lonbard, IL 60148 USA
Dist(s): **Lulu Pr., Inc.**

Jeremy's Things, *(978-0-9747878)* 410 Fifth Ave., 2nd Flr., Brooklyn, NY 11215 USA Tel 718-788-3987
E-mail: jeremy@jeremybullis.com
Web site: http://www.jeremybullis.com.

Jeriger Pr., *(978-1-59810)* P.O. Box 1249, Stafford, TX 77477-1249 USA Tel 888-447-5495 (phone/fax)
E-mail: info@jeriger.com
Web site: http://www.jeriger.com.

Jerome, Janice, *(978-0-9729741)* 273 Roy Huie Rd., Riverdale, GA 30274 USA
E-mail: feedback@providerhouse.com
Web site: http://www.providerhouse.com.

Jersey Classic Publishing, *(978-0-9765261)* 75 Locust Ave., Wallington, NJ 07057 USA.

Jerusalem Pubns., *(978-0-9707572; 978-0-9743911; 978-0-9761862; 978-0-9773885; 978-0-9792230; 978-0-9815567; 978-0-9844921; 978-0-9888958; 978-0-9863253; 978-0-9987055)* 4917 Ravenswood Dr., Apt. 513, San Antonio, TX 78232 USA Tel 732-901-3009; Fax: 732-901-4012
E-mail: rapaport@netvision.net.il
Web site: http://www.israelbookshop.com/; http://www.feldheim.com/
Dist(s): **Feldheim Pubs.**
Israel Bookshop Pubns.

JESSPress *See* **JESSPress/Susie Yakowicz**

JESSPress/Susie Yakowicz, *(978-0-9652546)* 4231 Wexford Way, Eagan, MN 55122 USA Tel 651-681-9537
E-mail: syakowicz@comcast.net
Web site: http://www.jesspress.com; susieyakowicz.com/blog.

Jester Bks., *(978-0-9723382)* 39 E. 12th St., 506, New York, NY 10003 USA Tel 212-529-9209 Do not confuse with companies with the same or similar names in Woodland Hills, CA, Orinda, CA
E-mail: davidmkom@earthlink.net.

Jesus Estanislado, *(978-0-9776291)* P.O. Box 6373, Lakewood, CA 90714 USA
E-mail: jesscortez01@gmail.com.

Jet City Comics *Imprint of* **Amazon Publishing**

JETM Publishing & Distribution *See* **I Am Your Playground LLC**

Jetpack Publishing, *(978-0-9898533)* 3 Maybrook Dr., Glenville, NY 12302 USA Tel 518-929-1895
E-mail: ethancrownberry@nycap.rr.com.

Jetway Geographer, LLC, *(978-0-9711640)* Orders Addr.: 431 S. Cooke, Helena, MT 59601 USA Tel 406-586-6879
E-mail: jgeographer@bresnan.net
Web site: www.jetwaygeographer.com.

Jew-El Pr. Co., *(978-0-9767618)* 40022 Milkmaid Ln., Murrieta, CA 92562 USA Tel 951-600-7054 (phone/fax)
E-mail: jew-el-press@verizon.net
Web site: http://www.jew-el-press.com.

Jewel Publishing, *(978-0-9744944)* P.O. Box 38, Chino Hills, CA 91709 USA Fax: 909-606-1092 Do not confuse with companies with the same or similar name in Baltimore, MD, Denver, CO, Detroit, MI, Cincinnati, OH E-mail: cmckee7721@aol.com.

Jewel Publishing LLC, *(978-0-9629715; 978-1-936499)* Orders Addr.: 6815 W. Floyd Ave., Denver, CO 80227 USA Tel 303-980-1957 Do not confuse with companies with similar names in Cincinnati, OH, New York, NY, Baltimore, MD, Detroit, MI, Chino Hills, CA E-mail: sandy7lardinois@gmail.com; sandy@jewelpublishing.com Web site: http://jewelpublishing.com.

Jewell Histories, *(978-0-9678413)* 143 Breckenridge St., Gettysburg, PA 17325 USA Tel 717-420-5344 E-mail: jewellhistories@superpa.net.

Jewish Community Federation of Rochester, NY, Inc., *(978-0-9710686)* 441 East Ave., Rochester, NY 14607 USA Tel 585-461-0490; Fax: 585-461-0912 E-mail: bappelbaum@jewishrochester.org Web site: http://www.jewishrochester.org *Dist(s):* **Wayne State Univ. Pr.**

Jewish Educational Media, *(978-1-931607; 978-1-932349; 978-0-9890522)* 784 Eastern Pkwy., Suite 403, Brooklyn, NY 11213 USA Tel 718-774-6000; Fax: 718-774-3402 E-mail: eli@jemedia.org Web site: http://www.jemedia.org *Dist(s):* **Kehot Pubn. Society.**

Jewish Learning Group, The, *(978-1-891293)* 6 Tokay Ln., Monsey, NY 10952-1701 USA Toll Free: 888-565-3276 E-mail: info@jewishlearninggroup.com Web site: http://www.jewishlearninggroup.com.

Jewish Lights Publishing *Imprint of* **LongHill Partners, Inc.**

†Jewish Pubn. Society, *(978-0-8276)* Orders Addr.: 22883 Quicksilver Dr., Dulles, VA 20166 USA (SAN 253-9446) Tel 703-661-1165; 703-661-1529; Fax: 703-661-1501; Toll Free: 800-355-1165; Edit Addr.: 2100 Arch St., 2nd Flr., Philadelphia, PA 19103-1399 USA Tel 215-832-0600 E-mail: marketing@jewishpub.org Web site: http://www.jewishpub.org *Dist(s):* **Ebsco Publishing MyiLibrary Univ. of Nebraska Pr.;** *CIP.*

JFA Productions, *(978-0-9723024)* 806 Homestead Ave., Maybrook, NY 12543 USA Tel 845-427-5008 E-mail: carrdero@warwick.net.

Jfalcock, *(978-0-9890111)* 4262 Althea Way, Palm Beach Gardens, FL 33410 USA Tel 561-252-3350 E-mail: jfalcock@gmail.com.

JFAR Bks., *(978-0-615-45886-1)* Orders Addr.: P.O. Box 331621, West Hartford, CT 06133 USA Tel 617-388-2489 E-mail: J_Farquharson@yahoo.com Web site: www.PlaytimetoBedtime.com.

JFK Online Studios, LLC, *(978-0-9742249)* 293 2nd Ave., West Haven, CT 06516-5127 USA Web site: http://www.jfkonlinestudios.com.

JFW, Ltd., *(978-0-9710071)* 400 N. Church St., Unit 602, Charlotte, NC 28202 USA Tel 704-277-8378 (phone/fax) E-mail: create2000@earthlink.net; jfwbird@earthlink.com.

JG Pr. *Imprint of* **World Pubns. Group, Inc.**

JGC/United Publishing Corps, *(978-0-910941)* 1717 Harlem Blvd., Rockford, IL 61103 USA (SAN 270-5109) Tel 815-968-6601 E-mail: mailbox@jgcunited.com Web site: http://www.jgcunited.com.

J.G.R. Enterprises, *(978-0-9758746)* 100 Oak St., Patchogue, NY 11772 USA Tel 631-790-0932 E-mail: joannros12@aol.com.

JGracia Publishing, *(978-0-9837403)* 2998 Valley View Cir., Powder Springs, GA 30127 USA Tel 678-668-6286 E-mail: jgraciaenterprises@gmail.com *Dist(s):* **Lulu Pr., Inc.**

JIMAPCO, Inc., *(978-1-56914)* Orders Addr.: P.O. Box 1137, Clifton Park, NY 12065 USA Fax: 518-899-5093; Toll Free: 800-627-7123; Edit Addr.: 2095 Rte. 9, Round Lake, NY 12151 USA Tel 518-899-5091 E-mail: cfisk@jimapco.com *Dist(s):* **Benchmark LLC Langenscheidt Publishing Group Rand McNally.**

Jimmy Patterson *Imprint of* **Little Brown & Co.**

Jimmy Patterson *Imprint of* **Grand Central Publishing**

Jimsam Incorporated *See* **Jimsam Inc. Publishing**

Jimsam Inc. Publishing, *(978-0-9790768; 978-0-9816914; 978-0-9820587; 978-0-9841074; 978-0-615-57183-6; 978-0-615-66583-2; 978-0-615-67879-5)* P.O. Box 3363, Riverview, FL 33569 USA Tel 813-748-9523 E-mail: contact@jimsaminc.com; ms1free@aol.com Web site: http://www.jimsam-inc.com.

Jinks, Elizabeth Schneider, *(978-0-9666312)* 7624 W. Mauna Loa Ln., Peoria, AZ 85381-4388 USA Tel 602-486-5362 E-mail: ee_jinks@qwest.net.

JINKS Studio Art & Publishing, *(978-0-9749672)* Orders Addr.: 9421 Woodlief Rd., Wake Forest, NC 27587-8993 USA E-mail: jinksstudio@comcast.net Web site: http://www.jinksstudio.com.

Jiovanie, *(978-0-578-10152-1)* 503 La Costa, Leander, TX 78641 USA.

JIST Life *Imprint of* **JIST Publishing**

†JIST Publishing, *(978-0-942784; 978-1-56370; 978-1-57112; 978-1-59357; 978-1-63332)* Div. of EMC Publishing, 875 Montreal Way, Saint Paul, MN 55102 USA (SAN 240-2351) Tel 651-290-2800 Toll Free Fax: 800-547-8329; *Imprints:* KIDSRIGHTS (Kidsrts); JIST Works (JIST Works); JIST Life (JIST Lfe) E-mail: info@jist.com Web site: http://www.jist.com *Dist(s):* **Cardinal Pubs. Group Ebsco Publishing Follett School Solutions Linx Educational Publishing, Inc. MyiLibrary;** *CIP.*

JIST Works *Imprint of* **JIST Publishing**

JIST Works, Incorporated *See* **JIST Publishing**

Jitterbug Bks., *(978-0-9763031; 978-0-615-49452-4)* 25 Whale Rock Rd., Jamestown, RI 02835 USA Tel 401-423-2823 E-mail: jitterbugbooks@cox.net.

JJ Bks. (GBR) *(978-0-9569212; 978-1-909661) Dist. by* **Casemate Pubs.**

J.K.H. Enterprises, *(978-0-9761422)* MSC 5033, Busch Student Center 20 N. Grand Blvd., Saint Louis, MO 63103 USA E-mail: juliushunter@slu.edu Web site: http://juliushunter.tripod.com.

JL Thomas Pub., *(978-0-9786537)* 1287 Hadaway Trl., Lawrenceville, GA 30043-4670 USA E-mail: jlthomas@jlthomas-author.com Web site: http://jlthomas-author.com.

JLM CD-ROM Publishing Co., *(978-0-9749905)* 150 Idora Ave., San Francisco, CA 94127-1016 USA (SAN 255-9552) Web site: http://www.jlmcd-rompublishing.com.

JM2 Publishing Co., *(978-0-9767210)* 6316 Monte Cresta, Richmond, CA 94806 USA Fax: 510-237-4305 E-mail: jeanmock@comcast.net.

JMC Printing, *(978-0-9638586)* Div. of JMC Marketing, Orders Addr.: 6730 W. 84th Cir. Suite 88, Arvada, CO 80003 USA Tel 303-564-1606 mobile E-mail: jmcpublishing@aol.com.

JMG Studio, *(978-0-9771117)* Div. of John-Marc Grob Studios, 6 Southwind Dr., Flanders, NJ 07836 USA (SAN 256-8691) Tel 973-347-5399 E-mail: johnmarc@jmgstudio.net Web site: http://www.jmgstudio.net.

JMK Music Publishing, *(978-0-9743218)* 22 Maple Ln., Northborough, MA 01532 USA Web site: http://www.jmkmusicpub.com.

Jo Fletcher Books *Imprint of* **Quercus NA**

JoAnn Vergona Krapp & Gene Zaner, *(978-0-9722576)* 94 Sunset Ave., Farmingdale, NY 11735 USA E-mail: jkrapp1940@aol.com.

Joanne Faye Pr., *(978-0-9747375)* c/o Goblin Fern Pr., Inc., 852 Hemlock Dr., Verona, WI 53593 USA Tel 608-835-5523; Fax: 608-442-0212 E-mail: jritland@mac.com Web site: http://www.loveybooks.com.

Joanne Frances Pr., *(978-0-9777640)* Orders Addr.: 210 Piney Hill Rd., Oakland, MI 48363-1449 USA Toll Free: 800-960-2347 Web site: http://www.JoanneFrancesPress.com.

JoAnne/Horatio Books *See* **Gumbo Multimedia Entertainment**

JoBen Books, LLC *See* **Unveiled Media, LLC**

Jodan Collections, *(978-0-9747181)* Orders Addr.: 2716 N. Univ. Rd., Spokane, WA 99206 USA Tel 509-927-1882; Edit Addr.: 6405 S. Dishman Mica Rd., Spokane, WA 99206 USA E-mail: joanne@inlandbindery.com Web site: http://www.inlandbindery.com.

Jodaviste Publishing, *(978-0-9789016)* P.O. Box 473444, Charlotte, NC 28247 USA (SAN 851-920X) E-mail: jodavistepublishing@earthlink.net Web site: www.margosmagictrunk.com.

Joe Bks. Inc. (CAN) *(978-1-926516; 978-1-987955; 978-1-77275) Dist. by* **HachBkGrp.**

Joe Girl Ink, *(978-0-9766080)* 111S. Morgan, No. 502, Chicago, IL 60607 USA.

Joewolf Pubs., *(978-0-9671344)* Orders Addr.: P.O. Box 80127, Conyer, GA 30013 USA Tel 770-922-6655; Fax: 770-388-0521 E-mail: joewolf@bellsouth.net.

Joey Publishing, *(978-0-9799444)* 300 Atlantic St., Suite 500, Stamford, CT 06902 USA Fax: 203-363-7825 E-mail: jeanne@joeypublishing.com.

Johannesen Printing & Publishing, *(978-1-881084)* Orders Addr.: P.O. Box 24, Whitethorn, CA 95589 USA Tel 707-986-7465; Fax: 707-986-1656 E-mail: books@johannesen.com Web site: http://www.johannesen.com.

Johnny Sundby Photography, *(978-0-9747152)* 4780 Easy St., Rapid City, SD 57702 USA Tel 605-343-5646; Fax: 605-342-0139 E-mail: dsp@rap.midco.net Web site: http://www.johnnysundby.com.

Johnson, Anthony, *(978-0-9773760)* P.O. Box 731, Burbank, CA 91503-0731 USA (SAN 257-4187) Fax: 818-558-6771 E-mail: leedobug@hotmail.com.

Johnson Bks. *Imprint of* **Bower Hse.**

Johnson, Bonnie, *(978-0-9769756)* Orders Addr.: 6 Son Ct., Valley Center, KS 67147-2659 USA.

Johnson, Colleen, *(978-0-9785002)* 2500 63rd St NW, Minot, ND 58703 USA Tel 701-839-5768 E-mail: gchristi@minot.com Web site: http://icecreamforbreakfastbook.com.

Johnson, Earl Photography, *(978-0-9649645; 978-0-9779024)* Orders Addr.: P.O. Box 870165, Stone Mountain, GA 30087 USA Tel 678-476-3950; Fax: 678-476-3951 E-mail: books@earljohnsontruckbooks.com Web site: http://earljohnsontruckbooks.com.

Johnson, Gary, *(978-0-9791794)* 938 E. Lois Ln., Phoenix, AZ 85020-1189 USA (SAN 852-6931) Tel 602-944-7517 (phone/fax); Toll Free: 888-665-2762 E-mail: gjohnson@molarman.com Web site: http://www.molarman.com.

Johnson, James *See* **Strategies Publishing Co.**

Johnson, Jenna Elizabeth, *(978-0-9976442)* 729 Calle Bendita, Arroyo Grande, CA 93420 USA Tel 805-478-0244 E-mail: authorjejohnson@gmail.com Web site: www.jennaelizabethjohnson.com.

Johnson, Suzanne, *(978-0-9968220)* 814 Chickasaw Ave., Auburn, AL 36830 USA Tel 504-301-6414 E-mail: suzannej3523@gmail.com Web site: http://www.suzannejohnsonauthor.com.

Johnson Tribe Publishing, *(978-0-9896733; 978-0-692-30715-1; 978-0-9977522)* 1484 Uncle Ben Dr., Powder Springs, GA 30127 USA Tel 770-815-6477 E-mail: johnsontribepublishing@gmail.com Web site: johnsontribepublishing@gmail.com.

Johnston, Ann, *(978-0-9656776)* Orders Addr.: P.O. Box 388, Ashland, OH 44805 USA Toll Free: 800-247-6553 (ordering & shipping information); Edit Addr.: P.O. Box 944, Lake Oswego, OR 97034 USA (SAN 852-9043) Tel 503-635-6791; Fax: 503-675-0366 E-mail: order@bookmaster.com Web site: http://www.annjohnston.net *Dist(s):* **CreateSpace Independent Publishing Platform.**

Johnston, Ann, *(978-0-9796010)* 2409 Crest St., Alexandria, VA 22302 USA Tel 703-629-2175 E-mail: growhealthy@gmail.com.

Johnston, Don Inc., *(978-1-893376; 978-1-58702; 978-1-4105)* Orders Addr.: 26799 W. Commerce Dr., Volo, IL 60073 USA Tel 847-740-0749; Fax: 847-740-7326; Toll Free: 800-999-4660 Web site: http://www.donjohnston.com.

Johnston, Lissa, *(978-0-9973068)* 721 Wildwood Rd., Leesville, SC 29070 USA Tel 803-487-9385 E-mail: lissajohnston@gmail.com.

Johnston-Brown, Anne Publishing Co. *See* **Retriever Pr.**

Joint Committee on Printing *Imprint of* **United States Government Printing Office**

Joint Heir Multimedia, *(978-0-9796148)* P.O. Box 108, Edgewater, NJ 07020 USA Web site: http://www.jointheirmultimedia.net.

Joint Publishing Co. (HKG) *(978-962-04) Dist. by* **China Bks.**

Joint Publishing Co. (HKG) *(978-962-04) Dist. by* **Chinasprout.**

Jokar Productions, LLC *See* **Save Our Seas, Ltd.**

Jolly Fish Pr. *Imprint of* **North Star Editions**

Jolly Geranium, Inc., *(978-0-9644524)* 2953 E. Pawnee Dr., Sierra Vista, AZ 85635-8511 USA Tel 520-321-4747.

Jolly Learning, Ltd. (GBR) *(978-1-870946; 978-1-903619; 978-1-84414) Dist. by* **Am Intl Dist.**

Jolt, *(978-0-9831498)* Orders Addr.: P.O. Box 201013, Montgomery, AL 36120 USA Tel 256-390-3722 E-mail: information@jolt-books.com Web site: http://www.jolt-books.com.

†Jones & Bartlett Learning, LLC, *(978-0-7637; 978-0-86720; 978-1-4496; 978-1-284)* 5 Wall St., Burlington, MA 01803 USA (SAN 285-0893) Toll Free: 800-832-0034 Web site: http://www.jblearning.com *Dist(s):* **Ebsco Publishing Rittenhouse Bk. Distributors ebrary, Inc.;** *CIP.*

Jones & Bartlett Publishers, Incorporated *See* **Jones & Bartlett Learning, LLC**

Jones, Augustine R., *(978-0-9743223)* 4213 N. Knoll Ridge Rd. Apt. B2, Peoria, IL 61614-7439 USA.

Jones, Bob University Press *See* **BJU Pr.**

Jones Bks., *(978-0-9721217; 978-0-9763539; 978-0-9790475)* 3 Loon Ln., Madison, WI 53717-1854 USA E-mail: info@jonesbooks.com Web site: http://www.jonesbooks.com.

Jones, Kirk, *(978-0-9759688)* P.O. Box 74702, Richmond, VA 23236 USA E-mail: kirkjonesillustrations@juno.com.

Jones, Linda, *(978-0-9776450)* 2700 Woodland Park Dr. Apt. 705, Houston, TX 77082-6605 USA E-mail: amiasthefirst@aol.com.

JonesHarvest Publishing, *(978-0-9794455; 978-1-60388)* 5400 E. State Rd. 45, Bloomington, IN 47408 USA Tel 812-323-2330; Fax: 812-323-2339; Toll Free: 877-400-0075 E-mail: jonesharvest@sbcglobal.net Web site: http://www.jonesharvest.com.

Jonquil Books *See* **Miglior Pr.**

Jon'taar Graphxs, *(978-0-9764385)* 75 Lantern Chase Dr., Delaware, OH 43015 USA Tel 740-972-6321 E-mail: msuplicki@jontaar.com; information@mirthburdz.com Web site: http://www.jontaar.com; http://www.mirthburdz.com.

Jordan Music Productions, Inc., *(978-1-895523; 978-1-894262; 978-1-55386)* M.P.O. Box 490, Niagara Falls, NY 14302-0490 USA E-mail: sjordan@sara-jordan.com Web site: http://www.sara-jordan.com; http://www.SongsThatTeach.com; http://www.edu-mart.com *Dist(s):* **Follett Media Distribution iLeon.**

Jordan Publishing Hse., *(978-1-890875)* Orders Addr.: P.O. Box 671, Columbia, CA 95310 USA Fax: 209-532-5503; Edit Addr.: 22620 Parrotts Ferry Rd., Columbia, CA 95310 USA Do not confuse with companies with the same name in Las Vegas, NV, Nappanee, IN, Reston, VA, Phoenix, AZ, Prescott, AZ E-mail: gpview@erli.net.

Jordan, Sara Publishing, *(978-1-895523; 978-1-894262; 978-1-55386)* Div. of Jordan Music Productions, Inc., Orders Addr.: M.P.O. Box 490, Niagara Falls, NY 14302-0490 USA (SAN 118-959X) Tel 416-760-7664; Fax: 416-762-2770; Toll Free Fax: 800-229-3855; Toll Free: 800-567-7733 E-mail: sjordan@sara-jordan.com Web site: http://www.edu-mart.com; http://www.sara-jordan.com; http://www.songsthatteach.com *Dist(s):* **Follett School Solutions.**

Jordan Valley Heritage Hse., *(978-0-939810)* P.O. Box 99, Stayton, OR 97383-0099 USA (SAN 216-7425) Tel 503-769-4236 E-mail: jvhh5@wvi.com.

Jorge Pinto Bks., *(978-0-9742615; 978-0-9774724; 978-0-9790766; 978-0-9795576; 978-0-9801147; 978-1-934978)* 6216 Vorlich Ln., Bethesda, MD 20816 USA (SAN 853-7526); *Imprints:* Illustrated Books (Illus Bks) Web site: http://www.pintobooks.com; jpintobooks.com *Dist(s):* **D.A.P./Distributed Art Pubs.**

Jorlan Publishing *See* **Jorlan Publishing, Inc.**

Jorlan Publishing, Inc., *(978-0-9710696; 978-1-933830)* P.O. Box 2882, Cedar City, UT 84721-2882 USA Web site: http://www.jorlanpublishing.com.

Joseph, Dr. Angela Banner, *(978-1-943945)* 37-29 104th Street, Apt. 3D, Corona, NY 11368 USA Tel 347-669-0151 *Dist(s):* **CreateSpace Independent Publishing Platform.**

Joseph Henry Pr. *Imprint of* **National Academies Pr.**

Joseph Pubns., *(978-0-9773243)* P.O. Box 401, Killington, VT 05751 USA Tel 917-502-7328 Web site: http://www.josephpublications.com *Dist(s):* **Independent Pubs. Group.**

Joseph's Coat Publishing *See* **Breezy Reads**

Joseph's Heartprint, *(978-0-9787035)* 728 Creek Rd., Carlisle, PA 17013 USA Tel 717-258-8796; Fax: 717-243-4254 E-mail: george@catholicartworks.com Web site: http://www.catholicartworks.com.

Joseph's Labor, *(978-0-9729800)* P.O. Box 176265, Covington, KY 41017-6265 USA Tel 859-578-8112 E-mail: JosephsLabor@aol.com.

Joshua Pr., Inc. (CAN) *(978-1-894400) Dist. by* **Gabriel Res.**

Joshua Tree Publishing, *(978-0-9710954; 978-0-9768677; 978-0-9778311; 978-0-9823703; 978-0-9845904; 978-0-9829803; 978-0-9886577; 978-1-941049)* 3 Golf Ctr. No. 201, Hoffman Estates, IL 60169 USA Tel 312-893-7525; 3 Golf Ctr. No. 201, Hoffman Estates, IL 60169 Tel 312-893-7525 Do not confuse with companies with the same or similar names in Mentor, OH, Lake San Marcos, CA E-mail: info@joshuatreepublishing.com Web site: http://joshuatreepublishing.com; http://centaurbooks.com; http://chiralhouse.com.

Jossey-Bass *Imprint of* **Wiley, John & Sons, Inc.**

Jostens Bks., *(978-0-9759530; 978-0-9788398)* 116 Independence Dr., Indian Trail, NC 28079-9452 USA Toll Free: 800-458-0319 E-mail: sherry.clontz@jostens.com Web site: http://www.jostens.com.

Jots & Tittles Publishing, *(978-0-9894379)* 310 W. 39th St., Vancouver, WA 98660 USA Tel 360-566-2781 E-mail: ghost@writingasaghost.com.

Journals Unlimited, Inc., *(978-1-892033; 978-0-9818414; 978-0-9842578; 978-0-9832414; 978-0-9859025; 978-0-9907307; 978-0-9973031)* P.O. Box 1882, Bay City, MI 48707 USA Tel 989-686-3377; Fax: 989-686-3380; Toll Free Fax: 800-897-8529; Toll Free: 800-897-8528 E-mail: barb@journalsunlimited.com; tech@journalsunlimited.com Web site: http://www.journalsunlimited.com.

Journalstone, *(978-0-9828119; 978-1-936564; 978-1-940161; 978-1-942712; 978-1-945373; 978-1-947654)* 1261 Peachwood Ct., San Bruno, CA 94066 USA Tel 415-235-6734 E-mail: christophercpayne@journalstone.com Web site: http://journalstone.com.

Journey of a Dream Pr., *(978-0-9749876; 978-0-9818251; 978-0-9839777; 978-0-9897142)* 2888 Winchester Ct., Duluth, GA 30096 USA Tel 770-789-9796 E-mail: journeyofadream@comcast.net Web site: www.journeyofadream.com.

Journey Pubns., LLC, *(978-0-9728716; 978-0-9748087; 978-0-9772078; 978-0-9798171)* Orders Addr.: P.O. Box 2442, Warminster, PA 18974-2442 USA (SAN 255-1675) Do not confuse with companies with the same or similar names in Woodstock, NY, Savannah, GA, Avon Park, FL, Metairie, LA, Lacey, WA E-mail: journeypubs@aol.com Web site: http://www.journeypublications.com.

Journey Stone Creations, LLC, *(978-0-9758709; 978-1-59958)* 3533 Danbury Rd., Fairfield, OH 45014 USA Fax: 513-860-0176; *Imprints:* A.W.A. Gang (AWA Gang) E-mail: pat@journeystonecreations.com Web site: http://www.journeystonecreations.com; http://www.myezbookclub.com; http://www.jscbooks.com.

JourneyForth *Imprint of* **BJU Pr.**

Journeys Press *See* **Whirlwind Publishing Group**

Journique Publishing Group, Inc., *(978-0-9795586)* P.O. Box 524, Knightdale, NC 27545 USA Fax: 407-796-6394 E-mail: pjordan@journique.com Web site: http://www.journique.com *Dist(s):* **Lightning Source, Inc.**

Joy of my Youth Pubns., The, *(978-0-9774345)* P.O. Box 128702, Cincinnati, OH 45212 USA Tel 513-531-2709 E-mail: thejoyofmyyouth@netzero.net Web site: http://www.thejoyofmyyouth.com.

J.O.Y. Pubns., *(978-0-9762975)* 186 Gatewood Ave., Rochester, NY 14624-1737 USA Do not confuse with companies with the same or similar name in Santa Maria, CA Gardena, CA, Pittsboro, NC, Woburn, MA E-mail: rainbowvillagecc@yahoo.com; rainbowvillage@homewithGod.net Web site: www.our.homewithGod.com/rainbowvillage/.

J.O.Y. Publishing, *(978-0-9755454)* Orders Addr.: P.O. Box 540912, Merritt Island, FL 32954-0912 USA; *Imprints:* Laughing Zebra - Books for Children (Laugh Zebra) E-mail: jdelgado@laughing-zebra-children-books.com Web site: http://zooprisepartyfiestazoorpresa.blogspot.com; http://www.laughing-zebra-children-books.com.

JoyceHerzog.com, Incorporated *See* **Herzog, Joyce**

Joyful Learning Publications, LLC, *(978-0-9836580)* 3148 Plainfield Ave NE suite 153, Grand Rapids, ME 49525-3285 USA Tel 207-693-5257 E-mail: sandyjane05@yahoo.com.

Joyful Learning Publishing *See* **Joyful Learning Publications, LLC**

Joyful Noise, (978-0-9772109) 312 Stonewall Rd., Concord, VA 24538 USA (SAN 257-0149)
E-mail: j.b.designs@att.net.

JoyRox, LLC, (978-0-9754972) 11585 Hooker St., Westminster, CO 80031-7121 USA
E-mail: info@joy-rox.com
Web site: http://www.joy-rox.com.

JoySoul Corp., (978-0-9727786) Orders Addr.: 1214 Rose St., Lisbon, ND 58054-0071 USA
E-mail: jscontact@joysoul.com
Web site: http://www.joysoul.com.

JoZanephine Originals *Imprint of* **Gamoke, John**

JPA Assocs., (978-0-9727125) 11026 Maple Rd., Lafayette, CO 80026 USA Tel 303-665-6764.

JR Comics (KOR) (978-89-94208; 978-89-92836; 978-89-98341) *Dist. by* **Lerner Pub.**

Jr Imagination, (978-0-9837404; 978-0-9893189) 17310 Trosa St., Granada Hills, CA 91344 USA Tel 818-366-4194; Fax: 818-366-2134
E-mail: marty@jrimagination.com
Web site: http://www.jrimagination.com; http://www.sarnatart.com; http://www.doublemgraphics.com.

JRP Ringier Kunstverlag AG (CHE) (978-2-940271; 978-3-905701; 978-3-905770; 978-3-03764; 978-3-905829) *Dist. by* **Dist Art Pubs.**

JRV Publishing, (978-0-9771250) P.O. Box 82, West Simsbury, CT 06092 USA
E-mail: jverney1@jrvpublishing.com.

JSP Bks., (978-0-9728519) 6886 Hickory Lake Cove, Memphis, TN 38119 USA Tel 901-757-0694
E-mail: contact@jspbooks.com
Web site: http://www.jspbooks.com.

Juba Bks. *Imprint of* **NetNia Publishing Co.**

Judah Bks., Inc., (978-0-9767469) 3535 W. Tierra Buena Ln., Apt. No. A273, Phoenix, AZ 85053 USA.

Judaica Pr., Inc., The, (978-0-910818; 978-1-880582; 978-1-932443; 978-1-60763) 123 Ditmas Ave., Brooklyn, NY 11218 USA (SAN 204-9856) Tel 718-972-6200; Fax: 718-972-6204; Toll Free: 800-972-6201; *Imprints:* Shayach Comics (Shayach Comics)
E-mail: info@judaicapress.com
Web site: http://www.judaicapress.com.

JuDe Publishing, (978-0-9712585) Orders Addr.: P.O. Box 264 s lacienega blvd #1283, beverly hills, CA 90211 USA Tel 310-600-9729
E-mail: judepublishing@yahoo.com
Dist(s): **Bookazine Co., Inc.**

†Judson Pr., (978-0-8170) Div. of American Baptist Churches, U.S.A., P.O. Box 851, Valley Forge, PA 19482-0851 USA (SAN 201-0348) Tel 610-768-2118; Fax: 610-768-2107; Toll Free: 800-458-3766
Web site: http://www.judsonpress.com
Dist(s): **A & B Distributors & Pubs. Group**
Afrikan World Bk. Distributor
Anchor Distributors
Appalachian Bible Co.
Partners Bk. Distributing, Inc.
Send The Light Distribution LLC
Sociedad Biblica de Puerto Rico
Spring Arbor Distributors, Inc.
Wizard Works; *CIP.*

Juice & Berriesr, The *Imprint of* **Asiana Media**

Julenda Enterprises, (978-0-9747994) 219 E. El Valle, Green Valley, AZ 85614-2903 USA Tel 520-393-0071
E-mail: judylgarcia@aol.com
Web site: http://www.judylenore.com.

Julie Andrews Collection *Imprint of* **HarperCollins Pubs.**

Julio C. Malone *See* **Editorial Miglo Inc.**

Julson, D. K., (978-0-9746564; 978-0-615-11699-0) 28704 County Hwy B., Richland Ctr, WI 53581-6721 USA.

July Publishing Inc., (978-0-9704379; 978-0-9968906) Orders Addr.: P.O. Box 5301, Herndon, VA 20172-5301 USA; Edit Addr.: P.O. Box 5301, Herndon, VA 20172-5301 USA; *Imprints:* Social Motion Publishing (SocialMotion)
E-mail: mailbox@julypublishing.com; andrew@socialmotionpublishing.com
Web site: http://www.JulyPublishing.com; http://www.SocialMotionPublishing.com.

July-Eight Publishing *See* **Three Socks Publishing**

Jump at the Sun *Imprint of* **Hyperion Bks. for Children**

Jump! Inc., (978-1-62031; 978-1-62496; 978-1-64128) 5357 Penn Ave. S., Minneapolis, MN 55419 USA (SAN 920-8143) Tel 888-960-1346; *Imprints:* Bullfrog Books (BullfrogBks); Pogo (Pogo)
E-mail: casie@jumplibrary.com
Web site: http://www.jumplibrary.com
Dist(s): **Follett School Solutions.**

Jump Pr., (978-0-9754902; 978-0-9980733) P.O. Box 600743, Newtonville, MA 02460-2210 USA
E-mail: emily@emilysper.com
Web site: http://blueirisdesign.com
Dist(s): **Bookmasters Distribution.**

Jump Start Performance Programs, (978-1-893962) P.O. Box 3448, Van Nuys, CA 91407 USA Toll Free Fax: 800-990-9667; Toll Free: 800-450-0432
E-mail: scott@scottgreenberg.com
Web site: http://www.scottgreenberg.com.

Jumping Cow Pr., (978-0-9801433; 978-0-9980010) P.O. Box 8982, Scarborough, NY 10510-8982 USA (SAN 855-305X) Tel 914-373-9816
E-mail: jumpingcowpress@gmail.com
Web site: http://www.JumpingCowPress.com.

Jumping Jack Pr., (978-0-9795441; 978-1-60580; 978-1-62348) Div. of Up With Paper, LLC, 6049 Hi-Tek Ct., Mason, OH 45040 USA Tel 513-759-7473; Fax: 513-336-3119
E-mail: info@upwithpaper.com; georgew@upwithpaper.com
Web site: http://www.jumpingjackpress.com
Dist(s): **Ingram Publisher Services.**

June & The Wolves Publishing, (978-0-615-74511-4; 978-0-615-89550-5; 978-0-692-36512-0) 148 E St. RD 177, FEASTERVILLE, PA 19053 USA Tel 480-999-1877
Dist(s): **CreateSpace Independent Publishing Platform.**

June Bks., LLC, (978-0-9835558) 408 W. Lotta St. Suite No. 1, Sioux Falls, SD 57105 USA Tel 512-630-3380
E-mail: trevor@junebooks.com; hello@junebooks.com
Web site: http://www.junebooks.com.

Junebug Bks. *Imprint of* **NewSouth, Inc.**

JuneOne Publishing Hub, (978-0-9763082) 27762 Antonio Pkwy., L1-404, Ladera Ranch, CA 92694 USA Tel 949-364-6179; Fax: 757-299-4407; *Imprints:* A JuneOne Production (A JuneOne Prod)
E-mail: info@juneonehub.com
Web site: http://www.juneonehub.com.

Junge, Michael, (978-0-692-75722-2; 978-0-692-75723-9; 978-0-692-77029-0) 10 Algerwood, LADERA RANCH, CA 92694 USA Tel 949-887-6085.

Jungle Communications, Incorporation *See* **Allergic Child Publishing Group**

Jungle Hse. Pubns., (978-0-9769332) Orders Addr.: 736 Cardium St., Sanibel, FL 33957-6704 USA Tel 239-395-4518
E-mail: junglehousepub@yahoo.com
Web site: http://junglehousepublications.com.

Jungle Jeep Press *See* **Jungle Wagon Pr.**

Jungle Wagon Pr., (978-0-9834092; 978-0-9904271) 5116 Didier Ave., Rockford, IL 61101 USA (SAN 920-6426) Tel 815-988-9048
E-mail: junglewagonpress@gmail.com
Web site: http://www.junglewagonpress.com.

Junior History Pr., (978-0-9744556) Orders Addr.: P.O. Box 157, Summerville, SC 29484-0157 USA Tel 843-873-8117; Edit Addr.: 1311 Jahnz Ave., Summerville, SC 29485 USA
E-mail: gteaster@juniorhistory.com
Web site: http://www.juniorhistory.com.

Junior League of Central Westchester, (978-0-615-16563-9) 1039 Post Rd., Scarsdale, NY 10583 USA Tel 914-723-6139; Fax: 914-723-6016
E-mail: jlcw@verizon.net
Web site: http://www.jlcentralwestchester.org.

Junior League of Grand Rapids Michigan, Inc., (978-0-9611316; 978-0-9634927) 25 Sheldon Blvd., Suite 124, Grand Rapids, MI 49503 USA (SAN 282-9452) Tel 616-451-0452; Fax: 616-451-1936
E-mail: juniorleague@iserv.net
Web site: http://www.juniorleagiegr.com.

Junior League of Tyler, Inc., The, (978-0-9607122) 1919 S. Donnybrook, Tyler, TX 75701 USA (SAN 238-9975) Tel 903-593-8141; Fax: 903-595-1362.

Juniper Berry Pr., (978-0-9760076) 6609 Cornelia Dr., Edina, MN 55435 USA Tel 952-285-4447
E-mail: gjudso@aol.com
Web site: http://www.juniperberrypress.com.

Juniper Grove, (978-1-60355) 2129 E. Stearns, Fayetteville, AR 72703 USA (SAN 853-5078)
E-mail: JuniperGrove@gmail.com
Web site: http://www.junipergrove.com
Dist(s): **CreateSpace Independent Publishing Platform.**

Juping Horse Pr., (978-0-615-55671-0; 978-0-615-75585-4) 845 N. 27th St., Philadelphia, PA 19130 USA Tel 215-978-0844
E-mail: karin@jumpinghorsepress.com
Web site: http://www.jumpinghorsepress.com.

Jupiter Coins *See* **Adventure in Discovery**

Jupiter Kids (Childrens & Kids Fiction) *Imprint of* **Speedy Publishing LLC**

juputer2 bks., (978-0-9779404) 309 Claymille Pl., Nashville, TN 37207 USA
Web site: http://www.juputer2books.com.

Just Be Publishing, Inc., (978-0-9668219) 746 E. Rosemore Ct., Salt Lake City, UT 84107 USA (SAN 299-7479) Tel 801-265-3435 (phone/fax)
E-mail: bl_ehrler@att.net
Web site: http://www.justbepublishing.com.

Just Chill Pubns., (978-0-9726548) P.O. Box 5990, Chicago, IL 60680 USA
E-mail: chill1960@comcast.net; contact@justchill.org; contact@communityaccesstoresources.org
Web site: http://www.justchill.org; http://www.communityaccesstoresources.org.

Just Enjoyable Memorable Story Bks., (978-0-9724472) 8258 Balsam Way, Arvada, CO 80005 USA
E-mail: jemsbooks@hotmail.com.

Just For Kids Pr., LLC, (978-1-934650; 978-1-935498; 978-1-935747; 978-1-936918; 978-1-937962) 360 Hurst St., Linden, NJ 07036 USA
E-mail: ssullivan@justforkidspress.com.

Just Like Me, Inc., (978-1-928889) P.O. Box 4494, Washington, DC 20017 USA Tel 202-526-1725; 525 Tailgate Terr., Landover, MD 20785
E-mail: yb1922@yahoo.com
Web site: http://www.justlikemebooks.com.

Just Me Productions, (978-0-9821118) 4255 Us 1 S., Suite 18-212, Saint Augustine, FL 32086 USA Tel 904-797-7242
Web site: http://www.justmeproductions.com.

Just Think Bks. *Imprint of* **Canary Connect Pubns.**

Just Us Bks., Inc., (978-0-940975; 978-1-933491) 356 Glenwood Ave., 3rd Flr., East Orange, NJ 07017-2108 USA (SAN 664-7413) Tel 973-672-7701; *Imprints:* Sankofa Books (Sankofa Bks)
E-mail: justusbook@aol.com
Web site: http://www.justusbooks.com.

Just Write Bks., (978-0-9722839; 978-0-9766533; 978-0-9777614; 978-0-9788628; 978-1-934949; 978-1-944386) Just Write Communications, 14 MUNROE LN, TOPSHAM, ME 04086 USA (SAN 855-5109) Tel 207-729-3600; Fax: 207-729-4600
E-mail: jstwrite@jstwrite.com
Web site: http://www.jstwrite.com.

Justice Link Publishing, (978-0-692-00612-2) P.O. Box 3144, Glendale, CA 91221 USA.

Juvenescent Research Corp., (978-0-9600148; 978-1-884996) 807 Riverside Dr., Apt. 1F, New York, NY 10032 USA (SAN 206-7250) Tel 212-795-3749
Dist(s): **Barnes & Noble, Inc.**

Juventud, Editorial (ESP) (978-84-261) *Dist. by* **Continental Bk.**

Juventud, Editorial (ESP) (978-84-261) *Dist. by* **Lectorum Pubns.**

Juventud, Editorial (ESP) (978-84-261) *Dist. by* **AIMS Intl.**

Juventud, Editorial (ESP) (978-84-261) *Dist. by* **Distribks Inc.**

JVED Publishing, (978-0-9768833) 18140 Zane St., NW No. 410, Elk River, MN 55330 USA
Web site: http://www.jvedpublishing.org.

JVGray, (978-0-9982387) 71 Snowden Ave, Ossining, NY 10562 USA Tel 914-713-4104
E-mail: jvgray01@gmail.com
Web site: jvgray.com.

JWall Publishing, (978-0-9760518) 287 Jones Rd., Statham, GA 30666 USA Tel 770-725-7465.

JWD Publishing, (978-0-9843365; 978-0-9846315; 978-1-941574) P.O. Box 32, Sylvania, GA 30467 USA Tel 912-564-2427
E-mail: jwpublishing@gmail.com
Web site: http://www.revolutionarydisciples.com; www.jaribooks.com.

JYZ Books, LLC *See* **JYZ Bks., LLC**

K and K Publishing, (978-0-9828886) P.O. Box 20517, Carson City, NV 89721 USA Tel 775-885-7986
E-mail: okmarge@charter.net; marge@kankpublishing.com
Web site: http://kankpublishing.com.

K. F. Enterprises *See* **Production Assocs., Inc.**

K T Graphics, (978-0-9755259) 5300 Standing Rock Pl., Las Vegas, NV 89130 USA Tel 702-808-3773
Web site: http://www.ktgraphicsolutions.com.

K12, (978-1-931728; 978-1-60153) 2300 Corporate Park Dr., Herndon, VA 20171 USA Tel 703-483-7000; Fax: 703-483-7330
Web site: http://www.k12.com.

K-Twelve MicroMedia Publishing, Inc., (978-0-943646; 978-1-56419) 16 McKee Dr., Mahwah, NJ 07430 USA (SAN 286-990X) Tel 201-529-4500; Fax: 201-529-5282; Toll Free: 800-292-1997
E-mail: sales@k12mmp.com
Web site: http://www.k12mmp.com.

KA Productions, LLC, (978-1-888018) Orders Addr.: P.O. Box 21, Alexandria, VA 22313-0021 USA Tel 703-371-4325 (phone/fax); *Imprints:* Word of Mouth Books (Word of Mouth Bks)
E-mail: stephanie@bookinaday.com
Web site: http://www.kwamealexander.com
Dist(s): **SPD-Small Pr. Distribution.**

Kabet Pr. (GBR) (978-0-948662) *Dist. by* **Empire Pub Srvs.**

Kadima Pr., (978-0-9723229) 410 Pine St. No., 802 C, Abilene, TX 79601-5163 USA Fax: 501-636-7425
E-mail: KadimaPress@juno.com
Web site: http://www.kadimapress.com; http://www.AuntLaya.com
Dist(s): **Bks. West.**

Kaeden Bks. *Imprint of* **Kaeden Corp.**

Kaeden Corp., (978-1-57874; 978-1-879835; 978-1-61181; 978-1-63584; 978-0-9747360; 978-1-64132) Orders Addr.: P.O. Box 16190, Rocky River, OH 44116 USA Tel 440-617-1400; Fax: 440-617-1403; Toll Free: 800-890-7323; *Imprints:* Kaeden Books (Kaeden)
E-mail: info@kaeden.com
Web site: http://www.kaeden.com
Dist(s): **Follett School Solutions.**

Kagan Cooperative Learning *See* **Kagan Publishing**

Kagan Publishing, (978-1-879097; 978-1-933445) Div. of Resources for Teachers, Orders Addr.: P.O. Box 72008, San Clemente, CA 92673 USA Tel 949-545-6300; Fax: 949-545-6301; Toll Free: 800-933-2667
E-mail: carol@kaganonline.com; parker@kaganonline.com; Hannah@KaganOnline.com
Web site: http://www.kaganonline.com.

kahla, bob, (978-1-882820; 978-0-692-75067-4) P.O. Box 134, Stowell, TX 77661 USA Tel 409-201-4614
E-mail: poss1108@msn.com.

Kahley, Glenn, (978-0-9788914) 1575 England Dr., Columbus, OH 43240 USA
E-mail: kahley.1@osu.edu.

Kaimanu Prodns., Ltd., (978-0-9764474) 135-A Kaimanu Pl., Kihei, HI 96753 USA Tel 808-268-9092; Fax: 808-442-0013
E-mail: customerservice@kaimanu.net
Web site: http://www.kaimanu.net
Dist(s): **Booklines Hawaii, Ltd.**

Kaio Pubns., Inc., (978-0-9960430) 2119 Autumn Cove Cir., Fleming Island, FL 32003 USA Tel 615-828-4363
E-mail: joe@kaiopublications.org
Web site: www.kaiopublications.org.

Kairos Publishing, (978-0-9665831; 978-0-9818864; 978-0-615-92130-3; 978-0-692-65816-1; 978-0-692-67177-1) Orders Addr.: P.O. Box 450, Clarence, NY 14031 USA Tel 716-759-1058; Edit Addr.: 10501 Main St., Clarence, NY 14031 USA Do not confuse with Kairos Publishing in Llano de San Juan, NM
E-mail: office@eagleswings.to
Web site: http://www.eagleswings.to
Dist(s): **Destiny Image Pubs.**
Send The Light Distribution LLC.

KAK, (978-0-615-40229-1) 776 Highland Hills Dr., Howard, OH 43028 USA Tel 740-294-3202
E-mail: saucie776@yahoo.com.

Kalandraka Catalunya, Edicions, S.L. (ESP) (978-84-95730) *Dist. by* **IPG Chicago.**

Kalandraka Ediciones Andalucia, S.L. (ESP) (978-84-96388; 978-84-933755; 978-84-933759; 978-84-933780) *Dist. by* **Lectorum Pubns.**

Kalandraka Editora, S.L. (ESP) (978-84-8464; 978-84-923553; 978-84-95123) *Dist. by* **Mariuccia Iaconi Bk Imports.**

Kalandraka Editora, S.L. (ESP) (978-84-8464; 978-84-923553; 978-84-95123) *Dist. by* **Lectorum Pubns.**

Kalawantis Computer Services, Incorporated *See* **Kalawantis Publishing Services, Inc.**

Kalawantis Publishing Services, Inc, (978-0-9665909) Orders Addr.: P.O. Box 25004, Charlotte, NC 28227 USA Tel 704-754-1108
E-mail: publisher@kalawantis.com
Web site: http://www.kalawantis.com.

Kalcom Publishing, (978-0-9797530) 84-01 Lefferts Blvd., Kew Gardens, NY 11415 USA Tel 718-805-5555
E-mail: yek@kalcom.com.

Kaleta Publishing, LLC, (978-0-615-39881-5; 978-0-9830222) 161 Trail E., Pataskala, OH 43062 USA Tel 614-352-3583
E-mail: mindyjkaleta@gmail.com
Dist(s): **MyiLibrary.**

KALEXT Productions, LLC, (978-0-9617451; 978-0-9748792) 12795 75th Lane N., West Palm Beach, FL 33412 USA (SAN 664-0613) Tel 561-310-4338; Fax: 561-790-6294 Call 561-310-4338 first
E-mail: xela319@comcast.net
Web site: http://www.bilingualgames.com; http://www.biznizgames.com.

Kalindi Pr., (978-1-935826; 978-0-9838455) 2508 Shadow Valley Ranch Rd., Prescott, AZ 86305 USA Tel 928-636-3759
E-mail: balazuccarello@gmail.com
Web site: http://www.kalindipress.com
Dist(s): **SCB Distributors.**

Kaliyan Publishing, (978-0-9762065) P.O. Box 473, Stephens City, VA 22655-9998 USA.

†Kalmbach Publishing Co., Bks. Div., (978-0-8238; 978-0-87116; 978-0-89024; 978-0-89778; 978-0-913135; 978-0-933168; 978-1-62700) Orders Addr.: P.O. Box 1612, Waukesha, WI 53186 USA (SAN 201-0399) Tel 262-796-8776 Toll Free: 800-533-6644 (customer sales); 800-446-5489 (customer service); 800-558-1544 (trade sales); Edit Addr.: 21027 Crossroads Cir., Waukesha, WI 53186 USA Tel 262-796-8776
E-mail: customerservice@kalmbach.com
Web site: http://corporate.kalmbach.com/; http://kalmbach.com
Dist(s): **Publishers Group West (PGW)**
Watson-Guptill Pubns., Inc.; *CIP.*

Kalmia Publishing, (978-0-9676620) Orders Addr.: 826 Amiford Dr., San Diego, CA 92107 USA Tel 619-222-7074 (phone/fax)
E-mail: pixieh@mymailstation.com; folsom@islc.net
Web site: http://www.islc.net/~folsom/language.

Kaloustian, Varak, (978-0-9987773) 13903 Otsego St., Sherman Oaks, CA 91423 USA Tel 818-383-0621; *Imprints:* TLOV Publishing (MYID_H_TLOV PU)
E-mail: info@thelegendofv.com
Web site: thelegendofv.com.

KAM Publishing, (978-0-9795474) Orders Addr.: 1716 Worley St., Durant, OK 74701-2468 USA
E-mail: sharonm@llibs.com
Web site: http://www.llibs.com
Dist(s): **Library Integrated Solutions & Assocs.**

Kamahoi Pr. *Imprint of* **Bishop Museum Pr.**

KAMAL Pubns., (978-0-9651552; 978-1-59236-028-4) 445C E. Cheyenne Mountain Blvd., No. 243, Colorado Springs, CO 80906 USA Tel 719-579-9777; Fax: 719-579-8221; Toll Free: 800-231-9341
E-mail: creative.organizing@worldnet.att.net; kitaos@aol.com.

Kamaron Institute Pr., Div. of Kamaron Institute for Rapid Business Results, 104 Strawflower Path, Peachtree City, GA 30269 USA
E-mail: info@kamaron.org; kamaroninstitute@earthlink.net
Web site: http://www.kamaron.org.

†Kamehameha Publishing, (978-0-87336) 567 S. King St., Suite 118, Honolulu, HI 96813 USA Tel 808-534-8205; Fax: 808-541-5305
E-mail: publishing@ksbe.edu
Web site: http://www.kamehamehapublishing.org
Dist(s): **Bess Pr., Inc.**
Booklines Hawaii, Ltd.
Follett School Solutions
Native Bks.; *CIP.*

Kamehameha Schools Press *See* **Kamehameha Publishing**

Kana'i Records, (978-0-9754567) 95-1168 Makaikai St. Apt. 113, Mililani, HI 96789-4392 USA
E-mail: bhelemano@aol.com
Dist(s): **Booklines Hawaii, Ltd.**

K&B Products, (978-0-9646181; 978-0-9740841; 978-0-9772372; 978-1-935122) P.O. Box 548, Yellville, AR 72687 USA Toll Free Fax: 888-871-5856; Toll Free: 800-700-5096
E-mail: brmp@aol.com
Web site: http://www.thecompletepet.com; http://www.whitehallpublishing.com
Dist(s): **Western International, Inc.**

Kane, Kimberly Brougham, (978-0-615-17610-9; 978-0-578-04556-6) 1406 Campfire Rd., Lake Charles, LA 70611 USA
Web site: http://www.mommysheart.com
Dist(s): **Lulu Pr., Inc.**

†Kane Miller, (978-0-916291; 978-1-929132; 978-1-933605; 978-1-935279; 978-1-61067) Div. of EDC Publishing, Orders Addr.: P.O. Box 470663, Tulsa, OK 74146 USA (SAN 295-8945) Tel 858-456-0540; Fax: 858-456-9641; Edit Addr.: P.O. Box 8515, La Jolla, CA 92038 USA Tel 858-456-0540
E-mail: info@kanemiller.com
Web site: http://www.kanemiller.com; http://www.edcpub.com
Dist(s): **EDC Publishing**; *CIP.*

Kane Press, Inc., *(978-1-57565; 978-0-9819697; 978-1-940947; 978-1-63592)* 300 Park Ave., New York, NY 10022-7402 USA Tel 650-862-2566
E-mail: ndmattia@kanepress.com; info@kanepress.com
Web site: http://www.kanepress.com
Dist(s): **Follett School Solutions**
Lerner Publishing Group
MyiLibrary.
Kane Press, The *See* **Kane Press, Inc.**
Kane/Miller#Book Publishers, Incorporated *See* **Kane Miller**
Kanlearn, Inc., *(978-0-9772077)* 8950 W. Olympic Blvd., No. 128, Beverly Hills, CA 90211 USA Tel 310-430-6806
E-mail: mattie3rd@yahoo.com
Web site: www.thekanlearnfoundation.com.
Kansas Alumni Assoc., *(978-0-9742918)* 1266 Oread Ave., Lawrence, KS 66044 USA
Web site: http://www.kualumni.org.
Kansas City Guidebooks, *(978-0-9763873)* P.O. Box 14082, Parkville, MO 64152 USA
Web site: http://www.kckidsguide.com.
Kansas City Star Bks., *(978-0-9604884; 978-0-9679519; 978-0-9709131; 978-0-9712920; 978-0-9717080; 978-0-9722739; 978-0-9740009; 978-0-9746012; 978-0-9754804; 978-0-9764021; 978-1-933466; 978-1-935362; 978-1-61169)* Cypress Media L L P, Orders Addr.: 1729 Grand Blvd., Kansas City, MO 64108 USA; Edit Addr.: 1729 Grand Blvd., Kansas City, MO 64108 USA Tel 816-234-4292; *Imprints:* Rockhill Books (Rockhill Bks)
E-mail: weaver@kcstar.com
Web site: www.TheKansasCityStore.com
Dist(s): **National Bk. Network**
Partners Bk. Distributing, Inc.
Kanto Productions, LLC, *(978-1-929956)* P.O. Box 630435, Simi Valley, CA 93063 USA Tel 805-584-9639; Fax: 310-507-0142; Toll Free: 800-335-2686
E-mail: info@atophill.com
Web site: http://www.atophill.com.
†Kaplan Publishing, *(978-0-7931; 978-0-88462; 978-0-913864; 978-0-936894; 978-0-942103; 978-1-57410; 978-1-60714; 978-1-60978; 978-1-61865; 978-1-62523; 978-1-5062)* 395 Hudson St., New York, NY 10014 USA (SAN 211-2280); 395 Hudson St., New York, NY 10014; *Imprints:* Dearborn Real Estate Education (Dearbn Real Est Ed)
E-mail: deb.darrock@kaplan.com; shayna.webb@kaplan.com; alexander.noya@kaplan.com
Web site: http://www.kaplanpublishing.com
Dist(s): **BookBaby**
Cranbury International
Dearborn Financial Publishing, Inc.
JAGCO & Associates Inc.
LibreDigital
MBI Distribution Services/Quayside Distribution
Simon & Schuster
Simon & Schuster, Inc.; *CIP.*
Kapp Bks. LLC, *(978-1-60346; 978-1-64035)* Orders Addr.: 204-Mohan complex , H block Market Phase 1, New Delhi, 110052 IND; Edit Addr.: 3602 Rocky Meadow Ct., Fairfax, VA 22033 USA Fax: 703-621-7162
E-mail: pravin@kappbooks.com; sundeep@macawbooks.com
Web site: http://www.kappbooks.com; http://www.macawbooks.com/.
Karadi Tales Co. Pvt, Ltd. (IND) *(978-81-8190) Dist. by* **Consort Bk Sales.**
Karadjian, Kayl, *(978-0-692-79862-1; 978-0-9989635)* 14324 Lake Price Dr., ORLANDO, FL 32826 USA Tel 954-551-8169.
Kar-Ben Publishing *Imprint of* **Lerner Publishing Group**
Kardec, Allan Educational Society, *(978-0-9649907)* 5020 N. Eighth St., Philadelphia, PA 19120 USA Tel 215-329-4010 (phone/fax)
E-mail: akesbooks@cox.net
Web site: http://www.allan-kardec.org.
Karen Pokras Toz *See* **Grand Daisy Pr.**
Karenzo Media, *(978-0-9798164; 978-0-9899318)* 5695 E. Great Marsh Church Rd., Saint Pauls, NC 28384 USA Tel 910-633-9358
E-mail: karenzomedia@gmail.com; khsilvestri@live.com
Web site: http://www.karenzomedia.com; http://www.publishersmarketplace.com/members/kazsilvestri/; http://www.writingyourlifetales.com.
Karina Library Pr., *(978-0-9824491; 978-1-937902)* P.O. Box 35, Ojai, CA 93024-9302 USA Tel 805-500-4535
E-mail: michael@karinalibrary.com; sails@karinalibrary.com
Web site: http://www.karinalibrary.com.
Karma Kollection LLC, *(978-0-9896966; 978-0-692-33207-8; 978-0-692-33208-5)* 549 W. Eugenie St., Chicago, IL 60614 USA Tel 312-952-0776
E-mail: roopaweber@gmail.com
Web site: www.messypenny.com.
Karma Valley Music, *(978-0-9746011)* 505 Lovins Ln., Somerset, KY 42503 USA Tel 606-274-5194
E-mail: flo@floydlovins.com.
Karnak Co., *(978-0-9630951)* Orders Addr.: P.O. Box 497-158, Chicago, IL 60649-7158 USA Tel 773-684-5298; Edit Addr.: 1616 E. 50th Pl., No. 5-C, Chicago, IL 60615 USA
E-mail: t.greer57@yahoo.com.
Karosa Publishing, *(978-0-9706312)* 4636 Almond Ln., Boulder, CO 80301 USA Tel 303-484-8856 Do not confuse with companies with same or similar name in Lower Burnell, PA, Paradise Valley, AZ, Sheffield, PA, hailey, ID
E-mail: karpub@comcast.net
Web site: http://www.spadesbook.com.
Karsonkina, Tatiana, *(978-0-9779672)* P.O. Box 191, Brooklyn, NY 11223 USA.
Karuna Press *See* **Utopia Pr.**
Karyn Henley Resources *Imprint of* **Child Sensitive Communication, LLC**
Kaseberg, W. G. Publishing, *(978-0-9761138)* 49 Red Bud Ln., Glen Carbon, IL 62034 USA Tel 618-288-5269; Fax: 618-288-0712
E-mail: wgkasebergpub@empowering.com.
Kasian Publishing, *(978-1-943207)* 15582 Eastbrook Ln., Apple Valley, MN 55124 USA Tel 612-414-9173
E-mail: kristin@kristinvanrisseghem.com
Web site: www.kristinvanrisseghem.com.
Kasson Publishing, *(978-0-9729435)* 201 E. St., Elmo Rd., Austin, TX 78745-1217 USA Tel 512-447-1988 (phone/fax)
E-mail: publishing@kassonscastings.com
Web site: http://www.kassonscastings.com.
Kasten, Victoria, *(978-0-9788850; 978-1-937363)* 5465 Glencoe Ave., Webster, MN 55088 USA Tel 952-652-6065
E-mail: rkasten@integra.net
Web site: http://www.epicscrolls.com.
Kat Tales Publishing *See* **EMC Publishing**
Kat Tales Publishing, *(978-0-9744330)* 2515 Clarkson St., Denver, CO 80205 USA Tel 303-394-6380
E-mail: alluptojah@aol.com.
KAtastroPHE, *(978-0-9769698)* 6389 Florio St., Oakland, CA 94618 USA Tel 510-601-9631
E-mail: info@katastrophemusic.com
Web site: http://www.katastrophemusic.com.
Kathy Dawson Books *Imprint of* **Penguin Young Readers Group**
Kathy's Pen, *(978-0-9777034)* 24 Ridgewood Pkwy, Newport News, VA 23608 USA Tel 757-872-6258
E-mail: regmcc@cox.net
Web site: http://www.kathyspen.com.
Kati Bee & Friends Publishing, *(978-0-9793760)* 8304 Limonite Ave. Suite D-3, Riverside, CA 92509 USA (SAN 853-2818) Tel 951-685-7256; Fax: 951-332-0436
E-mail: ContactKati@katibeeandfriends.com
Web site: http://www.katibeeandfriends.com.
Katie Cook, *(978-0-9883554)* 1201 Kenwood Dr., Nashville, TN 37216 USA Tel 615-430-8128
E-mail: cookontv@comcast.net.
Katrina Denise, *(978-0-692-77541-7; 978-0-692-84082-5)* 26 Pickersgill Sq., Owings Mills, MD 21117 USA Tel 443-416-5177
Dist(s): **CreateSpace Independent Publishing Platform.**
Kat's Kids Kreation, A, *(978-0-9749516)* 413 Fairlawn Ave., Saint Louis, MO 63119-2614 USA Fax: 314-963-0494
E-mail: katbuck123@aol.com.
Katsoris, Nicholas C. *See* **NK Pubns.**
Kattan, Peter I., *(978-0-615-15334-6; 978-0-615-18718-1; 978-0-578-03642-7)* 147-29 182nd St. Box AMM 2232, Springfield Gardens, NY 11413 USA Tel 718-553-8740
E-mail: info@kindergardensudoku.com; info@petrabooks.com
Web site: http://www.kindergardensudoku.com
Dist(s): **Lulu Pr., Inc.**
Katydid Pubns., *(978-1-879945)* Orders Addr.: P.O. Box 526, Point Lookout, MO 65726 USA; Edit Addr.: Acacia Club Rd., Hollister, MO 65672 USA Tel 417-335-8134
E-mail: mgcameron@aol.com; kay@camerons-crag.com
Web site: http://www.katydid-publications.com.
Katydid Publishing LLC, *(978-0-9724272)* 5845 Eldorado, San Joaquin, CA 93660 USA Tel 559-693-4565 Do not confuse with Latydid Publishing in Mincie, IN.
Kaukini Ranch Pr., *(978-0-9643674)* P.O. Box 2462, Wailuku, HI 96793 USA Tel 808-244-3371; Fax: 808-395-0738.
Kav Books, Incorporated *See* **Royal Fireworks Publishing Co.**
Kawainui Pr., *(978-0-943357)* P.O. Box 163, Captain Cook, HI 96704 USA (SAN 668-6427) Tel 808-328-9126 (phone/fax)
E-mail: herbkane@kona.net
Web site: http://www.hitrade.com
Dist(s): **Booklines Hawaii, Ltd.**
Kay, Janet Consulting, *(978-0-9768786)* 115 Brighton Pk., Battle Creek, MI 49015 USA.
Kay Productions LLC, *(978-0-9707201)* Orders Addr.: 1115 W. Lincoln Ave., Suite 107, Yakima, WA 98902 USA Tel 509-853-0860; Fax: 509-853-0861; Toll Free: 800-619-4345; Edit Addr.: 732 Summitview Ave., Suite 628, Yakima, WA 98902 USA Do not confuse with Kay Productions, San Rafael, CA
E-mail: marketing@kayproductions.com
Web site: http://www.kayproductions.com.
Kay, Sjoukje, *(978-0-9789698)* 4500 Broadway Suite 6i, New York, NY 10040 USA
E-mail: pdolan@fairpoint.net
Web site: http://www.thedonutyogi.com.
Kaya Production *See* **Muae Publishing, Inc.**
KayStar Publishing, *(978-0-9749886)* P.O. Box 571, Saddle River, NJ 07458 USA Fax: 201-825-3912.
Kazi Pubns., Inc., *(978-0-933511; 978-0-935782; 978-1-56744; 978-1-871031; 978-1-930637)* 3023 W. Belmont Ave., Chicago, IL 60618 USA (SAN 162-3397) Tel 773-267-7001; Fax: 773-267-7002
E-mail: info@kazi.org
Web site: http://www.kazi.org.
KB Bks. & More, *(978-0-9761128; 978-1-934486)* Orders Addr.: P.O. Box 56, Channing, TX 79018 USA Tel 806-235-2665; Fax: 866-282-1658; 715 Sante Fe, Channing, TX 79018 Fax: 866-282-1658
E-mail: kbbooks@windstream.net
Dist(s): **Follett School Solutions.**
KB Publishing, *(978-0-9768129)* 11 Running Fox Rd., Columbia, SC 29223 USA.
KBA, LLC, *(978-1-880931)* P.O. Box 3673, Carbondale, IL 62902 USA Tel 618-549-2893
E-mail: thriving@colorado.net
Web site: http://www.benziger.org.
KBR Mutti's Pubns., *(978-0-9762664)* P.O. Box 907431, Santa Barbara, CA 93190 USA
E-mail: kbrmuttis@cox.net
Web site: http://www.matthewsbox.com.
K.C. Fox Publishing, *(978-0-9767078)* Div. of The Kerr Co., P.O. Box 5446, Takoma Park, MD 20913 USA Tel 301-434-9191
E-mail: publisher@kcfoxpublishing.com
Web site: http://www.poutorpurpose.com; http://www.kcfoxpublishing.com.
KC13 Corp., *(978-1-945918)* 5440 Strand No. 203, Hawthorne, CA 90250 USA Tel 909-576-7002
E-mail: kccorp13@gmail.com.
KCI Sports *See* **KCI Sports Publishing**
KCI Sports Publishing, *(978-0-9758769; 978-0-9798729; 978-0-9843882; 978-0-9831985; 978-0-9837337; 978-0-9885458; 978-1-940056)* 3340 Whiting Ave., Suite 5, Stevens Point, WI 54481 USA Fax: 715-344-2668; Toll Free: 800-697-3756
Web site: http://www.kcisports.com
Dist(s): **Partners Bk. Distributing, Inc.**
K.Co.Kids, LLC, *(978-0-9801423)* 6804 Peter's Path, Colleyville, TX 76034 USA (SAN 855-3092) Tel 817-886-8402
E-mail: kristine@kcokids.com
Web site: http://www.kcokids.com; http://www.katieandthemagicumbrella.com
Dist(s): **Midpoint Trade Bks., Inc.**
Keaster, Diane W. *See* **ZC Horses Series of Children's Bks.**
Keenan Tyler Paine, *(978-0-9740907)* 1715 Brae Burn Rd., Altadena, CA 91001 USA (SAN 255-3414)
E-mail: pmgoddard@earthlink.net.
Keene Publishing, *(978-0-9724853; 978-0-9766805; 978-0-9792371; 978-0-9815972)* P.O. Box 54, Warwick, NY 10990-0054 USA (SAN 254-8631) Tel 845-987-7750; Fax: 845-987-7845; *Imprints:* Moo Press (Moo)
E-mail: dtinney@KeeneBooks.com; info@KeeneBooks.com; mbrowne@KeeneBoooks.com
Web site: http://www.KeeneBooks.com.
Keen's Martial Arts Academy, *(978-0-9702958; 978-1-60243)* Orders Addr.: P.O. Box 144, Tannersville, PA 18372-0144 USA (SAN 852-3002)
E-mail: LOHON6@msn.com
Web site: http://www.kmaa.info.
Keenspot Entertainment, *(978-0-9722350; 978-1-932775)* Orders Addr.: P.O. Box 110, Cresbard, SD 57435 USA Tel 605-324-3332; Toll Free: 888- 533-6776
E-mail: TeriCrosby@gmail.com
Web site: http://www.keenspot.com.
Keep Bks., *(978-1-893986)* Div. of The Ohio State Univ., 1100 Kinnear Rd., Columbus, OH 43212 USA Tel 800-678-6484; Fax: 614-688-3452; Toll Free: 800-678-6484
E-mail: keepbooks@osu.edu
Web site: http://www.keepbooks.org.
Keep Coming Back *See* **Puddledancer Pr.**
Keep Empowering Yourself Successfully, *(978-0-9762009)* 5630 S. Division, Grand Rapids, MI 49548 USA Tel 616-261-3000; Fax: 616-261-3355
E-mail: monicaharris@grar.com
Web site: http://www.successfulkeys.com.
Keep Hope Alive, *(978-1-887831)* P.O. Box 270041, West Allis, WI 53227 USA Tel 414-545-6539; Fax: 414-329-0653
E-mail: khope@access4less.net
Web site: http://www.keephopealive.org
Dist(s): **New Leaf Distributing Co., Inc.**
Keep Me Company Publishing Co., *(978-0-9718632)* 214 Blue Ridge Rd., Plymouth Meeting, PA 19462 USA Tel 610-828-2641.
Keepers of Wisdom and Peace Bks., *(978-0-9844079)* P.O. Box 1314, Woodstock, NY 12498 USA (SAN 859-3159) Tel 845-679-9258
E-mail: KeepersofWisdomandPeace@gmail.com
Web site: http://KeepersofWisdomandPeace.com
Dist(s): **Ingram Publisher Services.**
Keepsake Productions *Imprint of* **Keepsake Productions**
Keepsake Productions, *(978-0-615-63929-1; 978-0-9882979)* 2485 W. Mericrest Way, Queen Creek, AZ 85142-6066 USA Tel 480-659-9682; *Imprints:* Keepsake Productions (KeepsakeProdns)
Dist(s): **CreateSpace Independent Publishing Platform.**
Keepworthy Creations LLC, *(978-0-9833155)* P.O. Box 3529, Peoria, IL 61612 USA
E-mail: bob@keepworthy.com
Web site: www.keepworthy.com.
Kehot Pubn. Society, *(978-0-8266)* Div. of Merkos L'Inyonei Chinuch, Orders Addr.: 291 Kingston Ave., Brooklyn, NY 11213 USA Tel 718-778-0226; Fax: 718-778-4148; Toll Free: 877-463-7567 (877-4MERKOS); Edit Addr.: 770 Eastern Pkwy., Brooklyn, NY 11213 USA (SAN 220-7060) Tel 718-604-2785
E-mail: orders@kehotonline.com; info@kehot.com
Web site: http://www.kehotonline.com
Dist(s): **Follet Higher Education Grp**
Follett School Solutions.
Keira Pr., *(978-0-9824506)* P.O. Box 815, Joliet, IL 60434 USA Tel 815-726-4200
Web site: http://www.keirapress.com.
Keith Pubns., LLC, *(978-1-936372; 978-1-62882)* Orders Addr.: 1526 W. Sea Haze Dr., Gilbert, AZ 85233 USA
E-mail: KeithPublications@cox.net; mary@keithpublications.com
Web site: http://www.keithpublications.com.
Kelley, James *See* **Lypton Publishing**
Kelley, Mark, *(978-1-880865; 978-0-9744053)* Orders Addr.: P.O. Box 32077, Juneau, AK 99803 USA Tel 907-586-1993; Fax: 907-586-1201; Edit Addr.: PO Box 32077, Juneau, AK 99803 USA
E-mail: photos@markkelley.com
Web site: http://www.markkelley.com.
KelleyGreenworks Publishing, *(978-0-9791029)* Orders Addr.: 607 Woodsman Way, Crownsville, MD 21032 USA
Web site: http://www.readysetgo-organic.com.
Kelly Bear Pr., Inc., *(978-0-9621054)* 20493 Pine Vista, Bend, OR 97702 USA (SAN 250-5746) Fax: 541-330-6846; Toll Free: 800-431-1934 (orders only)
E-mail: kellybear@bendcable.com
Web site: http://www.kellybear.com
Dist(s): **Sunburst Visual Media.**
Kelly, D Scott, *(978-0-9755442)* 208 W. Lincoln, Charlevoix, MI 49720 USA Tel 231-547-1144; Fax: 231-547-4970
E-mail: info@basesteencenter.org
Web site: http://www.basesteencenter.org.
Kelly, Jason Pr., *(978-0-9664387)* 15 Ken Pratt Blvd. Suite 200, Longmont, CO 80501 USA Tel 303-772-7209
E-mail: jason@jasonkelly.com
Web site: http://www.JasonKelly.com
Dist(s): **BookBaby.**
Kelly, Katherine, *(978-0-9773481)* 4203 Cty. Rd., 3100, Lubbock, TX 79403-7869 USA
E-mail: kellytomkat@sptc.net
Web site: www.informationsleuth.wordpress.com.
Kelly, Kimberly, *(978-0-9747363)* 9801 E. Homestead Rd., Poplar, WI 54864 USA
E-mail: kimkellykimkelly@yahoo.com
Dist(s): **Partners Bk. Distributing, Inc.**
Kelly, Matthew Foundation, The *See* **Beacon Publishing**
Kelly, Tiffany, *(978-0-692-83022-2)* 9001 Bramblewood Way, Elk Grove, CA 95758 USA Tel 916-877-0378; Fax: 916-877-0378
E-mail: TiffanyKelly616@yahoo.com.
Kelsey Enterprises Publishing *See* **Cheval International**
†Kelsey Street Pr., *(978-0-932716)* 2824 Kelsey St., Berkeley, CA 94705-2302 USA (SAN 212-6729)
E-mail: kelseyst@sirius.com
Web site: http://www.kelseyst.com
Dist(s): **BookMobile**
SPD-Small Pr. Distribution; *CIP.*
Kelton, Inc., *(978-0-692-86206-3)* 200 2nd Ave SE, Sleepy Eye, MN 56085 USA Tel 715-533-5880
E-mail: jediblender1986@gmail.com.
Kempston, Megan, *(978-0-9975660)* 19275 Hidden Springs Ln., Boulder Creek, CA 95006 USA Tel 520-904-0546
E-mail: megankempston@gmail.com.
Kemtec Educational Corp., *(978-1-877960)* 4780 Interstate Dr., Cincinnati, OH 45246-1112 USA Toll Free: 877-536-8321
E-mail: prekem@kemtecscience.com
Web site: http://www.kemtecscience.com.
Ken Pr., *(978-1-928771)* 4001 N. Paseo de los Rancheros, Tucson, AZ 85745 USA (SAN 299-9714) Tel 520-743-3200; Fax: 520-743-3210
E-mail: office@kenpress.com
Web site: http://www.kenpress.com
Dist(s): **Distributors, The.**
Kenamar, Inc., *(978-0-9753207)* P.O. Box 689, West Dundee, IL 60110-0689 USA
E-mail: kenamarpublish@aol.com.
Kendahl Hse. Pr. *Imprint of* **Youngs, Bettie Bks.**
Kendall Hunt Publishing Co., *(978-0-7872; 978-0-8403; 978-0-7575; 978-1-4652; 978-1-5249)* Orders Addr.: P.O. Box 1840, Dubuque, IA 52004-1840 USA; Edit Addr.: 4050 Westmark Dr., Dubuque, IA 52002 USA (SAN 203-9184) Tel 563-589-1000; Fax: 563-589-1046; Toll Free Fax: 800-772-9165; Toll Free: 800-228-0810
E-mail: orders@kendallhunt.com; kkelly@kendallhunt.com
Web site: http://www.kendallhunt.com
Dist(s): **Smashwords.**
Kendar Publishing Company *See* **Kendar Publishing, Inc.**
Kendar Publishing, Inc., *(978-1-889506)* 310 5th St., Suite 101, Racine, WI 53403 USA Tel 262-632-4070; Fax: 262-632-7089; Toll Free: 866-632-7040.
Kendu Films, *(978-0-615-19233-8; 978-0-9825050; 978-0-9977328)* Orders Addr.: 27068 la paz rd, No. 543, Aliso Viejo, CA 92656 USA
Web site: http://www.kendufilms.com
Dist(s): **Publishers Services.**
Kenilworth Pr., Ltd. (GBR) *(978-0-600; 978-0-901366; 978-1-872082; 978-1-872119; 978-1-905693; 978-1-910016) Dist. by* **IPG Chicago.**
Kennebec Large Print *Imprint of* **Cengage Gale**
Kennedy Christian Publishing, *(978-0-9743136)* P.O. Box 5385, Texarkana, TX 75505-5385 USA
E-mail: knndytgr@aol.com.
Kennedy Enterprises, LLC, *(978-0-9836230)* 600 Baver St., Clarksburg, WV 26301 USA Tel 304-685-1239
E-mail: kennedykonnection@yahoo.com
Dist(s): **Lulu Pr., Inc.**
Kenneth B. White, *(978-0-9979291)* 1108 Wellesley Ave., Modesto, CA 95350 USA Tel 209-567-0600.
Kensington Bks. *Imprint of* **Kensington Publishing Corp.**
Kensington Publishing Corp., *(978-0-7860; 978-0-8065; 978-0-8184; 978-0-8217; 978-1-55817; 978-1-57566; 978-0-7582; 978-1-4201; 978-1-59983; 978-1-60183; 978-0-9817144; 978-0-9818905; 978-0-9824170; 978-0-9841132; 978-1-61650; 978-1-61773; 978-1-4967; 978-1-5161; 978-1-63573) 119 W. 40th St., New York, NY 10018 USA Tel 212-407-1500; Fax: 212-935-0699; Toll Free: 800-221-2647; 499 North Canon Dr., Beverly Hills, CA 90210 Tel 310-887-7082; Imprints:* Kensington Books (Knsington); Dafina (Dafina); K-Teen (K-TEEN); K-Teen/Dafina (K-TEEN/DAFINA); Urban Renaissance (Urban Renais)
E-mail: jmclean@kensingtonbooks.com; melley@kensingtonbooks.com
Web site: http://www.kensingtonbooks.com
Dist(s): **Ebsco Publishing**
MyiLibrary
Penguin Random Hse. LLC
Penguin Publishing Group
Random Hse., Inc.
Worldwide Media Service, Inc.
Kent Communications, Ltd., *(978-0-9627106; 978-1-888206; 978-0-9830963)* Orders Addr.: 25 Poplar

Plain Rd., Westport, CT 06880 USA Tel 203-454-9646; *Imprints:* Kent Press (Kent Pr)
E-mail: mhoule@gbiplaw.com
Dist(s): **Independent Pubs. Group**
MyiLibrary
National Bk. Network
Small Pr. United.

Kent Fine Art *See* **Kent Gallery**

Kent Gallery, (*978-1-878607*) P.O. Box 684, New York, NY 10012-0013 USA
E-mail: info@kentfineart.net
Web site: http://www.kentfineart.net.

Kent Pr. *Imprint of* **Kent Communications, Ltd.**

†Kent State Univ. Pr., (*978-0-87338; 978-1-60635; 978-1-61277; 978-1-63101*) Orders Addr.: c/o BookMasters, Inc., 30 Amberwood Pkwy., Ashland, OH 44805 USA Tel 419-281-1802; Fax: 419-281-6883; Toll Free: 800-247-6553; Edit Addr.: 1118 Univ. Library Bldg. 1125 Risman Dr., Kent, OH 44242-0001 USA (SAN 201-0437) Tel 330-672-7913; Fax: 330-672-3104; *Imprints:* Black Squirrel Books (Blck Squir)
E-mail: scash@kent.edu
Web site: http://www.kentstateuniversitypress.com
Dist(s): **BookMasters, Inc.**
Follett School Solutions
MyiLibrary
Partners Bk. Distributing, Inc.
ebrary, Inc.; *CIP.*

Keogh, Anne, (*978-1-938993*) 132 S. Battery St., Charleston, SC 29401 USA Tel 843-722-7350
E-mail: akeogh98@hotmail.com
Web site: www.annetoddbooks.com.

Kepler Pr., (*978-0-9713770*) Orders Addr.: P.O. Box 400326, Cambridge, MA 02140 USA (SAN 255-6014) Tel 617-413-7204
E-mail: ealex@keplerpress.com
Web site: http://www.keplerpress.com
Dist(s): **Lightning Source, Inc.**

Keriouspyeseries LLC, (*978-0-615-45033-9; 978-0-615-55447-1; 978-0-9899654; 978-0-692-88383-9*) 12437 N. Portland Ave., Mequon, WI 53092 USA Tel 262-243-1299
E-mail: keriouspyeseries@att.net.

Kerpluggo Bks. LLC, (*978-0-9762429*) 1015 W. Webster Ave., Suite 3, Chicago, IL 60614 USA Tel 773-665-8075
E-mail: mbwillian2@yahoo.com.

Kerr, Alex, (*978-0-9753076*) 145 Lincoln Rd. Apt. 2L, Brooklyn, NY 11225-4017 USA
E-mail: alexkerr@earthlink.net.

Kerr, Charles H. Publishing Co., (*978-0-88286*) 1726 W. Jarvis Ave., Chicago, IL 60626 USA (SAN 207-7043) Tel 773-465-7774 (orders); 847-328-2132 (orders); Fax: 773-472-7857 (orders)
E-mail: arcane@ripco.com
Web site: http://www.charleshkerr.net
Dist(s): **SPD-Small Pr. Distribution.**

Kerr Company, The *See* **K.C. Fox Publishing**

Kerr, Justin & Shelley, (*978-0-9766408*) 10735 Atascadero Ave., Atascadero, CA 93422-5723 USA
Web site: http://www.kirra-rincon.com.

Kessinger Publishing Company *See* **Kessinger Publishing, LLC**

Kessinger Publishing, LLC, (*978-0-7661; 978-0-922802; 978-1-56459; 978-1-4179; 978-1-4191; 978-1-4192; 978-1-4253; 978-1-4254; 978-1-4286; 978-1-4304; 978-1-4325; 978-1-4326; 978-0-548; 978-1-4365; 978-1-4366; 978-1-4367; 978-1-4368; 978-1-4369; 978-1-4370; 978-1-4371; 978-1-4372; 978-1-4373; 978-1-4374; 978-1-104; 978-1-120; 978-1-160; 978-1-161; 978-1-162; 978-1-163; 978-1-164; 978-1-165; 978-1-166; 978-1-167; 978-1-168; 978-1-169) Orders Addr.: P.O. Box 1404, Whitefish, MT 59937 USA (SAN 251-4621) Fax: 406-897-7825*
E-mail: kpreply55@runbox.com
Web site: http://www.kessinger.net
Dist(s): **Lightning Source, Inc.**

Kesterson & Associates *See* **Big Valley Publishing**

Kestrel Pubns., (*978-0-9628472; 978-0-9881925*) 1811 Stonewood Dr., Dayton, OH 45432-4002 USA Tel 937-426-5110; Fax: 937-320-1832; Toll Free: 800-314-4678 (orders only)
E-mail: invisiblei@aol.com.

Keszler, E., (*978-0-615-19548-3; 978-0-615-36360-8*) 6779 Sienna Club Pl., Lauderhill, FL 33319 USA
E-mail: uniqueart613@gmail.com.

Ketabe Gooya Publishing LLC, (*978-1-933429*) Orders Addr.: 6400 Canoga Ave., Suite 355, Woodland Hills, CA 91367 USA Tel 818-346-8338; Toll Free: 800-515-0069
E-mail: nasser@farrokh.us
Web site: http://www.ketabegooya.com.

Ketman Publishing *See* **Wooster Bk. Co., The**

Kevin W W Blackley Bks., LLC, (*978-0-9960839*) 3 Longcroft Rd., Lockport, NY 14094 USA Tel 716-316-6336
E-mail: kevin.blackley@gmail.com.

Kew Publishing (GBR) (*978-0-947643; 978-1-900347; 978-0-85521; 978-1-84246*) *Dist. by* **Chicago Distribution Ctr.**

Key Answer Products, Inc., (*978-0-9642823*) 108 S. Third St., Suite 4, Bloomingdale, IL 60108 USA (SAN 255-805X) Tel 630-893-4007; Fax: 630-893-4030; Toll Free: 800-539-1233
E-mail: dcowhey@ci-inc.com
Web site: http://www.ci-inc/what/what.htm.

Key Education Publishing Company, LLC *Imprint of* **Carson-Dellosa Publishing, LLC**

Key of David Publishing, (*978-1-886987*) Subs. of House of David, Orders Addr.: PO Box 947, Palatka, FL 32178 USA Tel 800-829-8777 (phone/fax); Toll Free: 800-829-8777 Do not confuse with Key of David Publishing, Poughquag, NY
E-mail: info@redeemedisrael.com
Web site: http://www.keyofdavidpublishing.com.

Key Publishers, Incorporated *See* **City Creek Pr., Inc.**

Key Publishing Hse., Inc., The (CAN) (*978-0-9782526; 978-0-9780431; 978-0-9811606; 978-1-926780*) *Dist. by* **Bookmasters.**

Keyboarding First, LLC, (*978-0-9768426*) 6919 Prairie Dr., Middleton, WI 53562-5356 USA Tel 608-836-4404 (phone/fax); Fax: 608-836-4405
E-mail: psm.janet@tds.net.

KEYGARD, (*978-0-9767086*) Orders Addr.: 7887 Broadway, Suite 506, San Antonio, TX 78209 USA Tel 210-829-5074; Fax: 210-829-5132
E-mail: bhkeyser@aol.com.

Keyhole Pr., (*978-0-9821512; 978-0-615-59031-8; 978-0-615-61927-9; 978-0-692-83815-0*) Div. of Dzanc Bks.,
E-mail: info@keyholepress.com
Web site: http://www.keyholepress.com
Dist(s): **Consortium Bk. Sales & Distribution**
CreateSpace Independent Publishing Platform
MyiLibrary
Smashwords.

Keys For Kids Publishing Company *See* **Amazing Drama Anointed Voices Original Music**

Keysquake Music, (*978-0-9760837*) 42 Blackfoot Ct., Guilford, CT 06437 USA
E-mail: bgillie48@yahoo.com
Web site: http://www.briangillie.com.

Keystone Bks. *Imprint of* **Stone Arch Bks.**

Keytochange Publishing, Inc., (*978-0-9729798*) 7484 University Ave. Ste. T, La Mesa, CA 91941-6030 USA
E-mail: sjones@keytochange.com
Web site: http://www.keytochange.com.

Keywords Press *Imprint of* **Atria Bks.**

Khanna, Rachel, (*978-0-9779568*) 163 John St., Greenwich, CT 06831 USA (SAN 850-7260)
Web site: http://www.liveeatcookhealthy.com
Dist(s): **Partners Pubs. Group, Inc.**

Khesed Foundation, (*978-0-9785077*) Orders Addr.: 633 S. Plymouth Ct, Chicago, IL 60605-6060 USA Tel 615-792-1449; Edit Addr.: 1030 Trouble Ct., No. 1005, Ashland City, TN 37015-6060 USA (SAN 850-7236)
E-mail: hankbo@juno.com.

Khunum Productions, Inc., (*978-0-9797010*) Khunum Productions, Inc. 149 Bainbridge St., Suite 3, Brooklyn, NY 11233 USA Tel 718-924-8779
E-mail: Khunumproductions@gmail.com; Nehprii@msn.com
Web site: http://www.NehpriiAmenii.com.

Kick The Ball, (*978-0-9790396; 978-1-934372; 978-1-61320*) Orders Addr.: 8595 Columbus Pike Suite 197, Lewis Center, OH 43035 USA
E-mail: pfwilson@triviagamebooks.com; tprippey@triviagamebooks.com
Web site: http://www.triviagamebooks.com; http://www.bythenumberbook.com
Dist(s): **Partners Bk. Distributing, Inc.**

Kickapoo Farms *See* **Genuine Prints, LLC**

Kicks and Giggles Today, (*978-0-615-20924-1; 978-0-615-54874-6*) P.O. Box 1023, Ross, CA 94957 USA
Web site: http://www.kicksandgigglestoday.com.

Kid by Kid, Incorporated, (*978-0-9745496*) 54249 Myrica Dr., Macomb, MI 48042 USA Tel 586-781-2345 (phone/fax)
E-mail: kidbykid@comcast.net
Web site: http://www.crystalkids.net.

Kid Niche Christian Bks., (*978-0-9852712; 978-0-9904626; 978-0-9994837*) 9958 Edgewood Ave, Traverse City, MI 49686-5845 USA.

Kid Niche Publishing *See* **Kid Niche Christian Bks.**

Kid Prep, Inc., (*978-1-58312*) 6942 FM 1960 E-132, Humble, TX 77346 USA Tel 281-852-5261; Fax: 281-852-4901; *Imprints:* Little Chameleon Books (Little Chameleon)
E-mail: customerservice@kidprep.com
Web site: http://www.kidprep.com.

KiD Sounds, (*978-0-9767650*) P.O. Box 13888, Las Vegas, NV 89112-1888 USA
Web site: http://www.kid-sounds.com.

kid2kid publishing, (*978-0-615-48783-0; 978-0-692-58147-6; 978-1-63393-444-3*) 2577 Cove Point Pl., Virginia Beach, VA 23455 USA Tel 757-375-5020
E-mail: kfk1313@yahoo.com
Dist(s): **CreateSpace Independent Publishing Platform.**

KidBiz 3000 *See* **Achieve3000**

KidBookInk Publishing, LLC, (*978-0-9776772*) Orders Addr.: 25809 Nichols Rd., Columbia Station, OH 44028 USA (SAN 257-9103) Tel 440-725-7587; Fax: 440-236-5356; Toll Free: 888-978-1669
E-mail: dbvanhorn@yahoo.com
Web site: http://www.kidbookink.com; http://www.storyboard4kidz.com.

Kidder, Clark, (*978-0-615-15313-1; 978-0-692-58895-6; 978-0-692-82942-4*) 1620 Sienna Crossing, Janesville, WI 53546 USA
Web site: http://www.clarkkidder.com.

Kidderature Publishing, (*978-0-9729703*) P.O. Box 612, Hammondsport, NY 14840 USA Tel 607-292-3026
E-mail: bobhicks@citlink.net
Web site: http://www.kidderature.com.

Kiddy Chronicles Publishing (CAN) (*978-0-9699203; 978-0-9733994*) *Dist. by* **Firefly Bks Limited.**

KID-E Bks. *Imprint of* **Word Prodns.**

Kidhaven *Imprint of* **Cengage Gale**

KidHaven Publishing *Imprint of* **Cengage Gale**

KidHaven Publishing *Imprint of* **Greenhaven Publishing LLC**

Kidible *Imprint of* **iCharacter.org**

Kidpub Pr., (*978-0-9840807; 978-1-936184; 978-1-61018*) P.O. Box 724, North Attleboro, MA 02761 USA (SAN 858-365X) Tel 401-466-4176; Toll Free: 800-252-5224 (orders/editorial)
E-mail: pd@kidpub.com; orders@kidpub.com
Web site: http://bookstore.kidpub.com; http://www.kidpub.com.

Kidrich Corp., (*978-0-9761051*) 347 5th Ave., Suite 610, New York, NY 10016 USA Tel 718-767-5135; Toll Free: 800-231-7385
Web site: http://www.kidrich.com.

Kids 4 Ever, (*978-0-9764433*) P.O. Box 1784, Holland, MI 49422 USA Tel 616-566-1231
E-mail: kids4ever@charter.net
Web site: http://www.kids4everbooks.com.

Kids Ahead Bks. *Imprint of* **WND Bks, Inc.**

Kids At Heart Publishing & Books *See* **Kids At Heart Publishing, LLC**

Kids At Heart Publishing, LLC, (*978-0-615-36340-0; 978-0-9828109; 978-0-9836641; 978-0-9855202; 978-0-9886360; 978-0-9899472; 978-0-9905734; 978-0-9964962; 978-0-9969574; 978-1-946171*) P.O. Box 492, Milton, IN 47357 USA Tel 765-478-5873
Dist(s): **Davis/Books Distribution.**

Kids At Our House, Inc., The, (*978-0-9705773; 978-1-942390*) Orders Addr.: 47 Stoneham Pl., Metuchen, NJ 08840 USA Tel 732-548-1779
E-mail: info@dannyandkim.com
Web site: www.dannyandkim.com
Dist(s): **Follett School Solutions**
Indig, Stanley M. Specialty Pubn.

Kids Can *Imprint of* **Proactive Publishing**

Kids Can Pr., Ltd. (CAN) (*978-0-919964; 978-0-921103; 978-1-55074; 978-1-55337; 978-1-894786; 978-1-55453; 978-1-77138*) *Dist. by* **HachBkGrp.**

Kids Children & Teens World 2000 & Beyond, (*978-0-9747543*) Orders Addr.: P.O. Box 385, Brandywine, MD 20613 USA Fax: 301-372-9979; Edit Addr.: 8300 Belding Ct., Brandywine, MD 20613 USA
E-mail: djospeh301@aol.com.

Kid's Creative Classics *Imprint of* **BrassHeart Music**

Kids, Critters & Country Publishing, (*978-0-9755200*) P.O. Box 866874, Plano, TX 75086-6874 USA
E-mail: jlarsen@chasewest.com
Web site: http://www.kidscrittersandcountry.com.

Kids Donate, Inc., (*978-0-9754131*) 221 Chesley Ln., Chapel Hill, NC 27514 USA Tel 919-967-0882.

Kids For Health, Inc., (*978-0-9759517; 978-1-933847*) P.O. Box 326, Springdale, AR 72763 USA Tel 479-756-9551; Fax: 479-756-0949.

Kids Go Europe, Inc., (*978-0-9772699*) P.O. Box 4014, Menlo Park, CA 94026 USA Tel 650-743-7404
E-mail: info@kidsgoeurope.com
Web site: http://www.kidsgoeurope.com.

Kids in Ministry International, (*978-0-9767647; 978-0-9815940*) P.O. Box 549, Mandan, ND 58554-0549 USA
Web site: http://www.kidsinministry.com.

Kids Life Pr., (*978-0-9755348; 978-0-9903172*) P.O. Box 3484, Pismo Beach, CA 93448-3484 USA Fax: 805-888-2838; Toll Free: 800-262-8973
E-mail: tuzee@charter.net.

Kid's Shelf, (*978-0-9729339*) 19600 Baker Rd., Gambier, OH 43022 USA Tel 740-247-2427.

Kids Think Big LLC, (*978-0-9797362*) P.O. Box 11013, Greenwich, CT 06831 USA (SAN 854-2597)
E-mail: info@kidsthinkbig.com
Web site: http://www.kidsthinkbig.com
Dist(s): **Distributors, The**
Follett School Solutions.

Kids Write On, LLC, (*978-0-615-23574-5*) Orders Addr.: P.O. Box 700924, Dallas, TX 75370 USA Tel 972-862-7257; Fax: 972-862-0194; Toll Free: 877-596-7257
Web site: http://www.thestaplercaper.com.

Kids1st Bks. *Imprint of* **BC Publishing**

Kidsafety of America, (*978-1-884413*) 6288 Susana St., Chino, CA 91710 USA
E-mail: peter@kidsafetystore.com
Web site: http://www.kidsafetystore.com
Dist(s): **Follett School Solutions.**

Kidsbooks, Incorporated *See* **Kidsbooks, LLC**

Kidsbooks, LLC, (*978-0-942025; 978-1-56156; 978-1-58865; 978-1-62885*) 3535 W. Peterson Ave., Chicago, IL 60659 USA (SAN 666-3729)
E-mail: sales@kidsbooks.com
Web site: http://www.kidsbooks.com
Dist(s): **Independent Pubs. Group.**

KidsCanPublish.Org, (*978-0-692-76150-2; 978-0-692-77349-9; 978-0-692-78442-6; 978-0-692-84092-4*) 1020 Brookview Ct., Morgan Hill, CA 95037 USA Tel 408-607-0986
E-mail: kidscanpublish@gmail.com
Web site: www.KidsCanPublish.Org.

Kidscope, Inc., (*978-0-9647798*) 2045 Peachtree Rd NE Ste. 150, Atlanta, GA 30309-1405 USA.

KidsDiscuss.com, (*978-0-9749244*) PCS, Orders Addr.: P.O. Box 6102, Edmonds, WA 98026 USA
E-mail: JeanTracy@KidsDiscuss.com
Web site: http://www.KidsDiscuss.com.

KidsGive, LLC, (*978-0-9792912; 978-0-9845910*) 5757 W. Century Blvd., Suite 800, Box 8, Los Angeles, CA 90045 USA (SAN 853-0297) Tel 310-665-9777; Fax: 310-665-9494
E-mail: lmuniz@kidsgive.com
Web site: http://www.kidsgive.com.

Kidskills America *Imprint of* **Kidskills International**

Kidskills International, (*978-0-9710641*) Div. of Creekside Creations, 1031 Cahoon Rd., Westlake, OH 44145-1232 USA Tel 440-835-5071 (phone/fax); *Imprints:* Kidskills America (Kidskills Amer)
E-mail: kidskills@wowway.com; diane@kidskills.com
Web site: http://www.kidskills.com.

KIDSRIGHTS *Imprint of* **JIST Publishing**

Kidsrights, 10100 Park Cedar Dr., Charlotte, NC 28210 USA (SAN 299-2809) Tel 704-541-0100; Fax: 704-541-0113; Toll Free: 888-970-5437 Do not confuse with Kidsrights, Mount Dora, FL.

Kidstalk, LLC, (*978-0-9776144*) P.O. Box 520, Sherman, TX 75091 USA (SAN 257-7992) Tel 903-436-0858; Fax: 903-893-1614
E-mail: kidstalk@cableone.net
Web site: http://www.kidstalkmag.com.

Kidstory Pr., (*978-0-9772231*) P.O. Box 75, Brighton, MI 48116-0075 USA Tel 517-204-9030
E-mail: kidstorypress@comcast.net
Web site: http://www.kidstorypress.home.comcast.net.

Kidwick Bks., (*978-0-9703809*) 363 S. Saltair Ave., First Fl., Los Angelas, CA 90049 USA Tel 310-471-2472; Fax: 310-861-8111
E-mail: mail@kidwick.com
Web site: http://www.kidwick.com
Dist(s): **National Bk. Network.**

Kidz & Katz Publishing Co., (*978-1-883371*) 752 Brandon Pl., Wheeling, IL 60090 USA Fax: 708-860-0513.

Kidz By Dezign Pr., Inc., (*978-0-9771030*) 1881 Kingston Way, Lawrenceville, GA 30044 USA (SAN 256-7121) Tel 770-962-2181; Fax: 678-615-2247; Toll Free: 800-719-5439
E-mail: info@slumbergirls.com
Web site: http://www.slumbergirls.com.

Kidz Entertainment, Inc., (*978-0-9795049; 978-0-9891954*) P.O. Box 0301, Baldwin, NY 11510 USA Fax: 516-223-6546
E-mail: dcorrado@optonline.net
Web site: http://www.chanteusemusic.com.

Kidz Krave Inc., (*978-0-9764144*) P.O. Box 88350, Houston, TX 77288 USA
Web site: http://www.prettypainful.com.

Kidzpoetz Publishing, (*978-0-9760220*) P.O. Box 621, New City, NY 10956 USA Tel 845-536-5505; Fax: 845-323-4272
E-mail: robertkurkela@kidzpoetz.com
Web site: http://www.kidzpoetz.com
Dist(s): **Quality Bks., Inc.**

Kidzup Productions, (*978-1-894281; 978-1-894677*) 555 VT Rte. 78, Suite 146, Box 717, Swanton, VT 05488 USA Toll Free: 888-321-5437 (888-321-KIDS)
E-mail: info@kidzup.com
Web site: http://www.kidzup.com
Dist(s): **Penton Overseas, Inc.**

Kieliszewski, Shelia, (*978-0-615-25575-0; 978-0-578-00002-2*) 2192 Willow Springs Dr., Stevens Point, WI 54481 USA
E-mail: sheilabrt@yahoo.com
Dist(s): **Lulu Pr., Inc.**

Kies Publishing Co., (*978-0-9767437*) Orders Addr.: P.O. Box 923572, Sylmar, CA 91392-3572 USA Tel 818-367-8416
E-mail: kies@kies.org
Web site: http://www.kies.org.

Kila Springs Pr., (*978-0-9716481*) Div. of Kila Springs Group, 4231 Oak Meadow Rd., Placerville, CA 95667 USA Tel 530-621-2297; Fax: 206-202-1309
E-mail: press@kilasprings.net
Web site: http://kilasprings.net/KSPress.html.

Killer Sports Publishing, (*978-1-933135*) Orders Addr.: P.O. Box 862, Berea, OH 44017 USA Tel 440-239-1854; Edit Addr.: 201 S. Rocky River Rd., Berea, OH 44017 USA
Web site: http://www.killersports.com.

Killingbeck, Dale, (*978-0-9762758*) 18300 Tustin Rd., Tustin, MI 49677 USA Tel 231-829-3084.

Kilsby, Raymond *See* **RK Enterprises, Inc.**

Kimball, Jane A., (*978-0-9755971*) 1 Reno Rd., Santa Fe, NM 87508-2132 USA
Dist(s): **Bookmasters Distribution.**

Kimber Stories, (*978-0-9767773*) Orders Addr.: P.O. Box 143, Woodlake, CA 93286 USA; Edit Addr.: 37811 Millwood Dr., Woodlake, CA 93286 USA
E-mail: kimberstories@yahoo.com.

Kimberlite Publishing Co., (*978-0-9632675*) 44091 Olive Ave., Hemet, CA 92544-2609 USA Tel 951-927-7726 Do not confuse with Kimberlite Publishing, Ventura, CA
E-mail: frumpypapa@yahoo.com.

Kimberly Pr., LLC, (*978-0-9668611*) 100 Westport Ave., Norwalk, CT 06851 USA (SAN 251-2483) Tel 203-750-6101; Fax: 203-846-3472.

Kimble, George J., (*978-0-9767024*) 4941 Hickory Woods E., Antioch, TN 37013 USA
Web site: http://www.theroadpoet.com.

Kind Critter Junction, (*978-0-9752842*) P.O. Box 30249, Indianapolis, IN 46220 USA Toll Free: 888-366-3525
E-mail: info@kindcritterjunction.com
Web site: http://www.kindcritterjunction.com.

KinderBach L.L.C., (*978-0-9773005*) P.O. Box 336, Hudson, IA 50643 USA (SAN 257-2397) Toll Free: 866-988-9814
E-mail: info@kinderbach.com
Web site: http://www.kinderbach.com.

Kinderhaus Publishing Co., (*978-0-578-05104-8*) 2970 Edgewick Dr., Glendale, CA 91206 USA
E-mail: bettyfritz@kinderhauspublishing.com.

Kindermusik International, (*978-0-945613; 978-1-931127; 978-1-58987*) Orders Addr.: P.O. Box 26575, Greensboro, NC 27415 USA (SAN 247-3747) Tel 336-273-3363; Fax: 336-273-2023; Toll Free: 800-628-5687; Edit Addr.: 6204 Corporate Park Dr., Browns Summit, NC 27214 USA (SAN 247-3755)
E-mail: info@kindermusik.com
Web site: http://www.kindermusik.com.

Kindness Queen's Empire, The, (*978-0-9889060*) 7850 Wildwood Rd., Jacksonville, FL 32211-6046 USA Tel 904-723-0116
E-mail: dbsmith10@comcast.net.

Kindred Press *See* **Kindred Productions**

Kindred Productions, (*978-0-921788; 978-0-919797*) Orders Addr.: 315 S. Lincoln St., Hillsboro, KS 67063 USA Tel 316-947-3151; Fax: 316-947-3266; Toll Free: 800-545-7322
E-mail: kindred@mbconf.ca
Web site: http://www.mbconf.org/kindred.htm
Dist(s): **Spring Arbor Distributors, Inc.**

Kinfolk Research Pr., (*978-0-9712564*) P.O. Box 6303, Plymouth, MI 48170 USA Tel 734-454-1883
E-mail: KinfolkPress@aol.com
Web site: http://cheekfamilychronicles.homestead.com/CheekFamilyChronicles.html.

King Joe Educational Enterprises, Inc., (*978-0-9728596; 978-0-9773902*) Orders Addr.: P.O. Box 86, Los Alamitos,

Publisher Name Index

CA 90720 USA Tel 562-430-8600; Fax: 562-598-5940; Toll Free: 866-818-5464 (866-818-KING); Edit Addr.: 3112 Inverness Dr., Los Alamitos, CA 90720 USA
E-mail: lindarodgers@kingjoe.com
Web site: http://www.kingjoe.com.

King, Joel, *(978-0-9787820)* 547 McLean Ave., Hopkinsville, KY 42240 USA
E-mail: joelk3@bellsouth.net.

King, Julia, *(978-0-615-34585-7; 978-0-615-37032-3; 978-0-9839827)* 13565 Watsonville Rd., Morgan Hill, CA 95037 USA Tel 408-591-6465
E-mail: wyethia3@yahoo.com.

King, Laurence Publishing (GBR) *(978-1-85669; 978-1-898113; 978-1-78067)* *Dist. by* **HachBkGrp.**

King, Marcy, *(978-0-9850752)* 4107 Sunset Ave., Chester, VA 23831 USA Tel 804-683-0517
E-mail: marcy.king@yahoo.com.

King Production, A, *(978-0-9755811; 978-0-9843325; 978-0-9860045; 978-0-9913890; 978-1-942217)* P.O. Box 912, Collierville, TN 38017 USA Tel 917-279-1363; Fax: 201-624-7225
E-mail: joyking1993@yahoo.com
Web site: www.joydejaking.com.

King St Bks./Stabler-Leadbeater Apothecary Museum, *(978-0-9763945)* 410 S Fairfax St., Alexandria, VA 22314 USA Fax: 703-456-7890
Web site: http://apothecarymuseum.org.

King, Terri Ann *See* **Paulus Publishing**

Kingdom Builders Pubn., *(978-0-578-12048-5; 978-0-578-13238-9; 978-0-578-13304-1; 978-0-578-13488-8; 978-0-578-13932-6; 978-0-578-13991-3; 978-0-578-14385-9; 978-0-578-14627-0; 978-0-578-14843-4; 978-0-578-14903-5; 978-0-578-14909-7; 978-0-578-15487-9; 978-0-692-38109-0; 978-0-692-38120-5; 978-0-692-38123-6; 978-0-692-39146-4; 978-0-692-40038-8; 978-0-578-15969-0; 978-0-692-41566-5; 978-0-692-45673-6; 978-0-692-45674-3; 978-0-692-45975-1; 978-0-692-50699-8; 978-0-692-52648-4; 978-0-692-53342-0; 978-0-692-53343-7;) 1641 Omarest Dr., Columbia, SC 29210 USA*
Web site: www.kingdombuilderspublications.com
Dist(s): **CreateSpace Independent Publishing Platform.**

Kingdom Kaught Publishing LLC, *(978-0-9824550; 978-0-9964040; 978-0-9982100; 978-1-947741)* 1350 Blair Dr., Odenton, MD 21113 USA (SAN 858-2033)
E-mail: kingdompublishingllc@gmail.com
Web site: http://www.kingdompublishingllc.com.

Kingdom Publishers *See* **Cathedral of the Holy Spirit**

Kingdom Publishing Co., *(978-0-9765636)* 17100 Halsted St., Harvey, IL 60426-6131 USA.

Kingdom Publishing Group, Inc., *(978-0-9745324; 978-0-9772964; 978-0-9792074; 978-0-9796130; 978-0-9801564; 978-0-9817706; 978-0-9821411; 978-0-9824084; 978-0-9825104; 978-0-9825849; 978-0-9826370; 978-0-9827484; 978-0-9829775; 978-0-9831452; 978-0-9833651; 978-0-9835721; 978-0-9839090; 978-0-9848940; 978-0-9852679; 978-0-9854693; 978-0-9896581; 978-0-9862492; 978-0-9962629; 978-0-9971518)* *P.O. Box 3273, Henrico, VA 23228-9705 USA*
Web site: http://www.kingdompublishing.org.

Kingdom Sound Pubs., *(978-0-9662666; 978-0-9856206)* Orders Addr.: P.O. Box 371917, Decatur, GA 30037 USA Tel 404-384-3795; Edit Addr.: 3622 Summit Trace, Suite 400, Decatur, GA 30034 USA
E-mail: kvjackson@yahoo.com.

Kingdom Talk Publishing, Incorporated *See* **Rapha Publishing**

Kingfisher *Imprint of* **Roaring Brook Pr.**

Kingfisher Bks., *(978-0-9662218)* Orders Addr.: P.O. Box 4628, Helena, MT 59604 USA Tel 406-442-2168; Toll Free: 800-879-4576; Edit Addr.: 2480 Broadway, No. 18D, Helena, MT 59601 USA
Dist(s): **Houghton Mifflin Harcourt Trade & Reference Pubs.**
Partners/West Book Distributors.

KingMaker Bks. LLC, *(978-0-9744870)* 13315 E. Cindy St., Chandler, AZ 85225 USA
E-mail: mbogumill@juno.com.

King's Kids Trading Cards, Inc., *(978-0-9703880)* P.O. Box 923271, Sylmar, CA 91392-3271 USA Fax: 818-364-2443; Toll Free: 800-910-2690
E-mail: visioninprint@brandx.net
Web site: http://www.kingskidscards.com.

King'S Land Pr. Inc,

King's Treasure Box Ministries, The, *(978-0-9910841)* 7735 Castle Combe Ct., Cumming, GA 30040 USA Tel 678-455-3710
E-mail: roy.nancyj@gmail.com
Web site: www.kingstreasurebox.org.

King's Way Pr., *(978-0-9814748; 978-0-615-22720-7; 978-0-615-29920-4; 978-0-692-67787-2; 978-0-692-70065-5; 978-0-692-70141-6; 978-0-692-70487-5; 978-0-692-71717-2; 978-0-9988367)* 3721 New Macland Rd. Suite 200-141, Powder Springs, GA 30127 USA (SAN 855-6539) Tel 404-642-5113
E-mail: publisher@kings-way-press.com
Web site: http://www.kwp-books.com
Dist(s): **CreateSpace Independent Publishing Platform.**

Kingston Pr. (CAN) *(978-1-894997)* *Dist. by* **SCB Distributo.**

Kingsway Pubns. (GBR) *(978-0-85476; 978-0-86065; 978-0-902088; 978-1-84291)* *Dist. by* **STL Dist.**

KiniArt Publishing, *(978-0-578-06335-5)* 658 SE Jerome St., Oak Harbor, WA 98277 USA
E-mail: publishing@kiniart.com
Dist(s): **Lulu Pr., Inc.**

KINJIN Global, *(978-0-9759152)* 4960 SW 32nd Ave., Dania Beach, FL 33312 USA Tel 347-826-6272
E-mail: i@dangoldman.net
Web site: http://dangoldman.net; http://redlightproperties.com.

Kinkachoo Pr., The, *(978-0-9729285)*
Web site: http://www.zhibit.org/bolan.

Kinkajou Pr. *Imprint of* **Artemesia Publishing, LLC**

Kip Kids of New York, *(978-0-9789384)* 85 Christopher St., Suite No. 5B, New York, NY 10014 USA
E-mail: KipKids@aol.com
Web site: http://www.KipKids.com.

Kirin Rise Studios, LLC, *(978-1-946003)* 120 e. anita ave, mount prospect, IL 60056 USA Tel 847-800-9679
E-mail: info@kirinrise.com
Web site: kirinrise.com.

Kirkham, Sharon Birlson, *(978-0-9767100)* 1530 Michigan Ave., La Porte, IN 46350 USA
Dist(s): **INscribe Digital.**

KIRKLAND, JUSTIN B., *(978-0-615-81456-8)* 906 BENDLETON TRACE, ALPHARETTA, GA 30004 USA Tel 404-434-8035
E-mail: KIRKLANDJUSTIN@YMAIL.COM.

Kiss A Me Productions, Inc., *(978-1-890343)* 90 Garfield Ave., Sayville, NY 11782 USA Tel 516-589-4886; Fax: 516-218-8927; Toll Free: 888-547-7263.

KISSFAQ.COM Publishing, *(978-0-9722253; 978-0-9822537; 978-0-9977658)* P.O. Box 210686, San Francisco, CA 94121-0686 USA
E-mail: kissfaq@outlook.com
Web site: http://www.kissfaq.com/
Dist(s): **CreateSpace Independent Publishing Platform.**

Kitanie Bks., *(978-0-9821262; 978-0-9841195; 978-1-935734)* P.O. Box 97, Saratoga Springs, NY 12866 USA (SAN 857-3263)
Web site: http://www.kitanie.com.

Kitanie Coloring Books *See* **Kitanie Bks.**

Kitchen Table Pubs., *(978-0-9707685)* Orders Addr.: 136 Cook-McDonald Rd., Collins, MS 39428 USA Tel 601-765-8329; Edit Addr.: 802 S. Cherry St., Collins, MS 39428 USA Tel 601-765-8329
E-mail: knight3230@bellsouth.net.

Kite Tales Publishing, *(978-1-935332)* 9122 N Tennyson Dr, Milwaukee, WI 53217 USA Tel 414-803-9259
E-mail: cbohlen@wi.rr.com
Web site: http://kitetalespublishing.com.

Kitsune Bks., *(978-0-9792700; 978-0-9819495; 978-0-9827409; 978-0-9840058; 978-0-9840059)* P.O. Box 1154, Crawfordville, FL 32326-1154 USA (SAN 852-9760) Tel 850-926-3464
E-mail: anne@kitsunebooks.com; contact@kitsunebooks.com
Web site: http://www.kitsunebooks.com
Dist(s): **Bella Distribution**
Smashwords.

Kitsune Inc., *(978-0-692-53331-4; 978-0-9978028; 978-0-9989942)* 10610 S. 48th St. 2090, Phoenix, AZ 85044 USA Tel 480-235-8151
Web site: http://varnellbrandon.wix.com/brandon-author
Dist(s): **CreateSpace Independent Publishing Platform.**

Kittyco Pr., *(978-1-937922)* 6D Auburn Ct., Alexandria, VA 22305 USA Tel 703-684-3699
E-mail: kittyerussell@comcast.net.

Kiva Publishing, Inc., *(978-1-885772)* 21731 E. Buckskin Dr., Walnut, CA 91789 USA Tel 909-595-6833; Fax: 909-860-5424; Toll Free: 800-634-5482
E-mail: kivapub@aol.com
Web site: http://www.kivapub.com
Dist(s): **Canyonlands Pubns.**
New Leaf Distributing Co., Inc.
Quality Bks., Inc.
Rio Nuevo Pubs.

Kivel, Lee, *(978-0-9774999)* 6010 E. Paseo Santa Teresa, Tucson, AZ 85750 USA Tel 520-529-2802
E-mail: ghostriver@gainusa.com.

KiwE Publishing, Ltd., *(978-1-931195; 978-1-933973)* 2980 Glacier St., Anchorage, AK 99508 USA Tel 907-333-5493
E-mail: kiwe@kiwepublishing.com
Web site: http://www.kiwepublishing.com.

Kiwi Media Group, Inc., *(978-0-9743319)* P.O. Box 493, Hopkinton, MA 01748 USA Tel 508-435-4986; Fax: 508-435-0378.

Kiwi Publishing *See* **Kiwi Media Group, Inc.**

KJ Pubns., *(978-0-9792383)* 7069 Middlebury Dr., Boynton Beach, FL 33436 USA
E-mail: contactus@kidshyperspace.com
Web site: http://www.thenutrigang.com.

Kjasen, *(978-0-692-68195-4; 978-0-692-69120-5; 978-0-692-70341-0; 978-0-692-71040-1; 978-0-692-71147-7; 978-0-692-71188-0; 978-0-692-71192-7; 978-0-692-71675-5; 978-0-692-72916-8; 978-0-9977621)* 2215 Rippling Rill St, San Antonio, TX 78232 USA Tel 210-788-0452; Toll Free: 210-788-0452
Dist(s): **CreateSpace Independent Publishing Platform.**

Kjelberg & Sons, Incorporated *See* **Kjellberg, Inc.**

Kjellberg, Inc., *(978-0-912868)* 805 W. Liberty Dr., Wheaton, IL 60187-4844 USA (SAN 201-5102) Tel 630-653-2244; Fax: 630-653-6233; *Imprints:* Kjellberg Publishers (Kjellberg Pubs)
E-mail: wsc@kjellbergprinting.com
Web site: http://kjellbergprinting.com.

Kjellberg Pubs. *Imprint of* **Kjellberg, Inc.**

KK, *(978-1-940689)* 149 Amapola Ave, Pacifica, CA 94044 USA Tel 650-284-3303
E-mail: kk@kk.org
Web site: http://www.kk.org.

Klapheke, Alisha, *(978-0-9987379)* 3975 New Hwy. 96 W, Franklin, TN 37064 USA Tel 615-440-3717
E-mail: alisha@alishaklapheke.com.

Klare & Taylor Publishing Company *See* **Klare Taylor Pubs.**

Klare Taylor Pubs., *(978-0-9764403)* P.O. Box 637, Ashland, OR 97520 USA
Web site: http://www.klaretaylorpublishers.com; http://www.pacificwestcom.com/klare; http://www.pacificwestcom.com/amazon; http://www.pacificwestcom.com/shipsofchildren; http://www.pacificwestcom.com/richardpoem.

K,L.Corgliano, *(978-0-615-56735-8)* 926 Holly hills Ct., Keller, TX 76248 USA Tel 817-914-2344
E-mail: corgliano@verizon.net.

Klemm, Rebecca Charitable Foundation *See* **NumbersAlive! Pr.**

Klett, Ernst, Verlag GmbH (DEU) *(978-3-12)* *Dist. by* **Continental Bk.**

Klett, Ernst, Verlag GmbH (DEU) *(978-3-12)* *Dist. by* **Intl Bk Import.**

Kline, Tom, *(978-0-9863364)* 3034 Cullens Dr, Graham, NC 27253 USA Tel 336-270-3757
E-mail: tom@todera.net.

KLITZNER, IRENE *See* **Attitude Pie Publishing**

KLS LifeChange Ministries *Imprint of* **Skinner, Kerry L.**

KLT & Assocs., *(978-0-9799119)* 11829 E. Parkview Ln., Scottsdale, AZ 85255 USA Tel 480-342-9638.

Kluis Publishing, LLC, *(978-0-9776878; 978-0-9830382)* Orders Addr.: 901 Twelve Oaks Ctr. Dr. Suite 907, Wayzata, MN 55391 USA Tel 952-767-5504; Toll Free: 888-345-2855
E-mail: info@kluispublishing.com; kt@alkluis.com
Web site: http://www.alkluis.com.

Klutz, *(978-0-932592; 978-1-57054; 978-1-878257; 978-1-59174)* Div. of Scholastic, Inc., 450 Lambert St., Palo Alto, CA 94306 USA (SAN 212-7539) Tel 650-857-0888; Fax: 650-857-9110; Toll Free: 800-737-4123; *Imprints:* Chicken Socks (Chick Socks); Klutz Certified (Klutz Cert)
E-mail: thefolks@klutz.com
Web site: http://www.klutz.com
Dist(s): **Scholastic, Inc.**

Klutz Certified *Imprint of* **Klutz**

Klutz Latino (MEX) *Dist. by* **IPG Chicago.**

KMR Scripts, *(978-1-932240)* P.O. Box 189, Webster City, IA 50595 USA
Web site: http://www.kmrscripts.com.

KnackPacks, Inc., *(978-0-9726619)* P.O. Box 3716, Oak Park, IL 60303-3716 USA Tel 708-358-1760
E-mail: comments@knackpacks.com
Web site: http://www.knackpacks.com.

KnausWorks, *(978-0-9758742)* 4160-87 Jade St., Capitola, CA 95010 USA
E-mail: ltrsfmspace@aol.com.

Knee-High Adventures, *(978-0-615-16825-8)* 13450 Oak Hollow, Cypress, TX 77429 USA
Web site: http://www.davidsdonkeytales.com
Dist(s): **Lulu Pr., Inc.**

Knickerbocker Pr. *Imprint of* **Book Sales, Inc.**

Knight Publishing, *(978-0-9740535)* P.O. Box 7452, Fremont, CA 94537-7452 USA Tel 209-743-7390; Fax: 510-818-1166
E-mail: knightpublishing@sbcglobal.net; childrenbooks@sbcglobal.net.

Knights of Soul Publishing, *(978-0-615-21482-5; 978-0-615-32994-9)* P.O. Box 715, Las Vegas, NV 89133 USA
E-mail: Paul@Dhunami.com
Web site: http://www.dhunami.com.

KNK Books *See* **California Is Me**

KnockKnock LLC, *(978-1-60106; 978-1-68349)* 1635-B Electric Ave., Venice, CA 90291 USA Tel 310-396-4132; Fax: 310-396-4385; Toll Free: 800-656-5662
E-mail: kk1@knockknockstuff.com
Web site: http://www.knockknockstuff.com.

†Knoll, Allen A. Pubs., *(978-0-9627297; 978-1-888310)* 200 W. Victoria St., Santa Barbara, CA 93101 USA (SAN 299-0539) Tel 805-564-3377 (orders); Fax: 805-966-6657 (orders); Toll Free: 800-777-7623 (orders)
E-mail: accounts@knollpublishers.com
Web site: http://www.knollpublishers.com
Dist(s): **Brodart Co.**
Follett School Solutions; *CIP.*

†Knopf, Alfred A. Inc., *(978-0-394)* Div. of The Knopf Publishing Group, Orders Addr.: 400 Hahn Rd., Westminster, MD 21157 USA Tel 410-848-1900; Toll Free: 800-726-0600 (orders); Edit Addr.: 1745 Broadway, New York, NY 10019 USA (SAN 202-5825) Tel 212-782-9000; Toll Free: 800-726-0600; *Imprints:* Knopf Books for Young Readers (Knop)
E-mail: customerservice@randomhouse.com
Web site: http://www.randomhouse.com/knopf
Dist(s): **Libros Sin Fronteras**
MyiLibrary
Penguin Random Hse. LLC
Random Hse., Inc.; *CIP.*

Knopf Bks. for Young Readers *Imprint of* **Knopf, Alfred A. Inc.**

Knopf Bks. for Young Readers *Imprint of* **Random Hse. Children's Bks.**

Knopf Canada (CAN) *(978-0-394; 978-0-676)* *Dist. by* **Peng Rand Hse.**

†Knopf Doubleday Publishing Group, Div. of Doubleday Broadway Publishing Group, Orders Addr.: 400 Hahn Rd., Westminster, MD 21157 USA (SAN 281-6083) Tel 410-848-1900; Toll Free: 800-726-0600; Edit Addr.: 1745 Broadway, New York, NY 10019 USA (SAN 201-0089) Tel 212-782-9000; 212-572-4961 Bulk orders; Toll Free Fax: 800-659-2436 Electronic orders only; Toll Free: 800-669-1536 Electronic orders; 800-726-0600 Customer service; *Imprints:* Doubleday (Double); Flying Dolphin Press (FDP); Everyman's Library (Everymns Lib); Pantheon (Pantheon); Schocken (Schocken); Vintage (Vin Bks); Anchor (AncKPG); Vintage Espanol (VintageEsp)
E-mail: ddaypub@randomhouse.com
Web site: http://www.doubleday.com
Dist(s): **Follett School Solutions**
MyiLibrary
Penguin Random Hse. LLC
Random Hse., Inc.; *CIP.*

Knosis, LLC *See* **SkyMark Corp.**

Knot Garden Pr., *(978-0-9655018)* 7712 Eagle Creek Dr., Dayton, OH 45459 USA Tel 937-433-2592 (phone/fax)
E-mail: marthaboice@aol.com.

Knott, Joan, *(978-0-9779895)* 132 W. High St., Jackson, MI 49203 USA.

Know Me Pubn. LLC, *(978-0-9790934)* Orders Addr.: 1679 Valdosta Cir., Pontiac, MI 48340 USA Tel 248-212-0204
E-mail: knowmepub@yahoo.com
Web site: http://www.cwren.bravehost.com.

Know Wonder Publishing, LLC, *(978-0-615-18112-7)* 12832 71st Ave., Kirkland, WA 98034 USA
Dist(s): **Publishers Services.**

Knowing Pr., The, *(978-0-936927)* Orders Addr.: 400 Sycamore, McAllen, TX 78501 USA (SAN 658-361X) Tel 956-686-4033
E-mail: janseale@rgv.rr.com.

Knowledge Box Central, *(978-1-61625; 978-1-62472)* 403 N. Jodie St., Shreveport, LA 71007 USA Tel 318-207-2454
Web site: http://www.knowledgeboxcentral.com.

Knowledge College Planning, *(978-0-9761218)* P.O. Box 321, Stockbridge, GA 30281 USA Tel 770-331-0739
Web site: http://www.kcplan.com.

Knowledge Kids Enterprises, Incorporated *See* **LeapFrog Enterprises, Inc.**

Knowledge Power Communications, *(978-0-9818790; 978-0-9854107; 978-0-9888644; 978-0-9907199; 978-0-9967162; 978-0-9976622; 978-0-9981701; 978-0-9993455)* 25379 Wayne Mills Dr., Suite 131, Valencia, CA 91355 USA (SAN 856-8189) Tel 661-513-0308
Web site: http://www.knowledgepowerinc.com.

Knowledge Quest, *(978-1-932786)* P.O. Box 474, Boring, OR 97009-0474 USA Tel 503-663-1210; Fax: 503-663-0670 Do not confuse with Knowledge Quest, Dieterich, IL
E-mail: orders@knowledgequestmaps.com; terri@knowledgequestmaps.com
Web site: http://www.knowledgequestmaps.com.

Knowledge Wand, LLC, *(978-0-9766680)* 100 Kennewyck Cir., Slingerlands, NY 12159 USA Tel 518-456-3110; Fax: 518-456-6990; Toll Free: 800-376-5669
E-mail: djahnel@gmail.com
Web site: http://www.knowledgewand.com.

KnowledgeGain Inc., *(978-0-9779844)* 3936 Hwy 52 N, Suite 121, Rochester, MN 55901 USA (SAN 850-802X) Tel 507-398-2384; Fax: 928-832-6568
E-mail: Publisher@KnowledgeGain.com
Web site: http://www.KnowledgeGain.com.

Knowtivate, LLC, *(978-0-9787021)* Orders Addr.: 116 Milton St., Lake Mills, WI 53551-5355 USA Tel 920-478-3936; Edit Addr.: N7894 Cty. Rd., O, Waterloo, WI 53594-5355 USA
Web site: http://www.knowtivate.com.

Knox, John Press *See* **Westminster John Knox Pr.**

KO Kids Books, *(978-0-9723946)* 16 Baytree Rd., San Rafael, CA 94903-3801 USA
Web site: http://www.kokidsbooks.com
Dist(s): **Publishers Group West (PGW).**

Koala Jo Publishing, *(978-0-9764698)* Orders Addr.: 352 N. El Camino Real, San Mateo, CA 94401 USA
Web site: http://www.koalajo.com.

KOBZ, *(978-0-9772222)* 2230 Rockingham Dr., Maryville, TN 37803 USA Tel 865-980-7755.

Koch, Chris, *(978-0-9764338)* 3344 Louisville Rd., Harrodsburg, KY 40330-9190 USA.

Kochevar, Steven, *(978-0-9763546)* 7 Beth Lee Dr., Grafton, MA 01519-1139 USA.

†Kodansha America, Inc., *(978-0-87011; 978-1-56836; 978-1-935429; 978-1-61262; 978-1-63236)* 451 Park Ave S. Flr. 7, New York, NY 10016-7390 USA (SAN 201-0526) Toll Free: 800-451-7556; *Imprints:* Vertical (Vertical)
E-mail: t-sumi@kodansha-usa.com; ka-koide@kodansha.co.jp
Web site: http://kodanshacomics.com/; www.kodanshausa.com
Dist(s): **Oxford Univ. Pr., Inc.**
Penguin Random Hse. LLC
Random Hse., Inc.; *CIP.*

Kodansha International (JPN) *(978-4-7700)* *Dist. by* **Cheng Tsui.**

Kodansha International (JPN) *(978-4-7700)* *Dist. by* **Kodansha.**

Kodansha USA Publishing *See* **Kodansha America, Inc.**

Kodel Group, LLC, The, *(978-0-9844784; 978-0-9850142; 978-1-62485)* Orders Addr.: P.O. Box 38, Grants Pass, OR 97528-0003 USA (SAN 859-4961) Tel 541-471-1234; Edit Addr.: 132 NW 6th St., Grants Pass, OR 97528 USA; *Imprints:* Empire Holdings (Empire Holds); Empire Holdins - Literary Division for Young Readers (EH LDYR)
E-mail: info@kodelgroup.com
Web site: stevietenderheart.com; kodelempire.com.

Koenisha Pubns., *(978-0-9700458; 978-0-9718758; 978-0-9741685; 978-0-9759621; 978-0-9800098)* 3196-53rd St., Hamilton, MI 49419 USA
E-mail: koenisha@macatawa.org
Web site: http://www.koenisha.com.

Kofford, Greg Books, Inc., *(978-1-58958)* P.O. Box 1362, Draper, UT 84020 USA (SAN 253-5882) Tel 801-572-7417; Fax: 801-576-0583
E-mail: gregk@koffordbooks.com
Web site: http://www.gregkofford.com.

Kogan Page, Ltd. (GBR) *(978-0-7494; 978-0-85038; 978-1-85091)* *Dist. by* **IngramPubServ.**

Koho Pono, LLC, *(978-0-9845424; 978-1-936282; 978-1-941379)* 15024 SE Pinegrove Loop, Clackamas, OR 97015-7629 USA (SAN 859-6956) Tel 503-723-7392
E-mail: burns@kohopono.com
Web site: http://kohopono.com.

Kokopelli Pr., *(978-0-9759270)* 9611 Paseo del Rey NE, Albuquerque, NM 87111-1649 USA Do not confuse with companies with the same name in Las Cruces, NM, Sedona, AZ.

Koldarana Pubns., *(978-1-884993)* Orders Addr.: P.O. Box 973, Dover, AR 72837 USA; Edit Addr.: 958 SR 164 E., Dover, AR 72837 USA
E-mail: ctn47496@yahoo.com.
Kollath-Stensaas Pubs., *(978-0-9673793; 978-0-9792006; 978-1-936571)* 394 Lake Ave., S., Suite 406, Duluth, MN 55802 USA Tel 218-341-3350
E-mail: sparkystensaas@hotmail.com
Web site: http://www.kollathstensaas.com
Dist(s): **Adventure Pubns.**
Kolluri, Alina M., *(978-0-9787319)* 10124 Queens Park Dr., Tampa, FL 33647-3179 USA
E-mail: alinakolluri@yahoo.com.
Komikwerks, LLC, *(978-0-9742803; 978-0-9778809; 978-1-933925)* 1 Ruth St., Worcester, MA 01602 USA; *Imprints:* Actionopolis (Actionopolis); Agent of Danger (AgentofDanger)
E-mail: patrick@komikwerks.com; shannon@komikwerks.com; kristendenton@gmail.com
Web site: http://www.komikwerks.com; http://www.actionopolis.com.
Kommon Cents, Inc., *(978-0-9745982)* Orders Addr.: P.O. Box 313274, Jamaica, NY 11431-3274 USA Tel 917-541-8568; Toll Free: 877-566-2368
E-mail: info@kommoncents.com
Web site: http://www.kommoncents.com.
Kommon Cents Publishing Company *See* **Kommon Cents, Inc.**
Konaa Publishing *See* **Smallbag Bks.**
Konecky & Konecky *Imprint of* **Konecky, William S. Assocs., Inc.**
Konecky, William S. Assocs., Inc., *(978-0-914427; 978-1-56852)* 72 Ayers Point Rd., Old Saybrook, CT 06475-4301 USA (SAN 663-2432) Tel 860-388-0878; Fax: 860-388-0273; *Imprints:* Konecky & Konecky (Konecky & Konecky)
E-mail: seankon@comcast.net.
Konkori International, *(978-0-9647012)* P.O. Box 102441, Denver, CO 80250 USA Tel 303-744-6318; Fax: 303-296-9113; *Imprints:* Dawn of a New Day Publications, The (Dawn of a New Day)
E-mail: dabdulai@yahoo.com
Dist(s): **Emery-Pratt Co.**
Konopka, Ann Marie, *(978-0-615-18598-9)* 20 Palmer Rd., Kendall Pk., NJ 08824 USA Tel 732-821-5415
E-mail: annmkonopka@yahoo.com
Dist(s): **Lulu Pr., Inc.**
Kontis, Alethea, *(978-1-942541)* PO Box 512, Mims, FL 32754 USA
E-mail: akontis@gmail.com
Web site: http://www.aletheakontis.com.
Kookalook Publishing, *(978-0-9706323)* 53 Garden Pl., Brooklyn, NY 11201-4501 USA
E-mail: kookypubs@hotmail.com.
Korab, Kat *See* **Purple Unicorn Pr.**
Korean Culture Research, Inc., *(978-0-9762990)* 38 W. 32nd St., Suite 1112, New York, NY 10001 USA Tel 212-563-5763; Fax: 212-563-6707
E-mail: leekle@sprynet.com
Web site: http://www.learnkoreannow.com.
Korero Books LLP (GBR) *(978-0-9553398; 978-0-9558336; 978-1-907621) Dist. by* **IPG Chicago.**
Kores, Michelle, *(978-0-692-78763-2; 978-0-692-78765-6)* 633 Montrose Ave., Delano, MN 55328 USA Tel 701-446-7048.
Koroknay, Thomas, *(978-0-9749705)* 3718 Lindsey Rd., Lexington, KY 44904 USA Tel 419-884-0222.
Kotzig Publishing, Inc., *(978-0-9715411; 978-0-9767163)* 1109 NW 16th St., Delray Beach, FL 33444 USA
E-mail: susan@kotzigpublishing.com
Web site: http://www.kotzigpublishing.com
Dist(s): **Independent Pubs. Group.**
Kountz Marketing Group *See* **Texas Pride Publishing**
Kovels Antiques, Inc., *(978-0-9646683; 978-0-9970825)* 22000 Shaker Blvd., Shaker Heights, OH 44122 USA Tel 216-752-2252; Fax: 216-752-3115; Toll Free: 800-303-1996
E-mail: kkovel@kovels.com
Web site: www.kovels.com.
Koyama Pr. (CAN) *(978-0-9784810; 978-0-9879630; 978-0-9868739; 978-1-927668) Dist. by* **Consort Bk Sales.**
KP Bks., *(978-0-9748549)* 354 Sequoia Ct., Antioch, IL 60002-2600 USA
E-mail: pudaitem@sbcglobal.net; bluehorizon1@sbcglobal.net; marylpk625@me.com.
Kraemer, Jean, *(978-0-9897694)* 28627 Essex St., Roseville, MI 48066 USA Tel 586-777-0113
E-mail: jeangirlk60@att.net.
Kramer, H.J. Inc., *(978-0-915811; 978-1-932073)* P.O. Box 1082, Tiburon, CA 94920 USA (SAN 294-0833) Fax: 415-435-5364; Toll Free: 800-972-6657
E-mail: hjkramer@jps.net
Web site: http://www.newworldlibrary.com
Dist(s): **New Leaf Distributing Co., Inc.**
New World Library
Publishers Group West (PGW).
Kranichfeld, Andrew, *(978-0-692-51647-8; 978-0-692-51648-5; 978-0-692-51649-2; 978-0-692-52541-8; 978-0-692-61529-4; 978-0-692-84206-5)* 3425 Kingsbridge Ave. Apt. 606, BRONX, NY 10463 USA Tel 914-227-0645.
Kraszewski, Terry, *(978-0-9821989)* 2162 Avenida De La Playa, La Jolla, CA 92037 USA (SAN 857-5223) Tel 858-456-9283; Fax: 858-456-9551
E-mail: ricswave@cox.net
Web site: http://www.surfangelbook.com.
Krause, Claudia, *(978-0-9655689)* P.O. Box 7083, Capistrano Beach, CA 92624 USA Tel 714-492-7778.
Kravec & Kravec & Associates *See* **Bellaboozle Books, Inc.**
Krazy Duck Productions, *(978-0-9776739; 978-0-9961622)* Orders Addr.: P.O. Box 105, Danville, KY 40423 USA Tel 606-787-2571; Fax: 606-787-8207; Edit Addr.: 2227 Wood Creek Rd., Liberty, KY 42539 USA
E-mail: KrazyduckProductions@msn.com
Web site: http://www.krazyduck.com.
KRBY Creations, LLC, *(978-0-9745715)* 2 Leeds Ct., Brick, NJ 08724-4011 USA
E-mail: krbyenterprises@comcast.net
Web site: http://www.krbycreations.com.
Kreations, *(978-0-9766621)* 19842 Needles St., Chatsworth, CA 91311 USA
E-mail: kreations@socal.rr.com
Web site: http://www.skelanimals.com.
Kreativ Kaos, *(978-0-9790572)* P.O. Box 27955, Anaheim Hills, CA 92809 USA (SAN 852-310X)
E-mail: admin@kreativkaos.com
Web site: http://www.kreativkaos.com.
Kreative Character Kreations, Inc., *(978-0-9641381)* 9 Endicott Dr., Huntington, NY 11743 USA Tel 516-673-8230; Fax: 516-346-6620.
Kreative X-Pressions Pubns., *(978-0-9798536; 978-0-9800552)* Orders Addr.: 87 Kennedy Dr., Colchester, CT 06415-1315 USA (SAN 854-5561) Tel 860-537-2673
E-mail: novelwriter@comcast.net
Web site: http://www.kreativexpressionsonline.com.
KreativeMindz Prodns. LLC, P.O. Box 2413, New York, NY 10108 USA Tel 212-222-3069
E-mail: KLB@kreativemindzproductions.com
Web site: http://www.kreativemindzproductions.
Kreder, Mary Ellen DeLuca, *(978-0-615-92430-4; 978-0-9913232)* 364 Quaker St., Wallkill, NY 12589 USA Tel 845-853-2803
E-mail: MaryEd4466@verizon.net.
†**Kregel Pubns.**, *(978-0-8254)* Div. of Kregel, Inc., Orders Addr.: P.O. Box 2607, Grand Rapids, MI 49501-2607 USA (SAN 206-9792) Tel 616-451-4775; Fax: 616-451-9330; Toll Free: 800-733-2607; Edit Addr.: 733 Wealthy St., SE., Grand Rapids, MI 49503-5553 USA (SAN 298-9115); *Imprints:* Editorial Portavoz (Edit Portavoz)
E-mail: kregelbooks@kregel.com; acquisitions@kregel.com
Web site: http://www.kregel.com
Dist(s): **Faith Alive Christian Resources**
INscribe Digital
Send The Light Distribution LLC
Spring Arbor Distributors, Inc.; *CIP.*
Kreizel Enterprises, Inc., *(978-0-9729232)* P.O. Box 224, Monsey, NY 10952 USA; 26 Charles Ln., Spring Valley, NY 10977-3330
E-mail: info@kreizelplating.com; books@kreizelplating.com.
Kremer Pubns, Inc., *(978-0-9707591; 978-0-9745631; 978-0-9817272)* 12615 W. Custer Ave., Butler, WI 53007 USA Toll Free: 800-669-0887
E-mail: info@kremerpublications.com
Web site: http://www.kremerpublications.com.
Krickle Forest Adventures, *(978-0-9855997)* 4081 Jeri Rd., Interlochen, MI 49643 USA Tel 231-753-6025
E-mail: customerservice@krickleforest.com
Web site: http://www.krickleforest.com.
Kringle Enterprises Company *See* **North Pole Pr.**
Krisaran Publishing Co., *(978-0-9773146)* 850 NC 55 E., Mount Olive, NC 28365 USA (SAN 257-3903)
E-mail: bjackson@esn.net; brenda@krisaran.com
Web site: http://www.krisaran.com.
Krishnamurti Pubns., *(978-1-888004; 978-1-934989)* Orders Addr.: Krishnamurti Foundation Of America 134 Besant Rd., Ojai, CA 93024-1560 USA Toll Free: 866-552-6651; Krishnamurti Foundation Trust Brockwood Pk., Bramdean, SO24 0LQ
E-mail: info@kpublications.com; publications@brockwood.org.uk
Web site: http://www.jkrishnamurti.org/info
Dist(s): **MyiLibrary**
SCB Distributors.
Krishnan, Laura, *(978-0-692-78397-9)* 13560 NE 54th PL, BELLEVUE, WA 98005 USA Tel 832-687-3560.
KRO Publishing *See* **Preschool Prep Co.**
Kruger, Wolfgang Verlag, GmbH (DEU) *(978-3-8105) Dist. by* **Intl Bk Import.**
Kruger, Wolfgang Verlag, GmbH (DEU) *(978-3-8105) Dist. by* **Distribks Inc.**
Krullstone Publishing, LLC, *(978-0-9833237; 978-0-9882170; 978-0-9889578; 978-1-941851)* 8751 Clayton Cove Rd., Springville, AL 35146 USA (SAN 860-1240) Tel 205-681-9455; Fax: 205-681-3774
E-mail: charlotte@krullstonepublishing.com
Dist(s): **Krullstone Distributing, LLC**
Smashwords.
K's Kids Publishing, *(978-0-9797208)* 12706 SW 94 Ct., Miami, FL 33176 USA (SAN 854-1892) Tel 305-969-5570
E-mail: ks_kids@bellsouth.net.
†**Ktav Publishing Hse., Inc.**, *(978-0-87068; 978-0-88125; 978-1-60280; 978-965-524)* Orders Addr.: 930 Newark Ave. 4th Flr., Jersey City, NJ 07306 USA (SAN 201-0038) Tel 201-963-9524; Fax: 201-963-0102; Toll Free Fax: 800-626-7517 (orders)
E-mail: orders@ktav.com; editor@ktav.com; questions@ktav.com
Web site: http://www.ktav.com
Dist(s): **eBookit.com**; *CIP.*
K-Teen *Imprint of* **Kensington Publishing Corp.**
K-Teen/Dafina *Imprint of* **Kensington Publishing Corp.**
ktf-writers-studio, *(978-0-615-41134-7; 978-0-615-44161-0; 978-3-9523908; 978-0-578-10595-6; 978-0-9913395; 978-0-9969890; 978-0-9986927)* 5712 Ashley Sq. S., Memphis, TN 38120 USA Tel 901-683-4210; 478 W. Racquet Club Pl., Memphis, TN 38117
E-mail: frigonormfr@aol.com; ktf-writers-studio@hotmail.com
Web site: www.ktf-writers-studio.ch
Dist(s): **Bookmasters Distribution.**
KTH Investment Group, *(978-0-692-85894-3)* 592 N Peppercorn Ln., Rossville, GA 30741 USA Tel 423-463-2720
E-mail: jeffwcrawford5+LVP0003448@gmail.com; jeffwcrawford5+LVP0003448@gmail.com.
Kube Publishing Ltd. (GBR) *(978-1-84774) Dist. by* **Consort Bk Sales.**
Kulupi Pr., *(978-0-9661867; 978-0-9817653)* 5082 Warm Springs Rd., Glen Ellen, CA 95442 USA Tel 707-996-1149
E-mail: kulupi@vom.com
Web site: http://www.kulupi.com
Dist(s): **Partners Bk. Distributing, Inc.**
Kumon Publishing North America, Inc., *(978-1-933241; 978-4-7743; 978-1-934968; 978-1-935800; 978-1-941082; 978-0-692-47466-2; 978-0-692-57875-9; 978-0-692-59884-9; 978-0-692-67737-7; 978-0-692-69890-7; 978-0-692-74109-2; 978-0-692-76435-0; 978-0-692-76436-7; 978-0-692-76437-4; 978-0-692-76438-1; 978-0-692-76658-3; 978-0-692-76659-0; 978-0-692-76660-6; 978-0-692-76661-3; 978-0-692-76662-0; 978-0-692-86678-8; 978-0-692-86679-5; 978-0-9989219) Glenpointe Ctr. E., Suite 6 300 Frank W. Burr Blvd., Teaneck, NJ 07666 USA Tel 201-836-2105; Fax: 201-836-1559; Toll Free: 800-657-7970; Goban-cho Grand, Bldg. 3F 3-1 Goban-cho Chiyoda-ku, Tokyo, 102-8180 Tel 0081 0332343485; Fax: 0081 0332344018*
E-mail: books@kumon.com
Web site: http://www.kumonbooks.com
Dist(s): **Bookazine Co., Inc.**
Ingram Publisher Services
Sterling Publishing Co., Inc.
Kumon U.S.A., Inc., *(978-0-9702092)* 300 Frank W. Burr Blvd., Teaneck, NJ 07666 USA
E-mail: falcbooks@home.com.
Kunce, Craig LLC *See* **Windhill Bks. LLC**
Kung, Jeannie M., *(978-0-578-18737-2)* 815 S. Songbird Cir., Anaheim Hills, CA 92808 USA Tel 714-809-5634
E-mail: jeanniekung@sbcglobal.net.
Kunz, Matt, *(978-0-9976298)* 730 Sable Pointe Rd, Milton, GA 30004 USA Tel 404-386-0354
E-mail: mkunz59@hotmail.com.
Kuperman, Marina, *(978-0-9801109)* 8 Forge Rd., Hewitt, NJ 07421 USA Tel 973-728-0835
E-mail: marinakuperman@yahoo.com
Web site: http://turtlefeetsurfersbeat.com.
Kupu Kupu Pr., *(978-0-9883448)* 1710 Franklin No. 300, Oakland, CA 94612 USA Tel 510-452-1912
E-mail: inno@designaction.org
Web site: http://aisforactivist.com.
Kurban, Mary, *(978-0-692-67003-3; 978-0-692-67648-6; 978-0-692-70535-3; 978-0-692-71575-8; 978-0-692-77582-0; 978-0-692-77604-9)* 1310 N. Avon St., BURBANK, CA 91505 USA Tel 818-848-3108
E-mail: makurban@hotmail.com.
Kurdyla, E L Publishing LLC, *(978-1-61751)* Orders Addr.: P.O. Box 958, Bowie, MD 20718-0958 USA Tel 301-805-2191; Fax: 301-805-2192; Edit Addr.: P.O. Box 958, Bowie, MD 20718-0958 USA Tel 301-805-2191; Fax: 301-805-2192; *Imprints:* 4th Division Press (FourthDiv)
E-mail: publisher@kurdylapublishing.com
Web site: http://www.kurdylapublishing.com.
Kurtz Art Studio Inc, *(978-0-9982674)* 64 Austin Storey Cir., Newnan, GA 30263 USA Tel 404-435-3647
E-mail: kurtzartwork@gmail.com
Web site: johnkurtzart.com.
Kurz, Ron, *(978-0-939829)* P.O. Box 95551, Las Vegas, NV 89193 USA (SAN 663-8333) Tel 702-837-6395 (phone/fax); 3060 Sunrise Heights Dr., Henderson, NV 89052 (SAN 663-8341) Tel 702-870-5968
E-mail: ronkurz@earthlink.net
Web site: http://www.ronkurz.com.
Kush Univ. Pr., *(978-1-893731)* Orders Addr.: 8247 S. Oglesby Ave., Chicago, IL 60617 USA Tel 773-598-5707; *Imprints:* Mandolin House (MandolinHse)
E-mail: esmith334@kushuniversitypress.net
Web site: http://kushuniversitypress.net/opencart/; http://kushuniversitypress.net/KU_press.html.
Kutie Kari Bks., Inc., *(978-1-884149)* 4189 Ethan Dr., Eagan, MN 55123 USA Tel 651-450-7427
E-mail: gharbo@garyharbo.com
Web site: http://www.garyharbo.com.
Kvale Good Natured Games LLC, *(978-0-9793583)* 771 Parkview Ave., Saint Paul, MN 55117-4045 USA Tel 651-204-6781; Fax: 651-204-6966
E-mail: admin@kvalegames.com
Web site: http://www.kvalegames.com.
Kvalvasser, Leonid, *(978-0-9753110)* 1124 Blake Ct. # 1A, Brooklyn, NY 11235-5219 USA.
Kwazy Kitty Publishing Co., *(978-0-9770012)* Orders Addr.: P.O. Box 178, Monkton, MD 21111-0178 USA.
Kwela Bks. (ZAF) *(978-0-7957) Dist. by* **IPG Chicago.**
KWIP, Inc., *(978-0-9790267; 978-0-692-25867-5)* 1400 Broadway Blvd., Polk City, FL 33868 USA
E-mail: stevec@fantasyofflight.com.
Kwist, Karla, *(978-0-9795046)* 2420 Golden Arrow, Las Vegas, NV 89120 USA Tel 702-768-8406
E-mail: karlakk@aol.com
Web site: http://www.karlakwist.com.
Kylie Jean *Imprint of* **Picture Window Bks.**
Kyoodoz, *(978-0-9771172)* Orders Addr.: P.O. Box 5431, Beaverton, OR 97006-0431 USA
E-mail: customerservice@kyoodoz.com; sales@kyoodoz.com
Web site: http://www.kyoodoz.com.
L A 411 Publishing Company *See* **Reed Business Information**
L. A. Eng Bks., *(978-0-9748598)* 231 W. Hillcrest Blvd., Inglewood, CA 90301 USA
E-mail: luis_arevalo@lennox.k12.ca.us.
L. A. Media, LLC *See* **Mardi Gras Publishing, LLC**
L & L Enterprises, *(978-0-9760046)* 6960 W. Peoria Ave. LOT 132, Peoria, AZ 85345-6038 USA
Web site: https://www.latinandlanguage.com.
L & R Publishing, LLC, *(978-1-55571)* Subs. of Publishing Services, Inc., P.O. Box 3531, Ashland, OR 97520 USA (SAN 218-9240) Tel 541-973-5154; *Imprints:* Hellgate Press (Hellgate Pr); Grid Press (Grid Pr); Paloma Books (PalomaBks)
E-mail: harley@hellgatepress.com
Web site: http://www.hellgatepress.com
Dist(s): **Midpoint Trade Bks., Inc.**
MyiLibrary
ebrary, Inc.
L. C. D., *(978-0-941414)* 663 Calle Miramar, Redondo Beach, CA 90277 USA (SAN 239-0035) Tel 310-375-6336
E-mail: lenduncan@earthlink.net
Web site: http://www.phonicsplus.com.
LED Publishing, *(978-1-885674)* Div. of Logical Expression In Design, 1730 M St. NW, Suite 407, Washington, DC 20036 USA Tel 703-558-0100; Fax: 703-558-4970.
L G Productions *See* **L G Publishing**
L G Publishing, *(978-0-9768486)* Orders Addr.: 281 Fielding, Ferndale, MI 48220 USA
E-mail: admin@lgproductions.info
Web site: http://www.lgproductions.info.
L L Teach, *(978-0-9676545; 978-1-931104)* 709 Country Club Rd., Bridgewater, NJ 08807-1601 USA Tel 908-575-8830; Fax: 908-704-1730; Toll Free: 800-575-7670
E-mail: ann4480@aol.com; llteach5757670@aol.com
Web site: http://www.LLteach.com.
LMA Publishing, *(978-1-892426)* Div. of Lifestyle Management Assocs., 111 Grove St., Apt. 1, West Roxbury, MA 02132 USA Tel 617-325-6752 (phone/fax)
E-mail: pentzj@ix.netcom.com
Web site: http://www.lifestylemanagement.com.
L P D Enterprises *See* **LPD Pr.**
L W S Bks., *(978-0-9704361)* 227 Bayshore Dr., Hendersonville, TN 37075 USA Tel 615-826-3871; Fax: 615-826-3883; Toll Free: 800-643-4718
E-mail: clazzy@mindspring.com
Web site: http://www.janethan.com; http://www.imsonofman.com.
L W S Publishers *See* **L W S Bks.**
La Caille Nous Publishing Co., *(978-0-9647635; 978-0-9718191)* 328 Flatbush Ave, Suite 240, Brooklyn, NY 11238 USA Tel 212-726-1293; Fax: 212-591-6465
E-mail: gcadet@lcnpub.com.
La Di La Dah, *(978-0-9816629)* 5508 Vantage Point Rd., Columbia, MD 21044-2631 USA
E-mail: r.higgins@xs4all.net
Dist(s): **Lulu Pr., Inc.**
La Frontera Publishing, *(978-0-9785634; 978-0-9857551; 978-0-9974757)* 1712 Pioneer Ave., Suite 181, Cheyenne, WY 82001 USA (SAN 851-0180) Tel 307-778-4752 general office number
E-mail: company@lafronterapublishing.com
Web site: http://www.lafronterapublishing.com
Dist(s): **Univ. of New Mexico Pr.**
La Galera, S.A. Editorial (ESP) *(978-84-246; 978-84-7515; 978-84-85297) Dist. by* **Lectorum Pubns.**
La Galera, S.A. Editorial (ESP) *(978-84-246; 978-84-7515; 978-84-85297) Dist. by* **AIMS Intl.**
La Librairie Parisienne, *(978-0-615-54542-4; 978-0-9886058)* 17844 Porto Marina Way, Pacific Palisades, CA 90272 USA Tel 310-392-2143
E-mail: JACKIEMANCUSO@GMAIL.COM; jackie@parischienbook.com
Web site: http://www.jackiemancuso.com/la-librairie-parisienne
Dist(s): **Independent Pubs. Group.**
La Luz Comics, *(978-0-9755193)* 1516 10th Ave. S., No. 6, Minneapolis, MN 55404-1795 USA
E-mail: sam@samhiti.com
Web site: http://www.samhiti.com.
La Mancha Publishing Group, *(978-1-890701)* 14534 Victory Blvd., Van Nuys, CA 91411 USA Tel 818-994-8195.
La Montagne Secrete (CAN) *(978-2-923163) Dist. by* **IPG Chicago.**
La Oferta Publishing Co., *(978-0-9665876; 978-0-9791624)* 1376 N. Fourth St., San Jose, CA 95112 USA Tel 408-436-7850; Fax: 408-436-7861; Toll Free: 800-336-7850
E-mail: sales@laoferta.com; mary@laoferta.com
Web site: http://www.laoferta.com
Dist(s): **Bilingual Pubns. Co., The**
Lectorum Pubns., Inc.
Libros Sin Fronteras
SPD-Small Pr. Distribution.
LA Ruocco, *(978-0-9743454; 978-1-941593)* Orders Addr.: 31 Lake St., Brooklyn, NY 11223 USA
E-mail: laruocco@cs.com.
Laasya Design, *(978-0-9774147)* 400 N. Catalina St., Burbank, CA 91505 USA
E-mail: info@laasyadesign.com
Web site: http://www.laasyadesign.com.
Lab-Aids, Inc., *(978-1-887725; 978-1-933298; 978-1-60301; 978-1-63093)* 17 Colt Ct., Ronkonkoma, NY 11779 USA Tel 631-737-1133; Fax: 631-737-1286; Toll Free Fax: 800-381-8003
E-mail: lab-aids@lab.aids.com.
Labarco, *(978-0-9762439)* P.O. Box 1734, Alief, TX 77411 USA
Web site: http://www.cushcity.com; http://www.Amazon.com.
L'Abeille Publishing Incorporated *See* **Orndee Omnimedia, Inc.**
Label Buster, Incorporated *See* **Block System, The**
Labor, Editorial S. A. (ESP) *(978-84-335) Dist. by* **Continental Bk.**
Labosh Publishing, *(978-0-9744341)* P.O. Box 588, East Petersburg, PA 17520-0588 USA Tel 717-898-3813 (phone/fax)
E-mail: laboshpublishing@msn.com
Web site: http://laboshpublishing.com.

Lab-Volt Systems, Inc., *(978-0-86657; 978-1-60533)* Orders Addr.: P.O. Box 686, Farmingdale, NJ 07727 USA (SAN 238-7050) Tel 732-938-2000 Toll Free: 800-522-8658
E-mail: us@labvolt.com; Ivanbrug@labvolt.com
Web site: http://www.labvolt.com.

Lacey Productions, *(978-0-9771076)* 611 Druid Rd., Suite 705, Clearwater, FL 33767 USA
E-mail: sherry@laceyproductions.com
Web site: http://www.laceyproductions.com.

Lacey Publishing Co., *(978-0-9709249)* 29 Bounty Rd W., Benbrook, TX 76132-1003 USA Tel 817-738-3185 (phone/fax)
E-mail: jamesb50@charter.net
Web site: http://www.marfalightsresearch.com
Dist(s): **MyiLibrary**
ebrary, Inc.

LaChrisAnd Productions, *(978-0-9765063)* P.O. Box 969, Desert Hot Springs, CA 92240 USA Tel 760-309-2263
Web site: http://www.lachrisandproductions.com.

Lackner, William *See* **Digging Clams n Oregon**

Ladd, David Pr., *(978-0-9774563)* 56 Coolidge Ave., South Portland, ME 04106 USA Tel 207-767-2836
E-mail: davidladdpress@yahoo.com.

LaDow Publishing, *(978-0-9723623)* 308 Reynolds Ln., West Chester, PA 19380-3300 USA Tel 219-689-4565; Fax: 610-918-9571
E-mail: wmladow@aol.com
Web site: http://www.wmladow.com.

Lady Hawk Pr., *(978-0-9829082)* 3831 Abbey Ct., Newbury Park, CA 91320 USA Tel 310-460-8744
Web site: ladyhawkpress.com
Dist(s): **ebrary, Inc.**

Lady Illyria Pr., *(978-0-9765572)* 30 Lamprey Ln., Lee, NH 03824 USA Tel 603-659-3826
E-mail: patricia.emison@unh.edu.

Laffin Minor Pr., *(978-0-9770516)* P.O. Box 273, Alma, CO 80420 USA Tel 970-409-8857; Fax: 207-967-5492
E-mail: lydia@laffinminorpress.com
Web site: http://www.laffinminorpress.com.

Lagesse Stevens *Imprint of* **Martell Publishing Co**

Laguna Press/BTI *See* **Cerebral Press International**

Lainez, Stephanie, *(978-0-9820358)* P.O. Box 1471, La Mirada, CA 90637-1471 USA (SAN 857-068X)
E-mail: storyhousebooks@yahoo.com.

Lake 7 Creative, LLC, *(978-0-9774122; 978-0-9821187; 978-0-9883662; 978-1-940647)* 3419 Vincent Ave. N., Minneapolis, MN 55412 USA (SAN 257-5167) Tel 612-412-5493; *Imprints:* Getchu Books (Getchu Bks)
E-mail: ryan@lake7creative.com
Web site: http://www.lake7creative.com
Dist(s): **Adventure Pubns.**

Lake Isle Pr., Inc., *(978-0-9627403; 978-1-891105)* 16 W. 32nd St., Suite 10B, New York, NY 10001 USA Tel 212-273-0796; Fax: 212-273-0198; Toll Free: 800-462-6420 (Orders only)
E-mail: lakeisle@earthlink.net; hiroko@lakeislepress.com
Web site: http://www.lakeislepress.com
Dist(s): **National Bk. Network.**

Lake Limericks, *(978-0-9761711)* P.O. Box 478, Lake Waccamaw, NC 28450 USA Tel 910-646-4998; Fax: 910-371-1133
E-mail: aldrich@weblnk.net.

Lake Street Pr., *(978-1-936181)* 4918 N Oakley Ave., Chicago, IL 60625 USA
Web site: http://www.lakestreetpress.com
Dist(s): **Lightning Source, Inc.**
Partners Pubs. Group, Inc.
Quality Bks., Inc.

Lake Street Pubs., *(978-1-58417)* Orders Addr.: 4537 Chowen Ave S., Minneapolis, MN 55410-1364 USA
E-mail: compass@sd.cybernex.net.

Lake Superior Port Cities, Inc., *(978-0-942235; 978-1-938229)* Orders Addr.: P.O. Box 16417, Duluth, MN 55816-0417 USA Tel 218-722-5002; Fax: 218-722-4096; Toll Free: 888-244-5253; Edit Addr.: 310 E. Superior St. #125, Duluth, MN 55802-3134 USA (SAN 666-9980)
E-mail: reader@lakesuperior.com
Web site: http://www.lakesuperior.com
Dist(s): **Partners Bk. Distributing, Inc.**
TNT Media Group, Inc.

Lakefront Research LLC, *(978-0-9764665)* P.O. Box 667, East Hampstead, NH 03826-0667 USA.

Lakeshore Curriculum Materials Company *See* **Lakeshore Learning Materials**

Lakeshore Learning Materials, *(978-1-929255; 978-1-58970; 978-1-59746; 978-1-60666)* Orders Addr.: 2695 E. Dominguez St., Carson, CA 90895 USA (SAN 630-0251) Toll Free: 800-421-5354; Edit Addr.: 2695 E. Dominguez St., Carson, CA 90895 USA Tel 310-537-8600; Fax: 310-632-8314
E-mail: ubeckham@lakeshorelearning.com
Web site: http://www.lakeshorelearning.com.

Lakeside Pr., *(978-1-879653; 978-0-9978959)* Do not confuse with companies with the same name in Anacortes, WA, Tamarac, FL
E-mail: larry.martin@roadrunner.com.

Lakeview Pr., *(978-0-9749677)* c/o Jan Devereux, 255 Lakeview Ave., Cambridge, MA 02138 USA Do not confuse with Lake View Press in New Orleans, LA, Mooresville, NC, Lake Oswego, OR.

Lakin, Laqwacia, *(978-0-9891103)* 3290 Osterley Way, Cumming, GA 30041 USA Tel 678-237-8495
E-mail: llakin.consulting@gmail.com.

Lakota Language Consortium, Inc., *(978-0-9761082; 978-0-9821107; 978-0-9834363; 978-1-941461)* 2620 N Walnut St. Suite 1280, Bloomington, IN 47404 USA Tel 812-961-0140; Fax: 812-961-0141; Toll Free: *888-525-6828*
E-mail: orders@lakhota.org; sales@lakhota.org
Web site: http://www.lakhota.org; http://www.languagepress.com; http://www.llcbookstore.com.

Lamar, Mel Ministries *See* **Lamar, Melvin Productions**

Lamar, Melvin Productions, *(978-0-9716068)* 900 Downtowner Blvd., Apt. 89, Mobile, AL 36609-5409 USA
E-mail: melvinelamar@att.net; melvinlamar31@gmail.com.

Lamb, Wendy Bks. *Imprint of* **Random Hse. Children's Bks.**

Lambda Pubs., Inc., *(978-0-915361; 978-1-55774)* 3709 13th Ave., Brooklyn, NY 11218-3622 USA (SAN 291-0640) Tel 718-972-5449; Fax: 718-972-6307
E-mail: judaica@email.msn.com.

Lambert Bk. Hse., Inc., *(978-0-89315)* 4139 Parkway Dr., Florence, AL 35630-6347 USA (SAN 180-5169) Tel 256-764-4098; 256-764-4090; Fax: 256-766-9200; Toll Free: 800-551-8511
E-mail: Info@lambertbookhouse.com
Web site: http://www.lambertbookhouse.com.

LaMothe, Karin, *(978-0-9728763)* P.O. Box 672, Belleville, MI 48112-0672 USA
Web site: http://www.angelslullaby.com.

Lamp Post Inc., *(978-0-9708587; 978-1-933428; 978-1-60039)* 29348 Ariel St., Murrieta, CA 92563 USA
E-mail: burner@lamppostpubs.com
Web site: http://www.lamppostpubs.com
Dist(s): **Diamond Comic Distributors, Inc.**
Diamond Bk. Distributors.

Lamp Post Publishing, Inc., *(978-1-892135)* 1741 Tallman Hollow Rd., Montoursville, PA 17754 USA (SAN 253-4681) Tel 570-435-2804; Fax: 570-435-2803; Toll Free: 800-326-9273
E-mail: lamppostp@aol.com
Web site: http://www.lamppostpublishing.com; http://www.beyondthegloesmur.com; http://www.heartstringsbio.com.

Lampo Licensing, LLC *See* **Ramsey Pr.**

Lampstand Pr., Ltd., *(978-1-935301)* Orders Addr.: P.O. Box 5798, Derwood, MD 20855 USA Tel 301-963-0808; Fax: 301-963-1868; Toll Free: 800-705-7487; Edit Addr.: 8073 Snouffer School Rd., Derwood, MD 20855 USA
Web site: http://www.lampstandpress.com.

LaMuth Publishing Company *See* **Fairhaven Bk. Pubs.**

Lamweg Publishing, *(978-0-9801146)* 176 W. 100 S., Kouts, IN 46347 USA Tel 219-766-2174.

Landauer Corporation *See* **Landauer Publishing, LLC**

Landauer Publishing, LLC, *(978-0-9646870; 978-1-890621; 978-0-9770166; 978-0-9793711; 978-0-9800688; 978-0-9818040; 978-0-9825586; 978-1-935726; 978-1-947163)* 3100 100th St., Urbandale, IA 50322 USA (SAN 915-2334) Tel 515-287-2144; Fax: 515 276 5102; Toll Free: 800-557-2144; 3100 100th St., Urbandale, IA 50322 (SAN 915-2334) Tel 515-287-2144; Fax: 515 276 5102; Toll Free: 800-557-2144
E-mail: info@landauercorp.com; jeramy@landauercorp.com; acounting@landauercorp.com
Web site: http://www.landauerpub.com
Dist(s): **American Wholesale Bk. Co.**
Baker & Taylor Bks.
Bookazine Co., Inc.
Brodart Co.

Landfall Co., The, *(978-0-9747445)* 18640 Mack Ave., P.O. Box 36551, Grosse Pointe Farms, MI 48236 USA Fax: 313-886-6250
E-mail: mhslandfall@landfallcompany.com.

Landmark Editions, Incorporated *See* **landmark Hse., Ltd.**

landmark Hse., Ltd., *(978-0-933849; 978-0-9822874)* 1949 Foxridge Dr., Kansas City, KS 66106 USA
Web site: http://www.landmarkhouse.com.

Landmark Publishing Inc., *(978-0-9726738)* P.O. Box 46403, Minneapolis, MN 55446 USA (SAN 254-9689) Tel 763-694-8907; Fax: 763-694-8909
E-mail: info@brainerdbound.com
Web site: http://www.brainerdbound.com.

Landstrider Pr., *(978-0-9969936)* 2944 NE Sawdust Hill Rd, Poulsbo, WA 98370 USA Tel 206-498-7944
E-mail: bors.vesterby@gmail.com.

Lane, Sondra Corp., *(978-0-9743874)* 2436 N. Federal Hwy., No. 300, Lighthouse Point, FL 33064 USA
Web site: http://www.hallelujahkids.com.

Lane, Veronica Bks., *(978-0-9637597; 978-0-9762743; 978-0-9826513; 978-0-9910083; 978-0-9992573)* Orders Addr.: 2554 Lincoln Blvd., Suite 142, Venice, CA 90291 USA (SAN 298-1157) Toll Free: 800-651-1001 (phone/fax)
E-mail: etan@veronicalanebooks.com
Web site: http://www.veronicalanebooks.com
Dist(s): **Bored Feet Pr.**
DeVorss & Co.
Follett School Solutions
INscribe Digital
Integral Yoga Pubns.
New Leaf Distributing Co., Inc.

Lang Graphics, Ltd., *(978-0-933617; 978-1-55962; 978-1-57832; 978-0-7412)* Div. of Perfect Timing, Inc., Orders Addr.: P.O. Box 1605, Waukesha, WI 53188 USA; Edit Addr.: 514 Wells St., Delafield, WI 53018 USA (SAN 692-4689) Tel 414-646-3399; Fax: 414-646-2224; Toll Free: 800-262-2611
E-mail: support@shop.lang.com
Web site: http://www.lang.com
Dist(s): **TNT Media Group, Inc.**

†Lang, Peter Publishing, Inc., *(978-0-8204; 978-1-4331; 978-1-4539; 978-1-4540; 978-1-4541; 978-1-4542)* Subs. of Verlag Peter Lang AG (SZ), 29 Broadway, New York, NY 10006 USA (SAN 241-5534) Tel 212-647-7700; 212-647-7706 (Outside USA); Fax: 212-647-7707; Toll Free: 800-770-5264
E-mail: customerservice@plang.com
Web site: http://www.peterlangusa.com
Dist(s): **MyiLibrary**
ebrary, Inc.; *CIP.*

Langenscheidt Publishing Group, *(978-0-88729; 978-1-58573)* Subs. of Langenscheidt KG, Orders Addr.: 15 Tyger River Dr., Duncan, SC 29334 USA Fax: 888-773-7979; Toll Free: 800-432-6277; Edit Addr.: 36-36 33rd St., Long Island City, NY 11106 USA
Web site: http://www.americanmap.com; http://www.langenscheidt.com
Dist(s): **Bilingual Pubns. Co., The**
Ingram Publisher Services.

Lange-Patton, Lorraine, *(978-0-9752874)* P.O. Box 96811, Las Vegas, NV 89193-6811 USA.

Langille, Cody, *(978-0-692-87818-7; 978-0-692-87819-4)* 1808 S 2095 W, Woods Cross, UT 84087 USA Tel 801-358-8934
E-mail: jeffwcrawford5+LVP0003669@gmail.com; jeffwcrawford5+LVP0003669@gmail.com.

Langley, Jan *See* **Captain & Harry LLC, The**

LangMarc Publishing, *(978-1-880292)* Orders Addr.: P.O. Box 90488, Austin, TX 78709 USA (SAN 297-519X) Tel 512-394-0989; Fax: 512-394-0829; Toll Free: 800-864-1648 (orders only); Edit Addr.: 7500 Shadowridge Run, No. 28, Austin, TX 78749 USA
E-mail: langmarc@booksails.com
Web site: http://www.langmarc.com.

Language 911, Inc., *(978-1-933451)* 12924 Calais Cir., Palm Beach Gardens, FL 33410 USA.

Language Adventure Pubns., *(978-0-9671053; 978-0-9976698)* 2311 E. Stadium Blvd., Suite 105 N, Ann Arbor, MI 48104 USA Tel 734-763-8378; Fax: 734-769-8409
E-mail: andrearojo@aol.com.

Language Quest Corp., *(978-0-9744691)* 1 Tartan Lakes, Westmont, IL 60559 USA.

Language Research Educational Series, *(978-0-9609446)* 4309 20th St., NE, Washington, DC 20018 USA (SAN 260-0927) Tel 202-636-9306
E-mail: lresduke@gmail.com.

Language Resource Manual for Schools *Imprint of* **Language Treasures**

Language Transformer Bks. *Imprint of* **Velichko, Vera**

Language Treasures, *(978-0-9765293)* 2141 SE 113th Ave., Portland, OR 97216 USA; *Imprints:* Language Resource Manual for Schools (L R M S)
E-mail: vrisk@comcast.net
Web site: http://www.languagetreasures.com.

Language Workshop for Children, The, *(978-0-9754205; 978-0-9755659; 978-0-9759664; 978-0-9819458)* 888 Lexington Ave., 2nd Flr., New York, NY 10065 USA (SAN 256-0704)
E-mail: info@professortoto.com
Web site: http://www.professortoto.com
Dist(s): **China Books & Periodicals, Inc.**

Lanico Media Hse., *(978-0-9886772; 978-0-9862057; 978-0-9967799; 978-0-9986520)* 206 Curve Dr. No. 13, Monroe, LA 71203 USA Tel 318-805-6589
E-mail: lacresha.hayes@gmail.com
Web site: www.lanicomediahouse.com.

LANIUS Software *See* **PassionQuest Technologies, LLC**

Lanphier Pr., *(978-0-9762151; 978-0-9786039; 978-1-934570)* Div. of Corporate Chaplains of America, 1300 Corporate Chaplain Dr., Wake Forest, NC 27587-6596 USA
E-mail: dwhite@chaplain.org
Dist(s): **Send The Light Distribution LLC.**

Lantern Bks., *(978-1-930051; 978-1-59056)* Div. of Booklight, Inc., 128 2nd Pl., Brooklyn, NY 11231-4102 USA
E-mail: martin@booklightinc.com
Web site: http://www.booklightinc.com
Dist(s): **Smashwords**
SteinerBooks, Inc.

Lapid, Yosef, *(978-0-9973899; 978-0-9993361)* 928 Raleigh Rd., Las Cruces, NM 88005 USA Tel 575-524-3201
E-mail: ioji158@gmail.com.

LAPOP (Latin American Public Opinion Project), *(978-0-9777042; 978-0-9792178; 978-0-9817299; 978-0-9821456; 978-0-9846260; 978-0-9846303; 978-1-939186)* 230 Appleton Pl, PMB 505 PSCI Dept at Vanderbily Univ., Nashville, TN 37203 USA
E-mail: liz.zechmeister@vanderbilt.edu
Web site: http://vanderbilt.edu/lapop.

Laramie, Charles, *(978-0-9769536)* 11 W. St., Fair Haven, VT 05743 USA Tel 802-265-3538
E-mail: chucklaramie@adelphia.net.

†Laredo Publishing Co., Inc., *(978-1-56492)* 465 Westview Ave., Englewood, NJ 07631 USA Tel 201-408-4048; Fax: 201-408-5011
E-mail: info@laredopublishing.com
Web site: http://www.laredopublishing.com; *CIP.*

Large Print Bk. Co., The, *(978-1-59688)* P.O. Box 970, Sanbornville, NH 03872-0970 USA Tel 603-569-4215.

Large Print Pr. *Imprint of* **Thorndike Pr.**

Lark Bks., *(978-0-937274; 978-1-57990; 978-1-887374; 978-1-60059; 978-1-4547)* Div. of Sterling Publishing Co., Inc., 67 Broadway St., Asheville, NC 28801-2919 USA (SAN 219-9947)
E-mail: info@larkbooks.com
Web site: http://www.larkbooks.com
Dist(s): **Hachette Bk. Group**
Hearst Bks.
Sterling Publishing Co., Inc.

†Larksdale, *(978-0-89896)* P.O. Box 801222, Houston, TX 77280 USA (SAN 220-0643) Tel 713-461-7200; Fax: 713-467-4770 (purchase orders); Toll Free: 877-461-7200; *CIP.*

Larousse, Ediciones, S. A. de C. V. (MEX) *(978-968-6042; 978-968-6147; 978-968-6347; 978-970-607; 978-970-22)* *Dist. by* **Continental Bk.**

Larousse, Ediciones, S. A. de C. V. (MEX) *(978-968-6042; 978-968-6147; 978-968-6347; 978-970-607; 978-970-22)* *Dist. by* **HM.**

Larousse, Ediciones, S. A. de C. V. (MEX) *(978-968-6042; 978-968-6147; 978-968-6347; 978-970-607; 978-970-22)* *Dist. by* **Giron Bks.**

Larousse, Editions (FRA) *(978-2-03)* *Dist. by* **HM.**

Larousse Kingfisher Chambers, Inc., *(978-0-7534; 978-1-85697)* 215 Park Ave., S., New York, NY 10003 USA (SAN 297-7540); 181 Ballardvale St., Wilmington, MA 01887
Dist(s): **Macmillan.**

Larry Huch Ministries, *(978-0-9745301)* Orders Addr.: P.O. Box 2197, Mansfield, TX 76063-0039 USA
E-mail: cory@larryhuchministries.com
Web site: http://www.larryhuchministries.com
Dist(s): **Anchor Distributors.**

Lars Muller Pubs. (CHE) *(978-3-907044; 978-3-906700; 978-3-907078; 978-3-03778)* *Dist. by* **Peng Rand Hse.**

Larson Learning, Inc., *(978-0-9639121; 978-1-58123; 978-1-887050)* Div. of Larson Texts, Inc., 1762 Norcross Rd., Erie, PA 16510-3838 USA Tel 814-824-6365; Fax: 814-824-6377; Toll Free: 800-530-2355
Web site: http://www.larsonlearning.com.

Larson Pubns., *(978-0-943914; 978-1-936012)* 4936 Rte. 414, Burdett, NY 14818 USA (SAN 241-130X) Tel 607-546-9342; Fax: 607-546-9344; Toll Free: 800-828-2197 Do not confuse with Larson Pubns., Joliet, IL
E-mail: larson@lightlink.com
Web site: http://www.larsonpublications.org
Dist(s): **National Bk. Network**
New Leaf Distributing Co., Inc.
Red Wheel/Weiser
ebrary, Inc.

Larstan Publishing, Inc., *(978-0-9764266; 978-0-9776895; 978-0-9789182)* 209 Canterbury Ct., Blue Bell, PA 19422 USA (SAN 256-3460) Fax: 707-922-7280
E-mail: sgenkin@larstan.net
Web site: http://www.theblackbooks.com.

Laser Productions *See* **Global Publishing**

Lash & Assocs. Publishing/Training, Inc., *(978-1-931117)* Orders Addr.: 100 Boardwalk Dr. Suite 150, Youngsville, NC 27596 USA Tel 919-556-0300 phone; Fax: 919-556-0900 fax
E-mail: mlyn@lapublishing.com
Web site: http://www.lapublishing.com.

Last Gasp Eco-Funnies, Incorporated *See* **Last Gasp of San Francisco**

Last Gasp of San Francisco, *(978-0-86719)* Orders Addr.: 777 Florida St., San Francisco, CA 94110 USA (SAN 216-8308); Edit Addr.: 777 Florida St., San Francisco, CA 94110-2025 USA (SAN 170-3242) Tel 415-824-6636; Fax: 415-824-1836; Toll Free: 800-366-5121
E-mail: colin@lastgasp.com
Web site: http://www.lastgasp.com
Dist(s): **SCB Distributors.**

Last Knight Publishing *See* **Last Knight Publishing Co.**

Last Knight Publishing Co., *(978-0-9720442)* P.O. Box 270006, Fort Collins, CO 80527 USA Tel 970-391-6857
Web site: http://www.lastknightpublishing.com
Dist(s): **Bks. West.**

Last Play Publishing, *(978-0-9760181)* 17931 Inverness Ave., Baton Rouge, LA 70810 USA Tel 225-751-6419
E-mail: djones@dow.com.

Lasting Bks. Publishing Co., *(978-0-9767511)* 8433 Briggs Dr., Roseville, CA 95747-5951 USA
E-mail: director@lastingbooks.com
Web site: http://www.lastingbooks.com.

Lata de Sal Editorial S.L. (ESP) *(978-84-940584; 978-84-941136; 978-84-941784; 978-84-942451; 978-84-942867)* *Dist. by* **Lectorum Pubns.**

Latinarte *See* **I.Om.Be Pr.**

Latino, Frank Publishing Co., *(978-0-9640474)* 6806 Newport Lake Cir., Boca Raton, FL 33496 USA Tel 561-241-3880; Fax: 561-995-6975; Toll Free: 800-922-8565
E-mail: frank@hollyboy.com
Web site: http://www.hollyboy.com.

Latino Literacy Press *See* **Lectura Bks.**

Latitude 20 *Imprint of* **Univ. of Hawaii Pr.**

Lauco Pr., *(978-0-692-32492-9; 978-0-692-48432-6; 978-0-9976422)* 8206 Kittama Dr., Clinton, MD 20735 USA Tel 3018683221; Toll Free: 3018683221
Dist(s): **CreateSpace Independent Publishing Platform.**

Laudati, Joe, *(978-0-615-20324-9; 978-0-578-06902-9)* 425 E. 76th St., No. 9B, New York, NY 10021-2516 USA Tel 212-737-3515
E-mail: joelaudati33@earthlink.net
Web site: http://www.joelaudati.com
Dist(s): **Lulu Pr., Inc.**

Laugh-A-Lot Bks., *(978-0-615-28469-9)* 25 W. Broadway, Apt. 310, Long Beach, NY 11561 USA
Web site: http://www.laughalotpoetry.com; http://www.laughalotbooks.com.

Laughing Baby Pubns., *(978-0-615-18948-2)* 3662 Big Spring Rd., Lake Almanor, CA 96137 USA Tel 530-596-4397
E-mail: jennifer@babyinspirations.net
Web site: http://www.laughingbabypublications.com.

Laughing Elephant, *(978-0-9621131; 978-1-883211; 978-1-59583; 978-1-5149)* Orders Addr.: 3645 Interlake Ave., N., Seattle, WA 98103 USA Tel 206-447-9229; Fax: 206-447-9189; Toll Free: 800-354-0400 (orders only); Edit Addr.: 4649 Sunnyside Ave., N., Seattle, WA 98103 USA (SAN 250-7722) Tel 206-632-7075; Fax: 206-632-0466; *Imprints:* Darling & Company (Darling & Comp); Green Tiger Press (Grn Tiger Pr)
E-mail: laughingelephant@laughingelephant.com
Web site: http://www.laughingelephant.com
Dist(s): **Ingram Publisher Services.**

Laughing Gull Pr., *(978-0-9726699)* P.O. Box 23272, Brooklyn, NY 11202-3272 USA
E-mail: laughinggullpress@earthlink.net.

Laughing Rhino Bks., *(978-0-9859603)* 23830 25th Dr. SE, Bothell, WA 98021 USA Tel 425-420-8144
E-mail: gordon.glessner@gmail.com
Web site: www.laughinrhinobooks.com.

Laughing Zebra - Bks. for Children *Imprint of* **J.O.Y. Publishing**

Laurel *Imprint of* **Random House Publishing Group**

Laurel & Herbert, Inc., *(978-0-9619155)* P.O. Box 440266, Sugarloaf Shores, FL 33044 USA (SAN 243-4687) Tel 305-745-3506; Fax: 305-745-9070.

Laurel Leaf *Imprint of* **Random Hse. Children's Bks.**

Laurel Press *See* **Laurel & Herbert, Inc.**

Laurel Valley Graphics, Inc., *(978-0-9717475; 978-0-9853454)* 1511 Monastery Dr., Latrobe, PA 15650 USA Fax: 724-532-1957
Web site: http://www.lvgraphics.net.

Lauren Elizabeth Design, *(978-0-9779594)* 2002 Duboin Rd, New Iberia, LA 70560 USA
E-mail: chad@turnkeybid.com.

Lauren Simone Publishing Co., *(978-0-9979520; 978-1-948071)* 41 Henderson Dr., East Hartford, CT 06108 USA Tel 860-478-3897
E-mail: laurensimonepubs@gmail.com
Web site: http://laurensimonepubs.weebly.com/.

Laurob Pr., *(978-0-9787376)* 4204 Anjou Ct., Chico, CA 95973 USA.

Laurus Bks., *(978-0-9841680; 978-0-9826957; 978-0-9847683; 978-1-938526; 978-1-943523)* Orders Addr.: 1410 Rotherwood Dr., Johnson City, TN 37601 USA Tel 423-262-8389; Edit Addr.: 3101 Browns Mill Rd. Ste. 6-145, Johnson City, TN 37604 USA Tel 423-262-8389 Toll Free: 800-596-7370
E-mail: info@thelauruscompany.com; bookstore@thelauruscompany.com; nancywilliams@thelauruscompany.com
Web site: http://www.TheLaurusCompany.com; http://www.LaurusBooks.com; www.BookShelfDepot.com
Dist(s): **Laurus Co., The.**

Laurus Company, The *See* **Laurus Bks.**

Laurus Co., The, Orders Addr.: 524 Guinevere Court, McDonough, GA 30252 USA (SAN 858-608X) Tel 678-814-4047; Fax: 678-272-7255; Toll Free: 800-596-7370
E-mail: thelaurusco@charter.net
Web site: http://www.thelauruscompany.com.

LaVa Pubns., *(978-0-9638838; 978-0-9714261; 978-0-9761449; 978-0-9792400)* Div. of Field O Dreams Farm, Orders Addr.: P.O. Box 9372, Dothan, AL 36303 USA (SAN 255-2027)
E-mail: spharr@centurytel.net.

Lavender Bks., *(978-0-9742739)* Orders Addr.: P.O. Box 3555, Culver City, CA 90231-3555 USA; Edit Addr.: 11111 Jefferson Blvd., Culver City, CA 90230 USA
E-mail: lavender_books33@aol.com; kc_kang@yahoo.com; lavenderbooks33@aol.com.

Lavoie, Louis, *(978-0-9791018)* 1300 W. Medicine Lake Dr., No. 211, Plymouth, MN 55441 USA
E-mail: lavoielouis6@hotmail.com.

Law Offices of Harry Glick, *(978-0-9717419)* 100 Quentin Rossevelt Blvd. No. 511, Garden City, NY 11530 USA Tel 516-456-1088; Fax: 805-473-9025
Web site: http://www.harryglick.com
Dist(s): **BookMasters, Inc.**

Lawe Street Bks., *(978-0-9713179)* 1818 S. Lawe St., Appleton, WI 54915 USA Tel 920-739-4577
E-mail: stedjee@aol.com.

Lawells Publishing, *(978-0-934981)* P.O. Box 1338, Royal Oak, MI 48068-1338 USA (SAN 694-602X) Tel 248-543-5297
E-mail: lawells@tm.net
Web site: http://www.lawells.net.

Lawrence Educational Services, Inc., *(978-1-932959; 978-1-59699)* Orders Addr.: P.O. Box 6256, Bridgewater, NJ 08807 USA Tel 908-575-8830; Fax: 908-704-1730; Toll Free: 800-575-7670; Edit Addr.: 674 Rte. 202-206 N, Suite 4, Bridgewater, NJ 08807 USA
E-mail: llteach5757670@aol.com
Web site: http://www.llteach.com.

Lawrence Publishing, *(978-0-9716039)* Div. of Educational Services & Publications, 2935 E. Rose Ln., Phoenix, AZ 85016 USA Tel 602-912-9553 Do not confuse with companies with the same or similar names in Flower Mound, TX, Van Nuys, CA, Los Angeles, CA, Wichita, KS, Baton Rouge, LA
E-mail: llawre2222@aol.com; walton90@alltel.net.

Lawson, Archie B., *(978-0-9762660)* 1168 Shashas Way, Riverton, UT 84065-4111 USA Tel 801-302-0440
E-mail: archiebl@msn.com.

Layne Morgan Media, Inc., *(978-0-9762904; 978-0-9772007; 978-0-9774803; 978-1-4265)* 2101 W. Chesterfield Blvd. Ste. A102, Springfield, MO 65807-8672 USA
E-mail: kimberlym@laynemorgan.com
Web site: http://www.laynemorgan.com.

L,B Kids *Imprint of* **Hachette Bk. Group**

LBF Bks., LLC, *(978-0-9754533; 978-0-9773082)* Orders Addr.: P.O. Box 7989, Pittsburgh, PA 15216 USA; Edit Addr.: 1537 Dormont Ave., Pittsburgh, PA 15216 USA
E-mail: lbf@lbfbooks.com.

LBF/Hadrosaur *Imprint of* **Hadrosaur Pr.**

L'Chaim Pubns., *(978-0-9766946)* 521 Fifth Ave., Suite 1740, New York, NY 10175 USA
E-mail: lchaim@att.biz
Web site: http://lchaimpublications.com/.

LD Bks., Inc., *(978-0-9772669; 978-0-9765897; 978-1-939048; 978-1-940281; 978-1-943387)* 8313 NW 68th St., Miami, FL 33166 USA (SAN 631-8088) Tel 305-406-2292; Fax: 305-406-2293
E-mail: vilmac@ldbooks.com; sales@ldbooks.com
Web site: http://www.sinlimites.net; http://www.ldbooks.com.

LD Coach, LLC, *(978-0-9745938; 978-0-9764112)* 1401 Johnson Ferry Rd., Suite 328-C13, Marietta, GA 30062-5241 USA Toll Free: 888-848-6224
E-mail: bill.allen@ldcoach.com
Web site: http://www.ldcoach.com.

LDS & Assocs., *(978-1-883574)* Orders Addr.: 13681 Newport Ave., Suite 8 #831, Tustin, CA 92780 USA Toll Free: 800-331-3610
E-mail: trainers@ldsassoc.com
Web site: http://www.ldsassoc.com.

Le Bk. Moderne, LLC, *(978-0-9768450)* 2849 W. 23rd Ave., Denver, CO 80211 USA Tel 303-523-6401; *Imprints:* Giggletins (Gigglet)
E-mail: michael@lebookmoderne.com
Web site: http://www.lebookmoderne.com.

Le Petit Chien, *(978-0-9717019)* 2415 Daybreaker Dr., Park City, UT 84098 USA.

Le Reve Enterprises, LLC *See* **13th & Joan**

Le Robert (FRA) *(978-2-85036; 978-2-84902) Dist. by* **Continental Bk.**

Le Robert (FRA) *(978-2-85036; 978-2-84902) Dist. by* **Distribks Inc.**

Le Rue Publishing, *(978-0-9985437)* 320 S. Boston Ave., Ste. 1030, Tulsa, OK 74103 USA Tel 918-216-0180
E-mail: robertsdenton@gmail.com
Web site: www.leruepublishing.com.

Lead Life Pr., LLC, *(978-0-9762408)* The Lead Life Institute, 2111 Deerfield Dr., New Hope, PA 18938 USA Tel 215 794 8516; Fax: 215 794 8532
E-mail: mdec@leadlifeinstitute.com.

Leaderbrook, *(978-0-9719079)* P.O. Box 864, Amherst, OH 44001-0864 USA Tel 440-985-5844
E-mail: timothy@clevelandceo.com
Web site: http://www.leaderbrook.com.

Leadership Horizons, LLC, *(978-0-9668868)* 959 Keystone Way, Carmel, IN 46032-2823 USA Tel 317-844-5587; Fax: 317-581-9226; Toll Free: 888-262-2477
E-mail: ron@leadershiphorizons.com.

Leadership Institute for Urban Education, *(978-0-615-27502-4)* 1302 N. 32nd St., Omaha, NE 68131 USA.

Leadership Loft, The *See* **Green Owl, Inc.**

LeaderTreks NFP, *(978-1-934577; 978-1-939031)* 25w560 Geneva Rd. #30, Carol Stream, IL 60188 USA Tel 630-668-0936; Fax: 630-668-0980; Toll Free: 800-502-0699
E-mail: danc@leadertreks.com; angie@leadertreks.com
Web site: http://www.leadertreks.com; http://www.leadertreks.org.

Leading Lady Pubns., *(978-0-9776746; 978-0-9798084; 978-0-9802468; 978-0-9818753)* Orders Addr.: P.O. Box 35, Worton, MD 21678 USA Toll Free: 800-597-9428; Edit Addr.: 306 Sunrise Ave., Ridgely, MD 21660 USA
Web site: http://www.publishyourchristianbook.com
Dist(s): **CreateSpace Independent Publishing Platform**
Lushena Bks.

Leadline Publishing, *(978-0-9801464)* Orders Addr.: 2101 NW Corporate Blvd Ste 206, Boca Raton, FL 33431 USA
Web site: http://www.teamfroglogic.com.

Leaf & Vine Bks, *(978-0-9786087; 978-0-615-18762-4)* 387 Ivy St., San Francisco, CA 94102 USA
E-mail: editor@leafvinebooks.com
Dist(s): **Lulu Pr., Inc.**

Leaf Storm Pr., *(978-0-9914105; 978-0-9970207; 978-1-945652)* P.O. Box 4670, Santa Fe, NM 87502 USA (SAN 920-7406)
E-mail: LeafStormPress@gmail.com
Web site: http://leafstormpress.com
Dist(s): **Legato Pubs. Group.**

Leafcollecting.com Publishing Co., *(978-0-9747654)* 189 N. Jefferson Ave., Bradley, IL 60915-1829 USA Tel 815-932-0850; *Imprints:* Egap Gifa Books (Egap Gifa Bks)
E-mail: Darlene@leafcollecting.com; Thegreatlakes189@yahoo.com
Web site: http://www.leafcollecting.com.

Leafwood Pubs. *Imprint of* **Abilene Christian Univ. Pr.**

Lean Pr., *(978-1-932475)* Div. of Hopefuls, Inc., Orders Addr.: P.O. Box 80334, Portland, OR 97280-1334 USA (SAN 255-6286) Tel 503-708-4415; Fax: 503-626-9098
E-mail: sean@leanpress.com; mike@leanpress.com
Web site: http://www.leanpress.com.

Leap Bks., *(978-1-61603)* P.O. Box 112, Reidsville, NC 27320-0112 USA (SAN 858-5431)
E-mail: leapbks@gmail.com
Web site: http://www.leapbks.com.

Leap Forward Pubns., *(978-0-9743664)* 12108 Scribe Dr., Austin, TX 78759-3133 USA
E-mail: mjanthony@sbcglobal.net.

L.E.A.P. (Learning through an Expanded Arts Program, Inc), *(978-0-9713649)* 441 W. End Ave., Suite 2G, New York, NY 10024 USA Tel 212-769-4160; Fax: 212-724-4479
E-mail: leap@leapnyc.org
Web site: http://www.leapnyc.org.

LeapFrog Enterprises, Inc., *(978-1-58605; 978-1-932256; 978-1-59319; 978-1-60685)* 6401 Hollis St., Suite 125, Emeryville, CA 94608 USA Tel 510-420-5000; Fax: 510-596-6821; *Imprints:* LeapFrog School House (LeapSchHse)
E-mail: crymer@leapfrog.com; leo_lui@vtech.com
Web site: http://www.leapfrog.com.

Leapfrog Pr., *(978-0-9654578; 978-0-9679520; 978-0-9728984; 978-0-9796415; 978-0-9815148; 978-1-935248)* Orders Addr.: P.O. Box 2110, Teaticket, MA 02536 USA; Edit Addr.: 59 Tanglewood Dr., Teaticket, MA 02536 USA Do not confuse with Leapfrog Pr., Wyandotte, MI
E-mail: books@leapfrogpress.com; lisa@leapfrogpress.com
Web site: http://www.leapfrogpress.com
Dist(s): **Consortium Bk. Sales & Distribution**
MyiLibrary
SPD-Small Pr. Distribution.

Leapfrog Press, Incorporated, The *See* **Leapfrog Pr.**

LeapFrog Schl. Hse. *Imprint of* **LeapFrog Enterprises, Inc.**

Leaping Antelope Productions, *(978-0-9659222; 978-0-9762059)* Div. of Armadillo Pr., Orders Addr.: 101 Industrial Way Ste. 10, Belmont, CA 94002-8207 USA (SAN 253-7974) Toll Free: 888-909-5327
E-mail: print123@leapingantelope.com
Web site: http://www.leapingantelope.com
Dist(s): **Distributors, The**
Quality Bks., Inc.

Learn & Sign Funtime *See* **Learn & Sign Funtime Bks.**

Learn & Sign Funtime Bks., *(978-0-9753717)* Orders Addr.: 0255 E. Yellowstone Trail, Hamlet, IN 46532 USA Tel 219-775-7080; Fax: 888-308-2606; 0255 E. Yellowstone Trail Hamlet, In 46532, Hamlet, IN 46532
E-mail: learnandsign@aol.com; jujub121@aol.com.

Learn As You Grow, L.L.C., *(978-0-9824652)* P.O. Box 103, Mount Horeb, WI 53572 USA
E-mail: chad.lindley@learnasyougrow.com.

Learn2study, *(978-0-9729557)* 1935 Columbia Pike No. 24, Arlington, VA 22204 USA
Web site: http://www.learn2study.org.

Learning Abilities Bks., *(978-0-9658653; 978-0-9720267)* 166 Glyndale Cir., Brunswick, GA 31520 USA (SAN 850-3087) Tel 912-264-5308; Fax: 775-305-0063; Toll Free: 800-779-5088
E-mail: contactlab@gate.net
Web site: http://www.gate.net/~labooks.

Learning All About Me, LLC, *(978-0-9763961)* Orders Addr.: P.O. Box 161923, Boiling Springs, SC 29316 USA; Edit Addr.: 8 Montford Ave., Boiling Springs, SC 29316 USA.

Learning Challenge, Inc., *(978-1-59203)* 36 Washington St., Wellesley, MA 02481 USA Tel 781-239-9900; Fax: 781-239-3273
Web site: http://www.learningchallenge.com.

Learning Connection, The, *(978-1-56831)* Orders Addr.: 4100 Silver Star Rd. Ste. D, Orlando, FL 32808-4618 USA Toll Free: 800-218-8489
Web site: http://www.tlconnection.com.

Learning Curve Brands, Incorporated *See* **TOMY International, Inc.**

Learning Fasten-Ations, Inc., *(978-0-9673268; 978-0-9729476)* 5014-16th Ave., Suite 195, Brooklyn, NY 11204 USA Tel 718-854-3808; Fax: 718-854-9436; Toll Free: 800-252-8152
Web site: http://www.velcroboards.com.

Learning in Motion, *(978-1-889775)* 113 Cooper St., Santa Cruz, CA 95060-4526 USA Toll Free: 800-560-5670 Do not confuse with Learning in Motion, Mount Laurel, NJ
Web site: http://www.learn.motion.com.

Learning Links Inc., *(978-0-7675; 978-0-88122; 978-0-934048; 978-1-56982)* Orders Addr.: 26 Haypress Road, Cranbury, NJ 08512 USA (SAN 241-3302) Tel 516-437-9071; Fax: 516-437-5392; Toll Free: 800-724-2616
E-mail: info@learninglinks.com
Web site: http://www.learninglinks.com; http://www.novel-ties.com/estore/search/.

Learning Management Systems *See* **Active Learning Corp.**

Learning Net, The, *(978-1-887946)* 567 Catnip Rd., Cullowhee, NC 28723 USA Tel 828-293-2542.

Learning Parent, The, *(978-0-9708770; 978-0-9777685; 978-0-9785859; 978-0-9860433)* 2430 Sunnymeade Rd., Rustburg, VA 24588 USA Tel 434-845-8345; Fax: 434-845-3020
E-mail: learningparent@aol.com
Web site: http://www.thelearningparent.com.

Learning Props, *(978-0-9741549; 978-0-9768706; 978-1-935292)* P.O. Box 774, Racine, WI 53401 USA Toll Free: 877-776-7750
E-mail: bev@learningprops.com
Web site: http://www.learningprops.com
Dist(s): **Follett School Solutions.**

Learning Research Associates, Incorporated *See* **National Reading Styles Institute, Inc.**

Learning Resources, Inc., *(978-1-56911)* 380 N. Fairway Dr., Vernon Hills, IL 60061 USA (SAN 630-057X) Tel 847-573-8400; Fax: 847-573-8425
E-mail: info@learningresources.com
Web site: http://www.learningresources.com.

Learning Series Pr., *(978-0-9769701)* P.O. Box 590812, Fort Lauderdale, FL 33359 USA (SAN 256-6060) Tel 954-552-4855
E-mail: mdgeddes@comcast.net
Web site: http://www.learningtodream.com.

Learning to Give, *(978-0-9774155)* 16924 Buchanan St., Grand Haven, MI 49417-8625 USA
Web site: http://www.learningtogive.org.

Learning Together, *(978-1-931840)* 5509b W. Friendly Ave. Ste. 201, Greensboro, NC 27410-4279 USA
E-mail: wtlecl@aol.com.

Learning Tools Co., *(978-0-938017)* Orders Addr.: P.O. Box 657, Berkeley Springs, WV 25411 USA (SAN 692-7297) Tel 304-258-1304; Edit Addr.: 714 Rockwell St., Berkeley Springs, WV 25422 USA.

Learning Wood, LLC, *(978-1-933577)* 3535 W. Peterson Ave., Chicago, IL 60659 USA Tel 773-509-0707; Fax: 773-509-0404.

Learning Works, The *Imprint of* **Creative Teaching Pr., Inc.**

Learning Wrap-Ups, Inc., *(978-0-943343; 978-1-59204)* 1660 West Gordon Ave., No. 4, Layton, UT 84041 USA (SAN 668-3975) Tel 801-497-0050; Fax: 801-497-0063; Toll Free: 800-992-4966
E-mail: info@learningwrapups.com
Web site: http://www.learningwrapups.com.

Learning ZoneXpress, *(978-1-57175)* Orders Addr.: P.O. Box 1022, Owatonna, MN 55060 USA Tel 507-455-9076; Fax: 507-455-3380; Toll Free: 888-455-7003
E-mail: customerservice@learningzonexpress.com
Web site: http://www.learningzonexpress.com
Dist(s): **Follett School Solutions.**

LearningExpress, LLC, *(978-1-57685; 978-1-61103)* 2 Rector St., Flr. 26, New York, NY 10006-3754 USA Tel 646-274-6453; 800-295-9556
E-mail: info@learnatest.com; customerservice@learnatest.com
Web site: http://www.learnatest.com
Dist(s): **MyiLibrary**
National Bk. Network
ebrary, Inc.

LearningSuccess Pr., *(978-0-9772350)* 1147 E. Main St., Ventura, CA 93001 USA (SAN 257-0726) Tel 805-648-1739
Web site: http://www.learningsuccessinstitute.com.

Learnovation, LLC, *(978-0-9705790; 978-0-9796434; 978-0-9969528)* Orders Addr.: P.O. Box 502150, Indianapolis, IN 46250 USA (SAN 255-4577); Edit Addr.: 10831 Thistle Ridge, Fishers, IN 46038 USA Tel 317-577-1190; Fax: 317-598-0816; Toll Free: 888-577-1190
E-mail: anna@learnovation.com; karen@learnovation.com
Web site: http://learnovation.com.

Leatherbound Bestsellers, *(978-1-62715)* Orders Addr.: 20325 N. 51st. Ave. Suite 134, Glendale, AZ 85308 USA Tel 602-616-4334
E-mail: leatherboundbestsellers@gmail.com
Web site: www.leatherboundbestsellers.com.

Leatherbound Booksellers *See* **Leatherbound Bestsellers**

Leatherman, Diane *See* **Bounty Project, The**

Leathers Publishing, *(978-0-9646898; 978-1-890622; 978-1-58597)* Div. of Ad Ctr., 4500 College Blvd., Overland Park, KS 66211-1760 USA Tel 913-498-2625; Fax: 913-498-1561; Toll Free: 888-888-7696
E-mail: barbara@leatherspublishing.com
Web site: http://www.leatherspublishing.com.

Leatherwood Press *See* **Walnut Springs Bks.**

Leatherwood Publishing, *(978-0-9741725)* 20395 Cty. 86, Long Prairie, MN 56347 USA Tel 320-732-2879
E-mail: tann0042@umn.edu
Web site: http://www.alexweb.net/whimsy/index.htm.

Leave No Sister Behind Pubns., *(978-0-9787004)* Orders Addr.: 13 Pecan Ln., Long Beach, MS 39560 USA (SAN 851-3759)
E-mail: info@leavenosisterbehind.net
Web site: http://www.leavenosisterbehind.net
Dist(s): **Lightning Source, Inc.**

LeBlanc, Terry Leonard, *(978-0-9755913)* Orders Addr.: P.O. Box 387, Loyalton, CA 96118 USA; Edit Addr.: 805 Mill St., Loyalton, CA 96118 USA
E-mail: terrythetrashman@owo.com.

Lectorum Pubns., Inc., *(978-0-9625162; 978-1-880507; 978-1-930332; 978-1-933032; 978-1-941802; 978-1-63245)* Orders Addr.: 205 Chubb Ave, Lyndhurst, NJ 07071 USA (SAN 990-0802) Tel 201-559-2232; Edit Addr.: 205 Chubb Ave., Lyndhurst, NJ 07071 USA (SAN 860-0597) Tel 201-559-2200; Fax: 201-559-2201; Toll Free Fax: 877-532-8676; Toll Free: 800-345-5946
E-mail: acorrea@lectorum.com
Web site: http://www.lectorum.com; http://www.librerialectorum.com
Dist(s): **Libros Sin Fronteras**
MyiLibrary
Perfection Learning Corp.

Lectorum, S.A. de C.V. (MEX) *(978-968-7748; 978-968-5270; 978-970-732) Dist. by* **LD Bks Inc.**

Lectura Bks., *(978-0-9716580; 978-0-9772852; 978-1-60448)* 1107 Fair Oaks Ave., Suite 225, South Pasadena, CA 91030 USA
E-mail: info@lecturabooks.com
Web site: http://www.lecturabooks.com.

Lectura Colaborativa (ARG) *(978-987-45) Dist. by* **IPG Chicago.**

L'Edge Pr., *(978-0-9762014; 978-1-935256)* P.O. Box 2567, Boone, NC 28607 USA
E-mail: jeffhendley@charter.net
Web site: http://www.upsidedownministries.com.

LeDor Publishing, *(978-0-9747382)* 4885 McKnight Rd., No. 350, Pittsburgh, PA 15237 USA Tel 888-624-9094; Fax: 412-421-1628; Toll Free: 888-624-9094
E-mail: drichman@ledorgroup.com
Web site: http://www.ledorgroup.com.

Lee & Low Bks., Inc., *(978-0-89239; 978-1-880000; 978-1-885008; 978-1-58430; 978-1-60060; 978-1-62014)* 95 Madison Ave., New York, NY 10016 USA (SAN 920-7546) Tel 212-779-4400 (General info./Editorial); Fax: 212-683-1894 (orders); Toll Free: 888-320-3190 (ext. 28, orders); *Imprints:* Tu Books (Tu Books); Children's Book Press (ChilBkPr); Shen's Books (ShensBks)
E-mail: clow@leeandlow.com
Web site: http://www.leeandlow.com
Dist(s): **Follett School Solutions**
Lectorum Pubns., Inc.
Perfection Learning Corp.

Lee Bks., *(978-0-9660653)* Orders Addr.: 514 Jamacha Rd., No. 16J, El Cajon, CA 92019 USA Tel 619-447-8789 Do not confuse with other companies with the same or similar names in San Anselmo, CA, Columbia, SC
E-mail: leebooks@juno.com
Web site: http://www.readatleebooks.com.

Lee, Collin, *(978-0-692-82896-0; 978-0-692-82897-7)*
E-mail: jeffwcrawford5+LVP0003213@gmail.com; jeffwcrawford5+LVP0003213@gmail.com.

Lee, Deborah I, *(978-0-9858839)* 3800 Bexley Sq., Reno, NV 89503 USA Tel 775-848-7797
E-mail: debbaleereno@yahoo.com.

Lee, Howard, *(978-0-9766137)* 191 Lorraine Dr., Berkeley Heights, NJ 07922 USA.

Lee Instruments, *(978-0-9704913)* Orders Addr.: P.O. Box 460-999, Leeds, UT 84746 USA; Edit Addr.: 555 E. 900 N., Leeds, UT 84746 USA; 1050 N. Main, Leeds, UT 84746 Tel 435-879-6907
E-mail: leeinst@infowest.com; violguy@infowest.com
Web site: http://kevinleeluthier.com.

Lee, J. & L. Co., *(978-0-934904)* P.O. Box 5575, Lincoln, NE 68505 USA (SAN 213-8557) Tel 402-488-4416; Fax: 402-489-2770; Toll Free: 888-665-0999
E-mail: leebooks@radiks.net
Web site: http://www.leebooksellers.com
Dist(s): **Big River Distribution.**

Lee, James V. *See* **Salado Pr., LLC**

Lee, Keith Russel Publishing *See* **Lee, Keith Russel Publishing Hse.**

Lee, Keith Russel Publishing Hse., *(978-0-9768684)* Orders Addr.: P.O. Box 630, Hazel Crest, IL 60429 USA
E-mail: keith@keithrlee.com
Web site: http://www.keithrlee.com.

Lee, Michael, *(978-0-9766830)* 5503 Harvard, Detroit, MI 48224 USA.

Lee, Quentin Daschel, *(978-0-9789007)* 4949 Harris Ave., Las Vegas, NV 89110 USA (SAN 851-867X) Tel 702-463-9692.

Lee, Shelley, *(978-0-9786757)* Orders Addr.: 441 Frazee Ave., Suite A, Bowling Green, OH 43402-1834 USA Tel 419-354-4673
E-mail: bgpc@wcnet.org
Web site: http://BeforeIKnewYou.com.

Leelanau Pr., *(978-0-9742068; 978-0-9785465)* 6898 MacFarlane Rd., Glen Arbor, MI 49636 USA
Web site: leelanaupress.com
Dist(s): **Partners Bk. Distributing, Inc.**

Leeth, Dawna, *(978-0-9799184)* Orders Addr.: 400 W. Bay Dr., Largo, FL 33770 USA Fax: 727-536-6863.

Leeway Pubs., *(978-0-9744929)* Div. of Leeway Artisans, Orders Addr.: P.O. Box 1577, Laurel, MD 20707 USA Tel 301-404-3355
E-mail: info@LeewayArtisans.com
Web site: http://www.LeewayArtisans.com.

Lefall & Co., Inc., *(978-0-9761778)* 2020 Edmondson Ave., Baltimore, MD 21223 USA (SAN 256-2596)
E-mail: lefallandco@aol.com
Web site: http://www.jockobook.com.

Leffler, Susan, *(978-0-9906244)* P.O. Box 4352, Tumwater, WA 98501 USA Tel 360-866-1841
E-mail: whitestarloghome@hotmail.com.

Left Brain Craft Brain, *(978-0-692-78236-1)* 516 Balra Dr., EL CERRITO, CA 94530 USA Tel 510-909-4971.

Left Field,Angel Gate,

Left Hand Publishing Co., *(978-0-9744799)* P.O. Box 253, Moose Lake, MN 55767 USA
E-mail: nemadji@computerpro.com
Web site: http://computerpro.com/~nemadji.

Left Paw Pr., *(978-0-9818360; 978-0-615-17884-4; 978-0-9829132; 978-0-9838044; 978-1-943356)* Orders Addr.: P.O. Box 133, Greens Fork, IN 47345 USA; Edit Addr.: 17 Washington Blvd., Greens Fork, IN 47345 USA
E-mail: lauren@laurenoriginals.com
Web site: http://www.leftpawpress.com
Dist(s): **Lulu Pr., Inc.**

Left Shoe Lost, *(978-0-9986932)* 66 Maple Ave, Maplewood, NJ 07040 USA Tel 310-614-0693
E-mail: daelo@me.com.

Legacies & Memories, *(978-0-9759533; 978-0-9972523)* 5 Willard Dr., No. 644, Saint Augustine, FL 32086 USA
E-mail: info@legaciesandmemories.com
Web site: http://www.legaciesandmemories.com.

Legacy *Imprint of* **WordWright.biz, Inc.**

Legacy Book Publishing, Incorporated *See* **Legacy Family History, Inc.**

Legacy Family History, Inc., *(978-0-9655835; 978-0-9716705)* 5902 Woodshire Ln., Highland, UT 84003 USA Tel 801-763-1686 (phone/fax)
E-mail: tristantolman@comcast.net
Dist(s): **Send The Light Distribution LLC.**

Legacy Group Productions, LLC, *(978-0-9740585)* 3980 Greenmount Rd., Harrisonburg, VA 22802-0504 USA Toll Free: 877-227-6027
E-mail: cheryl@legacymatters.org
Web site: http://www.legacymatters.org.

Legacy Planning Partners, LLC, *(978-0-9719177; 978-0-9823220)* 254 Plaza Dr., Suite B, Oviedo, FL 32765 USA Tel 407-977-8080; Fax: 407-977-8078
E-mail: peggy@hoytbryan.com.

Legacy Pr. *Imprint of* **Rainbow Pubs. & Legacy Pr.**

Legacy Pr., *(978-0-9653198; 978-0-9777897)* 11381 Mallard Dr., Rochester, IL 62563 USA Tel 217-498-8159; Fax: 217-498-7178 Do not confuse with companies with the same or similar name in Pensacola, FL, Fort Lauderdale, FL, Columbus, GA, Thinelander, WI, Sacremento, CA, Hollywood, FL, Fairfax, VA, Argle, TX
E-mail: legacypressbooks@aol.com
Web site: http://legacypress.homestead.com.

Legacy Pubns., *(978-0-933101)* Subs. of Pace Communications, Inc., Orders Addr.: 1301 Carolina St., Greensboro, NC 27401 USA (SAN 860-4495) Tel 800-248-3204; Fax: 336-378-8271 Do not confuse with companies with the same or similar name in Tumon GU, Overland KS, Brentwood TN, Canyon TX, Irving TX, Lilburn GA, Midlothian, VA
E-mail: legacy.publications@paceco.com
Web site: http://www.legacypublications.com.

Legacy Pubs., *(978-1-932957)* 1866 Oak Harbor Dr., Ocean Isle Beach, NC 28469 USA Tel 910-755-6873 Do not confuse with Legacy Publishers in Natural Bridge, VA, Austin, TX
E-mail: mtdixon@atmc.net.

Legacy Pubs., *(978-0-9754685)* 12126 Trotwood Dr., Austin, TX 78753 USA Tel 512-837-5366 Do not confuse with Legacy Publishers in Snellville GA, Natural Bridge VA
E-mail: legacypublishers@austin.rr.com.

Legacy Pubs. International, *(978-1-880809)* P.O. Box 9690, Rcho Santa Fe, CA 92067-4690 USA (SAN 257-0718)
E-mail: Michele@LegacyPublishersInternational.com; dmiller@hccweb.org
Web site: http://www.LegacyPublishersInternational.com
Dist(s): **Destiny Image Pubs.**

Legacy Publishing Services, Inc., *(978-0-9628733; 978-0-9708395; 978-0-9764982; 978-0-9776777; 978-1-934449; 978-1-937952)* 1883 Lee Rd. Ste. B, Winter Park, FL 32789-2108 USA Tel 407-647-3787 Do not confuse with companies with the same or similar name in Ojai, CA, Berkeley, CA, Atlanta, GA, West Chester, OH, Birmingham, AL, Daty, TX, Fort Meyers, Fl, Baton Rouge, LA
E-mail: legacybookpublishing@yahoo.com; legacypublishing@earthlink.net
Web site: http://www.legacybookpublishing.com
Dist(s): **BookBaby**
Bookmasters Distribution.

Legacy Tree, LLC, *(978-0-9974834)* 19537 Lake Rd., Rocky River, OH 44116 USA Tel 216-509-2828
E-mail: ckozak@scratchoffworks.com
Web site: www.thejesusfamilytree.com
Dist(s): **Ingram Publisher Services**
Spring Arbor Distributors, Inc.

Legend eXpress Publishing, *(978-0-9773648; 978-0-9846324; 978-0-9982261)* 3831 E. Clovis Ave., Mesa, AZ 85206-8520 USA Tel 480-664-1047; Fax: 800-528-0295
E-mail: jc@lxpaz.com
Web site: http://www.lxpaz.com.

Legend Publishing Co., *(978-0-615-22552-4; 978-0-615-22553-1; 978-0-615-22554-8; 978-0-9821687; 978-0-9909373; 978-0-9991813)* Orders Addr.: P.O. Box 429, Garden City, MI 48136 USA Tel 734-595-0663; Edit Addr.: 33807 Calumet Ct., Westland, MI 48186 USA
E-mail: bobwilly81897@Yahoo.com.

Legendary Comics, *(978-1-937278; 978-1-68116)* 2900 W Alameda Ave. 15th Flr., Suite 1500, Burbank, CA 91522 USA
E-mail: bschreck@legendary.com
Web site: www.legendary.com
Dist(s): **Penguin Random Hse. LLC**
Random Hse., Inc.

Legenderry.com, *(978-0-9776967)* 6154 Meadowbrook Dr., Morrison, CO 80465 USA Fax: 720-222-0490
Web site: http://www.legenderry.com.

LegendMaker Scriptoria, *(978-0-9759355)* 9400 Wade Blvd. #817, Frisco, TX 75035 USA Tel 413-313-9127
E-mail: scriptoria@legendmaker.com
Web site: http://legendmaker.com.

Legends in Their Own Lunchbox *Imprint of* **Capstone Classroom**

Legends of the West Publishing Co., *(978-0-9786904)* 174 Santa Rosa Ave., Sausalito, CA 94965-2060 USA (SAN 851-2825) Do not Copnfuse with Know DeFeet Publishing Company 2 Different companies. LD
E-mail: knowdefeet@aol.com.

Legler, Caroline, *(978-0-9771233)* Orders Addr.: 1930 Bonanza Ct., Winter Park, FL 32792 USA
E-mail: glegler@cfl.rr.com.

Legwork Team Publishing, *(978-0-578-00665-9; 978-0-578-00666-6; 978-0-578-01705-1; 978-0-578-01865-2; 978-0-578-01866-9; 978-0-578-01999-4; 978-0-578-02016-7; 978-0-578-02310-6; 978-0-578-02407-3; 978-0-578-02845-3; 978-0-9841535; 978-0-9843539; 978-0-9827337; 978-1-935905) 4 Peacock Ln., Commack, NY 11725 USA*
Web site: http://www.legworkteam.com
Dist(s): **Follett School Solutions.**

leharperwilliamsdesign group, *(978-0-615-37424-6)* 3819 Wake Forest Rd., Decatur, GA 30034 USA Tel 770-593-4687; Fax: 770-593-5466
E-mail: lhwdesign@me.com
Web site: http://leharperwilliamsdesign.com.

Lehman Publishing, *(978-0-9792686)* 15997 Hough, Allenton, MI 48002 USA
E-mail: dlehman@iwarp.net; dana@lehmanpublishing.com
Web site: http://www.lehmanpublishing.com
Dist(s): **Partners Bk. Distributing, Inc.**

Lehmann, Peter Publishing, *(978-0-9788399)* P.O. Box 11284, Eugene, OR 97440-3484 USA Tel 541-345-9106; Fax: 541-345-3737; Toll Free: 877-623-7743
E-mail: info@peter-lehmann-publishing.com
Web site: http://www.peter-lehmann-publishing.com.

Lehua, Inc., *(978-0-9647491)* P.o. Box 25548, Honolulu, HI 96825-0548 USA
E-mail: lehua@ohia.com
Web site: http://www.lehuainc.com
Dist(s): **Booklines Hawaii, Ltd.**

Leigh, Kimbra, *(978-0-9718851)* P.O. Box 20255, Rochester, NY 14602 USA
Web site: http://www.kimbraleigh.com.

Leisure Arts, Inc., *(978-0-942237; 978-1-57486; 978-1-60140; 978-1-60900; 978-1-4647)* Orders Addr.: 5701 Ranch Dr., Little Rock, AR 72223 USA (SAN 666-9565) Tel 501-868-8800; Fax: 501-868-1001; Toll Free Fax: 877-710-5603; Toll Free: 800-643-8030 (customer service); 800-526-5111
E-mail: hermine_linz@leisurearts.com
Web site: http://www.leisurearts.com
Dist(s): **Checker Distributors**
Midpoint Trade Bks., Inc.
Notions Marketing.

Leisure Time Pr., *(978-0-9890270)* 27259 Prescott Way, Temecula, CA 92591 USA Tel 951-219-3168
E-mail: j13m@aol.com
Web site: www.leisuretimepress.com.

Lekha Pubs., LLC, *(978-0-9725901; 978-1-937675)* 4204 Latimer Ave., San Jose, CA 95130 USA
Web site: http://www.lekhapublishers.com.

LeLeu, Lisa Puppet Show Bks. *Imprint of* **LeLeu, Lisa Studios! Inc.**

LeLeu, Lisa Studios! Inc., *(978-0-9710537; 978-0-9770299)* 100 Mechanics St., Doylestown, PA 18901 USA Tel 215-345-1233; Fax: 215-348-5378; *Imprints:* LeLeu, Lisa Puppet Show Books (L LeLeu Puppet)
E-mail: lisa.leleu@lisaleleustudios.com; Frederic.Leleu@LisaLeLeuStudios.com
Web site: http://www.LisaLeLeuStudios.com.

Lemniscaat *Imprint of* **Boyds Mills Pr.**

Lemniscaat USA, *(978-1-935954)* 413 Sixth Ave., New York, NY 11215 USA Tel 718-768-3696; Fax: 718-369-0844
E-mail: janetta@lemniscaat.nl
Web site: http://www.lemniscaatusa.com/
Dist(s): **Ingram Publisher Services.**

Lemon Grove Pr., *(978-0-9815240)* 1158 26th St. #502, Santa Monica,, CA 90403 USA Tel 310-471-1740; Fax: 310-476-7627
E-mail: info@lemongrovepress.com
Web site: http://www.lemongrovepress.com
Dist(s): **BookMasters, Inc.**
Bookmasters Distribution
Brodart Co.
MyiLibrary
ebrary, Inc.

Lemon Pr. LLC, *(978-0-9844183; 978-1-936617)* Orders Addr.: P.O. Box 459, Emerson, GA 30137 USA (SAN 859-3477) Tel 404-791-7742
E-mail: lemonpresspublishing@gmail.com
Web site: http://www.lemonpresspublishing.com
Dist(s): **Smashwords.**

Lemon Shark Pr., *(978-0-9741067)* 1604 Marbella Dr., Vista, CA 92081-5463 USA Tel 760-727-2850 [phone after 9AM PCT]
E-mail: lemonsharkpress@yahoo.com
Web site: http://www.lemonsharkpress.com
Dist(s): **Coutts Information Services**
Eastern Bk. Co.
Yankee Bk. Peddler, Inc.

Lemon Sherbet Pr., *(978-0-9897411)* 87 Guernsey St., Roslindale, MA 02131 USA Tel 781-799-5412
E-mail: lemonsherbetpress@gmail.com.

Lemon Vision Productions, *(978-1-934789)* 27475 Ynez Rd., No. 642, Temecula, CA 92591 USA (SAN 854-9346) Tel 951-526-2942 Toll Free: 866-580-1675
E-mail: info@lemonvision.com
Web site: http://www.lemonvision.com.

Lemondrop Pr., *(978-0-9704718)* 19210 Ambiance Way, Franklin, TN 37067 USA Tel 615-599-6765
E-mail: dplj@bellsouth.net
Web site: http://www.mistertubby.com.

Lemonflavor Productions, *(978-0-9740169)* 100 Pk. Ave., 18th Flr. (Dept. MSM), New York, NY 10017 USA Tel 212-316-4278; Fax: 212-937-2211
E-mail: info@lemonflavor.com
Web site: http://www.lemonflavor.com.

Lemur Conservation Foundation, *(978-0-9766009; 978-0-9856728; 978-0-615-97588-7)* P.O. Box 249, Myakka City, FL 34251 USA Tel 941-322-8494; Fax: 941-322-9264
Web site: http://www.lemurreserve.org.

Leni Bks., *(978-0-9828173)* 11036 S. Tripp, Oak Lawn, IL 60453 USA Tel 708-712-4021; Fax: 708-398-1546
E-mail: ntalty@me.com
Web site: http://cilie-yack-is-under-attack.com.

Leo Publishing, *(978-0-9834735; 978-1-941157)* 303 Augusta Cir., Saint Augustine, FL 32086 USA Tel 310-598-8943
E-mail: lp10leo@gmail.com.

Leo Publishing Works, Inc., *(978-0-615-35488-0)* 3 Monroe Pkwy., Suite P455, Lake Oswego, OR 97035 USA Tel 800-675-7564; Fax: 888-362-5891
E-mail: bethany@leopublishingworks.com
Web site: http://www.LeoPublishingWorks.com.

Leonard, Dennis Publications *See* **Legacy Pubs. International**

†Leonard, Hal Corp., *(978-0-634; 978-0-7935; 978-0-87910; 978-0-87930; 978-0-88188; 978-0-931340; 978-0-9607350; 978-1-56516; 978-1-57467; 978-1-4234; 978-1-936098; 978-1-61713; 978-1-61774; 978-1-61780; 978-1-4584; 978-1-4768; 978-1-4803; 978-1-62906; 978-1-4950; 978-1-5400) Orders Addr.: P.O. Box 13819, Milwaukee, WI 53213-0819 USA Tel 414-774-3630; Fax: 414-774-3259; Toll Free: 800-524-4425; Edit Addr.: 7777 W. Bluemound Rd., Milwaukee, WI 53213 USA (SAN 239-250X) Tel 414-777-3630; Fax: 414-774-4176; Imprints:* G Schirmer, Incorporated (G Schirmer); Limelight Editions (LimelightEd); Amadeus Press (AmadeusPress); Applause Theatre & Cinema (ApplauseTheatr)
E-mail: halinfo@halleonard.com
Web site: http://www.halleonard.com
Dist(s): **Follett School Solutions**
Giron Bks.
Hachette Bk. Group
MyiLibrary
Penguin Random Hse. LLC
Penguin Publishing Group; *CIP.*

Leonard Pr., *(978-0-9769114; 978-1-934223)* P.O. Box 752, Bolivar, MO 65613-0752 USA Tel 417-326-5001
Web site: http://www.leonardpress.com.

Leonardo Press *See* **Firenze Pr.**

Leonard's, Stew Holdings, LLC *See* **Kimberly Pr., LLC**

Leopard Bks. LLC, *(978-1-946525)* 3085 Ave. U, Brooklyn, NY 11229 USA Tel 917-353-7520
E-mail: leopardbooksllc@gmail.com.

Lerner Digital *Imprint of* **Lerner Publishing Group**

†Lerner Publishing Group, *(978-0-7613; 978-0-8225; 978-0-87406; 978-0-87614; 978-0-929371; 978-0-930494; 978-1-57505; 978-1-58013; 978-1-58196; 978-1-4677; 978-1-5124; 978-1-5415)* Orders Addr.: 1251 Washington Ave. N., Minneapolis, MN 55401 USA (SAN 256-0283) Tel 612-332-3344; Fax: 612-204-9208; Edit Addr.: 241 First Ave., N., Minneapolis, MN 55401 USA (SAN 201-0828) Tel 612-332-3344; Fax: 612-215-6230; Toll Free Fax: 800-332-1132; Toll Free: 800-328-4929; *Imprints:* First Avenue Editions (First Ave Edns); Lerner Publications (Lerner Publctns); Blackbirch Press, Incorporated (Blackbirch Pr); Carolrhoda Books (Carolrho Bks); Ediciones Lerner (EdiciLerner); Millbrook Press (Millbrok Pr); Twenty-First Century Books (TwentFrstCent); Graphic Universe™ (Graphic Univ); Kar-Ben Publishing (Kar-Ben); Carolrhoda Lab™ (CarolrhodaLAB); Darby Creek (DarbyCreek); Lerner Digital (LernerDigital); Hungry Tomato r (Hungry Tomato)
E-mail: info@lernerbooks.com; custserve@lernerbooks.com
Web site: http://www.lernerbooks.com; http://www.karben.com
Dist(s): **Ebsco Publishing**
Follett School Solutions
Ingram Publisher Services
MyiLibrary
Open Road Integrated Media, Inc.
Perfection Learning Corp.; *CIP.*

Lerner Pubns. *Imprint of* **Lerner Publishing Group**

LERN-LEARN, *(978-0-9763195)* 340 Vallejo Dr., Suite 82, Millbrae, CA 94030 USA.

Lerue Pr., LLC, *(978-0-9797460; 978-1-938814)* Orders Addr.: 280 Greg St., #10, Reno, NV 89502 USA Tel 775-849-3814
E-mail: janiceh@lerurpress.com; custserv@leruepress.com
Web site: http://www.leruepress.com; http://www.lrpnv.com.

Les Lurn Pubs., *(978-0-9792000)* 5451 Bancroft Ave., Oakland, CA 94601 USA (SAN 852-7512).

Les Penseurs, *(978-0-9764999; 978-0-9820676)* 309 Weatherstone Ln., Marietta, GA 30068 USA Tel 678-575-7052; Fax: 678-560-1580
E-mail: jsands@lespenseurs.com
Web site: http://www.lespenseurs.com.

Lesen Pub., *(978-0-9767200)* 2207 Shermont Pl., Brandon, FL 33511 USA Tel 813-857-6629; Fax: 813-684-7876
E-mail: jem2207@aol.com.

Leslie, Beverly J., *(978-0-9769722)* 1911 Patton Pl., Lithonia, GA 30058 USA Tel 770-987-8769; Fax: 770-987-8018
E-mail: bjleslie1@comcast.net; Beverly@lesliegraphicdesigns.com
Web site: http://LeslieGraphicDesigns.com.

Less is More Publishing, LLC, *(978-0-9769618)* 405 N. Woodlawn Ave., Kirkwood, MO 63122 USA
Web site: http://www.aboutheaven.net
Dist(s): **Big River Distribution.**

Less Pr., *(978-0-9657367)* 100 Hannah Niles Way, Braintree, MA 02184-7261 USA Tel 781-848-0555.

Lesson Ladder, *(978-0-9848657; 978-0-9884499; 978-0-9964067)* 21 Orient Ave, Melrose, MA 02176 USA Tel 800-301-4647; Fax: 617-583-5552
E-mail: accounting@xamonline.com
Dist(s): **Ingram Publisher Services.**

Lessons From The Vine *Imprint of* **Hutchings, John Pubs.**

Let Freedom Ring *Imprint of* **Capstone Press of Coughlan Cos.**

LeTay Publishing, *(978-0-9753434; 978-0-9830731)* Div. of LeTay Corp., Orders Addr.: P.O. Box 170233, Atlanta, GA 30317 USA Tel 404-667-2810
E-mail: booksales@letaypublishing.com; publisher@letaypublishing.com
Web site: http://www.letaypublishing.com
Dist(s): **Lightning Source, Inc.**

Lethe Pr., *(978-1-59021)* 118 Heritage Ave., Maple Shade, NJ 08052 USA Tel 609-410-7391
E-mail: lethepress@aol.com; editor@lethepressbooks.com
Web site: http://www.lethepressbooks.com
Dist(s): **Bookazine Co., Inc.**
Smashwords.

Letona, Oscar, *(978-0-615-24938-4)* 51 Cedar Pl., Yonkers, NY 10705 USA
E-mail: mrletona@thetrojancurse.com; mrletona@hotmail.com
Web site: http://www.thetrojancurse.com.

Lets Go Publish, *(978-0-9899957; 978-0-9962454; 978-0-9977667; 978-0-9980848; 978-0-9982683; 978-0-9986282; 978-0-9988111; 978-1-947402)* 11 Marjorie Ave., Wilkes Barre, PA 18702 USA Tel 570-829-5926
E-mail: jmac@kellyconsulting.com; bkelly@kellyconsulting.com
Web site: http://letsgopublish.com; http://www.bookhawkers.com
Dist(s): **BookHawkers Internet BookSeller.**

Let's Learn Library of Knowledge Series, *(978-0-9771015)* P.O. Box 9910, Canoga Park, CA 91309-9910 USA (SAN 256-7849)
E-mail: letslearn@letslearnlibrary.net
Web site: http://www.letslearnlibrary.net.

Let's Think-kids Foundation, Inc., *(978-1-58237)* 3925 Blackburn Ln., Burtonsville, MD 20866 USA Toll Free: 800-841-2883
E-mail: thinkkids@aol.com; sftierno@aol.com
Web site: http://www.LTKF.org.

Letter Bks. *Imprint of* **Capstone Press of Coughlan Cos.**

Level 4 Press, Inc., *(978-0-9768001; 978-1-933769)* 13518 Jamul Dr., Jamul, CA 91935 USA Tel 619-669-3100; Fax: 619-374-7311
E-mail: sales@level4press.com
Web site: http://www.level4press.com
Dist(s): **Follett School Solutions**
Midpoint Trade Bks., Inc.
MyiLibrary.

Level Green Bks., *(978-0-9788771)* 11 Level Green Rd., Brooktondale, NY 14817 USA (SAN 851-8319).

Level Ground Pr., *(978-0-9773461)* 2810 San Paula Ave., Dallas, TX 75228 USA Tel 214-796-2135
Web site: http://www.levelgroundfilms.com.

Levenger Pr., *(978-1-929154)* 420 S. Congress Ave., Delray Beach, FL 33445 USA Tel 561-276-2436; Fax: 561-276-3584
E-mail: mvogel@levenger.com
Web site: http://www.levenger.com.

Leverage Factory, *(978-0-9773000)* 38 Rogerson Dr., Chapel Hill, NC 27517-4037 USA (SAN 257-2710)
E-mail: info@leveragefactory.com
Web site: http://www.beawriter.us; http://www.leveragefactory.com
Dist(s): **Independent Pubs. Group.**

Levi Bass Publishing, *(978-0-9835651)* PO Box 608355, Orlando, FL 32860 USA Tel 407-709-0578; Fax: 407-271-8552
E-mail: carolyndenise@ymail.com
Web site: www.carolyndenise.com.

Levine, Arthur A. Bks. *Imprint of* **Scholastic, Inc.**

Levine, Bette M., *(978-0-9721094)* 4605 Regiment Way, Manlius, NY 13104 USA
E-mail: rampa505@aol.com.

Levity Pr., *(978-0-615-64986-3; 978-0-615-68151-1; 978-0-615-70890-4; 978-0-615-70893-5; 978-1-939896)* 10170 Palm Glen Dr. No. 46, Santee, CA 92071 USA
Web site: www.englishcorner.me
Dist(s): **CreateSpace Independent Publishing Platform.**

Lewis & Clark Bicentennial Corps of Discovery Arch, *(978-0-9763970)* 1907 NE 75th Ave., Portland, OR 97213 USA Tel 503-201-2494
E-mail: faith.ruffing@bicencorpsarchive.com
Web site: http://www.bicencorpsarchive.com.

Lewis International, Inc., *(978-0-9666771; 978-1-930983)* 2201 NW 102nd Pl., No. 1, Miami, FL 33172 USA Tel 305-436-7984; Fax: 305-436-7985; Toll Free: 800-259-5962.

Lewis Lynn Bks., *(978-0-9745544)* 1143 N. Carey Ave., Clovis, CA 93611-7371 USA Fax: 559-322-9038
E-mail: cconn@cwnet.com
Web site: http://www.borainiansector.com.

Lewis-Thornton, Rae, *(978-0-9747983)* 1507 E. 53rd St., Suite 315, Chicago, IL 60615 USA Tel 773-643-4316; Fax: 773-643-4356
E-mail: rae_lewis_thornton@hotmail.com
Web site: http://www.raelewisthornton.org.

Lexicon Marketing Corporation *See* **Lexicon Marketing, LLC**

Lexicon Marketing, LLC, *(978-1-59172)* 6380 Wilshire Blvd. Ste. 1400, Los Angeles, CA 90048-5018 USA
E-mail: Jbelletti@lexiconmarketing.com; icruz@lexiconmarketing.com.

Lexingford Publishing, *(978-0-9844938; 978-0-9859480; 978-0-9863343; 978-0-9963948; 978-0-9981665; 978-0-9986060; 978-1-947373)* 165 Backwoods Rd., Colton, NY 13625 USA (SAN 859-5674) Tel 415-328-5465
E-mail: abell@clarkson.edu.

Lexington Bks., *(978-0-7391; 978-1-4985)* Div. of Rowman & Littlefield Publishing Group, Inc., Orders Addr.: 15200 NBN Way, Blue Ridge Summit, PA 17214 USA Tel 717-794-3800 (Sales, Customer Service, MIS, Royalties, Inventory Mgmt., Dist., Credit & Collections); Fax: 717-794-3803 (Customer Service &/or orders only); 717-794-3857 (Sales & MIS); 717-794-3856 (Royalties, Inventory Mgmt., & Dist.); Toll Free Fax: 800-338-4550 (Customer Service &/or orders); Toll Free: 800-462-6420 (Customer Service &/or orders); 67 Mowat Ave., Suite 241, Toronto, ON M6K 3E3 Tel 416-534-1660; Fax: 416-534-3699; Edit Addr.: 4501 Forbes Blvd., Blvd., Ste. 200, Lanham, MD 20706 USA Tel 301-459-3366; Fax: 301-429-5749; Toll Free: 1-800-462-6420 Short Discount, contact rlpgsales@rowman.com
E-mail: custserv@rowman.com; edebusk@rowman.com; lexingtonbooks@rowman.com
Web site: http://www.lexingtonbooks.com; http://www.rlpgbooks.com; http://www.rowman.com
Dist(s): **CreateSpace Independent Publishing Platform**
Ebsco Publishing
Follett School Solutions
MyiLibrary
National Bk. Network
Rowman & Littlefield Publishers, Inc.
Send The Light Distribution LLC
Transaction Pubs.
ebrary, Inc.

Lexington Pubs., *(978-1-933361)* P.O. Box 750018, Arlington Heights, MA 02475 USA
E-mail: lexingtonpublishers@gmail.com.

Leyva, Barbara, *(978-0-9729056)* P.O. Box 3295, Clewiston, FL 33440-3295 USA; *Imprints:* Balticbard Publishing (Balticbard Pub)
E-mail: balticbard@yahoo.com
Web site: http://www.geocities.com/balticbard/index.html.

L.G. Publishing, *(978-0-615-16242-3)* P.O. Box 5098, Sarasota, FL 34277 USA Tel 941-312-4725
E-mail: glickmanfamily@aol.com.

LGE Performance Systems, Inc., *(978-0-9778776)* 9757 Lake Nona Rd., Orlando, FL 32827 USA (SAN 850-5055) Tel 407-438-9911; Fax: 407-438-6667.

LGR Productions *See* **LGR Publishing, Inc.**

LGR Publishing, Inc., *(978-0-9657610)* 3219 NW C St., Richmond, IN 47374 USA Tel 765-939-8924 (phone/fax)
E-mail: jwilde@indiana.edu; mcphd@infocom.com
Web site: http://www.angerchillout.com.

Lóguez Ediciones (ESP) *(978-84-85334; 978-84-89804; 978-84-96646) Dist. by* **Lectorum Pubns.**

LH Pubns. & Productions, *(978-0-9749013)* Orders Addr.: P.O. Box 914, Center Harbor, NH 03226 USA
E-mail: mcat_lh@yahoo.com
Web site: http://www.laurahickey.com.

LHC Publishing, *(978-0-615-71668-8; 978-0-615-86013-8; 978-0-615-93103-6; 978-0-692-02397-6; 978-0-692-47441-9; 978-0-692-47443-3; 978-0-9970254)* 5817 S. 3rd St., Tampa, FL 33611 USA Tel 9135655777
E-mail: yvijones@hotmail.com
Web site: www.LHCpublishing.com
Dist(s): **CreateSpace Independent Publishing Platform.**

Li, Richard T., *(978-0-9675988)* 4554 Rose Tree Ct., Fort Worth, TX 76137 USA Tel 817-656-5178; Fax: 817-656-4138.

LiArt-Literature & Art, *(978-1-931481)* P.O. Box 245686, Pembroke Pines, FL 33024-5686 USA Tel 954-986-6886 (phone/fax)
E-mail: liartpe@aol.com.

Libertary Company *See* **Booktrope**

Liberties Pr., Ltd. (IRL) *(978-0-9545335; 978-1-905483; 978-1-907593; 978-1-909718) Dist. by* **Casemate Pubs.**

Liberty Artists Management, *(978-0-9785427)* Orders Addr.: 31 Liberty St., Catskill, NY 12414-1442 USA
E-mail: admin@libertyartists.com
Web site: http://www.beckyblume.com; http://www.libertyartists.com.

Liberty Communications House *See* **JB Information Station**

Liberty Fund, Inc., *(978-0-86597; 978-0-913966; 978-1-61487)* Orders Addr.: c/o Total Response, Inc., 5804 Churchman By-Pass, Indianapolis, IN 46203 USA; Edit Addr.: 8335 Allison Pointe Trail, No. 300, Indianapolis, IN 46250-1684 USA (SAN 202-6740) Tel 317-842-0880; Fax: 317-579-6060; Toll Free: 800-866-3520; 800-955-8335 (customer service)
E-mail: webmaster@libertyfund.org
Web site: http://www.libertyfund.org
Dist(s): **Chicago Distribution Ctr.**
MyiLibrary
ebrary, Inc.

Liberty Manuals Co., *(978-0-9710748; 978-0-9820955; 978-1-940069)* Orders Addr.: P.O. Box 453, Rumson, NJ 07760 USA Tel 732-842-3000; Fax: 732-741-5820.

Liberty Publishing Group, *(978-1-893095; 978-1-946291)* Div. of The Holton Consulting Group, Inc., Orders Addr.: 1405 Autumn Ridge Dr., Durham, NC 27712-2680 USA Tel 919-767-9620; Toll Free Fax: 866-500-7697; Toll Free: 877-819-7489
E-mail: bil@holtonconsulting.com; cher@holtonconsulting.com
Web site: http://www.holtonconsulting.com; http://www.prosperityPublishing.com; http://www.themetaphysicalwebsite.com
Dist(s): **Prosperity Publishing Hse.**
Smashwords.

Liberty St. *Imprint of* **Time Inc. Bks.**

Liberty University Press, *(978-0-9819357; 978-1-935986; 978-0-9976828)* 1971 University Blvd., Lynchburg, VA 24502 USA Tel 434-592-3100
E-mail: libertyuniversitypress@liberty.edu.

Librado Pr., *(978-1-879571)* 11223 Leatherwood Dr., Reston, VA 22091 USA Tel 703-476-0516 Do not confuse with Librad Press in San Francisco, CA.

Librairie du Liban Pubns. (FRA) *Dist. by* **Intl Bk Ctr.**

Librairie Larousse (FRA) *(978-2-03) Dist. by* **Distribks Inc.**

Libraries Unlimited *Imprint of* **ABC-CLIO, LLC**

Library Assn. of La Jolla, *(978-0-9744804; 978-0-9828289)* 1008 Wall St., La Jolla, CA 92037-4418 USA Tel 858-454-5872; Fax: 858-454-5835; *Imprints:* Athenaeum Music & Arts Library (Athenaeum Music)
E-mail: Athlibrary@pacbell.net; kpeterson@ljathenaeum.org.

Library of America, The, *(978-0-940450; 978-1-883011; 978-1-931082; 978-1-59853)* Div. of Literary Classics of the U. S., Inc., 14 E. 60th St., New York, NY 10022 USA (SAN 286-9918) Tel 212-308-3360; Fax: 212-750-8352
E-mail: info@loa.org
Web site: http://www.loa.org
Dist(s): **MyiLibrary**
Penguin Random Hse. LLC
Penguin Publishing Group
Random Hse., Inc.

Library Reprints, Inc., *(978-0-7222)* Orders Addr.: P.O. Box 890820, Temecula, CA 92589-0820 USA (SAN 254-0258) Fax: 951-767-1803; 951-767-0133
E-mail: newbookorders@gmail.com.

Library Sales of N.J., *(978-1-888032)* Orders Addr.: P.O. Box 335, Garwood, NJ 07027-0335 USA Tel 908-232-1446; Edit Addr.: 607 S. Chestnut St., Westfield, NJ 07090-1369 USA
E-mail: Librarysalesofnj@aol.com.

LIBRI Bks., Division of Seasons & A Muse, Incorporated *See* **LIBRI Pubs.**

LIBRI Pubs., *(978-0-9763952)* P.O. Box 5849, Playa Del Rey, CA 90296-5849 USA Tel 310-827-6495; Fax: 310-827-8166
E-mail: libri@seasonsandamuse.com
Web site: http://www.seasonsandamuse.com.

Libris Draconis Pr., *(978-0-9728124)* PMB 279 1296 E. Gibson Rd., Suite A, Woodland, CA 95776 USA (SAN 255-1179)
Dist(s): **BookMasters, Inc.**

Libros Desafio, *(978-0-939125; 978-1-55883; 978-1-55955)* Subs. of CRC Pubns., 2850 Kalamazoo Ave., SE, Grand Rapids, MI 49560 USA (SAN 248-9775) Tel 616-224-0785; Fax: 616-224-0834; Toll Free: 800-333-8300
E-mail: info@librosdesafio.org
Web site: http://www.librosdesafio.org.

Libros, Encouraging Cultural Literacy, *(978-0-9675413; 978-0-9710860)* Orders Addr.: P.O. Box 453, Long Beach, NY 11561 USA Tel 516-889-6077; Fax: 516-889-6365; Toll Free: 800-260-9915; Edit Addr.: 160 LaFayette Blvd., Long Beach, NY 11561 USA (SAN 253-374X)
E-mail: librospress@msn.com
Web site: http://www.librospress.com.

Libros in Spanish, LLC, 1941 NE 147th Terr., North Miami, FL 33181 USA Tel 786-274-1556; Fax: 305-948-0333
E-mail: admin@librosinspanish.com.

Libros Liguori *Imprint of* **Liguori Pubns.**

Libros Para Ninos *Imprint of* **Libros Para Ninos**

Libros Para Ninos, Div. of Simon & Schuster Children's Publishing, 1230 Ave. of the Americas, New York, NY 10020 USA; *Imprints:* Libros Para Ninos (LibPara)
Dist(s): **Simon & Schuster**
Simon & Schuster, Inc.

Libros Publishing, *(978-0-9837458; 978-0-9851769; 978-0-9906713; 978-0-9987031)* 24040 Camino Del Avion No. A225, Monarch Beach, CA 92629 USA Tel 949-201-9477; Fax: 949-661-9098
E-mail: librospublishing@cox.net
Dist(s): **BookMasters, Inc.**
Bookmasters Distribution
Follett School Solutions
ebrary, Inc.

Libros Sin Fronteras, P.O. Box 2085, Olympia, WA 98507 USA Tel 360-357-4332; Fax: 360-357-4964
E-mail: info@librossinfronteras.com
Web site: http://www.librossinfronteras.com.

Libros-Latin American Treasures For Kids *See* **Libros, Encouraging Cultural Literacy**

Librujas, *(978-0-9771566)* 4335 Van Nuys Blvd., Suite 117, Sherman Oaks, CA 91403 USA (SAN 256-887X) Tel 818-905-7221
E-mail: jamie@librujas.com; patricia@librujas.com
Web site: http://www.librujas.com
Dist(s): **Quality Bks., Inc.**

Liburdi, Marlana *See* **Happy Hearts Family, The**

Lickel, Lisa Publishing, also operating as Five Loaves *See* **Fox Ridge Pubns.**

Life Action Inc., *(978-0-940110; 978-0-9667124; 978-1-934718)* Orders Addr.: P.O. Box 31, Buchanan, MI 49107 USA Tel 269-697-8600; Fax: 269-695-2974; Toll Free: 800-321-1538; Edit Addr.: 2727 Niles Buchanan Rd., Buchanan, MI 49107 USA (SAN 220-2859)
Web site: http://www.lifeaction.org; http://www.ReviveOurHearts.com.

Life Action Publishing *See* **Life Action Inc.**

LIFE Bks. *Imprint of* **Time Inc. Bks.**

Life by Design Youth Leadership Resources *See* **Youthleadership.com**

Life Changers International Church *See* **Dickow, Gregory Ministries**

Life force, *(978-0-9985790)* 7007 W. indian school Rd., Phoenix, AZ 85033 USA Tel 845-200-4962
E-mail: maryamnisajudan@gmail.com.

Life Force Bks., *(978-0-9795331; 978-0-9896540; 978-0-9962386)* P.O. Box 302, Bayside, CA 95524 USA; *Imprints:* Zardoz Press (ZardozPr)
E-mail: jjsemple@suddenlink.net; jjsemple@lifeforcebooks.com
Web site: http://www.lifeforcebooks.com; http://www.goldenflowermeditation.com; http://www.commonsensekundalini.com; http://www.kundaliniconsortium.org/
Dist(s): **Smashwords.**

Life Letters Publishing, *(978-0-9746022)* P.O. Box 360111, Strongsville, OH 44136 USA
E-mail: lifeletter@aol.com
Web site: http://www.lifeletter.net.

Life Line, Inc., *(978-0-9647089)* P.O. Box 7990, New York, NY 10116-8715 USA Tel 212-947-0661; Fax: 212-947-0681 Do not confuse with Life Lines, Rimrock, AZ
E-mail: lifel@aol.com.

Life Line Publishing, *(978-0-9761604)* P.O. Box 1482, Bridgeport, CT 06601-1482 USA Do not confuse with Life Line Publishing in Franklin, VA.

Life Link Worldwide Pubs., *(978-1-880608)* 175 Raymond Ct., Fayetteville, GA 30214 USA Tel 770-994-1683.

Life Pubs. International, *(978-0-7361; 978-0-943258; 978-1-890219)* 1625 N. Robberson Ave., Springfield, MO 65803 USA (SAN 213-5817) Tel 417-831-7766; Fax: 417-831-6445; Toll Free: 888-776-2425
E-mail: info@lifepublishers.org
Dist(s): **Bookmasters Distribution.**

Life Rich Publishing *Imprint of* **AuthorHouse**

Life Story Publishing, LLC *See* **Wizard Academies, LLC**

Lifeforce Enterprises, Inc., *(978-0-9709796)* 250 Pacific Ave., Suite 326, Long Beach, CA 90802 USA Tel 562-366-2617; Toll Free: 866-543-3367
E-mail: ajyager@entertheforce.com
Web site: http://www.entertheforce.com
Dist(s): **Midpoint Trade Bks., Inc.**

Lifegate Publishing LLC, *(978-1-941632)* 1110 C Parkside Green Dr., Greenacres, FL 33415 USA Tel 561-602-0089
E-mail: lifegatepublishing@yahoo.com.

Lifelight Bks., *(978-0-9743801)* 2629 262nd Pl SE, Sammamish, WA 98075-7900 USA (SAN 850-8070)
E-mail: lynne@lifelightbooks.com
Web site: http://www.lifelightbooks.com.

LifeLine Studios, Inc., *(978-0-9714753)* 1390 W. Main St., Lancaster, TX 75146 USA Tel 972-275-0468; Fax: 972-275-0469
E-mail: afoutsjr@lifelinestudios.com
Web site: http://www.lifelinestudio.com.

Lifelong Friends Pub., *(978-0-9971221)* po box 483, Mansfield Center, CT 06250 USA Tel 860-428-7691
E-mail: ssptbp@charter.net
Web site: www.lifelongfriends.com.

Lifepac *Imprint of* **Alpha Omega Pubns., Inc.**

Liferays Publishing, *(978-0-9795397)* 5390 Elliott Rd., Powder Springs, GA 30127-3803 USA Tel 770-943-6123
E-mail: liferays@bellsouth.net
Web site: http://liferays02.googlepages.com/home.

LifeReloaded *See* **LifeReloaded Specialty Publishing LLC**

LifeReloaded Specialty Publishing LLC, *(978-0-9776414; 978-1-60800)* 2256 Huber Dr., Manheim, PA 17545 USA; *Imprints:* American Literary Publishing (Amer Literary)
E-mail: admin@lifereloaded.com; Editor@LifeReloaded.com; Sales@LifeReloaded.com; Publisher@LifeReloaded.com
Web site: http://www.LifeReloaded.com; http://www.GhostTrainToFreedom.com; http://www.MooKittyFindsAHome.Com; http://www.JMPMysterySeries.com.

Life's Journey of Hope Pubns., *(978-0-9747815)* Orders Addr.: P.O. Box 1277, Groton, MA 01450 USA (SAN 255-7789) Tel 978-448-1252; Edit Addr.: 90 Martins Pond Rd., Groton, MA 01450 USA
E-mail: LLeonard@lifesjourneyofhope.com; lifesjourneyofhope@hotmail.com
Web site: http://www.lifesjourneyofhope.com.

Lifeskills Press *See* **Uplift Pr.**

LifeSong Pubs., *(978-0-9718306; 978-0-9799116)* Orders Addr.: P.O. Box 183, Somis, CA 93066-0183 USA Tel 805-504-3916; Toll Free: 866-266-6917
Web site: http://www.lifesongpublishers.com
Dist(s): **Send The Light Distribution LLC.**

Lifestage, Inc., *(978-0-9799905)* 496 Smithtown ByPass, Suite 202, Smithtown, NY 11787 USA (SAN 854-9192) Tel 631-366-4265
E-mail: lifestage_2000@yahoo.com
Web site: http://www.lifestage.org.

LifeStory Publishing, *(978-0-9758988)* 5328 Runnymede Rd., Jackson, MS 39211 USA Tel 601-978-3478
E-mail: maxwell@thewellpublishing.org.

LifeTime Media, Inc., *(978-0-9675967; 978-0-9816368; 978-0-9822171; 978-0-9823975)* 352 Seventh Ave., 7th Flr., New York, NY 10001 USA (SAN 856-0978) Tel 212-631-7524; Fax: 212-631-7529
E-mail: sales@lifetimemedia.com; jgrace@lifetimemedia.com
Web site: http://www.lifetimemedia.com
Dist(s): **Two Rivers Distribution.**

Lifetime Relationship Center *See* **Intralife Systems Publishing**

Lifetrack Resources, *(978-0-9743826)* 709 Univ. Ave. W., Saint Paul, MN 55104-4804 USA Tel 651-227-8471; Fax: 651-227-0621
E-mail: familiestogether@lifetrackresources.org
Web site: http://www.lifetrackresources.org.

Lifevest *Imprint of* **Lifevest Publishing, Inc.**

Lifevest Publishing, Inc., *(978-0-9724680; 978-1-932338; 978-1-59879)* 4910 E. Dry Creek Rd., Suite 170, Centennial, CO 80122 USA Tel 303-221-1007; Fax: 303-771-1166; Toll Free Fax: 877-843-1007; *Imprints:* Lifevest (Livevst)
E-mail: ric.simmons@lifevestpublishing.com; publisher@lifevestpublishing.com
Web site: http://www.lifevestpublishing.com.

LifeWay Christian Resources, *(978-0-7673; 978-0-633; 978-1-4158; 978-1-4300; 978-1-5359)* Div. of The Southern Baptist Convention, One Lifeway Plaza, Nashville, TN 37234 USA Tel 615-251-2000; Fax: 615-277-8221 (product info., ordering, order tracking); 615-251-2626 (shipping/transportation); Toll Free Fax: 800-296-4036; Toll Free: 800-458-2772 (product info., ordering); 800-251-3225; *Imprints:* Serendipity House (Serendip Hse)
E-mail: customerservice@lifeway.com; support.lifeway.com
Web site: http://www.lifewaystores.com; http://www.lifeway.com; http://www.bhpublishinggroup.com
Dist(s): **Spring Arbor Distributors, Inc.**

Liffey Pr., The (IRL) *(978-1-904148; 978-1-905785; 978-1-908308) Dist. by* **Dufour.**

Lift Every Voice *Imprint of* **Moody Pubs.**

Light & Life Publishing Co., *(978-0-937032; 978-1-880971; 978-1-933654)* Orders Addr.: 4808 Park Glen Rd., Minneapolis, MN 55416 USA (SAN 213-8565) Tel 952-925-3888; Fax: 888-925-3918; Toll Free Fax: 888-925-3918
E-mail: ivy@light-n-life.com
Web site: http://www.light-n-life.com.

Light Bugs Publishing, *(978-0-9765514)* 1400 Champions Green Dr., Gulf Breeze, FL 32563 USA Tel 850-932-9325
E-mail: allen911@bellsouth.net; russ@lightbugspublishing.com; jan@lightbugspublishing.com
Web site: http://www.lightbugspublishing.com.

Light Energy Bks., *(978-0-9740480)* 731 Mandana Blvd., Oakland, CA 94610 USA Tel 510-268-9999.

Light Incorporated, The *See* **Tughra Bks.**

Light Internal Publishing, *(978-0-9823732)* Orders Addr.: 6130 E. Fair Ave., Centennial, CO 80111 USA (SAN 857-9822)
E-mail: marnie@lightinternal.com
Web site: http://www.lightinternal.com.

Light Line, *(978-0-9773244)* 353 E. Pittsfield St., Pennsville, NJ 08070 USA (SAN 257-2540) Toll Free: 877-427-8271
E-mail: jlidadf@comcast.net.

Light Messages Publishing, *(978-0-9679937; 978-0-9800756; 978-1-61153)* 5216 Tahoe Dr., Durham, NC 27713 USA (SAN 920-9298) Tel 919-361-5041; Toll Free Fax: 866-585-4635
E-mail: books@lightmessages.com
Web site: http://www.lightmessages.com
Dist(s): **INscribe Digital**
Independent Pubs. Group
New Leaf Distributing Co., Inc.

Light of Logos Pr., *(978-0-615-82703-2; 978-0-9896356)* 15 Fairfield Rd, Wayland, MA 01778 USA
E-mail: yuegang_zhang@yahoo.com.

Light Pubns., *(978-0-9702642; 978-0-9824707; 978-1-940060)* Orders Addr.: P.O. Box 2462, Providence, RI 02906 USA Tel 401-272-8707; Edit Addr.: 393 Morris Ave., Providence, RI 02906 USA (SAN 852-7407) Tel 401-272-8707
E-mail: info@lightpublications.com
Web site: http://www.lightpublications.com.

Light Sword Publishing, LLC *See* **LSP Digital, LLC**

Light Works Publishing *Imprint of* **I.M. Enterprises**

Light24, *(978-0-9700002)* Orders Addr.: 85-42 160th St., Jamaica Queens, NY 11432 USA Tel 718-526-7021 Do not confuse with companies with the same name in Worthington, OH, Kirkland, WA.

Light-Beams Publishing, *(978-0-9708104; 978-0-9766289; 978-1-941506)* Orders Addr.: 36 Blandings Way, Biddeford, ME 04005 USA Tel 603-659-1300
E-mail: mforman@light-beams.com; info@light-beams.com
Web site: http://www.light-beams.com
Dist(s): **Independent Pubs. Group**
Library Video Co.
Midwest Tape
MyiLibrary
NewSound, LLC.

Publisher Name Index

LightBurst Media, (978-0-692-59600-5; 978-0-692-63807-1; 978-0-692-63810-1; 978-0-692-63813-2; 978-0-692-64039-5; 978-0-692-64283-2; 978-0-692-65893-2; 978-0-692-66096-6; 978-0-692-67320-1; 978-0-692-70346-5; 978-0-692-70858-3; 978-0-692-70961-0; 978-0-692-71084-5; 978-0-692-73769-9; 978-0-9979389) 3226 se gladstone st, portland, OR 97202 USA Tel 347-551-3121
Web site: www.lightburstmedia.com
Dist(s): **CreateSpace Independent Publishing Platform.**

Lighted Lamp Pr., (978-1-888350) Orders Addr.: P.O. Box 1234, Wheat Ridge, CO 80034 USA; Edit Addr.: 4945 Gray St., Denver, CO 80212 USA (SAN 298-8348)
E-mail: robertjinye@msn.com.

Lighthearted Pr., Inc., (978-0-9659225) Orders Addr.: P.O. Box 90125, Portland, OR 97290 USA Tel 503-786-3085; Fax: 503-786-0315; Edit Addr.: 10585 SE Fairway Dr., Portland, OR 97266 USA
E-mail: davis@lightheartedpress.com
Web site: http://www.lightheartedpress.com.

Lighthouse Bk. Publishing, (978-0-9791168) Orders Addr.: P.O. Box 310534, Houston, TX 77231 USA Toll Free: 800-247-9100
E-mail: book@journeytoseetheking.com
Web site: http://www.journeytoseetheking.com.

Lighthouse Christian Products Co., (978-0-9712894) 1050 Remington Rd., Schaumburg, IL 60173-4518 USA
Web site: http://lcpgifts.com.

Lighthouse eBooks *See* **Lighthouse Publishing**

Lighthouse for Leaders, (978-0-9820576) P.O. Box 1990, San Benito, TX 78586 USA; *Imprints*: Lighthouse for Leaders, A (LighthseforLea)
Web site: http://www.LighthouseforLeaders.com.

Lighthouse for Leaders, A *Imprint of* **Lighthouse for Leaders**

Lighthouse Point Pr., (978-0-9637966; 978-0-9792998) Div. of Yearick-Millea, Inc., 7412 Lighthouse Point, Pittsburgh, PA 15221 USA Tel 412-242-9382; Fax: 412-242-9382
Web site: http://lighthousepointpress.com.

LightHouse Pr., (978-0-9703823; 978-0-9724442; 978-0-9747189; 978-0-9762898; 978-0-9791372; 978-0-9823218) 2053 Williams Valley Dr., Madison, TN 37115-7610 USA Do not confuse with companies with the same or similar names in Culver City, CA, Millersburg, OH, York, ME, Marblehead, MA, Deerfield Beach, FL, La Junta, CO, Rochester, NY, San Mateo, CA.

Lighthouse Pr., Inc., (978-0-9677347; 978-0-9795392) 5448 Apex Peakway #230, Apex, NC 27502-3924 USA (SAN 253-0961) Do not confuse with companies with the same or similar names in York, ME, Marblehead, MA, La Junta, CO, Deerfield Beach, FL, San Mateo, CA, Sanford, MI, Minneapolis, MN, Millersburg, OH
E-mail: swagner@lighthouse-press.com
Web site: http://www.lighthouse-press.com
Dist(s): **Midpoint Trade Bks., Inc.**

Lighthouse Publications *See* **I AM Foundation, The**

Lighthouse Publishing, (978-0-9773766; 978-0-9797863; 978-1-935079; 978-0-9981577) 754 Roxholly Walk, Buford, GA 30518 USA (SAN 257-4330)
E-mail: andyoverett@lighthousechristianpublishing.com
Web site: http://www.lighthouseebooks.com; http://www.lighthousechristianpublishing.com; http://www.loneoakpublishing.com
Dist(s): **CreateSpace Independent Publishing Platform.**

Lighthouse Publishing of the Carolinas, (978-0-9822065; 978-0-9833196; 978-0-9847655; 978-1-938499; 978-0-615-89890-2; 978-1-941103; 978-1-946016) Div. of Christian Devotions Ministries, Orders Addr.: 2333 Barton Oaks Dr., Raleigh, NC 27614 USA
E-mail: aground@mindspring.com
Web site: lighthousepublishingofthecarolinas.com
Dist(s): **CreateSpace Independent Publishing Platform**
Spring Arbor Distributors, Inc.

Lightly Pr., (978-0-9794452) 26 Quay Ct., No. 65, sacramento, CA 95831-1540 USA Tel 916-427-7840
E-mail: regdown@hotmail.com.

Lightning Bug Flix, (978-1-933262) 1126 S. 70th St., Suite N601, Milwaukee, WI 53214 USA Tel 414-475-4445; Fax: 414-475-3621
E-mail: vicky@lightningbugflix.com
Web site: http://www.lightningbugflix.com.

Lightning Bug Learning Corporation *See* **Lightning Bug Learning Pr.**

Lightning Bug Learning Pr., (978-0-9817826; 978-0-9832098) Reviewer Relations Dept. 316 Mid Valley Ctr., #130, Carmel, CA 93923 USA (SAN 856-5449) Tel 831-250-1866; Fax: 971-250-2582; Toll Free: 877-695-7312
E-mail: mail@lightningbuglearning.com
Web site: http://www.lightningbuglearning.com; http://www.lightningbuglearningpress.com
Dist(s): **Book Clearing Hse.**

Lightning Creek *See* **Perceval Pr.**

Lightning Fast Bk. Publishing, (978-0-9916682; 978-0-9965411; 978-0-9974925; 978-0-9994653) 1812 Hollydale Rd., Fort Washington, MD 20744 USA Tel 240-605-1106
E-mail: matt@matthewchorne.com
Web site: www.lfbookpublishing.com.

Lightning Source, Inc., Orders Addr.: 1246 Heil Quaker Blvd., LaVergne, TN 37086 USA (SAN 179-6976) Tel 615-213-4595; Fax: 615-213-4426; 150 Fieldcrest Ave. Lightning Source, Edison, NJ 08837 (SAN 920-4288)
E-mail: terri.jones@lightningsource.com.

LightningBolt Pr., (978-0-9746398) 1481 Applegate Dr. Suite 101, Naperville, IL 60565-1225 USA Tel 630-778-7310; Fax: 630-778-7890
E-mail: info@mygreatdebate.net
Web site: http://www.greatdebate.net.

Lightwatcher Publishing *See* **Illumina Publishing**

Liguori Pubns., (978-0-7648; 978-0-89243) One Liguori Dr., Liguori, MO 63057-9999 USA (SAN 202-6783) Tel 636-464-2500; Fax: 636-464-8449; Toll Free Fax: 800-325-9526; Toll Free: 800-325-9521 (orders); *Imprints*: Libros Liguori (Libros Liguori)
E-mail: liguori@liguori.org
Web site: http://www.liguori.org
Dist(s): **ACTA Pubns.**
Follett School Solutions
MyiLibrary.

LikeMinds Pr., (978-0-9764724; 978-0-9915853) Orders Addr.: 3151 Airway Ave. Suite K-205 Suite K-205, Costa Mesa, CA 92626 USA Fax: 714-556-2354
E-mail: shendl@cox.net
Web site: http://www.likemindspress.com.

Lilac Pr., (978-0-9662568) Orders Addr.: P.O. Box 1356, Scottsdale, AZ 85252-1356 USA Fax: 480-368-5551; Edit Addr.: 6268 N. 85th St., Scottsdale, AZ 85250 USA
E-mail: lilacp@cholesterolnodiet.com; lilacp@frontiernet.net
Web site: http://www.cholesterolnodiet.com.

Lilacs in Liteartue, (978-0-692-74509-0; 978-0-692-74510-6; 978-0-9981958) 3014 Coventry Ct., Cocoa, FL 32926 USA Tel 321-525-9612
E-mail: wandalu64@gmail.com
Web site: www.wandaluthman.wordpress.com.

Lillenas Publishing Co., (978-0-8341) Div. of Nazarene Publishing Hse., P.O. Box 419527, Kansas City, MO 64141 USA (SAN 298-7619) Tel 816-931-1900; Fax: 816-753-4071; Toll Free Fax: 800-849-9827; Toll Free: 800-877-0700 (Orders Only)
E-mail: music@lillenas.com
Web site: http://www.lillenas.com
Dist(s): **Leonard, Hal Corp.**
Nazarene Publishing Hse.
Spring Arbor Distributors, Inc.

Lillian Press *See* **Smith & Assocs.**

Lillis, Holly, (978-0-9762733) P.O. Box 1082, Aptos, CA 95001-0000 USA.

Lill-Till Pr., (978-0-9742808) 15305 Walvem Blvd., Maple Heights, OH 44137 USA.

Lily & Co. Publishing, (978-1-929265) Orders Addr.: 15 Willow Rd., Greenville, RI 02828 USA
E-mail: erinesquedesign@mac.com
Web site: http://www.lilycopublishing.com.

Lily Wish Factory, (978-0-9792472) 44 W. Main St., Mystic, CT 06355 USA (SAN 852-8861) Tel 860-245-0629
E-mail: shipandshimmer@aol.com
Web site: http://shipandshimmer.com.

Lima Bear Pr LLC, The, (978-1-933872) 2305 MacDonough Rd., Wilmington, DE 19805 USA
E-mail: lbp.books@yahoo.com
Web site: http://www.limabearpress.com.

Limelight Editions *Imprint of* **Leonard, Hal Corp.**

Limerock Bks., (978-0-9746589) 15 Mechanic St., Thomaston, ME 04861 USA Tel 207-354-8191 Do not confuse with Limerock Books, Inc., New Canaan, CT
E-mail: limebks@midcoast.com
Web site: http://www.ChristopherFahy.com
Dist(s): **Brodart Co.**

Limitless Ink Press, LLC, (978-1-939672; 978-0-615-93665-9; 978-1-947218) P.O. Box 8802, Erie, PA 16505 USA Tel 913-271-7804
E-mail: patricemichelle@gmail.com.

Limitless Publishing, LLC, (978-0-615-68509-0; 978-0-615-76957-8; 978-0-615-78296-6; 978-0-615-78347-5; 978-1-68058; 978-1-64034) 701 N. Kalaheo, Kailua, HI 96734 USA
E-mail: jennifer@limitlesspublishing.com
Web site: www.limitlesspublishing.com
Dist(s): **CreateSpace Independent Publishing Platform.**

Lincoln Bks., (978-0-9910560) 406 Diana Ct., Highland Heights, OH 44124 USA Tel 440-813-0274
E-mail: robthomas@hotmail.com
Web site: Rob Thomas.

Lincoln, Emma *See* **Awesome Bk. Publishing**

Lincoln Library Pr., Inc., The, (978-0-912168) Orders Addr.: 812 Huron Rd., SE, Suite 401, Cleveland, OH 44115-1126 USA (SAN 205-5953) Fax: 216-781-9559 (phone/fax); Toll Free: 800-516-2656
E-mail: tgall@thelincolnlibrary.com
Web site: http://www.thelincolnlibrary.com
Dist(s): **Follett School Solutions**
INscribe Digital.

Lincoln Public Schls., (978-0-9671920) P.O. Box 82889, Lincoln, NE 68501 USA (SAN 508-9964) Tel 401-436-1628; Fax: 401-436-1638
E-mail: dpeters@lps.org
Web site: http://www.lps.org.

Linda Cardillo, Author *See* **Bellastoria Pr.**

Linda Hall Library, (978-0-9763590) 5109 Cherry St., Kansas City, MO 64110-2498 USA Tel 816-363-4600; Fax: 816-926-8790
E-mail: bradleyb@lindahall.org
Web site: http://www.lindahall.org.

Linda Kaye's Birthdaybakers, Partymakers, (978-0-9759161) 195 East 76th St., New York, NY 10021 USA Tel 212-288-7112; Fax: 212-879-6785
E-mail: lindak@partymakers.com
Web site: http://www.partymakers.com.

Lindaloo Enterprises, (978-0-9800923; 978-1-937564) P.O. Box 90135, Santa Barbara, CA 93190 USA; *Imprints*: Classic Bookwrights (ClassicBook)
E-mail: sales@lindaloo.com
Web site: http://www.lindaloo.com; http://www.tporigami.com
Dist(s): **Lightning Source, Inc.**

Linden Hill Publishing, (978-0-9704754; 978-0-9820153) Subs. of Arcadia Productions, 11923 Somerset Ave., Princess Anne, MD 21853 USA Tel 410-651-0757 (phone/fax)
E-mail: lindenhill2@comcast.net
Web site: http://www.lindenhill.net.

Linden Publishing Co., Inc., (978-0-941936; 978-1-933502; 978-1-61035) 2006 S. Mary, Fresno, CA 93721 USA (SAN 238-6089) Tel 559-233-6633 (phone/fax); Toll Free: 800-345-4447 (orders only) Do not confuse with LInden Publishing in Avon, NY
E-mail: richard@lindenpub.com
Web site: http://www.lindenpub.com
Dist(s): **CreateSpace Independent Publishing Platform**
Independent Pubs. Group
Ingram Publisher Services
Quality Bks., Inc.
Smashwords.

Lindisfarne Bks. *Imprint of* **SteinerBooks, Inc.**

Lindsay Pubns., Inc., (978-0-917914; 978-1-55918) Orders Addr.: P.O. Box 12, Bradley, IL 60915 USA (SAN 209-9462) Tel 815-935-5353; Fax: 815-935-5477.

Lindsley, David Studio, (978-0-9796008) P.O. Box 431, Springville, UT 84663 USA.

Line By Lion Pubns. *Imprint of* **3 Fates Pr.**

Linear Wave Publishing, (978-0-9767196) P.O. Box 177, Liberty, KY 42539-0177 USA Tel 606-787-8189
E-mail: blaine.staat@linearwavepublishing.com
Web site: http://www.linearwavepublishing.com.

Lingenfelser, Lynda L., (978-0-615-13290-7; 978-0-615-14072-8) 3284 Spruce Creek Glen, Daytona Beach, FL 32198 USA; P.O. Box 290714, Port Orange, FL 32129
Dist(s): **Lulu Pr., Inc.**

Linger Longer Books *See* **Artists' Orchard, LLC, The**

Lingo Pr. LLC, (978-0-9777419) 1020 Janet Dr., Lakeland, FL 33805 USA (SAN 850-119X) Tel 863-868-5996 (phone/fax)
E-mail: customerservice@lingopress.com
Web site: http://www.lingopress.com.

Linguatechnics Publishing, (978-0-9767837) 2114 Pauline Blvd., Ann Arbor, MI 48103 USA Tel 734-662-0434; Fax: 734-662-0248
E-mail: info@linguatechnics.com
Web site: http://www.linguatechnics.com.

LinguaText, Limited *See* **LinguaText, LLC**

LinguaText, LLC, (978-0-936388; 978-0-942566; 978-1-58871; 978-1-58977) Orders Addr.: 103 Walker Way, Newark, DE 19711-6119 USA (SAN 238-0307) Tel 302-453-8695
E-mail: text@linguatextltd.com
Web site: http://www.LinguatextLtd.com; http://www.EuropeanMasterpieces.com; http://www.JuandelaCuesta.com.

LinguiSystems, Inc., (978-0-7606; 978-1-55999) 3100 Fourth Ave., East Moline, IL 61244-9700 USA Tel 309-755-2300; Fax: 309-755-2377; Toll Free Fax: 800-776-4332; 800-577-4555
E-mail: kmicka@linguisystems.com
Web site: http://www.linguisystems.com.

Linhardt, Mitch, (978-0-578-13379-9; 978-0-578-17373-3; 978-0-578-18616-0; 978-0-578-18748-8) 921 Union Pl., Herculaneum, MO 63048 USA Tel 314-229-8689
E-mail: mclinhardt@yahoo.com.

Linive Kreyol Publishing, (978-0-9720954) 339 Howell Dr. SE, Suite 3-F, Atlanta, GA 30316 USA.

Link & Rosie Pr., (978-0-9762434) Orders Addr.: c/o Goblin Fern Press, Inc., 1118 Sequoia Trail, Madison, WI 53713 USA Tel 608-335-0542; Fax: 608-210-7235
E-mail: ssharron@sbcglobal.net
Web site: http://www.linkandrosie.com.

Linky & Dinky Enterprises, (978-0-9768588) P.O. Box 418, Oldsmar, FL 34677 USA
E-mail: uncle-url@linkydinky.com
Web site: http://www.linkydinky.com.

Linmore Publishing, Inc., (978-0-916591; 978-1-934472) Orders Addr.: P.O. Box 1545, Palatine, IL 60078 USA (SAN 662-2291) Fax: 612-729-9125; Toll Free: 800-336-3656
E-mail: linmore@linmore.com
Web site: http://www.linmore.com.

Linwood Hse. Publishing, (978-0-9753098) 843 Cypress Pkwy., No. 338, Kissimmee, FL 34759 USA Tel 407-595-6220
E-mail: zippityzem@comcast.net.

Linworth Publishing, Inc. *Imprint of* **ABC-CLIO, LLC**

Linx Educational Publishing, Inc., (978-1-891818; 978-0-9797510) P.O. Box 50009, Jacksonville Beach, FL 32240 USA Tel 904-241-1861; Fax: 904-241-3279; Toll Free Fax: 888-546-9338; Toll Free: 800-717-5469
E-mail: mimi@lixedu.com; info@linxedu.com
Web site: http://www.linxedu.com
Dist(s): **American Assn. for Vocational Instructional Materials**
Films Media Group
Follett School Solutions
JIST Publishing
S V E & Churchill Media.

†**Lion Bks.**, (978-0-87460) 235 Garth Rd. Apt. D5A, Scarsdale, NY 10583-3994 USA (SAN 241-7529)
Dist(s): **BookMasters, Inc.**; *CIP.*

Lion Forge, LLC, The, (978-0-9913324; 978-1-941302; 978-1-5493) 6600 Manchester Ave, Saint Louis, MO 63139 USA Tel 314-786-0800
E-mail: jen@lionforge.com; erika@lionforge.com
Web site: http://www.lionforge.com
Dist(s): **Diamond Comic Distributors, Inc.**
Diamond Bk. Distributors.

Lion Hudson PLC (GBR) (978-0-7459; 978-0-85648; 978-0-85721) *Dist. by* **Trafalgar.**

Lion Hudson PLC (GBR) (978-0-7459; 978-0-85648; 978-0-85721) *Dist. by* **Kregel.**

Lion Hudson PLC (GBR) (978-0-7459; 978-0-85648; 978-0-85721) *Dist. by* **IPG Chicago.**

Lion Prints Publishing, (978-0-9797699) Rhodes Ln., Suite 480, West Hempstead, NY 11552-1155 USA Tel 646-240-1633
E-mail: lesleynu@mac.com
Dist(s): **Lulu Pr., Inc.**

Lion Stone Bks., (978-0-9658486; 978-0-9859618) Orders Addr.: 4921 Aurora Dr., Kensington, MD 20895 USA Tel 301-949-3204; Fax: 301-949-3860
E-mail: lionstone@juno.com
Dist(s): **Book Wholesalers, Inc.**
Brodart Co.
Follett School Solutions.

Lioness Publishing, (978-0-9961606) 2120 W.96th St., Los Angeles, CA 90047 USA Tel 323-477-3530
E-mail: livia.latrice@gmail.com.

Lionheart Foundation, The, (978-0-9644933; 978-0-9799338) P.O. Box 194, Boston, MA 02117 USA Tel 781-444-6667; Fax: 781-444-6855
E-mail: judith@lionheart.org
Web site: http://www.lionheart.org.

Lionheart Pr., (978-0-9964246) 3711 Fews Ford Ln., Durham, NC 27712 USA Tel 919-812-6204
E-mail: hejafred@gmail.com
Web site: www.timberhowligan.com.

Lion's Crest Pr., (978-0-9763798) 1900 S. Rock Rd., Suite 5205, Wichita, KS 67207 USA Tel 316-305-5813.

Lions Den Publishing, LLC, (978-0-9786786) P.O. Box 91254, Washington, DC 20090-1254 USA (SAN 851-2477) Tel 202-256-0508
Dist(s): **Independent Pubs. Group.**

Lion's Tale Pr., LLC, (978-0-9748478) 4895 Kings Valley Dr., Suite 200, Roswell, GA 30075 USA Tel 770-998-3302; Fax: 770-998-3874
E-mail: ebbenator@mindspring.com.

LionX Publishing, (978-0-9716085) 24988 Blue Ravine Rd., #108-113, Folsom, CA 95630 USA (SAN 254-2021) Tel 916-939-9422; Fax: 916-939-9424
E-mail: info@lionxpublishing.com
Web site: http://www.lionxpublishing.com.

LIP Publishing LLC, (978-0-9771114) 903 Oakridge Dr, Suite 100, Round Rock, TX 78681 USA
E-mail: thelifeip@yahoo.com
Web site: http://www.thelifeip.com.

Lipp, G. Douglas & Assocs., (978-0-9707648) 3927 Edgevale Ct., Fair Oaks, CA 95628 USA Tel 916-962-1231; Fax: 916-962-0424
E-mail: pam@douglipp.com
Web site: http://douglipp.com.

†**Lippincott Williams & Wilkins**, (978-0-316; 978-0-397; 978-0-683; 978-0-7817; 978-0-8067; 978-0-8121; 978-0-88167; 978-0-89004; 978-0-89313; 978-0-89640; 978-0-911216; 978-1-881063; 978-1-60547; 978-1-60831; 978-1-60929; 978-1-4698) Orders Addr.: P.O. Box 1620, Hagerstown, MD 21741 USA Fax: 301-223-2400; Toll Free: 800-638-3030; Edit Addr.: 530 Walnut St., Philadelphia, PA 19106-3621 USA (SAN 201-0933) Tel 215-521-8300; Fax: 215-521-8902; Toll Free: 800-638-3030; 351 W. Camden St., Baltimore, MD 21201 Tel 410-528-4000; 410-528-4209
E-mail: custserv@lww.com; orders@lww.com
Web site: http://www.lww.com
Dist(s): **Igaku-Shoin Medical Pubs.**
MyiLibrary; *CIP.*

Lippincott-Raven Publishers *See* **Lippincott Williams & Wilkins**

Liquid Space Publishing, (978-0-9710366) 37 Endicott St., Salem, MA 01970 USA Tel 978-745-5529
E-mail: donniedives@earthlink.net
Web site: http://www.home.earthlink.net/~donniedives.

Lire Bks., (978-0-9849323; 978-1-939652) 7 Debaun Pl., Spring Valley, NY 10977 USA Tel 845-659-2018
E-mail: raedanbocs@gmail.com
Web site: lirebooks.com; http://simplylire.com.

Lisa Loucks Christenson Publishing, LLC, (978-1-878569; 978-0-9725311; 978-1-877275; 978-1-932542; 978-1-59819; 978-0-9771365) Orders Addr.: P.O. Box 9177, Rochester, MN 55903 USA; *Imprints*: Pickled Eggs Press (TM) (P E P); Waiting Room to Heaven (Wait Room Hvn); Cybereditions (TM) (MYID_A_CYBERED)
E-mail: lcpbooks@gmail.com; lisawtts@gmail.com; lisalc@protonmail.com
Web site: http://lisalc.com; http://bowwowdetectives.com; www.badgerbooks.com; www.entreepressllc.com; http://meowmeowdetectives.com; http://cybereditions.com; http://waubesapress.com; http://lisaloucksChristensonpublishing.com
Dist(s): **Ecompass Business Ctr.**

Lisa The Weather Wonder Inc., (978-0-9740997) 187 Summer Lake Dr., Marietta, GA 30060 USA
Web site: http://www.lisamozer.com.

Lisboa, David, (978-0-9752740) 9060 Palisade Ave., Apt. 307, North Bergen, NJ 07047 USA Tel 201-869-3494.

Listen & Live Audio, Inc., (978-1-885408; 978-1-931953; 978-1-59316) Orders Addr.: P.O. Box 817, Roseland, NJ 07068 USA Tel 201-558-9000; Fax: 201-558-9800; Toll Free: 800-653-9400; Edit Addr.: 1700 Manhattan Ave., Union City, NJ 07087-5473 USA
E-mail: Alfred@Listenandlive.com
Web site: http://www.listenandlive.com
Dist(s): **Audible.com**
Ebsco Publishing
Findaway World, LLC
Follett School Solutions
OverDrive, Inc.
Smashwords.

Listening Library *Imprint of* **Random Hse. Audio Publishing Group**

Listening Library (Audio) *Imprint of* **Penguin Random House Audio Publishing Group**

Lister, Tresina, (978-0-9791171) 541 S. Staunton Dr., Tucson, AZ 85710 USA Tel 520-751-8630.

Lit Torch Publishing, (978-1-887357) 4204 Danmire Dr., Richardson, TX 75082 USA Tel 312-239-8633 (phone/fax)
E-mail: littorch@gmail.com
Web site: http://www.littorch.com.

Lit Verlag (DEU) (978-3-8258; 978-3-89473; 978-3-88660; 978-3-643) *Dist. by* **Intl Spec Bk.**

Literacy Resources, Inc., *(978-0-9759575; 978-1-947260)* 143 Franklin Ave., River Forest, IL 60305-2113 USA Tel 708-366-5947; Fax: 708-366-9149
E-mail: tcorless@literacyresourcesinc.com
Web site: http://www.literacyresourcesinc.com.

Literal Publishing Inc., *(978-0-9770287; 978-0-9897957; 978-1-942307)* 5425 Renwick Dr., Houston, TX 77081 USA Tel 713-626-1433.

Literally Speaking Publishing Hse., *(978-1-929642)* 2020 Pennsylvania Ave., NW, No. 406, Washington, DC 20006 USA (SAN 852-8896) Tel 202-491-5774; Fax: 202-403-3535
E-mail: Distribution@LiterallySpeaking.com; bookinfo@literallyspeaking.com
Web site: http://www.literallyspeaking.com.

Literary Architects, LLC, *(978-1-933669)* 1427 W. 86th St., Suite 324, Indianapolis, IN 46260 USA Tel 317-462-6329
E-mail: info@literaryarchitects.com
Web site: http://www.literaryarchitects.com.

Literary Lessons *Imprint of* **HomeScholar Bks.**

Literary Licensing, LLC, *(978-1-258; 978-1-4940; 978-1-4941; 978-1-4978; 978-1-4979; 978-1-4980; 978-1-4981)* P.O. Box 1404, Whitefish, MT 59937 USA Fax: 406-897-7825
E-mail: literarylicensing@runbox.com
Web site: http://www.literarylicensing.com.

Literary Works Specialist, *(978-0-9746687)* P.O. Box 58908, New Orleans, LA 70158-8908 USA
E-mail: rdomio@aol.com
Web site: http://www.lwspublishing.net.

Literate Chigger Pr., Ink, Inc., The, *(978-0-9759042; 978-0-615-56517-0)* 1175 Queen Anne Rd., Teaneck, NJ 07666 USA Tel 201-741-6529
E-mail: emily@hipbo.org.

Literations, *(978-0-943514)* Div. of Dan Valenti Communications, P.O. Box 1845, Pittsfield, MA 01202 USA (SAN 240-706X) Tel 413-499-1459; *Imprints:* Raven Books (Raven Bks)
Dist(s): **Orca Bk. Pubs. USA.**

Literature Dramatization Pr., *(978-0-9644186)* 1089 Sunset Cliffs Blvd., San Diego, CA 92107-4037 USA Tel 619-222-2462
Dist(s): **Educational Bk. Distributors**
Empire Publishing Service
Lectorum Pubns., Inc.

LITHBTH Educational Services, *(978-0-9744920)* P.O. Box 55495, Hayward, CA 94545-5495 USA
E-mail: teachingkids@mindspring.com
Web site: http://www.home.mindspring.com/~teachingkids.

Litho Tech, LLC, *(978-0-9742791)* 3045 Highland Ave., Grants Pass, OR 97526 USA Tel 541-479-8905; Fax: 541-474-6937
E-mail: gpprint@charterinternet.com; lithotech541@charter.net.

Litkus Pr., *(978-1-932629)* P.O. Box 34785, Los Angeles, CA 90034 USA Tel 310-391-5629
E-mail: litkuspress@earthlink.net.

Little Acorn Assocs., Inc., *(978-0-9741579; 978-0-9844010; 978-1-937257; 978-1-946557)* P.O. Box 8787, Greensboro, NC 27419-8787 USA
E-mail: lilacorn@bellsouth.net.

Little Acorn LLC, *(978-0-9766703; 978-0-9964448)* Orders Addr.: 112 W. Calista Dr., Tahlequah, OK 74464-7446 USA
E-mail: info@littleacornkids.net
Web site: http://www.littleacornkids.net.

Little Adventures *Imprint of* **Amberjack Publishing Co.**

Little Balloon Pr., *(978-0-9843922)* 988 Belmont Terr., No. 2, Sunnyvale, CA 94086 USA (SAN 859-2721)
Web site: http://www.littleballoonpress.com.

Little Band Man Co., LLC, The, *(978-0-615-12596-1)* 1415 Easy St., New Iberia, LA 70560 USA Tel 337-365-4136; Fax: 337-365-4137
E-mail: jady@littlebandman.com
Web site: http://www.littlebandman.com.

Little Bay Pr., *(978-0-9745192)* 40 Salmon Beach, Tacoma, WA 98407 USA Tel 253-756-0987
E-mail: kcampbell@littlebaypress.com
Web site: http://www.littlebaypress.com.

Little Bee Books Inc., *(978-1-4998)* Div. of Bonnier Publishing USA, 251 Park Ave. S., 12th Flr., New York, NY 10016 USA Tel 917-280-6600; Toll Free: 844-321-0237
E-mail: info@littlebeebooks.com
Web site: http://www.littlebeebooks.com
Dist(s): **Simon & Schuster, Inc.**

Little Big Tomes, 1275 Trail Ridge Dr., Canyon Lake, TX 78133 USA Tel 830-899-6888
E-mail: cottage@gvtc.com.

Little Bigfoot *Imprint of* **Sasquatch Bks.**

Little Bird Bks., *(978-0-615-66291-6; 978-0-9913003)* 585 Mountain View Rd., Santa Cruz, CA 95065 USA
E-mail: masperling@gmail.com.

Little Bird Publishing, *(978-0-9728838)* 285 W. 8th St., Ship Bottom, NJ 08008 USA Tel 609-494-7485; Fax: 609-494-9569
E-mail: gwennhotaling@aol.com
Web site: http://www.gwennhotaling.com.

Little Blue Flower Pr. *Imprint of* **Grey Gate Media, LLC**

Little Blue Pr., *(978-0-9725584)* 14403 Little Blue Rd., Kansan City, MO 64136 USA Tel 816-455-1110
E-mail: littlebluepress@softhome.net.

Little Bookstore Who Could, The, *(978-0-9746997)* 1303 Windsong Way, Augusta, GA 30907 USA Tel 706-868-0075
E-mail: vickyharperselah@yahoo.com; vicky@thelittlebookstorethatcould.com
Web site: http://www.thelittlebookstorethatcould.coom.

Little Boost *Imprint of* **Picture Window Bks.**

Little Boots Publishing, *(978-0-9767230)* P.O. Box 3110, Pawtucket, RI 02861 USA Tel 401-475-5852 (phone/fax)
E-mail: Info@littlebootspublishing.com
Web site: http://www.littlebootspublishing.com.

Little Britches Childrens Bks., *(978-0-9798189)* P.O. Box 1188, Willow, AK 99688-1188 USA.

†**Little Brown & Co.**, *(978-0-316; 978-0-8212; 978-0-7595)* Div. of Hachette Bk. Group, Orders Addr.: 3 Center Plaza, Boston, MA 02108-2084 USA (SAN 630-7248) Tel 617-227-0730; Toll Free Fax: 800-286-9471; Toll Free: 800-759-0190; Edit Addr.: 237 Park Ave., New York, NY 10017 USA (SAN 200-2205) Tel 212-364-0600; Fax: 212-364-0952; *Imprints:* Back Bay Books (Back Bay); Mulholland Books (Mulholland Bk); Jimmy Patterson (JimmyPat)
E-mail: customer.service@hbgusa.com
Web site: http://www.hachettebookgroup.com
Dist(s): **Blackstone Audio, Inc.**
Continental Bk. Co., Inc.
Follett School Solutions
Grand Central Publishing
Hachette Bk. Group
Hastings Bks.
Lectorum Pubns., Inc.
MyiLibrary
Rounder Kids Music Distribution
Beeler, Thomas T. Pub.
TextStream
Thorndike Pr.; *CIP.*

Little, Brown Book Group Ltd. (GBR) *(978-0-09; 978-0-316; 978-0-349; 978-0-351; 978-0-7088; 978-0-7474; 978-0-7499; 978-0-7515; 978-0-8212; 978-0-86188; 978-0-948164; 978-1-85004; 978-1-85487; 978-1-85703; 978-1-85018; 978-1-84119; 978-0-7221; 978-0-86007; 978-0-9536151; 978-1-903608; 978-1-84529; 978-1-84528; 978-1-84901; 978-1-4087; 978-1-908974)* *Dist. by* **IPG Chicago.**

Little, Brown Book Group Ltd. (GBR) *(978-0-09; 978-0-316; 978-0-349; 978-0-351; 978-0-7088; 978-0-7474; 978-0-7499; 978-0-7515; 978-0-8212; 978-0-86188; 978-0-948164; 978-1-85004; 978-1-85487; 978-1-85703; 978-1-85018; 978-1-84119; 978-0-7221; 978-0-86007; 978-0-9536151; 978-1-903608; 978-1-84529; 978-1-84528; 978-1-84901; 978-1-4087; 978-1-908974)* *Dist. by* **HachBkGrp.**

Little, Brown Bks. for Young Readers, *(978-0-316; 978-0-8212; 978-0-7595; 978-0-7596)* Div. of Hachette Bk. Group, 1271 Ave. of the Americas, New York, NY 10020 USA Tel 212-522-8700; Fax: 212-522-2067; Toll Free: 800-343-9204; 3 Center Plaza, Boston, MA 02108-2084 USA Tel 617-227-0730; Toll Free Fax: 800-286-9471; Toll Free: 800-759-0190; *Imprints:* Tingley, Megan Books (Megan Tingley Bks); Poppy (Poppy)
Dist(s): **Blackstone Audio, Inc.**
Follett School Solutions
Grand Central Publishing
Hachette Bk. Group
Lectorum Pubns., Inc.
Little Brown & Co.
MyiLibrary.

Little Brown Children's Books *See* **Little, Brown Bks. for Young Readers**

Little Bunny Bks., *(978-0-615-46734-4; 978-0-615-58595-6; 978-0-615-66757-7; 978-0-692-48194-3)* P.O. Box 151, Cabin John, MD 20818 USA Tel 978-712-8669
E-mail: littlebunnybooks@gmail.com
Dist(s): **CreateSpace Independent Publishing Platform.**

Little Buzz Bk. Club, *(978-0-9975981; 978-1-947099-46-3)* 2146 Roswell Rd., Marietta, GA 30062 USA Tel 770-744-9390; Fax: 770-744-9390
E-mail: membership@littlebuzzbookclub.com
Web site: www.littlebuzzbookclub.com.

Little Chameleon Bks. *Imprint of* **Kid Prep, Inc.**

Little Clive Pr., *(978-0-615-58866-7; 978-0-615-69435-1; 978-0-615-79920-9; 978-0-9911479)* 306 N. 19th Ave., Kelso, WA 98626 USA Tel 503-381-3923
E-mail: bendertzu@yahoo.com; joey.wardell@gmail.com
Web site: www.littleclivepress.com.

Little Cottonwood River Bks., *(978-0-9884268)* 2918 71st St., Dundee, MN 56131 USA Tel 507-274-5316
E-mail: paplowp@gmail.com.

Little Creek Bks. *Imprint of* **Jan-Carol Publishing, INC.**

Little Creek Press, *(978-0-9828023; 978-0-9849245; 978-0-9896431; 978-0-9899780; 978-0-9899784; 978-1-942586)* Div. of Kristin Mitchell Design, LLC, 5341 Sunny Ridge Rd., Mineral Point, WI 53565 USA (SAN 920-2862) Tel 608-987-3370
E-mail: info@littlecreekpress.com
Web site: www.littlecreekpress.com.

Little Cubans, LLC, *(978-1-934113)* P.O. Box 260944, Pembroke Pines, FL 33026-7944 USA
E-mail: littlecubans@bellsouth.net
Web site: http://www.littlecubans.com.

Little, Cynthia M. *See* **Sleepless Warrior Publishing**

Little Deer Pr., *(978-1-891360)* P.O. Box 1220, Rainier, WA 98576 USA Tel 360-894-3459
E-mail: mollypiper@hotmail.com
Web site: http://www.focusbloom.com.

Little Devil Bks., *(978-0-9858280; 978-0-9911534)* 5139 Maxon Terr., Sanford, FL 32771 USA Tel 407-443-6494
E-mail: dave@littledevilbooks.com
Web site: www.littledevilbooks.com
Dist(s): **Lightning Source, Inc.**
Smashwords.

Little Dixie Publishing Co., *(978-0-9628099)* Orders Addr.: P.O. Box 215, Wynnewood, OK 73098 USA Tel 405-665-4811 Do not confuse with Rebel Pr., Chino, CA
E-mail: LittleDixie@itlnet.net
Web site: www.michaelandrewgrissom.com.

Little Dog Pubns., *(978-0-9774143)* P.O. Box 8680, Kansas City Missouri, MO 64114-0680 USA (SAN 257-5051)
E-mail: jeffr@littledogpress.net
Web site: http://littledogpress.net.

Little Fiddle Co., Inc., The, *(978-0-9700489; 978-0-9798643)* 700 Kinderkamack Rd., Oradell, NJ 07649 USA Fax: 201-265-6499; Toll Free: 888-678-5636
E-mail: info@minimaestro.com; jeofficemgr@osen.us
Web site: http://www.minimaestro.com
Dist(s): **Penton Overseas, Inc.**

Little Germ That Could..Creations, Inc., The, *(978-0-9763233; 978-0-9960186)* 6815 Edgewater Dr., No.108, Coral Gables, FL 33133 USA Tel 305-775-0281
Web site: www.littlegerm.com.

Little Guardians, Inc., *(978-0-9660879)* 111 Melody Dr., Metairie, LA 70001 USA Tel 504-837-3328; Fax: 504-835-9993; Toll Free: 800-582-4923.

Little Hands Bk. Co., LLC, *(978-0-9814878)* 32094 Vintage Way, Afton, OK 74331-5600 USA
Web site: http://www.littlehandsbook.com.

Little Hare Bks. (AUS) *(978-1-877003; 978-1-921049; 978-1-921272; 978-1-921541; 978-1-921714; 978-1-921894)* *Dist. by* **IPG Chicago.**

Little Hat Bks., *(978-0-9980763)* 13216 Mira Mar Dr, Sylmar, CA 91342 USA Tel 818-632-2909
E-mail: cloudgirlbook@gmail.com.

Little Hero, *(978-0-9769057)* P.O. Box 771371, Orlando, FL 32877 USA
E-mail: whitlockmatt@hotmail.com
Web site: http://www.littlehero.net.

Little Hill Pubs., *(978-0-9835048)* Orders Addr.: P.O. Box 282, Ashland, MA 01721 USA; Edit Addr.: 18 Pennock Rd., Ashland, MA 01721 USA Tel 508-881-0011
E-mail: contact@littlehillpublishers.com.

Little Hound Publishing *Imprint of* **E M McIntyre**

Little Hse. Pr., *(978-0-9773812)* 3618 Bayshore Rd., Sarasota, FL 34234 USA
Dist(s): **Independent Pubs. Group**
MyiLibrary.

Little Hse. Site Tours LLC, *(978-0-9765951)* 2430 Marlette Rd., Applegate, MI 48401 USA Tel 810-633-9973; Fax: 810-633-9027
E-mail: lhsitetours@email.com
Web site: http://www.lhsitetours.homestead.com.

Little Island (IRL) *(978-1-84840; 978-1-908195; 978-1-910411; 978-1-910031)* *Dist. by* **IPG Chicago.**

Little League Pr., *(978-0-9747883)* P.O. Box 249, Stanleytown, VA 24168 USA
E-mail: hooneybgood@adelphia.net
Dist(s): **Bassett Printing Corp.**

Little Light Pr., *(978-0-9755374)* Orders Addr.: 549 Broadway, Bethpage, NY 11714 USA Tel 516-938-3343 Do not confuse with Little Light Press in Oklahoma City, OK
E-mail: littlelightpress@yahoo.com
Web site: http://www.littlelightpress.biz.

Little Linguists Press, *(978-0-9777085)* P.O. Box 169, Owings Mills, MD 21117 USA.

Little Lion Pr., *(978-0-9796393)* 4911 Cumberland Ave., Chevy Chase, MD 20815 USA Tel 301-980-4344; Fax: 301-656-0086.

Little Lyrics Pubns., *(978-1-893429)* 12310 Old Barn Rd., Elbert, CO 80106 USA Tel 719-495-4941
E-mail: littlelyrics@prodigy.com
Web site: http://www.littlelyrics.com.

little m Bks., *(978-0-9830487)* 756 Pompton Ave., Cedar Grove, NJ 07009 USA Tel 201-704-7886
E-mail: wmadsen@me.com.

Little Mai Pr., *(978-1-893237)* 102 River Dr., Lake Hiawatha, NJ 07034 USA Tel 973-331-9648; Fax: 973-331-1856; Toll Free: 800-438-2719
E-mail: lmaipress@aol.com; f1promo@aol.com
Web site: http://www.littlemaipress.com.

Little Melody Pr. *Imprint of* **Brighter Minds Children's Publishing**

Little Moose Pr., *(978-0-9720227; 978-0-9786049; 978-0-9841021; 978-0-9841441; 978-0-9831161; 978-0-9838386; 978-0-9893988)* Orders Addr.: 269 S. Beverly Dr. #1065, Beverly Hills, CA 90212 USA (SAN 254-9778) Tel 310-862-2574; 310-862-2575; Toll Free: 866-234-0626
E-mail: ellen@littlemoosepresspub.com; bookshep@mac.com
Web site: http://www.littlemoosepresspub.com; www.louisegaylordauthor.com; www.pippinpb.com
Dist(s): **Book Clearing Hse.**
Pathway Bks.
Smashwords.

Little Munchkin Bks., *(978-0-9773936)* 2893 Rockefeller Rd., Willoughby Hills, OH 44092-1423 USA (SAN 257-411X) Tel 440-585-4950
E-mail: tara_tabernik@yahoo.com
Web site: http://www.littlemunchkinbooks.com.

Little Noggin LLC, *(978-0-9743760)* 1350 Grand Summit Dr., Suite 288, Reno, NV 89523 USA Tel 916-435-9737; Fax: 530-673-9680
E-mail: info@akidatart.com
Web site: http://www.akidatart.com.

Little Ones *Imprint of* **Port Town Publishing**

Little P Pr. Co., *(978-0-9853430)* 6387 Camp Bowie Blvd Ste B PMB No. 292, Fort Worth, TX 76116 USA Tel 817-501-8229
E-mail: pitch129@aol.com
Web site: ChazzKids.com.

Little Patriot Pr. *Imprint of* **Regnery Publishing, Inc., An Eagle Publishing Co.**

Little Paws Pr *Imprint of* **Veillette, Roseanne**

Little Pear Pr., *(978-0-9746911)* P.O. Box 343, Seekonk, MA 02771-1409 USA
Web site: http://www.littlepearpress.com.

Little Pemberley Pr., *(978-0-9763359)* Orders Addr.: 1528 Tulane St., Suite F, Houston, TX 77008-4146 USA Tel 713-862-8542; Fax: 713-862-6399
E-mail: littlepemberleypress@hotmail.com
Web site: http://www.giraffeofmontana.com; http://www.littlepemberleypress.com.

Little People Bks., *(978-0-9764114)* 2 Victor Ave., Worcester, MA 01603 USA Tel 508-963-2004.

Little Petals *Imprint of* **Roses Are READ Productions**

Little Pickle Press LLC *See* **March 4th, Inc.**

Little Pigeon Bks., *(978-0-9818976)* 5354 Washington St., Downers Grove, IL 60515 USA Tel 630-541-3700
Dist(s): **ebrary, Inc.**

Little Prince Publishing, *(978-0-615-46053-6; 978-0-615-46977-5; 978-0-615-47049-8; 978-0-9835220; 978-0-615-58516-1; 978-0-615-59301-2; 978-0-615-59908-3; 978-0-615-59909-0; 978-1-939947; 978-0-692-56834-7)* 7942 Indica Ct., North Charleston, SC 29418 USA
E-mail: sybilnelson@hotmail.com
Web site: www.sybilnelson.com; www.littleprincepublishing.com
Dist(s): **CreateSpace Independent Publishing Platform**
Dummy Record Do Not USE!!!!
Smashwords.

Little Red Acorns *Imprint of* **Little Red Tree Publishing LLC**

Little Red Cat Publishing, *(978-0-9726375)* 939A Terra Bella Ave., Mountainview, CA 94043 USA (SAN 254-9549) Tel 650-960-4040; Fax: 650-960-1040
E-mail: email@comprintingco.com; e-mail@comprintingco.com.

Little Red Tree Publishing LLC, *(978-0-9789446; 978-1-935656)* 509 W 3rd St., North Platte, NE 69101 USA (SAN 852-0143) Tel 860-287-1660; *Imprints:* Little Red Acorns (LR Acorns)
E-mail: mikelinnard@yahoo.co.uk
Web site: http://www.littleredtree.com.

Little Redhaired Girl Publishing, Inc., *(978-0-9729264)* 120 Riverside Blvd., #2e, New York, NY 10069 USA (SAN 857-6041) Fax: 225-410-6739; *Imprints:* Books for Brats (Books for Brats)
E-mail: booksforbrats@aol.com
Web site: http://www.booksforbrats.com.

Little River Bookshelf, *(978-0-9769856)* 2707 Silver Leaf Ct., Grapevine, TX 76051 USA Tel 817-308-2510
E-mail: mark.storer@usa.net.

Little Santa Bks., Inc., *(978-0-615-17411-2)* P.O. Box 806, Buffalo, NY 14220 USA Tel 716-316-1545
E-mail: sergioroguez@gmail.com
Web site: http://www.littlesantaclaus.com.

Little Scribblers Bks., LLC, *(978-0-9747689)* 2545 NW 55th Pl., Oklahoma City, OK 73112-7101 USA Tel 405-615-8662
E-mail: littlescribblers@cox.net
Web site: http://www.littlescribblers.com.

Little Shepherd *Imprint of* **Scholastic, Inc.**

Little Simon *Imprint of* **Little Simon**

Little Simon, *(978-0-671; 978-0-689; 978-1-4169)* Div. of Simon & Schuster Children's Publishing, 1230 Ave. of the Americas, New York, NY 10020 USA; *Imprints:* Little Simon (LSimon)
Dist(s): **Simon & Schuster**
Simon & Schuster, Inc.

Little Simon Inspirations *Imprint of* **Little Simon Inspirations**

Little Simon Inspirations, Div. of Simon & Schuster Children's Publishing, 1230 Ave. of the Americas, New York, NY 10020 USA; *Imprints:* Little Simon Inspirations (LSimonInsp)
Dist(s): **Simon & Schuster, Inc.**

Little Soundprints *Imprint of* **Soundprints**

Little Sprout Publishing Hse., *(978-0-9779194)* Orders Addr.: 520 Berry Way, La Habra, CA 90631 USA; *Imprints:* Psalms for Kidz (Psalms for Kidz)
Web site: http://psalmsforkidz.com.

Little Thoughts For Little Ones Publishing, Inc., *(978-0-9748884; 978-0-9861870)* Orders Addr.: P.O. Box 665, Tavernier, FL 33070 USA Fax: 305-852-4274
E-mail: vhandelsman@att.net
Web site: http://www.littlethoughtspublishing.net.

Little Tiger Pr., *(978-1-888444; 978-1-58431)* Div. of Futech Interactive Products, 39 S. La Salle St. Ste. 1410, Chicago, IL 60603-1706 USA Toll Free: 800-541-2205 Do not confuse Little Tiger Press in San Francisco, CA
E-mail: jody@futechsales.com
Dist(s): **Futech Educational Products, Inc.**
Lectorum Pubns., Inc.
MyiLibrary.

Little Treasure Bks., *(978-0-9639838; 978-0-9814571)* P.O. Box 362, Bensalem, PA 19020-0362 USA
Web site: http://www.littletreasurebooks.com.

Little Treasure Publications, Incorporated *See* **Little Treasure Bks.**

Little T's Corner *See* **Zadunajsky, Donna M.**

Little Tule Bks., *(978-0-9773133)* P.O. Box 549, Carmel Valley, CA 93924-0549 USA (SAN 257-2311) Tel 831-659-0107; Fax: 831-659-0106
E-mail: bill@littletulebooks.com
Web site: http://www.littletulebooks.com.

Little Vegan Monsters Publishing, *(978-0-9787590)* P.O. Box 9258, New Haven, CT 06533 USA
E-mail: Lourdes@littleveganmonsters.com
Web site: http://www.littleveganmonsters.com.

Little Way Pr., *(978-0-9764691)* 18252 Little Fuller Rd., Twain Harte, CA 95383 USA
Web site: http://www.littlewaypress.com
Dist(s): **Catholic Heritage Curricula.**

Little Willow Tree Bks., *(978-0-9743795)* 4900 Dodd St., Lynchburg, VA 24502 USA Do not confuse with Willow Tree Press in Monsey, NY
E-mail: willowtreebooks@yahoo.com.

Little Wooden Bks., *(978-0-929949)* 11001 S. Degray Ln., Spokane, WA 99224 USA (SAN 250-7943) Tel 509-932-4729.

Little Worm Publishing, *(978-0-9911382)* 920 Litchfield Pl., Roswell, GA 30076 USA Tel 706-258-8925
E-mail: hetheringtonlin@gmail.com
Web site: http://www.littlewormpub.com.

Littletonhouse Publishing, *(978-0-9746849)* Orders Addr.: P.O. Box 2954, Littleton, CO 80161-2954 USA (SAN 256-3371) Tel 303-740-2003; Fax: 303-771-0305
E-mail: info@thesecretcovebook.com; treis@littletonhousepublishing.com
Web site: http://www.thesecretcovebook.com; http://www.virobacter.com.

Liturgical Pr. Bks. *Imprint of* **Liturgical Pr.**

†**Liturgical Pr.**, *(978-0-8146; 978-0-916134)* Div. of Order of St. Benedict, Inc., Orders Addr.: a/o St. Johns Abbey, P.O. Box 7500, Collegeville, MN 56321-7500 USA (SAN 202-2494) Tel 320-363-2213; 612 363 2326; Fax:

Publisher Name Index

320-363-3299; Toll Free Fax: 800-445-5899; Toll Free: 800-858-5450; *Imprints:* Liturgical Press Books (Liturg Pr Bks)
E-mail: sales@litpress.org; bwoods@csbsju.edu
Web site: http://www.litpress.org; http://sjbible.org; http://cistercianpublications.com
Dist(s): **BookMobile**
Metapress
MyiLibrary; *CIP.*

Liturgy Training Pubns., *(978-0-929650; 978-0-930467; 978-1-56854; 978-1-61671; 978-1-61833)* Div. of Archdiocese of Chicago, 3949 S. Racine Ave., Chicago, IL 60609-2523 USA (SAN 670-9052) Toll Free Fax: 800-933-7094 (orders); Toll Free: 800-933-1800 (orders); *Imprints:* Catechesis of the Good Shepherd (Catechesis Good Shepherd)
E-mail: lguzman@ltp.org
Web site: http://www.ltp.org
Dist(s): **Faith Alive Christian Resources.**

Live Oak Games, *(978-0-9764394)* P.O. Box 780932, Orlando, FL 32878 USA Toll Free Fax: 800-214-4632 (phone/fax)
E-mail: sales@liveoakgames.com
Web site: http://www.liveoakgames.com.

Live Oak Media, *(978-0-87499; 978-0-941078; 978-1-59112; 978-1-59519; 978-1-4301)* Orders Addr.: P.O. Box 652, Pine Plains, NY 12567-0652 USA (SAN 217-3921) Tel 518-398-1010; Fax: 518-398-1070; Toll Free: 800-788-1121
E-mail: info@liveoakmedia.com
Web site: http://www.liveoakmedia.com
Dist(s): **AudioGO**
Ebsco Publishing
Findaway World, LLC
Follett School Solutions
Greathall Productions, Inc.
Lectorum Pubns., Inc.
Lerner Publishing Group.

†**Liveright Publishing Corp.,** *(978-0-87140; 978-1-63149)* Subs. of W. W. Norton Co., Inc., 500 Fifth Ave., New York, NY 10110 USA (SAN 201-0976) Tel 212-354-5500; Fax: 212-869-0856; Toll Free Fax: 800-458-6515; Toll Free: 800-233-4830
Web site: http://www.wwnorton.com
Dist(s): **Penguin Random Hse. LLC**; *CIP.*

Liverpool Univ. Pr. (GBR) *(978-0-85323; 978-1-84631; 978-1-78138) Dist. by* **OUP.**

Living Bks. Pr., *(978-0-9790876; 978-0-9818093; 978-1-938192)* 5497 S. Gilmore Rd., Mount Pleasant, MI 48858 USA (SAN 852-4114) Toll Free: 888-331-3481
E-mail: lbcinfo@livingbookscurriculum.com
Web site: http://www.livingbookscurriculum.com.

Living Dead Pr., *(978-1-935458; 978-1-61199)* 58 Dedham St., Revere, MA 02151 USA
Dist(s): **Smashwords.**

Living History Pr., *(978-0-9664925)* 7426 Elmwood Ave., Middleton, WI 53562 USA Tel 608-836-7426; Fax: 608-836-0176 Do not confuse with Living History Pr., Bellevue, WA
E-mail: pferd@itis.com
Web site: http://www.inwave.com/Milton/MiltonHouse/.

Living in Grace, *(978-0-9659319)* 10051 Siegen Ln., Baton Rouge, LA 70810 USA Tel 504-769-8844; Fax: 504-767-5655; Toll Free: 800-484-2046 ext. 9506
E-mail: QRBC@aol.com.

Living Ink Bks. *Imprint of* **AMG Pubs.**

Living Language *Imprint of* **Diversified Publishing**

Living Library Pr., *(978-0-692-74615-8; 978-0-692-81047-7; 978-0-692-83664-4; 978-0-692-87488-2)* 318 Meadow Dr., BRISTOL, VA 24201 USA Tel 276-644-9169.

Living Life Publishing Co., *(978-0-9768773; 978-0-9769166; 978-0-9774499; 978-1-934796)* Div. of Bianca Productions, LLC, 24165 IH-10, W., Suite 217-474, San Antonio, TX 78257 USA (SAN 256-5684) Tel 210-698-6392; Fax: 210-698-1754
E-mail: livinglifepublishing@msn.com
Web site: http://www.livinglifepublishing.com; http://www.biancaproductions.com.

Living Ministry, Inc., *(978-0-9763167)* 800 Prospect Blvd., Pasadena, CA 91103 USA Tel 626-356-9491; Fax: 626-584-0290
Web site: http://www.livingministry.com.

Living Stone Arts, *(978-0-9763901)* 3806 Owl Dr., Rolling Meadows, IL 60008 USA
Web site: http://www.livingstonearts.com.

Living Stream Ministry, *(978-0-7363; 978-0-87083; 978-1-57593; 978-1-5360)* 2431 W. La Palma Ave., Anaheim, CA 92801 USA (SAN 253-4266) Tel 714-236-6001; 714-991-4681; Fax: 714-991-4685; Toll Free: 800-549-5164
E-mail: books@lsm.org
Web site: http://www.lsm.org
Dist(s): **Anchor Distributors**
Spring Arbor Distributors, Inc.

Living the Good News *Imprint of* **Church Publishing, Inc.**

Living Water Pubns., *(978-1-59521)* P.O. Box 4653, Rockford, IL 61110-4653 USA Fax: 815-394-0140 Do not confuse with Living Water Publications in Edwardsville, KS
E-mail: lwministry@aol.com
Web site: http://www.livingwaterpublications.org.

Living Waters Publishing Co., *(978-0-9798154; 978-0-9814532; 978-0-9821153)* P.O. Box 1361, Marion, AR 72364-1361 USA
E-mail: administration@livingwaterspc.com
Web site: http://www.livingwaterspc.com
Dist(s): **Lightning Source, Inc.**

Livingston Pr., *(978-0-930501; 978-0-942979; 978-1-931982; 978-1-60489)* Div. of Univ. of West Alabama, Univ. of West Alabama, Sta. 22, Livingston, AL 35470 USA (SAN 851-917X) Tel 205-652-3470; Fax: 205-652-3717; Toll Free: 800-959-3245 Do not confuse with Livingston Pr., Anaheim, CA
E-mail: jwt@uwa.edu
Web site: http://www.livingstonpress.uwa.edu
Dist(s): **SPD-Small Pr. Distribution.**

Livingstone Corporation *See* **Barton-Veerman Co.**

Livraria Martins Editora (BRA) *(978-85-336) Dist. by* **Distribks Inc.**

LizStar Bks, *(978-0-9779753)* 2648 Jolly Acres Rd., White Hall, MD 21161 USA Tel 410-557-9388
E-mail: tracy@lizstarbooks.com
Web site: http://www.lizstarbooks.com.

Lizzy Anne's Adventures, *(978-0-9845887; 978-0-9835168)* P.O. Box 97, Monrovia, MD 21770-0097 USA (SAN 859-8320)
Web site: http://www.lizzyannesadventures.com.

LJK Publishing LLC, *(978-0-9771476)* P.O. Box 993, Springer, NM 87747 USA Tel 505-483-2451 (fax as well - phone to turn on)
E-mail: chieftalkjaw@aol.com.

LJM Publishing, *(978-0-615-46906-5; 978-0-615-48518-8; 978-0-9897175; 978-0-615-92333-8; 978-0-9861946)* 2597 CR 2101, Palestine, TX 75801 USA Tel 214-956-5656; 817-703-1844
Web site: www.RachelsLittleQuoteBook.org
Dist(s): **CreateSpace Independent Publishing Platform.**

Llama Press *See* **Birchall Publishing**

†**Llewellyn Pubns.,** *(978-0-7387; 978-0-87542; 978-1-56718)* Div. of Llewellyn Worldwide, Ltd., Orders Addr.: 2143 Wooddale Dr., Woodbury, MN 55125-2989 USA Tel 651-291-1970; Fax: 651-291-1908; Toll Free: 800-843-6666; *Imprints:* Flux (FluxUSA)
E-mail: sales@llewellyn.com
Web site: http://www.llewellyn.com; http://www.midnightinkbooks.com
Dist(s): **Follett School Solutions**
Lectorum Pubns., Inc.
Libros Sin Fronteras
Llewellyn Worldwide Ltd.
New Leaf Distributing Co., Inc.
Partners/West Book Distributors
Perrone; *CIP.*

Llumina Christian Bks. *Imprint of* **Aeon Publishing Inc.**

Llumina Kids *Imprint of* **Aeon Publishing Inc.**

Llumina Pr. *Imprint of* **Aeon Publishing Inc.**

LM Azpiazu, *(978-0-692-58185-8; 978-0-692-59170-3)* 3519 Woodlawn Dr., HONOLULU, HI 96822 USA Tel 808-988-6158.

LM Digital, *(978-0-9760770)* 4501 Mirador Dr., Pleasanton, CA 94566-7435 USA
E-mail: luke@lm-digital.com
Web site: http://www.lm-digital.com.

LMA Publishing, *(978-0-692-63132-4)* 8635 W Sahara Ave, Las Vegas, NV 89117 USA Tel 310-402-8677
E-mail: mzabner08@gmail.com.

LMS Bks., *(978-0-9764185)* 1007 Manor Dr., Ripon, CA 95366 USA Tel 209-599-4685.

LMW Works, *(978-1-889584)* 85 St. Michael Way NE., Hanceville, AL 35077 USA Tel 716-946-1060
E-mail: lynne@lmwworks.com; pviverito@yahoo.com
Web site: http://www.lmwworks.com.

LOA Quantum Growth LLC, *(978-0-9786158)* 7805 Tylerton Dr., Raleigh, NC 27613-1554 USA Tel 919-368-8041; Fax: 919-571-8769
E-mail: publisher@loaquantumgrowth.com
Web site: http://www.loaquantumgrowth.com
Dist(s): **Bookmasters Distribution.**

Lobster Pr. (CAN) *(978-1-894222; 978-1-897073) Dist. by* **Orca Bk Pub.**

Local Color Pr., *(978-0-9716607; 978-0-578-18575-0; 978-0-578-18576-7)* 526 W. 26th St., Studio No. 506, New York, NY 10001 USA Tel 212-242-2660; Fax: 212-242-2661
E-mail: localcolorpress@aol.com
Web site: http://www.localcolorpress.com.

Local History Co., The, *(978-0-9711835; 978-0-9744715; 978-0-9770429)* Orders Addr.: 112 N. Woodland Rd., Pittsburgh, PA 15232 USA (SAN 257-5264); *Imprints:* Towers Maguire Publishing (Towers Mag)
E-mail: Sales@TheLocalHistoryCompany.com; Sales@TowersMaguire.com
Web site: http://www.TheLocalHistoryCompany.com; http://www.TowersMaguire.com.

Lock & Mane, *(978-0-615-20562-5; 978-0-615-30969-9; 978-0-615-62282-8)* 2012 Spring Garden St., No. 3, Philadelphia, PA 19130 USA.

Lockman, James Consulting, *(978-0-9759988)* P.O. Box 278, Gorham, ME 04038-0278 USA
E-mail: james@jameslockman.com
Web site: http://www.jameslockman.com.

Lockman, Vic, *(978-0-936175)* 233 Rogue River Hwy No. 360, Grants Pass, OR 97527 USA (SAN 697-2063) Fax: 541-472-1083
E-mail: vlockman@budget.net.

Lodestone Pr., *(978-0-9678922)* 17 Appleby Rd., Suite B-2, Wellesley, MA 02482 USA
E-mail: books@lodestone.nu
Web site: http://www.lodestone.nu.

Loew-Cornell, Inc., *(978-0-9776925; 978-0-9794445)* Div. of Jarden Corporation, 2834 Schoeneck Rd., Macungie, PA 18062-9679 USA
E-mail: joleary@loew-cornell.com
Web site: http://www.loew-cornell.com
Dist(s): **Watson-Guptill Pubns., Inc.**

Loewe Verlag GmbH (DEU) *(978-3-7855; 978-3-8390) Dist. by* **Distribks Inc.**

LoewenHerz-Creative *See* **LHC Publishing**

LOF Publishing, *(978-0-9764441)* Orders Addr.: 7500 Bellerive, Suite 412, Houston, TX 77036 USA Tel 832-251-6867
E-mail: pslam144ym@aol.com; info@lofpublishing.com
Web site: http://www.lofpublishing.com; http://www.mbridges05.com.

Log Cabin Bks., *(978-0-9755548; 978-0-9848911; 978-0-9973251)* 6607 Craine Lake Rd., Hamilton, NY 13346 USA Tel 315-750-9157
Web site: http://www.logcabinbooks.us/; http://www.logcabinbooks.com/.

Logan Bks., *(978-0-9728691)* P.O. Box 21451, Columbia Heights, MN 55421 USA
Web site: http://www.loganbooks.com.

Logan Hse., *(978-0-9674123; 978-0-9769935)* Orders Addr.: Rte. 1, Box 154, Winside, NE 68790 USA Tel 402-286-4891; Edit Addr.: Rte. 1 Box 154, Winside, NE 68790 USA
E-mail: jim@loganhousepress.com
Web site: http://www.loganhousepress.com.

Logos Productions, Inc., *(978-0-9618891; 978-1-885361)* 6160 Carmen Ave., E., Inver Grove Heights, MN 55076-4422 USA Tel 612-451-9945; Fax: 612-457-4617; Toll Free: 800-328-0200 Do not confuse with Logos Productions, Carmel, CA
E-mail: lpstaff@mn.uswest.net
Web site: http://www.1logos.com.

LOGOS System Assocs., *(978-0-9727146; 978-0-9752605; 978-0-9768168)* 1405 Frey Rd., Pittsburgh, PA 15235 USA Tel 412-372-1341; Fax: 412-372-8447; Toll Free: 877-937-2572
E-mail: patjanssen@logos-system.org
Web site: http://www.logos-system.org.

Logos-Rhema Publishing *See* **Triumph Publishing**

Lollipop Media Productions, LP, *(978-0-9815111; 978-0-9824926; 978-0-9909073)* 3600 S. Harbor Blvd. Apt No. 81 Apt. No. 81, Channel Islands Harbor, CA 93035 USA
E-mail: Suzy@keopu.com.

Lollipop Publishing, LLC, *(978-0-9709793; 978-1-931737)* P.O. Box 6354, Chesterfield, MO 63006-6354 USA Tel 314-434-6011; Fax: 314-434-6040; Toll Free: 800-383-7767
E-mail: jbenigas@aol.com
Web site: http://www.lollipoppublishing.com.

Lollipop Publishing, LLC, *(978-0-615-30165-5)* 10710 Moore Cir., Westminster, CO 80021 USA.

Loma, LLC, *(978-0-9769460)* 6 Bryan Valley Ct., O'Fallon, MO 63366-3465 USA
E-mail: dudleytg@aol.com.

London Publishing, *(978-0-578-15413-8; 978-0-578-16496-0; 978-0-578-16507-3)* 84 Red Alder Court, Danville, CA 94506 USA
E-mail: jrespanosa@yahoo.com
Web site: http://www.myspiffykids.com
Dist(s): **Outskirts Pr., Inc.**

London Town Pr., *(978-0-9666490; 978-0-9766134; 978-0-9799759)* 2026 Hilldale Dr., La Canada, CA 91011 USA
E-mail: martin@londontownpress.com
Web site: http://www.londontownpress.com
Dist(s): **Publishers Group West (PGW).**

Lone Butte Pr., *(978-0-9666860; 978-0-9893518)* 32 S. Fork Extended, Santa Fe, NM 87508 USA Tel 505-424-3574; Fax: 505-473-1227
E-mail: wilddogbooks@cnsp.com
Dist(s): **Wild Dog Bks.**

Lone Cypress Pubs., *(978-0-9741413)* 3588 Hwy. 138 S.E., No. 193, Stockbridge, GA 30281 USA Tel 404-421-7445
E-mail: graysenwalles@yahoo.com
Web site: http://www.lonecypresspublishers.com.

Lone Dragonfly Bks., *(978-0-9967350)* 5565 Seminary Rd. Apt. 105, Falls Church, MD 22041 USA Tel 443-824-6854
E-mail: geoff@lonedragonflybooks.com
Web site: http://lonedragonflybooks.com.

Lone Oak Pr., Ltd. *Imprint of* **Finney Co., Inc.**

Lone Pine Publishing USA, Orders Addr.: 1808 B St., NW Suite 140, Auburn, WA 98001 USA (SAN 859-0427) Tel 253-394-0400; Fax: 253-394-0405; Toll Free Fax: 800-548-1169; Toll Free: 800-518-3541; *Imprints:* Ghost House Books (Ghost Hse Bks)
E-mail: mikec@lonepinepublishing.com
Web site: http://www.lonepinepublishing.com; http://www.companyscoming.com/; http://overtimebooks.com; http://www.folklorepublishing.com/.

Lone Star Pubns., *(978-0-9766157)* P.O. Box 810872, Dallas, TX 75381 USA Do not confuse with Lone Star Publication in Dallas, TX
E-mail: info@lonestarpublications.com
Web site: http://www.lonestarpublications.com.

Lone Star Publishing Co., *(978-0-9777274)* 906 SW St., Lucie W. Blvd., Port Saint Lucie, FL 34986 USA Tel 772-486-3214; Fax: 772-785-8496 do not confuse with companies with the same name in Paradise, TX, Amarillo, TX, Bryan, TX.

Lone Wolf Productions *See* **Canis Lupus Productions**

Lonejack Mountain Pr., *(978-0-9729101)* P.O. Box 28424, Bellingham, WA 98228-0424 USA.

Lonely Child Pr., *(978-0-9969401)* 16200 Mitchell Creek Dr., Fort Bragg, CA 95437 USA Tel 707-964-6810
E-mail: grorby@mcn.org
Web site: www.ginnyrorby.org.

Lonely Planet Pubns., *(978-1-55992)* Orders Addr.: 150 Linden St., Oakland, CA 94607 USA (SAN 659-6541) Tel 510-893-8555; Fax: 510-893-8572; Toll Free: 800-275-8555 (orders, 9am - 5pm Pacific Time)
E-mail: orders@lonelyplanet.com; customerservice@lonelyplanet.com
Web site: http://www.lonelyplanet.com.

Lonely Swan Bks. *Imprint of* **Cosmic Gargoyle Creative Solutions**

Lonestar Abilene Publishing *Imprint of* **LoneStar Abilene Publishing, LLC**

LoneStar Abilene Publishing, LLC, *(978-0-9749725)* 402 Cedar St., Suite 208, Abilene, TX 79601 USA Tel 325-676-9800; Fax: 325-676-2790; *Imprints:* Lonestar Abilene Publishing (LoneStarAbil)
E-mail: michael@yrbks.com
Web site: http://www.yrbks.com/LoneStar.html.

Long Beach City Schl. District, *(978-0-9677925)* 235 Lido Blvd., Lido Beach, NY 11561 USA Tel 516-897-2104; Fax: 516-897-2107
E-mail: RLF@li.net.

Long Dash Publishing, *(978-1-59899)* 49 Orchard St., Hackensack, NJ 07601-4806 USA
E-mail: longdash@gmail.com
Web site: http://www.longdash.com.

Long, George Children's Books, *(978-0-9844946)* P.O. Box 3672, Irmo, SC 29063 USA Tel 803-781-5528
E-mail: GL@GeorgeLongChildrensBooks.com
Web site: www.GeorgeLongChildrensBooks.com.

Long Life Publishing Co., *(978-0-9725836)* P.O. Box 1564, Escondido, CA 92033 USA.

Long Riders' Guild Pr., The, *(978-1-59048)* 2201 Coyle Ln., Walla Walla, WA 99362-8873 USA
E-mail: longriders@thelongridersguild.com
Web site: http://www.thelongridersguild.com.

Long Stories LLC, *(978-0-615-15295-0; 978-0-615-18961-1)* N3865 County Rd. H, Lake Geneva, WI 53147 USA
E-mail: chad@lycanjournal.com
Web site: http://www.lycanjournal.com.

Longevity Publishing, LLC, *(978-0-9777323)* Orders Addr.: 10179 E. Pinewood Ave., Englewood, CO 80111 USA Tel 720-489-7243
E-mail: info@longevitypublishing.com
Web site: http://www.longevitypublishing.com
Dist(s): **Partners Bk. Distributing, Inc.**

LongHill Partners, Inc., *(978-0-943763; 978-1-58023; 978-1-879045; 978-1-893361; 978-1-59473; 978-0-9904152)* P.O. Box 237, Woodstock, VT 05091 USA; *Imprints:* Jewish Lights Publishing (JewishLights); Skylight Paths Publishing (SkylightPaths)
E-mail: production@longhillpartners.com
Dist(s): **Ingram Publisher Services.**

Longhorn Creek Pr., *(978-0-9714358; 978-0-9764026; 978-0-615-99574-8)* 3780 County Road 4317., De Kalb, TX 75559-5681 USA
E-mail: editor@longhorncreekpress.com; Ron@longhorncreekpress.com
Web site: http://www.longhorncreekpress.com
Dist(s): **CreateSpace Independent Publishing Platform**
Wilson & Assocs.

Longman Publishing, *(978-0-02; 978-0-06; 978-0-13; 978-0-201; 978-0-205; 978-0-321; 978-0-582; 978-0-673; 978-0-7248; 978-0-8013; 978-1-57322; 978-0-7339)* 75 Arlington St., Boston, MA 02116 USA Tel 617-848-7500
Web site: http://www.aw-bc.com
Dist(s): **Giron Bks.**
Libros Sin Fronteras
Pearson Education.

†**Longman Publishing Group,** *(978-0-13; 978-0-201; 978-0-321; 978-0-582; 978-0-8013)* Div. of Addison Wesley Longman, Inc., The Longman Bldg., 10 Bank St., White Plains, NY 10606-1951 USA (SAN 202-6856) Tel 914-993-5000; Fax: 914-997-8115 800-922-0579 (college, bkstores, customer service only)
Web site: http://www.pearsonlongman.com
Dist(s): **Coronet Bks.**
Giron Bks.
MyiLibrary
Pearson Education
Pearson Technology Group
Sourcebooks, Inc.
Trans-Atlantic Pubns., Inc.; *CIP.*

Longoria, Eugene R., *(978-0-9796818)* 2222 W. Central Ave., Coolidge, AZ 85228 USA (SAN 854-1116)
E-mail: ElJunior@ElJunior.com
Web site: http://eljunior.com; http://eugenelongoria.com.

Longs Peak Publishing, Incorporated *See* **Crossing Guard Bks., LLC**

Longseller S.A. (ARG) *(978-987-550; 978-987-9481; 978-987-98516) Dist. by* **Bilingual Pubns.**

Longseller S.A. (ARG) *(978-987-550; 978-987-9481; 978-987-98516) Dist. by* **Libros Fronteras.**

LongTale Publishing, LLC, *(978-0-9818054; 978-0-9854705; 978-1-941515)* P.O. Box 266597, Houston, TX 77207-6597 USA Fax: 713-896-9701
Web site: http://www.iggytheiguana.com.

Look Again Pr., LLC, *(978-0-9801113)* 2461 Mountain Vista Dr., Birmingham, AL 35243 USA (SAN 855-2266) Tel 205-823-8556
Web site: www.lookagainpress.com
Dist(s): **CreateSpace Independent Publishing Platform.**

Look, Learn & Do Pubns., *(978-1-893327)* 24 Highland Blvd., Kensington, CA 94707 USA Fax: 510-524-7577
E-mail: professor@lldkids.com
Web site: http://www.lookleamanddo.com
Dist(s): **Ten Speed Pr.**

Look-About Bks., *(978-0-9800208)* P.O. Box 1907, Nampa, ID 83653 USA (SAN 854-9869) Tel 208-466-6260
E-mail: lpowersraptor@msn.com
Web site: http://www.look-aboutbooks.com.

Looking Glass Library *Imprint of* **ABDO Publishing Co.**

Looking Glass Library *Imprint of* **Magic Wagon**

Looking Glass Library- Nonfiction *Imprint of* **Magic Wagon**

Loon Song Publishing, *(978-0-9965070)* P.O. Box 14663, Portland, OR 97293 USA Tel 503-267-6339
E-mail: nick@nvasilieff.com
Web site: www.nvasilieff.com.

Loonfeather Pr., *(978-0-926147)* Orders Addr.: P.O. Box 1212, Bemidji, MN 56619 USA
E-mail: books@loonfeatherpress.com
Web site: http://www.loonfeatherpress.com.

Loose Cannon, *(978-0-9851292; 978-1-939812; 978-1-944476)* 444 Sutter St., Petaluma, CA 94954 USA Tel 530-762-7002
E-mail: stevhutch@loose-cannon.com.

Loose Change, *(978-0-944707)* 936 Sixth St., Los Banos, CA 93635 USA (SAN 244-9692) Tel 209-826-3797; Fax: 209-826-1514
E-mail: nco4242@sbcglobal.net.

Loose In The Lab, *(978-0-9660965; 978-1-931801)* 9462 S. 560 W., Sandy, UT 84070 USA Tel 801-568-9596; Fax: 801-568-9586; Toll Free: 888-403-1189
E-mail: mail@looseinthelab.com
Web site: http://www.looseinthelab.com.

Loose Leaves Publishing, *(978-1-62432)* 4218 E. Allison Rd, Tucson, AZ 85712 USA Tel 520-310-7528
E-mail: Talminia@gmail.com.

Looseleaf Law Pubns., Inc., *(978-0-930137; 978-1-889031; 978-1-932777; 978-1-60885)* Orders Addr.: P.O. Box 650042, Fresh Meadows, NY 11365-0042 USA Tel 718-359-5559; Fax: 718-539-0941; Toll Free: 800-647-5547
E-mail: info@looseleaflaw.com; lynette@looseleaflaw.com
Web site: http://www.looseleaflaw.com.

Loosey Goosey Pr., *(978-0-9820991)* 120 Daven Dr., Hopkinsville, KY 42240 USA (SAN 857-2623)
Web site: http://www.ganderpress.com.

Lopez, David, *(978-0-9744097)* 3441 Twinberry Ct., Bonita Springs, FL 34134 USA Tel 239-947-2532 (phone/fax)
E-mail: jazzpop@aol.com
Web site: http://www.maddiesmagicmarkers.com.

Loquacious Publishing Co., *(978-0-9763811)* 2115 Wintermere Pointe Dr., Winter Garden, FL 34787-5439 USA.

Loqueleo *Imprint of* **Santillana USA Publishing Co., Inc.**

LORE Mountain Productions, *(978-0-9970294; 978-1-946807)* 20875 Jerusalem Grade, Lower Lake, CA 95457 USA Tel 707-987-8577; *Imprints:* MonkeyBear Publishing (MonkeyBear Pub)
E-mail: info@loremountain.com
Web site: www.gracieandmonkeybear.com; www.loremountain.com.

Lorenz Corp., The, *(978-0-7877; 978-0-88335; 978-0-89328; 978-1-55863; 978-1-57310; 978-1-885564; 978-1-4291)* 501 E. Third St., Dayton, OH 45401-0802 USA (SAN 208-7413) Tel 937-228-6118; Fax: 937-223-2042; Toll Free: 800-444-1144
E-mail: service@lorenz.com
Web site: http://www.lorenz.com.

Lorian Assn., The, *(978-0-936878)* P.O. Box 1368, Issaquah, WA 98027 USA (SAN 666-6663) Tel 425-427-9071
E-mail: info@lorian.org
Web site: http://www.lorian.org.

Lorian Press *See* **Lorian Assn., The**

Lorimer & Pine Press *See* **Lorimer Pr.**

Lorimer, James & Co., Ltd., Pubs. (CAN) *(978-0-88862; 978-1-55028; 978-1-55277; 978-1-4594) Dist. by* **Orca Bk Pub.**

Lorimer, James & Co., Ltd., Pubs. (CAN) *(978-0-88862; 978-1-55028; 978-1-55277; 978-1-4594) Dist. by* **Casemate Pubs.**

Lorimer Pr., *(978-0-9704651; 978-0-9789342; 978-0-9826171; 978-0-9838936; 978-0-9897885; 978-0-9961884)* Div. of LBR Holdings, Orders Addr.: 619 Lorimer Rd., Davidson, NC 28036 USA; Edit Addr.: P.O. Box 1013, Davidson, NC 28036 USA Tel 704-896-8998
E-mail: leslie.b@att.net
Dist(s): **Midpoint Trade Bks., Inc.**
Partners Pubs. Group, Inc.

Lorito Bks., Inc., *(978-0-9815686; 978-0-9842981; 978-0-9835197; 978-0-9883561; 978-0-9904930)* 10395 W. 74th Pl., Arvada, CO 80005 USA (SAN 855-8876) Fax: 303-425-3277; Toll Free: 800-420-6936
Web site: http://www.loritobooks.com
Dist(s): **Follett School Solutions.**

Lormax Communications, *(978-0-9641239)* P.O. Box 40304, Raleigh, NC 27629 USA Tel 919-878-9108.

Los Alamos Historical Society Publications *See* **Bathtub Row Pr.**

Los Andes Publishing Co., *(978-0-9637065; 978-1-57159)* P.O. Box 190, Chino Hills, CA 91709 USA Tel 562-789-1540; Toll Free: 800-532-8872
E-mail: losandes@losandes.com
Web site: http://www.losandes.com
Dist(s): **Lectorum Pubns., Inc.**

Los Perros Publishing Co., *(978-0-9764685)* 3565 Parches Cove, Union Grove, AL 35175-8422 USA
E-mail: jr@losperros.com; mrgsd@hiwaay.net
Web site: http://www.mrgsd.com.

Losantiville Pr., Inc., *(978-0-9794946)* Orders Addr.: P.O. Box 42604, Cincinnati, OH 45242-6040 USA; Edit Addr.: 7012 Beech Hollow Dr., Cincinnati, OH 45236 USA
E-mail: losantivillepress@fuse.net.

Lost Candy Bar Pr., LLC, *(978-0-9786794)* P.O. Box 5193, Madison, WI 53705-0193 USA Tel 608-233-5690; Fax: 608-231-2312
Web site: http://www.lostcandybarpress.com.

Lost Classic Bks.,
Dist(s): **National Bk. Network.**

Lost Classics Bk. Co., *(978-0-9652735; 978-1-890623)* Orders Addr.: P.O. Box 1756, Fort Collins, CO 80522 USA Tel 970-493-3793 (Distribution Center); Toll Free Fax: 888-211-2665 (Libraries & Schools); Toll Free: 888-611-2665 (credit card orders only); Edit Addr.: P.O. Box 3429, Lake Wales, FL 33859-3429 USA Tel 863-678-3149; Fax: 863-678-0802
E-mail: mgeditor@lostclassicsbooks.com
Web site: http://lcbcbooks.com; http://www.lcbcbooks.com/homeright.htm
Dist(s): **National Bk. Network.**

Lost Coast Pr., *(978-1-882897; 978-1-935448)* 155 Cypress St., Fort Bragg, CA 95437 USA Tel 707-964-9520; Fax: 707-964-7531; Toll Free: 800-773-7782
E-mail: forms@cypresshouse.com
Web site: http://www.cypresshouse.com
Dist(s): **Continental Bk. Co., Inc.**
Cypress Hse.
New Leaf Distributing Co., Inc.
Partners/West Book Distributors.

Lost Hills Bks., *(978-0-9798535)* P.O. Box 3054, Duluth, MN 55803 USA (SAN 854-5553)
Web site: http://www.losthillsbks.com.

Lost Lake Pr., *(978-0-9906450; 978-0-9981736)* N7130 N. Lost Lake Rd., Randolph, WI 53956 USA Tel 920-326-5554
E-mail: LostLakePress@gmail.com
Web site: http://www.LostLakePress.com.

Lost Scout Pr., *(978-0-9741310)* P.O. Box 86, Loveland, OH 45140-0086 USA (SAN 255-7193) Fax: 719-457-5952; 1283 Sand Trap Ct., Loveland, OH 45140-6060
E-mail: hq@lostscout.com
Web site: http://www.lostscout.com.

Lotti, Marc, *(978-1-932341)* P.O. Box 5841, Carefree, AZ 85377-5841 USA
E-mail: mlotti@mandragore.com.

Lotus Art Works Inc., *(978-0-9800637)* 11833 Mississippi Ave., Suite 200, Los Angeles, CA 90025 USA Tel 310-442-3335.

Lotus Blossom Bks., *(978-0-9801414)* 1220 Rosecrans St., No. 325, San Diego, CA 92106 USA (SAN 855-3181) Tel 619-224-7771
E-mail: publisher@lotusblossombooks.com
Web site: http://www.lotusblossombooks.com
Dist(s): **BookBaby.**

Lotus Lights Publications *See* **Lotus Pr.**

Lotus Petal Publishing, *(978-0-9787672; 978-0-9820949)* Div. of Lotus Petal, P.O. Box 1394, Nashville, IN 47448-1394 USA Tel 812-988-1250; Toll Free Fax: 800-867-4851
E-mail: info@lotuspetalpublishing.com
Web site: http://www.lotuspetalpublishing.com.

Lotus Pond Media, *(978-0-9791021)* 176 Broadway, Suite 9C, New York, NY 10038 USA Tel 212-608-3329
E-mail: scgrant@goatkids.net; scgrant@customerresearchcenter.com
Web site: http://www.goatkids.net; http://www.highimpactquality.com.

Lotus Pr., *(978-0-910261; 978-0-914955; 978-0-940676; 978-0-940985; 978-0-941524; 978-1-60869)* Div. of Lotus Brands, Inc., P.O. Box 325, Twin Lakes, WI 53181 USA (SAN 239-1120) Tel 262-889-2461; Fax: 262-889-8591; Toll Free: 800-824-6396 Do not confuse with companies with the same or similar name in Lotus, CA, Westerville, OH, Bokeelia, FL, Brattleboro, VT, Detroit, MI, Tobyhanna, PA
E-mail: lotuspress@lotuspress.com
Web site: http://www.lotuspress.com
Dist(s): **National Bk. Network.**

Lotus Publications *See* **Johnson, Earl Photography**

Louck, Cheryl, *(978-0-9744230)* 2708 Avalon Ln., Montgomery, IL 60538 USA Tel 630-853-0653
Web site: http://www.cheryllouck.com.

Loughton Bks., *(978-0-9704974)* 101 W. 23rd St., New York, KS 37215 USA Do not confuse with companies with similar names in Newport, RI, San Diego, CA, Mary Esther, FL,
E-mail: mbraden@loghtonbooks.com
Web site: http://www.loughtonbooks.com.

Louisana (DNK) *(978-87-90029; 978-87-91607) Dist. by* **Dist Art Pubs.**

Louisiana Ladybug Pr., *(978-0-9753435)* 210 Pinecrest Rd., Arcadia, LA 71001 USA
Web site: http://www.LouisianaPotpourriFromAtoZ.com.

†Louisiana State Univ. Pr., *(978-0-8071)* 3990 W. Lakeshore Dr., Baton Rouge, LA 70808 USA Tel 225-578-6294; Fax: 225-578-6461; Toll Free Fax: 800-272-6817; Toll Free: 800-848-6224
E-mail: lsupress@lsu.edu
Web site: http://lsupress.org/
Dist(s): **Ebsco Publishing**
Longleaf Services
ebrary, Inc.; *CIP.*

Love + Lifestyle Media Group (CAN) *(978-0-9920874; 978-1-77210) Dist. by* **Bookmasters.**

Love & Blessings, *(978-0-9644765)* P.O. Box 55116, Valencia, CA 91385 USA Tel 661-288-1711; Toll Free: 800-906-3629
E-mail: vloveland@babybonding.com; vloveland@earthlink.net
Web site: http://www.babybonding.com
Dist(s): **New Leaf Distributing Co., Inc.**

Love Bug Bks., *(978-0-9787174)* 1117 Ariana Rd., Suite 102, San Marcos, CA 92069-8122 USA Tel 760-798-9415; Fax: 760-798-9415
E-mail: rolwink@cox.net
Web site: http://www.lovebugbooks.com.

Love Cultivating Editions, *(978-0-9744999)* 2665 Reed Rd., Hood River, OR 97031-9609 USA
Web site: http://www.lovecultivatingeditions.com.

Love II Learn Bks., *(978-0-9796679)* 860 Johnson Ferry Rd., Suite 140-345, Atlanta, GA 30342 USA (SAN 854-0535) Tel 404-808-0458
Web site: http://www.booksbykobie.com; http://www.loveiilearbooks.com
Dist(s): **BookMasters, Inc.**

Love Ink LLC, *(978-1-940426)* 65257 Solar Rd, Montrose, CO 81403 USA
E-mail: Love_Ink_LLC@yahoo.com.

Love Language Pubns., *(978-0-9749924)* 2111 E. Santa Fe, No. 268, Olathe, KS 66062 USA
E-mail: anne@lovelanguageforbabies.com
Web site: http://www.lovelanguageforbabies.com.

Love Your Life, *(978-0-9664806; 978-0-9798554; 978-0-9820477)* Orders Addr.: P.O. Box 2, Red Lion, PA 17356 USA (SAN 256-1387) Tel 717-200-2852; Fax: 310-496-0716; Edit Addr.: 755 Conndly Dr., Red Lion, PA 17356 USA Tel 717-200-2852; Fax: 310-496-0716
E-mail: publish@loveyourlife.com
Web site: http://www.loveyourlife.com
Dist(s): **Ingram Publisher Services.**

Loveland Pr., LLC, *(978-0-9662696; 978-0-9744851)* P.O. Box 7001, Loveland, CO 80537-0001 USA Tel 970-593-9557 Toll Free: 800-593-9557
E-mail: info@lovelandpress.com
Web site: http://www.lovelandpress.com.

LoveLight Media, *(978-0-9893181)* 216 Regina Dr., Fort Collins, CO 80525 USA Tel 970-218-2592
E-mail: Deidre@lovelightmedia.com
Web site: None yet.

Love's Creative Resources, *(978-1-929548)* Orders Addr.: P.O. Box 44306, Charlotte, NC 28215 USA Tel 704-563-7469
E-mail: ml9734@yahoo.com.

Lovestruck Literary, *(978-0-9833980; 978-0-9856574; 978-0-9960356)* 1643 Rodney Dr. APT 1, Los Angeles, CA 90027 USA
E-mail: afletcher@lovestruckliterary.com
Web site: lovestruckliterary.com
Dist(s): **Smashwords.**

Lovin Ovens, Inc., *(978-0-9617468)* 57 Chof Trail, Flagstaff, AZ 86001 USA (SAN 664-1180) Tel 928-525-1527
E-mail: GandCFox@msn.com.

Loving Guidance, Inc., *(978-1-889609)* P.O. Box 622407, Oviedo, FL 32762 USA Tel 407-366-0233; 407-977-8862; Fax: 407-366-4293; Toll Free: 800-842-2846; 50 Smith St., Oviedo, FL 32765-9608
E-mail: bryan@lovingguidance.com; kate@lovingguidance.com; becky.bailey@consciousdiscipline.com
Web site: http://www.beckybailey.com; http://www.consciousdiscipline.com
Dist(s): **Gryphon Hse., Inc.**

Loving Healing Pr., Inc., *(978-1-932690; 978-1-61599)* 5145 Pontiac Trail, Ann Arbor, MI 48105-9279 USA (SAN 255-7770) Tel 734-662-6864; Fax: 734-663-6861; Toll Free: 888-761-6268; *Imprints:* Marvelous Spirit Press (MarvelousSpir)
E-mail: info@lovinghealing.com
Web site: http://www.beyondtrauma.com/; http://www.TurtleDolphinDreams.com; http://www.TIRbook.com; http://www.LifeSkillsBook.com; http://www.VictorianHeritage.com; http://www.PhysicalLoss.com; http://www.gotparts.org; http://www.lovinghealing.com
Dist(s): **New Leaf Distributing Co., Inc.**
Quality Bks., Inc.
ebrary, Inc.

Lovstad, Joel Publishing, *(978-0-9749058)* 701 Henry St., No. 203, Waunakee, WI 53597 USA
E-mail: jlfred@chorus.net
Web site: http://www.joellovstad-books.com.

Low Fat Express, Incorporated *See* **Learning ZoneXpress**

†Lowell Hse., *(978-0-7373; 978-0-8092; 978-0-929923; 978-1-56565)* 2020 Avenue of the Stars, Suite 300, Los Angeles, CA 90067-4704 USA (SAN 250-863X) Tel 310-552-7555; Fax: 310-552-7573
Dist(s): **Independent Pubs. Group**
McGraw-Hill Trade; *CIP.*

Lowell Hse. Juvenile, *(978-0-7373; 978-0-929923; 978-1-56565)* 2020 Avenue of the Stars, No. 300, Los Angeles, CA 90067 USA Tel 310-552-7555; Fax: 310-552-7573; *Imprints:* Roxbury Park Juvenile (Roxbury Pk Juvenile)
Dist(s): **McGraw-Hill Trade.**

†Lowell Pr., The, Gallion Communications, *(978-0-913504; 978-0-932845)* Orders Addr.: P.O. Box 411877, Kansas City, MO 64141-1877 USA (SAN 207-0774) Tel 816-753-4545; Fax: 816-753-4057; Toll Free: 800-736-7660 Do not confuse with Lowell Pr. in Eugene, OR
E-mail: plowell@accessus.net; sales@thelowellpress.com
Web site: http://www.thelowellpress.com; *CIP.*

Lowell, Shelley, *(978-0-9765344)* Orders Addr.: c/o Montage Gallery, 925 South Charles St., Baltimore, MD 21230 USA.

Lower Kuskokwim Schl. District, *(978-1-58084)* Orders Addr.: P.O. Box 305, Bethel, AK 99559 USA Tel 907-543-4928; Fax: 907-543-4935
E-mail: catalog@fc.lksd-do.org
Web site: http://www.lksd.org/catalog.

Lower Lane Publishing LLC, *(978-0-9797790)* 2105 Carehill Rd., Vienna, VA 22181 USA.

†Loyola Pr., *(978-0-8294)* 3441 N. Ashland Ave., Chicago, IL 60657 USA (SAN 211-6537) Tel 773-281-1818; Fax: 773-281-0555; Toll Free: 800-621-1008
E-mail: customerservice@loyolapress.com
Web site: http://www.loyolabooks.org
Dist(s): **Spring Arbor Distributors, Inc.**; *CIP.*

L.Patrick Publishing, *(978-0-9774418)* 2710 W. 76th St., Inglewood, CA 90305 USA.

LPD Pr., *(978-0-9641542; 978-1-890689; 978-1-936744; 978-1-943681)* 925 Salamanca, NW, Los Ranchos, NM 87107-5647 USA Tel 505-344-9382; Fax: 505-345-5129; *Imprints:* Rio Grande Books (Rio Grande Bks)
E-mail: LPDPress@q.com
Web site: http://www.nmsantos.com
Dist(s): **Smashwords.**

LRS, *(978-1-58118)* 14214 S. Figueroa St., Los Angeles, CA 90061-1034 USA Tel 310-354-2610; Fax: 310-354-2601; Toll Free: 800-255-5002
E-mail: lrsprint@aol.com
Web site: http://www.lrs-largeprint.com
Dist(s): **Beeler, Thomas T. Pub.**

LSG Pubns., *(978-1-933532)* 29165 Clover Ln., Big Pine Key, FL 33043-6046 USA
E-mail: lisagaljanic@optonline.net
Web site: http://www.lsgpublications.com.

LSP *Imprint of* **LSP Digital, LLC**

LSP Digital, LLC, *(978-0-9792030; 978-0-9800733; 978-0-9817654)* P.O. Box 851556, Westland, MI 48185 USA Tel 734-355-3733; Fax: 734-261-0155; *Imprints:* LSP (LSP USA)
E-mail: admin@lspdigital.com
Web site: http://www.lspdigital.com.

LTI Publishing, *(978-0-9743048)* Div. of Let's Talk Interactive, Inc., P.O. Box 371, Huntersville, NC 28070 USA
E-mail: art@LTIPublishing.net
Web site: http://www.letstalkinterctive.com; http://www.FathersTouch.com; http://www.SexualAbuse.ws; http://www.ChildHoodItShouldNotHurt.com; http://www.ChildHoodShouldNotHurt.com; http://www.AgainstSexualAbuse.org; http://www.LetsTalkCounseling.com.

LTL Media LLC, *(978-0-9785744)* P.O. Box 12766, Tempe, AZ 85284 USA
Web site: http://www.mylittlethinkers.com.

Lu, Melissa Productions, *(978-0-9726832)* 5356 Rose Ridge Ln., Colorado Springs, CO 80917 USA Fax: 719-594-6993
E-mail: patsy@melissalu.com
Web site: http://www.melissalu.com.

Lua Publishing, *(978-0-9746304)* P.O. Box 3250, Fairfield, CA 94533 USA Tel 707-426-9480
E-mail: info@luapublishing.com
Web site: http://www.luapublishing.com
Dist(s): **New Leaf Distributing Co., Inc.**

Luath Pr. Ltd. (GBR) *(978-0-946487; 978-1-84282; 978-1-905222; 978-1-906307; 978-1-906817; 978-1-908373; 978-1-910021) Dist. by* **Midpt Trade.**

Luath Pr. Ltd. (GBR) *(978-0-946487; 978-1-84282; 978-1-905222; 978-1-906307; 978-1-906817; 978-1-908373; 978-1-910021) Dist. by* **IngramPubServ.**

Lubbers, Theresa *See* **Mr. Emmett Publishing**

Lucas Co., *(978-0-9715916)* P.O. Box 9245, Moscow, ID 83843 USA
Web site: http://www.lucasco.com.

Lucas Enterprises, *(978-0-9770611)* P.O. Box 9201, Chico, CA 95927 USA
E-mail: lucasent1@earthlink.net.

Lucas, Mattie, *(978-0-9762456)* P.O. Box 47070, Windsor Mills, MD 21244 USA Fax: 410-944-2597
E-mail: bishop@digc.org.

Lucas Violet *Imprint of* **Clocktower Hill Research & Publishing Group, LLC**

†Luce, Robert B. Pubs., *(978-0-88331)* Owned by Renaisance Book Services Corp., 2490 Black Rock Tpke., Fairfield, CT 06432 USA Tel 203-372-0300; Fax: 203-374-4766; Toll Free: 800-786-5427
E-mail: info@aslanpublishing.com
Web site: http://www.aslanpublishing.com
Dist(s): **APG Sales & Distribution Services**; *CIP.*

Lucent Bks. *Imprint of* **Cengage Gale**

Lucent Interpretations, LLC, *(978-0-9787849; 978-1-935146)* P.O. Box 3931, Lisle, IL 60532-8831 USA (SAN 856-6364)
E-mail: salmahammad@hotmail.com.

Lucent Pr. *Imprint of* **Greenhaven Publishing LLC**

Lucia Pubs., *(978-0-9762297)* Orders Addr.: P.O. Box 3, Churubusco, IN 46723-0003 USA Tel 260-693-0852; Fax: 260-693-0082; Edit Addr.: 209C S. Main St., Churubusco, IN 46723 USA
E-mail: diannegg@peoplepc.com; giannakeff@iquest.net
Web site: http://www.luciapublishers.com.

Lucky & Me Productions, Inc., *(978-0-9721256; 978-0-615-71754-8)* Orders Addr.: 410 East 74th St., 6H, New York, NY 10021-3918 USA (SAN 255-0873) Tel 212-288-7203; Fax: 401-783-7815 call before faxing/not always on
E-mail: writermyst@aol.com
Web site: http://www.dearjohnlennon.com
Dist(s): **CreateSpace Independent Publishing Platform.**

Lucky Bamboo Crafts, *(978-0-9884648)* P.O. Box 1022, Yarmouth, ME 04096 USA Tel 207-310-8101
E-mail: info@luckybamboocrafts.com
Web site: http://www.luckybamboocrafts.com
Dist(s): **Independent Pubs. Group.**

Lucky Bear Pubns., *(978-0-9729938)* 1144 Langwood Dr., Gallatin, TN 37066 USA Tel 615-452-3242 (phone/fax)
E-mail: perryluckybear@comcast.net
Web site: http://www.myluckybear.com.

Lucky Duck Designs, *(978-0-9790632)* P.O. Box 2192, Petaluma, CA 94953-2192 USA
E-mail: stuart@lucky-duck.com
Web site: http://www.lucky-duck.com.

Lucky Publications *See* **Covered Wagon Publishing LLC**

Lucky Red Pr., LLC, *(978-0-9790690)* 10061 Riverside Dr., Suite 812, Toluca Lake, CA 91602 USA Tel 818-795-2388; Fax: 818-566-4995
E-mail: Susan@frankiespals.com
Web site: http://www.frankiespals.com.

Lucky 3 Ranch, Inc., *(978-1-928624)* 2457 S. County Rd. 19, Loveland, CO 80537-9044 USA Tel 970-663-0066; Fax: 970-663-0676; Toll Free: 800-816-7566
E-mail: meredith@luckythreeranch.com
Web site: http://www.luckythreeranch.com/
Dist(s): **MediaTech Productions.**

LuckySports, *(978-0-935938)* 39844 Somerset Ave., Palm Desert, CA 92211 USA (SAN 213-7453) Tel 760-861-2174 (cell)
E-mail: chuck@LuckySports.net
Web site: http://www.bogiegolf.com; http://www.sportcartoonbooks.com; http://www.LuckySports.net.

Lucy Rose Publishing LLC, *(978-0-9789386; 978-0-9821936)* P.O. Box 3034, Fort Polk, LA 71459 USA
E-mail: admin@lucyrosepublishing.com
Web site: http://www.lucyrosepublishing.com.

Lueck Studios, *(978-0-9774547)* 8353 11th Ave. NW, Seattle, WA 98117 USA (SAN 257-6023)
E-mail: jenny@lueckstudios.com
Web site: http://www.chicabee.com
Dist(s): **BookMasters, Inc.**

Luisalchemy, *(978-0-9975433)* 10442 s artesian, Chicago, IL 60655 USA Tel 773-732-7722
E-mail: luisr124@gmail.com.

Luke & Lori Bks., *(978-0-9747792)* Orders Addr.: 5908 90th St., Lubbock, TX 79424 USA Tel 806-783-9941; Fax: 806-783-3099
E-mail: Melissa@lukeandlori.com
Web site: http://www.LukeAndLori.com.

Lulilite Productions, *(978-0-9759631)* P.O. Box 20847, Sedona, AZ 86341-0847 USA Tel 928-284-5442 (phone/fax) E-mail: ariamagi@npgcable.com Web site: http://www.lulilites.com.

Lulu Enterprises Inc. *See* **Lulu Pr., Inc.**

Lulu Pr., Inc., *(978-1-4116; 978-1-84728; 978-1-4303; 978-1-4357; 978-1-60552; 978-0-557; 978-1-4583; 978-1-257; 978-1-105; 978-1-300; 978-1-4834; 978-1-304; 978-1-312; 978-1-329; 978-1-365; 978-1-5342)* 627 Davis Dr. Suite 300, Morrisville, NC 27560 USA; 26-28 Hammersmith Grove, London, W6 7BA E-mail: sparker@lulu.com *Dist(s)*: **Booklines Hawaii, Ltd. Copyright Clearance Ctr., Inc. CreateSpace Independent Publishing Platform Lightning Source, Inc. Smashwords Valjean Pr.**

Lulu.com (GBR) *(978-1-84753; 978-1-4092; 978-1-4461; 978-1-4457; 978-1-4452; 978-1-84799; 978-1-4476; 978-1-4466; 978-1-4467; 978-1-4475; 978-1-4477; 978-1-4478; 978-1-4709; 978-1-4710; 978-1-291; 978-1-4717; 978-1-4716; 978-1-326; 978-1-387)* *Dist. by* **LuluCom.**

Lumadix Pr., *(978-0-9981647)* 1615 Buck St, West Linn, OR 97068 USA Tel 503-707-1438 E-mail: rio4koviak@gmail.com Web site: www.riokoviak.com.

Lumen (ARG) *(978-950-724; 978-950-9017; 978-987-00)* *Dist. by* **Lectorum Pubns.**

LUMEN-US Pubns., *(978-0-9703611; 978-0-9787788; 978-0-9794862; 978-0-9815359; 978-0-9819935; 978-1-936405)* 234 Main St., Park Forest, IL 60466-2098 USA Toll Free: 866-219-9637 E-mail: Lumenuspubl@aol.com Web site: http://www.lumen-us.com *Dist(s)*: **BookBaby.**

Lumina Pr. LLC, *(978-0-9708442)* P.O. Box 1106, Wrightsville Beach, NC 28480-1106 USA Do not confuse with Lumina Press in Springfield, MO E-mail: david@luminapress.com *Dist(s)*: **Two Rivers Distribution.**

Luminare Pr., LLC, *(978-1-937303; 978-1-944733)* 467 W. 17th Ave., Eugene, OR 97401 USA Tel 541-554-7574 E-mail: pmarshall17@comcast.net.

Luminary Media Group *Imprint of* **Pine Orchard, Inc.**

Luminate 7 Publishing, *(978-0-9765496)* 676 A 9th Ave., No. 142, New York, NY 10036 USA Tel 917-647-6740; Fax: 212-957-9191 E-mail: luminate7@aol.com.

Luminations Media Group, Inc., *(978-0-9821199; 978-1-61222)* P.O. Box 538, Monterey Park, CA 91754 USA Tel 626-571-0115 E-mail: office@luminationsmedia.com Web site: http://www.LuminationsMedia.com.

Luminis Bks., Inc., *(978-1-935462; 978-1-941311)* 13245 Blacktern Way, Carmel, IN 46033 USA (SAN 857-8125) Tel 317-250-9539 E-mail: publisher@luminisbooks.com Web site: http://www.luminisbooks.com *Dist(s)*: **Independent Pubs. Group MyiLibrary ebrary, Inc.**

Lumpkin, Carol *See* **Peace Rug Company, Inc., The**

Luna Publishing, *(978-0-9791785)* Orders Addr.: 5815 82nd St., No. 145, PMB 137, Lubbock, TX 79424 USA Tel 806-687-3479; Fax: 806-687-3401 Do not confuse with Luna PUblishing Company in Los Angeles, CA E-mail: ccmgr2@nts-online.net Web site: http://www.lunapublish.com.

Luna, Rachel Nickerson *See* **Howard, Emma Bks.**

Luna Rising *Imprint of* **Northland Publishing**

Lunada Pr., LLC, *(978-0-937176)* 2510 W. 237th, Suite 100, Torrence, CA 90505 USA Tel 435-632-8349 E-mail: jeannemaree@charter.net *Dist(s)*: **Lightning Source, Inc.**

Lunar Donut Pr., *(978-0-9725638)* P.O. Box 692625, Orlando, FL 32869 USA Tel 407-298-7779; Fax: 407-298-7779 E-mail: caricatureconnection@cfl.rr.com Web site: http://www.caricatureconnection.com.

Lunasea Studios, *(978-0-9799290)* 9450 Mira Mesa Blvd., Suite B-107, San Diego, CA 92126 USA Web site: http://www.lunasea-studios.com/.

Lunatic Pr., *(978-0-9772590)* P.O. Box 4571, West Hills, CA 91308 USA Web site: http://www.lunaticpress.com *Dist(s)*: **Independent Pubs. Group.**

Lunchbox Lessons, *(978-1-60507)* 970 E. Broadway, Suite 406, Jackson, WY 83001 USA (SAN 854-9540) Tel 307-462-4173 E-mail: info@lunchboxlessons.com Web site: http://www.lunchboxlessons.com.

Lunchbox Stories Inc., *(978-0-9798059)* 20425 NW Quail Hollow Dr., Portland, OR 97229 USA Web site: http://www.lunchboxstories.com.

Luse, Sandra I., *(978-0-615-22394-0)* P.O. Box 431, Wilber, NE 68465 USA Tel 402-821-2641.

Lushena Bks., *(978-1-930097; 978-1-63182)* 607 Country Club Dr., Unit E, Bensenville, IL 60106 USA (SAN 630-5105) Tel 630-238-8708; Fax: 630-238-8824 E-mail: Lushenabks@yahoo.com Web site: http://www.lushenabks.com/.

Lutherworth Pr., The (GBR) *(978-0-7188)* *Dist. by* **CasemateAcad.**

Lutz, William G., *(978-0-615-15622-4; 978-0-615-18287-2; 978-0-615-21273-9)* 10248 Ramm Rd., Whitehouse, OH 43571 USA *Dist(s)*: **Lulu Pr., Inc.**

Luv U Bks., *(978-0-9715322)* P.O. Box 42037, Cincinnati, OH 45242-0037 USA E-mail: luvubooks@fuse.net Web site: http://www.luvubooks.com.

Luvlife Publishing, *(978-0-9764316)* Orders Addr.: 69 Shore Dr., Old Lyme, CT 06371 USA Tel 860-434-0723 E-mail: mistilove@earthlink.net Web site: http://www.snakesofnewengland.com.

LuvLuv *Imprint of* **Aurora Publishing, Inc.**

L.W. Communications, *(978-0-9723378)* 16815 Victory Blvd. #226, Van Nuys, CA 91406-5550 USA Tel 818-787-9550 (phone, fax - call first) E-mail: lancecoach@aol.com Web site: http://www.lancecoach.com.

Lyceum Books, Incorporated *See* **Follmer Group, The**

Lychgate Pr., *(978-0-615-65502-4; 978-0-9882887; 978-0-9976116)* 529 N.W. 31st St., Corvallis, OR 97330 USA Tel 541-752-5211 Web site: editor@fullcitypress.com *Dist(s)*: **CreateSpace Independent Publishing Platform.**

Lynch, Marietta & Patricia Perry, *(978-0-9610962)* 240 Atlantic Rd., Gloucester, MA 01930 USA (SAN 265-2722) Tel 508-283-6322.

Lynn Tyner Mitchum & James Rogers, *(978-0-9745191)* P.O. Box 5799, Sevierville, TN 37864 USA Web site: http://jamesrogersonline.com.

Lynne Ellen, Inc., *(978-0-9748889)* 670 N. Stiles Dr., Charleston, SC 29412 USA Tel 843-817-2530 E-mail: lynne@metoommomy.com.

Lynn's Bookshelf, *(978-0-9618608)* Orders Addr.: P.O. Box 2224, Boise, ID 83701 USA (SAN 667-1314) Tel 208-331-1987 (phone/fax); Edit Addr.: 3423 Scenic Dr., Boise, ID 83703 USA E-mail: decker.barbara@ymail.com; lynnsbooks@cableone.net.

†Lynx Hse. Pr., *(978-0-89924)* 420 W. 24th Ave., Spokane, WA 99203-1922 USA (SAN 250-3344) Tel 309-624-4594; Fax: 309-623-4238 E-mail: cnhowell@mail.ewu.edu *Dist(s)*: **SPD-Small Pr. Distribution Univ. of Washington Pr.**; *CIP.*

Lyon, Ernest Media Productions, *(978-0-9741328; 978-0-9991661)* P.O. Box 26101, San Francisco, CA 94126-6101 USA (SAN 255-7460) Tel 415-387-5569 (phone/fax) E-mail: davidlyon@mindspring.com.

Lyons Pr. *Imprint of* **Globe Pequot Pr., The**

Lypton Publishing, *(978-0-9752780)* 35409 S. Fairbank Point, Drummond Island, MI 49726 USA (SAN 256-0143).

Lyrical Learning, *(978-0-9646367; 978-0-9741635; 978-0-692-37347-7; 978-0-692-38790-0; 978-0-9964731)* 8008 Cardwell Hill, Corvallis, OR 97330 USA Tel 541-754-3579 (phone/fax); Toll Free: 800-761-0906 Web site: http://www.lyricallearning.com.

Lyrically Korrect Publishing, *(978-0-9727776)* 5402 Belle Vista Ave., Baltimore, MD 21206 USA; *Imprints*: Book Her Publications (Bk Hr Pubns) Web site: http://www.lyricallykorrect.com.

M & B Publishing, *(978-0-9758580)* 930 Edgecliffs Dr., Langley, WA 98260 USA E-mail: wistful@whidbey.com.

M & D Publishing, Inc., *(978-0-9768667)* 2980 SE Fairway W., Stuart, FL 34997 USA Tel 772-286-9781; Fax: 772-286-5169 Do not confuse with M & D Publishing in Phoenix, AZ E-mail: manddpublishing@bellsouth.net.

M D C T Publishing, *(978-0-9674491)* 31990 SW Village Crest Ln., Wilsonville, OR 97070-8427 USA E-mail: mdundy@teleport.com *Dist(s)*: **Partners/West Book Distributors.**

M G L S, Inc., *(978-0-9601682; 978-1-888833)* 700 S. First St., Marshall, MN 56258 USA (SAN 212-2170) Tel 507-532-4311; Fax: 507-532-4313 E-mail: carberry@mgls.com.

M K L Publishing, *(978-0-9746204)* Orders Addr.: P.O. Box 407, Ballston Spa, NY 12020 USA; Edit Addr.: 5019 Fairground Ave., Ballston Spa, NY 12020 USA E-mail: mklpublishing@aol.com.

MM Co., *(978-1-883473)* 15007 Avon St., Independence, MO 64055 USA Tel 816-246-6365.

M Q Pubns., *(978-1-84072; 978-1-897954; 978-1-84601; 978-0-9797400)* 12 The Ivories 6-8 Northampton St., London, N1 2HY GBR Tel 020 7359 2244; Fax: 020 7359 1616; 49 W. 24th St., 8th Flr., New York, NY 10010 Tel 212-223-2320; Fax: 212-675-8026; Toll Free: 800-398-2848 E-mail: mail@mqpublications.com Web site: http://www.mqpublications.com *Dist(s)*: **Advanced Global Distribution Services Hachette Bk. Group Ingram Publisher Services Mercedes Distribution Ctr., Inc. Sterling Publishing Co., Inc. Wybel Marketing Group.**

M R L, Inc., *(978-1-892860)* 1445 Cannon St., Louisville, CO 80027-1453 USA Tel 303-666-8164 E-mail: moyazena@aol.com.

M T E, Ltd., *(978-1-888679)* 3095 S. Trenton St., Denver, CO 80231-4164 USA Tel 303-696-0935.

M2M Partners, *(978-0-9768884)* P.O. Box 60923, Phoenix, AZ 85082-0923 USA Toll Free: 800-658-8790 Web site: http://www.mamaroses.com; http://www.printserve.net; http://www.nonnieskitchen.com *Dist(s)*: **Partners/West Book Distributors.**

MAAT Resources, Inc., *(978-0-9624096; 978-1-893447)* 130 East Grand Ave., South San Francisco, CA 94080 USA Tel 650-871-4449; 650-871-4111; Fax: 650-871-4551; *Imprints*: Bilingual Language Materials (Biling Lang) E-mail: info@blmteachaids.com Web site: http://www.blmteachaids.com/; http://www.transparentpower.com/.

Mabbul Publishing Co., *(978-0-9762860)* 915 Hunting Horn Way, Evans, GA 30809 USA Web site: http://www.mabbul.com.

Mabrey, Chris, *(978-0-9979042)* 5410 Nighthawk Dr, Indianapolis, IN 46254 USA Tel 317-513-6413 E-mail: cmabrey@comcast.net.

MAC Productions, *(978-1-878591)* P.O. Box 84, Duvall, WA 98019 USA Tel 425-256-2652; Fax: 425-749-7065 E-mail: macproductions1@verizon.net Web site: http://www.macsgolfguides.com *Dist(s)*: **Partners/West Book Distributors.**

MacAdam/Cage Publishing, Inc., *(978-1-878448; 978-0-9673701; 978-1-931561; 978-1-59692)* 155 Sansome St., Suite 550, San Francisco, CA 94104 USA (SAN 299-9730) Tel 415-986-7503; Fax: 415-986-7414 E-mail: david@macadamcage.com Web site: http://www.macadamcage.com.

Macalester Park Publishing Co., Inc., *(978-0-910924; 978-0-930286; 978-1-886158)* 24558 546th Ave., Austin, MN 55912 USA (SAN 110-8077) Tel 507-396-0135; Toll Free: 800-407-9078 E-mail: macalesterpark@macalesterpark.com Web site: http://www.macalesterpark.com *Dist(s)*: **Bookmen, Inc. Spring Arbor Distributors, Inc.**

Macaronic Pr., *(978-0-9766859; 978-1-59864)* P.O. Box 1542, Sebastopol, CA 95473-1542 USA Tel 707-813-7047; Toll Free: 888-364-8253 E-mail: vivienka@msn.com Web site: http://www.macaronicpress.com.

Macaulay, David Studio *Imprint of* **Roaring Brook Pr.**

Macauley, Myron Christian, *(978-0-578-05300-4)* 106 Monroe St., No. 2, Brooklyn, NY 11216 USA E-mail: danae@kgn6.com.

Macaw Books LLC *See* **Kapp Bks. LLC**

MacBride, E. J. Pubn., Inc., *(978-1-892511)* 129 W. 147th St., No. 20B, New York, NY 10039 USA; *Imprints*: Disposition Sketch Books (Disposition Sketch).

MacGill, William V. & Company, *(978-0-9744720)* 1000 N. Lombard Rd., Lombard, IL 60148-1232 USA Tel 800-323-2841; Toll Free Fax: 800-727-3433 E-mail: macgill@macgill.com; nickh@macgill.com Web site: http://www.macgill.com.

MacGregor, Doug, *(978-0-9654843)* 1578 Rosada Way, Fort Myers, FL 33901 USA Tel 941-337-3980 E-mail: dmacgregor@news-press.com.

MacHillock Publishing, *(978-0-9744996)* 2537 Pine Cove Dr., Tucker, GA 30084 USA E-mail: sdh@mindspring.com *Dist(s)*: **Independent Pubs. Group MyiLibrary.**

MacIntyre & Purcell Publishing (CAN) *(978-0-9738063; 978-0-9784784; 978-0-9810941; 978-1-926916; 978-1-927097; 978-1-77276)* *Dist. by* **IPG Chicago.**

Mackenzie Smiles, LLC, *(978-0-9790347; 978-0-9815761)* P.O. Box 1373, Sausalito, CA 94965 USA Toll Free: 888-800-5978; P.O. Box 1373, Sausalito, CA 94965 Web site: http://www.mackenziesmiles.com.

Mackie, Valencia *See* **CRE Lease Talk, Incorporated**

Mackin, Dan, *(978-0-615-12303-5)* 8395 SE Palm St., Hobe Sound, FL 33455 USA Tel 772-546-3008; Fax: 772-546-5374 E-mail: danmackinartist@aol.com Web site: http://www.danmackin.com.

Mackinac Island Press, Inc. *Imprint of* **Charlesbridge Publishing, Inc.**

Mackinac Island State Park Commission *See* **Mackinac State Historic Parks**

Mackinac State Historic Parks, *(978-0-911872)* Orders Addr.: P.O. Box 873, Mackinaw City, MI 49701 USA; Edit Addr.: 207 W. Sinclair, Mackinaw City, MI 49701 USA (SAN 202-5981) Tel 231-436-5564; Fax: 231-436-4210.

MackStorm Productions, Inc., *(978-0-9753078)* 1410 Prairie Crossing Dr., West Chicago, IL 60185 USA Tel 630-231-3998 E-mail: marilee@americanslidechart.com.

MacMenamin Pr., *(978-0-9761414)* P.O. Box 133, Zionsville, PA 18092 USA Tel 610-739-9527 E-mail: sales@macmenaminpress.com Web site: http://www.macmenaminpress.com.

Macmillan, *(978-0-374; 978-1-4668; 978-1-68274)* Div. of Holtzbrinck Publishing, Orders Addr.: 16365 James Madison Hwy., Gordonsville, VA 22942 USA (SAN 631-5011) Tel 540-672-7600; Fax: 540-672-7664; 540-672-7540 (Customer Service); Toll Free Fax: 800-672-2054 (Order Dept.); Toll Free: 888-330-8477; Edit Addr.: 175 Fifth Ave., 20th Flr., New York, NY 10010 USA Tel 212-674-5151; Fax: 212-677-6487; Toll Free Fax: 800-258-2769; Toll Free: 800-488-5233 E-mail: customerservice@mpsvirginia.com Web site: http://www.macmillan.com *Dist(s)*: **Follett School Solutions ebrary, Inc.**

Macmillan Audio, *(978-0-940687; 978-1-55927; 978-1-893564; 978-1-59397; 978-1-59768; 978-1-4272)* Div. of Macmillan, Orders Addr.: 16365 James Madison Hwy., Gordonsville, VA 22942-8501 USA Toll Free Fax: 800-672-2054; Toll Free: 888-330-8477; Edit Addr.: 175 Fifth Ave., Suite 315, New York, NY 10010 USA (SAN 665-1275) Tel 646-307-5000; Fax: 917-534-0980; Toll Free: 800-221-7945 E-mail: audio@hbpub.com Web site: http://www.macmillanaudio.com *Dist(s)*: **AudioGO Findaway World, LLC Follett School Solutions Landmark Audiobooks MPS Macmillan.**

Macmillan Caribbean (GBR) *(978-0-333; 978-1-4050)* *Dist. by* **Interlink Pub.**

Macmillan Education, Ltd. (GBR) *(978-0-333; 978-1-4050)* *Dist. by* **Players Pr.**

Macmillan Pubs., Ltd. (GBR) *(978-0-330; 978-0-333; 978-1-4050)* *Dist. by* **Trafalgar.**

Macmillan Pubs., Ltd. (GBR) *(978-0-330; 978-0-333; 978-1-4050)* *Dist. by* **IPG Chicago.**

Macmillan Pubs., Ltd. (GBR) *(978-0-330; 978-0-333; 978-1-4050)* *Dist. by* **Trans-Atl Phila.**

Macmillan Reference USA *Imprint of* **Cengage Gale**

Macmillan/McGraw-Hill Schl. Div., *(978-0-02)* Div. of The McGraw-Hill Education Group, Orders Addr.: 220 E. Daniel Dale Rd., DeSoto, TX 75115 USA Fax: 972-228-1982; Toll Free: 800-442-9685 *Dist(s)*: **McGraw-Hill Cos., The.**

Macro Publishing Group, *(978-0-9702699; 978-0-9754130; 978-0-9826829)* 6700 Oglesby, Suite 1101, Chicago, IL 60649 USA Toll Free: 888-854-8823 (phone/fax) E-mail: lissawoodson@aol.com *Dist(s)*: **INscribe Digital.**

Macromedia Education *Imprint of* **Macromedia, Inc.**

Macromedia, Inc., *(978-0-9742273; 978-1-932719)* 600 Townsend St., San Francisco, CA 94103 USA Tel 415-252-2000; Fax: 415-832-5555; Toll Free: 800-457-1774; *Imprints*: Macromedia Education (Macromedia Educ) Do not confuse with Macromedia, Inc. in Lake Placid, NY Web site: http://www.macromedia.com/education.

Macy, Carolyn, *(978-0-9988838; 978-0-9989127)* 6227 81st Ave. N.E., Norman, OK 73026 USA Tel 405-401-2012 E-mail: cmacy2@aol.com.

MAD *Imprint of* **DC Comics**

Mad Dash Co., The, *(978-0-9975965)* 111 Windermere Way, Warwick, RI 02886 USA Tel 401-527-5700 E-mail: lumpybones@gmail.com.

Mad Island Communications LLC, *(978-0-9677458; 978-0-9910109)* P.O. Box 153, La Pointe, WI 54850-0153 USA Tel 715-209-5471 E-mail: barbwith@gmail.com Web site: http://www.barbarawith.com; http://partyof12.wordpress.com/ *Dist(s)*: **Lightning Source, Inc.**

Mad Island Publishing *See* **Mad Island Communications LLC**

Mad Libs *Imprint of* **Penguin Young Readers Group**

Mad Yak Pr., *(978-0-9717995)* 8232 Styers Ct., Laurel, MD 20723-2100 USA Tel 301-317-8817 *Dist(s)*: **Diamond Comic Distributors, Inc. Diamond Bk. Distributors.**

Madame Cat Publishing, *(978-0-9983859)* 6491 Smooth Thorn Ct, Jacksonville, FL 32258 USA Tel 904-955-9967 E-mail: meldow14@gmail.com.

Madame Fifi Pubns., *(978-0-9667418; 978-0-9762900; 978-0-9821707)* P.O. Box 310967, Newington, CT 06131-0967 USA Web site: http://www.madamefifi3.com.

Madd Mindz Publishing, Inc., *(978-0-9802262)* P.O. Box 20437, Brooklyn, NY 11202-0437 USA Tel 347-661-4030; Fax: 718-425-9919 E-mail: C.Brandon@MaddMindzPublishing.com Web site: http://www.maddmindzpublishing.com.

Maddness, Inc., *(978-0-9761619)* P.O. Box 76551, Oklahoma City, OK 73147-2551 USA E-mail: osheashamir@aol.com Web site: http://www.osheashamir.com.

Mader, Lothar, *(978-0-615-24577-5; 978-0-578-05621-0)* 2130 Professional Dr., Suite 240, Roseville, CA 95661 USA *Dist(s)*: **Lulu Pr., Inc.**

Madison, Dr. Ron *See* **Ned's Head Productions**

Maerkle Pr., *(978-0-9721966; 978-0-9819479)* 66 E. Shore Blvd., Timberlake, OH 44095 USA Tel 440-269-8653; Fax: 440-269-8035 Web site: http://www.maerklepress.com.

Maerov, Jeffrey, *(978-0-578-11402-6; 978-0-578-11504-7)* 24 Fecamp, Newport Coast, CA 92657 USA.

Maestro Classics, *(978-1-932684)* Div. of Simon & Simon, LLC, Orders Addr.: 1745 Broadway 17th Fl, New York, NY 10019 USA Tel 212-519-9847 E-mail: bsimon@maestroclassics.com Web site: http://www.MaestroClassics.com *Dist(s)*: **CD Baby Follett School Solutions.**

Maestro Learning, *(978-0-9740533)* 24 Chilton St., Cambridge, MA 02138-6802 USA E-mail: peter@maestrolearning.com Web site: http://www.maestrolearning.com.

MaestroMedia Pr., *(978-0-9773731)* 408 Pearl St., Richmond, IN 47374 USA Tel 765-962-8380 E-mail: rosecitysp@msn.com.

Maeva, Ediciones, S.A. (ESP) *(978-84-86478; 978-84-95354; 978-84-92695; 978-84-96231; 978-84-96748; 978-84-15120; 978-84-15532; 978-84-15893)* *Dist. by* **Lectorum Pubns.**

Magabala Bks. (AUS) *(978-0-9588101; 978-1-875641; 978-1-921248; 978-0-7316-0335-0; 978-0-7316-1622-0; 978-0-7316-1623-7; 978-0-7316-1736-4; 978-0-7316-3328-9; 978-0-646-22120-5; 978-0-646-26784-5; 978-1-922142; 978-1-925360)* *Dist. by* **IPG Chicago.**

Mage Pubs., Inc., *(978-0-934211; 978-1-933823)* 1408 35th St., NW, Washington, DC 20007 USA (SAN 693-0476) Tel 202-342-1642; Fax: 202-342-9269; Toll Free: 800-962-0922 (orders only) E-mail: as@mage.com Web site: http://www.mage.com.

Magee, Burke & Glenna, *(978-0-9748424)* Orders Addr.: P.O. Box 581, Carnation, WA 98014 USA; Edit Addr.: 2015 290th Ave., NE, Carnation, WA 98014 USA E-mail: rtg@returntogod.com Web site: http://www.returntogod.com.

MaggieMooseTracks, *(978-0-9895205)* 1766 Sand Hill Rd., No. 102, Palo Alto, CA 94304 USA Tel 650-322-8860 E-mail: girlfins@aol.com.

Magic Crystal Pr., *(978-0-9986487)* 727 W. 7th St. Suite 503, Los Angeles, CA 90017 USA Tel 949-278-8005 E-mail: jrc@magiccrystalpress.com Web site: www.magiccrystalpress.com.

Magic Factory, LLC, The, *(978-1-938155)* Orders Addr.: 3818 Somerset Dr., Durham, NC 27707 USA Tel

310-943-6972; Edit Addr.: 3818 Somerset Dr., Durham, NC 27707 USA Tel 310-943-6972 (Tel/Fax)
E-mail: orders@magicfactory.com; orders@magicfactory.com; info@magicfactory.com; books@magicfactory.com
Web site: http://magicfactory.com; http://signofthesandman.com; http://rangerbaldy.com.

Magic Lamp Pr., (*978-1-56891; 978-1-882629*) Div. of Magic Lamp Productions, 1838 Washington Way, Venice, CA 90291-4704 USA (SAN 256-1670) Tel 310-822-2985; Fax: 310-827-9123; Toll Free: 800-367-9661
E-mail: videopage@earthlink.net
Web site: http://www.magiclamppress.com
Dist(s): **Smashwords.**

Magic Lamp Productions *See* **Magic Lamp Pr.**

Magic of African Rhythm (TMOAR), The, (*978-0-9820926*) Orders Addr.: P.O. Box 14724, Raleigh, NC 27620-4724 USA Tel 919-828-1906; Fax: 419-781-8209
E-mail: shabutaso@gmail.com.

Magic Penny Pr., (*978-0-9982777*) 3336 Lone Hill Ln, Encinitas, CA 92024 USA Tel 858-367-8541
E-mail: massiveart@gmail.com.

Magic Penny Reading, (*978-0-9761987; 978-0-9899114*) 61 Wehrle Dr., Amherst, NY 14225 USA Tel 800-873-0396; Fax: 888-728-0754
E-mail: sandyschneider@magicpennyreading.org
Web site: http://magicpennyreading.org.

Magic Picture Frame Studio, LLC, (*978-0-9749269*) Orders Addr.: P.O. Box 2603, Issaquah, WA 98027 USA Tel 425-222-7562
E-mail: publisher@magicpictureframe.com; mvm@magicpictureframe.com; class@magicpictureframe.com
Web site: http://www.magicpictureframe.com
Dist(s): **BookMasters, Inc.**

Magic Propaganda Mill, (*978-0-9760117*) Please Send All Correspondence To: Info@mpmill.com, Brooklyn, NY 11238 USA
E-mail: info@mpmill.com
Web site: http://www.magicpropagandamill.com.

Magic Valley Pubs., (*978-0-9716681; 978-0-9774833; 978-0-9785509; 978-0-9800879; 978-0-9821496; 978-0-9845275*) 6390 E. Willow St., Long Beach, CA 90815 USA Tel 562-795-0289; Fax: 562-795-0490 Do not confuse with Magic Valley Publishers in Burly, ID
Web site: http://www.magicvalleypub.com.

Magic Wagon, (*978-1-60270; 978-1-61641*) Div. of ADBO Publishing Group, Orders Addr.: P.O. Box 398166, Minneapolis, MN 55439-8166 USA Fax: 952-831-1632; Toll Free: 800-458-8399; Edit Addr.: 8000 W. 78th St., Suite 310, Edina, MN 55439 USA Toll Free: 800-458-8399; *Imprints*: Looking Glass Library (LookngGlassLib); Graphic Planet (Graphic Planet); Short Tales (Short Tales); Calico Chapter Books (CalicoChap Bks); Looking Glass Library- Nonfiction (LOOKING GLASS) ; Calico Chapter Books (CalicoChapter)
E-mail: info@abdopublishing.com
Web site: http://www.abdopublishing.com
Dist(s): **ABDO Publishing Co.**
Follett School Solutions
MyiLibrary.

Magic Woman Pubns., (*978-0-9760062*) 1527 Veteran Ave., Suite 7, Los Angeles, CA 90024-5566 USA Tel 310-478-7743; Fax: 310-478-9892
E-mail: artdivin@yahoo.com
Web site: http://www.magicwomanpublications.com.

Magic Wordweaver Pr., (*978-0-9754116; 978-0-615-12456-8*) Orders Addr.: P.O. Box 1315, Conifer, CO 80433 USA (SAN 255-8459) Tel 303-838-7515 (phone/fax); Edit Addr.: 29580 S. Sunset Trail, Conifer, CO 80433 USA
E-mail: premalee108@yahoo.com.

Magic Works Publishing & Production, (*978-0-9799545*) 27 Greenmoor, Irvine, CA 92614 USA Tel 714-309-4824; Fax: 949-651-8895
E-mail: selina@superachievement.net
Web site: http://SuperAchievement.net.

Magical Beginnings, (*978-0-692-54966-7; 978-0-692-59310-3; 978-0-692-61084-8; 978-0-692-61356-6; 978-0-692-62334-3; 978-0-9973594; 978-0-692-65326-5; 978-0-692-71224-5*) 10940 S. Parker Rd. No. 791, Parker, CO 80134-7440 USA
Web site: www.FairyVillageBooks.com
Dist(s): **CreateSpace Independent Publishing Platform.**

Magical Child Bks. *Imprint of* **Shades of White**

Magical Creations, (*978-0-9744879*) P.O. Box 324, Chicago Park, CA 95712 USA Tel 530-477-7429
E-mail: doris_rainville@hotmail.com.

Magical Mischief Maker, (*978-0-9754004*) P.O. Box 1075, Douglasville, GA 30133 USA
Web site: http://www.magicalmischiefmaker.com.

MagicStar Inc., (*978-0-9821387*) 2021 Midwest Rd., Suite 200, Oak Brook, IL 60523 USA (SAN 857-3336) Tel 510-740-4045
E-mail: publisher@magicstarpub.com
Web site: http://www.magicstarpub.com.

Magill's Choice *Imprint of* **Salem Pr., Inc.**

Magination, (*978-1-881597*) 3579 E. Foothill Blvd., No. 330, Pasadena, CA 91107 USA Tel 626-306-1190; Fax: 626-306-1193.

Magination Pr. *Imprint of* **American Psychological Assn.**

Magiscule Publishing Group, L.L.C., (*978-0-9772232*) 12 Armstrong Ave., Suite 3 W., Providence, RI 02903 USA Fax: 401-861-7030
E-mail: Krystalstream@excite.com.

Magna Large Print Bks. (GBR) (*978-0-7505; 978-0-86009; 978-1-84137; 978-1-85057; 978-1-78502*) *Dist. by* **Ulverscroft US.**

Magnatic Music, (*978-0-9719897*) 13806 Delaney Rd., Dale City, VA 22193 USA
E-mail: alstonsongs@aol.com.

Magner Publishing *See* **Magner Publishing & American Binding & Publishing**

Magner Publishing & American Binding & Publishing, (*978-1-929416; 978-1-60080*) P.O. Box 60049, Corpus Christi, TX 78466 USA Tel 361-658-4221; Toll Free: 800-863-3708
E-mail: rmmagner@pyramid3.net
Web site: http://www.americanbindingpublishing.com.

Magness, Robert Pubns., LLC, (*978-0-9774577*) 1412 Kent St., Sturgis, MI 49091-2334 USA Tel 269-651-7473
E-mail: sengam@netzero.com.

Magnetar Venture Group, LLC, (*978-0-692-37543-3; 978-0-9861212*) P.O. Box 540324, Houston, TX 77254 USA Tel 5127632652
Dist(s): **CreateSpace Independent Publishing Platform.**

Magnetic Image, Inc., (*978-0-9678542*) 900 SW 13th St., Boca Raton, FL 33486 USA
E-mail: info@magneticimageinc.com
Web site: http://www.magneticimageinc.com.

Magni Co., The, (*978-1-882330; 978-1-937026*) 7106 Wellington Point Rd., McKinney, TX 75070 USA Tel 972-540-2050; Fax: 972-540-1057
E-mail: sales@magnico.com; info@magnico.com
Web site: http://www.magnico.com
Dist(s): **Book Publishing Co.**
INscribe Digital.

Magnificat, Inc., (*978-0-9676186; 978-0-9798086; 978-1-936260; 978-1-941709*) Div. of Groupe Fleurus, P.O. Box 822, Yonkers, NY 10702 USA
E-mail: a.depinay@magnificat.com
Web site: http://www.magnificat.com; http://www.magnifikid.com
Dist(s): **BookBaby**
Ignatius Pr.

Magnificat USA LLC *See* **Magnificat, Inc.**

Magpie Press *See* **Magpie Pr., Pine Mountain Club, CA**

Magpie Pr., Pine Mountain Club, CA, Orders Addr.: P.O. Box 6434, Pine Mountain Club, CA 93222-6434 USA Tel 661-242-1265 (phone/fax) Do not confuse with Magpie Pr. in Wallington, NJ
E-mail: MagSmith1265@msn.com
Web site: www.magpiepress.com.

Magrane, Etna International, (*978-0-9741167*) 8 Hill Point Ave., San Francisco, CA 94117 USA Tel 415-681-5157; Fax: 415-681-5820
E-mail: emagrane@aol.com.

Magsimba Pr., (*978-1-932956*) 1821 Bruce Rd., NE, Atlanta, GA 30329-2508 USA Tel 404-633-9153
E-mail: info@magsimba.org
Web site: http://www.magsimba.org; http://www.tagalog1.com/Ordinary/Learn_Filipino.jsp
Dist(s): **Quality Bks., Inc.**

MAHVL Publishing, (*978-0-9790072*) P.O. Box 134, Deerfield, IL 60015-0134 USA
Web site: http://michaelslewismd.com
Dist(s): **Chicago Distribution Ctr.**
Independent Pubs. Group
Ingram Publisher Services.

Mailbox Bks., The *Imprint of* **Education Ctr., Inc.**

Main Asset Pubns., (*978-0-9667617*) P.O. Box 1153, Teaneck, NJ 07666 USA Tel 201-837-6400; Fax: 201-837-8842
E-mail: mathispublishing@aol.com
Web site: http://www.whyarentumarried.com.

Main Coon Publishing, (*978-0-9983035*) 58 St. George Rd., Wingdale, NY 12594 USA Tel 845-832-6076
E-mail: osusanna@outlook.com.

Main Event Pr., (*978-0-9774129*) 1714 Boxwood Cir., Saint Cloud, MN 56303-0148 USA.

Main Frame Pr., (*978-0-615-49914-7; 978-0-9856790*) 858 Third Ave. No. 320, Chula Vista, CA 91911 USA Tel 619-253-4312
E-mail: gilbert@gilbertklein.com
Web site: www.football101.net.

Main Street Pubns., (*978-0-9745033*) 11810 Dice Rd., Freeland, MI 48623 USA.

Main Street Publishing, Inc. *See* **Main St Publishing, Inc.**

Main St Publishing, Inc., (*978-0-9666676; 978-0-9710470; 978-0-9741294; 978-0-9748591; 978-0-9760414; 978-0-9765369; 978-0-9776480; 978-0-9785934; 978-0-9791154; 978-1-934615; 978-1-939999*) 206 E. Main, Suite 207, Jackson, TN 38301 USA Fax: 731-427-7380; Toll Free: 866-457-7379; *Imprints*: MSP (MSP) Do not confuse with companies with same or similar names in Kingston, NJ, Shorewood, WI, Osage Beach MO,
E-mail: editor@mainstreetpublishing.com
Web site: http://www.mainstreetpublishing.com.

Mainstay, LLC, (*978-0-9798854*) 4134 W. View Pointe Dr., Highland, UT 84003 USA
Web site: http://www.MainstayEducation.com.

Mainstay Publishing, (*978-0-9832901; 978-0-9899479*) Mainstay Publishing P.O. Box 293, Middletown, DE 19709 USA Tel 302-223-6636
E-mail: denise@mainstaypublishing.com.

Mainstream Ctr., Schl. for the Deaf, The, (*978-0-9797287*) 48 Round Hill Rd., Northampton, MA 01060-2124 USA Tel 413-582-1121; Fax: 413-586-6654
E-mail: akot@clarkeschool.org
Web site: http://www.clarkeschool.org.

Mainstream Connections Publishing, (*978-1-60336*) 10103 Queens Cir., Ocean City, MD 21842 USA Tel 410-213-7861 fax or email requests; *Imprints*: Adventures of Everyday Geniuses, The (Adv Evryday)
E-mail: barb.esham@mainstreamconnections.org; lisa.spielman@mainstreamconnections.org
Web site: http://www.mainstreamconnections.org
Dist(s): **Brodart Co.**
Emery-Pratt Co.
Follett School Solutions
Quality Bks., Inc.
Yankee Bk. Peddler, Inc.

Mainstreet Systems & Software Inc., (*978-0-9726871*) P.O. Box 577, Harleysville, PA 19438-0577 USA (SAN 255-335X) Toll Free: 800-257-4535
E-mail: epwhelan@netcarrier.com
Web site: http://www.promotecopyrights.com.

Maire, Lucy Bedoya, (*978-0-9768436*) Orders Addr.: P.O. Box 2632, Westport, CT 06880 USA Tel 203-454-5204; Fax: 203-454-5204; Edit Addr.: 19 River Oak Rd., Westport, CT 06880 USA
E-mail: twelvetreasures@yahoo.com
Dist(s): **Raimond Graphics Inc.**

Majestic Eagle Publishing, (*978-0-9797495*) Div. of James J. Brown & Assoc., Inc., 6649 Navajo, Lincolnwood, IL 60712 USA Tel 847-679-3447; Fax: 847-679-6191
E-mail: jola1@aol.com.

Majestic Publishing, LLC, (*978-0-9755314; 978-1-942156*) Orders Addr.: P.O. Box 1560, Lithonia, GA 30058 USA Tel 770-482-9129 Do not confuse with Majestic Publishing, LLC in Santa Barbara, CA
E-mail: majpublish@gmail.com
Web site: http://www.majesticpublishing.net.

Majesty Publishing, (*978-0-9754839*) 12 Paddock Ln., Hampton, VA 23669 USA
E-mail: customerservice@faithfrontier.com
Web site: http://www.faithfrontier.com.

Major, Christina, (*978-0-692-02524-6; 978-0-692-46530-1*) 1910 Yosemite Ave. No. 205, Simi Valley, CA 93063 USA Tel 818-517-1076
E-mail: delphina2k@gmail.com
Web site: http://www.horizonscape.com.

Majority Press, Incorporated, The *See* **Majority Pr., The**

Majority Pr., The, (*978-0-912469*) Orders Addr.: 46 Development Rd., Fitchburg, MA 01420 USA (SAN 249-3012) Tel 978-342-9676; Fax: 978-348-1233; Edit Addr.: P.O. Box 538, Dover, MA 02030 USA (SAN 265-2757) Tel 508-744-6097 (phone/fax)
E-mail: tmpress@earthlink.net
Web site: http://www.themajoritypress.com
Dist(s): **A & B Distributors & Pubs. Group**
Lexicon Pubns., Inc.

Majzik, Bill *See* **Mill Creek Metro Publishing**

Makai Concepts, LLC, (*978-0-9744035*) Orders Addr.: 3 King William Ct., Hilton Head Island, SC 29926 USA (SAN 255-6219)
E-mail: betsys@hargray.com.

Makdan Publishing, (*978-0-9819283*) P.O. Box 7560, Bonney Lake, WA 98391 USA Tel 253-720-1059
E-mail: jimlandgraf@hotmail.com.

Make Believe Ideas (GBR) (*978-1-905051; 978-1-84610; 978-1-84879; 978-1-78065; 978-1-78235; 978-1-78393; 978-1-78598*) *Dist. by* **Nelson.**

Make Me A Story Pr., (*978-1-878847*) 1737 N. 2580 E. Rd., Sheldon, IL 60966 USA Tel 815-429-3501 (phone/fax)
E-mail: info@earthesquirrel.com
Web site: http://www.earthesquirrel.com.

Maker, Azmaira H. *See* **Aspiring Families Press**

Maker Media, Inc,
Dist(s): **Ingram Publisher Services**
O'Reilly Media, Inc.

Malachite Quills Publishing *See* **MQuills Publishing**

Malamih Publishing Hse., (*978-0-9820804*) 4311 Jamboree Rd., No. 170, Newport Beach, CA 92660 USA.

Malamute Pr., (*978-0-9722180*) Orders Addr.: P.O. Box W, Aspen, CO 81612 USA; Edit Addr.: P.O. Box W, Aspen, CO 81612-7424 USA
E-mail: info@dodogsvote.com; sales@malamutepress.com
Web site: http://www.malamutepress.com.

Malbrough, Michael, (*978-0-9758883*) 163-167 N. Pk. St., Apt. 5, East Orange, NJ 07019 USA.

Malibu Bks. for Children, (*978-1-929084*) Div. of Malibu Films, Inc., 48 Broad St., No. 134, Red Bank, NJ 07701 USA Tel 732-933-0446 (phone/fax); Toll Free: 888-629-9947 (phone/fax)
E-mail: malibuinc@aol.com
Web site: http://www.malibubooks.com.

Malik, Sakinah A. *See* **EDR**

Mallon Publishing (AUS) (*978-1-875696*) *Dist. by* **D C D.**

Malone-Ballard Book Publishers, (*978-0-9729484*) 160 S. Third St., Lansing, IA 52151 USA Tel 319-389-7174 (phone/fax)
Web site: http://www.malone-ballard.com
Dist(s): **Partners Bk. Distributing, Inc.**

Malor Bks. *Imprint of* **I S H K**

Malpaso Ediciones SL (ESP) (*978-84-15996; 978-84-16420*) *Dist. by* **IPG Chicago.**

Mama Incense Publishing, (*978-0-9761523*) P.O. Box 4635, Long Beach, CA 90804-9998 USA Tel 310-490-9097
E-mail: mama@mamaincense.com
Web site: http://www.mamaincense.com.

Mama Specific Productions, (*978-0-9749480*) P.O. Box 110393, Cleveland, OH 44111-0393 USA Tel 440-396-1963; Fax: 801-640-2494; *Imprints*: MSPpress (MSPpr)
E-mail: info@msppress.com; trula@MSPpress.com
Web site: http://www.msppress.com.

Mama's Boyz, Inc., (*978-0-9796132*) 304 Main Ave. #114, Norwalk, CT 06851 USA (SAN 854-1914)
E-mail: jerrycraft@aol.com
Web site: http://www.jerrycraft.net
Dist(s): **Follett School Solutions.**

MaMbabooks.com, (*978-0-9817448; 978-0-9887867*) Div. of Mamba Books & Publishing, 355 Liberty St., Dendron, VA 23839 USA
E-mail: mambabooks@gmail.com
Web site: http://www.mambabooks.com; http://www.mambabooks.biz.

Mammoth, Math, (*978-1-942715*) 915 Lounds St., Inverness, FL 34450 USA Tel 813-728-9831
E-mail: maria_miller@mathmammoth.com
Web site: www.mathmammoth.com.

Mamoo Hse., (*978-1-933014*) 17 W. Browning Rd., Collingswood, NJ 08108 USA Tel 856-858-6616
E-mail: melisma@earthlink.net
Web site: http://www.mamoohouse.com.

MAMP Creations, (*978-0-9772210*) P.O. Box 4253, Hopkins, MN 55343 USA Tel 952-938-9320 (phone/fax); *Imprints*: Phil the Pill & Friends (Phil PillFrnds)
E-mail: mampcreations@aol.com
Web site: http://www.cafepress.com/mampcreations.

Management Services, (*978-0-9747418*) 302 S. 2nd St. Apt. 711, Champaign, IL 61820-4141 USA Do not confuse with Managment Services Incorporated in Atlanta, GA
E-mail: aepelbaum@yahoo.com
Web site: http://moscowtechchicago.com.

Manassas Museum, The, (*978-1-886826*) Orders Addr.: P.O. Box 560, Manassas, VA 20108 USA Tel 703-368-1873; Edit Addr.: 9101 Prince William St., Manassas, VA 201110-5615 USA
Web site: http://www.manassasmuseum.org.

Manchester Univ. Pr. (GBR) (*978-0-7190; 978-1-84779; 978-1-5261; 978-1-78499; 978-1-78170*) *Dist. by* **OUP.**

Mandala Publishing, (*978-0-945475; 978-1-886069; 978-1-932771; 978-1-60109*) 3160 Kerner Blvd. Ste. 108, San Rafael, CA 94901-5454 USA Toll Free: 800-688-2218 (orders only); *Imprints*: Earth Aware Editions (Earth Aware)
E-mail: info@mandala.org
Web site: http://www.mandala.org; http://earthawareeditions.com/catalog/
Dist(s): **MyiLibrary**
Simon & Schuster, Inc.

Mandala Publishing Group *See* **Mandala Publishing**

Mandell, Ted, (*978-0-9749156*) 2232 Pine Creek Ct., South Bend, IN 46628 USA Tel 574-631-6953
E-mail: tmandell@nd.edu.

Mandeville, Terry M., (*978-0-9762475*) 7933 NE 124th St., Kirkland, WA 98034 USA
E-mail: terrymand@aol.com.

M&J Southwest, Inc., (*978-0-9744534*) 4402 E. Desert Willow Rd., Phoenix, AZ 85044 USA Tel 480-940-4046
E-mail: michaelc@gotwords.com
Web site: http://www.gotwords.com.

Mandolin House *See* **Kush Univ. Pr.**

Mandolin Hse. *Imprint of* **Kush Univ. Pr.**

Mandracchia Bks. *Imprint of* **Mandracchia, Charles**

Mandracchia, Charles, (*978-0-9721957*) 7914 Rockaway Beach Blvd. Apt. 6L, Rockaway Beac, NY 11693-2081 USA; *Imprints*: Mandracchia Books (Mandracchia Bks)
E-mail: charlesmandracchia@yahoo.com
Web site: http://www.kungfoogrannys.com; http://www.showtoonz.com.

Mandragora (ITA) (*978-88-7461; 978-88-85957*) *Dist. by* **Natl Bk Netwk.**

Mandy & Andy Bks., Inc., (*978-0-9772757*) 124 Meridian Ave., Poinciana, FL 34759-3241 USA (SAN 257-1765) Tel 407-319-3880; 863-427-4643
E-mail: wadams23@cfl.rr.com
Web site: http://mandyandandybooks.com.

Mandy & Pandy Bks., LLC, (*978-0-9800156; 978-0-9834411*) 2590 Cook Creek Ct., Ann Arbor, MI 48103 USA Tel 734-904-1916
E-mail: tsinkule@heulegordon.com
Dist(s): **China Books & Periodicals, Inc.**

Manga 18 *Imprint of* **Central Park Media Corp.**

Manga Punk, (*978-0-9748966*) P.O. Box 966, Meadows of Dan, VA 24120 USA
Web site: http://www.mangapunk.com.

MANGACANDY, LLC, (*978-0-9785891*) 13937 W. 73rd St., Shawnee, KS 66216 USA Tel 913-638-9940
E-mail: nami.bunny@gmail.com
Web site: http://www.mangacandy.com.

Mango (FRA) (*978-2-7404; 978-2-84270; 978-2-910635*) *Dist. by* **Distribks Inc.**

Mango Tree Pr., (*978-0-9708571*) Orders Addr.: P.O. Box 853, Mackinaw City, MI 49701 USA Tel 231-627-7322 (phone/fax); Edit Addr.: 2562 Pinewood Cir., Cheboygan, MI 49721 USA
E-mail: ids@mangotreepress.com; lds@mangotreepress.com
Web site: http://www.mangotreepress.com
Dist(s): **Partners Bk. Distributing, Inc.**

Mangrove Seed Expressions *Imprint of* **Mangrove Seed, Inc.**

Mangrove Seed, Inc., (*978-0-9797158*) Orders Addr.: P.O. Box 2, Sarasota, FL 34230-0002 USA Toll Free: 866-549-1549 to contact publisher; P.O. Box 02, Sarasota, FL 34230; *Imprints*: Mangrove Seed Expressions (Mangve Seed)
E-mail: dan@mangroveseed.org
Web site: http://www.mangroveseed.org; http://www.mangroveseedchronicles.com.

Mangrum, Kaylea J., (*978-0-9883009*) 1521 Carrick Dr., Murfreesboro, TN 37128 USA Tel 615-579-3663
E-mail: donmangrum@yahoo.com; phillipmangrum@mac.com.

Mangrum-Strichart Learning Resources, (*978-0-9745999; 978-0-9797723; 978-0-9978079*) 2634 Glendale Dr., Loveland, CO 80538 USA Tel 970-593-1586; Fax: 970-962-0057; Toll Free: 866-409-0585
E-mail: study@mangrum-strichart.com
Web site: http://www.mangrum-strichart.com.

Manhattan Academia, (*978-0-615-16120-4; 978-0-615-18454-8; 978-0-615-18503-3; 978-1-936581*) 26 Norwood Terr., Millburn, NJ 07041 USA
Web site: http://www.manhattanacademia.com
Dist(s): **Lulu Pr., Inc.**

Manic D Pr., (*978-0-916397; 978-1-933149; 978-1-945665*) Orders Addr.: P.O. Box 410804, San Francisco, CA 94141 USA (SAN 670-6932) Tel 415-648-8288 (phone/fax); Edit Addr.: 250 Banks St., San Francisco, CA 94110 USA
E-mail: info@manicdpress.com
Web site: http://www.manicdpress.com
Dist(s): **Consortium Bk. Sales & Distribution**
Last Gasp of San Francisco
MyiLibrary
SPD-Small Pr. Distribution.

Manifest Pubns., (*978-0-9627896; 978-1-929354*) Orders Addr.: P.O. Box 429, Carpinteria, CA 93014 USA Tel

805-684-4905; Fax: 805-684-3100; Edit Addr.: P.O. Box 429, Carpinteria, CA 93014-0429 USA
E-mail: editor@manifestpub.com; publisher@manifestpub.com
Web site: http://www.manifestpub.com
Dist(s): **Sunbelt Pubns., Inc.**

Maninge Mali, *(978-0-9729698)* 204 Garden Pl., Radnor, PA 19087 USA (SAN 255-4623) Tel 610-254-0846
E-mail: maningemali@aol.com.

Manis, Shirley, *(978-0-9839286)* 2205 Francesco Cr., Capitola, CA 95010 USA Tel 831-462-4126
E-mail: smanis@cruzio.com.

Manitowish River Pr., *(978-0-9656763)* 4245 Hwy. 47, Mercer, WI 54547 USA Tel 715-476-2828; Fax: 715-476-2818
E-mail: manitowish@centuryinter.net
Dist(s): **Adventure Pubns.**

Mankamyer, Laura, *(978-0-9728431)* 343 Stonebrook Dr., Canonsburg, PA 15317-3409 USA.

Mann Publishing Group, *(978-0-9726888; 978-1-932577; 978-1-933673)* 710 Main St., 6th Flr., Rollinsford, NH 03869 USA (SAN 255-5409) Tel 603-601-0325; Fax: 603-601-0334; Toll Free: 877-877-6266; *Imprints*: BookMann Press (BkMann Pr)
E-mail: tmann@mannpublishing.com
Web site: http://www.askopus.com; http://www.rationalpress.com; http://www.agilitypress.com; http://www.incpress.com; http://www.mannpublishing.com.

Mann Publishing Inc. *See* **Mann Publishing Group**

Manners Toy Co., LLC, *(978-0-615-17967-4)* Orders Addr.: 2546 Lochness Rd, Richmond, VA 23235 USA Tel 804-307-5154
E-mail: mmadore@mannerstoycompany.com.

Mannheim Steamroller L.L.C., *(978-0-9656909; 978-0-9754149)* 9130 Mormon Bridge Rd., Omaha, NE 68152 USA Tel 402-457-4341; Fax: 402-457-4332
Web site: http://www.amgram.com; www.mannheimsteamroller.com.

Manning, Laurie, *(978-1-892686)* Orders Addr.: 2640 Violet, Glenview, IL 60025 USA
E-mail: chinaqi888@aol.com.

Manning Pubns. Co., *(978-1-884777; 978-1-930110; 978-1-932394; 978-1-933988; 978-1-935182; 978-1-61729; 978-1-63343)* 180 Broad St. Apt. #1323, Saintmpford, CT 06901 USA; 178 S. Hill Dr., Westamptomn, NJ 08060 Tel 609-835-2793
E-mail: kidi@manning.com
Web site: http://www.manning.com
Dist(s): **Ebsco Publishing**
Independent Pubs. Group
Ingram Publisher Services
O'Reilly Media, Inc.

Manoa Pr., *(978-1-891839)* 2702 Menoa Rd., Honolulu, HI 96822 USA Tel 808-988-4904
Dist(s): **Native Bks.**

Manor Hse. Publishing Co., Inc., *(978-0-9645844; 978-0-9796239; 978-0-9836634; 978-0-9858774)* 880 Louis Dr., Warminster, PA 18974-2819 USA Tel 215-259-1700 Toll Free: 800-768-3222
E-mail: rdean@mgadvertising.com
Web site: http://www.poolspaliving.com.

Mansfield, J. Hse. Publishing Co., *(978-0-9707428)* P.O. Box 191575, Los Angeles, CA 90019 USA Fax: 323-935-6169
E-mail: jlmansfield@usa.net.

Mansion Publishing, Ltd., *(978-0-9675941)* c/o The Maggiore Companies, 60 Myopia Rd., Winchester, MA 01890 USA Tel 781-729-7210; 781-718-2003; Fax: 781-729-6444
E-mail: mansionpub@aol.com
Web site: http://wdressingthewholeperson.com.

Mantra Lingua (GBR) *(978-1-85269; 978-0-947679; 978-1-84444; 978-1-84611) Dist. by* **Chinasprout.**

Manual In Truth, A, *(978-0-9763252)* P.O. Box 541486, Miami, FL 33054 USA
E-mail: customersupport@amanualintruth.com
Web site: http://www.amanualintruth.com.

Manufacturing Application Konsulting Engineering (MAKE)in, *(978-1-62495)* 705 W. Azure Ln., Litchfield PArk, AZ 85340 USA Tel 469-265-8212
E-mail: trythaiketco@gmail.com
Web site: www.trythaiketco.com
Dist(s): **Lulu Pr., Inc.**

Many Kites Pr., *(978-0-9618469; 978-0-9729002)* Orders Addr.: P.O. Box 711, Cass Lake, MN 56633 USA Tel 605-341-4232 (phone/fax); Toll Free: 800-486-8940; Edit Addr.: 6511 160th St. NW, Cass Lake, MN 56633 USA
E-mail: info@manykites.com; jamie@manykites.com
Web site: http://www.manykites.com; http://www.manykites.org
Dist(s): **Independent Pubs. Group**
Smashwords.

Many Voice Pr., *(978-0-9795185; 978-0-9833679)* Flathead Valley Community College 777 Grandview Dr., Kalispell, MT 59901 USA (SAN 853-6686) Tel 406-756-3907; Fax: 406-756-3815 Do not confuse with companies with the same name in Long Islanf City, NY, Cincinnati, OH
E-mail: jjaegermontana@hotmail.com
Dist(s): **SPD-Small Pr. Distribution.**

Manzanita Falls Pubs., *(978-0-9763916)* P.O. Box 991920, Redding, CA 96099-1920 USA (SAN 256-3347)
Web site: http://www.manzanitafallspublishers.com.

MAP Creative LLC, *(978-0-9856967)* Orders Addr.: 128 Hamilton Rd, Bloomfield Hills, MI 48301 USA Tel 248-731-7065
E-mail: mattdamman@gmail.com
Web site: www.thesmallsports.com.

Mapin Publishing Pvt. Ltd (IND) *(978-81-85822; 978-81-88204) Dist. by* **Natl Bk Netwk.**

Maple Bend Farms Pr., *(978-0-9740799)* 4804 Laurel Canyon Blvd., Suite 224, Valley Village, CA 91607 USA
E-mail: ocsage@aol.com
Web site: http://www.maplebend.com.

Maple Canyon Co., *(978-0-9669760; 978-0-9787164)* P.O. Box 565, Mapleton, UT 84663 USA Tel 801-489-8948
E-mail: chuckclifton@maplecanyon.com; customerservice@maplecanyon.com
Web site: http://www.maplecanyon.com.

Maple Corners Press *Imprint of* **Attic Studio Publishing Hse.**

Maple Creek Media, *(978-0-9837967; 978-0-9859678; 978-0-9895471; 978-0-9912442; 978-0-9907392; 978-1-942914)* 1194 N. Carroll St., Hampstead, MD 21074 USA Tel 410-259-8295
E-mail: craig.schenning@maplecreekmedia.com
Web site: http://www.maplecreekmedia.com.

Maple Lane Writing & Desktop Publishing, *(978-0-9667527)* 16821 W. County Hill Rd., Hayward, WI 54843 USA Tel 715-634-9600; Fax: 715-634-1871
E-mail: mapleln@win.bright.net.

Maple Leaf Ctr., *(978-0-9759850; 978-0-9827210)* 167 N. Main St., Wallingford, VT 05773 USA Tel 802-446-3601; Fax: 802-446-3801
E-mail: mapleleaf@vermontel.net
Web site: http://www.mapleleafcenter.com.

Maple Leaf Publishing *See* **Spreeda Publishing**

Maple Road Publishing, Inc., *(978-0-9844453)* Orders Addr.: P.O. Box 10143, McLean, VA 22102 USA
Web site: http://www.mapleroadpublishing.com.

Maps For Kids Inc., *(978-0-9759433)* 1550 Poly Dr., Billings, MT 59102 USA Tel 406-238-7131; Fax: 406-259-4021; Toll Free: 877-897-7131
E-mail: banjo@floberg.com
Web site: http://www.mapsforkids.com.

Maps.com, *(978-1-930194)* 120 Cremona Dr. Ste. H, Goleta, CA 93117-5564 USA (SAN 254-4180) Toll Free: 800-929-4627
E-mail: info@maps.com
Web site: http://www.maps.com
Dist(s): **Cram, George F. Co., Inc.**

Marable, Justin, *(978-0-9831104)* 136 SW Kendall Ave., Topeka, KS 66606 USA Tel 785-286-7944
E-mail: justinmarableks@gmail.com.

Marak, Michael, *(978-0-9795866)* 6205 Daffan Ln., Austin, TX 78724-1501 USA
E-mail: sue@rezulting.com.

Marandu, Thobias L., *(978-0-9767605)* 2913 Columbiana Rd. Apt. B, Birmingham, AL 35216-3537 USA
E-mail: tlekundayo@yahoo.com.

Marble Hse. Editions, *(978-0-9677047; 978-0-9786745; 978-0-9815345; 978-0-9834030; 978-0-9966224)* 96-09 66th Ave., Suite 1d, Rego Park, NY 11374 USA (SAN 253-6536); 96-09 66th Ave., Suite 1d, Rego Park, NY 11374 (SAN 253-6536)
E-mail: elizabeth.uhlig@yahoo.com
Web site: http://www.marble-house-editions.com/.

Marble Mountain Pr., *(978-0-9748552)* PMB 214, 2019 Aero Way, Suite 103, Medford, OR 97504 USA Tel 530-926-2473
E-mail: marblemountain@snowcrest.net
Web site: http://www.rvinnz.com.

Marcabru Publishing, *(978-0-615-61495-3)* 108 E. 38th St., New York, NY 10016 USA Tel 917-596-0650
Web site: www.glennberger.net
Dist(s): **CreateSpace Independent Publishing Platform.**

Marcasa Bks., *(978-0-9763015)* Paloma del Lago No. 67, Campolago, Cidra, PR 00739-9361 USA Tel 787-960-3517 (phone/fax)
E-mail: mmartinezpr@gmail.com.

March 4th, Inc., *(978-0-9840806; 978-0-9829938; 978-1-939775)* 3701 Sacramento St. #494, San Francisco, CA 94118 USA (SAN 858-3641) Fax: 415-366-1520; Toll Free: 877-415-4488
E-mail: info@littlepicklepress.com
Web site: http://www.littlepicklepress.com
Dist(s): **Ingram Publisher Services**
MyiLibrary
Sourcebooks, Inc.

March Media, Inc., *(978-0-9634824)* 1114 Oman Dr., Brentwood, TN 37027 USA Tel 615-377-1146; Fax: 615-373-1705
E-mail: etta.wilson@comcast.net.

March Street Pr., *(978-0-9624453; 978-1-882983; 978-0-9745909; 978-1-59661)* 3413 Wilshire Dr., Greensboro, NC 27408-2923 USA Fax: 336-282-9754 prefer orders by email (rbixby@earthlink.net)
E-mail: rbixby@earthlink.net
Web site: http://www.marchstreetpress.com
Dist(s): **Bottom Dog Pr.**

Marcia's Menagerie, *(978-0-9777359)* 2960 W. Stuart St., A-203, Fort Collins, CO 80526 USA Tel 970-493-6373
E-mail: tangome27@hotmail.com.

Marcinson Pr., *(978-0-9893732; 978-0-9967207; 978-1-946932)* 11111-70 San Jose Blvd. Suite 136, Jacksonville, FL 32223 USA Tel 352-263-0910
E-mail: editor@marcinsonpress.com.

Marco Bk. Co., *(978-0-9710756; 978-0-9729765)* 60 Industrail Rd., Lodi, NJ 07644 USA Tel 973-458-0485; Fax: 973-458-5289; Toll Free: 800-842-4234; *Imprints*: Everbind (Everbind)
E-mail: everbind5@aol.com
Dist(s): **Bks. & Media, Inc.**

MAR*CO Products, Inc., *(978-1-57543; 978-1-884063)* Orders Addr.: 1443 Old York Rd., Warminster, PA 18974 USA Tel 215-956-0313; Fax: 215-956-9041; Toll Free: 800-448-2197
E-mail: csfunk@marcoproducts.com; marcoproducts@comcast.net
Web site: http://www.store.yahoo.com/marcoproducts; http://www.marcoproducts.com.

Marcoux, Tom Media, LLC, *(978-0-9624660; 978-0-9800511; 978-0-615-78342-0; 978-0-615-78657-5; 978-0-615-80157-5; 978-0-615-80934-2; 978-0-615-81302-8; 978-0-615-83582-2; 978-0-615-91576-0; 978-0-615-92869-2; 978-0-615-97539-9; 978-0-615-99188-7; 978-0-692-21096-3; 978-0-692-22704-6; 978-0-692-22972-9; 978-0-692-23525-6; 978-0-692-33069-2; 978-0-692-35850-4; 978-0-692-38436-7; 978-0-692-45951-5; 978-0-692-52718-4; 978-0-692-56195-9; 978-0-692-60115-0; 978-0-692-60208-9; 978-0-692-63808-8; 978-0-692-64737-0; 978-0-69) 674 Morse Ave. Unit F, Sunnyvale, CA 94085 USA Tel 415-572-6609*
Dist(s): **CreateSpace Independent Publishing Platform.**

Mardi Gras Publishing, LLC, *(978-0-9787262; 978-0-9789024; 978-0-9789986; 978-0-9790649; 978-0-9791570; 978-1-934329)* 6845 Hwy. 90 E. Suite 255, Daphne, AL 36526 USA
E-mail: contactlamedia@gmail.com
Web site: http://lamediaonline.com.

Mardick Pr., *(978-1-940413)* P.O. Box 10701, Houston, TX 77206 USA Tel 713-254-7285; *Imprints*: Blackbirch Press, Incorporated (Blackbirch Pr)
E-mail: publisher@mardickpress.com.

Marduk Publishing Inc., *(978-1-893138)* Orders Addr.: a/o Marduk Publishing Inc., P.O. Box 480608, Delray Beach, FL 33448 USA (SAN 256-3053) Tel 561-638-6070; 516 695-8077; Toll Free: 888-462-7385 (phone/fax)
E-mail: docbloc@marduk1.com; docbloc@marpub.com; docbloc@hotmail.com
Web site: http://www.marpub.com; http://www.marduk1.com; http://www.all-a.us; http://www.all-ace.com.

Marn Green Publishing, Inc., *(978-1-934277)* 5630 Memorial Ave N. # 3, Stillwater, MN 55082-1087 USA (SAN 852-4920) Toll Free: 800-287-1512
E-mail: toddsnow@marengreen.com
Web site: http://www.marengreen.com.

Maresca, Wendi, *(978-0-9772897)* 6130 Murifield Dr., Gurnee, IL 60031-5357 USA.

Margaret Weis Productions, Ltd., *(978-1-931567; 978-1-936685)* P.O. Box 1131, Williams Bay, WI 53191 USA Fax: 866-668-5730 Do not confuse with Sovereign Pr. in Rochester, WA
E-mail: margaret@margaretweis.com; christi@margaretweis.com
Web site: http://www.margaretweis.com
Dist(s): **Diamond Comic Distributors, Inc.**
Diamond Bk. Distributors
PSI (Publisher Services, Inc.).

Margolis, Amy Publishing, *(978-0-9776692)* Orders Addr.: 31 Saddle Ln., Old Brookville, NY 11545 USA (SAN 257-9294)
E-mail: Amy@ButterfliesandMagicalWings.com
Web site: http://www.ButterfliesandMagicalWings.com.

Margolis, Marion, *(978-0-9753184)* 1 W. 72nd St., Apt. No. 95, New York, NY 10023 USA Tel 212-595-7555
E-mail: chasmargolis@aol.com
Dist(s): **Xlibris Corp.**

Marhouse, Inc., *(978-0-9752703)* Orders Addr.: a/o Marhouse Inc., P.O. Box 150605, Altamonte Springs, FL 32715 USA Tel 407-499-5307 (phone/fax)
E-mail: marhouse12@yahoo.com
Web site: http://www.adventurefox.com.

Marian Pr., *(978-0-944203; 978-1-932773; 978-1-59614)* Marian Helpers Ctr., Eden Hill, Stockbridge, MA 01263-0004 USA (SAN 243-1548) Tel 413-298-3691; Fax: 413-298-1356; Toll Free: 800-462-7426
E-mail: marianpress@marian.org
Web site: http://www.marian.org
Dist(s): **Send The Light Distribution LLC.**

Marianist Pr., *(978-0-9628309)* Orders Addr.: 1116 Imperial Blvd., Kettering, OH 45419-2434 USA Tel 937-298-8509; Edit Addr.: 233 E. Helena St., Dayton, OH 45404-1003 USA.

Marianne Richmond Studios, Inc. *Imprint of* **Sourcebooks, Inc.**

Marilux Pr., *(978-0-9710281)* 4100 Corporate Sq., Suite 161, Naples, FL 34104 USA Tel 239-398-7018; Fax: 917-591-0387
E-mail: sales@mariluxpress.com
Web site: http://www.MariluxPress.com.

Marimba Bks. *Imprint of* **Hudson Publishing Group, The**

Marinaro, Stacy, *(978-0-615-20684-4; 978-0-615-20807-7; 978-0-615-20883-1; 978-0-615-21988-2; 978-0-578-02365-6)* 420 Matthews St., Bristol, CT 06010 USA
E-mail: stacymarinaro@yahoo.com
Dist(s): **Lulu Pr., Inc.**

Mariner Publishing, *(978-0-9768238; 978-0-9776841; 978-0-9800077; 978-0-9820172; 978-0-9841128; 978-0-9833478; 978-0-9835565; 978-0-9849214; 978-0-9909653; 978-0-9975226; 978-0-9992885)* Div. of Mariner Media, Inc., 131 W. 21st St., Buena Vista, VA 24416 USA Tel 540-264-0021; Fax: 540-261-1881 Do not confuse with Mariner Publishing in Tampa, FL Oklahoma City, OK
E-mail: andy@marinermedia.com
Web site: http://www.marinermedia.com
Dist(s): **Virginia Pubns.**

Marion Street Pr., LLC, *(978-0-9665176; 978-0-9710050; 978-0-9729937; 978-1-933338; 978-1-936863)* 4207 SE. Woodstock Blvd. #168, Portland, OR 97206 USA Tel 503-888-4624; Toll Free Fax: 866-571-8359
E-mail: info@acornguild.com; acornguild@yahoo.com
Web site: http://www.acornguild.com; http://www.marionstreetpress.com
Dist(s): **Independent Pubs. Group.**

Maritime Kids Quest Pr., *(978-0-9761178)* P.O. Box 700, Manteo, NC 27954 USA Tel 252-473-6933
E-mail: maritimekidsquest@earthlink.net.

Maritime Museum Assn. of San Diego, *(978-0-944580)* 1492 N. Harbor Dr., San Diego, CA 92101 USA (SAN 279-5027) Tel 619-234-9153; Fax: 619-234-8345
E-mail: museumstore@sdmaritime.com
Web site: http://www.sdmaritime.com/mains'lhaul
Dist(s): **Sunbelt Pubns., Inc.**

Marker, Margaret Penfield, *(978-0-9716721)* 64 Colonial Dr., Rancho Mirage, CA 92270-1600 USA
E-mail: tmlrmarker@aol.com.

Market 1 Group Inc., *(978-0-9748109)* 118 Worthington Business Ctr. 1550 Douglas Ave., Charleston, IL 61920 USA Tel 217-345-8281
E-mail: bmcelwee@consolidated.net
Web site: http://www.familyjourneys.net.

Market Management Group, *(978-0-9861953; 978-0-9969111; 978-1-944589)* 300 E Bellevue Dr. Unit 208, Pasadena, CA 91101 USA Tel 888-859-0792; *Imprints*: Incorgnito Publishing Press (MYID_H_INCORGN)
E-mail: mconant@incorgnitobooks.com
Dist(s): **Midpoint Trade Bks., Inc.**

Markins Enterprises, *(978-0-937729)* 2039 SE 45th Ave., Portland, OR 97215 USA (SAN 659-3224) Tel 503-235-1036.

Markowitz, Darryl, *(978-0-9818469)* 354 Park Blvd., Worthington, OH 43085 USA Tel 412-613-1733; *Imprints*: FaithWalker Publishing (FaithWalker)
Web site: http://www.thefaithwalkerseries.com.

Marks, Ginger *See* **DocUmeant Publishing**

Marks, William *See* **MPC Pr. International**

Markwin Pr., *(978-0-9740793)* Orders Addr.: P.O. Box 1143, Silver Springs, NV 89429 USA Tel 775-577-0676; Edit Addr.: 3220 E. 9th St., Silver Springs, NV 89429 USA
E-mail: softgaits@wildblue.com
Web site: www.TheFabulousFloatingHorses.com.

Marlor Pr., Inc., *(978-0-943400; 978-1-892147)* 4304 Brigadoon Dr., Saint Paul, MN 55126 USA (SAN 240-7140) Tel 651-484-4600; Fax: 651-490-1182; Toll Free: 800-669-4908
E-mail: marlor@minn.net
Dist(s): **Independent Pubs. Group**
MyiLibrary.

MarMooWorks,LLC, *(978-0-9853579; 978-0-9853580)* 318 Beverly Dr., Erie, PA 16505 USA Tel 814-454-1888
E-mail: mamoodey@gmail.com
Web site: jason@conveyorarts.org.

MarniPosa Services and Productions, *(978-0-9727687)* P.O. Box 812, Middletown, DE 19709 USA
E-mail: niamaebrown@gmail.com
Web site: http://www.marniwilliams.com; http://www.nia22.zumba.com; http://www.nia22.com.

Maroma Bks., *(978-0-9796465)* 5615 Kirby Dr., Suite 820, Houston, TX 77005 USA Toll Free Fax: 800-525-0910; Toll Free: 888-627-6628
E-mail: molly@maromabooks.com
Web site: http://www.maromabooks.com
Dist(s): **Lightning Source, Inc.**

Marquand Bks., Inc., *(978-0-9706394; 978-0-9744202; 978-0-9778028; 978-0-9815762; 978-0-615-22812-9; 978-0-615-27788-2; 978-0-615-31547-8; 978-0-615-31690-1; 978-0-615-33169-0; 978-0-615-35171-1; 978-0-615-35172-8; 978-0-615-36404-9; 978-0-615-39016-1; 978-0-615-39126-7; 978-0-615-39579-1; 978-0-615-41782-0; 978-0-615-45883-0; 978-0-615-47180-8; 978-0-615-55154-8; 978-0-615-56154-7; 978-0-615-56155-4; 978-0-615-56156-1; 978-0-615-56210-0; 978-0-615-56585-9; 978-0-9849864; 978-0-615-59005-9; 978-0-615-59427-9; 9) 1400 2nd Ave, Seattle, WA 98101 USA Tel 206-624-2030; Fax: 206-624-1821*
E-mail: Adrian@luciamarquand.com
Web site: http://www.luciamarquand.com
Dist(s): **Antique Collectors' Club**
D.A.P./Distributed Art Pubs.
National Bk. Network
Two Rivers Distribution
Univ. of Oklahoma Pr.
Univ. of Washington Pr.

Marquette Bks., LLC, *(978-0-922993; 978-0-9816018; 978-0-9826597; 978-0-9833476)* Orders Addr.: 16421 N. 31 Ave., Phoenix, AZ 85053 USA (SAN 251-5261) Tel 509-290-9240; Fax: 602-464-9675
E-mail: books@marquettebooks.com
Web site: http://www.marquettebooks.com
Dist(s): **Ambassador Bks. & Media**
Bk. Hse., The
Brodart Co.
Coutts Information Services
Eastern Bk. Co.
Emery-Pratt Co.
Levant USA, Inc.
Midwest Library Service
Blackwell.

Marquise Publishing, *(978-0-9745264)* Orders Addr.: 11459 Mayfield Rd Suite 338, Cleveland, OH 44106 USA
E-mail: marquisepublishing@gmail.com
Web site: http://www.marquisepublishing.com.

Marrero, Rafael, *(978-0-9747569)* 2121 Red Rd., Ave., Coral Gables, FL 33155-2232 USA Tel 305-267-0163
E-mail: rafelitomarrero@hotmail.com.

Marriwell Publishing, *(978-0-9742891)* P.O. Box 116, Center Valley, PA 18034 USA Tel 610-282-6807; Fax: 610-282-0909
Web site: http://www.marriwell.com.

Mars Media Publishers *See* **Audio Holdings, LLC**

Marsh, Carole Bks. *Imprint of* **Gallopade International**

Marsh, Carole Family CD-Rom *Imprint of* **Gallopade International**

Marsh, Carole Mysteries *Imprint of* **Gallopade International**

Marsh Creek Pr., *(978-0-937750)* Div. of Don Aslett, Inc., Orders Addr.: P.O. Box 700, Pocatello, ID 83204 USA (SAN 216-1028) Tel 208-232-3535; Fax: 208-235-5481; Edit Addr.: 311 S. Fifth Ave., Pocatello, ID 83201 USA
E-mail: Tobih@aol.com
Web site: http://www.aslett.com.

Marsh Media *See* **Witcher Productions**

Marsh, Thomas E. Inc., *(978-0-9633682)* 914 Franklin Ave., Youngstown, OH 44502 USA Tel 216-743-8600; Toll Free: 800-845-7930.

Marshall Cavendish (GBR) *(978-0-7614; 978-0-86307; 978-1-85435; 978-0-9533784; 978-1-902741; 978-0-462; 978-0-85080; 978-1-905992)* *Dist. by* **Marshall C.**

†Marshall Cavendish Corp., *(978-0-7614; 978-0-85685; 978-0-86307; 978-1-85435; 978-1-60870)* Member of Times Publishing Group, 99 White Plains Rd., Tarrytown, NY 10591-9001 USA (SAN 238-437X) Tel 914-332-8888; Fax: 914-332-8882; Toll Free: 800-821-9881; *Imprints:* Benchmark Books (Benchmark NY); Marshall Cavendish Reference Books (M C Ref Bks); Cavendish Children's Books (Cav Child Bks)
E-mail: npalazzo@marshallcavendish.com
Web site: www.MCEducation.us
Dist(s): **BookBaby**
Ebsco Publishing
Follett School Solutions
Fujii Assocs.
Lectorum Pubns., Inc.
MyiLibrary; *CIP.*

Marshall Cavendish International (Asia) Private Ltd. (SGP) *(978-981-204; 978-981-232; 978-2-85700; 978-981-261; 978-981-4302; 978-981-4312; 978-981-4328; 978-981-4346; 978-981-4351; 978-981-4361; 978-981-4382; 978-981-4398; 978-981-4408; 978-981-4426; 978-981-4430; 978-981-4433; 978-981-4435; 978-981-4484; 978-981-4516; 978-981-4561; 978-981-4771)* *Dist. by* **Natl Bk Netwk.**

Marshall Cavendish Reference Bks. *Imprint of* **Marshall Cavendish Corp.**

Marshall, George Publishing, *(978-0-9729403)* P.O. Box 375, Bedford, VA 24523 USA.

Marshall, John High Schl. Alumni Assn., *(978-0-9759618)* 347 Pineview Cir., Berea, OH 44017 USA
E-mail: jmhalumni@ameritech.com
Web site: http://www.jmhalumni.com.

Martell Publishing Co, *(978-1-893181; 978-1-930200)* P.O. Box 83554, San Diego, CA 92138-3554 USA Toll Free Fax: 800-805-3329; *Imprints:* Lagesse Stevens (LagesseS)
E-mail: martell@martellpublishing.com.

Martella, Liz, *(978-0-615-14941-7; 978-0-615-25506-4)* 393 Lathrop Rd., Lathrop, CA 95330 USA
E-mail: lizmartella@yahoo.com
Web site: http://www.lulu.com/lizmartella
Dist(s): **Lulu Pr., Inc.**

Marti Bks., *(978-0-9766006)* Orders Addr.: P.O. Box 603, West Tisbury, MA 02575 USA Tel 508-696-7496 (phone/fax); Edit Addr.: 635 State Rd., West Tisbury, MA 02575 USA
E-mail: fferr2@aol.com
Web site: http://www.martibooks.com.

Martin, Amy, *(978-0-9882051)* 2733 Braden Way, Lexington, KY 40509 USA Tel 859-797-0156
E-mail: amart71@rocketmail.com.

Martin & Brothers, *(978-0-9719842; 978-0-9767500)* Orders Addr.: P.O. Box 122, Abbott, TX 76621 USA Tel 254-235-8588; Edit Addr.: 101 Bordon, Abbott, TX 76621 USA
E-mail: martinbrothers@aol.com.

Martin, Carolyn, *(978-0-9746808)* 1890 N. 36th St., Galesburg, MI 49053-9528 USA Tel 269-665-9953 Do not confuse with Carolyn Martin in Philadelphia, PA
E-mail: carmartin@earthlink.net
Web site: http://www.finefrets.com/metalhorses.

Martin, Elizabeth B., *(978-0-578-12912-9; 978-0-578-12913-6; 978-0-9910543; 978-0-9904213)*
E-mail: elizabeth@elizabethbmartin.com
Dist(s): **Lulu Pr., Inc.**

Martin, Jack & Assocs., *(978-0-9649530)* Orders Addr.: 9422 S. Saginaw, Grand Blanc, MI 48439 USA Tel 810-694-5698; Fax: 810-694-7851
E-mail: jdmart@tir.com
Web site: http://www.Pre-Apprenticetraining.com.

Martin, James Jr., *(978-0-9799465)* P.O. Box 4207, Greenwitch, CT 06831 USA Fax: 516-060-1177
E-mail: JMJ723@optonline.com
Web site: http://williamthegarbagetruck.com.

Martin, Kevin, *(978-0-578-10705-9)* 7450 Globe Rd., Lenoir, NC 28645 USA.

Martin Publishing, *(978-0-9753992)* 1600 S. 30th, Lot 36, Escanaba, MI 49829 USA Do not confuse with companies with the same or similar name in Fort Morgan, CO; Tampico, IL; La Mesa, CA; Perry, OK; Cowpens, SC; Lincoln, ME.

Martinez, Leroy F., *(978-0-9748002)* 4045 E. 3rd St. Unit 111, Long Beach, CA 90814-2883 USA Tel 562-443-7727
Web site: http://leroymartinez.com.

†Martingale & Co., *(978-0-943574; 978-1-56477; 978-1-60468; 978-1-68356)* Orders Addr.: 19021 120th Ave. NE. Suite 102, Bothell, WA 98011 USA (SAN 665-7923) Tel 425-483-3313; Fax: 425-486-7596; Toll Free: 800-426-3126; *Imprints:* That Patchwork Place (That Patchwrk Pl)
E-mail: ssanta@martingale-pub.com; mburns@martingale-pub.com; info@martingale-pub.com
Web site: http://www.martingale-pub.com
Dist(s): **Bookazine Co., Inc.**; *CIP.*

Martino Fine Bks., *(978-1-57898; 978-1-888262; 978-1-61427; 978-1-68422)* P.O. Box 913, Eastford, CT 06242 USA Tel 860-974-2277; 118 Westford Rd., Eastford, CT 06242
E-mail: martinofinebooks@hotmail.com
Web site: http://www.martinofinebooks.com.

Martino Publishing *See* **Martino Fine Bks.**

Martin's *See* **Green Pastures Pr.**

Marvel Enterprises, Incorporated *See* **Marvel Worldwide, Inc.**

Marvel Pr. *Imprint of* **Disney Publishing Worldwide**

Marvel Worldwide, Inc., *(978-0-7851; 978-0-87135; 978-0-939766; 978-0-9604146; 978-1-4695; 978-1-302)* Subs. of The Walt Disney Co, 135 W. 50th St., New York, NY 10020 USA (SAN 216-9088); c/o Marvel Enterprises Japan, Inc., Hill House B, 9-10 Hachiyama-cho Sibuya, Tokyo, 150-0034
E-mail: mail@marvel.com; amorales@marvel.com
Web site: http://www.marvel.com
Dist(s): **Hachette Bk. Group.**

Marvelous Dream, *(978-0-9771016)* Div. of Marvelous World LLC, P.O. Box 252, Bloomfield, NJ 07003-9998 USA (SAN 256-7857).

Marvelous Spirit Pr. *Imprint of* **Loving Healing Pr., Inc.**

MarWel Enterprises, Inc., *(978-0-9759582)* P.O. Box 31227, Washington, DC 20030 USA
E-mail: marwel@earthlink.net.

Marx Group, The, *(978-0-9773962; 978-1-935309)* 2111 Jefferson Davis Hwy. 303N., Arlington, VA 22202 USA Tel 703-418-1956; Fax: 703-418-0224
E-mail: don@themarxgroup.com
Web site: http://www.the marxgroup.com.

Marx, Jeff, *(978-0-9667824; 978-0-9793134)* 3160 N. 35th St., Hollywood, FL 33021-2630 USA (SAN 853-1021)
E-mail: JeffMarx@schoolelection.com
Web site: http://www.schoolelection.com
Dist(s): **Independent Pubs. Group.**

Mary B./French, *(978-0-9852821)* 1355 Pine St. # 5, San Francisco, CA 94109 USA Tel 415-931-8691.

Maryknoll Fathers & Brothers *See* **Maryknoll Missioners**

Maryknoll Missioners, *(978-0-941395)* P.O. Box 308, Maryknoll, NY 15054-0308 USA (SAN 219-3752) Tel 914-941-7590; Toll Free: 800-227-8523
E-mail: jgoldbeck@maryknoll.org.

†Maryland Historical Society, *(978-0-938420; 978-0-9842135; 978-0-9965944)* 201 W. Monument St., Baltimore, MD 21201 USA (SAN 203-9788) Tel 410-685-3750; Fax: 410-385-2105
E-mail: panderson@mdhs.org
Web site: http://www.mdhs.org
Dist(s): **Hood, Alan C. & Co., Inc.**
Johns Hopkins Univ. Pr.; *CIP.*

Maryland Secretarial Services, Inc., *(978-0-692-31692-4; 978-0-692-31693-1; 978-0-692-31694-8; 978-0-692-56468-4)* 12105 Whiston Ct, Bowie, MD 20715 USA Tel 3013527927.

Maryruth Bks., Inc., *(978-0-9713518; 978-0-9720295; 978-0-9746475; 978-1-933624; 978-1-62544)* 18660 Ravenna Rd. Bldg. 2, Chagrin Falls, OH 44023 USA Tel 440-834-1105; Toll Free Fax: 800-951-4077
E-mail: admin@maryruthbooks.com
Web site: http://www.maryruthbooks.com.

Marzetta Bks., *(978-0-9657033)* P.O. Box 274, Lombard, IL 60148 USA Tel 630-424-1403
E-mail: marzetta@concentric.net.

Masalai Pr., *(978-0-9714127)* 368 Capricorn Ave., Oakland, CA 94611-2058 USA
E-mail: THSlone@yahoo.com
Web site: http://THSlone.tripod.com/masalaipress.html.

Mascot Bks., Inc., *(978-0-9743442; 978-1-932888; 978-1-934878; 978-1-936319; 978-1-937406; 978-1-62086; 978-1-63177; 978-1-68401)* Orders Addr.: 560 Herndon Pkwy. Suite 120, Herndon, VA 20170 USA Tel 703-437-3584; Fax: 703-437-3554; Toll Free: 877-862-7568
E-mail: info@mascotbooks.com; josh@mascotbooks.com; naren@mascotbooks.com; laura@mascotbooks.com; kristin@mascotbooks.com
Web site: http://www.mascotbooks.com
Dist(s): **Partners Bk. Distributing, Inc.**

Masha, Segun Inc., *(978-0-9755927)* Div. of SEGUN MASHA, INC., Orders Addr.: 1035 Franklin Rd. SE. #c04, Marietta, GA 30067 USA
E-mail: segunmasha@gmail.com
Web site: http://www.faith365.org; www.marketplacemissions.com.

Mashack, Jonathan *See* **Mashack Productions**

Mashack Productions, *(978-0-9773407; 978-0-615-83382-8)* 3321 Hugo Ln., Timmonsville, SC 29161 USA Tel 843-229-4641
E-mail: ralphy_jmm@yahoo.com; ollyaga@gmail.com.

Mason Crest, *(978-1-59084; 978-1-59482; 978-1-4222)* Div. of Highlights Inc., Orders Addr.: 450 Parkway Dr., Suite D, Broomall, PA 19008-0914 USA Tel 610-543-6200; Fax: 610-543-3878; Toll Free: 866-627-2665 (866-MCP-Book)
E-mail: gbaffa@masoncrest.com
Web site: http://www.masoncrest.com
Dist(s): **Follett School Solutions**
Simon & Schuster, Inc.
Smashwords.

Mason Crest Publishers *See* **Mason Crest**

Massachusetts Continuing Legal Education, Inc., *(978-0-944490; 978-1-57589; 978-1-68345)* 10 Winter Pl., Boston, MA 02108 USA (SAN 226-3033) Tel 617-482-2205; Fax: 617-482-9498; Toll Free: 800-966-6253
Web site: http://www.mcle.org.

Massey Publishing, *(978-0-9640883)* P.O. Box 8945, Atlanta, GA 31106-0945 USA Tel 404-406-5034 (phone/fax)
E-mail: galemassey7@aol.com
Dist(s): **New Leaf Distributing Co., Inc.**

Master Bks., *(978-0-89051; 978-1-61458)* P.O. Box 726, Green Forest, AR 72638-0726 USA (SAN 205-6119) Tel 870-438-5288; Fax: 870-438-5120; Toll Free: 800-999-3777
E-mail: nlp@newleafpress.net
Web site: http://www.masterbooks.net; NLPG.com
Dist(s): **MyiLibrary**
Spring Arbor Distributors, Inc.

Master Communications, Inc., *(978-1-888194; 978-1-60480)* 2692 Madison Rd., Suite N1-307 N1-307, Cincinnati, OH 45208 USA (SAN 299-2140) Tel 513-563-3100; Fax: 513-563-3105; Toll Free: 800-765-5885
E-mail: sales@master-comm.com
Web site: http://www.worldculturemedia.com; http://www.master-comm.com
Dist(s): **Follett School Solutions.**

Master Pr., *(978-0-9646543; 978-0-9759049; 978-0-9790296; 978-0-9834326; 978-0-9885057; 978-0-9913121; 978-0-9993750)* 318 SE. 4th Terrace, Cape Coral, FL 33990 USA Tel 239-772-0634 (phone/fax); Fax: 239-772-0634; Toll Free: 800-325-9136
E-mail: neil@ezraproject.org.

Master Publishing, Inc., *(978-0-945053)* 6019 W. Howard St., Niles, IL 60714-4801 USA (SAN 245-8829)
E-mail: pete@w5yi.com
Web site: http://www.MasterPublishing.com; http://www.ForrestMims.com; http://www.w5yi.org
Dist(s): **WFiveYI Group, Inc., The.**

Master Strategies Publishing, *(978-0-9766485)* 5806 Chatsworth Ct., Arlington, TX 76018 USA Toll Free: 888-792-5105.

Masterpiece Creations Graphics & Publishing, *(978-0-615-23057-3; 978-0-9842171)* 305 Friendship Ln., Suite 100, Gettysburg, PA 17325 USA (SAN 858-7507) Tel 717-337-1829
E-mail: dj@masterpiececreations.biz
Web site: http://www.masterpiececreations.biz.

MasterVision, *(978-1-55919)* 969 Park Ave., New York, NY 10028 USA Tel 212-879-0448
E-mail: stadin1@aol.com
Web site: http://www.mastervision.com/.

Mastery Education Corporation *See* **Charlesbridge Publishing, Inc.**

Mastery For Strings Pubns., *(978-0-9753919)* 1005 Meriden Ln., Austin, TX 78703 USA Tel 512-474-8196
E-mail: musipro@aol.com.

Mastery Learning Systems, *(978-1-888976)* 532 N. School St., Ukiah, CA 95482 USA Fax: 707-462-9307; Toll Free: 800-433-4181 (phone/fax)
E-mail: mastery@pacific.net
Web site: http://www.masterylearningsystems.com.

Masthof Pr., *(978-1-883294; 978-1-930353; 978-1-932864; 978-1-60126)* 219 Mill Rd., Morgantown, PA 19543-9701 USA Tel 610-286-0258; Fax: 610-286-6860
E-mail: mast@masthof.com
Web site: http://www.masthof.com.

Mateboer, Johannes Aart, *(978-0-9759487)* Div. of Captain's Publishing, 6514 Wakehurst Rd., Charlotte, NC 28226 USA Tel 704-540-7617 (phone/fax)
E-mail: hlmateboer@hotmail.com
Web site: http://www.captainspublishing.com
Dist(s): **eBookit.com.**

Math Essentials, *(978-0-9666211; 978-0-9821901; 978-0-9843629; 978-0-9994433)* P.O. Box 1723, Los Gatos, CA 95031 USA Fax: 408-358-3738; Toll Free: 866-444-6284; 265 Carlton Ct., Los Gatos, CA 95032
E-mail: rickwfisher@yahoo.com
Web site: http://www.mathessentials.com.

Math in Motion *See* **Crane Bks.**

Math Solutions, *(978-0-941355; 978-1-935099)* Div. of Marilyn Burns Education Assocs., Orders Addr.: 150 Gate 5 Rd., Sausalito, CA 94965 USA (SAN 665-5424) Tel 415-332-4181; Fax: 415-331-1931; Toll Free Fax: 877-942-8837; Toll Free: 800-868-9092
E-mail: info@mathsolutions.com; jcross@mathsolutions.com; jwayland@mathsolutions.com
Web site: http://www.mathsolutions.com
Dist(s): **MyiLibrary**
Scholastic, Inc.

Math Solutions Publications *See* **Math Solutions**

Math Studio, The, *(978-1-929362)* 271 Lafayette St., Salem, MA 01970-5404 USA
E-mail: cdraper@mathstudio.com
Web site: http://www.mathstudio.com.

Mathematical Assn. of America, *(978-0-88385; 978-0-9835005; 978-1-61444; 978-1-939512)* Orders Addr.: P.O. Box 91112, Washington, DC 20090-1112 USA; Edit Addr.: 1529 18th St., NW, Washington, DC 20036 USA (SAN 203-9737) Tel 301-617-7800; Fax: 301-206-9789; Toll Free: 800-331-1622
E-mail: cbaxter@maa.org; swebb@maa.org
Web site: http://www.maa.org
Dist(s): **Cambridge Univ. Pr.**
ebrary, Inc.

Mathematical Sciences Research Institute, *(978-0-9639903; 978-0-9824800)* 17 Gauss Way, Berkeley, CA 94720-5070 USA Tel 510-642-0143; Fax: 510-642-8609
E-mail: librarian@msri.org
Web site: http://www.msri.org/.

Mathematical Solutions Publishing Company *See* **Twianie Roberts Consulting**

Mathis, Stefan, *(978-0-692-89659-4)* 420 Somerset Dr, AUBURNDALE, FL 33823 USA Tel 863-585-9621
Dist(s): **Lightning Source, Inc.**

MathisJones Communications, LLC, *(978-0-9799482; 978-0-9840117; 978-0-9850542; 978-0-9853093; 978-0-9889643; 978-0-9964948)* Orders Addr.: P.O. Box 569, Chesterfield, MO 63006-0569 USA (SAN 854-8102) Tel 636-938-1100; Fax: 636-349-1100; Edit Addr.: 1 Putt Ln., Eureka, MO 63025-2828 USA
E-mail: info@mathisjones.com
Web site: www.monographpublishing.com
Dist(s): **eBookit.com.**

Mathis-Njie, Joan J. *See* **Anointed Pubs.**

MATHSTORY.COM, *(978-0-9702641)* Div. of Rak Productions, P.O. Box 20226, New York, NY 10025-1511 USA Tel 212-864-5462
E-mail: mathstory2000@aol.com
Web site: http://mathstory.com.

MathWord Pr., LLC, *(978-0-9840425; 978-1-939431)* 97 Fennbrook Dr., Hamden, CT 06517 USA Tel 203-288-8114
E-mail: mathwordpress@aol.com
Web site: mwpenn.com.

Matinicus Pr., *(978-0-9765689)* 734 Cleveland Ave., Brackenridge, PA 15014-1501 USA.

Matter of Africa America Time, *(978-0-9760523)* 2114 Vincent Ave. N., Minneapolis, MN 55411 USA.

Matting Leah Publishing Co., *(978-0-9761528; 978-0-9905764)* P.O. Box 265, Warwick, NY 10990-0265 USA
Web site: http://www.mattingleahpublishing.com.

Matzah Ball Bks., *(978-0-9753629)* 1830 Walgrove Ave., Los Angeles, CA 90066-2233 USA
E-mail: asneram@gmail.com
Web site: http://www.matzahballbooks.com.

Mau, C. Publishing Co., *(978-0-9778843)* Orders Addr.: P.O. Box 30084, Edmond, OK 73003-0002 USA
E-mail: cmaupublishing@cox.net.

Maui Arthoughts Co., *(978-0-945045)* P.O. Box 967, Wailuku, HI 96793-0967 USA (SAN 245-8799) Tel 808-244-0156; Toll Free: 800-403-3472
E-mail: books@maui.net
Web site: http://www.booksmaui.com
Dist(s): **Quality Bks., Inc.**

Maupin Hse. Publishing, *(978-0-929895; 978-1-934338; 978-1-936700; 978-1-937412; 978-1-4966)* Div. of Capstone Press, Incorporated, Orders Addr.: 1710 Roe Crest Dr., North Mankato, MN 56003 USA (SAN 250-7676) Toll Free Fax: 888-262-0705; Toll Free: 800-747-4992 (orders)
E-mail: k.monyhan@coughlancompanies.com
Web site: http://www.maupinhouse.com; http://www.capstoneclassroom.com.

Maval Medical Education *See* **Maval Publishing, Inc.**

Maval Publishing, Inc., *(978-1-884083; 978-1-59134)* Div. of Maval Printing Co., 5335 Victoria Cir., Firestone, CO 80504 USA Tel 303-682-9424
E-mail: info@jejerre.com
Web site: http://www.jejerre.com
Dist(s): **Majors Scientific Bks., Inc.**
Matthews Medical Bk. Co.

Maven Of Memory Publishing, *(978-0-9768042; 978-0-9833277; 978-0-9864412)* P.O. Box 398, Hurst, TX 76053-0398 USA Fax: 817-282-0000
Web site: http://www.mavenofmemory.com.

MavenMark Books, LLC *See* **HenschelHAUS Publishing**

Maverick Bks. *Imprint of* **Trinity Univ. Pr.**

Maverick Bks., *(978-0-9672355)* P.O. Box 897, Woodstock, NY 12498 USA (SAN 253-9284) Toll Free: 866-478-9266 (phone/fax) Do not confuse with Maverick Books, Perryton, TX
E-mail: maverickbooks@aol.com; hank1@ptsi.net.

Maverick Bks., Inc., *(978-0-916941; 978-0-9608612; 978-1-59188)* Orders Addr.: P.O. Box 549, Perryton, TX 79070 USA (SAN 240-7183) Tel 806-435-7611; Fax: 806-435-2410; Edit Addr.: 14492 N.W. Loop 143, Perryton, TX 78070 USA Do not confuse with Maverick Books, Woodstock, NY
E-mail: hank1@ptsi.net
Web site: http://www.hankthecowdog.com
Dist(s): **Follett School Solutions**
Ingram Publisher Services.

Maverick Press *See* **Maverick Bks.**

Mawco, Inc., *(978-0-9853523)* 22172 Bakers Mill Rd., Dacula, GA 30019 USA Tel 404-202-7615
E-mail: a1missy@aol.com.

Mawi, Inc., *(978-0-9743901)* P.O. Box 471666, Chicago, IL 60647-6525 USA
E-mail: info@mawibooks.com
Web site: http://www.mawibooks.com.

Max & Zoe *Imprint of* **Picture Window Bks.**

Max Publication, Inc., *(978-0-9633577; 978-0-9799882; 978-0-692-76992-8)* Div. of DL Services, Inc., Orders Addr.: 825 Malvern Hill, Alpharetta, GA 30022 USA Tel 770-851-0935; Fax: 770-740-0188
E-mail: info@mrandmrsitaly.com
Web site: www.mrandmrsitaly.com; www.mrandmrsitaly.com.

Maxim Pr., *(978-0-9767096)* 6947 Coal Creek Pkwy. SE, No. 137, Newcastle, WA 98059-3159 USA
E-mail: lg@maximpress.com
Web site: http://www.maximpress.com/.

Maximilian Pr. Pubs., *(978-0-9668650; 978-1-930211; 978-0-9827717)* Orders Addr.: P.O. Box 64841, Virginia Beach, VA 23467-4841 USA Tel 757-482-2273; Fax: 757-482-0325; Edit Addr.: 920 S. Battlefield Blvd., No. 100, Chesapeake, VA 23322 USA
E-mail: mp-publishing@inter-source.org
Web site: http://www.maximilianpressbookpublishers.com/.

Maximus Publishing, *(978-0-9792439)* P.O. Box 4455, Whitefish, MT 59937-4455 USA (SAN 852-8829)
E-mail: MaximusPublishing@bresnan.net
Web site: http://www.maximuspublishing.com.

Maxwell, Andre, *(978-0-578-10115-6; 978-0-578-10116-3; 978-0-9881811)* 722 Sawyer St. SE, Olympia, WA 98501 USA Tel 253-509-4022
E-mail: aleighmaxwell@gmail.com
Dist(s): **Follett School Solutions.**

Maxwell, Joseph *See* **LifeStory Publishing**

May 3rd Bks., Inc., *(978-0-692-72921-2; 978-1-945891)* 616 Corporate Way Ste 2-5577, Valley Cottage, NY 10989 USA Tel 202-740-5137
E-mail: info@may3rdbooks.com
Web site: www.may3rdbooks.com.

May, Cynthia D., *(978-0-615-12578-7)* 7720 W. 14 Rd., Mesick, MI 49668-9792 USA.

May, L. B. & Assocs., 3517 Neal Dr., Knoxville, TN 37918 USA Tel 865-922-7490; Fax: 865-922-7492
E-mail: lbmay@aol.com.

Maya & Me Pubns., *(978-0-692-47111-1; 978-0-9972566)* 12060 Cty. Line Rd Suite J No. 197, Madison, AL 35756 USA Tel 520-241-6559
E-mail: efalva@yahoo.com
Web site: www.maya-and-me.com.

Mayhaven Publishing, Inc., *(978-1-878044; 978-1-932278; 978-1-939695)* P.O. Box PO Box 557, Mahomet, IL 618530557 USA Tel 217-586-4493; *Imprints:* Wild Rose (Wild Rose)
E-mail: mayhavenpublishing@mchsi.com
Web site: http://www.mayhavenpublishing.com
Dist(s): **Brodart Co.**
Deseret Bk. Co.
Distributors, The
Follett School Solutions

Publisher Name Index

Mumford Library Bks., Inc.
Quality Bks., Inc.

Mayhem Bks., *(978-0-9770055)* P.O. Box 313, Bon Secour, AL 36511 USA
E-mail: sweetzer@gulftel.com.

Maylin, Grace, *(978-0-9792384)* 204 S. Roycroft Blvd., Cheektowaga, NY 14225 USA
E-mail: gmds@adelphia.net.

Maynestream Pr., *(978-0-9715183)* 3189 Cocoplum Cir., Coconut Creek, FL 33063 USA
E-mail: contact@maynestream.com
Web site: http://www.weirdthings.com.

Mayo, Jerry, *(978-0-9985792)* 7524 Via Desierto NE, Albuquerque, NM 87113 USA Tel 505-344-1857
E-mail: Mayo505@gmail.com.

Mayo, Johnny, *(978-0-9765918)* P.O. Box 5484, Columbia, SC 29250 USA Tel 803-767-6756
E-mail: k9heroes@att.net
Web site: http://www.bucksheroes.com.

Mayreni *Imprint of* **Mayreni Publishing**

Mayreni Publishing, *(978-0-9653718; 978-1-931834)* P.O. Box 5881, Monterey, CA 93944-5881 USA Tel 831-655-4377 (phone/fax); *Imprints:* Mayreni (Mayreni)
E-mail: mayrenipublishing@comcast.net; vatcheg@gmail.com
Web site: http://www.mayreni.com.

Maytag Messerschmitt Media Concern, *(978-0-9768470)* 931 W. 19th St., Santa Ana, CA 92706 USA.

Mazaa, LLC, *(978-0-9849624)* 1555 Botelho Dr., No. 433, Walnut Creek, CA 94596 USA Tel 925-954-7182
E-mail: jofarrell@mazaallc.com.

Maze Creek Studio, *(978-0-9742285)* Orders Addr.: 1495 E. Thirteenth St., Carthage, MO 64836-9507 USA Tel 417-359-8787
E-mail: studio@andythomas.com
Web site: http://www.andythomas.com.

Mazeology, *(978-0-9793043)* 284 W. 12th St., No. 2, New York, NY 10014-6000 USA Tel 212-929-0734
E-mail: mazeology@yahoo.com
Web site: http://www.mazeology.net.

Mazie, Bernard *See* **Pangus Publishing**

Mazo Pubs., *(978-965-90462; 978-965-7344; 978-1-936778; 978-1-946124)* P.O. Box 10474, Jacksonville, FL 32247 USA Tel 815-301-3559 (phone/fax)
E-mail: mazopublishers@gmail.com; cm@mazopublishers.com
Web site: http://htttp://www.mazopublishers.com
Dist(s): **Smashwords.**

Mazur, Kathy *See* **Spring Ducks Bks., LLC**

MB Publishing, LLC, *(978-0-9624166; 978-0-9850814; 978-0-9913646; 978-0-9908430; 978-0-9994463)* 7831 Woodmont Ave., Pmb 312, Bethesda, MD 20814 USA Toll Free: 866-530-4732
Web site: http://www.mbpublishing.com
Dist(s): **BWI**
BookBaby
Quality Bks., Inc.

MBT, *(978-0-9768419)* P.O. Box 215, Guilford, CT 06437 USA.

MC Basset, LLC, *(978-0-9774800)* P.O. Box 241, Asbury, NJ 08802 USA Tel 908-537-6410 (phone/fax)
E-mail: mkuderka@mcbasset.com.

MC Math Comics, *(978-0-9728453)* 720 Sutton Dr., Carlisle, PA 17013 USA Tel 717-243-4470
E-mail: clarkcherry@aol.com
Web site: http://plusman.org.

MC Publishing & Design Group, *(978-0-578-00109-8; 978-0-9966696)* 4207 Forest Ln., Nacogdoches, TX 75965 USA Toll Free: 800-781-4890.

MC Wheeler Enterprises, *(978-0-692-68048-3; 978-0-692-80814-6)* 657 Highland Ave., FALL RIVER, MA 02720 USA Tel 401-835-2718.

MC123 *See* **Taven Hill Studio**

MCA Denver, *(978-0-692-76221-9; 978-0-692-76318-6; 978-0-692-78930-8; 978-0-692-87222-2)* 1485 Delgany St., Denver, CO 80202 USA Tel 720-236-1813
E-mail: zoel@mcadenver.org
Web site: www.mcadenver.org.

McArdle, Donald, *(978-0-615-14212-8)* 11556 110th Ter., Largo, FL 33778-3716 USA
Web site: http://www.santaandbugsy.com
Dist(s): **Lulu Pr., Inc.**

McBook Pubs., LLC, *(978-0-9705777)* Orders Addr.: P.O. Box 35513, Tulsa, OK 74005 USA Tel 918-671-6656
E-mail: jdokla@cableone.net.

McBride Collection of Stories LLC, *(978-0-692-81414-7; 978-0-692-82418-4; 978-0-692-84474-8; 978-0-692-85606-2)* 70-02 Parsons Blvd, No. 7c, Fresh Meadows, NY 11365 USA Tel 917-771-4463
E-mail: mcbridestories@gmail.com
Dist(s): **CreateSpace Independent Publishing Platform.**

McBride, Heddrick, *(978-0-615-70075-5; 978-0-615-70923-9; 978-0-615-71693-0; 978-0-615-72059-3; 978-0-615-72339-6; 978-0-615-78846-3; 978-0-615-86353-5; 978-0-615-91076-5; 978-0-615-95937-5; 978-0-692-68651-5)* 70-02 parsons blvd. apt 7c, Flushing, NY 11365 USA Tel 917-771-4463
Web site: www.mcbride-collection-of-stories.com
Dist(s): **CreateSpace Independent Publishing Platform.**

McCall, Philip Lee II, *(978-0-9822656; 978-0-615-77486-2; 978-0-615-77543-2)* 11381 SW 17th Ct., Miramar, FL 33025 USA Tel 305-206-3699; *Imprints:* Mythix Studios (Mythix Stud)
E-mail: phil.mccalllii@gmail.com
Web site: plmii.com
Dist(s): **CreateSpace Independent Publishing Platform**
INscribe Digital.

McCarthy, Maria Skantzaris, *(978-0-9755844)* P.O. Box 1308, Westford, MA 01886 USA
E-mail: msmccarthy@mindspring.com.

McCarthy, Sally Studios, *(978-0-9898968)* 7 Patriot Ln., Whitman, MA 02382 USA Tel 781-771-3394
E-mail: sallyjm@comcast.net.

McClain Printing Co., *(978-0-87012)* Orders Addr.: P.O. Box 403, Parsons, WV 26287-0403 USA (SAN 203-9478) Tel 304-478-2881; Fax: 304-478-4658; Toll Free: 800-654-7179
E-mail: mcclain@mcclainprinting.com; mmckinnie@mcclainprinting.com
Web site: http://www.McClainPrinting.com.

McClanahan Publishing Hse., Inc., *(978-0-913383; 978-1-934898; 978-0-9829785; 978-0-615-40157-7; 978-0-9836687; 978-0-9847933; 978-0-9895424; 978-0-9897078)* P.O. Box 100, Kuttawa, KY 42055 USA (SAN 285-8371) Tel 270-388-9388; Fax: 270-388-6186; Toll Free: 800-544-6959
E-mail: books@kybooks.com
Web site: http://www.kybooks.com
Dist(s): **Partners Bk. Distributing, Inc.**

McClelland & Stewart (CAN) *(978-0-396; 978-0-7710) Dist. by* **Random.**

McClelland & Stewart (CAN) *(978-0-396; 978-0-7710) Dist. by* **Peng Rand Hse.**

McClenney Publishing *See* **First Associates Publishing**

McCourtie, Anne, *(978-0-9744448)* 15700 154th Rd., Mayetta, KS 66509 USA.

McCowan, Linda, *(978-0-9814596)* 1739 S. Hwy., 89 A, Kanab, UT 84741 USA.

McCray, Kathy *See* **Kathy's Pen**

McDaniel, Megan Faux *See* **25 Dreams Educational Media**

McDonald & Woodward Publishing Co., The, *(978-0-939923; 978-1-935778)* Orders Addr.: 431-B E. College St., Granville, OH 43023-1319 USA (SAN 663-6977) Tel 740-321-1140; Fax: 740-321-1141; Toll Free: 800-233-8787
E-mail: mwpubco@mwpubco.com
Web site: http://www.mwpubco.com.

McDonald Publishing Co., *(978-1-55708; 978-1-934256; 978-1-937664; 978-1-943600)* 567 Hanley Industrial Ct., Saint Louis, MO 63144 USA (SAN 249-5813) Tel 314-781-7400; Toll Free: 800-722-8080
E-mail: janet@mcdonaldpublishing.com.

McDougal Littell Incorporated *See* **Holt McDougal**

McDougal Publishing Co., *(978-1-58158; 978-1-884369)* Orders Addr.: P.O. Box 3595, Hagerstown, MD 21742-3595 USA (SAN 856-8286) Tel 301-797-6637; Fax: 301-733-2767; Toll Free: 800-962-3684
E-mail: publishing@mcdougal.org
Web site: http://www.mcdougalpublishing.com
Dist(s): **Anchor Distributors**
Spring Arbor Distributors, Inc.

McDowell Health-Science Bks., LLC, *(978-0-9741238)* P.O. Box 81, Lafayette, CO 80026 USA Tel 303-570-7231; Fax: 303-604-0773
E-mail: McDPubCo@mcdowellpublishing.com; McDPubCo@aol.com; healthscience@mcdowellpublishing.com
Web site: http://www.mcdowellpublishing.com.

McElderry, Margaret K. Bks. *Imprint of* **McElderry, Margaret K. Bks.**

McElderry, Margaret K. Bks., Div. of Simon & Schuster Children's Publishing, 1230 Ave. of the Americas, New York, NY 10020 USA; *Imprints:* McElderry, Margaret K. Books (MMcElderry)
Dist(s): **Simon & Schuster, Inc.**

McElreath, K.M., *(978-0-9769271)* 10420 Rivertown Rd., Fairburn, GA 30213 USA Tel 770-969-1718; Fax: 770-969-0183
E-mail: tmcelreath@bellsouth.net.

McElroy & Assocs., *(978-0-9673917)* 6651 Avignon Blvd., Falls Church, VA 22043-1724 USA Tel 703-237-5993; Fax: 703-237-5994
E-mail: roland@mcelroyassoc.com
Web site: http://www.mcelroyassoc.com.

McEvoy, N. L., *(978-0-615-95144-7; 978-0-9908933)* 3767 Winding Lake Cir., Orlando, FL 32835 USA Tel 8477369375
Dist(s): **CreateSpace Independent Publishing Platform.**

McEwen, Judith A., *(978-0-9780693)* 22342 Chimayo Bend, San Antonio, TX 78258 USA Tel 210-630-9226; Fax: 210-595-7490
E-mail: chickensonthego@hotmail.com
Web site: http://www.chickensonthego.com.

McFadden, Linnea, *(978-0-9984681)* 1740 Alden Ln., Wyomissing, PA 19610 USA Tel 610-656-9173
E-mail: lbqtmm@gmail.com.

†**McFarland & Co., Inc. Pubs.**, *(978-0-7864; 978-0-89950; 978-1-4766)* Orders Addr.: P.O. Box 611, Jefferson, NC 28640 USA (SAN 215-093X) Tel 336-246-4460; Fax: 336-246-5018; 336-246-4403; Toll Free: 800-253-2187 (orders only); Edit Addr.: 960 Hwy., 88 W., Jefferson, NC 28640 USA
E-mail: info@mcfarlandpub.com
Web site: http://www.mcfarlandpub.com
Dist(s): **Ebsco Publishing**
Follett School Solutions
Metapress
MyiLibrary
ebrary, Inc.; *CIP.*

McGab Publishing, *(978-0-9788092)* 12438 Prather Ave., Pt Charlotte, FL 33981-1352 USA
Web site: http://weirdobook.com.

McGovern, Matthew /700acres Communications, *(978-0-9749445)* 27 McGovern Dr., Buxton, ME 04093 USA
E-mail: matt@mattmcgovern.com
Web site: http://www.mattmcgovern.com.

McGraw, Jason A., *(978-0-615-13681-3)* 254 Westminster Rd., Rochester, NY 14607 USA Tel 585-771-7777
E-mail: jaymcgraw18@aol.com
Dist(s): **Lulu Pr., Inc.**

†**McGraw-Hill Cos., The**, *(978-0-07)* 6480 Jimmy Carter Blvd., Norcross, GA 30071-1701 USA (SAN 254-881X) Tel 614-755-5637; Fax: 614-755-5611; Orders Addr.: 860 Taylor Station Rd., Blacklick, OH 43004-0545 USA (SAN 200-254X) Fax: 614-755-5645; Toll Free: 800-722-4726 (orders & customer service); 800-338-3987 (college); 800-525-5003 (subscriptions); 800-352-3566 (books - US/Canada orders); P.O. Box 545, Blacklick, OH 43004-0545 USA Fax: 614-759-3759; Toll Free: 877-833-5524
E-mail: customer.service@mcgraw-hill.com
Web site: http://www.mcgraw-hill.com; http://www.ebooks.mcgraw-hill.com/
Dist(s): **Cambridge Univ. Pr.**
Ebsco Publishing
Libros Sin Fronteras
McGraw-Hill Osborne
McGraw-Hill Create (TM)
MyiLibrary
Sams Technical Publishing, LLC
ebrary, Inc.; *CIP.*

McGraw-Hill Education (GBR) *(978-0-07) Dist. by* **McGraw.**

McGraw-Hill Education, *(978-1-259; 978-1-260; 978-1-264; 978-1-265; 978-1-266)* Two Penn Plaza, New York, NY 10121-2298 USA Tel 212-904-2000; a/o The Mcgraw-Hill Companies, 8787 Orion Pl., Columbus, OH 43240 (SAN 256-3908) Tel 614-755-5637; Fax: 614-755-5611
E-mail: customer.service@mcgraw-hill.com
Web site: http://www.mheducation.com/custserv.html; http://www.mcgraw-hill.com
Dist(s): **Brilliance Publishing, Inc.**
McGraw-Hill Cos., The
MyiLibrary
ebrary, Inc.

McGraw-Hill Higher Education, *(978-0-07; 978-1-121)* Orders Addr.: P.O. Box 545, Blacklick, OH 43004-0545 USA Toll Free: 800-338-3987; Edit Addr.: 1333 Burr Ridge Pkwy., 3rd Flr., Burr Ridge, IL 60527 USA; *Imprints:* McGraw-Hill/Dushkin (Dshkn McG-Hill); McGraw-Hill Science, Engineering & Mathematics (McG-H Sci Eng)
E-mail: customer.service@mcgraw-hill.com
Web site: http://www.mhhe.com
Dist(s): **Follett School Solutions**
McGraw-Hill Cos., The
MyiLibrary
Oxford Univ. Pr., Inc.
ebrary, Inc.

McGraw-Hill Osborne, *(978-0-07; 978-0-88134; 978-0-931988)* Div. of The McGraw-Hill Professional, 160 Spear St. Flr. 7, San Francisco, CA 94105-1544 USA (SAN 274-3450) Toll Free: 800-227-0900
E-mail: customer.service@mcgraw-hill.com
Web site: http://www.osborne.com
Dist(s): **Ebsco Publishing**
McGraw-Hill Cos., The
MyiLibrary
ebrary, Inc.

McGraw-Hill Professional Book Group *See* **McGraw-Hill Schl. Education Group**

McGraw-Hill Professional Publishing, *(978-0-07)* Div. of McGraw-Hill Higher Education, Orders Addr.: P.O. Box 545, Blacklick, OH 43004-0545 USA Fax: 614-755-5645; Toll Free: 800-722-4726; Edit Addr.: 2 Penn Plaza, New York, NY 10121-2298 USA Tel 212-904-2000; *Imprints:* International Marine/Ragged Mountain Press (Inter Mar/Rag)
Dist(s): **Amacom**
American Pharmacists Assn.
Berrett-Koehler Pubs., Inc.
Ebsco Publishing
Entrepreneur Media Inc/Entrepreneur Pr.
Harvard Business Review Pr.
McGraw-Hill Cos., The
McGraw-Hill Medical Publishing Div.
McGraw-Hill Trade
MyiLibrary
ebrary, Inc.

McGraw-Hill Schl. Education Group, *(978-0-07; 978-0-7602; 978-0-8306; 978-0-911314; 978-0-917253; 978-1-55738; 978-1-307)* Div. of The McGraw-Hill Companies, Orders Addr.: P.O. Box 545, Blacklick, OH 43004-0545 USA Fax: 614-755-5645; Toll Free: 800-442-9685 (customer service); 800-722-4726; Edit Addr.: 8787 Orion Pl., Columbus, OH 43240 USA Tel 614-430-4000; Toll Free: 800-344-7344; c/o Grand Rapids Distribution Center, 3195 Wilson NW, Grand Rapids, MI 49544 (SAN 253-6420) Fax: 614-755-5611
E-mail: customer.service@mcgraw-hill.com
Web site: http://www.accessmedbooks.com; http://www.MHEducation.com
Dist(s): **Ebsco Publishing**
McGraw-Hill Cos., The
Urban Land Institute
ebrary, Inc.

McGraw-Hill Science, Engineering & Mathematics *Imprint of* **McGraw-Hill Higher Education**

McGraw-Hill Trade, *(978-0-07; 978-0-658; 978-0-8442)* Div. of McGraw-Hill Professional, Orders Addr.: P.O. Box 545, Blacklick, OH 43004-0545 USA Tel 800-722-4726; Fax: 614-755-5645; Edit Addr.: 2 Penn Plaza, New York, NY 10121 USA Tel 212-904-2000; *Imprints:* Passport Books (Passport Bks)
E-mail: Jeffrey_Krames@mcgraw-hill.com
Web site: http://www.books.mcgraw-hill.com
Dist(s): **Ebsco Publishing**
McGraw-Hill Cos., The
MyiLibrary
ebrary, Inc.

McGraw-Hill/Contemporary, *(978-0-658; 978-0-8092; 978-0-8325; 978-0-8442; 978-0-88499; 978-0-89061; 978-0-913327; 978-0-940279; 978-0-941263; 978-0-9630646; 978-1-56626; 978-1-56943; 978-1-57028)* Div. of McGraw-Hill Higher Education, Orders Addr.: P.O. Box 545, Blacklick, OH 43004-0545 USA Toll Free Fax: 800-998-3103; Toll Free: 800-621-1918; Edit Addr.: 4255 W. Touhy Ave., Lincolnwood, IL 60712 USA (SAN 169-2208) Tel 847-679-5500; Fax: 847-679-2494; Toll Free Fax: 800-998-3103; Toll Free: 800-323-4900; *Imprints:* National Textbook Company (Natl Textbk Co)
E-mail: ntcpub@tribune.com
Web site: http://www.ntc-cb.com
Dist(s): **Continental Bk. Co., Inc.**
Ebsco Publishing
Giron Bks.
Libros Sin Fronteras
McGraw-Hill Cos., The
ebrary, Inc.

McGraw-Hill/Dushkin *Imprint of* **McGraw-Hill Higher Education**

McHay, Micki, *(978-0-9786826)* 8212 Dolphin Bay Ct., Las Vegas, NV 89128 USA (SAN 854-655X).

McIntyre, Connie *See* **Grannie Annie Family Story Celebration, The**

McKatlib Pr., *(978-0-9745440)* P.O. Box 76693, Atlanta, GA 30358-1693 USA
Web site: http://www.bethanyadventures.com.

†**McKay, David Co., Inc.**, *(978-0-679; 978-0-88326; 978-0-89440)* Subs. of Random Hse., Inc., Orders Addr.: 400 Hahn Rd., Westminster, MD 21157 USA Tel 410-848-1900; Toll Free: 800-733-3000 (orders only); Edit Addr.: 201 E. 50th St., MD 4-6, New York, NY 10022 USA (SAN 200-240X) Tel 212-751-2600; Fax: 212-872-8026
Dist(s): **Libros Sin Fronteras**; *CIP.*

McKellen-Caffey, *(978-0-9794191)* 15543 Sprig St., Chino Hills, CA 91709-2853 USA (SAN 853-4144) Tel 909-393-0894
E-mail: mckellencaffey@yahoo.com
Web site: http://chiselhedgehog.com.

McKenna, Mark, *(978-0-9727681)* P.O. Box 633, Florida, NY 10921 USA.

McKenna Publishing Group, *(978-0-9713659; 978-1-932172)* 425 Poa Pl., San Luis Obispo, CA 93405 USA Tel 805-550-1667; Fax: 805-783-2317
E-mail: ric@mckennapubgrp.com
Web site: http://www.mckennapubgrp.com
Dist(s): **Booklines Hawaii, Ltd.**

McKenny, Stephanie L. *See* **J & J Publishing Co.**

McKinney, David, *(978-0-692-42801-6; 978-0-692-60111-2; 978-0-692-86325-1)* 7311 E 64 St, Tulsa, OK 74133 USA Tel 918-252-2360 Do not confuse with David McKinney in Phoenix, AZ
E-mail: sardsfamily@cox.net.

McKinnon, Robert Scott, *(978-0-9651943)* 1608 Seventh St., S., Great Falls, MT 59405 USA Tel 406-452-3500
E-mail: maddog526@bresnan.net
Web site: http://home.bresnan.net/~maddog526/.

McLellan Bks., *(978-0-9747536)* Orders Addr.: P.O. Box 341, Claymont, DE 19703-0341 USA Tel 302-798-4006; Fax: 302-798-2567
E-mail: richardmclellan@dca.net; richard@mclellanbooks.com
Web site: http://www.mclellanbooks.com.

MCM Prime, Inc., *(978-0-9742351)* 6355 E. Duke Ranch Rd., Pearce, AZ 85625-6113 USA Tel 520-824-4051; Fax: 775-249-9133
E-mail: paulmc@vtc.net
Web site: http://www.mcmprime.pair.com/mcmpindx.htm.

McMillan, Carol, *(978-0-9907106)* 12 Marigold Dr, Bellingham, WA 98229 USA Tel 509-429-0293
E-mail: sylvanease@msn.com.

McMillen Publishing, *(978-0-9635812; 978-1-888223)* Orders Addr.: 304 Main St., Ames, IA 50010 USA (SAN 254-9085) Tel 515-232-0208; Fax: 515-232-0402 (orders); Toll Free: 800-750-6997 (In Iowa); 800-453-3960 (Outside Iowa)
E-mail: denise.sunvold@sigler.com
Web site: http://www.mcmillenbooks.com.

McMurtrey, Martin A., *(978-0-9623961)* 808 Camden, San Antonio, TX 78215 USA Tel 210-223-9680.

McNair Publishing, *(978-0-9976408)* 1751 Mizell Ave., Winter Park, FL 32789 USA Tel 407-644-5662
E-mail: TrudyMcNair@outlook.com
Web site: www.mcnairpublishing.com.

McNatmar Ventures LLC, *(978-0-9787540)* P.O. Box 1324, Clover, SC 29710-7533 USA Tel 803-222-4043
E-mail: rhcisjdm@comporium.net
Web site: http://www.mcnatmar.com.

McNeil & Richards, *(978-0-9825602)* 2715 N. Wisconsin Ave., Peoria, IL 61603 USA.

McNeill, Lance, *(978-0-692-75992-9; 978-0-692-75994-3)* 6200 Honey Dew Ct., AUSTIN, TX 78749 USA Tel 512-964-6040.

McPhaul Publisher *See* **CJ Publishing Co.**

McPugh, Kathleen, *(978-0-9742062)* Orders Addr.: P.O. Box 8372, Fresno, CA 93747 USA; Edit Addr.: P.O. Box 2552, Fallbrook, CA 92088-2552 USA
Web site: http://home.att.net/~kathfreeman/book.html; http://home.att.net/~kathfreeman
Dist(s): **Lightning Source, Inc.**

McQueen Publishing Co., *(978-0-917186)* 1211 S. Osceola Ave., Orlando, FL 32806-2223 USA (SAN 203-9516).

McRae Bks. Srl (ITA) *(978-88-89272; 978-88-6098; 978-88-88166; 978-88-900466; 978-88-900126) Dist. by* **IPG Chicago.**

McRitchie, Mike, *(978-0-578-03644-1)* 109 Falcon Creek Dr., McKinney, TX 75070 USA Tel 972-540-6800
E-mail: mmcritchie@tx.rr.com
Dist(s): **Lulu Pr., Inc.**

Mcruffy Pr., *(978-1-59269)* P.O. Box 212, Raymore, MO 64083 USA Tel 816-331-2500; Fax: 816-331-3868; Toll Free Fax: 888-967-1300; Toll Free: 888-967-1200
E-mail: brian@mcruffy.com
Web site: http://www.mcruffy.

McSweeney's Books *See* **McSweeney's Publishing**

McSweeney's Publishing, *(978-0-9703355; 978-0-9719047; 978-1-932416; 978-1-934781; 978-1-936365; 978-1-938073; 978-1-940450; 978-1-944211)* Orders

Addr.: 849 Valencia St., San Francisco, CA 94110-1736 USA (SAN 254-3184)
E-mail: custservice@mcsweeneys.net
Web site: http://www.mcsweeneys.net
Dist(s): **MyiLibrary**
Publishers Group West (PGW).

MCW Publishing, *(978-0-9753773)* 50 Brookdale Ave., Rochester, NY 14621 USA Tel 585-317-5780
E-mail: itm2000@hotmail.com.

McWilliams Mediation Group Ltd., *(978-0-9768663)* P.O. Box 6216, Denver, CO 80206 USA (SAN 257-5442) Tel 303-830-0171
E-mail: joan@peacefinder.com
Web site: http://www.peacefinder.com
Dist(s): **ebrary, Inc.**

McWitty Pr., Inc., *(978-0-9755618; 978-0-9852227; 978-0-9977554)* 1835 NE Miami Gardens Dr. 150, MIAMI, FL 33179 USA Tel 305-466-0652
E-mail: jo@momentumtours.com
Web site: http://www.mcwittypress.com
Dist(s): **MyiLibrary**
Publishers Group West (PGW).

McWong Ink, *(978-0-9820881)* 440 Kent Ave., Apt. PH1B, Brooklyn, NY 11211 USA
Web site: http://www.gordonandlili.com
Dist(s): **Emerald Bk. Co.**

m.d. hughes, *(978-0-9788541)* 9 Pasadena Rd., Branford, CT 06405 USA
Web site: http://www.cryofthefalcon.com.

Avitable Pub., *(978-0-9769794; 978-0-578-09899-9)* P.O. Box 38, East Meadow, NY 11554 USA Fax: 516-826-6843
E-mail: milliemsrd@aol.com
Web site: http://www.CaloriestheBottomLine.com.

ME Media LLC *See* **Tiger Tales**

Mead, Brian Publishing, *(978-0-9717509)* 203 E. Grove Rd., Long Grove, IA 52756 USA (SAN 255-2329)
E-mail: meadpub@juno.com; mattedeye@aol.com.

Mead Lommen Publishing *See* **Calaroga Publishing**

†Meadowbrook Pr., *(978-0-88166; 978-0-915658)* 5451 Smetana Dr., Minnetonka, MN 55343 USA (SAN 207-3404) Tel 612-930-1100; Fax: 612-930-1940; Toll Free: 800-338-2232
E-mail: mballard@meadowbrookpress.com
Web site: http://www.meadowbrookpress.com
Dist(s): **Simon & Schuster**
Simon & Schuster, Inc.
Simon & Schuster Children's Publishing; *CIP.*

Meadowview Pubs., *(978-0-9741218)* Orders Addr.: P.O. Box 444, Portland, CT 06480 USA Tel 860-342-2646; Edit Addr.: 221 E. Cotton Hill Rd., Portland, CT 06480 USA
E-mail: marketbase@peoplepc.com.

MEAR LLC, *(978-0-9787628)* 636 Twp. Rd., 2724, Loudonville, OH 44842 USA Tel 419-994-3462 (phone/fax)
E-mail: mearllc@gmail.com
Web site: www.twralphabetbook.com.

MEC Publishing, *(978-0-9746865)* 1923 W. 17th St., Santa Ana, CA 92706 USA (SAN 256-405X)
E-mail: mecpublishing@aol.com
Web site: http://www.mecpublishing.com.

Mechanech Pubns., *(978-0-9702861; 978-0-9856497)* 4 Kaser Terr., Monsey, NY 10952 USA Tel 914-352-1926.

Mechling Bookbindery, *(978-0-9703825; 978-0-9744657; 978-0-9760563; 978-0-9793772; 978-0-9841400; 978-1-938184)* Div. of Mechling Associates, Inc., Orders Addr.: 1124 Oneida Valley Rd., Route 38, Chicora, PA 16025-3820 USA Tel 724-287-2120; Fax: 724-285-9231; Toll Free: 800-941-3735
E-mail: sales@mechlingbooks.com
Web site: http://www.mechlingbooks.com.

Medal Bks., *(978-0-9764300; 978-0-9785667)* P.O. Box 7231, Clearwater, FL 33758-7231 USA
E-mail: ronan@ronanblaze.com
Web site: http://www.ronanblaze.com.

Medallion Pr., Inc., *(978-0-9743639; 978-1-932815; 978-1-933836; 978-1-934755; 978-1-60542; 978-1-942546)* Orders Addr.: 4222 Meridian Pkwy. Ste 110, Aurora, IL 60504 USA (SAN 255-5360) Tel 630-513-8316; Fax: 630-513-8362; *Imprints:* Gold Medallion (Gold Medallion)
E-mail: jeanne@medallinmediagroup.com
Web site: http://www.medallionmediagroup.com
Dist(s): **Legato Pubs. Group**
MyiLibrary.

Medernach, T.K. *See* **ThunderBolt Pubns.**

Media Alert!, *(978-0-9676616)* P.O. Box 735, Littleton, CO 80160-0735 USA Toll Free: 800-986-5560 (code 02)
E-mail: CNFsueLS@aol.com.

Media Angels, Inc. *See* **Knowledge Box Central**

Media Angels, Inc., *(978-0-9700385; 978-1-931941)* Orders Addr.: 15720 S. Pebble Ln., Fort Myers, FL 33912-2341 USA
E-mail: felice@mediaangels.com
Web site: http://www.mediaangels.com
Dist(s): **Send The Light Distribution LLC.**

Media Assocs., *(978-0-918501)* Orders Addr.: P.O. Box 1221, Galt, CA 95632 USA (SAN 657-3207) Tel 916-529-8247; Toll Free: 800-373-1897; *Imprints:* Archives Pr. (Archives Pr) Do not confuse with Media Assocs., Marina Del Rey, CA
E-mail: zendogg@gmail.com
Web site: www.hankharrison.com.

Media Blasters, Inc., *(978-1-890228; 978-1-58655; 978-1-59883)* 132 W. 36th St. Rm. 401, New York, NY 10018-8837 USA (SAN 859-5712)
E-mail: info@media-blasters.com
Web site: http://www.media-blasters.com; http://www.kittymedia.com
Dist(s): **Diamond Comic Distributors, Inc.**
Diamond Bk. Distributors
Follett School Solutions.

Media Creations, Incorporated *See* **Aeon Publishing Inc.**

Media For Life, *(978-0-9675068)* 300 Main St. No. 540, Madison, NJ 07940 USA Fax: 603-250-8553
E-mail: EduFun@aol.com.

Media Magic New York, *(978-0-9744211)* 15 W. 39th St., 13th Flr., New York, NY 10018 USA Tel 212-926-5575
E-mail: mediamagicny@aol.com; info@mediamagic-ny.com.

Media Man! Productions *Imprint of* **Fairwood Pr.**

Media Publishing Group, The, *(978-0-692-82027-8)* 11 Penn plaza 5th Flr., NEW YORK, NY 10001 USA Tel 718-473-9819
E-mail: Syffronia.king@mail.com; Syffronia.king@mail.com.

Media Rodzina (POL) *(978-83-7278; 978-83-85594) Dist. by* **Distribks Inc.**

Medical Alternative Pr., *(978-0-9660882)* 4173 Fieldbrook Rd., West Bloomfield, MI 48323 USA Tel 248-851-3372; Fax: 248-851-0421; Toll Free: 888-647-5616 Do not confuse with Medical Alternative Pr., Colleyville, TX
E-mail: alselko@hotmail.com
Web site: http://www.drbrownstein.com.

Medical Manor Bks., *(978-0-934232)* Subs. of Manor Hse. Pubns., Inc., 3501 Newberry Rd., Philadelphia, PA 19154 USA (SAN 217-2526) Tel 800-343-8464; Fax: 215-440-9255; Toll Free: 800-343-8464
E-mail: info@diet-step.com; sales@diet-step.com; sales@medicalmanorbooks.com; marketing@diet-step.com; DrWalk@diet-step.com; info@medicalmanorbooks.com
Web site: http://www.medicalmanorbooks.com/; http://www.peace-healingbooks.com; http://www.manorhousepublications.com
Dist(s): **Bookmasters Distribution**
Distributors, The
Follett School Solutions
Quality Bks., Inc.
Unique Bks., Inc.
ebrary, Inc.

Medici Publishing, Inc., *(978-0-9743791; 978-0-9823853)* P.O. Box 282, Beulah, CO 81023 USA Tel 719-485-1167
E-mail: marcprat@juno.com
Web site: http://www.medicibooks.org.

Medicine Woman Inc., The, *(978-0-9771906)* Orders Addr.: P.O. Box 613, Cascade, ID 83611 USA Tel 208-382-6653; Edit Addr.: 843 S. Main Hwy. 55, Cascade, ID 83611 USA
E-mail: tmw@ctcweb.net
Web site: http://www.themedicinewoman.com.

Medicus Pr., Inc., *(978-0-9787727)* P.O. Box 284, Leonia, NJ 07605-0284 USA (SAN 851-5905) Tel 201-816-7363; Fax: 201-266-0537
E-mail: medicuspress@yahoo.com.

Medina Publishing, Ltd. (GBR) *(978-0-9570233; 978-1-909339; 978-0-9564170; 978-0-9567081) Dist. by* **Casemate Pubs.**

Medio Media *See* **Medio Media Publishing**

Medio Media Publishing, *(978-0-9666941; 978-0-9725627; 978-1-933182)* 627 N. 6th Ave., Tucson, AZ 85705-8330 USA Toll Free: 800-324-8305
E-mail: JoeD846136@aol.com; meditate@mediomedia.org
Web site: http://www.mediomedia.org
Dist(s): **Continuum International Publishing Group, Inc.**
Macmillan
National Bk. Network.

Medley, *(978-1-890034)* 1620 Los Alamos, SW, Albuquerque, NM 87104 USA Tel 505-247-3921; *Imprints:* Medley Publications (Medley Pubns)
E-mail: litchman@unm.edu.

Medley Pubns. *Imprint of* **Medley**

MedPress & Quality Publishers *See* **Quality Pubs.**

Medusa Road Pr., *(978-0-9779295)* 6 Rte. 75, Norton Hill, NY 12083 USA Tel 518-966-5281
E-mail: MedusaRoadStudio@aol.com
Web site: http://CarolynsWebsite.net.

Medwag Publishing, *(978-0-9654963)* P.O. Box 36037, Richmond, VA 23235 USA Tel 804-794-8186
E-mail: alrx1@juno.com.

Meehl Foundation Pr., *(978-0-9767049)* P.O. Box 2089, Brazoria, TX 77422-2089 USA Tel 979-798-7972
E-mail: meehlfou@meehlfoundation.org
Web site: http://www.meehlfoundation.org.

MeeraMasi, Inc., *(978-0-9773645; 978-0-9797191)* 449 London Pk. Ct., San Jose, CA 95136 USA Tel 408-365-8044; Fax: 408-225-8586
E-mail: info@meeramasi.com; sonali@meeramasi.com
Web site: http://www.meeramasi.com.

Meerkat Pr., *(978-0-692-37854-0; 978-0-9966262; 978-1-946154)* 200 River Vista Dr. Suite 522, Atlanta, GA 30339 USA Tel 678-439-7675
Web site: www.meerkatpress.com
Dist(s): **CreateSpace Independent Publishing Platform**
Midpoint Trade Bks., Inc.

Meerkat's Adventures Bks., *(978-0-9778072)* 510 Diamond St, Suite A, San Francisco, CA 94114 USA (SAN 850-2862)
Web site: http://www.meerkatsadventures.com.

Meet Bks., LLC, *(978-0-615-31579-9; 978-0-615-38973-8)* 806 Seale Ave., Palo Alto, CA 94303 USA.

Meet the Author *Imprint of* **Owen, Richard C. Pubs., Inc.**

Mefford, David, *(978-0-9762143)* 274 W. 700 N., American Fork, UT 84003 USA
E-mail: david@mefford.org.

Meg and Lucy Bks. (GBR) *Dist. by* **IPG Chicago.**

Megami Pr. LLC, *(978-0-615-39156-4; 978-0-615-40446-2; 978-0-9853471)* P.O. Box 128557, Nashville, TN 37212 USA
E-mail: Megamipress@gmail.com
Web site: http://www.megamipress.com.

Megyeri, Graham Bks., *(978-0-9711971; 978-0-9791994)* 439 Lakeview Blvd., Albert Lea, MN 56007 USA Tel 507-377-1255; Toll Free: 866-755-5942
E-mail: minnmemory@aol.com
Web site: http://www.minnesotamemories.com
Dist(s): **Partners Bk. Distributing, Inc.**

Mehr Iran Publishing Co. *See* **Mehriran Publishing Co.**

Mehriran Publishing Co., *(978-0-9633129)* 14900 Talking Rock Ct., Suite B, N. Potomac, MD 20878 USA Tel 301-279-6778; Fax: 301-738-2174
E-mail: pirnia@pirnia.com
Web site: http://www.pirnia.com.

Mehta Publishers (IND) *(978-93-83222) Dist. by* **Midpt Trade.**

MEIER Enterprises Inc., *(978-0-9726808)* 8697 Gage Blvd., Kennewick, WA 99336 USA Tel 509-735-1589; Fax: 509-783-5075; Toll Free: 800-239-7589
E-mail: sranderson@meierinc.com; info@learningtowrite.com
Web site: http://www.meierinc.com; http://www.learningtowrite.comw.

Meirovich, Igal, *(978-0-9820556; 978-1-60796)* 6408 Elray Dr., Apt. E, Baltimore, MD 21209 USA Tel 410-764-6423
E-mail: lightoncds@gmail.com
Dist(s): **BookBaby**
Lulu Pr., Inc.

Meister-Home, Inc., *(978-0-9702497)* P.O. Box 471250, Charlotte, NC 28247-1250 USA (SAN 256-1794) Tel 704-968-6741; Fax: 704-544-2034; *Imprints:* Meister-Home Press (Meister-Home Pr)
E-mail: ragilmartin@hotmail.com; rgilmartin@meister-home.com
Web site: http://www.meister-home.com.

Meister-Home Pr. *Imprint of* **Meister-Home, Inc.**

Mel Bay Pubns., Inc., *(978-0-7866; 978-0-87166; 978-1-56222; 978-1-60974; 978-1-61065; 978-1-61911; 978-1-5134)* 1734 Gilsinn Ln., Fenton, MO 63026 USA (SAN 657-3630) Tel 636-257-3970; Fax: 636-257-5062; Toll Free: 800-863-5229
E-mail: email@melbay.com; sharon@melbay.com
Web site: http://www.melbay.com; www.melbaydealers.com
Dist(s): **Alfred Publishing Co., Inc.**

Melanie, *(978-0-692-64200-9)* 208 Stimson St, Herkimer, NY 13350 USA Tel 315-219-1316
E-mail: melanie.lopata@yahoo.com.

Melanin Grace Publishing, LLC, *(978-0-692-87205-5; 978-0-692-87206-2)* 7440 Maple Spice Ave, CANAL WINCHESTER, OH 43110 USA Tel 614-946-6475
E-mail: jeffwcrawford5+LVP0003584@gmail.com; jeffwcrawford5+LVP0003584@gmail.com.

Melbourne Univ. Publishing (AUS) *(978-0-522; 978-0-646-05507-7) Dist. by* **IPG Chicago.**

Melbournestyle Bks. (AUS) *(978-0-9757047; 978-0-9924917) Dist. by* **IPG Chicago.**

Melissa Productions, Inc., *(978-0-9842394; 978-0-9834751; 978-0-9898293)* 2003 Arundale Ln., Matthews, NC 28104 USA (SAN 858-8252) Tel 704-246-7304
E-mail: melissa@melissaproductions.com
Web site: http://www.melissaproductions.com.

MELJAMES, Inc., *(978-0-9755195; 978-1-933419)* 107 Suncreek Dr., Suite 300, Allen, TX 75013 USA
Web site: http://www.meljamesinc.com.

†Mellen, Edwin Pr., The, *(978-0-7734; 978-0-88946; 978-0-935106; 978-0-7799; 978-1-4955)* Orders Addr.: P.O. Box 67, Queenston, ON L0S 1L0 CAN; Edit Addr.: P.O. Box 450, Lewiston, NY 14092-0450 USA (SAN 207-110X) Tel 716-754-2266; 716-754-2788; Fax: 716-754-1860
E-mail: sales@mellenpress.com
Web site: http://www.mellenpress.com; *CIP.*

Melton Hill Media, *(978-0-9816793; 978-0-9990919)* 9119 Solway Ferry Rd., Oak Ridge, TN 37830 USA (SAN 856-2288)
E-mail: wendy@meltonhillmedia.com
Web site: http://www.meltonhillmedia.com.

Melzee's Production, *(978-0-9722738)* P.O. Box 394, Hawthorne, CA 90251-0394 USA Tel 310-263-7804
E-mail: melzee3@juno.com.

Me+Mi Publishing, *(978-0-9679748; 978-1-931398)* 400 Knoll St. Ste. B, Wheaton, IL 60187-4557 USA Toll Free: 888-251-1444
E-mail: m3@memima.com
Web site: http://www.memima.com
Dist(s): **Lectorum Pubns., Inc.**
Quality Bks., Inc.

Memoir Bks., *(978-0-9793387; 978-1-937748)* Div. of Heidelberg Graphics, Orders Addr.: 2 Stansbury Ct., Chico, CA 95928 USA Tel 530-342-6582
Web site: http://www.heidelberggraphics.com.

Memoirs Publishing (GBR) *(978-1-86151; 978-1-909020; 978-1-908223; 978-1-909304; 978-1-909544; 978-1-909874) Dist. by* **Casemate Pubs.**

Memoria Pr., *(978-1-930953; 978-1-61538; 978-1-5477)* Orders Addr.: 4603 Poplar Level Rd., Louisville, KY 40213-2337 USA Toll Free: 877-862-1097
E-mail: magister@memoriapress.com
Web site: http://www.memoriapress.com
Dist(s): **Chicago Distribution Ctr.**

Memories Publishing, *(978-0-9748984)* P.O. Box 82516, Austin, TX 78708 USA Tel 512-907-1821
E-mail: mindyred@aol.com.

Mennonite Board of Missions *See* **Mennonite Mission Network**

Mennonite Mission Network, *(978-1-877736; 978-1-933845)* 500 S. Main St., P.O. Box 370, Elkhart, IN 46515-0370 USA Tel 219-294-7523; Fax: 574-294-8669; Toll Free: 866-866-2872
E-mail: Beyond@MennoniteMission.net
Web site: http://www.mennonitemission.net
Dist(s): **Follett School Solutions**
Herald Pr.

Mennonite Pr. Inc., *(978-0-9772745; 978-0-692-03234-3)* Orders Addr.: P.O. Box 867, Newton, KS 67114 USA Tel 316-283-4680; Fax: 316-283-2068; Toll Free: 800-536-4686; Edit Addr.: 532 N. Oliver Rd., Newton, KS 67114 USA
E-mail: reliability@mennonitepress.com
Web site: http://www.mennonitepress.com.

Mental Health Historic Preservation Society Of Central Illinois, *(978-0-9748742)* 209 Arnold Ave., East Peoria, IL 61611 USA Tel 309-699-3051
E-mail: aparr12345@aol.com
Dist(s): **Partners Bk. Distributing, Inc.**

Mental Wellness Publishing House *See* **Wellness pH**

Mentoring Minds, LP, *(978-0-9763559; 978-0-9767940; 978-1-935123; 978-1-938935; 978-1-62763)* P.O. Box 8843, Tyler, TX 75711 USA Fax: 800-838-8186; Toll Free: 800-585-5258
E-mail: gavin@mentoringminds.com
Web site: http://www.mentoring-minds.com.

MentorSource, LLC, *(978-0-9773324)* P.O. Box 24436, Minneapolis, MN 55424 USA Tel 612-269-8242
E-mail: gianna_bl@msn.com
Web site: http://www.rosyproses.com.

Mentzer Printing Ink, *(978-0-9746705; 978-0-9786276; 978-0-9797502; 978-0-9894927)* 1054 Virginia Ave., Indianapolis, IN 46203-1754 USA Toll Free: 800-514-6017
E-mail: info@m2print.com
Web site: http://www.m2print.com.

Menucha Pubs. Inc., *(978-1-61465)* 250 44th St. Suite No. B2, Brooklyn, NY 11232 USA (SAN 860-2115) Tel 718-232-0856; Fax: 718-232-0856
E-mail: hirshmt@hotmail.com.

†Mercer Univ. Pr., *(978-0-86554; 978-0-88146)* 1501 Mercer Univ. Dr., Macon, GA 31207 USA (SAN 220-0716) Tel 478-301-2880; Fax: 478-301-2585; Toll Free: 866-895-1472
E-mail: mupressorders@mercer.edu
Web site: http://www.mupress.org; *CIP.*

Merchant Bks. *Imprint of* **Rough Draft Printing**

Mercier Pr., Ltd., The (IRL) *(978-0-85342; 978-1-85635; 978-1-86023; 978-1-78117) Dist. by* **Dufour.**

Mercury Publishing, Inc., *(978-0-9778793)* Orders Addr.: 35 Fieldstone Way, Alpharetta, GA 30005 USA (SAN 850-5020)
E-mail: goga7n@gmail.com
Dist(s): **BCH Fulfillment & Distribution.**

Mercy Place, Inc., *(978-0-9677402; 978-0-9707919)* P.O. Box 134, Shippensburg, PA 17257 USA Tel 717-532-6899; Fax: 717-532-8646; Toll Free: 800-722-6774
E-mail: mpm@reapernet.com
Web site: http://mercyplace.com
Dist(s): **Destiny Image Pubs.**

†Meredith Bks., *(978-0-696; 978-0-89721; 978-0-917102)* Div. of Meredith Corp., Orders Addr.: 1716 Locust St., LN-110, Des Moines, IA 50309-3023 USA (SAN 202-4055) Tel 515-284-2363; 515-284-2126 (sales); Fax: 515-284-3371; Toll Free: 800-678-8091; *Imprints:* Food Network Kitchens (Food Net) Do not confuse with Meredith Pr. in Skaneateles, NY
E-mail: John.OBannon@meredith.com
Web site: http://www.bhgstore.com
Dist(s): **Follett School Solutions**
MyiLibrary
Sterling Publishing Co., Inc.; *CIP.*

Meredith Group Ltd., The, *(978-0-9765341)* Orders Addr.: 24 N. Bryn Mawr Ave., Box117, Bryn Mawr, PA 19010 USA (SAN 256-4920) Tel 610-642-0199; Edit Addr.: 71 Eden View Rd. # 6, Elizabethtown, PA 17022-3124 USA
E-mail: mmbellamy1@verizon.net
Web site: http://www.goldiesbook.com.

Meridia Pubs. LLC, *(978-0-615-40498-1; 978-0-9832330; 978-0-9904031)* 29439 Sayle Dr., Willoughby Hills, OH 44092 USA Tel 440-944-8047
E-mail: al.ruksenas@gmail.com
Dist(s): **BookBaby**
Smashwords.

Meridian Creative Group *See* **Larson Learning, Inc.**

Meritage Publishing, *(978-0-9769866)* Orders Addr.: 12339 Meritage Ct., Rancho Cucamonga, CA 91739 USA
E-mail: meritagepub@charter.net
Dist(s): **Quality Bks., Inc.**

Meriwether Publishing *Imprint of* **Meriwether Publishing, Ltd.**

Meriwether Publishing, Ltd., *(978-0-916260; 978-1-56608)* Orders Addr.: P.O. Box 7710, Colorado Springs, CO 80933 USA (SAN 208-4716) Tel 719-594-4422; Fax: 719-594-9916; P.O. Box 4267, Englewood, CO 80155 (SAN 990-2856) Tel 303-779-4035; Fax: 303-779-4315; Edit Addr.: 885 Elkton Dr., Colorado Springs, CO 80907 USA Tel 719-594-4422; 9707 E. Easter Ln. Suite A, Englewood, CO 80112 Tel 303-779-4035; *Imprints:* Meriwether Publishing (MeriwetherPub)
E-mail: mzapel@aol.com; books@pioneerdrama.com; wholesale@pioneerdrama.com
Web site: http://www.meriwetherpublishing.com; https://www.christianpub.com/; http://www.pioneerdrama.com
Dist(s): **Follett School Solutions**
Ingram Publisher Services.

Merkos L'Inyonei Chinuch, *(978-0-8266)* 291 Kingston Ave., Brooklyn, NY 11213 USA Tel 718-778-0226; Fax: 718-778-4148
E-mail: yonason@kehot.net
Web site: http://www.kehotonline.com.

Merlin, Debbi, *(978-0-9793568)* 12339 Scarcella Ln., Stafford, TX 77477-1609 USA (SAN 853-232X)
E-mail: merlin@merlinmagic.cc
Web site: http://www.merlinmagic.cc.

Merlin Enterprises, *(978-0-9761017)* Orders Addr.: 11881 S. Fortuna Rd., No. 451, Yuma, AZ 85367 USA
E-mail: napuff@gmail.com
Web site: http://cafepress.com/npuff.

Merlot Group, LLC, The, *(978-0-9816123; 978-0-9887117)* P.O. Box 302, Covington, KY 41012-0302 USA Tel 859-743-1003
Web site: http://www.merlotgroup.com
Dist(s): **Lulu Pr., Inc.**

Meroe Publishing, *(978-0-9768306)* P.O. Box 664, Cusseta, GA 31805 USA
E-mail: tonieshort@meroepublishing.com
Web site: http://www.meroepublishing.com.

Merriam-Webster *Imprint of* **Merriam-Webster, Inc.**

Merriam-Webster, Inc., *(978-0-87779; 978-1-68150)* Subs. of Encyclopaedia Britannica, Inc., Orders Addr.: 47 Federal St., Springfield, MA 01102 USA (SAN 202-6244) Tel 413-734-3134; Fax: 413-731-5979; 413-734-2014; Toll Free: 800-828-1880; *Imprints:* Merriam-Webster (Merriam-Webstr)
E-mail: sales@Merriam-Webster.com; orders@Merriam-Webster.com; jsantoro@Merriam-Webster.com
Web site: http://www.WordCentral.com; http://www.Merriam-Webster.com
Dist(s): **CENGAGE Learning**
Delmar Cengage Learning
Perfection Learning Corp.

Merril Pr., *(978-0-936783)* 12500 NE Tenth Pl., Bellevue, WA 98005 USA (SAN 699-9387) Tel 425-454-7009; Fax: 425-451-3959
E-mail: editor@merrilpress.com
Web site: http://www.merrilpress.com
Dist(s): **Midpoint Trade Bks., Inc.**

Merrimack Bk. Works, *(978-0-9799090)* 23 Pleasant St., No. 508, Newburyport, MA 01950-2632 USA (SAN 854-7424) Tel 978-417-9277
E-mail: mary@maryleemattison.com
Web site: http://www.maryleemattison.com.

Merrimack Media, *(978-1-939166; 978-1-945756)* 665 Washington St. No. 2507, Boston, MA 02111 USA Tel 508-932-0865
E-mail: jenny@merrimackmedia.com
Web site: http://merrimackmedia.com.

Merritt Publishing *See* **Silver Lake Publishing**

Merriwell, Frank Inc., *(978-0-8373)* Subs. of National Learning Corp., 212 Michael Dr., Syosset, NY 11791 USA (SAN 209-259X) Tel 516-921-8888; Toll Free: 800-645-6337.

Merry Dissonance Pr., *(978-1-939919)* 3113 Soaring Eagle Ln., Castle Rock, CO 80109 USA Tel 213-448-7701
E-mail: donnamazzitelli@gmail.com
Web site: merrydissonancepress.com.

Merry Lane Pr., *(978-0-9744307)* 18 E. 16th St., 7th Flr., New York, NY 10003 USA Tel 212-633-6505; Fax: 212-242-6077
E-mail: alan@merrylanepress.com
Web site: http://www.merrylanepress.com.

Merry Tales Publishing, *(978-0-9845471)* 209 Bobbitt Rd., Clayton, NC 27520-6557 USA (SAN 859-709X) Tel 919-550-0107.

Merryant Pubs., *(978-1-877599)* P.O. Box 1921, Vashon, WA 98070-1921 USA Toll Free: 800-228-8958
E-mail: jmboule@aol.com.

Merrybooks & More, *(978-0-9615407; 978-1-882607)* 1214 Rugby Rd., Charlottesville, VA 22903 USA (SAN 695-5053) Tel 804-979-3658; Fax: 804-296-8446; Toll Free: 800-959-2665.

Mesorah Pubns., Ltd., *(978-0-89906; 978-1-57819; 978-1-4226)* 4401 Second Ave., Brooklyn, NY 11232 USA (SAN 213-1269) Tel 718-921-9000 Toll Free: 800-637-6724; *Imprints:* ArtScroll Series (ArtScroll Series); Shaar Press (Shaar Pr)
E-mail: info@ArtScroll.com
Web site: http://www.artscroll.com.

Mesquite Tress Pr., LLC, *(978-0-9729835)* Orders Addr.: P.O. Box 17513, Louisville, KY 40217 USA; Edit Addr.: 212 W. Ormsby Ave, Louisville, KY 40203 USA
Web site: http://www.onetinytwig.com; http://www.mesquitetreepress.com; http://bluegrassbreeze.com.

Mess Hall Writers, *(978-1-885531)* P.O. Box 1551, Jeffersonville, IN 47130 USA Tel 812-288-9888; Fax: 812-288-9695
E-mail: fooddudes2@aol.com.

Message In a Bottle Translators *See* **Pangloss Publishing**

Messiah Publishing - Pearables, *(978-0-9792446)* P.O. Box 272000, Fort Collins, CO 80527 USA (SAN 852-8837) Tel 719-549-0662
Web site: http://www.pearables.com.

Messianic Perspectives, *(978-0-9674319; 978-0-9882120; 978-0-9898240)* Orders Addr.: P.O. Box 345, San Antonio, TX 78292-0345 USA Tel 210-226-0421; Fax: 210-226-2140; Toll Free: 800-926-5397; Edit Addr.: 611 Broadway St., San Antonio, TX 78215 USA
E-mail: info@cjfm.org
Web site: http://www.cjfm.org.

Messineo, Joe *See* **Socrates Solutions Incorporated**

Meta Adventures *See* **Meta Adventures Publishing & DIA Publishing**

Meta Adventures Publishing & DIA Publishing, *(978-0-9721202)* Orders Addr.: P.O. Box 1894, Sedona, AZ 86339 USA (SAN 254-6183) Tel 928-204-1560
E-mail: info@dreamsinaction.us; publishing@dreamsinaction.us; orderinfo@dreamsinaction.us
Web site: http://www.dreamsinaction.us; http://www.MrSedona.com
Dist(s): **Dreams in Action Distribution.**

Metacognition Pr., *(978-0-9859707)* 48 Michael Ln., Orinda, CA 94563 USA Tel 925-360-9159
E-mail: Metacognitionblog@yahoo.com.

Metal Lunchbox Publishing, *(978-0-9843437)* 5257 Buckeystown Pike #508, Frederick, MD 21704 USA (SAN 859-1202) Tel 412-916-0211
E-mail: info@metallunchboxpublishing.com
Web site: http://www.metallunchboxpublishing.com.

Metalmark Pr., *(978-0-9767239)* 7116 New Sharon Church Rd., Rougemont, NC 27572 USA
E-mail: birdcr@concentric.net
Web site: http://www.rlephoto.com.

Metamedix, Incorporated *See* **Science2Discover, Inc.**

Metamorphosis, *(978-0-9774589)* 100 State St S., Kirkland, WA 98033-6667 USA
E-mail: christinemerritt@earthlink.net
Web site: http://www.iahp.com/metamorphosis.

Metaphors 4 Life, *(978-0-9817291)* P.O. Box 270812, West Hartford, CT 06127 USA (SAN 856-3772)
E-mail: writeme@danarondel.com
Web site: http://www.danarondel.com; http://www.metaphors4life.org.

Metaphrog (GBR) *(978-0-9534932; 978-0-9545984) Dist. by* **D C D.**

Metapublishing, *(978-0-9654522)* 500 Center Ave. Apt. 211, Westwood, NJ 07675-1677 USA Do not confuse with Metapublishing, North Miami Beach, FL
Dist(s): **New Leaf Distributing Co., Inc.**

Metchnikoff, Elie Memorial Library, *(978-0-9634067)* 230 Orange St., No. 6, Oakland, CA 94610-4139 USA Tel 510-444-3435; Fax: 510-642-7175
E-mail: jbibel@arg.org.

Metric Moon Press *See* **Graphite Pr.**

Metro Bks., *(978-0-9752732)* 1706 W. Jarvis, 1W, Chicago, IL 60626 USA.

Metropolitan Bks. *Imprint of* **Holt, Henry & Co.**

Metropolitan Museum of Art, The, *(978-0-87099; 978-1-58839)* 1000 Fifth Ave., New York, NY 10028 USA (SAN 202-6279) Tel 212-879-5500; Fax: 212-396-5062
Web site: http://www.metmuseum.org
Dist(s): **California Princeton Fulfillment Services**
Casemate Academic
Chicago Distribution Ctr.
Continental Bk. Co., Inc.
Princeton Univ. Pr.
Yale Univ. Pr.

Metropolitan Teaching & Learning Co., *(978-0-928415; 978-1-58120; 978-1-58830)* 317 Madison Ave., New York, NY 10017 USA Tel 212-475-8826; Fax: 212-475-8311; Toll Free: 800-235-6931
Web site: http://metrotlc.com.

Meyer & Meyer Sport, Ltd. (GBR) *(978-1-84126; 978-1-78255) Dist. by* **Lewis Intl Inc.**

Meyer & Meyer Sport, Ltd. (GBR) *(978-1-84126; 978-1-78255) Dist. by* **Cardinal PubGr.**

Meyer Enterprises *See* **Western New York Wares, Inc.**

Meyer, Tjaden, *(978-0-9744536)* Orders Addr.: P.O. Box 230015, Saint Louis, MO 63123 USA Tel 314-352-2253; Edit Addr.: 7045 Parkwood St., Saint Louis, MO 63116 USA
E-mail: klmeyer@worldnet.att.net.

Meza, Marti, *(978-0-615-16571-4)* 1515 W. 7th St., Apt. 4-D, Brooklyn, NY 11204 USA
Dist(s): **Lulu Pr., Inc.**

MF Unlimited, *(978-0-9712278)* P.O. Box 55346, Atlanta, GA 30308 USA
Web site: http://www.mfunews.com
Dist(s): **Lightning Source, Inc.**

Mfg Application Konsulting Engineering, *(978-0-9762208)* 1071 E. 425 N., Ogden, UT 84404 USA.

M-Graphics *Imprint of* **M-Graphics Publishing**

M-Graphics Publishing, *(978-0-9753075; 978-0-9777003; 978-0-9792808; 978-1-934881; 978-1-940220)* One Dead Eye Rd., Swampscott, MA 01907 USA Tel 781-990-8778 Weekdays 9AM - 4 PM; *Imprints:* M-Graphics (M-Grap)
E-mail: mgraphics.books@gmail.com
Web site: http://www.mgraphics-publishing.com.

M.H. Gill & Co. U. C. (IRL) *(978-0-7171) Dist. by* **Dufour.**

MHC Ministries, *(978-0-9895422)* 1170 NE 133rd St., North Miami, FL 33161 USA Tel 786-286-5210
E-mail: mmuc31@gmail.com
Web site: www.mhcministries.com.

Mia Sharon, Inc., *(978-0-9759098)* 600 Academy Dr., No. 130, Northbrook, IL 60062 USA Tel 847-826-8196
Web site: http://www.miasharon.com.

†Micah Pubns., *(978-0-916288)* 255 Humphrey St., Marblehead, MA 01945 USA (SAN 209-1577) Tel 781-631-7601; Fax: 781-639-0772; Toll Free: 877-268-9963
E-mail: micah@micahbooks.com
Web site: http://www.micahbooks.com
Dist(s): **Book Publishing Co.**
David, Jonathan Pubs., Inc.; *CIP.*

Miceli, *(978-0-9888654)* P.O. Box 2027, Danvers, MA 01923 USA Tel 978-626-1429
E-mail: mary_miceli@comcast.net.

Miceli, Mary Anne, *(978-0-578-08747-4; 978-0-578-10145-3; 978-0-578-10979-4)* 10 Daniels Rd., Wenham, MA 01984 USA; P.O. Box 2027, Danvers, MA 01923
E-mail: mary_miceli@comcast.net
Web site: bostonnorthshorestoriesandpoems.com.

Micelle Pr., Inc., *(978-0-9608752; 978-1-870228)* Orders Addr.: P.O. Box 1519, Port Washington, NY 11050-0306 USA Tel 516-767-7171; Fax: 516-944-9824
E-mail: micellepress@googlemail.com
Web site: http://www.scholium.com
Dist(s): **Scholium International, Inc.**

MiceWorks, *(978-0-9764719)* 544 13th Ave., W., Kirkland, WA 98033 USA.

Michael Neugebauer Bks. *Imprint of* **North-South Bks., Inc.**

Michael-Christopher Bks., *(978-0-9710398)* Orders Addr.: P.O. Box 75313, Washington, DC 20013-0313 USA Tel 301-927-3179
E-mail: mc@michael-christopher.com
Web site: http://www.michael-christopher.com
Dist(s): **BookBaby.**

MichaelsMind LLC *See* **Right Stuff Kids Bks.**

Michaelson Entertainment, *(978-0-9727702; 978-1-932530; 978-1-60730)* 36 Cabrillo Terr., Aliso Viejo, CA 92656 USA Tel 949-916-0575 phone; Fax: 949-916-0574 fax; *Imprints:* 101 Book (101 Bk); ABC Book (ABCBk)
E-mail: brad@michaelsonentertainment.com
Web site: http://www.michaelsonentertainment.com
Dist(s): **Partners Bk. Distributing, Inc.**

Michalek, Curtis, *(978-0-9786177)* P.O. Box 403, Montezuma, IA 50171 USA Tel 641-623-3368
E-mail: c.a.michalek@hotmail.com
Web site: www.aluris.com.

Michele, Mary, *(978-0-615-25486-9)* 27838 N. 45th Way, Cave Creek, AZ 85331 USA Tel 602-952-8604
E-mail: scriptsrelief@cox.net
Dist(s): **Lulu Pr., Inc.**

Michelle, Patrice *See* **Limitless Ink Press, LLC**

michelle s lazurek-author, *(978-0-692-89435-4)* 3 alliance ave, coudersport, PA 16915 USA Tel 814-274-9298
E-mail: michellelazurek@yahoo.com
Web site: www.michellelazurek.com.

Michelle's A & E (KOR) *(978-89-954869) Dist. by* **APG.**

Michelle's Bks. & More, Ltd. Co., *(978-0-9763080)* 800 Fabric X-Press Way, Dallas, TX 75234 USA Tel 972-625-1444; Fax: 972-406-1321
E-mail: michelle@michellesbooks.com
Web site: http://www.michellesbooks.com.

Michelle's Designs, *(978-0-9789694; 978-0-9817663; 978-0-9842520)* 3702 Sandpoint Ct, Carlsbad, CA 92010 USA Tel 760-720-4335; Fax: 802-609-2629
E-mail: patterns@michelles-designs.com; jen@condormedia.com
Web site: http://www.michelles-designs.com.

Michigan Publishing, *(978-0-9745109; 978-1-4181; 978-1-4255; 978-1-60785)* Div. of University of Michigan Library, 1210 Buhr Bldg. 839 Greene St., Ann Arbor, MI 48109 USA (SAN 255-9889)
E-mail: spo.pod@umich.edu; lib.pod@umich.edu
Web site: http://www.lib.umich.edu/michigan-publishing.

Michigan State Univ., Julian Samora Research Institute, *(978-0-9650557)* 301 Nisbet Bldg., 1407 S. Harrison, East Lansing, MI 48823-586 USA Tel 517-432-1317; Fax: 517-432-2221
E-mail: info@jsri.msu.edu
Web site: http://jsri.msu.edu.

†Michigan State Univ. Pr., *(978-0-87013; 978-0-937191; 978-1-60917; 978-1-61186; 978-1-938065; 978-1-62895; 978-1-62896; 978-1-941258; 978-0-9967252; 978-1-68430; 978-1-947134)* Orders Addr.: 1405 S. Harrison Rd. Suite 25, East Lansing, MI 48823-5245 USA (SAN 202-6295) Tel 517-884-6901; Fax: 517-432-2611; Toll Free: 800-621-2736; 800-621-8476
E-mail: msupress@msupress.org
Web site: http://www.msupress.org
Dist(s): **Chicago Distribution Ctr.**; *CIP.*

mickego art, *(978-0-692-89076-9)* 12257 hill rd, SWARTZ CREEK, MI 48473 USA Tel 989-277-1585
Dist(s): **Lightning Source, Inc.**

Micro Publishing Media, Inc., *(978-0-9827716; 978-1-936517; 978-1-944068)* 29 Pk. St., Stockbridge, MA 01262 USA; *Imprints:* Pop Pop Press (Pop Pop Pr)
E-mail: Deborah@micropublishingmedia.com
Web site: http://www.micropublishingmedia.com.

Microcosm Publishing, *(978-0-9726967; 978-0-9770557; 978-0-9788665; 978-1-934620; 978-1-62106)* 636 SE. 11th Ave., Portland, OR 97214 USA Tel 503-232-3666 joe@microcosmpublishing.com; Toll Free Fax: 888-503-0599; *Imprints:* Elly Blue Publishing (Elly Blue); Into Action Publications (Into Action)
E-mail: joe@microcosmpublishing.com
Web site: http://www.microcosmpublishing.com
Dist(s): **AK Pr. Distribution**
Follett School Solutions
Legato Pubs. Group
MyiLibrary
Publishers Group West (PGW).

Microsoft Pr. *Imprint of* **Pearson Education**

†Microsoft Pr., *(978-0-7356; 978-0-914845; 978-0-925550; 978-1-55615; 978-1-57231; 978-1-879021)* Orders Addr.: 3 Center Plaza, Boston, MA 02108-2084 USA Toll Free: 800-677-7377; Edit Addr.: One Microsoft Way, Redmond, WA 98052-6399 USA (SAN 264-9969) Tel 425-882-8080; 206-882-8080; 425-703-0942; Fax: 425-936-7329 Do not confuse with Microsoft Pr., Dunmore, PA
E-mail: msporder@msn.com; duanedr@microsoft.com; chriscai@microsoft.com
Web site: http://www.microsoft.com/mspress/
Dist(s): **Follett School Solutions**
Pearson Education; *CIP.*

Mid-Atlantic Highlands Publishing *Imprint of* **Publishers Place, Inc.**

Middelhauve Verlags GmbH (DEU) *(978-3-7876) Dist. by* **Distribks Inc.**

†Middle Atlantic Pr., *(978-0-912608; 978-0-9705804; 978-0-9754419)* 400 Pond View Dr., Moorestown, NJ 08057 USA Tel 856-273-9062; Fax: 856-273-7526
E-mail: blake@middleatlanticpress.com; info@middleatlanticpress.com
Web site: http://www.middleatlanticpress.com
Dist(s): **Partners Bk. Distributing, Inc.**; *CIP.*

Middle River Pr., *(978-0-9785656; 978-0-9817036; 978-0-9846071; 978-0-9838203; 978-0-9857295; 978-0-9896724; 978-0-9964086; 978-1-946886)* 1498 NE 30th Ct., Oakland Park, FL 33334-4414 USA Tel 954-630-8192
E-mail: info@middleriverpress.com
Web site: http://www.middleriverpress.com.

Middleburry Hse. Publishing, *(978-0-9792067)* 3225 Middleburry Ln., Charleston, SC 29414 USA
Web site: http://www.rwridley.com; http://www.choytcaldwell.com.

Middleton Classics *See* **Middleton Publishing**

Middleton Publishing, *(978-0-9787871; 978-1-935702; 978-1-63104)* P.O. Box 226, Williamstown, NY 13493 USA (SAN 851-6308)
Web site: http://www.middletonpublishing.com.

Midnight Hologram, LLC, *(978-1-938516)* 1180 Beacon Hill Crossing, Alpharetta, GA 30005 USA Tel 678-393-0420
E-mail: yvet77@comcast.net
Web site: www.midnighthologram.com.

Midpoint Trade Bks., Inc., *(978-1-940416)* Orders Addr.: 1263 Southwest Blvd., Kansas City, KS 66103 USA (SAN 631-3736) Tel 913-831-2233; Fax: 913-362-7401; Toll Free: 800-742-6139 (consumer orders); Edit Addr.: 27 W. 20th St., No. 1102, New York, NY 10011 USA (SAN 631-1075) Tel 212-727-0190; Fax: 212-727-0195
E-mail: info@midpointtrade.com
Web site: http://www.midpointtrade.com; http://www.midpointtradebooks.com/
Dist(s): **Ingram Bk. Co.**
ebrary, Inc.

MidRun Pr., *(978-0-9664095; 978-0-9824397)* 90 Larch Row, Wenham, MA 01984-1624 USA Tel 978-468-9953 (phone/fax)
E-mail: midrunpress@aol.com
Web site: http://www.midrunpress.com.

Midwest Christian Center *See* **Family Harvest Church**

Midwest Cylinder Management, Inc., *(978-0-9729026)* 1203 Paramount Pkwy., Batavia, IL 60510-1458 USA Tel 630-673-9770; Fax: 630-406-9922
E-mail: prminalt@yahoo.com
Web site: http://www.kidsmenus.com.

Midwest Graphics, Inc., *(978-0-9776893)* 180 N. Wacker Dr., Suite 104, Chicago, IL 60606 USA Tel 312-641-2236; Fax: 312-641-2256
E-mail: mark@mwgchicago.com
Web site: http://www.mwgchicago.com.

Midwest Screen and Media Production, *(978-0-9719665)* P.O. Box 133, Greeley, KS 66033 USA (SAN 254-5527)
Web site: http://www.msmediaproduction.com.

Midwest Writng, *(978-0-9778290; 978-0-9818089; 978-0-9834116; 978-0-9906190)* 225 E.2nd St., Suite 303, Davenport, IA 52801 USA Tel 563-324-1410; Fax: 563-324-1410
Web site: http://www.mwcqc.org.

Mielcarek, David, *(978-0-9785480)* 3387 Ocean Beach Hwy, Longview, WA 98632 USA
E-mail: thebook@timeforyourmind.com
Web site: http://timeforyourmind.com.

Mighty Kids Media, *(978-0-9765953; 978-0-9770455; 978-1-933934; 978-0-9884241)* 4201 Congress St, Suite 451, Charlotte, NC 28209 USA Toll Free Fax: 877-723-3388 Do not confuse with companies with the same name in Dobbs Ferry, NY, Medofrd, OR, Lanett, AL
Web site: http://www.dangerrangers.com.

Mighty Lion Ventures, *(978-0-615-30860-9; 978-0-9831449)* P.O. Box 2950, Cypress, TX 77410 USA.

Mighty Media Junior Readers *Imprint of* **Mighty Media Pr.**

Mighty Media Kids *Imprint of* **Mighty Media Pr.**

Mighty Media Pr., *(978-0-9765201; 978-0-9798249; 978-0-9824584; 978-0-9830219; 978-1-938063)* Div. of Mighty Media, 1201 Currie Ave., Minneapolis, MN 55403 USA Tel 612-455-0252; Fax: 612-338-4817; *Imprints:* Mighty Media Junior Readers (MMJrRead); Mighty Media Kids (MMKids)
E-mail: info@scarlettapress.com; josh@scarlettapress.com
Web site: http://www.mightymediapress.com
Dist(s): **Continental Enterprises Group, Inc. (CEG)**
MyiLibrary
Publishers Group West (PGW).

Mighty Publishing, LLC, *(978-0-9966739)* 701 Niagara St, Denver, CO 80220 USA Tel 303-355-3120
E-mail: kbcinspires@gmail.com.

Miglior Pr., *(978-0-9827614; 978-0-9836484)* P.O. Box 7487, Athens, GA 30604 USA Tel 706-338-0017
E-mail: info@migliorpress.com
Web site: http://migliorpress.com.

Mijade Editions (BEL) *(978-2-87142) Dist. by* **Distribks Inc.**

Mikaya Pr., *(978-0-9650493; 978-1-931414)* 12 Bedford St., New York, NY 10014 USA Tel 212-647-1831; Fax: 212-727-0236
E-mail: Waldman@Mikaya.com
Web site: http://www.mikaya.com
Dist(s): **Firefly Bks., Ltd.**

Mikazuki Jujitsu *See* **Mikazuki Publishing Hse.**

Mikazuki Publishing Hse., *(978-0-615-47311-6; 978-0-615-48054-1; 978-0-9835946; 978-1-937981; 978-0-9910285; 978-1-942825)* 530 E. 8th St. Suite 400, Los Angeles, CA 90014 USA Tel 010-982-2379
E-mail: kambizmostofizadeh1@gmail.com
Web site: http://www.MikazukiPublishingHouse.com
Dist(s): **BookBaby**
Lightning Source, Inc.

Mike-Auri Bks., *(978-0-9747587)* P.O. Box 420966, Del Rio, TX 78842 USA Tel 830-774-2789
E-mail: dfitzgibbon@stx.rr.com
Web site: http://www.texasredhen.com; http://www.mikeauri.com.

Mike-Mike Distribution, *(978-0-9741043)* 1003 N., Fifth St., Champaign, IL 61820 USA Tel 217-352-4215.

Mikenzi's Kardz & Bks. Llc., *(978-0-9792647)* 1115 S. Alhambra Cir., Coral Gables, FL 33146-3711 USA
E-mail: sgbarrow@hotmail.com.

Milano, Jacque & Assocs., *(978-0-9728432)* 700 N. Dobson Rd., No. 15, Chandler, AZ 85224 USA; *Imprints:* Carefree Publishing (Carefree Pubng)
Web site: http://www.carefreepublishing.com.

Mile High Pr., Ltd., *(978-1-885331)* Div. of Briles Group, Inc., Orders Addr.: P.O. Box 460880, Aurora, CO 80046 USA Tel 303-627-9179; Fax: 303-627-9184; Toll Free: 800-594-0800; Edit Addr.: 14160 E. Bellewood Dr., Aurora, CO 80015 USA Tel 303-745-4590
E-mail: info@milehighpress.com; milehighpress@aol.com.

Mile Oak Publishing, Inc. (CAN) *(978-1-896819) Dist. by* **Austin and Co.**

Miles & Assocs., *(978-0-9778623)* P.O. Box 15566, Phoenix, AZ 85060 USA Tel 386-446-9291
E-mail: drlinda03@aol.com
Web site: http://www.thenewmarriage.com.

Miles, Linda *See* **Miles & Assocs.**

Miles Music, *(978-0-9710446)* Div. of Miles Enterprises, 3060 Larson Rd., Weippe, ID 83553 USA Tel 208-435-4600; Fax: 208-435-1116
E-mail: milesmusic@idamall.com
Web site: http://www.idamall.com.

For full information on wholesalers and distributors, refer to the Wholesaler and Distributor Name Index

Milestone Pr., Inc., *(978-0-9631861; 978-1-889596)* Orders Addr.: P.O. Box 158, Almond, NC 28702 USA Tel 828-488-6601 (phone/fax)
E-mail: maryellenhammond@milestonepress.com
Web site: http://www.milestonepress.com
Dist(s): **America's Cycling Pubns.**
Common Ground Distributors, Inc.

Milestones Publishing, *(978-0-9786154)* P.O. Box 1556, Wylie, TX 75098 USA Tel 214-403-9852; Fax: 972-442-1613
E-mail: kaylasadams@hotmail.com
Web site: http://www.kaylaadams.net.

Milet Publishing, *(978-1-84059)* P.O. Box 2459, Chicago, IL 60690-2459 USA
E-mail: info@milet.com
Web site: http://www.milet.com
Dist(s): **Chinasprout, Inc.**
Independent Pubs. Group
Tuttle Publishing.

Milk & Cookies *Imprint of* **ibooks, Inc.**

Milk Mug Publishing, *(978-0-9721882)* 9190 W. Olympic Blvd., Suite 253, Beverly Hills, CA 90212 USA Tel 310-278-1153 (phone/fax)
E-mail: orders@thehoopsterbook.com
Web site: http://www.thehoopsterbook.com
Dist(s): **SCB Distributors.**

Milken Family Foundation, *(978-0-9646425)* 1250 Fourth St., 4th Flr., Santa Monica, CA 90404-1353 USA Tel 310-998-2825; Fax: 310-998-2899
E-mail: jboone@mff.org
Web site: http://www.milkenexchange.org.

Milkweed Editions, *(978-0-915943; 978-1-57131)* 1011 Washington Ave. S., Suite 300, Minneapolis, MN 55415-1246 USA (SAN 294-0671) Tel 612-332-3192; Fax: 612-215-2550; Toll Free: 800-520-6455
E-mail: market@milkweed.org
Web site: http://www.milkweed.org;
http://www.worldashome.org
Dist(s): **MyiLibrary**
Publishers Group West (PGW).

Mill City Press, Inc *Imprint of* **Salem Author Services**

Mill Creek Metro Publishing, *(978-0-9741989)* P.O. Box 90134, Youngstown, OH 44509 USA Tel 330-797-0024
E-mail: ianjcue@ianjcue.com
Web site: http://www.ianjcue.com
Dist(s): **Book Clearing Hse.**

Mill Park Publishing, *(978-0-9728225; 978-0-9883980; 978-0-9975871)* E & M Group, LLC, Orders Addr.: 981 W. Cherry Bello Dr., Eagle, ID 83616 USA Tel 208-890-8122
E-mail: elaine@elaineambrose.com;
elaine@millparkpublishing.com
Web site: http://www.Elaineambrose.com;
www.millparkpublishing.com
Dist(s): **Lulu Pr., Inc.**

Mill Street Forward, The, *(978-0-9654628)* 15 1/2 Van Houten St., Apt. 117, Paterson, NJ 07505 USA Tel 973-345-9539.

Millbrook Pr. *Imprint of* **Lerner Publishing Group**

Millennial Mind Publishing *Imprint of* **American Bk. Publishing Group**

Millennium Marketing & Publishing, *(978-1-886161)* 2455 Glen Hill Dr., Indianapolis, IN 46240-3460 USA Tel 317-815-9828; Fax: 317-815-9829
E-mail: MMPbooks@comcast.net
Web site: http://www.chicksguidetofootball.com
Dist(s): **Cardinal Pubs. Group**
Independent Pubs. Group
Journey Pubns., LLC
Quality Bks., Inc.

Millennium Workshop Production, *(978-0-9725344)* 11501 Maple Ridge Rd., Reston, VA 20190-3604 USA (SAN 255-1624) Tel 703-925-0610 (phone/fax)
E-mail: victor@millenniumworkshop.com
Web site: http://www.millenniumworkshop.com.

Miller, Ann *See* **Jaylil Publishing Co.**

Miller, Bruce, *(978-0-9765598)* 10011 Bridgeport Way SW., Suite 1500 PMB128, Lakewood, WA 98499 USA Tel 253-227-2292
E-mail: warofpowers@comcast.net.

Miller, Deanna, *(978-0-9725424)* 12215 Fuller St., Silver Spring, MD 20902 USA
E-mail: info@deannamiller.com
Web site: http://www.deannamiller.com.

Miller, Debra Juanita, *(978-0-9706782; 978-0-9776014)* P.O. Box 20593, Chicago, IL 60620 USA
E-mail: monogrambooklets@yahoo.com;
djpmspinsstories@yahoo.com.

Miller, Don G., *(978-0-615-12836-8)* 5051 S. 172nd. St., Omaha, NE 68135 USA.

Miller, J. Cris & Assocs., *(978-0-9725308)* 10555 W. 74th St., Countryside, IL 60525 USA Tel 708-579-1707 (phone/fax)
E-mail: jcmtales@hotmail.com.

Miller, J. Garnet Ltd. (GBR) *(978-0-85343) Dist. by* **Empire Pub Srvs.**

Miller, Michael, *(978-0-9723474; 978-0-9743522; 978-0-9825155; 978-0-9839356)* 2418 Hagerman St., Colorado Springs, CO 80904 USA Tel 719-635-0017; Fax: 501-421-1495
E-mail: michael@mail.sabineundmichael.com
Web site: http://www.sabineundmichael.com.

Miller, Peter Mitchell *See* **Silver Print Pr., Inc.**

Miller, Randy, *(978-0-9770530)* 17 N. Rd., Alstead, NH 03602 USA Tel 603-835-7889
E-mail: jrmiller@sover.net
Web site: http://www.randymillerprints.com.

Miller, Smit Enterprises, *(978-0-9769433)* 112 Misty Creek Dr., Colorado Springs, CO 80132-6032 USA
E-mail: dawn@dawnsmit.com.

MillerWords, *(978-0-615-94052-6; 978-0-692-41237-4; 978-0-692-48617-7; 978-0-692-56102-7; 978-0-692-61478-5; 978-0-692-63441-7; 978-0-692-65983-0; 978-0-692-66359-2; 978-0-692-74074-3; 978-0-692-74075-0; 978-0-692-74141-2; 978-0-9982986)* P.O. Box 1622, Mount Dora, FL 32756 USA Tel 352-385-4499
E-mail: mark@millerwords.com
Web site: www.millerwords.com
Dist(s): **CreateSpace Independent Publishing Platform.**

MillerWrite, Inc., *(978-0-9723948)* 2875-F Northtowne Ln., No. 302, Reno, NV 89512-2062 USA Tel 775-673-2152
E-mail: chrisshelton78@msn.com;
jmiller@millerwrite.com
Web site: http://www.millerwrite.com.

Millfree Mursaps Media, *(978-0-9904093)* Orders Addr.: P.O. Box 52772, New Orleans, LA 70152 USA Tel 504-233-3369
E-mail: ryan@millfreemursaps.com
Web site: millfreemursaps.com
Dist(s): **Independent Pubs. Group.**

Milligan Books *See* **Professional Publishing Hse. LLC**

Millman, Selena, *(978-0-9793058; 978-0-9794584; 978-0-9795756; 978-0-9798417; 978-0-9798603; 978-0-9802400; 978-0-615-15137-3; 978-0-615-23804-3; 978-0-578-00466-2; 978-0-578-00564-5)* 4984 Ridgebury, Lyndhurst, OH 44124 USA
Web site: http://www.freewebs.com/heal4michael
Dist(s): **Lulu Pr., Inc.**

Millmark Education, *(978-1-4334; 978-1-61618)* Orders Addr.: 7272 Wisconsin Ave, Suite 300, Bethesda, MD 20814-2081 USA (SAN 852-4912) Tel 301-941-1974; Fax: 301-656-0183; Edit Addr.: 7272 Wisconsin Ave. Suite 300, Suite 300, Bethesda, MD 20814-2081 USA
E-mail: rachel.moir@millmarkeducation.com;
info@millmarkeducation.com
Web site: http://www.millmarkeducation.com/.

Mills & Morris Publishing Corporation *See* **Bluebonnets, Boots & Bks. Pr.**

Milner Crest Publishing, LLC, *(978-0-9820651)* P.O. Box 10754, Portland, OR 97296-0754 USA (SAN 857-1376)
E-mail: danielbruton@gmail.com
Web site: http://www.milnercrestpublishing.com
Dist(s): **BookBaby.**

Milo Educational Bks. & Resources, *(978-1-933668; 978-1-60698)* P.O. Box 41353, Houston, TX 77241-1353 USA Tel 713-466-6456; Fax: 713-896-6456
E-mail: milo_books@yahoo.com
Web site: http://www.miloeducationalbooks.com.

Milstein & Hauptman Publishing *See* **Wonderful Publishing**

Miltenberg, Robert Allen, *(978-0-615-63925-3; 978-0-615-66467-5; 978-0-615-77522-7; 978-0-9893031)* 210 LIME KEY Ln., NAPLES, FL 34114 USA Tel 310-994-2407
E-mail: Rmiltenberg@yahoo.com
Web site: www.blurb.com; www.artworq.com.

MiMar Publishing, *(978-0-9754241; 978-0-615-16688-9; 978-0-615-16689-6)* 714 Enchanted Rock Trail, Georgetown, TX 78633 USA
Web site: http://www.bakerstreetbunch.com
Dist(s): **Lulu Pr., Inc.**

Mimaxion, *(978-1-68321)* 40 E. Main St., Newark, DE 19711 USA (SAN 990-0896)
E-mail: cedric.dufay@gmail.com;
admin@speedypublishing.com
Web site: http://www.mimaxion.com/.

Mimi Bee Pubns., *(978-0-9745944)* Orders Addr.: P.O. Box 188, Accord, NY 12404 USA
E-mail: mimibee@att.com
Web site: http://mrallergyhead.com.

Minardi Photography, *(978-1-878444)* 5501 Harvest Scene Ct., Columbia, MD 21044 USA Tel 410-964-5403; Fax: 410-964-5643.

Minch, John Publishing, *(978-0-9631090; 978-0-9990251)* 27441 Betanzos, Mission Viejo, CA 92692 USA Tel 714-501-4162
E-mail: jmainc@earthlink.net.

Mind - Stretch, *(978-0-9676409)* 3124 Landrum Rd., Columbus, NC 28722 USA Tel 828-863-4235; Fax: 828-863-2584; Toll Free: 888-538-8911
E-mail: marklevin@alltel.net
Web site: http://www.mindstretch.com.

Mind Candy, LLC, *(978-0-9786929)* P.O. Box 2185, Garden City, NY 11531-2185 USA (SAN 851-3392) Tel 516-318-4433
Web site: http://mindcandymedia.com.

Mind Trip Press *See* **Big Ransom Studio**

Mindanao Publishing Co., *(978-0-9710841)* 1222 Hazel St., N., Saint. Paul, MN 55119-4500 USA Tel 651-274-6602; Fax: 651-771-9772
E-mail: jararick@worldnet.att.net
Web site: http://www.sanpedrocollege.org;
http://www.eslseminarschina.org;
http://www.eslseminars.org; http://www.ielts4nurses.org.

Mind/Body Workshops, *(978-0-9748548)* 131 S. Euclid, Westfield, NJ 07090 USA Tel 718-273-3682
Web site: http://www.kickoutstress.com.

Mindcastle Bks., Inc., *(978-0-9677204)* Orders Addr.: P.O. Box 3005, Woodinville, WA 98072 USA Tel 425-424-8860; Fax: 425-398-1354
E-mail: vanessa@mindcastle.com
Web site: http://www.mindcastle.com.

MindCatcher Pr., *(978-0-9724113)* 284 Mattison Dr., Concord, MA 01742 USA Tel 978-369-7868
E-mail: marian@mindcatcherpress.com
Web site: http://www.mindcatcherpress.com;
http://www.readylady.com.

Mindfull Publishing, *(978-0-9669551)* 177 W. Norwalk Rd., Norwalk, CT 06850 USA Tel 203-831-0855
E-mail: mindfullpub@hotmail.com
Web site: http://www.homestead.com/mindfullpublishing/.

Mindfull Publishing Co., *(978-0-9720308)* Orders Addr.: P.O. Box 34, Clairton, PA 15025 USA Toll Free: 888-946-0816; Edit Addr.: 329 Mitchell Ave., Clairton, PA 15025 USA
E-mail: gbberryauthor@yahoo.com.

MindMaze Publishing Co., *(978-0-9747668)* P.O. Box 251278, Woodbury, MN 55125 USA
E-mail: mindmaze@comcast.net.

Mindo Pr., *(978-0-9747971)* P.O. Box 34, Danielsville, PA 18038-9754 USA
E-mail: rshade@fast.net.

MindOH! Foundation, The, *(978-0-9773689)* 2525 Robinhood St., Houston, TX 77005 USA (SAN 257-3741) Tel 713-533-1138 Toll Free: 866-646-3641
Web site: http://www.mindohfoundation.org.

Mindsong Math, *(978-0-9758592)* 7757 N. Basin Way, Boise, ID 83714 USA Tel 208-371-7668
E-mail: karlalaland@gmail.com
Web site: http://www.thewhaleslibrary.com.

MindsOrb, Inc., *(978-0-9741877)* P.O. Box 162706, Austin, TX 78716 USA
Web site: http://www.mindsorb.com.

Mindstir Media, *(978-0-9819648; 978-0-9836771; 978-0-9853650; 978-0-9858398; 978-0-9883162; 978-0-9885180; 978-0-9886409; 978-0-9889595; 978-0-9890288; 978-0-9892711; 978-0-9894748; 978-0-9897168; 978-0-9898820; 978-0-9910324; 978-0-9911512; 978-0-9913190; 978-0-9914884; 978-0-9916230; 978-0-9903626; 978-0-9906106; 978-0-9908137; 978-0-9862149; 978-0-9863057; 978-0-9961434; 978-0-9962872; 978-0-9964615; 978-0-9967294; 978-0-9969689; 978-0-9970334; 978-0-9972233; 978-0-9973575; 978-0-9975435; 978-0-9977466;) 1931 Woodbury Ave. No. 182, Portsmouth, NH 03801 USA*
Dist(s): **Smashwords.**

MindWare Holdings, Inc., *(978-0-9648481; 978-1-892069; 978-1-933054; 978-1-936300)* 2100 County Rd. C W., Roseville, MN 55113 USA (SAN 859-9157) Fax: 651-582-0556; Toll Free: 800-999-0398
Web site: http://mindware.com.

Mindwing Concepts, Inc., *(978-0-9761393; 978-0-9769527; 978-0-9791307; 978-0-9792917; 978-0-9793185; 978-0-9816818)* 1 Federal St. Bldg. 103-1, Springfield, MA 01105 USA Toll Free: 888-228-9746
Web site: http://www.mindwingconcepts.com.

MindWorks Pr., *(978-1-886554)* 4019 Westerly Pl., Suite 108, Newport Beach, CA 92660 USA (SAN 850-4873) Tel 949.266.3714; Fax: 949.266.3770; Toll Free: 800-626-2720
E-mail: mindworkspress@aol.com;
sposs@amenclinic.com
Web site: http://www.mindworkspress.com
Dist(s): **Lulu Pr., Inc.**

Minecraft Interactive *See* **Interactive Stories**

Minerva Bks., *(978-0-9620125)* Div. of Hulbert Performance Rating, Inc., 316 Commerce St., Alexandria, VA 22314 USA (SAN 247-493X) Tel 703-683-5905 Do not confuse with companies with the same or similar name in Palo Alto, CA, New York, NY, Louisville, KY.

Minerva Bks., Ltd., *(978-0-8056)* 30 W. 26th St., New York, NY 10010 USA (SAN 205-8367) Tel 212-675-0465; Fax: 212-675-0573 Do not confuse with companies with the same or similar name in Alexandria, VA, Palo Alto, CA, Louisville, KY
Dist(s): **Continental Bk. Co., Inc.**
Lectorum Pubns., Inc.

Mini Enterprises - M.E. *See* **AGB Publishing**

Minikin Pr., *(978-0-9772320)* P.O. Box 528, Barrington, RI 02806-0280 USA (SAN 257-0076) Tel 401-245-7960
E-mail: jill@minikinpress.com
Web site: http://www.minikinpress.com
Dist(s): **Independent Pubs. Group.**

Minimal Pr., The, *(978-0-9742516; 978-0-615-25627-6; 978-0-615-25629-0; 978-0-9824665)* 406 Colchester Ave., Burlington, VT 05401 USA
Dist(s): **Lulu Pr., Inc.**

Minna Pr., *(978-0-9829680)* 8015 Stoneham Ct., Matthews, NC 28105 USA Tel 704-817-0343
E-mail: lj1838@gmail.com
Dist(s): **BookBaby.**

Minnesota Assn. for Children's Mental Health, *(978-0-9820482)* 165 Western Ave., N., Suite 2, Saint Paul, MN 55102 USA Tel 651-644-7333; Fax: 651-644-7391; Toll Free: 800-528-4511
E-mail: info@macmh.org
Web site: http://www.macmh.org.

Minnesota Department of Economic Security *See* **Minnesota Dept. Employment & Economic Development**

Minnesota Dept. Employment & Economic Development, *(978-0-9670505; 978-0-9845780; 978-0-615-50484-1)* 332 Minnesota St. Ste. E200, Saint Paul, MN 55101-1349 USA Toll Free: 888-234-1114
E-mail: Amy.yerkes@state.mn.us
Web site: http://www.positivelyminnesota.com.

†Minnesota Historical Society Pr., *(978-0-87351; 978-1-68134)* Orders Addr.: 11030 S. Langley Ave., Chicago, IL 60628 USA Toll Free Fax: 800-621-8476; Toll Free: 800-621-2736; Edit Addr.: 345 Kellogg Blvd., W., Saint Paul, MN 55102-1906 USA (SAN 202-6384) Tel 651-297-2221; 651-259-3202; Fax: 651-297-1345; Toll Free: 800-647-7827; *Imprints:* Borealis Book (Borealis Book)
E-mail: greg.britton@mnhs.org
Web site: http://www.mnhs.org/mhspress; mnhspress.org
Dist(s): **BookMobile**
Chicago Distribution Ctr.
Ingram Publisher Services; *CIP.*

Minnesota Humanities Ctr., *(978-0-9629298; 978-1-931016; 978-0-578-03464-5; 978-0-9884539)* 987 E. Ivy Ave., Saint Paul, MN 55106-2046 USA Tel 651-774-0105 Toll Free: 866-268-7293
E-mail: info@minnesotahumanities.org
Web site: http://www.minnesotahumanities.org.

Minnesota Humanities Commission *See* **Minnesota Humanities Ctr.**

Minnesota's Bookstore, *(978-0-9647451; 978-0-9754338)* 660 Olive St., Saint Paul, MN 55155 USA Tel 651-297-3000; Fax: 651-215-5733; Toll Free: 800-657-3757
E-mail: mnbookstore@state.mn.us
Web site: http://www.minnesotasbookstore.com
Dist(s): **Univ. of Texas Pr.**

Minnewaska Pr., *(978-0-9799410)* 24535 165th St., Glenwood, MN 56334 USA
E-mail: minnewaskapress@yahoo.com
Web site: http://www.debmercier.com.

Minnie Troy Pubs., *(978-0-9727480)* Div. of Historically Speaking, 309 Union St., Murfreesboro, NC 27855 USA Tel 252-398-5098; Fax: 252-398-5098 ext 51
E-mail: lion5098@aol.com.

Minon, S.A. (ESP) *(978-84-355) Dist. by* **Lectorum Pubns.**

Minotaur Bks. *Imprint of* **St. Martin's Pr.**

Minotauro Ediciones (ESP) *(978-84-450) Dist. by* **Lectorum Pubns.**

Minotauro Ediciones (ESP) *(978-84-450) Dist. by* **Distribks Inc.**

Minotauro Ediciones (ESP) *(978-84-450) Dist. by* **Planeta.**

Minted Prose, LLC, *(978-0-9744287; 978-0-9905721; 978-0-9965454)* 176 Broadway, Suite 11A, New York, NY 10038 USA (SAN 255-6138) Tel 646-789-7368; Fax: 347-493-3545
E-mail: linda@mintedprose.com
Web site: http://www.mintedprose.com;
http://www.traitordachshund.com
Dist(s): **CreateSpace Independent Publishing Platform**
Independent Pubs. Group
MyiLibrary.

Minton, Art, *(978-0-615-15948-5)* Orders Addr.: P.O. Box 16294, Jackson, MS 39236-6294 USA Tel 601-966-6699; Fax: 206-202-3329; Edit Addr.: 1939 Cherokee Dr., jackson, MS 39211 USA
E-mail: rentjackson@gmail.com
Web site: http://birdingforchildren.com.

Minuteman Press of Green Bay *See* **EPS Digital**

Minx *Imprint of* **DC Comics**

Mira Pr., The, *(978-0-9762947)* P.O. Box 590207, Newton Centre, MA 02459 USA.

Miracle Pr., *(978-0-929889)* 2808 W. Lexington Way, Edmond, OK 73003-4224 USA (SAN 250-975X) Tel 405-359-0369; Fax: 703-883-1861
E-mail: miraclepress@cox.net.

Miraculous Fingerprints Pubs., *(978-1-886134)* 74565 Dillon Rd., MH 15, Desert Hot Springs, CA 92241 USA Tel 760-251-3037.

Miramax Bks., *(978-0-7868; 978-1-4013; 978-1-4464)* Div. of Walt Disney Productions, 11 Beach St., 5th Flr., New York, NY 10013 USA Fax: 212-625-5075
Web site: http://www.miramax.com
Dist(s): **Disney Publishing Worldwide**
Hachette Bk. Group
Hyperion Pr.

MiraQuest, *(978-0-9748329; 978-0-615-26973-3; 978-0-9819958)* Orders Addr.: P.O. Box 29722, Los Angeles, CA 90029-0722 USA
Web site: http://www.islandlili.com
Dist(s): **Lightning Source, Inc.**

Mirhady, Farhad, *(978-0-9760323)* 2055 Beverly Beach Dr NW, Olympia, WA 98502-3427 USA
E-mail: fmirhady@comcast.net
Web site: http://www.poeticliterature.com.

MIROGLYPHICS, *(978-0-9773064; 978-0-9801073)* Orders Addr.: 5734 N. 4th St., Philadelphia, PA 19120 USA (SAN 257-2451) Tel 215-224-2486; *Imprints:* Romoulous (Romoulous)
E-mail: germic2008@gmail.com; mnik1972@aol.com
Web site: http://www.miroglyphics.biz
Dist(s): **Lightning Source, Inc.**

Mirror Pond Publishing, *(978-0-9777683)* 63090 Casey Pl., Bend, OR 97701 USA Tel 541-385-6927
E-mail: speedyread@hotmail.com.

Mirror Publishing, *(978-0-9796519; 978-0-9800675; 978-0-9815904; 978-0-9817521; 978-0-9821171; 978-0-9822560; 978-1-936046; 978-1-936352; 978-1-61225)* 6434 W. Dixon St., Milwaukee, WI 53214-1750 USA Tel 414-763-1034
E-mail: info@pagesofwonder.com
Web site: http://www.pagesofwonder.com
Dist(s): **Lightning Source, Inc.**

Mirrorstone *Imprint of* **Wizards of the Coast**

MirthMarks Publishing, *(978-0-9789591)* 675 Deis Dr., STE 123, Fairfield, OH 45014 USA
E-mail: flymaster@coppershoo.com.

Misfit Mous *See* **Misfit Mouse**

Misfit Mouse, *(978-0-578-11067-7; 978-0-578-12084-3; 978-0-578-15002-4; 978-0-692-42251-9; 978-0-692-48383-1; 978-0-9972406)* 3382 Habersham Rd. NW, Atlanta, GA 30305 USA
Web site: www.misfitmouse.com.

Missing Lid Bk.Hse., *(978-0-9838068)* 13526 Omega Cir., Littleton, CO 80124 USA Tel 303-799-8982
E-mail: tjterbush@yahoo.com.

Missing Piece Pr., *(978-0-9703729; 978-0-9977959)* 37042 S. Hollygreen Dr., Tucson, AZ 857398 USA Tel 520-338-2582
E-mail: Questions@MissingPiecePress.com
Web site: http://www.missingpiecepress.com
Dist(s): **Reveal Entertainment, Inc.**

Mission City Pr., Inc., *(978-1-928749; 978-1-934306)* 8122 Datapoint Dr. Ste. 1000, San Antonio, TX 78229-3273 USA Toll Free: 800-840-2641
E-mail: busaffair@missioncitypress.com
Web site: http://www.alifeoffaith.com
Dist(s): **Zondervan.**

Mission Creek Studios, *(978-0-929702)* 1040 Mission Canyon Rd., Santa Barbara, CA 93105-2122 USA (SAN 249-9630) Tel 805-682-6724; Fax: 805-682-6761
E-mail: dave@missioncreek.com
Web site: http://www.missioncreek.com.

Publisher Name Index

Mission Manuscripts, Inc., *(978-0-9768880)* 1000 Jorie Blvd., Suite 206, Oak Brook, IL 60523 USA Tel 630-990-0220; Fax: 630-990-2556
E-mail: kathy.hill@arends-inc.com.

Mission Mill Museum, *(978-0-9753484)* 1313 Mill St., SE, Salem, OR 97301 USA Tel 503-585-7012; Fax: 503-588-9902
E-mail: info@missionmill.org
Web site: http://www.missionmill.org.

Mision Ridge Pr., *(978-0-9763956)* 4660 Eastus Dr., San Jose, CA 95129 USA.

†Mississippi Museum of Art, *(978-1-887422)* 380 S. Lamar St., Jackson, MS 39201-4007 USA (SAN 279-6198)
E-mail: rpb@netdoor.com
Web site: http://www.msmuseumart.org
Dist(s): **Pennsylvania State Univ. Pr.**
Univ. Pr. of Mississippi
Univ. of Washington Pr.; *CIP.*

Missouri Historical Society Pr., *(978-1-883982)* Orders Addr.: P.O. Box 11940, Saint Louis, MO 63112-0040 USA Fax: 314-746-4548
E-mail: jstevens@mohistory.org
Web site: http://www.mohistory.org
Dist(s): **Chicago Distribution Ctr.**
SPD-Small Pr. Distribution
Univ. of Missouri Pr.
Univ. of New Mexico Pr.
Wayne State Univ. Pr.

Mister C Music, *(978-0-9755333)* P.O. Box 28, Rochester, PA 15074 USA Toll Free: 877-687-4258
E-mail: misterc437@aol.com
Web site: http://www.mistercmusic.com.

†MIT Pr., *(978-0-262; 978-0-89706)* Orders Addr.: c/o Triliteral LLC, 100 Maple Ridge Dr., Cumberland, RI 02864 USA Tel 401-531-2800; Fax: 401-531-2801; Toll Free Fax: 800-406-9145; Toll Free: 800-405-1619; Edit Addr.: One Rogers St., Cambridge, MA 02142-1209 USA (SAN 202-6414) Tel 617-253-5646; Fax: 617-253-6779
E-mail: orders@triliteral.org
Web site: http://mitpress.mit.edu
Dist(s): **Ebsco Publishing**
MyiLibrary
Wiley, John & Sons, Inc.
ebrary, Inc.; *CIP.*

Mitchell, Carol *See* **CaribbeanReads**

Mitchell, Damien Pardow, *(978-0-615-18469-2)* 13834 Doolittle Dr., San Leandro, CA 94577 USA
Web site: http://jarvisprinting.com
Dist(s): **Publishers Services.**

Mitchell, Karan, *(978-0-9763793)* 79 Baruch Dr., Apt.5E, New York, NY 10002-3659 USA Tel 212-982-7977
E-mail: mtchlkrn@aol.com.

Mitchell Lane Pubs., Inc., *(978-1-883845; 978-1-58415; 978-1-61228; 978-1-68020)* 2001 SW 31st Ave, Hallandale, FL 33009 USA (SAN 858-3749) Tel 954-985-9400; Fax: 954-987-2200; Toll Free: 800-814-5484
E-mail: Phil@mitchellane.com
Web site: http://www.mitchellane.com.

Mitchell, P. S., *(978-0-615-80354-8)* 3682 King St. Unit 16831, Alexandria, VA 22302 USA Tel 571-214-4805
E-mail: psmitchellbook@gmail.com.

Mitchell Publishing, Incorporated *See* **Teaching & Learning Co.**

Mitchell Publishing, Inc., *(978-0-938188)* 160 Spear St. Ste. 700, San Francisco, CA 94105-1562 USA (SAN 215-7896) Toll Free: 800-435-2665 Do not confuse with companies with the same or similar names in Spokane, WA, Medina, NY, Medicine Lodge, KS.

Mitre's Touch Gallery, The, *(978-0-9764384)* 1414 Adams Ave., La Grande, OR 97850 USA Tel 541-963-3477
E-mail: weframe@eoni.com.

Mitten Pr. *Imprint of* **Ann Arbor Editions LLC**

Mixta Publishing Co., *(978-0-9675951)* 3179 San Francisco Ave., Long Beach, CA 90806 USA Tel 562-427-4270
E-mail: michael.archuleta@gte.net; michael@mixtapublishing.com
Web site: http://www.mixtapublishing.com; http://www.mixtapublishing.net
Dist(s): **Leonard, Hal Corp.**

Mizzou Media - University BookStores *See* **Mizzou Publishing - The Mizzou Store**

Mizzou Publishing - The Mizzou Store, *(978-1-61600)* Div. of University of Missouri, Mu Student Ctr. 911 E. Rollins St., Columbia, MO 65211 USA Tel 573-882-8567; Fax: 573-884-8050
E-mail: mizzoupublishing@missouri.edu
Web site: http://www.themizzoustore.com/t-Espresso-About.aspx.

MJ Brooks Co., *(978-0-9787864)* 767 N. Pine St., Colville, WA 99114 USA Tel 808-347-1311
E-mail: amakihi@startmail.com.

MJA Creative, LLC, *(978-0-9910894)* P.O. Box 3997, Covington, LA 70434 USA Tel 985-875-9413
E-mail: mike@mikeartell.com
Web site: www.mikeartell.com.

MJS Music & Entertainment, LLC, *(978-0-9762917; 978-0-9817451)* 9699 W. Fort Island Trail, Crystal River, FL 34429 USA Tel 352-257-3261; Fax: 352-795-1658 Do not confuse with comapnies with the same or similar name in Boyertown, PA, Searsport, ME
E-mail: msternal@mjspublications.com; wriverroad@aol.com
Web site: http://www.mjspublications.com
Dist(s): **Dumont, Charles Son, Inc.**
Omnibus Pr.
TNT Media Group, Inc.

MJS Music Publications *See* **MJS Music & Entertainment, LLC**

MJS Publishing Group LLC, *(978-0-9764336)* P.O. Box 6582, Evanston, IL 60204-6582 USA Tel 847-869-5901; Fax: 847-745-0219
E-mail: mjspg@ameritech.net
Web site: http://www.mjspub.com
Dist(s): **Bookmasters Distribution.**

MK Publishing, *(978-0-9720484; 978-0-9747147; 978-0-9760534; 978-0-9763271; 978-0-9770933; 978-0-9785081)* 25123 22nd Ave. S., Saint Cloud, MN 56301 USA; P.O. Box 945, St Cloud, MN 56302 (SAN 256-4092) Tel 320-252-1023; Fax: 320-252-4574
Web site: http://www.yourbookpublisher.net
Dist(s): **Closet Case Bks.**
J & N Creations, LLC
JMS Distribution
Main Trail Productions
Ozark Bk. Distributors
Perfume River Pubns.
Puzzle Piece Pubns.

MKADesigns, *(978-0-9745839)* 131 Frankie Ln., Madison, AL 35757-6922 USA Tel 256-721-0200; *Imprints:* Fun to Read Books with Royally Good Morals (Fun to Read Bk)
E-mail: mike.dozier@mkadesigns.com
Web site: http://www.mkadesigns.com.

ML Publishing, *(978-0-9786347)* Div. of MIHP, 31500 Dequindre Rd., Warren, MI 48092-1057 USA Tel 586-268-6942
E-mail: smclaughlin@mihp.net
Web site: http://mlpublishing.com.

MLM Ranch Publishing, *(978-0-9743098)* P.O. Box 910251, St. George, UT 84791 USA.

MLR Pr., LLC, *(978-0-9793110; 978-1-934531; 978-0-615-13459-8; 978-1-60820; 978-1-944770; 978-1-64122)* 3052 Gaines Waterport Rd., Albion, NY 14411 USA (SAN 853-1013) Tel 585-589-7831
E-mail: mlrpress@gmail.com
Web site: http://www.mlrpress.com
Dist(s): **Lulu Pr., Inc.**

MMB Enterprises, LLC, *(978-0-9747443; 978-0-615-57676-3)* Orders Addr.: P.O. Box 5887, Santa Barbara, CA 93150 USA
E-mail: pabujack@me.com
Web site: http://www.michellemadridbranch.com.

MMG Technology Corp., *(978-0-9754886)* 379 Amherst St., Suite 204, Nashua, NH 03063 USA
Web site: http://www.the-common.com.

MMJ Foundation, *(978-0-9827972)* 4350 Von Karman, 4th Flr., Newport Beach, CA 92660 USA Tel 949-244-5544
E-mail: mjanavs@hotmail.com.

M-m-mauleg Publishing, *(978-0-9790111)* Orders Addr.: P.O. Box 5258, Mangilao, GU 96923 USA; Edit Addr.: 303 University Dr., Mangila, GU 96923-5258 USA
E-mail: millhoff@uog.edu.

MMP *See* **Millennium Marketing & Publishing**

MNMC, *(978-0-9728518; 978-0-9763532)* 17 Old Shelter Rock Rd., Danbury, CT 06810 USA Tel 203-798-6936; Toll Free: 866-210-0004
E-mail: order@muslimplanet.com
Web site: http://www.muslimpublisher.com.

Mo Peanuts Publishing, *(978-0-9971513)* 1019 Ft. Salonga Rd., Northport, NY 11768 USA Tel 631-682-1768
E-mail: trelfp@gmail.com
Web site: www.TheAlienClub.com.

Mobius Communications, Ltd., *(978-1-891304; 978-1-928583)* Div. of Publication Services, Inc., 1802 S. Duncan Rd., Champaign, IL 61822-5222 USA Fax: 217-398-3923; Toll Free: 800-662-4875
Web site: http://www.8-mobius.com.

Mocha Enterprises, *(978-0-9707163)* 6322 Chesapeake Cir., Stockton, CA 95219 USA (SAN 253-620X) Tel 209-478-0635 (phone/fax); 209-946-3064
E-mail: mochaenterprises@aol.com
Web site: http://www.welcometotheprofessionalwork.com.

Mockingbird Cottage Pr., *(978-0-692-68327-9; 978-0-9983519)* 1014 Richland Ct, Ashland City, TN Bell USA Tel 615-473-2757
Dist(s): **CreateSpace Independent Publishing Platform.**

Mockingbird Lane Pr., *(978-0-9856906; 978-0-9889542; 978-0-9893105)* 2441 Washington Rd., Maynard, AR 72444 USA Tel 870-647-2137
E-mail: mockingbirdlanepress@gmail.com.

Mockingbird Publishing, *(978-0-9828528)* Orders Addr.: P.O. Box 442, Fairhope, AL 36533 USA Tel 334-546-0710
E-mail: ashley@mockingbirdpublishing.com
Web site: http://www.mockingbirdpublishing.com.

Modern Curriculum Pr. *Imprint of* **Pearson Schl.**

†Modern Curriculum Pr., *(978-0-7652; 978-0-8136; 978-0-87895)* Div. of Pearson Education, Orders Addr.: P.O. Box 2500, Lebanon, IN 46052-3009 USA (SAN 206-6572) Toll Free: 800-526-9907 (Customer Service)
Web site: http://www.pearsonlearning.com
Dist(s): **Follett School Solutions**
Lectorum Pubns., Inc.
Pearson Learning; *CIP.*

Modern Evil Pr., *(978-1-934516)* 913 S 2nd Ave, Phoenix, AZ 85003-2511 USA Tel 602-999-6449
E-mail: teel@modernevil.com
Web site: http://modernevil.com/
Dist(s): **Smashwords.**

Modern Learning Pr., *(978-0-935493; 978-1-56762)* P.O. Box 167, Rosemont, NJ 08556 USA Tel 609-397-2214; Fax: 845-277-3548; Toll Free Fax: 888-558-7350; Toll Free: 800-627-5867
E-mail: Rlow@tasa.com.

Modern Library *Imprint of* **Random House Publishing Group**

Modern Living Media *See* **Pirouz, Raymond**

Modern Publishing, *(978-0-7666; 978-0-87449; 978-1-56144)* Div. of Unisystems, Inc., 155 E. 55th St., New York, NY 10022 USA (SAN 253-2921) Tel 212-826-0850; Fax: 212-759-9096
E-mail: info@modernpublishing.com
Web site: http://www.modernpublishing.com.

MoGho Bks., LLC, *(978-0-9712559; 978-0-615-11888-8)* Box 200, 9801 Hartley Rd., Hallsville, MO 65255 USA Tel 573-696-3537 (phone/fax)
E-mail: moghobks@tranquility.net
Dist(s): **Cowley Distributing, Inc.**
Univ. of Missouri Pr.

Mogul Comics, *(978-0-9657723)* 102 6th Ave. 2nd Flr., WaterVliet, NY 12189 USA.

Mohsena Memorial Foundation, Inc., *(978-0-9617273)* P.O. Box 2309, Princeton, NJ 08543 USA (SAN 663-5075) Tel 609-799-6545; Fax: 609-799-7311.

Mohsena Memorial Trust *See* **Mohsena Memorial Foundation, Inc.**

MoJo InkWorks, *(978-0-9820381)* 16 Foxglove Row, Riverhead, NY 11901 USA Tel 516-695-6690
E-mail: maureensullivan@gmail.com
Web site: http://www.maureensullivancommunications.com.

Molino, Editorial (ESP) *(978-84-272) Dist. by* **Continental Bk.**

Molino, Editorial (ESP) *(978-84-272) Dist. by* **Lectorum Pubns.**

Molino, Editorial (ESP) *(978-84-272) Dist. by* **Santillana.**

Molino, Editorial (ESP) *(978-84-272) Dist. by* **AIMS Intl.**

Molino, Editorial (ESP) *(978-84-272) Dist. by* **Distribks Inc.**

Molino RBA,
Dist(s): **Lectorum Pubns., Inc.**

Molly Brave, *(978-1-61245)* 3682 Quiet Pond Ln., Sarasota, FL 34235 USA Tel 941-955-0091
E-mail: mollybrave@gmail.com
Web site: http://www.mollybrave.com.

Momentpoint Media, *(978-0-9710448)* 2385 Friesian Rd., York, PA 17406 USA Tel 717-848-4528 (phone/fax) Do not confuse with Moment Point Press Inc. of NH/ME.
E-mail: momentpoint@suscom.net
Web site: http://www.momentpointmedia.com.

Momentum Books, Limited *See* **Momentum Bks., LLC**

Momentum Bks., LLC, *(978-0-9618726; 978-1-879094; 978-1-938018)* Div. of Hour Media, LLC, 117 W. Third St., Royal Oak, MI 48067 USA (SAN 668-7067) Tel 248-691-1800; Fax: 248-691-4531
E-mail: info@momentumbooks.com
Web site: http://www.momentumbooks.com
Dist(s): **Partners Bk. Distributing, Inc.**
TNT Media Group, Inc.

Mometrix Media LLC, *(978-1-60971; 978-1-61072; 978-1-61073; 978-1-61402; 978-1-61403; 978-1-62120; 978-1-62733; 978-1-63094; 978-1-5167)* 3827 Phelan No. 179, Beaumont, TX 77707 USA (SAN 860-0430) Tel 800-673-8175.

MomGeek.com *Imprint of* **Wood Designs, Inc.**

Mommy Has Tattoos, *(978-0-9770232)* P.O. Box 231059, New York, NY 10023-0023 USA
E-mail: info@mommyhastattoos.com
Web site: http://www.mommyhastattoos.com.

Mommy Workshop Bks., *(978-0-9817565)* P.O. Box 265, Doylestown, PA 18901 USA (SAN 856-4655) Tel 215-489-8649; Fax: 480-393-5692
E-mail: kristie@mommyworkshop.com
Web site: http://www.mommyworkshop.com/.

Momosa Publishing LLC, *(978-0-9844804; 978-0-9970808; 978-0-9986531; 978-0-9994151)* Orders Addr.: 765 Front St., Hellertown, PA 18055 USA (SAN 859-5224)
E-mail: mommymdguides@yahoo.com
Dist(s): **National Bk. Network.**

Momotombo Pr., *(978-0-9710465; 978-0-9797446)* Institute for Latino/University of Notre Dame, Notre Dame, IN 46556 USA; Inst. for Latino Studies Univ. of Notre Dame 230 McKenna Hall, Notre Dame, IN 46556
E-mail: faragon@nd.edu
Web site: http://www.momotombopress.com
Dist(s): **SPD-Small Pr. Distribution.**

Mom's Pride Enterprises, *(978-0-9720549)* 16521 N. 69th Dr., Peoria, AZ 85382 USA Tel 623-487-7589; Fax: 623-487-1504
E-mail: mrsb4kids@yahoo.com
Web site: http://www.mrsbstorytime.com.

Monacelli Pr., Inc., *(978-1-58093; 978-1-885254)* 1745 Broadway., New York, NY 10019-4305 USA Tel 212-782-9000
E-mail: info@monaddcellipress.com
Web site: http://www.monacellipress.com
Dist(s): **MyiLibrary**
Penguin Random Hse. LLC
Penguin Publishing Group
Random Hse., Inc.

Monarch Baby Publishing, *(978-0-9749499)* Orders Addr.: P.O. Box 22, Salem, VA 24153 USA Tel 504-669-1044
E-mail: monarchbaby@blackbutterflyrecords.com
Web site: http://blackbutterflyrecords.com\monarch_baby_publishing.thml.

Monarch Pubs., *(978-0-9774038; 978-0-615-12659-3)* Orders Addr.: 305 Holly Tree Ln., Simpsonville, SC 29681 USA
E-mail: joconnor@uscupstate.edu
Web site: http://www.monarchpublishers.com
Dist(s): **Follett School Solutions**
Parnassus Bk. Distributors
Bryan, R. L.

Monarch Publishing Hse., *(978-0-9797861)* 2573 Lake Cir., Jackson, MS 39211-6630 USA (SAN 859-4627) Tel 601-982-1233.

Monarchs in the Classroom, *(978-0-9800653)* 1980 Folwell Ave., 200 Hodson Hall, Saint Paul, MN 55108 USA Tel 612-624-8706; Fax: 612-625-5299
E-mail: oberh001@umn.edu
Web site: http://www.monarchlab.org.

Mondadori (ITA) *(978-88-04; 978-88-356; 978-88-86372; 978-88-520; 978-88-521) Dist. by* **Distribks Inc.**

Mondial, *(978-1-59569)* 203 W 107th St., No. 6C, New York, NY 10025 USA
E-mail: contact@mondialbooks.com
Web site: http://www.mondialbooks.com
Dist(s): **Smashwords.**

Mondo Fax Publishing, *(978-0-9710095)* 26235 Ravenhill Rd., Suite M, Santa Clarita, CA 91350-4754 USA Tel 661-250-0990; Fax: 661-251-4452
E-mail: argapc@socal.rr.com
Web site: http://mondofax.com.

Mondo Publishing, *(978-1-57255; 978-1-879531; 978-1-58653; 978-1-59034; 978-1-59336; 978-1-60201; 978-1-60715; 978-1-61736; 978-1-62889; 978-1-63060; 978-1-63061; 978-1-68156; 978-1-64064)* Div. of Music Plus, Inc., 980 6th Ave., New York, NY 10018 USA Toll Free: 888-268-3560
E-mail: ckracuna@mondopub.com
Web site: http://www.mondopub.com.

Money Management Books *See* **Prism Hse. Media**

Mongoose Pr., *(978-0-9791482; 978-1-936277)* 1005 Boylston St., Suite 324, Newton Highlands, MA 02461 USA Tel 617-875-6298
E-mail: info@mongoosepress.com
Web site: http://www.MongoosePress.com
Dist(s): **MyiLibrary**
National Bk. Network
ebrary, Inc.

Mongoose Publishing (GBR) *(978-1-903980; 978-1-904577; 978-1-904854; 978-1-905176; 978-1-905476; 978-1-905471; 978-1-905850; 978-1-906103; 978-1-906508; 978-1-907218) Dist. by* **Diamond Book Dists.**

Monique Patrice Hall *See* **Hall, Monique P. Productions**

Monkey Barrel Pr., *(978-0-9802000)* 4738 Andrea Way, Union City, CA 94587 USA
Web site: http://www.monkeybarrelpress.com.

Monkey Business *See* **Monkeying Around**

MonkeyBear Publishing *Imprint of* **LORE Mountain Productions**

MonkeyGod Enterprises, *(978-0-9708094; 978-0-9717729; 978-0-9728197)* Div. of Face 2 Face Games Publishing, 36 The Arcade, 65 Weybosset St., Providence, RI 02903 USA Tel 401-351-0362 (phone/fax)
E-mail: fmf@pipeline.com
Web site: http://www.monkeygodenterprses.com.

Monkeying Around, *(978-0-9700437; 978-0-9799753; 978-0-9975907)* P.O. Box 10131, Rochester, NY 14610 USA Tel 585-256-2660; Fax: 585-442-2965
E-mail: info@monkeyingaround.com
Web site: http://www.monkeyingaround.com.

Monkeyshines Publishers *See* **Allosaurus Pubs.**

Monkeytoes Pr., *(978-0-615-12555-8)* 125 Sycamore Rd., Braintree, MA 02184-7318 USA
E-mail: jvgandkdlarson@comcast.net
Web site: http://www.monkeytoespress.com.

Monkfish Bk. Publishing Co., *(978-0-9726357; 978-0-9749359; 978-0-9766843; 978-0-9789427; 978-0-9798828; 978-0-9823246; 978-0-9824530; 978-0-9825255; 978-0-9826441; 978-0-9830517; 978-0-9833589; 978-1-936940; 978-1-939681; 978-1-944037)* Orders Addr.: 22 E. Market St. Suite 304, Rhinebeck, NY 12572 USA; *Imprints:* Epigraph Books (Epigraph Bks)
E-mail: paul@monkfishpublishing.com
Web site: http://www.monkfishpublishing.com; http://www.epigraphps.com
Dist(s): **Consortium Bk. Sales & Distribution**
Lightning Source, Inc.
MyiLibrary
SPD-Small Pr. Distribution.

Monnin, Philip, *(978-0-9969639; 978-0-9982907)* 5220 Creekmonte Dr, Oakland Township, MI 48306 USA Tel 248-701-1995
E-mail: pmonnin@yahoo.com.

Monogram Booklets *See* **Miller, Debra Juanita**

Monolith Graphics, *(978-0-9675756; 978-0-9788857; 978-0-9824899)* Orders Addr.: P.O. Box 360801, Strongsville, OH 44136 USA
E-mail: goth@monolithgraphics.com; nox@noxarcana.com
Web site: http://www.monolithgraphics.com; http://www.noxarcana.com.

Monroe Educational Media, *(978-0-9721146)* 2965 Taylor Rd., Reynoldsburg, OH 43068 USA Tel 614-866-4289; Fax: 740-927-9131
E-mail: jon@gooddebt.com
Web site: http://www.monroemedia.com.

Monroe, Guy, *(978-0-9742443)* P.O. Box 2325, Newport, OR 97365-0171 USA Toll Free: 877-562-3866
Web site: http://www.pinerystreet.com.

Monroe Media *See* **Monroe Educational Media**

Monsoon Bks. Pte. Ltd. (SGP) *(978-981-05; 978-981-4358; 978-981-4423; 978-981-4625) Dist. by* **Tuttle Pubng.**

Monsoon Bks. Pte. Ltd. (SGP) *(978-981-05; 978-981-4358; 978-981-4423; 978-981-4625) Dist. by* **Natl Bk Netwk.**

Monster Street *Imprint of* **Picture Window Bks.**

MonsterHaven, *(978-0-615-38690-4)* 385 Camino dos Palos, Thousand Oaks, CA 91360 USA Tel 805-208-8383
E-mail: marmaxdesigns@hotmail.com
Web site: http://www.monsterhaven.com.

Monsters in My Head, LLC, The, *(978-0-9792860; 978-0-9914952)* 344 Grove St. #119, Jersey City, NJ 07302 USA (SAN 853-0254) Tel 917-881-8326
E-mail: info@worrywoos.com
Web site: http://www.worrywoos.com.

Montag Pr., *(978-0-9822809; 978-1-940233)* 1066 47th Ave., Unit #9, Oakland, CA 94601 USA Tel 916-806-8341
E-mail: c.lanfranco@gmail.com
Dist(s): **SPD-Small Pr. Distribution.**

Montana Historical Society Pr., *(978-0-917298; 978-0-9721522; 978-0-9759196; 978-0-9801292; 978-1-940527)* P.O. Box 201201, Helena, MT 59620 USA (SAN 208-7693) Toll Free: 800-243-9900
E-mail: mholz@mt.gov
Web site: http://www.montanahistoricalsociety.org
Dist(s): **Globe Pequot Pr., The**
National Bk. Network
Univ. of Nebraska Pr.

Montana Publishing Group *See* **Loughton Bks.**

Montanha Pr., *(978-0-9743380)* 1547 Palos Verdes Mall, Suite 139, Walnut Creek, CA 94597 USA.

Monte Nido Pr., *(978-0-9742663)* Rm 9L19, 1240 Mission Rd., Los Angeles, CA 90033 USA Tel 323-226-3406; Fax: 323-226-3440
E-mail: hoppenbrou@earthlink.net
Web site: http://www.toke.hoppenbrouwers.net.

Montemayor Pr., (*978-0-9674477; 978-1-932727*) P.O. Box 526, Millburn, NJ 07041 USA Tel 973-761-1341
E-mail: mail@montemayorpress.com
Web site: http://www.montemayorpress.com.

†**Monterey Bay Aquarium**, (*978-1-878244*) 886 Cannery Row, Monterey, CA 93940 USA Tel 831-648-4942; 408-648-4800; 831-648-4847; Fax: 831-644-7568; Toll Free: 877-665-2665
E-mail: mmckenzie@mbayaq.org
Web site: http://www.montereybayaquarium.org; *CIP*.

Monterey Bay Sancturary Foundation, (*978-0-9742810*) 299 Foam St., Monterey, CA 93940 USA
E-mail: info@mbnmsf.org
Web site: http://www.mbnmsf.org
Dist(s): **Sunbelt Pubns., Inc.**

Montessori Advantage, (*978-0-9766453*) Orders Addr.: P.O. Box 272, Wickatunk, NJ 07765 USA Toll Free: 888-946-2114; Edit Addr.: 257 Rt. 79N, Wickatunk, NJ 07765 USA.

Montevallo Historical Pr., Inc., (*978-0-9658624*) 1727 West 17th St., Davenport, OH 52804 USA Tel 563-823-5749
E-mail: dean@mhpress.com
Web site: http://www.mhpress.com.

Montgomery County Historical Society, (*978-0-9720965*) 1000 Carillon Blvd., Dayton, OH 45409-2023 USA Do not confuse with Montgomery County Historical Society in Rockville MD, Fort Johnson NY
Web site: http://www.daytonhistory.org.

Montlake Romance *Imprint of* **Amazon Publishing**

Montville Pr., (*978-0-9706527*) P.O. Box 4304, Greensboro, NC 27410-4304 USA Tel 336-292-8268; Fax: 336-218-0410
E-mail: bas236@aol.com.

Moo Pr. *Imprint of* **Keene Publishing**

Moo Press, Incorporated *See* **Keene Publishing**

†**Moody Pubs.**, (*978-0-8024*) Div. of Moody Bible Institute, Orders Addr.: 210 W. Chestnut, Chicago, IL 60610 USA; Edit Addr.: 820 N. LaSalle, Chicago, IL 60610 USA (SAN 202-5604) Tel 312-329-2101; Fax: 312-329-2144; Toll Free: 800-678-8812; *Imprints:* Lift Every Voice (LEV)
E-mail: mpcustomerservice@moody.edu
Web site: http://www.moodypublishers.com
Dist(s): **BJU Pr.**
Follett School Solutions; *CIP*.

Moody Valley, (*978-1-59513*) 475 Church Hollow Rd., Boone, NC 28607 USA Tel 828-963-5331; Fax: 828-963-4101
E-mail: moodyvalley@skybest.com
Web site: http://www.moodyvalley.com
Dist(s): **Partners Bk. Distributing, Inc.**

Moody, William, (*978-0-9762556*) 301 Willard Hall, Univ. of Delaware, Newark, DE 19711 USA Tel 302-831-1658; Fax: 302-831-0591
E-mail: wmoody@udel.edu
Web site: http://www.udel.edu/educ/solveit.htm.

Mookind Pr., (*978-0-9792761*) 1600 S. Eads St., Suite 822N, Arlington, VA 22202 USA Tel 703-920-1884
E-mail: cnadel999@yahoo.com.

Moombaya Bks., (*978-0-9766799*) 2118 Wilshire Blvd., Suite 528, Santa Monica, CA 90403-9040 USA
E-mail: diponzagroup@aol.com.

Moon, Alice *See* **PeachMoon Publishing**

Moon Bear Pr., (*978-0-944164*) P.O. Box 468, Velarde, NM 87582 USA (SAN 242-9144) Tel 505-852-4897
E-mail: orders@moonbearpress.com
Web site: http://www.moonbearpress.com
Dist(s): **New Leaf Distributing Co., Inc.**

Moon Mountain Publishing, Inc., (*978-0-9677929; 978-1-931659*) P.O. Box 188, West Rockport, ME 04865 USA Tel 207-236-0958; Fax: 978-719-6290; Toll Free: 800-353-5877
E-mail: hello@moonmountainpub.com
Web site: http://www.moonmountainpub.com.

Moon Over Mountains Publishing (M.O.M.), (*978-1-891665*) Div. of Gallery of Diamonds Jewelers, 1528 Brookhollow Dr. Suite 200, Santa Ana, CA 92705 USA (SAN 299-5492) Tel 714-549-2000; Fax: 714-545-8000; Toll Free: 800-667-4440
E-mail: info@galleryofdiamonds.com
Web site: http://www.whymomdeservesadiamond.com.

Moon Pie Pr., (*978-0-9761744*) 53 Faye Dr., Smithfield, VA 23430 USA Tel 757-356-1690
E-mail: cathyk@visi.net
Web site: http://www.moonpiepress.net.

Moon Trail Bks., (*978-0-9773140*) 24 W. 4th St., Bethlehem, PA 18015-1604 USA (SAN 850-6922) Tel 610-866-6482
E-mail: pnmca21@aol.com.

Moon Valley Productions, (*978-0-934290*) P.O. Box 1342, Healdsburg, CA 95448 USA (SAN 221-2900) Tel 707-823-9340; 707-523-8525
E-mail: zaksartandsoul@yahoo.com
Web site: http://www.zakzaikine.com.

Moonbow Pr., LLc, (*978-0-9789092*) P.O. Box 95, Bethel, OH 45106 USA (SAN 851-9110).

Moondance *Imprint of* **Quarto Publishing Group USA**

Moondance Publishing, (*978-0-9671865; 978-1-931524*) Orders Addr.: P.O. Box 16, Upper Black Eddy, PA 18972 USA Tel 610-442-1951; Fax: 610-982-5331; Edit Addr.: 1525 Oak Ln., Upper Black Eddy, PA 18972 USA (SAN 254-5101) Tel 610-442-1951
E-mail: caravan@moondancepublishing.com
Web site: http://www.moondancepublishing.com.

Moonjar, LLC, (*978-0-9724282; 978-0-9764231*) 612 19th Ave., E., Seattle, WA 98112 USA Fax: 206-726-0769; Toll Free: 888-323-0001
E-mail: contact@moonjar.com
Web site: http://www.moonjar.com
Dist(s): **Ten Speed Pr.**

Moonlight Publishing, Ltd. (GBR) (*978-0-907144; 978-1-85103*) *Dist. by* **IPG Chicago.**

MoonRattles, (*978-0-9790920*) P.O. Box 939, Carmel, CA 93921 USA; 70 Dapplegray Rd., Bell Canyon, CA 91307 (SAN 854-2201) Fax: 818-932-9631; Toll Free: 800-961-6073
E-mail: info@moonrattles.com
Web site: http://www.moonrattles.com.

Moons & Stars Publishing For Children, (*978-1-929063*) Div. of Moon Star Unlimited, Inc., P.O. Box 1763, Pasadena, TX 77505 USA Tel 713-473-7120; Fax: 713-473-1105
E-mail: services@dorpexpress.com
Web site: http://www.dorpexpress.com.

Moonshell Bks., Inc. *Imprint of* **Shelley Adina**

Moonshine Cove Publishing LLC, (*978-1-937327; 978-1-945181*) 150 Willow Pt., Abbeville, SC 29620 USA Tel 864-446-7570
E-mail: publisher@moonshinecovepublishing.com
Web site: http://moonshinecovepublishing.com
Dist(s): **Lightning Source, Inc.**

MoonStar Pr., (*978-0-9672107*) 4360 E. Main St., Suite 408, Ventura, CA 93003 USA Tel 805-648-7753
E-mail: toutzhag@earthlink.net
Dist(s): **New Leaf Distributing Co., Inc.**

Moonstone, (*978-0-9710129; 978-0-9712937; 978-0-9721668; 978-0-9726443; 978-0-9748501; 978-1-933076; 978-1-936814; 978-1-944017*) Div. of Amazing Fantasy Comic Shop Ltd., 582 Torrence Ave., Calumet City, IL 60409 USA Fax: 708-891-0644
E-mail: afbooks_frankfort@sbcglobal.net
Web site: http://www.moonstonebooks.com
Dist(s): **Diamond Comic Distributors, Inc.**
Diamond Bk. Distributors.

Moonstone Pr., LLC, (*978-0-9707768; 978-0-9727697; 978-0-9769542; 978-0-9834983*) 4816 Carrington Cir., Sarasota, FL 34243 USA (SAN 852-5625) Tel 301-765-1081; Fax: 301-765-0510
E-mail: mazeprod@erols.com
Web site: http://www.moonstonepress.net
Dist(s): **Independent Pubs. Group**
Lectorum Pubns., Inc.
PSI (Publisher Services, Inc.).

Moonview Pr., (*978-0-9828987*) 5460 Linda Ln., Santa Rosa, CA 95404 USA Tel 707-578-2269
E-mail: ctmarkee@gmail.com
Web site: http://www.charlesmarkee.comzbandit
Dist(s): **Smashwords.**

Moonwater Products, (*978-0-9769033*) 63 Roycroft Dr., Rochester, NY 14621 USA
E-mail: djed_ra_maat@yahoo.com.

Moore, Ammanuel, (*978-0-9744060*) P.O. Box 3295, Baltimore, MD 21228 USA Tel 410-788-7271
E-mail: info@acmoorebooks.com
Web site: http://www.acmoorebooks.com.

Moore, Evans, (*978-0-9709762*) P.O. Box 30311, Washington, DC 20030 USA Tel 202-889-3648
E-mail: evansmoore@hotmail.com.

Moore, Greg Publishing, (*978-0-9639495*) Orders Addr.: 6202 Wallina Ct., SE, Salem, OR 97309 USA Tel 503-749-1393; Fax: 503-588-7707
E-mail: yoyo@tdn.com.

†**Moore, Hugh Historical Park & Museums, Inc.**, (*978-0-930973*) 30 Centre Sq., Easton, PA 18042-7743 USA (SAN 678-8831) Tel 610-559-6617; 610-559-6613; Fax: 610-559-6690; *Imprints:* Canal History & Technology Press (Canal Hist Tech)
E-mail: ncm@canals.org
Web site: http://www.canals.org; *CIP*.

Moore, Hullihen, (*978-0-9785775*) P.O. Box 116, Oldhams, VA 22529 USA (SAN 850-9468).

Moore, Lonnie W. *See* **I & L Publishing**

Moore Publishing, (*978-0-9800791*) 646 Beautiful Run Rd., Madison, VA 22727 USA.

Moose Hill Bks., Inc., (*978-0-9728627*) P.O. Box 222271, Anchorage, AK 99522 USA (SAN 255-1616)
E-mail: publisher@moosehillbooks.com
Web site: http://www.moosehillbooks.com.

Moose Run Productions, (*978-0-9766315*) 22010 Highview, Clinton Township, MI 48036 USA Tel 586-718-7700
Web site: http://www.moose-run.com.

Morals & Values Pr., (*978-0-9754191; 978-0-9842140; 978-0-9898501*) P.O. Box 23804, Baltimore, MD 21203 USA
Web site: http://www.greatnessnow.org.

Moran, Kristyna, (*978-0-692-79225-4*) 5016 Thorne Dr. #14, LA MESA, CA 91942 USA Tel 619-787-3785.

Morari Specialties Inc., (*978-0-9770618*) 13901 SW 22nd St., Miami, FL 33175-7006 USA
Web site: http://www.morarispecialties.com.

Morcan, Dorina, (*978-0-9763663*) P.O. Box 1564, Malvern, AR 72104 USA Fax: 501-262-4127
E-mail: dmorcan@ix.netcom.com.

More Books Press *See* **SCOJO ENTERTAINMENT**

More, Frances International Teaching Systems *See* **Frances More International Teaching Systems**

More, Francisco J., (*978-0-9747851*) 221 Majorca Ave., No. 207, Coral Gables, FL 33134-4429 USA Tel 305-448-5081.

More Heart Than Talent Publishing, Incorporated *See* **Golden Mastermind Seminars, Inc.**

More Pr., (*978-0-9743394*) Div. of More Consulting Co., 1634 E. 53rd St., Chicago, IL 60615-4389 USA
E-mail: shaharimoore@aol.com.

M.O.R.E. Pubs., (*978-0-9719984; 978-0-9758549; 978-0-9801647; 978-0-9820354; 978-0-9830325; 978-0-692-27449-1; 978-1-945344*) Orders Addr.: P.O. Box 621, Collierville, TN 38027-0621 USA; Edit Addr.: 4466 Elvis Presley Blvd. 1st Memphis Plaza - Suite 103, Memphis, TN 38116 USA (SAN 255-1055)
E-mail: stlouiswpguild@aol.com; MOREPublishersCO@AOL.com
Web site: http://www.MOREPublishers.biz; http://www.TheScaleMagazine.MagCloud.com.

More to Life Publishing, (*978-0-9632564; 978-0-9766971; 978-0-9825746; 978-9949-9251*) 1549 22nd St N, Arlington, VA 22209 USA; Aarekoidu tee 10 Alliku Kula, Saue vald, Harjumaa, 76403 Tel 372 50 81 944
E-mail: kimismore@gmail.com; morepublish@gmail.com
Web site: http://www.askrealjesus.com; http://www.morepublish.com
Dist(s): **SCB Distributors.**

Morelmasters LLC, (*978-0-615-12829-0*) Orders Addr.: 6294 Reynolds Ridge Rd., Potosi, WI 53820 USA Tel 608-732-2175; Fax: 608-763-2799
E-mail: morelmasters@tds.net
Web site: http://www.morelmasters.com.

Morgan & Claypool Pubs., (*978-1-59829; 978-1-60845; 978-1-62705; 978-1-970001; 978-1-68173; 978-1-68174; 978-1-947487*) Orders Addr.: a/o c/o. bLogistics, 82 Winter Sport Ln., Williston, VT 05495 USA (SAN 256-5153) Tel 888-822-9942; Edit Addr.: 1210 5th Ave. Suite 250, San Rafael, CA 94901 USA Tel 415-785-8003; Fax: 415-785-2507
E-mail: info@morganclaypool.com
Web site: http://www.morganclaypool.com
Dist(s): **American International Distribution Corp.**
ebrary, Inc.

Morgan, E. A., (*978-0-9631975*) Orders Addr.: P.O. Box 7452, Naples, FL 34101 USA Fax: 941-598-9809
E-mail: rhymetime@mailstation.com.

Morgan Foundation Pubs.: International Published Innovations, (*978-1-885679*) Orders Addr.: 182 Fourth St., Ashland, OR 97520 USA Fax: 815-550-4456
E-mail: morganfoundation@earthlink.net
Web site: http://www.morganfoundationpublishers.com.

Morgan James Publishing, (*978-0-9746133; 978-0-9758570; 978-0-9760901; 978-0-9768491; 978-1-933596; 978-1-60037; 978-0-9815058; 978-0-9817906; 978-0-9820750; 978-0-9823793; 978-0-9846170; 978-0-9828590; 978-0-9833715; 978-0-9835013; 978-1-61448; 978-0-9837125; 978-0-9840316; 978-1-938467; 978-1-63047; 978-1-63195; 978-1-68350; 978-0-9985823) Div. of Morgan James, LLC, 23rd Flr. 5 Penn Plaza, New York, NY 10001 USA*
Web site: http://www.morganjamespublishing.com
Dist(s): **Ingram Publisher Services**
Lightning Source, Inc.
Lulu Pr., Inc.
MyiLibrary.

Morgan Publishing Co., (*978-0-9639940*) Orders Addr.: P.O. Box 28718, San Jose, CA 95159 USA (SAN 298-1432) Fax: 408-637-1674; Edit Addr.: 338 Fifth St., Hollister, CA 95023 USA Tel 408-637-7031.

Morgan Publishing, Incorporated *See* **Augustine Pr.**

Morgan Rice *Imprint of* **Morgan Rice Bks.**

Morgan Rice Bks., Div. of Lukeman Literary Management Ltd., 157 Bedford Ave., Brooklyn, NY 11211 USA Tel 718-599-8988; Fax: 718-264-2189; *Imprints:* Morgan Rice (MYID_X_MORGAN)
Dist(s): **Lukeman Literary Management, Ltd.**
MyiLibrary.

Moriah Ministries, (*978-0-9728454; 978-0-9774836*) P.O. Box 23823, Chagrin Falls, OH 44023 USA Tel 440-543-9304 (phone/fax)
E-mail: info@davidicdance.com; info@moriahministries.org
Web site: http://www.davidicdance.com; http://www.moriahministries.org.

Mormon Comics, (*978-0-9764965*) 435 N. 150 W., Blackfoot, ID 83221 USA Tel 208-785-4558 (phone/fax)
E-mail: info@mormoncomics.com
Web site: http://www.mormoncomics.com.

Mornin' Light Media, (*978-0-9763534*) Orders Addr.: 31203 N. Course View, Franklin, TN 37067 USA; *Imprints:* Mornin'Light Media (MorninLight)
E-mail: shawnsurber@comcast.net; hopebook@bellsouth.net
Web site: http://www.thehopebook.com.

†**Morning Glory Pr., Inc.**, (*978-0-930934; 978-1-885356; 978-1-932538; 978-0-9844283*) 6595 San Haroldo Way, Buena Park, CA 90620 USA (SAN 211-2558) 888-327-4362; Toll Free: 888-612-8254 Do not confuse with Morning Glory Press in Nashua, NH
E-mail: jwl@morningglorypress.com; info@morningglorypress.com
Web site: http://www.morningglorypress.com
Dist(s): **Independent Pubs. Group**
MyiLibrary; *CIP*.

Morning Glory Pubns., (*978-0-9762929*) Orders Addr.: 1104 Blue ridge Dr., Clarkston, MI 48348 USA
E-mail: klinejane@hotmail.com.

Morning Joy Media, (*978-0-9826102; 978-1-937107*) 359 Bridge St., Spring City, PA 19475 USA Tel 610-256-2906
E-mail: debbie@morningjoymedia.com
Web site: http://www.morningjoymedia.com
Dist(s): **BookBaby.**

Morning Star Music Pubs., (*978-0-944529*) 1727 Larkin Williams Rd., Fenton, MO 63026 USA (SAN 243-8496)
E-mail: morningstar@morningstarmusic.com
Web site: http://www.morningstarmusic.com
Dist(s): **BookBaby.**

Morning Sun Bks., Inc., (*978-0-9619058; 978-1-58248; 978-1-878887*) 9 Pheasant Ln., Scotch Plains, NJ 07076 USA (SAN 243-1157) Tel 908-755-5454; Fax: 908-755-5455
E-mail: morningsunbooks@comcast.net
Web site: http://www.morningsunbooks.com
Dist(s): **Walthers, William K. Inc.**

MorningGlory Publishing, (*978-0-9705090*) Orders Addr.: P.O. Box 15523, Plantation, FL 33318-5523 USA Tel 954-370-7205; Fax: 954-370-6817; Edit Addr.: 9951 NW Sixth Ct., Plantation, FL 33324 USA
E-mail: tandtsm@aol.com.

Morningside Publishing, LLC, (*978-1-936210*) 1705 W Riley Rd, Payson, AZ 85541 USA (SAN 858-835X)
Web site: http://www.morningsidepublishing.com
Dist(s): **Smashwords.**

Morningstar Christian Chapel, (*978-0-9715733; 978-0-9729477; 978-0-9842943; 978-1-940198; 978-0-9964131*) 16241 Leffingwell Rd., Whittier, CA 90603 USA Tel 562-943-0297; Fax: 562-943-3608
E-mail: jacobeelen@morningstarcc.org
Web site: http://www.morningstarcc.org.

MorningStar Pubns., Inc., (*978-1-878327; 978-1-929371; 978-1-59933; 978-1-60708*) Div. of MorningStar Fellowship Church, Orders Addr.: 375 Star Light Dr., Fort Mill, SC 29715 USA Fax: 704-285-7251; Toll Free: 800-542-0278 (orders only); Edit Addr.: 1605 Industrial Dr., Wilkesboro, NC 28697 USA Do not confuse with Morningstar Pubns., Boulder, CO
E-mail: info@morningstarministries.org
Web site: http://www.morningstarministries.org
Dist(s): **Anchor Distributors**
Destiny Image Pubs.
Whitaker Hse.

Morningtide Pr., (*978-0-9790395*) P.O. Box 312, St. Augustine, FL 32085-0312 USA
Web site: http://www.morningtidepress.com
Dist(s): **Quality Bks., Inc.**

Mornin'Light Media *Imprint of* **Mornin' Light Media**

Morris Publishing, (*978-0-7392; 978-0-9631249; 978-1-57502; 978-1-885591; 978-0-9863567*) Orders Addr.: P.O. Box 2110, Kearney, NE 68848 USA Fax: 308-237-0263; Toll Free: 800-650-7888 Do not confuse with companies with the same Wesley Chapel, FL, Elkhart, IN
Web site: http://www.morrispublishing.com.

Morris, Tami *See* **2B Pr.**

Morrison-Andrews, Sharalyn, (*978-0-9962889; 978-0-9974305; 978-0-9975343*) P.O. Box 2829, South Portland, ME 04116 USA Tel 207-799-3664
E-mail: sharalynlovesanimals@gmail.com
Web site: sharalynlovesanimals.com.

Morrow, William Cookbooks *Imprint of* **HarperCollins Pubs.**

Morrow, William & Co. *Imprint of* **HarperCollins Pubs.**

Morten Moore Publishing, (*978-0-9672576; 978-0-9991108*) Div. of K & M Marketing, 415 E. Mohawk, Flagstaff, AZ 86001 USA Tel 928-380-4982; Fax: 000-000-0000
Dist(s): **Canyonlands Pubns.**

Morton Arts Media, (*978-0-9796868*) P.O. Box 233, Cornelius, NC 28031 USA.

Morton Bks., (*978-1-929188*) 47 Stewart Ave., Irvington, NJ 07111 USA Tel 973-374-8327; Fax: 973-374-1125
E-mail: rmo1033555@aol.com
Web site: http://www.mortonbooks.com.

MOS, Inc., (*978-0-9778570*) 5271 E MANN RD, Pekin, IN 47165-8807 USA Tel 812-967-2531; Fax: 812-967-2980; Toll Free: 800-451-3993
E-mail: info@joyfulcatholic.com
Web site: http://www.traditionalcatholicpublishing.com/.

Mo's Nose, LLC, (*978-0-9816255*) 222 Palisades Ave., Santa Monica, CA 90402-2734 USA (SAN 856-0811) Tel 310-451-8125
Web site: http://www.mosnose.com
Dist(s): **Independent Pubs. Group**
Midpoint Trade Bks., Inc.

Mosaic Paradigm Group, LLC, (*978-0-578-07392-7; 978-0-9852542*) 3 Pasco Ct., Pikesville, MD 21208 USA (SAN 920-2889) Tel 877-733-7308
E-mail: info@mpg-publishing.com
Web site: http://www.mpg-publishing.com.

Mosaic Pr. (CAN) (*978-0-88962; 978-1-77161*) *Dist. by* **IPG Chicago.**

Mosaic Publishing *See* **Branded Black Publishing**

Mosby *Imprint of* **Elsevier - Health Sciences Div.**

Moscow Ballet *Imprint of* **Sports Marketing International, Inc.**

Mosdos Pr., (*978-0-9671009; 978-0-9742160; 978-0-9801670; 978-0-9858078; 978-0-9888286*) Div. of Mosdos Ohr Hatorah, 1508 Warrensville Ctr. Rd., Cleveland, OH 44121 USA Tel 216-291-4158; Fax: 216-291-4169
E-mail: mosdospress@moh1.org; jfactor@moh1.org
Web site: http://www.mosdospress.com.

Moselle Productions, Inc., (*978-0-9701289*) P.O. Box 1304, League City, TX 77574 USA Tel 732-623-9908; Toll Free: 800-598-2519
Web site: http://www.mangoeandmarlie.com.

Mosely, Winifred, (*978-0-9769610*) 6600 E. River Rd., Tucson, AZ 85750 USA Tel 520-327-3681
E-mail: njmosely@comcast.net.

Moshire Pr., (*978-0-615-39082-6*) 2355 Carlysle Cove, Lawrenceville, GA 30044 USA Tel 404-784-5987
Web site: http://www.moshirepress.com.

Mosley, Kim, (*978-0-9663215*) 1312 W. 40th St., Austin, TX 78756-3615 USA Tel 512-762-6790
E-mail: mrkimmosley@gmail.com
Web site: http://kimmosley.com/workbook.

Moss, Michael, (*978-0-9763003*) 610 Prestwick Dr., Frankfort, IL 60423 USA Tel 312-437-7827 (312-437-STAR)
Web site: http://www.5starpc.com.

Moss Press Publishing, (*978-0-578-12603-6*) 616 Corporate Way Suite 2-4348, Valley Cottage, NY 10989 USA.

Mosscovered Gumbo Barn, (*978-0-9725853*) 15960 Highland Rd., Baton Rouge, LA 70810 USA
Dist(s): **Greenleaf Book Group.**

Mossy Moot, (*978-0-9977134*) 127 KINGS HWY, HACKETTSTOWN, NJ 07840 USA Tel 908-852-7050
E-mail: Susimage66@gmail.com.

Mostats, Marie C., (*978-0-9742848*) Orders Addr.: P.O. Box 230053, Las Vegas, NV 89123-0001 USA; Edit Addr.: 608 NW 29th St., Wilton Manors, FL 33311-2443 USA.

Mother Goose Programs, (*978-0-9753985; 978-0-9841366; 978-1-935784*) P.O. Box 423, Chester, VT 05143-0423 USA
E-mail: debbi@mothergooseprograms.org
Web site: http://www.mothergooseprograms.org
Dist(s): **National Bk. Network.**

Mother Lode Pr. LLC, (*978-0-615-34241-2; 978-0-692-78184-5*) P.O. Box 2526, Bay Saint Louis, MS 39521 USA Tel 571-926-3443
E-mail: jonfaust@helicopterharry.com.

Mother Moose Pr., (*978-0-9724570*) Orders Addr.: 21010 Southbank St., PMB No. 435, Potomac Falls, VA 20165 USA Tel 571-223-6472
E-mail: books@mothermoosepress.com
Web site: http://www.mothermoosepress.com.

Mother Necessity Inc., *(978-0-9796579)* P.O. Box 2135, Bonita Springs, FL 34133 USA
E-mail: cfergus@mothernecessity.com
Web site: http://www.mothernecessity.com.

M.O.T.H.E.R. Publishing Co., Inc., The, *(978-0-9718431)* Orders Addr.: P.O. Box 477, Rock Springs, WY 82902 USA Tel 307-382-5027; Fax: 307-382-6492; Edit Addr.: 616 Elias Ave., Rock Springs, WY 82901 USA
E-mail: motherpublishing@wyoming.com
Web site: http://www.motherpublishing.com.

Motherboard Bks., *(978-0-9749653; 978-0-692-42438-4; 978-0-692-42562-6; 978-0-692-43162-7)* P.O. Box 430041, Saint Louis, MO 63143 USA
E-mail: info@motherboardbooks.com
Web site: http://motherboardbooks.com
Dist(s): **CreateSpace Independent Publishing Platform.**

Motherhood Printing & Etc., *(978-1-60225)* Orders Addr.: 45973 Rd. 795, Ansley, NE 68814-5126 USA (SAN 852-1212) Tel 308-880-1021; Fax: 308-732-3280
E-mail: motherhoodprinting@nctc.net; mary@motherhoodprinting.com
Web site: http://motherhoodprinting.com.

Motherly Way Enterprises, *(978-0-9671428)* P.O. Box 11, Marylhurst, OR 97036-0011 USA Tel 503-723-2879; Toll Free: 877-666-7929
E-mail: julie@motherlyway.com
Web site: http://www.motherlyway.com.

Mother's Love Publishing, A, *(978-0-9777022)* 4962 Bristol Rock Rd, Florissant, MO 63033 USA (SAN 257-9707)
Dist(s): **Lushena Bks.**

Mothwing Pr. *Imprint of* **Mothwing.com**

Mothwing.com, *(978-0-9724528)* 80 Sheffield Rd., Waltham, MA 02451-2374 USA Tel 781-899-8153; *Imprints:* Mothwing Press (Mothwng Pr)
E-mail: mothwingpress@mothwing.com; andylevesque@rcn.com
Web site: http://www.mothwing.com/mothwingpress.

Motion Fitness LLC, *(978-0-9744568)* P.O. Box 2179, Palatine, IL 60078-2179 USA
E-mail: sales@motionfitness.com
Web site: http://www.motionfitness.com.

Motivision Media, *(978-0-9722332)* 9528 Blossom Valley Rd., El Cajon, CA 92021 USA
E-mail: dehaven@motivisionmedia.com; dehaven1@cox.net
Web site: http://www.motivisionmedia.com; http://www.MyFootballMentor.com.

Motorbooks *Imprint of* **Quarto Publishing Group USA**

Motorbooks *Imprint of* **Quarto Publishing Group USA**

†Mott Media, *(978-0-88062; 978-0-915134; 978-0-940319)* 1130 Fenway Cir., Fenton, MI 48430 USA (SAN 207-1460) Tel 810-714-4280; Fax: 810-714-2077 Do not confuse with Mott Media in Stamford, CT
E-mail: sales@mottmedia.com; bill@mottmedia.com
Web site: http://www.mottmedia.com
Dist(s): **Spring Arbor Distributors, Inc.**; *CIP.*

Mottley, William, *(978-0-9769216)* 428 N. Genito Rd., Burkeville, VA 23922 USA Tel 434-767-5594
E-mail: emottley@ceva.net
Web site: http://www.narrowstrip.com.

Moulton, Shirley, *(978-0-615-97740-9; 978-0-9983137)* 8663 Equinox Cir, Bingham Canyon, UT 84037-2039 USA Tel 385-319-4871
Dist(s): **CreateSpace Independent Publishing Platform.**

Mount Baldy Pr., Inc., *(978-0-9715863)* P.O. Box 469, Boulder, CO 80306-0469 USA (SAN 254-2625) Tel 415-413-8052; Fax: 303-532-1007
E-mail: simeon@mountbaldy.com
Web site: http://www.mountbaldy.com
Dist(s): **New Leaf Distributing Co., Inc.**
Quality Bks., Inc.

Mount Helicon Pr. *Imprint of* **Rock, James A. & Co. Pubs.**

Mount Olive College Pr., *(978-0-9627087; 978-1-880994; 978-1-59761)* Mount Olive College, Administration Bldg. 634 Henderson St., Mount Olive, NC 28365 USA (SAN 297-7729) Tel 919-658-2502; Toll Free Fax: 800-653-0854.

Mount Rushmore Bookstores, *(978-0-9646798; 978-0-9752617; 978-0-9798823; 978-0-692-63993-1)* Div. of Mount Rushmore National Memorial Society, 13030 Hwy. 244, Keystone, SD 57751 USA Tel 605-341-8883; Fax: 605-341-0433; Toll Free: 800-699-3142
E-mail: debbie_ketel@mtrushmore.org
Web site: http://www.mountrushmoresociety.com
Dist(s): **Partners Distributing.**

Mount Rushmore History Association *See* **Mount Rushmore Bookstores**

†Mount Vernon Ladies' Assn. of the Union, *(978-0-931917)* Orders Addr.: P.O. Box 110, Mount Vernon, VA 22121 USA (SAN 225-3976); Edit Addr.: 3200 Mount Vernon Memorial Hwy., Mount Vernon, VA 22121 USA
E-mail: ajohnson@mountvernon.org
Web site: http://www.mountvernon.org
Dist(s): **University of Virginia Pr.**
Wimmer Cookbooks; *CIP.*

Mountain Air Bks., *(978-0-615-24940-7; 978-0-615-24941-4; 978-0-615-26703-6; 978-0-615-29319-6; 978-0-615-29829-0; 978-0-615-41620-5; 978-0-615-56237-7; 978-0-615-64830-9)* 1045 University Ave. Apt. 2, Rochester, NY 14607-1624 USA
E-mail: scottkny@yahoo.com; mairbooks123@yahoo.com.

Mountain Bk. Co., P.O. Box 778, Broomfield, CO 80038-0778 USA Tel 303-436-1982; Fax: 917-386-2769
E-mail: wordguise@aol.com
Web site: http://www.mountainbook.org.

Mountain Girl Press *See* **Jan-Carol Publishing, INC.**

Mountain Maid *See* **Light Messages Publishing**

Mountain Memories Bks. *Imprint of* **Quarrier Pr.**

Mountain Ministries, *(978-0-9787761)* 18055 100th St., Lindsay, OK 73052-3308 USA Do not confuse with Mountain Ministries Sitka, Alaska.

Mountain n' Air Bks., *(978-1-879415)* Div. of Mountain n' Air Sports, Inc., Orders Addr.: P.O. Box 12540, La Crescenta, CA 91224 USA (SAN 630-5598) Tel 818-248-9345; Toll Free Fax: 800-303-5578; Toll Free: 800-446-9696; Edit Addr.: 2947-A Hololulu Ave., La Crescenta, CA 91214 USA (SAN 631-4198); *Imprints:* Bearly Cooking (Bearly Cooking)
E-mail: books@mountain-n-air.com
Web site: http://mountain-n-air.com
Dist(s): **Alpenbooks Pr. LLC**
CreateSpace Independent Publishing Platform
Partners/West Book Distributors.

Mountain Path Pr., *(978-0-9653149)* 111 Bank St., Ste 152, Grass Valley, CA 95945 USA Toll Free: 888-224-9997
E-mail: Info@MountainPathPress.com
Web site: http://www.mountainpathpress.com
Dist(s): **Bks. West**
Integral Yoga Pubns.
New Leaf Distributing Co., Inc.
Partners Bk. Distributing, Inc.

Mountain Path Publications *See* **Mountain Path Pr.**

†Mountain Pr. Publishing Co., Inc., *(978-0-87842)* Orders Addr.: P.O. Box 2399, Missoula, MT 59806-2399 USA (SAN 202-8832) Tel 406-728-1900; Fax: 406-728-1635; Toll Free: 800-234-5308; Edit Addr.: 1301 S. Third West, Missoula, MT 59801 USA (SAN 662-0868)
E-mail: jrimel@mtnpress.com; info@mtnpress.com; anne@mtnpress.com
Web site: http://www.mountain-press.com
Dist(s): **Bks. West**
Partners Bk. Distributing, Inc.; *CIP.*

Mountain States Specialties, *(978-0-9726022)* 1671 Valtec Ln., Boulder, CO 80301 USA Tel 303-444-6186 Toll Free: 800-353-2147.

Mountain Stream Publishing, *(978-0-615-89002-9; 978-0-692-22188-4; 978-0-692-26072-2; 978-0-692-28524-4; 978-0-692-33655-7; 978-0-692-33933-6; 978-0-692-35039-3; 978-0-692-37723-9; 978-0-692-52377-3; 978-0-692-76014-7)* 5327 W. HILL Rd., BOISE, ID 83703 USA Tel 2088639839
Dist(s): **CreateSpace Independent Publishing Platform.**

Mountain Thunder Publishing, *(978-0-615-69738-3; 978-0-9887625)* P.O. Box 6264, Snowmass Village, CO 81615 USA Tel 6462836884
Dist(s): **CreateSpace Independent Publishing Platform.**

Mountain Valley Publishing, LLC, *(978-1-59453; 978-1-60002; 978-1-934940)* Orders Addr.: 1420 Maple Ct., Martinsville, IN 46151 USA Tel 765-349-8908; Fax: 765-349-8908
E-mail: bdenton308@comcast.net
Web site: http://www.mountainvalleypublishing.com.

Mountain Voices Pubs., *(978-0-9671908)* Orders Addr.: 2 Junaluska Rd., Andrews, NC 28901 USA Tel 828-321-5553; Fax: 828-321-2446
E-mail: MountainTeller@mountainvoice.com
Web site: http://www.mountainvoice.com.

Mountain World Media LLC, *(978-0-9763309)* Orders Addr.: P.O. Box 687, Telluride, CO 81435 USA Tel 970-729-0289; Edit Addr.: 135 Hillside Ln., Telluride, CO 81435 USA
E-mail: damon@mountainworldmedia.com
Web site: http://www.mountainworldmedia.com
Dist(s): **Alpenbooks Pr. LLC**
Bks. West.

Mountaintop Pr., *(978-0-9711106)* Orders Addr.: P.O. Box 550, Cary, NC 27512-0550 USA Tel 919-567-9550; Fax: 919-567-9694; Edit Addr.: 201-D Foliage Cir., Cary, NC 27511 USA
Dist(s): **Send The Light Distribution LLC.**

MountainView *Imprint of* **Treble Heart Bks.**

Mountan Creek Pubns., *(978-0-615-52752-9; 978-0-615-55170-8; 978-0-9853574)* 80 Post Ave., Rochester, NY 14619 USA Tel 585-966-9669
E-mail: nailahbaniti@gmail.com
Web site: Mountaincreekpublications.com.

Mountz Media & Publishing, *(978-0-9840673; 978-0-9891429)* Orders Addr.: P.O. Box 702398, Tulsa, OK 74170 USA; Edit Addr.: 5721 E. 101st Pl., Tulsa, OK 74137 USA
E-mail: mamountz@cox.net.

Mouse Prints Pr. (NLD) *(978-90-818368; 978-94-91613) Dist. by* **IngramPubServ.**

Mouse! Publishing, *(978-0-9643512)* Orders Addr.: P.O. Box 1674, Honolulu, HI 96806 USA Tel 808-625-7522; Fax: 808-284-5516; Edit Addr.: 419 South St., Suite 133, Honolulu, HI 96813 USA
Dist(s): **Booklines Hawaii, Ltd.**

Mouse Works, *(978-0-7364; 978-1-57082)* Div. of Disney Bk. Publishing, Inc., A Walt Disney Co., 114 Fifth Ave., New York, NY 10011 USA (SAN 298-0797) Tel 212-633-4400; Fax: 212-633-4811
Web site: http://www.disneybooks.com
Dist(s): **Random Hse., Inc.**

Mousetime Bks. *Imprint of* **Mousetime Media LLC**

Mousetime Media LLC, *(978-0-9723213)* 7960-B Soquel Dr., No. 297, Aptos, CA 95003 USA; *Imprints:* Mousetime Books (Msetime Bks)
E-mail: books@mousetime.com
Web site: http://www.mousetime.com.

Move Bks., LLC, *(978-0-9854810; 978-0-9970513; 978-0-692-73732-3)* 10 N. Main St., Beacon Falls, CT 06403 USA Tel 203-709-0490
Web site: http://www.move-books.com
Dist(s): **Independent Pubs. Group**
MyiLibrary
Small Pr. United.

Movement Makers International, *(978-0-9766930)* P.O. Box 3940, Broken Arrow, OK 74013-3940 USA
Web site: http://www.j12.com.

Movies for the Ear, LLC, *(978-1-935793)* 8362 Tamarack Village No. 119-327, St. Paul, MN 55125 USA Tel 612-209-3884
E-mail: moviesfortheear@comcast.net
Web site: www.CreepersMysteries.com
Dist(s): **Lightning Source, Inc.**

Mowery, Julia, *(978-0-9710529)* 6308 Starfish Ave, North Port, FL 34291 USA
E-mail: storyteller2000@msn.com; storytellerjm@aol.com
Web site: http://dobiebookpublishing.com.

†Moyer Bell, *(978-0-918825; 978-1-55921)* 549 Old North Rd., Kingston, RI 02881-1220 USA (SAN 630-1762) Tel 401-783-5480; Fax: 401-284-0959; Toll Free: 888-789-1945
Web site: http://www.moyerbellbooks.com/
Dist(s): **Acorn Alliance**
Midpoint Trade Bks., Inc.
MyiLibrary
ebrary, Inc.; *CIP.*

Moznaim Publishing Corp., *(978-0-940118; 978-1-885220)* 4304 12th Ave., Brooklyn, NY 11219 USA (SAN 214-4123) Tel 718-438-7680; Fax: 718-438-1305; Toll Free: 800-364-5118.

MP Publishing Ltd. (GBR) *(978-0-9555792; 978-1-84982) Dist. by* **Midpt Trade.**

MP2ME Enterprise, *(978-0-9717947; 978-0-9776679; 978-0-9841360)* 16754 SE 45th St., Issaquah, WA 98027 USA Tel 425-957-9459
E-mail: mpighin1@comcast.net
Dist(s): **Lightning Source, Inc.**

MPC Pr. International, *(978-0-9628453; 978-0-9715541)* P.O. Box 26142, San Fransisco, CA 94126-6142 USA
E-mail: info@laughingcookiejar.com
Web site: http://www.laughingcookiejar.com.

MPR Publishing, *(978-0-9831857)* 3550 N. Daisy Dr., Rialto, CA 92377 USA Tel 323-259-2884
E-mail: sales@mprpublishing.com.

MPublishing *See* **Michigan Publishing**

MQuills Publishing, *(978-0-615-55835-6; 978-0-615-56307-7; 978-0-615-63989-5; 978-1-62375)* 4179 Choteau Cir., Rancho Cordova, CA 95742 USA Tel 916-205-6999; *Imprints:* Caliburn Books (Caliburn Bks); Paramance (Paramance)
E-mail: mquills@mquills.com
Web site: www.mquills.com
Dist(s): **CreateSpace Independent Publishing Platform**
Lightning Source, Inc.

Mr Do It All, Inc., *(978-0-9722038)* 2212 S. Chickasaw Trail, No. 220, Orlando, FL 32825 USA Toll Free: 800-425-9206
E-mail: info@planet-heller.com
Web site: http://www.planet-heller.com.

Mr. Emmett Publishing, *(978-0-9759346)* 37 Harleston Pl., Charleston, SC 29401 USA Tel 843-853-5728
E-mail: talubbers@comcast.net.

Mr. Theodore Bear, *(978-0-9862968)* 5720 Belaire cir, Granbury, TX 76048 USA Tel 8174080634; Toll Free: 8174080634
Web site: http://mrtheobear.blogspot.com/
Dist(s): **CreateSpace Independent Publishing Platform.**

Mracek, Ann, *(978-0-9766488)* 22 Morwood Ln., Creve Coeur, MO 63141 USA (SAN 257-0009) Tel 314-432-5713; Fax: 314-569-2202
E-mail: anmracek@springmail.com.

MrDuz.com, *(978-0-9796226)* 1325 W. Sunshine No. 515, Springfield, MO 65807 USA (SAN 853-9332) Tel 417-831-9898; Fax: 417-863-6655 (please include To: MrDuz.com on cover pg.); Toll Free: 866-966-7389
E-mail: patrick@patrickwellman.com; patrick@mrduz.com
Web site: http://www.mrduz.com; http://www.patrickwellman.com.

MrExcel.com Publishing *See* **Tickling Keys, Inc.**

MRG Professional Services, *(978-0-9760310)* 6255 Cherry Ln. Farm Dr., West Chester, OH 45069 USA
E-mail: kgillis85@gmail.com.

MRN Pubns., *(978-0-9630495)* 1417 Noble St., Longwood, FL 32750 USA Tel 407-831-2947 (phone/fax)
E-mail: marjorie@partnersinlearning.com
Web site: http://www.partnersinglelearning.com.

Mroczka Media, *(978-0-9846800; 978-1-938397; 978-0-692-54800-4; 978-0-692-55469-2; 978-0-692-56464-6)* 2531 Southwick St., Houston, TX 77080 USA Fax: 832-365-7982; *Imprints:* Pagan Writers Press (PaganWriters)
E-mail: angie@paganwriters.com
Web site: http://www.paganwriterspress.com
Dist(s): **CreateSpace Independent Publishing Platform.**

Mrs. L's Reading Room, *(978-0-9767278)* Orders Addr.: 110 Wedgefield Dr., Hilton Head Island, SC 29926 USA Tel 843-682-2820 (telephone/fax)
Web site: http://www.readroom.com.

M.S.C. Bks. *Imprint of* **Mustard Seed Comics**

MSJ Music Publighing, *(978-0-9764521)* P.O. Box 3185, Rancho Santa Fe, CA 92067-3185 USA.

MSP *Imprint of* **Main St Publishing, Inc.**

MSPpress *Imprint of* **Mama Specific Productions**

MsRevenda.com, *(978-0-9768538)* P.O. Box 370109, Decatur, GA 30037 USA
Web site: http://www.msrevenda.com.

M.T. Publishing Co., Inc., *(978-1-932439; 978-1-934729; 978-1-938730; 978-1-945306)* Orders Addr.: P.O. Box 6802, Evansville, IN 47719-6802 USA Toll Free: 888-263-4702; Edit Addr.: 209 NW 8th St., Evansville, IN 47708 USA
Web site: http://www.mtpublishing.com.

mTrellis Publishing, Inc., *(978-0-9663281; 978-1-930650)* Orders Addr.: P.O. Box 280, New York Mills, MN 56567 USA (SAN 299-6669) Fax: 218-385-3708; Toll Free: 800-513-0115
E-mail: trellis2@aol.com; mary@trellispublishing.com
Web site: http://www.trellispublishing.com
Dist(s): **Independent Pubs. Group**
MyiLibrary
Small Pr. United.

MTV Bks. *Imprint of* **MTV Books**

MTV Books, 1230 Ave. of the Americas, New York, NY 10020 USA; *Imprints:* MTV Books (MTV Imp)
Dist(s): **Simon & Schuster, Inc.**

Mu Alpha Theta, National High Schl. Mathematics Club, *(978-0-940790)* 601 Elm Ave., Rm. 423, Norman, OK 73019 USA (SAN 204-0077) Tel 405-325-4489; Fax: 405-325-7184
E-mail: matheta@ou.edu
Web site: http://www.mualphatheta.org.

Muae Publishing, Inc., *(978-1-885030; 978-1-935717)* c/o 3620 S Vermont Ave KAP 462, Los Angeles, CA 90089 USA
E-mail: sunyoung@panix.com; kaya@kaya.com
Web site: http://www.kaya.com
Dist(s): **D.A.P./Distributed Art Pubs.**
SPD-Small Pr. Distribution
Two Rivers Distribution.

Mud Pie Pr., *(978-0-9714941)* 4201 Morrow Ave., Waco, TX 76710 USA Tel 254-716-3193
E-mail: bjelmore@msn.com; belmore1@hot.rr.com
Web site: http://www.mudpiepress.com
Dist(s): **Quality Bks., Inc.**

Mud Puddle, Inc., *(978-1-59412; 978-1-60311)* 54 W. 21st St., Suite 601, New York, NY 10010 USA Tel 212-647-9168.

Muddy Boots Pr., *(978-1-63076; 978-0-692-44652-2)* 421 Ponderosa Dr, Harker Heights, TX 76548 USA Tel 240-515-1042
Web site: www.muddybootspress.com
Dist(s): **CreateSpace Independent Publishing Platform**
National Bk. Network.

Mudpuppy Pr., *(978-0-7353; 978-0-929648; 978-0-939456; 978-1-56155)* Div. of Galison Bks., 28 W. 44th St., Suite 1411, New York, NY 10036 USA (SAN 216-3888) Tel 212-354-8840
Dist(s): **Hachette Bk. Group.**

Mugsy and Sugar Pressed, *(978-0-9798886)* 1117 Nobb Hill Dr., West Chester, PA 19380 USA
E-mail: tlaurento@comcast.net.

Mukund Pubns., *(978-0-9663831)* 3033 Arbor Bnd., Birmingham, AL 35244-1573 USA
E-mail: pratibhakhare@hotmail.com
Web site: http://www.learnhindi.com.

Mulholland Books *Imprint of* **Little Brown & Co.**

Mulholland Teacher Resources *See* **Sonic Sword Productions**

Mullen, Peter, *(978-0-692-77226-3; 978-0-692-77229-4)* 440 Dixon Landing Rd. Apt# I-306, MILPITAS, CA 95035 USA Tel 408-691-6581.

Mullings Media, *(978-0-9767657)* P.O. Box 934, Woodbridge, NJ 07095 USA.

Mullins Pubns. & Apparel, LLC, *(978-0-9760160)* 6600 Plaza Dr., No.2000, New Orleans, LA 70127 USA.

Multables, Inc., *(978-0-9645004)* 6398 S. Louthan St., Littleton, CO 80120 USA Tel 303-794-0786; Toll Free: 800-320-6857.

Multicultural Pubns., *(978-0-9634932; 978-1-884242)* 936 Slosson St., Akron, OH 44320 USA Tel 330-865-9578; Fax: 330-734-0737; Toll Free: 800-238-0297
E-mail: multiculturalpub@prodigy.net
Web site: http://www.multiculturalpub.net
Dist(s): **Brodart Co.**
Follett School Solutions.

Multi-Language Pubns., *(978-0-9703210; 978-1-931891)* 2500 George Dieter, El Paso, TX 79936 USA Tel 915-857-5852; Fax: 915-857-7644; Toll Free: 800-876-1388
E-mail: paul.hartman@wels.net; jan.gamble@wels.net.

Multi-Language Publications Program *See* **Multi-Language Pubns.**

Multnomah *Imprint of* **Doubleday Religious Publishing Group, The**

Multnomah Bks. *Imprint of* **Crown Publishing Group**

Mumblefish Bks., *(978-0-9759649)* Orders Addr.: P.O. Box 139, Point Pleasant, PA 18950-0139 USA Tel 215-297-5002; Fax: 215-297-5299
E-mail: info@mumblefishbooks.com
Web site: http://mumblefishboooks.com.

Mumford Institute, *(978-0-615-25457-9; 978-0-692-00349-7)* 330 Shore Dr., Unit C5, Highlands, NJ 07732 USA Tel 732-291-8243.

Mundania Pr. *Imprint of* **Mundania Pr.**

Mundania Pr., *(978-0-9723670; 978-1-59426; 978-1-60659)* 6470A Glenway Ave., No. 109, Cincinnati, OH 45211 USA (SAN 255-013X) Tel 513-490-2822; Fax: 513-598-9220; *Imprints:* Mundania Press (MundPr)
E-mail: bob@mundania.com; books@mundania.com
Web site: http://www.mundania.com; http://www.phaze.com
Dist(s): **Lightning Source, Inc.**

Munson, Craig *See* **Fleur De Lis Publishing, LLC**

Murdoch Bks. Pty Ltd. (AUS) *(978-0-86411; 978-1-74045; 978-1-921259; 978-1-921208; 978-1-74196; 978-1-74266; 978-0-7316-4258-8; 978-0-646-32800-3; 978-1-74325; 978-1-74336) Dist. by* **HachBkGrp.**

Murdock, Bob E., *(978-0-9754363)* 352 Carly Ln., Rock Hill, SC 29732-7750 USA Tel 803-366-2666 (phone/fax)
E-mail: pbmurdock@comporium.net
Web site: http://www.sermonsforchildren.com.

Murdock Publishing Co., *(978-0-9743359; 978-1-934102)* Orders Addr.: 127 Belk Ct., Clayton, NC 27520 USA Tel 919-934-2393; Fax: 919-938-2394
Web site: http://www.murdockmedia.com.

Murine Press *See* **Ancient Wisdom Pubns.**

Murphey, Hiromi, *(978-0-9761350)* 4049 Madison Ave. Apt. 102, Culver City, CA 90232-3246 USA
Web site: http://www.nabiland.com.

Publisher Name Index

Murphy, Indera *See* **Tolana Publishing**
Murphy's Bone Publishing, *(978-0-9748226)* P.O. Box 56835, Sherman Oaks, CA 91413-6835 USA Toll Free: 877-811-2663
E-mail: murphysbone@aol.com
Web site: http://www.murphysbone.com.
Murray, David M., *(978-0-9729807)* Orders Addr.: ., Seekonk, MA 02916 USA; Edit Addr.: 30 Wnterberry Ln., Seekink, MA 02771-4816 USA.
Murray Hill Bks., LLC, *(978-0-9719697; 978-1-935139)* 7 Evergreen Ln., Woodstock, NY 12498 USA (SAN 256-3622) Tel 845-679-6749
E-mail: robinsegal@earthlink.net; info@murrayhillbooks.com
Web site: http://www.murrayhillbooks.com
Dist(s): **Independent Pubs. Group**
Learning Connection, The.
Murray, Regina Waldron, *(978-0-9636918; 978-0-9664042)* 300 Hollinshead Spring Rd. Apt. AL137, Skillman, NJ 08558-2049 USA
E-mail: reginawmurray@yahoo.com.
Musa Publishing, *(978-1-61937; 978-1-68009)* 4815 Iron Horse Trail, Colorado Springs, CO 80917 USA Tel 719-393-2398
E-mail: kerry@musapublishing.com
Web site: www.musapublishing.com.
Muscatello Publishing, *(978-0-9722774)* P.O. Box 620011, Orlando, FL 32862-0011 USA Tel 407-888-3060; Fax: 407-650-3222; Toll Free: 877-888-3060
E-mail: info@muscatellopublishing.com
Web site: http://www.muscatellopublishing.com.
Museum Mysteries *Imprint of* **Stone Arch Bks.**
†**Museum of Fine Arts, Boston,** *(978-0-87846)* 465 Huntington Ave., Boston, MA 02115-4401 USA (SAN 202-2230) Tel 617-369-3438; Fax: 617-369-3459
E-mail: kmullins-mitchell@mfa.org
Web site: http://www.mfa.org
Dist(s): **Casemate Academic**
Brown, David Bk. Co.
D.A.P./Distributed Art Pubs.
ISD
MyiLibrary
Two Rivers Distribution; *CIP.*
Museum of Fine Arts, Houston, *(978-0-89090)* P.O. Box 6826, Houston, TX 77265-6826 USA (SAN 202-2559) Tel 713-639-7300
Dist(s): **D.A.P./Distributed Art Pubs.**
Texas A&M Univ. Pr.
Two Rivers Distribution
Univ. of Texas Pr.
Yale Univ. Pr.
Museum of Glass, *(978-0-9726649; 978-0-692-46250-8; 978-0-692-78193-7)* 1801 Dock St., Tacoma, WA 98402 USA Toll Free: 866-468-7386 (866-4-MUSEUM)
Web site: http://www.museumofglass.org
Dist(s): **Univ. of Washington Pr.**
Museum of Glass: International Center for Contemporary Art *See* **Museum of Glass**
Museum of Modern Art, *(978-0-87070; 978-1-63345)* 11 W. 53 St., New York, NY 10019-5497 USA (SAN 202-5809) Tel 212-708-9700; Fax: 212-333-1127; Toll Free: 800-447-6662 (orders)
E-mail: MoMA_Publications@moma.org
Web site: http://www.moma.org/publications
Dist(s): **Abrams, Inc.**
D.A.P./Distributed Art Pubs.
Hachette Bk. Group.
Museum of New Mexico Pr., *(978-0-89013)* Div. of New Mexico Department of Cultural Affairs, Orders Addr.: 1312 Basehart Rd. SE, Albuquerque, NM 87106-4363 USA (SAN 202-2575) 505-272-7778; Toll Free: 800-249-7737; Edit Addr.: P.O. Box 2087, Santa Fe, NM 87504-2087 USA
E-mail: custserv@upress.unm.edu
Web site: http://www.mnmpress.org
Dist(s): **Univ. of New Mexico Pr.**
Museum of Science *See* **Engineering is Elementary**
Museum of Texas Tech Univ., *(978-0-9640188; 978-1-929330)* Div. of Texas Tech Univ., 3301 4th St., Box 43191, Lubbock, TX 79409-3191 USA Tel 806-742-2442; Fax: 806-742-1136
E-mail: museum.texastech@ttu.edu
Web site: http://www.museum.ttu.edu.
Museyon, *(978-0-9822320; 978-0-9846334; 978-1-938450; 978-1-940842)* Orders Addr.: 1177 Ave. Of The Americas, 5th Flr., New York, NY 10036 USA (SAN 857-6033)
E-mail: chiba@museyon.com
Web site: http://www.museyon.com
Dist(s): **Independent Pubs. Group**
MyiLibrary.
Museyon Guides *See* **Museyon**
Mushgush Pr., *(978-0-9795818)* 335 Cantlegate Close, Johns Creek, GA 30022 USA
Web site: http://tidalpress.com.
Mushroom Cloud Pr. of Orlando, *(978-0-9679552)* 278 Leslie Ln., Lake Mary, FL 32746 USA Tel 407-328-7311
E-mail: mushroomcloudpress@hotmail.com.
Music Awareness, *(978-0-9753599)* P.O. Box 188, Amherst, MA 01004 USA Tel 413-253-4216; Fax: 413-253-1397
E-mail: pwb@valinet.com
Web site: http://www.musicawareness.com.
Music Bks. & Games, *(978-0-9744427)* P.O. Box 97, McNeil, TX 78651 USA
E-mail: info@musicbooksandgames.com
Web site: http://www.musicbooksandgames.com/.
Music City Publishing, *(978-1-933215)* P.O. Box 41696, Nashville, TN 37204-1696 USA (SAN 256-288X)
E-mail: manager@musiccitypublishing.com
Web site: http://www.musiccitypublishing.com.
Music for Little People, Inc., *(978-1-56628; 978-1-877737)* 390 Lake Benbow Dr., No. C, Garberville, CA 95542 USA Tel 707-923-3991; Fax: 707-923-3241; Toll Free: 800-346-4445
Web site: http://www.musicforlittlepeople.com
Dist(s): **Educational Record Ctr., Inc.**
Follett School Solutions
Goldenrod Music, Inc.
Linden Tree Children's Records & Bks.
Music Design, Inc.
New Leaf Distributing Co., Inc.
Rounder Kids Music Distribution
Western Record Sales.
Music Institute of California, *(978-0-9624062; 978-1-883993)* Orders Addr.: P.O. Box 3535, Vista, CA 92085-3535 USA (SAN 297-5955) Tel 760-891-0226
Dist(s): **BookBaby**
Brodart Co.
Music, Movement & Magination Bks., *(978-0-9818635; 978-1-935572)* 3165 S. Alma School Rd., Suite 29-195, Chandler, AZ 85248 USA (SAN 856-7662) Tel 480-247-3129; Fax: 480-634-7148; Toll Free: 888-637-1313
E-mail: info@MMMKids.com
Web site: http://www.MMMKids.com.
Music Resources International *See* **Kindermusik International**
Music Sales Corp., *(978-0-7119; 978-0-8256; 978-1-84609)* Orders Addr.: 445 Bellvale Rd., P.O. Box 572, Chester, NY 10918 USA (SAN 662-0876) Tel 845-469-2271; Fax: 845-469-7544; Toll Free Fax: 800-345-6842; Toll Free: 800-431-7187; Edit Addr.: 257 Park Ave., S., 20th Flr., New York, NY 10010 USA (SAN 282-0277) Tel 212-254-2100; Fax: 212-254-2103; *Imprints:* Amsco Music (Amsco Music); Chester Music (Chester Music)
E-mail: info@musicsales.com
Web site: http://www.musicroom.com; http://www.musicsales.com
Dist(s): **Beekman Bks., Inc.**
Dumont, Charles Son, Inc.
Chesbro Music Co.
Leonard, Hal Corp.
Ingram Publisher Services
Quality Bks., Inc.
Musical Linguist, The, *(978-0-9706829)* Orders Addr.: 14419 Greenwood Ave. N., Suite A, No. 354, Seattle, WA 98133 USA Fax: 509-693-4160; Toll Free: 866-297-2128
E-mail: mlinguist@aol.com
Web site: http://www.musicalspanish.com.
Musictech College Pr., *(978-0-9729879)* 19 Exchange St., E., Saint Paul, MN 55101 USA Tel 651-291-0177; Fax: 651-291-0366; Toll Free: 800-594-9500
E-mail: dsmith@musictech.com
Web site: http://www.musictech.com.
MusicWorks, *(978-0-9763194; 978-0-9820900)* Orders Addr.: P.O. Box 1971, Maryland Heights, MO 63043 USA; Edit Addr.: 13233 Amiot Dr., Saint Louis, MO 63146 USA; P.O. Box 1971, Saint Louis, MO 63043 (SAN 857-2291) Tel 314-439-5334 Do not confuse with MusicWorks in Marietta, GA
Web site: http://www.the-music-works.com; http://www.the-music-works.net.
MusiKinesis, *(978-0-9701416)* 3734 Cross Bow Ct., Ellicott City, MD 21042 USA Fax: 410-465-8472
E-mail: monicadale@musikinesis.com
Web site: http://www.musikinesis.com.
Muslim Writers Publishing, *(978-0-9767861; 978-0-9793577; 978-0-9819770; 978-0-9854638)* 2821-B O'Kelly St., Raleigh, NC 27607 USA Tel 919-817-8656
E-mail: debmcnichol@gmail.com
Web site: http://www.muslimwriterspublishing.com
Dist(s): **Smashwords.**
Mustang BKS, *(978-0-9766270)* P.O. Box 1193, Crooked River Ranch, OR 97760 USA Tel 541-504-9620.
Mustard Hill Pr., *(978-0-9977897)* 492 Pala Way, Sacramento, CA 95819 USA Tel 916-455-2797
E-mail: caron@caronvikre.com.
Mustard Seed Comics, *(978-0-9769819; 978-0-9826975; 978-0-9964631)* 1609 Stoney Grove Church Rd., Warrenton, GA 30828 USA Tel 706-466-1633; *Imprints:* M.S.C. Books (MSCBks)
E-mail: mail@mustardseedcomics.com; benitomsc@yahoo.com
Web site: http://www.mustardseedcomics.com.
Mustard Seed Pr., *(978-0-9797703)* 263 Northampton Rd., Amherst, MA 01002 USA
Web site: http://www.bagelsbuddyandme.com.
Muszynski, James A., *(978-0-9766461)* 1446 Yoder Rd., Manister, MI 49660 USA Tel 231-723-6500 (phone/fax)
E-mail: lsmuszyk@hotmail.com
Web site: http://www.jaminjimbooks.com.
Mutual Publishing LLC, *(978-0-935180; 978-1-56647; 978-1-939487; 978-0-9971305)* 1215 Center St., Suite 210, Honolulu, HI 96816 USA (SAN 222-6359) Tel 808-732-1709; Fax: 808-734-4094
E-mail: info@mutualpublishing.com
Web site: http://www.mutualpublishing.com
Dist(s): **Booklines Hawaii, Ltd.**
Islander Group
Mel Bay Pubns., Inc.
MVCD, Inc., *(978-0-9753617)* 4711 E. Falcon Dr., Suite 251, Mesa, AZ 85215 USA.
MVmedia, *(978-0-9800842; 978-0-9960167; 978-0-9992789)* 145 Ridgewood Dr., Fayetteville, GA 30215 USA.
MX No Fear, *(978-0-9766918)* 2251 Faraday Ave., Suite A, Carlsbad, CA 92008 USA Toll Free: 866-787-3691
Web site: http://www.mxnofear.com.
My Ancestors, My Heroes *Imprint of* **Parker-Wallace Publishing Co., LLC**
My Campus Adventure, Inc., *(978-1-935159)* Orders Addr.: 7705 Orly Ct., Plano, TX 75025 USA (SAN 856-6690)
E-mail: kim@mycampusadventure.com
Web site: http://www.mycampusadventure.com.
My Children Publishing Inc., *(978-0-9799376)* 17410 Vinwood Ln., Yorba Linda, CA 92886 USA (SAN 854-7890)
Web site: http://www.mychildrenpublishing.com.
My Darling-Tots Pubns., *(978-0-9797674)* 8593 Pantherburn Trace, Cordova, TN 38018 USA
E-mail: hdarling30@yahoo.com
Web site: http://www.helendarling.com.
My First Classic Story *Imprint of* **Picture Window Bks.**
My First Graphic Novel *Imprint of* **Stone Arch Bks.**
My Grandma & Me Pubs., *(978-0-9742732)* 1275 E. Parks Rd., Saint Johns, MI 48879 USA
E-mail: info@mygrandmaandme.com; janemarysinke@gmail.com
Web site: http://www.mygrandmaandme.com
Dist(s): **Partners Pubs. Group, Inc.**
My Heart Yours Publishing, *(978-1-932721)* P.O. Box 4975, Wheaton, IL 60187 USA (SAN 255-6774)
E-mail: tanya@myheartyours.com; jeannine@myheartyours.com
Web site: http://www.myheartyours.com.
My Journey Bks., *(978-0-9766295)* P.O. Box 1169, Olney, MD 20830-1169 USA Toll Free: 877-965-2665
E-mail: KGF@billiesworld.com; KGF@myjourneybooks.com
Web site: http://www.billiesworld.com; http://www.myjourneybooks.com.
My Little Jessie Pr., *(978-0-9740743)* Orders Addr.: P.O. Box 529, Bethel, VT 05032 USA (SAN 255-321X) Tel 802-234-9725; Edit Addr.: One Cushing Ave., Bethel, VT 05032 USA
E-mail: jhaywardburnham@aol.com.
My Little One, Incorporated *See* **Mylo Publishing**
My Little Planet *Imprint of* **Picture Window Bks.**
My Lyric's Hse., *(978-0-9761446)* 593 Vanderbilt Ave., No. 135, Brooklyn, NY 11238 USA Tel 347-408-7786
E-mail: itsmeisha@yahoo.com.
My Purple Toes, LLC, *(978-0-9844556; 978-0-9834778)* P.O. Box 826, Mt. Pleasant, SC 29465 USA
E-mail: blair@blairhahnbooks.com
Web site: http://www.blairhahnbooks.com; http://www.mypurpletoes.com
Dist(s): **Emerald Bk. Co.**
My Second Language Publishing, USA, *(978-0-615-23709-1; 978-0-615-24460-0; 978-0-615-26150-8; 978-0-615-26238-3; 978-0-615-26239-0; 978-0-615-26240-6; 978-0-578-00208-8; 978-0-578-00209-5; 978-0-578-02214-7)* 165 River Hills Dr., Clayton, NC 27527 USA
E-mail: publisher@mysecondlanguagepublishingusa.com
Web site: http://www.mysecondlanguagepublishingusa.com
Dist(s): **Lulu Pr., Inc.**
My Special Thoughts, *(978-0-9743019)* P.O. Box 150747, Nashville, TN 37215 USA Fax: 615-297-3138
Web site: http://www.myspecialthoughts.com.
My Student-Athlete, Inc., *(978-0-9767250)* P.O. Box 15, Redan, GA 30074 USA Tel 770-981-3000
Web site: http://www.morethanvictories.com.
My Sunshine Bks., *(978-0-9749561)* 1370 Little Brier Creek Rd., Warrenton, GA 30828 USA Toll Free: 800-765-4663.
My Three Sisters Publishing, *(978-0-615-73283-1; 978-0-615-73697-6; 978-0-615-73769-0; 978-0-615-74341-7; 978-0-615-74542-8; 978-0-615-74664-7; 978-0-615-74890-0; 978-0-615-74922-8; 978-0-615-75048-4; 978-0-615-75245-7; 978-0-615-75261-7; 978-0-615-75276-1; 978-0-615-75367-6; 978-0-615-75421-5; 978-0-615-75460-4; 978-0-615-75518-2; 978-0-615-75534-2; 978-0-615-75556-4; 978-0-615-75716-2; 978-0-615-75752-0; 978-0-615-75770-4; 978-0-615-75825-1; 978-0-615-75897-8; 978-0-615-75904-3; 978-0-615-75910-4; 978-0-615-75938-8;) 13817 W. Rovey Ave., Litchfield Park, AZ 85340 USA Tel 847-769-9824*
E-mail: Jenniseco@aol.com
Dist(s): **CreateSpace Independent Publishing Platform.**
My Time Pubns., *(978-0-9820530; 978-0-9843257; 978-0-9830518)* 2984 Spring Falls Dr., West Carrollton, OH 45449 USA Tel 937-344-4805
E-mail: leila@mytimepublications.com; ljeff25@yahoo.com
Web site: http://www.mytimepublications.com.
MyBoys3 Pr., *(978-0-9893414; 978-0-9861473; 978-1-947881)* P.O. Box 2555, Midlothian, VA 23113 USA
E-mail: steve@myboys3.com
Web site: www.stevensawyerbooks.com; www.myboys3.com.
Myers, Connie Ellis *See* **Say Out Loud, LLC**
Myers, Jack Ministries, Inc., *(978-0-9720928)* P.O. Box 158, Orland Park, IL 60462-0158 USA
E-mail: jmm.revival@juno.com
Web site: http://www.jackmyersministries.com.
Myers Publishing Co., *(978-0-9729381)* 1426 Vermont Ave., Tarpon Springs, FL 34689-3871 USA Tel 727-938-6855; Fax: 727-934-4562 Do not confuse with Myers Publishing Company in Sacramento, CA
E-mail: kmyers2@tampabay.rr.com.
Myers Publishing Co., *(978-0-9745210; 978-0-9745929)* Orders Addr.: 207 Shelley Ct., Roseville, CA 95747 USA Tel 916-987-7668 (phone/fax) Do not confuse with Myers Publishing Company in Tarpon Springs, FL
E-mail: myerspubco@myerspublishing.com
Web site: http://www.myerspublishing.com.
MyHandiwork, *(978-0-9742555)* 7520 Walker St., Saint Louis Park, MN 55426-4042 USA Fax: 952-935-2840
E-mail: myhandiwork@earthlink.net
Web site: http://www.myhandiwork.com.
MYHRECO, *(978-0-9753704)* 9033 1/2 Hubbard St., Culver City, CA 90232-2508 USA.
Mylo Publishing, *(978-0-9910341)* 10052 E. Gelding Dr., Scottsdale, AZ 85260 USA Tel 682-465-6845
E-mail: znscurry@hotmail.com
Web site: www.mylopublishing.com.
Mymilou Pr., *(978-0-615-93163-0; 978-0-692-79069-4)* 2923 Bighom Dr., Corona, CA 92881 USA Tel 714-390-6139
E-mail: amarestaing@hotmail.com.
Myrddin Publishing Group, *(978-0-9883828; 978-1-939296; 978-1-68063)* 54 Mill Pond Rd., Jackson, NJ 08527 USA Tel 732-822-8920
E-mail: alisondeluca@hotmail.com; cjjasp@gmail.com
Dist(s): **Lulu Pr., Inc.**
MyReportLinks.com Bks. *Imprint of* **Enslow Pubs., Inc.**
Myrin Institute, Incorporated *See* **Orion Society, The**
Myrtle Learns, *(978-1-930694)* Orders Addr.: P.O. Box 3645, Rancho Cucamonga, CA 91729 USA Fax: 909-428-2401 (phone/fax); Edit Addr.: 14034 Fort Ross Ct., Fontana, CA 92336 USA Tel 909-428-2401
E-mail: jaajdeem@aol.com
Web site: http://myrtlelearns.com.
MySheri Enterprises, LLC, *(978-0-9766782)* P.O. Box 141111, Detroit, MI 48214 USA.
Myst of the Oracle Corp., *(978-0-9786812)* P.O. Box 133, Piney Creek, NC 28663 USA
E-mail: administrator@mystoftheoracle.com
Web site: http://www.mystoftheoracle.com.
Mysteries by Vincent, LLC, *(978-1-932169)* Orders Addr.: 2707 Mountain Green Trail, Kingwood, TX 77345 USA Tel 281-312-0120; Toll Free: 866-946-3864 1-866-WHODUNIT
E-mail: robert@mysteriesbyvincent.com; cindy@mysteriesbyvincent.com
Web site: http://www.mysteriesbyvincent.com; http://www.buckleyandbogey.com; http://www.whodunitpress.com.
Mystery & Suspense Pr. *Imprint of* **iUniverse, Inc.**
Mystery Writers of America Presents *Imprint of* **iUniverse, Inc.**
Mystic Arts, LLC, *(978-0-9771700)* P.O. Box 1110, Riverton, UT 84065 USA (SAN 256-8217)
Web site: http://www.reading-with-kids.com.
Mystic Hippo Media Publishing, *(978-0-9848694)* 5 Bald Hill Ct., Saint Peters, MO 63304 USA Tel 636-922-3593
E-mail: 88fingerslouie@att.net.
Mystic Jaguar Publishing, *(978-0-9792294)* 10821 Margate Rd., Suite A, Silver Spring, MD 20901-1615 USA (SAN 852-8365)
E-mail: Mysticjaguar@verizon.net.
Mystic Night Bks. *Imprint of* **Pink Stucco Pr.**
Mystic Pubs., Inc., *(978-0-9727840; 978-1-934051; 978-1-941271)* 614 Mosswood Dr., Henderson, NV 89002 USA; *Imprints:* Ink & Quill Publishers (Ink&Quill)
E-mail: richard@themackennasaga.com
Web site: http://www.mysticpublishers.com; www.iqpublishing.com; www.newlinkpublishing.com
Dist(s): **ebrary, Inc.**
Mystic Publishing, *(978-0-9747454)* 16613 195th Ave., Mystic, IA 52574-8678 USA Do not confuse with Mystic Publishing in North, VA
E-mail: sharon@freddiethefrog.com; sharon@freddiethefrogbooks.com
Dist(s): **Leonard, Hal Corp.**
Mystic Ridge Bks., *(978-0-9672182; 978-0-9742845)* Div. of Mystic Ridge Productions, Inc., 222 Main St., Sutie 142, Farmington, CT 06032 USA (SAN 853-9898)
E-mail: mysticridge@att.net
Web site: http://www.mysticridgebooks.com; http://www.blackjacktoday.com; http://www.helixeye.com.
Mystic River Ink, *(978-0-9724752)* P.O. Box 441357, Somerville, MA 02144 USA
Web site: http://www.mysticriverink.com.
Mystic Seaport Museum, Inc., *(978-0-913372; 978-0-939510)* 75 Greenmanville Ave., Mystic, CT 06355-0990 USA (SAN 213-7550) Tel 860-572-5347; Fax: 860-572-5348; Toll Free: 800-248-1066
E-mail: publications@mysticseaport.org; wholesale@mysticseaport.org
Web site: http://www.mysticseaport.org
Dist(s): **Peabody Essex Museum**
Univ. Pr. of New England.
Mystic Waters Publishing, *(978-0-9824498)* 402 N. Fredericksburg Ave., Margate City, NJ 08402 USA
E-mail: stevenwinkelstein@gmail.com.
Mystic World Pr., *(978-0-9854289)* 115 San Jose Ave. No. 2, San Francisco, CA 94110 USA Tel 415-373-8533
E-mail: william@mysticworldpress.com.
Mystical Willow Productions, *(978-0-9763205)* P.O. Box 95, Wheaton, IL 60189 USA
E-mail: mysticalwillow@comcast.net.
MysticMountain Pr., *(978-0-9905938)* 483 Apache Rd., Arrey, NM 87930 USA Tel 505-550-5530
E-mail: sheilaofthejungle@yahoo.com.
Mystique International, Ltd., *(978-0-9745333)* 2533 N. Carson St., Suite 593, Carson City, NV 89706-0147 USA
E-mail: metamind@eznet.net.
Myth Breakers *See* **Happy About**
Mythix Studios *Imprint of* **McCall, Philip Lee II**
Myth-O-Mania *Imprint of* **Stone Arch Bks.**
MythSeries, *(978-0-9776472)* P.O. Box 211, Millville, MN 55957 USA (SAN 257-8743) Tel 507-798-2450
E-mail: lisa@mythseries.com
Web site: http://mythseries.com.
Mz. Rosa Notions, *(978-0-9740267)* P.O. Box 114, Turlock, CA 95380 USA
E-mail: ninarule62@aol.com.
N A L Trade *Imprint of* **Penguin Publishing Group**
NAPSAC Reproductions, *(978-0-934426; 978-1-932747; 978-0-615-45573-0)* Rte. 4, Box 646, Marble Hill, MO 63764 USA (SAN 222-4607) Tel 573-238-4846; Fax: 573-238-2010
E-mail: napsac@clas.net
Dist(s): **Send The Light Distribution LLC.**
N&N Publishing Co., Inc., *(978-0-9606036; 978-0-935487)* 18 Montgomery St., Middletown, NY 10940 USA (SAN 216-4221) Tel 845-342-1677; Fax: 845-342-6910; Toll

Free: 800-664-8398; *Imprints:* STAReviews (STAReviews); X-treme Reviews (X-treme Reviews)
E-mail: info@nandnpublishing.com; sales@nandnpublishing.com
Web site: http://www.nandnpublishing.com; http://www.nn4text.com; http://www.starreview.com; http://www.big8review.com.

N Gallerie Pr. LLC, *(978-0-9818347; 978-0-9962748)* Div. of N Gallerie Studios, LLC, Orders Addr.: 1213 Culbreth Dr. Suite 233, Wilmington, NC 28405 USA Tel 910-398-6411
E-mail: sales@ngallerie.com
Web site: http://www.ngallerie.com.

N2Print *Imprint of* **New Age World Publishing**

N8TIVE, *(978-0-9769575)* 620 S. 19th St., Philadelphia, PA 19146 USA
Web site: http://www.n8tve.com.

NA (CAP) *Imprint of* **Capstone Press of Coughlan Cos.**

Na Kamalei Koolauloa Early Education Program, *(978-0-9773495; 978-0-9760892; 978-1-935111)* P.O. Box 900, Hauula, HI 96717 USA Tel 808-237-8500; Fax: 808-237-8501; *Imprints:* Ho'ulu Hou Project: Stories Told by Us (Houlu Hou)
E-mail: nkpublishing@nakamalei.org
Web site: http://www.nakamalei.org.

Nabors, Murray W., *(978-0-615-38301-9; 978-0-615-40572-8; 978-0-615-49157-8; 978-0-615-85999-6)* 3051 NE State Rte. W., Saint Joseph, MO 64507 USA Tel 816-244-0354
E-mail: mnabors@missouriwestern.edu.

Nabu Pr. *Imprint of* **Creative Media Partners, LLC**

NACSCORP, Incorporated *See* **.**

Nadores Publishing & Research, *(978-0-9797847)* Orders Addr.: P.O. Box 1202, Gilroy, CA 95021-1202 USA
E-mail: regulo-zapata@Verizon.net
Web site: http://www.nadorespublishing.com.

Nags Head Art, Inc., *(978-0-9616344; 978-1-878405)* Orders Addr.: P.O. Box 2149, Manteo, NC 27954 USA (SAN 200-9145) Tel 252-441-7480; Fax: 252-475-9893; Toll Free Fax: 800-246-7014; Toll Free: 800-541-2722; Edit Addr.: 7728 Virginia Dare Trail, Manteo, NC 27954 USA (SAN 658-8107)
E-mail: suzannetate@yahoo.com
Web site: http://www.suzannetate.com
Dist(s): **Florida Classics Library**
Mistco, Inc.

NA-h *Imprint of* **Heinemann-Raintree**

NAHSH M'ISTAH Pub., *(978-0-9665427)* 8614 E. Dahlia Dr., Scottsdale, AZ 85260 USA Tel 480-998-8189
E-mail: nashmista@aol.com.

Naim, Deborah, *(978-0-9762828)* 20801 Biscayne Blvd., Suite 403, Aventura, FL 33180 USA
E-mail: dnaim@mercadeoecologico.com.

Nakota Publishing, *(978-0-9882442)* 7240 W Shaw Butte, Peoria, AZ 85345 USA Tel 602-750-3662
E-mail: vltreude@cox.net.

Namaste Publishing, Inc. (CAN) *(978-0-9682364; 978-0-9736512; 978-0-9738436; 978-1-897238) Dist. by* **PerseuPGW.**

Nambennett Publishing, *(978-0-9742208)* 11748 Fremont Ave. N., Seattle, WA 98133 USA
E-mail: kelly@nambennett.com
Web site: http://www.nambennett.com.

namelos llc, *(978-1-60898)* 133 Main Ave., South Hampton, NH 03827 USA Tel 828-221-
E-mail: roxburgh@namelos.com
Web site: http://www.namelos.com.

Nana's Stories, *(978-0-9857362)* 22 St. Nicholas Ave., Worcester, MA 01606 USA Tel 508-560-5888
E-mail: kfinneron@yahoo.com.

Nancy Becklean Tobin *See* **Thalian Bks.**

Nancy Paulsen Books *Imprint of* **Penguin Young Readers Group**

Nancy's Artworks, *(978-0-9748074)* Orders Addr.: 6185 Faxon Ct., Colorado Spgs, CO 80922-1839 USA
E-mail: sales@nancyweb.com
Web site: http://www.multcamp.com; http://www.nancyweb.com; http://www.seanotes.net.

NANUQ Publishing, *(978-0-9795400)* 111 Linwood Ave., Williamsville, NY 14221 USA Tel 716-634-4379
E-mail: cralt37@yahoo.com.

NAO Pubns., *(978-0-9760836)* 35895 Conroy Rd., Suite 1015, Orlando, FL 32839 USA
E-mail: bbgwyn12@netzero.net; briangwyn@bellsouth.net
Web site: http://www.notanotheroverdraft.com; http://notanotheroverdraft.blogspot.com.

NAPNAP, *(978-0-9749769)* 20 Brace Rd., Suite 200, Cherry Hill, NJ 08034-2634 USA Tel 856-857-9700; Fax: 856-857-1600
E-mail: info@napnap.org
Web site: http://www.napnap.org.

Napue & Tucker Publishing, L.L.C. *See* **NT Publishing, L.L.C.**

NA-r *Imprint of* **Heinemann-Raintree**

Narragansett Graphics, *(978-0-615-12390-5)* P.O. Box 1492, Coventry, RI 02816-0029 USA
E-mail: lsousa@narragansettgraphics.com
Web site: http://www.narragansettgraphics.com.

NarraGarden LLC, *(978-0-9907434)* P.O. Box 409259, Chicago, IL 60640-0029 USA Tel 872-220-7220
E-mail: info@narragarden.com; bradley.blankenship@gmail.com
Web site: www.papadadandme.com; www.narragarden.com.

Nastari, Nadine, *(978-0-9798387)* 8408 Salerno Rd., Fort Pierce, FL 34951-4506 USA
Web site: http://www.three-leggedcat.com.

NASW Pr. *Imprint of* **National Assn. of Social Workers/NASW Pr.**

Natavi Guides, *(978-0-9719392; 978-1-932204)* 44 Pine St., West Newton, MA 02465-1425 USA
E-mail: info@nataviguides.com
Web site: http://www.nataviguides.com.

Nathan, Fernand (FRA) *(978-2-09) Dist. by* **Distribks Inc.**

Nathaniel Max Rock, *(978-0-9749392; 978-1-59980)* 1418 S. Orange Ave., Monterey Park, CA 91755 USA
Web site: http://rockmath.com.

†**National Academies Pr.,** *(978-0-309)* Orders Addr.: 8700 Spectrum Dr., Landover, MD 20785 USA; Edit Addr.: 500 Fifth St., NW Lockbox 285, Washington, DC 20001 USA (SAN 202-8891) Tel 202-334-3313; Fax: 202-334-2451; Toll Free: 888-624-7654; *Imprints:* Joseph Henry Press (Joseph Henry Pr)
E-mail: zjones@nas.edu
Web site: http://www.nap.edu
Dist(s): **Ebsco Publishing**
MyiLibrary
ebrary, Inc.; *CIP.*

National Academy Press *See* **National Academies Pr.**

†**National Archives & Records Administration,** *(978-0-911333; 978-1-880875)* Orders Addr.: 700 Pennsylvania Ave., NW, Washington, DC 20408 USA (SAN 210-363X) Tel 301-713-6800; Fax: 310-713-6169; Toll Free: 800-234-8861
E-mail: katherine.coram@nara.gov
Web site: http://www.nara.gov
Dist(s): **United States Government Printing Office**; *CIP.*

National Assn. for Humane & Environmental Education, *(978-0-941246)* Div. of Humane Society of the U.S., P.O. Box 362, East Haddam, CT 06423 USA (SAN 285-0680) Tel 860-434-8666; Fax: 860-434-9579; *Imprints:* Humane Society Press (Humane Soc Pr)
E-mail: nahee@nahee.org
Web site: http://www.nahee.org.

National Assn. for Visually Handicapped, *(978-0-89064)* 3201 Balboa St., San Francisco, CA 94121 USA (SAN 202-0971) Tel 415-221-3201; Fax: 415-221-8754; 111 E. 59th St. # 6, New York, NY 10022-1202 (SAN 669-1870)
E-mail: staff@navh.org
Web site: http://www.navh.org.

†**National Assn. of Social Workers/NASW Pr.,** *(978-0-87101)* Orders Addr.: P.O. Box 431, Annapolis Junction, MD 20701 USA Fax: 301-206-7989; Toll Free: 800-227-3590; Edit Addr.: 750 First St., NE, Suite 700, Washington, DC 20002-4241 USA (SAN 202-893X) Tel 202-408-8600; Fax: 202-336-8312; Toll Free: 800-638-8799; *Imprints:* N A S W Press (NASW Pr)
E-mail: press@naswdc.org
Web site: http://www.naswpress.org; *CIP.*

National Assn. of Speed & Explosion, *(978-0-938074)* P.O. Box 1784, Kill Devil Hills, NC 27948 USA (SAN 215-6148) Tel 252-441-1185; Fax: 252-449-4125
E-mail: naseinc@aol.com.

National Bk. Network, Div. of Rowman & Littlefield Pubs., Inc., Orders Addr.: 15200 NBN Way, Blue Ridge Summit, PA 17214 USA (SAN 630-0065) Tel 717-794-3800; Fax: 717-794-3828; Toll Free Fax: 800-338-4550 (Customer Service); Toll Free: 800-462-6420 (Customer Service); a/o Les Petriw, 67 Mowat Ave., Suite 241, Toronto, ON M6P 3K3 Tel 416-534-1660; Fax: 416-534-3699
E-mail: custserv@nbnbooks.com
Web site: http://www.nbnbooks.com.

National Braille Pr., *(978-0-939173)* Orders Addr.: 88 St. Stephen St., Boston, MA 02115 USA (SAN 273-0952) Tel 617-266-6160; Fax: 617-437-0456; Toll Free: 800-548-7323
E-mail: orders@nbp.org
Web site: http://www.nbp.org.

National Ctr. For Youth Issues, *(978-1-931636; 978-1-937870)* Orders Addr.: P.O. Box 22185, Chattanooga, TN 37422-2185 USA Tel 423-899-5714; Fax: 423-899-4547; Toll Free: 800-477-8277; Edit Addr.: 6101 Preservation Dr., Chattanooga, TN 37416 USA (SAN 990-1590)
E-mail: info@ncyi.org
Web site: http://www.ncyi.org
Dist(s): **Follett School Solutions**
MAR*CO Products, Inc.
Youthlight, Inc.

National Children's Book Project *See* **Public Square Bks.**

National Conference of State Legislatures, *(978-0-941336; 978-1-55516; 978-1-58024)* 7700 E. First Pl., Denver, CO 80230-7143 USA (SAN 225-1000) Tel 303-364-7700; Fax: 303-364-7800
E-mail: rita.morris@ncsl.org
Web site: http://www.ncsl.org.

†**National Council of Teachers of English,** *(978-0-8141)* Orders Addr.: 1111 W. Kenyon Rd., Urbana, IL 61801-1096 USA (SAN 202-9049) Tel 217-328-3870 Main Switchboard; Fax: 217-328-0977 Editorial Fax; 217-328-9645 Customer Service Fax; Toll Free: 800-369-6283 Main Switchboard Toll Free Tel; 877-369-6283 Customer Service Toll Free Tel
E-mail: kaustin@ncte.org; orders@ncte.org
Web site: http://www.ncte.org
Dist(s): **APG Sales & Distribution Services**; *CIP.*

†**National Council of Teachers of Mathematics,** *(978-0-87353; 978-1-68054)* 1906 Association Dr., Reston, VA 20191-1502 USA (SAN 202-9057) Tel 703-620-9840; Fax: 703-476-2970; 703-715-9536; Toll Free Fax: 800-220-8483; Toll Free: 800-235-7566 (orders only)
E-mail: info@nctm.org; cnoddin@nctm.org
Web site: http://www.nctm.org; *CIP.*

National Crime Prevention Council, *(978-0-934513; 978-1-929888; 978-1-59686)* 2345 Crystal Dr. Suite 500, Arlington, VA 22202 USA (SAN 693-8574) Tel 202-466-6272; Fax: 202-296-1356; Toll Free: 800-627-2911 (orders only) Do not confuse with The National Crime Prevention Assn., also in Washington, D.C.
E-mail: kirby@ncpc.org; demenno@ncpc.org
Web site: http://www.ncpc.org; http://www.mcgruff.org.

National Dance Education Organization, *(978-1-930798)* 8609 2nd Ave. Ste. 203B, Silver Spring, MD 20910-6359 USA
E-mail: ndeo@erols.com
Web site: http://www.ndeo.org
Dist(s): **Chicago Distribution Ctr.**

National Deacons Association *See* **Tommy Bks. Pubng.**

†**National Education Assn.,** *(978-0-8106)* Orders Addr.: P.O. Box 404846, Atlanta, GA 30384-4846 USA (SAN 203-7262) Tel 202-822-7208; Fax: 202-822-7377; Toll Free: 800-229-4200; Edit Addr.: 1201 16th St., NW. Suite 514, Washington, DC 20036 USA Tel 770-280-4080; Fax: 770-280-4134
E-mail: nea-orders@pbd.com
Web site: http://www.nea.org/books; *CIP.*

National Educational Systems, Inc., *(978-1-893493)* P.O. Box 691450, San Antonio, TX 78269-1450 USA Toll Free: 800-442-2604.

National Film Network LLC, *(978-0-8026)* Orders Addr.: 4501 Forbes Blvd., Lanham, MD 20706 USA (SAN 630-1878) Tel 301-459-8020 ext 2066
E-mail: info@nationalfilmnetwork.com
Web site: http://www.nationalfilmnetwork.com.

National Foundation for Teaching Entrepreneurship, The, *(978-1-890859)* Orders Addr.: 120 Wall St., 29th Flr., New York, NY 10005 USA Tel 212-232-3333; Fax: 212-232-2244; Toll Free: 800-367-6383
E-mail: nfte@nfte.com
Web site: http://www.nfte.com.

National Gallery of Australia (AUS) *(978-0-646-30472-4) Dist. by* **U of Wash Pr.**

National Gallery of Victoria (AUS) *(978-1-925432) Dist. by* **Antique Collect.**

National Gallery of Victoria (AUS) *(978-1-925432) Dist. by* **Natl Bk Netwk.**

National Geographic *Imprint of* **National Geographic Society**

National Geographic Children's Bks. *Imprint of* **National Geographic Society**

National Geographic School Publishing, Inc., *(978-0-7362; 978-0-917837; 978-1-56334)* Div. of CENGAGE Learning, Orders Addr.: 10650 Toebben Dr., Independence, KY 41051 USA Tel 859-282-5700; Toll Free Fax: 800-487-8488; Toll Free: 800-354-9706; 888-915-3276; Edit Addr.: 1 Lower Ragsdale Dr., Bldg. 1, Suite 200, Monterey, CA 93940 USA
Web site: http://www.hampton-brown.com
Dist(s): **CENGAGE Learning.**

†**National Geographic Society,** *(978-0-7922; 978-0-87044; 978-1-4262; 978-1-4263)* 1145 17th St., NW, Washington, DC 20036 USA (SAN 202-8956) Tel 202-857-7000; Fax: 301-921-1575; Toll Free: 800-647-5463; 800-548-9797 (TTD users only); *Imprints:* National Geographic Children's Books (NGCB); National Geographic (NatiGeo)
E-mail: askngs@nationalgeographic.com
Web site: http://nationalgeographic.com
Dist(s): **Benchmark LLC**
Follett Media Distribution
Follett School Solutions
Lectorum Pubns., Inc.
MyiLibrary
Penguin Random Hse. LLC
Rand McNally
Random Hse., Inc.; *CIP.*

National Honor Roll, LLC, *(978-0-9714201; 978-0-9721652; 978-0-9729406; 978-1-932654)* 777 Sunrise Hwy. Ste. 300, Lynbrook, NY 11563-2950 USA Toll Free: 800-416-2185
Web site: http://www.nationalhonorroll.org.

National Horseman Publishing Inc., The, *(978-0-9762854)* 16101 N. 82nd St., Suite 10, Scottsdale, AZ 85260-1830 USA Tel 480-922-5202
Web site: http://www.tnh1865.com.

National Institute for Trauma & Loss in Children (TLC), The, *(978-1-931310)* Div. of Starr Global Learning Network, 900 Cook Rd., Grosse Pointe Woods, MI 48236 USA Tel 313-885-0390; Fax: 313-885-1861; Toll Free: 877-306-5256
E-mail: info@starr.org
Web site: http://www.starr.org/tlc.

National Institute on Alcohol Abuse & Alcoholism *Imprint of* **United States Government Printing Office**

National Marfan Foundation, The, *(978-0-918335)* 22 Manhasset Ave., Prt Washington, NY 11050-2023 USA (SAN 657-2855) Toll Free: 800-862-7326
E-mail: staff@marfan.org
Web site: http://www.marfan.org.

National Marine Fisheries Service *Imprint of* **United States Government Printing Office**

National Maritime Museum (GBR) *(978-0-905555; 978-0-948065; 978-0-9501764; 978-1-906367) Dist. by* **IPG Chicago.**

National Maritime Museum (GBR) *(978-0-905555; 978-0-948065; 978-0-9501764; 978-1-906367) Dist. by* **Casemate Pubs.**

National Museum of Australia (AUS) *(978-1-876944; 978-1-921953) Dist. by* **IPG Chicago.**

National Network of Digital Schls., *(978-0-9816745; 978-1-935193; 978-1-936318; 978-1-938165; 978-1-943303; 978-1-944075; 978-1-68379)* 294 Massachusetts Ave., Rochester, PA 15074 USA Toll Free: 866-990-6637
Web site: http://www.nndsonline.org; linconlearningsolutions.org.

†**National Park Service Div. of Pubns.,** *(978-0-912627)* Harpers Ferry Ctr., Harpers Ferry, WV 25425 USA (SAN 282-7980) Tel 304-535-6018; Fax: 304-535-6144
Dist(s): **United States Government Printing Office**; *CIP.*

National Professional Resources, Inc., *(978-1-887943; 978-1-934032; 978-0-9819919; 978-1-935609; 978-1-938539)* 1455 Rail Head Blvd. Suite 6, Naples, FL 34110 USA Tel 800-453-7461; Fax: 239-631-2259; Toll Free: 800-453-7461; *Imprints:* Dude Publishing (Dude Pubng)
E-mail: lhanson@NPRinc.com; lkehoe@nprinc.com
Web site: http://www.NPRinc.com
Dist(s): **Baum & Beaulieu Assocs.**
CEC: Council for Exceptional Children
Complete Book & Media Supply
Follett School Solutions
Master Teacher
National School Products
Park Pl.
QEP, Inc. Professional Bks.

National Reading Styles Institute, Inc., *(978-0-929192; 978-1-883186; 978-1-933533)* Orders Addr.: P.O. Box 737, Syosset, NY 11791 USA (SAN 248-8191) Tel 516-921-5500; Fax: 516-921-5591; Toll Free: 800-331-3117; Edit Addr.: 179 Lafayette Dr., Syosset, NY 11791 USA (SAN 248-8205)
E-mail: readingstyle@nrsi.com
Web site: http://www.literacy.org; http://www.nrsi.com.

National Rehabilitation Services *See* **Northern Speech Services**

National Review, Inc., *(978-0-9627841; 978-0-9758998; 978-0-9847650)* 215 Lexington Ave., 4th Flr., New York, NY 10016 USA (SAN 226-1685) Tel 212-679-7330; Fax: 212-696-0340
E-mail: jfowler@nationalreview.com
Web site: http://www.nationalreview.com
Dist(s): **Chicago Distribution Ctr.**

National Science Resources Center (NSRC) *See* **Smithsonian Science Education Ctr. (SSEC)**

†**National Science Teachers Assn.,** *(978-0-87355; 978-1-933531; 978-1-935155; 978-1-936137; 978-1-936959; 978-1-938946; 978-1-941316; 978-1-68140)* 1840 Wilson Blvd., Arlington, VA 22201 USA (SAN 203-7173) 703-243-7177; Toll Free Fax: 888-433-0526 (orders); Toll Free: 800-277-5300 (orders); 800-722-6782
E-mail: pubsales@nsta.org; dyudkin@nsta.org
Web site: http://www.nsta.org/store
Dist(s): **Ebsco Publishing**
Independent Pubs. Group
MyiLibrary
ebrary, Inc.; *CIP.*

National Self-Esteem Resources & Development Ctr., *(978-0-9632276)* 851 Irwin St., Suite 205, San Rafael, CA 94901-3343 USA Tel 415-457-4411; Fax: 415-457-0356.

National Society of Professional Engineers, *(978-0-915409)* 1420 King St., Alexandria, VA 22314-2715 USA (SAN 225-168X) Tel 703-684-2800; Fax: 703-836-4875; Toll Free: 888-285-6773
E-mail: customer.service@nspe.org
Web site: http://www.nspe.org.

National Textbook Co. *Imprint of* **McGraw-Hill/Contemporary**

National Training Network, Inc., *(978-1-57290)* Orders Addr.: P.O. Box 36, Summerfield, NC 27358 USA
Web site: http://www.algebraicthinking.com.

National Trust, Aylesbury (GBR) *(978-0-7078; 978-0-900562) Dist. by* **IPG Chicago.**

National Writers Pr., The, *(978-0-88100)* Div. of National Writers Assn., 17011 Lincoln Ave., No. 421, Parker, CO 80134 USA (SAN 240-320X) Tel 720-851-1944; Fax: 303-841-2607
E-mail: natlwritersassn@hotmail.com
Web site: http://www.nationalwriters.com.

National Writing Institute, *(978-1-888344)* PMB 248, 624 W. University Dr., Denton, TX 76201-1889 USA Tel 940-382-0044; Fax: 940-383-4414; Toll Free Fax: 888-663-7855; Toll Free: 800-688-5375
E-mail: info@writingstrands.com
Web site: http://www.writingstrands.com.

Nations Hope, Inc., The, *(978-0-9761415)* P.O. Box 691446, Orlando, FL 32869-1446 USA
Web site: http://www.nationshope.org.

Native American Pubns., *(978-0-9745867)* Orders Addr.: P.O. Box 9, Dulac, LA 70353-0009 USA Tel 985-223-3857; Edit Addr.: 443 Ashland Dr., Houma, LA 70363-7283 USA
E-mail: ccbilliot@aol.com.

Native Nature *See* **Niche Publishing & Marketing**

Native Sun Pr., *(978-0-9746848)* Orders Addr.: P.O. Box 1139, Summerland, CA 93067 USA (SAN 255-6839) Tel 805-969-2234 (phone/fax); Edit Addr.: 2240 Banner Ave., Summerland, CA 93067 USA.

Native Voices *Imprint of* **Book Publishing Co.**

Natl Bk. Network,
Dist(s): **Perfection Learning Corp.**

NaTroy Publishing Co., *(978-0-9755246)* Orders Addr.: P.O. Box 93442, Cleveland, OH 44101 USA Tel 216-376-4810.

Natural Genius Bks., *(978-0-9765070)* P.O. Box 191088, Sacramento, CA 95819 USA Toll Free: 800-917-9321
E-mail: mjsee3@earthlink.net
Web site: http://www.naturalgeniusbooks.com.

Natural History Museum Pubns. (GBR) *(978-0-565) Dist. by* **IPG Chicago.**

Natural Learning Concepts, Inc., *(978-0-9778866; 978-0-9800300)* 21 Gallatin Dr., Suite B, Dix Hills, NY 11746 USA Tel 631-858-0188 (phone/fax); Toll Free: 800-823-3430
E-mail: sales@nlconcepts.com
Web site: http://www.nlconcepts.com.

Natural Math *See* **Delta Stream Media**

Naturally You Can Sing, *(978-0-9708397)* 3026 South St., East Troy, WI 53120 USA (SAN 255-4712)
E-mail: mary@flowformsamerica.com
Web site: http://www.maturallyyoucansing.com
Dist(s): **SteinerBooks, Inc.**

Nature Works Press, *(978-0-915965)* Orders Addr.: P.O. Box 469, Talent, OR 97540 USA (SAN 293-9738) Tel 541-535-3189; Toll Free Fax: 866-749-3077
E-mail: irene@natureworkspress.com; natureworks1@gmail.com
Web site: http://www.natureworkspress.com
Dist(s): **Bks. West**
Partners/West Book Distributors.

Naturegraph Pubs., Inc., *(978-0-87961; 978-0-911010)* Box 1047, 3543 Indian Creek Rd., Happy Camp, CA 96039

USA (SAN 202-8999) Tel 530-493-5353; Fax: 530-493-5240; Toll Free: 800-390-5353
E-mail: nature@sisqtel.net
Web site: http://www.naturegraph.com
Dist(s): **American West Bks.**
Gem Guides Bk. Co.
New Leaf Distributing Co., Inc.
Sunbelt Pubns., Inc.

NaturEncyclopedia *Imprint of* **Stemmer Hse. Pubs.**

Natures Beauty Publishing, *(978-0-9754701)* P.O. Box 107, Oxford, MI 48371-0107 USA Tel 248-236-9314; Fax: 248-236-9315
E-mail: Ron@Naturesbeautyphotography.com
Web site: http://www.naturesbeautyphotography.com.

Nature's Hopes & Heroes, *(978-0-9822942)* 265 Kings Hwy., Boulder Creek, CA 95006 USA Tel 831-423-8973
E-mail: jimcruz@cruzers.com
Dist(s): **Bookmasters Distribution.**

Nature's Pr., *(978-0-9741883)* Orders Addr.: P.O. Box 371, Mercer, WI 54547 USA
Web site: http://www.naturespressbooks.com.

Naumann, Jennifer, *(978-0-9883902)* 2777 420th Ave, Elmore, MN 56027 USA Tel 507-943-3673
E-mail: jen.naumann@yahoo.com.

†**Naval Institute Pr.**, *(978-0-87021; 978-1-55750; 978-1-59114; 978-1-61251; 978-1-68247; 978-1-68269)* Orders Addr.: 291 Wood Rd, Annapolis, MD 21402-5034 USA (SAN 662-0930) Tel 410-268-6110; Fax: 410-295-1084; Toll Free: 800-233-8764; Edit Addr.: 291 Wood Rd., Beach Hall, Annapolis, MD 21402-5034 USA (SAN 202-9006)
E-mail: tskord@usni.org; books@usni.org
Web site: http://www.usni.org
Dist(s): **Fujii Assocs.**
MyiLibrary
Publishers Group West (PGW); *CIP.*

NavPress Publishing Group, *(978-0-89109; 978-1-57683; 978-1-60006; 978-1-61521; 978-1-61747; 978-1-61291; 978-1-63146; 978-1-64158)* 3820 N. 30th St., Colorado Springs, CO 80904 USA Fax: 719-260-7223; Toll Free Fax: 800-343-3902; Toll Free: 800-366-7788; *Imprints*: Th1nk Books (Th1nk Bks)
Web site: http://www.navpress.com
Dist(s): **Follett School Solutions**
Tyndale Hse. Pubs.

Nay Vogel Photography & Design, *(978-0-692-80195-6; 978-0-692-81723-0)*.

Naynay Bks *See* **Naynay Bks.**

Naynay Bks., *(978-0-9769589)* 122 Arbor Rd., NW, Minerva, OH 44657 USA
E-mail: naynaybooks@aol.com
Web site: http://www.naynaybooks.com.

Naypree Enterprises, LLC, *(978-0-9786565)* P.O. Box 31602, Aurora, CO 80041 USA (SAN 851-237X) Tel 303-856-3354
E-mail: dana@naypree-enterprises.com
Web site: http://www.naypree-enterprises.com.

Nazarene Publishing Hse., *(978-0-8341)* Orders Addr.: 2923 Troost Ave., Kansas City, MO 64109 USA (SAN 253-0902); Edit Addr.: P.O. Box 419527, Kansas City, MO 64141 USA (SAN 202-9022) Tel 816-931-1900; Fax: 816-531-0923; Toll Free Fax: 800-849-9827; Toll Free: 800-877-0700
E-mail: heather@nph.com
Web site: http://www.bhillkc.com; http://www.nph.com
Dist(s): **LifeWay Christian Resources**
Lorenz Corp., The
Spring Arbor Distributors, Inc.

NBM Publishing Co., *(978-0-918348; 978-1-56163; 978-1-68112)* Orders Addr.: 40 Exchange Pl., Suite 1308, New York, NY 10005 USA (SAN 210-0835) Tel 212-643-5407; Fax: 212-643-1545; Toll Free: 800-886-1223; Edit Addr.: 160 Broadway, Suite. 700, E. Wing, New York, NY 10038 USA Tel 646-559-4681; Fax: 212-643-1545; Toll Free: 800-886-1223; *Imprints*: Comics Lit (Comics Lit); Amerotica (Amerotica)
E-mail: catalog@nbmpublishing.com
Web site: http://www.nbmpub.com
Dist(s): **Independent Pubs. Group**
MyiLibrary.

N'Deeo Beauty *See* **N'Deeo, LLC**

N'Deeo, LLC, *(978-0-9724203; 978-0-9753811)* Orders Addr.: P.O. Box 460574, Aurora, CO 80046 USA Tel 770-896-6606; P.O. Box 1425, Mableton, GA 30126; Edit Addr.: 20511 E. Union Ave., Aurora, CO 80015 USA
E-mail: cservice@ndeeo.com
Web site: http://www.ndeeo.com.

Ndegwa, Catherine W., *(978-0-9742688)* Orders Addr.: P.O. Box 220411, Saint Louis, MO 63122-0411 USA; Edit Addr.: 119 Oakside Ln., Saint Louis, MO 63122-0411 USA
E-mail: catherine@varietystl.com.

NdueCzon Publishing Group, *(978-0-9755679)* P.O. Box 341825, Tampa, FL 33694 USA Tel 813-269-9351; Fax: 813-968-1941
E-mail: ndueczon@aol.com
Dist(s): **Culture Plus Bk. Distributors.**

Neal, Ann-Marie F, *(978-0-9747734; 978-0-9862096)* 903 Dale St., Edgewater, MD 21037 USA Tel 401-662-2411
E-mail: sunflower683@reagan.com
Web site: http://www.clarencethefrog.com.

Neal Morgan Publishing, *(978-0-9786117)* 51 Arrowgate Dr., Randolph, NJ 07869 USA Tel 973-598-9601; Fax: 973-927-8722
E-mail: Daleb6@aol.com.

†**Neal-Schuman Pubs., Inc.**, *(978-0-918212; 978-1-55570)* Div. of American Library Assn., 100 William St., Suite 2004, New York, NY 10038 USA (SAN 210-2455) Tel 212-925-8650; Fax: 212-219-8916; Toll Free Fax: 800-584-2414
E-mail: info@neal-schuman.com
Web site: http://www.neal-schuman.com
Dist(s): **ebrary, Inc.**; *CIP.*

Nearaway Far Pubns., *(978-0-9969878)* 22330 Victory Blvd., Woodland Hills, CA 91367 USA Tel 805-300-0738
E-mail: thehopefulprince@gmail.com
Web site: thehopefulprince.com.

Nebador Archives, *(978-1-936253)* P.O. Box 592, Kelso, WA 98626 USA
E-mail: jzc23@nebador.com
Web site: http://www.nebador.com.

Nebbadoon Pr., *(978-1-891331)* Div. of Nebbadoon, Inc., Orders Addr.: 371 Hubbard St., Glastonbury, CT 06033 USA Toll Free: 800-500-9086
E-mail: george@4554.com
Web site: http://www.nebbadoonpress.com.

Nebe, Charles, *(978-0-9773091)* Orders Addr.: P.O. Box 631143, Irving, TX 75063-1143 USA
Web site: http://www.boonefiles.com.

Nebraska Wealth.com, *(978-0-9746206)* 1803 Stagecoach Rd., Grand Island, NE 68801 USA
Web site: http://www.nebraskawealth.com.

Necessary Evil Pr., *(978-0-9753635)* P.O. Box 178, Escanaba, MI 49829 USA
E-mail: info@necessaryevilpress.com
Web site: http://www.necessaryevilpress.com.

Nectar Pubns., *(978-0-9859986)* P.O. Box 6552, Savannah, GA 31404 USA Tel 912-631-9214
E-mail: contact@nectarpublications.com
Web site: www.nectarpublications.com.

Ned's Head Productions, *(978-1-887206)* 307 State St., Apt. B3, Johnstown, PA 15905 USA (SAN 253-8059) Tel 814-255-6646 (phone/fax)
E-mail: drron@charter.net
Web site: http://nedsheadbooks.com
Dist(s): **APG Sales & Distribution Services.**

Need To Know Publishing, *(978-1-940705)* 11019 N. 73rd St., Scottsdale, AZ 85260 USA Tel 888-377-3158; Fax: 888-377-3158
E-mail: brad@needtoknowpublishing.com
Dist(s): **MyiLibrary**
Publishers Group West (PGW).

Neely, Judy, *(978-1-893968)* 54505 NW Scofield Rd., Buxton, OR 97109 USA Tel 503-324-8222; Fax: 503-324-8252
E-mail: jneely@neelyranch.com
Web site: http://www.neelyranch.com.

Neema's Children Literature Assn., Inc., *(978-0-9740653)* Orders Addr.: P.O. Box 440073, Chicago, IL 60644-1937 USA Tel 773-378-0607; Fax: 773-378-0042; Edit Addr.: 5345 W. Ferdinand St., Chicago, IL 60644-1937 USA Tel 773-575-4639
E-mail: nclapub@gmail.com.

Nefu Bks. *Imprint of* **Africana Homestead Legacy Pubs., Inc.**

Negro Publishing LLC *Imprint of* **Negro Publishing, LLC**

Negro Publishing, LLC, *(978-0-9763583)* Orders Addr.: P.O. Box 78, Mableton, GA 30126 USA Tel 770-265-0822; Fax: 770-948-2460; *Imprints*: Negro Publishing LLC (Negro Pub)
E-mail: supadave@negropublishing.com; dhhorton_2000@yahoo.com
Web site: http://www.negropublishing.com
Dist(s): **Culture Plus Bk. Distributors.**

NEHA Training LLC, *(978-0-944111)* 720 S. Colorado Blvd. Ste. 1000N, Denver, CO 80246-1926 USA
E-mail: support@nehatraining.com
Web site: http://www.nehatraining.com.

Neighborhood Pubs., *(978-0-615-75249-5)* 3317 Manor Rd., Austin, TX 78723 USA Tel 512-291-2314
E-mail: johnatpbp@yahoo.com.

Nelsbok Publishing, *(978-0-9763072)* 3312 Cedar Ave S., Minneapolis, MN 55407-2335 USA
Web site: http://www.nelsbok.com.

Nelsen, Margie, *(978-0-615-22008-6; 978-0-615-25480-7)* 804 Spruce Pl., Saint Peter, MN 56082 USA
E-mail: margienelsen@mchsi.com
Web site: http://www.snugglebooks.com.

Nelson Publishing & Marketing, *(978-1-933916; 978-0-9785075; 978-1-938326)* 366 Welch Rd., Northville, MI 48167-1160 USA Tel 248-735-0418; *Imprints*: Ferne Press (Ferne Press)
E-mail: marian@nelsonpublishingandmarketing.com; kris@nelsonpublishingandmarketing.com
Web site: http://nelsonpublishingandmarketing.com
Dist(s): **Partners Pubs. Group, Inc.**

Nelson Publishing, LLC, *(978-0-9794171)* 15480 Annapolis Road, Suite No. 202-216, Bowie, MD 20715 USA; *Imprints*: Adventures of Hillary, The (AdventuresHillary)
E-mail: info@nelson-publishing.com
Web site: http://www.nelson-publishing.com.

Nelson, R. E. & Assoc., *(978-0-9749636)* 1535 SW Plass Ave., Topeka, KS 66604 USA Tel 785-235-3041
Web site: http://www.renelson.com.

Nelson, Roy *See* **Nelson, R. E. & Assoc.**

†**Nelson, Thomas Inc.**, *(978-0-529; 978-0-7852; 978-0-8407; 978-0-8499; 978-0-86605; 978-0-88113; 978-0-89840; 978-0-89922; 978-0-918956; 978-0-7180; 978-1-4002; 978-1-4003; 978-1-4016; 978-1-59145; 978-1-4041; 978-1-59554; 978-1-59555; 978-1-4185; 978-1-59951; 978-1-4261; 978-1-60255; 978-1-4845; 978-1-5000; 978-1-5314) Div. of HarperCollins Christian Publishing, Orders Addr.: P.O. Box 141000, Nashville, TN 37214-1000 USA (SAN 209-3820) Fax: 615-902-1866; Toll Free: 800-251-4000; Edit Addr.: 501 Nelson Pl., Nashville, TN 37214 USA*
Web site: http://www.harpercollinschristian.com
Dist(s): **Brilliance Publishing, Inc.**
Christian Bk. Distributors
CreateSpace Independent Publishing Platform
Follett School Solutions
Twentieth Century Christian Bks.; *CIP.*

Nelson Thornes Ltd. (GBR) *(978-0-17; 978-0-7487; 978-0-85950; 978-1-871402; 978-1-873732; 978-1-4085)* *Dist. by* **OUP.**

Nelson Thornes Ltd. (GBR) *(978-0-17; 978-0-7487; 978-0-85950; 978-1-871402; 978-1-873732; 978-1-4085)* *Dist. by* **Trans-Atl Phila.**

NEMESIS Enterprises, L.P., *(978-0-9713230)* Orders Addr.: 1048 S. Wardsboro Rd., Wardsboro, VT 05355 USA
E-mail: nemesis@myfairpoint.net
Web site: http://www.gophergo.com.

Nemo Publishing, LLC, *(978-0-9817132)* 86 Newbury St., Portland, ME 04101 USA (SAN 856-3381) Tel 207-761-0807; Fax: 207-775-5567
E-mail: tami@maine.rr.com
Web site: http://www.captneli.com
Dist(s): **Diamond Comic Distributors, Inc.**
Diamond Bk. Distributors.

Nemsi Bks., *(978-0-9718164; 978-0-9766400; 978-0-9794855; 978-0-9815313; 978-0-9821427; 978-0-9825011)* Div. of Morphtek.com, Inc., P.O. Box 191, Pierpont, SD 57468-0191 USA Fax: 605-325-3393
E-mail: psiccusa@dailypost.com
Web site: http://www.nemsi-books.net.

Neo-Tech Publishing Co., *(978-0-911752)* P.O. Box PO Box 531330, Henderson, NV 89053-1330 USA (SAN 202-3156)
E-mail: rapper@neo-tech.com
Web site: http://www.neo-tech.com; http://www.neo-tech.com/front/cservice.html.

Nerdel Co., The, *(978-0-9823357)* 1000 West McNab Road, Pompano Beach, FL 33069 USA (SAN 858-7205)
Web site: http://www.nerdel.com.

NERO International Holding Co., Inc., *(978-0-9700563)* Orders Addr.: P.O. Box 2763 nc highway 731 west, MOUNT GILEAD, NC 27306 USA Tel 914-628-9497; Edit Addr.: 2763 NC Hwy. 731 W., MOUNT GILEAD, NC 27306 USA
E-mail: jvalenti@nerolarp.com
Web site: http://www.nerolarp.com; http://nerolarponline.com.

NESFA Pr. *Imprint of* **New England Science Fiction Assn., Inc.**

Neshee Pubn., *(978-0-9747017; 978-0-9770907; 978-0-9785794; 978-0-9823053)* P.O. Box 48028, Philadelphia, PA 19144 USA
E-mail: info@nesheepublicaiton.com
Web site: http://www.nesheepublication.com.

Neshui Publishing, Inc., *(978-0-9652528; 978-1-931190)* 6310 Rosebury Ave. #2, Saint Louis, MO 63105 USA
E-mail: info@neshuipress.com
Web site: http://www.neshuipress.com
Dist(s): **Raven West Coast Distribution.**

NetClinger, *(978-0-9760308)* P.O. Box 38144, Houston, TX 77238-8144 USA
Web site: http://www.netclinger.com.

Netcomics, *(978-1-60009)* P.O. Box 16484, Jersey City, NJ 07306 USA
Dist(s): **Diamond Comic Distributors, Inc.**
Diamond Bk. Distributors.

NetNia Publishing Co., *(978-1-884163)* 9218 Rockbrook Dr., Dallas, TX 75220 USA; *Imprints*: Juba Books (Juba Bks)
E-mail: jeffery.bradley@outlook.com
Web site: http://www.howtogrowdreadlocks.com; http://www.netnia.com; http://www.africanamericanchildrenplays.com
Dist(s): **Lightning Source, Inc.**

NETroplex Books *See* **Yankee Cowboy**

Network CPU Learning Technologies, *(978-1-932257)* 172 Fifth Ave., Suite 37, Brooklyn, NY 11217-3504 USA (SAN 254-9298)
E-mail: roxceyluv@yahoo.com.

NETWORK Inc., The, *(978-1-878234)* Div. of NETWORK, Inc., 136 Fenno Dr., Rowley, MA 01969-1004 USA Tel 978-948-7764; Fax: 978-948-7836; Toll Free: 800-877-5400
E-mail: info@thenetworkinc.org
Web site: http://www.thenetworkinc.org.

Networlding, *(978-0-9883471; 978-1-944027)* 130 N. Garland Ct. No. 3205, Chicago, IL 60602 USA Tel 312-560-0982; Fax: 312-560-0982
E-mail: melissa@networlding.com
Web site: www.networlding.com.

Neuburger Publishing, *(978-0-9762419)* Orders Addr.: P.O. Box 3928, Tualatin, OR 97062-3928 USA Tel 503-925-0400; Edit Addr.: 24386 SW Baker Rd., Sherwood, OR 97140 USA
Web site: http://www.takethefearoutofmath.com.

Neugebauer, Michael (Publishing) Limited (HKG) *(978-988-8240)* *Dist. by* **IPG Chicago.**

Neumann Pr. *Imprint of* **TAN Bks.**

Neurosculpting Institute, *(978-0-692-80006-5)*
Dist(s): **CreateSpace Independent Publishing Platform.**

Nevaeh Publishing, LLC, *(978-0-9787899; 978-0-9839187)* P.O. Box 962, Redan, GA 30074-0962 USA (SAN 851-6111) Tel 770-363-5669
E-mail: dwanabrams1@aol.com
Web site: http://www.dwanabrams.com; http://www.nevaehpublishing.com
Dist(s): **Smashwords.**

Never Quit Productions, Inc., *(978-0-615-26231-4)* 4832 Wind Hill Ct. W., Fort Worth, TX 76179 USA
Dist(s): **Lulu Pr., Inc.**

Never Stop Reading Never Stop Learning, *(978-0-9741750)* 3221 S. Indiana St., Lakewood, CO 80228 USA Tel 303-829-8699
E-mail: neverstopreading@aol.com
Web site: http://www.jdmcdoll.com.

Neverland Publishing Co., LLC, *(978-0-9826971; 978-0-9888290; 978-0-9903148; 978-0-9965595)* 24 NW 102 St., Miami Shores, FL 33150 USA (SAN 990-0187) Tel 786-521-0731
E-mail: editor@neverlandpublishing.com
Web site: http://www.neverlandpublishing.com.

Nevruz, Cori, *(978-0-692-89979-3; 978-0-692-92312-2)* 1121 Military Cutoff, Wilmington, NC 28405 USA Tel 919-610-8532
E-mail: corinevruz@gmail.com.

New Academia Publishing, LLC, *(978-0-9744934; 978-0-9767042; 978-0-9777908; 978-0-9787713; 978-0-9794488; 978-0-9800814; 978-0-9818654; 978-0-9823867; 978-0-9844062; 978-0-9828061; 978-0-615-43269-4; 978-0-9832451; 978-0-9836899; 978-0-9845832; 978-0-9855698; 978-0-9860216; 978-0-9886376; 978-0-9899169; 978-0-9915047; 978-0-9904471; 978-0-9906939; 978-0-9864353; 978-0-9966484; 978-0-9974962; 978-0-9981477; 978-0-9986433) 4401-A Connecticut Ave. NW No. 236, Washington, DC 20008 USA; Imprints*: Vellum (Vellum)
Web site: http://www.newacademia.com
Dist(s): **Lightning Source, Inc.**
eBookit.com.

New Age Dimensions, Incorporated *See* **Adrema Pr.**

New Age World Publishing, *(978-1-59405)* 4071 San Pablo Dam Rd. # 141, El Sobrante, CA 94803-2903 USA Toll Free Fax: 888-739-6129; Toll Free: 877-411-8744; *Imprints*: N2Print (N2Print)
E-mail: NAWP@comcast.net
Web site: http://www.nawpublishing.com.

New & Living Way Publishing Co., *(978-0-910003)* P.O. Box 830384, Tuskegee, AL 36083-0384 USA (SAN 241-2314) Tel 334-727-5372
E-mail: nlwpc@bellsouth.net; clgpgt@bellsouth.net
Web site: http://www.clgpgt.org/NLW/nlw1.html.

New & Living Way Publishing House *See* **New & Living Way Publishing Co.**

New Art & Vision, LLC, *(978-0-9742322)* 1360 E. 300 N., Layton, UT 84040 USA Tel 801-543-3383
E-mail: bnybo@elmojackson.com
Web site: http://www.elmojackson.com.

New Awareness Network, Inc., *(978-0-9652855; 978-0-9711198; 978-0-9768978; 978-0-9849285; 978-0-9894058; 978-0-9960986; 978-0-9975404)* 86 Dennis St., Manhasset, NY 11030 USA Tel 516-869-9108; 516-365-1547; Fax: 516-365-1624
E-mail: sumari@sethcenter.com
Web site: http://www.sethcenter.com.

New Baby Productions, *(978-0-9818530)* Orders Addr.: 4143 Tanglewood Ct., Bloomfield Township, MI 48301 USA (SAN 856-7298)
E-mail: eric@elementalfources.com
Web site: http://www.ElementalFources.com
Dist(s): **Haven Distributors**
Lightning Source, Inc.

New Birth Publishing, *(978-0-9755489)* 1900 Preston Rd., No. 267, PMB 264, Plano, TX 75093 USA
Web site: http://www.newbirthpublishing.com.

New Buds Publishing Hse. (CHN) *(978-7-5307)* *Dist. by* **Chinasprout.**

New Canaan Publishing Co. LLC, *(978-1-889658)* 2384 N. Hwy. 341, Rossville, GA 30741 USA Tel 423-285-8672
E-mail: djm@newcanaanpublishing.com
Web site: http://www.newcanaanpublishing.com
Dist(s): **Send The Light Distribution LLC.**

New Castle Publishing Co., *(978-0-9740195)* 512 Wadsworth Dr., Richmond, VA 23236 USA
E-mail: newcastlepubl@aol.com.

New Century Pr., *(978-1-890035)* Orders Addr.: 1055 Bay Blvd., Suite C, Chula Vista, CA 91911-1628 USA (SAN 859-3760) Tel 619-476-7400; Fax: 619-476-7474; Toll Free: 800-519-2465 (orders) Do not confuse with companies with the same or similar name in Bermuda Dunes CA, New York NY
E-mail: sales@newcenturypress.com
Web site: http://www.newcenturypress.com.

New Century Pr., *(978-0-9748013)* P.O. Box 73381, Richmond, VA 23235-8040 USA Tel 804-897-2824 Do not confuse with companies with the same or similar name in Bermuda Dunes CA, Chula Vista CA, New York NY
E-mail: newcenturypress@aol.com.

New Century Publishing, LLC, *(978-0-9768052; 978-0-9820729; 978-0-9822344; 978-0-9824711; 978-0-9841819; 978-0-9843666; 978-0-9844661)* 1040 E. 86th St., Suite 42A, Indianapolis, IN 46240 USA Tel 317-663-8741; Fax: 317-663-8745
E-mail: dwcaswell@newcentrypublishing.org
Web site: http://www.newcenturypublishing.org.

New City Community Pr., *(978-0-9712996; 978-0-9819560; 978-0-9840429; 978-0-9887635; 978-0-692-83625-5)* 7715 Crittenden St., #222, Philadelphia, PA 191182 USA Tel 315-443-1912 Do not confuse with New City Press in Hyde Park, NY
E-mail: sjparks@syr.edu
Web site: http://www.newcitypress.org
Dist(s): **Chicago Distribution Ctr.**
SPD-Small Pr. Distribution.

New City Press *See* **New City Press of the Focolare**

New City Press *See* **New City Community Pr.**

†**New City Press of the Focolare**, *(978-0-911782; 978-1-56548)* 202 Comforter Blvd., Hyde Park, NY 12538 USA (SAN 203-7335) Tel 845-229-0335; Fax: 845-229-0351; Toll Free: 800-462-5980 (orders only)
E-mail: info@newcitypress.com
Web site: http://www.newcitypress.com; *CIP.*

New Classics Pr., *(978-0-9755704)* 2400 Ridgecroft SE, Grand Rapids, MI 49546 USA.

New Concepts Publishing, *(978-1-891020; 978-1-58608; 978-1-60394)* 5202 Humphreys Rd., Lake Park, GA 31636 USA Tel 229-257-0367; Fax: 229-219-1097
E-mail: newconcepts@newconceptspublishing.com; service@newconceptspublishing.com
Web site: http://www.newconceptspublishing.com
Dist(s): **Smashwords.**

New Dawn Pr., Inc., *(978-0-9729607; 978-1-932705; 978-1-904910)* 244 S. Randall Rd., No. 90, Elgin, IL 60123 USA
E-mail: maildrop@newdawnpress.com
Web site: http://www.newdawnpress.com
Dist(s): **Independent Pubs. Group.**

New Dawn Publishing, *(978-0-9721948)* P.O. Box 11151, Portland, ME 04104 USA Tel 207-839-8809 Do not confuse with companies with the same or similar name in Elk Mills, MD, Dexter, NY
Web site: http://www.mynewdawn.com.

Publisher Name Index

New Day Pr., *(978-0-913678)* c/o Karamu Hse., 2355 E. 89th St., Cleveland, OH 44106 USA (SAN 279-2664) Tel 216-795-7070 ext 228; Fax: 216-795-7073 Do not confuse with New Day Press in Las Vegas, NV
E-mail: editor@newdaypress.com.

New Day Publishing, Inc., *(978-0-9789056; 978-0-9798247)* 26 Bluff Ridge Ct., Greensboro, NC 27455 USA Tel 336-545-1545; Fax: 336-545-1640; Toll Free: 866-763-2977 Do not confuse with companies with the same or similar name in Winston-Salem, NC, Phoenix, AZ, North Miami, FL
E-mail: ateich@newdaypublishing.net
Web site: http://www.newdaypublishing.net.

†New Directions Publishing Corp., *(978-0-8112)* 80 Eighth Ave., New York, NY 10011 USA (SAN 202-9081) Tel 212-255-0230; Fax: 212-255-0231; Toll Free: 800-233-4830
E-mail: nd@ndbooks.com
Web site: http://www.ndpublishing.com
Dist(s): **Continental Bk. Co., Inc.**
Norton, W. W. & Co., Inc.
Penguin Random Hse. LLC
SPD-Small Pr. Distribution; *CIP.*

New Eden Publishing, *(978-0-9882368; 978-0-692-32667-1; 978-0-9980950)* 50513 W Esch Trail, Maricopa, AZ 85139 USA Tel 480-217-0776
E-mail: anitasmall3@gmail.com
Dist(s): **Lulu Pr., Inc.**

New England Science Fiction Assn., Inc., *(978-0-915368; 978-1-886778; 978-1-61037)* P.O. Box 809, Framingham, MA 01701-0809 USA (SAN 223-8187) Tel 508-653-7397; Fax: 617-776-3243; *Imprints:* N E S F A Press (NESFA Pr)
E-mail: press@nesfa.org
Web site: http://www.nesfa.org/press/.

New Europe Bks., *(978-0-9825781; 978-0-9850623; 978-0-9900043; 978-0-9973169)* 54 Arnold St., Williamstown, MA 01267 USA Tel 208-779-9660
E-mail: paul@neweuropebooks.com; info@neweuropebooks.com
Web site: http://www.NewEuropeBooks.com; http://www.NewEuropeBooks.com
Dist(s): **MyiLibrary**
Penguin Random Hse. LLC
Random Hse., Inc.

New Family Pr., *(978-0-9742008)* 389 Belmont St., Suite 105, Oakland, CA 94610 USA Tel 510-866-3984
E-mail: newfamilypress@yahoo.com
Dist(s): **Book Wholesalers, Inc.**

New Forums Pr., *(978-0-913507; 978-1-58107)* Orders Addr.: P.O. Box 876, Stillwater, OK 74076 USA (SAN 285-8673) Tel 405-372-6158; Fax: 405-377-2237; Toll Free: 800-606-3766; Edit Addr.: 1018 S. Lewis, Stillwater, OK 74074 USA
E-mail: dougdollar@provalue.net; design@newforums.com
Web site: http://www.newforums.com
Dist(s): **BookBaby.**

New Global Publishing, *(978-0-9762292; 978-0-9770043; 978-0-9785609; 978-0-9791748; 978-0-9830940; 978-0-9896334)* Orders Addr.: 2310 SE. Bordeaux Ct., Port Saint Lucie, FL 34952 USA
Web site: http://www.newglobalpublishing.com.

New Growth Pr., *(978-0-9762308; 978-0-9770807; 978-0-9785567; 978-1-934885; 978-1-935273; 978-1-936768; 978-1-938267; 978-1-939946; 978-1-942572; 978-1-945270)* Orders Addr.: P.O. Box 4485, Greensboro, NC 27404 USA Tel 3363787775; Toll Free: 877-647-2233; Edit Addr.: 533 Woodland Dr., Greensboro, NC 27408 USA Tel 336-378-7775; Fax: 336-464-2722
Web site: http://www.newgrowthpress.com
Dist(s): **Cook, David C.**

New Harbinger Pubns., *(978-0-934986; 978-1-57224; 978-1-879237; 978-1-60882; 978-1-62625; 978-1-68403)* Orders Addr.: 5674 Shattuck Ave., Oakland, CA 94609 USA (SAN 205-0587) Tel 510-652-2002; 510-652-0215; Fax: 510-652-5472; Toll Free: 800-652-1613; *Imprints:* Impact Publishers (ImpactPubs); Instant Help Books (Instant Help Bks)
E-mail: customerservice@newharbinger.com
Web site: http://www.newharbinger.com
Dist(s): **MyiLibrary**
ebrary, Inc.

New Holland Pubs., Ltd. (GBR) *(978-1-85368; 978-1-85974; 978-1-84330; 978-1-84636; 978-1-84537; 978-1-84773; 978-1-78009)* *Dist. by* **Sterling.**

New Holland Pubs. Pty. Ltd. (AUS) *(978-1-86436; 978-1-875580; 978-1-876334; 978-1-877069; 978-1-74110; 978-1-921024; 978-1-921073; 978-1-921072; 978-1-921517; 978-1-921580; 978-1-921655; 978-1-74257; 978-1-74268; 978-1-921740; 978-1-921836; 978-0-7316-1991-7; 978-0-646-15496-1; -1-74337; 978-1-925546)* *Dist. by* **Tuttle Pubng.**

New Holland Pubs. Pty. Ltd. (AUS) *(978-1-86436; 978-1-875580; 978-1-876334; 978-1-877069; 978-1-74110; 978-1-921024; 978-1-921073; 978-1-921072; 978-1-921517; 978-1-921580; 978-1-921655; 978-1-74257; 978-1-74268; 978-1-921740; 978-1-921836; 978-0-7316-1991-7; 978-0-646-15496-1; -1-74337; 978-1-925546)* *Dist. by* **Midpt Trade.**

New Hope *See* **Woman's Missionary Union**

New Hope Pubs., *(978-1-56309)* Orders Addr.: P.O. Box 830010, Birmingham, AL 35283 USA Tel 205-991-8100; Fax: 205-995-4825; Toll Free: 800-968-7301 Do not confuse with New Hope Publishers in New Hope, MN
E-mail: info@newhopepublishers.com
Web site: http://www.newhopepublishers.com
Dist(s): **B&H Publishing Group**
MyiLibrary
Send The Light Distribution LLC.

New Horizon Pr. Pubs., Inc., *(978-0-88282)* Orders Addr.: P.O. Box 669, Far Hills, NJ 07931 USA (SAN 677-119X) Tel 908-604-6311; Fax: 908-604-6330; Toll Free: 800-533-7978 (orders only); *Imprints:* Small Horizons (Small Horizons)
E-mail: nhp@newhorizonpressbooks.com
Web site: http://www.newhorizonpressbooks.com
Dist(s): **Kensington Publishing Corp.**
MyiLibrary
Penguin Publishing Group
Publishers Group West (PGW).

New Horizons Christian Ctr., *(978-0-9728532)* 16 Foxbriar Rd., Hilton Head, SC 29926 USA.

New Horizons Pr., *(978-0-9647933)* Orders Addr.: 26 Nottingham Dr., Cartersville, GA 30121 USA; Edit Addr.: 2815 New South Dr., Marietta, GA 30066 USA Do not confuse with companies with the same name in, Lake Mary, FL, Ferrisburgh, VT, Leesburg, VA, Orlando, FL.

New in Chess *Imprint of* **Continental Sales, Inc.**

New In Chess,Csi *Imprint of* **Continental Sales, Inc.**

New Internationalist Pubns., Ltd. (GBR) *(978-1-869847; 978-0-9540499; 978-1-904456; 978-1-906523; 978-1-78026)* *Dist. by* **Consort Bk Sales.**

New Island Books (IRL) *(978-1-85186; 978-1-874597; 978-1-902602; 978-1-904301; 978-1-905494)* *Dist. by* **Dufour.**

New Issues Poetry & Prose, Western Michigan Univ., *(978-0-932826; 978-1-930974; 978-1-936970)* 1903 West Michigan Ave. Western Michigan University, Kalamazoo, MI 49008 USA (SAN 276-6299) Tel 269-387-8185; Fax: 269-387-2562
E-mail: new-issues@wmich.edu
Web site: http://www.wmich.edu/newissues
Dist(s): **SPD-Small Pr. Distribution**
Univ. Pr. of New England.

New Kid Safety, *(978-0-9829371)* 4824 Smallwood Rd. Suite 214, Columbia, SC 29223 USA Tel 803-740-0861; Fax: 803-736-0223
E-mail: info@newkidsafety.com
Web site: http://www.newkidsafety.com.

New Leaf Bks. *Imprint of* **WigWam Publishing Co.**

New Leaf Education, Inc. *See* **New Leaf Educ., Inc.**

New Leaf Educ., Inc., *(978-0-9722452; 978-0-9764217; 978-1-933655)* Orders Addr.: P.O. Box 16230, Baltimore, MD 21210 USA Tel 410-467-7835; Fax: 410-951-0419; Edit Addr.: 2050 Rockrose Ave., Baltimore, MD 21211 USA
E-mail: contactus@newleafeducation.com
Web site: http://www.newleafeducation.com.

New Leaf Pr. *Imprint of* **New Leaf Pub. Group**

New Leaf Press, Incorporated *See* **New Leaf Pub. Group**

New Leaf Pub. Group, *(978-0-89221; 978-1-68344)* P.O. Box 726, Green Forest, AR 72638 USA (SAN 207-9518) Tel 870-438-5288; Fax: 870-438-5120 Toll Free: 800-643-9535; 800-999-3777; *Imprints:* New Leaf Press (NLP) Do not confuse with companies with the same or similar name in Los Angeles, CAStone Mountain, GA
E-mail: nlp@nlpg.com
Web site: http://www.nlpg.com; www.masterbooks.com
Dist(s): **MyiLibrary**
Spring Arbor Distributors, Inc.
ebrary, Inc.

New Learning Publishing, *(978-0-9793576)* 123 Wolcott Ave., Rochester, NY 14606 USA (SAN 853-2273) Tel 585-426-9454
E-mail: callen10@rochester.rr.com.

New Library Press LLC, *(978-0-7950)* Orders Addr.: 3419 Chapman Ave. #133, Orange, CA 92869 USA; Edit Addr.: P.O. Box 130, Murrieta, CA 92564 USA
E-mail: newbookorders@gmail.com.

New Line Bks., *(978-1-57717; 978-1-880908; 978-1-59764)* 245 Eighth Ave., No. 180, New York, NY 10011-1607 USA Toll Free Fax: 888-719-7723; Toll Free: 888-719-7722
E-mail: info@newlinebooks.com
Web site: http://www.newlinebooks.com.

New Line International *See* **New Line Publishing Inc.**

New Line Publishing Inc., *(978-0-9657469)* 916 Spencer Ave., Santa Rosa, CA 95404-3814 USA (SAN 253-7583) Tel 707-545-1848.

New Millenium Pr., The, *(978-0-9706728)* 311 E. Seventh St., Tama, IA 52339 USA Tel 515-484-2313 Do not confuse with New Millennium Press in Augusta, GA.

New Millennium Bks., *(978-0-9672333)* c/o Gail Mathabane, 901 SW King St. Suite 1006, Portland, OR 97205 USA Tel 503-758-2628 Do not confuse with New Millennium Bks., Petersburg, VA
E-mail: gem@mathabane.com
Web site: http://www.mathabane.com.

New Monic Bks., *(978-0-9652422; 978-0-9840966)* P.O. Box 511314, Punta Gorda, FL 33951-1314 USA Toll Free: 800-741-1295
E-mail: bburchers@earthlink.net
Web site: www.vocabularycartoons.com.

New Montgomery Pr., *(978-0-692-77662-9)* 2422 Dundee Rd, Louisville, KY 40205 USA Tel 502-767-9312
Web site: http://louisrats.wixsite.com/witchrabbit
Dist(s): **CreateSpace Independent Publishing Platform.**

New Native Pr., *(978-1-883197)* P.O. Box 661, Cullowhee, NC 28723 USA Tel 828-293-9237
E-mail: newnativepress@hotmail.com
Dist(s): **SPD-Small Pr. Distribution.**

New Orleans Stories, *(978-0-9758996)* 7401 Slaughter Ln., PMB 5015, Austin, TX 78739 USA Tel 512-923-5015
E-mail: sean@neworleansstories.com
Web site: http://neworleansstories.com
Dist(s): **Forest Sales & Distributing Co.**

New Page Bks. *Imprint of* **Career Pr., Inc.**

New Paradigm Bks., *(978-1-892138)* 22491 Vistawood Way, Boca Raton, FL 33428 USA Tel 561-482-5971; Fax: 561-852-8322; Toll Free: 800-808-5179
E-mail: darbyc@earthlink.net
Web site: http://www.newpara.com
Dist(s): **New Leaf Distributing Co., Inc.**

New Paradigm Pubns., *(978-0-615-35944-1; 978-0-9827673)* 12 Cherokee St., Dover, NH 03820 USA (SAN 860-2255) Tel 603-742-4162
E-mail: jim@mastromedia.com; info@newparadigmpublications.com
Web site: http://www.newparadigmpublications.com.

New Poets Series, Incorporated/Chestnut Hills Press/Stonewall *See* **BrickHouse Bks., Inc.**

New Pr., The, *(978-1-56584; 978-1-59558; 978-1-62097)* 38 Greene St., 4th Flr., New York, NY 10013 USA Tel 212 629 8802; Fax: 212 629 8617; Toll Free Fax: 800 458 6515; Toll Free: 800 233 4830
E-mail: newpress@thenewpress.com
Web site: http://www.thenewpress.com
Dist(s): **China Books & Periodicals, Inc.**
MyiLibrary
ebrary, Inc.

New Publications, *(978-0-692-52964-5; 978-1-944156; 978-0-9933594-1-5)* 5 Bradley Rd., Enfield, NH 03585 USA Tel 603-838-6444
E-mail: darin@theinspiragroup.com
Dist(s): **CreateSpace Independent Publishing Platform.**

New Shelves Bks., *(978-1-935355; 978-0-692-73191-8)* Orders Addr.: 20 Office Pkwy. No. 126, Pittsford, NY 13534 USA (SAN 857-3700) Tel 518-261-1300; Fax: 518-633-1211
Web site: http://www.newshelves.com.

New Shelves Distribution, 103 Remsen St., Cohoes, NY 12047 USA Tel 518-391-2300; Fax: 518-391-2365
Web site: http://www.newshelvesdistribution.com.

New Song Publishing Co., *(978-0-942925)* Div. of Al Menconi Ministries, Orders Addr.: P.O. Box 131147, Carlsbad, CA 92013 USA (SAN 667-8475) Tel 760-591-4696; Toll Free: 800-786-8742; Edit Addr.: 1635 S. Rancho Santa Fe Rd., Suite 105, San Marcos, CA 92069 USA (SAN 667-8483)
E-mail: patty@almenconi.com; al@almenconi.com
Web site: http://www.AlMenconi.com.

New Star Bks., Ltd. (CAN) *(978-0-919573; 978-0-919888; 978-0-921586; 978-1-55420)* *Dist. by* **SPD-Small Pr Dist.**

New Strategist Pr., LLC, *(978-0-9628092; 978-1-885070; 978-1-933588; 978-1-935114; 978-1-935775; 978-1-937737; 978-1-940308)* Orders Addr.: P.O. Box 635, Amityville, NY 11701 USA Tel 631-608-8795; Edit Addr.: 26 Austin Ave., Amityville, NY 11701 USA (SAN 860-4002) Tel 800-848-0842; 631-608-8795; Fax: 631-691-1770
E-mail: accounting@newstrategist.com
Web site: http://www.newstrategist.com
Dist(s): **MyiLibrary.**

New Sweden Pr., *(978-0-9702646)* 10509 Schmidt Ln., Manor, TX 78653 USA Fax: 512-278-1251 Do not confuse with New Sweden Pr., South Saint Paul, MN
E-mail: shrout@mail.utexas.edu.

New Tribes Mission, Inc., *(978-1-890040; 978-1-61565; 978-0-9968348)* 1000 E. First St., Sanford, FL 32771-1487 USA Tel 407-323-3430; Fax: 407-330-0376; 407-547-2450; Toll Free: 800-321-5375
E-mail: ntm@ntm.org; doug_lotz@ntm.org
Web site: http://www.ntm.org.

New Village Pr., *(978-0-9766054; 978-0-9815593; 978-1-61332)* Div. of Architects/Designers/Planners for Social Responsibility, 400 Central Pk. W, 12B, New York, NY 10025 USA Tel 510-717-3101
E-mail: hello@newvillagepress.net
Web site: http://www.newvillagepress.net
Dist(s): **Consortium Bk. Sales & Distribution**
MyiLibrary.

New Virginia Pubns., *(978-0-9755030)* 9185 Matthew Dr., Manassas Park, VA 20111 USA (SAN 256-0453) Tel 703-928-8316; Fax: 703-331-0577
E-mail: lab49@att.net.

New Vision Entertainment, LLC, *(978-0-9778310)* Orders Addr.: 30 Estuary Trail, Clearwater, FL 33759 USA
E-mail: jim@newvisionentertainment.us.

New Voices Publishing Co., *(978-0-931642)* Div. of KidsTerrain, Inc., P.O. Box 560, Wilmington, MA 01887 USA (SAN 253-9047) Tel 978-658-2131; Fax: 978-988-8833 Do not confuse with companies with the same or similar names in Sarasota, FL, Flushing, NY
E-mail: egilmartin@kidsterrain.com
Web site: http://www.newvoicespublishing.com; http://www.kidsterrain.com.

New Wave Bks. & CD, *(978-0-9727753; 978-0-9741493)* Orders Addr.: 7850 S. Normandie Ave., Apt. 69, Los Angeles, CA 90044 USA; Edit Addr.: 11050 Bryant St., No. 292, Yucaipa, CA 92399 USA.

New Wave Internet Services Incorporated *See* **Healthy Life Pr., Inc.**

New Wave Pubns., *(978-0-9749674; 978-0-9786660; 978-0-9800452)* 1419 New York Ave., Rm 3A, New York, NY 11210-1221 USA Do not confuse with New Wave Publications in Lincoln, NE.

†New Win Publishing, *(978-0-8329; 978-0-87691)* 9682 Telstar Ave., Suite 110, El Monte, CA 91731 USA (SAN 217-1201) Tel 626-448-4422; *Imprints:* Z Health Books (Z Hlth Bks)
E-mail: info@AcademicLearningCompany.com
Web site: http://www.newwinpublishing.com; *CIP.*

†New World Library, *(978-0-931432; 978-0-945934; 978-1-57731; 978-1-880032; 978-1-60868)* 14 Pamaron Way, Novato, CA 94949 USA (SAN 211-8777) Tel 415-884-2100; Fax: 415-884-2199; Toll Free: 800-972-6657 (retail orders only) Do not confuse with New World Library Publishing Co., Los Altos, CA
E-mail: escort@nwlib.com
Web site: http://www.newworldlibrary.com
Dist(s): **Brilliance Publishing, Inc.**
Ebsco Publishing
Islander Group
Landmark Audiobooks
New Leaf Distributing Co., Inc.
Publishers Group West (PGW); *CIP.*

New World Publishing, *(978-0-9771939; 978-0-9776818; 978-0-9787112; 978-0-9796815; 978-0-9821528)* 4540 State Rd., Cleveland, OH 44109 USA Tel 216-635-1671 Do not confuse with New World Publishing in Riverdale, GA, Scottsdale, AZ and Auburn, CA
E-mail: rkisner5@sbcglobal.net
Web site: http://www.silverquillpoetry.net.

New World Revelation Pr., *(978-0-9762105)* Orders Addr.: P.O. Box 839, Ellijay, GA 30540 USA Tel 706-635-7720; Fax: 706-635-8170
E-mail: fess1944@etcmail.com; office@awakeandlive.org
Web site: http://www.awakeandlive.org
Dist(s): **Lightning Source, Inc.**

New Worlds Press *See* **Institute for Economic Democracy Pr., Inc.**

New Year Publishing, *(978-0-9671565; 978-0-9760095; 978-0-9799885; 978-1-935547; 978-1-61431)* 144 Diablo Ranch Ct., Danville, CA 94506 USA Tel 925-348-0481; Fax: 425-984-7256 Do not confuse with New Year Publishing in Oceanside, CA
E-mail: dmorris@newyearpublishing.com
Web site: http://www.newyearpublishing.com
Dist(s): **Distributors, The**
Innovative Logistics.

New York Review of Bks., Inc., The, *(978-0-940322; 978-1-59017; 978-1-68137)* 435 Hudson St., 3rd Flr. Suite 300, New York, NY 10014 USA (SAN 220-3448) Tel 212-757-8070; Fax: 212-333-5374; *Imprints:* NYR Children's Collection (NY Rev Child); NYRB Classics (NYRB Class); NYRB Kids (NYRB Kids)
E-mail: mail@nybooks.com; nyrb@nybooks.com
Web site: http://www.nyrb.com
Dist(s): **MyiLibrary**
Penguin Random Hse. LLC
Random Hse., Inc.

†New York Univ. Pr., *(978-0-8147; 978-1-4798)* Div. of New York Univ., Orders Addr.: 838 Broadway, 3rd Flr., New York, NY 10003-4812 USA (SAN 658-1293) Tel 212-998-2575; Fax: 212-995-3833; Toll Free: 800-996-6987 (ordering)
E-mail: orders@nyupress.org
Web site: http://www.nyupress.org
Dist(s): **CreateSpace Independent Publishing Platform**
Ebsco Publishing
Ingram Publisher Services
ebrary, Inc.; *CIP.*

Newburyport Pr., *(978-1-882266)* Orders Addr.: P.O. Box 389, Newburyport, MA 01950 USA Tel 978-465-5751; Fax: 978-462-2043; Toll Free: 800-491-4700 (in Massachusetts only); Edit Addr.: 477 Commerce Blvd., Oldsmar, FL 34677-2809 USA
E-mail: mail@newburyportpress.com
Dist(s): **D.A.P./Distributed Art Pubs.**

Newburyport Press, Incorporated *See* **Newburyport Pr.**

NeWest Pubs., Ltd. (CAN) *(978-0-920316; 978-0-920897; 978-1-896300; 978-1-897126; 978-1-927063)* *Dist. by* **Strauss Cnslts.**

NewLife Publications *See* **Campus Crusade for Christ**

Newman Educational Publishers *See* **Newman Educational Publishing Co.**

Newman Educational Publishing Co., *(978-0-938990)* P.O. Box 461, Glen Ellyn, IL 60138 USA (SAN 239-8273) Tel 630-668-7027
E-mail: bizfootstep@aol.com
Web site: http://www.ugrr.illinois.com.

Newmark Learning LLC, *(978-1-60719; 978-1-61269; 978-1-4788)* 629 Fifth Ave., Pelham, NY 10803 USA Tel 1-877-279-8388; 1-877-280-0375
E-mail: bhaggerty@benchmarkeducation.com
Dist(s): **Follett School Solutions.**

Newmarket for It Bks. *Imprint of* **HarperCollins Pubs.**

†Newmarket Pr., *(978-0-937858; 978-1-55704)* Div. of Newmarket Publishing & Communications Corp., 18 E. 48th St., New York, NY 10017 USA (SAN 217-2585) Tel 212-832-3575; Fax: 212-832-3629; Toll Free Fax: 800-458-6515 (trade orders); Toll Free: 800-233-4830 (trade orders)
E-mail: mailbox@newmarketpress.com
Web site: http://www.newmarketpress.com
Dist(s): **MyiLibrary**
Two Rivers Distribution
Worldwide Media Service, Inc.
ebrary, Inc.; *CIP.*

Newport Valley Pr, *(978-0-9778602)* P.O. Box 32, Solon, IA 52333-0032 USA Tel 319-351-8854.

NewSage Pr., LLC, *(978-0-939165)* Orders Addr.: P.O. Box 607, Troutdale, OR 97060-0607 USA (SAN 662-8370) Tel 503-695-2211
E-mail: info@newsagepress.com
Web site: http://www.newsagepress.com
Dist(s): **MyiLibrary**
Publishers Group West (PGW).

NewsChannelChurch *See* **Asiana Media**

NewSound, LLC, 81 Demeritt Pl., Waterbury, VT 05676 USA Tel 802-244-7858; Fax: 802-244-1808; Toll Free: 800-342-0295 (wholesale orders)
E-mail: sales@newsoundmusic.com.

NewSouth Bks. *Imprint of* **NewSouth, Inc.**

NewSouth, Inc., *(978-1-58838; 978-1-60306)* P.O. Box 1588, Montgomery, AL 36102-1588 USA Tel 334-834-3556; Fax: 334-834-3557; Toll Free: 866-639-7688; *Imprints:* NewSouth Books (NewSouth AL); Junebug Books (Junebug Bks)
E-mail: info@newsouthbooks.com
Web site: http://www.newsouthbooks.com
Dist(s): **Blair, John F. Pub.**
Ingram Publisher Services
ebrary, Inc.

NewSouth Publishing (AUS) *(978-0-86840; 978-0-909465; 978-0-908237; 978-1-921410; 978-1-74223; 978-1-74224; 978-0-646-09872-2; 978-0-646-27463-8)* *Dist. by* **IPG Chicago.**

Newton, J. Britt *See* **Twelve Stones Publishing LLC**

Newtonian Golf & Particle Physics, Inc., *(978-0-9725355)* 107 Bordeaux Ln., Cary, NC 27511 USA Tel 919-469-0180
E-mail: sales@saintmulligan.com
Web site: http://www.stmulligan.com.

New-York Historical Society, *(978-0-916141)* Two W. 77th St., New York, NY 10024 USA (SAN 294-975X) Tel 212-873-3400
Dist(s): **Ingram Publisher Services.**

Next Century Foundation *See* **Next Century Publishing Co.**

Next Century Publishing *See* **Pilot Communications Group, Inc.**

Next Century Publishing Co., *(978-0-9632937)* Orders Addr.: P.O. Box 3020, Carefree, AZ 85377 USA; Edit Addr.: 8548 Silver Saddle Dr., Carefree, AZ 85377 USA Tel 602-488-9600
Dist(s): **Midpoint Trade Bks., Inc.**

Next Chapter Pr., *(978-0-9816265)* P.O. Box 1937, Boca Grande, FL 33921 USA.

Next Generation Pr., *(978-0-9762706; 978-0-9815595)* P.O. Box 603252, Providence, RI 02906 USA Tel 401-247-7665; Fax: 401-245-6428
E-mail: info@nextgenerationpress.org
Web site: http://www.nextgenerationpress.org.

Next Page Pr., The, *(978-0-9749826)* Orders Addr.: 1915 W. Wakeham Pl., Santa Ana, CA 92704-7147 USA Tel 714-432-1729
E-mail: raday@pngusa.net
Web site: http://www.womeninrailroading.com
Dist(s): **Capstone Pub.**

Next Step Magazine, Inc., The, *(978-0-9752926)* 86 W. Main St., Victor, NY 14564 USA Tel 585-742-1260; Fax: 585-742-1263; Toll Free: 800-771-3117
Web site: http://www.nextstepmagazine.com.

Next Step Pr., *(978-1-892876)* Sub. of New Wisdom, Inc., 1201 Delta Glen Ct., Vienna, VA 22182-1320 USA Tel 703-757-7945; Fax: 703-757-7946
E-mail: Wyattwooodsmall@compuserve.com
Web site: http://www.peoplepatterns.com; http://www.mindcoach.org
Dist(s): **Two Rivers Distribution.**

Next Stop Publishing, *(978-1-942144)* 3225 McLeod Dr. Suite 100, Las Vegas, NV 89121 USA Tel 702-998-2837; Fax: 702-989-4627
E-mail: info@nextstopinc.com
Web site: www.nextstopinc.com.

Nextpos Corporation *See* **Aldelo Systems Inc.**

Neyborhood Enterprises, *(978-0-578-19088-4; 978-0-578-19089-1; 978-0-9989848)* 178 Maya Ct., St. Augustine, FL 32086 USA.

NF Publishing *See* **SouthWest Pubns.**

Ni, Kaiyao, *(978-0-692-89319-7)* 713 churchill rd, chester springs, PA 19425 USA Tel 517-420-7984
E-mail: nikaiyao@gmail.com.

Nia Publishing Company, Incorporated *See* **Urban Spirit!**

Nicassio, J. E., *(978-0-692-72812-3; 978-0-692-77187-7)* 1002 Attilio Ct, Harrison City, PA 15636 USA Tel 724-640-8877.

Nicco Boss, LLC, *(978-0-9891635)* 524 Cala Morlanda St., Las Vegas, NV 89138 USA Tel 702-595-4884
E-mail: niccoboss@yahoo.com.

Nicewood Imagined, *(978-0-9720334)* 6823 NW 52nd Ln., Gainesville, FL 32653 USA Tel 352-271-3306 (phone/fax)
E-mail: nicewoodimagined@yahoo.com
Web site: http://www.macecora.com.

Niche Publishing & Marketing, *(978-0-9726628)* 3310 Bexley Park Rd., Columbus, OH 43213 USA Tel 614-338-0783
E-mail: sairapriest@me.com; svpmba@aol.com
Web site: http://www.nichepublishing.us.

NicheMarket.com *See* **Passion Profit Co., The/NicheMarket**

Nicho The Tiger LLC, *(978-0-9820801)* 43-31 223 St., Bayside, NY 11361 USA Tel 347-853-2694.

Nichols, Brady, *(978-0-692-78919-3)* 605 Capricorn Ln., Madison, WI 53718 USA Tel 608-335-3775
E-mail: bnichols07@hotmail.com.

Nick Of Time Media, Inc., *(978-1-940775)* 8661 NW 16th St., Pembroke Pines, FL 33024 USA Tel 888-540-7593
E-mail: Bsamarel33414@yahoo.com
Web site: http://www.nickoftime.us.

Nick The Cat, LLC, *(978-1-936193)* 26541 Dundee Rd., Huntington Woods, MI 48070 USA Tel 313-570-7996
Dist(s): **Bookmasters Distribution.**

Nickel Pr., *(978-1-57122; 978-1-879424)* Div. of S.R. Jacobs & Assocs., 107 Knob Hill Pk. Dr., Reisterstown, MD 21136 USA Do not confuse with Nickel Press, Inc., Enterprise, AL.

Nicolin Fields Publishing, Inc., *(978-0-9637077; 978-1-892066)* 861 Lafayette Rd., Unit 2A, Hampton, NH 03842-1232 USA Toll Free: 800-431-1579 (orders only)
E-mail: nfp@nh.ultranet.com
Web site: http://www.nicolinfields.com
Dist(s): **Alpenbooks Pr. LLC**
Peregrine Outfitters
Quality Bks., Inc.
Univ. Pr. of New England.

Nicoll Creations, *(978-0-9747527)* 5608 Evergreen, Midland, MI 48642 USA Tel 989-839-8293
E-mail: hgnicoll@sbcglobal.net.

Nicolo Whimsey Pr., *(978-1-935550)* 14411 Baden Westwood Rd., Brandywine, MD 20613 USA
Dist(s): **Consortium Bk. Sales & Distribution**
MyiLibrary.

Nicolosi, Gaetano, *(978-0-9763828)* 74 W. Fountain Ave., Delaware, OH 43015-1629 USA
E-mail: ciaogaetano@yahoo.com.

Nielsen, Lester *See* **Eaglesquest Publishing**

Nielsen-Bks., *(978-0-9701670)* 11 Greenway Plaza, No. 2700, Houston, TX 77046 USA Tel 713-963-8740; Fax: 713-572-7728
Web site: http://nielsen-books.com.

Night After Night Pubns., Inc. *Imprint of* **Hebler, Michael**

Night Howl Productions, *(978-0-9702176)* P.O. Box 1, Clay Center, NE 68933 USA Tel 402-984-2566
E-mail: dirtytricksforchicks@yahoo.com
Dist(s): **AK Pr. Distribution.**

Night Light Pubns., LLC, *(978-0-9740418; 978-0-9743785)* 6101 E. Wethersfield Rd., Scottsdale, AZ 85254 USA Tel 480-948-2607; Fax: 480-948-9921
E-mail: reg@nightlightpublications.com
Web site: http://www.nightlightpublications.com.

Night Sky Bks., *(978-1-59014)* Div. of North-South Books, Inc., 11 E. 26th St., 17th Flr., New York, NY 10010 USA Tel 212-706-4545; Fax: 212-706-4546; Toll Free: 800-282-8257 Do not confuse with companies with the same name in Santa Fe, NM
E-mail: nightsky@northsouth.com
Web site: http://www.northsouth.com
Dist(s): **Ingram Publisher Services**
Lectorum Pubns., Inc.

Night Sky, LLC, *(978-0-9888901)* 4 Buckskin Heights Dr., Danbury, CT 06811 USA Tel 203-826-9690
E-mail: jrivot@yahoo.com.

Nightengale Pr., *(978-0-9743348; 978-0-9761289; 978-1-933449; 978-1-935993; 978-1-945257)* Div. of Nightengale Media LLC, 370 S. Lowe Ave. Suite A-122, Cookeville, TN 38501 USA Tel 931-854-1390; Fax: 866-830-2624
E-mail: publisher@nightengalepress.com
Web site: http://www.nightengalemedia.com.

Nightwood Editions (CAN) *(978-0-88971) Dist. by* **Midpt Trade.**

NIIS Publishing, *(978-0-9745013; 978-0-615-11294-7)* 7349 Milliken, No. 140164, Rancho Cucamonga, CA 91730 USA.

Nile Publishing, *(978-0-9768485)* 213 Hancock St., Brooklyn, NY 11216 USA Tel 718-810-1148 Do not confuse with Nile PUblishing in Cincinnati, OH
E-mail: wale1@hotmail.com.

Nilsson Media, *(978-0-9724771)* Box 1371, Brentwood, TN 37024-1371 USA Tel 615-776-2593; Fax: 615-776-3193; Toll Free: 888-801-5190; *Imprints:* Nilsson, Troy (Troy Nilsson)
E-mail: books@nilssonmedia.org
Web site: http://www.nilssonmedia.com.

Nilsson, Troy *Imprint of* **Nilsson Media**

Nimble Bks. LLC, *(978-0-9754479; 978-0-9765406; 978-0-9777424; 978-0-9788138; 978-0-9799205; 978-1-934840; 978-1-60888)* 1521 Martha Ave., Ann Arbor, MI 48103 USA
E-mail: wfz@nimblebooks.com
Web site: http://www.nimblebooks.com
Dist(s): **Smashwords.**

Nimbus Publishing, Ltd. (CAN) *(978-0-919380; 978-0-920852; 978-0-921054; 978-1-55109; 978-1-77108) Dist. by* **Natl Bk Netwk.**

Nimbus Publishing, Ltd. (CAN) *(978-0-919380; 978-0-920852; 978-0-921054; 978-1-55109; 978-1-77108) Dist. by* **Orca Bk Pub.**

Nine Petal Pr., *(978-0-9984256)* 702 Keywe Pl., Duncanville, TX 75116 USA Tel 214-226-9352
E-mail: unity9@sbcglobal.net
Web site: www.NinePetalPress.com.

Ninety & Nine Records *See* **Blooming Twig Books LLC**

Ninos Aprenden Ingles Corp., *(978-1-934665)* 15476 NW 77 Ct., No. 360, Miami Lakes, FL 33016 USA (SAN 854-249X)
E-mail: ar@childrenlearninglanguages.com
Web site: http://www.ChildrenLearningLanguages.com.

Ninth Planet Pr., *(978-0-615-41386-0; 978-0-615-54486-1; 978-0-615-60901-0; 978-0-692-26010-4; 978-0-692-41572-6; 978-0-9983351)* 402 Buckeye Trail, Austin, TX 78746 USA Tel 512-330-1726; Fax: 512-289-0595; 909 Live Oak Ridge Rd., Austin, TX 78746
E-mail: bmccandless@austin.rr.com.

Nistraman Consulting, *(978-0-9706387)* P.O. Box 1314, Brookline, MA 02446 USA
E-mail: alex_belenky@lycos.com.

Nithyananda Univ., *(978-0-9790806; 978-1-934364; 978-1-60607)* 9720 Central Ave., Montclair, CA 91763 USA Tel 909-625-1400
E-mail: galleriaorders@yahoo.com
Web site: http://www.lifeblissfoundation.org.

Nithyananda Yoga & Meditation University *See* **Nithyananda Univ.**

NJL College Preparation, *(978-0-9753913)* 880 Willis Ave., Albertson, NY 11507 USA Tel 516-741-3550
E-mail: njlcp@aol.com
Dist(s): **Topical Review Bk Co., Inc.**

NJM *See* **Allen-Ayers Bks.**

nJoy Bks., *(978-0-9769959)* Orders Addr.: 18 S. 2nd St., Madison, WI 53704 USA
E-mail: office@njoybooks.com
Web site: http://www.njoybooks.com.

NK nPrint *See* **nVision Publishing**

NK Pubns., *(978-0-9705100; 978-0-9841610)* P.O. Box 1735, New York, NY 10101-1735 USA
E-mail: nkatsoris@aol.com
Dist(s): **Michigan State Univ. Pr.**
Midpoint Trade Bks., Inc.

NLAlex Publishing *See* **Joe Girl Ink**

NMS Enterprises Ltd. - Publishing (GBR) *(978-0-948636; 978-0-900733; 978-1-901663; 978-1-905267) Dist. by* **Natl Bk Netwk.**

No Dream Too Big LLC, *(978-0-9745717; 978-0-9838415)* Div. of AsAMan Thinketh.net LLC, P.O. Box 1220, Melrose, FL 32666 USA
E-mail: ebooks@asamanthinketh.net
Web site: http://www.asamanthinketh.net
Dist(s): **CreateSpace Independent Publishing Platform.**

No Frills Buffalo, *(978-0-578-04711-9; 978-0-578-08224-0; 978-0-615-48945-2; 978-0-615-51315-7; 978-0-615-54031-3; 978-0-615-56207-0; 978-0-615-58847-6; 978-0-615-59426-2; 978-0-615-61034-4; 978-0-615-62237-8; 978-0-615-62696-3; 978-0-615-66171-1; 978-0-615-66520-7; 978-0-615-66821-5; 978-0-615-70800-3; 978-0-615-70801-0; 978-0-615-72411-9; 978-0-615-72567-3; 978-0-615-75542-7; 978-0-615-75973-9; 978-0-615-78493-9; 978-0-615-78813-5; 978-0-615-81005-8; 978-0-615-81239-7; 978-0-615-82396-6; 978-0-615-83012-4;) 119 Dorchester, Buffalo, NY 14213 USA*
E-mail: contact@nofrillsbuffalo.com
Web site: http://nofrillsbuffalo.com
Dist(s): **CreateSpace Independent Publishing Platform**
Lightning Source, Inc.

No Frills Press Buffalo *See* **No Frills Buffalo**

No Greater Joy Ministries, Inc., *(978-1-892112; 978-0-9786372; 978-1-934794; 978-1-935370; 978-1-61644)* 1000 Pearl Rd., Pleasantville, TN 37033 USA (SAN 914-5958) Toll Free: 866-292-9936
E-mail: ngj@nogreaterjoy.org; cjoyner@nogreaterjoy.org
Web site: http://www.nogreaterjoy.org
Dist(s): **BookMasters, Inc.**
Bookmasters Distribution
Follett School Solutions
MyiLibrary
Send The Light Distribution LLC
ebrary, Inc.

No Limits Communications, *(978-0-9712842)* P.O. Box 220, Horsham, PA 19044 USA Tel 215-675-9133; Fax: 215-675-9376.

No Limitz Productions, Inc., *(978-0-9766942)* 3257 Primera Ave., Los Angeles, CA 90068 USA Tel 323-876-7149
E-mail: nolimitz@aol.com
Web site: http://www.suzannelopez.com.

No Starch Pr., Inc., *(978-1-886411; 978-1-59327)* 555 De Haro St., Suite 250, San Francisco, CA 94107 USA Tel 415-863-9900; Fax: 415-863-9950; Toll Free: 800-420-7240 Do not confuse with No Starch Pr., in Berkeley, CA
E-mail: info@nostarch.com
Dist(s): **Wiley & Sons, Inc., John**
Ebsco Publishing
Follett School Solutions
O'Reilly Media, Inc.
Penguin Random Hse. LLC.

No Voice Left Behind Publishing, *(978-0-9773513)* P.O. Box 1109, Ceres, CA 95307 USA Tel 209-968-3425
E-mail: fernando_pena@sbcglobal.net
Web site: http://www.nvlb.net.

N.O.A.H Bks., *(978-0-615-59068-4; 978-0-9859770)* 16022 Beechnut St., Houston, TX 77083 USA Tel 713-582-9153; Fax: 281-277-4298
E-mail: cheryl_hil@msn.com
Web site: http://www.empoweringchildrentoread.blogspot.com/.

Noah Educational Projects *See* **N.O.A.H Bks.**

Noble Hero Pr., *(978-0-9768410)* 3754 Salem Walk, No. A1, Northbrook, IL 60062 USA
E-mail: mike@nobleheropress.com
Web site: http://www.nobleheropress.com.

Noble, John A. Collection *See* **Noble Maritime Collection, The**

†**Noble Maritime Collection, The,** *(978-0-9623017)* 1000 Richmond Terr., Staten Island, NY 10301-1114 USA Tel 718-447-6490
E-mail: erinurban@earthlink.net; *CIP.*

Noble Publishing *See* **20/20 Publishing**

Noble Publishing Assocs., *(978-0-923463; 978-1-56857)* 1300 NE 131st Cir., Vancouver, WA 98685 USA (SAN 251-656X) Tel 360-258-3119; Fax: 360-258-3122; Toll Free: 800-225-5259; 1300 NE 131st St., Vancouver, WA 98685-3164
E-mail: noblebooks@noblepublishing.com
Web site: http://www.noblepublishing.com.

Nobrow Ltd. (GBR) *(978-1-907704; 978-0-9562135) Dist. by* **Consort Bk Sales.**

Nodin Pr., *(978-0-931714; 978-1-932472; 978-1-935666; 978-1-947237)* c/o The Bookmen, Inc., 530 N. Third St., Suite 120, Minneapolis, MN 55401 USA (SAN 204-398X) Tel 612-333-6300; Fax: 612-333-6303
Dist(s): **Adventure Pubns.**
Itasca Bks.

Noel, Jaren, *(978-0-9993015)* 8941 Miami St, Unit 2, Omaha, NE 68134 USA Tel 308-870-1157; Fax: 308-870-1157; *Imprints:* Contemporary Fiction (MYD_ FICTION)
E-mail: jaren.zimmerman@gmail.com.

Noesis, Inc., *(978-0-9742091)* 10530 Linden Lake Plaza, Manassas, VA 20109 USA Tel 703-369-2924; Fax: 703-392-7978
E-mail: fstilley@noesis-inc.com
Web site: http://www.noesis-inc.com/drydockhistory.

Noesis Publishing, *(978-0-9794328)* Div. of Noesis Communications International, Orders Addr.: 4425 S., Mo Pac Expway Suite 600, Austin, TX 78735 USA Tel 512-891-6100 Greenleaf Book Group; Edit Addr.: 5777 W. Century Blvd., Suite 200, Los Angeles, CA 90045 USA Tel 310-645-5604 Noesis Publishing; 512-891-6100 Greenleaf Book Group; Fax: 310-215-3018 Noesis Publishing
E-mail: diana@cmsbiz.com; candice@greenleafbookgroup.com
Web site: http://noesispublishing.com; http://www.greenleafbookgroup.com; http://www.kandide.com
Dist(s): **Greenleaf Book Group.**

Noguer y Caralt Editores, S. A. (ESP) *(978-84-217; 978-84-279) Dist. by* **Lectorum Pubns.**

Noixia's Reading Circle, *(978-0-9749122)* 8002 Avenida Navidad, San Diego, CA 92122 USA Tel 858-550-9519
E-mail: contact@noixia.com
Web site: http://www.noixia.com.

Noller, Gail, *(978-0-9744877)* 1416 Oakwood Dr., Anoka, MN 55303 USA Tel 763-427-6897
E-mail: nolle005@tc.umn.edu.

NOLO, *(978-0-87337; 978-0-917316; 978-1-4133)* Orders Addr.: 950 Parker St., Berkeley, CA 94710 USA (SAN 206-7935) Tel 510-549-1976; Fax: 510-548-5902; Toll Free Fax: 800-645-0895; Toll Free: 800-728-3555 (customer service); 800-955-4775 (trade orders only)
E-mail: tradecs@nolo.com
Web site: http://www.nolo.com
Dist(s): **Ebsco Publishing**
Ingram Publisher Services
MyiLibrary.

Nolo.com *See* **NOLO**

Nomad Pr., *(978-0-9659258; 978-0-9722026; 978-0-9749344; 978-0-9771294; 978-0-9785037; 978-0-9792268; 978-1-934670; 978-1-936313; 978-1-936749; 978-1-61930)* Div. of Nomad Communications, Inc., 2456 Christian St., White River Junction, VT 05001 USA Tel 802-649-1995; Fax: 802-649-2667 Do not confuse with Nomad Pr., Clewiston, FL, Fort Collins, CO
E-mail: rachel@nomadcom.com; rachel@nomadpress.net
Web site: http://www.nomadpress.net
Dist(s): **Ebsco Publishing**
Follett School Solutions
Legato Pubs. Group
MyiLibrary
Perseus Bks. Group.

Nonetheless Pr., *(978-1-932053)* 20332 W. 98th St., Lenexa, KS 66220-2650 USA Tel 913-254-7266; Fax: 913-393-3245
E-mail: mschutte@nonethelesspress.com
Web site: http://www.nonethelesspress.com; http://www.lookingglasspress.com
Dist(s): **Bookazine Co., Inc.**
Brodart Co.
Greenleaf Book Group
Midwest Library Service.

Nonfiction Picture Bks. *Imprint of* **Picture Window Bks.**

Non-ISBN Publisher, 630 Central Ave., New Providence, NJ 07974 USA.

Noodle Holdings LLC, *(978-0-615-41968-8)* Rood Hill Farm 53 Rood Hill Rd., Sandisfield, MA 01255 USA
E-mail: hoover205@gmail.com
Web site: http://www.stevehooverauthor.com.

Noodle Pr., *(978-0-9601022)* Orders Addr.: P.O. Box 42542, Washington, DC 20015 USA; Edit Addr.: P.O. Box 42542, Washington, DC 20015 USA (SAN 208-7871) Tel 202-363-5078; Fax: 202-364-0090
E-mail: Noodleprss@aol.com.

Nooni Publishing, *(978-0-9796832)* 1211 Garden Lake Dr., Riverdale, GA 30296 USA
E-mail: Nooni-pub@hotmail.com.

Noor Foundation-International, *(978-0-9632067; 978-0-9766972; 978-1-942043)* P.O. Box 758, Hockessin, DE 19707 USA (SAN 854-3712) Tel 302-234-8860; Fax: 208-279-5341; Toll Free: 888-937-2665; 249 Peoples Way, Hockessin, DE 19707
E-mail: cyrusomar@hotmail.com; alnoorfoundation@hotmail.com
Web site: http://www.islamusa.org.

Noorart, Inc., *(978-1-933269)* 577 Sterling Dr., Richardson, TX 75081 USA Tel 972-234-9108
E-mail: asaadeh1@hotmail.com
Web site: http://www.noorart.com.

NooVoo Publishing LLC, *(978-0-9767513)* 28257 Thornybrae, Farmington Hills, MI 48331 USA Tel 248-762-4858
E-mail: glennrader@noovoo.com.

Nora Hse., *(978-0-9752958)* 9122 White Eagle Ct., Raleigh, NC 27617 USA
E-mail: oren2a@yahoo.com.

Norcor Enterprises, *(978-0-9622469)* 6147 N. Sheridan Rd., Chicago, IL 60660 USA Tel 773-743-6792
E-mail: norcorent@juno.com.

Nordic Studies Pr., *(978-0-9772714)* 5226 N. Sawyer, Chicago, IL 60625-4716 USA (SAN 257-1498) Tel 773-610-4283
E-mail: cpeterson@igc.org
Web site: http://www.nordicstudiespress.com.

Nordskog Publishing, Inc., *(978-0-9796736; 978-0-9824929; 978-0-9827074; 978-0-9831957; 978-0-9882976; 978-0-9903774; 978-0-9974221; 978-1-946497)* Orders Addr.: 4562 Westinghouse St. Suite E., Ventura, CA 93003 USA; Edit Addr.: 2716 Sailor Ave., Ventura, CA 93001 USA
E-mail: Jerry@NordskogPublishing.com; staff@nordskogpublication.com
Web site: http://www.NordskogPublishing.com
Dist(s): **Bookmasters Distribution.**

Norfleet Pr., Inc., *(978-0-9649934)* 1 Gracie Ter. Apt. 4C, New York, NY 10028-7956 USA
Dist(s): **Continental Enterprises Group, Inc. (CEG)**
North Country Bks., Inc.

Norilana Bks., *(978-1-934169; 978-1-934648; 978-1-60762)* Orders Addr.: P.O. Box 224, Highgate Center, VT 05459-0224 USA (SAN 851-8556); Edit Addr.: 145 Dubois Dr., Highgate Center, VT 05459-0224 USA; *Imprints:* YA Angst (YA Angst)
E-mail: service@norilana.com; vnazarian@gmail.com
Web site: http://www.norilana.com/
Dist(s): **Smashwords.**

NORKY AMERICA, *(978-0-9769209)* Orders Addr.: 4712 Admiralty Way, No. 614, Marina Del Rey, CA 90292 USA Tel 310-985-3039
Web site: http://www.norky.com.

Norma S.A. (COL) *(978-958-04; 978-958-45) Dist. by* **Continental Bk.**

Norma S.A. (COL) *(978-958-04; 978-958-45) Dist. by* **Lectorum Pubns.**

Norma S.A. (COL) *(978-958-04; 978-958-45) Dist. by* **AIMS Intl.**

Norma S.A. (COL) *(978-958-04; 978-958-45) Dist. by* **Distr Norma.**

Publisher Name Index

Norman & Globus, Inc., *(978-1-886978)* Orders Addr.: P.O. Box 20533, El Sobrante, CA 94803 USA; Edit Addr.: 4130 Lakeside Dr., San Pablo, CA 94806-1941 USA
E-mail: info@electrowiz.com; drpenny@sciencewiz.com
Web site: http://www.electrowiz.com; http://www.sciencewiz.com.

Norman Bks., *(978-0-9708617)* 900 Euclid St., Suite 302, Santa Monica, CA 90403 USA Tel 310-899-9310; Fax: 503-961-9523
E-mail: normanbooks411@gmail.com
Web site: http://www.normanbooks.com
Dist(s): **Book Wholesalers, Inc.**
Follett School Solutions
Quality Bks., Inc.
Sunbelt Pubns., Inc.

Nortex Pr. *Imprint of* **Eakin Pr.**

North American International, *(978-0-88265)* P.O. Box 251, Penn Laird, VA 22846 USA (SAN 202-9200) Tel 540-435-6454; *Imprints:* Fine Art Editions (Fine Art Edtns)
E-mail: naibooks@yahoo.com; naibooks@gmail.com
Web site: http://emiehippo.ecrater.com; http://finekidsbooks.webs.com; http://kidsbook.zoomshare.com.

North American Mission Board, SBC, *(978-1-59312)* 4200 North Point Pkwy, Alpharetta, GA 30022-4176 USA Tel 770-410-6100; Fax: 770-410-6051; Toll Free: 866-407-6262
E-mail: marketing@namb.net
Web site: http://www.namb.net.

North American Vexillological Assoc. (NAVA), *(978-0-9747728)* 101 Belair Dr., New Milford, CT 06776 USA
E-mail: tmealf@aol.com
Web site: http://www.nava.org.

†North Atlantic Bks., *(978-0-913028; 978-0-938190; 978-0-942941; 978-1-55643; 978-1-883319; 978-1-58394)* Div. of The Society of the Study of Native Art & Science, Orders Addr.: P.O. Box 12327, Berkeley, CA 94712 USA (SAN 203-1655) Fax: 510-559-8277; Toll Free: 800-337-2665 (orders only); Edit Addr.: 1435 4th St. # A, Berkeley, CA 94710-1335 USA; *Imprints:* Frog Limited (Frog Ltd); Frog Children's Books (FrogChld)
E-mail: orders@northatlanticbooks.com
Web site: http://www.northatlanticbooks.com
Dist(s): **China Books & Periodicals, Inc.**
MyiLibrary
Nutri-Bks. Corp.
Penguin Random Hse. LLC
Random Hse., Inc.
SPD-Small Pr. Distribution; *CIP.*

North Bay Bks., *(978-0-9725200; 978-0-9749098)* Orders Addr.: P.O. Box 21234, El Sobrante, CA 94820-1234 USA Tel 510-758-4276; Fax: 510-758-4659; Toll Free: 800-870-3194; Edit Addr.: 3110 Whitecliff Ct., Richmond, CA 94803 USA Do not confuse with companies with the same name in El Sobrante, CA, Richmond, CA
Web site: www.northbaybooks.com.

North Bks., *(978-0-939495; 978-1-58287)* P.O. Box 1277, Wickford, RI 02852 USA (SAN 663-4052) Tel 401-294-3682; Fax: 401-294-9491
E-mail: north@ids.net.

North Cape Pubns., Inc., *(978-1-882391)* P.O. Box 1027, Tustin, CA 92781 USA Tel 714-832-3621; Fax: 714-832-5302; Toll Free: 800-745-9714
E-mail: ncape@ix.netcom.com
Web site: http://www.northcapepubs.com.

North Carolina State Univ. Humanities Extension Pubns./Program, *(978-1-881507; 978-1-885647)* North Carolina State Univ., Box 8101 026 Winston Hall, Raleigh, NC 27695 USA Tel 919-515-1334; Fax: 919-515-8738
Web site: http://www.ncsu.edu/chass/extension.

North Carolina Symphony Society, Inc., The, *(978-0-9618952)* 4361 Lassiter At North Hills A. Ste. 105, Raleigh, NC 27609-5781 USA (SAN 242-5378).

†North Country Bks., Inc., *(978-0-925168; 978-0-932052; 978-0-9601158; 978-1-59531)* 220 Lafayette Street, Utica, NY 13502 USA (SAN 110-828X) Tel 315-735-4877; Fax: (315) 738-4342
E-mail: ncbooks@verizon.net
Web site: http://www.northcountrybooks.com; *CIP.*

North Country Pr., *(978-0-945980; 978-1-943424)* P.O. Box 501, Unity, ME 04988 USA (SAN 247-9680) Tel 207-948-2208; Fax: 207-948-9000 Do not confuse with North Country Pr., White Cloud, MI
E-mail: info@northcountrypress.com
Web site: http://www.northcountrypress.com.

North Dakota Center for Distance Education *See* **State Historical Society of North Dakota**

North Dakota State University, Institute for Regional Studies *See* **North Dakota State Univ. Pr.**

North Dakota State Univ. Libraries, *(978-0-9629777; 978-1-891193)* Orders Addr.: NDSU Dept 2080, Fargo, ND 58105-6050 USA Tel 701-231-8416; Fax: 701-231-7138; Edit Addr.: 1201 Albrecht Blvd., Fargo, ND 58105 USA
E-mail: michael.miller@ndsu.edu; jeremy.kopp@ndsu.edu
Web site: http://library.ndsu.edu/grhc/.

North Dakota State Uiv. Pr., *(978-0-911042; 978-1-946163)* Div. of North Dakota Institute for Regional Studies, Orders Addr.: 1210 Albrecht Blvd., Fargo, ND 58108-6050 USA (SAN 203-1574) Tel 701-231-6848; Fax: 701-231-1047
E-mail: suzzanne.kelley@ndsu.edu
Web site: https://www.ndsu.edu/ahss/ndirs/; https://www.facebook.com/NDSUPress/.

North Gap Publishing, *(978-0-9677379)* 636 Golden Hill St., Cheyenne, WY 82009 USA Tel 307-778-8761
E-mail: twalkwyo@hotmail.com.

North Light Bks. *Imprint of* **F&W Media, Inc.**

North Loop Pr. *Imprint of* **Salem Author Services**

North Pole Chronicles, *(978-0-9636442)* 7306 Park Ln., Dallas, TX 75225-2462 USA Tel 214-696-1717; Fax: 214-696-5288.

North Pole Pr., *(978-0-9787129; 978-0-9992977)* 537 Belle Ave., Sevierville, TN 37862 USA Tel 865-360-5565
E-mail: santa@santaclausunplugged.com; mrsclaus@santaclausunplugged.com
Web site: http://santaclausunplugged.com; http://santaclausstories.com.

North River Press, Incorporated *See* **North River Pr. Publishing Corp., The**

†North River Pr. Publishing Corp., The, *(978-0-88427)* P.O. Box 567, Great Barrington, MA 01230 USA (SAN 202-1048) Tel 413-528-0034 (phone/fax); Toll Free Fax: 800-266-5329; Toll Free: 800-486-2665
E-mail: agallagher@northriverpress.com
Web site: http://www.northriverpress.com; *CIP.*

North Shore Records, Inc., *(978-0-9746229)* Orders Addr.: P.O. Box 1035, Los Alamos, CA 93440 USA (SAN 257-3733) Tel 800-771-7531
E-mail: info@jacirae.com
Web site: http://www.winningromance.com; http://www.christmaswithlove.com; http://www.theindieguide.com; http://www.winningpoints.net; http://www.jacirae.com; http://www.thequeenofgreen.com; http://www.pennymeals.com.

North Star Editions, *(978-0-9848801; 978-0-9886491; 978-1-939967; 978-1-63163; 978-1-63517; 978-1-63583)* Subs. of Big Timber Media, 1600 Cliff Rd. E, Burnsville, MN 55337 USA (SAN 990-2325) Tel 952-446-7222; *Imprints:* Flux (FluxUSA); Focus Readers (FocusRead); Jolly Fish Press (JollyFishPr)
E-mail: info@northstareditions.com
Web site: www.fluxnow.com; www.northstareditions.com; www.focusreaders.com
Dist(s): **Independent Pub.**
Llewellyn Pubns.

North Star Press of Saint Cloud *See* **North Star Pr. of St. Cloud**

†North Star Pr. of St. Cloud, *(978-0-87839; 978-1-68201)* P.O. Box 451, Saint Cloud, MN 56302-0451 USA (SAN 203-7491) Tel 320-558-9062; Toll Free: 888-820-1636
E-mail: info@northstarpress.com
Web site: http://www.northstarpress.com
Dist(s): **Midpoint Trade Bks., Inc.**
Partners Bk. Distributing, Inc.; *CIP.*

North Star Way *Imprint of* **Simon & Schuster**

Northampton Hse., *(978-1-937997)* 7018 Wildflower Ln., Franktown, VA 23354 USA Tel 757-442-3013
E-mail: nhp@poyer.com
Web site: www.northampton-house.com.

Northbooks, *(978-0-9653074; 978-0-9720604; 978-0-9789766; 978-0-9815193; 978-0-9830764; 978-0-9888954)* Orders Addr.: P.O. Box 671832, Chugiak, AK 99567 USA Tel 907-696-8973
E-mail: tg@northbooks.com
Web site: http://www.northbooks.com.

Northcote Hse. Publishers, Ltd. (GBR) *(978-0-7463) Dist. by* **CasemateAcad.**

†Northern Illinois Univ. Pr., *(978-0-87580; 978-1-60909)* 2280 Bethany Rd., DeKalb, IL 60115-2854 USA (SAN 202-8875) Tel 815-753-1826; Fax: 815-753-1845
E-mail: bberg@niu.edu
Web site: http://www.niu.edu/univ_press/
Dist(s): **Chicago Distribution Ctr.**; *CIP.*

Northern Publications, Incorporated *See* **Northern Publishing**

Northern Publishing, *(978-0-9639869; 978-0-9741684)* P.O. Box 871803, Wasilla, AK 99687 USA Tel 907-376-6474
E-mail: tony@tonyruss.com
Web site: http://www.tonyruss.com
Dist(s): **News Group, The**
Partners Bk. Distributing, Inc.
Partners/West Book Distributors.

Northern Speech Services, *(978-0-9708947; 978-0-9761967; 978-0-9765497; 978-0-9785581; 978-0-9799245; 978-0-9823449; 978-1-935578)* 325 Meecher Rd., Gaylord, MI 49735 USA Toll Free Fax: 888-696-9655; Toll Free: 888-337-3866; P.O. Box 1247, Gaylord, MI 49734
E-mail: tslominski@nss-nrs.com
Web site: http://www.nss-nrs.com
Dist(s): **BookBaby.**

Northern State Univ. Pr., *(978-1-883120)* Div. of NSU Foundation, Orders Addr.: Northern State Univ. 1200 S Jay St, Aberdeen, SD 57401 USA.

Northern Trails Pr., *(978-0-9651535)* Orders Addr.: 5353 Oliver Ave. S., Minneapolis, MN 55419-1054 USA
E-mail: northerntrails@comcast.net
Dist(s): **Adventure Pubns.**

Northern Virginia Writing Project, *(978-0-9759524)* GMU, MSN3E4, 4400 University Dr., Fairfax, VA 22030 USA Tel 703-993-1168; Fax: 703-993-1184
E-mail: sbaker@gmu.edu; contact@nvwp.org
Web site: http://www.nvwp.org.

Northfield Publishing, *(978-1-881273)* Div. of Moody Pr., 215 W. Locust, Chicago, IL 60610 USA (SAN 297-6404) Tel 312-329-2110; Fax: 312-329-8062; Toll Free: 800-678-8001
E-mail: michele.forrider@moody.edu
Web site: http://www.moodypublishers.com
Dist(s): **Moody Pubs.**

Northland Press *See* **Northland Publishing**

†Northland Publishing, *(978-0-87358)* Div. of Rowman & Littlefield Publishing Group, Orders Addr.: P.O. Box 15200 NBN Way, Blue Ridge Summit, PA 17214 USA Tel 301-459-3366; Fax: 301-429-5745; Toll Free Fax: 800-338-4550; Toll Free: 800-462-6420; *Imprints:* Rising Moon Books for Young Readers (Rising Moon Bks); Luna Rising (Luna Rising) Do not confuse with companies with the same or similar name in Memomonie, WI, Cleveland, OH
E-mail: dbreier@nbnbooks.com
Dist(s): **Fujii Assocs.**
Lectorum Pubns., Inc.
Libros Sin Fronteras
Learning Connection, The
National Bk. Network; *CIP.*

Northlight Communications, Inc. *See* **Sign2Me Early Learning / Northlight Communications, Inc.**

Northopolis, *(978-0-615-69125-1; 978-0-9898090)* 1105 Jasmine, Weslaco, TX 78596 USA Tel 956-373-1134
E-mail: rbanda@gmail.com
Web site: www.northopolis.com.

Northshire Pr., *(978-1-60571)* Orders Addr.: P.O. Box 2200, Manchester Center, VT 05255 USA; Edit Addr.: 4869 Main St., Manchester Center, VT 05255 USA Tel 802-362-3565; Fax: 802-362-1233; *Imprints:* Shires Press (Shires Pr)
Web site: http://www.northshire.com/printondemand.

†North-South Bks., Inc., *(978-0-7358; 978-1-55858; 978-1-58717)* 350 7th Ave. Rm. 1400, New York, NY 10001-5013 USA; *Imprints:* Michael Neugebauer Books (M Neugebauer Bks)
E-mail: mnavarro@northsouth.com
Web site: http://www.northsouth.com
Dist(s): **Continental Bk. Co., Inc.**
Ingram Publisher Services
Lectorum Pubns., Inc.
Libros Sin Fronteras
Simon & Schuster, Inc.; *CIP.*

Northstar Entertainment Group, LLC, *(978-0-9741544)* 9009 Danwood Manor Ter., Richmond, VA 23227-1269 USA; *Imprints:* Baby Faye Books (Baby Faye)
E-mail: northstarent2003@yahoo.com
Web site: http://www.northstarent.net.

Northwestern Publishing Hse., *(978-0-8100)* 2949 N. Mayfair Rd., Suite 200, Milwaukee, WI 53222 USA (SAN 206-7943) Tel 414-454-2100; Fax: 414-454-2170
E-mail: kuehlt@nph.wels.net; johnsonr@nph.wels.net
Web site: http://www.nph.net.

Northwestern Univ. Pr., *(978-0-8101)* Orders Addr.: c/o Univ. of Chicago Pr. Distribution Ctr., 11030 S. Langley Ave., Chicago, IL 60628 USA Tel 773-568-1550; Fax: 773-660-2235; Toll Free Fax: 800-621-8476; Toll Free: 800-621-2736; Edit Addr.: 629 Noyes St., Evanston, IL 60208-4210 USA (SAN 202-5787) Tel 847-491-5313; 847-491.2046; Fax: 847-491-8150
E-mail: nupress@northwestern.edu
Web site: http://www.nupress.northwestern.edu
Dist(s): **Chicago Distribution Ctr.**
MyiLibrary
Random Hse., Inc.
Univ. of Chicago Pr.
ebrary, Inc.

Northwind Sailing, Inc., *(978-0-9752700)* P.O. Box 973, Grand Marais, MN 55604-0973 USA.

NorthWord Bks. for Young Readers *Imprint of* **T&N Children's Publishing**

Norton, Frances M., *(978-0-9632938)* 1012 N. Wheaton Ave., Wheaton, IL 60187 USA Tel 630-665-0249.

†Norton, W. W. & Co., Inc., *(978-0-393; 978-0-88150; 978-0-914378; 978-0-936399; 978-0-942440; 978-1-58157; 978-1-324; 978-1-68268)* Orders Addr.: c/o National Book Company, 800 Keystone Industrial Pk., Scranton, PA 18512 USA (SAN 157-1869) Tel 570-346-2020; Fax: 570-346-1442; Toll Free: 800-233-4830; Edit Addr.: 500 Fifth Ave., New York, NY 10110-0017 USA (SAN 202-5795) Tel 212-354-5500; Fax: 212-869-0856; Toll Free: 800-223-2584
Web site: http://www.wwnorton.com
Dist(s): **US PubRep, Inc.**
Wiley, John & Sons, Inc.; *CIP.*

Norvik Pr. (GBR) *(978-1-870041) Dist. by* **Dufour.**

Norwen Pubns., *(978-0-9852869)* 820 West Shore Dr., Culver, IN 46511 USA.

Norwood Hse. Pr., *(978-1-59953; 978-1-60357; 978-1-68404)* Orders Addr.: P.O. Box 316598, Chicago, IL 60631 USA (SAN 257-1552) Tel 773-467-0837; Fax: 773-467-9686; Toll Free Fax: 866-565-2901; Toll Free: 866-565-2900
E-mail: customerservice@norwoodhousepress.com
Web site: http://www.norwoodhousepress.com
Dist(s): **Follett School Solutions.**

Nosey Trunk, *(978-0-9911454)* Orders Addr.: 240 Dolores St., No. 216, San Francisco, CA 94103 USA Tel 650-218-2986
E-mail: ranjani_krishnaswamy@hotmail.com.

Nosy Crow *Imprint of* **Candlewick Pr.**

Not Available Books *Imprint of* **Not Available Comics**

Not Available Comics, *(978-0-9744767)* Orders Addr.: 2627 Pulaski St., Hamtramck, MI 48212 USA; *Imprints:* Not Available Books (NotAvailBks)
E-mail: feazell038@comcast.net
Web site: http://www.cynicalman.com.

Not Home Yet Publishing, *(978-0-615-20928-9; 978-0-615-21258-6)* 8 Catamount Ln., Littleton, CO 80127 USA Tel 303-972-0895
E-mail: nothomeyetmin@msn.com.

Notgrass Co., *(978-1-933410; 978-1-60999)* Orders Addr.: 370 S Lowe Ave., Suite A PMB 211, Cookeville, TN 38501 USA Tel 800-211-8793; Fax: 800-891-8335; Toll Free: 800-211-8793
E-mail: books@notgrass.com
Web site: http://www.notgrass.com
Dist(s): **BookBaby.**

Nothing But The Truth, LLC, *(978-0-9883754; 978-0-615-73258-9; 978-0-9904652; 978-0-9963074; 978-0-9968999; 978-0-9972962; 978-1-946706)* 1010 Sir Francis Drake Blvd Suite 102, Kentfield, CA 94904 USA Tel 4157067067
Dist(s): **CreateSpace Independent Publishing Platform**
Publishers Group West (PGW).

Notion Pr., Inc., *(978-0-9975577; 978-1-945400; 978-1-945497; 978-1-945579; 978-1-945621; 978-1-945688; 978-1-945825; 978-1-945926; 978-1-946048; 978-1-946129; 978-1-946204; 978-1-946280; 978-1-946390; 978-1-946436; 978-1-946515; 978-1-946556; 978-1-946641; 978-1-946714; 978-1-946822; 978-1-946869; 978-1-946983; 978-1-947027; 978-1-947137; 978-1-947202; 978-1-947283; 978-1-947349; 978-1-947429; 978-1-947498; 978-1-947586; 978-1-947634; 978-1-947697; 978-1-947752; 978-1-947851; 978-1-947949; 978-1-947988; 978) 800 W. El Camino Real, Suite 180,, Mountain View, CA 94040 USA Tel 984-041-8723*
E-mail: editor@notionpress.com.

NouSoma Communications, Inc., *(978-0-9743604)* 500 Waldron Pk. Dr., Haverford, PA 19041-1932 USA Tel 610-658-5889; *Imprints:* GIRLS KNOW HOW (Girls Know How)
Web site: http://www.nousoma.com; http://girlsknowhow.com/
Dist(s): **Book Wholesalers, Inc.**
Brodart Co.

Nova Blue, Inc., *(978-0-9725584)* 14403 Little Blue Rd., Kansas City, MO 64136 USA Tel 816-737-8895
E-mail: novablueco@aol.com.

Nova Media, Inc., *(978-0-9618567; 978-1-884239)* 1724 N. State St., Big Rapids, MI 49307-9073 USA (SAN 668-0372) Tel 231-796-4637 (phone/fax)
E-mail: trund@netonecom.net
Web site: http://www.novamediainc.com.

Nova Pr., *(978-0-9637371; 978-1-889057; 978-0-692-38359-9; 978-1-944595)* Orders Addr.: 9058 Lloyd Pl., West Hollywood, CA 90069 USA (SAN 858-8317) Tel 310-275-3513; Fax: 310-281-5629; Toll Free: 800-949-6175
E-mail: novapress@aol.com
Web site: http://www.novapress.net
Dist(s): **CreateSpace Independent Publishing Platform**
Ebsco Publishing
Lightning Source, Inc.
ebrary, Inc.

†Nova Science Pubs., Inc., *(978-0-941743; 978-1-56072; 978-1-59033; 978-1-59454; 978-1-60021; 978-1-60456; 978-1-60692; 978-1-60741; 978-1-60876; 978-1-61668; 978-1-61728; 978-1-61761; 978-1-61122; 978-1-61209; 978-1-61324; 978-1-61470; 978-1-62100; 978-1-61942; 978-1-62081; 978-1-62257; 978-1-62417; 978-1-62618; 978-1-62808; 978-1-62948; 978-1-63117; 978-1-63321; 978-1-63463; 978-1-63482; 978-1-63483; 978-1-63484; 978-1-63485; 978-1-5361) 400 Oser Ave., Suite 1600, Hauppauge, NY 11788 USA (SAN 666-0266)*
E-mail: novascience@earthlink.net; novapublishers@earthlink.net; suzy@novapublishers.com; nova.main@novapublishers.com; cathy@novapublishers.com
Web site: http://www.novapublishers.com
Dist(s): **Ebsco Publishing**
ebrary, Inc.; *CIP.*

Novanglus Publishing, LLC, *(978-0-9837186)* Orders Addr.: 15 E. Putnam Avenue, No. 232, Greenwich, CT 06830 USA (SAN 920-4504) Tel 203-885-7476; 15 E. Putnam Ave., #232, Greenwich, CT 06830 Tel 203-885-7476; Fax: 203-724-1867
E-mail: mpeacockphd@gmail.com; michelle@novanglusbublishing.com
Web site: http://www.novanglusbublishing.com; http://fairandsquarebook.com.

Novel Units, Inc., *(978-1-56137; 978-1-58130; 978-1-60878)* Orders Addr.: 2709 Bulverde Rd., Bulverde, TX 78163 USA (SAN 253-9276) Tel 830-438-4262; Fax: 830-438-4263; Toll Free Fax: 877-688-3226; Toll Free: 800-688-3224; P.O. Box 97, Bulverde, TX 78163-0097
E-mail: lmammen@ecslearningsystems.com
Web site: http://www.ecslearningsystems.com.

Novello & Co., Ltd. (GBR) *(978-0-85360) Dist. by* **H Leonard.**

Novello Festival Pr., *(978-0-9708972; 978-0-9760963; 978-0-9815192; 978-0-615-15969-0; 978-0-615-16624-7)* Div. of Public Library of Charlotte & Mecklenburg County, 310 N. Tryon St., Charlotte, NC 28202 USA (SAN 254-3206) Tel 704-416-0706
Dist(s): **Blair, John F. Pub.**

November Media Publishing and Consulting Firm, *(978-0-692-76179-3; 978-0-9981622; 978-0-9990431)* 2212 123rd St., Unit 1, Blue Island, IL 60406 USA Tel 708-515-7114
E-mail: novmedia10@gmail.com
Web site: http://www.novembermediapublishing.com/
Dist(s): **CreateSpace Independent Publishing Platform.**

Novus Via Music Group Inc. (CAN) *(978-1-897379) Dist. by* **H Leonard.**

Now Age Knowledge, *(978-0-9729259)* Orders Addr.: 8315 Lake City Way, NE, Seattle, WA 98115 USA; Edit Addr.: 16626 6th Ave. W. #m301, Lynnwood, WA 98037 USA (SAN 255-2876) Do not confuse with Awaken Publishing in Houston, TX
E-mail: nowageknowledge@gmail.com
Web site: http://nowageknowledge.com.

Now I'm Reading! *Imprint of* **Random Hse. Children's Bks.**

Nowata Press Publishing Consultants, *(978-0-615-21595-2; 978-0-692-00130-1; 978-0-692-01778-4; 978-0-615-81419-3; 978-0-9907950)* 1338 Old Coach Road, SW, Marietta, GA 30008 USA
E-mail: dmyles3784@yahoo.com
Web site: http://nowatapress.wordpress.com/.

Nowlin, Roberta J, *(978-0-9862905)* 30744 Mainmast Dr., Agoura Hills, CA 91301 USA Tel 818-874-3134
E-mail: robertajeanmurphy@gmail.com.

NPG Newspapers, Inc., *(978-0-9724933)* Orders Addr.: P.O. Box 29, St Joseph, MO 64502-0029 USA Tel 816-271-8500; Fax: 816-271-8631; Toll Free: 800-779-6397; Edit Addr.: 825 Edmond St., St Joseph, MO 64502-0029 USA
E-mail: brucek@npgco.com.

NQSBks., *(978-0-9793168)* 477 Brentview Hills Dr., Nashville, TN 37220 USA Tel 615-832-1125
E-mail: nqsbooks@comcast.net
Web site: http://www.nqsbooks.com.

NRG Pubns., *(978-0-9741647)* 3510 Plum Brook, Missouri City, TX 77459 USA
E-mail: info@nrgpublications.com
Web site: http://www.nrgpublications.com.

NRS Enterprises, *(978-0-615-27983-1)* 2237 NW. Terr. Pines Dr., Bend, OR 97701 USA.

NSR Pubns., *(978-0-9761724)* 1482 51st Rd., Douglass, KS 67039 USA Tel 620-986-5472; Toll Free: 866-677-2624
E-mail: gumm@wheatstate.com
Web site: http://www.nsrpublications.com.

NT Publishing, L.L.C., *(978-0-9741864; 978-0-9787123)* P.O. Box 461540, Aurora, CO 80047 USA Tel 303-484-1071; Fax: 303-484-1072
E-mail: questions@ntpublishing.net
Web site: http://www.ntpublishing.net.

NTC/Contemporary Publishing Company *See* **McGraw-Hill/Contemporary**

Nu Energy Horizons *See* **SonoMagnetics**

NUA Multimedia, *(978-0-9777573)* Orders Addr.: 15480 Annapolis Rd., Suite 202, No. 422, Bowie, MD 20715 USA Tel 410-710-2700
E-mail: pr@nuamultimedia.com; orders@nuamultimedia.com
Web site: http://www.soniahayes.com
Dist(s): **Brodart Co.**
Follett School Solutions.

NuAngel, Inc., *(978-0-9626614)* 14717 Friend Rd., Athens, AL 35611 USA Tel 256-729-5000; Fax: 256-729-5111
E-mail: sales@nuangel.com
Web site: www.nuangel.com.

NuBaby, Incorporated *See* **NuAngel, Inc.**

NubeOcho Ediciones (ESP) *(978-84-942360; 978-84-942929) Dist. by* **Consort Bk Sales.**

Nubiangodess Publishing, *(978-0-9744291)* P.O. Box 12224, Columbus, GA 31917-2224 USA
E-mail: ngpublishing@cs.com; admin@nubiangodesspublishing.com
Web site: http://www.nubiangodesspublishing.com.

Nubiano Project, Inc., The, *(978-0-9762837)* P.O. Box 371, Chapel Hill, NC 27514 USA
E-mail: info@thenubianoproject.com.

Nude Son Publishing *See* **Canoed Sun Publishing, LLC**

Nuevo Bks., *(978-1-936745)* 925 Salamanca NW, Los Ranchos, NM 87107 USA Tel 505-344-9382; Fax: 505-345-5129
E-mail: paul@nmsantos.com
Web site: www.NuevoBooks.com.

Nuf-Love Publishing, *(978-0-9636109)* P.O. Box 120976, Clermont, FL 34712 USA
E-mail: ashersbooks@earthlink.net
Web site: http://www.ashersbooks.com.

Nui Media & Entertainment, LLC, *(978-0-9817388)* P.O. Box 364, Santa Monica, CA 90406 USA
E-mail: publishing@nui.com.

NUMA LLC, *(978-0-9977196)* P.O. Box 52, Mystic, CT 06355 USA Tel 860-501-3316
E-mail: msoni.author@gmail.com.

NumbersAlive! Pr., *(978-0-9853667)* 975 F St., NW., Washington, DC 20004-1454 USA Tel 202-652-1820; Fax: 202-667-5793
E-mail: rebecca@numbersalive.org
Web site: http://www.numbersalive.org.

Nu-Nature, *(978-0-9759008)* 858 Heritage Valley Rd., Norcross, GA 30093 USA Tel 404-376-8917
E-mail: nunatureinfo@aol.com
Web site: http://www.nu-nature.com.

Nunes, H. William, *(978-0-9646934; 978-0-9787994)* 3029 Mark Trail, Glen Carbon, IL 62034 USA Tel 618-288-5185; Fax: 618-205-3053
E-mail: bnunesbook@aol.com
Dist(s): **Big River Distribution**
Partners Bk. Distributing, Inc.

Nunes Productions, LLC, *(978-0-9748142)* 1314 Fairmont St., NW, Washington, DC 20009 USA Tel 202-387-1314; *Imprints:* Brand Nu Words (Brand Nu)
E-mail: charisse@nunesproductions.com
Web site: http://www.nunesproductions.com; http://www.brandnuwords.com
Dist(s): **Independent Pubs. Group.**

Nur Pubns., *(978-0-9764947)* Orders Addr.: 562 Sawmill River Rd., Millwood, NY 10546 USA
E-mail: s_nadimi@yahoo.com
Web site: http://www.nurpublications.com.

Nurse, Lesley *See* **Lion Prints Publishing**

Nursery Bks., *(978-0-9894505)* 119 Old Chester Rd., Haddam, CT 06438 USA Tel 860-308-4303
E-mail: sophie.helenek@gmail.com
Web site: http://www.nurserybooks.net.

Nurturing Your Children Pr., *(978-0-9767198)* P.O. Box 5066, Larkspur, CA 94977-5066 USA Tel 415-927-4839 (phone/fax)
E-mail: nurturingpress@aol.com
Web site: http://nurturingyourchildren.com
Dist(s): **Independent Pubs. Group.**

Nutrishare Publishing, *(978-0-9764116)* 10519 E. Stockton Blvd., Suite 110, Elk Grove, CA 95624 USA.

Nutrition Network Pubs., Inc., *(978-0-9898633)* 5 Arleigh Rd., Great Neck, NY 11021 USA Tel 516-773-4754
E-mail: daunlester@gmail.com.

Nutshell Publishing *See* **Enisen Publishing**

NuVision Pubns., LLC, *(978-1-932681; 978-1-59547; 978-1-61536)* 1504 E. 70th St N., Sioux Falls, SD 57104-9429 USA
E-mail: nuvisionpub@gmail.com
Web site: http://www.nuvisionpublications.com
Dist(s): **CreateSpace Independent Publishing Platform**
Lightning Source, Inc.

Nvision Publishing *Imprint of* **Power Play Media**

nVision Publishing, *(978-0-9766086)* Div. of Written by Nicole Kearney Enterprises, P.O. Box 88731, Indianapolis, IN 46208 USA Tel 317-724-8926
E-mail: nicolekearney@yahoo.com
Web site: http://www.nicolekearney.com.

NY Media Works, LLC, *(978-0-9890914)* 112 Franklin St. First Flr., New York, NY 10013 USA (SAN 920-5187) Tel 646-369-5681
E-mail: jgribble@nymediaworks.com
Web site: http://www.nymediaworks.com
Dist(s): **Brodart Co.**
Quality Bks., Inc.

NY Studio Gallery LLC, *(978-0-692-49726-5; 978-0-692-62127-1; 978-0-692-62269-8; 978-0-692-65367-8; 978-0-692-67000-2; 978-0-692-67277-8; 978-0-692-67300-3; 978-0-692-72251-0; 978-0-692-78710-6; 978-0-692-80005-8; 978-0-692-80410-0; 978-0-692-80916-7; 978-0-692-80920-4) 420 N. Ohioville Rd, NEW PALTZ, NY 12561 USA Tel 612-987-1473.*

Nye Products, *(978-0-9746665)* P.O. Box 177, Wexford, PA 15090-0177 USA Tel 724-935-8710
E-mail: nyeproducts@stargate.net
Web site: http://nyeproducts.com; http://www.beverlynye.com/.

Nyiwo, Festus *See* **Transigar Co. LLC**

NYR Children's Collection *Imprint of* **New York Review of Bks., Inc., The**

NYRB Classics *Imprint of* **New York Review of Bks., Inc., The**

NYRB Kids *Imprint of* **New York Review of Bks., Inc., The**

NyreePr. Literary Group, *(978-0-615-76536-5; 978-0-9890039; 978-0-615-83176-3; 978-0-9910489; 978-0-9915412; 978-0-9903486; 978-0-9906662; 978-0-9909652; 978-0-9860866; 978-0-9969105; 978-0-9972921; 978-1-945304)* 321 Mystic River Trail, Fort Worth, TX 76131 USA Tel 972-793-3736
E-mail: contact@nyreepress.com
Web site: www.nyreepress.com.

OSS Publishing Co., *(978-0-9660286)* Orders Addr.: P.O. Box 610, White Plains, NY 10603 USA Tel 914-946-6521; Fax: 914-949-5380; Toll Free: 888-677-6521
E-mail: OSSpublishing@att.net
Web site: http://www.osspublishing.com.

Oak Court Pr., *(978-0-9767696)* 34612 Oak Ct., Elizabeth, CO 80107 USA Tel 303-703-6633
E-mail: oakcourtpress@msn.com.

Oak Hill Studios, *(978-0-9848818)* 2150 Farnsworth Dr., O'Fallon, MO 63368 USA Tel 314-560-0041; Fax: 636-978-1135
E-mail: nealwriter1@charter.net
Web site: letterstomillie.com
Dist(s): **BookBaby.**

†Oak Knoll Pr., *(978-0-938768; 978-1-884718; 978-1-58456; 978-1-872116)* 310 Delaware St., New Castle, DE 19720 USA (SAN 216-2776) Tel 302-328-7232; Fax: 302-328-7274; Toll Free: 800-996-2556 Do not confuse with Oak Knoll Press in Hardy, VA
E-mail: oakknoll@oakknoll.com
Web site: http://www.oakknoll.com; *CIP.*

Oak Lake Pr., *(978-0-9744115)* Orders Addr.: 1432 Higuera, San Luis Obispo, CA 93406 USA Tel 916-791-2309; Edit Addr.: P.O. Box 529, Loomis, CA 95650 USA
E-mail: abowler@surewest.net
Web site: http://www.annmartinbowler.net.

Oak Leaf Systems, *(978-0-9659546; 978-0-9848809)* 2710 John Tyler Hwy., Williamsburg, VA 23185 USA Tel 757-208-0200 Landline; 757-634-1441 Mobile
E-mail: carolfeltman@gmail.com
Web site: ATruckNamedTravis.com.

Oak Manor Publishing, Inc., *(978-0-9747361; 978-0-9791757)* 161 Boutwell St., Manchester, NH 03102-2933 USA Tel 603-860-5551
E-mail: customerservice@aokmanorpublishing.com
Web site: http://www.oakmanorpublishing.com.

Oak Ridge Publishing, *(978-0-9814735; 978-0-9843270; 978-0-9851416)* P.O. Box 682, Lady Lake, FL 32158 USA Tel 352-259-7450
E-mail: ldridgley@comcast.net.

Oak Tree Publishing, *(978-1-892343; 978-1-61009)* Orders Addr.: 1820 W. Lacey Blvd. #220, Hanford, CA 93230 USA; *Imprints:* Acorn (AcornIL) Do not confuse with companies with the same or similar name in Virginia Beach, VA, Seminole, FL
E-mail: oaktreepub@aol.com; Publisher@oaktreebooks.com; info@oaktreebooks.com
Web site: http://www.oaktreebooks.com; http://www.otpblog.blogspot.com.

Oakana Hse., *(978-0-9762197)* Orders Addr.: P.O. Box 1680, Ramona, CA 92065 USA (SAN 257-5418)
Web site: http://OakanaHouse.com.

Oakdale Pr., *(978-0-9656364)* Orders Addr.: P.O. Box 555, Caulfield, MO 65626 USA Tel 417-284-3512; Fax: 417-284-3623 Do not confuse with companies with the same name in Lincoln., MA, Tallahassee, FL
E-mail: oakdale@webound.com
Web site: http://www.oakdalepress.com.

Oaklawn Marketing, Inc., *(978-0-9764628)* P.O. Box 190615, Dallas, TX 75219 USA Tel 713-542-7642; Fax: 832-550-2079
E-mail: admin@bookofcontext.com.

OakTara Publishing Group LLC, *(978-1-60290)* 2206 N. Main St., Suite 343, Wheaton, IL 60187 USA
E-mail: rtucker@oaktara.com
Web site: http://www.oaktara.com
Dist(s): **Follett School Solutions.**

Oakwood Solutions, LLC, *(978-1-893806; 978-1-933093)* 4 Brookwood Ct., Appleton, WI 54914-8618 USA
E-mail: bschmitz@conovercompany.com; sales@conovercompany.com
Web site: http://www.conovercompany.com.

Oasis, Producciones Generales de Comunicacion, S.L. (ESP) *(978-84-7871; 978-84-7901; 978-84-85351) Dist. by* **Lectorum Pubns.**

Oasis Pubns., *(978-0-9652736; 978-0-9837859)* 2344 Cambridge Dr., Sarasota, FL 34232 USA Tel 941-371-2223; Fax: 941-342-1228
E-mail: oasis.dianne@juno.com
Web site: http://www.nutrikid2.com
Dist(s): **Nelson's Bks.**
New Leaf Distributing Co., Inc.
Teva Nature.

Oasis Studios Inc, *(978-0-9785605)* Orders Addr.: 7701 Witherspoon Dr., Baltimore, OH 43105 USA Tel 740-862-8620
E-mail: ekayzer@hotmail.com
Web site: http://www.championoasisstudios.com
Dist(s): **Send The Light Distribution LLC.**

OASYS Pr., *(978-0-9863965)* 5916 E. Lake Pkwy. Suite 195, McDonough, GA 30253 USA Tel 678-561-5655; Fax: 877-720-8705
E-mail: alonzo@theoasysgroup.com
Web site: www.HiringMadeEasyasPIE.com; www.TheOASYSGroup.com.

†Oberlin College Pr., *(978-0-932440; 978-0-9973355)* 50 N. Professor St., Oberlin, OH 44074 USA (SAN 212-1883) Tel 440-775-8408; Fax: 440-775-8124
E-mail: oc.press@oberlin.edu
Web site: http://www.oberlin.edu/ocpress
Dist(s): **CUP Services**
Univ. Pr. of New England; *CIP.*

Oberon Bks., Ltd. (GBR) *(978-0-948230; 978-1-84002; 978-1-870259; 978-1-84943; 978-1-78319) Dist. by* **Consort Bk Sales.**

O'Brien, Gerard, *(978-0-9743850)* 115 Essex St., Indian Orchard, MA 01151-1409 USA Tel 413-543-5939
E-mail: gob@ifriendly.com.

O'Brien, Lara Publishing, *(978-0-9896752)* 47 Davis st, Vineyard Haven, MA 02568 USA Tel 774-563-0292
E-mail: laraeobrien@yahoo.com.

O'Brien Pr., Ltd., The (IRL) *(978-0-86278; 978-0-86322; 978-0-905140; 978-0-9502046; 978-1-902011; 978-1-84717) Dist. by* **Dufour.**

OBrien, Wiley Workspace, *(978-0-615-29492-6; 978-0-615-97038-7)* 125 Washington St., Canandaigua, NY 14424 USA
Web site: http://www.WonderlandBook.com.

Ocean Crest Publishing, LLC, *(978-0-9981322)* P.O. Box 842, Palm Beach, FL 33480 USA Tel 561-629-2528
E-mail: chelow@comcast.net
Web site: www.oceancrestpublishing.com.

Ocean Front Bk. Publishing, Inc., *(978-1-934190)* Orders Addr.: 9101 W. Sahara Ave. Suite 105-130, Las Vegas,, NV 89117 USA (SAN 852-0046) Tel 702-499-0608; 9101 W. Sahara Ave. Suite 105-130, Las Vegas,, NV 89117 (SAN 852-0046) Tel 702-499-0608
E-mail: jhorowitz@oceanfrontbooks.com
Web site: http://www.oceanfrontbooks.com.

Ocean World Photography, *(978-0-9766749)* 6461 Running Brook Rd., Manassas, VA 20112 USA
E-mail: wgregorybrown@comcast.net
Web site: http://www.wgregorybrown.com.

OceanAir Publishing *See* **Mayreni Publishing**

Oceano Grupo Editoria, S.A. (ESP) *(978-84-494; 978-84-7069; 978-84-7505; 978-84-7555; 978-84-7764; 978-84-85317; 978-84-9719) Dist. by* **Gale.**

Oceanus Bks. *Imprint of* **Warrington Pubns.**

Ocher Moon Pr., *(978-0-9765303)* 391 Joppa Mountain Rd., Rutledge, TN 37861 USA Tel 865-828-8280
E-mail: jeri@hopalonggreetings.com
Web site: http://www.hopalonggreetings.com.

OCRS, Incorporated *See* **River Pr.**

Octagon Pr., Ltd., *(978-0-86304; 978-0-900860)* Orders Addr.: P.O. Box 400541, Cambridge, MA 02140 USA; Edit Addr.: 171 Main St. No. 140, Los Altos , CA 94022 USA
Web site: http://www.octagonpress.com
Dist(s): **I S H K.**

Octagon Pr./ISHK Bk. Service *See* **I S H K**

Octane Pr., *(978-0-9821733; 978-0-9829131; 978-1-937747)* Orders Addr.: 809 S. Lamar Blvd Suite H, Austin, TX 78704 USA (SAN 920-9395) Tel 512-334-9441; Fax: 512-852-4737; 809 S. Lamar Blvd Suite H, Austin, TX 78704
E-mail: lee@octanepress.com; sales@octanepress.com; barbara@octanepress.com
Web site: octanepress.com
Dist(s): **Bookazine Co., Inc.**
Lightning Source, Inc.

Octavio Publishing, *(978-0-9822407)* P.O. Box 221322, Carmel, CA 93922 USA (SAN 857-6386)
Web site: http://www.louisoroberts.com.

OctiRam Publishing Co., *(978-0-9830423)* Orders Addr.: P.O. Box 5859, Vancouver, WA 98668 USA Tel 360-464-7670
E-mail: raski@comcast.net.

Octopoda Pr., *(978-0-9858506; 978-0-9908818)* P.O. Box 8943, Ketchikan, AK 99901 USA Tel 907-225-8212
E-mail: evon@evonzerbetz.com
Web site: octopodapress.com.

Octopus Publishing Co., *(978-0-9824433)* Div. of Octopus Enterprises LLC, 100 S. River Bend, Jackson, GA 30233-3204 USA
E-mail: rogerfen@bellsouth.net; geletaf@bellsouth.net.

Octopus Publishing Group (GBR) *(978-0-600; 978-0-905879; 978-1-84091; 978-1-86007; 978-1-84202; 978-1-84430; 978-1-904705; 978-1-84403; 978-1-84696; 978-1-905814; 978-1-84898; 978-1-908150; 978-1-907579; 978-1-78157; 978-1-78325) Dist. by* **HachBkGrp.**

Odd Duck Ink, Inc., *(978-1-933069)* P.O. Box 533, Norwell, MA 02061-0533 USA
E-mail: jennifer@oddduckink.com
Web site: http://www.oddduckink.com.

OddInt Media *Imprint of* **Greenwood Hill Pr.**

Oddo Publishing, Inc., *(978-0-87783)* Storybook Acres, Box 68, Fayetteville, GA 30214 USA (SAN 282-0757) Tel 770-461-7627.

Odds Bodkin Storytelling Library, The *Imprint of* **Rivertree Productions, Inc.**

Oden, Rachel, *(978-0-9729914)* 133 E. Graham Ave., Council Bluffs, IA 51503 USA Tel 712-323-7222 (phone/fax)
E-mail: cbmarketadmin@juno.com.

Odenwald Pr., *(978-0-9623216; 978-1-884363)* 6609 Brooks Dr., Temple, TX 76502 USA Tel 254-773-4884; Fax: 254-773-4884
E-mail: CSho777@aol.com
Dist(s): **SMMA Distributors.**

odod bks. *Imprint of* **Uncivilized Bks.**

Odyssey Bks. (AUS) *(978-0-9806909; 978-0-9872325; 978-1-922200; 978-1-925652) Dist. by* **LightSource CS.**

Off The Record *Imprint of* **College Prowler, Inc.**

Office of the Legal Adviser, Treaty Affairs Staff *Imprint of* **United States Government Printing Office**

Officer Byrd Publishing Co., *(978-0-9787322)* 15730 Williams Cir., Lake Mathews, CA 92570 USA (SAN 851-4712) Tel 951-334-6111
E-mail: officerbyrd@aol.com.

Officina Libraria srl (ITA) *(978-88-89854; 978-88-97737) Dist. by* **Natl Bk Netwk.**

Offshoot Pubns., *(978-0-910013)* 1280 Goodpasture Island Rd., Eugene, OR 97401 USA (SAN 241-3426) Tel 541-686-8266; Fax: 541-686-0910
E-mail: hgreer@greergardens.com
Dist(s): **National Bk. Network.**

OffTheBookshelf.com *See* **Micro Publishing Media, Inc.**

Oglethorpe Pr., Inc., *(978-1-891495)* 326 Bull St., Savannah, GA 31401 USA Tel 912-231-9900; Fax: 912-234-7258
E-mail: sjackel@comcast.net
Dist(s): **Parnassus Bk. Distributors.**

Ogma Pr., *(978-0-9785853)* 4717 Broad Rd., Syracuse, NY 13215 USA Tel 315-491-9339
E-mail: bernie@ogmapress.com
Web site: http://www.ogmapress.com.

Ogorek, Elchanan, *(978-0-692-76640-8)*.

Oh My Stars Publishing, *(978-0-615-20153-5)* 222 3rd St., Suite 4, Lemoyne, PA 17043 USA
Dist(s): **APG Sales & Distribution Services**
Lulu Pr., Inc.

OHC Group LLC, *(978-0-9763213)* P.O. Box 7839, Westlake Village, CA 91359 USA Tel 805-384-4800
Web site: http://www.onlyheartsclub.com.

Ohio Distinctive Publishing, Inc., *(978-0-9647934; 978-1-936772)* 6500 Fiesta Dr., Columbus, OH 43235 USA Tel 614-459-0453; Fax: 614-457-2488
E-mail: tim@ohio-distinctive.com
Web site: http://www.ohio-distinctive.com.

†Ohio Univ. Pr., *(978-0-8214)* Orders Addr.: 11030 S. Langley Ave., Chicago, IL 60628 USA Tel 773-702-7000; Fax: 773-702-7212; Toll Free Fax: 800-621-8476; Toll Free: 800-621-2736; Edit Addr.: 19 Circle Dr. The Ridges, Athens, OH 45701 USA (SAN 282-0773) Tel 740-593-1154; Fax: 740-593-4536
Web site: http://www.ohiou.edu/oupress/
Dist(s): **Chicago Distribution Ctr.**
Ebsco Publishing
Trajectory, Inc.
Univ. of Chicago Pr.
Univ. of Hawaii Pr.
ebrary, Inc.; *CIP.*

Ohnick Enterprises, *(978-0-9746222)* Orders Addr.: P.O. Box 969, Meade, KS 67864-0969 USA Tel 620-873-2900; Fax: 620-873-2603; Toll Free: 800-794-2356; Edit Addr.: 102 N. Fowler, Meade, KS 67864-0969 USA
E-mail: nancy@prairiebooks.com
Web site: http://backroomprinting.com.

Oka, Joseph *See* **Joseph's Labor**

Okasan & Me, *(978-0-9743613)* 829 N. Sixth St., San Jose, CA 95112 USA
Web site: http://www.okasanandme.com.

Oki, Blessed, *(978-0-9721336)* 2465 Heaton Dr., Suite A, East Point, GA 30344 USA
E-mail: blessiebeke@yahoo.com.

Oklahoma Energy Resources Board, *(978-0-615-19844-6; 978-0-615-39316-2; 978-0-692-63684-8)* 3555 NW 58th St., Suite 430, Oklahoma City, OK 73112 USA Tel 405-942-5323; Fax: 405-942-3435; Toll Free: 800-664-1301
Web site: http://www.oerb.com.

Oklahoma Heritage Assn., *(978-1-885596; 978-1-938923)* Orders Addr.: 1400 Classen Dr., Oklahoma City, OK 73106 USA Tel 405-235-4458; 405-523-3202; Fax: 405-235-2714; Toll Free: 888-501-2059
E-mail: gmc@oklahomaheritage.com
Web site: http://www.oklahomaheritage.com
Dist(s): **Partners Bk. Distributing, Inc.**

Olandar Pr. Ltd., *(978-0-9729502)* Orders Addr.: 2222 Parview Rd., Middleton, WI 53562 USA Tel 608-831-1222; Fax: 608-831-1647
Web site: http://www.leighmccloskey.com.

Ola's Hanalei LTD, *(978-0-9763907)* P.O. Box 488, Hanalei, HI 96714 USA
E-mail: olashanalei@hawaiiantel.net.

Old Bay Publishing, *(978-0-9745854)* 19 Meeting St., Huntsville, AL 35806-5230 USA
E-mail: msikes@hiwaay.net
Dist(s): **Partners Bk. Distributing, Inc.**

Old Bess Publishing Co., *(978-0-9631912; 978-0-9762132)* Orders Addr.: P.O. Box 277, Brunswick, ME 04011 USA Tel 207-725-8575; P.O. Box P.O. Box 277, Brunswick, ME 04011
E-mail: sbutcherr@mcn.net.

Old Bow Publishing, *(978-0-615-54029-0; 978-0-9853219)* 1816 Morgan Horse Farm Rd., Weybridge, VT 05753 USA Tel 410-456-7151
E-mail: achambleton@earthlink.net
Web site: www.oldbowpublishing.com
Dist(s): **Independent Pubs. Group.**

Old Farm Pr., *(978-0-9788227)* P.O. Box 20894, Oklahoma City, OK 73156-0894 USA (SAN 851-6995) Tel 405-748-7072; Fax: 405-748-7073
E-mail: spi@mbo.net
Web site: http://www.BobbyBrightBooks.com.

Old Farmer's Almanac *Imprint of* **Yankee Publishing, Inc.**

Old Hogan Publishing Co., (*978-0-9638851*) Orders Addr.: P.O. Box 91978, Tucson, AZ 85752 USA Tel 520-579-9321; Fax: 520-579-0502; Toll Free: 800-867-1506; Edit Addr.: 3600 W. Mesa Ridge Trail, Tucson, AZ 85742 USA
E-mail: mgaraway@juno.com
Web site: http://www.oldhogan.com
Dist(s): **Hispanic Bks. Distributors & Pubs., Inc.**
Rio Nuevo Pubs.

Old Hundredth Pr., (*978-0-9793911*) 2885 Gordon Rd., NW, Dover, OH 44622 USA.

O.L.D. Inc., (*978-0-9830470*) 118 N Ross St No. 6, Auburn, AL 36830 USA Tel 334-787-1713
E-mail: cwjones@oldinc.net.

Old Maps, (*978-0-911653; 978-0-9747639*) P.O. Box 54, West Chesterfield, NH 03466 USA (SAN 264-2689)
E-mail: daven@sover.net
Web site: http://www.old-maps.com.

Old Silver Pr., (*978-0-9800975*) 224 Coonamessett Cir., East Falmouth, MA 02536 USA
E-mail: OldSilverPress@yahoo.com.

Old Soldier Publishing, (*978-0-9764167*) Orders Addr.: P.O. Box 1113, Richmond, TX 77469 USA Tel 281-341-0781 (phone/fax); Edit Addr.: 1110 Pioneer Dr., Richmond, TX 77469 USA
Dist(s): **ebrary, Inc.**

Old St. Augustine Pubns., (*978-0-9833684; 978-0-692-38918-8*) P.O. Box 162056, Altamonte Springs, FL 32716 USA Fax: 407-774-8799
E-mail: doug@oldstaugustinepublications.com
Web site: http://www.oldstaugustinepublications.com
Dist(s): **Lightning Source, Inc.**

Old Stone Pr., (*978-1-938462*) 520 Old Stone Ln., Louisville, KY 40207 USA Tel 502-693-1506
E-mail: john@JHClarkandAssociates.com
Web site: OldStonePress.com
Dist(s): **Bookmasters Distribution.**

Old Time Stories, (*978-0-9792770*) 116 Beasley Rd., Cusseta, GA 31805-3206 USA.

Old Vine Oublishing Co., (*978-0-9794291*) P.O. Box 6774, Pine Mountain Club, CA 93222-6774 USA.

Old West Co., The, (*978-0-9654341; 978-0-9801743; 978-0-9898004*) Orders Addr.: 5118 Village Trail Dr., San Antonio, TX 78218-3831 USA; *Imprints:* Sweetwater Stagelines (Sweetwtr Stage)
E-mail: kirkwest@sbcglobal.net
Web site: http://lulu.com/sweetwater.

Oldcastle Bks., Ltd. (GBR) (*978-0-948353; 978-1-874061; 978-1-84243; 978-1-84344; 978-1-904915*) *Dist. by* **IPG Chicago.**

Oldcastle Publishing, (*978-0-932529*) Orders Addr.: P.O. Box 1193, Escondido, CA 92033 USA (SAN 297-9039) Tel 760-489-0336; Fax: 760-747-1198; Edit Addr.: 3415 Laredo Ln., Escondido, CA 92025 USA (SAN 297-9047)
E-mail: abcurtiss@cox.net
Web site: http://www.abcurtiss.com; http://www.depressionisachoice.com
Dist(s): **National Bk. Network.**

Olde Springfield Shoppe *See* **Masthof Pr.**

Olde Town Publishing, (*978-0-9755906*) 703 W. Main, Jonesborough, TN 37659 USA
Web site: http://www.drisbell.com.

Olde Towne Publishing, (*978-0-9794935*) P.O. Box 98, Old Mission, MI 49673 USA Do noty confuse with Olde Towne Publishing Company in Fredericksburg, VA
Web site: http://www.strolltraversecity.com
Dist(s): **Partners Bk. Distributing, Inc.**

Oleson, Susan, (*978-0-9779251*) 511 E Iowa St, Monona, IA 52159 USA
E-mail: sammytails@netins.net.

Olive Branch Publishing, LLC *See* **OlivesAngels Publishing, LLC**

Olive Grove Pubs., (*978-0-9752508*) 1420 King Rd., Hinckley, OH 44233 USA Tel 330-278-4028
E-mail: RSpirko@Roadrunner.com
Web site: http://www.atlasbooks.com
Dist(s): **American Wholesale Booksellers Assn.**
BookMasters, Inc.
Book$mart, Inc.
Bookmasters Distribution
New Leaf Distributing Co., Inc.
ebrary, Inc.

Olive Leaf Pubns., (*978-0-9761583*) 782 San Gabriel Loop, New Braunfels, TX 78132 USA (SAN 256-6206) Tel 830-626-7671
E-mail: sharon@oliveleafpublications.com
Web site: http://www.oliveleafpublications.com
Dist(s): **Lightning Source, Inc.**

Olive Pr. Pub., (*978-0-9790873; 978-0-9847111; 978-0-9855241; 978-1-941173*) P.O. Box 163, Copenhagen, NY 13626 USA Tel 315-941-6710.

Olive Pr., The, (*978-0-9769298*) Orders Addr.: P.O. Box 2056, Saintllwater, MN 55082 USA Tel 651-251-3063 Do not confuse with Olive Press i Ann Arbor, MI West Orange, NJ Estes Park, CO
E-mail: olivepressinc@yahoo.com
Web site: http://jumpstartfuture.com.

Olive Tree of Life, (*978-0-9768182*) P.O. Box 344, Tijeras, NM 87059 USA
Web site: http://www.olivetreeoflife.com.

Oliver Pr., Inc., (*978-1-881508; 978-1-934545*) Orders Addr.: 5707 W. 36th St., Minneapolis, MN 55416-2510 USA Tel 952-926-8981; Fax: 952-926-8965; Toll Free: 800-865-4837
E-mail: orders@oliverpress.com
Web site: http://www.oliverpress.com.

Oliver Pr. LLC, (*978-0-692-42047-8; 978-0-692-42048-5; 978-0-692-78667-3; 978-0-692-87956-6*) 1935 Chene Ct. Apt. 1505, Detroit, MI 48207 USA Tel 313-744-8543
E-mail: grimlyjane@yahoo.com
Dist(s): **CreateSpace Independent Publishing Platform**
Lightning Source, Inc.

Oliver, Sarah (GBR) (*978-0-9559820*) *Dist. by* **LuluCom.**

Oliver, Wade, (*978-0-9768030*) P.O. Box 1605, Logan, UT 84322-1605 USA
E-mail: wademan@cache.net
Web site: http://www.dovepage.com.

OlivesAngels Publishing, LLC, (*978-0-9793147*) P.O. Box 940725, Plano, TX 75094-0725 USA (SAN 853-0955) Tel 972-977-4881
E-mail: olivesangels@tx.rr.com.

Olivo, Andy, (*978-0-9743376*) 1807 Glengarry St., Carrollton, TX 75006 USA Tel 972-242-0924; Fax: 972-242-1754; *Imprints:* Brown Books (Brown BksTX).

OLLY Publishing Co., (*978-0-9720427*) 4335 Lake Michigan Dr., NW Suite H, Grand Rapids, MI 49544 USA (SAN 254-587X) Tel 616-735-0553
E-mail: diane@ollypublishing.com
Web site: http://www.ollypublishing.com.

Olms, Georg Verlag AG (DEU) (*978-3-487*) *Dist. by* **IPG Chicago.**

Olmstead LLC *See* **Olmstead Publishing LLC**

Olmstead Publishing LLC, (*978-0-9667696; 978-1-934194*) Orders Addr.: 2629 Grassmoor Lp, Apopka, FL 32712-5005 USA Tel 954-559-0192 (phone); Fax: 650-479-8273
E-mail: olmsteadpublishing@usa.com
Web site: http://www.olmsteadpublishing.com; http://https://squareup.com/market/olmstead-publishing-llc; http://www.facebook.com/olmsteadpublishing.

Olsen, Mary Bks., (*978-0-9715374*) P.O. Box 882, Eastsound, WA 98245-0882 USA
E-mail: mary@maryolsenbooks.com.

Olson, Robin, (*978-0-9818695*) P.O. Box 5294, Laytonsville, MD 20882 USA (SAN 856-7719)
E-mail: robin@robinsweb.com
Web site: http://www.robinsweb.com.

Oma Publishing Co., (*978-0-9747175*) 2217 Eden Rd., Seguin, TX 78155-0179 USA Tel 210-684-3200.

Omaha Bks., (*978-0-9745410; 978-0-9788429; 978-0-9908000*) Div. of Eventive Marketing, 5037 Parker St., Omaha, NE 68104 USA (SAN 857-1295) Tel 402-679-5854
E-mail: kristine.gerber@cox.net; jkgerber@cox.net
Dist(s): **Partners Bk. Distributing, Inc.**

O'Mara, Michael Bks., Ltd. (GBR) (*978-1-85479; 978-0-946429; 978-0-948397; 978-1-84317; 978-1-903840; 978-1-904613; 978-1-907151; 978-1-78243; 978-1-910552*) *Dist. by* **IPG Chicago.**

O'Mara, Michael Bks., Ltd. (GBR) (*978-1-85479; 978-0-946429; 978-0-948397; 978-1-84317; 978-1-903840; 978-1-904613; 978-1-907151; 978-1-78243; 978-1-910552*) *Dist. by* **Trans-Atl Phila.**

O'Mara, Michael Bks., Ltd. (GBR) (*978-1-85479; 978-0-946429; 978-0-948397; 978-1-84317; 978-1-903840; 978-1-904613; 978-1-907151; 978-1-78243; 978-1-910552*) *Dist. by* **IngramPubServ.**

Omega Hse. Publishing, (*978-0-9672519*) Div. of Spectrum Group, Inc., Orders Addr.: P.O. Box 68, Three Rivers, MI 49093 USA Tel 269-273-7070; Fax: 269-273-7026; Edit Addr.: 58690 US 131, Three Rivers, MI 49093 USA
E-mail: zendra@omega777.com.

Omega Pr., (*978-0-9626087; 978-0-9754923; 978-1-933951*) 5823 N. Mesa, No. 823, El Paso, TX 79912-3340 USA Tel 915-584-6844; Toll Free: 888-560-1243 Do not confuse with companies with the same name in Tustin, CA
E-mail: ken@kenhudnall.com
Web site: http://www.omegapress.us; http://www.kenhudnall.com; http://shop.kenhudnall.com.

Omega Prime, LLC, (*978-0-9897588*) 3521 Hartzdale Dr., Camp Hill, PA 17011-7231 USA Tel 717-579-0038
E-mail: SusanRShutt@OmegaPrime.net
Web site: http://www.loveoffizz.com; http://www.fortheloveoffizz.com; http://www.omegaprime.net.

Omega Publishing, (*978-0-9748494*) P.O. Box 53626, Lubbock, TX 79453 USA (SAN 255-8815) Tel 806-748-9880; Fax: 806-748-9870; Toll Free: 877-842-9880 do not confuse with companies iwth the same or similar name in Madisonville, KY, Stockton, GA, Snohomish, WA, Norcross, GA
E-mail: jpartin@omega-pub.com
Web site: http://www.omega-pub.com.

Omega Publishing Hse., (*978-1-886297*) Subs. of B. C. & G. Graphics, Orders Addr.: 2935 Glenwood Ave., Youngstown, OH 44511 USA Tel 330-881-1344; Fax: 330-782-7599
E-mail: omegapublishing@ymail.com; craiga2356@msn.com
Web site: http://omegapublishinghouse.com.

Omen Sky Pubns., (*978-0-9744192*) 3600 Brookewind Way, No. 1201, Lexington, KY 40515 USA Tel 859-543-2026 (phone/fax)
E-mail: omensky@qx.net.

Omni Arts Publishing *Imprint of* **Read Street Publishing, Inc.**

Omni Arts Publishing, Incorporated *See* **Read Street Publishing, Inc.**

Omnibus Publishing, (*978-0-9740599*) 3402 Beresford Ave., Belmont, CA 94002 USA Tel 650-622-9702; Fax: 650-240-3586
E-mail: yuhogan@omnibuspublishing.com
Web site: http://www.omnibuspublishing.com.

Omnific Publishing, (*978-1-936305; 978-1-62342*) P.O. Box 793871, Dallas, TX 75379 USA Fax: 214-975-4889
E-mail: publisher@omnificpublishing.com
Web site: http://www.omnificpublishing.com
Dist(s): **Ingram Publisher Services.**

†**Omnigraphics, Inc.**, (*978-0-7808; 978-1-55888*) Orders Addr.: P.O. Box 8002, Aston, PA 19014-8002 USA Tel 800-234-1340; Fax: 800-875-1340; Toll Free Fax: 800-875-1340 (orders & customer service); Toll Free: 800-234-1340 (orders & customer service); Edit Addr.: 615 Griswold, Suite 901, Detroit, MI 48226 USA (SAN 249-2520)
E-mail: info@omnigraphics.com; customerservice@omnigraphics.com
Web site: http://www.omnigraphics.com
Dist(s): **Ebsco Publishing**
Gale Virtual Reference Library
Independent Pubs. Group
Mackin Educational Resources
MyiLibrary
Rittenhouse Bk. Distributors
Visible Ink Pr.
ebrary, Inc.; *CIP.*

O'More Publishing, (*978-0-9717444; 978-0-9800285; 978-0-9822618; 978-0-9846244; 978-0-9860150; 978-0-9860244*) 423 S. Margin St., Franklin, TN 37064 USA Fax: 615-790-1662; 615-790-1666
E-mail: mhilliard@omorecollege.edu; jsexton@omorecollege.edu
Web site: http://www.omorepublishing.com.

On Cape Pubns., (*978-0-9653283; 978-0-9719547; 978-0-9758502; 978-0-9785766; 978-0-9913401*) Orders Addr.: 87 Barley Neck Rd., Orleans, MA 02638 USA Tel 508-385-2108 Toll Free: 877-662-5839
E-mail: chopi@goodnightbooks.com
Web site: http://www.oncapepublications.com
Dist(s): **Independent Pubs. Group.**

On The Ball Publishing, (*978-0-615-21079-7; 978-0-615-25047-2; 978-0-615-45284-5; 978-0-615-45296-8; 978-0-9834341*) 12821 Stratford Dr. Suite 114, Oklahoma City, OK 73120 USA Tel 405-549-1174
E-mail: admin@ontheballpublishing.com
Web site: http://www.ontheballpublishing.com
Dist(s): **Lulu Pr., Inc.**

On The Edge Pubns., (*978-0-9762360*) P.O. Box 690007, Stockton, CA 95269 USA Tel 209-473-8553
E-mail: ontheedgepublications@msn.com
Web site: http://www.ontheedgepublications.com.

On the Spot! Bks., (*978-0-9652998*) 1492 Tipperary St., Boulder, CO 80303 USA Tel 303-666-0550
E-mail: onthespotbooks@msn.com
Web site: www.kerryleemaclean.com
Dist(s): **Bks. West**
New Leaf Distributing Co., Inc.

On Tour Publishing, (*978-0-9767234*) Orders Addr.: 512 Northampton St., 151, 303, Edwardsville, PA 18704 USA
E-mail: otp@ontourpublishing.com.

ON Words Publishing, LLC, (*978-0-9787589*) 8720 Ferguson Ave., Savannah, GA 31406 USA.

Once Upon A Time in a Classroom *Imprint of* **Interactive Media Publishing**

Oncekids, (*978-0-9844207; 978-1-938806*) 119 Maono Pl., Honolulu, HI 96821 USA (SAN 859-3574)
E-mail: oncekids@gmail.com
Dist(s): **Bookmasters Distribution.**

Oncology Nursing Press, Incorporated *See* **Oncology Nursing Society**

Oncology Nursing Society, (*978-1-890504; 978-1-935864; 978-1-63593*) Subs. of Oncology Nursing Society, 125 Enterprise Dr., Pittsburgh, PA 15275-1214 USA (SAN 689-8041) Tel 412-859-6100
E-mail: jholmes@ons.org
Web site: http://www.ons.org.

One Arm Publishing, (*978-0-9746024*) 3344 Via La Selva, Palos Verdes Estates, CA 90274 USA
E-mail: mariana1969@hotmail.com
Web site: http://www.onearmpublishing.com.

One Armed Operation *See* **One Arm Publishing**

One Coin Publishing, LLC, (*978-0-615-31066-4*) 6876 Towhee, Portage, MI 49024 USA.

One Eyed Pr., (*978-0-9665430; 978-0-615-26684-8*) 272 Rd. 6RT, Cody, WY 82414 USA Tel 307-272-9628; 307-587-6136
E-mail: one_eyed_press@yahoo.com
Web site: http://www.one-eyed-press.com
Dist(s): **Bks. West**
CreateSpace Independent Publishing Platform
Todd Communications.

One Eyed Tiger Publishing, (*978-0-9971588*) 1420 NE Brockman Pl, Seattle, WA 98125 USA Tel 206-228-5954
E-mail: hindmank@gmail.com.

One Faithful Harp Publishing Co., (*978-0-9666701*) 138 N. 2nd St., Catawissa, PA 17820-1210 USA
E-mail: info@onefaithfulharp.com
Web site: http://www.onefaithfulharp.com.

One Horse Pr., (*978-0-9725650*) 963 Maple Hill Dr., Erie, PA 16509 USA Tel 814-923-4086
E-mail: stephanie@stephaniewincik.com
Web site: http://www.stephaniewincik.com.

One in Me, The, (*978-0-9898437*) 503 Wicklow Pl., Acworth, GA 30102 USA Tel 678-324-8750; Fax: 678-324-8750
E-mail: tgodoy@comcast.net.

One In The Son Publishing, (*978-0-9973723*) 16745 SE Division St. No. 127, Portland, OR 97236 USA Tel 503-730-4688
E-mail: littleredappletree@hotmail.com
Web site: oneintheson.com.

One Little Miracle, (*978-0-9743948*) 1449 Highland Ct., Stillwater, MN 55082 USA Tel 651-439-3250
E-mail: allieschield@hotmail.com
Web site: http://www.onelittlemiracle.com.

One Little Spark, (*978-0-615-53981-2; 978-0-578-12711-8*) 239 W. Lime Ave., Monrovia, CA 91016 USA Tel 818-621-3466; Fax: 626-486-9456
E-mail: vicki@onelilspark.com
Web site: onelilspark.com.

One Love Assn. Bks., (*978-0-9776603*) 306 Trillick Ct., Rolesville, NC 27571 USA (SAN 257-8654)
E-mail: ras@newkemet.com; gerald@newkemet.com
Web site: http://www.newkemet.com/gerald.

One Million Words, LLC, (*978-0-9910562*) 1122 Carriage Cir., Fond du Lac, WI 54935 USA Tel 920-904-5249
E-mail: onemillionwords@hotmail.com
Web site: www.david-michael-williams.com.

One Monkey Bks., (*978-0-9777082; 978-1-940722*) 156 Diamond St., San Francisco, CA 94114-2414 USA (SAN 850-0320).

One Night Bks. *Imprint of* **WordWright.biz, Inc.**

One of a Kind Books, Incorporated *See* **Webster Henrietta Publishing**

One Part Rain, (*978-0-692-79233-9*) 340 E. 4380 N., PROVO, UT 84604 USA Tel 801-420-8087.

One Peace Bks., Inc., (*978-0-9785084; 978-1-935548; 978-1-944937*) 43-32 22nd St. #204, Long Island City, NY 11101 USA (SAN 850-7430) Tel 718-482-9100; Fax: 718-482-9101
E-mail: mcguire@onepeacebooks.com
Web site: http://www.onepeacebooks.com
Dist(s): **SCB Distributors.**

One Pink Rose, (*978-0-9722991*) 111921 Rawson Rd., Red Bluff, CA 96080 USA
E-mail: pinkwhirlwind@cablespeed.com; squallsknight@yahoo.com
Web site: http://www.darkfedora.com.

One Rib Pubns., (*978-0-9722625; 978-0-9746191; 978-1-944414*) Orders Addr.: 1811 NW 51st St., Fort Lauderdale, FL 33309 USA Tel 954-489-0141; Edit Addr.: PMB 826, 2001 NW 51st St., Ft. Lauderdale, FL 33309 USA.

1 Sleeve Publishing, (*978-0-9729153*) Orders Addr.: P.O. Box 1865, North Mankato, MN 56002-1865 USA; Edit Addr.: 442 Belgrade Ave., No. 13, North Mankato, MN 56003 USA
E-mail: onesleeve@hotmail.com.

One Source Publishing, LLC, (*978-0-9779374*) 63 Gates St, White River Junction, VT 05001 USA Fax: 802-295-5338
E-mail: hphipps@onesourcefg.com.

One Too Tree Publishing, (*978-0-9820781*) 106 Calendar Ct., No. 108, La Grange, IL 60525-2325 USA (SAN 857-1732)
E-mail: publisher@onetootree.com
Web site: http://www.OneTooTree.com.

One Voice Recordings, (*978-0-9708022*) 16835 Halper St., Encino, CA 91436 USA Tel 818-501-8145 (phone/fax)
E-mail: ddavies858@aol.com.

One Way Bks., (*978-0-9800451; 978-1-936459*) Div. of Waht About You?, Inc., 2269 S. Univ. Dr. #330, Fort Lauderdale, FL 33324 USA Tel 954-680-9095
Web site: http://www.OneWayBooks.org
Dist(s): **MyiLibrary**
Send The Light Distribution LLC
ebrary, Inc.

One Way St., Inc., (*978-1-58302*) Orders Addr.: P.O. Box 5077, Englewood, CO 80155-5077 USA Tel 303-790-1188; Fax: 303-790-2159; Toll Free: 800-569-4537
E-mail: webmaster@onewaystreet.com
Web site: http://www.onewaystreet.com.

OneHope, (*978-1-890525; 978-1-931940; 978-1-59480; 978-1-63049*) 600 SW 3rd St., Pompano Beach, FL 33060-6936 USA Toll Free: 800-448-2425
E-mail: andreadragotas@onehope.net.

ONeill, Gene & Assoc., (*978-0-9747797*) 10163 Potter Rd., Des Plaines, IL 60016 USA.

O'Neill, Hugh & Assocs., (*978-0-9675919; 978-0-615-76348-4*) Orders Addr.: P.O. Box 1297, Nevada City, CA 95959 USA Tel 530-265-4196; Edit Addr.: 227 Prospect St., Nevada City, CA 95959 USA
E-mail: info@bydb.com
Web site: http://www.bydb.com
Dist(s): **CreateSpace Independent Publishing Platform.**

O'Neill, Jan, (*978-0-9746409*) 5681 Rives Junction Rd., Jackson, MI 49201-9413 USA.

O'Neill-Sheehan, Elizabeth, (*978-0-692-69931-7; 978-0-692-76666-8; 978-0-692-76678-1*) 30 Vreeland Ave, East Longmeadow, MA 01028 USA Tel 413-519-5393.

OneShare Educational Pr., (*978-0-9788438*) 3450 Third St. Bldg. 1-D, San Francisco, CA 94124 USA (SAN 851-7487) Tel 415-777-1777; Fax: 415-777-1677; Toll Free: 888-777-6919
Web site: http://www.oneshare.com.

Oneworld Pubns. (GBR) (*978-1-85168; 978-1-78074*) *Dist. by* **PerseuPGW.**

Oni Pr., Inc., (*978-0-9667127; 978-1-929998; 978-1-932664; 978-1-934964; 978-1-62010*) 1305 SE Martin Luther King Jr. Blvd., Suite A, Portland, OR 97214 USA Tel 503-233-1377; Fax: 503-233-1477
E-mail: joe@onipress.com
Web site: http://www.onipress.com
Dist(s): **Diamond Comic Distributors, Inc.**
Diamond Bk. Distributors.

Onion River Pr., (*978-0-9657144; 978-0-9976458*) 21 Essex Way No. 407, Essex Junction, VT 05452 USA (SAN 990-1736) Tel 802-872-7111 (phone/fax)
E-mail: michael@phoenixbooks.biz; rachelf@phoenixbooks.biz
Web site: http://www.onionriverpress.com; www.phoenixbooks.biz.

ONLY1EARTH, LLC, (*978-0-9763354*) 3146 The Alameda Suite 7, San Jose, CA 95126 USA
E-mail: only1earthinc@gmail.com
Web site: http://www.theturtlekey.com.

Onondaga Hill Publishing, (*978-0-9794908*) 4586 Bloomsbury Dr., Syracuse, NY 13215 USA Tel 315-420-3025
E-mail: mdunn@imsolv.com; matthew@matthewdunn.net
Web site: http://www.matthewdunn.net
Dist(s): **BookBaby.**

For full information on wholesalers and distributors, refer to the Wholesaler and Distributor Name Index

Onrise Pubns., *(978-0-9658228)* 1820 Korbel Ct., Box 77938, Stockton, CA 95210 USA Tel 209-473-7889; 209-992-0575
E-mail: tqadree@netzero.com
Web site: http://www.tamirqadree.com.

Onstage Publishing, LLC, *(978-0-9700752; 978-0-9753367; 978-0-9790857)* Orders Addr.: 190 Lime Quarry Rd., Suite 106 J, Madison, AL 35758 USA Tel 256-461-0661; Fax: 256-461-0661
E-mail: onstage123@knology.net
Web site: http://www.onstagepublishing.com.

ONTRAK, *(978-0-9765502)* P.O. Box 205, Bethel, CT 06801-0153 USA Do not confuse with Ontrak in Yorba Linda, CA
E-mail: plumtrees@snet.net.

ooli & tooli llc, *(978-0-9987126)* 65 crest Dr. N., cresskill, NJ 07626 USA Tel 551-206-5577; Fax: 551-206-5577
E-mail: pollak.ora@gmail.com
Web site: ooliandtooli.com.

Ooligan Pr., *(978-1-932010; 978-1-947845)* Div. of Portland State Univ., Dept. of English, Orders Addr.: Dept. of English Portland State Univ. P.O. Box 751, Portland, OR 97207 USA Tel 503-725-9410; Fax: 503-725-3561; Edit Addr.: 630 SW Mill St., 97201, Rm. Nh405, Portland, OR 97201 USA
E-mail: ooligan@ooliganpress.pdx.edu; agaterud@pdx.edu
Web site: http://www.ooliganpress.pdx.edu; http://www.publishing.pdx.edu
Dist(s): **Ingram Publisher Services.**

OPA Author Services, *(978-0-911041)* Div. of Optimum Performance Associates, 777 W. Chandler Blvd., No. 1322, Chandler, AZ 85225-2511 USA (SAN 254-9255) Tel 480-275-5270; 480-393-1646 (phone/fax)
Web site: http://www.opaauthorservices.com; http://www.opapublishing.com
Dist(s): **OPA Publishing & Distributing.**

OPA Publishing *See* **OPA Author Services**

Opacity, Inc., *(978-0-615-14266-1)* 7086 SW Iron Horse St., Wilsonville, OR 97070 USA
Dist(s): **Lulu Pr., Inc.**

Open Arms Publishing, *(978-0-9770841)* 607 Knob Ct., Fayetteville, NC 28303 USA Tel 910-258-3941
E-mail: sallymander66@earthlink.net; thoglenm@yahoo.com
Web site: http://www.oaim.net.

Open Bk. Publishing, *(978-0-9719167; 978-0-9740321; 978-1-932621)* Rte. 2, Box 2607, Birch Tree, MO 65438 USA Tel 573-292-3368; Fax: 573-292-8115 Do not confuse with Open Book Publising Company in Huntington beach, CA
E-mail: ifann@socket.net; ifann@socket.net
Web site: http://www.openbookpublishing.com.

Open Bk. Publishing Co., *(978-0-9753349)* P.O. Box 3602, Huntington Beach, CA 92649 USA Tel 714-264-7284; Fax: 714-846-6782 Do not confuse with Open Book Publishing in Birch Tree, MO
E-mail: k.cutt@verizon.net
Web site: http://www.openbookpublishingcompany.com.

Open City Bks., *(978-1-890447)* 270 Lafayette St. Ste. 1410, New York, NY 10012-3327 USA
E-mail: editors@opencity.org
Web site: http://www.opencity.org
Dist(s): **Grove/Atlantic, Inc.**
SPD-Small Pr. Distribution.

†Open Court, *(978-0-8126; 978-0-87548; 978-0-89688; 978-0-912050; 978-0-8126-9956-2)* Div. of S R A/McGraw-Hill, 220 E. Daniel Dale Rd., DeSoto, TX 75115 USA Fax: 972-228-1982; Toll Free: 888-772-4543; 800-442-9685 (orders)
Web site: https://www.sraonline.com
Dist(s): **Libros Sin Fronteras**
SRA/McGraw-Hill; *CIP.*

Open Court Publishing Co., *(978-0-8126; 978-0-87548; 978-0-89688; 978-0-912050)* Div. of Carus Publishing Co., Orders Addr.: c/o Publishers Group West, 1700 Fourth St., Berkeley, CA 94710 USA Fax: 510-528-3444; Toll Free: 800-788-3123; Edit Addr.: 70 E. Lake St. Ste. 300, Chicago, IL 60601-5945 USA Toll Free: 800-815-2280
E-mail: opencourt@caruspub.com
Web site: http://www.opencourtbooks.com
Dist(s): **Follett School Solutions**
MyiLibrary.

Open Door Pr., *(978-1-942264)* 42299 Chisolm Trail, Murrieta, CA 92562 USA Tel 951-461-9072
E-mail: khales@me.com
Web site: http://www.opendoor-press.com.

Open Door Publishers, Inc., *(978-0-9841721; 978-1-937138)* 2373 Rte. 9, Mechanicville, NY 12118 USA (SAN 858-625X) Tel 518-899-2097
E-mail: adamiszyn@hotmail.com; ladean@opendoorpublishers.com
Web site: http://www.ladeanwarner.com; http://opendoorpublishers.com/.

Open Gate Publishing, *(978-0-9717036; 978-1-937195)* Div. of Open Gate Sangha, Inc., Orders Addr.: P.O. Box 112107, Campbell, CA 95011-2107 USA; Edit Addr.: 1299 Del Mar Ave., Suite 200, San Jose, CA 95128-3548 USA
E-mail: jerilyn@adyashanti.org
Web site: http://www.adyashanti.org
Dist(s): **New Leaf Distributing Co., Inc.**

Open Gate Sangha Publishing *See* **Open Gate Publishing**

Open Hand Publishing, LLC, *(978-0-940880)* P.O. Box 20207, Greensboro, NC 27420 USA (SAN 219-6174) Tel 336-292-8585; Fax: 336-292-8588
E-mail: info@openhand.com
Web site: http://www.openhand.com.

Open Heaven Pubns., *(978-0-9752622)* P.O. Box 457, Moravian Falls, NC 28654 USA
Web site: http://www.garyoates.com.

Open Mind Pr., *(978-0-9755157)* P.O. Box 1338, Garden Grove, CA 92844 USA Tel 714-322-3049 Do not confuse with Open Mind Press in Garner, NC
E-mail: openmindpress@albalagh.net
Web site: http://www.openmindpress.com.

Open Pages Publishing, *(978-0-9785937)* Orders Addr.: P.O. Box 420788, Houston, TX 77242 USA (SAN 851-0822); Edit Addr.: 3130 Walnut Bend Ln., Unit No. 317, Houston, TX 77042-4778 USA
E-mail: goodstory@openpagespublishing.com.

Open Road Integrated Media, Inc., *(978-1-58586; 978-0-7592; 978-1-936317; 978-1-4532; 978-1-61756; 978-0-9832929; 978-1-937624; 978-1-937957; 978-1-938582; 978-0-615-65097-5; 978-1-62467; 978-1-4804; 978-1-4976; 978-1-5040)* 180 Varick St. Suite 816, New York, NY 10014 USA Tel 212-691-0900; Fax: 212-691-0901; 345 Hudson St., Suite 6C, New York, NY 10014 Tel 212-691-0900; Fax: 212-691-0901; *Imprints:* Open Road Young Readers (OPEN ROAD YOUN); Open Road Media E-riginal (OpenRdMedE-rig)
E-mail: acolvin@openroadmedia.com
Web site: http://www.openroadmedia.com
Dist(s): **Follett School Solutions**
Independent Pubs. Group
Ingram Publisher Services
MyiLibrary.

Open Road Media E-riginal *Imprint of* **Open Road Integrated Media, Inc.**

Open Road Young Readers *Imprint of* **Open Road Integrated Media, Inc.**

Open Spaces Publishing (Rupen), LLC, *(978-0-9768752; 978-0-9846494)* 1411 Timberlake Circle, Richardson, TX 75080 USA
E-mail: chistinerhoden@att.net.

Open Suitcase, *(978-0-9985496)* 461 Wildwood Dr., St. Augustine, FL 32086-2903 USA Tel 352-316-2355
E-mail: Myopensuitcase@gmail.com
Web site: Myopensuitcase.com.

Open Texture, *(978-0-9742391; 978-1-933900)* 9457 S. Univ. Blvd. #409, Highlands Ranch, CO 80126 USA Toll Free: 866-546-6459 (phone/fax)
E-mail: sales@opentexture.com
Web site: http://www.opentexture.com.

Open Vision Entertainment Corp., *(978-0-9721825)* 48 Summer St., Stoneham, MA 02180 USA Tel 781-438-7939; Fax: 781-438-8115
Web site: http://www.open-visions.com
Dist(s): **Fell, Frederick Pubs., Inc.**

Open Window Publishing, *(978-0-9798505)* P.O. Box 1436, Clarkston, MI 48347-1436 USA (SAN 854-5642).

Openvein, *(978-0-9764033)* 3760 SE Morrison St., Portland, OR 97214-3210 USA
Web site: http://www.openvein.com/.

Oppenheim Toy Portfolio, Inc., *(978-0-9664823; 978-0-9721050)* 40 E. Ninth St., Suite 14M, New York, NY 10003 USA (SAN 255-2175) Tel 212-598-0502; Fax: 212-598-9709
E-mail: stephanie@toyportfolio.com
Web site: http://www.toyportfolio.com
Dist(s): **Brodart Co.**

Opportune Independent Publishing Co., *(978-0-9965694; 978-1-945532)* 113 Live Oak St, Houston, TX 77003 USA Tel 832-792-8269
E-mail: info@opportunepublishing.com
Web site: www.opportunepublishing.com.

Opposable Thumb Pr., *(978-0-9786570)* P.O. Box 409107, Chicago, IL 60640 USA
E-mail: Dawn@opposablethumbpress.com
Web site: http://opposablethumbpress.com.

Options Galore, *(978-0-9801426)* 22890 S. Woodland Rd., Suite 100, Shaker Heights, OH 44122 USA Tel 216-965-8599.

Optiview Publishing, *(978-0-9723066)* 7725 Martin Mill Pike, Knoxville, TN 37920 USA
E-mail: mmediajohn@ao.com
Web site: http://www.optiviewpubs.com.

OPUS II Bks., *(978-0-9796210)* Orders Addr.: 1216 Purple Sage Loop, Castle Rock, CO 80104 USA (SAN 853-9367) Tel 720-371-1872
E-mail: egualberto@opusiibooks.com
Web site: http://www.opusiibooks.com.

Oracle Institute Pr., LLC, The, *(978-0-9773929; 978-1-937465)* Div. of The Oracle Institute, Orders Addr.: 88 Oracle Way, Independence, VA 24348 USA (SAN 257-4780) Tel 276-773-3308
E-mail: Laura@TheOracleInstitute.org; Eric@TheOracleInstitute.org
Web site: http://www.TheOracleInstitute.org
Dist(s): **Lightning Source, Inc.**
New Leaf Distributing Co., Inc.

Orage Publishing, *(978-0-9740901)* 1460 Wren Ct., Punta Gorda, FL 33950 USA Tel 941-639-6144
E-mail: ntoupsschmitt@comcast.net.

Orange Avenue Publishing *See* **Zest Bks.**

Orange County Historical Society, Inc., *(978-1-932547)* 130 Caroline St., Orange, VA 22960 USA Tel 540-672-5366 (Wednesday afternoon)
E-mail: info@orangecohist.org
Web site: http://www.orangecohist.org.

Orange Frazer Pr., *(978-0-9619637; 978-1-882203; 978-1-933197; 978-1-939710)* Orders Addr.: P.O. Box 214, Wilmington, OH 45177 USA (SAN 245-9299)
E-mail: ofrazer@erinet.com
Web site: http://www.orangefrazer.com
Dist(s): **Partners Bk. Distributing, Inc.**

Orange Hat Publishing, *(978-1-937165; 978-1-943331)* 2726 N. 88th St., Milwaukee, WI 53222 USA Tel 414-755-0515
E-mail: orangehatpublishing@gmail.com
Web site: www.orangehatpublishing.com.

Orange, Michael Nicholas, *(978-0-9758877)* Orders Addr.: P.O. Box 236, Half Moon Bay, CA 94019 USA; Edit Addr.: 646 Filbert St., Half Moon Bay, CA 94019-2112 USA.

Orange Ocean Pr., *(978-1-885021)* 127 Bennett Ave., Long Beach, CA 90803-2935 USA; *Imprints:* Tangerine Tide (Tang Tide)
E-mail: nextmag@aol.com.

Orange Spot Publishing, *(978-0-9785191)* P.O. Box 224, Freeland, WA 98249 USA
Web site: http://www.pugetsoundbackyardbirds.com.

OrangeFoot Publishing Co., *(978-0-9760651)* P.O. Box 3694, Pittsburgh, PA 15230-3694 USA
E-mail: orangefootpublishing@zoominternet.net; info@orangefootpublishing.com.

Oratia Media (NZL) *(978-1-877514; 978-0-473-17634-1; 978-0-947506)* *Dist. by* **Casemate Pubs.**

Orb Bks. *Imprint of* **Doherty, Tom Assocs., LLC**

Orbis Publications, Incorporated *See* **Bilingual Dictionaries, Inc.**

Orbit, *(978-89-527)* Div. of Hachette Book Group, 237 Park Ave., New York, NY 10017 USA; *Imprints:* Yen Press (YenOr)
Dist(s): **Blackstone Audio, Inc.**
Hachette Bk. Group
MyiLibrary.

Orca Bk. Pubs. USA, *(978-0-920501; 978-1-55143; 978-1-55469)* Orders Addr.: P.O. Box 468, Custer, WA 98240-0468 USA (SAN 630-9674) Tel 250-380-1229; Fax: 250-380-1892; Toll Free: 800-210-5277
E-mail: orca@orcabook.com
Web site: http://www.orcabook.com.

Orchard Bks. *Imprint of* **Scholastic, Inc.**

Orchard Bks. *Imprint of* **Scholastic Library Publishing**

Orchard House Press *See* **Blue Forge Pr.**

Orchard Pr. *Imprint of* **Point Publishing**

Orchid Isle Publishing Co., *(978-1-887916)* 131 Halai St., Hilo, HI 96720 USA.

Orchid Pr. (THA) *(978-974-8299; 978-974-8304; 978-974-86220; 978-974-87426; 978-974-89229; 978-974-87356; 978-974-89212; 978-974-89218; 978-974-89219; 978-974-89271; 978-974-89272; 978-974-524)* *Dist. by* **Natl Bk Netwk.**

Orchid Publishing Co., *(978-0-9740898)* 14906 SW 104 St., Miami, FL 33196 USA.

Orchid Publishing, Inc., *(978-0-9831641; 978-0-9838325)* 333 N. Michigan Ave. Suite 222, Chicago, IL 60601 USA Tel 312-332-7200
E-mail: efimova@russianpointe.com.

Oregon Ctr. for Applied Science, Inc., *(978-1-933698)* 260 E. 11th Ave., Eugene, OR 97401-3291 USA (SAN 850-5284) Toll Free: 888-349-5472
E-mail: orcas@orcasinc.com
Web site: http://www.orcasinc.com.

Oregon State Univ. Extension Service, *(978-1-931979)* Extension & Station Communications 422 Kerr Administration, Corvallis, OR 97331 USA Tel 541-737-0807; Fax: 541-737-0817
Web site: http://extension.oregonstate.edu/eesc/.

†Oregon State Univ. Pr., *(978-0-87071)* 500 Kerr Administration Bldg., Corvallis, OR 97331-2122 USA (SAN 202-8328) Tel 541-737-3166; Fax: 541-737-3170; Toll Free: 800-426-3797
E-mail: osu.press@oregonstate.edu
Web site: http://osupress.oregonstate.edu/
Dist(s): **American Society of Civil Engineers**
Chicago Distribution Ctr.
Partners Bk. Distributing, Inc.
University of Arizona Pr.
Univ. of Oklahoma Pr.; *CIP.*

O'Reilly & Associates, Incorporated *See* **O'Reilly Media, Inc.**

O'Reilly Media, Inc., *(978-0-937175; 978-1-56592; 978-3-89721; 978-3-930673; 978-4-900900; 978-0-596; 978-4-87311; 978-1-60033; 978-1-4493; 978-1-4919; 978-1-4920; 978-1-4571)* Orders Addr.: 1005 Gravenstein Hwy. N., Sebastopol, CA 95472 USA (SAN 658-5973) Fax: 707-829-0104; Toll Free: 800-998-9938; Edit Addr.: 10 Fawcett St. Ste. 4, Cambridge, MA 02138-1175 USA Toll Free: 800-775-7731; 4 Castle St, Farnham, GU9 7HR Tel 01252 71 17 76; Fax: 01252 73 42 11
E-mail: order@oreilly.com; information@oreilly.co.uk; nuts@ora.com
Web site: http://www.oreilly.com; http://www.editions-oreilly.fr; http://oreilly.co.uk; http://oreilly.com.tw; http://www.ora.com; http://www.oreilly.fr/; http://www.oreilly.com.cn/
Dist(s): **CreateSpace Independent Publishing Platform**
Ebsco Publishing
Follett School Solutions
Ingram Publisher Services
MyiLibrary
Wiley, John & Sons, Inc.

Oren Village, LLC, *(978-0-9777272)* P.O. Box 1111, Worthington, OH 43085 USA Tel 614-937-8513
E-mail: author@alanstjean.com
Web site: http://www.alanstjean.com.

Orenda Pr., LLC, *(978-0-9907453; 978-0-9967920)* P.O. Box 1445, Cedar Park, TX 78630 USA Tel 512-961-0531
E-mail: kristen@orendapress.com
Web site: Orendapress.com.

Oresjozef Pubns., *(978-1-885566)* 167 Canton St., Randolph, MA 02368 USA Tel 781-961-5855; Toll Free: 617-851-0100
E-mail: ojozef@massed.net
Dist(s): **Educa Vision Inc.**
Haitiana Pubns., Inc.

OrganWise Guys Inc., The, *(978-0-9648438; 978-1-931212; 978-0-9858048)* 450 Satellite Blvd. NE Suite M, Suwanee, GA 30024 USA Tel 770-844-8686; Fax: 770-844-6580; Toll Free: 800-786-1730 Do not confuse with Wellness, Inc., Boston, MA
E-mail: karen@organwiseguys.com
Web site: http://www.organwiseguys.com.

Orion Publishing Group, Ltd. (GBR) *(978-0-304; 978-0-460; 978-0-575; 978-0-7528; 978-1-85797; 978-1-85798; 978-1-85881; 978-1-86047; 978-1-84188; 978-1-84255; 978-1-905619; 978-1-4091; 978-1-78062; 978-0-85782; 978-1-4072; 978-1-4719)* *Dist. by* **Trafalgar.**

Orion Publishing Group, Ltd. (GBR) *(978-0-304; 978-0-460; 978-0-575; 978-0-7528; 978-1-85797; 978-1-85798; 978-1-85881; 978-1-86047; 978-1-84188; 978-1-84255; 978-1-905619; 978-1-4091; 978-1-78062; 978-0-85782; 978-1-4072; 978-1-4719)* *Dist. by* **HachBkGrp.**

Orion Society, The, *(978-0-913098)* Orders Addr.: 187 Main St., Great Barrington, MA 01230-1601 USA (SAN 204-0182) Tel 413-528-4422; Fax: 413-528-0676; Toll Free: 888-909-6568
E-mail: gagne@orionmagazine.org
Web site: http://www.orionmagazine.org.

Orion Wellspring, Inc., *(978-0-9794614)* 20 Blaine St., Seattle, WA 98109 USA Tel 206-931-4656; Fax: 206-374-2149
E-mail: tom.masters@orionwellspring.com; info@orionwellspring.com
Web site: http://www.orionwellspring.com.

Orion-Cosmos, *(978-0-9752725)* 3609 Candleknoll Cir., San Antonio, TX 78244 USA
E-mail: customerservice@orion-cosmos.com
Web site: http://www.orion-cosmos.com.

Orison Pubs., *(978-0-9763800; 978-0-9827944; 978-1-945169)*
E-mail: marsha@orisonpublishers.com
Web site: www.discovertheauthor.com; www.orisonpublishers.com.

Ormond, Jennifer, *(978-0-9792010)* 77 Pkwy., Quincy, MA 02169 USA
E-mail: jennormond@gmail.com
Web site: http://www.jenniferormond.com.

Orndee Omnimedia, Inc., *(978-0-9774260; 978-0-9822229)* 36 West 37th St. Penthouse, New York, NY 10018 USA Tel 212-203-0363
E-mail: Publishing@Orndee.com
Web site: http://www.Orndee.com.

ORO Editions, *(978-0-9746800; 978-0-9774672; 978-0-9793801; 978-0-9795395; 978-0-9814628; 978-0-9820607; 978-0-9819857; 978-0-9826226; 978-1-935935; 978-1-941806; 978-1-939621; 978-1-940743; 978-1-943532)* Orders Addr.: P.O. Box 150338, San Rafael, CA 94915 USA Tel 415-663-0678; Fax: 415-457-3650; Edit Addr.: 31 Commercial Blvd., Suite F, Novato, CA 94945 USA Tel 415-883-3300; Fax: 415-883-3309
E-mail: gordon@oroeditions.com; christy@oroeditions.com; info@oroeditions.com
Web site: http://www.oroeditions.com
Dist(s): **D.A.P./Distributed Art Pubs.**
Ingram Publisher Services.

Orpen Pr. (IRL) *(978-1-871305; 978-1-84218; 978-1-909895; 978-1-78605; 978-1-909518)* *Dist. by* **Dufour.**

Orr Bks., *(978-0-9800611; 978-0-9827764; 978-0-9851760)* 608 Seitz St., Easton, PA 18042-6544 USA Tel 610-258-5479
E-mail: derek@beachfrontpress.com; peter@beachfrontpress.com
Web site: http://www.orrbooks.net; http://www.beachfrontpress.com.

Orsini Pr., *(978-0-9797816)* 201 N. Carmelina Ave., Los Angeles, CA 90049 USA.

Ortells, Alfredo Editorial S.L. (ESP) *(978-84-7189)* *Dist. by* **Continental Bk.**

Ortiz, Enrique Publishing, *(978-0-615-25622-1; 978-0-615-25637-5; 978-0-615-26124-9; 978-0-578-00134-0; 978-0-578-00135-7)* 1538 Bullbush Way, Oviedo, FL 32765 USA
Dist(s): **Lulu Pr., Inc.**

Osage Bend Publishing Co., *(978-0-9626245; 978-1-58389)* 213 Belair Dr., Jefferson City, MO 65109 USA Tel 573-635-5580; Toll Free: 888-243-9772
E-mail: OBPC@Socket.net
Dist(s): **Follett School Solutions.**

Osborne Enterprises Publishing, *(978-0-932117)* P.O. Box 255, Port Townsend, WA 98368 USA (SAN 242-7567) Tel 360-385-1200; Toll Free: 800-246-3255 (orders only)
E-mail: jpo@olympus.net
Web site: http://www.jerryosborne.com.

Osborne Pr., *(978-1-928856)* Div. of David M. Osborne, Inc., 16726 Comstock, Livonia, MI 48154 USA Tel 734-464-7002; Fax: 734-464-6837
E-mail: osborne@mich.com
Web site: http://www.mich.com/~osborne.

Osborne/McGraw-Hill *See* **McGraw-Hill Osborne**

Oscar, Erica, *(978-0-9747262)* 20424 Packard, Detroit, MI 48234 USA.

Osherbert Bks., LLC, *(978-0-9885461)* P.O. Box 1591, Gig Harbor, WA 98335 USA Tel 253-651-8997
E-mail: seshell@gmail.com.

Osmosis, LLC, *(978-0-9727886; 978-0-9816281)* 8 Findlay Ave., Hartsdale, NY 10530-2613 USA Tel 914-328-8898; Fax: 914-328-1124; Toll Free: 866-676-6747
E-mail: osmosis@earthlink.net
Web site: http://www.learningbyosmosis.com; http://www.osmosis.tv.

Osprey *Imprint of* **Bloomsbury Publishing USA**

Osprey Pr., *(978-0-9673711)* 2107 Ibis Dr., Buffalo, MN 55313 USA Tel 763-682-4558 Do not confuse with companies with the same or similar names in St. Johnsbury, VT, Wiscasset, ME
E-mail: ospreypress@charter.net
Web site: http://www.planetearthhome.com
Dist(s): **Random Hse., Inc.**

Osteogenesis Imperfecta Foundation, *(978-0-9642189)* 804 W. Diamond Ave., Suite 210, Gaithersburg, MD 20878 USA Tel 301-947-0083; Fax: 301-947-0456; Toll Free: 800-981-2663
E-mail: bonelink@oif.org
Web site: http://www.oif.org.

Ostermeyer Photography, *(978-0-9794228; 978-0-615-74538-1; 978-0-692-02001-2)* 1813 Country Brook Ln., Allen, TX 75002 USA Tel 972-542-7065
E-mail: tim@ostermeyer-photography.com
Web site: http://www.ostermeyer-photography.com.

Ostrageous Publishing, *(978-0-9785144)* P.O. Box 2867, Hot Springs, AK 71914 USA Tel 501-525-4245.

Otago University Pr. (NZL) *(978-0-908569; 978-1-877133; 978-1-877276; 978-1-877372; 978-1-877578) Dist. by* **IPG Chicago.**

Otis & Randolph Pr., *(978-0-9752516)* 1229 Bishop's Lodge Rd., Santa Fe, NM 87501 USA.

Otis, Dorcas Marie *See* **Zion Publishing**

Otter Run Bks. LLC, *(978-0-9760796)* 16965 Nicolet Rd., Townsend, WI 54175 USA Tel 715-276-6515 (phone/fax)
E-mail: kathiemarsh@yahoo.com
Web site: http://www.otterrunbooks.com.

Otter-Barry Bks. (GBR) *(978-1-910959) Dist. by* **PerseuPGW.**

OTTN Publishing, *(978-1-59556)* 16 Risler Street, Stockton, NJ 08559 USA Tel 609-397-4005; Fax: 609-397-4007
E-mail: jgallagher@ottnpublishing.com
Web site: http://www.ottnpublishing.com.

Ouattara, Issoufou *See* **International Development Ctr.**

†Our Child Pr., *(978-0-9611872; 978-1-893516)* P.O. Box 4379, Philadelphia, PA 19118 USA (SAN 682-272X) Tel 610-308-8988
E-mail: ourchildpress@aol.com
Web site: http://www.ourchildpress.com; *CIP.*

Our Companions, Inc., *(978-0-9753257)* 84 N. Acoma Blvd., No. 100-33, Lake Havasu City, AZ 86403 USA Tel 928-486-4508.

Our Kids Pr., *(978-0-9660884; 978-0-9860290)* Orders Addr.: P.O. Box 486, Bellingham, WA 98227 USA Tel 360-734-2335; Edit Addr.: 3804 Ridgemont Way, Bellingham, WA 98227 USA
Web site: ourkidspress.com.

Our Lady of Victory Schl., *(978-1-931555)* 103 E. Tenth Ave., Post Falls, ID 83854 USA Tel 208-773-7265; Fax: 208-773-1951
E-mail: lepanto@olvs.org
Web site: http://www.olvs.org.

Our Little Secret Pr., *(978-0-9720978)* 1524 E. Park Rd., Grand Island, NY 14072 USA Tel 716-773-4866.

Our Story Pubns., *(978-0-9765554)* P.O. Box 7514, Round Rock, TX 78683 USA Tel 512-663-1471
E-mail: nicoleeutsey@ourstorypublications.com
Web site: http://www.ourstorypublications.com.

Our Sunday Visitor, Publishing Div., *(978-0-87973; 978-0-9707756; 978-1-931709; 978-1-59276; 978-1-61278; 978-1-68192)* 200 Noll Plaza, Huntington, IN 46750 USA (SAN 202-8344) Tel 260-356-8400; Fax: 260-359-9117; 260-356-8472; Toll Free: 800-348-2440
E-mail: osvbooks@osv.com; ntopp@osv.com
Web site: http://www.osv.com
Dist(s): **Baker & Taylor International**
MyiLibrary
Spring Arbor Distributors, Inc.

Our World of Books *See* **Good Night Bks.**

OurRainbow Pr., LLC, *(978-0-9752860; 978-1-934214)* Orders Addr.: 2600 Penrick Dr., Marietta, GA 30064-1809 USA Tel 770-514-8794; Toll Free: 877-600-7323
E-mail: publisher@ourrainbow.com; ameadows@ourrainbow.com; anthony.meadows@gmail.com; sheila.meadows@gmail.com
Web site: http://www.ourrainbowpress.com; http://orpbooks.com.

Out of the Box, *(978-0-9726849)* P.O. Box 24234, Minneapolis, MN 55424 USA Tel 612-822-5151; Fax: 612-823-4164
E-mail: info@ootbooks.com
Web site: http://www.ootbooks.com
Dist(s): **Brodart Co.**
Follett School Solutions
Quality Bks., Inc.

Out of the Box Publishing, Inc., *(978-0-9664517; 978-0-9708554; 978-0-9716729; 978-1-932359)* 609 Bennett Rd., Dodgeville, WI 53533 USA (SAN 760-5269) Toll Free: 800-540-4201 Do not confuse with Out of the Box Publishing, Cincinnati, OH
E-mail: sales@otb-games.com; brad@otb-games.com
Web site: http://www.otb-games.com.

Out of this World (GBR) *Dist. by* **CapstonePubs.**

Outcomes Unlimited Pr., Inc., *(978-0-925640)* P.O. Box 8013, Asheville, NC 28814-8497 USA
E-mail: drdossey@drdossey.com
Web site: http://www.drdossey.com.

Outdoor Originals LLC, *(978-0-9762971)* 1052 California Ave. W., Saint Paul, MN 55117 USA.

Outdoor Writing & Photography, Limited *See* **Visions Of Nature**

Outer Banks Pr., *(978-0-9713890; 978-0-9778924)* Div. of OBBC, Inc., P.O. Box 2829, Kitty Hawk, NC 27949 USA (SAN 254-3958) Tel 252-261-0612; Toll Free Fax: 800-215-9648
E-mail: linda@outerbankspress.com
Web site: http://www.outerbankspress.com
Dist(s): **Independent Pubs. Group.**

Outland Communications, LLC, *(978-0-9714102; 978-1-932820)* Orders Addr.: P.O. Box 534, Skaneateles, NY 13152 USA; Edit Addr.: 4022 Mill Rd., Skaneateles, NY 13152-9319 USA
Web site: http://www.outlandbooks.com.

Outlaw Bks., *(978-0-9656946)* 419 Centre St., Hereford, TX 79045 USA Tel 806-364-2838; Fax: 806-364-5522; Toll Free: 888-583-9408 Do not confuse with Outlaw Books, Bozeman, MT
Dist(s): **Hervey's Booklink & Cookbook Warehouse.**

Outlaw Pubns., *(978-1-886709)* Orders Addr.: P.O. Box 1424, Red Oak, TX 75154 USA Tel 972-504-6608; Edit Addr.: P.O. Box 3043, Desoto, TX 75115 USA.

Outlet Book Company, Incorporated *See* **Random Hse. Value Publishing**

Outlook Publishing, Inc., *(978-0-9711667; 978-0-9817755)* Orders Addr.: P.O. Box 278, Laurel, MT 59044 USA Tel 406-628-4412; Fax: 406-628-8260; Edit Addr.: 415 E. Main St., Laurel, MT 59044 USA
E-mail: publisher@laureloutlook.com
Web site: http://www.laureloutlook.com.

Outrival Publishing, *(978-0-9885603)* P.O. Box 130345, Houston, TX 77219 USA Tel 832-878-6162; Fax: 713-861-1501
E-mail: kimpedigo@gmail.com.

Outside the Box Publishing, LLC, *(978-0-9817398)* 326 2nd St. No. 3, Brooklyn, NY 11215 USA Tel 202-905-3442
E-mail: info@otbpublishing.com; dax@daxdevlonross.com; daxdevlonross@gmail.com
Web site: http://www.otbpublishing.com
Dist(s): **Lightning Source, Inc.**

Outskirts Pr., Inc., *(978-0-9725874; 978-1-932672; 978-1-59800; 978-1-4327; 978-0-615-20388-1; 978-1-4787; 978-1-9772)* 10940 S. Parker Rd. - 515, Parker, CO 80134 USA (SAN 256-5420)
Web site: http://www.OutskirtsPress.com
Dist(s): **Aardvark Global Publishing**
Smashwords.

Outskirts Press, Incorporation *See* **Outskirts Pr., Inc.**

Ovation Bks., *(978-1-933538; 978-0-9790275; 978-0-9814534)* 2100 Kramer Ln., Suite 300, Austin, TX 78758 USA Tel 512-478-2028; Fax: 512-478-2117
E-mail: awillis@bookpros.com; sboulden@ovationbooks.net
Web site: http://www.bookpros.com; http://www.ovationbooks.net.

Over the Rainbow *Imprint of* **Pearn & Assocs. Inc.**

Over The Rainbow Publishing, *(978-0-9793882)* 1810 New Palm Way, No. 410, Boynton Beach, FL 33435 USA Tel 561-704-6581
E-mail: famuffy@aol.com.

Over the Rainbow Productions, *(978-0-9661330)* 1715 Rosedale, Suite B, Houston, TX 77004 USA Tel 713-523-1276; Fax: 713-526-0571
E-mail: apb3@prodigy.net
Web site: http://www.imneecie.com.

Overcup Pr., *(978-0-9834917)* 4760 SE 58th Ave., Portland, OR 97206 USA Tel 503-453-0091
E-mail: pat@overcupbooks.com
Web site: www.overcupbooks.com
Dist(s): **SCB Distributors.**

Overdue Bks., *(978-0-9786850)* P.O. Box 259462, Madison, WI 53725 USA Do not confuse with Overdue Books in West Linn, OR
E-mail: theoverduebooks@yahoo.com.

Overlook Connection Pr., The, *(978-0-9633397; 978-1-892950; 978-1-62330)* Orders Addr.: P.O. Box 1934, Hiram, GA 30141 USA Tel 678-567-9777; Edit Addr.: 364 Valerie Cir., Hiram, GA 30141 USA
E-mail: overlookcn@aol.com
Web site: http://www.overlookconnection.com; http://www.overlookconnection.com
Dist(s): **Diamond Comic Distributors, Inc.**

†Overlook Pr., The, *(978-0-87951; 978-1-58567; 978-1-59020; 978-1-4683)* 141 Wooster St., 4th Flr., New York, NY 10012 USA (SAN 202-8360) Tel 212-673-2210; Fax: 212-673-2296
Web site: http://www.overlookpress.com
Dist(s): **MyiLibrary**
Norton, W. W. & Co., Inc.
Open Road Integrated Media, Inc.
Penguin Random Hse. LLC
Penguin Publishing Group; *CIP.*

Overmountain Pr., *(978-0-932807; 978-0-9644613; 978-1-57072; 978-1-935692)* P.O. Box 1261, Johnson City, TN 37605 USA (SAN 687-6641) Tel 423-926-2691; Fax: 423-232-1252; Toll Free: 800-992-2691 (orders only); *Imprints:* Silver Dagger Mysteries (Silver Dagger)
E-mail: beth@overmtn.com
Web site: http://www.silverdaggermysteries.com; http://www.overmountainpress.com
Dist(s): **Independent Pubs. Group**
Partners Pubs. Group, Inc.

Overstreet, Mae *See* **Overstreet Pub. & Mktg.**

Overstreet Pub. & Mktg., *(978-0-9746253)* P.O. Box 3808, Yountville, CA 94599 USA
Web site: http://www.bettyoverstreet.com.

Overview Publishing, *(978-0-9760685)* 1081 Crown River Pkwy., McDonough, GA 30252 USA Tel 678-583-0898
E-mail: cindy@overviewpublishing.com
Web site: http://www.overviewpublishing.com
Dist(s): **Quality Bks., Inc.**

Owen, Richard C. Pubs., Inc., *(978-0-913461; 978-1-57274; 978-1-878450)* P.O. Box 585, Katonah, NY 10536 USA (SAN 285-1814) Tel 914-232-3903; Fax: 914-232-3977; Toll Free: 800-336-5588 (orders); *Imprints:* Meet the Author (Meet Author); Books for Young Learners (Bks Yng Learn); Author at Work (Author at Work)
Web site: http://www.RCOwen.com.

Owens, David A., *(978-0-578-05417-9)* 4253 October Woods Dr., Antioch, TN 37013 USA.

Owensby, Legertha, *(978-0-9742789)* 6820 Chiffview Dr., No. E, Indianapolis, IN 46214 USA
E-mail: legethao@yahoo.com
Web site: http://earvino.tripod.com.

Owl About Books *See* **Owl About Bks. Pub., Inc.**

Owl About Bks. Pub., Inc., *(978-1-937752)* 1632 Royalwood Cir., Joshua, TX 76058 USA Tel 682-553-9078; Fax: 817-558-8983
E-mail: owlaboutbooks@gmail.com
Web site: http://www.owlaboutbooks.com
Dist(s): **Lightning Source, Inc.**

Owl Creek Farm Bks. *Imprint of* **Owl Tree Pr.**

Owl Creek Media Ltd., *(978-1-60404)* 490 Trego Rd., Waverly, OH 45690 USA Tel 740-493-1939; Toll Free: 800-305-0339 Please leave a message
E-mail: james@owlcreekmedia.com
Web site: http://www.owlcreekmedia.com; http://www.localbookproject.com.

Owl Hollow Publishing, *(978-0-9726826)* 13704 Lawrence 2187, Verona, MO 65769 USA Tel 417-498-6964
E-mail: zona@mo-net.com.

Owl of Minerva Press *See* **Minerva Bks.**

Owl Pals, *(978-0-9799196)* 10210 NE. 12th St. Unit C301, Bellevue, WA 98004 USA Tel 206-948-2629
Web site: http://www.owlpals.com.

Owl Tree Pr., *(978-1-929424)* P.O. Box 292, Saint Helens, OR 97051 USA Tel 503-397-3667; Fax: 503-397-3684; *Imprints:* Owl Creek Farm Books (Owl Creek Farm Bks)
E-mail: jdnyberg@ados.com
Web site: http://www.owltreepress.com.

Owlkids Bks. Inc. (CAN) *(978-0-919872; 978-0-920775; 978-1-895688; 978-2-920660; 978-1-894379; 978-2-89579; 978-1-77147) Dist. by* **PerseuPGW.**

Oxbow Bks., *(978-0-9771129)* 76 Presidio Dr., Novato, CA 94949 USA
E-mail: dchaller@horizoncable.com.

Oxfam Publishing (GBR) *(978-0-85598) Dist. by* **Stylus Pub VA.**

Oxford Museum Pr., *(978-1-930127)* 5790 Stillwell-Beckett Rd., Oxford, OH 45056 USA Tel 513-756-9386; Fax: 513-756-9123; Toll Free: 877-127-1941
E-mail: omp@oxfordmuseumpress.com
Web site: http://www.oxfordmuseumpress.com.

Oxford Univ. Pr. (GBR) *(978-0-19) Dist. by* **OUP.**

Oxford Univ. Pr., Inc., *(978-0-19)* Orders Addr.: 2001 Evans Rd., Cary, NC 27513 USA (SAN 202-5892) Tel 919-677-0977 (general voice); Fax: 919-677-1303 (customer service); Toll Free: 800-445-9714 (customer service - inquiry); 800-451-7556 (customer service - orders); Edit Addr.: 198 Madison Ave., New York, NY 10016-4314 USA (SAN 202-5884) Tel 212-726-6000 (general voice); Fax: 212-726-6440 (general fax)
E-mail: custserv@oup-usa.org; orders@oup-usa.org
Web site: http://www.oup.com/us
Dist(s): **Chicago Distribution Ctr.**
CreateSpace Independent Publishing Platform
Ebsco Publishing
Follett School Solutions
Hancock Hse. Pubs.
ISD
MyiLibrary
World Bank Pubns.
ebrary, Inc.

Oxfordshire Publishing Co., *(978-0-9745895)* 900 Lincoln Hwy., Box 180, East Mckeesport, PA 15035 USA Tel 412-823-1700
E-mail: blissman@pghmail.com.

Oxmoor Hse., Inc., *(978-0-376; 978-0-8487)* Orders Addr.: Leisure Arts 5701 Ranch Dr., Little Rock, AR 72223 USA; Edit Addr.: 2100 Lakeshore Dr., Birmingham, AL 35209 USA Tel 205-445-6000; Fax: 205-445-6078; Toll Free: 800-633-4910
E-mail: allison_lowery@timeinc.com
Web site: http://www.oxmoorhouse.com/
Dist(s): **Hachette Bk. Group**
Leisure Arts, Inc.
MyiLibrary
Two Rivers Distribution
ebrary, Inc.

Oxton Hse., Pubs., *(978-1-881929)* Orders Addr.: P.O. Box 209, Farmington, ME 04938 USA Tel 207-779-1923; Fax: 207-779-0623; Toll Free: 800-539-7323
E-mail: info@oxtonhouse.com
Web site: http://www.oxtonhouse.com
Dist(s): **Smashwords.**

Ozark Publishing, *(978-1-56763; 978-1-59381)* P.O. Box 228, Prairie Grove, AR 72753 USA (SAN 298-4318) Tel 214-649-0188; Fax: 501-846-2853; Toll Free: 800-321-5671
E-mail: srg304@aol.com
Web site: http://www.ozarkpublishing.com
Dist(s): **Central Programs**
Gumdrop Bks.

Ozone Publishing, Corp., *(978-0-9773285)* PMB 500, RR-8 Box 1995, Bayamon, PR 00956-9676 USA Tel 787-562-5200; Fax: 787-730-0987
E-mail: info@ozonepublishing.net
Web site: http://www.ozonepublishing.net.

Ozten, *(978-0-9752966)* 347 NW 87th St., Seattle, WA 98117 USA
E-mail: shout@ozten.com
Web site: http://www.ozten.com.

P & P Publishing LLC, *(978-0-9797020)* 4957 Lakemont Blvd., SE, Suite C-4, No. 316, Bellevue, WA 98006 USA Tel 425-557-0257 Do not confuse with companies with the same or similar name in Frankermuth, MI, Warren, MI, Temple, TX, Wauwatosa, WI.

P & R Publishing, *(978-0-87552; 978-1-59638; 978-1-62995)* Orders Addr.: 1102 Marble Hill Rd., Harmony, Phillipsburg, NJ 08865 USA (SAN 658-1463) Tel 908-454-0505; Fax: 908-859-2390; Toll Free: 800-631-0094 Do not confuse with P & R Publishing Co. in Sioux Center, IA
E-mail: tara@prpbooks.com; jesse@prpbooks.com
Web site: http://www.prpbooks.com
Dist(s): **CLC Pubns.**
Faith Alive Christian Resources.

P C I Education, *(978-1-884074; 978-1-58804; 978-1-61975)* 4560 Lockhill-Selma, Suite 100, San Antonio, TX 78265-4270 USA Tel 210-377-1999; Fax: 210-377-1121; Toll Free Fax: 888-259-8284; Toll Free: 800-594-4263
E-mail: lboulet@pcieducation.com
Web site: http://www.pcieducation.com
Dist(s): **Attainment Co., Inc.**

P C I Educational Publishing *See* **P C I Education**

P K I Ds, *(978-1-929524)* P.O. Box 5666, Vancouver, WA 98668 USA Tel 360-695-0293; Fax: 360-695-6941; Toll Free: 877-557-5437
E-mail: pkids@pkids.org
Web site: http://www.pkids.org.

P.O.W. (Pubns. of Worth), *(978-1-877898)* 2561 E. 1980 N., Layton, UT 84040-7928 USA.

PSI & Assocs., *(978-0-938261; 978-1-55993)* 9745 SW 125th Terr., Miami, FL 33176-4941 USA (SAN 659-834X).

P2 Publishing, *(978-0-9856336)* 10455 N. Central Expwy Suite 109-115, Dallas, TX 75231 USA Tel 214-223-0366
E-mail: pickleproductionspc@gmail.com
Web site: www.PiperandPickle.com.

P4K Publishing, *(978-0-9744570)* 5699 Kanan Rd., Suite 373, Agoura Hills, CA 91301 USA Tel 818-991-5764; Fax: 818-879-9646
E-mail: lori@prosperity4kids.com
Web site: http://www.prosperity4kids.com.

Paarmann, Al International, *(978-0-9715963)* 368 El Gaucho Rd., Santa Barbara, CA 93111 USA Tel 805-964-2830 (phone/fax)
E-mail: alpaarmann@aol.com.

Pace Products, Inc., *(978-1-58295; 978-1-880592)* P.O. Box 470970, Lake Monroe, FL 32747-0970 USA Toll Free: 800-541-7670
E-mail: PaceProd@aol.com
Web site: http://www.paceplace.com.

Pacesetters Bible School *See* **Energion Pubns.**

Pacific Bks., *(978-1-885375)* Orders Addr.: P.O. Box 3562, Santa Barbara, CA 93130 USA (SAN 630-2548) Tel 805-687-8340; Fax: 805-687-2514; Edit Addr.: 2573 Treasure Dr., Santa Barbara, CA 93105 USA; *Imprints:* Shore Line Press (Shore Line Pr).

Pacific Heritage Bks., *(978-0-9635906; 978-1-928753)* Orders Addr.: P.O. Box 998, Palos Verdes, CA 90274 USA Tel 310-541-8818; Fax: 310-791-9069; Toll Free: 888-810-9891; Edit Addr.: 532 Via del Monte, Palos Verdes Estates, CA 90274 USA
E-mail: amawong@worldnet.att.net
Web site: http://www.pacificheritagebooks.com
Dist(s): **Distributors, The**
Quality Bks., Inc.

Pacific Learning, Inc., *(978-1-59055; 978-1-60457; 978-1-61391; 978-1-59055-000-7)* Orders Addr.: P.O. Box 2723, Huntington Beach, CA 92647-0723 USA; Edit Addr.: 15342 Graham St., Huntington Beach, CA 92649 USA Tel 714-516-8307; Fax: 714-516-8369; Toll Free: 800-279-0737
E-mail: info@pacificlearning.com
Web site: http://www.pacificlearning.com
Dist(s): **Brightpoint Literacy.**

Pacific Moon Pubns., *(978-0-9729524)* Orders Addr.: 2334 Monroe Blvd. Suite 703, Ogden, UT 84401-1727 USA
Dist(s): **Lightning Source, Inc.**

Pacific Northwest Ballet, *(978-0-9745415)* 301 Mercer St., Seattle, WA 98109 USA Tel 206-441-9411; Fax: 206-441-2440
E-mail: kaolivier@mac.com
Web site: http://www.pnb.org.

Pacific Pr. Pubns., *(978-0-9678122)* 3260 Monument, Ann Arbor, MI 48108 USA Tel 734-975-1877 (phone/fax)
E-mail: hailstormx@aol.com.

†Pacific Pr. Publishing Assn., *(978-0-8163; 978-1-5180)* P.O. Box 5353, Nampa, ID 83653-5353 USA (SAN 202-8409) Tel 208-465-2500; Fax: 208-465-2531; Toll Free: 800-447-7377
E-mail: donlay@pacificpress.com
Web site: http://www.AdventistBookCenter.com; http://www.pacificpress.com; *CIP.*

Pacific Pubs., *(978-0-936521; 978-1-933120)* P.O. Box 480, Bolinas, CA 94924 USA (SAN 697-9335) Tel 415-868-2909; Fax: 415-868-9040
E-mail: tideguy@fastmail.fm
Web site: http://www.tidelog.com.

Pacific Raven Press *See* **Pacific Raven Pr.**

Pacific Raven Pr., *(978-0-9841228; 978-0-9840204; 978-0-9860755)* P.O. Box 195, Wailuku, HI 96793 USA (SAN 931-4946)
E-mail: pacificravenpress@gmail.com
Web site: http://www.pacificravenpress.com.

Pacific Ridge Press, LLC *See* **Parra Grande Pr.**

Pacific View Pr., *(978-1-881896)* 2864 Harrison St., San Francisco, CA 94110 USA Tel 415-285-8538; 510-849-4216; Fax: 415-285-2620; 510-843-5835
E-mail: pvp2@mindspring.com
Web site: http://www.pacificviewpress.com
Dist(s): **Cheng & Tsui Co.**
China Books & Periodicals, Inc.
Chinasprout, Inc.

Pacifica Island Art, Inc., *(978-0-9727594; 978-0-9758721; 978-1-933735)* Orders Addr.: P.O. Box 120, Haiku, HI 96708 USA Fax: 808-575-2072; Edit Addr.: 810 Haiku Rd., No. 331, Haiku, HI 96708 USA
E-mail: joseph@islandartcards.com
Web site: http://www.islandartcards.com.

Packard, Boyle & Jackson *See* **Apollo Pubns.**

Padah Pr., *(978-0-9721269)* Orders Addr.: P.O. Box 231285, Gresham, OR 97281 USA Tel 971-219-1861
E-mail: eileen@padah.net; eileen@eileenscott.com
Web site: http://www.eileenscott.com.

Paddle Wheel Publishing, *(978-0-9657612)* Div. of Arabia Steamboat Museum, 400 Grand Blvd., Kansas City, MO 64106 USA Tel 816-471-1856; Fax: 816-471-1616; Toll Free: 800-471-1856
E-mail: greghawley@comcast.net
Web site: http://www.1856.com.

Paddywhack Lane LLC., *(978-0-9794286; 978-1-936169)* 9849 Bluestar Dr., Parker, CO 80138 USA (SAN 858-6497) Tel 303-841-1163; Fax: 888-840-0169; Toll Free: 800-796-1163
E-mail: bob@paddywhacklane.com
Web site: http://www.paddywhacklane.com.

Padwolf Publishing, Inc., *(978-1-890096)* P.O. Box 117, Yulan, NY 12792-0117 USA Toll Free: 800-484-7284 ext. 7239
E-mail: padwolf@padwolf.com
Web site: http://www.padwolf.com.

Pagan Writers Pr. *Imprint of* **Mroczka Media**

Pagan Writers Press *See* **Mroczka Media**

Page Publishing *See* **Page Publishing Inc.**

Page Publishing Inc., *(978-0-9854504; 978-1-62838; 978-1-63417; 978-1-68139; 978-1-68213; 978-1-68289; 978-1-68348; 978-1-68409; 978-1-63568; 978-1-64027; 978-1-64082; 978-1-64138)* 101 Tyrellan Ave., Suite 100, New York, NY 10309 USA Toll Free: 866-315-2708
E-mail: accounts@pagepublishing.com
Web site: http://www.pagepublishing.com.

Page Street Publishing Co., *(978-1-62414)* 31 Forest Ave., Essex, MA 01929 USA Tel 978-768-0168
E-mail: williamkiester@gmail.com
Dist(s): **Macmillan.**

PageFree Publishing, Inc., *(978-1-929077; 978-1-930252; 978-1-58961)* P.O. Box 60, Otsego, MI 49078-0060 USA Toll Free: 1-866-GO BOOKS
E-mail: pagefreepublish@aol.com; publisher@pagefreepublishing.com
Web site: http://www.pagefreepublishing.com
Dist(s): **BookBaby**
Lightning Source, Inc.
Midpoint Trade Bks., Inc.
Univ. of Hawaii Pr.

PageMaster Publishing, *(978-0-9797759)* 2884 Britton Rd., B34, Perry, MI 48872 USA (SAN 854-3453)
E-mail: Gwen@pagemasterpublishing.com
Web site: http://www.pagemasterpublishing.com.

Pages of Life, *(978-0-615-24716-8; 978-0-615-48466-2; 978-0-615-48467-9)* Div. of Lavender Belle Enterprises, 6328 Joe Klustch Dr., Fort Washington, MD 20744 USA Tel 202-251-2210
E-mail: LavenderBelle@verizon.net
Web site: http://pagesoflife.wordpress.com.

PageSpring Publishing, *(978-1-939403)* 2671 Bristol Rd., Columbus, OH 43221 USA Tel 614-204-2548
E-mail: rseum@pagespringpublishing.com
Web site: www.pagespringpublishing.com; www.luckymarblebooks.com; www.cupofteabooks.com.

Pageturners Publishing Co., *(978-0-9755102)* Orders Addr.: P.O. Box 6, Jacksonville, FL 32234-0006 USA (SAN 256-1719) Tel 904-266-3393; Fax: 904-266-3394
E-mail: publisher@pageturnerspublishing.com
Web site: http://www.pageturnerspublishing.com.

Paginas de Espuma (ESP) *(978-84-95642; 978-84-931243; 978-84-8393)* *Dist. by* **Lectorum Pubns.**

Paidea Classics, *(978-0-9749900; 978-1-947816)* 304 Robinhood Dr., Irving, TX 75061 USA
E-mail: paideaclassics@aol.com
Web site: http://paideaclassics.org.

Paige Martin Bks., *(978-0-578-06864-0; 978-0-578-08272-1)* 11101 Silver Aspen Ct., Hampton, GA 30228 USA
Dist(s): **Smashwords.**

Paige Publishing, *(978-0-9769375)* 5708 Washington St., Downers Grove, IL 60516 USA Do not confuse with companies with the same or similar name in Lexington, OK, Mesa, AZ La Harba, CA San Antonio, TX .

Paigerac, Patricia & Allan Choi *See* **Paigerac, Patricia M.**

Paigerac, Patricia M., *(978-0-9801137)* 30110 Crown Valley Pkwy., Suite 103, Laguna Niguel, CA 92677 USA.

Paint Creek Press, Limited *See* **Archus Pr., LLC**

Paintbox Pr., *(978-0-9669433; 978-0-9777905)* 208 Glandon Dr., Chapel Hill, NC 27514 USA Tel 919-969-7512; Fax: 919-933-4199; Toll Free: 877-969-7512
E-mail: ppease@paintboxpress.com
Web site: http://www.paintboxpress.com
Dist(s): **Follett School Solutions.**

Paintbrush Tales Publishing, LLC, *(978-0-9846151)* 20 Webber Ave., Beverly, MA 01915 USA Tel 978-239-9895
E-mail: caustin36@yahoo.com.

Painted Daisies Inc., *(978-0-615-34491-1)* 3433 Hwy. 190 PMB 377, Mandeville, LA 70471 USA Tel 985-674-0398; Fax: 985-674-2965; 978 Bald Cypress Dr., Mandeville, LA 70448
E-mail: kborg95@gmail.com.

Painted Horse Pubns., Inc., *(978-0-9708066; 978-0-9729482)* 45 Wingate St., Haverhill, MA 01835 USA Tel 978-521-1740
E-mail: sully@stopforastory.com.

Painted Pony, Inc., *(978-0-9759806)* Orders Addr.: P.O. Box 661, Fort Washakie, WY 82514 USA Tel 307-335-7330; Fax: 307-335-7332; Edit Addr.: 47 N. Fork Rd., Fort Washakie, WY 82514 USA Do not confuse with companies with similar name in Atlanta, GA and La Conner, WA.
E-mail: ppi@wrdf.org.

Painted Quill Publishing, *(978-0-9909471)* 230 Parker Oaks Ln., Hudson Oaks, TX 76087 USA
E-mail: paintedquill@gmail.com.

Painted Sky Productions *See* **Emerald City Publishing**

Painted Turtle *Imprint of* **Wayne State Univ. Pr.**

Painted WORD Studios, *(978-0-9721845; 978-0-9771809; 978-0-9845644)* P.O. Box 1606, Crosby, TX 77532-1606 USA Tel 281-456-8810 Toll Free: 866-241-7510
E-mail: paintedwordstudios@gmail.com
Web site: http://www.paintedwordstudios.com.

Painter, Annie & Assocs., *(978-1-928875)* P.O. Box 2135, Sisters, OR 97759 USA Tel 541-549-9539 (phone/fax)
E-mail: painterannie@msn.com.

Painting the Pages Publishing, *(978-0-9843487)* 673 Potomac Station Dr., No. 628, Leesburg, VA 20176 USA (SAN 859-1393)
Web site: http://www.paintingthepages.com.

Painting With Words, *(978-0-9743080)* 10 B State St., Windsor, VT 05089 USA Tel 802-674-5514; Fax: 802-674-9810.

Pair'a Spurs Pr., *(978-0-9749518)* Rt. 2 Box 20, Hollis, OK 73550 USA.

Paisley Publishing, *(978-0-9761710)* 7240 Sagebrush Dr., Parker, CO 80138 USA Fax: 303-841-5229 Do not confuse with Paisley Publishing in Anchorage, AK
E-mail: mlheinze11@aol.com.

Paizo Inc., *(978-0-9770071; 978-0-9776778; 978-1-60125; 978-1-64078)* 7120 185th Ave. NE. Ste 120, Redmond, WA 98052-0577 USA
Web site: http://www.paizo.com
Dist(s): **Diamond Comic Distributors, Inc.**
Diamond Bk. Distributors.

Paizo Publishing, LLC *See* **Paizo Inc.**

Pajama Pr. (CAN) *(978-0-9869495; 978-1-927485)* *Dist. by* **IngramPubServ.**

Paje Publishing, *(978-0-9857768)* 267 Henley Rd., Wynnewood, PA 19096 USA Tel 484-437-3876
E-mail: pajepub@yahoo.com
Dist(s): **Bookmasters Distribution.**

PAJE Publishing Co., *(978-0-9753200)* 267 Henley Rd., Wynnewood, PA 19096 USA Tel 610-642-1729; Fax: 610-642-9891; Toll Free: 877-561-1377
E-mail: jay.scott@verizon.net
Dist(s): **Bookmasters Distribution**
Quality Bks., Inc.

Pakkins Presents, *(978-0-9700241)* Orders Addr.: P.O. Box 10503, Salinas, CA 93912 USA Tel 831-422-3442; Edit Addr.: 637 Carmelita Dr., No. 23, Salinas, CA 93901 USA
E-mail: Pakkins-Land@worldnet.att.net
Web site: http://www.pakkinsland.com.

Pak's Tang Soo Do Studio *See* **High Mountain Publishing**

Pal Toys, LLC, *(978-0-9726170; 978-0-9763648; 978-0-9841459)* P.O. Box 2531, Palos Verdes Peninsula, CA 90274 USA Tel 310-938-6125 Toll Free: 877-725-8880; 26 Santa Bella Rd., Rolling Hills Estates, CA 90274
E-mail: info@paltoys.com; marymoepal@cox.net
Web site: http://www.paltoys.com.

Palabra, Ediciones S.A. (ESP) *(978-84-7118; 978-84-8239)* *Dist. by* **Lectorum Pubns.**

Palace Press International *See* **ORO Editions**

Paladin Timeless *Imprint of* **Twilight Times Bks.**

Palari Publishing LLP, *(978-1-928662)* Orders Addr.: P.O. Box 9288, Richmond, VA 23227-0288 USA Tel 804-355-1035; Toll Free Fax: 866-570-6724 (on demand); Toll Free: 866-570-6724; *Imprints:* Richmondmom.com Publishing (Richmondmom)
E-mail: dave@palaribooks.com
Web site: http://www.palaribooks.com
Dist(s): **Bookazine Co., Inc.**
Smashwords.

Palazzo Editions, Ltd. (GBR) *(978-0-9545103; 978-0-9553046; 978-0-9564448; 978-0-9564942; 978-0-9571483; 978-1-78675)* *Dist. by* **IPG Chicago.**

Pale Horse Bks., *(978-1-939917)* 108 Maid Marion Pl., Williamsburg, VA 23185 USA Tel 757-220-0146
E-mail: jwconl@wm.edu
Web site: palehorsebooks.com.

Pale Silver Rainplop Pr., *(978-0-9794396; 978-0-615-14670-6)* P.O. Box 1285, Sioux City, IA 51102 USA
Web site: http://www.katieandkimbleblog.com
Dist(s): **Lulu Pr., Inc.**

Palgrave *See* **Palgrave Macmillan**

Palgrave Macmillan, *(978-0-312; 978-0-333; 978-1-4039; 978-0-230; 978-1-4472; 978-1-137; 978-1-349; 978-1-78632)* Orders Addr.: 16365 James Madison Hwy., Gordonsville, VA 22942-8501 USA Toll Free Fax: 800-672-2054; Toll Free: 888-330-8477; Edit Addr.: 175 Fifth Ave., New York, NY 10010 USA Tel 212-982-9300; Fax: 212-777-6359; Toll Free Fax: 800 672-2054 (Customer Service); Toll Free: 800-221-7945; 888-330-8477 (Customer Service)
E-mail: customerservice@vhpsva.com
Web site: http://www.palgrave.com
Dist(s): **China Books & Periodicals, Inc.**
Ebsco Publishing
Independent Pubs. Group
Libros Sin Fronteras
Macmillan
MyiLibrary
Springer
Trans-Atlantic Pubns., Inc.
ebrary, Inc.

Palgrave Macmillan Ltd. (GBR) *(978-0-312; 978-0-333; 978-1-4039; 978-0-230; 978-1-137)* *Dist. by* **Spri.**

PALH, *(978-0-9719458)* P.O. Box 5099, Santa Monica, CA 90409 USA
E-mail: palh@aol.com
Web site: http://www.palhbooks.com.

Palibrio, *(978-1-61764; 978-1-5065)* Div. of Author Solutions, Inc., 1663 Liberty Dr., Bloomington, IN 47403 USA Tel 812-674-9757; Fax: 812-355-1576; Toll Free: 877-407-5847
Web site: http://www.palibrio.com
Dist(s): **Author Solutions, Inc.**

Palladium Bks., Inc., *(978-0-916211; 978-1-57457)* 39074 Webb Ct., Westland, MI 48185-7606 USA (SAN 294-9504)
E-mail: palladiumbooks@palladiumbooks.com
Web site: http://www.PalladiumBooks.com.

Palm Canyon Pr., *(978-0-9960794)* 24 Crockett St., Rowayton, CT 06853 USA Tel 203-853-1512
E-mail: pmorrison101@gmail.com; pagemcbrier@gmail.com
Web site: www.abracadabratut.com; www.palmcanyonpress.com; www.pagemcbrier.com.

Palm Publishing LLC, *(978-0-9753548)* 1016 N. Dixie Hwy., West Palm Beach, FL 33401 USA Tel 561-833-6333; Fax: 561-833-0070
Web site: http://www.phfpbc.org.

Palm Tree Pubns., *(978-0-9787128; 978-0-9795480; 978-0-9799879; 978-0-9817054; 978-0-9822237; 978-0-9826954; 978-0-9846311; 978-0-9847653; 978-0-9857942; 978-0-9862033)* Div. of Palm Tree Productions, P.O. Box 122, Keller, TX 76244 USA; 4508 Willow Rock ln., Keller, TX 76244 Tel 817-431-8574 Do not confuse with Palm Tree Publications in Baton Rouge, LA
Web site: http://www.palmtreeproductions.net
Dist(s): **BookBaby.**

Palmer, Barbara A., *(978-0-9728228)* 486 Manitou Beach Rd., Hilton, NY 14468 USA Tel 585-392-3391; Fax: 585-392-1322
E-mail: bpforlkart@aol.com.

Palmer Enterprises *See* **Palmer Pr., The**

Palmer Lake Historical Society, *(978-0-9755989)* P.O. Box 662, Palmer Lake, CO 80133 USA.

Palmer Pr., The, *(978-0-912479)* P.O. Box 1347, Loomis, CA 95650 USA (SAN 215-1650) Tel 916-652-3225; Fax: 916-652-8665.

Palmer Publications, Incorporated/Amherst Press *See* **Amherst Pr.**

Palmer Publishing, *(978-0-9744410)* 604 4th N.W., Ardmore, OK 73401 USA Tel 580-504-2609 Do not confuse with companies with the same or similar name in Palmer, AK, Ocala, FL
E-mail: charlsie@duracom.net.

Palmer-Pletsch Assocs., *(978-0-935278; 978-1-61847)* 18200 NW Sauvie Island Rd., Portland, OR 97231 USA
E-mail: info@palmerpletsch.com; wisner.palmerpletsch@gmail.com
Web site: http://www.palmerpletsch.com
Dist(s): **Independent Pubs. Group**
MyiLibrary.

Palmetto Street Publishing, *(978-0-615-49043-4; 978-0-9848782)* 106 W. Augusta Pl., Greenville, SC 29605 USA Tel 864-242-3906
E-mail: gabbehoward@gmail.com
Web site: n/a.

Palmetto Tree Pr., *(978-0-9742532)* 821 Calhoun St., Columbia, SC 29201 USA (SAN 255-5832) Tel 803-771-9300; Fax: 803-407-0766
E-mail: follybeech@aol.com.

Palmland Publishing, *(978-0-9666942; 978-1-933678)* Orders Addr.: 7881 Barrancas Ave., Bokeelia, FL 33922 USA (SAN 299-7835) Tel 239-283-3975; Fax: 941-870-2589; Toll Free: 877-725-6782; P.O. Box 478, Pineland, FL 33922 Toll Free: 877-725-6782
Web site: http://www.palmlandpublishing.com.

Palmore, Julie, *(978-0-9722653)* 3203 Harwood, Tyler, TX 75701-7642 USA.

Palo Alto Bks. *Imprint of* **Glencannon Pr.**

Paloma Bks. *Imprint of* **L & R Publishing, LLC**

Palomina Publishing, *(978-0-9763393)* 338 Napa Rd., Sonoma, CA 95476 USA.

Palomino Publishing, *(978-1-892344)* Div. of Programs for the Arts, Inc., 1535 E. Broadway, Tucson, AZ 85719 USA Tel 520-623-4000; Fax: 520-623-9102
E-mail: madaras@worldnet.att.net
Dist(s): **TNT Media Group, Inc.**

Pamir LLC, *(978-0-9888649)* 460 Jameson Hill Rd., Clinton Corners, NY 12514 USA Tel 845-266-0064
E-mail: natasha_rafi@hotmail.com.

Pampa Publishing, *(978-0-9744675; 978-0-615-11346-3)* Orders Addr.: P.O. Box 3481, Olympia, WA 98509-3481 USA; Edit Addr.: 4613 Shincke Rd. NE, Olympia, WA 98506 USA
E-mail: pampapublishing@comcast.net; ma2ka@home.com.

Pan Asia Pubns. (USA), Inc., *(978-1-57227)* 29564 Union City Blvd., Union City, CA 94587 USA (SAN 173-685X) Tel 510-475-1185; Fax: 510-475-1489; Toll Free: 800-909-8088
E-mail: sales@panap.com; info@panap.com
Web site: http://www.panap.com; http://www.cjkv.com
Dist(s): **China Books & Periodicals, Inc.**
Chinasprout, Inc.
Follett School Solutions
Lectorum Pubns., Inc.

Pan Asian Pubns. (U S A), Inc., *(978-1-57227)* 29564 Union City Blvd., Union City, CA 94587 USA Tel 510-475-1185; Fax: 510-475-1489
E-mail: schiu@panap.com.

Pan Macmillan (GBR) *(978-0-283; 978-0-312; 978-0-330; 978-0-333; 978-0-7522; 978-1-85283; 978-1-4050; 978-1-904633; 978-1-904919; 978-1-905716; 978-1-907360; 978-1-4472; 978-1-909621)* *Dist. by* **Trafalgar.**

Pan Macmillan (GBR) *(978-0-283; 978-0-312; 978-0-330; 978-0-333; 978-0-7522; 978-1-85283; 978-1-4050; 978-1-904633; 978-1-904919; 978-1-905716; 978-1-907360; 978-1-4472; 978-1-909621)* *Dist. by* **IPG Chicago.**

Pan Macmillan (GBR) *(978-0-283; 978-0-312; 978-0-330; 978-0-333; 978-0-7522; 978-1-85283; 978-1-4050; 978-1-904633; 978-1-904919; 978-1-905716; 978-1-907360; 978-1-4472; 978-1-909621)* *Dist. by* **Trans-Atl Phila.**

Pan Macmillan (GBR) *(978-0-283; 978-0-312; 978-0-330; 978-0-333; 978-0-7522; 978-1-85283; 978-1-4050; 978-1-904633; 978-1-904919; 978-1-905716; 978-1-907360; 978-1-4472; 978-1-909621)* *Dist. by* **Macmillan.**

Panacea Pr., *(978-0-9791309; 978-0-9842147; 978-0-9893645; 978-0-9861012)* P.O. Box 292005, Nashville, TN 37229-2005 USA Tel 615-406-822
E-mail: king2dw@aol.com.

Panacea Publishing, *(978-0-9743432)* Orders Addr.: 5002 Barlow Dr., Round Rock, TX 78681 USA Tel 512-228-1388; Fax: 512-906-1579; Toll Free: 877-723-6110 Do not confuse with Panacea Publishing in North Attleboro MA, South Yarmouth MA
E-mail: sales@panaceabooks.com
Web site: http://www.panaceabooks.com
Dist(s): **Brodart Co.**
Midwest Library Service
Quality Bks., Inc.

Panama Hat Publishing, Ltd., *(978-0-9852202; 978-1-943317)* P.O. Box 343, Green Mountain Falls, CO 80819-0343 USA Tel 970-368-2665
E-mail: admin@panamahatpublishing.com
Web site: http://www.panamahatpublishing.com/.

Pan-American Publishing Co., *(978-0-932906)* P.O. Box 1505, Las Vegas, NM 87701 USA (SAN 212-5366).

Panamericana Editorial (COL) *(978-958-30)* *Dist. by* **Lectorum Pubns.**

Panda Bear Pr., *(978-0-9724699)* Orders Addr.: 612 Museum Rd., Reading, PA 19611-1427 USA (SAN 255-5328) Tel 610-374-7048; Fax: 610-478-7992
E-mail: HaileJohnJr@msn.com
Web site: http://www.caroljhaile.com
Dist(s): **Firenze Pr.**

PANDA BKS. PR., *(978-0-692-78668-0; 978-0-692-80099-7)* 47 bristol St., thomaston, CT 32968 USA Tel 772-766-6549
E-mail: kramer535@bellsouth.net
Web site: www.musicboxstory.com.

Panda Pubns., *(978-0-9818392)* P.O. Box 595, Wilkes Barre, PA 18703 USA
E-mail: pandapublications@verizon.net; antobianco@msn.com.

Panda Publishing, L.L.C., *(978-0-9740180; 978-1-932724)* Orders Addr.: P.O. Box 670608, Dallas, TX 75367 USA (SAN 255-8165) Toll Free: 800-807-1776; Edit Addr.: 6215 Rex Dr., Dallas, TX 75230 USA; *Imprints:* Bios for Kids (Bios for Kids)
E-mail: info@biosforkids.com.

Pandia Pr., *(978-0-9766057; 978-0-9798496; 978-0-9977963)* 18400 SE Hwy.42, Weirsdale, FL 32195 USA
Web site: http://www.PandiaPress.com.

Pandora *Imprint of* **Highland Pr. Publishing**

Pandora Pr. (GBR) *(978-0-04; 978-0-86358; 978-1-85489)* *Dist. by* **IPG Chicago.**

Pandora Press U. S. *See* **Cascadia Publishing Hse., LLC**

PANGAEA, *(978-0-9630180; 978-1-929165)* Orders Addr.: 226 Wheeler St., S., Saint Paul, MN 55105-1927 USA Tel 651-226-2032
E-mail: info@pangaea.org
Web site: http://www.pangaea.org
Dist(s): **Follett School Solutions.**

Pangaea Publishing *See* **PANGAEA**

Pangea Software, Inc., *(978-0-9761505)* 12405 John Simpson Ct., Austin, TX 78732-2112 USA Tel 512-266-9991
Web site: http://www.pangeasoft.net.

Pangloss Pr., *(978-0-9668784; 978-0-692-51345-3)* Orders Addr.: P.O. Box 2225, Ballston Spa, NY 12020 USA Tel 518-584-4034 phone/fax; Edit Addr.: 63 Franklin St., Saratoga, NY 12866 USA Do not confuse with Pangloss Pr., Malibu, CA
E-mail: tuckerb@global2000.net.

Pangloss Publishing, *(978-0-9768586; 978-0-615-12424-7)* 3904 Becker Ave., Austin, TX 78751-5209 USA Fax: 512-453-1486
E-mail: candide@grandecom.net.

Pangus Publishing, *(978-0-9769715)* Orders Addr.: 1637 S. Iseminger St., Philadelphia, PA 19148 USA; Edit Addr.: P.O. Box 15763, Philadelphia, PA 19148 USA.

Panigrahy, Sonia, *(978-0-9975956)* 129 W. 89th St., New York, NY 10024 USA Tel 646-648-1898
E-mail: sonia1211@gmail.com.

Pankratz Creations, *(978-0-9742637)* 355 S. Fairlane Dr., Tooele, UT 84074-2623 USA
E-mail: customerservice@pankratzcreations.com; pankratz@mstar2.net
Web site: http://www.pankratzcreations.com.

Panline U.S.A., Inc., *(978-0-9713507; 978-0-615-23938-5; 978-0-9822010; 978-0-9847127)* 251 Union St., Northvale, NJ 07647 USA (SAN 920-5772) Tel 201-750-8010; Fax: 201-750-8030
E-mail: info@alextoys.com
Web site: http://www.alextoys.com.

Pannonia Pr., *(978-0-9657793)* P.O. Box 1062, Palatine, IL 60078-1062 USA Tel 847-277-0806; Fax: 847-228-6847
E-mail: pannoniapress2000@sbcglobal.net
Web site: http://www.pannoniapress.com.

Pannycake Pubn., *(978-0-9769538)* 1710 Vallejo St., Unit B, Seaside, CA 93955 USA Tel 831-393-1358; Fax: 831-753-6085
E-mail: carmelalayne@yahoo.com.

Panoply Pubns., *(978-0-9818391)* P.O. Box 2329, North Hollywood, CA 91610-0329 USA Tel 818-761-8757
E-mail: panoplypub@aol.com
Web site: http://www.panoplypublications.com.

Panorama Pr., Inc., *(978-0-9768642)* P.O. Box 183, Boulder, CO 80306-0183 USA.

Pantheon *Imprint of* **Knopf Doubleday Publishing Group**

Panther Creek Pr., *(978-0-9678343; 978-0-9718361; 978-0-9747839; 978-0-9771797)* Orders Addr.: P.O. Box 130233, Spring, TX 77393-0233 USA (SAN 253-8520); Edit Addr.: 104 Plum Tree Ter. Apt. 115, Houston, TX 77077-5375 USA
E-mail: panthercreek3@hotmail.com; guidamj@juno.com
Web site: http://www.panthercreekpress.com.

Pants On Fire Pr., *(978-0-9827271; 978-0-9860373; 978-0-615-88989-4; 978-0-615-89685-4; 978-0-615-89931-2; 978-0-615-91719-1; 978-0-615-96453-9; 978-0-615-98402-5; 978-0-692-02170-5; 978-0-692-02171-2; 978-0-692-20585-3; 978-0-692-20941-7; 978-0-692-21000-0; 978-0-692-21001-7; 978-0-692-21003-1; 978-0-692-30738-0; 978-0-692-35957-0; 978-0-692-44415-3; 978-0-692-44416-0; 978-0-692-57238-2; 978-0-692-69868-6) 2062 Harbor Cove Way, Winter Garden, FL 34787 USA*
E-mail: david@pantsonfirepress.com; editor@pantsonfirepress.com
Web site: http://www.pantsonfirepress.com
Dist(s): **CreateSpace Independent Publishing Platform**
INscribe Digital
Ingram Publisher Services.

Paon Pubns., *(978-0-9711721)* 608 S. Webik Ave, Clawson, MI 48017 USA Tel 248-288-5621.

Papaloizos Pubns., Inc., *(978-0-932416)* 11720 Auth Ln., Silver Spring, MD 20902-1645 USA (SAN 220-9853) Tel 301-593-0652
E-mail: info@greek123.com
Web site: http://www.greek123.com.

Papas & Nellie Pr., *(978-0-9719925)* 2110 Lakeland Ave., Madison, WI 53704 USA Tel 608-661-0508
E-mail: papasandnellie@tds.net.

Papell, David, *(978-0-615-17531-7; 978-0-615-17931-5; 978-0-615-17932-2)* 5601 Riverdale Ave., Bronx, NY 10471 USA Tel 718-601-3771
E-mail: dpapell@earthlink.net
Web site: http://www.davidpapell.net
Dist(s): **Lulu Pr., Inc.**

Paper Crane Pr., *(978-0-9650833)* P.O. Box 29292, Bellingham, WA 98228-1292 USA Tel 360-676-0266; Toll Free: 800-356-9315
E-mail: carolrj@nas.com
Dist(s): **Brodart Co.**
New Leaf Distributing Co., Inc.
Unique Bks., Inc.
Upper Access, Inc.

Paper Doll Publishing, *(978-0-9748252)* Orders Addr.: a/o Orders, P.O. Box 72028, Phoenix, AZ 85050 USA (SAN 255-8084)
E-mail: michael@paperdollpublishing.com; books@paperdollpublishing.com
Web site: http://www.paperdollpublishing.com.

Paper Jam Publishing, *(978-1-888345)* Orders Addr.: P.O. Box 435, Eastsound, WA 98245 USA Tel 360-376-3200 (phone/fax); Toll Free: 877-757-2665; Edit Addr.: 531 Fern St., Eastsound, WA 98245 USA
E-mail: paperjam@rockisland.com
Web site: http://www.rockisland.com/~paperjam.

Paper Posie, *(978-0-9707944; 978-0-9774763)* Orders Addr.: 315a Meigs Rd., #167, Santa Barbara, CA 93109 USA Tel 805-569-2398; Fax: 805-563-0166; Toll Free: 800-360-1761
Web site: http://www.paperposie.com; http://www.kidsatweddings.com
Dist(s): **Greenleaf Book Group.**

Paper Studio Pr., *(978-0-9790668; 978-0-9795053; 978-1-935223; 978-1-942490)* Orders Addr.: P.O. Box 14, Kingfield, ME 04947 USA Tel 207-265-2500
Web site: http://paperstudiopress.com.

Paper Tiger, Incorporated, The *See* **Paper Tiger, The**

Paper Tiger, The, *(978-1-889439)* Orders Addr.: 722 Upper Cherrytown Rd., Kerhonkson, NY 12446 USA Tel 845-626-5354
E-mail: fredweiss@papertig.com
Web site: http://www.papertig.com.

Paperbacks for Educators, *(978-0-9702376; 978-1-59721)* 426 W. Front St., Washington, MO 63090 USA (SAN 103-3379) Tel 636-239-1999; Fax: 636-239-4515; Toll Free Fax: 800-514-7323; Toll Free: 800-227-2591
E-mail: paperbacks@usmo.com
Web site: http://www.any-book-in-print.com.

Papercutz, *(978-1-59707; 978-1-62991; 978-1-5458)* 160 Broadway, E. Wing Suite 700, New York, NY 10038 USA (SAN 850-9670) Tel 646-559-4681
E-mail: nantier@papercutz.com
Web site: http://www.papercutz.com
Dist(s): **Diamond Comic Distributors, Inc.**
Macmillan.

Papergraphics Printing, *(978-0-9773322)* 4 John Tyler St., Suite 1, Merrimack, NH 03054-3054 USA Tel 603-880-1835; Fax: 603-880-1751; Toll Free: 800-499-1835
E-mail: prepress@papergraphics.biz
Web site: http://www.papergraphics.biz.

Papillon Pr., *(978-1-884429)* Orders Addr.: P.O. Box 54502, Phoenix, AZ 85078-4502 USA Tel 602-931-0556
E-mail: firstchoiceent05@msn.com.

Papillon Pr., Inc., *(978-0-9667476)* 23 Seagull Pl., Vero Beach, FL 32960-5212 USA
Dist(s): **New Leaf Distributing Co., Inc.**

Papillon Publishing *Imprint of* **Blue Dolphin Publishing, Inc.**

Papillon Publishing, *(978-0-9651048)* P.O. Box 12044, Dallas, TX 75225 USA Tel 214-722-1297 (phone/fax) Do not confuse with Papillon Publishing in Rochester, MN
E-mail: ford.lawrence@sbcglobal.net.

PAPO Brand *Imprint of* **Planet Bronx Productions**

Papyrus & Pen, *(978-0-9770687)* 2923 Cecil B. Moore Ave., Suite 3, Philadelphia, PA 19121 USA Tel 267-539-7540
E-mail: dmccrary@papyrusandpen.com
Web site: http://www.papyrusandpen.com
Dist(s): **Ingram Publisher Services**
Lightning Source, Inc.

Papyrus Publishing, Inc., *(978-0-9675581; 978-0-9882883)* Orders Addr.: 7409 Edgewood Ave. N., Brooklyn Park, MN 55428 USA Tel 763-717-8854; Fax: 763-374-7737 Do not confuse with Papyrus Publishing in Missouri City, TX
E-mail: PapyrusPublishing@msn.com
Web site: http://www.mahmoudelkati.com; http://www.papyruspublishinginc.com.

Para-Anchors International, *(978-1-878832)* Orders Addr.: P.O. Box 19, Summerland, CA 93067 USA Tel 805-966-4837; Fax: 805-966-0782; Toll Free: 800-350-7070; Edit Addr.: 21 E. Canon Perdido, Suite 303, Santa Barbara, CA 93101 USA
E-mail: victor1pai@netscape.com; victor1cnp@netscape.com
Web site: http://www.jerustar.com
Dist(s): **Bookmasters Distribution**
Quality Bks., Inc.

†Parable Pr., *(978-0-917250)* P.O. Box 51, Vinalhaven, ME 04863-0051 USA (SAN 208-4449); *CIP.*

Parable Venture Partners, LLC, *(978-0-9728501)* 12946 SW 133 Ct., Suite B, Miami, FL 33186 USA Tel 305-252-0905; Fax: 305-245-9974
E-mail: info@ethansparables.com
Web site: http://www.ethansparables.com.

Parables & Bks., *(978-0-9833188; 978-1-939682)* 24 S. Front St., Bergenfield, NJ 07621 USA Tel 201-338-4953
E-mail: sandy@parablesandbooks.com
Web site: www.parablesandbooks.com.

Parabola Bks., *(978-0-930407)* 656 Broadway, Suite 615, New York, NY 10012-2317 USA (SAN 219-5763) Tel 212-505-6200; Fax: 212-979-7325; Toll Free: 800-560-6984
E-mail: ads-promo@parabola.org; orders@parabola.org; JoeKulin@aol.com; editors@parabola.org
Web site: http://www.parabola.org/; http://www.cinemaofthespirit.org
Dist(s): **Independent Pubs. Group**
New Leaf Distributing Co., Inc.

Parabola Magazine/Society for Study of Myth & Tradition *See* **Parabola Bks.**

Parachute Jump Publishing, *(978-0-9852469; 978-0-9888905; 978-0-9915405; 978-0-9903660)* 50 Brighton 1st Rd. Apt. 16D, Brooklyn, NY 11235 USA Tel 718-593-7717
E-mail: kpaulet@verizon.net
Dist(s): **BookBaby**
Lightning Source, Inc.

Parachute Press, Incorporated *See* **Parachute Publishing, LLC**

Parachute Publishing, LLC, *(978-0-938753; 978-1-57351)* 156 Fifth Ave., New York, NY 10010 USA (SAN 661-5554) Tel 212-691-1421; Fax: 212-645-8769
E-mail: ppibooks@aol.com.

Paraclete Pr., Inc., *(978-0-941478; 978-1-55725; 978-1-61261; 978-1-64060)* Orders Addr.: P.O. Box 1568, Orleans, MA 02653 USA (SAN 282-1508) Fax: 508-255-5705; Toll Free: 800-451-5006; Edit Addr.: 36 Southern Eagle Cartway, Brewster, MA 02631 USA (SAN 664-6239) Do not confuse with companies with the same or similar names in Indianapolis, IN, Pentwater, MI
E-mail: srmercy@paracletepress.com; miao@paracletepress.com
Web site: http://www.paracletepress.com
Dist(s): **BookMasters**
Follett School Solutions
Forward Movement Pubns.
MyiLibrary.

Paradigm Accelerated Curriculum, *(978-1-928629; 978-1-59476)* Div. of Paradigm Alternatives Centers, Inc., Orders Addr.: P.O. Box 200, Dublin, TX 76446-0200 USA Tel 254-445-4272; Fax: 254-445-3947; Edit Addr.: 112 S. Grafton, Dublin, TX 76446-0200 USA
E-mail: learn@pacworks.com
Web site: http://www.pacworks.com.

Paradigm Alternatives Centers, Incorporated *See* **Paradigm Accelerated Curriculum**

Paradigm Publishing, *(978-0-9746013)* Orders Addr.: P.O. Box 872, LaPorte, CO 80535 USA; Edit Addr.: 3106 Kintzley Ct., D, LaPorte, CO 80535 USA Do not confuse with companies with the same or similar name in Oklahoma City OK, San Dimas CA, Chicago IL, McFarland WI, Saint Paul MN, Midvale UT, Pembroke Pines FL, Pocatello ID, Brookline MA, Boulder CO, Laguna Park, TX , Washington, DC
E-mail: sales@paradigmpublish.com
Web site: http://www.paradigmpublish.com.

Paradise Cay Pubns., *(978-0-939837; 978-1-937196)* P.O. Box 29, Arcata, CA 95518-0029 USA (SAN 663-690X) Tel 707-822-9063; Fax: 707-822-9163; Toll Free: 800-736-4509 (orders only)
E-mail: jim@paracay.com
Web site: http://www.paracay.com
Dist(s): **Hale, Robert & Co., Inc.**

Paradise Copies, Inc., *(978-0-9836716)* 21 Conz St., Northampton, MA 01060 USA Tel 413-585-0414; Fax: 413-585-0417
E-mail: Carol@paradisecopies.com
Web site: http://paradisecopies.com.

Paradise Pr. & Assocs., LLC, *(978-0-9755970)* P.O. Box 783573, Winter Garden, FL 34778-3573 USA Tel 321-354-5881 (phone/fax)
E-mail: bbeehy@gmail.com
Web site: none.

Paradise Pr., Inc., *(978-1-57657; 978-1-884907; 978-1-4194)* 1776 N. Pine Island Rd. Ste. 218, Plantation, FL 33322-5223 USA Do not confuse with companies with the same or similar names in Crested Butte, CO Corte Madera, CA, Santa Monica, CA, Ridgefield, CA, Chicago, IL, Herdon, VA, Temple Terrace, FL
E-mail: buybooks@paradisepress.us.

Paradise Research Pubns., Inc., *(978-1-885803)* Orders Addr.: P.O. Box 837, Kihei, HI 96753-0837 USA Tel 808-874-4876 (phone/fax)
E-mail: dickb@dickb.com
Web site: http://www.dickb.com/index.html
Dist(s): **Globe Pequot Pr., The**
Good Bk. Publishing Co.

Paradox *Imprint of* **DC Comics**

Paradoxal Pr., *(978-0-9766132)* 28916 NE 34th Ct., Redmond, WA 98053-9114 USA
Web site: http://www.paradoxalpress.com.

Paradoxical Pr., The, *(978-0-9786663)* 48 Cranford Pl., Teaneck, NJ 07666 USA Tel 201-281-8112
E-mail: info@theparadoxicalpress.com
Web site: http://www.theparadoxicalpress.com.

Paraglyph, Inc., *(978-1-932111; 978-1-933097)* 3533 E. Friess Dr., Phoenix, AZ 85032-5318 USA; 3533 E. Friess Dr., Phoenix, AZ 85032-5318; *Imprints:* Paraglyph Press (Paraglyph Pr)
E-mail: ccaldwell@paraglyphpress.com; stevesayre@paraglyphpress.com
Web site: http://www.paraglyphpress.com
Dist(s): **Ingram Publisher Services**
O'Reilly Media, Inc.

Paraglyph Pr. *Imprint of* **Paraglyph, Inc.**

Paragon Agency, Pubs., The *Imprint of* **Paragon Agency, The**

Paragon Agency, The, *(978-1-891030; 978-0-9710012)* Orders Addr.: P.O. Box 1281, Orange, CA 92856 USA Tel 714-771-0652; *Imprints:* Paragon Agency, Publishers, The (PAP)
E-mail: Paragon@SpecialBooks.com
Web site: http://www.SpecialBooks.com.

†Paragon Hse. Pubs., *(978-0-88702; 978-0-89226; 978-0-913729; 978-0-943852; 978-1-55778; 978-1-885118; 978-1-61083)* Orders Addr.: 3600 Labore Rd., Suite 1, Saint Paul, MN 55110-4144 USA (SAN 286-1704) Tel 651-644-3087; Fax: 651-644-0997; Toll Free Fax: 800-494-0997; Toll Free: 800-447-3709
E-mail: paragon@paragonhouse.com
Web site: http://www.paragonhouse.com
Dist(s): **Bookmasters Distribution**; *CIP.*

Parallax, Inc., *(978-1-928982)* 599 Menlo Dr., No. 100, Rocklin, CA 95765-3708 USA Tel 916-624-8333; Fax: 916-624-8003; Toll Free: 888-512-1024
E-mail: info@parallaxinc.com
Web site: http://www.parallaxinc.com.

Parallax Pr., *(978-0-938077; 978-1-888375; 978-1-935209; 978-0-9846271; 978-1-937006; 978-1-941529; 978-1-946764)* Orders Addr.: P.O. Box 7355, Berkeley, CA 94707 USA (SAN 663-4494) Tel 510-525-0101; Fax: 510-525-7129; Toll Free: 800-863-5290; Edit Addr.: 2236 6th St., Berkeley, CA 94710-2219 USA; *Imprints:* Plum Blossom Books (Plum Blossom)
E-mail: orders@parallax.org
Web site: http://www.parallax.org
Dist(s): **MyiLibrary**
Penguin Random Hse. LLC
SPD-Small Pr. Distribution.

Paramance *Imprint of* **MQuills Publishing**

Paramount Market Publishing, Inc., *(978-0-9671439; 978-0-9725290; 978-0-9766973; 978-0-9766602; 978-0-9801745; 978-0-9819869; 978-0-9830436; 978-0-9851795; 978-1-941688)* 950 Danby Rd., Suite 136, Ithaca, NY 14850 USA (SAN 850-6612) Tel 607-275-8100 (phone/fax); Toll Free: 888-787-8100
E-mail: doris@paramountbooks.com
Web site: http://www.paramountbooks.com.

Paraphrase, LLC, *(978-0-9815879)* Orders Addr.: P.O. Box 56508, Sherman Oaks, CA 91413 USA (SAN 855-9643) Tel 818-219-4377; Toll Free Fax: 888-863-4377
Web site: http://www.paraphrasellc.com; http://www.espete.com.

Parascension, Inc., *(978-0-9729380; 978-0-615-18212-4)* 222 Oak Grove Rd., Suite 201, Bradfordwoods, PA 15015-1338 USA; *Imprints:* Parascension Press (Parascen)
E-mail: jameshayhurst@zoominternet.net
Web site: http://www.parascension.com; http://www.badcommandments.com; http://www.adventuresofmercurylane.com.

Parascension Pr. *Imprint of* **Parascension, Inc.**

Parent Brigade Company, The, *(978-0-9774998)* 530 New Los Angeles Ave., Suite 115-332, Moorpark, CA 93021 USA Fax: 805-523-0119.

Parent Child Pr., Inc., *(978-0-939195; 978-0-9601016)* Orders Addr.: 11 W 9th St, Santa Rosa, CA 95401 USA (SAN 208-4333) Tel 707-579-3003; Fax: 707-579-1604; Toll Free: 866-727-3682; Edit Addr.: 11 W 9th St, Santa Rosa, CA 95401 USA (SAN 662-7331)
E-mail: smcmath@montessoriservices.com
Web site: http://http://www.montessoriservices.com/parent-child-press.

Parent Perks, Inc., *(978-0-9822150)* 217 Bellevue St., Newton, MA 02458 USA (SAN 857-569X)
E-mail: parentperks@yahoo.com.

Parent Positive Pr., *(978-0-9721502)* 446 Willis Ave., No. 118, Williston Park, NY 11596-0118 USA (SAN 257-4438) Tel 516-997-0051
E-mail: Info@parentpositive.com
Web site: http://www.girlsonlyweightloss.com
Dist(s): **Independent Pubs. Group.**

Parental Interventional Tools, Inc, *(978-0-9778274)* P.O. Box 547, Southbury, CT 06488 USA Tel 203-264-1054
E-mail: pittools@aol.com
Web site: http://www.drketch.com; www.pit-inc.com.

†Parenting Pr., Inc., *(978-0-943990; 978-0-9602862; 978-1-884734; 978-1-936903)* Orders Addr.: P.O. Box 75267, Seattle, WA 98175 USA (SAN 215-6938) Tel 206-364-2900; Fax: 206-364-0702; Toll Free: 800-992-6657; Edit Addr.: P.O. Box 75267, Seattle, WA 98175 USA (SAN 699-5500)
E-mail: cthreadgill@ParentingPress.com
Web site: http://www.parentingpress.com
Dist(s): **Brodart Co.**
Follett School Solutions
Independent Pubs. Group
Midwest Library Service
MyiLibrary; *CIP.*

Parents Publishing Group *Imprint of* **Big Tent Bks.**

Parish, Alex (GBR) *(978-0-9561613) Dist. by* **LuluCom.**

Parity Pr., *(978-0-9762015)* 1450 W. Horizon Ridge Pkwy, B-304-226, Henderson, NV 89012-4480 USA Tel 702-260-8989; Fax: 702-364-8988; Toll Free: 877-260-8989
E-mail: info@paritypress.biz
Web site: http://www.ShiftingRings.com.

Pariyatti Publishing, *(978-0-9649484; 978-81-7414; 978-1-928706; 978-1-938754; 978-1-68172)* Div. of Pariyatti, 867 Larmon Rd., Onalaska, WA 98570 USA Tel 360-978-4998; Fax: 360-978-4557
E-mail: director@pariyatti.org; admin@pariyatti.org
Web site: http://www.pariyatti.org
Dist(s): **Independent Pubs. Group**
MyiLibrary.

Park Hse. Bks., *(978-0-9755097)* 838 N. 6th St., Saint Clair, MI 48079 USA
E-mail: parkhousebooks@yahoo.com; mmerkau@yahoo.com
Web site: http://www.familyunity.us.

Park Tutor Schl., *(978-0-9612740)* 7200 N. College Ave., Indianapolis, IN 46240 USA (SAN 289-7903) Tel 317-415-2700; Fax: 317-254-2714; Toll Free: 888-782-5861
E-mail: info@parktudor.pvt.org
Web site: http://www.parktudor.org.

Parker Girl Publishing, *(978-0-9855074)* 227 Shoreline Dr., Honey Brook, PA 19344 USA Tel 610-496-5070
E-mail: Huganursem@gmail.com.

Parker, Laurie, *(978-0-9729615; 978-0-9980060)* 111 Dunbrook Dr., Starkville, MS 39759 USA.

Parker Publishing Company *See* **Parker-Wallace Publishing Co., LLC**

Parker Publishing Inc., *(978-1-60043)* 12523 Limonite Ave. #440-438, Mira Loma, CA 91752 USA Fax: 681-685-8036
E-mail: miriam@parker-publishing.com
Web site: http://www.parker-publishing.com
Dist(s): **CreateSpace Independent Publishing Platform.**

Parker-Wallace Publishing Co., LLC, *(978-0-9654700; 978-1-893091)* Orders Addr.: P.O. Box 8654, Fort Lauderdale, FL 33310 USA; *Imprints:* My Ancestors, My Heroes (My Ancestors)
E-mail: thebusiness2@yahoo.com.

Parkhurst Brook Pubs., *(978-0-9615664)* 303 Perrin Rd., Potsdam, NY 13676 USA (SAN 695-9121) Tel 315-265-9037
E-mail: mhcharle@northnet.org.

Parkhurst Brothers, Inc., Pubs., *(978-1-935166; 978-1-62491)* Orders Addr.: 110 West Main, Marion, MI 49665 USA (SAN 856-7107) Tel 5015153224
E-mail: ted@parkhurstbrothers.com
Web site: www.parkhurstbrothers.com; http://www.parkhurstbrothers.com
Dist(s): **Chicago Distribution Ctr.**

Parkhurst, R.M., *(978-0-9770323)* Orders Addr.: P.O. Box 1033, Redwood City, CA 94064 USA; Edit Addr.: P.O. Box 1013, Atascadero, CA 93423-1013 USA
E-mail: parkhurst@bigfoot.com.

Parklane Publishing, *(978-1-59384)* Div. of Book Club of America, 100 Marcus Blvd. Ste. 8, Hauppauge, NY 11788-3749 USA
E-mail: lbaumert@bookclubusa.com
Web site: http://www.parklanepublishing.com.

Parks Publishing *Imprint of* **RBC Publishing Co., Inc.**

Parkside Pubns., Inc., *(978-0-9617266; 978-0-9820774)* 901 5th Ave. Ste. 4100, Seattle, WA 98164-2001 USA (SAN 663-4907) Do not confuse with Parkside Pubns., Inc., Davis, SD
E-mail: info@parksidepublications.com
Web site: http://www.parksidepublications.com
Dist(s): **Partners Bk. Distributing, Inc.**

Parkway Pr., Ltd., *(978-0-9826641; 978-0-9828089)* 330 Smith St., Niles, OH 44446-1735 USA Tel 330-505-8113
E-mail: dlbrown88@yahoo.com
Web site: www.parkwaypress.com.

Parkway Pubs., Inc., *(978-0-9635752; 978-1-887905; 978-1-933251)*
E-mail: parkwaypub@hotmail.com
Web site: http://www.parkwaypublishers.com
Dist(s): **Blair, John F. Pub.**
Julia Taylor Ebel.

Parkwest Pubns., Inc., *(978-0-88186)* P.O. Box 310251, Miami, FL 33231 USA (SAN 264-6846) Tel 305-256-7880; Fax: 305-256-7816
E-mail: parkwest@parkwestpubs.com; info@parkwestpubs.com
Web site: http://www.parkwestpubs.com
Dist(s): **Independent Pubs. Group.**

Parlance Publishing, *(978-0-9721032)* Orders Addr.: P.O. Box 841, Columbus, MS 39703-0841 USA (SAN 255-0806) Tel 662-327-4064; Fax: 662-327-4504; Edit Addr.: 1099 Southdown Pkwy., Columbus, MS 39701 USA
E-mail: parlancepub@aol.com; mail@abookery.com
Web site: http://www.parlancepublishing.com; http://www.abookery.com.

Parlor Pr., *(978-0-9724772; 978-1-932559; 978-1-60235)* Orders Addr.: 3015 Brackenberry Dr., Anderson, SC 29621 USA (SAN 254-8879) Tel 765-409-2649; Fax: 206-600-5076
E-mail: editor@parlorpress.com; sales@parlorpress.com
Web site: http://www.parlorpress.com
Dist(s): **Ebsco Publishing**
MBS Textbook Exchange, Inc.
SPD-Small Pr. Distribution
ebrary, Inc.

Parra Grande Pr., *(978-0-9815541; 978-0-615-19049-5)* 211 E. Carrillo St., No. 301, Santa Barbara, CA 93101 USA (SAN 855-8671) Tel 805-899-3210; Fax: 805-899-3211
E-mail: jb657@verizon.net.

Parragon, Inc., *(978-0-7525; 978-1-85813; 978-1-4054)* Div. of Parragon Publishing, 440 Park Ave. S, 13th Flr., New York, NY 10016 USA (SAN 256-7385) Tel 212-629-9773; Fax: 212-629-9756; *Imprints:* Exclusive Editions (Exclusive Editions); Bright Sparks (Bright Sparks)
Dist(s): **Central Programs.**

Parramon Ediciones S.A. (ESP) *(978-84-342) Dist. by* **Continental Bk.**

Parramon Ediciones S.A. (ESP) *(978-84-342) Dist. by* **Lectorum Pubns.**

Parramon Ediciones S.A. (ESP) *(978-84-342) Dist. by* **Distr Norma.**

Parrish, Fayrene, *(978-0-9826717)* 264 Country Club Dr., Avila Beach, CA 93424 USA Tel 805-500-5481
Dist(s): **CreateSpace Independent Publishing Platform.**

Parrot Pr., *(978-0-615-17122-7)* 6200 Vista Del Mar, Suite 313, Playa del Rey, CA 90293 USA Tel 310-574-0911
E-mail: mira@miramarmango.com
Web site: http://www.parrotstory.com
Dist(s): **Partners Pubs. Group, Inc.**

PARSEC Ink, *(978-0-9743231; 978-0-615-15280-6; 978-0-615-23540-0; 978-0-578-03103-3)* P.O. Box 3681, Pittsburgh, PA 15230-3681 USA
Web site: http://www.trfn.clpgh.org/parsec
Dist(s): **Lulu Pr., Inc.**

PARSEC Publishing *See* **PARSEC Ink**

Parson Place Pr., LLC, *(978-0-9786567; 978-0-9842163; 978-0-9888528)* 10701 Tanner Williams Rd., Mobile, AL 36608-8846 USA (SAN 851-254X); P.O. Box 8277, Mobile, AL 36689-0277 Tel 251-645-9803
E-mail: info@parsonplacepress.com; mlwhite@parsonplacepress.com
Web site: http://www.parsonplacepress.com
Dist(s): **Lightning Source, Inc.**
Spring Arbor Distributors, Inc.

Parsons Porch Bks., *(978-0-9826337; 978-0-9829413; 978-1-936912; 978-0-692-25814-9; 978-0-692-30031-2; 978-0-692-30040-4; 978-0-692-30872-1; 978-0-692-32034-1; 978-0-692-32056-3; 978-0-692-32058-7; 978-0-692-32063-1; 978-0-692-32066-2; 978-0-692-32067-9; 978-0-692-32776-0; 978-0-692-33452-2; 978-0-692-33526-0; 978-0-692-33625-0; 978-0-692-33626-7; 978-0-692-35217-5; 978-0-692-35889-4; 978-0-692-35891-7; 978-0-692-35894-8; 978-0-692-36083-5; 978-0-692-36086-6; 978-0-692-38065-9; 978-0-692-38067-3; 978-0-692-380) 121 Holly Trail NW, Cleveland, TN 37311 USA Tel 423-476-4122*
E-mail: dtullock@parsonsporch.com
Web site: http://www.parsonsporch.com
Dist(s): **CreateSpace Independent Publishing Platform.**

Parsons Technology, *(978-1-57264)* Subs. of The Learning Co., Orders Addr.: P.O. Box 100, Hiawatha, IA 52233-0100 USA (SAN 665-6161) Tel 319-395-9626; Fax: 319-378-0335; Toll Free: 800-833-3241
Dist(s): **Spring Arbor Distributors, Inc.**

Partae Pr., *(978-0-9662608)* 703 Ivinson Ave., Laramie, WY 82070 USA (SAN 254-1688) Tel 307-745-6893
E-mail: press@partae.com
Web site: http://www.partae.com.

Parthenon Pr., *(978-0-9718398)* 4839 Fullmoon Dr., El Sobrante, CA 94803-2139 USA Tel 510-223-6850 Do not confuse with Parthenon Pr., in New York, NY
E-mail: wakingthetiger@yahoo.com
Web site: http://expage.com/tigerspirit
Dist(s): **CreateSpace Independent Publishing Platform.**

Parthian Bks. (GBR) *(978-0-9521558; 978-1-902638; 978-1-905762; 978-1-906998; 978-1-907476) Dist. by* **IPG Chicago.**

Partners in Development *See* **Partners in Development Foundation**

Partners in Development Foundation, *(978-1-933835)* 2040 Bachelot St., Honolulu, HI 96817 USA Tel 808-595-2752; Fax: 808-595-4932
E-mail: admin@pidfoundation.org
Web site: http://www.pidfoundation.org
Dist(s): **Islander Group.**

Partners in Learning, Incorporated *See* **MRN Pubns.**

Partridge Pub., *(978-1-4828; 978-1-5437)* 1663 Liberty Dr., Bloomington, IN 47403 USA Tel 812-334-5223; Fax: 812-334-5223; Toll Free: 877-655-1722
E-mail: sfurr@authorsoultions.com; jburns@authorsolutions.com
Web site: http://www.partridgepublishing.com.

PartridgeIndia *Imprint of* **Author Solutions, Inc.**

Pascha Pr., *(978-0-9964045)* P.O. Box 944, Schererville, IN 46375 USA Tel 844-472-7242
E-mail: mkunch@paschapress.com
Web site: www.paschapress.com.

Pasco Scientific, *(978-1-886998; 978-1-937492)* 10101 Foothills Blvd., Roseville, CA 95678-8905 USA Tel 916-786-3800; Fax: 916-786-8905.

Pascualina Producciones S.A., 150 42nd Ave. E., Seattle, WA 98112 USA Tel 206-940-5412; Fax: 206-621-7956
E-mail: magdelenarossa@aol.com
Dist(s): **Independent Pubs. Group.**

Pasiteles Publishing Co., *(978-0-9785270)* 743 Belmont St., Belmont, MA 02478 USA
Web site: http://www.pasiteles.com.

Passage Publishing, *(978-0-9715926; 978-0-9724619; 978-0-9814833)* Div. of Art by Marianne, P.O. Box 148304, Nashville, TN 37214 USA Tel 615-828-3657 Do not confuse with Passage Publishing in Seattle, WA
E-mail: upcountrygirl@comcast.net; marsydotes1@live.com; upcountrygirl7@msn.com
Web site: http://www.upcountrycreations.com; http://www.artbymarianne.com.

Passion Profit Co., The/NicheMarket, *(978-0-9629202; 978-0-9745313; 978-0-9835808)* Div. of A Company Called W, Orders Addr.: P.O. Box 618, New York, NY 10008 USA Tel 646-219-3565; Fax: 212-658-9232
E-mail: orderdept@passionprofit.com
Web site: http://www.passionprofit.com.

Passionate Purpose, *(978-0-9898579)* 377 Carodon Dr., Ruckersville, VA 22968 USA Tel 850-890-2768
E-mail: wildcatdtt@yahoo.com.

PassionQuest Technologies, LLC, *(978-0-9679338; 978-0-9912611)* P.O. Box 912, Marysville, OH 43040 USA (SAN 254-4326) Tel 707-688-2848; 5055 Business Ctr. Dr. Suite 108, Pmb 110, Fairfield, CA 94534 Tel 707-688-2848; *Imprints:* Wings-on-Disk (Wings Disk)
E-mail: john@earnprofitsfromyourpassion.com
Web site: http://www.OnMyMountain.com.

Passkey Pubns., *(978-0-9818971; 978-0-9822660; 978-1-935664; 978-1-937361)* Orders Addr.: P.O. Box 580465, Elk Grove, CA 95758 USA (SAN 856-8782) Tel 916-712-7446; Fax: 916-427-5765; *Imprints:* Defiant Press (DefiantPr)
E-mail: admin@passkeypublications.com
Web site: http://www.passkeypublications.com; http://www.pineapplepublications.com; http://www.enrolledagentreview.com; http://www.defiantpress.com/
Dist(s): **CreateSpace Independent Publishing Platform**
Lightning Source, Inc.
Lulu Pr., Inc.

Passport Bks. *Imprint of* **McGraw-Hill Trade**

Pastime Pr., *(978-0-9711632; 978-1-932046)* Div. of CICA Industries, Inc., P.O. Box 741084, Boynton Beach, FL 33474 USA Tel 561-731-3400; Toll Free: 800-370-1174 Do not confuse with Pastime Press in Seattle, WA
E-mail: cicausadotcom@aol.com
Web site: http://www.pastimepress.com.

Pastime Pubns., *(978-0-9760276)* 1370 Trancas St., No. 372, Napa, CA 94558 USA Do not confuse with Pastime Publications in Walnut Creek, CA; Oakhill, VA; Herndon, VA
Web site: http://napavalleypastime.com.

Pastime Pubns., LLC, *(978-0-692-77305-5)* 1303 Waterfront Dr., Virginia Beach, VA 23451 USA Tel 724-961-2922
E-mail: scott@pastimepublicationsllc.com.

Pastorpreneur Ministries, *(978-0-9716489; 978-0-9831958)* Orders Addr.: 5214 Silver Peak Ln., Rocklin, CA 95765 USA Tel 916-872-5435
E-mail: john@pastorpreneur.com
Web site: http://www.pastorpreneur.com.

PastWays Inc., *(978-0-9671075)* Orders Addr.: P.O. Box 551, Farmington, MI 48332-0551 USA Tel 248-701-8112; Edit Addr.: 33414 Oakland, Suite 2, Farmington Hills, MI 48335-3571 USA
E-mail: bgolden@pastways.info
Web site: http://www.pastways.info.

Patagonia, *(978-0-9790659; 978-0-9801227; 978-1-938340)* 259 W. Santa Clara St., Ventura, CA 93001-2717 USA Tel 805-643-8616; Fax: 805-643-2367; Toll Free: 800-638-6464
E-mail: karla_olson@patagonia.com
Web site: http://www.Patagonia.com
Dist(s): **D.A.P./Distributed Art Pubs.**
MyiLibrary
Publishers Group West (PGW).

Patagonia Books *See* **Patagonia**

Patagonia Pr., *(978-1-882695)* P.O. Box 284, Bagdad, FL 32530 USA Tel 904-623-5790 Do not confuse with Patagonia Pr., Inc., Patagonia AZ
E-mail: Patagoniapress@aol.com.

Patchwork Pr., *(978-0-615-88322-9; 978-0-615-91877-8; 978-0-615-93512-6; 978-0-615-98429-2; 978-0-692-20253-1)* 7707 Red Maple Dr., Plainfield, IL 60586 USA Tel 815-416-8236
Dist(s): **CreateSpace Independent Publishing Platform.**

Paterson Museum for Italian Girls Press *See* **Mill Street Forward, The**

Path of Peace Inc., The, *(978-0-9766702)* 6610 Dorel St., Suite B, Philadelphia, PA 19142 USA Tel 215-681-6592
E-mail: blessbango@yahoo.com
Web site: http://www.thepathofpeace.net.

Pathfinder Equine Publications, *(978-0-9819240; 978-0-9915027)* 1908 Glade Rd., Farmington, NM 87401 USA
Dist(s): **Independent Pubs. Group**
MyiLibrary.

PathLight Bks. *Imprint of* **Sunesis Publishing Co.**

Pathway Pr., *(978-0-87148; 978-1-59684)* Div. of Church of God Publishing Hse., Orders Addr.: P.O. Box 2250, Cleveland, TN 37320-2250 USA (SAN 665-7567); Edit Addr.: 1080 Montgomery Ave., Cleveland, TN 37311 USA (SAN 202-8727) Tel 423-476-4512; Fax: 423-478-7616; Toll Free: 800-546-7590 (music only); 800-553-8506 (trade only) Do not confuse with Pathway Press, San Rafael, CA
E-mail: bill_george@pathwaypress.org
Web site: http://www.pathwaypress.org.

Pathways into Science, *(978-0-9779427)* 7417 River Falls Dr., Potomac, MD 20854 USA (SAN 850-5683) Tel 301-365-7593
Web site: http://pathwaysintoscience.com.

Patmos, Inc., *(978-0-9741748)* P.O. Box 124, Maple Hill, KS 66507-0124 USA
Web site: http://www.patmos.us.

Patmos Publishing, *(978-0-9768545)* 4591 Jernigan Rd., Milton, FL 32571-1921 USA Tel 850-994-0908 (phone/fax) Do not confuse with Patmos Publications in Bristol GBR
E-mail: patmosprinting@gmail.com
Web site: http://www.patmospublishing.com.

Patou Bks., LLC, *(978-0-9767756)* 1550 Larimer St., Suite 459, Denver, CO 80202-1602 USA.

Patrenialla Turner, Queen , *(978-0-578-14812-0)* .

Patria Pr., Inc., *(978-1-882859; 978-1-935731)* P.O. Box 752, Carmel, IN 46082 USA (SAN 153-7504) Tel 317-577-1321; Fax: 413-215-8030; Toll Free: 877-736-7930; *Imprints:* Young Patriots Series (Yng Patriots)
E-mail: info@patriapress.com
Web site: http://www.patriapress.com
Dist(s): **Ebsco Publishing**
Independent Pubs. Group
MyiLibrary.

Patrick Henry College Pr., *(978-0-9714458)* 1 Patrick Henry Cir., Purcellville, VA 20132 USA Tel 540-338-1776; Fax: 540-338-8707
E-mail: info@phc.edu
Web site: http://www.phc.edu.

PatrickGeorge (GBR) *(978-0-9562558; 978-1-908473) Dist. by* **IPG Chicago.**

†Patrick's Pr., *(978-0-944322; 978-0-9609412)* Orders Addr.: P.O. Box 5189, Columbus, GA 31906 USA (SAN 274-466X) Tel 706-322-1584; Fax: 706-322-5806; Toll Free: 800-654-1052; Edit Addr.: 2218 Wynnton Rd., Columbus, GA 31906 USA (SAN 243-2773)
E-mail: quizbowl@aol.com
Web site: http://www.patrickspress.com
Dist(s): **Peller, A. W. & Assocs.**; *CIP.*

Patriot Media, Inc., *(978-0-9791642; 978-0-9845777; 978-0-9846638; 978-0-9888930; 978-0-9905724)* Orders Addr.: P.O. Box 5414, Niceville, FL 32578 USA Tel 850-897-4204 (phone/fax)
E-mail: dari.bradleyceo@patriotmediainc.com; dari@patriotmediainc.com
Web site: http://www.patriotmediapublishing.com; http://www.patriotmediainc.com; http://www.patriotmediainternational.com; http://www.silentbattleground.com; http://www.dmulmer.com; http://www.staffmonkeys.com; http://www.paulsherbo.com; http://www.booksbynelson.com; http://www.those67blues.com
Dist(s): **CreateSpace Independent Publishing Platform.**

Patriot Media Publishing *See* **Patriot Media, Inc.**

Patriot Pr., *(978-0-9796000; 978-1-941020)* 1505 Knoxlyn Rd., Gettysburg, PA 17325 USA (SAN 853-8735)
E-mail: patriotpress@live.com
Web site: http://www.patriotpressbooks.com; http://www.jessicajamesbooks.com
Dist(s): **Independent Pubs. Group.**

Patriot Publishing, *(978-0-9789936)* Ernest Beath, III, 2216 Horn Point Rd., Cambridge, MD 21613-3379 USA Tel 410-228-5771
E-mail: docprb@bluecrab.org.

Patten Point Marketing Services, Incorporated *See* **Liberty Manuals Co.**

Pattern Pr., *(978-0-9729248; 978-1-935559; 978-1-941961)* Orders Addr.: P.O. Box 2737, Fallbrook, CA 92088 USA; Edit Addr.: 40521 De Luz Rd., Fallbrook, CA 92028 USA
E-mail: patternpress1@gmail.com
Web site: http://www.patternpress.com.

Patty's Blooming Words, *(978-0-615-78050-4; 978-0-9893303)* 693 Springlake Dr., Franklin, TN 37064 USA Tel 615-790-0109
E-mail: pattysbloomers@me.com.

†Pauline Bks. & Media, *(978-0-8198)* 50 St. Paul's Ave., Boston, MA 02130-3491 USA (SAN 203-8900) Tel 617-522-8911; Fax: 617-524-8035; Toll Free: 800-876-4463 (orders only)
E-mail: editorial@pauline.org; kcorina@paulinemedia.com
Web site: http://www.PAULINE.org
Dist(s): **MyiLibrary**
O'Reilly Media, Inc.
St Pauls/Alba Hse. Pubs.; *CIP.*

†Paulist Pr., *(978-0-8091; 978-1-893757; 978-1-58768; 978-1-61643)* 997 MacArthur Blvd., Mahwah, NJ 07430-2096 USA (SAN 202-5159) Tel 201-825-7300 (ext. 232); Fax: 201-825-8345; Toll Free Fax: 800-836-3161; Toll Free: 800-218-1903; *Imprints:* HiddenSpring (HidSpring); E T Nedder (ETNedder); Ambassador Books (Ambass Bks)
E-mail: info@paulistpress.com
Web site: http://www.paulistpress.com
Dist(s): **Bookazine Co., Inc.**
Spring Arbor Distributors, Inc.; *CIP.*

Paulsen, Marc Productions, Incorporated *See* **Stance Pubns.**

Paulus Publishing, *(978-0-9744863)* 6115 E. Hillview St., Mesa, AZ 85205 USA.

Pavilion Bks. (GBR) *(978-0-85177; 978-0-86101; 978-0-86283; 978-1-85470; 978-1-85585; 978-1-85753; 978-1-85833; 978-0-947553; 978-1-84138; 978-1-85561; 978-0-904609; 978-1-85028; 978-1-84065; 978-1-85600; 978-1-902616; 978-1-85993; 978-0-86288; 978-1-84333; 978-1-903954; 978-1-84411; 978-1-86222; 978-1-84340; 978-1-84458; 978-0-86124; 978-1-85841; 978-1-906388; 978-1-908449; 978-1-909397) Dist. by* **Trafalgar.**

Pavilion Bks. (GBR) *(978-0-85177; 978-0-86101; 978-0-86283; 978-1-85470; 978-1-85585; 978-1-85753; 978-1-85833; 978-0-947553; 978-1-84138; 978-1-85561; 978-0-904609; 978-1-85028; 978-1-84065; 978-1-85600; 978-1-902616; 978-1-85993; 978-0-86288; 978-1-84333; 978-1-903954; 978-1-84411; 978-1-86222; 978-1-84340; 978-1-84458; 978-0-86124; 978-1-85841; 978-1-906388; 978-1-908449; 978-1-909397) Dist. by* **Sterling.**

Pavilion Bks. (GBR) *(978-0-85177; 978-0-86101; 978-0-86283; 978-1-85470; 978-1-85585; 978-1-85753; 978-1-85833; 978-0-947553; 978-1-84138; 978-1-85561; 978-0-904609; 978-1-85028; 978-1-84065; 978-1-85600; 978-1-902616; 978-1-85993; 978-0-86288; 978-1-84333; 978-1-903954; 978-1-84411; 978-1-86222; 978-1-84340; 978-1-84458; 978-0-86124; 978-1-85841; 978-1-906388; 978-1-908449; 978-1-909397) Dist. by* **IPG Chicago.**

Pavilion Pr., Inc., *(978-1-4145)* 1213 Vine St., Philadelphia, PA 19107 USA Tel 215-569-9779; Fax: 215-569-8814
Web site: http://www.pavilionpress.com.

Pavilion Pubs., *(978-0-88432; 978-1-57970)* Div. of Pavilion Publishers, LLC, P.O. Box 1460, Guilford, CT 06437 USA (SAN 213-957X) Tel 518-605-5179; Toll Free: 800-243-1234
E-mail: Antonydaou@gmail.com; Mcgradylaura@gmail.com
Web site: http://www.audioforum.com
Dist(s): **Bolchazy-Carducci Pubs.**

Paw Print Pubns., *(978-0-9785473)* Orders Addr.: 4206 NE Newbury Ct., Lees Summit, MO 64064-1617 USA (SAN 850-9573) Toll Free: 877-267-9482; *Imprints:* Austin & Charlie Adventures (Austin & Charlie Adventures)
E-mail: lparker154@aol.com; pawfacts@aol.com; linda8000@sbcglobal.net
Web site: http://www.austincharlieadventures.com
Dist(s): **Book Clearing Hse.**

Paw Print Publishing, *(978-0-9770898)* Orders Addr.: P.O. Box 48309, Cumberland, NC 28331-8309 USA
Web site: www.k9fluffy.com.

Paw Prints *Imprint of* **Baker & Taylor, CATS**

Paw Prints Press *See* **Heather & Highlands Publishing**

Paws and Claws Publishing, LLC, *(978-0-9846724; 978-0-9906067; 978-1-946198)* 1586 Skeet Club Rd. Ste 102-175, High Point, NC 27265 USA Tel 336-297-9783
E-mail: jcappoen@pawsandclawspublishing.com
Web site: http://www.pawsandclawspublishing.com.

Paws in the Sand Publishing, *(978-0-9790057)* Orders Addr.: 4644 Pepper Mill St., Moorpark, CA 93021-9302 USA (SAN 852-193X) Fax: 805-553-9253
Web site: http://pawsinthesand.com.

Paxen Learning Corporation *See* **Paxen Publishing LLC**

Paxen Publishing LLC, *(978-1-934350)* 710 Atlantis Rd., Melbourne, FL 32904 USA Tel 321-724-1033; 800-247-2936; Fax: 321-951-1617
E-mail: sales@paxen.com
Web site: http://www.paxen.com.

Paycock Pr., *(978-0-931181; 978-0-9602424)* 3819 N. 13th St., Arlington, VA 22201 USA (SAN 212-5420) Tel 703-525-9296 phone/fax
E-mail: gargoyle@gargoylemagazine.com
Web site: http://www.gargoylemagazine.com.

Payne, Christine, *(978-0-9740643)* P.O. Box 951, Mountain Home, AR 72654-0951 USA.

Payne, Yadira V. Publishing, *(978-0-9747350)* 341 Lamplighter Ln., Martinez, GA 30907 USA Tel 706-414-9566
E-mail: yvppublishing@knology.net.

PAZ Publishing, *(978-0-942253)* Div. of PAZ Percussion, Orders Addr.: 2415 Bevington St. NW, North Canton, OH 44709-2221 USA (SAN 666-8100) Tel 330-493-6661 (phone/fax)
E-mail: PAZPublishing@aol.com
Web site: http://www.PAZPublishing.com.

PB&J OmniMedia *Imprint of* **Takahashi & Black**

PBD, Inc., *(978-0-9846038; 978-0-9837260; 978-1-62219)* 1650 Bluegrass Lakes Pkwy., Alpharetta, GA 30004 USA (SAN 126-6039) Tel 770-442-8633; Fax: 770-442-9742
Web site: http://www.pbd.com.

PBL Stories LLC, *(978-0-9792379)* Orders Addr.: P.O. Box 393, Lynn Haven, FL 32444-4272 USA Tel 850-348-0718; Fax: 850-265-9815; Edit Addr.: 1812 S. Hwy. 77, Suite. 115, Lynn Haven, FL 32444-4272 USA
E-mail: booksales@pblstories.com
Web site: http://www.pblstories.com.

PC Treasures, Inc., *(978-1-933796; 978-1-60072)* 1795 N. Lapeer Rd., Oxford, MI 48371-2415 USA (SAN 857-0930)
E-mail: lthomas@pctreasures.com; jbrandt@pctreasures.com; jadams@pctreasures.com
Web site: http://www.pctreasures.com.

PCS Edventures, Inc., *(978-0-9753193; 978-0-9827203)* 345 Bobwhite Ct., Suite 200, Boise, ID 83706 USA Tel 208-343-3110; Fax: 208-343-1321; Toll Free: 800-429-3110
E-mail: mwright@pcsedu.com; rgrover@pcsedu.com; agranger@pcsedu.com
Web site: http://www.edventures.com.

PD Hse. Holdings, LLC, *(978-0-9815333; 978-0-9984644)* 4704 Venice Rd., Sandusky, OH 44870 USA (SAN 855-806X)
E-mail: pjgron@pjgrondin.com
Web site: http://www.pjgrondin.com.

PDG *Imprint of* **Publishers Design Group, Inc.**

†Peabody Museum of Archaeology & Ethnology, Harvard Univ., Pubns. Dept., *(978-0-87365)* Orders Addr.: 11 Divinity Ave., Cambridge, MA 02138 USA (SAN 203-1426) Tel 617-496-9922; 617-495-3938; Fax: 617-495-7535
E-mail: ddickers@fas.harvard.edu
Web site: http://www.peabody.harvard.edu/publications
Dist(s): **Harvard Univ. Pr.**
Univ. Pr. of New England
Univ. of New Mexico Pr.; *CIP.*

Peace B Still Ministries Pr., *(978-0-9752665)* 205 Joel Blvd., Suite 107, Lehigh Acres, FL 33972-0202 USA
E-mail: gduncan316@aol.com.

Peace Education Foundation, *(978-1-878227; 978-1-934760)* 1900 Biscayne Blvd., Miami, FL 33132-1025 USA Tel 305-576-5075; Fax: 305-576-3106; Toll Free: 800-749-8838
Web site: http://www.peaceeducation.com.

Peace Evolutions, LLC, *(978-0-9753837; 978-0-9912489)* P.O. Box 458, Glen Echo, MD 20812-0458 USA (SAN 256-2146) Fax: 301-263-9280
E-mail: info@peace-evolutions.com; julie@peace-evolutions.com
Web site: http://www.peace-evolutions.com.

Peace Hill Press *See* **Well-Trained Mind Pr.**

Peace Love Karma Publishing, *(978-0-9743540)* Orders Addr.: 2360 Mendocino Ave. Ste. 2a, box 363, Santa Rosa, CA 95403 USA Tel 707-449-9990; Edit Addr.: 2360 Mendocino Ave. STe 2A -box 363, Santa Rosa, CA 95403 USA
E-mail: Carol@peacelovekarma.com; mail@peacelovekarma.com
Web site: http://www.peacelovekarma.com
Dist(s): **New Leaf Distributing Co., Inc.**

Peace of Mind LLC, *(978-0-692-53539-4; 978-0-9976954)* 5540 Nevada Ave. NW, Washington, DC 20015 USA Tel 202-494-2624; *Imprints:* Peace of Mind Press (P M P)
E-mail: teachpeacedc@gmail.com
Web site: www.teachpeaceofmind.com.

Peace of Mind Pr. *Imprint of* **Peace of Mind LLC**

Peace Power Pr., *(978-0-9824601)* 6044 Waterloo Rd., Dayton, OH 45402-3015 USA (SAN 858-2254) Tel 937-227-3223
Web site: http://daytonpeacemuseum.org.

Peace Rug Company, Inc., The, *(978-0-9763949)* 407 W. Emery St., Dalton, GA 30720 USA Tel 706-272-0200; Fax: 706-226-2296; Toll Free: 888-732-2378
E-mail: info@peacerug.com
Web site: http://www.peacerug.com.

Peaceable Kingdom Pr., *(978-1-56890; 978-1-59395)* 950 Gilman, Suite 200, Berkeley, CA 94710 USA Tel 510-558-2051; Fax: 510-558-2052; Toll Free: 800-444-7778 Do not confuse with Peaceable Kingdom Press in Greenville, VA
E-mail: djaffe@pkpress.com
Web site: http://www.pkpress.com.

Peaceable Productions, *(978-0-9709187)* Orders Addr.: P.O. Box 708, Center Hill, FL 33514 USA (SAN 254-4946) Tel 352-793-7516; Edit Addr.: 6698 SE 57th Rd., Center Hill, FL 33514 USA Tel 352-793-7516; Fax: 775-514-8681
E-mail: yvonne@atlantic.net.

Peaceful Daily, Inc., *(978-0-9884926; 978-0-9970143; 978-0-9982579)* 800 Village Walk Suite 103, Guilford, CT 06437 USA Tel 203-298-8077
E-mail: sandy@peacefuldaily.com
Web site: www.peacefuldaily.com.

Peaceful Thoughts Pr., (978-0-9725118) 598 Straton Chase SE, Marietta, GA 30067 USA
Web site: http://www.peacefulthoughts.net.

Peacemakers Press *See* **Positive Spin Pr.**

Peach Blossom Pubns., (978-0-941367) 120 E. Beaver Ave. Apt. 212, State College, PA 16801-4991 USA (SAN 665-4800)
E-mail: inezwaterson@prodigy.net
Dist(s): **Quality Bks., Inc.**

Peach Tree Pr., (978-0-9893120; 978-1-62910) 1321 Upland Dr., Houston, TX 77043 USA Tel 919-502-0151
E-mail: arpl.dropbox@gmail.com.

PeachMoon Publishing, (978-0-9795831) 3915 Bonnett Creek Ln., Hoschton, GA 30548-6204 USA (SAN 853-814X)
E-mail: Alice@peachmoonpublishing.com
Web site: http://luckythelizard.com; http://peachmoonpublishing.com.

Peachtree Junior *Imprint of* **Peachtree Pubs.**

†**Peachtree Pubs.**, (978-0-931948; 978-0-934601; 978-1-56145; 978-1-68263) 1700 Chattahoochee Ave., NW, Atlanta, GA 30318-2112 USA (SAN 212-1999) Tel 404-876-8761; Fax: 404-875-2578; Toll Free Fax: 800-875-8909; Toll Free: 800-241-0113; Imprints: Peachtree Junior (Peachtree); Freestone (Freestone)
E-mail: sales@peachtree-online.com; palermo@peachtree-online.com; McManus@peachtree-online.com
Web site: http://www.peachtree-online.com; www.cheshirecheesecat.com; www.christmasinthetrenches.info; www.14cowsforamerica.com
Dist(s): **Heinecken & Assoc., Ltd.**
Lectorum Pubns., Inc.
MyiLibrary
Open Road Integrated Media, Inc.; CIP.

Peachtree Publishers, Limited *See* **Peachtree Pubs.**

Peak City Publishing, LLC, (978-1-935711) 104B N. Salem St., Apex, NC 27502 USA Tel 919-758-9516
Web site: http://www.peakcitypublishing.com.

Peak Writing, LLC, (978-0-9717330; 978-0-9767961) Orders Addr.: P.O. Box 14196, Savannah, GA 31416 USA Tel 912-398-2987; Toll Free Fax: 888-226-4811; Edit Addr.: 12 Mercer Rd., Savannah, GA 31411 USA Do not confuse with Peak Writing in Frisco, CO
E-mail: info@peakwriting.com
Dist(s): **Quality Bks., Inc.**
Send The Light Distribution LLC
Spring Arbor Distributors, Inc.

Peaks Pr. LLC, (978-1-938032) 630 Race St., Denver, CO 80206 USA Tel 720-560-3779
E-mail: info@peakspress.com
Dist(s): **BookBaby.**

Peanut Butter Publishing, (978-0-89716; 978-1-59849) 2207 Fairview Ave. E., Houseboat No. 4, Seattle, WA 98102 USA (SAN 212-7881) Tel 206-860-4900 Toll Free: 877-728-8837
E-mail: ewolfpub@aol.com
Web site: http://www.peanutbutterpublishing.com.

Peapod Pr. *Imprint of* **PublishingWorks**

Peapod Publishing, Inc., (978-0-9729507; 978-0-9894591) P.O. Box 951599, Lake Mary, FL 32795-1599 USA Tel 407-333-3030
E-mail: info@peapodpublishing.com
Web site: http://www.adventureswithpawpaw.com; http://www.pawpawspals.org; http://www.peapodpublishing.com; http://www.borntoflybook.com; http://www.born2fly.org
Dist(s): **BookBaby.**

Pearl & Dotty, (978-0-9772441) Orders Addr.: P.O. Box 2162, Seattle, WA 98111-2162 USA
E-mail: pearlanddotty@gmail.com; holler@pearlanddotty.com
Web site: http://www.pearlanddotty.com.

Pearl Pr., (978-0-9674525) Orders Addr.: P.O. Box 266, Eastport, MI 49627 USA (SAN 299-9870) Tel 231-599-2372 (phone/fax); Edit Addr.: 6027 M-88 Hwy., Eastport, MI 49627 USA Do not confuse with Pearl Pr., Nazareth, PA, Sacramento CA
E-mail: Beebystudio@mailbug.com.

Pearl Pr., (978-0-9741332) 3104 O St., No. 175, Sacramento, CA 95816 USA Do not confuse with Pearl Press in Nazareth PA, Eastport MI
E-mail: info@pearlpress.net
Web site: http://www.pearlpress.net
Dist(s): **Quality Bks., Inc.**

Pearl Publishing, LLC, (978-0-9785264; 978-0-9826175; 978-1-937390) 2587c Southside Blvd., Melba, ID 83641 USA Tel 888-499-9666
E-mail: info@pearlpublishing.net
Web site: http://wupublishing.com; http://666america.com; http://pearlpublishing.net.

Pearlman, Beth, (978-0-9767527) 1773 Diane Rd., Mendota Heights, MN 55118 USA.

PearlStone Publishing, Inc., (978-0-9724586; 978-0-9816883; 978-0-9841899; 978-1-936513; 978-1-944348) 514-201 Daniels St., Raleigh, NC 27603 USA
E-mail: publish@pendiumpublishing.com
Web site: http://www.pendiumpublishing.com.

Pearn & Assocs. Inc., (978-0-9777318; 978-0-9841683; 978-0-9846523; 978-0-9897242) Orders Addr.: 1600 Edora Ct. Ste. D, Fort Collins, CO 80525-6016 USA; Imprints: Over the Rainbow (Over the Rain)
E-mail: happypoet@hotmail.com.

Pearson Education (GBR) (978-0-15; 978-0-515; 978-0-7466; 978-1-299) Dist. by **ABC-CLIO.**

Pearson Education, (978-0-13; 978-0-582; 978-0-7686; 978-1-5093) Orders Addr.: 200 Old Tappan Rd., Old Tappan, NJ 07675 USA (SAN 200-2175) Tel 201-767-5000 (Receptionist); Toll Free Fax: 800-445-6991; Toll Free: 800-428-5331; 800-922-0579; Edit Addr.: One Lake St., Upper Saddle River, NJ 07458 USA Tel 201-236-7000; 201-236-5321; Fax: 201-236-6549; 800 E. 96th St., Suite 300, Indianapolis, IN 46240 Toll Free: 800-571-4580; Imprints: Microsoft Press (MicrosoftPress)
E-mail: communications@pearsoned.com
Web site: http://www.pearsoned.com; www.pearson.com
Dist(s): **Gaunt, Inc.**
MyiLibrary
Trans-Atlantic Pubns., Inc.

Pearson Education Australia (AUS) (978-0-7248; 978-0-7342; 978-0-7312; 978-1-86391; 978-0-7339; 978-0-85859; 978-0-86462; 978-1-74009; 978-1-74140; 978-1-876209; 978-1-74085; 978-1-74103; 978-1-74091; 978-1-74081; 978-1-74206; 978-1-4425; 978-0-86911; 978-0-7316-1261-1; 978-0-646-24199-9; 978-0-646-29552-7; 978-0-646-30941-5; 978-0-646-31855-4; 978-0-646-32904-8; 978-0-646-32905-5; 978-1-4860) Dist. by **Cheng Tsui.**

Pearson Education, Ltd. (GBR) (978-0-201; 978-0-273; 978-0-321; 978-0-582; 978-0-673; 978-1-4058; 978-1-84479; 978-1-84658; 978-1-84959; 978-1-84878; 978-1-84776; 978-1-4479; 978-1-292) Dist. by **Trans-Atl Phila.**

Pearson Education, Ltd. (GBR) (978-0-201; 978-0-273; 978-0-321; 978-0-582; 978-0-673; 978-1-4058; 978-1-84479; 978-1-84658; 978-1-84959; 978-1-84878; 978-1-84776; 978-1-4479; 978-1-292) Dist. by **Pearson Educ.**

Pearson ESL, (978-0-582) Div. of Pearson International, 75 Arlington St., Boston, MA 02116 USA
Dist(s): **Pearson Education.**

Pearson Learning, (978-0-7652; 978-1-4284) Div of Pearson Education, Orders Addr.: P.O. Box 2500, Lebanon, IN 46052 USA Toll Free Fax: 800-393-3156; Toll Free: 800-321-3106; Edit Addr.: 1 Lake St., U Saddle Riv, NJ 07458-1813 USA Toll Free: 800-526-9907 (Customer Service)
E-mail: jeff.hoitsma@pearsonlearning.com
Web site: http://www.pearsonlearning.com
Dist(s): **Follett School Solutions.**

Pearson Schl., (978-1-59896; 978-1-60637) 75 Arlington St., Boston, MA 02116 USA; Imprints: Dominie Elementary (Dominie Elem); FEARON (FEARON); GLOBE (GLOBPS); Celebration Press (Celebration); Dale Seymour Publications (Dale Seymo); Modern Curriculum Press (Mod Curriculu); Scott Foresman (Scott Fores); SILVER BURDETT (SilvBurd); Prentice Hall (PHall).

Peartree r, (978-0-935343) P.O. Box 14533, Clearwater, FL 33766 USA Tel 727-531-4973 (phone/fax)
E-mail: peartreebooks@yahoo.com
Web site: http://www.peartree-books.com
Dist(s): **Brodart Co.**
Follett School Solutions
Quality Bks., Inc.

Pebble Beach Pr., Ltd., (978-1-883740) P.O. Box 1171, Pebble Beach, CA 93953-1171 USA Tel 408-372-5559; Fax: 408-375-4525.

Pebble Bks. *Imprint of* **Capstone Press of Coughlan Cos.**

Pebble Plus *Imprint of* **Capstone Press of Coughlan Cos.**

Pebble Plus Bilingue/Bilingual *Imprint of* **Capstone Press of Coughlan Cos.**

Pebbleton Pr., (978-0-9760011) P.O. Box 1894, Duxbury, MA 02331 USA
E-mail: pebbletonpress@comcast.net
Web site: http://www.pebbletonpress.com.

Pecci Educational Pubs., (978-0-943220) 440 Davis Ct., No. 405, San Francisco, CA 94111 USA (SAN 240-558X) Tel 415-391-8579; Fax: 970-493-8781
E-mail: pecci@sirius.com
Web site: http://www.onlinereadingteacher.com.

PeDante Pr., (978-0-9790199; 978-1-940844) 4 White Oak, Danbury, CT 06410 USA Tel 203-350-9288
E-mail: erikagrey@rocketmail.com
Web site: www.erikagrey.com.

Peddlers Group, (978-0-9802257; 978-0-9829177) 1127 Parrish Rd., Leesville, SC 29070 USA Tel 803-657-5324; Fax: 803-753-9824
E-mail: peddlersgroup@gmail.com
Web site: http://www.peddlersgroup.com.

Pedigree Bks., Ltd. (GBR) (978-1-874507; 978-1-904329; 978-1-906450; 978-1-907602; 978-1-908152) Dist. by **Diamond Book Dists.**

†**Pedipress, Inc.**, (978-0-914625) Orders Addr.: 125 Red Gate Ln., Amherst, MA 01002 USA (SAN 287-7570) Tel 413-549-7798 M - Thurs. 8:30 to 4:30 EST; Fax: 413-549-4095; Toll Free: 800-611-6081 M - Thurs. 8:30 to 4:30 EST
E-mail: tplautassistant@gmail.com
Web site: http://www.pedipress.com
Dist(s): **INscribe Digital**; CIP.

Pedro Pubns. (GBR) (978-0-9555971) Dist. by **CapstonePubs.**

Peebco Publishing Hse., The, (978-0-9644758) P.O. Box 45333, Saint Louis, MO 63145 USA (SAN 298-6760) Tel 636-346-7179
E-mail: Info@PeebcoPublishing.com
Web site: http://www.PeebcoPublishing.com.

Peek-A-Boo Publishing, (978-1-943154) 500 Montgomery St., Alexandria, VA 22314 USA Tel 703-348-9898; Imprints: See-Saw Publishing (See-SawPub)
E-mail: info@peekaboopublishing.com
Web site: peekaboopublishing.com
Dist(s): **Independent Pubs. Group.**

Peel Productions, Inc., (978-0-939217; 978-1-943158) 9415 NE Woodridge, Vancouver, WA 98664 USA; Imprints: Blackbirch Press, Incorporated (Blackbirch Pr)
E-mail: ddub@drawbooks.com
Web site: http://www.drawbooks.com; http://www.peelbooks.com; http://www.123draw.com; http://www.1-2-3.draw.com
Dist(s): **F&W Media, Inc.**
Pathway Bk. Service.

Peeler, Casey, (978-0-9906984; 978-0-9961521) 2424 Olan Dr., Shelby, NC 28152 USA Tel 704-472-9384
E-mail: caseypeelerauthor@gmail.com.

Peepal Tree Pr., Ltd. (GBR) (978-0-948833; 978-1-900715; 978-1-84523) Dist. by **IPG Chicago.**

Peeper & Friends *Imprint of* **Tree Of Life Publishing**

Peerless Publishing, L.L.C., (978-0-9666076) Orders Addr.: P.O. Box 20466, Ferndale, MI 48220 USA Tel 248-542-1930; Fax: 248-542-3895; Edit Addr.: 414 W. Lewiston, Ferndale, MI 48220 USA
E-mail: peerlesspublishing@ameritech.net
Web site: http://www.spannet.org/peerless/index.html.

Pegasus Bks. for Children, (978-0-9824095; 978-0-615-82835-0) P.O. Box 681, Flossmoor, IL 60422 USA Tel 708-990-8111; Fax: 708-747-4659
E-mail: stallionbooks@gmail.com
Web site: http://www.stallionbooks.com
Dist(s): **CreateSpace Independent Publishing Platform.**

Pegasus Pubns., (978-0-9747023) 1055 E., 16th St., Brooklyn, NY 11230 USA Do not confuse with companies with the same name in Point Reyes Statio, CA, San Antonio, TX.

Pegatha Press *See* **Rosasharn Pr.**

Peiffer, Trisha Cousineau *See* **Dream Ridge Pr.**

Peine, Jan *See* **Ashway Pr.**

Pelagia Pr. *Imprint of* **Calm Unity Pr.**

Pelican Book Group *See* **Pelican Ventures, LLC**

Pelican Lake Pr., (978-0-9649139) Div. of Healthy Lifestyle, Inc., 11442 Vista Ridge, San Diego, CA 92130 USA Tel 858-888-2278
E-mail: tomiselin@gmail.com
Web site: http://www.tomiselin.com.

Pelican Press *See* **booksonnet.com**

Pelican Pr., (978-0-9771102; 978-0-9911640) Div. of The Pelican Enterprise, LLC, Orders Addr.: 9121 Carabella St., Pensacola, FL 32514 USA Tel 850-475-8179; 850-206-4608 preferred Do not confuse with companies with the same name in Prather, CA, Santa Barbara, CA, Aptos, CA, Saint Augustine, FL, Belvedere, CA
E-mail: pelican.post@att.net
Dist(s): **BookBaby**
CreateSpace Independent Publishing Platform
Lulu Pr., Inc.

†**Pelican Publishing Co., Inc.**, (978-0-88289; 978-0-911116; 978-1-56554; 978-1-58980; 978-1-4556) Orders Addr.: 1000 Burmaster St., Gretna, LA 70053-2246 USA Tel 504-368-1175; Fax: 504-368-1195; Toll Free: 800-843-1724 ordering Do not confuse with companies with the same or similar names in Lowell, MA, Dallas, TX
E-mail: Sales@pelicanpub.com; promo@pelicanpub.com; editorial@pelicanpub.com
Web site: http://www.pelicanpub.com; CIP.

Pelican Ventures, LLC, (978-0-9712522; 978-0-9842968; 978-1-61116; 978-1-5223) Div.of Pelican Ventures LLC, Orders Addr.: P.O. Box 1738, Aztec, NM 87410 USA; Edit Addr.: 2307 E. Main St., Farmington, NM 87401 USA
Web site: http://www.harbourlightbooks.com; http://www.whiterosepublishing.com; http://www.pelicanbookgroup.com
Dist(s): **Independent Pubs. Group.**

Peller, A. W. & Associates, Incorporated *See* **Educational Impressions**

Pemblewick Pr., (978-0-9656557; 978-0-9718507) Orders Addr.: P.O. Box 321, Lincoln, MA 01773 USA (SAN 254-0886); Edit Addr.: 155 S. Great Rd., Lincoln, MA 01773 USA Tel 781-259-8832 (phone/fax); 617-259-8389; 617 259 8389
E-mail: pemblewick@aol.com
Web site: http://www.pemblewickpress.com.

Pembroke Pubs., Ltd. (CAN) (978-0-921217; 978-1-55138) Dist. by **Stenhsa Pubs.**

Pen & Pad Publishing, (978-0-9769050) P.o. Box 2995, Orcutt, CA 93457-2995 USA Tel 805-938-1307
E-mail: JBest@BestFamilyAdventures.com
Web site: http://BestFamilyAdventures.com
Dist(s): **Central Coast Bks.**

Pen & Paper Publishing, (978-0-9703876) 5450 Saluson Ave., PMB 15, Culver City, CA 90230 USA Fax: 323-933-3851; Toll Free: 800-662-9066 Do not confuse with Pen & Paper Publishing in Horn Lake, MS
E-mail: sixrags@earthlink.net
Web site: http://www.penandpaper.net.

Pen & Publish Inc., (978-0-9768391; 978-0-9779530; 978-0-9790446; 978-0-9800429; 978-0-9817264; 978-0-9823850; 978-0-9842258; 978-0-9844600; 978-0-9845751; 978-0-9846359; 978-0-9852737; 978-0-9859367; 978-1-941799) Orders Addr.: 4735 S. State Rd., No. 446, Bloomington, IN 47401 USA Tel 812-837-9226; Toll Free: 866-326-7768
E-mail: info@penandpublish.com; paul@penandpublish.com; info@brickmantelbooks.com
Web site: http://www.penandpublish.com; http://transformationmediabooks.com; http://openbookspress.com; http://brickmantelbooks.com
Dist(s): **Smashwords.**

Pen & Rose Pr. *Imprint of* **Harlin Jacque Pubns.**

Pen & Sword Bks. Ltd. (GBR) (978-0-7232; 978-0-85052; 978-1-84415; 978-1-84468; 978-1-84832; 978-1-84884; 978-1-78159; 978-1-78383; 978-1-4738) Dist. by **Casemate Pubs.**

Pen & Sword Publishing Co., The, (978-0-9745798) 522 N. Holly St., Philadelphia, PA 19104 USA
E-mail: nancy@theaalamgroup.com; nk81dove@yahoo.com; melodiog2003@hotmail.com.

Pen Row Productions, (978-0-9766695) 9461 Charleville Blvd., No. 506, Beverly Hills, CA 90212 USA Tel 310-924-9167
E-mail: bwasz1@verizon.net
Web site: http://www.penrowproductions.com.

Pencil Point Pr., Inc., (978-1-58108; 978-1-881641) P.O. Box 634, New Hope, PA 18938-0634 USA Toll Free: 800-356-1299
E-mail: penpoint@ix.netcom.com
Web site: http://www.pencilpointpress.com.

Pendentive Pubns., (978-0-9853817) 405 Serrano Dr., Apt. 9-K, San Francisco, CA 94132 USA Tel 415-586-1806
E-mail: mpowers2004@yahoo.com
Dist(s): **Lulu Pr., Inc.**

Pendleton Publishing, Inc., (978-0-9654480; 978-0-9711564) Orders Addr.: P.O. Box 5004, Laurel, MD 20726 USA Tel 301-604-4076; Fax: 301-317-5746; Edit Addr.: 3113 Burning Springs Rd., No.1A, Laurel, MD 20724 USA
E-mail: newauthorsandartists@msn.com; garnjampublishing@yahoo.com.

Pendulum Pr., Inc., (978-0-87232; 978-0-88301) Academic Bldg., Saw Mill Rd., West Haven, CT 06516 USA (SAN 202-8808) Tel 203-933-2551 Do not confuse with companies with same or similar names in Jacksonville, FL, Palm Coast, FL, Minneapolis, MN.

Penelope Pipp Publishing, (978-0-9882369) 38 McCreedy Dr., McHenry, MS 39561 USA Tel 601-928-4567
E-mail: admin@penelopepipp.com
Web site: www.penelopepipp.com.

Penfield Bks., (978-0-941016; 978-0-9603858; 978-1-57216; 978-0-9717025; 978-1-932043) 215 Brown St., Iowa City, IA 52245 USA Tel 319-337-9998; Fax: 319-351-6846
E-mail: penfield@penfieldbooks.com
Web site: http://www.penfieldpress.com; http://www.penfieldbooks.com
Dist(s): **Partners Bk. Distributing, Inc.**
Penfield Pr.

PenGame Publishing LLC, (978-0-9771444) Orders Addr.: P.O. Box 341361, Jamaica, NY 11434 USA (SAN 256-8802)
E-mail: PenGameLLC@aol.com
Web site: http://www.PenGamePublishing.com.

Penguin AudioBooks *Imprint of* **Penguin Publishing Group**

Penguin Bks., Ltd. (GBR) (978-0-14; 978-0-241; 978-0-670; 978-0-7232; 978-1-4059; 978-1-4093) Dist. by **IPG Chicago.**

Penguin Bks., Ltd. (GBR) (978-0-14; 978-0-241; 978-0-670; 978-0-7232; 978-1-4059; 978-1-4093) Dist. by **Diamond Book Dists.**

Penguin Bks., Ltd. (GBR) (978-0-14; 978-0-241; 978-0-670; 978-0-7232; 978-1-4059; 978-1-4093) Dist. by **D C D.**

Penguin Books *Imprint of* **Penguin Publishing Group**

Penguin Books *Imprint of* **Penguin Publishing Group**

Penguin Books *Imprint of* **Penguin Young Readers Group**

Penguin Books Australia (AUS) (978-0-14; 978-0-670; 978-0-86914; 978-0-7343; 978-1-920989; 978-1-921382; 978-1-921383; 978-1-921384; 978-1-921518; 978-1-74228; 978-1-74253; 978-1-74348; 978-0-85796; 978-0-85797; 978-1-74377; 978-1-76014) Dist. by **IPG Chicago.**

Penguin Canada (CAN) (978-0-14; 978-0-216; 978-0-451; 978-0-452; 978-0-453; 978-0-670; 978-1-55305; 978-0-7723) Dist. by **Peng Rand Hse.**

Penguin Classics *Imprint of* **Penguin Publishing Group**

Penguin Family Publishing, (978-0-9637985) P.O. Box 471, Orland, CA 95963 USA.

Penguin Global *Imprint of* **Penguin Publishing Group**

Penguin Group India (IND) (978-0-14; 978-0-670) Dist. by **Penguin Grp USA.**

Penguin Group New Zealand, Ltd. (NZL) (978-0-14; 978-0-670) Dist. by **IPG Chicago.**

Penguin Group (USA) Incorporated *See* **Penguin Publishing Group**

Penguin Publishing Group, (978-0-14; 978-0-399; 978-0-425; 978-0-452; 978-0-525; 978-0-698; 978-0-87477; 978-1-58542; 978-1-933438; 978-1-4295; 978-1-934511; 978-1-4362; 978-1-4406; 978-1-101; 978-1-937007) Orders Addr.: 405 Murray Hill Pkwy., East Rutherford, NJ 07073-2136 USA (SAN 282-5074) Fax: 201-933-2903 (customer service); Toll Free Fax: 800-227-9604; Toll Free: 800-526-0275 (reseller sales); 800-631-8571 (reseller customer service); 800-788-6262 (individual consumer sales); Edit Addr.: 375 Hudson St., New York, NY 10014 USA Tel 212-366-2000; Fax: 212-366-2666; 405 Murray Hill Pkwy., East Rutherford, NJ 07073 (SAN 852-5455) Tel 201-933-9292; Imprints: Ace Books (Ace Bks); Avery (Avr); Berkley (BerkBks); Dial (Dial); Dutton Adult (Dut); Dutton Juvenile (DuttJuv); Warne (Warne); Putnam Juvenile (PutnaJuv); Grosset & Dunlap (Gross-Dun); HP Trade (HPTrade); N A L Trade (NewTrade); Penguin AudioBooks (PengAudBks); Penguin Classics (PenClassics); Philomel (PhilPG); Planet Dexter (PlanDext); Plume (PlumPG); Portfolio Trade (PortfolTrade); Price Stern Sloan (PSS); Puffin (PufBks); Penguin Global (PenGlobal); Roc (Roc); Razorbill (Razrbl); Riverhead Books (Hardcover) (RivhdHC); Sentinel (Sent); Signet (SigBks); Viking Adult (VikiPG); Prentice Hall Press (PHPP); Speak (SpeakPeng); Puffin Books (PuffPeng); Blue Rider Press (Blue Rider Pr); Warne (WarneUSA); Dial Books (DialYoung); Viking Books for Young Readers (VikingBksforYR); Razorbill (RazorbillUSA); G.P. Putnam's Sons Books for Young Readers (GPPutnam); Philomel Books (PhilomelBks); G.P. Putnam's Sons (GPPutnams); Celebra Young Readers (Celebra Youn); Penguin Books (Penguin Bks); TarcherPerigee (TarcherPerigee); Penguin Books (PenguinYR); Dutton Caliber (DuttonCaliber)
E-mail: customer.service@us.penguingroup.com
Web site: http://penguingroup.custhelp.com; http://booksellers.penguingroup.com; http://www.penguinputnam.com
Dist(s): **Casemate Academic**
Ebsco Publishing
Follett School Solutions
Independent Pubs. Group
Lectorum Pubns., Inc.
MyiLibrary
Pearson Education
Penguin Random Hse. LLC
Perfection Learning Corp.
Viking Penguin
ebrary, Inc.

Penguin Random House Audio Publishing Group, (978-1-61176) 375 Hudson St., New York, NY 10014

USA Tel 212-366-2000; Fax: 212-366-2873; *Imprints:* Listening Library (Audio) (LLA)
Web site: www.penguin.com
Dist(s): **Follett School Solutions**
Penguin Random Hse. LLC
Penguin Publishing Group.

Penguin Random House Canada Young Readers (CAN) *Dist. by* **Peng Rand Hse.**

Penguin Random House Grupo Editorial (ESP) *Dist. by* **Casemate Pubs.**

Penguin Random House Grupo Editorial (ESP) *Dist. by* **TwoRivers.**

Penguin Random House Grupo Editorial, S.A. de C.V. (MEX) *(978-607-31; 978-607-429) Dist. by* **TwoRivers.**

Penguin Random Hse. LLC, *(978-1-101)* 375 Hudson St. 3rd Flr., New York, NY 10014 USA Tel 212-366-2424
E-mail: brittany.wienke@us.penguingroup.com
Web site: http://www.PenguinRandomHouse.com.

Penguin Workshop *Imprint of* **Penguin Young Readers Group**

Penguin Young Readers *Imprint of* **Penguin Young Readers Group**

Penguin Young Readers Group, 375 Hudson St., New York, NY 10014 USA; *Imprints:* Speak (SpeakPeng); Puffin Books (PuffPeng); Cartoon Network Books (Cartoon Net); Warne (WarneUSA); Dial Books (DialYoung); Viking Books for Young Readers (VikingBksforYR); Dutton Books for Young Readers (Dutt BksYR); Firebird (Firebird); Razorbill (RazorbillUSA); G.P. Putnam's Sons Books for Young Readers (GPPutnam); Grosset & Dunlap (GrosDunl); Kathy Dawson Books (Kathy Daws); Price Stern Sloan (PriceSternSloan); Philomel Books (PhilomelBks); Nancy Paulsen Books (NancyPaul); Penguin Young Readers (Penguin YR); Penguin Books (PenguinYR); Mad Libs (MadLibs); Penguin Young Readers Licenses (PenYngRead); Penguin Workshop (PenguinWrkshop)
Dist(s): **Penguin Random Hse. LLC**
Penguin Publishing Group.

Penguin Young Readers Licenses *Imprint of* **Penguin Young Readers Group**

Penknife Pr., *(978-0-9741949; 978-1-59997)* 1837 N. Oak Pk. Ave., Chicago, IL 60707 USA Tel 773-733-0830
E-mail: publisher@penknifepress.com
Web site: http://www.penknifepress.com
Dist(s): **Lightning Source, Inc.**

Pen-L Publishing, *(978-0-9851274; 978-1-940222; 978-1-942428; 978-1-68313)* 12 W. Dickson St., No. 4455, Fayetteville, AR 72702 USA
E-mail: duke@pen-l.com
Web site: Pen-L.com.

Penlight Pubns., *(978-0-9838685)* 572 Empire Blvd., Brooklyn, NY 11225 USA Tel 718-972-5449
E-mail: urim_pub@netvision.net.il
Web site: www.penlightpublications.com
Dist(s): **Independent Pubs. Group.**

Penman Publications *See* **Voice & Vision Pubns.**

Penman Publishing, Inc., *(978-0-9700486; 978-0-9707646; 978-0-9712808; 978-0-9720775; 978-1-932496)* Div. of Pathway Pr., Orders Addr.: P.O. Box 3933, Cleveland, TN 37320-2250 USA; Edit Addr.: 1705 Overhead Bridge Rd., Cleveland, TN 37312 USA Tel 423-478-7613
Web site: http://www.penmanpublishing.com.

Pen-Mar News Distributors *See* **Americana Souvenirs & Gifts**

Pennerllynn Publishing, *(978-0-9763025)* P.O. Box 7393, Naples, FL 34104 USA
E-mail: pennerlynn@msn.com
Web site: http://www.pennerlynn.com.

Pennie Rich Publishing, *(978-0-9820328; 978-0-9824960)* 4755 Cty. Rd. 27, Monte Vista, CO 81144-9314 USA (SAN 857-0884)
E-mail: pennierich@pennierich.com
Web site: http://www.pennierich.com.

Penny Candy Pr. *Imprint of* **Brighter Minds Children's Publishing**

Penny Laine Papers, Inc., *(978-1-890703)* 2211 Century Center Blvd. Ste. 110, Irving, TX 75062-4960 USA Toll Free: 800-456-6484; *Imprints:* Bookmates (Bkmates)
E-mail: cardwhiz1@mindspring.com.

Penny Lane Pubns., Inc., *(978-0-911211)* P.O. Box 3005, New York, NY 10012-0009 USA (SAN 274-4961) Tel 212-570-9666.

Penny Pr. *Imprint of* **Penny Pubns., LLC**

Penny Pubns., LLC, *(978-0-944422; 978-1-55956; 978-1-59238)* 6 Prowitt St., Norwalk, CT 06855 USA (SAN 243-6485); *Imprints:* Penny Press (Penny Pr)
E-mail: ltrutnau@pennypublications.net
Web site: http://www.pennydellpuzzles.com; http://www.analogsf.com; http://www.asimovs.com; http://www.themysteryplace.com; http://www.dellhoroscope.com; http://www.thecrosswordsclub.com.

Penny-Farthing Press, Incorporated *See* **Penny-Farthing Productions, Inc.**

Penny-Farthing Productions, Inc., *(978-0-9673683; 978-0-9719012; 978-0-9842143; 978-0-9991709)* One Sugar Creek Ctr. Blvd., Suite 820, Sugar Land, TX 77478 USA Tel 713-780-0300; Fax: 713-780-4004; Toll Free: 800-926-2669
E-mail: corp@pfproductions.com; edit@pfproductions.com; design@pfproductions.com
Web site: http://www.pfpress.com; http://www.pfproductions.com
Dist(s): **Diamond Comic Distributors, Inc.**

Pennypack Productions, Inc., *(978-0-9704184)* 21 Tree Farm Ct., Glen Arm, MD 21057 USA Tel 410-420-3828; Fax: 410-420-2243
E-mail: ppennypack@comcast.net
Web site: http://www.kinderfun.net.

Penny's Publishing *Imprint of* **Balloon Magic**

Pennywhistler's Pr., *(978-0-9623456; 978-0-9727516)* Orders Addr.: P.O. Box 2473, New York, NY 10108 USA Tel 212-247-3231 (phone/fax); Edit Addr.: 467 W. 46th St., New York, NY 10036 USA
E-mail: info@pennywhistle.com
Web site: http://www.pennywhistle.com
Dist(s): **Book Clearing Hse.**
Mel Bay Pubns., Inc.

Pennywise Pubns., Inc., *(978-0-9702944)* 10550 St. Rd. 84, L98, Davie, FL 33324 USA Tel 954-472-8776 (phone/fax)
E-mail: filmpeny@bellsouth.net.

Penrod/Hiawatha Co., *(978-0-942618; 978-1-893624; 978-1-940691)* 10116 M140, Berrien Center, MI 49102 USA (SAN 238-5546) Tel 269-461-6993; Fax: 269-461-4170; Toll Free: 800-632-2823
Web site: http://www.penrodhiawatha.com
Dist(s): **Partners Bk. Distributing, Inc.**

Pentacle Pr., *(978-0-9604760; 978-0-9763500; 978-0-9825047; 978-1-937313)* Orders Addr.: P.O. Box 9400, Scottsdale, AZ 85252 USA (SAN 255-4860) Tel 480-922-2759; Fax: 480-443-8333; Edit Addr.: 5432 E. Desert Jewel Dr., Paradise Valley, AZ 85253 USA
E-mail: djm543@cox.net
Web site: http://www.missionscalifornia.com; http://www.pentacle-press.com
Dist(s): **Sunbelt Pubns., Inc.**
Univ. of New Mexico Pr.

Pentatonic Pr., *(978-0-9773712)* 1232 Second Ave., San Francisco, CA 94122 USA Tel 415-564-1597; Fax: 415-566-6828
E-mail: Goodkindg@aol.com
Web site: http://www.douggoodkin.com
Dist(s): **Midpoint Trade Bks., Inc.**

Pen-Tech Professional, *(978-0-9820962)* P.O. Box 67, Greenville, WI 54942 USA Tel 920-203-0563
Web site: http://www.pentechprofessional.com.

Pentland Pr., Inc., *(978-1-57197)* 5122 Bur Oak Cir., Raleigh, NC 27612 USA (SAN 298-5063) Tel 919-782-0281; Fax: 919-781-9042; Toll Free: 800-948-2786; *Imprints:* Ivy House Publishing Group (Ivy Hse Pubng Grp)
E-mail: janetevans@ivyhousebooks.com
Web site: http://www.ivyhousebooks.com
Dist(s): **Independent Pubs. Group.**

Penton Kids *Imprint of* **Penton Overseas, Inc.**

Penton Overseas, Inc., *(978-0-939001; 978-1-56015; 978-1-59125; 978-1-60379)* 1958 Kellogg Ave., Carlsbad, CA 92008 USA (SAN 631-0826) Tel 760-431-0060; Fax: 760-431-8110; Toll Free: 800-748-5804; *Imprints:* Penton Kids (Penton Kids); Smart Kids (Smrt Kds)
E-mail: kellie@pentonoverseas.com; susan@pentonoverseas.com
Web site: http://www.pentonoverseas.com
Dist(s): **Ideals Pubns.**

Penury Pr., *(978-0-9676344)* 8701 Utah Ave S., Bloomington, MN 55438 USA Tel 952-829-1811
E-mail: penurypress@hotmail.com
Web site: http://www.penurypress.com
Dist(s): **Adventure Pubns.**
Adventures Unlimited Pr.
Partners Bk. Distributing, Inc.

People Bks. *Imprint of* **Time Inc. Bks.**

People, Incorporated *See* **People Ink Pr.**

People Ink Pr., *(978-0-9789476; 978-0-9845983)* 1219 N. Forest Rd., Williamsville, NY 14231 USA Tel 716-634-8132; Fax: 716-817-7558
Web site: http://www.people-inc.org.

People Ink Pr., *(978-0-9858052; 978-0-9893267; 978-0-9862182; 978-0-9977740)* 1219 N. Forest, Williamsville, NY 14223 USA Tel 716-629-3602
E-mail: scrocker@people-inc.org; npalumbo@people-inc.org.

People Skills International, *(978-1-881165)* Orders Addr.: 2910 Baily Ave., San Diego, CA 92105 USA Tel 619-262-9951; Fax: 619-262-0505
E-mail: idagreene@earthlink.net
Web site: http://www.idagreene.com.

People's Literature Publishing Hse. (CHN) *(978-7-02) Dist. by* **China Bks.**

People's Literature Publishing Hse. (CHN) *(978-7-02) Dist. by* **Chinasprout.**

Pep & Olie Publishing, *(978-0-9912023)* 1355 Hilda Ave. No. 6, Glendale, CA 91205 USA Tel 818-552-2642
E-mail: sahin@ersoz.com
Web site: www.pepandolie.com.

Peppermint Bks., *(978-0-9828852)* P.O. Box 16512, Edina, MN 55416 USA (SAN 859-9424) Tel 651-815-8137
E-mail: orders@peppermintbooks.com
Web site: http://www.peppermintbooks.com.

Peppernut Publishing, *(978-0-9796500)* P.O. Box 31126, Omaha, NE 68131-1126 USA Tel 402-556-5591
E-mail: evyboonyawiroj@yahoo.com.

Peppertree Pr., The, *(978-0-9778525; 978-0-9787740; 978-1-934246; 978-0-9814894; 978-0-9817572; 978-0-9818683; 978-0-9820479; 978-0-9821654; 978-0-9822540; 978-0-9823002; 978-1-936051; 978-1-936343; 978-1-61493)* 1269 First St., Suite 7, Sarasota, FL 34236-5518 USA
Web site: http://www.peppertreepublishing.com.

Peppery Pr., *(978-0-9764813)* 504 Springcreek Dr., Longwood, FL 32779 USA Tel 407-786-6113
E-mail: pruben@cfl.rr.com
Web site: http://www.pepperypress.com.

Per Aspera Pr., *(978-0-9745734; 978-1-941662)* Div. of Viridian City Media, Orders Addr.: 205 Grandview Dr., San Marcos, TX 78666 USA
E-mail: adastra@perasperapress.com
Web site: http://www.perasperapress.com/
Dist(s): **Brodart Co.**
Independent Pubs. Group
Partners/West Book Distributors.

Peralta Publishing, LLC, *(978-0-9798620)* 9908 E. Desert Trail Ln., Gold Canyon, AZ 85218 USA Tel 480-288-4306
E-mail: thomaspreiss@msn.com.

Perceval Pr., *(978-0-9721436; 978-0-9747078; 978-0-9763009; 978-0-9774869; 978-0-9819747; 978-0-9895616; 978-0-9969227)* 1223 Wilshire Blvd. No. F, Santa Monica, CA 90403 USA
E-mail: info@percevelpress.com; michele@percevalpress.com
Web site: http://www.percevalpress.com
Dist(s): **D.A.P./Distributed Art Pubs.**
SPD-Small Pr. Distribution.

Peregrine Communications *Imprint of* **Collins, Robert**

Perelandra Publishing Co., *(978-0-9640858)* Orders Addr.: P.O. Box 697, Cardiff, CA 92007 USA; Edit Addr.: 2387 Montgomery, Cardiff, CA 92007 USA Tel 760-753-4469.

Perennial Dreams Pubns., *(978-0-9764779)* P.O. Box 671, Lehi, UT 84043-0671 USA.

Perennis, Sophia, *(978-0-900588; 978-1-59731)* 84A Main St., Peterborough, NH 03458 USA Tel 415-509-6969; *Imprints:* Dawn Chorus Press (DawnChrous)
E-mail: jameswetmore@mac.com
Web site: http://www.sophiaperennis.com
Dist(s): **Lightning Source, Inc.**
SPD-Small Pr. Distribution.

Perennis, Sophia Et Universalis *See* **Perennis, Sophia**

Perfect 4 Preschool, *(978-0-9769239)* 428 N. Nelson St., Arlington, VA 22203 USA (SAN 850-0614) Tel 703-351-5843
E-mail: bjmischel@aol.com
Web site: http://www.perfect4preschool.

Perfect Bound Marketing, *(978-0-9769923; 978-0-9795588; 978-0-9887022; 978-1-939614)* P.O. Box 44545, Phoenix, AZ 85064 USA Tel 480-941-8202
E-mail: vickie@perfectboundmarketing.press
Web site: www.PerfectBoundMarketing.press
Dist(s): **eBookit.com.**

Perfect Page, The, *(978-0-692-54554-6)* 939 Palm Ave., No. 306, West Hollywood, CA 90069 USA Tel 310-652-8438
E-mail: jamesradford@hotmail.com.

Perfect Praise Publishing, *(978-0-9679240; 978-0-9915735)* 1228 Fourth Ave., E., Williston, ND 58801 USA
E-mail: perfectpraise@dia.net
Web site: http://www.perfect-praise.com.

Perfecting Parenting Pr., *(978-0-9790420)* 3943 Jefferson Ave, Emerald Hills, CA 94062-3437 USA Tel 650-364-4466; Fax: 650-364-2299
Web site: http://www.perfectingparentingpress.com.

Perfection Form Company, The *See* **Perfection Learning Corp.**

Perfection Learning Corp., *(978-0-7807; 978-0-7891; 978-0-8124; 978-0-89598; 978-1-56312; 978-0-7569; 978-1-60686; 978-1-61563; 978-1-61383; 978-1-61384; 978-1-62299; 978-1-62359; 978-1-62765; 978-1-62766; 978-1-62974; 978-1-63419; 978-1-68064; 978-1-68065; 978-1-68240; 978-1-5311) 1000 N. 2nd Ave., Logan, IA 51546 USA (SAN 221-0010) Tel 712-644-2831; Fax: 712-644-2392; Toll Free Fax: 800-543-2745; Toll Free: 800-831-4190; Imprints:* Covercraft (Covercraft)
E-mail: orders@perfectionlearning.com
Web site: http://www.perfectionlearning.com.

Pergot Pr., *(978-0-936865)* 19 Prospect Ave., Sausalito, CA 94965 USA (SAN 699-9441) Tel 415-332-0279; Fax: 415-332-5588.

Perinatal Loss *See* **Grief Watch**

Perio Reports, *(978-0-9659236)* Orders Addr.: P.O. Box 30367, Flagstaff, AZ 86003-0367 USA Tel 520-526-2523; Fax: 520-526-0852; Edit Addr.: 1640 N. Spyglass Way, Flagstaff, AZ 86004 USA
Dist(s): **Jenkins Group, Inc.**

Peripatetic Productions, LLC, *(978-0-578-02360-1; 978-0-9842385)* 4145 Joan Ave., Concord, CA 94521-2737 USA Tel 925-798-1311 (phone/fax)
Web site: http://www.peripateticproductions.com
Dist(s): **Lulu Pr., Inc.**

Periplus Editions (HK), Ltd. (HKG) *(978-0-945971; 978-962-593; 978-0-7946; 978-962-8734) Dist. by* **S and S Inc.**

PeriplusEdition *Imprint of* **Tuttle Publishing**

Periscope Film, LLC, *(978-0-9786388; 978-0-9816526; 978-1-935327; 978-1-935700; 978-1-937684; 978-1-940453)* P.O. Box 341474, Los Angeles, CA 90034 USA
E-mail: contact@periscopefilm.com
Web site: http://www.periscopefilm.com.

Periscope Pr., *(978-0-9718546)* 15736 Horton Ln., Overland Park, KS 66223-3491 USA (SAN 254-9700)
Web site: http://www.hearthisorg.com
Dist(s): **Midwest Library Service**
Quality Bks., Inc.

Periscopefilm.com *See* **Periscope Film, LLC**

Periwinkle Studios, *(978-0-9759385)* P.O. Box 5134, Roselle, IL 60172 USA
E-mail: periwinklestudios@comcast.net.

Perkins Crawford, *(978-0-9762935)* 2605 Treybume Ln., Owens Crossroads, AL 35763 USA Tel 256-536-5391
E-mail: e_vroom@bellsouth.net
Web site: http://www.perkinscrawford.com.

Perkins Miniatures, *(978-0-9759198)* 1708-59th St., Des Moines, IA 50322 USA Tel 515-279-6639
E-mail: gladon@earthlink.net.

Perkins Schl. for the Blind, *(978-0-9657170; 978-0-9743510; 978-0-615-26039-6; 978-0-9822721; 978-0-9881713; 978-0-692-69882-2; 978-0-9991766; 978-0-9992637; 978-1-947954)* a/o Publications Dept., 175 N. Beacon St., Watertown, MA 02472 USA
Web site: http://www.Perkins.org
Dist(s): **eBookit.com.**

Perkins-Stell, Crystal, *(978-0-9740705)* P.O. Box 8044, Edmond, OK 73013-8044 USA Tel 405-216-0224; Fax: 405-216-0224
E-mail: cleva@crystalstell.com
Web site: http://www.crystalstell.com.

Perks, Brad Lightscapes Photo Gallery, *(978-0-9788442)* 4055 Kimberly Pl., Concord, CA 94521-3359 USA
E-mail: bradperks@yahoo.com; bradperks@pcimagenetwork.com
Web site: http://pcimagenetwork.com; http://bradperks.com.

Perky Penguin Prs, *(978-0-578-18046-5; 978-0-578-18047-2)* 1808 E. Oxford Dr., Tempe, AZ 85283 USA.

Perlina Pr., *(978-0-9971333)* 20 Udine St., Arlington, MA 02476 USA Tel 781-643-3162
E-mail: irerasin@yahoo.com.

Perlycross Pubs., *(978-0-9741743)* Orders Addr.: a/o Bryce D. Gibby, P.O. Box 9725, Ogden, UT 84409 USA Tel 801-732-8600; Fax: 801-732-8602; Edit Addr.: 2711 Centerville Rd., Suite 120, PMB 5544, Wilmington, DE 19808 USA.

Perman, LeAnn, *(978-0-615-79750-2; 978-0-9892677)* 2295 S. Hiawassee Rd. Suite 208, Orlando, FL 32835 USA Tel 801-243-8463
Dist(s): **BookBaby**
CreateSpace Independent Publishing Platform.

Permanent Productions, Incorporated *See* **Permanent Productions Publishing**

Permanent Productions Publishing, *(978-0-9818204)* Orders Addr.: 904 Silver Spur Rd., No. 510, Rolling Hills Estates, CA 90274 USA (SAN 856-6348) Tel 310-366-4996; Fax: 310-521-9329; Toll Free: 866-698-7376
E-mail: c.jackson@permproductions.com
Web site: http://www.permproductions.com.

Permiso Por Favor Publishing Co., *(978-0-9747272)* 8568 Riverwood Farms, Cordova, TN 38016 USA Tel 901-756-0663
E-mail: permisoporfavor@hotmail.com.

Perpendicular Pr., *(978-0-9740234)* 64 Estabrook Rd., Carlisle, MA 01741-1724 USA
E-mail: info@perpendicularpress.com
Web site: http://www.perpendicularpress.com.

Perpetual Motion Machine Publishing, *(978-0-9887488; 978-0-9860594; 978-1-943720)* 152 Dew Fall Trail, Cibolo, TX 78108 USA Tel 210-573-7796
E-mail: pmmpublishing@gmail.com
Web site: www.perpetualpublishing.com.

Perri Tales Pubns., *(978-0-9763442)* Orders Addr.: 45 W. 132nd St., Suite 12K, New York City, NY 10037-3123 USA; Edit Addr.: 19601 Kings Hwy., Warrensville Heights, OH 44122 USA
E-mail: perrigaffney@aol.com
Web site: http://www.perritales.com.

Perrin & Kabel Publishing, *(978-0-9725364)* 145 Waverly Dr., Pasadena, CA 91105 USA Tel 626-577-1023; Fax: 626-577-1024
E-mail: perrinkabel@earthlink.net.

Perry Enterprises, *(978-0-941518)* 3907 N. Foothill Dr., Provo, UT 84604 USA (SAN 171-0281) Tel 801-226-1002.

Perry Heights Pr., *(978-0-9630181)* P.O. Box 102, Georgetown, CT 06829 USA Tel 203-767-6509; *Imprints:* A Road to Discovery Series Guide (Rd Discovery)
E-mail: contact@perryheightspress.com; contact@cttrips.com
Web site: http://www.cttrips.com.

Pers Publishing, *(978-1-932179)* Div. of Pers Corp., 5255 Stevens Creek Blvd., No. 232-5, Santa Clara, CA 95051-6664 USA (SAN 254-7716) Toll Free Fax: 800-505-7377
E-mail: info@pers.com
Web site: http://www.pers.com; http://www.pers.com/wholesale
Dist(s): **APG Sales & Distribution Services**
Brodart Co.
Emery-Pratt Co.
Quality Bks., Inc.

†**Persea Bks., Inc.,** *(978-0-89255)* 853 Broadway, Suite 604, New York, NY 10003 USA (SAN 212-8233) Tel 212-260-9256; Fax: 212-260-1902
E-mail: info@perseabooks.com
Web site: http://www.perseabooks.com
Dist(s): **Norton, W. W. & Co., Inc.**
Penguin Random Hse. LLC; *CIP.*

Perseus Bks. Group, *(978-0-7382; 978-0-938289; 978-1-58097; 978-1-882810; 978-1-903985; 978-1-78239)* Div. of Hachette Book Group, Orders Addr.: 2465 Central Ave., Suite 200, Boulder, CO 80301-5728 USA Toll Free: 800-343-4499 (customer service); Edit Addr.: 387 Park Ave., S., 12th Flr., New York, NY 10016-8810 USA Tel 212-340-8100; Fax: 212-340-8105; *Imprints:* Weinstein Books (WeinsteinBks)
Web site: http://www.perseusbooksgroup.com.

Perseus Distribution *See* **Two Rivers Distribution**

Perseus-PGW *See* **Publishers Group West (PGW)**

Personal, *(978-0-9856724)* P.O. Box 661, Monticello, IL 61856 USA Tel 217-649-1589
E-mail: flygrl78@gmail.com.

Personal Best Motivional Sciences, Inc., *(978-0-9769988)* P.O. Box 562, Social Circle, GA 30025-0562 USA
Web site: http://www.babysimplerecipe.com/.

Personal Genesis Publishing, *(978-0-9747395)* 110 Pacific Ave., No. 204, San Francisco, CA 9411 USA Toll Free: 888-337-7776
Web site: http://www.ForgottenFaces.org.

Personal Power Pr., *(978-0-9616046; 978-0-9772321; 978-0-9821568)* Div. of Institute for Personal Power, P.O. Box 547, Merrill, MI 48637 USA (SAN 698-0155) Tel 989-643-5059; Fax: 989-643-5156; Toll Free: 877-360-1477
E-mail: ipp57@aol.com
Web site: http://www.chickmoorman.com
Dist(s): **Austin & Company, Inc.**
Midpoint Trade Bks., Inc.
Partners Pubs. Group, Inc.

Personal Promise Bible, *(978-0-9759578)* 470 Heritage Hills Dr., Richland, WA 99352 USA Tel 509-627-2607; Fax: 775-402-2106; Toll Free: 866-968-7242
Web site: http://www.personalpromisebible.com.

Personal Security, *(978-0-9675357)* 24366 Falcon, Lake Forest, CA 92630 USA Tel 949-461-9552; Fax: 949-472-8018
E-mail: xwordshicklers@hotmail.com.

Personality Wise *See* **Uniquely You Resources**

Personhood Pr., *(978-1-932181)* P.O. Box 370, Fawnskin, CA 92333 USA Tel 909-866-2912; Fax: 909-866-2961; Toll Free: 800-662-9662
E-mail: blwjalmar@att.net; cathy_winch@charter.net; personhoodpress@att.net
Web site: http://www.personhoodpress.com
Dist(s): **Ebsco Publishing**
Independent Pubs. Group
MyiLibrary
ebrary, Inc.

Personify Pr., *(978-0-9797491)* 1959 Camino a los Cerros, Menlo Park, CA 94025 USA.

Perspective Publishing, Inc., *(978-0-9622036; 978-1-930085)* 2528 Sleepy Hollow Dr., No. A, Glendale, CA 91206 USA Tel 818-502-1270; Fax: 818-502-1272; Toll Free: 800-330-5851 Do not confuse with Perspective Publishing, Memphis, TN
E-mail: books@familyhelp.com
Web site: http://www.familyhelp.com
Dist(s): **Independent Pubs. Group**
Quality Bks., Inc.

Perspectives Pr., Inc., *(978-0-944934; 978-0-9609504)* P.O. Box 90318, Indianapolis, IN 46290-0318 USA (SAN 262-5059) Tel 317-872-3055
E-mail: patjohnston@perspectivespress.com
Web site: http://www.perspectivespress.com
Dist(s): **Smashwords.**

PES, Inc., *(978-0-9766962)* P.O. Box 5501, Virginia Bch, VA 23471-0501 USA
E-mail: sailingthroughbusiness@cox.net
Web site: http://www.sailingthroughbusiness.com.

Pesout, Christine, *(978-0-615-47220-1)* 14 Dinan Ct., Lake St. Louis, MO 63367 USA Tel 314-443-6319
E-mail: cpesout@hotmail.com.

Pet Pundit Publishing, *(978-0-9853752)* P.O. Box 91733, Austin, TX 78209-1733 USA Tel 512-358-4515
E-mail: cathy@petpundit.com
Web site: www.petpunditpublishing.com.

Petalous Publishing, LLC, *(978-0-9777811)* Orders Addr.: PO Box 285, Farmingdale, NJ 07727 USA.

Peter Pauper Pr. Inc., *(978-0-88088; 978-1-59359; 978-1-4413)* Orders Addr.: 202 Mamaroneck Ave., Suite 400, White Plains, NY 10601 USA (SAN 204-9449) Tel 914-681-0144; Fax: 914-681-0389
E-mail: orders@peterpauper.com; customerservice@peterpauper.com
Web site: http://www.peterpauper.com.

PeterCottonBks., *(978-0-692-57072-2)* 2736 Magnolia Woods Dr., Mount Pleasant, SC 29464 USA Tel 843-814-1872
E-mail: petercotto@gmail.com
Web site: www.petercottontales.com.

Peterman, Melvin G. *See* **Insight Technical Education**

Peters & Pardee Pubs., *(978-0-9626279)* Orders Addr.: 1039 NW Hwy. 101, Lincoln City, OR 97367 USA.

Petersburg Museums, The, *(978-0-9744824)* 15 W. Bank St., Petersburg, VA 23803 USA Tel 804-733-2402 Toll Free: 800-368-3595.

Peterson-Boyce, Linda, *(978-0-9766034)* P.O. Box 2942, North Babylon, NY 11703 USA.

†Peterson's, *(978-0-7689; 978-0-87866; 978-1-56079)* Div. of Nelnet, Orders Addr.: P.O. Box 67005, Lawrenceville, NJ 08648-6105 USA (SAN 200-2167); Edit Addr.: 2000 Lenox Dr., 3rd Flr., Lawrenceville, NJ 08648 USA (SAN 297-5661) Tel 609-896-1800; Fax: 609-896-1811; Toll Free: 800-338-3282 X5660;Customer Service; *Imprints:* Arco (Arco)
E-mail: custsvc@petersons.com
Web site: http://www.petersons.com
Dist(s): **Hachette Bk. Group**
MyiLibrary
Simon & Schuster; *CIP.*

Petey, Rock & Roo Children's Pubns., *(978-0-9789642)* Orders Addr.: 1657 Broadway, New York, NY 10019 USA (SAN 852-0585)
E-mail: tash@timessquarechurch.org
Web site: http://www.timessquarechurch.org.

Petit Chou Chou, LLC, *(978-0-615-54492-2; 978-0-9882306)* P.O. Box 470875, Fort Worth, TX 76147 USA Tel 817-793-2594
E-mail: jdrez@att.net
Web site: http://goodnightcowtown.com.

Petra Publishing *See* **Petra Publishing Co.**

Petra Publishing Co., *(978-0-9712429)* 385 S. Lemon Ave., Suite E314, Walnut, CA 91789 USA Tel 404-452-3374
E-mail: admin@petrapublishingcompany.com
Web site: http://www.petrapublishingcompany.com; http://www.positivemag.com.

Pet's Playground *See* **Singing Moon Pr.**

Pex Publishing Co., *(978-0-933767)* 8625 Boysenberry Dr., Tampa, FL 33635 USA (SAN 692-7645).

P.F.B. Publishing, *(978-0-9741273)* P.O. Box 149, Warren, OH 44482-0149 USA Fax: 330-373-0211
E-mail: pat@southparktitle.com.

Pflaum Publishing Group, *(978-0-89837; 978-0-937997; 978-1-933178; 978-1-935042; 978-1-939105; 978-1-947358)* Div. of Bayard, Inc., 3055 Kettering Blvd., Suite 100, Dayton, OH 45439 USA (SAN 661-2539) Fax: 937-293-1310; Toll Free Fax: 800-370-4450; Toll Free: 800-543-4383; 3055 Kettering Blvd., Suite 100, Dayton, OH 45439 (SAN 661-2539) Fax: 937-293-1310; Toll Free Fax: 800-370-4450; Toll Free: 800-543-4383
E-mail: service@pflaum.com
Web site: http://www.pflaum.com
Dist(s): **ACTA Pubns.**

P.F.P. Pubs., *(978-0-615-18028-1; 978-0-615-18027-4; 978-0-615-18157-8; 978-0-615-18343-5; 978-0-615-18415-9; 978-0-615-18648-1; 978-0-615-18873-7; 978-0-615-19123-2; 978-0-615-19266-6; 978-0-615-19773-9; 978-0-615-22198-4)* 35 Stone Ridge Blvd., Hermitage, PA 16148 USA
E-mail: p.f.p.publishers@gmail.com
Web site: http://www.pfpublishers.com
Dist(s): **Lulu Pr., Inc.**

PGC Publishing *See* **Hope of Vision Publishing**

PH Publishing, *(978-0-9835863; 978-0-9835863-7-1)* 3446 13th Ave. SW, Naples, FL 34117 USA Tel 239-352-1889
E-mail: pphayton@yahoo.com.

Phaidon Pr. Ltd. (GBR) *(978-0-7148) Dist. by* **HachBkGrp.**

Phaidon Pr., Inc., *(978-0-7148)* 180 Varick St., 14th Flr., New York, NY 10014-4606 USA (SAN 253-3367) Tel 212-652-5400; Fax: 212-652-5410; Toll Free Fax: 800-286-9471 (Orders only); Toll Free: 800-759-0190 (Orders only); 877-742-4366 (Editorial)
E-mail: ussales@phaidon.com
Web site: http://www.phaidon.com
Dist(s): **Hachette Bk. Group.**

Phantom Pubns., Inc., *(978-0-9625372)* 9451 Page Rd., Wattsburg, PA 16442-2005 USA
Dist(s): **Empire Publishing Service.**

Pharmasoft Publishing *See* **Hale Publishing**

phazelFOZ Co., LLC., The, *(978-0-9819645; 978-0-9834876; 978-0-9859333; 978-0-9960781; 978-0-692-61390-0; 978-0-9974257; 978-0-9988803)* 858 W. Armitage Ave., No. 365, Chicago, IL 60614 USA.

PHD Ink, *(978-0-9897278; 978-1-941104)* P.O. Box 4295, Sarasota, FL 34230 USA Tel 347-661-2073
E-mail: rkclark@aol.com.

Pheasant Tale Productions, *(978-0-9817001)* P.O. Box 73, Skamokawa, WA 98647-0073 USA (SAN 856-2814)
E-mail: rajj@iinet.com; adventureinborneo@gmail.com
Web site: http://https://sites.google.com/site/adventureinborneo/.

Phelps, Diane *See* **Red Rock Mountain Pr. LLC**

Phenomenal One Pr., *(978-0-9841989; 978-0-9850251; 978-0-9969195)* 1463 Akeke Pl., Kailua, HI 96734 USA
E-mail: lprstn@hotmail.com
Web site: http://www.phenomenalonepress.com
Dist(s): **Lightning Source, Inc.**
MyiLibrary.

Phi Sigma Omega, Alpha Kappa Alpha Sorority, Inc., *(978-0-9785269)* P.O. Box 1784, Gonzales, LA 70707-1784 USA Tel 225-936-1565
Web site: http://phisigmaomega2000.org.

Phidal Publishing, Inc./Editions Phidal, Inc. (CAN) *(978-2-89393; 978-2-920129; 978-2-7643) Dist. by* **AIMS Intl.**

Phil the Pill & Friends *Imprint of* **MAMP Creations**

Philadelphia Folklore Project, *(978-0-9644937)* 735 S. 50th St., Philadelphia, PA 19147 USA Tel 215-726-1106; Fax: 215-726-6250
E-mail: pfp@folkloreproject.org
Web site: http://www.folkloreproject.org; *CIP.*

Philadelphia Inquirer, The, *(978-1-58822)* Div. of Philadelphia Newspapers, Inc., 400 N. Broad St., Philadelphia, PA 19101 USA Tel 215-854-2000
Web site: http://www.philly.com.

†Philadelphia Museum of Art, *(978-0-87633)* 2525 Pennsylvania Ave., Philadelphia, PA 19130 USA (SAN 203-0969) Fax: 215-235-8715
Web site: http://www.philamuseum.org
Dist(s): **Antique Collectors' Club**
Art Media Resources, Inc.
D.A.P./Distributed Art Pubs.
ISD
National Bk. Network
Pennsylvania State Univ. Pr.
Yale Univ. Pr.; *CIP.*

Philio International *See* **Philio Publishing**

Philio Publishing, *(978-0-9622996; 978-0-9964356)* 1138 N. Germantown Pkwy. Suite 101-294, Cordova, TN 38018 USA Tel 901-201-4058
Dist(s): **Lulu Pr., Inc.**

Philipp, Cathy Publishing, *(978-0-9655848)* P.O. Box 1954, Thousand Oaks, CA 91358-1954 USA Tel 805-498-0611; Fax: 805-498-7331
E-mail: philifam@adelphia.net.

Philippine American Literary House *See* **PALH**

Philippine American Writers & Artists, Inc., *(978-0-9763316; 978-0-9968032; 978-0-9981792)* P.O. Box 31928, San Francisco, CA 94131-0928 USA
E-mail: pawa@pawainc.com
Web site: http://www.pawainc.com.

Philips, Fleur, *(978-0-9889299)* 250 N. College Pk. Dr. No. U33, Upland, CA 91786 USA Tel 909-908-3788
E-mail: fleurphilips@gmail.com
Dist(s): **BookBaby.**

Philograph *Imprint of* **Cascade, Inc.**

Philokalos Pr., *(978-0-9912472)* P.O. Box 3811, McLean, VA 22103 USA Tel 703-586-1353
E-mail: philokalospress@gmail.com
Web site: www.philokalospress.org.

Philomel *Imprint of* **Penguin Publishing Group**

Philomel Bks. *Imprint of* **Penguin Publishing Group**

Philomel Bks. *Imprint of* **Penguin Young Readers Group**

Philos Pr., *(978-0-9831075)* 22545 SW Miami Dr., Tualatin, OR 97062 USA Tel 503-885-8877; Fax: 503-885-1847
E-mail: maryandonian@yahoo.com.

†Philosophical Library, Inc., *(978-0-8022)* P.O. Box 1789, New York, NY 10010 USA (SAN 201-999X) Tel 212-886-1873; Fax: 212-873-6070
Dist(s): **Kensington Publishing Corp.**
MyiLibrary
Open Road Integrated Media, Inc.
Open Road Distribution
Rowman & Littlefield Publishers, Inc.; *CIP.*

Philothea Pr., *(978-0-9826867)* P.O. Box 1262, West Chester, OH 45071 USA Tel 513-805-6766.

Phlare, Inc., *(978-0-9741147)* 9565 W. 52nd Ave., Arvada, CO 80002 USA Tel 303-513-1565; Toll Free: 888-731-2398
Web site: http://www.phlare.com.

Phoenix Bks., Inc., *(978-1-59777; 978-1-60747; 978-1-61467)* 9465 Wilshire Blvd., Suite 840, Beverly Hills, CA 90212-2609 USA; *Imprints:* Pickwick Press (PickwickPr); Dove Books and Audio (Dove Bks)
Dist(s): **Ingram Publisher Services.**

Phoenix Films & Video, *(978-0-7919)* 2349 Chaffee Dr., Saint Louis, MO 63146 USA (SAN 653-5224) Tel 314-569-0211; Fax: 314-569-2834; Toll Free: 800-221-1274
E-mail: phoenixfilm@worldnet.att.net
Web site: http://www.phoenix-bfa-coronet.com
Dist(s): **Follett School Solutions**
Weston Woods Studios, Inc.

Phoenix International, Inc., *(978-0-9650485; 978-0-9713470; 978-0-9780007; 978-0-9824295; 978-0-9835615; 978-0-9899356)* 17762 Summer Rain Rd., Fayetteville, AR 72701 USA Tel 479-521-2204 Do not confuse with companies with the same or similar names in Oxon Hill, MD, Nampa, ID
E-mail: john@phoenixpub.com
Web site: http://www.phoenixbase.com
Dist(s): **Chicago Distribution Ctr.**
Univ. of Arkansas Pr.

Phoenix International Publications, Inc., *(978-0-7853; 978-1-4127; 978-1-60553; 978-1-4508; 978-1-5037)* 7373 N. Cicero Ave., Lincolnwood, IL 60712 USA; 7390 Lincoln Ave., Lincolnwood, IL 60712 (SAN 860-424X) Tel 847-676-3518; Fax: 847-676-3528; Toll Free: 800-860-6828
E-mail: ldolan@pikidsmedia.com
Dist(s): **Hachette Bk. Group.**

Phoenix Learning Resources, LLC, *(978-0-7915)* Orders Addr.: P.O. Box 510, Honesdale, PA 18431 USA (SAN 246-148X) Tel 570-251-6871; Fax: 570-253-3227; Toll Free: 800-228-9345
E-mail: rich@phoenixlr.com
Web site: http://www.phoenixlr.com.

Phoenix Publishing, *(978-1-928812)* Orders Addr.: P.O. Box 8231, Missoula, MT 59807 USA Fax: 406-721-6195; Toll Free: 800-549-8371; Edit Addr.: 309 SW Higgins, Missoula, MT 59803 USA Do not confuse with companies with the same or similar names in Redmond, WA, W. Kennebunk, ME, Rocklin, CA, Bloomington, IN, Miami, FL, Fairfield, FL, Tolono, IL, Newark, NJ, Lansing, MI, Alpharetta, GA, Custer, WA, Marina del Ray, CA, Half Moon Bay, CA, New York, NY
E-mail: phoenixl@phoenixpub.com
Web site: http://www.phoenixpub.com.

Phoenix Publishing, *(978-0-615-20417-8)* 308 W. Burnside Ave., Fairland, IN 46126 USA
E-mail: kphoenix_3@sbcglobal.net
Dist(s): **Lulu Pr., Inc.**

Phoenix Rising LLC, *(978-0-9800807)* 11684 Ventura Blvd., Suite 886, Studio City, CA 91604 USA (SAN 855-1464)
E-mail: phoenixrising@earthlink.net.

Phoenix Yard Bks. (GBR) *(978-1-907912) Dist. by* **IPG Chicago.**

Phonic Monic, *(978-1-943241)* 472 Trident Maple Terr., Fremont, CA 94539 USA Tel 510-573-1646
E-mail: cammieho123@gmail.com
Web site: www.phonicmonic.com
Dist(s): **Independent Pubs. Group.**

Phonics Readers *Imprint of* **Capstone Press of Coughlan Cos.**

Phosphene Publishing Co., *(978-0-9796968; 978-0-9851477; 978-0-9986316)* 4019 River Dr., Houston, TX 77017 USA.

PhotoGraphics Publishing, *(978-0-9643844; 978-0-9793813; 978-0-9829730)* 23 Cool Water Ct., Palm Coast, FL 32137 USA Tel 386-246-3672; Fax: 386-445-7365; *Imprints:* Doctor Dolittle's Library (Doctor Dolittle)
E-mail: joycehuber47@hotmail.com
Web site: http://www.photographicspublishing.com.

Photographs Naturally, Inc., *(978-0-9710343)* 57 Laurel Oak, Amelia Island, FL 32034 USA Tel 904-277-4403; Fax: 904-277-0749.

Photographs Naturally, Incorporated *See* **Photographs Naturally, Inc.**

PhotoHutch, *(978-0-9824925)* P.O. Box 482, Alamo, CA 94507 USA
Web site: http://www.bisforbufflehead.com; http://www.photohutch.com.

Photon Pubns., *(978-0-9744128; 978-0-615-11954-0)* 7532 Mason Dells Dr., Dallas, TX 75230-3246 USA
E-mail: j1jagger@aol.com
Dist(s): **BookMasters, Inc.**

Piano Pr, *(978-0-9673325; 978-1-931844)* Orders Addr.: P.O. Box 85, Del Mar, CA 92014-0085 USA Tel 619-884-1401; Fax: 858-755-1104; Edit Addr.: 1425 Ocean Ave., No. 17, Del Mar, CA 92014 USA Tel 619-884-1401
E-mail: eaxford@aol.com; pianopress@pianopress.com; lizaxford@pianopress.com
Web site: http://www.pianopress.com
Dist(s): **Book Wholesalers, Inc.**
Coutts Information Services
Blackwell
Wayland Audio-Visual.

Pianomouse Productions, *(978-0-9889068)* Orders Addr.: 8789 Auburn Folsom Rd. Ste. C416, Granite Bay, CA 95746 USA Tel 916-204-8110
E-mail: kathleen@pianomouse.com
Web site: www.pianomouse.com.

Piñata Books *Imprint of* **Arte Publico Pr.**

Picador, *(978-0-312)* Div. of Holtzbrinck Publishers, Orders Addr.: 16365 James Madison Hwy., Gordonsville, VA 22942-8501 USA Fax: 800-672-2054; Toll Free: 888-330-8477; Edit Addr.: 175 Fifth Ave., New York, NY 10010 USA Tel 212-674-5151; Fax: 540-672-7540 (customer service)
Web site: http://www.picadorusa.com
Dist(s): **Libros Sin Fronteras**
Macmillan.

Picaro Press *See* **One Eyed Pr.**

Piccadilly Bks., Ltd., *(978-0-941599; 978-1-936709)* P.O. Box 25203, Colorado Springs, CO 80936 USA (SAN 665-9969) Tel 719-550-9887
E-mail: info@piccadillybooks.com
Web site: http://www.piccadillybooks.com
Dist(s): **MyiLibrary**
New Leaf Distributing Co., Inc.
Nutri-Bks. Corp.

Piccolo Tales, *(978-0-9881889)* 10640 Riverlake Dr., Knoxville, TN 37922 USA Tel 865-966-0274; Fax: 865-966-0274
E-mail: bc2bls@yahoo.com.

Pick It Publishing, *(978-0-615-26122-5)* P.O. Box 284, Danville, IA 52623 USA
Dist(s): **Lulu Pr., Inc.**

Pick Me Up N Go Publishing Co., *(978-0-615-15832-7)* 10312 S. Prospect Ave., Chicago, IL 60643 USA
E-mail: felice@pickmeupngo.com
Dist(s): **Lulu Pr., Inc.**

Pickering, Todd, *(978-0-615-12910-5)* P.O. Box 907, Pt Reyes Sta, CA 94956-0907 USA
E-mail: todd@toddpickering.com
Web site: http://www.toddpickering.com
Dist(s): **SPD-Small Pr. Distribution.**

Pickett Fennell Group, The, *(978-0-615-31289-7; 978-0-9833864)* 619 Castlewood Dr., Upper Marlboro, MD 20774 USA
E-mail: pfgpublishing@gmail.com.

Pickett Publishing *See* **Pickett Fennell Group, The**

Pickled Eggs Press (TM) *Imprint of* **Lisa Loucks Christenson Publishing, LLC**

Pickled Herring Pr., *(978-0-9778276)* 2380 W. Hill Dr., Madison, WI 53711 USA.

Picklesisters, *(978-0-9767542)* 224 Red Oak Dr E. Apt. F, Sunnyvale, CA 94086-6612 USA
E-mail: editor@picklesisters.com
Web site: http://www.picklesisters.com.

Pickup, Terry Lowey *See* **Terry Lowey's Children's Stories, LLC**

Pickwick Pr. *Imprint of* **Phoenix Bks., Inc.**

Picnic Publishing Ltd. (GBR) *(978-0-9556105) Dist. by* **Trans-Atl Phila.**

Pictorial Legends, *(978-0-939031)* Subs. of Event Co., 435 Holland Ave., Los Angeles, CA 90042 USA (SAN 662-8486) Tel 213-254-4416
Dist(s): **Igram Pr.**

Picture Bk. *Imprint of* **Spotlight**

Picture Bk. Learning, Inc., *(978-0-9760725)* P.O. Box 270075, Louisville, CO 80027 USA
E-mail: todd@picturebooklearning.com
Web site: http://www.picturebooklearning.com.

Picture Entertainment *See* **Evening Sun Pr.**

Picture Me Books, Incorporated *See* **Playhouse Publishing**

Picture Window Bks., *(978-1-4048; 978-1-4795; 978-1-5158)* Div. of Coughlan Publishing, 1710 Roe Crest Dr., North Mankato, MN 56003 USA (SAN 254-8828) Toll Free Fax: 888-262-0705; *Imprints:* Chapter Readers (ChapReads); Easy Readers (Easy Readers); Fiction Picture Books (FictPicBks); Nonfiction Picture Books (Nonfiction Pict); My First Classic Story (MY FIRST CLASS); DC Super-Pets (DC SUPER-PETS); Little Boost (LITTLE BOOST); Kylie Jean (KYLIE JEAN); Monster Street (MONSTER STREET); Max & Zoe (MAX & ZOE); I See (I SEE); Henry Helps (HENRY HELPS); My Little Planet (MY LITTLE PLAN); Zeke Meeks (ZEKE MEEKS); Adventures at Hound Hotel (AdventHound); Charles Reasoners Little Cuddles (ChuckReas); Finley Flowers (FinFlower); Sofia Martinez (SofiMart)
E-mail: k.monyhan@coughlancompanies.com; customerservice@capstonepub.com
Web site: http://www.picturewindowbooks.com; http://www.capstonepub.com; http://www.capstoneclassroom.com
Dist(s): **Capstone Press of Coughlan Cos.**
Capstone Pub.

Pie in the Sky Publishing, LLC, *(978-1-893815)* 8031 E. Phillips Cir., Centennial, CO 80112 USA
E-mail: PieintheSkyPublishing@msn.com
Web site: http://www.pieintheskypublishing.com
Dist(s): **Bks. West.**

Pie Plate Publishing Co., *(978-0-9855906; 978-1-941175)* P.O. Box 760151, Lathrup Village, MI 48076 USA Tel 248-508-7749
E-mail: joddo@pieplatepublishing.com
Web site: www.pieplatepub.com.

Pieces of Learning, *(978-0-9623835; 978-1-880505; 978-1-931334; 978-1-934358; 978-1-937113)* Div. of Creative Learning Consultants, Inc., 1990 Market Rd., Marion, IL 62959 USA (SAN 298-461X) Tel 618-964-9426; Fax: 618-964-1897; Toll Free Fax: 800-844-0455; Toll Free: 800-729-5137
E-mail: piecesoflearning@frontier.com; stan@piecesoflearning.com
Web site: http://www.piecesoflearning.com.

Piedra Santa, Editorial (GTM) *(978-84-8377; 978-99922-1; 978-99922-58) Dist. by* **Libros Fronteras.**

PIEEYE Publishing, Inc., *(978-0-9759435)* 116 Consumer Sq., Suite 333, Plattsburgh, NY 12901 USA Tel 514-684-0434; Toll Free: 888-474-3393
E-mail: jocelyne@pieeyepublishing.com; info@pieeyepublishing.com
Web site: http://www.pieeyepublishing.com/.

Pier Media, *(978-0-9715980)* Div. of Pier Video, Inc., P.O. Box 190, Gardiner, NY 12525 USA Tel 212-481-0031; Fax: 212-481-0892
E-mail: joe514@aol.com
Web site: http://www.marcusantebi.com.

Pieras Inc. Editorial, *(978-0-9729719)* Div. of Pieras Inc., Y-9 México Ave. and Colorado St. Parkville Extension, Guaynabo, PR 00962-3923 USA (SAN 255-3112) Tel 787-299-4486
E-mail: jorge@elbien.org
Web site: http://www.wakebooks.com
Dist(s): **Lightning Source, Inc.**

Pieras Incorporated *See* **Pieras Inc. Editorial**
Pierce, Paul, *(978-0-9741819)* 1400 15th St., Columbus, GA 31901 USA
E-mail: prpierce@mindspring.com
Dist(s): **Parnassus Bk. Distributors.**
Pierce Pr., *(978-0-9776396; 978-0-9960975; 978-0-9970681)* P.O. Box 206, Arlington, MA 02746 USA Tel 339-368-5656; Fax: 339-368-5656
E-mail: charlotte@piercepress.com
Web site: http://www.piercepress.com; https://www.facebook.com/daytripperbooks; https://plus.google.com/+CharlottePierce; http://peeragogy.org
Dist(s): **Ingram Publisher Services.**
Pig Iron Pr., *(978-0-917530)* Orders Addr.: P.O. Box 237, Youngstown, OH 44501 USA (SAN 209-0937) Tel 330-747-6932; Fax: 330-747-0599; Edit Addr.: 26 N. Phelps, Youngstown, OH 44503 USA (SAN 241-8193)
E-mail: pigironpress@cboss.com.
Pike Road Productions *See* **STR8*UP Productions**
Pikes Peak Library District, *(978-1-56735)* 5550 N. Union, Colorado Springs, CO 80918 USA Tel 719-531-6333; Fax: 719-389-8161
E-mail: tblevins@ppld.org.
Pikku Publishing (GBR) *(978-0-9928050) Dist. by* **IPG Chicago.**
Pik-Ware Publishing, *(978-0-9744190)* P.O. Box 110, Crisfield, MD 21817 USA Tel 410-968-3873 (phone/fax)
E-mail: pat@funkyseagull.com
Web site: http://www.pik-ware.com.
PIL Kids *Imprint of* **Publications International, Ltd.**
Pilate, Victoria, *(978-0-9759665)* P.O. Box 75433, Washington, DC 20013 USA.
Pilgrim Press *See* **Kinfolk Research Pr.**
Pilgrim Pr., The/United Church Pr., *(978-0-8298)* Div. of United Church Board for Homeland Ministries, Orders Addr.: 226 Sheldon Rd., Berea, OH 44017-1234 USA Toll Free: 800-537-3394; Edit Addr.: 700 Prospect Ave. E., Cleveland, OH 44115-1100 USA Tel 216-736-3764; Fax: 216-736-2207
E-mail: ucpress@ucc.org; pilgrim@ucc.org
Web site: http://www.ucpress.com; http://www.pilgrimpress.com
Dist(s): **BookBaby**
Faith Alive Christian Resources
Women Ink.
Pilinut Pr., Inc., *(978-0-9779576; 978-1-944390)* 41 W. Lee Hwy., Suite 59, #808, Warrenton, VA 20186 USA.
Pill Bug Pr., *(978-0-9761623)* 1868 Bridgeport Ave., Claremont, CA 91711 USA Tel 909-624-9985 (phone/fax).
Pill Hill Pr., *(978-0-9842610; 978-1-61706)* 343 W. 4th St., Chadron, NE 69337 USA
E-mail: pillhillpress@gmail.com
Web site: http://www.pillhillpress.com
Dist(s): **BookBaby.**
Pillar of Enoch Ministry Bks., *(978-0-9759131)* 1708 N. 77th Ave., Elmwood Park, IL 60707-4107 USA
E-mail: helena@pillar-of-enoch.com
Web site: http://www.pillar-of-enoch.com
Dist(s): **Lightning Source, Inc.**
Pillar Rock Publishing, *(978-0-9764109)* P.O. Box 86571, Portland, OR 97286 USA
Web site: http://www.zoppa.com.
Pillowtalks Publishing, *(978-0-692-82809-0)* 105 Beverly Blvd., Hobart, IN 46342 USA Tel 219-942-1821; Fax: 219-942-1821
E-mail: sherryfinnerty@gmail.com.
Pilot Bks. *Imprint of* **Bellwether Media**
Pilot Communications Group, Inc., *(978-0-9791957; 978-0-9824967; 978-0-9826665; 978-1-936417; 978-1-939268; 978-1-62903)* 317 Appaloosa Trl., Woodway, TX 76712-8816 USA
Dist(s): **Midpoint Trade Bks., Inc.**
Pilumeli, Tanya *See* **FAVA Pr.**
Pinata Pubns., *(978-0-934925)* P.O. Box 13252, Oakland, CA 94611 USA (SAN 694-6062) Tel 510-336-0819 (phone/fax)
E-mail: bsalinas@ousd.k12.ca.us
Dist(s): **Lectorum Pubns., Inc.**
Libros Sin Fronteras
Teacher's Discovery.
Pinata Publishing (CAN) *(978-0-9685097; 978-0-9809163) Dist. by* **Midpt Trade.**
Pinchey Hse. Pr., *(978-0-9820342)* 1805 Mummasburg Rd., Gettysburg, PA 17325 USA (SAN 857-0655)
Web site: http://www.ofthewing.com
Dist(s): **Follett School Solutions.**
Pine Cone Pr., *(978-0-9791982; 978-0-692-20517-4)* 2870 Callie Still Rd., Lawrenceville, GA 30045 USA
E-mail: marty@donnellan.com
Web site: http://www.frendibles.com
Dist(s): **CreateSpace Independent Publishing Platform.**
Pine Hill Graphics, *(978-0-9714103; 978-0-9727279; 978-1-933150; 978-0-615-29527-5)* 85334 Lorane Hwy., Eugene, OR 97405 USA Tel 541-343-1364; Fax: 541-343-0568
E-mail: fred@pinehillgraphics.com
Dist(s): **Leonard, Hal Corp.**
Pine Hill Pr., *(978-1-57579)* Div. of Print Right Printing, 1808 N. K Ave., Sioux Falls, SD 57104 USA Tel 605-362-9200; Fax: 605-362-9222 Do not confuse with Pine Hill Pr., Lafayette, CA8
E-mail: print@pinehillpress.com
Web site: http://www.printrightprinting.com.
Pine Orchard, Inc., *(978-0-9645727; 978-1-930580)* Orders Addr.: 2850 Hwy 95 South. P.O. box 9184, Moscow, ID 83843 USA (SAN 253-4258) Tel 208-882-4838; Fax: 208-882-4845; Toll Free: 877-354-7433; *Imprints:* Ulyssian Publications (Ulyssian Pubns); Luminary Media Group (Luminary Media)
E-mail: orders@pineorchard.com; pineorch@pineorchard.com
Web site: http://www.pineorchard.com
Dist(s): **Brodart Co.**
Pine Orchard Press *See* **Pine Orchard, Inc.**
Pine View Pr., *(978-0-9740151)* Orders Addr.: 42 Central St., Southbridge, MA 01550 USA (SAN 255-3309) Tel 508-764-7415; Fax: 508-765-1963
E-mail: shawnpcormier@aol.com
Web site: http://www.pineviewpress.com
Dist(s): **Partners Bk. Distributing, Inc.**
Pineapple Pr., Inc., *(978-0-910923; 978-1-56164; 978-1-68334)* P.O. Box 3889, Sarasota, FL 34230-3889 USA (SAN 285-0850) Tel 941-739-2219; Fax: 941-739-2296; Toll Free: 800-746-3275 Do not confuse with companies with same or similar names in Saint Johns, MI, Middletown, RI, Northampton, MA, Wimberley, TX
E-mail: editorial@pineapplepress.com
Web site: http://www.pineapplepress.com
Dist(s): **American Wholesale Bk. Co.**
Ingram Publisher Services
MyiLibrary.
Pineapple Publishing and Consulting LLC, *(978-0-9794608; 978-1-938188)* 1046 W. 42nd St., Houston, TX 77018-4314 USA
Web site: http://www.pineapplepublishing.com.
Pineapple Study Guides *See* **Passkey Pubns.**
Pinefield Publishing, *(978-0-9746397)* 9801 Fall Creek Rd., Suite 318, Indianapolis, IN 46256 USA Tel 317-258-6211; Fax: 317-576-9154
E-mail: Pinefieldpublishing@comcast.net
Web site: http://www.Pinefieldpublishing.com.
Pines Publishing, *(978-0-9766820)* 9896 Lincoln Rd., Morrison, KY 61270-9498 USA
E-mail: info@pinespublishing.com
Web site: http://www.pinespublishing.com.
Pinetree Pubns., *(978-0-9709408)* 6523 Oregon Chickadee Rd., Weeki Wachee, FL 34613-8353 USA Tel 352-592-5292 (phone/fax)
E-mail: lwnorris@hitter.net; lwnorris@bellsouth.net.
Pink Elephant Pr. The, *(978-0-9772975)* P.O. Box 1153, Jonesboro, GA 30236-1153 USA (SAN 257-2532) Toll Free: 800-583-1439 (phone/fax)
E-mail: info@thepinkelephantpress.com
Web site: http://www.thepinkelephantpress.com.
Pink Granite Pr., *(978-0-9766737)* P.O. Box 231, Thousand Island Park, NY 13692-0231 USA Tel 613-549-6575.
Pink Hyacinth Press *See* **Kelly, Katherine**
Pink Kiss Publishing Co., *(978-0-615-29068-3; 978-0-9828795; 978-0-9835756; 978-0-9847455; 978-0-9851909; 978-0-9858299; 978-0-9885632; 978-0-9895580; 978-0-9904442; 978-0-9962965)* 2316 Greenway Dr., Gautier, MS 39553 USA
E-mail: pinkkisspublishing@pinkkisspublishing.com; glenda099@cableone.net
Web site: http://www.pinkkisspublishing.com.
Pink Lemonade, LLC, *(978-0-9799159)* 297 Sunset Pk. Dr., Prescott, AZ 86303 USA
E-mail: zuzu@cableone.net
Web site: http://www.thecupcakesclub.com.
Pink Pig Pr., *(978-0-9816360)* 980 Broadway, Suite 248, Thornwood, NY 10594 USA Tel 914-747-8188
Dist(s): **Bookmasters Distribution.**
Pink Stucco Pr., *(978-0-9717796)* 36 Dexter St., Waltham, MA 02453-5017 USA; *Imprints:* Mystic Night Books (Mystic Night Bks)
E-mail: publishing@pinkstucco.net
Web site: http://www.pinkstucco.net/psp/.
Pink&Brown Publishing, LLP, *(978-0-615-36448-3)* 35 E. Main St. Suite 373, Avon, CT 06001 USA Tel 860-674-0292
E-mail: marycashman@comcast.net
Dist(s): **West.**
Pinkney, Gail, *(978-0-9799320)* 1185 Collier Rd NW Apt. 10E, Atlanta, GA 30318-8218 USA
E-mail: pinkneycorey@yahoo.com
Web site: http://www.dreamteambook.com.
Pinkney Wilcox, JoAnn, *(978-0-9764191)* Orders Addr.: 4044 George Busbee Pkwy. #8304, Kennesaw, GA 30144 USA Tel 678-768-5644
E-mail: joannpwilcox@yahoo.com
Web site: http://www.booksbyjpw.com.
Pinkston, Anastasia, *(978-0-9790515)* 500 Moonraker Dr. Apt. 107, Chesapeake, VA 23320-4051 USA
E-mail: anapinkston@yahoo.com
Web site: http://www.cafepress.com/pinkston.
Pinnacle Press *See* **Capital Communications, Inc.**
Pinnacle Press *See* **Mountaintop Pr.**
Pinnacle Pr., *(978-0-9745542)* 25 Country Estates W., East Durham, NY 12423 USA Tel 518-239-8003 Do not confuse with companies with the same name in Little Rock, AR, Cary, NC, Spokane, WA, Nashville, TN, Franklin, TN, Saint Louis, MO
E-mail: foxykate2001@yahoo.com.
Pinninti Pubs., *(978-0-9703474)* 120 Carter Rd., Princeton, NJ 08540-2111 USA
E-mail: pkrao@dr.com
Web site: http://www.pinnintipublishers.com.
Pinpoint Color *See* **Pinpoint Printing**
Pinpoint Printing, *(978-0-9702324)* 5115 E. Highland Dr., Jonesboro, AR 72401 USA Tel 870-931-6200; Fax: 870-931-5800
E-mail: dkelley@mkbmarketing.com
Web site: http://www.pinpointprinting.com.
Pinter & Martin Ltd. (GBR) *(978-0-9530964; 978-1-905177; 978-1-78066) Dist. by* **Natl Bk Netwk.**
Pintos, Yoselem G., *(978-0-9800127; 978-1-61196)* 93-64 204th St., Hollis, NY 11423 USA Tel 646-634-9490
E-mail: yoselem@hotmail.com.
Pinup Vintage *See* **Pinup Vintage**
Pinup Vintage, *(978-0-692-76674-3; 978-0-692-76689-7)*.
Pinwheel Bks., *(978-0-9832577; 978-0-9854248; 978-1-940741)* Orders Addr.: PO BOX 491470, Key Biscayne, FL 33149 USA Tel 617-794-7976
E-mail: publisher@pinwheelbooks.com
Web site: www.pinwheelbooks.com.
Pinyon Publishing, *(978-0-9821561; 978-1-936671)* 23847 V66 Trail, Montrose, CO 81403 USA Tel 970-596-8676
E-mail: susanelliott@pinyon-publishing.com
Web site: http://www.pinyon-publishing.com.
Pinz, Shelley Music, *(978-0-9700251)* Orders Addr.: P.O. Box 275, Atlantic Beach, NY 11509 USA Tel 516-371-4437; Fax: 516-371-4437 (*51); Edit Addr.: 2100 Atlantic Blvd., Atlantic Beach, NY 11509 USA.
Pioneer Clubs, *(978-0-9743503; 978-1-934725; 978-0-9853008; 978-0-9885794)* Orders Addr.: P.O. Box 788, Wheaton, IL 60187-0788 USA (SAN 225-4891) Tel 630-293-1600; Fax: 630-293-3053; Toll Free: 800-694-2582; Edit Addr.: 27 W. 130 St. Charles Rd., Carol Stream, IL 60188-1999 USA (SAN 669-2419)
E-mail: info@pioneerclubs.org
Web site: http://www.pioneerclubs.org.
Pioneer Poet Publishing, *(978-0-615-55095-4; 978-0-615-65742-4)* 10651 MacGregor Dr., Pensacola, FL 32514 USA Tel 850-748-8895
E-mail: gincru@gmail.com
Dist(s): **CreateSpace Independent Publishing Platform**
Lulu Pr., Inc.
Pioneer Valley Bks. *Imprint of* **Pioneer Valley Bks.**
Pioneer Valley Bks., *(978-1-58453; 978-1-932570; 978-1-60343)* 155A Industrial Drive, Northhampton, MA 01060 USA Tel 4137273573; Fax: 4137278211; *Imprints:* Pioneer Valley Books (PioValley Bks)
E-mail: Christine@pvep.com; Shanique@pvep.com; lauri@pvep.com; gina@pvep.com; nick@pvep.com
Web site: http://www.pioneervalleybooks.com.
Pioneer Valley Educational Press, Incorporated *See* **Pioneer Valley Bks.**
Piper, J.G., *(978-0-9916561)* P.O. Box 14018, Columbus, OH 43214 USA Tel 614-262-7896
E-mail: books@jgpiper.com
Web site: http://jgpiper.com.
Piper Verlag GmbH (DEU) *(978-3-492; 978-3-89029; 978-3-8225; 978-3-89521; 978-3-921909) Dist. by* **Distribks Inc.**
Pippin & Maxx Arts & Entertain, LLC, *(978-0-9818747)* 533 Choctaw Rd., Jackson, MS 39206-3920 USA (SAN 856-7794) Tel 601-982-9394 (phone/fax)
E-mail: amile@pippinandmaxx.com
Web site: http://www.pippinandmaxx.com.
Pippin Pr., *(978-0-945912)* Orders Addr.: P.O. Box 1347, New York, NY 10028 USA (SAN 247-8366) Tel 212-288-4920; Fax: 732-225-1562; Edit Addr.: 229 E. 85th St., New York, NY 10028 USA.
Pipton Pr., *(978-0-9828203)* Orders Addr.: 1457 Capri Ave., Petaluma, CA 94954 USA; Edit Addr.: 2506 Castello St., Oakland, CA 94602 USA
E-mail: ginaartbooks@gmail.com.
Pirate Island Pr., *(978-0-9799326)* 3750-A Airport Blvd., No. 224, Mobile, AL 36608 USA (SAN 855-0026) Tel 251-650-4147; Fax: 251-928-9841; Toll Free: 877-689-6660
E-mail: pirateisland@bellsouth.net
Web site: http://www.thrivers.com; http://www.jihadgerm.com
Dist(s): **Bookmasters Distribution.**
Pirate Publishing International, *(978-0-9674081)* 6323 St. Andrews Cir., No. 5, Fort Myers, FL 33919-1719 USA Tel 941-939-4845
E-mail: SuperK@juno.com
Dist(s): **ebrary, Inc.**
Piroux, Raymond, *(978-0-9729815)* Orders Addr.: 2014 Holland Ave. #719, Port Huron, MI 48060 USA (SAN 255-3899)
Web site: http://www.raymondpiroux.com.
P.I.T. Pubns., *(978-0-9760608)* 120 Deweese Dr., Waggaman, LA 70094-2480 USA Tel 504-436-7012.
Pitcher, Jan, *(978-0-9795877)* 208 Tait Ave., Los Gatos, CA 95030 USA
E-mail: janpitcher@verizon.net.
Pitchstone LLC, *(978-0-9728875; 978-0-9844932; 978-0-9852815; 978-1-939578; 978-1-63431)* 848 Sedgefield St., Durham, NC 27705-4251 USA
Web site: http://www.pitchstonepublishing.com
Dist(s): **BookBaby**
Follett School Solutions
Independent Pubs. Group
MyiLibrary
ebrary, Inc.
Pitspopany Pr. *Imprint of* **Simcha Media Group**
Pittsburgh Literary Arts Network LLC, *(978-0-9727319)* P.O. Box 226, Oakmont, PA 15139 USA Tel 412-820-2507; *Imprints:* Blacktypewriter Press (Blacktypewriter Pr)
E-mail: info@blacktypewriter.com
Web site: http://www.blacktypewriter.com.
PitziGil Pr. *Imprint of* **PitziGil Pubns.**
PitziGil Pubns., *(978-0-9846397; 978-0-9914760; 978-0-9970488; 978-0-9985426)* Orders Addr.: P.O. Box 1315, Gaffney, SC 29342-1315 USA (SAN 860-1550) Tel 864-488-7320; *Imprints:* PitziGil Press (PitziGil Pr)
E-mail: pitzigil@yahoo.com; di@pitzigilpublications.com
Web site: www.pitzigilpublications.com.
Pivotal Force, *(978-0-9740473)* 632 Skyview Rd., Bellville, TX 77418 USA (SAN 256-4319) Tel 979-865-9213
E-mail: pivotalforce@evl.net
Web site: http://www.pivotalforce.com.
Pixel Mouse Hse., *(978-1-939322)* P.O. Box 20241, Huntington Station, NY 11746 USA Tel 631-850-3497
E-mail: info@pixelmousehouse.com
Web site: www.pixelmousehouse.com.
Pixelated Publishing *Imprint of* **Faithful Publishing**
Pixelpics Publishing, *(978-0-9747826)* 4801 Secret Harbor Dr., Jacksonville, FL 32257 USA
Web site: http://www.pixelpics.net.
Pixels Publishing, *(978-0-9728743)* P.O. Box 10, La Fox, IL 60147 USA
E-mail: customerservice@pixelspublishing.com
Web site: http://www.pixelspublishing.com.
Pixie Stuff LLC, *(978-0-9761421; 978-0-9795832; 978-0-9826081; 978-0-9833364; 978-0-9850897; 978-0-9850898; 978-0-9854666; 978-0-9890806; 978-0-9916167; 978-0-9862115; 978-0-9966836; 978-0-9974255; 978-0-9978570)* Orders Addr.: 18 Brighton Way, Saint Louis, MO 63105 USA Tel 314-721-4107; Fax: 314-721-4107
E-mail: jennifer@thumbsupjohnnie.com; jennifer@hiredink.com
Web site: http://www.thumbsupjohnnie.com; www.hiredink.com.
PixyJack Pr., Inc., *(978-0-9658098; 978-0-9773724; 978-1-936555)* Orders Addr.: P.O. Box 149, Masonville, CO 80541 USA Tel 303-810-2850; Toll Free Fax: 888-273-7499
E-mail: info@pixyjackpress.com
Web site: http://www.pixyjackpress.com.
Pizzazz Publishing, *(978-0-9744936)* Orders Addr.: P.O. Box 415, Victoria, MN 55386 USA Tel 952-368-1903; Fax: 952-944-0399
E-mail: psimenson@aol.com
Web site: http://www.pizzazzpublishing.com
Dist(s): **Quality Bks., Inc.**
PJR Assocs., Ltd., *(978-0-9790796)* Orders Addr.: P.O. Box 2482, Alexandria, VA 22301 USA Fax: 703-683-4348; Edit Addr.: 910 Junior St., Alexandria, VA 22301 USA
E-mail: patrichards@pjrassociates.com
Web site: http://www.pjrassociates.com.
PJs Corner, *(978-0-9745615; 978-1-933158)* P.O. Box 39, Taft, CA 93268 USA Tel 661-765-7216; Fax: 661-770-8608; *Imprints:* Twiglet The Little Christmas Tree (Twiglet)
E-mail: memories@pjscorner.net
Web site: http://www.pjscorner.net.
PJS Publishing, *(978-0-9743177; 978-0-615-40511-7)* 40344 Redbud Dr., Oakhurst, CA 93644 USA Tel 559-641-5994
E-mail: steve@tycooney.com.
PK Bks. Inc., *(978-0-9827347; 978-0-9846799; 978-0-9891177)* 512 Terrace Rd., Bayport, NY 11705-1528 USA
E-mail: jnewbauer6@hotmail.com
Dist(s): **Lightning Source, Inc.**
†Place In The Woods, The, *(978-0-932991)* 3900 Glenwood Ave., Golden Valley, MN 55422-5302 USA (SAN 689-058X) Tel 763-374-2120; Fax: 952-593-5593
E-mail: placewoods@aol.com; differentbooks@aol.com
Dist(s): **Social Studies Schl. Service**; *CIP.*
Placenames Press *See* **Back Channel Pr.**
Plaidswede Publishing, *(978-0-9626832; 978-0-9755216; 978-0-9790784; 978-0-9840650; 978-0-9837400; 978-0-9889176; 978-0-9962182)* P.O. Box 269, Concord, NH 03302-0269 USA Tel 603-226-1020; Toll Free: 800-267-9044
E-mail: gnews@empire.net
Web site: http://www.plaidswede.com.
Plain Vision Publishing, *(978-0-9761628; 978-0-9848234; 978-0-9910594; 978-0-9971664; 978-1-947820)* Eb#141 Paria Dr. Aripero Village Rousillac, La Brea, TTO Tel 868-704-6397; 984 Ashford St., Brooklyn, NY 11207 Tel 347-652-0883 Do not confuse with Plain Vision Publishing in Kihei, HI
E-mail: info@pvppress.com; eguadeloupe@pvppressl.com
Web site: http://www.pvppress.com
Dist(s): **Lightning Source, Inc.**
Plain White Pr., LLC, *(978-0-9760250; 978-0-9777383; 978-0-9815004; 978-0-9815964; 978-1-936005)* Orders Addr.: 17 Chadwick Rd., West Harrison, NY 10604-1802 USA (SAN 850-0886)
E-mail: julie@plainwhitepress.com
Web site: http://www.plainwhitepress.com.
Plan B Bks, *(978-0-9785798)* P.O. Box 300307, University City, MO 63130 USA
E-mail: abby@planbbooks.com
Web site: http://www.planbbooks.com.
Planet Bronx Productions, *(978-0-9765566)* P.O. Box 672146, Bronx, NY 10467-0803 USA; *Imprints:* PAPO Brand (PAPO)
E-mail: ivanvelezjr@planetbronx.com; admin@planetbronx.com
Web site: http://www.planetbronx.com.
Planet Dexter *Imprint of* **Penguin Publishing Group**
Planeta Mexicana Editorial S. A. de C. V. (MEX) *(978-968-406; 978-970-690) Dist. by* **Lectorum Pubns.**
Planeta Publishing *Imprint of* **Planeta Publishing Corp.**
Planeta Publishing Corp., *(978-0-9715256; 978-0-9719950; 978-0-9748724; 978-1-933169; 978-0-9795042)* 999 Ponce De Leon Blvd. Ste. 1045, Coral Gables, FL 33134-3047 USA; *Imprints:* Planeta Publishing (PlanPubng)
E-mail: mnorman@planetapublishing.com
Web site: http://www.planeta.es
Dist(s): **Ediciones Universal**
Ingram Publisher Services
Two Rivers Distribution.
Plankton Pr., *(978-0-9774074)* 5692 Kalanianaole Hwy., Honolulu, HI 96821 USA Tel 808-373-1016; Fax: 808-373-5381
Web site: www.planktonpress.com.
†Planned Parenthood Federation of America, Inc., *(978-0-934586; 978-1-930996; 978-1-935100)* 434 W. 33rd St., New York, NY 10001 USA (SAN 205-1281) Tel 212-541-4653
E-mail: julia.scheinbeim@ppfa.org
Web site: http://www.plannedparenthood.org/store; *CIP.*
Planning/Communications, *(978-0-9622019; 978-1-884587)* 7215 Oak Ave., River Forest, IL 60305-1935 USA (SAN

253-8717) Tel 708-366-5200; Fax: 708-366-5280; Toll Free: 888-366-5200 (orders only)
E-mail: info@planningcommunications.com; dl@planningcommunications.com
Web site: http://www.jobfindersonline.com; http://www.planningcommunications.com; http://www.dreamitdoit.net.

Plant Kingdom Communications, *(978-0-9834114)* 1503 Gates Ct., Morris Plains, NJ 07950 USA Tel 201-745-5494
E-mail: basia@plantkingdomcommunications.com
Web site: www.PlantKingdomCommunications.com.

Plant the Seed Publishing, *(978-0-9759790)* 4361 Fiesta Ln., Houston, TX 77004 USA Tel 713-747-0026
E-mail: rr4361@aol.com
Web site: http://hometown.aol.com/rr4361/myhomepage/business.

Plantain Pr., Inc., *(978-0-9816262)* P.O. Box 37, Cruz Bay, VI 00831-0037 USA (SAN 856-0838) Tel 340-344-6123
E-mail: info@vitaxhelp.com.

Plata Publishing, *(978-1-61268)* 4330 N. Civic Ctr. Plaza Suite 100, Scottsdale, AZ 85251 USA Tel 480-998-6971
E-mail: d.leong@richdad.com
Dist(s): **Ingram Publisher Services**
Smashwords
Two Rivers Distribution.

Plataforma Editorial SL (ESP) *(978-84-15115; 978-84-15577; 978-84-15750; 978-84-15880; 978-84-16096; 978-84-16256; 978-84-935962; 978-84-96981) Dist. by* **Lectorum Pubns.**

Platinum Bks., *(978-0-9746503)* P.O. Box 660876, Arcadia, CA 91066-0876 USA (SAN 255-7525) Do not confuse with companies with the same name in Alpharetta, GA, Washington, DC
E-mail: hongdenise@yahoo.com
Web site: http://www.happierkids.com.

Platinum Medallion Children's Bks., *(978-1-929489)* Div. of EDS Design & Animation, 2705 Ridge Rd., Huntingtown, MD 20639 USA Tel 410-535-6992; Fax: 410-535-7643
E-mail: doug@dougweb.com; edsdesign@dsmith.com
Web site: http://www.platinum-medallion.com.

Platinum Rose Publishing, *(978-0-9742948)* 16619 W. Sierra Hwy., Canyon Country, CA 91351 USA
Web site: http://www.platinumrose.com.

Platte Publishing *See* **Forsberg, Michael Photography**

Platypus Media, L.L.C., *(978-1-930775)* Orders Addr.: 725 Eighth St., SE, Washington, DC 20003 USA Tel 202-546-1674; Fax: 202-546-2356; Toll Free: 877-752-8977
E-mail: info@platypusmedia.com
Web site: http://www.platypusmedia.com
Dist(s): **MyiLibrary**
National Bk. Network.

Play Ball Publishing, *(978-0-615-17947-6)* 891 Juliana Cove, Collierville, TN 38017 USA Tel 901-240-1353
E-mail: tmanso9@aol.com.

Play Odyssey Inc., *(978-0-9799441; 978-0-9825931)* 3 Alan Rd., Spring Valley, NY 10977 USA (SAN 854-8463) Tel 520-400-5188; Fax: 310-575-8873
E-mail: mgill@playoi.com
Web site: http://playoi.com; http://worksheetlab.com.

Playdate Kids Publishing, *(978-1-933721)* 1901 Main St., Santa Monica, CA 90405 USA (SAN 257-571X) Toll Free: 800-587-1501
E-mail: info@fmrockskids.com
Web site: http://www.theplaydatekids.com/.

Player Piano Mouse Productions (PPMP), *(978-0-9797794)* 883 S. Iowa St., Suite 105, Dodgeville, WI 53533 USA.

Player Pr., *(978-0-9623966)* 139-22 Caney Ln., Rosedale, NY 11422 USA Tel 718-528-3285 Do not confuse with Player Press LLC in New York, NY.

Players Pr., Inc., *(978-0-88734)* P.O. Box 1132, Studio City, CA 91614-0132 USA (SAN 239-0213) Tel 818-789-4980
E-mail: Playerspress@att.net
Dist(s): **Empire Publishing Service.**

PlayGround *Imprint of* **Forest Hill Publishing, LLC**

Playground Pr., *(978-0-9790033)* 1951 W. Rochelle Ave., Glendale, WI 53209 USA (SAN 852-1832) Tel 414-352-1590
E-mail: trishwilliams@trishwilliams.net
Web site: http://www.trishwilliams.net.

Playhouse Publishing, *(978-1-57151; 978-1-878338)* 1566 Akron Peninsula Rd., Akron, OH 44313 USA Tel 330-762-6800; Fax: 330-762-2230; Toll Free: 800-762-6775
E-mail: info@playhousepublishing.com
Web site: http://www.nibble-me-books.com; http://www.playhousepublishing.com; http://www.littlelucyandfriends.com.

Playing Pig Pr., *(978-0-9788324)* 922 S. 87th Ave., Omaha, NE 68114 USA (SAN 851-7452) Tel 402-399-0516
E-mail: bettyhan@cox.net
Web site: http://FrecklesandMaya.com.

PlayinTime Productions, Inc., *(978-1-932895; 978-1-59860)* 19525 Valdez Dr., Tarzana, CA 91356-4946 USA Toll Free: 800-310-0087
E-mail: playintime@aol.com
Web site: http://www.playintime.com.

Playmore, Incorporated, Publishers *See* **Waldman Publishing Corp.**

Playor, Editorial, S.A. (ESP) *(978-84-359) Dist. by* **Continental Bk.**

Playscripts, Inc., *(978-0-9709046; 978-0-9819099; 978-1-62384; 978-1-68069)* 450 Fashion Ave. Ste. 809, New York, NY 10123-0805 USA Toll Free Fax: 866-203-4519
E-mail: info@playscripts.com
Web site: http://www.playscripts.com
Dist(s): **Consortium Bk. Sales & Distribution.**

Playscripts.com *See* **Playscripts, Inc.**

Playwrights Canada Pr. (CAN) *(978-0-88754; 978-0-919834; 978-1-55155) Dist. by* **Consort Bk Sales.**

Plaza & Janes Editories, S.A. (ESP) *(978-84-01) Dist. by* **Distribks Inc.**

Plaza Joven, S.A. (ESP) *(978-84-7655) Dist. by* **Lectorum Pubns.**

Pleasant Co. *Imprint of* **American Girl Publishing, Inc.**

Pleasant Company Publications *See* **American Girl Publishing, Inc.**

Pleasant Plains Pr., *(978-0-9790906)* 366 Kingsberry Dr, Suite 100, Annapolis, MD 21409 USA Tel 410-757-1318
E-mail: boaterbrenda@comcast.net
Web site: http://www.pleasantplainspress.com.

Pleasant St. Pr., *(978-0-9792035; 978-1-935025)* P.O. Box 520, Raynham Center, MA 02768 USA (SAN 852-7598) Tel 508-822-3075; Fax: 508-977-2498
E-mail: orders@pleasantstpress.com; info@pleasantstpress.com
Web site: http://www.pleasantstpress.com
Dist(s): **Independent Pubs. Group.**

Pleasure Boat Studio *See* **Pleasure Boat Studio: A Literary Pr.**

Pleasure Boat Studio: A Literary Pr., *(978-0-912887; 978-0-9651413; 978-1-929355)* 201 W. 89th St., New York, NY 10024 USA Tel 212-362-8563; Toll Free: 888-810-5308; 721 Mt. Pleasant Rd., Port Angeles, WA 98362 (SAN 299-0075)
E-mail: pleasboat@nyc.rr.com
Web site: http://www.pleasureboatstudio.com
Dist(s): **Brodart Co.**
Partners/West Book Distributors
SPD-Small Pr. Distribution
Smashwords.

Pleiness Publishing, *(978-0-9742472)* 45937 Duke Dr., Chesterfield Township, MI 48051 USA
E-mail: cpbusy@comcast.net.

PLEO, *(978-0-9660617)* 302 Park Tree Terr Bldg. 1311, Orlando, FL 32825-3474 USA Tel 407-277-3776; 321-297-5531.

pleo leonard productions *See* **PLEO**

Plexus Publishing, Ltd. (GBR) *(978-0-85965) Dist. by* **PerseuPGW.**

Plicata Pr. LLC, *(978-0-9828205; 978-0-9848400; 978-0-9903102)* P.O. Box 32, Gig Harbor, WA 98335 USA Tel 253-851-2444
E-mail: janwalker@centurytel.net; info@plicatapress.com
Web site: http://www.plicatapress.com.

PLMII LLC *See* **McCall, Philip Lee II**

Plouffe, Delci, *(978-0-692-84708-4)* 1102 Clark Ave, Lewistown, MT 59457 USA Tel 406-366-4174
E-mail: jeffwcrawford5+LVP0003374@gmail.com; jeffwcrawford5+LVP0003374@gmail.com.

†Plough Publishing Hse., *(978-0-87486)* 151 Bowne Dr., Walden, NY 12586 USA (SAN 202-0092) Tel 845-572-3455; Fax: 845-572-3472; Toll Free: 800-521-8011
E-mail: info@plough.com
Web site: http://www.plough.com
Dist(s): **Ingram Publisher Services**
MyiLibrary
Spring Arbor Distributors, Inc.; *CIP.*

Plowshare Media, *(978-0-9821145; 978-0-9860428)* P.O. Box 278, La Jolla, CA 92038 USA (SAN 857-2933) Tel 858-454-5446
E-mail: tt@plowsharemedia.com
Web site: http://www.plowsharemedia.com.

Pluegl Bks., *(978-0-9760868)* Orders Addr.: P.O. Box 16622, Chapel Hill, NC 27516-6622 USA; Edit Addr.: 114 Waverly Forest Ln., Chapel Hill, NC 27516 USA.

Plum Blossom Bks. *Imprint of* **Parallax Pr.**

Plum Tree Pr., *(978-0-9653535; 978-1-892476)* Orders Addr.: 531 Silcott Rd., Clarkston, WA 99403 USA Tel 509-758-2820; 509-332-1520 (Pine Orchard Distributors)
E-mail: bookinfo@pineorchard.com; gpducky@aol.com
Web site: http://www.pineorchard.com/plumtree; http://www.chinchinian.com
Dist(s): **Partners/West Book Distributors**
Pine Orchard, Inc.

Pluma Productions, *(978-1-889848)* Div. of Southern Dominican Province, USA, Orders Addr.: P.O. Box 1138, Los Angeles, CA 90078-1138 USA Tel 213-463-6488; Fax: 213-466-6645; Edit Addr.: 1977 Carmen Ave., Los Angeles, CA 90068 USA
E-mail: pluma@eathlink.net.

Plume *Imprint of* **Penguin Publishing Group**

Pluriverse Publishing, *(978-0-9846119)* P.O. Box 3305, Ponte Vedra Beach, FL 32004-3305 USA
E-mail: isbn-registration@epluriverse.com; information@ePluriverse.com
Web site: http://www.ePluriverse.com
Dist(s): **Smashwords.**

Plushy Feely Corp, *(978-0-9837668)* 11 San Rafael Ave., San Anselmo, CA 94960 USA Tel 415-454-4600 (Tel/Fax)
E-mail: kerri@kimochis.com
Web site: www.kimochis.com.

Pluteo Pleno, *(978-1-937847)* 5516 N Linder Ave., Chicago, IL 60630 USA Tel 815-459-2789
E-mail: pete@pluteopleno.com
Web site: http://www.pluteopleno.com.

Pluto Project, *(978-0-9662982)* 601 Van Ness, No. E3801, San Francisco, CA 94102-3200 USA Tel 415-647-5501; Fax: 415-840-0060; Toll Free: 888-227-5886
E-mail: walter@plutoproject.com
Web site: http://www.plutoproject.com
Dist(s): **Bookmasters Distribution**
New Leaf Distributing Co., Inc.
Quality Bks., Inc.

PM, INK, *(978-0-9753852)* 522 aNDERSON aVE., Rockville, MD 20850 USA (SAN 256-0275) Tel 301-424-0638 (phone/fax)
E-mail: pm.ink@verizon.net
Web site: http://www.pmink.net.

PM Moon Pubs., Ltd., *(978-0-9817777; 978-0-615-15573-9; 978-0-615-15734-4)* Orders Addr.: P.O. Box 110813, Cleveland, OH 44111 USA Tel 216-671-8445; Edit Addr.: 3308 W. 111th St., Cleveland, OH 44111-3642 USA
Dist(s): **Lulu Pr., Inc.**

PM Pr., *(978-1-60486; 978-1-62963)* P.O. Box 23912, Oakland, CA 94623 USA
Web site: http://www.pmpress.org
Dist(s): **AK Pr. Distribution**
Ebsco Publishing
Follett School Solutions
Independent Pubs. Group
ebrary, Inc.

P.M. Publishing, *(978-0-9798346)* Orders Addr.: P.O. Box 185, Lottsburg, VA 22511 USA (SAN 854-5200); Edit Addr.: 353 Walmsley Rd., Callao, VA 22435 USA
E-mail: pinkie_thecat@yahoo.com.

PMK Press *See* **Dancer's Publishing**

Pneuma Life Publishing, Inc., *(978-1-56229)* Orders Addr.: 12138 Central Ave. #251, Mitchellville, MD 20721 USA (SAN 297-3057); *Imprints:* Christian Living Books, Inc. (Christian Livng)
E-mail: info@pneumalife.com; info@christianlivingbooks.com
Web site: http://www.pneumalife.com; http://christianlivingbooks.com
Dist(s): **Anchor Distributors**
Lightning Source, Inc.
Smashwords
Spring Arbor Distributors, Inc.

POCEE Publishing, *(978-0-9824812)* 1260 Wesley Ave., Pasadena, CA 91104 USA Tel 626-794-8524.

Pocket Books, *(978-1-4165)* 1230 Avenue of the Americas, New York, NY 10020 USA
Dist(s): **Simon & Schuster, Inc.**

Pocket Books/Star Trek *Imprint of* **Pocket Bks./Star Trek**

Pocket Bks./Star Trek, 1230 Avenue of the Americas, New York, NY 10020 USA; *Imprints:* Pocket Books/Star Trek (PockBksStar)
Dist(s): **Simon & Schuster, Inc.**

Pocket Pr., Inc., *(978-1-884493; 978-1-61371)* P.O. Box 25124, Portland, OR 97298 USA Toll Free Fax: 877-643-3732; Toll Free: 888-237-2110
E-mail: sales@pocketpressinc.com
Web site: http://www.pocketpressinc.com.

Pocket Pubn., A, *(978-0-9721333)* 6701 Democracy Blvd., Suite 300, Bethesda, MD 20817 USA Tel 301-468-4905 Do not confuse with Pocket Publications in York, PA
E-mail: david_new@msn.com
Web site: http://www.home.talkcity.com/LibertySt/davidwnew.

PockitBook Publishing, Inc., *(978-0-9761716)* P.O. Box 6753, Athens, GA 30604-4120 USA Tel 706-354-8380
E-mail: pockitbook@bellsouth.net
Web site: http://www.pockitbook.com.

Pocol Pr., *(978-1-929763)* Orders Addr.: 6023 Pocol Dr., Clifton, VA 20124-1333 USA (SAN 253-6021) Tel 703-830-5862; Fax: 703-830-5862
E-mail: chrisandtom@erols.com
Web site: http://www.pocolpress.com.

Poet Tree Pubns., *(978-0-9658926)* P.O. Box 571444, Salt Lake City, UT 84157-1444 USA Tel 801-685-9398; Fax: 801-262-2324
Dist(s): **Tree Hse. Distribution.**

Poet's Passage Pr., The, *(978-0-9841252)* Calle Cruz 203, Old San Juan, PR 00901 USA (SAN 858-4826) Tel 787-567-9235
E-mail: ducart@yahoo.com.

Poets Wear Prada, *(978-0-9817678; 978-0-9841844; 978-0-615-60020-8; 978-0-615-60651-4; 978-0-615-65019-7; 978-0-615-76123-7; 978-0-615-81963-1; 978-0-615-83322-4; 978-0-615-84885-3; 978-0-615-86358-0; 978-0-615-87926-0; 978-0-615-88477-6; 978-0-615-91007-9; 978-0-615-97110-0; 978-0-615-98830-6; 978-0-692-22769-5; 978-0-692-28457-5; 978-0-692-30379-5; 978-0-692-45069-7; 978-0-692-67933-3; 978-0-9979811; 978-1-946116)* 533 Bloomfield St., 2nd Flr., Hoboken, NJ 07030 USA (SAN 856-5031) Tel 201-253-0561 office
E-mail: poetswearpradanj@att.net; roxy533@yahoo.com
Web site: http://thesmokingbook.blogspot.com; http://poetsweaprada.blogspot.com; http://twitter.com/pradapoet; http://pwpbooks.blogspot.com; http://issuu.com/pradapoet/; http://www.facebook.com/pages/Poets-Wear-Prada/4148 3895438
Dist(s): **CreateSpace Independent Publishing Platform.**

Pogo *Imprint of* **Jump! Inc.**

Pohl, J. Assocs., *(978-0-939332)* 307 N. Shady Ave., Houston, PA 15342 USA (SAN 220-181X) Tel 724-746-1178
E-mail: judepohl@comcast.net.

Pohrte, Dorey Publishing, Inc., *(978-0-9722296)* 917 Maple Rd., Buffalo, NY 14221 USA Tel 716-631-1256
E-mail: kathysue1@adelphia.net.

Point of Grace Entertainment Group, *(978-0-9706112; 978-0-9727644)* 3575 N. Beltline Rd., Suite 345, Irving, TX 75062 USA Tel 972-331-2538; Fax: 972-331-2569; Toll Free: 877-447-2233
E-mail: pgedist@yahoo.com.

Point of Life, Inc., *(978-0-9668069; 978-0-9819367)* 3032 E. Commercial Blvd., Ft. Lauderdale, FL 33308 USA
E-mail: mikmikl@aol.com
Web site: http://www.pointoflife.com.

Point Publishing, *(978-0-9663560)* Orders Addr.: 960 Sage Crest Dr., Wenatchee, WA 98801 USA Tel 509-670-6250; *Imprints:* Orchard Press (Orchard Press) Do not confuse with Point Publishing, Madison, WI
E-mail: thacken@genext.net
Dist(s): **Lulu Pr., Inc.**

Point To Point Publishing, *(978-0-9714147)* 5108 Brittany Dr., Old Hickory, TN 37138 USA Fax: 615-758-8495.

Poisoned Pen Pr., *(978-1-890208; 978-1-929345; 978-1-59058; 978-1-61595; 978-1-4642; 978-1-62886)* Orders Addr.: 6962 E. First Ave., Suite 103, Scottsdale, AZ 85251 USA (SAN 299-6898) Tel 480-945-3375; Fax: 480-949-1707; Toll Free: 800-421-3976
E-mail: info@poisonedpenpress.com; sales@poisonedpenpress.com
Web site: http://www.poisonedpenpress.com; www.thepoisonedpencil.com
Dist(s): **INscribe Digital**
Ingram Publisher Services
MyiLibrary.

Pokemon, USA, Inc., *(978-1-933743; 978-1-60438)* 777 108th Ave. NE, Suite 2000, Bellevue, WA 98004 USA
Web site: http://www.pokemon-tcg.com
Dist(s): **Diamond Bk. Distributors**
Simon & Schuster, Inc.

Pokeweed Pr. (CAN) *(978-1-894323) Dist. by* **IngramPubServ.**

Polaire Pubns., *(978-0-9708500; 978-0-9795218; 978-1-936315)* Div. of Polaire Entertainment Group, Inc., 422 Wolf Run Rd., Bartonville, TX 76226 USA (SAN 254-8291)
E-mail: chmeezepal@earthlink.net
Web site: http://www.animalcompanionsandtheirpeople.com
Dist(s): **DeVorss & Co.**

Polar Bear & Co., *(978-1-882190)* Orders Addr.: P.O. Box 311, Solon, ME 04979 USA (SAN 858-8902) Tel 207 643-2795; Edit Addr.: 8 Brook St., Solon, ME 04979 USA
E-mail: polarbear@polarbearandco.com
Web site: http://www.polarbearandco.com; http://www.polarbearandco.org
Dist(s): **Magazines, Inc.**

Polar Club Publishing, *(978-0-615-22038-3)* 635 Sandy Ridge Dr., Glen Burnie, MD 21061 USA
Dist(s): **Lulu Pr., Inc.**

Polar Surf Enterprises *See* **NORKY AMERICA**

Polaris Bks., *(978-0-9741443)* 11111 W. 8th Ave., Unit A, Lakewood, CO 80215-5516 USA Tel 303-980-0890; Fax: 303-980-0753
E-mail: zubrin@aol.com
Web site: http://www.polarisbooks.net.

Polark, Kelly *See* **Big Smile Pr., LLC**

Polebridge Pr., *(978-0-944344; 978-1-59815)* Orders Addr.: P.O. Box 7268, Santa Rosa, CA 95407 USA Tel 707-523-1323; Fax: 707-523-1350; Toll Free: 877-523-3545
E-mail: accounts@polebridgepress.com
Web site: http://www.polebridgepress.com
Dist(s): **Spring Arbor Distributors, Inc.**

Policy Studies Organization *See* **Westphalia Press**

Polis Bks., *(978-1-940610; 978-1-943818; 978-1-947993)* 1201 Hudson St. No. 211S, Hoboken, NJ 07030 USA
E-mail: jpinter@polisbooks.com
Web site: www.polisbooks.com
Dist(s): **MyiLibrary**
Publishers Group West (PGW).

Polistampa (ITA) *(978-88-8304; 978-88-85977) Dist. by* **CasemateAcad.**

Political Status Education Coordinating Commission *See* **Dept. of Chamorro Affairs**

Poll, Michael Publishing, *(978-1-887560; 978-1-934935; 978-1-61342)* Orders Addr.: P.O. Box 24652, New Orleans, LA 70184 USA; *Imprints:* Cornerstone Book Publishers (Cstone Bk Pubs)
E-mail: 1cornerstonebooks@gmail.com
Web site: http://www.cornerstonepublishers.com.

PollieMarieSolutions, *(978-0-578-18749-5)* 2111 E. Blue Lake Dr., Magnolia, TX 77354 USA.

PollyRhythm Productions, *(978-0-9701249)* Orders Addr.: P.O. Box 7707, New York, NY 10150 USA Tel 212 688 3900; Toll Free Fax: 800 701 7981
E-mail: prprd@attglobal.net
Web site: http://www.pollyrhythm.com.

Pollywog Bog Bks. (CAN) *(978-0-9810575) Dist. by* **IngramPubServ.**

Polychrome Publishing Corp., *(978-1-879965)* 4509 N. Francisco, Chicago, IL 60625-3808 USA Tel 773-478-4455; Fax: 773-478-0786
E-mail: polypub@earthlink.net
Web site: http://www.home.earthlink.net/~polypub.

Polyface, Inc., *(978-0-9638109)* 363 Shuey Rd., Swoope, VA 24479 USA Tel 540-885-3590; Fax: 540-885-5888
Dist(s): **Chelsea Green Publishing.**

Polyglot Pr., Inc., *(978-1-931927; 978-1-4115)* 111 Caenarvon Ln., Haverford, PA 19041-1049 USA Do not confuse with Polyglot Press in Fairfax, VA
E-mail: david@polyglotpress.com
Web site: http://www.polyglotpress.com.

Polygon Publishing, *(978-0-9764768)* 73 Sutton Pl. W., Palm Desert, CA 92211 USA (SAN 256-4521) Tel 760-346-0544; Fax: 760-406-9333
E-mail: polygnpublishing@aol.com
Web site: http://www.polygonpublishing.com/.

Polytope Pr., *(978-0-9670526)* Div. of Tarescent Synductions, Orders Addr.: P.O. Box 1349, Phoenix, AZ 85001 USA Tel 602-271-9922; Fax: 602-230-1991; Edit Addr.: 321 E. Portland, No. 6, Phoenix, AZ 85004 USA
E-mail: polytope@hotmail.com.

Pomegranate Communications, Inc., *(978-0-7649; 978-0-87654; 978-0-917556; 978-1-56640)* Orders Addr.: 19018 NE. Portal Way, Portland, OR 97230 USA (SAN 860-2077) Toll Free: 800-227-1428; Edit Addr.: 19018 NE. Portal Way, Portland, OR 97230 USA Tel 503-328-6500; Fax: 503-328-9330; Toll Free: 800-227-1428; *Imprints:* POMEGRANATE KIDS (POMEGRANATEKID)
E-mail: info@pomegranate.com
Web site: http://www.pomegranate.com.

POMEGRANATE KIDS *Imprint of* **Pomegranate Communications, Inc.**

Pomegranate Publishing, *(978-0-9767377)* P.O. Box 43, Carpinteria, CA 93014 USA Do not confuse with Pomegranate Publishing in Loma Linda, CA
Web site: http://www.pomegranatepublishing.com.

Pontrelli, Jeany, *(978-0-9778456)* 6156 Solstice Dr., Sparks, NV 89436 USA.

PONY *Imprint of* **Stabenfeldt Inc.**

Pony Rock Pr., *(978-0-9759598)* 23484 150th Ave. NE, Thief River Falls, MN 56701 USA.

Poodle Suit Publishing, *(978-0-9728429)* P.O. Box 9844, Phoenix, AZ 85068 USA (SAN 255-1608) Tel 602-943-6766 Toll Free: 800-547-8247
E-mail: lougold@cox.net
Web site: http://www.poodlesuit.com.

Poor Magazine, *(978-0-9742007)* 255 9th St., 3, San Francisco, CA 94103 USA Tel 415-863-6306; Fax: 415-865-1932
E-mail: alex@poormagazine.org
Web site: http://www.poormagazine.org.

PoorHse. Publishing LLC, *(978-0-9896335; 978-1-943468)* 905 Myrtle Ave., Big Bear City, CA 92314 USA (SAN 920-6027) Tel 909-272-0059
E-mail: info@poorhousepublishingllc.com
Web site: poorhousepublishingllc.com
Dist(s): **BookBaby**
Small Pr. United.

Pop Academy of Music, *(978-0-9887710; 978-0-692-39597-4; 978-0-9961631; 978-1-947029)* 4912 Bendahl valley Terr., Richmond, VA 23237 USA Tel 7576131097
Dist(s): **CreateSpace Independent Publishing Platform.**

Pop Pop Pr. *Imprint of* **Micro Publishing Media, Inc.**

Pop Sandbox, Inc. (CAN) *(978-0-9864884) Dist. by* **Diamond Book Dists.**

Pop the Cork Publishing, *(978-0-9741854)* 1629 McGilvra Blvd., E., Seattle, WA 98112 USA Tel 206-720-9779; Fax: 206-720-9771
E-mail: sallyv@isomedia.com
Dist(s): **Hara Publishing Group.**

Popol Vuh Press *See* **Talisman Pr.**

Poppy *Imprint of* **Little, Brown Bks. for Young Readers**

Poppy Blossom Pr., *(978-0-615-24059-6)* 8713 Glenbury Ct., S. Suite 102, Jacksonville, FL 32256 USA
E-mail: hello@poppyblossom.com.

Popstheclub.com, Inc., *(978-0-692-29061-3; 978-0-692-43666-0; 978-0-692-43667-7; 978-0-9988382)* 4160 Lyceum Ave., Los Angeles, CA 90066 USA Tel 3107092484.

Popular Kinetics Pr., *(978-0-9627752)* 6005 Yale Ave., Glen Echo, MD 20812 USA Tel 301-229-2213
E-mail: cbarton@mindspring.com
Web site: http://www.popularkinetics.com
Dist(s): **Independent Pubs. Group.**

Popular Truth, Inc., *(978-0-9631547)* P.O. Box 40656, Indianapolis, IN 76260 USA Toll Free: 888-342-8156
E-mail: anyike@netscape.net.

Porcupine Communications, *(978-0-9792809)* 309 College Ave., Beaver, PA 15009 USA (SAN 853-005X) Tel 412-972-0690
Web site: http://www.porcupinecommunications.com.

Port, Cynthia L., *(978-0-9912278)* 2513 E. Poplar Ct., Bloomington, IN 47401 USA Tel 812-322-7897
E-mail: cynthia.l.port@gmail.com.

Port Hole Pubns., *(978-0-9700274; 978-0-9768107; 978-0-9827627; 978-0-9882659; 978-0-9892608; 978-1-943119)* P.O. Box 205, Westlake, OR 97493-0205 USA
E-mail: porthole@digisys.net
Web site: http://www.ellentraylor.com.

Port Ludlow Bks., *(978-0-9729884)* 20 Keefe Ln., Port Ludlow, WA 98365 USA
E-mail: gldyerjr@waypt.com.

Port Town Publishing, *(978-0-9700544; 978-0-9716239; 978-0-9725990; 978-0-9740833; 978-1-59466)* 5832 Lamborn Ave., Superior, WI 54880-6231 USA; *Imprints:* Little Ones (Little Ones); Growing Years (Growing Years)
E-mail: porttownpublish@aol.com
Web site: http://www.porttownpublishing.bigstep.com.

Port Washington Public Library, *(978-0-9615059)* 1 Library Dr., Port Washington, NY 11050 USA (SAN 694-163X) Tel 516-883-4400.

Portable COO, The, *(978-1-940350)* P.O. Box PO Box 587, Beaverton, OR 97075-0587 USA
E-mail: KarenM@WordWeaverMedia.com.

Portable Pr. *Imprint of* **Readerlink Distribution Services, LLC**

Portable Press *See* **Akashic Bks.**

Portage & Main Pr. (CAN) *(978-0-919566; 978-0-920541; 978-0-9694264; 978-1-894110; 978-1-895411; 978-1-55379) Dist. by* **Orca Bk Pub.**

Portal Ctr. Pr., *(978-1-936902; 978-0-9834956)* P.O. Box 264, Gleneden Beach, OR 97388 USA; *Imprints:* SpiritBooks (SpiritBooks)
E-mail: editor@portalcenterpress.com; sales@portalcenterpress.com
Web site: portalcenterpress.com.

Portals Publishing, *(978-0-692-51890-8; 978-0-692-52862-4; 978-0-9970512; 978-1-946469)* Denouement Literary Agency PO Box 973, Eagle Lake, FL 33839 USA Tel 863-640-6709
Web site: http://BLISSBooksOnline.com; http://DenouementLit.com; http://portalspublishing.com
Dist(s): **CreateSpace Independent Publishing Platform.**

Porter, Inman, *(978-0-9979766)* 32 Leroy St., Apt. 10, New York, NY 10014 USA Tel 478-290-2815
E-mail: inmanporter@gmail.com
Web site: www.inmanporter.com.

Porter, Rosanna *See* **Raisykinder Publishing**

Portfolio Press *See* **Portfolio Pr. Corp.**

Portfolio Pr. Corp., *(978-0-942620)* Orders Addr.: 130 Wineow St., Suite 3, Cumberland, MD 21502 USA Tel 301-724-2795; Fax: 301-724-2796; Toll Free: 877-737-1200; Edit Addr.: 1107 Broadway, 12th Flr., New York, NY 10010 USA (SAN 238-5554) Tel 212-989-8700; Fax: 212-691-3073
E-mail: portfolio@hereintown.net
Web site: http://www.portfoliopress.com.

Portfolio Trade *Imprint of* **Penguin Publishing Group**

Portico Bks., *(978-0-9664867)* Orders Addr.: P.O. Box 6094, Chesterfield, MO 63006 USA Tel 636-527-2822 (phone/fax); Toll Free: 888-641-5353 (phone/fax); Edit Addr.: 1316 Rusticview Dr., Ballwin, MO 63011 USA
E-mail: info@grammarandmore.com
Web site: http://www.grammarandmore.com.

Portland Press, Incorporated *See* **Chihuly Workshop, Inc.**

Portland State University, Ooligan Press *See* **Ooligan Pr.**

Portland Studios, Inc., *(978-0-9797183)* The Point At Pk. Pl. 112 Poinsett Hwy., Greenville, SC 29609 USA (SAN 854-1744) Tel 864-241-0810; Fax: 864-241-0811
E-mail: jpeterson@portlandstudios.com
Web site: http://www.beowulfthebook.com; http://www.portlandstudios.com
Dist(s): **Pioneer Enterprises.**

Portrait Health Publishing, *(978-0-9853555)* Orders Addr.: 175 E Hawthorn Pkwy. Suite 235, Vernon Hills, IL 60061 USA Tel 847-236-0943
E-mail: info@portraithealthpublishing.com
Web site: http://www.portraithealthpublishing.com.

Portunus Publishing Co., *(978-0-9641330; 978-1-886440)* 27875 Berwick Dr., Carmel, CA 93923 USA Tel 831-622-0604; Fax: 310-399-5644
E-mail: service@portunus.net
Dist(s): **Lectorum Pubns., Inc.**

Positive Action For Christ, *(978-1-929784; 978-0-9719491; 978-1-59557)* 502 W. Pippen St., Whitakers, NC 27891 USA Tel 252-437-7771; Fax: 252-437-3297; Toll Free: 800-688-3008; *Imprints:* ProTeens (ProTeens)
Web site: http://www.positiveaction.org.

Positive Imaging, LLC, *(978-0-615-16787-9; 978-0-615-18693-1; 978-0-9842480; 978-0-9856876; 978-1-944071)* 9016 Palace Pwky., Austin, TX 78748 USA (SAN 858-8430) Tel 512-217-4803; 512-282-5717; Fax: 877-288-5496
E-mail: bill@positive-imaging.com; awbenitez@hotmail.com
Web site: http://www.positive-imaging.com; http://www.handyman-business-guide.com/; http://www.woodworking-business.com; http://www.selfpublishingworkbook.com; http://woodworking-biz-solutions.com; http://billbenitez.com; http://self-publish-your-writing.com; http://woodworkingbusinessbook.com; http://selfpublishingworkbook.com; http://woodworking-business-guide.com; http://notesonrelationship.com; http://awilliambenitez.com; http://goodrelationships101.com; http://self-publishing-suppo
Dist(s): **CreateSpace Independent Publishing Platform**
Lulu Pr., Inc.
Smashwords.

Positive Productions, *(978-1-928726)* 934 E. 84th Pl., Suite A, Chicago, IL 60619 USA Tel 773-846-6131; Fax: 773-846-6555; Toll Free: 800-306-3064.

Positive Spin Pr., *(978-0-9773096)* P.O. Box 653, Warren, MI 02885-9998 USA
E-mail: info@positivespinpress.com; lisa@studiocvr.com
Web site: http://www.thehalloweenfairy.com
Dist(s): **Independent Pubs. Group.**

Positive Strokes, *(978-0-9673490)* Orders Addr.: P.O. Box 97271, Raleigh, NC 27624 USA
E-mail: pstrokes@aol.com; healheartsbooks@aol.com.

Positively for Kids, Inc., *(978-0-9634650; 978-0-9765722; 978-0-9778237; 978-0-9786838)* P.O. Box 3283, Kirkland, WA 98083-3283 USA Toll Free: 800-600-5437
E-mail: customerservice@positivelyforkids.com
Web site: http://www.positivelyforkids.com
Dist(s): **American West Bks.**
Brodart Co.
Mackin Bk. Co.

Possum Products, *(978-0-615-12548-0)* 712 Warren Dr., Annapolis, MD 21403 USA Fax: 410-510-1003; 410-263-4473 (call 410-263-1847 first)
E-mail: possumpalette@aol.com.

Post Mortem Publications, Inc., *(978-0-615-30090-0; 978-0-9839074; 978-1-941880)* 146 E. Broad St., Groveland, FL 34736 USA.

Post Oak Hill, *(978-0-9636122)* 235 Shady Hill Ln., Double Oak, TX 75067-8270 USA Tel 817-430-1182.

Potenial Psychotherapy Counseling & Remedial Service, *(978-0-9759889)* 1525 E. 53rd St., Suite 516, 11-2, Chicago, IL 60615 USA.

Potential Developing Ministries, Inc., *(978-0-9745554)* 455 Grason Hwy., Suite 111 Box 153, Lawrenceville, GA 30045 USA
E-mail: pdm@winning.com.

Potential Unlimited Publishing, *(978-0-9740003)* 1400 N. Elmhurst Rd. Unit 416, Mount Prospect, IL 60056 USA Tel 630-728-6046
E-mail: screenwriter1914@gmail.com.

Potoma, Alison Elise, *(978-1-940602)* 6234 Avalon Dr., Wilmington, MA 01887 USA Tel 845-461-1065
E-mail: alisonpotoma@gmail.com
Web site: www.alisonpotoma.com.

Potter Assocs., *(978-0-9758672)* 2305 Jacob Dr., Santa Clara, UT 84765 USA Tel 435-986-3886; Fax: 435-986-3887; *Imprints:* Hot Page Press (HotPP)
E-mail: stanpot@sisna.com.

Potter Craft *Imprint of* **Potter/TenSpeed/Harmony**

Potter Publishing, *(978-0-9856350)* 100 Cherry Tree Hill Ln., Barton, VT 05822 USA Tel 802-525-3311 Do not confuse with Potter Publishing in Elmsford, NY
E-mail: info@cherryyarn.com.

Potters Publishing LLC, *(978-0-9745810)* Orders Addr.: 2204 Blackjack Oak St., Ocoee, FL 34761 USA Tel 407-877-7444
Web site: http://www.potterspublishing.com.

Potter/TenSpeed/Harmony, 1745 Broadway, New York, NY 10019 USA; *Imprints:* Clarkson Potter (Clarkso); Crossing Press (CrossingP); Celestial Arts (CelestialAs); Potter Craft (PotterCraft); Ten Speed Press (TenSpeedPr); Watson-Guptill (WatsonG)
Dist(s): **MyiLibrary**
Penguin Random Hse. LLC.

PottyMD LLC, *(978-0-9762877)* 2216 White Ave., Knoxville, TN 37916 USA Tel 865-525-0000; Fax: 865-525-0262; Toll Free: 877-769-8963
E-mail: support@pottymd.com
Web site: http://www.pottymd.com
Dist(s): **SCB Distributors.**

Poudre Landmarks Foundation, *(978-0-9753849)* 108 N. Meldrum St., Fort Collins, CO 80521 USA Tel 970-221-4220; 970-221-0553
Web site: http://www.poudrelandmarks.com.

Pounce To Success International, Inc., *(978-0-9776074)* 608 1/2 W. Park St., Lamar, CO 81052 USA (SAN 257-7364) Tel 719-201-7470; Toll Free: 800-768-6238.

Pounders Publishing, *(978-0-692-33113-2)* 4545 Barfield Rd, Memphis, TN 38117 USA Tel 901-278-6868
E-mail: pounders@anfa.com.

Pouring the Oil: Poetic Praise Pubns., *(978-0-9760734; 978-0-9841968)* Orders Addr.: P.O. Box 944, Brewster, NY 10509 USA; Edit Addr.: P.O. Box 253, Danbury, CT 06813-0253 USA
E-mail: pouringtheoil@yahoo.com; info@pouringtheoilpublications.com; spoken_word03@yahoo.com
Web site: http://www.pouringtheoilpublications.com.

Powell Hill Pr., *(978-0-9760648)* 8 Packett's Glen, Fairport, NY 14450 USA Tel 585-388-8622
E-mail: scoopwrite@aol.com
Web site: http://www.spiritwolf.info; http://www.powellhillpress.com
Dist(s): **North Country Bks., Inc.**

Power Play Media, *(978-0-9724003; 978-0-9741394; 978-1-934230)* P.O. Box 423, Brandywine, MD 20613 USA Tel 240-375-6908; Fax: 301-579-9913; *Imprints:* Nvision Publishing (NvisPub)
E-mail: tressa428@cs.com
Web site: http://www.nvisionpublishing.com/
Dist(s): **INscribe Digital.**

Power Pr., *(978-0-9748508; 978-0-9825568)* P.O. Box 622, Tyrone, GA 30290 USA Tel 770-486-0758; Fax: 770-486-6687 Do not confuse with Power Press in Torrance CA, Chico CA, Sonoma CA
E-mail: ratto@mindspring.com.

Power Pubns., Inc., *(978-0-9629858; 978-0-9724194; 978-0-615-40283-3; 978-0-615-41417-1)* 185 Randon Terr., Lake Mary, FL 32746 USA (SAN 254-6817) Tel 407-732-4322 (phone/fax) Do not confuse with Power Publications, Inc. in Phoenix, AZ, Mountain City, GA
E-mail: igilbert@cfl.rr.com.

Power Through Faith, *(978-0-9707320)* 1702 Capps St., Durham, NC 27707 USA Tel 919-596-7753.

Power Writings, *(978-0-9641640)* 9019 Wall St., 6F, North Bergen, NJ 07047 USA Fax: 201-869-9179
E-mail: fmelfa02@yahoo.com
Web site: http://www.pharmalanding.com.

Powerband, LLC, *(978-0-9746445)* 16199 Kennedy Rd., Los Gatos, CA 95032-9503 USA Fax: 408-402-0617; 16199 Kennedy Rd., Los Gatos, CA 95032-9503
E-mail: clelliott@mac.com
Web site: http://www.powerbandllc.com.

Power-Glide Foreign Language Courses, *(978-1-58204)* 1682 W. 820 N., Provo, UT 84601 USA Tel 801-373-3973; Fax: 801-343-3912; Toll Free: 800-596-0910
E-mail: deloyh@power-glide.com
Web site: http://www.power-glide.com.

powerHouse Bks. *Imprint of* **powerHouse Cultural Entertainment, Inc.**

powerHouse Cultural Entertainment, Inc., *(978-1-57687)* 37 Main St., Brooklyn, NY 11201 USA (SAN 850-5845); Mercedes Distribution Ctr. Bldg. 3 Brooklyn Navy Yard, Brooklyn, NY 11205 Tel 212-604-9074; Fax: 212-366-5247; *Imprints:* powerHouse Books (pwerHse Bks); PowerHouse Kids (PowerKids)
E-mail: info@powerhousebooks.com
Web site: http://www.powerhousebooks.com
Dist(s): **MyiLibrary**
Penguin Random Hse. LLC
Random Hse., Inc.

PowerHouse Kids *Imprint of* **powerHouse Cultural Entertainment, Inc.**

PowerKids Pr. *Imprint of* **Rosen Publishing Group, Inc., The**

PowerMark Productions, *(978-0-9705669; 978-0-9713412; 978-0-9717876; 978-0-9729135; 978-0-9747026; 978-0-9749339; 978-0-9795833; 978-0-9827990; 978-1-935980)* Div. of Quest Ministries International, 380 E. Hwy. Cc Suite E104, Nixa, MO 65714 USA Tel 417-724-1222; Fax: 417-724-0119; Toll Free: 877-769-2669
E-mail: linda@qminternational.com
Web site: http://www.powermarkcomics.com
Dist(s): **New Day Christian Distributors Gifts, Inc.**

PowerMoves, *(978-0-9748298)* P.O. Box 92907, Washington, DC 20090 USA Tel 202-568-9111
Web site: http://www.powermoves.org.

Powerstart Pr. *Imprint of* **Rosen Publishing Group, Inc., The**

PowWow Publishing, *(978-0-9819789; 978-0-9859577)* P.O. Box 31855, Tucson, AZ 85751 USA
E-mail: brent@powwowinc.com
Web site: http://www.powwowpublishing.com; http://www.katemathis.net.

P.R.A. Enterprises Incorporated *See* **P.R.A. Publishing**

P.R.A. Publishing, *(978-0-9727703; 978-0-9821407; 978-0-9840142; 978-1-941416)* Orders Addr.: P.O. Box 211701, Martinez, GA 30917 USA Tel 706-855-6173
E-mail: lucindaclark@phoenixrisingarts.com; info@prapublishing.com; ljclark08@gmail.com
Web site: http://www.prapublishing.com; http://www.phoenixrisingarts.com; http://www.phoenixrisingart.wordpress.com
Dist(s): **BookBaby**
Bookmasters Distribution
Lightning Source, Inc.

Practical Christianity Foundation, *(978-0-9705996; 978-1-932587; 978-1-60098)* 2514 Aloha Pl., Holiday, FL 34691 USA (SAN 254-4377) Tel 727-934-0927; Fax: 727-934-4241; Toll Free: 888-278-3300
E-mail: cseitz@greenkeybooks.com
Web site: http://www.greenkeybooks.com
Dist(s): **Send The Light Distribution LLC.**

PRACTICAL SOLUTIONS Writing, Editing, Consulting, *(978-0-615-19350-2; 978-0-615-19351-9; 978-0-615-32636-8)* P.O. Box 1484, Wake Forest, NC 27588 USA Tel 919-604-4585; Fax: 901-273-1852
E-mail: Jfaulk28@nc.rr.com
Web site: http://stores.lulu.com/store.php?fAcctID=1906985; http://www.jefferyafaulkerson.com
Dist(s): **Lulu Pr., Inc.**

Pragmatic Bookshelf, The *Imprint of* **Pragmatic Programmers, LLC, The**

Pragmatic Programmers, LLC, The, *(978-0-9745140; 978-0-9766940; 978-0-9776166; 978-0-9787392; 978-1-934356; 978-1-937785; 978-1-941222; 978-1-68050)* 9650 Strickland Rd., Suite 103, No. 255, Raleigh, NC 27615 USA; 2831 El Dorado Pkwy., No. 103-381, Frisco, TX 75033 Toll Free Fax: 800-699-7764; *Imprints:* Pragmatic Bookshelf, The (Pragmatic Bkshelf)
E-mail: andy@pragprog.com
Web site: http://www.pragmaticprogrammer.com
Dist(s): **Ingram Publisher Services**
O'Reilly Media, Inc.

Prairie Arts, Inc., *(978-0-9725382)* 3100 Birch Bark Ln., Oklahoma City, OK 73120 USA Tel 405-755-5432; 405-728-1350; Fax: 405-728-9813
E-mail: dgordonart@aol.com.

Prairie Heart Publishing, *(978-0-9793668)* 8967 W. Driftwood Dr., Coeur d'Alene, ID 83814 USA Tel 208-777-8079 (phone/fax)
E-mail: aprairieheart@earthlink.net; sdianewood@earthlink.net
Web site: http://www.prairievirtuedolls.com.

Prairie Hills Publishing, *(978-0-9821084)* 310 N. Washington St., B5, Groton, SD 57445 USA
Web site: http://www.prairiehillspublishing.com.

Prairie Shore Creative, Inc., *(978-0-9740542)* 2500 S. Corbett, Chicago, IL 60608 USA
E-mail: PSCreative@AOL.come
Web site: http://www.Prairieshorecreative.com.

Prairie Winds Publishing, *(978-0-9778240)* 15154 W. 231st St., Spring Hill, KS 66083 USA Tel 913-592-5002
E-mail: cyndi@gertrudemccluck.com
Web site: http://www.gertrudemccluck.com.

Prairieland Pr., *(978-0-9759829; 978-1-944132)* P.O. Box 2404, Fremont, NE 68026-2404 USA Tel 402-721-0241
E-mail: nlsharpwriter@gmail.com
Web site: http://www.prairielandpress.com; http://writesharp.com.

Pranayama Institute, Inc., The, *(978-0-9724450)* Orders Addr.: P.O. Box 40731, Albuquerque, NM 87196 USA Tel 706-889-5035 (phone/fax); Fax: 505-212-0097
E-mail: ssaranam@pranayama.org; publicity@pranayama.org
Web site: http://www.pranayama.org; http://www.godwithoutreligion.com.

Prancing Pony, The, *(978-0-9763555)* Orders Addr.: 104802 W. Foisy Rd., Prosser, WA 99350 USA
Web site: http://www.herbleonhard.com.

Pratt Ctr. The, *(978-0-9772835)* Orders Addr.: Four Main St., Suite 210, Los Altos, CA 94022 USA Tel 650-949-2997; Fax: 650-949-2442
E-mail: prattcenter@covad.net.

Praxis Pr., Inc., *(978-0-9754305; 978-1-934278)* 1515 Skelton Rd.5-100, Gainesville, GA 30504 USA Tel 770-846-5978
Web site: http://www.praxispress.com.

Prayer Bk. Pr., Inc., *(978-0-87677)* Subs. of Media Judaica, Inc., Orders Addr.: 1363 Fairfield Ave., Bridgeport, CT 06605 USA (SAN 207-0022) Tel 203-384-2284; Edit Addr.: 304 E. 49th St., New York, NY 10017 USA (SAN 282-1788) Tel 212-319-6666.

PRAZZ Pubns., *(978-0-9776356)* Orders Addr.: P.O. Box 636, Upper Marlboro, MD 20773-0636 USA (SAN 257-8212); Edit Addr.: 8419 Thornberry Dr., West Upper Marlboro, MD 20772 USA
E-mail: ycsmallwood@yahoo.com.

Precept Ministries, *(978-1-888655; 978-1-934884; 978-1-62119)* Orders Addr.: P.O. Box 182218, Chattanooga, TN 37422 USA Tel 423-892-6814; Fax: 423-894-2449; Toll Free: 800-763-8280; Edit Addr.: 7324 Noah Reid Rd., Chattanooga, TN 37421 USA
E-mail: info@precept.org; jbundy@precept.org
Web site: http://www.precept.org.

Precious Little Bks., *(978-0-9787235)* 9353 SE. Yardarm Terr., Hobe Sound, FL 33455-3214 USA (SAN 851-3813) Tel 561-307-2367; Fax: 772-545-4944
E-mail: clarke@preciouslittlebooks.com
Web site: http://www.preciouslittlebooks.com.

Precious Moments, Inc., *(978-0-9817159; 978-0-9819885; 978-0-9825809)* 2850 W. Golf Rd., Suite 250, Rolling Meadows, IL 60008 USA (SAN 856-3403)
Web site: http://www.preciousmoments.com
Dist(s): **Midpoint Trade Bks., Inc.**

Precioustymes Entertainment, LLC, *(978-0-9729325; 978-0-9776507)* 229 Governors Pl., No. 138, Bear, DE

19701 USA Tel 302-294-6980 (office line); Fax: 302-294-6980
E-mail: PrecioustymesEnt@aol.com
Web site: http://www.precioustymes.com; http://www.platinumteen.org
Dist(s): **A & B Distributors & Pubs. Group**
Afrikan World Bk. Distributor.

Precision Cad/Cam Systems, Inc., *(978-0-9707464)* 9564 Deereco Rd., Luthvle Timon, MD 21093-2119 USA
E-mail: info@cadcam4u.com
Web site: http://www.cadcam4u.com.

Preferred Enterprises, *(978-1-885143)* P.O. Box 848, Lakewood, NJ 08701-0848 USA.

Preferred Marketing *See* **American Historical Pr.**

PremaNations Publishing, *(978-1-892176)* Div. of PremaNations, Inc., P.O. Box 321447, Cocoa Beach, FL 32932-1447 USA (SAN 299-5808) Tel 310-417-9195; Fax: 407-784-5372; Toll Free Fax: 877-372-4660; Toll Free: 877-372-4664
E-mail: Paradigm@PremaNations.com
Web site: http://www.PremaNations.com
Dist(s): **New Leaf Distributing Co., Inc.**
Quality Bks., Inc.

Prematurely Yours, *(978-0-9614786)* Orders Addr.: P.O. Box 9141, Chesapeake, VA 23321 USA (SAN 692-9907) Tel 757-483-9879; Fax: 757-484-8267; Toll Free: 800-767-0023
E-mail: kbryant@prematurelyyours.com
Web site: http://www.prematurelyyours.com.

Premier Schl. Agendas, *(978-1-884272; 978-1-59923; 978-1-63080)* 400 Sequoia Dr., Ste. 200, Bellingham, WA 98226 USA Tel 360-734-1153; Fax: 360-734-3014; Toll Free Fax: 800-880-3287; Toll Free: 800-447-2034
E-mail: ruth.richardson@schoolspecialty.com; nancy.fosberg@schoolspecialty.com; arielle.bons@schoolspecialty.com; whitney.ochs@schoolspecialty.com
Web site: http://www.premier.us.

Premiere *Imprint of* **FastPrncil, Inc.**

Premio Publishing & Gozo Bks., LLC, *(978-0-9776065; 978-0-615-43691-3; 978-0-615-44230-3; 978-0-615-44305-8; 978-0-615-49278-0; 978-0-9853988; 978-0-615-68823-7; 978-0-615-68824-4; 978-0-615-69229-6; 978-0-615-85615-5; 978-0-615-85616-2; 978-0-615-85617-9; 978-0-615-87686-3; 978-0-692-22096-2; 978-0-692-22097-9; 978-0-692-22098-6; 978-0-692-22099-3; 978-0-692-40797-4; 978-0-692-42677-7; 978-0-692-43639-4; 978-0-692-64859-9) Div. of Premio Publishing, 648 W. Wasatch St., Midvale, UT 84047 USA Tel 801-953-3793; Imprints*: Gozo Books (Gozo Bks)
E-mail: karl@premiobooks.com; karlbx@gmail.com
Web site: http://Premiobooks.com; http://gozobooks.com; https://twitter.com/PremioBooks; http://premiopublishing.com; http://twitter.com/karlbeckstrand; http://karlbeckstrand.com
Dist(s): **CreateSpace Independent Publishing Platform**
Follett School Solutions
Smashwords.

Premium Pr. America, *(978-0-9637733; 978-1-887654; 978-1-933725)* Div. of Schnitzer Communications, Inc., Orders Addr.: P.O. Box 159015, Nashville, TN 37215-9015 USA Tel 615-256-8484; Fax: 615-256-8524; Toll Free: 800-891-7323; Edit Addr.: 2606 Eugenia Ave., Suite C, Nashville, TN 37211-2177 USA
E-mail: bbsgcs@aol.com
Web site: http://www.premiumpress.com
Dist(s): **Send The Light Distribution LLC.**

Prentice Hall *Imprint of* **Prentice Hall PTR**

Prentice Hall *Imprint of* **Pearson Schl.**

Prentice Hall Bks., *(978-0-13)* Orders Addr.: 200 Old Tappan Rd., Old Tappan, NJ 07675 USA Toll Free Fax: 800-445-6991; 800-835-5327; Toll Free: 800-223-1360; 800-282-0693 (Single-Copy Phone Orders)
Web site: http://www.prenhall.com
Dist(s): **Langenscheidt Publishing Group.**

Prentice Hall, ESL Dept., *(978-0-13; 978-0-88345)* 240 Frisch Ct., Paramus, NJ 07652-5240 USA Tel 201-236-7000; Fax: 201-592-0904; Toll Free: 800-922-0579
Dist(s): **Continental Bk. Co., Inc.**
Pearson Education.

Prentice Hall General Reference & Travel *See* **Prentice Hall Bks.**

Prentice Hall Pr. *Imprint of* **Penguin Publishing Group**

Prentice Hall Pr., *(978-0-13; 978-0-7352)* Orders Addr.: 200 Old Tappan Rd., Old Tappan, NJ 07675 USA; Edit Addr.: 240 Frisch Ct., Paramus, NJ 07652 USA Tel 201-909-6200; Fax: 201-909-6360; Toll Free: 800-288-4745; 800-223-2336 (customer service); a/o Prentice Hall Direct, P.O. Box 11075, Des Moines, IA 50336 Tel 515-284-6719; Toll Free: 800-947-7700
E-mail: pearsoned@eds.com
Web site: http://www.phdirect.com
Dist(s): **Pearson Education**
Penguin Random Hse. LLC
Penguin Publishing Group
ebrary, Inc.

†Prentice Hall PTR, *(978-0-13; 978-0-201; 978-0-672)* Div. of Pearson Technology Group, Orders Addr.: 200 Old Tappan Rd., Old Tappan, NJ 07675 USA Fax: 416-447-2819 (orders - Canada); Toll Free Fax: 800-835-5327 (individual single copy orders - US); 800-445-6991 (government orders); Toll Free: 800-282-0693 (individual single copy orders - US); 800-922-0579 (government orders); 800-567-3800 (orders - Canada); Edit Addr.: 405 Murray Hill Pkwy., E Rutherford, NJ 07073-2136 USA; *Imprints*: Prentice Hall (Prentice Hall)
Web site: http://www.phptr.com/
Dist(s): **Cambridge Bk. Co.**
Continental Bk. Co., Inc.
Ebsco Publishing
IFSTA
MyiLibrary
Pearson Education
Pearson Technology Group
Rittenhouse Bk. Distributors
Trans-Atlantic Pubns., Inc.; *CIP.*

Prentice Hall (Schl. Div.), *(978-0-13)* Div. of Pearson Education, Orders Addr.: P.O. Box 2500, Lebanon, IN 46052-3009 USA Toll Free: 800-848-9500; P.O. Box 2649, Columbus, OH 43216-2649; Edit Addr.: 160 Gould St. (Northeast Region), Needham Heights, MA 02194-2310 USA Tel 617-455-1300; 8445 Freeport Pkwy., Suite 400 (South Central Region), Irving, TX 75063 Tel 214-915-4255
Web site: http://www.phschool.com/
Dist(s): **Pearson Education.**

Prentice-Hall *See* **Prentice Hall PTR**

Prepare For Rain Pr., *(978-0-9889537)* 4366 S Wagon Train Ln., Boise, ID 83716 USA Tel 208-514-8607
E-mail: Joel@PrepareForRain.com.

Presbeau Publishing, Inc., *(978-0-9831380)* 6533 S. Ouray St., Aurora, CO 80016 USA Tel 303-690-1177
E-mail: carmens222@comcast.net
Web site: www.presbeaupublishing.com.

Presbyterian & Reformed Publishing Company *See* **P & R Publishing**

Presbyterian Publishing Corporation *See* **Curriculum Publishing, Presbyterian Church (U. S. A.)**

Preschool Prep Co., *(978-0-9767008; 978-0-9770215; 978-0-9801717; 978-0-9820331; 978-1-935610)* P.O. Box 1159, Danville, CA 94526 USA Tel 925-743-1400; Fax: 925-886-4843; Toll Free: 866-451-5600
Web site: http://www.preschoolprepco.com
Dist(s): **Follett School Solutions.**

Presence Publishing, *(978-0-9729676)* Orders Addr.: 25909 Plantation Ave., Denham Springs, LA 70726 USA
E-mail: presencepub@bellsouth.net; sharonelliott@bellsouth.net.

Preserving Memories, *(978-0-9742576; 978-0-9817835)* 5809 Stonebridge Ln., Waxhaw, NC 28173 USA
Web site: http://www.preservememories.net.

Presidential Publishing, *(978-0-9729095)* Orders Addr.: P.O. Box 221834, Sacramento, CA 95822 USA (SAN 255-1977) Tel 916-447-2460
E-mail: contactus@presidentialcookies.com; contactus@presidentialpublishing.com
Web site: http://www.presidentialcookies.com; http://www.presidentialpublishing.com.

Press Americana, *(978-0-9789041; 978-0-9829558; 978-0-9967779)* 7095 Hollywood Blvd, 1240, Hollywood, CA 90028-8903 USA (SAN 851-9013) Tel 818-370-1143; Fax: 818-760-1828
E-mail: editor@americanpopularculture.com
Web site: http://www.americanpopularculture.com.

Pr. & Brand Productions, *(978-0-615-25883-6)* 2515 34th St., No. 6, New York, NY 11103 USA Tel 718-267-8771
Dist(s): **Lulu Pr., Inc.**

Press North America, *(978-0-938271)* P.O. Box 105, Gustavus, AK 99826 USA (SAN 659-8285) Tel 907-697-2303 (phone/fax, press start); Fax: 907-697-2760.

Press of the Camp Pope Bookshop *See* **Camp Pope Publishing**

Press Release Group Corp., *(978-0-9764633)* Orders Addr.: P.O. Box 651, New York, NY 10276 USA
E-mail: info@prgroup.info
Web site: http://www.prgroup.info.

Pr. Room Editions LLC, *(978-1-62143; 978-1-63235; 978-1-63494)* 1686 Cliff Rd. E., Burnsville, MN 55337-1300 USA Tel 952-746-7867; Fax: 952-746-4287; *Imprints*: 12-Story Library (12-Story Lib)
E-mail: btemple@reditorial.com
Dist(s): **Amicus Publishing**
RiverStream Publishing.

Presses Pocket (FRA) *(978-2-266) Dist. by* **Distribks Inc.**

Prestel Publishing, *(978-3-7913)* Orders Addr.: c/o VNU, 575 Prospect St., Lakewood, NJ 08701 USA Tel 732-363-5679; Fax: 732-363-0338; Toll Free Fax: 877-227-6564; Toll Free: 888-463-6110; Edit Addr.: 900 Broadway, Suite 603, New York, NY 10003 USA Tel 212-995-2720; Fax: 212-995-2733
E-mail: sales@prestel-usa.com
Web site: http://www.prestel.com; http://www.die-gestalten.de; http://www.scalo.com
Dist(s): **VNU.**

Prestel Verlag GmbH & Co KG. (DEU) *(978-3-7913) Dist. by* **Peng Rand Hse.**

Preston-Speed Pubns., *(978-1-887159; 978-1-931587)* 51 Ridge Rd., Mill Hall, PA 17751 USA Tel 570-726-7844; Fax: 570-726-3547
E-mail: doug@prestonspeed.com
Web site: http://www.prestonspeed.com.

Prestwick Hse., Inc., *(978-1-58049; 978-1-60389; 978-1-60843; 978-1-935464; 978-1-935465; 978-1-935466; 978-1-935467; 978-1-935468; 978-0-9823095; 978-0-9823096; 978-0-9823097; 978-0-692-00136-3; 978-0-692-00137-0; 978-1-62019)* Orders Addr.: P.O. Box 658, Clayton, DE 19938 USA Fax: 302-734-0549; Toll Free: 800-932-4593; Edit Addr.: 58 Artisan Dr., Smyrna, DE 19977 USA (SAN 154-5523) Tel 800-983-4593; Fax: 302-659-2792
E-mail: info@prestwickhouse.com; keith@prestwickhouse.com
Web site: http://www.prestwickhouse.com.

Pretty Paper Pr., *(978-0-9746315; 978-0-9858814)* 14 Everett St., East Orange, NJ 07017 USA
E-mail: moody4u@verizon.net
Web site: http://www.moodyholiday.com.

Pretty Please Pr., Inc., *(978-0-9759378)* 105 E. 29th St., 6th Flr., New York, NY 10016 USA.

Prevention Through Puppetry, Inc., *(978-0-9768827)* 468 Boyle Rd., Port Jefferson Station, NY 11776 USA Tel 631-476-3099; Fax: 631-476-7680
Web site: http://www.sunshinepreventionctr.org.

Previn, Lovely Pubns., *(978-0-9847107)* 1810 S. El Camino Real Suite B101, Encinitas, CA 92024 USA Tel 760-632-8288 (phone/fax)
E-mail: lovelyprevinmusic@gmail.com
Web site: www.AliciaPrevin.com.

PRF Pubs., *(978-0-578-03405-8; 978-0-578-04719-5)* 221 Hopewell Amwell Rd., Hopewell, NJ 08525 USA
E-mail: s.schwinn1@verizon.net
Web site: http://www.henrythelamb.com.

Price, Diane Joan, *(978-0-9789637)* 10508 Courtney Cove, Las Vegas, NV 89144 USA
E-mail: dpcontact@netzero.net.

Price, Mathew Ltd., *(978-1-935021; 978-0-9844366)* 12300 Ford Rd. Ste. 455, Dallas, TX 75234-8136 USA (SAN 856-0471)
Web site: http://www.mathewprice.com.

Price Stern Sloan *Imprint of* **Penguin Publishing Group**

Price Stern Sloan *Imprint of* **Penguin Young Readers Group**

Price World Enterprises, LLC *See* **Price World Publishing**

Price World Publishing, *(978-0-9724102; 978-1-932549; 978-1-936910; 978-1-61984)* Orders Addr.: 3971 Hoover Rd, Columbus, OH 43123 USA Tel 888-234-6896; Fax: 216-803-0350; Toll Free: 888-234-6896; *Imprints*: BlogIntoBook.com (BlogIntoBook); Quintessential Press (MYID_L_QUINTES)
Web site: http://www.priceworldpublishing.com; http://www.GatekeeperPress.com
Dist(s): **Cardinal Pubs. Group**
INscribe Digital
MyiLibrary.

Priceless Ink Publishing Co., Inc., *(978-0-9778937)* Orders Addr.: P.O. Box 218538, Nashville, TN 37221 USA
E-mail: apricelessgiftcom@yahoo.com; audreylprice@yahoo.com
Web site: http://apricelessgift.com.

PricePoint+Publications, *(978-0-9661661; 978-0-9741627; 978-0-9772614; 978-0-9826838; 978-0-9838033)* P.O. Box 26, Alto, NM 88312 USA (SAN 257-067X) Tel 575-973-3277
E-mail: laura@pricepointcreative.com; laurareynoldsdesigner@gmail.com
Web site: http://www.ppcbookpublishing.com; http://www.pricepointcreative.com.

Prickly Pear Pr., *(978-0-9764323)* P.O. Box 69, Sahuarita, AZ 85629-0069 USA Tel 520-625-1587; Fax: 520-625-3655 Do not confuse with Pricly Pear Press in San Francisco CA, Cedar Park TX, Scottsdale AZ, Tucson AZ.
E-mail: pricklypearpress@msn.com
Web site: http://pricklypearpress.info.

Prickly Pr., *(978-1-893463)* 11695 Rosehill Rd, Overland Park, KS 66210 USA Tel 913-648-2034 (phone/fax)
E-mail: ikesmith@kc.rr.com
Web site: http://www.readwest.com/flouncesmith.thm.

Priddy Bks. *Imprint of* **St. Martin's Pr.**

Priest, Gerald L., *(978-0-9743871)* 4801 Allen Rd., Allen Park, MI 48101 USA Toll Free: 800-866-0111.

Prima Games *Imprint of* **Random Hse. Information Group**

Primary Concepts, Inc., *(978-1-893791; 978-1-60184)* 1338 Seventh St., Berkeley, CA 94710 USA
E-mail: info@primaryconcepts.com
Web site: http://www.primaryconcepts.com.

Primary Concepts/Concepts to Go *See* **Primary Concepts, Inc.**

Primary Sources, *(978-1-881849)* 16442 SE 42nd Pl., Issaquah, WA 98027 USA Tel 425-865-0409 (phone/fax)
E-mail: info@primary-sources.com
Web site: http://www.primary-sources.com/
Dist(s): **Smashwords.**

Prime, *(978-0-8095; 978-0-9668968; 978-1-930997; 978-1-894815)* Div. of Wildside Press, P.O. Box 301, Holicong, PA 18928 USA
E-mail: sean@wildsidepress.com
Web site: http://www.primebooks.net
Dist(s): **Diamond Comic Distributors, Inc.**
Diamond Bk. Distributors.

Primedia eLaunch LLC, *(978-1-62209; 978-1-62890; 978-0-615-88236-9; 978-0-615-88337-3; 978-0-615-88403-5; 978-1-63173; 978-1-63315; 978-1-63443; 978-1-942526; 978-1-942573; 978-1-942574; 978-1-942748; 978-1-942749; 978-0-692-36411-6; 978-1-942844; 978-1-942845; 978-1-942846; 978-1-943090; 978-1-943091; 978-1-943092; 978-1-943093; 978-1-943274; 978-1-943275; 978-1-943276; 978-1-943277; 978-1-943278; 978-1-943279; 978-1-943280; 978-1-943281; 978-0-692-42561-9; 978-1-943842; 978-1-943843; 978-1-943844; 978-1-943845) 3900 Swiss Ave. No. 205, Dallas, TX 75204 USA (SAN 935-4808) Tel 214-870-5515*
E-mail: josh@primediaelaunch.com
Web site: http://www.primediaelaunch.com
Dist(s): **BookBaby**
CreateSpace Independent Publishing Platform
Lulu Pr., Inc.
eBookit.com.

Primera Persona (ESP) *(978-84-95923) Dist. by* **IPG Chicago.**

Primordia, *(978-0-9759007)* P.O. Box 2455, Santa Barbara, CA 93120 USA (SAN 256-1018).

Primrose Layne Pr., *(978-0-692-85825-7)* 494 Landsdown Cir., ROHNERT PARK, CA 94928 USA Tel 707-664-8110
E-mail: jeffwcrawford5+LVP0003479@gmail.com; jeffwcrawford5+LVP0003479@gmail.com.

Primrose Pr., *(978-0-9673171)* Orders Addr.: P.O. Box 2577, Prescott, AZ 86302 USA (SAN 299-9331) Tel 520-445-4567; Fax: 520-445-0517; Edit Addr.: 815 Bertrand Ave., Prescott, AZ 86303 USA Do not confuse with companies with the same name in Antelope, CA, Alhambra, CA, San Francisco, CA.

Primrose Presses *See* **Scarlet Primrose Pr.**

Prince Motivation, *(978-0-692-88507-9)* 1033 SW 167th ave, Pembroke Pines, FL 33027 USA Tel 954-868-8102
E-mail: 954prince@gmail.com
Web site: http://www.instagram.com/IamPaulMompremier.

Princess Khrystle & Prince Michael, Inc., *(978-0-9772565)* Orders Addr.: P.O. Box 960176, Miami, FL 33296 USA; Edit Addr.: 14631 SW 104 Ct., Miami, FL 33176 USA
E-mail: khrystle19@aol.com
Web site: http://www.princesskhrystle.org.

Princeton Architectural Pr., *(978-0-910413; 978-0-9636372; 978-1-56898; 978-1-878271; 978-1-885232; 978-1-61689)* Div. of The McEvoy Group, 37 E. Seventh St., New York, NY 10003 USA (SAN 260-1176) Tel 212-995-9720; Fax: 212-995-9454; Toll Free: 800-722-6657
E-mail: sales@papress.com
Web site: http://www.papress.com
Dist(s): **Chronicle Bks. LLC**
Hachette Bk. Group
McEvoy Group, The
Metapress
ebrary, Inc.

Princeton Bk. Co. Pubs., *(978-0-87127; 978-0-916622)* Orders Addr.: P.O. Box 831, Hightstown, NJ 08520-0831 USA (SAN 630-1568) Tel 609-426-0602; Fax: 609-426-1344; Toll Free: 800-220-7149; 614 Rte. 130, Hightstown, NJ 08520 (SAN 244-8076); *Imprints*: Dance Horizons (Dance Horizons); Elysian Editions (Elysian Editions)
E-mail: pbc@dancehorizons.com; elysian@aosi.com
Web site: http://www.dancehorizons.com
Dist(s): **Ebsco Publishing**
Follett School Solutions
Independent Pubs. Group
MyiLibrary.

Princeton Health Pr., *(978-0-933665; 978-0-9835782; 978-1-940175)* 711 Westchester Ave., West Harrison, NY 10604-3504 USA (SAN 692-5391) Toll Free: 800-293-4969
E-mail: ksilloway@nhpamail.com
Web site: http://www.lifeskillstraining.com.

†Princeton Univ. Pr., *(978-0-691)* Orders Addr.: California-Princeton Fulfillment Services, 1445 Lower Ferry Rd., Ewing, NJ 08618 USA Tel 800-777-4726; Fax: 800-999-1958; Edit Addr.: 41 William St., Princeton, NJ 08540 USA (SAN 202-0254) Tel 609-258-4900; Fax: 609-258-6305; 3 Market Place, Woodstock, OX20 1SY Tel (0) 1993 814501; Fax: (0) 1993 814504
E-mail: webmaster@pupress.princeton.edu
Web site: http://www.press.princeton.edu
Dist(s): **California Princeton Fulfillment Services**
Casemate Academic
De Gruyter, Inc.
Ebsco Publishing
ISD
MyiLibrary
Ingram Academic
Two Rivers Distribution
Wiley, John & Sons, Inc.
ebrary, Inc.; *CIP.*

Prindle House *See* **Prindle Hse. Publishing Co.**

Prindle House Publishing Co. *Imprint of* **Prindle Hse. Publishing Co.**

Prindle Hse. Publishing Co., *(978-0-9759527; 978-0-9819372; 978-0-9826846; 978-0-9835320; 978-0-9889080)* Orders Addr.: P.O. Box 18761, Jacksonville, FL 32229 USA Tel 904-710-6529; Fax: 904-751-9338; Toll Free: 866-877-4635; Edit Addr.: 62 W. 27th St., Jacksonville, FL 32206 USA; *Imprints*: Prindle House Publishing Company (PrinHsePubCo)
E-mail: tp@prindlehouse.com; twylaprindle@yahoo.com
Web site: http://www.prindlehouse.com; http://www.twylaprindle.com; www.childanthology.com.

Printt Pr., *(978-0-932970)* 211 NW Seventh St., Richmond, IN 47374-4051 USA (SAN 212-680X) Tel 765-966-7130; Fax: 765-966-7131; Toll Free: 800-478-4885
Web site: http://www.printpress.com.

Printing Systems, *(978-0-9767595; 978-1-59916)* Orders Addr.: 2249 14th St SW, Akron, OH 44314-2007 USA Toll Free: 800-231-0521
E-mail: info@48HrBooks.com
Web site: http://www.48HrBooks.com.

Printmedia Bks., *(978-0-9778591; 978-0-9788447; 978-0-9790999; 978-1-934379)* Div. of The Printmedia Cos. of Southern California, 3355 E. Miraloma Ave., Bldg. 165, Anaheim, CA 92806 USA Tel 714-729-0789; Fax: 714-729-0790
E-mail: peter@printmediabooks.com; books@printmediabooks.com
Web site: http://www.printmediabooks.com.

printONDEMANDpublisher.com, *(978-0-9765725)* 325 W. Belden Ave., Chicago, IL 60614-3817 USA Tel 773-988-8619; Fax: 773-935-9967
E-mail: george@georgevalko.com
Web site: http://www.printondemandpublisher.com.

Prints By Mail, *(978-0-9740173)* 33 Jose I Garica Rd., Belen, NM 87002 USA; 33 Jose I Garcia Rd., Belen, NM 87002
E-mail: books@printsbymail.com
Web site: http://www.printsbymail.com.

Prioleau, Jivonne, *(978-0-615-25200-1; 978-0-578-00427-3; 978-0-578-08744-3)* 5701 Rafferty Ave., McClellan, CA 95652 USA
Dist(s): **Lulu Pr., Inc.**

Prion (GBR) *(978-1-85375) Dist. by* **IPG Chicago.**

Prioritybooks Pubns., *(978-0-9753634; 978-0-9792823; 978-0-9816483; 978-0-9819913; 978-0-9834860; 978-0-9896502)* P.O. Box 2535, Florissant, MO 63033 USA (SAN 853-0130) Tel 314-741-6789 (phone/fax); 314-306-2972; Fax: 314-475-5613
E-mail: rosbeav03@yahoo.com
Web site: http://www.prioritybooks.com
Dist(s): **Brodart Co.**
Follett Higher Education Grp

Lightning Source, Inc.
Lushena Bks.

Prism Comics, (978-0-9759164) 2621 E. Madison, Seattle, WA 98122-4711 USA Fax: 206-770-6137
Web site: http://www.prismcomics.org.

Prism Hse. Media, (978-0-9748088) Orders Addr.: 126 Quail Hollow Dr., San Jose, CA 95128 USA Tel 407-461-4999
E-mail: paulpelley@gmail.com
Dist(s): **Review & Herald Publishing Assn.**

Pristine Pubs., Inc., (978-0-9716633) 18 Buckthorn Cove, Jackson, TN 38305 USA (SAN 254-2420) Tel 731-660-3333 Toll Free: 866-565-3311
E-mail: Kathy@pristinepublishers.com
Web site: http://www.readysetgofitness.com; http://www.questforasdin.com; http://www.pristinepublishers.com; http://www.gabrielsmagicornament.com.

†Pritchett & Hull Assocs., Inc., (978-0-939838; 978-1-933638; 978-1-943234) 3440 Oakcliff Rd., NE, Suite 110, Atlanta, GA 30340 USA (SAN 216-9258) Tel 770-451-0602; Fax: 770-454-7130; Toll Free: 800-241-4925
E-mail: phsales@p-h.com
Web site: http://www.p-h.com/; *CIP.*

Privacy Trust Group, The, (978-0-9777457) Div. of JR The Trust Group Inc., Orders Addr.: 240 S. Elizabeth #h1-116, ELizabeth, CO 80107 USA (SAN 850-122X) Tel 303-648-3496; Fax: 303-648-3205; Toll Free: 877-648-0119; 240 S. Elizabeth #h1-116, Elizabeth, CO 80107 Tel 303-648-3496; Fax: 303-648-3205
Web site: http://www.privacytrustgroup.com.

Privateer Pr., Inc., (978-0-9706970; 978-1-933362; 978-1-939480; 978-1-943693) 13434 NE 16th St. Ste. 120, Bellevue, WA 98005-2335 USA Do not confuse with Privateer Pr. in New Orleans, LA
E-mail: mw@privateerpress.com
Web site: http://www.privateerpress.com
Dist(s): **Diamond Bk. Distributors**
PSI (Publisher Services, Inc.).

Privatgaeste Verlag, (978-0-9712545) c/o Ute Kruedewagen, 3168 Harrison St., No. 106, Oakland, CA 94611 USA
Web site: http://www.privatgaeste.com.

Privileged Communications, LLC, (978-0-9802302) 844 25th St., Santa Monica, CA 90403 USA Fax: 310-828-9590
E-mail: lester310@earthlink.net
Web site: http://www.theboywhowouldntsitstill.com.

PRL Publishing, (978-0-9743957) 2245 E. Colorado Blvd., No. 104 PMB 243, Pasadena, CA 91107 USA Tel 626-255-1743
E-mail: info@prldesigns.com
Web site: http://www.prlpub.com.

†Pro Lingua Assocs., Inc., (978-0-86647) Orders Addr.: P.O. Box 1348, Brattleboro, VT 05302 UMI (SAN 216-0579) Tel 802-257-7779; Fax: 802-257-5117; Toll Free: 800-366-4775; Edit Addr.: P.O. Box 1348, Brattleboro, VT 05302-1348 USA
E-mail: info@prolinguaassociates.com; orders@prolinguaassociates.com
Web site: http://www.prolinguaassociates.com; http://www.lexicarry.com
Dist(s): **Hood, Alan C. & Co., Inc.;** *CIP.*

Pro-Actif Communications (GBR) (978-0-9559121; 978-1-908211) *Dist. by* **IngramPubServ.**

Proactive Publishing, (978-0-9767324) 260 Gateway Dr., Suite 21-C, Bel Air, MD 21014 USA Tel 410-893-9016; Fax: 410-893-9380; *Imprints:* Kids Can (Kids Can)
Web site: http://www.proactive-solutions.net.

Process Inc U. S. *See* **Process Transition International, Inc.**

Process Transition International, Inc., (978-0-9646008) P.O. Box 1988, Annapolis, MD 21404 USA Tel 301-261-9921; Fax: 410-295-5037
E-mail: spi@processtransition.com
Web site: http://www.processtransition.com.

Proclaim Publishing, (978-1-885831) P.O. Box 415, Palmer, TX 75152-0415 USA
E-mail: jo@awake-ministries.org; mreaves872@earthlink.net.

Production 101, Inc., (978-0-9729706; 978-0-9767765)
E-mail: julie@smartkids101.com
Web site: http://www.smartkids101.com
Dist(s): **Big Kids Productions, Inc.**

Production Assocs., Inc., (978-1-887120) 1206 W. Collins Ave., Orange, CA 92867 USA Tel 714-771-6519; Fax: 714-771-2456; Toll Free: 800-535-8368
E-mail: mikec@production-associates.com
Web site: http://www.production-associates.com; http://signtospeak.com; http://www.wesign.com
Dist(s): **Brodart Co.**
Follett School Solutions
Independent Pubs. Group.

Products With A Purpose, (978-0-9641134) 16430 N. 34th Pl., Phoenix, AZ 85032 USA Tel 602-595-1188
E-mail: maryalice@ev1.net.

Profane Existence, (978-0-9662035) P.O. Box 8722, Minneapolis, MN 55408-0722 USA
E-mail: blackened@visi.com
Web site: http://www.propaneeexistence.com
Dist(s): **AK Pr. Distribution.**

Professional Book Distributors, Incorporated *See* **PBD, Inc.**

Professional Publishing Hse. LLC, (978-1-881524; 978-0-9719749; 978-0-9725941; 978-0-9742811; 978-0-9753504; 978-0-9759654; 978-0-9764690; 978-0-9767678; 978-0-9771082; 978-0-9786032; 978-0-9792016; 978-0-9799308; 978-0-9815783; 978-0-9824292; 978-0-9826704; 978-0-9834444; 978-0-9853259; 978-0-9891960; 978-0-9861557; 978-0-692-79600-9; 978-0-9983089) *1425 W. Manchester Ave., Suite B, Los Angeles, CA 90047 USA (SAN 852-7563) Tel 323-750-3592; Fax: 323-750-2886*
Web site: http://www.professionalpublishinghouse.com.

Professional Publishing Services *See* **WayaMedia**

Profile Bks. Ltd. (GBR) (978-1-86197; 978-0-9536969; 978-0-9535895; 978-0-9541303; 978-1-903942; 978-0-9547913; 978-1-84668; 978-0-9551384; 978-0-9551904; 978-1-84765; 978-0-9556476; 978-1-906994; 978-1-906507; 978-0-9873178; 978-1-78125; 978-1-908990) *Dist. by* **IPG Chicago.**

Profile Entertainment, Inc., (978-0-88013; 978-0-931064; 978-0-934551) 475 Park Ave., S., 8th Flr., New York, NY 10016 USA (SAN 212-1247) Tel 212-689-2830; Fax: 212-889-7933
E-mail: dee.erwine@starloggroup.com
Dist(s): **Kable Media Services.**

Profiles of the Presidents *Imprint of* **Compass Point Bks.**

Profit Publishing, (978-0-9773757) 39 W. Trace Creek Dr., Spring, TX 77381 USA.

Profitable Publishing *Imprint of* **Thornton Publishing, Inc.**

Profits Publishing, (978-1-933817) Orders Addr.: 1300 Boblett St., Unit A-218, Blaine, WA 98230 USA Fax: 604-944-7993; Toll Free: 866-492-6623
E-mail: bwburnham@gmail.com
Web site: http://www.profitspublishing.com
Dist(s): **Lightning Source, Inc.**
Whitewing Pr.

Profound Impact Group, Inc., (978-0-9760564; 978-0-9887900; 978-1-942151) Orders Addr.: P.O. Box 370567, Denver, CO 80237 USA Tel 303-437-7827
Web site: http://www.profoundgroup.com; http://www.BusterBlank.com; http://www.DomTesta.com
Dist(s): **Bks. West.**

Progeny Pr., (978-1-58609) Div of MG Publishers Group LLC, Orders Addr.: P.O. Box 223, Eau Claire, WI 54702-0223 USA Tel 715-838-0171; Fax: 715-836-0176; Toll Free: 877-776-4369; Edit Addr.: 133 S. State St., Box 100, Fall Creek, WI 54742 USA
E-mail: progeny@progenypress.com
Web site: http://www.progenypress.com.

Progreso Publishing Group , LLC, (978-1-930584) 2733 East Battlefield #283, Springfield, MO 65804 USA Tel 417-234-0084
E-mail: sanderson@progresopublishing.com
Web site: www.progresopublishing.com.

Progressive Language, Inc., (978-0-9758759; 978-0-9899749) 5804 Lost Dutchman Ave NE, Albuquerque, NM 87111-5901 USA
Web site: http://www.progresssivelangauge.com.

Progressive Rising Phoenix Pr., LLC, (978-1-940834; 978-1-944277; 978-1-946329) 100 Goldmine Ct., Aledo, IL 76008 USA Tel 817-757-7143
E-mail: contact@progressiverisingphoenix.com
Web site: www.progressiverisingphoenix.com
Dist(s): **Ingram Publisher Services.**

Project Management Excellence Ctr., Inc., The, (978-0-9726656; 978-0-9787468) Div. of Sturgeon Publishing, P.O. Box 30291, Phoenix, AZ 85046-0291 USA Tel 623-321-8068
E-mail: info@perfectscoresoftware.com
Web site: http://www.perfectscoresoftware.com.

Project WET Foundation, (978-1-888631; 978-0-9857384; 978-0-9903620; 978-0-9907148; 978-1-942416) 1001 W. Oak St. Suite 210, Bozeman, MT 59715 USA Tel 406-585-2236; Fax: 406-522-0394
E-mail: kristen.read@projectwet.org; linda.hveem@projectwet.org; sandra.deyonge@projectwet.org; stephanie.kaleva@projectwet.org
Web site: http://www.projectwet.org.

Prologo Pubns., (978-0-9764264) 4109 N. O Connor Rd., Irving, TX 75062-3748 USA
E-mail: layne@msu.edu; prologo@comcast.net
Web site: http://www.prologopublications.com.

Prom Girl Publishing. Inc., (978-0-9726917) 808 Broadway, Penthouse C, New York, NY 10003 USA
Web site: http://www.promgirl.com.

†Prometheus Bks., Pubs., (978-0-87975; 978-1-57392; 978-1-59102; 978-1-61592; 978-1-61614; 978-1-63388) Orders Addr.: 59 John Glenn Dr., Amherst, NY 14228-2197 USA (SAN 202-0289) Tel 716-691-0133; Fax: 716-691-0137; Toll Free: 800-421-0351; *Imprints:* Pyr Books (Pyr Bks)
Web site: http://www.prometheusbooks.com
Dist(s): **Casemate Academic**
MyiLibrary
Penguin Random Hse. LLC
Random Hse., Inc.; *CIP.*

Promocion Editorial Inca S.A., PEISA (PER) (978-9972-40; 978-9972-721) *Dist. by* **Mariuccia Iaconi Bk Imports.**

Promotora de prensa internacional S.A (ESP) (978-84-936408; 978-84-92810; 978-84-935438; 978-84-935881; 978-84-935608; 978-84-15967) *Dist. by* **Consort Bk Sales.**

ProNailTech.com, (978-0-9748796) P.O. Box 260515, Lakewood, CO 80226 USA Tel 720-935-1761
Web site: http://www.pronailtech.com.

Pronghorn Pr., (978-0-9714725; 978-1-932636; 978-0-9885533; 978-1-941052) Orders Addr.: P.O. Box 707, Greybull, WY 82426 USA; Edit Addr.: 335 2nd Ave., N., Greybull, WY 82426 USA
Web site: http://www.pronghornpress.org
Dist(s): **INscribe Digital.**

Pronoun, Inc., (978-0-9842977; 978-1-936321; 978-0-9846202; 978-1-936792; 978-1-61430; 978-1-62539; 978-1-62921; 978-1-63295; 978-1-63461; 978-1-68105; 978-1-5080; 978-1-5183; 978-1-5312; 978-1-5378) Orders Addr.: 229 W. 43rd St. Flr. 8, New York, NY 10036 USA
E-mail: distribution@pronoun.com; alex@pronoun.com
Web site: http://www.pronoun.com.

Prop-Abilities Inc., (978-0-9827461) 1502 Fairway Grn, Mamaroneck, NY 10543 USA Tel 914-309-4383.

Propeller Pr., (978-0-9678577) P.O. Box 729, Fort Collins, CO 80522 USA (SAN 253-1704) Tel 970-482-8807; Fax: 970-493-1240
E-mail: propress@frii.com
Web site: http://www.propellerpress.com.

Prophecy Pubns., (978-0-941241) P.O. Box 7000, Oklahoma City, OK 73153 USA (SAN 665-5319) Tel 405-634-1234; Fax: 405-636-1054; Toll Free: 800-245-5577.

Prophecy, The *Imprint of* **Simon & Son Publishing**

ProPress Bks., Inc., (978-0-9845197; 978-0-9915627; 978-0-9908641; 978-0-9969945; 978-0-9969946) 645 Franklin Ave., Massapequa, NY 11758 USA
E-mail: gmpro07@optonline.net
Web site: http://www.ProPressBooks.net.

ProQuest Information and Learning *See* **ProQuest LLC**

ProQuest LLC, (978-0-14; 978-0-608; 978-0-7837; 978-0-8357; 978-0-88692; 978-0-89093; 978-0-912380; 978-1-55655; 978-0-591; 978-0-9702937; 978-0-599; 978-1-931694; 978-1-59399; 978-0-496; 978-0-542; 978-1-4247; 978-0-9778091; 978-1-60205; 978-1-4345; 978-0-549; 978-1-109; 978-1-124; 978-1-267; 978-1-303; 978-1-321; 978-1-339; 978-1-369; 978-0-355) *5252 N. Edgewood Dr., Suite 125, Provo, UT 84604 USA Tel 801-765-1737; 789 Eisenhower Pkwy., Ann Arbor, MI 48106-1346 Tel 734-761-4700 Toll Free: 800-521-0600;* *Imprints:* CultureGrams World Edition (CultureGram Wrld)
E-mail: sales@csa.com
Web site: http://www.culturegrams.com; http://www.proquest.com/
Dist(s): **Cengage Gale.**

ProsePress, (978-0-9833073; 978-0-9851889; 978-0-9886194; 978-0-9893063; 978-1-941069) 75 Red Maple Dr., Pawleys Island, SC 29585 USA Tel 843-237-9929
E-mail: prose-cons@outlook.com
Web site: prosepress.biz.

Prospect Palo Alto Publishing, (978-0-9891043) 435 Tasso Street, Suite 200, Palo Alto, CA 94301 USA Tel 650-327-8800
E-mail: dschnell@prospectventures.com.

Prospect Park Bks., LLC, (978-0-9753939; 978-0-9844102; 978-0-9834594; 978-1-938849; 978-1-945551) Orders Addr.: 2359 Lincoln Ave., Altadena, CA 91001 USA
E-mail: colleen@prospectparkbooks.com
Web site: http://www.prospectparkbooks.com
Dist(s): **Consortium Bk. Sales & Distribution**
MyiLibrary.

Prospect Park Publishing *See* **Prospect Park Bks., LLC**

Prospecta Pr. *Imprint of* **Easton Studio Pr., LLC**

Prospective Pr., (978-1-943419; 978-1-63516) 1959 Peace Haven Rd No. 246, Winston Salem, NC 27106-4850 USA Tel 888-833-0360
E-mail: contact@prospectivepress.com
Web site: prospectivepress.com.

Prosperity & Profits Unlimited, Distribution Services, P.O. Box 416, Denver, CO 80201-0416 USA (SAN 200-4682) Tel 303-575-5676; Fax: 303-575-1187
E-mail: nonstopsuccess@gmail.com
Web site: http://www.breadpudding.net; http://www.contentprovidermedia.com; http://www.gumbomedia.com.

Prospero's Pr., (978-0-9727315) P.O. Box 4616, Boulder, CO 80306-4616 USA (SAN 255-0121) Tel 303-817-5622
Web site: http://www.ahouseforamouse.com.

Protar Hse., LLC, (978-0-9720910) 829 Ann St., East Lansing, MI 48823 USA Tel 517-974-7993
E-mail: info@protarhouse.com
Dist(s): **Partners Bk. Distributing, Inc.**

Protea Boekhuis (ZAF) (978-1-86919; 978-1-919825) *Dist. by* **Casemate Pubs.**

Protecting Our Diversity (POD), (978-0-9727714) P.O. Box 231598, Encinitas, CA 92023-1598 USA Tel 760-944-0852
E-mail: email@kidspod.com
Web site: http://www.kidspod.com.

Protective Hands Communications, (978-0-9787394; 978-0-9818990; 978-0-9845161; 978-0-615-57240-6; 978-0-615-60403-9; 978-0-615-63600-9; 978-0-9857105; 978-0-9892028; 978-0-692-32229-1; 978-0-692-40426-3; 978-0-692-46613-1; 978-0-9975272) Orders Addr.: 1668 Essex Ln., Riviera Beach, FL 33404 USA Toll Free: 866-457-1203
E-mail: info@protectivehands.com; steve@protectivehands.com
Web site: http://protectivehands.com.

ProTeens *Imprint of* **Positive Action For Christ**

ProTips(TM) Media, (978-0-9740600) 810 Adair Pl., Del Rey Oaks, CA 93940 USA
E-mail: tom@rivelli.com
Web site: http://www.protipsmedia.com.

Proton Arts, (978-0-9752647; 978-0-9905028; 978-1-945857) 5051 Grand Beech Ct., Haymarket, VA 20169-2586 USA
E-mail: info@protonarts.com
Web site: http://www.protonarts.com.

Proud Peacock Publishing, (978-0-9859437) 930 Palm Ave. Apt. 136, West Hollywood, CA 90069 USA Tel 925-520-5528
E-mail: marcelino.rosas@ymail.com.

Proud 2-B Me Publishing!, (978-0-9655726) 3653-F Flakes Mill Rd., PMB-F188, Decatur, GA 30034 USA Tel 770-808-2301.

Prous, J. R. S.A. (ESP) (978-84-499; 978-84-300; 978-84-401; 978-84-86973) *Dist. by* **Continental Bk.**

Providence Hse Pubs., (978-1-57736; 978-1-881576) 238 Seaboard Ln., Franklin, TN 37067 USA Tel 615-771-2020; Fax: 615-771-2002; Toll Free: 800-321-5692
E-mail: books@providencehouse.com
Web site: http://www.providencehouse.com.

Providence Publishing, (978-0-9651661; 978-0-9753004; 978-0-9819222; 978-1-60934) 9500 Tomahawk Trail, Fort Worth, TX 76244 USA; 1317 Ben Hur, Houston, TX 77055 Tel 713-480-7069 Do not confuse with companies with the same or similar name in Salt Lake City, UT, Martinez, CA
E-mail: info@providencepublishing.com; woodtee@aol.com
Web site: http://www.providencepublishing.com
Dist(s): **Wilson & Assocs.**

Providence Publishing Corporation *See* **Providence Hse Pubs.**

Provine Pr., (978-1-889883) 832 Cerrito St., Albany, CA 94706 USA Tel 510-528-7055
E-mail: jmbartlett@sbcglobal.net.

PRPublishing, (978-0-9712258) 2830 N. Fifth St., Kalamazoo, MI 49009 USA Tel 616-375-5909; Fax: 616-375-7649
E-mail: freelanceediting@ameritech.net.

PRS Inc., (978-0-9768441) PRS Ctr. Suite 200, PO Box 852, Latrobe, PA 15650 USA Tel 724-539-7820; Fax: 724-539-1388; Toll Free: 800-338-3688
E-mail: prsinfo@prsrx.com; alexr@prsrx.com
Web site: http://www.prsrx.com.

†Pruett Publishing Co., (978-0-87108) P.O. Box 2140, Boulder, CO 80306-2140 USA (SAN 205-4035) Toll Free: 800-592-9727 (orders)
Web site: http://www.pruettpublishing.com
Dist(s): **Bks. West**
Ingram Publisher Services; *CIP.*

Prufrock Pr., (978-1-882664; 978-1-59363; 978-1-61821) Orders Addr.: P.O. Box 8813, Waco, TX 76714-8813 USA Tel 254-756-3337; Fax: 254-756-3339; Toll Free Fax: 800-240-0333; Toll Free: 800-998-2208; Edit Addr.: 6898 Woodway Dr., Woodway, TX 76712-6158 USA (SAN 851-9188); 1935 Brookdale Rd, Ste 139, Naperville, IL 60563
E-mail: info@prufrock.com
Web site: http://www.prufrock.com
Dist(s): **Follett School Solutions**
MyiLibrary
Sourcebooks, Inc.

Pruggus Publishing, (978-0-9844037; 978-0-9900225) P.O. Box 1655, Taos, NM 87571 USA.

Prytania Pr., (978-0-9742602) Orders Addr.: P.O. Box 1892, Gray, LA 70359 USA Tel 225-346-8811
E-mail: ameliastreet@go.com.

Psalms for Kidz *Imprint of* **Little Sprout Publishing Hse.**

Pseudepigrapha Publishing, (978-1-931608) Div. of Chi Xi Stigma Publishing Co., LLC, 2113 Elmwood Ln., Pueblo, CO 81005-2724 USA Tel 719-564-3025 Do not confuse with Penny Dreadful Publishers in Jackson, MI
E-mail: hrothbeorht@hotmail.com.

PSI (Publisher Services, Inc.), 3095 Kingston Ct., Norcross, GA 30071-1231 USA Toll Free: 800-755-9653; 877-578-4774.

PSI Research *See* **L & R Publishing, LLC**

PT Publishing, (978-0-615-21675-1; 978-0-615-27677-9; 978-0-9839147) P.O. Box 2668, Oak Bluffs, MA 02557 USA
Dist(s): **Lulu Pr., Inc.**

PTO Pr., (978-0-9760187) P.O. Box 5394, Snowmass Village, CO 81615 USA.

P2 Educational Services, Inc., (978-1-885964) 4915 S. 146th Cir., Omaha, NE 68137-1402 USA Tel 712-727-3772.

Puarose Publishing, (978-1-933593) P.O. Box 1597, Gilroy, CA 95021 USA Tel 408-846-0116
E-mail: admin@puarosepublishing.com
Web site: http://www.puarosepublishing.com.

Public Education Foundation, The, (978-0-9788980; 978-0-9988332) 3360 W. Sahara Ave., Suite 160, Las Vegas, NV 89102 USA Tel 702-799-1042; Fax: 702-799-5247
E-mail: dkchristensen@interact.ccsd.net
Web site: http://www.thepef.org.

Public Ink, (978-0-9772371) 314 Sandpiper Ct., Novato, CA 94949 USA Fax: 415-883-7669
E-mail: sdunwell@earthlink.net.

Public Square Bks., (978-1-59497) 307 Seventh Ave., Suite 1601, New York, NY 10001 USA (SAN 255-8149) Tel 212-604-0415; Fax: 212-604-0390; Toll Free: 800-732-3321
Web site: http://www.publicsquarebooks.com
Dist(s): **Diamond Comic Distributors, Inc.**
Diamond Bk. Distributors.

Publicaciones Citem, S.A. de C.V. (MEX) (978-970-656; 978-968-6792; 978-968-7668) *Dist. by* **Lectorum Pubns.**

Publicaciones Educativas, Inc., (978-0-9767623; 978-0-9767624; 978-0-9779806) Orders Addr.: P.O. Box 192337, San Juan, PR 00919-2337 USA Tel 787-250-8252; Fax: 787-274-1671; Edit Addr.: 1117 Ave. Munoz Rivera, San Juan, PR 00925 USA Do not confuse with Publicaciones Educativas, Inc. in Hato Rey, PR, Rio Piedras, PR
E-mail: peduc@coqui.net
Web site: http://www.libreriaeducativapr.com.

Publicaciones Fher, S.A. (ESP) (978-84-243) *Dist. by* **AIMS Intl.**

Publicaciones Papelandia, (978-0-9759194; 978-0-9765805) 843 Waukee Pass, San Antonio, TX 78260-1919 USA
E-mail: wjconaway@yahoo.com
Web site: http://www.mexicowalkingtours.com.

Publicaciones Puertorriquenas, Inc., (978-0-929441; 978-1-881713; 978-1-881720; 978-1-932243; 978-1-933485; 978-1-934630; 978-1-935145; 978-1-935606; 978-1-62537) Orders Addr.: P.O. Box 195064, San Juan, PR 00919-5064 USA; Edit Addr.: 46 Mayaguez St., San Juan, PR 00917-4915 USA (SAN 249-4272) Tel 787-759-9673; Fax: 787-250-6498
Web site: http://www.publicacionespr.com.

Publicaciones Urbanas, (978-0-615-41660-1) Garden Hills PLaza PMB 359, Carr. 19, Guaynabo, PR 00966 USA Tel 787-793-1164 (phone/fax).

Publicaciones y Ediciones Salamandra, S.A. (ESP) (978-84-7888; 978-84-86033) *Dist. by* **Lectorum Pubns.**

Publicaciones y Ediciones Salamandra, S.A. (ESP) (978-84-9838) *Dist. by* **Spanish.**

PublicAffairs, (978-1-891620; 978-1-58648; 978-1-61039; 978-1-5417; 978-1-4789-2184-4) A Member of Perseus

Publisher Name Index

Books Group, 1290 Avune of the Americas, New York, NY 10104 USA Toll Free: 800-759-0190 (and fax)
E-mail: customer.service@hbgusa.com
Web site: http://www.hbgusa.com
Dist(s): **Blackstone Audio, Inc.**
Ebsco Publishing
Follett School Solutions
Hachette Bk. Group
MyiLibrary
ebrary, Inc.

Publication Consultants, *(978-0-9644809; 978-1-888125; 978-1-59433)* 8370 Eleusis Dr., Anchorage, AK 99502 USA Tel 907-349-2424; Fax: 907-349-2426; *Imprints*: Publishing Consultants (Pubng Consultants)
E-mail: evan@publicationconsultants.com
Web site: http://www.publicationconsultants.com
Dist(s): **INscribe Digital**
News Group, The
Todd Communications
Wizard Works.

Publications International, Ltd., *(978-0-7853; 978-0-88176; 978-1-56173; 978-1-4127; 978-1-60553; 978-1-4508; 978-1-68022; 978-1-64030)* 8140 Lehigh Ave., Morton Grove, IL 60053-2627 USA (SAN 263-9823) Tel 847-676-3470; Fax: 847-676-3671; Toll Free: 800-745-9299; *Imprints*: PIL Kids (PIL Kids)
E-mail: customer_service@pubint.com
Web site: http://www.pilbooks.com
Dist(s): **Penguin Publishing Group**
Send The Light Distribution LLC.

Publications Unltd, *(978-0-9767450)* Orders Addr.: P.O. Box 30752, Raleigh, NC 27622 USA Do not confuse with Publications Unlimited in Lake Worth, FL
E-mail: cfmajors@gmail.com
Web site: http://www.publicationsunltd.com.

Publish For Christ, Incorporated *See* **Nathaniel Max Rock**

Publish To Go Pubns., *(978-0-9669289; 978-0-9728923; 978-0-9745110)* Orders Addr.: 21539 Hollandaire Dr. E., Boca Raton, FL 33433 USA; Edit Addr.: 21539 Hollandaire Dr. E., Boca Raton, FL 33433 USA Tel 561-350-4770 (phone/fax)
E-mail: marknemcek@comcast.net.

PublishAmerica, Inc., *(978-1-893162; 978-1-58851; 978-1-59129; 978-1-59286; 978-1-4137; 978-1-4241; 978-1-60441; 978-1-60474; 978-1-60563; 978-1-60610; 978-1-60672; 978-1-60703; 978-1-60813; 978-1-60836; 978-1-60749; 978-1-61546; 978-1-61582; 978-1-4489; 978-1-4512;-1-4560; 978-1-4626; 978-1-62709; 978-1-63000; 978-1-63004; 978-1-62772; 978-1-62907; 978-1-63084)* Div. of America Hse. Bk. Pubs., Orders Addr.: P.O. Box 151, Frederick, MD 21705 USA Fax: 301-631-9073; Edit Addr.: 230 E Patrick St, Frederick, MD 21701 USA; 230 E. Patrick St., Frederick, MD 21701
E-mail: pratherm@publishamerica.com; support@publishamerica.com; tina@publishamerica.com; retta@publishamerica.com; alice@publishamerica.com
Web site: http://www.publishamerica.com
Dist(s): **America Hse. Bk. Pubs.**

Published by Westview, Inc., *(978-0-9819172; 978-0-9819325; 978-1-935271; 978-1-937763; 978-1-62880; 978-0-692-95380-8)* P.O. Box 210183, Nashville, TN 37082 USA Tel 615-646-6134; Fax: 615-662-0946.

Publisher Media Services *See* **Independent Publisher Services**

Publisher Page *Imprint of* **Headline Bks., Inc.**

Publisher Plus, *(978-1-888537)* Div. of Montana Ole Store, Orders Addr.: 200 Choteau St., Sun River, MT 59483 USA Tel 406-264-5953; Fax: 406-264-5672
E-mail: rebeccahel2000@yahoo.com
Web site: http://www.montanaolestore.com.

Publishers Design Group, Inc., *(978-1-929170)* Orders Addr.: P.O. Box 37, Roseville, CA 95678 USA Tel 916-784-0500; Fax: 916-773-7421; Toll Free: 800-587-6666; Edit Addr.: 1655 Booth Rd., Roseville, CA 95747 USA; *Imprints*: PDG (PDG)
E-mail: books@publishersdesign.com; orders@publishersdesign.com; admin@publishersdesign.com; marketing@publishersdesign.com
Web site: http://www.publishersdesign.com; http://www.tearoomguide.com
Dist(s): **Quality Bks., Inc.**
Send The Light Distribution LLC.

Publishers' Graphics, L.L.C., *(978-0-9663402; 978-1-930847; 978-1-933556; 978-1-934703; 978-1-935590)* 140 Della Ct., Carol Stream, IL 60188 USA (SAN 990-0241) Toll Free: 888-404-3769
Web site: http://www.pubgraphics.com.

Publishers Group West (PGW), Div. of Ingram Content Group, Orders Addr.: 1094 Flex Dr., Jackson, TN 38301-5070 USA (SAN 631-7715) Tel 731-423-1973; Toll Free Fax: 800-351-5073; Toll Free: 800-343-4499; Edit Addr.: 387 Park Avenue South, New York, NY 10016 USA (SAN 631-760X) Tel 212-340-8100; Fax: 212-340-8195
E-mail: info@pgw.com
Web site: http://www.pgw.com/home.

Publishers Place, Inc., *(978-0-9676051; 978-0-9744785; 978-0-9771978; 978-0-9840757; 978-0-9864267; 978-0-9994072)* Div. of Grace Associates, 821 4th Ave., Suite 201, Huntington, WV 25701 USA Tel 304-697-3236; Fax: 304-697-3399; *Imprints*: Mid-Atlantic Highlands Publishing (Mid Atlantic WV)
E-mail: publishersplace@gmail.com
Web site: http://www.publishersplace.org.

Publishers' Pr., *(978-0-943592)* Orders Addr.: P.O. Box 86421, Portland, OR 97286 USA (SAN 240-7558) Do not confuse with Publishers Pr., Salt Lake City, UT.

Publishers Quality Library Service, *(978-1-4844; 978-1-5364)* P.O. Box 159, Crete, IL 60417 USA Tel 708-946-4100; Fax: 708-946-4199; Toll Free Fax: 800-896-7213; Toll Free: 800-230-1279.

Publishers@TreeHouse, The, *(978-0-9708816)* 2658 Patapsco Rd., Finksburg, MD 21048 USA Tel 410-848-9306
E-mail: pix4u@qis.net.

Publishing Assocs., Inc., *(978-0-942683)* Subs. of Financial & Commercial Printing Services, 5020 Montcalm Dr., Atlanta, GA 30331 USA (SAN 667-2183) Tel 404-349-4678; Fax: 404-629-5533
E-mail: fcpublish@aol.com.

Publishing Consultants *Imprint of* **Publication Consultants**

Publishing Cooperative, The *Imprint of* **Publishing Factory, The**

Publishing Designs, Inc., *(978-0-929540; 978-1-945127)* Orders Addr.: P.O. Box 3241, Huntsville, AL 35810 USA (SAN 249-6372) Tel 256-533-4301; Fax: 256-533-4302; Edit Addr.: 517 Killingsworth Cove Rd., Gurley, AL 35748 USA (SAN 249-6380) Tel 205-859-9372
E-mail: info@publishingdesigns.com
Dist(s): **Send The Light Distribution LLC**
Twentieth Century Christian Bks.

Publishing Factory, The, *(978-0-9722741)* 1836 Blake St., Suite 200, Denver, CO 80202 USA Tel 303-297-1233; Fax: 303-297-3997; *Imprints*: Publishing Cooperative, The (Publishing Coop)
E-mail: editorinchief@penclay.com.

Publishing Hse. Gelany, *(978-0-9712665; 978-0-9728301; 978-0-9747248; 978-0-9777566; 978-0-9817529; 978-0-9827833)* Orders Addr.: P.O. Box 61472, Staten Island, NY 10306 USA Tel 718-668-1375; Edit Addr.: 34 Maple Terr., Staten Island, NY 10306 USA
E-mail: gelany@juno.com
Web site: http://www.zagorizontom20megsfree.com.

Publishing in Motion, *(978-1-61279)* 2502 Canada bld. No. 1, Glendale, CA 91208 USA Tel 818-547-1554
E-mail: publishinginmotion@yahoo.com
Web site: www.publishinginmotion.com.

Publishing Services @ Thomson-Shore, *(978-0-9841658; 978-1-936672; 978-1-943290)* 7300 W. Joy Rd., Dexter, MI 48130 USA Tel 734-426-6248; *Imprints*: Excite Kids Press (ExciteKids); Ignition Press (IgnitionPr)
E-mail: jerryf@tshore.com
Web site: http://thomsonshore.com/publishing/
Dist(s): **Seattle Bk. Co.**

Publishing Syndicate LLC,
Dist(s): **Independent Pubs. Group**
MyiLibrary.

PublishingWorks, *(978-0-9744803; 978-1-933002; 978-1-935557)* 151 Epping Rd., Exeter, NH 03833-4522 USA Toll Free: 800-333-9883; 151 Epping Rd., Exeter, NH 03833-4522 (SAN 850-4806) Toll Free: 800-333-9883; *Imprints*: Townsend, J. N. Publishing (JNTown); Peapod Press (PeapodPr) Do not confuse with The Publishing Works in Waldport, OR
E-mail: bookpub@worldpath.net; jeremy@publishingworks.com
Web site: http://www.publishingworks.com
Dist(s): **MyiLibrary.**

PublishNext *See* **Publishing Services @ Thomson-Shore**

Pucker Art Pubns. *Imprint of* **Pucker Gallery**

Pucker Gallery, *(978-0-9635318; 978-1-879985)* 240 Newbury St. 3rd Flr., Boston, MA 02116-2897 USA Tel 617-267-9473; Fax: 617-424-9759; *Imprints*: Pucker Art Publications (Pucker Art)
E-mail: contactus@puckergallery.com; destiny@puckergallery.com; jenny@puckergallery.com
Web site: http://www.puckergallery.com
Dist(s): **Longleaf Services**
Syracuse Univ. Pr.
Univ. Pr. of New England
Univ. of Washington Pr.

Pucker Safrai Gallery *See* **Pucker Gallery**

Puckett Publishing, Inc., *(978-0-9764936)* P.O. Box 528, Columbia, IL 62236 USA.

Puddinhead LLC, *(978-0-615-24552-2)* 6470 Fogle Ct., Westerville, OH 43082 USA Tel 614-899-6112.

Puddle Jump Pr., Ltd., *(978-0-9726487)* 763 Rte. 9W, Nyack, NY 10960 USA Tel 914-645-6551 (phone/fax)
E-mail: puddlejumppress@gmail.com
Web site: http://www.puddlejumppress.com
Dist(s): **Follett School Solutions.**

Puddledancer Pr., *(978-0-9647349; 978-1-892005; 978-1-934336)* Orders Addr.: P.O. Box 231129, Encinitas, CA 92023-1129 USA Toll Free: 877-367-2849; Edit Addr.: 3245 Rim Rock Cir., Encinitas, CA 92024 USA
E-mail: email@puddledancer.com; neill@puddledancer.com; meiji@puddledancer.com
Web site: http://www.puddledancer.com; http://www.nonviolentcommunication.com
Dist(s): **Ebsco Publishing**
Independent Pubs. Group
MyiLibrary
ebrary, Inc.

Puddletown Publishing Group, Inc., *(978-1-61413)* 4125 SE 63rd, Portland, OR 97206 USA Tel 503-320-1242
E-mail: lachance@puddletowngroup.com
Web site: puddletowngroup.com
Dist(s): **BookBaby.**

Puffin *Imprint of* **Penguin Publishing Group**

Puffin Books *Imprint of* **Penguin Publishing Group**

Puffin Books *Imprint of* **Penguin Young Readers Group**

Puget Sound Bks., *(978-0-9715019)* Div. of Angel Fire Pr., Orders Addr.: 14403 N. Silverado Dr., Fountain Hls, AZ 85268-3048 USA Tel 480-304-2948
E-mail: almoeblog@yahoo.com.

Pugh, Val, *(978-0-692-54429-7; 978-0-692-68624-9; 978-0-9982706)* 3536 Del Rio St., Shreveport, LA 71109 USA Tel 318-550-1272
E-mail: valerie@valpughlove.com
Web site: www.valpughlove.com.

Pulp Collector Press *See* **Adventure Hse.**

Pulte, Therese Marie, *(978-0-9746557)* 1278 Glenneyre St., Suite 39, Laguna Beach, CA 92651 USA; *Imprints*: Destination Publishers (Destin Pubs)
Web site: http://www.destinationpublishers.com.

Pumpkin Hill Productions, *(978-0-9793602)* P.O. Box 165, Hawleyville, CT 06440 USA
E-mail: nmroddas@aol.com.

Pumpkin House Company *See* **Pumpkin Hse., Ltd.**

Pumpkin Hse., Ltd., *(978-0-9646010)* 3508 La Rochelle Dr., Columbus, OH 43221 USA (SAN 255-0644) Fax: 614-557-9635
E-mail: pumpkinhouse@columbus.rr.com
Web site: http://www.pumpkinhouse.net
Dist(s): **Independent Pubs. Group.**

Pumpkin Patch Publishing, *(978-0-9754823)* 10911 E. Skinner Dr., Scottsdale, AZ 85262 USA.

Pumpkin Ridge Publishing, *(978-0-9754459)* P.O. Box 1668, North Plains, OR 97113-6157 USA (SAN 256-1379) Tel 503-647-5970
E-mail: prpublish@msn.com
Web site: http://www.factoryride.com.

Pumpkin Seed Pr., *(978-0-9700273)* 68335 355th Ave., Humphrey, NE 68642 USA Tel 402-923-1682; Fax: 402-923-9110; Toll Free Fax: 877-923-1682
E-mail: rjnoona@megavision.com; rjnoona@magavision.com
Web site: http://www.usedhomeschoolbooks.com/bgh.htm.

Pumpkin Seeds Pr., *(978-0-615-17159-3)* 24 Uranus Rd., Sewell, NJ 08080 USA
Dist(s): **Lulu Pr., Inc.**

Pumpkins Pansies Bunnies & Bears, *(978-0-9747367)* Orders Addr.: 19 Treevine Ct., The Woodlands, TX 77381 USA Tel 281-785-0755
E-mail: paklppbb@aol.com; tricialowenfield@gmail.com
Web site: http://www.tricialowenfielddesign.com.

Punch Press Publications *See* **New Growth Pr.**

Punkin Pr., *(978-1-60149)* 1221 S. Sherbourne Dr., Apt. No. 5, Los Angeles, CA 90035 USA
E-mail: punkinpress@hotmail.com
Web site: http://www.punkinpress.net.

Punta Gorda Pr., *(978-1-929528)* 2760 W. Marion Ave., Punta Gorda, FL 33950 USA
E-mail: joeinnovations@gmail.com
Web site: http://www.puntagordapress.com.

Punto de Lectura *Imprint of* **Santillana USA Publishing Co., Inc.**

Puppet Rescue, *(978-0-9799958)* 711 9th St., No. 2, Santa Monica, CA 90402 USA (SAN 854-9516) Tel 310-656-7738
E-mail: darinvents@adelphia.net
Web site: http://www.puppetrescue.com.

Puppetry in Practice, *(978-0-9720183)* 1923 Haring St., Brooklyn, NY 11229-3713 USA
E-mail: tovaa@aol.com
Web site: http://www.puppetryinpractice.com.

Puptattle Pr., Inc., *(978-0-9786947)* 21813 S. Embassy Ave., Carson, CA 90810 USA
Web site: http://www.puptattle.com.

†**Purdue Univ. Pr.,** *(978-0-911198; 978-1-55753; 978-1-61249)* Orders Addr.: P.O. Box 388, Ashland, OH 44805 USA Toll Free: 800-247-6553; Edit Addr.: 504 W. State St. Stewart Ctr. 370, West Lafayette, IN 47907-2058 USA (SAN 203-4026) Tel 765-494-2038; Fax: 765-496-2442 Do not confuse with Purdue Univ. Pubns., same address
E-mail: mchunt@purdue.edu
Web site: http://www.thepress.purdue.edu/
Dist(s): **BookMasters, Inc.**
Bookmasters Distribution
Ebsco Publishing
Follett School Solutions
MyiLibrary
Trajectory, Inc.; *CIP.*

Pure Joy Pubns., *(978-0-9749578)* P.O. Box 482, Wheat Ridge, CO 80034-0482 USA
E-mail: purejoypublications@comcast.net.

PureLight Pubns., *(978-0-9787597; 978-0-615-23432-8; 978-0-9825988)* Orders Addr.: P.O. Box 720193, Dallas, TX 75372 USA Tel 214-770-0206 weekdays 9am to 5 pm
E-mail: pl.publications@yahoo.com; seaonducote@aol.com
Web site: http://www.seaonducoteproductions.com; http://www.purelightpublications.org
Dist(s): **Lulu Pr., Inc.**

Pureplay Pr., *(978-0-9714366; 978-0-9765096)* 11353 Missouri Ave., Los Angeles, CA 90025-5553 USA (SAN 852-5404) Tel 310-479-8773; Fax: 310-473-9384
E-mail: editor@pureplaypress.com
Web site: http://www.pureplaypress.com
Dist(s): **BookMasters, Inc.**

pureplaypress.com *See* **Pureplay Pr.**

Purfect Promises, *(978-0-9759343)* 149 Summerhill Dr., Rockwall, TX 75032 USA Tel 972-771-9528; Fax: 972-772-5403
E-mail: purfectpromises@aol.com.

Purgatory Publishing, Inc., *(978-1-932867)* 904 Colonial Ct., Coatesville, PA 19320 USA; *Imprints*: West End Games (W End Games)
Web site: http://www.westendgames.com
Dist(s): **Century Pr.**
Diamond Distributors, Inc.

Purity Pr. Pubs., *(978-0-9728797)* P.O. Box 2896, Decatur, GA 30031 USA.

Purple Bear Bks., Inc., *(978-1-933327)* 300 Park Ave., Suite 1700, New York, NY 10022 USA.

Purple Cow Pr., *(978-0-9820983)* 14688 Denmark Ct., Apple Valley, MN 55124 USA Tel 952-322-1419
E-mail: wdwaibel@aol.com
Web site: http://www.rudyslittleworld.com.

Purple Crayon Studios, *(978-0-9706491)* 0-115 Luce, SW, Grand Rapids, MI 49055 USA Tel 616-822-3186; Toll Free Fax: 877-710-2368
E-mail: beryl@pca3d.com
Web site: http://www.mushtons.com.

Purple Haze Pr., *(978-0-9773200; 978-1-935183)* Orders Addr.: 2195 Malibu lake Cir., No. 1134, Naples, FL 34119 USA; Edit Addr.: 2430 Vanderbilt Beach Rd., No. 108, PMB 167, Naples, FL 34109 USA
E-mail: v@purpleV.com; p_tomasello@yahoo.com
Web site: http://www.purplehazepress.com
Dist(s): **Bookmasters Distribution**
ebrary, Inc.

Purple Hse. Pr., *(978-1-930900)* Orders Addr.: P.O. Box 787, Cynthiana, KY 41031 USA; Edit Addr.: 8100 US Hwy. 62 E., Cynthiana, KY 41031-6796 USA
E-mail: ray@purplehousepress.com
Web site: http://www.purplehousepress.com.

Purple Ink, Inc., *(978-0-9801002; 978-1-939119)* Orders Addr.: P.O. Box 41232, Houston, TX 77241 USA (SAN 855-1987) Tel 713-705-5530; Fax: 713-474-5529
E-mail: onediagage@purpleink.net
Web site: http://www.purpleink.net.

Purple Lady Productions, *(978-0-9714506)* P.O. Box 1277, Tiburon, CA 94920-4277 USA Tel 415-435-0720
E-mail: purpleladybythebay@earthlink.net.

Purple Lizard Pr. LLC, *(978-0-9762902)* Orders Addr.: P.O. Box 68883, Tucson, AZ 85737-7076 USA Tel 520-575-6660
E-mail: Julie@PurpleLizardPress.com
Web site: http://www.purplelizardpress.com.

Purple Mountain Pr., Ltd., *(978-0-916346; 978-0-935796; 978-1-930098)* Orders Addr.: P.O. Box 309, Fleischmanns, NY 12430-0309 USA (SAN 222-3716) Tel 845-254-4062; Fax: 845-254-4476; Toll Free: 800-325-2665; Edit Addr.: 1060 Main St., Fleischmanns, NY 12430 USA Do not confuse with Purple Mountain Pr., Carson City, NV
E-mail: purple@catskill.net
Web site: http://www.catskill.net/purple.

Purple Peaks Pr., *(978-0-9971266)* Orders Addr.: 145 Univ. Dr. No. 3048, Amherst, MA 01004 USA Tel 908-763-6397; Edit Addr.: 145 Univ. Dr. No. 3048, Amherst , MA 01004 USA Tel 908-763-6397
E-mail: mepsteinagain@comcast.net.

Purple Penguin Publishing, *(978-0-9765473)* 3929 Hummingbird Ln., Roanoke, VA 24018 USA Tel 540-400-7220; Toll Free: 800-788-3196
E-mail: tanyapenguin@aol.com
Web site: http://www.underragingskies.tanyaadams.com.

Purple People, Inc., *(978-0-9707793)* P.O. Box 3194, Sedona, AZ 86340-3194 USA Tel 928-204-6400; Fax: 928-282-1662
E-mail: info@purplepeople.com
Web site: http://www.purplepeople.com.

Purple Pig Publishing, *(978-0-9700380)* Orders Addr.: P.O. Box 1083, Bethel, CT 06801 USA Tel 203-797-1857; Edit Addr.: 7 Wixon Rd., Danbury, CT 06811 USA
E-mail: jshaboo@att.net.

Purple Plume Pr., *(978-0-9744923)* 5980 Peach Ave., Manteca, CA 95337 USA Tel 209-825-7602
E-mail: purpleplumepress@cs.com; purpleplumeprss@cs.com.

Purple Toad Publishing, Inc., *(978-1-62469)* 204 S. Union St., Kennett Square, PA 19348 USA Tel 610-444-8259
E-mail: cynthia@purpletoadpublishing.com.

Purple Unicorn Pr., *(978-0-692-36341-6; 978-0-692-64540-6)* 1635 35th Ave., Seattle, WA 98122 USA Tel 206-909-8562
E-mail: kat@hopmann.org.

PUSH *Imprint of* **Scholastic, Inc.**

Pushkin Children's Bks. *Imprint of* **Steerforth Pr.**

Pushkin Press *Imprint of* **Steerforth Pr.**

Putnam Juvenile *Imprint of* **Penguin Publishing Group**

Putschakap?n Pr., *(978-0-9978943)* 1720 Spruce St., Philadelphia, PA 19103 USA Tel 267-318-7297
E-mail: edmundweisberg@yahoo.com.

Putumayo World Music & Crafts, *(978-1-885265; 978-1-58759)* Div. of Putumayo, Inc., 324 Lafayette St., 7th Flr., New York, NY 10012 USA Tel 212-625-1400; Fax: 212-460-0095; Toll Free: 800-995-9588
E-mail: info@putumayo.com
Web site: http://www.putumayo.com
Dist(s): **Follett School Solutions**
Recorded Bks., Inc.
Rhino Entertainment Co, A Warner Music Group Co.
Rounder Kids Music Distribution.

Puumakaa Pr., *(978-0-9762387)* Orders Addr.: P.O. Box 500, Na'Alehu, HI 96772 USA; Edit Addr.: 94-6448 Mamalahoa Hwy., Na'Alehu, HI 96772 USA
E-mail: elizabeth@fastnethi.com
Web site: http://www.inka-online.com.

Puwaii International, LLC, *(978-0-9787949)* 7326 N. 61 St., Paradise Valley, AZ 85253 USA
E-mail: jerrelvanier@yahoo.com
Web site: http://www.puwaiiadventures.com.

Puzzlewright *Imprint of* **Sterling Publishing Co., Inc.**

PW.Co., *(978-0-9745102)* 774 Henry St., Apt. 1E, Brooklyn, NY 11231-3153 USA
E-mail: tregeryefim@aol.com.

PXL Media, LLC, *(978-0-9749322)* P.O. Box 99, LeClaire, IA 52753-0099 USA
E-mail: pxlmedia@aol.com.

Pyle, Robert Associates *See* **Avocus Publishing, Inc.**

Pyr Bks. *Imprint of* **Prometheus Bks., Pubs.**

Pyramid Dancer Pubns., *(978-0-9659913)* P.O. Box 5263, Colorado Spgs, CO 80931-5263 USA
E-mail: rjb@phoenixbonsai.com
Web site: http://www.phoenixbonsai.com.

Pyramid Educational Products, Inc., *(978-1-928598)* Div of Pyramid Educational Consultants, Incorporated, 13 Garfield Way, Newark, DE 19713-3450 USA
E-mail: dbittner@pyramidproducts.com
Web site: http://www.pyramidproducts.com.

Pyramid Publishing, Inc., *(978-1-885920; 978-1-934008)* Orders Addr.: P.O. Box 129, Zenda, WI 53195-0129 USA Tel 414-275-3384; Fax: 414-275-3584; P.O. Box 129, Zenda, WI 53195 Do not confuse with companies with the same name in Utica, NY, Montgomery, AL
E-mail: pyramid2mail@gmail.com.

Pyrola Publishing, *(978-0-9618348)* P.O. Box 80961, Fairbanks, AK 99708 USA (SAN 667-3503) Tel 907-455-6469 (phone/fax)
E-mail: mshields@mosquitonet.com
Web site: http://www.maryshields.com.

Pyxie Moss Press *See* **Fun Fitness Publishing**

Q & A Books *See* **Paradoxical Pr., The**

Q & J Bird Pr., LLC, *(978-0-615-16566-0)* 141 Morey Pl., Greensburg, PA 15601 USA
E-mail: icanbe@qandjbirdpress.com
Web site: http://www.qandjbirdpress.com.

QEB Publishing Inc., *(978-1-59566; 978-1-60992; 978-1-68297)* Div. of QED Publishing, 6 Orchard, Ste. 100, Lake Forest, CA 92630 USA Tel 949-380-7510
Web site: http://www.qed-publishing.co.uk; http://www.quarto.com
Dist(s): **Hachette Bk. Group**
Lerner Publishing Group
Scholastic Bk. Fairs.

QED Publishing *See* **QEB Publishing Inc.**

Quackenbush, Robert Studios, *(978-0-9612518; 978-0-9712757)* Orders Addr.: 460 E. 79th St., Suite 14E, New York, NY 10021 USA (SAN 656-0458) Tel 212-744-3822; Fax: 212-861-2761
E-mail: rqstudios@aol.com
Web site: http://www.rquackenbush.com.

Quackenworth Publishing, *(978-1-933211)* P.O. Box 4747, Culver City, CA 90230-4747 USA Tel 310-945-5634; Fax: 310-945-5709
E-mail: info@quackenworth.com
Web site: http://www.quackenworth.com.

Quad Cities' Learning, Incorporated *See* **Quad City Pr.**

Quad City Pr., *(978-0-9824448; 978-0-9863898; 978-0-692-52738-2)* 2127 3rd St., Suite B, East Moline, IL 61244-2409 USA (SAN 858-1819)
Web site: http://www.weeklywilson.com
Dist(s): **CreateSpace Independent Publishing Platform.**

QuadMama Pr., *(978-1-944701)* 538 Sinton Ave, Colorado Springs, CO 80906 USA Tel 719-391-8980
E-mail: MyBusinessTweets@outlook.com.

Quadradrillion, LLC - Publishing Division *See* **Transaltar Publishing**

Quail Ridge Pr., Inc., *(978-0-937552; 978-1-893062; 978-1-934193; 978-1-938879)* Orders Addr.: P.O. Box 123, Brandon, MS 39043 USA (SAN 257-8794) Tel 601-825-2063; Fax: 601-825-3091; Toll Free Fax: 800-864-1082; Toll Free: 800-343-1583
E-mail: lward@quailridge.com
Web site: http://www.quailridge.com
Dist(s): **Booklines Hawaii, Ltd.**
Gibson, Dot Pubns.
Forest Sales & Distributing Co.
Islander Group
Southwest Cookbook Distributors.

Quake *Imprint of* **Echelon Press Publishing**

Quaker Press of Friends General Conference *See* **QuakerPress**

QuakerPress, *(978-0-9620912; 978-1-888305; 978-1-937768)* Div. of Friends General Conference, 1216 Arch St., 2B, Philadelphia, PA 19107 USA (SAN 225-4484) Tel 215-561-1700; Fax: 215-561-0759; Toll Free: 800-966-4556
E-mail: publications@fgcquaker.org; bookstore@fgcquaker.org
Web site: http://www.fgcquaker.org/services/fgc-publications.

Quale Pr. LLC, *(978-0-9656161; 978-0-9700663; 978-0-9744503; 978-0-9792999; 978-1-935835; 978-1-939606)* 2 Hillcrest Rd., Niantic, CT 06357 USA Tel 860-739-9153 (phone/fax); P.O. Box 642, Niantic, CT 06357 Tel 860-739-9153
E-mail: central@quale.com
Web site: http://www.quale.com
Dist(s): **ConsuLogic Consulting Services**
SPD-Small Pr. Distribution.

Quality Nature Displays by Eddie Dunbar *See* **Insect Sciences Museum of California**

Quality of Life Publishing Co., *(978-0-9675532; 978-0-9816219; 978-0-9972612)* 6210 Shirley St., Suite 112, Naples, FL 34109-6258 USA Toll Free: 877-513-0099
Web site: http://www.qolpublishing.com
Dist(s): **Bookmasters Distribution.**

Quality Pubs., *(978-0-9671107)* Orders Addr.: P.O. Box 691546, San Antonio, TX 78269 USA Tel 210-699-9007; Fax: 210-641-6334; Edit Addr.: 11238 Jade Green, San Antonio, TX 78249 USA Toll Free: 888-633-9898
E-mail: aroman@qualitypublishers.com
Web site: http://www.medpress.com.

Quality Publishing Inc., *(978-0-9745741; 978-0-9759309)* 1005 E. Highland Ave., Rome, GA 30161 USA Fax: 706-290-1223; Toll Free: 800-262-4404
E-mail: bbmonday@comcast.net.

Quantum Manifestations Publishing, *(978-0-9718099; 978-1-933505)* 1360 University Ave., W. Suite #104-192, Saint Paul, MN 55104 USA Tel 678-227-3162
E-mail: pm@quantumdatingclub.com
Web site: http://www.quantummanifestationspublishing.com.

Quantum One Publishing, *(978-0-9755681)* 1728 Spruce Ln., Linton, IN 47441 USA Tel 812-847-8708; Fax: 812-847-8712
E-mail: jdsapara@iglide.net.

Quarrier Pr., *(978-0-938985; 978-0-9646197; 978-1-891852; 978-1-942294)* 1125 Central Ave., Charleston, WV 25302 USA Tel 304-342-1848; Fax: 304-343-0594; Toll Free: 888-982-7472; *Imprints:* Mountain Memories Books (Mtn Memories Bks)
E-mail: clemmtstate@gmail.com
Web site: http://www.wvbookco.com
Dist(s): **West Virginia Book Co., The.**

Quarry Bks. *Imprint of* **Indiana Univ. Pr.**

Quarry Bks. *Imprint of* **Quarto Publishing Group USA**

Quarry Books *Imprint of* **Quarto Publishing Group USA**

Quarry Pr. (CAN) *(978-0-919627; 978-1-55082; 978-1-894997) Dist. by* **SCB Distributo.**

Quarrystone Bond *See* **Club4Girls Publishing Co.**

Quarter Milestones Publishing, *(978-0-9748216)* Orders Addr.: P.O. Box 441, Milligan College, TN 37682-0441 USA Tel 423-542-0159; Fax: 423-542-9532; Edit Addr.: 1682 Powder Branch Rd., Johnson City, TN 37601-6220 USA
E-mail: qmp@preferred.com
Web site: http://www.quartermilestones.com
Dist(s): **Overmountain Pr.**

Quarterback Press *See* **Why Not Bks.**

Quarto Publishing Group UK (GBR) *(978-0-7112; 978-1-85410; 978-0-948149; 978-0-906053; 978-0-946544; 978-0-906459; 978-1-84092; 978-1-85076; 978-1-84543; 978-1-84507; 978-1-84538; 978-1-84513; 978-1-84780; 978-1-84835; 978-1-78131; 978-1-78171; 978-1-910277; 978-1-78493) Dist. by* **HachBkGrp.**

Quarto Publishing Group USA, *(978-0-7603; 978-0-86573; 978-0-89738; 978-0-912612; 978-0-929261; 978-0-9640392; 978-1-55832; 978-1-56010; 978-1-888608; 978-1-930604; 978-1-58923; 978-1-59186; 978-1-59233; 978-1-59253; 978-1-60058; 978-1-61673; 978-1-936309; 978-1-61058; 978-1-61059; 978-1-61060; 978-1-937994; 978-1-939581; 978-1-62788; 978-1-63106; 978-1-63159; 978-1-63322; 978-1-942875) Orders Addr.: Retail Order Dept., Quayside Publishing Group 18705 Lake Dr. E., Chanhassen, MN 55317 USA Tel 1-952-936-4700; Fax: 1-952-099-9101; Toll Free: 1-800-328-0590; Edit Addr.: 3 Wrigley Suite A, Irvine, CA 92618-2748 USA (SAN 249-051X) Toll Free: 800-426-0099; Imprints:* Motorbooks (Motorbks); Zenith Press (Zenith Press); Creative Publishing International (Creativ Pub); Rockport Publishers (Rockport Pub); Quarry Books (QuarryBks); Voyageur Press (VoyageurPr); Walter Foster (WalterFoster); Walter Foster Jr (WalterFostJr); Race Point Publishing (RacePtPub); Fair Winds Press (FairWindsPr); Motorbooks (Motorbooks); Zenith Press (ZenithPr); Quarry Books (QuarryBksUSA); Voyageur Press (VoyageurUSA); Creative Publishing International (CreatPubIntl); Rockport Publishers (Rockport); Moondance Press (Moondance); Seagrass Press (Seagrass)
E-mail: rebecca.razo@quartous.com
Web site: http://www.quartoknows.com/Walter-Foster
Dist(s): **Arcadia Publishing**
Hachette Bk. Group
Lerner Publishing Group
MyiLibrary.

Quatemion Pr., *(978-0-9672535)* P.O. Box 700564, San Antonio, TX 78270 USA Tel 210-497-1096.

Que, *(978-0-7897; 978-0-88022; 978-1-56529)* Div. of Pearson Technology Group, 201 W. 103rd St., Indianapolis, IN 46290-1094 USA Tel 317-581-3500; Toll Free: 800-428-5331 (orders); 800-858-7674 (customer service) Do not confuse with Que Software, also a division of Macmillan Computer Publishing, same address
E-mail: customerservice@macmillanUSA.com
Web site: http://www.quepublishing.com
Dist(s): **Alpha Bks.**
Ebsco Publishing
MyiLibrary
Pearson Education
Pearson Technology Group
Sams Technical Publishing, LLC.

Quebla, *(978-0-9772738)* P.O. Box 958073, Duluth, GA 30095 USA Tel 404-906-3993
E-mail: support@quebla.com
Web site: http://www.quebla.com.

Queen Adisa, *(978-0-9979672)* 443 Riverbend Apt, Riverside, AL 35135 USA Tel 205-362-5000
E-mail: adisasalim@gmail.com
Web site: www.queenadisa.com.

Queen Alexandra Foundation for Children (CAN) *(978-0-9880536) Dist. by* **Orca Bk Pub.**

Queen Pubns, *(978-0-9778377)* Orders Addr.: P.O. Box 496, Antioch, IL 60002 USA
E-mail: apascascio@comcast.net
Web site: http://www.queenpublications.com.

Queen's Knight, *(978-0-9752810)* 8741 Saline Waterwirks Rd., Saline, MI 48176 USA.

Queens Museum of Art, *(978-0-9604514; 978-1-929641)* New York City Bldg., Flushing Meadows Park, Queens, NY 11368-3398 USA (SAN 280-2147) Tel 718-592-9700; Fax: 718-592-5778
Web site: http://www.queensmuseum.org
Dist(s): **D.A.P./Distributed Art Pubs.**
Univ. Pr. of New England.

Quentin Road Ministries *See* **Victory In Grace Ministries**

Quercus (GBR) *(978-1-905204; 978-1-84724; 978-1-906694; 978-1-84916; 978-0-85705; 978-0-85738; 978-1-84866; 978-1-78087; 978-1-78206; 978-1-78429) Dist. by* **HachBkGrp.**

Quercus *Imprint of* **Quercus NA**

Quercus NA, *(978-1-62365; 978-1-63378; 978-1-68144; 978-1-63506)* Orders Addr.: 31 W. 57th St. 6th fl, New York, NY 10019 USA; Edit Addr.: 1290 Avenue of the Americas, Flr. 4, New York, NY 10104 USA; *Imprints:* Quercus (Querc); Jo Fletcher Books (Jo Fletcher Bks)
E-mail: nathmaru@gmail.com; eric.price@quercus.com
Dist(s): **Hachette Bk. Group**
MyiLibrary
Random Hse., Inc.

Quercus Pr., *(978-0-9793444)* P.O. Box 46163, Plymouth, MN 55446-0163 USA (SAN 853-1773)
Web site: http://www.windingoak.com.

Questmarc Publishing, *(978-0-9634251; 978-0-9755801; 978-0-9819946; 978-1-939532)* Orders Addr.: P.O. Box 340, Yankton, SD 57078 USA Tel 605-660-0335; Fax: 605-260-6873; Edit Addr.: 811 W. 8th, Yankton, SD 57078 USA Tel 605-660-0335
E-mail: questmarc@gmail.com
Web site: http://www.questmarc.com.

Quick Book Publishing *See* **FREOMM Publishing**

Quick Quest Pubns. LLC, *(978-0-9760372)* Orders Addr.: P.O. Box 9934, Alexandria, VA 22306 USA Toll Free Fax: 800-682-6576; Edit Addr.: P.O. Box 9934, Alexandria, VA 22304 USA Tel 978-726-5713
E-mail: nathanialportis@yahoo.com; mnportis@yahoo.com
Web site: http://www.quickquestpub.com.

Quick Wisdom Publishers *See* **Aylen Publishing**

Quickpresspublishing Incorporated *See* **Quick Quest Pubns. LLC**

Quiet Impact, Inc., *(978-0-9713749; 978-0-9754629)* 140 Cherry St., No. 388, Hamilton, MT 59840 USA Tel 406-375-9378; Fax: 406-363-5234; *Imprints:* Character-in-Action (Character-in-Action)
E-mail: elhamilton@quietimpact.com; elhamilton@character-in-action.com
Web site: http://www.character-in-action.com; http://www.quietimpact.com.

Quiet Man, *(978-0-9744251)* 28 W. 44th St., Suite 2105, New York, NY 10036-6600 USA (SAN 255-7150) Tel 212-921-4444; Fax: 212-921-4504
E-mail: dawn@quietman.net
Web site: http://www.quietman.net.

Quiet Man Publishing, *(978-0-9742829)* 27542 Berkshire Hills Pl., Valencia, CA 91354 USA
E-mail: jh1429@yahoo.com
Web site: http://www.Quietmanpublishing.com.

Quiet Owl Bks., *(978-0-615-54891-3; 978-0-615-59366-1; 978-0-615-64284-0; 978-0-615-64677-0; 978-0-615-65835-3; 978-0-9859443; 978-0-615-67800-9; 978-0-9898331)* 85 E. Point Rd., Montrose, PA 18801 USA Tel 323-253-1411; 570-278-6332
E-mail: books@quietowl.com
Web site: http://quietowl.com/
Dist(s): **CreateSpace Independent Publishing Platform**
Dummy Record Do Not USE!!!!.

Quiet Storm Publishing Group, *(978-0-9714296; 978-0-9728819; 978-0-9744084; 978-0-9749608; 978-0-9758571; 978-0-9770070; 978-0-9787528)* Orders Addr.: P.O. Box 1666, Martinsburg, WV 25401 USA; Edit Addr.: 1045 Needmore Rd., Martinsburg, WV 25401 USA
E-mail: quietstormbooks@yahoo.com
Web site: http://www.quietstormpublishing.com.

Quiet Time Pr. *Imprint of* **TKG Publishing**

Quiet Vision Publishing, *(978-1-57646; 978-1-891595; 978-1-60545)* Orders Addr.: 12155 Mountain Shadow Rd., Sandy, UT 84092-5812 USA Tel 801-572-4018; Fax: 801-571-8625; Toll Free: 800-442-4018
E-mail: john@quietvision.com; info@quietvision.com
Web site: http://www.quietvision.com.

Quiet Waters Pubns., *(978-0-9663966; 978-1-931475)* Orders Addr.: P.O. Box 0034, Bolivar, MO 65613-0034 USA Tel 417-326-5001; Fax: 617-249-0256; Edit Addr.: 1228 Northwood Cir., Bolivar, MO 65613 USA
E-mail: qwp@usa.net
Web site: http://www.quietwaterspub.com; http://www.fromthescholarsdesk.com.

Quigley, Karen, *(978-0-9800449)* P.O. Box 535, Blackwood, NJ 08012 USA (SAN 855-076X)
E-mail: loveelwood @comcast.net
Web site: http://www.EveryoneLovesElwood.com.

Quill & Hearth Publishing Hse., *(978-0-9984597)* 8 Hammer Ln., Rustburg, VA 24588 USA Tel 540-535-8952
E-mail: jessiebiggs@ymail.com.

Quiller Publishing, Ltd. (GBR) *(978-1-904057; 978-1-84689) Dist. by* **IPG Chicago.**

Quillpen, *(978-0-9673504)* 1520 Waverly Dr., Trenton, MI 48183 USA Tel 734-676-1285; Fax: 734-676-9822
E-mail: bfquillpen@msn.com.

Quillrunner Publishing LLC, *(978-0-9796330; 978-0-9851157)* 8423 Los Reyes Ct., NW, Albuquerque, NM 87120 USA (SAN 853-9669) Tel 505-890-0723
E-mail: khickman@comcast.net
Web site: http://www.quillrunner.com.

Quimby & Sneet Publications *See* **405 Pubns.**

Quindaro Pr., *(978-0-9669258; 978-0-9764434; 978-1-946248)* 3808 Genessee St., Kansas City, MO 64111 USA Tel 816-200-2276
E-mail: quindaropress@gmail.com
Web site: http://www.quindaropress.com
Dist(s): **Itasca Bks.**

Quindim *See* **KINJIN Global**

Quinlan Pr., *(978-0-933341; 978-0-9611268; 978-1-55770)* 1 Devonshire Pl., No. 3108, Boston, MA 02109-3515 USA (SAN 226-4641).

Quinn Entertainment, *(978-0-9773099)* 7535 Austin Harbour Dr., Cumming, GA 30041 USA (SAN 257-2575) Tel 770-356-3847; Fax: 770-886-1475
E-mail: stephaniequinn@bellsouth.net
Web site: http://www.startabusinessteachingkids.com.

Quinn Micheal Publishing, Incorporated *See* **Rhapsody Branding, Inc.**

†**Quintessence Publishing Co., Inc.**, *(978-0-86715; 978-0-931386; 978-1-85097; 978-1-883695)* 4350 Chandler Dr., Hanover Park, IL 60133-6763 USA (SAN 215-9783)
E-mail: service@quintbook.com
Web site: http://www.quintpub.com; *CIP.*

Quintessential Corp., *(978-0-9715298)* P.O. Box 9224, Mclean, VA 22102 USA Tel 703-734-4900
E-mail: info@qproductsarchery.com
Web site: http://qproductsarchery.com.

Quintessential Pr. *Imprint of* **Price World Publishing**

Quirk Bks., *(978-1-931686; 978-1-59474; 978-1-68369)* 215 Church St., Philadelphia, PA 19106 USA Tel 215-627-3581; Fax: 215-627-5220
E-mail: jane@quirkbooks.com
Web site: http://www.quirkbooks.com
Dist(s): **Hachette Bk. Group**
MyiLibrary
Penguin Random Hse. LLC
Random Hse., Inc.

Quirkles, The *Imprint of* **Creative 3, LLC**

†**Quite Specific Media Group, Ltd.**, *(978-0-89676)* Orders Addr.: 7373 Pyramid Pl., Hollywood, CA 90046-1312 USA (SAN 213-5752) Tel 323-851-5797; Fax: 323-851-5798; *Imprints:* Costume & Fashion Press (Costume & Fashion Pr)
E-mail: info@quitespecificmedia.com
Web site: http://www.quitespecificmedia.com; *CIP.*

Quixote Press *See* **Padwolf Publishing, Inc.**

Quixote Pr., *(978-1-57166; 978-1-878488)* 1854 345th Ave., Wever, IA 52658-9597 USA Tel 319-372-7480; Fax: 319-372-7485; Toll Free: 800-571-2665 Do not confuse with Quixote Pr., Houston, TX, Los Angeles, CA
E-mail: heartsntummies@hotmail.com
Dist(s): **Bookmen, Inc.**

Quoir, *(978-0-9765222; 978-0-9827446; 978-1-938480; 978-0-9913345)* 5927 E. Creekside Ave. Unit 46, Orange, CA 92869 USA Tel 714-403-1922
E-mail: rafael@quoir.com
Web site: www.quoir.com.

QuotationWorld Pubns., *(978-0-9741868)* 3035 Shannon Lakes Dr., N., Tallahassee, FL 32309 USA Tel 850-894-1903 (phone/fax)
E-mail: admin@quotationworld.com
Web site: http://www.quotationworld.com.

Quotidian, Incorporated *See* **Quotidian Pubs.**

Quotidian Pubs., *(978-0-934391)* Orders Addr.: 377 River Rd., Cushing, ME 04563-9502 USA (SAN 693-8094) Tel 207-354-7091
E-mail: judydownmaine@roadrunner.com.

Quranic Educational Society, *(978-0-9760681)* Orders Addr.: P.O. Box 597969, Chicago, IL 60659 USA; Edit Addr.: 6355 N Claremont Ave., Chicago, IL 60659 USA Tel 773-743-9345
E-mail: qeschicago@sbcglobal.net
Web site: http://www.qesonline.org.

R & D Educational Center *See* **Boarding House Publishing**

R & D Publishing of Lakeland, Florida, *(978-0-9797566)* 5709 LaSerena Ave., Lakeland, FL 33809-4262 USA Tel 863-859-2984.

R & J Publishing, *(978-0-615-15136-6)* 1136 5th Ave. S., Anoka, MN 55303-2726 USA
E-mail: bobhelf.1@juno.com.

R & R Advertising, *(978-0-9765225)* 3409 Executive Ctr. Dr., No. 202, Austin, TX 78731 USA Tel 512-342-0110; Fax: 512-342-0142
E-mail: info@rradinc.com
Web site: http://www.rradinc.com.

R & R Publishing, LLC, *(978-0-9764845; 978-0-615-34449-2; 978-0-9829599; 978-0-9830577)* Div. of GlutenFree Passport, Orders Addr.: 80 Burr Ridge Pkwy. Suite 141, Burr Rudge, IL 60527 USA Tel 312-244-3702; Fax: 312-276-8001 Do not confuse with companies with the same or similar name in Torrance, CA, Brimingham, AL, Shelton, WA, San Antonio, TX, Washington, DC, Baldwin City, KS
E-mail: info@rrpublishing.com; kkoeller@glutenfreepassport.com
Web site: http://www.glutenfreepassport.com.

R & S Bks. (SWE) *(978-91-29) Dist. by* **Macmillan.**

R & S Pubns., *(978-0-615-18520-0; 978-0-615-18814-0)* 6799 Durham Rd., Whitehall, MI 49461 USA
E-mail: beckywlt@charterinternet.com
Web site: http://www.rspublications.com
Dist(s): **Lulu Pr., Inc.**

RBC Publishing Co., Inc., *(978-0-9703178; 978-0-9721547)* Orders Addr.: P.O. Box 1330, Elk Grove, CA 95759 USA Tel 916-685-5578; Fax: 916-685-5958; Edit Addr.: 9107 Voos Ct., Elk Grove, CA 95624 USA; *Imprints:* Parks Publishing (Parks Publ)
E-mail: scituate@citlink.net
Web site: http://www.rbcpublishingco.com.

R.B. Media, Inc., *(978-0-9700021; 978-0-9797932)* 14064 Monterey Estates Dr., Delray Beach, FL 33446-2217 USA Tel 561-498-5922; Fax: 561-498-2369
E-mail: mabudnik@comcast.net
Web site: http://www.rbmediainc.com.

R. E. Farrellbooks, LLC, *(978-0-9759116; 978-0-9963587)* Orders Addr.: 18212 N. 130th Ave, Sun City West, AZ 85375-5015 USA
E-mail: ref40@msn.com
Web site: http://www.refarrellbooks.com.

REP Pubs., *(978-0-9604876)* Orders Addr.: 733 Turrentine Trail, St. Louis, MO 63141 USA (SAN 239-3786) Tel 314-434-1833
E-mail: Richard@reppublishers.com
Web site: www.reppublishers.com
Dist(s): **Unique Bks., Inc.**

R F T Publishing Company *See* **aha! Process, Inc.**

R.H. Boyd Publishing Corp., *(978-1-58942; 978-1-68167)* 6717 Centennial Blvd., Nashville, TN 37209-1049 USA Tel 615-350-8000; Fax: 615-350-9018
E-mail: dgroves@rhboyd.com
Web site: http://www.rhboydpublishing.com.

R. H. Publishing, *(978-0-9772460; 978-0-9976907; 978-1-945693)* 5021 S. 30th St., Lincoln, NE 68516 USA Tel 214-605-0162
Dist(s): **Lightning Source, Inc.**

R J Communications, LLC, *(978-0-9700741; 978-1-59664)* 51 E. 42nd St., Suite 1202, New York, NY 10017-5404 USA Tel 212-867-1331; Fax: 212-681-8002; Toll Free: 800-621-2556 (New York)
E-mail: ron@rjcom.com
Web site: http://www.selfpublishing.com; http://www.booksjustbooks.com.

R. N. M., Incorporated *See* **Onion River Pr.**

RSVP Pr., *(978-0-930865; 978-1-60209)* 619 Gay Rd., Monroe, NC 28112-8214 USA (SAN 657-6346)
E-mail: writernet@aol.com
Web site: http://www.rsvpbooks.com; http://www.members.aol.com/writernet/rsvp.htm.

R T A Pr., *(978-1-929768)* Div. of Rochester Teachers Assn., 30 N. Union St., Suite 301, Rochester, NY 14607 USA Tel 716-546-2681; Fax: 716-546-4123
E-mail: ddsigns@servtech.com.

RVS Bks., Inc., *(978-0-9634257)* P.O. Box 683, Lebanon, TN 37088-0683 USA (SAN 298-7325) Tel 615-449-6725; Fax: 615-449-6910.

Rabbit Ears Pr. & Co., *(978-0-9748922)* Orders Addr.: P.O. Box 1952, Davis, CA 95617 USA Tel 530-220-3289
Web site: http://www.rockythemudhen.com
Dist(s): **Partners Bk. Distributing, Inc.**

Rabbit Pubs., *(978-1-943785)* a/o Mr. Mark A. Poe, 1624 W. Northwest Hwy., Arlington Heights, IL 60004 USA Tel 858-513-7150
E-mail: plewis@smartfamilies.com
Web site: www.smartfamilies.com
Dist(s): **Diamond Comic Distributors, Inc.**

Rabbit's Foot Pr. *Imprint of* **Blue Mountain Arts Inc.**

Race Point Publishing *Imprint of* **Quarto Publishing Group USA**

Racehorse Publishing *Imprint of* **Skyhorse Publishing Co., Inc.**

Racemaker Pr., *(978-0-9766683; 978-1-935240)* 39 Church St., Boston, MA 02116 USA (SAN 256-4513) Tel 617-723-6533.

Rach, W. Dennis, *(978-0-9792579)* 9965 Portofino Dr., Orlando, FL 32832 USA (SAN 852-9299) Tel 407-625-8528
E-mail: dennis@rachfamily.com.

Racing to Joy Pr. LLC, *(978-0-9852488; 978-0-9908807)* 6103 Centerwood Dr., Crestwood, KY 40014 USA Tel 502-241-7574
E-mail: lindampenn@gmail.com.

Racom Communications, *(978-0-9704515; 978-1-933199)* 150 N. Michigan Ave. Ste. 2800, Chicago, IL 60601 USA (SAN 852-7210)
E-mail: rahagle@aol.com
Dist(s): **Bookmasters Distribution.**

Raconteurs, Inc., *(978-0-9621758)* 1305 W. Wisconsin Ave., No. 114, Oconomowoc, WI 53066-2646 USA (SAN 252-080X) Tel 414-567-4009.

Rada Press, Inc., *(978-0-9604212; 978-1-933011)* Orders Addr.: 1277 Fairmount Ave., Saint Paul, MN 55105-2701 USA Fax: 888-288-6401
E-mail: rm@radapress.com
Web site: http://www.radapress.com.

Radiance Pubs., *(978-0-918224)* Div. of S. K. Publications, Orders Addr.: 1042 Maple Ave., Lisle, IL 60532 USA Tel 630-577-7624
E-mail: 'nlarson@radiancepublishers.com
Web site: http://www.radiancepublishers.com.

Radical Reformation Bks., *(978-0-9818973)* 34 Cindia Ln, Ephrata, PA 17522 USA (SAN 856-8790) Tel 717-738-9099
E-mail: deantaylorfamily@gmail.com; dean@radicalreformation.net
Web site: http://www.radicalreformation.com.

Rae, Karyn Publishing, *(978-0-9960922; 978-1-946847)* 13 Colonel Hazzard Rd., Okatie, SC 29909 USA Tel 573-424-0155
E-mail: krp@karynraepublishing.com
Web site: www.karynraepublishing.com.

Raedan Bocs *See* **Lire Bks.**

Rafka Pr. LLC, *(978-0-9779628; 978-0-9911958)* P.O. Box 8099, Phoenix, AZ 85066 USA
Web site: http://www.rafkapress.com.

Rag Mag *See* **Black Hat Pr.**

Ragan, Jewel, *(978-0-9853809)* 24206 SE 248th St., Maple Valley, WA 98038 USA Tel 425-413-6032
E-mail: jewelragan@gmail.com.

Ragged Bears USA, *(978-1-929927)* Div. of Ragged Bears Publishing, Ltd., 413 Sixth Ave., Brooklyn, NY 11215-3310 USA Tel 718-768-3696; Fax: 718-369-0844
E-mail: publisher@raggedbears.com
Web site: http://www.raggedbears.com
Dist(s): **Chronicle Bks. LLC**
Independent Pubs. Group.

Ragged Sky Pr., *(978-0-9633092; 978-1-933974)* 270 Griggs Dr., Princeton, NJ 08540 USA
E-mail: ellen_foos@pupress.princeton.edu
Web site: http://Raggedsky.com.

Raging Bull Publishing, LLC *See* **Command Publishing, LLC**

Rai Publishing, *(978-0-9765641)* P.O. Box 918, Grover Beach, CA 93483 USA Tel 805-473-9025
E-mail: donrai@ix.netcom.com.

Raider Publishing International, *(978-0-9772054; 978-0-9790799; 978-1-934360; 978-1-935383; 978-1-61667)* 350 5th Ave., 59th Flr., New York, NY 10118 USA Tel 917-267-7912; Toll Free: 800-293-1653
E-mail: johnraider@hotmail.com; jraider@raiderpublishing.com
Web site: http://www.raiderpublishing.com.

Rain Tree Bks., *(978-0-9764129)* Orders Addr.: P.O. Box 1290, DeQueen, AR 71832 USA; Edit Addr.: 146 Treating Plant Rd., DeQueen, AR 71832 USA Tel 870-582-3565.

Rainbow Bks., Inc., *(978-0-935834; 978-1-56825)* P.O. Box 430, Highland City, FL 33846-0430 USA (SAN 213-5515) Tel 863-648-4420; Fax: 863-647-5951 Do not confuse with companies with the same or similar name in Middleburg, VT, Amstgerdam, NY, New York, NY, Sparks, NV
E-mail: RBIbooks@aol.com
Web site: http://www.RainbowBooksInc.com
Dist(s): **BCH Fulfillment & Distribution**
Book Clearing Hse.
Smashwords.

Rainbow Bridge Publishing, *(978-1-887923; 978-1-932210)* Div. of Carson-Dellosa Publishing Co., Inc., Orders Addr.: P.O. Box 571470, Salt Lake City, UT 84157-1470 USA Tel 801-268-8887; Fax: 801-268-2770; Toll Free: 800-598-1441; Edit Addr.: P.O. Box 571470, Salt Lake City, UT 84157-1470 USA
E-mail: danell@rbpbooks.com
Web site: http://www.rbpbooks.com
Dist(s): **Carson-Dellosa Publishing, LLC**
Midpoint Trade Bks., Inc.

Rainbow Communications, *(978-0-9725479; 978-0-9728737; 978-0-9888554)* 471 NW Hemlock Ave, Corvallis, OR 97330 USA Tel 541-753-3335
E-mail: varsell4@comcast.net.

†Rainbow Horizons Publishing, Inc., *(978-1-55319)* Orders Addr.: P.O. Box 19729, San Diego, CA 92159 USA Toll Free Fax: 800-663-3608; Toll Free: 800-663-3609; *Imprints:* Classroom Complete Press (Classrm Comp)
E-mail: paul@classroomcompletepress.com
Web site: http://www.ccpinteractive.com; http://www.rainbowhorizons.com; http://www.classroomcompletepress.com
Dist(s): **Follett School Solutions**
OverDrive, Inc.
ebrary, Inc.; *CIP.*

Rainbow Morning Music Alternatives, *(978-0-938663; 978-0-9615696)* 2121 Fairland Rd., Silver Spring, MD 20904 USA (SAN 218-2963) Tel 301-384-9207; Fax: 312-337-5985; Toll Free: 800-881-4741
E-mail: barrylou@ziplink.net
Web site: http://www.barrylou.com
Dist(s): **Independent Pubs. Group**
MyiLibrary.

Rainbow Pony Publishing, *(978-0-9728871)* 368 S. McCaslin Blvd., PMB No. 226, Louisville, CO 80027 USA.

Rainbow Pony Publising *See* **Rainbow Pony Publishing**

Rainbow Publishers *See* **Rainbow Pubs. & Legacy Pr.**

Rainbow Pubs. & Legacy Pr., *(978-0-937282; 978-1-885358; 978-1-58411)* Orders Addr.: P.O. Box 261129, San Diego, CA 92196 USA (SAN 256-4718) Tel 858-668-3260; Fax: 858-668-3328; Toll Free Fax: 800-331-0297; Toll Free: 800-323-7337; Edit Addr.: P.O. Box 70130, Richmond, VA 23255-0130 USA; *Imprints:* Legacy Press (Lgacy Pr)
E-mail: rainbowed@earthlink.net; drmiley@juno.com
Web site: http://www.rainbowpublishers.com
Dist(s): **Appalachian Bible Co.**
Spring Arbor Distributors, Inc.

Rainbow Reach, *(978-0-9829490)* 2340 Bedfordshire Cir., Reston, VA 20191 USA
E-mail: susan@rainbowreach.com
Web site: www.rainbowreach.com
Dist(s): **Lightning Source, Inc.**

Rainbow Resource Ctr., Inc., *(978-1-933407; 978-1-942446)* P.O. Box 391, Williamsfield, IL 61489 USA; *Imprints:* In the Think of Things (IntheThink).

Rainbow Star Bks., *(978-0-9802363)* P.O. Box 422, Centereach, NY 11720 USA (SAN 855-5680)
Web site: http://www.rainbowstarbooks.com.

Rainbow Star, Incorporated *See* **Rainbow Star Bks.**

Rainbow Valley Publishing Co., *(978-0-9748558)* 2189 Hwy. 90 W., Sulphur, LA 70663 USA Tel 337-528-1157.

Rainbows Within Reach, *(978-0-9705987; 978-0-578-03944-2; 978-0-578-06631-8)* 5765 Westbourne Ave., Columbus, OH 43213 USA
E-mail: debbie@rainbowswithinreach.com
Web site: http://www.rainbowswithinreach.com
Dist(s): **Follett School Solutions**
TNT Media Group, Inc.

Raincoast Bk. Distribution (CAN) *(978-0-920417; 978-1-55192; 978-1-895714; 978-1-894542) Dist. by* **PerseuPGW.**

Raindrop Bks., *(978-0-9766129)* 423 Hicks St., No. 6-H, Brooklyn, NY 11201 USA Tel 718-855-2918
E-mail: lgliessner@aol.com.

Raindrop Bks., *(978-0-9799677)* 10 Sunderland St., Melville, NY 11747 USA
Web site: http://www.learnalongwithlily.com; http://www.raindropbooks.com
Dist(s): **Big Tent Bks.**

Raining Popcorn Media, *(978-0-9797304)* P.O. Box 91244, San Antonio, TX 78209 USA Tel 210-320-0548; Toll Free: 866-503-3088
E-mail: info@rainingpopcorn.com; lisa@rainingpopcorn.com
Web site: http://www.RainingPopcorn.com.

Rainstorm Pr., *(978-0-615-47986-6; 978-0-615-49269-8; 978-0-615-53082-6; 978-1-937758; 978-1-4748-9005-2)* P.O. Box 391038, Anza, CA 92539 USA Tel 760-270-8641
E-mail: Lyle@rainstormpress.com
Web site: http://www.RainstormPress.com
Dist(s): **CreateSpace Independent Publishing Platform.**

Raintree Freestyle *Imprint of* **Heinemann-Raintree**

Raintree Freestyle Express *Imprint of* **Heinemann-Raintree**

Raintree Fusion *Imprint of* **Heinemann-Raintree**

Raintree Perspectives *Imprint of* **Heinemann-Raintree**

Raintree Steck-Vaughn Publishers *See* **Steck-Vaughn**

Rainy Day Entertainment, LLC *See* **Apologue Entertainment, LLC**

Rairarubia Bks., *(978-0-9712206)* 1000 San Diego Rd., Santa Barbara, CA 93103 USA Fax: 805-966-4697
E-mail: raira@silcom.com
Web site: http://www.rairarubia.com.

Raisykinder Publishing, *(978-0-615-21798-7; 978-0-615-27779-0; 978-0-9825530; 978-0-9907348; 978-0-9978111; 978-0-9992760)* 1713 Golden Ct., Bellingham, WA 98226 USA
E-mail: raisykinderpub@aol.com
Web site: http://www.raisykinderpublishing.com.

Rakha, Marwa *See* **Malamih Publishing Hse.**

Rakowski, Diane, *(978-0-9760194)* 11402 W. Parkhill Dr., Littleton, CO 80127-4716 USA
E-mail: dsjsit@juno.com.

Raku Bks., *(978-0-615-12445-2; 978-0-615-12561-9)* Orders Addr.: P.O. Box 51954, Palo Alto, CA 94303 USA
E-mail: rapimus@yahoo.com.

Raku Publishing, *(978-0-9770662)* 30799 Pinetree Rd., No. 411, Pepper Pike, OH 44124 USA Tel 216-299-0613
Dist(s): **BookBaby.**

Ralston Store Publishing, *(978-0-9822585; 978-1-938322)* P.O. Box 4513, Durango, CO 81302-4513 USA
Web site: http://www.ralstonstorepublishing.com
Dist(s): **Smashwords.**

Ramos, Raymond G., *(978-0-9855114)* 11600 Mendel Dr. Apt. 3, Orlando, FL 32826 USA Tel 407-756-5730
E-mail: congabuena@yahoo.com.

Ramsey Dean, Inc., *(978-0-9893372)* 1555 N. Dearborn Pkwy. No. 14A, Chicago, IL 60610 USA Tel 312-860-2021
E-mail: ramseydeaninc@gmail.com
Web site: www.ridingonabeamoflight.com.

Ramsey Pr., *(978-0-9635712; 978-0-9718554; 978-0-9720044; 978-0-9726323; 978-0-9753033; 978-0-9769630; 978-0-9774895; 978-0-9777767; 978-0-9785620; 978-0-9786577; 978-1-934629; 978-0-9800873; 978-0-9816839; 978-0-9829862; 978-1-936948; 978-1-937077; 978-1-938400; 978-1-942121)* 1749 *Mallory Ln., Brentwood, TN 37027 USA Tel 615-515-3223; 888-227-3223; Fax: 615-371-5007; Toll Free: 888-227-3223*
E-mail: preston.cannon@daveramsey.com; lauren.kallemeyn@daveramsey.com
Web site: http://www.daveramsey.com
Dist(s): **Ingram Publisher Services**
Nelson, Thomas Inc.

Ranch Gate Bks., *(978-0-9618660)* 2409 Dormarion, Austin, TX 78703 USA (SAN 668-4033) Tel 512-476-2185.

†RAND Corp., The, *(978-0-8330; 978-1-9774)* Orders Addr.: P.O. Box 2138, Santa Monica, CA 90407-2138 USA (SAN 218-9291) Tel 310-393-0411; Fax: 310-393-4818; Toll Free: 1-877-584-8642; Edit Addr.: 1776 Main St., Santa Monica, CA 90401-3208 USA (SAN 665-763X) Tel 310-393-0411; Fax: 412-802-4981
E-mail: jwarren@rand.org; correspondence@rand.org; randell@rand.org; cs@rand.org
Web site: http://www.rand.org
Dist(s): **CreateSpace Independent Publishing Platform**
Ebsco Publishing
MyiLibrary
National Bk. Network
ebrary, Inc.; *CIP.*

†Rand McNally, *(978-0-528)* Orders Addr.: 9855 Woods Dr., Skokie, IL 60077-1074 USA Toll Free Fax: 800-934-3479 (Orders); Toll Free: 800-333-0136 (ext. 4771); 800-678-7263 (Orders)
E-mail: Education@randmcnally.com
Web site: http://www.randmcnally.com
Dist(s): **Benchmark LLC**
Bryant Altman Map, Inc.; *CIP.*

Rand Media Co, *(978-0-9818935; 978-0-9824390; 978-0-9841393; 978-0-9844418; 978-0-692-01528-5; 978-0-9852818; 978-0-9988392)* Orders Addr.: 265 Post Rd. W., Westport, CT 06880 USA (SAN 925-4919) Tel 203-226-8727; Fax: 203-221-7677; *Imprints:* Skinny On (tm), The (Skinny on)
E-mail: dhardy@randmediaco.com; daveaweiner7@aol.com; awuqi@randmediaco.com
Web site: http://www.theskinnyon.com; http://randmediaco.com/money/money-book-1/; http://randmediaco.com/
Dist(s): **Lulu Pr., Inc.**

RAND Publishing *See* **Rand Media Co**

Randall, Charles Inc., *(978-0-9624736; 978-1-890379)* Orders Addr.: 30 Amberwood Pkwy., Ashland, OH 44805 USA Fax: 419-281-6883; Toll Free: 800-247-6553; Edit Addr.: P.O. Box 1656, Orange, CA 92856 USA (SAN 253-7737)
E-mail: peter@randallonline.com
Web site: http://www.randallonline.com; http://www.charlesrandall.com
Dist(s): **BookMasters, Inc.**
Bookmasters Distribution
Follett School Solutions
MyiLibrary
ebrary, Inc.

Randall, Cheri, *(978-0-9767213)* P.O. Box 2176, Belton, TX 76513 USA Tel 254-939-8776 (phone/fax)
E-mail: hrandallmail@aol.com
Web site: http://www.harveyrandall.org.

Randall Fraser Publishing *See* **RandallFraser Publishing**

Randall Hse. Pubns., *(978-0-89265; 978-1-61484)* 114 Bush Rd., Nashville, TN 37217 USA (SAN 207-5040) Tel 615-361-1221; Fax: 615-367-0535; Toll Free: 800-877-7030
E-mail: michelle.orr@randallhouse.com
Web site: http://www.randallhouse.com.

Randall International *See* **Randall, Charles Inc.**

†Randall, Peter E. Pub., *(978-0-914339; 978-1-931807; 978-0-9817898; 978-0-9828236; 978-1-937721; 978-0-692-22144-0; 978-1-942155; 978-0-692-51521-1; 978-0-9971567)* 5 Greenleaf Woods Dr., Unit 102, Portsmouth, NH 03801 USA (SAN 223-0496) Tel 603-431-5667; Fax: 603-431-3566
E-mail: deidre@perpublisher.com; media@perpublisher.com
Web site: http://www.perpublisher.com
Dist(s): **Bondcliff Bks.**
BookBaby
Enfield Publishing & Distribution Co., Inc.
MyiLibrary
National Bk. Network
Univ. Pr. of New England; *CIP.*

Randall, Robert E. *See* **Zander Pubns.**

RandallFraser Publishing, *(978-0-9745143)* 2082 Business Ctr. Dr., Suite 163, Irvine, CA 92612 USA Fax: 949-250-9020; Toll Free: 866-339-3999
E-mail: algreen51@comcast.net
Web site: http://www.Deweydooit.com
Dist(s): **National Bk. Network.**

R&B Trading Co., *(978-0-9718784)* 7619 Belmont Stakes Dr., Midlothian, VA 23112 USA (SAN 254-4741) Tel 804-739-8073; Fax: 775-243-6578
E-mail: dwindsofdestiny@aol.com
Web site: http://www.RnBtradingco.net/home.html.

Randle, Ian Pubs., Inc., *(978-0-9729358; 978-0-9742155; 978-0-9753529)* 25 SE Second Ave., Suite 1105, Miami, FL 33131 USA Tel 305-358-1588; Fax: 305-358-1589
E-mail: info@ianrandlepublishers.com
Web site: http://www.ianrandlepublishers.com
Dist(s): **Indiana Univ. Pr.**

R&N Productions, *(978-0-615-14376-7)* 698 Talbert Ave., Simi Valley, CA 93065 USA
E-mail: norm@kuvina.com
Web site: http://www.troublestreet.com
Dist(s): **Lulu Pr., Inc.**

Randolph Publishing, *(978-1-932258)* 4125 Braswell Church Rd., Good Hope, GA 30641-160 USA Do not confuse with companies with the same or similar names in Dunnellon, FL, Dallas, TX, Indianapolis, IN, Princeton, TX
E-mail: randolphpublishing@EarthLink.net
Web site: http://www.RandolphPublishing.com.

Random House *Imprint of* **Random House Publishing Group**

Random House Adult Trade Publishing Group *See* **Random House Publishing Group**

Random Hse. Audio Publishing Group, Div. of Random House, Inc., Orders Addr.: 400 Hahn Rd., Westminster, MD 21157 USA (SAN 201-3975) Tel 410-848-1900; Toll Free: 800-726-0600; Edit Addr.: 1745 Broadway, New York, NY 10036 USA Tel 212-782-9000; *Imprints:* Listening Library (Listening Lib)
Web site: http://www.randomhouse.com/audio
Dist(s): **Ebsco Publishing**
Follett School Solutions
Penguin Random Hse. LLC
Random Hse., Inc.

Random House Children's Books (GBR) *Dist. by* **Trafalgar.**

Random House Children's Books (GBR) *Dist. by* **Perfect Learn.**

Random House Children's Books (GBR) *Dist. by* **IPG Chicago.**

Random Hse. Children's Bks., Div. of Random Hse., Inc., Orders Addr.: 400 Hahn Rd., Westminster, MD 21157 USA Tel 410-848-1900; Toll Free: 800-726-0600; Edit Addr.: 1745 Broadway, 10th Flr., New York, NY 10019 USA Tel 212-782-8491; 212-782-9000; Fax: 212-782-9577; Toll Free: 800-200-3552; *Imprints:* Delacorte Books for Young Readers (Delacorte Bks); Lamb, Wendy Books (Wendy Lamb); Random House Para Ninos (ParaNinos); Crown Books For Young Readers (CBYR); Knopf Books for Young Readers (Knop); RH/Disney (RH Disney); Golden Books (Gold Bks); Random House Books for Young Readers (RHBYR); Bantam Books for Young Readers (BBYngRead); Doubleday Books for Young Readers (Doubleday Bk Yng); Yearling (Year); Dragonfly Books (Dragonfly Bks); Laurel Leaf (LaurelLeaf); Schwartz & Wade Books (Schwartz & Wade); Golden/Disney (Gold Disney); Robin Corey Books (Robin Corey); Golden Inspirational (Gold Inspir); Ember (Ember); Delacorte Press (DelacortePr); Bluefire (BluefireR); Sylvan Learning Publishing (Sylvan Lea); Tricycle Press (Tricycle); Now I'm Reading! (Now Im)
E-mail: pmuller@randomhouse.com; kids@random.com
Web site: http://www.randomhouse.com/kids/
Dist(s): **Follett School Solutions**
Libros Sin Fronteras
MyiLibrary
Penguin Random Hse. LLC
Random Hse., Inc.

Random House Espanol, 1745 Broadway, New York, NY 10019 USA Tel 212-782-9000; Fax: 212-302-7985
Web site: http://www.randomhouse.com/espanol/
Dist(s): **Penguin Random Hse. LLC**
Two Rivers Distribution.

Random House, Incorporated *See* **Random Hse., Inc.**

†Random Hse., Inc., *(978-0-307; 978-0-345; 978-0-375; 978-0-385; 978-0-394; 978-0-440; 978-0-449; 978-0-517; 978-0-553; 978-0-593; 978-0-609; 978-0-676; 978-0-679; 978-0-7364; 978-0-7366; 978-0-7615; 978-0-7679; 978-0-7704; 978-0-8041; 978-0-8052; 978-0-8129; 978-0-8230; 978-0-87637; 978-0-87665; 978-0-87788; 978-0-88070; 978-0-913369; 978-0-914629; 978-0-930014; 978-0-945564; 978-1-57082; 978-1-57673; 978-1-57856; 978-1-878867; 978-1-884536; 978-1-885305; 978-1-58836; 978-1-4000; 978-1-59052; 978-1-4159; 978-1-)* Div. *of Penguin Random House LLC, Orders Addr.: 400 Hahn Rd., Westminster, MD 21157 USA (SAN 202-5515) Tel 410 848 1900; Toll Free Fax: 800 659 2436; Toll Free: 800 726 0600 (customer service/orders); Edit Addr.: 1745 Broadway, New York, NY 10019 USA (SAN 202-5507) Tel 212 782 9000; Fax: 212 302 7985*
E-mail: customerservice@randomhouse.com
Web site: http://www.randomhouse.com
Dist(s): **Ebsco Publishing**
Follett School Solutions
Giron Bks.
Libros Sin Fronteras
MyiLibrary
Penguin Random Hse. LLC
Perfection Learning Corp.; *CIP.*

Random Hse. Information Group, Div. of Random Hse., Inc., Orders Addr.: 400 Hahn Rd., Westminster, MD 21157 USA Tel 410-848-1900; Toll Free: 800-726-0600; Edit Addr.: 1745 Broadway, New York, NY 10019 USA Tel 212-751-2600; Toll Free: 800-726-0600; *Imprints:* Random House Puzzles & Games (RHPG); Prima Games (PrimGames)
E-mail: customerservice@randomhouse.com
Web site: http://www.randomhouse.com/
Dist(s): **Bilingual Pubns. Co., The**
Ediciones Universal
Libros Sin Fronteras
MyiLibrary
Penguin Random Hse. LLC
Random Hse., Inc.
Simon & Schuster, Inc.

Random Hse. Large Print, Div. of Random House, Inc., Orders Addr.: 400 Hahn Rd., Westminster, MD 21157 USA Tel 410-848-1900 Toll Free: 800-726-0600 (customer service); Edit Addr.: 1745 Broadway, New York, NY 10019 USA Tel 212-782-9000
E-mail: editor@randomhouse.com; customerservice@randomhouse.com
Web site: http://www.randomhouse.com
Dist(s): **Libros Sin Fronteras**
MyiLibrary
Penguin Random Hse. LLC
Random Hse., Inc.
Thorndike Pr.

Random House Para Ninos *Imprint of* **Random Hse. Children's Bks.**

Random House Publishing Group, Orders Addr.: 400 Hahn Rd., Westminster, MD 21157 USA (SAN 852-5579) Tel 410-848-1900; 410-386-7560; Toll Free: 800-726-0600; Edit Addr.: 1745 Broadway, New York, NY 10019 USA Tel 212-751-2600; Fax: 212-572-4949; Toll Free: 800-726-0600; *Imprints*: Random House Trade Paperbacks (RH Trade Bks); Modern Library (Mod Lib); Villard Books (Villard Books); Random House (Random House); Del Rey (Del Rey); Ballantine Books (Ballantine Bks); Bantam (Bant); Delacorte Press (DelacorRHP); Laurel (LaureRH); Delacorte Press (DelacortePr)
E-mail: lstark@randomhouse.com
Dist(s): **Follett School Solutions**
Libros Sin Fronteras
MyiLibrary
Penguin Random Hse. LLC
Perfection Learning Corp.
Random Hse., Inc.

Random House Reference & Information Publishing *See* **Random Hse. Information Group**

†**Random Hse. Value Publishing,** Div. of Random House, Inc., Orders Addr.: 400 Hahn Rd., Westminster, MD 21157 USA Tel 410-848-1900 Toll Free: 800-726-0600 (Customer Service); Edit Addr.: 280 Park Ave., 11th Flr., New York, NY 10017 USA Tel 212 572 2400
Web site: http://www.randomhouse.com
Dist(s): **Penguin Random Hse. LLC**
Random Hse., Inc.; *CIP.*

Random Hse. (GBR) *(978-0-09; 978-0-224; 978-0-7126; 978-1-86046; 978-1-870516; 978-0-85265; 978-1-84413; 978-1-84657; 978-1-84655; 978-1-84853; 978-1-4881; 978-1-911215; 978-1-78089) Dist. by* **Trafalgar.**

Random Hse. (GBR) *(978-0-09; 978-0-224; 978-0-7126; 978-1-86046; 978-1-870516; 978-0-85265; 978-1-84413; 978-1-84657; 978-1-84655; 978-1-84853; 978-1-4881; 978-1-911215; 978-1-78089) Dist. by* **IPG Chicago.**

Random Hse. Australia (AUS) *(978-1-86359; 978-0-86824; 978-0-947189; 978-1-86325; 978-0-7338; 978-1-74051; 978-0-900882; 978-1-74166; 978-1-86471; 978-1-4230; 978-1-74274; 978-1-74275; 978-0-646-08769-6; 978-0-646-19362-5; 978-0-646-23850-0; 978-0-646-29047-8; 978-0-646-31636-9; 978-0-646-32934-5; 978-0-85798; 978-1-925324) Dist. by* **IPG Chicago.**

Random Hse. Bks. for Young Readers *Imprint of* **Random Hse. Children's Bks.**

Random Hse. of Canada (CAN) *(978-0-09; 978-0-307; 978-0-375; 978-0-394; 978-0-676; 978-0-679; 978-0-7704; 978-1-4000) Dist. by* **Random.**

Random Hse. Puzzles & Games *Imprint of* **Random Hse. Information Group**

Random Hse. Trade Paperbacks *Imprint of* **Random House Publishing Group**

R&R Blackburn Enterprises, *(978-0-9907603)* P.O. Box 27577, Fresno, CA 93729 USA Tel 559-287-4149
E-mail: rlb737@gmail.com
Web site: www.TwasWithATwist.com.

R&R Endeavors, Inc., *(978-0-9740444)* Orders Addr.: P.O. Box 301, Indianapolis, IN 46217 USA; Edit Addr.: 1350C W. Southport Rd., Indianapolis, IN 46217 USA
E-mail: editor@writerpublishing.com
Web site: http://www.writerpublishing.com.

Rang Jung Yshe Pubns. (HKG) *(978-962-7341) Dist. by* **PerseuPGW.**

RAPC - Sparkle & Shine Project, *(978-0-9760282)* 116 Jackson St., Sylva, NC 28779 USA Tel 828-586-0661; Fax: 828-586-0663
Web site: http://www.sparkle-shine.com.

RAPHA, Inc., *(978-0-9740081)* Orders Addr.: P.O. Box 1184, Groton, CT 06340 USA Tel 860-938-2599; Edit Addr.: 45 South Rd., Apt. 9A, Groton, CT 06340 USA Tel 860-514-7266
E-mail: joyindamornin@earthlink.net.

Rapha Publishing, *(978-0-9763686)* 431 Beechwood Ave., Carnegie, PA 15106 USA Tel 412-249-0669
E-mail: raphapublishing@yahoo.com
Web site: http://www.raphapublishing.com/.

Raphel Marketing, Inc., *(978-0-9624808; 978-0-9711542; 978-0-9826644; 978-1-938406)* Orders Addr.: 211 North Ave., St Johnsbury, VT 05819-1626 USA Tel 802-751-8802; *Imprints*: Compass (CompassUSA)
E-mail: neil@raphel.com
Web site: http://www.raphel.com; http://www.brigantinemedia.com; http://compasspublishing.org.

Rapids Christian Pr., Inc., *(978-0-915374)* P.O. Box 717, Ferndale, WA 98248-0717 USA (SAN 205-0986) Tel 360-384-1747
E-mail: gundersonwv@aol.com.

Rapier Publishing Co., LLC, *(978-0-9839483; 978-0-9966083; 978-0-9970307; 978-0-9977029; 978-1-946683)* 135 Lakeside Dr., Dothan, AL 36301 USA Tel 256-553-9410; Fax: 334-699-5550
E-mail: petefannie@aol.com.

R.A.R.E. TALES, *(978-0-9760303)* 14120 River Rd., Fort Myers, FL 33905-7436 USA
E-mail: kphchance@comcast.net
Web site: http://www.raretales.net.

Rarecity Pr., *(978-0-9760959)* 17 Yardley Dr., Medford, NJ 08055 USA Tel 201-788-9746
E-mail: jason@rarecity.com.

Rasa Music Co., *(978-0-9766219)* 409 Glenview Rd., Glenview, IL 60025-3262 USA Tel 847-486-0416; Fax: 847-657-9459
E-mail: lleifer@northpark.edu
Web site: http://www.admin.northpark.edu/lleifer/.

Rascal Treehouse Publishing, *(978-0-9759321)* 1523 Morris St. - Suite 330, Lincoln Park, MI 48146 USA
E-mail: lscoffman@lscoffman.com
Web site: http://www.lscoffman.com.

Raspberry Bks., *(978-0-9848749)* 4346 Mammoth Ave. No. 4, Sherman Oaks, CA 91423 USA Tel 818-633-9190
E-mail: tammy@tammylaframboise.com.

Ratatat Graphics LLC *See* **Studio Moonfall**

Ratna, Sagar Pvt. Ltd. (IND) *(978-81-7070; 978-81-8332) Dist. by* **Midpt Trade.**

Rattle OK Pubns., *(978-0-9626210; 978-1-883965)* Orders Addr.: P.O. Box 5614, Napa, CA 94581 USA (SAN 297-5475) Tel 707-253-9641; Edit Addr.: 296 Homewood Ave., Napa, CA 94558-5617 USA
Dist(s): **Gryphon Hse., Inc.**

Ratway, Michael, *(978-0-9724698)* 216 Midshipman Cir., Stafford, VA 22554-2421 USA
E-mail: yawtar@earthlink.net
Web site: http://www.earthlink.net/~yawtar.

Raven Bks. *Imprint of* **Literations**

Raven Bks. *Imprint of* **Raven Productions**

Raven House Media, *(978-0-9963624)* 1625 SW 173rd Ter, Beaverton, OR 97003 USA Tel 503-459-8547
E-mail: rmseidler@gmail.com
Web site: rmseidler.com.

Raven Mad Studios, *(978-0-9896269)* 16327 197th Ave. NE, Woodinville, WA 98077 USA Tel 206-310-7246
E-mail: randybriley@comcast.net.

Raven Press *See* **Raven House Media**

Raven Productions, *(978-0-9764091)* 325 E. 2550 N, Suite 117, North Ogden, UT 84414 USA Tel 801-782-0872; *Imprints*: Raven Books (RavenBks) Do not confuse with companies with the same or similar name in Delta Junction, AKEly, MN
E-mail: gshaw@post.harvard.edu
Dist(s): **MyiLibrary.**

Raven Productions, Inc., *(978-0-9677057; 978-0-9766264; 978-0-9794202; 978-0-9801045; 978-0-9819307; 978-0-9835189; 978-0-9883508; 978-0-9914157)* P.O. Box 188, Ely, MN 55731 USA Fax: 218-343-3423 Do not confuse with companies with the same or similar name in Delta Junction, AK, North Ogden, UT
E-mail: raven@ravenwords.com
Dist(s): **Adventure Pubns.**
MyiLibrary.

Raven Publishing *See* **Raven Publishing Inc. of Montana**

Raven Publishing Inc. of Montana, *(978-0-9714161; 978-0-9772525; 978-0-9820893; 978-0-9827377; 978-1-937849)* P.O. Box 2866, Norris, MT 59745 USA (SAN 254-5861) Tel 406-685-3545; Fax: 406-685-3599; Toll Free: 866-685-3545 Do not confuse with companies with the same or similar name in Bronx, NY, Pittsfield, MA
E-mail: janet@ravenpublishng.net
Web site: http://www.ravenpublishing.net
Dist(s): **Bks. West**
Distributors, The
Follett School Solutions
Partners/West Book Distributors
Quality Bks., Inc.
Smashwords
Wolverine Distributing, Inc.
Western International, Inc.

Raven Rocks Pr., *(978-0-9615961)* 53650 Belmont Ridge, Beallsville, OH 43716 USA (SAN 696-5679) Tel 740-926-1481 (phone/fax)
E-mail: jmrpress@1st.net.

Raven Tree Pr. *Imprint of* **Delta Systems Company, Inc.**

Raven Tree Pr. *Imprint of* **Continental Sales, Inc.**

Raven Tree Pr.,Csi *Imprint of* **Continental Sales, Inc.**

Ravenhawk Bks., *(978-1-893660)* Div. of The 6DOF Group, 7739 E. Broadway Blvd. Suite 95, Tucson, AZ 85710 USA Tel 520-886-9885 (phone/fax); Toll Free: 800-520-9885
E-mail: 76673.3165@compuserve.com
Web site: http://www.ravenhawk.org.

RavenMark, *(978-0-9713998; 978-0-615-55902-5)* 27 E. State St., Montpelier, VT 05602-3011 USA Tel 802-223-5507
E-mail: rebecca@ravenmark.com
Dist(s): **R. C. Brayshaw.**

Ravensburger Buchverlag Otto Maier GmbH (DEU) *(978-3-473) Dist. by* **Distribks Inc.**

Ravenstone Pr., *(978-0-9659712)* Orders Addr.: Ravenstone Press 2056 Berry Roberts Dr., Sun City Center, FL 33573-6130 USA Tel 813-633-5759; Fax: 813-633-5759; Edit Addr.: 2056 Berry Roberts Dr., Sun City Ctr, FL 33573-6130 USA
E-mail: writerjerri@gmail.com
Web site: http://www.ravenstonepress.com.

Ravenwood Publishing, *(978-0-9899275)* 133 Rob Rd., Brooklin, ME 04616 USA Tel 207-359-2451
E-mail: ruthjohnhowell@gmail.com.

Ravenwood Studios, *(978-0-9718604; 978-1-933420)* P.O. Box 197, Diamond Springs, CA 95619 USA
E-mail: ravenwoodstudios@me.com; maureenedgecomb@me.com; todd.ryan@comcast.net
Web site: http://www.maureenedgecomb.com; http://www.ravenwoodstudios.net; http://www.marcyinmanhattan.com.

Ravette Publishing, Ltd. (GBR) *(978-0-948456; 978-1-85304; 978-0-906710; 978-1-84161) Dist. by* **Parkwest Pubns.**

Raw Dog Screaming Pr., *(978-0-9745031; 978-1-933293; 978-1-935738; 978-1-947879)* 2802 Farris Ln., Bowie, MD 20715 USA (SAN 255-7673) Tel 301-262-4414
E-mail: books@rawdogscreaming.com
Web site: http://www.rawdogscreaming.com.

Raw Junior, LLC *See* **TOON Books / RAW Junior, LLC**

Ray Greer, Mary Lou, *(978-0-9749161)* P.O. Box 1740, Eagar, AZ 85925 USA Tel 520-850-6209.

Raynestorm Bks. *Imprint of* **Silver Rose Publishing**

Rayo *Imprint of* **HarperCollins Pubs.**

Rayve Productions, Inc., *(978-1-877810)* Orders Addr.: P.O. Box 726, Windsor, CA 95492 USA (SAN 248-4250) Tel 707-838-6200; Fax: 707-838-2220; Toll Free: 800-852-4890
E-mail: rayvepro@aol.com
Web site: http://www.rayveproductions.com; http://www.rayvepro.com
Dist(s): **Brodart Co.**
Follett School Solutions
Lippincott Williams & Wilkins
Quality Bks., Inc.
Unique Bks., Inc.

Razorbill *Imprint of* **Penguin Publishing Group**

Razorbill *Imprint of* **Penguin Publishing Group**

Razorbill *Imprint of* **Penguin Young Readers Group**

RBA Libros, S.A. (ESP) *(978-84-89662; 978-84-7871; 978-84-7901; 978-84-85351; 978-84-9867; 978-84-9006) Dist. by* **Lectorum Pubns.**

RBA Libros, S.A. (ESP) *(978-84-89662; 978-84-7871; 978-84-7901; 978-84-85351; 978-84-9867; 978-84-9006) Dist. by* **Santillana.**

RBTB Publishing, *(978-0-9977530)* P.O. Box 970131, Coconut Creek, FL 33097 USA Tel 973-303-9412
E-mail: kelly@reviewsbythebanks.com
Web site: www.reviewsbythebanks.com.

RCL Benziger Publishing, *(978-0-89505; 978-0-913592; 978-1-55924)* A Kendall Hunt Company, Orders Addr.: 8805 Governor's Hill, Suite 400, Cincinnati, OH 45249 USA (SAN 299-0628) Toll Free Fax: 800-688-8356; Toll Free: 877-275-4725
E-mail: customerservice@rclbenziger.com
Web site: http://www.rclweb.com/
Dist(s): **Spring Arbor Distributors, Inc.**

RDM Publishing, *(978-0-9766038)* 605 CR 1040E, Norris City, IL 62869 USA Tel 618-265-3225
E-mail: earthart@midwest.net.

RDR Bks., *(978-0-9636161; 978-1-57143)* 1487 Glen Ave., Muskegon, MI 49441-3101 USA; 960 S. Sherman, Muskegon, MI 49441
E-mail: books@rdrbooks.com
Web site: http://www.rdrbooks.com
Dist(s): **Alpen Bks**
American West Bks.
Book Wholesalers, Inc.
Bookazine Co., Inc.
Brodart Co.
Follett School Solutions
New Leaf Distributing Co., Inc.
Quality Bks., Inc.
Sunbelt Pubns., Inc.
Unique Bks., Inc.
Yankee Bk. Peddler, Inc.

Reaching Beyond, Inc., *(978-0-9741893)* Orders Addr.: P.O. Box 12364, Columbus, GA 31917-2364 USA Tel 706-573-5942; Edit Addr.: P.O. Box 12364, Columbus, GA 31917-2364 USA
E-mail: nccjohnson@hotmail.com
Web site: http://Www.charlotterjohnson.com
Dist(s): **Book Clearing Hse.**

Reachment Publications *See* **Southeast Media**

Read 2 Children, *(978-0-9755839)* P.O. Box 4113, Warren, NJ 07059 USA Tel 732-805-9073
Web site: http://www.read2children.com.

Read All Over Publishing, *(978-0-9728779)* 17705 Ingleside Rd., Cleveland, OH 44119 USA Tel 216-486-8615 ext. 3
E-mail: readallover@sbcglobal.net.

Read Me! *Imprint of* **Heinemann-Raintree**

Read More! Run More!, *(978-0-692-82924-0; 978-0-692-92465-5)* 3900 Woodchase Dr Apt152, HOUSTON, TX 77042 USA Tel 443-739-4339
E-mail: jeffwcrawford5+LVP0003230@gmail.com; jeffwcrawford5+LVP0003230@gmail.com.

Read Publishing, *(978-0-9762868)* Orders Addr.: 3918 Dorcas Dr., Nashville, TN 37215 USA Tel 615-279-9988; Fax: 615-385-2651
E-mail: snea5001@bellsouth.net; jennie0120@aol.com.

Read Street Publishing, Inc., *(978-0-942929)* 133 W. Read St., Baltimore, MD 21201 USA (SAN 667-8505) Tel 410-837-1116; Fax: 410-727-3174; *Imprints*: Omni Arts Publishing (Omni Arts Pubng)
E-mail: editor@omnititles.com; editor@tablespr.com; editor@readstreetpublishing.com
Web site: http://www.omnititles.com; http://www.tablespr.com; http://www.readstreetpublishing.com.

Read Together Bks., *(978-0-9822615)* 8045 230th St, Bellerose Manor, NY 11427-2105 USA Tel 917-757-5868
E-mail: mike@readtogetherbooks.com
Web site: http://www.readtogetherbooks.com
Dist(s): **Bookmasters Distribution.**

Read Us For Fun Publishing, *(978-0-9820363)* P.O. Box 623, Dover, MA 02030 USA Tel 508-523-9414
E-mail: mking426@msn.com
Web site: http://readusforfun.com.

Read Well Publishing Inc., *(978-0-9630539; 978-0-9703400; 978-1-933873)* Div. of Apodixis, Inc., Orders Addr.: P.O. Box 671053, Dallas, TX 75367 USA Tel 972-241-1366; Fax: 972-241-5345 (call first); Toll Free: 800-522-3341; Edit Addr.: 3975 High Summit Dr., Dallas, TX 75244 USA
E-mail: jillsmithusa@att.net
Web site: http://www.learning-apodixis.com.

ReadaClassic.com, *(978-1-61104)* Orders Addr.: P.O. Box 7, Cedar Lake, MI 48812 USA Tel 989-427-2790; Edit Addr.: 4769 Feather Trail, Cedar Lake, MI 48812 USA Tel 989-427-2790
E-mail: carjhaus@gmail.com
Web site: http://www.readaclassic.com; http://www.clearwords.org.

Reader Publishing Group, *(978-0-9837873)* 1900 E. Ocean Blvd. No. 1001, Long Beach, CA 90802 USA Tel 562-900-0953
E-mail: cunham@aol.com.

Readerlink Distribution Services, LLC, *(978-0-934429; 978-1-57145; 978-1-59223; 978-1-60710; 978-1-62686; 978-1-68412)* 10350 Barnes Canyon Rd. Suite 100, San Diego, CA 92121 USA (SAN 630-8090) Toll Free: 800-284-3580; *Imprints*: Thunder Bay Press (Thunder Bay); Silver Dolphin Books (Silver Dolph); Portable Press (Portable Pr)
E-mail: lnordland@readerlink.com
Web site: http://www.silverdolphinbooks.com; http://www.printersrowpublishinggroup.com; http://www.thunderbaybooks.com/; http://www.bathroomreader.com; http://www.readerlink.com
Dist(s): **Publishers Group West (PGW).**

Readers Are Leaders, *(978-0-9673625)* 908 Ashland Dr., Mesquite, TX 75149 USA Tel 972-288-5806 (phone/fax)
E-mail: rlgant@airmail.net.

Readers Are Leaders U.S.A., Inc., *(978-0-9768035; 978-0-9800397)* 2315 SW 5th Ave., Miami, FL 33129-1939 USA (SAN 855-0557)
Web site: http://www.readersareleadersusa.net.

†**Reader's Digest Assn., Inc., The,** *(978-0-7621; 978-0-89577; 978-0-86438; 978-1-60652)* One Bedford Rd., Pleasantville, NY 10570 USA (SAN 282-2091) Toll Free: 800-463-8820; 800-334-9599; 800-635-5006
Web site: http://www.readersdigest.com; http://www.rd.com
Dist(s): **Leonard, Hal Corp.**
Penguin Publishing Group
Simon & Schuster, Inc.
Tuttle Publishing; *CIP.*

Reader's Digest Children's Bks. *Imprint of* **Studio Fun International**

Reader's Digest Children's Publishing, Incorporated *See* **Studio Fun International**

Reader's Digest Young Families, Inc. *Imprint of* **Studio Fun International**

READERS to EATERS, *(978-0-9836615; 978-0-9984366)* 12437 SE 26th Pl., Bellevue, WA 98005 USA Tel 206-849-1962
E-mail: philip@readerstoeaters.com
Web site: www.ReadersToEaters.com
Dist(s): **Publishers Group West (PGW).**

Reading Co., The *Imprint of* **Rhoades & Assocs.**

Reading Power *Imprint of* **Rosen Publishing Group, Inc., The**

Reading Reading Bks., LLC, *(978-1-933727; 978-1-60892)* P.O. Box 6654, Reading, PA 19610 USA
E-mail: service@rrbooks.com; orangetabbycat2000@yahoo.com
Web site: http://www.rrbooks.com.

Reading Resc., *(978-0-9755561; 978-0-9795648)* 314 Knowles Hill Rd., Alexandria, NH 03222 USA (SAN 853-7771) Tel 603-744-5803 Do not confuse with Reading Resources, Inc. in Worthington, OH
E-mail: laberge001@gmail.com; readingrescources@metrocast.net.

Reading Rock Books *See* **Reading Rock, Inc.**

Reading Rock, Inc., *(978-1-929591)* P.O. Box 67, Athens, MI 49011 USA Tel 616-729-9440
Web site: http://www.Readingrockbook.com.

Reading Room Collection *Imprint of* **Rosen Publishing Group, Inc., The**

Reading Studio Pr., *(978-0-9767506)* 250 W. 90th St., Suite 12F, New York, NY 10024 USA Tel 212-724-6232
E-mail: readingstudio@aol.com
Web site: http://www.alphieandthealphabets.com.

Reading Tree Pr., *(978-0-615-92763-3; 978-0-692-38179-3)*
Dist(s): **CreateSpace Independent Publishing Platform.**

Reading with Rose, *(978-0-9891006)* 317 S. Elm St. Loft 313, Owosso, MI 48867 USA Tel 989-274-1053
E-mail: rlthof@gmail.com.

Reading's Fun/Books are Fun, Limited *See* **Bks. Are Fun, Ltd.**

Ready Blade *Imprint of* **Blooming Tree Pr.**

Ready Writer Publishing, LLC, *(978-0-9748748)* P.O. Box 18197, Shreveport, LA 71138 USA Tel 318-470-0538
E-mail: satbeau1@bellsouth.net.

ReadZone Bks. (GBR) *(978-1-78322) Dist. by* **IPG Chicago.**

Reagent Pr. Bks. for Young Readers *Imprint of* **RP Media**

Reagent Pr. Echo *Imprint of* **RP Media**

Reagent Pr. Signature Editions *Imprint of* **RP Media**

Reagent Press *See* **RP Media**

Reaktion Bks., Ltd. (GBR) *(978-0-948462; 978-1-86189; 978-1-78023) Dist. by* **Chicago Distribution Ctr.**

R.E.A.L. Pubns., *(978-0-9724503; 978-0-9748003)* 109 La Costa Dr., Georgetown, KY 40324 USA (SAN 255-867X) Tel 859-539-2463
E-mail: austinandbelinda@gmail.com
Web site: http://www.arealeducation.com.

R.E.A.L. Publishing *See* **R.E.A.L. Pubns.**

Real Reads Ltd. (GBR) *(978-1-906230; 978-1-911091) Dist. by* **Casemate Pubs.**

Real World Productions, *(978-1-60855; 978-1-60856)* 131 Ave. B, No. 1B, New York, NY 10009 USA.

Realistically Speaking Publishing Co., *(978-0-9727874)* 10808 Foothill Blvd. No. 160-260, Rancho Cucamonga , CA 91730 USA
E-mail: sherea@vejauan.com
Web site: http://www.vejauan.com.

Reality Living Publishing, Inc., *(978-0-9643021; 978-1-888220)* 8720 E. 55th St., Kansas City, MO 64129 USA Tel 816-358-1515 ext 2062; Fax: 816-358-3439 ext 2062
E-mail: sehle@kcbt.org
Web site: http://www.realityliving.org.

RealityIs Bks. *Imprint of* **RealityIsBooks.com, Inc.**

RealityIsBooks.com, Inc., *(978-0-9791317; 978-0-9817137; 978-0-9843883; 978-0-9847390)* 1327 Winslowe Dr., Unit 304, Palatine, IL 60074 USA Tel 847-305-4657; Toll

Publisher Name Index

Free: 866-534-3366; *Imprints:* Realityls Books (Realityls Bks); Green Lady Press, The (GreenLady)
E-mail: publish@realityisbooks.com
Web site: http://www.realityisbooks.com.

Really Big Coloring Bks., Inc., (*978-0-9727833; 978-0-9729753; 978-0-9763186; 978-1-935266; 978-1-61953*) 224 N. Meramec, Saint Louis, MO 63105 USA Tel 314-725-1452; Fax: 314-725-3553; Toll Free: 800-244-2665 (1-800-Big-Book)
E-mail: wayne@bigcoloringbooks.com; ken@bigcoloringbooks.com; derek@bigcoloringbooks.com
Web site: http://www.bigcoloringbook.com; http://www.spanishcoloringbooks.com; http://www.wholesalecoloringbooks.com; http://www.coloringbook.com; http://www.coloringbookpublishers.com
Dist(s): **MeadWestvaco.**

Realms *Imprint of* **Charisma Media**

RealWord Pubns., (*978-0-9743088*) Orders Addr.: P.O. Box 931461, Norcross, GA 30093-1461 USA Fax: 678-406-9178; Edit Addr.: 6450 Indian Acres Trail, Norcross, GA 30093 USA
E-mail: wrcomm@comcast.net
Web site: http://www.climbeveryobstacle.com.

Reasor, Teresa J., (*978-0-615-50243-4; 978-0-9850069; 978-0-9886627; 978-1-940047*) P.O. Box 124, Corbin, KY 40702 USA Tel 606-528-0819
Web site: http://www.teresareasor.com
Dist(s): **CreateSpace Independent Publishing Platform**
Smashwords.

Rebecca Hse., (*978-0-945522*) 1550 California St., Suite 330, San Francisco, CA 94109 USA (SAN 247-1361) Tel 415-752-1453; Toll Free: 800-321-1912 (orders only)
E-mail: Rebeccahse@aol.com
Dist(s): **New Leaf Distributing Co., Inc.**

Rebecca's Bks., (*978-0-9744346*) P.O. Box 644, Watertown, WI 53094 USA.

Rebel Press *See* **Little Dixie Publishing Co.**

Rebellion (GBR) (*978-1-904265; 978-1-906735; 978-1-907519; 978-1-84997; 978-1-907992; 978-1-78108*) *Dist. by* **S and S Inc.**

Recipe Pubs., (*978-0-9778057; 978-0-9816282; 978-0-9824801; 978-0-9826424; 978-0-9828531; 978-0-9898137*) Orders Addr.: 610 N. Elmwood Ave, Springfield, MO 65802 USA (SAN 930-8873) Tel 417-619-4939; Toll Free: 800-313-5121
E-mail: jec1963@sbcglobal.net; jec@recipepubs.com
Web site: http://www.recipepubs.com.

Reclam, Philip jun., Verlag GmbH (DEU) (*978-3-15*) *Dist. by* **Intl Bk Import.**

Reclamation Bureau *Imprint of* **United States Government Printing Office**

Recon Academy *Imprint of* **Stone Arch Bks.**

Record Stockman & Coyote Cowboy *See* **Coyote Cowboy Co.**

Recorded Bks., Inc., (*978-0-7887; 978-1-55690; 978-1-84197; 978-1-4025; 978-1-4193; 978-1-84505; 978-1-4281; 978-1-4361; 978-1-4407; 978-1-4498; 978-1-4561; 978-1-4618; 978-1-4640; 978-1-4703; 978-1-4906; 978-1-5019*) Subs. of W. F. Howes Limited, Orders Addr.: 270 Skipjack Rd., Prince Frederick, MD 20678 USA (SAN 111-3984) Fax: 410-535-5499; Toll Free: 800-638-1304; 7257 Pkwy. Dr., Hanover, MD 21076 (SAN 920-7414)
E-mail: thelvey@recordedbooks.com
Web site: http://www.recordedbooks.com
Dist(s): **Brilliance Publishing, Inc.**
Ebsco Publishing
Follett School Solutions
Ingram Publisher Services.

Recorded Books, LLC *See* **Recorded Bks., Inc.**

Rector Pr., Ltd., (*978-0-7605; 978-0-934393; 978-1-57205*) Orders Addr.: The Ledge House 130 Rattlesnake Gutter Rd. Suite 1000, Leverett, MA 01054-9726 USA (SAN 693-8108) Tel 413-367-0303 (International Book Sales); Fax: 413-367-2853
E-mail: info@rectorpress.com; info@runanywhere.com
Web site: http://www.rectorpress.com; http://twitter.com/Lewisxxxusa; http://twitter.com/Rectorpress.

Rector Tales, (*978-0-9969085*) 22154 Barrington Way, Santa Clarita, CA 91350 USA Tel 661-449-9103
E-mail: cuffsbyrector@gmail.com
Web site: RectorTales.com.

Recursos, Ediciones (ESP) (*978-84-89984; 978-84-921663*) *Dist. by* **IPG Chicago.**

Red & Black Pubs., (*978-0-9791813; 978-1-934941; 978-1-61001*) P.O. Box 7542, Saint Petersburg, FL 33734 USA
E-mail: info@redandblackpublishers.com
Web site: http://www.redandblackpublishers.com.

Red Barn Reading Inc., (*978-0-9753059*) P.O. Box 540, Alanson, MI 49706 USA
E-mail: thecathy@tm.net.

Red Brick Learning, (*978-0-7368*) Div. of Coughlan Publishing, 151 Good Counsel Dr., P.O. Box 669, Mankato, MN 56002-0669 USA Toll Free Fax: 888-574-5570; Toll Free: 888-262-6135; *Imprints:* High Five (High Five)
Dist(s): **Capstone Press of Coughlan Cos.**

Red Bud Publishing, (*978-0-9759421*) 2425 Lakeshore Ct., Lebanon, IN 46052 USA.

Red CalacArts Publications *Imprint of* **Calaca Pr.**

Red Carpet Publishing, (*978-0-9719657; 978-0-9722829*) P.O. Box 309, Noblesville, IN 46061-0309 USA (SAN 255-755X) Tel 317-847-9553; Fax: 317-773-5375
Web site: http://www.redcarpetpublishing.com.

Red Chair Pr., (*978-1-936163; 978-1-937529; 978-1-939656; 978-1-63440; 978-1-947159*) P.O. Box 333, South Egremont, MA 01258 USA (SAN 858-6209)
E-mail: redchairpress@gmail.com; info@redchairpress.com
Web site: http://www.redchairpress.com; http://www.lernerbooks.com
Dist(s): **Follett School Solutions**
Lerner Publishing Group
MyiLibrary.

†**Red Crane Bks., Inc.,** (*978-1-878610*) Orders Addr.: P.O. Box 33590, Santa Fe, NM 87954 USA; Edit Addr.: 2008 Rosina St., Suite C, Santa Fe, NM 87505 USA Tel 505-988-7070; Fax: 505-989-7476; Toll Free: 800-922-3392
E-mail: publish@redcrane.com
Web site: http://www.redcrane.com
Dist(s): **Continental Bk. Co., Inc.**
Libros Sin Fronteras; *CIP.*

Red Cygnet Pr., (*978-1-60108*) 2245 Enterprise St. Ste. 110, Escondido, CA 92029-2060 USA; *Imprints:* Bearing Books (Bearing Bks)
E-mail: info@redcygnet.com
Web site: http://www.redcygnet.com
Dist(s): **Rosen Publishing Group, Inc., The Soundprints.**

Red Deer Pr. (CAN) (*978-0-88995*) *Dist. by* **IngramPubServ.**

Red Door Pr., (*978-0-9763770*) 1704 Black Oak Ln., Silver Spring, MD 20910 USA Tel 301-588-7599; Fax: 301-838-9771 Do not confuse with Red Door Press in San Francisco, CA
E-mail: trishbaur@comcast.net.

Red Earth Publishing, (*978-0-9767748*) Orders Addr.: 104 Candace Dr., Ponca City, OK 74604 USA Tel 580-763-7003
E-mail: deborahjuckes@gmail.com
Web site: http://www.redearthpub.com.

Red Earth Publishing, (*978-0-9779993*) 2041 NW 20th St., Oklahoma City, OK 73106-1609 USA.

Red Engine Pr., (*978-0-9663276; 978-0-9743758; 978-0-9745652; 978-0-9785158; 978-0-9800064; 978-0-9800332; 978-0-9827923; 978-0-9834930; 978-1-937958; 978-1-943267*) 18942 State Hwy. 13, Suite F107, Branson West, MO 65737 USA Tel 417-230-5555
E-mail: riverroadpress@yahoo.com
Web site: http://www.redenginepress.com.

Red Feather *Imprint of* **Schiffer Publishing, Ltd.**

Red Fox Publishing, (*978-0-692-78504-1; 978-0-692-78506-5*) 19706 N Ramsey Rd, Rathdrum, ID 83858 USA Tel 208-709-7762.

Red Giant Entertainment *Imprint of* **Active Media Publishing, LLC**

Red Giant Publishing, (*978-0-9767661*) P.O. Box 5, San Mateo, CA 94401 USA
E-mail: questions@redgiantpublishing.com
Web site: http://www.redgiantpublishing.com.

†**Red Hen Pr.,** (*978-0-931093*) P.O. Box 454, Big Sur, CA 93920 USA (SAN 678-9420) Tel 831-667-2726 (phone/fax) Do not confuse with Red Hen Pr. in Casa Grande, AZ, Granada Hills, CA
E-mail: HopeHen@aol.com
Dist(s): **Book Wholesalers, Inc.**
Brodart Co.
Follett School Solutions; *CIP.*

Red Hills Writers Project, (*978-0-9759339*) 1509 Hasosaw Nene, Tallahassee, FL 32301 USA Tel 850-216-2016; Fax: 831-308-3285
E-mail: info@redhillswritersproject.org
Web site: http://www.redhillswritersproject.org.

Red Ink Pr., (*978-0-9788401*) 1914 N. Roan St., Suite 106-223, Johnson City, TN 37601 USA (SAN 851-724X) Tel 423-741-2835
Web site: http://www.redinkpress.com
Dist(s): **Book Hub, Inc.**

Red Jacket Pr., (*978-0-9748895*) 3099 Maqua Pl., Mohegan Lake, NY 10547-1054 USA
E-mail: info@redjacketpress.com
Web site: http://www.redjacketpress.com
Dist(s): **Pathway Bk. Service.**

Red Letter Pr., (*978-0-9661199; 978-0-9794420; 978-0-692-43517-5*) Orders Addr.: 6148 Rutledge Hill, Columbia, SC 29209-1315 USA Tel 843-344-2221 Do not confuse with Red Letter Pr., Seattle, WA
E-mail: redletterpress@gmail.com
Web site: http://redletterpress.googlepages.com
Dist(s): **CreateSpace Independent Publishing Platform.**

Red Letter Publishing & Media Group *See* **Potential Unlimited Publishing**

Red Men Interprises, (*978-0-9744682*) 8 Boton Rd., Lloyd Harbor, NY 11743 USA Tel 516-769-9720
E-mail: jason@drugfreeteen.com
Web site: http://www.drugfreeteen.com.

Red Mountain Creations, (*978-0-9759858; 978-0-9910804*) P.O. Box 172, High Ridge, MO 63049 USA Tel 636-677-3088; Toll Free: 866-732-4857
E-mail: redmountain@swbell.net
Web site: http://www.byronvonrosenberg.com.

Red Mud Pr., (*978-0-9672996*) Orders Addr.: P.O. Box 1257, Sedona, AZ 86336-4357 USA Tel 520-282-5285; Edit Addr.: 51 Remuda Rd., Sedona, AZ 86336 USA
E-mail: Crawford@sedona.net.

Red Owl Pubns., (*978-0-9754279*) 7857 Sedgewick Dr., Freeland, MI 48623 USA Tel 989-737-4486
E-mail: ckblack@redowlpublications.com
Dist(s): **MyiLibrary.**

Blue Pheonix Bks., (*978-0-9726290; 978-1-937781; 978-1-938969*) 809 W. Dike St., Glendora, CA 91740 USA
E-mail: Service@redphoenixbooks.com; cja@redphoenixbooks.com; claudia.alexander@gmail.com
Web site: http://www.redphoenixbooks.com
Dist(s): **Partners Pubs. Group, Inc.**

Red Planet Pictures, (*978-0-9719031*) 1800 S. Robertson Blvd., No. 153, Los Angeles, CA 90035 USA Tel 310-659-8386 (phone/fax)
E-mail: markm@laube.com
Dist(s): **Consortium Bk. Sales & Distribution.**

Red Pumpkin Pr., (*978-0-9711572; 978-0-9849284*) P.O. Box 40, Rutledge, TN 37861 USA Tel 865-828-3362; Fax: 865-828-4578
E-mail: centar123@aol.com.

Red River Pr. *Imprint of* **Red River Pr.**

Red River Pr., (*978-0-910653*) 3900 Roy Rd., Suite 37, Shreveport, LA 71107 USA (SAN 270-1774) Fax: 318-309-1653; *Imprints:* Red River Press (Red River Pr)
E-mail: rrp_asi@Bellsouth.net
Web site: http://www.ArchivalServicesInc.com.

Red Rock Mountain Pr. LLC, (*978-0-615-30253-9; 978-0-615-40473-8; 978-0-615-73121-6*) 560 Schnebly Rd., Sedona, AZ 86336 USA.

Red Rock Pr., Inc., (*978-0-9669573; 978-0-9714372; 978-1-933176*) 331 W. 57th. Street, suite 175, New York, NY 10019 USA Tel 212-362-8304; Fax: 212-362-6216; Toll Free: 800-488-8040
E-mail: richard@redrockpress.com
Web site: http://www.redrockpress.com
Dist(s): **MyiLibrary.**

Red Sage Publishing, (*978-0-9648942; 978-0-9754516; 978-1-60310*) Div. of Red Sage Publishing, Inc., P.O. Box 4844, Seminole, FL 33775 USA (SAN 859-0249) Tel 727-391-3847 (phone/fax)
E-mail: alekendall@aol.com
Web site: http://www.eRedSage.com
Dist(s): **Brodart Co.**
Cowley Distributing, Inc.
OverDrive, Inc.

Red Tail Publishing, (*978-0-9635757; 978-0-9847756; 978-1-941950*) Orders Addr.: P.O. Box 1477, Anderson, CA 96007 USA Tel 530-365-5863
E-mail: livingston@redtail.com; info@redtail.com
Web site: http://www.redtail.com.

Red Team Ink, (*978-0-9982349; 978-0-9984881*) 9480 W. River Beach Ln., Boise, ID 83714 USA Tel 208-870-8359; Fax: 208-870-8359
E-mail: Redteamink@gmail.com
Web site: www.redteamink.com.

Red Wagon *See* **Magic Wagon**

Red Wagon Bks. *Imprint of* **Harcourt Children's Bks.**

†**Red Wheel/Weiser,** (*978-0-87728; 978-0-943233; 978-1-57324; 978-1-57863; 978-1-59003; 978-1-60925; 978-1-61283; 978-1-61852; 978-1-61940; 978-1-938875; 978-1-63341; 978-1-942785*) Div. of Weiser Bks., Orders Addr.: 65 Parker St., Suite 7, Newburyport, MA 01950 USA (SAN 255-8610) Tel 978-465-0504; Fax: 978-465-0243; Toll Free Fax: 877-337-3309; Toll Free: 800-423-7087 (orders only)
E-mail: customerservice@redwheelweiser.com
Web site: http://www.redwheelweiser.com
Dist(s): **Abyss Distribution**
Ebsco Publishing
New Leaf Distributing Co., Inc.; *CIP.*

Redcay Publishing, (*978-0-615-17346-7*) 2953 Grandview Blvd ., West LAwn, PA 19609 USA Tel 610-678-5636
E-mail: mwkreltz@msn.com
Web site: http://www.divcothelittlemilktruck.com.

Redding, Marion T., (*978-0-9671701*) Orders Addr.: 684 Chaloupe St. SE., Palm Bay, FL 32909-4433 USA (SAN 254-4024) Tel 740-369-4952
E-mail: starbourne53@mac.com; marionredding@icloud.com
Web site: http://www.davidredding.net.

Redding Pr., (*978-0-9658879*) Orders Addr.: c/o Mary Mahony, P.O. Box 366, Belmont, MA 02178 USA Fax: 617-489-9476; Toll Free: 800-267-6012; Edit Addr.: P.O. Box 366, Belmont, MA 02178 USA
E-mail: mary@reddingpress.com
Web site: http://www.channel.com/users/msmahony; http://www.reddingpress.com
Dist(s): **Quality Bks., Inc.**

Redel, Nicole, (*978-0-9769738*) 2125 David Dr., Florissant, MO 63031-4321 USA Tel 314-839-3242
E-mail: gospelpitbull@sbcglobal.net
Web site: http://www.gospelpitbull.com.

Redemption Pr., (*978-1-63232; 978-1-68314*) 1730 Railroad St., Enumclaw, WA 98022 USA Tel 360-226-3488; Toll Free Fax: 855-498-6595; Toll Free: 888-305-2967
E-mail: athena@redemption-press.com; info@redemption-press.com
Web site: www.redemption-press.com.

Redhawk Publishing, (*978-0-9641861; 978-0-9769267*) Orders Addr.: 602 Pompa St., Carlsbad, NM 88220 USA Tel 505-885-1748; *Imprints:* RWP Books (RWP Bks)
E-mail: randy@rwpbooks.com
Web site: http://www.rwpbooks.com
Dist(s): **CreateSpace Independent Publishing Platform.**

RedJack, (*978-1-892619*) P.O. Box 633, Bayside, CA 95524 USA Tel 707-825-7817
E-mail: heidi@redjack.us
Web site: http://www.redjack.us.

Redleaf Pr., (*978-0-934140; 978-1-884834; 978-1-929610; 978-1-933653; 978-1-60554*) Div. of Resources for Child Caring, Inc., 10 Yorkton Ct., Saint Paul, MN 55117-1065 USA (SAN 212-8691) Toll Free Fax: 800-641-0115; Toll Free: 800-423-8309
E-mail: sales@redleafpress.org
Web site: http://www.redleafpress.org
Dist(s): **Capstone Press of Coughlan Cos.**
Capstone Pub.
Consortium Bk. Sales & Distribution
Gryphon Hse., Inc.
Lectorum Pubns., Inc.
MyiLibrary.

Redline Bks., (*978-0-9727440*) 2280 Jones Creek Rd., White Bluff, TN 37187 USA Tel 615-797-3043 (phone/fax)
E-mail: redlinebooks@bardyoung.com; bardyoung@bardyoung.com.

RedMEDIA, (*978-0-9721708*) 41 Schermerhorn St., No. 147, Brooklyn, NY 11201 USA Tel 718-857-6638; Fax: 718-857-6427
E-mail: rmedia3@aol.com
Web site: http://www.tgoodlife.com; http://www.ibrooklyn.com/redmedia.

Redmond, Pamela, (*978-0-9760767*) P.O. Box 169, Topping, VA 23169-0169 USA.

Reece, Kim Taylor Prodns. LLC, (*978-0-9660395; 978-1-59779*) 53-866 Kamehameha Hwy., Hauula, HI 96717 USA Tel 808-293-2000; Fax: 808-293-2136; Toll Free: 800-657-7966
E-mail: info@kimtaylorreece.com
Web site: http://www.kimtaylorreece.com
Dist(s): **Booklines Hawaii, Ltd.**
Islander Group.

Reed Business Information, (*978-0-9614276; 978-1-879930; 978-1-931625; 978-0-9764027; 978-0-9851869*) 5900 Wilshire Blvd. Ste. 3100, Los Angeles, CA 90036-5030 USA (SAN 687-3944) Toll Free: 800-545-2411
E-mail: nlongman@reedbusiness.com; steve.atinsky@reedbusiness.com
Web site: http://www.la411.com
Dist(s): **SCB Distributors.**

Reed, Robert D. Pubs., (*978-1-885003; 978-1-931741; 978-1-934759; 978-1-944297*) P.O. Box 1992, Bandon, OR 97411 USA Tel 541-347-9882; Fax: 541-347-9883
E-mail: 4bobreed@msn.com
Web site: http://www.rdrpublishers.com
Dist(s): **Midpoint Trade Bks., Inc.**
Todd Communications.

Reedswain, Inc., (*978-0-9651020; 978-1-890946; 978-1-59164*) Orders Addr.: 88 Wells Rd., Spring City, PA 19475-8628 USA Toll Free: 800-331-5191
E-mail: bryan@reedswain.com
Web site: http://www.reedswain.com
Dist(s): **Cardinal Pubs. Group.**

Reedy Pr., (*978-0-9753180; 978-1-933370; 978-1-935806; 978-1-68106*) Orders Addr.: P.O. Box 5131, Saint Louis, MO 63139 USA Toll Free Fax: 866-999-6916 fax
E-mail: jstevens@reedypress.com; dkorte@reedypress.com
Web site: http://www.reedypress.com
Dist(s): **Partners Bk. Distributing, Inc.**

Reel Productions, LLC, (*978-0-9675010; 978-0-9707422*) P.O. Box 1069, Monument, CO 80132 USA Toll Free: 800-964-0439
E-mail: support@reelproductions.net; jolene@explorationfilms.com
Web site: http://www.explorationfilms.com; http://www.reelproductions.net
Dist(s): **Exploration Films**
Send The Light Distribution LLC.

Reeves Bay Press, (*978-0-9860833*) 17 Huntington Lane, Flanders, NY 11901 USA.

Reeves, Emily, (*978-0-9821506*) P.O. Box 15861, Savannah, GA 31416 USA.

Reference Service Pr., (*978-0-918276; 978-1-58841*) 5000 Windplay Dr., Suite 4, El Dorado Hills, CA 95762 USA (SAN 210-2633) Tel 916-939-9620; Fax: 916-939-9626
E-mail: findaid@aol.com; info@rspfunding.com
Web site: http://www.rspfunding.com.

ReferencePoint Pr., Inc., (*978-1-60152; 978-1-68282*) P.O. Box 27779, San Diego, CA 92198 USA (SAN 858-6845) Tel 858-618-1314; Fax: 858-618-1730; Toll Free: 888-479-6436; 17150 Via Del Campo. Ste. 205, San Diego, CA 92127-2138
E-mail: dan@referencepointpress.com; orders@referencepointpress.com; info@referencepointpress.com
Web site: http://www.referencepointpress.com.

Refined Savage Editions / Ediciones El Salvaje Refinado, The, (*978-0-9713175; 978-0-9746855; 978-0-9761940; 978-0-9768868; 978-0-9791011; 978-0-9802008; 978-0-9816968*) 10 Delaware Ave., Charleston, WV 25302-1950 USA
E-mail: esrefinado@aol.com
Web site: http://www.esrefinado.net.

Reflection Pr., (*978-0-9671543*) 3430 W. 98th Pl. Unit A, Westminster, CO 80031 USA Tel 303-862-4868 Do not confuse with companies with the same name in Huntsville, AL, Berkeley, CA
E-mail: mbsmith48@gmail.com.

Reflection Pr., (*978-0-9843799; 978-1-945289*) 3543 18th St., Ste 17, San Francisco, CA 94110 USA
E-mail: info@reflectionpress.com; manager@reflectionpress.com
Web site: http://www.reflectionpress.com.

Reflection Publishing, (*978-0-9797618; 978-1-936629*) P.O. Box 2182, Citrus Heights, CA 95621-2182 USA Fax: 916-726-2768
E-mail: contact@reflectpublishing.com
Web site: http://www.reflectpublishing.com.

Reflection Publishing Company *See* **Imprints**

Reflection Publishing Co., (*978-0-9657561; 978-0-9712142*) 1813 4th St W., Palmetto, FL 34221-4303 USA (SAN 299-2787) Toll Free: 888-677-0101
E-mail: lakepm@msn.com
Web site: http://www.reflectionpublishing.com
Dist(s): **Brodart Co.**
Spring Arbor Distributors, Inc.

Reflections Publishing Hse., (*978-0-9837231; 978-0-9965296*) 925 N. Inglewood Ave No. 10, Inglewood, CA 90302 USA Tel 310-695-9800
E-mail: dabellis@sbcglobal.net
Web site: www.reflectionspublishings.net.

Reflections Publishing, Inc., (*978-0-9792132; 978-0-9840789*) P.O. Box 294, Inglewood, CA 90306 USA (SAN 858-2297) Tel 310-695-9800 Do not confuse with companies with the same or similar name in Odenton, MD, Cove, OR, Livingston, TX, Dallas, TX, Dunlap, TN, Hume, CA
E-mail: writray@aol.com
Web site: http://www.reflectionspublishings.net.

Reformation Herald Publishing Assn., *(978-0-9745295; 978-1-934308)* P.O. Box 7240, Roanoke, VA 24019-0240 USA
Web site: http://www.sdarm.org.

Reformation Heritage Bks., *(978-1-892777; 978-1-60178)* 2965 Leonard St., NE, Grand Rapids, MI 49525-5828 USA
E-mail: jay.collier@heritagebooks.org
Web site: http://www.heritagebooks.org
Dist(s): **Send The Light Distribution LLC**
christianaudio.

Reformation Pubs., *(978-1-933304; 978-1-60416)* 242 University Dr., Prestonsburg, KY 41653-1058 USA Tel 606-886-7222; Fax: 606-886-8222; Toll Free Fax: 800-765-2464
E-mail: rpublisher@aol.com
Web site: http://www.reformationpublishers.com
Dist(s): **Lightning Source, Inc.**

Reformed Church in America, Reformed Church Pr., *(978-0-916466)* 4500 60th St., SE, Grand Rapids, MI 49512-9670 USA Tel 616-698-7071; Fax: 616-698-6606; Toll Free: 800-968-7221 (orders); 475 Riverside Dr., 18th Flr., New York, NY 10115 (SAN 207-4508)
Dist(s): **Faith Alive Christian Resources.**

Reformed Free Publishing Assn., *(978-0-916206; 978-1-936054; 978-1-944555)* Orders Addr.: 1894 Georgetown Ctr. Dr., Jenison, MI 49428-7137 USA Tel 616-457-5970
E-mail: mail@rfpa.org; evelyn@rfpa.org
Web site: http://www.rfpa.org.

Refugee Pr., *(978-0-692-43628-8; 978-0-692-88712-7; 978-0-692-95136-1)* 2511 Buck Quarter Farm Rd., Hillsborough, NC 27278 USA Tel 919 625-4502
Dist(s): **CreateSpace Independent Publishing Platform.**

Regal Bks. *Imprint of* **Gospel Light Pubns.**

Regal Enterprises, *(978-0-9727771; 978-0-9729960)* 16310 Garfield Ave., Paramount, CA 90723-4806 USA (SAN 255-2477)
Dist(s): **Timberwolf Pr., Inc.**

ReganBooks *Imprint of* **HarperCollins Pubs.**

Regency Hse., Ltd., *(978-0-9716923)* 6538 Pardee, Taylor, MI 48180-1771 USA Tel 313-291-9242
Dist(s): **BookMasters, Inc.**

Regenold Publishing, *(978-0-9773085)* P.O. Box 621967, Littleton, CO 80162-1967 USA (SAN 257-2583) Tel 303-797-8881
Web site: http://www.regenoldpublishing.com.

Regent Pr., *(978-0-916147; 978-1-889059; 978-1-58790)* 2747 Regent St., Berkeley, CA 94705-1212 USA (SAN 294-9717) Tel 510-845-1196 Do not confuse with Regent Pr., Oxnard, CA
E-mail: regentpress@mindspring.com
Web site: http://www.regentpress.net
Dist(s): **Consortium Bk. Sales & Distribution**
Lightning Source, Inc.
New Village Pr.
Quality Bks., Inc.

Regina Orthodox Pr., *(978-0-9649141; 978-1-928653)* Orders Addr.: P.O. Box 5288, Salisbury, MA 01952 USA Fax: 978-462-5079; Toll Free: 800-636-2470; Edit Addr.: 6 Second St., Salisbury, MA 01952 USA
E-mail: reginaorthodoxpress@comcast.net
Web site: http://www.reginaorthodoxpress.com
Dist(s): **National Bk. Network.**

Regina Pr., Malhame & Co., *(978-0-88271)* Orders Addr.: P.O. Box 608, Melville, NY 11747-0608 USA (SAN 203-0853) Tel 631-694-8600; Edit Addr.: 10 Hub Dr., Melville, NY 11747 USA
E-mail: customerservice@malhame.com
Web site: http://www.malhame.com/.

Region IV Education Service Ctr., *(978-1-932524; 978-1-932797; 978-1-933049; 978-1-933521; 978-1-934950; 978-1-937403; 978-1-945615)* 7145 W. Tidwell, Houston, TX 77092-2096 USA Tel 713-462-7708; Fax: 713-744-6514
E-mail: dharvey@esc4.net
Web site: http://www.esc4.net
Dist(s): **Consortium Bk. Sales & Distribution.**

Regional Laboratory for Educational Improvement of the Northeast & Islands *See* **NETWORK Inc., The**

Regnery Gateway, Incorporated *See* **Regnery Publishing, Inc., An Eagle Publishing Co.**

Regnery Kids *Imprint of* **Regnery Publishing, Inc., An Eagle Publishing Co.**

†**Regnery Publishing, Inc., An Eagle Publishing Co.**, *(978-0-89526; 978-1-59698; 978-1-62157)* Div. of Caron Broadcasting, Inc., One Massachusetts Ave., NW, Suite 600, Washington, DC 20001 USA (SAN 210-5578) Tel 202-216-0600; *Imprints:* Little Patriot Press (LittlePatriot); Regnery Kids (REGNERY KIDS)
Web site: http://www.regnery.com
Dist(s): **Continental Bk. Co., Inc.**
Ingram Publisher Services
MyiLibrary
Send The Light Distribution LLC
ebrary, Inc.; *CIP.*

†**Regular Baptist Pr.**, *(978-0-87227; 978-1-59402; 978-1-60776; 978-1-62940)* Div. of General Assn. of Regular Baptist Churches, 1300 N. Meacham Rd., Schaumburg, IL 60173-4806 USA (SAN 205-2229) Tel 847-843-1600 (foreign orders); 708-843-1600; Fax: 847-843-3757; Toll Free: 800-727-4440 (orders only)
E-mail: rbporders@garbc.org
Web site: http://www.regularbaptistpress.org; *CIP.*

Reiki Blessings, *(978-0-9743679)* P.O. Box 2000, Byron, GA 31008-2000 USA (SAN 255-7045) Fax: 801-705-1802
E-mail: reikiblessings@earthlink.net
Web site: http://www.rbpress.com.

Reimann Bks., *(978-0-9820941; 978-0-9838148; 978-0-9852254; 978-1-938743)* Orders Addr.: 305 Parkton Dr, Richlands, NC 28574 USA
E-mail: reimannbooks@gmail.com
Web site: http://www.reimannbooks.com.

Reinoso, Marta, *(978-0-9676203)* World Educational Guild, Inc. 1330 E. 223rd., Suite 501, Carson, CA 90745 USA Tel 310-816-1100; Fax: 310-816-1103
E-mail: wegi@earthnet.com.

Reisman, Dave *See* **Jumping Cow Pr.**

Rejoyce Pubns., *(978-0-9661564)* 5205 Aryshire Dr., Dublin, OH 43017 USA Tel 614-766-2771; Fax: 614-766-1731.

Relationship Resources, Inc., *(978-0-9721726)* P.O. Box 63383, Colorado Springs, CO 80962 USA
E-mail: gaylyn@relationshipresources.org
Web site: http://www.relationshipresources.org
Dist(s): **Send The Light Distribution LLC.**

Relde Publishing, *(978-0-9701863)* Subs. of Solutions Training & Development LLC, P.O. Box 21304, Jackson, MS 39289 USA Tel 601-926-4375; Fax: 601-926-4374; Toll Free: 800-489-3439
E-mail: solut2000@aol.com.

Relevant Graces Productions, *(978-0-9822375)* 1044 Cresswood Dr., Richlands, VA 24641 USA.

Relevant Media Group, Inc., *(978-0-9714576; 978-0-9729276; 978-0-9746942; 978-0-9760357; 978-0-9763642; 978-0-9768175; 978-0-9776167; 978-0-9777480)* 1220 Alden Rd., Orlando, FL 32803-2546 USA; 600 Rinehart Rd., Lake Mary, FL 32746
E-mail: nick@relevantmediagroup.com
Web site: http://www.relevantbooks.com/
Dist(s): **Charisma Media.**

Relevant Pages Pr., *(978-0-615-82759-9; 978-0-615-87121-9; 978-0-692-31475-3; 978-0-692-50308-9; 978-0-692-56515-5; 978-0-692-58351-7; 978-0-692-58360-9; 978-0-692-58792-8; 978-0-692-64319-8; 978-0-9982211; 978-1-947303)* 3301 Heathland Way, Mt. Pleasant, SC 29466 USA Tel 843-813-0172
Web site: www.narthexacademyseries.com
Dist(s): **CreateSpace Independent Publishing Platform.**

Relevant Ventures, LLC, *(978-0-9760259)* 4279 Roswell Rd., Suite 102-273, Atlanta, GA 30342-4145 USA (SAN 256-4483) Tel 404-842-1930; Fax: 404-842-1021
E-mail: td3@mac.com; tom@relevantventures.com
Web site: http://www.relevantventures.com.

Reliant Energy, *(978-0-9791383)* 1000 Main St., Houston, TX 77002 USA
E-mail: jmolholt@reliant.com.

Religion Res. Institute, *(978-0-9765024)* P.O. Box 7505, Prospect Heights, IL 60070 USA Tel 773-396-0147
E-mail: info@religionresearchinstitute.org
Web site: http://www.religionresearchinstitute.org.

Reluctant Reader Bks. *Imprint of* **Cronus College**

Remarco Publishing, *(978-0-9770762)* P.O. Box 644, Ames, IA 50010 USA (SAN 256-6958) Tel 515-203-0358
Web site: http://www.remarcopublishing.com.

RemarkableMe, *(978-0-9776642)* 3905 W 10260 N, CEDAR HILLS, UT 84062 USA Tel 801-796-6486; Fax: 801-796-6486
E-mail: charless@utahweb.com
Web site: http://www.remarkableme.com.

Remedia Pubns., *(978-1-56175; 978-1-59639; 978-1-61394)* 15887 N. 76th St., Suite 120, Scottsdale, AZ 85260-1696 USA Tel 602-661-9900; Fax: 602-661-9901; Toll Free: 800-826-4740
E-mail: Becky@rempub.com
Web site: http://www.rempub.com.

Remey, Lisa, *(978-0-9855445)* PSC 2 Box 6496, APO, AE 85718 USA
E-mail: rlremey@aol.com.

Reminders Of Faith, Inc., *(978-0-9748160; 978-0-9763691)* 518 Overhead Dr., Moon Township, PA 15108 USA Fax: 412-264-7857
E-mail: kathyb@remindersoffaith.com
Dist(s): **Send The Light Distribution LLC.**

Remnant Pubns., Inc., *(978-1-883012; 978-1-933291; 978-0-9777445; 978-1-937718; 978-1-62913)* Orders Addr.: 649 E. Chicago Rd., Coldwater, MI 49036-9497 USA Tel 517-279-1304 (ext. 23); Fax: 517-279-1804; Toll Free: 800-423-1319
Web site: http://www.remnantpublications.com.

RemStar Ink, *(978-0-9988791)* 5209 Melvin Ave., Tarzana, CA 91356 USA Tel 818-977-3023
E-mail: remace@yahoo.com.

Renaissance Books *See* **New Millennium Bks.**

Renaissance Learning, Inc., *(978-0-9646404; 978-1-893751; 978-0-9708138; 978-1-931731; 978-1-931819; 978-1-932299; 978-1-59455)* 2911 Peach St., Wisconsin Rapids, WI 54494 USA Tel 715-424-3636; Toll Free: 800-338-4204; P.O. Box 8036, Wisconsin Rapids, WI 54495-8036
E-mail: answers@renlearn.com
Web site: http://www.renlearn.com.

Renaissance Printing *See* **Bookends Pr.**

Renaissance Pubns., *(978-1-929473)* Div. of Mission Renaissance, 5744 San Fernando Rd., Glendale, CA 91202-2104 USA Toll Free: 800-430-4278 Do not confuse with Renaissance Publications, Worthington, OH

Renegado Pr., The, *(978-0-9754616)* Orders Addr.: 29 Lynn Way, Indiana, PA 15701 USA Tel 724-388-3958
E-mail: mackelly@renegadopress.com
Web site: http://www.theavatarthenovel.com.

Reney Editions, Inc., *(978-0-9752688)* 35 Sands Brook Dr., New Hemstead, NY 10977 USA Tel 845-548-4029
E-mail: ethan@reney.com
Web site: http://www.reney.com.

Renovo Partners LLC, *(978-1-935310)* 8220 Jones Rd., Suite 100, Houston, TX 77065-5375 USA (SAN 857-1163) Tel 281-677-9568; Fax: 281-677-9480; Toll Free: 877-773-6686
E-mail: customers@renovopartners.com; barhorw@nationwide.com
Web site: http://www.renovopartners.com.

Repko, Marya *See* **ECity Publishing**

Repressed Publishing LLC, *(978-1-4622; 978-1-5042; 978-1-5222)* P.O. Box 1242, Provo, UT 84603 USA; 223 W. Bulldog Blvd., Number 420, Provo, UT 84604 Tel 385-204-4408
E-mail: orders@repressedpublishing; customerservice@repressedpublishing.com
Web site: http://www.repressedpublishing.com/.

†**Reprint Services Corp.**, *(978-0-7812; 978-0-932051; 978-1-4227)* P.O. Box 130, Murrieta, CA 92564-0130 USA (SAN 686-2640) Fax: 951-699-5065
E-mail: Reprintservices@gmail.com; *CIP.*

Requiem Pr., *(978-0-9758542; 978-0-9788687)* Orders Addr.: 3271 Timrod Rd., Bethune, SC 29009 USA Toll Free: 888-708-7675; P.O. Box 7, Bethune, SC 29009 Tel 843-334-6222; Toll Free: 888-708-7675
E-mail: info@requiempress.com
Web site: http://www.requiempress.com.

Research & Education Assn., *(978-0-7386; 978-0-87891)* Div. of Courier Corporation, Orders Addr.: 61 Ethel Rd., W., Piscataway, NJ 08854 USA (SAN 204-6814) Tel 732-819-8880; Fax: 732-819-8808; Toll Free: 800-822-0830
E-mail: jcording@rea.com; info@rea.com
Web site: http://www.rea.com
Dist(s): **Dover Pubns., Inc.**
INscribe Digital
MyiLibrary.

Research Evaluation & Statistics *See* **Image Cascade Publishing**

Research In Time Publications, *(978-0-9764341)* 101 Hotchkiss Grove Rd., No. 4, Branford, CT 06405 USA
E-mail: raradune@comcast.net
Dist(s): **Bookmasters Distribution.**

Research In Time Publishers *See* **Research In Time Publications**

Research Institute Pr., The, *(978-0-9752986)* 5000 Enighed Pmb 356, Saint John, VI 00830 USA Tel 340-998-9597
E-mail: asewer@triinformation.com; info@triinformation.com
Web site: www.triinformation.com.

Research Pr., *(978-0-87822)* Orders Addr.: P.O. Box 7886, Champaign, IL 61826-9177 USA (SAN 282-2490) Toll Free: 800-519-2707; Edit Addr.: 2612 N. Mattis Ave., Champaign, IL 61822 USA (SAN 282-2482) Tel 217-352-3273; Fax: 217-352-1221 Do not confuse with Research Pr., Prairie Village, KS
E-mail: products@researchpress.com; permissions@researchpress.com
Web site: http://www.researchpress.com.

Resolution Pr., *(978-0-9838886; 978-0-9982423-0-9)* 8301 SW 6th Ave., Portland, OR 97219 USA Tel 503-244-1121
E-mail: betsyshand@hotmail.com
Web site: www.survivingnaturaldisastersbook.com.

Resort Gifts Unlimited, Incorporated *See* **RGU Group, The**

ReSource Guides, Inc., *(978-0-9755370)* 13110 Vista del Mundo, San Antonio, TX 78216-2200 USA Tel 210-493-3974
E-mail: resource@resourceguides.com
Web site: http://www.resourceguides.com.

†**Resource Pubns., Inc.**, *(978-0-89390)* 160 E. Virginia St., No. 290, San Jose, CA 95112-5876 USA (SAN 209-3081) Tel 408-286-8505; Fax: 408-287-8748; Toll Free: 888-273-7782 Do not confuse with Resource Pubns. in Los Angeles, CA
E-mail: info@rpinet.com
Web site: http://www.rpinet.com
Dist(s): **Empire Publishing Service**
Feldheim Pubs.; *CIP.*

Resource Publishing, *(978-0-9706429; 978-0-615-22022-2; 978-0-692-49159-1)* 3736 Brookwood Rd., Birmingham, AL 35223 USA Tel 205-967-3446 Do not confuse company with same or similar name in Greensboro, NC, Baton Rouge, LA, San Francisco, CA
E-mail: hoytwilson1@charter.net.

Resource Pubns.(OR) *Imprint of* **Wipf & Stock Pubs.**

Resources for Children with Special Needs, Inc., *(978-0-9678365; 978-0-9755116)* 116 E. 16th St., 5th Flr., New York, NY 10003 USA
E-mail: dlittwin@resourcesnyc.org
Web site: http://www.resourcesnyc.org.

Resources for Christian Living *See* **RCL Benziger Publishing**

Resources on the Net Publishing, *(978-0-9722803)* 250 32 St., No. 307, Bellingham, WA 98225-0943 USA.

RESPONDER911, Inc., *(978-0-9746186)* 17011 Beach Blvd., Suite No. 900, Huntington Beach, CA 92647 USA Tel 714-375-6693; Fax: 714-375-6694
Web site: http://www.responder911.com.

Resurrected Pr. *Imprint of* **Intrepid Ink, LLC**

Resurrecting Faith, *(978-0-9729876)* P.O. Box 43217, Minneapolis, MN 55443-0217 USA
E-mail: admin@churchofminneapolis.org; cerise.lewis@comcast.net
Web site: http://www.resurrectingfaith.org; http://www.churchofminneapolis.org.

Resurrection Pr. *Imprint of* **Catholic Bk. Publishing Corp.**

Resurrection Resources LLC, *(978-0-9653723; 978-0-9710950; 978-0-9792338)* 8362 Tamarack Village, Ste. 119, Woodbury, MN 55125 USA
E-mail: editor@thefathersbooks.com; sales@thefathersbooks.com
Web site: http://www.thefathersbooks.com
Dist(s): **Send The Light Distribution LLC.**

Retriever Pr., *(978-0-9760718; 978-0-615-55790-8)* 3689 Ridge Line Dr., San Bernardino, CA 92407 USA.

Retro Recess, *(978-0-9785425)* 3939 Lavista Rd., Suite E, PMB 327, Tucker, GA 30084 USA
E-mail: retrorecess@comcast.net
Web site: http://www.retrorecess.net.

Return To The Word, *(978-0-9709763)* Div of LIFE Fellowship Family Bible Church, 11500 Sheridan Blvd., Westminster, CO 80020 USA Tel 303-451-5433; Fax: 303-469-1787
E-mail: truthquester@aol.com
Web site: http://www.returntotheworld.org.

Return to Titanic *Imprint of* **Stone Arch Bks.**

Retzlaff Publishing Co., *(978-0-9752525)* 1516 Piedmont Pl., Savannah, TX 76227 USA Tel 817-975-1115
E-mail: DonRetzlaff@gmail.com
Web site: http://RPC.macroenterprisesinc.com.

Revelation Products LLC, *(978-0-9792510)* 11746 Manhattan Ave., Saint Louis, MO 63131-4625 USA Tel 314-984-8180; Fax: 314-984-8194; Toll Free: 888-344-0606
E-mail: info@rpideas.com.

†**Revell**, *(978-0-8007)* Div. of Baker Publishing Group, Orders Addr.: P.O. Box 6287, Grand Rapids, MI 49516-6287 USA Toll Free Fax: 800-398-3111; Toll Free: 800-877-2665; Edit Addr.: 6030 E. Fulton, Ada, MI 49301 USA Tel 616-676-9185; Fax: 616-676-9573
E-mail: sharlow@bakerbooks.com
Web site: http://www.bakerbooks.com
Dist(s): **Baker Publishing Group**; *CIP.*

Revell, Fleming H. Company *See* **Revell**

Reverence Design Team Hair Salon, The *See* **D&C Publishing**

Reverence for Life, *(978-1-880757)* P.O. Box 222, Rectortown, VA 20140 USA Tel 540-364-1282; Fax: 540-364-7636
E-mail: sananda@erols.com
Web site: http://www.1spirit.com/sananda.

Reverie Publishing Co., *(978-1-932485)* Orders Addr.: 130 South Wineow St., Suite 3, Cumberland, MD 21502 USA Tel 301-722-2373; Fax: 301-722-2374; Toll Free: 888-721-4999; Edit Addr.: 127 West 96th St., 6-D, New York, NY 10025 USA Tel 212-662-7627
E-mail: info@reveriepublishing.com
Web site: http://www.reveriepublishing.com.

†**Review & Herald Publishing Assn.**, *(978-0-8127; 978-0-8280)* 55 W. Oak Ridge Dr., Hagerstown, MD 21740 USA (SAN 203-3798) Tel 301-393-3000
E-mail: smulkern@rhpa.org
Web site: http://www.reviewandherald.com/
Dist(s): **Spring Arbor Distributors, Inc.**; *CIP.*

Revival Waves of Glory, *(978-0-615-94231-5; 978-0-615-94271-1; 978-0-615-94272-8; 978-0-615-94273-5; 978-0-615-94286-5; 978-0-615-94292-6; 978-0-615-94831-7; 978-0-615-95143-0; 978-0-615-95145-4; 978-0-615-96815-5; 978-0-615-96817-9; 978-0-692-20785-7; 978-0-692-21429-9; 978-0-692-21499-2; 978-0-692-21554-8; 978-0-692-21663-7; 978-0-692-22184-6; 978-0-692-22285-0; 978-0-692-22331-4; 978-0-692-22921-7; 978-0-692-23397-9; 978-0-692-24064-9; 978-0-692-26625-0; 978-0-692-27285-5; 978-0-692-27996-0; 978-0-692-32262-8;) P.O. Box 596, Litchfield, IL 62056 USA Tel 217-851-0361*
E-mail: bill.vincent@yahoo.com
Web site: http://www.revivalwavesofgloryministries.com
Dist(s): **BookBaby**
Bookmasters Distribution
CreateSpace Independent Publishing Platform
Send The Light Distribution LLC.

Revivalist Pr., The, *(978-0-9749186; 978-0-9891979)* Div. of God's Bible School & College, 1810 Young St., Cincinnati, OH 45202 USA
E-mail: president@gbs.edu
Web site: http://www.gbs.edu.

Revolutionary Strategies, *(978-0-9769354; 978-0-9825493; 978-0-9883527; 978-0-9981269)* P.O. Box 900, Dripping Springs, TX 78620 USA Tel 512-858-0974
Web site: http://www.rickgreen.com.

Rexroad International, *(978-0-9817742; 978-1-946650)* Div. of Rexroad International, 616 Upham Pl. NW, Vienna, VA 22180 USA; *Imprints:* Rexroad Kids (MYID_G_REXROAD)
E-mail: fred@rexroad.us; fred_rexroad@yahoo.com; fred.rexroad@yahoo.com
Web site: http://Rexroad.International
Dist(s): **CreateSpace Independent Publishing Platform**
Lightning Source, Inc.

Rexroad Kids *Imprint of* **Rexroad International**

Reyes, Jose, *(978-0-9794731)* 422 Sabal Palm Ln., Pearland, TX 77584-7770 USA
E-mail: thelordsfield@sbcglobal.net; riff28@sbcglobal.net.

Reynolds & Hearn (GBR) *(978-1-903111; 978-1-905287)*
Dist. by **Trafalgar.**

Reynolds, Morgan Inc., *(978-1-883846; 978-1-931798; 978-1-59935)* 620 S. Elm St., Suite 223, Greensboro, NC 27406 USA (SAN 858-4680) Tel 336-275-1311; Fax: 336-275-1152; Toll Free Fax: 800-535-5725; Toll Free: 800-535-1504; *Imprints:* First Biographies (First Biographies)
E-mail: sales@morganreynolds.com; editorial@morganreynolds.com
Web site: http://www.morganreynolds.com
Dist(s): **Follett School Solutions.**

RG Mincey Group, LLC, The, *(978-0-9882039; 978-1-63498-451-5)* P.O. Box 1245, Bluffton, SC 29910 USA Tel 678-472-4740
E-mail: rgmincey@gmail.com.

RGC Pr., LLC, *(978-0-9728876; 978-0-9779886)* P.O. Box 2921, Indianapolis, IN 46206-2921 USA (SAN 255-4747) Tel 317-926-0541
E-mail: info@RGCPress.com
Web site: http://www.RGCPress.com.

RGU Group, The, *(978-1-891795)* 560 W. Southern Ave., Tempe, AZ 85282 USA (SAN 299-9366) Tel 480-736-9862; Fax: 480-736-9863; Toll Free: 800-266-5265
E-mail: mpagnozzi@theRGUgroup.com
Web site: http://www.thergugroup.com
Dist(s): **Send The Light Distribution LLC.**

RGZ Consulting, *(978-0-615-80196-4)* P.O. Box 153, South Woodstock, VT 05071 USA Tel 802-457-5861
E-mail: zamenhof@alum.mit.edu.

Rhapsody Branding, Inc., (*978-0-9667232*) Orders Addr.: 14027 N. Miami Ave., Miami, FL 33168 USA Tel 305-681-0489 E-mail: pumba66@yahoo.com; Don@notw8.com; Don@nightofthewitches.com Web site: http://www.nightofthewitches.com *Dist(s)*: **Bk. Warehouse Distributors, The Southern Bk. Service.**

RH/Disney *Imprint of* **Random Hse. Children's Bks.**

Rhea Leto Media Group, (*978-0-9904727; 978-1-947185*) 6854 Orcutt Ave., Long Beach, CA 90805 USA Tel 424-757-8134 E-mail: Rhea@rhealeto.com; phabb5live@gmail.com Web site: www.RheaLeto.Com.

Rhemalda Publishing, (*978-0-615-32885-0; 978-0-9827437; 978-1-936850*) P.O. Box 1790, Moses Lake, WA 98837 USA E-mail: emmaline@rhemalda.com Web site: http://www.rhemalda.com; http://shop.rhemalda.com/ *Dist(s)*: **MyiLibrary Smashwords.**

Rhino Entertainment Co, A Warner Music Group Co., (*978-0-7379; 978-0-930589; 978-1-56826; 978-0-9797278*) 3400 W. Olive Ave., Burbank, CA 91505 USA (SAN 677-5454) Tel 818-238-6110; Fax: 818-562-9239 E-mail: gladys.sanchez@wmg.com; tracie.bowers@wmg.com Web site: http://www.rhino.com.

Rhizoo Publishing, (*978-0-9762723*) P.O. Box 1249, Stephenville, TX 76401 USA.

Rhoades & Assocs., (*978-1-930006; 978-0-9841378*) 8070 19th St., No. 326, Alta Loma, CA 91701 USA (SAN 858-5369) Tel 909-297-3436; Fax: 909-657-5446; Toll Free: 888-699-0685; *Imprints*: Reading Company, The (Reading Co) E-mail: jacquie@readingcompany.us Web site: http://www.readingcompany.us.

Rhode Island State Council, International Reading Assn., (*978-0-9664455*) 4 Gardner Ave., North Providence, RI 02911 USA.

Rhode, Steve Inc., (*978-0-9742781; 978-1-59840*) 310 Watkins Pond Blvd., Rockville, MD 20850 USA E-mail: steve@steverhode.com Web site: http://www.steverhode.com.

Rhodes Educational Pubns., (*978-0-9743214*) P.O. Box 501155, Dallas, TX 75250 USA Web site: http://www.nativeamericanrhymes.com.

Rhodes, Edwin Books LLC *See* **Rhodes, EL. Bks., LLC**

Rhodes, EL. Bks., LLC, (*978-0-615-24550-8; 978-0-578-01988-8; 978-0-578-03719-6; 978-0-692-82552-5*) 7710 Tinkers Creek Dr., Clinton, MD 20735 USA.

RHS Consulting, (*978-0-9990937*) 104 Pine Lake Dr., Whispering Pines, NC 28327 USA Tel 910-633-1169 E-mail: rhsconsulting@outlook.com.

Rhymeglow LLC, (*978-0-9786912; 978-0-578-15239-4*) Orders Addr.: 14625 Baltimore Ave., #869, Laurel, MD 20707 USA; Edit Addr.: P.O. Box 869, Laurel, MD 20707 USA.

Rialp, Ediciones, S.A. (ESP) (*978-84-320; 978-84-321*) *Dist. by* **Lectorum Pubns.**

Ribbing, John, (*978-0-9987219*) 4866 Charles, Shelby Township, MI 48316 USA Tel 248-310-7551 E-mail: jribbing@yahoo.com.

Ric Design LLC, (*978-0-9758704; 978-0-9859684*) 2245 Stony Hill Rd., Boulder, CO 80305 USA Toll Free: 800-432-7346 (phone/fax) E-mail: ricdilz13@gmail.com *Dist(s)*: **Bookazine Co., Inc.**

R.I.C. Publications Asia Co, Inc. (JPN) (*978-4-902216*) *Dist. by* **CEG.**

R.I.C. Pubns. (AUS) (*978-1-86311; 978-1-74126; 978-1-921750; 978-1-922116; 978-1-925201; 978-1-925431; 978-1-925660; 978-1-925686; 978-1-925698*) *Dist. by* **SCB Distributo.**

Rich List *See* **Rich Register, The**

Rich Pr., (*978-1-933914*) 4330 N. Civic Center Plaza, #100, Scottsdale, AZ 85251 USA (SAN 850-5209) E-mail: kathy@richdad.com *Dist(s)*: **Ingram Publisher Services Two Rivers Distribution.**

Rich Publishing, (*978-0-9726670*) 4175 W. 5345 S., Salt Lake City, UT 84118 USA Tel 801-965-6200; Fax: 801-965-6199; Toll Free: 800-224-3221 Do not confuse with companies with the same or similar name in Houston, TX, Temecula, CA E-mail: milton@zeestlouis.com Web site: http://www.miltonrich.com.

Rich Register, The, (*978-0-9633933; 978-0-9831368*) P.O. Box 29955, Austin, TX 78755 USA Tel 512-477-8871 E-mail: jda@richregister.com Web site: www.richregister.com.

Richardson, Lilith, (*978-0-578-00920-9; 978-0-578-04792-8; 978-0-578-07481-8*) 360 Dusty Rd., St. Augustine, FL 32095 USA *Dist(s)*: **Lulu Pr., Inc.**

Richardson Production, Inc., (*978-0-9761222*) Orders Addr.: P.O. Box 543, Marietta, OH 45750 USA Tel 740-373-0861; Edit Addr.: 177 Acme St., Marietta, OH 45750 USA Web site: http://www.richardsonproductions.tv.

Richardson Publishing, Inc., (*978-0-9637991; 978-1-935683*) Orders Addr.: P.O. Box 162115, Altamonte Springs, FL 32716-2115 USA Tel 407-862-5037 E-mail: coachrik@aol.com Web site: http://www.gymnastictrainingtips.com; http://www.AmericanDreamPublishing.com.

Richer Life, LLC, (*978-0-9744617; 978-0-9855699; 978-0-9892884; 978-0-9899001; 978-0-9903291; 978-0-9863544; 978-0-9970831; 978-0-9988773*) 5725 S. 21st Pl., Phoenix, AZ 85040 USA Tel 602-708-4268; Fax: 602-772-4910 E-mail: earlcobb@earthlink.net; earlcobb1@gmail.com; earl@richerlifellc.com; charlotte@richerlifellc.com; cobbcare@yahoo.com Web site: http://www.richerlifellc.com.

Richer Life, LLC (dba RICHER Publications) *See* **Richer Life, LLC**

Richer Resources Pubns., (*978-0-9776269; 978-0-9797571; 978-0-9818162; 978-1-935238; 978-1-63464*) 1926 N. Woodrow St., Arlington, VA 22207-2410 USA (SAN 853-2931) Tel 800-856-3060; Fax: 703-276-0193 E-mail: info@richerresourcespublications.com; publisher@richerresourcespublications.com Web site: http://www.richerresourcespublications.com.

Riches Publishing Co., (*978-0-9728219*) P.O. Box 02232, Detroit, MI 48202 USA E-mail: klrich@sbcglobal.net Web site: http://www.klrich.com.

Richeson, John W., (*978-0-9675315*) P.O. Box 710371, San Diego, CA 92171 USA E-mail: john@VBAtech.com Web site: http://vbatech.com.

Richlee Publishing, (*978-0-9796265*) 2898 Morning Creek Rd., Chula Vista, CA 91914-4311 USA E-mail: jmacgregor@cadencemarketinggroup.com.

Richlyn Publishing, (*978-0-9722264*) 12045 W Brandt Pl, Littleton, CO 80127-4572 USA Tel 303-979-8609 E-mail: richlyn2@msn.com Web site: http://www.richlynpublishing.com.

Richmond *Imprint of* **Santillana USA Publishing Co., Inc.**

Richmondmom.com Publishing *Imprint of* **Palari Publishing LLP**

Rickshaw Press *See* **Ragged Sky Pr.**

Riddering, Marggie, (*978-0-9765977*) P.O. Box 770, Hormigueros, PR 00660 USA Fax: 787-833-2260.

Riddle Creek Publishing, (*978-0-9725894; 978-0-9835009*) 232 Cty. Rd. 19, Haleyville, AL 35565-7416 USA E-mail: riddlecreek@centurytel.net Web site: http://www.riddlecreekpublishing.com.

Rider Franklin Reynolds Publishing *See* **Belisarian Bks.**

Riders Elite Academy, Inc., (*978-0-9741628*) 23120 Garrison Rd., Corcoran, MN 55340-9103 USA Tel 763-498-6565 (phone/fax) E-mail: books@riderselite.com Web site: http://www.riderselite.com.

Ridge Rock Pr., (*978-0-9670177*) Div. of Ridge Rock, Inc., Orders Addr.: P.O. Box 255, Healy, AK 99743 USA (SAN 253-6595) Tel 907-322-8185 (cell); 907-683-7737 (phone/fax); Edit Addr.: Mile 261 Parks Hwy., Box 255, Healy, AK 99743 USA E-mail: ridgerock@gtemail.net *Dist(s)*: **Todd Communications.**

Ridge Row Press *See* **Univ. of Scranton Pr.**

Ridgewood Group, The, (*978-0-9716907*) P.O. Box 8011, Manchester, CT 06040 USA (SAN 254-3419) Tel 860-432-4537 (phone/fax); *Imprints*: Ridgewood Publishing (Ridgewd Pub) E-mail: info@theridgewoodgroup.com Web site: http://www.hermanthecrab.com.

Ridgewood Pr., (*978-0-9650434*) 2160 Aztec Dr., dyersburg, TN 38024 USA Do not confuse with Ridgewood Pr., Jefferson City, MO E-mail: bartonsn@mac.com.

Ridgewood Publishing *Imprint of* **Ridgewood Group, The**

†Rienner, Lynne Pubs., (*978-0-89410; 978-0-931477; 978-0-931816; 978-1-55587; 978-1-56549; 978-1-58826; 978-1-62637*) 1800 30th St., Suite 314, Boulder, CO 80301-1026 USA (SAN 683-1869) Tel 303-444-6684; Fax: 303-444-0824 E-mail: cservice@rienner.com; sglover@rienner.com; questions@rienner.com Web site: http://www.rienner.com; *CIP.*

Rigby Education, (*978-0-7635; 978-0-7578; 978-1-4189*) Div. of Houghton Mifflin Harcourt Supplemental Pubs., Orders Addr.: 6277 Sea Harbor Dr., 5th Flr., Orlando, FL 32887 USA Toll Free Fax: 877-578-2638; Toll Free: 888-363-4266; Edit Addr.: 10801 N. Mopac Expressway, Bldg. 3, Austin, TX 78759 USA Toll Free Fax: 800-699-9459; Toll Free: 800-531-5015 Web site: http://www.harcourtachieve.com *Dist(s)*: **Follett School Solutions Houghton Mifflin Harcourt Supplemental Pubs.**

Riggott, Dean Photography, (*978-0-9659875*) 831 10 1/2 St., SW, Rochester, MN 55902 USA Tel 507-285-5076; Fax: 253-540-6093 Web site: http://www.riggottphoto.com *Dist(s)*: **Partners Bk. Distributing, Inc.**

Riggs, Theresia, (*978-0-9746132*) 8910 Dogwood Dr., Tomball, TX 77375 USA Tel 281-351-2329 (phone/fax) E-mail: Ohringen@aol.com Web site: http://www.CosmicSisters.com.

Right On Programs, Inc., (*978-0-933426*) 522 E. Broadway, Suite 101, Glendale, CA 91205 USA (SAN 212-5099) Tel 818-240-1683; Fax: 818-240-2858.

Right Stuff Kids Bks., (*978-0-9704597; 978-1-932317*) 5600 Claire Rose Ln., Atlanta, GA 30327 USA E-mail: satiller@bellsouth.net Web site: http://www.michaelsmind.com.

Right Track Reading LLC, (*978-0-9763290*) P.O. Box 1952, Livingston, MT 59047 USA E-mail: mmgagen@earthlink.net.

Right-Away, Inc., (*978-0-9709095*) P.O. Box 741993, Riverdale, GA 30274 USA Tel 404-798-7508 E-mail: jakiharris2004@yahoo.com; rightaway1@hotmail.com.

Righteous Bks., (*978-0-9883634*) 2801 W. 83rd St., Chicago, IL 60652 USA Tel 773-744-8162 E-mail: righteousrayray@gmail.com.

Righter Publishing Co., Inc., (*978-0-9706823; 978-0-9747735; 978-0-9766032; 978-0-9778948; 978-0-9796209; 978-1-934936; 978-1-938527*) Orders Addr.: 410 River Oaks Pkwy., Timberlake, NC 27583 USA Fax: 336-597-8881 E-mail: righterpub@esinc.net Web site: http://www.righterbooks.com *Dist(s)*: **CreateSpace Independent Publishing Platform.**

Riker, Dale, (*978-0-9771621*) 6937 W. Country Club Dr. N, Unit 152, Sarasota, FL 34243-3507 USA.

Riley Pr., (*978-0-9728958*) P.O. Box 202, Eagle, MI 48822 USA Tel 517-626-7027 E-mail: rileypress@yahoo.com Web site: http://rileypress.hypermart.net.

Rilly Silly Bk. Co., The, (*978-0-9747054*) 11130 W. Heatherbrae Dr., Phoenix, AZ 85037 USA Tel 623-877-6020 Web site: http://www.rillysilly.com.

Rincon Publishing Co., (*978-0-9660858*) Orders Addr.: 1913 Skyline Dr., Orem, UT 84097 USA Tel 801-377-7657; Fax: 801-356-2733 E-mail: RinconPub@Utahtrails.com Web site: http://www.utahtrails.com *Dist(s)*: **Partners/West Book Distributors.**

Rind, Sherry, (*978-0-9674729*) Orders Addr.: 959 Evonshire Ln., Great Falls, VA 22066 USA; Edit Addr.: 8419 NE 144th St., Bothell, WA 98011-5055 USA E-mail: AIREBIRD@hotmail.com; KCBROOM@erols.com Web site: http://www.airedaleterriers.org.

Rindle Books Inc *See* **Rindle Bks. Inc.**

Rindle Bks. Inc., (*978-1-942214*) 1200 Westlake Ave. N, Seattle, WA 98109 USA Tel 206-430-6021 E-mail: mark@rindlebooks.com Web site: www.rindlebooks.com *Dist(s)*: **Bookmasters Distribution.**

Rinehart, Roberts Pubs., (*978-0-911797; 978-0-943173; 978-1-57098; 978-1-57140; 978-1-879373; 978-1-58979*) Div. of Rowman & Littlefield Pubs., Inc., Orders Addr.: 15200 NBN Way, Blue Ridge Summit, PA 17214 USA Tel 717-794-3800 (Customer Service &/or orders); Fax: 717-794-3803 (Customer Service &/or orders only); 717-794-3857 (Sales & MIS); 717-794-3856 (Royalties, Inventory Mgmt., & Dist.); Toll Free Fax: 800-338-4550 (Customer Service &/or orders); Toll Free: 800-462-6420 (Customer Service &/or orders); Edit Addr.: 4501 Forbes Blvd., Suite 200, Lanham, MD 20706 USA Tel 301-459-3366; Toll Free: 800-462-6420 E-mail: nrothschild@rowman.com Web site: http://www.robertsrinehart.com *Dist(s)*: **Ebsco Publishing Follett School Solutions National Bk. Network Rowman & Littlefield Publishers, Inc. ebrary, Inc.**

Rio Grande Bks. *Imprint of* **LPD Pr.**

Rio Nuevo Pubs., (*978-0-918080; 978-1-887896; 978-0-9700750; 978-1-933855; 978-1-940322*) Orders Addr.: P.O. Box 5250, Tucson, AZ 85703-0250 USA (SAN 209-3251) Tel 520-623-9558; Fax: 520-624-5888; Toll Free Fax: 800-715-5888; Toll Free: 800-969-9558; Edit Addr.: 451 N. Bonita Ave., Tucson, AZ 85745 USA Tel 602-623-9558; *Imprints*: Rio Nuevo Publishers (Rio Nuevo) E-mail: info@rionuevo.com; info@treasurechestbooks.com; suzang@rionuevo.com Web site: http://www.treasurechestbooks.com; http://www.rionuevo.com/ *Dist(s)*: **Treasure Chest Bks.**

Rio Nuevo Pubs. *Imprint of* **Rio Nuevo Pubs.**

Rio Wildflower Pubns., (*978-0-9786168*) P.O. Box 246, Almont, CO 81210 USA Tel 970-642-0272 E-mail: wildflowercd@peoplepc.com.

Rip Squeak, Inc., (*978-0-9672422; 978-0-9747825*) Orders Addr.: c/o Raven Tree Press, 1400 Miller Pkwy., McHenry, IL 60050 USA Tel 815-363-3582; Fax: 815-363-2948; Edit Addr.: 840 Capitolio Way, Suite B, San Luis Obispo, CA 93401-7130 USA Tel 805-594-0184; Fax: 805-543-5782; Toll Free: 800-251-0654; *Imprints*: Rip Squeak Press (Rip Squeak Pr) E-mail: Beda@RipSqueak.com; dawnj@delta-systems.com Web site: http://www.RipSqueak.com; http://www.raventreepress.com *Dist(s)*: **Delta Systems Company, Inc.**

Rip Squeak Pr. *Imprint of* **Rip Squeak, Inc.**

Ripley Entertainment, Inc., (*978-1-893951; 978-1-60991*) Div. of The Jim Pattison Group, 7576 Kingspointe Pkwy., Suite. 188, Orlando, FL 32819-6510 USA (SAN 299-9498) E-mail: meyer@ripleys.com; dula@ripleys.com Web site: http://www.ripleys.com *Dist(s)*: **Mint Pubs. Group Simon & Schuster, Inc.**

Riptide Pr., Inc., (*978-0-9723456*) 233 Walnut Creek Dr., Clayton, NC 27520 USA Tel 919-359-2852; Fax: 919-882-9924 Do not confuse with companies with the same or similar name in New York, NY, Fredericksburg, VA E-mail: info@riptidebooks.com; info@riptidepress.com Web site: http://www.riptidebooks.com; http://www.riptidepress.com.

Risa Publications, (*978-0-9771404*) 8424-A Santa Monica Blvd., Suite 175, West Hollywood, CA 90069 USA Web site: http://www.lisahaisha.com.

Risen Heart Pr., (*978-0-9764497*) 554 Bruns Dr., Rossford, OH 43460 USA Tel 419-666-6269 E-mail: rjbaden@wcnet.org.

Rising Bks., (*978-0-9644456*) P.O. Box 1408, Conyers, GA 30012 USA (SAN 298-5438) Tel 404-378-7464; Fax: 770-761-9865 E-mail: chadfoster@mindspring.com Web site: www.chadfoster.com.

Rising Moon Bks. for Young Readers *Imprint of* **Northland Publishing**

Rising Phoenix Pr., (*978-0-615-68352-2; 978-0-615-68666-0; 978-0-615-68667-7; 978-0-615-69091-9; 978-0-615-70515-6; 978-0-615-74990-7; 978-0-9888568*) 100 Goldmine Ct., Aledo, TX 68008 USA Tel 817-757-7143 Web site: www.progressiverisingphoenix.com *Dist(s)*: **CreateSpace Independent Publishing Platform.**

Rising Son International, Ltd., (*978-0-9915370; 978-0-9961358*) 218 Beach Rd., Washington, MA 01223 USA Tel 413-623-6112 E-mail: annieguthrie@risingsonrecords.com Web site: www.risingsonrecords.com.

Rising Star Publishers *See* **WeWrite LLC**

Rising Star Studios, LLC., (*978-1-936086; 978-1-936770*) 5251 W. 73rd St. Suite C, Edina, MN 55439 USA Tel 952-831-8532; Fax: 952-831-5809 E-mail: mark@risingstarstudios.com; info@risingstarstudios.com; sales@risingstarstudios.com Web site: http://www.risingstarstudios.com *Dist(s)*: **Follett School Solutions.**

Rising Sun Publishing, Inc., (*978-1-880463*) P.O. Box 70906, Marietta, GA 30007-0906 USA Tel 770-518-0369; Fax: 770-587-0862; Toll Free: 800-524-2813 Do not confuse with Rising Sun Pubng in Fairfield, OH E-mail: info@rspublishing.com; sholland@rspublishing.com Web site: http://www.rspublishing.com.

Rising Tide Pr., (*978-0-913844*) Div. of American-Canadian Pubs., Inc., P.O. Box 6136, Santa Fe, NM 87502-4595 USA (SAN 298-217X) Do not confuse with Rising Tide Pubs., Tucson, AZ.

Rissylyn, (*978-0-9894933*) 2 12th St. Apt. 1012, Hoboken, NJ 07030 USA Tel 917-859-4751 E-mail: info@dreambigacademy.com.

Ritchie, John Ltd. (GBR) (*978-0-946351; 978-1-904064; 978-1-907731; 978-1-909803; 978-1-910513*) *Dist. by* **Bookmasters.**

Ritchie Unlimited Pubns., (*978-0-939656*) 1427 Anderson Rd. Suite B, Springfield, OR 97477 USA (SAN 216-6461) Tel 541-741-0794 (phone/fax) E-mail: ralph-ritchie@comcast.net Web site: http://www.ritchieunlimitedpublications.com.

Rite Lite Limited, (*978-0-9772560*) 333 Stanley Ave., Brooklyn, NY 11207 USA Tel 718-498-1700; Fax: 718-498-1251; Toll Free: 800-942-0707 E-mail: mail@riteliteltd.com Web site: http://www.riteliteltd.com.

Rite Quest, (*978-0-9801484*) 1308 Turnberry Ct., Chesapeake, VA 23320-9445 USA.

Ritz, Lee Pubns., (*978-1-940840*) 2934 Ames St., Wheat Ridge, CO 80214 USA Tel 303-330-2477 E-mail: leeritz@leeritzpublications.com Web site: www.leeritzpublications.com.

Rivendell Bk. Factory, (*978-0-944353*) 217 Country Club Park Crestline Village, PMB321, Mountain Brook, AL 35213 USA Tel (205) 871-5915; Fax: (205) 871-5945 *Dist(s)*: **Cardinal Pubs. Group.**

River Canyon Pr., (*978-0-9815914; 978-0-9827531*) Orders Addr.: P.O. Box 191, Oakland, OR 97462 USA (SAN 855-9651) Tel 541-530-2061 Web site: http://www.rivercanyonpress.com *Dist(s)*: **CreateSpace Independent Publishing Platform River Canyon Distributing.**

River City Kids *Imprint of* **River City Publishing**

River City Pr., (*978-0-9706962; 978-0-9764232; 978-0-9776713*) 4301 Emerson Ave. N., Minneapolis, MN 55412 USA Tel 612-521-9633 (phone/fax); Toll Free: 888-234-3559 Do not confuse with River City Pr. in New Orleans, LA E-mail: bwolf@rivercitypress.net Web site: http://www.rivercitypress.net.

River City Publishing, (*978-0-913515; 978-0-9622815; 978-1-57966; 978-1-880216; 978-1-881320*) 1719 Mulberry St., Montgomery, AL 36106 USA (SAN 631-4910) Tel 334-265-6753; Fax: 334-265-8880; Toll Free: 877-408-7078; *Imprints*: River City Kids (River City Kids) Do not confuse with companies with the same or similar names in Richland, WA, South Bend, IN E-mail: sales@rivercitypublishing.com Web site: http://www.rivercitypublishing.com.

River Grove Bks., (*978-1-938416; 978-1-63299*) 4005 B Banister Ln. Three Pk. Pl., Austin, TX 78704 USA Tel 512-891-6100 E-mail: jgoff@greenleafbookgroup.com.

River Lake Pr., (*978-0-615-36951-8*) 1799 Ashland Ave., Saint Paul, MN 55104 USA Tel 651-646-2915 E-mail: bethanymasters@riverlakepress.com Web site: http://www.bethanymasters.com.

River of Life Publishing, (*978-0-9746345*) 3700 Chestnut Lake Ct., Jonesboro, GA 30236-5502 USA Do not confuse with River of Life Publishing in Kremmling, CO.

River Pointe Pubns., (*978-0-9758805; 978-0-9817258; 978-0-9848103*) 612 River Pointe Ct., Milan, MI 48160 USA Tel 734-439-8031 E-mail: riverptpub@sbcglobal.net.

River Pr., (*978-0-9725796; 978-0-9849909*) Div. of OCRS, Inc., Orders Addr.: 52 Tuscan Way Ste 202 # 404, Saint Augustine, FL 32092 USA (SAN 850-5098) Tel 904-563-6277; Fax: 904-940-5178; Edit Addr.: P.O. Box 551627, Jacksonville, FL 32255 USA E-mail: wrcsacriver@comcast.net Web site: http://randycribbsauthor.com.

River Road Pubns., Inc., (*978-0-938682*) 1433 Fulton St., Grand Haven, MI 49417-1572 USA (SAN 253-8172) Toll Free: 800-373-8762 E-mail: Pandex@prodigy.net Web site: http://www.riverroadpublications.com.

River Sanctuary Publishing, (*978-0-9841140; 978-1-935914*) P.O. Box 1561, Felton, CA 95018 USA (SAN 858-4532) Tel 831-335-7283 Web site: http://www.riversanctuarypublishing.com.

River Styx Publishing Co., *(978-0-9788997; 978-1-61704)* 1400 Ash St., Terre Haute, IN 47804 USA; P.O. Box 3246, Terre Haute, IN 47803
E-mail: pessy74@aol.com
Web site: http://fixitprogram.zoomshare.com.

Rivera Engineering, *(978-0-9801695)* 227 Brahan Blvd., San Antonio, TX 78215 USA (SAN 855-3874) Tel 210-771-2662; Fax: 210-226-9027
E-mail: alanegarivera@yahoo.com
Web site: http://www.rivera-engineering.com.

Riverbank Publishing, *(978-0-9753320)* 1917 Winterport Cluster, Reston, VA 20191 USA
Web site: http://www.riverbankpublishing.com.

Riverbend Publishing, *(978-1-931832; 978-1-60639)* Orders Addr.: P.O. Box 5833, Helena, MT 59604 USA Tel 406-449-0200; Fax: 406-449-0330; Toll Free: 866-787-2363; Edit Addr.: 1660 B St., Helena, MT 59601 USA (SAN 254-5020) Do not confuse with companies with the same or similar names in Elizabeth, CO, Marion, KY, Knoxville, TN
Web site: http://www.riverbendpublishing.com
Dist(s): **Bks. West**
High Peak Bks.
Partners Bk. Distributing, Inc.
Smashwords
TNT Media Group, Inc.
Wolverine Distributing, Inc.

Rivercity Pr. *Imprint of* **Amereon Ltd.**

RiverCreek Bks., Inc., *(978-0-9745171)* Orders Addr.: P.O. Box 1146, Buies Creek, NC 27506 USA Tel 910-893-8853.

Riverdale Bks. *Imprint of* **Riverdale Electronic Bks.**

Riverdale Electronic Books *See* **Riverdale Electronic Bks.**

Riverdale Electronic Bks., *(978-0-9712207; 978-1-932606)* 4420 Bonneville Dr., Cumming, GA 30041 USA Tel 770-891-2710; *Imprints*: Riverdale Books (RiverdBks)
E-mail: jtm@riverdalebooks.com
Web site: http://www.riverdaleebooks.com.

Riverdeep, Incorporated *See* **Houghton Mifflin Harcourt Learning Technology**

RiverEarth, *(978-0-9787722)* Orders Addr.: P.O. Box 245, Southern Pines, NC 28388 USA (SAN 851-5824) Tel 910-795-2285; Edit Addr.: P.O. Box 245, Southern Pines, NC 28388 USA
E-mail: bernie@riverearth.com
Web site: http://riverearth.com.

Riverhead Bks. (Hardcover) *Imprint of* **Penguin Publishing Group**

RiverPlace Development Corp., *(978-0-9785538)* Orders Addr.: P.O. Box 6218, Reading, PA 19610-0218 USA
E-mail: info@RiverPlacePA.com
Web site: http://www.RiverPlacePA.com.

RIVERRUN BOOKSTORE INC, *(978-0-9856073; 978-0-9885370; 978-1-939739; 978-1-944393)* 142 Fleet St, Portsmouth, NH 3801 USA Tel 603-431-2100
E-mail: riverrunbookstore@gmail.com.

Rivers, Swannee, *(978-0-9749216; 978-0-578-04160-5)* 1629 Index Ave. Se, Suite No. 400, Renton, WA 98058 USA Fax: 425-277-2950
E-mail: swanneerivers@mindspring.com
Web site: http://www.swanneerivers.com.

Riverside Art Museum, *(978-0-9802207; 978-0-692-41917-5)* 3425 Mission Inn Ave., Riverside, CA 92501-3304 USA
E-mail: mcarlson@riversideartmuseum.org
Dist(s): **D.A.P./Distributed Art Pubs.**

Riverstone Group Publishing, *(978-0-9706117; 978-0-9763092; 978-0-9906166)* 331 Laiken Dr., Jasper, GA 30143 USA; 331 Laiken Dr., Jasper, GA 30143 Tel 404-219-1008
E-mail: ep@rsgroup.us
Web site: http://www.riverstonegroup.com.

RiverStream Publishing, *(978-0-9834972; 978-1-62243)* 123 S. Broad St., Mankato, MN 56001 USA Tel 414-378-2480
E-mail: jstrick@hickorytech.net.

Rivertide Publishing, *(978-0-9826252)* 890 Kensington Ave., Astoria, OR 97103 USA Tel 503-325-8818
E-mail: karenleedom@q.com.

Rivertree Productions, Inc., *(978-1-882412)* P.O. Box 410, Bradford, NH 03221 USA Tel 603-938-5120; Fax: 603-938-5616; Toll Free: 800-554-1333; *Imprints*: Odds Bodkin Storytelling Library, The (Odds Bodkin)
E-mail: rivertree@conknet.com
Web site: http://www.oddsbodkin.com
Dist(s): **Penton Overseas, Inc.**

Riverview Foundation, *(978-0-9771639)* Orders Addr.: P.O. Box 310, Topsham, ME 04086 USA (SAN 256-8357) Tel 207-729-7399; Fax: 207-797-5676; Edit Addr.: 610 Augusta Rd., Tomsham, ME 04086 USA
E-mail: office@riverviewfoundation.com
Web site: http://www.riverviewfoundation.com.

Riverwood Bks. *Imprint of* **White Cloud Pr.**

Rivet Bks. *Imprint of* **Feral Pr., Inc.**

RIXKIN, *(978-0-9842069)* P.O. Box 11922, Atlanta, GA 30355 USA Tel 888-674-1679; Fax: 888-674-2577
E-mail: info@rixkin.com; pr@rixkin.com; orders@rixkin.com
Web site: http://www.rixkin.com
Dist(s): **Quality Bks., Inc.**

†Rizzoli International Pubns., Inc., *(978-0-8478; 978-0-88363; 978-0-941807; 978-1-932183; 978-1-59962)* Subs. of RCS Rizzoli Editore Corp., 300 Park Ave., S., 3rd Flr., New York, NY 10010 USA (SAN 111-9192) Tel 212-387-3400; Fax: 212-387-3535; *Imprints*: White Star (White Star NY); Rizzoli Universe Promotional Books (RUPB); Skira (Skira); Welcome Books (Welcome)
Web site: http://www.rizzoliusa.com/
Dist(s): **Casemate Academic**
Ingram Publisher Services
MyiLibrary
Penguin Random Hse. LLC
Random Hse., Inc.; *CIP.*

Rizzoli Universe Promotional Bks. *Imprint of* **Rizzoli International Pubns., Inc.**

R.J. Bob Chavez Images, *(978-0-9778110)* 5537 Lewis Ct. Unit 201, Arvada, CO 80002 USA Tel 303-423-6982
E-mail: rjbcimages@aol.com.

RJ Pubns., *(978-0-9769277; 978-0-9786373; 978-0-9817773; 978-0-9819998; 978-1-939284)* 290 Dune St., Far Rockaway, NY 11691-2714 USA (SAN 256-5919); P.O. Box 300771, Jamaica, NY 11430
Web site: http://www.rjpublications.com.

RJI Publishing, *(978-1-885184)* Orders Addr.: 2800 N. Roadrunner Pkwy. # 701, Las Cruces, NM 88011 USA Tel 575-521-1336
E-mail: rjipublishing@aol.com
Web site: http://www.rjipublishing.com.

RK Enterprises, Inc., *(978-0-9743775)* 22581 NE State Route 3., Belfair, WA 98528-9303 USA
E-mail: rkilsby@wavecable.com
Web site: http://www.gooshu.com.

RMA Publicity LLC dba Sigma's Bookshelf, *(978-0-9987157)* 13540 Knollway Dr. N, MINNETONKA, MN 55305 USA Tel 952-240-2513
E-mail: jeffwcrawford5+LVP0003359@gmail.com; jeffwcrawford5+LVP0003359@gmail.com.

Roach, Patricia, *(978-0-9817680)* 17 Hillside Ave., Winsted, CT 06098 USA.

Road Tunes Media, *(978-0-9721725)* Orders Addr.: 534 Hidden Way, Homer, AK 99603 USA (SAN 852-5188)
E-mail: roadtunes@gci.net
Web site: http://www.berniejones.com
Dist(s): **Follett School Solutions.**

Road West Publishing Co., *(978-0-9641402)* 1908 Dexter Ave., Cincinnati, OH 45206 USA Tel 513-861-6151 (phone/fax).

Roadracing World Publishing, Inc., *(978-0-9749615)* P.O. Box 1428, Lake Elsinore, CA 92531 USA Tel 951-245-6411 Toll Free: 800-464-8336
E-mail: custsvc@roadracingworld.com
Web site: http://www.roadracingworld.com.

Roadrunner Pr., *(978-0-9636346)* Orders Addr.: 2815 Lake Shore Dr., Michigan City, IN 46360-1619 USA Tel 219-879-0133; 2815 Lake Shore Dr., Michigan City, IN 46360-1619
E-mail: roadrunnerpress@comcast.net
Web site: http://www.halhigdon.com.

RoadRunner Pr., *(978-1-937054)* P.O. Box 2564, Oklahoma City, OK 73101 USA Tel 405-524-6205; Fax: 405-524-6312
E-mail: jeanne@theroadrunnerpress.com
Web site: www.TheRoadRunnerPress.com.

Roald Publishing, *(978-0-578-12595-4; 978-0-578-12602-9)* 1139 West Ave., J-9, Lancaster, CA 93534 USA.

Roane Ink LLC, *(978-0-9969750; 978-0-9976869)* 121 Arlette Dr, lafayette, LA 70503 USA Tel 337-278-0169
E-mail: GeorgeR728@aol.com.

Roane, Janice J. *See* **Roane Ink LLC**

Roaring Brook Pr., *(978-0-7613; 978-1-59643)* 115 West 18th Street, New York, NY 10011 USA Tel 212-886-1030; *Imprints*: First Second Books (First Second); Kingfisher (Kingfsh); Macaulay, David Studio (D Macaulay)
Web site: http://www.henryholt.com; http://us.macmillan.com/splash/publishers/roaring-brook-press.html
Dist(s): **Follett School Solutions**
Macmillan
MyiLibrary.

Robbie Dean Pr., *(978-0-9630608; 978-1-889743; 978-0-9892303; 978-0-9916017; 978-0-9982493)* 2910 E. Eisenhower Pkwy., Ann Arbor, MI 48108 USA Tel 734-973-9511; Fax: 734-973-9475
E-mail: fairyha@aol.com.

Robe Communications, Inc., *(978-0-9817403; 978-1-935831)* 5138 S. Clifton Ave., Springfield, MO 65810 USA Tel 417-887-8793
E-mail: krobe@mchsi.com
Web site: http://www.robbietherabbit.com.

Roberts & Ross Publishing, *(978-1-936449)* 3361 W. Monmouth Ave., Englewood, CO 80110-6336 USA Tel 303-762-1469; Fax: 303-993-5639
E-mail: Patricia@RobertsRossPublishing.com.

Roberts, Michele, *(978-0-9760188)* P.O. Box 271611, Houston, TX 77277-1611 USA.

Roberts Publishing Co., *(978-0-931764)* 738 32nd St., S. E., Grand Rapids, MI 49548 USA Tel 616-245-1560; Fax: 616-245-1561 (orders can be sent by fax) Do not confuse with companies with the same or similar names in Sacramento, CA, San Marcos, CA, Great Lake, WI, Blaine, WA
E-mail: robertspublishingco@juno.com
Web site: http://www.scoliosishelp.com; http://www.scoliosishelp.org; http://www.robertsbookshelf.comw.

Robertson, Deirdre, *(978-0-692-46152-5)* RT 5 Box 157, KEYSER, WV 26726 USA Tel 3048130345.

Robertson Publishing, *(978-0-9727721; 978-0-9796251; 978-0-9798633; 978-0-9801675; 978-1-935125; 978-1-61170)* 59 N. Santa Cruz Ave., Suite B, Los Gatos, CA 95030 USA Tel 408-354-5957 Toll Free: 888-354-5957
E-mail: alicia.r@robertsonpublishing.com
Web site: http://www.RobertsonPublishing.com.

Robillard, Kristy, *(978-0-9800870)* 15110 S Oakleigh Ln., Prairieville, LA 70769 USA Fax: 225-744-3276
E-mail: robillard1@eatel.net.

Robin Corey Bks. *Imprint of* **Random Hse. Children's Bks.**

Robinbook, Ediciones S.L. (ESP) *(978-84-7927; 978-84-9917) Dist. by* **Lectorum Pubns.**

Robins Lane Pr. *Imprint of* **Gryphon Hse., Inc.**

Robinson, Beth, *(978-0-9799092)* P.O. Box 100, New Deal, TX 79350 USA (SAN 854-7378)
Web site: http://www.drbethrobinson.com.

Robinson, Consuelo, *(978-0-9786767)* P.O. Box 8662, Delray Beach, FL 33482 USA (SAN 851-2868)
E-mail: math1on1@math1on1.com
Web site: www.math1on1.com.

Robinson, Francesca *See* **Francesca Studios**

Robison Gamble Creative, *(978-1-933497)* 402B W Mt Vernon 272, Nixa, MO 65714 USA Tel 417-581-6008; Fax: 417-581-4542; Toll Free: 877-335-2735
E-mail: carrie@robisoncreative.com
Web site: http://www.robisoncreative.com.

Robot Playground, Inc., *(978-0-615-51355-3; 978-0-615-57232-1; 978-0-615-67487-2; 978-0-9862926)* 5110 LONG MEADOW DR, FRANKLIN, OH 45005 USA Tel 937-371-1240
E-mail: rita@ritajwebb.com
Dist(s): **CreateSpace Independent Publishing Platform.**

Robus, Debbie, *(978-0-9762034)* 31 Timberline Dr., Heber Springs, AR 72543-9417 USA
E-mail: firecrackerbaby57@yahoo.com
Web site: http://firecrackerbaby57.blogspot.com; http://www.workamper.com
Dist(s): **Workamper Bookstore.**

Robyn Z Moon Publishing, *(978-0-615-15292-9; 978-0-615-20370-6)* 3021 Eads Ave., Saint Lois, MO 63104 USA Toll Free: 877-544-0102
E-mail: robynzmoon@gmail.com
Dist(s): **Lulu Pr., Inc.**

Roc *Imprint of* **Penguin Publishing Group**

Roca Bolsillo (ESP) *(978-84-96940; 978-84-92833; 978-84-15729; 978-84-16240) Dist. by* **Spanish.**

Roca Editorial (ESP) *(978-84-96284; 978-84-96544; 978-84-96791; 978-84-9918; 978-84-92429; 978-84-16700; 978-84-16867; 978-84-17092) Dist. by* **Ediciones.**

Roca Editorial (ESP) *(978-84-96284; 978-84-96544; 978-84-96791; 978-84-9918; 978-84-92429; 978-84-16700; 978-84-16867; 978-84-17092) Dist. by* **Spanish.**

Rocco, Editora, Ltda (BRA) *(978-85-325; 978-85-62500) Dist. by* **Distribks Inc.**

Rock & Learn Educational Products *See* **Rock 'N Learn, Inc.**

Rock Cliff Media, *(978-0-9791384)* 553 Staci Ct., Ogden, UT 84404 USA
E-mail: info@rockcliffmedia.com
Web site: http://www.rockcliffmedia.com.

Rock Hse. Method, The *Imprint of* **Russell, Fred Publishing**

Rock Ink, *(978-0-9726979)* 2826 Cory Creek Rd., Oroville, CA 95965 USA Tel 530-894-7743; Fax: 530-892-8293
E-mail: mlrock@mariarock.com
Web site: http://www.mariarock.com.

Rock, James A. & Co. Pubs., *(978-0-918736; 978-1-59663)* 900 S. Irby St., #508, Florence, SC 29505-6357 USA (SAN 211-4690) Toll Free: 800-411-2230; 9710 Traville Gateway Dr., No. 305, Rockville, MD 20850; *Imprints*: Castle Keep Press (Castle Keep Pr); Sense of Wonder Press (Sense of Wonder); Mount Helicon Press (Mt Helicon MD)
E-mail: jarrock@sprintmail.com
Web site: http://www.rockpublishing.com; http://www.senseofwonderpress.com.

Rock 'N Learn, Inc., *(978-1-878489; 978-1-934312; 978-1-941722)* Orders Addr.: P.O. Box 3595, Conroe, TX 77305-3595 USA Tel 936-539-2731; Fax: 936-539-2659; Toll Free Fax: 800-801-5481; Toll Free: 800-348-8445; Edit Addr.: 105 Commercial Cir., Conroe, TX 77304 USA
E-mail: info@rocknlearn.com
Web site: http://www.rocknlearn.com
Dist(s): **Big Kids Productions, Inc.**
Follett School Solutions
Rounder Kids Music Distribution.

Rock Village Publishing, *(978-0-9674204; 978-0-9721389; 978-0-9766356; 978-1-934400)* 41 Walnut St., Middleborough, MA 02346 USA Tel 508-946-4738
E-mail: rockvillage@verizon.net.

Rockbott'm *See* **Spring Hollow Bks., LLC**

Rocket Press Books Inc. *See* **Rocket Press Publishing, LLC**

Rocket Press Publishing, LLC, *(978-0-9891732; 978-1-5375-9865-9)* 139-B James Comeaux Rd. PMB No. 571, Lafayette, LA 70508 USA Tel 337-591-9845
E-mail: rocketpressbooks@gmail.com
Web site: www.rocketpressbooks.com.

Rocket Ride Bks., *(978-0-9823322)* P.O. Box 1046, Somerset, PA 15501 USA
E-mail: anthonyrotoolo@yahoo.com.

Rocket Science Productions, LLC, *(978-0-9821823; 978-0-9830725; 978-1-937121; 978-1-939954; 978-1-945355)* 5765-F Burke Centre Pkwy., No. 222, Burke, VA 22015 USA (SAN 857-4863) Tel 703-764-8000
E-mail: fmonahan@rsp-llc.com
Dist(s): **Smashwords.**

Rockhill Bks. *Imprint of* **Kansas City Star Bks.**

Rockland Press *See* **Peach Tree Pr.**

Rockmill Publishing Co., *(978-0-9764012)* Rockmill Management, Inc., 17360 Hunter Ct., Lake Oswego, OR 97035 USA (SAN 256-5722) Tel 503-989-2590 (phone/fax); 503-806-3970
E-mail: energiesinc@msn.com; tammystamermotsch@msn.com.

Rockon Publishing, *(978-0-9726255)* 210 Hy Rd., Buda, TX 78610 USA Tel 512-295-4889
E-mail: wermundj@mail.utexas.edu.

Rockport Publishers *Imprint of* **Quarto Publishing Group USA**

Rockport Publishers *Imprint of* **Quarto Publishing Group USA**

Rocksand, LLC, *(978-1-931552)* 238 Greenbrier Dr., Cape Girardeau, MO 63701 USA Tel 877-625-7263
E-mail: bethprints@ymail.com
Web site: http://www.rainbowindow.com.

Rockshow Comedy, Inc., *(978-0-9854699)* 130 Old Town Blvd. N., Argyle, TX 76226 USA Tel 817-915-4296
E-mail: todd@rockshowcomedy.com
Web site: www.rockshowcomedy.com.

RockTuff, *(978-0-9800754)* Orders Addr.: P.O. Box 133, Roscoe, SD 57471 USA (SAN 855-1308) Tel 605-287-4133; Fax: 605-287-4188; Edit Addr.: 34240 Hwy. 12, Roscoe, SD 57471 USA
E-mail: rocktuff@venturecomm.net
Web site: http://www.andreabeyers.com.

Rod & Staff Pubs., Inc., *(978-0-7399)* P.O. Box 3, 14193 Hwy. 172, Crockett, KY 41413 USA (SAN 206-7633) Tel 606-522-4348; Fax: 606-522-4896; Toll Free Fax: 800-643-1244
Web site: http://www.rodstaff.com/.

Rodaian Pr., *(978-1-935436; 978-0-9847167; 978-0-9847986; 978-0-9893251)* P.O. Box 3128, Palm Springs, CA 92263 USA
Web site: http://www.rodaian.com.

Rodale Kids *Imprint of* **Rodale Pr., Inc.**

†Rodale Pr., Inc., *(978-0-87596; 978-0-87857; 978-1-57954; 978-1-4050; 978-1-59486; 978-1-60529; 978-1-60961; 978-1-62336; 978-1-63565)* Orders Addr.: 16365 James Madison Hwy., Gordonsville, VA 22942-8501 USA Toll Free Fax: 800-672-2054; Toll Free: 888-330-8477; Edit Addr.: 400 S. Tentth St., Emmaus, PA 18098-0099 USA (SAN 200-2477) Tel 610-967-5171; Fax: 215-967-8961; Toll Free: 800-222-4997; *Imprints*: Rodale Kids (Rodale Kids)
E-mail: sara.cox@rodale.com
Web site: rodale.com
Dist(s): **Bilingual Pubns. Co., The**
Lectorum Pubns., Inc.
MBI Distribution Services/Quayside Distribution
Macmillan
Send The Light Distribution LLC
St. Martin's Pr.
TNT Media Group, Inc.; *CIP.*

Rodgers, Alan Bks., *(978-1-59818; 978-1-60312; 978-1-60664; 978-1-4638)* 23511 Aliso Creek Rd., No. 120, Alsio Viejo, CA 92656-1341 USA
E-mail: AlanRodg@aol.com; amysterlingcasil@gmail.com; lmdegange@yahoo.com
Web site: http://www.aegypan.com; www.chameleonpublishers.com; http://www.chameleonmedia.co.

Rodgers & Nelsen Publishing Company *See* **Loveland Pr., LLC**

Rodrigue & Sons Company *See* **Rodrigue & Sons Co./Double R Books Publishing**

Rodrigue & Sons Co./Double R Books Publishing, *(978-0-9749026; 978-0-9833975; 978-1-938319)* Orders Addr.: 740 N. H St., Suite 170, Lompoc, CA 93436 USA Tel 805-735-7103 10am - 5pm PST; Fax: 805-737-9846; 740 N. H St., Suite 170, Lompoc, CA 93436 Tel 805-735-7103 10am - 5pm PST; Fax: 805-737-9846; *Imprints*: DOUBLE-R BOOKS (DOUBLE-R); DOUBLE R BOOKS (MYID_E_DOUBLE)
E-mail: publisher@doubleRbooks.com
Web site: http://DoubleRbooks.com
Dist(s): **INscribe Digital**
Ingram Bk. Co.

Rodriguez, Estela, *(978-0-9772631)* Orders Addr.: 2050 NW 16th Terr., Apt. E111, Miami, FL 33125 USA Tel 305-549-3039; Edit Addr.: Jose Marti Stat. 27 & 4th St., Miami, FL 33135 USA
E-mail: colorama@bellsouth.net.

Rodriguez, Josue D., *(978-1-63587-619-2)* 34 Norwood Rd, NEW HAVEN, CT 06513 USA Tel 203-214-3981.

Rodriguez, Michelle, *(978-0-9900061)* 38-33 147th St., Flushing, NY 11354 USA Tel 646-217-9177
E-mail: maliperto1@gmail.com.

Rodriguez, Raul, *(978-0-9912750)* 9619 Judalon Ln, Houston, TX 77063 USA Tel 281-467-6992
E-mail: raul6992@yahoo.com.

Rodro, *(978-0-9744770)* 52 Richmond Blvd., No. 3B, Ronkonkoma, NY 11779-3629 USA
Web site: http://www.rodro.com.

Roedway Pr., *(978-0-9659650)* P.O. Box 903, La Quinta, CA 92253 USA Tel 760-771-9818; Fax: 760-771-9618; Toll Free: 888-694-2248.

Roehm, Nancy Jean, *(978-0-9745591)* 210 Stoney Ridge Dr., Alpharetta, GA 30022-7668 USA
E-mail: njroehm4116@aol.com.

Roger Dean Publishing Co., *(978-0-89328)* Div. of The Lorenz Corp., 501 E. Third St., Dayton, OH 45402-2118 USA Tel 937-228-6118; Toll Free: 800-444-1144
E-mail: order@lorenz.com
Web site: http://www.lorenz.com.

Rogers, Al M. Jr., *(978-0-9760159)* 48151 N. Laura Rogers Rd., Tickfaw, LA 70466 USA
Web site: http://www.lasttrumpgathering.com.

Rogers, Siobain K., *(978-0-615-13289-1)* 103 Harris Cir., Carthage, TX 75633 USA
Web site: http://www.lulu.com/siobainrogers
Dist(s): **Lulu Pr., Inc.**

Rogue Bear Pr., *(978-0-9789512)* PO Box #513, Ardsley, NY 10502 USA (SAN 852-0275)
Web site: http://monsterdetectiveagency.com
Dist(s): **Midpoint Trade Bks., Inc.**
Partners Pubs. Group, Inc.

Rogue Wave Publishing *See* **Tonepoet Publishing**

Rohrer Design, *(978-0-9721138)* 725-17th St., Kenosha, WI 53140-1329 USA
Web site: http://www.rohrer-design.com.

Roland & Eleanor Bergthold, *(978-0-9741193)* 9133 N. Stoneridge Ln., Fresno, CA 93720 USA Tel 559-434-4137
E-mail: rolbergthold@prodigy.net; embergthold@prodigy.net.

Rolemommy, *(978-0-9822974)* 36 Rutledge Rd., Scarsdale, NY 10583 USA
E-mail: beth@rolemommy.com; mail@plainwhitepress.com.

Rolest P. Inc., *(978-0-9786281; 978-0-9984275; 978-0-692-83116-8; 978-0-9986232)* 1503 Elberta Rd., No. 115, Warner Robins, GA 31093 USA Tel 478-442-6936
E-mail: rolest@juno.com.

Publisher Name Index

Rolling Hills Pr., *(978-0-943978)* 17 Olive Ave., Novato, CA 94945-3428 USA (SAN 282-2601) Do not confuse with Rolling Hills Pr., in Alexandria, VA
E-mail: rhpresslc@aol.com.

Romain, Trevor Co., The, *(978-0-9762843; 978-0-9787783; 978-1-934365; 978-0-9819804; 978-1-936407)* 4412 Spicewood Springs Rd. Suite 705, Austin, TX 78759-8567 USA Toll Free: 877-876-6246
E-mail: sabrina@trevorromain.com
Web site: http://www.TrevorRomain.com; http://www.comicalsense.com.

Roman Catholic Bks., *(978-0-912141; 978-1-929291; 978-0-9793540; 978-1-934888)* Div. of Catholic Media Apostolate, Orders Addr.: P.O. Box 2286, Fort Collins, CO 80522 USA Fax: 970-493-8781; Edit Addr.: 1331 Red Cedar Cir., Fort Collins, CO 80524 USA
Web site: http://www.booksforcatholics.com.

Roman, Teresa, *(978-0-9961545)* 5207 Arden Way, Carmichael, CA 95608 USA Tel 904-625-4310
E-mail: gayoba@gmail.com
Web site: teresaromanwrites.com.

Romancing Cathay, *(978-1-932592)* 10050 Montgomery Rd., No. 315, Cincinnati, OH 45242 USA Tel 513-290-7419; Fax: 949-266-8395
E-mail: business@romancingcathay.com
Web site: http://www.romancingcathay.com.

Romani, Gabriella *See* **BBM Bks.**

Romoulous *Imprint of* **MIROGLYPHICS**

Romoulous Enterprises *See* **MIROGLYPHICS**

Ronald, George Pub., Ltd., *(978-0-85398)* 8325 17th St., N., Saint Petersburg, FL 33702-2843 USA (SAN 679-1859); 3 Rosecroft Ln. Oaklands, Welwyn, AL6 0UB
E-mail: sales@grbooks.com
Web site: www.grbooks.com
Dist(s): **Cambridge Univ. Pr.**

Ronan Enterprises, Inc., *(978-0-9821110)* P.O. Box 574, Richmond, MI 48062 USA.

Rondo Books *See* **Parrish, Fayrene**

Ronin Publishing, *(978-0-914171; 978-1-57951)* P.O. Box 22900, Oakland, CA 94609 USA (SAN 287-5365) Tel 510-420-3669; Fax: 510-420-3672; Toll Free: 800-858-2665 (orders) Do not confuse with Ronin Publishing in Cambridge, MA
E-mail: orders@roninpub.com
Web site: http://www.roninpub.com
Dist(s): **MyiLibrary**
New Leaf Distributing Co., Inc.
Publishers Group West (PGW)
ebrary, Inc.

RonJon Publishing, Incorporated *See* **Hewell Publishing**

Ronsdale Pr. (CAN) *(978-0-921870; 978-1-55380) Dist. by* **SPD-Small Pr Dist.**

Roost Books *Imprint of* **Shambhala Pubns., Inc.**

Rooster Pubns., *(978-0-9792135)* Orders Addr.: 101 S. Page St., Morrisonville, IL 62546-6746 USA; Edit Addr.: 101 S. Page St., Morrisonville, IL 62546-6746 USA
E-mail: grandmotherstewart@msn.com.

RoosterBugglePue Bks. *Imprint of* **Eupanapue-Auntella's Rooster Pubns.**

Roots & Wings, *(978-0-9703319)* 20114 Illinois Rte. 16, Nokomis, IL 62075 USA Tel 217-594-7300; Fax: 217-563-2111 Do not confuse with companies with the same name in Lake Forest, IL, New Paltz, NY, Boulder, CO
E-mail: beltpulley@ccipost.net.

Roots, Robert, *(978-0-9715336)* 11820 Miramar Pkwy. No. 212, Miramar, FL 33025 USA
E-mail: rbroots22@yahoo.com; rr@robertroots.com
Web site: http://www.robertroots.com.

Rope Ferry Press *See* **Anemone Publishing**

Roque-Velasco, Dr. Ismael, *(978-0-9706319)* P.O. Box 432804, Miami, FL 3243 USA Tel 305-667-6230; 305-740-6724
E-mail: northemismael@aol.com
Web site: http://www.cubaforkids.com
Dist(s): **Lectorum Pubns., Inc.**

Rorschach Entertainment, *(978-0-9748654)* 15806 18th Ave W. Apt. F203, Lynnwood, WA 98087-8755 USA
E-mail: info@rorschachentertainment.com
Web site: http://www.rorschachentertainment.com.

Rosales, Irene, *(978-0-9824348)* PMB 154, 3118 FM 528, Webster, TX 77598 USA.

Rosasharn Pr., *(978-0-615-96746-2; 978-0-9916496; 978-0-692-50595-3)* 1011 Serenity Cir., Auburn, AL 36830 USA Tel 334-750-6280
E-mail: info@pegathapress.com.

Rose Art Industries, Inc., *(978-1-57041)* 6 Regent St., Livingston, NJ 07039 USA Toll Free: 800-272-9667.

Rose Bud Publishing Co. LLC, *(978-0-9836913)* 8245 N. 27th Ave., Apt. 1048, Phoenix, AZ 85051 USA Tel 602-501-4533.

Rose, Gary Publishing, *(978-0-9988777)* 4065 River Woods, Auburn, CA 95602 USA Tel 530-885-3067
E-mail: grose1@pacbell.net.

Rose Publishing, *(978-0-9655082; 978-1-890947; 978-1-59636; 978-1-62862)* 4733 Torrance Blvd., No. 259, Torrance, CA 90503-4100 USA (SAN 253-0120) Tel 310-353-2100; Fax: 310-353-2116; Toll Free: 800-532-4278 Do not confuse with companies with same or similar names in Flagtown, NJ, Arcadia, CA, Keystone Heights, FL, Salem, OR, Santa Cruz, CA, Tucson, AZ, Alameda, CA, Grand Rapids, MI, Little Rock, AR, Boulder, CO
Web site: http://www.rose-publishing.com
Dist(s): **Firebrand Technologies**
INscribe Digital
Spring Arbor Distributors, Inc.

Rose River Publishing Co., *(978-0-9707976)* P.O. Box 19864, Alexandria, VA 22320 USA Tel 703-768-2380 (phone/fax)
E-mail: herbpuscheck@cs.com.

Rose Valley Publishing, *(978-0-9765905)* 53762 Kristin Ct., Shelby Township, MI 48316 USA
E-mail: manitoumagic@aol.com
Web site: http://www.rosevalleypublishing.com.

Rose Water Cottage Pr., *(978-0-9853223; 978-0-9961393)* 308 Stewart St., Franklin, TN 37064 USA Tel 615-476-6717
E-mail: tray296@att.net.

Rose Wind Pr., *(978-0-9631232)* Div. of Compass Rose Corp., 1701 Broadway, No. 345, Vancouver, WA 98663 USA Tel 360-693-7742; Fax: 360-693-0950
E-mail: galenahk@aol.com
Web site: http://www.compassart.

RoseDog Bks. *Imprint of* **Dorrance Publishing Co., Inc.**

RoseFountain Pr., LLC, *(978-0-9768051)* 65 High Ridge Rd., No. 163, Stamford, CT 06905-3814 USA (SAN 858-4664)
Dist(s): **BookBaby**
Enfield Publishing & Distribution Co., Inc.

RoseKnows, Inc., *(978-0-9755889)* P.O. Box 5448, McLean, VA 22103-5448 USA
Web site: http://www.playgeist.com.

Rosemaling & Crafts, *(978-0-9674583)* Orders Addr.: 3208 Snowbrush Pl., Fort Collings, CO 80521 USA Tel 970-229-9846; Fax: 970-229-5683
E-mail: diaedwards@cs.com
Web site: http://www.nordic-arts.com.

Rosemont, Ltd., *(978-0-9635811)* 1620 Belmont St., Jackson, MS 39202-1203 USA Tel 601-355-1233.

Rosen & Assocs., Inc., *(978-0-9746811; 978-0-9778973)* P.O. Box 17173, Chapel Hill, NC 27516 USA Tel 919-264-5976; Fax: 919-929-7119
E-mail: info@cashworkbooks.com
Web site: http://www.cashworkbooks.com.

Rosen Central *Imprint of* **Rosen Publishing Group, Inc., The**

Rosen Classroom *Imprint of* **Rosen Publishing Group, Inc., The**

†**Rosen Publishing Group, Inc., The,** *(978-0-8239; 978-1-56696; 978-1-4042; 978-1-4358; 978-1-60851; 978-1-60852; 978-1-60853; 978-1-60854; 978-1-61511; 978-1-61512; 978-1-61513; 978-1-61514; 978-1-61530; 978-1-61531; 978-1-61532; 978-1-61533; 978-1-4488; 978-1-4777; 978-1-4824; 978-1-4994; 978-1-68048; 978-1-5081; 978-1-68416; 978-1-5382; 978-1-5383) a/o Dept. C234561, 29 E. 21st St., New York, NY 10010 USA (SAN 203-3720) Tel 212-777-3017; Fax: 212-358-9588; Toll Free Fax: 888-436-4643; Toll Free: 800-237-9932; Imprints:* Everett Press (Everett Pr); PowerKids Press (PowerKids Pr); Rosen Reference (RosenRef); Editorial Buenas Letras (EditBuenas); Powerstart Press (Powerstart Pr); Reading Power (Reading Power); Reading Room Collection (RRC); Dance & Movement Press (Dance); Rosen Classroom (RosenClassrm); Britannica Educational Publishing (BritEducPub); Rosen Young Adult (RosenYA); Windmill Books (WindmillBks); Rosen Central (RosenCent)
E-mail: info@rosenpub.com; customerservice@rosenpub.com; deang@rosenpub.com; hollyc@rosenpub.com
Web site: http://www.rosenpublishing.com; http://www.rosendigital.com; http://www.rosenclassroom.com
Dist(s): **Ebsco Publishing**
Follett School Solutions
Lectorum Pubns., Inc.
ebrary, Inc.; *CIP.*

Rosen Publishing Group, Incorporated, The *See* **Rosen Publishing Group, Inc., The**

Rosen Publishing, Inc., *(978-1-881930)* 3000 Chestnut Ave., Suite 300, Baltimore, MD 21211 USA Tel 800-237-9932; Fax: 410-889-1320.

Rosen Reference *Imprint of* **Rosen Publishing Group, Inc., The**

Rosen Young Adult *Imprint of* **Rosen Publishing Group, Inc., The**

Rosenberg, Harvey *See* **Go Jolly Bks.**

Rosenberg Publishing Pty. Ltd. (AUS) *(978-1-877058; 978-1-921719; 978-1-922013; 978-1-925078; 978-0-9945627; 978-0-6480439) Dist. by* **Intl Spec Bk.**

Rosenberger, Matthew, *(978-0-9760047; 978-0-9909415)* Div. of ABC Publishing for Kids, One Summit St., Philadelphia, PA 19118 USA (SAN 858-9887) Tel 215-242-4011; Fax: 215-242-9421
E-mail: mgr@kidstravelguides.com
Web site: http://www.kidstravelguides.com.

Roses Are READ Productions, *(978-0-9703489; 978-0-9755093)* P.O. Box 7844, Saint Paul, MN 55107 USA Tel 651-686-8418; Fax: 651-340-5333; *Imprints:* Little Petals (Little Petals)
E-mail: admin@rosesareread.cc.

Rosetta Stone Communications, *(978-0-9759331)* 1971 N. Nowak Ave., Thousand Oaks, CA 91360 USA (SAN 256-1549) Tel 805-370-0010; Fax: 805-435-1541
E-mail: johngriffith@maggio-associates.com
Web site: http://www.scientificgolfer.com.

Rosetta Stone Ltd., *(978-1-58022; 978-1-883972; 978-1-60391; 978-1-60717; 978-1-60829; 978-1-61716; 978-1-62821)* 135 W. Market St., Harrisonburg, VA 22801 USA Toll Free: 800-788-0822
E-mail: info@trstone.com; help@RosettaStone.com
Web site: http://www.rosettastone.com.

Rosmen-Izdat (RUS) *(978-5-8451) Dist. by* **Distribks Inc.**

Ross, Alan Publications *See* **Ross Pubns.**

Ross & Perry, Inc., *(978-1-931641; 978-1-931839; 978-1-932080; 978-1-932109; 978-0-9849531)* 3 S. Haddon Ave., Suite 4, Haddonfield, NJ 08003 USA (SAN 253-8555) Tel 856 427-6135; Fax: 856-427-6136
E-mail: grfisherii@gmail.com
Web site: http://www.rossperry.com; http://www.gporeprints.com
Dist(s): **TextStream.**

Ross, Cathy, *(978-0-9797832)* 1509 Cypress Rd., Olney, IL 62450 USA Tel 618-393-7732; Fax: 618-395-0123
E-mail: devspecinc@yahoo.com.

Ross, Jeanne, *(978-0-9850216)* PO Box 9011 PMB 308, Calexico, CA 92232 USA Tel 720-480-0121
E-mail: Raydiant1s@yahoo.com.

Ross Pubns., *(978-0-9617038)* 1438 W. Lantana Rd., No. 401, Lantana, FL 33462 USA (SAN 662-8230)
E-mail: alanross@aol.com
Web site: http://www.thegenuinejesus.com.

Rossi, Debra, *(978-0-9758982)* 813 Wentwood, Southlake, TX 76092 USA.

Rotaplast Pr., *(978-0-9706901)* Orders Addr.: P.O. Box 1100, Kennebunkport, ME 04046 USA Tel 207-967-0118; Edit Addr.: 4 East Ave., Kennebunkport, ME 04046 USA.

Roth Pubs., *(978-0-9832102; 978-1-938428)* P.O. Box 1058, Monsey, NY 10952 USA Tel 845-474-0022; Fax: 845-770-3382
E-mail: solomon@rothpublishers.com
Web site: www.rothpublishers.com.

Roth Publishing *See* **HELORO Publishing Group**

Rothwell Digital Imagery, *(978-0-615-18912-3)* Orders Addr.: P.O. Box 383, Westfield, NY 14787 USA Tel 716-326-4319; 716-969-4088 (cell)
E-mail: tiroth@fairpoint.net; tlrothwell@gmail.com; lewisthedragon@live.com
Web site: http://lewisthedragon.com
Dist(s): **R J Communications, LLC.**

Rough Draft Printing, *(978-1-933998; 978-1-60386)* 1280 Queen St., Seaside, OR 97138 USA; *Imprints:* Merchant Books (Merchant Bks).

Round Cow Media Group, *(978-0-9745218)* Orders Addr.: P.O. Box 87, Alpharetta, GA 30009-0087 USA Tel 678-762-9053; Edit Addr.: 2822 Ashleigh Ln., Alpharetta, GA 30004 USA; *Imprints:* Biz4Kids (Biz4Kids)
E-mail: christian@biz4kids.com
Web site: http://www.biz4kids.com.

Round Tower Pr., *(978-0-9765964)* P.O. Box 2942, Paradise, CA 95969-2942 USA Tel 530-872-9705; Fax: 530-872-7732; Toll Free: 888-737-9705
E-mail: thor@roundtowerpress.com
Web site: http://www.roundtowerpress.com.

Rounder Bks., *(978-1-57940)* 1 Rounder Way, Burlington, MA 01803-5157 USA Toll Free: 800-768-6337
E-mail: info@rounderbooks.com
Web site: http://www.rounderbooks.com/
Dist(s): **Leonard, Hal Corp.**

Roundsquare Pr., *(978-0-9717280)* 295 Marble St., Suite 303, Broomfield, CO 80020-2171 USA
E-mail: rs_press@msn.com.

Rourke Educational Media, *(978-0-86592; 978-0-86593; 978-0-86625; 978-1-55916; 978-1-57103; 978-1-58952; 978-1-59515; 978-1-60044; 978-1-60472; 978-1-60694; 978-1-61590; 978-1-61741; 978-1-61236; 978-1-61810; 978-1-62169; 978-1-62717; 978-1-63155; 978-1-63430; 978-1-68191; 978-1-68342; 978-1-64156) Orders Addr.: P.O. Box 643328, Vero Beach, FL 32964 USA (SAN 857-0825) Fax: 772-234-6622; Toll Free: 800-394-7055; Edit Addr.: 1701 Hwy. A1A S., Ste 300, Vero Beach, FL 32963 USA Toll Free Fax: 1-888-355-6270; Toll Free: 800-394-7055*
E-mail: rourke@rourkepublishing.com; rbrady@rourkepublishing.com; renee@rourkeeducationalmedia.com
Web site: http://www.rourkeeducationalmedia.com
Dist(s): **Findaway World, LLC**
Follett School Solutions
Ideals Pubns.
MyiLibrary.

Rourke Enterprises, Inc., *(978-0-86592)* Div. of Rourke Publishing Group, P.O. Box 3328, Vero Beach, FL 32964-3328 USA Tel 561-234-6001; Fax: 561-234-6622
E-mail: rourke@sunet.net
Web site: http://www.rourkepublishing.com.

Rourke Publishing, LLC *See* **Rourke Educational Media**

Rourke, Ray Publishing Company, Incorporated *See* **Rourke Enterprises, Inc.**

†**Routledge,** *(978-0-04; 978-0-413; 978-0-415; 978-0-7100; 978-0-87830; 978-1-317)* Member of Taylor & Frances Group, Orders Addr.: 7625 Empire Dr., Florence, KY 41042 USA Toll Free Fax: 800-248-4724 (orders, customer serv.); Toll Free: 800-634-7064 (orders, customer serv.); Edit Addr.: 270 Madison Ave. # 3, New York, NY 10016-0601 USA (SAN 213-196X)
E-mail: cserve@routledge-ny.com; info@routledge-ny.com
Web site: http://www.routledge-ny.com
Dist(s): **Chicago Distribution Ctr.**
Ebsco Publishing
MyiLibrary
Oxford Univ. Pr., Inc.
Taylor & Francis Group
Women Ink; *CIP.*

Rovakada, LLC, *(978-0-9845867)* P.O. Box 210324, San Francisco, CA 94121 USA Tel 415-290-6454
E-mail: order@rovakada.com
Web site: http://rovakada.com
Dist(s): **National Bk. Network.**

Rowe, Kysha, *(978-0-9769339)* 605 Crested View Ct., Loganville, GA 30052-8926 USA
E-mail: kysha_r@yahoo.com
Web site: http://www.whatcreaturesteachus.com; http://www.focusontheyouth.com.

Rowe Publishing and Design, *(978-0-9833971; 978-0-9851196; 978-1-939054)* 1080 15 Rd., Stockton, KS 67669 USA Tel 785-425-7350
E-mail: info@rowepublishingdesign.com
Web site: www.rowepublishingdesign.com
Dist(s): **Smashwords.**

Rowfant Pr., *(978-1-929731)* 2401 W. 27th St., N., Wichita, KS 67204 USA Tel 316-832-0309
E-mail: rowfant@hotmail.com
Web site: http://rowfantpress.com/.

Rowles, Louis, *(978-0-9708748)* 204 12th Ave., N., Amory, MS 38821-1206 USA Tel 662-256-3865
E-mail: glrowles@network-one.com.

Rowman & Littlefield Education, *(978-0-8108; 978-1-56676; 978-1-57886; 978-1-60709; 978-1-61048; 978-1-4758)* Orders Addr.: 15200 NBN Way, Blue Ridge Summit, PA 17214 USA Tel 717-794-3800 (Sales, Customer Service, MIS, Royalties Inventory); Fax: 717-794-3803 (Customer Service & orders only); 717-794-3857 (Sales & MIS); 717-794-3856 (Royalties, Inventory Mgmt. & Distribution); Toll Free Fax: 800-338-4550 (Customer Service & orders); Toll Free: 800-462-6420 (Customer Service & orders); Edit Addr.: 4501 Forbes Blvd., Suite 200, Lanham, MD 20706 USA Tel 301-459-3366; Fax: 301-459-5748; Toll Free Fax: 800-338-4550; Toll Free: 800-462-6420; 4501 Forbes Blvd Suite 200, Lanham, MD 20706 Short Discount, contact rlpgsales@rowman.com
E-mail: mmcmenamin@rowman.com; tkoerner@rowman.com
Web site: http://www.rlpgbooks.com; http://www.scarecroweducation.com; http://www.rowman.com
Dist(s): **CreateSpace Independent Publishing Platform**
Ebsco Publishing
Follett School Solutions
MyiLibrary
National Bk. Network
Rowman & Littlefield Publishers, Inc.
ebrary, Inc.

†**Rowman & Littlefield Publishers, Inc.,** *(978-0-8476; 978-0-87471; 978-0-9632978; 978-1-56699; 978-1-888052; 978-0-7425; 978-1-931890; 978-1-933494; 978-1-4422; 978-1-936283; 978-1-61281; 978-1-4616; 978-1-4617; 978-1-62093; 978-1-5381)* Mem. of Rowman & Littlefield Publishing Group, Inc., Orders Addr.: 15200 NBN Way, Blue Ridge Summit, PA 17214 USA Tel 717-794-3800 (Sales, Customer Service, MIS, Royalties, Inventory; Fax: 717-794-3803 (Customer Service & orders only); 717-794-3857 (Sales & MIS); 717-794-3856 (Royalties, Inventory Mgmt. & Distribution); Toll Free Fax: 800-338-4550 (Customer Service & orders); Toll Free: 800-462-6420 (Customer Service & orders); Edit Addr.: 4501 Forbes Blvd., Suite 200, Lanham, MD 20706 USA Tel 301-459-3366; Fax: 301-459-5749; Toll Free: 800-462-6420; *Imprints:* Gooseberry Patch (GooseberP) Short Discount, please contact rlpgsales@rowman.com
E-mail: rlpgsales@rowman.com; lweston@rowman.com
Web site: http://www.rowmanlittlefield.com; http://www.rlpgbooks.com/bookseller/index.shtml
Dist(s): **CreateSpace Independent Publishing Platform**
Ebsco Publishing
Follett School Solutions
MyiLibrary
National Bk. Network
National Film Network LLC
Send The Light Distribution LLC
Two Rivers Distribution
ebrary, Inc.; *CIP.*

Rowohlt Taschenbuch Verlag GmbH (DEU) *(978-3-499) Dist. by* **Continental Bk.**

Rowohlt Taschenbuch Verlag GmbH (DEU) *(978-3-499) Dist. by* **Distribks Inc.**

Roxbury Park Juvenile *Imprint of* **Lowell Hse. Juvenile**

Roxby Media Ltd. (GBR) *(978-1-900521; 978-0-9848539) Dist. by* **LaurusCo.**

Roy, Wendy, *(978-0-615-59502-3)* 18 Haviland St. No. 15, Boston, MA 02115 USA Tel 617-645-9018
E-mail: contactwendynow@yahoo.com
Web site: http://www.glamgranola.com.

Royal Brown Publishing, *(978-0-9978541; 978-0-9979611)* 12138 Central Ave., Bowie, MD 20721 USA Tel 301-262-3472
E-mail: tdroyal@gmail.com
Web site: www.royalbrownpublishing.com.

Royal Caliber Pubns., *(978-0-9860785; 978-0-9860824)* 4043 Cypress Landing E., Winter Haven, FL 33884 USA
Dist(s): **Bookmasters Distribution.**

Royal Council of the Real Fairyland, LLC, *(978-0-9841188)* 1332 Landfall Dr., Wilmington, NC 28405-2840 USA (SAN 858-4621)
Web site: http://www.therealtoothfairies.com.

Royal Financial Investment Group, *(978-0-578-16296-6; 978-0-578-16297-3; 978-0-578-16298-0; 978-0-9983860)* 1102-A Hwy 56 North, Waynesboro, GA 30830 USA
E-mail: info@royalfinancials.com
Web site: www.royalfinancials.com.

Royal Fireworks Publishing Co., *(978-0-88092; 978-0-89824)* Orders Addr.: P.O. Box 399, Unionville, NY 10988 USA (SAN 240-2394) Tel 845-726-4444; Fax: 845-726-3824; Edit Addr.: 1 First Ave., Unionville, NY 10988 USA
E-mail: rfpress@frontiernet.net
Web site: http://www.rfwp.com/
Dist(s): **Bridge Pubns., Inc.**

Royal Guard Dragon Society, The, *(978-0-9791733)* 706 Hall Ave., White Bear Lake, MN 55110 USA
E-mail: trgdspublications@trgds.com
Web site: http://trgds.com.

Royal Hse. Publishing, *(978-0-9772671)* 2315 Market Pl., Suite E, Huntsville, AL 35801 USA Tel 256-519-2291; Fax: 256-519-2292.

Royal Imprint Pr., Inc., *(978-0-9798624)* P.O. Box 342403, Austin, TX 78734 USA
Web site: http://http:www.TheRoyalYacht.net.

Royal Knight Inc., *(978-0-9777110)* 1204 Harbor Dr SE # 100, Rochester, MN 55904-5923 USA
Web site: http://www.royalknightresearch.com.

Royal Limited Partnership, *(978-0-9714798)* P.O. Box 448, Eugene, OR 97440-0448 USA
E-mail: fun@funnix.com
Web site: http://www.funnix.com.

Royal Peacock Publications *See* **Satin Finish Publishing**

Royal Penny Pr., The, *(978-0-9912370)* 9300 Colesville Rd., Silver Spring, MD 20901 USA Tel 240-372-1670
E-mail: sales@royalpennypress.com.

Royal Swan Enterprises, Inc., *(978-0-9793000; 978-0-9977720)* 201 Orchard Ln., Carrboro, NC

For full information on wholesalers and distributors, refer to the Wholesaler and Distributor Name Index

27510-2530 USA (SAN 853-0521); *Imprints:* Alazar Press (Alazar Pr)
E-mail: rse@nc.rr.com; alazar.press@gmail.com
Web site: http://www.royal-swan-enterprises.com; http://www.alazar-press.com
Dist(s): **Independent Pubs. Group**
MyiLibrary.

Royal Voice Productions *See* **Snow Waters Publishing**

Royall World Productions, *(978-0-9768115)* 1608 N. 13th St., Kansas City, KS 66102 USA Toll Free: 800-331-7668
E-mail: royallworldproductions@unoi.org.

Royalty Bks. International, Inc., *(978-0-9705458)* Orders Addr.: 2047 Gees Mill Rd. Suite 210, Conyers, GA 30013 USA
E-mail: royaltybooks@gmail.com
Web site: http://www.royaltybooksonline.com.

Royalty Company Two-Thousand, The *See* **Royalty Bks. International, Inc.**

Royalty Publishing Co., *(978-0-910487)* P.O. Box 2125, Bedford, IN 47421 USA (SAN 260-1265) Fax: 812-278-8785
E-mail: nitaspeaks@nitascoggan.com
Web site: http://www.the-maximum-zone.com.

Rozanski, Johnathan, *(978-0-9983327)* 471 E. Main St., Chicopee, MA 01020 USA Tel 413-594-3155
E-mail: mysteriousmisterenter@gmail.com.

RP Media, *(978-1-57545; 978-1-62716; 978-0-692-62456-2)* Div. of RP Bks., Orders Addr.: P.O. Box 362, East Olympia, WA 98540 USA; *Imprints:* Ruin Mist Publications (Ruin Mist Pubns); Reagent Press Signature Editions (Reagent Pr Sig Edns); Reagent Press Echo (Reagent Pr Echo); Reagent Press Books for Young Readers (RPBTR)
E-mail: sales@reagentpress.com; service@reagentpress.com; rights@reagentpress.com; emma.spring@reagentpress.com
Web site: http://www.reagentpress.com/; http://www.ruinmist.com/; http://books.reagentpress.com/; http://audio.reagentpress.com/; http://video.reagentpress.com/; http://graphics.reagentpress.com/; http://www.wizardsofskyhall.com/; http://www.ruinmistmovie.com/; http://www.themagiclands.com/; http://www.tvpress.com; http://www.bugvillecritters.com/
Dist(s): **CreateSpace Independent Publishing Platform**
EBSCO Media
Lightning Source, Inc.
MyiLibrary
OverDrive, Inc.
ebrary, Inc.

RPG Objects, *(978-0-9724826; 978-0-9743067; 978-1-935432)* 9275 Cedar Forest Rd., Eden Prairie, MN 55347 USA
E-mail: chris@rpgobjects.com
Web site: http://www.rpgobjects.com.

RPJ & Co., Inc., *(978-0-9761122; 978-0-615-27121-7; 978-0-9819980; 978-0-9828277; 978-1-937770)* 1080 Princewood Dr., Orlando, FL 32810-4542 USA; *Imprints:* SPC Books (SPCBks)
E-mail: kathy@rpjandco.com
Web site: http://www.rpjandco1417.com; http://www.rpjandco.com
Dist(s): **Advocate Distribution Solutions**
Ingram Content Group Inc.
Send The Light Distribution LLC
Smashwords.

RPM Publishing, *(978-0-9764085; 978-0-9795126; 978-0-692-58325-8; 978-0-692-59412-4; 978-0-9992743)* P.O. Box 1417, Maple Valley, WA 98038 USA Tel 425-890-3113
Web site: http://www.sarahgerdes.com
Dist(s): **CreateSpace Independent Publishing Platform.**

R.R Publishing Company *See* **Dara Publishing LLC**

RRJ Publishing, Inc., *(978-0-9857095)* 2073 SilverCrest Dr. unit C, Myrtle Beach, SC 29579 USA Tel 864-497-8392
E-mail: Mstnwright@yahoo.com.

RS Art Studio, *(978-0-9787729)* PO Box 64, Big Bear City, CA 92314 USA Tel 714-724-1480
E-mail: rsart@aol.com
Web site: http://www.rsartstudio.com.

RS Publishing *See* **JD Entertainment**

RTC Publishing, *(978-1-939418; 978-1-947564)* P.O. Box 511, Highland Park, IL 60035-0511 USA Tel 949.375.1006; Fax: 815.346.2398.

RTE Media, LLC, *(978-0-692-80787-3)* 6 Westhill Rd., Saddle River, NJ 07458 USA Tel 201-934-9675
E-mail: aforment@optonline.net
Web site: www.alisonashleyformento.com.

RTI Publishing, LLC, *(978-0-9769086)* 5685 S. Topaz Pl., Chandler, AZ 85249-5804 USA (SAN 256-6338)
E-mail: rtipublishing@cox.net.

RTMC Organization, LLC, *(978-1-934316)* P.O. Box 15105, Baltimore, MD 21282 USA (SAN 852-6923) Tel 410-900-7834
E-mail: Sales@RTMC.org
Web site: http://www.rtmc.org.

Ruano, José A., *(978-0-9792972)* 8909 NW 189 TE, Miami, FL 33018 USA (SAN 853-0610) Tel 305-829-2683; Fax: 305-829-2094
E-mail: jaruano@bellsouth.net.

Rubicon Bks., *(978-0-9771676)* P.O. Box 1167, Silver City, NM 88062-1167 USA Tel 505-388-4585 Do not confuse with companies with the same name in Montrose, CA, Glendale, AZ
E-mail: badarmstrong@signalpeak.net.

Ruby Tuesday Books Limited (GBR) *(978-1-909673; 978-1-910549; 978-1-911341) Dist. by* **Bearport Pubng.**

Ruddick, Jessica Bks. LLC, *(978-1-946164)* 515 Miami Dr., Chesapeake, VA 23323 USA Tel 757-548-0468; Fax: 757-548-0468
E-mail: jmruddick@gmail.com.

Rugg's Recommendations, *(978-0-9608934; 978-1-883062)* P.O. Box 417, Fallbrook, CA 92088-0417 USA (SAN 237-9694) Tel 760-728-4558; Fax: 760-728-4467
E-mail: frugg@thegrid.net
Web site: http://www.ruggsrecommendations.com.

Ruin Mist Pubns. *Imprint of* **RP Media**

Rule 2 Bks., *(978-0-9915511)* 2365 Rice Blvd, Houston, TX 77005 USA Tel 713-533-9300
E-mail: lchambers@brightskypress.com
Web site: www.rule2books.com
Dist(s): **Bright Sky Pr.**

Run With Me Publishing, *(978-0-9776835)* 15447 W. Monterey Ln., Kerman, CA 93630 USA Tel 559-846-6432
E-mail: runwithmepublishing@yahoo.com.

Runamuck Publishing, *(978-0-615-16220-1)* 221 Academy St., Mexico, NY 13114 USA
Dist(s): **Lulu Pr., Inc.**

Running Horse Pr., *(978-0-9908979; 978-1-945087)* 14819 W. Yosemite Dr., Sun City West, AZ 85375 USA Tel 575-650-2246
E-mail: ecellenb@gmail.com
Web site: www.ellenbuikema.com; www.runninghorsepress.com.

Running Moose Publications, *(978-0-9777210)* 42400 Garfield Road, Clinton Township, MI 48038 USA
Dist(s): **Adventure Pubns.**

Running Pr. *Imprint of* **Running Pr. Bk. Pubs.**

Running Pr. Kids *Imprint of* **Running Pr. Bk. Pubs.**

Running Pr. Minature Editions *Imprint of* **Running Pr. Bk. Pubs.**

†Running Pr. Bk. Pubs., *(978-0-7624; 978-0-89471; 978-0-914294; 978-1-56138)* Div. of Perseus Books Group, 125 S. 22nd St., Philadelphia, PA 19103-4399 USA (SAN 204-5702) Tel 215-567-5080; Fax: 215-568-2919; Toll Free Fax: 800-453-2884; Toll Free: 800-345-5359 customer service; *Imprints:* Running Press (RunPr); Running Press Kids (RunningKids); Running Press Miniature Editions (RunMinEdns)
E-mail: support@runningpress.com
Web site: http://www.runningpress.com
Dist(s): **Blackstone Audio, Inc.**
Hachette Bk. Group
MyiLibrary
Zondervan
ebrary, Inc.; *CIP.*

Runny Nose Press L.L.C., *(978-0-9788542)* 24111 Beierman, Warren, MI 48091-1714 USA
Web site: http://www.runnynosepress.com.

Rupa & Co. (IND) *(978-81-7167; 978-81-291) Dist. by* **S Asia.**

Rupanuga Vedic College, *(978-0-9650899; 978-0-9728372; 978-1-934405)* Div. of Iskcon Krishnafest, Inc., Orders Addr.: 5201 Paseo Blvd, Kansas City, MO 64110 USA Tel 224-558-8868; Edit Addr.: 5201 Paseo, Kansas City, MO 64110 USA Tel 816-924-5619; Fax: 816-924-5640
E-mail: eternityknowledgebliss@gmail.com; danavir.goswami@pamho.net
Web site: RVC.edu; DanavirGoswami.com; RVC.edu/RVC_BOOKS.html.

Rural Farm Productions, *(978-0-9753542)* 6538 Germanton Rd., Rural Hall, NC 27045 USA Tel 336-969-2202.

Rush, Ricki, *(978-0-9674292)* 123 Gregory Dr., Fairfax, CA 94930 USA Tel 415-457-6422; Fax: 415-456-4459
E-mail: rickicoach@aol.com
Web site: http://lifeworks-coaching.com.

Russell, Fred Publishing, *(978-0-9764347; 978-0-9789832; 978-0-9796229)* 52 Collis St., West Haven, CT 06516 USA Tel 203-934-2501; Fax: 203-934-8723; Toll Free: 866-968-7685; *Imprints:* Rock House Method, The (The Rock)
E-mail: jp@rockhousemethod.com
Web site: http://www.rockhousemethod.com
Dist(s): **Leonard, Hal Corp.**
Music Sales Corp.

Russet & Kensington Pr., *(978-1-940114)* 2066 Russet Dr. Suite 200, Troy, MI 48098 USA Tel 248-515-4247
E-mail: time4equilibrium@hotmail.com.

Russian Information & Business Center, Incorporated *See* **International Business Pubns., USA**

†Rutgers Univ. Pr., *(978-0-8135)* 106 Somerset St., Third Flr., New Brunswick, NJ 08901 USA (SAN 253-2115) Tel 848-445-7786
Web site: http://www.rutgersuniversitypress.org
Dist(s): **Ebsco Publishing**
Longleaf Services
MyiLibrary
ebrary, Inc.; *CIP.*

Ruth, A. Creations, *(978-0-9656306; 978-0-9907390)* 1860 Wynnewood Ln., Cincinnati, OH 45237 USA Tel 513-821-9027; Fax: 513-821-7762
E-mail: annieruth@fuse.net
Web site: http://www.annieruth.com.

Rutigliano, Joe, *(978-0-9767769)* 178 Ramona Ave., Staten Island, NY 10312-2717 USA.

Ruwanga Trading, *(978-0-9615102; 978-0-9701528)* P.O. Box 1027, Puunene, HI 96784 USA (SAN 694-2776)
Dist(s): **Booklines Hawaii, Ltd.**

Ruybal, Michael, *(978-0-9963959)* 4537 Azure Hills, Las Cruces, NM 88011 USA Tel 575-312-2581
E-mail: micru20@gmail.com.

RWP Bks. *Imprint of* **Redhawk Publishing**

Rx Humor, *(978-0-9639002; 978-1-892157)* 2272 Vistamont Dr., Decatur, GA 30033 USA Tel 404-321-0126; Fax: 404-633-9198
E-mail: nshulma@emory.edu.

Ryan Ave Publishing, *(978-0-9760759)* Div. of J. C. Melvin Seminars, Inc., 5738 Hedgeford Ct., Las Vegas, NV 89120 USA Tel 702-454-9822; Fax: 702-454-9821.

Ryan, Karlene Kay Author, *(978-0-9888843)* 5154 N. Woodson, Fresno, CA 93711 USA Tel 559-304-9737; Fax: 559-446-0565
E-mail: karleneryan@comcast.net
Web site: karleneryan.com
Dist(s): **Bookmasters Distribution.**

Ryan, Shirley, *(978-0-9754196)* 6480 Havenside Dr., Sacramento, CA 95831-1504 USA
E-mail: shirleyryanphd@gmail.com
Web site: http://www.shirleyryan.net.

Rye Grass Roots Publishing, *(978-0-9788713)* Orders Addr.: P.O. Box 291382, Port Orange, FL 32129-1382 USA (SAN 851-8289) Tel 386-212-1800
E-mail: jamesmhunt@ryegrassroots.com.

Ryherd, Tim Publishing, *(978-0-9749974)* 21479 FM 365, Beaumont, TX 77705 USA.

Ryland, John B. Publishing *See* **DJ Blues Publishing**

Ryland Peters & Small (GBR) *(978-1-84172; 978-1-900518; 978-1-872536; 978-1-903116; 978-1-904991; 978-1-84597; 978-1-906094; 978-1-906525; 978-1-907030; 978-1-84975; 978-1-907563; 978-0-9571409; 978-1-909313) Dist. by* **S and S Inc.**

Ryland Peters & Small (GBR) *(978-1-84172; 978-1-900518; 978-1-872536; 978-1-903116; 978-1-904991; 978-1-84597; 978-1-906094; 978-1-906525; 978-1-907030; 978-1-84975; 978-1-907563; 978-0-9571409; 978-1-909313) Dist. by* **WIPRO.**

Rymer Bks., *(978-0-934723; 978-0-9600792)* P.O. Box 153, Tollhouse, CA 93667-0153 USA (SAN 207-1010) Tel 209-298-8845.

Ryzewski, Deborah, *(978-0-9765302)* 240 Crabapple Ln., Valparaiso, IN 46383 USA.

R.Z. Enterprises of Florida, *(978-0-9792031)* 7640 Prospect Hill Cir., New Port Richey, FL 34654-6376 USA
Web site: http://www.RobertzHicks.com.

S & S Pr., *(978-0-615-14271-5; 978-0-615-14642-3; 978-0-615-14930-1; 978-0-615-14931-8; 978-0-615-14954-7)* 35221 SE Kinsey, Suite 101, Snoqualmie, WA 98065 USA
Web site: http://www.gloriabond.com
Dist(s): **Lulu Pr., Inc.**

SMS Cos., Inc., *(978-0-9669595)* P.O. Box 1184, Smyrna, GA 30081 USA Tel 678-339-0626; Fax: 678-339-0726
E-mail: JMBryant@bellsouth.net
Web site: http://www.smsbooks.com
Dist(s): **Follett School Solutions.**

S.O.C.O. Pubns., *(978-0-910119)* 276 Ward Rd., Mohawk, NY 13407 USA (SAN 241-5720) Tel 315-866-7445
E-mail: copress@borg.com.

S P I E-International Society for Optical Engineering *See* **SPIE**

S V E & Churchill Media, *(978-0-7932; 978-0-89290; 978-1-56357)* 6465 N. Avondale Ave., Chicago, IL 60631-1909 USA (SAN 208-3930) Toll Free Fax: 800-624-1678; Toll Free: 800-829-1900
E-mail: custserv@svemedia.com
Web site: http://www.svemedia.com
Dist(s): **Video Project, The**
Weston Woods Studios, Inc.

†SYDA Foundation, *(978-0-911307; 978-0-914602; 978-1-930939)* 371 Brickman Rd., South Fallsburg, NY 12779 USA (SAN 206-5649) Tel 845-434-2000 Toll Free Fax: 888-422-2339 (ordering); Toll Free: 888-422-3334 (ordering); P.O. Box 600, South Fallsburg, NY 12779
Web site: http://www.siddhayoga.org
Dist(s): **Bookpeople**
Independent Pubs. Group
New Leaf Distributing Co., Inc.; *CIP.*

S2 Services, *(978-0-9770928)* 9006 Friars Rd., Bethesda, MD 20817 USA (SAN 257-3377) Tel 301-493-4982
E-mail: socrtwo@s2services.com
Web site: http://www.socrtwo.info/portfolio.htm; http://people.lulu.com/users/index.php?fHomepage=179563; http://s2press.com
Dist(s): **CafePress.com**
Lulu Pr., Inc.

S.A. Kokinos (ESP) *(978-84-88342; 978-84-96629) Dist. by* **Lectorum Pubns.**

Sabeels Publishing, *(978-1-68376)* 40 E. Main St., Newark, DE 19711 USA Tel 902-457-9356
E-mail: isbn@speedy.partners.

Saberlee Bks., *(978-0-9815836; 978-0-9909606)* 171 N. Wilson Ave. Apt. 205, Pasadena CA, CA 91106 USA
E-mail: saberleebooks@yahoo.com
Web site: http://www.lisettebrodey.com; facebook.com/BrodeyAuthor.

Sable Creek Pr. LLC, *(978-0-9766823; 978-0-9828875; 978-0-9890667; 978-0-9974953; 978-0-9991157)*
E-mail: sablecreekpress@cox.net
Web site: http://www.sablecreekpress.com; http://www.sandrawaggoner.com; http://janetclarkshay.com.

Sabledrake Enterprises, *(978-0-9702189; 978-0-9771005; 978-0-9844032)* P.O. Box 30751, Seattle, WA 98113 USA Tel 425-317-9241; Fax: 772-673-2381
E-mail: tim@sabledrake.com
Web site: http://www.sabledrake.com.

Sabre Publishing Hse., Inc., *(978-0-9746213)* 201 Huff Lake Ct., Ortonville, MI 48462 USA Tel 248-627-1112; Fax: 248-627-1113
E-mail: mikeatsabre@aol.com.

Sabyr Pr., *(978-0-9746463)* 2999 Allmon Ln., Missouri Vly, IA 51555-5057 USA
E-mail: info@sabyr.com
Web site: http://www.sabyr.com.

Sachedina, Dr. Shenin Medical Education Products, *(978-0-9778648)* 2200 Glenwood Dr., Winter Park, FL 32792 USA (SAN 850-4377) Tel 407-740-5127
E-mail: Metuandlee@aol.com
Web site: http://www.metuandlee.com
Dist(s): **Bookmasters Distribution.**

Sacred Garden Fellowship, *(978-1-932746)* 333 Delaware Ave., Albany, NY 12208 USA Tel 802-363-5579
E-mail: sacredgf@gmail.com
Web site: www.sacredgardenfellowship.org.

Sacred Truth Publishing, *(978-1-58840)* Div. of Sacred Truth Ministries, Orders Addr.: P.O. Box 18, Mountain City, TN 37683 USA
E-mail: sacredtruthministries@mounet.com.

Saddle & Bridle, Inc., *(978-0-9655501)* 375 Jackson Ave., Saint Louis, MO 63130-4243 USA Tel 314-725-9115; Fax: 314-725-6440
E-mail: saddlebr@saddleandbridle.com
Web site: http://www.saddleandbridle.com.

Saddle Pal Creations, Inc., *(978-0-9663495; 978-1-931353)* Orders Addr.: P.O. Box 872127, Wasilla, AK 99687-2127 USA Tel 907-357-3235; Fax: 907-357-3446
Web site: http://www.alaskachildrensbooks.com
Dist(s): **Partners Bk. Distributing, Inc.**
Partners/West Book Distributors
Wizard Works.

Saddleback Educational Publishing *See* **Saddleback Educational Publishing, Inc.**

Saddleback Educational Publishing, Inc., *(978-1-56254; 978-1-59905; 978-1-60291; 978-1-61651; 978-1-61247; 978-1-62250; 978-1-62670; 978-1-63078; 978-1-68021)* 3120-A Pullman St., Costa Mesa, CA 92626-4564 USA (SAN 860-0902) Toll Free Fax: 888-734-4010; Toll Free: 800-637-8715
E-mail: contact@saddleback.com; amchugh@sdlback.com; cpizer@sdlback.com
Web site: http://www.saddlebackpublishing.com
Dist(s): **Findaway World, LLC**
Follett School Solutions
ebrary, Inc.

Sadie Bks., *(978-0-9816047; 978-0-615-55525-6; 978-0-615-74503-9)* 215 E. Camden Ave., H11, Moorestown, NJ 08057 USA (SAN 856-017X) Tel 856-234-2676; 856-313-0548
E-mail: info@sadie-books.com
Web site: http://www.sadie-books.com
Dist(s): **CreateSpace Independent Publishing Platform**
Dummy Record Do Not USE!!!!
Smashwords.

Sadlier *Imprint of* **Sadlier, William H. Inc.**

Sadlier, William H. Inc., *(978-0-8215; 978-0-87105; 978-1-4217)* 9 Pine St., New York, NY 10005-1002 USA (SAN 204-0948) Tel 212-227-2120; Fax: 212-267-8696; Toll Free: 800-221-5175; *Imprints:* Sadlier (Sadlier)
Web site: http://www.sadlier.com.

†SAE Intl., *(978-0-7680; 978-0-89883; 978-1-56091; 978-1-4686)* 400 Commonwealth Dr., Warrendale, PA 15096 USA (SAN 232-5721) Tel 724-776-4970; Fax: 724-776-0790
E-mail: customerservice@sae.org
Web site: http://www.sae.org; http://books.sae.org/; *CIP.*

Saeligstone, *(978-0-615-15984-3; 978-0-615-15985-0)* 13110 Moselle Forest, helotes, TX 78023 USA
E-mail: peirce1@saeligstone.com
Dist(s): **Lulu Pr., Inc.**

Safari, Ltd., *(978-1-881469)* Orders Addr.: P.O. Box 630685, Miami, FL 33163 USA Tel 305-621-1000; Fax: 305-621-6894; Toll Free: 800-554-5414; Edit Addr.: 1400 NW 159th St., Miami, FL 33169 USA
Web site: http://www.toydirectory.com.

Safari Pr., Inc., *(978-0-940143; 978-1-57157)* 15621 Chemical Ln., Suite B, Huntington Beach, CA 92649 USA (SAN 663-0723) Tel 714-894-9080; Fax: 714-894-4949; Toll Free: 800-451-4788 (orders only)
E-mail: info@safaripress.com
Web site: http://www.safaripress.com
Dist(s): **National Bk. Network.**

Safe Harbor Pubns., *(978-0-9760416)* P.O. Box 396, Titusville, FL 32781 USA
E-mail: admin@rikerbooks.com
Web site: http://www.rikerbooks.com.

Safeblade, Evelyn Collins, *(978-0-9670655)* W8504 Jellen Rd., Spooner, WI 54801 USA Tel 715-635-7536.

Safer Society Pr., *(978-1-884444; 978-1-940234)* Div. of Safer Society Foundation, Inc., Orders Addr.: P.O. Box 340, Brandon, VT 05733-0340 USA Tel 802-247-3132; Fax: 802-247-4233; Edit Addr.: 8-10 Conant Sq., Brandon, VT 05733-1121 USA
E-mail: Therearn@saver.net
Web site: http://www.safersociety.org.

Safety Always Matters, Inc., *(978-0-9620584; 978-1-883994)* 222 Wildwood Ct., Bloomingdale, IL 60108 USA (SAN 248-9759) Tel 630-894-1229
Dist(s): **Syndistar, Inc.**

Safeworld Publishing Co., *(978-0-9655604; 978-0-578-15130-4; 978-0-692-31823-2; 978-0-692-31827-0; 978-0-692-31835-5)* 3 Greenshire Ln., Owings Mills, MD 21117-4813 USA Tel 410-356-7233
E-mail: janisraf4@aol.com
Web site: www.declineandfallofallevil.org.

SAGA Press *Imprint of* **Simon & Schuster Bks. For Young Readers**

Sagaponack Bks., *(978-0-9668845; 978-0-9801336; 978-0-9983526; 978-0-9985673)* Orders Addr.: 101 South Walk Pl., Saint Augustine, FL 32086 USA Tel 904-429-7209
E-mail: fran@sagbooks.com
Web site: http://www.SagaponackBooks.com
Dist(s): **Follet Higher Education Grp**
Partners Bk. Distributing, Inc.

Sage, David, *(978-0-9894210)* 67 N. Piney PO Box 208, Story, WY 82842 USA Tel 303-883-4148
E-mail: davesageinstory@gmail.com.

Sage Hill Pubs., LLC, *(978-0-913205)* Orders Addr.: P.O. Box 866, Yerington, NV 89447 USA (SAN 283-0493) Tel 775-463-4188 (phone/fax)
E-mail: booksbysagehill@aol.com.

Sage Pr., *(978-0-9799972)* P.O. Box 981432, Park City, UT 84098 USA (SAN 854-9494) Tel 435-658-1238 Do not confuse with companies with similar name in Evergreen, CO, Phonenix, AZ, Murrieta, CA, Glenwood Springs, CO, San Diego, CA
E-mail: rudyandcoco@hotmail.com
Web site: http://www.rudyandcoco.com
Dist(s): **Itasca Bks.**

†SAGE Pubns., Inc., *(978-0-7619; 978-0-8039; 978-1-4129; 978-1-4522; 978-1-4462; 978-1-4833; 978-1-5063;*

Publisher Name Index

978-1-5443) 2455 Teller Rd., Thousand Oaks, CA 91360 USA (SAN 204-7217) Tel 800-818-7243; Fax: 800-583-2665; 805-499-0871
E-mail: info@sagepub.com; deborah.vaughn@sagepub.com
Web site: http://www.sagepub.com; http://www.sagepub.co.uk; http://www.pineforge.com; http://sagepub.com
Dist(s): **Ambassador Bks. & Media**
Coutts Information Services
Cranbury International
Ebsco Publishing
Emery-Pratt Co.
MBS Textbook Exchange, Inc.
Midwest Library Service
MyiLibrary
Blackwell
Yankee Bk. Peddler, Inc.
ebrary, Inc.
.; CIP.

SAGE Pubns., Ltd. (GBR) *(978-0-7619; 978-0-8039; 978-1-903300; 978-1-4129; 978-1-84445; 978-1-84641; 978-1-84860; 978-1-4462; 978-0-85725; 978-0-85702; 978-1-84787; 978-1-4739; 978-1-84920; 978-93-85985) Dist. by* **SAGE.**

Sagebrush Entertainment, Inc., *(978-0-9766557)* P.O. Box 261187, Encino, CA 91426-1187 USA Toll Free Fax: 800-881-4577; Toll Free: 800-711-4677
E-mail: info@hopalong.com
Web site: http://www.hopalong.com.

SageBrush Exchange, *(978-0-9762728)* P.O. Box 525, Buckner, MO 64016 USA Tel 816-305-6916
E-mail: toby@sagebrushexchange.com
Web site: http://www.prairielabyrinth.com; http://www.chakralabyrinth.com.

Sager Group, The, *(978-0-9881785; 978-0-9895241; 978-0-9916629; 978-0-9862679; 978-0-9964901; 978-0-9980793)* 5996 La Jolla Corona Dr, La Jolla, CA 92037 USA Tel 619-218-2109
E-mail: info@mikesager.com
Web site: www.TheSagerGroup.net.

Saint Andrew Pr., Ltd. (GBR) *(978-0-7152; 978-0-86153) Dist. by* **Westminster John Knox.**

Saint Anthony Messenger Press & Franciscan Communications *See* **Franciscan Media**

St. Augustine Pr., *(978-0-9819634)* 809 Copperhead Cir., St. Augustine, FL 32092 USA
Dist(s): **Chicago Distribution Ctr.**

St. Augustine's Pr., Inc., *(978-1-890318; 978-1-58731)* P.O. Box 2285, South Bend, IN 46680 USA Tel 574-291-3500; Fax: 574-291-3700; Toll Free: 888-997-4994
E-mail: bruce@staugustine.net
Web site: http://www.staugustine.net
Dist(s): **Chicago Distribution Ctr.**
Univ. of Chicago Pr.

St. Bob Pr., *(978-0-9796988)* 2095 Poplar Ave., Suite 54, Memphis, TN 38104 USA (SAN 854-1523) Tel 901-412-7362
E-mail: murff@saintbobpress.com
Web site: http://www.saintbobpress.com.

St. Clair Pubns., *(978-0-9801704; 978-0-9826302; 978-1-935786; 978-1-947514)* P.O. Box 727, Mc Minnville, TN 37111-0726 USA Tel 931-668-2860; Fax: 931-668-2861; Toll Free: 888-248-0192
E-mail: stan@stclair.net
Web site: http://stan.stclair.net/StClairPublications.html#books.

St. Clair Publishing, *(978-0-615-17629-1)* 3103 Fleece Flower, Austin, TX 78735 USA
Web site: http://www.richardshenderson.com.

Saint Mary's Press *See* **St. Mary's Pr. of MN**

St. Mary's Pr. of MN, *(978-0-88489; 978-1-59982; 978-1-64121)* 702 Terrace Heights, Winona, MN 55987-1320 USA (SAN 203-073X) Tel 507-457-7900; Fax: 507-457-7990; Toll Free Fax: 800-344-9225; Toll Free: 800-533-8095
E-mail: smpress@smp.org; hwilliams@smp.org
Web site: http://www.smp.org.

St. Nectarios Pr., *(978-0-913026)* 10300 Ashworth Ave., N., Seattle, WA 98133-9410 USA (SAN 203-3542) Tel 206-522-4471; Fax: 206-523-0550; Toll Free: 800-643-4233
E-mail: orders@stnectariospress.com; anneborozan@live.com
Web site: http://www.stnectariospress.com.

St. Nicholas Monastery, *(978-0-9773579)* 1340 Piney Rd., North Fort Myers, FL 33903-3822 USA.

Saint Paul Books & Media *See* **Pauline Bks. & Media**

Saint Paul Brotherhood, *(978-0-9721698; 978-0-9800065; 978-1-940661)* Div. of Coptic Orthodox Church - Diocese of Los Angeles, P.O. Box 4467, Diamond Bar, CA 91765 USA
E-mail: theophiluspaul@lacopts.org
Web site: http://www.lacopts.org.

St. Vincent Archabbey Pubns., *(978-0-9708216; 978-0-9773909; 978-0-9906855)* 300 Fraser Purchase Rd., Latrobe, PA 15650-2690 USA Tel 724-805-2601; Fax: 724-805-2775
E-mail: kim.metzgar@email.stvincent.edu
Web site: http://www.stvincentstore.com
Dist(s): **Distributors, The.**

St. Vincent College Ctr. for Northern Appalachian Studies, *(978-1-885851)* 300 Fraser Purchase Rd., Latrobe, PA 15650 USA Tel 724-805-2316; Fax: 724-537-4554
E-mail: rwissolik@stvincent.edu
Web site: http://www.stvincent.edu/napp.

†St. Vladimir's Seminary Pr., *(978-0-88141; 978-0-913836; 978-0-9618545; 978-0-9622536; 978-1-879038; 978-1-891295)* 575 Scarsdale Rd., Yonkers, NY 10707 USA (SAN 204-6296) Tel 914-961-8313 x 348; Fax: 914-961-5456 Bookstore fax; 914-961-4507 Press fax; Toll Free: 800-204-2665 Bookstore
E-mail: benedict@svots.edu; ghatrak@svots.edu
Web site: http://www.svspress.com; *CIP.*

Saints Of Glory Church, *(978-0-9673342)* Orders Addr.: P.O. Box 8957, Anaheim, CA 92812-0957 USA Tel 714-846-0401; Fax: 714-846-3395; Edit Addr.: 16102 Warmington Ln., Huntington Beach, CA 92649 USA
E-mail: sgcgow@aol.com.

Sakthi Bks., Inc., *(978-0-9752586)* Orders Addr.: 1507 Lone Oak Cir., Fairfield, IA 52556 USA
E-mail: pradheepkumar@hotmail.com
Web site: http://www.matrixjourney.com; http://www.rightawareness.com.

Sakura Pr., *(978-0-9660583)* Hesta Roach 227 Croatan Dr., Oriental, NC 28571 USA Tel 252-249-1929 (phone/fax) Do not confuse with Sakura Pr., Pleasant Hill, OR
E-mail: roachdj@hotmail.com.

Salaam Reads *Imprint of* **Simon & Schuster Bks. For Young Readers**

Salado Pr., LLC, *(978-0-9663870; 978-0-9835342; 978-0-9913118)* Orders Addr.: P.O. Box 470171, Fort Worth, TX 76147 USA Tel 972-215-6116
E-mail: lee@saladopress.com
Web site: http://www.saladopress.com.

Salani (ITA) *(978-88-7782; 978-88-8451) Dist. by* **Distribks Inc.**

Salaud Publishing, *(978-0-9713167)* P.O. Box 11681, Portland, OR 97211 USA Tel 919-963-9135
E-mail: jesse@hastardrecords.com; jesse@bastardrecords.com; jordan_lari@highcountrystudentpublishers.org
Web site: http://www.highcountrystudentpublishers.org; http://www.bastardrecords.com/salaud.htm.

Salch, Megan F., *(978-0-9776154)* 3106 Lawrence St., Houston, TX 77018 USA Tel 713-864-1344.

Salem Academy & College, *(978-0-9789608)* P.O. Box 10548, Winston-Salem, NC 27108 USA
Web site: http://www.salem.edu.

Salem Author Services, *(978-1-931232; 978-1-59160; 978-0-9723806; 978-0-9740030; 978-1-59467; 978-0-9744668; 978-0-9754803; 978-1-59781; 978-0-9764981; 978-0-9769668; 978-1-60034; 978-1-934248; 978-1-60266; 978-0-9798246; 978-0-9798467; 978-1-60477; 978-0-9799120; 978-1-934937; 978-1-934938; 978-0-9802455; 978-0-9802456; 978-1-60647; 978-1-935097; 978-1-935098; 978-1-935204; 978-0-9820938; 978-1-60791; 978-1-935456; 978-1-61579; 978-1-936107; 978-1-936183; 978-0-9841965; 978-1-936198; 978-1-60957; 978-1-936400; 9) Div. of Salem Media Group, 2301 Lucien Way, Suite 415, Maitland, FL 32751 USA Tel 407-339-4217; Fax: 407-339-9898; Toll Free: 866-381-2665; Imprints:* Mill City Press, Inc (Mill City); North Loop Press (MYID_T_NORTH L)
E-mail: sscott@christianpublishing.com; cclark@christianpublishing.com
Web site: http://www.salemauthorservices.com/
Dist(s): **INscribe Digital**
Itasca Bks.
eBookit.com.

†Salem Pr., Inc., *(978-0-89356; 978-1-58765)* Div. of EBSCO Publishing, Orders Addr.: 10 Estes St, IPSWICH, MA 01938 USA (SAN 241-841X) Tel 800-758-5995; Fax: 201-968-1411; Toll Free: 800-221-1592; *Imprints:* Magill's Choice (Magills Choice)
E-mail: csr@salempress.com
Web site: http://www.salempress.com; http://salempress.com/Store/pages/hwwilson.htm
Dist(s): **Ebsco Publishing**
Grey Hse. Publishing
MyiLibrary
ebrary, Inc.; *CIP.*

Salem Publishing Solutions, Incorporated *See* **Salem Author Services**

Salem Ridge Press LLC, *(978-0-9776786; 978-1-934671)* 4263 Salem Dr., Emmaus, PA 18049 USA
E-mail: customerservice@slaemridgepress.com.

Sales Effectiveness, Inc., *(978-0-9676255)* 570 W. Crossville Rd., Suite 103, Roswell, GA 30075 USA Tel 770-552-6612; Fax: 770-643-8205
E-mail: info@saleseffectiveness.com
Web site: http://www.saleseffectiveness.com.

Salih, Sara *See* **Harlan Rose Publishing**

Salina Bookshelf *See* **Salina Bookshelf Inc**

Salina Bookshelf Inc, *(978-0-9644189; 978-1-893354)* 1120 W. University Ave, Ste. 102, Flagstaff, AZ 86001 USA (SAN 253-0503) Tel 928-527-0070; Fax: 928-526-0386; Toll Free: 877-527-0070
E-mail: elockard@salinabookshelf.com
Web site: http://www.salinabookshelf.com.

Salish Kootenia College Pr., *(978-1-934594)* Orders Addr.: P.O. Box 70, Pablo, MT 59855 USA Tel 406-275-4882; Fax: 406-275-4801; Edit Addr.: 52000 Hwy.93, Pablo, MT 59855 USA
E-mail: bob-bigant@skc.edu
Dist(s): **Stoneydale Pr. Publishing Co.**
Univ. of Nebraska Pr.

Sally Ride Science, *(978-0-9753920; 978-1-933798; 978-1-940073; 978-1-941094)* 9191 Towne Centre Dr. Ste. L101, San Diego, CA 92122-6204 USA Tel 858-638-1432; Fax: 858-638-1419; Toll Free: 800-561-5161
E-mail: tam@sallyridescience.com; bleck@sallyridescience.com
Web site: http://www.sallyridescience.com.

Salmon Hole Poetry Press *See* **Minimal Pr., The**

Salmon Publishing (IRL) *(978-0-948339; 978-1-897648; 978-1-903392; 978-1-910669) Dist. by* **Dufour.**

Salmon Run Pr., *(978-0-9634000; 978-1-887573)* Orders Addr.: P.O. Box 672130, Chugiak, AK 99567-2130 USA Tel 907-688-4268
E-mail: salmonrp@aol.com
Dist(s): **Partners/West Book Distributors**
SPD-Small Pr. Distribution
Todd Communications
Wizard Works.

Salmon Run Publishing Company *See* **Salmon Run Pr.**

Salt City Books, *(978-0-9776332)* P.O. Box 6, Farmington, UT 84025-0006 USA (SAN 257-8522) Tel 801-309-7820; Fax: 801-485-2654
E-mail: saltcitybooks@msn.com.

Salt City Systems *See* **Salt Pubs.**

Salt of the Earth Pr., *(978-0-9816949; 978-0-9849183)* W. 4456 Hwy. 63, Springbrook, WI 54875 USA (SAN 856-2555) Fax: 715-318-6417
Web site: http://www.saltpress.com.

Salt Pubs., *(978-0-9709940; 978-0-9725804)* 6163 E. Molloy Rd., East Syracuse, NY 13057 USA Tel 315-437-1139; Fax: 315-463-2055; Toll Free: 800-324-2607
E-mail: salt@twcny.rr.com.

Salt Publishing (GBR) *(978-1-876857; 978-1-901994; 978-1-84471; 978-1-907773; 978-1-78463) Dist. by* **SPD-Small Pr Dist.**

SaltRiver *Imprint of* **Tyndale Hse. Pubs.**

Salty Dog, Inc., The, *(978-0-9793560)* Orders Addr.: a/o Mark Yarbrough, The Salty Dog Inc., 69 Arrow Rd., Hilton Head Island, SC 29928-2992 USA (SAN 853-2338)
Web site: http://www.saltydog.com.

Salty Pond Pubs., *(978-0-615-45705-5; 978-0-615-56089-2)* 10 Edward Kelly Rd., East Sandwich, MA 02537 USA Tel 781-715-5014; Fax: 508-833-8923
E-mail: jglinehan@comcast.net.

Salty Sea Publishing, *(978-0-692-78475-4)* 2400 NE 99th St., Vancouver, WA 98665 USA Tel 503-929-6941
E-mail: katebeeman@gmail.com
Web site: http://katebeeman.website.

Salvation Army, *(978-0-89216)* 440 W. Nyack Rd., West Nyack, NY 10994 USA (SAN 237-2649) Tel 845-620-7200 Do not confuse with Salvation Army Supplies, Southern, Des Plaines, IL (Southern Territory) or Salvation Army Supplies & Purchasing Dept., Des Plaines, IL or Salvation Army, Des Plaines, IL
Dist(s): **Bookmasters Distribution.**

Salvo Pr. *Imprint of* **Start Publishing LLC**

Saman Publishing, *(978-0-9728020)* 751 Lemonwood Ct., San Jose, CA 95120 USA.

Samantha's Stories Inc. *See* **Samantha's Stories Inc.**

Samantha's Stories Inc, *(978-1-5136-1171-6)* 115 G st spc 14, arcata, CA 95521 USA Tel 707-999-7334
Web site: http://samanthastories.us; http://weilandenglishtutor.com
Dist(s): **CreateSpace Independent Publishing Platform.**

Samara Pr., *(978-0-9577556)* c/o Trillium Hse., 241 Bonita, Los Trancos Woods, Portola Valley, CA 94028-8103 USA Tel 650-851-1847.

Sambodh Society, Inc., The, *(978-0-9785969)* 6363 N 24th St., Kalamazoo, MI 49004 USA (SAN 851-0849)
Web site: http://www.sambodh.us.

Samhain Publishing, LTD, *(978-1-59998; 978-1-60504; 978-1-60928; 978-1-61921; 978-1-61922; 978-1-61923; 978-1-5139; 978-1-61923-400-0; 978-1-61923-300-3)* Orders Addr.: 11821 Mason Montgomery Rd. 4B, Cincinnati, OH 45249 USA; Edit Addr.: 11821 Mason Montgomery Rd. Suite 4b, Cincinnati, OH 45249 USA (SAN 257-7488) Tel 513-453-4688; Fax: 513-583-0191
E-mail: contracts@samhainpublishing.com
Web site: http://www.samhainpublishing.com.

Samizdat Express, *(978-0-915232; 978-0-931968; 978-1-4553; 978-1-4554)* 33 Gould St., West Roxbury, MA 02132 USA (SAN 207-1037) Tel 617-469-2269
E-mail: seltzer@samizdat.com
Web site: http://www.samizdat.com/; http://store.yahoo.com/samizdat
Dist(s): **Smashwords.**

Sams, II, Carl R. Photography, Inc., *(978-0-9671748; 978-0-9770108; 978-0-9827625; 978-0-9989836)* 361 Whispering Pines, Milford, MI 48380-3807 USA (SAN 859-435X) Tel 248-685-2422; Fax: 248-685-1643; Toll Free: 800-552-1867
E-mail: carlsams@carlsams.com
Web site: http://www.carlsams.com; http://www.strangerinthewoods.com
Dist(s): **Follett School Solutions**
Partners Bk. Distributing, Inc.

San Diego Business Accounting Solutions a Non CPA Firm, *(978-0-9746093; 978-0-9794124)* Subs. of SDBAS Publishing, Orders Addr.: P.O. Box 7275, Loveland, CO 80537 USA Tel 970-776-8395; Fax: 970-692-2492
E-mail: julieaydlott@gmail.com
Web site: http://www.sdbas.biz; http://www.businessbudgetinghelp.com; http://www.messages-from-beyond.com
Dist(s): **Emery-Pratt Co.**
Midwest Library Service.

San Diego County Regional Airport Authority, *(978-0-9745294)* P.O. Box 82776, San Diego, CA 92138-2776 USA Tel 619-400-2400; Fax: 619-400-2866
Web site: http://www.san.org.

San Diego Museum of Man, *(978-0-937808)* 1350 El Prado, Balboa Pk., San Diego, CA 92101-1616 USA Tel 619-239-2001; Fax: 619-239-2749
E-mail: khedges@museumofman.org
Web site: http://www.museumofman.org
Dist(s): **Casemate Academic.**

San Francisco Art Commission, The, *(978-1-888048)* 800 Chestnut St., San Francisco, CA 94133 USA Tel 415-771-7020; Fax: 415-252-2595; *Imprints:* WritersCorps Books (WrtrsCorps Bks)
Dist(s): **SPD-Small Pr. Distribution.**

San Francisco Story Works, *(978-0-9774227)* 386 Union St., San Francisco, CA 94133-3516 USA (SAN 257-5248)
Web site: http://www.pengey.com.

San Francisco Study Ctr., *(978-0-936434; 978-1-888956)* 1663 Mission St. Suite310, San Francisco, CA 94103 USA (SAN 214-4654) Tel 415-626-1650; Fax: 415-626-7276; Toll Free: 888-281-3757; *Imprints:* Study Center Press (Study Ctr Pr)
E-mail: marjorie@studycenter.org
Web site: http://www.studycenter.org
Dist(s): **Parent Services Project.**

San Juan Publishing, *(978-0-9707399; 978-0-9858897)* Orders Addr.: P.O. Box 923, Woodinville, WA 98072 USA
E-mail: sanjuanbooks@yahoo.com
Dist(s): **Partners Bk. Distributing, Inc.**

San Val, Incorporated *See* **Turtleback Bks.**

Sananda Publications *See* **Reverence for Life**

Sancho Storybooks *See* **Joseph Pubns.**

Sanctuary Bks., *(978-0-9753334)* P.O. Box 1623, New York, NY 10028 USA Do not confuse with companies with the same or similar name in Mount Juliet, TN, Tampa, FL
E-mail: sanctuarybooks@earthlink.net
Web site: http://www.sanctuarybks.com.

Sanctuary Publishing, Inc., *(978-0-9746995; 978-0-9785334; 978-0-9843754; 978-0-9830018; 978-0-9840392)* 40 Red Butte Rd., Sedona, AZ 86351-7765 USA (SAN 920-1122) Tel 928-284-2269; 928-284-1154; Fax: 928-284-4782
Web site: http://www.SanctuaryPublications.com
Dist(s): **MyiLibrary.**

Sanctuary Publishing, Ltd. (GBR) *(978-1-86074; 978-1-898141) Dist. by* **H Leonard.**

Sand Dreams Pr., LLC, *(978-0-9798656)* P.O. Box 24, Whitehouse Station, NJ 08889-0024 USA (SAN 854-6134) Tel 908-256-4834
E-mail: imre@sanddreamspress.com
Web site: http://www.sanddreamspress.com.

Sand Sage Pr., *(978-0-9793474)* Orders Addr.: P.O. Box 60812, Canyon, TX 79016 USA (SAN 853-1935) Toll Free: 888-655-0875 (phone/fax)
E-mail: psallison@earthlink.net
Web site: http://www.SandSagePress.com.

Sandbox Bks., *(978-0-9755184)* 6561 Portage Rd., DeForest, WI 53532-0000 USA
Web site: http://www.sandboxbooks.com.

Sandbox Publishing, *(978-0-692-59788-0)* 4818 Jumano Ave., San Diego, CA 92117 USA Tel 858-437-1416
Dist(s): **CreateSpace Independent Publishing Platform**
Midpoint Trade Bks., Inc.

Sandbridge Sons Publishing, *(978-0-9796039)* 2577 Sandpiper Rd., Virginia Beach, VA 23456 USA.

SandCastle *Imprint of* **ABDO Publishing Co.**

Sandcastle Publishing, *(978-0-9627756; 978-1-883995)* Orders Addr.: P.O. Box 3070, South Pasadena, CA 91031-6070 USA Fax: 323-255-3616; Edit Addr.: 1723 Hill Dr., South Pasadena, CA 91030 USA Tel 213-255-3616 Do not confuse with Sandcastle Publishing, Orleans, MA
E-mail: info@sandcastle-online.com; rwhatley@sandcastle-online.com
Web site: http://www.sandcastle-online.com
Dist(s): **Quality Bks., Inc.**
Unique Bks., Inc.

†Sandlapper Publishing Co., Inc., *(978-0-87844)* Orders Addr.: P.O. Box 730, Orangeburg, SC 29115 USA (SAN 203-2678) Toll Free Fax: 800-337-9420 (orders); Toll Free: 800-849-7263 (orders); Edit Addr.: 1281 Amelia St., NE., Orangeburg, SC 29116 USA Tel 803-533-1658; Fax: 803-534-5223
E-mail: agallman1@bellsouth.net
Web site: http://www.sandlapperpublishing.com
Dist(s): **Follet Higher Education Grp;** *CIP.*

Sandner-Petersen International Bks., *(978-0-9744852)* 5112 Coronado Pkwy., No.11, Cape Coral, FL 33904 USA Tel 739-549-3028; Fax: 239-549-5547.

Sandpiper *Imprint of* **Houghton Mifflin Harcourt Trade & Reference Pubs.**

Sandramantos Publishing, *(978-0-9887848)* 1550 Alpine Trail, San Marcos, TX 78666 USA Tel 512-462-9670
E-mail: manager@Sandramantos.com
Web site: http://princessapril.com.

Sands, Monty, *(978-0-9788038; 978-0-615-25788-4; 978-0-578-15474-9)* P.O. Box 6463, Visalia, CA 93291 USA
E-mail: monger15@juno.com; montysands@yahoo.com.

S&S Publishing LLC, *(978-0-9794710)* 1609 Dublin Dr., Silver Spring, MD 20902 USA Tel 301-681-8729
E-mail: xsalinas21@gmail.com.

Sandvik Innovations, LLC, *(978-1-932915; 978-1-935868)* 460 E. Swedesford Rd., Suite 2030, Wayne, PA 19087 USA Tel 610-975-3585; Fax: 610-975-3587
Web site: http://www.sandvikinnovations.com.

Sandvik Publishing, *(978-1-58048; 978-1-881445)* Div. of Sandviks Bokforlag, Norway, 3729 Knights Rd., Bensalem, PA 19020-2908 USA Toll Free: 800-843-2445
E-mail: Nicole@sandvikpublishing.com; cust-serv@sandvikpublishing.com
Web site: http://www.sandviks.com.

Sandy Bay Publishing, *(978-0-9701285)* Orders Addr.: P.O. Box 580, Hatteras, NC 27943-0580 USA Tel 252-986-2195; Fax: 252-986-2372; Edit Addr.: 56187 Pamlico Dr., Hatteras, NC 27973-0580 USA Tel 252-986-2195
E-mail: joannewhale@earthlink.net.

Sandy Putter Pr., *(978-0-578-05153-6)* 9 Meadowview Rd., Asheville, NC 28804 USA.

SangFroid Pr., *(978-0-917939)* 34 Water St., Excelsior, MN 55331 USA (SAN 657-0178) Tel 952-474-6220; Fax: 952-474-6221 Do not confuse with Sang Froid in New York, NY
Dist(s): **Independent Pubs. Group.**

Sanitaryum, *(978-0-9983352)* 414 Terr. Cir., Lamesa, TX 79331 USA Tel 505-362-6990; *Imprints:* Bookify by Sanitaryum (MYID_R_BKIFY B)
E-mail: nathantafoya@gmail.com
Web site: http://sanitaryum.com/bookify-publishing/; www.sanitaryum.com.

Sankofa Bks. *Imprint of* **Just Us Bks., Inc.**

Sankofa Pr., *(978-0-9654009)* Orders Addr.: P.O. Box 3144, Jacksonville, FL 32206 USA Tel 904-355-0126 (phone/fax); Edit Addr.: 239 W. 40th St., Jacksonville, FL 32206 USA
E-mail: sankofa@leading.net
Web site: http://www.users.southeast.net/~sankofa.

Sankofa Productions *See* **Sankofa Pr.**

SanPaul Group, LLC, The, *(978-0-9670875)* 209 Josephine St., Detroit, MI 48202-1811 USA (SAN 253-6013)
E-mail: gtpspg@cs.com
Web site: http://www.qtpieworld.com.

Sanpitch Pr., *(978-0-9760607)* 141 S. Main, Manti, UT 84642 USA Tel 435-835-6271; Fax: 435-835-8431; Toll Free: 800-748-4660
E-mail: sanman@horseshoetrader.com.

Santa Ana River Pr., *(978-0-9747638)* P.O. Box 5473, Norco, CA 92860 USA (SAN 255-7568)
E-mail: admin@santaanariverpress.com
Web site: http://www.santaanariverpress.com
Dist(s): **Sunbelt Pubns., Inc.**

Santa Fe Writers Project, *(978-0-9776799; 978-0-9819661; 978-0-9882252; 978-1-939650)* No. 350, 369 Montezuma Ave., Santa Fe, NM 87501 USA (SAN 257-9588)
E-mail: agifford@sfwp.com
Web site: http://www.sfwp.com
Dist(s): **Ebsco Publishing**
Independent Pubs. Group
MyiLibrary
ebrary, Inc.

Santa Monica Pr., *(978-0-9639946; 978-1-891661; 978-1-59580)* Orders Addr.: P.O. Box 1076, Santa Monica, CA 90406 USA (SAN 298-1459) Tel 310-230-7759; Fax: 310-230-7761; Toll Free: 800-784-9553; Edit Addr.: 513 Wilshire Blvd., No. 321, Santa Monica, CA 90401 USA
E-mail: books@santamonicapress.com
Web site: http://www.santamonicapress.com
Dist(s): **Ebsco Publishing**
Independent Pubs. Group
Legato Pubs. Group
MyiLibrary
Perseus Bks. Group
ebrary, Inc.

Santacroce, John, *(978-0-615-76887-8; 978-0-9899916)* 2066 Rivers Edge Dr., Rio Rancho, NM 87144 USA Tel 505-450-7096
E-mail: johnpsantacroce@gmail.com.

Santiago, Claribel, *(978-0-9744726)* P.O. Box 25345, Tamarac, FL 33320 USA
E-mail: claribel_santiago@hotmail.com
Web site: http://www.claribelsantiago.com.

Santillana (COL) *(978-958-24) Dist. by* **Santillana.**

Santillana *Imprint of* **Santillana USA Publishing Co., Inc.**

Santillana Ecuador (ECU) *(978-9978-07; 978-9942-05; 978-9942-19; 978-9978-29) Dist. by* **Santillana.**

Santillana Ediciones Generales, S.A. de C.V. (MEX) *(978-607-11; 978-607-01) Dist. by* **Santillana.**

Santillana, Editorial, S.A. de C.V. (MEX) *(978-970-29; 978-968-430; 978-970-642) Dist. by* **Santillana.**

Santillana S. A. (URY) *(978-9974-590; 978-9974-671) Dist. by* **Santillana.**

Santillana USA Publishing Co., Inc., *(978-0-88272; 978-1-56014; 978-1-58105; 978-1-58986; 978-1-59437; 978-1-59820; 978-1-60396; 978-1-61605; 978-1-61435; 978-1-62263; 978-1-63113; 978-1-68292; 978-1-64101)* Div. of Grupo Santillana, 2023 NW 84th Ave., Doral, FL 33122 USA (SAN 205-1133) Tel 305-591-9522 Toll Free Fax: 888-248-9518 (orders); Toll Free: 800-245-8584; Av. Rio Mixcoac No. 274 Col. Acacias, C.P. 0324 Benito Juarez, Ciudad de Mexico, DF,; *Imprints:* Santillana (Santillana Imprint); Richmond (Richmond); Alfaguara (Alfaguara); Punto de Lectura (Punto de Lectura); Alfaguara Juvenil (AlfaguaraJuv); Loqueleo (Loqueleo)
E-mail: dpena@santillanausa.com; esanta@santillanausa.com; customerservice@santillanausa.com
Web site: http://www.santillanausa.com
Dist(s): **Barnes & Noble, Inc.**
Bilingual Pubns. Co., The
Continental Bk. Co., Inc.
CreateSpace Independent Publishing Platform
EMC/Paradigm Publishing
Follett School Solutions
Lectorum Pubns., Inc.
Libros Sin Fronteras
Two Rivers Distribution.

Santoon Bks., *(978-0-9744905)* 13533 1/2 Village Dr., Cerritos, CA 90703 USA Tel 562-926-3361; Fax: 562-802-7680
E-mail: santoon@santoon.com.

Santoon Productions, Incorporated *See* **Santoon Bks.**

Sapient Business Solutions *See* **Herobrine Publishing**

Sapphire Bks. Publishing, *(978-0-9828608; 978-1-939062; 978-1-943353)* P.O. Box 8142, Salinas, CA 93912 USA Tel 831-998-7145
E-mail: publisher@sapphirebooks.com; info@sapphirebooks.com
Web site: http://www.sapphirebooks.com.

Saqi Bks. (GBR) *(978-0-86356; 978-1-908906) Dist. by* **Consort Bk Sales.**

Sara Anderson Children's Bks., *(978-0-9702784; 978-0-9911933; 978-1-943459)* 1522 Post Alley No. 206, Seattle, WA 98101 USA Tel 206-285-1520
E-mail: sara@saranderson.com
Web site: http://www.saranderson.com/
Dist(s): **BWI.**

Saraband (Scotland) Ltd. (GBR) *(978-1-887354; 978-1-908643; 978-1-910192) Dist. by* **IPG Chicago.**

Sarah & David LLC, *(978-0-9761648; 978-0-9796785)* P.O. Box 5894, Englewood, NJ 07631-5894 USA Fax: 201-221-7879
Web site: http://www.sarahdavid.com.

SarahRose Children's Bks. *Imprint of* **SarahRose Publishing**

SarahRose Publishing, *(978-0-9745865)* Orders Addr.: 1220 Wing Point Way NE, Bainbridge Island, WA 98110 USA Tel 253-232-9561; Edit Addr.: 1220 Wing Point Way NE, Bainbridge Island, WA 98110 USA Tel 253-232-9561; *Imprints:* SarahRose Children's Books (SarahRose Child Bks)
E-mail: melodycurtiss@gmail.com
Web site: http://www.melodycurtiss.com; http://sarahrosepublishing.tumblr.com.

Sarah's Daughters Publishing *See* **Fidelity Heart Publishing**

Sarajames Poetry, Inc., *(978-0-9767395)* 88 Lawrence Ave., Brooklyn, NY 11230 USA Tel 718-972-2944
E-mail: jamestronan@yahoo.com.

Saranghay Studios, *(978-0-9887068)* 9 Brookside Dr., Foxboro, MA 02035 USA Tel 617-475-0563
E-mail: ray@saranghaystudios.com
Web site: www.saranghaystudios.com.

Saranjon Publishing, *(978-0-9665282)* Orders Addr.: P.O. Box 980, Homer, AK 99603-0980 USA Tel 907-235-8200; Fax: 907-235-8699; Edit Addr.: 385 E. Fairview St., Homer, AK 99603-0980 USA
E-mail: saranjon@alaska.net
Dist(s): **Wizard Works.**

Sarvis, Barbara, *(978-0-9831346)* 10 Northgate Dr., Ponte Vedra Beach, FL 32082 USA Tel 904-285-2196
E-mail: barbarasarvis@aol.com.

Saseen, Sharon, *(978-0-9748425)* 403 E. 46th St., Savannah, GA 31405 USA Tel 912-233-1341
E-mail: saseenart@aol.com
Web site: http://www.saseen.com.

Sasquatch Bks., *(978-0-912365; 978-1-57061; 978-0-9821188; 978-1-63217)* 1904 Third Avenue, Suite 710, Seattle, WA 98101 USA (SAN 289-0208) Toll Free: 800-775-0817; *Imprints:* Little Bigfoot (Little Bigfoot)
E-mail: custserv@SasquatchBooks.com
Web site: http://www.sasquatchbooks.com
Dist(s): **MyiLibrary**
Penguin Random Hse. LLC
Random Hse., Inc.

Sasscer, Abby, *(978-0-9854729)* 158 Nazareth Dr., Fort Valley, VA 22652 USA Tel 540-933-6496
E-mail: projectnazareth@yahoo.com.

Satellite Studio, *(978-0-9743968)* P.O. Box 32457, Knoxville, TN 37930-2457 USA Tel 865-691-1450; Fax: 865-691-2464
E-mail: dwilson@dannywilson.com.

Satin Finish Publishing, *(978-0-9764930; 978-0-9800209)* P.O. Box 481351, Kansas City, MO 64131 USA
E-mail: slfoster0826@kc.rr.com.

Satin Sheet Memoirs Publishing *See* **Nowata Press Publishing Consultants**

Saturn International, *(978-0-9764957)* 126 Herricks Rd., Mineola, NY 11501 USA Fax: 516-214-0154.

Satya Hse. Pubns., *(978-0-9729191; 978-0-9818720; 978-1-935874)* Orders Addr.: 22 Turkey St., Hardwick, MA 01037 USA; Edit Addr.: P.O. Box 122, Hardwick, MA 01037 USA Tel 413-477-8743
E-mail: julie@satyahouse.com
Web site: http://www.satyahouse.com; http://www.iseethesunbooks.com
Dist(s): **Midpoint Trade Bks., Inc.**
OverDrive, Inc.
Smashwords.

Sauerlander AG (CHE) *(978-3-7941) Dist. by* **Distribks Inc.**

Sauls, Lynn, *(978-0-615-74910-5; 978-0-615-78903-3; 978-0-9893216)* 14 Alexander St., Alexandria, VA 22314 USA Tel 703-549-5799
E-mail: lynnbsauls@aol.com.

Saunders Bk. Co. (CAN) *(978-1-895058; 978-1-897563; 978-1-926660; 978-1-926722; 978-1-926853; 978-1-77092; 978-1-77308) Dist. by* **Creative Co.**

Saunders Bk. Co. (CAN) *(978-1-895058; 978-1-897563; 978-1-926660; 978-1-926722; 978-1-926853; 978-1-77092; 978-1-77308) Dist. by* **RiverStream.**

Saur, Gregory, *(978-0-9964245; 978-0-692-80648-7)* 711 Old Wormley Creek Rd., Yorktown, VA 23692 USA Tel 757-898-1524
E-mail: imalepton@hotmail.com.

Sauvignon Pr., *(978-0-9889618)* 1459 Brookcliff Dr., Marietta, GA 30062 USA Tel 404-435-6507
E-mail: rewrites1@gmail.com.

Savage Books *See* **Blue Thunder Bks.**

Savage Pr., *(978-1-886028; 978-1-937706)* 14172 E Carlson Rd, Brule, WI 54820 USA Tel 218-391-3070 (phone/fax); 14172 E Carlson Rd., Brule, WI 54820 Tel 218-391-3070
E-mail: mail@savpress.com
Web site: http://www.savpress.com
Dist(s): **Baker & Taylor Bks.**
Partners Bk. Distributing, Inc.

Savanna Pr., *(978-0-9759440)* Orders Addr.: P.O. Box 777, Monte Vista, CO 81144 USA Tel 719-850-2255; Fax: 719-852-2211; Edit Addr.: 67 Gold Cir., Pagosa Springs, CO 81147 USA; P.O. Box 1806, Vryburg, 8600
E-mail: riovista@rmi.net.

Savannah College of Art & Design Exhibitions, *(978-0-9654682; 978-1-893974; 978-0-9797440; 978-0-615-22202-8)* Orders Addr.: P.O. Box 3146, Savannah, GA 31401-3146 USA Tel 912-525-5287; Fax: 912-525-4952; Edit Addr.: 212 W. Hall St., Garden Apt., Savannah, GA 31401 USA; *Imprints:* Design Press Books (Design Press Bks)
E-mail: asalgado@scad.edu
Web site: http://www.scadexhibitions.com
Dist(s): **D.A.P./Distributed Art Pubs.**

Savas, Bachtsoglou, *(978-0-9771020)* 139-02 97th Ave., Jamaica, NY 11435 USA Tel 718-793-0107
E-mail: avipremlall@gmail.com.

Savas Beatie, *(978-1-932714; 978-1-61121)* 989 Governor Dr., Suite 102, El Dorado Hills, CA 95762 USA Tel 916-941-6896; Fax: 916-941-6895
E-mail: sarahs@savasbeatie.com; editorial@savasbeatie.com
Web site: http://www.savasbeatie.com
Dist(s): **Casemate Pubs. & Bk. Distributors, LLC**
MBI Distribution Services/Quayside Distribution
MyiLibrary
ebrary, Inc.

Save Our Seas, Ltd., *(978-0-9800444)* 626 Elvira Ave., Redondo Beach, CA 90277-9027 USA Tel 310-792-0338; Fax: 310-792-9273
E-mail: jonr@jokarproductions.com
Web site: http://www.saveourseas.com
Dist(s): **National Bk. Network.**

Savor Publishing Hse., Inc., *(978-0-9708296)* 6020 Broken Bow Dr., Citrus Heights, CA 95621 USA Tel 718-846-7277
E-mail: Smarties@SavorPublishing.com; SavorPubHouse@aol.com
Web site: http://www.savorpublishing.com
Dist(s): **Book Clearing Hse.**
Book Wholesalers, Inc.
Follett School Solutions.

Savory Palate, Inc., *(978-1-889374)* 8174 S. Holly, No. 404, Centennial, CO 80122-4004 USA Tel 303-741-5408; Fax: 303-741-0339; Toll Free: 800-741-5418
E-mail: info@savorypalate.com
Web site: http://www.savorypalate.com
Dist(s): **Brodart Co.**
New Leaf Distributing Co., Inc.
Quality Bks., Inc.
Royal Pubns., Inc.

Savvy Cyber Kids, Inc., *(978-0-9827968)* 4780 Ashford Dunwoody Rd. Suite A 312, Atlanta, GA 30338 USA Tel 404-955-7233
E-mail: info@savvycyberkids.org
Web site: http://www.savvycyberkids.org.

Savvy Pr., *(978-0-9669877; 978-0-9826069; 978-0-9852115; 978-1-939113)* Orders Addr.: P.O. Box 63, Salem, NY 12865 USA Tel 518-633-4778; Fax: 815 346-2659
E-mail: info@savvypress.com; info@gowanusbooks.com
Web site: http://www.savvypress.com; http://www.sagasf.com; http://www.gowanusbooks.com
Dist(s): **Quality Bks., Inc.**

Sawmill Publishing, *(978-0-9749915)* 6444 E. Spring St., No. 215, Long Beach, CA 90815 USA
Web site: http://www.sawmillpublishing.com.

Sawmill Ridge Publishing, *(978-0-9761924)* 183 Post Oak Dr., Roanoke, VA 24019 USA Tel 540-966-5706.

Saxon Pubs., Inc., *(978-0-939798; 978-1-56577; 978-1-59141)* Div. of Houghton Mifflin Harcourt Supplemental Pubs., Orders Addr.: 6277 Sea Harbor Dr., 5th Flr., Orlando, FL 32887 USA Toll Free Fax: 877-578-2638; Toll Free: 888-363-4266; Edit Addr.: 10801 N. Mopac Expressway, Bldg. 3, Austin, TX 78759 USA (SAN 216-8960) Toll Free: 800-531-5015
Web site: http://www.saxonpublishers.com
Dist(s): **Follett School Solutions**
Houghton Mifflin Harcourt Publishing Co.

Say It Loud! Readers & Writers Series, *(978-0-9779499)* 1507 E. 53rd St., No. 841, Chicago, IL 60615 USA.

Say It Right, *(978-0-9723457; 978-0-9760490; 978-0-9770418; 978-1-934701)* Orders Addr.: P.O. Box 651, Tybee Island, GA 31328 USA Tel 912-228-4556; Fax: 912-480-4214; Toll Free: 888-811-0759
E-mail: jim@sayitright.org
Web site: http://www.sayitright.org.

Say Out Loud, LLC, *(978-0-9799127)* Orders Addr.: 885 Woodstock Rd. Suite 430-373, Roswell, GA 30075 USA (SAN 854-7483) Tel 404-428-7935; Fax: 404-506-9823
E-mail: author@wordstosayoutloud.com
Web site: http://www.wordstosayoutloud.com.

SBA Bks., LLC, *(978-0-9711404)* Orders Addr.: P.O. Box 3019, Daphne, AL 36526 USA Tel 251-232-9927; Fax: 251-621-1834; Edit Addr.: 12655-a Dominion Dr., Fairhope, AL 36532 USA
E-mail: sheila@sbabooks.com
Web site: http://www.sbabooks.com
Dist(s): **Emerald Bk. Co.**
Greenleaf Book Group.

SC & FC Publications, *(978-0-9860794)* P.O. Box 124, Interlochen, MI 49643 USA.

S.C. TreeHouse LLC, *(978-0-692-87157-7)* 183 Parker RD, BENTON, TN 37307 USA Tel 423-715-4694
E-mail: jeffwcrawford5+LVP0003605@gmail.com; jeffwcrawford5+LVP0003605@gmail.com.

Scafe, Claire, *(978-0-9787695)* 7918 John Dr., Cheyenne, WY 82009 USA Tel 307-632-1702
E-mail: skir2@aol.com.

Scandinavia Publishing Hse. (DNK) *(978-87-7247; 978-87-87732) Dist. by* **Destiny Image Pubs.**

Scandora,

†Scarecrow Pr., Inc., *(978-0-8108; 978-1-57886)* Div. of Rowman & Littlefield Publishing Group, Orders Addr.: 15200 NBN Way, Blue Ridge Summit, PA 17214 USA Tel 717-794-3800 (Sales, Customer Service, MIS, Royalties, Inventory Mgmt., Dist., Credit & Collection); Fax: 717-794-3803 (Customer Service &/or orders); 717-794-3857 (Sales & MIS); 717-794-3856 (Royalties, Inventory Mgmt. & Dist.); Toll Free Fax: 800-338-4550 (Customer Service &/or orders); Toll Free: 800-462-6420 (Customer Service &/or orders); Edit Addr.: 4501 Forbes Blvd., Suite 200, Lanham, MD 20706-4310 USA Tel 301-459-3366; Fax: 301-429-5747 Short Discount, please contact rlpgsales@rowman.com
E-mail: custserv@rowman.com
Web site: http://www.scarecrowpress.com; http://www.rlpgbooks.com
Dist(s): **CreateSpace Independent Publishing Platform**
Ebsco Publishing
Follett School Solutions
MyiLibrary
National Bk. Network
Rowman & Littlefield Publishers, Inc.
ebrary, Inc.; *CIP.*

ScarecrowEducation *See* **Rowman & Littlefield Education**

Scarlet Primrose Pr., *(978-0-9851678)* 308 Blue Heron Cir., Simpsonville, SC 29680 USA Tel 585-545-0032
E-mail: andreacefalo4@gmail.com; scarletprimrosepress@gmail.com
Web site: http://www.andreacefalo.com
Dist(s): **CreateSpace Independent Publishing Platform**
Lightning Source, Inc.
Smashwords.

Scarlett L Pr., *(978-0-615-60059-8; 978-0-9982452)* 7800 E Freeport Pl., Broken Arrow, OK 74014 USA Tel 918-520-5718
Dist(s): **CreateSpace Independent Publishing Platform.**

Scarletta *See* **Mighty Media Pr.**

Scars Pubns. & Design, *(978-1-891470)* 829 Brian Ct., Gurnee, IL 60031 USA
E-mail: Editor@scars.tv
Web site: http://scars.tv.

Scavenger's Pubns., *(978-0-9798792)* 3443 Remington Ct., Eau Claire, WI 54703 USA Tel 715-456-3909
E-mail: ggparadox@hotmail.com.

SCB Distributors, Orders Addr.: 15608 S. New Century Dr., Gardena, CA 90248-2129 USA (SAN 630-4818) Tel 310-532-9400; Fax: 310-532-7001; Toll Free: 800-729-6423 (orders only)
E-mail: info@scbdistributors.com
Web site: http://www.scbdistributors.com.

Schafer-Post Entomology Pubns., *(978-0-9766855)* Entomology Dept. Hultz Hall, North Dakota State Univ., Fargo, ND 58105 USA Tel 701-231-7582; Fax: 701-231-8557
E-mail: david.rider@ndsu.edu.

Schallert, Ann, *(978-0-578-03425-6)* 10047 Hwy. 104, Tucumcari, NM 88401 USA
E-mail: crossann@shipleysystems.com.

Schaub, Stephen M. Photography *See* **Indian Hill Gallery of Fine Photography**

Scheer Delight Publishing, *(978-0-9671761)* 4030 E. Christy, Wichita, KS 67220-2540 USA (SAN 253-908X) Tel 316-683-2001; Fax: 316-636-1268
E-mail: schdelight@cox.net
Web site: http://scheerdelightpub.com.

Schermerhorn, Walters Co., *(978-0-9741746; 978-0-9824987)* 740 Purdue Dr., Claremont, CA 91711-3418 USA Tel 909-398-1228
E-mail: lilly.walters@verizon.net
Web site: http://www.motivational-keynote-speakers.com.

Schiavi, Sherry *See* **Celltrition**

Schiffer Publishing, Ltd., *(978-0-7643; 978-0-87033; 978-0-88740; 978-0-89538; 978-0-916838; 978-0-9787278; 978-1-5073)* Orders Addr.: 4880 Lower Valley Rd., Atglen, PA 19310 USA (SAN 208-8428) Tel 610-593-1777; Fax: 610-593-2002; *Imprints:* Cornell Maritime Press/Tidewater Publishers (CornellTide); Schiffer Publishing Ltd (SCHIFFER PUBLI); Red Feather (RedFeather)
E-mail: info@schifferbooks.com; karen@schifferbooks.com
Web site: http://www.schifferbooks.com.

Schiffer Publishing Ltd *Imprint of* **Schiffer Publishing, Ltd.**

Schiffner, Frederick A., *(978-0-9765782)* P.O. Box 1047, Spring Mt., PA 19478 USA Tel 610-287-5827
E-mail: fschiffner@fast.net.

Schiller Institute, Inc., *(978-0-9621095; 978-1-882985)* Orders Addr.: P.O. Box 20244, Washington, DC 20041-0244 USA (SAN 250-4944) Tel 703-777-9451 ext 541; Fax: 703-771-3099
E-mail: swelsh@schillerinstitute.org
Web site: http://www.schillerinstitute.org.

Schleich, James, *(978-0-615-12142-0)* 105 Woodland Dr., Zelienople, PA 16063-9316 USA
E-mail: james@the-soundman.org
Web site: http://www.the-soundman.org.

Schlessinger Media, *(978-1-57225; 978-1-879151)* Div. of Library Video Co., Orders Addr.: P.O. Box 580, Wynnewood, PA 19096 USA Tel 610-645-4000; Fax: 610-645-4050; Toll Free: 800-843-3620; Edit Addr.: 7 Wynnewood Rd., Wynnewood, PA 19096 USA
E-mail: sales@libraryvideo.com
Web site: http://www.libraryvideo.com
Dist(s): **Follett School Solutions**
Library Video Co.
Video Project, The.

Schlessinger Video Productions *See* **Schlessinger Media**

Schley, Michael, *(978-0-9759645)* 2 Oak Pk. Ave., Darien, CT 06820 USA
E-mail: mike_schley@yahoo.com.

Schmitt, Steven E. *See* **Global Partnership, LLC**

Schmul Publishing Co., Inc., *(978-0-88019)* Orders Addr.: P.O. Box 716, Salem, OH 44460-0716 USA (SAN 180-2771) Tel 330-222-2249; Fax: 330-222-0001; Toll Free: 800-772-6657; Edit Addr.: 3583 Newgarden Rd., Salem, OH 44460 USA
E-mail: spchale@valunet.com
Web site: http://www.wesleyanbooks.com.

Schnitzelbank Press *See* **BeerBooks.com**

Schocken *Imprint of* **Knopf Doubleday Publishing Group**

Schoenberg & Assocs., *(978-0-9748208)* 8033 W. Sunset Blvd., No. 944, Los Angeles, CA 90046 USA
Web site: http://www.rdsphotos.com.

Schoenhof's Foreign Bks., Inc., *(978-0-87774)* 76a Mount Auburn St., Cambridge, MA 02138-5051 USA (SAN 212-0062)
E-mail: info@schoenhofs.com
Web site: http://www.schoenhofs.com.

Scholargy Custom Publishing, Incorporated *See* **Scholargy Publishing, Inc.**

Scholargy Publishing, Inc., *(978-1-58666; 978-1-59247)* 17855 N. Black Cnyon Hwy., Phoenix, AZ 85023 USA (SAN 254-7295) Tel 602-548-5833 (phone/fax); Fax: 602-353-0680
E-mail: stephanie@scholargy.com
Web site: http://www.scholargy.com.

Scholastic *Imprint of* **Scholastic, Inc.**

Publisher Name Index

Scholastic Canada, Ltd. (CAN) *(978-0-439; 978-0-590; 978-0-7791; 978-1-4431)* *Dist. by* **Scholastic Inc.**

Scholastic en Espanol *Imprint of* **Scholastic, Inc.**

Scholastic, Inc. *Imprint of* **Scholastic, Inc.**

†Scholastic, Inc., *(978-0-439; 978-0-590; 978-0-545; 978-1-338)* 557 Broadway, New York, NY 10012-3999 USA (SAN 202-5442) Fax: 212-343-6802; Toll Free: 800-325-6149 (customer service); *Imprints:* Cartwheel Books (Cartwheel); Scholastic Reference (Scholastic Ref); Blue Sky Press, The (Blue Sky Press); Scholastic (Scholastic); Levine, Arthur A. Books (A A Levine); Orchard Books (Orchard Bks); Scholastic Press (Scholastic Pr); Chicken House, The (Chick Hse); PUSH (PUSH); Scholastic en Espanol (Scholastic en Espanol); Scholastic Nonfiction (Schol Nonfic); Scholastic Paperbacks (Schol Pbk); Sidekicks TM (Sidekicks); Tangerine Press (Tang Pr Sch); Teaching Resources (Teach Res Sch); Graphix (Graphx); Scholastic, Incorporated (Schlnc); Teaching Strategies (TeachStrategi); Theory & Practice (Theory & Prac); Little Shepherd (Little Shepard); Di Capua, Michael (Michael DiCapua); WestBow Press (WestBowPr); Exhibit A (Exhibit A); Scholastic Professional (ScholProf)
E-mail: info@scholastic.com
Web site: http://www.scholastic.com
Dist(s): **Blackstone Audio, Inc.**
Brilliance Publishing, Inc.
Ebsco Publishing
Follett School Solutions
Hachette Bk. Group
HarperCollins Pubs.
INscribe Digital
Lectorum Pubns., Inc.
MyiLibrary
Open Road Integrated Media, Inc.
Perfection Learning Corp.; *CIP.*

Scholastic Institute Chokyi Gyaltsen Univ., *(978-0-9973275; 978-0-9990141)* 3433 N Druid Hills Rd. Apt M, Decatur, GA 30033 USA Tel 404-825-8898
E-mail: office@sicgu.org
Web site: www.sicgu.org.

Scholastic Library Publishing, *(978-0-516; 978-0-531; 978-0-7172; 978-1-60631; 978-1-5461)* 90 Old Sherman Tpke., Danbury, CT 06816 USA (SAN 253-8865); *Imprints:* Orchard Books (Orchard Bks); Grolier Online (Grolier Online); Children's Press (Childrens Pr); Grolier (Grolier Schol); Watts, Franklin (Frank Watts)
E-mail: agraham@grolier.com; kbreen@scholastic.com
Web site: http://librarypublishing.scholastic.com
Dist(s): **Booksource, The**
Hachette Bk. Group
Lectorum Pubns., Inc.

Scholastic Nonfiction *Imprint of* **Scholastic, Inc.**

Scholastic Paperbacks *Imprint of* **Scholastic, Inc.**

Scholastic Pr. *Imprint of* **Scholastic, Inc.**

Scholastic Professional *Imprint of* **Scholastic, Inc.**

Scholastic Reference *Imprint of* **Scholastic, Inc.**

Schonwalder, Helmut, *(978-0-9763287)* P.O. Box 1390, Monterey, CA 93940 USA Tel 831-375-7737
E-mail: helmut@schonwalder.org; helmut@schonwalder.com
Web site: http://www.schonwalder.com; http://www.gastronomical.net; http://www.kaufhouse.info.

School Age Notes *Imprint of* **Gryphon Hse., Inc.**

School Days, *(978-0-9744302)* Orders Addr.: P.O. Box 454, North Carrollton, MS 38947 USA
E-mail: schooldaysmemorybook@yahoo.com
Web site: http://www.schooldaysmemorybook.com
Dist(s): **Wimmer Cookbooks.**

†School for Advanced Research Pr./SAR Pr., *(978-0-933452; 978-1-930618; 978-1-934691; 978-1-938645)* P.O. Box 2188, Santa Fe, NM 87504-2188 USA (SAN 212-6222) Tel 505-954-7206; Fax: 505-954-7241; Toll Free: 888-390-6070
E-mail: press@sarsf.org
Web site: http://www.sarpress.sarweb.org
Dist(s): **Univ. of New Mexico Pr.**; *CIP.*

School of American Research Press *See* **School for Advanced Research Pr./SAR Pr.**

School of Color Publishing, *(978-0-9679628; 978-1-931780)* Div. of The Michael Wilcox School of Color, Inc., P.O. Box 4793, Pinehurst, NC 28374 USA Toll Free: 888-794-5269
E-mail: wilcoxschool@earthlink.net; anne.m.gardner@worldnet.att.net
Web site: http://www.schoolofcolor.com
Dist(s): **F&W Media, Inc.**

Schl. of Government, *(978-1-56011)* CB 3330 UNC Chapel Hill, Chapel Hill, NC 27599-3330 USA (SAN 204-8752) Tel 919-966-4119; Fax: 919-962-2707
E-mail: khunt@iogmail.iog.unc.edu
Web site: http://www.sog.unc.edu.

School of Music Publishing Hse. (RUS) *(978-5-9500)* *Dist. by* **Coronet Bks.**

Schl. Services of California, Inc., *(978-0-9708628; 978-0-9748487; 978-0-9848031)* 1121 L St., No. 1060, Sacramento, CA 95814 USA Tel 916-446-7517; Fax: 916-446-2011
E-mail: susanm@sscal.com
Web site: http://www.sscal.com.

Schl. Tools, *(978-0-9754578)* 23418 28th Ave. W, Brier, WA 98036 USA.

School Zone Publishing Co., *(978-0-88743; 978-0-938256; 978-1-58947; 978-1-60041; 978-1-60159; 978-1-68147)* 1819 Industrial Dr., Grand Haven, MI 49417 USA (SAN 289-8314) Tel 616-846-5030; Fax: 616-846-6181; Toll Free: 800-253-0564
E-mail: christyf@schoolzone.com; sharonw@schoolzone.com
Web site: http://www.schoolzone.com.

Schoolhouse Publishing, *(978-0-9758543; 978-0-9845335; 978-0-9834657)* Orders Addr.: 659 Schoolhouse Rd., Telford, PA 18969-2449 USA Toll Free: 877-747-4711
Web site: http://www.shpublishing.com.

Schoolside Pr, *(978-0-9785100)* 7039 Sacred Cir., Sparks, NV 89437 USA Tel 818-884-7349
E-mail: eamartonyi@schoolsidepress.com
Web site: http://Schoolsidpress.com
Dist(s): **Midpoint Trade Bks., Inc.**

Schooner Pubns., *(978-1-929234)* 1610-D Church St. Coastal Ctr., PMB 360, Conway, SC 29526 USA Tel 843-347-9792.

Schott Music Corp., *(978-0-930448)* 35 E 21st ST., 8th Flr., New York, NY 10010 USA
E-mail: scott.wollschleger@eamdllc.com
Dist(s): **Leonard, Hal Corp.**

Schott Musik International GmbH & Co. KG (DEU) *(978-3-7957; 978-3-95983)* *Dist. by* **H Leonard.**

Schrader, Racheal, *(978-0-9815274)* P.O. Box 15603, Colorado Springs, CO 80935-5603 USA
E-mail: inspired-ink@hotmail.com
Web site: http://inspired-ink.net.

Schroeder, Patrick A. Publications: Civil War Books *See* **Schroeder Pubns.: Civil War Bks.**

Schroeder Pubns.: Civil War Bks., *(978-1-889246)* Orders Addr.: 131 Tanglewood Dr., Lynchburg, VA 24502 USA Tel 434-525-4431; Fax: 434-525-7293
E-mail: civilwarbooks@yahoo.com
Web site: http://www.civilwar-books.com.

Schwarcz, Editora Ltda, Companhia das Letrinhas (BRA) *(978-85-7406)* *Dist. by* **Distribks Inc.**

Schwartau, Winn LLC, *(978-0-9628700; 978-0-9964019)* Orders Addr.: 545 Westport Dr., Old Hickory, TN 37138-1115 USA
E-mail: sherra@alwayschaos.com; winn@securityexperts.com
Web site: http://www.winnschwartau.com.

Schwartz & Wade Bks. *Imprint of* **Random Hse. Children's Bks.**

Schwartz, Arthur & Company, Incorporated/Woodstocker Books *See* **Woodstocker Books/Arthur Schwartz & Company**

Schwartz, Gary, *(978-0-9975860)* P.O. Box 1123, North Bend, WA 98045 USA Tel 425-831-5667
E-mail: gary@gary-schwartz.com
Web site: http://gary-schwartz.com.

Schwartz, Joel, *(978-0-9785885)* 1315 Cinnamon Dr., Fort Washington, PA 19034-2818 USA
E-mail: jshrink@comcast.net
Web site: http://www.stresslessshrink.com.

Schwartz Marketing, *(978-0-9893046)* 1234 Bloomfield St., Hoboken, NJ 07030 USA Tel 201-656-2223; Fax: 201-656-2223
E-mail: tomschwartz@earthlink.net.

Schwarz Pauper Pr., *(978-0-9621505)* 88 Winwood Dr., Barnstead, NH 03225 USA (SAN 251-4540) Tel 603-776-5680
E-mail: Granitesunset@aol.com.

Sci Fi-Arizona, Inc., *(978-1-929381)* 1931 E. Libra Dr., Tempe, AZ 85283 USA Tel 480-838-6558; *Imprints:* Third Millennium Publishing (Third Millen Pubng)
E-mail: mccollum@scifi-az.com
Web site: http://www.scifi-az.com; http://www.3mpub.com.

Science Academy Software, *(978-0-9623926)* 600 Baychester Ave., Apt 5B, Bronx, NY 10475-4457 USA Tel 718-561-4048.

Science & God, Inc., *(978-0-9745861)* P.O. Box 2036, Labelle, FL 33975-2036 USA Tel 239-218-4543.

Science & Humanities Pr., *(978-1-888725; 978-1-59630)* Subs. of Banis & Assocs., Orders Addr.: P.O. Box 7151, Chesterfield, MO 63006-7151 USA (SAN 299-8459) Tel 636-394-4950; Fax: 800-706-0585; P.O. Box 7151, Chesterfield, MO 63006-7151; Edit Addr.: 1023 Stuyvesant Ln., Manchester, MO 63011-3601 USA Tel 636-394-4950; Toll Free Fax: 800-706-0585; 1023 Stuyvesant Ln., Manchester, MO 63011-3601 Tel 636-394-4950; Toll Free Fax: 800-706-0585; *Imprints:* BeachHouse Books (BeachHouse Bks)
E-mail: banis@sciencehumanitiespress.com; banis@banis-associates.com
Web site: http://www.banis-associates.com; http://www.sciencehumanitiespress.com; http://www.macroprintbooks.com; http://www.stressmyth.com; http://www.normajeanebook.com; http://www.route66book.com; http://www.accessible-travel.com.

Science and Technology Concepts (STC) *Imprint of* **Smithsonian Science Education Ctr. (SSEC)**

Science Curriculum, Inc., *(978-1-882057)* Orders Addr.: 200 Union Blvd. Ste. G18, Lakewood, CO 80228-1845 USA (SAN 248-3637) Toll Free: 888-501-0957; 24 Stone Rd., Belmont, MA 04278
E-mail: marketing@sci-ips.com
Web site: http://www.sci-ips.com.

Science Enterprises, Inc., *(978-0-930116)* 402 N. Blackford St., Indianapolis, IN 46202-3272 USA (SAN 210-6639).

Science, Naturally!, *(978-0-9678020; 978-0-9700106; 978-1-938492)* 725 Eighth St., SE., Washington, DC 20003 USA Tel 202-465-4798; Fax: 202-558-2132; Toll Free: 866-724-9876
E-mail: dia@sciencenaturally.com
Web site: http://www.sciencenaturally.com
Dist(s): **MyiLibrary**
National Bk. Network
ebrary, Inc.

Science of Knowledge Pr., *(978-1-59620)* P.O. Box 324, Little Falls, NJ 07424 USA Fax: 973-272-1102
Web site: http://www.scienceok.com
Dist(s): **Majors, J. A. Co.**

Science of Mind Publishing, *(978-0-911336; 978-0-917849; 978-0-9727184)* Div. of United Church of Religious Science, Orders Addr.: 573 Park Point Dr., Golden, CO 80401-7042 USA (SAN 203-2570) Tel 720-279-1643; 720-496-1370; Fax: 303-526-0913
E-mail: dsimone@csl.org
Web site: http://www.scienceofmind.com; http://www.spirituallivingpress.com
Dist(s): **DeVorss & Co.**
Red Wheel/Weiser.

Science Pubs., *(978-0-9700733; 978-0-9716445; 978-0-9749755; 978-1-938024)* Div. of BrainMind.com, 677 Elm St., San Jose, CA 95126 USA Do not confuse with companies with the same name in Hudson, WI, Flushing, NY, San Francisco, CA, Missoula, MT, Wolf City, TX
E-mail: BookMoviesOrders@BrainMind.com
Web site: http://BrainMind.com; http://Cosmology.com
Dist(s): **MyiLibrary.**

Science Square Publishing, *(978-0-9740861)* 2845 Bowen St., Graton, CA 95444-9347 USA
E-mail: info@sciencesquare.com
Web site: http://www.sciencesquare.com.

Science2Discover, Inc., *(978-0-9673811)* P.O. Box 2435, Del Mar, CA 92014-1735 USA Fax: 858-793-0410; Toll Free: 888-359-6075; 2015 Seaview Ave., Del Mar, CA 92014 Do not confuse with MetaMetrix, Inc., Norcross, GA
E-mail: info@science2discover.com
Web site: http://www.science2discover.com.

Sciencenter, *(978-0-578-00196-8; 978-0-578-00197-5)* 601 First St., Ithaca, NY 14850 USA Tel 607-272-0600
Dist(s): **Lulu Pr., Inc.**

Scientia Est Vox Pr., *(978-0-578-02353-3; 978-0-578-05385-1; 978-0-578-07089-6; 978-0-578-12511-4; 978-0-578-16302-4; 978-0-578-18130-1; 978-0-578-19361-8)* 2338 8th Ave., Terre Haute, IN 47804 USA Tel 812-917-4182; 812-917-4384
E-mail: magicianofoz@hotmail.com
Web site: http://www.magicianofoz.blogspot.com
Dist(s): **Lulu Pr., Inc.**

Sci-Hi *Imprint of* **Heinemann-Raintree**

Scion Publishing Ltd. (GBR) *(978-1-904842; 978-1-907904)* *Dist. by* **Chicago Distribution Ctr.**

Scobre Pr. Corp., *(978-0-9708992; 978-0-9741695; 978-0-9741997; 978-0-9766240; 978-1-933423; 978-1-934713; 978-1-61570; 978-1-62920)* 2255 Calle Clara, La Jolla, CA 92037 USA Toll Free: 877-726-2734
E-mail: Scott@bookbuddyaudio.com
Web site: http://www.scobre.com
Dist(s): **MyiLibrary.**

SCOJO ENTERTAINMENT, *(978-0-9651306; 978-0-9786488)* Orders Addr.: P.O. Box 1225, New York, NY 10008 USA
Web site: theportalinthepark.com.

Scooby-Doo *Imprint of* **Stone Arch Bks.**

SCOPE Pubns., *(978-0-9759955)* Orders Addr.: 100 Lawrence Ave., Smithtown, NY 11787 USA Tel 631-360-0800; Fax: 631-360-8489 Do not confuse with Scope Publications, Fairfax, OK
E-mail: bkauffman@scopeonline.us
Web site: http://www.scopeonline.us.

Scotland Gate, Inc., *(978-0-9830084; 978-0-9837523; 978-0-9839550; 978-0-9888972; 978-0-9888973)* 176 Edgecliff Dr., Highland Park, IL 60035 USA Tel 847-432-1947
E-mail: mskemp@sbcglobal.net.

Scott, Cassandra Dr Ministries, *(978-0-9882936)* 3802 Hanberry, Pearland, TX 77584 USA Tel 713-550-3370
E-mail: cescott1@aol.com.

Scott, D.& F. Publishing, Inc., *(978-0-941037; 978-1-930566)* Orders Addr.: P.O. Box 821653, North Richland Hills, TX 76182-1653 USA (SAN 665-2875) Tel 817-788-2280; Fax: 817-788-9232; Toll Free: 888-788-2280; Edit Addr.: P.O. Box 821653, N Richlnd Hls, TX 76182-1653 USA; *Imprints:* WestWind Press (WstWind)
E-mail: info@dfscott.com
Web site: http://www.dfscott.com.

Scott Foresman *Imprint of* **Addison-Wesley Educational Pubs., Inc.**

Scott Foresman *Imprint of* **Addison-Wesley Educational Pubs., Inc.**

Scott Foresman *Imprint of* **Pearson Schl.**

Scott Foresman *Imprint of* **Addison Wesley Schl.**

Scott, J & N Pubs., *(978-0-9719868)* 10461 NW 20 St., Pembroke Pines, FL 33026 USA Tel 954-432-6578
E-mail: nscott2000@aol.com.

Scott, James *See* **Scott, J & N Pubs.**

Scott, Josephine, *(978-0-9718582; 978-0-9746600)* P.O. Box 55127, Bridgeport, CT 06610 USA
E-mail: jartist@optonline.net
Web site: http://www.ethnicitycards.com
Dist(s): **MyiLibrary**
ebrary, Inc.

†Scott Pubns., Inc., *(978-0-916809; 978-1-893625; 978-0-9787419)* 2145 W. Sherman Blvd., Muskegon, MI 49441-3434 USA Toll Free: 866-733-9382 Do not confuse with Scott Pubns. in Indianapolis, IN
E-mail: contactus@scottpublications.com
Web site: http://www.scottpublications.com; *CIP.*

Scott Publishing Co., *(978-0-9617626; 978-1-930043; 978-0-9908913; 978-0-9982386; 978-0-9991508)* Orders Addr.: P.O. Box 9707, Kalispell, MT 59901 USA (SAN 664-6948) Tel 406-755-0099; Fax: 406-756-0098; Edit Addr.: 1845 Helena Flats Rd., Kalispell, MT 59901-6525 USA (SAN 664-6956) Do not confuse with companies with the same or similar name in Sidney, OH, Houston, TX, Edmonds, WA
E-mail: scott@scottcompnay.net.

Scottish Children's Pr. (GBR) *(978-1-898218; 978-1-899827)* *Dist. by* **Wlsn Assocs.**

Scottish Christmas, *(978-0-9726114)* 2369 Joslyn Ct., Lake Orion, MI 48360 USA.

Scottwall Assocs., *(978-0-942087; 978-0-9612790; 978-0-578-01245-2)* 95 Scott St., San Francisco, CA 94117 USA (SAN 289-8322) Tel 415-861-1956; Fax: 415-863-7273
E-mail: scotwall@pacbell.net
Web site: http://www.scottwallpub.com
Dist(s): **Sunbelt Pubns., Inc.**
Todd Communications.

Scott-Waters, Marilyn, *(978-0-9759884)* 1589 Baker St., Costa Mesa, CA 92626 USA
E-mail: msw@scottwatersdesign.com
Web site: http://www.thetoymaker.com.

SCR, Inc., *(978-0-9747582; 978-1-63227)* Orders Addr.: P.O. Box 803338 #46673, Chicago, IL 60680 USA (SAN 255-7509) Tel 815-642-0848
E-mail: isbn@spamex.com
Web site: http://www.scrbooks.ocom
Dist(s): **Lulu Pr., Inc.**

SCR Publications *See* **SCR, Inc.**

S.C.R.A.P. Gallery, *(978-0-9708135)* 46-350 Arabia St., Indio, CA 92201 USA Tel 760-863-7777; Fax: 760-863-8973; Toll Free: 866-717-2727 (866-71-SCRAP)
E-mail: scrapgallery@earthlink.net
Web site: http://www.infoteam.com/nonprofit/scrapgallery.

Scrap Paper Pr., *(978-0-9745493)* 6 Manor Dr., Goldens Bridge, NY 10526 USA Tel 914-997-1692; Fax: 914-997-2253.

Scribble & Sons, *(978-0-615-93279-8; 978-0-615-93286-6; 978-0-615-93328-3; 978-0-615-93335-1; 978-0-615-93344-3; 978-0-9916352)* 720 W Idaho #28, Boise, ID 83702 USA Tel 970-556-3740
Web site: www.goodbookco.com
Dist(s): **CreateSpace Independent Publishing Platform**
Independent Pubs. Group.

Scribbler's Sword, *(978-0-9761186)* 1640 Halfacre Rd., Newberry, SC 29108 USA.

Scribe Publishing, *(978-0-9727077)* 842 S 2ND ST, Philadelphia, PA 19147 USA Do not confuse with companies with the same or similar name in King City, CA, Murray, UT, Welsh, LA, Seattle, WA, Redan, GA
E-mail: contact@scribenet.com
Web site: http://www.scribenet.com.

Scribe Publishing & Consulting Services, The, *(978-0-9793516)* Div. of TrueLight Ministries, P.O. Box 11013, Tacoma, WA 98411 USA Tel 253-312-9377; Fax: 253-238-6041; *Imprints:* Writing The Vision (Writing The Vision)
E-mail: missmillie59@yahoo.com
Web site: http://www.truelightmin.org.

Scribe Publishing Co., *(978-0-9859562; 978-1-940368; 978-0-9916021)* 29488 Woodward Suite 426, Royal Oak, MI 48073 USA Tel 248-259-0090
E-mail: jennifer@scribe-publishing.com
Web site: http://scribe-publishing.com
Dist(s): **Midpoint Trade Bks., Inc.**

Scribe's Closet Pubns., The, *(978-0-9801269; 978-0-9832570; 978-0-9884125; 978-0-9912487; 978-1-943058)* 702 South Missouri, Macon, MO 63552 USA
E-mail: scribescloset@gmail.com
Web site: http://www.thescribesclosetpublications.com.

Scribez, Scarebz & Vibez, *(978-0-9853406)* 689 Macon St., Brooklyn, NY 11233 USA Tel 646-267-1459
E-mail: bedstuybelle1@gmail.com.

Scribner *Imprint of* **Scribner**

Scribner, *(978-0-684; 978-0-7432)* Orders Addr.: 100 Front St., Riverside, NJ 08075 USA; Edit Addr.: 1230 Ave. of the Americas, New York, NY 10020 USA; *Imprints:* Scribner (ScribImp)
Dist(s): **Simon & Schuster**
Simon & Schuster, Inc.

Scribolin, *(978-0-9746226)* 10107 Copeland Dr., Manassas, VA 20109 USA Tel 703-257-7683
E-mail: books@scribolin.com
Web site: http://www.scribolin.com.

Scripts Publishing, *(978-1-889826)* Orders Addr.: 638 Hennepin Ter., Mcdonough, GA 30253-5965 USA
E-mail: AtaxiaBooks@aol.com
Web site: http://www.hometown.aol.com/pathamilto/myhomepage/profile.html.

Scripture Mastery Resources!, *(978-1-933589)* 1814 Cranberry Way, Springville, UT 84663-3930 USA
E-mail: scripturemastery@kenalford.com
Web site: http://www.kenalford.com.

Scripture Memory Fellowship International, *(978-1-880960)* Orders Addr.: P.O. Box 411551, Saint Louis, MO 63141 USA Tel 314-569-0244; Fax: 314-569-0025; Toll Free: 888-569-2560; Edit Addr.: P.O. Box 568, Hannibal, MO 63401-0568 USA
E-mail: memorize@stlnet.com
Web site: http://www.scripturememory.com.

Scripture Union (GBR) *(978-0-85421; 978-0-86201; 978-1-85999; 978-1-873824; 978-1-84427; 978-1-78506)* *Dist. by* **STL Dist.**

Scripture Union (GBR) *(978-0-85421; 978-0-86201; 978-1-85999; 978-1-873824; 978-1-84427; 978-1-78506)* *Dist. by* **Gabriel Res.**

†Scroll Pr., Inc., *(978-0-87592)* 2858 Valerie Ct., Merrick, NY 11566 USA (SAN 206-796X) Tel 516-379-4283; *CIP.*

Scroll Publishing Co., *(978-0-924722)* Orders Addr.: P.O. Box 4714, Tyler, TX 75712 USA; Edit Addr.: 22012 Indian Spring Tr., Amberson, PA 17210 USA Tel 717-349-7033; Fax: 717-349-7558
E-mail: customerservice@scrollpublishing.com
Web site: http://www.scrollpublishing.com.

Scrub Jay Journeys, *(978-0-9898122; 978-1-946253)* 205 Wiley Ln., Middleton, TN 38052 USA Tel 407-227-0540
E-mail: author@daviscrossing.com.

Scrumps Entertainment, Inc., *(978-0-9672279)* 19320 NW. 47th Ave., Miami, FL 33055 USA Tel 305-624-7231
E-mail: climbcrick@aol.com.

SDP Publishing, *(978-0-9824461; 978-0-9829256; 978-0-9885157; 978-0-9889381; 978-0-9899723; 978-0-9911597; 978-0-9913167; 978-0-9905596; 978-0-9862896; 978-0-9964345; 978-0-9968426;*

978-0-9972853; 978-0-9977224; 978-0-9981277; 978-0-9984240; 978-0-9986730; 978-0-9992839) Div. of SDP Publishing Solutions, LLC, Orders Addr.: P.O. Box 26, East Bridgewater, MA 02333 USA (SAN 858-1762)
E-mail: lross@SDPPublishing.com
Web site: http://www.sdppublishingsolutions.com; http://www.PublishAtSweetDreams.com; http://www.sdppublishing.com
Dist(s): **Lightning Source, Inc.**

SDP Publishing Solutions *See* **SDP Publishing**

SE PrinTech, *(978-0-615-33647-3; 978-0-615-48019-0; 978-0-9847344)* 315 E. Banks St., Glennville, GA 30427 USA Tel 912-654-3610
E-mail: bill@welovetoprint.com.

Se7enth Swan Publishing Group, LLC, *(978-0-615-14849-6)* P.O. Box 16874, Chapel Hill, NC 27516 USA
Web site: http://www.se7enthswan.com
Dist(s): **Lulu Pr., Inc.**

Sea Chest Bks., *(978-0-9742909)* 11573 Viking Ave., Northridge, CA 91326 USA
E-mail: info@beverlyhillsvideographer.com
Web site: http://www.seachestbooks.com.

Sea Keepers Publishing, *(978-0-9846251)* 936 N. Main St., Akron, OH 44310 USA.

Sea Lion Bks., *(978-0-578-06080-4; 978-0-9828186; 978-0-9836131; 978-0-9857691)* 6070 Autumn View Trail, Acworth, GA 30101 USA
E-mail: david@sealionbooks.com
Dist(s): **BookBaby**
Diamond Bk. Distributors.

Sea Oats Publishing, *(978-0-9798143)* 699-A Sterling Dr., James Island, SC 29412-9135 USA Tel 843-762-2606
E-mail: seaoatspublishing@yahoo.com.

Sea Raven Enterprises *See* **Sea Raven Pr.**

Sea Raven Pr., *(978-0-9768707; 978-0-9821899; 978-0-9827700; 978-0-9838185; 978-0-9858632; 978-0-9913779; 978-1-943737)* Orders Addr.: P.O. Box 1054, Franklin, TN 37065 USA Tel 615-349-1345; P.O. Box 1054, Franklin, TN 37065
E-mail: searavenpress@nii.net
Web site: http://www.searavenpress.com.

Seachild, *(978-0-9787881)* P.O. Box 2600, Petaluma, CA 94952 USA (SAN 851-6499) Tel 707-762-7316
E-mail: judiegerber@earthlink.net
Web site: http://www.seachild.net.

Seacoast Publishing, Inc., *(978-1-878561; 978-1-59421)* Orders Addr.: P.O. Box 991, Florence, AL 35631 USA Tel 256-367-4195; *Imprints:* Blackbirch Press, Incorporated (Blackbirch Pr) Do not confuse with companies with the same name in Monterey, CA, East Hampton, NY
E-mail: darren@seacoast.pub; info@seacoast.pub
Web site: http://www.seacoast.pub.

Seaforth Publishing, *(978-0-9725706)* 5818 Three Ponds Ct., West Bloomfield, MI 48324-3124 USA
Dist(s): **MyiLibrary.**

Seagrass *Imprint of* **Quarto Publishing Group USA**

Seagull Bks. (IND) *(978-81-7046) Dist. by* **Chicago Distribution Ctr.**

Seagull Books (GBR) *(978-1-905422; 978-1-906497; 978-0-85742) Dist. by* **Chicago Distribution Ctr.**

Seagull Pr., *(978-0-9753709)* 375-A Maxham Rd., No. 414, Austell, GA 30168 USA Fax: 770-944-3799 Do not confuse with companies with the same name in Oakland, CA, Owings, MD.

Seal Pr, *(978-0-931188; 978-1-58005; 978-1-878067)* Div. of Perseus Bks. Grp., 387 Park Ave., S., 12th Flr., New York, NY 10016-8810 USA Tel 212-340-8100
Dist(s): **Blackstone Audio, Inc.**
Ebsco Publishing
Follett School Solutions
Hachette Bk. Group
ebrary, Inc.

Seal Publishing, LLC, *(978-0-9774062)* P.O. Box 435, Odessa, FL 33556 USA
Web site: http://www.sealswimschool.com.

Seal Rock Publishing, LLC, *(978-0-9763778)* 834 Marshall Rd., Boulder, CO 80305-7337 USA
E-mail: sealrockpub@yahoo.com.

Sealaska Heritage Institute, *(978-0-9825786; 978-0-9853129; 978-0-9963698; 978-1-946019)* 105 S. Seward St. Suite 201, Juneau, AK 99801 USA
E-mail: nobu.koch@sealaska.com.

Seaman, P. David, *(978-0-9755066)* 2645 E. Southern Ave. Apt. A679, Tempe, AZ 85282-7532 USA.

Sean Tigh Pr., *(978-0-9851200)* 1799 Ivy Oak Sq., Reston, VA 20190 USA Tel 321-446-1483
E-mail: kristen@kristenandjoe.com.

Search Institute, *(978-1-57482)* 615 First Ave. NE, Suite 125, Minneapolis, MN 55413 USA Tel 612-376-8955; Fax: 612-376-8956; Toll Free: 800-888-7828
Web site: http://www.search-institute.org
Dist(s): **Ebsco Publishing**
Independent Pubs. Group
MyiLibrary
ebrary, Inc.

Searchlight Pr., *(978-0-9644609; 978-0-9824802; 978-1-936497)* Orders Addr.: 5634 Ledgestone Dr., Dallas, TX 75214-2026 USA Tel 214-662-5494; Toll Free: 888-896-6081
E-mail: searchlight@johncunyus.com; info@searchlight-press.com
Web site: http://www.johncunyus.com; http://www.searchlight-press.com.

SearlStudio Publishing, *(978-0-9883670; 978-0-9895062)* 18331 Pines Blvd., No. 322, Pembroke Pines, FL 33029 USA Tel 305-517-7261
E-mail: searlstudio@me.com
Web site: http://www.searlstudio.com.

Sears, M.A., *(978-0-9639785)* 16809 Superior, North Hills, CA 91343 USA; 555 W. Sierra Hwy., Acton, CA 93510 Tel 818-891-8632.

Sears, Stanley, *(978-0-9770067)* Rte. 1 Box 215, Hickman, NE 68372-9686 USA.

Seascape Pr., *(978-0-9769510)* P.O. Box 13132, Jekyll Island, GA 31527 USA Tel 912-635-3263; Fax: 912-635-3264 Do not confuse with Seascape Press, LLC in Santa Barbara, CA.

SeaScape Pr., Ltd., *(978-0-9669741; 978-0-9852381)* 5717 Tanner Ridge Ave., Westlake Vlg, CA 91362-5238 USA (SAN 299-8386) Tel 818-707-3080 Toll Free: 800-929-2906 do not confuse with Seascape Press in Jekyll Island, GA
E-mail: seapress@aol.com; llamensdor@aol.com
Web site: http://www.lenlamensdorf.com.

Seascay Productions, *(978-0-9764152)* 11 Ventnor Dr. Suite 906, Edison, NJ 08820 USA Tel 732-242-3902
E-mail: corporate@seascay.com
Web site: http://www.seascay.com.

Seashell Pr., The, *(978-0-9768866)* 28 Skytop Rd, Ipswich, MA 01938 USA
E-mail: mailbag@theseashellpress.com
Web site: http://www.theseashellpress.com.

Seaside Books *See* **Ladd, David Pr.**

Seasoning Quilting (Arts & Crafts), *(978-1-888413)* 806 Elvie St., Wilson, NC 27893-6116 USA Tel 919-291-7705.

SeaSquirt Pubns. (GBR) *(978-1-905470) Dist. by* **Basic Dist.**

SeaStar Bks. *Imprint of* **Chronicle Bks. LLC**

Seastory Pr., *(978-0-9673704; 978-0-9768370; 978-0-9799474; 978-0-9821151; 978-1-936818)* 305 Whitehead St., No. 1, Key West, FL 33040 USA Tel 305-296-5762; Toll Free: 877-454-6282
E-mail: sheri@seastorypress.com
Web site: http://www.seastorypress.com
Dist(s): **MyiLibrary**
ebrary, Inc.

Sea-To-Sea Pubns., *(978-1-932889; 978-1-59771)* Div. of Creative Co., 2140 Howard Dr., W., North Mankato, MN 56003 USA
Dist(s): **Creative Co., The**
RiverStream Publishing.

Seawall Bks., Inc., *(978-0-615-34226-9; 978-0-615-34240-5; 978-0-615-37353-9; 978-0-615-75068-2; 978-0-9893324)* 7 Summit Dr., Hingham, MA 02043 USA Tel 781-749-4284; Fax: 781-749-0977
E-mail: donhussey@aol.com
Web site: http://donhussey.com.

SeaWorld Education Dept. *Imprint of* **SeaWorld, Inc.**

SeaWorld, Inc., *(978-1-893698)* Div. of Anheuser-Busch Adventure Parks, 500 SeaWorld Dr., San Diego, CA 92109 USA (SAN 255-576X) Tel 619-225-4275; Fax: 619-226-3634; Toll Free: 800-237-4268; *Imprints:* SeaWorld Education Department (SeaWorld Educ)
E-mail: swc.education@seaworld.com; debbie.nuzzolo@seaworld.com
Web site: http://www.seaworld.org
Dist(s): **Book Wholesalers, Inc.**
Brodart Co.
Carolina Biological Supply Co.

Second Ark Pubns., *(978-1-889667)* 2907 Kevin Ln., Houston, TX 77043 USA.

Second Base Publishing, *(978-0-9793562; 978-0-9981709)* 6197 Hinterlong Ct, Lisle, IL 60532 USA (SAN 853-2206)
Dist(s): **Ebsco Publishing**
Independent Pubs. Group
MyiLibrary
ebrary, Inc.

Second Sight Enterprises, Inc., *(978-0-9785222)* P.O. Box 251248, Plano, TX 75025 USA (SAN 850-7996)
Web site: http://www.asktheinventors.com
Dist(s): **Independent Pubs. Group.**

Second Star Creations, *(978-0-9725977)* 12120 State Line Rd., No. 190, Leawood, KS 66209 USA Tel 913-681-2252
E-mail: jan@secondstar.us
Web site: http://www.secondstar.us.

Second Story Pr. (CAN) *(978-0-921299; 978-0-929005; 978-1-896764; 978-1-897187) Dist. by* **Orca Bk Pub.**

Second Time Media & Communications, *(978-0-9727498; 978-0-9815162; 978-0-9840660; 978-0-9831743)* P.O. Box 401367, Redford, MI 48240 USA Tel 800-377-7497
E-mail: secondtimemedia@yahoo.com
Web site: http://www.secondtimemedia.com.

Second Wind Creations, *(978-0-9848879)* 2142 Ivar Ave., Los Angeles, CA 90068 USA Tel 213-200-6030
E-mail: barbara@secondwindcreations.com
Web site: http://www.secondwindcreations.com.

Second Wind Publishing, LLC *See* **Indigo Sea Pr., LLC**

Secret Corners Publishing, *(978-0-615-24083-1; 978-0-615-24084-8)* 12917 Brookcrest Pl., Riverview, FL 33578 USA
E-mail: info@secret-corners.com
Web site: http://www.secret-corners.com.

Secret Garden Bookworks, *(978-0-9766283)* Orders Addr.: P.O. Box 1506, Oak Bluffs, MA 02557-1506 USA Tel 508-693-4759; Fax: 508-693-4867; Edit Addr.: 41 Circuit Ave., Oak Bluffs, MA 02557-1506 USA
E-mail: secretgardenmv@peoplepc.com
Web site: http://www.secretgardenbookworks.com.

Secret Passage Pr., *(978-1-888695)* 26 Tucker Hollow Rd., North Scituate, RI 02857 USA Tel 401-647-0440; Toll Free: 877-863-4622 (Orders Only)
E-mail: lucindalandon@verizon.net
Web site: http://www.megmackintosh.com
Dist(s): **Ebsco Publishing**
Enfield Publishing & Distribution Co., Inc.
Independent Pubs. Group
MyiLibrary.

Security Studies Pr., *(978-0-9797539)* 650 J St., Suite 405, Lincoln, NE 68508 USA
E-mail: rlund@securitystudies.us
Web site: http://www.securitystudies.us.

Sedell, Kirsten, *(978-0-9800838)* 3 John R's Bend, Berkley, MA 02779 USA
E-mail: ksedell@norton.k12.ma.us.

sedgewick eye Assocs., P.C., *(978-0-9968178)* 44121 harry byrd hwy, No. 175, ashburn, VA 20147 USA Tel 703-725-1698
E-mail: jrsedgewick@verizon.net
Web site: www.sedgewickeye.com.

Sedwick, Daniel Frank LLC, *(978-0-9820818)* P.O. Box 1964, Winter Park, FL 32790-1964 USA Tel 407-975-3325; Fax: 407-975-3327
E-mail: info@sedwickcoins.com
Web site: http://www.sedwickcoins.com.

See abc's LC, *(978-1-890566)* Orders Addr.: P.O. Box 276, Smithfield, UT 84335 USA; Edit Addr.: 9 S. 490 E., Smithfield, UT 84335 USA.

See Sharp Pr., *(978-0-9613289; 978-1-884365; 978-1-937276; 978-1-947071)* P.O. Box 1731, Tucson, AZ 85702-1731 USA (SAN 653-8134) Tel 520-628-8720 (phone/fax)
E-mail: info@seesharppress.com
Web site: http://www.seesharppress.com
Dist(s): **Ebsco Publishing**
Independent Pubs. Group
MyiLibrary
ebrary, Inc.

See The Wish, *(978-0-9822134; 978-0-9857676; 978-0-9986716)* 246 Main St., Cold Spring, NY 10516 USA Tel 845-797-9183
Web site: http://www.seethewish.com
Dist(s): **Follett School Solutions.**

Seed Faith Bks, *(978-1-60101)* P.O. Box 12227, Portland, OR 97212-0227 USA (SAN 850-6795)
Web site: http://seedfaithbooks.com.

SeeDEGA, *(978-0-9746586)* Orders Addr.: P.O. Box 588, Rhinebeck, NY 12572 USA Tel 845-876-0609
E-mail: info@seedega.com
Web site: http://seedega.com.

Seedling Pubns. *Imprint of* **Continental Pr., Inc.**

SeeHearDo Co., LLC, The, *(978-0-9788089)* 3011 E. 7145 S., Salt Lake City, UT 84121 USA.

Seelcraft Publishing, *(978-0-9728380)* 63 Church St., Suite 201, High Bridge, NJ 08829-1516 USA
Web site: http://www.seelcraft.com.

See-More's Workshop, *(978-1-882601)* Div. of Shadow Box Theatre, 325 West End Ave., New York, NY 10023 USA Tel 212-724-0677; Fax: 212-724-0767
E-mail: sbt@shadowboxtheatre.org
Web site: http://www.shadowboxtheatre.org
Dist(s): **Follett School Solutions**
Professional Media Service Corp.

See-Saw Publishing *Imprint of* **Peek-A-Boo Publishing**

Segal, Berty Inc., *(978-0-938395)* 1749 E. Eucalyptus St., Brea, CA 92821 USA (SAN 630-0553) Tel 714-529-5359; Fax: 714-529-3882
E-mail: bertytprsource@earthlink.net
Web site: http://www.tprsource.com
Dist(s): **Continental Bk. Co., Inc.**

Segal, Robin *See* **Murray Hill Bks., LLC**

Segarra, Angelo, *(978-0-9752664)* 422 Gregg Ave., Santa Fe, NM 87501-1600 USA
Dist(s): **Greenleaf Book Group.**

Seglie, Susan M., *(978-0-9747243)* 1 Deer Run Ln., Pittsburg, KS 66762 USA Fax: 620-232-5819.

Segue Pubs., *(978-0-9671796)* 527 arbor Rd., Cheltenham, PA 19012 USA Tel 215-277-5525 phone
E-mail: seguepublishing@aol.com; kbradford@seguepublishing.com
Web site: seguepublishing.com.

Seif, Daniel J., *(978-0-9983807)* 106 Kingfisher Ln., New Hartford, NY 13413 USA Tel 315-796-2751
E-mail: danseif@roadrunner.com.

Seigle Bks., *(978-0-9852819)* 235 County Rte. 627, Phillipsburg, NJ 08865 USA Tel 908-319-0384
E-mail: prepub@bookmasters.com.

Selah Publishing Group, LLC, *(978-0-9679371; 978-1-58930)* 162 Crescent Dr., Bristol, TN 37620 USA Toll Free Fax: 866-777-8909; Toll Free: 877-616-6451 Do not confuse with the same name in Kingston, NY, Berkley, MI
E-mail: garlen@selahbooks.com
Web site: http://www.selahbooks.com.

Selah Publishing, Incorporated *See* **Selah Publishing Group, LLC**

Selby Dean Ventures, Inc., *(978-0-9716479)* P.O. Box 246, Kure Beach, NC 28449 USA (SAN 852-7539) Tel 910-279-2486
E-mail: fishinstructor@aol.com
Web site: http://www.gullswatch.com; http://www.SelbyDeanVentures.com.

Select Bks., Inc., *(978-1-59079)* Orders Addr.: 87 Walker Street, Suite B1, New York, NY 10013 USA Tel 212-206-1997; Fax: 212-206-3815; Edit Addr.: One Union Sq. W. Suite 909, New York, NY 10003 USA Tel 212-206-1997; Fax: 212-206-3815 Do not confuse with companies with the same or similar name in Evanston, IL, San Francisco, CA, Mountain View, CA, Starke, FL
E-mail: kenzi@selectbooks.com; kenichi@selectbooks.com; info@selectbooks.com
Web site: http://www.selectbooks.com
Dist(s): **BookBaby**
Ingram Publisher Services
Two Rivers Distribution.

Selective Mutism Anxiety Research & Treatment Ctr., *(978-0-9714800)* 1130 Herkness Dr., Meadowbrook, PA 19046 USA Tel 215 -887-5748; Fax: 215-827-5722
E-mail: dreshiponblum@aol.com
Web site: http://www.selectivemutismcenter.org.

Selector, S.A. de C.V. (MEX) *(978-968-403; 978-970-643; 978-607-453) Dist. by* **Lectorum Pubns.**

Selector, S.A. de C.V. (MEX) *(978-968-403; 978-970-643; 978-607-453) Dist. by* **AIMS Intl.**

Selector, S.A. de C.V. (MEX) *(978-968-403; 978-970-643; 978-607-453) Dist. by* **Libros Fronteras.**

Self-Discovery LLC, *(978-0-9974831)* 22200 W. Eleven Mile Rd. Unit No. 4232, Southfiled, MI 48037 USA Tel 248-705-9074
E-mail: Info@SelfDiscoverySolutions.com
Web site: http://www.selfdiscoverysolutions.com/.

Self-Esteem Adventures Pr., *(978-0-9747597)* P.O. Box 2145, Universal City, TX 78148 USA Tel 210-595-6952
E-mail: daddybooks@grandecom.net
Web site: http://www.daddybooks.com.

Self-Mastery Press *See* **Love & Blessings**

Self-Realization Fellowship Pubs., *(978-0-87612)* Orders Addr.: 3208 Humboldt St., Los Angeles, CA 90031 USA (SAN 204-5788) Tel 323-276-6002; Fax: 323-276-6003; Toll Free: 888-773-8680; Edit Addr.: 3880 San Rafael Ave., Los Angeles, CA 90065 USA Tel 323-276 6000; 215 K. St., Encinitas, CA 92024 Tel 760-753-2888 ext 471; Fax: 323-276-6003
E-mail: sales@srfpublishers.org
Web site: http://www.srfpublishers.org
Dist(s): **Distributors, The**
TNT Media Group, Inc.

Sellers, Amy, *(978-0-9787632)* 5151 Round Lake Rd., Apopka, FL 32712 USA (SAN 851-5425)
E-mail: amycsellers@yahoo.com
Web site: http://www.amysellers.com.

Sellers Publishing, Inc., *(978-1-56906; 978-1-4162; 978-1-5319)* Orders Addr.: P.O. Box 818, Portland, ME 04104 USA (SAN 858-1258) Tel 207-772-6833; Fax: 207-772-6814; Toll Free: 800-625-3386 (800-MAKE-FUN); Edit Addr.: 161 John Roberts Rd., South Portland, ME 04106 USA
E-mail: rsp@rsvp.com
Web site: http://www.rsvp.com
Dist(s): **Bookazine Co., Inc.**
MBI Distribution Services/Quayside Distribution
New Leaf Distributing Co., Inc.
Partners Bk. Distributing, Inc.

Sellers, Ronnie Productions, Incorporated *See* **Sellers Publishing, Inc.**

Sem Fronteiras Pr., Ltd., *(978-0-9642333)* 1530 Palisade Ave., Suite 2F, Fort Lee, NJ 07024 USA (SAN 253-4959) Toll Free Fax: 800-433-5193
E-mail: semfront@superlink.net.

Sem, Gilmore, *(978-0-9742299)* 1822 Carl St., Lauderdale, MN 55113-5203 USA.

Semele Bks., *(978-0-9764937)* 40 Cedar Ln., Princeton, NJ 08540 USA Tel 609-924-6481; Fax: 609-924-0549; Toll Free: 866-967-3835
E-mail: eva@evasiroka.com
Web site: http://www.evasiroka.com.

Semper Studio, *(978-0-9778420)* 4416 Rte. 47, Delmont, NJ 08314 USA (SAN 850-3885) Tel 609-501-3341
E-mail: Catherine@semperstudiosus.com
Web site: http://www.semperstudiosus.com.

Send The Light Distribution LLC, *(978-0-9835608; 978-1-939900)* Orders Addr.: 129 Mobilization Dr., Waynesboro, GA 30830 USA (SAN 631-8894) Tel 706-554-5827; Toll Free Fax: 877-323-4551; Toll Free: 877-323-4550; 100 Biblica Way, Elizabethton, TN 37643-6070 (SAN 630-7388) Tel 423-547-5131 editorial Toll Free Fax: 800-759-2779
E-mail: Customerservice@stl.org
Web site: http://www.stl-publisherservices.com.

Seneca Mill Pr. LLC, *(978-0-9786986; 978-0-9899595)* P.O. Box 1423, Great Falls, VA 22066 USA
E-mail: senecamillpress@aol.com.

Sensational Bks., *(978-0-9770054)* P.O. Box 261085, Lakewood, CO 80226 USA (SAN 256-6265) Tel 303-238-4760; Fax: 303-205-0614
Web site: http://www.sensationalbooks.com.

Sensational Pubns., *(978-0-9888003; 978-0-9912808; 978-1-944948)* 1756 Cumberland Green Dr Unit 126, saint Charles, IL 60174 USA Tel 630-549-7226
E-mail: cindyjusino@ymail.com
Web site: www.cindyjusino.com; http://www.sensationalpublications.com.

Sensational Publishing *See* **Sensational Pubns.**

Sense of Wonder Pr. *Imprint of* **Rock, James A. & Co. Pubs.**

Senshu, Noriko *See* **Studio Cherry Publishing**

Sensory Resources, *(978-1-893601; 978-1-931615)* Div. of Future Horizons, Inc., P.O. Box 530790, Henderson, NV 89053-0790 USA (SAN 253-8288) Toll Free: 888-357-5867
E-mail: orders@sensoryresources.com
Web site: http://www.sensoryresources.com
Dist(s): **Ingram Publisher Services**
MyiLibrary.

Sentient Pubns., *(978-0-9710786; 978-1-59181)* 1113 Spruce St., Boulder, CO 80302 USA Tel 303-443-2188; Fax: 303-447-1511; Toll Free: 866-588-9846
E-mail: cshaw@sentientpublications.com; dialagzone@aol.com
Web site: http://www.sentientpublications.com/
Dist(s): **National Bk. Network.**

Sentinel *Imprint of* **Penguin Publishing Group**

Sentinel Publishing, *(978-0-9728291)* 1131 Rossiter Ln., Wayne, PA 19087-2812 USA Tel 610-687-5908; Fax: 610-687-5909 Do not confuse with Sentinel Publishing in Ogden, UT
E-mail: orchidman@snip.net
Web site: http://www.linenpostcards.com.

Sentry Bks. *Imprint of* **Great West Publishing**

Sentry Pr., Inc., *(978-1-889574)* 424 E. Call St., Tallahassee, FL 32301-7693 USA
E-mail: wwrogers@peoplepc.com
Web site: http://sentry-press.com/
Dist(s): **Polk County Historical Assn.**

Seoul Selection, *(978-1-62412)* 4199 Campus Dr., Suite 550, Irvine, CA 92612 USA Tel 949-509-6584; Fax: 949-509-6599
E-mail: sales@seoulselection.com
Web site: www.seoulselection.com
Dist(s): **SPD-Small Pr. Distribution.**

Publisher Name Index

Sephyrus *See* **Sephyrus Pr.**

Sephyrus Pr., (*978-0-615-23982-8; 978-0-9830137*) PO Box 72513, Phoenix, AZ 85050 USA Tel 203-414-5694
E-mail: rachel@sephyrus.com
Web site: http://sephyruspress.com.

SepSha Publishing, (*978-0-9727885*) P.O. Box 462075, Aurora, CO 80046 USA (SAN 255-3007)
Web site: http://www.endtimebooks.com.

Sequent Media, Inc., (*978-0-9746531*) P.O. Box 126325, San Diego, CA 92112 USA
Web site: http://www.sequentmedia.com.

Seraph Publishing, (*978-1-934948*) 7660 Fay Ave., La Jolla, CA 92037-4843 USA
E-mail: info@markmlittle.com.

Seraphemera Bks *See* **Seraphemera Bks.**

Seraphemera Bks., (*978-0-9778989; 978-0-9815516; 978-0-9844441; 978-0-9846464; 978-0-9971384; 978-0-9978698; 978-1-947406*) P.O. Box 73562, Houston, TX 77273-7727 USA Tel 832-515-9539
E-mail: three@seraphemera.org
Web site: http://www.seraphemera.org.

Seraphic Pr., (*978-0-9754382*) 1531 Cardiff Ave., Los Angeles, CA 90035 USA (SAN 256-0496) Tel 310-557-0132; Fax: 310-286-9534
E-mail: robert@seraphicpress.com; rjaprod@aol.com
Web site: http://www.seraphicpress.com
Dist(s): **David, Jonathan Pubs., Inc.**

Seraphim Pubns., (*978-0-615-21071-1*) 17641 Gilmore St., Van Nuys, CA 91406 USA
E-mail: toni@seraphimpublications.com
Web site: http://www.seraphimpublications.com.

Seraphina *Imprint of* **Bonita and Hodge Publishing Group**

Seren Bks. (GBR) (*978-0-907476; 978-1-85411; 978-1-78172*) *Dist. by* **IPG Chicago.**

Serena Bocchino/In His Perfect Time Collection, (*978-0-9767674; 978-0-9838660; 978-0-9961443*) 82 Haas Rd., Basking Ridge, NJ 07920 USA
E-mail: serena@serenaboochino.com
Web site: http://www.serenabocchino.com.

Serendib Pr., (*978-0-615-18889-8*) 1611 N. Bell, No. 3N, Chicago, IL 60647 USA
Dist(s): **Lulu Pr., Inc.**

Serendipity Hse. *Imprint of* **LifeWay Christian Resources**

Serenity Pr., (*978-0-9787981*) 500 SW. 21st Terr., Fort Lauderdale, FL 33312 USA (SAN 851-6251)
E-mail: marty@mwpr.com
Web site: http://www.mwpr.com/Splash.html.

Serenity Pubs. *Imprint of* **Arc Manor**

Serey/Jones Pubs., (*978-1-881276*) 7413 W. Oraibi Dr., Glendale, AZ 85308 USA Tel 623-561-0240; Fax: 623-561-8441
E-mail: info@sereyjones.com.

Serpent's Tale Natural History Bk. Distributors, Inc., (*978-1-885209*) Orders Addr.: P.O. Box 405, Lanesboro, MN 55949-0405 USA (SAN 630-6101) Tel 507-467-8734; Fax: 507-467-8735
E-mail: zoobooks@acegroup.cc
Web site: http://www.zoobooksales.com.

Serres, Ediciones, S. L. (ESP) (*978-84-88061; 978-84-95040; 978-84-8488*) *Dist. by* **Lectorum Pubns.**

Servant Bks. *Imprint of* **Franciscan Media**

Serve Man Pr., (*978-0-9768517*) P.O. Box 1445, Easthampton, MA 01027 USA Tel 413-209-1029
E-mail: rokaril@hotmail.com
Web site: http://www.seanwang.com; www.runnersuniverse.com.

Servilibro Ediciones, S.A. (ESP) (*978-84-7971*) *Dist. by* **Giron Bks.**

Serving Jesus Christ with Joy Ministries, (*978-0-9770078; 978-0-9774428*) Div. of Serving Jesus Christ with Joy, Orders Addr.: 316 E. Ajo, Tucson, AZ 85713 USA Tel 520-406-1674 (Publishing Phone) 520-889-0215 (Publishing Fax)
E-mail: pastorrandy@sjcwj.org; info@sjcwj.org
Web site: http://christianbooks1.com.

Serving One Lord Resources, (*978-0-9823137*) P.O. Box 98, Sewickley, PA 15143 USA
Web site: www.servingonelord.com.

Session Family, (*978-0-9658006*) Orders Addr.: P.O. Box 841, Florissaint, MO 63032 USA Tel 314-972-7705 (phone/fax); Edit Addr.: 16856 Heather Moor Dr., Florissant, MO 63034 USA
E-mail: denise.session@att.net
Web site: http://www.sessionfamily.com.

Set on a Hill, (*978-0-9971485*) 11152 Westheimer Rd No. 1115, Houston, TX 77042 USA Tel 832-900-9802
E-mail: info@setonahill.com
Web site: www.setonahill.com.

Seton Pr., (*978-1-60704*) 1350 Progress Dr., Front Royal, VA 22630 USA Tel 540-636-9990; Fax: 540-636-1602
Web site: http://setonhome.org.

Setubandh Pubns., (*978-0-9623674*) 1 Lawson Ln., Great Neck, NY 11023 USA Tel 516-482-6938
Web site: http://www.setubandh.com.

Seven C's Productions, Inc., (*978-0-9910345*) 311 W. 43rd St. Penthouse, New York, NY 10036 USA Tel 212-757-7555
E-mail: marc@7csproductions.com
Web site: www.7csproductions.com.

Seven Footer Pr., (*978-0-9740439; 978-0-9788178; 978-1-934734*) 184 Kendrick Pl., Apt. 28, Gaithersburg, MD 20878-5662 USA; 247 W. 30th St., New York, NY 10001-2824
E-mail: david@wouldyourather.com; jnheimberg@aol.com
Web site: http://www.wouldyourather.com; http://www.movieplotgenerator.com
Dist(s): **Publishers Group West (PGW).**

Seven Guns Pr., (*978-0-615-70006-9; 978-0-9884259; 978-0-615-82838-1; 978-0-9899461; 978-0-9974474; 978-0-9982177*) 2405 Jennieville Dr., Davidsonville, MD 21035 USA Tel 4433066691
Dist(s): **CreateSpace Independent Publishing Platform.**

†Seven Locks Pr., (*978-0-929765; 978-0-932020; 978-0-9615964; 978-1-931643; 978-0-9790950; 978-0-9795852; 978-0-9801270; 978-0-9822293; 978-0-9824957*) P.O. Box 25689, Santa Ana, CA 92799-5689 USA (SAN 211-9781) Toll Free: 800-354-5348
E-mail: sevenlocks@aol.com
Web site: http://www.sevenlockspublishing.com; *CIP.*

Seven Rivers Publishing, (*978-0-9728768; 978-0-615-63339-8*) P.O. Box 682, Crowley, TX 76036-0682 USA Toll Free: 800-544-3770 (Order line: Hendrick-Long)
E-mail: hendrick-long@att.net; djls@sevenriverspublishing.com; sales@sevenriverspublishing.com; seven-rivers@earthlink.net
Web site: http://www.hendricklongpublishing.com; http://www.sevenriverspublishing.com; http://www.smashwords.com/books/view/93148
Dist(s): **CreateSpace Independent Publishing Platform**
Hendrick-Long Publishing Co.
Lightning Source, Inc.
Smashwords.

Seven Seas Entertainment, LLC, (*978-1-933164; 978-1-934876; 978-1-935934; 978-1-937867; 978-1-62692*) 3463 State St., Suite 545, Santa Barbara, CA 93105 USA
Web site: http://www.gomanga.com
Dist(s): **Diamond Comic Distributors, Inc.**
Diamond Bk. Distributors
Macmillan.

Seven Stars Trading Co., (*978-0-9743999; 978-0-9863464*) 3543 Marvin St., Annandale, VA 22003 USA Tel 703-573-2939.

Seven Stories Pr., (*978-1-58322; 978-1-888363; 978-1-60980*) 140 Watts St., New York, NY 10013 USA Tel 212-226-8760; Fax: 212-226-1411; Toll Free: 800-596-7437; *Imprints:* Triangle Square (Triangle Sq)
E-mail: info@sevenstories.com
Web site: http://www.sevenstories.com
Dist(s): **Independent Pubs. Group**
MyiLibrary
Penguin Random Hse. LLC
Random Hse., Inc.

SevenHorns Publishing, (*978-0-9838427; 978-0-9976846*) P.O. Box 269, Randolph, MA 02368 USA Tel 856-269-2852
E-mail: admin@sevenhornspublishing.com
Web site: http://www.sonsofcaasi.com; http://www.biffprice.com; http://www.sevenhornspublishing.com; http://www.adventuresofjackandmax.com.

Seventh Street Pr., Div. of Malone-Ballard Book Pubs., 2215 6th Ave. Apt D, Moline, IL 61265 USA
E-mail: bookwoman1110@hotmail.com.

Severn Hse. Pubs., Ltd. (GBR) (*978-0-7278; 978-1-78029; 978-0-9560566; 978-1-78010; 978-1-4483*) *Dist. by* **IngramPubServ.**

Seymour, Dale Pubns., (*978-0-201; 978-0-7690; 978-0-86651; 978-1-57232*) Div. of Pearson Learning, Orders Addr.: P.O. Box 2500, Lebanon, OH 43216 USA Toll Free Fax: 800-393-3156; Toll Free: 800-321-3106 (Customer Service); Edit Addr.: 10 Bank St., White Plains, NY 10602-5026 USA (SAN 200-9781) Toll Free Fax: 800-393-3156; Toll Free: 800-237-3142
E-mail: pearson_learning2@prenhall.com
Web site: http://www.pearsonlearning.com; http://www.pearsonlearning.com/rightsPerm.rtf
Dist(s): **Addison-Wesley Educational Pubs., Inc.**

Seymour Institute for Advanced Christian Studies, (*978-0-9765717*) 411 Washington St., Dorchester, MA 02124 USA Tel 617-373-7273; Fax: 617-373-7575
E-mail: erivers@ntlf.org.

Seymour Institute for the Advancement of Christian *See* **Seymour Institute for Advanced Christian Studies**

Seymour Science LLC *See* **Isabella Products, Inc.**

SFT Pubns., (*978-0-9724384*) Orders Addr.: 3915 S. Cramer Cir., Bloomington, IN 47403 USA (SAN 254-8283) Tel 812-333-8902
E-mail: leilarandle@sbcglobal.net.

Sgian Enterprises, (*978-0-9771197; 978-0-615-12814-6*) 4349 W. Tomahawk Dr., Beverly Hills, FL 34465-4871 USA.

Shaar Pr. *Imprint of* **Mesorah Pubns., Ltd.**

Shade Bks. *Imprint of* **Stone Arch Bks.**

Shades of Me Publishing, (*978-0-9718307*) 3969 Strandhill Rd., Cleveland, OH 44128 USA
E-mail: marybury1927@msn.com.

Shades of White, (*978-0-9796834*) 301 Tenth Ave., Crystal City, MO 63019 USA Tel 314-740-0361; *Imprints:* Magical Child Books (Magical Child)
Web site: http://www.magicalchildbooks.com
Dist(s): **New Leaf Distributing Co., Inc.**

ShadeTree Publishing, LLC, (*978-0-9822632; 978-1-937331*) 1038 N. Eisenhower Dr., No. 274, Beckley, WV 25801 USA (SAN 857-6971)
E-mail: jennifer.minigh@shadetreepublishing.com
Web site: http://www.shadetreepublishing.com.

Shadow Canyon Graphics, (*978-0-9857420*) 454 Somerset Dr., Golden, CO 80401 USA Tel 303 278 0949; Fax: 303-279-5831
E-mail: dnshadow@earthlink.net.

Shadow Mountain *Imprint of* **Deseret Bk. Co.**

Shadow Mountain *Imprint of* **Shadow Mountain Publishing**

Shadow Mountain Publishing, (*978-0-87579; 978-1-57345; 978-1-59038; 978-1-60907*) Div. of Deseret Book Company, P.O. Box 30178, Salt Lake City, UT 84130 USA Tel 801-517-3223; *Imprints:* Shadow Mountain (ShadowMountain); Ensign Peak (EnsPeak)
E-mail: info@shadowmountain.com
Web site: http://www.shadowmountain.com
Dist(s): **Blackstone Audio, Inc.**
Deseret Bk. Co.

Shadow Pubns., (*978-0-9771424*) P.O. Box 1151, Valley Forge, PA 19482-1151 USA
Web site: http://www.olliedude.com.

ShadowPlay Pr., (*978-0-9638819*) P.O. Box 647, Forreston, IL 61030 USA Tel 815-938-3151; Fax: 815-371-1440
E-mail: sheilawelch@juno.com; ericwelch2@juno.com
Web site: http://www.shadowplay.userworld.com.

Shady Tree Productions, (*978-0-9747352*) 5383 Iron Pen Pl., Columbia, MD 21044 USA Tel 410-997-6337 (phone/fax)
E-mail: shadytreepro@hotmail.com; bigtree_75@msn.com; ronfullwood@returningsoldiers.us.

Shaffer, Dale E., (*978-0-915060*) 478 Jennings Ave., Salem, OH 44460-2732 USA (SAN 206-9067).

Shaffer, Earl Foundation, Inc., (*978-0-9795659*) 1635 Haft Dr., Reynoldsburg, OH 43068-3059 USA Tel 614-751-0029
E-mail: spur@mac.com
Web site: http://www.earlshaffer.org.

Shaffner, Randolph P. *See* **Faraway Publishing**

Shaggy Dog Pr., (*978-0-9722007*) P.O. Box 4436 Reeves Road, Ojai, CA 93023 USA Tel 805-646-1849
E-mail: shaggydogpress@gmail.com.

Shah, Meera, (*978-0-9774219*) 7003 Westminster Ln., Germantown, TN 38138 USA Tel 901-754-7197
E-mail: meeds_46@yahoo.com; merra.meeds46@gmail.com.

Shakalot High Entertainment, (*978-0-9721067; 978-0-9796219*) 20687 White Dove Ln., Bend, OR 97702 USA Tel 541-788-4011; 13019 SW 154th Ave., Tigard, OR 97223 Tel 503-548-3336; *Imprints:* Writing Wild & Crazy (Writing Wild)
E-mail: shakalothighentertainment@yahoo.com
Web site: http://www.shakalothigh.com
Dist(s): **Lulu Pr., Inc.**

Shake the Moon Bks., (*978-0-615-25125-7; 978-0-615-53638-5*) 6216 Denny Ave., N. Hollywood, CA 91606 USA Tel 818-903-4112
E-mail: scott@shakethemoonbooks.com
Web site: http://www.shakethemoonbooks.com
Dist(s): **Bookmasters Distribution.**

ShakeB Co., (*978-0-615-24232-3; 978-0-615-41353-2*) 1189 Masselin Ave., Los Angeles, CA 90019 USA.

Shakespeare Graphics *Imprint of* **Stone Arch Bks.**

Shalako Pr., (*978-0-9798898; 978-0-9830608; 978-0-9846811; 978-0-9892917; 978-0-9908878; 978-0-9964235; 978-0-9970679; 978-0-9990070*) P.O. Box 371, Oakdale, CA 95361-0371 USA (SAN 854-6622)
E-mail: major@majormitchell.net
Web site: http://www.shalakopress.com
Dist(s): **Smashwords.**

Shalhout, Ahlam LLC *See* **Expressions Woven**

Shamber Pubns., (*978-0-9771326*) P.O. Box 470321, Lake Monroe, FL 32747-0321 USA
E-mail: unbrokencirclebymcghee@gmail.com.

Shambhala Publications, Incorporated *See* **Shambhala Pubns., Inc.**

†Shambhala Pubns., Inc., (*978-0-8348; 978-0-87773; 978-0-937938; 978-0-9627138; 978-1-55939; 978-1-56957; 978-1-57062; 978-1-930485; 978-1-59030; 978-1-61180*) 4720 Walnut St., Boulder, CO 80301 USA (SAN 203-2481) Tel 303-222-9598; 978-829-2599 (international); Toll Free: 888-424-2329 (orders); *Imprints:* Weatherhill, Incorporated (Weathill); Trumpeter (Trumpeter); Roost Books (Roost Bks); Snow Lion Publications, Incorporated (SnowLion)
E-mail: editors@shambhala.com; support@shambhala.com; customercare@shambhala.com
Web site: http://www.shambhala.com
Dist(s): **MyiLibrary**
Penguin Random Hse. LLC
Random Hse., Inc.; *CIP.*

Shammah Ministries, (*978-0-9725944*) Orders Addr.: 1346 Oak Pk. Dr., Aransas Pass, TX 78336 USA Tel 361-226-4918
E-mail: tonia@shammah.org; twoolever@gmail.com
Web site: http://www.shammah.org.

Shamrock Pr., (*978-0-9675410*) Orders Addr.: P.O. Box 58186, Charleston, WV 25358 USA Tel 304-744-4259 (phone/fax) Do not confuse with Shamrock Pr. in Chattanooga, TN
E-mail: shamrockpress@frontier.com
Web site: www.shamrockpress.com.

Shamrock Publishing, Inc., (*978-0-9743244; 978-0-9759703*) 400 Corey Ave., Wachovia Bldg., 2nd Flr., Saint Pete Beach, FL 33706 USA Tel 727-363-4747; Fax: 727-363-4848; 1220 S. State St., Chicago, IL 60605 Tel 312-212-1143; Fax: 708-371-9576 Do not confuse with Shamrock Publishing, Incorporated in New Orleans, LA
E-mail: tpmac@sprynet.com; bksemmer@blueshamrockpublishing.com.

Shamus B. Publishing, (*978-0-9753671*) 18533 Pond Dr., Abingdon, VA 24211 USA.

Shan Jen Publishing Co., Ltd. (TWN) (*978-986-7517; 978-957-2041; 978-957-8298; 978-957-9658; 978-957-99079*) *Dist. by* **Chinasprout.**

Shanahan, John Francis Publishing, (*978-0-9618275*) 6727 N. Lightfoot Ave., Chicago, IL 60646 USA (SAN 667-0490) Tel 773-631-6344; Fax: 773-631-6372
E-mail: REPSbooks@aol.com.

Shanbhag, Arun, (*978-0-9790081*) 32 Chatham St., Arlington, MA 02474-2008 USA
E-mail: arun@shanbhag.org.

Shangri-La Pubns., (*978-0-9677201; 978-0-9714683; 978-0-9719496*) Orders Addr.: P.O. Box 65, Warren Center, PA 18851-0065 USA Toll Free: 866-966-6288; Edit Addr.: 3 Coburn Hill Rd., PMB 65, Warren Center, PA 18851 USA Tel 570-395-3423; Fax: 570-395-0146
E-mail: gosline@egypt.net; shangrila@egypt.net; shangri_la_book@hotmail.com
Web site: http://www.shangri-la.0catch.com/.

Shannon Road Pr., (*978-0-9788785; 978-0-9846101*) 16330 Shannon Rd., Los Gatos, CA 95032 USA
E-mail: info@shannonroadpress.com
Web site: http://www.shannonroadpress.com.

Shanti Publishing, (*978-0-615-86491-4; 978-0-615-88564-3; 978-0-615-93871-4; 978-0-692-32474-5; 978-0-692-35882-5; 978-0-692-36270-9; 978-0-692-38178-6; 978-0-692-38320-9; 978-0-692-44042-1; 978-0-692-47800-4; 978-0-9973754*) P.O. Box 6252, Pine Mountain Club, CA 93222 USA Tel 6613199977
Web site: www.ShantiPublishing.com
Dist(s): **CreateSpace Independent Publishing Platform.**

Shapato Publishing, LLC, (*978-0-9821058; 978-0-9826992; 978-0-9833526; 978-0-615-50457-5; 978-0-615-50918-1; 978-0-615-50920-4; 978-0-615-50921-1; 978-0-615-51306-5; 978-0-615-53431-2; 978-0-615-53435-0; 978-0-615-56643-6; 978-0-615-59791-1; 978-0-615-60650-7; 978-0-615-72638-0; 978-0-615-83271-5; 978-0-615-91943-0; 978-0-692-25479-0; 978-0-692-30027-5; 978-0-692-58092-9) Orders Addr.: P.O. Box 476, Everly, IA 51338 USA Tel 712-490-5165; Edit Addr.: 503 E 2nd St., Everly, IA 51338 USA*
E-mail: Jean@midwestwriter.com
Web site: http://www.shapatopublishing.com
Dist(s): **CreateSpace Independent Publishing Platform**
Smashwords.

Shar-Don & Associates, Incorporated *See* **Lovin Ovens, Inc.**

Share & Care Society, (*978-0-9722025*) 2105 55th Ln., NW, Olympia, WA 98502 USA Tel 760-819-9174; *Imprints:* True Lightening (True Lght)
E-mail: london_pain@hotmail.com
Web site: http://www.shareandcaresociety.org.

Share Publishing, (*978-0-9633705*) Orders Addr.: 313 Laurel Ave., Menlo Park, CA 94025 USA Tel 650-321-5947 (phone/fax)
E-mail: pamelalaw@sbcglobal.net
Web site: http://sharepublishing.com.

Sharif, Mboya *See* **Doses of Reality, Inc.**

Shark Press *See* **Lemon Shark Pr.**

†Sharp & Dunnigan, (*978-0-918495*) 2700 Richards Rd., Suite 110, Bellevue, WA 98005 USA (SAN 657-3029) Tel 425-467-6565; Fax: 425-467-6564
E-mail: ecovepress@aol.com
Web site: http://elfincovepress.com
Dist(s): **Elfin Cove Pr.**; *CIP.*

Sharp & Dunnigan, Publications, Incorporated *See* **Sharp & Dunnigan**

Sharp, Diana Consulting, (*978-0-9762626*) 5954 Fishhawk Crossing Blvd., Lithia, FL 33547-5878 USA.

SHARP Literacy, Inc., (*978-0-9770816; 978-0-9836222; 978-0-9986683*) 750 N. Lincoln Memorial Dr. Suite 311, Milwaukee, WI 53202 USA Tel 414-270-3388
Web site: http://www.sharpliteracy.org.

Sharpe, Jeannie W., (*978-0-9763117*) 373 Langford Rd., Blythewood, SC 29016 USA Fax: 803-786-4557
E-mail: jws415@aol.com.

Shauger, Daniel, (*978-0-9746114*) 12438 Moorpark St., No. 241, Studio City, CA 91605 USA Tel 818-693-6231
E-mail: dan@aperfectswing.com
Web site: http://www.aperfectswing.com.

Shaw, Dana, (*978-0-9791091*) Orders Addr.: P.O. Box 91, Franklin, ME 04634 USA (SAN 852-4815) Tel 207-565-4445; Edit Addr.: 206 Georges Pond Rd., Franklin, ME 04634 USA
E-mail: myfriendzundel@yahoo.com
Web site: http://myfriendzundel.com.

Shawnee Pr., Inc., (*978-0-8256; 978-0-9603394; 978-1-59235*) Subs. of Music Sales Corp., Orders Addr.: P.O. Box 1250, Marshalls Creek, PA 18335 USA Toll Free Fax: 800-345-6842; Toll Free: 800-962-8584; Edit Addr.: 9 Dartmouth Dr., Bldg. 4, Marshalls Creek, PA 18335 USA (SAN 202-084X) Tel 212-254-2100 (copyright & licensing information); 570-476-0550; Fax: 570-476-5247
E-mail: shawnee-info@shawneepress.com
Web site: http://www.shawneepress.com
Dist(s): **Leonard, Hal Corp.**
Music Sales Corp.

Shayach Comics *Imprint of* **Judaica Pr., Inc., The**

Shaymaa Publishing Corp., (*978-0-9719581*) P.O. Box 501, Lodi, NJ 07644-0501 USA (SAN 255-738X) Fax: 973-237-0537
E-mail: elhewiemf@juno.com; todaysgy@todaysgym.com; elhewie@lift-4-life.com
Web site: http://www.lift-4-life.com; http://www.todaysgym.com; http://www.shaymaa-publishing.com.

Shayne Publishing, (*978-0-9771192*) 4895 SE 40th St., Des Moines, IA 50320 USA (SAN 256-7997) Tel 515-263-2784
E-mail: dlhuston01@aol.com.

Shazak Productions *Imprint of* **Torah Excel**

†Shearer Publishing, (*978-0-940672*) 406 Post Oak Rd., Fredericksburg, TX 78624 USA Tel 830-997-6529; Fax: 830-997-9752; Toll Free: 800-458-3808
E-mail: shearer@shearerpub.com
Web site: http://www.shearerpub.com
Dist(s): **Bk. Marketing Plus**
Texas A&M Univ. Pr.; *CIP.*

Shechinah Third Temple, Inc., (*978-0-9723866; 978-0-9817212; 978-0-9895128*) 11583 Pamplona Blvd., Boynton Beach, FL 33437 USA Tel 561-735-7958; Fax: 561-738-1535
E-mail: thirdtemple@bellsouth.net; jerrypollock@bellsouth.net
Web site: http://www.shechinahthirdtemple.org.

Sheepdog Pr., (*978-0-9742205*) P.O. Box 60, Onancock, VA 23417 USA Tel 888-787-1951; Fax: 888-787-2675
E-mail: publisher@sheepdogpress.com
Web site: http://www.sheepdogpress.com.

Sheets, Judy, (*978-0-9726451*) 2526 Brune Rd., Farmington, MO 63640 USA Tel 573-756-6254
E-mail: judys@i1.net.
Shekinah Productions, (*978-0-9802250; 978-0-578-04316-6; 978-0-578-05243-4; 978-0-578-05610-4; 978-0-578-05834-4; 978-0-578-07417-7; 978-0-578-08092-5; 978-0-578-08093-2; 978-0-578-08094-9; 978-0-578-08182-3; 978-0-578-08415-2; 978-0-578-08869-3; 978-0-578-10324-2; 978-0-578-11645-7; 978-0-578-12000-3; 978-0-578-13210-5; 978-0-578-13328-7; 978-0-578-13499-4; 978-0-578-13962-3; 978-0-578-14057-5; 978-0-578-14114-5; 978-0-578-18040-3; 978-0-578-19525-4; 978-0-578-19715-9; 978-0-578-19716-6) 8111 Windersgate Drive, Olive Branch, MS 38654 USA Fax: 662-504-4234; P.O. Box 209, Olive Branch, MS 38654*
E-mail: shekinah.productions@yahoo.com
Web site: http://www.skpseminars.com.
Shekinah Publishing Hse., (*978-0-9700976; 978-1-940153*) Orders Addr.: P.O. Box 1118811, Carrollton, TX 75011 USA Tel 877-538-1363; Edit Addr.: P.O. Box 118811, Carrollton, TX 75011 USA Fax: 877-538-1363; *Imprints:* Shekinah Publishing House (Shek Pub Hse) Do not confuse with companies with the same or similar names in Cameron, NC, Cameron, NC
E-mail: lpbowk@thebwfg.com; author@shekinahpublishinghouse.com.
Shekinah Publishing Hse. *Imprint of* **Shekinah Publishing Hse.**
Shelby, Lloyd *See* **Painted WORD Studios**
Shelbykay Pubilshing Co., (*978-0-9744407*) 525 Greenhill Ln., Philadelphia, PA 19128 USA Tel 215-483-6688
E-mail: cdkae@aol.com.
Shelf-Life Bks., (*978-1-880042*) Div. of M.A.P.S., Inc., 2132 Fordem, Madison, WI 53704-0599 USA Tel 608-244-7767; Fax: 608-244-8394.
Shell Beach Publishing, LLC, (*978-0-9706732*) 677 Shell Beach Dr., Lake Charles, LA 70601-5732 USA Tel 433-439-2110
E-mail: kkblake@compuserve.com.
Shell Educational Publishing, (*978-1-4258*) 5301 Oceanus Dr., Huntington Beach, CA 92649 USA Tel 714-489-2080; Fax: 714-230-7070; Toll Free: 888-877-7606; 877-777-3450
E-mail: cmiller2@tcmpub.com; LShill@seppub.com; pkoehl@tcmpub.com; CMiller2@teachercreatedmaterials.com
Web site: http://www.seppub.com; http://www.tcmpub.com
Dist(s): **Follett School Solutions**
Lectorum Pubns., Inc.
Teacher Created Materials, Inc.
Shelle, Carole Creative Arts, (*978-0-9792641*) P.O. Box 52972, Irvine, CA 92619 USA (SAN 852-9493) Toll Free: 800-929-1634.
Shelley Adina, (*978-0-615-52095-7; 978-0-615-62675-8; 978-1-939087*) P.O. Box 752, Redwood Estates, CA 95044 USA Tel 408-761-1195; *Imprints:* Moonshell Books, Inc. (MoonshellBks)
Web site: http://www.shelleyadina.com
Dist(s): **CreateSpace Independent Publishing Platform.**
Shelly's Adventures LLC, (*978-0-9851845*) P.O. Box 2632, Land O Lakes, FL 34639 USA Tel 352-219-7199
E-mail: kentrell@shellysadventuresllc.com; kentrell.martin15@gmail.com; kentrell@shellysadventures.com
Web site: www.shellysadventuresllc.com; www.shellysadventures.com
Dist(s): **Partners Pubs. Group, Inc.**
Shelter Harbor Pr., (*978-0-9853230; 978-1-62795*) 605 W. 115th St. Suite 163, New York, NY 10025 USA Tel 212-864-0427; Fax: 212-316-6496
E-mail: Jeanette.Limondjian@gmail.com; info@shelterharborpress.com; jeanette@shelterharborpress.com.
Shelter of Flint, Inc., (*978-0-9740929*) 902 E. 6th St., Flint, MI 48503-2787 USA
E-mail: sof@shelterofflint.com
Web site: http://www.shelterofflint.com.
†Shelter Pubns., Inc., (*978-0-936070*) Orders Addr.: P.O. Box 279, Bolinas, CA 94924 USA (SAN 122-8463) Tel 415-868-0280; Fax: 415-868-9053; Toll Free: 800-307-0131; Edit Addr.: 285 Dogwood Rd, Bolinas, CA 94924 USA
E-mail: shelter@shelterpub.com
Web site: http://www.shelterpub.com
Dist(s): **Bk. Express**
Bookmen, Inc.
Distributors, The
Koen Pacific
Partners/West Book Distributors
Publishers Group West (PGW); *CIP.*
shelterpetsink, (*978-0-9740980*) 16457 Gledhill St., North Hills, CA 91343 USA Fax: 818-892-2112
E-mail: shelterpetsink@shelterpetsink.com; remilove2002@yahoo.com
Web site: http://www.shelterpetsink.com.
Shenandoah County Historical Society, Inc., (*978-0-9795924*) P.O. Box 506, Edinburg, VA 22824 USA Tel 540-465-5570
E-mail: adamsons@shentel.net.
Shenango River Bks., (*978-1-888836*) P.O. Box 631, Sharon, PA 16146 USA Tel 412-342-3811; Fax: 412-342-1583.
Shenanigan Bks., (*978-0-9726614; 978-1-934860*) 84 River Rd., Summit, NJ 07901-1443 USA (SAN 915-7085)
Web site: http://www.shenaniganbooks.com
Dist(s): **Jobson, Oliver H.**
Shenanigans Series,
Shen's Bks. *Imprint of* **Lee & Low Bks., Inc.**
Shepard Pubns., (*978-0-938497; 978-1-62035; 978-0-9849616; 978-0-9898649*) P.O. Box 280, Friday Harbor, WA 98250 USA (SAN 661-0536); *Imprints:* Skyhook Press (Skyhook Pr)
Web site: http://www.shepardpub.com
Dist(s): **CreateSpace Independent Publishing Platform**
Lightning Source, Inc.
Shepherd Mountain Pr., (*978-0-9749282*) 21 Cargill Rd., Liberty, ME 04949 USA Tel 207-589-4772.
Shepherd Pr. Inc., (*978-0-9663786; 978-0-9723046; 978-0-9767582; 978-0-9815400; 978-0-9824387; 978-0-9830990; 978-1-936908; 978-1-63342*) Orders Addr.: P.O. Box 24, Wapwallopen, PA 18660 USA Tel 570-379-2101; Fax: 570-379-2071; Toll Free: 800-338-1445; Edit Addr.: 437 S. River St., Wapwallopen, PA 18660 USA Do not confuse with companies with the same or similar names in Tappan, NJ, S. Hackensack, NJ, Birmingham, AL, Amityville, NY
E-mail: info@shepherdpress.com
Web site: http://www.shepherdpress.com.
Shepherd's Workshop, LLC, The, (*978-0-9752895*) 8213 Otis Ct., Arvada, CO 80003 USA Toll Free: 888-257-4673
E-mail: info@tsworkshop.com
Web site: http://www.tsworkshop.com.
Sheppard Publishing, (*978-0-9725286*) 3371 Old Forge Rd., Kent, OH 44240 USA Tel 330-325-9658
E-mail: sheppardpublishing@neo.rr.com.
Sher-A-Craft, (*978-0-9670612*) Div. of Bell Blueprint Co., Inc., 7888 Othello Ave., San Diego, CA 92111 USA Tel 619-278-4830; Fax: 619-278-6830; Toll Free: 877-235-5877.
Sheri McCulley Studio, (*978-0-9981591*) 5928 Hemlock St., Merriam, KS 66202 USA Tel 913-362-0560
E-mail: tseib@aol.com.
Sherian Publishing, (*978-0-9795676*) 2700 Braselton Hwy., Suite 10-390, Dacula, GA 30019-3207 USA Tel 888-276-6730; Fax: 888-209-8212; Toll Free: 888-276-6730
E-mail: sherri.sheusi@sherianinc.com
Web site: http://www.sherianinc.com.
Sheridan Books *See* **KEYGARD**
Sheridan County Historical Society Pr., (*978-0-9792871*) Orders Addr.: 850 Sibley Cir., Sheridan, WY 82801-9626 USA
Web site: http://www.sheridancountyhistory.org
Dist(s): **Greenleaf Book Group.**
Sherman Asher Publishing, (*978-0-9644196; 978-1-890932*) P.O. Box 31725, Santa Fe, NM 87594-1725 USA
E-mail: westernedge@santa-fe.net
Web site: http://www.shermanasher.com
Dist(s): **Partners/West Book Distributors**
SCB Distributors.
Sherman, Linda, (*978-0-615-16017-7*) 31557 W. 10 Mile Rd., Farmington, MI 48336 USA Tel 248-476-3433; Fax: 248-476-4307
E-mail: grandmalouie@hotmail.com
Web site: http://grandmalouie.com.
Sheron Enterprises, Inc., (*978-1-891877*) 1035 S. Carley Ct., N Bellmore, NY 11710-2051 USA
E-mail: sheron@concentric.net.
Sherrifmatt9 Publishing Company *See* **Second Time Media & Communications**
Sherry Gansle *See* **Little Big Tomes**
Sherwood Publishing LLC, (*978-0-9987872*) 16480 White Haven DR, Northville, MI 48168 USA Tel 734-420-6932
E-mail: jam@mipalmers.us.
Sheva, Marie, (*978-0-9741736*) 301 Main St., Apt. 8, East Greenwich, RI 02818 USA
E-mail: mariesheva@yearofthedogs.com
Web site: http://www.yearofthedogs.com.
ShiaGnosis, (*978-0-9975945; 978-1-946737; 978-1-946737-00-7*) 1115 Virginia Ave., Hagerstown, MD 21740 USA Tel 301-582-8743
E-mail: ddsodagar@gmail.com
Web site: www.shiagnosis.com; https://heavenlywise.com.
Shields, Kathleen J. *See* **Erin Go Bragh Publishing**
Shiloh Children's Bks., (*978-0-9777923; 978-0-615-81504-6*) P.O. Box 954, Polson, MT 59860 USA Tel 406-531-2281
E-mail: oxman@blackfoot.net.
Shiloh Group *See* **Shiloh Children's Bks.**
Shine On Pubns., (*978-0-9749806*) 12325 Kosich Pl., Saratoga, CA 95070 USA; 12325 Kosich Pl., Saratoga, CA 95070-3575
Web site: http://www.shineonpublications.com.
Shine Publishing Hse., (*978-0-9749467*) 1811 Abbey Oak Dr., Suite 12879, Vienna, VA 22182 USA (SAN 255-9269) Tel 571-432-8922; Fax: 703-448-8443
E-mail: sales@shinepublishing.com
Web site: http://www.shinepublishing.com
Dist(s): **CreateSpace Independent Publishing Platform**
Global Bk. Distributors.
Shine Time Records & Bks., (*978-0-9712398*) Orders Addr.: P.O. Box 331941, Nashville, TN 37203 USA Tel 615-242-9857 (phone/fax); Toll Free: 888-807-4463 (888-80-SHINE)
E-mail: chucwhit@usit.net; info@shinetime.com; info@littleststar.com
Web site: http://www.littleststar.com; http://www.shinetime.com.
Shining Hall *Imprint of* **Twelve Winters Pr.**
Shining Tramp Pr., (*978-0-9749352; 978-0-615-46043-7*) 2114 Harbor View Dr., Rocky Hill, CT 06067 USA Tel 860-563-1899
E-mail: kjmurphy@sbcglobal.net
Dist(s): **CreateSpace Independent Publishing Platform.**
Shiny Red Ball Publishing, (*978-0-9773608*) 105 Lakeover Dr., Athens, GA 30607 USA
Web site: http://www.shinyredball.com.
Shires Press *Imprint of* **Northshire Pr.**
Shirley's Girl Pubns., (*978-0-578-06605-9*) 2165 Silverado St., San Marcos, CA 92078 USA Tel 619-723-8492
E-mail: LVa2thpro@gmail.com.
Shirt Tales *Imprint of* **Brookteam Corp.**
Shively, Lisa Cookbooks, (*978-0-9766756*) P.O. Box 2123, Eden, NC 27289 USA
E-mail: loopi3@earthlink.net; kitchenhelpers@earthlink.net
Web site: http://www.fromourhometoyours.net; http://www.cookingwithlisa.com.
Shiver Hill Bks., (*978-0-9747417*) 1220 Tico Rd., Ojai, CA 93023 USA; 79 S Canyon Diablo Rd. Unit 11, Sedona, AZ 86351 Tel 805-908-1651
E-mail: geraldstanek@yahoo.com
Dist(s): **Lulu Pr., Inc.**
Shoetree Publishers, Inc., (*978-0-9785521*) P.O. Box 2122, Chandler, AZ 85244 USA (SAN 850-9859) Fax: 480-812-0182
Web site: http://www.shoetreepublishers.com.
Shogakukan (JPN) (*978-4-09*) *Dist. by* **S and S Inc.**
Shooting Star Edition *Imprint of* **American Literary Pr.**
Shooting Star Publishing, (*978-0-9762835*) 1305 E. Fort King St. # 100, Ocala, FL 34471-2443 USA Do not confuse with companies with the same name in Dearborn, MI, Moses Lake, WA
Web site: http://www.shottingstarpublishing.com.
Shope, Diann, (*978-0-9968988*) 1222 20th Ave E., Seattle, WA 98112 USA Tel 206-329-1178
E-mail: eshope12@msn.com
Web site: diannshope.com.
Shope, E. Raymond *See* **Flutter-By Productions**
Shore Line Pr. *Imprint of* **Pacific Bks.**
Shorebird Media, (*978-0-9745737*) Orders Addr.: P.O. Box 372, Mukilteo, WA 98275-0372 USA (SAN 255-6359)
E-mail: jeanie.james@verizon.net.
Shorefront N.F.P., (*978-0-9765232; 978-1-946717*) Orders Addr.: P.O. Box 1894, Evanston, IL 60204 USA Tel 847-864-7467; Edit Addr.: P.O. Box 1894, Evanston, IL 60204 USA
Web site: http://shorefrontlegacy.org
Dist(s): **Lulu Pr., Inc.**
Shoreline Pr., (*978-1-887671*) P.O. Box 555, Jamestown, RI 02835 USA Do not confuse with Shoreline Press in Soquel, CA
E-mail: kennethproudfoot@hotmail.com.
Shore Publishing Co., (*978-0-9746846*) PMB 123, 7485 Rush River Dr., Suite 710, Sacramento, CA 95831-5260 USA Tel 916-442-4883; Fax: 916-428-9542.
Shorey Publications *See* **Shorey's Bookstore**
Shorey's Bookstore, (*978-0-8466*) P.O. Box 77316, Seattle, WA 98177-0316 USA (SAN 204-5958) Tel 206-633-2990
E-mail: shorey@serv.net
Web site: http://www.serv.net/shorey.
Short Books *See* **Half-Pint Kids, Inc.**
Short Tales *Imprint of* **Magic Wagon**
Short Term Mission Language Program, (*978-0-9746182*) 3612 Mary Elizabeth Church Rd., Waxhaw, NC 28173-9273 USA
E-mail: info@missionlanguage.com
Web site: http://www.missionlanguage.com.
Shortbread Hill Bk. Co., (*978-0-9799162*) P.O. Box 1565, Veradale, WA 99037 USA (SAN 854-7599)
E-mail: shortbreadhill@hotmail.com.
Shortland Pubns. (U. S. A.) Inc., (*978-0-7699; 978-1-57257*) 19201 120th Ave NE Ste. 100, Bothell, WA 98011-9507 USA
Dist(s): **Heinemann-Raintree**
Wright Group/McGraw-Hill.
Show n' Tell Publishing,
Showcase Writers, (*978-0-9753340*) P.O. Box 13757, Richmond, VA 23225 USA Tel 804-398-1138
E-mail: editor@showcasewriters.com
Web site: http://www.showcasewriters.com.
Shrewsbury Publishing, (*978-0-9678182*) 3624 Livingston, New Orleans, LA 70118 USA Tel 504-488-5249.
Shulemite Christian Crusade, (*978-0-9714361*) 1420 Armstrong Valley Rd., Halifax, PA 17032-8383 USA (SAN 254-3931) Tel 717-896-8383; Fax: 717-896-8386
E-mail: sherrerd@epix.net
Web site: http://www.chrissherrerd.com.
Shulenberger Publishing, (*978-0-9767355*) 3912 NE 127th St., Seattle, WA 98125 USA (SAN 256-5935) Tel 206-367-5886
E-mail: ericshul@hotmail.com.
Shumpert, Sharon *See* **SYS Publishing**
ShuNu Publishing, (*978-0-9742329*) P.O. Box 2031, Stafford, TX 77497 USA Tel 713-401-8479
E-mail: kmitchellthomas@aol.com.
Shurley Instructional Materials, Inc., (*978-1-881940; 978-1-58561*) 366 Sim Dr., Cabot, AR 72023 USA Tel 501-843-3869; Fax: 501-843-0583; Toll Free: 800-566-2966; Ballad Rd., Cabot, AR 72023
E-mail: shurley@shurley.com
Web site: http://www.shurley.com.
SIA Publishing, LLC, (*978-0-9787344; 978-1-936820*) 204 Wyndom Ct., Goodlettsvile, TN 37072-2176 USA
E-mail: donbloomquist@siapublishing.com
Web site: http://www.siapublishing.com
Dist(s): **Smashwords.**
SIA Software, LLC *See* **SIA Publishing, LLC**
Sibyl Merritt, (*978-0-9824565*) 25 Western Ledge Rd., Corea, ME 04624 USA (SAN 858-2157)
E-mail: bparks@maine.edu
Web site: http://sibylmerritt.com
Dist(s): **Lightning Source, Inc.**
Side FX Partners, LLC, (*978-0-692-82883-0; 978-0-692-83666-8; 978-0-692-83799-3; 978-1-63587-711-3*) 5875 Collins Ave #1801, MIAMI BEACH, FL 33140 USA Tel 443-570-4942
E-mail: jeffwcrawford5+LVP0003227@gmail.com; jeffwcrawford5+LVP0003227@gmail.com.
Sidedoor Publishing LLC, (*978-0-9770248*) P.O. Box 18271, San Jose, CA 95158-8271 USA
E-mail: isbn@sidedoorpublishing.com
Web site: http://www.sidedoorpublishing.com.
Sidekicks TM *Imprint of* **Scholastic, Inc.**
Sidewalk Publishing, (*978-0-9766418*) Inform Design, 2809 Forest Hill Cir., SE, Olympia, WA 98501 USA Tel 360-570-9398
E-mail: informbarb@qwest.net
Web site: http://www.sidewalkpublishing.net.
Sidewalk Univ. Pr., (*978-0-9759962*) 1739 Springfield Ave., Maplewood, NJ 07040 USA Tel 973-885-0860
E-mail: sidewalku@msn.com
Web site: http://www.sidewalkuniversity.org.
Sidewinder Publishing LLC, (*978-0-914001*) 4609 Kinney St. SE, Albuquerque, NM 87105 USA Tel 505-998-8000
Web site: http://www.sidewinderpublishing.com/.
Sidran Institute Pr., (*978-0-9629164; 978-1-886968*) Div. of Sidran Institute, P.O. Box 436, Brooklandville, MD 21022 USA Tel 410-825-8888; Fax: 410-560-0134
E-mail: esther.giller@sidran.org
Web site: http://www.sidran.org
Dist(s): **New Leaf Distributing Co., Inc.**
Quality Bks., Inc.
Siebler Corp.,
Siegrist, Vicky, (*978-0-615-21676-8; 978-0-9820977; 978-0-9824444*) 1478 E. Buder Ave., Millington, MI 48529 USA
Web site: http://www.vicksiegrist.com
Dist(s): **Lulu Pr., Inc.**
Siemers, Robert, (*978-0-9744723*) P.O. Box 549, Koloa, HI 96756-0549 USA Toll Free: 888-233-8365
Web site: http://www.teok.com.
Siems, D.R., (*978-0-9794483*) Orders Addr.: P.O. Box 83, Daniel, WY 83115 USA; Edit Addr.: 19 School House Ln., Daniel, WY 83115 USA.
Sienna Bay Pr., (*978-0-9898438; 978-1-945527*) 1409 Timber Ridge Cir., Nashville, TN 37211 USA Tel 615-693-1568
E-mail: shannonlbrown@yahoo.com.
Sierra Club Bks. for Children, (*978-0-87156; 978-1-57805*) Div. of Sierra Club Bks., 85 Second Street, San Francisco, CA 94105 USA Tel 415-977-5500; Fax: 415-977-5792
E-mail: Books.Publishing@sierraclub.org
Web site: http://www.sierraclub.org/books
Dist(s): **Gibbs Smith, Publisher.**
Sierra Nevada Publishing Hse., (*978-0-9765697*) P.O. Box 50366, Henderson, NV 89016 USA Tel 702-991-1383; Fax: 702-953-8973; Toll Free: 800-254-6266
Web site: http://www.climbonsuccess.com.
Sierra Pr., (*978-0-939365; 978-0-9617651; 978-1-58071*) Div. of Panorama International Productions, Inc., Orders Addr.: 4988 Gold Leaf Dr., Mariposa, CA 95338 USA (SAN 662-6955) Tel 209-966-5071; Fax: 209-966-5073; Toll Free: 800-745-2631; *Imprints:* Wish You Were Here (Wish You Were Here)
E-mail: siepress@sti.net
Web site: http://www.nationalparksusa.com
Dist(s): **Smashwords.**
Sierra Raconteur Publishing, (*978-1-58365; 978-1-58582*) Orders Addr.: P.O. Box 97, Memphis, IN 47143 USA Tel 812-294-4693
E-mail: Lori_soard@yahoo.com.
Sierra Vista Junior High *See* **Sierra Vista Pubns.**
Sierra Vista Pubns., (*978-0-9711314; 978-0-615-11784-3*) Alpine Sports, Orders Addr.: P.O. Box 55391, Valencia, CA 91385 USA Fax: 661-259-8941; Toll Free: 800-330-7734; Edit Addr.: P.O. Box 186, Crystal Bay, NV 89402 USA (SAN 411-5961)
E-mail: alpinesport@earthlink.net
Web site: http://www.alpinebasketball.com
Dist(s): **American West Bks.**
Brigham Distribution.
Sigel Pr., (*978-1-905941*) Orders Addr.: 4403 Belmont Ct., Medina, OH 44256 USA (SAN 853-960X) Tel 330-722-2541 (phone/fax); 51a Victoria Rd., Cambridge, CB4 3BW Tel 01223 30 33 03
E-mail: tsigel@sigelpress.com
Web site: http://www.sigelpress.com
Dist(s): **MyiLibrary.**
Sights Productions, (*978-0-9629978; 978-1-886366*) Orders Addr.: 15130 Black Ankle Rd., Mount Airy, MD 21771 USA Tel 410-795-4582; Fax: 410-795-5054
E-mail: eric@sights-productions.com
Web site: http://sights-productions.com
Dist(s): **Brodart Co.**
Follett School Solutions
Kamkyi Bks.
New Leaf Distributing Co., Inc.
Quality Bks., Inc.
Sigil Publishing, (*978-0-9728461; 978-0-9785642; 978-0-9846528; 978-0-9860323*) P.O. Box 824, Leland, MI 49654- USA (SAN 255-1667)
Web site: http://www.knightscares.com; www.realheroesread.com
Dist(s): **Partners Bk. Distributing, Inc.**
Quality Bks., Inc.
Sigler Printing & Publishing, Incorporated *See* **McMillen Publishing**
Sigmar (ARG) (*978-950-11*) *Dist. by* **Continental Bk.**
Sigmar (ARG) (*978-950-11*) *Dist. by* **Mariuccia Iaconi Bk Imports.**
Sigmar (ARG) (*978-950-11*) *Dist. by* **Lectorum Pubns.**
Sigmar (ARG) (*978-950-11*) *Dist. by* **AIMS Intl.**
Sign Up Learning, Incorporated *See* **Language Quest Corp.**
Sign2Me *Imprint of* **Sign2Me Early Learning / Northlight Communications, Inc.**
Sign2Me Early Learning / Northlight Communications, Inc., (*978-0-9668367; 978-1-932354*) Orders Addr.: 11112 47th Ave. W., Mukilteo, WA 98275 USA (SAN 850-7902) Tel 425-493-1903; Fax: 425-493-1904; Edit Addr.: 11112 4th Ave. W., Mukilteo, WA 98275 USA Tel 425-493-1903; Fax: 425-493-1904; Toll Free: 877-744-6263; *Imprints:* Sign2Me (Sign Two Me)
E-mail: btarcea@sign2me.com; acrain@sign2me.com
Web site: http://sign2me.com
Dist(s): **American Wholesale Bk. Co.**

Publisher Name Index

Signal Fire Pr., *(978-0-9764128)* 25260 Terr. Grove Rd., Los Gatos, CA 95033 USA (SAN 256-4351)
Web site: http://www.signalfirepress.com.

Signator Publishing Group Inc., *(978-0-9728472)* 1725 I St. NW., Suite 300, Washington, DC 20006 USA Tel 202-349-3896; Fax: 202-349-3915
E-mail: info@signatorpublishing.com
Web site: http://www.signatorpublishing.com.

Signature Lives *Imprint of* **Compass Point Bks.**

Signet *Imprint of* **Penguin Publishing Group**

SignificantFaith.com *See* **Sincerity Publishing**

Sigueme, Ediciones, S.A. (ESP) *(978-84-301) Dist. by* **Augsburg Fortress.**

Sikes Sports Concepts *See* **Old Bay Publishing**

Sikh Research Institute, *(978-1-60411)* P.O. Box 690504, San Antonio, TX 78269 USA (SAN 854-0403)
E-mail: info@sikhri.org
Web site: http://www.sikhri.org.

Sikorski, Lorna D. & Associates *See* **LDS & Assocs.**

Silent Devil Productions, *(978-0-9752582; 978-0-9786451; 978-0-9789281; 978-0-9791192; 978-0-9796902)* 3777 Center Way, Fairfax, VA 22033 USA
E-mail: silentdevilproductions@hotmail.com
Web site: http://www.silentdevil.com.

Silent Hse. Pr., *(978-0-615-66700-3)* 115 Orange Tree Dr., Orange, OH 44022 USA Tel 216-970-1899
E-mail: sap2006@gmail.com.

Silent Moon Bks., *(978-0-9721457)* P.O. Box 1280, Seeley Lake, MT 59868 USA
E-mail: bschieber@yahoo.com.

Silhouette Pond Productions, *(978-0-9761169)* P.O. Box 778, Palm Harbor, FL 34682-0778 USA (SAN 256-3886) Tel 727-771-1691
E-mail: ceceenter@tampabay.rr.com
Web site: http://www.silhouettepond.com.

Silk Waters Mooney, *(978-0-9776608)* 316 E. El Paso St., Brackettville, TX 78832 USA Tel 830-563-3443; P.O. Box 393, Brackettville, TX 78832
E-mail: swmooney@pukathemoose.com.

Silly Goose Productions, LLC, *(978-0-9711500)* 525 Cutty Trl. Apt. A, Lakeway, TX 78734-4836 USA
E-mail: sallysue678@yahoo.com; sally@onmyown.com
Web site: http://www.starfishpublishing.com; http://www.onmyown.com
Dist(s): **Follett School Solutions.**

Silly String Media, *(978-0-615-25193-6)* P.O. Box 884, Ross, CA 94957 USA
Web site: http://www.sillystringmedia.com
Dist(s): **Lulu Pr., Inc.**

Sillygeese Publishing, LLC, *(978-0-9987112)* P.O. Box 1434, Elgin, TX 78621 USA Tel 512-695-4048
E-mail: mydragonbubbles@gmail.com.

Siloam Pr. *Imprint of* **Charisma Media**

Silver Bells Publishing Hse., *(978-0-9793517)* 19415 150th Ave., Tustin, MI 49688 USA Tel 231-829-3898
E-mail: dgbelleville@yahoo.com.

SILVER BURDETT *Imprint of* **Pearson Schl.**

†**Silver, Burdett & Ginn, Inc.**, *(978-0-382; 978-0-663; 978-1-4182)* Orders Addr.: P.O. Box 2500, Lebanon, IN 46052 USA Toll Free Fax: 800-841-8939; Toll Free: 800-552-2259; Edit Addr.: P.O. Box 480, Parsippany, NJ 07054 USA (SAN 204-5982); 108 Wilmot Rd., Suite 380, Midwest Div., Deerfield, IL 60015 (SAN 111-6517) Tel 708-945-1240
E-mail: customerservice@scottforesman.com
Web site: http://www.scottforesman.com/; *CIP.*

Silver Cloak Pubns., *(978-0-9777677)* P.O. Box 1027, Carpinteria, CA 93014-1027 USA
E-mail: SilverCloak@aol.com.

Silver Dagger Mysteries *Imprint of* **Overmountain Pr.**

Silver Dolphin Bks. *Imprint of* **Readerlink Distribution Services, LLC**

Silver Knight Publishing, LLC, *(978-0-615-55725-0; 978-0-615-58405-8; 978-1-938083)* PO Box 721254, Orlando, FL 32872 USA Tel 407-668-3103
Web site: http://www.silverknightpublishing.com
Dist(s): **CreateSpace Independent Publishing Platform.**

Silver Lake Publishing, *(978-0-930868; 978-1-56343)* 1119 N. Broadway St., Aberdeen, WA 98520-2433 USA (SAN 203-8110) Toll Free: 800-663-3091 Do not confuse with Silver Lake Publishing, Morton, PA
E-mail: publisher@silverlakepublishing.com; SCRIBERE@aol.com; mthorpe@silverlakepub.com
Web site: http://www.silverlakepub.com
Dist(s): **SCB Distributors.**

Silver Leaf Bks., LLC, *(978-0-9744354; 978-0-9787782; 978-1-60975)* Orders Addr.: P.O. Box 6460, Holliston, MA 01746 USA Tel 508-740-6270; Toll Free: 888-823-6450; Edit Addr.: 13 Temi Rd., Holliston, MA 01746 USA
E-mail: Sales@SilverLeafBooks.com
Web site: http://www.silverleafbooks.com.

Silver Linden Pr., *(978-0-9981354)* 1094 37th Pl. NE No. 112, Salem, OR 97301 USA Tel 503-586-8696
E-mail: patti.bowman@msn.com.

Silver Moon Pr., *(978-1-881889; 978-1-893110)* 400 E. 85th St. Apt. 15K, New York, NY 10028-6324 USA Toll Free: 800-874-3320
E-mail: mail@silvermoonpress.com
Web site: http://www.silvermoonpress.com.

Silver Print Pr., Inc., *(978-0-9628064; 978-0-9749890)* Div. of Peter Miller LLC, 20 Crossroad, Suite No. 1, Colbyville, VT 05676 USA (SAN 299-0350) Tel 802-272-8851
E-mail: peter@petermillerphotography.com
Web site: http://www.petermillerphotography.com.

Silver Rim Pr., *(978-1-878611)* 2759 Park Lake Dr., Boulder, CO 80301 USA Tel 303-666-4290 (phone/fax)
E-mail: Sybilset@aol.com.

Silver Rose Publishing, *(978-0-9778211)* P.O. Box 462174, Aurora, CO 80046 USA Tel 303-946-2183; Toll Free: 800-431-1579; *Imprints:* Raynestorm Books (Raynestorm Bks)
E-mail: contact@silverrosepublishing.com
Web site: http://www.silverrosepublishing.com; http://www.bookch.com
Dist(s): **BCH Fulfillment & Distribution.**

Silver Snowflake Publishing, *(978-0-9778476)* P.O. Box 1256, East Greenwich, RI 02818 USA (SAN 850-394X)
E-mail: exteriordesigner@cox.net
Web site: http://www.themagicsceptre.com; http://www.silversnowflakepublishing.com.

Silver Thread Publishing, *(978-0-9844129; 978-0-9858326; 978-0-9861864; 978-0-9991794)* 730 Vista Pacifica Cir., Pismo Beach, CA 93449 USA (SAN 859-3248)
E-mail: jeannie@asilverthread.com
Web site: http://www.asilverthread.com.

Silver Whistle *Imprint of* **Harcourt Trade Pubs.**

SilverBrown Bks., *(978-0-9840922)* 9355 54th Ave., S., Seattle, WA 98118 USA Tel 206-721-3794.

SilverhawkCorp., *(978-0-9772933)* 618 Draper Heights Way, Draper, UT 84020 USA.

Silverman, Toby, *(978-0-9793475)* 1611 Hemlock Farms, Lords Valley, PA 18428 USA
E-mail: tsilverman@noln.com.

Silvermine International Bks., LLC, *(978-0-692-35528-2)* 25 Perry Ave., Suite 11, Norwalk, CT 06850 USA (SAN 760-6338) Tel 203-451-2396
E-mail: jatkin@silvermineinternational.com
Dist(s): **INscribe Digital.**

Silvey Bk. Publishing, *(978-0-9762446)* P.O. Box 5171, Goodyear, AZ 85338-5171 USA Fax: 623-853-9172
E-mail: silveybooks@earthlink.net.

Simakan Group, The, *(978-0-9767812)* P.O. Box 492496, Atlanta, GA 30349 USA Fax: 770-981-1046
E-mail: info@playingyouragame.com
Web site: http://www.playingyourAgame.com.

Simba Publishing Co., *(978-0-9765982)* 5413 Whistler Dr., Tallahassee, FL 32317 USA (SAN 256-4270) Tel 850-878-7741
E-mail: gladys_gikiri@simbapublishingcompany.com
Web site: http://www.simbapublishingcompany.com.

Simba's Publishing, *(978-0-9765475)* P.O. Box 27634, Fresno, CA 93729-7634 USA.

Simcha Media Group, *(978-0-943706; 978-965-465; 978-1-930143; 978-1-932687; 978-1-934440; 978-1-936068)* 94 Dwight Pl., Englewood, NJ 07631 USA Tel 201-503-1151; Fax: 201-503-9761; *Imprints:* Devora Publishing (DevorPubng); Pitspopany Press (Pitspopany Pr)
Web site: http://www.pitspopany.com
Dist(s): **Coronet Bks.**
Lulu Pr., Inc.

Simmons, Kristina, *(978-0-9769843)* 40 Christopher Cir., Middletown, CT 06457 USA.

Simmons, Sukether Williams *See* **Shrewsbury Publishing**

Simms, Laura Storyteller, *(978-0-9911692)* 814 Broadway, New York, NY 10003 USA Tel 212-674-3479
E-mail: storymentor2010@gmail.com
Web site: http://www.laurasimms.com.

Simon & Barklee, Inc./ExplorerMedia, *(978-0-9704661; 978-0-9714502)* 2280 E. Whidbey Shores Rd., Langley, WA 98260 USA Tel 360-730-2360; Fax: 360-730-2355; *Imprints:* Explorer Media (Explorer Media)
E-mail: cwsch@whidbey.com
Web site: http://simonandbarklee.com
Dist(s): **Quality Bks., Inc.**

Simon & Brown, *(978-0-9814843; 978-1-936041; 978-1-61382)* 3140 N 52nd Ave, Hollywood, FL 33021 USA Tel 305-610-7128
E-mail: info@simonandbrown.com
Web site: http://www.simonandbrown.com.

Simon & Northrop of Cal, Incorporated *See* **Martell Publishing Co**

Simon & Schuster, *(978-0-671; 978-0-684; 978-0-689; 978-0-914676; 978-0-7432; 978-1-4165; 978-1-4391; 978-1-4516; 978-1-4767; 978-1-5011)* Div. of Simon & Schuster, Inc., Orders Addr.: 100 Front St., Riverside, NJ 08075 USA (SAN 200-2442) Toll Free Fax: 800-943-9831; Toll Free: 800-223-2336 (ordering); 800-223-2348 (customer service); Edit Addr.: a/o Subsidiary Rights, 11th Flr., 1230 Avenue of the Americas, New York, NY 10020 USA (SAN 200-2450) Tel 212-698-7000; Fax: 212-698-7007; 212-632-8099 (Rights & Permissions); 212-698-1269 (Pocket Bks. Rights & Permissions); Toll Free: 800-897-7650 (customer financial services); 100 Front St., Riverside, NJ 08075 (SAN 852-5471) Tel 856-824-2115; *Imprints:* Atria Books (Atria); North Star Way (NorthStarWay)
E-mail: ssonline_feedback@simonsays.com; consumer.customerservice@simonandschuster.com
Web site: http://www.simonsays.com; http://www.oasis.simonandschuster.com; http://www.simonandschuster.com/
Dist(s): **Cengage Gale**
Giron Bks.
Hachette Bk. Group
Libros Sin Fronteras
Simon & Schuster, Inc.
Studio Fun International
TextStream
Thorndike Pr.
Ulverscroft Large Print Bks., Ltd.

Simon & Schuster Audio, *(978-0-671; 978-0-7435; 978-1-4423)* Orders Addr.: 100 Front St., Riverside, NJ 08075 USA Toll Free Fax: 800-943-9831 (orders); Toll Free: 800-223-2336 (customer service); Edit Addr.: a/o Sub Rights Manager, 11th flr., 1230 Avenue of the Americas, New York, NY 10020 USA Tel 212-698-7000; Fax: 212-698-2370; 212-632-8091 (Rights & Permissions)
Web site: http://www.simonsays.com/subs/index.cfm?areaid=45
Dist(s): **Follett School Solutions**
Simon & Schuster
Simon & Schuster, Inc.

Simon & Schuster Bks. For Young Readers *Imprint of* **Simon & Schuster Bks. For Young Readers**

Simon & Schuster Bks. For Young Readers *Imprint of* **Simon & Schuster/Paula Wiseman Bks.**

Simon & Schuster Bks. For Young Readers, Div. of Simon & Schuster Children's Publishing, 1230 Ave. of the Americas, New York, NY 10020 USA; *Imprints:* Simon & Schuster Books For Young Readers (S&SBFYng); Simon & Schuster/Paula Wiseman Books (S&SPaulaW); SAGA Press (SAGA Press); Salaam Reads (SalaamReads)
Dist(s): **Simon & Schuster, Inc.**

Simon & Schuster Canada (CAN) *Dist. by* **S and S Inc.**

Simon & Schuster Children's Publishing, *(978-0-02; 978-0-671; 978-0-684; 978-0-689; 978-0-7434; 978-1-4169; 978-1-4424; 978-0-85707)* Orders Addr.: 100 Front St., Riverside, NJ 08075 USA Toll Free Fax: 800-943-9831; Toll Free: 800-223-2336; Edit Addr.: a/o Subsidiary Rights, 4th floor, 1230 Avenue of the Americas, New York, NY 10020 USA Tel 212-698-7200; Fax: 212-698-2797 (Rights & Permissions); *Imprints:* Aladdin Library (AlaLib); Atheneum Books for Young Readers (AthenSS); Atheneum/Anne Schwartz Books (Anne Schwart); Atheneum/Richard Jackson Books (Rich Jack); Simon & Schuster/Paula Wiseman Books (S&SPaulaW); Aladdin Paperbacks (AladdinPaperbcks); Atheneum/Caitlyn Dlouhy Books (Caitlyn Dlou); Aladdin (Aladdin)
Web site: http://www.simonsays.com
Dist(s): **Follett School Solutions**
Lectorum Pubns., Inc.
Simon & Schuster
Simon & Schuster, Inc.

†**Simon & Schuster, Inc.**, *(978-0-02; 978-0-671; 978-0-684; 978-0-689; 978-0-914676; 978-0-7432; 978-0-7434; 978-0-7435; 978-1-4165; 978-1-4169; 978-1-4391; 978-1-4423; 978-1-4424; 978-1-4516; 978-0-85707; 978-1-4814; 978-1-5082; 978-1-5344)* Div. of Viacom Co., Orders Addr.: 100 Front St., Riverside, NJ 08075 USA Toll Free Fax: 800-943-9831; Toll Free: 800-223-2336 (orders); 800-223-2348 (customer service); Edit Addr.: 1230 Ave. of the Americas, New York, NY 10020 USA Tel 212-698-7000
E-mail: Consumer.CustomerService@simonandschuster.com
Web site: http://www.simonsays.com; http://www.simonandschuster.com
Dist(s): **Follett School Solutions**; *CIP.*

Simon & Schuster, Ltd. (GBR) *(978-0-671; 978-0-684; 978-0-689; 978-0-7432; 978-0-7434; 978-1-84738; 978-1-84737; 978-0-85720; 978-0-85707; 978-1-84983; 978-1-4711) Dist. by* **IPG Chicago.**

Simon & Schuster, Ltd. (GBR) *(978-0-671; 978-0-684; 978-0-689; 978-0-7432; 978-0-7434; 978-1-84738; 978-1-84737; 978-0-85720; 978-0-85707; 978-1-84983; 978-1-4711) Dist. by* **S and S Inc.**

Simon & Schuster Trade *See* **Simon & Schuster**

Simon & Schuster/Paula Wiseman Bks. *Imprint of* **Simon & Schuster Children's Publishing**

Simon & Schuster/Paula Wiseman Bks. *Imprint of* **Simon & Schuster Bks. For Young Readers**

Simon & Schuster/Paula Wiseman Bks. *Imprint of* **Simon & Schuster/Paula Wiseman Bks.**

Simon & Schuster/Paula Wiseman Bks., Div. of Simon & Schuster Children's Publishing, 1230 Ave. of the Americas, New York, NY 10020 USA; *Imprints:* Simon & Schuster Books For Young Readers (S&SBFYng); Simon & Schuster/Paula Wiseman Books (S&SPaulaW)
Dist(s): **Simon & Schuster, Inc.**

Simon & Simon, LLC *See* **Maestro Classics**

Simon & Son Publishing, *(978-0-9773665)* 4995 Paist Rd., Doylestown, PA 18901 USA; *Imprints:* Prophecy, The (Prophecy)
E-mail: frankfsp1@comcast.net
Web site: http://www.simonsonpublishing.com.

Simon, Les, *(978-0-9761914)* Orders Addr.: P.O. Box 57274, Washington, DC 20037-0274 USA Tel 202-659-3639; Fax: 202-457-1155; Edit Addr.: 1400 20th St., NW, No. 805, Washington, DC 20036 USA
E-mail: lessim2003@yahoo.com.

Simon Peter Pr., Inc., *(978-0-9761533; 978-0-9777430; 978-1-936159)* P.O. Box 2187, Oldsmar, FL 34677 USA Fax: 727-772-0368
E-mail: theaben@aol.com
Web site: http://www.simonpeterpress.com
Dist(s): **eBookit.com.**

Simon Pulse *Imprint of* **F&W Media, Inc.**

Simon Pulse *Imprint of* **Simon Pulse**

Simon Pulse, Div.of Simon & Schuster Children's Publishing, 1230 Ave. of the Americas, New York, NY 10020 USA; *Imprints:* Simon Pulse (SimonPulse)
Dist(s): **Simon & Schuster, Inc.**

Simon Pulse/Beyond Words, 1230 Avenue of the Americas, New York, NY 10020 USA
Dist(s): **Simon & Schuster, Inc.**

Simon Pulse/Mercury Ink *Imprint of* **Simon Pulse/Mercury Ink**

Simon Pulse/Mercury Ink, 1230 Avenue of the Americas, New York, NY 10020 USA; *Imprints:* Simon Pulse/Mercury Ink (SimoPulseMer)
Dist(s): **Simon & Schuster, Inc.**

Simon Scribbles *Imprint of* **Simon Scribbles**

Simon Scribbles, Div. of Simon & Schuster Children's Publishing, 1230 Ave. of the Americas, New York, NY 10020 USA; *Imprints:* Simon Scribbles (SScribbles)
Dist(s): **Simon & Schuster, Inc.**

Simon Spotlight *Imprint of* **Simon Spotlight**

Simon Spotlight, Div. of Simon & Schuster Children's Publishing, 1230 Ave. of the Americas, New York, NY 10020 USA; *Imprints:* Simon Spotlight (SimonSpotlight)
Dist(s): **Simon & Schuster, Inc.**

Simon Spotlight/Nickelodeon *Imprint of* **Simon Spotlight/Nickelodeon**

Simon Spotlight/Nickelodeon, Div.of Simon & Schuster Children's Publishing, 1230 Ave. of the Americas, New York, NY 10020 USA; *Imprints:* Simon Spotlight/Nickelodeon (SSpotNick)
Dist(s): **Simon & Schuster, Inc.**

Simone, Julia, *(978-0-692-82697-3; 978-0-692-82698-0)*
E-mail: jeffwcrawford5+LVP0003217@gmail.com; jeffwcrawford5+LVP0003217@gmail.com.

Simone's Bks., *(978-0-615-18719-8; 978-0-615-20614-1)* 65 Winding Wood Dr., Apt. 4A, Sayreville, NJ 08872 USA
Dist(s): **Lulu Pr., Inc.**

Simpatico Bks., *(978-0-9771322)* P.O. Box 201, Heber Springs, AR 72543 USA Tel 501-362-2858
Web site: http://www.simpaticobooks.com.

Simple Faith Bks. *Imprint of* **Sunrise Mountain Bks.**

Simple Fish Bk. Co., LLC, *(978-0-9817598; 978-0-9837932)* 5500 Abercorn St., Suite 32, Savannah, GA 31405 USA
E-mail: bbrooks@simplefishbookco.com
Web site: http://www.simplefishbookco.com
Dist(s): **Bookmasters Distribution.**

Simple Ink, LLC, *(978-0-9794167)* P.O. Box 1825, Hays, KS 67601 USA
E-mail: gmarconette@simpleink.net; gameck@gmail.com
Web site: http://www.simpleink.net.

Simple Productions *See* **Shepard Pubns.**

Simple Thoughts Pr., LLC, *(978-0-9768557)* Orders Addr.: P.O. Box 759, Northfield, MN 55057 USA; Edit Addr.: 14345 Falk Ave., Northfield, NJ 55057 USA
Web site: http://www.backandforthjournal.com.

Simplemente Maria Pr., *(978-0-9766811)* 2611 Samarkand Dr., Santa Barbara, CA 93105 USA Tel 805-962-2497
E-mail: mary@maryheebner.com
Web site: http://www.simplementemariapress.com; http://www.maryheebner.com.

Simpler Life Pr., *(978-0-9619806)* 1599 S. Uinta Way, Denver, CO 80231 USA (SAN 246-5809) Tel 303-751-2454; Fax: 303-671-5200
E-mail: avs@vansteenhouse.com
Web site: http://www.vansteenhouse.com.

Simplex Pubns., *(978-0-9623113; 978-1-929304)* Orders Addr.: 575 Larkspur Plaza Dr., Unit 4, Larkspur, CA 94939-1476 USA
E-mail: gosmith@pacbell.net
Web site: http://www.simplexpublications.com
Dist(s): **Bookpeople.**

SimpliFun Studios, *(978-1-932839)* 2070 Stratford Dr., Milpitas, CA 95035 USA Tel 408-946-8632; Toll Free: 800-850-4-FUN
E-mail: mail@simplifun.com
Web site: http://www.childrenspartygames.com.

Simply Hooked, *(978-0-692-77545-5)* 12308 Marblehead Dr., Tampa, FL 33626 USA Tel 843-812-7686
E-mail: mwynnsc@hotmail.com
Web site: www.simplyhooked.co.

Simply Read Bks. (CAN) *(978-0-9688768; 978-1-894965; 978-1-897476; 978-1-927018) Dist. by* **IngramPubServ.**

Simply Silly Stories, *(978-0-9838964)* 3603 Forsythia Dr., Wylie, TX 75098 USA Tel 214-597-8999
E-mail: bewilson@simplysillystories.com.

SimplyCMB,LLC, *(978-0-9980042)* 1958 S. Cherry Blossom Ln., Suttons Bay, MI 49682 USA
E-mail: yroehler@bookpublishing.com.

Simpson, Charles B., *(978-0-9703818)* 234 Faulkner Ave., Hazard, KY 41701 USA Tel 606-436-4652
E-mail: cngsimpson@earthlink.net
Web site: http://www.appalachianwriter.com.

Simsand Publishing, *(978-0-9765580)* 8 Huntington Pl. Dr., Atlanta, GA 30350 USA Tel 678-458-0759
E-mail: timsanders01@aol.com.

Sinanan, Cindy, *(978-0-9769004)* 10169 New Hampshire Ave., No. 155, Silver Spring, MD 20903 USA
E-mail: mybook@mris.com.

Sincerity Publishing, *(978-0-9848314; 978-1-945915)* 450 Pine Flower Ct., Highlands Ranch, CO 80126 USA
E-mail: hwhitmore12@icloud.com
Web site: http://www.HughWhitmore.com.

Sinclair, A. E., *(978-0-692-78356-6)* 8518 OAK VIEW DR, Chattanooga, TN 37421 USA Tel 423-693-3597
E-mail: aprilsinclair355@gmail.com.

Sinclair, Loretta, *(978-0-615-24452-5; 978-0-615-40432-5; 978-0-9916159; 978-0-9992025)* P.O. Box 2052, Rancho Cordova, CA 95741 USA
E-mail: lori@sinclairinkspot.com
Web site: http://www.sinclairinkspot.com.

Sinclair/Polk, *(978-0-615-20281-5)* 1717 W. Green Tree Rd., No. 204, Glendale, WI 53209 USA Tel 414-704-3207
E-mail: janpolk@janpolk.com; margerysinclair@juno.com
Web site: http://www.janpolk.com; http://www.margerysinclair.com; http://www.ayearofgoodmanners.com
Dist(s): **Signature Bks., LLC.**

SingaporeMath.com, Inc., *(978-0-9741573; 978-1-932906; 978-1-947226)* 19535 SW 129th Ave., Tualatin, OR 97062 USA (SAN 255-6510) Tel 503-557-8100; Fax: 503-557-8103
E-mail: accounting@singaporemath.com; dthomas@singaporemath.com
Web site: http://www.singaporemath.com.

SingaporeMath.com, Incorporated *See* **SingaporeMath.com, Inc.**

Singing Moon Pr., *(978-0-9770497)* Singing Moon Press #239 2601 S. Minnesota Ave., Ste 105, Sioux Falls, SD 57105-4750 USA; *Imprints:* Itty Bitty Kitty (Itty Bitty Kitty)
E-mail: editor@singingmoonpress.com
Web site: http://www.singingmoonpress.com.

Singing River Pubns., *(978-0-9709575; 978-0-9759953; 978-0-9774831; 978-0-9789870; 978-0-9822596)* Orders Addr.: P.O. Box 72, Ely, MN 55731 USA (SAN 254-136X) Tel 218-365-3498; Fax: 218-365-5792; Edit Addr.: 3365 Wolf Lake Rd., Ely, MN 55731 USA
E-mail: cmoroni@singingriverpublications.com; info@singingriverpublications.com
Web site: http://www.singingriverpublications.com
Dist(s): **Adventure Pubns.**
Partners Bk. Distributing, Inc.

For full information on wholesalers and distributors, refer to the Wholesaler and Distributor Name Index

Singing Tree Pr., *(978-0-9708005)* P.O. Box 722, Auburn, CA 95604 USA (SAN 255-4011) Tel 530-823-9284
E-mail: editor@mail.singingtreepress.com; orders@singingtreepress.com
Web site: http://www.singingtreepress.com.

Singing Turtle Pr., *(978-0-9659113; 978-0-9846381)* 942 Vuelta Del Sur., Santa Fe, NM 87507-7755 USA Toll Free: 888-308-6284
E-mail: kathy@mathkits.com
Web site: http://www.mathkits.com
Dist(s): **Blessing Way Publishing Co. Midpoint Trade Bks., Inc.**

Singing Winds Pr., *(978-1-61955)* 1331 SE Ellis, Dallas, OR 97338 USA Tel 503-551-7241 (phone/fax)
E-mail: singingwindspress@gmail.com
Web site: www.singingwindspress.com.

Siniff Publishing *See* **Country Messenger Pr. Publishing Group, LLC**

Sinolingua (CHN) *(978-7-80052) Dist. by* **China Bks.**

Sinonexus Publishing Co., *(978-0-9787664)* 65 Wethersfield Rd., Bellingham, MA 02019-1045 USA Tel 508-966-4423
E-mail: sinonexus@yahoo.com
Web site: http://www.sinonexus.org.

Sinsinawa Dominicans, Inc., *(978-0-9774934)* 585 Cty. Rd., Z, Sinsinawa, WI 53824-9701 USA Tel 608-748-4411; Fax: 608-748-4491
E-mail: communication@sinsinawa.org
Web site: http://www.sinsinawa.org.

Sioux City Lewis & Clark Interpretive Ctr., The, *(978-0-9753860; 978-0-9785063)* 900 Larsen Pk. Rd., Sioux city, IA 51103 USA Tel 712-224-5242; Fax: 712-224-5244
E-mail: mpoole@siouxcitylcic.com
Web site: http://www.siouxcitylcic.com.

Sippel, Robert, *(978-0-692-84050-4)* 8745 Mcdowell Rd, Scottsdale, AZ 85257 USA Tel 928-254-0081
E-mail: rsippel@mail.com.

Sir Brody Bks., *(978-0-692-39979-8; 978-0-9978611)* 605 Sycamore Dr. NE, CLEVELAND, TN 37312 USA Tel 423-595-7005.

Sir Pigglesworth Publishing, Inc., *(978-1-68055)* 1515 N. Town East Blvd., Suite. 138-118, Mesquite, TX 75150 USA Tel 469-416-25
E-mail: bill.wagner@whereintheworldi ssitpi gleleswofih.com
Web site: www. whereintheworldissirpigglesworth. com.

Sir Wrinkles Pr., *(978-0-9766639)* 30692 Fox Run Ln., San Juan Capistrano, CA 92675 USA
Web site: http://www.sirwrinklesthebulldog.com.

Siren-BookStrand, Inc., *(978-1-933563; 978-1-60601; 978-1-61034; 978-1-61926; 978-1-62241; 978-1-62242; 978-1-62740; 978-1-62741; 978-1-63258; 978-1-63259; 978-1-68295; 978-1-64010)* 2500 S. Lamar Blvd., Austin, TX 78704 USA (SAN 256-6869) Toll Free: 866-887-4736
E-mail: diana.debalko@sirenpublishing.com
Web site: http://www.sirenpublishing.com; http://www.sirenbookstrand.com.

Sirius Entertainment, Inc., *(978-1-57989)* Orders Addr.: P.O. Box X, Unadilla, NY 13849 USA Tel 607-369-2620; Fax: 607-369-2623; Edit Addr.: P.O. Box X, Unadilla, NY 13849-0723 USA
E-mail: sirent@aol.com
Dist(s): **Diamond Comic Distributors, Inc. Diamond Bk. Distributors.**

SIRS Mandarin *See* **SIRS Publishing, Inc.**

†SIRS Publishing, Inc., *(978-0-89777; 978-0-9678914)* Div. of ProQuest Information and Learning, 5201 Congress Ave., Suite 250, Boca Raton, FL 33487 USA (SAN 222-8920) Tel 561-994-0079; Fax: 561-995-4074; Toll Free: 800-521-0600
Web site: http://www.proquestK12.com; *CIP.*

Siruela, Ediciones S.A. (ESP) *(978-84-7844; 978-84-85876; 978-84-15937) Dist. by* **Lectorum Pubns.**

Sistemas Tecnicos de Edicion, S.A. de C.V. (MEX) *(978-968-6579; 978-970-629; 978-968-6048; 978-968-6135; 978-968-6394) Dist. by* **AIMS Intl.**

Sisterhaus Publishing, *(978-0-578-05291-5)* 40555 La Colima Rd., Suite 100, Temecula, CA 92591 USA
E-mail: lisaharding4@yahoo.com.

Sisters of Providence, *(978-1-893789; 978-0-9897397)* a/o Ann Casper, SP, Sisters of Providence Owens Hall, Saint Mary-of-the-Woods, IN 47876 USA Tel 812-535-2800; Fax: 812-535-1009 Do not confuse with Sisters of Providence in Holyoke, MA
E-mail: acasper@spsmw.org
Web site: http://www.sistersofprovidence.org.

Sisters Three Publishing Inc., *(978-0-9787375)* 5026 SW. 94th Ave., Cooper City, FL 33328 USA Fax: 954-885-8007
Web site: http://www.sistersthreeseries.com.

Sisu Home Entertainment, Inc., *(978-1-56086; 978-1-884857)* 340 W. 39th St., 6th Flr., New York, NY 10018 USA Tel 212-779-1559; Fax: 212-779-7115; Toll Free Fax: 888-221-7478; Toll Free: 800-223-7478
E-mail: sisu@sisuent.com
Web site: http://www.sisuent.com
Dist(s): **Follett School Solutions.**

Sitare, Ltd., *(978-0-940178)* Orders Addr.: 1101 N. Rainbow Blvd., No. 52, Las Vegas, NV 89108 USA (SAN 217-0833) Tel 702-990-0688
E-mail: editor@dlvmagazine.com
Web site: http://www.dlvmagazine.com.

Six Seconds, *(978-0-9629123; 978-0-9716772; 978-0-9797343; 978-1-935667)* Orders Addr.: P.O. Box 1985, Freedom, CA 95019 USA Tel 831-763-1800
E-mail: staff@6seconds.org; jenny@6seconds.org
Web site: http://www.6seconds.org.

Six Suns Publishing, *(978-0-9654200)* P.O. Box 112852, Anchorage, AK 99511 USA Tel 907-344-2905
Dist(s): **Todd Communications Wizard Works.**

Sixth Avenue Bks. *Imprint of* **Grand Central Publishing**

Sixth&Spring Bks., *(978-1-931543; 978-1-933027; 978-1-936096)* 233 Spring St., 3rd Flr., New York, NY 10013 USA; *Imprints:* Hart, Chris Books (Chris Hart)
E-mail: wendy@sohopublishing.com
Web site: http://sixthandspringbooks.com
Dist(s): **Sterling Publishing Co., Inc.**

Skandisk, Inc., *(978-0-9615394; 978-1-57534)* 6667 W. Old Shakopee Rd., Suite 109, Bloomington, MN 55438-2622 USA (SAN 695-4405) Tel 952-829-8998; Fax: 952-829-8992; Toll Free: 800-468-2424 (orders)
E-mail: lhamnes@skandisk.com; tomten@skandisk.com
Web site: http://www.skandisk.com.

SkateRight Publishing, *(978-0-9798876)* 2913 Cummings, Berkley, MI 48072-4807 USA.

Skeete, D., *(978-0-9769012)* P.O. Box 737, New York, NY 10030 USA
E-mail: msdss@aol.com
Web site: http://www.hiphopwordsearch.com.

Skeezel Pr., *(978-0-9747217)* 2624 Lakeside Dr., Erie, PA 16511 USA
E-mail: pmerski@roadrunner.com; patricia@skeezelpress.com
Web site: http://www.skeezelpress.com
Dist(s): **Independent Pubs. Group MyiLibrary.**

Skeptical Guitarist Pubns., *(978-0-9665029; 978-0-9788609; 978-1-944210)* Orders Addr.: P.O. Box 5824, Raleigh, NC 27650-5824 USA Tel 919-834-2031; Edit Addr.: 714 Faircloth St., Raleigh, NC 27607-4013 USA
E-mail: bruceemery@mindspring.com
Web site: http://www.skepticalguitarist.com/.

Sketch Publishing, *(978-0-9726764)* 414 S. 43rd St, Philadelphia, PA 19104 USA Tel 215-243-0644
E-mail: msand227@aol.com.

Sketches From The Heart Publishing, *(978-0-9759300)* P.O. Box 3431, Boulder, CO 80307 USA
Web site: www.sketchesfromtheheart.com
Dist(s): **Bks. West Common Ground Distributors, Inc. Partners/West Book Distributors Quality Bks., Inc.**

Skinder-Strauss Assocs., *(978-1-57741)* Orders Addr.: P.O. Box 50, Newark, NJ 07101 USA Tel 973-642-1440; Fax: 973-242-1905; Toll Free: 800-444-4041; Edit Addr.: 240 Mulberry St., Newark, NJ 07101 USA
E-mail: ed@elaw.com
Web site: http://lawdiary.com; http://elaw.com.

Skinner Hse. Bks. *Imprint of* **Unitarian Universalist Assn.**

Skinner, Kerry L., *(978-0-9648743; 978-1-931080)* Div. of Think Life/Change, Orders Addr.: 67 N. Marshside Pl., The Woodlands, TX 77389 USA; *Imprints:* KLS LifeChange Ministries (KLS LifeChge)
E-mail: kerry@kerryskinner.com
Web site: http://www.kerryskinner.com.

Skinny On (tm), The *Imprint of* **Rand Media Co**

Skira *Imprint of* **Rizzoli International Pubns., Inc.**

Skirvan, Pamela, *(978-0-9742943)* P.O. Box 484, New Harbor, ME 04554-0484 USA.

Skookum Bks., *(978-0-692-79518-7; 978-0-9983078; 978-0-9985225)* 1 Manatee Ct, Simpsonville, SC 29681 USA Tel 864-552-1055; Toll Free: 864-552-1055
Dist(s): **CreateSpace Independent Publishing Platform.**

Sky Blue Pr., *(978-0-9652364; 978-0-9774851; 978-0-9889170; 978-0-9987246)* 4514 Spotted Oak Woods, San Antonio, TX 78249 USA Tel 505-603-5738
E-mail: orders@skybluepress.com; skybluepress@skybluepress.com
Web site: http://www.skybluepress.com
Dist(s): **Smashwords.**

Sky Carrier Pr., *(978-1-880589)* P.O. Box 442, Fayetteville, NY 13066 USA Tel 605-486-4310; 315-637-9511
E-mail: swagner711@aol.com.

Sky Pony Pr. *Imprint of* **Skyhorse Publishing Co., Inc.**

†Sky Publishing, *(978-0-933346; 978-1-931559; 978-0-615-38976-9)* Div. of New Track Media, 90 Sherman St. Ste. D, Cambridge, MA 02140-3264 USA (SAN 212-4556) Toll Free: 800-253-0245
E-mail: orders@SkyandTelescope.com
Web site: http://www.skyandtelescope.com
Dist(s): **F&W Media, Inc. Sterling Publishing Co., Inc.**; *CIP.*

Sky Publishing Corporation *See* **Sky Publishing**

Sky Rocket Pr., *(978-0-9724637)* Orders Addr.: 2104 Old York Dr., Keller, TX 76248-5497 USA Tel 817-498-4300; Fax: 757-299-3608
E-mail: robert@rocketvilletexas.com
Web site: http://www.rocketvilletexas.com.

Skyhook Pr. *Imprint of* **Shepard Pubns.**

Skyhorse Publishing Co., Inc., *(978-0-934672; 978-0-941873; 978-1-56148; 978-1-892389; 978-1-59780; 978-1-60239; 978-1-61608; 978-1-61145; 978-1-936697; 978-1-61321; 978-1-62087; 978-1-62153; 978-1-62636; 978-1-62872; 978-1-62873; 978-1-62914; 978-1-940456; 978-1-63144; 978-1-63158; 978-1-63220; 978-1-63450; 978-1-68099; 978-1-5107; 978-1-68358) 307 W. 36th Street, Flr. 11, New York, NY 10018 USA Tel 212-643-6816; 212-643-6819; Imprints:* Arcade Publishing (ARCADE PUBLISH); Sky Pony Press (SKY PONY PRESS); Allworth Press (Allwrth Pr); Yucca Publishing (Yucca Pub); Good Books (GoodBksUSA); Racehorse Publishing (Racehorse Pub)
E-mail: skyhorsepublishing@gmail.com
Web site: http://www.skyhorsepublishing.com
Dist(s): **Follett School Solutions INscribe Digital MBI Distribution Services/Quayside Distribution MyiLibrary Open Road Integrated Media, Inc. Publishers Group West (PGW) Random Hse., Inc. Sterling Publishing Co., Inc.**

Skylight Paths Publishing *Imprint of* **LongHill Partners, Inc.**

Skylight Publishing, *(978-0-9654853; 978-0-9727055; 978-0-9824775; 978-0-9972528)* Orders Addr.: 9 Bartlet St., Suite 70, Andover, MA 01810-3655 USA Tel 978-475-1431 (phone/fax); Toll Free: 888-476-1940
E-mail: support@skylit.com
Web site: http://www.skylit.com.

Skyline Pubn., *(978-0-9723493; 978-0-9815846; 978-0-9843602; 978-0-615-66773-7)* P.O. Box 295, Stormville, NY 12582-0295 USA; *Imprints:* Water Forest Press (Wtr Forest) Do not confuse with companies with the same or similar name in Lancaster, OH, Oakland Park, FL
E-mail: skylineeditor@aol.com
Web site: http://www.skylinemagazines.com
Dist(s): **CreateSpace Independent Publishing Platform.**

Skyline Publishing, *(978-0-918981)* Orders Addr.: P.O. Box 1118, Columbia Falls, MT 59912 USA (SAN 669-8662) Tel 406-892-5560; Fax: 406-892-1922; Edit Addr.: a/o Skyline Publishing, 3101 Hwy. 206, Columbia Falls, MT 59912 USA Do not confuse with companies with similar names in Londonderry, NH, Saint George, UT
E-mail: carolynj@rolandcheek.com
Web site: http://www.rolandcheek.com
Dist(s): **Partners/West Book Distributors.**

SkyMacSyd Publishing, *(978-0-9767244)* P.O. Box 56363, Little Rock, AR 72215 USA.

SkyMark Corp., *(978-0-9769873)* 7300 Penn Ave., Pittsburgh, PA 15208 USA Tel 412-371-0680; Fax: 412-371-0681
E-mail: marie.routledge@skymark.com
Web site: http://www.theseus.biz.

Skyrai Publishing, *(978-0-692-68252-4; 978-0-9978555)* 935 Carla Dr., Troy, IL 62294 USA Tel 309-338-7589
Dist(s): **CreateSpace Independent Publishing Platform.**

Skyscape *Imprint of* **Amazon Publishing**

Skyscraper Pr. (children's) *Imprint of* **Windy City Pubs.**

Skyward Bks., *(978-0-9777902)* Orders Addr.: P.O. Box 56734, Riverside, CA 92517 USA Tel 951-782-0711
E-mail: skywardbooks@msn.com.

Skyward Press *See* **Skyward Bks.**

Skyward Publishing Co., *(978-1-881554)* Div. of Paragon Media Corp., 813 Michael St., Kennett, MO 63857 USA (SAN 297-9705) Tel 573-888-5589
E-mail: nfo@skywardpublishing.com
Web site: http://www.skywardpublishing.com; http://www.bransonozarks.com; http://www.brandywineswar.com.

Skywater Publishing Co., *(978-0-9793081; 978-0-9818279; 978-1-938237)* Orders Addr.: 398 Goodrich Ave., Saint Paul, MN 55102 USA Tel 952-818-2178
E-mail: info@skywaterpublishing.com
Web site: http://www.solbooks.com
Dist(s): **Follett School Solutions Smashwords.**

Skyway Pictures LLC., *(978-0-692-84306-2)* 1700 ROBINSON DR N, SAINT PETERSBURG, FL 33710 USA Tel 321-578-0022; Fax: 727-201-2407
E-mail: tate_moghee@yahoo.com.

Skyword Pr., *(978-0-9740202)* Orders Addr.: P.O. Box 1714, Hood River, OR 97031 USA; Edit Addr.: 555 Highline Rd., Hood River, OR 97031 USA.

SL Conradt, LLC, *(978-0-615-37381-2)* N1685 Amies Ln., Greenville, WI 54942 USA Tel 920-427-0512
E-mail: shanaleeconradt@gmail.com
Web site: http://www.getfitwithfood.com.

SL Resources, *(978-1-935040; 978-1-935808)* Orders Addr.: P.O. Box 36040, Birmingham, AL 35236 USA Tel 205-985-0760; Fax: 205-403-3969; Toll Free: 800-718-2267; Edit Addr.: 2183 Pkwy. Lake Dr., Hoover, AL 35242 USA
E-mail: products@studentlife.net; bradford@studentlife.net
Web site: http://www.studentlifestore.com.

SLABYPRESS, *(978-0-9774118; 978-0-9792622)* W25952 State Rd., 95, Arcadia, WI 54612 USA Tel 608-323-7335
E-mail: slabypress@yahoo.com
Web site: http://www.jsiwicki.com.

SLACK, Inc., *(978-0-913590; 978-0-943432; 978-1-55642; 978-1-61711; 978-1-63091)* 6900 Grove Rd., Thorofare, NJ 08086-9447 USA (SAN 201-8632) Tel 856-848-1000; Fax: 856-853-5991; Toll Free: 800-257-8290
E-mail: orders@slackinc.com; lplummer@slackinc.com
Web site: http://www.slackbooks.com
Dist(s): **Barnes & Noble Bks.-Imports Coutts Information Services Ebsco Publishing Emery-Pratt Co. Holt, Henry & Co. Majors, J. A. Co. Macmillan Matthews Medical Bk. Co. Rittenhouse Bk. Distributors.**

Slangman Publishing, *(978-1-891888; 978-1-947601)* Orders Addr.: 12206 Hillslope St., Studio City, CA 91604 USA Tel 818-752-6462; Fax: 413-647-1589
E-mail: info@slangman.com
Web site: http://www.slangman.com
Dist(s): **Delta Systems Company, Inc.**

Slate Falls Pr., LLC, *(978-0-578-04697-6; 978-0-578-07199-2; 978-0-578-10560-4; 978-0-578-12468-1; 978-0-578-17224-8; 978-0-578-18544-6)* P.O. Box 7062, Loveland, CO 80537 USA
Web site: http://www.slatefallspress.com.

Slater Software. Inc., *(978-0-9743149)* 351 Badger Ln., Guffey, CO 80820-9106 USA Tel 719-479-2255 Toll Free: 877-306-6968
E-mail: jim@slatersoftware.com
Web site: http://www.slatersoftware.com.

Slater-Milligan, Joey, *(978-0-9979619)* 184 Franklin Street, D17, Brooklyn, NY 11222 USA Tel 631-339-4411
E-mail: joeyslatermilligan@gmail.com.

Slave Labor Bks., *(978-0-943151; 978-1-59362)* 577 S. Market St., San Jose, CA 95113 USA (SAN 668-1204) Tel 408-971-8929; Fax: 408-279-0451; Toll Free: 800-866-8929; *Imprints:* Slave Labor Graphics (Slave Labor Graph)
E-mail: dan@slavelabor.com
Web site: http://www.slavelabor.com
Dist(s): **Diamond Comic Distributors, Inc. Diamond Bk. Distributors.**

Slave Labor Graphics *Imprint of* **Slave Labor Bks.**

Slavens Enterprises & Marketing Services, LLP *See* **Slavens Enterprises, LLC.**

Slavens Enterprises, LLC., *(978-0-9740348)* 13335 SW Violet Ct., Beaverton, OR 97008-5015 USA Toll Free: 877-526-0904; *Imprints:* Special Editions — Customized Biographies (Special Edns)
E-mail: ricks@slavensmarketing.com.

Sleep Garden, Inc., *(978-0-9752988)* P.O. Box 2365, Menlo Park, CA 94025-2365 USA Toll Free: 877-475-3376
E-mail: marykelley@amsiventures.com
Web site: http://www.zzonesleep.com.

Sleeping Bear Pr., *(978-1-57504; 978-1-886947; 978-1-58536)* Orders Addr.: P.O. Box 20, Chelsea, MI 48118 USA (SAN 253-8466) Tel 734-475-4411; Fax: 734-475-0787; Toll Free: 800-487-2323; Edit Addr.: 27500 Drake Rd., Farmington Hills, MI 48331 USA
E-mail: customerservice@sleepingbearpress.com
Web site: http://www.sleepingbearpress.com
Dist(s): **Booklines Hawaii, Ltd. Cherry Lake Publishing Follett School Solutions Keith Distributors MyiLibrary Partners Bk. Distributing, Inc. Southern Bk. Service Urban Land Institute.**

Sleepless Warrior Publishing, *(978-0-9747707)* 14989 Grassy Knoll Ct., Woodbridge, VA 22193 USA (SAN 256-1069) Tel 703-897-9394; Fax: 703-897-0695
E-mail: cynthia.little@comcast.net
Web site: http://www.sleeplesswarrior.com.

Sleepy Creek Music, *(978-0-9754633)* P.O. Box 2652, Bloomington, IN 47402-2652 USA Tel 812-334-9901
E-mail: grey@greylarsen.com
Web site: http://www.greylarsen.com.

Sleepy Dog Publishing, *(978-0-9842560)* P.O. Box 2033, Turlock, CA 95381 USA
E-mail: swolsen@sbcglobal.net
Web site: http://sleepydogpublishing.com.

Sleepytown Pr., *(978-0-9826344; 978-0-9831738; 978-1-937260)* 1709 Valley Creek Rd., Anniston, AL 36207 USA Tel 256-365-1416
E-mail: artnbooks73@yahoo.com
Web site: http://www.sleepytownpress.com.

SLG, *(978-0-615-12907-5)* 128 C Main St., Agawam, MA 01001 USA
E-mail: slg_gallery@yahoo.com
Web site: http://geocities.com/slg_gallery/about.

Slhoetree Publishers, Incorporated *See* **Shoetree Publishers, Inc.**

Slice of Lime Publishing, *(978-0-9789475)* 1415 Easy St., New Iberia, LA 70560 USA Tel 337-365-4136; Fax: 337-365-4137
E-mail: jady@sliceoflime.net
Web site: http://www.sliceoflime.net
Dist(s): **Partners Bk. Distributing, Inc.**

Slim Goodbody Corp., *(978-1-887028; 978-0-9708230)* Orders Addr.: P.O. Box 242, Lincolnville, ME 04850 USA Tel 207-230-0399; Fax: 207-230-0795; Toll Free: 888-484-1100
E-mail: john@slimgoodbody.com
Web site: http://www.slimgoodbody.com
Dist(s): **INscribe Digital.**

Slippery Slope Press *See* **Ideate Prairie**

SLM Bk. Publishing, *(978-0-9830039)* Orders Addr.: 21204 Pontiac Trail, No. 16, South Lyon, MI 48178 USA
E-mail: joanna@slmbookpublishing.com
Web site: http://www.slmbookpublishing.com.

Slow on the Draw Productions, *(978-0-615-48469-3; 978-0-615-74591-6)* 12826 Ironstone Way No. 304, Parker, CO 80134 USA Tel 720-838-5176
E-mail: swpaulding@msn.com
Web site: lifelessonsfromandywink.com.

Sluser Publishing, *(978-0-578-03599-4; 978-0-578-03634-2; 978-0-578-04034-9; 978-0-578-06031-6; 978-0-578-08065-9; 978-0-578-10299-3; 978-0-578-10318-1; 978-0-578-12746-0; 978-0-578-12986-0)* 324 Stonegate Cir. N., Chambersburg, PA 17201 USA.

Slusser, Jan *See* **RiverCreek Bks., Inc.**

SM Ediciones (ESP) *(978-84-348; 978-84-404; 978-84-398; 978-84-675) Dist. by* **Continental Bk.**

SM Ediciones (ESP) *(978-84-348; 978-84-404; 978-84-398; 978-84-675) Dist. by* **Mariuccia Iaconi Bk Imports.**

SM Ediciones (ESP) *(978-84-348; 978-84-404; 978-84-398; 978-84-675) Dist. by* **Lectorum Pubns.**

SM Ediciones (ESP) *(978-84-348; 978-84-404; 978-84-398; 978-84-675) Dist. by* **AIMS Intl.**

SM Ediciones (ESP) *(978-84-348; 978-84-404; 978-84-398; 978-84-675) Dist. by* **IBD Ltd.**

Small Batch Bks., *(978-0-9829758; 978-1-937650)* 493 S. Pleasant St., Amherst, MA 01002 USA Tel 413-230-3943
E-mail: fred@smallbatchbooks.com
Web site: www.smallbatchbooks.com
Dist(s): **BookBaby Lightning Source, Inc.**

Small Bear Publishing, *(978-0-9801662)* P.O. Box 842, Livingston, MT 59047 USA
E-mail: BarringtonBear@q.com
Web site: http://www.travelswithbarrington.com.

Small Beer Pr., *(978-1-931520; 978-1-61873)* 150 Pleasant St. #306, Easthampton, MA 01027 USA Fax:

Publisher Name Index

413-203-1636; *Imprints:* Big Mouth House (BigMouthHse)
E-mail: info@smallbeerpress.com; info@bigmouthhouse.net; info@lcrw.net
Web site: http://www.smallbeerpress.com; http://www.bigmouthhouse.net; http://www.lcrw.net; http://www.weightlessbooks.com
Dist(s): **Consortium Bk. Sales & Distribution**
MyiLibrary
ebrary, Inc.

Small Fry Beginnings, *(978-0-9651690; 978-1-892703)* Affil. of LightVision Films, Inc., 6625 Hwy. 53 E. Suite No. 410-212, Dawsonville, GA 30534 USA Tel 770-451-7000
E-mail: dennis@smallfrybeginnings.com
Web site: http://www.smallfrybeginnings.com
Dist(s): **Follett School Solutions**
Ingram Entertainment, Inc.
VPD, Inc.
Valley Media, Inc.

Small Fry Productions *See* **Small Fry Beginnings**

Small Horizons *Imprint of* **New Horizon Pr. Pubs., Inc.**

Small New York LLC, *(978-0-578-16183-9; 978-0-9963985)* 676 Third Ave., New York, NY 10017 USA.

Small Press Distribution *See* **SPD-Small Pr. Distribution**

Small Pr., The, *(978-1-933651)* Div. of Brown Bks. Publishing Group, 16200 N. Dallay Pkwy., No. 170, Dallas, TX 75248 USA Tel 972-381-0009; Fax: 972-248-4336
Dist(s): **BookBaby.**

Small Waters Publishing, *(978-0-9765621)* 14251 75th Ave. SE, Atwater, MN 56209 USA Tel 320-894-7904; Fax: 320-235-6418
E-mail: markp@lakesideprintingandadvertising.com.

Small Wonder Publishing, *(978-0-9899964)* 130 Boniface Dr., Rochester, NY 14620 USA Tel 585-271-3492
E-mail: hdm@smallwonderpublishing.com.

Small Wonders Enterprises, *(978-0-9741888)* 12210 Fairfax Towne Ctr., PMB No. 901, Fairfax, VA 22033 USA Tel 703-352-0226 Do not confuse with Small Wonders Enterprises in Farmington, NM
E-mail: snickerdoodle@erols.com
Web site: http://www.snickerdoodleforkids.com.

Small World Toys, *(978-0-9774677; 978-0-9776034; 978-0-9795081)* P.O. Box 3620, Culver City, CA 90231-3620 USA
Web site: http://www.smallworldtoys.com.

Smallbag Bks., *(978-0-9761631)* Orders Addr.: 2000 Del Sol, Bowie, MD 20721 USA
E-mail: konaapub@yahoo.com
Web site: http://www.younganddebtfree.com.

Smallfellow Pr. *Imprint of* **Tallfellow Pr.**

SmallHorse Pr. *Imprint of* **Equine Graphics Publishing Group**

Smallwood, Edward, *(978-0-9741282)* 1609 Mountain Ashe Ct., Matthews, NC 28105 USA
Web site: http://www.jfrankles.com.

Smart & Smarter Publishing, *(978-0-9713530)* P.O. Box 1815, Zillah, WA 98953 USA (SAN 255-3104) Tel 877-807-3703 (phone/fax)
E-mail: daviddunham@smartandsmarter.com; services@smartandsmarter.com
Web site: http://www.smartandsmarter.com.

Smart Apple Media *Imprint of* **Black Rabbit Bks.**

Smart Data Processing, Inc., *(978-0-9718439)* 14 Molly Pitcher Dr., Manalapan, NJ 07726 USA Tel 732-598-4027; Fax: 732-409-1364
E-mail: info@smartdataprocessing.com
Web site: http://www.smartdataprocessing.com.

Smart Kids *Imprint of* **Penton Overseas, Inc.**

Smart Kids Publishing *See* **Smart Kidz Media, Inc.**

Smart Kidz Media, Inc., *(978-1-891100; 978-1-939658)* 2460 Hobbit Ln., Fallbrook, CA 92028 USA Tel 760-468-1891
Dist(s): **APG Sales & Distribution Services.**

smart Life Ministries, Inc., The, *(978-0-9741091)* 1649 Springhill St., Chillicothe, MO 64601 USA.

Smart Love Pr., LLC, *(978-0-9838664)* 400 E. Randolph St. Suite 1905, Chicago, IL 60601 USA Tel 312-970-9846; Fax: 312-278-0441
E-mail: smartlovepress@gmail.com; marthahpieper@smartlovepress.com
Web site: http://www.smartlovepress.com; http://www.jillysterribletempertantrums.com; http://www.mommydaddyihadabaddream.com
Dist(s): **Brigham Distributing.**

Smart Picks, Inc., *(978-0-9764785)* P.O. Box 771440, Lakewood, OH 44107 USA Tel 216-226-6173; Fax: 216-226-5413
E-mail: games@smartpicks.com.

Smart Poodle Publishing, *(978-0-9800307)* 3436 Pierce St., Hollywood, FL 33021 USA
E-mail: debbie.glade@comcast.net
Web site: http://www.smartpoodlepublishing.com.

Smart Publishing, *(978-0-9761819)* P.O. Box 410894, Chicago, IL 60641 USA Tel 773-616-0267
E-mail: halfbakedsistas@aol.com
Web site: http://www.halfbakedsistas.com.

Smart Smiles Co., The, *(978-0-9722792; 978-0-9723727; 978-0-9762740; 978-0-9763328)* 380 S. Mizner Blvd., No. 1709, Boca Raton, FL 33432 USA Tel 561-347-3075; *Imprints:* Flat Kids (Flat Kids)
Web site: http://www.smartsmilescompany.com.

SmartBook Media, Inc., *(978-1-5105)* 350 5th Ave, 59th Floor, New York, NY 10118 USA Toll Free Fax: 866-449-3445; Toll Free: 866-649-3445
E-mail: linda@weigl.com; samantha.nugent@weigl.com
Web site: http://www.asmartbook.com.

Smartinbooks, Inc., *(978-0-9761765)* Orders Addr.: P.O. Box 729, Paducah, KY 42002-0729 USA; Edit Addr.: 1441 HC Mathis Dr., Paducah, KY 42001 USA
E-mail: hmartin@paducah.com
Web site: http://www.smartinbooks.com.

SmartInk Bks., LLC, *(978-1-932403)* 413 6th Ave., Brooklyn, NY 11215 USA Tel 718-768-3696; Fax: 718-369-0844
E-mail: publisher@smartinkbooks.com
Web site: http://www.smartinkbooks.com
Dist(s): **Hachette Bk. Group**
Ideals Pubns.
Penton Overseas, Inc.

SmartiPantz Publishing, *(978-0-9747563)* P.O. Box 24014, Minneapolis, MN 55424 USA (SAN 256-0720).

SmartLab *Imprint of* **becker&mayer! books**

S.M.A.R.T.S. Learning System, *(978-0-9709634)* 3208 Eldon Ln., Waco, TX 76710-1204 USA Fax: 254-776-3136
E-mail: edavis5024@worldnet.att.net
Dist(s): **Capstone Pub.**

SMARTseeds Co., LLC, The, *(978-0-9790931)* P.O. Box 100828, Cudahy, WI 53110 USA (SAN 852-4068) Tel 414-433-0500
E-mail: carlos@thesmartseedscompany.com; info@thesmartseedscompany.com
Web site: http://www.thesmartseedscompany.com.

Smartypants Bks., *(978-0-9773550)* P.O. Box 1014, Logandale, NV 89021-1014 USA (SAN 257-3423)
Web site: http://www.smartypants-books.com.

Smartypants Publishing, *(978-0-9792897)* Orders Addr.: P.O. Box 1548, Buckley, WA 98321 USA Tel 253-278-6612
E-mail: christa@smartypantspublishing.com
Web site: http://smartypantspublishing.com.

SmatteringsBks., *(978-0-9800130)* P.O. Box 556, Clarence, NY 14031 USA (SAN 854-9931) Tel 716-818-0324
Web site: http://smatteringsbooks.com/books.html.

SMC Pubns., LLC, *(978-0-9729546)* P.O. Box 2684, Branchville, NJ 07826 USA Tel 973-948-7441 (phone/fax) Do not confuse with companies with the same name in Houston, TX, Garden Grove, CA, Corona, CA, West Long Branch, NJ
E-mail: smcpublications@embarqmail.com
Web site: http://www.magi-call.com.

SMC Publishing *See* **SMC Pubns., LLC**

Smethwick Publishing LLC *See* **Oliver Pr. LLC**

Smile Time Publishing, *(978-0-9785961)* P.O. Box B, Del Mar, CA 92014 USA
E-mail: ps@peterstrunk.com
Web site: http://www.smile-time.com.

Smile-a-Lot, LLP, *(978-0-9785132)* 1050 Walnut St. #201, Boulder, CO 80302 USA Tel 303-443-2006; Fax: 303-443-9475; *Imprints:* Smiletown Books (Smiletown Bks)
E-mail: chris@smiletownbooks.com
Web site: http://smiletownbooks.com.

SMiles Productions (SMP), LLC, *(978-0-9768456)* 14241 NE Woodinville-Duvall Rd., Woodinville, WA 98072 USA Tel 425-481-8817; Fax: 425-481-8179
E-mail: language@smilesprod.com
Web site: http://www.smilesprod.com.

Smiletown Bks. *Imprint of* **Smile-a-Lot, LLP**

Smiley Co., *(978-0-9629001)* 401 Anglin St., Smiley, TX 78159-0099 USA (SAN 297-4045) Tel 830-587-6623; Fax: 830-587-6113; Toll Free: 800-584-3655
E-mail: npattesonsmiley@the-cia.net.

Smiley Originals *See* **Smiley Co.**

Smith & Assocs., *(978-0-9790817)* 70 Goodwin Cir., Hartford, CT 06105 USA (SAN 852-3886) Tel 860-543-0279; Fax: 860-586-8718
Web site: http://www.morningdovepress.com
Dist(s): **Connecticut River Pr.**

Smith & Daniel, *(978-0-9630463; 978-1-889668)* P.O. Box 8097, Jacksonville, FL 32239-0097 USA Toll Free: 800-330-1325.

Smith & Kraus Pubs., Inc., *(978-0-9622722; 978-1-57525; 978-1-880399; 978-1-936232; 978-1-937738; 978-1-943511; 978-1-970012)* Orders Addr.: P.O. Box 127, Lyme, NH 03768 USA (SAN 255-1454) Tel 603-643-6431; Toll Free: 877-866-8680; Edit Addr.: 177 Lyme Rd., Hanover, NH 03755 USA
E-mail: marisasmithkraus@gmail.com; boda@sover.net
Web site: http://www.smithandkraus.com.

Smith, Andrea Joy, *(978-0-9764396)* 2447 Mission Ave, Suite B, Carmichael, CA 95608 USA
E-mail: smithfamdent@aol.com
Web site: http://smileagainnow.com; http://inthechairwithdrsmith.com.

Smith, Barbara Maxine, *(978-0-578-11939-7; 978-0-615-85722-0)* 21103 Gary Dr., Apt 114, Castro Valley, CA 94546 USA.

Smith, Bill O., *(978-0-615-56972-7; 978-0-9895238)* 8489 Timbers Trail, Traverse City, MI 49685 USA Tel 313-515-4328
E-mail: bill@billosmith.com.

Smith, Brenda J. Few *See* **Tall Through Bks.**

Smith, C. Brandt, *(978-0-9768020)* 1910 Scenic Rd., Jonesboro, AR 72401-0220 USA Tel 870-933-1908
E-mail: brandt@walnutstreetbaptist.org.

Smith, Deanna *See* **Annade Publishing**

Smith, Debra, *(978-0-9747754)* 1934 Donna Dr., Coupeville, WA 98239 USA.

Smith, Ernest, *(978-0-9729154)* Orders Addr.: 3155 Sharpe Ave. Apt. 304, Memphis, TN 38111-3784 USA
E-mail: ernest725@Hotmail.com.

Smith, Florence B. *See* **Prickly Pr.**

Smith, George Publishing, *(978-0-9740434)* Orders Addr.: 11 Amberwinds Ct., Lakewood, NJ 08701 USA (SAN 255-3716)
E-mail: customer_support@georgesmithpublishing.com
Web site: http://www.georgesmithpublishing.com
Dist(s): **Mountain Bk. Co.**

Smith, Gibbs Publisher *See* **Gibbs Smith, Publisher**

Smith Island Foundation, *(978-0-9754170)* 44108 Bristow Cir., Ashburn, VA 20147 USA Tel 703-729-4462 Phone/Fax
E-mail: books@smithislandfoundation.org; heather@pneumabooks.com
Web site: http://www.smithislandfoundation.org.

Smith, Jennifer W. *See* **Apple House Publishing**

Smith, Joseph L., *(978-0-9754985)* 38118 Village 38, Camarillo, CA 93012 USA
E-mail: cayusekid@earthlink.net.

Smith, Kasper, *(978-0-9744519)* 4251 Fischer, Detroit, MI 48214 USA Tel 313-922-1728
E-mail: pastorsmith@dominionintl.org
Web site: http://www.dominionintl.org.

Smith, Keith Bks., *(978-0-9637682; 978-0-9740764)* 1115 E. Main St., Suite 219, Box 8, Rochester, NY 14609 USA Tel 585-473-6776; Fax: 585-482-2496
E-mail: keith@keithsmithbooks.com
Web site: http://www.keithsmithbooks.com.

Smith, Mason, *(978-0-692-02010-4)* 107 Southland Dr., Richmond, KY 40475-2413 USA Tel 859-582-5960
E-mail: mason.smith@eku.edu.

Smith, Michael *See* **East West Discovery Pr.**

Smith, Mildred C., *(978-0-9778641; 978-0-692-60783-1)* 4200 Cathedral Ave, NW, Apt. 610, Washington, DC 20016 USA Tel 202-363-5352
E-mail: mcs29@georgetown.edu.

Smith Novelty Co., Inc., *(978-0-938765; 978-1-59099; 978-1-934954)* Div. of Smith News Co., Inc., 460 Ninth St., San Francisco, CA 94103-4478 USA (SAN 216-2326) Tel 415-861-4900; Fax: 415-861-5683
E-mail: ken@smithnovelty.com; matt@smithnovelty.com
Web site: http://www.smithnovelty.com.

Smith, Peter Pub., Inc., *(978-0-8446)* Five Lexington Ave., Magnolia, MA 01930 USA (SAN 206-8885) Tel 978-525-3562; Fax: 978-525-3674.

Smith, Ronald J. Sr., *(978-0-9749390)* 1123 S. Thomas St., Apt. 22, Arlington, VA 22204-3640 USA
E-mail: ronaldjay50@gmail.com
Dist(s): **Morris Publishing.**

Smith, S. Pubns., *(978-0-9769320)* P.O. Box 122, Severna Park, MD 21146 USA Tel 410-271-0837; Fax: 410-544-0059
E-mail: stew@stewsmith.com
Web site: http://www.stewsmith.com.

Smith, Sharon, *(978-0-9817615)* 13611 SW 285th Terr., Homestead, FL 33033 USA Tel 786-317-0267
E-mail: dexavior1@msn.com.

Smith, Tyjauna, *(978-0-9760112)* P.O. Box 2230 Misty Woods Rd., Lake Cormorant, MS 38641 USA
E-mail: tyjauna@bellsouth.net
Web site: http://www.authorsden.com/tyjaunalsmith.

Smith, Viveca Publishing, *(978-0-9740551)* PMB No. 131, 3001 S. Hardin Blvd., Suite 110, McKinney, TX 75070-9028 USA Tel 214-793-0089; Fax: 972-562-7559
E-mail: vsmithpublishing@aol.com
Web site: http://www.vivecasmithpublishing.com
Dist(s): **BookBaby**
ebrary, Inc.

Smithfield Capital Corp., *(978-0-9764670)* 219 S. D. St., Hamilton, OH 45013 USA
E-mail: smithfieldcap@msn.com.

Smithfield Press *See* **Princeton Health Pr.**

Smithsonian Bks. *Imprint of* **Smithsonian Institution Scholarly Pr.**

†Smithsonian Institution Pr., *(978-0-87474; 978-1-56098; 978-1-58834)* Div. of Smithsonian Institution, Orders Addr.: 22883 Quicksilver Dr., Dulles, VA 20166 USA (SAN 253-3383); Edit Addr.: 750 Ninth St. NW, Suite 4300, Washington, DC 20560-0950 USA (SAN 206-8044) Tel 202-275-2300; Fax: 202-275-2245; 202-275-2274; Toll Free: 800-233-4830 (orders)
Web site: http://www.sipress.si.edu/
Dist(s): **CreateSpace Independent Publishing Platform**
Ebsco Publishing
MyiLibrary
Penguin Random Hse. LLC
Random Hse., Inc.
Rowman & Littlefield Publishers, Inc.
Wittenborn Art Bks.; *CIP.*

Smithsonian Institution Scholarly Pr., *(978-0-9788460; 978-1-935623; 978-1-944466; 978-0-9992662; 978-0-9992663)* Orders Addr.: P.O. Box 37012, MRC 957, Washington, DC 20013 USA Tel 202-633-3017; Fax: 202-633-3017; *Imprints:* Smithsonian Books (SmithsonBks)
E-mail: schol.press@si.edu
Web site: http://www.scholarlypress.si.edu/
Dist(s): **MyiLibrary**
National Bk. Network
Penguin Random Hse. LLC
Random Hse., Inc.
Rowman & Littlefield Publishers, Inc.

Smithsonian National Museum of the American Indian, *(978-0-9719163; 978-1-933565)* MRC 590 PO Box 37012, Washington, DC 20013-7012 USA; 4th St. & Independence Ave., SW, Washington, DC 20024
E-mail: nmai-pubs@si.edu
Web site: http://www.americanindian.si.edu
Dist(s): **Consortium Bk. Sales & Distribution**
D.A.P./Distributed Art Pubs.
Fulcrum Publishing.

Smithsonian Science Education Ctr. (SSEC), *(978-1-933008; 978-0-9985286; 978-0-9985287)* 901 D St. SW, Suite 704B, Washington, DC 20024 USA Tel 202-633-2992; *Imprints:* Science and Technology Concepts (STC) (Sci & Tech)
E-mail: marohnp@si.edu
Web site: http://www.nsrconline.org; http://carolinacurriculum.com
Dist(s): **Carolina Biological Supply Co.**

Smokestack Bks. (GBR) *(978-0-9548691; 978-0-9551061; 978-0-9554028; 978-0-9575747; 978-0-9571722; 978-0-9927409; 978-0-9560341; 978-0-9564175; 978-0-9568144; 978-0-9929581) Dist. by* **Dufour.**

Smooth Sailing Pr., LLC, *(978-1-933660; 978-0-578-01793-8; 978-1-61899)* Orders Addr.: 20519 Sunshine Ln. Suite B, Spring, TX 77388 USA (SAN 257-2680) Tel 281-826-4026 (phone/fax); *Imprints:* Tadpole Press 4 Kids (Tadpole Pr)
E-mail: fwilmoth@smoothsailingpress.com; cmcginnis@smoothsailingpress.com
Web site: http://www.smoothsailingpress.com
Dist(s): **Follet Higher Education Grp.**

SMPR, *(978-0-9767898)* 4800 S. Westshore Blvd., Suite 411, Tampa, FL 33611 USA Tel 813-831-8206 (phone/fax); Toll Free Fax: 866-958-1323 (phone/fax)
E-mail: sonja.moffett@smpr.info
Web site: http://www.smpr.info.

Snake Country Publishing, *(978-0-9635828)* 16748 W. Linden St., Caldwell, ID 83607-9270 USA Tel 208-459-9233
E-mail: snakecountry@mindspring.com
Dist(s): **Caxton Pr.**

Snake Goddess Bks., *(978-0-9744910)* 11431/2 Gladsy Ave., Long Beach, CA 90804 USA.

Snap Bks. *Imprint of* **Capstone Press of Coughlan Cos.**

Snaptail Pr. *Imprint of* **Images Unlimited Publishing**

Snelsonbks.com, *(978-0-9723935)* 355 N. Diamond Ave., Canon City, CO 81212 USA
E-mail: bs@ris.net
Web site: http://www.snelsonbooks.com.

SNL Publishing, *(978-0-615-48221-7; 978-0-9848368)* 9 Spring Hill Ave., Norwalk, CT 06850 USA Tel 914-671-2252
E-mail: davidalara@aol.com; snlpublishing@aol.com.

Snodgrass, Ruth M., *(978-0-9754867)* 160 Polaris Dr., Dover, OH 44622 USA.

Snojoy Publishing, *(978-0-9743913)* 4509 14th St., Greeley, CO 80634 USA
E-mail: snojoy1@hotmail.com; gnojoy1@hotmail.com.

Snow In Sarasota Publishing, *(978-0-9663335; 978-0-9824611; 978-0-9830362; 978-0-9837685; 978-0-9893840; 978-0-9862979; 978-0-9977126)* 5170 Central Sarasota Pkwy., No.309, Sarasota, FL 34238 USA Tel 941-923-9201; Fax: 941-926-8739
E-mail: sarasota58@aol.com
Web site: http://www.snowinsarasota.com
Dist(s): **Bookmasters Distribution**
Follett School Solutions
MyiLibrary
ebrary, Inc.

Snow Leopard Publishing, *(978-1-944361)* 171 Durham Rd., Dover, NH 03820 USA (SAN 990-1183) Tel 603-343-8107
E-mail: info@snowleopardpublishing.com
Web site: SnowLeopardPublishing.com.

Snow Lion Publications, Inc, *Imprint of* **Shambhala Pubns., Inc.**

Snow Tree Bks., *(978-0-9749006)* Orders Addr.: P.O. Box 546, Peabody, MA 01960-7564 USA (SAN 255-965X) Tel 781-592-9866
E-mail: info@snowtreebooks.com
Web site: http://snowtreebooks.com.

Snow Waters Publishing, *(978-0-9792713)* 1302 E. 30th St., Suite A, Texarkana, AR 71854 USA Tel 870-216-2243 (phone/fax)
E-mail: teaching2win@gmail.com.

Snowbound Bks., *(978-0-9722570)* Orders Addr.: P.O. Box 281327, Lamoille, NV 89828 USA; Edit Addr.: 1291 Country Ln., Lamoille, NV 89828 USA.

Snowbound Pr., Inc., *(978-1-932362)* P.O. Box 698, Littleton, CO 80160-0698 USA Tel 303-347-2869; Fax: 303-386-3232
E-mail: info@snowboundpress.com
Web site: http://www.snowboundpress.com
Dist(s): **Independent Pubs. Group**
Quality Bks., Inc.

Snowman Learning Center, The, *(978-0-9674666)* 6 Carver St., Plymouth, MA 02360-3301 USA Tel 508-746-5993; Fax: 508-746-8097
E-mail: S.Snowmanph.d@worldnet.att.net.

Snowy Day Distribution & Publishing, A, *(978-0-9844681; 978-1-936615)* P.O. Box 2014, Merrimack, NH 03054 USA Tel 603-493-2276
E-mail: salspiritosr@asnowyday.com
Web site: http://www.asnowyday.com.

Snowy Night Pub., *(978-0-9860324)* 44240 Riverview Ridge Dr., Clinton Township, MI 48038 USA
E-mail: yroehler@bookpublishing.com.

Snowy Plains, *(978-0-9791367)* 270 Flodin Rd., Gwinn, MI 49841 USA
E-mail: jwsnowyplains@yahoo.com.

Snuggle Up Bks., *(978-0-9655530)* 3145 Claremore Ave., Long Beach, CA 90808-4421 USA
E-mail: judybelshe@aol.com.

SnuggleBugzzz Pr., *(978-0-615-38169-5)* 21328 Independence Ave., Lakeville, MN 55044 USA Tel 612-910-0190; Fax: 952-985-4151
E-mail: kathylucilejohnson@att.net
Web site: http://www.snugglebugzzz.com
Dist(s): **West.**

Snyder, Ted, *(978-0-9965019)* 8100 Valley Creek Dr., Choctaw, OK 73020 USA Tel 405-590-0794
E-mail: tedsnyder@reagan.com.

Snyder, Vicki, *(978-0-9773187)* 4349 Cimarron Ct., NW, Rochester, MN 55901 USA
E-mail: cctraining@prodigy.net.

Snyder-Winston Pr., *(978-0-9752749)* 23679 Calabasas Rd., No. 186, Calabasas, CA 91302 USA Tel 818-876-0188; Fax: 818-876-0133
E-mail: tedafed@earthlink.net
Web site: http://www.midaskids.com.

SNZ Publishing, *(978-0-9758815)* P.O. Box 32190, Cincinnati, OH 45232 USA (SAN 256-1255)
E-mail: doug@snzpublishing.com
Web site: http://www.snzpublishing.com.

So Pretty In Pink LLC *See* **King Production, A**

So Simple Learning, *(978-0-9772158)* 12463 Rancho Bernardo Rd., PMB 253, San Diego, CA 92128 USA Tel 858-530-5055
E-mail: info@sosimplelearning.com
Web site: http://www.sosimplelearning.com.

Soar Publishing, LLC, *(978-0-9721142; 978-0-9825450; 978-0-9838220; 978-0-9888650; 978-0-9962052; 978-0-9992960)* 16 Austree Ct., Columbia, SC 29229-7581 USA (SAN 255-4437) Tel 803-699-0633 phone; Fax: 803-699-0634 (phone/fax)
E-mail: smithser@bellsouth.net; smithser1@bellsouth.net
Web site: http://www.soarpublishing.com; http://www.titlewave.com; http://titletales.com
Dist(s): **Follett School Solutions.**

Soaring Sparrow Pr., *(978-1-891262)* 11795 SW Crater Loop, Beaverton, OR 97008 USA Tel 503-644-5960
E-mail: sparrowman@earthlink.net
Web site: www.marvinmallard.com.

Soccer Poet LLC, *(978-0-9896977)* 245 Falling Shoals Dr., Athens, GA 30605 USA Tel 706-201-3858
E-mail: soccerpoet@gmail.com
Web site: www.soccerpoet.com.

Soccertowns LLC, *(978-0-692-27681-5; 978-0-692-29319-5; 978-0-692-29448-2; 978-0-9908808; 978-0-9863584; 978-1-943255)* 4504 W. Memphis St, Broken Arrow, OK 74012 USA Tel 918-893-3121
E-mail: andresvarela@hotmail.com
Web site: www.soccertowns.com.

Social Motion Publishing *Imprint of* **July Publishing Inc.**

Social Skill Builder, Inc., *(978-0-9819585)* P.O. Box 2430, Leesburg, VA 20177 USA.

Social Studies Collections *Imprint of* **Capstone Press of Coughlan Cos.**

Social Studies Schl. Service, *(978-1-56004; 978-1-57596)* Orders Addr.: 10200 Jefferson Blvd., P.O. Box 802, Culver City, CA 90232-0802 USA (SAN 168-9592) Tel 310-839-2436; Fax: 310-839-2249; Toll Free: 800-421-4246
E-mail: access@socialstudies.com
Web site: http://socialstudies.com
Dist(s): **Follett School Solutions.**

Sociedad de San Pablo (COL) *(978-958-607) Dist. by* **St Pauls Alba.**

Sociedad de San Pablo (ESP) *Dist. by* **St Pauls Alba.**

Sociedad General Espanola de Libreria (ESP) *(978-84-7143; 978-84-9778) Dist. by* **Continental Bk.**

Sociedad General Espanola de Libreria (ESP) *(978-84-7143; 978-84-9778) Dist. by* **Distribks Inc.**

Society for Developmental Education *See* **Staff Development for Educators**

Society For The Understanding Of Early Child Development, *(978-0-9762509)* 39741 Lynn St., Canton, MI 48187 USA (SAN 256-260X) Tel 734-416-0480; Fax: 734-459-5280
E-mail: rsawhney@infotreeservice.com.

Society for Visual Education, Incorporated *See* **S V E & Churchill Media**

Society of Automotive Engineers, Incorporated *See* **SAE Intl.**

Society of Young Inklings, *(978-0-615-42953-3; 978-0-9839568; 978-0-9910031; 978-0-9981849)* 16 Muller Pl., San Jose, CA 95126 USA Tel 650-861-0508
E-mail: naomi@younginklings.org; info@younginklings.org
Web site: www.younginklings.org
Dist(s): **Lulu Pr., Inc.**

Socrates Solutions Incorporated, *(978-0-692-00121-9; 978-0-615-52175-6; 978-0-9905501)* P.O. Box 18457, San Jose, CA 95158 USA Tel 408-448-4018
E-mail: joemessineo@yahoo.com.

Sofia Martinez *Imprint of* **Picture Window Bks.**

Soft Saints, Inc., *(978-0-9769519)* 5753-G Santa Ana Canyon Rd., No. 378, Anaheim Hills, CA 92807 USA Tel 714-505-3127; Fax: 714-838-5857
E-mail: teri@softsaints.com
Web site: http://www.softsaints.com.

Softlight Pr. LLC, *(978-0-9983623)* P.O. Box 242, Wilton, CT 06897 USA Tel 203-554-8509
E-mail: abbymsmith@icloud.com.

SoftPlay, Inc., *(978-1-931312; 978-1-59292)* 3535 W. Peterson Ave., Chicago, IL 60659 USA (SAN 858-4982) Tel 773-509-0707; Fax: 773-509-0404
E-mail: sales@softplayforkids.com
Web site: http://www.softplayforkids.com.

SoGo Creation, *(978-0-9852052; 978-1-941006; 978-1-944425)* 6830 Via Marinero, Carlsbad, CA 92009 USA Tel 760-710-7144
E-mail: sogocreation@yahoo.com.

Soho Crime *Imprint of* **Soho Pr., Inc.**

Soho Pr., Inc., *(978-0-939149; 978-1-56947; 978-1-61695; 978-1-64129)* 853 Broadway Ste. 1402, New York, NY 10003 USA (SAN 662-5088) Tel 212-260-1900; Fax: 212-260-1902; *Imprints:* Soho Crime (Soho Crime); Soho Teen (Soho Teen)
E-mail: soho@sohopress.com
Web site: http://www.sohopress.com
Dist(s): **MyiLibrary**
Penguin Random Hse. LLC
Random Hse., Inc.

Soho Publishing Company *See* **Sixth&Spring Bks.**

Soho Teen *Imprint of* **Soho Pr., Inc.**

Soil Science Society of America *See* **ASA-CSSA-SSSA**

SoJam Pr., *(978-0-9761477)* P.O. Box 25163, Woodbury, MN 55125-9998 USA (SAN 256-2359)
E-mail: sojam@comcast.net
Web site: http://www.sojampress.com.

Sojourner Publishing, Inc., *(978-0-9701726; 978-0-9773156; 978-0-9824741)* Orders Addr.: P.O. Box 1575, Wake Forest, NC 27588 USA; Edit Addr.: 1208 Chilmark Ave., Wake Forest, NC 27587 USA Do not confuse with companies with the same name in Arlington, WA, Clarkston, MI
E-mail: wandam123@yahoo.com
Web site: http://www.thepaperjourney.com.

Sojourner Stories, *(978-0-9896660)* 4225 Piedmont Mesa Rd., Claremont, CA 91711 USA Tel 562-305-9119
E-mail: sojournerstories@gmail.com.

Sol de Oro Pubns., *(978-0-9754261)* 1004 S. Quinn Ct., Gilbert, AZ 85296-8818 USA Tel 480-892-0582
E-mail: SoldeOroPublications@yahoo.com
Web site: http://www.SoldeOroPublications.50megs.com.

Solar Publishing LLC, *(978-0-9785326)* P.O. Box 2116, Ellicott City, MD 21041 USA (SAN 850-8089) Tel 410-493-1872
E-mail: robyn@solarpub.com
Web site: http://www.solarpub.com
Dist(s): **BookBaby.**

Sole Bks., *(978-0-9844257; 978-1-938591)* P.O. Box 10445, Beverly Hills, CA 90213 USA Tel 424-283-4299
E-mail: info@wildsoccer.com; sales@solebooks.com; tally@wildsoccer.com
Web site: http://www.wildsoccerbunch.com; http://www.solebooks.com.

Solebury Press *See* **Thompson Mill Pr.**

Solel Pubns., *(978-0-9748332)* 309 Concord Ave., Oceanside, NY 11572 USA Tel 516-678-9778.

Solemn Word Publishing, *(978-0-9759717)* P.O. Box 301, Grant City, MO 64456 USA
E-mail: cjblanchard@solemnword.com
Web site: http://www.solemnword.com.

Soler, Michael, *(978-0-9795469)* 74 Sashington Heights Rd., Washington, NH 03280 USA (SAN 853-6996).

Solibros, *(978-0-9755945)* 2215 Peachtree N. Ct., Atlanta, GA 30338 USA
Web site: http://www.solibros.com.

Solid Ground Christian Bks., *(978-0-9710169; 978-1-932474; 978-1-59925)* Orders Addr.: P.O. Box 660132, Vestavia Hills, AL 35266 USA Tel 205-443-0311; Fax: 775-822-5917; Toll Free: 877-666-9469; Edit Addr.: 715 Oak Grove Rd., Birmingham, AL 35209-6503 USA
E-mail: solid-ground-books@juno.com; solid_ground_books@yahoo.com; scgbclassics@juno.com; sgcb@charter.net
Web site: http://www.solid-ground-books.com.

Solid Rock Bks. *Imprint of* **Trumpet In Zion Publishing**

Solid Rock Publishing *See* **Trumpet In Zion Publishing**

SolidA, Inc., *(978-0-9677328)* 9339 Paradise Rd., Kewaskum, WI 53040 USA Tel 262-692-9609
E-mail: deanne@solida.net
Web site: http://www.solida.net.

Solitude Pr., *(978-1-928874)* 212 Brooks St., Williamsburg, VA 23185 USA Tel 757-564-1365
E-mail: zander67@cox.net.

Solomon Schechter Day Schl. of Greater Boston, *(978-0-9836623)* 60 Stein Cir., Newton, MA 02459 USA Tel 617-964-7765
E-mail: amy.bardack@ssdsboston.org
Web site: www.ssdsboston.org.

Solomon Waterwine, LLC *See* **Tinsley Phelps, LLC**

Solomon's Bks., *(978-0-9763871; 978-0-9827949; 978-0-9838687; 978-0-615-67340-0)* 885 New Hope Dr., Suite 100, Hampton, GA 30228 USA.

Solovisions *Imprint of* **Comic Library International**

Solsidan Hse., *(978-0-9741620)* Orders Addr.: 104 7th St., Colorado Springs, CO 80906 USA; Edit Addr.: 475 Sunnyside Ave., Eugene, OR 97404 USA
E-mail: solsidanhouse@yahoo.com
Web site: http://www.solsidanhouse.com.

Solutionary Stories Pr., *(978-0-692-79987-1)* 3761 Portland Ct., Carlsbad, CA 92010 USA Tel 760-729-7383
E-mail: writermeeg@gmail.com.

Solutions for Human Services, LLC, *(978-0-9764802)* 25 Vernon Dr., Warren, PA 16365 USA Tel 814-726-1228
E-mail: lindab@westpa.net.

Solving Light Bks., *(978-0-9705438; 978-0-692-26013-5)* 727 Mountalban Dr., Annapolis, MD 21409-4646 USA Tel 410-757-4630
E-mail: rbowiej@comcast.net; nancygjohnson@comcast.net
Web site: http://www.solvinglight.com; http://www.theparthenoncode.com
Dist(s): **BookBaby**
CreateSpace Independent Publishing Platform
Send The Light Distribution LLC.

Some Kids I Know, *(978-0-9768230)* Div. of Some Kids I Know, LLC, W323 N8164 Northcrest Dr., Hartland, WI 53029 USA Tel 262-966-2582
E-mail: thorst@wi.rr.com.

Some Kids I Know, LLC, *(978-0-9768230)* W323 N8164 Northcrest Dr., Hartland, WI 53029 USA.

Someday Ranch, *(978-0-9910180)* P.O. Box 414, Wauna, WA 98395 USA Tel 253-380-0663
E-mail: zookeeper99@comcast.net.

†Somerset Pubs., Inc., *(978-0-403)* 1532 State St., Santa Barbara, CA 93101 USA (SAN 204-6105) Toll Free: 800-937-7947
Dist(s): **North American Bk. Distributors**; *CIP.*

Somerville Hse. Bks., Ltd. (CAN) *(978-0-921051; 978-1-58184; 978-1-895897; 978-1-55286; 978-1-894042) Dist. by* **Penguin Grp USA.**

Sonfire Media, LLC, *(978-0-9825773; 978-0-9891064)* 974 E. Stuart Dr. Suite D, PMB 232, Galax, VA 24333 USA; *Imprints:* Taberah Press (Taberah Pr)
Web site: http://www.sonfiremedia.com.

Song Revival Fellowship & Ministries, *(978-0-9673093; 978-0-9823344)* Div. of LaVerne Tripp Ministries, Orders Addr.: P.O. Box 899, Gallatin, TN 37066 USA Tel 615-230-7577; Fax: 615-230-7939; Edit Addr.: 2105 Cages Bend Rd., Gallatin, TN 37066 USA
E-mail: kim@lavernetripp.com
Web site: http://www.lavernetripp.com.

Songadh, Jain Swadhyay Mandir, *(978-0-9748681)* 304 Tall Oak Trail, Tarpon Springs, FL 34688 USA Tel 602-863-1073; 727-376-7290; Fax: 602-863-3557; 727-843-8157
E-mail: kahanguru@hotmail.com.

Songbird Pr., *(978-0-9720913)* Orders Addr.: P.O. Box 99, Freeport, ME 04032 USA Fax: 207-373-1128
Web site: http://www.songbirdpress.biz.

Sonic Sword Productions, *(978-0-9797715)* 1089-A Alice Dr., Suite 327, Sumter, SC 29150 USA Tel 803-983-5084
E-mail: john@jhollandbooks.com
Web site: http://jhollandbooks.com; http://rjwargames.com.

Sonnenschein Bks. *Imprint of* **Black Forest Pr.**

Sono Nis Pr. (CAN) *(978-0-919203; 978-0-919462; 978-0-9690282; 978-1-55039) Dist. by* **Orca Bk Pub.**

SonoMagnetics, *(978-1-930216)* P.O. Box 22, Rumney, NH 03266-0022 USA Tel 603-204-5273
E-mail: bap@sonomagnetics.com
Web site: http://www.nuenergy.org; http://www.sonomagnetics.com.

Son-Rise Pubns. & Distribution Co., *(978-0-936369)* 51 Greenfield Rd., New Wilmington, PA 16142 USA (SAN 698-0031) Tel 724-946-9057; Fax: 724-946-8700; Toll Free: 800-358-0777
Web site: http://www.softspace.com/steelvalley; http://www.sonrisepublications.com.

Sonrise Publishing, *(978-0-9724458; 978-0-9845663; 978-0-9914347)* 131 Galleon St. # 2B, Marina Dl Rey, CA 90292-5973 USA (SAN 254-8348) Do not confuse with companies with the same or similar names in Corte Madera, CA, Ashland, OH
E-mail: annsonrise@aol.com
Web site: http://www.sonrisepublishing.com; http://www.annhamiltonwallace.com
Dist(s): **BookMasters, Inc.**

Sonship Pr. *Imprint of* **21st Century Pr.**

†Sophia Institute Pr., *(978-0-918477; 978-1-928832; 978-1-933184; 978-1-62282)* Orders Addr.: P.O. Box 5284, Manchester, NH 03108 USA (SAN 657-7172) Tel 603-641-9344; Fax: 603-641-8108; Toll Free: 800-888-9344 Do not confuse with Sophia Pr., Durham, NH
E-mail: production@sophiainstitute.com
Web site: http://www.sophiainstitute.com
Dist(s): **eBookit.com**; *CIP.*

Sophie's Tales, LLC, *(978-0-578-03818-6; 978-0-9851575)* 665 S Skinker Blvd, Saint Louis, MO 63105 USA Tel 516-242-1466
E-mail: mpaticoff@sophiestales.com
Web site: www.sophiestales.com.

Sophrose Entertainment Inc., *(978-0-9800736)* P.O. Box 1989, Cape Canaveral, FL 32920-1989 USA (SAN 855-1286) Tel 321-459-3442 Toll Free: 888-599-7483
E-mail: mail@sophrose.com
Web site: http://www.sophrose.com.

Sopris West Educational Services *See* **Cambium Education, Inc.**

Sora Publishing, *(978-0-9765756)* 1800 Atlantic Blvd., A-405, Key West, FL 33040-5708 USA (SAN 256-4157) Tel 305-296-6699
E-mail: sorapublishing@comcast.net
Web site: http://www.sorapublishing.com.

Sorcerer's Pr., The, *(978-0-9667747)* 6 Berks St., Catasauqua, PA 18032-1532 USA.

Sorella Bks., *(978-0-9767351)* P.O. Box 454, Plantsville, CT 06479 USA
E-mail: sorellabooks@yahoo.com
Web site: http://www.sorellabooks.com.

Sorenson, E. Randy, *(978-0-615-16939-2)* 3053 Frederick Pl., West Valley City, UT 84119 USA
Web site: http://www.firstreindeer.com.

Sortis Publishing, *(978-0-9772025; 978-0-9827986)* 2193 E. Claxton Ave., Gilbert, AZ 85297 USA (SAN 256-923X) Tel 480-310-8316; Fax: 480-279-5851
E-mail: tradewebb@wydebeam.com
Web site: http://www.sortispublishing.com.

Soul Attitude Press, *(978-0-578-06870-1; 978-1-939181; 978-1-946338)* P.O. Box 1656, Pinellas Park, FL 33782 USA
Web site: http://www.johnrehg.com.

Soul Family Travels *See* **SFT Pubns.**

Soul Mate Publishing, *(978-1-61935; 978-1-68291)* P.O. Box 24, Macedon, NY 14502 USA Tel 315-986-4571
Web site: http://www.soulmatepublishing.com.

Soul Pubns., *(978-0-937327)* 232 Rockford St., Mt. Airy, NC 27030 USA (SAN 658-8050) Tel 336-786-4118 (phone/fax); 3220 Lazelle St. #114, STURGIS, SD 57785 Tel 605-720-0986
Dist(s): **Lulu Pr., Inc.**

Soul Vision Works Publishing, *(978-0-9659538; 978-0-9816254)* P.O. Box 360063, Brooklyn, NY 11236 USA Tel 718-493-7981; Toll Free: 888-789-6757; *Imprints:* Vision Works Publishing (Vis Wrks)
E-mail: info@visionworksonline.net
Web site: http://www.visionworksonline.net.

Soulful Storytellers, Inc., *(978-0-9851628)* 3263 Ave. H, Brooklyn, NY 11210 USA Tel 718-781-7560
E-mail: soulmuze@gmail.com.

Soulo Communications, *(978-0-9778209; 978-0-9825607)* Div. of Soulo Communications, Orders Addr.: 2112 Broadway St., NE Suite 100, Minneapolis, MN 55413-3036 USA Tel 612-788-4341; Fax: 612-788-4347
E-mail: tomh@soulocommunications.com
Web site: http://www.soulocommunications.com
Dist(s): **Partners Pubs. Group, Inc.**

SoulSong Publishing, *(978-0-9793113)* Div. of SoulSong Enterprises, Orders Addr.: P.O. Box 715, Crestone, CO 81131 USA
E-mail: soulsongpublishing@yahoo.com
Web site: http://www.soulsong.org.

Sound Concepts, Inc., *(978-1-887938; 978-1-933057; 978-1-936631)* 782 S. Automall Dr. Unit A, American Fork, UT 84003 USA Tel 801-225-9520; Fax: 801-343-3301; Toll Free: 800-544-7044
E-mail: mjo@soundconcepts.com; jca@soundconcepts.com; jason@soundconcepts.com; vs@soundconcepts.com; edr@soundconcepts.com
Web site: http://www.soundconcepts.com.

Sound Craft Designs, *(978-0-9771357)* P.O. Box 1563, Poway, CA 92074-1563 USA Tel 858-842-1985
E-mail: info@exploreguitar.com
Web site: http://www.exploreguitar.com.

Sound Library *Imprint of* **AudioGO**

Sound Reading *Imprint of* **Sound Reading Solutions**

Sound Reading Solutions, *(978-0-9704183; 978-0-9742485; 978-0-9743384)* 379 Turkey Hill Rd., Ithaca, NY 14850 USA Tel 607-273-1370 (phone/fax); Toll Free: 800-801-1954; *Imprints:* Sound Reading (Sound Read)
E-mail: info@soundreading.com
Web site: http://www.soundreading.com.

Sound Room Pubs., Inc., *(978-1-883049; 978-1-58472)* Orders Addr.: P.O. Box 3168, Falls Church, VA 22043 USA Tel 540-722-2535; Fax: 540-722-0903; Toll Free: 800-643-0295; Edit Addr.: 100 Weems Ln., Winchester, VA 22601 USA; *Imprints:* In Audio (In Aud)
E-mail: commuterslib@worldnet.att.net
Web site: http://www.inaudio.biz/
Dist(s): **Distributors, The**
Findaway World, LLC
Follett Media Distribution
Follett School Solutions.

Sound View Press *See* **Falk Art Reference**

Soundprints, *(978-0-924483; 978-1-56899; 978-1-931465; 978-1-59249; 978-1-60727)* Div. of Trudy Corp., 353 Main Ave., Norwalk, CT 06851 USA Fax: 203-846-1776; Toll Free: 800-228-7839; *Imprints:* Blackbirch Press, Incorporated (Blackbirch Pr); Little Soundprints (Little Sound)
Web site: http://www.soundprints.com
Dist(s): **Follett School Solutions**
Cengage Gale
Learning Connection, The.

Sounds Devine, *(978-0-9745249)* P.O. Box 251, Arabi, LA 70032 USA Do not confuse with Calliope Publishing in Steamboat Springs, CO
Web site: http://www.soundsdevine.com.

Sounds True, Inc., *(978-1-56455; 978-1-59179; 978-1-60407; 978-1-62203; 978-1-68364)* Orders Addr.: P.O. Box 8010, Boulder, CO 80306-8010 USA; Edit Addr.: 413 S. Arthur Ave., Louisville, CO 80027 USA (SAN 850-3532) Tel 303-665-3151; Fax: 303-665-5292; Toll Free: 800-333-9185
Web site: http://www.soundstrue.com.

Sounds Write Productions, Inc., *(978-0-9626286; 978-1-890161)* 6685 Norman Ln., San Diego, CA 92120 USA Tel 619-697-6120; Fax: 619-697-6124; Toll Free: 800-976-8639
E-mail: soundswrite@aol.com; info@soundswrite.com
Web site: http://www.soundswrite.com.

SourceAid, LLC, *(978-0-9771957)* Orders Addr.: P.O. Box 430, Osterville, MA 02655 USA Tel 508-428-3150 Toll Free: 877-687-2324; Edit Addr.: 1284 A Main St., Osterville, MA 02655 USA
E-mail: info@sourceaid.com
Web site: http://www.sourceaid.com
Dist(s): **Independent Pubs. Group.**

Sourcebook Project, The, *(978-0-915554; 978-0-9600712)* P.O. Box 107, Glen Arm, MD 21057 USA (SAN 201-7652) Tel 410-668-6047
Web site: http://www.science-frontiers.com.

Sourcebooks Casablanca *Imprint of* **Sourcebooks, Inc.**

†Sourcebooks, Inc., *(978-0-942061; 978-0-9629162; 978-0-9629803; 978-1-57071; 978-1-57248; 978-1-58182; 978-1-883518; 978-1-887166; 978-1-888952; 978-1-4022; 978-1-932783; 978-1-62047; 978-1-4926)* 1935 Brookdale Rd., Suite 139, Naperville, IL 60563 USA (SAN 666-7864) Tel 630-961-3900; Fax: 630-961-2168; Toll Free: 800-727-8866; *Imprints:* Sourcebooks Casablanca (Casablanca); Sourcebooks Landmark (Sourcebks Land); Sourcebooks MediaFusion (MediaFusion); Sourcebooks Jabberwocky (Srcbks Jabber); Marianne Richmond Studios, Incorporated (MarianneRich); Cumberland House (Cumberland)
E-mail: info@sourcebooks.com
Web site: http://www.sourcebooks.com/
Dist(s): **Ebsco Publishing**
Follett School Solutions
Ingram Publisher Services
MyiLibrary
Source Bk. Pubns.; *CIP.*

Sourcebooks Jabberwocky *Imprint of* **Sourcebooks, Inc.**

Sourcebooks Landmark *Imprint of* **Sourcebooks, Inc.**

Sourcebooks MediaFusion *Imprint of* **Sourcebooks, Inc.**

South Asia Bks., *(978-0-8364; 978-0-88386)* P.O. Box 502, Columbia, MO 65205 USA (SAN 207-4044) Tel 573-474-0116; Fax: 573-474-8124
E-mail: sabooks@juno.com
Web site: http://www.southasiabooks.com.

South Carolina Geographic Alliance, *(978-0-9768247)* Ctr. of Excellence for Geographic Education, Orders Addr.: Department of Geography, Univ. of S. C., Columbia, SC 29208 USA Toll Free: 888-895-2023
Web site: http://www.cas.sc.edu/cege/.

South Dakota State Historical Society Pr. *Imprint of* **South Dakota State Historical Society Pr.**

South Dakota State Historical Society Pr., *(978-0-9622621; 978-0-9715171; 978-0-9749195; 978-0-9777955; 978-0-9798940; 978-0-9822749; 978-0-9845041; 978-0-9846505; 978-0-9852817; 978-0-9852905; 978-0-9860355; 978-1-941813)* 900 Governors Dr., Pierre, SD 57501 USA; *Imprints:* South Dakota State Historical Society Press (S Dak St Hist Soc Pr)
E-mail: sdshspress@state.sd.us; rodger.hartley@state.sd.us
Web site: http://www.sdshspress.com
Dist(s): **BookBaby.**

South Florida Art Ctr., Inc., *(978-0-9719492)* 924 Lincoln Rd., Suite 205, Miami Beach, FL 33139-2609 USA
Web site: http://www.artcentersf.org.

South Hadley Publishing, *(978-0-9761844)* Orders Addr.: P.O. Box 681, South Hadley, MA 01075 USA Tel 413-433-6456; Edit Addr.: 18 Maria Dr., South Hadley, MA 01075 USA
E-mail: price@bookshappen.com
Web site: http://bookshappen.com.

South River Pr., *(978-0-9770764)* P.O. Box 392, Indianola, IA 50125-5012 USA (SAN 256-6982) Tel 515-962-9375.

Southall, Twyla, *(978-0-9765501)* 5837 Karric Sq. Dr., Dublin, OH 43016 USA
E-mail: twyla@tsouthall.com
Web site: http://www.tsouthall.com.

Southeast Media, *(978-1-888141)* 87 Piedmont Dr., Palm Coast, FL 32164-7085 USA
E-mail: Reachment@msn.com
Web site: http://www-gout-haters.com.

Southern Acres Academy, *(978-0-615-17522-5)* 4955 Hwy. 4, Davenport, NE 68335ed USA
Dist(s): **Lulu Pr., Inc.**

Southern Girl Media, *(978-0-9744423)* Orders Addr.: P.O. Box 373, Festus, MO 63028 USA Tel 760-535-2640
Web site: http://www.masonweaver.com
Dist(s): **Tremendous Life Bks.**

Southern Lion Bks., *(978-0-9662454; 978-0-9794203; 978-1-935272)* 1070 Jordan Rd., Madison, GA 30650 USA Tel 706-474-1667 (Tel. & Fax)
E-mail: taniamcclain@yahoo.com; mcclain2@bellsouth.net
Web site: http://www.southernlionbooks.com.

Southern Yellow Pine (SYP) Publishing LLC, *(978-1-59616; 978-0-9857062; 978-1-940869)* 4351 Natural Bridge Rd., Tallahassee, FL 32305 USA Tel 850-421-7420; *Imprints:* SYP Kids (SYP Kids)
E-mail: tgerrell@syppublishing.com
Web site: www.syppublishing.com.

Southfarm Pr., *(978-0-913337)* Div. of Haan Graphic Publishing Services, Ltd., P.O. Box 1296, Middletown, CT 06457 USA (SAN 283-4146) Tel 860-346-8798
E-mail: southfar@ix.netcom.com
Web site: http://www.war-books.com; http://www.wandahaan.com.

Southgate Pubs. (GBR) *(978-1-85741) Dist. by* **Parkwest Pubns.**

Southpaw Books LLC, *(978-0-9777720)* Southpaw Books LLC, Maplewood, NJ 07040 USA (SAN 850-1017) Tel 973-313-0843; Fax: 973-313-0843
E-mail: info@southpawbooks.com
Web site: http://southpawbooks.com.

Southport Historical Society, Inc., *(978-1-892444)* P.O. Box 10014, Southport, NC 28461-0014 USA Tel 910-457-6940
E-mail: Furstenau@earthlink.net.

Southwest guns & stuff, *(978-0-9747407)* 4212 Lanshire Ct., Grand Prairie, TX 75052-3164 USA.

Southwest Legal Services, *(978-0-9644908; 978-0-9843383)* Div. of Charlynn Publishing Co., Inc., Orders Addr.: P.O. Box 57091, Tucson, AZ 85732 USA Tel 520-795-1414; Edit Addr.: 4152 E. Fifth St., Tucson, AZ 85711 USA
E-mail: swlsorders@yahoo.com
Web site: http://www.southwestlegalservices.com; http://www.bustedbythefeds.com
Dist(s): **Charlynn Publishing Co., Inc.**

Southwest Parks & Monuments Association *See* **Western National Parks Assn.**

SouthWest Pubns., *(978-1-934345)* Div. of NF Publishing, P.O. Box 782, Kingsport, TN 37662 USA Tel 423-765-1416; Fax: 800-807-9203; Toll Free Fax: 800-807-9203; Toll Free: 800-807-9203
Web site: http://www.southwestpublications.net.

Southwestern Pr., Inc, *(978-0-923176)* Orders Addr.: P.O. Box 4297, Carlsbad, CA 92018-4297 USA (SAN 251-5601) Tel 760-434-8858; Fax: 760-434-8888
E-mail: sharon@southwesternpress.com
Web site: http://www.southwesternpress.com/.

†Southwestern Publishing Group, Inc., *(978-0-87197; 978-1-935442; 978-1-941800; 978-1-943198)* A member of the Southwestern Family of Companies, Orders Addr.: P.O. Box 305142, Nashville, TN 37230 USA (SAN 204-1197) Tel 615-391-2944; Fax: 615-391-2656; Toll Free: 800-798-1780; Edit Addr.: 2451 Atrium Way, Nashville, TN 37214 USA Fax: 615-391-2815; Toll Free: 800-269-6839; *Imprints:* Beckon Books (BeckonBks) Do not confuse with Favorite Recipes in Vernal, UT
E-mail: info@frpbooks.com; kconnelly@swpublishinggroup.com
Web site: http://www.frpbooks.com; http://www.beckonbooks.com; http://www.swpublishinggroup.com; http://www.greenwichpublishing.com
Dist(s): **Cookbook Marketplace, The;** *CIP.*

Souvenir Pr. Ltd. (GBR) *(978-0-285) Dist. by* **IPG Chicago.**

Sovereign Grace Pubs., Inc., *(978-1-878442; 978-1-58960)* P.O. Box 4998, Lafayette, IN 47903-4998 USA (SAN 299-6847) Toll Free: 800-447-9142 Do not confuse with Sovereign Grace Pubns., Lexington, KY
E-mail: jaygreenxx@iquest.net
Web site: http://www.sovgracepub.com.

Sovereign Press *See* **Margaret Weis Productions, Ltd.**

Sow Forth Publishing LLC, *(978-0-9822262)* P.O. Box 303, Lewis Center, OH 43035-9462 USA (SAN 857-7358)
E-mail: sowforth@insight.rr.com.

Sowash, Rick Publishing Co., *(978-0-9762412)* 338 Milton St. # 1, Cincinnati, OH 45202-0971 USA Toll Free: 888-255-2764
E-mail: rick@sowash.com
Web site: http://www.sowash.com.

Soxwings Publishing, *(978-0-615-20974-6)* 414 Executive Ctr. Blvd., Suite 105, El Paso, TX 79902 USA Tel 915-533-3827; Fax: 915-533-3745; Toll Free: 866-416-3827
E-mail: bobtjr@yahoo.com.

SP Family Productions, LLC, *(978-0-9773134)* 5 Knute Drive, Andover, NJ 07821-3912 USA Tel 973-479-6111
E-mail: seancanning@hotmail.com
Web site: http://www.seancanning.com.

Space Penguins *Imprint of* **Stone Arch Bks.**

Spalding Education International, *(978-1-935289)* 23335 N. 18th Dr., Suite 102, Phoenix, AZ 85027-6301 USA (SAN 857-0310) Tel 623-434-1204; Fax: 623-434-1208
E-mail: jsexton@spalding.org; kporter@spalding.org
Web site: http://www.spalding.org.

Spanish Language Texts, Inc., *(978-0-9710710)* Orders Addr.: P.O. Box 1088, New York, NY 10040 USA; Edit Addr.: 19 Seaman Ave. 2M, New York, NY 10034 USA
Web site: http://www.spanishlanguagetexts.com
Dist(s): **Lectorum Pubns., Inc.**

Spanish Pubs., LLC, 8871 SW 129 Terr., Miami, FL 33176 USA Tel 305-233-3365; Fax: 305-251-1310
E-mail: mariela@spanishpublishers.net
Web site: www.spanishpublishers.net.

Spanish-Live, *(978-0-9816973)* 1033 Imperial Dr., Morgantown, WV 26508 USA
E-mail: lorena@spanish-live.com
Web site: http://www.spanish-live.com.

Spann Productions, *(978-0-9772209)* P.O. Box 10412, Bakersfield, CA 93389 USA Tel 661-832-2135 (phone/fax)
E-mail: spannlake@aol.com.

SpanPress, Inc., *(978-1-58045; 978-1-887578)* 5722 S. Flamingo Rd., Suite 277, Cooper City, FL 33330 USA Tel 305-592-7913; Fax: 305-477-5632; Toll Free: 800-585-8384
Dist(s): **Continental Bk. Co., Inc.**
Lectorum Pubns., Inc.

Spark Hse., *(978-1-936174)* Div. of Augsburg Fortress, Pubs., 100 S. 5th St., Suite 600, Minneapolis, MN 55402 USA Tel 612-330-3305; Fax: 612-330-3514; Toll Free: 800-426-0115; *Imprints:* Sparkhouse Press (Sparkhouse)
E-mail: irene.crooks@augsburgfortress.org
Dist(s): **Augsburg Fortress, Pubs.**

Spark Notes *Imprint of* **Sterling Publishing Co., Inc.**

Spark Publishing Group *Imprint of* **Sterling Publishing Co., Inc.**

Sparkhouse Family *Imprint of* **Augsburg Fortress, Pubs.**

Sparkhouse Pr. *Imprint of* **Spark Hse.**

Sparkledoll Productions, *(978-0-9747832)* P.O. Box 56173, Virginia Beach, VA 23456 USA Tel 757-718-3095
E-mail: books@sparkledoll.com
Web site: http://www.sparkledoll.com/publishing.

Sparklesoup LLC, *(978-0-9714776; 978-1-932379; 978-1-59748; 978-1-61814)* 11700 W. Charleston Blvd., Ste. 170-95, Las Vegas, NV 89135 USA; *Imprints:* The Edge (TheEdge)
E-mail: sparklesoup@aol.com
Web site: http://www.sparklesoup.com; http://www.theedgebooks.com; http://www.kailingowbooks.com
Dist(s): **CreateSpace Independent Publishing Platform**
Lightning Source, Inc.

Sparklesoup Studios, Incorporated *See* **Sparklesoup LLC**

Sparkling Bks. (GBR) *(978-1-907230) Dist. by* **Silvermine Int.**

Sparkling Pr., *(978-0-9774855)* 137 E. Curtice St., St. Paul, MN 55107 USA Tel 651-227-5248.

SparkNotes *Imprint of* **Barnes & Noble, Inc.**

Sparkplug Bks., *(978-0-9742715; 978-0-9797465; 978-0-9854150)* P.O. Box 10952, Portland, OR 97296-0952 USA
E-mail: virginia@sparkplugcomicbooks.com
Web site: http://www.sparkplugcomicbooks.com
Dist(s): **Consortium Bk. Sales & Distribution.**

Sparkplug Comic Books *See* **Sparkplug Bks.**

SparkPr. (a Bks.parks Imprint), *(978-1-940716; 978-1-943006)* 688 W. First St. Ste. 5, TEMPE, AZ 85281 USA Tel 480-650-1688
E-mail: Publishing@sparkpointstudio.com
Web site: http://booksparkspr.com/
Dist(s): **Ingram Publisher Services.**

Sparks Fly, *(978-0-9789445)* 609 Myrtle Ave., Apt 3A, Brooklyn, NY 11205-1470 USA Toll Free: 866-556-2432
E-mail: info@sparksfly.org
Web site: http://www.sparksfly.org.

Sparrow Media Group, Inc., *(978-0-9719304; 978-0-9786018; 978-0-9829526)* P.O. Box 44272, Eden Prairie, MN 55344-4272 USA Tel 952-953-9166
Web site: http://www.sparrowmediagroup.com.

SPC Bks. *Imprint of* **RPJ & Co., Inc.**

SPCK Publishing (GBR) *(978-0-281; 978-0-7459; 978-0-85969; 978-1-902694) Dist. by* **Pilgrim OH.**

SPD-Small Pr. Distribution, *(978-0-914068)* 1341 Seventh St., Berkeley, CA 94710-1409 USA (SAN 204-5826) Tel 510-524-1668; Fax: 510-524-0852; Toll Free: 800-869-7553 (orders)
E-mail: orders@spdbooks.org
Web site: http://www.spdbooks.org.

Speak *Imprint of* **Penguin Publishing Group**

Speak *Imprint of* **Penguin Young Readers Group**

Speak Out Ministry, *(978-0-578-02848-4; 978-0-692-86807-2; 978-0-9993791)* 13844 Carter House Way, Silver Spring, MD 20904 USA Tel 202-412-7957
E-mail: aileencunningham15@gmail.com
Web site: http://www.alphathetaomega.com.

Speakeasy Comics (CAN) *(978-0-9737039; 978-0-9738388) Dist. by* **Diamond Book Dists.**

Speak-Easy Publishing, LLC, *(978-0-9714433; 978-0-9754977)* Orders Addr.: P.O. Box 11377, Takoma Park, MD 20913 USA Tel 202-723-1317
E-mail: jgduarte@speakeasypublishing.com; info@speakeasypublishing.com
Web site: http://www.speakeasypublishing.com
Dist(s): **Lyrical Liquor Productions.**

Speaking Volumes, LLC, *(978-1-935138; 978-1-61232; 978-1-62815)* 21 Sleeping Dog Rd., Santa Fe, NM 87508 USA (SAN 856-5880) Tel 505-466-4318; 888-777-8204
E-mail: kurt@speaking-volumes.com
Web site: http://www.speaking-volumes.com/indexfish.asp; http://.www.speakingvolumes.us
Dist(s): **Follett School Solutions.**

Special Edition Studios, Inc., *(978-0-9759013)* P.O. Box 7216, Sebring, FL 33872-0104 USA
Web site: http://www.sestudios.com.

Special Editions — Customized Biographies *Imprint of* **Slavens Enterprises, LLC.**

Special Kids Company, Incorporated *See* **Anythings Possible, Inc.**

Special Reads for Special Needs, *(978-0-9702698; 978-0-9795922)* 12025 Merganser Dr., Cincinnati, OH 45246-1542 USA Tel 513-541-7617; Fax: 513-541-2543; Toll Free: 866-553-2042
E-mail: specialreads@aol.com
Web site: http://www.specialreads.com.

Specialized Printing, LLC, *(978-0-615-38944-8)* 2430 NW Broadway St., Albany, OR 97321 USA Tel 800-282-6621
E-mail: ericbrunsvold@gmail.com.

Specialized Quality Pubns., *(978-0-9634906; 978-0-9789582)* 921 11th St., S., Wisconsin Rapids, WI 54494 USA (SAN 299-299X) Tel 715-423-7476; *Imprints:* SQP (SQP)
Web site: http://www.specializedqualitypublications.com/index.htm.

Specialty Educational Pubs., *(978-0-9718488)* P.O. Box 161, New Oxford, PA 17350 USA
E-mail: specialtypublishers@hotmail.com.

Specialty Greetings, *(978-0-9860024)* 2225 Grant St., Eugene, OR 97405 USA Tel 541-344-6400
E-mail: orders@specialtygreetings.com
Web site: http://www.SpecialtyGreetings.com.

Specialty Pr., Inc., *(978-0-9621629; 978-1-886941; 978-1-937761)* 300 NW 70th Ave., Suite 102, Plantation, FL 33317 USA (SAN 251-6977) Tel 954-792-8100; Fax: 954-792-8545; Toll Free: 800-233-9273 Do not confuse with Specialty Pr., Inc., in Ocean, NJ
E-mail: sales@addwarehouse.com
Web site: http://www.addwarehouse.com
Dist(s): **Ebsco Publishing**
Independent Pubs. Group
MyiLibrary.

Specialty Publishing Co., *(978-0-9755199)* 135 E. Saint Charles Rd., Carol Stream, IL 60188 USA (SAN 256-0569) Tel 630-933-0844; Fax: 630-933-0845
Web site: http://www.specialtypub.com.

Spectacle Films, Inc., *(978-0-9767771)* 2021 Commonwealth Ave. #2, Boston, MA 02135 USA Tel 212-807-0290
E-mail: spectaclefilms@gmail.com; csoling@gmail.com
Web site: http://www.Rumpleville.com; http://www.SpectacleFilms.com.

Spectre Publishing, *(978-0-9709191)* 22316 Haig St., Taylor, MI 48180 USA
E-mail: publisher@spectrepublishing.com
Web site: http://www.spectrepublishing.com
Dist(s): **CreateSpace Independent Publishing Platform.**

Spectrum *Imprint of* **Carson-Dellosa Publishing, LLC**

Spectrum Films, Inc., *(978-0-9760906)* 4319 Salisbury Rd., Suite 4, Jacksonville, FL 32216 USA
Web site: http://www.spectrumfilms.tv.

SpeculativeFictionReview.com, *(978-0-9785232)* 22281 Letur, Mission Viejo, CA 92691-1406 USA
Web site: http://www.speculativefictionreview.com.

Speech Bin, Inc., The, *(978-0-937857)* 1965 25th Ave., Vero Beach, FL 32960 USA (SAN 630-1657) Tel 772-770-0007; Fax: 772-770-0006
E-mail: info@speechbin.com
Web site: http://www.speechbin.com.

Speech Kids Texas Pr., *(978-1-933319)* 3802 Beaconsdale Dr., Austin, TX 78727-2951 USA (SAN 256-4122)
E-mail: info@speechkidstexaspress.com
Web site: http://www.speechkidstexaspress.com.

Speech Place Publishing, The, *(978-0-9794102)* 1810-A York Rd., No. 432, Lutherville, MD 21093 USA (SAN 853-3679) Tel 410-517-9026
E-mail: cs@thespeechplace.com
Web site: http://www.thespeechplace.com.

Speech Publishing Hse., *(978-0-9770483)* 1115 Cordova St., Suite 318, Pasadena, CA 91106-3013 USA Tel 626-372-1195
E-mail: jonandspeech@prodigy.net.

Speedwitch Media, *(978-0-9749508; 978-0-9987341)* 645 Tanner Marsh Rd., Guilford, CT 06437-2106 USA
Web site: http://www.speedwitchmedia.com.

Speedy Kids (Children's Fiction) *Imprint of* **Speedy Publishing LLC**

Speedy Publishing Books (General) *Imprint of* **Speedy Publishing LLC**

Speedy Publishing LLC, *(978-1-939643; 978-1-62884; 978-1-63022; 978-1-63187; 978-1-63287; 978-1-63383; 978-1-63428; 978-1-68032; 978-1-63501; 978-1-68127; 978-1-68145; 978-1-68185; 978-1-68212; 978-1-68260; 978-1-68280; 978-1-68305; 978-1-68326; 978-1-68368; 978-1-5419) 7914 Raven Creek Ln., Cypress, TX 77433 USA (SAN 920-6620) Tel 954-379-7796; Fax: 954-379-7796; 40 E. Main St., Newark, DE 19733; Imprints:* Speedy Kids (Children's Fiction) (Speedy Kids); Baby Professor (Education Kids) (Baby Profes); Jupiter Kids (Childrens & Kids Fiction) (Jupiter Kids); Speedy Publishing Books (General) (SpeedyPub)
Web site: http://www.speedypublishing.co
Dist(s): **Lulu Pr., Inc.**

Speight, Theresa , L.L.C. *See* **Complete in Christ Ministries, Inc.**

Spellbound River Pr., *(978-0-9911914; 978-1-945017)* P.O. Box 161081, Austin, TX 78716 USA Tel 617 233 6143
E-mail: bondsam@hotmail.com.

†Speller, Robert & Sons, Pubs., Inc., *(978-0-8315)* Orders Addr.: P.O. Box 411, New York, NY 10159 USA (SAN 203-2295) Tel 646-334-8008; P.O. Box 461, New York, NY 10108 (SAN 203-2309); *CIP.*

Spence City *Imprint of* **Spencer Hill Pr.**

Spence Publishing Co., *(978-0-9653208; 978-1-890626)* 5646 Milton St. Ste. 314, Dallas, TX 75206-3923 USA (SAN 257-9383) Toll Free: 888-773-6782
E-mail: tspence@spencepublishing.com
Web site: http://www.spencepublishing.com
Dist(s): **Chicago Distribution Ctr.**
Vigilante, Richard Bks.

Spence, Stephen Mark, *(978-0-9705324)* 211 Moore Ave., Buffalo, NY 14223 USA Tel 716-836-5178
E-mail: spence@buffalo.edu
Web site: http://www.acsu.buffalo.edu/~spence/.

Spencer Hill Contemporary *Imprint of* **Spencer Hill Pr.**

Spencer Hill Middle Grade *Imprint of* **Spencer Hill Pr.**

Spencer Hill Pr., *(978-0-9845311; 978-0-9831572; 978-1-937053; 978-1-939392; 978-1-63392)* 27 W. 20th St., New York, NY 10011 USA (SAN 859-6573); *Imprints:* Spence City (Spence City); Spencer Hill Contemporary (SpencerHill); Spencer Hill Middle Grade (SpencHill Middl)
E-mail: karen@beaufortbooks.com
Web site: http://www.spencerhillpress.com; http://www.spencecity.com/
Dist(s): **INscribe Digital**
Midpoint Trade Bks., Inc.

Spencer, Russell & Kathlynn, *(978-0-9664055)* Orders Addr.: 2484 Dewberry Ln., Oxnard, CA 93030 USA Tel 805-981-2820
E-mail: RSpencer@windshieldadventures.com
Web site: http://www.windshieldadventures.com
Dist(s): **Gem Guides Bk. Co.**

Spencer's Mill Pr., *(978-0-9771666)* 555 Church St. No. 1501, Nashville, TN 37219 USA (SAN 256-8225) Tel 615 477-2044
E-mail: trudychoices@aol.com
Web site: http://www.spencersmillpress.com
Dist(s): **BookBaby.**

Spending Solutions Pr., *(978-0-9729732)* 4347 W. NW Hwy., Suite 120, PMB 283, Dallas, TX 75220-3864 USA
Web site: http://www.spendingsolutions.com.

Sper, Emily *See* **Jump Pr.**

Speranza's Pr., *(978-0-9800327)* P.O. Box 2404, Glenview, IL 60025 USA.

Sphinx Publishing, *(978-0-9725951; 978-0-9762875; 978-0-9770912; 978-0-9776711; 978-1-934144; 978-1-935921)* 7400 Airport Dr., Macon, GA 31216 USA Toll Free: 866-311-9578; *Imprints:* Blue Marble Books (Blu Marble Bks)
E-mail: gpulliam@indigopublishing.us
Web site: http://www.indigopublishing.us
Dist(s): **American Wholesale Bk. Co.**
Parnassus Bk. Distributors.

SPI Bks., *(978-0-944007; 978-1-56171)* 99 Spring St., 3rd Flr., New York, NY 10012 USA Tel 212-431-5011; Fax: 212-431-8646
E-mail: ian@spibooks.com
Web site: http://www.spibooks.com
Dist(s): **APG Sales & Distribution Services**
Two Rivers Distribution.

Spica Bks., *(978-0-9728531)* 9742 N. 105th Dr., Sun City, AZ 85351 USA Tel 623-583-6764 (phone/fax)
E-mail: marilyn@dreamlady.com
Web site: http://www.dreamlady.com.

Spicka, Jana Incorporated *See* **Tree of Life Pr.**

Spider Comics, *(978-0-9859884)* 1489 Wallace Dr., Springville, UT 84663 USA Tel 678-386-5550
E-mail: michael@spidercomics.com
Web site: www.spidercomics.com.

SPIE, *(978-0-8194; 978-0-89252; 978-1-62841; 978-1-5106)* Orders Addr.: P.O. Box 10, Bellingham, WA 98227-0010 USA (SAN 224-1706) Tel 360-676-3290; Fax: 360-647-1445; Edit Addr.: 1000 20th St., Bellingham, WA 98225 USA (SAN 669-1323) Tel 360-676-3290; Fax: 360-647-1445; Toll Free: 888-504-8171
E-mail: spie@spie.org; kerryg@spie.org; marysu@spie.org
Web site: http://www.spie.org/bookstore
Dist(s): **Wiley, John & Sons, Inc.**
ebrary, Inc.

Spineless Bks., *(978-0-9724244; 978-0-9801392; 978-0-9853578)* P.O. Box 91, Urbana, IL 61803 USA Tel 217-722-1033
E-mail: william@spinelessbooks.com
Web site: http://www.spinelessbooks.com.

Spinelli, Patti, *(978-0-9742328)* 87 Portland Ave., Dover, NH 03820-3525 USA
E-mail: pasbug1010@aol.com.

Spinifex Pr. (AUS) *(978-1-875559; 978-0-908205; 978-1-876756; 978-1-74219; 978-0-646-04196-4; 978-1-925581) Dist. by* **IPG Chicago.**

Spinner Bks., *(978-1-59653)* 2030 Harrison St., San Francisco, CA 94110-1310 USA Tel 415-503-1600; Fax: 415-503-0085.

Spinner Pubns., Inc., *(978-0-932027)* 164 William St., New Bedford, MA 02740-6022 USA (SAN 686-0826) Tel 508-994-4564; Fax: 508-994-6925; Toll Free: 800-292-6062
E-mail: spinner@spinnerpub.com
Web site: http://www.spinnerpub.com.

Spinning Horse Publishing, *(978-0-9842832)* 6320 Cty. Rd. K, Omro, WI 54963 USA Tel 920-685-2094.

Spinning Wheel Pr., *(978-0-9978532)* 5008 T St., Sacramento, CA 95819 USA Tel 512-250-8546
E-mail: ruthyballard@adminismith.com
Dist(s): **Independent Pubs. Group.**

SpinSmart Software, *(978-0-9743434)* Orders Addr.: 4717 S. Hydraulic, Wichita, KS 67216 USA
E-mail: support@spinsmart.com
Web site: http://www.spinsmart.com.

Spinsters Ink *See* **Spinsters Ink Bks.**

†Spinsters Ink Bks., *(978-1-883523; 978-1-935226)* Div. of Southern Belle Bks., P.O. Box 242, Midway, FL 32343 USA (SAN 212-6923) Tel 850-576-2370; Fax: 850-576-3498; Toll Free: 800-301-6860
E-mail: Linda@SpinstersInk.com
Web site: http://www.spinstersink.com
Dist(s): **Bella Distribution**
SPD-Small Pr. Distribution
Two Rivers Distribution; *CIP.*

Spirit & Life Productions, *(978-0-9788928)* Orders Addr.: 2260 Grand Ave., Baldwin, NY 11510 USA Tel 866-430-3801.

Spirit Arm Publishing *See* **Solemn Word Publishing**

Spirit of Americar *Imprint of* **Child's World, Inc., The**

Spirit Pr. *Imprint of* **Bendon, Inc.**

Spirit Pr., LLC, *(978-1-893075)* Orders Addr.: 1520 NE. 21st Ave. #101, Portland, OR 97232 USA Tel 503-954-0012 suzannedeak@gmail.com Do not confuse with companies with the same name in Santa Cruz, CA, Raleigh, NC
E-mail: suzannedeak@gmail.com; onespiritpress@gmail.com; spiritpresspublishing@gmail.com
Web site: http://www.onespiritpress.com
Dist(s): **CreateSpace Independent Publishing Platform**
Lightning Source, Inc.

Spirit Publishing LLC, *(978-0-9770967)* 819 Marcy Ave., Brooklyn, NY 11216 USA (SAN 256-7636) Tel 718-230-5605.

SpiritBooks *Imprint of* **Portal Ctr. Pr.**

Spiritbuilding, *(978-0-9774754; 978-0-9821376; 978-0-9829811; 978-0-9990684)* 15591 N. State Rd., 9, Summitville, IN 46070 USA Tel 765-623-2238
E-mail: mcmurray@spiritbuilding.com
Web site: http://www.SpiritBuilding.com.

Spirited Presentations, *(978-0-9790017)* 4249 Peak Ln., Grand Rapids, MI 49525 USA
E-mail: Kathey@spiritedpresentations.com
Web site: http://Spiritedpresentations.com.

Spirited Publishing, LLC, *(978-0-9768513)* Orders Addr.: P.O. Box 1796, Appleton, WI 54912-1796 USA Tel 920-419-3340
E-mail: kris@spiritedpublishing.com
Web site: http://www.spiritedpublishing.com.

Spiritpoint Press *See* **Bitty Book Pr.**

Spiritual Hse. Pr., The, *(978-0-9656847)* 24 Old Milford Rd., Brookline, NH 03033 USA Tel 603-672-8550
E-mail: blueskies@myfairpoint.net
Web site: http://www.TheSpiritualHouse.com.

Spitzer, Lance, *(978-0-615-72525-3)* 226 Crestmoor Cir., Pacifica, CA 94044 USA Tel 650-922-8554
E-mail: lancesherwood@comcast.net.

Spizzirri Pr., Inc., *(978-0-86545)* P.O. Box 9397, Rapid City, SD 57709 USA (SAN 215-2851) Tel 605-348-2749; Fax: 605-348-6251 (orders); Toll Free: 800-325-9819; 800-322-9819
E-mail: spizzpub@aol.com
Web site: http://www.spizzirri.com.

Splendid Benedict, *(978-0-615-90023-0; 978-0-9910809)* 5094 N Agave Trl, Flagstaff, AZ 86001 USA Tel 303-455-1835
Dist(s): **CreateSpace Independent Publishing Platform.**

Splendid Torch, *(978-0-9788027; 978-0-615-16717-6; 978-0-615-16784-8)* 2000 St. Regis Dr. #6d, Lombard, IL 60148 USA (SAN 851-6588)
Web site: http://www.puglish.com
Dist(s): **Lulu Pr., Inc.**

Splendors Publishing, *(978-0-9717228)* P.O. Box 1155, Soquel, CA 95073 USA Fax: 831-464-1854
E-mail: lalo@lalofiorelli.com
Web site: http://www.lalofiorelli.com.

Split Level of the Blessed Suburbs Publishing, *(978-0-9761515)* 56 Arbor St., Hartford, CT 06106-1201 USA Tel 860-586-8448 (phone/fax)
Web site: http://www.tedpaulsen.com.

Spoken Arts, Inc., *(978-0-8045)* 195 S. White Rock Rd., Holmes, NY 12531-5406 USA (SAN 205-079X) Toll Free: 800-326-4090
Web site: http://www.spokenartsmedia.com/home.htm
Dist(s): **AudioGO**
Follett Media Distribution
Follett School Solutions
Lectorum Pubns., Inc.
Weston Woods Studios, Inc.

Spoken Word, The, *(978-0-9637644)* 1031 Michigan Ave. NE, No. 205, Washington, DC 20017 USA Tel 202-832-2368 Do not confuse with Spoken Word, The, Arlington, TX.

SpokenVizions Entertainment Group, LLC, *(978-0-9773834)* P.O. Box 373, Florissant, MO 63032 USA Tel 314-517-8764
E-mail: info@spokenvizions.com
Web site: http://www.spokenvizions.com.

Spoon Publishing Hse., *(978-0-615-11213-8)* Div. of A Corpus Polymedia Monolith, 440 E. Broadway, Executive Suite 51, Salt Lake City, UT 84111-2651 USA
E-mail: spoonpublishing@corpuspolymedia.com
Web site: http://www.corpuspolymedia.com/spoonpublishing/; http://www.spoonpublishing.com.

Spoonbender Bks., *(978-0-9725750)* Div. of Holahan, Inc., 419 N. Larchmont Blvd., No. 4, Los Angeles, CA 90004 USA (SAN 254-9123) Tel 323-933-0253 (phone/fax)
E-mail: jgrist@mac.com; publisher@spoonbenderbooks.com
Web site: http://www.spoonbenderbooks.com
Dist(s): **Follett School Solutions**
Quality Bks., Inc.
SCB Distributors.

Spooners Publishing, *(978-0-9766179)* 98 Onteora Ct., Shokan, NY 12481-5610 USA Tel 845-657-8737
E-mail: ecurts@hvc.rr.com.

Spork *Imprint of* **Clear Fork Publishing**

Sport Story Publishing, *(978-0-9702216)* 740 Lakeview Dr., Palm Harbor, FL 34683 USA Fax: 727-447-3587
E-mail: thoover@tampabay.rr.com.

Sport Workbooks, *(978-0-9787458)* P.O. Box 1623, Pacifica, CA 94044 USA (SAN 851-5093) Tel 650-270-3200
E-mail: baseballmath@hotmail.com.

Sport Your Stuff Corp., *(978-1-931746)* 5025 Longbrook Rd., Winston Salem, NC 27105 USA.

SportAmerica, *(978-1-879498)* P.O. Box 95030, South Jordan, UT 84095 USA Tel 801-253-3360; Fax: 801-253-3361; Toll Free: 800-467-7885
Web site: http://www.sportamerica.com.

Sportime International, *(978-0-9793506)* 3175 Northwoods Pkwy. # A, Norcross, GA 30071-1539 USA
E-mail: dkissel@sportime.com
Web site: http://www.sportime.com.

Sports Challenge Network, *(978-0-615-15195-3; 978-0-615-21091-9; 978-0-578-00861-5; 978-0-9819861; 978-1-935592)* Orders Addr.: 1420 Locust St., No. 10F, Philadelphia, PA 19102 USA (SAN 913-4190) Tel 1-267-847-9018
E-mail: elik@sportschallengenetwork.com
Web site: www.sportschallengenetwork.com.

Sports Illustrated For Kids, *(978-0-316; 978-0-553; 978-1-886749; 978-1-930623)* Div. of Time, Inc., 135 W. 50th St. ., New York, NY 10020-1393 USA Tel 212-522-1212; Fax: 212-522-0926
E-mail: joe_nunziata@sikids.com
Web site: http://www.sikids.com
Dist(s): **Hachette Bk. Group.**

Sports In Mind, *(978-0-9745066; 978-0-9765074)* 3603 Palm Harbor Blvd., Unit C, Palm Harbor, FL 34683 USA Fax: 727-942-3339
Web site: http://www.ravesystems.com.

Sports Marketing International, Inc., *(978-0-9743082)* 27 E. Housatonic St., Pittsfield, MA 01201-4121 USA Tel 413-499-1733; Fax: 413-499-3820; Toll Free: 800-320-1733; *Imprints:* Moscow Ballet (Moscow Ballet)
E-mail: smi@nutcracker.com
Web site: http://www.nutcracker.com.

Sports Masters, *(978-1-58382)* Div. of Sports Publishing, Inc., 804 N. Neil St., Champaign, IL 61820 USA Tel 217-363-2072; Fax: 217-363-2073; Toll Free: 877-424-2665
E-mail: choffman@sagamorepub.com
Dist(s): **Ingram Publisher Services.**

Sports Publishing, LLC, *(978-1-57167; 978-1-58261; 978-1-58382; 978-1-59670)* 804 N. Neil St., Champaign, IL 61820 USA Tel 217-363-2072; Fax: 217-353-2073; Toll Free: 877-424-2665 Do not confuse with Sports Publishing, Champaign, IL
E-mail: info@sportspublishingllc.com
Web site: http://www.sportspublishingllc.com
Dist(s): **Hachette Bk. Group**
Ingram Publisher Services
MyiLibrary.

Sports Touch *See* **Sports Touch/Kate Montgomery**

Sports Touch/Kate Montgomery, *(978-1-878069)* 1625 E. Jackson Blvd., Elkhart, IN 46516 USA
E-mail: kate@sportstouch.com; katemontgomery@mac.com
Web site: http://www.lulu.com; http://www.sportstouch.com; http://www.createspace.com
Dist(s): **Lulu Pr., Inc.**

Sportsman's Connection, *(978-1-885010)* Div. of Sportsman's Marketing, Inc., Orders Addr.: P.O. Box 852, Lake Elmo, MN 55042 USA Tel 800-264-0474; Fax: 651-773-3320; Toll Free: 800-777-7461; Edit Addr.: 1810 N. 16th St. Ste. 1, Superior, WI 54880-2597 USA
E-mail: info@sportsmansconnection.com
Web site: http://www.sportsmansconnection.com
Dist(s): **Partners Bk. Distributing, Inc.**

SportsZone *Imprint of* **ABDO Publishing Co.**

Spotlight *Imprint of* **ABDO Publishing Co.**

Spotlight, *(978-1-59961)* Div. of ABDO Publishing Group, Orders Addr.: P.O. Box 398166, Edina, MN 55439-8166 USA Fax: 952-831-1632; Toll Free: 877-877-5939; Edit Addr.: 8000 W. 78th St., Suite 310, Edina, MN 55439 USA; *Imprints:* Chapter Books (ChapterBks); Graphic Novels (GraphNvls); Picture Book (PicBook)
E-mail: info@abdopublishing.com
Web site: http://www.abdopublishing.com
Dist(s): **ABDO Publishing Co.**

Spotlight Books *See* **Hannacroix Creek Bks., Inc.**

Spotlight News Publications *See* **Autumn Hse. Publishing**

Spotted Dog Pr., Inc., *(978-0-9647530; 978-1-893343)* Orders Addr.: P.O. Box 1721, Bishop, CA 93515 USA (SAN 257-9936) Tel 760-872-1524; Fax: 800-872-0681; Toll Free: 800-417-2790 Do not confuse with Spotted Dog Pr., Ashland, OR
E-mail: wbenti@spotteddogpress.com; store@spotteddogpress.com
Web site: http://www.spotteddogpress.com
Dist(s): **Gem Guides Bk. Co.**
Partners/West Book Distributors
Treasure Chest Bks.

Spreeda Publishing, *(978-0-9748979)* Div. of SPREEDA, 14204 W. 72nd St., Shawnee, KS 66216 USA Do not confuse with Maple Leaf Publishing in Minneapolis, MN
E-mail: karen@spreeda.com
Web site: http://www.spreeda.com.

Spriitelee Enterprises, *(978-0-9773460)* P.O. Box 207, Westwood, MA 02090 USA.

Spring Arbor Distributors, Inc., Subs. of Ingram Industries Inc., 4271 Edison Ave., Chino, CA 91710 USA; 7315 Innovation Blvd., Fort Wayne, IN 46818-1371; Edit Addr.: 1 Ingram Blvd., La Vergne, TN 37086-1976 USA Fax: 615-213-5192; Toll Free: 800-395-4340; 800-395-7234 (customer service)
E-mail: orders@springarbor.com.

Spring Creek Bk. Co., *(978-1-932898; 978-0-9960974; 978-1-944657)* P.O. Box 1013, Rexburg, ID 83440 USA Tel 801-669-4368
Web site: http://www.springcreekbooks.com
Dist(s): **Brigham Distribution.**

Spring Ducks Bks., LLC, *(978-0-9761076)* Orders Addr.: P.O. Box 44847, Madison, WI 53744-4847 USA Toll Free: 800-342-4404; Edit Addr.: 222 Carillon Dr., Madison, WI 53705 USA
E-mail: kathy@springducks.com
Web site: http://www.springducks.com.

Spring Harbor Pr., *(978-0-935891)* Div. of Spring Harbor, Ltd., Orders Addr.: P.O. Box 346, Delmar, NY 12054 USA (SAN 695-9768) Tel 518-478-7817 (phone/fax)
E-mail: springharbor@springharborpress.com; info@springharborpress.com
Web site: http://www.springharborpress.com.

Spring Hollow Bks., LLC, *(978-0-9665389)* P.O. Box 115, Cave Spring, GA 30124-0115 USA Tel 706-235-5113; Fax: 706-235-0742 Do not confuse with Spring Hollow Bks., Richfield, MN
E-mail: jbcjmc@aol.com.

Spring Tide Publishing, *(978-0-9765578)* 1281 N. Ocean Dr. Suite 151, Singer Island, FL 33404 USA Tel 561-632-2278
E-mail: delores@springtidepublishing.com
Web site: www.springtidepublishing.com.

Spring Tree Pr., *(978-0-9785007)* P.O. Box 461, Atlantic Highlands, NJ 07716 USA (SAN 850-8429) Tel 732-872-8002; Fax: 732-872-6967
Web site: http://www.springtreepress.com
Dist(s): **New Leaf Distributing Co., Inc.**

†Springer, *(978-0-387; 978-0-8176; 978-3-211; 978-3-540; 978-3-7908; 978-4-431; 978-1-85233; 978-1-84628; 978-1-4419; 978-1-4612; 978-1-4613; 978-1-4614; 978-1-4615; 978-1-4684; 978-1-4757; 978-1-4899; 978-1-4939; 978-1-5041)* Subs. of Springer Science+Business Media, Orders Addr.: P.O. Box 2485, Secaucus, NJ 07096-2485 USA Tel 201-348-4033; Fax: 201-348-4505; Toll Free: 800-777-4643; Edit Addr.: a/o Springer Nature, 233 Spring St., New York, NY 10013-1578 USA (SAN 203-2228) Tel 212-815-0249; 212-460-1500; Fax: 212-460-1575; Toll Free: 800-777-4643 Thomson Delmar Learning Distributes Blanchard & Loeb Nursing Videos Only
E-mail: Slu@Springer-ny.com; service-ny@springer.com; customerservice@springernature.com.com
Web site: http://www.springeronline.com; http://www.springer.com
Dist(s): **Ebsco Publishing**
Metapress
MyiLibrary
Rittenhouse Bk. Distributors
ebrary, Inc.; *CIP.*

†Springer Publishing Co., Inc., *(978-0-8261; 978-0-939957; 978-1-888799; 978-1-932603; 978-0-9771597; 978-1-933864; 978-1-935281; 978-1-936287; 978-1-936303; 978-1-61705; 978-1-62070)* 11 W. 42nd St., 15th Fl., New York, NY 10036 USA (SAN 203-2236) Tel 212-431-4370; Fax: 212-941-7842; Toll Free: 877-687-7476
E-mail: Springer@springerpub.com; journals@springerpub.com; Editorial@springerpub.com; cs@springerpub.com
Web site: http://www.springerpub.com
Dist(s): **CreateSpace Independent Publishing Platform**
Ebsco Publishing
Independent Pubs. Group
MyiLibrary
Rittenhouse Bk. Distributors
ebrary, Inc.; *CIP.*

Springer-Verlag New York, Incorporated *See* **Springer**

SpringTree *Imprint of* **Forest Hill Publishing, LLC**

Sprite Pr., *(978-0-9706654; 978-0-9764295)* 2118 Sycamore Cove Cir., Miamisburg, OH 45343 USA Tel 740-767-2470
E-mail: spritepress@aol.com
Web site: http://www.members.aol.com/spritepress.

Sproing Books *See* **Gripper Products**

Sprouting Peanut Pubs., *(978-0-615-22222-6)* P.O. Box 2606, Gilroy, CA 95021 USA
Web site: http://www.whatsupwillie.com.

Spruce Gulch Pr., *(978-0-9625714; 978-0-9841259)* Orders Addr.: P.O. Box 4347, Rome, NY 13442-4347 USA (SAN 297-3014) Tel 315-337-3626
E-mail: SprGulch@aol.com
Dist(s): **North Country Bks., Inc.**

Spuyten Duyvil Publishing, *(978-0-923389; 978-0-9661242; 978-1-881471; 978-0-9720662; 978-1-933132; 978-1-941550; 978-1-944682; 978-1-947980)* 42 St. Johns Pl., Brooklyn, NY 11217 USA (SAN 237-9481) Toll Free: 800-886-5304 (phone/fax)
E-mail: editors@spuytenduyvil.net
Web site: http://www.spuytenduyvil.net
Dist(s): **SPD-Small Pr. Distribution.**

SpyGirls Pr., *(978-0-9852273; 978-0-9979545)* P.O. Box 1537, Fairfax, VA 22038 USA Tel 571-213-1586
E-mail: melissamahle@verizon.net
Web site: www.anatoliasteppe.com.

Spyrou-Andriotis, Vicky, *(978-0-615-24795-3; 978-0-9821808)* 3919 Old Town Rd., Bridgeport, CT 06606 USA
E-mail: info@vickyandriotis.com
Web site: http://www.vickyandriotis.com.

SQP *Imprint of* **Specialized Quality Pubns.**

Square Circle Pr., LLC *See* **Square Circle Pr. LLC**

Square Circle Pr. LLC, *(978-0-9789066; 978-0-9833897; 978-0-9856926; 978-0-9989670)* P.O. Box 913, Schenectady, NY 12301 USA (SAN 851-9145) Tel 518-432-6657 Do not confuse with Square Circle Press in Corte Madera, CA
E-mail: bookinfo@squarecirclepress.com
Web site: http://www.squarecirclepress.com
Dist(s): **Lightning Source, Inc.**
North Country Bks., Inc.

Square Deal Pr., *(978-0-9754941)* 368 S. McCaslin Blvd., Box 206, Louisville, CO 80027 USA.

Square Fish, *(978-0-312)* 175 Fifth Ave., New York, NY 10010 USA Tel 646-307-5770
E-mail: squarefish.market@hbpub.com
Web site: http://www.squarefishbooks.com
Dist(s): **Macmillan.**

Square Halo Bks., *(978-0-9658798; 978-0-9785097; 978-1-941106)* Orders Addr.: P.O. Box 18954, Baltimore, MD 21206 USA Tel 410-485-6227; Edit Addr.: 4310 Southern Ave., Baltimore, MD 21206 USA
E-mail: square_halo@yahoo.com; ned@squarehalobooks.com
Web site: http://www.squarehalobooks.com.

Square One Pubs., *(978-0-9664202; 978-0-7570; 978-0-9792746)* 115 Herricks Rd., Garden City Park, NY 11040 USA Tel 516-535-2010; Fax: 516-535-2014; *Imprints:* Vital Health Publishing (Vital Hlth)
E-mail: sq1info@aol.com
Web site: http://squareonepublishers.com
Dist(s): **Athena Productions, Inc.**

Squarey Head, Inc., *(978-0-9742003)* 6362 W. Cross Dr., Littleton, CO 80123 USA Tel 303-798-1877; Fax: 303-794-4639.

Squid Works, *(978-0-9755041; 978-0-9972813)* Orders Addr.: 2132 E. 97th Dr., Thornton, CO 80229 USA
E-mail: squidworkscomics@gmail.com
Web site: http://www.squidworkscomics.com
Dist(s): **Mascot Bks., Inc.**

Squires Publishing, *(978-0-9816048)* 7224 S. Yates Blvd., Suite 3N, Chicago, IL 60649 USA Tel 773-667-0039
E-mail: tanyacloud@comcast.net.

SRA/McGraw-Hill, *(978-0-07; 978-0-383)* Div. of The McGraw-Hill Education Group, Orders Addr.: 220 E. Daniel Dale Rd., DeSoto, TX 75115-2490 USA Fax: 972-228-1982; Toll Free: 800-843-8855; Edit Addr.: 8787 Orion Pl., Columbus, OH 43240-4027 USA Tel 614-430-6600; Fax: 614-430-6621; Toll Free: 800-468-5850
E-mail: sra@mcgraw-hill.com
Web site: https://www.sraonline.com
Dist(s): **Libros Sin Fronteras**
Weston Woods Studios, Inc.

Sri Ramakrishna Math (IND) *(978-81-7120; 978-81-86465; 978-81-7823) Dist. by* **Vedanta Pr.**

Sroda, George, *(978-0-9604486)* P.O. Box 97, Amherst Junction, WI 54407 USA (SAN 210-8607) Tel 715-824-3868; Fax: 715-824-5344.

SRT Publishing, *(978-0-9771248)* 530 Moon Clinton Rd., Moon Township, PA 15108 USA Tel 412-741-0581; Fax: 412-264-1103
E-mail: merch@silverringthing.com
Web site: http://www.silverringthing.com.

Sruvis Publishing, *(978-0-9889907)* 2219 Pear Blossom, San Antonio, TX 78247 USA Tel 210-219-2156; Fax: 210-494-1994
E-mail: lyndasdavis8@aol.com.

Ssorgsoft, LLC, *(978-0-9765240)* P.O. Box 771192, Orlando, FL 32877 USA.

St. Aidan Pr., Inc., *(978-0-9719230)* 96 Dunlap Dr., Charles Town, WV 25414 USA
E-mail: michael_rabjohns@hotmail.com
Web site: http://www.staidanpress.com.

St. Augustine Academy Pr., *(978-1-936639; 978-1-64051)* 12050 Rambling Rd., Homer Glen, IL 60491 USA Tel 708-645-4691
E-mail: Lbergman2@sbcglobal.net
Web site: www.staugustineacademypress.com.

St. Bernard Publishing, LLC, *(978-0-9741269)* P.O. Box 2218, Bay City, MI 48707-2218 USA Tel 989-892-1348 (phone/fax)
E-mail: bcgirl@charter.net
Web site: http://www.lifeongrannysfarm.com/.

St. Germain, Mark *See* **Three Cups, LLC**

St. Hope Academy, *(978-0-9759548)* Orders Addr.: P.O. Box 5447, Sacramento, CA 95817 USA Tel 916-649-7900; Fax: 916-452-7177; Edit Addr.: 3400 3rd Ave., Sacramento, CA 95817 USA
Web site: http://40acresartgallery.org.

St. John's Pr., *(978-0-9710551; 978-0-615-83132-9; 978-0-9916014)* Orders Addr.: 5318 Torri Park Dr., Cottondale, AL 35453 USA Tel 205-242-4422; Fax: 205-553-9459 Do not confuse with Saint John's Press in Los Angeles, CA
E-mail: charleysix@gmail.com.

St. Martin's Griffin *Imprint of* **St. Martin's Pr.**

St. Martin's Paperbacks *Imprint of* **St. Martin's Pr.**

†St. Martin's Pr., *(978-0-312; 978-0-8050; 978-0-940687; 978-0-9603648; 978-1-55927; 978-1-58063; 978-1-58238; 978-1-4299; 978-1-250)* Div. of Holtzbrinck Pubs., Orders Addr.: 16365 James Madison Hwy., Gordonville, VA 22942 USA Tel 540-672-7600; Fax: 540-672-7540 (customer service); Toll Free Fax: 800-672-2054; Toll Free: 888-330-8477; Edit Addr.: 175 Fifth Ave., 20th Flr., New York, NY 10010 USA (SAN 200-2132) Tel 212-674-5151 (Trade Div.); 212-726-0200 (College Div.); Fax: 212-674-3179 (Trade Div.); 212-686-9491 (College Div.); Toll Free: 800-221-7945 (Trade Div.); 800-470-4767 (College Div.); *Imprints:* Saint Martin's Griffin (St Martin Griffin); Saint Martin's Paperbacks (St Martins Paperbacks); Dunne, Thomas Books (Thomas Dunne); Minotaur Books (Minotaur); Golden Books Adult Publishing Group (Golden Adult); Golden Guides from Saint Martin's Press (Gldn Guides); Priddy Books (Priddy); Wednesday Books (Wednesday Bks)
E-mail: webmaster@stmartins.com; enquiries@stmartins.com
Web site: http://www.stmartins.com; http://www.smpcollege.com
Dist(s): **Comag Marketing Group**
Cambridge Univ. Pr.
CreateSpace Independent Publishing Platform
Ediciones Universal
Kaplan Publishing
Libros Sin Fronteras
Macmillan
MyiLibrary
ebrary, Inc.; *CIP.*

St Mary's Church, *(978-0-9763902)* 429 Central Ave., Sandusky, OH 44870 USA Tel 419-625-7465
Web site: http://www.stmarysandusky.org.

St. Michael's Abbey, *(978-0-9742298)* 19292 El Toro Rd., Silverado, CA 92676-9710 USA
E-mail: fmorbertw@yahoo.com
Web site: http://www.abbeynews.com.

St. Nicholas Pr. *Imprint of* **CrossBearers Publishing**

St. Pauls *Imprint of* **St Pauls/Alba Hse. Pubs.**

St Pauls Pubns. (AUS) *(978-0-909986; 978-0-949080; 978-1-875570; 978-1-876295; 978-1-921032;*

Publisher Name Index

978-1-921472; 978-1-921963; 978-1-925494) *Dist. by* **St Pauls Alba.**

†**St Pauls/Alba Hse. Pubs.**, *(978-0-8189)* Div. of Society of St. Paul, 2187 Victory Blvd., Staten Island, NY 10314-6603 USA (SAN 201-2405) Tel 718-761-0047; Fax: 718-761-0057; 718-698-8390; Toll Free: 800-343-2522; *Imprints:* Saint Pauls (Saint Pauls)
E-mail: albabooks@aol.com
Web site: http://www.albahouse.org; *CIP.*

St. Roux Pr., *(978-0-9718433)* 308 Montmartre St., Folsom, LA 70437 USA
E-mail: faucheux@msn.com.

Stabenfeldt Inc., *(978-1-933343; 978-1-934983)* Orders Addr.: 225 N. Main St., Bristol, CT 06011 USA Toll Free: 800-410-4145; *Imprints:* PONY (Pny)
Web site: http://www.pony4kids.com.

Stacey Alysson Yoga, *(978-0-692-83320-9)* 234 s gale Dr. #109, BEVERLY HILLS, CA 90211 USA Tel 424-333-6771
E-mail: jeffwcrawford5+LVP0003257@gmail.com; jeffwcrawford5+LVP0003257@gmail.com.

Stacey Publishing (GBR) *(978-1-906768)* *Dist. by* **Casemate Pubs.**

†**Stackpole Bks.**, *(978-0-8117)* 5067 Ritter Rd., Mechanicsburg, PA 17055 USA (SAN 202-5396) Tel 717-796-0411; Fax: 717-796-0412; Toll Free: 800-732-3669
E-mail: ccraley@stackpolebooks.com
Web site: http://www.stackpolebooks.com/
Dist(s): **MyiLibrary**
National Bk. Network; *CIP.*

Staff Development for Educators, *(978-0-9627389; 978-1-884548; 978-1-934026; 978-1-935502; 978-1-63133)* Div. of Highlights for Children, Orders Addr.: P.O. Box 577, Peterborough, NH 03458 USA Tel 603-924-9621; Fax: 603-924-6688; Toll Free Fax: 800-337-9929; Toll Free: 800-321-0401; Edit Addr.: 10 Sharon Rd., Peterborough, NH 03458 USA; *Imprints:* Crystal Springs Books (Crystal Spgs)
E-mail: dfredericks@sde.com
Web site: http://www.sde.com; http://www.crystalsprings.com; http://www.barnesandnoble.com
Dist(s): **Follett School Solutions**
Stenhouse Pubs.

Stafford House, *(978-0-9822587; 978-0-9981070)* P.O. Box 291, Pacific Palisades, CA 90272 USA
Web site: http://www.abcyogaforkids.com; www.kidsyogaday.com.

Stagecast Software, Inc., *(978-1-929721)* 580 College Ave., Palo Alto, CA 94306 USA Tel 650-354-0735; Fax: 650-354-0739; Toll Free: 888-782-4322
E-mail: info@stagecast.com
Web site: http://www.stagecast.com.

Stahl Pubns., *(978-0-9755174)* P.O. Box 201, Ashley, IN 46705-0201 USA.

Staige Productions, *(978-0-9641375)* 290 Orrin St., Winona, MN 55987-2083 USA Tel 507-452-3627.

Stairway Pubns., *(978-0-9740061)* P.O. Box 518, Huntington, NY 11743-0518 USA (SAN 255-3422) Fax: 631-351-2142
E-mail: publisher@stairwaypub.com
Web site: http://www.stairwaypub.com
Dist(s): **Quality Bks., Inc.**

Stairway Publishing, *(978-0-9761953)* 1332 Anacapa St., Suite 200, Santa Barbara, CA 93101 USA; 230 E Pedregosa St., Santa Barbara, CA 93101 (SAN 256-761X) Tel 805-451-5070; Fax: 805-962-1404 Do not Confuse with Shoreline Publishing in Bayside, NY
E-mail: pumoff@seedmackall.com.

Stampley, C. D. Enterprises, Inc., *(978-0-915741; 978-1-58087)* Orders Addr.: P.O. Box 33172, Charlotte, NC 28233 USA (SAN 294-1325) Tel 704-333-6631; Fax: 704-336-6932; Edit Addr.: 6100 Orr Rd., Charlotte, NC 28213 USA
E-mail: info@stampley.com; rick@stampley.com
Web site: http://www.stampley.com
Dist(s): **Follett School Solutions**
Giron Bks.

Stance Pubns., *(978-0-615-18108-0; 978-0-9821047)* 4510 Seashore Dr., #A, Newport Beach, CA 92663-2520 USA
E-mail: marcpent@msn.com
Web site: http://www.stancepublications.com
Dist(s): **Lightning Source, Inc.**

Standard International Media, *(978-1-58279; 978-1-888777; 978-1-86091; 978-1-60081)* Orders Addr.: 568 9th St. South, Suite 201, Naples, FL 34105 USA Tel 239-595-5516; Fax: 239-649-5832
E-mail: orders@standardinternationalmedia.com
Web site: http://www.standardinternationalmedia.com.

Standard Pubns., Inc., *(978-0-9709788; 978-0-9722691; 978-1-59462; 978-1-60424; 978-1-60597; 978-1-4385; 978-1-61742)* P.O. Box 2226, Champaign, IL 61825 USA (SAN 912-9251) Tel 217-898-7825; Fax: 630-214-0564; *Imprints:* Book Jungle (Book Jungle)
E-mail: spi@standardpublications.com
Dist(s): **MyiLibrary.**

†**Standard Publishing**, *(978-0-7847; 978-0-87239; 978-0-87403; 978-0-933657; 978-1-58170)* 8805 Governors Hill Dr. Ste. 400, Cincinnati, OH 45249-3319 USA (SAN 110-5515) Toll Free Fax: 877-867-5751 (customer service); Toll Free: 800-543-1301; 800-543-1353 (customer service); *Imprints:* Bean Sprouts (Bean Sprouts) Do not confuse with Standard Publishing Corp., Boston, MA
E-mail: customerservice@standardpub.com; trolfes@standardpub.com; dlewis@standardpub.com
Web site: http://www.standardpub.com
Dist(s): **B&H Publishing Group**
Cook, David C.; *CIP.*

Standard Publishing Company *See* **Standard Publishing**

Standing For Christ, Inc., *(978-0-9754834)* P.O. Box 28468, Cleveland, OH 44128 USA Tel 216-299-4523
E-mail: kelvinsfc@yahoo.com
Web site: http://www.standingforchrist.org.

Stanek, Mary Beth, *(978-0-9747556)* 291 Lothrop Rd., Grosse Pointe, MI 48236 USA.

Stanfield, James Co., *(978-1-56304; 978-1-941264)* P.O. Box 41058, Santa Barbara, CA 93140 USA Tel 805-897-1185; Fax: 805-897-1187; Toll Free: 800-421-6534
E-mail: maindesk@stanfield.com
Web site: http://www.stanfield.com.

Stanford Center for Research in Disease Prevention (S C R D P) *See* **Stanford Prevention Research Ctr.**

Stanford Prevention Research Ctr., *(978-1-879552)* Div. of Stanford Univ. Schl. of Medicine, Hoover Pavilion, Rm. N 229 211 Quarry Rd., Stanford, CA 94305-5705 USA Tel 650-723-0003; Fax: 650-498-4828
E-mail: askhpro@med.stanford.edu
Web site: http://hprc.stanford.edu.

Stanger, Robert *See* **Club Pro Products**

Stanley, Donna Lacy, *(978-0-9766894)* 244 Sunset Dr., Waynesboro, VA 22980 USA Tel 540-949-5474
E-mail: dlstanle@yahoo.com.

Stanley, Shirley, *(978-0-9747318)* Orders Addr.: 1116 20th St. S., No. 216, Birmingham, AL 35205 USA Tel 205-663-6674.

Stansbury Publishing, *(978-0-9708922; 978-0-9766269; 978-1-935807)* Subs. of Heidelberg Graphics, Orders Addr.: 2 Stansbury Ct., Chico, CA 95928 USA
E-mail: spublishing@heidelberggraphics.com
Web site: http://www.heidelberggraphics.com.

Stanton & Harper Bks., *(978-0-9630151)* Orders Addr.: P.O. Box 21585, Greensboro, NC 27420 USA; Edit Addr.: 291 Buckhorn Trail, Reidsville, NC 27320 USA Tel 910-951-1234; Fax: 910-951-9966.

Star Bible & Tract Corp., *(978-0-933672; 978-0-940999; 978-1-56794)* Orders Addr.: P.O. Box 821220, Fort Worth, TX 76182 USA (SAN 203-3518) Tel 817-416-5889; Fax: 817-251-0129; Toll Free: 800-433-7507; Edit Addr.: P.O. Box 821220, N Richind His, TX 76182-1220 USA (SAN 664-6247)
E-mail: starbible@starbible.com
Web site: http://www.starbible.com
Dist(s): **Twentieth Century Christian Bks.**

Star Bright Bks., Inc., *(978-1-887734; 978-1-932065; 978-1-59572)* Orders Addr.: 30-19, 48th Ave., Long Island City, NY 11101 USA (SAN 254-5225) Tel 718-784-9112; Fax: 718-784-9012; Toll Free: 800-788-4439
E-mail: info@starbrightbooks.com
Web site: http://www.starbrightbooks.com.

Star Cross'd Destiny *Imprint of* **Bohemian Trash Studios**

Star Dome Publishing, LLC, *(978-0-9766662)* P.O. Box 411300, Melbourne, FL 32941 USA
E-mail: fcavalli@bellsouth.net
Web site: http://www.stardomepublishing.com.

Star Gem Publishing, *(978-0-615-54730-5; 978-0-9978384)* 4101 California Ave #44, Bakersfield, CA 93309 USA Tel 661-932-0573
Dist(s): **CreateSpace Independent Publishing Platform**
Dummy Record Do Not USE!!!!.

Star Light Pr., *(978-1-879817)* 1811 S. First St., Austin, TX 78704-4299 USA Tel 512-441-0588; 512-441-0062 (phone/fax); *Imprints:* Children (Children)
E-mail: info@starlightpress.com
Web site: http://www.starlightpress.com
Dist(s): **Book Wholesalers, Inc.**
iLeon.

Star Pr., The, *(978-0-9676189)* Div. of Indiana Newspapers, Inc., Orders Addr.: P.O. Box 2408, Muncie, IN 47307-0408 USA (SAN 169-2437) Tel 765-213-5799; Fax: 765-213-5703; Toll Free: 800-783-7827; Edit Addr.: 345 S. High St., Muncie, IN 47305 USA
E-mail: rfarmer@thestarpress.com
Web site: http://www.thestarpress.com.

Star Publish LLC, *(978-1-932993; 978-1-935188)*
E-mail: tcmcmullen@starpublishllc.com
Web site: http://www.starpublishllc.com
Dist(s): **Smashwords.**

Star Quest Publishing Phx, *(978-0-9767035)* 3030 E. Shangri-La Rd., Phoenix, AZ 85028 USA Tel 602-621-3431; Fax: 602-926-2484
E-mail: karen@starquestpublishingphx.com
Web site: http://www.starquestpublishing.com.

Star Write Creations, *(978-0-9743851)* P.O. Box G, Birnamwood, WI 54414 USA Toll Free: 888-999-6609.

Starbell Bks., *(978-0-9747774)* 2507 LaBrecque Dr., Plainfield, IL 60544 USA Tel 815-254-9495
E-mail: starbellbooks@comcast.net
Web site: http://www.starbellbooks.com.

Starborne House *See* **Redding, Marion T.**

Starbound Bks. *Imprint of* **Wheatmark, Inc.**

Starbound Publishing Company *See* **Collectors Pr., Inc.**

Starbucks Coffee Co., *(978-0-9726394)* 2401 Utah Ave. S., Seattle, WA 98134 USA Tel 206-447-1575; Toll Free: 800-235-2883
E-mail: info@starbucks.com
Web site: http://www.starbuckscollectibles.com.

Stardust Stables *Imprint of* **Stone Arch Bks.**

STAReviews *Imprint of* **N&N Publishing Co., Inc.**

Starfall Education, *(978-1-59577)* Div. of Pancil, LLC, P.O. Box 359, Boulder, CO 80306 USA Toll Free Fax: 800-943-6666; Toll Free: 888-857-8990
Web site: http://www.starfall.com
Dist(s): **Blue Mountain Arts Inc.**

Starfall Publications *See* **Starfall Education**

Starfish Aquatics Institute, *(978-0-9746613; 978-0-578-13105-4; 978-0-578-13448-2; 978-0-578-13449-9)* 10 Ramshorn Ct., Savannah, GA 31411 USA Tel 912-692-1173
E-mail: sara@sai-intl.org; jill@sai-intl.org
Web site: http://www.starfishaquatics.org.

Starfish Bay Publishing Pty Ltd. (AUS) *(978-1-76036)* *Dist. by* **IPG Chicago.**

Stargazer Publishing Co., *(978-0-9643853; 978-0-9713756; 978-1-933277)* Orders Addr.: P.O. Box 77002, Corona, CA 92877-0100 USA (SAN 298-6566) Tel 951-898-4619; Fax: 951-898-4633; Toll Free: 800-606-7895; Edit Addr.: 958 Stanislaus Dr., Corona, CA 92881 USA Do not confuse with Stargazer Publishing in Neenah, WI
E-mail: stargazer@stargazerpub.com
Web site: http://www.stargazerpub.com.

Stark Productions Inc., *(978-1-936592)* 109 Orange Ave., St. Cloud, FL 34769 USA Tel 407-957-8502 (Tel/Fax) Do not confuse with Stark Productions Inc in OaklandCA
E-mail: stark109@hotmail.com
Web site: www.starkproductioninc.com.

Starks, Shirley *See* **Inspirational Hse. of America**

StarLineage Pubns., *(978-1-885226)* P.O. Box 1630, McCloud, CA 96057-1630 USA Tel 530-964-2496.

Starling Publishing, *(978-0-9857394; 978-0-9976390)* 1011 Paintbrush Ave., Kimberly, ID 83341 USA Tel 435-881-4812
E-mail: amberargyle@yahoo.com.

Starlit Publishing LLC, *(978-0-9792946)* 1750 Powder Springs Rd. Suite 190, Marietta, GA 30064 USA.

Starlog Group, Incorporated *See* **Profile Entertainment, Inc.**

StarProse Corp., *(978-0-9721071)* 17445 Roosevelt Rd., Hemlock, MI 48626 USA
E-mail: webmaster@starprose.com
Web site: http://www.starprose.com.

Starr, Joyce *See* **Dr. Joyce STARR Publishing**

StarryBks., *(978-0-9882113; 978-0-692-27075-2; 978-0-692-34543-6)* P.O. Box 1788, Yelm, WA 98597 USA Tel 360-894-3592
E-mail: dreamscapes@ywave.com
Dist(s): **CreateSpace Independent Publishing Platform.**

Starscape *Imprint of* **Doherty, Tom Assocs., LLC**

Starseed & Urantian Schools of Melchizedek Publishing *See* **Global Community Communications Publishing**

Starshell Pr., Ltd., *(978-0-9707110)* 210 Ridge Rd., Watchung, NJ 07069 USA Tel 908-755-7050; Fax: 212-983-5271
E-mail: starshellpress@yahoo.com
Web site: http://www.starshellpress.com.

Starshow Pubns., *(978-0-9966665; 978-0-9989245)* 122 Woodland St., BURKESVILLE, KY 42717 USA Tel 6153069481.

Start Publishing LLC, *(978-0-9664520; 978-1-930486; 978-1-60977; 978-1-62558; 978-1-62793; 978-1-63355; 978-1-68146; 978-1-68299; 978-1-63596)* 101 Hudson St., 37th Flr., Ste. 3705, Jersey City, NJ 07302 USA; *Imprints:* Salvo Press (SalvoPr)
E-mail: weisfeld@start-media.com; start-publishing.com
Web site: http://www.start-publishing.com
Dist(s): **MyiLibrary**
Red Wheel/Weiser
Simon & Schuster, Inc.

StarWalk Kids Media *Imprint of* **Isabella Products, Inc.**

Starward Publishing, *(978-0-9862099)* 18552 Ocean Mist Dr, Boca Raton, FL 33498 USA Tel 561-482-9812
E-mail: info@starwardpublishing.com.

Stash Bks. *Imprint of* **C & T Publishing**

State Historical Society of North Dakota, *(978-1-891419; 978-0-9796796; 978-0-9801993)* Orders Addr.: 612 E. Blvd. Ave., Bismarck, ND 58505-0830 USA Tel 701-205-7802; Fax: 701-328-3710
E-mail: nhowe@nd.gov
Web site: http://www.history.nd.gov.

State Historical Society of Wisconsin *See* **Wisconsin Historical Society**

State Hse. Pr., *(978-0-938349; 978-1-880510; 978-1-933337)* S. 14th & Sayles Blvd., Austin, TX 79697 USA (SAN 660-966X); McMurry University, Box 637, Abilene, TX 79697-0637 Tel 325-793-4697; Fax: 325-793-4754 Do not confuse with State House Publishing in Madison, WI
E-mail: ckahl@mcm.edu
Web site: http://www.mcwhiney.org
Dist(s): **Encino Pr.**
Texas A&M Univ. Pr.

State of Growth Publishing Co., *(978-0-9740289)* P.O. Box 38633, Colorado Springs, CO 80937 USA
Web site: http://www.stateofgrowth.com.

State Standards Publishing, LLC, *(978-1-935077; 978-1-935884; 978-1-938813; 978-1-946400)* P.O. Box 68, Athens, GA 30603 USA (SAN 856-292X) Tel 706-621-5225; Fax: 706-621-5226; Toll Free: 866-740-3056; *Imprints:* Everett Press (Everett Pr)
E-mail: jward@statestandardspublishing.com
Web site: http://www.statestandardspublishing.com.

State Street Pr. *Imprint of* **Borders Pr.**

†**State Univ. of New York Pr.**, *(978-0-7914; 978-0-87395; 978-0-88706; 978-1-4384)* Orders Addr.: P.O. Box 960, Herndon, VA 20172-0960 USA (SAN 203-3496) Tel 703-661-1575; Fax: 703-996-1010; Toll Free Fax: 877-204-6074; Toll Free: 877-204-6073 (customer service); Edit Addr.: 22 Corporate Woods Blvd., 3rd Flr., Albany, NY 12211-2504 USA (SAN 658-1730) Tel 518-472-5000; Fax: 518-472-5038; Toll Free: 866-430-7869; *Imprints:* Suny Press (Suny Pr)
E-mail: info@sunypress.edu; suny@presswarehouse.com
Web site: http://www.sunypress.edu
Dist(s): **Books International, Inc.**
CreateSpace Independent Publishing Platform
Ebsco Publishing
Pegasus Pr.
SPD-Small Pr. Distribution
TNT Media Group, Inc.
ebrary, Inc.; *CIP.*

Station Hill Press *See* **Barrytown/Station Hill Pr.**

Staying Healthy Media, Inc., *(978-0-9763237)* 4409 Summer Grape Rd., Pikesville, MD 21208 USA Tel 410-484-0457
E-mail: healthy@stayinghealthymedia.com
Web site: http://www.stayinghealthymedia.com.

Steam Crow Pr., *(978-0-9774173)* 7233 W. Cottontail Ln., Peoria, AZ 85383 USA
E-mail: sales@steamcrow.com
Web site: http://www.steamcrow.com.

Steam, Karl, *(978-1-63578)* 1012 Pk. Ave. NW., Willmar, MN 56201 USA Tel 320-293-7702; Fax: 320-293-7702
E-mail: karlsteambooks@gmail.com.

Steam Passages Pubns., *(978-0-9758584)* 508 Lakeview Ave., Wake Forest, NC 27587 USA
E-mail: sdegaetano@steampassages.com
Web site: http://www.dlrcad.com/book.

STEAM Publishing, LLC, *(978-0-9984337)* 2125 E STANFORD DR, TEMPE, AZ 85283 USA Tel 480-777-2621
E-mail: scolsen.writer@gmail.com.

†**Steck-Vaughn**, *(978-0-8114; 978-0-8172; 978-0-8393; 978-0-7398; 978-1-4190)* Div. of Houghton Mifflin Harcourt Supplemental Pubs., Orders Addr.: 6277 Sea Harbor Dr., 5th Flr., Orlando, FL 32887 USA Toll Free Fax: 877-578-2638; Toll Free: 888-363-4266; Edit Addr.: 10801 N. Mopac Expressway, Bldg. 3, Austin, TX 78759 USA (SAN 658-1757) Toll Free: 800-531-5015
E-mail: ecare@harcourt.com
Web site: http://www.harcourtachieve.com
Dist(s): **Follett School Solutions**
Houghton Mifflin Harcourt Publishing Co.
Houghton Mifflin Harcourt Supplemental Pubs.; *CIP.*

Stedjee Publishing *See* **Lawe Street Bks.**

Steel Bridge Pr., *(978-0-9764415)* 610 Briarcliff, Bardstown, KY 40004-8941 USA Tel 502-348-7447; Fax: 502-350-1126
E-mail: john@steelbridgepress.com.

Steele, Eugene *See* **E-BookTime LLC**

Steele Studios, *(978-0-9716811)* Orders Addr.: P.O. Box 3093, Glenwood Springs, CO 81602 USA (SAN 254-3230); Edit Addr.: 125 Ctr. Dr., No.18, Glenwood Springs, CO 81601 USA.

Steerforth Pr., *(978-0-944072; 978-1-58195; 978-1-883642; 978-1-58642)* 45 Lyme Rd. # 208, Hanover, NH 03755-1219 USA; *Imprints:* Campfire (Campf); Pushkin Press (Pushkin P); Elsewhere Editions (ElsewhereEd); Pushkin Children's Books (PushkinChld); Young Europe Books (YngEurBks)
E-mail: helga@steerforth.com; info@steerforth.com
Web site: http://www.steerforth.com
Dist(s): **MyiLibrary**
Penguin Random Hse. LLC
Random Hse., Inc.
Red Wheel/Weiser.

†**SteinerBooks, Inc.**, *(978-0-8334; 978-0-88010; 978-0-89345; 978-0-910142; 978-1-58420; 978-1-85584; 978-0-9701097; 978-0-9831984; 978-1-62148; 978-1-62151; 978-1-938685; 978-0-9969211)* Orders Addr.: P.O. Box 960, Herndon, VA 20172-0960 USA Tel 703-661-1594 (orders); Fax: 702-661-1501; Toll Free Fax: 800-277-7947 (orders); Toll Free: 800-856-8664 (orders); Edit Addr.: 610 Main St., Suite 1, Great Barrington, MA 01230 USA Tel 413-528-8233; Fax: 413-528-8826; Fulfillment Addr.: 22883 Quicksilver Dr., Dulles, VA 20166 USA (SAN 253-9519) Tel 703-661-1529; Fax: 703-996-1010; *Imprints:* Bell Pond Books (Bell Pond); Lindisfarne Books (Lindisfarne)
E-mail: service@steinerbooks.org
Web site: http://www.steinerbooks.org
Dist(s): **New Leaf Distributing Co., Inc.**
Red Wheel/Weiser; *CIP.*

Steingart, Nathan Publishing, *(978-0-9769321)* 617 N. Kensington Dr., No. 1, Appleton, WI 54915 USA
E-mail: nathansteingart@new.rr.com
Web site: http://www.santastories.net.

Steinschneider, Bernadetta, *(978-0-9790026)* 205 Georgetown Rd., Weston, CT 06883 USA Tel 203-454-8907; Fax: 203-227-0184
E-mail: swigutb@gmail.com.

Stejskal, Susan M., *(978-0-615-13395-9; 978-0-615-81867-2)* 15095 S. 18th St., Vicksburg, MI 49097 USA.

Stella Bks, Inc., *(978-0-9746932)* P.O. Box 4707, Edwards, CO 81632-4707 USA Tel 970-926-7827 (phone/fax)
E-mail: info@astellabook.com
Dist(s): **Partners/West Book Distributors.**

Stellar Learning, *(978-0-9763833)* P.O. Box 64, Guildrind Ctr, NY 12085-0064 USA
E-mail: admin@stellarlearn.com
Web site: http://www.stellarlearn.com.

Stellar Pubns., *(978-0-9761224)* 3767 Forest Ln., Suite 124 - MBX 1231, Dallas, TX 75244 USA Toll Free: 866-840-4378
E-mail: info@stellarpublishers.com; maymathis@msn.com
Web site: http://www.stellarpublishers.com.

Stellar Publishing, *(978-0-9703041; 978-0-9849660)* Div. of M & M Enterprises, Orders Addr.: 2114 S. Live Oak Pkwy., Wilmington, NC 28403 USA (SAN 860-2298) Tel 910-269-7444
E-mail: info@stellar-publishing.com
Web site: http://www.stellar-publishing.com
Dist(s): **Distributors, The.**

Stellinga, Mark, *(978-0-9762011; 978-0-9796421; 978-0-9817101)* 42 Lancester Pl., Iowa City, IA 52240 USA Tel 319-354-7287
E-mail: mark@writerofbooks.com
Web site: http://www.writerofbooks.com.

Stellium Pr., *(978-1-883376)* P.O. Box 82834, Portland, OR 97282-0834 USA.

Stelucan Pr., *(978-0-9601454)* 2129 State Hwy. 79 S., Wichita Falls, TX 76302 USA (SAN 221-3176).

†**Stemmer Hse. Pubs.**, *(978-0-88045; 978-0-916144)* P.O. Box 89, Gilsum, NH 03448 USA (SAN 207-9623) Tel 603-357-0236; Fax: 603-357-2073; *Imprints:* NaturEncyclopedia (Naturencyclop)
E-mail: pbs@pathwaybook.com
Web site: http://stemmer.com
Dist(s): **Pathway Bk. Service**; *CIP.*

Stenhouse Pubs., *(978-1-57110; 978-1-62531)* Div. of Highlights for Children, Orders Addr.: P.O. Box 11020, Portland, ME 04104-7020 USA (SAN 298-1580) Tel

207-253-1600; Fax: 207-253-5121; Toll Free Fax: 800-833-9164; Toll Free: 800-988-9812 (orders)
E-mail: jkilburn@stenhouse.com
Web site: http://www.stenhouse.com
Dist(s): **Ebsco Publishing**
Follett School Solutions
MyiLibrary.

Stensland Bks., *(978-0-9759456)* 6011 S. 102 St., Omaha, NE 68127 USA
E-mail: info@stenslandbooks.com
Web site: http://www.stenslandbooks.com.

Stephi /Lee, *(978-0-578-11938-0)* 2884 Blairmont Dr., Danville, VA 24540 USA
Web site: http://www.wheredomyprayersgo.com; http://www.stephileebooks.com.

Steps To Literacy, LLC, *(978-0-9728803; 978-1-59564; 978-1-60015; 978-1-60881; 978-1-60923; 978-1-61267; 978-1-62038; 978-1-63395; 978-1-63502; 978-1-68136; 978-1-68288; 978-1-68432)* Orders Addr.: P.O. Box 6737, Bridgewater, NJ 08807 USA (SAN 858-3005) Toll Free: 800-895-2804
E-mail: sales@stepstoliteracy.com
Web site: http://www.stepstoliteracy.com.

stepup strategies *See* **Stepup Strategies**

Stepup Strategies, *(978-0-9964109; 978-1-947276)* 116 Hazley Ave., Rochelle Park, NJ 07662 USA Tel 561-601-9871
E-mail: trevorscrane@gmail.com.

Sterli Publishing, *(978-0-9790014)* 986 Gable Cove, Collierville, TN 38017 USA (SAN 852-1638) Tel 352-753-4335 (sales office)
E-mail: admin@sterlipublishing.com
Web site: http://www.sterlipublishing.com.

Sterling & Ross Pubs., *(978-0-9766372; 978-0-9779545; 978-0-9787213; 978-0-9814535; 978-0-9814536; 978-0-9821391; 978-0-9821392; 978-0-9827588; 978-1-937802)* 1221 Ave. of the Americas Suite 4200, New York City, NY 10020 USA; *Imprints*: Cambridge House Press (CambridgeHse)
E-mail: contact@sterlingandross.com
Web site: http://www.sterlingandross.com.

Sterling Innovation *Imprint of* **Sterling Publishing Co., Inc.**

Sterling Investments I, LLC DBA Twins Magazine, *(978-0-9636745; 978-0-9655442; 978-1-891846)* 30799 Pinetree Rd., #256, Cleveland, OH 44124 USA Tel 855-758-9467; Fax: 855-758-9467; Toll Free: 855-758-9467; *Imprints*: Twins Books (Twins Bks)
E-mail: bill@twinsmagazine.com
Web site: http://www.twinsmagazine.com; http://www.twinsmagazine.com/theBookshelf.shtml.

Sterling Pr., Inc., *(978-0-9637735)* 6811 Old Canton Rd., Apt. 3802, Ridgeland, MS 39157-1248 USA Tel 602-957-9265 Do not confuse with companies with similar names in Bulverde, TX, Chicago, IL, Marysville, WA, Bedford, TX, Kihei,HI.

†**Sterling Publishing Co., Inc.**, *(978-0-8069; 978-1-4027; 978-1-60582; 978-1-4549; 978-1-61837)* 387 Park Ave., S., New York, NY 10016-8810 USA (SAN 211-6324) Tel 212-532-7160 212-213-2495; Toll Free Fax: 800-775-8736 (warehouse); *Imprints*: Sterling/Main Street (Sterling-Main St); Chapelle (Chapelle); Balloon Books (Balloon Books); Sterling Innovation (SterInnov); Puzzlewright (Puzzlewright); Fall River (FallRiver); Spark Notes (Spark Notes); Spark Publishing Group (SparkPubng) Do not confuse with companies with similar names in Falls Church, VA, Fallbrook, CA, Lewisville, TX
E-mail: custservice@sterlingpub.com; tradesales@sterlingpub.com
Web site: http://www.sterlingpublishing.com/
Dist(s): **Booklines Hawaii, Ltd.**
Follett School Solutions
Hachette Bk. Group
MBI Distribution Services/Quayside Distribution
Music Sales Corp.
MyiLibrary
Partners Bk. Distributing, Inc.; *CIP.*

Sterling Test Prep, *(978-0-9892925; 978-0-9977782; 978-1-947556)* 276 Washington St. No. 305, Boston, MA 02108 USA Tel 617-777-5936
E-mail: info@onlinemcatprep.com
Web site: www.onlinemcatprep.com.

Sterling/Main St. *Imprint of* **Sterling Publishing Co., Inc.**

Stern, Frederick *See* **Stern Math, LLC**

Stern Math, LLC, *(978-0-9779132; 978-0-9845392)* 754 N. Hollow Rd., Box 172, Rochester, VT 05767 USA (SAN 850-6027) Tel 212-874-4530
E-mail: sternmath@gmail.com; fredstern@gmail.com; emilyalison@gmail.com
Web site: http://sternmath.com.

Sterner, Hilda, *(978-0-615-22164-9)* P.O. Box 713071, Santee, CA 92072-3071 USA
E-mail: hilda@momsauthenticassyrianrecipes.com
Web site: http://www.momsauthenticassyrianrecipes.com.

Stevens, Andrew, *(978-0-9848340)* 8409 Lee Hwy., Merrifield, VA 22116-0613 USA Tel 703-222-3790
E-mail: alstevans@cox.net.

Steve Diet Goedde, *(978-1-890836)* 2807 W. Sunset Blvd., Los Angeles, CA 90026 USA Tel 323-377-0235
E-mail: stevedg@gmail.com
Web site: http://www.stevedietgoedde.com.

Steveedee Publishing Co,

Stevens, Gareth Incorporated *See* **Stevens, Gareth Publishing LLLP**

†**Stevens, Gareth Publishing LLLP**, *(978-0-8368; 978-0-918831; 978-1-55532; 978-1-4339)* Orders Addr.: P.O. Box 360140, Strongsville, OH 44136-0140 USA Fax: 877-542-2596; Toll Free: 800-542-2595; Edit Addr.: 111 East 14th St., Suite 349, New York, NY 10003 USA (SAN 696-1592) Toll Free: 877-444-0210; *Imprints*: World Almanac Library (Wrld Almanac Lib); Weekly Reader Leveled Readers (Weekly Read); Gareth Stevens Secondary Library (G S Sec Lib); Gareth Stevens Learning Library (G S Lrning Lib); Gareth Stevens Hi-Lo Must Reads (G S Hi-Lo)
E-mail: customerservice@gspub.com; hollyc@rosenpub.com
Web site: http://www.garethstevens.com; http://www.garethstevensclassroom.com
Dist(s): **Bound to Stay Bound Bks.**
Davidson Titles, Inc.
Follett School Solutions
Lectorum Pubns., Inc.; *CIP.*

Stevens Publishing, *(978-0-9632054; 978-1-885529)* Orders Addr.: P.O. Box 160, Kila, MT 59920 USA Tel 406-756-0307; Fax: 406-257-5051; Edit Addr.: 1550 Rogers Ln. Rd., Kila, MT 59920 USA Do not confuse with Stevens Publishing Corp. in Waco, TX.

Stevenson, Ian Author, *(978-0-9984836)* 2221 Eye St. NW, Washington, DC 20037 USA Tel 202-774-4596
E-mail: jim@getstyle.com
Web site: vocabularymoose.com.

Steward & Wise Publishing *See* **Acclaim Pr., Inc.**

Stewart Education Services, *(978-0-9764154)* 3722 Bagely Ave., No. 19, Los Angeles, CA 90034-4113 USA Tel 310-838-6247; Fax: 310-838-6769
E-mail: info@stewarteducationservices.com
Web site: http://www.stewarteducationservices.com.

Stewart, Mary *See* **Rooster Pubns.**

Stewart, R. J. Bks., *(978-0-9791402; 978-0-9819246; 978-0-9856006)* P.O. Box 507, milton, WA 98354 USA (SAN 852-5382)
E-mail: rjspeak@gmail.com
Web site: http://www.rjstewart.net.

†**Stewart, Tabori & Chang**, *(978-0-941434; 978-0-941807; 978-1-55670; 978-1-899791; 978-1-58479)* Div. of Harry N. Abrams, Inc., 115 W. 18th St., 5th Flr., New York, NY 10011 USA (SAN 293-4000) Tel 212-519-1200; Fax: 212-519-1210
E-mail: trudi@stcbooks.com
Web site: http://www.abramsbooks.com
Dist(s): **Abrams, Inc.**
Hachette Bk. Group
MyiLibrary
Open Road Integrated Media, Inc.; *CIP.*

Stickysoft Corp., *(978-0-9740384)* Orders Addr.: P.O. Box 7855, Buffalo Grove, IL 60089 USA Tel 847-229-9999; Fax: 847-808-8777; Toll Free: 800-366-8448; Edit Addr.: 620 Silver Rock Ln., Buffalo Grove, IL 60089 USA
E-mail: euclid@stickysoft.com
Web site: http://www.blackjack678.com.

Still Water Publishing, *(978-0-9740855)* Orders Addr.: 1093 Kiva Cir., Windsor, CO 80550 USA
E-mail: chein8@attbi.com
Web site: http://www.stillwaterpublishing.com.

Stillman, Steve, *(978-0-9740508)* 251 Green St., Shrewsbury, MA 01545-4708 USA.

STL Distribution North America *See* **Send The Light Distribution LLC**

Stockade Bks., *(978-0-9731570; 978-0-9863983; 978-0-9973879)* P.O. Box 30, Woodsville, NH 03785 USA Toll Free: 866-799-4500
E-mail: orders@stockadebooks.com
Web site: http://www.stockadebooks.com.

Stockcero, Inc., *(978-1-934768)* 3785 NW 82nd Ave. Suite 302, Doral, FL 33166 USA Tel 305-722-7628; Fax: 305-477-5794
E-mail: pagrest@stockcero.com; stockcero@stockcero.com
Web site: http://www.stockcero.com.

Stockwell Publishing, *(978-0-9785594)* 84 State St. Suite 300, Boston, MA 02109 USA Tel 617-290-3039; Fax: 617-720-0761
E-mail: pel.stockwell@lpl.com
Web site: http://www.followthefox.com.

Stogo, Malcolm Assocs., *(978-0-9712703; 978-0-615-28965-6; 978-0-9966586)* 79 Edgewood Ave., West Orange, NJ 07052 USA
Web site: www.icecreamuniversity.org
Dist(s): **Bookmasters Distribution.**

Stoke Bks.,

Stone Acres Publishing Co., *(978-0-9765478; 978-1-937480)* P.O. Box 407, Waverly, PA 18471-0407 USA (SAN 850-0940) Fax: 570-319-1655
E-mail: gmiltony@yahoo.com
Web site: http://www.stoneacrespublishing.com.

Stone & Scott Pubs., *(978-0-9627031; 978-1-891135)* Orders Addr.: P.O. Box 56419, Sherman Oaks, CA 91413-1419 USA (SAN 297-3030) Tel 818-904-9088; Fax: 818-787-1431
E-mail: Friday@StoneandScott.com; BostonLesPaul@adelphia.net
Web site: http://www.stoneandscott.com.

Stone, Anne Publishing, *(978-0-9858811)* 1158 26th St. Suite 440, Santa Monica, CA 90403 USA Tel 310-418-4674; Fax: 310-828-8057
E-mail: JulieK.AnneStone@gmail.com
Web site: www.annestonepublishing.com.

Stone Arch Bks., *(978-1-59889; 978-1-4342; 978-1-4965)* Div. of Coughlan Publishing, Orders Addr.: 1710 Roe Crest Dr., North Mankato, MN 56003 USA (SAN 257-3148) Tel 800-747-4992; Fax: 888-262-0705; Edit Addr.: 5050 Lincoln Dr, Edina, MN 55436 USA Fax: 952-933-2410; Toll Free: 1-888-517-8977; 1710 Roe Crest Dr., North Mankato, MN 56003; *Imprints*: Claudia Cristina Cortez (CCCortez); David Mortimore Baxter (DMB); Graphic Flash (Graphic Flash); Graphic Quest (Graph Quest); Graphic Revolve (GraRevolve); Graphic Sparks (GraphiSparks); Impact Books (ImpacBks); Keystone Books (KeystonBks); Shade Books (Shade Bks); Vortex Books (Vortex Bks); Zone Books (ZoneBks); After Happily Ever After (After Happily); DC Super Heroes (DC Super Hero); My First Graphic Novel (First Graph Nov); Recon Academy (Recon Acad); Graphic Revolve en Español (GRAPHIC REVOLV); Shakespeare Graphics (SHAKESPEARE GR); Team Cheer (TEAM CHEER); Good vs Evil (GOOD VS EVIL); Myth-O-Mania (MYTH-O-MANIA); Tony Hawk's 900 Revolution (TONY HAWKS 900); Stone Arch Novels (STONE ARCH NOV); Graphic Spin en Español (GRAPHIC SPIN E); Bilingual Stone Arch Readers (BILINGUAL STON); DC Super-villains (DC SUPER-VILLA); Return to Titanic (RETURN TO TITA); Troll Hunters (TROLL HUNTERS); Faerieground (FAERIEGROUND); Claudia & Monica: Freshman Girls (CLAUDIA & MONI); Echo & the Bat Pack (ECHO & THE BAT); Connect (Connect2); Dino-Mike! (Dino-Mike); Far Out Fairy Tales (Far Out FT); Museum Mysteries (Museum Myst); Scooby-Doo (Scooby-Doo2); Space Penguins (Space Peng); Stardust Stables (Stardust Stabl) Do not confuse with Stone Arch Books in Afton, MN
E-mail: k.monyhan@coughlancompanies.com; customerservice@capstonepub.com
Web site: http://stonearchbooks.com; http://www.capstonepub.com
Dist(s): **Capstone Press of Coughlan Cos.**
Capstone Pub.
Follett School Solutions.

Stone Arch Novels *Imprint of* **Stone Arch Bks.**

Stone Arrow Bks., *(978-0-9825528)* P.o. Box 221, Draper, UT 84020 USA Tel 801-699-2844
E-mail: komarkris@gmail.com
Dist(s): **Coutts Information Services**
Lightning Source, Inc.
Spring Arbor Distributors, Inc.

Stone Castle Publishing, *(978-0-578-00171-5)* 2602 Skyline Dr., Sedalia, MO 65301 USA
Dist(s): **Lulu Pr., Inc.**

Stone Cottage Bks., *(978-0-9822503)* Orders Addr.: P.O. Box 962497, Riverdale, GA 30296 USA (SAN 857-6734)
E-mail: info@stonecottagebooks.com; orders@stonecottagebooks.com
Web site: http://www.stonecottagebooks.com; http://www.bigandgrown.com; http://www.bigandgrown.com.

Stone Pine Pr., *(978-0-9728929)* Orders Addr.: P.O. Box 585, Marcola, OR 97454-0585 USA; Edit Addr.: 92985 Marcola Rd., Marcola, OR 97454 USA.

Stone Publishing Co., *(978-1-880991)* Orders Addr.: P.O. Box 711, Mendocino, CA 95460 USA Tel 707-937-0239; Edit Addr.: 10491 Wheeler St., Mendocino, CA 95460 USA.

Stone Ridge Publishing, *(978-0-9760313; 978-0-9909158)* 2515 Garthus Rd., Wrenshall, MN 55797 USA Tel 218-341-0181
E-mail: sparkystensaas@hotmail.com
Dist(s): **Adventure Pubns.**

Stone Skin Pr. (GBR) *(978-1-908983) Dist. by* **IPG Chicago.**

Stonebridge Pubns., *(978-0-9896904; 978-1-940473)* 25036 Meadowdale Ln., Veneta, OR 97487 USA Tel 626-629-0195 Do not confuse with Stonebridge Publications in Chesapeake, VA
E-mail: stonebridgepublications@outlook.com.

Stonechester, Inc., *(978-0-9759014)* 4894 Lone Mountain Rd., No. 311, Las Vegas, NV 89130-2239 USA.

StoneGarden.net Publishing, *(978-0-9765426; 978-1-60076)* 3851 Cottonwood Dr., Danville, CA 94506 USA Tel 925-984-7867
E-mail: theshop@stonegarden.net
Web site: http://www.stonegarden.net.

Stonehorse Publishing, LLC, *(978-0-9764199)* Orders Addr.: 6528 E. 101st St. S., Ste D1 Rm. 296, Tulsa, OK 74133 USA (SAN 256-3797) Toll Free Fax: 888-867-1927; Toll Free: 888-867-1927
E-mail: generalinfo@stonehorsepublishing.com
Web site: http://www.stonehorsepublishing.com
Dist(s): **Educational Distribution Corp.**

StoneHouse Ink, *(978-0-9826078; 978-0-9827705; 978-0-615-52573-0; 978-0-615-52575-4; 978-0-615-53802-0; 978-0-615-54333-8; 978-0-615-54337-6; 978-0-615-54696-4; 978-0-615-54711-4; 978-0-615-54901-9; 978-0-615-56858-4; 978-0-615-56861-4; 978-0-615-56900-0; 978-0-615-57160-7; 978-0-615-57163-8; 978-0-615-57164-5; 978-0-615-57165-2; 978-0-615-57168-3; 978-0-615-57222-2; 978-0-615-57225-3; 978-0-615-57624-4; 978-0-615-58014-2; 978-0-615-61352-9; 978-0-615-61354-3; 978-0-615-61786-2; 978-1-938426; 978-0-615-626) 12235 W. Briarwood Dr, Boise, ID 83713 USA Tel 208-514-6631*
E-mail: Pattersonbooks@hotmail.com; stonehousepress@hotmail.com; StoneHouseMgr@gmail.com
Web site: http://www.stonegateink.com/; http://www.stonehouseink.net
Dist(s): **CreateSpace Independent Publishing Platform**
Smashwords
Wesscott Marketing, Inc.

StonesThrow Publishing, LLC, *(978-0-9793823)* P.O. Box 1898, Mount Dora, FL 32756 USA Tel 208-610-0431
Web site: http://stonesthrowpublishing.com.

Stoneydale Pr. Publishing Co., *(978-0-912299; 978-1-931291; 978-1-938707)* Orders Addr.: P.O. Box 188, Stevensville, MT 59870 USA Tel 406-777-2729; Fax: 406-777-2521; Toll Free: 800-735-7006; Edit Addr.: 523 Main St., Stevensville, MT 59870 USA (SAN 265-3168)
E-mail: stoneydale@stoneydale.com
Web site: http://www.stoneydale.com
Dist(s): **Partners Bk. Distributing, Inc.**

Stony Meadow Publishing, *(978-0-9787925; 978-0-9834335; 978-0-9850290; 978-0-9885569; 978-0-9894090; 978-0-9962834)* 3412 Imperial Palm Dr., Largo, FL 33771 USA
E-mail: stonymeadowbooks@aol.com; darkmoondigest@gmail.com
Web site: http://www.stonymeadowpublishing.com; http://www.inspiration4songwriters.net; http://www.books4songwriters.com; http://htto://www.darkmoondigest.com.

Stop N Go Fitness, *(978-0-9800091)* 13518 L St., Omaha, NE 68137 USA Fax: 413-669-8870
E-mail: angelinsights@conciergemarketing.com
Web site: http://www.anangeltowatchover.com.

Storer, Mark *See* **Little River Bookshelf**

Storey Books *See* **Storey Publishing, LLC**

†**Storey Publishing, LLC**, *(978-0-88266; 978-1-58017; 978-0-9674717; 978-1-60342; 978-1-61212; 978-1-63586)* Subs. of Workman Publishing Co., Inc., Orders Addr.: 210 Mass Moca Way, North Adams, MA 01247 USA (SAN 203-4158) Fax: 413-346-2198; Toll Free Fax: 800-865-3429; Toll Free: 800-827-7444; c/o Workman Publishing, 225 Varick St., New York, NY 10014-4381 Tel 212-614-7700; Toll Free Fax: 800-521-1832; Toll Free: 800-722-7202
E-mail: info@storey.com; sales@storey.com
Web site: http://www.storey.com
Dist(s): **MBI Distribution Services/Quayside Distribution**
Workman Publishing Co., Inc.; *CIP.*

Stori Tyme Huggggs, Inc., *(978-1-890925)* Div. of T.L.B. Publishing, 827 N. Hollywood, #202, Burbank, CA 91505 USA Tel 770-987-5547; 894 Roberts Way, Lawrenceville, GA 30043
E-mail: tenabrown@thejpak.com.

Storie Tree, Inc., The, *(978-0-9679014)* Orders Addr.: P.O. Box 441048, Aurora, CO 80044-1048 USA Tel 303-690-6493; Fax: 303-758-7792; Edit Addr.: 3952 S. Joplin Way, Aurora, CO 80044-1048 USA.

Stories From Four Publishing Co., *(978-0-9742288)* 558 N. Nash St., Hortonville, WI 54944 USA Tel 920-779-9995
E-mail: fourinspirations@aol.com
Web site: http://www.storiesfromfour.com.

Stories of My Life, The, *(978-0-9741215)* Div. of Frontsiders Marketing Strategists, P.O. Box 1478, Summerland, CA 93067 USA Tel 805-969-3597
Web site: http://www.thestoriesofmylife.com.

Storm Leaf, *(978-0-9858325)* 6041 S Valdai Way, Aurora, CO 80015 USA Tel 303-408-3838
E-mail: david@stormleaf.com
Web site: www.stormleaf.com.

Storm Moon Pr., LLC, *(978-0-9827008; 978-1-937058; 978-1-62757)* 5705 Fishermans Dr., Bradenton, FL 34209 USA
E-mail: editor@stormmoonpress.com
Web site: http://www.stormmoonpress.com
Dist(s): **Smashwords.**

Storm Peak Pr., *(978-0-9641357; 978-1-928990)* 2502 4th Ave N., Seattle, WA 98109-2149 USA.

Story and Logic Media Group, *(978-0-615-72436-2; 978-0-615-74806-1; 978-0-9897549; 978-1-941622)* 12386 W. National Rd., New Carlisle, OH 45344 USA Tel 9374783002
E-mail: sharonalavy1@gmail.com
Web site: http://storyandlogic.blogspot.com/
Dist(s): **CreateSpace Independent Publishing Platform.**

Story Direction, *(978-0-9675940)* 39650 Us Hwy. 19 N. Apt. 583, Tarpon Spgs, FL 34689-3950 USA Tel 727-939-8466
E-mail: angelface12@earthlink.net.

Story of Your Life Publishing Co., The, *(978-0-9771667)* 528 Palisades Dr., No. 711, Pacific Palisades, CA 90272 USA (SAN 256-8241) Tel 310-230-8510.

Story Plant, The, *(978-0-9816087; 978-0-9819568; 978-0-9841905; 978-1-61188)* P.O. Box 4331, Stamford, CT 06907 USA (SAN 856-0234)
Web site: http://www.thestoryplant.com
Dist(s): **MyiLibrary**
National Bk. Network
Two Rivers Distribution.

Story Road Publishing, Inc., *(978-1-939898)* 16564 SW 47th Ter., Miami, FL 33185 USA Tel 818-590-3991
E-mail: zachary@zcbolger.com.

Story Store Collection Publishing, *(978-0-9764798)* 11040 Hickman Rd. # 226, Clive, IA 50325-3740 USA.

Story Stuff, Inc., *(978-1-928811)* P.O. Box 501372, Indianapolis, IN 46250-6372 USA Fax: 317-913-1777
E-mail: jmferrone@storystuff.com
Web site: http://www.storystuff.com.

Story Time Stories That Rhyme, *(978-1-56820)* P.O. Box 416, Denver, CO 80201-0416 USA Tel 303-575-5676; *Imprints*: folder leaf (folder leaf)
E-mail: emailstreet@gmail.com
Web site: http://www.storytimestoriesthatrhyme.net; http://www.storytimestoriesthatrhyme.com/; http://www.storytimestoriesthatrhyme.org; http://www.storiesforschools.com; http://www.kidsrhymenewsletter.com.

Storybook Acres, *(978-0-9761675)* 4309 Creek Rd., Conneaut, OH 44030 USA (SAN 256-2219) Tel 440-593-2780 (phone/fax)
E-mail: storybookacres@adelphia.net
Web site: http://storybookacres.org.

Storybook Meadow Publishing, *(978-0-9704621; 978-0-9845236)* 7700 Timbers Trail, Traverse City, MI 49684 USA; *Imprints*: Bower Books (Bower Bks)
E-mail: garybower@charter.net
Web site: http://www.bowerbooks.com
Dist(s): **Partners Bk. Distributing, Inc.**

Storybook Pr. & Productions, *(978-1-887683)* 467 Central Park W., Apt. 6E, New York, NY 10025 USA Tel 212-975-2473; 212-749-7178 (phone/fax); Fax: 212-975-2026; Toll Free: 800-779-4341
E-mail: storybookp@aol.com.

Storycraft Publishing, *(978-0-9638339)* Orders Addr.: P.O. Box 205, Masonville, CO 80541-0205 USA Tel 970-669-3755 (phone/fax); Edit Addr.: 8600 Firethorn Dr., Loveland, CO 80538 USA
E-mail: Vivian@storycraft.com
Web site: http://www.storycraft.com
Dist(s): **Book Wholesalers, Inc.**
Brodart Co.

Follett School Solutions
Quality Bks., Inc.
Unique Bks., Inc.
Storydog, Inc., *(978-0-9722690)* 3510 N. Bell Ave., Chicago, IL 60618 USA (SAN 254-9786) Tel 773-327-1588
Web site: http://www.storydog.com.
StoryGirl Productions, LLC, *(978-0-9762587)* 213 W. Montebello, Phoenix, AZ 85013 USA
E-mail: jaime@ding-a-lings.net
Web site: http://www.ding-a-lings.net.
StoryMaster Pr., *(978-0-9761179)* 15420 Memorial Dr., Suite M -141, Houston, TX 77079 USA Tel 281-920-0443; Fax: 281-920-1629
E-mail: info@storymasterpress.com
Web site: http://www.storymasterpress.com.
StoryRobin Co., *(978-1-937489)* 849 Durshire Way, Sunnyvale, CA 94087 USA Tel 408-905-7543
E-mail: suechen78@gmail.com
Web site: www.storyrobin.com.
StoryScapes, *(978-0-9975202; 978-0-9979283)* P.O. Box 116, Sebastopol, CA 95473 USA Tel 707-332-8100
E-mail: erik@permacultureartisans.com
Web site: storyscapes.us.
Storytime Ink International, *(978-0-9628769; 978-0-9897371)* P.O. Box 470505, Broadview Heights, OH 44147 USA Tel 440-584-0018; Fax: 270-573-4913; 10001 Gatewood Dr., Brecksville, OH 44141
E-mail: storytimeink@att.net
Web site: http://storytimeink.com.
Storytime Pr., Inc., *(978-0-9754942)* 427 W. Main, Suite D, Brighton, MI 48116 USA
E-mail: monroestudio@yahoo.com
Web site: http://www.michaelglennmonroe.com
Dist(s): **Ann Arbor Editions LLC.**
Storytime Works, *(978-0-9886984)* 904 Winter Dr., El Paso, TX 79912 USA Tel 915-248-9658
E-mail: storytimeworks@gmail.com
Web site: www.storytimeworks.com
Dist(s): **Greenleaf Book Group.**
StoryTime World Publishing Hse., *(978-0-9792800)* 5268g Nicholson Ln., Suite 380, Kensington, MD 20895 USA Tel 301-672-4296
Web site: http://storytimeworld.com.
StoryTyme Publishing, *(978-0-9753699)* 7909 Walergra Rd., Suite 112, PMB 178, Antelope, CA 95843 USA (SAN 256-0763)
Web site: http://www.storytymepublishing.com.
Stott, Darrel Ministry, *(978-0-9755564)* 1885 Nancy Ave., Central Point, OR 97502-1627 USA Tel 541-840-7171
E-mail: Dstottmin@yahoo.com
Web site: www.DarrelStott.com.
Stourbridge Distributors, Inc., *(978-0-9753758)* 812 Ct. St., Honesdale, PA 18431-1965 USA
E-mail: rich@stourbridgedist.com
Web site: http://www.stourbridgedist.com
Dist(s): **Phoenix Learning Resources, LLC.**
Stout, William Inc., *(978-0-9712716; 978-0-9743838)* 1468 Loma Vista St., Pasadena, CA 91104-4709 USA Tel 626-798-6490; Fax: 626-798-3756
E-mail: wmstout@altrionet.com
Web site: http://www.williamstout.com.
STR8*UP Productions, *(978-0-9795862)* Orders Addr.: P.O. Box 640173, Pike Road, AL 36064 USA.
Strack, Beth, *(978-0-9898991)* 2594 Hastings Ave., Redwood City, CA 94061 USA Tel 650-368-6158
E-mail: hummingbirdhmmmm@aol.com.
Straight Edge Pr., The, *(978-1-883043)* Subs. of Straight Edge, Inc., 386 Clinton St., Brooklyn, NY 11231-3603 USA (SAN 254-9395) Toll Free: 800-732-3628
E-mail: info@straightedgeinc.com
Web site: http://www.straightedgeinc.com.
Straight Forward Technologies, *(978-0-9718515)* P.O. Box 102, Valley Center, KS 67147 USA Tel 316-207-3211; Toll Free Fax: 877-766-8566
E-mail: info@straightforwardtech.com
Web site: http://www.bakingwithmommy.com; http://www.straightforwardtech.com; http://www.gardeningwithmommy.com.
Straight From The Heart Publishing, *(978-0-692-78740-3)* 2600 W Ina Rd. Apt 135, Tucson, AZ 85741 USA Tel 310-739-9348
E-mail: Straight From The Heart Publishing jimmydanelli@aol.com.
Straight Paths Pr., *(978-0-9759871)* 17450 SW Viking St., Beaverton, OR 97007 USA (SAN 256-1468) Tel 503-259-9764 (phone/fax); Toll Free: 800-348-2346 ext. 23
E-mail: info@straightpathspress.com
Web site: http://www.straightpathspress.com.
Strang Communications Company *See* **Charisma Media**
StrangeDays Publishing, *(978-0-9747581)* P.O. Box 587, Merton, WI 53056 USA.
Stranger Comics, *(978-0-578-03139-2; 978-0-578-03140-8; 978-0-578-03141-5; 978-0-578-04111-7; 978-0-578-07612-6; 978-0-578-08000-0; 978-0-578-11087-5; 978-1-939834)* 4121 Redwood Ave. Suite 101, Los Angeles, CA 90066 USA
E-mail: sebjones3@gmail.com; stranger@strangercomics.com
Web site: http://www.strangercomics.com
Dist(s): **Ingram Publisher Services.**
Strategic Bk. Publishing *Imprint of* **Strategic Book Publishing & Rights Agency (SBPRA)**
Strategic Book Publishing & Rights Agency (SBPRA), *(978-0-9795935; 978-1-934925; 978-1-60693; 978-1-60911; 978-1-60976; 978-1-61204; 978-1-61897; 978-1-62212; 978-1-62516; 978-1-62857; 978-1-63135; 978-1-63410; 978-1-943204; 978-1-68181; 978-1-946539; 978-1-946540)* 2450 Louisiana St., Houston, TX 77006 USA (SAN 853-8492) Toll Free: 888-808-6187; *Imprints:* Eloquent Books (Eloquent Bks); Strategic Book Publishing (Strat Bk)
E-mail: payroll@sbpra.net; support@sbpra.net; katie@sbpra.net
Web site: http://sbpra.net.
Strategic Educational Tools, *(978-0-9842863)* 293 Center St., East Aurora, NY 14052 USA (SAN 858-9666) Tel 716-445-9609.
Strategic Media Group, *(978-0-9824157)* 9800 De Soto Ave., Chatsworth, CA 91311 USA (SAN 858-0979)
Web site: http://www.hospitalcritterz.com.
Strategic Partners Press *See* **Strategic Media Group**
Strategic Visions, Inc. *See* **TAOH Inspired Education, LLC**
Strategies Publishing Co., *(978-0-9769662)* Orders Addr.: P.O. Box 5588, Cary, NC 27512 USA Do not confuse with companies with the same or similar name in Sahuarita, AZ, Tampa, FL, New Augusta, MS
E-mail: jjohnson0710@yahoo.com; strategiespublishing@nc.rr.com.
Strathmoor *Imprint of* **Tabby Hse. Bks.**
Strathmoor Pr., *(978-0-9740718)* 1710 Tyler Pkwy., Louisville, KY 40204 USA Tel 502-479-3287.
Stratten, Lou, *(978-0-9747173)* Orders Addr.: 3144 S. Barrington Ave. #c, Los Angeles, CA 90066 USA; Edit Addr.: 3144 S. Barrington Ave. Apt. C, Los Angeles, CA 90066-1146 USA.
Straub, Rick, *(978-0-9793269; 978-0-9842209; 978-0-9913726)* Orders Addr.: 493 Ridgecrest Dr., Blairsville, GA 30512 USA Tel 706-781-6551
E-mail: csddata@windstream.net
Web site: http://www.straubpublishing.com/.
Strauberry Studios, *(978-0-9830321)* 11000 NE 10th St. No. 230, Bellevue, WA 98004 USA Tel 425-821-7007
E-mail: susan@strauberrystudios.com
Web site: http://www.strauberrystudios.com.
Straus, Jane, *(978-0-9667221)* Orders Addr.: P.O. Box 472, Mill Valley, CA 94942 USA (SAN 253-8202) Toll Free: 800-644-3222
E-mail: jane@grammarbook.com
Web site: http://www.grammarbook.com; http://www.thebluebooks.com.
Strauss Consultants, 48 W. 25th St., 11th Flr., New York, NY 10010-2708 USA Toll Free Fax: 888-528-8273; Toll Free: 800-236-7918
E-mail: strausscon@aol.com
Dist(s): **Smashwords.**
Strawbery Banke, Incorporated *See* **Strawbery Banke Museum**
Strawbery Banke Museum, *(978-0-9603896)* Orders Addr.: P.O. Box 300, Portsmouth, NH 03802-0300 USA (SAN 221-6515) Tel 603-433-1100; Fax: 603-433-1115; Edit Addr.: 454 Court St., Portsmouth, NH 03802-0300 USA
E-mail: deidre@perpublisher.com
Web site: http://www.strawberybanke.org
Dist(s): **Univ. Pr. of New England.**
Stray Dog Pr., LLC, *(978-0-9898831)* 1030 Bowen Creek Rd., Niangua, MO 65713 USA Tel 417-473-1136; *Imprints:* Fun 4 Kids Publishing (Fun four Kids)
E-mail: susankeenebooks@gmail.com.
Streamline Brands, *(978-0-9855732; 978-0-692-86750-1)* 80 So. Highland Ave. The Holyoke-Manhattan blg, Ossining, NY 10562 USA Tel 914-941-5668
E-mail: jacollen@collenip.com.
Streams Publishing Co., *(978-1-933358)* P.O. Box 260, Sidney, OH 45365-0260 USA Tel 937-492-4586; Fax: 937-492-7633
E-mail: budford@bright.net
Web site: http://www.cityreaching.net.
Strebor Bks. *Imprint of* **Strebor Bks.**
Strebor Bks., *(978-0-9674601; 978-0-9711953; 978-1-59309)* 1230 Ave. of the Americas, New York, NY 10020 USA; *Imprints:* Strebor Books (Strebor Imp)
Dist(s): **Simon & Schuster, Inc.**
Streetside Stories, Inc., *(978-0-9646977; 978-0-9710606)* 3130 20th St. Ste. 311, San Francisco, CA 94110-2700 USA
E-mail: contact@streetside.org
Web site: http://www.streetside.org.
StreetTalk Publishing Co., *(978-0-9770009)* 187 N. Garfield Ave., Columbus, OH 43203 USA
E-mail: amazingteistreet@gmail.com.
Strelecky, John *See* **Aspen Light Publishing**
Stress Free Kids *See* **Stress Free Pubs.**
Stress Free Pubs., *(978-0-9708633; 978-0-9787781; 978-0-9800328; 978-0-9836256; 978-1-937985)* 2561 Chimney Springs Dr, Marietta, GA 30062 USA
E-mail: rick@StressFreeKids.com
Web site: www.stressfreepublishers.com
Dist(s): **Ingram Publisher Services**
Lightning Source, Inc.
Strickland, Wilton, *(978-0-9747035)* 618 Pk. Ave., Goldsboro, NC 27530 USA (SAN 255-8114) Tel 919-734-2830 (phone/fax)
E-mail: wilton@esn.net
Web site: http://www.wiltonstrickland.com.
Striking Presence Pubns., *(978-0-9724925)* Orders Addr.: P.O. Box 475, Moorestown, NJ 08057 USA Tel 609-936-7278; Fax: 609-936-9651; Edit Addr.: 49-13 Quail Ridge Dr., Plainsboro, NJ 08536 USA
E-mail: jc@strikingpresence.com
Web site: http://www.strikingpresence.com.
String of Beads Pubns., *(978-0-9672012)* 9297 Avignon Pl., West Jordan, UT 84088 USA Fax: 801-566-0406
E-mail: jepp@fiber.net
Web site: http://www.stringofbeads.com.
Strong Corner Publishing, LCC, *(978-0-9754755)* 5331 Talavero Pl., Parker, CO 80134-2799 USA
E-mail: spencerj@broncos.nfl.com.
Strong, Louise dev, *(978-0-9770950)* P.O. Box 197, Morristown, NY 13664 USA Tel 315-375-4238
E-mail: riverstrong@gisco.net.
Strother, Rosemarie, *(978-0-692-00131-8)* 4880 Coral Wood Dr., Naples, FL 34119 USA Tel 239-353-4919.
Structured Learning, *(978-0-9787800; 978-0-9845881; 978-0-9893690; 978-1-942101)* 27062 Lost Colt, Laguna Hills, CA 92653 USA
Web site: http://www.structuredlearning.net.
Struggle Against the Odds, *(978-0-9778318)* 3929 Clay Pl., NE, Washington, DC 20019 USA Tel 202-397-5310 (phone/fax)
E-mail: satocommunications@rcn.com
Web site: http://www.satocommunication.com.
Struik Christian Media (ZAF) *(978-1-4153) Dist. by* **Casemate Pubs.**
Stryker Illustrations, *(978-0-9821038)* 18011 Biscayne Blvd. Apt. 1901, Aventura, FL 33160-5239 USA Toll Free: 888-710-2513
E-mail: strykercards@bellsouth.net.
STS Publishing, *(978-0-9798806)* 1125 E. Second St., Casper, WY 82601 USA Tel 307-577-4227.
Stuart & Weitz Publishing Group, *(978-0-9769949)* Div. of EQ Pubns., Orders Addr.: 674 Triunfo Canyon Rd., Westlake Village, CA 91361 USA
E-mail: contact@stuartweitzpublishing.com
Web site: http://www.stuartweitzpublishing.com
Dist(s): **BookBaby.**
Stuart, Jesse Foundation, The, *(978-0-945084; 978-1-931672; 978-1-938471)* 1645 Winchester Ave., Ashland, KY 41101 USA (SAN 245-8845)
Web site: http://www.jsfbooks.com.
Stubblefield, Jean A, *(978-0-692-80292-2)* 2716 Inman Bend Rd, Morristown, TN 37814 USA Tel 423-307-3173
E-mail: craigjeanie@bellsouth.net.
Student Pr. Initiative, *(978-1-932948)* 509 W. 121st St., Suite 406, New York, NY 10027 USA Tel 212-678-8339; Fax: 212-678-3746
E-mail: epg10@columbia.edu.
Studio 37 Pubns., *(978-0-615-73166-7; 978-0-615-79740-3; 978-0-615-92329-1)* 502 Leonard St, Madison, WI 53711 USA Tel 503-449-2821
Dist(s): **CreateSpace Independent Publishing Platform.**
Studio 403, *(978-0-9633943; 978-1-933129)* 399 Shoreland Dr., Lopez Island, WA 98261-8412 USA Tel 360-468-4347
E-mail: mark@studio403.com
Web site: http://www.studio403.com.
Studio 9 Bks. and Music, 162 Margaret St., Plattsburgh, NY 12901 USA Tel 518-298-8595
E-mail: studio9@rdppub.com.
Studio Cherry Publishing, *(978-0-9793360)* 3697 Rt.75, Huntington, WV 25704-9011 USA Tel 304-697-2051
E-mail: studio_cherry@verizon.net.
Studio Foglio, LLC, *(978-1-889061; 978-1-890856)* 2400 NW 80th St., Suite 129, Seattle, WA 98117-4449 USA (SAN 254-5128) Tel 206-782-8739; Fax: 206-783-3931
E-mail: foglio@studiofoglio.com; savannah@studiofoglio.com; foglio@xxxenophile.com
Web site: http://www.studiofoglio.com
Dist(s): **Berkeley Game Distributors**
Chessex
Cold Cut Comics Distribution
Diamond Comic Distributors, Inc.
Diamond Bk. Distributors
FM International
Rip Off Pr.
Syco Distribution.
Studio Fun International, *(978-0-276; 978-0-7621; 978-0-88705; 978-0-88850; 978-0-89577; 978-1-57584; 978-1-57619; 978-0-7944)* Subs. of Reader's Digest Assn., Inc., Reader's Digest Rd., Pleasantville, NY 10570-7000 USA (SAN 283-2143) Tel 914-244-4800; Fax: 914-244-4841; *Imprints:* Reader's Digest Children's Books (RD Childrens); Reader's Digest Young Families, Incorporated (RDYF)
Web site: http://www.readersdigestkids.com; http://www.studiofun.com/
Dist(s): **Continental Bk. Co., Inc.**
MyiLibrary
Simon & Schuster, Inc.
Simon & Schuster Children's Publishing
Simon & Schuster Children's Publishing.
Studio Indiana, *(978-0-9745186)* 430 N. Sewell Rd., Bloomington, IN 47408 USA Tel 812-223-5073 (phone/fax)
E-mail: john@studioindiana.com
Web site: http://www.studioindiana.com.
Studio Ironcat L.L.C. *See* **International Comics & Entertainment L.L.C.**
Studio Moonfall, *(978-0-9841746; 978-1-942811)* 5605 Sheridan Rd. No. 1172, Kenosha, WI 53141-1172 USA
Web site: http://www.fearandsunshine.com; http://www.ratatatgraphics.com
Dist(s): **Lightning Source, Inc.**
Studio Mouse LLC, *(978-1-59069)* 353 Main Ave., Norwalk, CT 06851 USA Tel 203-846-2274; Fax: 203-846-1776; Toll Free: 800-228-7839
E-mail: chelsea.shriver@soundprints.com
Dist(s): **Soundprints.**
Studio See *See* **Studio See Publishing, LLC**
Studio See Publishing, LLC, *(978-0-9796974)* P.O. Box 7013, Sheridan, WY 82801 USA Tel 307-673-1207
E-mail: psee@fiberpipe.net
Web site: http://www.studiosee.com.
StudioLine Photo *Imprint of* **H&M Systems Software, Inc.**
Studios West Publications *See* **Ritchie Unlimited Pubns.**
Study Ctr. Pr. *Imprint of* **San Francisco Study Ctr.**
Stuff on Paper, *(978-0-578-01210-0; 978-0-578-05355-4; 978-0-578-13881-7)* 21849 Erdahl Ct. NE, Tenstrike, MN 56683 USA
Dist(s): **Aardvark Global Publishing.**
Stull, Judy, *(978-0-9765738)* 16401 96th St., Lexington, OK 73051-8208 USA Tel 405-527-7467
E-mail: puppetlady@valornet.com.
Stunt Publishing, *(978-0-9745930)* 22287 Mulholland Why, No. 281, Calabasas, CA 91302 USA Tel 818-312-5157
E-mail: stuntpublishing@earthlink.net
Dist(s): **Independent Pubs. Group.**
Stuttering Foundation of America *See* **Stuttering Foundation, The**
Stuttering Foundation, The, *(978-0-933388; 978-1-930244)* Orders Addr.: P.O. Box 11749, Memphis, TN 38111-0749 USA (SAN 282-3330) Tel 901-452-7343; Fax: 901-452-3931; Toll Free: 800-992-9392
E-mail: stutter@stutteringhelp.org
Web site: http://www.stutteringhelp.org.
Stylewriter Pubns., *(978-0-9718288; 978-0-9721653; 978-0-9729411; 978-0-9748771)* Div. of Stylewriter, Inc., 4395 N. Windsor Dr., Provo, UT 84604-6301 USA Toll Free: 866-802-7888
E-mail: customerservice@spllc.rog
Web site: http://www.spllc.org.
Stylus Publishing, LLC, *(978-1-57922; 978-1-887208; 978-0-9729394; 978-1-62036)* Orders Addr.: P.O. Box 605, Herndon, VA 20172-0605 USA; Edit Addr.: 22883 Quicksilver Dr., Sterling, VA 20166-2012 USA (SAN 299-1853) Tel 703-661-1581; Fax: 703-661-1501 Do not confuse with companies with the same name in Sunnyvale, CA, Quakertown, PA
E-mail: stylusmail@presswarehouse.com; jean.westcott@styluspub.com
Web site: http://www.styluspub.com
Dist(s): **ebrary, Inc.**
Subcomission Literature Christiana *See* **Libros Desafio**
Subterranean Pr., *(978-0-9649890; 978-1-892284; 978-1-931081; 978-1-59606)* P.O. Box 190106, Burton, MI 48519 USA Tel 810-232-1489; Fax: 810-232-1447 Do not confuse with Subterranean Pr., San Francisco, CA
E-mail: subpress@gmail.com
Web site: http://www.subterraneanpress.com
Dist(s): **Diamond Comic Distributors, Inc.**
Diamond Bk. Distributors.
Success Empowering Techniques, Inc., *(978-0-9753415)* 5500 S. Eastern Ave., Las Vegas, NV 89119 USA Tel 702-893-0042
E-mail: set@setsuccess.com
Web site: http://www.setsuccess.com.
Success for All Foundation, *(978-0-9767850; 978-1-941010)* 300 E. Joppa Rd. 5th Flr., Baltimore, MD 21286 USA Tel 800-548-4998; Fax: 410-324-4458
E-mail: jworrell@successforall.org; tkoromah@successforall.org
Web site: http://www.successforall.org.
Suckerfish Bks., *(978-0-9764659)* 23700 NW Skyline Blvd., North Plains, OR 97133 USA Tel 503-957-1554
Web site: http://www.suckerfishbooks.com.
Sugar Creek Publishing, *(978-0-9712571)* 4126 N. London Rd., Fairland, IN 46126 USA Tel 727-399-0342.
Sugar Ducky Bks., Inc., *(978-0-9727388)* P.O. Box 56954, Jacksonville, FL 32241-6954 USA (SAN 255-1403)
E-mail: service@sugarduckybooks.com
Web site: http://www.sugarduckybooks.com.
Sugar Goblin LLC, The, *(978-0-9860859)* 2566 Delaware Ave., Sunfish Lake, MN 55118 USA.
Sulby Hall Publishing, *(978-0-615-84593-7; 978-0-615-86133-3; 978-0-615-89846-9)* P.O. Box 8687, Malibu, CA 90264 USA Tel 310-457-0439
Dist(s): **CreateSpace Independent Publishing Platform.**
Sullivan, Kayla , *(978-0-578-18078-6)* 2909 Springdale Ln, San Ramon, CA 94583 USA.
Sullivan, Kelley Enterprises, *(978-0-9728556)* c/o L. Leon, KSE, P.O. Box 1843, Lemon Grove, CA 91946-1843 USA
E-mail: ll@mykse.com
Web site: http://www.mykse.com.
Suma de Letras, S.L. (ESP) *(978-84-663; 978-84-95501; 978-84-96463) Dist. by* **Distribks Inc.**
Summa Bks., *(978-0-932423)* P.O. Box 2095, Darien, IL 60561-6895 USA (SAN 687-4096).
Summa Publishing Company *See* **Summa Bks.**
Summer Camp Stories LLC, *(978-0-9863743)* 35 Toilsome Brook Rd., Stamford, CT 06905 USA Tel 203-705-1600
E-mail: elliotsloyer@yahoo.com
Web site: www.summercampstories.com.
Summer Day Publishing, LLC, *(978-0-9768653)* 14747 San Marsala Ct., Tampa, FL 33626 USA Tel 727-224-9874; Fax: 813-926-8215
E-mail: baflorida@aol.com
Web site: http://www.thebreakawaykid.com.
Summer Street Pr., *(978-0-9766367; 978-0-9822541)* 460 Summer St., Stamford, CT 06901 USA Tel 203-325-2217; Fax: 203-325-2218 Do not confuse with Summer Street Press in Santa Barbara, CA
E-mail: Cathy@summerstreetpress.com
Web site: http://www.summerstreetpress.com.
Summerbook Co., *(978-1-933055)* 305 Lyndale Dr., Hartsville, SC 29550 USA Tel 843-383-5554 (phone/fax)
E-mail: angela@summerbookcompany.com
Web site: http://www.summerbookcompany.com.
Summerdale Pubs. (GBR) *(978-1-84024; 978-1-873475; 978-1-84953; 978-0-85764; 978-0-85765; 978-1-78372) Dist. by* **IPG Chicago.**
Summerhill Pr., *(978-0-9801861)* P.O. Box 79684, Fort Worth, TX 76179 USA; *Imprints:* Summertime Books (Summertime Bk) Do not confuse with Summerhill Pr., Naperville, IL
E-mail: summerhillpress@charter.net
Web site: http://www.summertimebooks.com.
Summerland Publishing, *(978-0-9794585; 978-0-9794863; 978-0-9795444; 978-0-9824870; 978-0-9837923; 978-0-9891121; 978-0-9893996; 978-0-9905886; 978-0-9963736; 978-0-9986451)* Orders Addr.: 887 Hanson St, Bozeman, MT 97470 USA (SAN 853-4497) Tel 307-399-7744
E-mail: summerlandpublishing@gmail.com
Web site: http://www.SummerlandPublishing.com.
Summerside Lane, *(978-0-9777570)* 179 Highlands Dr., Williston, VT 05495 USA (SAN 850-1793)
Web site: http://www.Summersidelane.com.
Summerthought Publishing Ltd. (CAN) *(978-0-919934; 978-0-9782375; 978-0-9811491; 978-1-926983) Dist. by* **Alpen Bks.**
Summertime Bks. *Imprint of* **Summerhill Pr.**
Summertime Books *See* **Summerhill Pr.**

Summit Hse. Pubs., *(978-0-9746735)* Orders Addr.: P.O. Box 15478, Chicago, IL 60615 USA Tel 847-379-8822 (phone/fax); *Imprints:* Ijiwola Press, Gregory (G Ijiwola Pr)
Web site: http://www.summitpublishers.com; http://thecitylight.org.

Summit Interactive, *(978-1-57458)* Orders Addr.: 302 Albany Ave., Shreveport, LA 71105 USA Tel 318-865-8232; Fax: 318-865-6227; Toll Free: 877-843-0277
E-mail: mhenry@sieducation.com; scavel@sieducation.com; kbriley@sieducation.com
Web site: http://www.sieducation.com; http://www.AscendEdu.com.

Sun Break Publishing, *(978-0-9815557; 978-1-60916)* 1037 NE 65th St., No. 164, Seattle, WA 98115 USA
Web site: http://sunbreakpublishing.com
Dist(s): **Smashwords.**

Sun Cuisine Concepts LLC, *(978-0-692-61118-0)* 12200 SW 70th Ct., Miami, FL 33156 USA Tel 305-510-1569
E-mail: delius@ortaniquerestaurants.com
Dist(s): **Bookmasters Distribution.**

Sun on Earth Bks., *(978-1-883378)* P.O. Box 704, Heathsville, VA 22473 USA Tel 804-435-5195
E-mail: books@sunonearth.com
Web site: http://www.sunonearth.com.

Sun Pubns., *(978-0-9665932; 978-1-931034)* Div. of Success Unleashed, Inc., 300 Carlsbad Village Dr., Suite 108A-7B, Carlsbad, CA 92008 USA (SAN 253-4444) Tel 619-884-7505; Fax: 760-434-7076 Do not confuse with Sun Publications, Charlottesville, VA
E-mail: eagles10@pacbell.net
Dist(s): **Insight Publishing.**

Sun Rose Pubs., *(978-0-9712781)* P.O. Box 2314, East Orange, NJ 07019 USA
E-mail: carolineilo@yahoo.com; eph-llogienboh@worldnet.att.net.

Sun Sings Pubns., *(978-0-9721429; 978-0-9832053)* 4144 Lafayette Pl., Culver City, CA 90232-2818 USA Tel 310-837-1313; Fax: 802-609-2959
E-mail: alan-alanlindgren@hotmail.com.

Sun Sprite Publishing, *(978-0-9745712)* 19 Milton Ave, Cranston, RI 02905 USA Toll Free: 877-883-4798
E-mail: kwanyin@ureach.com
Web site: http://www.mykwanyin.com/sunsprite.html.

Sunbelt Media, Incorporated *See* **Eakin Pr.**

†Sunbelt Pubns., Inc., *(978-0-916251; 978-0-932653; 978-0-9606704; 978-0-9620402; 978-1-941384)* 1256 Fayette St., El Cajon, CA 92020-1511 USA (SAN 630-0790) Tel 619-258-4911; Fax: 619-258-4916; Toll Free: 800-626-6579
E-mail: info@sunbeltpub.com; sales@sunbeltpub.com; dyoung@sunbeltpub.com; mail@sunbeltpub.com
Web site: http://www.sunbeltpub.com; http://www.sunbeltbooks.com
Dist(s): **Pacific Bks.**
Quality Bks., Inc.; *CIP.*

Sunburst *Imprint of* **Farrar, Straus & Giroux**

Sunbury Press, Inc., *(978-0-9760925; 978-1-934597; 978-1-62006)* Orders Addr.: 1602 W Lisburn Rd, Boiling Springs, PA 17007-0548 USA Tel 1-855-338-8359
E-mail: orders@sunburypress.com
Web site: http://www.sunburypress.com.

Sundance Entertainment, *(978-0-9729847)* P.O. Box 418, New York, NY 10035 USA Tel 646-431-9334.

Sundance Media Group, Inc./VASST, *(978-0-9762380)* P.O. Box 3, Stockton, UT 84071 USA Tel 435-882-8494; Fax: 435-882-8508
E-mail: info@sundancemediagroup.com
Web site: http://www.vasst.com.

SunDance Press *See* **Bk. Pubs. of El Paso**

Sundance/Newbridge Educational Publishing, *(978-0-7608; 978-0-88741; 978-0-940146; 978-1-56784; 978-1-56801; 978-1-58273; 978-1-4007; 978-1-4207)* P.O. Box 740, Northborough, MA 01532 USA (SAN 169-3484) Tel 888-200-2720; Fax: 508-303-2015; Toll Free: 800-343-8204
E-mail: info@sundancepub.com; lroman@sundancepub.com
Web site: http://www.sundancepub.com; http://www.newbridgeonline.com.

Sunday School Board of the Southern Baptist Convention *See* **LifeWay Christian Resources**

Sunday School Publishing Board *See* **Townsend Pr. - Sunday Schl. Publishing Board**

SundaySchoolNetwork.com, *(978-0-9665124)* Div. of SA Keith of Creative Imaginations, 438 E. Ilex Dr., Lake Park, FL 33403-2606 USA Tel 561-281-5033
E-mail: orders@Bible-4-Life.com; orders@SundaySchoolNetwork.com; orders@christiancrafters.com
Web site: http://www.christiancrafters.com; http://www.Bible-4-Life.com; http://www.SundaySchoolNetwork.com; http://www.creativeimaginations.net.

Sundback, Ruth, *(978-0-9776850)* 10430 Perla Bello Ct., Las Vegas, NV 89135 USA (SAN 850-9719)
E-mail: ruthslv@earthlink.net.

Sundie Enterprises, *(978-0-9859811; 978-0-9991261)* P.O. Box 1274, Provo, UT 84603-1274 USA Tel 801-995-9342
E-mail: sundieents@gmail.com.

SunDog Enterprises, *(978-0-9854677)* 119 Persimmon Ridge Rd., Cleveland, SC 29635 USA Tel 864-836-2668
E-mail: gail.mcdiarmid@furman.edu.

Sundog, Ltd., *(978-1-932203; 978-1-59744)* Orders Addr.: 35 W. 92nd St., 5e, New York, NY 10025 USA.

Sunergos Bible Studies, *(978-1-932934)* 2485 Morse Rd., Sebastopol, CA 95472 USA Tel 707-829-2956
E-mail: rich@sunergosbible.org; jan@sunergosbible.org
Web site: http://www.sunergosbible.org.

Sunesis Publishing Co., *(978-0-9716487)* 424 S. Mckinley Maddox Rd., Perry, FL 32347 USA Tel 850-838-3909 (phone/fax); *Imprints:* PathLight Books (PathLight Bks) Do not confuse with Compass Publishing in Savannah, GA
Web site: http://www.sunesispublishing.com.

Sunflower Education, *(978-1-937166)* 15044 Haley Hollow, Austin, TX 78728 USA Tel 512-310-2215
E-mail: cynthia.hannon@gmail.com
Web site: sunflowereducation.net.

Sunflower Pr., *(978-0-9616586; 978-0-9768507; 978-0-9832659)* P.O. Box 750733, Forest Hills, NY 11375 USA (SAN 659-7785) Fax: 718-830-9616
E-mail: order@chutaichi.com.

Sunflower Publishing *See* **Growing Field Bks.**

Sunflower Seeds Pr., *(978-0-9743627; 978-0-9830089)* 9470 Hwy 96 W., Franklin, TN 37064 USA
E-mail: bill@rondafriend.com
Web site: http://www.sunflowerseedspress.com; http://www.downonfriendlyacres.com.

Sunflower Univ. Pr., *(978-0-89745)* Subs. of Journal of the West, Inc., 2961 Nevada St., Manhattan, KS 66502-2355 USA (SAN 218-5075) Toll Free: 800-258-1232 (orders)
E-mail: pub@sunflower-univ-press.org
Web site: http://www.sunflower-univ-press.org.

SunHill Pubs., *(978-0-9673189)* Orders Addr.: P.O. Box 4921, Atlanta, GA 30302 USA Tel 404-627-9025; Fax: 678-623-8237 Do not confuse with Hill Publishing in Marina, CA
E-mail: ehill111@comcast.net.

Sunlight Publishing, *(978-0-9818190)* 339 E. Weller St., Ansonia, OH 45303 USA (SAN 924-7130) Tel 937-671-8511; 419-925-4121; *Imprints:* Candy Cane Books (CandyCane).

Sunny & The Chocolate Dog, LLC, *(978-0-9725945)* 5 Palm Row, Saint Augustine, FL 32084 USA Tel 904-808-7144; Fax: 904-808-7142
E-mail: josh@sunnyandthechocolatedog.com
Web site: http://www.sunnyandthechocolatedog.com.

Sunny Bks. *Imprint of* **J B Communications, Inc.**

Sunny Day Publishing, LLC, *(978-0-9825480; 978-0-9903823; 978-0-9978006)* 3365 Crestwood Cir., Cuyahoga Falls, OH 44223 USA (SAN 920-8232) Tel 330-414-2760 Do not confuse with Sunny Day Publishing in Richardson, TX
E-mail: sales@sunnydaypublishing.com; stacie@sunnydaypublishing.com
Web site: http://www.sunnydaypublishing.com.

Sunny Future Pr., *(978-0-9754980)* 890 Bruce Dr., Wantagh, NY 11793-1116 USA
E-mail: canivan@optonline.net
Web site: http://www.jc-solarhomes.com.

Sunny Hollow Pr., *(978-0-9755818)* 2517 N. 62nd St., Mesa, AZ 85215 USA Tel 480-830-7634; Toll Free: 800-442-0046
E-mail: rjvb@sunnyhollowpress.com
Web site: http://www.sunnyhollowpress.com.

Sunny Palms Pr., *(978-1-942073)* P.O. Box 230348, Encinitas, CA 92023 USA Tel 760-902-6502
E-mail: janmoran123@gmail.com.

Sunnycroft Bks., *(978-0-9904320)* 4110 SE Hawthorne Blvd. No. 749, Portland, OR 97214 USA Tel 503-867-3085
E-mail: sunnycroftbooks@gmail.com.

Sunnyfields Publishing, *(978-0-578-06095-8; 978-0-578-06541-0; 978-0-578-06574-8; 978-0-615-75133-7; 978-0-615-76128-2; 978-0-615-76235-7)* 1746 N. Gramercy Pl., No. 15, Los Angeles, CA 90028 USA Tel 323-960-2563
E-mail: Daviddayan666@aol.com.

Sunnyside Pr., *(978-0-9742566)* 902 E. 10th St., Jeffersonville, IN 47130 USA Tel 812-282-8832; Fax: 812-282-4057 Do not confuse with companies with the same or similar name in Saint Johnsville, NY, San Marcos, CA, Washington, DC
E-mail: bprintcenter@cs.com.

Sunphone, Ltd., *(978-0-9652458)* 427 Sippewissett Rd., Falmouth, MA 02540 USA Tel 508-540-6899; Fax: 508-540-8226
E-mail: sunfal@aol.com.

Sunraehealing, *(978-0-9896218; 978-0-9908374)* 3906 Cherrywood Rd., Austin, TX 78722 USA Tel 512-547-2454
E-mail: raedoman@hotmail.com.

SunRaSon Production Co., *(978-0-9677644)* 882 E. 57th St., Brooklyn, NY 11234 USA
E-mail: info@sunrason.com
Web site: http://www.sunrason.com.

Sunray Publishing, *(978-1-934478)* 25123 22nd Ave., Saint Cloud, MN 56301 USA Tel 320-253-8808; Fax: 320-253-9683; Toll Free: 888-253-8808
E-mail: jwindschitl@sunrayprinting.com
Web site: http://www.sunrayprinting.com
Dist(s): **Partners Bk. Distributing, Inc.**

Sunrise Bks., *(978-0-940652)* P.O. Box 7003, Eureka, CA 95502-7003 USA (SAN 665-7893) Do not confuse with with companies with the same name in Lebanon, VA, Lake Bluff, IL
E-mail: Sunrise-2004@sbcglobal.net.

Sunrise Mountain Bks., *(978-0-9842362; 978-1-940728)* Div. of Sunrise Services Distributing, LLC, 13347 W. Tapatio Dr., Boise, ID 83713 USA (SAN 858-8139) Fax: 208-938-8338; *Imprints:* Simple Faith Books (SimpleFaith)
Web site: http://www.sunrisemountainbooks.com; http://www.sunrisedistrib.com; http://www.youcandoitart.com.

Sunrise Publications *See* **Prematurely Yours**

SunRise Publishing, *(978-0-9644552; 978-1-57636)* Orders Addr.: P.O. Box 1001, Orem, UT 84059 USA Tel 801-860-2665; Fax: 801-705-0124; Edit Addr.: P.O. Box 1001, Orem, UT 84059-1001 USA Do not confuse with companies with the same or similar names in Lake Forest, IL, Niagara Falls, NY, Lincoln City, OR, Santa Barbara, CA, Hatfield, PA, Maryland Heights, MD, Austinburg, OH, Inman, SC, Fort Lauderdale, FL, Albuquerque, NM
E-mail: brian@sunrisebooks.com
Web site: http://www.sunrisebooks.com
Dist(s): **Granite Publishing & Distribution**
Village Marketing.

Sunrise Publishing Co., *(978-0-9722262; 978-0-615-18943-7)* 1110 N. Sheridan Rd., Lake Forest, IL 60045 USA Tel 847-295-1093; Fax: 847-615-0102 Do not confuse with companies with the same or similar names in Orem, UT, Niagara Falls, NY, Lincoln City, OR, Santa Barbara, CA, Hatfield, PA, Maryland Heights, MD, Austinburg, OH, Inman, SC, Fort Lauderdale, FL
E-mail: pat@themcdonnellcompany.com.

Sunrise Selections, *(978-0-9656307)* Orders Addr.: P.O. Box 51602, Provo, UT 84605-1602 USA Tel 801-852-6141; Fax: 801-489-9517; Edit Addr.: 1102 N. Main, Mapleton, UT 84664 USA
E-mail: bbriggs@provo.utah.gov
Web site: http://www.sunrise-selections.com
Dist(s): **Granite Publishing & Distribution.**

SunriseHouse Pubs., *(978-0-9770783)* 5181 Blackpool Rd., Westminster, CA 92683 USA
E-mail: dawn@dawnwilliams.net
Web site: http://www.sunrisehousepublishers.com.

Sunseri, Heather, *(978-0-9887153; 978-1-943165)* P.O. Box 1264, Versailles, KY 40383 USA
E-mail: heather@heathersunseri.com.

Sunset Beach Music, *(978-0-9639279)* P.O. Box 159, Haleiwa, HI 96712 USA
E-mail: msmusic@hula.net.

Sunset Readers Publishing, *(978-0-9749333)* 220 W., 400 N., American Fork, UT 84003-1567 USA
E-mail: beb1@sisna.com
Web site: http://www.bennettbracken.com.

Sunshine Bks. for Children, *(978-0-9745116)* 8127 E. Weldon Ave., Scottsdale, AZ 85251 USA.

Sunshine Center, Incorporated *See* **Prevention Through Puppetry, Inc.**

Sunshine In My Soul Publishing, *(978-1-68327)* 7380 Park Ridge Blvd. No. 124, San Diego, CA 92120 USA (SAN 990-0969) Tel 619-788-9612
E-mail: admin@speedypublishing.com; bowe@sunshineinmysoulpublishing.com.

Sunshine Publishing, *(978-0-9749844)* 1421 Washington St., Lincoln, NE 68502-2455 USA Do not confuse with companies with the same or similar names in Carthage, NY, Buffalo Grove, IL, Bristol, TN, Columbus, GA, Raleigh, NC, Ft Worth, TX.

Sunshine53 Pr., *(978-0-9855233)* 18008 NW Sylvania Ln., Portland, OR 97229 USA Tel 503-747-2658
E-mail: coryell5150@comcast.net.

SunSprouts *Imprint of* **ETA hand2mind**

Sunstar Publishing *Imprint of* **1st World Publishing, Inc.**

†Sunstone Pr., *(978-0-86534; 978-0-913270; 978-1-61139; 978-1-63293)* Div. of The Sunstone Corporation, Orders Addr.: 239 Johnson St., Santa Fe, NM 87504-2321 USA; Edit Addr.: P.O. Box 2321, Santa Fe, NM 87504-2321 USA (SAN 214-2090) Tel 505-988-4418; Fax: 505-988-1025; Toll Free: 800-243-5644 (Orders Only); *Imprints:* Blackbirch Press, Incorporated (Blackbirch Pr)
E-mail: jsmith@sunstonepress.com
Web site: http://www.sunstonepress.com
Dist(s): **Brodart Co.**
Lightning Source, Inc.
New Leaf Distributing Co., Inc.
Quality Bks., Inc.
Rio Nuevo Pubs.; *CIP.*

Suny Pr. *Imprint of* **State Univ. of New York Pr.**

Super Dentists, The, *(978-0-9798506)* 2226 Otay Lakes Rd., Chula Vista, CA 91915 USA (SAN 854-5650)
Web site: http://www.thesuperdentists.com.

Super Duper Pubns., *(978-1-58650; 978-1-60723)* Div. of Super Duper, Inc., Orders Addr.: P.O. Box 24997, Greenville, SC 29616 USA Tel 864-288-3536; Fax: 864-288-3380; Toll Free: 800-277-8737; Edit Addr.: 5201 Pelham Rd., Greenville, SC 29615-5723 USA
E-mail: lgranger@superduperinc.com
Web site: http://www.superduperinc.com; http://www.handyhandouts.com; http://www.hearbuilder.com; http://www.superduperlearning.com.

Super SandCastle *Imprint of* **ABDO Publishing Co.**

Super Smart Science Stuff, *(978-0-9843848; 978-0-9911472; 978-1-941775)* 5813 Anselm Ct, Austin, TX 78739-7873 USA Tel 512-203-6919; Fax: 512-288-0208
E-mail: april@supersmartsciencestuff.com.

Super Source The *Imprint of* **ETA hand2mind**

SuperKids Nutrition Inc., *(978-0-9801148)* 375 S. Grand Oaks Ave., Pasadena, CA 91107 USA (SAN 855-2436) Tel 626-818-6299
E-mail: melissa@superkidsnutrition.com
Web site: http://www.superkidsnutrition.com.

Supreme Art, *(978-1-942912)* 6425 Reseda Blvd., Reseda, CA 91335 USA Tel 818-438-9779
E-mail: info@supremeart.org
Web site: www.supremeArt.org.

Supreme Design, LLC, *(978-0-9816170; 978-1-935721)* P.O. Box 10887, Atlanta, GA 30310 USA Tel 404-759-8799
E-mail: sujandass@ymail.com
Web site: http://www.supremedesignllc.com.

SuProCo, *(978-0-9906567)* 1300 Army Navy Dr. No. 1101, Arlington, VA 22202 USA Tel 703-271-8889
E-mail: SuProCo@aol.com.

Surber, Shawn-Michelle *See* **Mornin' Light Media**

Surface Communications LLC *See* **Books by Kids LLC**

Surfing Group, The, *(978-0-9770730)* Primedia, 236 Avenida Fabricante. Ste. 201, San Clemente, CA 92672-7557 USA
E-mail: ross.garrett@primedia.com.

Sur-Mount Pubs., *(978-0-9673517; 978-0-9740107)* P.O. Box 99396, Emeryville, CA 94662-9396 USA Tel 510-559-8797
E-mail: cs@surmountpublishersincorporated.com; sales@surmountpublishersincorporated.com
Web site: http://www.surmountpublishersincorporated.com.

Suromex, Ediciones, S.A. (MEX) *(978-968-855) Dist. by* **Giron Bks.**

Susaeta Ediciones, S.A. (ESP) *(978-84-305; 978-84-677) Dist. by* **Lectorum Pubns.**

Susaeta Ediciones, S.A. (ESP) *(978-84-305; 978-84-677) Dist. by* **IPG Chicago.**

Susaeta Ediciones, S.A. (ESP) *(978-84-305; 978-84-677) Dist. by* **AIMS Intl.**

Susaeta Ediciones, S.A. (ESP) *(978-84-305; 978-84-677) Dist. by* **Giron Bks.**

Susan Palavics Publishing, *(978-0-692-78458-7)* 51760 Becker Rd., Bigfork, MN 56628 USA Tel 218-743-3458
E-mail: thewildernesslodge1@gmail.com.

Susi B. Marketing, Inc., *(978-0-9773653)* 188 Wentworth St., Charleston, SC 29401 USA Tel 843-822-7676; Fax: 843-958-8444
Web site: http://www.angietheant.com.

Susquehanna Univ. Pr., *(978-0-941664; 978-0-945636; 978-1-57591)* Affil. of Associated Univ. Presses, Orders Addr.: 2010 Eastpark Blvd., Cranbury, NJ 08512 USA Tel 609-655-4770; Fax: 609-655-8366
Web site: http://www.susqu.edu/su_press
Dist(s): **Associated Univ. Presses**
Rowman & Littlefield Publishers, Inc.
ebrary, Inc.

Sussman Sales Co., *(978-0-9755367; 978-1-934211; 978-1-61717; 978-1-68265)* 250 E. 54th St. Suite 8A, New York, NY 10022 USA Toll Free Fax: 212-371-8882; Toll Free: 800-350-7180
E-mail: info@sussmansales.com
Web site: http://www.sussmansales.com.

Susy Dorn Productions, LLC, *(978-0-9764010)* P.O. Box 111393, Campbell, CA 95011-1393 USA
Web site: http://www.juguemosenespanol.com.

Sutton, Robin, *(978-0-9755098)* P.O. Box 79174, Saginaw, TX 76179 USA
Web site: http://www.therobinsnestbooks.com.

Suzalooz Pr., *(978-0-9660350)* 139 S. Eighth St., Brooklyn, NY 11211 USA Tel 718-387-3384; Fax: 212-475-4442
E-mail: zhour@inx.net.

Suzeteo Enterprises *See* **Athanatos Publishing Group**

Suzuki *Imprint of* **Alfred Publishing Co., Inc.**

Susy & Livy Pubns., *(978-0-9727757)* Orders Addr.: P.O. Box 449, Virginia City, NV 89440 USA Tel 775-847-0454; Fax: 775-847-9010; Edit Addr.: 111 S. C St., Virginia City, NV 89440-0449 USA
E-mail: info@marktwainbooks.com
Web site: http://www.marktwainbooks.com.

Svoboda, David *See* **BooksbyDave Inc.**

†Swallow Pr., *(978-0-8040)* Ohio Univ. Pr., Scott Quadrangle, Athens, OH 45701 USA (SAN 202-5663) Tel 740-593-1158; Fax: 740-593-4536; Toll Free: 800-621-2736
E-mail: arnold@ohio.edu
Web site: http://www.ohio~.edu/oupress/
Dist(s): **Chicago Distribution Ctr.**
Ohio Univ. Pr.
Univ. of Chicago Pr.
ebrary, Inc.; *CIP.*

Swampland Publishing Co., *(978-0-9754785)* P.O. Box 1311, Larose, LA 70373 USA
E-mail: alces@cajunswampland.com.

Swan Creek Pr., *(978-0-9753216)* 3736 Linden Green Dr., Toledo, OH 43614 USA Tel 419-381-0115
E-mail: swancreekpress@buckeye-express.com
Dist(s): **Lightning Source, Inc.**

Swan Hill Pr. (GBR) *(978-1-84037; 978-1-85310; 978-0-906393; 978-0-9504543; 978-1-904057) Dist. by* **IPG Chicago.**

Swan-Jones Production, *(978-1-882238)* 8362 San Cristobal Dr., Dallas, TX 75218 USA Tel 214-319-7049.

Swannee Rivers *See* **Rivers, Swannee**

Swanson, David, *(978-0-9830830; 978-0-9980859)* 707 Gillespie Ave., Charlottesville, VA 22902 USA Tel 434-296-4228
E-mail: david@davidswanson.org.

SWC Editions *Imprint of* **Wayne, Steven Co.**

Sweden Trade, Inc., *(978-0-9744088)* 9-11 South Blvd. of Presidents, Sarasota, FL 34236 USA; *Imprints:* Sweden Trade Publishing (Sweden Trd Pub)
Web site: http://TheRoadToHappinessBook.com.

Sweden Trade Publishing *Imprint of* **Sweden Trade, Inc.**

Swedenborg Foundation, Inc., *(978-0-87785)* 320 N. Church St., West Chester, PA 19380 USA (SAN 111-7920) Tel 610-430-3222; Fax: 610-430-7982
E-mail: editor@swedenborg.com
Web site: http://www.swedenborg.com
Dist(s): **Chicago Distribution Ctr.**

Sweet 76 Bakery, *(978-0-615-80672-3)* 8709 58th Ave. SW Apt. D, Lakewood, WA 98499 USA Tel 253-205-1373
E-mail: dineensmith@yahoo.com.

Sweet Grin Bks., *(978-0-9905402)* 1305 SE 3rd St., Cape Coral, FL 33990 USA Tel 239-478-0255
E-mail: befranz@yahoo.com.

Sweet, Joanne, *(978-0-9774881)* 228 Westin Hls., New Braunfels, TX 78132-2328 USA.

Sweet, Joanne, *(978-1-936660)* 228 Westin Hills, New Braunfels, TX 78132 USA Tel 830-624-4560
E-mail: store1@jhsweet.com
Web site: www.jhsweet.com.

Sweet Potato Brown, *(978-0-9788158)* Orders Addr.: 5208 S. Drexel Ave., 2w, Chicago, IL 60615 USA Tel 773-752-3521
E-mail: sofiapenelopebrown@sbcglobal.net
Web site: http://www.at3619.com
Dist(s): **Lulu Pr., Inc.**

Sweet Punkin Pr., *(978-0-9755078)* 43 Riverside Ave., No. 405, Medford, MA 02155-4605 USA Tel 781-389-0693; Fax: 781-396-8052
E-mail: cvenez@aol.com
Web site: http://www.sweetpunkinpress.com.

Sweet Spot Publishing, *(978-0-9907739; 978-0-9863890)* 11370 Twelve Oaks Way, North Palm Beach, FL 33408 USA Tel 561-818-6700
E-mail: d.abis77@gmail.com.

Publisher Name Index

Sweet Success Pr., *(978-0-9700127)* P.O. Box 351564, Westminster, CO 80035-1564 USA
E-mail: Vkrudwig@aol.com
Web site: http://www.members.aol.com/vkrudwig
Dist(s): **Bks. West.**

Sweetbriar Crafts & Pubns., *(978-0-9802015)* 3390 40th St., Mandan, ND 58554 USA Tel 701-663-6941
E-mail: swcandp@gmail.com.

Sweetgrass Bks. *Imprint of* **Farcountry Pr.**

Sweetwater Bks. *Imprint of* **Cedar Fort, Inc./CFI Distribution**

Sweetwater Pr., *(978-1-58173; 978-1-889372; 978-1-60196)* Div. of Books-A-Million, Orders Addr.: 3608 Clairmont Ave., Birmingham, AL 035222 USA Do not confuse with companies with the same name in Ault, CO, Raleigh, NC Miami FL, Little Rock AR
Dist(s): **Independent Pubs. Group.**

Sweetwater Stagelines *Imprint of* **Old West Co., The**

Swift Learning Resources, *(978-0-944991; 978-1-56861)* Div. of Swift Printing Corp., 1520 N. State St., Lehi, UT 84043-1079 USA (SAN 245-6737) Toll Free: 800-292-2831
E-mail: swift@swift-net.com
Web site: http://www.swiftlearning.com.

Swingset Pr., LLC, *(978-0-9658167; 978-1-930680)* Orders Addr.: P.O. Box 18701, Encino, CA 91416-8701 USA Tel 818-779-1413; Fax: 818-779-1411; Toll Free: 888-543-9966; Edit Addr.: 5987 S. High Dr., Morrison, CO 80465-2608 USA
E-mail: info@swingsetpress.com
Web site: http://www.swingsetpress.com.

Swiss Creek Pubns., *(978-0-9702276)* Orders Addr.: 15565 Swiss Creek Ln., Cupertino, CA 95014-5452 USA Tel 408-741-5809; Fax: 408-741-5231
E-mail: bob@zeidman.net
Web site: http://www.zeidman.net.

Switch Pr., *(978-1-63079)* Div. of Capstone Publishers, Orders Addr.: 1710 Roe Crest Dr., North Mankato, MN 56003 USA; Edit Addr.: 5050 Lincoln Dr., Edina, MN 55436 USA Tel 952-224-0558.

Switzer Land Enterprises, *(978-0-9642663)* Orders Addr.: P.O. Box 3800, Estes Park, CO 80517 USA Tel 303-586-4624; Fax: 907-577-0775; Edit Addr.: 1236 Glacier View, Estes Park, CO 80517 USA
E-mail: philalpaca@aol.com.

Sword of the Lord Pubs., *(978-0-87398)* Orders Addr.: P.O. Box 1099, Murfreesboro, TN 37133 USA (SAN 203-5642) Tel 615-893-6700; Fax: 615-895-7447
E-mail: cpenland@swordofthelord.com
Web site: http://www.swordbooks.com/; http://www.swordofthelord.com/
Dist(s): **Dake Publishing.**

Sword of the Spirit Publishing, *(978-0-615-20617-2; 978-0-615-20810-7; 978-0-615-21223-4; 978-0-615-21437-5; 978-0-615-22183-0; 978-0-615-22348-3; 978-0-615-24292-7; 978-0-578-01560-6; 978-0-578-03282-5; 978-0-9825870; 978-0-9838836; 978-1-939219)* Orders Addr.: 219 Lakewood Dr., Crossville, TN 38558 USA Tel 931-287-0280
E-mail: scaramouche9999@yahoo.com
Web site: http://www.swordofspirit.net
Dist(s): **Lulu Pr., Inc.**
Send The Light Distribution LLC.

Swordfish Communications, LLC, *(978-0-9741955)* Orders Addr.: 1748 Ohlen Rd. #67, Austin, TX 78757 USA
E-mail: orders@swordfishcommunications.com
Web site: http://www.swordfishcommunications.com.

Sy Publishing, *(978-0-9761613)* 7720 E. Redfield Rd., Suite No. 7, Scottsdale, AZ 85260 USA Tel 480-596-9226; Fax: 480-967-8736
E-mail: devinsper@yahoo.com
Web site: http://www.devinsper.com.

Sybertooth, Inc. (CAN) *(978-0-9688024; 978-0-9739505; 978-0-9810244; 978-0-9864974; 978-1-927592) Dist. by* **LightSource CS.**

Sycuan Pr., *(978-0-9790951)* 5401 Sycuan Rd., El Cajon, CA 92019 USA Tel 619-445-6917; Fax: 619-445-5176
E-mail: jbathke@sycuan.org.

Sydney Pr., LLC, *(978-0-9724577)* Orders Addr.: 2035 Fanning Ct., Leland, NC 28451 USA Tel 910-632-7778
E-mail: buckaloha@gmail.com.

Syentek Books Company, Incorporated *See* **Syentek, Inc.**

Syentek, Inc., *(978-0-914082)* P.O. Box 26588, San Francisco, CA 94126 USA (SAN 202-7534) Tel 415-928-0471.

Sylables, *(978-0-9724394)* 2105 Sheldon Rd., Saint Albans, VT 05478 USA (SAN 255-1500) Tel 802-524-0262
E-mail: sylables@earthlink.net
Web site: http://www.sylables.com.

Syllabets, LLC, *(978-0-9794543)* 3740 30th Ave. S., Suite 307, Grand Forks, ND 58201-5820 USA (SAN 853-4632)
Web site: http://www.syllabets.com.

Syllogism Pr., *(978-0-9638001)* 875 Emory Shield Rd., Murphy, NC 28906 USA Tel 732-290-7901
E-mail: spress@dnet.net.

Sylph Pubns., *(978-0-9673004; 978-0-9760742)* 1248 E. Edison St., W., Tucson, AZ 85719 USA Tel 520-882-3794
E-mail: eliotbooks@aol.com
Web site: http://www.eliotbooks.com.

Sylvan Dell Publishing *See* **Arbordale Publishing**

Sylvan Learning Publishing *Imprint of* **Random Hse. Children's Bks.**

Sylvestre, Gibson Publishing, *(978-0-615-21166-4; 978-0-578-01878-2; 978-0-578-01879-9; 978-0-578-03784-4; 978-0-578-04150-6)* P.O. Box 934741, Margate, FL 33093 USA
E-mail: info@mylifeonpurpose.org
Web site: http://www.mylifeonpurpose.org.

Symmetry Learning Systems, *(978-1-58447)* Div. of Symmetry Research, Inc., 5 Bretton Rd., Dover, MA 02030 USA (SAN 299-7967)
E-mail: info@symmetrylearning.com; prberget@symmetrylearning.com
Web site: http://www.symmetrylearning.com.

Symtalk, Inc., *(978-1-932770; 978-1-933209)* 875 Montreal Way, Saint Paul, MN 55102-4245 USA Toll Free: 877-796-8255
E-mail: info@symtalk.com
Web site: http://www.symtalk.com.

Symtext Media, *(978-0-9768379)* 21538 N. 65th Ave., Glendale, AZ 85308-6410 USA Tel 623-362-1947
E-mail: fullschedule@symtextmedia.com
Web site: http://www.symtextmedia.com.

Synapse, Edition (JPN) *(978-4-901481; 978-4-931444; 978-4-86166) Dist. by* **Taylor and Fran.**

Synaptic Wammy Works *See* **Loose In The Lab**

Synaxis Pr., *(978-0-911523)* P.O. Box 689, Lynden, WA 98264 USA (SAN 685-4338) Tel 604-826-9336; Fax: 604-820-9758.

Syndistar, Inc., *(978-1-56230)* P.O. Box 3027, Hammond, LA 70404-3027 USA (SAN 298-007X) Toll Free: 800-841-9532
E-mail: webmaster@syndistar.com
Web site: http://www.syndistar.com.

SynergEbks., *(978-1-929017; 978-0-7443; 978-0-9702385; 978-1-931540)* Orders Addr.: 948 New Hwy 7, Columbia, TN 38401 USA (SAN 254-4962) Tel 931-548-2494
E-mail: synergebooks@aol.com
Web site: http://www.synergebooks.com; http://www.yourspecs.media.

Synergetic Pubns., Inc., *(978-0-9632248)* Orders Addr.: P.O. Box 1506, Hendersonville, TN 37075 USA (SAN 297-6129) Tel 615-264-3405; Edit Addr.: 205 Applewood Valley Dr., Hendersonville, TN 37075 USA.

SYP Kids *Imprint of* **Southern Yellow Pine (SYP) Publishing LLC**

†Syracuse Univ. Pr., *(978-0-8156; 978-0-615-28768-3; 978-1-68445)* 621 Skytop Rd., Suite 110, Syracuse, NY 13244-5290 USA (SAN 206-9776) Tel 315-443-5534; Fax: 315-443-5545
E-mail: supress@syr.edu; arpfeiff@syr.edu
Web site: http://www.SyracuseUniversityPress.syr.edu
Dist(s): **Gryphon Hse., Inc.**
Longleaf Services
ebrary, Inc.; *CIP.*

Syren Bk. Co., *(978-0-929636)* Orders Addr.: 5120 Cedar Lake Rd., S., Minneapolis, MN 55416 USA (SAN 249-7719) Tel 763-398-0030; Fax: 763-398-0198; Toll Free: 800-901-3480 Do not confuse with BookMobile in Port Ludlow WA
E-mail: dleeper@bookmobile.com; jogren@bookmobile.com
Web site: http://www.itascabooks.com
Dist(s): **BookMobile**
Itasca Bks.

SYS Publishing, *(978-0-9794871)* P.O. Box 868, Montclair, NJ 07042 USA Tel 973-951-7490; 2142 Blackwolf Run Ln., Raleigh, NC 27604 Toll Free: 800-994-3683
E-mail: SYSPublishing@aol.com
Web site: http://www.sadieshero.com.

Systems Group, Inc., The, *(978-0-9847740)* 4618 Granite Rock Ct., Chantilly, VA 20151 USA Tel 703-378-4193
E-mail: Oliver.Franklin@verizon.net.

Szydlowski, Mary Vigliante, *(978-0-9965622; 978-0-9983869)* 37 Normanside Dr., Albany, NY 12208 USA Tel 518-453-3613
E-mail: maszyd@aol.com
Web site: http://www.maryviglianteszydlowski.com/.

†TAB Bks., Div. of The McGraw-Hill Cos., 11 W. 19th St., New York, NY 10011 USA (SAN 202-568X)
E-mail: bookstore@mcgraw-hill.com; customer.service@mcgraw-hill.com
Web site: http://www.mcgraw-hill.com/; *CIP.*

T. A. S. Enterprises, Incorporated *See* **Lit Torch Publishing**

T & T Roberts Publishing, *(978-0-9723868)* 3105 S. Trenton Cir., Sioux Falls, SD 57103 USA
E-mail: tom.roberts@chssd.org
Web site: http://www.chssd.org/books.

TBM, Inc., *(978-0-9647096)* 280 N. Latah St., Boise, ID 83706 USA Tel 208-853-0555; Fax: 208-383-9010; 9295 Esterbrook, Boise, ID 83703
E-mail: realbows@aol.com
Web site: http://www.tradbow.com.

TCR Pr., *(978-0-9714465)* P.O. Box 12011, Raleigh, NC 27605 USA
E-mail: newplants@angelfire.com
Web site: http://www.tcrpress.com.

T. E. Publishing, Inc., *(978-0-9722036)* P.O. Box 823, Bath, NY 14810 USA Tel 607-76-1307
E-mail: pcarlton@tepublishing.com.

THINC Corp., *(978-0-9655026)* Orders Addr.: P.O. Box 14, Batesville, MS 38606 USA Tel 601-563-1162; Fax: 601-563-6640; Toll Free: 888-837-7606; Edit Addr.: 150 Hwy. 35 N., Batesville, MS 38606 USA.

TM Photography, Inc., *(978-0-9660144)* 82 King St., Charleston, SC 29401 USA Tel 843-577-3237.

T.Y.M. Publishing, *(978-0-9641274)* 409 Melville Ave., Palo Alto, CA 94301 USA Tel 415-325-1130.

Tabby Hse. Bks., *(978-0-9627974; 978-1-881539)* Orders Addr.: P.O. Box 544, Mineral, VA 23117 USA Tel 540-895-9093 (phone/fax); Edit Addr.: 12004 Sycamore Shoals Dr. Bumpass, Va 23034, Bumpass, VA 23024 USA; *Imprints:* Strathmoor (Strathmoor)
E-mail: tabbyhouse@gmail.com; publisher@tabbyhouse.com
Web site: http://www.tabbyhouse.com
Dist(s): **Distributors, The.**

Taberah Pr. *Imprint of* **Sonfire Media, LLC**

Table Rock Bks., *(978-0-9726869)* 69 Woodland Ave., Smithfield, RI 02917 USA.

Tabor Pr., *(978-0-9745799)* Orders Addr.: P.O. Box 470842, Brookline Village, MA 02447 USA Tel 617-784-6561; Edit Addr.: 278 Warren St., Brookline, MA 02445 USA
E-mail: ephraim541@hotmail.com.

Tackett, Viti, *(978-0-9769963)* 85 Pond St., Cabot, AR 72023-3741 USA Toll Free: 877-518-9575.

Tacoma Historical Society, *(978-0-9846234)* P.O. Box 1865, Tacoma, WA 98401 USA Tel 253-472-3738
E-mail: info@tacomahistory.org
Web site: www.tacomahistory.org.

Tadpole Pr. 4 Kids *Imprint of* **Smooth Sailing Pr., LLC**

TAE Nazca Resources, *(978-0-9749745)* P.O. Box 7592, Broomfield, CO 80021 USA
E-mail: anitajg5@aol.com
Web site: http://www.nazcaresources.com
Dist(s): **Mountain Bk. Co.**

Taffey Pop Kids Publishing, *(978-0-9771438)* Div. of Taffey Pop Kids Educational Services LLC, Orders Addr.: P.O. Box 571973, Dallas, TX 75357-1973 USA Tel 214-434-9024
E-mail: info@taffeyhpopkids.org
Web site: http://www.taffeypopkids.org.

TAG Publishing, LLC, *(978-1-934606)* Orders Addr.: P.O. Box 8975, Amarillo, TX 79109 USA (SAN 853-9251); Edit Addr.: 2618 Lipscomb, Amarillo, TX 79109 USA Do not confuse with companies with the same name in Hanover, VA, Camerillo, CA
E-mail: deaitra@suddenlink.net
Web site: http://www.tagbookpublishing.com.

Tahrike Tarsile Quran, Inc., *(978-0-940368; 978-1-879402)* 80-08 51st Ave., Elmhurst, NY 11373 USA (SAN 658-1870) Tel 718-446-6472; Fax: 718-446-4370
E-mail: read@koranusa.org
Web site: http://www.koranusa.org
Dist(s): **BookBaby**
Publishers Group West (PGW).

Tai Chi Chuan Center of New York *See* **Sunflower Pr.**

Taiji Arts Publishing, *(978-0-9728192)* 50 Bates Rd., Hillsborough, CA 94010-7016 USA
E-mail: ben@TaijiArts.com
Web site: http://www.TaijiArts.com
Dist(s): **China Books & Periodicals, Inc.**

Tail Wagging Productions, *(978-0-9752887)* P.O. Box 1357, Brea, CA 92822-1357 USA
E-mail: contact@tailwaggingproductions.us
Web site: http://www.tailwaggingproductions.us.

Tailwind Press, *(978-0-9799473)* 58 Brookshire Dr., Warrenton, VA 20186-3033 USA
E-mail: loribakewell@gmail.com.

Taj Bks. International LLC, *(978-1-62732)* 219 Great Lake Dr., Cary, NC 27519 USA Tel 919-650-1719; *Imprints:* Bellagio Press (BellagioPr)
E-mail: suneel@tajbooks.com
Dist(s): **Casemate Pubs. & Bk. Distributors, LLC**
MyiLibrary.

Takahashi & Black, *(978-0-9723247)* Orders Addr.: 8725 Roswell Rd., Suite 0-129, Atlanta, GA 30350 USA; *Imprints:* PB&J OmniMedia (PB&J)
E-mail: orders@pbjomnimedia.com; credit@pbjomnimedia.com; returns@pbjomnimedia.com; domo@takahashiblack.com
Web site: http://www.pbjomnimedia.com
Dist(s): **Book Wholesalers, Inc.**
Brodart Co.

Takatuka (ESP) *(978-84-936766; 978-84-16003; 978-84-92696) Dist. by* **Lectorum Pubns.**

Take Charge Books *See* **Take Charge Bks.**

Take Charge Bks., *(978-0-9815818; 978-0-9883866; 978-0-9961589; 978-0-9982658)* 392 Sunny Acre Ln., Brevard, NC 28712 USA Tel 828-883-5695
E-mail: kathleen@kathleenbarnes.com
Web site: http://www.kathleenbarnes.com
Dist(s): **BookBaby.**

Take Five Pubs., *(978-0-930099)* P.O. Box 1094, Arlington, IL 60006 USA (SAN 670-1884) Tel 847-253-4370
E-mail: m.shaughnessy@comcast.net.

Take2CreativeStorywriters, *(978-0-9982801)* 161 W. Hanford Armona Rd Suite 133, Lemoore, CA 93245 USA Tel 559-696-0401
E-mail: r.rose@take2creativestorywriters.com; roxyrvt@gmail.com
Web site: www.take2creativestorywriters.com.

Takhar's, Jodi Spilt Milk Collection, *(978-1-886000)* Orders Addr.: P.O. Box 1005, Bemidji, MN 56601 USA Tel 218-759-2089; Fax: 218-759-2088; Edit Addr.: 403 4th St., NW, No. 200, Bemidji, MN 56601 USA.

Taking Grades Publishing Co., *(978-1-934538)* 1110 4th St., Dr., S.E., Conover, NC 28613-1825 USA Tel 866-511-8378; Fax: 828-466-0025; Toll Free: 866-511-8378
E-mail: takinggrades@charter.net
Web site: http://www.takinggrades.com
Dist(s): **Follett School Solutions.**

Taku Graphics, *(978-0-9717820; 978-0-9772297; 978-0-9801616; 978-0-9823450; 978-0-9846318; 978-0-9899679)* 5763 Glacier Hwy., Juneau, AK 99801 USA Tel 907-780-6310; Fax: 907-780-6314; Toll Free: 800-278-3291
E-mail: adele@takugraphics.com
Web site: http://www.takugraphics.com.

Talaris Research Institute, *(978-0-9742761; 978-0-615-40953-5)* P.O. Box 45040, Seattle, WA 98145 USA Tel 206-859-5604; Fax: 206-859-5699
E-mail: tinam@talaris.org
Web site: http://www.talaris.org.

Ta-La-Vue Pub., *(978-0-9797521)* 316 Rowan Alley, Apt. 6, Pottstown, PA 19464 USA (SAN 854-2376).

Tale Weaver Pr., *(978-0-692-66880-1)* 10942 Canyon Mesa Ln., San Diego, CA 92126 USA Tel 619-200-3836
E-mail: lisadavis92127@gmail.com.

Talented *See* **Cantemos-bilingual bks. and music**

Tales Alive *See* **Words & Music**

Talicor, Inc., *(978-1-57057; 978-0-9674871)* 901 Lincoln Pkwy., Plainwell, MI 49080 USA (SAN 253-0406) Tel 269-685-2345; Fax: 269-685-6789; Toll Free: 800-433-4263
E-mail: webmaster@talicor.com; orders@talicor.com
Web site: http://www.talicor.com.

Talisman Pr., *(978-0-9670848)* 7036 Lyndale Cir., Elk Grove, CA 95758 USA Tel 916-683-1749
E-mail: talismanpress@aol.com.

TALK, *(978-0-9741182)* Orders Addr.: P.O. Box 9226, Peoria, IL 61612 USA Tel 309-224-9665; Edit Addr.: 5001 N. Big Hollow Rd., Peoria, IL 61615 USA Tel 309-694-5444
E-mail: dsymo92699@aol.com
Web site: http://www.doristalk.com.

TALKAIDS, Inc., *(978-0-9659046)* Orders Addr.: P.O. Box 112, New York, NY 10113 USA Tel 212-465-2646; Fax: 212-675-7291; Edit Addr.: 305 W. 13th St., 1K, New York, NY 10014 USA
E-mail: talkaids@aol.com.

Talking Crow Publishing, *(978-0-9860287)* P.O. Box 1356, Haines, AK 99827 USA.

Talking Drum Pr., Ltd., *(978-0-9662428)* Div. of Oversoul Theater Collective, Inc., P.O. Box 190028, Roxbury, MA 02119 USA
E-mail: talkingdrumpress@gmail.com.

Talking Drum Press/OTC, Incorporated *See* **Talking Drum Pr., Ltd.**

Talking Hands, Incorporated *See* **Time to Sign, Incorporated**

TalkTools/Innovative Therapists International, *(978-1-932460; 978-0-9979204)* 2209 Mechanic St., Charleston, SC 29405 USA Tel 843-789-3672; Fax: 843-206-0590; Toll Free: 888-529-2879
E-mail: info@talktools.com
Web site: http://www.talktools.com.

Tall Tails Publishing Hse., *(978-0-9823519)* 902 Arlington Box 113, Ada, OK 74820 USA (SAN 857-9288)
E-mail: talltailspublishing@gmail.com
Web site: http://www.talltailspublishing.com.

Tall Tales, *(978-0-9973641; 978-0-9979540; 978-1-947543)* P.O. Box 1262, Lynnwood, WA 98046 USA Tel 425-744-0580
E-mail: kizeliz@gmail.com
Web site: www.kizziejones.com.

Tall Through Bks., *(978-0-9744549)* P.O. Box 6723, Virginia Beach, VA 23456 USA Tel 757-635-6174; Fax: 757-563-8277
E-mail: tallthroughbooks@aol.com
Web site: http://www.tallthroughbooks.com.

Tallfellow Pr., *(978-0-9676061; 978-1-931290)* 9454 Wilshire Blvd. Ste. 550, Beverly Hills, CA 90212-2905 USA; *Imprints:* Smallfellow Press (Smallfellow Pr)
E-mail: Tallfellow@pacbell.net
Web site: http://TallfellowPress.com
Dist(s): **Parklane Publishing**
SCB Distributors.

Tallulah & Bear (GBR) *(978-0-9559752) Dist. by* **LuluCom.**

Talmage Publishing, *(978-0-9773010)* 4820 Strack Rd., Houston, TX 77069 USA (SAN 257-2370) Tel 281-440-1106.

Talonbooks, Ltd. (CAN) *(978-0-88922) Dist. by* **Consort Bk Sales.**

Tamaja Pr., *(978-0-9841260; 978-0-9863753)* Div. of Arteees / Tamaja, Orders Addr.: P.O. Box 3796, Gulfport, MS 39505 USA; Edit Addr.: Gloria Tillman 11111 Highland No. 315 Gulfport, MS 39503, Gulfport, MS 39505 USA
E-mail: tam3artees@yahoo.com.

Tameme, Inc., *(978-0-9674093)* 199 First St. Suite 335, Los Altos, CA 94022 USA Tel 650-941-2037; Fax: 650-941-5338
E-mail: Sales@tameme.org
Web site: http://www.tameme.org.

Tamerac Publishing, *(978-0-9621292)* 402 Conestoga Dr., Moscow, ID 83843 USA (SAN 250-9466) Tel 208-883-7761
Web site: www.tameracpub.com
Dist(s): **Lightning Source, Inc.**

Tamerac Publishing Company *See* **Tamerac Publishing**

Tamos Bks., Inc. (CAN) *(978-1-895569) Dist. by* **Sterling.**

TAN Bks., *(978-0-89555; 978-0-911845; 978-0-9675978; 978-1-930873; 978-1-939094)* Div. of Saint Benedict Press, LLC, 13315 Carowinds Blvd Suite Q, Charlotte, NC 28273 USA; *Imprints:* Neumann Press (Neumann NC)
E-mail: rick@tanbooks.com; mara@tanbooks.com
Web site: https://tanbooks.com/; https://neumann.benedictpress.com/
Dist(s): **BookMasters, Inc.**
Bookmasters Distribution
Saint Benedict Pr.

Tana Lake Publishing, *(978-0-9651007)* P.O. Box 44595, Fort Washington, MD 20749 USA Tel 301-292-3636; P.O. Box P.O. Box 44595, Fort Washington, MD 20749
E-mail: xnate333@aol.com
Web site: http://www.tanalakepublishing.com
Dist(s): **Evanston Publishing, Inc.**

T&N Children's Publishing, *(978-1-55971; 978-1-58728)* Div. of Rowman & Littlefield Publishing Group, Orders Addr.: 8500 Normandale Lake Blvd., Minneapolis, MN 55437-3813 USA Toll Free: 888-255-9989; Fulfillment Addr.: SDS-12-2462, P.O. Box 86, Minneapolis, MN 55486-2462 USA; *Imprints:* NorthWord Books for Young Readers (NrthWrd Bks); Two-Can Publishing (TCan Pubng)
E-mail: sales@tnkidsbooks.com
Web site: http://www.tnkidsbooks.com
Dist(s): **Follett School Solutions**
National Bk. Network.

Tandora's Box Pr., *(978-0-9627337)* Orders Addr.: P.O. Box 8073, Vallejo, CA 94590 USA
E-mail: barbara@tangrammit.com
Web site: http://www.tangrammit.com.

Tangela Publishing, *(978-0-615-18297-1)* 8093 Miller Cir., Arvada, CO 80005 USA
E-mail: a.newell@comcast.net.

Tangerine Pr. *Imprint of* **Scholastic, Inc.**

Tangerine Tide *Imprint of* **Orange Ocean Pr.**

TangleTown Media Inc., *(978-0-9724022)* 713 Minnehaha Ave. E. Suite 210, Saint Paul, MN 55106 USA (SAN 254-8054)
E-mail: todd.berntson@tangletownmedia.com
Web site: http://www.tangletownmedia.com.

Tanglewood Pr., *(978-0-9749303; 978-1-933718; 978-1-939100)* P.O. Box 3009, Terre Haute, IN 47803

USA Do not confuse with Tanglewood Press in Portland, OR, Raleigh, NC
E-mail: ptierney@tanglewoodbooks.com
Web site: http://www.tanglewoodbooks.com
Dist(s): **Lectorum Pubns., Inc.**
MyiLibrary
Publishers Group West (PGW).

Tango Bks. (GBR) *(978-1-85707) Dist. by* **IPG Chicago.**

Tango Latin, *(978-0-9663572)* 325 N. Maple Dr., Beverly Hills, CA 90209 USA Tel 213-381-5820; P.O. Box 16111, Beverly Hills, CA 90209
E-mail: tangomediagroup@yahoo.com.

Tango Publishing International, Incorporated *See* **Tango Latin**

TankerToys, *(978-0-615-16200-3)* 387 C Bergin Dr., Monterey, CA 93940 USA
E-mail: tanker@tankertoys.com
Web site: http://www.tankertoys.com
Dist(s): **Lulu Pr., Inc.**

Tanner, David, *(978-0-9767287; 978-0-578-00817-2)* P.O. Box 140, Avon, CT 06001-0140 USA; 3 David Dr., Simsbury, CT 06070
E-mail: collectiblesodacans@comcast.net
Web site: http://www.collectiblesodacans.com.

Tanner, Matt J., *(978-0-9885253)* 27 Amherst Dr., Basking Ridge, NJ 07920 USA Tel 908-581-9822
E-mail: mtanner07@msn.com.

Tanner, Ralph Assocs., Inc., *(978-0-942078)* P.O. Box 3400, Prescott, AZ 86302-3400 USA (SAN 239-9857).

TanosBooks Publishing, *(978-0-9764666; 978-0-9788520; 978-0-9815522; 978-0-9822543; 978-0-9844865; 978-0-9846540)* 1110 W. 5th St., Coffeyville, KS 67337 USA
Web site: http://www.tanosbookspublishing.com.

Tantan Publishing, 4005 W Olympic Blvd., Los Angeles, CA 90019-3258 USA
Dist(s): **Independent Pubs. Group.**

Tao of Golf *See* **DVTVFilm**

TAOC (AUS) *(978-0-9803455; 978-0-646-46214-1; 978-0-9808435) Dist. by* **Consort Bk Sales.**

TAOH Inspired Education, LLC, *(978-0-9769069)* Orders Addr.: 99 Palatine Rd., Pittsgrove, NJ 08318 USA
E-mail: taohinspirededucation@gmail.com
Web site: http://www.taohinspirededucation.com.

Tapis & Assocs., Inc., *(978-0-9729610; 978-0-9741172)* 1950 N. 6900 E., Croydon, UT 84018-9707 USA Tel 801-829-3295; Fax: 509-984-2718
E-mail: info@tapisinc.com
Web site: http://www.tapisinc.com.

Tapper Records Inc., *(978-0-9747465)* P.O. Box 5241, Hollywood, FL 33083-5241 USA Tel 954-483-5093; Fax: 954-961-9049
E-mail: thespeakingsax@juno.com
Web site: http://www.thespeakingsax.com.

Tapper Seminars *See* **Tapper Records Inc.**

Taqwa Images *See* **Early Rise Pubns.**

Tara Books Agency (IND) *(978-81-85403; 978-81-907546) Dist. by* **PerseuPGW.**

Tara Publishing (IND) *(978-81-86211; 978-81-906756) Dist. by* **Consort Bk Sales.**

Tarbutton Pr., *(978-0-9714086; 978-1-933094)* 951 Snug Harbor St., Salinas, CA 93906 USA (SAN 254-4989) Tel 831-443-5694
E-mail: info@tarbuttonpress.com
Web site: http://www.tarbuttonpress.com
Dist(s): **CreateSpace Independent Publishing Platform**
Lightning Source, Inc.

TarcherPerigee *Imprint of* **Penguin Publishing Group**

targa 7 inc, *(978-0-692-84875-3; 978-0-692-84876-0)* 704 1st Ave. N., safety harbor, FL 34695 USA Tel 727-799-4891
E-mail: patriciastewart@tampabay.rr.com
Web site: www.patbrooksbooks.com.

Targum Pr., Inc., *(978-0-944070; 978-1-56871)* 22700 W. Eleven Mile Rd., Southfield, MI 48034 USA (SAN 242-8997) Tel 248-355-2266; Toll Free Fax: 888-298-9992
E-mail: targum@elronet.co.il
Web site: http://www.targum.com
Dist(s): **Feldheim Pubs.**
Lulu Pr., Inc.
SPD-Small Pr. Distribution.

Targum Press USA Incorporated *See* **Menucha Pubs. Inc.**

TARK Classic Fiction *Imprint of* **Arc Manor**

Tarquin Pubns. (GBR) *(978-0-906212; 978-1-899618; 978-1-907550; 978-1-911093) Dist. by* **Parkwest Pubns.**

Tarver, Monroe, *(978-0-9743568)* 7904 Calibre Crossing Dr. Apt. 205, Charlotte, NC 28227-6781 USA
E-mail: monroetarver@msn.com
Web site: http://www.worldoftarver.com.

TASCHEN (DEU) *(978-3-8228; 978-3-89450; 978-3-8365) Dist. by* **IngramPubServ.**

Tastica, Suanne Creations Inc., *(978-0-9769348)* 1621 25th St., PMB No. 337, San Pedro, CA 90732 USA.

Tasty Minstrel Games, *(978-0-9841558; 978-1-938146; 978-1-947941)* P.O. Box 64794, Tucson, AZ 85728 USA Tel 520-275-8913
E-mail: michael@playtmg.com; daniel@playtmg.com
Web site: http://playtmg.com.

Tate Publishing, Ltd. (GBR) *(978-0-900874; 978-0-905005; 978-1-85437; 978-0-946590; 978-1-84976) Dist. by* **Abrams.**

Tate Publishing, Ltd. (GBR) *(978-0-900874; 978-0-905005; 978-1-85437; 978-0-946590; 978-1-84976) Dist. by* **HachBkGrp.**

Tattered Essence Publishing LLC, *(978-0-9766130)* P.O. Box 290996, Nashville, TN 37229 USA Tel 615-360-6117
E-mail: info@cinderellasrebellion.com
Web site: http://www.tatteredessence.com.

Tau Publishing *See* **Vesuvius Pr. Inc.**

Tau Publishing *Imprint of* **Vesuvius Pr. Inc.**

†Taunton Pr., Inc., *(978-0-918804; 978-0-942391; 978-1-56158; 978-1-60085; 978-1-62113; 978-1-62710; 978-1-63186; 978-1-64155)* 63 S. Main St., P. O. Box 5506, Newtown, CT 06470-5506 USA (SAN 210-5144) Tel 203-426-8171; Fax: 203-426-7184; Toll Free: 800-477-8727 (orders)
E-mail: tt@taunton.com; cmandarano@taunton.com
Web site: http://www.taunton.com
Dist(s): **Ingram Publisher Services**
Linden Publishing Co., Inc.
Simon & Schuster, Inc.; *CIP.*

Tauszik, Karleen, *(978-0-9846830; 978-0-9904899)* 622 Lemonwood Dr., Oldsmar, FL 34677 USA Tel 727-543-4158
E-mail: karleen@karleent.com.

Taven Hill Studio, *(978-0-9765321)* 5214n 325w, LaPorte, IN 46350 USA
E-mail: mhill@mc123.com
Web site: http://www.tavenhill.com.

Tavine'ra Publishing, LLC, *(978-0-9713953)* 270 Doug Baker Blvd Suite 700-316, Birmingham, AL 35242 USA Tel 205-218-7678; Toll Free: 888 234-7256
E-mail: tahiera@gmail.com
Web site: www.tahieramoniquebrown.com.

Tawa Productions, *(978-0-9718741)* Orders Addr.: 2186 Buffalo Dr., Grand Junction, CO 81503 USA
E-mail: information@peopal.com
Web site: http://www.poepal.com.

Tawnsy Publishing, *(978-0-9887612)* 1212 N. Wuthering Hills Dr., Janesville, WI 53546 USA Tel 608-754-2024
E-mail: tawnsy@charter.net.

Tayes Bks., *(978-0-9743207)* Orders Addr.: P.O. Box 50973, Fort Myers, FL 33994-0973 USA; Edit Addr.: 813 Dellena Ln., Fort Myers, FL 33905 USA
E-mail: tayesbooks@yahoo.com
Web site: http://www.tayesbooks.com.

Tayler Corp., The, *(978-0-9779074; 978-0-9835746; 978-1-945120)* Orders Addr.: 1066 N. 440 W., Orem, UT 84057 USA Tel 801-426-5714
Web site: http://www.schlockmercenary.com.

Taylor & Francis Group (GBR) *(978-0-389; 978-0-7484; 978-0-85066; 978-0-905273; 978-1-85000; 978-1-85728; 978-1-84142; 978-0-901286; 978-1-902653; 978-0-203; 978-1-904350; 978-1-906540; 978-1-905981; 978-1-907975; 978-1-84872; 978-1-907625; 978-1-907747; 978-1-909662; 978-1-134; 978-1-136; 978-1-910887; 978-1-910526) Dist. by* **Taylor and Fran.**

†Taylor & Francis Group, *(978-0-335; 978-0-415; 978-0-8448; 978-0-85066; 978-0-89116; 978-0-903796; 978-0-905273; 978-1-56032; 978-1-85000; 978-1-59169; 978-1-315)* Orders Addr.: 7625 Empire Dr., Florence, KY 41042-2919 USA Toll Free Fax: 800-248-4724; Toll Free: 800-634-7064; 74 Rolark Dr., Scarborough, ON M1R 4G2 Tel 416-299-5388; Fax: 416-299-7531; Toll Free: 877-226-2237; Edit Addr.: 325 Chestnut St., Philadelphia, PA 19106 USA (SAN 241-9246) Tel 215-625-8900; Fax: 215-625-2940; 270 Madison Ave., 4th Flr., New York, NY 10016-0601
Web site: http://www.routledge-ny.com; http://www.crcpress.com; http://www.garlandscience.com; http://www.taylorandfrancis.com
Dist(s): **CRC Pr. LLC**
Ebsco Publishing
MyiLibrary
Oxford Univ. Pr., Inc.; *CIP.*

Taylor & Francis, Incorporated *See* **Taylor & Francis Group**

Taylor and Seale Publishers *See* **Taylor and Seale Publishing, LLC**

Taylor and Seale Publishing, LLC, *(978-0-9846558; 978-0-9887836; 978-1-940224; 978-1-943789)* Orders Addr.: 2 Oceans West Blvd. Unit 406, Daytona Beach Shores, FL 32118 USA Tel 386-760-8987.

Taylor, Ann, *(978-0-9800059)* 4319 Candlewood Ln., Ponce Inlet, FL 32127 USA
E-mail: taboka@aol.com; anntaylor@cfl.rr.com.

Taylor, Dale *See* **Barton Publications**

Taylor, Dorothy Loring, *(978-0-9610640)* R. R. 2, Box 152, Virginia, IL 62691 USA (SAN 265-3567) Tel 217-458-2506.

Taylor Productions *Imprint of* **G R M Assocs.**

Taylor Publishing Company *See* **Taylor Trade Publishing**

Taylor Publishing Grp., *(978-0-9762933)* 1605 E. Elizabeth St., Pasadena, CA 91104 USA Tel 626-398-2341
E-mail: tp@finishthetask.org
Web site: http://www.taylorpublishing.info.

Taylor Street Publishing LLC, *(978-0-9892854; 978-0-9911621)* 575 O'Farrell St. Suite 904, San Francisco, CA 94102 USA Tel 415-374-4846
E-mail: timhewtson@gmail.com
Web site: www.taylorstreetbooks.com.

†Taylor Trade Publishing, *(978-0-87833; 978-0-925190; 978-1-57749; 978-1-58979; 978-1-63076)* Orders Addr.: 15200 NBN Way, Blue Ridge Summit, PA 17214 USA Tel 717-794-3800 (Sales, Customer Service, MIS, Royalties, Inventory Mgmt., Dist., Credit & Collections); Fax: 717-794-3803 (Customer Service &/or orders only); 717-794-3857 (Sales & MIS); 717-794-3856 (Royalties, Inventory Mgmt. & Dist.); Toll Free Fax: 800-338-4550 (Customer Service &/or orders); Toll Free: 800-462-6420 (Customer Service &/or orders); Edit Addr.: 4501 Forbes Blvd., Suite 200, Lanham, MD 20706 USA Tel 301-459-3366; Fax: 301-459-5743 Do not confuse with companies with the same or similar names in Rochester, MI, Bellingham, WA, St. Petersburg, FL, Owatonna, MN, Eureka, CA
Web site: http://www.rlpgbooks.com; http://www.taylortradepublishing.com
Dist(s): **Ebsco Publishing**
Follett School Solutions
MyiLibrary
National Bk. Network
Rowman & Littlefield Publishers, Inc.
Smashwords
ebrary, Inc.; *CIP.*

Taylor, Y. H., *(978-0-9788386)* P.O. Box 9618, Philadelphia, PA 19131-3315 USA.

Taylor-Dth Publishing, *(978-0-9712923; 978-0-9727583; 978-0-9747532; 978-0-9774431; 978-0-9834780; 978-0-9988935)* Orders Addr.: P.O. Box 216, Fairfax, CA 94978 USA Tel 415-299-1087
E-mail: ncardinali@taylor-dth.com
Web site: http://www.taylor-dth.com.

TaySysCo Publishing, *(978-0-9773236)* 808 White Ivy Pl. NE, Cedar Rapids, IA 52402 USA
E-mail: taysysco@msn.com
Web site: http://taysysco.com.

TazTales, *(978-0-9742178)* P.O. Box 48031, Oak Park, MI 48237-5731 USA
E-mail: taztales@lycos.com
Web site: http://www.taztales.com.

TBCN Inc., *(978-0-938447)* 1680 Keylake Dr, Suwanee,, GA 30024 USA Tel 470-239-7375
E-mail: Fred@bookfunmagazine.com
Web site: http://www.bookfun.org.

TBG.LLC *See* **Gilliam, T. & Associates, LLC**

Tbooks Publishing Co., *(978-0-9789449)* 324 E. 2nd St., Benicia, CA 94510-3249 USA (SAN 852-0135) Tel 707-342-2280
E-mail: terrie@tbookspublishing.com
Web site: http://tbookspublishing.com.

TBSM Publishing, *(978-0-9860056)* P.O. Box 6314, Traverse City, MI 49686 USA.

T.C. McSears Publishing, *(978-0-9787015)* P.O. Box 341, Linconton, NC 28093 USA
E-mail: tryloc@tryloc.com
Web site: http://www.tryloc.com
Dist(s): **Big Tent Bks.**

TCB-Cafe Publishing, *(978-0-9674898; 978-0-9767682; 978-0-9798640; 978-0-9822200; 978-0-9911208)* Orders Addr.: P.O. Box 471706, San Francisco, CA 94147 USA Tel 415-263-6800
Web site: http://www.cafeandre.com; http://www.tastetv.com
Dist(s): **Quality Bks., Inc.**

TdB Pr. LLC, *(978-0-9740494)* P.O. Box 6348, Altadena, CA 91003-6348 USA (SAN 255-3147)
E-mail: mail@tdbpress.com
Web site: http://www.tdbpress.com.

TDG Communications, Inc., *(978-0-9793584)* 93 Sherman St., Deadwood, SD 57732-5773 USA (SAN 853-2478) Tel 605-722-7111; Fax: 605-722-7112
Web site: http://www.tdgcommunications.com.

TDO Enterprises, *(978-0-9787624)* Orders Addr.: 92 N. Yale St., Nampa, ID 83651-2347 USA (SAN 851-6553)
E-mail: jscott@tdoent.com
Web site: http://www.tdoent.com; http://www.booksbyjeffscott.com.

Te Papa Pr. (NZL) *(978-0-909010; 978-0-908953; 978-0-9582371; 978-0-9582432; 978-1-877385; 978-0-9941041) Dist. by* **IPG Chicago.**

Tea Party Pr., *(978-0-9749173)* P.O. Box 767425, Atlanta, GA 30076 USA Tel 770-649-4434 Do not confuse with Tea Party Press in Cincinnati, OH
E-mail: paula_taylor@bellsouth.net
Web site: http://www.teapartypress.com.

Tea with Mrs. B, *(978-0-9863560)* 6703 Lumsden St., McLean, VA 22101 USA Tel 202-448-2930
E-mail: r@czfamily.com
Web site: www.TeawithMrsB.com.

Teach Me Tapes, Inc., *(978-0-934633; 978-1-59972)* P.O. Box 698, Mequon, WI 53092 USA (SAN 693-9309) Tel 262-518-6060; Toll Free: 800-456-4656
E-mail: renee@teachmetapes.com
Web site: http://www.teachmetapes.com
Dist(s): **Ingram Publisher Services.**

TEACH Ministries, *(978-0-9740328)* Orders Addr.: 891 Ted Ln., Elgin, IL 60120 USA
E-mail: marylou@empoweringdiversity.com
Web site: http://www.empoweringdiversity.com/anna.

Teach My Children Pubns., *(978-0-9668891)* 258 Bahia Ln., E., Litchfield Park, AZ 85340-4728 USA Tel 602-935-0386
E-mail: oldbaha@goodnet.com.

Teach Services *See* **TEACH Services, Inc.**

TEACH Services, Inc., *(978-0-945383; 978-1-57258; 978-1-4796)* P.O. Box 954, Ringgold, GA 30736 USA (SAN 246-9863) Tel 706-504-9187; Fax: 866-757-6023; Toll Free: 800-367-1844; 8300 Highway 41, Unit 107, Ringgold, GA 30736 Tel 800-367-1844; Fax: 866-757-6023; *Imprints:* Aspect Book (AspectBk)
E-mail: publisher@teachservices.com
Web site: http://www.teachservices.com; http://www.AspectBooks.com.

Teacher Created Materials, Inc., *(978-0-87673; 978-0-7439; 978-1-4333; 978-1-60401; 978-1-4807; 978-1-4938; 978-1-5164)* 5301 Oceanus Dr., Huntington Beach, CA 92649 USA (SAN 665-5270) Tel 714-891-2273; Fax: 714-230-7070; Toll Free Fax: 888-877-7606; Toll Free: 800-858-7339
E-mail: sozbat@tcmpub.com
Web site: http://www.tcmpub.com; http://www.teachercreated.com
Dist(s): **Ebsco Publishing**
Follett School Solutions
Lectorum Pubns., Inc.
MyiLibrary
Shell Educational Publishing.

Teacher Created Resources, Inc., *(978-1-55734; 978-1-57690; 978-1-4206; 978-1-4570)* 12621 Western Ave., Garden Grove, CA 92841 USA Tel 714-891-1690; Fax: 800-525-1254; Toll Free: 800-662-4321
E-mail: dlytle@teachercreated.com; custserv@teachercreated.com
Web site: http://www.teachercreated.com
Dist(s): **Austin & Company, Inc.**
Follett School Solutions
Partners Pubs. Group, Inc.

Teacher Press, Incorporated *See* **Teaching Point, Inc.**

†Teachers College Pr., Teachers College, Columbia Univ., *(978-0-8077)* Orders Addr.: c/o AIDC, P.O. Box 20, Williston, VT 05495-0020 USA (SAN 248-3904) Fax: 802-864-7626; Toll Free: 800-575-6566; Edit Addr.: 1234 Amsterdam Ave., New York, NY 10027 USA (SAN 282-3985) Tel 212-678-3929; Fax: 212-678-4149
E-mail: tcpress@tc.columbia.edu
Web site: http://www.teacherscollegepress.com
Dist(s): **American International Distribution Corp.**
Ebsco Publishing
MyiLibrary; *CIP.*

Teachers' Curriculum Institute, *(978-1-58371; 978-1-934534)* 4009 Miranda Ave. Ste. 100, Palo Alto, CA 94304-1227 USA Toll Free: 800-497-6138; P.O. Box 1327, Rancho Cordova, CA 95741 Toll Free: 800-343-6828
E-mail: info@teachtci.com
Web site: http://www.teachtci.com.

Teacher's Discovery, *(978-1-884473; 978-0-7560)* Div. of American Eagle Co., Inc., 2741 Paldan Dr., Auburn Hills, MI 48326 USA (SAN 631-4570) Tel 248-340-7210; Fax: 248-340-7212; Toll Free: 800-832-2437
Web site: http://www.teachersdiscovery-science.com; http://www.teachersdiscovery-english.com; http://www.teachersdiscovery-social studies.com; http://www.teachersdiscovery-foreignlanguage.com; http://www.teachersdiscovery.com
Dist(s): **American Eagle Pubns., Inc.**
Follett School Solutions.

Teacher's Friend Pubns., Inc., *(978-0-943263; 978-1-57882)* Div. of Scholastic, inc., 2155 Chicago Ave. Ste. 304, Riverside, CA 92507-2209 USA (SAN 668-3177) Toll Free Fax: 800-307-8176; Toll Free: 800-343-9680
E-mail: info@teachersfriend.com
Web site: http://www.teachersfriend.com
Dist(s): **Scholastic, Inc.**

Teachers' Handbooks, *(978-0-9634938)* P.O. Box 2778, San Rafael, CA 94912 USA (SAN 297-8326) Tel 415-461-0871; Fax: 415-461-5357.

Teacher's Treasure *See* **Perfect 4 Preschool**

Teaching & Learning Co., *(978-1-57310)* Div. of Lorenz Corp., 501 E. Third St., Dayton, OH 45401 USA Tel 937-228-6118; Fax: 937-223-2042; Toll Free: 800-444-1144
E-mail: customerservice@teachinglearning.com
Web site: http://www.teachinglearning.com.

Teaching Christ's Children Publishing, *(978-0-9855423; 978-0-615-80614-3; 978-0-692-20138-1; 978-0-692-20142-8; 978-0-692-20166-4; 978-0-692-61203-3)* 7404 Forrest Ave., Parkville, MD 21234 USA Tel 410-665-2655
E-mail: teachingchristschildren@yahoo.com
Web site: www.teachingchristschildren.com
Dist(s): **CreateSpace Independent Publishing Platform.**

Teaching Point, Inc., *(978-0-9629357; 978-1-931680; 978-1-59657)* Orders Addr.: 6950 Philips Hwy. Ste. 46, Jacksonville, FL 32216-6087 USA Toll Free: 877-494-0550; *Imprints:* Expert Systems for Teachers (Expert Systms Teach)
Web site: http://www.teaching-point.net.

Teaching Resources *Imprint of* **Scholastic, Inc.**

Teaching Strategies *Imprint of* **Scholastic, Inc.**

Teaching Strategies, Incorporated *See* **Teaching Strategies, LLC**

Teaching Strategies, LLC, *(978-0-9602892; 978-1-879537; 978-1-933021; 978-1-60617)* 4500 East W. Highway, Suite 300, Bethesda, MD 20814 USA (SAN 222-240X) Tel 301-634-0818; Fax: 301-657-0250; Toll Free: 800-637-3652
E-mail: MatthewM@teachingstrategies.com; jow@teachingstrategies.com
Web site: http://www.teachingstrategies.com; http://www.EdPro.com; http://www.MindNurture.com
Dist(s): **Delmar Cengage Learning**
Gryphon Hse., Inc.

Teahouse of Danger, *(978-0-9801054)* P.O. Box 1361, Tucson, AZ 85702 USA (SAN 855-2193) Toll Free: 877-663-3324
E-mail: teahouseofdanger@gmail.com
Web site: http://www.teahouseofdanger.com.

Team B Creative LLC, *(978-0-9774119; 978-1-937665)* 9864 E. Grand River, Suite 110, No. 244, Brighton, MI 48116 USA
E-mail: mickmorrisinfo@yahoo.com; teambcreative@yahoo.com; karen@teambcreative.com
Web site: http://www.mickmorris.net; http://www.ghostboardposse.com; http://www.mickmorris.com; http://www.totallyunrehearsed.com
Dist(s): **Follett School Solutions**
Partners Bk. Distributing, Inc.

Team Cheer *Imprint of* **Stone Arch Bks.**

Team Dawg Productions, Inc., *(978-0-9749378)* Orders Addr.: P.O. Box 105, Nesconset, NY 11767 USA Tel 718-926-5984; Edit Addr.: 1 Mayfair Rd., Apt. 1, Nesconset, NY 11767 USA
E-mail: bobby@teamdawg.com
Web site: http://www.teamdawg.com.

Team EEK!, *(978-0-9767646)* Orders Addr.: 413 Bella St., Hollidaysburg, PA 16648 USA Tel 814-695-7631
E-mail: gimmygum@gimmygum.com
Web site: http://www.gimmygum.com.

Team Kidz, Inc., *(978-0-9793833)* P.O. Box 2111, Voorhees, NJ 08043-8111 USA Tel 856-768-2181
E-mail: jgkeega@aol.com.

Team Kreskin Productions, LLC, *(978-0-9859882)* P.O. Box 216, Simsbury, CT 06070 USA Tel 860-658-4010; Fax: 860-658-4011
E-mail: wwklaw@aol.com
Dist(s): **ebrary, Inc.**

Team Reach, Inc., *(978-0-9767610)* 8448 Summit St., Lenexa, KS 66215-5388 USA Fax: 913-312-8872
E-mail: troy@krystal-planet.com; troy@troyhelming.com
Web site: http://www.troyhelming.com; http://www.teamreach.com.

TechArts International LLC, *(978-0-9726326)* 7638 S. Carroll Rd., Indianapolis, IN 46259 USA; P.O. Box 6983, Great Falls, MT 59405.

Technical Data Freeway, Inc., *(978-0-9841600)* P.O. Box 308, Poway, CA 92074 USA.

Technology & Imagination Pr., *(978-0-9798991; 978-1-944273)* 1970 Chalon Glen Ct., Livermore, CA 94550-8206 USA (SAN 854-7068) Tel 925-606-1285; Fax: 925-606-1297
E-mail: books@siliconmap.net.

Technology Education Concepts Inc., *(978-0-9740796; 978-0-9777525)* 32 Commercial St., Concord, NH 03301-5031 USA Tel 603-224-8324; Fax: 603-225-7766; Toll Free: 800-338-2238
E-mail: justyn@tecedu.com
Web site: http://www.tecedu.com.

Tecki-Corp, Ltd., *(978-0-9724178)* P.O. Box 866, Bettendorf, IA 52722-1955 USA Tel 563-359-4388; Fax: 563-359-4671
E-mail: patrickm@studentsafe.com
Web site: http://www.studentsafe.com.

Tecolote, Ediciones, S.A. de C.V. (MEX) *(978-968-7381)* *Dist. by* **Mariuccia Iaconi Bk Imports.**

Tecolote, Ediciones, S.A. de C.V. (MEX) *(978-968-7381)* *Dist. by* **Lectorum Pubns.**

Tectum B.V.B.A. (BEL) *(978-90-76886; 978-90-79761) Dist. by* **InnovativeLog.**

Teddy Bear Pr., Inc., *(978-1-880017)* 5470 Van Ness, Bloomfield Hills, MI 48302 USA Tel 248-851-8607 Do not confuse with Teddy Bear Pr., Las Vegas, NV.

Teddy Traveler Co., *(978-0-9748954)* P.O. Box 3223, Manhattan Beach, CA 90266 USA
Web site: http://www.teddytraveler.com
Dist(s): **Beyda for Bks., LLC.**

Tedesco, James *See* **JBT Publishing**

Teen Winners, LLC, *(978-0-9740356)* 19 Quail Run, Berlin, CT 06037 USA Tel 860-829-2067; Fax: 860-829-8067
E-mail: info@teenwinners.com
Web site: http://www.teenwinners.com.

Teeter, Diana, *(978-0-692-88078-4)* 6620 108th St Apt 1L, FOREST HILLS, NY 11375 USA Tel 248-895-9097
E-mail: jeffwcrawford5+LVP0003691@gmail.com; jeffwcrawford5+LVP0003691@gmail.com.

TEG Publishing, *(978-0-9707208; 978-0-9727410)* Orders Addr.: P.O. Box 12737, Tempe, AZ 85284 USA Tel 310-919-3013
E-mail: microlawyers@aol.com; tegpublishing@wwsws.com
Web site: http://www.tegpublishing.com.

Tegen, Katherine Bks *Imprint of* **HarperCollins Pubs.**

Tehabi Bks., *(978-1-887656; 978-1-931688)* 4920 Carroll Canyon Rd., Suite 200, San Diego, CA 92121 USA Tel 858-450-9100; Fax: 858-450-9146; Toll Free: 800-243-7259
E-mail: Emily.Henning@tehabi.com
Web site: http://www.tehabi.com.

Telemachus Pr., LLC, *(978-0-9841083; 978-1-935670; 978-1-937387; 978-1-937698; 978-1-938135; 978-1-938701; 978-1-939337; 978-1-939927; 978-1-940745; 978-1-941536; 978-1-942899; 978-1-945330; 978-1-948046)* Orders Addr.: 7551 Ashford Ct., Dublin, OH 43017 USA (SAN 858-4508) Tel 941-993-5816; 941-993-5987; Fax: 941-296-7873; 7551 Ashford Ct., Dublin, OH 43017 (SAN 858-4508) Tel 941-993-5816; 941-993-5987; Fax: 941-296-7873
E-mail: Steve.himes@telemachuspress.com
Web site: http://www.telemachuspress.com
Dist(s): **Lightning Source, Inc.**
Smashwords.

Tell Me Pr., LLC, *(978-0-9816453; 978-0-9819835; 978-0-9829421; 978-0-9906453)* 98 Mansfield St., New Haven, CT 06511 USA (SAN 857-8508) Tel 203-562-4215; Fax: 203-562-4225
E-mail: lisa@tellmepress.com
Web site: http://www.tellmepress.com
Dist(s): **Greenleaf Book Group.**

Tell My Story Publishing, LLC, *(978-0-9729363)* Orders Addr.: 898 Mahogany Dr., Kaysville, UT 84037-4409 USA
E-mail: tellmystory@msn.com.

Tell-a-Vision Bks., *(978-0-9727706)* Orders Addr.: P.O. Box 396, Lexington, VA 24450 USA; Edit Addr.: 272 Dogwood Rise, Lexington, VA 24450 USA
Web site: http://www.tell-a-visionbooks.com.

Telling Family Tales, *(978-1-940379)* 12129 S. 2160 W., Riverton, UT 84065 USA Tel 801-787-5673
E-mail: raelyn@tellingfamilytales.com.

Temenos Pr., *(978-0-9701319)* Orders Addr.: P.O. Box 477, Ashfield, MA 01330 USA Tel 413-625-9148; Edit Addr.: 989 Apple Valley Rd., Ashfield, MA 01330 USA Do not confuse with Temenos Pr., in Cloverdale, CA.

Tempest Bk. Shop, *(978-0-9632484)* Orders Addr.: 5031 Main St., Waitsfield, VT 05673-7111 USA Tel 802-496-2022; Fax: 802-496-3299
E-mail: rayfieldvt@aol.com.

Tempest Pr., *(978-0-9790232)* P.O. Box 3504, New York, NY 10008-3504 USA (SAN 852-2340)
E-mail: info@tempestpress.com
Web site: http://www.tempestpress.com
Dist(s): **Greenfield Distribution, Inc.**

Templar *Imprint of* **Candlewick Pr.**

Temple Care: Body, Mind & Spirit, *(978-0-9773759)* P.O. Box 1221 Ring Bill Loop, Upper Marlboro, MD 20774-7170 USA Tel 301-218-5941; Fax: 719-218-5948
E-mail: templecare@verizon.com.

Temple Street Pr., *(978-0-9896231)* P.O. Box 7071, Halcyon, CA 93421 USA Tel 805-243-8144
E-mail: eva@templestreetpress.com
Web site: http://templestreetpress.com.

†Temple Univ. Pr., *(978-0-87722; 978-1-56639; 978-1-59213; 978-1-4399)* 1601 N. Broad St., Univ. Services Bldg., Rm. 305, Philadelphia, PA 19122-6099 USA (SAN 202-7666) Tel 215-204-3389; Fax: 215-204-4719; Toll Free: 800-447-1656
E-mail: charles.ault@temple.edu
Web site: http://www.temple.edu/tempress
Dist(s): **Chicago Distribution Ctr.**
Ebsco Publishing
Follett School Solutions
Fordham Univ. Pr.
MyiLibrary
Univ. of Chicago Pr.
ebrary, Inc.; *CIP.*

Templeton Foundation Press *See* **Templeton Pr.**

Templeton Pr., *(978-1-890151; 978-1-932031; 978-1-59947)* Div. of John Templeton Foundation, 300 Conshohocken State Rd., Conshohocken, PA 19428-3801 USA
E-mail: info@templetonpress.org; lbarrett@templeton.org
Web site: http://www.templetonpress.org
Dist(s): **Chicago Distribution Ctr.**
Ebsco Publishing
MyiLibrary
ebrary, Inc.

Temporal Mechanical Pr., *(978-1-928878)* Div. of Enos Mills Cabin, Orders Addr.: 6760 Hwy. 7, Estes Park, CO 80517-6404 USA Tel 970-586-4706
E-mail: info@enosmills.com
Web site: http://www.enosmills.com.

Tempus (ESP) *(978-84-92567; 978-84-936181) Dist. by* **IPG Chicago.**

Ten Gallon Pr., *(978-0-615-69261-6; 978-0-9883021; 978-0-9991217)* 2896 Bardy Rd., Santa Rosa, CA 95404 USA Tel 415-713-8386
E-mail: helen@helensedwick.com
Web site: www.tengallonpress.com
Dist(s): **CreateSpace Independent Publishing Platform.**

Ten Minas Publishing, *(978-0-9716786)* P.O. Box 8984, Reston, VA 20195 USA Fax: 703-834-1176
Web site: http://www.crowsofhiddencreek.

Ten Speed Pr. *Imprint of* **Potter/TenSpeed/Harmony**

†Ten Speed Pr., *(978-0-89815; 978-0-913668; 978-1-58008; 978-1-60774)* Div. of Crown Publishing Group, Orders Addr.: P.O. Box 7123, Berkeley, CA 94707 USA (SAN 202-7674) Fax: 510-559-1629 (orders); Toll Free: 800-841-2665; 555 Richmond St., W. Suite 405, Box 702, Toronto, ON M5V 3B1 Tel 416-703-7775; Fax: 416-703-9992; *Imprints:* Tricycle Press (TricyclePress)
E-mail: order@tenspeed.com; alan@tenspeed.ca
Web site: http://www.tenspeed.com
Dist(s): **Fujii Assocs.**
MyiLibrary
Penguin Random Hse. LLC
Random Hse., Inc.; *CIP.*

Ten Story Bks., LLC, *(978-0-9916348; 978-1-945131)* P.O. Box 701561, Dallas, TX 75370 USA Tel 972-345-0734
E-mail: info@tenstorybooks.com.

Tender Heart Pr., *(978-0-9741401)* 15448 S. Jasper, Bldg. G, Odessa, TX 79766 USA
Web site: http://www.tenderheartpress.com.

Tender Learning Concepts, *(978-0-9708796)* 5362 Rockledge Dr., Buena Pk., CA 90621 USA Tel 714 739 2145; 714-739-2145; Fax: 714-739-0593; Toll Free: 877 886-7091; *Imprints:* TLConcepts, Incorporated (TLCPTS)
E-mail: whm@iqboosters.com
Web site: http://www.iqboosters.com; http://tenderlearning.econgo.com.

Tendril Pr., LLC, *(978-0-9763706; 978-0-9802190; 978-0-9822394; 978-0-9841543; 978-0-9831587; 978-0-9858933)* Orders Addr.: P.O. Box 441110, Aurora, CO 80044 USA Tel 303-696-9227; Fax: 303-873-6766; 2215 S. Oakland Way, Aurora, CO 80014 Tel 720-275-8371 Direct
E-mail: publisher@tendrilpress.com
Web site: http://www.tendrilpress.com
Dist(s): **Brigham Distribution.**

teNeues Publishing Co., *(978-3-570; 978-3-8238; 978-3-929278; 978-3-8327; 978-1-933427; 978-1-60160; 978-1-62325)* 7 W. 18th St., New York, NY 10011 USA (SAN 245-176X) Tel 212-627-9090; Fax: 212-627-9511; Toll Free: 800-352-0305; 12 Ferndene Rd., London, SE24 0AQ
E-mail: tnp@teneues-usa.com
Web site: http://www.teneues.com.

Tengan, G. Shay Service Group, *(978-0-9883478)* 2229 Orange Grove Pl., Escondido, CA 92027 USA Tel 760-443-9069
E-mail: stengan@cox.net.

Tennessee Valley Publishing, *(978-1-882194; 978-1-932604)* Orders Addr.: P.O. Box 52527, Knoxville, TN 37950-2527 USA Tel 865-584-5235; Fax: 865-584-0113; Toll Free: 800-762-7079; Edit Addr.: 5227 N. Middlebrook Pike., Knoxville, TN 37921-5963 USA
E-mail: info@tvp1.com
Web site: http://www.tvp1.com
Dist(s): **Chicago Distribution Ctr.**

Tenney, Bob Solutions, LLC, *(978-0-9916435)* 160 Hamburg Mountain Rd., Weaverville, NC 28787-9432 USA
E-mail: bobtenney@earthlink.net
Web site: http://www.tenneypubs.com.

Tensaw Pr., Inc., The, *(978-0-9746444)* 158 S. Jefferson St., Mobile, AL 36602-1119 USA Fax: 251-438-4545
E-mail: tensawpress@aol.com.

Teora USA LLC, *(978-1-59496)* Orders Addr.: 505 Hampton Park Blvd. Ste. G, Capitol Hgts, MD 20743-3862 USA (SAN 256-1220)
E-mail: welcome@teora.com
Web site: http://www.teorausa.com.

Terabyte Pr. LLC, *(978-0-9839877)* 223A S. Durkee Hill Ln., Southbury, CT 06488 USA Tel 203-448-8142
E-mail: cbaileysims@gmail.com.

Terminal Pr., LLC, *(978-0-9753683)* 27 June Walk., Long Beach, NY 11561-2884 USA
E-mail: bferrara@terminalpress.com
Web site: http://www.terminalpress.com.

Terra Denuo, Inc., *(978-1-933232)* P.O. Box 485, Rocklin, CA 95677 USA
E-mail: mark@terradenuo.com
Web site: http://www.terradenuo.com.

Terra Linda Publishing, *(978-0-9746710)* 593 Tamarack Dr., San Rafael, CA 94903 USA Tel 415-491-1042
E-mail: meolson@earthlink.net
Web site: http://www.terralindapublishing.com.

Terra Niños *See* **Solibros**

Terra Nova Publishing Company *See* **Dream Ship Publishing Co.**

Terra Tales, *(978-0-9771804)* 101 Lattice Ln., Collegeville, PA 19426-3374 USA.

Terrapin Pr., *(978-0-9753087)* 2094 Arthur St., Eugene, OR 97405-1519 USA Do not confuse with companies with the same name in Marina del Rey, CA, Aiken, SC.

Terrific Science Pr., *(978-1-883822)* Miami Univ. Middletown, 4200 E. University Blvd., Middletown, OH 45042 USA Fax: 513-727-3328
E-mail: cse@muohio.edu
Web site: http://www.terrificscience.org
Dist(s): **Carolina Biological Supply Co.**
Nasco Math Eighty-Six
Science Kit & Boreal Labs
Teacher's Discovery.

Terrific Twins LLC, *(978-0-9769910)* 659 Kensington Ave., Severna Park, MD 21146 USA Tel 410-647-8923 (phone/fax)
E-mail: carpenterzyla@hotmail.com
Web site: http://terrifictwins.com.

Terry Lowey's Children's Stories, LLC, *(978-0-9792695)* 1325 Airmotive Way, Suite 175, Reno, NV 89502 USA Tel 775-322-1924; Fax: 775-322-1937
Web site: http://www.lifeisamagicaljourney.com.

Tertulia Pubns., *(978-0-9785988)* P.O. Box 2450, Nevada City, CA 95959 USA (SAN 851-0962)
Web site: http://www.tertuliapress.com.

Terumah Publishing, *(978-0-9744277)* Orders Addr.: 5 Pipe Hill Ct., Unit C, Baltimore, MD 21209 USA Tel 410-486-0950
E-mail: info@terumah.com
Web site: http://www.terumah.com.

Tesoro Publishing, *(978-0-9797419; 978-1-941346)* P.O. Box 528, Fullerton, CA 92836 USA (SAN 854-2279)
E-mail: Info@Tesoropublishing.com
Web site: http://www.TesoroPublishing.com.

Tetoca Pr., *(978-0-9788085)* P.O. Box 337, Puyallup, WA 98371 USA Tel 253-845-1256; 253-845-5090; Toll Free: 888-483-8622
E-mail: thhunter@earthlink.net; tetoca@tetocapress.net
Web site: http://www.tetocapress.net
Dist(s): **Pathway Bk. Service**
Quality Bks., Inc.

Tetrahedron, Incorporated *See* **Tetrahedron Publishing LLC**

Tetrahedron Publishing LLC, *(978-0-923550; 978-0-9609386)* Orders Addr.: c/o Healthy World Distributing, LLC, 206 N. Fourth Ave., Suite 147, Sandpoint, ID 83864 USA Tel 208-265-2575; Fax: 208-265-2775; Toll Free: 888-508-4787; Edit Addr.: P.O. Box 2033, Sandpoint, ID 83864-0906 USA (SAN 260-2717) Toll Free: 888-508-4787 (orders)
E-mail: tetra@tetrahedron.org
Web site: http://www.tetrahedron.org
Dist(s): **New Leaf Distributing Co., Inc.**

Texas A&M AgriLife Extension Service, *(978-0-9672990; 978-0-9721049)* c/o Texas A & M University, 2112 TAMU, College Station, TX 77843-2112 USA Fax: 979-862-1202
E-mail: d-bowen@tamu.edu
Dist(s): **Texas A&M Univ. Pr.**

†Texas Christian Univ. Pr., *(978-0-87565; 978-0-912646; 978-0-87565-510-9)* P.O. Box 298300, Fort Worth, TX 76129 USA (SAN 202-7690) Tel 817-257-7822; Fax: 817-257-5075
E-mail: j.alter@tcu.edu; s.petty@tcu.edu
Web site: http://www.prs.tcu.edu
Dist(s): **Ebsco Publishing**
MyiLibrary
Texas A&M Univ. Pr.
ebrary, Inc.; *CIP.*

Texas Cooperative Extension *See* **Texas A&M AgriLife Extension Service**

Texas Pride Publishing, *(978-0-9859601)* 9802 Dibsworth Ln. D9802, Dallas, TX 75238 USA Tel 214-326-4356
E-mail: theamazingcharity@gmail.com
Web site: http://www.charitymarie.com.

†Texas State Historical Assn., *(978-0-87611)* 2-306 Richardson Hall, University Sta., Austin, TX 78712 USA (SAN 202-7704) Tel 512-471-1525; Fax: 512-471-1551; Toll Free: 800-687-8132
Web site: http://www.tshaonline.org
Dist(s): **MyiLibrary**
Texas A&M Univ. Pr.
ebrary, Inc.; *CIP.*

†Texas Tech Univ. Pr., *(978-0-89672; 978-1-68283)* Affil. of Texas Tech Univ., P.O. Box 41037, Lubbock, TX 79409-1037 USA (SAN 218-5989) Tel 806-742-2982; Fax: 806-742-2979; Toll Free: 800-832-4042
E-mail: ttup@ttu.edu; barbara.brannon@ttu.edu
Web site: http://www.ttup.ttu.edu; http://www.ttupress.org
Dist(s): **Chicago Distribution Ctr.**
MyiLibrary; *CIP.*

†Texas Woman's Univ. Pr., *(978-0-9607488; 978-0-9712104)* Orders Addr.: P.O. Box 425858, Denton, TX 76204 USA (SAN 238-4833) Tel 940-898-3123; Fax: 940-898-3127; Edit Addr.: 1200 Frame St., Denton, TX 76205 USA
E-mail: wbenson@twu.edu; *CIP.*

Text 4m Publishing, *(978-0-9779207; 978-0-9795691)* P.O. Box 12586, Milwaukee, WI 53212-0586 USA (SAN 850-6299)
E-mail: info@text4mpublishing.com; teresarae@msn.com
Web site: http://www.text4mpublishing.com.

Text N Tone, Inc., *(978-0-9764429)* 1500 King William Woods Rd., Midlothian, VA 23113-9119 USA
E-mail: mchekel@dslextreme.com.

Text Publishing Co. (AUS) *(978-1-875847; 978-1-876485; 978-1-86372; 978-1-877008; 978-1-920885; 978-1-921145; 978-1-921351; 978-1-921520; 978-1-921656; 978-1-921758; 978-1-921776; 978-1-921799; 978-1-921834; 978-1-921921; 978-1-921922; 978-1-921961; 978-0-85786; 978-1-922079; 978-1-922147; 978-1-922148; 978-1-922182; 978-1-925095; 978-1-922253; 978-1-925240; 978-1-925355; 978-1-925410; 978-1-925498; 978-1-925570; 978-1-925603; 978-1-925626) Dist. by* **Consort Bk Sales.**

Textbook Pubs., *(978-0-7581; 978-1-60630; 978-1-62583)* Orders Addr.: 17853 Santiago Blvd. Suite 107-133, Villa Park, CA 92861 USA Fax: 951-767-0133
E-mail: reprintservices@gmail.com.

Textbooks On Demand *See* **Reprint Services Corp.**

Textorium Publishing, *(978-0-9988194)* P.O. Box 62385, Virginia Beach, VA 23466 USA Tel 757-270-5590
E-mail: textoriumpublishing@yahoo.com.

Texture Pr., *(978-0-9641837; 978-0-9712061; 978-0-9797573; 978-0-9850081; 978-0-615-69474-0; 978-0-615-71148-5; 978-0-615-71503-2; 978-0-615-75380-5; 978-0-615-77101-4; 978-0-615-78283-6; 978-0-615-81691-3; 978-0-615-82399-7; 978-0-615-85856-2; 978-0-615-87735-8; 978-0-615-90534-1; 978-0-615-95462-2; 978-0-615-95463-9; 978-0-692-21272-1; 978-0-692-30003-9; 978-0-692-30004-6; 978-0-692-31702-0; 978-0-692-35682-1; 978-0-692-35683-8; 978-0-692-36138-2; 978-0-692-39578-3; 978-0-692-40157-6; 978-0-692-52042-) 1108 Westbrooke Terr., Norman, OK 73072 USA Tel 405-314-7730; Fax: 405-310-6617*
E-mail: susan@beyondutopia.com; texturepress@beyondutopia.com
Web site: http://www.texturepress.org; http://beyondutopia.net/texturepress/
Dist(s): **SPD-Small Pr. Distribution.**

TFG, *(978-0-9884132)* P.O. Box 91452, Portland, OR 97291 USA Tel 503-629-5045; Fax: 503-531-9175
E-mail: kimball@kimballfisher.com; info@thefishergroup.com
Web site: www.kimballfisher.com; www.thefishergroup.com.

TFG Pr., *(978-0-9743521; 978-0-9748553)* 244 Madison Ave., No. 254, New York, NY 10016 USA Tel 877-822-2504 do nto confuse with TGF Press in New York, NY.

†TFH Pubns., Inc., *(978-0-7938; 978-0-86622; 978-0-87666; 978-1-85279)* Orders Addr.: One TFH Plaza, Third & Union Aves., Neptune City, NJ 07753 USA (SAN 202-7720) Tel 732-988-8400; Fax: 732-988-5466; Toll Free: 800-631-2188 (outside New Jersey); Edit Addr.: P.O. Box 427, Neptune, NJ 07753 USA (SAN 658-1862)
E-mail: info@tfh.com
Web site: http://www.tfh.com; *CIP.*

Th1nk Bks. *Imprint of* **NavPress Publishing Group**

Th3rd World Studios, *(978-0-9818694; 978-0-9832161; 978-0-9895744)* 290 Powell Cir., Berlin, MD 21811 USA
Web site: http://www.th3rdworld.com
Dist(s): **Diamond Comic Distributors, Inc.**
Diamond Bk. Distributors.

Thacker Hse. Enterprises, *(978-0-9801919)* 1840 Thacker Ave., Jacksonville, FL 32207 USA Tel 904-398-8332
E-mail: 22dwebb@comcast.net
Web site: http://www.debrawebbrogers.com.

Thalian Bks., *(978-0-9884868; 978-0-9961317)* 271B Heritage Village, Southbury, CT 06488 USA Tel 203-262-1558
E-mail: becklean@gmail.com.

Thames & Hudson, *(978-0-500)* 500 Fifth Ave., New York, NY 10110 USA Tel 212-354-3763; Fax: 212-398-1252; Toll Free: 800-233-4830 (orders)
E-mail: bookinfo@thames.wwnorton.com
Web site: http://www.thamesandhudsonusa.com
Dist(s): **Hachette Bk. Group**
ISD
MyiLibrary
Norton, W. W. & Co., Inc.
Penguin Random Hse. LLC.

Thameside Press *See* **Chrysalis Education**

Thandi's Place, A Billo Communication Company *See* **Youth Popular Culture Institute, Inc.**

Tharpa Pubns. (GBR) *(978-0-948006; 978-1-899996; 978-0-9548790; 978-1-906665; 978-0-9558667; 978-84-15849-24-7) Dist. by* **IngramPubServ.**

That Patchwork Place *Imprint of* **Martingale & Co.**

That's Life, Incorporated *See* **That's Life Publishing, Inc.**

That's Life Publishing, Inc., *(978-0-9722304)* 3431 Thunderbird Rd., No. 200, Phoenix,, AZ 85053 USA Toll Free: 877-896-9500; *Imprints:* ZZ Dogs Press (ZZ Dogs Pr)
Web site: http://www.zzdogs.com.

That's Me Publishing, LLC, *(978-1-933843)* Hc 62 Box 488., Salem, MO 65560-8819 USA
E-mail: mary@thatsmepublishing.com
Web site: http://www.thatsmepublishing.com.

ThatsMyLife Co., *(978-0-9760419)* 5516 Challis View Ln., Charlotte, NC 28226 USA Tel 704-752-0935; Toll Free: 866-752-0935
E-mail: customerservice@thatsmytale.com
Web site: http://www.thatsmytale.com.

The 101 Group, Inc., *(978-0-9772313; 978-0-9817033; 978-0-9848624)* Orders Addr.: N7112 Cty. Rd. P, Watertown, WI 53094 USA; Edit Addr.: P.O. Box 12, Watertown, WI 53094 USA
Web site: http://www.the101group.com.

The Argonauts *See* **Argonauts, The**

The Art of Jessycka Drew, *(978-0-692-85164-7; 978-0-9987596)* 81 Westford St, HAVERHILL, MA 01832 USA.

The Bookworm of Edwards, *(978-0-692-81222-8; 978-0-692-86242-1)* 295 Main Street, C101, EDWARDS, CO 81632 USA Tel 970-926-7323
E-mail: events@bookwormofedwards.com; events@bookwormofedwards.com.

The Edge *Imprint of* **Sparklesoup LLC**

Mincing Mockingbird, The,

The Old West Company *See* **Old West Co., The**

The Publishing Place LLC, *(978-0-9754307; 978-0-9760129; 978-0-9763423; 978-0-9776554; 978-0-9788002; 978-0-9840555; 978-0-9845794; 978-0-9835095;*

978-0-9849172) 2330 Hickory Ridge, Ashland, KY 41101 USA Do not confuse with Avant-garde Publishing Company in Mableton, GA
E-mail: info@avantgardepublishing.com
Web site: http://www.avantgardepublishing.com
Dist(s): **Smashwords.**

The Richard Janes Co., *(978-0-692-77834-0)* 12856 Walsh Ave, Los Angeles, CA 90066 USA Tel 310-801-2661
Dist(s): **Independent Pub.**

The Rolling Acorn Pr., *(978-0-692-31870-6; 978-0-692-37782-6; 978-0-692-79386-2)* 4730 Castle Rd, LA CANADA, CA 91011 USA Tel 818-434-2395.

The Wisdom Pages, Inc., *(978-0-9706482)* Div. of Bullies to Buddies, Inc., 65 Fraser St., Staten Island, NY 10314 USA (SAN 255-1217) Tel 718-983-1333; Fax: 718-983-3851
E-mail: miriam@bullies2buddies.com; izzy@bullies2buddies.com
Web site: http://www.bullies2buddies.com; http://www.thewisdompages.com.

†Theatre Communications Group, Inc., *(978-0-88754; 978-0-913745; 978-0-930452; 978-1-55936; 978-1-84002; 978-1-85459; 978-1-870259; 978-1-899791)* 355 Lexington Ave., New York, NY 10017-6603 USA (SAN 210-9387) Tel 212-697-5230; Fax: 212-983-4847
Web site: http://www.tcg.org
Dist(s): **Abraham Assocs. Inc.**
Consortium Bk. Sales & Distribution
MyiLibrary
ebrary, Inc.; *CIP.*

Theatre of Innocence, A, L.L.C., *(978-0-9760283)* 1212 Hull St., No. 1, Louisville, KY 40204 USA.

Theee Hole Punch Publishing, *(978-0-9771678)* P.O. Box 4488, Midlothian, VA 23112 USA
E-mail: threeholepunchpublishing@verizon.net; vzentja9@verizon.net
Web site: http://threeholepunchpublishing.com.

Theisen, Patricia, *(978-0-9793076)* 10520 11th Ave. NW, Seattle, WA 98177 USA
E-mail: ptheisen@gmail.com.

Them Potatoes, *(978-0-9772564)* 7318 21st Ave NW, Seattle, WA 98117-5623 USA (SAN 257-1285)
E-mail: kbrown@thempotatoes.com
Web site: http://www.thempotatoes.com.

Theme Perks, Inc., *(978-0-9729777)* 3300 S. Hiawassee Rd., Bldg. 105, Orlando, FL 32835 USA (SAN 852-6435) Tel 407-296-5800; Fax: 407-296-5801
E-mail: salcom@alcom.com
Web site: http://www.themeperks.com
Dist(s): **Smashwords.**

TheNetworkAdministrator.com, *(978-0-9744630; 978-1-937485)* Orders Addr.: 201 W. Cottesmore Cir., Longwood, FL 32779 USA
E-mail: douglaschick@thenetworkadministrator.com
Web site: http://www.thenetworkadministrator.com.

Theodore Berlin Publishing, *(978-0-9769196)* Div. of Theodore Berlin LLC, Orders Addr.: 8221 Provident St., Philadelphia, PA 19150 USA Tel 215-327-8212; Fax: 615-704-4422
E-mail: berlintheodore@yahoo.com.

Theory & Practice *Imprint of* **Scholastic, Inc.**

ThePaintedWord, Ltd., *(978-0-9846473)* P.O. Box 4132, Lutherville, MD 21094 USA.

Theragogy.com, *(978-0-9749862)* 301 1/2 Crescent NE, Grand Rapids, MI 49503 USA
E-mail: drperkins@theragogy.com
Web site: http://www.theragogy.com.

Therapeutae Pr., *(978-0-9675575)* Orders Addr.: P.O. Box 1557, Bothell, WA 98041 USA Tel 206-783-8028; Edit Addr.: 11112 E. Riverside Dr., Bothell, WA 98041 USA
E-mail: nedwolf@rcia.com.

TheWhippetyWood, *(978-0-9897216)* S9305 Slotty Rd., Prairie du Sac, WI 53578 USA Tel 608-544-2242
E-mail: pj.pixie1@gmail.com
Web site: www.theWhippetyWood.com.

Thewordverve, *(978-0-9857157; 978-0-9889264; 978-0-9896979; 978-1-941251; 978-0-9989052; 978-0-9992479)* 163 Mountain Vista Blvd., Canton, GA 30115 USA Tel 678-710-4353
E-mail: jan@thewordverve.com
Web site: www.bookswithverve.com; www.thewordverve.com.

Thimble Mouse Publishing, Inc., *(978-0-9794522)* 1619 Saddle Creek Cir., No. 1312, Arlington, TX 76015 USA (SAN 853-4942).

ThingsAsian Pr., *(978-0-9715940; 978-1-934159)* 3230 Scott St., San Francisco, CA 94123 USA Tel 415-921-1316; Fax: 415-921-3432
E-mail: info@thingsasian.com; albert@thingsasian.com
Web site: http://www.thingsasianpress.com; http://www.toasiawithlove.com; http://www.thingsasian.com
Dist(s): **Ingram Publisher Services.**

Thinking Ink Pr., *(978-1-942480)* P.O. Box 1411, Campbell, CA 95009-1411 USA Tel 408-507-1990
E-mail: editorial@thinkinginkpress.com
Web site: www.thinkinginkpress.com.

Thinking Kids *Imprint of* **Carson-Dellosa Publishing, LLC**

Think-Outside-the-Book Publishing, Inc., *(978-0-9770751; 978-0-9896781; 978-0-9985471)* 311 N. Robertson Blvd., Suite 323, Beverly Hills, CA 90211 USA
Web site: http://www.thinkoutsidethebook.com.

Thinkus Pubs., *(978-0-9818449)* Orders Addr.: 13109 SW 43rd St., Davie, FL 33330 USA
E-mail: loriflorido@aol.com
Web site: http://www.Dezzerthebook.com; http://www.HugothePunk.com
Dist(s): **Brodart Co.**
Follet Higher Education Grp
Quality Bks., Inc.

Third Axe Publishing, *(978-0-9765547)* 1150 McFarland, HR 26, Morristown, TN 37814 USA Tel 423-736-0884
E-mail: thirdaxepub@yahoo.com
Web site: http://www.brotherhoodofdwarves.com.

Third Dimension Publishing, *(978-0-9777041)* Div. of Third Dimension Group, Inc., Orders Addr.: P.O. Box 1845, Calhoun, GA 30703-1845 USA Tel 706-602-0398; Fax: 706-625-8712; Edit Addr.: 167 Richardson Rd., Calhoun, GA 30701 USA
E-mail: jeffcompton@msn.com
Web site: http://www.areyouawriter.com; http://www.thirddimensiongroup.com; http://www.thirddimensionpublishing.com.

Third Millennium Pr., *(978-0-9795608; 978-0-9833308)* 1845 Avondale Dr., Baton Rouge, LA 70808-1913 USA (SAN 853-7496) Tel 805-217-3109; Toll Free: 800-891-0390
E-mail: ellenhbrown@gmail.com
Web site: http://www.webofdebt.com; http://www.forbiddenmedicine.org; http://www.ellenbrown.com
Dist(s): **Lightning Source, Inc.**

Third Millennium Pubns., *(978-1-932657; 978-1-934805; 978-1-947483)* Sci Fi - Arizona, Inc., 1931 E. Libra Dr., Tempe, AZ 85283-5117 USA Tel 602-740-0569; Fax: 480-619-6202
E-mail: mccollum@3mpub.com
Web site: http://www.3mpub.com; http://www.scifi-az.com.

Third Millennium Publishing *Imprint of* **Sci Fi-Arizona, Inc.**

3rd Party Publishing Co., *(978-0-89914)* Div. of Third Party Assocs., Inc., P.O. Box 13306, Oakland, CA 94661-0306 USA (SAN 127-7294) Tel 510-339-2323; Fax: 510-339-6729; Toll Free: 888-339-2323
E-mail: paulmico@tpaserver.com
Web site: http://www.tpaserver.com.

Third Week Bks., *(978-0-9712816; 978-0-9829948)* 1112 W. 66th St., No.1, Richfield, MN 55423-2280 USA Tel 612-990-6011
E-mail: TheBabyReader@yahoo.com
Web site: http://ThirdWeekBooks.com.

Third World Games, Inc., *(978-0-9728526)* P.O. Box 667, Westminster, CA 92684-0667 USA Tel 714-357-2967
E-mail: companyisbn-dir@thirdworldgames.com
Web site: http://www.thirdworldgames.com.

Third World Press, *(978-0-88378)* P.O. Box 19730, Chicago, IL 60619 USA (SAN 202-778X) Tel 773-651-0700; Fax: 773-651-7286
E-mail: TWPress3@aol.com
Web site: http://www.thirdworldpressinc.com
Dist(s): **Austin & Company, Inc.**
Chicago Distribution Ctr.
Independent Pubs. Group
Ingram Publisher Services.

Thirsty(?) *Imprint of* **Tyndale Hse. Pubs.**

Thirsty Horse LLC, *(978-0-9723127)* 1220 N. Market St., Suite 606, Wilmington, DE 19801-2598 USA (SAN 254-7767) Tel 302-428-1222
E-mail: orders@thirsty-horse.com
Web site: http://www.thirsty-horse-media.com.

Thirsty Sponge Publishing Co., *(978-0-9797960)* 898 Southgate Dr., Cookeville, TN 38501 USA.

Thirty-Three Hundred Pr., *(978-0-9646017)* 3300 Mission St., San Francisco, CA 94110 USA Tel 415-826-6886; 300 Vicksburg St., No. 5, San Francisco, CA 94114
Dist(s): **SPD-Small Pr. Distribution.**

This Joy Bks., *(978-0-9821835; 978-0-9834546; 978-0-692-78357-3)* 1117 S. Milwaukee Ave., Suite A4, Libertyville, IL 60048 USA Tel 847-247-4350
E-mail: info@thisjoybooks.com
Web site: http://www.thisjoybooks.com.

Thistle Publishing, *(978-1-879403)* 11985 Cherokee Cir., Shelby Township, MI 48315 USA Tel 586-781-7039; Fax: 586-589-6011.

Thistledown Pr., Ltd. (CAN) *(978-0-920066; 978-0-920633; 978-1-895449; 978-1-894345; 978-1-897235; 978-1-77187) Dist. by* **IngramPubServ.**

Thistlewood Publishing, *(978-0-9821507; 978-0-9853600)* 92 Wayside Ln., Apalachin, NY 13732 USA
E-mail: gnw@stny.rr.com; gwestover@thistlewoodpublishing.com
Web site: http://www.thistlewoodpublishing.com.

Thomas & Kay, LLC, *(978-0-9729505)* N37w26805 Kopmeier Dr., Pewaukee, WI 53072 USA (SAN 255-7576) Tel 414-581-0449
E-mail: susan@solutionsbysusan.com
Web site: http://www.solutionsbysusan.com.

Thomas & Mercer *Imprint of* **Amazon Publishing**

Thomas & Sons Bks., *(978-0-9758800)* 33 Greenwich Ave., Suite 7L, New York, NY 10014 USA
E-mail: willysthom@rcn.com.

Thomas, Brandis, *(978-0-9792526)* P.O. Box 690162, Houston, TX 77269 USA.

†Thomas, Charles C. Pub., Ltd., *(978-0-398)* 2600 S. First St., Springfield, IL 62704 USA (SAN 201-9485) Tel 217-789-8980; Fax: 217-789-9130; Toll Free: 800-258-8980
E-mail: books@ccthomas.com; dmccarty@ccthomas.com; editorial@ccthomas.com
Web site: http://www.ccthomas.com
Dist(s): **Follett School Solutions**
MyiLibrary
ebrary, Inc.; *CIP.*

Thomas, Duerre, *(978-0-9793877; 978-0-9857798)* 23505 Ferndale Ave., Port Charlotte, FL 33980 USA
E-mail: d_jacel@yahoo.com; madpastor1@gmail.com
Web site: http://www.madpastor.tripod.com.

Thomas Expressions, Incorporated *See* **Thomas Expressions, LLC**

Thomas Expressions, LLC, *(978-0-9713573; 978-0-9771059)* Orders Addr.: 390 S. Tyndall Pkwy., #294, Panama City, FL 32404 USA Fax: 850-785-6408; Toll Free: 866-570-5560
E-mail: thomasexpressions@gmail.com
Web site: http://www.thomasexpressions.com; http://www.didyano.com
Dist(s): **Follett School Solutions.**

Thomas, Frederic Inc., *(978-0-9747133; 978-1-933443)* 5621 Strand Blvd. Ste. 301, Naples, FL 34110-7307 USA (SAN 255-8157); *Imprints:* Values to Live By Classic Stories (ValLiveByClass)
E-mail: freimer@fredericthomas.com; bmichalowski@fredericthomas.com
Web site: http://fredericthomas.com; http://www.healthylivingforkids.com; http://www.valuestoliveby.com.

Thomas, Kevin *See* **Catch 22 Publishing Inc.**

Thomas Max Publishing, *(978-0-9764052; 978-0-9788571; 978-0-9799950; 978-0-9822189; 978-0-9842626; 978-0-9846347; 978-0-9972920)* P.O. Box 250054, Atlanta, GA 30325-1054 USA Tel 404-794-6588
E-mail: LeeC@thomasmax.com; bee.ell.cee@comcast.net
Web site: http://www.thomasmax.com.

Thomas More Publishing, *(978-0-692-75285-2).*

Thomas Pubns., *(978-0-939631; 978-1-57747)* 3245 Fairfield Rd., Gettysburg, PA 17325 USA (SAN 663-7213) Tel 717-642-6600; Fax: 717-642-5555; Toll Free: 800-840-6782 Do not confuse with companies with the same name in Austin, TX, La Crescenta, CA
E-mail: info@thomaspublications.com
Web site: http://www.thomaspublications.com.

Thomas, R. E., *(978-0-9761077)* P.O. Box 53091, Houston, TX 77052 USA.

Thomas, Richard Kayeen *See* **MarWel Enterprises, Inc.**

Thomas, Sheldon Wade, *(978-0-9670539)* 1091 Thomas S. Boyland St., Brooklyn, NY 11236 USA Tel 718-495-6002 (phone/fax).

Thomas, Thomas C. II, *(978-0-692-80928-0; 978-0-692-84277-5)* 249 Santa Rita Ave., PALO ALTO, CA 94301 USA Tel 917-428-3322.

Thomastar Publishing, *(978-0-615-17087-9)* 14241 NE Wood-Duvall Rd Suite 406, Woodinville, WA 98072 USA Tel 425-703-8807
E-mail: thomastar.publishing@hotmail.com
Dist(s): **Lulu Pr., Inc.**

Thompson, Alyce C. Books, Inc., *(978-0-9746411)* Orders Addr.: 6105 W.master St., Philadelphia, PA 19151-0827 USA; Edit Addr.: P.O. Box 664, Havertown, PA 19083 USA
E-mail: emailalyce8@aol.com; info@alycecthompsonbooksinc.com
Web site: http://alycecthompsonbooksinc.com; http://www.myspace.com/alycecthompson; http://www.myspace.com/alycecthompsonbooksinc
Dist(s): **A & B Distributors & Pubs. Group**
Afrikan World Bk. Distributor
Culture Plus Bk. Distributors
Lushena Bks.

Thompson, Angela Bolden, *(978-0-615-14774-1)* 9501 W. 171st St. Ste. Q, Tinley Park, IL 60487 USA
Web site: http://angelathompson1.tripod.com/
Dist(s): **Lulu Pr., Inc.**

Thompson Mill Pr., *(978-0-9883269; 978-0-9971239)* 2110 S. Eagle Rd., No. 368, Newtown, PA 18940 USA
E-mail: bob.regan@thompsonmillpress.com
Web site: http://www.thompsonmillpress.com; http://www.KobeeManatee.com
Dist(s): **Independent Pubs. Group.**

Thompson Original Productions LLC, *(978-0-9799216)* 11997 Youngtree Ct., Bristow, VA 20136 USA (SAN 854-7203)
E-mail: tracyathompson@hotmail.com
Web site: http://www.chickenboybooks.com.

Thomsen, Keith Stuart II, *(978-0-692-55783-9; 978-0-692-79741-9)* 2417 Courtland Ave, HENDERSON, NV 89074 USA Tel 702-610-3662.

Thomson Custom Solutions *See* **CENGAGE Learning Custom Publishing**

Thomson, D.C. & Co., Ltd. (GBR) *(978-0-85116; 978-1-84535) Dist. by* **APG.**

Thomson Delmar Learning *See* **Delmar Cengage Learning**

Thomson ELT, *(978-1-4240; 978-1-4282)* 25 Thomson Pl., 5th Flr., Boston, MA 02210 USA Tel 617-289-7700 Toll Free: 800-237-0053
E-mail: reply@heinle.com
Web site: http://www.elt.thomson.com
Dist(s): **CENGAGE Learning.**

Thomson Gale *See* **Cengage Gale**

Thomson, J P, *(978-0-9754365)* P.O. Box 377, Exton, PA 19341 USA Tel 610-594-1707; Fax: 610-594-1866
E-mail: montanapino@comcast.net.

Thomson Learning *See* **CENGAGE Learning**

Thomson Peterson's *See* **Peterson's**

Thomson South-Western *See* **Cengage South-Western**

Thornapple Farms, LLC, *(978-0-9749728)* 13010 W. Darrow Rd., Vermilion, OH 44089 USA Tel 440-967-2680; Fax: 440-967-2696
E-mail: ashar@hbr.net
Web site: http://www.thornapplefarms.com.

Thorncrown Publishing *Imprint of* **Yorkshire Publishing Group**

†Thorndike Pr., *(978-0-7838; 978-0-7862; 978-0-8161; 978-0-89621; 978-1-56054; 978-1-4104)* Div. of Gale Group, 295 Kennedy Memorial Dr., Waterville, ME 04901 USA Tel 207-859-1053; 207-859-1020; 207-859-1000; Toll Free Fax: 800-558-4676; Toll Free: 800-223-1244 (ext. 15); 800-877-4253 (customer resource ctr.); *Imprints:* Large Print Press (Lrg Print Pr)
E-mail: jamie.knobloch@gale.com; barb.littfield@galegroup.com; Betsy.M.Brown@thomson.com; jamie.knobloch@cengage.com
Web site: http://www.gale.com/thorndike
Dist(s): **Cengage Gale**; *CIP.*

Thornton Publishing, *(978-1-882913)* 1504 Howard St., New Iberia, LA 70560 USA Tel 337-364-2752; Fax: 318-365-0316; Toll Free: 800-551-3076 Do not confuse with companies with the same or similar names in Littleton, CO, Forest Grove, OR, Burley, ID.

Thornton Publishing, Inc., *(978-0-9670242; 978-0-9719597; 978-0-9723309; 978-1-932344; 978-0-9774761; 978-0-9779960; 978-0-9801941; 978-0-9820838; 978-0-9824705; 978-0-9844838; 978-0-9845417; 978-0-9846342; 978-0-9856151; 978-0-9889816)* 17011 Lincoln Ave., No. 408, Parker, CO 80134 USA Tel 303-794-8888; Fax: 720-863-2013; *Imprints:* Profitable Publishing (Profitable Pubng); Books To Believe In (Bks To Believe In) Do not confuse with companies with the same or similar names in New Iberia, LA, Forest Grove, OR, Burley, ID
E-mail: publisher@bookstobelievein.com
Web site: http://bookstobelievein.com; http://www.getting-published.com
Dist(s): **Follett School Solutions.**

Thorogood (GBR) *(978-1-85418) Dist. by* **Stylus Pub VA.**

Thorpe, Sandy, *(978-0-9764147)* 20205 NE 3rd Ct., No. 3, N. Miami Beach, FL 33179 USA
E-mail: sthorpe@trekstuff.com.

Thotsup LLC, *(978-0-9883420)* Orders Addr.: 305 NE 6th St. Suite 588, Grants Pass, OR 97526 USA Tel 541-792-0212.

ThoughtRockets, Inc., *(978-0-9766793)* 2033 Ralston Ave., No. 114, Belmont, CA 94002 USA Tel 650-592-3169 (phone/fax)
E-mail: laura@thoughtrockets.com
Web site: http://www.thoughtrockets.com.

Threatt, Cedric L., *(978-0-9720543)* Div. of Ahava Publishing, LLC, 65 Twisted Oak Cir., Odenville, AL 35120 USA
E-mail: cl3tt@windstream.net
Web site: http://www.Ahavapublishing.org.

Three Angels Broadcasting Network, *(978-0-9718083; 978-0-9720888; 978-1-934869; 978-1-942455)* Orders Addr.: P.O. Box 220, West Frankfort, IL 62896 USA Tel 618-627-4651; Edit Addr.: 3391 Charley Good Rd., West Frankfort, IL 62896 USA
Web site: http://www.3abn.org
Dist(s): **Pacific Pr. Publishing Assn.**

Three Bean Pr., *(978-0-9767276; 978-0-9882212; 978-0-9903315)* P.O. Box 301711, Jamaica Plain, MA 02130 USA (SAN 256-5137) Tel 617-584-5759; 617-827-2042
E-mail: seneca@threebeanpress.com
Web site: http://www.threebeanpress.com
Dist(s): **Partners Bk. Distributing, Inc.**

Three Cents Publishing, *(978-0-9746697)* Orders Addr.: 177 Ocean St.: PO Box 339 Brant Rock Ma02020 Usa, Boston, MA 02020 USA.

Three Conditions Pr., *(978-0-9721241)* Drawer H, Baltimore, MD 21228 USA
Web site: http://www.marylandpoetry.org.

Three Crows Media (NZL) *(978-1-927136) Dist. by* **RiverStream.**

Three Cups, LLC, *(978-0-9794563)* 36 S. Pennsylvania St. Suite 190, Indianapolis, IN 46204 USA Tel 317-633-1456
E-mail: trt@hokansoninc.com; Scott@360GroupOnline.com
Web site: http://www.3cupsbook.com
Dist(s): **Ingram Publisher Services.**

Three Flower Farm Pr., *(978-0-615-67849-8)* 24 Brooks Rd, Wayland, MA 01778 USA Tel 508-653-9307
E-mail: kjlin306@gmail.com.

Three Four Three Publishing Co., *(978-0-9675286)* 3738 Victoria Dr., West Palm Beach, FL 33406 USA Tel 917-407-2270
E-mail: paulnison@mindspring.com
Web site: http://www.rawlife.com.

Three Hermits Pr., *(978-0-9753906)* P.O. Box 99099, Bennington, VT 05201 USA
E-mail: threehermits@mail.com.

Three Moons Media, *(978-0-9725164; 978-0-9747440; 978-1-933514)* 1610 Valley Brook Ln., Longview, TX 75605-2676 USA
E-mail: marilyn@threemoonsmedia.com
Web site: http://www.threemoonsmedia.com
Dist(s): **CreateSpace Independent Publishing Platform.**

Three Part Harmony LLC, *(978-0-9800577)* Orders Addr.: 538 Eagle Blvd., Kingsland, GA 31548 USA (SAN 855-0972) Tel 386-717-4583; 912-882-7008
E-mail: threepartharmony@earthlink.net.

Three Pebble Pr., LLC, *(978-0-9799289; 978-0-9960219)* 10040 SW 25th Ave., Portland, OR 97219-6325 USA (SAN 854-7777) Tel 503-977-0944
E-mail: info@yogacalm.org
Web site: http://www.threepebblepress.com
Dist(s): **Follett School Solutions**
Independent Pubs. Group
MyiLibrary.

Three Ring Circus Publishing Hse., Inc. *Imprint of* **405 Pubns.**

Three River Rambler, *(978-0-615-20131-3)* 422 W. Cumberland Ave., Knoxville, TN 37901 USA Tel 865-524-9411; Fax: 865-546-3717
E-mail: kac@gulfandohio.com
Web site: http://threeriversrambler.com.

Three Rivers Council, BSA, Incorporated *See* **Alchemy Creative, Inc.**

Three Rooms Pr., *(978-0-9840700; 978-0-9835813; 978-0-9884008; 978-0-9895125; 978-1-941110)* Orders Addr.: 561 Hudson Street, No. 33, New York, NY 10014 USA
E-mail: info@threeroomspress.com
Web site: http://threeroomspress.com; http://threeroomspress.blogspot.com
Dist(s): **MyiLibrary**
Publishers Group West (PGW).

Three Sisters Communication, LLC, *(978-0-9771204)* P.O. Box 280, Star, ID 83669-5015 USA (SAN 256-7970)
E-mail: sfunk624@heritagewifi.com.

Three Sisters Pr., *(978-0-9722999)* P.O. Box 17061, Golden, CO 80402 USA Tel 720-231-6540; Fax: 303-561-0626 Do not confuse with Three Sisters Pr., in Washington, DC
E-mail: violeta134@hotmail.com; sjbrehm@comcast.net.

Three Sisters Publishing Hse., Ltd., *(978-0-9785570)* 32104 Cty. Rd., 1, Saint Cloud, MN 56303 USA Tel 320-654-0001.

Three Socks Publishing, *(978-0-9789631)* 3351 Charlotte, Brighton, MI 48114 USA.

Publisher Name Index

Three Spots Productions, *(978-0-9744509)* 67 Rutz St., Stamford, CT 06906 USA
E-mail: rarruzza@optonline.net; rarruzza@sparkyswalk.com
Web site: http://www.sparkyswalk.com.

Three Trees, Inc., *(978-0-9789426)* P.O. Box 92, Cottleville, MO 63368-6336 USA Tel 636-561-9184; Fax: 636-561-9184
Web site: http://Petalwinkthefairy.com.

Three Willows Pr., *(978-0-9770279)* 4680 S. 1000 W., Rensselaer, IN 47978 USA.

Three Wishes Publishing Co., *(978-0-9796380)* 26500 W. Agoura Rd., Suite 102-754, Calabasas, CA 91302 USA Tel 818-878-0902; Fax: 818-878-1805
E-mail: alva710@aol.com
Web site: http://www.alvasachs.com; http://www.threewishespublishing.com.

Three-D Vision Productions *See* **Soul Vision Works Publishing**

Threshold Editions *Imprint of* **Threshold Editions**

Threshold Editions, Div. of Simon & Schuster, 1230 Ave. of the Americas, New York, NY 10020 USA; *Imprints:* Threshold Editions (ThresholdEdit)
Dist(s): **Simon & Schuster, Inc.**

Thriving Churches International *See* **Pastorpreneur Ministries**

Throwback Publishing, *(978-0-9771630)*
Web site: http://www.throwbackpublishing.com.

Thule Ediciones, S. L. (ESP) *(978-84-933734; 978-84-96473) Dist. by* **IPG Chicago.**

Thumbprint Publishing, *(978-0-9741833)* P.O. Box 9972, Cincinnati, OH 45209 USA Tel 513-207-7550 Do not confuse with Thumbprint Publishing in Studio City, CA
E-mail: rdavis_art@fuse.net
Web site: http://www.connectionssp.org/.

Thumbs Up Pr., *(978-0-9772513)* 3731 Reed's Landing Cir., Midlothian, VA 23113 USA Tel 804-320-8331
E-mail: thumbsuppress@earthlink.net.

Thunder Bay Pr. *Imprint of* **Readerlink Distribution Services, LLC**

Thunder Bay Pr., *(978-1-882376; 978-1-933272; 978-1-62026)* 4503 S. M-76, West Branch, MI 48661 USA Tel 989-701-2430; Fax: 989-345-9452
E-mail: sspeigel@partners-east.com; thunderbaypressmichigan@gmail.com
Web site: http://www.thunderpressmichigan.com
Dist(s): **Midpoint Trade Bks., Inc.**
Partners Bk. Distributing, Inc.

Thunder Enlightening, *(978-0-9832491)* 11 Cherokee Camp Trail No. 20451, JASPER, GA 30143 USA Tel 706-692-2199
E-mail: chrisrumble@gmail.com
Web site: www.chrisrumble.com.

Thunder Mountain Bks., Co., *(978-0-9968565)* 7946 E. 35th Ave, Denver, CO 80238 USA Tel 303-506-1667
E-mail: anthony@aakerr.com
Web site: www.thundermountainbooks.com.

ThunderBolt Pubns., *(978-0-615-16040-5; 978-0-578-00692-5)* 14785 Kay Ln., Atlanta, GA 30306 USA
E-mail: medernach@bellsouth.net
Web site: http://www.kenmedernach.com
Dist(s): **Lulu Pr., Inc.**

Thunderbolt Publishing *See* **We Do Listen Foundation**

ThunderBolt Publishing, *(978-0-9799671)* 113 14th Ave. S., Nampa, ID 83651 USA Tel 208-466-0122; Fax: 208-466-5294
E-mail: arlette@thunder-bolt.com.

ThunderHousePress, *(978-0-9771154)* Div. of ThunderHouse Entertainment, 6709 La Tijera Blvd., No. 141, Los Angeles, CA 90045 USA
E-mail: reggiecook@yahoo.com
Web site: http://www.thunderhousepress.com.

Thundermist Consulting and Research Co., *(978-0-9759494)* P.O. Box 7023, Cumberland, RI 02864-7023 USA
E-mail: book-sales@thundermist.com
Web site: http://www.thundermist.com; http://thundermist.blogspot.com.

Thurman Hse., LLC, *(978-1-58989)* 5 Park Ctr. Ct., Suite 300, Owings Mills, MD 21117 USA Tel 410-902-9100; Fax: 410-902-7210
E-mail: thurmanhouse@ottenheimerpub.com.

Thynne, Garry R. *See* **Garry & Donna, LLC**

Tianjin Education Pr.,
Dist(s): **Chinasprout, Inc.**

Tiaanya Literature Pr., *(978-0-9768679; 978-1-60508)* 613 151st St. Pl., NE, Bellevue, WA 98007 USA
E-mail: tianyapress@hotmail.com
Web site: http://www.tianyapress.com.

Tiara Bks. LLC, *(978-0-9729846)* 62 Birchall Dr., Scarsdale, NY 10583-4503 USA Tel 914-723-9133.

Tickling Keys, Inc., *(978-0-9724258; 978-1-932802; 978-1-61547)* 13386 Judy Ave., NW, Uniontown, OH 44685 USA Tel 330-715-2875; Fax: 707-220-4510; *Imprints:* Holy Macro! Books (Holy Macro Bks)
E-mail: consult@mrexcel.com; pub@mrexcel.com
Web site: http://www.holymacrobooks.com
Dist(s): **Ebsco Publishing**
Independent Pubs. Group
MyiLibrary
ebrary, Inc.

TICO Publishing, *(978-0-9777688)* 25045 Jaclyn Ave., Moreno Valley, CA 92557 USA (SAN 850-167X) Tel 562-292-0796
E-mail: tjerin@yahoo.com; books@ticopublishing.com.

Tidal Press, Incorporated *See* **Mushgush Pr.**

Tidal Wave Bks., *(978-0-9724770)* 4476 Wedgewood Dr., Pleasant Grove, UT 84062 USA Tel 801-785-5555; Fax: 801-785-9676
E-mail: sgraham@tidalwavebooks.com
Web site: http://www.tidalwavebooks.com
Dist(s): **Send The Light Distribution LLC.**

Tidal Wave Productions *See* **Black, Judith Storyteller**

Tide-Mark Pr., Ltd, *(978-0-936846; 978-1-55949; 978-1-59490; 978-1-63114)* Orders Addr.: 22 Prestige Park Cir., East Hartford, CT 06108-1917 USA (SAN 222-1802) Tel 860-683-4499; Fax: 860-683-4055; Toll Free: 800-338-2508; Edit Addr.: 22 Prestige Park Cir., East Hartford, CT 06108-1917 USA (SAN 665-794X)
E-mail: carol@tide-press.com
Web site: http://www.tidemarkpress.com
Dist(s): **BookBaby.**

Tiedeman, Leia *See* **Indigo Hse. Publishing, LLC**

Tiffin Pr. of Maine, *(978-0-9646018)* Div. of Tiffin Pr., 110 Jones Point Rd., Brooksville, ME 04617-3570 USA Tel 207-326-0916
E-mail: tiffinpress@yahoo.com; joanmacc45@gmail.com
Dist(s): **Bilingual Pubns. Co., The.**

Tiger Iron Pr., *(978-0-9787263; 978-0-9851745)* Orders Addr.: 4 Hopscotch Ln., Savannah, GA 31411 USA Tel 478-474-2323
E-mail: Sales@TigerIronPress.com
Web site: http://www.TigerIronPress.com; http://Http://www.TI-Holdings.com
Dist(s): **TI-Holdings Distribution Co.**

Tiger Lily Publishing, *(978-1-880883)* Six Swift Ct., Newport Beach, CA 92663 USA Tel 949-645-5907; Toll Free: 800-950-3237 (800-950-DADS)
E-mail: janedrew@home.com.

Tiger Publishing *See* **Tiger Tale Publishing Co.**

Tiger Stripe Publishing, *(978-0-9905895)* 5215 S. Drexel Ave. No. 2S, Chicago, IL 60615 USA Tel 773-505-4232
E-mail: jet@tigerstripepub.com.

Tiger Tale Publishing Co., *(978-0-9787533; 978-0-9859579)* 522 N. Grant Ave., Odessa, TX 79761 USA Tel 432-337-8511; Fax: 432-337-1035
E-mail: cynthia.l.clack@gmail.com
Dist(s): **BookBaby.**

Tiger Tales, *(978-1-58925; 978-1-68010; 978-1-944530)* Orders Addr.: P.O. Box 411037, Kansas City, MO 64141-1037 USA Fax: 913-362-7401; Toll Free: 888-454-0097; *Imprints:* 360 Degrees (360 Degrees)
E-mail: barbknight@tigertalesbooks.com
Web site: http://www.tigertalesbooks.com
Dist(s): **Midpoint National, Inc.**

Tiger Tales Pubns., *(978-0-9610576)* 103 Monte Cresta, Oakland, CA 94611 USA (SAN 264-4347) Tel 510-653-8422.

Tigermoth Pubns., *(978-0-9844785)* P.O. Box 4367, Tulsa, OK 74159 USA (SAN 859-4953)
Web site: http://www.tigermothpublications.com.

Tightrope Bks. (CAN) *(978-0-9738645; 978-1-926639) Dist. by* **IPG Chicago.**

TIGO & Co., *(978-0-9761167)* P.O. Box 210066, Dallas, TX 75211-0066 USA Tel 214-330-4420
E-mail: thekingskid1982@sbcglobal.net.

Tike Time, Inc., *(978-0-9729093)* Orders Addr.: 872 S. Milwaukee, No. 125, Libertyville, IL 60048 USA (SAN 255-3058)
E-mail: info@tiketime.com
Web site: http://www.tiketime.com.

Tiki Machine, LLC, *(978-0-615-39785-6; 978-0-615-49510-1; 978-0-615-54715-2; 978-0-615-65028-9; 978-0-9894507; 978-0-692-22851-7)* 160 W. Foothill Pkwy. Suite 105 No. 171, Corona, CA 92882 USA Tel 818-237-6325
Web site: www.tikimachine.blogspot.com; www.tikimachine.com.

Tiki Tales, *(978-0-9740582)* P.O. Box 1194, Haiku, HI 96708 USA
Dist(s): **Booklines Hawaii, Ltd.**

Tikva Corp., *(978-0-615-12595-4)* 40 W. 23rd St., New York, NY 10010-5215 USA
E-mail: emilyl@mkugodessa.org.

Tilbury Hse. Pubs., *(978-0-88448; 978-0-937966; 978-1-937644)* 12 Starr St., Thomaston, ME 04861 USA Toll Free: 800-582-1899 (orders)
E-mail: tilbury@tilburyhouse.com; mariellen@tilburyhouse.com
Web site: http://www.tilburyhouse.com
Dist(s): **INscribe Digital**
Lectorum Pubns., Inc.
Norton, W. W. & Co., Inc.
SPD-Small Pr. Distribution
Univ. Pr. of New England.

†Timber Pr., Inc., *(978-0-88192; 978-0-917304; 978-0-931146; 978-0-931340; 978-1-60469)* Div. of Workman Publishing Co., Inc., 133 SW Second Ave., Suite 450, Portland, OR 97204-3527 USA (SAN 216-082X) Tel 503-227-2878; Fax: 503-227-3070; Toll Free: 800-327-5680; 20 Lonsdale Rd Swavesey, London, NW6 6RD Tel (01954) 232959; Fax: (01954) 206040
E-mail: info@timberpress.co.uk; publicity@timberpress.com
Web site: http://www.timberpress.com
Dist(s): **Ebsco Publishing**
Meredith Bks.
Workman Publishing Co., Inc.; *CIP.*

Timberwood Pr., *(978-0-9745454)* 112 NW 156th St., Shoreline, WA 98177 USA Tel 206-295-6186
E-mail: kearney@timberwoodpress.com
Web site: http://www.timberwoodpress.com
Dist(s): **Partners Bk. Distributing, Inc.**

Timbuktu Labs, Inc., *(978-0-9978958)* 1051 Elkgrove Ave, APT. 2, Venice, CA 90291 USA Tel 415-528-0207
E-mail: francesca@timbuktu.me.

Time & Chance Publishing, *(978-0-9748274)* Orders Addr.: P.O. Box 488, New York, NY 10116 USA Tel 718-370-3655 [phone/fax]
E-mail: tandchpublishing@yahoo.com; timeandchancepublishing@yahoo.com
Dist(s): **Culture Plus Bks.**

Time Bks. *Imprint of* **Time Inc. Bks.**

Time Dancer Press *See* **5 Star Stories, Inc.**

Time for Kids Inc (AUS) *(978-0-646-53813-6) Dist. by* **CapstonePubs.**

Time Home Entertainment, Incorporated *See* **Time Inc. Bks.**

Time Inc. Bks., *(978-1-883013; 978-1-929049; 978-1-931933; 978-1-932273; 978-1-932994; 978-1-933405; 978-1-933821; 978-1-60320; 978-1-61893; 978-1-68330; 978-1-5478)* Div. of Time, Inc., 1271 Avenue of the Americas, New York, NY 10020-1201 USA (SAN 227-3209); 225 Liberty St., New York, NY 10281; *Imprints:* Time Books (Time Bks); People Books (People Bks); LIFE Books (LIFEBooks); Liberty Street (LibertySt)
Dist(s): **Hachette Bk. Group**
MyiLibrary
National Bk. Network.

Time to Organize, *(978-0-9786733)* 1414 Willow Creek Ln., Shoreview, MN 55126 USA Tel 651-717-1284
E-mail: sara@time2organize.net.

Time to Sign, Incorporated, *(978-0-9713666; 978-0-9765364)* Orders Addr.: P.O. Box 110308, Palm Bay, FL 32911 USA Tel 321-723-6997; Fax: 321-723-6896; Edit Addr.: 426 Olsmar St., Palm Bay, FL 32908 USA Do not confuse with Talking Hands, Inc., in Bangor, ME
E-mail: contact@timetosign.com
Web site: http://www.timetosign.com.

Time Warner Book Group *See* **Hachette Bk. Group**

Time Warner Custom Publishing, *(978-1-931722; 978-1-59995)* 1271 Ave. of the Americas, New York, NY 10020 USA Tel 212-522-7381
Dist(s): **Hachette Bk. Group.**

†Timeless Bks., *(978-0-931454; 978-1-932018)* Div. of Assn. for the Development of Human Potential, Orders Addr.: P.O. Box 3543, Spokane, WA 99220-3543 USA (SAN 211-6502) Fax: 509-838-6652; Toll Free: 800-251-9273; P.O. Box 9, Kootenay Bay, BC V0B 1X0 Tel 250-227-9224 (Business Office); Fax: 250-227-9494 (orders); Toll Free: 800-661-8711 (orders) Do not confuse with Timeless Books in Pickerington, OH
E-mail: info@timeless.org; orders@timeless.org; bookstore@timeless.org; Contact@timeless.org
Web site: http://timeless.org
Dist(s): **Lulu Pr., Inc.**
New Leaf Distributing Co., Inc.; *CIP.*

Timeless Voyager Pr., *(978-1-892264)* Orders Addr.: 249 Iris Ave., Goleta, CA 93117 USA; Edit Addr.: P.O. Box 6678, Santa Barbara, CA 93160 USA (SAN 253-9233) Tel 805-455-8895; Fax: 805-683-4456; Toll Free: 800-576-8463
E-mail: bsh@timelessvoyager.com
Web site: http://www.timelessvoyager.com.

Time-Life Education, Inc., *(978-0-7054; 978-0-7370; 978-0-7835; 978-0-8094)* Orders Addr.: P.O. Box 85026, Richmond, VA 23285-5026 USA Toll Free Fax: 800-449-2011; Edit Addr.: 2000 Duke St., Alexandria, VA 22314 USA Tel 703-838-7000; Fax: 703-518-4124; Toll Free: 800-449-2010
E-mail: education@timelifecs.com
Web site: http://www.timelifeedu.com/
Dist(s): **Hachette Bk. Group.**

†Time-Life, Inc., *(978-0-7835; 978-0-8094)* Div. of Time Warner Co., Orders Addr.: Three Center Plaza, Boston, MA 02108-2084 USA Toll Free Fax: 800-308-1083; 800-286-9471; Toll Free: 800-277-8844; 800-759-0190; Edit Addr.: 8280 Willow Oaks Corporate Dr., Fairfax, VA 22031-4511 USA (SAN 202-7836) Toll Free: 800-621-7026
Web site: http://www.timelifeedu.com
Dist(s): **Hachette Bk. Group**
Time-Life Publishing Warehouse
Worldwide Media Service, Inc.; *CIP.*

Times Bks. *Imprint of* **Holt, Henry & Co.**

Times Square Church *See* **Petey, Rock & Roo Children's Pubns.**

Time-Together Pr., *(978-1-888384)* Orders Addr.: P.O. Box 11689, Saint Paul, MN 55111 USA Tel 612-827-1639; Fax: 612-823-6404.

T.I.M.M.-E. Co., Inc., *(978-0-9718232)* Div. of NYC Department of Education, 230 E. 25th St, Suite 2E, New York, NY 10010 USA
E-mail: tbellavia@weareallthesameinside.com; tools4tolerance@aol.com
Web site: http://www.weareallthesameinside.com
Dist(s): **Bookazine Co., Inc.**

Timothy Lane Pr., *(978-0-9744751)* 3211 Rosewood Dr., Hattiesburg, MS 39401-4517 USA
Web site: http://www.robynjackson.com.

Timshel Literature, *(978-0-9708317)* P.O. Box 751, Portsmouth, RI 02871 USA Tel 401-835-7156
E-mail: jkatz@timshelarts.com
Web site: http://www.timshelarts.com.

Timtu Ink., *(978-0-9742460)* 11 Via Acuatica, Rancho Santa Margarita, CA 92688-1482 USA (SAN 255-6146); 31441 Santa Margarita Pkwy., Suite A, No. 341, Rancho Santa Margarita, CA 92688
E-mail: timtuink@dslextreme.com
Web site: http://www.dragonopolis.com; http://www.dragonia.net.

Timun Mas, Editorial S.A. (ESP) *(978-84-480; 978-84-7176; 978-84-7722) Dist. by* **Lectorum Pubns.**

Timun Mas, Editorial S.A. (ESP) *(978-84-480; 978-84-7176; 978-84-7722) Dist. by* **AIMS Intl.**

Tin Hse. Bks., LLC, *(978-0-9773127; 978-0-9776989; 978-0-9794198; 978-0-9802436; 978-0-9820539; 978-0-9825030; 978-0-9825048; 978-0-9825691; 978-1-935639; 978-0-9850469; 978-0-9857869; 978-1-941040; 978-1-947793)* 2601 NW Thurman St., Portland, OR 97210 USA (SAN 257-2273) Tel 503-219-0622; Fax: 971-222-2548
E-mail: meg@tinhouse.com
Web site: http://www.tinhouse.com
Dist(s): **MyiLibrary**
Norton, W. W. & Co., Inc.
Penguin Random Hse. LLC.

Tingley, Megan Bks. *Imprint of* **Little, Brown Bks. for Young Readers**

TINK INK Publishing, *(978-0-9840916)* 6817 W. Lariat Ln., Peoria, AZ 85383 USA Toll Free: 888-829-5117
Web site: http://www.tinkinkpublishing.com.

Tinkertown Museum, *(978-0-9793124)* Orders Addr.: P.O. Box 303, Sandia Park, NM 87047 USA (SAN 853-1161) Tel 505-281-5233; Edit Addr.: 121 Sandia Crest Rd., Sandia Park, NM 87047-0303 USA
E-mail: tinker4u@tinkertown.com
Web site: http://www.tinkertown.com.

Tino Turtle Travels, LLC, *(978-0-9793158; 978-0-9816297)* 8550 W. Charleston Blvd., Suite 102-398, Las Vegas, NV 89117 USA (SAN 853-0920) Tel 702-499-4477; Toll Free Fax: 800-656-4641
E-mail: info@tinoturtletravels.com
Web site: http://www.tinoturtletravels.com.

Tinsley Phelps, LLC, *(978-1-934195)* 30 Westgate Pkwy. Suite No. 359, Asheville, NC 28806 USA
E-mail: tinsleyphelps@gmail.com
Web site: http://www.tinsleypheps.com.

Tintagel Publications, *(978-0-9743718)* 45 Lapeer St., Lake Orion, MI 48362 USA.

Tintinatie Publishing Hse., *(978-0-9842625; 978-0-9830884; 978-0-9966540)* 32315 Corte Zamora, Temecula, CA 92592 USA Tel 888-998-4684
E-mail: natalie.tinti@tintinatie.com
Web site: http://tintinatiepublishing.com; http://www.sewingafriendship.com
Dist(s): **Lightning Source, Inc.**
Smashwords.

Tiny Stachel Pr., *(978-0-9845318; 978-0-9849146)* 311 W. Seymour St., Philadelphia, PA 19144 USA Tel 215-266-9587
E-mail: TinySatchelPress@gmail.com
Web site: http://www.TinySatchelPress.com
Dist(s): **Two Rivers Distribution.**

Tiny Tales, *(978-0-9627661)* P.O. Box 12212, Wilmington, DE 19850 USA
Dist(s): **Capstone Pub.**

Tiny Tortoise Publishing, LLC, *(978-0-9787477)* Orders Addr.: P.O. Box 752123, Las Vegas, NV 89136 USA Tel 702-798-6646.

Tip-Of-The-Moon Publishing Co., *(978-0-9657047; 978-0-9746372; 978-0-9829121; 978-0-692-93276-6)* Orders Addr.: 175 Crescent Rd., Farmville, VA 23901 USA; Edit Addr.: c/o Francis E. Wood, Jr., Rte. 2, Box 1725, Farmville, VA 23901 USA Tel 434-392-4195; Fax: 434-392-5724
E-mail: fewwords@moonstar.com
Web site: http://www.tipofthemoon.com.

Tisdale, Edward W., *(978-0-9744166)* 3420 SW 1st Pl., Cape Coral, FL 33914 USA.

Tish & Co. LLC, *(978-0-9793419)* 10 Twin Pines Ln. No. 205, Belmont, CA 94002-3889 USA (SAN 853-182X)
Web site: http://www.tishandcompany.com
Dist(s): **Big Tent Bks.**
Music, Bks. & Business, Inc.

Tishomingo Tree Pr., The, *(978-0-9768861; 978-0-9986961)* 606 Bay St., Hattiesburg, MS 39401 USA
E-mail: info@tishomingotree.com
Web site: http://www.tishomingotree.com.

Titan Bks. Ltd. (GBR) *(978-0-907610; 978-1-84023; 978-1-85286; 978-1-900097; 978-1-84576; 978-1-84856; 978-0-85768; 978-1-78116; 978-1-78329; 978-1-78585; 978-1-78565) Dist. by* **Peng Rand Hse.**

Titan Publishing, *(978-0-9770680)* P.O. Box 2457, Glen Allen, VA 23058 USA (SAN 256-6737)
E-mail: sales@titan-media.com
Web site: http://www.titan-media.com.

Titletown Publishing, LLC, *(978-0-9820009; 978-0-9837547; 978-0-9888605; 978-0-9910699; 978-0-9911938)* Orders Addr.: P.O. Box 12093, Green Bay, WI 54304 USA Tel 920-737-8051; Edit Addr.: 1581 Forest Glen Dr., Green Bay, WI 54304 USA
E-mail: tracy.ertl@titletownpublishing.com
Web site: http://www.titletownpublishing.com
Dist(s): **Midpoint Trade Bks., Inc.**
MyiLibrary.

Titlewaves Publishing, *(978-1-57077)* 1579 Kuhio Hwy., Suite 104, Kapaa, HI 96746 USA (SAN 152-1357) Tel 808-822-7449; Fax: 808-822-2312; Toll Free: 800-835-0583
E-mail: transform@hshawaii.com
Web site: http://www.bestbookshawaii.com; http://www.writersdirect.com.

Titus Institute of California, *(978-0-9747452)* P.O. Box 77023, Corona, CA 92877 USA
E-mail: titusbooks@titusinstitute.com
Web site: http://www.titusinstitute.com.

Tiville Press *See* **MiraQuest**

Tixlini Scriptorium, Inc., *(978-0-9723720)* 681 Grove St., San Luis Obispo, CA 93401 USA Tel 805-543-3540; Fax: 805-543-5195
E-mail: tixlini@yahoo.com.

Tizbit Books, LLC, *(978-0-9760553)* 304 Rte. 22 W., Springfield, NJ 07081 USA Tel 973-564-7200; Fax: 973-564-8895
E-mail: jill@tizbitbooks.com
Web site: http://www.tizbitbooks.com.

T.J. Publishing, *(978-0-9760811)* 1099 E. Champlain, Suite A, No. 152, Fresno, CA 93720 USA Tel 559-297-5559
E-mail: tjpub@aol.com.

TJ Studios Ltd,
Dist(s): **Bookmasters Distribution.**

TJG Management Publishing Services, Inc., *(978-0-9762347; 978-1-62193)* 7909 Delbonita Ave., Las Vegas, NV 89147 USA Tel 702-349-7718
E-mail: tjgmanage@gmail.com
Web site: http://www.theresagonsalves.com
Dist(s): **BCH Fulfillment & Distribution.**

TJG Management Services, Incorporated *See* **TJG Management Publishing Services, Inc.**

TJMF Publishing, *(978-0-9759314; 978-0-9789705; 978-0-9801003; 978-0-9829447; 978-0-9910671)* P.O. Box 2923, Clarksville, IN 47131-2923 USA Tel 812-288-7597; Fax: 812-288-1329
E-mail: jimf@dialinn.com
Web site: http://www.tjmfpublishing.com.

TJMF Publishing Daylight Enterprises *See* **TJMF Publishing**

Tkac, John Enterprises LLC, *(978-0-9794454)* Orders Addr.: P.O. Box 7813, Delray Beach, FL 33482 USA Tel 954-632-6360; Fax: 561-330-6917; Edit Addr.: 1095 Hibiscus Ln., Delray Beach, FL 33444 USA
E-mail: adstkac@aol.com
Web site: http://www.jtack.com.

TKG Publishing, *(978-1-884743; 978-0-9755812; 978-0-9825090)* 1800 S. Robertson Blvd., Suite 125, Los Angeles, CA 90035 USA Tel 310-827-9060; Fax: 310-827-9460; *Imprints:* Quiet Time Press (QuietTimePr)
E-mail: cgreco@earthlink.net
Web site: http://www.buyamilliondollars.com.

TLC, *(978-0-9853560)* 12 W. End Ave., Old Greenwich, CT 06870 USA Tel 203-344-9548
E-mail: tanyalceco@optonline.net.

TLC Information Services, *(978-0-9771594)* Orders Addr.: P.O. Box 944, Yorktown Heights, NY 10598 USA Tel 914-248-6770; Edit Addr.: 3 Louis Dr., Katonah, NY 10536-3122 USA
E-mail: ifaywanli@yahoo.com
Web site: http://www.mwsearch.com.

TLC Publishing, *(978-0-9721517)* c/o Tiller Lactation Consulting, 5221 Rushbrook Dr., Centreville, VA 20120 USA Tel 703-266-3823 Do not confuse with TLC Publishing in Paonia, CO
E-mail: stiller@breastfeeding101.com
Web site: http://www.breastfeeding101.com.

TLConcepts, Inc. *Imprint of* **Tender Learning Concepts**

TLK Pubns., *(978-0-9752558; 978-0-9970438)* Div. of TLK Enterprise, 762 Heather Ln., Easton, PA 18040 USA Tel 973-906-2814
E-mail: ugochuik@yahoo.com
Web site: http://www.tlkenterprise.com
Dist(s): **Lulu Pr., Inc.**

TLM Publishing Hse., *(978-0-9748829)* P.O. Box 123, Ozark, MO 65721 USA
E-mail: booksellers@tlmpublishinghouse.com
Web site: http://tlmpublishinghouse.com.

TLOV Publishing *Imprint of* **Kaloustian, Varak**

TLS Consulting *See* **TLS Publishing**

TLS Publishing, *(978-0-9716244)* P.O. Box 403, Dobbs Ferry, NY 10522 USA Tel 914-674-2257 Do not confuse with TLS Publishing in Irvine, CA
E-mail: tls@nvbb.net.

TMD Enterprises, *(978-0-9789297; 978-0-9842980)* 76 E. Blvd., Suite 11, Rochester, NY 14610-1536 USA (SAN 851-9617)
E-mail: dbeerse@tmd-enterprises.com
Web site: www.tmd-enterprises.com.

TNJ Ministries, *(978-0-9762770)* 8214 SW 52nd Ln., Gainesville, FL 32608 USA Tel 352-376-8930
E-mail: tnj_ministries@yahoo.com
Web site: http://www.wtswlg.bravehost.com.

TNMG Publishing, *(978-0-9768297)* P.O. Box 1032, Winter Park, FL 32790-1032 USA
Web site: http://www.tnmg.ws.

TNT Bks., *(978-1-885227)* Orders Addr.: 3657 Cree Dr., Salt Lake City, UT 84120-2867 USA
E-mail: twixom@msn.com.

TNT Publishing *See* **Reasor, Teresa J.**

TNT Publishing Co., *(978-0-9800860)* P.O. Box 456, Richmond, CA 94808-9991 USA (SAN 855-1634) Tel 510-334-2533
E-mail: tanithtyler@yahoo.com
Web site: http://tntpublishing.com.

To The Stars.., *(978-1-943272)* 1051 s. coast hwy 101, encinitas, CA 92024 USA Tel 760-645-1045
E-mail: kari@tothestarsinc.com
Web site: www.tothestarsinc.com
Dist(s): **INscribe Digital**
Simon & Schuster, Inc.

Toasted Coconut Media LLC, *(978-1-934906)* 200 Second Ave., 4th Flr., Suite 40, New York, NY 10003 USA (SAN 855-4862) Fax: 646-434-1102
E-mail: donuts@toastedcoconutmedia.com; sales@toastedcoconutmedia.com
Web site: http://www.toastedcoconutmedia.com
Dist(s): **Diamond Comic Distributors, Inc.**
Diamond Bk. Distributors.

Toby & Tutter Publishing, *(978-0-9847812)* 817 W. End Ave. No. 5E, New York, NY 10025-5319 USA (SAN 920-6868) Tel 212-663-8416; Fax: 212-663-8715
E-mail: laura@lauradwightphoto.com
Web site: http://www.tobyandtutter.com.

Todd Communications, *(978-1-57833; 978-1-878100)* 611 E. 12th Ave. Ste. 102, Anchorage, AK 99501-4663 USA (SAN 298-6280)
E-mail: info@toddcom.com
Dist(s): **Ingram Publisher Services**
Wizard Works.

Toe The Line, *(978-0-9792820)* 7071 Warner Ave., Suite F-497, Huntington Beach, CA 92647-5495 USA
E-mail: toetheline@earthlink.net
Web site: http://Toetheline.org.

Tofte Literary Enterprises *See* **Creative Quill Publishing, Inc.**

Together in the Harvest Ministries, Incorporated *See* **Together in the Harvest Pubns./Productions**

Together in the Harvest Pubns./Productions, *(978-0-9637090; 978-1-892853)* Div. of Together In The Harvest Ministries, Inc., Orders Addr.: P.O. Box 612288, Dallas, TX 75261 USA Tel 817-849-8773; Fax: 888-800-1509
E-mail: contact@stevehill.org
Web site: http://www.stevehill.org.

Together, Inc., *(978-0-9764572; 978-1-933463)* 3205 Roosevelt St., NE, Saint Anthony, MN 55418 USA Tel 612-706-7836; Fax: 612-789-8008
E-mail: info@togetherinc.com; pesellors@minn.net
Web site: http://www.togetherinc.com.

Toki Productions, *(978-0-9729527)* P.O. Box 88216, Los Angeles, CA 90009-6888 USA
Web site: http://www.betteroffthan.com.

TokoBooks, LLC, *(978-0-9720436)* 1863c Brattleboro Ct., Kettering, OH 45440 USA (SAN 254-573X) Tel 937-231-4193.

Tokyopop Adult *Imprint of* **TOKYOPOP, Inc.**

TOKYOPOP, Inc., *(978-1-892213; 978-1-931514; 978-1-59182; 978-1-59532; 978-1-59816; 978-1-4278)* Div. of Mixx Entertainment, Inc., 9420 Reseda Blvd Suite 555, Northridge, CA 91324 USA Tel 323-920-5967; *Imprints:* TOKYOPOP Manga (Tokyopop Manga); Tokyopop Kids (TokyoKids); Tokyopop Adult (TokyoAdult)
Web site: http://www.tokyopop.com/
Dist(s): **Diamond Comic Distributors, Inc.**
Diamond Bk. Distributors
MyiLibrary.

Tokyopop Kids *Imprint of* **TOKYOPOP, Inc.**

TOKYOPOP Manga *Imprint of* **TOKYOPOP, Inc.**

Tokyopop Press *See* **TOKYOPOP, Inc.**

Tolana Publishing, *(978-0-9773912; 978-1-935208)* Orders Addr.: P.O. Box 719, Teaneck, NJ 07666 USA
E-mail: tolanapub@yahoo.com
Web site: http://www.tolanapublishing.com
Dist(s): **CreateSpace Independent Publishing Platform**
Lightning Source, Inc.

Toledo Zoo, The, *(978-0-9776974)* P.O. Box 140130, Toledo, OH 43614 USA Tel 419-385-5721; Fax: 419-724-0068
E-mail: tzgift@toledozoo.org
Web site: http://www.toledozoo.org.

Tolstoy Dom Press, LLC *See* **Vernissage Pr., LLC**

Tom & Susan Allen *See* **Dean's Bks., Inc.**

Tomato Enterprises, *(978-0-9617357)* P.O. Box 73892, Davis, CA 95617 USA (SAN 664-0427) Tel 530-750-1832; Fax: 530-759-9741
E-mail: info@tomatoenterprises.com
Web site: http://www.tomatoenterprises.com.

Tommy Bks. Pubng., *(978-0-9762690)* Div. of C4 Kids, 1220 N. Las Palmas, No. 201, Los Angeles, CA 90038 USA Tel 323-974-8249
E-mail: renegadepic@earthlink.net
Web site: http://www.tommybooks.net
Dist(s): **C4 Kids.**

Tommye-music Corp. DBA Tom eMusic, *(978-1-62321)* 157-17 Willets Point Blvd., Whitestone, NY 11357 USA Tel 718-609-9420
E-mail: office@tommye-music.com.

Tomoka Pr., *(978-0-9657211)* Orders Addr.: 115 Coquina Ave., Ormond Beach, FL 32174 USA Tel 386-677-4219
E-mail: yvonnewpunnett@aol.com
Web site: http://www.tomokapress.com.

Tomorrow's Forefathers, Inc., *(978-0-9719405; 978-1-940793)* Orders Addr.: P.O. Box 11451, Cedar Rapids, IA 52410-1451 USA
E-mail: info@tomorrowsforefathers.com
Web site: http://www.tomorrowsforefathers.com
Dist(s): **Send The Light Distribution LLC.**

TOMY International, Inc., *(978-1-887327; 978-1-890647)* Orders Addr.: 2021 9th St., SE, Dyersville, IA 52040 USA Tel 563-875-5653; Fax: 563-875-5633; Edit Addr.: 1111 W. 22nd St., Oak Brook, IL 60523-1940 USA
E-mail: rcs@rc2corp.com; credit@rc2corp.com
Web site: http://www.learningcurve.com.

Tonepoet Publishing, *(978-0-922224)* 3069 Alamo Dr., Suite 146, Vacaville, CA 95687 USA (SAN 250-3654)
E-mail: tonepoet@jackshiner.com
Web site: http://www.jackshiner.com.

Tongue Untied Publishing, *(978-0-9745783)* Orders Addr.: P.O. Box 822, Jackson, GA 30233 USA; Edit Addr.: 2571 Hwy. 36 E., Jackson, GA 30233 USA
E-mail: maseyree2001@yahoo.com
Web site: http://www.tongueuntiedpublishing.com
Dist(s): **A & B Distributors & Pubs. Group**
Culture Plus Bk. Distributors.

Tony Franklin Cos., The, *(978-0-9714280)* 521 Ridge Rd., Lexington, KY 40503-1229 USA (SAN 254-2145)
E-mail: tff3c@aol.com; ed@crystalcommunications.biz
Web site: www.thetonyfranklin.com.

Tony Hawk's 900 Revolution *Imprint of* **Stone Arch Bks.**

Tony Tales, *(978-0-9791362)* 6024 Cottontail Cove, Las Vegas, NV 89130 USA (SAN 852-5285) Tel 702-245-8624; Fax: 702-898-1359
E-mail: barbarites@aol.com
Web site: www.Tony.

Too Fun Publishing, *(978-0-9773317)* P.O. Box 2098, Vashon Island, WA 98070 USA; 1055 SW 178th St., Vashon Island, WA 98070
E-mail: toofunpublishing@gmail.com.

Too Licky LLC, *(978-0-692-88872-8)* 937 Saratoga Dr., JACKSONVILLE, FL 32207 USA Tel 310-927-5345
Dist(s): **Lightning Source, Inc.**

Toobeez Project-Connect Joint Venture, *(978-0-9765670)* Div. of Connectable Color Tubes, LLC, Orders Addr.: Project Connect JV 1204 Thomas Rd., Wayne, PA 19087 USA Tel 610-975-0102 (phone/fax)
E-mail: jdonahue@toobeez.com
Web site: http://www.toobeez.com; http://www.project-connect.net.

Toodle-oo Innovative Products, *(978-0-9793145)* 2166 E. Wellington Ave., Santa Ana, CA 92701 USA (SAN 853-0890) Tel 714-558-9537
E-mail: w.kawamoto@cox.net; suszanales@adelphia.net
Web site: http://www.makebubblesgrow.com.

Tool Kits For Kids LLC, *(978-0-9819483)* Orders Addr.: P.O. Box 173, Glen Rock, NJ 07452 USA
Web site: http://www.toolkitsforkids.com.

Tools For Young Historians *Imprint of* **BrimWood Pr.**

TOON Books / RAW Junior, LLC, *(978-0-9799238; 978-1-935179; 978-1-943145)* 27 Greene St., New York, NY 10013 USA (SAN 854-7246) Tel 212-226-0146; Fax: 212-343-9296
E-mail: raw.junior@gmail.com
Web site: http://www.toon-books.com
Dist(s): **Consortium Bk. Sales & Distribution**
Diamond Comic Distributors, Inc.
Diamond Bk. Distributors.

Toonhound Studios, LLC, *(978-0-615-37908-1; 978-0-9833944)* 2761 Peach Dr., Little Elm, TX 75068 USA Tel 214-726-2875
E-mail: kurtz@pvponline.com
Web site: http://www.pvponline.com
Dist(s): **Diamond Comic Distributors, Inc.**

Tootle Time Publishing Co., *(978-0-9721706)* Orders Addr.: P.O. Box 62, Cade, LA 70519 USA Tel 337-364-6410; Fax: 337-364-6415; Edit Addr.: 1031 Mary Rd., New Iberia, LA 70560 USA
E-mail: marycelesteclement@yahoo.com.

Tootsiepup Pr., *(978-0-9970290)* 415 Camino de la Tierra, Corrales, NM 87048 USA Tel 505-440-3208
E-mail: liajesse@yahoo.com
Web site: tootsiesvision.org.

TOP *Imprint of* **Top Pubns., Ltd.**

Top5 Co., The, *(978-0-9746760)* Div. of Bucc Wild LLC, Orders Addr.: 785 E. Tibet Rd., Columbus, OH 43211 USA Tel 614-372-3367
E-mail: bzumfelde@hotmail.com.

Top Choice Pr., LLC., *(978-0-9761396)* 28 Worcester Sq., Unit No. 1, Boston, MA 02118-2943 USA Tel 617-424-9726; Fax: 617-262-0702
E-mail: tberkan@mindspring.com
Web site: http://topchoicebooks.com.

Top Pubns., Ltd., *(978-0-9666366; 978-1-929976; 978-1-935722)* Div. of Top Ventures, Ltd., Orders Addr.: 12221 Merit Dr., Suite 950, Dallas, TX 75251 USA; Edit Addr.: 3100 Independence Pkwy., No. 311-349, Plano, TX 75075-9152 USA Tel 972-960-2240; Fax: 972-233-0713; *Imprints:* TOP (TOP USA)
E-mail: bill@toppub.com
Web site: http://toppub.com.

Top Quality Pubns., *(978-0-9726311)* Orders Addr.: 3925 Americana Dr., Tampa, FL 33634 USA
E-mail: parfisher@yahoo.com
Web site: http://www.topqualitypublications.org.

Top Shelf *Imprint of* **Jawbone Publishing Corp.**

Top Shelf Productions, *(978-1-891830; 978-1-60309)* Orders Addr.: P.O. Box 1282, Marietta, GA 30061-1282 USA Fax: 770-427-6395; Edit Addr.: 1109 Grand Oaks Glen, Marietta, GA 30064 USA Fax: 770-427-6395
E-mail: staros@bellsouth.net; chris@topshelfcomix.com
Web site: http://www.topshelfcomix.com
Dist(s): **Consortium Bk. Sales & Distribution**
Diamond Comic Distributors, Inc.
Diamond Bk. Distributors
Penguin Random Hse. LLC.

Top Shelf Publishing, *(978-0-9770443)* 4124 W. Fremont Rd., Spokane, WA 99224 USA
Web site: http://www.melodramerica.com/html/grammar_keys.html.

Top That! Publishing PLC (GBR) *(978-1-902973; 978-1-84229; 978-1-84510; 978-1-904748; 978-1-905359; 978-1-84666; 978-1-84956; 978-1-78244; 978-1-78445)* *Dist. by* **IPG Chicago.**

TopNotch Pr., *(978-0-930037)* P.O. Box 1185, Merchantville, NJ 08109 USA (SAN 669-7798) Tel 609-364-6902; Fax: 856-488-0291
E-mail: maryann@maryanndiorio.com
Web site: http://www.maryanndiorio.com.

Tor Bks. *Imprint of* **Doherty, Tom Assocs., LLC**

Tor Fantasy *Imprint of* **Doherty, Tom Assocs., LLC**

Tor Romance *Imprint of* **Doherty, Tom Assocs., LLC**

Tor Science Fiction *Imprint of* **Doherty, Tom Assocs., LLC**

Tor Teen *Imprint of* **Doherty, Tom Assocs., LLC**

†Torah Aura Productions, *(978-0-933873; 978-1-891662; 978-1-934527)* 4423 Fruitland Ave., Los Angeles, CA 90058 USA (SAN 692-7025) Fax: 323-585-0327; Toll Free: 800-238-6724
E-mail: jane@torahaura.com
Web site: http://torahaura.com; *CIP.*

Torah Excel, *(978-1-930925)* 6415 N. Sacramento, Chicago, IL 60645 USA Tel 773-743-7915; Fax: 773-508-9874; *Imprints:* Shazak Productions (Shazak Prods)
E-mail: torahxl@megsinet.com
Web site: http://torahxl.com.

Torah Institute of Baltimore, *(978-0-9767505)* 35 Rosewood Ln., Owings Mills, MD 21117-3704 USA Tel 410-654-3500 ext. 3; Fax: 443-394-5999
E-mail: tibexec@comcast.net
Web site: http://www.torahinstitute.org.

Torah Umesorah Pubns., *(978-0-914131; 978-1-878895)* 1090 Coney Island Ave. 3rd Flr., Brooklyn, NY 11230 USA (SAN 218-9992) Tel 718-259-1223; Fax: 718-259-1795.

Torch Flame Media, *(978-0-9988161)* 7162 Beverly Blvd, No. 225, Los Angeles, CA 90036 USA Tel 310-619-4251; Fax: 310-619-4251
E-mail: helena@girlunfiltered.com.

Torch Legacy Pubns., *(978-0-9763487; 978-0-9785333; 978-0-615-26544-5; 978-0-615-30182-2; 978-0-615-30191-4; 978-0-615-37024-8; 978-0-9830141; 978-0-9849441)* P.O. Box 165046, Irving, TX 75016 USA
E-mail: torchlegacypublications@msn.com
Web site: http://www.torchlegacy.com
Dist(s): **Send The Light Distribution LLC**
Smashwords.

Torchlight Publishing, *(978-1-887089; 978-0-9779785; 978-0-9817273; 978-1-937731)* Orders Addr.: P.O. Box 52, Badger, CA 93603 USA Tel 559-337-2200; Fax: 559-337-2354; Toll Free: 888-867-2458 Do not confuse with Torchlight Publishing in Colorado Springs, CO
E-mail: torchlightpublishing@yahoo.com
Web site: http://www.torchlight.com
Dist(s): **BookMasters**
Bookmasters Distribution.

Torgerson Meadows Publishing, *(978-0-9767116)* 37492 Outpost Rd., NW, Grygla, MN 56727 USA Tel 218-294-6644
E-mail: sstorg@webtv.net
Web site: http://www.taolc.com.

Tornado Creek Pubns., *(978-0-9652219; 978-0-9740881; 978-0-9821529)* P.O. Box 8625, Spokane, WA 99203-8625 USA Tel 509-838-7114; Fax: 509-455-6798; 1308 E. 29th Ave., Spokane, WA 99203 Tel 509-838-7114; Fax: 509-445-6798
E-mail: tcpoffice@comcast.net
Web site: http://www.tornadocreekpublications.com.

Torque Bks. *Imprint of* **Bellwether Media**

Torres, Eliseo & Sons, *(978-0-88303)* P.O. Box 2, Eastchester, NY 10709 USA (SAN 207-0235).

Tortuga Pr., *(978-1-889910)* Orders Addr.: PMB 181, 2777 Yulupa Ave., Santa Rosa, CA 95405 USA (SAN 299-1756) Tel 707-544-4720; Fax: 707-544-5609; Toll Free: 866-4 TORTUGA
E-mail: info@tortugapress.com
Web site: http://www.tortugapress.com
Dist(s): **Follett School Solutions**
Independent Pubs. Group.

Total Career Resources, *(978-0-615-24214-9; 978-0-9849970)* 2000 Bering Dr., Suite 460, Houston, TX 77057 USA Tel 713-784-3197.

Total Outreach for Christ Ministries, Inc., *(978-0-9745834)* 3411 Asher Ave., Little Rock, AR 72204 USA Tel 501-663-0362; Fax: 501-663-0390
E-mail: tofchristm@aol.com
Web site: http://theonenewman.org.

Total Publishing & Media *Imprint of* **Yorkshire Publishing Group**

Total Recall Learning, Inc., *(978-0-9716238)* 3944 Murphy Canyon Rd., Suite C203, San Diego, CA 92123 USA Tel 858-268-8875; *Imprints:* ExamWise (ExamWise)
Web site: http://www.totalrecalllearning.com.

Total Wellness *See* **Total Wellness Publishing**

Total Wellness Publishing, *(978-0-9744585)* 14545 Glenoak Pl., Fontana, CA 92337 USA
E-mail: micheleiqbal@netzero.net
Web site: http://www.Totalwellnesspublishing.com; http://www.micheleiqbal.com
Dist(s): **Distributors, The.**

Totally Outdoors Publishing, Inc., *(978-0-9726653)* 7284 Raccoon Rd., Manning, SC 29102 USA
Web site: http://www.totallyoutdoorspublishing.com.

TotalRecall Pubns., *(978-0-9704684; 978-1-59095)* P.O. Box 1497, Friendswood, TX 77549 USA Tel 281-992-3131
E-mail: corby@totalrecallpress.com
Web site: http://www.totalrecallpress.com
Dist(s): **Bookmasters Distribution**
MyiLibrary
ebrary, Inc.

Totem Tales Publishing, *(978-0-9843228)* 219 Salzedo St., Royal Palm Beach, FL 33411 USA Tel 561-537-2522
E-mail: books@totemtales.com; danbodenstein@yahoo.com
Web site: http://www.totemtales.com
Dist(s): **BookBaby.**

Toucan Pr., Inc., *(978-0-9744926)* 307 Sweet Bay Pl., Carrboro, NC 27510-2378 USA.

Toucan Valley Pubns., Inc., *(978-0-9634017; 978-1-884925)* Orders Addr.: P.O. Box 15520, Fremont, CA 94539-2620 USA Tel 510-498-1009; Fax: 510-498-1010; Toll Free Fax: 888-391-6943; Toll Free: 800-236-7946
E-mail: ben@toucanvalley.com; query@toucanvalley.com
Web site: http://www.toucanvalley.com
Dist(s): **Grey Hse. Publishing.**

Touch Books, Incorporated *See* **Minardi Photography**

Touch the Music, *(978-0-9837585)* 110 Konner Ave., Pine Brook, NJ 07058 USA (SAN 860-2794) Tel 973-220-9785
E-mail: Claudia@Touchthemusic.us
Web site: www.Touchthemusic.us.

TouchSmart Publishing, LLC, *(978-0-9765060; 978-0-9787517)* 167 Old Richmond Rd., Swanzeyti, NH 03446 USA (SAN 256-3835) Tel 603-352-7282; a/o Touchsmart Publishing (Distributor), LLC, 6522 Waldorf Pl., Cincinnati, OH 45230 (SAN 631-8703) Tel 513-225-8765; Fax: 206-666-4856
E-mail: ccardine@touchsmart.net
Web site: http://www.touchsmart.net.

Touchstone *Imprint of* **Touchstone**

Touchstone, *(978-0-7432)* 1230 Avenue of the Americas, New York, NY 10020 USA; *Imprints:* Touchstone (TouchImp)
Dist(s): **Simon & Schuster, Inc.**

Touchstone Center for Children, Incorporated, The *See* **Touchstone Ctr. Pubns.**

Touchstone Ctr. Pubns., *(978-1-929299)* Div. of Touchstone Center for Children, Inc., Orders Addr.: 141 E. 88th St., New York, NY 10028 USA (SAN 265-3664) Tel 212-831-7717
E-mail: rlewis212@aol.com
Web site: http://www.touchstonecenter.net
Dist(s): **Bookmasters Distribution**
State Univ. of New York Pr.

Touchstone Communications, *(978-0-9790775; 978-0-9973569)* Orders Addr.: P.O. Box 396, Oneonta, NY 13820-0396 USA (SAN 852-3835); 291 Chestnut St., Box 396, Oneonta, NY 13820
E-mail: Touchstonecom@stny.rr.com; bd@bookpublishguide.com
Web site: http://Touchstone-com.com.

Touchstones Discussion Project, *(978-1-878461; 978-1-937742)* PO Box 2329, Annapolis, MD 21404-2329 USA Toll Free: 800-456-6542
Web site: http://www.touchstones.org.

Toure, Khari, *(978-0-692-82465-8)* .

Tower Pr., *(978-0-615-67490-2)* 7211 Brickyard Rd., Potomac, MD 20854 USA Tel 202 944 3810; Fax: 202 944 3826
Dist(s): **CreateSpace Independent Publishing Platform.**

Towers Maguire Publishing *Imprint of* **Local History Co., The**

Town & Country Reprographics, *(978-0-9725808; 978-0-9754383; 978-0-9771894; 978-0-9794860; 978-0-9801439; 978-0-9825067; 978-0-9835219;*

978-0-9896702; 978-0-9968302) 230 N. Main St., Concord, NH 03301 USA (SAN 254-959X)
Web site: http://www.reprographic.com
Dist(s): **Smashwords.**

Towne, Russ, *(978-0-692-56808-8; 978-0-692-56837-8; 978-0-692-57310-5; 978-0-692-57313-6; 978-0-692-57322-8; 978-0-692-57325-9; 978-0-692-57597-0; 978-0-692-57600-7; 978-0-692-57656-4; 978-0-692-57660-1; 978-0-692-57663-2; 978-0-692-60270-6; 978-0-692-70008-2; 978-0-692-70460-8; 978-0-692-70932-0; 978-0-692-72351-7; 978-0-692-74214-3; 978-0-692-77261-4; 978-0-692-80418-6; 978-0-692-80423-0; 978-0-692-81855-8; 978-0-692-90776-4; 978-0-692-94549-0) 1114 Bucknam Av, CAMPBELL, CA 95008 USA Tel 408-364-6987.*

Towne Woman Creations, *(978-0-9981499)* 2805 Mowrey Dr., Bloomington, IL 61704 USA Tel 360-485-8078
E-mail: Tammychewe@msn.com.

Townsend, Diana, *(978-0-615-15882-2; 978-0-615-16214-0)* 3432 Briaroaks Dr., Garland, TX 75044 USA Tel 214-703-9718
E-mail: dianatownsend@aol.com
Dist(s): **Lulu Pr., Inc.**

Townsend, J. N. Publishing *Imprint of* **PublishingWorks**

Townsend Pr., *(978-0-944210; 978-1-59194)* 439 Kelly Dr., West Berlin, NJ 08091-9284 USA (SAN 243-0444) Toll Free Fax: 800-225-8894; Toll Free: 800-772-6410
E-mail: townsendcs@aol.com; orderstp@aol.com; emily@townsend.press
Web site: http://www.townsendpress.com.

Townsend Pr. - Sunday Schl. Publishing Board, *(978-0-910683; 978-1-932972; 978-1-939225; 978-1-945356)* 330 Charlotte Ave., Nashville, TN 37201-1188 USA (SAN 275-8598) Tel 615-256-2480; Fax: 615-242-4929; Toll Free: 800-359-9398
E-mail: bavant@sspbnbc.com.

Toy Box Productions, *(978-1-887729; 978-1-932332)* Div. of CRT, Custom Products, Inc., 7532 Hickory Hills Ct., Whites Creek, TN 37189 USA Tel 615-299-0822; 615-876-5490; Fax: 615-876-3931; Toll Free: 800-750-1511
E-mail: leeann@crttoybox.com
Dist(s): **Christian Bk. Distributors.**

Toy Quest, *(978-0-9767325; 978-0-9786246)* Manley, 2229 Barry Ave., Los Angeles, CA 90064-1401 USA.

Toy Rocket Studios, LLC, *(978-0-615-23521-9; 978-0-578-15192-2)* Orders Addr.: 5410 Fallen Timbers Dr., West Chester, OH 45069 USA; Edit Addr.: 814 St.Clair Ave, Hamilton, OH 45015 USA
E-mail: ToyRocketLaunch@gmail.com
Web site: http://www.ToyRocketStudiosLLC.com; http://www.ToyRocketLaunch.com.

Toy Truck Publishing, *(978-0-9764983)* 4602 Lilac Ln., Lake Elmo, MN 55042 USA (SAN 256-3754) Tel 612-716-8383; Fax: 651-275-1279
E-mail: sales@toytruckpublishing.com
Web site: http://www.toytruckpublishing.com.

Toys 'n Things Press *See* **Redleaf Pr.**

Tpprince Esquire *See* **Tpprince Esquire International**

Tpprince Esquire International, *(978-0-9790110; 978-0-692-22159-4; 978-1-63365)* 6429 Printz Ct. Apt 237, Saint Louis, MO 63116 USA (SAN 852-2219) Tel 41794299891 (swiss portable); 41218821971 (swiss main office); 314-843-0451 st.Louis, Mo. USA; Cretillon 9, Froideville, ch 1055 Fax: +41218821971
E-mail: tpprince_esq@yahoo.com; dan.sekarski@bluewin.ch; tpprince@tpprince-esquire.com; dan.sekarski@bluewin.ch; sandrinesekarski@bluewin.ch
Web site: http://stores.lulu.com/tpprince_esquire; http://tpprince-esquire.com.

TPRS Publishing, Inc., *(978-0-9777911; 978-1-934958; 978-1-935575; 978-1-940408; 978-1-945956)* P.O. Box 11624, Chandler, AZ 85248 USA Tel 480-821-8608; Fax: 480-963-3463; Toll Free: 800-877-4738
E-mail: patgaab@gmail.com
Web site: http://www.tprstorytelling.com.

TR Bks., *(978-0-9788969)* 2430 N. Penn Ave., Independence, KS 67301 USA (SAN 851-8882) Tel 620-331-4486; *Imprints:* Exhibit A (Exhibit A).

Tracepaper Bks. Inc., *(978-0-9792728)* 68 Ridgewood Ave., Selden, NY 11784 USA
Web site: http://www.tracepaper.net.

Trachtman, Joseph, *(978-0-9795170)* 5008 Pullman Ave. NE, Seattle, WA 98105 USA.

Tracks Publishing, *(978-1-884654; 978-1-935937)* 140 Brightwood Ave., Chula Vista, CA 91910 USA Tel 619-476-7125; Fax: 619-476-8173; Toll Free: 800-443-3570
E-mail: tracks@cox.net
Web site: http://www.startupsports.com
Dist(s): **Ebsco Publishing**
Independent Pubs. Group
MyiLibrary
ebrary, Inc.

Tractor Mac Inc., *(978-0-9788496; 978-0-9826870; 978-0-9888329)* 121 Transylvania Rd., Roxbury, CT 06783 USA Tel 860-210-9805; Fax: 260-210-9805
E-mail: bsteers@tractormac.com
Web site: http://tractormac.com.

Tracy, Jean A. *See* **KidsDiscuss.com**

TracyTrends, *(978-0-9708226; 978-0-9814737; 978-0-615-11462-0)* 7710-C Somerset Bay, Indianapolis, IN 46240-3336 USA Toll Free: 800-840-6118
E-mail: tracytrends@aol.com
Web site: http://www.tracytrends.com.

Tradewind Bks. (CAN) *(978-1-896580; 978-1-926890) Dist. by* **Orca Bk Pub.**

Tradition Publishing, *(978-0-9789969)* 1823 Hart Leonard Rd., Cornerville, TN 37047 USA (SAN 852-1603)
Web site: http://www.carouselcarving.com.

Trafalgar Square Bks., *(978-0-943955; 978-1-57076)* Orders Addr.: P.O. Box 257, North Pomfret, VT 05053 USA Tel 802-457-1911; Fax: 802-457-1913; Edit Addr.: Howe Hill Rd., North Pomfret, VT 05053 USA
E-mail: kimcook@sover.net
Web site: http://www.horseandriderbooks.com; http://www.trafalgarbooks.com/
Dist(s): **Follett School Solutions**
Legato Pubs. Group
MyiLibrary
Perseus Bks. Group.

Trafalgar Square Publishing, *(978-0-943955; 978-1-57076)* Orders Addr.: P.O. Box 257, North Pomfret, VT 05053-0257 USA (SAN 213-8859) Tel 802-457-1911; Fax: 802-457-1913; Toll Free: 800-423-4525; Edit Addr.: 388 Howe Hill Rd., North Pomfret, VT 05053 USA Tel 802-423-4525; 802-457-1913
E-mail: tsquare@sover.net
Web site: http://www.trafalgarbooks.com; http://www.horseandriderbooks.com
Dist(s): **Independent Pubs. Group**
MyiLibrary.

Trafford Publishing, *(978-1-55212; 978-1-55369; 978-1-55395; 978-1-4120; 978-1-4122; 978-1-4251; 978-1-4269; 978-1-4669; 978-1-4907)* 1663 Liberty Dr., Suite 200, Bloomington, IN 47403 USA Tel 812-334-5345; 888-232-4444; Fax: 812-339-6554
E-mail: orders@trafford.com; editorial@trafford.com; info@trafford.com
Web site: http://www.trafford.com
Dist(s): **Author Solutions, Inc.**
Bookmasters Distribution
CreateSpace Independent Publishing Platform
DecisionPro, Inc.
Ediciones Universal
Wizard Works
Zondervan.

Trahan, Virginia A. - Author, *(978-0-692-74059-0; 978-0-692-78996-4; 978-0-692-80854-2; 978-0-692-89332-6; 978-0-692-90547-0)* 1649 Sugar Loaf Ln., SAINT AUGUSTINE, FL 32092 USA Tel 904-940-9193; *Imprints:* CVTrahan Publishing, LLC (CVTrahan).

Trail, George (GBR) *(978-0-9559927) Dist. by* **LuluCom.**

Trail Trotters Bk. Ranch, *(978-0-9763209)* 616 N. Aurelius Rd., Mason, MI 48854 USA Tel 517-244-0727
E-mail: rosewoodbouz@aol.com
Web site: http://www.ponypointers.com.

Trails Bks. *Imprint of* **Bower Hse.**

Trails of Discovery, *(978-0-9788926)* 31071 Marbella Vista, San Juan Capistrano, CA 92675 USA.

Training Grounds, *(978-0-9729057)* P.O. Box 5631, Tucson, KY 85703 USA
E-mail: sjrose@plantagriculture.org
Web site: http://www.plantagriculture.org.

Train-Up A Child, LLC, *(978-0-9703069)* P.O. Box 1122, Jenks, OK 74037 USA Tel 918-299-8178 (phone/fax)
E-mail: TrainUpStudies@aol.com
Web site: http://www.trainupstudies.com.

Traitor Dachshund, LLC *See* **Minted Prose, LLC**

Trammel, Crystal, *(978-0-9746327)* 133 Montego Dr., Mesquite, TX 75149-1708 USA
E-mail: minc34@hotmail.com.

Tranquility Publishing *See* **Tranquility Ranch Publishing**

Tranquility Ranch Publishing, *(978-0-9747425)* 25796 Tranquility Ln., Magnolia, TX 77355 USA
E-mail: gcadwalder@aol.com.

†Transaction Pubs., *(978-0-7658; 978-0-87855; 978-0-88738; 978-1-56000; 978-1-4128)* Raritan Ctr., 300 McGaw Dr., Edison, NJ 08837 USA; Edit Addr.: 10 Corporate Pl., S., Piscataway, NJ 08854 USA (SAN 202-7941) Toll Free: 888-999-6778
E-mail: orders@transactionpub.com
Web site: http://www.transactionpub.com
Dist(s): **MyiLibrary**
ebrary, Inc.; *CIP.*

Transaltar Publishing, *(978-0-9771802; 978-0-615-20263-1; 978-0-615-20419-2; 978-0-615-20678-3; 978-0-615-20814-5)* 5517 E St., Sacramento, CA 95819 USA
E-mail: publisher@transaltar.com
Web site: http://www.transaltar.com; http://www.heathbuckmaster.com/
Dist(s): **CreateSpace Independent Publishing Platform**
Lulu Pr., Inc.

Transatlantic Arts, Inc., *(978-0-693)* P.O. Box 6086, Albuquerque, NM 87197 USA (SAN 202-7968) Tel 505-898-2289 Do not confuse with Trans-Atlantic Pubns., Inc., Philadelphia, PA.
E-mail: books@transatlantic.com
Web site: http://www.transatlantic.com/direct
Dist(s): **MyiLibrary.**

Trans-Atlantic Pubns., Inc., 311 Bainbridge St., Philadelphia, PA 19147 USA (SAN 694-0234) Tel 215-925-5083; Fax: 215-925-1912 Do not confuse with Transatlantic Arts, Inc., Albuquerque, NM
E-mail: order@transatlanticpub.com
Web site: http://www.transatlanticpub.com.

Transcontinental Education Inc., *(978-0-692-84805-0; 978-0-692-94946-7)* 11612 Brigit Ct, BOWIE, MD 20720 USA Tel 202-380-7738
E-mail: jeffwcrawford5+LVP0003383@gmail.com; jeffwcrawford5+LVP0003383@gmail.com.

Transcontinental Music Pubns., *(978-0-8074)* Div. of URJ, 633 Third Ave., 6th Flr., New York, NY 10017-6778 USA Tel 212-650-4101; Fax: 212-650-4109
E-mail: tmp@uahc.org
Web site: http://www.eTranscon.com
Dist(s): **Leonard, Hal Corp.**

Transfuzion Publishing *See* **Caliber Comics**

Trans-Galactic Pubns., *(978-0-9616078)* 20 Sunnyside Ave. Suite A134, Mill Valley, CA 94941 USA (SAN 698-0899)
E-mail: transpubls@aol.com.

Transigar Co. LLC, *(978-0-9800466)* Orders Addr.: P.O. Box 5957, Dayton, OH 45405 USA (SAN 855-0735) Tel 937-389-1956
E-mail: festme@yahoo.com; info@transigar.com
Web site: http://www.transigar.com.

Transitional Pr., *(978-0-9960369)* 8679 SW 51st St., Cooper City, FL 33328 USA Tel 954-298-8178
E-mail: Mortlaitner@bellsouth.net.

Transworld Publishers Ltd. (GBR) *(978-0-552; 978-0-85752) Dist. by* **IPG Chicago.**

Trapper Creek Museum Sluice Box Productions, *(978-0-9718302)* Orders Addr.: P.O. Box 13011, Trapper Creek, AK 99683 USA Tel 907-733-2555; Edit Addr.: Mile 3/4 Petersville Rd., Trapper Creek, AK 99683 USA
E-mail: info@trappercreekmuseum.com
Web site: http://www.trappercreekmuseum.com; http://www.sluiceboxproductions.com.

Trash, Steve Enterprises, *(978-0-9652542)* 975 Old Dirt Rd., Spruce Pine, AL 35585 USA.

Travel 4 Life !, *(978-0-9749441)* 2040 E. 22nd St., Box 911, Fremont, NE 68025 USA Tel 402-727-1559
E-mail: deanjcbs4u@yahoo.com
Web site: http://www.travel4life.org.

Travel America Bks., *(978-0-9795867)* 64 Vanderbilt Ave., Floral Park, NY 11001 USA Tel 516-354-2615
E-mail: shajovin@aol.com.

TravelBrains, Inc., *(978-0-9705809; 978-1-933763)* 14 Tether Rd, Bedford, NH 03110-5660 USA
Web site: http://www.travelbrains.com.

Traveler's Trunk Publishing LLC, *(978-0-9841496)* 15071 Hanna Ave. NE, Cedar Springs, MI 49319 USA (SAN 858-558X) Tel 937-903-9233
E-mail: amanda@travelerstrunkpublishing.com
Web site: http://www.travelerstrunkpublishing.com/.

Trawick, Gary E., *(978-0-615-66181-0)* 202 N. McNeil St., Burgaw, NC 28425 USA Tel 910-602-0993
E-mail: jenningstrawick@hotmail.com.

Traylor, Waverley Publishing, *(978-0-9715068)* Div. of Waverley Traylor Photography, 3407 Longwood Dr., Smithfield, VA 23430 USA Tel 757-356-9119 (phone/fax)
E-mail: wlfoto@aol.com.

Treadle Pr., *(978-0-935143)* Div. of Binding & Printing Co., Box D, Sheperdstown, WV 25443 USA (SAN 695-2070) Tel 304-876-2557.

Treasure Bay, Inc., *(978-1-891327; 978-1-60115)* 5 Ash Ct., Novato, CA 94949 USA (SAN 859-0958)
E-mail: customerservice@webothread.com; donpanec@comcast.net
Web site: http://www.webothread.com.

Treasure Chest Books *See* **Rio Nuevo Pubs.**

Treasure Hunt Adventures, Inc., *(978-0-9749809)* P.O. Box 1049, Carmel, NY 10512-9998 USA Tel 845-225-2539
E-mail: info@treasurehuntadventures.com
Web site: http://www.treasurehuntadventures.com.

Treasure Trove, Inc., *(978-0-9760618; 978-0-9772314)* P.O. Box 459, Pound Ridge, NY 10576 USA Fax: 203-801-0099
Web site: http://www.atreasuretrove.com.

Treasured Images, *(978-0-9728770)* P.O. Box 361, Milton, WA 98354-0361 USA
E-mail: snspubs@aol.com.

Treasured Legacies, *(978-0-9819217)* 1589 Althouse Rd., Cochranville, PA 19330 USA Tel 610-593-2053
E-mail: arjoy@epix.net.

Treasures Media Incorporated *See* **BroadStreet Publishing**

Treasures of Glory Ministries, *(978-0-9916112; 978-1-946162)* P.O. Box 23743, San Diego, CA 92193 USA Tel 858-254-1868
E-mail: treasuresofgloryministries@gmail.com.

Treble Heart Bks., *(978-0-9711882; 978-1-931742; 978-1-932695; 978-1-936127; 978-1-938370)* 1284 Overlook Dr., Sierra Vista, AZ 85635-5512 USA (SAN 254-7120) Tel 520-458-5602; Fax: 520-459-0162; *Imprints:* MountainView (MtnView)
Web site: http://www.trebleheartbooks.com
Dist(s): **Smashwords.**

Tree Branch Publishing, *(978-0-9772578)* Orders Addr.: P.O. Box 421004, Summerland Key, FL 33042 USA Tel 305-872-4600; Fax: 305-832-0156; Toll Free: 866-454-6525; Edit Addr.: 19769 Date Palm Dr., Summerland Key, FL 33042 USA
E-mail: info@treeoflifepublishing.com.

Tree Musketeers, Inc., *(978-0-9770196)* Orders Addr.: 136 Main St., El Segundo, CA 90245 USA
E-mail: gail@treemusketeers.org
Web site: http://www.treemusketeers.org.

Tree of Life Pr., *(978-0-9727103)* 7212 Dogwood Dr., Knoxville, TN 37919-8828 USA
E-mail: jana@janaspicka.com
Web site: http://www.janaspicka.com.

Tree Of Life Publishing, *(978-0-9745052)* P.O. Box 421004, Summerland Key, FL 33042 USA Tel 305-744-0330; Fax: 305-744-0320; Toll Free: 866-454-6525; *Imprints:* Peeper & Friends (Peep & Friends)
E-mail: peeper@peeperandfriends.com
Web site: http://www.peeperandfriends.com.

Tree of Life Publishing Hse., *(978-0-9801357; 978-0-9822060)* 730 Gladstone St., La Verne, CA 91750 USA Tel 626-825-5539
E-mail: shaynah@treeoflifepublishinghouse.com
Web site: http://www.treeoflifepublishinghouse.com.

Tree Tunnel Pr., *(978-0-9841037)* P.O. Box 733, Capitola, CA 95010 USA (SAN 931-3931) Tel 831-427-5551; Toll Free: 800-213-1885
E-mail: contact@treetunnelpress.com
Web site: http://www.treetunnelpress.com.

Treehaus Communications, Inc., *(978-0-929496; 978-1-886510)* Orders Addr.: P.O. Box 249, Loveland, OH 45140 USA (SAN 249-5325) Tel 513-683-5716; Fax: 513-683-2882; Toll Free: 800-638-4287; Edit Addr.: 906 W. Loveland Ave., Loveland, OH 45140 USA (SAN 249-5333)
E-mail: treehaus1@fuse.net
Dist(s): **ACTA Pubns.**

TreeHse. Publishing Group, *(978-0-9892079; 978-0-9963901)* Div. of Amphorae Publishing Group, 3963 Flora Pl., St. Louis, MO 63110 USA Tel 314-363-4546
E-mail: kbmakansi@blankslatecommunications.com
Web site: http://www.treehousepublishinggroup.com
Dist(s): **Midpoint Trade Bks., Inc.**

Trefry, Deana, *(978-0-9798193)* 587 Essex St., Beverly, MA 01915 USA
E-mail: deanat@comcast.net.

Tremendous Leadership *Imprint of* **Tremendous Life Bks.**

Tremendous Life Bks., *(978-0-937539; 978-1-933715; 978-1-936354)* Div. of Life Management Services, Inc., 206 West Allen St., Mechanicsburg, PA 17055-6240 USA (SAN 156-5419) Tel 717-766-9499; Fax: 717-766-6565; Toll Free: 800-233-2665; *Imprints:* Tremendous Leadership (TremendLrdship)
E-mail: JLiller@TremendousLifeBooks.com
Web site: http://www.TremendousLifeBooks.com
Dist(s): **Send The Light Distribution LLC.**

Trend Enterprises, Inc., *(978-1-889319; 978-1-58792; 978-1-60912; 978-1-62807)* Orders Addr.: P.O. Box 64073, Saint Paul, MN 55164 USA Tel 651-631-2850; Fax: 651-582-3500; Toll Free Fax: 800-845-4832; Toll Free: 800-328-5540; Edit Addr.: 300 Ninth Ave., SW, New Brighton, MN 55112 USA
Web site: http://www.trendenterprises.com.

Trend Factor Pr., *(978-0-9818669)* 8101 Timber Valley Ct., Dunn Loring, VA 22027 USA (SAN 856-7468) Tel 571-723-5645
E-mail: publisher@trendfactorpress.com; avanderbilt@vanderbilt-consulting.com
Web site: http://www.trendfactorpress.com
Dist(s): **Blu Sky Media Group.**

Trenton Creative Enterprises, *(978-0-9754958)* 731 Springdale Dr., Spartanburg, SC 29302 USA
E-mail: trentoncreativeenterprises@charter.net
Web site: http://www.vintagegastonia.com.

Trent's Prints, *(978-0-9728872; 978-0-9762389; 978-0-9773723; 978-1-934035; 978-1-937000)* 3754 Willard Norris Rd., Pace, FL 32571 USA Tel 850-994-1421 Toll Free: 866-275-7124
Web site: http://www.trentsprints.com.

Treorca Pr., *(978-0-9766559)* 1718 W. 102nd St., Chicago, IL 60643-2147 USA
E-mail: joga9@aol.com
Web site: http://www.treorcapress.com.

Tres Canis Publishing Co., *(978-0-9659065)* P.O. Box 163, Nanticoke, PA 18634 USA Tel 570-735-0328
E-mail: rjanosov@verizon.net.

Tres Clavas Pr., *(978-0-615-37077-4; 978-0-9855731)* 626 N. 6th Ave., Tucson, AZ 85705 USA Tel 480-433-0597
E-mail: zaa@dexterandstray.com
Web site: http://dexterandstray.com.

Trevor Romain Company, The *See* **Romain, Trevor Co., The**

TRI LIFE Pr., *(978-0-9755938)* P.O. Box 2174, Clinton, MD 20735 USA Tel 602-561-1354; Toll Free: 888-786-7526
Web site: http://www.byrongarrett.com.

Tri Valley Children's Publishing, *(978-0-9790962)* 512 Briarwood Ct., Livermore, CA 94551 USA Tel 925-413-0546
E-mail: stephanierutledge@comcast.net.

†Triad Publishing Co., *(978-0-937404)* Imprint of Triad Communications, Inc., Orders Addr.: P.O. Box 13355, Gainesville, FL 32604 USA (SAN 205-4574) Tel 352-373-5800 editorial office; Toll Free Fax: 352-373-1488 editorial office; Toll Free Fax: 800-854-4947 orders & queries Do not confuse with companies iwth the same or similar name in Tujuga, CA, Sequim, WA, Parker, CO, Marlton, NJ, West Hartford, CT,Raleigh, NC , Sarasota, Fl
E-mail: lorna@triadpublishing.com
Web site: http://www.triadpublishing.com; *CIP.*

Tri-Ad veterans League, Inc., *(978-0-9720404)* 31 Heath St., Jamaica Plain, MA 02130-1650 USA
E-mail: triadveterans@hotmail.com
Web site: http://www.triadveteransleague.org.

Trialtea USA, LLC, *(978-0-9741482; 978-0-9778295; 978-0-9796067; 978-0-9821418; 978-0-9841136; 978-0-9828388; 978-1-939645; 978-1-68165)* 7955 NW 12th St., Suite 115, Miami, FL 33126 USA Toll Free: 800-210-0344
E-mail: info@trialtea.com
Web site: http://www.trialtea.com
Dist(s): **INscribe Digital.**

Triangle Square *Imprint of* **Seven Stories Pr.**

Triarchy Press (GBR) *(978-0-9550081; 978-1-909470; 978-1-911193) Dist. by* **Intl Spec Bk.**

Tribal Eye Productions, *(978-0-9800272; 978-0-692-78018-3; 978-0-692-95151-4; 978-0-692-95640-3)* P.O. Box 1123, Santa Ynez, CA 93460 USA
E-mail: garyd1123@gmail.com.

Tribute Bks., *(978-0-9765072; 978-0-9795045; 978-0-9814619; 978-0-9822565; 978-0-9837418; 978-0-9857922)* P.O. Box 95, Archbald, PA 18403 USA (SAN 256-4416) Tel 570-876-2416 (phone/fax)
E-mail: info@tribute-books.com
Web site: http://www.tribute-books.com
Dist(s): **Lightning Source, Inc.**

Trice, B.E. Publishing, *(978-0-9631925; 978-1-890885)* 2727 Prytania St., New Orleans, LA 70130 USA Tel 504-895-0111
E-mail: betbooks@aol.com.

Trickle Creek Bks., *(978-0-9640742; 978-1-929432)* Orders Addr.: 500 Andersontown Rd., Mechanicsburg, PA 17055 USA Tel 717-766-2638; Fax: 717-766-1343; Toll Free: 800-353-2791
E-mail: tonialbert@aol.com
Web site: http://www.TrickleCreekBooks.com.

Tricolor Bks., *(978-0-9754641)* P.O. Box 24811, Tempe, AZ 85285 USA
E-mail: tricolorbrian@hotmail.com
Web site: http://www.mountainkingsnake.com.

Tricycle Pr. *Imprint of* **Ten Speed Pr.**

Tricycle Pr. *Imprint of* **Random Hse. Children's Bks.**
Trident, Inc., *(978-1-887801; 978-1-58978)* Orders Addr.: 885 Pierce Butler Rte., Saint Paul, MN 55104 USA; *Imprints:* Atlas Games (Atlas Games)
E-mail: info@atlas-games.com
Web site: http://www.atlas-games.com
Dist(s): **PSI (Publisher Services, Inc.).**
Trident Press International *See* **Standard International Media**
TriEclipse, Inc., *(978-0-9704512; 978-0-9976342)* P.O. Box 7763, Jacksonville, FL 32238 USA Tel 904-778-0372
E-mail: vtaylor4@bellsouth.net
Web site: http://www.trieclipse.com.
Trigger Memory Systems, *(978-0-9762024; 978-0-9863000)* P.O. Box 24, Waitsburg, WA 99361 USA
E-mail: timestalesmj@msn.com
Web site: http://www.triggermemorysystem.com.
Trillas Editorial, S. A. (MEX) *(978-968-24) Dist. by* **Continental Bk.**
Trillas Editorial, S. A. (MEX) *(978-968-24) Dist. by* **Lectorum Pubns.**
Trilogy Pubns. LLC, *(978-0-9772799; 978-0-615-80854-3)* Orders Addr.: 560 Sylvan Ave. Suite 1240, Englewood Cliffs, NJ 07632 USA (SAN 257-2044) Tel 201-816-1211; Fax: 201-816-8424
Web site: http://www.trilogypublications.com.
Trinity Bks., *(978-0-9743669)* P.O. Box 401, Cascade, ID 83611 USA.
†Trinity Univ. Pr., *(978-0-911536; 978-0-939980; 978-0-9651507; 978-1-893271; 978-1-59534)* One Trinity Pl., San Antonio, TX 78212 USA (SAN 205-4590) Tel 210-999-8881; Fax: 210-999-8182; *Imprints:* Maverick Books (MaverickBks) Do not confuse with Trinity University Press in Bannockburn, IL
E-mail: sarah.nawrocki@trinity.edu
Dist(s): **Bilingual Pr./Editorial Bilingue**
MyiLibrary
Publishers Group West (PGW); *CIP.*
Triple Crown Pubns., *(978-0-9702472; 978-0-9778895; 978-0-9762349; 978-0-9767894; 978-0-9778804; 978-0-9799517; 978-0-9820996; 978-0-9825888; 978-0-9832095)* P.O. Box 247378, Columbus, OH 43219 USA (SAN 914-3815) Tel 614-478-9402
E-mail: editor@triplecrownpublications.com
Web site: http://www.triplecrownpublications.com
Dist(s): **Ambassador Bks. & Media**
Brodart Co.
MyiLibrary.
Triple Exposure Publishing, Incorporated *See* **T. E. Publishing, Inc.**
Triple Seven Pr., *(978-0-9710486)* P.O. Box 70552, Las Vegas, NV 89170-0552 USA Do not confuse with Triple Seven International, Gaston, IN
E-mail: wendy@777press.com
Web site: http://www.777press.com.
Triple Tail Publishing *See* **Farcountry Pr.**
Triple Tulip Pr., *(978-0-9754825; 978-0-615-11380-7)* Orders Addr.: P.O. Box 250, Sanbornville, NH 03872 USA Tel 603-522-3398; Fax: 603-218-6502; 2717 Wakefield Rd., Sanbornville, NH 03872 Tel 603-522-3398; Fax: 603-218-6502
E-mail: tripletulip@roadrunner.com
Web site: http://www.tripletulippress.com.
TripleCrown Pubns. *See* **Triple Crown Pubns.**
Trisar, Inc., *(978-1-886386)* 804 W. Town & Country Rd., Orange, CA 92868-4712 USA.
TRISTAN Publishing, Inc., *(978-0-931674; 978-0-9726504; 978-1-939881)* 2355 Louisiana Ave N. Ste. 2, Minneapolis, MN 55427-3646 USA Toll Free: 866-545-1383; *Imprints:* Waldman House Press (WaldmanHse)
E-mail: bwaldman@tristanpublishing.com; swaldman@tristanpublishing.com
Web site: http://www.tristanpublishing.com.
Tristar Cos., *(978-0-9906595)* 13397 Lakefront Dr., Earth City, MO 63045 USA Tel 314-292-5312
E-mail: chudgens@tristarcompanies.net.
Tritium Pr., *(978-0-9761726)* 8690 Aero Dr., No. 339, San Diego, CA 92123 USA
E-mail: tritium@n2.net.
Triumph Bks., *(978-0-9624436; 978-1-57243; 978-1-880141; 978-1-60078; 978-1-61749)* Orders Addr.: 542 S. Dearborn St., Suite 750, Chicago, IL 60605 USA (SAN 852-6826) Tel 312-939-3330; Fax: 312-663-3557; Toll Free: 800-335-5323; Edit Addr.: c/o Kaplan Logistics, 901 Bilter Rd., Aurora, IL 60502 USA
E-mail: Ordering@TriumphBooks.com; J_Martini@triumphbooks.com; s_kaufman@triumphbooks.com; orders@triumphbooks.com; w.swanson@triumphbooks.com
Web site: http://www.triumphbooks.com
Dist(s): **Detroit Free Pr., Inc.**
Independent Pubs. Group
MyiLibrary.
Triumph Publishing, *(978-1-890430)* 10415 219th St., Queens Village, NY 11429-2020 USA Do not confuse with companies with a similar name in Omal, WA, College park, GA.
Triumphant Living Enterprises, Inc., *(978-0-9786681; 978-0-9852789)* Orders Addr.: P.O. Box 691223, Orlando, FL 32869-1223 USA Tel 407-614-5176; Fax: 407-614-5200
E-mail: LHarris@chpublishing.org
Web site: http://www.chpublishing.org; http://www.facebook.com/chpublishing; http://www.twitter.com/ch_publishing; http://lorettafaithharris.com/products/.
Trivium Pubns., *(978-0-9713671)* Orders Addr.: Dept. of Humanities & Human Sciences Point Park Univ., 201 Wood St., Pittsburgh, PA 15222 USA (SAN 254-5152) Tel 716-982-8591
E-mail: bdeanrob@janushead.org
Web site: http://www.janushead.org.
Trivium Pursuit, *(978-0-9743616; 978-1-933228)* 429 Lake Park Blvd., PMB 168, Muscatine, IA 52761 USA Tel 309-537-3641
E-mail: bluedorn@triviumpursuit.com
Web site: http://www.triviumpursuit.com
Dist(s): **Send The Light Distribution LLC.**
Troika Bks. (GBR) *(978-0-9573013; 978-1-909991) Dist. by* **IPG Chicago.**
Troll Hetta Publishing Company *See* **SBA Bks., LLC**
Troll Hunters *Imprint of* **Stone Arch Bks.**
Trolley (GBR) *(978-0-9542079; 978-0-9542648; 978-1-904563; 978-1-907112) Dist. by* **Dist Art Pubs.**
Trolley Press *See* **Ignite Reality**
Trotman, Kay L., *(978-0-615-13350-8)* P.O. Box 1501, Lake Elsinore, CA 92531 USA Tel 951-898-6094; Fax: 951-898-6094
E-mail: njeri@mac.com
Web site: www.onsafariwithkay.com.
Troublemaker Publishing, LP, *(978-1-933104)* P.O. Box 608, Spicewood, TX 78669 USA Tel 512-334-7777.
Tru Publishing, *(978-0-9890985; 978-1-941420)* 2952 S. Goshen Way, Boise, ID 83709 USA Tel 612-423-1052; Fax: 888-854-7690
E-mail: Kevin@TruPublishing.com
Web site: www.TruPublishing.com.
truckerkidzPr., *(978-0-9856770)* 121 Overhill Rd., Warwick, RI 02818 USA Tel 401-480-3403
E-mail: ckmellor@cox.net
Web site: http://www.grandpaandthetruck.com.
Trudgian, Sherri *See* **Little Sprout Publishing Hse.**
True Exposures Publishing, Inc., *(978-0-9642595; 978-0-9771762)* Orders Addr.: P.O. Box 5066, Brandon, MS 39047 USA Tel 601-829-1222; Fax: 601-829-1656; Toll Free: 800-323-3398; Edit Addr.: 106 Shenandoah Estates Cir., Brandon, MS 39047 USA
E-mail: trueexposures@bellsouth.net
Web site: http://www.trueexposures.com.
True Friends Bk. Club, LLC, *(978-0-9797165)* 3708 142nd Pl. NE, Bellevue, WA 98007 USA (SAN 854-1833) Tel 425-556-4319
E-mail: laurawreeves@yahoo.com
Web site: http://www.truefriendsbookclub.com.
True Gifts Publishing, *(978-0-9796701)* 14 Clark St., Belmont, MA 02478 USA (SAN 854-056X) Fax: 617-741-4013
Web site: http://truegifts.net.
True Horizon Publishing, *(978-0-9818396)* 12306 Fox Lake Pl., Fairfax, VA 22033 USA Toll Free: 866-601-4106 (phone/fax)
E-mail: montgomerylm@gmail.com
Web site: http://www.truehorizonpublishing.com.
True Light Publishing, *(978-0-9656670)* Orders Addr.: P.O. Box 1284, Boulder, CO 80308-0734 USA Tel 303-447-2547; Fax: 303-443-4373; Edit Addr.: 411 Wild Horse Cir., Boulder, CO 80304-0459 USA Do not confuse with True Light Publishing in Homewood, IL
E-mail: tlpub@ecentral.com; orders@truelightpub.com; amber@truelightmusic.com
Web site: http://www.truelightpub.com; http://www.truelightpublishing.com; http://www.truelightmusic.com
Dist(s): **New Leaf Distributing Co., Inc.**
Gangaji Foundation, The.
True Lightening *Imprint of* **Share & Care Society**
True North Studio, *(978-0-9845798)* 518 W. 8th St., Traverse City, MI 49684 USA.
True Path Pubs., *(978-0-9830978)* 9620 Smoot Ln., Argyle, TX 76226 USA Tel 817-879-8229
E-mail: ronda@ronda-ray.com.
True Perspective Publishing Hse., *(978-0-9832399; 978-0-9846672; 978-0-9852094; 978-0-9859892; 978-0-9894026; 978-0-9910561; 978-0-9904624; 978-0-9864305; 978-0-9975539; 978-0-9990755)* 2811 Imperial Point Terr., Clermont, FL 34711 USA Tel 407-383-3356; Fax: 352-394-4443
E-mail: seancort3839@yahoo.com
Web site: www.thepowerofperspective.net.
True Vine Publishing Co., *(978-0-9760914; 978-0-9786088; 978-0-9822087; 978-0-9826694; 978-0-9894869; 978-0-9905326; 978-0-9989239)* P.O. Box 22448, Nashville, TN 37202 USA Tel 615-585-0143
E-mail: timbond@truevinepublishing.org
Web site: http://www.truevinepublishing.org.
True You Inc,
Truman Pr., Inc., *(978-0-9637846; 978-0-9798599)* 5 NW. Ave., Fayetteville, AR 72701 USA Tel 479-521-4999; Fax: 479-575-9393; *Imprints:* Hannover House (Hann Hse)
E-mail: hannoverhouse@aol.com
Web site: http://www.HannoverHouse.com
Dist(s): **Follett School Solutions**
National Bk. Network.
Truman State Univ. Pr., *(978-0-943549; 978-1-931112; 978-1-935503; 978-1-61248)* 100 E. Normal Ave., Kirksville, MO 63501-4221 USA (SAN 253-4231) Tel 660-785-7336; Fax: 660-785-4480; Toll Free: 800-916-6802
E-mail: tsup@truman.edu
Web site: http://tsup.truman.edu
Dist(s): **INscribe Digital**
ISD
Longleaf Services.
Trumpet In Zion Publishing, *(978-0-9716355)* Div. of Spring of Hope Church of God in Christ, P.O. Box 51163, Indian Orchard, MA 01151 USA Tel 413-733-1032; Fax: 413-241-6132; *Imprints:* Solid Rock Books (Solid Rock Bks).
Trumpeter *Imprint of* **Shambhala Pubns., Inc.**
Truth Bk. Pubs., *(978-0-9778261; 978-0-9794861; 978-0-9815203; 978-1-935298; 978-1-937089; 978-1-940725; 978-1-946598)* 824 Bills Rd., Franklin, IL 62638 USA (SAN 912-2834) Tel 217-243-8880
E-mail: faithprinting77@yahoo.com; truthbookpublishers@yahoo.com
Web site: http://www.faithprinting.net; http://www.itseasywithjesus-printing.com; http://www.truthbookpublishers.com
Dist(s): **BCH Fulfillment & Distribution**
BookBaby
eBooks2go Inc.
Truth For Eternity Ministries, *(978-1-889520)* Div. of Reformed Baptist Church of Grand Rapids, 860 Peachcrest Ct NE, Grand Rapids, MI 49505-6435 USA
E-mail: office@girbc.org
Web site: www.girbc.org.
Truth Pr., *(978-0-692-59377-6; 978-0-9974331)* 306 Hideaway Ln. Central, Hideaway Lakes, TX 75771 USA Tel 903-780-1236
Dist(s): **CreateSpace Independent Publishing Platform.**
Truth Publishers *See* **Truth Bk. Pubs.**
Truthful Pr. Publishing, *(978-0-9799707)* P.O. Box 240, Statesville, NC 28687 USA Tel 704-287-8378; Fax: 704-878-8972
E-mail: author@daphinerobinson.com
Web site: http://www.daphinerobinson.com.
Tsaba Hse., *(978-0-9725486; 978-1-933853)* 2252 12th St., Reedly, CA 93654 USA (SAN 254-9441) Tel 559-643-8575; Fax: 559-638-2640
E-mail: ps@tsabahouse.com
Web site: http://www.tsabahouse.com
Dist(s): **Send The Light Distribution LLC.**
T.S.I. Strategies, LLC, *(978-0-9772609)* 140 SE 8th St., Cape Coral, FL 33990 USA Fax: 866-761-4233
E-mail: jim@jamesroach.com
Web site: http://www.producevideos.com.
TSM Publishing Group, LLC *See* **Autumn Publishing Group, LLC**
Tsui Wong-Avery, Sally, *(978-0-9798874; 978-0-9819358; 978-0-9855246)* 2618 W. Canyon Ave., San Diego, CA 92123 USA.
Tu Bks. *Imprint of* **Lee & Low Bks., Inc.**
Tualen (GBR) *(978-0-9556798) Dist. by* **LuluCom.**
Tubbs, Stephen P., *(978-0-9659446; 978-0-9819753)* 1344 Firwood Dr., Pittsburgh, PA 15243-1861 USA Tel 412-279-4866
E-mail: electrpow@aol.com
Web site: http://www.members.aol.com/electrpow/power.htm.
Tucker, Peggy *See* **Heritage Publishing**
Tucker, Peter E. *See* **PT Publishing**
Tucker, Terra, *(978-0-9794578)* P.O. Box 2792 Americus Dr, Thompson Station, TN 37179 USA (SAN 853-5027).
Tucson Botanical Gardens, *(978-0-9792253)* 2150 N. Alvernon Way, Tucson, AZ 85712 USA Tel 520-326-9686; Fax: 520-324-0166
E-mail: execdirector@tucsonbotanical.org
Web site: http://www.tucsonbotanical.org.
Tucu Pr., *(978-0-9766572)* Orders Addr.: P.O. Box 447, Bozeman, MT 59771-0447 USA Tel 406-586-5084 (phone/fax); Edit Addr.: 3150 Graf St., No. 8, Bozeman, MT 59715 USA
E-mail: anndiberardinis@msn.com.
Tudor Assocs. Pr., *(978-0-9760939)* P.O. Box 1804, Payson, AZ 85547-1804 USA Tel 928-978-5799
E-mail: press@tudorassociates.com
Web site: http://www.tudorassociates.com.
Tudor Hse. (GBR) *(978-0-9530676) Dist. by* **Orca Bk Pub.**
Tudor Pubs., Inc., *(978-0-936389; 978-0-9778026)* Orders Addr.: P.O. Box 38366, Greensboro, NC 27438 USA; Edit Addr.: 3109 Shady Lawn Dr., Greensboro, NC 27408 USA (SAN 697-3035) Tel 336-288-5395
E-mail: tudorpublishers@triad.rr.com
Dist(s): **Brodart Co.**
Tuesday's Child, *(978-0-9772795)* Orders Addr.: P.O. Box 2512, Cookeville, TN 38502-2512 USA (SAN 257-2060)
E-mail: tuesdayschildpub@charter.net
Web site: http://tuesdayschildpub.com.
Tughra Bks., *(978-0-9720654; 978-1-932099; 978-1-59784; 978-1-68236)* 345 Clifton Ave., Clifton, NJ 07011 USA Tel 973-777-2704; Fax: 973-457-7334 Do not confuse with Light, Inc., in Lemont, IL
E-mail: info@tughrabooks.com; senturk@tughrabooks.com
Web site: http://www.tughrabooks.com/
Dist(s): **Independent Pubs. Group**
National Bk. Network.
Tulip & Petunia Publishing, *(978-0-692-82983-7)* 3800 Buchtel Blvd #103191, DENVER, CO 80250 USA Tel 720-474-0591
E-mail: jeffwcrawford5+LVP0003235@gmail.com; jeffwcrawford5+LVP0003235@gmail.com.
Tulip Books (GBR) *(978-1-900149) Dist. by* **IPG Chicago.**
Tullycrine, LLC, *(978-0-9746554)* P.O. Box 178, Heisson, WA 98622-0178 USA
E-mail: tullycrineinc@aol.com; tullycrinellc@aol.com
Web site: http://www.tullycrine.com; http://www.book.traditionalcats.com.
Tumblehome Learning, *(978-0-9850008; 978-0-9897924; 978-0-9907829; 978-1-943431)* P.O. Box 171386, Boston, MA 02117-3225 USA Tel 781-924-5036
E-mail: info@tumblehomelearning.com
Web site: http://www.tumblehomelearning.com
Dist(s): **Independent Pubs. Group.**
Tumbleweed Publishing, *(978-0-9720132)* P.O. Box 194, Valley City, OH 44280 USA Do not confuse with Tumbleweed Publishing Company in Eugene, OH
E-mail: tumbleweedbooks@aol.com.
Tundra Bks. (CAN) *(978-0-88776; 978-0-89541; 978-0-912766; 978-1-77049) Dist. by* **Random.**
Tundra Bks. (CAN) *(978-0-88776; 978-0-89541; 978-0-912766; 978-1-77049) Dist. by* **Peng Rand Hse.**
Tuned in to Learning, *(978-0-9768881)* P.O. Box 221016, San Diego, CA 92192 USA (SAN 256-5803) Tel 858-453-0590; Fax: 858-777-3626
E-mail: mlazar@coastmusictherapy.com
Web site: http://www.tunedintolearning.com.
Turley, Sandy *See* **Helps4Teachers**
Turman, E., *(978-0-9753042)* 1321 Singingwood Ct., No. 1, Walnut Creek, CA 94595 USA Tel 925-944-5743
E-mail: shihtze1@msn.com.
Turn the Page Publishing, *(978-0-9832148; 978-1-938501)* Memorial Sta., Upper Montclair, NJ 07043 USA (SAN 860-0864) Tel 973-202-8979
E-mail: rlentin@turnthepagepublishing.com
Web site: www.turnthepagepublishing.com
Dist(s): **Lightning Source, Inc.**
Turnapaige & Reed Moore, *(978-0-9725231)* P.O. Box 412, Scottsdale, AZ 85252 USA
E-mail: reedmoore@turnapaige.com
Web site: http://www.turnapaige.com.
Turnaround Bk. Publishing Corp., *(978-0-9753028)* 5047 W. Main St., Suite 212, Kalamazoo, MI 49001 USA.
Turnberry Pr., *(978-0-9971477)* 150 Crest Rd., Southern Pines, NC 28387 USA Tel 910-693-9906
E-mail: annieh@microcare.com
Web site: www.AnnabellesReadingCorner.com.
Turner, Barbara, *(978-0-9747019)* P.O. Box 893493, Temecula, CA 92589 USA Tel 951-699-3933
E-mail: adayinsanfrancisco@yahoo.com
Dist(s): **Lulu Pr., Inc.**
Turner, Blaine, *(978-0-615-25688-7; 978-0-578-00165-4; 978-0-578-00497-6; 978-0-578-09035-1; 978-0-578-12843-6; 978-0-578-14952-3)* 26626 Lily Lake Inn Rd., Webster, WI 54893 USA
E-mail: blaine_turner@tsco.org
Dist(s): **Lulu Pr., Inc.**
Turner Publishing Co., *(978-0-89793; 978-0-938021; 978-0-940069; 978-1-56311; 978-1-59652; 978-1-61858; 978-1-62045; 978-1-63026; 978-1-68162; 978-1-68336; 978-1-68442)* 200 4th Ave N. Ste. 950, Nashville, TN 37219-2145 USA; 424 Church St., Suite 2240, Nashville, TN 37209 Tel 615-255-2665; Fax: 615-255-5081; *Imprints:* Hunter House (HunterHse) Do not confuse with companies with the same or similar name in Atlanta, GA, Eastchester, NY, Houston, TX
E-mail: editorial@turnerpublishing.com
Web site: http://www.turnerpublishing.com
Dist(s): **Ingram Publisher Services**
MyiLibrary
Partners Bk. Distributing, Inc.
Turner, Rich Photographs, *(978-0-9762410)* 305 Fyffe Ave., Suite 158, Stockton, CA 95203 USA Tel 209-460-1050; Fax: 209-460-1051
E-mail: richt@turnerphoto.com
Web site: http://www.turnerphoto.com.
Turngroup Technologies, LLC, *(978-0-9794377)* 2811 Locust St., Saint Louis, MO 63103-1308 USA
Web site: http://www.hisforhopebooks.com
Dist(s): **Big River Distribution.**
Turning a New Page, *(978-0-9762030)* Orders Addr.: P.O. Box 91603, Tucson, AZ 85752-1603 USA Tel 520-579-7183; Fax: 520-407-6524
E-mail: rick4758@turninganewpage.com
Web site: http://www.turninganewpage.com.
Turning Point LLC, *(978-0-9745745)* 1339 Indiana Ave., Connersville, IN 47331 USA Tel 765-825-9835; 765-265-3207 (Mobile)
E-mail: lsfitzg@aol.com
Web site: http://www.stellarstar.biz.
Turning Point Pubns., LLC, *(978-0-9752742; 978-0-9840986)* Orders Addr.: 2822 Cashwell Dr., No. 233, Goldsboro, NC 27534 USA Tel 615-562-1540 Order books at www.turningpointstore.org Do not confuse with Turning Point Publications in Eureka, CA
E-mail: info@turningpointpublications.com
Web site: http://www.turningpointpublications.com.
Turnstyle, *(978-0-9668541)* Orders Addr.: P.O. Box 810, Portland, IN 47371 USA; Edit Addr.: 1601 W. 100 S., Portland, IN 47371 USA
E-mail: rogdomingo@gmail.com.
Turquoise Lake *See* **FireFly Lights**
Turquoise Morning Pr., *(978-1-935817; 978-1-937389; 978-1-62237)* PO Box 43958, Louisville, KY 40253 USA Tel 859-940-6816
E-mail: kim@turquoisemorning.com; kim.tmpress@gmail.com
Web site: http://www.maddiejames.com; http://www.bellamasters.com
Dist(s): **Smashwords.**
Turtle Bks. *Imprint of* **Jason & Nordic Pubs.**
Turtle Bks., *(978-1-890515)* 897 Boston Post Rd., Madison, CT 06443-3155 USA
E-mail: turtlebook@aol.com
Web site: http://www.turtlebooks.com
Dist(s): **Lectorum Pubns., Inc.**
Turtle Gallery Editions, *(978-0-9626935)* P.O. Box 219, Deer Isle, ME 04627-0219 USA Tel 207-348-9977 (phone/fax)
E-mail: person@turtlegallery.com
Web site: http://www.turtlegallery.com.
Turtle Point Pr., *(978-0-9627987; 978-1-885586; 978-1-885983; 978-1-933527)* 233 Broadway, Rm. 946, New York, NY 10279 USA Tel 212-285-1019 (phone/fax)
E-mail: countomega@aol.com
Web site: http://www.turtlepoint.com
Dist(s): **Consortium Bk. Sales & Distribution**
Lightning Source, Inc.
MyiLibrary
SPD-Small Pr. Distribution
Sprout, Inc.
Turtle Pr., *(978-1-880336; 978-1-934903; 978-1-938585; 978-0-9895971)* Orders Addr.: 500 N Washington St No. 1545, Rockville, MD 20849 USA Toll Free: 800-778-8785 (orders only)
E-mail: orders@turtlepress.com; turtlepress@gmail.com
Web site: http://www.turtlepress.com.
Turtle Press Corporation *See* **Turtle Pr.**

Turtle Time Bks., *(978-0-9770957)* P.O. Box 809, San Luis Obispo, CA 93406 USA.

Turtleback *Imprint of* **Turtleback Bks.**

Turtleback Bks., *(978-0-613; 978-0-7857; 978-0-8085; 978-0-8335; 978-0-88103; 978-1-4176; 978-1-4177; 978-1-4178; 978-0-606)* Sub. of GL group, Inc., 1230 Macklind Ave., Saint Louis, MO 63110-1432 USA (SAN 159-947X) Tel 314-644-6100; Fax: 314-647-2845; Toll Free: 800-458-8438; *Imprints:* Turtleback (TurtleMO)
E-mail: info@sanval.com; rheflin@turtleback.com
Web site: http://www.Turtleback.com
Dist(s): **Booksource, The**
MyiLibrary.

Tuscarora Publishing Company, *(978-0-9860321)* 3199 Sherman Rd, Mansfield, OH 44903 USA Tel 419-529-5596.

Tush People, The, *(978-0-9722514)* P.O. Box 950100, Mission Hills, CA 91395 USA Tel 661-298-2293; 818-897-1734; Fax: 818-899-4455
E-mail: dfav218@aol.com.

Tuttle Publishing, *(978-0-8048; 978-1-4629)* Orders Addr.: 364 Innovation Dr., North Clarendon, VT 05759 USA (SAN 213-2621) Tel 802-773-8930; Fax: 802-773-6993; Toll Free Fax: 800-329-8885; Toll Free: 800-526-2778; *Imprints:* PeriplusEdition (PeriplEdns)
E-mail: info@tuttlepublishing.com
Web site: http://www.tuttlepublishing.com
Dist(s): **Cheng & Tsui Co.**
MyiLibrary
Publishers Group West (PGW)
Simon & Schuster
Simon & Schuster, Inc.
ebrary, Inc.

Tuvott Publishing, *(978-0-9723974)* P.O. Box 18276, Erlanger, KY 41018 USA (SAN 255-3341) Tel 859-341-6004; Fax: 859-341-6033
E-mail: tuvott@fuse.net
Web site: http://www.trinityunveiled.com
Dist(s): **Book Clearing Hse.**
Spring Arbor Distributors, Inc.

Tuxedo Blue, LLC, *(978-0-9754056)* Orders Addr.: P.O. Box 2008, Lenox, MA 01240 USA Tel 413-637-2190; Edit Addr.: 455 W. 43rd St., No. 1A, New York, NY 10036 USA Tel 212-262-5113
E-mail: billiamsw@earthlink.net
Web site: http://www.spacenicks.com.

Tuxedo Pr., *(978-0-9774486; 978-1-936161)* 546 E. Springville Rd., Carlisle, PA 17015 USA
E-mail: info@Tuxedo-Press.com
Web site: http://Tuxedo-Press.com.

TV Acres Bks., *(978-0-9794133; 978-0-615-14014-8)* Div. of TV Acres.com, 1965 Broadway St., Saintckport, OH 43787 USA
Web site: http://www.tvacres.com
Dist(s): **CreateSpace Independent Publishing Platform**
Lulu Pr., Inc.

Twain, Mark Media, Inc. Pubs., *(978-1-58037)* 100 E. Main St., Lewistown, MO 63452 USA Tel 573-497-2202; Fax: 573-497-2507
Dist(s): **Carson-Dellosa Publishing, LLC.**

Twain's Huckleberry Press *See* **Huckleberry Pr.**

Tweener Pr. *Imprint of* **Baker Trittin Pr.**

Twelve Star Pr., *(978-0-9797232)* 1105 2nd Ave. NE, Clarion, IA 50525 USA Tel 515-689-9157
E-mail: duncalfj@goldfieldaccess.net.

Twelve Stones Publishing LLC, *(978-0-9712363; 978-0-692-30050-3; 978-0-692-65064-6)* Orders Addr.: P.O. Box 921, Eufaula, AL 36072 USA Tel 334-687-4491 Do not confuse with Twelve Stones Publishing in Grandville, MI
E-mail: brittbooks@msn.com
Web site: http://www.poemsfromthefast.com
Dist(s): **CreateSpace Independent Publishing Platform.**

Twelve Winters Pr., *(978-0-9895151; 978-0-9861597; 978-0-9987057)* P.O. Box 414, Sherman, IL 62684 USA Tel 217-502-2570; *Imprints:* Shining Hall (ShiningHALL)
E-mail: xii.winters@gmail.com
Web site: twelvewinters.com; shininghall.com.

Twentieth Century Christian Bks., *(978-0-89098)* 2809 Granny White Pike, Nashville, TN 37204 USA (SAN 206-2550) Tel 615-383-3842.

Twenty First Century Bks., *(978-0-9636012; 978-1-893817)* P.O. Box 2001, 507 SCR 528, Breckenridge, CO 80424-2001 USA (SAN 298-248X) Tel 970-453-9293; Fax: 970-453-6692; Toll Free: 877-453-9293 Do not confuse with Twenty First Century Bks., Inc. in New York, NY
E-mail: order_desk03@tfcbooks.com; g.peterson@tfcbooks.com
Web site: http://www.tfcbooks.com; http://www.teslabooks.com
Dist(s): **MyiLibrary.**

Twenty-First Century Bks. *Imprint of* **Lerner Publishing Group**

Twenty-First Century Co., The, *(978-0-933451; 978-1-888264)* 2201 Rockbrook Dr., No. 1916, Lewisville, TX 75067-3830 USA Tel 972-459-6327 (phone/fax)
E-mail: t21cenco@flash.net
Web site: http://www.cleareducation.com.

Twenty-fourth Street Bks, LLC, *(978-0-9726939)* 215 E. 24th St., New York, NY 10010 USA
E-mail: cz@yiddishcat.com
Web site: http://www.yiddishcat.com.

Twenty-Third Pubns./Bayard, *(978-0-89622; 978-1-58595; 978-1-62785)* 1 Montauk Ave. No. 20, New London, CT 06320-4967 USA (SAN 658-2052) Toll Free Fax: 800-572-0788; Toll Free: 800-321-0411
E-mail: kerry.moriarty@bayard-inc.com
Web site: http://www.23rdpublications.com
Dist(s): **Forward Movement Pubns.**

twhiteart, *(978-0-9639670)* 5290 Meadville St., Excelsior, MN 55331-8792 USA Tel 952-474-2083
E-mail: madonna@twhiteart.com
Web site: http://www.twhiteart.com.

Twianie Roberts Consulting, *(978-0-9718019; 978-0-9815629)* P.O. Box 70236, Rosedale, MD 21237 USA (SAN 855-8787) Fax: 301-965-8249
Web site: http://walkintheworddc.com/index.html.

Twice As Good Productions, LLC, *(978-0-9960696)* 1105 S. Rio Vista Blvd., Fort Lauderdale, FL 33316 USA Tel 305-778-2775
E-mail: johnathan@twiceasgoodshow.com
Web site: www.twiceasgoodshow.com
Dist(s): **Cookbook Marketplace, The.**

Twiglet The Little Christmas Tree *Imprint of* **PJs Corner**

Twilight Tales, Inc., *(978-0-9711309; 978-0-9779856)* Orders Addr.: 331 Berkshire Terrace, Roselle, IL 60172 USA Tel 630-351-9311 Sales; Edit Addr.: 2339 N. Commonwealth, No. 4C, Chicago, IL 60614 USA (SAN 851-772X) Tel 773-472-8722
E-mail: sales@twilighttales.com
Web site: http://www.twilighttales.com.

Twilight Times Bks., *(978-1-931201; 978-1-933353; 978-1-60619)* Orders Addr.: P.O. Box 3340, Kingsport, TN 376643340 USA; *Imprints:* Paladin Timeless (PalaTimeless)
E-mail: publisher@twilighttimes.com
Web site: http://www.twilighttimesbooks.com
Dist(s): **Book Clearing Hse.**

Twin Flame Productions, *(978-1-880765; 978-0-692-24690-0; 978-1-68323)* 358 SE Sena Ct., Bend, OR 97702 USA (SAN 990-0934)
E-mail: admin@twinflameproductions.us; admin@speedypublishing.com
Web site: http://twinflameproductions.us; https://www.creativeplaybooks.com
Dist(s): **CreateSpace Independent Publishing Platform.**

Twin Guardian Publishing, *(978-0-9858953)* 8821 W. Oklahoma Ave. No. 301, Milwaukee, WI 53227 USA Tel 414-477-5975
E-mail: debh1913@live.com
Web site: www.dperduehenderson.com.

Twin Lights Pubs., Inc., *(978-1-885435; 978-1-934907)* 8 Hale St., Rockport, MA 01966 USA (SAN 257-8867) Tel 978-546-7398; Fax: 978-546-5803; 6 Tide St., Boston, MA 02210
E-mail: info@twinlightspub.com; orders@twinlightspub.com
Web site: http://www.twinlightspub.com
Dist(s): **Strisik, Nancy**
Windhover Performing Arts Ctr.

Twin Monkeys Pr., *(978-0-9768602)* 146 First St., Dunellen, NJ 08812 USA Tel 732-752-3285
E-mail: storytellerjt@optonline.net
Web site: http://www.twinmonkeyspress.com.

Twin Peaks Publishing, Inc., *(978-0-9722259)* 4708 Mountain Vista Ct., Loveland, CO 80537 USA
E-mail: Twinpeakspublish@aol.com
Web site: http://www.bookmasters.com/marktplc/rr00979.htm; http://www.atlasbooks.com/authorspotlight/asdmiller.htm; http://hometown.aol.com/TwinPeaksPublish/TwinPeaks.htm.

Twin Sisters IP, LLC, *(978-0-9632249; 978-1-57583; 978-1-882331; 978-1-59922; 978-1-61938; 978-1-62002; 978-1-62581; 978-1-64033)* Orders Addr.: 1653 Merriman Rd. Suite L-1, Akron, OH 44313 USA (SAN 859-8460) Toll Free: 800-248-8946; 800-480-8946
E-mail: doug.kline@twinsisters.com; melissa.chase@twinsisters.com.

Twin Sisters Productions, LLC *See* **Twin Sisters IP, LLC**

Twin Sisters Publishing Co., *(978-0-615-23714-5; 978-0-615-24258-3; 978-0-578-00651-2)* 1805 Breckenridge Dr., Del City, OK 73115 USA Tel 405-882-9606
E-mail: twinsisterspublishing@yahoo.com
Web site: http://www.oklahomawriter/tripod.com
Dist(s): **Lulu Pr., Inc.**

TwinAtaa Studio, *(978-1-889926)* P.O. Box 1162, Stone Mountain, GA 30086 USA Tel 770-469-5138; Fax: 770-469-5139
E-mail: twinataa@twinataa.com; srw@twinataa.com
Web site: http://www.twinataa.com.

TwinAtaa/Sanaa Village Publications *See* **TwinAtaa Studio**

Twinbrook Publishing, *(978-0-9759086)* P.O. Box 355, Bedminster, NJ 07921 USA Tel 908-534-6799
Web site: http://www.pleasantdreaming.com/.

Twinkle Bks., *(978-0-9792992)* 1415 Riverbank St., Lincoln Park, MI 48146-3880 USA (SAN 853-0483) Tel 313-381-2082
E-mail: Treasurecloud@msn.com
Web site: http://Twinkleblink.com.

Twinkle Twinkle Little Bks., *(978-0-9771447)* 131 E. Wilson St., Centre Hall, PA 16828-8703 USA Tel 814-364-2237
E-mail: nicole@twinkletwinklelittlebooks.com
Web site: http://www.twinkletwinklelittlebooks.com.

Twins Bks. *Imprint of* **Sterling Investments I, LLC DBA Twins Magazine**

TwinsBooks, *(978-0-615-35370-8; 978-0-615-60112-0)* 14590 Ludlow St., Oak Park, MI 48237 USA Tel 248-968-2135
E-mail: deanna41969@hotmail.com.

Twisted Key Publishing, LLC, *(978-1-947744; 978-1-365-60988-6)* 165 Bedford Rd., Lincoln, MA 01773 USA Tel 954-864-9405
E-mail: gimjarquin@gmail.com.

Twisted Spice, *(978-0-9893075)* 2873 SW 85th Ave., Miramar, FL 33025 USA Tel 954-391-7520
E-mail: Crimpy79@hotmail.com.

Twisted Tree Pr, *(978-0-9778865)* 1232 Grant Rd, Harlem, GA 30814 USA Tel 706-306-9503
E-mail: twisted_tree_press@hotmail.com.

Twister Publishing Co., *(978-0-9749744)* Orders Addr.: HCR 2, Box 6228, Keaau, HI 96749-9304 USA Tel 808-982-7058; Edit Addr.: 15-1915 2nd St., Keaau, HI 96749 USA
E-mail: anxwiz@greensand.net
Web site: http://anomalonministry.panacea.com.

Two Bear Publishing *See* **Cracker the Crab LLC**

Two Chicks, *(978-0-9899544)* 2063 White Horse Rd, Berwyn, PA 19312 USA Tel 610-408-8688
E-mail: ayfriday@gmail.com.

Two Dogz, *(978-0-9767072)* Orders Addr.: 775 Lefort By Pass Rd., Thibodaux, LA 70301 USA
E-mail: zsagabby@yahoo.com
Web site: http://www.two-dogz.com.

Two Dolphins Publishing Group, *(978-0-615-47819-7; 978-0-9836920)* 28494 Westinghouse Pl. No. 201, Valencia, CA 91355 USA Tel 818-266-8210
E-mail: info@twodolphinspublishing.com
Web site: www.twodolphinspublishing.com; www.wendylewisbooks.com.

Two Lakes Pr., Inc., *(978-1-59885)* P.O. Box 384, Saint Joseph, MN 56374-0384 USA Tel 616-822-1865
E-mail: s@twolakespress.com
Web site: http://www.twolakespress.com.

Two Lands, *(978-1-933984)* 1631 Lakefield North Ct., Wellington, FL 33414-1066 USA
E-mail: twolandsoffice@yahoo.com.

Two Lions *Imprint of* **Amazon Publishing**

Two Little Birds Bks., *(978-0-9912935)* 58 Cutts Rd., Kittery, ME 03904 USA Tel 603-828-7343
E-mail: birdie@twolittlebirdsbooks.com
Web site: www.twolittlebirdsbooks.com
Dist(s): **Ingram Publisher Services**
Univ. Pr. of New England.

Two Little Hands Productions LLC, *(978-1-933543; 978-1-936859)* Orders Addr.: 870 E. 7145 S., Midvale, UT 84047 USA
E-mail: rose@signingtime.com
Web site: http://www.signingtime.com.

Two Little Pubs., *(978-0-692-76235-6; 978-0-692-79163-9; 978-0-692-82284-5)* 2447 Stately Oaks Dr., Raleigh, NC 27614 USA Tel 803-622-0319
E-mail: globalpartners202@gmail.com.

Two Lives Publishing, *(978-0-9674468)* Orders Addr.: 2500 Painter Ct., Annapolis, MD 21401 USA; Edit Addr.: 2500 Painter Ct., Annapolis, MD 21401 USA
E-mail: bcombs@TwoLives.com
Web site: http://www.TwoLives.com
Dist(s): **Book Wholesalers, Inc.**
Brodart Co.

Two Pens and a Grind Pubns., *(978-0-615-92288-1; 978-0-9978304)* 5915 Quantrell Ave, Alexandria, VA 22312 USA Tel 8509808678; Fax: 7039976332
Dist(s): **CreateSpace Independent Publishing Platform.**

Two Rivers Distribution, Div. of Ingram Content Group, Orders Addr.: 210 American Dr., Jackson, TN 38301 USA Toll Free Fax: 800-351-5073 (Customer Service); Toll Free: 866-400-5351 (Customer Service); 800-343-4499
E-mail: pd_orderentry@ingramcontent.com; ips@ingramcontent.com
Web site: http://www.tworiversdistribution.com/.

Two Saints Publishing, *(978-0-9625782)* 615 Mennonite Church Rd., Kalispell, MT 59901-7753 USA Tel 406-756-1959.

Two Seed Planters Inc., *(978-0-9755789)* 141 Tall Pines Dr., Leesburg, GA 31763-3143 USA
E-mail: twoseedplanters@aol.com
Web site: http://www.twoseedplanters.com.

Two Small Fish Pubns., *(978-0-9826582; 978-0-9971972)* 109 W. Market St., Freeburg, PA 17827 USA Tel 570-374-1363
E-mail: brendakhendricks@verizon.net
Web site: http://www.twosmallfish.org.

Two Sons Pr., Inc., *(978-0-9748995)* 14 Red Tail Dr., Highlands Ranch, CO 80126-5001 USA Tel 303-346-3003; Fax: 303-791-2226
E-mail: McAdamfam@aol.com.

Two Tired Teachers Connection, Inc., The, *(978-0-9786835)* 151 Michael Ln., Aberdeen, NC 28315 USA (SAN 851-3090) Tel 910-944-8857
E-mail: bevlashley@nc.rr.com
Web site: http://www.twotiredteachers.com.

Two Way Bilingual, Inc., *(978-0-941911)* Cond The Falls, No. 405, Guaynabo, PR 00657 USA (SAN 666-0169).

Two-Can Publishing *Imprint of* **T&N Children's Publishing**

TwoDot *Imprint of* **Globe Pequot Pr., The**

TwoMorrows Publishing, *(978-1-893905; 978-1-60549)* Div. of TwoMorrows Advertising & Design, 10407 Bedfordtown Dr., Raleigh, NC 27614-8058 USA Tel 919-449-0344; Fax: 919-449-0327
E-mail: twomorrow@aol.com
Web site: http://www.twomorrows.com
Dist(s): **Diamond Comic Distributors, Inc.**
Diamond Bk. Distributors.

TwoPenny Pubns., *(978-0-9755671)* 205 Rainbow Dr., No. 10503, Livingston, TX 77399-2005 USA
E-mail: samnalice@twopennytravels.com
Web site: http://www.79scenario.com.

Two's Company, *(978-0-9742862)* Div. of Threaded Images, 303 Wrenn Ave., New Paris, OH 45347 USA Tel 937-437-0095; 513-933-9207; Toll Free Fax: 877-217-0700; Toll Free: 800-487-0095
E-mail: sgray6@cinci.rr.com; timages@aol.com
Web site: http://www.twos-company.biz.

Two-Ten Bk. Pr., *(978-0-578-05661-6; 978-0-9827799; 978-0-9884642; 978-0-9896216; 978-1-941208; 978-1-946218)* 5 Gibson Kees Way, Sissonville, WV 25320 USA; P.O. Box 4215, Charleston, WV 25364 Tel 304-419-4169
Web site: http://www.thedarkslayer.com; http://www.thedarkslayer.net
Dist(s): **Smashwords.**

TyBook, *(978-0-9779631)* 5504 Nieman Rd., Shawnee, KS 66203 USA Tel 503-407-1217
E-mail: clayme@claytonpixton.com
Web site: http://www.tybookinc.com.

TYL Publishing, *(978-0-9753902)* 1902 Spillers Ln., Houston, TX 77043 USA Tel 713-647-9501; Fax: 713-647-9410
E-mail: tylnwt@gmail.com
Dist(s): **Partners/West Book Distributors**
Quality Bks., Inc.

Tyler, J. Publishing *See* **Crush Publishing**

Tyndale Entertainment *Imprint of* **Tyndale Hse. Pubs.**

Tyndale Espanol *Imprint of* **Tyndale Hse. Pubs.**

†**Tyndale Hse. Pubs.**, *(978-0-8423; 978-1-4143; 978-1-4964)* Orders Addr.: 370 Executive Dr., Carol Stream, IL 60188 USA; Edit Addr.: 351 Executive Dr., Carol Stream, IL 60188 USA (SAN 206-7749) Tel 630-668-8310; Fax: 630-668-3245; Toll Free: 800-323-9400; *Imprints:* Tyndale Kids (Tyndale Kids); Tyndale Entertainment (Tyndale Ent); Thirsty(?) (Thirsty); SaltRiver (SaltRiver); Tyndale Espanol (Tyndale Espanol); Tyndale Momentum (TyndaleMomentum); Happy Day (HappyDay)
E-mail: international@tyndale.com; permission@tyndale.com
Web site: http://www.tyndale.com
Dist(s): **Anchor Distributors**
Brodart Co.
Christian Bk. Distributors
Cokesbury
CreateSpace Independent Publishing Platform
Editorial Unilit
Follett School Solutions
Ingram Entertainment, Inc.
Spring Arbor Distributors, Inc.; *CIP.*

Tyndale Kids *Imprint of* **Tyndale Hse. Pubs.**

Tyndale Momentum *Imprint of* **Tyndale Hse. Pubs.**

Type F, *(978-0-9768733)* P.O. Box 1045, Lodi, CA 95241-1045 USA
E-mail: info@enduranceguide.com
Web site: http://www.enduranceguide.com.

Tyr Publishing, *(978-0-9723473)* P.O. Box 19895, Fountain Hills, AZ 85269-9895 USA (SAN 254-7775) Tel 480-836-4261
E-mail: info@tyrpublishing.com
Web site: http://www.tyrpublishing.com
Dist(s): **Midpoint Trade Bks., Inc.**

Tyson, Sandi *See* **Christiangela Productions**

Tytam Publishing, *(978-0-9758602)* 111 Lincoln Ave., Suite A-9, Newark, NJ 07104-4607 USA
E-mail: Tygoode1@aol.com
Web site: http://www.tygoode.com.

Tzipora Pubns., Inc., *(978-0-9722595)* Orders Addr.: P.O. Box 115, New York, NY 10185 USA Tel 347-562-8727; Toll Free Fax: 775-414-2940
E-mail: tziporapub@msn.com
Web site: http://www.tziporapub.us.

U A H C Press *See* **URJ Pr.**

U H H Hale Kuamo'o Hawaiian Language Center *See* **Hale Kuamo'o Hawaiian Language Ctr. at UHH**

U. S. Capitol Historical Society, *(978-0-916200)* 200 Maryland Ave., NE, Washington, DC 20002 USA (SAN 226-6601) Tel 202-543-8919; Fax: 202-544-8244; Toll Free: 800-887-9318
E-mail: uschs@uschs.org
Web site: http://www.uschs.org
Dist(s): **University of Virginia Pr.**

U. S. ISBN Agency, *(978-0-317; 978-0-318; 978-0-614; 978-0-615; 978-0-685; 978-0-686; 978-0-615-17190-6; 978-0-578; 978-0-692)* R. R. Bowker, 630 Central Ave., New Providence, NJ 07974 USA Fax: 908-219-0188; Toll Free: 877-310-7333
E-mail: ISBN-SAN@Bowker.com
Web site: http://www.isbn.org.

Ubaviel's Gifts, *(978-0-9713589)* 1550 Scenic View Dr., Loudon, TN 37774 USA
Web site: http://www.angelicgift.com.

UBUS Communications Systems, *(978-1-56411)* Div. of Khalifah's Booksellers & Associates, Orders Addr.: 26070 Barhams Hill Rd., Drewryville, VA Southhampton 23844 USA (SAN 630-6748) Tel 434-378-2140; 704-390-0663; *Imprints:* CB Publishing & Design (CB Pubng & Design)
E-mail: khalifah@khabooks.com
Web site: http://www.khabooks.com; http://www.khabooks.com; http://www.blackbooksaward.com; http://www.black-e-books.com; http://www.black-e-books.com
Dist(s): **Khalifah's Booksellers & Assocs.**

Uccello Rosso, *(978-0-9819187)* 328 Windsor St., Reading, PA 19601-2124 USA (SAN 856-955X)
E-mail: mail@uccellorosso.com
Web site: http://uccellorosso.com.

UFO Photo Archives, *(978-0-934269; 978-0-9608558)* 27341 Stanford St., Hemet, CA 92544 USA (SAN 240-7949) Tel 520-907-0102
Web site: http://www.UFOPhotoArchives.com.

Ufodike, Ekwutosi, *(978-0-9800538)* 3987 Nemours Trail, Kennesaw, GA 30152 USA Tel 404-574-0193
E-mail: tosi.ufodike@ge.com.

Uitti, Daniel, *(978-0-9708430; 978-0-9819478)* Div. of DaSum Company LLC, 223 Buckingham St., Oakville, CT 06779 USA Tel 860-274-9065; Fax: 860-417-0609
E-mail: dan@uitti.net
Web site: http://www.uitti.net/DaSum/.

UK Abrams Bks. for Young Readers,
Dist(s): **Abrams, Inc.**

Ullstein-Taschenbuch-Verlag (DEU) *(978-3-548) Dist. by* **Distribks Inc.**

Ultimacy Pr., *(978-0-9760205)* 11409 Parkside Pl., Bradenton, FL 34202 USA Tel 941-753-6560; Fax: 941-753-6561
E-mail: info@ultimatefinancialadvisor.com
Web site: http://www.ultimatefinancialadvisor.com.

Ultimate Bks., *(978-0-9725953; 978-0-9788430)* 104 Oakhill Key Ct., Valrico, FL 33594 USA Do not confuse with Ultimate Bks., in Glendale, CA
E-mail: info@opynyon.com
Web site: http://www.opynyon.com.

Ultimate Martial Arts CD, The *See* **Black Belt Training**

Ulverscroft Large Print Bks. (GBR) *(978-0-7089; 978-0-85456; 978-1-84395; 978-1-84617) Dist. by* **Ulverscroft US.**

Ulverscroft Large Print Bks., Ltd., *(978-0-7089; 978-1-84617)* Orders Addr.: P.O. Box 1230, West Seneca, NY 14224-1230 USA; Edit Addr.: 950 Union Rd., West Seneca, NY 14224-3438 USA (SAN 208-3035) Toll Free: 800-955-9659
E-mail: enquiries@ulverscroft.co.uk; sales@ulverscroft.com
Web site: http://www.ulverscroft.co.uk.

Ulysses Pr., *(978-0-915233; 978-1-56975; 978-1-61243)* Orders Addr.: P.O. Box 3440, Berkeley, CA 94703-3440 USA (SAN 289-8764) Tel 510-601-8301; Fax: 510-601-8307; Toll Free: 800-377-2542; Edit Addr.: 3286 Adeline St., Suite 1, Berkeley, CA 94703 USA (SAN 289-8772)
E-mail: ulysses@ulyssespress.com
Web site: http://www.ulyssespress.com
Dist(s): **Ingram Publisher Services**
MyiLibrary
Publishers Group West (PGW)
Two Rivers Distribution
ebrary, Inc.

Ulyssian Pubns. *Imprint of* **Pine Orchard, Inc.**

Umbrelly Bks., *(978-0-9791127; 978-0-615-14064-3; 978-0-615-14065-0; 978-0-615-15448-0; 978-0-615-20654-7; 978-0-692-53594-3)* P.O. Box 2703, Saratoga, CA 95070-5608 USA
E-mail: umbrelly_books@yahoo.com
Web site: http://www.umbrellybooks.com
Dist(s): **Lulu Pr., Inc.**

UMI *Imprint of* **UMI (Urban Ministries, Inc.)**

UMI (Urban Ministries, Inc.), *(978-0-940955; 978-1-932715; 978-1-934056; 978-1-60352; 978-1-60997; 978-1-63038; 978-1-68353)* 1551 Regency Ct., Calumet City, IL 60409-5448 USA (SAN 665-2247) Fax: 708-868-7105; Toll Free: 800-860-8642; *Imprints:* UMI (UMI)
Web site: http://www.urbanministries.com
Dist(s): **Midpoint Trade Bks., Inc.**

Umina, Lisa M. *See* **Halo Publishing International**

Unaluna Ediciones (ARG) *(978-987-1296) Dist. by* **Lectorum Pubns.**

Unbridled Bks., *(978-1-932961; 978-1-936071; 978-1-60953)* 2000 Wadsworth Blvd., No. 195, Lakewood, CO 80214 USA Toll Free: 888-732-3822 (phone/fax)
E-mail: alexa@unbridledbooks.com; swallace@unbridledbooks.com
Web site: http://www.unbridledbooks.com
Dist(s): **Intrepid Group, Inc., The**
MyiLibrary
Publishers Group West (PGW).

Unchained Spirit Enterprises, *(978-0-9717790; 978-0-615-94962-8)*
Dist(s): **CreateSpace Independent Publishing Platform.**

Uncivilized Bks., *(978-0-9846814; 978-0-9889014; 978-1-941250)* 3336 30th Ave. S, Minneapolis, MN 55406 USA Tel 917-495-8637; *Imprints:* odod books (odod bks)
E-mail: chief@uncivilizedbooks.com
Web site: http://www.uncivilizedbooks.com/
Dist(s): **Consortium Bk. Sales & Distribution**
MyiLibrary.

Uncle Dave's Bks., *(978-0-692-68564-8; 978-0-692-84581-3; 978-0-9989598)* 164 Lawrence ave, Washington, PA 15301 USA Tel 724-833-1289
Web site: www.uncledavesbooks.com; www.uncledavehoward.com
Dist(s): **Independent Pub.**

Uncle Henry Bks., *(978-1-932568)* P.O. Box 41310, Long Beach, CA 90853-1310 USA Tel 562-987-9165; Fax: 562-439-5924
E-mail: unclehenrybooks@aol.com.

Uncle Jim's Publishing, *(978-0-9800764)* Orders Addr.: c/o Potomac Adventist Bookstore, 12004 Cherry Hill Rd., Silver Spring, MD 20904 USA Tel 301-572-0700; Toll Free: 800-325-8492; P.O. Box 410, Chino Valley, AZ 86323 Tel 928-636-9419 (wholesale orders only); Fax: 928-636-1216 (wholesale orders only)
E-mail: soonchin@freezees.com
Web site: http://www.freezees.com; http://www.potomacabc.com.

Under License from Andrews UK *See* **New Publications**

Under the Green Umbrella, *(978-1-929701)* 5808 Westmont Dr., Austin, TX 78731-3836 USA Tel 512-454-2414
E-mail: janesbauld@aol.com
Web site: http://www.uts.cc.utexas.edu/~jbauld.

Understanding For Life Ministries, Inc., *(978-0-9714584; 978-0-9721504; 978-0-9749019; 978-0-9797019; 978-0-9822938; 978-0-9833673; 978-0-9850813; 978-0-9904982; 978-0-9970699)* 3665 Kirby Pkwy., Suite 6, Memphis, TN 38115 USA Tel 901-844-3962; Fax: 901-844-3944
E-mail: info@understandingforlife.org
Web site: http://www.understandingforlife.org
Dist(s): **BookBaby.**

Understanding Nutrition, PC, *(978-0-9764002; 978-0-9800334)* Orders Addr.: 505 N. College St., McKinney, TX 75069 USA Tel 214-503-7100
E-mail: info@understandingnutrition.com; jessica@understandingnutrition.com
Web site: http://www.understandingnutrition.com.

Underwood Books, *(978-0-88733; 978-0-934438; 978-1-887424; 978-1-59929)* Orders Addr.: P.O. Box 1919, Nevada City, CA 95945 USA Tel 530-470-9095; Fax: 530-470-9049; Edit Addr.: 12514 Cavanaugh Ln., Navada City, CA 95959 USA
E-mail: tim@underwoodbooks.com; contact@underwoodbooks.com
Web site: http://www.underwoodbooks.com
Dist(s): **Publishers Group West (PGW).**

Unicorn Castle Bks., *(978-0-615-56949-9; 978-0-9890340)* 1110 Pack Rd., White Bluff, TN 37187 USA Tel 615-477-4097; 509-999-4551
E-mail: unicorncastle@bellsouth.net
Web site: http://www.kerrydking.com.

Unicorn Pr., *(978-0-937004)* 3300 Chestnut St., Reading, PA 19605 USA Tel 610-929-8306 Do not confuse with Unicorn Pr. in Northville, MI
E-mail: kthynoll@aol.com
Web site: http://hometown.aol.com/kthynoll.

Uniformology, *(978-0-9815078; 978-1-935344)* 105 Coates Trail, Weatherford, TX 76087 USA Tel 817-629-9205
E-mail: uniformology@mac.com
Web site: http://www.uniformology.com.

Union Creek Communications, Inc., *(978-0-9721404)* P.O. Box 1811, Bryson City, NC 28713 USA Tel 828-488-3596; Fax: 828-488-1018
E-mail: info@researchpaperstation.com
Web site: http://researchpaperstation.com.

Unique Executive Pubs., *(978-0-9744978)* Div. of Unique Executive.com, 1653 Georgia Hwy. 257, Suite A, Cordele, GA 31015 USA Tel 229-273-8121; Fax: 229-273-7289; *Imprints:* Healthful Living Books (Living Books)
E-mail: harvardg@sowega.net
Web site: http://upublish.uniquexecutive.com.

Uniquely You Resources, *(978-0-9627245; 978-1-888846)* P.O. Box 490, Blue Ridge, GA 30513 USA Tel 706 492 4709; 706-492-5490
E-mail: drmels@myuy.com
Web site: http://www.myuy.com; http://www.uyprofiler.com
Dist(s): **Send The Light Distribution LLC.**

Unisystems, Inc., *(978-0-7666; 978-0-87449; 978-1-56144)* 155 55th St., New York, NY 10022 USA Tel 212-826-0850; Fax: 212-758-4166
Web site: http://www.modernpublishing.com.

†Unitarian Universalist Assn., *(978-0-933840; 978-1-55896; 978-1-946169)* 25 Beacon St., Boston, MA 02108-2800 USA (SAN 225-4840) Tel 617-742-2100; Fax: 617-742-7025; Toll Free: 800-215-9076; *Imprints:* Skinner House Books (Skinner Hse)
Web site: http://www.uua.org
Dist(s): **Red Wheel/Weiser**; *CIP.*

United Bible Societies Association Inc., *(978-1-57697; 978-1-930564; 978-1-931471; 978-1-931952; 978-1-932507; 978-1-933218; 978-1-59877)* 1989 NW 88th Ct., Miami, FL 33172 USA Tel 305-702-1824; Fax: 305-702-0424 Do not confuse with United Bible Societies, New York, NY
E-mail: Pteixeira@sbb.org.br; Bdehoyos@biblesocieties.org
Web site: http://www.labibliaweb.com
Dist(s): **American Bible Society.**

United Bible Societies/Americas Service Center *See* **United Bible Societies Association Inc.**

United Christian Fellowship of Chapel Hill, North Carolina *See* **Armour of Light Publishing**

United Comics, *(978-0-9743086)* Div. of Obsidian Entertainment, P.O. Box 401, Milford, CT 06460-0401 USA Toll Free: 800-546-3249 (phone/fax)
E-mail: unitedcomicworks@gmail.com
Web site: http://www.unitedcomicworks.com.

United Educators, Inc., *(978-0-87566)* 900 W. North Shore Dr. Ste. 279, Lake Bluff, IL 60044-2210 USA (SAN 204-8795).

United InnoWorks Academy, *(978-0-9771380; 978-1-936478)* 9721 Conestoga Way, Potomac, MD 20854-4711 USA
E-mail: executive@innoworks.org; staff@innoworks.org
Web site: http://www.innoworks.org.

United Nation of Islam, The, *(978-0-9768502)* 1608 N. 13th St., Kansas City, KS 66102 USA Tel 913-342-0758; Fax: 913-342-0340; Toll Free: 800-331-7668
E-mail: unoi@unoi.org
Web site: http://www.unoi.org.

United Network for Organ Sharing, *(978-1-886651)* Orders Addr.: P.O. Box 2484, Richmond, VA 23218 USA Tel 804-782-4800; Edit Addr.: 700 N. 4th St., Richmond, VA 23219 USA
Web site: http://www.unos.org.

United Optical Publishing Co., *(978-0-9764337)* 9147 Millbranch Rd., Southaven, MS 38671 USA
Web site: http://www.steelguitarbyhughjeffreys.com.

United Research Publishers, *(978-0-9614924; 978-1-887053)* Div. of Solor Products, Inc., 2233 Faraday Ave., Suite G, Carlsbad, CA 92008-7214 USA (SAN 693-5834) Tel 760-930-8937; Fax: 760-930-4291 Do not confuse with United Research, Black Mountain, NC
Web site: http://www.unitedresearchpubs.com.

†United States Government Printing Office, *(978-0-16; 978-0-18)* Orders Addr.: P.O. Box 371954, Pittsburgh, PA 15250-7954 USA (SAN 658-0785) Tel 202-512-1800; Fax: 202-512-2250; Toll Free: 866-512-1800; Edit Addr.: USGPO Stop SSMB, Washington, DC 20401 USA (SAN 206-152X) Tel 202-512-1705 (bibliographic information only); 202-512-2268 (book dealers only); Fax: 202-512-1655; *Imprints:* Defense Department (Defense Dept); Environmental Protection Agency (Envir Protect); Interior Department (Interior Dept); Department of the Army (Dept Army); Federal Emergency Management Agency (F E M A); Food Safety & Inspection Service (F S I S); Forest Service (Forest Service); Joint Committee on Printing (Joint ComPrint); National Institute on Alcohol Abuse & Alcoholism (NIAAA); National Marine Fisheries Service (NMFS); Office of the Legal Adviser, Treaty Affairs Staff (LegalAdvTreaty); Reclamation Bureau (ReclamBur)
E-mail: orders@gpo.gov; rdavis@gpo.gov; ContactCenter@gpo.gov
Web site: http://bookstore.gpo.gov; http://www.gpoaccess.gov/index.html
Dist(s): **Bernan Assocs.**
MyiLibrary
Rowman & Littlefield Publishers, Inc.
Trucatriche
ebrary, Inc.; *CIP.*

United States Judo Federation, Inc., *(978-0-9729790)* P.O. Box 338, Ontario, OR 97914-0338 USA Tel 541-889-8753; Fax: 541-889-5836
E-mail: natofc@usjf.com
Web site: http://www.usjf.com.

United States Power Squadrons, *(978-1-891148; 978-1-938405)* Orders Addr.: P.O. Box 30423, Raleigh, NC 27622 USA Tel 919-821-0281; Fax: 919-836-0813; Toll Free: 888-367-8777; Edit Addr.: 1504 Blue Ridge Rd., Raleigh, NC 27607 USA
Web site: http://www.usps.org.

United States Trotting Association, *(978-0-9793891)* 750 Michigan Ave., Columbus, OH 43215 USA Tel 614-224-2291 Toll Free: 877-800-8782 (ext. 3260)
E-mail: jamie.rucker@ustrotting.com; HRCNews@ustrotting.com
Web site: http://www.ustrotting.com.

United Synagogue of America Bk. Service, *(978-0-8381)* Subs. of United Synagogue of America, 820 2nd Ave., New York, NY 10017-4504 USA (SAN 203-0551)
E-mail: booksvc@uscj.org
Web site: http://www.uscj.org/booksvc.
Dist(s): **Rowman & Littlefield Publishers, Inc.**

United Writers Pr., *(978-0-9725197; 978-0-9760824; 978-1-934216; 978-1-945338)* Orders Addr.: 17 Willow Tree Run, Asheville, NC 28803 USA
E-mail: vsharpe@unitedwriterspress.com
Web site: http://www.unitedwriterspress.com.

Unitrust Design, *(978-0-9752775)* P.O. Box 653, Loma Linda, CA 92354 USA
E-mail: unitrustdesign@aol.com
Web site: http://www.unitrustdesign.com.

Unity Books & Multimedia Publishing (Unity School of Christianity) *See* **Unity Schl. of Christianity**

Unity Hse. *Imprint of* **Unity Schl. of Christianity**

Unity Schl. of Christianity, *(978-0-87159)* Orders Addr.: 1901 NW Blue Pkwy., Unity Village, MO 64065-0001 USA (SAN 204-8817) Tel 816-524-3550; 816 251-3571 (ordering); Fax: 816-251-3551; *Imprints:* Unity House (Unity Hse)
E-mail: unity@unityworldhq.org
Web site: http://www.unity.org
Dist(s): **BookBaby**
DeVorss & Co.
New Leaf Distributing Co., Inc.

Univ. of Alberta Pr. (CAN) *(978-0-88864; 978-0-919058; 978-1-55195; 978-1-896445; 978-1-77212) Dist. by* **Wayne St U Pr.**

Univ. of Ottawa Pr./Presses de l'Universite d'Ottawa (CAN) *(978-0-7766; 978-2-7603) Dist. by* **TwoRivers.**

Univ. of Queensland Pr. (AUS) *(978-0-7022; 978-1-875491; 978-0-646-96356-3) Dist. by* **IPG Chicago.**

Universal Flag Publishing, *(978-1-933426)* Div. of Universal Flag Cos., 1440 W. Maple Ave., Suite 6B, Lisle, IL 60532 USA Tel 630-245-8500
E-mail: publishing@universalflag.com
Web site: www.universalflag.com.

Universal Handwriting *See* **Universal Publishing**

Universal Life Matters, Incorporated *See* **Quality of Life Publishing Co.**

Universal Marketing Media, Inc., *(978-0-9764272)* Orders Addr.: P.O. Box 7575, Pensacola, FL 32534-0575 USA Toll Free: 877-437-7811
E-mail: sales@universalmarketingmedia.com
Web site: http://www.universalmarketingmedia.com.

Universal Messengers Pubns., *(978-0-9768879)* P.O. Box 9039, Wilmington, DE 19809 USA Tel 302-764-4293; Toll Free: 866-207-9301
E-mail: phdfoxx@msn.com; phdfoxx@verizon.net
Web site: http://mysite.verizon.net/vze0488v.

Universal Pubs., *(978-0-9658564; 978-1-58112; 978-1-59942; 978-1-61233; 978-1-62734)* Orders Addr.: 200 Spectrum Ctr. #300, Irvine, CA 92618-5004 USA Tel 949-416-5590
E-mail: bookorders@upublish.com; bookorders@universal-publishers.com
Web site: http://www.dissertation.com; http://www.universal-publishers.com; http://www.BrownWalker.com.

Universal Publishing, *(978-1-883421; 978-1-931181; 978-1-934732)* Subs. of Gutenberg, Inc., 100 4th St., Honesdale, PA 18431 USA Tel 570-251-0260; Fax: 570-251-0264; Toll Free: 800-940-2270 Do not confuse with companies with the same or similar name in Ecino, CA, Egg Harbor Township, NJ, Gainesville, FL, Newport Beach, CA, Stoughton, MA, Pasadena, CA, Oak Park, IL, Jacksonville, FL
E-mail: tom@upub.net; larry@upub.net
Web site: http://www.upub.net; http://www.universalpublishing.net.

Universal Publishing LLC, *(978-0-9840456)* P.O. Box 99491, Emeryville, CA 94606 USA Tel 510-485-1183
E-mail: universalpublishingllc@gmail.com
Web site: www.universalpublishingllc@gmail.com.

Universal Reference Pubns. *Imprint of* **Grey Hse. Publishing**

Universal Values Media, LLC, *(978-0-9729821; 978-1-60210)* 3800 Powell Ln., No. 823, Falls Church, VA 22041 USA
Web site: http://www.onceandfuturebooks.com.

Universe Publishing, *(978-0-7893; 978-0-87663; 978-1-55550)* Div. of Rizzoli International Pubns., Inc., 300 Park Ave. S., 3rd Flr., New York, NY 10010 USA (SAN 202-537X) Tel 212-387-3400; Fax: 212-387-3444 Do not confuse with similar names in North Hollywood, CA, Englewood, NJ, Mendocino, CA
Dist(s): **Andrews McMeel Publishing**
Ingram Publisher Services
MyiLibrary
Penguin Random Hse. LLC
Random Hse., Inc.
Rizzoli International Pubns., Inc.

Univ. At Buffalo, Child Care Ctr., *(978-0-9712349)* Butler Annex A, 3435 Main St., Buffalo, NY 14214-3011 USA Tel 716-829-2226
E-mail: rorrange@buffalo.edu.

Univ. Editions, *(978-0-9711659; 978-0-615-11379-1; 978-0-692-63610-7)* 1003 W. Centennial Dr., Peoria, IL 61614-2828 USA Tel 309-692-0621; Fax: 309-693-0628 Do not confuse with University Editions in Huntington, WV
E-mail: mikruc@aol.com
Web site: http://www.terrythetractor.com.

Univ. Games, *(978-0-935145; 978-1-57528)* 2030 Harrison St., San Francisco, CA 94110-1310 USA (SAN 695-2321) Tel 415-503-1600; Fax: 415-503-0085
E-mail: info@ugames.com
Web site: http://www.ugames.com.

†Univ. of Alabama Pr., *(978-0-8173)* Orders Addr.: 11030 S. Langley, Chicago, IL 60628 USA Tel 773-702-7000; Toll Free: 800-621-2736; Edit Addr.: P.O. Box 870380, Tuscaloosa, AL 35487-0380 USA (SAN 202-5272) Tel 205-348-5180; Fax: 205-348-9201
Web site: http://www.uapress.ua.edu
Dist(s): **Casemate Academic**
Chicago Distribution Ctr.
Univ. of Chicago Pr.
ebrary, Inc.; *CIP.*

Univ. of Alaska Pr., *(978-0-912006; 978-1-889963; 978-1-60223)* P.O. Box 756240, Fairbanks, AK 99775-6240 USA (SAN 203-3011) Tel 907-474-5831; Fax: 907-474-5502; Toll Free: 888-252-6657
E-mail: fypress@uaf.edu; sue.mitchell@alaska.edu
Web site: http://www.alaska.edu/uapress
Dist(s): **Chicago Distribution Ctr.**
Wizard Works
ebrary, Inc.

Univ. of Arizona, Poetry Ctr., Arizona Board of Regents, *(978-0-9727635)* c/o Univ. of Arizona Poetry Ctr.,, 1216 N. Cherry Ave., Tucson, AZ 85719 USA Tel 520-626-3765; Fax: 520-621-5566
E-mail: poetry@u.arizona.edu
Web site: http://www.poetrycenter.arizona.edu.

†University of Arizona Pr., *(978-0-8165; 978-1-941451)* 355 S. Euclid Ave., Suite 103, Tucson, AZ 85719 USA (SAN 205-468X) Tel 520-621-1441; Fax: 520-621-8899; Toll Free: 800-426-3797 (orders)
E-mail: orders@uapress.arizona.edu
Web site: http://www.uapress.arizona.edu
Dist(s): **Casemate Academic**
Chicago Distribution Ctr.
Continental Bk. Co., Inc.
Many Feathers Bks. & Maps
MyiLibrary
Univ. of Chicago Pr.
Univ of Arizona Critical Languages Program
ebrary, Inc.; *CIP.*

†Univ. of Arkansas Pr., *(978-0-938626; 978-1-55728; 978-1-61075; 978-1-68226)* 105 N. McIlroy Ave., Fayetteville, AR 72701 USA (SAN 239-3972) Tel 479-575-7544; Fax: 479-575-6044; Toll Free: 800-626-0090
E-mail: info@uapress.com
Web site: http://www.uapress.com; http://www.uark.edu/~uaprinfo
Dist(s): **Chicago Distribution Ctr.**
MyiLibrary
Yankee Peddler Bookshop
ebrary, Inc.; *CIP.*

Univ. of California, Berkeley, Lawrence Hall of Science, *(978-0-912511; 978-0-924886; 978-1-931542)* U of CA, Lawrence Hall of Science, Berkeley, CA 94720-5200 USA (SAN 271-9754) Tel 510-642-7771; Fax: 510-643-0309; *Imprints:* GEMS (GEMS); EQUALS (EQUALS)
E-mail: gems@berkeley.edu
Web site: http://www.lhs.berkeley.edu; http://www.lhsgems.org
Dist(s): **Distributors, The.**

†Univ. of California Pr., *(978-0-520)* 155 Grand Ave., Suite 400, Oakland, CA 94612-3758 USA Tel 510-883-8232 (Books & Journals); Fax: 510-836-8910
E-mail: journals@ucpress.edu; orders@cpfsinc.com; askucp@ucpress.edu
Web site: http://www.ucpress.edu
Dist(s): **California Princeton Fulfillment Services**
Ebsco Publishing
Facts On File, Inc.
ISD
MyiLibrary
Oxford Univ. Pr., Inc.
Ingram Academic
Two Rivers Distribution
Wiley, John & Sons, Inc.
ebrary, Inc.; *CIP.*

†Univ. of Chicago Pr., *(978-0-226; 978-0-89065; 978-0-943056; 978-1-892850)* Orders Addr.: 11030 S. Langley Ave., Chicago, IL 60628 USA (SAN 202-5280) Tel 773-702-7000; Fax: 773-702-7212; Toll Free Fax: 800-621-8476 (US & Canada); Toll Free: 800-621-2736 (US & Canada); Edit Addr.: 1427 E. 60th St., Chicago, IL 60637 USA (SAN 202-5299) Tel 773-702-7700; 773-702-7748 (Marketing & Sales); Fax: 773-702-9756
E-mail: general@press.uchicago.edu; kh@press.uchicago.edu; custserv@press.uchicago.edu; sales@press.uchicago.edu; marketing@press.uchicago.edu; publicity@press.uchicago.edu
Web site: http://www.press.uchicago.edu
Dist(s): **Chicago Distribution Ctr.**
CreateSpace Independent Publishing Platform
Ebsco Publishing
Giron Bks.
MyiLibrary
Oxford Univ. Pr., Inc.
TNT Media Group, Inc.

Wiley, John & Sons, Inc.
ebrary, Inc.; *CIP.*

Univ. of Denver, Ctr. for Teaching International Relations Pubns., *(978-0-943804)* 2201 S. Gaylord St., Denver, CO 80208 USA (SAN 241-0877) Tel 303-871-2697; Fax: 303-871-2456
E-mail: ctir-press@du.edu; pubsinfo@du.edu
Web site: http://www.du.edu/ctir
Dist(s): **Lightning Source, Inc.**
Social Studies Schl. Service
Teacher's Discovery.

†Univ. of Georgia, Carl Vinson Institute of Government, *(978-0-89854)* 201 N. Milledge Ave., Athens, GA 30602 USA (SAN 212-8012) Tel 706-542-2736; Fax: 706-542-6239
E-mail: pou@cviog.uga.edu
Web site: http://www.cviog.uga.edu; *CIP.*

†Univ. of Georgia Pr., *(978-0-8203)* Orders Addr.: 4435 Atlanta Hwy. West Dock, Athens, GA 30602 USA; Edit Addr.: Main Library, Third Flr. 320 S. Jackson St., Athens, GA 30602 USA (SAN 203-3054) Fax: 706-542-2558; Toll Free: 800-266-5842
E-mail: books@uga.edu
Web site: http://www.ugapress.org
Dist(s): **Ebsco Publishing**
Longleaf Services
MyiLibrary
ebrary, Inc.; *CIP.*

Univ. of Guam, Micronesian Area Research Ctr., *(978-1-878453; 978-0-9800331; 978-1-935198)* 303 University Dr., UOG Sta., Mangilao, GU 96923 USA Tel 671-735-2150; Fax: 671-734-7403
Web site: http://www.uog.edu/marc.

†Univ. of Hawaii Pr., *(978-0-8248; 978-0-87022)* Orders Addr.: 2840 Kolowalu St., Honolulu, HI 96822-1888 USA (SAN 202-5353) Tel 808-956-8255; Fax: 808-988-6052; Toll Free Fax: 800-650-7811; Toll Free: 888-847-7377; *Imprints:* Latitude 20 (Latitude Twenty)
E-mail: uhpmkt@hawaii.edu; uhpbooks@hawaii.edu
Web site: http://www.uhpress.hawaii.edu
Dist(s): **Booklines Hawaii, Ltd.**
De Gruyter, Inc.; *CIP.*

†Univ. of Iowa Pr., *(978-0-87745; 978-1-58729; 978-1-60938)* Div. of The University of Iowa, Orders Addr.: c/o Chicago Distribution Ctr. 11030 S. Langley Ave., Chicago, IL 60628 USA Toll Free Fax: 800-621-8476; Toll Free: 800-621-2736; Edit Addr.: 100 Kuhl Hse. 119 W. Park Rd., Iowa City, IA 52242-1000 USA (SAN 203-3070) Tel 319-335-2000; Fax: 319-335-2055 Do not confuse with Univ. of Iowa, Pubns. Dept. at same address
E-mail: uipress@uiowa.edu
Web site: http://www.uiowapress.org
Dist(s): **Chicago Distribution Ctr.**
Ebsco Publishing
Univ. of Chicago Pr.
ebrary, Inc.; *CIP.*

University of Louisiana at Lafayette *See* **Univ. of Louisiana at Lafayette Pr.**

Univ. of Louisiana at Lafayette Pr., *(978-0-940984; 978-1-887366; 978-1-935754; 978-1-946160)* P.O. Box 40831, Lafayette, LA 70504 USA (SAN 630-9755) Tel 337-482-6027; Fax: 337-482-6028
E-mail: cls@louisiana.edu
Web site: http://www.ulpress.org
Dist(s): **Forest Sales & Distributing Co.**

†Univ. of Michigan Pr., *(978-0-472)* Orders Addr.: c/o Chicago Distribution Center, Perseus Distribution 1094 Flex Dr., Jackson, TN 38301 USA (SAN 282-4884) Toll Free Fax: 800-351-5073; Toll Free: 800-343-4499 , ext. 165; Edit Addr.: 839 Greene St., Ann Arbor, MI 48104-3209 USA Tel 734-764-4388; Fax: 734-615-1540
E-mail: um.press@umich.edu
Web site: http://www.press.umich.edu/
Dist(s): **Chicago Distribution Ctr.**
Ebsco Publishing
MyiLibrary
Palgrave Macmillan
ebrary, Inc.; *CIP.*

†Univ. of Minnesota Pr., *(978-0-8166; 978-1-4529; 978-1-5179)* Affil. of Univ. of Minnesota, 111 Third Ave. S., Suite 290, Minneapolis, MN 55401-2520 USA (SAN 213-2648) Tel 612-627-1970; Fax: 612-627-1980
E-mail: ump@umn.edu
Web site: http://www.upress.umn.edu
Dist(s): **Chicago Distribution Ctr.**
Ebsco Publishing
MyiLibrary
Univ. of Chicago Pr.
ebrary, Inc.; *CIP.*

Univ. of Missouri, Extension, *(978-0-933842)* c/o Extension Pubns., Univ. of Missouri, 2800 Maguire Blvd., Columbia, MO 65211 USA (SAN 688-427X) Tel 573-882-7216; Fax: 573-884-5038; Toll Free: 800-292-0969; 2800 Maguire Blvd., Columbia, MO 65211
E-mail: extpubs@missouri.edu; umccafnrexplore@missouri.edu; muextensionweb@missouri.edu
Web site: http://www.muextension.missouri.edu/xplor.

†Univ. of Missouri Pr., *(978-0-8262)* 2910 LeMone Blvd., Columbia, MO 65201 USA (SAN 203-3143) Tel 573-882-7641; Fax: 573-884-4498; Toll Free: 800-828-1894 (orders only)
E-mail: rennerk@umsystem.edu; deandj@umsystem.edu
Web site: http://press.umsystem.edu
Dist(s): **Chicago Distribution Ctr.**
East-West Export Bks.
Ebsco Publishing
Lulu Pr., Inc.
Univ. of Chicago Pr.
ebrary, Inc.; *CIP.*

Univ. of Montana Pr., The, *(978-0-9754009; 978-0-9815760; 978-0-9837259; 978-0-9894031; 978-0-9909748; 978-0-9983438)* Div. of The Univ. of Montana, The University of Montana 32 Campus Dr. Todd Bldg., Lower Level, Missoula, MT 59812-0792 USA (SAN 255-9994) Tel 406-243-2711; Fax: 406-243-2615
E-mail: ken.price@umontana.edu
Web site: http://www.umt.edu/printingandgraphics.com.

†Univ. of Nebraska Pr., *(978-0-8032; 978-1-4962; 978-1-64012)* Orders Addr.: 1111 Lincoln Mall, Lincoln, NE 68588-0630 USA Tel 402-472-3581; 402-472-7702; Fax: 402-472-6214; Toll Free Fax: 800-526-2617; Toll Free: 800-755-1105; Edit Addr.: P.O. Box 880630, Lincoln, NE 68588-0630 USA (SAN 202-5337); *Imprints:* Bison Books (Bison Books)
E-mail: pressmail@unl.edu
Web site: http://www.nebraskapress.unl.edu; http://www.bisonbooks.com
Dist(s): **Continental Bk. Co., Inc.**
Ebsco Publishing
Longleaf Services
MyiLibrary
ebrary, Inc.; *CIP.*

Univ. of Nebraska-Lincoln, GPN, *(978-0-7941)* Orders Addr.: P.O. Box 80669, Lincoln, NE 68501-0669 USA (SAN 179-1699) Tel 402-472-2007; Fax: 402-472-4076; Toll Free: 800-228-4630; Edit Addr.: 1800 N. 33rd St., Lincoln, NE 68583 USA
E-mail: gpn@unl.edu
Web site: http://gpn.unl.edu; http://shopgpn.com/.

†Univ. of New Mexico Pr., *(978-0-8263; 978-0-9766839)* Orders Addr.: 1312 Basehart Rd., SE, Albuquerque, NM 87106-4363 USA (SAN 213-9588) Tel 505-277-2346; 505-272-7777 (orders); Toll Free Fax: 800-622-8667; Toll Free: 800-249-7737 (orders)
E-mail: unmpress@unm.edu
Web site: http://www.unmpress.com
Dist(s): **Bks. West**
Casemate Academic
Continental Bk. Co., Inc.
D.A.P./Distributed Art Pubs.
MyiLibrary
Rio Nuevo Pubs.
ebrary, Inc.; *CIP.*

†Univ. of North Carolina Pr., *(978-0-8078; 978-1-4696)* c/o Longleaf Services, 116 S. Boundary sT., Chapel Hill, NC 27514-3808 USA (SAN 203-3151) Tel 919-966-3561; Fax: 919-966-3829; Toll Free Fax: 800-272-6817; Toll Free: 800-848-6224
E-mail: uncpress@unc.edu
Web site: http://www.uncpress.unc.edu
Dist(s): **CreateSpace Independent Publishing Platform**
Ebsco Publishing
Longleaf Services
Oxford Univ. Pr., Inc.
ebrary, Inc.; *CIP.*

†Univ. of Oklahoma Pr., *(978-0-8061)* Orders Addr.: 2800 Venture Dr., Norman, OK 73069-8218 USA Tel 405-325-2000; Fax: 405-364-5798; Toll Free Fax: 800-735-0476; Toll Free: 800-627-7377
E-mail: presscs@ou.edu
Web site: http://www.oupress.com
Dist(s): **Ebsco Publishing**
ebrary, Inc.; *CIP.*

†Univ. of Pennsylvania Pr., *(978-0-8122; 978-1-5128)* Orders Addr.: c/o Hopkins Fulfillment Srvc., Hopkins Fulfillment Service, Baltimore, MD 21211-4370 USA Tel 410-516-6948; Fax: 410-516-6998; Toll Free: 800-537-5487; Edit Addr.: 3905 Spruce St., Philadelphia, PA 19104-4112 USA (SAN 202-5345) Tel 215-898-6261; Fax: 215-898-0404; Toll Free: 800-537-5487 (book orders)
E-mail: custserv@pobox.upenn.edu
Web site: http://www.upenn.edu/pennpress
Dist(s): **Capstone Pub.**
De Gruyter, Inc.
Hopkins Fulfillment Services
MyiLibrary
TNT Media Group, Inc.; *CIP.*

†Univ. of Pittsburgh Pr., *(978-0-8229)* 3400 Forbes Ave., Eureka Bldg., Fifth Flr., Pittsburgh, PA 15260 USA (SAN 203-3216) Tel 412-383-2456; Fax: 412-383-2466
E-mail: press@pitt.edu
Web site: http://www.upress.pitt.edu
Dist(s): **Chicago Distribution Ctr.**
MyiLibrary; *CIP.*

†Univ. of Puerto Rico Pr., *(978-0-8477)* Subs. of Univ. of Puerto Rico, Orders Addr.: P.O. Box 23322, Rio Piedras, PR 00931-3322 USA (SAN 208-1245) Tel 787-250-0435 Administrative Offices; 787-250-8996 Administrative Offices; 787-758-8345 Sales Office and Warehouse; 787-751-8251 Sales Office and Warehouse; 787-934-3400 Sales Office and Warehouse; Fax: 787-753-9116 Administrative Offices; 787-751-8785 Sales/Warehouse, Ordering fax
E-mail: info@laeditorialupr.com
Web site: http://www.laeditorialupr.com
Dist(s): **Ediciones Universal**
Lectorum Pubns., Inc.
Libros Sin Fronteras; *CIP.*

Univ. of Rhode Island, Sea Grant Pubns. Unit, *(978-0-938412)* Narragansett Bay Campus, Narragansett, RI 02882-1197 USA (SAN 209-0708) Tel 401-874-6800
E-mail: tkennedy@gso.uri.edu
Web site: http://www.seagrant.gso.uri.edu/riseagrant
Dist(s): **Chicago Distribution Ctr.**

Univ. of Scranton Pr., *(978-0-940866; 978-1-58966)* Orders Addr.: c/o Univ. of Scranton Pr., St. Thomas Hall, Linden & Monroe Sts., Scranton, PA 18510 USA Toll Free Fax: 800-941-8804; Toll Free: 800-941-3081; Edit Addr.: Linden & Monroe Sts., Scranton, PA 18510 USA (SAN 688-4067) Tel 570-941-7955; Fax: 570-941-4309
E-mail: richard.rousseau@uofs.edu
Web site: http://www.scrantonpress.com
Dist(s): **Associated Univ. Presses**
Chicago Distribution Ctr.

†Univ. of South Carolina Pr., *(978-0-87249; 978-1-57003; 978-1-61117)* Orders Addr.: 718 Devine St., Columbia, SC 29208 USA Tel 803-777-1774; Fax: 803-777-0026; Toll Free Fax: 800-868-0740; Toll Free: 800-768-2500; Edit Addr.: 1600 Hampton St., 5th Flr., Columbia, SC 29208 USA (SAN 203-3224) Tel 803-777-5243; Fax: 803-777-0160; Toll Free Fax: 800-868-0740; Toll Free: 800-768-2500
E-mail: jhaupt@sc.edu
Web site: http://www.sc.edu/uscpress/
Dist(s): **Ebsco Publishing**
MyiLibrary
ebrary, Inc.; *CIP.*

Univ. St. Mary of the Lake, Mundelein Seminary, *(978-0-9774733)* 1000 E. Maple Ave., Mundelein, IL 60060 USA Tel 847-566-6401; Fax: 847-566-7330
E-mail: info@usml.edu
Web site: http://www.usml.edu.

University of Tampa *See* **Univ. of Tampa Pr.**

Univ. of Tampa Pr., *(978-1-879852; 978-1-59732)* 401 W. Kennedy Blvd., Tampa, FL 33606 USA Tel 813-253-6266; Fax: 813-258-7593
E-mail: utpress@ut.edu
Web site: http://utpress.ut.edu.

Univ. of Temecula Pr., Inc., *(978-0-936283)* 42730 De Luz Ave., Murrieta, CA 92362-7214 USA (SAN 697-9793) Tel 951-698-0059; Fax: 951-698-3676; *Imprints:* UTP (UTP)
E-mail: mikeray@utem.com
Web site: http://www.utem.com.

†Univ. of Texas Pr., *(978-0-292; 978-1-4773)* Orders Addr.: P.O. Box 7819, Austin, TX 78713-7819 USA (SAN 212-9876) Tel 512-471-7233; Fax: 512-232-7178; Toll Free: 800-252-3206; Edit Addr.: University of Texas at Austin 2100 Comal, Austin, TX 78722 USA
E-mail: info@utpress.utexas.edu
Web site: http://www.utexas.edu/utpress
Dist(s): **Continental Bk. Co., Inc.**
Ebsco Publishing
Urban Land Institute
ebrary, Inc.; *CIP.*

Univ. of Toledo Pr., *(978-0-615-99400-0; 978-0-692-35470-4; 978-0-692-67712-4; 978-0-692-73061-4; 978-0-692-90809-9; 978-0-692-95666-3)* 2801 W. Bancroft MS 509, Toledo, OH 43606 USA Tel 419-530-2311
E-mail: utoledopress@utoledo.edu
Web site: http://utoledopress.com.

†Univ. of Utah Pr., *(978-0-87480; 978-1-60781)* 1795 E. South Campus Dr., Rm. 101, Salt Lake City, UT 84112-9402 USA (SAN 220-0023) Tel 801-581-6771; Fax: 801-581-3365; Toll Free: 800-773-6672
E-mail: info@upress.utah.edu
Web site: http://www.upress.utah.edu
Dist(s): **Casemate Academic**
Chicago Distribution Ctr.
Partners Bk. Distributing, Inc.
Rio Nuevo Pubs.
ebrary, Inc.; *CIP.*

†University of Virginia Pr., *(978-0-8139; 978-0-912759; 978-1-57814)* Orders Addr.: P.O. Box 400318, Charlottesville, VA 22904-4318 USA (SAN 202-5361) Tel 804-924-3468; Fax: 804-982-2655
E-mail: upress@virginia.edu
Web site: http://www.upress.virginia.edu
Dist(s): **Ediciones Universal**
Fordham Univ. Pr.
Longleaf Services
MyiLibrary; *CIP.*

†Univ. of Washington Pr., *(978-0-295; 978-1-902716)* Orders Addr.: P.O. Box 50096, Seattle, WA 98145-5096 USA (SAN 212-2502) Tel 206-543-4050; Fax: 206-543-3932; Toll Free Fax: 800-669-7993; Edit Addr.: P.O. Box 50096, Seattle, WA 98145-5096 USA Toll Free: 800-669-7993; 1126 N. 98th St., Seattle, WA 98103
E-mail: uwpord@u.washington.edu
Web site: http://www.washington.edu/uwpress
Dist(s): **Ebsco Publishing**
Hopkins Fulfillment Services
MyiLibrary
Partners Bk. Distributing, Inc.
Urban Land Institute
ebrary, Inc.; *CIP.*

Univ. of West Florida Foundation, Inc., *(978-0-9659142; 978-0-9798292)* 11000 University Pkwy., Pensacola, FL 32514 USA
E-mail: cmarse@uwf.edu.

†Univ. of Wisconsin Pr., *(978-0-299)* Orders Addr.: c/o Chicago Dist Ctr., 11030 S. Langley Ave., Chicago, IL 60628 USA Tel 773-568-1550; Fax: 773-660-2235; Toll Free Fax: 800-621-8476 (orders only); Toll Free: 800-621-2736 (orders only); Edit Addr.: 1930 Monroe St., 3rd Flr., Madison, WI 53711 USA Tel 608-263-1110; Fax: 608-263-1132
E-mail: uwiscpress@uwpress.wisc.edu
Web site: http://www.wisc.edu/wisconsinpress/
Dist(s): **Chicago Distribution Ctr.**
East-West Export Bks.
Ebsco Publishing
Follett School Solutions
MyiLibrary
ebrary, Inc.; *CIP.*

†Univ. Pr. of America, Inc., *(978-0-7618; 978-0-8191; 978-1-879691)* Member of Rowman & Littlefield Publishing Group, Inc., Orders Addr.: 15200 NBN Way, Blue Ridge Summit, PA 17214-0190 USA Tel 717-794-3800 (Sales, Customer Service, MIS, Royalties, Inventory Mgmt, Dist., Credit & Collections); Fax: 717-794-3803 (Customer Service & orders); 717-794-3857 (Sales & MIS); 717-794-3856 (Royalties, Inventory Mgmt. & Dist.); Toll Free Fax: 800-338-4550 (Customer Service & /or orders); Toll Free: 800-462-6420 (Customer Service &/or orders); Edit Addr.: 4501 Forbes Blvd., Suite 200, Lanham, MD 20706 USA Tel 301-459-3366; Fax: 301-459-5748 Short Discount, please contact rlpgsales@rowman.com
E-mail: custserv@rowman.com
Web site: http://www.univpress.com; http://www.rlpgbooks.com
Dist(s): **CreateSpace Independent Publishing Platform**
Ebsco Publishing
MyiLibrary
National Bk. Network
Rowman & Littlefield Publishers, Inc.
Yale Univ. Pr.
ebrary, Inc.; *CIP.*

Univ. Pr. of Colorado, *(978-0-87081; 978-0-87421; 978-1-60732)* Orders Addr.: 2800 Venture Dr., Norman, OK 73069-8218 USA Toll Free Fax: 800-735-0476; Toll Free: 800-627-7377; c/o Utah State University Press, 3078 Old Main Hill, Logan, UT 84322 (SAN 202-9294) Toll Free: 800-621-2736; Edit Addr.: 5589 Arapahoe Ave., Suite 206C, Boulder, CO 80303 USA (SAN 658-0343) Tel 720-406-8849
Web site: http://www.upcolorado.com; http://www.usupress.org
Dist(s): **Bks. West**
Chicago Distribution Ctr.
Ctr. for Literary Publishing, Colorado State Univ.
Ebsco Publishing
Follett School Solutions
MyiLibrary
O'Reilly Media, Inc.
Univ. of Oklahoma Pr.
ebrary, Inc.

†Univ. Pr. of Florida, *(978-0-8130; 978-0-942084; 978-0-9760555; 978-1-61610; 978-1-942852; 978-1-68340)* Orders Addr.: 15 NW 15th St., Gainesville, FL 32611-0279 USA (SAN 207-9275) Tel 352-392-1351; Fax: 352-392-7302; Toll Free Fax: 800-680-1955; Toll Free: 800-226-3822; *Imprints:* Gatorbytes (Gatorbytes)
E-mail: press@upf.com; orders@upf.com
Web site: http://www.upf.com
Dist(s): **Casemate Academic**
Ebsco Publishing
MyiLibrary
Oxford Univ. Pr., Inc.
TNT Media Group, Inc.
ebrary, Inc.; *CIP.*

†Univ. Pr. of Kentucky, *(978-0-8131; 978-0-912839; 978-0-916968)* Orders Addr.: P.O. Box 4680, Lexington, KY 40544-4680 USA Tel 859-257-8400; Fax: 859-257-8481; Toll Free: 800-839-6855; Edit Addr.: 663 S. Limestone St., Lexington, KY 40508-4008 USA (SAN 203-3275) Tel 859-257-5200; Fax: 859-323-4981; Toll Free Fax: 800-870-4981
Web site: http://www.kentuckypress.com
Dist(s): **Ebsco Publishing**
MyiLibrary
Oxford Univ. Pr., Inc.
ebrary, Inc.; *CIP.*

†Univ. Pr. of Mississippi, *(978-0-87805; 978-1-57806; 978-1-934110; 978-1-60473; 978-1-61703; 978-1-62103; 978-1-62674; 978-1-62846; 978-1-4968)* 3825 Ridgewood Rd., Jackson, MS 39211-6492 USA (SAN 203-1914) Tel 601-432-6205; Fax: 601-432-6217; Toll Free: 800-737-7788 (orders only)
E-mail: kburgess@ihl.state.ms.us; press@mississippi.edu
Web site: http://www.upress.state.ms.us
Dist(s): **CreateSpace Independent Publishing Platform**
East-West Export Bks.
Ebsco Publishing
MyiLibrary
ebrary, Inc.; *CIP.*

†Univ. Pr. of New England, *(978-0-87451; 978-0-915032; 978-1-58465; 978-1-61168; 978-1-5126)* Orders Addr.: One Court St., Suite 250, Lebanon, NH 03755 USA Tel 603-448-1533 (ext. 255); Fax: 603-448-9429; Toll Free: 800-421-1561
E-mail: University.Press@Dartmouth.edu
Web site: http://www.upne.com
Dist(s): **Casemate Academic**
MyiLibrary
Smashwords
ebrary, Inc.; *CIP.*

Univ. Pr. of the Pacific, *(978-0-89875; 978-1-4102)* 4440 NW 73rd Ave., PTY 362, Miami, FL 33166-6437 USA Tel 407-650-2537 (phone/fax)
E-mail: bip@universitypressofthepacific.com
Web site: http://www.universitypressofthepacific.com.

University Publishing Associates, Incorporated *See* **National Film Network LLC**

Univ. Publishing Co., *(978-0-8346)* P.O. Box 80298, Lincoln, NE 68501 USA (SAN 206-0582) Tel 402-476-2761.

University Readers *See* **Cognella, Inc.**

Univ. Science Bks., *(978-0-935702; 978-1-891389; 978-1-938787; 978-1-940380)* 20 Edgehill Rd., Mill Valley, CA 94941-1113 USA (SAN 213-8085); 111 Prospect Pl., South Orange, NJ 07079 Tel 973-378-3900; Fax: 973-378-3925
E-mail: univscibks@igc.org; bjellis@igc.org; deskcopy@uscibooks.com
Web site: http://www.uscibooks.com
Dist(s): **RedShelf.**

UniversityPress.Info *See* **Science Pubs.**

Unlimited Horizons, *(978-0-9753817)* 427 S. Fraser Dr., Mesa, AZ 85204-2605 USA.

Unlimited Possibilities Publishing, LLC, *(978-0-9724621)* Orders Addr.: 110 WALTER WAY No. 2635, STOCKBRIDGE, GA 30281 USA
E-mail: info@unlimitedpossibilitiespublishing.com
Web site: http://www.unlimitedpossibilitiespublishing.com.

Unlimited Potential Publishing, *(978-0-9899212; 978-0-9979879)* 122 Camberley Ct., Columbia, SC 29223 USA Tel 706-399-4916; Fax: 803-865-9271
E-mail: will8149@bellsouth.net
Dist(s): **Lightning Source, Inc.**

Unlimited Publishing LLC, *(978-0-9677649; 978-1-58832)* P.O. Box 3007, Bloomington, IN 47402 USA Fax: 425-928-5465
E-mail: jaymasp@aol.com; paradoxofthesoul@aol.com
Web site: http://www.unlimitedpublishing.com
Dist(s): **CreateSpace Independent Publishing Platform**
TextStream.

Unlock A Bk. Pubs., LLC, *(978-0-9796456)* 225 S. Bishop, San Angelo, TX 76901 USA
Web site: http://unlockabook.com.

Unmistakably C K C, *(978-0-9742064)* 3244 Kingswood Glen, Decatur, GA 30034 USA Tel 404-244-8113; 404-242-2690; Fax: 678-418-3056
E-mail: info@billyzany.com
Web site: http://www.billyzany.com.

Unseen Gallery, *(978-0-9795206)* Orders Addr.: P.O. Box 6065, Albuquerque, NM 87197 USA Tel 505-232-2161
E-mail: webmaster@unseengallery.com
Web site: http://www.unseengallery.com.

Unshackled Publishing, *(978-0-9708688)* Orders Addr.: P.O. Box 44216, Indianapolis, IN 46244 USA; P.O. Box 44216, Indianapolis, IN 46244
E-mail: lexthewriter@yahoo.com; treks-journey@yahoo.com
Web site: http://www.unshackledpublishing.com; http://www.alexusrhone.com.

Unspeakable Joy Pr., *(978-0-9761538)* Orders Addr.: 499 Adams St., #252, Milton, MA 02186 USA; Edit Addr.: 233 Eliot St., Milton, MA 02186 USA
E-mail: roybue@aol.com; adoptionis@aol.com
Web site: http://www.adoptionis.com.

Untreed Reads Publishing, LLC, *(978-1-61187; 978-1-945447)* 506 Kansas St., San Francisco, CA 94107 USA Tel 415-621-0465; Toll Free Fax: 800-318-6037
E-mail: jhartman@untreedreads.com; kdsullivan@untreedreads.com
Web site: http://www.untreedreads.com.

Unveiled Media, LLC, *(978-0-9776385)* P.O. Box 930463, Verona, WI 53593 USA (SAN 257-8093); *Imprints:* Cotton Candy Press (CottonCandy Pr)
Web site: http://www.unveiledmedia.com
Dist(s): **Consortium Bk. Sales & Distribution**
CreateSpace Independent Publishing Platform
Lightning Source, Inc.

UP *See* **Infobus, Inc.**

Upcentral Publishing, *(978-0-9897466)* 29 Braeside Rd., Baldwinsville, NY 13027 USA Tel 315-720-4684
E-mail: garypluff@yahoo.com.

UPfirst.com Bks., *(978-0-9800222)* Div. of UPfirst.com, 2803 Us Hwy. 41 W. Suite 100, Marquette, MI 49855-2291 USA (SAN 855-0271)
E-mail: michaeleen@upfirst.com
Web site: http://www.upfirst.com.

UPfirst.com Picture Books for Children *See* **UPfirst.com Bks.**

Upheaval Media, Inc., *(978-0-615-19321-2; 978-0-578-03360-0; 978-0-615-36266-3; 978-0-9829610)* P.O. Box 241488, Detroit, MI 48224 USA Tel 877-429-2370; Fax: 313-556-1669; Toll Free: 877-429-2370
E-mail: ida@upliftinc.org
Web site: http://www.upheavalmedia.net
Dist(s): **Lulu Pr., Inc.**

Upland Avenue Productions, *(978-0-578-10367-9; 978-0-615-92673-5; 978-0-9960401; 978-0-692-53123-5; 978-0-692-53124-2; 978-0-692-53125-9; 978-0-692-53127-3; 978-0-692-54731-1; 978-0-692-77111-2; 978-0-692-80419-3; 978-0-692-85300-9)* Orders Addr.: 1405 Vegas Verdes Suite 312, Santa Fe, NM 87507 USA
Web site: http://www.uplandpublish.com
Dist(s): **CreateSpace Independent Publishing Platform**
Lulu Pr., Inc.

Upland Public Library Foundation *See* **Citrus Roots - Preserving Citrus Heritage Foundation**

Uplift Pr., *(978-0-9622834)* 295 Lenox Ave., #105, Oakland, CA 94610 USA Do not confuse with Uplift Pr. in Los Angeles, CA.

Upper Deck Co., LLC,The, *(978-1-931860; 978-1-932241; 978-1-932669; 978-1-932825; 978-1-932939; 978-1-933103; 978-1-933252; 978-1-933489; 978-1-59945; 978-1-60806)* 5909 Sea Otter Pl., Carlsbad, CA 92010 USA Tel 760-929-6500; Fax: 760-929-6548; Toll Free: 800-873-7332
Web site: http://www.upperdeck.com
Dist(s): **Diamond Bk. Distributors.**

Upper Room Bks. *Imprint of* **Upper Room Bks.**

Upper Room Bks., *(978-0-8358; 978-0-88177; 978-1-935205)* Div. of The Upper Room, 1908 Grand Ave., Nashville, TN 37212 USA (SAN 203-3364) Tel 615-340-7256; Toll Free: 800-972-0433 (customer service, orders); *Imprints:* Upper Room Books (UpperRmBks); Discipleship Resources (DiscipleshipRes) Do not confuse with Upper Room Education for Parenting, Inc. in Derry, NH
E-mail: jneely@gbod.org; lbruner@gbod.org; atrudel@gbod.org
Web site: http://www.upperroom.org; http://books.upperroom.org; http://bookstore.upperroom.org
Dist(s): **Abingdon Pr.**
Smashwords.

Upper Strata Ink, Incorporated *See* **Crowder, Jack L.**

Upside Down Tree Publishing, *(978-0-9802329)* 1605 N. Grand Ave., Maryville, MO 64468 USA.

Upstart Bks. *Imprint of* **Highsmith Inc.**

Upstart Pr. (NZL) *(978-1-927262; 978-1-927262-02-3; 978-1-927262-53-5; 978-1-988516) Dist. by* **IPG Chicago.**

UpTree Publishing, *(978-0-9787248)* P.O. Box 212863, Columbia, SC 29221 USA (SAN 851-447X) Toll Free: 800-905-2157 (phone/fax)
E-mail: sales@uptreepublishing.com; info@uptreepublishing.com
Web site: http://www.uptreepublishing.com.

Upublish.com *See* **Universal Pubs.**

Upword Pr., *(978-0-9654140)* Orders Addr.: P.O. Box 974, Atmore, AL 36504-0974 USA; 1879 Old Bratt Rd., Atmore, AL 36504 Tel 251-609-2918 Do not confuse with Upword Pr., Yelm, WA
Web site: http://www.scattersunshine.com
Dist(s): **American Wholesale Bk. Co.**

Urban Advocacy, *(978-0-9745122)* 917 Columbia Ave. Suite 123, Lancaster, PA 17603 USA Tel 717-490-6148
E-mail: vuuhu02@yahoo.com
Web site: http://www.urbanadvocacy.org.

Urban Edge Publishing Co., *(978-0-9743781)* 16209 Victory Blvd., Suite 207, Van Nuys, CA 91406 USA Tel 818-786-3700; Fax: 818-786-3737
E-mail: willcon@pacbell.net.

Urban, Keith Studios, *(978-0-9815370)* P.O. Box 4572, Wayne, NJ 07474 USA (SAN 855-8280)
Web site: http://www.keithurban.com.

Urban Ministries, Incorporated *See* **UMI (Urban Ministries, Inc.)**

Urban Moon Publishing, *(978-0-9787913; 978-0-9800101)* 931 Monroe Dr., Suite 276, Atlanta, GA 30308 USA Toll Free: 866-205-9228
E-mail: kinglistens@aol.com.

Urban Renaissance *Imprint of* **Kensington Publishing Corp.**

Urban Spirit!, *(978-0-9638127; 978-0-9845359; 978-0-9846480; 978-0-9881958; 978-0-9884572)* 753 Walden Blvd., Atlanta, GA 30349 USA Tel 770-969-7891
E-mail: melbanks2002@yahoo.com
Web site: http://www.urbanspirit.biz.

Urbanik, Karen L., *(978-0-9759031)* 2285 Marsh Hawk Ln. Apt. 302, Orange Park, FL 32003-6366 USA.

Ure, Daylene, *(978-0-615-25326-8)* 160 E. 200 S., Washington, UT 84780 USA
Dist(s): **Lulu Pr., Inc.**

Urim Pubns. (ISR) *(978-965-7108; 978-965-524) Dist. by* **Coronet Bks.**

Urim Pubns. (ISR) *(978-965-7108; 978-965-524) Dist. by* **IPG Chicago.**

Urim Pubns. (ISR) *(978-965-7108; 978-965-524) Dist. by* **Lambda Pubs.**

†URJ Pr., *(978-0-8074)* 633 Third Ave., New York, NY 10017 USA (SAN 203-3291) Tel 212-650-4120; Fax: 212-650-4119; Toll Free: 888-489-8242
E-mail: press@urj.org
Web site: http://www.urjbooksandmusic.com
Dist(s): **Leonard, Hal Corp.**
MyiLibrary; *CIP.*

URON Entertainment Corp. (CAN) *(978-0-9738652; 978-0-9781386; 978-1-897376; 978-1-926778; 978-1-927925) Dist. by* **Diamond Book Dists.**

URON Entertainment Corp. (CAN) *(978-0-9738652; 978-0-9781386; 978-1-897376; 978-1-926778; 978-1-927925) Dist. by* **D C D.**

Ursu Pubns., *(978-0-9741634)* PMB 429, 5250 Grand Ave., Suite 14, Gurnee, IL 60031-1877 USA
E-mail: info@grandmaursu.com
Web site: http://www.grandmaursu.com.

Urtext, *(978-0-9790573; 978-1-940121)* 39 Longwood Dr., San Rafael, CA 94901-1026 USA (SAN 852-3061).

U.S. Games Systems, Inc., *(978-0-88079; 978-0-913866; 978-1-57281)* 179 Ludlow St., Stamford, CT 06902 USA (SAN 158-6483) Tel 203-353-8400; Fax: 203-353-8431; Toll Free: 800-544-2637
E-mail: usgames@aol.com
Web site: http://www.usgamesinc.com
Dist(s): **New Leaf Distributing Co., Inc.**

Usborne *Imprint of* **EDC Publishing**

Usera, Christian, *(978-0-615-14618-8; 978-0-615-14645-4; 978-0-615-31319-1)* 7818 S. Zeno St., Centennial, CO 80016-1849 USA
Dist(s): **Lulu Pr., Inc.**

Utopia Pr., *(978-0-9661060)* 126 1/2 E. Front St., Traverse City, MI 49684 USA Tel 231-922-2234 editorial office
E-mail: pub@fimg.net.

UTP *Imprint of* **Univ. of Temecula Pr., Inc.**

Utterly Global, *(978-0-9891338)* 44 Lenhome Dr., Cranford, NJ 07016 USA Tel 908-272-0631
E-mail: info@antibullyingprograms.com
Web site: www.antibullyingprograms.com.

UWA Publishing (AUS) *(978-0-85564; 978-0-86422; 978-0-909751; 978-1-875560; 978-1-876268; 978-1-920694; 978-0-9802964; 978-0-9802965; 978-1-921401; 978-1-920964; 978-1-74258; 978-0-7316-0213-1; 978-0-7316-1196-6; 978-0-7316-1212-3; 978-0-7316-3945-8; 978-0-646-15226-4; 978-0-646-31692-5; 978-0-646-39116-8; 978-0-646-43446-9) Dist. by* **Intl Spec Bk.**

UXL *Imprint of* **Cengage Gale**

Uxor Pr., Inc., *(978-0-932555)* One Blackfield Dr. #174, Tiburon, CA 94920 USA Tel 415-383-8481
E-mail: bobzimmerman@usa.com.

V Bks., *(978-0-9972031)* 7801 NW 37th St., Doral, FL 33166-6503 USA Tel 305-592-0839
E-mail: myarobarts@gmail.com
Web site: https://www.facebook.com/MyaRobartsBooks/.

V V C Publishing *See* **Vic-Vincent Publishing**

Vabella Publishing, *(978-0-9712204; 978-0-9834332; 978-1-938230; 978-1-942766)* Orders Addr.: P.O. Box 1052, Carrollton, GA 30112 USA (SAN 920-1858) Tel 770-328-8355; Edit Addr.: 222 Hampton Way, Carrollton, GA 30116 USA (SAN 860-1682) Tel 770-328-8355
E-mail: belljg@aol.com
Web site: www.vabella.com.

Vacation Spot Publishing, *(978-0-9637688; 978-1-893622)* Orders Addr.: P.O. Box 1723, Lorton, VA 22199-1723 USA Tel 703-684-8142; Fax: 703-684-7955; Toll Free: 800-441-1949; Edit Addr.: 1903 Duffield Ln., Alexandria, VA 22307 USA; *Imprints:* VSP Books (VSP Bks)
E-mail: mail@VSPBooks.com
Web site: http://www.vspbooks.com
Dist(s): **Follett School Solutions.**

Vadeboncoeur, Jim, *(978-0-9724697)* 3809 Laguna Ave., Palo Alto, CA 94306-2629 USA Fax: 650-493-1145
E-mail: images@bpib.com
Web site: http://www.bpib.com/images.htm.

Valenti, Robert A., *(978-0-9773119)* 3500 Galt Ocean Dr.2401, Fort Lauderdale, FL 33308-6809 USA Tel 954-563-0069; Fax: 954-563-4503
E-mail: rvalenti@bellsouth.net.

Valerie Bendt, *(978-1-885814)* Orders Addr.: 333 W. Rio Vista Ct., Tampa, FL 33604 USA
E-mail: ValerieBendt@verizon.net; ValeneBendt@gmail.com
Web site: http://www.ValerieBendt.com
Dist(s): **Follett School Solutions.**

Vallentine Mitchell Pubs. (GBR) *(978-0-85303; 978-1-910383) Dist. by* **Intl Spec Bk.**

Valley Pr., *(978-0-9748447)* P.O. Box 427, Vienna, VA 22183-1427 USA Fax: 703-281-2994 Do not confuse with companies with the same name in Bradenton, FL, Lyndhurst, NJ, GreenBay, WI, Mill Valley, CA.

Valley Publishing *See* **Karosa Publishing**

Values of America Co., *(978-0-9765868)* P.O. Box 1534, Merchantville, NJ 08109 USA Toll Free: 866-467-7304
E-mail: orders@quipman.com
Web site: http://www.quipman.com.

Values to Live By Classic Stories *Imprint of* **Thomas, Frederic Inc.**

Van der Westhuizen, Kevin Ministries International, Incorporated *See* **JMC Printing**

van der Zande, Irene, *(978-0-9796191)* P.O. Box 1212, Santa Cruz, CA 95061 USA Tel 831-426-4407 Toll Free: 800-467-6997
E-mail: safety@kidpower.org
Web site: http://www.kidpower.org
Dist(s): **Romeii LLC.**

Van Steenhouse, Andrea L. *See* **Simpler Life Pr.**

Vandalia Pr. *Imprint of* **West Virginia Univ. Pr.**

Vandam Pr., Inc., *(978-0-9702383; 978-1-937010)* P.O. Box 155, Brooklyn, NY 11230 USA Tel 212-969-0286; Fax: 212-858-5720
E-mail: publisher@vandampress.com
Web site: http://www.vandampress.com.

Vandamere Pr., *(978-0-918339)* Subs. of AB Assocs., Orders Addr.: P.O. Box 149, St. Petersburg, FL 33731 USA (SAN 657-3088) Tel 727-556-0950; Fax: 727-556-2560; Toll Free: 800-551-7776
Web site: www.vandamere.com.

V&R Editoras,
Dist(s): **Lectorum Pubns., Inc.**

Vanguard Pr., *(978-1-59315)* 425 Madison Ave., 3rd Flr., New York, NY 10017 USA Do not confuse with CDS Books in Paso Robles, CA Durham, NC
Dist(s): **Ebsco Publishing**
Hachette Bk. Group
ebrary, Inc.

Vanguard Productions, *(978-1-887591; 978-1-934331)* 186 Center St., Suite 200, Clinton, NJ 08809 USA Tel 732-748-8895
E-mail: vanguardpub@att.net
Web site: http://vanguardproductions.net
Dist(s): **Innovative Logistics**
Watson-Guptill Pubns., Inc.

Vanir Bks., *(978-0-615-28865-9)* 351 Salem St., No. 2, Glendale, CA 91203 USA Tel 818-669-4070
Web site: http://rickandbobo.com.

Vanishing Horizons, *(978-0-9823445)* Orders Addr.: 1018 Cedarcrest Dr., Pueblo, CO 81005 USA Tel 719-561-0993
E-mail: vanishinghorizons1@me.com
Web site: http://www.vanishinghorizons.com.

Vanissery, Matthew, *(978-0-9759906)* P.O. Box 1056, Guasti, CA 91743-1056 USA; 175 Mountain View Ave., Scotch Plains, NJ 07076 Tel 908-889-7930; Fax: 908-889-6281
E-mail: chemplavil@aol.com.

VanitaBooks, *(978-0-9800162; 978-0-9819714; 978-0-9826366)* 3875 Embassy Pkwy., Suite 250, Akron, OH 44333 USA
Web site: http://www.vanitabooks.com
Dist(s): **Ingram Publisher Services.**

Vanwell Publishing, Ltd. (CAN) *(978-0-920277; 978-1-55068; 978-1-55125) Dist. by* **Casemate Pubs.**

Varas, Reny, *(978-0-9726946)* 918 Cortney Dr., Carpentersville, IL 60110 USA (SAN 255-3333) Tel 847-428-7852; Fax: 847-428-7880
E-mail: lionan2@msn.com.

Variance Publishing, LLC, *(978-1-935142)* P.O. Box 612, Cabot, AR 72023-7577 USA (SAN 856-6259) Tel 501-259-6102; *Imprints:* Breakneck Books (Breakneck)
E-mail: tpaulschulte@variancepublishing.com
Web site: http://www.variancepublishing.com
Dist(s): **Bookazine Co., Inc.**
Smashwords.

Varida Publishing & Resources, *(978-1-937046)* P.O. Box 688, Woodinville, WA 98072 USA Tel 425-830-2909
E-mail: president@varida.com
Web site: varida.com.

Vaughan, Christopher, *(978-0-9863101)* 203 Southbrook Pkwy., Kearney, MO 64060 USA Tel 816-728-5718
E-mail: Ljcv125@hotmail.com.

Vaughanworks *Imprint of* **Vaughanworks Publishing**

Vaughanworks Publishing, *(978-0-9771160)* Div. of Vaughanworks, Orders Addr.: P.O. Box 44224, West Allis, WI 53214 USA; *Imprints:* Vaughanworks (Vaughanworks)
E-mail: vaughanworks@sbcglobal.net
Web site: http://www.vaughanworks.com.

Vaughn, Jerry T., *(978-0-9772507)* 1921 Ashford Cir., Longmout, CO 80501 USA Tel 303-776-9134
E-mail: vaughn.jc@gmail.com.

Vecchia Publishing, *(978-0-9860470; 978-1-944906)* 41 Grand Ave., Suite 101, River Edge, NJ 07661 USA.

Vedanta Pr., *(978-0-87481)* Div. of Vedanta Society of Southern California, Orders Addr.: 1946 Vedanta Pl., Hollywood, CA 90068-3996 USA (SAN 202-9340) Tel 323-960-1728 (general manager); 323-960-1727 (orders and customer service); Fax: 323-465-9568 (orders)
E-mail: bob@vedanta.com; vpress@vedanta.com
Web site: http://www.vedanta.com.

vegaslocal.com, *(978-0-9752804)* 4329 Talofa Ave., Toluca Lake, CA 91602-2917 USA
E-mail: info@vegaslocal.com
Web site: http://www.vegaslocal.com.

Veillette, Roseanne, *(978-0-9843705; 978-0-9977504)* Orders Addr.: 40 Tutherly Ave., Claremont, NH 03743 USA (SAN 859-2128) Tel 603-372-7390; *Imprints:* Little Paws Press (LittlePaws)
E-mail: roseanneveillette@comcast.net
Web site: http://www.buckandben.com.

Veillette, Sally *See* **Pop the Cork Publishing**

Velazquez de Leon, Mauricio *See* **Duo Pr. LLC**

Velesquious Studios, *(978-0-9754232)* P.O. Box 72, Blakeslee, PA 18610-0072 USA Tel 610-360-8946
E-mail: webmaster@velesquious.com
Web site: http://www.velesquious.com.

Velichko, Vera, *(978-0-9754433)* Orders Addr.: 12671 SE 169th Pl., Renton, WA 98058 USA Tel 253-237-2271; Fax: 253-444-4916; *Imprints:* Language Transformer Books (LangTransforBks)
E-mail: talkinrussian@gmail.com
Web site: http://www.lulu.com/talkinrussian1; http://www.languagetransformer.com/.

Velikanje, Kathryn *See* **Levity Pr.**

Vellum *Imprint of* **New Academia Publishing, LLC**

VeloPress, *(978-0-9622630; 978-1-884737; 978-1-931382; 978-1-934030)* Div. of Inside Communications, Inc., 1830 N. 55th St., Boulder, CO 80301-2700 USA Tel 303-440-0601; Fax: 303-444-6788; Toll Free: 800-811-4210
E-mail: velopress@7dogs.com
Web site: http://www.velogear.com
Dist(s): **Ingram Publisher Services.**

Velvet Pony Stories, *(978-0-615-26652-7; 978-0-692-80080-5)*
Dist(s): **Independent Pub.**

Velázquez Pr., *(978-1-59495)* Div. of Academic Learning Co., LLC, 9682 Telstar Ave., Suite 110, El Monte, CA 91731-3009 USA (SAN 255-786X) Tel 626-448-3448; Fax: 626-602-3817
E-mail: info@academiclearningcompany.com
Web site: http://www.academiclearningcompany.com.

Vendera Publishing, *(978-0-9749411; 978-1-936307)* 61 Big Pete Rd., Franklin Furnace, OH 45629 USA Tel 740-531-2122; *Imprints:* 711Press (SevenElev)
E-mail: admin@venderapublishing.com
Web site: http://www.venderapublishing.com.

Vengco, Aletha Fulton, *(978-0-578-00613-0; 978-0-578-00778-6; 978-0-578-00890-5; 978-0-578-02728-9)* 2224 O St., Apt. 4, Sacramento, CA 95816 USA
Dist(s): **Lulu Pr., Inc.**

Venture Development Group, *(978-0-9748030)* 1114 Blue Lake Sq., Mountain View, CA 94040-4561 USA Tel 650-967-3403; Fax: 650-965-0320.

Venture Publishing, *(978-0-9761694)* 750 Tabor St., No. 64, Golden, CO 80401 USA Tel 303-239-6531 (phone/fax).

Venture Publishing, Inc., *(978-0-910251; 978-1-892132; 978-1-939476)* 1999 Cato Ave., State College, PA 16801 USA (SAN 240-897X) Tel 814-234-4561; Fax: 814-234-1651 Do not confuse with companies with the same name in Andover, MA, Ho-Ho-Kus, NJ
E-mail: vpublish@venturepublish.com
Web site: http://www.venturepublish.com.

Verbal Images Pr., *(978-0-9625136; 978-1-884281; 978-0-9821982)* 46 Duncott Rd., Fairport, NY 14450-3150 USA
Web site: http://www.verbalimagespress.com
Dist(s): **Gryphon Hse., Inc.**
Independent Pubs. Group.

Veritas Pr., Inc., *(978-1-930710; 978-1-932168; 978-1-936648)* 1829 William Penn Way, Lancaster, PA 17601 USA (SAN 255-9617) Tel 717-519-1974; Fax: 717-519-1978; Toll Free: 800-922-5082 Do not confuse with companies with same name in Santa Barbara CA, Santa Monica CA, Bronx NY, Clearwater Fl, Sioux Falls SD, West Hartford CT, West Allis,MI
E-mail: info@veritaspress.com
Web site: http://www.veritaspress.com.

Veritas Publishing, *(978-0-9643261; 978-0-9715007; 978-1-933297; 978-0-9765742; 978-1-933391; 978-1-933885; 978-1-938033)* Orders Addr.: P.O. Box 3516, Sedona, AZ 86340 USA (SAN 254-3613) Tel 928-282-8722; Fax: 928-282-4789 Do not confuse with companies with the same or similar names in Cranbrook, WA, Rockwall, TX, McMinnville, MN, Mountain View, CA, Prescott, AZ
E-mail: veritaspublish@postmark.net; info@veritaspub.com; eventcoordinator@veritaspub.com
Web site: http://www.veritaspub.com
Dist(s): **Bookmasters Distribution**
DeVorss & Co.
Hay Hse., Inc.
New Leaf Distributing Co., Inc.
Partners Bk. Distributing, Inc.

Veritas Pubns. (IRL) *(978-1-85390; 978-0-901810; 978-0-905092; 978-0-86217; 978-1-84730) Dist. by* **Dufour.**

Verlag Wilhelm Heyne (DEU) *(978-3-453) Dist. by* **Distribks Inc.**

Publisher Name Index

Vermont Bookworks, *(978-0-9745931)* 12 Perry Ln., Rutland, VT 05701 USA
E-mail: digbysworld@comcast.net
Web site: http://www.digbysworld.com
Dist(s): **North Country Bks., Inc.**

Vermont Council on the Arts, Incorporated *See* **Vermont Folklife Ctr.**

†**Vermont Folklife Ctr.,** *(978-0-916718; 978-0-692-00433-3)* Orders Addr.: 88 Main St., Middlebury, VT 05753 USA (SAN 208-9092) Tel 802-388-4964; Fax: 802-388-1844
E-mail: bbjorkman@vermontfolklifecenter.org
Web site: http://www.vermontfolklifecenter.org
Dist(s): **Thistle Hill Pubns.**
Univ. Pr. of New England; *CIP.*

†**Vermont Life Magazine,** *(978-0-936896; 978-1-931389; 978-1-941730)* Div. of State of Vermont, Agency on Development & Community Affairs, 1 National Life Drive, 6th fl, Montpelier, VT 05620-0501 USA (SAN 215-8213) Tel 802-828-3241; Fax: 802-828-3366; Toll Free: 800-455-3399
E-mail: info@vtlife.com; products@vtlife.com; subs@vtlife.com
Web site: http://www.vermontlife.com; http://www.VermontLifeCatalog.com
Dist(s): **Hood, Alan C. & Co., Inc.**
TNT Media Group, Inc.; *CIP.*

Vernacular Pr., *(978-0-9740266)* 197 Grand St. Ste. 2W, New York, NY 10013-3859 USA (SAN 255-3945)
E-mail: hthamann@vernacularpress.com; cvecoli@vernacularpress.com
Web site: http://www.vernacularpress.com.

Verney, Jeff *See* **JRV Publishing**

Vernier Software *See* **Vernier Software & Technology**

Vernier Software & Technology, *(978-0-918731; 978-1-929075; 978-1-948008)* 13979 SW Millikan Way, Beaverton, OR 97005-2886 USA (SAN 293-1753) Tel 503-277-2299; Fax: 503-277-2440
E-mail: info@vernier.com
Web site: http://www.vernier.com.

Vernissage Pr., LLC, *(978-0-9725027)* 2200 Central Ave., Boulder, CO 80301 USA Tel 303-440-8102; Toll Free: 888-849-8697
E-mail: info@vernissagepress.com
Web site: http://www.vernissagepress.com.

Verona (Bk.) Publishing, Inc., *(978-0-9667037; 978-0-9769031)* P.O. Box 24071, Edina, MN 55426 USA
Web site: http://www.veronapublishing.com.

Versalt Pr. LLC, *(978-0-9746810)* P.O. Box 644332, Vero Beach, FL 32964-4332 USA
E-mail: info@versaitpress.com
Web site: http://VersaitPress.com.

Versal Editorial Group *See* **Cambridge BrickHouse, Inc.**

Versal Technologies, Inc., *(978-0-9749460)* One Cranberry Hill, Suite 102, Lexington, MA 02421 USA.

Versary Pubns., *(978-0-9641429)* 984 Brownsville Rd., Wernersville, PA 19565 USA Tel 610-693-5920.

Verso Bks. (GBR) *(978-0-86091; 978-0-902308; 978-1-85984; 978-1-84467; 978-1-78168; 978-1-78478; 978-1-78663)* *Dist. by* **Peng Rand Hse.**

Vertical *Imprint of* **Kodansha America, Inc.**

Vertical *Imprint of* **Vertical, Inc.**

Vertical Connect Pr., *(978-0-9769087)* 120 N. Magnolia St., Summerville, SC 29483-6836 USA; *Imprints:* Grand Kidz, The (Grand Kidz)
E-mail: kate@verticalconnectpress.com
Web site: http://www.verticalconnectpress.com.

Vertical, Inc., *(978-1-932234; 978-1-934287; 978-1-935654; 978-1-939130; 978-1-941220; 978-1-942993; 978-1-945054; 978-1-947194)* 451 Park Ave. S. 7th Flr., New York, NY 10016 USA; *Imprints:* Vertical (Vrtical)
E-mail: info@vertical-inc.com
Web site: http://www.vertical-inc.com.
Dist(s): **MyiLibrary**
Penguin Random Hse. LLC
Random Hse., Inc.

Vertigo *Imprint of* **DC Comics**

Vertigo Publishing, *(978-0-9764463)* P.O. Box 2683, Dearborn, MI 48123 USA
E-mail: vertigopublish@cs.com
Web site: http://www.vertigopublishing.com.

Vescori, Laura, *(978-0-9762965)* 28 Fir Tree Dr., Bradford, CT 06405 USA.

Vesper Enterprises, Inc., *(978-0-9663730)* Orders Addr.: P.O. Box 565, Hingham, MA 02043 USA Tel 781-749-5378; Fax: 781-740-2391; Edit Addr.: 102 Central St., Hingham, MA 02043 USA.

Vessel Ministries, *(978-0-9713345; 978-0-9816463; 978-0-615-11148-3)* 1974 E. Mcandrews Rd., Medford, OR 97504-5510 USA
E-mail: vesselmin@cox.net
Dist(s): **Todd Communications.**

Vesta Bks., LLC, *(978-0-9791065)* 3624 Lone Wolf Trail, Saint Augustine, FL 32086-5316 USA.

Vesta Publishing, *(978-1-60481)* 3750 Priority Way S. Dr., Suite 114, Indianapolis, IN 46240 USA
E-mail: customerservice@vestapublishing.com
Web site: http://www.vestapublishing.com.

Vested Owl, *(978-0-9767926)* Div. of IRM, 3217 Wisconsin Ave., NW #5c, Washington, DC 20016 USA
E-mail: nino@irm360.com
Web site: http://www.vestedowl.com; http://www.kit4marketing.com.

Vesuvius Pr. Inc., *(978-0-9719921; 978-0-9796766; 978-0-9815190; 978-1-935257; 978-1-61956)* Orders Addr.: 4727 N. 12th St., Phoenix, AZ 85014 USA (SAN 255-2981) Tel 602-651-1873; Fax: 602-651-1875; *Imprints:* Tau Publishing (TauPubng)
E-mail: jeffcampbell@vesuviuspress.com
Web site: http://www.taupublishing.com; http://Amordeus.com; http://http:/WellnessandEducation.com; http://Vesuviuspressincorporated.com; http://VesuviusPress.com.

VG Publishing, *(978-0-9785900)* 51613 Sass Rd., Chesterfield, MI 48047-5935 USA (SAN 851-0482)
Web site: http://www.voyagergroupllc.com.

Via Media, Incorporated *See* **Via Media, Pr.**

Via Media, Pr., *(978-0-9646362)* 3112 James St., San Diego, CA 92106 USA Tel 619-884-6440
E-mail: via_media_press@pacbell.net.

Viaduct Music, *(978-0-9831629)* 711 Broadway E. Apt. 9, Seattle, WA 98102-4680 USA Tel 206-322-3187
E-mail: theramster@gmail.com
Dist(s): **BookBaby.**

Vibatorium LLC, *(978-0-9742495)* 419 N. Larchmont Blvd., No. 3265, Los Angeles, CA 90004 USA Tel 323-460-4441; Fax: 323-935-0225
E-mail: info@backyardwonders.com
Web site: http://www.vibatorium.com; http://www.backyardwonders.com.

Vibrante Pr., *(978-0-935301)* P.O. Box 51853, Albuquerque, NM 87181-1853 USA (SAN 696-2351)
E-mail: Lonnie@vibrante.com
Web site: http://www.vibrante.com.

Vice Press Publishing Company *See* **Ascension Education**

Vicens-Vives, Editorial, S.A. (ESP) *(978-84-316)* *Dist. by* **Lectorum Pubns.**

Vickery Bks., *(978-1-928531)* 3012 Anchor Dr., Ormond Beach, FL 32176-2304 USA
E-mail: kvv145@gte.net.

Vic's Lab, LLC, *(978-1-942178)* P.O. Box 10865, Danville, VA 24543 USA Tel 512-842-7552
E-mail: vicslabpublishing@gmail.com
Web site: VicsLab.com.

Victoria Univ. Pr. (NZL) *(978-0-86473; 978-1-77656; 978-1-77656-063-9; 978-1-77656-058-5; 978-1-77656-064-6; 978-1-77656-047-9; 978-1-77656-071-4)* *Dist. by* **IPG Chicago.**

Victor's Crown Publishing, *(978-0-9761188)* 3322 N. 900 E., Ogden, UT 84414 USA Fax: 801-782-3864
E-mail: steve@victorscrown.com
Web site: http://www.victorscrown.com.

Victory Belt Publishing, *(978-0-9777315; 978-0-9815044; 978-0-9825658; 978-1-936608; 978-1-62860)* 32245 Old Ranch Pk. Ln., Auberry, CA 93602 USA (SAN 850-0819) Tel 559-355-4188
Web site: http://www.victorybelt.com
Dist(s): **Simon & Schuster**
Simon & Schuster, Inc.
Tuttle Publishing.

Victory by Any Means Games, *(978-0-9764048; 978-1-935074)* Orders Addr.: P.O. Box 329, Lusk, WY 82225-0329 USA Tel 307-334-3190; Edit Addr.: 315 S. Iron, Lusk, WY 82225-0329 USA
E-mail: tyrel@vbamgames.com
Web site: http://www.vbamgames.com.

Victory Graphics & Media *See* **Yorkshire Publishing Group**

Victory Hse. Pr., *(978-1-935571)* 3836 Tradition Dr., Fort Collins, CO 80526 USA Tel 970-226-1078.

Victory In Grace Ministries, *(978-0-9679145; 978-0-9719262; 978-0-9858764)* 60 Quentin Rd., Lake Zurich, IL 60047 USA Tel 847-438-4494 ext 1071; Fax: 847-438-4232; Toll Free: 800-784-7223
E-mail: feedback@victoryingrace.org
Web site: http://www.victoryingrace.org.

Victory Pr., *(978-0-9753818)* P.O. Box 118, Massillon, OH 44648 USA Do not confuse with companies with the same name in Carlton OR, Chesterfield MO, Monterey CA
E-mail: rabteach2001@aol.com
Web site: http://www.ruthann.faithweb.com.

Victory Publishing Co., *(978-0-9778925)* 3797 N. Ashley Ct., Decatur, IL 62526 USA (SAN 850-4458) Do not confuse with companies with the same or similar name in Hampton, VA, Redwood City, CA, MOunt Pleasant, SC, Inglewood, CA, Banco, VA, Pama, ID, New Orleans, LA, Littleton, CO
E-mail: edmar84@aol.com.

Victory WW 2 Publishing Ltd., *(978-0-9700567)* 18140 Zane St. NW - 200, Elk River, MN 55330 USA (SAN 253-2476) Tel 763-753-5200; Fax: 763-753-2862
E-mail: victorypub@aol.com
Dist(s): **MyiLibrary**
ebrary, Inc.

Vic-Vincent Publishing, *(978-0-9646817)* Div. of Vic-Vincent Corp., Orders Addr.: 362 Gulf Breeze Pkwy., Suite 151, Gulf Breeze, FL 32561 USA (SAN 257-4039) Tel 850-476-7673; Toll Free: 800-772-3343
E-mail: inventorz@aol.com
Web site: http://www.inventorsfreehelp.com
Dist(s): **Distributors, The.**

Vida Life Publishers International *See* **Vida Pubs.**

Vida Pubs., *(978-0-8297)* 8410 NW 53rd Ter. Ste. 103, Miami, FL 33166-4510 USA Toll Free: 800-843-2548
E-mail: vidapubsales@harpercollins.com
Web site: http://www.editorialvida.com
Dist(s): **Follett School Solutions**
Zondervan.

Vidro, Kenneth *See* **Gilbert Square Bks.**

Vidya Bks., *(978-1-878099)* P.O. Box 7788, Berkeley, CA 94707-0788 USA Tel 510-527-9932.

Vidyaranayam, *(978-0-692-71703-5)* 3218 Sharpton Dr., DULUTH, GA 30096 USA Tel 617-899-9122.

Viet Baby, LLC, *(978-0-9776482)* Orders Addr.: P.O. Box 750074, Las Vegas, NV 89136-0074 USA Tel 702-234-5127
E-mail: an@viet-baby.com
Web site: http://www.viet-baby.com.

Vietnamese International Poetry Society, *(978-0-9746300)* Orders Addr.: P.O. Box 246958, Sacramento, CA 95824 USA; Edit Addr.: 3067 Harrison St., NW, Washington, DC 20015 USA.

Viewpoint Pr., *(978-0-943962)* Orders Addr.: P.O. Box 1090, Tehachapi, CA 93581 USA Tel 661-821-5110; Fax: 661-821-7515; Edit Addr.: 785 Tucker Rd., Apt. G400, Tehachapi, CA 93561 USA Do not confuse with companies with the same name in San Diego, CA, Portland, ME
E-mail: joie99@aol.com.

Viewpoints Research Institute, Inc., *(978-0-9743131)* 1209 Grand Central Ave., Glendale, CA 91201 USA
Web site: http://www.viewpointsresearch.org.

Vikasam, *(978-0-615-46456-5)* 23355 N. Empress Dr., Hawthorn Woods, IL 60047 USA Tel 847-815-1978
E-mail: dollysap@gmail.com.

Viking Adult *Imprint of* **Penguin Publishing Group**

Viking Books for Young Readers *Imprint of* **Penguin Publishing Group**

Viking Books for Young Readers *Imprint of* **Penguin Young Readers Group**

VILA Group, Inc., The, *(978-0-9635047)* V2947 S. Atlantic Ave., Apt. 1906, Daytona Beach, FL 32118-6029 USA Tel 904-767-8245.

Vilasa Pr., *(978-0-9762809; 978-1-937927)* Orders Addr.: 2835 Long Valley Rd., Santa Ynez, CA 93460 USA (SAN 256-2995) Tel 805-688-6116; Fax: 805-456-3340
E-mail: vilasapress@gmail.com
Web site: http://www.vilasapress.com; http://sandynathan.com
Dist(s): **BookBaby**
Lightning Source, Inc.
Smashwords.

Villa Wisteria Pubns., *(978-0-615-52506-8)* 6103 Hoochaneetsa Pl. N., Cochiti Lake, NM 87083 USA Tel 505-465-0361
E-mail: mlpbadarak@villawisteria.com
Web site: http://www.villawisteria.com.

Village Earth Pr. *Imprint of* **Harding Hse. Publishing Sebice Inc.**

Village Monkey LLC, The, *(978-0-9789633)* 7760 McWhorter Rd., Martinsville, IN 46151 USA Tel 765-352-1718
E-mail: zenmonkey@thevillagemonkey.com
Web site: http://www.thevillagemonkey.com.

Village Monkey, The *See* **Village Monkey LLC, The**

Village Museum, *(978-0-9740091)* Orders Addr.: 401 Pinckney St., McClellanville, SC 29458 USA Tel 843-887-3030; Edit Addr.: P.O. Box 595, McClellanville, SC 29458 USA Tel 843-887-3030
Web site: http://www.villagemuseum.com.

Village Publishing, *(978-0-9857741; 978-0-9981196-0-1)* 2924 W.132nd Pl., Gardena, CA 90249 USA Tel 310-922-6562
E-mail: wwilson150@gmail.com.

Village Tales Publishing, *(978-0-9753609; 978-0-9853625; 978-1-945408)* 662 Lookout Point, Lawrenceville, GA 30043 USA
E-mail: publisher@villagetalespublishing.com; villagetalespublishing@yahoo.com; villagetalespub@gmail.com
Web site: http://villagetalespublishing.com; http://www.villagetalespublishing.com.

Villager Bk. Publishing, *(978-1-934643)* Orders Addr.: P.O. Box 222 W. Las Colinas Blvd, Suite 1650, Irving, TX 75039 USA (SAN 854-0969)
E-mail: semerick@villagerdustbunnies.com; jbloom@villagerdustbunnies.com; lrinn@villagerdustbunnies.com; jfox@villagerdustbunnies.com
Web site: http://villagerpublishers.com; http://www.villagerdustbunnies.com.

Villard Bks. *Imprint of* **Random House Publishing Group**

Vilnius Pr., *(978-0-615-80054-7; 978-0-615-80223-7; 978-1-940136)* 152 Ct. St. Suite 2E, Portsmouth, NH 03801 USA Tel 8552607535
Web site: http://vilnius-press.com/
Dist(s): **CreateSpace Independent Publishing Platform.**

Vincent, Thomas J. Foundation Inc., *(978-0-9759284)* 44-447 Kaneohe Bay Dr., Kaneohe, HI 96744 USA
E-mail: vincentfoundation@yahoo.com.

Vincero Enterprises, *(978-0-9675329)* 490 Marin Oaks Dr., Novato, CA 94949 USA Tel 800-715-1492; Fax: 415-883-4115; Toll Free: 800-715-1492
E-mail: heritage1492@earthlink.net
Web site: http://www.italianheritage.net; http://www.hispaniclatino.net.

Vindof Publishing, *(978-0-9759310)* 410 N. 3rd St., Ft. Atkinson, WI 53538 USA.

Vineyard Publishing, LLC *See* **Ampelon Publishing, LLC**

Vineyard Stories, *(978-0-9771384; 978-0-615-26606-0; 978-0-615-34267-2; 978-0-9827146; 978-0-9849136; 978-0-9915028; 978-0-692-40086-9; 978-0-692-73037-9; 978-0-692-86175-2)* Orders Addr.: RR 1, Box 65-B9, Edgartown, MA 02539 USA Tel 598-221-2338; Fax: 508-627-6909; Edit Addr.: 52 Bold Meadow Rd., Edgartown, MA 02539 USA
Web site: http://www.vineyardstories.com
Dist(s): **Ingram Publisher Services.**

Vinland Pr., *(978-0-9721410)* P.O. Box 927, North Bend, OR 97459 USA Tel 541-751-1566
E-mail: s_coons@charter.net.

Vinland Publishing, *(978-0-9801601; 978-0-9889455)* 661 Tamarron Dr., Grand Jct, CO 81506-4911 USA (SAN 855-3564)
E-mail: jahunsinger@vinlandpublishing.com; info@vinlandpublishing.com
Web site: http://www.vinlandpublishing.com
Dist(s): **Follett School Solutions**
MyiLibrary
ebrary, Inc.

Vinspire Publishing LLC, *(978-0-9752868; 978-0-9770107; 978-0-9785368; 978-0-9793327; 978-0-9815592; 978-0-9819896; 978-0-9834198; 978-0-9851232; 978-0-9890632; 978-0-9903042; 978-0-9964423; 978-0-9971732)* P.O. Box 1165, Ladson, SC 29456 USA
Web site: http://www.vinspirepublishing.com.

Vintage *Imprint of* **Knopf Doubleday Publishing Group**

Vintage Espanol *Imprint of* **Knopf Doubleday Publishing Group**

Vintage Romance Publishing, LLC *See* **Vinspire Publishing LLC**

Vintage Wild, *(978-0-9862627; 978-0-9986293)* 10070 n.w. 9 St. Cir. 204, Miami, FL 33172 USA Tel 7863026680.

Violet Bks., *(978-0-615-19128-7)* 306 Edgewater Dr., Anderson, SC 29626 USA
Dist(s): **Lulu Pr., Inc.**

Violette Editions (GBR) *(978-1-900828)* *Dist. by* **Dist Art Pubs.**

VIP INK Publishing Group, Inc., *(978-0-615-59125-4; 978-0-615-59946-5; 978-0-9886428; 978-0-9911719; 978-0-9861340; 978-0-9965701; 978-0-9970016; 978-0-9978116)* 4623 branch Ct., lithonia, GA 30038 USA
E-mail: AANDE46461@yahoo.com; Lenny@Printhousebooks.com
Web site: http://www.Printhousebooks.com
Dist(s): **Lightning Source, Inc.**
eBookit.com.

VIP Ink Publishing, L.L.C., *(978-1-939670)* 140 Belle Terre Dlvd. Ste. D 211, LaPlace, LA 70068 USA Tel 985-359-2337
E-mail: info@vipinkpublishing.com
Web site: http://www.vipinkpublishing.com.

Vipassana Research Publications *See* **Pariyatti Publishing**

Viper Comics, *(978-0-9754193; 978-0-9777883; 978-0-9793680; 978-0-9802385; 978-0-9827117; 978-0-9833670)* Div. of Viper Entertainment Inc., 9400 N. MacArthur Blvd., Suite 124-215, Irving, TX 75063 USA Tel 214-638-1400; 469-682-9331; Fax: 817-741-3758
E-mail: jessie@vipercomics.com
Web site: http://www.vipercomics.com
Dist(s): **Diamond Comic Distributors, Inc.**

Virginia Museum of Natural History, *(978-0-9625801; 978-1-884549)* 21 Starling Ave., Martinsville, VA 24112-2921 USA
E-mail: dgreytak@vmnh.org.

Virginia Publishing Corp., *(978-0-9631448; 978-1-891442; 978-0-9914806)* P.O. Box 4538, Saint Louis, MO 63108 USA Tel 314-367-6612 (ext. 22); Fax: 314-367-0727 Do not confuse with Virginia Publishing Co. in Lynchburg, VA
E-mail: jfister@westendword.com
Web site: http://www.stl-books.com; http://bluebirdbookpub.com
Dist(s): **Big River Distribution**
Partners Bk. Distributing, Inc.

Virginian Pilot, *(978-0-9648308)* Div. of Landmark Communcations, Inc., 150 W. Brambleton Ave., Norfolk, VA 23501 USA Tel 757-481-4777; Fax: 757-446-2963
E-mail: linda.hollingsworth@pilotonline.com; pam.smithrodden@pilotonline.com
Dist(s): **Parnassus Bk. Distributors.**

VirTru Powers, *(978-0-9778798; 978-0-9779497)* Orders Addr.: P.O. Box 9404, Tavernier, FL 33070 USA; Edit Addr.: 10S073 Clarendon Hills Rd., Willowbrook, IL 60527 USA (SAN 850-492X) Tel 630-986-5262; Fax: 630-986-5262
E-mail: nomorewast@aol.com.

Virtual Baby Nurse LLC, *(978-0-9755180)* P.O. Box 881296, Port Saint Lucie, FL 34988-1296 USA (SAN 256-1239)
Web site: http://www.virtualbabynurse.com.

Virtual Tales *See* **BRP Publishing Group**

Virtual Word Publishing, *(978-0-9787930)* 1660 Cathedral Dr., Margate, FL 33063 USA Tel 954-971-4025; Fax: 954-971-4025
E-mail: diana@virtualwordpublishing.com
Web site: http://www.virtualwordpublishing.com.

Virtualbookworm.com Publishing, Inc., *(978-0-9703682; 978-1-58939; 978-1-60264; 978-1-62137; 978-1-947532)* P.O. Box 9949, College Station, TX 77842 USA (SAN 852-6575) Toll Free: 877-376-4955 (phone/fax)
E-mail: info@virtualbookworm.com
Web site: http://www.virtualbookworm.com.

Virtue Bks., *(978-0-9746440)* Div. of Virtue Products, Inc., 197 Woodland Pkwy., No. 104-476, San Marcos, CA 92069 USA Tel 760-471-5511; Fax: 760-471-5515; Toll Free: 800-201-5200
E-mail: kenwilcox3@cox.net; ken@virtueproducts.com
Web site: http://www.virtueproducts.com.

Viselman, Kenn Presents.., *(978-0-9722361)* P.O. Box 195, New York, NY 10113 USA (SAN 254-7783) Tel 212-929-1234
E-mail: viselmanpresents@aol.com.

Visible Ink Pr., *(978-0-7876; 978-0-8103; 978-1-57859)* Orders Addr.: 1094 Flex Dr., Jackson, TN 38301-5070 USA Toll Free Fax: 800-351-5073; Toll Free: 800-343-4499; Edit Addr.: 43311 Joy Rd., Canton, MI 48187-2075 USA (SAN 860-2271) Tel 734-667-3211; Fax: 734-667-4311
E-mail: inquiries@visibleink.com
Web site: http://www.visibleink.com
Dist(s): **Ebsco Publishing**
Follett School Solutions
Legato Pubs. Group
Mint Pubs. Group
MyiLibrary
Perseus Bks. Group.

Visikid Bks. *Imprint of* **GSVQ Publishing**

Vision *Imprint of* **Grand Central Publishing**

Vision & Voice Publishing LLC, *(978-0-692-77452-6)* 13102 Creek Bridge Ln., Alpharetta, GA 30004 USA Tel 718-598-3076; Fax: 800-387-9075
E-mail: traceyworthen@aol.com.

Vision Book Company *See* **G.E. Bks.**

Vision Chapters Publishing Co., *(978-0-9860169)* 932 Homestead Park Dr., Apex, NC 27502 USA.

Vision Forum, Inc., The, *(978-0-9665233; 978-1-929241; 978-0-9755263; 978-0-9787559; 978-1-934554)* 4719 Blanco Rd., San Antonio, TX 78212 USA Tel 210-340-5250; Fax: 210-340-8577; Toll Free: 800-440-0022
E-mail: orders@visionforum.com
Web site: http://www.visionforum.com
Dist(s): **Send The Light Distribution LLC.**

For full information on wholesalers and distributors, refer to the Wholesaler and Distributor Name Index

Vision Harmony Publishing, *(978-0-9748715)* 4195 Chino Hills Pkwy., #393, Chino Hills, CA 91709 USA Tel 951-505-2503; Toll Free Fax: 866-855-1476
E-mail: info@visionharmony.com
Web site: http://www.visionharmony.com.

Vision Pubns., *(978-0-9746161; 978-1-933260)* P.O. Box 71532, Marietta, GA 30007-1532 USA Fax: 770-973-9446; Toll Free: 800-862-5264 Do not confuse with companies with the same name in Southfield, MI, Saint Louis, MO, Boise, ID
E-mail: visionpublications@earthlink.net; dvandewalker@earlink.net.

Vision Publishers, Incorporated *See* **Vision Pubs., LLC**

Vision Pubs., LLC, *(978-0-9717054; 978-1-932676; 978-1-63100)* Orders Addr.: P.O. Box 190, Harrisonburg, VA 22803 USA Fax: 540-437-1969; Toll Free: 877-488-0901; Edit Addr.: 755 Cantrell Ave., Suite C, Harrisonburg, VA 22801 USA Do not confuse with Vision Publishers, Fort Lauderdale, FL
E-mail: visionpubl@ntelos.net
Web site: www.vision-publishers.com
Dist(s): **Bookmasters Distribution**
ebrary, Inc.

Vision Publishing, *(978-0-9651783; 978-0-9762730)* Orders Addr.: P.O. Box 11166, Carson, CA 90746-1166 USA Tel 310-537-0791; Toll Free: 800-478-7925; Edit Addr.: 20123 Harlan Ave., Carson, CA 90746 USA Tel 310-367-0641 Do not confuse with companies with the same name in Sandy, UT, Huntsville, AL, Ramona, CA, Southfield, MI, Griffen, GA, Phoenix, MD, Detroit, MI
E-mail: visionpub@rcn.com
Web site: http://www.visionpublishing.net
Dist(s): **Send The Light Distribution LLC**
Smashwords.

Vision Tree, Ltd., The, *(978-1-933334)* 216 Waterbury Cir., Lake Villa, IL 60046 USA (SAN 256-5072) Tel 847-833-2546; Fax: 847-356-3783
E-mail: jo@thevisiontree.com
Web site: http://www.thevisiontree.com.

Vision Unlimited Pr., *(978-0-9746385)* 3832 Radnor Ave., Long Beach, CA 90808 USA Tel 562-537-1397 Do not confuse with Vision Unlimited in Spartanburg, SC
E-mail: joachung@msn.com; susan@newhopegrief.org.

Vision Video, *(978-1-56364)* Orders Addr.: P.O. Box 540, Worcester, PA 19490 USA Tel 610-584-3500; Fax: 610-584-4610; Toll Free: 800-523-0226; Edit Addr.: 2030 Wentz Church Rd., Worcester, PA 19490 USA (SAN 298-7392)
E-mail: info@gatewayfilms.com; info@visionvideo.com
Web site: http://www.gatewayfilms.com
Dist(s): **BJU Pr.**
Christian Bk. Distributors
Follett Media Distribution
Follett School Solutions
Midwest Tape
Spring Arbor Distributors, Inc.
Tapeworm Video Distributor, Inc.

Vision Works Publishing *Imprint of* **Soul Vision Works Publishing**

Visionary Consulting Services, LLC, *(978-0-692-84351-2; 978-0-692-84352-9; 978-0-692-89967-0)* 9024 PENNINGTON PLACE, MONTGOMERY, AL 36117 USA Tel 334-277-8937
E-mail: jeffwcrawford5+LVP0003343@gmail.com; jeffwcrawford5+LVP0003343@gmail.com.

Visionary Play Pr., *(978-0-615-21946-2; 978-0-615-40324-3)* 5098 Reed Rd., Columbus, OH 43220 USA
Web site: http://www.InspiredFlyiing.com
Dist(s): **Lightning Source, Inc.**

VisionQuest Kids *Imprint of* **GSVQ Publishing**

Visions Given Life Publishing Co., *(978-0-9842468)* 1514 Parker Pointe Blvd., Odessa, FL 33556-4022 USA Tel 724-561-9426
E-mail: gdgregdixon@gmail.com.

Visions Of Nature, *(978-0-9656051; 978-0-9749570)* 460 E. 56th St., Suite A, Anchorage, AK 99518 USA Tel 907-561-4062
E-mail: robolson@gci.com
Web site: http://robertolson.com.

Visit to Hawaii, A, *(978-0-9772200)* 445 Kaiolu St., No. 807, Honolulu, HI 55303 USA Tel 808-921-2440
E-mail: hawaiiholm@aol.com
Dist(s): **Booklines Hawaii, Ltd.**

Visor Bks., *(978-0-9771994)* 62 W. Gaslight Pl., The Woodlands, TX 77382 USA (SAN 256-9752)
E-mail: rosszilla@sbcglobal.net
Web site: http://www.visorbooks.com.

Visor Libros (ESP) *(978-84-7522) Dist. by* **AIMS Intl.**

Vista Italia, *(978-0-9820672)* P.O. Box 92, La Mirada, CA 90637 USA (SAN 857-1643).

Vista Press Ventures, Incorporated *See* **Eaglemont Pr.**

Vister Bks., *(978-0-9983337)* 429 Visser Dr., Blackwater, VA 24221 USA Tel 276-346-1650
E-mail: circlevisser@gmail.com.

Visual Education Productions, *(978-1-56918)* 1020 SE Loop 289, Lubbock, TX 79404 USA Tel 806-745-8820; Toll Free: 800-922-9965
E-mail: cev@cevmultimedia.com
Web site: http://www.cevmultimedia.com
Dist(s): **Follett School Solutions.**

Visual Manna, *(978-0-9677386; 978-0-9715970; 978-0-9816093)* Orders Addr.: P.O. Box 553, Salem, MO 65560 USA Tel 573-729-2100; Edit Addr.: 1403 Dent County Rd., 502A, Salem, MO 65560 USA
E-mail: visualmanna@gmail.com.

Visual Velocity, *(978-0-9884679)* 22106 Chesapeake Cir., Commerce Twp., MI 48390 USA Tel 248-345-0789
E-mail: visualvelocityllc@gmail.com.

Vital Health Publishing *Imprint of* **Square One Pubs.**

Vital Link Orange County, *(978-0-9765880)* Orders Addr.: P.O. Box 12064, Costa Mesa, CA 92627 USA Tel 949-646-2520; Fax: 949-646-2523; Edit Addr.: 1701 E. 16th St., Newport Beach, CA 92663 USA
E-mail: kathy@vitallinkoc.org
Web site: http://www.vitallinkoc.org.

Vital Links, *(978-0-9717653)* 6613 Seybold Rd., Suite E, Madison, WI 53719 USA Tel 608-270-5424; Fax: 608-278-9363; Toll Free: 866-829-6331
Web site: http://vitallinks.net.

Vital Narrative Pr., *(978-0-692-38692-7; 978-0-692-39642-1; 978-0-692-39747-3; 978-0-692-40643-4; 978-0-692-40899-5; 978-0-692-46199-0; 978-0-692-46406-9; 978-0-9983364)* 1296 Sessions Ct S, Memphis, TN 38119 USA Tel 9196961665; Toll Free: 9196961665
Dist(s): **CreateSpace Independent Publishing Platform.**

Vitale, Mary Ann, *(978-0-9981359; 978-0-9981359-1-5)* 23550 Hall Rd., Woodhaven, MI 48183 USA Tel 734-675-7946; Fax: 734-675-7946
E-mail: nvitale1@comcast.net.

Vitally Important,
Dist(s): **SPD-Small Pr. Distribution.**

Vives, Luis Editorial (Edelvives) (ESP) *(978-84-263) Dist. by* **Lectorum Pubns.**

Viz Comics *Imprint of* **Viz Media**

Viz Communications, Incorporated *See* **Viz Media**

Viz Media, *(978-0-929279; 978-1-56931; 978-1-59116; 978-1-4215; 978-1-9747)* Subs. of Shogakukan, Inc., 295 Bay St., San Francisco, CA 94133 USA (SAN 248-8604) Tel 415-546-7073; Fax: 415-546-7086; P.O. Box 77010, San Francisco, CA 94107 Fax: 415-546-7086; *Imprints:* Viz Comics (Viz Comics)
E-mail: scott@viz.com; info@info@viz.com
Web site: http://www.viz.com
Dist(s): **AAA Anime Distribution**
Diamond Comic Distributors, Inc.
Follett School Solutions
Simon & Schuster, Inc.
Simon & Schuster Children's Publishing.

Vizione Productions Inc., *(978-0-9758863)* P.O. Box 54838, Atlanta, GA 30312 USA (SAN 256-1158) Tel 404-538-9424.

VK Publishing, Inc., *(978-0-9777171)* 464 Ridgewood Ln., Buffalo Grove, IL 60089 USA (SAN 850-0509)
E-mail: vkofman@vkpublishing.com.

Vocal Power Inc., *(978-0-934419)* 2123 N. Topanga Canyon Blvd., Topanga, CA 90290 USA (SAN 693-4471) Toll Free: 800-829-7664
E-mail: info@vocalpowerinc.com
Web site: http://www.vocalpowerinc.com
Dist(s): **Alfred Publishing Co., Inc.**

Vocalis, Ltd., *(978-0-9665743; 978-0-9709948; 978-1-932653)* 100 Avalon Cir., Waterbury, CT 06710 USA Tel 203-753-5244; Fax: 203-574-5433
E-mail: vocalis@sbcglobal.net; info@VocalisESL.com
Web site: http://www.vocalisltd.com; http://www.vocalisesl.com; http://www.vocalis.com
Dist(s): **Follett School Solutions**
ebrary, Inc.

Vogel, Robert, *(978-0-9768455)* P.O. Box 551, Chesterton, IN 46304 USA Tel 219-688-5895; Toll Free: 800-815-7685 (phone/fax) Do not confuse with Robert Vogel in South Burlington, VT
E-mail: contact@azarovmemories.com
Web site: http://www.garrythegroundhog.com.

Voice & Vision Pubns., *(978-1-888251)* 902 Fletcher Ave., Indianapolis, IN 46203 USA Tel 317-262-4030; Fax: 317-262-4029
E-mail: voicevision@apostolic.edu.

Voice Connection/Vendera Publishing, The *See* **Vendera Publishing**

Voice of Light Pubns., *(978-0-9785623)* P.O. Box 1437, Fair Oaks, CA 95628 USA (SAN 850-9905) Tel 916-965-3046
E-mail: voiceoflight@comcast.net.

Voice of Truths Publishing, *(978-0-9666777; 978-0-9742357; 978-0-9818992; 978-0-9916280)* P.O. Box 34, Donalds, SC 29638-9039 USA
E-mail: publishers@charter.net; robert@voiceoftruths.com
Web site: http://www.voiceoftruths.com.

Voigt, J. M. Incorporated *See* **MindWare Holdings, Inc.**

Volare, LLC *See* **Dividion Group, LLC, The**

†volcano pr., *(978-0-912078; 978-1-884244)* Orders Addr.: P.O. Box 270, Volcano, CA 95689 USA (SAN 220-0015) Tel 209-296-4991; Fax: 209-296-4995; Toll Free: 800-879-9636; Edit Addr.: 21496 National St., Volcano, CA 95689 USA
E-mail: info@volcanopress.com; sales@volcanopress.com; adam@volcanopress.com
Web site: http://www.volcanopress.com
Dist(s): **New Leaf Distributing Co., Inc.**
Quality Bks., Inc.; *CIP.*

Volo *Imprint of* **Hyperion Bks. for Children**

Volunteers of the Colorado Historical Society, *(978-0-9770423)* 1560 Broadway. Ste. 400, Denver, CO 80202-5133 USA
E-mail: angela.caudill@chs.state.co.us.

von Buchwald, Martin Farina, *(978-0-9777266)* 1158 5th Ave., New York, NY 10029 USA Tel 212-348-5580
E-mail: martin@farina.com.

Von Curtis Publishing, *(978-0-9749939)* 1278 Glenneyre, Suite 96, LaGuna Beach, CA 92651 USA Tel 800-459-4007; Fax: 949-497-7163
E-mail: info@beniceorelse.com
Web site: http://www.beniceorelse.com.

von Klan, Laurene, *(978-0-578-00322-1)* 4532 N. Albany, Chicago, IL 60625 USA
E-mail: chicagoriver@hotmail.com
Dist(s): **Lulu Pr., Inc.**

Vook Inc. *See* **Pronoun, Inc.**

Vorndran, Judith Clay, *(978-0-9772439)* 6431 Antoinette Dr., Mentor, OH 44060-3431 USA
E-mail: jclayvorndran05@sbcglobal.net; jclayvorndran@aol.com
Web site: http://www.hometown.aol.com/jclayvorndran/myhomepage.

Vorpal Words, LLC, *(978-0-9881969)* 2840 W Hwy. 101, Wellsville, UT 84339 USA Tel 435-764-7052
E-mail: dcolemanbooks@gmail.com
Web site: www.dcolemanbooks.com.

Vortex Bks. *Imprint of* **Stone Arch Bks.**

Voss, Dawn L., *(978-0-615-15324-7; 978-0-615-15581-4)* 481 Hallman St., Berlin, WI 54923 USA
E-mail: wr1t3r@yahoo.com
Dist(s): **Lulu Pr., Inc.**

Vox Dei *Imprint of* **Booktrope**

Voyageur Pr *Imprint of* **Quarto Publishing Group USA**

Voyageur Pr. *Imprint of* **Quarto Publishing Group USA**

VSP Bks. *Imprint of* **Vacation Spot Publishing**

WAMY International, Inc., *(978-1-882837)* P.O. Box 8096, Falls Church, VA 22041-8096 USA Tel 703-916-0924; Fax: 703-916-0925.

WCS Corp., *(978-0-9639350)* Orders Addr.: P.O. Box 900, Lander, WY 82520 USA Tel 307-332-2881; Fax: 307-332-9332; Toll Free: 800-656-8762.

WGBH Boston Video, *(978-0-9636881; 978-1-57807; 978-1-884738; 978-1-59375)* Orders Addr.: P.O. Box 2284, South Burlington, VT 05407-2284 USA Fax: 802-864-9846; 617-300-1050; Toll Free: 800-255-9424
Web site: http://www.wgbh.org
Dist(s): **Follett School Solutions**
Midwest Tape.

W.J. Fantasy, Inc., *(978-1-56021)* 120 Long Hill Cross Rd., Shelton, CT 06484-6125 USA Toll Free Fax: 800-200-3000; Toll Free: 800-222-7529
E-mail: wjfantasy@erols.com.

WJH Publishing, *(978-0-9674864)* 1445 Ross St., Suite 5400, Dallas, TX 75202-2785 USA Tel 214-978-8520; Fax: 214-978-8526.

W M Books *See* **Sierra Raconteur Publishing**

W M C Publishing *See* **Milestone Pr., Inc.**

WP Pr., Inc., *(978-0-9633019; 978-1-884837)* 525 N. Norris Ave., Tucson, AZ 85719-5239 USA.

W Q E D Multimedia, *(978-0-9713080; 978-0-9769936; 978-0-9816697)* 4802 Fifth Ave., Pittsburgh, PA 15213 USA
Web site: http://www.wqed.org.

W Q E D Pittsburgh *See* **W Q E D Multimedia**

W S Publishing, *(978-0-9773520)* 213 Levant Way, Oceanside, CA 92057 USA (SAN 257-3180)
E-mail: elaine@elaineswann.com
Web site: http://www.elaineswann.com.

W. St. James Pr., *(978-0-9672818)* 2683 W. St. James Pkwy., Cleveland Heights, OH 44106 USA Tel 216-932-0290 (phone/fax)
E-mail: marcjaffe@aol.com.

WW West, Inc., *(978-0-9653924; 978-0-9727921; 978-0-9758960)* 20875 Sholes Rd., Bend, OR 97702 USA (SAN 299-2574) Tel 541-385-8911 (phone/fax)
E-mail: wwwest@bendbroadband.com
Web site: http://www.nationalparkspopup.com
Dist(s): **Farcountry Pr.**

W Y Publishing *See* **Bluewood Bks.**

W3 Publishing, *(978-0-9801322)* P.O. Box 1255, Suitland, MD 20752-2075 USA Tel 240-354-7077
E-mail: kellum_ent@verizon.net.

W5YI Group, Incorporated, The *See* **Master Publishing, Inc.**

Wachob, Chuck , *(978-0-578-15467-1)* 311 Rigas Ct, Americas, GA 31709 USA.

Wack, Nancy, *(978-0-615-16634-6)* 600 Fairwick Dr., saint Louis, MO 63129 USA
Dist(s): **Lulu Pr., Inc.**

Wackophoto, *(978-0-9798532)* P.O. Box 14843, Richmond, VA 23221 USA (SAN 854-5529)
E-mail: info@coolingthesouth.com
Web site: http://www.wackophoto.com; http://www.coolingthesouth.com.

Wacky World Studios LLC, *(978-0-9742997)* 148 E. Douglas Rd., Oldsmar, FL 34677-2939 USA Tel 813-818-8277; Fax: 813-818-8396; Toll Free: 877-429-2259
E-mail: info@wackyworld.tv
Web site: http://www.wackyworld.tv.

Wade & Kayak Fishing Bks., *(978-0-9742253)* 702 Balmoral Ct., Friendswood, TX 77546 USA
E-mail: flyfisher@ev1.net
Web site: http://www.texascoastalfishingbooks.com/pages/1/index.htm.

Wade, John Pub., *(978-0-9623934; 978-1-882425)* Orders Addr.: P.O. Box 303, Phillips, ME 04966 USA Tel 207-639-2501 (phone/fax); 1413 Hwy. 17 S., PMB 154, Surfside Beach, SC 29575 Tel 843-215-1097; Edit Addr.: 193 Weld Rd., Phillips, ME 04966 USA
E-mail: wadecjs@yahoo.com
Web site: http://www.johnwadepublisher.com.

Wadhams! Pr., *(978-0-9754987)* c/o Cordelia Sand, P.O. Box 264, Essex, NY 12936 USA.

Wading River Bks., LLC., *(978-0-9791463)* P.O. Box 361, Calverton, NY 11933 USA Tel 516-527-6283
E-mail: robert@wrbooks.com
Web site: http://www.wrbooks.com.

†Wadsworth, *(978-0-15; 978-0-314; 978-0-534; 978-0-8185; 978-0-8273; 978-0-942728; 978-1-928916; 978-1-4163; 978-0-495)* Div. of CENGAGE Learning, Orders Addr.: 7625 Empire Dr., Florence, KY 41042-2978 USA (SAN 200-2663) Tel 859 525 2230; Toll Free Fax: 800-487-8488; Toll Free: 800 354 9706; 10650 Toebben Dr., Independence, KY 41051 Toll Free Fax: 800-487-8488; Toll Free: 800-354-9706; Edit Addr.: 10 Davis Dr., Belmont, CA 94002 USA Tel 650 595 2350; Fax: 606 592 9081
Web site: http://www.brookscole.com; http://www.wadsworth.com
Dist(s): **CENGAGE Learning**
Follett School Solutions
MyiLibrary; *CIP.*

Wadsworth Publishing *See* **Wadsworth**

Wagging Tails Publishing *See* **Wagging Tales Publishing**

Wagging Tales Publishing, *(978-0-9715224)* 727 Lincoln Ave., Carbondale, CO 81623 USA.

Wagner Entertainment, *(978-0-9754515)* Orders Addr.: 3640 Loadstone Dr., Sherman Oaks, CA 91403-4558 USA
Web site: http://www.wagnerentertainment.com.

WainWave Media, *(978-0-9789319)* P.O. Box 11037, Lexington, KY 40512-1037 USA (SAN 853-6953) Tel 859-294-9033; Fax: 859-233-1999
E-mail: dougwain@earthlink.net
Web site: http://www.waragainstviolence.com.

WainWave Publishing *See* **WainWave Media**

Waiting Room to Heaven *Imprint of* **Lisa Loucks Christenson Publishing, LLC**

Wajsbort, Rochel, *(978-0-9749491)* 1431 E9, Brooklyn, NY 11230 USA Tel 718-339-5070; Fax: 718-998-1615.

Wakefield Connection, The, *(978-0-9703632)* 5201 Kingston Pike, Suite 6-302, Knoxville, TN 37919-5026 USA Tel 304-624-3901
E-mail: richard@wakefieldconnection.com; wendy@wakefieldconnection.com
Web site: http://www.wakefieldconnection.com
Dist(s): **Independent Pubs. Group.**

Wakinglion Studio, *(978-0-9767413)* P.O. Box 624, Bayfield, CO 81122 USA.

Walch Education, *(978-0-8251)* 40 Walch Dr., Portland, ME 04103 USA (SAN 669-6562) Fax: 207-828-8818; Toll Free Fax: 888-991-5755; Toll Free: 800-341-6094
E-mail: customerservice@walch.com
Web site: http://www.walch.com
Dist(s): **Follett School Solutions.**

Walch Publishing *See* **Walch Education**

Waldenhouse Pubs., Inc., *(978-0-9705214; 978-0-9761033; 978-0-9779189; 978-0-9793712; 978-0-9814996; 978-1-935186; 978-1-947589)* 100 Clegg St., Signal Mountain, TN 37377 USA (SAN 856-8111) Toll Free: 888-222-8228
E-mail: karenstone@waldenhouse.com
Web site: http://waldenhouse.com
Dist(s): **eBookit.com.**

Waldman House Pr. *Imprint of* **TRISTAN Publishing, Inc.**

Waldman Publishing Corp., *(978-0-86611; 978-1-59060; 978-1-60340)* P.O. Box 1587, New York, NY 10028-0013 USA (SAN 219-340X)
E-mail: info@waldmanbooks.com
Web site: http://www.waldmanbooks.com/.

Waldon Pond Pr. *Imprint of* **HarperCollins Pubs.**

Waldorf Early Childhood Assn. Of North America, *(978-0-9722238; 978-0-9796232; 978-0-9816159; 978-1-936849)* 285 Hungry Hollow Rd., Chestnut Ridge, NY 10977 USA Tel 845-352-1690
E-mail: mlyons@wardolfearlychildhood.org; publications@waldorfearlychildhood.org.

Waldorf Publications, *(978-0-9623978; 978-1-888365; 978-1-936367; 978-1-943582)* Div. of Research Institute for Waldorf Education, Orders Addr.: Publications Office 38 Main St., Chatham, NY 12037 USA Tel 303-545-9486; Edit Addr.: 575 Quail Cir., Boulder, CO 80304 USA
E-mail: ann_erwin@hotmail.com
Web site: http://www.whywaldorfworks.org; http://www.waldorfeducation.org; http://www.waldorfreasearchinstitute.org
Dist(s): **Midpoint Trade Bks., Inc.**
SteinerBooks, Inc.

Waldorf Publishing, *(978-0-578-19693-0)* 2140 Hall Johnson Rd. 102-345, Grapevine, TX 76051 USA Tel 972-674-3131
E-mail: barbara@waldorfpublishing.com
Web site: http://www.waldorfpublishing.com
Dist(s): **Bookmasters Distribution.**

Walkabout Publishing, *(978-0-9802086; 978-0-9821799)* P.O. Box 151, Kansasville, WI 53139 USA Tel 262-878-0448
E-mail: publisher@walkaboutpublishing.com
Web site: http://www.walkaboutpublishing.com
Dist(s): **Smashwords.**

†Walker & Co., *(978-0-8027)* 175 Fifth Ave., New York, NY 10010 USA (SAN 202-5213) Tel 646-438-6056; Fax: 212-780-0115 (orders); Toll Free Fax: 800-218-9367; Toll Free: 800-289-2553 (orders); *Imprints:* Bloomsbury USA Childrens (Bloom Child)
Web site: http://www.walkerbooks.com
Dist(s): **Macmillan**
Perfection Learning Corp.
Beeler, Thomas T. Pub.; *CIP.*

Walker, Esther, *(978-0-9716071)* 80-000 Ave. 48, Suite 131, Indio, CA 92201 USA Tel 760-347-4352
E-mail: strwalkr@easyfeed.com.

Walker, Fay Alice *See* **Favortwou Publishing**

Walker, J.W. Ministries *See* **LightHouse Pr.**

Walker Large Print *Imprint of* **Cengage Gale**

Walker Publishing Company *See* **Walker & Co.**

Walking Elk Pubns., *(978-1-59648; 978-0-615-41705-9; 978-0-9881775)* 81 Portsmouth Ave. No. 5, Stratham, NH 03885 USA Tel 603-772-9300
E-mail: ajkitt@kripara.com.

Walking the Line Pubns., *(978-0-9714540; 978-0-9816247; 978-0-9846299)* 4612 S. Jordan Pkwy., South Jordan, UT 84009 USA
E-mail: kclawson@walkingthelinebooks.com
Web site: http://www.walkingthelinebooks.com.

Walking Tree, Inc., *(978-0-9749832)* P.O. Box 468, Crystal Beach, FL 34681 USA Tel 727-784-5016
E-mail: art@halstowers.com
Web site: http://www.halstowers.com; http://www.lifeblending.com.

Wall, Mary Joanne, *(978-0-9644283)* 601 Ingomar Rd., Pittsburgh, PA 15237-4983 USA Tel 412-364-2598; Fax: 412-314-0862.

Walling, Emma *See* **Emma's Pantry**

Walls Tumbling Down Publishing, *(978-0-9770098)* Manhttanville Station, 871, New York, NY 10027-9998 USA Tel 212-865-6008
E-mail: antonioj365@aol.com
Web site: http://www.hometown.aol.com.

wallymeets, *(978-0-9843648)* Div. of wallymeets ltd., Orders Addr.: Hans Memlingdreef 50, LOMMEL, 3920 BEL
Web site: http://wallymeets.com/.

Publisher Name Index

Walnut Cracker Publishing, LLC, *(978-0-9800571)* Orders Addr.: P.O. Box 2707, Loveland, CO 80539 USA
E-mail: mwalker@walnutcrackerpublishing.com
Web site: http://www.walnutcrackerpublishing.com
Dist(s): **Independent Pubs. Group.**

Walnut Springs Bks., *(978-1-933317; 978-1-59992; 978-1-934393; 978-1-935217)* 4110 Highland Dr. Ste. 300, Salt Lake Cty, UT 84124-2676 USA
E-mail: editorial@leatherwoodpress.com
Web site: http://www.leatherwoodpress.com
Dist(s): **Brigham Distribution**
Deseret Bk. Co.
Independent Pubs. Group.

Walsh, Joseph, *(978-0-9818019)* P.O. Box 34105, Granada Hills, CA 91394 USA
Web site: http://www.gambleronthe loose.com.

Walt Disney Home Video, 3333 N. Pagosa Ct., Indianapolis, IN 46226 USA Tel 317-890-3030; Fax: 818-560-1930
Web site: http://disney.go.com/DisneyVideos/
Dist(s): **Buena Vista Home Video**
Critics' Choice Video
Follett Media Distribution
Midwest Tape.

Walt Disney Records, *(978-0-7634; 978-1-55723)* Div. of Walt Disney Co., 3333 N. Pagosa Ct., Indianapolis, IN 46226 USA Tel 317-890-3030; Fax: 317-897-4614
Web site: http://disneymusic.disney.go.com/index.html
Dist(s): **Follett School Solutions**
Ingram Publisher Services
Rounder Kids Music Distribution.

Walter Foster *Imprint of* **Quarto Publishing Group USA**

Walter Foster Jr *Imprint of* **Quarto Publishing Group USA**

Water Shoe Pr., *(978-0-9759499)* P.O. Box 928, Langley, WA 98260 USA.

Walter, Wendy D., *(978-0-9857147)* 301 Hillcrest Rd., San Carlos, CA 94070 USA Tel 650-598-0178; *Imprints:* Angry Bicycle (AngryBicycle)
Web site: ambrils-tale.com.

Walterick Pubs., Inc., *(978-0-937396; 978-1-884838)* Orders Addr.: P.O. Box 2216, Kansas City, KS 66110-0216 USA (SAN 211-9366) Tel 913-334-0100; Fax: 913-334-0153; Toll Free: 800-255-4097 (US only); Edit Addr.: 6549 State Ave., Kansas City, KS 66110 USA Toll Free: 800-648-0443 (Canada only).

Walters, Jack C., *(978-0-9754658)* 2850 Airport Rd., No. 1, Carson City, NV 89706 USA Tel 775-882-0518
E-mail: waltersjc@charter.net.

Walters, Steve Ministries, *(978-0-9719767)* 3633 Corners Way, Norcross, GA 30092 USA Tel 770-409-1633; Fax: 770-300-9636; *Imprints:* Crowned Warrior Publishing (Crowned Warr)
E-mail: holyspiritinfo@stevewaltersministries.com
Web site: http://www.stevewaltersministries.com.

Waltower Publishing, *(978-0-9905422)* 6405 E. 129th Pl., Grandview, MO 64030 USA Tel 816-695-0541
E-mail: acwaltower@yahoo.com.

Wampum Bks., LLC, *(978-0-9842012)* 115a Pine St., Greenwich, CT 06830 USA (SAN 858-7116) Tel 203-531-8111
E-mail: sgalfas@itoinc.net.

Wan Lee Publishing, *(978-0-9858042)* 2860 Fenton Rd., Hartland, MI 48353 USA Tel 248-408-7103; Fax: 248-889-3647
E-mail: wayne@wanleepublishing.com
Web site: www.wanleepublishing.com.

Wand In Magic, *(978-0-9761921)* P.O. Box 58068, Nashville, TN 37205 USA Fax: 615-269-6820.

Wander Twins, The, *(978-0-9985434)* 2803 SE 87th Ave., Portland, OR 97266 USA Tel 707-267-1848
E-mail: wesleynickerman@gmail.com.

Wandering Sage Bookstore & More, LLC *See* **Wandering Sage Pubns., LLC**

Wandering Sage Pubns., LLC, *(978-0-9725230; 978-1-933300)* Orders Addr.: 614 Rivers Bend Estates Dr., Saint Charles, MO 63303 USA Tel 314-623-6647
E-mail: valkpub@yahoo.com
Web site: http://www.wanderingsagebooks.com
Dist(s): **Valkyrie Distribution.**

WannaBees Media LLC, *(978-0-9767670)* 118 E. 25th St., Suite LL, New York, NY 10010 USA Tel 212-253-9874
E-mail: kdonovan@nvmagazine.com
Web site: http://www.theDobees.com.

Wanniarichchige, Somiruwan, *(978-0-615-17026-8)* 20700 San Jose Hills Rd., Suite 115, Walnut, CA 91789 USA
E-mail: ruwangotu@hotmail.com
Dist(s): **Lulu Pr., Inc.**

Warbelow, Willy Lou, *(978-0-9618314)* P.O. Box 252, Tok, AK 99780 USA (SAN 667-2639) Tel 907-883-2881.

Warbranch Pr., Inc., *(978-0-9667114; 978-0-692-52275-2)* 329 Warbranch Rd., Central, SC 29630 USA Tel 864-654-6180
E-mail: kspalmer@aol.com; salley.ouellette@gmail.com; jhpalmer42@aol.com
Web site: http://www.warbranchpress.com
Dist(s): **Follett School Solutions**
Partners Bk. Distributing, Inc.

Warburton and Gorman Publishing *See* **BareBones Publishing**

Ward, Jason E., *(978-0-9662366)* P.O. Box 719, Bronx, NY 10475 USA Tel 718-379-6285
E-mail: Jason@aiyahlevene.com.

Ward, John H., *(978-0-615-21017-9; 978-0-9834038)* 6606 Deerwood Dr., Crystal Lake, IL 60012 USA.

Warehousing & Fulfillment Specialists, LLC (WFS, LLC), *(978-1-57102; 978-1-58029; 978-1-59093)* 7344 Cockrill Bend Blvd., Nashville, TN 37209-1043 USA Toll Free Fax: 800-510-3650; Toll Free: 800-327-5113; *Imprints:* Eager Minds Press (Eager Minds)
E-mail: vhill@apgbooks.com
Web site: http://www.apgbooks.com
Dist(s): **APG Sales & Distribution Services.**

Warne *Imprint of* **Penguin Publishing Group**

Warne *Imprint of* **Penguin Publishing Group**

Warne *Imprint of* **Penguin Young Readers Group**

Warner Books, Incorporated *See* **Grand Central Publishing**

Warner Bros. Pubns. *Imprint of* **Alfred Publishing Co., Inc.**

Warner Brothers Records, *(978-1-880528)* Div. of Creative Enterprises, 3300 Warner Blvd., Burbank, CA 91505 USA Tel 818-953-3467; Fax: 818-953-3797.

†Warner Pr., Inc., *(978-0-87162; 978-1-59317; 978-1-68434)* Orders Addr.: P.O. Box 2499, Anderson, IN 46018-2499 USA (SAN 691-4241) Tel 765-648-2116; Fax: 765-622-9511; Toll Free: 800-848-2464; Edit Addr.: 2902 Enterprise Dr., Anderson, IN 46013 USA (SAN 111-8110) Tel 765-644-7721; Fax: 765-640-8005; Toll Free: 800-741-7721 (orders only)
E-mail: jallison@warnerpress.org; wporders@warnerpress.org; rjackson@warnerpress.org
Web site: http://www.warnerpress.org; http://www.francisasburypress.org
Dist(s): **Anchor Distributors**
Lightning Source, Inc.
OverDrive, Inc.
Potter's House Book Service
SPD-Small Pr. Distribution
Send The Light Distribution LLC
Spring Arbor Distributors, Inc.; *CIP.*

Warner Press Publishers *See* **Warner Pr., Inc.**

Warren Machine Co., *(978-0-9729410; 978-1-934866)* 3 Taylor St., Portland, OR 04102 USA
E-mail: ari.meil@warren-machine.com
Web site: http://www.warren-machine.com
Dist(s): **Independent Pubs. Group.**

Warren Publishing, Inc., *(978-1-886057; 978-0-9853094; 978-0-9884170; 978-0-9894814; 978-0-9960506; 978-0-9908136; 978-1-943258)* 3440 Toringdon Way Suite 205, CHARLOTTE, NC 28277 USA Tel 704-992-2829 Do not confuse with companies with the same or similar name in Indianapolis, IN, Pomona, CA, Washington, DC, Loomis, CA, Roseville, CA, , Chesterfield, VA
E-mail: warrenpublish@gmail.com
Web site: http://warrenpublishing.net
Dist(s): **BookBaby.**

Warrington Pubns., *(978-0-9889698; 978-0-9890974; 978-0-9984331)* 11100 SE Petrovitsky Apt. A-104, Renton, WA 98055 USA Tel 425-793-9629; *Imprints:* Oceanus Books (Oceanus Bks)
E-mail: WarringtonPress@aol.com
Web site: WarringtonPublications.com.

Warrior Schl. Pr., *(978-0-9715289)* P.O. Box 768, Sonoita, AZ 85637 USA
E-mail: info@warriorschool.com
Web site: http://www.warriorschool.com.

Warwick Hse. Publishing, *(978-0-9638455; 978-1-890306; 978-0-9786369; 978-0-9790367; 978-0-9795258; 978-0-9801315; 978-0-9823004; 978-0-9842516; 978-0-9845166; 978-1-936553; 978-0-9978020; 978-0-9994023)* 720 Court St., Lynchburg, VA 24504 USA Tel 434-846-1200
E-mail: whp720@aol.com
Web site: http://www.warwickpublishers.com.

Warwick Publishing (CAN) *(978-1-894020; 978-1-895629; 978-1-894622) Dist. by* **TwoRivers.**

Washington Pubs., *(978-0-9715721)* P.O. Box 12517, Tallahassee, FL 32317-2517 USA (SAN 254-2366) Do not confuse with Washington Publishers in Renton, WA
E-mail: info@washingtonpublishers.com
Web site: http://www.washingtonpublishers.com.

†Washington State Univ. Pr., *(978-0-87422)* P.O. Box 645910, Pullman, WA 99164-5910 USA (SAN 206-6688) Tel 509-335-3518; Fax: 509-335-8568; Toll Free: 800-354-7360
E-mail: wsupress@wsu.edu; lawton@wsu.edu
Web site: http://wsupress.wsu.edu
Dist(s): **Ebsco Publishing**
MyiLibrary
Partners Bk. Distributing, Inc.
Todd Communications; *CIP.*

Washington University, Gallery of Art *See* **Washington Univ., Mildred Lane Kemper Art Museum**

Washington Univ., Mildred Lane Kemper Art Museum, *(978-0-936316)* Campus Box 1214, 1 Brookings Dr., Saint Louis, MO 63130 USA (SAN 214-4859) Tel 314-935-7460; Fax: 314-935-7282
E-mail: Jane_Neidhardt@wustl.edu
Web site: http://www.kemperartmuseum.wustl.edu
Dist(s): **Chicago Distribution Ctr.**
D.A.P./Distributed Art Pubs.
Univ. of Chicago Pr.

WasiWorks Studio LLC, *(978-0-9845203)* 6109 Piping Rock Rd., Madison, WI 53711 USA Tel 608-239-2526
E-mail: odalo@wasiworks.com
Web site: http://www.wasiworks.com.

Wasteland Pr., *(978-0-9715811; 978-0-9724289; 978-0-9729186; 978-0-9740725; 978-0-9742342; 978-0-9744368; 978-0-9746290; 978-0-9748230; 978-1-932852; 978-1-933265; 978-1-60047; 978-1-68111)* Orders Addr.: 18 Village Plz Pmb 177, Shelbyville, KY 40065 USA
Dist(s): **Lightning Source, Inc.**
SPD-Small Pr. Distribution.

Watch & Learn, Inc., *(978-1-893907; 978-1-940301)* 1882 Queens Way, Atlanta, GA 30341 USA Tel 404-762-7760; Fax: 770-457-2132; Toll Free: 800-416-7088
E-mail: bc@cvls.com
Web site: http://www.cvls.com
Dist(s): **Music, Bks. & Business, Inc.**

Watch Me Grow Kids, *(978-1-932555)* P.O. Box 4405, Carson, CA 90749 USA (SAN 255-5093) Fax: 310-532-4536
E-mail: panderson@watchmegrowkids.com
Web site: http://www.watchmegrowkids.com.

Watchmaker Publishing *Imprint of* **Wexford College Pr.**

Water Daughter Publishing, *(978-0-9753089)* Orders Addr.: 108 Academy St., POUGHKEEPSIE, NY 12601 USA Tel 845-397-7157; Toll Free: 888-778-2928
E-mail: omikemi@hotmail.com
Web site: http://www.waterdaughter.com.

Water Forest Pr. *Imprint of* **Skyline Pubn.**

Water Lily Pr., Inc., *(978-0-9772168; 978-0-9860394)* 17214 Hillview Ln., Spring, TX 77379 USA
E-mail: hfwynn@outlook.com
Web site: waterlilypress.com.

WaterBrook Pr. *Imprint of* **Crown Publishing Group**

Waterbrook Press *See* **Doubleday Religious Publishing Group, The**

Watercourse, The *See* **Project WET Foundation**

Waterfall Ridge, *(978-0-9725485)* 40497 Cty. Rd. 20, Saint Peter, MN 56082 USA.

Waterford Pr., Inc., *(978-0-9640225; 978-1-58355; 978-1-889903)* 1123 Overcash Dr., Dunedin, FL 34698 USA Tel 602-681-3333
E-mail: info@waterfordpress.com
Web site: http://www.waterfordpress.com
Dist(s): **Legato Pubs. Group**
Perseus Bks. Group.

Waterford Press, Limited *See* **Waterford Pr., Inc.**

Waterfront Productions, *(978-0-9759185; 978-0-692-26375-4; 978-0-692-29262-4; 978-0-9976140)* Orders Addr.: P.O. Box 607085, Chicago, IL 60660 USA
E-mail: jb@johnborowski.com
Web site: http://www.hhholmesthefilm.com; http://www.johnborowski.com; http://www.albertfishfilm.com; http://www.panzram.com; http://www.serialkillerculture.com.

Waterhouse Publishing, *(978-0-9764082)* 40 Sheridan Ave., Congers, NY 10920 USA Tel 646-391-6669; Toll Free Fax: 877-260-5758 Do not confuse with Waterhouse Publishing in Scottsdale, AZ
E-mail: dfighter@msn.com
Web site: http://www.devonharris.com.

Watering Can, *(978-0-9759868; 978-0-9826416; 978-0-9984488)* 351 W. 19th St., New York, NY 10011 USA
E-mail: info@wateringcanpress.com
Web site: http://www.wateringcanpress.com.

Watering the Seed Productions *See* **Grace & Mercy Publishing**

Waterleaf Pubns., *(978-0-9816846)* 17710 151st Ave. SE, Suite 7A, Renton, WA 98058 USA (SAN 856-2210) Tel 425-572-6374; Fax: 866-863-5364
E-mail: info@waterleafpublications.com
Web site: http://www.waterleafpublications.com.

Watermark Cruises, *(978-0-9754400)* P.O. Box 3350, Annapolis, MD 21403 USA
Web site: http://www.watermarkcruises.com.

WaterMark, Inc., *(978-1-882077)* 5281 Mount Juliet Farm, Crozet, VA 22932 USA (SAN 248-2010) Fax: 434-823-1187; Toll Free: 888-490-0100 Do not confuse with Watermark Assocs. in New York, NY or Watermark Pr., Inc. in Wichita, KS
E-mail: agary242@aol.com
Web site: http://www.picture-book.com; http://wmibooks.com/.

Watermark Publishing, LLC, *(978-0-9631154; 978-0-9705787; 978-0-9720932; 978-0-9742672; 978-0-9753740; 978-0-9779143; 978-0-9790647; 978-0-9796769; 978-0-9815086; 978-0-9821698; 978-0-9844212; 978-1-935690; 978-1-948011)* Orders Addr.: 1000 Bishop St., Suite 806, Honolulu, HI 96813 USA (SAN 253-7427) Tel 808-587-7766; Fax: 808-521-3461; Toll Free: 866-900-2665 (866-900-BOOK) Do not confuse with confuse with companies with the same or similar names in San Diego, CA, Beverly Hills, CA, Seattle, WA
E-mail: info@bookshawaii.net
Web site: http://www.bookshawaii.net
Dist(s): **Booklines Hawaii, Ltd.**
Islander Group.

Waterside Productions, Inc., *(978-0-9627145; 978-1-939116; 978-1-941768; 978-1-943625; 978-1-945390; 978-1-945949; 978-1-947637)* 2055 Oxford Ave., Cardiff-by-the-Sea, CA 92007-1719 USA
Dist(s): **Blackstone Audio, Inc.**
INscribe Digital
Midpoint Trade Bks., Inc.
Two Rivers Distribution.

Waterside Publishing, *(978-0-9766801; 978-1-933754)* 2376 Oxford Ave., Cardiff-by-the-Sea, CA 92007 USA
E-mail: admin@waterside.com
Web site: http://www.waterside.com
Dist(s): **Ingram Publisher Services.**

Waterwood Publishing Group, *(978-0-9769044)* Orders Addr.: P.O. Box 12540, Charlotte, NC 28220 USA (SAN 257-1072) Tel 704-477-0708
Web site: http://www.waterwoodpublishing.com.

Watkins Media Limited (GBR) *(978-1-900131; 978-1-903296; 978-1-84293; 978-1-904292; 978-1-84483; 978-1-906787; 978-0-85766; 978-1-907486; 978-1-78028; 978-1-84899) Dist. by* **Peng Rand Hse.**

Watling St., Ltd. (GBR) *(978-1-904153) Dist. by* **Trafalgar.**

Watling St., Ltd. (GBR) *(978-1-904153) Dist. by* **IPG Chicago.**

Watosh Publishing, *(978-0-9611954)* P.O. Box 11231, Las Vegas, NV 89111 USA (SAN 286-1976) Tel 702-896-4108
E-mail: gecfly@aol.com
Web site: http://www.watoshpublishing.com; http://www.angietheaviator.com.

Watson Publishing, *(978-0-615-44576-2; 978-0-473-40077-4)* 8937 S Cornell Ave., Chicago, IL 60617 USA Tel 239-603-3121; Fax: 239-791-1260
E-mail: geraldcwatson@comcast.net.

Watson-Guptill *Imprint of* **Potter/TenSpeed/Harmony**

†Watson-Guptill Pubns., Inc., *(978-0-8230; 978-1-60569)* Div. of Crown Publishing Grp., 575 Prospect St., Lakewood, NJ 08701 USA Tel 732-363-5679; Toll Free Fax: 877-227-6564; Edit Addr.: 1745 Broadway # 124, New York, NY 10019-4305 USA (SAN 282-5384)
E-mail: aalexander@watsonguptill.com
Web site: http://www.watsonguptill.com
Dist(s): **Follett School Solutions**
Leonard, Hal Corp.
MyiLibrary
Penguin Random Hse. LLC
Random Hse., Inc.
ebrary, Inc.; *CIP.*

Watts, Franklin *Imprint of* **Scholastic Library Publishing**

Watts, Katherine (GBR) *(978-0-9556878) Dist. by* **LuluCom.**

Waugh Wright, *(978-0-9989586)* 919 Englewood Ave., Durham, NC 27701 USA Tel 215-715-8549
E-mail: waughwright@gmail.com.

Wave Publishing, *(978-0-9642359; 978-0-9722430)* Div. of Caroy, Inc., 4 Yawl St., Venice, CA 90292 USA (SAN 298-3788) Tel 310-306-0699; Fax: 310-822-4921 Do not confusw with Wave Publishing in Virginia Beach, VA.

WaveCloud Corp., *(978-1-62217; 978-1-5356)* 3190 S. Vaughn Way, Denver, CO 80016 USA; *Imprints:* Evergreen House Publishing LLC (EvergreenHse)
E-mail: Bill.VanOrsdel@WaveCloud.com; publishing.manager@bookfuel.com
Web site: www.WaveCloud.com; http://www.bookfuel.com.

Waves of Bliss, *(978-0-9821302)* 6909 VT Rt. 15, Jeffersonville, VT 05464 USA
E-mail: nasrin@nasrinsafai.com
Web site: http://www.wavesofbliss.com.

Wawa Pr. *Imprint of* **Adisoft, Inc.**

Way Out Comics, *(978-0-9742386)* P.O. Box 642218, Los Angeles, CA 90064 USA
E-mail: julieyeh@sbcglobal.net
Web site: http://www.wayoutcomics.com.

Way With Words Publishing Company *See* **W3 Publishing**

WayaMedia, *(978-0-9765700)* 391 Watson Br. Rd., Cullowhee, NC 28723 USA (SAN 256-503X) Do not confuse with PPS Publishing Inc. in Lake in the Hills, IL
Web site: http://www.wayamedia.com.

Wayfarer Pr., LLC, *(978-0-9789965)* P.O. Box 948, Union Lake, MI 48387-0948 USA Do not confuse with Wayfarer Press in Plymouth, NH
E-mail: wayfarerpress@sbcglobal.net
Web site: http://www.wayfarerbooks.com.

Wayland Historical Society, *(978-0-9762756)* Orders Addr.: P.O. Box 56, Wayland, MA 01778 USA Tel 508-358-7959; Edit Addr.: 12 Cochituate Rd., Wayland, MA 01778 USA
E-mail: jane_sciacca@comcast.net
Web site: http://j.w.d.home.comcast.net/whs.

†Wayne State Univ. Pr., *(978-0-8143)* Leonard N. Simons Bldg., 4809 Woodward Ave., Detroit, MI 48201-1309 USA (SAN 202-5221) Tel 313-577-6120; Fax: 313-577-6131; Toll Free: 800-978-7323 (customer orders); *Imprints:* Great Lakes Books (Great Lks Bks); Painted Turtle (Painted Turtle)
E-mail: theresa.martinelli@wayne.edu; Kristina.Stonehill@wayne.edu
Web site: http://wsupress.wayne.edu
Dist(s): **East-West Export Bks.**
INscribe Digital
ebrary, Inc.; *CIP.*

Wayne, Steven Co., *(978-0-9713154; 978-0-9727696)* 3940 Laurel Canyon Blvd., No. 698, Studio City, CA 91604 USA Tel 323-654-9339; Fax: 323-656-7324; Toll Free: 866-446-1201; *Imprints:* SWC Editions (SWC Editions)
E-mail: wschoenfeld@stevenwaynecompany.com; schoenfeld@swceditions.com
Web site: http://www.stevenwaynecompany.com; http://www.swceditions.com.

Wayside Pubns., *(978-0-9749749)* P.O. Box 318, Goreville, IL 62939 USA (SAN 255-898X)
E-mail: belletrist.1@gmail.com.

Wayside Publishing, *(978-1-877653; 978-1-938026; 978-1-942400; 978-1-944876; 978-1-64159)* Orders Addr.: 262 US Rte 1, Ste 2, Freeport, ME 04032 USA Toll Free: 888-302-2519
E-mail: sales@waysidepublishing.com
Web site: http://www.waysidepublishing.com.

Waywiser Pr., The (GBR) *(978-1-904130) Dist. by* **Dufour.**

Wayword Pr. Bks., *(978-0-692-79523-1; 978-0-9990515)* 101 Pinyon Ln., COPPELL, TX 75019 USA Tel 406-369-0902.

WCI Pr., *(978-0-9745480)* 6161 7th Ave N., St Petersburg, FL 33710-7015 USA
E-mail: clauberfl@aol.com
Web site: http://www.SoccerDreamsBook.com.

WD/GBGM Bks. *Imprint of* **General Board of Global Ministries, The United Methodist Church**

We Do Listen *Imprint of* **We Do Listen Foundation**

We Do Listen Foundation, *(978-0-9715390; 978-0-9826165; 978-0-9910777)* 1750 Ben Franklin Dr. #11g, Sarasota, FL 34236 USA (SAN 254-8119); *Imprints:* We Do Listen (WE DO LISTEN)
E-mail: howardb@wedolisten.com
Web site: http://www.wedolisten.org
Dist(s): **Lerner Publishing Group.**

We the People *Imprint of* **Compass Point Bks.**

Wealth of Wisdom LLC, A, *(978-0-9843125; 978-1-941635)* P.O. Box 390038, Keauhou, HI 96739 USA Tel 808-896-3950
Web site: http://www.awealthofwisdom.com.

Weapons of Mass Instruction, *(978-0-9766978; 978-0-9769266)* P.O. Box 1299, Freedom, CA 95019 USA Tel 831-728-0600
Web site: http://www.bilingualnation.com.

Wear-A-Book *Imprint of* **Capstone Young Readers of Coughlan Cos.**

Weatherhill, Inc. *Imprint of* **Shambhala Pubns., Inc.**

Weatherstock, Inc., *(978-0-9728107)* P.O. Box 31808, Tucson, AZ 85751 USA.

Weaver *Imprint of* **Alpha Omega Pubns., Inc.**

Weaver, Jack R. Company, *(978-0-9773370)* 375 A. Donald Rd., Canton, GA 30114 USA Tel 770-479-1342
E-mail: jackweaver426@tds.net.

Web of Life Children's Bks., *(978-0-9773795; 978-0-9777539; 978-0-9883302; 978-0-9883303)* P.O. Box 2726, Berkeley, CA 94702-0726 USA
E-mail: mdunphy@weboflifebooks.com
Web site: http://www.weboflifebooks.com
Dist(s): **Publishers Group West (PGW).**

Web Wise Services, Inc., *(978-0-9748237; 978-1-933404)* 305 Woodstock Rd, Eastlake, OH 44095 USA Tel 440-953-2443; Toll Free: 866-232-7032
Web site: http://www.webwiseseniors.com.

Webb, Dirk E, *(978-0-578-01867-6; 978-0-578-05527-5)* 3367 E. 150 N., Anderson, IN 46012 USA Tel 765-378-7025
E-mail: dirk.webb@comcast.net
Web site: http://lulu.com/dirkwebb
Dist(s): **Lulu Pr., Inc.**

Webb, Genie, *(978-0-692-86133-2)* 1414 W. Lawn Ave, RACINE, WI 53405 USA Tel 262-497-0059
E-mail: jeffwcrawford5+LVP0003504@gmail.com; jeffwcrawford5+LVP0003504@gmail.com.

Webb, Jack, *(978-0-9640275; 978-0-9719906; 978-0-615-99047-7; 978-0-692-69771-9; 978-0-692-86917-8)* Div. of San Diego State Univ. Research Foundation, Orders Addr.: 7618 Stevenson, San Diego, CA 92120 USA Tel 619-723-5371
E-mail: jackwebb1@cox.net
Web site: http://www.bordervoices.com.

Webb Ministries, Inc., *(978-0-9632226)* Orders Addr.: P.O. Box 520729, Longwood, FL 32752-0729 USA Tel 407-834-5233; Fax: 407-332-6277
E-mail: Webbministries@cfl.rr.com
Dist(s): **CreateSpace Independent Publishing Platform**
Spring Arbor Distributors, Inc.

WebbWorks, *(978-0-9791076)* P.O. Box 985, Semmes, AL 36575-0985 USA (SAN 852-4629)
E-mail: duet2sisters@bellsouth.net.

WebCartoons, LLC, *(978-0-9743215)* 3727 W. Magnilia Blvd., Suite No. 141, Burbank, CA 91510 USA Tel 818-620-4256; Fax: 818-598-1842
E-mail: jerryching@earthlink.net
Web site: http://www.thegreatestkingbok.com.

WeBeANS Corp., *(978-0-9740115)* 466 S. Spruce Ave., Galloway, NJ 08205 USA Tel 609-652-5778; Fax: 877-589-3184; Toll Free Fax: 877-589-3184; Toll Free: 888-867-8838
E-mail: john@webeans.net
Web site: http://www.webeans.net.

Webster Henrietta Publishing, *(978-0-9728222)* P.O. Box 50044, Myrtle Beach, SC 29579 USA Tel 843-251-8867; Fax: 843-236-0260
E-mail: mhetzer@websterhenrietta.com
Web site: http://www.websterhenrietta.com
Dist(s): **Independent Pubs. Group.**

Webster House Publishing LLC, *(978-1-932635)* 309 Florida Hill Rd., Ridgefield, CT 06877 USA Tel 203-438-0345; Fax: 203-438-0379
E-mail: fred@websterhousepub.com
Web site: http://www.websterhousepub.com.

Wedding Solutions Publishing, Incorporated *See* **WS Publishing**

Wedgeworth, Anthony G., *(978-0-615-20879-4; 978-0-615-25816-4; 978-0-615-26007-5; 978-0-578-00695-6; 978-0-578-03617-5; 978-0-578-04710-2; 978-0-578-05827-6; 978-0-578-06337-9)* Orders Addr.: P.O. Box 621, Monona, IA 52159-0621ed USA; Edit Addr.: 104 N. Anderson St., Monona, IA 52159-0621 USA
E-mail: anthonywedgeworth@hotmail.com; thorlk@alteredcreatures.com
Web site: http://www.anthonywedgeworth.com
Dist(s): **Lulu Pr., Inc.**
Smashwords.

Wednesday Bks. *Imprint of* **St. Martin's Pr.**

WeDream.com, *(978-0-9764351)* P.O. Box 6020, Dillon, CO 80435-6020 USA
E-mail: climbing@wedream.com
Web site: http://www.wedream.com; http://discgolfguides.com.

Wee Creek Pr. LLC, *(978-1-942922)* P.O. Box 51052, casper, WY 82605-1052 USA Tel 307-265-8585; Fax: 307-265-4640
E-mail: weecreekpress@gmail.com
Web site: www.weecreekpress.com.

Wee Read Publishing, *(978-0-9723122)* 2269 Ginger Hill Loop., Lincoln, CA 95648-8719 USA
E-mail: lindamarchus@yahoo.com; vmarchus@hotmail.com
Web site: http://www.weereadpublishing.com.

Weebie Publishing *See* **Susi B. Marketing, Inc.**

Weekly Reader Corp., *(978-0-8374)* Affil. of WRC Media, Orders Addr.: P.O. Box 120023, Stamford, CT 06912-0023 USA (SAN 207-060X) Tel 203-705-3569; Fax: 203-705-3483; Toll Free: 800-446-3355; 3001 Cindel Dr., Delran, NJ 08370 (SAN 207-0618); Edit Addr.: 1 Readers Digest Rd., Pleasantville, NY 10570-7000 USA
E-mail: cpekar@weeklyreader.com
Web site: http://www.weeklyreader.com.

Weekly Reader Leveled Readers *Imprint of* **Stevens, Gareth Publishing LLLP**

Weekly Reader Teacher's Pr *Imprint of* **iUniverse, Inc.**

Weeks, Kermit *See* **KWIP, Inc.**

Weeley Pr., *(978-0-692-84235-5)* 1500 Bay Area Blvd, Suite 324, Houston, TX 77058 USA Tel 832-805-1691; Fax: 832-805-1691
E-mail: phil.roiz@yahoo.com.

Weem, Nadia *See* **Weems, Madia**

Weems, Madia, *(978-0-615-19289-5)* 1343 Stevens Rd. SE, Washington, DC 20020 USA Tel 202-889-5239
E-mail: thewriter1115@yahoo.com.

Weeping Willow Publishing, *(978-0-9789227)* Orders Addr.: 405 Redwater Rd., Wake Village, TX 75501 USA Tel 903-293-4433; 2416 Connecticut Ln. Ste. A, Dallas, TX 75214
E-mail: tomcgreer@gmail.com
Web site: http://www.tomcgreer.com.

Wehner, Adrienna, *(978-0-9653866)* P.O. Box 6196, San Jose, CA 95150-6196 USA
E-mail: Awehner408@hotmail.com.

Wehr Animations, *(978-0-9748093)* 3890 CloverLeaf Dr., Boulder, CO 80304 USA
Web site: http://www.wehranimations.com.

Wehrley, Susan K. & Associates, Incorporated *See* **Thomas & Kay, LLC**

Weight Loss Buddy, Inc., *(978-0-9754448)* P.O. Box 488, Tenafly, NJ 07670 USA Toll Free: 877-283-3987
Web site: http://www.weightlossbuddy.com.

Weightman, Bud, *(978-0-9821035)* PMB#103, 5315 FM 1960 W., Suite B, Houston, TX 77069 USA (SAN 857-247X) Tel 281-444-4950; Fax: 281-966-1769
E-mail: budqsi@isoconsultants.com; piggytales.press@gmail.com
Web site: http://www.piggytalespress.com.

Weigl Pubs., Inc., *(978-1-930954; 978-1-59036; 978-1-60596; 978-1-61690; 978-1-61913; 978-1-62127; 978-1-4896)* Orders Addr.: 350 5th Ave., Suite 3304, PMB 6G 59th Flr., New York, NY 10118 USA Tel 866-649-3445; Fax: 866-449-3445; 6325 Tenth St., SE, Calgary, AB T2H 2ZP Tel 403-233-7747; Fax: 403-233-7769; *Imprints*: AV2 by Weigl (AVTwo Weigl)
E-mail: editorial3@weigl.com
Web site: http://www.weigl.com
Dist(s): **Follett School Solutions**
MyiLibrary.

Weinstein Bks. *Imprint of* **Perseus Bks. Group**

Wei's Publishing Co., *(978-0-9747284)* 116 W. Donald St., South Bend, IN 46613 USA
E-mail: liuwei82@hotmail.com
Web site: http://www.weispublishing.com.

Weiser, Samuel Incorporated *See* **Red Wheel/Weiser**

Weiss, Janet Bruschetti, *(978-0-9747716)* P.O. Box 8411, Longboat Key, FL 34228 USA
E-mail: jentajean@aol.com.

Welcome Bks *Imprint of* **Rizzoli International Pubns., Inc.**

Weldon Owen, Inc., *(978-1-875137; 978-1-892374; 978-1-61628; 978-1-68188)* Div. of Bonnier Publishing USA, 1045 Sansome St. Suite 100, San Francisco, CA 94117 USA Tel 415-291-0111 Do not confuse with Weldon Owen Reference, Inc. also at the same address
E-mail: info@weldonowen.com; customer_service@weldonowen.info
Web site: http://www.weldonowen.com/
Dist(s): **Chain Sales Marketing, Inc.**
INscribe Digital
MyiLibrary
Simon & Schuster, Inc.

Weldon Pubns., Inc., *(978-0-9724175)* 432 Pennsylvania Ave., Waverly, NY 14892 USA
E-mail: weldon@cqservices.com; sales@cqservices.com
Web site: http://www.Marchintotheendlessmountains.com.

Well Fire Pubns., *(978-0-9701912; 978-0-615-11133-9; 978-0-615-11146-9)* Orders Addr.: 100 Markley St., Port Reading, NJ 07064-1897 USA Tel 732-636-2060; Fax: 732-636-2538
E-mail: sherryross@home.com
Web site: http://www.sherryross.com.

WellFire Publications *See* **Well Fire Pubns.**

Wellfleet *Imprint of* **Book Sales, Inc.**

Wellman, Patrick *See* **MrDuz.com**

Wellness, Incorporated *See* **OrganWise Guys Inc., The**

Wellness Institute, Incorporated *See* **Wellness Institute/Self-Help Bks., LLC**

Wellness Institute/Self-Help Bks., LLC, *(978-0-9617202; 978-1-58741)* 515 W. N. St., Pass Christian, MS 39571 USA (SAN 663-382X) Tel 228-452-0770; Fax: 228-452-0775 YES NAME CHANGE CORRECT H DAWLEY
E-mail: publisher@selfhelpbooks.com
Web site: http://www.selfhelpbooks.com.

Wellness pH, *(978-1-933559)* P.O. Box 27, Greer, SC 29652 USA (SAN 256-6753) Tel 864-371-0753
E-mail: stroblechristine@gmail.com.

Wellness Pubn., *(978-0-9701490; 978-0-9748581; 978-0-9906147)* 624 Marsat Ct., Chula Vista, CA 91911-4646 USA Toll Free: 800-755-4656; *Imprints*: Bayport Press (Bayport Pr) Do not confuse with companies with the same or similar name in Rockport, TX, Omaha, NE, Holland, MI, Ft. Lauderdale, FL, Santa Barbara, CA
E-mail: malan1208@sbcglobal.net; ted@soriano.com
Web site: http://www.drjwallach.com.

Well-Trained Mind Pr., *(978-0-9714129; 978-0-9728603; 978-1-933339; 978-1-942968; 978-1-945841)* 18021 The Glebe Ln., Charles City, VA 23030-3828 USA (SAN 254-1726)
E-mail: ptbuff@peacehillpress.net
Web site: http://www.peacehillpress.com
Dist(s): **Norton, W. W. & Co., Inc.**
Penguin Random Hse. LLC.

Welt, Rich & Assocs., *(978-0-9706529)* 8401 Heron Cir., Huntington Beach, CA 92646 USA Tel 866-742-4935
E-mail: richwelt@aol.com
Web site: http://richwelt.com.

Wenner Bks., *(978-1-932958)* 1290 Ave. of the Americas, 2nd Flr., New York, NY 10104 USA Tel 212-484-1696; Fax: 212-484-3433
E-mail: kate.rockland@wennermedia.com.

Wentworth Pr. *Imprint of* **Creative Media Partners, LLC**

We-Publish.com, *(978-1-931335)* 6311 Gulf Freeway #4201, Houston, TX 77023 USA Tel 713-448-0720 phone
E-mail: admin@banmex.com
Web site: http://www.we-publish.com.

WeShine Pr. Co., *(978-0-9818113)* 12 Lake Mist Dr., Sugar Land, TX 77479 USA
Web site: www.weshinepress.com.

Wesleyan Publishing Hse., *(978-0-89827; 978-1-63257; 978-0-692-88620-5; 978-0-692-92243-9)* Div. of The Wesleyan Church, P.O. Box 50434, Indianapolis, IN 46250-0434 USA (SAN 162-7104) Tel 317-774-3853; Fax: 317-774-3860; Toll Free Fax: 800-788-3535; Toll Free: 800-493-7539 (orders only)
E-mail: wph@wesleyan.org; lebarons@wesleyan.org
Web site: http://www.wesleyan.org/wph
Dist(s): **Faith Alive Christian Resources.**

West Alden Publishing, LLC, *(978-0-9976002)* 208 Biltmore Dr., Colonial Heights, VA 23834 USA Tel 804-520-8866
E-mail: scnorkus@gmail.com.

West Barnstable Pr., *(978-0-9816873; 978-0-9828122; 978-0-9978182)* 21 Meadow Ln., West Barnstable, MA 02668 USA (SAN 856-2490).

West Coast Learning Development Center, *(978-0-615-19154-6; 978-0-615-19269-7; 978-0-578-12128-4)* P.O. Box 194, Torrance, CA 90507 USA
E-mail: westcoastlearningdevelopmentcenter@yahoo.com
Web site: http://www.westcoastlearningdevelopmentcenter.org
Dist(s): **R J Communications, LLC.**

West, Dave Corporation *See* **Aztec 5 Publishing**

West End Games *Imprint of* **Purgatory Publishing, Inc.**

West End Games, Inc., *(978-0-87431)* Subs. of Bucci Imports, R.D. 3, Box 2345, Honesdale, PA 18431 USA (SAN 687-8466) Tel 717-253-6990; Fax: 717-253-5104
E-mail: dspweg@hotmail.com
Web site: http://www.westendgames.net.

West Highland Pr., *(978-0-9721486)* P.O. Box 10040, Alexandria, VA 22310 USA
E-mail: westhighlandpress@earthlink.net
Web site: http://www.westhighlandpress.com.

West, Mary, *(978-0-578-02740-1)* 733 Avenida Tercera, Apt 109, Clermont, FL 34714 USA
E-mail: sales@hecalledianswered.com
Web site: http://www.hecalledianswered.com
Dist(s): **Lulu Pr., Inc.**

West Ridge Farm Publishing, *(978-0-9845582; 978-0-9892282)* 535 Glendale St., Hampden, MA 01036 USA Tel 413-566-5366
E-mail: luvfisk@yahoo.com; sanj535@charter.net
Web site: http://www.westridgefarmpublishing.com; http://www.angelsclubkids.com.

West Virginia Univ. Pr., *(978-0-937058; 978-1-933202; 978-1-935978; 978-1-938228; 978-1-940425; 978-1-943665; 978-1-946684)* Orders Addr.: P.O. Box 6295, Morgantown, WV 26506-6295 USA (SAN 205-5163) Tel 304-293-8400; Fax: 304-293-6585; Toll Free: 866-988-7737; *Imprints*: Vandalia Press (Vandalia Pr)
E-mail: carrie.mullen@mail.wvu.edu
Web site: http://www.wvupress.com
Dist(s): **BookMobile**
Chicago Distribution Ctr.
MyiLibrary
ebrary, Inc.

West Winds Pr. *Imprint of* **Graphic Arts Ctr. Publishing Co.**

West Woods Pr., *(978-0-9776837)* 3905 Westwood Cir., Flagstaff, AZ 86001 USA (SAN 257-9375)
Web site: http://www.WestWoodsPress.com.

WestBow Pr. *Imprint of* **Scholastic, Inc.**

WestBow Pr. *Imprint of* **Author Solutions, Inc.**

Westchester Publishing, *(978-0-9891504)* 280 Mamaroneck Ave., White Plains, NY 10605 USA Tel 914-761-1894
E-mail: dhampton@newshelves.com.

Westcliffe Pubs. *Imprint of* **Bower Hse.**

Westcom Press *See* **Cathedrall Pr./Encycloware**

Western Images Pubns., Inc., *(978-0-9627600; 978-1-887302)* 2249 Marion St., Denver, CO 80205 USA.

Western Michigan University, New Issues Press *See* **New Issues Poetry & Prose, Western Michigan Univ.**

Western National Parks Assn., *(978-0-911408; 978-1-877856; 978-1-58369)* 12880 N. Vistoso Village Dr., Tucson, AZ 85755 USA (SAN 202-750X) Tel 520-622-1999; Fax: 520-623-9519
E-mail: abby@wnpa.org; derek@wnpa.org
Web site: http://www.wnpa.org
Dist(s): **Canyonlands Pubns.**
Rio Nuevo Pubs.
Sunbelt Pubns., Inc.

Western New York Wares, Inc., *(978-0-9620314; 978-1-879201)* Orders Addr.: P.O. Box 733, Buffalo, NY 14205 USA (SAN 248-6911) Tel 716-832-6088; Edit Addr.: 419 Parkside Ave., Buffalo, NY 14216 USA (SAN 248-692X) Tel 716-832-6088
E-mail: wnywares@gateway.net.

Western Psychological Services, *(978-0-87424)* Div. of Manson Western Corp., 12031 Wilshire Blvd., Los Angeles, CA 90025 USA (SAN 160-8002) Tel 310-478-2061; Fax: 310-478-7838; Toll Free: 800-648-8857
E-mail: weinberg@wpspublish.com
Web site: http://www.wpspublish.com.

Western Reflections Publishing Co., *(978-1-890437; 978-1-932738; 978-1-937851)* Orders Addr.: P.O. Box 1149, Lake City, CO 81235 USA Tel 970-944-0110 Toll Free: 800-993-4490
Web site: http://www.westernreflectionspub.com
Dist(s): **Bks. West**
Hinsdale County Historical Society
Lake City Downtown Improvement and Revitalization Team
Partners/West Book Distributors
Quality Bks., Inc.
Rio Nuevo Pubs.

Westie Pr., *(978-0-578-18653-5; 978-0-578-18956-7)* 26616 Pepperidge Cove, Millsboro, DE 19966 USA
Web site: www.customadultcoloring.com.

Westigan Review Press *See* **Ephemeron Pr.**

†Westminster John Knox Pr., *(978-0-664; 978-0-8042; 978-1-61164; 978-1-947888)* Div. of Presbyterian Publishing Corp., Orders Addr.: 100 Witherspoon St., Louisville, KY 40202 USA (SAN 202-9669) Tel 502-569-5052 (outside U.S. for ordering); Fax: 502-569-5113 (outside U.S. for faxed orders); Toll Free Fax: 800-541-5113 (toll-free U.S. faxed orders); Toll Free: 800-227-2872 (customer service)
E-mail: orders@wjkbooks.com
Web site: http://www.wjkbooks.com
Dist(s): **Faith Alive Christian Resources**
MyiLibrary
Presbyterian Publishing Corp.; *CIP.*

Weston Priory, *(978-0-9763005)* 58 Priory Hill Rd., Weston, VT 05161-6400 USA Tel 802-824-5409; Fax: 802-824-3573
E-mail: brjohn@westonpriory.org
Web site: http://www.westonpriory.org.

Weston Woods Studios, Inc., *(978-0-7882; 978-0-89719; 978-1-55592; 978-1-56008)* Div. of Scholastic, Inc., 143 Main St., Norwalk, CT 06851 USA (SAN 630-3838) Tel 203-845-0197; Fax: 203-845-0498; Toll Free: 800-243-5020
E-mail: questions@Scholastic.com
Web site: http://www.scholastic.com/westonwoods
Dist(s): **Findaway World, LLC**
Follett School Solutions.

Westphalia Press, *(978-0-918592; 978-0-944285; 978-1-935907; 978-1-941472; 978-1-941755; 978-1-63391)* 1527 New Hampshire Ave. NW, Washington, DC 20036 USA Tel 202-349-9282
E-mail: dgutierrezs@ipsonet.org
Web site: http://ipsonet.org.

Westphalia Thoroughbreds, LLC, *(978-0-9754103)* 1231 Latigo Ln., Flower Mound, TX 75022 USA Tel 817-368-6981
E-mail: arazielf@yahoo.com
Web site: http://www.westphaliathoroughbreds.com.

Westrim Crafts, *(978-0-9819053)* 7855 Hayvenhurst Ave., Van Nuys, CA 91406 USA Fax: 469-362-8016
E-mail: lisa.groshek@creativityinc.com
Web site: http://www.creativityinc.com.

Westry Wingate Group, Inc., *(978-1-935323)* 2708 Wet Stone Way Unit 108, Charlotte, NC 28208-4794 USA (SAN 857-183X)
E-mail: gabriel@westrywingate.com
Web site: http://www.westrywingate.com.

Westside Bks., *(978-1-934813)* Div. of Marco Bk. Co., 60 Industrial Rd., Lodi, NJ 07644 USA (SAN 855-0166) Tel 973-458-0485; Fax: 973-458-5289; Toll Free: 800-842-4234
Web site: http://www.westside-books.com
Dist(s): **Bks. & Media, Inc.**
Marco Bk. Co.
MyiLibrary.

Westside Press *See* **Wordsmith Pr.**

Westside Studio, *(978-0-9786147)* P.O. Box 703, Trumansburg, NY 14886-0703 USA.

†Westview Pr., *(978-0-8133; 978-0-86531; 978-0-89158)* A Member of Perseus Books Group, 2465 Central Ave. Ste. 200, Boulder, CO 80301-5728 USA (SAN 219-970X) Toll Free: 800-343-4499 orders only
E-mail: westview.orders@perseusbooks.com; meegan.finnegan@perseusbooks.com
Web site: http://www.perseusbooksgroup.com; http://www.westviewpress.com
Dist(s): **Hachette Bk. Group**
MyiLibrary
ebrary, Inc.; *CIP.*

Westview Publishing Co., Inc., *(978-0-9744322; 978-0-9748730; 978-0-9755646; 978-0-9764940; 978-0-9773179; 978-0-9776207; 978-1-933912; 978-0-9816172; 978-0-692-69338-4)* P.O. Box 210183, Nashville, TN 37221 USA
Web site: http://www.westviewpublishing.com.

Westview Publishing, Incorporated *See* **Westview Publishing Co., Inc.**

WestWind Pr. *Imprint of* **Scott, D.& F. Publishing, Inc.**

Westwood Pr., Inc., *(978-0-936159)* 116 E. 16th St., New York, NY 10003-2112 USA (SAN 696-7183) Tel 212-420-8008 Do not confuse with Westwoods Press, Darien, CT.

Wever Books *See* **Red Engine Pr.**

WeWrite LLC, *(978-1-57635; 978-1-884987)* Orders Addr.: P.O. Box 593, Ben Lomond, CA 95005 USA Tel 831-336-3382; Fax: 831-336-8592; Toll Free: 800-295-9037; Edit Addr.: 11040 Alba Rd., Ben Lomond, CA 95005-9220 USA
E-mail: info@wewrite.net
Web site: http://www.wewrite.net.

Wexford College Pr., *(978-0-9709917; 978-0-9721786; 978-0-9726596)* 401 Merito Pl., Journalism Bldg., Palm Springs, CA 92262 USA; *Imprints*: Watchmaker Publishing (Watchmaker Pub)
E-mail: books@wexfordcollegepress.com
Web site: http://www.wexfordcollegepress.com.

WGH Arts LLC, *(978-0-9776562)* P.O. Box 215, Lisbon, IA 52253-0215 USA
E-mail: bill@wgharts.com
Web site: http://www.wgharts.com.

WHA Publishing, *(978-0-9773228)* P.O. Box 20818, Wickenburg, AZ 85358 USA Tel 520-877-7860; Fax: 520-877-7869
E-mail: jerry@datssoftware.com.

Whale Tale Pr., *(978-0-9824784)* 343 Hertford Cir., Decatur, GA 30030 USA
Web site: http://www.whaletalepress.com
Dist(s): **Bookmasters Distribution.**

Whaleback Publishing, *(978-0-9725938)* 4 Captain's Way, Exeter, NH 03833 USA Fax: 603-772-5416; Toll Free: 800-207-2580
Web site: http://www.whalebackpublishing.com.

Whale's Jaw Publishing, *(978-0-9740778)* 11 Dennison St., Gloucester, MA 01930 USA Tel 978-281-9684
E-mail: info@whalesjaw.com; chetbrg@comcast.net
Web site: http://www.whalesjaw.com.

Whale's Library, The *See* **Mindsong Math**

What on Earth Bks (GBR) *(978-0-9565936; 978-0-9929249; 978-0-9932847; 978-0-9930199) Dist. by* **IngramPubServ.**

What The Flux Media, Incorporated *See* **Ark Watch Holdings LLC**

Whatever Publishing, Incorporated *See* **New World Library**

Wheat State Media LLC, *(978-0-9882892)* 21606 W. 52nd St., Shawnee, KS 66226 USA Tel 816-668-8400
E-mail: bhowell@wheatstatemedia.com
Web site: http://www.wheatstatemedia.com
Dist(s): **Anchor Distributors.**

Wheatmark, Inc., *(978-1-58736; 978-1-60494; 978-1-62787)* 2030 E. Speedway Blvd., Suite 106, Tucson, AZ 85719 USA (SAN 253-1054) Tel 520-798-0888; Fax: 520-798-3394; Toll Free: 888-934-0888; *Imprints:* Starbound Books (Starbound Bks)
E-mail: bookstore@wheatmark.com; atilla@wheatmark.com; sam@wheatmark.com
Web site: http://www.wheatmark.com
Dist(s): **INscribe Digital.**

Wheaton-Smith, Simon, *(978-0-9765286)* 810 W. 6th St., Silver City, NM 88061 USA
E-mail: illustratingshadows@yahoo.com
Web site: http://www.illustratingshadows.com/.

WHEEL Council, Inc., The, *(978-0-9656732; 978-0-9728889)* P.O. Box 22517, Flagstaff, AZ 86002 USA Tel 928-214-0120
E-mail: info@wheelcouncil.org
Web site: http://www.wheelcouncil.org.

Wheeler Publishing, Inc. *Imprint of* **Cengage Gale**

When I Grow Up Publishing, Inc., *(978-0-9795117)* 3721 Chelton Rd., Shaker Hts., OH 44120 USA
E-mail: erinn@theblackcrayon.com
Web site: http://www.theblackcrayon.com.

Where? Pr., Inc., *(978-0-9719144)* Orders Addr.: P.O. Box 154, Paintsville, KY 41240 USA Tel 606-789-9423; Edit Addr.: 830 Robin Ct., Paintsville, KY 41240 USA
E-mail: wherepress@mail.com
Web site: http://www.wherepress.netfirms.com.

Where-I-Live / Foster Pr., *(978-0-9764893)* 430 91st Ave., NE, Suite 3, Everett, WA 98205 USA Tel 425-334-9317; Fax: 425-334-8155
E-mail: vern@fosterpress.com
Web site: http://www.fosterpress.com.

Whimble Designs, *(978-0-9773523)* 1540/42 Monroe Dr., NE, Atlanta, GA 30324 USA.

WhipperSnapper Bks., *(978-0-9657218)* P.O. Box 3186, Los Altos, CA 94024 USA 925-249-0709 (orders/general); Toll Free: 800-910-4482.

Whippoorwill, LLC, *(978-0-9741968)* 9601 Linden St., Overland Park, KS 66207 USA (SAN 255-6553) Tel 913-341-7104; Fax: 913-385-2453
E-mail: schase@mischomeloans.com.

Whirling Dirvish Publishing, *(978-0-9768870)* 26895 Aliso Creek Rd., Suite B591, Aliso Viejo, CA 92656 USA Tel 949-643-1865; Fax: 949-606-7180; Toll Free: 800-993-1291
E-mail: info@whirlingdirvish.com
Web site: http://www.whirlingdirvish.com/.

Whirlwhim, *(978-0-9800274)* 12930 Ventura Blvd., Studio City, CA 91604 USA
E-mail: whirlwhim@yahoo.com
Web site: http://www.blunderbrothers.com.

Whirlwind Publishing Group, *(978-0-9882643)* 2506 Bridal Wreath Ln., Dallas, TX 75233 USA Tel 858-220-2917
E-mail: lolahawk@hotmail.com
Web site: www.whirlwindpublishinggroup.com
Dist(s): **CreateSpace Independent Publishing Platform.**

Whiskey Creek Pr. *Imprint of* **Whiskey Creek Pr., LLC**

Whiskey Creek Pr., LLC, *(978-1-59374; 978-1-60313; 978-1-61160)* Orders Addr.: 609 Greenwich St. 6th Fl, New York, NY 10014 USA Tel 212-431-5455; Fax: 917-464-6394; *Imprints:* Whiskey Creek Press (Whisk Creek Pr)
E-mail: publishing@start-media.com
Web site: http://www.whiskeycreekpress.com; http://www.whiskeycreekpresstorrid.com
Dist(s): **All Romance Ebooks, LLC**
OverDrive, Inc.
Simon & Schuster, Inc.

Whiskey Creek Restorations, *(978-0-9625756)* 7205 68th Ave., S.W., Elgin, ND 58533 USA Tel 218-354-2253.

Whispering Pine Press, Incorporated *See* **Whispering Pine Pr. International, Inc.**

Whispering Pine Pr. International, Inc., *(978-0-9679368; 978-1-930948; 978-1-59210; 978-1-59434; 978-1-59649; 978-1-59808)* Orders Addr.: P.O. Box 70, Greenacres, WA 99016-0070 USA (SAN 253-200X) Tel 509-928-7888; Fax: 509-922-9949; Edit Addr.: 1710 N. Aladdin Rd., Liberty Lake, WA 99016 USA
E-mail: whisperingpinepress@outlook.com
Web site: http://www.whisperingpinepress.com; http://www.whisperingpinepressbookstore.com.

Whispering Wind Publishing Inc., *(978-0-9721640)* Orders Addr.: 11089 Utica Ct., Westminster, CO 80031-2057 USA Tel 303-717-6442
E-mail: KaKillam@cs.com; publisher@whisperingwind.org
Web site: http://www.whisperingwind.org
Dist(s): **Quality Bks., Inc.**

Whistle Pr., The, *(978-0-9624893)* P.O. Box 1006, Petal, MS 39465-8618 USA Tel 601-544-8486 (phone/fax)
E-mail: contact@whistlepress.com
Web site: www.whistlepress.com.

Whitaker Hse., *(978-0-88368; 978-1-60374; 978-1-62911; 978-1-64123)* Div. of Whitaker Corp., 1030 Hunt Valley Cir., New Kensington, PA 15068 USA (SAN 203-2104) Tel 724-334-7000 Whitaker House/Anchor Distributors; Fax: 724-334-1200 Anchor Distributors; Toll Free Fax: 866-773-7001 Whitaker House; 800-765-1960 Anchor Distributors; Toll Free: 877-793-9800 Whitaker House; 800-444-4484 Whitaker House/Anchor Distributors
E-mail: sales@whitakerhouse.com
Web site: http://www.whitakerhouse.com/; http://www.anchordistributors.com/; http://www.amazon.com/
Dist(s): **Anchor Distributors.**

Whitaker, Thurston Information Services, LLC, *(978-0-9758940; 978-0-9892525)* P.O. Box 271743, West Hartford, CT 06127-1743 USA Tel 860-922-4719
E-mail: gwhit@twisbiz.com
Web site: http://www.thurstonwhitaker.com.

Whitcombe, Renee *See* **Budding Family Publishing**

White Cloud Pr., *(978-1-883991; 978-0-9745245; 978-0-9793840; 978-1-935952; 978-1-940468)* Orders Addr.: P.O. Box 3400, Ashland, OR 97520 USA; Edit Addr.: 300 E. Hersey St., #11, Ashland, OR 97520-6200 USA Fax: 541-482-7708; Toll Free: 800-380-8286; *Imprints:* Riverwood Books (RiverwoodBks) Do not confuse with White Cloud Pr. in Hobbs, NM
Web site: http://www.whitecloudpress.com
Dist(s): **MyiLibrary**
Publishers Group West (PGW).

White Dharma Ltd., *(978-0-9907781)* P.O. Box 390251, Cambridge, MA 02139 USA Tel 617-299-0883
E-mail: whitedharmaltd@gmail.com.

White Dog Pr., Ltd, *(978-0-9741027; 978-0-615-43844-3; 978-0-9855823; 978-0-615-93256-9; 978-0-692-48522-4)* 321 High School Rd., No. 393, Bainbridge Island, WA 98110-2977 USA Tel 206-661-5946
E-mail: whitedogpress@aol.com.

White Dog Studio, *(978-0-9667266; 978-0-9897882)* Orders Addr.: P.O. Box 189, Louisville, TN 37777 USA Tel 865-776-9886; Edit Addr.: 3825 Island Path, Louisville, TN 37777 USA
E-mail: jprince1@mac.com
Web site: http://www.newcooksinamerica.com; www.missjanetsglutenfreeamerica.

White Eagle Publishing Trust (GBR) *(978-0-85487) Dist. by* **DeVorss.**

White Feather Press, LLC, *(978-0-9766083; 978-0-9822487; 978-0-9831751; 978-1-61808)* 579 119th Ave, Martin, MI 49070 USA
E-mail: skip@whitefeatherpress.com
Web site: http://www.whitefeatherpress.com
Dist(s): **Smashwords.**

White Feather Publishing, *(978-0-9740413)* 5595 White Feather Way, Placerville, CA 95667 USA
E-mail: whitefeather@directcom.net.

White Hat Communications, *(978-0-9653653; 978-1-929109; 978-0-615-62872-1)* Orders Addr.: P.O. Box 5390, Harrisburg, PA 17110-0390 USA Tel 717-238-3787; Fax: 717-238-2090; Edit Addr.: 2793 Old Post Rd., Suite 13, Harrisburg, PA 17110 USA
E-mail: Linda.grobman@paonline.com; lindagrobman@gmail.com
Web site: http://www.whitehatcommunications.com; http://www.socialworker.com
Dist(s): **CreateSpace Independent Publishing Platform**
Smashwords.

White Heat Ltd., *(978-0-9740149; 978-0-9799108)* 901 N. Mcdonald St. Ste. 503, Mckinney, TX 75069-2166 USA
E-mail: info@whiteheatltd.com
Web site: http://www.whiteheatltd.com.

White Horse Bks., *(978-0-9744860; 978-0-9801406)* 1347 Glenmare St., Salt Lake Cty, UT 84105-2707 USA
Web site: http://www.whitehorsebooks.net.

White, Howard Ray, *(978-0-9746875; 978-0-9837192)* Orders Addr.: 6012 Lancelot Dr., Charlotte, NC 28270 USA Tel 704-846-4411 Ask for Howard
E-mail: howardraywhite@gmail.com
Web site: http://www.southernhistorians.org; http://www.amazon.com.

White, James C., *(978-0-9747752)* 7020 E. 28th Ter., Kansas City, MO 64129-1209 USA Do not confuse with James C. White in Ruston, LA
E-mail: jcwhite08@yahoo.com
Web site: http://www.jcwhite08.com.

White Kiser, Dolores, *(978-0-9766648)* 212 Quail Creek Rd., Durant, OK 74701-7543 USA
E-mail: wobblywh@yahoo.com.

White Knight Printing and Publishing, *(978-0-9725916)* 187 E. 670 S., Kamas, UT 84036 USA (SAN 853-3539) Tel 801-955-4504; Fax: 801-955-5324
E-mail: johnmsimmons@whiteknightpublish.com; brigdist@sisna.com; careenlancaster@whiteknightpublish.com
Web site: http://www.brighamdistributing.com; http://www.whiteknightpublish.com
Dist(s): **Brigham Distribution.**

White Line Productions Inc., *(978-0-9729965)* P.O. Box 248411, Coral Gables, FL 33124 USA Tel 305-663-3235
E-mail: lcoll@bewaretheunknown.com
Web site: http://www.bewaretheunknown.com.

White Lion Pr., *(978-0-9615707; 978-1-886942)* 225 E. Fifth St., No. 4D, New York, NY 10003 USA (SAN 695-7919) Tel 212-982-5518; Toll Free: 800-243-9642
Dist(s): **New Leaf Distributing Co., Inc.**

White Mane Kids *Imprint of* **White Mane Publishing Co., Inc.**

White Mane Publishing Co., Inc., *(978-0-942597; 978-1-57249)* Orders Addr.: P.O. Box 708, Shippensburg, PA 17257 USA (SAN 667-1926) Tel 717-532-2237; Fax: 717-532-6110; Toll Free: 888-948-6263; *Imprints:* White Mane Kids (WM Kids)
E-mail: marketing@whitemane.com
Web site: http://www.whitemane.com.

White Oak Creative, *(978-0-9763562)* 26415 W. Stonebriar Way, Channahon, IL 60410-8740 USA Tel 815-922-2890; Fax: 815-521-0042 Do not confuse with White Oak Publishing in Reed Springs, MO; Galena, MO; Sewickley, PA; Portland, OR
E-mail: kashmir37@aol.com.

White Owl Publishing, *(978-1-891691)* P.O. Box 1180, Redding, CA 96001 USA Tel 530-241-1921 Do not confuse with White Owl Publishing, Wellington, KS,
E-mail: editor@whiteowlweb.com
Web site: http://whiteowlweb.com
Dist(s): **Smashwords.**

White Pelican Pr., *(978-0-9625544)* 1805 Cedar Ridge Dr., Austin, TX 78741 USA Tel 512-477-5211 Do not confuse with companies with the same name in Windsor, CO, Sharpsburg, GA.

White Phoenix, *(978-0-9886472)* 405 Litchfield Dr., Moore, SC 29369 USA Tel 847-848-6307
E-mail: ghallium50@yahoo.com.

White Rhino Pr., *(978-0-9704122)* Div. of The Patnaude Corp., Orders Addr.: 6068 Windsor Farm Rd., Summerfield, NC 273589053 USA Tel 336-253-8987; Fax: 336-644-7849
E-mail: joy@patnaude.com.

White Rhino Publishing *See* **White Rhino Pr.**

White, Russ, *(978-0-9742885)* 122 E. Oak Hill Dr., Florence, AL 35633 USA.

White Stag Pr., *(978-0-9792583; 978-0-9828216)* Div. of Publishers Design Group, Inc., P.O. Box 37, Roseville, CA 95678 USA (SAN 852-9353) Tel 916-784-0500; Fax: 916-773-7421; Toll Free: 800-587-6666
E-mail: orders@publishersdesign.com
Web site: http://www.publishersdesign.com.

White Star (ITA) *(978-88-8095; 978-88-544; 978-88-7844; 978-88-540) Dist. by* **Random.**

White Star *Imprint of* **Rizzoli International Pubns., Inc.**

White Star (ITA) *(978-88-8095; 978-88-544; 978-88-7844; 978-88-540) Dist. by* **Sterling.**

White Stone Bks., *(978-1-59379)* P.O. Box 35035, Tulsa, OK 74153 USA Toll Free: 866-253-8622 Do not confuse with White Stone Books in Atlanta, MI
E-mail: amandap@whitestonebooks.com
Web site: http://www.whitestonebooks.com
Dist(s): **Distributors, The**
Harrison House Pubs.

White Stone Publications *See* **Fair Havens Pubns.**

White, T. *See* **twhiteart**

White, Terry, *(978-0-9755835)* P.O. Box 760399, Southfield, MI 48076-0399 USA.

White Tiger Pr. *Imprint of* **Homes for the Homeless Institute, Inc.**

White Tulip Publishing, *(978-0-9746890)* Orders Addr.: P.O. Box 645, Brewster, NY 10509 USA Tel 917-514-7701
E-mail: wtime2write@aol.com
Web site: http://www.whitetulippublishing.com
Dist(s): **Quality Bks., Inc.**

White Turtle Bks., *(978-1-933482)* P.O. Box 2113, North Mankato, MN 56003 USA Tel 605-770-5385
E-mail: info@whiteturtlebooks.com.

White Wolf Publishing, Inc., *(978-0-9627790; 978-1-56504; 978-1-58846)* 2075 W. Park Place Blvd. Ste. G, Stone Mtn, GA 30087-3542 USA (SAN 299-1349) Toll Free: 800-454-9653 Do not confuse with White Wolf Publishing, Cresson, TX
E-mail: dianez@white-wolf.com
Web site: http://www.white-wolf.com
Dist(s): **PSI (Publisher Services, Inc.).**

White Wolf Studio, Inc., *(978-0-9760654)* P.O. Box 490, Windermere, FL 34786 USA Tel 407-909-0889; Fax: 407-876-8462
E-mail: whitewolfstudio@aol.com
Web site: http://www.whitewolfstudio.com.

White-Boucke Publishing, *(978-0-9625006; 978-1-888580)* Orders Addr.: P.O. Box 1463, Oakhurst, CA 93644 USA Tel 559-641-5444
E-mail: orders@white-boucke.com
Web site: http://www.white-boucke.com.

Whitecap Bks., Ltd. (CAN) *(978-0-920620; 978-0-921061; 978-0-921396; 978-1-55110; 978-1-895099; 978-1-55285; 978-1-77050) Dist. by* **Wizard Works.**

Whitecaps Media, *(978-0-9758577; 978-0-9826353; 978-0-9836825; 978-0-9883628; 978-1-942732)* P.O. Box 680568, Houston, TX 77268-0568 USA
Web site: http://www.whitecapsmedia.com
Dist(s): **Partners Bk. Distributing, Inc.**

Whitedove Pr., *(978-0-9714908; 978-0-615-11118-6; 978-0-615-11600-6)* Orders Addr.: 401 Thornton Rd, Lithia Springs, GA 30112 USA Tel 800-326-2665; Edit Addr.: 2728 Davie Blvd. 226, Fort Lauderdale, FL 33312 USA Tel 954-981-2828; 954-981-2828; 2728 Davie Blvd No. 226, fort Lauderdale, FL 33312 Tel 954-981-2828
E-mail: mail@michelleWhitedove.com
Web site: http://www.michellewhitedove.com
Dist(s): **New Leaf Distributing Co., Inc.**

Whitegate Bks., *(978-0-9767570)* The Appletree, 903 26 Rd., Grand Junction, CO 81506 USA
E-mail: lyn@appletreedesigns.com
Web site: http://www.appletreedesigns.com.

Whitehead, D. Literature, *(978-0-9972943)* 14854 depot Dr., Neosho, MO 64850 USA Tel 417-389-2773
E-mail: plantatree.doug@gmail.com
Web site: www.whiteheadliterature.com.

Whitehead, Judith, *(978-0-615-23987-3)* 5686 Fieldbrook Dr., East Amherst, NY 14051 USA Tel 716-238-5547
E-mail: juju8451@yahoo.com
Web site: http://myspace.com.

Whitehouse Publishing, *(978-0-9644171)* 6556 Mckenna Way, Alexandria, VA 22315-5571 USA Do not confuse with Whithouse Publishing in Corning, NY
E-mail: erw192@hotmail.com
Web site: http://users.starpower.net/whitee/bookcover/treasure.html

Whitehouse Publishing, *(978-1-933031)* P.O. Box 16, Corning, NY 14830 USA Toll Free: 800-784-0537 Do not confuse with Whitehouse Publishing in Alexandria, VA
E-mail: elizabeth@whitehouse-publishing.com
Web site: http://www.whitehouse-publishing.com.

Whitepoint Pr., *(978-0-615-51020-0; 978-0-615-51021-7; 978-0-615-51022-4; 978-0-615-74499-5; 978-0-615-77099-4; 978-0-615-79369-6; 978-0-615-84585-2; 978-0-9898971; 978-1-944856)*
Web site: www.whitepointpress.com
Dist(s): **CreateSpace Independent Publishing Platform**
Dummy Record Do Not USE!!!!
Smashwords.

WhiteWalls, Inc., *(978-0-945323)* Orders Addr.: P.O. Box 8204, Chicago, IL 60647 USA (SAN 246-9952); Edit Addr.: 2845 W. Altgeld, Chicago, IL 60647 USA (SAN 246-9960)
E-mail: aeelms@aol.com
Web site: http://www.whitewalls.org
Dist(s): **Chicago Distribution Ctr.**
SPD-Small Pr. Distribution.

Whitis, Cindy, *(978-0-615-17079-4)* 9018 Imperial Dr., Indianapolis, IN 46239 USA
E-mail: jim.whitis@sbcglobal.net.

Whitline Ink, Inc., *(978-1-930154)* Orders Addr.: P.O. Box 668, Boonville, NC 27011 USA Tel 336-367-6914; Fax: 336-367-6913; Edit Addr.: Hwy. 601 S., Boonville, NC 27011 USA
E-mail: whitlineink@yadtel.net
Dist(s): **Parnassus Bk. Distributors.**

†Whitman, Albert & Co., *(978-0-8075)* 250 S. Northwest Hwy. # 320, Park Ridge, IL 60068-4237 USA (SAN 201-2049) Toll Free: 800-255-7675
E-mail: mail@awhitmanco.com
Web site: http://www.albertwhitman.com
Dist(s): **Follett School Solutions**
Independent Pubs. Group
MyiLibrary
Open Road Integrated Media, Inc.
Open Road Distribution
Perfection Learning Corp.; *CIP.*

Whitman Publishing LLC, *(978-0-937458; 978-1-930849; 978-0-7948)* Div. of Anderson Press Inc., Orders Addr.: 4001 Helton Dr., Florence, AL 35030 USA Tel 256-246-1166; Toll Free: 800-528-3992; Edit Addr.: 3101 Clairmont Rd., NE, Suite C, Atlanta, GA 30329 USA (SAN 253-522X) Tel 404-214-4300; Fax: 404-214-4391; Toll Free: 800-528-3992
E-mail: info@whitmanbooks.com
Web site: http://www.whitmanbooks.com.

†Whitmore Publishing Co., *(978-0-87426)* 1144 Riverview Ln., West Conshohocken, PA 19428-2964 USA (SAN 203-2112)
E-mail: production@whitmorepublishing.com; *CIP.*

Whittet Bks., Ltd. (GBR) *(978-0-905483; 978-1-873580) Dist. by* **Diamond Farm Bk.**

Whike, Traudl, *(978-1-68377)* 40 Main St., Newark, DE 19711 USA Toll Free: 888-248-4521
E-mail: colinwfscott@gmail.com.

Who Am I Pr., *(978-0-9774174)* 4444 Hazeltine Ave., No. 229, Sherman Oaks, CA 91423 USA Tel 818-501-5908
E-mail: lea@godwhoami.com
Web site: http://www.godwhoami.com.

Who Chains You, *(978-0-615-19983-2; 978-0-615-21952-3; 978-0-578-01626-9; 978-0-9842897; 978-0-692-71696-0; 978-0-692-74473-4; 978-1-946044)* P.O. Box 581, Amissville, VA 20106 USA Tel 757-474-5474
Web site: http://www.whochainsyou.com
Dist(s): **CreateSpace Independent Publishing Platform.**

Whole Heart Ministries, *(978-1-888692)* Orders Addr.: P.O. Box 3445, Monument, CO 80132-8506 USA; *Imprints:* Whole Heart Press (WholeHeart)
E-mail: whm@wholeheart.org; admin@wholeheart.org
Web site: http://www.wholeheart.org/
Dist(s): **BookBaby.**

Whole Heart Pr. *Imprint of* **Whole Heart Ministries**

Whole Spirit Pr., *(978-1-892857)* 1905 S. Clarkson St., Denver, CO 80210 USA Tel 303-979-5820; 303-246-9554; Fax: 303-979-6151; Toll Free: 877-488-3774
E-mail: sales@wholespiritpress.com
Web site: http://www.wholespiritpress.com.

Whole Systems Support *See* **WiseWoman Pr.**

Wholemovement Pubns., *(978-0-9766773)* Orders Addr.: 4606 N. Elston No. 3, Chicago, IL 60630 USA Tel 773-794-9764
E-mail: bradhs@interaccess.com
Web site: http://www.wholemovement.com.

Wholesome Pr., *(978-1-943449)* 892 Cabaniss Cres, Pensacola, FL 32508 USA
E-mail: hello@wholesome.press
Web site: wholesome.press.

Wholesome Puppy Tales, *(978-0-9762466)* 13432 San Pasqual Rd., Escondido, CA 92025-7834 USA
E-mail: cmodicagraphics@aol.com
Web site: http://www.wholesomepuppytales.com.

Whorl Bks., *(978-0-9778850; 978-0-615-70205-6; 978-0-615-71111-9; 978-0-615-72898-8; 978-0-615-99191-7; 978-0-692-21281-3; 978-0-692-30046-6; 978-0-692-37390-3; 978-0-692-47723-6)* 5658 NW Pioneer Cir., Norman, OK 73072 USA (SAN 850-5713); *Imprints:* Dark Passages (Dark Passages); WhorlBooks Thumbprints (WhorlBks)
E-mail: whorlbooks@gmail.com; marilynahudson@yahoo.com
Web site: http://www.freewebs.com/whorlbooks/
Dist(s): **CreateSpace Independent Publishing Platform.**

WhorlBooks Thumbprints *Imprint of* **Whorl Bks.**

Who's There, Incorporated *See* **KnockKnock LLC**

Who's Who In Sports *Imprint of* **Guidry Assocs., Inc.**

Why Mom Deserves a Diamond, Incorporated *See* **Moon Over Mountains Publishing (M.O.M.)**

Why Not Bks., *(978-0-9849919; 978-0-9962422; 978-0-9978808)* 831 Spruce Ave., Pacific Grove, CA 93950 USA Tel 831-238-1849
E-mail: info@whynotbooks.com; amyherzog@sbcglobal.net
Web site: http://www.bradherzog.com; http://www.whynotbooks.com
Dist(s): **Midpoint Trade Bks., Inc.**

Wickenburg Healthcare Alliance *See* **WHA Publishing**

Wicker Park Pr., Ltd., *(978-0-9789676; 978-1-936679)* 334 Hawthorn Ave,, Glencoe, IL 60022 USA Tel 773-391-1199
E-mail: eric@3ibooks.com
Web site: http://www.wickerparkpress.us.

Wicks, Valerie, *(978-0-615-71556-8; 978-0-9912594)* 831 1/2 Silver Lake Blvd., Los Angeles, CA 90026 USA Tel 678 3613895
Web site: www.sevenspectral.com
Dist(s): **CreateSpace Independent Publishing Platform.**

Wide World Publishing/Tetra, *(978-0-933174; 978-1-884550)* Orders Addr.: P.O. Box 476, San Carlos, CA 94070 USA (SAN 211-1462) Tel 650-593-2839; Fax: 650-595-0802
E-mail: wwpbl@aol.com
Web site: http://www.wideworldpublishing.com
Dist(s): **Booklines Hawaii, Ltd.**
Islander Group
Publishers Group West (PGW).

WideThinker Bks., *(978-0-9728195)* P.O. Box 30144, Philadelphia, PA 19146 USA Tel 215-985-0322; Toll Free: 866-236-1077
E-mail: wtb@widethinker.com
Web site: http://www.widethinkerbooks.com.

WiDo Publishing, *(978-0-9796070; 978-0-9830238; 978-1-937178; 978-1-947966)* Orders Addr.: 840 S W. TEMPLE APT 2, Salt Lake City, UT 84101 USA (SAN 853-8786) Tel 801-532-2343
E-mail: information@widopublishing.com
Web site: http://www.widopublishing.com.

†**Wiener, Markus Pubs., Inc.**, *(978-0-910129; 978-0-945179; 978-1-55876)* 231 Nassau St., Princeton, NJ 08542 USA (SAN 282-5465) Tel 609-921-1141; Fax: 609-921-1140
E-mail: publisher@markuswiener.com
Web site: http://www.markuswiener.com; *CIP.*

Wiese, Michael Productions, *(978-0-941188; 978-1-932907; 978-1-61593)* 6049 37th Ave. NE, Seattle, WA 98115 USA (SAN 237-9716) Tel 206-283-2948; Fax: 206-283-2072; Toll Free: 800-833-5738 (24 hours); 800-379-8808
E-mail: mwpsales@earthlink.net; kenlee@mwp.com
Web site: http://www.mwp.com
Dist(s): **Follett School Solutions**
Ingram Publisher Services
MyiLibrary
Elsevier Science & Technology Bks.

Wiggies, Piggy, *(978-1-939076)* 150 Ocean Pk. Blvd. Ste 418, Santa Monica, CA 90405 USA Tel 310-666-0069
E-mail: emma@emmalouisebooks.com.

Wiggles Pr., *(978-0-9823906; 978-1-935706)* Orders Addr.: 23 Athens St. Suite 2, Cambridge, MA 02138 USA Tel 617-895-7698; 617-981-0285
E-mail: rochelle.thorpe@yahoo.com.

Wighita Pr., *(978-0-9786648)* P.O. Box 30399, Little Rock, AR 72260-0399 USA
E-mail: info@wighitapress.com
Web site: www.wighitapress.com.

Wigu Publishing *Imprint of* **Wigu Publishing**

Wigu Publishing, *(978-1-939973)* 4327 N. Nines Ridge Ln., Boise, ID 83702 USA; *Imprints:* Wigu Publishing (WiguPubng)
E-mail: beressler59@gmail.com
Web site: www.wigupublishing.com; www.whenigrowupbooks.com.

Wigwam Publishing, *(978-0-9721022)* Orders Addr.: P.O. Box 574, Weyauwega, WI 54983 USA; Edit Addr.: 410 S. Harlon St., No. 2, Weyauwega, WI 54983 USA Do not confuse with companies with the same or similar names in Villa Park, IL, Cheyenne, WY.

WigWam Publishing Co., *(978-1-930076)* Orders Addr.: P.O. Box 6992, Villa Park, IL 60181 USA; *Imprints:* New Leaf Books (New Leaf Books) Do not confuse with companies with the same or similar names in Weyauwega, WI, Cheyenne, WY
E-mail: info@newleafbooks.net
Web site: http://www.newleafbooks.net.

Wilander Publishing Co., *(978-0-9628335)* Orders Addr.: P.O. Box 56121, Portland, OR 97238 USA.

Wild About Coloring, *(978-0-692-91040-5)* P.O. Box 94, KEELER, CA 93530 USA Tel 760-608-7245
E-mail: elmirafoley@gmail.com
Dist(s): **Lightning Source, Inc.**

Wild About Learning, Inc., *(978-0-9789880)* 964 John St., Joliet, IL 60435 USA Tel 815-740-1173; Fax: 815-740-1174
E-mail: info@wildaboutlearning.org
Web site: http://wildaboutlearning.org.

Wild Animal Publishing, *(978-0-9769555)* 246 Meridian St., Westerly, RI 02891 USA
E-mail: sciarrajb@aol.com; keith@wildanimalpublishing.com
Web site: http://www.wildanimalpublishing.com.

Wild Child Publishing, *(978-0-9771314; 978-1-934069; 978-1-935013; 978-1-936222; 978-1-61798)* P.O. Box 4897, Culver City, CA 90231 USA
E-mail: mgbaun@wildchildpublishing.com; mbaun@freyasbower.com
Web site: http://www.wildchildpublishing.com; http://www.freyasbower.com/
Dist(s): **All Romance Ebooks, LLC.**

Wild Earth, *(978-0-9719807)* P.O. Box 407, Charlottesville, VA 22902-0407 USA Tel 434-977-4615 Toll Free: 800-871-5647
Web site: http://www.animalessence.com/.

Wild Flower USA, *(978-0-9646698)* 26614 Oak Ridge Dr., Suite 110, The Woodlands, TX 77380 USA Tel 281-363-2360; Fax: 281-367-4480.

Wild Goose Publishing, *(978-0-9792657; 978-0-9799255)* Orders Addr.: P.O. Box 386, Charlotte, MI 48813 USA
E-mail: wildgoosepub@sbcglobal.net.

Wild Hare Collective, *(978-0-692-90631-6)* 1981 Deep Woods Trail, NASHVILLE, TN 37214 USA Tel 260-908-1908
E-mail: jandra@jandralee.com
Dist(s): **Lightning Source, Inc.**

Wild Hare Publishing, *(978-0-9772096)* P.O. Box 2144, Ridgeland, MS 39158-2144 USA (SAN 256-9639) Tel 601-853-8120; Fax: 601-853-8121
E-mail: dgibbes@wildharepublishing.com.

Wild Heart Ranch, Inc., *(978-0-9761768)* 1385 Gulf Rd., Suite 102, Point Roberts, WA 98281 USA Toll Free Fax: 866-735-3518; Toll Free: 888-889-9215
E-mail: dawn@wildheartranch.com
Web site: http://www.wildheartranch.com; http://www.iseahorses.com.

Wild Horses Publishing Co., *(978-0-937148; 978-0-9601088)* Orders Addr.: P.O. Box 1373, Los Altos, CA 94022 USA (SAN 211-8289)
E-mail: pwalatka@earthlink.net
Dist(s): **TNT Media Group, Inc.**

Wild Iris Publishing, *(978-1-936607)* 4538 Hastings-Newville Rd., Bellville, OH 44813-9143 USA Tel 419-892-2900
E-mail: davefitzsimmons@yahoo.com
Dist(s): **Independent Pubs. Group.**

Wild Mind Creations, *(978-0-615-15138-0)* P.O. Box 1935, Fairview, OR 97024-1806 USA
E-mail: jmm1965mionda_4@msn.com.

Wild Plum Woods Bks., *(978-0-9745581)* 39042 Ruann Ct., Zephyrhills, FL 33540 USA.

Wild Rose *Imprint of* **Mayhaven Publishing, Inc.**

Wild Rose Pr., Inc., The, *(978-1-60154; 978-1-61217; 978-1-62830; 978-1-5092)* P.O. Box 708, Adams Basin, NY 14410 USA Tel 585-880-0819
E-mail: info@thewildrosepress.com
Web site: http://www.thewildrosepress.com.

Wilde Art, *(978-0-9974828)* 21807 el Coyote Dr., Sonora, CA 95370 USA Tel 209-533-1261
E-mail: kwilde55@gmail.com
Web site: wilde-art.com.

Wilder Pubns., Corp., *(978-0-9773040; 978-1-934451; 978-1-60459; 978-1-61720; 978-1-62755; 978-1-63384; 978-1-5154)*.

Wilder Publications, Limited *See* **Wilder Pubns., Corp.**

Wildfire Enterprises, *(978-0-9771969)* Orders Addr.: P.O. Box 402, Viola, AR 72583-0402 USA Tel 870-458-3600 (phone/fax); Edit Addr.: P O Box 402, Viola, AR 72583-0402 USA
E-mail: wfenterprises@hotmail.com
Web site: http://www.wildfireenterprises.iceryder.net.

Wildflower Pr., The, *(978-0-9714343; 978-0-9779933)* P.O. Box 4757, Albuquerque, NM 87196-4757 USA Tel 505-296-0691; Fax: 505-296-6124 Do not confuse with companies with the same or similar name in Oceanside, CA ,Phoenix, AZ ,Littleton, CO
E-mail: jspoetry@aol.com
Dist(s): **Smashwords.**

Wildflower Run, *(978-0-9667086)* Orders Addr.: P.O. Box 9656, College Station, TX 77842 USA Tel 979-764-0166
E-mail: atmgold@aol.com
Web site: http://www.aggiegoose.com.

Wildlife Education, Ltd., *(978-0-937934; 978-1-888153; 978-1-932396; 978-1-938811; 978-1-946318)* 1260 Audubon Rd., Park Hills, KY 41011-1904 USA (SAN 215-8299) Toll Free: 800-477-5034; *Imprints:* Zoo Books (Zoo Bks); Critters Up Close (Critters Up Close)
E-mail: sales@zoobooks.com
Web site: http://www.zoobooks.com.

Wildlife Tales Publishing, *(978-0-9793207)* Div. of Ark R.A.I.N. Wildlife Sanctuary, Inc., P.O. Box 721, Brownsville, TN 38012-0721 USA Toll Free: 877-352-6657
E-mail: books@wildlifetalespublishing.com
Web site: http://www.wildlifetalespublishing.com.

Wildly Austin, *(978-0-9753990)* P.O. Box 161987, Austin, TX 78716-1987 USA
E-mail: vikki@wildlyaustin.com; vl@intersourcesearch.com
Web site: http://www.wildlyaustin.com.

Wildot Pr., *(978-0-9789043; 978-0-9797933)* 4402 W. Creedance Blvd., Glendale, AZ 85310-3921 USA Tel 623-434-2636
E-mail: wildotpress@cox.net
Web site: http://ww.wildotpress.com.

Wildside Pr., LLC, *(978-0-8095; 978-0-913960; 978-1-880448; 978-1-58715; 978-1-59224; 978-1-4344; 978-1-4794)* Orders Addr.: 9710 Traville Gateway Dr., No. 234, Rockville, MD 20850 USA Tel 301-762-1305; Fax: 301-762-1306
E-mail: customerservice@wildsidepress.com; wildsidepress@gmail.com
Web site: http://www.wildsidepress.com; http://www.weirdtales.net; http://www.wildsidebooks.com
Dist(s): **Diamond Comic Distributors, Inc.**
Diamond Bk. Distributors
MyiLibrary

Wildstone Media, *(978-1-882467)* Orders Addr.: P.O. Box 511580, Saint Louis, MO 63151 USA Tel 314-482-8472; Fax: 314-487-1910; Toll Free: 800-296-1918
E-mail: wildstone@mlc.net
Web site: http://www.wildstonemedia.com
Dist(s): **Anderson News, LLC**
Big River Distribution
BookBaby.

Wildstorm *Imprint of* **DC Comics**

WildWest Publishing, *(978-0-9721800)* P.O. Box 11658, Olympia, WA 98508 USA
E-mail: clamityJan@aol.com
Web site: http://www.CalamityJan.com.

Wiley *Imprint of* **Wiley, John & Sons, Inc.**

†**Wiley, John & Sons, Inc.**, *(978-0-470; 978-0-471; 978-0-7645; 978-0-7821; 978-0-8260; 978-0-87605; 978-0-88422; 978-0-937721; 978-0-939246; 978-1-55828; 978-1-56561; 978-1-56884; 978-1-57313; 978-1-58245; 978-1-878058; 978-1-118; 978-1-119)* Orders Addr.: c/o John Wiley & Sons, Inc., United States Distribution Ctr., 1 Wiley Dr., Somerset, NJ 08875-1272 USA Tel 732-469-4400; Fax: 732-302-2300; Toll Free Fax: 800-597-3299; Toll Free: 800-225-5945 (orders); Edit Addr.: 111 River St., Hoboken, NJ 07030 USA (SAN 200-2272) Tel 201-748-6000; 201-748-6276 (Retail and Wholesale); Fax: 201-748-6088; 201-748-8641 (Retail and Wholesale); *Imprints:* Wiley-VCH (Wiley-VCH); Jossey-Bass (Jossey-Bass); For Dummies (For Dummies); Howell Book House (HBH); Capstone (CapstW); Wiley (JWiley); Wiley-Blackwell (WileyBlack)
E-mail: compbks@wiley.com; bookinfo@wiley.com; custserv@wiley.com
Web site: http://www.wiley.com/compbooks; http://www.interscience.wiley.com; http://www.wiley.com
Dist(s): **Ebsco Publishing**
Follett School Solutions
Leonard, Hal Corp.
Ingram Publisher Services
Lightning Source, Inc.
Lippincott Williams & Wilkins
MBI Distribution Services/Quayside Distribution
Mastery Education
Mel Bay Pubns., Inc.
MyiLibrary
Pearson Education
TNT Media Group, Inc.
Urban Land Institute
ebrary, Inc.; *CIP.*

Wiley OBrien Worksapce *See* **OBrien, Wiley Workspace**

Wiley-Blackwell *Imprint of* **Wiley, John & Sons, Inc.**

Wiley-VCH *Imprint of* **Wiley, John & Sons, Inc.**

Wilfrid Laurier Univ. Pr. (CAN) *(978-0-88920; 978-0-921821; 978-1-55458; 978-1-77112) Dist. by* **IngramPubServ.**

Wilkes Publishing Co., Inc., *(978-0-9747755)* P.O. Box 340, Washington, GA 30673 USA Tel 706-678-2636; Fax: 706-678-3857
E-mail: editor@news-reporter.com
Web site: http://www.news-reporter.com.

Wilkins Farago Pty. Ltd. (AUS) *(978-0-9585571; 978-0-9804165; 978-0-9806070; 978-0-9871099; 978-0-6480091) Dist. by* **IPG Chicago.**

Wilkinson Publishing (AUS) *(978-0-9775457; 978-0-9802818; 978-1-921332; 978-1-921667; 978-1-921804; 978-1-922178; 978-1-925265; 978-1-925642) Dist. by* **IPG Chicago.**

Will Hall Bks., *(978-0-9630310; 978-0-9801257)* 611 Oliver Ave., Fayetteville, AR 72701 USA
E-mail: rharriso@uark.edu
Web site: http://www.willhallbooks.com.

Will to Print Pr., *(978-0-9772985)* 234 Hyde St., San Francisco, CA 94102-3324 USA Tel 415-474-0508; Fax: 415-673-1027
E-mail: willtoprintpress@faithfulfools.org
Web site: http://www.faithfulfools.org.

WillGo Pr., *(978-0-9828231)* 2874 Arcade St., Maplewood, MN 55109 USA Tel 651-774-2558
E-mail: gdesigns@comcast.net.

William Askel Art, *(978-0-9752528)* 21665 Wallace Dr., Southfield, MI 48075-7570 USA
E-mail: waksel@provide.net
Web site: http://fieldguidetomonsters.com.

William M. Gaines Agent, INC. *Imprint of* **Diamond Bk. Distributors**

William Morrow Paperbacks *Imprint of* **HarperCollins Pubs.**

William Works, Inc., *(978-0-9745244)* P.O. Box 2709, Washington, DC 20013 USA Toll Free: 877-535-2057.

Williams, Angela Claudette, *(978-0-615-15833-4; 978-0-615-16052-8; 978-0-615-16098-6; 978-0-615-16138-9; 978-0-615-17571-3; 978-0-615-17889-9)* 3645 Watkins Ridge Ct., Raleigh, NC 27616 USA
E-mail: claudetteexpressiona@yahoo.com
Web site: http://www.claudetteexpressions.com
Dist(s): **Lulu Pr., Inc.**

Williams, Benjamin Publishing, *(978-0-9764945; 978-0-9796180; 978-0-9802398; 978-0-9850233; 978-0-9909650)* 18525 S. Torrence Ave. Suite D3, Lansing, IL 60438 USA Tel 1-888-757-0007
E-mail: ben@bwpublishing.com
Web site: http://www.bwpublishing.com.

Williams, Benny Publishing *See* **Williams, Benjamin Publishing**

Williams, Darnell *See* **Williams, Darnell L. Foundation, The**

Williams, Darnell L. Foundation, The, *(978-0-9747771)* 2402 Magnolia Dr., Harrisburg, PA 17104 USA Tel 717-233-1511
E-mail: WDarn44243@aol.com.

Williams, David Michael *See* **One Million Words, LLC**

Williams, Dontez *See* **MySheri Enterprises, LLC**

Williams Enterprises, Inc., *(978-0-9755478)* 500 5th Ave., N., Greybull, WY 82426 USA.

Williams, Gary, *(978-0-9743000)* 574 Falcon Fork Way, Jacksonville, FL 32259 USA
Web site: http://www.fbcofmand.org.

Williams, Geoffrey T., *(978-0-9771381; 978-0-9801671)* 3119 Redwood St., San Diego, CA 92104 USA
Web site: http://wildvoices.com
Dist(s): **Audible.com**
Smashwords.

Williams, James E., *(978-0-9746310)* P.O. Box 6921, Atlanta, GA 30315-0921 USA Fax: 404-691-0726.

Williams, Michael, *(978-0-9761503)* 1324 Lake Grove Ln., Desoto, TX 75115-3326 USA.

Williams, Morgan, *(978-0-9762768)* 3243 Cloverwood Dr., Nashville, TN 37214-3428 USA
E-mail: mandj@magiclink.com
Web site: http://www.thestandards.com.

Williams, Rozalia *See* **Hidden Curriculum Education**

Williams, Thomas, *(978-0-9763633)* 358 Homestead Rd., NW, Willis, VA 24380 USA Tel 540-789-4295
E-mail: tomwill@swva.net
Web site: http://www.santacares.org.

Williamson County Public Library, *(978-0-9911915; 978-0-9970690)* Williamson Cty. Public Library, Franklin, TN 37064 USA Tel 615-595-1240; *Imprints:* Academy Park Press (AcadParkPr)
E-mail: dgreenwald@williamson-tn.org
Web site: wcpltn.org.

Williamspublishing, *(978-0-615-19121-8)* 317 E. Oakgrove, Kalamazoo, MI 49004 USA
E-mail: starowl1@hotmail.clm
Dist(s): **Lulu Pr., Inc.**

Willby-Walker, Debra June, *(978-0-692-70291-8; 978-0-692-85861-5)* 12018 Ingleside Rd., Oakvale, WV 24739 USA Tel 304-396-9105
E-mail: debbeejune@gmail.com.

Willie & Willie, *(978-0-9754126)* P.O. Box 26071, Saint Louis, MO 63136 USA.

Willis, E.B. Bks., *(978-0-9976634)* 209 Braxberry Way, Holly Springs, NC 27540 USA Tel 919-656-5893
E-mail: bethwillis@nc.rr.com
Web site: www.ebwillis.com.

Willis Music Co., *(978-0-87718)* Orders Addr.: P.O. Box 548, Florence, KY 41022-0548 USA (SAN 294-6947) Tel 606-283-2050 859; Fax: 606-283-1784; Toll Free: 800-354-9799; Edit Addr.: 7380 Industrial Rd., Florence, KY 41040 USA
E-mail: willis@willis-music.com; orderdpt@willis-music.com
Web site: http://www.willismusic.com
Dist(s): **Leonard, Hal Corp.**

Willow Bend Publishing, *(978-0-9709002; 978-0-9831138)* 111 West St., P.O. Box 304, Goshen, MA 01032 USA Tel 413-230-1514 Do not confuse with Willow Bend Publishing in Lakeland, FL
E-mail: info@willowbendpublishing.com
Web site: http://www.willowbendpublishing.com.

Willow Brook Publishing, *(978-0-9817636)* 19600 W. Shore Dr., Suite 101, Mundelein, IL 60060 USA (SAN 856-4914)
E-mail: Info@willowBrookPublishing.com
Web site: http://www.willowbrook-publishing.com/
Dist(s): **Pathway Bk. Service.**

†**Willow Creek Pr., Inc.**, *(978-0-932558; 978-1-57223; 978-1-59543; 978-1-60755; 978-1-62343; 978-1-68234; 978-1-5492)* Orders Addr.: P.O. Box 147, Minocqua, WI 54548-0147 USA (SAN 255-4038) Tel 715-358-7010; Fax: 715-358-2807; Toll Free: 800-850-9453; P.O. Box 147 / EDI Orders, Minoqua, WI 54548 (SAN 920-8070) Tel 715-358-7010; Fax: 715-358-2807; Edit Addr.: 9931 Hwy. 70 W., Minocqua, WI 54548 USA Tel 715-358-7010; Fax: 715-358-2807; Toll Free: 800-850-9453; 9931 Hwy 70 W, Minocqua, WI 54548 Toll Free: 800-850-9453 Do not confuse with Willowcreek Pr. in Aloha, OR
E-mail: info@willowcrewpress.com; info@wcpretail.com
Web site: http://www.wcpretail.com
Dist(s): **MyiLibrary**
Strauss Consultants
Two Rivers Distribution; *CIP.*

Willow Creel Publishing Co., *(978-0-9729655)* 35 Willow Creek, 820 9th Ave. S., North Myrtle Beach, SC 29582 USA Tel 843-272-1096 Do not confuse with Willow Creek Publishing in Canton, MI, Pine River, MN
E-mail: grayfox.43@att.net
Web site: http://www.chinquawhere.com.

Willow Dance Pubns., *(978-0-9768750)* Orders Addr.: P.O. Box 71, Hillsdale, WY 82060 USA Tel 307-631-0236; Edit Addr.: 1370 CR 142, Hillsdale, WY 82060 USA
E-mail: willowdancepublishing@yahoo.com.

Willow Publishing, *(978-0-9825212)* 1000 Kinsley Ave., No. 32, Winslow, AZ 86047 USA Toll Free Fax: 800-643-9527.

Willow Tree Books *See* **Apricot Pr.**

Willow Tree Press *See* **Little Willow Tree Bks.**

Willowgate Pr., *(978-1-930008)* P.O. Box 6529, Holliston, MA 01746 USA (SAN 253-0376); 120 Brook Rd., Port Jefferson, NY 11777-1665
E-mail: willowgatepress@yahoo.com
Web site: http://www.willowgatepress.com.

WillowSpring Downs, *(978-0-9648525; 978-0-9742716)* 1582 N. Falcon, Hillsboro, KS 67063 USA Tel 620-367-8432; Fax: 620-367-8218; Toll Free: 888-551-0973
E-mail: willowspringdowns@juno.com.

WillowTree Pr., L.L.C., *(978-0-9678221; 978-0-9794533; 978-1-937778)* Orders Addr.: P.O. Box 1195, High Ridge, MO 63049 USA Tel 314-740-7791; Edit Addr.: P.O. Box 1195, High Ridge, MO 63049 USA (SAN 253-1178); *Imprints:* Full Circle Press (Full Circle MO)
E-mail: info@willowtreepress.com
Web site: http://www.willowtreepress.com
Dist(s): **Smashwords.**

Willy Waw wees, LLC, *(978-0-9785103)* Orders Addr.: PO Box 390593, Deltona, FL 32739 USA
E-mail: artgallerymeris@aol.com
Web site: http://www.willywawwees.com.

Wilmington Today LLC, *(978-0-9729573; 978-0-9916642)* 1213 Culbreth Dr., Wilmington, NC 28405 USA Tel 910-509-7195
E-mail: hwjones@wilmingtontoday.com
Web site: http://www.wilmingtontoday.com.

Wilshire House of Arkansas *See* **Ozark Publishing**

Wilson & Assocs., *(978-0-9710427)* P.O. Box 2569, Alvin, TX 77512 USA Tel 281-388-0196; Fax: 413-683-8503 Do not confuse with Wilson & Associates, Gig Harbor, WA
E-mail: john@wilsonpublishing.com; pwilson@wilsonpublishing.com
Web site: http://www.orsapress.com; http://www.thebookdistributor.com; http://www.wilsonpublishing.com.

Wilson, Gerrard (IRL) *(978-0-9561553) Dist. by* **LuluCom.**

†**Wilson, H.W.**, *(978-0-8242)* 950 University Ave., Bronx, NY 10452-4224 USA (SAN 203-2961) Tel 718-588-8400; Fax: 718-681-1511 (Outside of the U.S. & Canada); Toll Free: 800-367-6770 ext 2272
E-mail: custserv@hwwilson.com
Web site: http://www.hwwilson.com
Dist(s): **Ebsco Publishing**
Grey Hse. Publishing
MyiLibrary; *CIP.*

Wilson Language Training, *(978-1-56778)* 47 Old Webster Rd., Oxford, MA 01540-2705 USA Toll Free: 800-899-8454.

Wilson Place Comics, *(978-0-9744235)* P.O. Box 435, Oceanside, NY 11572 USA
E-mail: Wilplace@optonline.net
Web site: http://www.wjhc.com
Dist(s): **Brodart Co.**
Diamond Comic Distributors, Inc.
Diamond Bk. Distributors
Follett School Solutions
Mackin Library Media
Midwest Library Service.

Wilson, Rebecca, *(978-0-9760569)* 450 Massachusetts Ave NW Apt. 1004, Washington, DC 20001-6222 USA
E-mail: info@sunfishmanuals.com
Web site: http://www.sunfishmanuals.com.

Wilson, W. Shane, *(978-0-578-00301-6; 978-0-578-00634-5; 978-0-578-00797-7; 978-0-578-01639-9; 978-0-578-02119-5; 978-0-578-02550-6; 978-0-578-03095-1; 978-0-578-03299-3)* 7600 NE 64th Cir., Vancouver, WA 98662 USA Tel 360-521-1584
E-mail: redtimberwolf67@yahoo.com
Web site: http://stores.lulu.com/shanesbooks
Dist(s): **Lulu Pr., Inc.**

Wilson-Barnett Publishing, *(978-1-888840)* P.O. Box 345, Tustin, CA 92781-0345 USA Tel 949-380-5748; Fax: 714-730-6140
E-mail: mrcalc@usa.net.

Wilson-Crawford & Co., *(978-0-9752948)* P.O. Box 809, Island Lake, IL 60042-0809 USA Fax: 847-487-1591
E-mail: freecellmax@aol.com
Web site: http://www.freecellsecrets.com.

Wilstonian, *(978-0-9772122)* 3603 Whitaker Dr., Melvindale, MI 48122 USA (SAN 257-0106)
Web site: http://www.wilstonian.com.

Wilt, Lisa, *(978-0-9770053)* Orders Addr.: 1072 Frye Rd., Jeannette, PA 15644-4717 USA
E-mail: thankyoumousie@comcast.net.

Wiltshire Bks., *(978-0-9831685; 978-0-9970240)* 1924 Wiltshire Blvd., Huntington, WV 25701 USA Tel 304-730-0798
E-mail: WiltshireBookLLC@aol.com.

Wimabi Pr., *(978-0-578-02359-5; 978-0-578-03340-2; 978-0-578-05718-7)* 7102 Lakewood Dr., Richmond, VA 23229 USA
E-mail: inquiries@wimabi.com
Web site: http://www.wimabi.com
Dist(s): **Lulu Pr., Inc.**

Win Publishing, LLC, *(978-0-9826865)* 35 E. Main St., Suite 337, Avon, CT 06001 USA Tel 860-651-6859; Fax: 203-413-4409
Dist(s): **Outskirts Pr., Inc.**

Winchester Pr., *(978-0-9745279)* P.O. Box 711, Hollis, NH 03049-0711 USA Tel 603-880-9559 Do not confuse with companies with the same or similar name in Southhampton, NY, Howell, NJ, LaFox, IL.

Wincik, Stephanie *See* **One Horse Pr.**

Wind Pubns., *(978-0-9636545; 978-1-893239; 978-1-936138)* Orders Addr.: 600 Overbrook Dr., Nicholasville, KY 40356 USA
E-mail: books@windpub.com
Web site: http://www.windpub.com.

Windblown Enterprises, *(978-0-9752576)* 12207 243rd Pl NE, Redmond, WA 98053-5685 USA
E-mail: windblowne@msn.com.

Windblown Media, *(978-0-9647292; 978-1-935170; 978-1-61871)* 4680 Calle Norte, Newbury Park, CA 91320 USA Tel 805-498-2484; Fax: 805-499-4260
E-mail: office@windblownmedia.com
Web site: http://www.windblownmedia.com
Dist(s): **Hachette Bk. Group.**

Windcall Enterprises *See* **Windcall Publishing**

Windcall Publishing, *(978-0-9745884; 978-0-9845934; 978-0-9847607)* Div. of Windcall Enterprises, Orders Addr.: 75345 Rd. 317, Venango, NE 69168 USA Tel 308-447-5566 (phone/fax); Fax: 308-447-5566
E-mail: windcall@chase3000.com
Web site: http://www.windcallenterprises.com; http://www.windcallpublishing.com
Dist(s): **Smashwords.**

Windchimes Publishing, *(978-0-9763253)* P.O. Box 1433, Palm City, FL 34991-6433 USA Tel 772-285-5429
E-mail: wchimes@gate.net
Web site: http://www.wchimes.com.

Windfeather Pr., *(978-0-9620122)* 4545 W. Heart Rd., Bismarck, ND 58504-4257 USA (SAN 247-7246); 1203 N. 27th St., Bismarck, ND 58501 (SAN 247-7254) Tel 701-258-5047
Dist(s): **Duebbert, Harold F.**

Windham Pr., *(978-1-62845)* 11240 Plantation Oaks Ln, Lumberton, TX 77657 USA Tel 409-790-3812 Do not confuse with Windham Press in New Rochelle, NY, Miami, FL
E-mail: pmorrison@gmail.com.

Windhill Bks. LLC, *(978-0-9844828; 978-1-944734)* 939 Windhill St., Onalaska, WI 54650-2081 USA (SAN 859-5135)
E-mail: jeanna@windhillbooks.com
Web site: http://www.windhillbooks.com.

Windhorse Bks., *(978-0-9973745)* 5429 SW 80 St., Gainesville, FL 32608 USA Tel 352-336-5888
E-mail: barbaragresbach@gmail.com
Web site: windhorsebooks.com.

Winding Road Pubs., *(978-0-615-21989-9; 978-0-578-04819-2; 978-0-578-07274-6; 978-0-578-09900-2; 978-0-578-10413-3; 978-0-578-10703-5; 978-0-578-10929-9; 978-0-578-11074-5; 978-0-578-11693-8; 978-0-578-12821-4; 978-0-578-13843-5)* 2904 Giles St., West Des Moines, IA 50265 USA Tel 515-226-1179
Dist(s): **Lulu Pr., Inc.**

Windjammer Adventure Publishing, *(978-0-9768477; 978-0-615-29130-7; 978-0-615-33790-6; 978-0-615-36411-7; 978-0-615-38745-1; 978-0-9831300; 978-0-9898232; 978-0-9978807; 978-0-9994812)* 289 S. Franklin St., Chagrin Falls, OH 44022-3449 USA Tel 440-247-6610
E-mail: windjammerpub@mac.com
Web site: http://windjammerpublishing.com.

Windmill Bks. *Imprint of* **Rosen Publishing Group, Inc., The**

Windmill Bks. Ltd. (GBR) *(978-1-78121) Dist. by* **Black Rab.**

Windmill Bks., *(978-1-60754; 978-1-62275)* 303 Pk. Ave. S., Suite No. 1280, NEW YORK, NY 10010-3657 USA Tel 646-205-7415
Dist(s): **Rosen Publishing Group, Inc., The.**

Window Bks., *(978-1-889829)* Orders Addr.: 1425 Broadway #513, Seattle, WA 98122 USA Tel 206-351-9993
E-mail: orders@windowbooksonline.com
Web site: http://www.meetmarcadams.com; http://www.windowbooksonline.com.

Window Box Pr. LLC, *(978-0-9793738)* Orders Addr.: 13516 Fillmore Ct., Thornton, CO 80241-1330 USA (SAN 853-2958) Tel 303-255-9432
E-mail: windowboxpress@q.com
Web site: http://windowboxpress.com
Dist(s): **Independent Pubs. Group.**

Window Seat Publishing, *(978-0-9721949)* 82 Marlborough Rd., West Hempstead, NY 11552 USA Tel 516-481-5969
E-mail: aferrant@optonline.net.

Windows of Discovery, *(978-0-9785399)* P.O. Box 9085, Spokane, WA 99209-9085 USA
Web site: http://theprofessorstelescope.com.

Windrad Press *See* **Pinwheel Bks.**

WinDruid Publishing, *(978-0-9758943)* Orders Addr.: 220 Walworth Dr., St. Louis, MO 63125-5008 USA; Edit Addr.: P.O. Box 25008, Saint Louis, MO 63125-5008 USA
E-mail: orders@LukeCarter.com; info@windruidpublishing.com; susan@windruidpublishing.com
Web site: http://www.LukeCarter.com; http://www.windruidpublishing.com
Dist(s): **Book Clearing Hse.**
Quality Bks., Inc.

Windsong Publishing Co., *(978-0-9655078)* P.O. Box 588, Rimrock, AZ 86335 USA Do not confuse with companies with the same or similar names in Eugene, OR, San Diego, CA, Staunton, VA, Lake Patagonia, AZ
Dist(s): **New Leaf Distributing Co., Inc.**

Windsor Media Enterprises, Inc., *(978-0-9765304; 978-0-9777297; 978-1-934229)* 5412 Wolf St., Longmont, CO 80504-3432 USA Toll Free: 877-947-2665
E-mail: collins@wmebooks.com
Web site: http://www.wmebooks.com.

WindSpirit Publishing, *(978-0-9643407)* Orders Addr.: 220 Compass Ave., Beachwood, NJ 08722-2919 USA Fax: 732-240-7860
E-mail: windspiritpub@earthlink.net
Web site: http://www.windspiritpublishing.net.

Windsurf Publishing LLC, *(978-1-936509)* 14 Ctr. Dr., Old Greenwich, CT 06870 USA Tel 203-698-2975
E-mail: m.lagana@att.net.

Windswept Productions, *(978-0-9764825)* Orders Addr.: P.O. Box 167, Felton, PA 17322-0167 USA Tel 717-244-7700; Edit Addr.: 11525 High Point Rd., Felton, PA 17322 USA
E-mail: wpebs@earthlink.net.

Windward Publishing *Imprint of* **Finney Co., Inc.**

Windward Publishing, *(978-0-9758897)* 112 N. St., New Bedford, MA 02740-6513 USA Do not confuse with Windward Publishing in Minneapolis, MN
E-mail: windwardpublish@aol.com; josettefernandes@hotmail.com.

Windy City Pubs., *(978-0-9819505; 978-1-935766; 978-1-941478)* 2118 Plum Grove Rd., No. 349, Rolling Meadows, IL 60008 USA Tel 888-673-7126; *Imprints:* Skyscraper Press (children's) (Skyscraper Pr)
E-mail: dawn@windycitypublishers.com
Dist(s): **BookBaby.**

Windy City Publishing *See* **Windy City Pubs.**

Windy Hill Pr., *(978-0-9662983)* Orders Addr.: 22 Hilltop Ave., Barrington, RI 02806 USA Tel 401-247-2707 Do not confuse with Windy Hill Pr., in Menlo Park, CA
E-mail: windyhillpress@cox.net
Web site: http://www.windyhillpress.net.

Windy Hills Press *See* **Old Stone Pr.**

Windy Press International Publishing Hse., LLC, *(978-1-890568)* 29W 424 Tanglewood Ln, Warrenville, IL 60555-2663 USA; P.O. Box 5131, Wheaton, IL 60189-4383 Fax: 630-604-0490; Toll Free Fax: 888-508-5577; *Imprints:* A-BA-BA-HA-LA-MA-HA Publishers (A-BA-BA-HA-LA-MA-HA)
E-mail: interhouse@comcast.net
Web site: http://www.snowqueen.us.

Wineries by County, *(978-0-615-18047-2)* 3373 Silver Rapids Rd., Valley Spgs, CA 95252-9573 USA
E-mail: info@wineriesbycounty.com
Web site: http://www.wineriesbycounty.com.

Winfrey Inc., *(978-0-9818526)* Orders Addr.: 14525 SW. Millikan Way #23515, Beaverton, OR 970052343 USA (SAN 856-7263) Tel 404-993-0532; 228 Pk. Ave. S. #23515, New York, NY 10003; Edit Addr.: 4480 S. Cobb Dr. Ste H Pmb 451, Smyrna, GA 30080 USA
E-mail: info@shakeetawinfrey.com
Web site: http://www.shakeetawinfrey.com
Dist(s): **APG Sales & Distribution Services**
BCH Fulfillment & Distribution
Bella Distribution
Book Hub, Inc.
Bks. Plus, U.S.A.
C & B Bk. Distribution
Cardinal Pubs. Group
Greenleaf Book Group
Independent Pubs. Group
Lightning Source, Inc.
Midpoint Trade Bks., Inc.
Mint Pubs. Group
New Leaf Distributing Co., Inc.
Partners Bk. Distributing, Inc.
Penton Overseas, Inc.
Quality Bks., Inc.
SCB Distributors
SPD-Small Pr. Distribution
Send The Light Distribution LLC
Two Rivers Distribution.

Wing Dam Pr., *(978-0-9758615)* P.O. Box 200, Ferryville, WI 54628 USA Tel 608-734-3292 (phone/fax)
E-mail: nlichter@mwt.net.

Wing Lane Pr., *(978-0-9792430)* 19 Exeter Ln., Morristown, NJ 07960 USA
E-mail: tazni@optonline.net.

Winged Willow Pr., *(978-0-9664805)* Orders Addr.: P.O. Box 92, Carrboro, NC 27510 USA Tel 919-942-4689; Fax: 919-933-3555
E-mail: info@sudierakusin.com
Web site: http://www.sudierakusin.com
Dist(s): **Parnassus Bk. Distributors.**

WingedChariot Pr. (GBR) *(978-1-905341) Dist. by* **IPG Chicago.**

Winger Publishing, P.O. Box 20991, Juneau, AK 99802 USA
E-mail: wingerpublishing@gmail.com.

Wings Above, *(978-0-9768403)* 1607 Market St., Galveston, TX 77550 USA Tel 409-750-9176.

Wings ePress, Inc., *(978-1-59088; 978-1-59705; 978-1-61309)* 403 Wallace Crt., Richmond, KY 82225 USA; 3000 N. Rock Rd., Newton, KS 67114 Tel 316-283-0981 Do not confuse with companies with the same or similar name in Northhampton, MA, Union, ME, San Antonio, TX
E-mail: mkapp2@roadrunner.com; publisherwingsepress@gmail.com
Web site: http://www.wings-press.com; http://www.books-by-wings-epress.com/
Dist(s): **CreateSpace Independent Publishing Platform**
Smashwords.

Wings, Inc., *(978-0-9705018)* 4790 Caughlin Pkwy., Suite 143, Reno, NV 89509 USA
E-mail: glebeck@wingsnv.com
Web site: http://www.wingsnv.com.

Wings Pr., *(978-0-916727; 978-0-930324; 978-1-60940)* 627 E. Guenther, San Antonio, TX 78210 USA (SAN 209-4975) Tel 210-271-7805 Do not confuse with companies with the same or similar name in Northhampton, MA, UNion, ME, Lusk, WY
E-mail: milligan@wingspress.com
Web site: http://www.wingspress.com
Dist(s): **Brodart Co.**
Ebsco Publishing
Follett School Solutions
Independent Pubs. Group
MyiLibrary
SCB Distributors
ebrary, Inc.

Wings Press, Limited *See* **Wings ePress, Inc.**

Wings-on-Disk *Imprint of* **PassionQuest Technologies, LLC**

Wingspan Pr. *Imprint of* **WingSpan Publishing**

WingSpan Publishing, *(978-1-59594)* P.O. Box 2085, Livermore, CA 94551 USA Toll Free: 866-735-3782; *Imprints:* Wingspan Press (Wingspan Pr)
E-mail: info@wingspanpress.com
Web site: http://www.wingspanpress.com
Dist(s): **BookBaby**
CreateSpace Independent Publishing Platform.

WingSpread Publishers, *(978-1-60066)* Div. of Zur LTD, 820 N. LaSalle, Chicago, IL 60610 USA Tel 312-329-2101; Fax: 312-329-2144; Toll Free: 800-678-8812
E-mail: pbrossman@zurltd.com
Web site: http://www.wingspreadpublishers.com
Dist(s): **Anchor Distributors**
Moody Pubs.
Send The Light Distribution LLC.

Wink Publishing, *(978-0-9702572)* P.O. Box 9957, Richmond, VA 23228 USA.

Winking Moon Pr., *(978-0-9764175)* 4130 S. Splendor Ct., Gilbert, AZ 85297 USA Do not confuse with Winking Moon Press in Cleveland OH.

Winn, Lynnette, *(978-0-9791884)* 2617 Claudia Dr., Leander, TX 78641 USA (SAN 852-7040)
Web site: http://www.butterpodjerome.com.

Winnow Pr., *(978-0-9764726)* 3505 El Dorado Trail, Suite A, Austin, TX 78739 USA (SAN 256-4017) Tel 512-280-4483
E-mail: publisher@winnowpress.com
Web site: http://winnowpress.com.

Winoca Bks. & Media, *(978-0-9755910; 978-0-9789736; 978-1-935619)* 1923 29th St., Suite 2, Lubbock, TX 79411-1515 USA
E-mail: barbaralubbock@gmail.com
Web site: http://www.winocapress.com; www.Bookadelphia.com; www.winoca.com; www.BoldfaceBooks.com
Dist(s): **Parnassus Bk. Distributors.**

Winoca Press *See* **Winoca Bks. & Media**

Winslow's Art, *(978-0-9748505)* P.O. Box 2099, Avalon, CA 90704-2099 USA Tel 310-510-1613 (phone/fax)
E-mail: winslow@catalinaisp.com.

Winsor Corporation *See* **Winsor Learning, Inc.**

Winsor Learning, Inc., *(978-1-891602; 978-1-935450)* 1620 W. Seventh St., Saint Paul, MN 55102 USA Tel 651-222-3922; Fax: 651-222-3969; Toll Free: 800-321-7585
E-mail: sondaysystem@winsorcorp.net
Web site: http://www.sondaysystem.com.

Winstead Pr., Ltd., *(978-0-940787)* 202 Slice Dr., Stamford, CT 06907 USA (SAN 664-6913) Tel 203-322-4941
E-mail: winstead.press@gte.net.

Winter Goose Publishing, *(978-0-9836764; 978-0-9851548; 978-0-9881845; 978-0-9889049; 978-0-9894792; 978-1-941058)* 2701 Del Paso Rd., 130-92, Sacramento, CA 95835 USA Tel 530-771-7058
E-mail: jordan@wintergoosepublishing.com
Web site: wintergoosepublishing.com; graceinspiredpress.com
Dist(s): **Lightning Source, Inc.**

Winter Light Bks., Inc., *(978-0-9797372)* 734 Franklin Ave., No. 675, Garden City, NY 11530-4525 USA (SAN 854-2163)
Web site: http://www.winterlightbooks.com; http://www.winterlightbooks.org.

Wintergreen Orchard Hse., *(978-1-933119; 978-1-936035; 978-1-945520)* Div. of Carnegie Communications, 2 Lan Dr., Suite 100, Westford, MA 01886 USA Tel 978-692-9708; Fax: 978-692-2304
E-mail: info@wintergreenorchardhouse.com; cglennon@carnegiecomm.com
Web site: http://www.wintergreenorchardhouse.com.

Winterhouse Editions, *(978-1-884381)* Orders Addr.: P.O. Box 159, Falls Village, CT 06031 USA Tel 860-824-5040; Fax: 860-824-1065
E-mail: desk@winterhouse.com
Web site: http://www.winterhouse.com
Dist(s): **Chicago Distribution Ctr.**
Columbia Univ. Pr.
SPD-Small Pr. Distribution
Univ. of Chicago Pr.

Wintermantel Group, LLC, The, *(978-0-9767418)* 316 Saddle Back Dr., Saint Louis, MO 63129-3449 USA
Web site: http://www.theangelchildren.com.

Winters Publishing, *(978-0-9625329; 978-1-883651)* Orders Addr.: P.O. Box 501, Greensburg, IN 47240 USA (SAN 298-1645) Tel 812-663-4948 (phone/fax); Toll Free: 800-457-3230; Edit Addr.: 705 E. Washington, Greensburg, IN 47240 USA Do not confuse with Winters Publishing, Wichita, KS
E-mail: tmwinters@juno.com
Web site: http://www.winterspublishing.com
Dist(s): **Partners Bk. Distributing, Inc.**
Partners/West Book Distributors
Send The Light Distribution LLC
Spring Arbor Distributors, Inc.

Winterwolf Publishing, *(978-0-9744831; 978-0-9752711; 978-0-9762471; 978-0-9772632)* Orders Addr.: P.O. Box 1373, Westerville, OH 43086-1373 USA; Edit Addr.: 5446 Highbrook Ct., Westerville, OH 43081 USA
Web site: http://www.winterwolfpublishing.com.

Wipf and Stock *Imprint of* **Wipf & Stock Pubs.**

Wipf & Stock Pubs., *(978-0-9653517; 978-1-55635; 978-1-57910; 978-1-59244; 978-1-59752; 978-1-60608; 978-1-60899; 978-1-61097; 978-1-62032; 978-1-62189; 978-1-62564; 978-1-63087; 978-1-4982; 978-1-5326)* Orders Addr.: 199 W 8th Ave Ste 3, Eugene, OR 97401 USA (SAN 990-3038) Tel 541-344-1528; Fax: 541-344-1506; Edit Addr.: 199 W 8th Ave Ste 3, Eugene, OR 97401 USA Tel 541-344-1528; Fax: 541-344-1506; *Imprints:* Resource Publications (OR) (Resource Pubcns); Wipf and Stock (Wipf and Stock)
Web site: http://wipfandstock.com/; http://slantbooks.com
Dist(s): **CreateSpace Independent Publishing Platform**
MyiLibrary
Spring Arbor Distributors, Inc.

WIPRO, 2 Christie Heights St., Leonia, NJ 07605 USA Tel 201-840-4755.

Wire Rim Bks., *(978-0-9802253; 978-0-615-15357-5; 978-1-935236)* 188 Spring Valley St., Hutto, TX 78634 USA (SAN 913-5960)
E-mail: hmelton@mac.com
Web site: http://www.wirerimbooks.com.

Wisconsin Dept. of Public Instruction, *(978-1-57337)* Orders Addr.: Drawer 179, Milwaukee, WI 53293-0179 USA Tel 608-266-2188; Fax: 608-267-9110; Toll Free: 800-243-8782; Edit Addr.: 125 S. Webster St., Box 7841, Madison, WI 53702 USA
Web site: http://www.dpi.state.wi.us.

†**Wisconsin Historical Society**, *(978-0-87020; 978-1-9766)* 816 State St., Madison, WI 53706 USA (SAN 203-350X) Tel 608-264-6584; Fax: 608-264-6486
E-mail: diane.drexler@wisconsinhistory.org; whspress@wisconsinhistory.org
Web site: http://www.wisconsinhistory.org
Dist(s): **Chicago Distribution Ctr.**
Hoover Institution Pr.
Univ. of Chicago Pr.; *CIP.*

Wisdom Audio-Books *Imprint of* **BloomingFields**

Wisdom Foundation Publishing, *(978-1-932590)* 796 Isenberg St., Suite 19E, Honolulu, HI 96826 USA Tel 808-944-3113; Fax: 808-988-4212
E-mail: wisdomfactors@hawaii.rr.com.

†**Wisdom Pubns.**, *(978-0-86171; 978-1-61429)* 199 Elm St., Somerville, MA 02144 USA (SAN 246-022X) Tel 617-776-7416 ext 24; Fax: 617-776-7841; Toll Free Fax: 800-338-4550 (orders only); Toll Free: 800-462-6420 (orders only)
E-mail: marketing@wisdompubs.org
Web site: http://www.wisdompubs.org
Dist(s): **MyiLibrary**
Simon & Schuster, Inc.; *CIP.*

Wisdom Tales *Imprint of* **World Wisdom, Inc.**

Wisdom Tree (IND) *(978-81-86685; 978-81-8328) Dist. by* **SCB Distributo.**

Wisdom Tree Records *See* **Rivertree Productions, Inc.**

Wisdon Hse. Bks., *(978-0-9984145; 978-0-9984145-1-5)* 412 Parker Rd.,, Mount Airy, NC 27030 USA Tel 336-786-4922; Fax: 336-786-4922
E-mail: dretjdt1987@gmail.com
Web site: www.wisdomhousebooks.com.

Wise Guides, LLC, *(978-0-9768772; 978-1-935237)* 1924 W. Montrose, PMB No. 206, Chicago, IL 60613 USA Toll Free: 866-262-3842
E-mail: info@wiseguidebooks.com
Web site: http://www.wiseguidebooks.com
Dist(s): **Zagat Survey.**

Wise Owl Printing Plus, Incorporated *See* **Deziner Media International**

Wise Pubns. (GBR) *(978-0-7119; 978-0-86001) Dist. by* **Music Sales.**

Wise Words Publications *See* **EPI Bks.**

Wisecracker Press, Inc., *(978-0-9752657)* 2735 April Hill Ln., Dallas, TX 75287 USA
Web site: http://www.wisecrackerpress.com.

Wisehearted Warrior Enterprises, *(978-0-9972797)* 1606 Arrowhead Trail, Neptune Beach, FL 32266 USA Tel 904-307-1941
E-mail: deborajscott@aol.com.

WiseMind Educational Services LLC, *(978-0-692-78691-8; 978-0-692-78692-5)* 1757 Schoolhouse Ct NW, SALEM, OR 97304 USA Tel 541-325-2195.

WiseWoman Pr., *(978-0-945385)* 1521 N. Jantzen Ave., No. 143, Portland, OR 97217 USA (SAN 247-0039) Tel 1-800-603-3005; 1408 NE 65th St., Vancouver, WA 98665 Tel 503 310-0105
E-mail: web@wisewomanpress.com
Web site: http://www.wisewomanpress.com
Dist(s): **DeVorss & Co.**
Lulu Pr., Inc.

Wish Publishing, *(978-1-930546; 978-0-9835754; 978-0-615-74522-0)* P.O. Box 10337, Terre Haute, IN 47801 USA (SAN 253-4320) Fax: 928-447-1836
E-mail: holly@wishpublishing.com
Web site: http://www.wishpublishing.com
Dist(s): **Cardinal Pubs. Group**
Lightning Source, Inc.

Wish You Were Here *Imprint of* **Sierra Pr.**

Wishful Penny Books *See* **See The Wish**

Wishing Star Children's Bks., *(978-0-615-16077-1; 978-0-615-16078-8; 978-0-615-16079-5)* 12755 Eurels Rd., Southgate, MI 48195 USA Tel 734-754-3168
E-mail: mgrazi@wowway.com
Web site: http://www.wishingstarchildrensbooks.com
Dist(s): **Lulu Pr., Inc.**

Wishing U Well Publishing, *(978-0-9769524)* 1560 Gulf Blvd., Unit 1202, Clearwater, FL 33767 USA.

Wishingstone Enterprises *See* **Wishingstone Publishing**

Wishingstone Publishing, *(978-0-9779701)* 1640 Hartley Ave., Henderson, NV 89052 USA Tel 702-612-7325
E-mail: dapwishingstone@earthlink.net.

Witcher Productions, *(978-0-925159; 978-1-55942)* Div. of Marsh Film Enterprises, Inc., P.O. Box 8082, Shawnee Mission, KS 66208 USA Tel 816-523-1059; Fax: 816-333-7421; Toll Free: 800-821-3303 (for orders/customer service only)
E-mail: info@marshmedia.com
Web site: http://www.marshmedia.com
Dist(s): **Follett School Solutions.**

Witherspoon Pr. *Imprint of* **Curriculum Publishing, Presbyterian Church (U. S. A.)**

Within Reach, Inc., *(978-0-9718864)* P.O. Box 6217, Harrisburg, PA 17112 USA Tel 717-657-8689
E-mail: wreach@epix.net
Web site: http://www.boatingsidekicks.com.

WithinU Life Coaching LLC *See* **A Different Kind of Safari LLC**

Witness Impulse *Imprint of* **HarperCollins Pubs.**

Witness Productions, *(978-0-9627653; 978-1-891390)* Box 34, Church St., Marshall, IN 47859 USA Tel 765-597-2487.

Wittman, Natasha, *(978-0-9904091)* 708 Littler Pl., Edmond, OK 73034 USA Tel 405-432-8989
E-mail: natasha2036@gmail.com.

Witty Bit World, Inc., *(978-0-9770548)* 1009 Basil Dr., New Bern, NC 28562 USA
E-mail: deborah@wittybitworld.com
Web site: http://www.wittybitworld.com.

Witty Fools Productions, *(978-0-9745179)* 19 Le Grande Ave., No.14, Greenwich, CT 06830 USA Toll Free: 877-733-0528 (phone/fax)
E-mail: wittyfools@aol.com; fierlp@bww.com
Web site: http://www.wittyfools.com; http://www.prayerlaughterandbroccoli.com.

Witty Publishing, *(978-0-9785571)* 2875 F Northtowne, Box 232, Reno, NV 89512 USA Toll Free: 866-948-8948.

Witwatersrand Univ. Pr. (ZAF) *(978-0-85494; 978-1-86814) Dist. by* **IPG Chicago.**

Wiyd, Lewis, *(978-0-9650637)* 47 Glen Park Rd., East Orange, NJ 07017-1813 USA Tel 973-673-0094; Fax: 973-673-0095.

Wizard Academies, LLC, *(978-0-615-18398-5; 978-0-615-18505-7; 978-0-615-18594-1; 978-0-615-18712-9; 978-0-615-18713-6)* 57485 170th St., Ames, IA 50010-9425 USA
E-mail: rivals@interdrama.com
Web site: http://www.interdrama.com/wiz/
Dist(s): **Lulu Pr., Inc.**

Wizard Academy Pr., *(978-0-9714769; 978-1-932226; 978-0-9987523)* 16621 Crystal Hills Dr., Austin, TX 78737 USA Tel 512-295-5700; Fax: 512-295-5701; Toll Free: 800-425-4769
E-mail: publisher@wizardofads.com; sean@wizardofads.com
Web site: http://www.wizardacademypress.com
Dist(s): **BookBaby.**

Wizard Works, *(978-0-9621543; 978-1-890692)* Orders Addr.: P.O. Box 1125, Homer, AK 99603-1125 USA Toll Free: 877-210-2665
E-mail: wizard@xyz.net
Web site: http://www.xyz.net/~wizard.

Wizarding World Pr., *(978-0-9723936)* 8926 N. Greenwood Ave., Suite 133, Niles, IL 60714 USA
E-mail: wizardingworld@waycoolstuffonline.com
Web site: http://www.wizardingworldpress.com
Dist(s): **SCB Distributors.**

Wizard's Mark Pr., *(978-0-9915720)* 27 Ash Street, Dover, NH 03820 USA Tel 603-866-2466
E-mail: kerrydoherty001@gmail.com.

Wizards of the Coast *Imprint of* **Wizards of the Coast**

Wizards of the Coast, *(978-0-7869; 978-1-57530; 978-1-880992; 978-0-7430)* Subs. of Hasbro, Inc., Orders Addr.: P.O. Box 707, Renton, WA 98057-0709 USA Toll Free: 800-821-8028; Edit Addr.: 1801 Lind Ave., SW, Renton, WA 98055 USA (SAN 299-4410) Tel 425-226-6500; *Imprints:* Mirrorstone (Mirrorstone); Wizards of the Coast (Wiz Coast)
E-mail: angella@wizards.com
Web site: http://www.wizards.com
Dist(s): **Diamond Bk. Distributors**
MyiLibrary
PSI (Publisher Services, Inc.)
Penguin Random Hse. LLC
Random Hse., Inc.
Doherty, Tom Assocs., LLC.

Wizdominc, *(978-0-9764829; 978-0-9767958; 978-0-9768053; 978-0-9778512; 978-0-9785170; 978-0-9786574; 978-0-9820173; 978-0-9840885)* Orders Addr.: 273 Candlelight Dr., Santa Rosa, CA 95403 USA Tel 707-578-1866; Fax: 707-578-4978; Toll Free: 866-607-4510
E-mail: aswan@wizdominc.com
Web site: http://www.wizdominc.com.

WizKids, LLC, *(978-0-9703934; 978-1-931462; 978-1-59041)* Subs. of Topps Europe Ltd., 2002 156th Ave. NE, #300, Bellevue, WA 98007-3827 USA
E-mail: jenny@wizkidsgames.com; customerservice@wizkidsgames.com
Web site: http://www.mageknight.com
Dist(s): **Diamond Bk. Distributors.**

Wms-Ashe, Marcella *See* **Allecram Publishing**

WND Bks, Inc., *(978-0-9746701; 978-0-9767269; 978-0-9778984; 978-0-9790451; 978-0-9792671; 978-1-935071; 978-1-936488; 978-1-938067; 978-1-942475; 978-1-944212; 978-1-944229; 978-1-946918)* Orders Addr.: 845 Alder Creek, Medford, OR 97504 USA (SAN 255-7304) Tel 541-474-1776; Fax: 541-474-1770; Edit Addr.: 2020 Pennsylvania Ave., NW No. 351, Washington, DC 20006 USA Tel 571-612-8600; Fax: 571-612-8619; *Imprints:* Kids Ahead Books (Kids Ahead)
E-mail: marketing@wndbooks.com; gstone@wnd.com
Web site: http://www.wnd.com; http://www.wndbooks.com
Dist(s): **Follett School Solutions**
McLemore, Hollern & Assocs.
Midpoint Trade Bks., Inc.
MyiLibrary
Quality Bks., Inc.
REKO
ebrary, Inc.

Wobble Hill Pr., *(978-0-9975892)* 2400 Johnson Ave., Bronx, NY 10463 USA Tel 347-907-2292
E-mail: estherk777@gmail.com
Web site: wobblehillpress.com.

Wobblefoot Ltd., *(978-0-9747149)* 1662 Mars Ave., Lakewood, OH 44107-3825 USA
E-mail: wblft1@sbcglobal.net
Web site: http://wobblefoot.com.

Wocto Publishing, *(978-1-934867)* 7486 La Jolla Blvd., Pmb 559, La Jolla, CA 92037 USA (SAN 855-2754) Tel 858-551-5585; Fax: 858-731-4082; Toll Free: 888-551-5010
E-mail: lin@wocto.com; sales@wocto.com
Web site: http://www.wocto.com.

Wohlers Assocs., Inc., *(978-0-9754429; 978-0-9913332)* OakRidge Business Pk., 1511 River Oak Dr., Fort Collins, CO 80525-5537 USA
Web site: http://www.wohlersassociates.com.

Wold Creative Group, *(978-0-615-24135-7)* 1392 S. 1100 E., Suite 201, Salt Lake City, UT 84105 USA Tel 801-783-4502
Web site: http://www.woldcreative.com
Dist(s): **Lulu Pr., Inc.**

Wold, Kelly, *(978-0-9768944)* 398 Ricketts Rd. Apt. D, Monterey, CA 93940-7420 USA
E-mail: kmwold@hotmail.com.

Wolf Creek Publishing, *(978-0-9768983)* 193 Tenby Chase Dr., Apt. S-233, Delran, NJ 08075 USA
Web site: http://www.photosfromthewild.com.

Wolf Jump Publications, *(978-0-9820440)* 2217 Princess Anne St., Suite 101-1A c/o R.R.R., Fredericksburg, VA 22401 USA
E-mail: rr@marstel-day.com.

Wolf Pirate Publishing, *(978-0-9798372; 978-0-9822343)* 337 Lost Lake Dr., Divide, CO 80814 USA
E-mail: cmrudy337@gmail.com
Web site: http://www.wolf-pirate.com.

Wolfenden, *(978-0-9642521; 978-0-9786951; 978-0-9973513)* 780-a Redwood Dr., Garberville, CA 95542 USA (SAN 298-4571)
E-mail: dai@asis.com
Web site: http://wolfendenpublishing.com.

Wolfhound Pr. (IRL) *(978-0-86327; 978-0-905473; 978-0-9503454) Dist. by* **Irish Bks Media.**

Wolfhound Pr. (IRL) *(978-0-86327; 978-0-905473; 978-0-9503454) Dist. by* **Interlink Pub.**

Wolfhound Pr. (IRL) *(978-0-86327; 978-0-905473; 978-0-9503454) Dist. by* **Irish Amer Bk.**

Wolfmont, LLC, *(978-0-9778402; 978-1-60364)* 238 Park Dr., NE, Ranger, GA 30734 USA Fax: 702-543-8386; P.O. Box 205, Ranger, GA 30734; *Imprints:* Honey Locust Press (Honey Locust)
E-mail: tony@wolfmont.com; editor@honeylocustpress.com
Web site: http://www.wolfmont.com; http://www.honeylocustpress.com
Dist(s): **Smashwords.**

Wolfmont Publishing *See* **Wolfmont, LLC**

Wolfs Corner Publishing, *(978-0-9779921)* 20 Primrose Ln., Sparta, NJ 07871 USA (SAN 856-4191) Tel 973-579-5305
E-mail: jmd_inc007@hotmail.com
Web site: http://www.wolfscornerpublishing.com.

Wollaston Pr., *(978-0-9657005)* Div. of Ctr. for Learning Abilities, 4013 Coyte Ct., Marietta, GA 30062 USA Tel 678-318-3518; Fax: 208-474-9521
E-mail: morewords@comcast.net.

Wolsak & Wynn Pubs., Ltd. (CAN) *(978-0-919897; 978-1-894987; 978-1-928088) Dist. by* **IPG Chicago.**

Wolter, Russel II, *(978-0-692-84564-6)* 7200 Carmel Valley Rd., Carmel, CA 93923 USA Tel 831-915-6798
E-mail: rwolterii@yahoo.com
Dist(s): **Independent Pub.**

Woman's Missionary Union, *(978-0-936625; 978-1-56309; 978-1-59669; 978-1-62591)* Orders Addr.: c/o Carol Causey, P.O. Box 830010, Birmingham, AL 35283 USA (SAN 699-7015) Tel 205-991-8100; Fax: 205-995-4825; Toll Free: 800-968-7301; Edit Addr.: 100 Missionary Ridge, Birmingham, AL 35242 USA (SAN 699-7023)
E-mail: cwhite@wmu.org
Web site: http://www.wmu.com
Dist(s): **Send The Light Distribution LLC.**

Wombacher, Michael, *(978-0-9713033)* 2412 Valley St., Berkeley, CA 94702-2136 USA
E-mail: michael_wombacher@excite.com
Web site: http://www.doggonegood.org.

Women & Addiction Counseling & Educational Services, *(978-0-9663144)* 43522 Modena Dr., Temecula, CA 92592-9235 USA Tel 951-303-0235 (phone/fax)
E-mail: info@wacespublishing.com
Web site: http://www.wacespublishing.com.

Women in Aviation, International, *(978-0-9749190)* 3647 State Route 503 S., W Alexandria, OH 45381-9354 USA
Web site: http://www.wai.org.

Women's Pr., Ltd., The (GBR) *(978-0-7043) Dist. by* **Trafalgar.**

Wonder Chess LLC, *(978-0-9771787)* 2622 10th Ave E., Seattle, WA 98102-3901 USA
E-mail: info@wonderchess.com
Web site: http://www.wonderchess.com.

Wonder Forge, Inc., *(978-0-9797123; 978-0-9819248; 978-1-935595)* 300 E. Pike St., Seattle, WA 98122 USA
E-mail: brant@thewonderforge.com
Web site: http://www.thewonderforge.com.

Wonder Forge LLC, The *See* **Wonder Forge, Inc.**

Wonder Readers *Imprint of* **Capstone Press of Coughlan Cos.**

Wonder Toast Arts, Incorporated *See* **WonderToast**

Wonder Workshop, *(978-1-56919)* Div. of Stephens Group, Inc., 1123 Brookstone Blvd., Mount Juliet, TN 37122-3274 USA Toll Free: 800-627-6874.

Wonderbooks Publishing, *(978-0-9773809)* P.O. Box 770741, Orlando, FL 32877 USA (SAN 257-4535)
Web site: http://www.wonderbookspublishing.com.

Wonderful Publishing, *(978-0-9798421)* 150 Brewster Rd., Scarsdale, NY 10583 USA (SAN 854-5006)
Web site: http://www.madelineart.com
Dist(s): **Partners Pubs. Group, Inc.**

Wonderstrand Pr., *(978-0-9818295)* P.O. Box 156, North Eastham, MA 02651-0156 USA (SAN 856-6585) Tel 508-240-0432; Fax: 508-240-0432
E-mail: michael@successonyourownterms.com
Web site: http://www.wonderstrandpress.com.

WonderToast, *(978-0-9761606)* Orders Addr.: 3075 E. Bates Ave., Denver, CO 80210 USA Tel 303-330-4770
E-mail: anna@wondertoast.com
Web site: http://www.wondertoast.com.

Wood Designs, Inc., *(978-0-9729454)* P.O. Box 1790, New Waverly, TX 77358-1790 USA Toll Free Fax: 877-612-8306; Toll Free: 877-612-8306; *Imprints:* MomGeek.com (MomGeek.com)
E-mail: sales@pegrack.com
Web site: http://www.flamencoguide.com.

Wood, Ella Sue, *(978-0-9774937)* 3229 Regatta Pointe Ct., Midlothian, VA 23112 USA.

Wood, Katy Lynn, *(978-0-692-88033-3; 978-0-692-88034-0)* 6620 Finecrest Dr., COLORADO SPRINGS, CO 80923 USA Tel 720-822-0598
E-mail: jeffwcrawford5+LVP0003688@gmail.com; jeffwcrawford5+LVP0003688@gmail.com.

Wood Lake Publishing, Inc. (CAN) *(978-0-919599; 978-0-929032; 978-0-929599; 978-1-55145; 978-1-895562) Dist. by* **Westminster John Knox.**

Woodberry International Publishing, *(978-0-615-73339-5; 978-0-615-73423-1; 978-0-9916537)* 3758 Riverchase way, Decatur, GA 30034 USA Tel 4042415864.

†Woodbine Hse., *(978-0-933149; 978-1-890627; 978-1-60613)* 6510 Bells Mill Rd., Bethesda, MD 20817 USA (SAN 630-4052) Tel 301-897-3570; Fax: 301-897-5838; Toll Free: 800-843-7323
E-mail: info@woodbinehouse.com
Web site: http://www.woodbinehouse.com; *CIP.*

Woodburn Graphics, Inc., *(978-0-9707547)* P.O. Box 490, Terre Haute, ID 47807 USA Tel 812-232-0323; Fax: 812-232-2733; Toll Free: 800-457-0674
E-mail: len@woodburngraphics.com
Web site: http://www.woodburngraphics.com.

Wooded Hill Productions, *(978-1-886635)* Orders Addr.: 7480 Esplin Way, Flagstaff, AZ 86004 USA Tel 928-522-0058 (phone/fax)
E-mail: sig@boloz.com; sigmund.boloz@nau.edu
Web site: http://www.boloz.com.

Wooden Nickel Pr., *(978-0-615-25177-6; 978-0-9882891)* 2189 N. 55th St., Milwaukee, WI 53208 USA
Web site: http://www.woodennickelpress.com.

Wooden Shoe Pr., *(978-0-9762852)* N3566 Cty. Rd., GG, Hancock, WI 54943 USA Do not confuse with Wooden Shoe Press in Philadelphia, PA
E-mail: woodenshoepress@yahoo.com
Web site: http://www.woodenshoepress.com.

WoodenBoat Pubns., *(978-0-937822; 978-1-934982)* P.O. Box 78, Brooklin, ME 04616 USA Tel 207-359-4651; Fax: 207-359-2058; Toll Free: 800-273-7447
E-mail: books@woodenboat.com; wbstore@woodenboat.com
Web site: http://www.woodenboat.com.

Woodglen Publishing LLC, *(978-0-9827951)* P.O. Box 122, Califon, NJ 07830 USA Tel 908-638-5338; Fax: 908-638-0368
E-mail: stephanie@woodglenpublishing.com
Web site: http://www.woodglenpublishing.com
Dist(s): **Bookmasters Distribution.**

Woodland Health Books *See* **Woodland Publishing, Inc.**

Woodland Pr., *(978-0-9755822)* 605 Timber Ln., Lake Forest, IL 60045-3117 USA Tel 847-295-3514; 847-924-0324 Do not confuse with companies with the same name in Minneapolis, MN, Lapeer MI, Salt Lake City, UT.

Woodland Pr., LLC, *(978-0-9724867; 978-0-9793236; 978-0-9824939; 978-0-9829937; 978-0-9852640; 978-0-9912301)* 118 Woodland, Suite 1102, Chapmanville, WV 25508 USA (SAN 254-9999) Tel 304-752-7500; Fax: 304-752-9002 Do not confuse with companies with the same or similar names in Minneapolis, MN, Lapeer, MI, Salt Lake City, UT, Florance, AL, Moscow, ID
E-mail: info@woodlandpress.com; woodlandpresslc@mac.com; fkeithdavis@me.com
Web site: http://www.woodlandpress.com
Dist(s): **New Day Christian Distributors Gifts, Inc.**
Quality Bks., Inc.
West Virginia Book Co., The
Woodland Distribution.

Woodland Publishing, Inc., *(978-0-913923; 978-1-58054; 978-1-885670)* Orders Addr.: 1500 Kearns Blvd., Park City, UT 84060-7226 USA (SAN 286-9063) Toll Free: 800-777-2665
E-mail: hpackham@woodlandpublishing.com
Web site: http://www.woodlandpublishing.com
Dist(s): **Integral Yoga Pubns.**
New Leaf Distributing Co., Inc.
Nutri-Bks. Corp.
Royal Pubns., Inc.

Woodland Scenics, *(978-1-887436)* Div. of Osment Models, Inc., Orders Addr.: P.O. Box 98, Linn Creek, MO 65052 USA Tel 573-346-5555; Toll Free: 800-346-6642; Edit Addr.: 101 E. Valley Dr., Linn Creek, MO 65052 USA
E-mail: sales@woodlandscenics.com.

Woodruff, David Roberts, *(978-0-9716806)* 4075 Carmel View Rd., No.9, San Deigo, CA 92130 USA
E-mail: drbts@att.net.

Woodruff, Paul, *(978-0-9764327)* 58048 Inglewood Ln., Glenwood, IA 51534 USA.

Woods, Emmett L., *(978-0-615-12589-3)* 4016 Monterey Ct., Montgomery, AL 36116 USA Tel 334-288-1380.

Woods N' Water, Incorporated *See* **Woods N' Water Pr., Inc.**

Woods N' Water Pr., Inc., *(978-0-9707493; 978-0-9722804; 978-0-9769233; 978-0-9795131; 978-0-9820414; 978-0-9828228; 978-0-615-38124-4)* Orders Addr.: P.O. Box 10, South New Berlin, NY 13843 USA (SAN 254-3869) Tel 607-548-4011; Fax: 607-548-4013; Toll Free: 800-652-7527; Edit Addr.: 3312 State Hwy. 8, South New Berlin, NY 13843 USA Tel 607-548-4011; Fax: 607-548-4013; Toll Free: 800-652-7527
E-mail: kate@fiduccia.com
Web site: http://www.woodsnwaterpress.com; http://www.atabooks.com
Dist(s): **Cardinal Pubs. Group.**

Woodstocker Books/Arthur Schwartz & Company, *(978-1-879504)* 15 Meads Mountain Rd., Woodstock, NY 12498-1016 USA (SAN 630-0464) Tel 845-679-4024; Fax: 845-679-4093; Toll Free: 800-669-9080 (orders only)
E-mail: woodstockerbooks@woodstockerbooks.com
Web site: http://www.aschwartzbooks.com
Dist(s): **Antique Collectors' Club**
National Bk. Network.

Woolfolk Publications *See* **Gye Nyame Hse.**

Woolley Family Studios, *(978-0-9909391)* 34 Hadley St., Cambridge, MA 02140 USA Tel 310-909-4329
E-mail: jakegpanda@gmail.com
Web site: www.endangeredfiles.com.

Wooster Bk. Co., The, *(978-1-888683; 978-1-59098)* 205 W. Liberty St., Wooster, OH 44691-4831 USA Tel 330-262-1688; Fax: 330-264-9753; Toll Free: 800-982-6651 (800-WUBook-1)
E-mail: mail@woosterbook.com
Web site: http://www.woosterbook.com.

Wo-Pila Publishing, *(978-1-886340)* Orders Addr.: P.O. Box 8966, Erie, PA 16505-0966 USA Tel 814-868-5331; Fax: 814-868-1711; Toll Free: 888-567-8267; Edit Addr.: 3324 Charlotte St., Erie, PA 16508-2224 USA
E-mail: WopilaPublishing@aol.com
Web site: http://www.MannyTwofeathers.com.

Word Aflame Pr., *(978-0-912315; 978-0-932581; 978-1-56722; 978-0-7577)* Subs. of Pentecostal Publishing Hse., 8855 Dunn Rd., Hazelwood, MO 63042 USA (SAN 212-0046) Tel 314-837-7300; Fax: 314-837-6574
E-mail: pph@upci.org
Web site: http://www.upci.org/pph.

Word Among Us Pr., *(978-0-932085; 978-1-59325)* 7115 Guilford Dr. Suite 100, Frederick, MD 21704 USA (SAN 686-4651) Tel 301-831-1262; Fax: 301-831-1188; Toll Free: 800-775-9673
E-mail: pmm@wall.org
Web site: http://www.wau.org
Dist(s): **Spring Arbor Distributors, Inc.**

Word Assocs., Inc., *(978-0-939153; 978-1-57265)* 3226 Robincrest Dr., Northbrook, IL 60062 USA (SAN 679-7792) Tel 847-291-1101; Fax: 847-291-0931
E-mail: microlm@aol.com
Web site: http://www.wordassociates.com.

Word Association Pubs., *(978-1-891231; 978-1-932205; 978-1-59571; 978-1-63385)* 205 Fifth Ave., Tarentum, PA

15084 USA Tel 724-226-4526; Fax: 724-226-3974; Toll Free: 800-827-7903
E-mail: publish@wordassociation.com
Web site: http://www.wordassociation.com
Dist(s): **Chicago Distribution Ctr.**

Word Distribution *See* **Word Entertainment**

Word Entertainment, *(978-0-9644619; 978-1-933876)* 25 Music Sq. W., Nashville, TN 37203 USA Tel 615-726-7900; Toll Free Fax: 800-671-6601; Toll Free: 800-876-9673; *Imprints:* Word Music (Word Music)
E-mail: matt.taylor@wordentertainment.com
Web site: http://www.wordentertainment.com
Dist(s): **Christian Bk. Distributors.**

Word For Word Publishing Co., *(978-1-889732)* 144 Quincy St. Apt. 1, Brooklyn, NY 11216-1393 USA; *Imprints:* A & E Sivells Publications (A & E Sivells Pubns)
E-mail: word4wrd@aol.com.

Word Gift Pubns., *(978-0-9788381)* 6641 Cty. Rd. 912, Joshua, TX 76058 USA (SAN 851-7223)
E-mail: peregrina@wordgift.org
Web site: http://www.wordgift.org.

Word Music *Imprint of* **Word Entertainment**

Word of Life Fellowship, Inc., *(978-1-931235; 978-1-935475)* Orders Addr.: P.O. Box 600, Schroon Lake, NY 12870-0600 USA Fax: 518-494-6312; Toll Free: 888-932-5827; Edit Addr.: 71 Olmstedville Rd., Pottersville, NY 12860 USA Do not confuse with Word of Life Fellowship, Sand Springs, OK
E-mail: timf@wol.org; DReichard@wol.org
Web site: http://www.wol.org.

Word of Mouth Bks. *Imprint of* **KA Productions, LLC**

Word of Mouth Pr., *(978-0-615-24213-2; 978-0-578-03631-1; 978-0-578-05051-5; 978-0-578-05113-0; 978-0-578-12825-2)* 406 Shelby St., Kingsport, TN 37660 USA Tel 423-245-1199
E-mail: electragraphics@earthlink.net.

Word on Da Street Publishing, *(978-0-615-52643-0; 978-0-615-64869-9; 978-0-9885056)* 252 W. Westfield Ave. 252 W. Westfield Ave, Roselle Park, NJ 07204 USA Tel 973-445-1690
E-mail: llperry803@gmail.com.

Word Prodns., *(978-0-9728590; 978-0-9765010; 978-0-9827998; 978-0-9909245; 978-0-9978373)* Orders Addr.: P.O. Box 11865, Albuquerque, NM 87192 USA Tel 505-750-2748; *Imprints:* KID-E Books (KID-E Bks)
E-mail: media@wordproductions.org
Web site: http://www.wordproductions.org
Dist(s): **CreateSpace Independent Publishing Platform.**

Word Prostitute, *(978-0-9728465)* 3434 SE 13th Ave., Portland, OR 97202 USA
E-mail: kalabjoster@wordprostitute.com
Web site: http://www.wordprostitute.com.

Word Riot Pr., *(978-0-9728200; 978-0-9779343)* P.O. Box 414, Middletown, NJ 07748 USA
E-mail: editor@wordriot.org
Web site: http://www.wordriot.org
Dist(s): **Pathway Bk. Service.**

Word Seed Publishing, *(978-0-9755232)* 650 NE 2nd St., Hermiston, OR 97838 USA Tel 541-567-0886; Fax: 541-481-7500
E-mail: hashcraftz1@charter.net.

Word Supremacy Pr., *(978-0-9747231)* 910 St., Paul St., No. C, Baltimore, MD 21202 USA Tel 443-414-4600; Fax: 877-504-3140
E-mail: taalam@aol.com
Web site: http://www.taalamacey.com.

Word Weaver Bks., Inc., *(978-0-9670600)* 9743 W. Bray Creek St., Star, ID 83669-5815 USA
E-mail: tidegirl32@aol.com
Web site: http://www.wordweaverbooks.com.

Word Weaver Media *See* **Portable COO, The**

Word with You Pr., A, *(978-0-9843064; 978-0-9829094; 978-0-9884646)* 802 S. Tremont St., Oceanside, CA 92054 USA Tel 760-500-5409; 310 E. A St. Suite B, Moscow, ID 83843 Tel 760-500-5409
E-mail: thom@awordwithyoupress.com
Web site: http://awordwithyoupress.com.

Word Wright International *See* **WordWright.biz, Inc.**

Wordcraft of Oregon, LLC, *(978-1-877655; 978-0-9964371)* P.O. Box 3235, La Grande, OR 97850 USA Do not confuse with Wordcraft, Oakland, CA
E-mail: info@wordcraftoforegon.com
Web site: http://www.wordcraftoforegon.com.

WordFire, Incorporated *See* **WordFire Pr.**

WordFire Pr. *Imprint of* **WordFire Pr.**

WordFire Pr., *(978-0-9673548; 978-1-61475; 978-1-68057)* P.O. Box 1840, Monument, CO 80132-1840 USA; *Imprints:* WordFire Press (WrdFire Pr)
E-mail: reb@wordfire.com
Web site: http://wordfire.com; http://wordfirepress.com.

WordMaster Publishing, *(978-0-9740410)* 4317 W. Farrand Rd., Clio, MI 48420 USA (SAN 255-3325) Tel 810-686-2047; Fax: 810-564-9929
E-mail: wordmasterpub@aol.com.

Wordminder Pr., *(978-0-9729103)* Orders Addr.: 1008 Norview Ave., Norfolk, VA 23513-3410 USA Tel 757-853-4775
E-mail: sma@wordminderpress.com; wp@wordminderpress.com
Web site: http://www.wordminderpress.com
Dist(s): **CreateSpace Independent Publishing Platform.**

WordPlay Multimedia, LLC, *(978-0-9755444)* Orders Addr.: P.O. Box 9303, Jacksonville, FL 32208 USA Tel 904-683-8032
E-mail: jjfrederick98@aol.com
Web site: http://www.frederickpreston.com
Dist(s): **A & B Distributors & Pubs. Group.**

Words & Music, *(978-0-9800880; 978-0-615-15540-1)* 13967 Amber Pl., San Diego, CA 92130 USA Do not confuse with Words & Music, Gig Harbor, CA
E-mail: info@talesalive.com
Web site: http://www.talesalive.com.

Words & Pictures Publishing, Inc., *(978-0-9621280)* P.O. Box 61444, Honolulu, HI 96839 USA (SAN 250-9326) Tel 808-955-4742; Fax: 808-951-6541
E-mail: gecko@aloha.net
Web site: http://www.brucehale.com
Dist(s): **Booklines Hawaii, Ltd.**
Sunbelt Pubns., Inc.

Words of Essence Publishing, *(978-0-9768133)* P.O. Box 13182, Durham, NC 27709 USA Tel 919-624-4138
E-mail: godslove232@yahoo.com
Web site: http://www.wordsofessence.com.

words4u, *(978-0-9740419)* P.O. Box 641257, San Francisco, CA 94164-1257 USA
E-mail: info@words4u.com
Web site: http://www.words4u.com.

WordsBright, *(978-1-940229)* 501-I S. Reino Rd, No. 365, Newbury Park, CA 91320 USA Tel 805-413-4525
E-mail: contactus@wordsbright.com
Web site: www.wordsbright.com
Dist(s): **Pathway Bk. Service.**

Wordshed, *(978-0-942684)* 5118 Glendale St., Duluth, MN 55804-1107 USA (SAN 239-6246) Tel 218-525-3266.

Wordsmith Bks., *(978-1-882646)* Orders Addr.: 157 Chris St., Hollidaysburg, PA 16648 USA Tel 814-317-5314 Do not confuse with Wordsmith Bks. in Auburn, AL
E-mail: catalano.tom@gmail.com.

Wordsmith Pr., *(978-1-893972)* 11462 East Ln., Whitmore Lake, MI 48189 USA Tel 810-231-5435
E-mail: info@thewordsmithpress.com
Web site: http://www.thewordsmithpress.com.

Wordsmiths, *(978-0-9632774; 978-1-886061)* 1355 Ferry Rd., Grants Pass, OR 97526 USA Tel 541-476-3080; Fax: 541-474-9756 Do not confuse with the Wordsmiths in Evergreen, CO
E-mail: frodej@chatlink.com
Web site: http://www.jsgrammar.com.

Wordsong *Imprint of* **Boyds Mills Pr.**

Wordsworth Editions, Ltd. (GBR) *(978-1-85326; 978-1-84022; 978-1-84870) Dist. by* **LBMayAssocs.**

WORDSWORTH Publishing Co., *(978-0-9672491; 978-0-9754351)* Orders Addr.: P.O. Box 7132, Santa Rosa, CA 95407 USA Tel 707-829-2316 (phone/fax); Edit Addr.: 2524 S. Edison St., Graton, CA 95444 USA
E-mail: wwinfo@getyourwordsworth.com
Web site: http://www.getyourwordsworth.com.

WordThunder Pubns., *(978-0-9745268; 978-1-59790)* P.O. Box 540931, Merritt Island, FL 32954 USA (SAN 256-3770)
E-mail: books@wordthunder.com
Web site: http://wordthunder.com/books/.

Wordwhittler Bks., *(978-0-9895487)* 3073 Cypress Creek Dr. N., Ponte Vedra Beach, FL 32082 USA Tel 904-285-8531
E-mail: sscalfee@aol.com.

Wordwindow LLC, *(978-0-9774484)* 2125 Jackson Bluff Rd. Apt. V-204, Tallahassee, FL 32304 USA Toll Free: 877-967-3946
Web site: http://www.wordwindow.com.

WordWorks Publishing, *(978-0-9831557)* 1081 Rosedale Dr., Atlanta, GA 30306 USA Tel 404-664-5256 Do not confuse with WordWorks Publishing in Austin, TX, Westfield, IN
E-mail: laurelannd@gmail.com
Dist(s): **BookBaby.**

Wordwright Communications, *(978-0-9718838)* 4900 Randall Pkwy. Ste. F, Wilmington, NC 28403-2831 USA Toll Free: 888-235-0248.

WordWright.biz, Inc., *(978-0-9700615; 978-0-9713832; 978-0-9717868; 978-1-932196; 978-1-934335)* P.O. Box 1785, Georgetown, TX 78627 USA Fax: 512-260-3080 (phone/fax); *Imprints:* Legacy (Lgcy TX); One Night Books (One Night Bks)
E-mail: joan@wordwright.biz; snwriter@earthlink.net; jnwriter@aol.com
Web site: http://www.wordwright.biz.

Workhouse Road Productions, *(978-0-615-74249-6; 978-0-615-78551-6; 978-0-692-41154-4; 978-0-692-55532-3)* 1321 S. CLOVERDALE AVE, LOS ANGELES, CA 90019 USA Tel 323-528-7495
E-mail: Bettykbynum@gmail.com
Web site: www.theimagirlcollection.com
Dist(s): **Midpoint Trade Bks., Inc.**

Working Parents, LLC, *(978-0-9711040)* P.O. Box 715, Santa Clara, CA 95052-0715 USA Tel 408-554-0280 (phone/fax)
E-mail: info@workingparents.com
Web site: http://www.workingparents.com.

Working Title Publishing, *(978-1-59344; 978-0-9776440)* P.O. Box 384, Lodi, CA 95241 USA
Web site: http://www.workingtitlepublishing.com.

Working Words & Graphics *See* **Lockman, James Consulting**

†**Workman Publishing Co., Inc.,** *(978-0-7611; 978-0-89480; 978-0-911104; 978-1-56305; 978-1-5235)* Orders Addr.: 225 Varick St., New York, NY 10014-4381 USA (SAN 203-2821) Tel 212-254-5900; Fax: 212-254-8098; Toll Free: 800-722-7202
E-mail: info@workman.com
Web site: http://www.workman.com; *CIP.*

World Ahead Media *See* **WND Bks, Inc.**

World Almanac Bks. *Imprint of* **Facts On File, Inc.**

World Almanac Library *Imprint of* **Stevens, Gareth Publishing LLLP**

World Audience Pubs., *(978-0-9788086; 978-1-934209; 978-0-9820540; 978-1-935444)* 303 Pk. Ave. S., Suite 1440, New York, NY 10010 USA
E-mail: worldaudience@gmail.com; mstefanstrozier@gmail.com
Web site: http://www.worldaudience.org; http://www.worldaudience.mobi; http://www.worldaudience.co.uk.

World Awake Bks., *(978-0-615-26795-1)* 15508 W. Bell Rd., Suite 101,, Surprise, AZ 85374 USA.

†**World Bank Pubns.,** *(978-0-8213; 978-1-4648)* Orders Addr.: P.O. Box 960, Herndon, VA 20172-0960 USA Toll Free: 800-645-7247; Edit Addr.: 1818 H St., NW, Mail Stop: U11-1104, Washington, DC 20433 USA (SAN 219-0648) Tel 703-661-1580; 202-473-1000 (Head Office); Fax: 202-614-1237
E-mail: books@worldbank.org
Web site: http://www.worldbank.org/publications
Dist(s): **Bernan Assocs.**
Ebsco Publishing
Independent Pubs. Group
MyiLibrary
Oxford Univ. Pr., Inc.
Rowman & Littlefield Publishers, Inc.
ebrary, Inc.; *CIP.*

World Bk., Inc., *(978-0-7166)* Div. of Scott Fetzer Co., 233 N. Michigan, Suite 2000, Chicago, IL 60601 USA (SAN 201-4815) Tel 312-729-5800; Fax: 312-729-5600; 312-729-5614; Toll Free Fax: 800-433-9330 (US orders); 888-690-4002 (Canadian orders); Toll Free: 800-975-3250 (US orders); 800-967-5325; 800-837-5365 (Canadian orders)
Web site: http://www.worldbook.com
Dist(s): **MyiLibrary.**

World CARP, *(978-0-9722946)* 4 W. 43rd St., New York, NY 10036-7408 USA
E-mail: yyk21@worldcarp.org
Web site: http://www.worldcarp.org.

World Cycling Pr., *(978-0-9745842)* 3910 Chapman St., San Diego, CA 92110-5694 USA Tel 619-224-1050; Fax: 619-224-0530
E-mail: team_mallory@hotmail.com.

World Famous Children's Bks., *(978-0-9725398)* 4455 Torrance Blvd, No. 153, Torrance, CA 90503 USA
Web site: http://www.worldfamouschildrensbooks.com
Dist(s): **Quality Bks., Inc.**

World Health Organization, *(978-0-11)* Orders Addr.: 49 Sheridan Ave., Albany, NY 12210 USA (SAN 221-6310) Tel 518-436-9686; Fax: 518-436-7433; Edit Addr.: Av Appia, Geneva, 1211 CHE Tel 41-22) 7912111; Fax: 41-22) 7910746
E-mail: publications@who.int
Web site: http://www.who.ch
Dist(s): **Balogh International, Inc.**
Bernan Assocs.
MyiLibrary
Stylus Publishing, LLC
Women Ink.

World Leisure Marketing Ltd (GBR) *(978-1-84006; 978-1-899026) Dist. by* **Midpt Trade.**

World Library Pubns., *(978-0-937690; 978-1-58459)* Div. of J. S. Paluch Co., Inc., 3708 River Rd. Suite 400, Franklin Park, IL 60131-2158 USA (SAN 203-0306) Tel 847-233-2767; Toll Free Fax: 888-957-3291; Toll Free: 800-621-5197
E-mail: wlpcs@jspaluch.com
Web site: http://www.wlpmusic.com
Dist(s): **Ingram Publisher Services**
Spring Arbor Distributors, Inc.

World Nouveau, *(978-0-9828865; 978-1-938208)* P.O. Box 571, Torrance, CA 90508 USA Tel 310-776-5510
E-mail: WorldNouveau@Gmail.com
Web site: http://www.WorldNouveau.com.

World of Angels, A, *(978-0-9743964)* 97 Main St., Belfast, ME 04915 USA Tel 207-338-8900
E-mail: aworldofangels@prexar.com
Web site: http://www.aworldofangels.com.

World of Empowerment *See* **Twin Flame Productions**

World of Imagination, *(978-0-9761228)* 200 N. Maryland Ave., Suite 101, Glendale, CA 91206 USA Tel 818-547-5541; Fax: 818-543-1889; Toll Free: 800-266-5255.

World of Learning Publishing *See* **Swift Learning Resources**

World of Reading, Ltd., P.O. Box 13092, Atlanta, GA 30324-0092 USA Tel 404-233-4042; Fax: 404-237-5511; Toll Free: 800-729-3703.

World of Whimsy Productions, LLC, *(978-0-9702675)* 409 N. Pacific Coast Hwy., No. 594, Redondo Beach, CA 90277 USA (SAN 256-1077) Fax: 310-542-9297; Toll Free: 1-888-4-WHIMSY
E-mail: info@worldofwhimsy.com
Web site: http://worldofwhimsy.com.

World Pubns. Group, Inc., *(978-0-7669; 978-0-9640034; 978-1-57215; 978-0-7429; 978-1-4132; 978-1-4279; 978-1-4376; 978-1-4513; 978-1-4643; 978-1-4785)* Orders Addr.: P.O. Box 509, East Bridgewater, MA 02333 USA (SAN 631-7014); *Imprints:* JG Press (JG Pr)
E-mail: sales@wrldpub.net
Web site: http://www.wrldpub.com
Dist(s): **Hachette Bk. Group.**

World Publications, Incorporated *See* **World Pubns. Group, Inc.**

World Quest Learning, *(978-1-933248)* P.O. Box 654, Lewis Center, OH 43035 USA Tel 740-548-3857; Toll Free Fax: 866-722-7521; Toll Free: 866-722-7520
E-mail: info@worldquestlearning.com
Web site: http://www.worldquestlearning.com.

World Revealed Ink, *(978-0-615-47813-5; 978-0-9854594)* 5419 Hollywood Blvd. C226, Los Angeles, CA 90027 USA Tel 708-415-6753
E-mail: worldrevealed@gmail.com
Dist(s): **MyiLibrary.**

World Thoughts Publishing, Co., *(978-0-9711018)* P.O. Box 3206, Saint Augustine, FL 32084-3206 USA
E-mail: beebes@aug.com
Web site: http://www.energeticawakening.com; http://www.worldthoughts.com.

World Tribune Pr., *(978-0-915678; 978-1-932911; 978-1-935523; 978-1-944604; 978-1-946635)* Orders Addr.: 8811 Aviation Blvd., Inglewood, CA 90301 USA Tel 310-337-0055; Fax: 310-642-4625; Toll Free: 800-626-1313; Edit Addr.: 606 Wilshire Blvd., Santa Monica, CA 90401 USA (SAN 683-230X) Tel 310-260-8900; Fax: 310-260-8910
E-mail: dmcneill@sgi-usa.org
Dist(s): **PCE International.**

World Wide Distributors, Limited *See* **Island Heritage Publishing**

World Wisdom, Inc., *(978-0-941532; 978-1-933316; 978-1-935493; 978-1-936597; 978-1-937786)* Orders Addr.: P.O. Box 2682, Bloomington, IN 47402-2682 USA (SAN 239-1406) Tel 812-330-3232; Fax: 812-333-1642; Toll Free: 888-992-6651; Edit Addr.: 1501 E. Hillside Dr., Bloomington, IN 47401 USA; *Imprints:* Wisdom Tales (WisdomTales)
Web site: http://www.worldwisdom.com
Dist(s): **Follett School Solutions**
MyiLibrary
National Bk. Network
New Leaf Distributing Co., Inc.
Send The Light Distribution LLC
ebrary, Inc.

Worlds In Ink *See* **Worlds In Ink Publishing, Inc.**

Worlds In Ink Publishing, Inc., *(978-0-9745568)* 4812 Ridgecrest Cir SE, Albuquerque, NM 87108-4435 USA
E-mail: info@WorldsInInk.com
Web site: http://www.WorldsInInk.com.

WorldTrek Publishing, *(978-1-936376)* 121 E. Vermijo, Colorado Springs, CO 80903 USA (SAN 859-7154).

Worldview Publishing, Inc., *(978-1-889995)* 521 Herchel Dr., Tampa, FL 33617 USA Tel 813-985-9344; Fax: 813-985-4505; Toll Free: 800-987-9444 Do not confuse with companies with same or similar names in Tiburon, CA, Colorado Springs, CO
E-mail: drlindahf@aol.com
Web site: http://www.worldviewpub.com.

Worldwide Publishing Group, *(978-0-692-20798-7; 978-0-692-21343-8; 978-0-692-23202-6; 978-0-692-26528-4; 978-0-692-28543-5; 978-0-692-33975-6; 978-0-692-34486-6; 978-0-692-34654-9; 978-0-692-35794-1; 978-0-692-35819-1; 978-0-692-36089-7; 978-0-692-38604-0; 978-0-692-40727-1; 978-0-692-41000-4; 978-0-692-41425-5; 978-0-692-41942-7; 978-0-692-46338-3; 978-0-692-47708-3; 978-0-692-49561-2; 978-0-692-49566-7; 978-0-692-49571-1; 978-0-692-50705-6; 978-0-692-50706-3; 978-0-692-50707-0; 978-0-692-50708-7; 978-0-692-50709-4;) P.O. Box 596, Litchfield, IL 62056 USA Tel 217-851-0361*
E-mail: rwgcontact@yahoo.com
Web site: http://www.worldwidepublishinggroup.com/
Dist(s): **CreateSpace Independent Publishing Platform.**

Worldwide United Publishing *See* **Pearl Publishing, LLC**

Worthwhile Bks. *Imprint of* **Idea & Design Works, LLC**

Worthy Media, Incorporated *See* **Worthy Publishing**

Worthy Publishing, *(978-0-8249; 978-0-89542; 978-0-9640955; 978-1-58334; 978-1-887655; 978-0-9794446; 978-0-9796938; 978-1-934770; 978-1-60587; 978-1-935416; 978-1-936034; 978-1-60936; 978-1-61795; 978-1-63326; 978-1-68397; 978-1-945470)* Div. of Worthy Media, Inc., Orders Addr.: One Franklin Park 6100 Tower Cir., Suite 210, Franklin, TN 37067 USA Tel 615-932-7600; *Imprints:* F/S (F/S); Ideals Publications (IdealsPubns) Do not confuse with Worthy Publishing in Birmingham, AL
E-mail: jeana@worthymedia.com; leeannan@worthypublishing.com
Web site: http://worthypublishing.com/
Dist(s): **Capitol Christian Distribution**
CreateSpace Independent Publishing Platform
EMI CMG Distribution
MyiLibrary.

Worthy Shorts, *(978-1-935340; 978-1-937503; 978-1-937504; 978-1-937505; 978-1-937506; 978-1-937507)* P.O. Box 177, Malden on Hudson, NY 12453 USA Tel 845-246-2336; 15 Bostan Rd., Malden on Hudson, NY 12453
Web site: http://www.worthyshorts.com
Dist(s): **Smashwords.**

Wowza World LLC,

WowZee Works Inc, *(978-0-9778858)* 2217 Green Mountain Ct., Las Vegas, NV 89135 USA (SAN 850-5128).

WPR Publishing, *(978-1-889379)* 3445 Catalina Dr., Carlsbad, CA 92010 USA Tel 760-434-1223; Fax: 760-434-7476 Do not confuse with WPR Publishing, Dillon, MT
E-mail: kirk@whisler.com
Web site: http://www.WPRbooks.com
Dist(s): **Lightning Source, Inc.**

WRB Pub., *(978-0-9844198; 978-0-9838832; 978-0-9856762; 978-0-9896247; 978-0-9909040)* 1260 SW 25 LN, Palm City, FL 34990 USA Tel 772-463-0928; Fax: 267-220-1541
E-mail: wrb1174@att.net
Dist(s): **Ingram Publisher Services**
Smashwords.

WRDSMTH Productions, *(978-0-9744562)* Orders Addr.: P.O. Box 1406, Lawton, OK 73502-1406 USA (SAN 255-7282) Tel 580-353-4710; Fax: 580-357-9787; Toll Free: 800-357-9854; Edit Addr.: 130 SW B Ave., Lawton, OK 73501 USA
E-mail: oktelier@juno.com
Web site: http://www.stringfigurestore.com.

Wren Song Pr., *(978-0-9769827)* 233 Poors Mill Rd., Belfast, ME 04915 USA Toll Free: 800-943-7664 Do not confuse with Wren Song Press in Ripton, VT
E-mail: jennifer@jenniferarmstrong.com
Web site: http://www.jenniferarmstrong.com.

Wren's Nest Publishing, Inc., *(978-0-9744111)* 177 Rabbit Farm Trail, Advance, NC 27006 USA Tel 336-998-2858
E-mail: rickyp@yadtel.net.

Wright Bk. Publishing, *(978-0-615-23176-1; 978-0-9822822)* 4188 Defoors Farm Dr., Powder Springs, GA 30127 USA
Web site: http://www.wrightbookpublishing.com; http://www.earthsavergirl.com.

For full information on wholesalers and distributors, refer to the Wholesaler and Distributor Name Index

Wright, Dr. Author O., *(978-0-9679676)* 4524 Portland Ave., S., Minneapolis, MN 55407-3550 USA Tel 612-822-8032
E-mail: Awright@email.usps.gov.

Wright Group/McGraw-Hill, *(978-0-322; 978-0-7802; 978-0-940156; 978-1-55624; 978-1-55911; 978-1-4045)* Div. of Mcgraw-Hill School Education Group, Orders Addr.: P.O. Box 545, Blacklick, OH 43004-0545 USA Tel 614-755-5645; Toll Free: 800-722-4726; 800-442-9685 (customer service)
Web site: http://www.wrightgroup.com/.

Wright, Lacie, *(978-0-615-20657-8; 978-0-615-20658-5)* 413 Acorn Grove Ln. Apt. C, Chesapeake, VA 23320-6561 USA
E-mail: paulndlacie@gmail.com
Dist(s): **Lulu Pr., Inc.**

Wright Publishing, Inc., *(978-0-935087; 978-0-9652368)* Orders Addr.: P.O. Box 1956, Fayetteville, GA 30214 USA Tel 770-460-5525; Fax: 770-460-8998; Edit Addr.: 320 Devilla Trace, Fayetteville, GA 30214 USA (SAN 695-0507) Do not confuse with companies with same or similar name in Los Angeles, CA, Virgina Beach, VA, West Seneca, NY, Torrance, CA.

Wright, Robert, *(978-0-9763223)* 272 Horse Hill Rd., Ashford, CT 06278 USA.

Wright's Way Inc., *(978-0-9767483)* 210 Henderson Dr., Jacksonville, NC 28540 USA Tel 910-989-0000 (phone/fax)
E-mail: sensei@bizec.rr.com
Web site: http://www.wrightskarate.com.

Write Away, *(978-0-615-26181-2)* 242 Hyle Ave., Murfreesboro, TN 37128 USA Tel 615-848-0247.

Write Bloody Publishing, *(978-0-9789989; 978-0-9815213; 978-0-9821488; 978-0-9842515; 978-0-9845031; 978-1-935904; 978-1-938912)* 235 E. Broadway, Sixth Flr., No. 609, Long Beach, CA 90802 USA
E-mail: writebloody@gmail.com
Web site: http://www.writebloody.com
Dist(s): **SCB Distributors.**

Write Designs, Limited *See* **PricePoint+Publications**

Write Integrity Pr., *(978-0-9839485; 978-1-938092; 978-1-944120)* 4475 Trinity Mills Rd, Dallas, TX 75370 USA (SAN 920-0673) Tel 678-600-4617 (Tel/Fax)
E-mail: writeintegrity@gmail.com; marji.laine@gmail.com
Web site: http://www.writeintegrity.com; http://MarjiLaine.com.

Write On!, *(978-0-9753870; 978-0-9825722; 978-0-9890688)* Orders Addr.: 704 Norwalk Ct., Nashville, TN 37214 USA Tel 615-415-9861 Do not confuse with companies with a similar name in Albuquerque, NM, Estes Park, CO
E-mail: writer@yvonneperry.net
Web site: http://writersinthesky.com; http://weare1inspirit.com/bookstore.htm.

Write Way Publishing, *(978-1-885173)* Orders Addr.: P.O. Box 441278, Aurora, CO 80044 USA Tel 303-617-0497; Fax: 303-617-1440; Toll Free: 800-680-1493 Do not confuse with Write Way Publishing, Charleston, WV
E-mail: staff@writewaypub.com; writewy@aol.com
Web site: http://www.writewaypub.com.

Write Way Publishing Co. LLC, *(978-0-9976076; 978-1-946425)* 322 Fox Hollow Dr, Clayton, NC 27527 USA Tel 919-606-2618
E-mail: kevin@writewaypublishingcompany.com; lee@writewaypublishing.com
Web site: writewaypublishingcompany.com.

Write Words, Inc., *(978-0-9706152; 978-1-59431; 978-1-61386)* 2934 Old Rte. 50, Cambridge, MD 21613 USA (SAN 254-0304) Fax: 410-221-7510; *Imprints:* Cambridge Books (CB); Ebooks On The Net (Ebks on the net) Do not confuse with The Write Words Inc., in Arlington, VA
E-mail: arline@mail.com; ArlineChase@comcast.net
Web site: http://www.ebooksonthe.net; http://www.cambridgebooks.us
Dist(s): **CreateSpace Independent Publishing Platform.**

Write World, Inc., *(978-0-9722173)* 3839 McKinney Ave. No. 155-373, Dallas, TX 75204 USA (SAN 254-8445)
E-mail: writeworld@cs.com.

Write Your Way Through Publishing *See* **Urban Moon Publishing**

WriteGirl Pubns., *(978-0-9741251; 978-0-9837081; 978-0-692-88728-8)* 1330 Factory Pl. Unti 104, Los Angeles, CA 90013 USA Tel 213-253-2655
E-mail: info@writegirl.org
Web site: http://www.writegirl.org
Dist(s): **SPD-Small Pr. Distribution.**

WriteLife Publishing *Imprint of* **Boutique of Quality Books Publishing Co., Inc.**

WRITER for HIRE!, *(978-0-9701356; 978-0-9854623)* Orders Addr.: P.O. Box 1143, Decatur, GA 30031 USA Tel 404-315-7740 (9am-5pm EST); Fax: 770-454-0029 (24 hour)
E-mail: angeladurden@msn.com
Web site: http://www.angeladurden.com; http://www.mikeandhisgrandpa.com.

Writers Advantage Pr. *Imprint of* **iUniverse, Inc.**

Writers Cafe Pr., The, *(978-1-934284)* 418 S. Brookfield Dr., Lafayette, IN 47905-7299 USA (SAN 852-5498)
E-mail: admin@thewriterscafe.com
Web site: http://www.thewriterscafe.com.

Writers Club Pr. *Imprint of* **iUniverse, Inc.**

Writer's Coffee Shop, The, *(978-1-61213)* P.O. Box 2116, Waxahachie, TX 75168 USA (SAN 860-0112)
E-mail: publishing@thewriterscoffeeshop.com; amhayward@thewriterscoffeeshop.com
Web site: http://www.thewriterscoffeeshop.com; http://ph.thewriterscoffeeshop.com/
Dist(s): **Lulu Pr., Inc.**

Writers Collective, The *Imprint of* **Day to Day Enterprises**

Writers' Collective, The, *(978-0-9716734; 978-1-932133; 978-1-59411)* 780 Reservoir Ave., Suite 243, Cranston, RI 02910 USA Toll Free: 800-497-0037
E-mail: factotum@writerscollective.org
Web site: http://www.writerscollective.org
Dist(s): **Midpoint Trade Bks., Inc.**

Writer's Cramp, Inc., *(978-0-9645983)* 711 San Juan Dr., Coral Gables, FL 33143-6224 USA
E-mail: JandyPF@aol.com.

Writers in the Schools (WITS), *(978-0-9747704)* 1523 W. Main, Houston, TX 77006 USA
E-mail: mail@writersintheschools.org
Web site: http://www.writersintheschools.org.

Writer's Ink. Studios, Inc., *(978-0-9704460)* P.O. Box 952, Windermere, FL 34786 USA Tel 407-876-3399; Fax: 270-964-5984; Toll Free: 888-229-9200
E-mail: cat@brownbagbooks.com; writersinkstudios@cfl.rr.com
Web site: http://www.brownbagbooks.com.

Writers Marketplace:Consulting, Critiquing & Publishing, *(978-1-928632)* P.O. Box 21218, Carson City, NV 89721 USA Tel 775-544-0909; Fax: 775-884-3103.

Writer of the Round Table Pr., *(978-0-9814545; 978-0-9822206; 978-1-61066)* P.O. Box 511, Highland Park, IL 60035-0511 USA (SAN 855-6067)
Web site: http://www.writersoftheroundtable.com
Dist(s): **National Bk. Network.**

Writer's Publishing Cooperative *Imprint of* **Beech River Bks.**

Writer's Showcase Pr. *Imprint of* **iUniverse, Inc.**

WritersCorps Bks. *Imprint of* **San Francisco Art Commission, The**

Writing as a Ghost *See* **Jots & Tittles Publishing**

Writing Bench LLC., The, *(978-0-9818374)* P.O. Box 775037, Saint Louis, MO 63177-5037 USA
E-mail: backwardkingdom@yahoo.com.

Writing Center, The *See* **Full Court Pr.**

Writing etc. *See* **Etcetera Pr. LLC**

Writing for the Lord Ministries, *(978-0-9705902; 978-0-9883038; 978-0-9893188)* 6400 Shannon Ct., Clarksville, MD 21029 USA
E-mail: kevin@writingforthelord.com; kgj27@aol.com
Web site: http://www.writingforthelord.com; http://www.writingforthelord.org.

Writing The Vision *Imprint of* **Scribe Publishing & Consulting Services, The**

Writing Wild & Crazy *Imprint of* **Shakalot High Entertainment**

Writing-Right, *(978-0-9772196)* 27 Somerset Dr., Holbrook, NY 11741 USA
E-mail: lori@writing-right.org.

Written By Clark, Publishing, *(978-0-9795102)* Orders Addr.: P.O. Box 874023, Vancouver, WA 98687 USA Tel 323-447-9676
E-mail: jthomasclark@gmail.com; info@writtenbyclark.com
Web site: http://www.writtenbyclark.com
Dist(s): **Lightning Source, Inc.**

Written Expressions Enterprise, Inc., *(978-0-9728674)* 2276 Griffin Way, Suite 105-161, Corona, CA 92879 USA Tel 951-371-0160.

Written Images, Inc., *(978-0-9705721)* 1300 E. Lafayette, Suite 1104, Detroit, MI 48207 USA (SAN 253-7591) Tel 248-356-8310; Fax: 248-356-8311 Do not confuse with Written Image, The in Lancaster, NY
E-mail: writtenimages@aol.com
Web site: http://www.adiaryofjoseph.com.

Written in Black Publishing *See* **WordPlay Multimedia, LLC**

Written World Communications, *(978-0-9829377; 978-1-938679)* Orders Addr.: 4725 Splendid Cir. S., Colorado Springs, CO 80917 USA (SAN 859-9696) Tel 719-947-2181
E-mail: kristinepratt@gmail.com
Web site: http://www.writtenworldcommunications.com/.

WS Publishing, *(978-0-9639654; 978-1-887169; 978-1-934386; 978-1-936061; 978-1-61351)* 7290 Navajo Rd., Suite 207, San Diego, CA 92119 USA Tel 619-589-1919
E-mail: sarah@weddingsolutions.com; info@wspublishinggroup.com
Web site: http://wspublishinggroup.com
Dist(s): **Ingram Publisher Services**
Two Rivers Distribution.

Wu Li Turtle Corp., *(978-0-9741176)* 3885 S. Decatur Blvd., Suite 2010, Las Vegas, NV 89103 USA Tel 703-864-3769; Fax: 702-920-8118; Toll Free: 888-381-6864
E-mail: rbraye@wuliturtle.com
Web site: http://www.wuliturtle.com.

Wunderlannd Pr., *(978-0-615-62918-6; 978-0-9893166)* 3141 Elmer St., Sarasota, FL 34231 USA Tel 443-742-7039
E-mail: wunderlanndpress@hotmail.com.

www.margaretmouse.com publishing co., *(978-0-9761326)* Orders Addr.: 41953 20th St., W., Palmdale, CA 93551-0000 USA Please allow four weeks for delivery. Shipments come direct from printer in China. Invoiced at order. Shipping free for all orders over 5000. Dolls are available as well. Please contact me direct at email Lparnold@verizon.net or call US 661-943-0275 with any questions or concerns or special orders.
E-mail: info@margaretmouse.com
Web site: http://www.margaretmouse.com
Dist(s): **Follett School Solutions.**

www.pmptools.com *See* **Project Management Excellence Ctr., Inc., The**

www.underdogpublishing.com, *(978-0-9754420)* 124 Titleist Cir., Savannah, GA 31419 USA; P.O. Box 638, Tybee Island, GA 31328 Tel 912-596-5532
Web site: http://www.underdogpublishing.com.

Wyatt Hse. Publishing, *(978-0-9882209; 978-0-9896119; 978-0-9915798; 978-0-9977422)* 399 Lakeview Dr. W., Mobile, AL 36695 USA Tel 251-421-1296
E-mail: editor@wyattpublishing.com
Web site: http://www.wyattpublishing.com.

Wyatt Pr., *(978-0-9718161)* 15005 W. 167th Terr., Olathe, KS 66062 USA Tel 913-768-1917; Fax: 913-768-4307.

Wyatt-MacKenzie Publishing, *(978-0-9673025; 978-1-932279; 978-0-9743832; 978-0-9820518; 978-1-936214; 978-1-939288; 978-1-942545; 978-1-948018)* 15115 Hwy. 36, Deadwood, OR 97430-9700 USA (SAN 990-1191) Tel 541-964-3314; Fax: 541-964-3315
E-mail: info@wymacpublishing.com; nancy@wyattmackenzie.com
Web site: http://www.wymacpublishing.com.

Wycliffe Bible Translators, *(978-0-938978)* P.O. Box 628200, Orlando, FL 32862-8200 USA (SAN 211-5484)
Web site: http://www.wycliffe.org.

Wyer Pearce Press *See* **SangFroid Pr.**

Wyland Galleries *See* **Wyland Worldwide, LLC**

Wyland Worldwide, LLC, *(978-0-9631793; 978-1-884840; 978-1-60586)* 6 Mason, Irvine, CA 92618 USA Tel 949-643-7070; Fax: 949-643-7082
E-mail: valeries@wyland.com
Web site: http://www.wyland.com
Dist(s): **Booklines Hawaii, Ltd.**

Wynden *Imprint of* **Canmore Pr.**

Wyoming Historical & Geological Society, *(978-0-937537)* 49 S. Franklin St., Wilkes-Barre, PA 18701 USA (SAN 281-2061) Tel 717-823-6244; Fax: 717-823-9011
E-mail: lchs@epix.net
Web site: http://www.luzernecountyhistory.com.

Wyson, Dan, *(978-0-9771522)* 1173 S. 250 W. Suite 305, Saint George, UT 84770 USA Tel 435-229-6713 Toll Free: 877-827-0710.

Wysteria, Limited *See* **Wysteria Publishing**

Wysteria Publishing, *(978-0-9651162; 978-0-9677839; 978-1-932412)* P.O. Box 1250, Bellmore, NY 11710 USA Toll Free Fax: 888-434-7979; Toll Free: 888-997-8300
E-mail: wysteria@wysteria.com
Web site: http://www.wysteria.com.

X, Y, & Me LLC, *(978-0-9755028; 978-0-9773441)* 21409 138th St., Webster, IA 52355-9079 USA
E-mail: customerservice@xyandme.com
Web site: http://www.xyandme.com.

Xanadu Metaphysical *See* **Xanadu New Age Products & Services, LLC**

Xanadu New Age Products & Services, LLC, *(978-0-9759752)* Orders Addr.: 1011 S. Lake St., Neenah, WI 54956 USA; Edit Addr.: 1011 S. Lake St., Neenah, WI 54956 USA
E-mail: parisdrake@parisdrake.com
Web site: http://www.parisdrake.com.

xbks publishing, *(978-0-9626458)* c/o Arturo Watlington Station, P.O. Box 568, Saint Thomas, VI 00804 USA
E-mail: llrush@viaccess.net; mail@xbkspublishing.net
Web site: http://www.xbkspublising.net.

Xbooks *See* **xbks publishing**

Xerces Society, The, *(978-0-9744475)* 4828 SE Hawthorne Blvd., Portland, OR 97215 USA Tel 503-232-6639; Fax: 503-233-6794
E-mail: mdshepherd@xerces.org
Web site: http://www.xerces.org.

Xist Publishing, *(978-0-615-49153-0; 978-0-9838428; 978-1-62395; 978-1-68195; 978-1-5324)* 16604 Sonora St., Tustin, CA 92782 USA Tel 949-842-5296; 949-478-2568; P.O. Box 61593, Irvine, CA 92692
E-mail: calee@xistpublishing.com; info@xistpublishing.com
Web site: http://xistpublishing.com
Dist(s): **CreateSpace Independent Publishing Platform**
Follett School Solutions
Ingram Publisher Services
Mackin Educational Resources.

Xlibris, 1663 Liberty Dr., Bloomington, IN 47403 USA Tel 888-795-4274
E-mail: Johnnyline.Jagdon@xlibris.com
Web site: http://www2.xlibris.com/.

Xlibris Corporation *See* **Xlibris Corp.**

Xlibris Corp., *(978-0-7388; 978-0-9663501; 978-1-4010; 978-1-4134; 978-1-59926; 978-1-4257; 978-1-4363; 978-1-4415; 978-1-4500; 978-1-4535; 978-1-4568; 978-1-4628; 978-1-4653; 978-1-4691; 978-1-4771; 978-1-4797; 978-1-4836; 978-1-4931; 978-1-4990; 978-1-5035; 1-5144; 978-1-5245; 978-1-4990-9726-9; 978-1-4990-9725-2; 978-1-4990-9724-5; 978-1-5434) Orders Addr.: 1663 S. Liberty Dr. Suite 200, Bloomington, IN 47403 USA (SAN 299-5522) Tel 812-334-5223; Fax: 812-334-5223; Toll Free: 888-795-4274*
E-mail: info@xlibris.com; orders@xlibris.com; dave.weinman@xlibris.com; customersupport@xlibris.com; digitalcontent@authorsolutions.com
Web site: http://www2.xlibris.com
Dist(s): **Author Solutions, Inc.**
Bookmasters Distribution
CreateSpace Independent Publishing Platform
International Pubns. Service
Lulu Pr., Inc.
Smashwords
TextStream.

Xophix, *(978-0-9754173)* P.O. Box 12081, Scottsdale, AZ 85267 USA Fax: 586-461-1712
E-mail: books@xophix.com
Web site: http://www.xophix.com.

X-treme Reviews *Imprint of* **N&N Publishing Co., Inc.**

Y Lolfa (GBR) *(978-0-86243; 978-0-904864; 978-0-9500178; 978-0-9555272; 978-1-84771; 978-0-9567031; 978-0-9560125; 978-1-78461) Dist. by* **Dufour.**

YA Angst *Imprint of* **Norilana Bks.**

YA Bks., *(978-0-615-72187-3; 978-0-615-79766-3; 978-0-9899934)* 211 Oxford St., Martin, TN 38237 USA Tel 7315875993
Web site: merrybrown.com
Dist(s): **CreateSpace Independent Publishing Platform.**

Yabitoon Bks., *(978-0-578-05342-4)* 1679 Bluffhill Dr., Monterey Park, CA 91754 USA.

Yacos Pubns., *(978-0-9653734)* Orders Addr.: 90-20 169th St., Apt. 4D, Jamaica, NY 11432 USA Tel 718-523-8911 (phone/fax)
E-mail: Drltgrant@yahoo.com
Web site: http://www.yacos.org.

Yad Vashem Pubns. (ISR) *(978-965-308) Dist. by* **Coronet Bks.**

Yadda Yadda Pr., *(978-0-9791387)* 1748 Donwell Dr., South Euclid, OH 44121-3734 USA
E-mail: williamecook@gmail.com
Web site: http://www.yaddayaddapress.com.

Yadeeda.com, *(978-0-9747122)* P.O. Box 38642, Colorado Springs, CO 80937 USA Tel 719-520-5125
E-mail: yadeeda@hotmail.com
Web site: http://www.yadeeda.com.

†**Yale Univ. Pr.,** *(978-0-300)* Orders Addr.: c/o Triliteral LLC, 100 Maple Ridge Dr., Cumberland, RI 02864 USA Tel 401-531-2800; Fax: 401-531-2801; Toll Free Fax: 800-406-9145; Toll Free: 800-405-1619; Edit Addr.: 302 Temple St., New Haven, CT 06511 USA (SAN 203-2740) Tel 203-432-0960; Fax: 203-432-0948
E-mail: yupmkt@yale.edu
Web site: http://www.yale.edu/yup/; http://www.yale.edu/yup/index.html
Dist(s): **Casemate Academic**
Cheng & Tsui Co.
De Gruyter, Inc.
Ebsco Publishing
ISD
MyiLibrary
TriLiteral, LLC
Wiley, John & Sons, Inc.
Yale Univ., Far Eastern Pubns.
ebrary, Inc.; *CIP.*

Yali Bks., *(978-0-9890615)* 24 C Hollandale Ln., Clifton Park, NY 12065 USA Tel 574-606-9154
E-mail: Yalibooks@gmail.com
Web site: Www.yalibooks.wordpress.com.

Yam Hill Publishing, *(978-0-692-50620-2; 978-0-692-83700-9; 978-0-692-84230-0)* 2926 NE Redwood Dr., McMinnville, OR 97128 USA Tel 503-857-5355
Web site: www.jim-gullo.com
Dist(s): **CreateSpace Independent Publishing Platform.**

Yana's Kitchen, *(978-0-9670982)* 5256 Pizzo Ranch Rd., La Canada, CA 91011 USA Tel 818-790-8381 (phone/fax)
E-mail: yana119@yahoo.com
Web site: http://yanasplace.com.

Yang, Jennifer, *(978-0-578-06384-3; 978-0-578-09356-7; 978-0-578-12358-5; 978-0-578-14107-7)* P.O. Box 22204, San Francisco, CA 94122 USA
E-mail: jenniyang@aol.com
Dist(s): **Lulu Pr., Inc.**

Yankee Cowboy, *(978-0-9708530; 978-0-9836149)* P.O. Box 123, Keller, TX 76244 USA Tel 800-557-8166; Toll Free: 800-557-8166
E-mail: publisher@yankeecowboy.com
Web site: http://www.yankeecowboy.com; http://www.watchdognation.com; http://www.davelieber.org
Dist(s): **BCH Fulfillment & Distribution.**

Yankee Publishing, Inc., *(978-0-89909; 978-1-57198)* Orders Addr.: P.O. Box 520, Dublin, NH 03444 USA Tel 603-563-8111; Fax: 603-563-8252; Edit Addr.: Main St., Dublin, NH 03444 USA; *Imprints:* Old Farmer's Almanac (OldFarmers) Do not confuse with Yankee Publishing, Saint Petersburg, FL
E-mail: almanac@yankeepub.com
Web site: http://www.almanac.com
Dist(s): **Houghton Mifflin Harcourt Publishing Co.**
Houghton Mifflin Harcourt Trade & Reference Pubs.
MyiLibrary.

Yarbrough Hse. Publishing, *(978-0-9970132)* 3596 Greensport Rd., Ashville, AL 35953 USA Tel 205-594-5338
E-mail: elizabethl.sorrell@gmail.com
Web site: http://www.elizabethleesorrell.com.

Yard Dog Pr., *(978-1-893687; 978-0-9824704; 978-1-937105; 978-1-945941)* 710 W. Redbud Ln., Alma, AR 72921 USA Tel 479-632-4693
Web site: http://www.yarddogpress.com
Dist(s): **Smashwords.**

Yari Publishing, *(978-0-578-06838-1)* P.O. Box 142624, Austin, TX 78714-2624 USA.

Yaroslavskaya, Lyudmila, *(978-0-9791248)* 600 W. Diversey Parkaway, Rm. 1410, Chicago, IL 60614 USA.

Yarrow Pr., *(978-0-9741562)* Orders Addr.: P.O. Box 665, Rainelle, WV 25962 USA Tel 304-438-1040 Do not confuse with Yarrow Press in Pelham, NY
E-mail: kate@yarrowpress.com
Web site: http://www.yarrowpress.com.

Yasgur, Abigail *See* **Change the Universe Pr.**

Yasram Global Industries, LLC, *(978-0-692-36502-1; 978-0-692-56482-0; 978-0-692-79807-2)* 2019 Fox Hill Glenn, Bldg. 18, Apt. 12, Grand Blanc, MI 48439 USA Tel 810-610-1040; Fax: 810-780-4268
Web site: www.keiraandme.info
Dist(s): **CreateSpace Independent Publishing Platform.**

YAV, *(978-0-9790221; 978-1-937449)* Orders Addr.: 1950 Hendersonville Rd. No. 243, Skyland, NC 28776 USA
E-mail: books@yav.com
Web site: http://InterestingWriting.com; http://ScienceOfWriting.com; http://YAVpublications.com.

Yawn's Bks. & More, Inc., *(978-0-9818673; 978-0-9830190; 978-1-936815; 978-1-940395; 978-1-943529; 978-1-947773)* 198 North St., Canton, GA 30114 USA (SAN 856-7476) Tel 678-880-1922; Fax: 678-880-1923
E-mail: fyawn@yawnsbooks.com
Web site: http://www.yawnspublishing.com.

YBK Pubs., Inc., *(978-0-9703923; 978-0-9764359; 978-0-9790972; 978-0-9800508; 978-0-9824012; 978-1-936411)* 39 Crosby St. Apt. 2N, New York, NY 10013-3254 USA
E-mail: obarz@ybkpublishers.com
Web site: http://www.ybkpublishers.com.

Publisher Name Index

Ye Hedge Schl., *(978-0-9723239; 978-0-9825521)* Orders Addr.: 24934 478 Ave., Garretson, SD 57030 USA E-mail: mod61047@alliancecom.net Web site: http://www.hedgeschool.com.

Ye Olde Font Shoppe, *(978-1-889289)* Orders Addr.: P.O. Box 8328, New Haven, CT 06708 USA Tel 203-575-9385; Edit Addr.: 35 Ferndale, Waterbury, CT 06708 USA Tel 860-870-9741 E-mail: varivas@yahoo.com Web site: http://www.yeolde.org.

Yearling *Imprint of* **Random Hse. Children's Bks.**

Yehuda, Ben Pr., *(978-0-9769862; 978-0-9789980; 978-1-934730)* 122 Ayers Ct. No. 1B, Teaneck, NJ 07666 USA Tel 201-833-5145; Fax: 201-917-1278 E-mail: yudel@benyehudapress.com Web site: http://www.BenYehudaPress.com.

Yellow Brick Road Publishing, *(978-0-615-24159-3)* 35 Fiske St., No. 1, Waltham, MA 02451 USA.

Yellow Daffodil Pr., *(978-0-9824943)* 17939 Chatsworth St., No. 241, Granada Hills, CA 91344 USA E-mail: mdesannoy@gmail.com.

Yellow Umbrella Bks. *Imprint of* **Capstone Press of Coughlan Cos.**

Yellow Umbrella en espanol *Imprint of* **Capstone Press of Coughlan Cos.**

Yellowstone Association for Natural Science, History & Education, Incorporated *See* **Yellowstone Forever**

Yellowstone Forever, *(978-0-934948)* P.O. Box 117, Yellowstone National Park, WY 82190 USA (SAN 214-4921) Tel 406-848-2454; Fax: 406-848-2453 E-mail: dcollins@yellowstone.org Web site: http://www.YellowstoneAssociation.org *Dist(s):* **Outskirts Pr., Inc.**

Yen Pr. *Imprint of* **Orbit**

Yen Press *See* **Yen Pr. LLC**

Yen Pr. LLC, *(978-0-7595; 978-89-527; 978-1-9753)* Div. of Hachette Book Group, 1290 Avenue of the Americas, New York, NY 10104 USA E-mail: customer.service@hbgusa Web site: http://www.yenpress.com *Dist(s):* **Hachette Bk. Group MyiLibrary.**

Yeoman Hse., *(978-0-9754676; 978-0-9822659; 978-0-9852537)* 10 Old Bulgarmarsh Rd., Tiverton, RI 02878 USA Tel 401-816-0061 E-mail: yeomanhouse@cox.net Web site: http://www.yeomanhouse.com.

YES - Your Emergency Safety, *(978-0-9740670)* 1302 W. Adams Ave., Saint Louis, MO 63122 USA Tel 314-822-8895; Fax: 775-458-7717 E-mail: info@youremergencysafety.org Web site: http://www.youremergencysafety.org.

Yesterday's Classics, *(978-1-59915; 978-1-63334)* Orders Addr.: P.O. Box 3418, Chapel Hill, NC 27515 USA Tel 919-967-3119; Toll Free: 866-497-3729 (phone/fax); Edit Addr.: 1705 Audubon Rd., Chapel Hill, NC 27514 USA Web site: http://www.yesterdaysclassics.com.

Yestermorrow, Inc., *(978-1-56723)* Orders Addr.: P.O. Box 700, Princess Anne, MD 21853 USA.

Yewtree Pr. LLC, *(978-1-933029)* P.O. Box 110 671, Brooklyn, NY 11211 USA Toll Free: 800-939-7404 E-mail: info@yewtreepress.com Web site: http://www.yewtreepress.com.

Yhabbut Publishing, *(978-0-9724292)* Orders Addr.: P.O. Box 23032, Seattle, WA 981 USA; Edit Addr.: 2111 15th Ave., S., Suite A, Seattle, WA 98144-4271 USA E-mail: benthoven@qwest.net Web site: http://www.1stbooks.com/bookview/20054.

Y-IREAD Publishing, *(978-0-9728549)* Orders Addr.: P.O. Box 33248, Indianapolis, IN 46203 USA Tel 317-294-3423 E-mail: kenyawash@sbcglobal.net.

Yisrael, Sean Publishing Co., *(978-0-9772424)* 11769 Kenn Rd., Cincinnati, OH 45240 USA Tel 513-266-1158 E-mail: syisrael@dps.k12.oh.us.

YNR Media L.L.C., *(978-0-9753262)* 338 Streeter Dr., McCook Lake, SD 57049 USA Tel 310-422-1662.

Yo Puedo Publishing, *(978-0-9714533)* P.O. Box 940895, Houston, TX 77094 USA (SAN 254-3729) Tel 281-496-2015; 866-YO-PUEDO; Fax: 281-558-3773 E-mail: kathryn@yopuedo.com Web site: http://www.yopuedo.com.

Yofi Bk. Publishing, Inc., *(978-1-931387; 978-1-60046)* 199 Lee Ave. Unit #397, Brooklyn, NY 11211 USA Tel 718-694-9040; Fax: 718-694-9062 E-mail: yofi@yeshivanet.com.

Yoga Life *See* **Love Your Life**

YOLT Publishing, *(978-0-9982931)* 13518 L St., Omaha, NE 68137 USA Tel 402-884-5995 E-mail: yolt@conciergemarketing.com.

yomitobi, *(978-0-9799470)* 403 Knight Dr., Apt 9, Statesboro, GA 30458 USA E-mail: yoko_6@hotmail.com Web site: http://www.yomitobi.com.

Yonay, Shahar, *(978-0-927580; 978-0-9616783)* 126 Dover St., Brooklyn, NY 11235 USA (SAN 661-0544) Tel 718-615-0027.

Yoon-il Auh/Intrepid Pixels, *(978-1-882858)* 820 West End Ave., No. 9E, New York, NY 10025 USA Tel 212-662-6891.

Yoot Pr., *(978-0-9764611)* 17-47 Chandler Dr., Fair Lawn, NJ 07410 USA Web site: http://www.yootpress.com.

York House Pr., Ltd., *(978-0-9791956; 978-0-9855508)* 1266 E. Main St, suite 700R,, Stamford, CT 06902 USA Tel 203-539-6180; Fax: 914-764-5159 E-mail: pholt@yorkhousepress.com *Dist(s):* **Lightning Source, Inc.**

Yorkshire Publishing Group, *(978-0-88144; 978-1-936750; 978-0-9883786; 978-0-9889281; 978-0-9896518; 978-1-942451; 978-1-946977; 978-1-947247; 978-1-947491; 978-1-947825)* Orders Addr.: 9731 E. 54th St., Tulsa, OK 74147 USA (SAN 260-0285) Tel 918-394-2665; *Imprints:* Thorncrown Publishing (Thorncrown); Total Publishing & Media (Total Pubng) E-mail: todd.rutherford@yorkshirepublishing.com Web site: http://www.yorkshirepublishing.com *Dist(s):* **BookBaby INscribe Digital.**

Yorkville Pr., *(978-0-9729427; 978-0-9767442)* Orders Addr.: 1202 Lexington Ave., No. 315, New York, NY 10028 USA (SAN 255-3139) Tel 212-650-9154; Fax: 212-650-9157; 1202 Lexington Ave. # 315, New York, NY 10028 Tel 212-650-9154 E-mail: editors@yorkvillepress.com Web site: http://www.yorkvillepress.com.

Yoroson Publishing *See* **Young-Robinson, Christine**

Yosemite Assn., *(978-0-939666; 978-1-930238)* Orders Addr.: P.O. Box 230, El Portal, CA 95318 USA (SAN 662-197X) Tel 209-379-2648; Fax: 209-379-2486; Edit Addr.: 5020 El Portal Rd., El Portal, CA 95318 USA E-mail: dguy@yosemite.org Web site: http://www.yosemite.org *Dist(s):* **MyiLibrary Publishers Group West (PGW) Sunbelt Pubns., Inc.**

Yosoy Publishing, *(978-0-9763503)* 4141 Linden Ave, Long Beach, CA 90807 USA Tel 714-271-7667; Fax: 562-989-2031 E-mail: goodbooks@yeomanhouse.com Web site: http://www.ginaspoems.com; http://www.yosoypublishing.com.

Yost-Haynes, Melissa, *(978-0-9760909)* RR1, 115C, Ravenswood, WV 26164 USA.

You Can Do It! Productions, *(978-0-9744306)* 106 Paradise Rd., Havana, FL 32333-4236 USA E-mail: infinipede@juno.com Web site: http://www.infinipede.com.

You Can Do It! ART Publications *See* **Sunrise Mountain Bks.**

You Choose Bks. *Imprint of* **Capstone Press of Coughlan Cos.**

You Come Too Publishing, *(978-0-9816836)* 3138 NW Colonial Dr., Bend, OR 97701 USA Tel 541-317-4912 (phone/fax) E-mail: imkehoe@msn.com Web site: http://youcometoo.com *Dist(s):* **Smashwords.**

You Publishing Group, *(978-0-9764472)* 2500 S. Lamar Blvd., Austin, TX 78704 USA.

Young Advent Pilgrim's Bookshelf *See* **Barnes Printing**

Young, Beth, *(978-0-9760180)* 124 Chestnut St. Apt. 201, Englewood, OH 45322-1410 USA E-mail: 369beth@bellsouth.net Web site: http://www.saintlukespress.com.

Young Createers, *(978-0-9980893)* 4901 E. Kelton Ln, Scottsdale, AZ 85254 USA Tel 480-228-3988 E-mail: lisabenger@hotmail.com Web site: youngcreateers.com.

Young, Estrell III, *(978-0-692-90306-3; 978-0-692-91185-3)* 2764 Pkwy. Cove, LITHONIA, GA 30058 USA Tel 678-485-8864 E-mail: just.estrell@gmail.com *Dist(s):* **Lightning Source, Inc.**

Young Europe Bks. *Imprint of* **Steerforth Pr.**

Young Patriots Series *Imprint of* **Patria Pr., Inc.**

Young Patronesses of the Opera, The, *(978-0-9785364; 978-0-9795725; 978-0-9993895)* P.O. Box 3471616, Miami, FL 33234-7616 USA Tel 305-665-3470; Fax: 305-667-9265 E-mail: education@YPO-Miami.org Web site: www.ypo-miami.org.

Young Readers Publications, *(978-0-9789525)* 47 W. Schuyler St., Oswego, NY 13126 USA E-mail: sabistonart@yahoo.com Web site: http://jguntherphotography.com.

Young Scholars Pr., *(978-0-9787138)* 354 1/2 Calle Loma Norte, Santa Fe, NM 87501 USA Tel 505-989-7116; Fax: 505-820-2367 E-mail: MsAnnett1@aol.com Web site: http://oneworldmanypeople.com.

Young Women Books *See* **Harper Kids Hse.**

Young Women Programming *Imprint of* **Harper Kids Hse.**

Young Writer's Contest Foundation *See* **Miracle Pr.**

Youngheart Music, *(978-0-945267; 978-1-57471)* Affil. of Creative Teaching Pr., Orders Addr.: P.O. Box 2723, Huntington, CA 92647-0723 USA Tel 714-895-5047; Fax: 714-895-5087; Toll Free Fax: 800-229-9929; Toll Free: 800-444-4287; Edit Addr.: 15342 Graham St., Huntington Beach, CA 92649-1111 USA E-mail: webmaster@creativeteaching.com; rebecca.cleland@creativeteaching.com Web site: http://www.youngheartmusic.com; http://www.creativeteaching.com *Dist(s):* **Creative Teaching Pr., Inc. Follett School Solutions Rounder Kids Music Distribution.**

Youngheart Records *See* **Youngheart Music**

Young-Robinson, Christine, *(978-0-9706985)* 10120 Two Notch Rd., No. 143, Columbia, SC 29223 USA Fax: 803-865-9001 E-mail: miraclewriter4u@aol.com Web site: http://www.christineyoungrobinson.com.

Youngs, Bettie Bks., *(978-0-9843081; 978-1-936332; 978-0-9836045; 978-0-9882848; 978-1-940784)* Div. of Bettie Youngs Book Publishers, 532 1/2 Via De La Valle No. C Suite C, Solana Beach, CA 92075 USA Tel 858-350-6360; *Imprints:* Kendahl House Press (KendahlHse) E-mail: Bettie@BettieYoungs.com Web site: http://www.BettieYoungsBooks.com *Dist(s):* **Brodart Co. Coutts Information Services Lightning Source, Inc. Quality Bks., Inc. Smashwords.**

Youngs, C. R., *(978-0-9760451)* 11687 Sugar Creek Ave., Mount Carmel, IL 62863 USA E-mail: ronyoungs@davidbook.com Web site: http://www.davidbook.com/.

Your Culture Gifts, *(978-0-9797637)* P.O. Box 1245, Ellicott City, MD 21041 USA (SAN 854-3208) Tel 410-461-5799 E-mail: info@yourculturegifts.com Web site: http://www.yourculturegifts.com.

Your Story Hour Recordings, P.O. Box 511, Medina, OH 44258 USA Tel 216-725-5767; 717 St. Jospeh Dr. #254, Saint Joseph, MI 49085 Tel 269-471-3701 Web site: http://www.yourstoryhour.org.

You're On!, Inc., *(978-0-9760280)* P.O. Box 101071, Fort Worth, TX 76185 USA.

Youth Communication - New York Center, *(978-0-9661256; 978-1-933939; 978-1-935552; 978-1-938970)* 244 W. 27th St., 2nd Flr., New York, NY 10001 USA Tel 212-279-0708 ext. 115; Fax: 212-279-8856 E-mail: khefner@youthcomm.org Web site: http://www.youthcomm.org *Dist(s):* **Follett School Solutions.**

Youth Cultural Publishing Co. (CHN) *(978-957-530; 978-957-574) Dist. by* **Chinasprout.**

Youth Development & Research Fund, *(978-0-9659130)* P.O. Box 2188, Germantown, MD 20875-2188 USA E-mail: ed@ydrf.com Web site: http://www.ydrf.com.

Youth Inkwell Publishing, *(978-0-9773451)* 155 S. El Molino Ave., Suite 102, Paadena, CA 91101 USA Tel 626-449-6884; Fax: 626-449-6885 E-mail: info@youthinkwell.org Web site: http://youthinkwell.org; http://www.youthinkwell.org.

Youth Popular Culture Institute, Inc., *(978-1-887191)* 8906 Fox Park Rd., Clinton, MD 20735 USA Tel 301-877-1525.

Youth Quest Institute, *(978-0-9748994)* 5515 Azalea Trail Ln., Sugar Land, TX 77479 USA Web site: http://youthquestinstitute.com; http://getagripbooks.com.

Youthleadership.com, *(978-0-9677981)* 5593 Golf Course Dr., Morrison, CO 80465 USA Tel 303-358-1563; Fax: 303-393-9066 E-mail: support@youthleadership.com; mariam@youthleadership.com Web site: http://www.youthleadership.com.

Youthlight, Inc., *(978-1-889636; 978-1-59850)* Orders Addr.: P.O. Box 115, Chapin, SC 29036 USA (SAN 256-6400) Tel 803-345-1070; Fax: 803-345-0888; Toll Free: 800-209-9774; Edit Addr.: 105 Fairway Pond Dr., Chapin, SC 29036 USA E-mail: yl@sc.rr.com; yl@youthlightbooks.com Web site: http://www.youthlight.com; http://www.youthlightbooks.com.

YouthPlays, *(978-1-62088; 978-1-62088-584-0)* 7125 De Longpre Ave. No. 209, Los Angeles, CA 90046 USA Tel 424-703-5315 E-mail: info@youthplays.com Web site: http://youthplays.com.

Ysanti *See* **Lion's Crest Pr.**

Yucca Publishing *Imprint of* **Skyhorse Publishing Co., Inc.**

Yudcovitch, Lorne, *(978-0-9749781)* 6905 S.W. 7th Ave., Portland, OR 97219 USA Tel 503-293-6923 E-mail: yudcovil@pacificu.edu.

Yumcha Studios LLC, *(978-0-9881899)* 33-59 Farrington St., 2nd Flr., Flushing, NY 11354 USA Tel 917-332-8931; Fax: 917-332-8931 E-mail: yenyen@dimsumwarriors.com; colin@dimsumwarriors.com Web site: www.dimsumwarriors.com *Dist(s):* **Diamond Comic Distributors, Inc. Diamond Bk. Distributors.**

YWAM Publishing, *(978-0-927545; 978-0-9615534; 978-1-57658)* Div. of Youth With A Mission International, P.O. Box 55787, Seattle, WA 98155 USA (SAN 248-4021) E-mail: customerservice@ywampublishing.com Web site: http://www.ywampublishing.com *Dist(s):* **christianaudio.**

ZEM Pr., *(978-0-9634168)* 8220 Stone Trail Dr., Bethesda, MD 20817-4556 USA Tel 301-365-4585; Fax: 301-365-4586 E-mail: zem@wbh.com Web site: http://www.wb4.com.

Z Health Bks. *Imprint of* **New Win Publishing**

Z Pr., *(978-0-615-14380-4)* P.O. Box 6556, Woodland Hills, CA 91365 USA Tel 717-337-9968 E-mail: amy@amyleecoy.com *Dist(s):* **Lulu Pr., Inc.**

Z2 Comics, *(978-1-940878)* 527 Madison Ave., NEW YORK, NY 10022 USA Tel 718-440-6576 E-mail: zipcomic@gmail.com Web site: z2comics.com *Dist(s):* **Diamond Comic Distributors, Inc. Diamond Bk. Distributors.**

Zaccheus Entertainment Co., *(978-0-692-53734-3; 978-0-9969964; 978-0-9981972; 978-0-9985191; 978-0-9994571)* 136 Morrison Ave., Mt. Prospect, IL 60056 USA Tel 847-894-5574 E-mail: chiefcreta@att.net.

Zach Feuer Gallery, *(978-0-9768533)* 530 W 24th St., New York, NY 10011 USA Tel 212-989-7700 E-mail: zach@zachfeuer.com Web site: http://www.zachfeuer.com *Dist(s):* **D.A.P./Distributed Art Pubs.**

Zachmeyer, Mary L., *(978-0-9646864)* 1008 County Road 105., Columbus, TX 78934-1606 USA.

Zack Zombie Publishing *Imprint of* **Herobrine Publishing**

Zadunajsky, Donna M., *(978-0-9842397; 978-1-938037)* Orders Addr.: 17344 S. Parker Rd., Homer Glen, IL 60491 USA (SAN 858-821X) Tel 708-548-9829 E-mail: dmzadunajsky@gmail.com; 72allshookup@gmail.com Web site: http://www.donnazadunajskymalacina.blogspot.com; http://www.donnazadunajsky.com *Dist(s):* **BookBaby MyiLibrary ebrary, Inc.**

Zagat Survey, *(978-0-943421; 978-0-9612574; 978-1-57006; 978-1-60478)* 4 Columbus Cir., New York, NY 10019 USA (SAN 289-4777) Tel 212-977-6000; Fax: 212-765-9438; Toll Free: 866-999-0991 E-mail: tradesales@justzagat.com; theinz@zagat.com Web site: http://www.zagat.com *Dist(s):* **Ingram Publisher Services Two Rivers Distribution.**

Zagorski, Steve, *(978-0-578-05364-6)* Orders Addr.: P.O. Box 50196, Austin, TX 78763 USA Tel 517-789-3259; Edit Addr.: 1009 W. 6th St., Suite 206, Austin, TX 78703 USA E-mail: swzagorski@gmail.com.

Zaharko, Mary, *(978-0-692-59295-3)* 70 Mohawk Dr., West Hartford, CT 06117 USA Tel 860-463-0700 E-mail: jmintonq@comcast.net.

Zahir Publishing, *(978-0-9741311; 978-0-9786041; 978-0-9831090)* 315 S. Coast Hwy. 101, Suite U8, Encinitas, CA 92024 USA Web site: http://www.zahirtales.com.

Zahrob Publishing Co., *(978-0-9753641)* Orders Addr.: P.O. Box 5825, Rochester, MN 55903-5825 USA; Edit Addr.: 1445 Valley High Dr., NW, Rochester, MN 55903-5825 USA.

Zaloli, LLC, *(978-0-9857047; 978-0-9897380)* 4065 Sleeping Indian Ln., Colorado Springs, CO 80904 USA Tel 719-685-6505 E-mail: goldflagstudios@gmail.com.

Zander Pubns., *(978-0-578-01907-9; 978-0-578-01908-6; 978-0-578-02012-9; 978-0-578-02076-1; 978-0-578-04264-0; 978-0-578-05322-6; 978-0-578-05695-1; 978-0-9834052)* 2351 Sunset Blvd., Suite 170-433, Rocklin, CA 95765 USA Tel 916-624-1578 E-mail: randall@ips.net; contact@zanderpublications.com Web site: http://www.zanderpublications.com *Dist(s):* **Lulu Pr., Inc.**

Zaner-Bloser, Inc., *(978-0-7367; 978-0-88085; 978-0-88309; 978-1-4531)* Subs. of Highlights for Children, Orders Addr.: P.O. Box 16764, Columbus, OH 43216-6764 USA (SAN 282-5678) Tel 614-486-0221; Fax: 614-487-2263; Toll Free Fax: 800-992-6087; Toll Free: 800-421-3018; 1201 Dublin Rd., Columbus, OH 43215-1026 Web site: http://www.zaner-bloser.com/.

Zangadoo Entertainment, *(978-0-9847428)* 14101 19th Dr. SE, Mill Creek, WA 98102 USA Tel 206-234-8123 E-mail: dean@zangadoo.com Web site: www.zangadoo.com.

Zangadoo LLC *See* **Zangadoo Entertainment**

Zany Angel Projects LLC, *(978-0-9769234)* P.O. Box 1411, New York, NY 10159 USA Tel 212-686-4206.

Zardoz Pr. *Imprint of* **Life Force Bks.**

Zarraonandia, Anne, *(978-0-9741070)* P.O. Box 151435, San Rafael, CA 94915 USA Tel 415-456-4070; Toll Free: 877-892-6974 (phone/fax) E-mail: annezarra@aol.com Web site: http://www.cowboyluke.com.

Zarrella, Sharon *See* **Lizzy Anne's Adventures**

Zarrika, Ltd., *(978-0-9758663; 978-1-934252)* P.O. Box 488, Unionville, PA 19375 USA Fax: 610-486-6501; Toll Free: 888-369-3366 Web site: http://www.zarrika.com.

ZC Horses Series of Children's Bks., *(978-0-9721496; 978-0-9791719)* 8 Hokanson Ln., Salmon, ID 83467 USA Tel 208-756-7947 E-mail: zchorses@hotmail.com Web site: http://www.zchorses.com.

ZCR Pr., *(978-0-9763926)* 4912 Woodman Ave., No. 3, Sherman Oaks, CA 91423 USA (SAN 256-3479) Tel 818-995-3032 (phone/fax) E-mail: zaldy80@aol.com.

Zebra Ginkgo, *(978-0-9891510)* 310 Frieda Ave., Kirkwood, MO 63122 USA Tel 314-292-9452 E-mail: edchen7@zebraginkgo.com Web site: www.zebraginkgo.com.

Zeezok Publishing *See* **Zeezok Publishing, LLC**

Zeezok Publishing, LLC, *(978-0-9746505; 978-1-933573; 978-1-61006)* P.O. Box 1960, Elyria, OH 44036 USA (SAN 179-4493) Fax: 440-323-9494; Toll Free: 800-749-1681 E-mail: info@zeezok.com Web site: http://www.zeezok.com.

Zeidman Consulting *See* **Swiss Creek Pubns.**

Zeke & Me Bks., *(978-0-9883042)* 2415 Outlook St., Kalamazoo, MI 49001 USA Tel 269-344-7757 E-mail: sstamm625@gmail.com.

Zeke Meeks *Imprint of* **Picture Window Bks.**

Zellmann Publishing, LLC, *(978-0-9763325)* 420 Springwood Ct., Canton, GA 30115-8287 USA Tel 770-345-7265; Fax: 770-345-7265 E-mail: zellmann@zellmannpublishing.com.

Zelma's Farm, *(978-0-9989774)* 1351 Fulton Rd., E. Corinth, VT 05040 USA Tel 802-439-5126 E-mail: bdod@sover.net Web site: zelmasfarm.com.

Zemek, Alan, *(978-0-9960921)* 1316 LaClair Ave., Pittsburgh, PA 15218 USA Tel 412-508-1491 E-mail: zemeka27@verizon.net.

Zemi Comics, *(978-0-9745825)* SDQ 17, 4440 NW, 73rd Ave., Miami, FL 33166 USA Tel 787-748-4567 E-mail: fans@zemicomics.com Web site: http://www.zemicomics.com.

Zendrera Zariquiey, Editorial (ESP) *(978-84-89675; 978-84-8418) Dist. by* **Marluccia Iaconi Bk Imports.**

Zendrera Zariquiey, Editorial (ESP) *(978-84-89675; 978-84-8418) Dist. by* **Lectorum Pubns.**

Zenescope Entertainment, *(978-0-9786874; 978-0-9817550; 978-0-9823630; 978-0-9825826; 978-0-9827507; 978-0-615-40679-4; 978-0-9830404; 978-1-937068; 978-0-9853378; 978-1-939683; 978-1-942275)* 433 Caredean Dr Suite C, Horsham, PA 19044 USA (SAN 851-2760)
E-mail: jbrusha@zenscope.com
Web site: http://www.zenescope.com
Dist(s): **Diamond Comic Distributors, Inc.**
Diamond Bk. Distributors.

Zenga Publishing, *(978-0-9765484)* Orders Addr.: P.O. Box 39, New York, NY 10113 USA; Edit Addr.: 48 W. 22nd St., Suite 2, New York, NY 10010 USA
E-mail: zenga@nyc.rr.com
Web site: http://www.zengapublishing.com.

Zenith Pr. *Imprint of* **Quarto Publishing Group USA**

Zenith Pr. *Imprint of* **Quarto Publishing Group USA**

Zephyr Pr. *Imprint of* **Chicago Review Pr., Inc.**

Zephyr Pr., *(978-0-939010; 978-0-9815521; 978-0-9832970; 978-1-938890)* 50 Kenwood St., No. 2, Brookline, MA 02446 USA (SAN 239-7668) Do not confuse with companies with the same name in New York, NY, Tucson, AZ, Kansas City, MO, Canton, OH
E-mail: editors@zephyrpress.org
Web site: http://www.zephyrpress.org
Dist(s): **Consortium Bk. Sales & Distribution**
MyiLibrary
SPD-Small Pr. Distribution.

Zero To Three Pr., *(978-0-943657; 978-1-934019; 978-1-938558)* Div. of Zero To Three: National Ctr. for Infants, Toddlers & Families, Orders Addr.: P.O. Box 960, Herndon, VA 20172 USA Toll Free: 800-899-4301; Edit Addr.: 1255 23RD St. NW, Suite 350, Washington, DC 20037 USA (SAN 242-5084) Tel 202-638-1144; Fax: 202-638-0851
E-mail: n.guadagno@zerotothree.org; jenniferli@zerotothree.org
Web site: http://www.zerotothree.org.

Zeromayo Studios, LLP, *(978-0-9661985)* Orders Addr.: P.O. Box 417, Haydenville, MA 01039 USA Tel 413-584-9372; Fax: 413-665-2312; Edit Addr.: 16 Market St., Northampton, MA 01060 USA; *Imprints:* Empty Sky (Empty Sky)
E-mail: planetrace@aol.com
Web site: http://www.ninjaturtles.com
Dist(s): **Diamond Comic Distributors, Inc.**

ZeroTo Three: National Center for Instants, Toddlers & Families *See* **Zero To Three Pr.**

Zest Bks., *(978-0-9772660; 978-0-9790173; 978-0-9800732; 978-0-9819733; 978-0-9827322; 978-1-936976; 978-1-942186)* 35 Stillman St., Suite 121, San Francisco, CA 94107 USA
Web site: http://zestbooks.net
Dist(s): **Books International, Inc.**
Houghton Mifflin Harcourt Publishing Co.
Houghton Mifflin Harcourt Trade & Reference Pubs.
Hachette Bk. Group
Independent Pubs. Group
MyiLibrary.

Zest Publishing, *(978-0-9758861)* Orders Addr.: P.O. Box 484, Edgar, NE 68935-0484 USA; Edit Addr.: R.R. 1, Edgar, NE 68935-0484 USA Do not confuse with Zest Publishing Company in Southfield, MI.

Zeus Media LLC, *(978-0-9765840)* 12900 Canterbury, Leawood, KS 66209 USA
Web site: http://www.wisdomofzeus.com.

Zeus Sports Florida LLC, *(978-0-9777437)* Orders Addr.: 2312 SE 23rd Rd., Homestead, FL 33035-1900 USA Tel 786-417-9197
E-mail: habbook@msn.com.

JYZ Bks., LLC, *(978-0-9743272; 978-0-9906905)* Orders Addr.: 5816 White Pebble Path, Clarksville, MD 21029 USA (SAN 990-1868) Tel 443-535-2541; Fax: 703-485-2970
E-mail: jianyi.zhang66@gmail.com.

Zhang, Shiyu, *(978-0-692-90983-6)* 888 O'Farrell St APT E509, San Francisco, CA 94109 USA Tel 612-636-7385
E-mail: fishjump_000ya@hotmail.com
Dist(s): **Lightning Source, Inc.**

Zhera Pubns., *(978-0-9618904)* Orders Addr.: 2605 E. Flora Pl., Denver, CO 80210-6827 USA (SAN 242-231X) Tel 303-753-0384
E-mail: Zhera@msn.com; zhera@msn.com.

Ziert, Paul Assocs., Inc., *(978-0-9666104)* Orders Addr.: P.O. Box 721020, Norman, OK 73070 USA Tel 405-447-9988; Fax: 405-447-5810; Edit Addr.: 3214 Bart Conner Dr., Norman, OK 73072 USA
E-mail: paul@intlgymnast.com; IGDwight@aol.com.

Zig the Pig, *(978-0-9761700)* 815 Poinsettia St., Columbia, SC 29205 USA.

Ziggy Owl Pr., *(978-0-9963747)* 24 Canal St., Medford, MA 02155 USA Tel 781-396-8470
E-mail: johngarp@aol.com.

Ziker, Andrew, *(978-0-9762147)* 1788 E. Indigo St., Gilbert, AZ 85298-3222 USA.

Zilber, Jeremy, *(978-0-9786688)* P.O. Box 5543, Madison, WI 53705 USA
E-mail: jzilber@littledemocrats.net
Web site: http://www.littledemocrats.net.

Zimmerman, W. Frederick *See* **Nimble Bks. LLC**

Zindel Publishing *See* **Graymalkin Media**

Zinka Pr., Inc., *(978-0-9647171)* 1480 Pulaski Ln., Wayne, PA 19087 USA Tel 610-688-2113; Fax: 610-688-0753
E-mail: zinkapress@aol.com
Web site: http://www.zinkapress.com.

Zino Pr. Children's Bks., *(978-1-55933)* Div. of Knowledge Unlimited, Inc., P.O. Box 52, Madison, WI 53701-0052 USA Tel 608-836-6660; Fax: 608-831-1570; Toll Free Fax: 800-618-1570; Toll Free: 800-356-2303
E-mail: madzino@zinopress.com
Web site: http://www.zinopress.com
Dist(s): **Brodart Co.**
Follett School Solutions.

Zion Natural History Assn., *(978-0-915630)* Zion National Pk., Springdale, UT 84767 USA (SAN 205-9959) Tel 435-772-3264; Fax: 435-772-3908; Toll Free: 800-635-3959
E-mail: znha@infowest.com
Web site: http://zionpark.org
Dist(s): **Chicago Distribution Ctr.**

Zion Publishing, *(978-0-9627147; 978-0-9979841)* 1500 Crown Colony Ct., Suite 540, Des Moines, IA 50315 USA Tel 515-282-5940; Toll Free: 800-996-2777 Do not confuse with companies with the same name in Monarch Beach, CA, Vallejo, CA
E-mail: maryenilsen@aol.com
Web site: http://www.zionpublishing.org.

Zion Publishing, *(978-0-9714844)* 17 Harding Ln., Sumiton, AL 35148 USA Tel 205-648-6741
E-mail: driverdm@aol.com.

Zip Line Publishing, *(978-0-9883792)* P.O. Box 78134, Charlotte, NC 28271 USA Tel 704-516-4287
E-mail: bethsmith@zipintoreading.com
Web site: zipintoreading.com
Dist(s): **Independent Pubs. Group.**

Zo Publishing, *(978-0-938465)* Orders Addr.: P.O. Box 61335, Honolulu, HI 96839 USA (SAN 660-9864) Tel 808-988-7111; Edit Addr.: 2918 Manoa Rd., Honolulu, HI 96822 USA (SAN 660-9872)
E-mail: dyen@lava.net.

Zoe Life Publishing, *(978-0-9748251; 978-0-9779445; 978-1-934363; 978-1-938807)* P.O. Box 871066, Canton, MI 48187 USA (SAN 256-1735) Tel 734-404-5485; Fax: 734-981-0251; Toll Free: 877-841-3400
E-mail: info@zoelifepub.com
Web site: http://www.zoelifepub.com
Dist(s): **Send The Light Distribution LLC.**

Zolie Zi Empire, *(978-0-692-89897-0; 978-0-692-92967-4)* 200 S. Ryan Dr. #11207, RED OAK, TX 75154 USA Tel 469-892-8816
E-mail: zoliezi@yahoo.com; zoliezi@yahoo.com.

Zonderkidz, *(978-0-310)* Div. of Zondervan, 5300 Patterson Ave., SE, Grand Rapids, MI 49530 USA Tel 1-800-727-3480
E-mail: zprod@zondervan.com
Web site: http://www.zondervan.com
Dist(s): **Nelson, Thomas Inc.**
Zondervan.

†**Zondervan,** *(978-0-00; 978-0-310; 978-0-937336)* Div. of HarperCollins Christian Publishing, Orders Addr.: c/o Zondervan XNET Ordering Dept., 5249 Corporate Grove, Grand Rapids, MI 49512 USA (SAN 298-9107); Edit Addr.: 5300 Patterson Ave., SE, Grand Rapids, MI 49530 USA (SAN 203-2694) Tel 616-698-6900; Fax: 616-698-3439
Web site: http://www.zondervan.com
Dist(s): **Brilliance Publishing, Inc.**
Ebsco Publishing
Follett School Solutions
Send The Light Distribution LLC
Vida Pubs.; *CIP.*

Zondervan bibles *See* **Zondervan Bibles**

Zondervan Bibles, *(978-0-310)* 5300 Patterson Ave., SE, Grand Rapids, MI 49530 USA Tel 800-727-3480
E-mail: zprod@zondervan.com
Web site: http://www.zondervan.com
Dist(s): **Zondervan.**

Zondervan Bks., *(978-0-310)* 5300 Patterson Ave., SE, Grand Rapids, MI 49530 USA Tel 1-800-727-3480
E-mail: zprod@zondervan.com
Web site: http://www.zondervan.com
Dist(s): **Zondervan.**

Zondervan Publishing House *See* **Zondervan**

Zone Bks. *Imprint of* **Stone Arch Bks.**

Zonk Galleries *See* **Zonk Galleries and Pubns.**

Zonk Galleries and Pubns., *(978-0-9706537)* 2909 Hansen Rd., Hayward, CA 94541 USA (SAN 254-3443) Tel 510-530-2681
E-mail: davidhoobler@sbcglobal.net
Web site: http://zonktheturtle.com.

Zoo Bks. *Imprint of* **Wildlife Education, Ltd.**

Zoombird Bks., *(978-0-615-32691-7)* Orders Addr.: 2734 Carisbrook Dr., Oakland, CA 94611 USA Tel 510-530-2737
Web site: http://www.zoombirdbooks.com.

Zoo-phonics, Inc., *(978-0-9617342; 978-1-886441)* Orders Addr.: 20950 Ferretti Rd., Groveland, CA 95321 USA (SAN 663-8589) Tel 209-962-5030; Fax: 209-962-4320; Toll Free: 800-622-8104
E-mail: zoo-info@zoo-phonics.com; shirley@zoo-phonics.com
Web site: http://www.zoo-phonics.com.

Zora, *(978-0-9714039; 978-1-59898)* Orders Addr.: 450 Stedman Pl., Monrovia, CA 91016 USA Tel 626-359-6071
E-mail: emil@zorapubs.com.

Zottola Publishing, Inc., *(978-0-9725880; 978-0-9823907)* Orders Addr.: 4212 Boone Ave. N., New Hope, MN 55428-0001 USA
E-mail: zottolaj@comcast.net
Web site: http://www.zotpub.com.

zReyomi Publishing, *(978-0-9670712)* Div. of Reyomi Global Media Group, Inc., P.O. Box 51928, Durham, NC 27717 USA Tel 919-321-2573; Fax: 919-489-3913
E-mail: Reyomi@aol.com
Dist(s): **Bk. Hse., The**
Brodart Co.

Zu Bks., *(978-0-615-15267-7)* 1813 Comet, Altus, OK 73521 USA Tel 580-477-0819
Web site: http://zuopolis.com
Dist(s): **Lulu Pr., Inc.**

'Zubaan Bks. (IND) *(978-93-81017) Dist. by* **Chicago Distribution Ctr.**

Zuber Publishing, *(978-0-9785551)* 52180 Tammy Dr., Granger, IN 46530 USA Tel 574-272-8914
E-mail: admin@zuberpublishing.com
Web site: http://www.zuberpublishing.com
Dist(s): **Distributors, The.**

Zuiho, *(978-0-9743474)* 11628 82nd Ave. NE, Kirkland, WA 98034-3400 USA.

Zulema Enterprises Publishing, *(978-1-881223)* 7715 Yardley Dr., Tamarac, FL 33321 USA Tel 954-724-5204
E-mail: peopleteachers@aol.com
Web site: http://www.zulemabooks.com.

Zulu Planet Pubs. (ZAF) *(978-1-920070; 978-1-920153) Dist. by* **APG.**

Zumaya Embraces *Imprint of* **Zumaya Pubns. LLC**

Zumaya Otherworlds *Imprint of* **Zumaya Pubns. LLC**

Zumaya Pubns. LLC, *(978-1-894869; 978-1-894942; 978-1-55410; 978-1-934135; 978-1-934841; 978-1-936144; 978-1-61271)* Orders Addr.: 3209 S. Interstate 35 APT 1086, Austin, TX 78741-6905 USA Tel 512-537-3145; 512-931-4594; Fax: 512-276-6745; *Imprints:* Zumaya Otherworlds (Zumaya Otherworlds); Zumaya Embraces (Zumaya Embraces); Zumaya Thresholds (ZumThresh)
E-mail: production@zumayapublishing.com; business@zumayapublishing.com
Web site: http://www.zumayapublications.com; http://www.zumayapublishing.com.

Zumaya Thresholds *Imprint of* **Zumaya Pubns. LLC**

Zy Iman Pubng, *(978-0-9779130)* P.O. Box 367, Brooklyn, NY 11221 USA
Web site: http://www.ucanspeakup.com.

Zygote Games LLC, *(978-0-9770419)* 100 Venture Way, Flr. 3, Suite 4, Hadley, MA 01035 USA Tel 413-303-9031; Fax: 253-540-5054
E-mail: orders@zygotegames.com
Web site: http://www.zygotegames.com.

Zyrro, Roggen, *(978-0-9762580)* 5841 Wornall Rd., Kansas City, MO 64113 USA
Web site: http://www.bunsta.com.

ZZ Dogs Pr. *Imprint of* **That's Life Publishing, Inc.**

Publisher Name Index

WHOLESALER & DISTRIBUTOR NAME INDEX

1stBooks Library, *See* **AuthorHouse**

26799Bernan Associates, *See* **Bernan Assocs.**

2Learn-English, (*978-0-9627878; 978-1-891077; 978-1-934637*) Div. of Authors & Editors, Orders Addr.: 10736 Jefferson Blvd., No. 604, Culver City, CA 90230-4969 USA Tel 310-251-3931 Arthur Rubin; 310-836-2014 General/Messages; Fax: 310-836-1845
E-mail: info@2learn-english.com
Web site: http://www.2learn-english.com.

3M Sportsman's Video Collection, 3M Ctr., Bldg. 223-4NE-05, Saint Paul, MN 55144-1000 USA (SAN 159-8929) Tel 612-733-7412; Fax: 612-736-7479; Toll Free: 800-940-8273 (orders only).

A & B Books, *See* **A & B Distributors & Pubs. Group**

A & B Distributors & Pubs. Group, (*978-1-881316; 978-1-886433*) Div. of A&B Distributors, 1000 Atlantic Ave., Brooklyn, NY 11238 USA (SAN 630-9216) Tel 718-783-7808; Fax: 718-783-7267; Toll Free: 877-542-6657; 146 Lawrence St., Brooklyn, NY 11201 (SAN 631-385X)
E-mail: maxtay@webspan.net.

A & M Church Supplies, 3535 Bay Rd., Saginaw, MI 48603-2464 USA (SAN 157-0145) Toll Free: 800-345-4694.

A B C-Clio Information Services, *See* **ABC-CLIO, LLC**

A B S Corporation, *See* **Budgetext**

A K J Educational Services, Incorporated, *See* **AKJ Bks.**

AAA Anime Distribution, 4509 Shirley Ave., Unit D, El Mone, CA 91731 USA Tel 626-575-8922
E-mail: vince@aaaanime.com.

Aardvark Global Publishing, (*978-0-9770328; 978-1-933570; 978-1-59971; 978-1-4276*) 9587 S. Grandview Dr., Sandy, UT 84092 USA Do not confuse with Aardvark Global Publishing, Atlanta, GA
E-mail: info@eckohousepublishing.com
Web site: http://eckohousepublishing.com/; http://aardvarkglobalpublishing.com/; http://eckobooks.com.

ABC-CLIO, LLC, (*978-0-275; 978-0-313; 978-0-8371; 978-0-86569; 978-0-87287; 978-0-87436; 978-0-89789; 978-0-89930; 978-0-903450; 978-0-938865; 978-1-56308; 978-1-56720; 978-1-57607; 978-1-85109; 978-1-58683; 978-1-59158; 978-0-9742537; 978-1-59884; 978-1-4408; 978-1-61069*) *130 Cremona Dr., Santa Barbara, CA 93117 USA (SAN 301-5467) Tel 805-968-1911; Fax: 805-685-9685; Toll Free: 800-368-6868; P.O. Box 93116, Goleta, CA 93116 (SAN 857-7099)*
E-mail: customerservice@abc-clio.com; service@abc-clio.com; salesuk@abc-clio.com
Web site: http://www.abc-clio.com.

ABC'S Bk. Supply, Inc., 7319 W. Flagler St., Miami, FL 33144 USA Toll Free: 877-383-4240
E-mail: abcbooks@abcbooks.com.

Abdo & Daughters Publishing, *See* **ABDO Publishing Co.**

ABDO Publishing Co., (*978-0-939179; 978-1-56239; 978-1-57765; 978-1-59197; 978-1-59679; 978-1-59928; 978-1-59961; 978-1-60270; 978-1-60453; 978-1-61613; 978-1-61714; 978-1-61758; 978-1-61783; 978-1-61784; 978-1-61785; 978-1-61786; 978-1-61787; 978-1-61478; 978-1-61479; 978-1-61480; 978-1-62401; 978-1-62402; 978-1-62403; 978-1-62968; 978-1-62969; 978-1-62970; 978-1-68076; 978-1-68077; 978-1-68078; 978-1-68079; 978-1-68080; 978-1-5321*) *Div. of ABDO Publishing Group, Orders Addr.: 8000 W. 78th St. Suite 310, Edina, MN 55439 USA (SAN 662-9172) Tel 952-831-2120; Fax: 952-831-1632; Toll Free Fax: 800-862-3480; Toll Free: 800-800-1312*
E-mail: info@abdopublishing.com
Web site: http://www.abdopublishing.com.

Abel Love, Inc., Orders Addr.: P.O. Box 2250, Newport News, VA 23609 USA (SAN 158-4081) Tel 757-877-2939; Toll Free: 800-520-2939; Edit Addr.: 935 Lucas Creek Rd., Newport News, VA 23608 USA Fax: 804-877-2939.

Abingdon Pr., (*978-0-687; 978-1-4267; 978-1-63088; 978-1-5018*) Div. of United Methodist Publishing House, Orders Addr.: P.O. Box 801, Nashville, TN 37202-3919 USA (SAN 201-0054) Tel 615-749-6409; Fax: 615-749-6056; Toll Free: 800-627-1789; Edit Addr.: 201 Eighth Ave., S., Nashville, TN 37202 USA (SAN 699-9956) Tel 615-749-6000; Toll Free Fax: 800-445-8189; Toll Free: 800-672-1789
E-mail: cokes_serv@cokesbury.com
Web site: http://www.abingdonpress.com/; http://www.umph.org.

Abraham Assocs. Inc., 5120-A Cedar Lake Rd., Minneapolis, MN 55416 USA Tel 952-927-7920; Fax: 952-927-8089; Toll Free: 800-701-2489
E-mail: stu@abrahamassociatesinc.com.

Abrams, Harry N. Incorporated, *See* **Abrams, Inc.**

Abrams, Inc., (*978-0-8109; 978-1-4197; 978-1-61769; 978-1-61312; 978-1-68335*) Orders Addr.: The Market Building Third Floor, 72-82 Rosebery Ave., London, EC1R 4RW GBR Tel 020 7713 2060; Fax: 020 7713 2061; Edit Addr.: 115 West 18th St., New York, NY 10011 USA (SAN 200-2434) Tel 212-206-7715; Fax: 212-519-1210
E-mail: webmaster@abramsbooks.com
Web site: http://www.abramsbooks.com.

Abrams Learning Trends, Orders Addr.: 16310 Bratton Ln., Suite 250, Austin, TX 78728 USA Tel 512-735-2863
E-mail: billt@abramslearningtrends.com.

Abyss Distribution, (*978-1-932548*) P.O. Box 48, Middlefield, MA 01243-0048 USA (SAN 630-9925) Tel 413-623-2155; Fax: 413-623-2156; Toll Free: 800-326-0804
E-mail: abyssdist@aol.com
Web site: http://www.azuregreen.om.

Academic Bk. Ctr., Inc., P.O. Box 1320, Lake Oswego, OR 97035-0320 USA (SAN 169-7145) Toll Free: 800-547-7704
E-mail: orders@acbc.com
Web site: http://www.abc.com.

Academic Bk. Services, Inc., 5490 Fulton Industrial Blvd., Atlanta, GA 30336 USA (SAN 631-0591) Tel 404-344-8317; Fax: 404-349-2127.

Academi-Text Medical Wholesalers, P.O. Box 1080, Monroe, MI 48161-6080 USA (SAN 135-2415) Toll Free: 800-552-8398 (out of state)
E-mail: dyourist@academi-text.com.

ACCESS Pubs. Network, 6893 Sullivan Rd., Grawn, MI 49637 USA.

Acorn Alliance, 549 Old North Rd., Kingston, RI 02881-1220 USA Tel 401-783-5480; Fax: 401-284-0959; Fulfillment Addr.: Client Distribution Services 193 Edwards Dr., Jackson, TN 38301 USA Toll Free Fax: 800-351-5073; Toll Free: 800-343-4499
E-mail: moyerbellbooks@yahoo.com
Web site: http://www.moyerbellbooks.com.

ACTA Pubns., (*978-0-87946; 978-0-914070; 978-0-915388*) 5559 Howard St., Skokie, IL 60077-2621 USA (SAN 204-7489) Toll Free Fax: 800-397-0079; Toll Free: 800-397-2282; 4848 N. Clark St., Chicago, IL 60640
E-mail: actapublications@aol.com
Web site: http://www.actapublications.com.

Action Products International, Inc., 344 Cypress Rd., Ocala, FL 34472-3108 USA (SAN 630-8805) Tel 352-687-4961; Toll Free: 800-772-2846
E-mail: sales@apii.com.

Activated Ministries, P.O. Box 462805, Escondido, CA 92046-2805 USA Toll Free: 877-862-3228
E-mail: sales@activatedministries.org.

ACW Pr., (*978-0-9656749; 978-1-892525; 978-1-932124; 978-1-934668*) Orders Addr.: P.O. Box 110390, Nashville, TN 37222 USA Tel 615-834-0450; Toll Free: 800-219-7483; Edit Addr.: 4854 Aster Dr., Nashville, TN 37211 USA
E-mail: regaforder@aol.com.

Adams Bk. Co., Inc., 140 58th Street, Unit 6G, Box 39, Brooklyn, NY 11220-2523 USA (SAN 107-7171) Tel 718-875-5464; Fax: 718-852-3212; Toll Free: 800-221-0909
E-mail: sales@adamsbook.com
Web site: http://www.adamsbook.com.

Adams News, 1555 W. Galer St., Seattle, WA 98119 USA (SAN 169-8842) Tel 206-284-7617; Fax: 206-284-7599; Toll Free: 800-533-7617.

Adams, Robert Henry Fine Art, (*978-0-9713010*) 2146 W. Sunnyside Ave., Chicago, IL 60625-1626 USA (SAN 159-6918)
E-mail: info@adamsfineart.com
Web site: http://www.adamsfineart.com.

Addicus Bks., (*978-1-886039; 978-1-936374; 978-1-938803; 978-1-940495; 978-1-943886; 978-0-692-67011-8*) Orders Addr.: P.O. Box 45327, Omaha, NE 68145 USA Tel 402-330-7493; Fax: 402 330-1707; Toll Free: 800-352-2873; Edit Addr.: 814 N. Franklin St., Chicago, IL 60610 USA
E-mail: addicusbks@aol.com; info@addicusbooks.com
Web site: http://www.AddicusBooks.com.

Addison-Wesley Educational Pubs., Inc., (*978-0-321; 978-0-328; 978-0-673*) Div. of Addison Wesley Longman, Inc., 75 Arlington St., Boston, MA 02116 USA Tel 617-848-7500; Toll Free: 800-447-2226
Web site: http://www.awl.com.

Addison-Wesley Longman, Inc., (*978-0-201; 978-0-321; 978-0-582; 978-0-673; 978-0-8013; 978-0-8053; 978-0-9654123*) Orders Addr.: 200 Old Tappan Rd., Old Tappan, NJ 07675 USA (SAN 299-4739) Toll Free: 800-922-0579; Edit Addr.: 75 Arlington St., Suite 300, Boston, MA 02116 USA (SAN 200-2000) Tel 617-848-7500; Toll Free: 800-447-2226
E-mail: pearsoned@eds.com; orderdeptnj@pearsoned.com
Web site: http://www.awl.com.

Addison-Wesley Publishing Company, Incorporated, *See* **Addison-Wesley Longman, Inc.**

Adelman, Joseph, 530 N. 40th St., Allentown, PA 18104-4558 USA (SAN 285-8002).

Adler, Leo, P.O. Box 10308, Eugene, OR 97440-2308 USA (SAN 169-7021).

Adler's Foreign Bks., Inc., (*978-0-8417*) 915 Foster St., Evanston, IL 60201 USA (SAN 111-3089) Tel 847-864-0664; Fax: 847-864-0804; Toll Free: 800-235-3771
E-mail: info@afb-adlers.com
Web site: http://www.afb-adlers.com.

Advanced Global Distribution Services, 5880 Oberlin Dr., San Diego, CA 32121 USA Toll Free Fax: 800-499-3822; Toll Free: 800-284-3580.

Adventure Pubns., (*978-0-934860; 978-1-885061; 978-1-59193*) Div. of Keen Communications, Orders Addr.: 820 Cleveland St., S., Cambridge, MN 55008 USA (SAN 212-7199) Tel 763-689-9800; Fax: 763-689-9039; Toll Free Fax: 877-374-9016; Toll Free: 800-678-7006
E-mail: orders@adventurepublications.net; custservice@adventurepublications.net
Web site: http://www.adventurepublications.net.

Adventures Unlimited Pr., (*978-0-932813; 978-1-931882; 978-1-935487; 978-1-939149*) Orders Addr.: P.O. Box 74, Kempton, IL 60946 USA (SAN 630-1126) Tel 815-253-6390; Fax: 815-253-6300; Edit Addr.: 303 Main St., Kempton, IL 60946 USA (SAN 250-3484)
E-mail: auphq@frontiernet.net
Web site: http://www.adventuresunlimitedpress.com.

Advertising Specialties, Inc., 4920 River Rd., Pascagoula, MS 39567 USA (SAN 108-6316) Tel 601-769-7904
Web site: http://www.advmkt.com; http://www.advantagebooksonline.com.

Advocate Distribution Solutions, Div. of Send The Light Distribution LLC, 100 Biblica Way, Elizabethton, TN 37643 USA Tel 423-767-1100; Fax: 423-547-5199; Toll Free Fax: 800-759-2779; Toll Free: 800-289-2772
Web site: http://www.stl-distribution.com; http://www.advocatedistribution.com.

Affiliated Bk. Distributor, Div. of North Shore Distributors, Inc., 1200 N. Branch St., Chicago, IL 60622 USA (SAN 169-2267).

Africa World Pr., (*978-0-86543; 978-1-59221*) 541 W. Ingham Ave., Suite B, Trenton, NJ 08638 USA (SAN 692-3925) Tel 609-695-3200; Fax: 609-695-6466
E-mail: customerservice@africaworldpressbooks.com
Web site: http://www.africaworldpressbooks.com.

African World Bks., 2217 Pennsylvania Ave., Baltimore, MD 21217 USA (SAN 631-3868) Tel 410-383-2006.

Afrikan World Bk. Distributor, Orders Addr.: P.O. Box 16447, Baltimore, MD 21217 USA; Edit Addr.: 2217 Pennsylvania Ave., Baltimore, MD 21217 USA (SAN 631-2020) Tel 410-383-2006.

Afro-American Bk. Distributor, 2537 Prospect, Houston, TX 77004 USA (SAN 169-8257).

Agencia de Publicaciones de Puerto Rico, GPO Box 4903, San Juan, PR 00936 USA (SAN 169-9296).

Agritech Publishing Group, Inc., Div. of Agritech Corp., 825 W. Samalayuca Dr., Tucson, AZ 85704-3912 USA (SAN 174-612X) Tel 520-544-2542.

AHA, Inc., (*978-0-918545*) P.O. Box 8405, Santa Cruz, CA 95061-8405 USA (SAN 295-5059) Tel 408-458-9119.

AIMS International Bks., Inc., (*978-0-922852*) 7709 Hamilton Ave., Cincinnati, OH 45231-3103 USA (SAN 630-270X) Tel 513-521-5590; Fax: 513-521-5592; Toll Free: 800-733-2067
E-mail: aimsbooks@fuse.net
Web site: http://www.aimsbooks.com.

A-K News Company, *See* **Aramark Magazine & Bk. Co.**

AK Pr. Distribution, (*978-1-873176; 978-1-902593; 978-0-9830597; 978-1-939202*) 370 Ryan Ave, Unit 100, Chico, CA 95973 USA (SAN 298-2234) Tel 510-208-1708; Fax: 510-208-1701
E-mail: akpress@akpress.org
Web site: http://www.akpress.org.

AKJ Bks., 4702 Benson Ave., Halethorpe, MD 21227-1411 USA (SAN 170-5431) Toll Free: 800-922-6066
E-mail: info@akjbooks.com
Web site: www.akjbooks.com; http://store.akjbooks.com; www.akjebooks.com.

Alabama Bookstore, Orders Addr.: P.O. Box 1279, Tuscaloosa, AL 35401-1626 USA Tel 205-758-4532; Fax: 205-758-5525; Toll Free: 800-382-2665 (orders only)
E-mail: ABS@AlabamaBook.com
Web site: http://www.AlabamaBook.com.

Alamo Square Distributors, P.O. Box 14543, San Francisco, CA 94114 USA Fax: 415-863-7456
E-mail: alamosqdist@earthlink.net.

Alba House, *See* **St Pauls/Alba Hse. Pubs.**

Alexander News Company, *See* **Blue Ridge News Co.**

Alfonsi Enterprises, 8621 Gavinton Ct., Dublin, OH 43017-9615 USA (SAN 169-4227).

Alfred Publishing Co., Inc., (*978-0-7390; 978-0-87487; 978-0-88284; 978-1-58951; 978-1-4574; 978-1-4706*) Orders Addr.: P.O. Box 10003, Van Nuys, CA 91410-0003 USA; Edit Addr.: 123 Dry Rd., Oriskany, NY 13424 USA Tel 315-736-1572; Fax: 315-736-7281
E-mail: customerservice@alfred.com; permissions@alfred.com; submissions@alfred.com
Web site: http://www.alfred.com.

Alibris, (*978-0-9702763*) 1250 45th St., Suite 100, Emeryville, CA 94608 USA Fax: 510-550-6052; Toll Free: 877-254-2747 (877-ALIBRIS, option 1)
E-mail: libraries@alibris.com
Web site: http://www.alibris.com/library.

Alive Books, *See* **Books Alive**

All Electronics Corp., 14928 Oxnard St., Van Nuys, CA 91411 USA.

All Romance Ebooks, LLC, (*978-1-936387; 978-1-943576; 978-1-945193; 978-1-946297*) 6252 Commercial Way No. 145, Weeki Wachee, FL 34613 USA
E-mail: info@allromanceebooks.com.

Allegro New Sound Distribution, Subs. of Allegro Distribution, 20048 NE San Rafael St., Portland, OR 97230-7459 USA.

Allentown News Agency, Inc., Orders Addr.: P.O. Box 446, Allentown, PA 18105 USA; Edit Addr.: 719-723 Liberty

St., Allentown, PA 18105 USA (SAN 169-7226) Tel 610-432-4441; Fax: 610-432-2708.

Alliance Bk. Co., P.O. Box 7884, Hilton Head, SC 29938-7884 USA
E-mail: alliancebk@mindspring.com.

Alliance Game Distributors, Centennial Dr., Fort Wayne, IN 46808 USA Tel 260-482-5490 (ext. 253); Fax: 260-471-9539
E-mail: jjh@alliance-games.com
Web site: http://www.alliance-games.com.

Alliance Hse., Inc., *(978-0-9665234)* 220 Ferris Ave., Suite 201, White Plains, NY 10603 USA Tel 914-328-5456; Fax: 914-946-1929
E-mail: alliancehs@aol.com.

Alonso Bk. & Periodical Services, Inc., 2316 2nd St S., Arlington, VA 22204-2010 USA (SAN 170-7035).

Alpen Bks, 4602 Chennault Beach Rd. Ste. B1, Mukilteo, WA 98275-5016 USA.

Alpenbooks, *See* **Alpenbooks Pr. LLC**

Alpenbooks Pr. LLC, *(978-0-9669795)* 4602 Chennault Beach Rd, B1, Mukilteo, WA 98275 USA (SAN 113-5309) Tel 425-415-4560; Fax: 425-493-6381
E-mail: rkoch@alpenbooks.com
Web site: http://www.alpenbooks.com.

Alpha & Omega Distributor, P.O. Box 36640, Colorado Springs, CO 80936-3664 USA (SAN 169-0515).

Alpha Bks., *(978-0-02; 978-0-672; 978-0-7357; 978-0-7897; 978-1-56761; 978-1-57595; 978-0-7431; 978-1-59257; 978-1-61564)* Div. of Pearson Technology Group, 800 E 96th St., 3rd Flr., Indianapolis, IN 46290 USA (SAN 219-6298) Tel 317-581-3500 Toll Free: 800-571-5840 (orders)
Web site: http://www.idiotsguides.com.

Alpine News Distributors, Div. of Mountain States Distributors, 0105 Marand Rd., Glenwood Springs, CO 81601 USA Tel 970-945-2269; Fax: 970-945-2260.

Alta Book Center Publishers, *See* **Alta English Publishers**

Alta English Publishers, *(978-1-878598; 978-1-882483; 978-1-932383)* 1775 E. Palm Canyon Dr. Suite 110-275, Palm Springs, CA 92264 USA (SAN 630-9240) Tel 760-459-2603; Fax: 760-464-0588
E-mail: info@altaenglishpublishers.com
Web site: http://www.altaenglishpublishers.com; http://www.altaenglishonline.com.

Amacom, *(978-0-7612; 978-0-8144)* Div. of American Management Association, Orders Addr.: 600 AMA Way, Saranac Lake, NY 12983 USA (SAN 227-3578) Tel 518-891-5510; Fax: 518-891-2372; Toll Free: 800-250-5308 (orders & customer service); Edit Addr.: 1601 Broadway, New York, NY 10019-7420 USA (SAN 201-1670) Tel 212-586-8100; Fax: 212-903-8168; 1 Ingram Blvd., La Vergne, TN 37086
E-mail: pubservice@amanet.org
Web site: http://www.amacombooks.org.

Amarillo Periodical Distributors, P.O. Box 3823, Lubbock, TX 70404 USA (SAN 156-4986) Tel 806-745-6000.

Amato, Frank Pubns., Inc., *(978-0-936608; 978-1-57188; 978-1-878175)* Orders Addr.: P.O. Box 82112, Portland, OR 97282 USA (SAN 214-3372) Tel 503-653-8108; Fax: 503-653-2766; Toll Free: 800-541-9498; Edit Addr.: 4040 SE Wister St., Milwaukie, OR 97222 USA (SAN 858-5741)
E-mail: wholesale@amatobooks.com; Lorraine@amatobooks.com
Web site: http://www.amatobooks.com.

Amazon.Com, *(978-1-58060)* 1200 12th Ave. S., Suite 1200, Seattle, WA 98144 USA (SAN 179-4205) Tel 206-266-6817; Orders Addr.: P.O. Box 80387, Seattle, WA 98108-0387 USA (SAN 156-143X) Tel 206-622-2335; Fax: 206-622-2405; 1 Centerpoint Blvd., non-carton, New Castle, DE 19720 (SAN 155-3992); 1 Centerpoint Blvd., carton, New Castle, DE 19720 (SAN 156-1405); 520 S. Brandon, non-carton, Seattle, WA 98108 (SAN 152-6642); 520 S. Brandon, carton, Seattle, WA 98108 (SAN 156-1383); 1600 E. Newlands Dr., carton, Fernley, NV 89408 (SAN 156-5982); 1600 E. Newlands Dr., non-carton, Fernley, NV 89408 (SAN 156-6008); Edit Addr.: 520 Pike St., Seattle, WA 98101 USA (SAN 155-3984); P.O. Box 81226, Seattle, WA 98108-1226; 705 Boulder Dr. Carton, Breinigsville, PA 18031
E-mail: catalog-dept@amazon.com
Web site: http://www.amazon.com.

Ambassador Bks. & Media, 42 Chasner St., Hempstead, NY 11550 USA (SAN 120-064X) Tel 516-489-4011; Fax: 516-489-5661; Toll Free: 800-431-8913
E-mail: ambassador@absbook.com
Web site: http://www.absbook.com.

Ambassador Book Service, *See* **Ambassador Bks. & Media**

America Hse. Bk. Pubs., *(978-1-893162; 978-1-58851; 978-1-59129)* Orders Addr.: P.O. Box 151, Frederick, MD 21705-0151 USA; Edit Addr.: 113 E. Church St., Frederick, MD 21701 USA
Web site: http://www.publishamerica.com.

American Assn. for Clinical Chemistry, Inc., *(978-0-915274; 978-1-890883; 978-1-59425)* Orders Addr.: 1850 K St NW Ste. 625, Washington, DC 20006-2215 USA (SAN 214-2813) Toll Free: 800-892-1400
E-mail: info@aacc.org
Web site: http://www.aaccdirect.org.

American Assn. for Vocational Instructional Materials, *(978-0-89606; 978-0-914452)* 220 Smithonia Rd., Winterville, GA 30683 USA (SAN 225-8811) Tel 706-742-5355; Fax: 706-742-7005; Toll Free: 800-228-4689
E-mail: ksseab@aavim.com; sales@aavim.com
Web site: http://www.aavim.com.

American Bible Society, *(978-0-8267; 978-1-58516; 978-1-937628; 978-1-941448; 978-1-941449)* Orders Addr.: 6201 E. 43rd St., Tulsa, OK 74135-6562 USA (SAN 662-7129) Toll Free Fax: 866-570-2877; Edit Addr.: 1865 Broadway, New York, NY 10023-9980 USA (SAN 203-5189) Tel 212-408-1200; Fax: 212-408-1305; 700 Plaza Dr., 2nd Flr., Secaucus, NJ 07094
E-mail: info@americanbible.org
Web site: http://www.bibles.org; http://www.americanbible.org.

American Buddhist Shim Gum Do Assn., Inc., *(978-0-9614427)* 203 Chestnut Hill Ave., Brighton, MA 02135 USA (SAN 113-2873) Tel 617-787-1506; Fax: 617-787-2708
E-mail: marystackhouse@shimgumdo.org
Web site: http://www.shimgumdo.org.

American Business Systems, Inc., 315 Littleton Rd., Chelmsford, MA 01824 USA (SAN 264-8229) Tel 508-250-9600; Fax: 508-250-8027; Toll Free: 800-356-4034.

American Eagle Pubns., Inc., *(978-0-929408)* Orders Addr.: P.O. Box 5111, Sun City West, AZ 85376 USA (SAN 249-2415) Tel 623-556-2925; Fax: 623-556-2926; Toll Free: 866-764-2925; Edit Addr.: 12647 Crystal Lake Dr., Sun City West, AZ 85375 USA
E-mail: custservice@ameaglepubs.com
Web site: http://www.ameaglepubs.com.

American Education Corp., The, *(978-0-87570; 978-1-58636; 978-0-9841672; 978-0-9841972)* 7506 N. Broadway, Suite 505, Oklahoma City, OK 73116-9016 USA (SAN 654-6250) Tel 405-840-6031; Toll Free: 800-222-2811
E-mail: jamesr@amered.com
Web site: http://www.amered.com.

American Educational Computer, Incorporated, *See* **American Education Corp., The**

American Heritage Magazine, 90 Fifth Ave., New York, NY 10011 USA.

American International Distribution Corp., Orders Addr.: P.O. Box 574, Williston, VT 05495-0020 USA Tel 800-390-3149; Fax: 802-864-7626; Toll Free: 888-822-9942; Edit Addr.: 50 Winter Sport Ln., Williston, VT 05495 USA (SAN 630-2238) Toll Free: 800-488-2665
E-mail: jmacon@aidcvt.com
Web site: http://www.aidcvt.com/Specialty/Home.asp.

American Kennel Club Museum of the Dog, *(978-0-9615072)* 1721 S. Mason Rd., Saint Louis, MO 63131 USA (SAN 110-8751) Tel 314-821-3647; Fax: 314-821-7381.

American Magazine Service, *See* **Prebound Periodicals**

American Marketing & Publishing Company, *See* **Christian Publishing Network**

American Mathematical Society, *(978-0-8218; 978-0-8284; 978-1-4704)* Orders Addr.: 201 Charles St., Providence, RI 02904 USA (SAN 250-3263) Tel 401-455-4000; Fax: 401-331-3842; Toll Free: 800-321-4267
E-mail: las@ams.org
Web site: http://www.ams.org.

American Micro Media, 19 N. Broadway, Box 306, Red Hook, NY 12571 USA (SAN 653-9920) Tel 914-758-5567.

American Overseas Bk. Co., Inc., 550 Walnut St., Norwood, NJ 07648 USA (SAN 169-4863) Tel 201-767-7600; Fax: 201-784-0263
E-mail: books@aobc.com
Web site: http://www.aobc.com.

American Pharmacists Assn., *(978-0-914768; 978-0-917330; 978-1-58212)* 2215 Constitution Ave., NW, Washington, DC 20037-2907 USA (SAN 202-4446) Tel 202-628-4410; Fax: 202-783-2351; Toll Free: 800-878-0729
E-mail: kanderson@aphanet.org
Web site: http://www.pharmacist.com.

American Society of Agronomy, *(978-0-89118)* 5585 Guilford Rd., Fitchburg, WI 53711-5801 USA (SAN 107-5683)
Web site: http://www.agronomy.org.

American Society of Civil Engineers, *(978-0-7844; 978-0-87262)* 1801 Alexander Bell Dr., Reston, VA 20191-4400 USA (SAN 204-7594) Tel 703-295-6300; Fax: 703-295-6211; Toll Free: 800-548-2723
E-mail: pubsful@asce.org
Web site: http://www.asce.org/bookstore.

American Technical Pubs., Inc., *(978-0-8269)* 10100 Orland Pkwy., Orland Park, IL 60467-5756 USA (SAN 206-8141) Toll Free: 800-323-3471
E-mail: service@americantech.net
Web site: http://www.americantech.net.

American West Bks., Orders Addr.: 14190 N. Washington Hwy., Ashland, VA 23005 USA (SAN 920-5233); Edit Addr.: 1254 Commerce Way, Sanger, CA 93657 USA (SAN 630-8570) Toll Free: 800-497-4909 Do not confuse with American West Bks., Albuquerque, NM
E-mail: JBM12@CSUFresno.edu.

American Wholesale Bk. Co., Subs. of Books-A-Million, Orders Addr.: 402 Industrial Ln., Birmingham, AL 35211-4465 USA (SAN 631-7391).

American Wholesale Booksellers Assn., *(978-0-9664715)* 702 S. Michigan St., South Bend, IN 46601 USA Tel 219-232-8500; Fax: 303-265-9292
E-mail: pwalsh@awba.com
Web site: http://www.awba.com.

Americana Publishing, Inc., *(978-1-58807; 978-1-58943)* 195 Us Highway 9. Ste. 204, Englishtown, NJ 07726-8294 USA Toll Free: 888-883-8203; 303 San Mateo Blvd, Ne, Albuquerque, NM 87108
E-mail: editor@americanabooks.com
Web site: http://www.americanabooks.com.

Americana Souvenirs & Gifts, *(978-1-890541)* 206 Hanover St., Gettysburg, PA 17325-1911 USA (SAN 169-7366) Toll Free: 800-692-7436.

America's Cycling Pubns., 6425 Capitol Ave., Suite F, Diamond Springs, CA 95619 USA.

America's Hobby Ctr., 146 W. 22nd St., New York, NY 10011 USA (SAN 111-0403) Tel 212-675-8922.

Ames News Agency, Inc., 2110 E. 13th St., Ames, IA 50010 USA (SAN 169-2550).

Amicus Educational, *See* **Amicus Publishing**

Amicus Publishing, *(978-1-60753; 978-1-68151)* P.O. Box 1329, Mankato, MN 56002 USA Tel 507-388-5164; Fax: 507-388-4797
E-mail: info@amicuspublishing.us
Web site: http://www.amicuspublishing.us.

Amigos Book Co., Orders Addr.: 5401 Bissonnet, Houston, TX 77081-6605 USA.

Amoskeag News Agency, 92 Allard Dr., Manchester, NH 03102 USA (SAN 169-4537) Tel 603-623-5343.

AMS Pr., Inc., *(978-0-404)* Brooklyn Navy Yard Bldg. 292, Suite 417, 63 Flushing Ave., New York, NY 11205 USA (SAN 106-6706) Tel 718-875-8100; Fax: 212-995-5413 Do not confuse with companies with the same or similar name in Los Angeles, CA, Pittsburgh, PA
E-mail: amserve@earthlink.net
Web site: http://www.amspressinc.com/.

Analos Magazine, 475 Park Ave. S., New York, NY 10016 USA.

Anchor Distributors, 1030 Hunt Valley Cir., New Kensington, PA 15068 USA (SAN 631-077X) Tel 724-334-7000; Fax: 724-334-1200; Toll Free: 800-444-4484
E-mail: customerservice@anchordistributors.com
Web site: http://www.anchordistributors.com.

Anderson Merchandisers, 421 E. 34th St., Amarillo, TX 79103 USA (SAN 169-8028) Tel 806-376-6251
E-mail: hanleyg@amerch.com.

Anderson News - Tacoma, 9914 32nd Ave., S., Lakewood, WA 98499 USA (SAN 108-1322) Tel 253-581-1940; Fax: 253-584-5941; Toll Free: 800-552-2000 (in Washington).

Anderson News, LLC, 211 Industrial Dr., Roanoke, VA 24019 USA (SAN 168-9223); 6016 Brookvale Ln. Ste. 110B, Knoxville, TN 37919-4003 (SAN 168-9363); 2541 Westcott Blvd., Knoxville, TN 37931 Tel 423-966-7575; 3911 Volunteer Dr., Chattanooga, TN 37416 (SAN 169-7862) Tel 423-894-3945; 6301 Forbing Rd., Little Rock, AR 72219 Tel 501-562-7360; 1185a Commerce Blvd., Midway, FL 32343-6629; 1857 W. Grant Rd., Tucson, AZ 85745-1203; 5184 Sullivan Gardens Pkwy., Kingsport, TN 37660-8104 (SAN 241-6131); 390 Exchange St., Box 1624, New Haven, CT 06506 (SAN 241-6158) Tel 203-777-5545; 5000 Moline St., Denver, CO 80239-2622 Tel 303-321-1111; 1709 N. East St., Flagstaff, AZ 86002 (SAN 168-9290) Tel 520-774-6171; Fax: 520-779-1958; 6016 Brookvale Ln. Ste. 110B, Knoxville, TN 37919-4003; P.O. Box 22968, Chattanooga, TN 37422; P.O. Box 36003, Knoxville, TN 37930-6003; P.O. Box 280077, Memphis, TN 38168-0077; P.O. Box 6660, Pensacola, FL 32503 Do not confuse with Anderson News Company, Pinellas Park, FL.

Anderson-Austin News Co., LLC, 808 Newtown Cir., No. B, Lexington, KY 40511-1230 USA (SAN 169-2836) Tel 606-254-2765; Fax: 606-254-3328.

Andich Brothers News Company, *See* **Tobias News Co.**

Andrews McMeel Publishing, *(978-0-8362; 978-0-939251; 978-1-57939; 978-0-7407; 978-1-4494; 978-1-5248)* Orders Addr.: c/o Simon & Schuster, Inc., 100 Front St., Riverside, NJ 08075 USA Toll Free Fax: 800-943-9831; Toll Free: 800-943-9839 (Customer Service); 800-897-7650 (Credit Dept.); Edit Addr.: 1130 Walnut St., Kansas City, MO 64106-2109 USA (SAN 202-540X) Toll Free: 800-851-8923
Web site: http://www.AndrewsMcMeel.com.

Andrzejewski's Marian Church Supply, *See* **A & M Church Supplies**

Angler's Bk. Supply, 1380 W. Second Ave., Eugene, OR 97402 USA (SAN 631-4546) Tel 541-342-8355; Fax: 541-342-1785; Toll Free: 800-260-3869.

Anglo-American Book Company, Limited (UK), *See* **Crown Hse. Publishing**

Ann Arbor Editions LLC, *(978-1-58726)* 2500 S. State St., Ann Arbor, MI 48104 USA Tel 734-913-1302; Fax: 734-913-1249; 1094 Flex Dr., Jackson, TN 38301
E-mail: ljohnson@aaeditions.com
Web site: http://www.annarbormediagroup.com; http://www.mittenpress.com; http://www.aaeditions.com.

Ann Arbor Media Group, LLC, *See* **Ann Arbor Editions LLC**

answers period, inc., *(978-0-917875)* Orders Addr.: P.O. Box 427, Goliad, TX 77963 USA (SAN 112-6431) Tel 361-645-2268; Toll Free: 800-852-4752
Web site: http://www.answersbook.com.

Anthracite News Company, *See* **Great Northern Distributors, Inc.**

Anthroposophic Press, Incorporated, *See* **SteinerBooks, Inc.**

Antipodes Bks. & Beyond, 9707 Fairway Ave., Silver Spring, MD 20901-3001 USA Tel 301-602-9519; Fax: 301-565-0160
E-mail: Antipode@antipodesbooks.com
Web site: http://www.antipodesbooks.com.

Antiquarian Bookstore, The, 1070 Lafayette Rd., Portsmouth, NH 03801 USA (SAN 158-9938) Tel 603-436-7250.

Antique Collectors' Club, *(978-0-902028; 978-0-907462; 978-1-85149)* Orders Addr.: Eastworks, 116 Pleasant St., Easthampton, MA 01027 USA (SAN 630-7787) Tel 413-529-0861; Fax: 413-529-0862; Toll Free: 800-252-5231 (orders)
E-mail: info@antiquecc.com; sales@antiquecc.com
Web site: http://www.antiquecollectorsclub.com.

AOAC International, *(978-0-935584)* 481 N. Frederick Ave., Suite 500, Gaithersburg, MD 20877-2417 USA (SAN 260-3411) Tel 301-924-7077; Fax: 301-924-7089; Toll Free: 800-379-2622
E-mail: aoac@aoac.org
Web site: http://www.aoac.org.

A-One Bk. Distributors, Inc., 1555 Ocean Ave. Ste. D, Bohemia, NY 11716-1933 USA (SAN 630-7981).

APG Sales & Distribution Services, Div. of Warehousing and Fulfillment Specialists, LLC (WFS, LLC), 7344 Cockrill Bend Blvd., Nashville, TN 37209-1043 USA (SAN 630-818X) Toll Free: 800-327-5113
E-mail: sswift@agpbooks.com
Web site: http://www.apgbooks.com.

APG Sales & Fulfillment, *See* **APG Sales & Distribution Services**

Apollo Bks., *(978-0-938290)* 91 Market St., Wappingers Falls, NY 12590-2333 USA (SAN 170-0928).

Apollo Library Bk. Supplier, 865 Kent Ln., Philadelphia, PA 19115 USA (SAN 159-8031).

Appalachian Bible Co., *(978-1-889049)* Orders Addr.: 522 Princeton Rd., Johnson City, TN 37605 USA (SAN 169-7889) Tel 423-282-9475; Fax: 423-282-9110; Toll Free: 800-289-2772; Edit Addr.: P.O. Box 1573, Johnson City, TN 37601 USA
E-mail: appainc@aol.com.

Appalachian Bk. Distributors, Div. of Send The Light Distribution LLC, Orders Addr.: 100 Biblica Way, Elizabethton, TN 37643-6070 USA Toll Free Fax: 800-759-2779; Edit Addr.: 506 Princeton Rd., Johnson City, TN 37601 USA.

Appalachian, Incorporated, *See* **Appalachian Bible Co.**

Applause Learning Resources, *(978-0-9655052; 978-0-9786746; 978-0-9788527; 978-0-9790091; 978-1-60713)* 85 Fernwood Ln., Roslyn, NY 11576 USA Tel 516-625-1145; Fax: 516-625-7392; Toll Free Fax: 877-365-7484; Toll Free: 800-277-5287
E-mail: info@applauselearning.com
Web site: http://www.applauselearning.com.

Applause Productions, *See* **Applause Learning Resources**

Apple Bk. Co., Div. of Scholastic Bk. Fairs, Inc., Orders Addr.: P.O. Box 217156, Charlotte, NC 28221-0156 USA Tel 704-596-6641; Fax: 704-599-1738; Toll Free: 800-331-1993; Edit Addr.: 5901 N. Northwoods Business Pkwy., Charlotte, NC 28269 USA (SAN 108-4569).

Applewood Bks., *(978-0-918222; 978-1-55709; 978-1-889833; 978-1-933212; 978-1-4290; 978-0-9819430; 978-1-60889; 978-0-9844156; 978-0-9836416; 978-1-938700; 978-0-9882885; 978-1-941216; 978-1-5162; 978-1-944038; 978-1-945187)* 1 River Rd., Carlisle, MA 01741-1820 USA (SAN 210-3419) Toll Free: 800-277-5312; 1 Ingram Blvd., La Vergne, TN 37086
E-mail: applewood@awb.com; svec@awb.com
Web site: http://www.awb.com.

Aquarian Concepts Publishing & Distribution, *(978-0-9666593)* Orders Addr.: HC Box 81-L, Payson, AZ 85541 USA (SAN 299-7215) Tel 520-474-0816; Toll Free: 888-539-8069; Edit Addr.: 62 Switchman Ln., Payson, AZ 85541 USA
E-mail: concepts1@cybertrails.com.

Arabic & Islamic Univ. Pr., 4263 Fountain Ave., Los Angeles, CA 90029 USA (SAN 107-6299) Tel 323-665-1000; Fax: 323-665-3107.

Aramark, 18825 67th Ave., NE, Arlington, WA 98223-9656 USA (SAN 631-3507) Tel 360-435-2524; Fax: 360-435-6805 Do not confuse with Aramark, Albuquerque, NM.

Aramark Magazine & Bk. Co., P.O. Box 25489, Oklahoma City, OK 73125 USA (SAN 169-6971) Tel 405-843-9383; Fax: 405-843-0379 Do not confuse with Aramark Magazine & Bk. Services, Inc., Norfolk, VA.

Aramark Magazine & Bk. Services, Inc., P.O. Box 2240, Norfolk, VA 23501 USA (SAN 169-8680) Do not confuse with Aramark Magazine & Book Co., Oklahoma City, OK.

Arbit Bks., Inc., *(978-0-930038)* 8050 N. Port Washington Rd., Milwaukee, WI 53217 USA (SAN 169-913X) Tel 414-352-4404.

Arcadia Publishing, *(978-0-7385; 978-1-58973; 978-1-59629; 978-1-4396; 978-1-60949; 978-1-61423; 978-1-4671; 978-1-62584; 978-1-62585; 978-1-62619; 978-0-9903765; 978-1-944313; 978-1-5316; 978-1-5402; 978-1-64111; 978-1-64112)* Orders Addr.: 420 Wando Park Blvd., Mount Pleasant, SC 29464 USA (SAN 255-268X) Tel 843-853-2070; Fax: 843-853-0044; Toll Free: 888-313-2665 Do not confuse with Arcadia Publishing in Greenwood Village, CO
E-mail: sales@arcadiapublishing.com
Web site: http://www.arcadiapublishing.com.

Ardic Bk. Distributors, Inc., 331 High St., 2nd Flr., Burlington, NJ 08016-4411 USA (SAN 170-5415).

Argus International Corp., Subs. of ICS International Group, Skypark Business Pk., P.O. Box 4082, Irvine, CA 92716-4082 USA (SAN 681-9761) Tel 714-552-8494 (phone/fax).

Aries Pr., *(978-0-933646)* P.O. Box 30081, Chicago, IL 60630 USA (SAN 111-9168) Tel 312-725-8300.

Aries Productions, Inc., *(978-0-910035)* Orders Addr.: P.O. Box 29396, Sappington, MO 63126 USA (SAN 669-0009); Edit Addr.: 6935 Tholozan Ave., Saint Louis, MO 63109-1130 USA (SAN 241-2004)
E-mail: uspsisquad@aol.com
Web site: http://ww.ussisquad.com.

Arizona Periodicals, Inc., P.O. Box 5780, Yuma, AZ 85366-5780 USA Tel 520-782-1822.

Arkansas Bk. Co., 1207 E. Second St., Little Rock, AR 72202-2732 USA (SAN 168-9460) Tel 501-375-1184.

Arlington Card Co., Bk. Dept., 140 Gansett Ave., Cranston, RI 02910 USA (SAN 108-5794) Tel 401-942-3188.

Armstrong, J. B. News Agency, *See* **News Group, The**

Arrow, G. H. Co., P.O. Box 676, Bala Cynwyd, PA 19004 USA (SAN 111-3771) Tel 215-227-3211; Fax: 215-221-0631; Toll Free: 800-775-2776.

Arrowhead Magazine Co., Inc., P.O. Box 5947, San Bernardino, CA 92412 USA (SAN 169-0094) Tel 909-799-8294; Fax: 909-799-3774; 1055 Cooley Ave., San Bernardino, CA 92408 (SAN 249-2717) Tel 909-370-4420.

Ars Obscura, *(978-0-9623780)* P.O. Box 4424, Seattle, WA 98104-0424 USA (SAN 113-5368) Tel 206-324-9792.

Art Institute of Chicago, *(978-0-86559)* Orders Addr.: a/o Museum Shop Mail Order Dept., 950 N. North Branch

St., Chicago, IL 60622-4276 USA; Edit Addr.: 111 S. Michigan Ave., Chicago, IL 60603-6110 USA (SAN 204-479X) Tel 312-443-3540; Fax: 312-443-1334
Web site: http://www.artic.edu.

Art Media Resources, Inc., *(978-1-878529; 978-1-58886)* 1507 S. Michigan Ave., Chicago, IL 60605 USA (SAN 253-8199) Tel 312-663-5351; Fax: 312-663-5177
E-mail: info@artmediaresources.com
Web site: http://www.artmediaresources.com.

ARVEST, P.O. Box 200248, Denver, CO 80220 USA (SAN 159-8694) Tel 303-388-8486; Fax: 303-355-4213; Toll Free: 800-739-0761
E-mail: copy@concentric.net.

Asia Bk. Corp. of America, *(978-0-940500)* 45-77 157th St., Flushing, NY 11355 USA (SAN 214-493X) Tel 718-762-7204; Fax: 718-460-5030.

ASM International, *(978-0-87170; 978-1-61503; 978-1-62708)* 9639 Kinsman Rd., Materials Park, OH 44073-0002 USA (SAN 204-7586) Tel 440-338-5151; Fax: 440-338-4634; Toll Free: 800-336-5152 Do not confuse with ASM International, Inc., Fort Lauderdale, FL
E-mail: memberservicecenter@asminternational.org
Web site: http://www.asminternational.org.

ASP Wholesale, c/o A&A Quality Shipping Services 3623 Munster Ave, Unit B, Hayward, CA 94545 USA Tel 510-732-6521 (Voice).

Aspen West Publishing, *(978-0-9615390; 978-1-885348)* P.O. Box 522151, Salt Lake Cty, UT 84152-2151 USA (SAN 112-7993) Toll Free: 800-222-9133 (orders only)
E-mail: kent@aspenwest.com
Web site: http://www.aspenwest.com.

Assn. of Energy Engineers, Orders Addr.: P.O. Box 1026, Liburn, GA 30048 USA Tel 770-925-9558; Fax: 770-381-9865; Edit Addr.: 4025 Pleasantdale Rd., Suite 420, Atlanta, GA 30340 USA Tel 770-447-5083.

Associated Univ. Presses, *(978-0-8453)* 2010 Eastpark Blvd., Cranbury, NJ 08512 USA (SAN 281-2959) Tel 609-655-4770; Fax: 609-655-8366
E-mail: aup440@aol.com
Web site: http://www.aupresses.com.

Association of Official Analytical Chemists, *See* **AOAC International**

Astran, Inc., 6995 NW 82nd Ave. Ste. 40, Miami, FL 33166-2783 USA (SAN 169-1082) Toll Free: 800-431-4957
E-mail: sales@astranbooks.com
Web site: http://www.astranbooks.com.

ATEXINC, Corp., *(978-0-9702332; 978-1-60405)* Orders Addr.: 17738 Vintage Oak Dr., Glencoe, MO 63038-1478 USA (SAN 631-774X) Toll Free Fax: 866-346-9515 Do not confuse with Atex, Inc., Bedford, MA
E-mail: mail@atexinc.com
Web site: http://www.atexinc.com; http://www.thetextilekit.com; http://www.itextiles.com.

Athelstan Pubns., *(978-0-940753)* Orders Addr.: 5925 Kirby Dr. Suite E. 464, Houston, TX 77005 USA (SAN 663-5318) Tel 713-371-2107; Fax: 713-524-1159
E-mail: info@athel.com; barlow@athel.com
Web site: http://www.athel.com.

Athena Productions, Inc., 5500 Collins Ave., No. 901, Miami Beach, FL 33140 USA Tel 305-868-8482; Fax: 305-868-8891.

Atlas Bks., 2541 Ashland Rd., Ashland, OH 44905 USA.

Atlas News Co., Div. of Hudson News Co., P.O. Box 779, Boylston, MA 01505-0779 USA (SAN 169-3360).

Atlas Publishing Co., *(978-0-930575)* 1464 36th St., Ogden, UT 84403 USA (SAN 110-3873) Tel 801-627-1043.

AtlasBooks Distribution, *See* **Bookmasters Distribution**

Attainment Co., Inc., *(978-0-934731; 978-1-57861; 978-1-943148; 978-1-944315)* Orders Addr.: P.O. Box 930160, Verona, WI 53593 USA (SAN 694-1656) Tel 608-845-7880; Fax: 608-845-8040; Toll Free: 800-327-4269; Edit Addr.: 504 Commerce Pkwy., Verona, WI 53953 USA (SAN 631-6174)
E-mail: info@attainmentcompany.com; sue@attainmentcompany.com; ameyer@attainmentcompany.com
Web site: http://www.attainmentcompany.com/.

Audible.com, One Washington Pk., Newark, NJ 07102 USA Tel 973-820-0400 (International); Fax: 973-890-2442; Toll Free: 888-283-5051 (USA & Canada)
E-mail: content-requests@audible.com
Web site: http://www.audible.com.

Audio Bk. Co., *(978-0-89926)* 235 Bellefontaine St., Pasadena, CA 91105-2921 USA (SAN 158-1414) Toll Free: 800-423-8273
E-mail: sales@audiobookco.com
Web site: http://www.audiobookco.com.

AudioGO, *(978-0-563; 978-0-7540; 978-0-7927; 978-0-89340; 978-1-55504; 978-1-60283; 978-1-60998; 978-1-62064; 978-1-62460; 978-1-4815; 978-1-4821)* Orders Addr.: c/o Perseus, 1094 Flex Dr., Jackson, TN 38301 USA; Edit Addr.: 42 Whitecap Dr., North Kingstown, RI 02852-7445 USA (SAN 858-7701) Toll Free: 800-621-0182
E-mail: laura.almeida@audiogo.com
Web site: http://www.audiogo.com/us/.

Audubon Prints & Bks., 9720 Spring Ridge Ln., Vienna, VA 22182 USA (SAN 111-820X).

Augsburg Fortress Publishers, Publishing House of The Evangelical Lutheran Church in America, *See* **Augsburg Fortress, Pubs.**

Augsburg Fortress, Pubs., *(978-0-8006; 978-0-8066; 978-1-4514; 978-1-5064)* Orders Addr.: P.O. Box 1209, Minneapolis, MN 55440-1209 USA (SAN 169-4081) Toll Free Fax: 800-722-7766; Toll Free: 800-328-4648 (orders only); Edit Addr.: 510 Marquette 8th Fl., Minneapolis, MN 55402 USA Tel 800-328-4648 800-722-7766
E-mail: customerservice@augsburgfortress.org; info@augsburgfortress.org; subscriptions@augsburgfortress.org; copyright@augsburgfortress.org; international@augsburgfortress.org
Web site: http://www.augsburgfortress.org.

Augusta News Co., 25 Second St., Apt. 124, Hallowell, ME 04347-1481 USA (SAN 169-3026).

Auromere, Inc., *(978-0-89744)* 2621 W. US Hwy. 12, Lodi, CA 95242-9200 USA (SAN 169-0043) Fax: 209-339-3715; Toll Free: 800-735-4691
E-mail: sasp@lodinet.com
Web site: http://www.auromere.com.

Austin & Company, Inc., *(978-0-9657153)* 104 S. Union St., Suite 202, Traverse City, MI 49684 USA (SAN 631-1466) Tel 231-933-4649; Fax: 231-933-4659
E-mail: aandn@aol.com
Web site: http://www.austinandcompanyinc.com.

Austin & Nelson Publishing, *See* **Austin & Company, Inc.**

Austin Management Group, Orders Addr.: P.O. Box 3206, Paducah, KY 42002-3206 USA (SAN 135-3349); Edit Addr.: P.O. Box 300, Paducah, KY 42002-0300 USA (SAN 249-6844).

Author Solutions, Inc., Div. of Penguin Group (USA) Inc., 1663 Liberty Dr., Bloomington, IN 47403 USA Tel 812-334-5223; Toll Free: 877-655-1722
E-mail: sfurr@authorsolutions
Web site: http://www.authorsolutions.com.

AuthorHouse, *(978-1-58500; 978-0-9675669; 978-1-58721; 978-1-58820; 978-0-7596; 978-1-4033; 978-1-4107; 978-1-4140; 978-1-4184; 978-1-4208; 978-1-4259; 978-1-4343; 978-1-4389; 978-1-4490; 978-1-4520; 978-1-61764; 978-1-4567; 978-1-4582; 978-1-4624; 978-1-4633; 978-1-4634; 978-0-9846457; 978-1-4670; 978-1-4678; 978-1-4685; 978-1-4772; 978-1-4817; 978-1-4918; 978-1-4969; 978-1-5049; 978-1-5065; 978-1-5246; 978-1-5462)* Div. of *Author Solutions, Inc., 1663 Liberty Dr., Suite 200, Bloomington, IN 47403 USA (SAN 253-7605) Fax: 812-336-5449; Toll Free: 888-519-5121*
E-mail: authorsupport@authorhouse.com; emilyguldin@yahoo.com; sfurr@authorsolutions.com; jburns@authorsolutions.com
Web site: http://www.facebook.com/daveywizzletooth1; http://www.authorhouse.com.

Authors & Editors, *See* **2Learn-English**

Auto-Bound, Inc., 909 Marina Village Pkwy., No. 67B, Alameda, CA 94501-1048 USA (SAN 170-0782) Tel 510-521-8655; Fax: 510-521-8755; Toll Free: 800-523-5833.

Avanti Enterprises, Inc., P.O. Box 3563, Hinsdale, IL 60522-3563 USA (SAN 158-3727) Toll Free: 800-799-6464.

Avenue Bks., 2270 Porter Way, Stockton, CA 95207-3339 USA (SAN 122-4158).

Avery BookStores, Inc., 516 Asharoken Ave., Northport, NY 11768-1176 USA (SAN 169-510X).

Aviation Bk. Co., *(978-0-911720; 978-0-911721; 978-0-916413)* 7201 Perimeter Rd., S., No. C, Seattle, WA 98108-3812 USA (SAN 120-1530) Tel 206-767-5232; Fax: 206-763-3428; Toll Free: 800-423-2708
E-mail: sales@aviationbook.com.

Avonlea Bks., Inc., Orders Addr.: P.O. Box 74, White Plains, NY 10602-0074 USA (SAN 680-4446) Tel 914-946-5923; Fax: 914-761-3119; Toll Free: 800-423-0622
E-mail: avonlea@bushkin.com
Web site: http://www.bushkin.com.

B. P. I. Communications, *See* **VNU**

B T P Distribution, 4135 Northgate Blvd., Suite 5, Sacramento, CA 95834-1226 USA (SAN 631-2489) Tel 916-567-2496; Fax: 916-441-6749.

Baggins Bks., 3560 Meridian St., Bellingham, WA 98225-1731 USA (SAN 156-501X).

Baha'i Distribution Service, *(978-0-87743)* Orders Addr.: P.O. Box 1759, Powder Springs, GA 30127-7522 USA (SAN 213-7496) Toll Free: 800-999-9019; Edit Addr.: 415 Linden Ave., Wilmette, IL 60091 USA Tel 847-251-1854; Fax: 847-251-3652
E-mail: bds@usbnc.org.

Baker & Taylor Bks., *(978-0-8480; 978-1-222; 978-1-223)* Orders Addr.: Commerce Service Ctr., 251 Mt. Olive Church Rd., Commerce, GA 30599 USA (SAN 169-1503) Tel 404-335-5000; Toll Free: 800-775-1200 (customer service); 800-775-1800 (orders); Reno Service Ctr., 1160 Trademark Dr., Suite 111, Reno, NV 89511 (SAN 169-4464) Tel 775-850-3800; Fax: 775-850-3826 (customer service); Toll Free Fax: 800-775-1700 (orders); Edit Addr.: Bridgewater Service Ctr. 1120 US Hwy. 22, E., Bridgewater, NJ 08807 USA (SAN 169-4901) Toll Free: 800-775-1500 (customer service); Momence Service Ctr., 501W. Gladiolus St., Momence, IL 60954-1799 (SAN 169-2100) Tel 815-472-2444 (international customers); Fax: 815-472-9886 (international customers); Toll Free: 800-775-2300 (customer service, academic libraries)
E-mail: btinfo@btol.com
Web site: http://www.btol.com.

Baker & Taylor Fulfillment, Inc., 2550 W. Tyvola Rd., Suite 370, Charlotte, NC 28217 USA (SAN 760-8772) Tel 704-236-9553
E-mail: johnsod@btol.com.

Baker & Taylor International, 1120 US Hwy. 22 E., Box 6885, Bridgewater, NJ 08807 USA (SAN 200-6804) Tel 908-541-7000; Fax: 908-729-4037.

Baker & Taylor Publishing Group, *See* **Readerlink Distribution Services, LLC**

Baker Bks., *(978-0-8010; 978-0-913686)* Div. of Baker Publishing Group, Orders Addr.: P.O. Box 6287, Grand Rapids, MI 49516-6287 USA (SAN 299-1500) Toll Free Fax: 800-398-3111 (orders only); Toll Free: 800-877-2665 (orders only); Edit Addr.: 6030 E. Fulton, Ada, MI 49301 USA (SAN 201-4041) Tel 616-676-9185; Fax: 616-676-9573
Web site: http://www.bakerpublishinggroup.com.

Baker Book House, Incorporated, *See* **Baker Publishing Group**

Baker Publishing Group, *(978-0-8007; 978-0-8010; 978-1-58743; 978-1-4412; 978-1-4934; 978-1-68196; 978-1-5409)* Orders Addr.: P.O. Box 6287, Grand Rapids, MI 49516-6287 USA Tel 616-676-9573; Toll Free Fax: 800-398-3111 (orders only); Toll Free: 800-877-2665 (orders only); Edit Addr.: 6030 E. Fulton, Ada, MI 49301 USA Tel 616-676-9185; Fax: 616-676-9573; Toll Free Fax: 800-398-3111; Toll Free: 800-877-2665
E-mail: webmaster@bakerpublishinggroup.com
Web site: http://www.bakerbooks.com; http://www.bakerpublishinggroup.com.

Balogh International, Inc., *(978-1-878762; 978-1-891770)* 1911 N. Duncan Rd., Champaign, IL 61822 USA (SAN 297-2344) Tel 217-355-9331; Fax: 217-355-9413
E-mail: balogh@balogh.com
Web site: http://www.balogh.com.

Balogh Scientific Books, *See* **Balogh International, Inc.**

Balzekas Museum of Lithuanian Culture, 6500 S. Pulaski Rd., Chicago, IL 60629 USA (SAN 110-8522) Tel 773-582-6500; Fax: 773-582-5133.

Banner of Truth, The, *(978-0-85151)* Orders Addr.: P.O. Box 621, Carlisle, PA 17013 USA Tel 717-249-5747; Fax: 717-249-0604; Toll Free: 800-263-8085; Edit Addr.: 63 E. Louther St., Carlisle, PA 17013 USA (SAN 112-1553)
E-mail: info@banneroftruth.org
Web site: http://www.banneroftruth.co.uk.

Banta Packaging & Fulfillment, 1071 Willow Spring Rd., Harrisonburg, VA 22801 USA (SAN 631-7731) Tel 540-442-1333; Fax: 540-434-3541; N9234 Lake Park Rd., Appleton, WI 54915 (SAN 631-8290) Tel 920-969-6400; Fax: 920-751-7794
E-mail: jfair@banta.com.

Banyan Tree Bks., *(978-0-9604320)* 1963 El Dorado Ave., Berkeley, CA 94707 USA (SAN 207-3862) Fax: 510-524-2690
E-mail: banyan@uclink.berkeley.edu.

Barbour & Company, Incorporated, *See* **Barbour Publishing, Inc.**

Barbour Publishing, Inc., *(978-0-916441; 978-1-55748; 978-1-57748; 978-1-58660; 978-1-59310; 978-1-59789; 978-1-60260; 978-1-60742; 978-1-61626; 978-1-62029; 978-1-62416; 978-1-62836; 978-1-63058; 978-1-63409; 978-1-944836; 978-1-68322)* Orders Addr.: P.O. Box 719, Uhrichsville, OH 44683 USA (SAN 295-7094) Fax: 740-922-5948; Toll Free Fax: 800-220-5948; Toll Free: 800-852-8010
E-mail: info@barbourbooks.com
Web site: http://www.barbourbooks.com.

Barnes & Noble Bks.-Imports, *(978-0-389)* 4720 Boston Way, Lanham, MD 20706 USA (SAN 206-7803) Tel 301-459-3366; Toll Free: 800-462-6420.

Barnes & Noble, Inc., *(978-0-7607; 978-0-88029; 978-1-4028; 978-1-4114; 978-1-4351; 978-1-61551; 978-1-61552; 978-1-61553; 978-1-61554; 978-1-61555; 978-1-61556; 978-1-61557; 978-1-61558; 978-1-61559; 978-1-61560; 978-1-61679; 978-1-61680; 978-1-61681; 978-1-61682; 978-1-61683; 978-1-61684; 978-1-61685; 978-1-61686; 978-1-61687; 978-1-61688; 978-1-970008) 76 Ninth Ave., 9th Flr., New York, NY 10011 USA (SAN 141-3651) Tel 212-414-6385; 122 Fifth Ave., New York, NY 10011*
E-mail: smcculloch@bn.com.

Barnes&Noble.com, *(978-1-4005; 978-1-4006)* c/o Merch Accounts Payable/NR Dept., 76 Ninth Ave., 9th Flr., New York, NY 10011 USA (SAN 192-6551) Tel 212-414-6000
Web site: http://www.bn.com.

Basic Crafts Co., 6001 66th Ave., No. 10, Riverdale, MD 20737-1717 USA (SAN 169-5622) Toll Free: 800-847-4127 (outside New York).

Basin News Co., P.O. Box 300, Paducah, KY 42002-0300 USA (SAN 169-2860).

Bassett Printing Corp., *(978-0-9632415)* Orders Addr.: P.O. Box 866, Bassett, VA 24055 USA Fax: 540-629-3416; Toll Free: 800-336-5102 (outside Virginia); Edit Addr.: 101 Main St., Bassett, VA 24055 USA Tel 540-629-2541.

Baum & Beaulieu Assocs., 46 O'Connell Ct., Great River, NY 11749 USA Tel 631-277-3249; Toll Free: 800-923-2444; P.O. Box 582, Great River, NY 11739-0582 Toll Free: 800-923-2444.

Bay News, Inc., 3333 NW 35th Ave., Portland, OR 97210 USA Tel 503-219-3001; Fax: 503-241-1877.

Bayou Bks., 1005 Monroe St., Gretna, LA 70053 USA (SAN 120-1913) Tel 504-368-1171; Toll Free: 800-843-1724.

BBC Audiobooks America, *See* **AudioGO**

BCH Fulfillment & Distribution, 46 Purdy St., Harrison, NY 10528 USA
E-mail: info@bookch.com
Web site: http://www.bookch.com/.

Beagle Bay Bks., *(978-0-9679591; 978-0-9749610)* Div. of Beagle Bay, Inc., 2325 Homestead Pl., Reno, NV 89509-3657 USA
E-mail: info@beaglebay.com
Web site: http://www.beaglebay.com.

Beaver News Co., Inc., 230 W. Washington St., Rensselaer, IN 47978 USA (SAN 630-8864).

Beck's Bk. Store, 4520 N. Broadway, Chicago, IL 60640 USA (SAN 159-8139) Tel 773-784-7963; Fax: 773-784-0066
E-mail: rsvitrd@aol.com
Web site: http://www.aol.members/becks.html.

Beechwood Pubns., Inc., P.O. Box 1158, Kennett Square, PA 19348 USA (SAN 107-5853) Tel 610-444-5991; Fax: 215-566-4178.

Beekman Bks., Inc., *(978-0-8464)* 300 Old All Angels Hill Rd., Wappingers Falls, NY 12590 USA (SAN 170-1622) Tel 845-297-2690; Fax: 845-297-1002
E-mail: manager@beekmanbooks.com
Web site: http://www.beekmanbooks.com.

Beeler, Thomas T. Pub., *(978-1-57490)* Orders Addr.: P.O. Box 310, Rollinsford, NH 03869 USA Toll Free Fax: 888-222-3396; Toll Free: 800-818-7574; Edit Addr.: 710 Main St., Suite 300, Rollinsford, NH 03869 USA Tel 603-749-0392; Fax: 603-749-0395
E-mail: tombeeler@beelerpub.com
Web site: http://www.beelerpub.com.

Before Columbus Foundation, 655 13th St. Ste. 302, Oakland, CA 94612-1225 USA (SAN 159-2955).

Beijing Bk. Co., Inc., 701 E. Linden Ave., Linden, NJ 07036-2495 USA (SAN 169-5673) Tel 908-862-0909; Fax: 908-862-4201.

Bell Magazine, Orders Addr.: P.O. Box 1957, Monterey, CA 93940 USA (SAN 159-7221); Edit Addr.: 3 Justin Ct., Monterey, CA 93940 USA (SAN 169-0353) Tel 408-642-4668.

Bella Distribution, Orders Addr.: P.O. Box 10543, Tallahassee, FL 32302 USA; Edit Addr.: 1041 Aenon Church Rd., Tallahassee, FL 32304 USA Fax: 850-576-3498; Toll Free: 800-533-1973
E-mail: info@belladistribution.com
Web site: http://www.belladistribution.com.

Benchmark LLC, *(978-0-7834; 978-0-929591)* 559 San Ysidro Rd. Suite I, Santa Barbara, CA 93108 USA (SAN 249-7522) Tel 805-565-8911; Toll Free: 888-797-9377
E-mail: bridger@benchmarkmaps.com; teri@benchmarkmaps.com; curtis@benchmarkmaps.com
Web site: http://www.benchmarkmaps.com.

Benjamin News Group, Orders Addr.: 2131 International St., Columbus, OH 43228 USA (SAN 660-9406) Tel 614-777-9768; Fax: 7=614-777-9766; Edit Addr.: 1701 Rankin St., Missoula, MT 59808-1629 USA (SAN 169-4391) Tel 406-721-7801; Fax: 406-721-7802.

Bennett & Curran, Inc., *(978-1-879607)* 1280 Cherryville Rd., Greenwood Vlg, CO 80121-1222 USA
E-mail: Jeff@bennettandcurran.com.

Berkeley Educational Paperbacks, 2480 Bancroft Way, Berkeley, CA 94704 USA (SAN 168-9509) Tel 510-848-7907.

Berkeley Game Distributors, 5850 Hollis St., Emeryville, CA 94608-2016 USA (SAN 631-2934) Toll Free: 800-424-4263; 1164 E. Sandhill Ave., Carson, CA 90746
E-mail: bgdnorth@ix.netcom.com.

Bernan Assocs., *(978-0-400; 978-0-527; 978-0-89059; 978-1-59610; 978-1-59888; 978-1-60175; 978-1-60946; 978-1-63005; 978-1-64143)* Div. of Kraus Organization, The, Orders Addr.: 15200 NBN Way, P.O. Box 190, Blue Ridge Summit, PA 17214 USA (SAN 169-3182) Tel 301-459-7666; Fax: 301-459-6988; Toll Free Fax: 800-865-3450; Toll Free: 800-865-3457; Edit Addr.: 4501 Forbes Blvd., Suite 200, Lanham, MD 20706 USA (SAN 760-7253) Tel 301-459-2255; Fax: 301-459-0056; Toll Free: 800-416-4385; 15200 Nbn Way, Blue Ridge Summ, PA 17214
E-mail: query@bernan.com; order@bernan.com; info@bernan.com; jkemp@bernan.com; jculley@rowman.com
Web site: www.rowman.com.

Berrett-Koehler Pubs., Inc., *(978-1-57675; 978-1-58376; 978-1-881052; 978-1-60509; 978-1-60994; 978-1-62656; 978-1-5230)* Orders Addr.: c/o AIDC, P.O. Box 565, Williston, VT 05495 USA Fax: 802-864-7626 (orders); Toll Free: 800-929-2929 (orders); Edit Addr.: 1333 Broadway, Suite 1000, Oakland, CA 94612 USA Tel 510-817-2277; Fax: 415-362-2512
E-mail: bkpub@bkpub.com
Web site: http://www.bkconnection.com.

Bess Pr., Inc., *(978-0-935848; 978-1-57306; 978-1-880188; 978-0-615-50460-5; 978-0-615-56510-1)* 3565 Harding Ave., Honolulu, HI 96816 USA (SAN 239-4111) Tel 808-734-7159; Fax: 808-732-3627
E-mail: kelly@besspress.com
Web site: http://www.besspress.com.

Best Bk. Ctr., Inc., 1016 Ave. Ponce De Leon, San Juan, PR 00926 USA (SAN 132-4403) Tel 809-727-7945; Fax: 809-268-5022.

Best Continental Bk. Co., Inc., P.O. Box 615, Merrifield, VA 22116 USA (SAN 107-3737) Tel 703-280-1400.

Bethany Hse. Pubs., *(978-0-7642; 978-0-87123; 978-1-55661; 978-1-56179; 978-1-57778; 978-1-880089; 978-1-59066)* Div. of Baker Publishing Group, Orders Addr.: P.O. Box 6287, Grand Rapids, MI 49516-6287 USA Toll Free Fax: 800-398-3111 (orders); Toll Free: 800-877-2665 (orders); Edit Addr.: 11400 Hampshire Ave., S., Bloomington, MN 55438-2455 USA (SAN 201-4416) Tel 952-829-2500; Fax: 952-996-1393
E-mail: orders@bakerbooks.com
Web site: http://www.bethanyhouse.com.

Better Homes & Gardens Books, *See* **Meredith Bks.**

Betty Segal, Inc., 1749 Eucalyptus St., Brea, CA 92621 USA Tel 714-529-5359; Fax: 714-529-3882
E-mail: BertySegal@aol.com
Web site: http://www.agoralang.com/trp-bertysegal.html.

Beyda & Associates, Incorporated, *See* **Beyda for Bks., LLC**

Beyda for Bks., LLC, P.O. Box 2535, Montclair, CA 91763-1035 USA (SAN 169-0426) Toll Free: 800-422-3932 (orders only)
E-mail: info@beydaforbooks.com
Web site: http://www.beydaforbooks.com.

B&H Publishing Group, *(978-0-8054; 978-0-87981; 978-1-55819; 978-1-58640; 978-0-8400; 978-1-4336)* Div. of LifeWay Christian Resources of the Southern Baptist Convention, One LifeWay Plaza MSN 114, Nashville, TN 37234-0114 USA (SAN 201-937X) Tel 615-251-2520; Fax: 615-251-5026 (Books Only); 615-251-2036 (Bibles Only); 615-251-2413 (Gifts/Supplies Only); Toll Free: 800-725-5416; 800-251-3225 (retailers); 800-296-4036 (orders/returns); 800-448-8032 (consumers); 800-458-2772 (churches)
E-mail: broadmanholman@lifeway.com; heather.counsellor@bhpublishinggroup.com; wes.banks@bhpublishinggroup.com; laurene.martin@lifeway.com
Web site: http://www.bhpublishinggroup.com; http://www.lifeway.com.

BHB Fulfillment, Div. of Weatherhill, Inc., 41 Monroe Tpke., Trumbull, CT 06611 USA.

BHB International, Incorporated, *See* **Continental Enterprises Group, Inc. (CEG)**

Wholesaler & Distributor Name Index

Bibliotech, Inc., P.O. Box 720459, Dallas, TX 75372-0459 USA (SAN 631-8312) Tel 214-221-0002; Fax: 214-221-1794
E-mail: metatron@airmail.net
Web site: http://www.bibliotechincorporated.com.

Biddy Bks., 1235 168 Model Rd., Manchester, TN 37355 USA (SAN 157-8561) Tel 931-728-6967.

Big Kids Productions, Inc., *(978-1-885627)* 2120 Oxford Ave., Austin, TX 78704-4014 USA (SAN 631-340X) Toll Free: 800-477-7811
E-mail: customerservice@bigkidsvideo.com
Web site: http://www.awardvids.com.

Big River Distribution, *(978-0-9795944; 978-0-9823575; 978-0-9845519)* Orders Addr.: 8214 Exchange Way, Saint Louis, MO 63144 USA (SAN 631-9114) Tel 314-918-9800; Fax: 314-918-9804
E-mail: info@bigriverdist.com; randy@bigriverdist.com
Web site: http://www.bigriverdist.com.

Big Tent Bks., *(978-1-60131)* 115 Bluebill Dr., Savannah, GA 31419 USA (SAN 851-1136)
E-mail: admin@dragonpencil.com; admin@bigtentbooks.com
Web site: http://www.bigtentbooks.com.

Bilingual Educational Services, Inc., *(978-0-86624; 978-0-89075)* 2514 S. Grand Ave., Los Angeles, CA 90007 USA (SAN 218-4680) Tel 213-749-6213; Fax: 213-749-1820; Toll Free: 800-448-6032
E-mail: sales@besbooks.com
Web site: http://www.besbooks.com.

Bilingual Pr./Editorial Bilingue, *(978-0-916950; 978-0-927534; 978-1-931010; 978-1-939743)* Orders Addr.: Hispanic Research Ctr. Arizona State Univ. P.O. Box 875303, Tempe, AZ 85287-5303 USA (SAN 208-5526) Fax: 480-965-8309; Toll Free: 800-965-2280; Edit Addr.: Bilingual Review Pr. Administration Bldg. Rm. B-255 Arizona State Univ., Tempe, AZ 85281 USA
E-mail: brp@asu.edu
Web site: http://www.asu.edu/brp.

Bilingual Pubns. Co., The, 270 Lafayette St., New York, NY 10012 USA (SAN 164-8993) Tel 212-431-3500; Fax: 212-431-3567 Do not confuse with Bilingual Pubns., in Denver, CO
E-mail: lindagoodman@juno.com; spanishbks@aol.com.

Birdlegs Christian Apparel, P.O. Box 189, Duluth, GA 30136-0189 USA (SAN 631-3280) Toll Free: 800-545-0790.

BJU Pr., *(978-0-89084; 978-1-57924; 978-1-59166; 978-1-60682; 978-1-62856)* 1700 Wade Hampton Blvd., Greenville, SC 29614 USA (SAN 223-7512) Tel 864-242-5731; 864-370-1800 (ext. 4397; Fax: 864-298-0268; Toll Free Fax: 800-525-8398; Toll Free: 800-845-5731
E-mail: bjup@bjup.com
Web site: http://www.bjupress.com.

Bk. Box, Inc., 3126 Purdue Ave., Los Angeles, CA 90066 USA (SAN 243-2285) Tel 310-391-2313.

Bk. Buy Back, 5150 Candlewood St., No. 6, Lakewood, CA 90712 USA (SAN 631-7251) Tel 562-461-9355; Fax: 562-461-9445.

Bk. Co., The, 145 S. Glencoe St., Denver, CO 80222-1152 USA (SAN 200-2809).

Bk. Distribution Ctr., *(978-0-941722)* Div. of Free Islamic Literatures, Inc., Orders Addr.: P.O. Box 35844, Houston, TX 77235 USA (SAN 241-6395); Edit Addr.: P.O. Box 31669, Houston, TX 77231 USA (SAN 226-2770).

Bk. Distribution Ctr., Inc., Orders Addr.: P.O. Box 64631, Virginia Beach, VA 23467-6431 USA (SAN 134-8019) Tel 757-456-0005; Fax: 757-552-0837; Edit Addr.: 5321 Cleveland St., No. 203, Virginia Beach, VA 23462-6552 USA (SAN 169-8672)
E-mail: sales@bookdist.com
Web site: http://www.bookdist.com.

Bk. Dynamics, Inc., *(978-0-9612440)* 18 Kennedy Blvd., East Brunswick, NJ 08816 USA (SAN 169-5649) Tel 732-545-5151; Fax: 732-545-5959; Toll Free: 800-441-4510.

Bk. Express, *(978-0-9612322; 978-1-890308)* Orders Addr.: P.O. Box 1249, Bellflower, CA 90706 USA (SAN 289-1301) Tel 562-865-1226; Edit Addr.: 12122 E. 176th St., Artesia, CA 90701-4013 USA
E-mail: carbks4u@escapenet.net.

Bk. Home, The, 119 E. Dale St., Colorado Springs, CO 80903-4701 USA (SAN 249-3055) Tel 719-634-5885.

Bk. Hse., Inc., The, 208 W. Chicago St., Jonesville, MI 49250-0125 USA (SAN 169-3859) Tel 517-849-2117; Fax: 517-849-9716; Toll Free Fax: 800-858-9716; Toll Free: 800-248-1146
E-mail: bhinfo@thebookhouse.com.

Bk. Hse., The, 9719 Manchester Rd., Saint Louis, MO 63119 USA Toll Free: 800-513-4491.

Bk. Margins, Inc., 7100 Valley Green Rd., Fort Washington, PA 19034-2206 USA (SAN 106-7788) Tel 215-223-5300
E-mail: paul.gross@bookmargins.com
Web site: http://www.bookmargins.com.

Bk. Marketing Plus, 406 Post Oak Rd., Fredericksburg, TX 78624 USA (SAN 630-6543) Tel 830-997-4776; Fax: 830-997-9752; Toll Free: 800-356-2445.

Bk. Mart, The, 1153 E. Hyde Pk., Inglewood, CA 90302 USA (SAN 168-969X).

Bk. Service of Puerto Rico, 102 De Diego, Santurce, PR 00907 USA (SAN 169-9326) Tel 809-728-5000; Fax: 809-726-6131
E-mail: bellbook@coqui.net
Web site: http://home.coqui.net/bellbook.

Bk. Service Unlimited, P.O. Box 31108, Seattle, WA 98103-1108 USA (SAN 169-877X) Toll Free: 800-347-0042.

Bk. Services International, Orders Addr.: P.O. Box 1434-SMS, Fairfield, CT 06430 USA (SAN 157-9541) Tel 203-374-4939; Fax: 203-384-6099; Toll Free: 800-243-2790.

Bk. Shelf, The, 222 Crestview Dr., Fort Dodge, IA 50501-5708 USA (SAN 169-2658).

Bk. Warehouse, 5154 NW 165th St., Hialeah, FL 33014-6335 USA.

Bk. World, 311 Sagamore Pkwy., N., Lafayette, IN 47904 USA (SAN 135-4051) Tel 765-448-1131 Do not confuse with companies with the same or similar name in Sun Lakes, AZ, Roanoke, VA
E-mail: fsjintl@pworld.net.ph.

Bks. & Media, Inc., *(978-0-7848; 978-0-88483; 978-1-55744)* Div. of Marco Bk. Co., Orders Addr.: P.O. Box 695, Lodi, NY 07644 USA (SAN 206-3352) Tel 973-458-8153; Fax: 973-458-5289; Toll Free: 800-901-8150; Edit Addr.: 60 Industrail Rd., Lodi, NJ 07644 USA.

Bks. & Research, Inc., 145 Palisade St. Ste. 389, Dobbs Ferry, NY 10522-1628 USA (SAN 130-1101)
E-mail: brinc@ix.netcom.com
Web site: http://www.books-and-research.com.

Bks. Are Fun, Ltd., *(978-0-9649777; 978-1-58209; 978-1-890409; 978-1-59795; 978-1-60626)* 1 Readers Digest Rd., Pleasantville, NY 10570-7000 USA
E-mail: msmall@booksarefun.com
Web site: http://www.booksarefun.com.

Bks. Plus, U.S.A., 20171 Kelso Rd., Walnut, CA 91789-1922 USA (SAN 630-8473).

Bks. to Grow On, 826 S. Aiken Ave., Pittsburgh, PA 15232 USA (SAN 128-438X); 210 S. Highland Ave., Pittsburgh, PA 15206 Fax: 412-621-5324.

Bks. West, 11111 E. 53rd Ave., Unit D2, Boulder, CO 80239 USA (SAN 631-4724) Tel 303-449-5995; Fax: 303-449-5951; Toll Free: 800-378-4188; 6340 E. 58Th Ave, Commerce City, CO 80022 Do not confuse with Books West, San Diego, CA
E-mail: wnack@rmi.net
Web site: http://www.bookswest.net/.

Black Box Corp., 1000 Park Dr., Lawrence, PA 15055 USA (SAN 277-1985) Tel 412-746-5500; Fax: 412-746-0746.

Black Christian Bk. Distributors, 1169 North Burleson Blvd. Suite 107-246, Burleson, TX 76028 USA.

Black Magazine Agency, 4515 Fleur Dr. Ste. 301, Des Moines, IA 50321-2369 USA (SAN 107-0819) Toll Free: 800-782-9787.

Black Rabbit Bks., *(978-1-58340; 978-1-887068; 978-1-59920; 978-1-77092; 978-1-62310; 978-1-62588; 978-1-68071; 978-1-68072)* Orders Addr.: P.O. Box 3263, Mankato, MN 56002 USA (SAN 925-4862); Edit Addr.: 123 S. Broad St., Mankato, MN 56001 USA (SAN 858-902X)
E-mail: info@blackrabbitbooks.com; production@blackrabbitbooks.com
Web site: http://www.blackrabbitbooks.com.

Blackburn News Agency, P.O. Box 1039, Kingsport, TN 37662 USA (SAN 169-7900).

Blackstone Audio Books, Incorporated, *See* **Blackstone Audio, Inc.**

Blackstone Audio, Inc., *(978-0-7861; 978-1-4332; 978-1-4417; 978-1-4551; 978-1-4708; 978-1-4829; 978-1-4830; 978-1-5046; 978-1-5047; 978-1-5384; 978-1-5385)* 31 Mistletoe Rd., Ashland, OR 97520 USA (SAN 173-2811) Fax: 800-482-9294; Toll Free Fax: 800-482-9294; Toll Free: 800-729-2665
E-mail: Orders@blackstoneaudio.com; megan.wahrenbrock@blackstoneaudio.com
Web site: http://www.blackstoneaudio.com.

Blackwell, *(978-0-913262; 978-0-916472)* Orders Addr.: 6024 SW Jean Rd., Bldg. G, Lake Oswego, OR 97034 USA (SAN 169-7048) Tel 503-684-1140; Fax: 503-639-2481; Toll Free: 800-547-6426 (in Oregon); Edit Addr.: 100 University Ct., Blackwood, NJ 08012 USA (SAN 169-4596) Tel 856-228-8900; Toll Free: 800-257-7341
Web site: http://www.blackwell.com/.

Blackwell North America, *See* **Blackwell**

Blair, John F. Pub., *(978-0-89587; 978-0-910244)* Orders Addr.: 1406 Plaza Dr., Winston-Salem, NC 27103 USA (SAN 201-4319) Tel 336-768-1374; Fax: 336-768-9194; Toll Free: 800-222-9796
E-mail: sutton@blairpub.com
Web site: http://www.blairpub.com.

Blessing Way Publishing Co., *(978-0-9627324)* 1131 Villa Dr., Suite 003, Atlanta, GA 30306-2593 USA (SAN 297-3251).

Bloomington News Agency, P.O. Box 3757, Bloomington, IL 61702-3757 USA (SAN 169-1732).

Bloomsbury Academic & Professional, *See* **Bloomsbury Academic & Professional**

Bloomsbury Publishing USA, *(978-1-58234; 978-1-59691; 978-1-59990; 978-1-60819; 978-1-84706; 978-1-61963; 978-1-62040; 978-1-62356; 978-1-62892; 978-1-63286; 978-1-5013; 978-1-68119; 978-1-63557; 978-1-5476)* Orders Addr.: 16365 James Madison Hwy., Gordonsville, VA 22942-8501 USA Tel 888-330-8477; Toll Free: 888-330-8477; Edit Addr.: 175 Fifth Ave., Suite 300, New York, NY 10010 USA Toll Free: 888-330-8477; 1385 Broadway, New York, NY 10018 Tel 212-419-5300
E-mail: bloomsbury.kids@bloomsburyusa.com; nathaniel.knaebel@bloomsbury.com; mike.o'connor@bloomsbury.com
Web site: http://www.bloomsburyusa.com.

Blu Sky Media Group, P.O. Box 10069, Murfreesboro, TN 37129-0002 USA
Web site: http://www.bluskymediagroup.com.

Blue Cat, *(978-0-932679; 978-0-936200)* 469 Barbados, Walnut, CA 91789 USA (SAN 214-0322) Tel 909-594-3317.

Blue Mountain Arts Inc., *(978-0-88396; 978-1-58786; 978-1-59842; 978-1-68088)* Orders Addr.: P.O. Box 4549, Boulder, CO 80306 USA (SAN 299-9609) Tel 303-449-0536; Fax: 303-417-6434; 303-417-6496; Toll Free Fax: 800-943-6666; 800-545-8573; Toll Free: 800-525-0642
Web site: http://www.sps.com/.

Blue Mountain Arts (R) by SPS Studios, Incorporated, *See* **Blue Mountain Arts Inc.**

Blue Ridge News Co., 21 Westside Dr., No. B, Asheville, NC 28806-2846 USA (SAN 169-6335).

BMI Educational Services, *(978-0-922443; 978-1-60884; 978-1-60933; 978-1-63071; 978-1-5367)* Orders Addr.: 26 Haypress Rd., Cranbury, NJ 08512 USA (SAN 760-7032); Edit Addr.: P.O. Box 800, Dayton, NJ 08810-0800 USA (SAN 169-4669) Tel 732-329-6991; Fax: 732-329-6994; Toll Free Fax: 800-986-9393 (orders only); Toll Free: 800-222-8100 (orders only)
E-mail: info@bmionline.com
Web site: http://www.bmionline.com/.

Bolchazy-Carducci Pubs., *(978-0-86516; 978-1-61041)* 1570 Baskin Rd., Mundelein, IL 60060-4474 USA (SAN 219-7685) Toll Free: 800-392-6453
E-mail: jcull@bolchazy.com
Web site: http://www.bolchazy.com.

Boley International Subscription Agency, Inc., 1001 Fries Mill Rd., Blackwood, NJ 08012 USA (SAN 159-6225) Tel 609-629-2500.

Bolinda Publishing, Inc., Orders Addr.: 186 S. Long Swamp Rd., Jackson, ME 04921-3154 USA Toll Free Fax: 877-864-8307; Toll Free: 888-235-2019
E-mail: karen@bolinda.com
Web site: http://www.bolinda.com.

Bondcliff Bks., *(978-0-9657475; 978-1-931271)* Orders Addr.: P.O. Box 385, Littleton, NH 03561 USA Toll Free: 800-859-7581; Edit Addr.: 8 Bluejay Ln., Littleton, NH 03561 USA
E-mail: bondclif@ncia.net.

Bonneville News Co., 965 Beardsley Pl., Salt Lake City, UT 84119 USA Tel 801-972-5454; Fax: 801-972-1075; Toll Free: 800-748-5453.

Book Clearing Hse., 46 Purdy St., Harrison, NY 10528 USA (SAN 125-5169) Tel 914-835-0015; Fax: 914-835-0398; Toll Free: 800-431-1579
E-mail: bookch@aol.com.

Book Gallery, *(978-1-878382)* 632 S. Quincy Ave., Apt. 1, Tulsa, OK 74120-4635 USA (SAN 630-9321).

Book Hub, Inc., 903 Pacific Ave., Suite 207A, Santa Cruz, CA 95060 USA Tel 831-466-0145; Fax: 831-515-5955.

Book Publishing Co., *(978-0-913990; 978-1-57067; 978-0-9669317; 978-0-9673108; 978-0-9779183; 978-1-939053)* P.O. Box 99, Summertown, TN 38483 USA (SAN 202-439X) Tel 931-964-3571; Fax: 931-964-3518; Toll Free: 888-260-8458
E-mail: info@bookpubco.com
Web site: http://www.bookpubco.com.

Book Sales, Inc., *(978-0-7628; 978-0-7858; 978-0-89009; 978-1-55521; 978-1-57715; 978-1-4161)* Orders Addr.: 400 1st Ave N. Ste. 300, Minneapolis, MN 55401-1721 USA (SAN 169-488X) Toll Free: 800-526-7257; Edit Addr.: 276 Fifth Ave., Suite 206, New York, NY 10001 USA (SAN 299-4062) Tel 212-779-4972; Fax: 212-779-6058
E-mail: sales@booksalesusa.com
Web site: http://www.booksalesusa.com/.

Book Wholesalers, Inc., *(978-0-7587; 978-1-4046; 978-1-4131; 978-1-4155; 978-1-4156; 978-1-4287)* 1847 Mercer Rd., Lexington, KY 40511-1001 USA (SAN 135-5449) Toll Free: 800-888-4478
E-mail: jcarrico@bwibooks.com; lison@bwibooks.com
Web site: http://www.bwibooks.com.

Bookazine Co., Inc., 75 Hook Rd., Bayonne, NJ 07002 USA (SAN 169-5665) Tel 201-339-7777; Fax: 201-339-7778; Toll Free: 800-221-8112.

Bookazine Company, Incorporated, *See* **Bookazine Co., Inc.**

BookBaby, *(978-1-60984; 978-1-61792; 978-1-61842; 978-1-62095; 978-1-62309; 978-1-62488; 978-1-62675; 978-1-4835; 978-1-5439; 978-0-692-95466-9)* 7905 N. Rt 130, Pennsauken, NJ 08110 USA Toll Free: 877-961-6878; 13909 NE. Airport Way, Portland, OR 97230 Toll Free: 877-961-6878
E-mail: info@bookbaby.com; support@bookbaby.com; jburton@bookbaby.com; jfoley@bookbaby.com
Web site: http://www.bookbaby.com.

BookHawkers Internet BookSeller, P.O. Box 2094, Wilkes-Barre, PA 18703 USA
Web site: http://www.bookhawkers.com.

Bookhouse, The, 10505 N. May Ave., Oklahoma City, OK 73120-2611 USA (SAN 200-8467) Tel 405-755-0020.

Booklegger, The, *(978-0-936421)* Orders Addr.: P.O. Box 2626, Grass Valley, CA 95945 USA (SAN 697-9548); Edit Addr.: 13100 Grass Valley Ave., Suite D, Grass Valley, CA 95945 USA (SAN 120-6125) Tel 530-272-1556; Fax: 530-272-2133; Toll Free Fax: 800-250-2199; Toll Free: 800-262-1556
E-mail: order@booklegger.com
Web site: http://www.booklegger.com/.

Bookline, Div. of Michiana News Service, Inc., 2232 S. 11th St., Niles, MI 49120 USA (SAN 169-3948) Tel 616-684-3013; Fax: 616-684-8740.

Booklines Hawaii, Ltd., *(978-1-929844; 978-1-58849; 978-1-60274)* Div. of Islander Group, 269 Pali'i St., Mililani, HI 96789 USA (SAN 630-6624) Tel 808-676-0116; Fax: 808-676-0634
E-mail: customerservice@booklines.com
Web site: http://www.booklineshawaii.com.

BookLink, *(978-0-9797436)* 465 Broad Ave., Leonia, NJ 07605-1637 USA (SAN 854-2473) Tel 201-947-3471; Fax: 201-947-6321
E-mail: booklink@es1booklink.com.

BookLink, Inc., 444 Broad St., Camden, SC 29020 USA (SAN 631-5291) Tel 803-432-5169; Fax: 803-424-8418
E-mail: sam@thebooklink.com
Web site: http://www.thebooklink.com.

Bookman Bks., 138 Elena St., Santa Fe, NM 87501 USA (SAN 630-933X) Tel 505-982-5964.

Bookmark, Inc., The, 1445 N. Winchester St., Olathe, KS 66061-5881 USA (SAN 131-4017) Toll Free: 800-642-1288.

Book$mart, Inc., *(978-1-885051)* Div. of Books-A-Million, 602 John Aldridge Dr., Tuscumbia, AL 35674-3002 USA Tel 256-314-4466 Do not confuse with Booksmart in Irondale, AZ
E-mail: brad@roses-4u.com.

BookMasters, 6745 FM 2738, Burleson, TX 76028-1167 USA (SAN 630-8406) Do not confuse with BookMasters Inc., Ashland, OH.

Bookmasters Distribution, Div. of BookMasters, Inc., Orders Addr.: 30 Amberwood Pkwy., Ashland, OH 44805 USA (SAN 631-936X) Fax: 419-281-6883; Toll Free: 800-247-6553; 800-537-6727; 800-266-5564
E-mail: orders@atlasbooks.com
Web site: http://www.bookmasters.com/.

BookMasters, Inc., *(978-0-917889)* Orders Addr.: P.O. Box 388, Mansfield, OH 44903 USA (SAN 631-3566) Tel 419-281-1802; Fax: 419-281-6883; Toll Free: 800-247-6553; 30 Amberwood Pkwy., Ashland, OH 44805 (SAN 760-9264) Tel 419-281-1802; Fax: 419-281-6886 Do not confuse with BookMasters, Burleson, TX
E-mail: info@bookmasters.com; order@bookmaster.com
Web site: http://www.bookmasters.com.

Bookmen, Inc., Orders Addr.: 2300 Louisiana Ave N. # B, Minneapolis, MN 55427-3631 USA (SAN 169-409X) Toll Free Fax: 800-266-5636; Toll Free: 800-328-8411 (customer service)
Web site: http://www.bookmen.com.

BookMobile, Orders Addr.: 5120 Cedar Lake Rd., Saint Louis Park, MN 55416 USA (SAN 760-7245) Fax: 763-398-0198
E-mail: dieeper@bookmobile.com
Web site: http://www.bookmobile.com.

BookPartners, Inc., *(978-0-9622269; 978-1-58151; 978-1-885221)* Orders Addr.: P.O. Box 345, Portland, OR 97205 USA; Edit Addr.: 620 SW Main, Portland, OR 97205 USA Tel 503-225-9900; Fax: 503-225-9901
Web site: http://www.amicapublishing.com.

Books Alive, *(978-0-920470; 978-1-55312)* Div. of Book Publishing Co., Orders Addr.: P.O. Box 99, Summertown, TN 38483 USA (SAN 115-7078) Tel 931-964-3571; Fax: 931-964-3518; Toll Free: 888-260-8458 (orders and customer service)
E-mail: Cynthia@bookpubco.com
Web site: http://www.bookpubco.com.

Books International, Inc., *(978-1-891078)* Orders Addr.: P.O. Box 605, Herndon, VA 20172-0605 USA (SAN 131-761X) Tel 703-661-1500; Fax: 703-661-1501
E-mail: bimail@presswarehouse.com.

Booksellers Order Service, 828 S. Broadway, Tarrytown, NY 10591-5112 USA (SAN 106-5181) Tel 914-591-2665; Fax: 914-591-2720; Toll Free: 800-637-0037.

Booksmith Promotional Co., 100 Paterson Plank Rd., Jersey City, NJ 07307 USA (SAN 664-5364) Tel 201-659-2768; Fax: 201-659-3631.

Booksource, The, *(978-0-7383; 978-0-8335; 978-0-911891; 978-0-9641084; 978-1-886379; 978-1-890760; 978-0-7568; 978-1-4117; 978-1-4178; 978-1-60446; 978-1-4364)* Div. of GL group, Inc., Orders Addr.: 1230 Macklind Ave., Saint Louis, MO 63110-1432 USA (SAN 169-4324) Tel 314-647-0600 Toll Free Fax: 800-647-1923; Toll Free: 800-444-0435
E-mail: shankins@booksource.com
Web site: http://www.booksource.com.

BookWorksUSA, 385 Freeport Blvd., Suite 3, Sparks, NV 89431 USA
E-mail: bookworksusa@mac.com.

Bookworld Cos., P.O. Box 2260, Sarasota, FL 34230-2260 USA.

Bookworm, 14 Griffin St., Northport, ME 04849-4446 USA (SAN 170-8074).

Bookworm Bookfairs, P.O. Box 306, Simsbury, CT 06070-0306 USA (SAN 156-5621).

Bookworm, The, 417 Monmouth Dr., Cherry Hill, NJ 08002 USA (SAN 120-9531) Tel 609-667-5884.

Borchardt, G. Inc., 136 E. 57th St., New York, NY 10022 USA (SAN 285-8614) Tel 212-753-5785; Fax: 212-838-6518.

Borders, Inc., 9910 N. By NE Blvd., Bldg. 4, Fishers, IN 46038 USA (SAN 152-5352); Space 497, 1st Level 525 F D Roosevelt Ave. Plaza Las Americas, Hato Rey, PR 00917 (SAN 193-2314); 455 Industrial Blvd., Suite E, La Vergne, TN 37086 (SAN 156-6474); Edit Addr.: 100 Phoenix Dr., Ann Arbor, MI 48108 USA (SAN 152-3546) Tel 734-477-1100; Fulfillment Addr.: a/o Fullfillment Center, 100 Phoenix Dr., Ann Arbor, MI 48108-2202 USA (SAN 197-0917).

Bored Feet Pr., *(978-0-939431)* Orders Addr.: P.O. Box 1832, Mendocino, CA 95460 USA (SAN 661-6992) Tel 707-964-6629; Fax: 707-964-5953; Edit Addr.: 16630 Mitchell Creek Dr., Fort Bragg, CA 95437 USA (SAN 663-3226)
E-mail: Boredft@mcn.org.

Bored Feet Publications, *See* **Bored Feet Pr.**

Bottman Design, Inc., *(978-1-884741)* 1081 S. 300 W., No. A, Salt Lake City, UT 84101 USA (SAN 860-2166) Tel 801-487-1949; Fax: 801-973-6746; Toll Free: 800-365-5564.

Bottom Dog Pr., *(978-0-933087; 978-1-933964; 978-1-947504)* c/o Firelands College, P.O. Box 425, Huron, OH 44839 USA (SAN 689-5492) Tel 419-433-3573; Fax: 419-616-3966
E-mail: LSmithDog@aol.com; lsmithdog@smithdocs.net
Web site: https://www.facebook.com/BottomDogPress/?ref=bookmarks; http://smithdocs.net; http://smithdocs.net/recent_bottom_dog_press_titles.

Bound to Stay Bound Bks., *(978-0-9718238)* 1880 W. Morton Rd., Jacksonville, IL 62650 USA (SAN 169-1996) Toll Free Fax: 800-747-2872; Toll Free: 800-637-6586
Web site: http://www.btsb.com.

Bowers & Merena Galleries, Inc., *(978-0-943161)* Orders Addr.: P.O. Box 1224, Wolfeboro, NH 03894 USA (SAN 168-9746) Tel 603-569-5095; Fax: 603-569-5319; Toll Free: 800-222-5993; Edit Addr.: 18061 Fitch., Irvine, CA 92614-6018 USA (SAN 668-2561).

Bowker LLC, R. R., *(978-0-8352; 978-0-911255; 978-0-641; 978-0-9856945; 978-1-941808)* Subs. of Proquest LLC, Orders Addr.: P.O. Box 32, New Providence, NJ 07974 USA Tel 908-286-1090; Fax: 908-219-0098; Toll Free:

888-269-5372; Edit Addr.: 630 Central Ave., New Providence, NJ 07974 USA (SAN 214-1191); 630 Central Ave., B&T box, New Providence, NJ 07974 (SAN 857-8516)
E-mail: info@bowker.com; pad@bowker.com; customerservice@bowker.com; specialtytitles@bowker.com
Web site: http://www.bowker.com.

Bowling Green State University, Philosophy Documentation Center, *See* **Philosophy Documentation Ctr.**

Boydell & Brewer, Inc., *(978-0-85115; 978-0-85991; 978-0-907239; 978-0-938100; 978-1-57113; 978-1-58046; 978-1-85566; 978-1-870252; 978-1-878822; 978-1-879751; 978-1-900639; 978-1-84384; 978-1-84383; 978-1-64014)* Div. of Boydell & Brewer Group, Ltd., Orders Addr.: 668 Mount Hope Ave., Rochester, NY 14620-2731 USA (SAN 013-8479) Tel 585-275-0419; Fax: 585-271-8778
E-mail: boydell@boydellusa.net; boydell@boydell.co.uk
Web site: http://www.boydellandbrewer.com.

Boyds Mills Pr., *(978-1-56397; 978-1-878093; 978-1-886910; 978-1-59078; 978-1-932425; 978-1-62091; 978-1-62979; 978-0-9961172; 978-0-9961173; 978-1-943283; 978-1-68238; 978-1-68329; 978-1-68437)* Div. of Highlights For Children, Inc., 815 Church St., Honesdale, PA 18431 USA (SAN 852-3177) Tel 570-251-4513 Toll Free: 800-490-5111 Admin line; 877-512-8366; 800-874-8817 Cust Svc Columbus, OH
E-mail: admin@boydsmillspress.com; honesdale-cs@boydsmillspress.com; marketing@boydsmillspress.com
Web site: http://www.boydsmillspress.com; http://www.wordsongpoetry.com; http://www.calkinscreekbooks.com; http://www.frontstreetbooks.com.

BPDI, 1000 S. Lynndale Dr., Appleton, WI 54914 USA (SAN 631-6859) Tel 920-830-7897; Fax: 920-830-3857.

Bridge Pubns., Inc., *(978-0-88404; 978-1-57318; 978-1-4031; 978-1-61177; 978-1-4572)* Orders Addr.: 5600 E. Olympic Blvd., Commerce, CA 90022 USA (SAN 208-3884) Tel 323-888-6200; Fax: 323-888-6210; Toll Free: 800-722-1733; Edit Addr.: 4751_Fountain Ave., Los Angeles, CA 90029 USA
E-mail: annarnow@bridgepub.com; daniellem@bridgepub.com; donarnow@bridgepub.com
Web site: http://www.bridgepub.com; http://www.clearbodyclearmind.com; http://www.scientology.org; http://www.dianetics.org.

Bridge-Logos Foundation, *See* **Bridge-Logos, Inc.**

Bridge-Logos, Inc., *(978-0-88270; 978-0-912106; 978-0-9841034; 978-1-61036)* Orders Addr.: 14260 W. Newberry Rd, Newberry, FL 32669 USA (SAN 253-5254) Tel 352-727-9324; Toll Free: 800-935-6467 (orders only); 800-631-5802 (orders only)
E-mail: SWooldridge@bridgelogos.com
Web site: http://www.bridgelogos.com.

Brigham Distributing, *(978-0-578-09711-4; 978-0-578-14054-4)* 330 South 150 E., Burley, ID 83318 USA; 110 S 800 W., Brigham City, UT 84302.

Brigham Distribution, 110 S. 800 W., Brigham City, UT 84302 USA (SAN 760-7652) Tel 435-723-6611; Fax: 435-723-6644
E-mail: brigdist@sisna.com.

Brigham, Kay, Orders Addr.: 9500 Old Cutler Rd., Miami, FL 33156 USA Tel 305-666-3844; Fax: 305-661-4843
Web site: http://www.kaybrigham.com.

Brigham Young Univ. Print Services, 205 UPB, Provo, UT 84602 USA Tel 801-378-2809; Fax: 801-378-3374
E-mail: denise@upb.byu.edu
Web site: http://www.upb.byu.edu.

Bright Horizons Specialty Distributors, Inc., 206 Riva Ridge Dr., Fairview, NC 28730-9764 USA (SAN 110-4101) Toll Free: 800-437-3959 (orders only).

Bright Sky Pr., *(978-0-9704729; 978-0-9709987; 978-1-931721; 978-1-933979; 978-1-936474; 978-1-939055; 978-1-942945)* Orders Addr.: 2365 Rice Blvd., Suite 202, Houston, TX 77005 USA Tel 713-533-9300; Fax: 713-528-2432 Do not confuse with Breakaway Bks., Halcottsville, NY
Web site: http://www.brightskypress.com.

Brightpoint Literacy, 299 Market St., Saddle Brook, NJ 07663 USA Tel 201-708-6498.

Brill, E. J. U. S. A., Incorporated, *See* **Brill USA, Inc.**

Brill USA, Inc., *(978-0-916846)* Subs. of Brill Academic Publishing Co., The Netherlands, 2 Liberty Square, Eleventh Flr., Boston, MA 02109 USA (SAN 254-6922) Tel 617-263-2323; Fax: 617-263-2324; Toll Free: 800-962-4406
E-mail: cs@brillusa.com; brillonline@brillusa.com
Web site: http://www.brill.nl.

Brilliance Publishing, *See* **Brilliance Publishing, Inc.**

Brilliance Publishing, Inc., *(978-0-930435; 978-1-56100; 978-1-56740; 978-1-58788; 978-1-59086; 978-1-59355; 978-1-59600; 978-1-59710; 978-1-59737; 978-1-4233; 978-1-4418; 978-1-61106; 978-1-4558; 978-1-4692; 978-1-4805; 978-1-4915; 978-1-5012; 978-1-5113; 978-1-5226; 978-1-5318; 978-1-5366; 978-1-5436; 978-1-9786) Orders Addr.: P.O. Box 887, Grand Haven, MI 49417 USA (SAN 690-1395) Tel 616-846-5256; Fax: 616-846-0630; Toll Free: 800-648-2312 (phone/fax, retail & library orders); Edit Addr.: 1704 Eaton Dr., Grand Haven, MI 49417 USA (SAN 858-138X) Toll Free: 800-648-2312 x330*
E-mail: sales@brillianceaudio.com; customerservice@brillianceaudio.com; jcraig@brilliancepublishing.com
Web site: http://www.brilliancepublishing.com.

Brisco Pubns., *(978-0-9603576)* P.O. Box 2161, Palos Verdes Peninsula, CA 90274 USA (SAN 133-0268) Tel 310-534-4943; Fax: 310-534-8437.

Bristlecone Publishing Co., 2560 Brookridge Ave., Golden Valley, MN 55422 USA
E-mail: davej@jblcompanies.com.

Broadman & Holman Publishers, *See* **B&H Publishing Group**

Brodart Co., *(978-0-87272; 978-1-62844; 978-1-63546)* Orders Addr.: 500 Arch St., Williamsport, PA 17705 USA (SAN 169-7684) Tel 570-326-2461 (International); Fax: 570-326-1479; 717-326-2461; 519-759-1144 (Canada); Toll Free Fax: 800-999-6799; Toll Free: 800-233-8467 (US & Canada)
E-mail: bookinfo@brodart.com
Web site: http://www.brodart.com.

Brookes, Paul H. Publishing Company Incorporated, *See* **Brookes Publishing**

Brookes Publishing, *(978-0-933716; 978-1-55766; 978-1-59857; 978-1-68125)* Orders Addr.: P.O. Box 10624, Baltimore, MD 21285-0624 USA (SAN 212-730X) Tel 410-337-9580; Fax: 410-337-8539; Toll Free: 800-638-3775 (customer service/ordering/billing/fulfillment); Edit Addr.: 409 Washington Ave., Suite 500, Baltimore, MD 21204 USA (SAN 666-6485)
E-mail: custserv@brookespublishing.com
Web site: http://www.brookespublishing.com.

Brotherhood of Life, Inc., *(978-0-914732)* P.O. Box 46306, Las Vegas, NV 89114-6306 USA (SAN 111-3674) Fax: 702-319-5577
E-mail: brotherhoodoflife@hotmail.com
Web site: http://www.brotherhoodoflife.com.

Brown Bks., *(978-0-9668452; 978-0-9717197)* Div. of Personal Profiles, Inc., 16200 Dallas Pkwy., Suite 170, Dallas, TX 75248-2616 USA Do not confuse with companies with the same or similar names in Allen, TX, Redway, CA, Montrose, CO, Plano, TX
Web site: http://www.brownbooks.com.

Brown, David Book Company, The, *See* **Casemate Academic**

Brown Enterprises, Inc., *(978-0-9711451)* P.O. Box 11447, Durham, NC 27703 USA Tel 919-680-2288 Do not confuse with companies with the same or similar names in Pasadena, CA, Bellingham, WA
E-mail: brown.enterprisesinc@verizon.net.

Brunner News Agency, 217 Flanders Ave., P.O. Box 598, Lima, OH 45801 USA (SAN 169-6777) Tel 419-225-5826; Fax: 419-225-5537; Toll Free: 800-998-1727
E-mail: brunnews@aol.com
Web site: http://www.readmoreshallmark.com.

Bryan, R. L., *(978-0-934870)* P.O. Box 368, Columbia, SC 29202 USA Tel 803-779-3560.

Bryant Altman Map, Inc., Endicott St., Bldg. 26, Norwood, MA 02062 USA (SAN 630-2475) Tel 781-762-3339; Fax: 781-769-9080
E-mail: JPG63@aol.com.

Bryant-Altman Book & Map Distributors, *See* **Bryant Altman Map, Inc.**

Buckeye News Co., 6800 W. Central Ave., Suite F, Toledo, OH 43617-1157 USA (SAN 169-6874).

Budget Bk. Service, Inc., Div. of LDAP, Inc., 386 Park Ave. S., Suite 1913, New York, NY 10016-8804 USA (SAN 169-5762) Fax: 212-679-2247.

Budget Marketing, Inc., P.O. Box 1805, Des Moines, IA 50306 USA (SAN 285-8754).

Budgetext, Orders Addr.: P.O. Box 1487, Fayetteville, AR 72702 USA (SAN 111-3321) Tel 501-443-9205; Fax: 501-442-3064; Toll Free: 800-643-3432; Edit Addr.: 1936 N. Shiloh Dr., Fayetteville, AR 72704 USA (SAN 249-3330)
E-mail: wmorgan@absc.com; scaldwell@budgetext.com
Web site: http://www.budgetext.com.

Buena Vista Home Video, *(978-0-7888; 978-1-55890)* Div. of Walt Disney Studios, 500 S. Buena Vista St., Burbank, CA 91521-1120 USA (SAN 249-2342) Tel 818-295-4841; Fax: 818-972-2845; Toll Free: 800-723-4763
Web site: http://www.disney.com.

Burlington News Agency, 382 Hercules Dr., Colchester, VT 05446-5836 USA (SAN 169-8583).

Burns News Agency, P.O. Box 1211, Rochester, NY 14603-1211 USA (SAN 169-5320).

B.W. Bks. on Wings, Orders Addr.: 581 Market St., San Francisco, CA 94105-2847 USA.

BWI, 1340 Ridgeview Dr., Mchenry, IL 60050-7047 USA.

Byeway Bks., *(978-1-85997; 978-1-904586; 978-1-933581; 978-1-934004; 978-1-60176)* 15941 W. 65th St., Shawnee, KS 66217-9342 USA Toll Free Fax: 866-426-3929; Toll Free: 866-429-3929
E-mail: customerservice@byewaybooks.com
Web site: http://www.byewaybooks.com/how_to_order.html.

Byrrd Enterprises, Inc., *(978-1-886715)* 1302 Lafayette Dr., Alexandria, VA 22308 USA (SAN 169-8605) Tel 703-765-5626; Fax: 703-768-4086; Toll Free: 800-628-0901
E-mail: byrrdbooks@aol.com.

C & B Bk. Distribution, 65-77 160th St., Flushing, NY 11365 USA Tel 718-591-4525
Web site: http://www.cbbooksdistribution.com.

C & B Bk. Hse., 21 Oak Ridge Rd., Monroe, CT 06468 USA (SAN 159-8279).

C & H News Co., P.O. Box 2768, Corpus Christi, TX 78403-2768 USA (SAN 169-8249).

C & T Publishing, *(978-0-914881; 978-1-57120; 978-1-60705; 978-1-61745)* Orders Addr.: 1651 Challenge Dr., Concord, CA 94520 USA (SAN 289-0720) Tel 925-677-0377; Fax: 925-617-0374; Toll Free: 800-284-1114
E-mail: ctinfo@ctpub.com
Web site: http://www.ctpub.com.

C R C Publications, *See* **Faith Alive Christian Resources**

C4 Kids, Orders Addr.: 1220 N. Las Palmas, No. 201, Los Angeles, CA 90038 USA.

Cadmus Communications, a Cenveo Co., Publisher Services Group 136 Carlin Rd., Conklin, NY 13748 USA Tel 607-762-5555; Fax: 607-762-6774.

Cafepress, 127 Brockmoore Dr., East Amherst, NY 14051 USA.

CafePress.com, *(978-1-4148)* 1850 Gateway Dr. Ste. 300, Foster City, CA 94404-4061 USA Toll Free: 877-809-1659
E-mail: mystore@cafepress.com
Web site: http://www.cafepress.com.

Calico Subscription Co., P.O. Box 640337, San Jose, CA 95164-0337 USA (SAN 285-9173) Tel 408-432-8700; Fax: 408-432-8813; Toll Free: 800-952-2542.

California Princeton Fulfillment Services, 1445 Lower Ferry Rd., Ewing, NJ 08618 USA (SAN 630-639X) Tel 609-883-1759 ext 536; Toll Free: 800-777-4726
E-mail: donnaw@cpfs.pupress.princeton.edu.

Calliope Bks., *(978-0-9620187)* 2115 Chadbourne Ave., Madison, WI 53705 USA (SAN 247-9370) Tel 608-238-9258 Do not confuse with Calliope Books in Santa Barbara, CA
E-mail: wcoleman@facstaff.wisc.edu; calliopebooks@hotmail.com
Web site: http://www.execpc.com/~calliope.

Calvary Chapel Resources, *(978-0-936728; 978-1-931713; 978-1-932941; 978-1-59751)* Div. of Calvary Chapel Costa Mesa, Orders Addr.: P.O. Box 8000, Costa Mesa, CA 92628 USA (SAN 110-8379) Tel 714-825-9673 Toll Free: 800-272-9673; Edit Addr.: 3232 W. MacArthur Blvd., Santa Ana, CA 92704 USA (SAN 214-2260) Tel 714-825-9673 Toll Free: 800-272-9637
E-mail: cathyr@twft.com
Web site: http://www.twft.com; cccm.com.

Cambium Education, Inc., *(978-0-944584; 978-1-57035; 978-1-59318; 978-1-932282; 978-1-4168; 978-1-60218; 978-1-60697)* 4093 Specialty Pl., Longmont, CO 80504 USA (SAN 243-945X) Tel 303-651-2829; Fax: 303-907-8694; Toll Free: 800-547-6747 (orders only)
E-mail: publishing@sopriswest.com; customerservice@cambiumlearning.com
Web site: http://www.sopriswest.com.

Cambridge Bk. Co., *(978-0-8428)* Div. of Simon & Schuster, Inc., 4350 Equity Dr., Box 249, Columbus, OH 43216 USA (SAN 169-5703) Toll Free: 800-238-5833
Web site: http://www.simonsays.com/.

Cambridge Univ. Pr., *(978-0-521; 978-0-511)* Orders Addr.: 100 Brook Hill Dr., West Nyack, NY 10994-2133 USA (SAN 281-3769) Tel 845-353-7500; Fax: 845-353-4141; Toll Free: 800-872-7423 (orders, returns, credit & accounting); 800-937-9600; Edit Addr.: 32 Avenue of the Americas, New York, NY 10013-2473 USA (SAN 200-206X) Tel 212-924-3900; Fax: 212-691-3239
E-mail: customer_service@cup.org; orders@cup.org; information@cup.org
Web site: http://www.cambridge.org/.

Canyonlands Pubns., *(978-0-9702595)* Orders Addr.: P.O. Box 16175, Bellemont, AZ 86015-6175 USA (SAN 114-3824) Tel 520-779-3888; Fax: 520-779-3778; Toll Free: 800-283-1983; Edit Addr.: 4860 N. Ken Morey, Bellemont, AZ 86015 USA
E-mail: books@infomagic.com.

Cape Cod Scribe, 5 Camelot Ln., Bourne, MA 02532 USA Tel 508-415-1295.

Cape News Co., P.O. Box 568680, Rockledge, FL 32955 USA Tel 407-636-5909.

Capital Business Systems, Div. of Capital Business Service, Orders Addr.: P.O. Box 2088, Napa, CA 94558 USA (SAN 698-3146) Tel 707-252-8844; Fax: 707-252-6368; Edit Addr.: 2033 First St., Napa, CA 94558 USA.

Capital News Co., 961 Palmyra, Jackson, MS 39203 USA Tel 601-355-8341; Fax: 601-352-1343.

Capitol Christian Distribution, Orders Addr.: P.O. Box 5084, Brentwood, TN 37024-5084 USA Tel 800-877-4443
E-mail: ccmgdistribution@umusic.com.

Capitol News Agency, P.O. Box 7886, Richmond, VA 23231 USA (SAN 249-2768); 5203 Hatcher St., Richmond, VA 23231-0271 Tel 804-222-7252.

Capper Pr., 1503 SW 42nd, Topeka, KS 66609 USA (SAN 285-8886) Tel 913-274-4324; Fax: 913-274-4305; Toll Free: 800-678-5779 (ext. 4324).

Capstone Press, Incorporated, *See* **Capstone Press of Coughlan Cos.**

Capstone Press of Coughlan Cos., *(978-0-7368; 978-1-56065; 978-1-4296; 978-1-62065; 978-1-4765; 978-1-4914; 978-1-5157; 978-1-5435)* Div. of Coughlan Publishing, 1905 Lookout Dr., North Mankato, MN 55003 USA Tel 507-385-8215; Fax: 507-388-3752; Orders Addr.: 1710 Roe Crest Dr., North Mankato, MN 56003 USA (SAN 254-1815) Toll Free Fax: 888-262-0705; Toll Free: 800-747-4992; Edit Addr.: 5050 Lincoln Dr Suite 200, Edina, MN 55436 USA Fax: 952-933-2410; Toll Free: 888-517-8977 Do not confuse with Capstone Pr., Inc. in Decatur, IL
E-mail: customerservice@capstonepub.com
Web site: http://www.capstone-press.com; http://www.capstonepub.com; http://www.capstoneclassroom.com.

Cardinal Pubs. Group, 2402 N. Shadeland Ave. Ste. A, Indianapolis, IN 46219-1746 USA (SAN 631-7936)
E-mail: tdoherty@in.net.

Cards Bks. N Things, 1446 St., Rd. 2 West, La Porte, IN 46350 USA (SAN 159-8295).

Carlex, Orders Addr.: 1545 W. Hamlin, Rochester Hills, MI 48309 USA (SAN 631-5615) Tel 810-852-5422; Fax: 810-852-7142.

Carolina Biological Supply Co., *(978-0-89278; 978-1-4350)* 2700 York Rd., Burlington, NC 27215-3398 USA (SAN 249-2784) Tel 336-584-0381; Fax: 910-584-3399; Toll Free Fax: 800-222-7112; Toll Free: 800-334-5551
E-mail: carolina@carolina.com
Web site: http://www.carolina.com/.

Carolina Cassette Distributors, Orders Addr.: P.O. Box 429, New Bern, NC 28560 USA (SAN 110-8395) Fax: 919-638-1291; Edit Addr.: 2600 Oaks Rd., New Bern, NC 28560 USA (SAN 659-2155) Tel 919-638-5583.

Carolina News Co., Orders Addr.: P.O. Box 10, Fayetteville, NC 28302 USA; Edit Addr.: 245 Tillinghast St., Fayetteville, NC 28301 USA Tel 910-483-4135.

Carson-Dellosa Publishing Company, Incorporated, *See* **Carson-Dellosa Publishing, LLC**

Carson-Dellosa Publishing, LLC, *(978-0-88724; 978-1-57156; 978-1-57332; 978-1-59441; 978-1-60022; 978-1-60418; 978-1-936022; 978-1-936023; 978-1-936024; 978-0-9823625; 978-0-9823626; 978-0-9823627; 978-0-692-00200-1; 978-1-60996; 978-1-62057; 978-1-62223; 978-1-62399; 978-1-62442; 978-1-62648; 978-1-4838) Orders Addr.: P.O. Box 35665, Greensboro, NC 27425 USA Tel 336-632-0084; Fax: 336-808-3249; Toll Free: 800-321-0943*
Web site: http://www.carsondellosa.com.

Casa Del Libro, Orders Addr.: P.O. Box 3853, La Mesa, CA 91944-3853 USA.

Cascade News, Inc., 1055 Commerce Ave., Longview, WA 98632 USA (SAN 169-8761) Tel 360-425-2450; Fax: 360-425-2451.

Casemate Academic, *(978-0-9774094; 978-1-935488)* Orders Addr.: P.O. Box 511, Oakville, CT 06779 USA (SAN 630-9461) Tel 860-945-9329; Fax: 860-945-9468; Toll Free: 800-791-9354; Edit Addr.: 20 Main St., Oakville, CT 06779 USA
E-mail: queries@dbbconline.com
Web site: http://www.oxbowbooks.com.

Casemate Pubs. & Bk. Distributors, LLC, *(978-0-9711709; 978-1-932033; 978-1-935149; 978-1-61200)* Orders Addr.: 1950 Lawrence Rd., Havertown, PA 19083 USA; 22883 Quicksilver Dr., Herndon, VA 20166 (SAN 631-9386) Tel 703-661-1500; Edit Addr.: 180 Varick St. Suite 816, New York, NY 10014 USA
E-mail: casemate@casematepublishing.com
Web site: http://www.casematepublishing.com.

Casino Distributors, Orders Addr.: P.O. Box 849, Pleasantville, NJ 08232 USA (SAN 169-457X) Tel 609-646-4165; Fax: 609-645-0152; Edit Addr.: 10 Canale Dr., Pleasantville, NJ 08234 USA (SAN 249-3276).

Casper Magazine Agency, P.O. Box 2340, Casper, WY 82602 USA (SAN 159-8325).

Cassette Book Company, *See* **Audio Bk. Co.**

Castlebridge Distribution, 115 Bluebill Dr., Savannah, GA 31419 USA Toll Free: 888-300-1961 (phone/fax)
E-mail: orders@castlebridgedistribution.com.

Catholic Bookrack Service, 700 E. Elm St., La Grange, IL 60525 USA (SAN 169-2178) Tel 708-482-0044; Fax: 708-482-9644.

Catholic Heritage Curricula, *(978-0-9788376; 978-0-9824585; 978-0-9836832; 978-0-9851642; 978-0-9858343; 978-0-9883797; 978-0-9913264; 978-1-946207)* 2505 Texas Drive, Suite 102, Irving, TX 75062 USA
Web site: https://www.chcweb.com.

Catholic Literary Guild, Inc., 200 Hamilton Ave., White Plains, NY 10601 USA (SAN 285-8908) Tel 914-949-4444.

Catholic Univ. of America Pr., *(978-0-8132)* Orders Addr.: c/o Hopkins Fulfillment Services, P.O. Box 50370, Baltimore, MD 21211-4370 USA (SAN 203-6304) Tel 410-516-6953; Fax: 410-516-6998; Toll Free: 800-537-5487; Edit Addr.: 620 Michigan Ave., NE, Washington, DC 20064 USA (SAN 203-6290) Tel 202-319-5052; Fax: 202-319-4985
E-mail: cua-press@cua.edu
Web site: http://cuapress.cua.edu/.

Catweasel Productions, *See* **Ars Obscura**

Caxton Pr., *(978-0-87004)* Div. of Caxton Printers, Ltd., 312 Main St., Caldwell, ID 83605-3299 USA (SAN 201-9698) Tel 208-459-7421; Fax: 208-459-7450; Toll Free: 800-657-6465
E-mail: publish@caxtonprinters.com; wcornell@caxtonpress.com; sgipson@caxtonpress.com
Web site: http://www.caxtonpress.com.

Caxton Printers, Limited, *See* **Caxton Pr.**

CBLS Pubs., *(978-1-878907; 978-1-59529)* 119 Brentwood St., Marietta, OH 45750 USA (SAN 169-5517) Tel 740-374-9458; Fax: 740-374-8029
E-mail: cbls@cbls.com
Web site: http://www.cbls.com.

CD Baby, Orders Addr.: 5925 NE 80th Ave., Portland, OR 97218-2891 USA Tel 503-595-3000; Fax: 503-296-2370; Toll Free: 800-289-6923 (CD orders only)
E-mail: cdbaby@cdbaby.com
Web site: http://www.cdbaby.com.

CD Distributing, Inc., P.O. Box 4965, Missoula, MT 59806-4965 USA (SAN 169-4367) Fax: 406-454-0415.

CEC: Council for Exceptional Children, 2900 Crystal Dr., Suite 1000, Arlington, VA 22202-9466 USA
Web site: http://www.cec.sped.org/.

Cedar Fort, Inc./CFI Distribution, *(978-0-88290; 978-0-934126; 978-1-55517; 978-1-59955; 978-1-4621)* 2373 West 700 South, Springville, UT 84663 USA (SAN 170-2858) Tel 801-489-4084; Fax: 801-489-1097; Toll Free: 800-759-2665
E-mail: skybook@cedarfort.com
Web site: http://www.cedarfort.com.

Cedar Graphics, *See* **Igram Pr.**

Cengage Gale, *(978-0-13; 978-0-7876; 978-0-8103; 978-0-936474; 978-1-57302; 978-1-878623; 978-1-59413; 978-1-59414; 978-1-59415; 978-1-4144; 978-1-4205; 978-1-59722; 978-1-4328; 978-1-5358)* Subs. of Cengage Learning, Orders Addr.: P.O. Box 9187, Farmington Hills, MI 48333-9187 USA Toll Free Fax: 800 414 5043; Toll Free: 800 877 4253; Edit Addr.: 27500 Drake Rd., Farmington Hills, MI 48331 USA (SAN 213-4373) Tel 248-699-8495 Toll Free: 800-877-4253; a/o Wheeler Publishing, 295 Kennedy Memorial Dr., Waterville, ME 04901 Toll Free: 800 223 1244
E-mail: gale.salesassistance@thomson.com
Web site: http://www.gale.com.

CENGAGE Learning, Orders Addr.: 10650 Toebben Dr., Independence, KY 41051 USA (SAN 200-2213) Tel

859-525-6620; Fax: 859-525-0978; Toll Free Fax: 800-487-8488; Toll Free: 800-354-9706
Web site: http://www.cengage.com/.

Centennial Pubns., 1400 Ash Dr., Fort Collins, CO 80521 USA (SAN 630-494X) Tel 970-493-2041 Do not confuse with Centennial Pubns., Grand Junction, CO.

Central Arizona Distributing, 4932 W. Pasadena Ave., Glendale, AZ 85301 USA (SAN 170-6128) Tel 602-939-6511.

Central Coast Bks., 1195 Al Sereno Ln., Los Osos, CA 93402-4413 USA Tel 805-534-0307 (phone/fax)
E-mail: ccbooks@charter.net.

Central European Univ. Pr., *(978-1-85866; 978-963-9116; 978-963-9241; 978-963-7326; 978-963-9776; 978-1-61055; 978-615-5053; 978-615-5225; 978-615-5211; 978-963-386)* Orders Addr.: c/o Books International, P.O. Box 605, Herndon, VA 20172 USA; Edit Addr.: 2 River Rd. Apt. 18, Highland Park, NJ 08904 USA Tel 732-763-8816; Október 6 utca 14, Budapest, 1051 Tel 36-1-327-3000; Fax: 36-1-327-3183
E-mail: abel.meszaros@gmail.com; ceupress@ceu.hu; MeszarosA@ceu.hu
Web site: http://www.ceupress.com.

Central Illinois Periodicals, P.O. Box 3757, Bloomington, IL 61701 USA (SAN 630-8945) Tel 309-829-9405.

Central Kentucky News Distributing Company, *See* **Anderson-Austin News Co., LLC**

Central News of Sandusky, 5716 McCartney Rd., Sandusky, OH 44870-1538 USA (SAN 169-684X).

Central Programs, 802 N. 41st St., Bethany, MO 64424 USA Tel 660-425-7777.

Central South Christian Distribution, 3730 Vulcan Dr., Nashville, TN 37211 USA (SAN 631-2543) Tel 615-833-5960; Toll Free Fax: 800-220-0194; Toll Free: 800-757-0856.

Centralia News Co., 232 E. Broadway, Centralia, IL 62801 USA (SAN 159-8341) Tel 618-532-5601.

CentroLibros de Puerto Rico, Inc., Santa Rosa Unit, Bayamon, PR 00960 USA (SAN 631-1245) Tel 787-275-0460; Fax: 787-275-0360.

Century Bk. Distribution, 814 Boon, Traverse City, MI 49686 USA Tel 231-933-6405 (phone/fax).

Century Pr., *(978-0-9659417)* Div. of Conservatory of American Letters, P.O. Box 298, Thomaston, ME 04861 USA Tel 207-354-0998; Fax: 207-354-8953 Do not confuse with companies with the same name in Arroyo Seco, NM, Oklahoma City, OK
E-mail: cal@americanletters.org
Web site: http://www.americanletters.org.

Ceramic Book & Literature Service, *See* **CBLS Pubs.**

Chain Sales Marketing, Inc., *(978-1-55836)* 149 Madison Ave., Suite 810, New York, NY 10016 USA (SAN 245-1328) Tel 212-696-4230; Fax: 212-696-4391.

Chambers Kingfisher Graham Publishers, Incorporated, *See* **Larousse Kingfisher Chambers, Inc.**

Champaign-Urbana News Agency, Orders Addr.: P.O. Box 793, Champaign, IL 61824 USA (SAN 630-8953) Tel 217-351-7047; Edit Addr.: 503 Kenyon, Champaign, IL 61820 USA.

Charisma Media, *(978-0-88419; 978-0-930525; 978-1-59185; 978-1-59979; 978-1-61638; 978-1-62136; 978-1-62998; 978-1-62999)* Div. of Creation House Pr., 600 Rinehart Rd., Lake Mary, FL 32746 USA (SAN 677-5640) Tel 407-333-0600; Fax: 407-333-7100; Toll Free: 800-283-8494
Web site: http://www.charismamedia.com/.

Charlesbridge Publishing, Inc., *(978-0-88106; 978-0-935508; 978-1-57091; 978-1-58089; 978-1-879085; 978-1-60734; 978-0-9822939; 978-0-9823064; 978-1-936140; 978-1-63289)* Orders Addr.: c/o Penguin Random House, 400 Hahn Rd., Westminster, MD 21157 USA Toll Free Fax: 800-669-1536; Toll Free: 800-733-3000; Edit Addr.: 85 Main St., Watertown, MA 02472 USA (SAN 240-5474) Tel 617-926-0329; Fax: 617-926-5720; Toll Free Fax: 800-926-5775; Toll Free: 800-225-3214
E-mail: orders@charlesbridge.com
Web site: http://www.charlesbridge.com.

Charlynn Publishing Co., Inc., 4152 E. Fifth St., Tucson, AZ 85711 USA.

Checker Distributors, 400 W. Dussel Dr. Ste. B, Maumee, OH 43537-1636 USA (SAN 631-1431) Toll Free: 800-537-1060.

Chelsea Green Publishing, *(978-0-930031; 978-1-890132; 978-1-931498; 978-1-933392; 978-1-60358)* Orders Addr.: P.O. Box 428, White River Junction, VT 05001 USA (SAN 669-7631) Tel 802-295-6300; Fax: 802-295-6444; Toll Free: 800-639-4099; Edit Addr.: 85 N. Main St., Suite 120, White River Junction, VT 05001 USA
E-mail: info@chelseagreen.com
Web site: http://www.chelseagreen.com.

Cheng & Tsui Co., *(978-0-88727; 978-0-917056; 978-1-62291)* 25 West St., Boston, MA 02111-1213 USA (SAN 169-3387) Tel 617-988-2401; Fax: 617-426-3669
E-mail: service@cheng-tsui.com
Web site: http://www.cheng-tsui.com.

Cherry Lake Publishing, *(978-1-60279; 978-1-61080; 978-1-62431; 978-1-62753; 978-1-63137; 978-1-63188; 978-1-63362; 978-1-63470; 978-1-63471; 978-1-63472; 978-1-5341)* 1215 Overidgeview Ct., Ann Arbor, MI 48103 USA Tel 248-705-2045; 1750 Northway Dr., Suite 101, North Mankato, MN 56003 (SAN 858-9275) Tel 866-918-3956; Toll Free Fax: 866-489-6490; 2395 S. Huron Prkwy Ste. 200, Ann Arbor, MI 48104
E-mail: customerservice@cherrylakepublishing.com; benmondloch@me.com; lois.hume@sleepingbearpress.com
Web site: http://cherrylakepublishing.com; www.sleepingbearpress.com.

Chesbro Music Co., 327 Broadway, Idaho Falls, ID 83403 USA (SAN 631-0850) Tel 208-522-8691.

Chicago Distribution Ctr., Orders Addr.: 11030 S. Langley Ave., Chicago, IL 60628 USA (SAN 630-6047) Tel 773-702-7000 (International); Fax: 773-702-7212 (International); Toll Free Fax: 800-621-8476 (USA/Canada); Toll Free: 800-621-2736 (USA/Canada); 800-621-8471 (credit & collections)
E-mail: custserv@press.uchicago.edu; orders@press.uchicago.edu
Web site: http://www.press.uchicago.edu; http://www.press.uchicago.edu/presswide/cdc/.

Chicago Review Pr., Inc., *(978-0-89733; 978-0-912777; 978-0-913705; 978-0-914090; 978-0-914091; 978-0-915864; 978-1-55652; 978-1-56976; 978-1-61373; 978-1-61374; 978-1-64160)* 814 N. Franklin St., Chicago, IL 60610 USA (SAN 213-5744) Tel 312-337-0747; Toll Free: 800-888-4741 (orders only)
E-mail: frontdesk@chicagoreviewpress.com; orders@ipgbook.com
Web site: http://www.ipgbook.com; http://www.chicagoreviewpress.com.

Chico News Agency, P.O. Box 690, Chico, CA 95927 USA (SAN 168-9533) Tel 530-895-1000; Fax: 530-895-0158.

Children's Bookfair Co., The, 700 E. Grand Ave., Chicago, IL 60611-3472 USA (SAN 630-6705) Tel 312-477-7323; 837 W. Altgeld St., Chicago, IL 60614 (SAN 630-6713).

Children's Plus, Inc., 1387 Dutch American, Beecher, IL 60401 USA Tel 708-946-4100; Fax: 709-946-4199
E-mail: danw@childrensplusinc.com
Web site: http://www.childrensplusinc.com.

China Books & Periodicals, Inc., *(978-0-8351)* 360 Swift Ave., Suite 48, South San Francisco, CA 94080 USA (SAN 145-0557) Tel 650-872-7718; 650-872-7076; Fax: 650-872-7808
E-mail: chris@chinabooks.com
Web site: http://www.chinabooks.com.

China Cultural Ctr., 3535 Dunn Dr. Apt. 303, Los Angeles, CA 90034-4977 USA (SAN 111-8161).

China House Gallery, China Institute in America, *See* **China Institute Gallery, China Institute in America**

China Institute Gallery, China Institute in America, *(978-0-9654270; 978-0-9774054; 978-0-9893776; 978-0-692-93086-1)* Div. of China Institute in America, 100 Washington St., New York, NY 10006 USA (SAN 110-8743) Tel 212-744-8181; Fax: 212-628-4159
E-mail: gallery@chinainstitute.org
Web site: http://www.chinainstitute.org.

Chinasprout, Inc., *(978-0-9707332; 978-0-9747302; 978-0-9820227; 978-1-945947)* 110 W. 32nd St., Flr. 6, New York, NY 10001-3205 USA Toll Free: 800-644-2611
E-mail: info@chinasprout.com
Web site: http://www.chinasprout.com.

Chinese American Co., 44 Kneeland St., Boston, MA 02111 USA (SAN 159-7248) Fax: 617-451-2318.

Christian Bk. Distributors, Orders Addr.: P.O. Box 7000, Peabody, MA 01961 USA (SAN 630-5458) Tel 978-977-5000; Fax: 978-977-5010
Web site: http://www.christianbook.com.

Christian Literature Crusade, Incorporated, *See* **CLC Pubns.**

Christian Printing Service, 4861 Chino Ave., Chino, CA 91710-5132 USA (SAN 108-2647) Tel 714-871-5200.

Christian Publishing Network, *(978-0-9628406)* P.O. Box 405, Tulsa, OK 74101 USA (SAN 631-2756) Tel 918-296-4673 (918-296-HOPE); Toll Free: 888-688-8125
E-mail: vpsales@olp.net.

christianaudio, *(978-1-59644; 978-1-61045; 978-1-61843; 978-1-63389; 978-1-68366; 978-1-5459)* 2235 Enterprise ,Ste. 140, Escondido, CA 92029 USA (SAN 851-4577) Tel 760-745-2411; Fax: 760-745-3462
E-mail: jeannette@christianaudio.com; roberta@christianaudio.com; customerservice@christianaudio.com
Web site: http://christianaudio.com.

Chronicle Bks. LLC, *(978-0-8118; 978-0-87701; 978-0-938491; 978-1-4521)* Div. of The McEvoy Group, Orders Addr.: 680 Second St., San Francisco, CA 94107 USA (SAN 202-165X) Tel 415-537-4200; Fax: 415-537-4460; Toll Free Fax: 800-286-9471; Toll Free: 800-759-0190 (orders only); Edit Addr.: 3 Center Plaza, Boston, MA 2108 USA
E-mail: order.desk@hbgusa.com; customer.service@hbgusa.com
Web site: http://www.chroniclebooks.com.

Chulain Publishing Corp., Orders Addr.: 8241 Sweet Water Rd., Lone Tree, CO 80124-3017 USA.

Church Hymnal Corporation, *See* **Church Publishing, Inc.**

Church of Scientology Information Service-Pubns., *(978-0-915598)* c/o Bridge Pubns., Inc., 1414 N. Catalina, Los Angeles, CA 90029 USA (SAN 268-9774).

Church Publishing, Inc., *(978-0-89869; 978-1-59627; 978-1-59628; 978-1-64065)* Orders Addr.: 19 E. 34th St., New York, NY 10016 USA (SAN 857-0140) Tel 212-592-1800; Fax: 212-779-3392; Toll Free: 800-242-1918; Edit Addr.: 19 East 34th st, New York, NY 10016 USA
E-mail: rmasteller@cpg.org; lsimonello@cpg.org
Web site: http://www.churchpublishing.org.

Church Richards Co., 10001 Roosevelt Rd., Westchester, IL 60154 USA (SAN 285-8975) Toll Free: 800-323-0227.

Circa Pubns., Inc., 415 Fifth Ave., Pelham, NY 10803-0408 USA (SAN 169-6122) Tel 914-738-5570; Toll Free: 800-582-5952 (orders only).

Circle Bk. Service, Inc., *(978-0-87397)* P.O. Box 626, Tomball, TX 77377 USA (SAN 158-2526) Tel 281-255-6824; Fax: 281-255-8158; Toll Free: 800-227-1591
E-mail: orders@circlebook.com
Web site: http://www.circlebook.com.

City News Agency, Orders Addr.: P.O. Box 561129, Charlotte, NC 28256-1129 USA (SAN 169-782X); Edit Addr.: P.O. Box 2069, Newark, OH 43055 USA (SAN 169-6947); 220 Cherry Ave., NE, Canton, OH 44702-1198 (SAN 169-6602); 303 E. Lasalle St., South Bend, IN 46617 (SAN 159-9992); 417 S. McKinley, Harrisburg, IL 62946 (SAN 169-1961).

Clarks Out of Town News, 303 S. Andrews Ave., Fort Lauderdale, FL 33301 USA (SAN 159-8384) Tel 954-467-1543.

Class Pubns., Inc., *(978-0-913031)* 71 Bartholomew Ave., Hartford, CT 06106 USA (SAN 283-0302) Tel 860-951-9200.

Classroom Reading Service, P.O. Box 2708, Santa Fe Spgs, CA 90670-0708 USA (SAN 131-3959) Toll Free: 800-422-6657
E-mail: crsbooks@aol.com.

CLC Pubns., *(978-0-87508; 978-1-936143; 978-1-61958)* Div. of CLC Ministries International, Orders Addr.: P.O. Box 1449, Fort Washington, PA 19034-8449 USA Tel 215-542-1242; Fax: 215-542-7580; Toll Free: 800-659-1240; 701 Pennsylvania Ave., Fort Washington, PA 19034 (SAN 169-7358) Tel 215-542-1242; Fax: 215-542-7580; Toll Free: 800-659-1240
E-mail: orders@clcpublications.com; churd@clcpublications.com; ckelly@clcpublications.com
Web site: http://www.clcusa.org; http://www.clcpublications.com.

CLEARVUE/eav, Inc., 6465 N. Avondale Ave., Chicago, IL 60631-1996 USA (SAN 204-1669) Tel 773-775-9433; Fax: 773-775-9855; Toll Free Fax: 800-444-9855 (24 Hours); Toll Free: 800-253-2788 (8:00 am to 4:30 pm Central Time M-F); P.O. Box 2284, S Burlington, VT 05407-2287
E-mail: custserv@clearvue.com
Web site: http://www.clearvue.com.

Closet Case Bks., P.O. Box 16116, Saint Paul, MN 55116 USA
Web site: http://www.closetcasebooks.com.

Clover Bk. Service, 1220 S. Monroe St., Covingtons, LA 70433-3639 USA (SAN 106-472X) Tel 504-875-0038.

Cobblestone Publishing Co., *(978-0-382; 978-0-942389; 978-0-9607638)* Div. of Cricket Magazine Group, 30 Grove St., Suite C, Peterborough, NH 03458 USA (SAN 237-9937) Tel 603-924-7209; Fax: 603-924-7380; Toll Free: 800-821-0115; P.O. Box 487, Effingham, IL 62401
E-mail: custsvc@cobblestone.mv.com
Web site: http://www.cobblestonepub.com.

Cogan Bks., *(978-0-940688)* P.O. Box 579, Hudson, OH 44236-0579 USA (SAN 168-9649) Toll Free: 800-733-3630.

Cokesbury, 201 Eighth Ave., S., Nashville, TN 37203 USA (SAN 200-6863) Tel 615-749-6409; Toll Free: 800-672-1789
Web site: http://www.cokesbury.com.

Cold Cut Comics Distribution, 475-D Stockton Ave., San Jose, CA 95126 USA (SAN 631-6409) Tel 408-293-3844; Fax: 408-293-6645
E-mail: comics@coldcut.com
Web site: http://www.coldcut.com.

Cole, Bill Enterprises, Inc., P.O. Box 60, Randolph, MA 02368-0060 USA (SAN 685-6373) Tel 617-986-2653.

Collector Bks., *(978-0-89145; 978-1-57432; 978-1-60460)* Div. of Schroeder Publishing Co., Inc., Orders Addr.: P.O. Box 3009, Paducah, KY 42003 USA (SAN 157-5368) Tel 270-898-6211; 270-898-7903; Fax: 270-898-8890; 270-898-1173; Toll Free: 800-626-5420 (orders only); Edit Addr.: 5801 Kentucky Dam Rd., Paducah, KY 42003 USA (SAN 200-7479)
E-mail: Info@collectorbooks.com; info@AQSquilt.com
Web site: http://www.collectorbooks.com; http://www.americanquilter.com/.

College Bk. Co. of California, Inc., 181 W. Orangethorpe Ave. Ste. C, Placentia, CA 92870-6931 USA (SAN 269-0802).

Collegedale Distributors, *See* **Tree of Life Midwest**

Colonial Williamsburg Foundation, *(978-0-87935; 978-0-910412)* P.O. Box 3532, Williamsburg, VA 23187-3532 USA (SAN 128-4630) Fax: 757-565-8999 (orders only); Toll Free: 800-446-9240 (orders only)
Web site: http://www.colonialwilliamsburg.com.

Colorado Periodical Distributor, Inc., 1227 Pitkin St., Grand Junction, CO 81502 USA Tel 970-242-3865; Fax: 970-242-3760.

Colorado State University, Center for Literary Publishing, *See* **Ctr. for Literary Publishing, Colorado State Univ.**

Columbia County News Agency, Inc., 49 Bender Blvd., Ghent, NY 12075-3327 USA (SAN 169-5339).

Columbia Univ. Pr., *(978-0-231)* Orders Addr.: 61 W. 62nd St., New York, NY 10023-7015 USA (SAN 212-2480) Toll Free Fax: 800-944-1844; Toll Free: 800-944-8648 x 6240 (orders); Edit Addr.: 61 W. 62nd St., New York, NY 10023 USA (SAN 212-2472) Tel 212-459-0600; Fax: 212-459-3678; 387 Pk. Ave., S., New York, NY 10016; 1094 Flex Dr., Jackson, TN 38301
E-mail: cupbooks@columbia.edu
Web site: http://www.columbia.edu/cu/cup.

Comag Marketing Group, 1790 Broadway, Suite 401, New York, NY 10019 USA (SAN 169-5800) Tel 212-841-8365; Fax: 212-977-9401.

Comics Hawaii Distributors, *See* **Hobbies Hawaii Distributors**

Common Ground Distributors, Inc., Orders Addr.: P.O. Box 25249, Asheville, NC 28813-1249 USA Toll Free: 800-654-0626; Edit Addr.: 115 Fairview Rd., Asheville, NC 28803-2307 USA (SAN 113-8006) Tel 828-274-5575; Fax: 828-274-1955
E-mail: orders@comground.com.

Communication Service Corporation, *See* **Gryphon Hse., Inc.**

Communications Technology, Inc., *(978-0-918232)* P.O. Box 209, Rindge, NH 03461 USA (SAN 159-8198) Tel 603-899-6957.

Complete Book & Media Supply, 1200 Toro Grande Dr., Suite 200, Cedar Park, TX 78613 USA Fax: 512-616-0400; 512-616-0410; Toll Free: 800-986-1775
E-mail: books@completebook.com; bradm@completebook.com.

Computer & Technical Bks., 6338 Ranchview Ln., N., Osseo, MN 55311-3924 USA (SAN 630-8120).

Conde Nast Pubns., Inc., *(978-1-878494)* Four Times Sq., 20th Flr., New York, NY 10036 USA (SAN 285-905X) Tel 212-880-8800; Fax: 212-880-8289.

Connecticut River Pr., *(978-0-9706573)* 111 Holmes Rd., Newington, CT 06111 USA Tel 860-666-1200; 203-254-0147; Fax: 860-594-6037
E-mail: wolftalk@ziplink.net.

Consortium Bk. Sales & Distribution, Div. of Ingram Content Group, Orders Addr.: 1094 Flex Dr., Jackson, TN 38301-5070 USA; Edit Addr.: 34 13th Ave NE, Suite 100, Minneapolis, MN 55413-1007 USA (SAN 200-6049) Toll Free: 800-283-3572 (orders)
E-mail: info@cbsd.com
Web site: http://www.cbsd.com/.

ConsuLogic Consulting Services, 276 Longhouse Ln., Slingerlands, NY 12159-3012 USA Tel 518-452-9228; Fax: 518-452-9216.

Contemporary Arts Pr., *(978-0-931818)* Div. of La Mamelle, Inc., P.O. Box 3123, San Francisco, CA 94119-3123 USA (SAN 170-5423) Tel 415-282-0286.

Continental Bk. Co., Inc., *(978-0-9626800)* Eastern Div., 80-00 Cooper Ave., Bldg. No. 29, Glendale, NY 11385 USA (SAN 169-5436) Tel 718-326-0560; Fax: 718-326-4276; Toll Free: 800-364-0350; Western Div., 625 E. 70th Ave., No. 5, Denver, CO 80229 (SAN 630-2882) Tel 303-289-1761; Fax: 303-289-1764
E-mail: hola@continentalbook.com; esl@continentalbook.com; bonjour@continentalbook.com; tag@continentalbook.com
Web site: http://www.continentalbook.com.

Continental Enterprises Group, Inc. (CEG), Orders Addr.: 108 Red Row St., Easley, SC 29640-2820 USA (SAN 631-0915)
E-mail: ContactUs@centerprisesgrp.com.

Continental Sales, 213 W. Main St., Barrington, IL 60010-0010 USA Tel 847-381-6530.

Cook, David C., *(978-0-7814; 978-0-88207; 978-0-89191; 978-0-89693; 978-0-912692; 978-1-55513; 978-1-56476; 978-1-4347)* 4050 Lee Vance View, Colorado Springs, CO 80918 USA (SAN 206-0981) Tel 719-536-0100; Fax: 719-536-3244; Toll Free: 800-708-5550; 800-323-7543 (Customer Service)
E-mail: wendi.lord@davidccook.com
Web site: http://www.davidccook.com.

Cook, David C. Publishing Company, *See* **Cook, David C.**

Cookbook Marketplace, The, P.O. Box 305142, Nashville, TN 37230 USA (SAN 631-4201) Tel 615-391-2656; Toll Free: 800-358-0560.

Coos Bay Distributors, 131 N. Schoneman St., Coos Bay, OR 97420 USA (SAN 169-7064) Tel 541-888-5912.

Copper Island News, 1010 Wright St., Marquette, MI 49855-1834 USA (SAN 169-3824).

Copyright Clearance Ctr., Inc., 222 Rosewood Dr, Danvers, MA 01923 USA Tel 978-750-8400; Fax: 978-750-4343
Web site: http://www.copyright.com.

Cornell Univ. Pr., *(978-0-8014; 978-0-87546; 978-1-5017)* Orders Addr.: P.O. Box 6525, Ithaca, NY 14851 USA (SAN 281-5680) Tel 607-277-2211; Toll Free Fax: 800-688-2877; Toll Free: 800-666-2211; Edit Addr.: Sage House, 512 E. State St., Ithaca, NY 14851 USA (SAN 202-1862) Tel 607-277-2338
E-mail: cupressinfo@cornell.edu; orders@nbninternational.com; cupress-sales@cornell.edu
Web site: http://www.cornellpress.cornell.edu.

Coronet Bks., *(978-0-89563)* 311 Bainbridge St., Philadelphia, PA 19147 USA (SAN 210-6043) Tel 215-925-2762; Fax: 215-925-1912 Do not confuse with Coronet Bks. & Pubns., Eagle Point, OR
E-mail: ronsmolin@earthlink.net; order@coronetbooks.com
Web site: http://www.coronetbooks.com.

Country News Distributors, Div. of Bakers, Inc., P.O. Box 1258, Brattleboro, VT 05302-1258 USA (SAN 169-8575).

Countryside Bks., *(978-0-88453)* 2430 Estancia Blvd. Ste. 100, Clearwater, FL 33761-2644 USA (SAN 107-4415).

Coutts Information Services, Div. of ProQuest LLC, Orders Addr.: 7309 Innovation BLVD, Fort Wayne, IN 46818 USA (SAN 920-6779); Edit Addr.: 7309 Innovation BLVD, Fort Wayne, IN 46818 USA (SAN 169-5401) Toll Free: 800-263-1686.

Coutts Library Service, Incorporated, *See* **Coutts Information Services**

Cove Distributors, 6325 Erdman Ave., Baltimore, MD 21205 USA (SAN 158-9814) Toll Free: 800-622-5656 (Orders).

Cowley Distributing, Inc., 732 Heisinger Rd., Jefferson City, MO 65109 USA (SAN 169-426X) Tel 573-636-6511; Fax: 573-636-6262; Toll Free: 800-346-5950 (orders).

Cox Subscriptions, Inc., 201 Village Rd., Shallotte, NC 28470 USA (SAN 107-0061) Tel 800-571-9554; Fax: 877-755-6274; Toll Free: 800-553-8088
E-mail: dknox@wtcox.com
Web site: http://www.wtcox.com.

CQ Products, 507 Industrial St., Waverly, IA 50677 USA (SAN 631-5216) Tel 319-352-2086; Fax: 319-352-5338
E-mail: gifts@cqproducts.com
Web site: http://www.cqproducts.com.

Crabtree Publishing, *(978-0-937070)* P.O. Box 3451, Federal Way, WA 98063 USA (SAN 214-3615) Tel 253-925-9300; 59Th Flr., New York, NY 10118 Do not confuse with Crabtree Publishing Co. in New York, NY.

Cram, George F. Co., Inc., *(978-0-87448)* 301 S. LaSalle St., P.O. Box 426, Indianapolis, IN 46201 USA (SAN 204-2630) Tel 317-635-5564; Fax: 317-635-2720; Toll Free: 800-227-4199
E-mail: cram-services@iquest.net.

Cranbury International, Orders Addr.: 7 Clarendon Ave., Suite 2, Montpelier, VT 05602 USA.

CRC Pr. LLC, *(978-0-8493; 978-0-87762; 978-0-87819; 978-0-935184; 978-1-56676; 978-1-57491; 978-1-58488; 978-1-58716; 978-1-4200; 978-1-4398; 978-1-4665; 978-1-4822; 978-1-4987; 978-1-351)* Subs. of Taylor &

Francis, Inc., Orders Addr.: 6000 Broken Sound Pkwy., NW, Ste. 300, Boca Raton, FL 33487 USA Tel 800-272-7737 Toll Free Fax: 800-374-3401; Edit Addr.: 270 Madison Ave., New York, NY 10016 USA
E-mail: orders@crcpress.com; Theresa.Gutierrez@taylorandfrancis.com
Web site: http://www.crcpress.com; http://www.taylorandfrancis.com.

CreateSpace, *See* **CreateSpace Independent Publishing Platform**

CreateSpace Independent Publishing Platform, *(978-1-58898; 978-1-5423; 978-1-59109; 978-1-59456; 978-1-59457; 978-1-4196; 978-1-4348; 978-1-4382; 978-1-4392; 978-1-4404; 978-1-4414; 978-1-4421; 978-1-61550; 978-1-4486; 978-1-4495; 978-1-4499; 978-1-4505; 978-1-4515; 978-1-4528; 978-1-4536; 978-1-4537; 978-1-4538; 978-1-4563; 978-1-4564; 978-1-4565; 978-1-61789; 978-1-4609; 978-1-4610; 978-1-4611; 978-1-61396; 978-1-61397; 978-1-4635; 978-1-4636; 978-1-4637; 978-1-4662; 978-1-4663; 978-1-4664; 978-1-61914; 978-1-61915; 978-1-61916; 978) Orders Addr.: 4900 LaCross Rd., North Charleston, SC 29406 USA (SAN 255-2132) Tel 843-225-4700 (Ask for ordering department); Fax: 843-577-7506; Toll Free: 866-308-6235; 4900 LaCross Rd., North Charleston, SC 29406*
E-mail: info@createspace.com
Web site: http://www.createspace.com.

Creative Co., The, *(978-0-87191; 978-0-88682; 978-0-89812; 978-1-56660; 978-1-56846; 978-1-58341; 978-1-60818; 978-1-62832; 978-1-68277; 978-1-64000; 978-1-64026)* 123 S. Broad St., Mankato, MN 56001 USA Tel 507-388-6273; Fax: 507-388-4797; Toll Free: 800-445-6209 Do not confuse with The Creative Co., Lawrenceburg, IN
E-mail: info@thecreativecompany.us; kate.riggs@thecreativecompany.us
Web site: http://www.thecreativecompany.us.

Creative Homeowner, *(978-0-932944; 978-1-58011; 978-1-880029)* Div. of Courier Corporation, 24 Park Way, Upper Saddle River, NJ 07458-9960 USA (SAN 213-6627) Tel 201-934-7100; Fax: 201-934-8971; Toll Free: 800-631-7795
E-mail: info@creativehomeowner.com
Web site: http://www.creativehomeowner.com.

Creative Teaching Pr., Inc., *(978-0-88160; 978-0-916119; 978-1-57471; 978-1-59198; 978-1-60689; 978-1-61601; 978-1-62186; 978-1-63445; 978-1-68310)* Orders Addr.: P.O. Box 2723, Huntington Beach, CA 92647-0723 USA Tel 714-895-5047; Fax: 714-895-6547; Toll Free Fax: 800-444-4287; Edit Addr.: 6262 Katella Ave., Cypress, CA 90630 USA (SAN 294-9180) Tel 714-895-5047; Toll Free Fax: 800-229-9929; Toll Free: 800-444-4287
E-mail: webmaster@creativeteaching.com; we.listen@creativeteaching.com
Web site: http://www.creativeteaching.com; http://www.thelearningworks.com; http://www.learntoreadkidsclub.com.

Crescent Imports & Pubns., *(978-0-933127)* P.O. Box 7827, Ann Arbor, MI 48107-7827 USA (SAN 111-3976) Tel 734-665-3492; Fax: 734-677-1717; Toll Free: 800-521-9744
E-mail: crescentus@aol.com
Web site: http://www.crescentimports.com.

Crescent International, Inc., 2238 Otranto Rd., Charleston, SC 29418 USA (SAN 110-0777) Tel 803-797-6363; Fax: 803-797-6367.

Critics' Choice, *See* **Critics' Choice Video**

Critics' Choice Video, *(978-1-932566; 978-1-933240)* 900 N. Rohlwing Rd., Itasca, IL 60143 USA Tel 630-775-3300; Fax: 603-775-3340
E-mail: rterry@ccvideo.com
Web site: http://www.ccvideo.com.

Cromland, 964 Marcon Blvd, Suite 190, Allentown, PA 18109 USA (SAN 254-6736) Tel 610-266-6610; Fax: 610-266-8987; Toll Free: 800-944-5554 (U.S. & Canada)
Web site: http://www.cromland.com.

CrossLife Expressions, *(978-0-9636049; 978-1-57838)* Div. of Exchanged Life Ministries, Inc., 10610 E. Bethany Dr., Suite A, Aurora, CO 80014 USA (SAN 169-0590) Tel 303-750-0440; Fax: 303-750-1228; Toll Free: 800-750-6818
E-mail: info@crosslifebooks.com
Web site: http://www.crosslifebooks.com.

Crowley Distributors, *See* **Sunburst Bks., Inc., Distributor of Florida Bks.**

Crowley, Inc., 16120 U.S. Hwy. 19 N., Suite 220, Clearwater, FL 34624-6862 USA (SAN 285-9130) Tel 813-531-5889.

Crown Agents Service, Ltd., 3100 Massachusetts Ave., NW, Washington, DC 20008 USA (SAN 285-919X).

Crown Hse. Publishing, *(978-1-899836; 978-1-904424; 978-1-84590; 978-0-9823573; 978-1-935810; 978-1-78135; 978-1-78583)* Orders Addr.: P.O. Box 2223, Williston, VT 05495 USA Fax: 802-864-7626; Toll Free: 877-925-1213; Edit Addr.: Crown Bldg., Bancyfelin, Carmarthen, Dyfed SA33 5ND GBR Tel 01267 211345; 01267 211880; Fax: 01267 211882; 01267 211593; 6 Trowbridge Dr., Suite 5, Bethel, CT 06801 Tel 203-778-1300; Fax: 203-778-9100; Toll Free: 866-272-8497
E-mail: books@crownhouse.co.uk; info@CHPUS.com
Web site: http://www.crownhouse.co.uk/; http://www.CHPUS.com; http://www.crownhousepublishing.com.

Ctr. for Literary Publishing, Colorado State Univ., *(978-1-885635)* Center for Literary Publishing, Department of English, Colorado State University, Fort Collins, CO 80523 USA Tel 970-491-5449; Fax: 970-491-0283
E-mail: creview@colostate.edu
Web site: http://coloradoreview.colostate.edu/.

Cultural Hispana/Ameriketako Liburuak, Orders Addr.: P.O. Box 7729, Silver Spring, MD 20907 USA (SAN 159-2823); Edit Addr.: 1413 Crestridge Dr., Silver Spring, MD 20910 USA (SAN 249-3063) Tel 301-585-0134
E-mail: mokordo@erols.com
Web site: http://www.coloquio.com/libros.html.

Culture Plus Bk. Distributors, 44 Willoughby St., Brooklyn, NY 11201-5200 USA.

Culture Plus Bks., 209 N. La Brea Ave., Inglewood, CA 90301-1247 USA (SAN 631-3876).

CUP Services, 750 Cascadilla St., Ithaca, NY 14851 USA (SAN 630-6519) Tel 607-277-2211; Fax: 607-277-6292; Toll Free: 800-666-2211.

Curran Assocs., Inc., *(978-1-60423; 978-1-60560; 978-1-61567; 978-1-61738; 978-1-61782; 978-1-61839; 978-1-62276; 978-1-62748; 978-1-62993; 978-1-63266; 978-1-63439; 978-1-5108)* 57 Morehouse Ln., Red Hook, NY 12571 USA Tel 845-758-0400; Fax: 845-758-2633
E-mail: curran@proceedings.com
Web site: http://www.proceedings.com.

Curreri, Michelle Morrow, 3 Eagle Ln., Beverly, MA 01915 USA Tel 978-921-8020; Fax: 978-921-7577
E-mail: michelle@curreriworldsvs.net.

Curtis, Ralph Books, *See* **Curtis, Ralph Publishing**

Curtis, Ralph Publishing, *(978-0-88359)* P.O. Box 349, Sanibel, FL 33957 USA (SAN 121-1323) Tel 239-454-0010; Fax: 239-395-2727; Toll Free: 888-454-0011
E-mail: rcurtisbks@yahoo.com
Web site: http://www.ralphcurtisbooks.com.

CustomFlix Labs, Inc., *(978-0-9774415)* 100 Enterprise Way Ste. A200, Scotts Valley, CA 95066-3266 USA.

Cybernetics Technology Corp., *(978-0-923458)* 1370 Port Washington Blvd., Port Washington, NY 11050-2628 USA (SAN 295-933X) Tel 516-883-7676.

Cypress Bk. Co., Inc., *(978-0-934643)* Subs. of China International Bk. Trading Corp., 360 Swift Ave. Ste. 42, S San Fran, CA 94080-6220 USA (SAN 112-1162) Toll Free: 800-383-1688
E-mail: sales@cypressbook.com; info@cypressbook.com; cypbook@pacbell.net
Web site: http://www.cypressbook.com.

Cypress Hse., *(978-1-879384; 978-0-9987854)* 155 Cypress St., Fort Bragg, CA 95437 USA (SAN 297-9004) Tel 707-964-9520; Fax: 707-964-7531; Toll Free: 800-773-7782
E-mail: cypresshouse@cypresshouse.com; forms@cypresshouse.com
Web site: http://www.cypresshouse.com.

D & H News Co., Inc., 79 Albany Post Rd., Montrose, NY 10548 USA (SAN 169-5533) Tel 914-737-3152.

D & J Bk. Distributors, *(978-1-883080)* 229-21B Merrick Blvd., Laurelton, NY 11413 USA (SAN 630-5091) Tel 718-949-5400; Fax: 718-949-6161; Toll Free: 800-446-4707.

D K Publishing, Incorporated, *See* **Dorling Kindersley Publishing, Inc.**

Daedalus Bks., 9645 Gerwig Ln., Columbia, MD 21046-1520 USA (SAN 158-9202) Tel 410-309-2700
E-mail: tstock@daedalus-books.com; custserv@daedalus-books.com
Web site: http://www.daedalus-books.com.

Dahlstrom, Carol Field Inc., *(978-0-9679764; 978-0-9768446)* 7952 NE. Berwick Dr., Ankeny, IA 50021 USA Tel 515-964-1777; Fax: 515-964-1788
E-mail: braveink@aol.com
Web site: http://www.braveink.com.

Dake Bible Sales, *See* **Dake Publishing**

Dake Publishing, *(978-0-9655968; 978-1-55829)* Orders Addr.: P.O. Box 1050, Lawrenceville, GA 30046 USA (SAN 212-0828) Tel 770-963-1611; Fax: 770-963-7700; Toll Free: 800-241-1239; Edit Addr.: 764 Martins Chapel Rd., Lawrenceville, GA 30246 USA (SAN 243-2684)
E-mail: derrick@dake.com
Web site: http://www.dake.com.

Dakota News, Inc., 221 Petro Ave., Box 1310, Sioux Falls, SD 57101 USA (SAN 169-7854) Tel 605-336-3000; Fax: 605-336-7279; Toll Free: 800-658-5498.

Dakota West Bks., P.O. Box 9324, Rapid City, SD 57701 USA (SAN 630-351X) Tel 605-348-1075; Fax: 605-348-0615.

Danforth Bk. Distribution, Orders Addr.: 3220 228th St., S. E., Bothell, WA 98021 USA Tel 206-351-5872
E-mail: Danfothbookdist@gmail.com.

D.A.P./Distributed Art Pubs., *(978-1-881616; 978-1-891024; 978-1-933045; 978-1-935202; 978-1-938922; 978-1-942884)* Orders Addr.: 75 Broad St., Suite 630, New York, NY 10004 USA (SAN 630-6446) Tel 212-627-1999; Fax: 212-627-9484; Toll Free Fax: 800-478-3128; Toll Free: 800-338-2665
E-mail: dap@dapinc.com
Web site: http://www.artbook.com/.

Darr Subscription Agency, P.O. Box 575, Louisburg, KS 66053-0575 USA (SAN 285-9149) Toll Free: 800-850-3741
E-mail: lgriff@midusa.net.

David, Jonathan Pubs., Inc., *(978-0-8246)* 68-22 Eliot Ave., Middle Village, NY 11379 USA (SAN 169-5274) Tel 718-456-8611; Fax: 718-894-2818
E-mail: jondavpub@aol.com
Web site: http://www.jdbooks.com.

Davidson Titles, Inc., *(978-1-884756)* Orders Addr.: 2345 Dr. F.E. Wright Dr., Jackson, TN 38303 USA; Edit Addr.: P.O. Box 3538, Jackson, TN 38303-3538 USA (SAN 255-9129) Tel 731-988-5333; Fax: 731-988-5080; Toll Free Fax: 800-787-7935; Toll Free: 800-433-3903 Do not confuse with companies of the same name in Sugar Hill NH, Windsor CT, Redmond & Kirkland WA, Newark NJ, Fairfield & Reddick FL, East Lansing MI, Rocklin CA, Tolono IL, Missoula MT, Ann Arbor MI, Half Moon Bay CA
E-mail: brian@davidsontitles.com
Web site: http://www.davidsontitles.com.

Davis/Books Distribution, 215 W. Main, Cambridge City, IN 47357 USA Tel 765-478-5773.

Dawson Subscription Service, *See* **Faxon Illinois Service Ctr.**

Day School Magazine Service, P.O. Box 262, Brooklyn, NY 11219 USA (SAN 285-9157) Tel 718-871-1486; Fax: 718-435-2342
E-mail: Elciv@juno.com.

De Gruyter, Inc., *(978-0-89925; 978-1-56445; 978-1-934078; 978-1-61451; 978-1-5015; 978-1-5473)* Subs. of Walter de Gruyter & GmbH & Co. KG, Orders Addr.: P.O. Box 960, Herndon, VA 20172-0960 USA Tel 703-661-1589; Fax: 703-661-1501; Toll Free: 800-208-8144; Edit Addr.: 121 High St., Third Flr., Boston, MA 02110 USA Tel 857-284-7073; Fax: 857-284-7358
E-mail: info@deGruyterny.com; kruehle@degruyterny.com; USinfo@degruyter.com; info@degruyter.com
Web site: http://www.degruyter.com; http://www.mouton-publishers.com; http://www.mouton-online.com; www.degruyter.com.

De Gruyter, Walter Incorporated, *See* **De Gruyter, Inc.**

De Vore Group/Carla Bks. & More, Orders Addr.: P.O. Box 10276, San Juan, PR 00922 USA (SAN 159-8309) Tel 809-721-7645; Fax: 809-722-9216; Edit Addr.: 1409 Ave. Ponce De Leon, San Juan, PR 00907-4023 USA (SAN 249-2776).

Dearborn Financial Publishing, Inc., *(978-0-7931; 978-0-88462; 978-0-913864; 978-0-936894; 978-1-57410)* 30 South Wacker Dr., Chicago, IL 60606-1719 USA (SAN 201-3622) Tel 312-836-4400 ext 282429; Fax: 312-836-1021
Web site: http://www.dearborn.com.

Dearborn Trade, A Kaplan Professional Company, *See* **Kaplan Publishing**

DeBoer, Bernhard Inc., 113 E. Centre St., Nutley, NJ 07110 USA (SAN 282-1990) Tel 973-667-9300; Fax: 973-667-0086
E-mail: stout@javanet.com
Web site: http://www.javanet.com/-stout/pannus.

DecisionPro, Inc., 2452 General Potter Hwy., Centre Hall, PA 16828-9022 USA.

DeHoff Christian Bookstore, *(978-1-933965)* 749 N. W. Broad St., Murfreesboro, TN 37129-3797 USA (SAN 184-4202) Tel 615-893-8322; Fax: 615-896-7447; Toll Free: 800-695-5385
E-mail: dehoff@bellsouth.net; fakesb@yahoo.com
Web site: http://www.dehoffbooks.com.

Dehoff Publications, *See* **DeHoff Christian Bookstore**

Delmar Cengage Learning, *(978-0-314; 978-0-7668; 978-0-7693; 978-0-8273; 978-0-87350; 978-0-916032; 978-0-944132; 978-0-9653629; 978-1-56253; 978-1-56593; 978-1-56930; 978-1-4018; 978-1-4180; 978-1-4283; 978-1-4354)* Div. of Cengage Learning, Orders Addr.: c/o Thomson Learning Order Fulfilment, P.O. Box 6904, Florence, KY 41022 USA Toll Free Fax: 800 487 8488; Toll Free: 800 347 7707; c/o Thomson Delmar Learning Clinical Health Care Series, P.O. Box 3419, Scranton, PA 18505-0419 Fax: 570-347-9072; Toll Free: 888-427-5800; Edit Addr.: P.O. Box 15015, Albany, NY 12212-5015 USA (SAN 206-7544) Tel 518-348-2300; Fax: 518-373-6345; Toll Free: 800-998-7498; 5 Maxwell Dr., Clifton Park, NY 12065- (SAN 658-0440) Tel 518-348-2300; Fax: 518-881-1256; Toll Free: 800-998-7498
E-mail: matthew.grover@thomson.com; clinicalmanuals@thomson.com
Web site: http://www.delmarlearning.com; http://www.clinicalmanuals.com/.

Delmar News Agency, Inc., P.O. Box 7169, Newark, DE 19714-7169 USA (SAN 169-0892) Tel 302-455-9922; Toll Free: 800-441-7025.

DeLong Subscription Agency, P.O. Box 806, Lafayette, IN 47902 USA (SAN 285-9246) Toll Free: 800-992-2092.

Delphi Distribution Inc., Orders Addr.: 1263 SW Blvd., Kansas City, KS 66103 USA (SAN 760-7989) Tel 913-362-7400; Fax: 913-362-7401
E-mail: kent@delphidistribution.com; linda@midpt.com.

Delta Education, Incorporated, *See* **Delta Education, LLC**

Delta Education, LLC, *(978-0-87504; 978-1-58356; 978-1-59242; 978-1-59821; 978-1-60395; 978-1-60902; 978-1-62571; 978-1-64011)* 80 Northwest Blvd., Nashua, NH 03063 USA (SAN 630-1711) Toll Free: 800-442-5444
E-mail: ngosselin@delta-edu.com
Web site: http://www.delta-education.com.

Delta Systems Company, Inc., *(978-0-937354; 978-1-887744; 978-1-932748; 978-1-934960; 978-1-936299; 978-1-936402; 978-1-62167)* Orders Addr.: 1400 Miller Pkwy., McHenry, IL 60050-7030 USA (SAN 220-0457) Tel 815-363-3582; Fax: 815-363-2948; Toll Free Fax: 800-909-9901; Toll Free: 800-323-8270
E-mail: d.patchin@DeltaPublishing.com; L.Bruell@DeltaPublishing.com; j.patchin@deltapublishing.com
Web site: http://www.deltapublishing.com; http://www.raventreepress.com.

Deltiologists of America, *(978-0-913782)* P.O. Box 8, Norwood, PA 19074 USA (SAN 170-3072) Tel 610-485-8572.

Derstine, Roy Bk. Co., 14 Birch Rd., Kinnelon, NJ 07405 USA (SAN 130-822X) Tel 973-838-1109.

DeRu's Fine Arts, *(978-0-939370)* 9100 E. Artesia Blvd., Bellflower, CA 90706 USA (SAN 159-3862) Tel 562-920-1312; Fax: 562-920-3077
E-mail: derusgal@aol.com
Web site: http://www.derusfinearts.com.

Deseret Bk. Co., *(978-0-87579; 978-0-87747; 978-1-57345; 978-1-59038; 978-1-60641; 978-1-60907; 978-1-60908; 978-1-62972; 978-1-62973)* Div. of Deseret Management Corp., P.O. Box 30178, Salt Lake City, UT 84130 USA (SAN 150-763X) Tel 801-517-3165 (Wholesale Dept.); 801-534-1515; Fax: 801-517-3338; Toll Free: 800-453-3876
E-mail: wholesale@deseretbook.com; dbwhsale@deseretbook.com
Web site: http://www.deseretbook.com; http://www.shadowmountain.com.

Destiny Image Pubs., *(978-0-7684; 978-0-914903; 978-1-56043; 978-0-9716036)* 167 Walnut Bottom Rd., Shippensburg, PA 17257 USA (SAN 253-4339) Tel 717-532-3040; Fax: 717-532-9291; Toll Free: 800-722-6774
E-mail: dnj@destinyimage.com
Web site: http://www.destinyimage.com.

Detroit Free Pr., Inc., *(978-0-937247; 978-0-9605692)* Div. of Gannett, 615 W. Lafayette Blvd., Detroit, MI 48226 USA (SAN 239-6998) Tel 313-223-4575; Fax: 313-222-5982; Toll Free: 800-678-6400
E-mail: ajhartley@freepress.com; ldelves@freepress.com
Web site: http://www.freep.com.

Devin-Adair Pubs., Inc., *(978-0-8159)* P.O. Box A, Old Greenwich, CT 06870 USA (SAN 112-062X) Tel 203-531-7755; Fax: 718-359-8568.

DeVorss & Co., *(978-0-87516)* Orders Addr.: P.O. Box 1389, Camarillo, CA 93011-1389 USA (SAN 168-9886) Tel 805-322-9010; Fax: 805-322-9011; Toll Free: 800-843-5743; Edit Addr.: 553 Constitution Ave., Camarillo, CA 93012-8510 USA
E-mail: service@devorss.com
Web site: http://www.devorss.com.

Diamond Bk. Distributors, *(978-1-64031)* Div. of Diamond Comic Distributors, Inc., Orders Addr.: 1966 Greenspring Dr., Suite 300, Timonium, MD 21093 USA (SAN 110-9502) Tel 410-560-7100; Fax: 410-560-2583; Toll Free: 800-452-6642
E-mail: books@diamondbookdistributors.com
Web site: http://www.diamondcomics.com; http://www.diamondbookdistributors.com/.

Diamond Book Distributors Inc., *See* **Diamond Comic Distributors, Inc.**

Diamond Comic Distributors, Inc., *(978-1-59396; 978-1-60584)* 1966 Greenspring Dr., Suite 300, Timonium, MD 21093 USA Tel 410-560-7100; Fax: 410-560-2583; Toll Free: 800-452-6642
E-mail: books@diamondbookdistributors.com
Web site: http://www.diamondbookdistributors.com/.

Diamond Distributors, Inc., Orders Addr.: 1966 Greenspring Dr., Suite 300, Timonium, MD 21093 USA Tel 410-560-7100.

Digital Manga Distribution, *See* **Digital Manga Publishing**

Digital Manga Publishing, *(978-1-56970)* Div. of Digital Manga, Inc., 1487 W. 178th St. Ste. 300, Gardena, CA 90248-3253 USA (SAN 111-817X) Toll Free: 866-897-7300
E-mail: contact@emanga.com
Web site: http://www.dmpbooks.com/.

Dillon Bk., Subs. of Harold Dillon, Inc., 460 S. Marion Pkwy., Apt. 851B, Denver, CO 80209-2508 USA (SAN 169-0493) Tel 303-442-5323; Toll Free: 800-525-0842.

Discount Bk. Distributors, 1854 Wallace School Rd., No. E, Charleston, SC 29407-4822 USA (SAN 107-2250) Tel 843-556-6582.

Disney Publishing Worldwide, *(978-1-892309; 978-1-931580; 978-1-4231; 978-1-4847; 978-1-368; 978-1-368-01377-2)* Subs. of Walt Disney Productions, 44 S. Broadway, 10th Flr., White Plains, NY 10601 USA Tel 914-288-4316; 1101 Flower St., Glendale, CA 91201
Web site: http://www.disney.go.com; http://www.hyperionbooksforchildren.com; books.disney.com.

Distribooks, Inc., Div. of MED, Inc., 8124 N. Ridgeway, Skokie, IL 60076 USA (SAN 630-9763) Tel 847-676-1596; Fax: 847-676-1195
E-mail: info@distribooks.com.

Distribuidora Escolar, Inc., 2250 SW 99th Ave., Miami, FL 00165-7569 USA (SAN 169-1104).

Distribuidora Norma, Inc., *(978-1-881700; 978-1-935164)* Div. of Carvajal International, Orders Addr.: P.O. Box 195040, San Juan, PR 00919-5040 USA Tel 787-788-5050; Fax: 787-788-7161; Edit Addr.: Carretera 869 Km 1.5 Barrio Palmas Royal Industrial, Catano, PR 00962 USA
Web site: http://www.norma.com.

Distribuidora Plaza Mayor, 1500 Ave. Ponce de Leon Local 2 El Cinco, San Juan, PR 1 USA.

Distribution Solutions Group, 1120 Rte. 22 E., Bridgewater, NJ 08807-0885 USA Toll Free: 866-374-4748.

Distributors International, Div. of Dennis-Landman Pubs., 1150 18th St., Santa Monica, CA 90403 USA (SAN 129-8089) Tel 310-828-0680
E-mail: info@moviecraft.com
Web site: http://www.moviecraft.com.

Distributors, The, *(978-0-942520)* 702 S. Michigan, South Bend, IN 46601 USA (SAN 169-2488) Tel 574-232-8500; Fax: 312-803-0887; Toll Free: 800-348-5200
E-mail: info@thedistributors.com
Web site: http://thedistributors.com/.

Diversion Books, *See* **Diversion Publishing Corp.**

Diversion Publishing Corp., *(978-0-9845151; 978-0-9829050; 978-0-9833371; 978-0-9838395; 978-0-9839885; 978-1-938120; 978-1-62681; 978-1-68230; 978-1-63576)* 443 Park Aveue S., Ste. 1008, New York, NY 10016 USA (SAN 990-6304) Tel 212-675-5556; 212-961-6390
E-mail: info@diversionbooks.com; charles@efit.com
Web site: http://www.diversionbooks.com.

Divine, Inc., *(978-0-87305)* 1600 Providence Hwy., Walpole, MA 02081-2553 USA (SAN 159-8619) Toll Free: 800-766-0039
E-mail: pubservices@faxon.com; helpdesk@faxon.com
Web site: http://www.faxon.com.

Dixie News Co., P.O. Box 561129, Charlotte, NC 28256-1129 USA (SAN 169-636X) Tel 704-376-0140; Fax: 704-335-8604; Toll Free: 800-532-1045.

DKE Toys, *(978-0-9915790)* 8568 Walnut Dr., Los Angeles, CA 90046 USA Tel 323-656-3262
E-mail: dkelemer@aol.com
Web site: dketoys.com.

Docustar, 1325 Glendale-Milford Rd., Cincinnati, OH 45215 USA Tel 513-772-5400; Fax: 513-772-5410.

Dog Museum, The, *See* **American Kennel Club Museum of the Dog**

Doherty, Tom Assocs., LLC, *(978-0-312; 978-0-7653; 978-0-8125)* Div. of Holtzbrinck Publishers, Orders Addr.: 16365 James Madison Hwy., Gordonsville, VA 22942-8501 USA Toll Free Fax: 800-672-2054; Toll Free: 888-330-8477; Edit Addr.: 175 Fifth Ave., New York, NY 10010 USA Tel 212-674-5151; Fax: 540-672-7540 (customer service)
E-mail: inquiries@tor.com
Web site: http://www.tor.com/.

Donars Spanish Bks., P.O. Box 808, Lafayette, CO 80026 USA (SAN 108-1586) Tel 303-666-9175; Toll Free: 800-552-3316
E-mail: donars@prolynx.com.

Dorling Kindersley Publishing, Inc., *(978-0-7894; 978-1-56458; 978-1-879431; 978-0-7566; 978-1-4654)* Div. of Penguin Publishing Group, 375 Hudson St., 2nd Flr., New York, NY 10014 USA (SAN 253-0791) Tel 212-213-4800; Fax: 212-213-5240; Toll Free: 877-342-5357 (orders only)
E-mail: Annemarie.Cancienne@dk.com; customer.service@dk.com
Web site: http://www.dk.com.

Dot Gibson Distribution, Div. of Dot Gibson Pubns., P.O. Box 117, Waycross, GA 31502 USA Tel 912-285-2848.

Dover Pubns., Inc., *(978-0-486; 978-1-60660)* Div. of Courier Corporation, 31 E. Second St., Mineola, NY 11501 USA (SAN 201-338X) Tel 516-294-7000; Fax: 516-873-1401 (orders only); Toll Free: 800-223-3130 (orders only)
E-mail: rights@doverpublications.com
Web site: http://www.doverdirect.com; http://www.doverpublications.com.

Downtown Bk. Ctr., Inc., *(978-0-941010)* 247 SE First St., Suites 236-237, Miami, FL 33131 USA (SAN 169-1112) Tel 305-377-9941
E-mail: raxdown@aol.com.

Draft2Digital, *(978-1-4977; 978-1-4989; 978-1-5014; 978-1-5022; 978-1-5070; 978-1-5130; 978-1-5163; 978-1-5199; 978-1-5242; 978-1-5337; 978-1-5365; 978-1-5401; 978-1-386)* 5629 SE 67th St., Oklahoma City, OK 73135 USA Fax: 866-358-6413; Toll Free Fax: 866-358-6413; Toll Free: 866-336-5099
E-mail: support@draft2digital.com
Web site: www.draft2digital.com.

Dreams in Action Distribution, P.O. Box 1894, Sedona, AZ 86339 USA Tel 928-204-1560; 70 Yucca St., Sedona, AZ 86351
E-mail: sales@dreamsinaction.us; pamela@deamsinaction.us.

Drown News Agency, P.O. Box 2080, Folsom, CA 95763-2080 USA (SAN 169-0450).

Duebbert, Harold F., P.O.B. 629 E. Adolphus Ave., Fergus Falls, MN 56537 USA Tel 218-736-4312.

Dufour Editions, Inc., *(978-0-8023)* Orders Addr.: P.O. Box 7, Chester Springs, PA 19425-0007 USA (SAN 201-341X) Tel 610-458-5005; Fax: 610-458-7103; Toll Free: 800-869-5677
E-mail: info@dufoureditions.com
Web site: http://www.dufoureditions.com.

Dumont, Charles Son, Inc., *(978-1-61727)* 1085 Dumont Cir. PO Box 1017, Voorhees, NJ 08043 USA (SAN 631-0842) Tel 856-346-9100; Fax: 856-346-3452; Toll Free: 800-257-8283
E-mail: info@dumontmusic.com
Web site: http://www.dumontmusic.com.

Durst, Sanford J., *(978-0-915262; 978-0-942666; 978-1-886720)* 106 Woodcleft Ave., Freeport, NY 11520 USA (SAN 211-6987) Tel 516-867-3333; Fax: 516-867-3397
E-mail: sjdbooks@verizon.net.

Duval News Co., Orders Addr.: P.O. Box 61297, Jacksonville, FL 32203 USA (SAN 169-1015); Edit Addr.: 5638 Commonwealth Ave., Jacksonville, FL 32205 USA (SAN 249-2865) Tel 904-783-2350.

Duval-Bibb Publishing Co., *(978-0-937713)* Div. of Mareeco Enterprises, Inc., Orders Addr.: P.O. Box 24168, Tampa, FL 33623-4168 USA (SAN 111-8641) Tel 813-281-0091; Fax: 813-282-0220; 1808 B St. NW, Suite 140, Auburn, WA 98001 Toll Free Fax: 800-548-1169; Toll Free: 800-518-3541
E-mail: reese.cop@gte.net
Web site: http://lonepinepublishing.com/ordering.

E Learn Aid, Orders Addr.: P.O. Box 39545, Los Angeles, CA 90039-0545 USA Fax: 323-665-8875.

E M C Publishing, *See* **EMC/Paradigm Publishing**

Eagle Business Systems, *(978-0-928210)* P.O. Box 1240, El Toro, CA 92630-1240 USA (SAN 285-7510) Tel 714-859-9622.

Eagle Feather Trading Post, Inc., 168 W. 12th St., Ogden, UT 84404 USA (SAN 630-8996) Tel 801-393-3991; Fax: 801-745-0903; Toll Free: 800-547-3364 (orders only).

Eaglecrafts, Orders Addr.: 168 W. 12th St., Ogden, UT 84404 USA (SAN 630-6381) Tel 801-393-3991; Fax: 801-745-0903; Toll Free: 800-547-3364 (orders only)
E-mail: porsturbo@aol.com.

EAL Enterprises, Inc., Div. of Ambassador Bk. Service, 42 Chasner St., Hempstead, NY 11550 USA (SAN 169-6645) Toll Free: 800-431-8913.

East Kentucky News, Inc., 416 Teays Rd., Paintsville, KY 41240 USA (SAN 169-2879) Tel 606-789-8169.

East Texas Distributing, 7171 Grand Blvd., Houston, TX 77054 USA (SAN 169-8265) Tel 713-748-2520; Fax: 713-748-2504.

Eastern Bk. Co., Orders Addr.: P.O. Box 4540, Portland, ME 04112-4540 USA Fax: 207-774-0331; Toll Free Fax: 800-214-3895; Toll Free: 800-937-0331; Edit Addr.: 55 Bradley Dr., Westbrook, ME 04092-2013 USA (SAN 169-3050)
E-mail: info@ebc.com
Web site: http://www.ebc.com.

Eastern News Distributors, Subs. of Hearst Corp., 250 W. 55th St., New York, NY 10019 USA (SAN 169-5738) Tel 212-649-4484; Fax: 212-265-6239; Toll Free: 800-221-3148; 1 Media Way, 12406 Rte. 250, Milan, OH 44846-9705 (SAN 200-7711); 227 W. Trade St., Charlotte, NC 28202 (SAN 631-600X) Tel 704-348-8427
E-mail: enews@hearst.com.

Eastern Subscription Agency, 231 Moria Ct., Aston, PA 19014-1264 USA (SAN 285-9467).

Easton News Co., 2601 Dearborn St., Easton, PA 18042 USA (SAN 169-7315).

Eastview Editions, *(978-0-89860)* P.O. Box 247, Bernardsville, NJ 07924 USA (SAN 169-4952) Tel 908-204-0535.

East-West Export Bks., c/o Univ. of Hawaii Pr., 2840 Kolowalu St., Honolulu, HI 96822 USA Tel 808-956-8830; Fax: 808-988-6052
E-mail: royden@hawaii.edu
Web site: http://eastwestexportbooks.wordpress.com.

Eastwind Bks. & Arts, Inc., 1435-A Stockton St., San Francisco, CA 94133 USA (SAN 127-3159) Tel 415-772-5888; Fax: 415-772-5885
E-mail: info@eastwindsf.com
Web site: http://www.eastwindsf.com.

Eau Claire News Co., Inc., 8100 Partridge Rd., Eau Claire, WI 54703-9646 USA (SAN 169-9059) Tel 715-835-5437.

eBookIt.com, *(978-1-4566)* Div. of Archieboy Holdings, LLC, 365 Boston Post Rd., No. 311, Sudbury, MA 01776 USA
Web site: http://www.ebookit.com.

eBooks2go, *See* **eBooks2go Inc**

eBooks2go Inc, *(978-1-61813; 978-1-5457)* 1111 N. Plaza Dr., Ste. 300, Schaumburg, IL 60173 USA Tel 847-598-1150
E-mail: ram@ebooks2go.net
Web site: www.gantecpublishing.com; http://www.ebooks2go.com/.

ebrary, Inc., Div. of Proquest LLC, 318 Cambridge Ave., Palo Alto, CA 94306 USA (SAN 760-7741) Tel 650-475-8700; Fax: 650-475-8881
E-mail: info@ebrary.com
Web site: http://www.ebrary.com.

ebrary.com, *See* **ebrary, Inc.**

EBS, Inc. Bk. Service, 290 Broadway, Lynbrook, NY 11563 USA (SAN 169-5487) Tel 516-593-1195; Fax: 516-596-2911.

EBSCO Media, *(978-1-885860)* Div. of EBSCO Industries, Inc., 801 Fifth Ave., S., Birmingham, AL 35233 USA Tel 205-323-1508; Fax: 205-226-8400; Toll Free: 800-765-0852
Web site: http://www.ebsco.com.

Ebsco Publishing, *(978-1-882248; 978-0-585; 978-1-4175; 978-1-4237; 978-1-4294; 978-1-4298; 978-1-4356; 978-1-4416; 978-1-4619)* Orders Addr.: 10 Estes St., Ipswich, MA 01938 USA (SAN 253-9497) Tel 978-356-6500; 800-653-2726; Fax: 978-356-6565
E-mail: information@ebscohost.com
Web site: http://www.ebscohost.com.

EBSCO Subscription Services, 5724 Hwy. 280 E., Birmingham, AL 35242-6818 USA (SAN 285-9394) Tel 205-991-6000; Fax: 205-991-1479
E-mail: jacomo@ebsco.com
Web site: http://www.ebsco.com.

Ecompass Business Ctr., 3125 Wellner Dr. NE, Rochester, MN 55906 USA Tel 507-280-0787.

Economical Wholesale Co., 6 King Philip Rd., Worcester, MA 01606 USA (SAN 169-3646).

EDC Publishing, *(978-0-7460; 978-0-86020; 978-0-88110; 978-1-58086; 978-0-7945; 978-1-60130)* Orders Addr.: P.O. Box 470663, Tulsa, OK 74147-0663 USA (SAN 658-0505); Edit Addr.: 10302 E. 55th Pl., Tulsa, OK 74146-6515 USA (SAN 107-5322) Tel 918-622-4522; Fax: 918-665-7919; Toll Free Fax: 800-747-4509; Toll Free: 800-475-4522
E-mail: edc@edcpub.com
Web site: http://www.edcpub.com.

Ediciones del Norte, *(978-0-910061)* P.O. Box 5130, Hanover, NH 03755 USA (SAN 241-2993).

Ediciones Enlace de PR, Inc., *(978-0-9904869)* 159 Calle Las Flores, San Juan, PR 00911-2223 USA Tel 787-725-7252; Fax: 787-725-7231
E-mail: info@edenlacepr.com; gramirez@edenlacepr.com
Web site: www.edenlacepr.com.

Ediciones Universal, *(978-0-89729; 978-1-59388)* Orders Addr.: P.O. Box 450353, Miami, FL 33245-0353 USA (SAN 658-0548); Edit Addr.: 3090 SW Eighth St., Miami, FL 33135 USA (SAN 207-2203) Tel 305-642-3355; Fax: 305-642-7978
E-mail: marta@ediciones.com; ediciones@ediciones.com
Web site: http://www.ediciones.com.

Editorial Betania, *See* **Grupo Nelson**

Editorial Cernuda, Inc., 1040 27th Ave., SW, Miami, FL 33135 USA (SAN 158-8850) Tel 305-264-9400.

Editorial Cultural, Inc., *(978-1-56758; 978-84-399)* Orders Addr.: P.O. Box 21056, San Juan, PR 00928 USA; Edit Addr.: Calle Robles, No. 51, San Juan, PR 00928 USA
E-mail: angiev@editorialculturalpr.com; alamo48@gmail.com
Web site: http://www.editorialculturalpr.com.

Editorial Unilit, *(978-0-7899; 978-0-945792; 978-1-56063)* Div. of Spanish Hse., Inc., 1360 NW 88th Ave., Miami, FL 33172-3093 USA (SAN 247-5979) Tel 305-592-6136; Fax: 305-592-0087; Toll Free: 800-767-7726
E-mail: sales1@unidial.com
Web site: http://www.editorialunilit.com/.

Educa Vision Inc., *(978-1-881839; 978-1-58432; 978-1-62632)* 7550 NW 47th Ave., Coconut Creek, FL 33073 USA (SAN 760-873X) Tel 954-968-7433; Fax: 954-970-0330
E-mail: educa@aol.com
Web site: http://www.educavision.com; http://www.educabrazil.org; http://www.caribbeanstudiespress.com; www.educalanguage.com.

Education Guide, Inc., *(978-0-914880)* P.O. Box 421, Randolph, MA 02368 USA (SAN 201-4580) Tel 617-376-0066; Fax: 617-376-0067.

Educational Audio Visual, Incorporated, *See* **CLEARVUE/eav, Inc.**

Educational Bk. Distributors, P.O. Box 2510, Novato, CA 94948 USA (SAN 158-2259) Tel 415-883-3530; Fax: 415-883-4280; Toll Free: 800-761-5501
E-mail: PblshrSvcs@aol.com.

Educational Development Corporation, *See* **EDC Publishing**

Educational Distribution Corp., 10302 E. 55th Pl., Tulsa, OK 74146 USA Tel 918-622-4522.

Educational Media Corp., *(978-0-932796; 978-1-930572)* Orders Addr.: 1443 Old York Rd., Warminster, PA 18974 USA Fax: 215-956-9041; Toll Free: 800-448-2197; Edit Addr.: 4256 Central Ave. NE, Minneapolis, MN 55421-2920 USA (SAN 212-4203) Tel 763-781-0088; Fax: 763-781-7753; Toll Free: 800-966-3382
E-mail: emedia@educationalmedia.com
Web site: http://www.educationalmedia.com.

Educational Record Ctr., Inc., 3233 Burnt Mill Dr., Suite 100, Wilmington, NC 28403-2698 USA (SAN 630-592X) Tel 910-251-1235; Fax: 910-343-0311; Toll Free Fax: 888-438-1637; Toll Free: 800-438-1637
E-mail: info@erc-inc.com
Web site: http://www.erc-inc.com.

Educational Resources, 1550 Executive Dr., Elgin, IL 60123 USA (SAN 631-5674) Tel 847-888-8300; Toll Free: 800-624-2926 Do not confuse with companies with same or similar name in Shawnee Mission, Columbia, SC, Saint Paul, MN
E-mail: gmhardeman@aol.com.

Educational Showcase, 3571 Newgate Dr., Troy, MI 48084-1042 USA Toll Free: 800-213-3671.

Edumate-Educational Materials, Inc., P.O. Box 711174, San Diego, CA 92171-1174 USA (SAN 630-2955)
E-mail: GusBus@aol.com.

Edu-Tech Corp., The, 65 Bailey Rd., Fairfield, CT 06432 USA (SAN 157-5392) Tel 203-374-4212; Fax: 203-374-8050; Toll Free: 800-338-5463
E-mail: edutcorp@aoc.com.

Edward Weston Graphic, Incorporated, *See* **Weston, Edward Fine Arts**

Eisenbrauns, Inc., *(978-0-931464; 978-1-57506)* Orders Addr.: P.O. Box 275, Winona Lake, IN 46590-0275 USA (SAN 200-7835) Tel 574-269-2011; Fax: 574-269-6788; Edit Addr.: 600 N. Bay Dr., Warsaw, IN 46580 USA
E-mail: ghannah@eisenbrauns.com; Orders@eisenbrauns.com
Web site: http://www.eisenbrauns.com.

El Qui-Jote Bk., Inc., 12651 Monarch, Houston, TX 77047 USA (SAN 107-8666) Tel 713-433-3388.

Elder's Bk. Store, 2115 Elliston Pl., Nashville, TN 37203 USA (SAN 112-6091) Tel 615-327-1867.

Elkins, C. J., 400 S. Beverly Dr. Suite 214, Beverly Hills, CA 90212 USA Toll Free: 800-769-2120
E-mail: sitare@aol.com; sitare@zwallet.com.

Ellis News Co., Affil. of L-S Distributors, 130 E. Grand Ave., South San Francisco, CA 94080 USA (SAN 169-0183) Tel 415-873-2094; Fax: 415-873-4222; Toll Free: 800-654-7040 (orders only).

ELS Educational Services, *(978-0-87789; 978-0-89285; 978-0-89318)* Orders Addr.: 200 Old Tappan Rd., Old Tappan, NJ 07675 USA; Edit Addr.: 1357 Second St., Santa Monica, CA 90401-1102 USA (SAN 281-6326).

Elsevier, *(978-0-444; 978-0-7204; 978-0-916086; 978-1-85617; 978-1-59278; 978-0-08; 978-1-4831; 978-1-4832; 978-1-4933)* Orders Addr.: P.O. Box 945, New York, NY 10159-0945 USA (SAN 251-2564) Toll Free: 888-437-4636; P.O. Box 28430, Saint Louis, MO 63146-0930 Toll Free Fax: 800-535-9935; Toll Free: 800-460-3110 (Outside US); 800-545-2522; Edit Addr.: 360 Park Ave S. Flr. 11, New York, NY 10010-1710 USA (SAN 200-2051); 525 B St., Suite 1800, San Diego, CA 92101-4475 Tel 800-894-3434; 1-619-231-6616
E-mail: usinfo-f@elsevier.com; custserv@elsevier.com; d.gomez@elsevier.com
Web site: http://www.elsevier.com.

Elsevier - Health Sciences Div., *(978-0-323; 978-0-443; 978-0-444; 978-0-7020; 978-0-7216; 978-0-7234; 978-0-7236; 978-0-7506; 978-0-8016; 978-0-8151; 978-0-920513; 978-0-932883; 978-1-55664; 978-1-56053; 978-1-898507; 978-1-932141; 978-1-4160; 978-1-4377; 978-1-4557)* Subs. of Elsevier Science, Orders Addr.: a/o Customer Service, 3251 Riverport Ln., Maryland Heights, MO 63043 USA Tel 314-453-7010; Fax: 314-447-8030; Toll Free Fax: 800-535-9935; Toll Free: 800-545-2522; 800-460-3110 (Customers Outside US); 1799 Highway 50, Linn, MO 65051 (SAN 200-2280); Edit Addr.: 1600 John F. Kennedy Blvd., Suite 1800, Philadelphia, PA 19103-2899 USA Tel 215-239-3900; Fax: 215-239-3990; Toll Free: 800-523-4069
E-mail: usbkinfo@elsevier.com
Web site: http://www.elsevier.com; http://www.us.elsevierhealth.com/.

Elsevier Science, *See* **Elsevier**

Elsevier Science - Health Sciences Division, *See* **Elsevier - Health Sciences Div.**

Elsevier Science & Technology Bks., Orders Addr.: P.O. Box 28430, Saint Louis, MO 63146-0930 USA Toll Free Fax: 800-535-9935; Toll Free: 800-545-2522; 800-460-3110 (Customers Outside US); Edit Addr.: 525 B St., Suite 1900, San Diego, CA 92101 USA Toll Free: 1-800-894-3434; 200 Wheeler Rd., 6th Flr., Burlington, MA 01803 Tel 781-313-4700
E-mail: bookstore.orders@elsevier.com
Web site: http://www.elsevier.com/; http://www.syngress.com.

EMC/Paradigm Publishing, *(978-0-7638; 978-0-8219; 978-0-88436; 978-0-912022; 978-1-56118; 978-1-5338)* Div. of EMC Corp., 875 Montreal Way, Saint Paul, MN 55102 USA (SAN 201-3800) Toll Free Fax: 800-328-4564; Toll Free: 800-328-1452
E-mail: publish@emcp.com; educate@emcp.com
Web site: http://www.emcp.com.

Emerald Bk. Co., *(978-1-934572; 978-1-937110)* Div. of Greenleaf Bk. Group, 4425 Mo Pac Expy., Suite 600, Austin, TX 78735 USA.

Emery-Pratt Co., Orders Addr.: 1966 W. M 21, Owosso, MI 48867-1397 USA (SAN 170-1401) Tel 989-723-5291; Fax: 989-723-4677; Toll Free Fax: 800-523-6379; Toll Free: 800-762-5683 (library orders only); 800-248-3887 (customer service only) Distributor to Libraries & Hospitals
E-mail: custserv@emery-pratt.com
Web site: http://www.emery-pratt.com.

Empire Comics, 375 Stone Rd., Rochester, NY 14616 USA (SAN 110-943X) Tel 716-442-0371; Fax: 716-442-7807
E-mail: empires@frontiernet.net.

Empire News of Jamestown, Foot Ave. & Extension St., Box 2029, Sta. A, Jamestown, NY 14702 USA (SAN 169-5371).

Empire Publishing Service, *(978-1-58690)* P.O. Box 1344, Studio City, CA 91614-0344 USA (SAN 630-5687) Tel 818-784-8918
E-mail: empirepubsvc@att.net.

Empire State News Corp., Orders Addr.: P.O. Box 1167, Buffalo, NY 14240-1167 USA Tel 716-681-1100; Fax: 716-681-1120; Toll Free: 800-414-6247; Edit Addr.: 316 Forestview Dr., Buffalo, NY 14221-1461 USA (SAN 169-5177)
Web site: http://www.esnc.com.

Empowerment Technologies, *See* **Empowerment Technologies/Neuro-Semantics Publns.**

Empowerment Technologies/Neuro-Semantics Publns., *(978-1-890001; 978-1-899836)* Orders Addr.: P.O. Box 8, Clifton, CO 81520 USA Tel 704-864-3585; Fax: 970-523-5790; Edit Addr.: P.O. Box 9231, Grand Junction, CO 81501 USA Tel 970-523-7877
E-mail: meta@acsol.net
Web site: http://www.neurosemantics.com.

Encino Pr., *(978-0-88426)* 510 Baylor St., Austin, TX 78703 USA (SAN 201-3843) Tel 512-476-6821; Fax: 512-476-9393.

Enfield Publishing & Distribution Co., Inc., *(978-0-9656184; 978-1-893598)* Orders Addr.: P.O. Box 699, Enfield, NH 03748 USA Tel 603-632-7377; Fax: 603-632-5611; Edit Addr.: 234 May St., Enfield, NH 03748 USA
E-mail: info@enfieldbooks.com
Web site: http://www.enfielddistribution.com; http://www.enfieldbooks.com.

Entrepreneur Media Inc/Entrepreneur Pr., *(978-0-916378; 978-1-55571; 978-1-891984; 978-1-932156; 978-1-932531; 978-1-59918; 978-1-61308)* 2445 McCabe Way, Suite 400, Irvine, CA 92614-6244 USA Tel 949-261-2325; Fax: 949-261-7729; Toll Free: 800-864-6864
E-mail: jmctigue@entrepreneur.com
Web site: http://www.entrepreneur.com; http://www.entrepreneurpress.com.

Entrepreneur Press, *See* **Entrepreneur Media Inc/Entrepreneur Pr.**

Entrepreneur Start a Business Store, 9114 River Look Ln., Fair Oaks, CA 95628-6565 USA (SAN 133-1485) Fax: 916-863-0361.

Epic Book Promotions, 914 Nolan Way, Chula Vista, CA 91911-2408 USA Tel 619-498-8547; Fax: 619-498-8540
E-mail: gvjack@pacbell.net.

Epicenter Pr., Inc., *(978-0-945397; 978-0-9708493; 978-0-9724944; 978-0-9745014; 978-0-9790470; 978-0-9800825; 978-1-935347; 978-1-941890)* Orders Addr.: 6524 NE 181st ST No. 2, Kenmore, WA 98028 USA; Edit Addr.: 6524 NE 181st ST No. 2, Kenmore, WA 98028 USA (SAN 246-9405) Do not confuse with companies with similar names in Kanehoe, HI, Long Beach, CA, Oakland, CA
E-mail: info@epicenterpress.com; phil@epicenterpress.com; aubrey@epicenterpress.com
Web site: http://www.epicenterpress.com.

E-Pros DG, 32 N. Goodwin Ave., Elmsford, NY 10523 USA Toll Free: 866-377-6700
E-mail: sales@e-pros.ws.

Epson Mid-Atlantic, Subs. of Epson America, Inc., 8 Neshaminy Interplex, Suite 319, Trerose, PA 19053 USA (SAN 285-7243) Tel 215-245-2180.

Equinox, Ltd., 1307 Park Ave., Williamsport, PA 17701 USA.

Eriksson Enterprises, 126 Sunset Dr., Farmington, UT 84025-3426 USA (SAN 110-5892).

Erlbaum, Lawrence Assocs., Inc., *(978-0-8058; 978-0-86377; 978-0-89859; 978-1-880393; 978-1-4106)* 270 Madison Ave. Flr. 4, New York, NY 10016-0601 USA (SAN 213-960X) Toll Free: 800-926-6579 (orders only)
E-mail: orders@erlbaum.com
Web site: http://www.erlbaum.com.

ETA hand2mind, *(978-0-7406; 978-0-914040; 978-0-923832; 978-0-938587; 978-1-57162; 978-1-57452; 978-1-63406)* Div. of A. Daigger & Company, 500 Greenview Ct., Vernon Hills, IL 60061 USA (SAN 285-7553) Tel 847-816-5050; Fax: 847-816-5066; Toll Free: 800-445-5985
E-mail: info@hand2mind.com
Web site: http://www.hand2mind.com.

ETAhand2mind, *See* **ETA hand2mind**

ETD KroMar Temple, P.O. Box 535695, Grand Prairie, TX 75053-5625 USA (SAN 169-8435) Tel 254-778-5261; Fax: 254-778-5267.

European Bk. Co., Inc., 925 Larkin St., San Francisco, CA 94109 USA (SAN 169-0191) Tel 415-474-0626; Fax: 415-474-0630; Toll Free: 877-746-3666
E-mail: info@europeanbook.com.

European Press Service - PBD America Wholesalers, 30 Edison Dr., Wayne, NJ 07470-4713 USA (SAN 630-7825).

Evans Bk. Distribution & Pubs., Inc., *(978-0-9654884; 978-1-56684)* 895 W. 1700 S., Salt Lake City, UT 84104 USA.

Evans Book, *See* **Evans Bk. Distribution & Pubs., Inc.**

Evanston Publishing, Inc., *(978-1-879260)* 4824 Brownsboro Ctr. Arcade, Louisville, KY 40207-2342 USA Tel 502-899-1919; Fax: 502-896-0246; Toll Free: 800-594-5190
E-mail: EvanstonPB@aol.com; info@evanstonpublishing.com
Web site: http://www.EvanstonPublishing.com.

Everbind/Marco Book Company, *See* **Marco Bk. Co.**

Excaliber Publishing Co., *(978-1-881353)* 7954 W. Bury Ave., San Diego, CA 92126 USA (SAN 297-6412) Tel 619-695-3091; Fax: 619-695-3095.

Exciting Times, 17430C Crenshaw Blvd., Torrance, CA 90504 USA (SAN 114-4642) Tel 310-515-2676; Fax: 310-515-1382.

Executive Books, *See* **Tremendous Life Bks.**

Exploration Films, P.O. Box 1069, Monument, CO 80132 USA Tel 719-481-4599; Fax: 719-481-1399; Toll Free: 800-964-0439
E-mail: jolene@explorationfilms.com
Web site: http://www.explorationfilms.com.

Explorations, 360 Interlocken Blvd., Suite 300, Broomfield, CO 80021 USA Toll Free Fax: 800-456-1139; Toll Free: 800-720-2114
E-mail: customerservice@gaiam.com
Web site: http://www.gaiam.com.

Express Media, *(978-0-9723163)* 127 Rankin Rd., Columbia, MS 37202 USA Tel 615-360-6400
Web site: http://www.authorsexpress.com.

Faber & Faber, Inc., *(978-0-571)* Affil. of Farrar, Straus & Giroux, LLC, Orders Addr.: c/o Van Holtzbrinck Publishing Services, 16365 James Madison Hwy., Gordonsville, VA 22942 USA Fax: 540-572-7540; Toll Free: 888-330-8477; Edit Addr.: 19 Union Sq., W, New York, NY 10003-3304 USA (SAN 218-7256) Tel 212-741-6900; Fax: 212-633-9385
E-mail: sales@fsgbooks.com
Web site: http://www.fsgbooks.com.

Facts On File, Inc., *(978-0-8160; 978-0-87196; 978-1-60413; 978-1-4381; 978-1-61753)* Orders Addr.: 132 W. 31st St., 17th Flr., New York, NY 10001-2006 USA (SAN 201-4696) Tel 212-967-8800; 212-896-4296 (customer service); Fax: 917-339-0325; 917-339-0323; Toll Free Fax: 800-678-3633; Toll Free: 800-322-8755
E-mail: custserv@factsonfile.com; Sales@ChelseaHouse.com
Web site: http://www.factsonfile.com; http://www.fergpubco.com; http://www.chelseahouse.com.

Fairfield Bk. Service Co., 150 Margherita Lawn, Stratford, CT 06615 USA (SAN 131-0976) Tel 203-375-7607.

Faith Alive Christian Resources, *(978-0-930265; 978-0-933140; 978-1-56212; 978-1-59255; 978-1-62025)* 2850 Kalamazoo Ave., SE, Grand Rapids, MI 49560 USA (SAN 212-727X) Tel 616-224-0784; Fax: 616-224-0834; Toll Free Fax: 888-642-8606; Toll Free: 800-333-8300; P.O. Box 5070, Burlington, ON L7R 3Y8 Toll Free Fax: 888-642-8606; Toll Free: 800-333-8300
E-mail: sales@faithaliveresources.org
Web site: http://www.faithaliveresources.org.

Falk Bks. Inc., W.E., 7491 N. Federal Hwy., PMB 267, Boca Raton, FL 33487 USA.

Falk, W. E., *See* **Falk Bks. Inc., W.E.**

Fall River News Co., Inc., 144 Robeson St., Fall River, MA 02720-4925 USA (SAN 169-3425) Tel 508-679-5266.

Family History World, P.O. Box 129, Tremonton, UT 84337 USA (SAN 159-673X) Fax: 801-250-6727; Toll Free: 800-377-6058
E-mail: genealogy@utahlinx.com
Web site: http://www.genealogical-institute.com.

Family Reading Service, 1601 N. Slappey Blvd., Albany, GA 31701-1431 USA (SAN 169-1376).

Fantaco Pubns., *(978-0-938782)* Affil. of Fantaco Enterprises, Inc., 17810 Poppy Trails Ln., Houston, TX 77084-1070 USA (SAN 158-5134).

Far West Bk. Service, 3515 NE Hassalo, Portland, OR 97232 USA (SAN 107-6760) Tel 503-234-7664; Fax: 503-231-0573; Toll Free: 800-964-9378.

Farcountry Pr., *(978-0-938314; 978-1-56037; 978-1-59152)* Orders Addr.: P.O. Box 5630, Helena, MT 59604 USA (SAN 220-0732) Tel 406-422-1263; Fax: 406-443-5480; Toll Free: 800-821-3874; 2750 Broadwater, Helena, MT 59602
E-mail: books@farcountrypress.com
Web site: http://www.farcountrypress.com.

Farrar, Straus & Giroux, *(978-0-374)* Div. of Holtzbrinck Publishers, Orders Addr.: c/o Holtzbrinck Publishers, 16365 James Madison Hwy., Gordonsville, VA 22942 USA Toll Free Fax: 800-672-2054; Toll Free: 888-330-8477; Edit Addr.: 18 W. 18th St., New York, NY 10011-4607 USA (SAN 206-782X)
E-mail: sales@fsgee.com; fsg.editorial@fsgee.com
Web site: http://www.fsgbooks.com/.

Faxon Company, The, *See* **Divine, Inc.**

Faxon Illinois Service Ctr., Affil. of Dawson Holdings PLC, 1600 Providence Hwy., Walpole, MA 02081-2553 USA (SAN 286-0147) Toll Free: 800-852-7404
E-mail: postmaster@dawson.com; sandy.nordman@dawson.com
Web site: http://www.faxon.com.

Fayette County News Agency, Orders Addr.: P.O. Box 993, Uniontown, PA 15401 USA Tel 724-437-1181; Edit Addr.: Cherry Tree Square 42 Matthew Dr., Uniontown, PA 15401 USA (SAN 169-765X).

FEC News Distributing, 2201 Fourth Ave., N., Lake Worth, FL 33461-3835 USA (SAN 169-1341) Tel 407-547-3000; Fax: 407-547-3080.

Feldheim, Philipp Incorporated, *See* **Feldheim Pubs.**

Feldheim Pubs., *(978-0-87306; 978-1-58330; 978-1-59826; 978-1-68025)* 208 Airport Executive Park., Nanuet, NY 10954-5262 USA (SAN 106-6307) Toll Free: 800-237-7149
E-mail: sales@feldheim.com; eli@feldheim.com
Web site: http://www.feldheim.com.

Fell, Frederick Pubs., Inc., *(978-0-8119; 978-0-88391; 978-0-936320)* Orders Addr.: 1403 Shoreline Way, Hollywood, FL 33019-5007 USA (SAN 215-0670)
Web site: http://www.fellpub.com.

Fennell, Reginald F. Subscription Service, 1002 W. Michigan Ave., Jackson, MI 49202 USA (SAN 159-6071) Tel 517-782-3132; Fax: 517-782-1109.

FEP, A Booksource Co., 1230 Macklind Ave., Saint Louis, MO 63110 USA (SAN 169-1317) Tel 314-647-0600; Fax: 314-647-6850; Toll Free: 800-444-0435
Web site: http://www.booksource.com.

Fiddlecase Bks., HC 63 Box 104, East Alstead, NH 03602 USA (SAN 200-7495) Tel 603-835-7889.

Fiesta Bk. Co., *(978-0-88473)* P.O. Box 490641, Key Biscayne, FL 33149 USA (SAN 201-8470) Tel 305-858-4843.

Fiesta Publishing Corporation, *See* **Fiesta Bk. Co.**

Films for the Humanities & Sciences, *See* **Films Media Group**

Films Media Group, *(978-0-7365; 978-0-89113; 978-1-56950; 978-1-4213; 978-1-60467)* Div. of Infobase Learning, Orders Addr.: 132 W. 31st St., 17th Flr., New York, NY 10001 USA (SAN 653-2705) Toll Free Fax: 800-678-3633; Toll Free: 800-322-8755
E-mail: mgallo@infobaselearning.com
Web site: http://www.films.com.

Findaway World, LLC, *(978-1-59895; 978-1-60252; 978-1-60514; 978-1-60640; 978-1-60775; 978-1-60812; 978-1-60847; 978-1-61545; 978-1-61574; 978-1-61587; 978-1-61637; 978-1-61657; 978-1-61707; 978-1-4676; 978-1-5094)* 31999 Aurora Rd., Solon, OH 44139 USA (SAN 853-8778)
Web site: http://www.findawayworld.com; http://www.playawaydigital.com.

Fine Assocs., One Farragut Sq., S., Washington, DC 20006 USA (SAN 169-0914) Tel 202-628-2609.

Finn News Agency, Inc., 4415 State Rd. 327, Auburn, IN 46706-9542 USA (SAN 169-2356).

Finney Co., Inc., *(978-0-89317; 978-0-912486; 978-0-933855; 978-0-9617767; 978-0-9639705; 978-1-880654; 978-1-893272)* Orders Addr.: 8075 215th St. W., Lakeville, MN 55044 USA (SAN 206-412X) Tel 952-469-6699; Fax: 952-469-1968; Toll Free Fax: 800-330-6232; Toll Free: 800-846-7027
E-mail: feedback@finneyco.com
Web site: http://www.finneyco.com; http://www.ecopress.com; http://www.pogopress.com; http://www.astragalpress.com.

Fire Protection Publications, *See* **IFSTA**

Firebird Distributing, LLC, 1945 P St., Eureka, CA 95501-3007 USA (SAN 631-1229) Toll Free: 800-353-3575
E-mail: sales@firebirddistributing.com
Web site: http://www.firebirddistributing.com.

Firebrand Technologies, 44 Merrimac St., Newburyport, MA 01950 USA.

Firefly Bks., Ltd., *(978-0-920668; 978-1-55209; 978-1-895565; 978-1-896284; 978-1-55297; 978-1-55407)* Orders Addr.: c/o Frontier Distributing, 1000 Young St., Suite 160, Tonawanda, NY 14150 USA (SAN 630-611X) Tel 203-222-9700; Toll Free Fax: 800-565-6034; Toll Free: 800-387-5085; Edit Addr.: 8514 Long Canyon Dr., Austin, TX 78730-2813 USA
E-mail: service@fireflybooks.com
Web site: http://www.fireflybooks.com/.

Firenze Pr., *(978-0-9711236)* Orders Addr.: P.O. Box 6892, Wyomissing, PA 19610-0892 USA (SAN 254-315X); Edit Addr.: 612 Museum Rd., Reading, PA 19610-0892 USA Tel 610-374-7048; Fax: 610-478-7992 Do not confuse with Leonardo Pr., Camden, ME
E-mail: hailejohnjr@msn.com; HaileJohnJr@msn.com; InkPenCJH@msn.com
Web site: http://caroljhaile.com.

Fischer, Carl LLC, *(978-0-8258)* Orders Addr.: 588 N. Gulph Rd. Ste. B, King Of Prussa, PA 19406-2831 USA Toll Free: 800-762-2328; Edit Addr.: 65 Bleeker St., New York, NY 10012-2420 USA (SAN 107-4245) Tel 212-772-0900; Fax: 212-477-6996; Toll Free: 800-762-2328
E-mail: cf-info@carlfischer.com
Web site: http://www.carlfischer.com.

Fish, Enrica Medical Bks., 1208 W. Minnehaha Pkwy., Minneapolis, MN 55419-1163 USA (SAN 157-8588) Toll Free: 800-728-8398.

Fisher King Bks., 316 Mid Valley Ctr., #194, Carmel, CA 93923 USA Tel 831-238-7799; Toll Free: 800-228-9316 (Canada & US).

Flannery Co., 16430 Beaver Rd., Adelanto, CA 92301-3904 USA (SAN 168-9754) Toll Free: 800-456-3400.

Flannery, J. F. Company, *See* **Flannery Co.**

Fleming, Robert Hull Museum, *(978-0-934658)* Div. of Univ. of Vermont, Univ. of Vermont, 61 Colchester Ave., Burlington, VT 05405 USA (SAN 110-8824) Tel 802-656-0750; Fax: 802-656-8059
Web site: www.uvm.edu.

Flora & Fauna Bks., P.O. Box 15718, Gainesville, FL 32604 USA (SAN 133-1221) Tel 352-373-5630; Fax: 352-373-3249
E-mail: ffbks@aol.com
Web site: http://www.ffbooks.com.

Florida Academic Pr., *(978-1-890357)* P.O. Box 540, Gainesville, FL 32602-0540 USA (SAN 299-3643) Tel 352-332-5104; Fax: 352-331-6003
E-mail: fapress@worldnet.att.net.

Florida Classics Library, *(978-0-912451)* P.O. Drawer 1657, Port Salerno, FL 34992-1657 USA (SAN 265-2404) Tel 561-546-9380 (orders); Fax: 561-546-7545 (orders).

Florida Schl. Bk. Depository, 1125 N. Ellis Rd., Jacksonville, FL 32236 USA (SAN 161-8423) Tel 904-781-7191; Fax: 904-781-3486; Toll Free: 800-447-7957
Web site: http://www.fsbd.com.

Flury & Co., 322 First Ave S., Seattle, WA 98104 USA (SAN 107-5748) Tel 206-587-0260.

FM International, P.O. Box 91, Waunakee, WI 53597-0091 USA.

Fodor's Travel Guides, *See* **Fodor's Travel Pubns.**

Fodor's Travel Pubns., Div. of Random Hse., Information Group, Orders Addr.: 400 Hahn Rd., Westminster, MD 21157 USA Tel 410-848-1900; Toll Free: 800-726-0600; Edit Addr.: 1745 Broadway, New York, NY 10019 USA Tel 212-782-9000
Web site: http://www.fodors.com.

Follet Higher Education Grp, P.O. Box 3488, Oak Brook, IL 60522-3488 USA Tel 630-279-0123.

Follett Audiovisual Resources, *See* **Follett Media Distribution**

Follett Library Resources, *See* **Follett School Solutions**

Follett Media Distribution, 1847 Mercer Rd., Lexington, KY 40511-1001 USA (SAN 631-7316) Toll Free: 888-281-1216.

Follett School Solutions, *(978-0-329; 978-0-88153; 978-0-924917; 978-1-4898; 978-1-5160; 978-1-5181; 978-1-5379; 978-1-5444; 978-1-5490)* Div. of the Follett Corp., Orders Addr.: a/o McHenry Warehouse, 1340 Ridgeview Dr., McHenry, IL 60050 USA (SAN 169-1902) Toll Free: 888-511-5114; a/o Patti Hall: R & R Bindery Services, 499 Rachel Rd., Girard, IL 62640 (SAN 155-8412) Tel 815-759-1700; a/o Formerly FES, 1433 Internationale Pkwy. DOCK Door 30, Woodridge, IL 60517 (SAN 631-7901) Tel 630-972-5600; Fax: 630-972-4673; Toll Free: 800-621-4272; a/o Russell Henning (Formerly FSC), 1391 Corporate Dr., McHenry, IL 60050-7041 (SAN 298-587X) Fax: 815-344-8774; a/o Formerly FLR, 1340 Ridgeview Dr., Suite EDI, McHenry, IL 60050-0000 (SAN 760-7164)
Web site: http://www.follett.com.

Fondo de Cultura Economica USA, 2293 Verus St., San Diego, CA 92154 USA (SAN 860-1380) Tel 619-429-0455; Fax: 619-651-9684; Toll Free: 800-532-3872
E-mail: orders@fceusa.com; drazo@fceusa.com; fondosales@fceusa.com
Web site: http://www.fceusa.com.

Fordham Univ. Pr., *(978-0-8232; 978-1-5315)* Joseph A. Martino Hall 45 Columbus Ave., New York, NY 10023 USA (SAN 201-6516) Tel 718-817-4795; Fax: 718-817-4785
E-mail: kasweeney@fordham.edu
Web site: http://www.fordhampress.com.

Forest Hse. Publishing Co., Inc., *(978-1-56674; 978-1-878363)* P.O. Box 738, Lake Forest, IL 60045 USA Tel 847-295-8287; Fax: 847-295-8201; Toll Free: 800-394-7323.

Forest Sales & Distributing Co., *(978-0-9712183)* 139 Jean Marie St., Reserve, LA 70084 USA (SAN 157-5511) Toll Free: 800-347-2106
E-mail: tbooks2@juno.com.

Forsa Editores, *(978-1-881714)* Orders Addr.: P.O. Box 11249, San Juan, PR 00922-1249 USA Tel 787-707-1792; Fax: 787-707-1797; Toll Free: 888-225-8984; Edit Addr.: No. 1594 J.T. Pinero Ave., Caparra Heights, PR 00920 USA
E-mail: forsa@forsaeditores.com
Web site: http://www.forsaeditores.com.

Forsyth Travel Library, Inc., *(978-0-9614539)* 1750 E. 131st St., P.O. Box 480800, Kansas City, MO 64148-0800 USA (SAN 169-2755) Tel 816-942-9050; Fax: 816-942-6969; Toll Free: 800-367-7984 (orders only)
E-mail: forsyth@gvi.net
Web site: http://www.forsyth.com.

Forward Movement Pubns., *(978-0-88028)* 300 West Fourth St., Cincinnati, OH 45202 USA (SAN 208-3841) Tel 513-721-6659; Fax: 513-721-0729; Toll Free: 800-543-1813 (orders only)
E-mail: Orders@forwarddaybyday.com
Web site: http://www.forwardmovement.org.

Four Winds Trading Co., *(978-0-9672383)* 6355 Joyce Dr., Golden, CO 80403-7568 USA (SAN 631-1989) Toll Free: 800-456-5444
E-mail: Paul@Fourwinds-trading.com; sales@fourwinds-trading.com
Web site: http://www.fourwinds-trading.com.

Franklin Bk. Co., Inc., P.O. Box 451, Newtown Sq, PA 19073-0451 USA (SAN 121-4160)
E-mail: service@franklinbook.com
Web site: http://www.franklinbook.com.

Franklin Readers Service, P.O. Box 662, Dunn Loring, VA 22027-0662 USA (SAN 285-9599).

Franklin Square Overseas, 17-19 Washington St., Tenafly, NJ 07670-2084 USA (SAN 285-9637) Tel 201-569-2500; Fax: 201-569-5141
E-mail: esstn@ebsco.com.

Fraser Publishing Co., *(978-0-87034; 978-0-918632)* Div. of Alvin Q. Garbanzo, Inc., Orders Addr.: P.O. Box 217, Flint Hill, VT 22747 USA (SAN 213-9537)
E-mail: info@fraserpublishing.com
Web site: http://www.fraserpublishing.com.

Freeman Family Ministries, Orders Addr.: P.O. Box 593, Waldo, FL 32694 USA Tel 352-468-2785
E-mail: freemanfamily9@msn.com.

Freihofer, A. G., 175 Fifth Ave., New York, NY 10010 USA (SAN 285-9602) Tel 272-460-7500; Fax: 272-473-6272.

French & European Pubns., Inc., *(978-0-320; 978-0-7859; 978-0-8288; 978-1-5479)* 425 E. 58th St., Suite 27D, New York, NY 10022-2379 USA (SAN 206-8109) Fax: 212-265-1094
E-mail: livresny@gmail.com; frenchbookstore@aol.com
Web site: http://www.frencheuropean.com.

Fresno Bk. Fairs, 1030 Bonita Ave., La Verne, CA 91750 USA (SAN 630-6225) Tel 909-593-0697; 1650 W. Orange Grove Ave., Pomona, CA 91768-2153 (SAN 299-2434)
Web site: http://www.mrsnelsons.com.

Friendly Hills Fellowship, *See* **Health and Growth Assocs.**

Fris News Co., 194 River Ave., Holland, MI 49423 USA (SAN 159-8643).

Frontline Communications, *See* **YWAM Publishing**

FRP Cookbook Marketplace, *See* **Cookbook Marketplace, The**

Fujii Assocs., 1400 W. 47th St. Ste. 4, La Grange, IL 60525-6148 USA (SAN 631-5305).

Fulcrum Publishing, *(978-0-912347; 978-1-55591; 978-1-56373; 978-1-936218; 978-1-938486; 978-1-68275)* Orders Addr.: 4690 Table Mountain Dr. Suite 100, Golden, CO 80403 USA (SAN 200-2825) Toll Free Fax: 800-726-7112; Toll Free: 800-992-2908
E-mail: info@fulcrumbooks.com
Web site: http://www.fulcrumbooks.com.

Fulmont News Co., Affil. of Rubin Periodical Group, P.O. Box 1211, Rochester, NY 14603-1211 USA (SAN 169-5029) Tel 518-843-2421.

Fultz News Agency, 2008 Woodbrook, Denton, TX 76205 USA (SAN 169-8168).

Futech Educational Products, Inc., *(978-0-9627001; 978-1-889192)* 2999 N. 44th St., Suite 225, Phoenix, AZ 85018-7248 USA Tel 602-808-8765; Fax: 602-278-5667; Toll Free: 800-597-6278.

F&W Media, Inc., *(978-0-89134; 978-0-89879; 978-0-932620; 978-1-55870; 978-1-58180; 978-1-58297; 978-1-884910; 978-1-892127; 978-1-59963; 978-1-60061; 978-1-4402; 978-1-4403; 978-0-578-03300-6; 978-1-940038)* Orders Addr.: 10151 Carver Rd., Ste 200, Blue Ash, OH 45242 USA Tel 513-531-2690; Fax: 513-531-1843; Toll Free Fax: 888-590-4082; Toll Free: 800-289-0963; Edit Addr.: Brunel House Forde Close, Newton Abbot, TQ12 4PU GBR Tel 01626 323200; Fax: 01626 323319
E-mail: amber.ziegler@fwmedia.com; mark.griffin@fwmedia.com
Web site: http://www.artistsmagazine.com; http://www.artistsnetwork.com; http://www.davidandcharles.co.uk; http://www.krause.com; http://www.familytreemagazine.com; http://www.howdesign.com; http://www.idonline.com; http://www.memorymakersmagazine.com; http://www.popularwoodworking.com; http://www.writersdigest.com; http://www.writersmarket.com; http://www.writersonlineworkshops.com; http://www.fwpublications.com; http://www.fwmedia.co.uk.

F+W Media, Incorporated, *See* **F&W Media, Inc.**

G A M Printers & Grace Christian Bookstore, *See* **GAM Pubn.**

Gabriel Resources, Orders Addr.: P.O. Box 1047, Waynesboro, GA 30830 USA Tel 706-554-1594; Fax: 706-554-7444; Toll Free: 800-732-6657 (8MORE-BOOKS); Edit Addr.: 129 Mobilization Dr., Waynesboro, GA 30830 USA.

Galda Library Services, Inc., 33 Richdale Ave., Cambridge, MA 02140 USA (SAN 630-5806) Tel 617-864-8232.

Gale Virtual Reference Library, 27500 Drake Rd., Farmington Hills, MI 48331 USA Toll Free: 800-877-4253
Web site: http://www.gale.cengage.com/servlet/GvrlMS?msg=ma.

Galesburg News Agency, Inc., Five E. Simmons St., Galesburg, IL 61401 USA (SAN 169-1945).

Galveston News Agency, P.O. Box 7608, San Antonio, TX 78207-0608 USA (SAN 169-8230).

GAM Pubn., P.O. Box 25, Sterling, VA 20167 USA (SAN 158-7218) Tel 703-450-4121; Fax: 703-450-5311.

Gamboge International, Inc., 18 Brittany Ave., Trumbull, CT 06611 USA (SAN 631-046X) Tel 203-261-2130; Fax: 203-452-0180
E-mail: gamboge@pcaet.com.

Gangaji Foundation, The, *(978-0-9632194; 978-1-887984)* P.O. Box 716, Ashland, OR 97520-0024 USA Toll Free: 800-267-9205
E-mail: order@Gangaji.org; info@gangaji.org
Web site: http://www.gangaji.org.

Gannon Distributing Co., *(978-0-88307)* 100 La Salle Cir., No. A, Santa Fe, NM 87505-6916 USA (SAN 201-5889).

Gardner's Bk. Service, 11226 N. 23rd Ave., Ste. 103, Phoenix, AZ 85029 USA (SAN 106-9322) Tel 602-863-6000; Fax: 602-863-2400 (orders only); Toll Free: 800-851-6001 (orders only)
E-mail: gbsbooks@bgsbooks.com
Web site: http://www.gbsbooks.com.

Gardner's Book Service, *See* **Gardner's Bk. Service**

Garrett Educational Corp., *(978-0-944483; 978-1-56074)* Orders Addr.: P.O. Box 1588, Ada, OK 74820 USA (SAN 169-6955) Tel 580-332-6884; Fax: 580-332-1560; Toll Free: 800-654-9366; Edit Addr.: 130 E. 13th St., Ada, OK 74820 USA (SAN 243-2722)
E-mail: mail@garrettbooks.com
Web site: http://www.garrettbooks.com.

Gasman News Agency, 2211 Third Ave., S., Escanaba, MI 49829 USA (SAN 169-3794).

Gaunt, Inc., *(978-0-912004; 978-1-56169; 978-1-60449)* 3011 Gulf Dr., Holmes Beach, FL 34217-2199 USA (SAN 202-9413) Tel 941-778-5211; Fax: 941-778-5252
E-mail: info@gaunt.com; sales@gaunt.com
Web site: http://www.gaunt.com.

Gaunt, William W. & Sons, Incorporated, *See* **Gaunt, Inc.**

GBGM Service Ctr., P.O. Box 691328, Cincinnati, OH 45269 USA.

Gefen Bks., *(978-0-86343)* 11 Edison Pl., Springfield, NJ 07081 USA (SAN 856-8065)
E-mail: gefenny@gefenpublishing.com
Web site: http://www.gefenpublishing.com.

Gem Guides Bk. Co., *(978-0-935182; 978-0-937799; 978-1-889786)* Orders Addr.: 1275 W. 9th St., Upland,

CA 91786 USA (SAN 221-1637) Tel 626-855-1611; Fax: 626-855-1610
E-mail: info@gemguidesbooks.com
Web site: http://www.gemguidesbooks.com.

Gemini Enterprises, P.O. Box 8251, Stockton, CA 95208 USA (SAN 128-1402).

Genealogical Sources, Unlimited, *(978-0-913857)* 407 Ascot Ct., Knoxville, TN 37923-5807 USA (SAN 170-8058) Tel 865-690-7831.

Genealogy Digest, 960 N. 400 E., North Salt Lake, UT 84054-1920 USA (SAN 110-389X); 420 S. 425 W., Bountiful, UT 84010 (SAN 243-2439).

General Medical Pubs., *(978-0-935236)* P.O. Box 210, Venice, CA 90294-0210 USA (SAN 215-689X) Tel 310-392-4911.

Generic Computer Products, Inc., *(978-0-918611)* P.O. Box 790, Marquette, MI 49855 USA (SAN 284-8856) Tel 906-226-7600; Fax: 906-226-8309.

GenPop Bks., *(978-0-9823594; 978-0-9985126)* Orders Addr.: P.O. Box 189, Grafton, VT 05146 USA
Web site: http://www.genpopbooks.com.

Geographia Map Co., Inc., *(978-0-88433)* 75 Moore St., Hackensack, NJ 07601-7107 USA (SAN 132-5566).

Gerold International Booksellers, Inc., 35-23 Utopia Pkwy., Flushing, NY 11358 USA (SAN 129-959X) Tel 718-358-4741; Fax: 718-358-3688.

Gibbs Smith, Publisher, *(978-0-87905; 978-0-941711; 978-1-58685; 978-1-4236)* Orders Addr.: P.O. Box 667, Layton, UT 84041 USA (SAN 201-9906) Tel 801-544-9800; Fax: 801-544-5582; Toll Free Fax: 800-213-3023 (orders); Toll Free: 800-748-5439 (orders); 800-835-4993 (Customer Service order only); Edit Addr.: 1877 E. Gentile St., Layton, UT 84040 USA Tel 801-544-9800; Fax: 801-546-8853
E-mail: info@gibbs-smith.com; tradeorders@gibbs-smith.com
Web site: http://www.gibbs-smith.com.

Gibson, Dot Pubns., *(978-0-941162)* Orders Addr.: P.O. Box 117, Waycross, GA 31502-0117 USA (SAN 200-4143) Tel 912-285-2848; Fax: 912-285-0349; Toll Free: 800-336-8095; Edit Addr.: 383 Bonneyman Rd., Blackshear, GA 31516 USA (SAN 200-9676)
E-mail: info@dotgibson.com
Web site: http://www.dotgibson.com.

Gilmore-Howard, P.O. Box 1268, Arlington, TX 76004-1268 USA (SAN 157-485X).

Giron Bks., *(978-0-9741393; 978-0-9915442)* 2141 W. 21st St., Chicago, IL 60608-2608 USA Tel 773-847-3000; Fax: 773-847-9197; Toll Free: 800-405-4276
E-mail: juanmanuel@gironbooks.com
Web site: http://www.gironbooks.com.

G-Jo Institute/DeerHaven Hills, *(978-0-916878)* P.O. Box 1460, Columbus, NC 28722-1460 USA (SAN 111-0004)
E-mail: officesupport@g-jo.com
Web site: http://www.g-jo.com.

G-Jo Institute/Falkyn, Incorporated, *See* **G-Jo Institute/DeerHaven Hills**

GL Services, 4588 Interstate Dr., Cincinnati, OH 45246 USA Tel 805-677-6815.

Global Bk. Distributors, P.O. Box 192629, Dallas, TX 75219 USA.

Global Engineering Documents-Latin America, 3909 NE 163rd St., Suite 110, North Miami Beach, FL 33160 USA (SAN 630-7868) Tel 305-944-1099; Fax: 305-944-1028
E-mail: global.csa@ihs.com.

Global Info Centres, *See* **Global Engineering Documents-Latin America**

Global Publishing Associates, Inc., *See* **Jobson, Oliver H.**

Globe Pequot Pr., The, *(978-0-7627; 978-0-87106; 978-0-88742; 978-0-914788; 978-0-933469; 978-0-934802; 978-0-941130; 978-1-56440; 978-1-57034; 978-1-58574; 978-1-59228; 978-1-59921; 978-1-4779; 978-1-4930)* Orders Addr.: P.O. Box 480, Guilford, CT 06437-0480 USA (SAN 201-9892) Tel 888-249-7586; Toll Free Fax: 800-820-2329 (in Connecticut); Toll Free: 800-243-0495 (24 hours); 800-336-8334; Edit Addr.: 246 Goose Ln., Guilford, CT 06437 USA Tel 203-458-4500; Fax: 203-458-4600; Toll Free Fax: 800-336-8334
E-mail: info@globepequot.com
Web site: http://www.globepequot.com.

Gluesing & Gluesing, *(978-0-9631357)* 10301 Bren Rd W. Ste. 165, Hopkins, MN 55343-9129 USA (SAN 630-0022) Toll Free: 800-747-0227.

GOBI Library Solutions from EBSCO, 999 Maple St., Contocook, NH 03229 USA Tel 603-746-3102; Toll Free: 800-258-3774
Web site: http://www.gobi.ebsco.com.

Goldberg, Louis Library Bk. Supplier, 45 Belvidere St., Nazareth, PA 18064 USA (SAN 169-7536) Tel 610-759-9458; Fax: 610-759-8134.

Goldenrod Music, Inc., 1310 Turner Rd., Lansing, MI 48906-4342 USA (SAN 630-5962) Tel 517-484-1777
E-mail: music@goldenrod.com
Web site: http://www.goldenrod.com.

Goldenrod/Horizon Distribution, *See* **Goldenrod Music, Inc.**

Goldman, S. Otzar Hasefarim, Inc., 125 Ditmas Ave., Brooklyn, NY 11218 USA (SAN 169-5770) Tel 718-972-6200; Fax: 718-972-6204; Toll Free: 800-972-6201.

Good Bk. Publishing Co., *(978-1-881212)* P.O. Box 837, Kihei, HI 96753-0837 USA (SAN 297-9578) Tel 808-874-4876 (phone/fax)
E-mail: dickb@dickb.com
Web site: http://www.dickb.com/index.shtml.

Good News Magazine Distributors, 6332 Saunders St., Rego Park, NY 11374-2031 USA (SAN 113-7271) Toll Free: 800-624-7257.

Gopher News Co., 9000 10th Ave N., Minneapolis, MN 55427-4322 USA (SAN 169-4138).

Gopher News Company, *See* **St. Marie's Gopher News Co.**

Gospel Light Pubns., *(978-0-8307)* Orders Addr.: 1957 Eastman Ave., Ventura, CA 93003 USA (SAN 299-0873) Tel 805-644-9721; Fax: 805-289-0200; Toll Free: 800-446-7735 (orders only) Do not confuse with companies with similar names in Brooklyn, NY, Delight, AR
E-mail: info@gospellight.com; kyleloffelmacher@gospellight.com
Web site: http://www.gospellight.com.

Gospel Mission, Inc., *(978-1-62813)* Orders Addr.: P.O. Box 318, Choteau, MT 59422 USA (SAN 170-3196) Tel 406-466-2311; Edit Addr.: 316 First St., NW, Choteau, MT 59422 USA (SAN 243-2455).

Gospel Publishing Hse., *(978-0-88243; 978-1-60731)* Div. of General Council of the Assemblies of God, 1445 N. Boonville Ave., Springfield, MO 65802-1894 USA (SAN 206-8826) Tel 417-862-2781; Fax: 417-862-5881; Toll Free Fax: 800-328-0294; Toll Free: 800-641-4310 (orders only)
E-mail: webmaster@gph.com
Web site: http://www.gospelpublishing.com.

Goyescas Corp. of Florida, P.O. Box 524207, Miami, FL 33152-4207 USA (SAN 169-1120).

Graham Services, Inc., 180 James Dr., E., Saint Rose, LA 70087-9481 USA (SAN 169-2895) Tel 504-467-5863; Fax: 504-464-6196; Toll Free: 800-457-7323 (in Los Angeles only)
E-mail: gsi@aol.com.

Grand Central Publishing, *(978-0-445; 978-0-446; 978-0-7595; 978-1-4555; 978-1-5387; 978-1-5460)* Orders Addr.: c/o Little Brown & Co., 3 Center Plaza, Boston, MA 02108-2084 USA Toll Free Fax: 800-286-9471; Toll Free: 800-759-0190; Edit Addr.: 237 Park Ave., New York, NY 10017 USA (SAN 281-8892) Fax: 800-331-1664; Toll Free Fax: 800-759-0190; 1290 Avenue of the Americas, New York, NY 10104
E-mail: renee.supriano@twbg.com; customer.service@hbgusa.com
Web site: http://www.hbgusa.com.

Granite Publishing & Distribution, *(978-1-890558; 978-1-930980; 978-1-932280; 978-1-59936)* 868 N. 1430 W., Orem, UT 84057 USA (SAN 631-0605) Tel 801-229-9023; Fax: 801-229-1924; Toll Free: 800-574-5779 Do not confuse with companies with same or similar names in Madison, WI, Columbus, NC
E-mail: granite@granitepublishing.biz; gregg@granitepublishing.biz
Web site: http://granitepublishing.biz.

Graphic Arts Ctr. Publishing Co., Orders Addr.: P.O. Box 10306, Portland, OR 97296-0306 USA (SAN 201-6338) Tel 503-226-2402; Fax: 503-223-1410 (executive & editorial); Toll Free Fax: 800-355-9685 (sales office); Toll Free: 800-452-3032
E-mail: sales@gacpc.com
Web site: http://www.gacpc.com.

Great American Book Fairs, *See* **Scholastic Bk. Fairs**

Great Lakes Reader's Service, Inc., Orders Addr.: P.O. Box 1078, Detroit, MI 48231 USA (SAN 285-9912) Tel 313-965-4577; Fax: 313-965-2445.

Great Northern Distributors, Inc., 634 South Ave., Rochester, NY 14620-1316 USA (SAN 169-7676) Tel 717-342-8159.

Greathall Productions, Inc., *(978-1-882513; 978-1-940916)* Orders Addr.: P.O. Box 5061, Charlottesville, VA 22905-5061 USA Tel 434-296-4288; Fax: 434-296-4490; Toll Free: 800-477-6234
E-mail: greathall@greathall.com
Web site: http://www.greathall.com.

Green Dragon Bks., *(978-0-89334; 978-1-62386)* 2875 S. Ocean Blvd. Ste 200, Palm Beach, FL 33480 USA (SAN 658-0882) Toll Free Fax: 888-874-8844; Toll Free: 800-874-8844 Do not confuse with Humanics ErgoSystems, Inc., Reseda, CA
E-mail: info@greendragonbooks.com
Web site: http://www.greendragonbooks.com; http://www.humanicslearning.com; http://www.humanicsdealer.com.

Green Gate Bks., 6700 W. Chicago St., Chandler, AZ 85226 USA (SAN 169-6785) Tel 480-961-5176; Fax: 480-961-5256; Toll Free: 800-228-3816
E-mail: ggb@wcoil.com
Web site: http://www.greengatebooks.com.

Greenfield Distribution, Inc., Orders Addr.: c/o IDS, 400 Bedford St., Suite 322, Manchester, NH 03101 USA Tel 413-772-2976; Edit Addr.: 20 Blaine St., Manchester, NH 03102 USA
E-mail: Findlkzade1@aol.com; Gdibooks@aol.com
Web site: http://www.gdibooks.com.

Greenleaf Book Group, *(978-0-9665319; 978-1-929774; 978-0-9790842; 978-1-60832; 978-1-61486; 978-1-62634)* Orders Addr.: 4005-B Banister Ln., Austin, TX 78704 USA Tel 512-891-6100; Fax: 512-891-6150; Toll Free: 800-932-5420; Edit Addr.: P.O. Box 91869, Austin, TX 78709 USA
E-mail: tanya@greenleafbookgroup.com
Web site: http://www.greenleafbookgroup.com.

Grey Hse. Publishing, *(978-0-939300; 978-1-891482; 978-1-930956; 978-1-59237; 978-1-61925; 978-1-68217)* 4919 Rte. 22, Amenia, NY 12501 USA Tel 518-789-8700; Fax: 518-789-0556; Toll Free: 800-562-2139; 4919 Rte. 22, Amenia, NY 12501 Tel 518-789-8700; Fax: 518-789-0556; Toll Free: 800-562-2139; 4919 Rte. 22, Amenia, NY 12501 Tel 518-789-8700; Fax: 518-789-0556; Toll Free: 800-562-2139
E-mail: books@greyhouse.com
Web site: http://www.greyhouse.com.

Grey Owl Indian Craft Co., Inc., 132-05 Merrick Blvd., P.O. Box 468, Jamaica, NY 11434 USA (SAN 132-9979) Tel 718-341-4000.

Grolier Americana, 1111 Crandon Blvd., Apt. C501, Key Biscayne, FL 33149-2734 USA (SAN 108-1764) Tel 305-551-6711.

Grove/Atlantic, Inc., *(978-0-8021; 978-0-87113; 978-1-55584; 978-1-61185)* 841 Broadway, 4th Flr., New York, NY 10003-4793 USA (SAN 201-4890) Tel 212-614-7850; Fax: 212-614-7886; Toll Free: 800-521-0178
Web site: http://www.groveatlantic.com/.

Grupo Nelson, *(978-0-8499; 978-0-88113; 978-0-89922; 978-1-60255)* Div. of Thomas Nelson, Inc., 501 Nelson Pl., Nashville, TN 37217 USA (SAN 240-6349) Tel 615-889-9000; Fax: 615-883-9376; Toll Free: 800-251-4000
Web site: http://www.editorialcaribe.com.

Gryphon Hse., Inc., *(978-0-87659; 978-0-917505; 978-1-58904)* Orders Addr.: 6848 Leon's Way, Lewisville, NC 27023 USA (SAN 169-3190) Tel 800-638-0928; Fax: 800-638-7576; Toll Free: 800-638-0928
E-mail: info@ghbooks.com
Web site: http://www.gryphonhouse.com.

GSG & Assocs., *(978-0-945001; 978-1-933355)* Orders Addr.: P.O. Box 590, San Pedro, CA 90733 USA (SAN 245-7792) Tel 310-548-3455; Fax: 310-548-5802; Edit Addr.: 831 S. Palos Vereds St., San Pedro, CA 90731 USA
E-mail: gsgbooks@earthlink.net.

Guardian Bk. Co., P.O. Box 202, Ottawa Lake, MI 49267-0202 USA (SAN 163-7355).

Gulf States Book Fairs, *See* **Gulf States Educational Bks.**

Gulf States Educational Bks., Orders Addr.: 368 Laurel Dr., Satsuma, AL 36572 USA (SAN 158-7870) Toll Free: 800-533-1189.

Gumdrop Bks., Div. of Central Programs, Inc., Orders Addr.: P.O. Box 505, Bethany, MO 64424 USA (SAN 631-4988) Tel 660-425-3923; Fax: 660-425-3970; Toll Free: 800-821-7199; Edit Addr.: P.O. Box 505, Bethany, MO 64424-0505 USA (SAN 131-0860)
E-mail: wecare@gumdropbooks.com
Web site: http://www.gumdropbooks.com.

H & H Distribution, 1634 Stilesgate, Grand Rapids, MI 49508 USA Tel 616-248-7990; Fax: 616-248-0016.

Hachette Bk. Group, *(978-0-446; 978-1-60941; 978-1-61113; 978-1-61969; 978-1-4789)* Div. of Hachette Group Livre, Orders Addr.: 3 Center Plaza, Boston, MA 02108 USA (SAN 852-5463) Tel 617-263-1828; Toll Free Fax: 800-286-9471; Toll Free: 800-759-0190; Edit Addr.: P.O. Box 2146, Johannesburg, 2196 ZAF Tel 2711 783-7565; Fax: 2711 883-6866
Web site: http://www.hachettebookgroup.com.

Hagerstown News Distributors, *See* **Mid-States Distributors**

Haitiana Pubns., Inc., *(978-0-944987)* 3740 81st St. Apt. B3, Jackson Hts, NY 11372-6947 USA (SAN 245-7059)
E-mail: haitiana@idt.net
Web site: http://www.idtnet/haitiana/.com.

Halalco Bks., 108 E. Fairfax St., Falls Church, VA 22046 USA
E-mail: halalco@halalco.com.

Hale, Robert & Co., Inc., 1803 132nd Ave., NE, Suite 4, Bellevue, WA 98005 USA (SAN 200-6995) Tel 425-881-5212; Fax: 425-881-0731; Toll Free: 800-733-5330.

Half Halt Pr., *(978-0-939481)* Orders Addr.: P.O. Box 67, Boonsboro, MD 21713-0067 USA (SAN 663-270X) Tel 301-733-7119; Fax: 301-733-7408
E-mail: mail@halfhaltpress.com
Web site: http://www.halfhaltpress.com.

Ham Radio's Bookstore, *See* **Radio Bookstore**

Hamakor Judaica, Inc., 7777 Merrimac Ave., Niles, IL 60714 USA (SAN 169-1791) Tel 847-966-4040; Fax: 847-966-4033; Toll Free: 800-552-4088.

Hamel, Bernard H. Spanish Bk. Corp., 10977 Santa Monica Blvd., Los Angeles, CA 90025 USA (SAN 111-8862) Tel 310-475-0453; Fax: 310-473-6132
E-mail: spanish@primenet.com
Web site: http://www.BernardHamel.com; http://www.SpanishBooksUSA.com.

Hamilton News Co., Ltd., 41 Hamilton Ln., Glenmont, NY 12077 USA (SAN 169-5312) Tel 518-463-1135; Fax: 518-463-3154.

Hammond, Incorporated, *See* **Hammond World Atlas Corp.**

Hammond Publishing Co., Inc., *(978-1-883882)* P.O. Box 279, G7166 N. Saginaw St., Mount Morris, MI 48458 USA (SAN 185-142X) Tel 810-686-8881; Fax: 810-686-0561; Toll Free: 800-521-3440 (orders only)
E-mail: hammondpub@juno.com.

Hammond World Atlas Corp., *(978-0-7230; 978-0-8437)* Subs. of Langenscheidt Pubs., Inc., 193 Morris Ave., Springfield, NJ 07081-1211 USA (SAN 202-2702)
E-mail: rstrung@americanmap.com
Web site: http://www.Hammondmap.com.

Hamon, Gerard Incorporated, *See* **Lafayette Bks.**

Hancock Hse. Pubs., *(978-0-88839; 978-0-919654; 978-1-55205)* 1431 Harrison Ave., Blaine, WA 98230-5005 USA (SAN 665-7079) Tel 604-538-1114; Fax: 604-538-2262; Toll Free Fax: 800-983-2262; Toll Free: 800-938-1114; 19313 Zero Ave., Surrey, BC V3S 9R9 (SAN 115-3730)
E-mail: sales@hancockhouse.com
Web site: http://www.hancockhouse.com.

Handleman, 500 Kirts Blvd., Troy, MI 48084-5225 USA (SAN 106-4886).

Handler News Agency, P.O. Box 27007, Omaha, NE 68127-0007 USA (SAN 169-4405).

Hansen Hse., 1842 West Ave., Miami Beach, FL 33139 USA (SAN 200-7908) Tel 305-532-5461; Toll Free: 800-327-8202.

Harcourt Achieve, *See* **Houghton Mifflin Harcourt Supplemental Pubs.**

Harcourt Brace & Company, *See* **Harcourt Trade Pubs.**

Harcourt Trade Pubs., *(978-0-15)* Div. of Houghton Mifflin Harcourt Trade & Reference Pubs., Orders Addr.: 6277 Sea Harbor Dr., Orlando, FL 32887 USA (SAN 200-285X) Tel 619-699-6707; Toll Free Fax: 800-235-0256; Toll Free: 800-543-1918 (trade orders, inquiries, claims); Edit Addr.: 15 E. 26th St., New York, NY 10010 USA Tel 212-592-1000; Fax: 212-592-1011; 525 B St., Suite 1900, San Diego, CA 92101-4495 (SAN 200-2736) Tel 619-231-6616
E-mail: andrewporter@harcourt.com
Web site: http://www.HarcourtBooks.com.

Harness, Miller, 750 Route 73 S. Ste. 110, Marlton, NJ 08053-4142 USA (SAN 169-5789) Toll Free: 800-526-6310.

HarperCollins Pubs., *(978-0-00; 978-0-06; 978-0-380; 978-0-688; 978-0-690; 978-0-694; 978-0-87795; 978-1-55710)* Div. of News Corp., Orders Addr.: 1000 Keystone Industrial Pk., Scranton, PA 18512-4621 USA (SAN 215-3742) Tel 570-941-1500; Toll Free Fax: 800-822-4090; Toll Free: 800-242-7737 (orders only); Edit Addr.: 10 E. 53rd St., New York, NY 10022-5299 USA (SAN 200-2086) Tel 212-207-7000
Web site: http://www.harpercollins.com; http://www.harpercollinschildrens.com.

Harrisburg News Co., 980 Briarsdale Rd., Harrisburg, PA 17109 USA (SAN 169-7420) Tel 717-561-8377; Fax: 717-561-1466
E-mail: jmurphy@harrisburgnewsco.com
Web site: http://www.harrisburgnewsco.com.

Harrison House, Incorporated, *See* **Harrison House Pubs.**

Harrison House Pubs., *(978-0-89274; 978-1-57794; 978-1-60683; 978-1-68031)* Orders Addr.: P.O. Box 35035, Tulsa, OK 74153 USA (SAN 208-676X) Tel 918-523-5700; Toll Free Fax: 800-830-5688; Toll Free: 800-888-4126; Edit Addr.: 7498 E. 46th Pl., Tulsa, OK 74145 USA Tel 918-523-5700; Toll Free Fax: 800-830-5688; Toll Free: 800-888-4126
E-mail: lisad@harrisonhouse.com; juliew@harrisonhouse.com
Web site: http://www.harrisonhouse.com.

Harry-Young Pubn. Services Agency, Inc., 6261 Manchester Blvd., Buena Park, CA 90621-2259 USA (SAN 110-8832).

Harvard Assocs., Inc., *(978-0-924346)* 10 Holworthy St., Cambridge, MA 02138 USA (SAN 170-2939) Tel 617-492-0660; Fax: 617-492-4610; Toll Free: 800-774-5646
E-mail: info@harvassoc.com
Web site: http://www.harvassoc.com.

Harvard Business Review Pr., *(978-0-87584; 978-1-57851; 978-1-59139; 978-1-4221; 978-1-62527; 978-1-63369)* 60 Harvard Way, Boston, MA 02163 USA (SAN 202-277X) Tel 617-783-7400; 617 495 6181; Fax: 617-783-7492; Toll Free: 888-500-1016 6-19-01 faxed 2nd prefix app, charge, KC
E-mail: corpcustserv@hbsp.harvard.edu
Web site: http://www.hbsp.harvard.edu; http://www.harvardbusinessonline.com.

Harvard Business School Press, *See* **Harvard Business Review Pr.**

Harvard Univ. Art Museums Shop, 32 Quincy St., Cambridge, MA 02138 USA (SAN 111-3372) Tel 617-495-8286; Fax: 617-495-9985
E-mail: appleyar@fas.harvard.edu
Web site: http://www.artmuseums.harvard.edu.

Harvard Univ. Pr., *(978-0-674; 978-0-916724; 978-0-935617)* Orders Addr.: c/o Triliteral LLC, 100 Maple Ridge Dr., Cumberland, RI 02864 USA Tel 401-531-2800; Fax: 401-531-2801; Toll Free Fax: 800-406-9145; Toll Free: 800-405-1619; 800-448-2242; Edit Addr.: 79 Garden St., Cambridge, MA 02138 USA (SAN 200-2043) Tel 617-495-2600; Fax: 617-495-5898
E-mail: contact_hup@harvard.edu
Web site: http://www.hup.harvard.edu.

Harvest Distributors, *See* **ARVEST**

Hastings Bks., *(978-0-940846)* 116 N. Wayne Ave., Wayne, PA 19087 USA (SAN 205-048X).

Haven Distributors, 5456 N. Damen Ave., Chicago, IL 60625 USA.

Hawaiian Magazine Distributor, 3375 Koapaka St., No. D180, Honolulu, HI 96819-1865 USA (SAN 169-1619).

Hay Hse., Inc., *(978-0-937611; 978-0-945923; 978-1-56170; 978-1-891751; 978-1-58825; 978-1-4019)* Orders Addr.: P.O. Box 5100, Carlsbad, CA 92018-5100 USA (SAN 630-477X) Tel 760-431-7695 ext 112; Fax: 760-431-6948; Toll Free Fax: 800-650-5115 (orders only); Toll Free: 800-654-5126 (orders only); 2776 Loker Ave. W, Carlsbad, CA 92010 (SAN 257-3024) Tel 800-654-5126; Fax: 800-650-5115; 2776 Loker Ave. W., Carlsbad, CA 92010
E-mail: kjohnson@hayhouse.com; pcrowe@hayhouse.com
Web site: http://www.hayhouse.com.

Hazelden, *(978-0-89486; 978-0-89638; 978-0-935908; 978-0-942421; 978-1-56246; 978-1-56838; 978-1-59285; 978-1-61649)* 15251 Pleasant Valley Rd., P.O. Box 176, Center City, MN 55012-0176 USA (SAN 209-4010) Fax: 651-213-4044; Toll Free: 800-328-9000; P.O. Box 176, RW4, Center City, MN 55012 Tel 651-213-4000; Toll Free: 800-328-9000
E-mail: bosterbauer@hazelden.org
Web site: http://www.hazelden.org.

Hazelden Publishing & Educational Services, *See* **Hazelden**

Health and Growth Assocs., *(978-0-9630266)* Orders Addr.: 28195 Fairview Ave., Hemet, CA 92544 USA Tel 951-927-1768; Fax: 951-927-1548
E-mail: flloomis@earthlink.net.

Health Communications, Inc., *(978-0-932194; 978-1-55874; 978-0-7573; 978-0-9910732)* Orders Addr.: 3201 SW 15th St., Deerfield Beach, FL 33442-8190 USA (SAN 212-100X) Tel 954-360-0909; Fax: 954-360-0034; Toll Free: 800-441-5569 Do not confuse with Health Communications, Inc., Edison, NJ
E-mail: terip@hcibooks.com; lorig@hcibooks.com
Web site: http://www.hcibooks.com.

Hearst Distribution Group, Incorporated, Book Division, *See* **Comag Marketing Group**

Heartland Bk. Co., 10195 N. Lake Ave., Olathe, KS 66061 USA (SAN 631-2497) Tel 913-829-1784.

Heffernan Audio Visual, Orders Addr.: P.O. Box 5906, San Antonio, TX 78201-0906 USA Tel 210-732-4333; Fax: 210-732-5906; Edit Addr.: 435 Isom Rd. Ste. 210, San Antonio, TX 78216-5144 USA (SAN 166-8722) E-mail: sales@heffernanav.com Web site: http://www.heffernanav.com.

Heffernan School Supply, *See* **Heffernan Audio Visual**

Heinecken & Assoc., Ltd., 1733 N. Mohawk, Chicago, IL 60614 USA Toll Free Fax: 800-947-5694; Toll Free: 800-449-0138.

.Heinemann-Raintree, *See* **Heinemann-Raintree**

Heinemann-Raintree, (*978-0-431; 978-1-57572; 978-1-58810; 978-1-4034; 978-1-4109; 978-1-4329; 978-1-4846*) Div. of Capstone, Orders Addr.: 1710 Roe Crest Dr., North Mankato, MN 56003 USA Toll Free Fax: 888-844-5329; Toll Free: 800-747-4992; Halley Court Freepost PO Box 1125, Oxford, OX2 8YY E-mail: k.monyhan@coughlancompanies.com; customerservice@capstonepub.com Web site: http://www.heinemannlibrary.com/; http://www.capstonepub.com; http://www.capstoneclassroom.com.

Heirloom Bible Pubs., (*978-0-9817263*) Orders Addr.: P.O. Box 118, Wichita, KS 67201-0118 USA (SAN 630-2793) Fax: 316-267-1850; Toll Free: 800-676-2448; Edit Addr.: 9020 E. 35th St. N., Wichita, KS 67226-2017 USA.

Helix, 310 S. Racine St., Chicago, IL 60607 USA (SAN 111-915X) Tel 312-421-6000; Fax: 312-421-1586.

Hemed Books, Incorporated, *See* **Lambda Pubs., Inc.**

Hendrick-Long Publishing Co., (*978-0-937460; 978-1-885777*) Orders Addr.: 10635 Tower Oaks, Suite D, Houston, TX 77070 USA (SAN 281-7756) Toll Free: 800-544-3770; Edit Addr.: 10635 Tower Oaks Blvd., Houston, TX 77070-5927 USA (SAN 281-7748) E-mail: hendrick-long@worldnet.att.net Web site: http://www.hendricklongpublishing.com.

Herald Pr., (*978-0-8361; 978-1-5138*) Div. of MennoMedia, Inc., Orders Addr.: 1251 Virginia Ave., Harrisonburg, VA 22802 USA (SAN 202-2915) Fax: 1-316-283-0454; Toll Free: 1-800-245-7894; 800-631-6535 (Canada only) Do not confuse with Herald Pr., Charlotte, NC E-mail: info@mennomedia.org Web site: http://www.mennomedia.org.

Herald Publishing Hse., (*978-0-8309*) Orders Addr.: P.O. Box 390, Independence, MO 64051-0390 USA Tel 816-521-3015; Fax: 816-521-3066 (customer services); Toll Free: 800-767-8181; Edit Addr.: 1001W. Walnut St., Independence, MO 64051-0390 USA (SAN 111-7556) Tel 816-257-0200 E-mail: sales@HeraldHouse.org Web site: http://www.heraldhouse.org.

Heritage Bookstore, Orders Addr.: P.O. Box 6007, Springfield, MO 65801-6007 USA (SAN 111-7696).

Hertzberg-New Method Inc., 617 E. Vandalia Rd., Ebooks, Jacksonville, IL 62650 USA (SAN 780-0479) Tel 217-243-5451.

Hervey's Booklink & Cookbook Warehouse, P.O. Box 831870, Richardson, TX 75083 USA (SAN 630-9747).

Hesteria Records & Publishing Co., 124 Hagar Ct., Santa Cruz, CA 95064 USA Tel 831-459-2575; Fax: 831-457-2917 E-mail: alissa@aainnovators.com Web site: http://www.aainnovators.com.

Hi Jolly Library Service, 150 N. Gay St., Susanville, CA 96130-3902 USA (SAN 133-5944).

Hibel, Edna Studio, P.O. Box 9967, Riviera Beach, FL 33419 USA (SAN 111-1574) Tel 561-848-9640; Toll Free: 800-275-3426.

Hicks News Agency, Incorporated, *See* **NEWSouth Distributors**

High Peak Bks., (*978-1-884709*) Orders Addr.: P.O. Box 703, Wilson, WY 83014 USA (SAN 299-4232); Edit Addr.: 355 N. Bar Y Rd., Jackson, WY 83011 USA Tel 307-739-0147 Do not confuse with High Peak Pr. in Schenectady, NY.

Hill City News Agency, Inc., 3228 Odd Fellow Rd., Lynchburg, VA 24501 USA (SAN 169-8656) Tel 804-845-4231; Fax: 804-845-0864.

Hillsboro News, Orders Addr.: P.O. Box 25738, Tampa, FL 33622-5738 USA Tel 813-622-8087; Edit Addr.: 7002 Parke E. Blvd., Tampa, FL 33610 USA.

Himber Bks., Div. of F. C. Himber & Son's, Inc., 1380 W. Second Ave., Eugene, OR 97402 USA Tel 541-686-8003; Toll Free: 800-888-5904.

Himber, F. C., *See* **Himber Bks.**

Hinrichs, E. Louis, P.O. Box 1090, Lompoc, CA 93438-1090 USA (SAN 133-1493) Tel 805-736-7512 E-mail: booklompoc@aol.com.

Hinsdale County Historical Society, P.O. Box 353 130 N. Silver St., Lake City, CO 81235 USA Tel 970-944-2050.

Historic Aviation Bks., 121 Fifth Ave., Suite 300, New Brighton, MN 55112 USA (SAN 129-5284) Tel 651-635-0100; Fax: 651-635-0700.

Historic Cherry Hill, (*978-0-943366*) 523 1/2 S. Pearl St., Albany, NY 12202 USA (SAN 110-8859) Tel 518-434-4791; Fax: 518-434-4806.

Hobbies Hawaii Distributors, 4420 Lawehana St., No. 3, Honolulu, HI 96818 USA (SAN 630-8619) Tel 808-423-0265; Fax: 808-423-1635.

Holiday Enterprises, Inc., 3328 US Hwy. 123, Rochester Bldg., Greenville, SC 29611 USA (SAN 169-779X) Tel 864-220-3161; Fax: 864-295-9757.

Holt, Henry & Co., (*978-0-03; 978-0-8050*) Div. of Holtzbrinck Publishers, Orders Addr.: 16365 James Madison Hwy., Gordonsville, VA 22942-8501 USA Toll Free Fax: 800-672-2054; Toll Free: 888-330-8477; Edit Addr.: 115 W. 18th St., 5th Flr., New York, NY 10011 USA (SAN 200-6472) Tel 212-886-9200; Fax: 540-672-7540 (customer service) E-mail: info@hholt.com Web site: http://www.henryholt.com.

Holtzbrinck Publishers, *See* **Macmillan**

Holyoke News Co., Inc., 720 Main St., P.O. Box 990, Holyoke, MA 01041 USA (SAN 169-3468) Tel 413-534-4537; Fax: 413-538-7161; Toll Free: 800-628-8372 E-mail: sales@holyoke-news.com.

Homestead Book Co., (*978-0-930180*) Orders Addr.: P.O. Box 31608, Seattle, WA 98103 USA (SAN 662-037X); Edit Addr.: 6101 22nd Ave., NW, Seattle, WA 98107 USA (SAN 169-8796) Tel 206-782-4532; Fax: 206-784-9328; Toll Free: 800-426-6777 (orders only) E-mail: info@homesteadbook.com Web site: http://www.homesteadbook.com.

Homestead Book, Incorporated, *See* **Homestead Book Co.**

Hood, Alan C. & Co., Inc., (*978-0-911469*) P.O. Box 775, Chambersburg, PA 17201 USA (SAN 270-8221) Tel 717-267-0867; Fax: 717-267-0572; Toll Free Fax: 888-844-9433; 4501 Forbes Blvd., Lanham, MD 20706 E-mail: hoodbooks@pa.net Web site: http://www.hoodbooks.com.

Hoover Institution Pr., (*978-0-8179*) Stanford Univ., Stanford, CA 94305-6010 USA (SAN 202-3024) Tel 650-723-3373; Fax: 650-723-8626; Toll Free: 800-935-2882 E-mail: scott.harrison@stanford.edu Web site: http://www.hooverpress.org.

Hopkins Fulfillment Services, P.O. Box 50370, Baltimore, MD 21211-4370 USA Fax: 410-516-6998; Toll Free: 800-537-5487.

Hotho & Co., P.O. Box 9738, Fort Worth, TX 76147-2738 USA (SAN 169-8192).

Houghton Mifflin Company, *See* **Houghton Mifflin Harcourt Publishing Co.**

Houghton Mifflin Company Trade & Reference Division, *See* **Houghton Mifflin Harcourt Trade & Reference Pubs.**

Houghton Mifflin Harcourt Publishing Co., (*978-0-395; 978-0-87466; 978-0-9631591; 978-1-57630; 978-1-881527; 978-0-618; 978-0-544; 978-0-547; 978-1-328; 978-0-358*) Orders Addr.: 9205 Southpark Ctr. Loop, Orlando, FL 32819 USA Toll Free: 800-225-3362; Edit Addr.: 222 Berkeley St., Boston, MA 02116 USA (SAN 215-3793) Tel 617-351-5000; 125 High St., Boston, MA 02110 Web site: http://www.hmco.com.

Houghton Mifflin Harcourt Supplemental Pubs., (*978-1-60032; 978-1-60277*) 10801 N. Mopac Expressway, Bldg. 3, Austin, TX 78759 USA Web site: www.harcourtachieve.com.

Houghton Mifflin Harcourt Trade & Reference Pubs., (*978-0-395; 978-0-89919; 978-0-618*) Orders Addr.: 9205 Southpark Ctr. Loop, Orlando, FL 32819 USA Tel 978-661-1300; Toll Free: 800-225-3362; Edit Addr.: 222 Berkeley St., Boston, MA 02116 USA (SAN 200-2388) Tel 617-351-5000; Fax: 617-227-5409; 215 Park Ave S., 12th Flr., New York, NY 10003-1621 E-mail: trade_sub_rights@hmco.com Web site: http://www.hmco.com/; http://www.houghtonmifflinbooks.com.

Houston Paperback Distributor, 4114 Gairloch Ln., Houston, TX 77025-2912 USA (SAN 169-8273).

Hovel Audio, Incorporated, *See* **christianaudio**

How-2 Bks., P.O. Box 5793, Denver, CO 80217 USA (SAN 631-1369) Tel 303-778-8383; Toll Free: 800-279-7323.

HPK Educational Resource Ctr., (*978-0-89895*) Div. of H. P. Koppelmann, Inc., 140 Van Block Ave., Hartford, CT 06141 USA (SAN 169-071X) Tel 860-549-6210; Toll Free: 800-243-7724.

Hubbard, P.O. Box 100, Defiance, OH 43512 USA (SAN 169-6726) Tel 419-784-4455; Fax: 419-782-1662; Toll Free: 800-582-0657 E-mail: hubbard@bright.net.

Hudson County News Co., 1305 Paterson Plank Rd., North Bergen, NJ 07047 USA (SAN 169-4782) Tel 201-867-3600.

Hudson Hills Pr. LLC, (*978-0-933920; 978-0-9646042; 978-1-55595*) Orders Addr.: P.O. Box 205, Manchester, VT 05254 USA; Edit Addr.: 74-2 Union St., Manchester, VT 05254 USA (SAN 213-0815) Tel 802-362-6450; Fax: 802-362-6459 E-mail: artbooks@hudsonhills.com Web site: http://www.hudsonhills.com/.

Hudson Hills Press, Incorporated, *See* **Hudson Hills Pr. LLC**

Hudson Valley News Distributors, P.O. Box 1236, Newburgh, NY 12550 USA (SAN 169-6084) Tel 914-562-3399; Fax: 914-562-6010.

Humanics Publishing Group, *See* **Green Dragon Bks.**

Hyperion Pr., (*978-0-7868; 978-1-56282; 978-1-4013*) Div. of Disney Bk. Publishing, Inc., A Walt Disney Co., Orders Addr.: c/o HarperCollins Publishers, 1000 Keystone Industrial Park, Scranton, PA 18512-4621 USA Toll Free: 800-242-7737; Edit Addr.: 114 Fifth Ave., New York, NY 110011 USA Tel 917-661-2000 Web site: http://www.hyperionbooks.com.

i. b. d., Ltd., (*978-0-88431*) 24 Hudson St., Kinderhook, NY 12106 USA (SAN 630-7779) Tel 518-758-1755; Fax: 518-758-6702 E-mail: lankhof@ibdltd.com Web site: http://www.ibdltd.com.

I S H K, (*978-0-86304; 978-0-900860; 978-1-883536; 978-1-933779; 978-1-942698; 978-1-944493; 978-1-946270; 978-1-948013*) Div. of Institute for the Study of Human Knowledge, Orders Addr.: P.O. Box 400541, Cambridge, MA 02140 USA (SAN 226-4536) Tel 617-497-4124; Fax: 617-500-0268; Toll Free Fax: 800-223-4200; Toll Free: 800-222-4745; Edit Addr.: Ishk-hoopoe 171 Main St. #140, Los Altos, CA 94022 USA Tel 650-948-9428 E-mail: ishkbooks@aol.com; ishkadm@aol.com Web site: http://www.ishkbooks.com; http://www.hoopoekids.com.

Iaconi, Mariuccia Bk. Imports, (*978-0-9628720*) P.O. Box 77023, San Francisco, CA 94107-0023 USA (SAN 161-1364) Toll Free: 800-955-9577 E-mail: mibibook@ixnetcom.com Web site: http://www.mibibook.com.

ICG Muse, Inc., 420 W. 42nd St. Apt. 35B, New York, NY 10036-6863 USA (SAN 631-7200).

Icon Distribution, 3325 Donnell Dr., Forestville, MD 20747 USA.

ID International Bk. Service, 126 Old Ridgefield Rd., Wilton, CT 06897-3017 USA (SAN 630-8074) Tel 203-834-2272; Fax: 203-762-9725 E-mail: orders@idintl.com.

Idaho News Agency, 2710 Julia St., Coeur D'Alene, ID 83814 USA (SAN 169-1651) Tel 208-664-3444.

Ideal Foreign Bks., Inc., 132-10 Hillside Ave., Richmond Hill, NY 11418 USA (SAN 169-6173) Tel 718-297-7477; Fax: 718-297-7645; Toll Free: 800-284-2490 (orders only).

IFSTA, (*978-0-87939; 978-1-56916*) Orders Addr.: c/o Oklahoma State Univ., Fire Protection Pubns., 930 N. Willis, Stillwater, OK 74078-8045 USA Tel 405-744-5723; Fax: 405-744-8204; Toll Free: 800-654-4055 (orders only) Web site: http://www.ifsta.org/.

Ignatius Pr., (*978-0-89870; 978-1-58617; 978-1-62164; 978-1-68149*) Orders Addr.: P.O. Box 1339, Fort Collins, CO 80522-1339 USA (SAN 855-3556) Tel 970-221-3920; Fax: 970-221-3964; Toll Free Fax: 800-278-3566; Toll Free: 877-320-9276 (bookstore orders); 800-651-1531 (credit card orders, no minimum, individual orders); Edit Addr.: 1348 10th Ave., San Francisco, CA 94122 USA (SAN 214-3887) Toll Free: 800-651-1531 E-mail: info@ignatius.com Web site: http://www.ignatius.com.

Igram Pr., (*978-0-911119; 978-1-930279*) 311 Parsons Dr., Hiawatha, IA 52233 USA (SAN 263-1709) Tel 319-393-3600; Fax: 319-393-3934; Toll Free: 800-393-2399 E-mail: clabarr@cedargraphicsinc.com.

Illinois News Service, *See* **News Group - Illinois, The**

Ilmhouse Inc., P.O. Box 74, Haverford, PA 19041-0074 USA E-mail: admin@ilmhouse.com Web site: http://www.ilmhouse.com.

Image Processing Software, Inc., (*978-0-924507*) 6409 Appalachian Way, Madison, WI 53705 USA (SAN 265-5977) Tel 608-233-5033; 4414 Regent St., Madison, WI 53705 (SAN 249-3020).

Impact Photographics, (*978-0-918327; 978-1-56540; 978-1-60068*) 4961 Windplay Dr., Eldorado Hills, CA 95630 USA (SAN 657-3126) Tel 916-939-9333; Fax: 916-939-9334; Toll Free: 800-950-0110 E-mail: juliem@impactphotographics.com Web site: http://www.impactphotographics.com.

Imperial News Co., Inc., 5131 Post Rd., Dublin, OH 43017-1160 USA (SAN 169-5509) Fax: 516-752-8515.

Imported Bks., Orders Addr.: St., Dallas, TX 75208 USA (SAN 169-8095) Tel 214-941-6497.

In Between Bks., (*978-0-935430; 978-0-9802007*) P.O. Box 790, Sausalito, CA 94966 USA (SAN 213-6236) Tel 415-383-8447; Fax: 415-381-1938; 415-381-3513 E-mail: inbetweenbooks@atthebutterflytree.com; karla@inbetweenbooks.com; juno@inbetweenbooks.com Web site: http://www.atthebutterflytree.com.

Incor Periodicals, 32150 Hwy. 34, Tangent, OR 97389-9704 USA (SAN 169-7072) Tel 541-926-8889; Fax: 541-926-9553.

Independent Magazine Co., 2970 N. Ontario St., Burbank, CA 91504-2016 USA (SAN 159-8783).

Independent Pub., (*978-1-4243; 978-1-59975; 978-1-60402; 978-1-60461; 978-1-60530; 978-1-60585; 978-1-60643; 978-1-60702; 978-1-60725; 978-1-60743; 978-1-61539; 978-1-61584; 978-1-61623; 978-1-61658; 978-1-4507; 978-1-4675; 978-1-4951; 978-0-9927847; 978-1-5323;-1-5323-0640-2) Div. of Bar Code Graphics, 875 N. Michigan Ave., Suite 2650, Chicago, IL 60615 USA Fax: 312-595-0725; Toll Free: 800-662-0701; 65 E. Wacker Pl., 18th Flr., Chicago, IL 60601 Tel 312-595-0600; Toll Free: 800-662-0703 Do not confuse with Independent Publishers in Bountiful, UT* E-mail: pubserv@barcode-us.com Web site: http://www.publisherservices-us.com; http://www.isbn-us.com.

Independent Pubs. Group, (*978-1-4956; 978-1-5136-1835-7*) Subs. of Chicago Review Pr., 814 N. Franklin, Chicago, IL 60610 USA (SAN 201-2936) Tel 312-337-0747; Fax: 312-337-5985; Toll Free: 800-888-4741 E-mail: frontdesk@ipgbook.com Web site: http://www.ipgbook.com; http://www.trafalgarsquarepublishing.com.

Indiana Periodicals, Inc., 2120 S. Meridian St., Indianapolis, IN 46225 USA (SAN 169-2380) Tel 317-786-1488; Fax: 317-782-4999.

Indiana Univ. Pr., (*978-0-253; 978-0-86196*) 601 N. Morton St., Bloomington, IN 47404-3797 USA (SAN 202-5647) Fax: 812-855-7931; Toll Free: 800-842-6796 E-mail: iuporder@indiana.edu Web site: http://www.iupress.indiana.edu.

Indig, Stanley M. Specialty Pubn., (*978-0-945815; 978-1-57767*) 2173 E. 38th St., Brooklyn, NY 11234 USA (SAN 248-0719) Tel 718-692-0648; Fax: 718-677-9542 E-mail: indigpublishing@yahoo.com; indigpublishing@aol.com Web site: http://www.indigpublishing.com.

Infobase Learning, (*978-0-8160*) 132 West 31st St., 17th Flr., New York, NY 10001 USA.

Infobase Publishing Company, *See* **Infobase Learning**

Ingenix, Incorporated, *See* **OptumInsight, Inc.**

Ingham Publishing, Inc., (*978-0-9611804; 978-1-891130*) Orders Addr.: P.O. Box 12642, Saint Petersburg, FL 33733-2642 USA Tel 813-343-4811; Fax: 813-381-2807; Edit Addr.: 5650 First Ave., N., Saint Petersburg, FL 33710 USA (SAN 112-8930) E-mail: ftreflex@concentric.net.

Ingram Academic, Div. of Ingram Content Group, Orders Addr.: c/o Perseus Books Group, 210 American Dr., Jackson, TN 38301 USA Toll Free Fax: 800-351-5073; Toll Free: 800-343-4499; c/o Publishers Group Canada, 76 Stafford St., Unit 300, Toronto, ON M6J 2S1 Tel 416-934-9900; Fax: 416-934-1410; Toll Free Fax: 800-565-3770; Toll Free: 800-663-5714 E-mail: academicorders@perseusbooks.com; client.info@perseusbooks.com Web site: http://www.perseusacademic.com.

Ingram Bk. Co., (*978-1-61522; 978-1-60894*) Subs. of Ingram Industries, Inc., Orders Addr.: 1 Ingram Blvd., P.O. Box 3006, La Vergne, TN 37086-1986 USA (SAN 169-7978) Tel 615-213-5000; Fax: 615-213-3976 (Electronic Orders); Toll Free Fax: 800-285-3296 (fax inquiry US & Canada); 800-876-0186 (orders); 877-663-5367 (Canadian orders); Toll Free: 800-937-8000 (orders only); 800-937-8200 (customer service US & Canada); 800-289-0687 (Canadian orders only customer service); 800-234-6737 (electronic orders US & Canada)) Do not confuse with Ingram Pr., Sacramento, CA E-mail: flashback@ingrambook.com; customerservice@ingrambook.com; ics-sales@ingrambook.com Web site: http://www.ingrambook.com.

Ingram Content Group Inc., Sub. of Ingram Industries Inc., 1 Ingram Blvd., La Vergne, TN 37086 USA Tel 615-793-5000; Toll Free: 800-937-8000 (option 3) E-mail: inquiry@ingramcontent.com; customerservice@ingramcontent.com Web site: http://www.ingramcontent.com.

Ingram Entertainment, Inc., Two Ingram Blvd. (Corp. Headquarters), La Vergne, TN 37089-7006 USA (SAN 630-6780) Tel 615-287-4000; Fax: 615-287-4995; Toll Free: 800-759-5000; 12000 Ridgemont Dr., Urbandale, IA 50323-2317 (SAN 630-6950); 26391 Curtiss Wright Pkwy. Ste. 106, Cleveland, OH 44143-4401 (SAN 630-6896) Toll Free: 800-621-1333; 15002 Sommermeyer, Houston, TX 77041-5333 (SAN 630-7000) Tel 713-937-3600; Fax: 713-466-4316; 382 E. Lies Rd., Carol Stream, IL 60188-9418 (SAN 630-690X) Toll Free: 800-621-1333; 7911 NE 33rd Dr., Suite 270, Portland, OR 97211-1920 (SAN 630-7116) Tel 503-281-2673; Fax: 503-284-6046; 23 Monte Vista Ave., Larkspur, CA 94939-2120 (SAN 630-6993) Toll Free: 800-621-1333; 2611 S. Roosevelt, Suite 102, Tempe, AZ 85282-2017 (SAN 630-7094) Tel 602-966-6691; Fax: 602-894-0329; 4703 Fulton Industrial Blvd., Atlanta, GA 30336-2017 (SAN 630-6845) Tel 404-691-6280; Fax: 404-696-3944; 400 Airport Executive Pk., Spring Valley, NY 10977-7404 (SAN 630-7078) Tel 914-425-3191; Fax: 914-425-7521; 7949 Woodley Blvd., Van Nuys, CA 91406 (SAN 630-7183) Tel 818-375-5027; Fax: 818-375-5001; 1293 Heil Quaker Blvd., Suite B, P.O. Box 7006, La Vergne, TN 37086-7006 (SAN 630-7051) Fax: 615-793-6196; Toll Free: 800-688-3110; 3675 Crestwood Pkwy NW Ste. 105, Duluth, GA 30096-5045 (SAN 630-6853) Toll Free: 800-876-0832; 3114 S. 24th St., Kansas City, KS 66106-4709 (SAN 630-7027) Tel 913-362-0391; Fax: 913-362-0605; Toll Free: 800-621-1333; 6635 NE 59th Pl., Portland, OR 97218-2709 (SAN 630-7124) Tel 503-284-3313; Fax: 503-284-3876; Toll Free: 800-876-0834; 7319 Innovation Blvd., Fort Wayne, IN 46818-1371 (SAN 630-6985) Fax: 219-489-8850; Toll Free: 800-759-5588; 8779 Greenwood Pl., Savage, MD 20763 (SAN 630-7019) Tel 301-490-1166; Fax: 301-490-0031; Toll Free: 800-621-1333; 1521 W. Copans Rd., Suite 105, Pompano Beach, FL 33064 (SAN 630-7108) Tel 954-971-5412; Fax: 954-971-3113; Toll Free: 800-888-3876; 20435 E. Business Pkwy., Walnut, CA 91789-2999 (SAN 630-7191) Tel 714-594-6569; Fax: 714-595-0735; Toll Free: 800-759-4422; 2 Ingram Blvd., La Vergne, TN 37086-3638 (SAN 630-6837) Toll Free: 800-621-1333; 1349 Charwood Rd., Hanover, MD 21076-3114 (SAN 630-6861) Tel 410-850-9191; Fax: 410-850-9229; 110 Shawmut Rd., Canton, MA 02021-1412 (SAN 630-687X) Tel 617-575-9585; Fax: 617-575-9586; 100 Dobbs Ln., Suite 206, Cherry Hill, NJ 08034-1435 (SAN 630-6888) Tel 609-428-8668; Fax: 609-428-8536; Toll Free: 800-288-7565; 11235 Knott Ave., Suite C, Cypress, CA 90630-5401 (SAN 630-6918) Tel 714-373-8855; Fax: 714-373-8858; Toll Free: 800-759-4422; 1430 Bradley Ln., No. 102, Carrollton, TX 75007-4855 (SAN 630-6926) Tel 214-245-6088; Fax: 214-323-3890; Toll Free: 800-621-1333; 2259 Merritt Dr., Garland, TX 75041-6138 (SAN 630-6934) Tel 214-840-6621; Fax: 214-840-3357; Toll Free: 800-727-0688; 10990 E. 55th Ave., Denver, CO 80239-2007 (SAN 630-6942) Tel 303-371-8372; Fax: 303-373-4583; 35245 Schoolcraft, Livonia, MI 48150-1209 (SAN 630-6969) Tel 313-422-9955; Fax: 313-422-1171; 3540 NW 56th St., Fort Lauderdale, FL 33309-2260 (SAN 630-6977) Tel 305-733-7440; Fax: 305-735-7752; 6733 S. Sepulveda, Suite 108, Los Angeles, CA 90045-1525 (SAN 630-7035) Tel 213-410-4067; Fax: 213-410-0919; Toll Free: 800-759-4422; 9549 Penn Ave S. Ste. 200, Minneapolis, MN 55431-2565 (SAN 630-7043) Toll Free: 800-825-3112; 25 Branca Rd., East Rutherford, NJ 07073-2121 (SAN 630-706X) Tel 201-933-9797; Fax: 201-933-5139; Toll Free: 800-621-1333; 5576 Inland Empire Blvd, Bldg. G, Suite A, Ontario, CA 91764-5117 (SAN 630-7086) Tel 714-948-7998; Fax: 714-948-9778; Freeport Ctr., Bldg. H-12 N., P.O. Box 1387, Clearfield, UT 84016-1387 (SAN 630-7132) Tel 801-775-0555; Fax: 801-773-8172; 2700 Merchantile Dr., Suite 100, Rancho Cordova, CA 95742-6574 (SAN 630-7140) Tel 916-638-8090; Fax: 916-638-8021; Toll Free: 800-866-1568; 4660 Viewridge Ave., Suite B, San Diego, CA 92123-1638 (SAN 630-7159) Tel 619-569-9816; Fax: 619-569-1542; Toll Free: 800-365-5229; 6411 S. 216th, Bldg. F, Kent, WA 98032-1392 (SAN 630-7167) Tel 206-395-3515; Fax: 206-395-0650; 445 W. Freedom Ave., Orange, CA 92865 (SAN 630-7175) Tel

714-282-1232; Fax: 714-282-2245; 201 Ingram Dr., Roseburg, OR 97470; 12600 SE Hwy. 212, Bldg. B, Clackamas, OR 97015-9081 Tel 615-287-4000
Web site: http://www.ingramentertainment.com.

Ingram Publisher Services, Orders Addr.: Customer Services, Box 512 1 Ingram Blvd., LaVergne, TN 37086 USA Toll Free Fax: 800-838-1149; Edit Addr.: 1 Ingram Blvd., LaVergne, TN 37086 USA (SAN 631-8630) Tel 615-793-5000; Fax: 615-213-5811
E-mail: customer.service@ingrampublisherservices.com; Publisher@ingrampublisherservices.com; Retailer@ingrampublisherservices.com
Web site: http://www.ingrampublisherservices.com.

Ingram Software, Subs. of Ingram Distribution Group, Inc., 1759 Wehrle, Williamsville, NY 14221 USA (SAN 285-760X) Toll Free: 800-828-7250; 900 W. Walnut Ave., Compton, CA 90220 (SAN 285-7073).

INgrooves, *See* **INscribe Digital**

Inland Empire Periodicals, *See* **Incor Periodicals**

Inner Traditions International, Ltd., *(978-0-89281; 978-1-59477; 978-1-62055)* Orders Addr.: P.O. Box 388, Rochester, VT 05767-0388 USA Tel 802-767-3174; Fax: 802-767-3726; Toll Free Fax: 800-246-8648; Edit Addr.: One Park St., Rochester, VT 05767 USA (SAN 208-6948) Tel 802-767-3174; Fax: 802-767-3726
E-mail: customerservice@innertraditions.com; info@innertraditions.com
Web site: http://www.innertraditions.com.

Innovative Logistics, Orders Addr.: 575 Prospect St., Lakewood, NJ 08701 USA (SAN 760-6532) Tel 732-534-7001; 732-363-5679; Fax: 732-363-0338
E-mail: innlogorders@innlog.net
Web site: http://www.innlog.net.

INscribe Digital, *(978-1-61750; 978-1-62517)* Div. of IPG, 55 Francisco St. Suite 710, San Francisco, CA 94105 USA
E-mail: digitalpublishing@ingrooves.com
Web site: http://www.INscribeDigital.com.

Insight Guides, *(978-0-88729; 978-1-58573)* 46-35 54th Rd., Maspeth, NY 11378 USA Tel 718-784-0055; Fax: 718-784-1246
E-mail: customerservice@americanmap.com
Web site: http://www.americanmap.com.

Insight Publishing, *(978-0-9663550)* Orders Addr.: P.O. Box 32383, Jacksonville, FL 32237 USA Tel 904-262-9975; Fax: 904-262-3220; Edit Addr.: 5417 Autumnbrook Trail, N., Jacksonville, FL 32258 USA Do not confuse with companies with the same name in Yreka, CA, Parker, CO, Woodbridge, VA, Salt Lake City, UT, Tulsa, OK
E-mail: 102502.2561@compuserve.com.

Instructional Video, 2219 C St., Lincoln, NE 68502 USA (SAN 631-6115) Tel 402-475-6570; 402 475 6570; Fax: 402-475-6500; Toll Free: 800-228-0164 Do not confuse with Instructional Video in Golden, CO
E-mail: Kathy@insvideo.com
Web site: http://www.insvideo.com.

Integral Yoga Pubns., *(978-0-932040; 978-1-938477)* Satchidananda Ashram-Yogaville, 108 Yogaville Way, Buckingham, VA 23921 USA (SAN 285-0338) Tel 434-969-3121 ex 102; Fax: 434-969-1303; Toll Free: 800-262-1008 (orders)
Web site: http://www.yogaville.org.

Interlink Publishing Group, Inc., *(978-0-940793; 978-1-56656; 978-1-62371)* 46 Crosby St., Northampton, MA 01060-1804 USA (SAN 664-8908) Tel 413-582-7054; Fax: 413-582-6731; Toll Free: 800-238-5465
E-mail: info@interlinkbooks.com; editor@interlinkbooks.com
Web site: http://www.interlinkbooks.com.

InterMountain Periodical Distributors, *See* **Majic Enterprises**

International Bk. Ctr., Inc., *(978-0-86685; 978-0-917062)* 2007 Laurel Dr., P.O. Box 295, Troy, MI 48099 USA (SAN 169-4014) Tel 248-879-7920; 586-254-7230; Fax: 586-254-7230
E-mail: ibc@ibcbooks.com
Web site: http://www.ibcbooks.com.

International Magazine Service, Div. of Periodical Pubs. Service Bureau, 1 N. Superior St., Sandusky, OH 44870 USA (SAN 285-9955) Tel 419-626-0623.

International Networking Assn., 4130 Citrus Ave., Suite 5, Rocklin, CA 95677 USA (SAN 631-1857).

International Periodical Distributors, 674 Via de la Valle, Suite 204, Solana Beach, CA 92075 USA (SAN 250-5290) Tel 619-481-5928; Toll Free: 800-999-1170; 800-228-5144 (in Canada).

International Pubns. Service, *(978-0-8002)* Div. of Taylor & Francis, Inc., Orders Addr.: 325 Chestnut St., 8th Flr., Levittown, PA 19057-4700 USA Fax: 215-785-5515; Toll Free: 800-821-8312.

International Readers League, Div. of Periodical Pubs. Service Bureau, 1 N. Superior St., Sandusky, OH 44870 USA (SAN 285-9971) Tel 419-626-0633.

International Service Co., International Service Bldg., 333 Fourth Ave., Indialantic, FL 32903-4295 USA (SAN 169-5134) Tel 407-724-1443 (phone/fax).

International Specialized Book Services, *See* **ISBS Publisher Services**

International Thomson Computer Pr., *(978-1-85032)* Orders Addr.: 7625 Empire Dr., Florence, KY 41042-2978 USA Tel 606-525-6600; Fax: 606-525-7778; Toll Free: 800-842-3636; Edit Addr.: 20 Park Plaza, 13th Flr., Boston, MA 02116 USA Fax: 617-695-1615
E-mail: itcp@itp.thomson.com
Web site: http://www.itcpmedia.com.

Internet Systems, Inc., Subs. of Internet Systems, Inc., 20250 Century Blvd., Germantown, MD 20874 USA (SAN 129-9611) Tel 301-540-5100; Fax: 301-540-5522; Toll Free: 800-638-8725
Web site: http://www.pwl.com/Internet.

Interstate Distributors, 150 Blackstone River Rd. Ste. 4, Worcester, MA 01607-1455 USA (SAN 170-4885) Toll Free: 800-365-6430.

Interstate Periodical Distributors, 201 E. Badger Rd., Madison, WI 53713 USA (SAN 169-9105) Tel 608-277-2407; Fax: 608-277-2410; Toll Free: 800-752-3131.

Intertech Bk. Services, Inc., 25971 Sarazen Dr., South Riding, VA 20152-1741 USA (SAN 630-5253).

Intrepid Group, Inc., The, 1331 Red Cedar Cir., Fort Collins, CO 80524 USA (SAN 631-5429) Tel 970-493-3793; Fax: 970-493-8781
E-mail: intrepid@frii.com.

Iowa & Illinois News, 8645 Northwest Blvd., Davenport, IA 52806-6418 USA (SAN 169-2607).

Irish American Bk. Co., Subs. of Roberts Rinehart Pubs., Inc., P.O. Box 666, Niwot, CO 80544-0666 USA Tel 303-652-2710; Fax: 303-652-2689; Toll Free: 800-452-7115
E-mail: irishbooks@aol.com
Web site: http://www.irishvillage.com.

Irish Bks. & Media, Inc., *(978-0-937702)* Orders Addr.: 2904 41st Ave S., Minneapolis, MN 55406-1814 USA (SAN 111-8870) Toll Free: 800-229-3505 Do not confuse with Irish Bks. in New York, NY
E-mail: Irishbook@aol.com
Web site: http://www.irishbook.com.

Ironside International Pubs., Inc., *(978-0-935554)* Orders Addr.: P.O. Box 1050, Lorton, VA 22199-1050 USA (SAN 206-2380) Tel 703-493-9120; Fax: 703-493-9424; Edit Addr.: P.O. Box 1050, Lorton, VA 22199-1050 USA (SAN 663-656X)
E-mail: info@ironsidepub.com.

ISBS Publisher Services, 920 NE 58th Ave., Suite 300, Portland, OR 97213-3786 USA (SAN 169-7129) Tel 503-287-3093; Fax: 503-280-8832; Toll Free: 800-944-6190
E-mail: info@isbs.com
Web site: http://www.isbs.com.

ISD, 70 Enterprise Dr., Suite 2, Bristol, CT 06010 USA Tel 860-584-6546; Fax: 860-540-1001
E-mail: orders@isdistribution.com
Web site: https://www.isdistribution.com/.

Islamic Bk. Service, 1209 Cleburne, Hoston, TX 77004 USA (SAN 169-2453) Tel 713-528-1440; Fax: 713-528-1085.

Island Heritage Publishing, *(978-0-89610; 978-0-931548; 978-1-59700)* Div. of The Madden Corp., 94-411 Koaki St., Waipahu, HI 96797 USA (SAN 211-1403) Tel 808-564-8800; Fax: 808-564-8888; Toll Free: 800-468-2800
E-mail: ihorders@welcometotheislands.com
Web site: http://www.welcometotheislands.com.

Islander Group, 269 Pali'i St., Mililani, HI 96789 USA Tel 808-676-0116.

Israel Book Shop, *See* **Israel Bookshop Pubns.**

Israel Bookshop Pubns., *(978-0-9670705; 978-1-931681; 978-1-60091)* 501 Prospect St., No. 97, Lakewood, NJ 08701 USA Tel 732-901-3009; Fax: 732-901-4012; Toll Free: 888-536-7427
E-mail: sales@israelbookshoppublications.com
Web site: http://www.israelbookshoppublications.com.

Itasca Bks., *(978-0-9767054)* Orders Addr.: 5120 Cedar Lake Rd. S., Minneapolis, MN 55416 USA (SAN 855-3823) Tel 952-345-4488; Fax: 952-920-0541; Toll Free: 800-901-3480
E-mail: mjung@itascabooks.com
Web site: http://www.itascabooks.com.

iUniverse, Inc., *(978-0-9665514; 978-1-58348; 978-0-9668591; 978-1-893652; 978-0-595; 978-0-9795279; 978-1-60528; 978-1-4401; 978-1-936236; 978-1-4502; 978-1-4620; 978-1-4697; 978-1-4759; 978-1-4917; 978-1-5320)* Orders Addr.: 1663 Liberty Dr., Suite 300, Bloomington, IN 47403 USA (SAN 254-9425) Toll Free: 800-288-4677
E-mail: post.production@iuniverse.com; book.orders@iuniverse.com; bethany.dirks@iuniverse.com
Web site: http://www.iUniverse.com; http://iuniverse.com.

iUniverse.com, Incorporated, *See* **iUniverse, Inc.**

J & J Bk. Sales, 24871 Pylos Way, Mission Viejo, CA 92691-4668 USA (SAN 253-8075)
E-mail: jacki@hydrasystems.com
Web site: http://www.divanet.com/matilda.

J & L Bk. Co., Orders Addr.: P.O. Box 13100, Spokane, WA 99213 USA (SAN 129-6817) Fax: 509-534-0152; 509-534-7713; Toll Free: 800-288-9756; Edit Addr.: 1710 Trent, Spokane, WA 99220 USA (SAN 243-2145).

J & N Creations, LLC, 48 First St., N., Sauk Centre, MN 56304 USA Tel 320-352-6260.

Jacobob Pr. Distributing, 11035 Ridge Forest Ct., Saint Louis, MO 63126 USA.

JAGCO & Associates Inc., Orders Addr.: 596 Indian Trail Rd. South #227, Indian Trail, NC 28079 USA Tel 802-223-6565.

Jalmar Pr., *(978-0-915190; 978-0-935266; 978-1-880396; 978-1-931061)* Subs. of B. L. Winch & Assocs., P.O. Box 370, Fawnskin, CA 92333-0370 USA (SAN 113-3640) Toll Free: 800-662-9662 (orders)
E-mail: jalmarpress@att.net
Web site: http://jalmarpress.com.

James & Law Co., Orders Addr.: P.O. Box 2468, Clarksburg, WV 26302-2468 USA (SAN 169-894X); Edit Addr.: Middletown Mall I-79 & U. S. 250, Fairmont, WV 26554 USA (SAN 169-8966) Tel 304-624-7401.

James Trading Group, Limited, The, 13 Highview Ave., Orangeburg, NY 10962-2125 USA Toll Free: 800-541-5004
E-mail: sales@thejamestradinggroup.com.

Janway, 11 Academy Rd., Cogan Station, PA 17728 USA (SAN 108-3708) Tel 717-494-1239; Fax: 717-494-1350; Toll Free: 800-877-5242.

Jawbone Publishing Corp., *(978-0-9702959; 978-1-59094)* 1540 Happy Valley Cir., Newnan, GA 30263-4035 USA (SAN 253-5335)
E-mail: marketing@jawbonepublishing.com
Web site: http://www.jawbonepublishing.com.

Jeanies Classics, *(978-0-9609672)* Orders Addr.: 2123 Oxford St., Rockford, IL 61103 USA (SAN 271-7409); Edit Addr.: 2123 Oxford St., Rockford, IL 61103 USA (SAN 271-7395) Tel 815-968-4544.

Jean's Dulcimer Shop & Crying Creek Pubs., P.O. Box 8, Hwy. 32, Cosby, TN 37722 USA (SAN 249-9282) Tel 423-487-5543.

Jech Distributors, 674 Via De La Valle, No. 204, Solana Beach, CA 92075-2462 USA (SAN 107-0258) Tel 619-452-7251.

Jellyroll Productions, *See* **Osborne Enterprises Publishing**

Jenkins Group, Inc., *(978-1-890587; 978-0-9860224)* 121 E. Front St., 4th Flr., Traverse City, MI 49684 USA Tel 231-933-0445; Fax: 231-933-0448; 1129 Woodmere Ave., Traverse City, MI 49686
Web site: http://www.bookpublishing.com.

JIST Publishing, *(978-0-942784; 978-1-56370; 978-1-57112; 978-1-59357; 978-1-63332)* Div. of EMC Publishing, 875 Montreal Way, Saint Paul, MN 55102 USA (SAN 240-2351) Tel 651-290-2800 Toll Free Fax: 800-547-8329
E-mail: info@jist.com
Web site: http://www.jist.com.

JIST Works, Incorporated, *See* **JIST Publishing**

JMS Distribution, 2017 San Mateo St., Richmond, CA 94804 USA.

Jobson, Oliver H., *(978-0-9764988)* 12171 SW 123rd Pl., Miami, FL 33186 USA (SAN 256-5463) Tel 954-260-4914
E-mail: ojobson@gmail.com
Web site: http://www.gpaonline.com.

Johns Hopkins Univ. Pr., *(978-0-8018; 978-1-4214)* Div. of Johns Hopkins Univ., Orders Addr.: P.O. Box 50370, Baltimore, MD 21211-4370 USA; Edit Addr.: 2715 N. Charles St., Baltimore, MD 21218-4319 USA (SAN 202-7348) Fax: 410-516-4189; Toll Free: 800-537-5487
E-mail: webmaster@press.jhu.edu
Web site: http://muse.jhu.edu/; http://www.press.jhu.edu/books/.

Johnson News Agency, P.O. Box 9009, Moscow, ID 83843 USA (SAN 169-1678).

Johnson, Walter J. Inc., *(978-0-8472)* 1 New York Plaza 28th Flr., New York, NY 10004-1901 USA (SAN 209-1828).

Jones, Bob University Press, *See* **BJU Pr.**

Joseph Ruzicka, Incorporated, *See* **Southeast Library Bindery, Inc.**

Journey Pubns., LLC, *(978-0-9671696)* 6709 Ave. A, New Orleans, LA 70124 USA; 1441 Canal St. Suite 318, New Orleans, LA 70112 Do not confuse with companies with the same or similar names in Woodstock, NY, Summerland, CA, Savannah, GA, Avon Park, FL, lacey, WA
E-mail: msl3393@yahoo.com; mlewis@simmonswhite.com.

Joyce Media, Inc., *(978-0-917002)* P.O. Box 57, Acton, CA 93510 USA (SAN 208-7197) Tel 805-269-1169; Fax: 805-269-2139
E-mail: joycemed@pacbell.net
Web site: http://joycemedia.com.

JPL Fulfillment, 3883 Linden Ave., Suite E, Wyoming, MI 49548 USA Toll Free: 877-683-6935
E-mail: orders@jplbooks.com
Web site: https://www.jplfulfillment.com/.

Julia Taylor Ebel, P.O. Box 11, Jamestown, NC 27282 USA
E-mail: ebel@northstate.net.

Junior League of Greensboro Pubns., *(978-0-9605788)* 3101 W. Friendly Ave., Greensboro, NC 27408-7801 USA (SAN 112-9597)
E-mail: Jlgso@aol.com.

Just Us Bks., Inc., *(978-0-940975; 978-1-933491)* 356 Glenwood Ave., 3rd Flr., East Orange, NJ 07017-2108 USA (SAN 664-7413) Tel 973-672-7701
E-mail: justusbook@aol.com
Web site: http://www.justusbooks.com.

K. F. Enterprises, *See* **Production Assocs., Inc.**

K. M. R. Enterprises, *(978-0-9656379)* 5731 Pony Express Trail, Pollock Pines, CA 95726 USA (SAN 299-237X) Tel 530-644-1410.

Kable Media Services, Subs. of AMREP Corp., 505 Park Ave. 7th Fl., New York, NY 10022 USA Tel 212-705-4600; Fax: 212-705-4666; Toll Free: 800-223-6640
E-mail: info@kable.com
Web site: http://www.kable.com/.

Kable News Company, Incorporated, *See* **Kable Media Services**

Kalispell News Agency, P.O. Box 4965, Missoula, MT 59806-4965 USA (SAN 169-4383) Toll Free: 800-955-1266.

Kamkin, Victor, P.O. Box 34583, Bethesda, MD 20827-0583 USA Toll Free: 800-852-6546; 925 Broadway, New York, NY 10010 (SAN 113-7395) Tel 212-673-0776; Fax: 212-673-2473.

Kamkyi Bks., *(978-0-9675031)* Div. of Source International Technology Corp., 939 E. 156th St., Bronx, NY 10455 USA (SAN 630-8392) Tel 718-378-3878 (phone/fax); Toll Free: 888-729-5117
E-mail: source.Intl.Tech@erols.com
Web site: http://www.kamkyibooks.

Kampmann, Kump & Bell, LLC, Orders Addr.: 27 W. 20th St., Suite 1102, New York, NY 10011 USA Tel 212-727-0190; Fax: 212-727-0195
E-mail: midpointny@aol.com.

Kane Miller, *(978-0-916291; 978-1-929132; 978-1-933605; 978-1-935279; 978-1-61067)* Div. of EDC Publishing, Orders Addr.: P.O. Box 470663, Tulsa, OK 74146 USA (SAN 295-8945) Tel 858-456-0540; Fax: 858-456-9641; Edit Addr.: P.O. Box 8515, La Jolla, CA 92038 USA Tel 858-456-0540
E-mail: info@kanemiller.com
Web site: http://www.kanemiller.com; http://www.edcpub.com.

Kane/Miller#Book Publishers, Incorporated, *See* **Kane Miller**

Kansas City Periodical Distributing, Orders Addr.: P.O. Box 14948, Lenexa, KS 66285-4948 USA (SAN 107-9433); Edit Addr.: 9605 Dice Ln., Lenexa, KS 66215 USA Tel 913-541-8600.

Kansas State Reading Circle, 715 W. Tenth St., C-170, Topeka, KS 66601 USA (SAN 169-2771).

Kaplan Publishing, *(978-0-7931; 978-0-88462; 978-0-913864; 978-0-936894; 978-0-942103; 978-1-57410; 978-1-60714; 978-1-60978; 978-1-61865; 978-1-62523; 978-1-5062)* 395 Hudson St., New York, NY 10014 USA (SAN 211-2280); 395 Hudson St., New City, NY 10014
E-mail: deb.darrock@kaplan.com; shayna.webb@kaplan.com; alexander.noya@kaplan.com
Web site: http://www.kaplanpublishing.com.

Kaybee Montessori, Inc., 157 Lagrange Ave., Rochester, NY 14613-1511 USA (SAN 133-1256) Toll Free: 800-732-9304.

Kazi Pubns., Inc., *(978-0-933511; 978-0-935782; 978-1-56744; 978-1-871031; 978-1-930637)* 3023 W. Belmont Ave., Chicago, IL 60618 USA (SAN 162-3397) Tel 773-267-7001; Fax: 773-267-7002
E-mail: info@kazi.org
Web site: http://www.kazi.org.

Kehot Pubn. Society, *(978-0-8266)* Div. of Merkos L'Inyonei Chinuch, Orders Addr.: 291 Kingston Ave., Brooklyn, NY 11213 USA Tel 718-778-0226; Fax: 718-778-4148; Toll Free: 877-463-7567 (877-4MERKOS); Edit Addr.: 770 Eastern Pkwy., Brooklyn, NY 11213 USA (SAN 220-7060) Tel 718-604-2785
E-mail: orders@kehotonline.com; info@kehot.com
Web site: http://www.kehotonline.com.

Keith Distributors, 1230 Macklind Ave., Saint Louis, MO 63110-1432 USA (SAN 112-6377) Toll Free: 800-373-2366
E-mail: keithsbooks@juno.com.

Kensington Publishing Corp., *(978-0-7860; 978-0-8065; 978-0-8184; 978-0-8217; 978-1-55817; 978-1-57566; 978-0-7582; 978-1-4201; 978-1-59983; 978-1-60183; 978-0-9817144; 978-0-9818905; 978-0-9824170; 978-0-9841132; 978-1-61650; 978-1-61773; 978-1-4967; 978-1-5161; 978-1-63573)* 119 W. 40th St., New York, NY 10018 USA Tel 212-407-1500; Fax: 212-935-0699; Toll Free: 800-221-2647; 499 North Canon Dr., Beverly Hills, CA 90210 Tel 310-887-7082
E-mail: jmclean@kensingtonbooks.com; melley@kensingtonbooks.com
Web site: http://www.kensingtonbooks.com.

Kent News Agency, Inc., P.O. Box 1828, Scottsbluff, NE 69363-1828 USA (SAN 169-4448) Tel 303-286-9694; 308-635-2225; Fax: 308-635-1563; Toll Free: 877-290-4740
E-mail: kentrob@prairieweb.com.

Keramos, P.O. Box 7500, Ann Arbor, MI 48107 USA (SAN 169-3670) Tel 313-439-1261.

Kerem Publishing, *(978-1-889727)* 723 N. Orange Dr., Los Angeles, CA 90038 USA (SAN 299-1209).

Kerhulas News Co., P.O. Box 751, Union, SC 29379 USA (SAN 169-7838).

Ketab Corp., *(978-1-883819; 978-1-59584)* Orders Addr.: 1419 Westwood Blvd., Los Angeles, CA 90024 USA (SAN 107-7791) Tel 310-477-7477; Fax: 310-444-7176; Toll Free: 800-367-4726
E-mail: ketab@ketab.com
Web site: http://www.ketab.com.

Key Bk. Service, Inc., *(978-0-934636)* P.O. Box 1434, Fairfield, CT 06430 USA (SAN 169-0671) Tel 203-374-4939; Fax: 203-384-6099.

Keystone Bks. & Media LLC, 12526 Cutten Rd., Suite C, Houston, TX 77066 USA (SAN 990-0160) Tel 281-893-2665; 888-670-2665; Fax: 281-549-2500; Toll Free: 888-670-2665
E-mail: books@keystonebooksmedia.com; matthew@keystonebooksmedia.com
Web site: http://www.keystonebooksmedia.com/.

Khalifah's Booksellers & Assocs., Orders Addr.: 210 East Arrowhead Dr. #2, Charlotte, NC 28213 USA.

Kidsbooks, Inc., 220 Monroe Tpke., No. 560, Monroe, CT 06468-2247 USA (SAN 169-0795).

King Electronics Distributing, 1711 Southeastern Ave., Indianapolis, IN 46201-3990 USA (SAN 107-6795) Tel 317-639-1484; Fax: 317-639-4711.

Kingdom, Inc., P.O. Box 506, Mansfield, PA 16933 USA.

Kinokuniya Bookstores of America Co., Ltd., 1581 Webster St., San Francisco, CA 94115 USA (SAN 121-8441) Tel 415-567-7625; Fax: 415-567-4109.

Kinokuniya Pubns. Service of New York, 1075 Avenue Of The Americas., New York, NY 10018-3701 USA (SAN 157-5414)
E-mail: kinokuniya@kinokuniya.com
Web site: http://www.kinokuniya.com.

Kirkbride, B.B. Bible Co., Inc., *(978-0-88707; 978-0-934854)* P.O. Box 606, Indianapolis, IN 46206-0606 USA (SAN 169-2372) Tel 317-633-1900; Fax: 317-633-1444; Toll Free: 800-428-4385
E-mail: hyperbible@aol.com
Web site: http://www.kirkbride.com.

Kitrick Management Co., Ltd., P.O. Box 15523, Cincinnati, OH 45215 USA (SAN 132-6236) Tel 513-782-2930; Fax: 513-782-2936
E-mail: bachb@aol.com.

Klein's Booklein, Orders Addr.: P.O. Box 968, Fowlerville, MI 48836 USA (SAN 631-3329) Tel 517-223-3964; Fax: 517-223-1314; Toll Free: 800-266-5534; Edit Addr.: One Klein Dr., Fowlerville, MI 48836 USA (SAN 631-3337).

Knopf, Alfred A. Inc., *(978-0-394)* Div. of The Knopf Publishing Group, Orders Addr.: 400 Hahn Rd., Westminster, MD 21157 USA Tel 410-848-1900; Toll Free: 800-726-0600 (orders); Edit Addr.: 1745 Broadway,

New York, NY 10019 USA (SAN 202-5825) Tel 212-782-9000; Toll Free: 800-726-0600
E-mail: customerservice@randomhouse.com
Web site: http://www.randomhouse.com/knopf.

Knox, John Press, *See* **Westminster John Knox Pr.**

KOCH Entertainment, LLC, *(978-0-9721700; 978-1-4172)* 740 Broadway, New York, NY 10003 USA Tel 212-353-8800; Fax: 212-505-3095; 22 Harbor Park Dr., Port Washington, NY 11050 Tel 516-484-1000; Fax: 516-484-4746; Toll Free: 800-332-7553
E-mail: nives@kochent.com; videosales@kochent.com
Web site: http://www.kochvision.com; http://www.kochlorberfilms.com; http://www.kochentertainment.com.

Kodansha America, Inc., *(978-0-87011; 978-1-56836; 978-1-935429; 978-1-61262; 978-1-63236)* 451 Park Ave S. Flr. 7, New York, NY 10016-7390 USA (SAN 201-0526) Toll Free: 800-451-7556
E-mail: t-sumi@kodansha-usa.com; ka-koide@kodansha.co.jp
Web site: http://kodanshacomics.com/; www.kodanshausa.com.

Kodansha USA Publishing, *See* **Kodansha America, Inc.**

Koen Pacific, Orders Addr.: P.O. Box 600, Moorestown, NJ 08057-0600 USA (SAN 631-5593) Toll Free: 800-995-4840
E-mail: info@koenpacific.com.

Kraus Reprint, *See* **Periodicals Service Co.**

Kregel Pubns., *(978-0-8254)* Div. of Kregel, Inc., Orders Addr.: P.O. Box 2607, Grand Rapids, MI 49501-2607 USA (SAN 206-9792) Tel 616-451-4775; Fax: 616-451-9330; Toll Free: 800-733-2607; Edit Addr.: 733 Wealthy St., SE., Grand Rapids, MI 49503-5553 USA (SAN 298-9115)
E-mail: kregelbooks@kregel.com; acquisitions@kregel.com
Web site: http://www.kregel.com.

Krullstone Distributing, LLC, 8751 Clayton Cove Rd., Springville, AL 35146 USA
E-mail: charlotte@krullstonepublishing.com
Web site: http://www.krullstonepublishing.com.

KSG Distributing, 1121 W. Flint Meadow Dr., Kaysville, UT 84037 USA.

Kurian, George Reference Bks., *(978-0-914746)* Orders Addr.: P.O. Box 519, Baldwin Place, NY 10505 USA (SAN 203-1981); Edit Addr.: 3689 Campbell Ct., Yorktown Heights, NY 10598 USA (SAN 110-6236) Tel 914-962-3287.

Kurtzman Bk. Sales Co., 17348 W. 12 Mile Rd., Southfield, MI 48076 USA (SAN 114-0787) Tel 248-557-7230; Fax: 248-557-8705; Toll Free: 800-869-0505.

Kuykendall's Pr., Bookstore Div., P.O. Box 627, Athens, AL 35612-0627 USA (SAN 168-9185) Tel 256-232-1754; Toll Free: 800-781-1754.

L I M Productions, LLC, *(978-1-929617)* 3553 Northdale St., NW, Uniontown, OH 44685-8004 USA Toll Free: 877-628-4532
E-mail: customerservice@limproductions.com
Web site: http://www.limproductions.com.

L L Co., *(978-0-937892)* 1647 Manning Ave., Los Angeles, CA 90024 USA (SAN 110-0009) Tel 310-615-0116; Fax: 310-640-6863; Toll Free: 800-473-3699
E-mail: wallacelab@aol.com.

L M C Source, P.O. Box 720400, San Jose, CA 95172-0400 USA (SAN 631-189X) Tel 408-630-0589; Fax: 408-634-1456; Toll Free: 800-873-3043
E-mail: lmcs@pacbell.net
Web site: http://www.csn.net/~davidl/.

L P C Group, c/o CDS, 193 Edwards Dr., Jackson, TN 38305 USA (SAN 630-5644) Fax: 731-423-1973; 731-935-7731; Toll Free Fax: 800-351-5073; Toll Free: 800-343-4499
E-mail: lpc-info@lpcgroup.com
Web site: http://www.lpcgroup.com.

La Belle News Agency, 814 University Blvd., Steubenville, OH 43952 USA (SAN 169-6858) Tel 740-282-9731.

La Cite French Bks., Div. of The La Cite Group, Inc., P.O. Box 64504, Los Angeles, CA 90064-0504 USA (SAN 168-9789)
E-mail: lacite@aol.com.

La Moderna Poesia, Inc., 5739 NW 7th St., Miami, FL 33126-3105 USA (SAN 169-1139).

Lafayette Bks., P.O. Box 758, Mamaroneck, NY 10543-0758 USA (SAN 135-292X) Tel 914-833-0248.

Lake City Downtown Improvement and Revitalization Team, P.O. Box 973 231 N. Silver St., Lake City, CO 81235 USA Tel 970-944-3478
E-mail: ed@lakecitydirt.com.

Lakeport Distributors, Inc., 139 W. 18th St., P.O. Box 6195, Erie, PA 16501 USA (SAN 169-734X).

Lambda Pubs., Inc., *(978-0-915361; 978-1-55774)* 3709 13th Ave., Brooklyn, NY 11218-3622 USA (SAN 291-0640) Tel 718-972-5449; Fax: 718-972-6307
E-mail: judaica@email.msn.com.

Lambert Bk. Hse., Inc., *(978-0-89315)* 4139 Parkway Dr., Florence, AL 35630-6347 USA (SAN 180-5169) Tel 256-764-4098; 256-764-4090; Fax: 256-766-9200; Toll Free: 800-551-8511
E-mail: info@lambertbookhouse.com
Web site: http://www.lambertbookhouse.com.

Landmark Audiobooks, 4865 Sterling Dr., Boulder, CO 80301 USA Fax: 303-443-3775
Web site: http://www.landmarkaudio.com.

Landmark Bk. Co., *(978-0-929194)* 131 Hicks St., Brooklyn, NY 11201-2318 USA (SAN 169-5843).

Lang, Peter Publishing, Inc., *(978-0-8204; 978-1-4331; 978-1-4539; 978-1-4540; 978-1-4541; 978-1-4542)* Subs. of Verlag Peter Lang AG (SZ), 29 Broadway, New York, NY 10006 USA (SAN 241-5534) Tel 212-647-7700; 212-647-7706 (Outside USA); Fax: 212-647-7707; Toll Free: 800-770-5264
E-mail: customerservice@plang.com
Web site: http://www.peterlangusa.com.

Langenscheidt Publishing Group, *(978-0-88729; 978-1-58573)* Subs. of Langenscheidt KG, Orders Addr.: 15 Tyger River Dr., Duncan, SC 29334 USA Fax: 888-773-7979; Toll Free: 800-432-6277; Edit Addr.: 36-36 33rd St., Long Island City, NY 11106 USA
Web site: http://www.americanmap.com; http://www.langenscheidt.com.

Larousse Kingfisher Chambers, Inc., *(978-0-7534; 978-1-85697)* 215 Park Ave., S., New York, NY 10003 USA (SAN 297-7540); 181 Ballardvale St., Wilmington, MA 01887.

Las Vegas News Agency, 2312 Silver Bluff Ct., Las Vegas, NV 89134-6092 USA.

Lash Distributors, 7106 Geoffrey Way, Frederick, MD 21704 USA (SAN 169-3131).

Last Gasp Eco-Funnies, Incorporated, *See* **Last Gasp of San Francisco**

Last Gasp of San Francisco, *(978-0-86719)* Orders Addr.: 777 Florida St., San Francisco, CA 94110 USA (SAN 216-8308); Edit Addr.: 777 Florida St., San Francisco, CA 94110-2025 USA (SAN 170-3242) Tel 415-824-6636; Fax: 415-824-1836; Toll Free: 800-366-5121
E-mail: colin@lastgasp.com
Web site: http://www.lastgasp.com.

Laster, Larry D. Old & Rare Bks., Prints & Maps, 2416 Maplewood Ave., Winston-Salem, NC 27103 USA (SAN 112-9600) Tel 336-724-7544; Fax: 336-724-9055.

Latcorp, Ltd., 10 Norden Ln., Huntington Station, NY 11746 USA (SAN 159-8910) Tel 516-271-0548; Fax: 516-549-8849.

Latin American Book Source, Inc., 681 Anita St., Suit 102, Chula Vista, CA 91911-4663 USA
Web site: http://www.latambooks.com/.

Latin Trading Corp., 539 H St., Chula Vista, CA 91910 USA (SAN 630-2963) Tel 619-427-7867; Fax: 619-476-1817; Toll Free: 800-257-7248
E-mail: info@latintradingbooks.com
Web site: http://www.latintradingbooks.com.

Latta, J. S. Incorporated, *See* **Latta's**

Latta's, 1502 Fourth Ave., P.O. Box 2668, Huntington, WV 25726 USA (SAN 169-8982) Fax: 304-525-5038; Toll Free: 800-624-3501.

Laurus Co., The, Orders Addr.: 524 Guinevere Court, McDonough, GA 30252 USA (SAN 858-608X) Tel 678-814-4047; Fax: 678-272-7255; Toll Free: 800-596-7370
E-mail: thelaurusco@charter.net
Web site: http://www.thelauruscompany.com.

LD Bks., Inc., *(978-0-9772669; 978-0-9785897; 978-1-939048; 978-1-940281; 978-1-943387)* 8313 NW 68th St., Miami, FL 33166 USA (SAN 631-8088) Tel 305-406-2292; Fax: 305-406-2293
E-mail: vilmac@ldbooks.com; sales@ldbooks.com
Web site: http://www.sinlimites.net; http://www.ldbooks.com.

LEA Bk. Distributors (Libros Espana y America), *(978-1-883110)* 170-23 83rd Ave., Jamaica Hills, NY 11432 USA (SAN 170-5407) Tel 718-291-9891; Fax: 718-291-9830
E-mail: leabook@idt.net
Web site: http://www.leabooks.com.

Learning Collection, The, 145 S. Glencoe St., Denver, CO 80246-1152 USA (SAN 630-8287).

Learning Connection, The, *(978-1-56831)* Orders Addr.: 4100 Silver Star Rd. Ste. D, Orlando, FL 32808-4618 USA Toll Free: 800-218-8489
Web site: http://www.tlconnection.com.

Learning Services, 2095 Laura St. Ste. H, Springfield, OR 97477-2285 USA Toll Free: 800-877-3278.

Lectorum Pubns., Inc., *(978-0-9625162; 978-1-880507; 978-1-930332; 978-1-933032; 978-1-941802; 978-1-63245)* Orders Addr.: 205 Chubb Ave, Lyndhurst, NJ 07071 USA (SAN 990-0802) Tel 201-559-2232; Edit Addr.: 205 Chubb Ave., Lyndhurst, NJ 07071 USA (SAN 860-0597) Tel 201-559-2200; Fax: 201-559-2201; Toll Free Fax: 877-532-8676; Toll Free: 800-345-5946
E-mail: acorrea@lectorum.com
Web site: http://www.lectorum.com; http://www.librerialectorum.com.

Lee Bks., *(978-0-939818)* Div. of Lee S. Cole & Assocs., Inc., 524 San Anselmo Ave., No 215, San Anselmo, CA 94960-2614 USA (SAN 110-649X) Tel 415-456-4388; Fax: 415-456-7532; Toll Free: 800-828-3550 Do not confuse with other companies with the same or similar names in Jacksonville, FL, Columbia, SC
E-mail: lcs@lsc-associates.com
Web site: http://www.lsc-associates.com.

Left Bank Bks., 92 Pike St., Seattle, WA 98101 USA
Web site: http://www.leftbankbooks.com.

Left Bank Books Distribution & Publishing, *See* **Left Bank Distribution**

Left Bank Distribution, *(978-0-939306)* 92 Pike St., Seattle, WA 98101-2025 USA (SAN 216-5368)
E-mail: leftbank@leftbankbooks.com
Web site: http://www.leftbankbooks.com.

Legato Pubs. Group, Orders Addr.: 1700 4th St., Berkeley, CA 94710 USA Toll Free: 800-343-4499
Web site: http://www.legatopublishersgroup.com/.

Leisure Arts, Inc., *(978-0-942237; 978-1-57486; 978-1-60140; 978-1-60900; 978-1-4647)* Orders Addr.: 5701 Ranch Dr., Little Rock, AR 72223 USA (SAN 666-9565) Tel 501-868-8800; Fax: 501-868-1001; Toll Free Fax: 877-710-5603; Toll Free: 800-643-8030 (customer service); 800-526-5111
E-mail: hermine_linz@leisurearts.com
Web site: http://www.leisurearts.com.

Leman Pubns., Inc., *(978-0-943721; 978-0-9602970)* Div. of Rodale Pr. Co., Box 4100, 741 Corporate Cir., Suite A, Golden, CO 80401-5622 USA (SAN 213-3415) Fax: 303-277-0370; Toll Free: 800-877-3775.

Leonard, Hal Corp., *(978-0-634; 978-0-7935; 978-0-87910; 978-0-87930; 978-0-88188; 978-0-931340; 978-0-9607350; 978-1-56516; 978-1-57467; 978-1-4234; 978-1-936098; 978-1-61713; 978-1-61774; 978-1-61780; 978-1-4584; 978-1-4768; 978-1-4803; 978-1-62906; 978-1-4950; 978-1-5400)* Orders Addr.: P.O. Box 13819, Milwaukee, WI 53213-0819 USA Tel 414-774-3630; Fax: 414-774-3259; Toll Free: 800-524-4425; Edit Addr.: 7777 W. Bluemound Rd., Milwaukee, WI 53213 USA (SAN 239-250X) Tel 414-777-3630; Fax: 414-774-4176
E-mail: halinfo@halleonard.com
Web site: http://www.halleonard.com.

Leonardo Press, *See* **Firenze Pr.**

Lerner Publishing Group, *(978-0-7613; 978-0-8225; 978-0-87406; 978-0-87614; 978-0-929371; 978-0-930494; 978-1-57505; 978-1-58013; 978-1-58196; 978-1-4677; 978-1-5124; 978-1-5415)* Orders Addr.: 1251 Washington Ave. N., Minneapolis, MN 55401 USA (SAN 256-0283) Tel 612-332-3344; Fax: 612-204-9208; Edit Addr.: 241 First Ave., N., Minneapolis, MN 55401 USA (SAN 201-0828) Tel 612-332-3344; Fax: 612-215-6230; Toll Free Fax: 800-332-1132; Toll Free: 800-328-4929
E-mail: info@lernerbooks.com; custserve@lernerbooks.com
Web site: http://www.lernerbooks.com; http://www.karben.com.

Levant Distributors, Incorporated, *See* **Levant USA, Inc.**

Levant USA, Inc., 145 Hook Creek Blvd. BLDG B6B3, Valley Stream, NY 11581-2223 USA (SAN 631-1970)
E-mail: levantusa@cs.com.

Levine, J. Religious Supplies, Five W. 30th St., New York, NY 10001 USA (SAN 169-5878) Tel 212-695-6888; Fax: 212-643-1044
E-mail: sales@levine.judica.com.

Levy, Charles Company, *See* **Levy Home Entertainment, Ltd.**

Levy Home Entertainment, *See* **Readerlink Distribution Services, LLC**

Levy Home Entertainment, Ltd., Div. of Charles Levy Co., 1420 Kensington Rd. Ste. 300, Oak Brook, IL 60523-2164 USA (SAN 159-835X).

Lewis International, Inc., *(978-0-9666771; 978-1-930983)* 2201 NW 102nd Pl., No. 1, Miami, FL 33172 USA Tel 305-436-7984; Fax: 305-436-7985; Toll Free: 800-259-5962.

Lewis, John W. Enterprises, 168 Perez St., P.O. Box 3375, Santurce, PR 00936 USA (SAN 169-9334) Tel 809-722-0104.

Lexicon Pubns., Inc., P.O. Box 1737, Danbury, CT 06810 USA (SAN 205-664X) Tel 203-796-2540.

LEXIS Law Publishing, *See* **LEXIS Publishing**

LEXIS Publishing, *(978-0-327; 978-0-406; 978-0-409; 978-0-672; 978-0-87215; 978-0-87473; 978-0-88063; 978-0-930273; 978-1-55834; 978-1-56257)* Div. of Reed Elsevier, Orders Addr.: P.O. Box 7587, Charlottesville, VA 22906-7587 USA Tel 434-972-7600; Fax: 434-972-7686; Toll Free Fax: 800-643-1280; Toll Free: 800-446-3410; Edit Addr.: 701 E. Water St., Charlottesville, VA 22902 USA Do not confuse with Lexis Publishing, Malabar, FL
Web site: http://www.lexisnexis.com.

Liberation Distributors, *(978-0-89928)* P.O. Box 5341, Chicago, IL 60680 USA (SAN 169-880X) Tel 773-248-3442.

Library & Educational Services, P.O. Box 288, Berrien Springs, MI 49103 USA Tel 269-695-1800; Fax: 616-695-8500
E-mail: libraryanded@juno.com.

Library Bk. Selection Service, P.O. Box 277, Bloomington, IL 61702-0277 USA (SAN 169-1740).

Library Integrated Solutions & Assocs., P.O. Box 6189, Mckinney, TX 75071-5105 USA
Web site: http://www.llibs.com.

Library Sales of N.J., *(978-1-888032)* Orders Addr.: P.O. Box 335, Garwood, NJ 07027-0335 USA Tel 908-232-1446; Edit Addr.: 607 S. Chestnut St., Westfield, NJ 07090-1369 USA
E-mail: Librarysalesofnj@aol.com.

Library Video Co., *(978-1-4171)* P.O. Box 580, Wynnewood, PA 19096 USA (SAN 631-3205) Fax: 610-645-4050; Toll Free: 800-843-3620
E-mail: cs@libraryvideo.com
Web site: http://www.libraryvideo.com.

LibreDigital, 1835-B Kramer Ln. Suite 150, Austin, TX 78758 USA; 18 Soho Sq., London, W1D3QL
E-mail: support@libredigital.com.

Libreria Bereana, 1825 San Alejandro, Urb San Ignacio, Rio Piedras, PR 00927-6819 USA (SAN 169-9288) Tel 809-764-6175.

Libreria Distribuidora Universal, 3090 SW 8th St., Miami, FL 33135 USA Tel 305-642-3234.

Libreria Universal, Inc., *(978-1-881375)* Orders Addr.: P.O. Box 1480, Mayaguez, PR 00680 USA; Edit Addr.: 55 N. Post St., Mayaguez, PR 00680 USA Tel 787-832-6041; Fax: 787-832-8477
E-mail: colom@coqui.net; nikkynicole2004@gmail.com.

Libros de Espana y America, *See* **LEA Bk. Distributors (Libros Espana y America)**

Libros Sin Fronteras, P.O. Box 2085, Olympia, WA 98507 USA Tel 360-357-4332; Fax: 360-357-4964
E-mail: info@librossinfronteras.com
Web site: http://www.librossinfronteras.com.

LifeWay Christian Resources, *(978-0-7673; 978-0-633; 978-1-4158; 978-1-4300; 978-1-5359)* Div. of The Southern Baptist Convention, One Lifeway Plaza, Nashville, TN 37234 USA Tel 615-251-2000; Fax: 615-277-8221 (product info., ordering, order tracking); 615-251-2626 (shipping/transportation); Toll Free Fax: 800-296-4036; Toll Free: 800-458-2772 (product info., ordering); 800-251-3225
E-mail: customerservice@lifeway.com; support.lifeway.com
Web site: http://www.lifewaystores.com; http://www.lifeway.com; http://www.bhpublishinggroup.com.

Light & Life Publishing Co., *(978-0-937032; 978-1-880971; 978-1-933654)* Orders Addr.: 4808 Park Glen Rd., Minneapolis, MN 55416 USA (SAN 213-8565) Tel 952-925-3888; Fax: 888-925-3918; Toll Free Fax: 888-925-3918
E-mail: ivy@light-n-life.com
Web site: http://www.light-n-life.com.

Light Impressions Corp., *(978-0-87992)* Orders Addr.: P.O. Box 940, Rochester, NY 14603-0940 USA (SAN 169-619X) Toll Free Fax: 800-826-5539; Toll Free: 800-828-6216; Edit Addr.: P.O. Box 22708, Rochester, NY 14692-2708 USA
Web site: http://www.lightimpresionsdirect.com.

Light Technology Publishing, *See* **Light Technology Publishing, LLC**

Light Technology Publishing, LLC, *(978-0-929385; 978-1-891824; 978-1-62233)* Orders Addr.: P.O. Box 3540, Flagstaff, AZ 86003 USA (SAN 249-1389) Tel 928-526-1345; Toll Free: 800-450-0985; Edit Addr.: 4030 E. Huntington Dr., Flagstaff, AZ 86004 USA (SAN 990-0101)
E-mail: publishing@lighttechnology.net; art@lighttechnology.net; newmedia@lighttechnology.com; jon.campbell@lighttechnology.com
Web site: http://www.sedonajournal.com; http://lighttechnology.com.

Lightning Source, Inc., Orders Addr.: 1246 Heil Quaker Blvd., LaVergne, TN 37086 USA (SAN 179-6976) Tel 615-213-4595; Fax: 615-213-4426; 150 Fieldcrest Ave. Lightning Source, Edison, NJ 08837 (SAN 920-4288); 4260 Port Union Rd. No. 100 Lightning Source, Fairfield, OH 45011 (SAN 920-4296); 150 Fieldcrest Ave Ingram Book - IBC, Edison, NJ 08837 (SAN 920-430X) Tel 615-413-4476; 4260 Port Union Rd. No. 100 Ingram Book - IBC, Fairfield, OH 45011 (SAN 920-4318); 150 Fieldcrest Ave Ingram Publisher Services, Edison, NJ 08837 (SAN 920-4431); 4260 Port Union Rd. No 100 Ingram Publisher Services, Fairfield, OH 45011 (SAN 920-444X); 860 Nestle Way - IBC, Breinigsville, PA 18031 (SAN 920-6264); 860 Nestle Way-IPS, Breinigsville, PA 18031 (SAN 920-6272); 3145 S. Northpointe Dr. N. Pointe Business Pk., Fresno, CA 93725 (SAN 920-6280); 3145 S Northpointe Dr - IPS, Fresno, CA 93725 (SAN 920-7937); 3145 S Northpointe Dr - IBC, Fresno, CA 93725 (SAN 920-7945)
E-mail: terri.jones@lightningsource.com.

Liguori Pubns., *(978-0-7648; 978-0-89243)* One Liguori Dr., Liguori, MO 63057-9999 USA (SAN 202-6783) Tel 636-464-2500; Fax: 636-464-8449; Toll Free Fax: 800-325-9526; Toll Free: 800-325-9521 (orders)
E-mail: liguori@liguori.org
Web site: http://www.liguori.org.

Likely Story Bookfairs, A, 7210 SW 57th Ave., Suite 207-A, South Miami, FL 33143 USA (SAN 631-1210) Tel 305-668-9183; Fax: 305-667-3323.

Lilly News Agency, P.O. Box 280077, Memphis, TN 38168-0077 USA (SAN 168-9452).

Limerock Bks., Inc., P.O. Box 57, New Canaan, CT 06840 USA (SAN 630-8708) Tel 203-322-5352; Fax: 203-322-2182 Do not confuse with Limerock Books, Thomaston, ME
E-mail: limerockbk@aol.com
Web site: http://www.netpocus.com/limerock.

Linden Publishing Co., Inc., *(978-0-941936; 978-1-933502; 978-1-61035)* 2006 S. Mary, Fresno, CA 93721 USA (SAN 238-6089) Tel 559-233-6633 (phone/fax); Toll Free: 800-345-4447 (orders only) Do not confuse with Linden Publishing in Avon, NY
E-mail: richard@lindenpub.com
Web site: http://www.lindenpub.com.

Linden Tree Children's Records & Bks., 265 State St., Los Altos, CA 94022 USA (SAN 131-744X) Tel 415-949-3390; Fax: 415-949-0346.

Linden Tree Children's Records & Books, *See* **Linden Tree Children's Records & Bks.**

Lindsay News & Photo Service, Inc., 868 Lockport Rd., Youngstown, NY 14174-1139 USA (SAN 169-6092).

Ling's International Bks., Orders Addr.: P.O. Box 82684, San Diego, CA 92138 USA (SAN 169-0116) Tel 619-292-8104; Fax: 619-292-8207; Edit Addr.: 3396 Via Cabo Verde., Escondido, CA 92029-7459 USA.

Linx Educational Publishing, Inc., *(978-1-891818; 978-0-9797510)* P.O. Box 50009, Jacksonville Beach, FL 32240 USA Tel 904-241-1861; Fax: 904-241-3279; Toll Free Fax: 888-546-9338; Toll Free: 800-717-5469
E-mail: mimi@lixedu.com; info@linxedu.com
Web site: http://www.linxedu.com.

Lippincott Williams & Wilkins, *(978-0-316; 978-0-397; 978-0-683; 978-0-7817; 978-0-8067; 978-0-8121; 978-0-88167; 978-0-89004; 978-0-89313; 978-0-89640; 978-0-911216; 978-1-881063; 978-1-60547; 978-1-60831; 978-1-60929; 978-1-4698)* Orders Addr.: P.O. Box 1620, Hagerstown, MD 21741 USA Fax: 301-223-2400; Toll Free: 800-638-3030; Edit Addr.: 530 Walnut St., Philadelphia, PA 19106-3621 USA (SAN 201-0933) Tel 215-521-8300; Fax: 215-521-8902; Toll Free: 800-638-3030; 351 W. Camden St., Baltimore, MD 21201 Tel 410-528-4000; 410-528-4209; 345 Hudson St., 16th Flr., New York, NY 10014 Tel 212-886-1200; 16522 Hunters Green Pkwy., Hagerstown, MD 21740 Tel 301-223-2300; Fax: 301-223-2398; Toll Free: 800-638-3030
E-mail: custserv@lww.com; orders@lww.com
Web site: http://www.lww.com.

Lippincott-Raven Publishers, *See* **Lippincott Williams & Wilkins**

Listen & Live Audio, Inc., *(978-1-885408; 978-1-931953; 978-1-59316)* Orders Addr.: P.O. Box 817, Roseland, NJ 07068 USA Tel 201-558-9000; Fax: 201-558-9800; Toll Free: 800-653-9400; Edit Addr.: 1700 Manhattan Ave., Union City, NJ 07087-5473 USA
E-mail: Alfred@Listenandlive.com
Web site: http://www.listenandlive.com.

Literal Bk. Distributors: Bks. in Spanish, Orders Addr.: P.O. Box 7113, Langley Park, MD 20787 USA; Edit Addr.: 7705 Georgia Ave. NW, Suite 102, Washington, DC

20012 USA (SAN 113-2784) Tel 202-723-8688; Fax: 202-882-6592; Toll Free: 800-366-8680.

Little Brown & Co., *(978-0-316; 978-0-8212; 978-0-7595)* Div. of Hachette Bk. Group, Orders Addr.: 3 Center Plaza, Boston, MA 02108-2084 USA (SAN 630-7248) Tel 617-227-0730; Toll Free Fax: 800-286-9471; Toll Free: 800-759-0190; Edit Addr.: 237 Park Ave., New York, NY 10017 USA (SAN 200-2205) Tel 212-364-0600; Fax: 212-364-0952
E-mail: customer.service@hbgusa.com
Web site: http://www.hachettebookgroup.com.

Little Dania's Juvenile Promotions, Div. of Booksmith Promotional Co., 100 Paterson Plank Rd., Jersey City, NJ 07307 USA (SAN 169-5681) Tel 201-659-2317; Fax: 201-659-3631
E-mail: hochberga@aol.com.

Little Professor Bk. Ctrs., Inc., P.O. Box 3160, Ann Arbor, MI 48106-3160 USA (SAN 144-2503) Toll Free: 800-899-6232.

Llewellyn Pubns., *(978-0-7387; 978-0-87542; 978-1-56718)* Div. of Llewellyn Worldwide, Ltd., Orders Addr.: 2143 Wooddale Dr., Woodbury, MN 55125-2989 USA Tel 651-291-1970; Fax: 651-291-1908; Toll Free: 800-843-6666
E-mail: sales@llewellyn.com
Web site: http://www.llewellyn.com; http://www.midnightinkbooks.com.

Llewellyn Worldwide Ltd., Orders Addr.: 2143 Wooddale Dr., Woodbury, MN 55125-2989 USA Tel 651-291-1970; Fax: 651-291-1908
E-mail: sales@llewellyn.com
Web site: http://www.llewellyn.com.

Login Fulfillment Services, *See* **L P C Group**

Lone Pine Publishing USA, Orders Addr.: 1808 B St., NW Suite 140, Auburn, WA 98001 USA (SAN 859-0427) Tel 253-394-0400; Fax: 253-394-0405; Toll Free Fax: 800-548-1169; Toll Free: 800-518-3541
E-mail: mikec@lonepinepublishing.com
Web site: http://www.lonepinepublishing.com; http://www.companyscoming.com/; http://overtimebooks.com; http://www.folklorepublishing.com/.

Long Beach Bks., Inc., P.O. Box 179, Long Beach, NY 11561-0179 USA (SAN 164-632X) Tel 718-471-5934.

Longleaf Services, Orders Addr.: P.O. Box 8895, Chapel Hill, NC 27515-8895 USA Tel 800-848-6224; Fax: 800-272-6817; 919-962-2704 (24 hours)
E-mail: customerservice@longleafservices.org; orders@longleafservices.org
Web site: http://www.longleafservices.org/.

Longstreet Pr., Inc., *(978-0-929264; 978-1-56352)* Subs. of Cox Newspapers, Inc., 325 N. Milledge Ave., Athens, GA 30601-3805 USA (SAN 248-7640)
E-mail: scottbard@gmail.com.

Looseleaf Law Pubns., Inc., *(978-0-930137; 978-1-889031; 978-1-932777; 978-1-60885)* Orders Addr.: P.O. Box 650042, Fresh Meadows, NY 11365-0042 USA Tel 718-359-5559; Fax: 718-539-0941; Toll Free: 800-647-5547
E-mail: info@looseleaflaw.com; lynette@looseleaflaw.com
Web site: http://www.looseleaflaw.com.

Lord's Line, *(978-0-915952)* 1065 Lomita Blvd., No. 434, Harbor City, CA 90710-1944 USA (SAN 169-0051).

Lorenz Corp., The, *(978-0-7877; 978-0-88335; 978-0-89328; 978-1-55863; 978-1-57310; 978-1-885564; 978-1-4291)* 501 E. Third St., Dayton, OH 45401-0802 USA (SAN 208-7413) Tel 937-228-6118; Fax: 937-223-2042; Toll Free: 800-444-1144
E-mail: service@lorenz.com
Web site: http://www.lorenz.com.

Los Angeles Mart, The, 1933 S. Broadway, Suite 665, Los Angeles, CA 90007 USA (SAN 168-9797) Tel 213-748-6449; Fax: 714-523-0796.

Lotus Lights Publications, *See* **Lotus Pr.**

Lotus Pr., *(978-0-910261; 978-0-914955; 978-0-940676; 978-0-940985; 978-0-941524; 978-1-60869)* Div. of Lotus Brands, Inc., P.O. Box 325, Twin Lakes, WI 53181 USA (SAN 239-1120) Tel 262-889-2461; Fax: 262-889-8591; Toll Free: 800-824-6396 Do not confuse with companies with the same or similar name in Lotus, CA, Westerville, OH, Bokeelia, FL, Brattleboro, VT, Detroit, MI, Tobyhanna, PA
E-mail: lotuspress@lotuspress.com
Web site: http://www.lotuspress.com.

Louisville Distributors, *See* **United Magazine**

Louisville News Co., P.O. Box 36, Columbia, KY 42728 USA (SAN 169-281X) Tel 502-384-3444; Fax: 502-384-9324.

Lubrecht & Cramer, Ltd., *(978-0-934454; 978-0-945345)* P.O. Box 3110, Port Jervis, NY 12771-0176 USA; Orders Addr.: 2749 Albany Post Rd., Montgomery, NY 12549 USA (SAN 214-1256) Toll Free: 800-920-9334; Edit Addr.: 350 Fifth Ave., Suite 3304, New York, NY 10118-0069 USA
E-mail: lubrecht@frontiernet.net; books@lubrechtcramer.com
Web site: http://www.lubrechtcramer.com.

Luciano Bks., 13111 NW Le Jeune, Opa Locka, FL 33054 USA (SAN 631-2829) Tel 305-769-3103.

Ludington News Co., 1600 E. Grand Blvd., Detroit, MI 48211-3195 USA (SAN 169-3751) Tel 313-929-7600.

Lukeman Literary Management, Ltd., *(978-0-9829537; 978-0-9839778; 978-0-9849753; 978-1-939416; 978-1-63291; 978-1-64029)* 157 Bedford Ave., Brooklyn, NY 11211 USA Tel 718-599-8988; Fax: 775-264-2189.

Lulu Enterprises Inc., *See* **Lulu Pr., Inc.**

Lulu Pr., Inc., *(978-1-4116; 978-1-84728; 978-1-4303; 978-1-4357; 978-1-60552; 978-0-557; 978-1-4583; 978-1-257; 978-1-105; 978-1-300; 978-1-4834; 978-1-304; 978-1-312; 978-1-329; 978-1-365; 978-1-5342)* 627 Davis Dr. Suite 300, Morrisville, NC 27560 USA; 26-28 Hammersmith Grove, London, W6 7BA
E-mail: sparker@lulu.com.

Lushena Bks., *(978-1-930097; 978-1-63182)* 607 Country Club Dr., Unit E, Bensenville, IL 60106 USA (SAN 630-5105) Tel 630-238-8708; Fax: 630-238-8824
E-mail: Lushenabks@yahoo.com
Web site: http://www.lushenabks.com/.

Lyrical Liquor Productions, Orders Addr.: 7212 15th Ave., Takoma Park, MD 20912 USA Tel 202-723-1317
E-mail: llp@speakeasypublishing.com.

M & J Bk. Fair Service, 2307 Sherwood Cir., Minneapolis, MN 55431 USA (SAN 169-4030).

M & M News Agency, Orders Addr.: P.O. Box 1129, La Salle, IL 61301 USA (SAN 169-2062) Fax: 815-223-2828; Toll Free: 800-245-6247.

M L E S, *See* **Pathway Bk. Service**

Ma'ayan, *See* **WellSpring Bks.**

MacGregor News Agency, 1733 Industrial Park Dr., Mount Pleasant, MI 48858 USA (SAN 169-3921) Toll Free: 800-626-1982.

Mackin Bk. Co., 615 Travelers Trail W., Burnsville, MN 55337 USA (SAN 631-3442).

Mackin Educational Resources, *(978-1-62170; 978-1-62353)* 3505 CR 42 W., Burnsville, MN 55306 USA Tel 800-245-9540
E-mail: developers@mackin.com
Web site: http://www.mackin.com/.

Mackin Library Media, 3505 County Rd. 42 W., Burnsville, MN 55306-3804 USA (SAN 134-8795) Toll Free: 800-245-9540
E-mail: mackin@mackin.com
Web site: http://www.mackin.com.

Macmillan, *(978-0-374; 978-1-4668; 978-1-68274)* Div. of Holtzbrinck Publishing, Orders Addr.: 16365 James Madison Hwy., Gordonsville, VA 22942 USA (SAN 631-5011) Tel 540-672-7600; Fax: 540-672-7664; 540-672-7540 (Customer Service); Toll Free Fax: 800-672-2054 (Order Dept.); Toll Free: 888-330-8477; Edit Addr.: 175 Fifth Ave., 20th Flr., New York, NY 10010 USA Tel 212-674-5151; Fax: 212-677-6487; Toll Free Fax: 800-258-2769; Toll Free: 800-488-5233
E-mail: customerservice@mpsvirginia.com
Web site: http://www.macmillan.com.

Macmillan USA, *See* **Alpha Bks.**

MacRae's Indian Bk. Distributor, 1605 Cole St., P.O. Box 652, Enumclaw, WA 98022 USA (SAN 157-5473) Tel 360-825-3737.

Madden Corp., The, *(978-1-61710)* 94-411 Koaki St., Waipahu, HI 96797 USA.

Madison Art Ctr., Inc., *(978-0-913883)* 222 W. Washington Ave. Ste. 350, Madison, WI 53703-2719 USA
E-mail: mac@itis.com
Web site: http://www.madisonartcenter.org.

Magazine Distributors, Inc., 15 Sparks St., Plainville, CT 06062 USA (SAN 169-0817).

Magazines, Inc., 1135 Hammond St., Bangor, ME 04401 USA (SAN 169-3034) Tel 207-942-8237; Fax: 207-942-9226; Toll Free: 800-649-9224 (in Maine)
E-mail: pam@mint.net.

Mahoning Valley Distributing Agency, Inc., 2556 Rush Blvd., Youngstown, OH 44507 USA Tel 330-788-6162; Fax: 330-788-9046.

Main Trail Productions, P.O. Box 365, Clearwater, MN 55320 USA.

Maine Writers & Pubs. Alliance, *(978-0-9618592)* P.O. Box 9301, Portland, ME 04104-9301 USA (SAN 224-2303).

Majic Enterprises, 2232 S. 11th St., Niles, MI 49120-4410 USA (SAN 169-8508).

Majors, J. A. Co., Orders Addr.: 1401 Lakeway Dr., Lewisville, TX 75057 USA (SAN 169-8117) Tel 972-353-1100; Fax: 972-353-1300; Toll Free: 800-633-1851
E-mail: dallas@majors.com
Web site: http://www.majors.com.

Majors Scientific Bks., Inc., P.O. Box 35705, Dallas, TX 75235-0705 USA Toll Free: 800-633-1851
E-mail: dallas@majors.com
Web site: http://www.majors.com.

Manchester News Co., Inc., P.O. Box 4838, Manchester, NH 03108-4838 USA (SAN 169-4480).

Manhattan Publishing Co., Div. of U.S. & Europe Bks., Inc., P.O. Box 850, Croton-on-Hudson, NY 10520 USA (SAN 113-7476) Tel 914-271-5194; Fax: 914-271-5856
Web site: http://www.manhattanpublishing.com.

Manitowoc News Agency, 907 S. Eighth St., Manitowoc, WI 54220 USA (SAN 159-9046).

Manning's Bks. & Prints, 580M Crespi Dr., Pacifica, CA 94044 USA (SAN 157-5384) Fax: 650-355-1851
E-mail: manningsbks@aol.com
Web site: http://www.printsoldandrare.com.

Many Feathers Bks. & Maps, 2626 W. Indian School Rd., Phoenix, AZ 85017 USA (SAN 158-8877) Tel 602-266-1043; Toll Free: 800-279-7652.

Map Link, *See* **Benchmark LLC**

Maple Press Co., 1000 Strickler Rd., Mount Joy, PA 17552 USA Tel 717-653-5483; Edit Addr.: P.O. Box 2695, York, PA 17406 USA Tel 717-764-5911; Fax: 717-764-4702; 480 Willow Springs Ln., York, PA 17406.

Marangio, Charles F. Distribution, Orders Addr.: P.O. Box 3643, Sonoro, CA 95370 USA (SAN 631-3965) Tel 209-533-0997; Edit Addr.: 659 Sanguinetti Rd., Sonoro, CA 95370 USA (SAN 631-3973).

Marco Bk. Co., *(978-0-9710756; 978-0-9729765)* 60 Industrail Rd., Lodi, NJ 07644 USA Tel 973-458-0485; Fax: 973-458-5289; Toll Free: 800-842-4234
E-mail: everbind5@aol.com.

Marco Bk. Distributors, *(978-0-88298)* 60 Industrial Rd., Lodi, NJ 07644 USA (SAN 169-5142) Tel 973-458-0485; Fax: 973-458-5289; Toll Free: 800-842-4234
Web site: http://www.everbind.com.

MAR*CO Products, Inc., *(978-1-57543; 978-1-884063)* Orders Addr.: 1443 Old York Rd., Warminster, PA 18974 USA Tel 215-956-0313; Fax: 215-956-9041; Toll Free: 800-448-2197
E-mail: csfunk@marcoproducts.com; marcoproducts@comcast.net
Web site: http://www.store.yahoo.com/marcoproducts; http://www.marcoproducts.com.

Marcus Wholesale, P.O. Box 1618, R49 E. Hwy. 4, Murphys, CA 95247 USA (SAN 185-0296).

Mardelva News Co., Inc., 8999 Ocean Hwy., Delmar, MD 21875 USA (SAN 169-3247) Tel 410-742-8613; Fax: 410-742-2616.

Mariposa Pr., *(978-0-9666899)* 551 W. Cordova Rd., Santa Fe, NM 87501 USA Tel 505-471-7846; Fax: 505-986-0690 Do not confuse with companies with same or similar names in Gainesville, FL, Chicago, IL, Hurleyville, NY, Boulder, CO, Abilene TX .

Marshall Cavendish Corp., *(978-0-7614; 978-0-85685; 978-0-86307; 978-1-85435; 978-1-60870)* Member of Times Publishing Group, 99 White Plains Rd., Tarrytown, NY 10591-9001 USA (SAN 238-437X) Tel 914-332-8888; Fax: 914-332-8882; Toll Free: 800-821-9881
E-mail: npalazzo@marshallcavendish.com
Web site: www.MCEducation.us.

Marshall-Mangold Distribution Co., Inc., 4805 Nelson Ave., Baltimore, MD 21215-2507 USA (SAN 169-3115) Toll Free: 800-972-2665.

Marvin Law Bk., 11020 27th Ave., S., Burnsville, MN 55337 USA (SAN 163-898X) Tel 612-644-2236.

Mascot Bks., Inc., *(978-0-9743442; 978-1-932888; 978-1-934878; 978-1-936319; 978-1-937406; 978-1-62086; 978-1-63177; 978-1-68401)* Orders Addr.: 560 Herndon Pkwy. Suite 120, Herndon, VA 20170 USA Tel 703-437-3584; Fax: 703-437-3554; Toll Free: 877-862-7568
E-mail: info@mascotbooks.com; josh@mascotbooks.com; naren@mascotbooks.com; laura@mascotbooks.com; kristin@mascotbooks.com
Web site: http://www.mascotbooks.com.

Master Bks., *(978-0-89051; 978-1-61458)* P.O. Box 726, Green Forest, AR 72638-0726 USA (SAN 205-6119) Tel 870-438-5288; Fax: 870-438-5120; Toll Free: 800-999-3777
E-mail: nlp@newleafpress.net
Web site: http://www.masterbooks.net; NLPG.com.

Master Communications, Inc., *(978-1-888194; 978-1-60480)* 2692 Madison Rd., Suite N1-307 N1-307, Cincinnati, OH 45208 USA (SAN 299-2140) Tel 513-563-3100; Fax: 513-563-3105; Toll Free: 800-765-5885
E-mail: sales@master-comm.com
Web site: http://www.worldculturemedia.com; http://www.master-comm.com.

Master Teacher, One Leadership Ln., Manhattan, KS 66505-1207 USA
Web site: http://www.masterteacher.com.

Mastery Education, *(978-1-56256; 978-1-58984; 978-1-4138; 978-1-61526; 978-1-61527; 978-1-936025; 978-1-936026; 978-1-936027; 978-1-936028; 978-1-936029; 978-1-936030; 978-1-936031; 978-0-692-00207-0; 978-0-692-00208-7; 978-0-692-00209-4; 978-0-692-00210-0; 978-1-61602; 978-1-61734; 978-1-60979; 978-1-64090) Orders Addr.: P.O. Box 513, Saddle Brook, NJ 07633 USA Tel 201-712-0090; Fax: 201-712-1534; Toll Free: 800-822-1080; Edit Addr.: 299 Market St. Suite 240, Saddle Brook, NJ 07663 USA (SAN 857-9873)*
E-mail: solvier@peoplesed.com; sales@peoplesed.com; customersupport@peoplesed.com; editorial@peoplesed.com
Web site: http://www.masteryeducation.com/.

Mastery Education Corporation, *See* **Charlesbridge Publishing, Inc.**

Matagiri Sri Aurobindo Ctr., *(978-0-89071)* 2288 Fulton St., No. 310, Berkeley, CA 94704-1449 USA (SAN 169-5541).

Matthews Medical Bk. Co., Orders Addr.: 10 Old Bloomfield Ave., Pine Brook, NJ 07058 USA; 11559 Rock Island Ct., Maryland Heights, MO 63043 (SAN 146-4655) Tel 314-432-1400; Fax: 314-432-7044
E-mail: mlc@mattmccoy.com
Web site: http://www.mattmccoy.com.

Maus Tales, 77-490 Loma Vista, La Quinta, CA 92253 USA Fax: 760-564-6669
E-mail: maustales@aol.com.

Maxwell Scientific International, Inc., *(978-0-8277)* Div. of Pergamon Pr., Inc., 1345 Ave. of the Americas, No. 1036C, New York, NY 10105-0302 USA (SAN 169-524X) Tel 914-592-9141.

May, L. B. & Assocs., 3517 Neal Dr., Knoxville, TN 37918 USA Tel 865-922-7490; Fax: 865-922-7492
E-mail: lbmay@aol.com.

MBI Distribution Services/Quayside Distribution, *(978-0-7603; 978-0-87938; 978-0-912612; 978-1-85010)* Div. of MBI Publishing Co. LLC, Orders Addr.: P.O. Box 1, Osceola, WI 54020-0001 USA (SAN 169-9164) Toll Free: 800-458-0454; Edit Addr.: 400 First Ave., N, Suite 300, Minneapolis, MN 55401 USA Toll Free: 800-328-0590
Web site: http://www.motorbooks.com.

MBS Textbook Exchange, Inc., Orders Addr.: 2711 W. Ash St., Columbia, MO 65203-4613 USA (SAN 140-7015) Tel 573-445-2243; Fax: 573-446-5254; Toll Free: 800-325-0929 (orders); 800-325-0530 (customer service); Edit Addr.: 2711 W. Ash St., Columbia, MO 65203 USA
E-mail: kyates@mbsbooks.com
Web site: http://www.mbsbooks.com.

McCaslin, Boyce, 3 Greenbriar Dr., Saint Louis, MO 63124-1819 USA (SAN 110-8298).

McCoy Church Goods, 1010 Howard Ave., San Mateo, CA 94401 USA (SAN 107-2315) Tel 415-342-0924.

McCrory's Books, *See* **McCrory's Wholesale Bks.**

McCrory's Wholesale Bks., Orders Addr.: P.O. Box 2032, Alexandria, LA 71301 USA (SAN 108-5999); Edit Addr.: 1808 Rapides Ave., Alexandria, LA 71301 USA.

McEvoy Group, The, 680 Second St., San Francisco, CA 94107 USA Tel 415-537-4300
E-mail: info@mcevoygroup.com
Web site: http://mcevoygroup.com.

McGraw-Hill Cos., The, *(978-0-07)* 6480 Jimmy Carter Blvd., Norcross, GA 30071-1701 USA (SAN 254-881X) Tel 614-755-5637; Fax: 614-755-5611; Orders Addr.: 860 Taylor Station Rd., Blacklick, OH 43004-0545 USA (SAN 200-254X) Fax: 614-755-5645; Toll Free: 800-722-4726 (orders & customer service); 800-338-3987 (college); 800-525-5003 (subscriptions); 800-352-3566 (books - US/Canada orders); P.O. Box 545, Blacklick, OH 43004-0545 Fax: 614-759-3759; Toll Free: 877-833-5524; a/o General Customer Service, P.O. Box 182604, Columbus, OH 43272 Fax: 614-759-3759; Toll Free: 877-833-5524
E-mail: customer.service@mcgraw-hill.com
Web site: http://www.mcgraw-hill.com; http://www.ebooks.mcgraw-hill.com.

McGraw-Hill Create (TM), *(978-0-390)* Div. of McGraw-Hill Higher Education, 148 Princeton-Hightstown Rd., Hightstown, NJ 08520-1450 USA Tel 609-426-5721; Toll Free: 800-962-9342
Web site: http://www.mhhe.com.

McGraw-Hill Health Professions Division, *See* **McGraw-Hill Medical Publishing Div.**

McGraw-Hill Medical Publishing Div., *(978-0-07)* Div. of The McGraw-Hill Cos., Orders Addr.: P.O. Box 545, Blacklick, OH 43004-0545 USA Fax: 614-755-5645 (customer service); Toll Free: 800-262-4729 (customer service); 800-722-4726 (bookstores & libraries)
E-mail: customerservice@mcgraw-hill.com
Web site: http://www.mghmedical.com.

McGraw-Hill Osborne, *(978-0-07; 978-0-88134; 978-0-931988)* Div. of The McGraw-Hill Professional, 160 Spear St. Flr. 7, San Francisco, CA 94105-1544 USA (SAN 274-3450) Toll Free: 800-227-0900
E-mail: customer.service@mcgraw-hill.com
Web site: http://www.osborne.com.

McGraw-Hill Primis Custom Publishing, *See* **McGraw-Hill Create (TM)**

McGraw-Hill Professional Publishing, *(978-0-07)* Div. of McGraw-Hill Higher Education, Orders Addr.: P.O. Box 545, Blacklick, OH 43004-0545 USA Fax: 614-755-5645; Toll Free: 800-722-4726; Edit Addr.: 2 Penn Plaza, New York, NY 10121-2298 USA Tel 212-904-2000.

McGraw-Hill Trade, *(978-0-07; 978-0-658; 978-0-8442)* Div. of McGraw-Hill Professional, Orders Addr.: P.O. Box 545, Blacklick, OH 43004-0545 USA Tel 800-722-4726; Fax: 614-755-5645; Edit Addr.: 2 Penn Plaza, New York, NY 10121 USA Tel 212-904-2000
E-mail: Jeffrey_Krames@mcgraw-hill.com
Web site: http://www.books.mcgraw-hill.com.

McGraw-Hill/Contemporary, *(978-0-658; 978-0-8092; 978-0-8325; 978-0-8442; 978-0-88499; 978-0-89061; 978-0-913327; 978-0-940279; 978-0-941263; 978-0-9630646; 978-1-56626; 978-1-56943; 978-1-57028)* Div. of McGraw-Hill Higher Education, Orders Addr.: P.O. Box 545, Blacklick, OH 43004-0545 USA Toll Free Fax: 800-998-3103; Toll Free: 800-621-1918; Edit Addr.: 4255 W. Touhy Ave., Lincolnwood, IL 60712 USA (SAN 169-2208) Tel 847-679-5500; Fax: 847-679-2494; Toll Free Fax: 800-998-3103; Toll Free: 800-323-4900
E-mail: ntcpub@tribune.com
Web site: http://www.ntc-cb.com.

McKay, David Co., Inc., *(978-0-679; 978-0-88326; 978-0-89440)* Subs. of Random Hse., Inc., Orders Addr.: 400 Hahn Rd., Westminster, MD 21157 USA Tel 410-848-1900; Toll Free: 800-733-3000 (orders only); Edit Addr.: 201 E. 50th St., MD 4-6, New York, NY 10022 USA (SAN 200-240X) Tel 212-751-2600; Fax: 212-872-8026.

McKnight Sales Co., P.O. Box 4138, Pittsburgh, PA 15202 USA (SAN 169-7587) Tel 412-761-4443; Fax: 412-761-0122; Toll Free: 800-208-8078
E-mail: sales@mscmags.com
Web site: http://www.mscmags.com.

McLemore, Hollern & Assocs., 3538 Maple Park Dr., Kingwood, TX 77339 USA Tel 281-360-5204.

McMillen Bk. Distributors, 304 Main St., Ames, IA 50010 USA Fax: 515-232-0402; Toll Free: 866-385-2027.

MeadWestvaco, Orders Addr.: 4751 Hempstead Sta., Kettering, OH 45429 USA Tel 937-495-6323
Web site: http://us.meadwestvaco.com.

MediaTech Productions, *(978-0-9702309)* 917 E. Prospect Rd. Unit B, Fort Collins, CO 80525-1364 USA Toll Free: 800-816-7566 Do not confuse with companies with the same or similar name in Chicago, IL
E-mail: maury@mediatechproductions.com
Web site: http://mediatechproductions.com.

Medicina Biologica, 2937 NE Flanders St., Portland, OR 97232 USA (SAN 113-0226) Tel 503-287-6775; Fax: 503-235-3520
E-mail: med_bio@imagina.com.

Mel Bay Pubns., Inc., *(978-0-7866; 978-0-87166; 978-1-56222; 978-1-60974; 978-1-61065; 978-1-61911; 978-1-5134)* 1734 Gilsinn Ln., Fenton, MO 63026 USA (SAN 657-3630) Tel 636-257-3970; Fax: 636-257-5062; Toll Free: 800-863-5229
E-mail: email@melbay.com; sharon@melbay.com
Web site: http://www.melbay.com; www.melbaydealers.com.

Melton Book Company, Incorporated, *See* **Nelson Direct**

Menasha Ridge Pr., Inc., *(978-0-89732; 978-1-63404)* Div. of Keen Communications, 2204 First Ave., S., Suite 102, Birmingham, AL 35233 USA (SAN 219-7294) Tel 205-322-0439; Fax: 205-326-1012
E-mail: info@menasharidge.com
Web site: http://www.menasharidge.com.

Mentor Bks., 5318 Lowell Blvd., Denver, CO 80221 USA Fax: 303-975-1936; Toll Free: 800-795-6198
E-mail: blair@mentorbooks.com.

Merced News Co., 1324 Coldwell Ave., Modesto, CA 95350-5702 USA (SAN 168-9894) Tel 209-722-5791.

Mercedes Book Distributors Corporation, *See* **Mercedes Distribution Ctr., Inc.**

Mercedes Distribution Ctr., Inc., Brooklyn Navy Yard, Bldg. No. 3, Brooklyn, NY 11205 USA (SAN 169-5150) Tel 718-534-3000; Fax: 718-935-9647; Toll Free: 800-339-4804
E-mail: contact@mdist.com.

Meredith Bks., *(978-0-696; 978-0-89721; 978-0-917102)* Div. of Meredith Corp., Orders Addr.: 1716 Locust St., LN-110, Des Moines, IA 50309-3023 USA (SAN 202-4055) Tel 515-284-2363; 515-284-2126 (sales); Fax: 515-284-3371; Toll Free: 800-678-8091 Do not confuse with Meredith Pr. in Skaneateles, NY
E-mail: John.OBannon@meredith.com
Web site: http://www.bhgstore.com.

Merkos Pubns., Div. of Merkos L'Inyonei Chinuch, 291 Kingston Ave., Brooklyn, NY 11213 USA (SAN 631-1040) Tel 718-778-0226; Fax: 718-778-4148.

Merry Thoughts, *(978-0-88230)* 364 Adams St., Bedford Hills, NY 10507 USA (SAN 169-5061) Tel 914-241-0447; Fax: 914-241-0247.

Meta Co., LLC, P.O. Box 2667, Columbia, MD 21045 USA.

Metamorphosis Publishing Company, *See* **Metamorphous Pr., Inc.**

Metamorphous Pr., Inc., *(978-0-943920; 978-1-55552)* Orders Addr.: P.O. Box 10616, Portland, OR 97296-0616 USA (SAN 110-8786) Tel 503-228-4972; Fax: 503-223-9117; Toll Free: 800-937-7771 (orders only); Edit Addr.: P.O. Box 10616, Portland, OR 97296-0616 USA
E-mail: metabooks@metamodels.com
Web site: http://www.metamodels.com.

Metro Systems, 3381 Stevens Creek Blvd., Suite 209, San Jose, CA 95117 USA (SAN 631-1016) Tel 408-247-4050; Fax: 408-247-4236.

Metropolitan News Co., 47-25 34th, Long Island City, NY 11101 USA (SAN 159-9089) Do not confuse with Metropolitan News Co. in Los Angeles, CA.

Mi Lybro, 9775 Marconi Dr., Suite D, San Diego, CA 92154 USA Tel 619-900-7624
E-mail: sales@milybro.com.

Miami Bks., Inc., 17842 State Rd. 9, Miami, FL 33162 USA (SAN 106-8997) Tel 305-652-3231.

Miami Valley News Agency, 2127 Old Troy Pike, Dayton, OH 45404 USA (SAN 169-6718) Fax: 513-233-8544; Toll Free: 800-791-5137.

Michiana News Service, 2232 S. 11th St., Niles, MI 49120 USA (SAN 110-5051) Tel 616-684-3013; Fax: 616-684-8740.

Michigan Church Supply, P.O. Box 279, Mount Morris, MI 48458-0279 USA (SAN 184-413X) Toll Free: 800-521-3440.

Michigan State Univ. Pr., *(978-0-87013; 978-0-937191; 978-1-60917; 978-1-61186; 978-1-938065; 978-1-62895; 978-1-62896; 978-1-941258; 978-0-997252; 978-1-68430; 978-1-947134)* Orders Addr.: 1405 S. Harrison Rd. Suite 25, East Lansing, MI 48823-5245 USA (SAN 202-6295) Tel 517-884-6901; Fax: 517-432-2611; Toll Free: 800-621-2736; 800-621-8476
E-mail: msupress@msupress.org
Web site: http://www.msupress.org.

Mickler's Bks., Inc., 61 Alafaya Woods Blvd., No. 197, Oviedo, FL 32765 USA Tel 407-365-8500; Toll Free Fax: 800-726-0585
E-mail: orders@micklers.com
Web site: http://www.micklers.com.

Micklers Floridiana, Incorporated, *See* **Mickler's Bks., Inc.**

Microdistributors International, Inc., *(978-0-918025)* Subs. of Medcomp Technologies, Inc., 34 Maple Ave., P.O. Box 8, Armonk, NY 10504 USA (SAN 296-158X) Tel 914-273-6480.

Mid Penn Magazine Agency, 100 Eck Cir., Williamsport, PA 17701 USA (SAN 169-7692).

Mid South Manufacturing Agency, Incorporated, *See* **Mid-South Magazine Agency, Inc.**

Mid-Cal Periodical Distributors, P.O. Box 245230, Sacramento, CA 95824-5230 USA (SAN 169-0078).

Midpoint National, Inc., 1263 Southwest Blvd., Kansas City, MO 66103-1901 USA (SAN 630-9860) Tel 913-831-2233; Fax: 913-362-7401; Toll Free: 800-228-4321.

Midpoint Trade Bks., Inc., *(978-1-940416)* Orders Addr.: 1263 Southwest Blvd., Kansas City, KS 66103 USA (SAN 631-3736) Tel 913-831-2233; Fax: 913-362-7401; Toll Free: 800-742-6139 (consumer orders); Edit Addr.: 27 W. 20th St., No. 1102, New York, NY 10011 USA (SAN 631-1075) Tel 212-727-0190; Fax: 212-727-0195
E-mail: info@midpointtrade.com
Web site: http://www.midpointtrade.com; http://www.midpointtradebooks.com/.

Mid-South Magazine Agency, Inc., P.O. Box 4585, Jackson, MS 39296-4585 USA (SAN 286-0163) Toll Free: 800-748-9444.

Mid-State Periodicals, Inc., P.O. Box 3455, Quincy, IL 62305-3455 USA Tel 217-222-0833; Fax: 217-222-1256.

Mid-States Distributors, P.O. Box 1374, Chambersburg, PA 17201-5374 USA (SAN 169-3166).

Midtown Auto Bks., 212 Burnet Ave., Syracuse, NY 13203 USA (SAN 169-6289).

Midwest European Pubns., 915 Foster St., Evanston, IL 60201 USA (SAN 169-1937) Tel 847-866-6289; Fax: 847-866-6290; Toll Free: 800-380-8919
E-mail: info@mep-eli.com
Web site: http://www.mep-eli.com.

Midwest Library Service, 11443 St. Charles Rock Rd., Bridgeton, MO 63044-2789 USA (SAN 169-4243) Tel 314-739-3100; Fax: 314-739-1326; Toll Free Fax: 800-962-1009; Toll Free: 800-325-8833
E-mail: hudson@midwestls.com.

Midwest Tape, Orders Addr.: P.O. Box 820, Holland, OH 43528-0820 USA (SAN 254-9913) Toll Free Fax: 800-444-6645; Toll Free: 800-875-2785
E-mail: randys@midwesttapes.com
Web site: http://www.midwesttapes.com.

MightyWords, Inc., *(978-1-58895; 978-0-7173; 978-1-4036)* 2850 Walsh Ave., Santa Clara, CA 95051 USA Tel 408-845-0100; Fax: 408-845-0425; Toll Free: 877-328-2724
Web site: http://www.mightywords.com.

Mightywords.com, *See* **MightyWords, Inc.**

Military History Assocs., 407B E. Sixth St., No. 200, Austin, TX 78701-3739 USA (SAN 111-7866).

Miller Educational Materials, *(978-1-934274)* Orders Addr.: P.O. Box 2428, Buena Park, CA 90621 USA Fax: 714-562-0237; Toll Free: 800-636-4375; Edit Addr.: 3294 Cherry Ave., Long Beach, CA 90807-5214 USA (SAN 631-5445)
E-mail: MillerEdu@aol.com
Web site: http://www.millereducational.com.

Miller Trade Bk. Marketing, 363 W. Erie St. Ste. 700E, Chicago, IL 60610-6996 USA (SAN 631-4287)
E-mail: millertrade@sbcglobal.net.

Milligan News Co., Inc., 150 N. Autumn St., San Jose, CA 95110 USA (SAN 169-0272) Tel 408-286-7604; Fax: 408-298-0235; Toll Free: 800-873-2387.

Millmark Education, *(978-1-4334; 978-1-61618)* Orders Addr.: 7272 Wisconsin Ave, Suite 300, Bethesda, MD 20814-2081 USA (SAN 852-4912) Tel 301-941-1974; Fax: 301-656-0183; Edit Addr.: 7272 Wisconsin Ave. Suite 300, Suite 300, Bethesda, MD 20814-2081 USA
E-mail: rachel.moir@millmarkeducation.com; info@millmarkeducation.com
Web site: http://www.millmarkeducation.com/.

Mind Trip Pr., P.O. Box 489, Georgetown, TX 78626 USA Tel 513-428-9278.

Minerva Science Bookseller, Inc., 175 Fifth Ave., New York, NY 10010 USA (SAN 286-0171).

Mint Pubs. Group, Orders Addr.: 62 June Rd., Suite 241, North Salem, NY 10560 USA Tel 914-276-6576; Fax: 914-276-6579; Edit Addr.: 1220 Nicholson Rd., Newmarket, ON I3Y 7VI CAN Toll Free Fax: 800-363-2665; Toll Free: 800-399-6858
E-mail: info@mintpub.com
Web site: http://www.mintpub.com.

Mission Resource Ctr., 1221 Profit Dr., Dallas, TX 75247 USA Toll Free: 800-305-9857.

Mississippi Library Media & Supply Co., P.O. Box 108, Brandon, MS 39043-0108 USA (SAN 169-4189) Tel 601-824-1900; Fax: 601-824-1999; Toll Free: 800-257-7566 (in Mississippi).

Mistco, Inc., P.O. Box 694854, Miami, FL 33269 USA (SAN 630-8384) Tel 305-653-2003; Fax: 305-653-2037; Toll Free: 800-552-0446
E-mail: mistco@worldnet.att.net
Web site: http://www.mistco.com.

Mobile News Co., 1118 14th St., Tuscaloosa, AL 35401-3318 USA (SAN 168-924X) Tel 334-479-1435.

Modern Curriculum Pr., *(978-0-7652; 978-0-8136; 978-0-87895)* Div. of Pearson Education, Orders Addr.: P.O. Box 2500, Lebanon, IN 46052-3009 USA (SAN 206-6572) Tel 800-526-9907 (Customer Service)
Web site: http://www.pearsonlearning.com.

Modesto News Co., 1324 Coldwell Ave., Modesto, CA 95350-5702 USA (SAN 168-9908) Tel 209-577-5551.

Montfort Pubns., *(978-0-910984)* Div. of Montfort Missionaries, 26 S. Saxon Ave., Bay Shore, NY 11706-8993 USA (SAN 169-5053) Tel 631-665-0726; Fax: 631-665-4349
E-mail: montfort@optonline.net
Web site: http://www.montfortmissionaries.com; http://www.montfortmissionaries.org; http://www.montfortpublications.com.

Moody Pubs., *(978-0-8024)* Div. of Moody Bible Institute, Orders Addr.: 210 W. Chestnut, Chicago, IL 60610 USA; Edit Addr.: 820 N. LaSalle, Chicago, IL 60610 USA (SAN 202-5604) Tel 312-329-2101; Fax: 312-329-2144; Toll Free: 800-678-8812
E-mail: mpcustomerservice@moody.edu
Web site: http://www.moodypublishers.com.

Mook & Blanchard, P.O. Box 4177, La Puente, CA 91747-4177 USA (SAN 168-9703) Toll Free: 800-875-9911
E-mail: mookbook@ix.netcom.com
Web site: http://www.mookandblanchard.com.

Moon Over the Mountain Publishing Company, *See* **Leman Pubns., Inc.**

More, Thomas Assn., 205 W. Monroe St., 5th Flr., Chicago, IL 60606-5097 USA (SAN 169-1880) Tel 312-609-8880; Toll Free: 800-835-8965.

Morlock News Co., Inc., 496 Duanesburg Rd., Schenectady, NY 12306 USA (SAN 169-6246).

Morris Publishing, *(978-0-7392; 978-0-9631249; 978-1-57502; 978-1-885591; 978-0-9863567)* Orders Addr.: P.O. Box 2110, Kearney, NE 68848 USA Fax: 308-237-0263; Toll Free: 800-650-7888 Do not confuse with companies with the same Wesley Chapel, FL, Elkhart, IN
Web site: http://www.morrispublishing.com.

Moshy Brothers, Inc., 127 W. 25th St., New York, NY 10001 USA (SAN 169-5886) Tel 212-255-0613.

Mother Lode Distributing, 17890 Lime Rock Dr., Sonora, CA 95370-8707 USA (SAN 169-0361).

Motorbooks International Wholesalers & Distributors, *See* **MBI Distribution Services/Quayside Distribution**

Mountain Bk. Co., P.O. Box 778, Broomfield, CO 80038-0778 USA Tel 303-436-1982; Fax: 917-386-2769
E-mail: wordguise@aol.com
Web site: http://www.mountainbook.org.

Mountain n' Air Bks., *(978-1-879415)* Div. of Mountain n' Air Sports, Inc., Orders Addr.: P.O. Box 12540, La Crescenta, CA 91224 USA (SAN 630-5598) Tel 818-248-9345; Toll Free Fax: 800-303-5578; Toll Free: 800-446-9696; Edit Addr.: 2947-A Hololulu Ave., La Crescenta, CA 91214 USA (SAN 631-4198)
E-mail: books@mountain-n-air.com
Web site: http://mountain-n-air.com.

Mountain Pr. Publishing Co., Inc., *(978-0-87842)* Orders Addr.: P.O. Box 2399, Missoula, MT 59806-2399 USA (SAN 202-8832) Tel 406-728-1900; Fax: 406-728-1635; Toll Free: 800-234-5308; Edit Addr.: 1301 S. Third West, Missoula, MT 59801 USA (SAN 662-0868)
E-mail: jrimel@mtnpress.com; info@mtnpress.com; anne@mtnpress.com
Web site: http://www.mountain-press.com.

Mountain States News Distributor, P.O. Drawer P, Fort Collins, CO 80522 USA Tel 970-221-2330; Fax: 970-221-1251.

Mouse Works, *(978-0-7364; 978-1-57082)* Div. of Disney Bk. Publishing, Inc., A Walt Disney Co., 114 Fifth Ave., New York, NY 10011 USA (SAN 298-0797) Tel 212-633-4400; Fax: 212-633-4811
Web site: http://www.disneybooks.com.

MPS, 16365 James Madison Hwy., Gordonsville, VA 22942-8501 USA Toll Free Fax: 800-672-2054; Toll Free: 888-330-8477.

Mr. Paperback/Publishers News Co., 6030 Fostoria Ave., Findlay, OH 45840 USA (SAN 169-393X) Tel 419-424-6774; Fax: 419-420-1805; Toll Free: 800-872-0031.

M-S News Co., Inc., P.O. Box 13278, Wichita, KS 67213-0278 USA Fax: 316-267-5405.

Mullare News Agency, Inc., P.O. Box 578, Brockton, MA 02401 USA (SAN 169-3379) Tel 508-580-1000; Fax: 508-586-0968.

Multi-Cultural Bks. & Videos, Inc., *(978-0-9656274)* 30007 John R. Rd., Madison Hts, MI 48071-2526 USA (SAN 760-6796) Toll Free: 800-567-2220
E-mail: service@multiculbv.com
Web site: http://www.multiculbv.com.

Multilingual Bks., Orders Addr.: P.O. Box 440632, Miami, FL 33144 USA (SAN 169-1155) Tel 305-471-9847 Do not confuse with Multilingual Bks., Seattle, WA.

Mumford Library Bks., Inc., 7847 Bayberry Rd., Jacksonville, FL 32256 USA (SAN 156-7721) Fax: 904-730-8913; Toll Free: 800-367-3927.

Mumford Library Book Sales, *See* **Mumford Library Bks., Inc.**

Murr's Library Service, 4045 E. Palm Ln., No. 5, Phoenix, AZ 85008-3116 USA (SAN 107-3222) Fax: 602-273-1217; Toll Free: 888-273-0279.

Music, Bks. & Business, Inc., Orders Addr.: 4305 32nd St W Suite A, Bradenton, FL 34205 USA (SAN 760-5986) Fax: 941-752-8994; Toll Free: 888-876-7716
E-mail: info@musicbooksbusiness.com
Web site: http://www.musicbooksbusiness.com.

Music Design, Inc., 4650 N. Port Washington Rd., Milwaukee, WI 53212 USA (SAN 200-7649) Tel 414-961-8380; Fax: 414-961-8381; Toll Free: 800-862-7232
E-mail: order@musicdesign.com
Web site: http://www.musicdesign.com.

Music in Motion, P.O. Box 869231, Plano, TX 75086-9231 USA (SAN 631-4589) Fax: 972-943-8906; Toll Free Fax: 866-943-8906; Toll Free: 800-445-0649 Do not confuse with Music In Motion, Ithaca, NY
Web site: http://www.musicmotion.com.

Music is Elementary, *(978-0-9721085; 978-0-9910656; 978-0-9966913; 978-0-692-90589-0)* P.O. Box 24263, Cleveland, OH 44124 USA Tel 440-442-4475; Fax: 440-461-3631; Toll Free: 800-888-7502
E-mail: music@en.com
Web site: http://www.musiciselementary.com.

Music Sales Corp., *(978-0-7119; 978-0-8256; 978-1-84609)* Orders Addr.: 445 Bellvale Rd., P.O. Box 572, Chester, NY 10918 USA (SAN 662-0876) Tel 845-469-2271; Fax: 845-469-7544; Toll Free Fax: 800-345-6842; Toll Free: 800-431-7187; Edit Addr.: 257 Park Ave., S., 20th Flr., New York, NY 10010 USA (SAN 282-0277) Tel 212-254-2100; Fax: 212-254-2103
E-mail: info@musicsales.com
Web site: http://www.musicroom.com; http://www.musicsales.com.

Musicart West, P.O. Box 1900, Orem, UT 84059-1900 USA (SAN 110-1250) Tel 801-225-0859; Toll Free: 800-950-1900 (orders only).

MVP Wholesales, 9301 W. Hwy. 290, No. D, Austin, TX 78736-7817 USA (SAN 630-9550) Tel 512-416-1452; Toll Free: 800-328-7931 (phone/fax).

MyiLibrary, *(978-1-280; 978-1-281; 978-1-282; 978-1-283; 978-1-299; 978-1-306; 978-1-322; 978-1-336)* Div. of Coutts Information Services, 14 Ingram Blvd., La Vergne, TN 37086 USA Tel 615-213-5400; Fax: 615-213-5111
E-mail: wendell.lotz@ingramcontent.com.

myON, 5050 Lincoln Dr., Suite 200, Edina, MN 55436 USA Toll Free: 800-864-3899.

NACSCORP, Incorporated, *See* .

Najarian Music Co., Inc., 236 Partridge Ln., Concord, MA 01742-2651 USA (SAN 169-3344).

Napa Book Company, *See* **Napa Children's Bk. Co.**

Napa Children's Bk. Co., 1239 First St., Napa, CA 94559 USA (SAN 122-2732) Tel 707-224-3893; Fax: 707-224-1212.

Nasco Math Eighty-Six, 901 Janesville Ave., Fort Atkinson, WI 53538 USA (SAN 679-7512).

National Academies Pr., *(978-0-309)* Orders Addr.: 8700 Spectrum Dr., Landover, MD 20785 USA; Edit Addr.: 500 Fifth St., NW Lockbox 285, Washington, DC 20001 USA (SAN 202-8891) Tel 202-334-3313; Fax: 202-334-2451; Toll Free: 888-624-7654
E-mail: zjones@nas.edu
Web site: http://www.nap.edu.

National Academy Press, *See* **National Academies Pr.**

National Assn. of the Deaf, *(978-0-913072)* 8630 Fenton St. Ste. 820, Silver Spring, MD 20910-3819 USA (SAN 159-4974)
E-mail: donna.morris@nad.org
Web site: http://www.nad.org.

National Bk. Co., Keystone Industrial Pk., Scranton, PA 18512 USA Tel 717-346-2020; Toll Free: 800-233-4830 Do not confuse with National Book Company, Portland, OR.

National Bk. Network, Div. of Rowman & Littlefield Pubs., Inc., Orders Addr.: 15200 NBN Way, Blue Ridge Summit, PA 17214 USA (SAN 630-0065) Tel 717-794-3800; Fax: 717-794-3828; Toll Free Fax: 800-338-4550 (Customer Service); Toll Free: 800-462-6420 (Customer Service); a/o Les Petriw, 67 Mowat Ave., Suite 241, Toronto, ON M6P 3K3 Tel 416-534-1660; Fax: 416-534-3699
E-mail: custserv@nbnbooks.com
Web site: http://www.nbnbooks.com.

National Catholic Reading Distributor, 997 Macarthur Blvd., Mahwah, NJ 07430 USA (SAN 169-4855) Tel 201-825-7300; Fax: 201-825-8345; Toll Free: 800-218-1903
E-mail: paulistp@pipeline.com.

National Educational Systems, Inc., *(978-1-893493)* P.O. Box 691450, San Antonio, TX 78269-1450 USA Toll Free: 800-442-2604.

National Film Network LLC, *(978-0-8026)* Orders Addr.: 4501 Forbes Blvd., Lanham, MD 20706 USA (SAN 630-1878) Tel 301-459-8020 ext 2066
E-mail: info@nationalfilmnetwork.com
Web site: http://www.nationalfilmnetwork.com.

National Health Federation, Box 688, Monrovia, CA 91016 USA (SAN 227-9266) Tel 626-357-2181; Fax: 818-303-0642
E-mail: nhf@earthlink.net
Web site: http://www.healthfreedom.net.

National Learning Corp., *(978-0-8293; 978-0-8373)* 212 Michael Dr., Syosset, NY 11791 USA (SAN 206-8869) Tel 516-921-8888; Fax: 516-921-8743; Toll Free: 800-645-6337
E-mail: sales@passbooks.com.

National Magazine Service, Orders Addr.: P.O. Box 834, Mars, PA 16046 USA (SAN 169-7595); Edit Addr.: 535 Linden Way, Pittsburgh, PA 15202 USA Tel 412-898-0001.

National Organization Service, Inc., P.O. Box 2007, Birmingham, AL 35201-2007 USA (SAN 107-1548) Toll Free: 800-747-3032.

National Rifle Assn., *(978-0-935998)* a/o Office of the General Counsel, 11250 Waples Mill Rd., Fairfax, VA 22030 USA (SAN 213-859X) Tel 703-267-1250; Fax: 703-267-3985; Toll Free: 800-672-3888
E-mail: ndowd@nrahq.org.

National Sales, Inc., 1818 W. 2300 South, Salt Lake City, UT 84119 USA (SAN 159-9127) Tel 801-972-2300; Fax: 801-972-2883.

National School Products, 1523 Old Niles Ferry Rd., Maryville, TN 37803 USA
Web site: http://nationalschoolproducts.com/.

National Technical Information Service, U.S. Dept. of Commerce, *(978-0-934213; 978-1-935239)* Orders Addr.: 5285 Port Royal Rd., Springfield, VA 22161 USA (SAN 205-7255) Tel 703-605-6000; Fax: 703-605-6900; Toll Free: 800-553-6847
E-mail: orders@ntis.gov; info@ntis.gov
Web site: http://www.ntis.gov; http://wnc.fedworld.gov.

Native Bks., P.O. Box 37095, Honolulu, HI 96837 USA (SAN 631-1121) Tel 808-845-8949; Fax: 808-847-6637; Toll Free: 800-887-7751.

Naval Institute Pr., *(978-0-87021; 978-1-55750; 978-1-59114; 978-1-61251; 978-1-68247; 978-1-68269)* Orders Addr.: 291 Wood Rd, Annapolis, MD 21402-5034 USA (SAN 662-0930) Tel 410-268-6110; Fax: 410-295-1084; Toll Free: 800-233-8764; Edit Addr.: 291 Wood Rd., Beach Hall, Annapolis, MD 21402-5034 USA (SAN 202-9006)
E-mail: tskord@usni.org; books@usni.org
Web site: http://www.usni.org.

Nazarene Publishing Hse., *(978-0-8341)* Orders Addr.: 2923 Troost Ave., Kansas City, MO 64109 USA (SAN 253-0902); Edit Addr.: P.O. Box 419527, Kansas City, MO 64141 USA (SAN 202-9022) Tel 816-931-1900; Fax: 816-531-0923; Toll Free Fax: 800-849-9827; Toll Free: 800-877-0700
E-mail: heather@nph.com
Web site: http://www.bhillkc.com; http://www.nph.com.

Neal-Schuman Pubs., Inc., *(978-0-918212; 978-1-55570)* Div. of American Library Assn., 100 William St., Suite 2004, New York, NY 10038 USA (SAN 210-2455) Tel 212-925-8650; Fax: 212-219-8916; Toll Free Fax: 800-584-2414
E-mail: info@neal-schuman.com
Web site: http://www.neal-schuman.com.

Neeland Media, LLC, 3921 Harvard Rd., Lawrence, KS 66049 USA Tel 913-548-6825.

Neighborhood Periodical Club, Inc., P.O. Box 830, Clementon, NJ 08021-0860 USA (SAN 285-9262).

Nelson Direct, P.O. Box 140300, Nashville, TN 37214 USA (SAN 169-8133) Toll Free: 800-441-0511 (sales); 800-933-9673
E-mail: csalazar@thomasnelson.com
Web site: http://www.nelsondirect.com.

Nelson News, Inc., P.O. Box 27007, Omaha, NE 68127-0007 USA (SAN 169-443X) Tel 402-734-3333; Fax: 402-731-0516.

Nelson, Thomas Inc., *(978-0-529; 978-0-7852; 978-0-8407; 978-0-8499; 978-0-86605; 978-0-88113; 978-0-89840; 978-0-89922; 978-0-918956; 978-0-7180; 978-1-4002; 978-1-4003; 978-1-4016; 978-1-59145; 978-1-4041; 978-1-59554; 978-1-59555; 978-1-4185; 978-1-59951; 978-1-4261; 978-1-60255; 978-1-4845; 978-1-5000; 978-1-5314) Div. of HarperCollins Christian Publishing, Orders Addr.: P.O. Box 141000, Nashville, TN 37214-1000 USA (SAN 209-3820) Fax: 615-902-1866;*

Wholesaler & Distributor Name Index

Toll Free: 800-251-4000; Edit Addr.: 501 Nelson Pl., Nashville, TN 37214 USA
Web site: http://www.harpercollinschristian.com.

Nelson's Bks., *(978-0-9612188)* P.O. Box 2302, Santa Cruz, CA 95063 USA (SAN 289-4858) Tel 831-465-9148.

Ner Tamid Bk. Distributors, P.O. Box 10401, Riviera Beach, FL 33419-0401 USA (SAN 169-135X) Tel 561-686-9095.

Net Productions, 210 Elm Cir., Colorado Springs, CO 80906-3348 USA (SAN 159-9143).

NetLibrary, Incorporated, *See* **Ebsco Publishing**

NetSource Distribution, Orders Addr.: 675 Dutchess Tpke., Poughkeepsie, NY 12603 USA Tel 845-463-1100 x314; Fax: 845-463-0018; Toll Free: 800-724-1100
Web site: http://www.hudsonhousepub.com.

New Alexandrian Bookstore, 110 N Cayuga St., Ithaca, NY 14850-4331 USA (SAN 159-4958) Tel 607-272-1163.

New Concepts Bks. & Tapes Distributors, Orders Addr.: P.O. Box 55068, Houston, TX 77255 USA (SAN 114-2682) Tel 713-465-7736; Fax: 713-465-7106; Toll Free: 800-842-4807; Edit Addr.: 9722 Pine Lake, Houston, TX 77055 USA (SAN 630-7531).

New Day Christian Distributors, *See* **New Day Christian Distributors Gifts, Inc.**

New Day Christian Distributors Gifts, Inc., 124 Shivel Dr., Hendersonville, TN 37075 USA (SAN 631-2551) Tel 615-822-3633; Fax: 615-822-5829; Toll Free: 800-251-3633; 126 Shivel Dr., Hendersonville, TN 37075 (SAN 920-6604).

New England Bk. Service, Inc., 7000 Vt Route 17 W., Vergennes, VT 05491-4408 USA (SAN 170-0952) Toll Free: 800-356-5772
E-mail: nebs@together.net.

New England Mobile Bk. Fair, 82 Needham St., P.O. Box 610159, Newton Highlands, MA 02461 USA (SAN 169-3530) Tel 617-527-5817; Fax: 617-527-0113.

New Jersey Bk. Agency, Orders Addr.: P.O. Box 144, Morris Plains, NJ 07950 USA (SAN 106-861X) Tel 973-267-7093; Fax: 973-292-3177; Edit Addr.: 7 Somerset Hills Ct. Apt. D, Bernardsville, NJ 07924-2619 USA (SAN 243-2307).

New Jersey Bks., Inc., 59 Market St., Newark, NJ 07102 USA Tel 973-624-8070; Toll Free: 800-772-3678.

New Leaf Distributing Co., Inc., *(978-0-9627209)* Div. of Al-Wali Corp., 401 Thornton Rd., Lithia Springs, GA 30122-1557 USA (SAN 169-1449) Tel 770-948-7845; Fax: 770-944-2313; Toll Free Fax: 800-326-1066; Toll Free: 800-326-2665
E-mail: santoshk@msn.com; alimt@bellsouth.net
Web site: http://www.NewLeaf-dist.com.

New Leaf Press, Incorporated, *See* **New Leaf Pub. Group**

New Leaf Pub. Group, *(978-0-89221; 978-1-68344)* P.O. Box 726, Green Forest, AR 72638 USA (SAN 207-9518) Tel 870-438-5288; Fax: 870-438-5120 Toll Free: 800-643-9535; 800-999-3777 Do not confuse with companies with the same or similar name in Los Angeles, CAStone Mountain, GA
E-mail: nlp@nlpg.com
Web site: http://www.nlpg.com; www.masterbooks.com.

New Leaf Resources, 2102 Button Ln., Unit 2, Lagrange, KY 40031 USA Toll Free: 800-346-3087
E-mail: info@newleaf-resources.com
Web site: http://www.newleaf-resources.com.

New Life Foundation, *(978-0-911203; 978-1-934162)* P.O. Box 2230, Pine, AZ 85544-2230 USA (SAN 170-3986) Tel 928-476-3224; Fax: 928-476-4743; Toll Free: 800-293-3377 (wholesale only)
E-mail: info@anewlife.org
Web site: http://www.anewlife.org.

New Shelves Distribution, 103 Remsen St., Cohoes, NY 12047 USA Tel 518-391-2300; Fax: 518-391-2365
Web site: http://www.newshelvesdistribution.com.

New Tradition Bks., *(978-0-9728473; 978-1-932420; 978-0-9845418)* 627 Brickle Ridge Rd., Decatur, TN 37322 USA
E-mail: newtraditionbooks@yahoo.com.

New Village Pr., *(978-0-9766054; 978-0-9815593; 978-1-61332)* Div. of Architects/Designers/Planners for Social Responsibility, 400 Central Pk. W, 12B, New York, NY 10025 USA Tel 510-717-3101
E-mail: hello@newvillagepress.net
Web site: http://www.newvillagepress.net.

New World Library, *(978-0-931432; 978-0-945934; 978-1-57731; 978-1-880032; 978-1-60868)* 14 Pamaron Way, Novato, CA 94949 USA (SAN 211-8777) Tel 415-884-2100; Fax: 415-884-2199; Toll Free: 800-972-6657 (retail orders only) Do not confuse with New World Library Publishing Co., Los Altos, CA
E-mail: escort@nwlib.com
Web site: http://www.newworldlibrary.com.

New World Resource Ctr., P.O. Box 25310, Chicago, IL 60625-0310 USA (SAN 169-1848).

New York Periodical Distributors, P.O. Box 29, Massena, NY 13662-0029 USA (SAN 169-6149).

New York Univ. Pr., *(978-0-8147; 978-1-4798)* Div. of New York Univ., Orders Addr.: 838 Broadway, 3rd Flr., New York, NY 10003-4812 USA (SAN 658-1293) Tel 212-998-2575; Fax: 212-995-3833; Toll Free: 800-996-6987 (ordering)
E-mail: orders@nyupress.org
Web site: http://www.nyupress.org.

Newborn Enterprises, Inc., P.O. Box 1713, Altoona, PA 16603 USA (SAN 169-7242) Tel 814-944-3593; Fax: 814-944-1881; Toll Free: 800-227-0285 (in Pennsylvania).

NewLife Bk. Distributors, 2969 Spalding Dr., Suite 100, Atlanta, GA 30350 USA (SAN 169-121X) Tel 404-207-5280
E-mail: lifebooks@mindspring.com
Web site: http://www.newlifebookdistributors.com.

News Group, 15 N. Spring St., #2, Bloomfield, NJ 07003 USA.

News Group - Illinois, The, 1301 SW Washington St., Peoria, IL 61602 USA (SAN 169-216X) Tel 309-673-4549; Fax: 309-673-8883.

News Group, The, 325 W. Potter Dr., Anchorage, AK 99518 USA (SAN 168-9274) Tel 907-563-3251; Fax: 907-261-8523 Do not confuse with companies with the same name in Winston-Salem, NC, Elizabeth, NC.

News Supply Co., 216 S. La Huerta Cir., Carlsbad, NM 88220-9620 USA (SAN 159-9151).

Newsdealers Supply Co., Inc., P.O. Box 3516, Tallahassee, FL 32315-3516 USA.

NewSound, LLC, 81 Demeritt Pl., Waterbury, VT 05676 USA Tel 802-244-7858; Fax: 802-244-1808; Toll Free: 800-342-0295 (wholesale orders)
E-mail: sales@newsoundmusic.com.

NEWSouth Distributors, P.O. Box 61297, Jacksonville, FL 32236-1297 USA (SAN 159-8732).

Newsstand Distributors, 155 W. 14th St., Ogden, UT 84404 USA (SAN 169-8494) Fax: 810-621-7336; Toll Free: 800-283-6247; 800-231-4834 (in Utah).

Ng Hing Kee, 648 Jackson St., San Francisco, CA 94133 USA (SAN 107-1084) Tel 415-781-8330; Fax: 415-397-9766.

Niagara County News, 70 Nicholls St., Lockport, NY 14094 USA (SAN 169-541X) Tel 716-433-6466.

Noelke, Carl B., 529 Main, Box 563, La Crosse, WI 54602 USA (SAN 111-8315) Tel 608-782-8544.

Nonagon, 1556 Douglas Dr., El Cerrito, CA 94530 USA (SAN 654-0503) Tel 510-237-5290.

Nonetheless Pr., *(978-1-932053)* 20332 W. 98th St., Lenexa, KS 66220-2650 USA Tel 913-254-7266; Fax: 913-393-3245
E-mail: mschutte@nonethelesspress.com
Web site: http://www.nonethelesspress.com; http://www.lookingglasspress.com.

Nor-Cal News Co., 2040 Petaluma Blvd., P.O. Box 2508, Petaluma, CA 94953 USA (SAN 169-0035) Tel 707-763-2606; Fax: 707-763-3905.

Norfolk SPCA, 916 Ballentine Blvd., Norfolk, VA 23504 USA Tel 757-622-3319
Web site: http://www.norfolkspca.com.

North American Bk. Distributors, P.O. Box 510, Hamburg, MI 48139 USA (SAN 630-4680) Tel 810-231-3728.

North Carolina News Co., P.O. Box 1051, Durham, NC 27702-1051 USA Tel 919-682-5779.

North Carolina Schl. Bk. Depository, Inc., P.O. Box 950, Raleigh, NC 27602-0950 USA (SAN 169-6467) Tel 919-833-6615.

North Central Bk. Distributors, N57 W13636 Carmen Ave., Menomonee Falls, WI 53051 USA (SAN 173-5195) Tel 414-781-3299; Fax: 414-781-4432; Toll Free: 800-966-3299.

North Country Bks., Inc., *(978-0-925168; 978-0-932052; 978-0-9601158; 978-1-59531)* 220 Lafayette Street, Utica, NY 13502 USA (SAN 110-828X) Tel 315-735-4877; Fax: (315) 738-4342
E-mail: ncbooks@verizon.net
Web site: http://www.northcountrybooks.com.

North Shore Distributors, 1200 N. Branch, Chicago, IL 60622 USA (SAN 169-2275).

North Shore News Co., Inc., 150 Blossom St., Lynn, MA 01902 USA (SAN 169-3492).

North Texas Periodicals, Inc., Orders Addr.: P.O. Box 3823, Lubbock, TX 79452 USA Tel 806-745-6000; Fax: 806-745-7028; Edit Addr.: 118 E. 70th St., Lubbock, TX 79404 USA
E-mail: ntp@hts-online.net.

Northern News Co., P.O. Box 467, Petoskey, MI 49770-0467 USA (SAN 169-3964) Toll Free: 800-632-7138 (Michigan only).

Northern Schl. Supply Co., P.O. Box 2627, Fargo, ND 58108 USA (SAN 169-6548) Fax: 800-891-5836.

Northern Sun, 2916 E. Lake St., Minneapolis, MN 55406 USA (SAN 249-9290) Tel 612-729-2001; Fax: 612-729-0149; Toll Free: 800-258-8579
Web site: http://www.northernsun.com/.

Northern Sun Merchandising, *See* **Northern Sun**

North-South Bks., Inc., *(978-0-7358; 978-1-55858; 978-1-58717)* 350 7th Ave. Rm. 1400, New York, NY 10001-5013 USA
E-mail: rnavarro@northsouth.com
Web site: http://www.northsouth.com.

Northwest News, 1560 NE First St., No. 13, Bend, OR 97701 USA (SAN 111-8587) Tel 541-382-6065; 3100 Merriman Rd., Medford, OR 97501 Tel 541-779-5225.

Northwest News Company, Incorporated, *See* **Benjamin News Group**

Northwest Textbook Depository, Orders Addr.: P.O. Box 5608, Portland, OR 97228 USA Toll Free: 800-676-6630; Edit Addr.: 17970 SW McEwan Rd., Portland, OR 97224 USA (SAN 631-4481) Tel 503-639-3193; Fax: 503-639-2559.

Norton News Agency, 905 Kelly Ln., Dubuque, IA 52003-8526 USA (SAN 169-2631); 1467 Service Dr., Winona, MN 55987 (SAN 156-4889).

Norton, W. W. & Co., Inc., *(978-0-393; 978-0-88150; 978-0-914378; 978-0-936399; 978-0-942440; 978-1-58157; 978-1-324; 978-1-68268)* Orders Addr.: c/o National Book Company, 800 Keystone Industrial Pk., Scranton, PA 18512 USA (SAN 157-1869) Tel 570-346-2020; Fax: 570-346-1442; Toll Free: 800-233-4830; Edit Addr.: 500 Fifth Ave., New York, NY 10110-0017 USA (SAN 202-5795) Tel 212-354-5500; Fax: 212-869-0856; Toll Free: 800-223-2584
Web site: http://www.wwnorton.com.

Notions Marketing, 1500 Buchanan Ave., SW, Grand Rapids, MI 49507-1613 USA.

NTC/Contemporary Publishing Company, *See* **McGraw-Hill/Contemporary**

Nueces News Agency, 5130 Commerce Pkwy., San Antonio, TX 78218-5523 USA (SAN 169-8079).

Nueva Vida Distributors, 4300 Montana Ave., El Paso, TX 79903-4503 USA (SAN 107-8615) Tel 915-565-6215; Fax: 915-565-1722.

Nutri-Bks. Corp., Div. of Royal Pubns., Inc., 790 W. Tennessee Ave., P.O. Box 5793, Denver, CO 80223 USA Tel 303-778-8383; Fax: 303-744-9383; Toll Free: 800-279-2048 (orders only).

Oak Knoll Pr., *(978-0-938768; 978-1-884718; 978-1-58456; 978-1-872116)* 310 Delaware St., New Castle, DE 19720 USA (SAN 216-2776) Tel 302-328-7232; Fax: 302-328-7274; Toll Free: 800-996-2556 Do not confuse with Oak Knoll Press in Hardy, VA
E-mail: oakknoll@oakknoll.com
Web site: http://www.oakknoll.com.

Octagon Pr./ISHK Bk. Service, *See* **I S H K**

Ohio Periodical Distributors, P.O. Box 145449, Cincinnati, OH 45250-5449 USA (SAN 169-6904) Fax: 513-853-6245; Toll Free: 800-777-2216.

Ohio Univ. Pr., *(978-0-8214)* Orders Addr.: 11030 S. Langley Ave., Chicago, IL 60628 USA Tel 773-702-7000; Fax: 773-702-7212; Toll Free Fax: 800-621-8476; Toll Free: 800-621-2736; Edit Addr.: 19 Circle Dr. The Ridges, Athens, OH 45701 USA (SAN 282-0773) Tel 740-593-1154; Fax: 740-593-4536
Web site: http://www.ohiou.edu/oupress/.

Oil City News Co., 112 Innis St., Oil City, PA 16301-2930 USA (SAN 169-7501).

Oleand Pubns., P.O. Box 375, Lyons, WI 53148 USA Tel 262-342-0018 (phone/fax)
E-mail: wings@oleand.com.

Ollis Bk. Corp., Orders Addr.: P.O. Box 258, Steger, IL 60475 USA (SAN 658-1323); Edit Addr.: 28 E. 35th St., Steger, IL 60475 USA (SAN 169-2224) Tel 312-755-5151; Fax: 708-755-5153; Toll Free: 800-323-0343.

Olson, D & Company, *See* **Nelson's Bks.**

Olson News Agency, P.O. Box 129, Ishpeming, MI 49849 USA (SAN 169-3832).

Omega Pubns., Inc., *(978-0-930872; 978-1-941810)* 34 Amity Pl., Amherst, MA 01002-2255 USA (SAN 214-1493) Toll Free: 888-443-7107 (orders only) Do not confuse with companies with the same name in Medford, OR, Indianapolis, IN
E-mail: sufibooks@omegapub.com
Web site: http://www.omegapub.com.

Omnibooks, 456 Vista Del Mar Dr., Aptos, CA 95003-4832 USA (SAN 168-9487) Tel 408-688-4098; Toll Free: 800-626-6671.

Omnibus Pr., *(978-0-7119; 978-0-8256; 978-0-86001; 978-1-84449)* Div. of Music Sales Corp., Orders Addr.: 445 Bellvale Rd., Chester, NY 10918-0572 USA Tel 845-469-4699; Fax: 845-469-7544; Toll Free Fax: 800-345-6842; Toll Free: 800-431-7187; Edit Addr.: 257 Park Ave., S., 20th Flr., New York, NY 10010 USA Tel 212-254-2100; Fax: 212-254-2013 Do not confuse with Omnibus Pr., Menasha, WI
E-mail: info@musicsales.com
Web site: http://www.musicsales.com.

One Small Voice Foundation, P.O. Box 644, Elmhurst, IL 60126 USA Tel 630-620-6634
E-mail: onesmallvoice@earthlink.net
Web site: http://www.onesmallvoicefoundation.org.

Onondaga News Agency, P.O. Box 6445, Syracuse, NY 13217-6445 USA (SAN 169-6297).

OPA Publishing & Distributing, Orders Addr.: P.O. Box 1764, Chandler, AZ 85244-1764 USA; Edit Addr.: 777 W. Chandler Blvd., Suite 1322, Chandler, AZ 85244-1764 USA.

Open Road Distribution, Div. of Open Road Integrated Media, Inc., 345 Hudson St., Suite 6C, New York, NY 10014 USA Tel 212-691-0900; Fax: 212-691-0901.

Open Road Integrated Media, Inc., *(978-1-58586; 978-0-7592; 978-1-936317; 978-1-4532; 978-1-61756; 978-0-9832929; 978-1-937624; 978-1-937957; 978-1-938582; 978-0-615-65097-5; 978-1-62467; 978-1-4804; 978-1-4976; 978-1-5040)* 180 Varick St. Suite 816, New York, NY 10014 USA Tel 212-691-0900; Fax: 212-691-0901; 345 Hudson St., Suite 6C, New York, NY 10014 Tel 212-691-0900; Fax: 212-691-0901
E-mail: acolvin@openroadmedia.com
Web site: http://www.openroadmedia.com.

Options Unlimited, 550 Swan Creek Ct., Suwanee, GA 30174 USA (SAN 631-3949) Tel 770-237-3282 Do not confuse with Options Unlimited, Inc., Green Bay, WI.

OptumInsight, Inc., *(978-1-56329; 978-1-56337; 978-1-60151; 978-1-62254)* 2525 Lake Park Blvd., West Valley City, UT 84120 USA (SAN 630-5482) Tel 801-982-3000; Toll Free: 800-464-3649 (phone/fax)
E-mail: jeni.smith@ingenix.com; chris.smith@ingenix.com; jean.parkinson@ingenix.com
Web site: http://www.ingenix.com; http://www.IngenixOnline.com.

Orange News Company, *See* **Anderson News, LLC**

Orbit Bks. Corp., 43 Timberline Dr., Poughkeepsie, NY 12603 USA (SAN 169-6157) Tel 914-462-5653; Fax: 914-462-8409.

Orca Bk. Pubs. USA, *(978-0-920501; 978-1-55143; 978-1-55469)* Orders Addr.: P.O. Box 468, Custer, WA 98240-0468 USA (SAN 630-9674) Tel 250-380-1229; Fax: 250-380-1892; Toll Free: 800-210-5277
E-mail: orca@orcabook.com
Web site: http://www.orcabook.com.

Oregon State Univ. Pr., *(978-0-87071)* 500 Kerr Administration Bldg., Corvallis, OR 97331-2122 USA (SAN 202-8328) Tel 541-737-3166; Fax: 541-737-3170; Toll Free: 800-426-3797
E-mail: osu.press@oregonstate.edu
Web site: http://osupress.oregonstate.edu/.

O'Reilly & Associates, Incorporated, *See* **O'Reilly Media, Inc.**

O'Reilly Media, Inc., *(978-0-937175; 978-1-56592; 978-3-89721; 978-3-930673; 978-4-900900; 978-0-596; 978-4-87311; 978-1-60033; 978-1-4493; 978-1-4919; 978-1-4920; 978-1-4571)* Orders Addr.: 1005 Gravenstein Hwy. N., Sebastopol, CA 95472 USA (SAN 658-5973) Fax: 707-829-0104; Toll Free: 800-998-9938; Edit Addr.: 10 Fawcett St. Ste. 4, Cambridge, MA 02138-1175 USA Toll Free: 800-775-7731; 4 Castle St, Farnham, GU9 7HR Tel 01252 71 17 76; Fax: 01252 73 42 11; c/o Madeleine Fakhoury Editions O'Reilly, 18, rue Seguier, Paris, F-75006 Tel 33 1 40 51 52 30; Fax: 33 1 40 51 52 31; c/o Michelle Chen, SIGMA Building, Suite B809 No. 49 Zhichun Rd. Haidian District, Beijing, 100080 Tel 86-10-88097476; 86-10-88097475; Fax: 86-10-88097463; c/o O'Reilly Verlag, Gerd Miske, Balthasarstr. 81, Köln, D-50670 Tel 49 221 973160 0; Fax: 49 221 973160 8; 1Fl, No. 21, Lane 295 Section 1, Fu-Shing South Rd., Taipei, Tel 886 2 27099669; Fax: 886 2 27038802; Intelligent Plaza Bldg. 1F 26 Banchi 27, Sakamachi, Shinjuku-ku, Tokyo, 160-0002 Tel 81 3 3356 5227; Fax: 81 3 3356 5261
E-mail: order@oreilly.com; information@oreilly.co.uk; nuts@ora.com
Web site: http://www.oreilly.com; http://www.editions-oreilly.fr; http://oreilly.co.uk; http://oreilly.com.tw; http://www.ora.com; http://www.oreilly.fr/; http://www.oreilly.com.cn/.

Original Pubns., *(978-0-942272)* Subs. of Maximo, Inc., 129 Forest Dr., Jericho, NY 11753-2324 USA (SAN 133-0225) Toll Free: 888-622-8581.

Osborne Enterprises Publishing, *(978-0-932117)* P.O. Box 255, Port Townsend, WA 98368 USA (SAN 242-7567) Tel 360-385-1200; Toll Free: 800-246-3255 (orders only)
E-mail: jpo@olympus.net
Web site: http://www.jerryosborne.com.

Osborne/McGraw-Hill, *See* **McGraw-Hill Osborne**

Osiander Bk. Trade, 7483H Candlewood Rd., Hanover, MD 21076-3102 USA (SAN 130-0970).

Outbooks, Incorporated, *See* **Vistabooks**

Outdoorsman, The, Orders Addr.: P.O. Box 268, Boston, MA 02134 USA (SAN 169-3352).

Outskirts Pr., Inc., *(978-0-9725874; 978-1-932672; 978-1-59800; 978-1-4327; 978-0-615-20388-1; 978-1-4787; 978-1-9772)* 10940 S. Parker Rd. - 515, Parker, CO 80134 USA (SAN 256-5420)
Web site: http://www.OutskirtsPress.com.

Outskirts Press, Incorporation, *See* **Outskirts Pr., Inc.**

OverDrive, Inc., Valley Tech Ctr. 8555 Sweet Valley Dr., Cleveland, OH 44125-4210 USA (SAN 245-0658) Tel 216-573-6886; Fax: 216-573-6888
Web site: http://www.overdrive.com.

OverDrive Systems, Incorporated, *See* **OverDrive, Inc.**

Overmountain Pr., *(978-0-932807; 978-0-9644613; 978-1-57072; 978-1-935692)* P.O. Box 1261, Johnson City, TN 37605 USA (SAN 687-6641) Tel 423-926-2691; Fax: 423-232-1252; Toll Free: 800-992-2691 (orders only)
E-mail: beth@overmtn.com
Web site: http://www.silverdaggermysteries.com; http://www.overmountainpress.com.

Oxford Univ. Pr., *(978-0-19)* Orders Addr.: 2001 Evans Rd., Cary, NC 27513 USA (SAN 202-5892) Tel 919-677-0977 (general voice); Fax: 919-677-1303 (customer service); Toll Free: 800-445-9714 (customer service - inquiry); 800-451-7556 (customer service - orders); Edit Addr.: 198 Madison Ave., New York, NY 10016-4314 USA (SAN 202-5884) Tel 212-726-6000 (general voice); Fax: 212-726-6440 (general fax)
E-mail: custserv@oup-usa.org; orders@oup-usa.org
Web site: http://www.oup.com/us.

Oxmoor Hse., Inc., *(978-0-376; 978-0-8487)* Orders Addr.: Leisure Arts 5701 Ranch Dr., Little Rock, AR 72223 USA; Edit Addr.: 2100 Lakeshore Dr., Birmingham, AL 35209 USA Tel 205-445-6000; Fax: 205-445-6078; Toll Free: 800-633-4910
E-mail: allison_lowery@timeinc.com
Web site: http://www.oxmoorhouse.com/.

Ozark Bk. Distributors, 1802 Van Buren Ave., Mountain Home, AR 72653 USA.

Ozark Magazine Distributing, Incorporated, *See* **Ozark News Distributor, Inc.**

Ozark News Agency, Inc., P.O. Box 1150, Fayetteville, AR 72702 USA.

Ozark News Distributor, Inc., 1630 N. Eldon Ave., Springfield, MO 65803 USA (SAN 169-4332) Tel 417-862-9224; Fax: 417-862-6642; Toll Free: 800-743-0380.

P & G Wholesale, P.O. Box 1548, Fargo, ND 58102 USA (SAN 156-4536).

P & R Publishing, *(978-0-87552; 978-1-59638; 978-1-62995)* Orders Addr.: 1102 Marble Hill Rd., Harmony, Phillipsburg, NJ 08865 USA (SAN 658-1463) Tel 908-454-0505; Fax: 908-859-2390; Toll Free: 800-631-0094 Do not confuse with P & R Publishing Co. in Sioux Center, IA
E-mail: tara@prpbooks.com; jesse@prpbooks.com
Web site: http://www.prpbooks.com.

P C I Education, *(978-1-884074; 978-1-58804; 978-1-61975)* 4560 Lockhill-Selma, Suite 100, San Antonio, TX 78265-4270 USA Tel 210-377-1999; Fax: 210-377-1121; Toll Free Fax: 888-259-8284; Toll Free: 800-594-4263
E-mail: lboulet@pcieducation.com
Web site: http://www.pcieducation.com.

P C I Educational Publishing, *See* **P C I Education**

P. D. Music Headquarters, Inc., Orders Addr.: P.O. Box 252, New York, NY 10014 USA (SAN 282-5880) Tel 212-242-5322.

Pacific Bks., *(978-1-885375)* Orders Addr.: P.O. Box 3562, Santa Barbara, CA 93130 USA (SAN 630-2548) Tel 805-687-8340; Fax: 805-687-2514; Edit Addr.: 2573 Treasure Dr., Santa Barbara, CA 93105 USA.

Pacific Island Bks., 2802 E. 132nd Cir., Thornton, CO 80241 USA Fax: 603-368-6628; Toll Free: 888-492-6657 (888-49-BOOKS)
E-mail: pacificbks@aol.com
Web site: http://www.pacificisiandbooks.com.

Pacific Learning, Inc., *(978-1-59055; 978-1-60457; 978-1-61391; 978-1-59055-000-7)* Orders Addr.: P.O.

Box 2723, Huntington Beach, CA 92647-0723 USA; Edit Addr.: 15342 Graham St., Huntington Beach, CA 92649 USA Tel 714-516-8307; Fax: 714-516-8369; Toll Free: 800-279-0737
E-mail: info@pacificlearning.com
Web site: http://www.pacificlearning.com.

Pacific Magazine-Bk. Wholesaler, 1515 NW 51st St., Seattle, WA 98107 USA (SAN 274-3884) Tel 206-789-5333.

Pacific Periodical Services, LLC, *See* **Anderson News - Tacoma**

Pacific Pr. Publishing Assn., *(978-0-8163; 978-1-5180)* P.O. Box 5353, Nampa, ID 83653-5353 USA (SAN 202-8409) Tel 208-465-2500; Fax: 208-465-2531; Toll Free: 800-447-7377
E-mail: donlay@pacificpress.com
Web site: http://www.AdventistBookCenter.com; http://www.pacificpress.com.

Pacific Trade Group, 68-309 Crozier Dr., Waialua, HI 96791 USA (SAN 169-1635) Tel 808-636-2300; Fax: 808-636-2301.

Paladin Pr., *(978-0-87364; 978-1-58160; 978-1-891268; 978-1-61004)* Orders Addr.: c/o Gunbarrel Tech Ctr., 7077 Winchester Cir., Boulder, CO 80301 USA (SAN 662-1066) Tel 303-443-7250; Fax: 303-442-8741; Toll Free: 800-392-2400 (Credit Card Orders Only)
E-mail: sales@paladin-press.com; editorial@paladin-press.com; service@paladin-press.com
Web site: http://www.paladin-press.com; http://www.flying-machines.com; http://www.sycamoreisland.com.

Palgrave, *See* **Palgrave Macmillan**

Palgrave Macmillan, *(978-0-312; 978-0-333; 978-1-4039; 978-0-230; 978-1-4472; 978-1-137; 978-1-349; 978-1-78632)* Orders Addr.: 16365 James Madison Hwy., Gordonsville, VA 22942-8501 USA Toll Free Fax: 800-672-2054; Toll Free: 888-330-8477; Edit Addr.: 175 Fifth Ave., New York, NY 10010 USA Tel 212-982-9300; Fax: 212-777-6359; Toll Free Fax: 800 672-2054 (Customer Service); Toll Free: 800-221-7945; 888-330-8477 (Customer Service)
E-mail: customerservice@vhpsva.com
Web site: http://www.palgrave.com.

Palmer News Co., Inc., 534 S. Kansas Ave. Ste. 700, Topeka, KS 66603-3429 USA.

Palmer News, Inc., 9605 Dice Ln., Lenexa, KS 66215 USA Tel 913-541-8600; Fax: 913-541-9413
E-mail: palmerco@oni.com.

Palmetto News Co., 200 Sunbelt Ct., Greer, SC 29650-9349 USA.

Pan American Publishing, Inc., *(978-1-889867)* 420 E. Ohio St., Suite 4-F, Chicago, IL 60611-3355 USA (SAN 299-1977) Tel 773-404-7282.

Pan Asia Pubns. (USA), Inc., *(978-1-57227)* 29564 Union City Blvd., Union City, CA 94587 USA (SAN 173-685X) Tel 510-475-1185; Fax: 510-475-1489; Toll Free: 800-909-8088
E-mail: sales@panap.com; info@panap.com
Web site: http://www.panap.com; http://www.cjkv.com.

Pan De Vida Distributors, *(978-1-934811)* 5507 Brooks St., Montclair, CA 91763 USA (SAN 631-0753) Tel 909-510-5219; 909-510-5200; Fax: 909-510-5210
Web site: http://www.pandevida.com.

Panamericana Publishing LLC, 12902 SW 133 Ct., Suite D, Miami, FL 33186 USA (SAN 256-1409) Tel 305-278-2648; Fax: 305-436-7264
E-mail: operez@panamericana.com.co
Web site: http://panamericanaeditorial.com.

Pantheon Bks., *(978-0-375; 978-0-394; 978-0-676; 978-0-679)* Orders Addr.: 400 Hahn Rd., Westminster, MD 21157 USA Toll Free: 800-733-3000 (orders); Edit Addr.: 299 Park Ave, New York, NY 10171 USA (SAN 202-862X).

Paperback Books, Incorporated, *See* **Bk. Distribution Ctr., Inc.**

Paperbacks for Educators, *(978-0-9702376; 978-1-59721)* 426 W. Front St., Washington, MO 63090 USA (SAN 103-3379) Tel 636-239-1999; Fax: 636-239-4515; Toll Free Fax: 800-514-7323; Toll Free: 800-227-2591
E-mail: paperbacks@usmo.com
Web site: http://www.any-book-in-print.com.

Paradise Cay Pubns., *(978-0-939837; 978-1-937196)* P.O. Box 29, Arcata, CA 95518-0029 USA (SAN 663-690X) Tel 707-822-9063; Fax: 707-822-9163; Toll Free: 800-736-4509 (orders only)
E-mail: jim@paracay.com
Web site: http://www.paracay.com.

Parent Services Project, 79 Belvedere St., Suite 101, San Rafael, CA 94901 USA Tel 415-454-1870
E-mail: family@parentservices.org.

Park Pl., 1601 Rio Grande, Suite 455, Austin, TX 78701 USA
Web site: http://www.ed311.com.

Parklane Publishing, *(978-1-59384)* Div. of Book Club of America, 100 Marcus Blvd. Ste. 8, Hauppauge, NY 11788-3749 USA
E-mail: lbaumert@bookclubusa.com
Web site: http://www.parklanepublishing.com.

Parkwest Pubns., Inc., *(978-0-88186)* P.O. Box 310251, Miami, FL 33231 USA (SAN 264-6846) Tel 305-256-7880; Fax: 305-256-7816
E-mail: parkwest@parkwestpubs.com; info@parkwestpubs.com
Web site: http://www.parkwestpubs.com.

Parliament News Co., Inc., P.O. Box 910, Santa Clarita, CA 91380-9010 USA (SAN 168-9924).

Parnassus Bk. Distributors, 200 Academy Way, Columbia, SC 29206-1445 USA (SAN 631-0680) Tel 803-782-7748; Toll Free: 800-782-7760.

Partners Distributing, Orders Addr.: 13089 Root Rd., Columbia Station, OH 44028 USA Tel 216-236-3744.

Pathfinder Pr., *(978-0-87348; 978-0-913460; 978-1-60488)* Orders Addr.: P.O. Box 162767, Atlanta, GA 30321-2767 USA Tel 404-669-0600 (voice mail only); Fax: 707-667-1141; Pathfinder Books/Livres Pathfinder 6362 Fraser St. Suite 264, VANCOUVER, BC V5W 0A1 Tel 888-692-4939; Fax: 029-718-9698; Unit 4, 125 Grafton Rd., London, E2 6DG; P.O. Box 10130,75723, Paris, Cedex 15 FRANCE Tel 014-010-2837; Fax: 014-010-2837; Australia Pathfinder Level 1, 3/281-287 Beamish St., Campsie, NSW, NSW 2194 Tel 029-718-9698; Fax: 029-718-9698; Unit 4, 125 Grafton Rd., Grafton, Auckland, none; Edit Addr.: 306 W. 37th St., 10th Flr., New York, NY 10018 USA (SAN 202-5906) Do not confuse with companies with the same or similar names in Alameda, CA, Battle Ground, WA, Elicott City, MD, Midland, MI
E-mail: pathfinder@pathfinderpress.com; permissions@pathfinderpress.com; orders@pathfinderpress.com
Web site: http://www.pathfinderpress.com.

Pathway Bk. Service, Div. of MLES, Inc., Orders Addr.: 4 White Brook Rd., Gilsum, NH 03448 USA (SAN 170-0545) Tel 603-357-0236; Fax: 603-357-2073; Toll Free: 800-345-6665; P.O. Box 89, Gilsum, NH 03448
E-mail: pbs@pathwaybook.com
Web site: http://www.pathwaybook.com.

Pathway Bks., *(978-0-935538)* P.O. Box 27790, Golden Valley, MN 55427-0790 USA (SAN 213-4241) Tel 612-694-9434; Toll Free: 800-958-3375 (Pin 32) Do not confuse with Pathway Books, Gilsum, NH
E-mail: shermjim@aol.com
Web site: http://www.caregiver911.com.

Paul & Co. Pubs. Consortium, Inc., Div. of Independent Publishers Group, Orders Addr.: 814 N. Franklin St., Chicago, IL 60610 USA Tel 312-337-0747; Fax: 312-337-5985; Toll Free: 800-888-4741
E-mail: frontdesk@ipgbook.com
Web site: http://www.ipgbook.com.

Paulsen, G. Co., 27 Sheep Davis Rd., Pembroke, NH 03275 USA (SAN 169-4499) Tel 603-225-9787.

PBD, Inc., *(978-0-9846038; 978-0-9837260; 978-1-62219)* 1650 Bluegrass Lakes Pkwy., Alpharetta, GA 30004 USA (SAN 126-6039) Tel 770-442-8633; Fax: 770-442-9742
Web site: http://www.pbd.com.

PCE International, 8811 Aviation Blvd., Inglewood, CA 90301 USA Tel 310-337-0055; Fax: 310-642-4625; Toll Free: 800-626-1313.

Peabody Essex Museum, *(978-0-87577; 978-0-88389)* Orders Addr.: East India Sq., Salem, MA 01970 USA Tel 978-745-9500 ext 3047; Fax: 978-740-3622; Toll Free: 800-745-4054 ext 3047
E-mail: wholesale@pem.org
Web site: http://www.pem.org.

Pearson Education, *(978-0-13; 978-0-582; 978-0-7686; 978-1-5093)* Orders Addr.: 200 Old Tappan Rd., Old Tappan, NJ 07675 USA (SAN 200-2175) Tel 201-767-5000 (Receptionist); Toll Free Fax: 800-445-6991; Toll Free: 800-428-5331; 800-922-0579; Edit Addr.: One Lake St., Upper Saddle River, NJ 07458 USA Tel 201-236-7000; 201-236-5321; Fax: 201-236-6549; 800 E. 96th St., Suite 300, Indianapolis, IN 46240 Toll Free: 800-571-4580
E-mail: communications@pearsoned.com
Web site: http://www.pearsoned.com; www.pearson.com.

Pearson Learning, *(978-0-7652; 978-1-4284)* Div of Pearson Education, Orders Addr.: P.O. Box 2500, Lebanon, IN 46052 USA Toll Free Fax: 800-393-3156; Toll Free: 800-321-3106; Edit Addr.: 1 Lake St., U Saddle Riv, NJ 07458-1813 USA Toll Free: 800-526-9907 (Customer Service)
E-mail: jeff.hoitsma@pearsonlearning.com
Web site: http://www.pearsonlearning.com.

Pearson Technology Group, One Lake St., Upper Saddle River, NJ 07458 USA.

Pee Dee News Co., 2321 Lawrens Cir., Florence, SC 29501-9408 USA.

Pegasus Pr., *(978-1-889818)* 2641 S. Emerson St., Chandler, AZ 85248-3248 USA Do not confuse with companies with the same name in Vashon Island, WA, San Diego, CA, Kerrville, TX, Lake Forest, IL
E-mail: pegpress@hotmail.com
Web site: http://www.pegpress.org.

Pegram, Christine, 1901 Upper Cove Terr., Sarasota, FL 33581 USA (SAN 110-0254) Tel 941-921-2467.

Pekin News Agency, 1637 Monroe St., Madison, WI 53711-2021 USA (SAN 169-2151).

Pelican Publishing Co., Inc., *(978-0-88289; 978-0-911116; 978-1-56554; 978-1-58980; 978-1-4556)* Orders Addr.: 1000 Burmaster St., Gretna, LA 70053-2246 USA Tel 504-368-1175; Fax: 504-368-1195; Toll Free: 800-843-1724 ordering Do not confuse with companies with the same or similar names in Lowell, MA, Dallas, TX
E-mail: Sales@pelicanpub.com; promo@pelicanpub.com; editorial@pelicanpub.com
Web site: http://www.pelicanpub.com.

Peller, A. W. & Assocs., 210 Sixth Ave., P.O. Box 106, Hawthorne, NJ 07507-0106 USA (SAN 631-1563) Tel 973-423-4666; Fax: 973-423-5569; Toll Free: 800-451-7450
E-mail: awpeller@worldnet.att.net
Web site: http://www.awpeller.com.

Pen Notes, Inc., *(978-0-939564)* 10111 NW 24th Pl. Apt. 201, Sunrise, FL 33322-6882 USA (SAN 107-3621)
E-mail: pennotes@worldnet.att.net.

Penguin Group (USA) Incorporated, *See* **Penguin Publishing Group**

Penguin Publishing Group, *(978-0-14; 978-0-399; 978-0-425; 978-0-452; 978-0-525; 978-0-698; 978-0-87477; 978-1-58542; 978-1-933438; 978-1-4295; 978-1-934511; 978-1-4362; 978-1-4406; 978-1-101; 978-1-937007)* Orders Addr.: 405 Murray Hill Pkwy., East Rutherford, NJ 07073-2136 USA (SAN 282-5074) Fax: 201-933-2903 (customer service); Toll Free Fax: 800-227-9604; Toll Free: 800-526-0275 (reseller sales); 800-631-8571 (reseller customer service); 800-788-6262 (individual consumer sales); Edit Addr.: 375 Hudson St., New York, NY 10014 USA Tel 212-366-2000; Fax: 212-366-2666; 405 Murray Hill Pkwy., East Rutherford, NJ 07073 (SAN 852-5455) Tel 201-933-9292
E-mail: customer.service@us.penguingroup.com
Web site: http://penguingroup.custhelp.com; http://booksellers.penguingroup.com; http://www.penguinputnam.com.

Penguin Random Hse. LLC, *(978-1-101)* 375 Hudson St. 3rd Flr., New York, NY 10014 USA Tel 212-366-2424
E-mail: brittany.wienke@us.penguingroup.com
Web site: http://www.PenguinRandomHouse.com.

Peniel Productions, 73 Smith Hill Rd., Monsey, NY 10952-4131 USA (SAN 631-2837).

Pen-Mar News Distributors, *See* **Americana Souvenirs & Gifts**

Penmarch Publishing, 3932 S. Willow Ave., Sioux Falls, SD 57105 USA Toll Free: 800-282-2399.

Penn News Co., 944 Franklin St., Johnstown, PA 15905 USA (SAN 169-7390).

Pennsylvania State Univ. Pr., *(978-0-271)* Orders Addr.: 820 N. University Dr., USB-1 Suite C, University Park, PA 16802 USA (SAN 213-5760) Tel 814-865-1327; Fax: 814-863-1408; Toll Free Fax: 877-778-2665 (orders only); Toll Free: 800-326-9180 (orders only)
E-mail: info@psupress.org; log-ins@press.psu.edu
Web site: http://www.psupress.org.

Pentecostal Publishing Hse., *(978-0-912315)* Subs. of United Pentecostal Church International, 8855 Dunn Rd., Hazelwood, MO 63042-2299 USA (SAN 219-3817) Tel 314-837-7300; (314) 837-7300; Fax: 314-837-4503
E-mail: PPHpublish@aol.com.

Penton Overseas, Inc., *(978-0-939001; 978-1-56015; 978-1-59125; 978-1-60379)* 1958 Kellogg Ave., Carlsbad, CA 92008 USA (SAN 631-0826) Tel 760-431-0060; Fax: 760-431-8110; Toll Free: 800-748-5804
E-mail: kellie@pentonoverseas.com; susan@pentonoverseas.com
Web site: http://www.pentonoverseas.com.

Peoples Education, *See* **Mastery Education**

Peregrine Outfitters, Orders Addr.: P.O. Box 1500, Williston, VT 05495 USA (SAN 631-1059) Tel 802-860-2977; Fax: 802-860-2978; Toll Free: 800-222-3088; Edit Addr.: 25 Omega Dr., Suite A, Williston, VT 05482 USA.

Perelandra, Ltd., *(978-0-927978; 978-0-9617713)* Orders Addr.: P.O. Box 3603, Warrenton, VA 20188 USA (SAN 665-0198) Tel 540-937-2153; Fax: 540-937-3360; Toll Free: 800-960-8806
E-mail: email@perelandra-ltd.com
Web site: http://www.perelandra-ltd.com.

Perfection Form Company, The, *See* **Perfection Learning Corp.**

Perfection Learning Corp., *(978-0-7807; 978-0-7891; 978-0-8124; 978-0-89598; 978-1-56312; 978-0-7569; 978-1-60686; 978-1-61563; 978-1-61383; 978-1-61384; 978-1-62299; 978-1-62359; 978-1-62765; 978-1-62766; 978-1-62974; 978-1-63419; 978-1-68064; 978-1-68065; 978-1-68240; 978-1-5311)* 1000 N. 2nd Ave., Logan, IA 51546 USA (SAN 221-0010) Tel 712-644-2831; Fax: 712-644-2392; Toll Free Fax: 800-543-2745; Toll Free: 800-831-4190
E-mail: orders@perfectionlearning.com
Web site: http://www.perfectionlearning.com.

Perfume River Pubns., 1420 2nd Ave., N., Suite 304, Sauk Rapids, MN 56379 USA Tel 320-761-1229.

Periodical Distributors, Incorporated, *See* **North Texas Periodicals, Inc.**

Periodical Marketing Services, 1065 Bloomfield Ave., Clifton, NJ 07012 USA (SAN 250-5304) Tel 201-342-6334.

Periodical Pubs. Service Bureau, One N. Superior St., Sandusky, OH 44870 USA (SAN 285-9351) Tel 419-626-0623.

Periodicals Service Co., *(978-0-527; 978-0-8115; 978-3-262; 978-3-601)* 11 Main St., Germantown, NY 12526 USA (SAN 164-8608) Tel 518-537-4700; Fax: 518-537-5899
E-mail: psc@periodicals.com
Web site: http://www.periodicals.com.

Perma-Bound Bks., *(978-0-605; 978-0-7804; 978-0-8000; 978-0-8479)* Div. of Hertzberg-New Method, Inc., 617 E. Vandalia Rd., Jacksonville, IL 62650 USA (SAN 169-202X) Tel 217-243-5451; Fax: 217-243-7505; Toll Free Fax: 800-551-1169; Toll Free: 800-637-6581 (customer service)
E-mail: books@permabound.com
Web site: http://www.perma-bound.com.

Perrone, Calle 11. #372-A Urb. Hill Brothers, San Juan, PR 00924 USA Tel 787-764-6112; Fax: 787-754-2374 Do not confuse with Perrone in Franklin, TN
E-mail: ecruz@perroneimporters.com
Web site: http://www.perroneimporters.com.

Perry Enterprises, *(978-0-941518)* 3907 N. Foothill Dr., Provo, UT 84604 USA (SAN 171-0281) Tel 801-226-1002.

Perseus Academic, *See* **Ingram Academic**

Perseus Bks. Group, *(978-0-7382; 978-0-938289; 978-1-58097; 978-1-882810; 978-1-903985; 978-1-78239)* Div. of Hachette Book Group, Orders Addr.: 2465 Central Ave., Suite 200, Boulder, CO 80301-5728 USA Toll Free: 800-343-4499 (customer service); Edit Addr.: 387 Park Ave., S., 12th Flr., New York, NY 10016-8810 USA Tel 212-340-8100; Fax: 212-340-8105
Web site: http://www.perseusbooksgroup.com.

Perseus Distribution, *See* **Two Rivers Distribution**

Perseus-PGW, *See* **Publishers Group West (PGW)**

Peterson Publishing Co., Inc., *(978-0-9709033)* 1660 Commerce Dr., Suite 1, North Mankato, MN 56003 USA Tel 507-625-4803 Do not confuse with Peterson Publishing Co. in Gunnison, CO.

Peterson's, *(978-0-7689; 978-0-87866; 978-1-56079)* Div. of Nelnet, Orders Addr.: P.O. Box 67005, Lawrenceville, NJ 08648-6105 USA (SAN 200-2167); Edit Addr.: 2000 Lenox Dr., 3rd Flr., Lawrenceville, NJ 08648 USA (SAN 297-5661) Tel 609-896-1800; Fax: 609-896-1811; Toll Free: 800-338-3282 X5660;Customer Service
E-mail: custsvc@petersons.com
Web site: http://www.petersons.com.

Petterson Antiques, 379 Clayton Dr., Charleston, SC 29414-5048 USA (SAN 114-2399).

Philosophy Documentation Ctr., *(978-0-912632; 978-1-889680; 978-1-63435)* Orders Addr.: P.O. Box 7147, Charlottesville, VA 22906-7147 USA (SAN 218-6586) Tel 434-220-3300; Fax: 434-220-3301; Toll Free: 800-444-2419
E-mail: order@pdcnet.org
Web site: http://www.pdcnet.org.

Phoenix Distributors, Orders Addr.: P.O. Box 1589, Blaine, WA 98231 USA Toll Free Fax: 800-298-4422.

Phoenix Learning Resources, LLC, *(978-0-7915)* Orders Addr.: P.O. Box 510, Honesdale, PA 18431 USA (SAN 246-148X) Tel 570-251-6871; Fax: 570-253-3227; Toll Free: 800-228-9345
E-mail: rich@phoenixlr.com
Web site: http://www.phoenixlr.com.

Phoenix Rising Pr., *(978-0-9840521; 978-1-936429)* PO BOX 18809, Asheville, NC 28814 USA (SAN 631-838X)
E-mail: support@phoenixrisingpress.com; lynnames@lynnames.com
Web site: http://www.phoenixrisingpress.com.

Pictorial Histories Distribution, *See* **West Virginia Book Co., The**

Pilgrim Pr., The/United Church Pr., *(978-0-8298)* Div. of United Church Board for Homeland Ministries, Orders Addr.: 226 Sheldon Rd., Berea, OH 44017-1234 USA Toll Free: 800-537-3394; Edit Addr.: 700 Prospect Ave. E., Cleveland, OH 44115-1100 USA Tel 216-736-3764; Fax: 216-736-2207
E-mail: ucpress@ucc.org; pilgrim@ucc.org
Web site: http://www.ucpress.com; http://www.pilgrimpress.com.

Pine Orchard, Inc., *(978-0-9645727; 978-1-930580)* Orders Addr.: 2850 Hwy 95 South. P.O. box 9184, Moscow, ID 83843 USA (SAN 253-4258) Tel 208-882-4838; Fax: 208-882-4845; Toll Free: 877-354-7433
E-mail: orders@pineorchard.com; pineorch@pineorchard.com
Web site: http://www.pineorchard.com.

Pine Orchard Press, *See* **Pine Orchard, Inc.**

Pioneer Enterprises, W10085 Pike Plain Rd., Dunbar, WI 54119 USA.

Pitsco Education, 1002 E. Adams St., Pittsburg, KS 66762-6050 USA Tel 620-231-0010.

Pittsfield News Co., Inc., 6 Westview Rd., Pittsfield, MA 01201 USA (SAN 124-2768) Tel 413-445-5682; Fax: 413-445-5683.

PixyJack Pr., Inc., *(978-0-9658098; 978-0-9773724; 978-1-936555)* Orders Addr.: P.O. Box 149, Masonville, CO 80541 USA Tel 303-810-2850; Toll Free Fax: 888-273-7499
E-mail: info@pixyjackpress.com
Web site: http://www.pixyjackpress.com.

Plains Distribution Service, P.O. Box 931, Moorhead, MN 56561 USA (SAN 169-6556).

Planeta Publishing Corp., *(978-0-9715256; 978-0-9719950; 978-0-9748724; 978-1-933169; 978-0-9795042)* 999 Ponce De Leon Blvd. Ste. 1045, Coral Gables, FL 33134-3047 USA
E-mail: mnorman@planetapublishing.com
Web site: http://www.planeta.es.

Plank Road Publishing, Orders Addr.: 3540 J N. 126 St., Brookfield, WI 53005 USA Tel 262-790-5210; Fax: 262-781-8818.

Players Pr., Inc., *(978-0-88734)* P.O. Box 1132, Studio City, CA 91614-0132 USA (SAN 239-0213) Tel 818-789-4980
E-mail: Playerspress@att.net.

Plough Publishing Hse., *(978-0-87486)* 151 Bowne Dr., Walden, NY 12586 USA (SAN 202-0092) Tel 845-572-3455; Fax: 845-572-3472; Toll Free: 800-521-8011
E-mail: info@plough.com
Web site: http://www.plough.com.

Plymouth Press, Limited, *See* **Plymouth Toy & Book**

Plymouth Toy & Book, *(978-1-882663)* 101 Panton Rd., Vergennes, VT 05491 USA Tel 802-877-2150; Fax: 802-877-2116; Toll Free: 800-350-1007 Do not confuse with Plymouth Pr. in Miami Beach, FL
E-mail: plymouth@together.net
Web site: http://www.plymouthtoyandbook.com.

PMG Bks. Ltd., P.O. Box 7608, San Antonio, TX 78207-0608 USA (SAN 631-3183).

Polk County Historical Assn., c/o UrbanDog Communications, Inc., P.O. Box 25474, Tampa, FL 33622 USA Tel 813-832-4538; Fax: 813-832-1759
E-mail: cbrownfl@earthlink.net.

Polybook Distributors, Orders Addr.: P.O. Box 109, Mount Vernon, NY 10550 USA Tel 914-664-1633; Fax: 904-428-3953; Edit Addr.: 501 Mamaroneck Ave., White Plains, NY 10605 USA (SAN 169-5568) Tel 914-328-6364
E-mail: mainstreetbook@gmail.com.

Pomona Valley News Agency, 10736 Fremont Ave., Ontario, CA 91762 USA (SAN 169-0019) Tel 909-591-3885.

Pop-M Company, *See* **Bk. Margins, Inc.**

Popular Subscription Service, P.O. Box 1566, Terre Haute, IN 47808 USA (SAN 285-9386) Tel 812-466-1258; Fax: 812-466-9443; Toll Free: 800-466-5038
E-mail: info@popularsubscriptionsvc.com
Web site: http://www.popularsubscriptionsvc.com.

Portland News Co., Orders Addr.: P.O. Box 6970, Scarborough, ME 04070-6970 USA (SAN 169-3093) Toll Free: 800-639-1708 (in Maine); Edit Addr.: 18 Hutcherson Dr., Gorham, ME 04038-2643 USA.

Potter's House Book Service, *(978-1-928717)* 1658 Columbia Rd., NW, Washington, DC 20009 USA Tel 202-232-5483; Fax: 202-328-7483
E-mail: pottershse@aol.com
Web site: http://www.pottershousebooks.com.

Potter's House Church, *See* **Potter's House Book Service**

Powells.com, Orders Addr.: 2720 NW 29th Ave., Portland, OR 97210 USA Tel 800-291-2676
Web site: http://www.powells.com/.

powerHouse Cultural Entertainment, Inc., *(978-1-57687)* 37 Main St., Brooklyn, NY 11201 USA (SAN 850-5845); Mercedes Distribution Ctr. Bldg. 3 Brooklyn Navy Yard, Brooklyn, NY 11205 Tel 212-604-9074; Fax: 212-366-5247
E-mail: info@powerhousebooks.com
Web site: http://www.powerhousebooks.com.

Practice Ring, *(978-0-929758)* Div. of Beeman Jorgensen, Inc., 7510 Allisonville Rd., Indianapolis, IN 46250 USA (SAN 630-6144) Tel 317-841-7677; Toll Free: 800-553-5319.

Pratz News Agency, Orders Addr.: P.O. Box 892, Deming, NM 88030 USA (SAN 159-9275).

Prebound Periodicals, 631 SW Jewell Ave., Topeka, KS 66606-1606 USA (SAN 285-8037).

Premier Pubs., Inc., *(978-0-915665)* P.O. Box 330309, Fort Worth, TX 76163 USA (SAN 292-5966) Tel 817-293-7030; Fax: 817-293-3410.

Presbyterian & Reformed Publishing Company, *See* **P & R Publishing**

Presbyterian Publishing Corp., *(978-0-664)* 100 Witherspoon St., Louisville, KY 40202-1396 USA Tel 502-569-5052; Fax: 502-569-8308; Toll Free Fax: 800-541-5113; Toll Free: 800-227-2872
E-mail: rpinotti@presbypub.com; customer_service@presbypub.com
Web site: http://www.ppcbooks.com.

Prestel Publishing, *(978-3-7913)* Orders Addr.: c/o VNU, 575 Prospect St., Lakewood, NJ 08701 USA Tel 732-363-5679; Fax: 732-363-0338; Toll Free Fax: 877-227-6564; Toll Free: 888-463-6110; Edit Addr.: 900 Broadway, Suite 603, New York, NY 10003 USA Tel 212-995-2720; Fax: 212-995-2733
E-mail: sales@prestel-usa.com
Web site: http://www.prestel.com; http://www.die-gestalten.de; http://www.scalo.com.

Princeton Bk. Co. Pubs., *(978-0-87127; 978-0-916622)* Orders Addr.: P.O. Box 831, Hightstown, NJ 08520-0831 USA (SAN 630-1568) Tel 609-426-0602; Fax: 609-426-1344; Toll Free: 800-220-7149; 614 Rte. 130, Hightstown, NJ 08520 (SAN 244-8076)
E-mail: pbc@dancehorizons.com; elysian@aosi.com
Web site: http://www.dancehorizons.com.

Princeton Univ. Pr., *(978-0-691)* Orders Addr.: California-Princeton Fulfillment Services, 1445 Lower Ferry Rd., Ewing, NJ 08618 USA Tel 800-777-4726; Fax: 800-999-1958; Edit Addr.: 41 William St., Princeton, NJ 08540 USA (SAN 202-0254) Tel 609-258-4900; Fax: 609-258-6305; 3 Market Place, Woodstock, OX20 1SY Tel (0) 1993 814501; Fax: (0) 1993 814504
E-mail: webmaster@pupress.princeton.edu
Web site: http://www.press.princeton.edu.

Print & Ship, 1412 Greenbrier Pkwy., Suite 145-B, Norfolk, VA 23320 USA Tel 757-424-5868.

Printed Matter, Inc., *(978-0-89439)* 195 10th Ave. FRNT, New York, NY 10011-4739 USA (SAN 169-5924)
E-mail: Keith@printedmatter.org; Max@printedmatter.org
Web site: http://www.printedmatter.org.

Production Assocs., Inc., *(978-1-887120)* 1206 W. Collins Ave., Orange, CA 92867 USA Tel 714-771-6519; Fax: 714-771-2456; Toll Free: 800-535-8368
E-mail: mikec@production-associates.com
Web site: http://www.production-associates.com; http://signtospeak.com; http://www.wesign.com.

Productivity, Incorporated, *See* **Productivity Pr.**

Productivity Pr., *(978-0-527; 978-0-915299; 978-1-56327)* Orders Addr.: 7625 Empire Dr., Florence, KY 41042-2919 USA (SAN 290-036X) Toll Free Fax: 800-248-4724; Toll Free: 800-634-7064 (orders).

PRO-ED, Inc., *(978-0-88744; 978-0-89079; 978-0-933014; 978-0-936104; 978-0-944480; 978-1-4164)* Orders Addr.: 8700 Shoal Creek Blvd., Austin, TX 78757-6897 USA (SAN 222-1349) Tel 512-451-3246 Toll Free Fax: 800-397-7633; Toll Free: 800-897-3202; Edit Addr.: P.O. Box 679029, Dallas, TX 75267-9029 USA
E-mail: cheri@proedinc.com
Web site: http://www.proedinc.com.

Professional Book Distributors, Incorporated, *See* **PBD, Inc.**

Professional Media Service Corp., 1160 Trademark Dr., Suite 109, Reno, NV 89511 USA (SAN 630-5776) Toll Free Fax: 800-253-8853; Toll Free: 800-223-7672.

Project Patch, 2404 E. Mill Plain Blvd., Vancouver, WA 98661-4334 USA.

ProQuest Information and Learning, *See* **ProQuest LLC**

ProQuest LLC, *(978-0-14; 978-0-608; 978-0-7837; 978-0-8357; 978-0-88692; 978-0-89093; 978-0-912380; 978-1-55655; 978-0-591; 978-0-9702937; 978-0-599; 978-1-931694; 978-1-59399; 978-0-496; 978-0-542; 978-1-4247; 978-0-9778091; 978-1-60205; 978-1-4345; 978-0-549; 978-1-109; 978-1-124; 978-1-267; 978-1-303; 978-1-321; 978-1-339; 978-1-369; 978-0-355)* *5252 N. Edgewood Dr., Suite 125, Provo, UT 84604 USA Tel 801-765-1737; 789 Eisenhower Pkwy., Ann Arbor, MI 48106-1346 Tel 734-761-4700 Toll Free: 800-521-0600; 7500 Old Georgetown Rd. Suite 1400, Bethesda, MD 20814*
E-mail: sales@csa.com
Web site: http://www.culturegrams.com; http://www.proquest.com/.

Prosperity Publishing Hse., 1405 Autumn Ridge Dr., Durham, NC 27712 USA Tel 919-767-9620.

Provident Music Distribution, 1 Maryland Farms, Brentwood, TN 37027 USA Tel 615-373-3950; Fax: 615-373-0386; Toll Free: 800-333-9000
E-mail: gmiller@pmgsonybmg.com
Web site: http://www.providentmusic.com.

PSI (Publisher Services, Inc.), 3095 Kingston Ct., Norcross, GA 30071-1231 USA Toll Free: 800-755-9653; 877-578-4774.

Public Lands Interpretive Assn., *(978-1-879343; 978-0-9863666)* 6501 Fourth St., NW, No. 1, Albuquerque, NM 87107-5800 USA (SAN 133-3119) Tel 505-345-9498; Fax: 505-344-1543.

Publication Consultants, *(978-0-9644809; 978-1-888125; 978-1-59433)* 8370 Eleusis Dr., Anchorage, AK 99502 USA Tel 907-349-2424; Fax: 907-349-2426
E-mail: evan@publicationconsultants.com
Web site: http://www.publicationconsultants.com.

Publications Unlimited, 7512 Coconut Dr., Lake Worth, FL 33467-6511 USA (SAN 285-9432) Tel 407-434-4688 Do not confuse with Publications Unlimited in Raleigh, NC.

Publishers Business Service, Inc., P.O. Box 25674, Chicago, IL 60625 USA (SAN 285-9459) Tel 312-561-5552.

Publishers Clearing Hse., 382 Channel Dr., Port Washington, NY 11050 USA (SAN 285-9440) Tel 516-883-5432.

Publishers Continental Sales Corp., 613 Franklin Sq., Michigan City, IN 46360 USA (SAN 285-9475) Tel 219-874-4245; Fax: 219-872-8961.

Publishers' Graphics, L.L.C., *(978-0-9663402; 978-1-930847; 978-1-933556; 978-1-934703; 978-1-935590)* 140 Della Ct., Carol Stream, IL 60188 USA (SAN 990-0241) Toll Free: 888-404-3769
Web site: http://www.pubgraphics.com.

Publishers Group International, Inc., *(978-0-9633653)* 1506 27th St. NW, No. 1, Washington, DC 20007 USA Tel 202-342-0886; Fax: 202-338-1940
E-mail: issbooks@aol.com.

Publishers Group West (PGW), Div. of Ingram Content Group, Orders Addr.: 1094 Flex Dr., Jackson, TN 38301-5070 USA (SAN 631-7715) Tel 731-423-1973; Toll Free Fax: 800-351-5073; Toll Free: 800-343-4499; Edit Addr.: 387 Park Avenue South, New York, NY 10016 USA (SAN 631-760X) Tel 212-340-8100; Fax: 212-340-8195
E-mail: info@pgw.com
Web site: http://www.pgw.com/home.

Publishers Media, *(978-0-934064)* 1447 Valley View Rd., Glendale, CA 91202-1716 USA (SAN 159-6683) Tel 818-548-1998.

Publishers News Company, *See* **Mr. Paperback/Publishers News Co.**

Publishers Services, Orders Addr.: P.O. Box 2510, Novato, CA 94948 USA (SAN 201-3037) Tel 415-883-3530; Fax: 415-883-4280.

Publishers Storage & Shipping, 46 Development Rd., Fitchburg, MA 01420 USA Tel 978-345-2121; 660 S. Mansfield Dr., Ypsilanti, MI 48197 Tel 734-487-9720
Web site: http://www.pssc.com.

Publishers Wholesale Assocs., Inc., Orders Addr.: P.O. Box 2078, Lancaster, PA 17608-2078 USA (SAN 630-7450) Fax: 717-397-9253; Edit Addr.: 231 N. Shippen St., Lancaster, PA 17608 USA.

Puerto Rico Postcard, P.O. Box 79710, Carolina, PR 00984-9710 USA.

Pulley Learning Assocs., 210 Alpine Meadow Rd., Winchester, VA 22602-6701 USA (SAN 133-1434).

Pura Vida Bks., Inc., P.O. Box 2002, Salinas, PR 00751 USA Tel 787-824-3763
E-mail: info@puravidabooks.com.

Purple Unicorn Bks., *(978-0-931998)* 1928 W. Kent Rd., Duluth, MN 55812-1154 USA (SAN 111-0071) Tel 218-525-4781 Do not confuse with Purple Unicorn in Augusta, ME.

Puzzle Piece Pubns., 846 36th Ave., N., Saint Cloud, MN 56303 USA Tel 320-656-5361.

QEP, Inc. Professional Bks., 3273 Independence Pkwy., Plano, TX 75086-4964 USA Toll Free: 800-323-6787.

Quality Bks., Inc., *(978-0-89196)* 1003 W. Pines Rd., Oregon, IL 61061-9680 USA (SAN 169-2127) Tel 815-732-4450; Fax: 815-732-4499; Toll Free: 800-323-4241 (libraries only)
E-mail: info@quality-books.com.

Quality Book Fairs, 5787 Ryan Rd., Medina, OH 44256-8823 USA (SAN 630-7752).

Quality Schl. Plan, Inc., P.O. Box 10203, Des Moines, IA 50381-0001 USA (SAN 285-953X).

R & W Distribution, Inc., 87 Bright St., Jersey City, NJ 07302 USA (SAN 169-4723) Tel 201-333-1540; Fax: 201-333-1541
E-mail: rwmag@mail.idt.net.

R. C. Brayshaw, P.O. Box 91, Warner, NH 03278 USA Tel 603-456-3101.

R J Communications, LLC, *(978-0-9700741; 978-1-59664)* 51 E. 42nd St., Suite 1202, New York, NY 10017-5404 USA Tel 212-867-1331; Fax: 212-681-8002; Toll Free: 800-621-2556 (New York)
E-mail: ron@rjcom.com
Web site: http://www.selfpublishing.com; http://www.booksjustbooks.com.

R T R Publishing Company, *See* **Red Toad Road Co.**

Radio Bookstore, P.O. Box 209, Rindge, NH 03461-0209 USA (SAN 111-3496) Tel 603-899-6957 Do not confuse with Radio Bookstore Pr., Bellevue, WA.

Raimond Graphics Inc., Orders Addr.: 360 Sylvan Ave., Englewd Clfs, NJ 07632-2712 USA.

Rainbow Bk. Co., *(978-1-932834; 978-1-60117; 978-1-60447)* 500 E. Main St., Lake Zurich, IL 60047 USA (SAN 920-2935) Tel 800-255-0965; Fax: 847-726-9935 Do not confuse with Rainbow Book Company in Mt. Mourne, NC
E-mail: mike@rainbowbookcompany.com
Web site: http://www.rainbowbookcompany.com.

Rainbow Re-Source Ctr., P.O. Box 491, Kewanee, IL 61443 USA (SAN 631-4007) Tel 309-937-3385; Fax: 309-937-3382
E-mail: rainbowres@aol.com.

Rainier News, Inc., 3400-D Industry Dr., E., Fife, WA 98424-1853 USA (SAN 169-8745) Toll Free: 800-843-2995 (in Washington).

RAM Pubns. & Distribution, *(978-0-9630785; 978-0-9703860; 978-0-9897315)* Bergamot Sta., 2525 Michigan Ave., No. A2, Santa Monica, CA 90404 USA (SAN 298-2641) Tel 310-453-0043; Fax: 310-264-4888
E-mail: rampub@gte.net.

Rand McNally, *(978-0-528)* Orders Addr.: 9855 Woods Dr., Skokie, IL 60077-1074 USA Toll Free Fax: 800-934-3479 (Orders); Toll Free: 800-333-0136 (ext. 4771); 800-678-7263 (Orders)
E-mail: Education@randmcnally.com
Web site: http://www.randmcnally.com.

Random House Adult Trade Publishing Group, *See* **Random House Publishing Group**

Random House, Incorporated, *See* **Random Hse., Inc.**

Random House Publishing Group, Orders Addr.: 400 Hahn Rd., Westminster, MD 21157 USA (SAN 852-5579) Tel 410-848-1900; 410-386-7560; Toll Free: 800-726-0600; Edit Addr.: 1745 Broadway, New York, NY 10019 USA Tel 212-751-2600; Fax: 212-572-4949; Toll Free: 800-726-0600
E-mail: lstark@randomhouse.com.

Random Hse. Bks. for Young Readers, *(978-0-375; 978-0-394; 978-0-517; 978-0-679; 978-1-4000)* Orders Addr.: 400 Hahn Rd., Westminster, MD 21157 USA; Edit Addr.: 1540 Broadway, New York, NY 10036 USA.

Random Hse., Inc., *(978-0-307; 978-0-345; 978-0-375; 978-0-385; 978-0-394; 978-0-440; 978-0-449; 978-0-517; 978-0-553; 978-0-593; 978-0-609; 978-0-676; 978-0-679; 978-0-7364; 978-0-7366; 978-0-7615; 978-0-7679; 978-0-7704; 978-0-8041; 978-0-8052; 978-0-8129; 978-0-8230; 978-0-87637; 978-0-87665; 978-0-87788; 978-0-88070; 978-0-913369; 978-0-914629; 978-0-930014; 978-0-945564; 978-1-57082; 978-1-57673; 978-1-57856; 978-1-878867; 978-1-884536; 978-1-885305; 978-1-58836; 978-1-4000; 978-1-59052; 978-1-4159; 978-)* *Div. of Penguin Random House LLC, Orders Addr.: 400 Hahn Rd., Westminster, MD 21157 USA (SAN 202-5515) Tel 410 848 1900; Toll Free Fax: 800 659 2436; Toll Free: 800 726 0600 (customer service/orders); Edit Addr.: 1745 Broadway, New York, NY 10019 USA (SAN 202-5507) Tel 212 782 9000; Fax: 212 302 7985*
E-mail: customerservice@randomhouse.com
Web site: http://www.randomhouse.com.

Raven West Coast Distribution, 767 W. 18th St., Costa Mesa, CA 92627 USA
E-mail: ken@ravenwcd.com.

Read News Agency, 2501 Greensboro Ave., Tuscaloosa, AL 35401-6520 USA Tel 205-752-3515.

Readerlink Distribution Services, LLC, *(978-0-934429; 978-1-57145; 978-1-59223; 978-1-60710; 978-1-62686; 978-1-68412)* 10350 Barnes Canyon Rd. Suite 100, San Diego, CA 92121 USA (SAN 630-8090) Toll Free: 800-284-3580
E-mail: lnordland@readerlink.com
Web site: http://www.silverdolphinbooks.com; http://www.printersrowpublishinggroup.com; http://www.thunderbaybooks.com/; http://www.bathroomreader.com; http://www.readerlink.com.

Reader's Digest Assn., Inc., The, *(978-0-7621; 978-0-89577; 978-0-86438; 978-1-60652)* One Bedford Rd., Pleasantville, NY 10570 USA (SAN 282-2091) Toll Free: 800-463-8820; 800-334-9599; 800-635-5006
Web site: http://www.readersdigest.com; http://www.rd.com.

Reader's Digest Children's Publishing, Incorporated, *See* **Studio Fun International**

Readex Bk. Exchange, Box 1125, Carefree, AZ 85377 USA (SAN 159-9291).

Reading Circle, The, 7858 Industrial Pkwy., Plain City, OH 43064-9468 USA (SAN 169-670X).

Reading Matters, Inc., *(978-1-930654)* 806 Main St., Akron, PA 17501 USA Tel 717-859-5608; Fax: 717-859-3469; Toll Free: 888-255-6665 Do not confuse with companies with the same name in Brookline, MA, Denver, CO
E-mail: office@readingmatters.net
Web site: http://readingmatters.net.

Reading Peddler Bk. Fairs, 10580 3/4 W. Pico Blvd., Los Angeles, CA 90064 USA (SAN 157-9770) Tel 310-559-2665.

Reading's Fun/Books are Fun, Limited, *See* **Bks. Are Fun, Ltd.**

Readmor, Orders Addr.: P.O. Box 7264, Grand Rapids, MI 49508 USA (SAN 169-3875); Edit Addr.: 301 S. Rath Ave., Ludington, MI 49431 USA Tel 231-843-2537.

Readmore Academic Services, Orders Addr.: P.O. Box 1459, Blackwood, NJ 08012 USA (SAN 630-5741) Tel 609-227-1100; Fax: 609-227-8322; Toll Free: 800-645-6595; Edit Addr.: 700 Black Horse Pike, Suite 207, Blackwood, NJ 08012 USA.

Readmore, Inc., 22 Cortlandt St., New York, NY 10007 USA (SAN 159-9313) Tel 212-349-5540; Fax: 212-233-0746; Toll Free: 800-221-3306.

Recorded Bks., Inc., *(978-0-7887; 978-1-55690; 978-1-84197; 978-1-4025; 978-1-4193; 978-1-84505; 978-1-4281; 978-1-4361; 978-1-4407; 978-1-4498; 978-1-4561; 978-1-4618; 978-1-4640; 978-1-4703; 978-1-4906; 978-1-5019)* Subs. of W. F. Howes Limited, Orders Addr.: 270 Skipjack Rd., Prince Frederick, MD 20678 USA (SAN 111-3984) Fax: 410-535-5499; Toll Free: 800-638-1304; 7257 Pkwy. Dr., Hanover, MD 21076 (SAN 920-7414)
E-mail: thelvey@recordedbooks.com
Web site: http://www.recordedbooks.com.

Recorded Books, LLC, *See* **Recorded Bks., Inc.**

Red Sea Pr., *(978-0-932415; 978-1-56902)* Affil. of Africa World Pr., 541 W. Ingham Ave., Suite B, Trenton, NJ 08638 USA (SAN 630-1983) Tel 609-695-3200; Fax: 609-695-6466
E-mail: awprsp@verizon.net
Web site: http://www.africaworldpressbooks.com.

Red Toad Road Co., *(978-1-889287)* Orders Addr.: P.O. Box 642, Havre de Grace, MD 21078 USA Tel 410-939-4092; Fax: 410-939-5614; Edit Addr.: 223 Heather Way, Havre de Grace, MD 21078 USA
E-mail: redtoadroad@aol.com
Web site: http://www.amazon.com/shops/redtoadroad.

Red Wheel/Weiser, *(978-0-87728; 978-0-943233; 978-1-57324; 978-1-57863; 978-1-59003; 978-1-60925; 978-1-61283; 978-1-61852; 978-1-61940; 978-1-938875; 978-1-63341; 978-1-942785)* Div. of Weiser Bks., Orders Addr.: 65 Parker St., Suite 7, Newburyport, MA 01950 USA (SAN 255-8610) Tel 978-465-0504; Fax: 978-465-0243; Toll Free Fax: 877-337-3309; Toll Free: 800-423-7087 (orders only)
E-mail: customerservice@redwheelweiser.com
Web site: http://www.redwheelweiser.com.

RedShelf, Orders Addr.: 500 North Dearborn St., Suite 1200, Chicago, IL 60654 USA Tel 312-878-8586
E-mail: help@virdocs.com
Web site: http://www.redshelf.com/.

Redwing Bk. Co., Orders Addr.: 202 Bendix Dr., Taos, NM 87571 USA Tel 505-758-7758; Fax: 505-758-7768; Toll Free: 800-873-3946 (USA); 888-873-3947 (Canada); Edit Addr.: P.O. Box 470688, Brookline Vlg, MA 02447-0688 USA (SAN 163-3597) Toll Free: 800-873-3946
E-mail: bob@redwingbooks.com
Web site: http://www.redwingbooks.com.

Reference Bk. Ctr., 175 Fifth Ave., New York, NY 10010 USA (SAN 159-9356) Tel 212-677-2160; Fax: 212-533-0826.

Regent Bk. Co., Inc., Orders Addr.: P.O. Box 750, Lodi, NJ 07644-0750 USA Tel 973-574-7600; Fax: 973-574-7605; Toll Free: 800-999-9554; Edit Addr.: 101 E. Main St. BLDG 5, Little Falls, NJ 07424-1659 USA (SAN 169-4715)
E-mail: info@regentbook.com
Web site: http://www.regentbook.com.

REKO, P.O. Box 4005, Joplin, MO 64803 USA Tel 417-626-0402.

Renaissance News, 5232 Clairton Blvd., Pittsburgh, PA 15236 USA Tel 412-881-4848; Fax: 412-881-5422.

Replica Books, *See* **TextStream**

Representaciones Borinquenas, Inc., *(978-0-9727750; 978-0-9755107)* P.O. Box 139, Aguas Buenas, PR 00703-0139 USA Tel 787-309-9047; Fax: 787-780-5835
E-mail: rborinquenas@centennialpr.net.

Reprint Services Corp., *(978-0-7812; 978-0-932051; 978-1-4227)* P.O. Box 130, Murrieta, CA 92564-0130 USA (SAN 686-2640) Fax: 951-699-5065
E-mail: Reprintservices@gmail.com.

Research Bks., Inc., P.O. Box 555, Old Saybrook, CT 06475-0555 USA
E-mail: info@researchbooks.com.

Resource Software International, Inc., *(978-0-87539)* Affil. of Datamatics Management, 330 New Brunswick Ave., Fords, NJ 08863 USA (SAN 264-8628) Tel 732-738-8500; Fax: 732-738-9603; Toll Free: 800-673-0366
E-mail: info@datamaticsinc.com
Web site: http://www.tc-1.com.

Resurgam Publishing Company, *See* **Blessing Way Publishing Co.**

Reveal Entertainment, Inc., *(978-0-9712633)* 1250 Petroleum Dr. Ste. B6, Abilene, TX 79602-7957 USA
E-mail: revealgames@aol.com
Web site: http://www.revealgames.com.

Review & Herald Publishing Assn., *(978-0-8127; 978-0-8280)* 55 W. Oak Ridge Dr., Hagerstown, MD 21740 USA (SAN 203-3798) Tel 301-393-3000
E-mail: smulkern@rhpa.org
Web site: http://www.reviewandherald.com/.

Revolution Booksellers, 60 Winter St., Exeter, NH 03833 USA Tel 603-772-7200; Fax: 603-772-7200; Toll Free: 800-738-6603.

Rhinelander News Agency, 314 Courtney, Crescent Lake, WI 54501 USA (SAN 159-9372) Tel 715-362-6397.

Rhino Entertainment Co, A Warner Music Group Co., *(978-0-7379; 978-0-930589; 978-1-56826; 978-0-9797278)* 3400 W. Olive Ave., Burbank, CA 91505 USA (SAN 677-5454) Tel 818-238-6110; Fax: 818-562-9239
E-mail: gladys.sanchez@wmg.com; tracie.bowers@wmg.com
Web site: http://www.rhino.com.

Rhodes News Agency, *See* **Treasure Valley News**

Richardson's Bks., Inc., 2014 Lou Ellen Ln., Houston, TX 77018 USA (SAN 169-829X) Tel 713-688-2244; Fax: 713-688-8420; Toll Free: 800-392-8562.

Richardson's Educators, *See* **Richardson's Bks., Inc.**

Right Start, Inc., 5388 Sterling Center Dr., Suite C, Westlake Village, CA 91361-4687 USA (SAN 631-7022).

Rio Grande Bk. Co., P.O. Box 2795, McAllen, TX 78502-2795 USA (SAN 169-8354).

Rio Nuevo Pubs., *(978-0-918080; 978-1-887896; 978-0-9700750; 978-1-933855; 978-1-940322)* Orders Addr.: P.O. Box 5250, Tucson, AZ 85703-0250 USA (SAN 209-3251) Tel 520-623-9558; Fax: 520-624-5888; Toll Free Fax: 800-715-5888; Toll Free: 800-969-9558; Edit Addr.: 451 N. Bonita Ave., Tucson, AZ 85745 USA Tel 602-623-9558
E-mail: info@rionuevo.com; info@treasurechestbooks.com; suzang@rionuevo.com
Web site: http://www.treasurechestbooks.com; http://www.rionuevo.com/.

Rip Off Pr., *(978-0-89620)* Orders Addr.: P.O. Box 4686, Auburn, CA 95604 USA (SAN 207-7671) Tel 530-885-8183; Toll Free: 800-468-2669
E-mail: mail@ripoffpress.com
Web site: http://www.ripoffpress.com.

Rishor News Co., Inc., 109 Mountain Laurel Dr., Butler, PA 16001-3921 USA (SAN 159-9402).

Rittenhouse Bk. Distributors, *(978-0-87381)* Orders Addr.: P.O. Box 61565, Kng Of Prussa, PA 19406-0965 USA (SAN 213-4454) Toll Free Fax: 800-223-7488; Toll Free: 800-345-6425
E-mail: alan.yockey@rittenhouse.com; joan.townshend@rittenhouse.com
Web site: http://www.rittenhouse.com.

Ritter Bk. Co., 7011 Foster Pl., Downers Grove, IL 60516-3446 USA (SAN 169-1856).

River Canyon Distributing, P.O. Box 70643, Eugene, OR 97401 USA.

River Road Recipes Cookbook, 9523 Fenway Dr., Baton Rouge, LA 70809 USA (SAN 132-7852) Tel 504-924-0300; Fax: 504-927-2547; Toll Free: 800-204-1726.

RiverStream Publishing, *(978-0-9834972; 978-1-62243)* 123 S. Broad St., Mankato, MN 56001 USA Tel 414-378-2480
E-mail: jstrick@hickorytech.net.

Rizzoli International Pubns., Inc., *(978-0-8478; 978-0-88363; 978-0-941807; 978-1-932183; 978-1-59962)* Subs. of RCS Rizzoli Editore Corp., 300 Park Ave., S., 3rd Flr., New York, NY 10010 USA (SAN 111-9192) Tel 212-387-3400; Fax: 212-387-3535
Web site: http://www.rizzoliusa.com/.

Roadrunner Library Service, c/o Kerbs, 700 Highview Ave., Glen Ellyn, IL 60137-5504 USA.

Roberts, F.M. Enterprises, *(978-0-912746)* P.O. Box 608, Dana Point, CA 92629-0608 USA (SAN 201-4688) Tel 714-493-1977; Fax: 714-493-7124.

Rockbottom Bks., Pentagon Towers, P.O. Box 398166, Minneapolis, MN 55439 USA (SAN 108-4402) Tel 612-831-2120.

Rockland Catskill, Inc., 26 Church St., Spring Valley, NY 10977 USA (SAN 169-6254) Tel 914-356-1222; Fax: 914-356-8415; Toll Free: 800-966-6247.

Rocky Mount News Agency, Two Great State Ln., Rocky Mount, NC 27801 USA.

Rodale Institute Bookstore, *(978-0-9652477)* 611 Siegfriedale Rd., Kutztown, PA 19530 USA Tel 610-683-6009; Fax: 610-683-8548; Toll Free: 800-832-6285
E-mail: ribooks@fast.net
Web site: http://www.rodaleinstitute.org.

Rogue Valley News Agency, Inc., 550 Airport Rd., Medford, OR 97504-4156 USA (SAN 169-7137).

Rohr, Hans E., 76 State St., Newburyport, MA 01950-6616 USA (SAN 113-8804).

Roig Spanish Bks., 146 W. 29th St., No. 3W, New York, NY 10001-5303 USA (SAN 165-1021) Fax: 212-695-6811.

Romeii LLC, *(978-0-9830484; 978-1-937391)* 1050 Sommers St. N, Hudson, WI 54016 USA Tel 651-204-3753
E-mail: steve@romeii.com
Web site: Romeii.com.

Rosen Publishing Group, Inc., The, *(978-0-8239; 978-1-56696; 978-1-4042; 978-1-4358; 978-1-60851; 978-1-60852; 978-1-60853; 978-1-60854; 978-1-61511; 978-1-61512; 978-1-61513; 978-1-61514; 978-1-61530; 978-1-61531; 978-1-61532; 978-1-61533; 978-1-4488; 978-1-4777; 978-1-4824; 978-1-4994; 978-1-68048; 978-1-5081; 978-1-68416; 978-1-5382; 978-1-5383) a/o Dept. C234561, 29 E. 21st St., New York, NY 10010 USA (SAN 203-3720) Tel 212-777-3017; Fax: 212-358-9588; Toll Free Fax: 888-436-4643; Toll Free: 800-237-9932*
E-mail: info@rosenpub.com; customerservice@rosenpub.com; deang@rosenpub.com; hollyc@rosenpub.com
Web site: http://www.rosenpublishing.com; http://www.rosendigital.com; http://www.rosenclassroom.com.

Rosen Publishing Group, Incorporated, The, *See* **Rosen Publishing Group, Inc., The**

Rosenblum's, *See* **Rosenblum's World of Judaica, Inc.**

Rosenblum's World of Judaica, Inc., 2906 W. Devon Ave., Chicago, IL 60659 USA (SAN 169-1864) Tel 773-262-1700; Fax: 773-262-1930; Toll Free: 800-626-6536.

Rosewood Foundation, The, Orders Addr.: P.O. Box 252, Archer, FL 32618 USA Tel 352-495-2197; Fax: 352-495-8313
E-mail: lizziePRJ@aol.com.

Rounder Kids Music Distribution, Orders Addr.: P.O. Box 516, Montpelier, VT 05602 USA (SAN 630-6675) Tel 802-223-5825; Fax: 802-223-5303; Toll Free: 800-223-6357; Edit Addr.: 80 W. Harvey Farm Rd., Waterbury Ctr, VT 05677-7132 USA
E-mail: Pauls@rounder.com.

Rowman & Littlefield Publishers, Inc., *(978-0-8476; 978-0-87471; 978-0-9632978; 978-1-56699; 978-1-888052; 978-0-7425; 978-1-931890; 978-1-933494; 978-1-4422; 978-1-936283; 978-1-61281; 978-1-4616; 978-1-4617; 978-1-62093; 978-1-5381)* Mem. of Rowman & Littlefield Publishing Group, Inc., Orders Addr.: 15200 NBN Way, Blue Ridge Summit, PA 17214 USA Tel 717-794-3800 (Sales, Customer Service, MIS, Royalties, Inventory; Fax: 717-794-3803 (Customer Service & orders only); 717-794-3857 (Sales & MIS); 717-794-3856 (Royalties, Inventory Mgmt. & Distribution); Toll Free Fax: 800-338-4550 (Customer Service & orders); Toll Free: 800-462-6420 (Customer Service & orders); Edit Addr.: 4501 Forbes Blvd., Suite 200, Lanham, MD 20706 USA Tel 301-459-3366; Fax: 301-459-5749; Toll Free: 800-462-6420 Short Discount, please contact rlpgsales@rowman.com
E-mail: rlpgsales@rowman.com; lweston@rowman.com
Web site: http://www.rowmanlittlefield.com; http://www.rlpgbooks.com/bookseller/index.shtml.

Royal Pubns., Inc., *(978-0-918738)* Orders Addr.: P.O. Box 5793, Denver, CO 80217 USA (SAN 244-7193) Tel 303-778-8383; Toll Free: 800-279-2048 (orders only); Edit Addr.: 790 W. Tennessee Ave., Denver, CO 80223 USA (SAN 169-054X).

Rumpf, Raymond & Son, Orders Addr.: P.O. Box 319, Sellersville, PA 18960 USA (SAN 631-5259).

Rushmore News, Inc., 924 East St. Andrew, Rapid City, SD 57701 USA (SAN 169-7846) Tel 605-342-2617; Fax: 605-342-9091; Toll Free: 800-423-0501
E-mail: afreese911@aol.com.

Russell News Agency, Inc., P.O. Box 158, Sarasota, FL 33578 USA (SAN 169-1287).

Russica Bk. & Art Shop, Inc., 799 Broadway, New York, NY 10003 USA (SAN 165-1072) Tel 212-473-7480; Fax: 212-473-7486.

S & L Sales Co., Inc., Orders Addr.: P.O. Box 2067, Waycross, GA 31502 USA (SAN 107-413X) Tel 912-283-0210; Fax: 912-283-0261; Toll Free: 800-243-3699 (orders only).

S & S News & Greeting, 5304 15th Ave., S., Minneapolis, MN 55417-1812 USA (SAN 159-9453) Tel 612-224-8227; Toll Free: 800-346-9892.

S & W Distributors, Inc., 1600-H E. Wendover Ave., Greensboro, NC 27405 USA.

S. A. V. E. with Victor Hotho, *See* **S.A.V.E. Suzie & Vic Enterprises**

S V E & Churchill Media, *(978-0-7932; 978-0-89290; 978-1-56357)* 6465 N. Avondale Ave., Chicago, IL 60631-1909 USA (SAN 208-3930) Toll Free Fax: 800-624-1678; Toll Free: 800-829-1900
E-mail: custserv@svemedia.com
Web site: http://www.svemedia.com.

SAAN Corp., 189-01 Springfield Ave., Suite 201, Flossmoor, IL 60422 USA (SAN 631-0419) Tel 708-799-5225; Fax: 708-799-8713.

Saddleback Educational Publishing, *See* **Saddleback Educational Publishing, Inc.**

Saddleback Educational Publishing, Inc., *(978-1-56254; 978-1-59905; 978-1-60291; 978-1-61651; 978-1-61247; 978-1-62250; 978-1-62670; 978-1-63078; 978-1-68021)* 3120-A Pullman St., Costa Mesa, CA 92626-4564 USA (SAN 860-0902) Toll Free Fax: 888-734-4010; Toll Free: 800-637-8715
E-mail: contact@saddleback.com; amchugh@sdlback.com; cpizer@sdlback.com
Web site: http://www.saddlebackpublishing.com.

Sadler, Dale, 209 Foster Dr., White House, TN 37188 USA.

Safari Museum Pr., 111 N. Lincoln Ave., Chanute, KS 66720 USA Tel 630-431-2730; Fax: 630-431-3848.

SAGE Pubns., Inc., *(978-0-7619; 978-0-8039; 978-1-4129; 978-1-4522; 978-1-4462; 978-1-4833; 978-1-5063; 978-1-5443)* 2455 Teller Rd., Thousand Oaks, CA 91360 USA (SAN 204-7217) Tel 800-818-7243; Fax: 800-583-2665; 805-499-0871
E-mail: info@sagepub.com; deborah.vaughn@sagepub.com
Web site: http://www.sagepub.com; http://www.sagepub.co.uk; http://www.pineforge.com; http://sagepub.com.

Sagebrush Pr., *(978-0-930704)* P.O. Box 87, Morongo Valley, CA 92256 USA (SAN 113-387X) Tel 760-363-7398 Do not confuse with companies with same name in Cedarville, CA, Salt Lake City, UT.

Saint Benedict Pr., Div. of Saint Benedict Press, LLC, Orders Addr.: P.O. Box 410487, Charlotte, NC 28241 USA Toll Free: 800-437-5876
Web site: https://books.benedictpress.com/.

Saint George Book Service, Incorporated, *See* **Steiner, Rudolf College Pr./St. George Pubns.**

Saks News, Inc., P.O. Box 1857, Bismarck, ND 58502 USA (SAN 169-653X).

Sams Technical Publishing, LLC, *(978-0-7906; 978-0-578-12070-6)* 9850 E. 30th St., Indianapolis, IN 46229 USA Toll Free Fax: 800-552-3910; Toll Free: 800-428-7267
E-mail: samstech@samswebsite.com
Web site: http://www.samswebsite.com.

San Diego Museum of Art, *(978-0-937108; 978-0-9845555)* Orders Addr.: P.O. Box 122107, San Diego, CA 92112-2107 USA Tel 619-696-1970; Fax: 619-232-9367
E-mail: sward@sdmart.org
Web site: http://www.sdmart.org.

San Francisciana, *(978-0-934715)* P.O. Box 590955, San Francisco, CA 94159 USA (SAN 161-1607) Tel 415-751-7222.

San Val, Incorporated, *See* **Turtleback Bks.**

Sandlapper Publishing Co., Inc., *(978-0-87844)* Orders Addr.: P.O. Box 730, Orangeburg, SC 29115 USA (SAN 203-2678) Toll Free Fax: 800-337-9420 (orders); Toll Free: 800-849-7263 (orders); Edit Addr.: 1281 Amelia St., NE., Orangeburg, SC 29116 USA Tel 803-533-1658; Fax: 803-534-5223
E-mail: agallman1@bellsouth.net
Web site: http://www.sandlapperpublishing.com.

Sandvik Publishing, *(978-1-58048; 978-1-881445)* Div. of Sandviks Bokforlag, Norway, 3729 Knights Rd., Bensalem, PA 19020-2908 USA Toll Free: 800-843-2445
E-mail: Nicole@sandvikpublishing.com; cust-serv@sandvikpublishing.com
Web site: http://www.sandviks.com.

Santa Barbara Botanic Garden, *(978-0-916436)* 1212 Mission Canyon Rd., Santa Barbara, CA 93105 USA (SAN 208-8398) Tel 805-682-4726; Fax: 805-563-0352
E-mail: info@sbbg.org
Web site: http://www.sbbg.org.

Santa Barbara News Agency, 725 S. Kellogg Ave., Goleta, CA 93117-3806 USA (SAN 168-9665) Tel 805-564-5200.

Santa Monica Software, Inc., 30018 Zenith Point Rd., Malibu, CA 90265-4264 USA (SAN 630-6764) Tel 310-457-8381; Fax: 310-395-7635.

Santillana USA Publishing Co., Inc., *(978-0-88272; 978-1-56014; 978-1-58105; 978-1-58986; 978-1-59437; 978-1-59820; 978-1-60396; 978-1-61605; 978-1-61435; 978-1-62263; 978-1-63113; 978-1-68292; 978-1-64101)* Div. of Grupo Santillana, 2023 NW 84th Ave., Doral, FL 33122 USA (SAN 205-1133) Tel 305-591-9522 Toll Free Fax: 888-248-9518 (orders); Toll Free: 800-245-8584; Av. Rio Mixcoac No. 274 Col. Acacias, C.P. 0324 Benito Juarez, Ciudad de Mexico, DF,
E-mail: dpena@santillanausa.com; esanta@santillanausa.com; customerservice@santillanausa.com
Web site: http://www.santillanausa.com.

Saphrograph Corp., *(978-0-87557)* 5409 18th Ave., Brooklyn, NY 11204 USA (SAN 110-4128) Tel 718-331-1233; Fax: 718-331-8231
E-mail: saphrograph@verizon.net.

Sathya Sai Bk. Ctr. of America, *(978-1-57836)* 305 W. First St., Tustin, CA 92780 USA (SAN 111-3542) Tel 714-669-0522; Fax: 714-669-9138
Web site: http://www.sathyasaibooks.com.

Satsang Press, *See* **Gangaji Foundation, The**

S.A.V.E. Suzie & Vic Enterprises, 303 N. Main, P.O. Box 30, Schulenburg, TX 78956 USA (SAN 630-6365) Tel 409-743-4145; Fax: 409-743-4147.

SCB Distributors, Orders Addr.: 15608 S. New Century Dr., Gardena, CA 90248-2129 USA (SAN 630-4818) Tel 310-532-9400; Fax: 310-532-7001; Toll Free: 800-729-6423 (orders only)
E-mail: info@scbdistributors.com
Web site: http://www.scbdistributors.com.

Schmul Publishing Co., Inc., *(978-0-88019)* Orders Addr.: P.O. Box 716, Salem, OH 44460-0716 USA (SAN 180-2771) Tel 330-222-2249; Fax: 330-222-0001; Toll Free: 800-772-6657; Edit Addr.: 3583 Newgarden Rd., Salem, OH 44460 USA
E-mail: spchale@valunet.com
Web site: http://www.wesleyanbooks.com.

Schoenhof's Foreign Bks., Inc., *(978-0-87774)* 76a Mount Auburn St., Cambridge, MA 02138-5051 USA (SAN 212-0062)
E-mail: info@schoenhofs.com
Web site: http://www.schoenhofs.com.

Scholar's Bookshelf, *(978-0-678; 978-0-945726; 978-1-60105)* Orders Addr.: 110 Melrick Rd., Cranbury, NJ 08512 USA (SAN 110-8360) Tel 609-395-6933; Fax: 609-395-0755
E-mail: books@scholarsbookshelf.com
Web site: http://www.scholarsbookshelf.com.

Scholastic Bk. Fairs, P.O. Box 958411, Lake Mary, FL 32795-8411 USA (SAN 173-7457) Tel 407-829-2600.

Scholastic, Inc., *(978-0-439; 978-0-590; 978-0-545; 978-1-338)* 557 Broadway, New York, NY 10012-3999 USA (SAN 202-5442) Fax: 212-343-6802; Toll Free: 800-325-6149 (customer service)
E-mail: info@scholastic.com
Web site: http://www.scholastic.com.

Scholium International, Inc., *(978-0-87936)* P.O. Box 1519, Port Washington, NY 11050-0306 USA (SAN 169-5282) Tel 516-767-7171; Fax: 516-944-9824
E-mail: info@scholium.com
Web site: http://www.scholium.com.

School Aid Co., *(978-0-87385)* 911 Colfax Dr., P.O. Box 123, Danville, IL 61832 USA (SAN 158-3719) Tel 217-442-6855; Toll Free: 800-447-2665.

School Aids, 9335 Interline Ave., Baton Rouge, LA 70809-1910 USA (SAN 169-2909) Tel 504-926-4498.

School Bk. Service, 3650 Coral Ridge Dr., Suite 112, Coral Springs, FL 33065-2559 USA (SAN 158-6963) Tel 954-341-7207; Fax: 954-341-7303; Toll Free: 800-228-7361
E-mail: compedge@ix.netcom.com.

School of Metaphysics, 163 Moonvalley Rd., Windyville, MO 65783 USA (SAN 159-5423) Tel 417-345-8411; Fax: 417-345-6668
E-mail: som@som.org
Web site: http://www.som.org.

Schroeder News Company, *See* **Merced News Co.**

Schroeder's Bk. Haven, 104 Michigan Ave., League City, TX 77573 USA (SAN 122-7998) Tel 281-332-5226; Fax: 281-332-1695; Toll Free: 800-894-5032
E-mail: schroedr@interloc.com.

Schulze News Co., 2451 Eastman Ave., Suite 13, Oxnard, CA 93030-5193 USA (SAN 169-0434) Tel 805-642-9759.

Schuylkill News Service, 1801 W. Market St., Pottsville, PA 17901-2001 USA (SAN 159-9518).

Schwartz, Arthur & Company, Incorporated/Woodstocker Books, *See* **Woodstocker Books/Arthur Schwartz & Company**

Schwartz Brothers, Inc., 822 Montgomery Ave., No. 204, Narberth, PA 19072-1937 USA (SAN 285-7529) Fax: 301-459-6418; Toll Free: 800-638-0243.

Science Kit & Boreal Labs, P.O. Box 5003, Tonawanda, NY 14151-5003 USA (SAN 631-2314)
E-mail: sk@sciencekit.com.

Scientific & Medical Pubns. of France, Inc., P.O. Box 3490, New York, NY 10163-3490 USA (SAN 169-5940).

SCPBooks, *See* **Phoenix Rising Pr.**

Seaboard Sub Agency, 215 S. Ott St., Allentown, PA 18104-6147 USA (SAN 285-9718).

Seaburn Bks., P.O. Box 2085, Long Island City, NY 11102 USA (SAN 631-2799) Tel 718-274-7040
E-mail: info@seaburn.com.

Seattle Bk. Co., Orders Addr.: P.O. Box 2222, Poulsbo, WA 98370 USA Tel 206-922-0418; Edit Addr.: 18864 Front St., Suite 200, Poulsbo, WA 98370 USA
E-mail: sales@seattlebookcompany.com.

Selective Bks., Inc., *(978-0-912584)* P.O. Box 1140, Clearwater, FL 34617 USA (SAN 204-577X) Tel 813-447-0100.

Selective Publishers, Incorporated, *See* **Selective Bks., Inc.**

Semler News Agency, Orders Addr.: P.O. Box 350, New Castle, PA 16101 USA (SAN 169-7471); Edit Addr.: P.O. Box 526, Morgantown, WV 26505 USA (SAN 169-8990).

Send The Light Distribution LLC, *(978-0-9835608; 978-1-939900)* Orders Addr.: 129 Mobilization Dr., Waynesboro, GA 30830 USA (SAN 631-8894) Tel 706-554-5827; Toll Free Fax: 877-323-4551; Toll Free: 877-323-4550; 100 Biblica Way, Elizabethton, TN 37643-6070 (SAN 630-7388) Tel 423-547-5131 editorial Toll Free Fax: 800-759-2779
E-mail: Customerservice@stl.org
Web site: http://www.stl-publisherservices.com.

Seneca News Agency, 800 Pre Emption Rd., Geneva, NY 14456-2010 USA (SAN 169-5304).

Sentai Distributors, 8839 Shirley Ave., Northridge, CA 91324 USA (SAN 168-9959) Tel 818-886-3113; Fax: 818-886-0423
Web site: http://www.plasticmodels.com.

Sepher-Hermon Pr., *(978-0-87203)* 1153 45th St., Brooklyn, NY 11219 USA (SAN 169-5959) Tel 718-972-9010; Fax: 718-972-6935.

Serendipity Couriers, Inc., P.O. Box 5897, Vallejo, CA 94591-5897 USA (SAN 169-0329) Toll Free: 800-459-4005 (Bay area only)
E-mail: dipity@14.netcom.com.

Serpent's Tale Natural History Bk. Distributors, Inc., *(978-1-885209)* Orders Addr.: P.O. Box 405, Lanesboro, MN 55949-0405 USA (SAN 630-6101) Tel 507-467-8734; Fax: 507-467-8735
E-mail: zoobooks@acegroup.cc
Web site: http://www.zoobooksales.com.

Service News Co., 1306 N. 23rd St., Wilmington, NC 28406 USA (SAN 169-6491) Tel 910-762-0837; Fax: 910-762-9539; Toll Free: 800-552-8238; P.O. Box 5027, Macon, GA 31208; Pope's Island, Box D-629, New Bedford, MA 02742 (SAN 169-3514).

Seven Locks Pr., *(978-0-929765; 978-0-932020; 978-0-9615964; 978-1-931643; 978-0-9790950; 978-0-9795852; 978-0-9801270; 978-0-9822293; 978-0-9824957)* P.O. Box 25689, Santa Ana, CA 92799-5689 USA (SAN 211-9781) Toll Free: 800-354-5348
E-mail: sevenlocks@aol.com
Web site: http://www.sevenlockspublishing.com.

Seymour, Dale Pubns., *(978-0-201; 978-0-7690; 978-0-86651; 978-1-57232)* Div. of Pearson Learning, Orders Addr.: P.O. Box 2500, Lebanon, OH 43216 USA Toll Free Fax: 800-393-3156; Toll Free: 800-321-3106 (Customer Service); Edit Addr.: 10 Bank St., White Plains, NY 10602-5026 USA (SAN 200-9781) Toll Free Fax: 800-393-3156; Toll Free: 800-237-3142
E-mail: pearson_learning2@prenhall.com
Web site: http://www.pearsonlearning.com; http://www.pearsonlearning.com/rightsPerm.rtf.

Shambhala Publications, Incorporated, *See* **Shambhala Pubns., Inc.**

Shambhala Pubns., Inc., *(978-0-8348; 978-0-87773; 978-0-937938; 978-0-9627138; 978-1-55939; 978-1-56957; 978-1-57062; 978-1-930485; 978-1-59030; 978-1-61180)* 4720 Walnut St., Boulder, CO 80301 USA (SAN 203-2481) Tel 303-222-9598; 978-829-2599 (international); Toll Free: 888-424-2329 (orders)
E-mail: editors@shambhala.com; support@shambhala.com; customercare@shambhala.com
Web site: http://www.shambhala.com.

Sharon News Agency Co., 527 Silver St., Sharon, PA 16146 USA (SAN 169-7633).

Sharpe, M.E. Inc., *(978-0-7656; 978-0-87332; 978-1-56324)* 80 Business Park Dr., Armonk, NY 10504 USA (SAN 202-7100) Tel 914-273-1800; Fax: 914-273-2106; Toll Free: 800-541-6563
Web site: http://www.mesharpe.com.

Shea Bks., 1563 Solano Ave., Suite 206, Berkeley, CA 94707 USA (SAN 159-9720) Tel 510-528-5201; Fax: 510-528-4987.

Shell Educational Publishing, *(978-1-4258)* 5301 Oceanus Dr., Huntington Beach, CA 92649 USA Tel 714-489-2080; Fax: 714-230-7070; Toll Free: 888-877-7606; 877-777-3450
E-mail: cmiller2@tcmpub.com; LShill@seppub.com; pkoehl@tcmpub.com; CMiller2@teachercreatedmaterials.com
Web site: http://www.seppub.com; http://www.tcmpub.com.

Shelter Pubns., Inc., *(978-0-936070)* Orders Addr.: P.O. Box 279, Bolinas, CA 94924 USA (SAN 122-8463) Tel 415-868-0280; Fax: 415-868-9053; Toll Free: 800-307-0131; Edit Addr.: 285 Dogwood Rd, Bolinas, CA 94924 USA
E-mail: shelter@shelterpub.com
Web site: http://www.shelterpub.com.

Shenanigan Bks., *(978-0-9726614; 978-1-934860)* 84 River Rd., Summit, NJ 07901-1443 USA (SAN 915-7085)
Web site: http://www.shenaniganbooks.com.

Shoppers Guide Pr., 706 N. Fifth, Alpine, TX 79830 USA (SAN 159-9550) Tel 915-837-7426.

Sierra News Co., 2136 Pony Express Ct., Stockton, CA 95215-7946 USA (SAN 169-4472).

Signature Bks., LLC, *(978-0-941214; 978-1-56085)* 564 W. 400 N., Salt Lake City, UT 84116-3411 USA (SAN 217-4391) Tel 801-531-1483; Fax: 801-531-1488; Toll Free: 800-356-5687 (orders only)
E-mail: people@signaturebooks.com
Web site: http://www.signaturebooks.com.

Silky Way, Inc., 1227 38th Ave., San Francisco, CA 94122-1334 USA (SAN 169-3328).

Silver Bow News Distributing Co., Inc., 219 E. Park St., Butte, MT 59701 USA (SAN 169-4359) Tel 406-782-6995.

Silver, Burdett & Ginn, Inc., *(978-0-382; 978-0-663; 978-1-4182)* Orders Addr.: P.O. Box 2500, Lebanon, IN 46052 USA Toll Free Fax: 800-841-8939; Toll Free: 800-552-2259; Edit Addr.: P.O. Box 480, Parsippany, NJ 07054 USA (SAN 204-5982); 108 Wilmot Rd., Suite 380, Midwest Div., Deerfield, IL 60015 (SAN 111-6517) Tel 708-945-1240; 1925 Century Blvd. NE, Suite 14,

Southeast Div., Atlanta, GA 30345 (SAN 111-6509); 8445 Freeport Pkwy., Suite 400, South Div., Irving, TX 75063 (SAN 108-0458) Tel 214-915-4200; 2001 The Alameda, West Div., San Jose, CA 95126 (SAN 111-6525) Tel 408-248-6854; 160 Gould St., East Div., Needham Heights, MA 02194-2310; 1900 E. Lake Ave., Glenview, IL 60025
E-mail: customerservice@scottforesman.com
Web site: http://www.scottforesman.com/.

Simon & Schuster, *(978-0-671; 978-0-684; 978-0-689; 978-0-914676; 978-0-7432; 978-1-4165; 978-1-4391; 978-1-4516; 978-1-4767; 978-1-5011)* Div. of Simon & Schuster, Inc., Orders Addr.: 100 Front St., Riverside, NJ 08075 USA (SAN 200-2442) Toll Free Fax: 800-943-9831; Toll Free: 800-223-2336 (ordering); 800-223-2348 (customer service); Edit Addr.: a/o Subsidiary Rights, 11th Flr., 1230 Avenue of the Americas, New York, NY 10020 USA (SAN 200-2450) Tel 212-698-7000; Fax: 212-698-7007; 212-632-8099 (Rights & Permissions); 212-698-1269 (Pocket Bks. Rights & Permissions); Toll Free: 800-897-7650 (customer financial services); 100 Front St., Riverside, NJ 08075 (SAN 852-5471) Tel 856-824-2115
E-mail: ssonline_feedback@simonsays.com; consumer.customerservice@simonandschuster.com
Web site: http://www.simonsays.com; http://www.oasis.simonandschuster.com; http://www.simonandschuster.com/.

Simon & Schuster Children's Publishing, *(978-0-02; 978-0-671; 978-0-684; 978-0-689; 978-0-7434; 978-1-4169; 978-1-4424; 978-0-85707)* Orders Addr.: 100 Front St., Riverside, NJ 08075 USA Toll Free Fax: 800-943-9831; Toll Free: 800-223-2336; Edit Addr.: a/o Subsidiary Rights, 4th floor, 1230 Avenue of the Americas, New York, NY 10020 USA Tel 212-698-7200; Fax: 212-698-2797 (Rights & Permissions)
Web site: http://www.simonsays.com.

Simon & Schuster, Inc., *(978-0-02; 978-0-671; 978-0-684; 978-0-689; 978-0-914676; 978-0-7432; 978-0-7434; 978-0-7435; 978-1-4165; 978-1-4169; 978-1-4391; 978-1-4423; 978-1-4424; 978-1-4516; 978-0-85707; 978-1-4814; 978-1-5082; 978-1-5344)* Div. of Viacom Co., Orders Addr.: 100 Front St., Riverside, NJ 08075 USA Toll Free Fax: 800-943-9831; Toll Free: 800-223-2336 (orders); 800-223-2348 (customer service); Edit Addr.: 1230 Ave. of the Americas, New York, NY 10020 USA Tel 212-698-7000
E-mail: Consumer.CustomerService@simonandschuster.com
Web site: http://www.simonsays.com; http://www.simonandschuster.com.

Simon & Schuster Trade, *See* **Simon & Schuster**

Skandisk, Inc., *(978-0-9615394; 978-1-57534)* 6667 W. Old Shakopee Rd., Suite 109, Bloomington, MN 55438-2622 USA (SAN 695-4405) Tel 952-829-8998; Fax: 952-829-8992; Toll Free: 800-468-2424 (orders)
E-mail: lhamnes@skandisk.com; tomten@skandisk.com
Web site: http://www.skandisk.com.

Sky Oaks Productions, Inc., *(978-0-940296; 978-1-56018)* P.O. Box 1102, Los Gatos, CA 95031 USA (SAN 217-5843) Tel 408-395-7600; Fax: 408-395-8440
E-mail: TRPWorld@aol.com
Web site: http://www.tpr-world.com.

Slatner, Thomas & Co., Inc., 193 Palisade Ave., 3rd Flr., Jersey City, NJ 07306-1112 USA (SAN 130-9862) Tel 201-420-6700; Fax: 201-420-6787.

Slavica Pubs., *(978-0-89357)* c/o Indiana University, 2611 E. Tenth St., Bloomington, IN 47408-2618 USA (SAN 208-8576) Tel 812-856-4186; Fax: 812-856-4187
E-mail: slavica@indiana.edu
Web site: http://www.slavica.com.

Sleeper, Dick Distribution, 18680-B Langensand Rd., Sandy, OR 97055-6426 USA (SAN 631-0273) Tel 503-668-3454; Fax: 503-668-5314; Toll Free: 800-699-9911
E-mail: sleepydick@bigfoot.com.

Sleuth Pubns., Ltd., *(978-0-915341)* 3398 Washington, San Francisco, CA 94118 USA (SAN 130-9374) Tel 415-771-2689.

Small Pr. United, Div. of Independent Pubs. Group, 814 N. Franklin St., Chicago, IL 60610 USA Tel 312-337-0747 (ext. 274)
Web site: http://www.smallpressunited.com.

Small Press Distribution, *See* **SPD-Small Pr. Distribution**

Smashwords, *(978-1-4523; 978-1-4524; 978-1-4580; 978-1-4581; 978-1-4657; 978-1-4658; 978-1-4659; 978-1-4660; 978-1-4661; 978-1-4760; 978-1-4761; 978-1-4762; 978-1-4763; 978-1-4764; 978-1-301; 978-1-310; 978-1-311; 978-1-370)* 15951 Gatos Blvd., Suite 16, Los Gatos, CA 95032 USA Tel 408-358-1824; ziya gokalp mah. cimen sk. no:1/1 ikitelli koyu, basaksehir-istanbul, 34306 Tel 90 0538 8939727
Web site: http://www.smashwords.com.

Smith, Gibbs Publisher, *See* **Gibbs Smith, Publisher**

Smith News Agency, 118 S. Mitchell St., Cadillac, MI 49601 USA (SAN 169-3727).

SMMA Distributors, 6609 Brooks Dr., Temple, TX 76502 USA Tel 254-773-4884.

Snyder Magazine Agency, 3050 S. 9th Terr., Kansas City, KS 66103-2629 USA (SAN 285-9750).

Social Studies Schl. Service, *(978-1-56004; 978-1-57596)* Orders Addr.: 10200 Jefferson Blvd., P.O. Box 802, Culver City, CA 90232-0802 USA (SAN 168-9592) Tel 310-839-2436; Fax: 310-839-2249; Toll Free: 800-421-4246
E-mail: access@socialstudies.com
Web site: http://socialstudies.com.

Sociedad Biblica de Puerto Rico, Orders Addr.: P.O. Box 2548, Bayamon, PR 00960-2548 USA; Edit Addr.: Carr. 167, Km 14.7 Bo, Bayamon, PR 00960-2548 USA.

Society for Visual Education, Incorporated, *See* **S V E & Churchill Media**

Sopris West Educational Services, *See* **Cambium Education, Inc.**

Sort Card Co., The, 400 S. Summit View Dr., Fort Collins, CO 80524-1424 USA (SAN 159-9607).

Soundprints, *(978-0-924483; 978-1-56899; 978-1-931465; 978-1-59249; 978-1-60727)* Div. of Trudy Corp., 353 Main Ave., Norwalk, CT 06851 USA Fax: 203-846-1776; Toll Free: 800-228-7839
Web site: http://www.soundprints.com.

Sounds True, Inc., *(978-1-56455; 978-1-59179; 978-1-60407; 978-1-62203; 978-1-68364)* Orders Addr.: P.O. Box 8010, Boulder, CO 80306-8010 USA; Edit Addr.: 413 S. Arthur Ave., Louisville, CO 80027 USA (SAN 850-3532) Tel 303-665-3151; Fax: 303-665-5292; Toll Free: 800-333-9185
Web site: http://www.soundstrue.com.

Source Bk. Pubns., *(978-1-887137)* 1814 Franklin St., Suite 820, Oakland, CA 94612 USA Tel 510-839-5471; Fax: 510-547-3245.

Source Bks., *(978-0-940147; 978-0-85650)* Orders Addr.: 204 E. Fourth St., Suite O, Santa Ana, CA 92701 USA (SAN 248-2231) Tel 714-558-8944 (phone/fax); Toll Free: 800-695-4237 Do not confuse with Source Bks., Nashville, TN
E-mail: studio185@earthlink.net.

Source International Technology Corporation, *See* **Kamkyi Bks.**

Sourcebooks, Inc., *(978-0-942061; 978-0-9629162; 978-0-9629803; 978-1-57071; 978-1-57248; 978-1-58182; 978-1-883518; 978-1-887166; 978-1-888952; 978-1-4022; 978-1-932783; 978-1-62047; 978-1-4926)* 1935 Brookdale Rd., Suite 139, Naperville, IL 60563 USA (SAN 666-7864) Tel 630-961-3900; Fax: 630-961-2168; Toll Free: 800-727-8866
E-mail: info@sourcebooks.com
Web site: http://www.sourcebooks.com/.

South Asia Bks., *(978-0-8364; 978-0-88386)* P.O. Box 502, Columbia, MO 65205 USA (SAN 207-4044) Tel 573-474-0116; Fax: 573-474-8124
E-mail: sabooks@juno.com
Web site: http://www.southasiabooks.com.

South Atlantic News, Orders Addr.: P.O. Box 61297, Jacksonville, FL 32236-1297 USA; Edit Addr.: 1426 NE Eighth Ave., Ocala, FL 32678 USA.

South Carolina Bookstore, Orders Addr.: P.O. Box 4767, West Columbia, SC 29171 USA (SAN 131-2294) Tel 803-796-8200; Fax: 803-794-6927; Toll Free: 800-845-8200; Edit Addr.: 523 Jasper St., West Columbia, SC 29169 USA (SAN 243-2390).

South Central Bks., Inc., 1106 S. Strong Blvd., McAlester, OK 74501-6952 USA (SAN 108-1144) Tel 405-275-4522; Toll Free: 800-548-9858.

South Eastern Bk. Co., Inc., 3333 Hwy. 641 N., P.O. Box 309, Murray, KY 42071 USA (SAN 630-4869) Tel 270-753-0732; Fax: 270-759-4742; Toll Free Fax: 800-433-6966 (orders); Toll Free: 800-626-3952 (orders)
E-mail: orders@sebook.com
Web site: http://www.sebook.com.

South Louisiana News Company, *See* **Southern Periodicals, Inc.**

Southeast Library Bindery, Inc., P.O. Box 35484, Greensboro, NC 27425-5484 USA (SAN 159-9445) Tel 336-931-0800
E-mail: 70304.3023@compuserve.com
Web site: http://www.webmasters.net/bookbinding/.

Southeast Periodical & Bk. Sales, Inc., 10100 NW 25th St., Box 520155-Biscayne Annex, Miami, FL 33152 USA.

Southeastern Educational Toy & Bk. Distributors, Orders Addr.: 3215 Wellington Court Suite 113, Raleigh, NC 27615 USA (SAN 630-8104) Tel 704-364-6988; Edit Addr.: 4217 Park Rd., Charlotte, NC 28209 USA Tel 704-527-1921; Fax: 704-527-1653.

Southeastern Library Service, Subs. of Haskins Hse., P.O. Box 44, Gainesville, FL 32602-0044 USA (SAN 159-9615) Tel 352-372-3823.

Southern Bk. Service, *(978-0-9663836)* 5154 NW 165th St., Palmetto Lakes Industrial Pk., Hialeah, FL 33014-6335 USA (SAN 169-0981) Tel 305-624-4545; Fax: 305-621-0425; Toll Free: 800-766-3254.

Southern Cross Pubns., 1734 W. Roseberry Rd., P.O. Box 717, Donnelly, ID 83615 USA (SAN 110-8549) Tel 208-325-8606; Fax: 208-325-3400
E-mail: scp@cyberhighway.net
Web site: http://www.thoughtlines.com/southerncross/.

Southern Library Bindery Co., 2952 Sidco Dr., Nashville, TN 37204 USA (SAN 169-7986).

Southern Michigan News Co., 2571 Saradan, P.O. Box 908, Jackson, MI 49204 USA (SAN 169-3697) Tel 517-784-7163; Toll Free: 800-248-2213 (in Michigan); 800-828-2140.

Southern Periodicals, Inc., P.O. Box 407, Rayne, LA 70578-0407 USA (SAN 113-2520); 180 James Dr E., Saint Rose, LA 70087-4005.

Southern Tier News Co., P.O. Box 2128, Elmira Heights, NY 14903 USA (SAN 169-5223).

Southern Wisconsin News, 58 Artisan Dr., Edgerton, WI 53534 USA (SAN 169-9121) Tel 608-884-2600; Fax: 608-756-2357
E-mail: ndewar@southernwisconsinnews.com.

Southwest Cookbook Distributors, Orders Addr.: P.O. Box 707, Bonham, TX 75418 USA (SAN 200-4925) Tel 903-583-8898; Fax: 903-583-2522; Toll Free: 800-725-8898 (orders); Edit Addr.: P.O. Box 707, Bonham, TX 75418-0707 USA (SAN 630-8325).

Southwest Natural Cultural Heritage Association, *See* **Public Lands Interpretive Assn.**

Southwest News Co., Box 5465, Tucson, AZ 85704 USA (SAN 159-9631).

Southwestern Bk. Distributors, c/o Kerbs, 700 Highview Ave., Glen Ellyn, IL 60137-5504 USA (SAN 160-2373).

Sovereign News Company, *See* **Trans World News**

Spama, Inc., 78 Lake St., Jersey City, NJ 07306-3407 USA (SAN 169-5967).

Spanish & European Bookstore, Inc., 3102 Wilshire Blvd., Los Angeles, CA 90010 USA Tel 213-739-8899; Fax: 213-739-0087.

Spanish Bookstore-Wholesale, The, 10977 Santa Monica Blvd., Los Angeles, CA 90025-4538 USA (SAN 168-9835) Tel 310-475-0453; Fax: 310-473-6132
E-mail: BernardHamel@SpanishbooksUSA.com
Web site: http://www.BernardHamel.com.

Spanish Hse. Distributors, 1360 NW 88th Ave., Miami, FL 33172-3093 USA (SAN 169-1171) Tel 305-592-6136; Fax: 305-592-0087; Toll Free: 800-767-7726.

Spanish Language Bk. Services, Inc., Orders Addr.: 7855 N.W. 12th St., Suite 211, Miami, FL 33126 USA.

Spanish Pubs., LLC, 8871 SW 129 Terr., Miami, FL 33176 USA Tel 305-233-3365; Fax: 305-251-1310
E-mail: mariela@spanishpublishers.net
Web site: www.spanishpublishers.net.

Spanishtech, Inc., Div. of Editor's Bureau, Ltd., P.O. Box 68, Westport, CT 06881 USA (SAN 289-9620) Tel 203-452-7655.

SPD-Small Pr. Distribution, *(978-0-914068)* 1341 Seventh St., Berkeley, CA 94710-1409 USA (SAN 204-5826) Tel 510-524-1668; Fax: 510-524-0852; Toll Free: 800-869-7553 (orders)
E-mail: orders@spdbooks.org
Web site: http://www.spdbooks.org.

SpeakWare, 2836 Stephen Dr., Richmond, CA 94803 USA Tel 510-222-2455
E-mail: leds@speakware.com
Web site: http://www.speakware.com.

Specialized Bk. Service, Inc., 307 Autumn Ridge Rd., Fairfield, CT 06432-1003 USA (SAN 166-9788) Tel 203-377-6510; Fax: 203-377-4792.

Specialty Bk. Services, 1150 N. San Francisco, Flagstaff, AZ 86001 USA (SAN 130-8114) Tel 520-779-7843.

Specialty Promotions, 4516 S. Vincennes Ave. # 1S, Chicago, IL 60653-3470 USA (SAN 110-9987).

Speech Bin, Inc., The, *(978-0-937857)* 1965 25th Ave., Vero Beach, FL 32960 USA (SAN 630-1657) Tel 772-770-0007; Fax: 772-770-0006
E-mail: info@speechbin.com
Web site: http://www.speechbin.com.

Speedimpex U.S.A., Inc., 35-02 48th Ave., Long Island City, NY 11101-2421 USA (SAN 169-5479) Tel 718-392-7477; Fax: 718-361-0815
E-mail: nsalvatore@speedimpex.com
Web site: http://www.speedimpex.com.

Spencer Museum of Art, *(978-0-913689)* Affil. of Univ. of Kansas, Univ. of Kansas 1301 Mississippi St., Lawrence, KS 66045-7500 USA (SAN 111-347X) Tel 785-864-4710; Fax: 785-864-3112
E-mail: spencerart@ku.edu
Web site: http://www.spencerart.ku.edu.

SPI Bks., *(978-0-944007; 978-1-56171)* 99 Spring St., 3rd Flr., New York, NY 10012 USA Tel 212-431-5011; Fax: 212-431-8646
E-mail: ian@spibooks.com
Web site: http://www.spibooks.com.

Spirit Filled Pr., Inc., *(978-0-9656668)* 2549 Tallavana Trail, Havana, FL 32333 USA Tel 850-539-3843 (phone/fax)
E-mail: 2549@bellsouth.net
Web site: http://www.mindspring.com/~spiritfilled.

Spirit Rising, c/o Nicole Heyward, 1505 Hadley St., Houston, TX 77002 USA Tel 713-772-5175; Fax: 713-772-3034
E-mail: nicole.heyward@musicworldent.com.

Spring Arbor Distributors, Inc., Subs. of Ingram Industries Inc., 4271 Edison Ave., Chino, CA 91710 USA; 7315 Innovation Blvd., Fort Wayne, IN 46818-1371; 201 Ingram Dr., Roseburg, OR 97470-7148; Newbury Rd., East Windsor, CT 06088; 25420 Weakley Rd., Petersburg, VA 23803; 11333 E. 53rd Ave., Denver, CO 80239-2108; Edit Addr.: 1 Ingram Blvd., La Vergne, TN 37086-1976 USA Fax: 615-213-5192; Toll Free: 800-395-4340; 800-395-7234 (customer service)
E-mail: orders@springarbor.com.

Springer, *(978-0-387; 978-0-8176; 978-3-211; 978-3-540; 978-3-7908; 978-4-431; 978-1-85233; 978-1-84628; 978-1-4419; 978-1-4612; 978-1-4613; 978-1-4614; 978-1-4615; 978-1-4684; 978-1-4757; 978-1-4899; 978-1-4939; 978-1-5041)* Subs. of Springer Science+Business Media, Orders Addr.: P.O. Box 2485, Secaucus, NJ 07096-2485 USA Tel 201-348-4033; Fax: 201-348-4505; Toll Free: 800-777-4643; Edit Addr.: a/o Springer Nature, 233 Spring St., New York, NY 10013-1578 USA (SAN 203-2228) Tel 212-815-0249; 212-460-1500; Fax: 212-460-1575; Toll Free: 800-777-4643 Thomson Delmar Learning Distributes Blanchard & Loeb Nursing Videos Only
E-mail: Slu@Springer-ny.com; service-ny@springer.com; customerservice@springernature.com.com
Web site: http://www.springeronline.com; http://www.springer.com.

Springer-Verlag New York, Incorporated, *See* **Springer**

Springwater Bks., Orders Addr.: P.O. Box 194, Springwater, NY 14560-0194 USA (SAN 111-8900); Edit Addr.: Main St. & East Ave., Springwater, NY 14560-0194 USA (SAN 243-2412) Tel 716-669-2450.

Sprout, Inc., Orders Addr.: 430 Tenth St., NW, Suite 007, Atlanta, GA 30318 USA Tel 404-892-9600; Fax: 404-881-1383.

Square Deal Records, 303 Higuera St., San Luis Obispo, CA 93401-4209 USA (SAN 170-6799) Tel 805-543-3636; Fax: 805-543-3938; Toll Free: 800-253-4114
E-mail: sdrsslo@aol.com.

SRA/McGraw-Hill, *(978-0-07; 978-0-383)* Div. of The McGraw-Hill Education Group, Orders Addr.: 220 E. Daniel Dale Rd., DeSoto, TX 75115-2490 USA Fax: 972-228-1982; Toll Free: 800-843-8855; Edit Addr.: 8787 Orion Pl., Columbus, OH 43240-4027 USA Tel 614-430-6600; Fax: 614-430-6621; Toll Free: 800-468-5850
E-mail: sra@mcgraw-hill.com
Web site: https://www.sraonline.com.

Sri Aurobindo Association, Incorporated, *See* **Matagiri Sri Aurobindo Ctr.**

St. Marie's Gopher News Co., 9000 Tenth Ave., N., Minneapolis, MN 55427 USA (SAN 169-4103) Tel 612-546-5300; Fax: 612-546-1487.

St. Martin's Pr., *(978-0-312; 978-0-8050; 978-0-940687; 978-0-9603648; 978-1-55927; 978-1-58063; 978-1-58238; 978-1-4299; 978-1-250)* Div. of Holtzbrinck Pubs., Orders Addr.: 16365 James Madison Hwy., Gordonville, VA 22942 USA Tel 540-672-7600; Fax: 540-672-7540 (customer service); Toll Free Fax: 800-672-2054; Toll Free: 888-330-8477; Edit Addr.: 175 Fifth Ave., 20th Flr., New York, NY 10010 USA (SAN 200-2132) Tel 212-674-5151 (Trade Div.); 212-726-0200 (College Div.); Fax: 212-674-3179 (Trade Div.); 212-686-9491 (College Div.); Toll Free: 800-221-7945 (Trade Div.); 800-470-4767 (College Div.)
E-mail: webmaster@stmartins.com; enquiries@stmartins.com
Web site: http://www.stmartins.com; http://www.smpcollege.com.

St. Mary Seminary Bookstore, 28700 Euclid Ave., Wyckliffe, OH 44092 USA (SAN 169-667X) Tel 216-943-7600.

St Pauls/Alba Hse. Pubs., *(978-0-8189)* Div. of Society of St. Paul, 2187 Victory Blvd., Staten Island, NY 10314-6603 USA (SAN 201-2405) Tel 718-761-0047; Fax: 718-761-0057; 718-698-8390; Toll Free: 800-343-2522
E-mail: albabooks@aol.com
Web site: http://www.albahouse.org.

Stackpole Bks., *(978-0-8117)* 5067 Ritter Rd., Mechanicsburg, PA 17055 USA (SAN 202-5396) Tel 717-796-0411; Fax: 717-796-0412; Toll Free: 800-732-3669
E-mail: ccraley@stackpolebooks.com
Web site: http://www.stackpolebooks.com/.

Star Bright Bks., Inc., *(978-1-887734; 978-1-932065; 978-1-59572)* Orders Addr.: 30-19, 48th Ave., Long Island City, NY 11101 USA (SAN 254-5225) Tel 718-784-9112; Fax: 718-784-9012; Toll Free: 800-788-4439
E-mail: info@starbrightbooks.com
Web site: http://www.starbrightbooks.com.

StarCrossed Productions, *(978-0-9668483)* 14552 NW., 88 Pl., Miami, FL 33018 USA Tel 305-828-2619 Phone/Fax
E-mail: tinami@msn.com
Web site: http://www.cookiesisters.com.

Starkmann, Inc., 25-u Olympia Ave., Woburn, MA 01801 USA (SAN 126-6128) Tel 781-938-9643; Fax: 781-938 9647
E-mail: biggs@starkmann.co.uk.

Starmaster Co., 6911 Haverhill Dr., Knoxville, TN 37909 USA (SAN 108-1217) Tel 423-588-6661.

StarWalk Kids, 15 Cutter Mill Rd., Suite 242, Great Neck, NY 11021 USA.

State News Agency, 2750 Griffith Rd., Winston Salem, NC 27103-6418 USA (SAN 169-6424).

State Univ. of New York Pr., *(978-0-7914; 978-0-87395; 978-0-88706; 978-1-4384)* Orders Addr.: P.O. Box 960, Herndon, VA 20172-0960 USA (SAN 203-3496) Tel 703-661-1575; Fax: 703-996-1010; Toll Free Fax: 877-204-6074; Toll Free: 877-204-6073 (customer service); Edit Addr.: 22 Corporate Woods Blvd., 3rd Flr., Albany, NY 12211-2504 USA (SAN 658-1730) Tel 518-472-5000; Fax: 518-472-5038; Toll Free: 866-430-7869
E-mail: info@sunypress.edu; suny@presswarehouse.com
Web site: http://www.sunypress.edu.

Steerforth Pr., *(978-0-944072; 978-1-58195; 978-1-883642; 978-1-58642)* 45 Lyme Rd. # 208, Hanover, NH 03755-1219 USA
E-mail: helga@steerforth.com; info@steerforth.com
Web site: http://www.steerforth.com.

Steiner, Rudolf College Pr./St. George Pubns., *(978-0-916786; 978-0-945803; 978-0-9818095)* 9200 Fair Oaks Blvd., Fair Oaks, CA 95628 USA (SAN 208-8371) Tel 916-961-3722; Fax: 916-961-3032
E-mail: claude.julien@steinercollege.edu; cblatch@comcast.net
Web site: http://www.steinercollege.edu.

SteinerBooks, Inc., *(978-0-8334; 978-0-88010; 978-0-89345; 978-0-910142; 978-1-58420; 978-1-85584; 978-0-9701097; 978-0-9831984; 978-1-62148; 978-1-62151; 978-1-938685; 978-0-9969211)* Orders Addr.: P.O. Box 960, Herndon, VA 20172-0960 USA Tel 703-661-1594 (orders); Fax: 702-661-1501; Toll Free Fax: 800-277-7947 (orders); Toll Free: 800-856-8664 (orders); Edit Addr.: 610 Main St., Suite 1, Great Barrington, MA 01230 USA Tel 413-528-8233; Fax: 413-528-8826; Fulfillment Addr.: 22883 Quicksilver Dr., Dulles, VA 20166 USA (SAN 253-9519) Tel 703-661-1529; Fax: 703-996-1010
E-mail: service@steinerbooks.org
Web site: http://www.steinerbooks.org.

Stenhouse Pubs., *(978-1-57110; 978-1-62531)* Div. of Highlights for Children, Orders Addr.: P.O. Box 11020, Portland, ME 04104-7020 USA (SAN 298-1580) Tel 207-253-1600; Fax: 207-253-5121; Toll Free Fax: 800-833-9164; Toll Free: 800-988-9812 (orders)
E-mail: jkilburn@stenhouse.com
Web site: http://www.stenhouse.com.

Sterling Publishing Co., Inc., *(978-0-8069; 978-1-4027; 978-1-60582; 978-1-4549; 978-1-61837)* 387 Park Ave., S., New York, NY 10016-8810 USA (SAN 211-6324) Tel 212-532-7160 212-213-2495; Toll Free Fax: 800-775-8736 (warehouse) Do not confuse with companies with similar names in Falls Church, VA, Fallbrook, CA, Lewisville, TX
E-mail: custservice@sterlingpub.com; tradesales@sterlingpub.com
Web site: http://www.sterlingpublishing.com/.

Stevens, Gareth Incorporated, *See* **Stevens, Gareth Publishing LLLP**

Stevens, Gareth Publishing LLLP, *(978-0-8368; 978-0-918831; 978-1-55532; 978-1-4339)* Orders Addr.:

P.O. Box 360140, Strongsville, OH 44136-0140 USA Fax: 877-542-2596; Toll Free: 800-542-2595; Edit Addr.: 111 East 14th St., Suite 349, New York, NY 10003 USA (SAN 696-1592) Toll Free: 877-444-0210
E-mail: customerservice@gspub.com; hollyc@rosenpub.com
Web site: http://www.garethstevens.com; http://www.garethstevensclassroom.com.

Stevens International, Orders Addr.: P.O. Box 126, Magnolia, NJ 08049 USA (SAN 631-3612) Tel 856-435-1555; Edit Addr.: 706 N. White Horse Pike, Magnolia, NJ 08049 USA
Web site: http://www.stevenshobby.com.

Stevens, Mark Industries, Div. of Christian World, Inc., 304 N. Meridian Ave., Suite 6, Oklahoma City, OK 73107 USA (SAN 631-127X) Toll Free: 800-654-6760.

STL Distribution North America, *See* **Send The Light Distribution LLC**

Stoneydale Pr. Publishing Co., *(978-0-912299; 978-1-931291; 978-1-938707)* Orders Addr.: P.O. Box 188, Stevensville, MT 59870 USA Tel 406-777-2729; Fax: 406-777-2521; Toll Free: 800-735-7006; Edit Addr.: 523 Main St., Stevensville, MT 59870 USA (SAN 265-3168)
E-mail: stoneydale@stoneydale.com
Web site: http://www.stoneydale.com.

Storey Books, *See* **Storey Publishing, LLC**

Storey Publishing, LLC, *(978-0-88266; 978-1-58017; 978-0-9674717; 978-1-60342; 978-1-61212; 978-1-63586)* Subs. of Workman Publishing Co., Inc., Orders Addr.: 210 Mass Moca Way, North Adams, MA 01247 USA (SAN 203-4158) Fax: 413-346-2198; Toll Free Fax: 800-865-3429; Toll Free: 800-827-7444; c/o Workman Publishing, 225 Varick St., New York, NY 10014-4381 Tel 212-614-7700; Toll Free Fax: 800-521-1832; Toll Free: 800-722-7202
E-mail: info@storey.com; sales@storey.com
Web site: http://www.storey.com.

Strang Communications Company, *See* **Charisma Media**

Strauss Consultants, 48 W. 25th St., 11th Flr., New York, NY 10010-2708 USA Toll Free Fax: 888-528-8273; Toll Free: 800-236-7918
E-mail: strausscon@aol.com.

Streamwood Distribution, P.O. Box 91011, Mobile, AL 36691 USA Tel 334-665-0022; Fax: 334-665-0570.

Strelow, James C., 12588 Ivy Glen Ln., Garden Grove, CA 92841-4563 USA (SAN 132-4144).

Strisik, Nancy, 10 Main St., Rockport, MA 01966 USA Tel 978-546-7653.

Studio 2 Publishing, Inc., *(978-0-9763601; 978-0-9792455; 978-0-9815281; 978-0-9819874; 978-0-9826427; 978-0-9828175; 978-1-937013; 978-1-944413)* 1722 Louisville Dr. Suite A, Knoxville, TN 37921 USA Tel 865-212-3797
E-mail: contact@studio2publishing.com
Web site: http://www.studio2publishing.com.

Studio Fun International, *(978-0-276; 978-0-7621; 978-0-88705; 978-0-88850; 978-0-89577; 978-1-57584; 978-1-57619; 978-0-7944)* Subs. of Reader's Digest Assn., Inc., Reader's Digest Rd., Pleasantville, NY 10570-7000 USA (SAN 283-2143) Tel 914-244-4800; Fax: 914-244-4841
Web site: http://www.readersdigestkids.com; http://www.studiofun.com/.

Stylus Publishing, LLC, *(978-1-57922; 978-1-887208; 978-0-9729394; 978-1-62036)* Orders Addr.: P.O. Box 605, Herndon, VA 20172-0605 USA; Edit Addr.: 22883 Quicksilver Dr., Sterling, VA 20166-2012 USA (SAN 299-1853) Tel 703-661-1581; Fax: 703-661-1501 Do not confuse with companies with the same name in Sunnyvale, CA, Quakertown, PA
E-mail: stylusmail@presswarehouse.com; jean.westcott@styluspub.com
Web site: http://www.styluspub.com.

Subscription Account, 84 Needham, Newton Highlands, MA 02161 USA (SAN 285-9424).

Subscription Hse., Inc., 209 Harvard St., Suite 407, Brookline, MA 02146-5005 USA (SAN 285-9343).

Subterranean Co., Orders Addr.: P.O. Box 160, Monroe, OR 97456 USA Fax: 541-847-6018
E-mail: subco@clipper.net.

Success Education Assn., Box 175, Roanoke, VA 24002 USA (SAN 159-9690).

Suite 3 Productions, 90 W. 100 N., Suite 13, Provo, UT 84501 USA Tel 801-472 — 6024.

Sun Life, *(978-0-937930)* 2399 Cool Springs Rd., Thaxton, VA 24174 USA (SAN 240-8333) Tel 540-586-4898.

Sunbelt Pubns., Inc., *(978-0-916251; 978-0-932653; 978-0-9606704; 978-0-9620402; 978-1-941384)* 1256 Fayette St., El Cajon, CA 92020-1511 USA (SAN 630-0790) Tel 619-258-4911; Fax: 619-258-4916; Toll Free: 800-626-6579
E-mail: info@sunbeltpub.com; sales@sunbeltpub.com; dyoung@sunbeltpub.com; mail@sunbeltpub.com
Web site: http://www.sunbeltpub.com; http://www.sunbeltbooks.com.

Sunburst Bks., Inc., Distributor of Florida Bks., 700 S. John Rodes Blvd., #D8, West Melbourne, FL 32904 USA Tel 321-409-0225; Fax: 321-728-2742
Web site: http://www.sunburstbooks.com.

Sunburst Communications, Inc., *(978-0-7805; 978-0-911831; 978-1-55636; 978-1-55826)* 400 Columbus Ave., Valhalla, NY 10595-1335 USA (SAN 213-5620) Toll Free: 800-431-1934
E-mail: webmaster@nysunburst.com
Web site: http://www.sunburst.com.

Sunburst Visual Media, *(978-1-59520)* Orders Addr.: P.O. Box 4455, Scottsdale, AZ 85261 USA Toll Free: 800-262-8837; Edit Addr.: P.O. Box 9120, Plainview, NY 11803-9020 USA
Web site: http://www.schoolspecialty.com.

Sunday School Board of the Southern Baptist Convention, *See* **LifeWay Christian Resources**

Sundaykool Bulletins, *(978-1-888824)* Div. of Griffin Publishing Co., 18022 Cowan, Suite 202, Irvine, CA 92614 USA (SAN 631-5046) Toll Free: 800-472-9741
E-mail: griffinbooks@earthlink.net
Web site: http://www.griffinpublishing.com.

Sunshine Harbor, 825 Glen Arden Way, Altamonte Springs, FL 32701 USA (SAN 159-6640) Tel 407-339-0401.

Swedenborg Foundation, Inc., *(978-0-87785)* 320 N. Church St., West Chester, PA 19380 USA (SAN 111-7920) Tel 610-430-3222; Fax: 610-430-7982
E-mail: editor@swedenborg.com
Web site: http://www.swedenborg.com.

Swenson, Jim, 2610 Riverside Ln., NE, Rochester, MN 55901 USA (SAN 285-9505).

Swift News Agency, Orders Addr.: P.O. Box 160, Poncha Springs, CO 81242 USA (SAN 282-3810); Edit Addr.: 338 E. Hwy. 50, Poncha Springs, CO 81242 USA (SAN 169-0639).

Syco Distribution, 9208A Venture Ct., Manassas, VA 20111-4804 USA.

Symmes Systems, *(978-0-916352; 978-0-9907312)* 3977 Briarcliff Rd., NE, Atlanta, GA 30345-2647 USA (SAN 169-1465) Tel 404-876-7260.

Syndistar, Inc., *(978-1-56230)* P.O. Box 3027, Hammond, LA 70404-3027 USA (SAN 298-007X) Toll Free: 800-841-9532
E-mail: webmaster@syndistar.com
Web site: http://www.syndistar.com.

Syracuse Univ. Pr., *(978-0-8156; 978-0-615-28768-3; 978-1-68445)* 621 Skytop Rd., Suite 110, Syracuse, NY 13244-5290 USA (SAN 206-9776) Tel 315-443-5534; Fax: 315-443-5545
E-mail: supress@syr.edu; arpfeiff@syr.edu
Web site: http://www.SyracuseUniversityPress.syr.edu.

T A Bookstore, *See* **Shea Bks.**

Taku Graphics, *(978-0-9717820; 978-0-9772297; 978-0-9801616; 978-0-9823450; 978-0-9846318; 978-0-9899679)* 5763 Glacier Hwy., Juneau, AK 99801 USA Tel 907-780-6310; Fax: 907-780-6314; Toll Free: 800-278-3291
E-mail: adele@takugraphics.com
Web site: htto://www.takugraphics.com.

Tales of Wonder.com, 3037 Summer Oak Pl., Buford, GA 30518 USA (SAN 920-1246) Tel 770-904-2221; 770-904-2221; Toll Free: 866-796-6337
E-mail: service@towdistribution.com; rob@towdistribution.com
Web site: www.talesofwonder.com; http://www.towdistribution.com.

Tallahassee News Co., Inc., 3777 Hartsfield Rd., Tallahassee, FL 32303-1120 USA.

Tapeworm Video Distributor, Inc., 27833 Avenue Hopkins, Unit 6, Valencia, CA 91355-3407 USA (SAN 630-8767) Tel 805-257-4904; Fax: 805-257-4820; Toll Free: 800-367-8437
E-mail: sales@tapeworm.com
Web site: http://www.tapeworm.com.

Tatnuck BookSeller, The, 335 Chandler St., Worcester, MA 01602-3402 USA (SAN 169-3654) Tel 508-756-7644.

Tattered Cover Bookstore, 1628 16th St., Denver, CO 80202-1308 USA (SAN 631-0214) Toll Free: 800-833-9327 (ext. 250)
E-mail: roy@tatteredcover.com.

Taylor & Francis Group, *(978-0-335; 978-0-415; 978-0-8448; 978-0-85066; 978-0-89116; 978-0-903796; 978-0-905273; 978-1-56032; 978-1-85000; 978-1-59169; 978-1-315)* Orders Addr.: 7625 Empire Dr., Florence, KY 41042-2919 USA Toll Free Fax: 800-248-4724; Toll Free: 800-634-7064; 74 Rolark Dr., Scarborough, ON M1R 4G2 Tel 416-299-5388; Fax: 416-299-7531; Toll Free: 877-226-2237; Edit Addr.: 325 Chestnut St., Philadelphia, PA 19106 USA (SAN 241-9246) Tel 215-625-8900; Fax: 215-625-2940; 270 Madison Ave., 4th Flr., New York, NY 10016-0601
Web site: http://www.routledge-ny.com; http://www.crcpress.com; http://www.garlandscience.com; http://www.taylorandfrancis.com.

Taylor & Francis, Incorporated, *See* **Taylor & Francis Group**

TBN Enterprises, *See* **Ironside International Pubs., Inc.**

Teacher Created Materials, Inc., *(978-0-87673; 978-0-7439; 978-1-4333; 978-1-60401; 978-1-4807; 978-1-4938; 978-1-5164)* 5301 Oceanus Dr., Huntington Beach, CA 92649 USA (SAN 665-5270) Tel 714-891-2273; Fax: 714-230-7070; Toll Free Fax: 888-877-7606; Toll Free: 800-858-7339
E-mail: sozbat@tcmpub.com
Web site: http://www.tcmpub.com; http://www.teachercreated.com.

Teacher Created Resources, Inc., *(978-1-55734; 978-1-57690; 978-1-4206; 978-1-4570)* 12621 Western Ave., Garden Grove, CA 92841 USA Tel 714-891-1690; Fax: 800-525-1254; Toll Free: 800-662-4321
E-mail: dlytle@teachercreated.com; custserv@teachercreated.com
Web site: http://www.teachercreated.com.

Teacher's Discovery, *(978-1-884473; 978-0-7560)* Div. of American Eagle Co., Inc., 2741 Paldan Dr., Auburn Hills, MI 48326 USA (SAN 631-4570) Tel 248-340-7210; Fax: 248-340-7212; Toll Free: 800-832-2437
Web site: http://www.teachersdiscovery-science.com; http://www.teachersdiscovery-english.com; http://www.teachersdiscovery-social studies.com; http://www.teachersdiscovery-foreignlanguage.com; http://www.teachersdiscovery.com.

Technical Bk. Co., P.O. Box 25934, Los Angeles, CA 90025-8994 USA (SAN 168-9851) Toll Free: 800-233-5150.

Techno Mecca, Inc., 4201 Wilshire Blvd., No. 620, Los Angeles, CA 90019 USA (SAN 631-7812) Tel 323-634-1650; Fax: 323-634-1655
E-mail: tjkim@tmecca.com
Web site: http://www.tmecca.com.

Temme Haus Pr., *(978-0-9727036)* 1784 Palm Ave., Stockton, CA 95205 USA (SAN 253-1925) Fax: 209-463-5527
E-mail: temmehans1953@sbcglobal.net.

Temple News Agency, *See* **ETD KroMar Temple**

Tempo Bookstore, 4905 Wisconsin Ave., NW, Washington, DC 20016 USA Tel 202-363-6683; Fax: 202-363-6686
E-mail: Tempobookstore@usa.net; tempobookstore@usa.net.

Ten Speed Pr., *(978-0-89815; 978-0-913668; 978-1-58008; 978-1-60774)* Div. of Crown Publishing Group, Orders Addr.: P.O. Box 7123, Berkeley, CA 94707 USA (SAN 202-7674) Fax: 510-559-1629 (orders); Toll Free: 800-841-2665; 555 Richmond St., W. Suite 405, Box 702, Toronto, ON M5V 3B1 Tel 416-703-7775; Fax: 416-703-9992
E-mail: order@tenspeed.com; alan@tenspeed.ca
Web site: http://www.tenspeed.com.

teNeues Publishing Co., *(978-3-570; 978-3-8238; 978-3-929278; 978-3-8327; 978-1-933427; 978-1-60160; 978-1-62325)* 7 W. 18th St., New York, NY 10011 USA (SAN 245-176X) Tel 212-627-9090; Fax: 212-627-9511; Toll Free: 800-352-0305; 12 Ferndene Rd., London, SE24 0AQ
E-mail: tnp@teneues-usa.com
Web site: http://www.teneues.com.

Territory Titles, 22 Camino Real, Sandia Park, NM 87047 USA.

Tesla Bk. Co., *(978-0-914119; 978-0-9603536)* P.O. Box 121873, Chula Vista, CA 91912-6573 USA (SAN 241-8703) Tel 619-585-8487; Toll Free: 800-398-2056
E-mail: bfeuling@teslabook.com.

Teva Nature, 2344 Black Oak Ct., Sarasota, FL 34232 USA (SAN 631-4619) Tel 941-377-7414; Fax: 941-371-6237; Toll Free: 800-924-8382.

Texas A&M Univ. Pr., *(978-0-89096; 978-1-58544; 978-1-60344; 978-1-62349)* 4354 TAMU John H. Lindsey Bldg., Lewis St., College Station, TX 77843-4354 USA (SAN 658-1919) Tel 979-458-3978; Fax: 979-847-8752; Toll Free Fax: 888-617-2421 (orders); Toll Free: 800-826-8911 (orders)
E-mail: tamupresscontact@gmail.com
Web site: http://www.tamupress.com.

Texas Art Supply, 2001 Montrose Blvd., Houston, TX 77006 USA (SAN 169-8303) Tel 713-526-5221; Fax: 713-524-7474; Toll Free: 800-888-9278
E-mail: info@texasart.com
Web site: http://www.texasart.com.

Texas Bk. Co., Orders Addr.: 2601 King, Greenville, TX 75401 USA (SAN 103-4308) Tel 903-455-6969; Fax: 903-454-4775; US Naval Academy/TBC, 5th Wing Bancroft Hall/Textbook, 101 Wilson Rd., Anapolis, MD 21402 (SAN 920-8461) Tel 903-455-6969 ext 642; TBC-NWLTC Bookstore-810 8501 Technology Cir. - Unit 810, Greenville, TX 75402 (SAN 920-9050) Tel 903-455-6969; TBC - #820 Sowela Bookstore 3824 Sen. J. Bennett Johnston Ave., Lake Charles, LA 70615 (SAN 920-9069); TBC-Trenholm State Tech. Coll Bookstore-830 8501 Technology Circle-Unit 830, Greenville, TX 75402 (SAN 920-9077) Tel 903-455-6969; TBC-Drake State Tech College Bookstore-831 8501 Technology Circle-Unit 831, Greenville, TX 75402 (SAN 920-9085) Tel 903-455-6969; Edit Addr.: P.O. Box 212, Greenville, TX 75403 USA Fax: 903-454-2442; Toll Free: 800-527-1016
E-mail: monica@texasbook.com; diana@texasbook.com; molson@texasbook.com.

Texas Bookman, The, *(978-1-931040)* 2700 Lone Star Dr., Dallas, TX 75212-6209 USA (SAN 106-875X) Toll Free: 800-566-2665
E-mail: texas.bookman@halfpricebooks.com.

Texas Hill Country Cookbook, P.O. Box 126, Round Mountain, TX 78663 USA (SAN 110-831X) Tel 210-825-3242; Fax: 210-825-3244; Toll Free: 800-231-3553.

Texas Library Bk. Sales, 1408 West Koenig Lane, Austin, TX 78756 USA (SAN 169-8044) Tel 512-452-4140.

Textbooks On Demand, *See* **Reprint Services Corp.**

TextStream, *(978-0-7351)* Div. of Baker & Taylor Bks., Orders Addr.: c/o Baker & Taylor Digital Media Services, 1120 US Hwy., 22 E., Bridgewater, NJ 08807 USA Tel 908-541-7035; Toll Free Fax: 800-648-0541; Toll Free: 800-775-1800; Edit Addr.: P.O. Box 6885, Bridgewater, NJ 08807-0885 USA
E-mail: btinfo@baker-taylor.com
Web site: http://www.baker-taylor.com/textstream.

TFH Pubns., Inc., *(978-0-7938; 978-0-86622; 978-0-87666; 978-1-85279)* Orders Addr.: One TFH Plaza, Third & Union Aves., Neptune City, NJ 07753 USA (SAN 202-7720) Tel 732-988-8400; Fax: 732-988-5466; Toll Free: 800-631-2188 (outside New Jersey); Edit Addr.: P.O. Box 427, Neptune, NJ 07753 USA (SAN 658-1862)
E-mail: info@tfh.com
Web site: http://www.tfh.com.

Thames Bk. Co., 1 Quarry Rd., Mystic, CT 06355-3200 USA (SAN 169-0760).

Theme Stream, Inc., P.O. Box 142, Broomfield, CT 06002 USA Tel 860-243-5200
Web site: http://www.themestream.com.

Theological Bk. Service, P.O. Box 509, Barnhart, MO 63012 USA (SAN 631-6662) Tel 636-464-2500; Fax: 636-464-8449; Toll Free Fax: 800-325-9526; Toll Free: 877-484-1600
E-mail: tbs@execpc.com
Web site: http://www.theobooks.org.

Thieme Medical Pubs., Inc., *(978-0-86577; 978-0-913258; 978-1-58890; 978-1-60406; 978-1-62623; 978-1-68420)* Subs. of Georg Thieme Verlag Stuttgart, 333 Seventh Ave., 18th Flr., New York, NY 10001 USA (SAN 169-5983) Tel 212-760-0888; Fax: 212-947-1112; Toll Free: 800-782-3488 (orders only)
E-mail: customerservice@thieme.com
Web site: http://www.thieme.com.

Thieme-Stratton, Inc., *See* **Thieme Medical Pubs., Inc.**

Thinkers' Pr., Inc., *(978-0-938650; 978-1-888710)* Orders Addr.: P.O. Box 8, Davenport, IA 52805-0008 USA Tel 319-323-1226; Fax: 319-323-0511; Toll Free: 800-397-7117 (orders only); Edit Addr.: 1524 Leclaire St., Davenport, IA 52803-4428 USA (SAN 162-7759)
E-mail: tpi@chessco.com
Web site: http://www.chessco.com.

Thistle Hill Pubns., *(978-0-9705511)* 477 Thistle Hill Rd., North Pomfret, VT 05053-0307 USA Tel 802-457-2050; Fax: 802-457-3653; Fulfillment Addr.: P.O. Box 428, White River Junction, VT 05001 USA
E-mail: thp@together.net
Web site: http://www.thistlehillpub.com.

Thomas Brothers Maps, *(978-0-88130; 978-1-58174)* Div. of Rand McNally & Co., 17731 Cowan, Irvine, CA 92614 USA (SAN 158-8192) Fax: 949-757-1564; Toll Free: 800-899-6277
Web site: http://www.thomas.com.

Thompson Schl. Bk. Depository, Orders Addr.: P.O. Box 60160, Oklahoma City, OK 73146 USA (SAN 159-9747) Tel 405-525-9458; Fax: 405-524-5443; Edit Addr.: 39 NE 24th St., Oklahoma City, OK 73143 USA.

Thomson Delmar Learning, *See* **Delmar Cengage Learning**

Thomson Gale, *See* **Cengage Gale**

Thomson Learning, *See* **CENGAGE Learning**

Thomson, Linda, P.O. Box 1225, Orem, UT 84059-1225 USA (SAN 110-3881) Tel 801-226-0155; Fax: 801-226-0166; Toll Free: 800-226-0155.

Thomson Peterson's, *See* **Peterson's**

Thomson West, *See* **West**

Thorndike Pr., *(978-0-7838; 978-0-7862; 978-0-8161; 978-0-89621; 978-1-56054; 978-1-4104)* Div. of Gale Group, 295 Kennedy Memorial Dr., Waterville, ME 04901 USA Tel 207-859-1053; 207-859-1020; 207-859-1000; Toll Free Fax: 800-558-4676; Toll Free: 800-223-1244 (ext. 15); 800-877-4253 (customer resource ctr.)
E-mail: jamie.knobloch@gale.com; barb.littfield@galegroup.com; Betsy.M.Brown@thomson.com; jamie.knobloch@cengage.com
Web site: http://www.gale.com/thorndike.

Tiffin News Agency, 34 Kennat Blvd., Tiffin, OH 44883-4604 USA (SAN 169-6866).

Tiger Bk. Distributors, Ltd., 328 S. Jefferson, Chicago, IL 60661 USA (SAN 631-0672) Tel 312-382-1160; Fax: 312-382-0323.

TI-Holdings Distribution Co., 4 Hopscotch Ln., Savannah, GA 31411 USA.

Timber Pr., Inc., *(978-0-88192; 978-0-917304; 978-0-931146; 978-0-931340; 978-1-60469)* Div. of Workman Publishing Co., Inc., 133 SW Second Ave., Suite 450, Portland, OR 97204-3527 USA (SAN 216-082X) Tel 503-227-2878; Fax: 503-227-3070; Toll Free: 800-327-5680; 20 Lonsdale Rd Swavesey, London, NW6 6RD Tel (01954) 232959; Fax: (01954) 206040
E-mail: info@timberpress.co.uk; publicity@timberpress.com
Web site: http://www.timberpress.com.

Time Home Entertainment, Incorporated, *See* **Time Inc. Bks.**

Time Inc. Bks., *(978-1-883013; 978-1-929049; 978-1-931933; 978-1-932273; 978-1-932994; 978-1-933405; 978-1-933821; 978-1-60320; 978-1-61893; 978-1-68330; 978-1-5478)* Div. of Time, Inc., 1271 Avenue of the Americas, New York, NY 10020-1201 USA (SAN 227-3209); 225 Liberty St., New York, NY 10281.

Time Warner Book Group, *See* **Hachette Bk. Group**

Time-Life Publishing Warehouse, 5240 W. 76th, Indianapolis, IN 43268-4137 USA (SAN 631-1504) Fax: 717-348-6409; Toll Free: 800-277-8844
Web site: http://www.timelifecs.com; http://www.timelifeedu.com.

TIS, Inc., *(978-0-89917; 978-1-56581; 978-0-7421)* Orders Addr.: P.O. Box 669, Bloomington, IN 47402 USA Tel 812-332-3307; Fax: 812-331-7690; Toll Free: 800-367-4002; Edit Addr.: 5005 N. State Rd. 37 Business, Bloomington, IN 47404 USA.

Titan Bookstore, P.O. Box 34080, Fullerton, CA 92634-9480 USA (SAN 106-4851).

Title Bks., Inc., 3013 Second Ave. S, Birmingham, AL 35233 USA (SAN 168-9207) Tel 205-324-2596.

Tobias News Co., 130 18th St., Rock Island, IL 61201 USA (SAN 169-2186) Tel 309-788-7517.

Todd Communications, *(978-1-57833; 978-1-878100)* 611 E. 12th Ave. Ste. 102, Anchorage, AK 99501-4663 USA (SAN 298-6280)
E-mail: info@toddcom.com.

Topical Review Bk Co., Inc., *(978-1-929099; 978-1-939246)* P.O. Box 328, Onsted, MI 49265 USA Tel 517-547-8072; Fax: 517-547-7512
E-mail: topicalrbc@aol.com
Web site: www.topicalrbc.com.

Total Information, Inc., 844 Dewey Ave., Rochester, NY 14613 USA (SAN 123-7373) Tel 716-254-0621.

T.R. Bks., Orders Addr.: P.O. Box 310279, New Braunfels, TX 78131 USA (SAN 630-4885) Tel 830-625-2665; Fax: 830-620-0470; Toll Free: 800-659-4710; Edit Addr.: P.O. Box 310279, New Braunfels, TX 78131-0279 USA
E-mail: trbooks@trbooks.com
Web site: http://www.trbooks.com.

T.R. Trading Co., *See* **T.R. Bks.**

Tracor Technology Resources (TTR), Specialized Bk. Distributors, 1601 Research Blvd., Rockville, MD 20850 USA (SAN 169-3220) Tel 301-251-4970.

Trafalgar Square Bks., *(978-0-943955; 978-1-57076)* Orders Addr.: P.O. Box 257, North Pomfret, VT 05053 USA Tel 802-457-1911; Fax: 802-457-1913; Edit Addr.: Howe Hill Rd., North Pomfret, VT 05053 USA
E-mail: kimcook@sover.net
Web site: http://www.horseandriderbooks.com; http://www.trafalgarbooks.com/.

Trafalgar Square Publishing, *(978-0-943955; 978-1-57076)* Orders Addr.: P.O. Box 257, North Pomfret, VT 05053-0257 USA (SAN 213-8859) Tel 802-457-1911; Fax: 802-457-1913; Toll Free: 800-423-4525; Edit Addr.: 388 Howe Hill Rd., North Pomfret, VT 05053 USA Tel 802-423-4525; 802-457-1913
E-mail: tsquare@sover.net
Web site: http://www.trafalgarbooks.com; http://www.horseandriderbooks.com.

Trajectory, Inc., *(978-1-62028; 978-1-62665; 978-1-62978; 978-1-63209; 978-1-68100; 978-1-68124)* 50 Doaks Lane, Marblehead, MA 01945 USA Tel 781-476-2100
E-mail: info@trajectory.com; bob@trajectory.com
Web site: http://www.trajectory.com.

Trans World News, 3700 Kelley Ave., Cleveland, OH 44114-4533 USA (SAN 169-6688) Tel 216-391-4800; Fax: 216-391-9911; Toll Free: 800-321-9858.

Transaction Pubs., *(978-0-7658; 978-0-87855; 978-0-88738; 978-1-56000; 978-1-4128)* Raritan Ctr., 300 McGaw Dr., Edison, NJ 08837 USA; Edit Addr.: 10 Corporate Pl., S., Piscataway, NJ 08854 USA (SAN 202-7941) Toll Free: 888-999-6778
E-mail: orders@transactionpub.com
Web site: http://www.transactionpub.com.

Transamerican & Export News Co., 12345 World Trade Dr., San Diego, CA 92128-3743 USA (SAN 169-0140).

Trans-Atlantic Pubns., Inc., 311 Bainbridge St., Philadelphia, PA 19147 USA (SAN 694-0234) Tel 215-925-5083; Fax: 215-925-1912 Do not confuse with Transatlantic Arts, Inc., Albuquerque, NM
E-mail: order@transatlanticpub.com
Web site: http://www.transatlanticpub.com.

Traveler Restaurant, 741 Buckley Hwy., Union, CT 06076 USA (SAN 111-8218) Tel 860-684-4920.

Treasure Chest Bks., P.O. Box 5250, Tucson, AZ 85703-0250 USA Tel 520-623-9558; Fax: 520-624-5888; Toll Free Fax: 800-715-5888; Toll Free: 800-969-9558.

Treasure Chest Books, *See* **Rio Nuevo Pubs.**

Treasure Valley News, 4242 S. Eagleson Rd. Ste. 108B, Boise, ID 83705-4985 USA.

Tree Frog Trucking Co., 7983 SE 13th Ave., Portland, OR 97202-6665 USA (SAN 169-7188).

Tree Hse. Distribution, 1007 Perrywill Ave., Salt Lake City, UT 84124-2428 USA (SAN 631-6603) Fax: 801-262-2324; Toll Free: 888-299-7895.

Tree of Life Midwest, P.O. Box 2629, Bloomington, IN 47402-2629 USA (SAN 169-7994) Toll Free: 800-999-4200.

Tremendous Life Bks., *(978-0-937539; 978-1-933715; 978-1-936354)* Div. of Life Management Services, Inc., 206 West Allen St., Mechanicsburg, PA 17055-6240 USA (SAN 156-5419) Tel 717-766-9499; Fax: 717-766-6565; Toll Free: 800-233-2665
E-mail: JLiller@TremendousLifeBooks.com
Web site: http://www.TremendousLifeBooks.com.

Tres Americas Bks., Orders Addr.: 4336 N. Pulaski Rd., Chicago, IL 60641 USA Tel 773-481-9090.

T-Rex Products, 2391 Boswell Rd., Chula Vista, CA 91914-3509 USA.

Triangle News Co., Inc., 3498 Grand Ave., Pittsburgh, PA 15225 USA (SAN 169-7447).

Tri-County News Co., Inc., 1376 W. Main St., Santa Maria, CA 93458 USA (SAN 169-0345) Tel 805-925-6541; Fax: 805-925-3565
E-mail: trico2000@aol.com
Web site: http://tri-countynews.com.

TriLiteral, LLC, 100 Maple Ridge Dr., Cumberland, RI 02864-1796 USA (SAN 631-8126) Tel 401-531-2800; 401-531-2804 (Credit & Collections); Fax: 401-531-2801; 401-531-2803 (Credit & Collections); Toll Free Fax: 800-406-9145; Toll Free: 800-405-1619
E-mail: rich.swafford@triliteral.org; customer.care@Triliteral.org.

Trinity Pr. International, *(978-0-567; 978-1-56338)* Orders Addr.: P.O. Box 1321, Harrisburg, PA 17105-1321 USA; Edit Addr.: 4775 Linglestown Rd., Harrisburg, PA 17112 USA (SAN 253-8156).

Triple Tail Publishing, *See* **Farcountry Pr.**

Tri-State News Agency, P.O. Box 778, Johnson City, TN 37601 USA (SAN 169-7897) Tel 423-926-8159; 604 Rolling Hills Dr., Johnson City, TN 37601 (SAN 282-4744).

Tri-State Periodicals, Inc., Orders Addr.: P.O. Box 1110, Evansville, IN 47706-1110 USA Tel 812-867-7416; Edit Addr.: 9844 Heddon Rd., Evansville, IN 47711 USA (SAN 241-7537) Tel 812-867-7419.

Trucatriche, Orders Addr.: 3800 Main St., Suite 8, Chula Vista, CA 91911 USA Tel 619-426-2690; Fax: 619-426-2695
E-mail: info@trucatriche.com
Web site: http://www.trucatriche.com.

Truth Pubns., Orders Addr.: 8105 NW 23rd Ave., Gainesville, FL 32606 USA Tel 352-376-6320; Fax: 352-376-7105 Do not confuse with companies with the same or similar name in Paris, TX, Lombard, IL, Philadelphia, PA, Springfield, MO, Woodstock, MO
E-mail: upgflorida@juno.com.

Tulare County News, 13595 El Nogal Ave., Visalia, CA 93292-9352 USA (SAN 169-0442) Toll Free: 800-479-6006.

Turner Subscription Agency, Subs. of Dawson Holdings PLC, 15 S. West Park., Westwood, MA 02090-1524 USA (SAN 107-7112) Toll Free: 800-847-4201
E-mail: postmaster@dawson.com.

Turtleback Bks., *(978-0-613; 978-0-7857; 978-0-8085; 978-0-8335; 978-0-88103; 978-1-4176; 978-1-4177; 978-1-4178; 978-0-606)* Sub. of GL group, Inc., 1230 Macklind Ave., Saint Louis, MO 63110-1432 USA (SAN 159-947X) Tel 314-644-6100; Fax: 314-647-2845; Toll Free: 800-458-8438
E-mail: info@sanval.com; rheflin@turtleback.com
Web site: http://www.Turtleback.com.

Tuttle Publishing, *(978-0-8048; 978-1-4629)* Orders Addr.: 364 Innovation Dr., North Clarendon, VT 05759 USA (SAN 213-2621) Tel 802-773-8930; Fax: 802-773-6993; Toll Free Fax: 800-329-8885; Toll Free: 800-526-2778
E-mail: info@tuttlepublishing.com
Web site: http://www.tuttlepublishing.com.

Twentieth Century Christian Bks., *(978-0-89098)* 2809 Granny White Pike, Nashville, TN 37204 USA (SAN 206-2550) Tel 615-383-3842.

Twenty First Century Pubns., *(978-0-933278)* Orders Addr.: P.O. Box 702, Fairfield, IA 52556-0702 USA Tel 515-472-5105; Fax: 515-472-8443; Toll Free: 800-593-2665; Edit Addr.: 401 N. Fourth St., Fairfield, IA 52556 USA Do not confuse with Twenty First Century Pubns., Tolland, CT
E-mail: books21st@lisco.com
Web site: http://www.21stbooks.com.

Twenty-First Century Antiques, Orders Addr.: P.O. Box 70, Hatfield, MA 01038 USA (SAN 110-8085); Edit Addr.: 11 1/2 Main St., Hatfield, MA 01038 USA (SAN 243-248X) Tel 413-247-9396.

Twenty-Third Pubns./Bayard, *(978-0-89622; 978-1-58595; 978-1-62785)* 1 Montauk Ave. No. 20, New London, CT 06320-4967 USA (SAN 658-2052) Toll Free Fax: 800-572-0788; Toll Free: 800-321-0411
E-mail: kerry.moriarty@bayard-inc.com
Web site: http://www.23rdpublications.com.

Twin City News Agency, Inc., P.O. Box 466, Lafayette, IN 47902-0466 USA Tel 765-742-1051.

Two Rivers Distribution, Div. of Ingram Content Group, Orders Addr.: 210 American Dr., Jackson, TN 38301 USA Toll Free Fax: 800-351-5073 (Customer Service); Toll Free: 866-400-5351 (Customer Service); 800-343-4499
E-mail: pd_orderentry@ingramcontent.com; ips@ingramcontent.com
Web site: http://www.tworiversdistribution.com/.

Tyndale Hse. Pubs., *(978-0-8423; 978-1-4143; 978-1-4964)* Orders Addr.: 370 Executive Dr., Carol Stream, IL 60188 USA; Edit Addr.: 351 Executive Dr., Carol Stream, IL 60188 USA (SAN 206-7749) Tel 630-668-8310; Fax: 630-668-3245; Toll Free: 800-323-9400
E-mail: international@tyndale.com; permission@tyndale.com
Web site: http://www.tyndale.com.

Ubiquity Distributors, Inc., 607 Degraw St., Brooklyn, NY 11217 USA (SAN 200-7428) Tel 718-875-5491; Fax: 718-875-8047.

Ultra Bks., P.O. Box 945, Oakland, NJ 07436 USA (SAN 112-9074) Tel 201-337-8787.

Ulverscroft Large Print Bks., Ltd., *(978-0-7089; 978-1-84617)* Orders Addr.: P.O. Box 1230, West Seneca, NY 14224-1230 USA; Edit Addr.: 950 Union Rd., West Seneca, NY 14224-3438 USA (SAN 208-3035) Toll Free: 800-955-9659
E-mail: enquiries@ulverscroft.co.uk; sales@ulverscroft.com
Web site: http://www.ulverscroft.co.uk.

Unarius Academy of Science Pubns., *(978-0-932642; 978-0-935097)* Orders Addr.: 145 S. Magnolia Ave., El Cajon, CA 92020-4522 USA (SAN 168-9614) Tel 619-444-7062; Fax: 619-444-9637; Toll Free: 800-475-7062
E-mail: uriel@unarius.org
Web site: http://www.unarius.org.

Underground Railroad, The, 2769 Club House Rd., Mobile, AL 36605-4373 USA (SAN 630-7892) Tel 334-432-8811.

Unifacmanu International Trading Co., Inc., 22 Cross Ridge Rd., Chappaqua, NY 10514 USA (SAN 631-743X)
E-mail: unifacmanu@att.net
Web site: http://www.bookvariety.com.

Unique Bks., Inc., 5010 Kemper Ave., Saint Louis, MO 63139 USA (SAN 630-0472) Tel 314-776-6695; Fax: 314-776-0841; Toll Free: 800-533-5446.

United Magazine, Orders Addr.: P.O. Box 36, Columbia, KY 42728-0036 USA (SAN 169-2852) Tel 502-384-3444; Fax: 502-384-9324; Edit Addr.: 361 Industrial Park Rd., Louisville, KY 42728-0036 USA (SAN 250-3336).

United Methodist Publishing Hse., *(978-1-63088)* 201 Eighth Ave., S., Nashville, TN 37203 USA Tel 615-749-6000; Fax: 615-749-6079; Toll Free Fax: 800-836-7802; Toll Free: 800-672-1789 (orders only)
Web site: http://www.umph.org; http://www.abingdonpress.com.

United Nations Pubns., *(978-0-680; 978-0-89714; 978-92-1; 978-952-9520)* 300 E. 42nd St., 9th Flr., New York, NY 10017 USA (SAN 206-6718) Tel 212-963-8302; 212-963-7680 UN Bookshop; Fax: 212-963-3489; 212-963-4910 UN Bookshop; Toll Free: 800-253-9646 (bookshop orders); 800-553-3210 UN Bookshop
E-mail: publications@un.org
Web site: https://unp.un.org/.

United News Co., Inc., 111 Lake St., P.O. Box 3426, Bakersfield, CA 93305 USA (SAN 169-7579) Tel 805-323-7864.

United Society of Shakers, *(978-0-915836)* 707 Shaker Rd., New Gloucester, ME 04260 USA (SAN 158-619X) Tel 207-926-4597; Fax: 207-926-3559
E-mail: sdlshakers@aol.com
Web site: http://www.shaker.lib.me.us.

United States Government Printing Office, *(978-0-16; 978-0-18)* Orders Addr.: P.O. Box 371954, Pittsburgh, PA 15250-7954 USA (SAN 658-0785) Tel 202-512-1800; Fax: 202-512-2250; Toll Free: 866-512-1800; Edit Addr.: USGPO Stop SSMB, Washington, DC 20401 USA (SAN 206-152X) Tel 202-512-1705 (bibliographic information only); 202-512-2268 (book dealers only); Fax: 202-512-1655
E-mail: orders@gpo.gov; rdavis@gpo.gov; ContactCenter@gpo.gov
Web site: http://bookstore.gpo.gov/; http://www.gpoaccess.gov/index.html.

United Subscription Service, 527 Third Ave., No. 284, New York, NY 10016-4100 USA (SAN 286-0104).

Univ of Arizona Critical Languages Program, 1230 N. Park Ave., Suite 102, Tucson, AZ 85719 USA.

Univ. of Arkansas Pr., *(978-0-938626; 978-1-55728; 978-1-61075; 978-1-68226)* 105 N. McIlroy Ave., Fayetteville, AR 72701 USA (SAN 239-3972) Tel 479-575-7544; Fax: 479-575-6044; Toll Free: 800-626-0090
E-mail: info@uapress.com
Web site: http://www.uapress.com; http://www.uark.edu/~uaprinfo.

Univ. of California Pr., *(978-0-520)* 155 Grand Ave., Suite 400, Oakland, CA 94612-3758 USA Tel 510-883-8232 (Books & Journals); Fax: 510-836-8910
E-mail: journals@ucpress.edu; orders@cpfsinc.com; askucp@ucpress.edu
Web site: http://www.ucpress.edu.

Univ. of Chicago Pr., *(978-0-226; 978-0-89065; 978-0-943056; 978-1-892850)* Orders Addr.: 11030 S. Langley Ave., Chicago, IL 60628 USA (SAN 202-5280) Tel 773-702-7000; Fax: 773-702-7212; Toll Free Fax: 800-621-8476 (US & Canada); Toll Free: 800-621-2736 (US & Canada); Edit Addr.: 1427 E. 60th St., Chicago, IL 60637 USA (SAN 202-5299) Tel 773-702-7700; 773-702-7748 (Marketing & Sales); Fax: 773-702-9756
E-mail: general@press.uchicago.edu; kh@press.uchicago.edu; custserv@press.uchicago.rdu; sales@press.uchicago.edu; marketing@press.uchicago.edu; publicity@press.uchicago.edu
Web site: http://www.press.uchicago.edu.

Univ. of Georgia Pr., *(978-0-8203)* Orders Addr.: 4435 Atlanta Hwy. West Dock, Athens, GA 30602 USA; Edit Addr.: Main Library, Third Flr. 320 S. Jackson St., Athens, GA 30602 USA (SAN 203-3054) Fax: 706-542-2558; Toll Free: 800-266-5842
E-mail: books@uga.edu
Web site: http://www.ugapress.org.

Univ. of Hawaii Pr., *(978-0-8248; 978-0-87022)* Orders Addr.: 2840 Kolowalu St., Honolulu, HI 96822-1888 USA (SAN 202-5353) Tel 808-956-8255; Fax: 808-988-6052; Toll Free Fax: 800-650-7811; Toll Free: 888-847-7377
E-mail: uhpmkt@hawaii.edu; uhpbooks@hawaii.edu
Web site: http://www.uhpress.hawaii.edu.

Univ. of Missouri Pr., *(978-0-8262)* 2910 LeMone Blvd., Columbia, MO 65201 USA (SAN 203-3143) Tel 573-882-7641; Fax: 573-884-4498; Toll Free: 800-828-1894 (orders only)
E-mail: rennerk@umsystem.edu; deandj@umsystem.edu
Web site: http://press.umsystem.edu.

Univ. of Nebraska Pr., *(978-0-8032; 978-1-4962; 978-1-64012)* Orders Addr.: 1111 Lincoln Mall, Lincoln, NE 68588-0630 USA Tel 402-472-3581; 402-472-7702; Fax: 402-472-6214; Toll Free Fax: 800-526-2617; Toll Free: 800-755-1105; Edit Addr.: P.O. Box 880630, Lincoln, NE 68588-0630 USA (SAN 202-5337)
E-mail: pressmail@unl.edu
Web site: http://www.nebraskapress.unl.edu; http://www.bisonbooks.com.

Univ. of New Mexico Pr., *(978-0-8263; 978-0-9766839)* Orders Addr.: 1312 Basehart Rd., SE, Albuquerque, NM 87106-4363 USA (SAN 213-9588) Tel 505-277-2346; 505-272-7777 (orders); Toll Free Fax: 800-622-8667; Toll Free: 800-249-7737 (orders)
E-mail: unmpress@unm.edu
Web site: http://www.unmpress.com.

Univ. of Oklahoma Pr., *(978-0-8061)* Orders Addr.: 2800 Venture Dr., Norman, OK 73069-8218 USA Tel 405-325-2000; Fax: 405-364-5798; Toll Free Fax: 800-735-0476; Toll Free: 800-627-7377
E-mail: presscs@ou.edu
Web site: http://www.oupress.com.

Univ. of Pennsylvania Pr., *(978-0-8122; 978-1-5128)* Orders Addr.: c/o Hopkins Fulfillment Srvc., Hopkins Fulfillment Service, Baltimore, MD 21211-4370 USA Tel 410-516-6948; Fax: 410-516-6998; Toll Free: 800-537-5487; Edit Addr.: 3905 Spruce St., Philadelphia, PA 19104-4112 USA (SAN 202-5345) Tel 215-898-6261; Fax: 215-898-0404; Toll Free: 800-537-5487 (book orders)
E-mail: custserv@pobox.upenn.edu
Web site: http://www.upenn.edu/pennpress.

Univ. of Tennessee Pr., *(978-0-87049; 978-1-57233; 978-1-62190)* Div. of Univ. of Tennessee & Member of Assn. of American Univ. Presses, Orders Addr.: 11030 S. Langley, Chicago, IL 60628 USA Tel 773-568-1550; Toll Free Fax: 800-621-8471; Toll Free: 800-621-2736 (orders only); Edit Addr.: 110 Conference Ctr. Bldg., Knoxville, TN 37996-0325 USA (SAN 212-9930) Tel 865-974-3321; Fax: 865-974-3724
E-mail: tpost@utk.edu
Web site: http://www.utpress.org.

Univ. of Texas Pr., *(978-0-292; 978-1-4773)* Orders Addr.: P.O. Box 7819, Austin, TX 78713-7819 USA (SAN 212-9876) Tel 512-471-7233; Fax: 512-232-7178; Toll Free: 800-252-3206; Edit Addr.: University of Texas at Austin 2100 Comal, Austin, TX 78722 USA
E-mail: info@utpress.utexas.edu
Web site: http://www.utexas.edu/utpress.

Univ. of Washington Pr., *(978-0-295; 978-1-902716)* Orders Addr.: P.O. Box 50096, Seattle, WA 98145-5096 USA (SAN 212-2502) Tel 206-543-4050; Fax: 206-543-3932; Toll Free Fax: 800-669-7993; Edit Addr.: P.O. Box 50096, Seattle, WA 98145-5096 USA Toll Free Fax: 800-669-7993; 1126 N. 98th St., Seattle, WA 98103
E-mail: uwpord@u.washington.edu
Web site: http://www.washington.edu/uwpress.

Univ. of Wisconsin Pr., *(978-0-299)* Orders Addr.: c/o Chicago Dist Ctr., 11030 S. Langley Ave., Chicago, IL 60628 USA Tel 773-568-1550; Fax: 773-660-2235; Toll Free Fax: 800-621-8476 (orders only); Toll Free: 800-621-2736 (orders only); Edit Addr.: 1930 Monroe St., 3rd Flr., Madison, WI 53711 USA Tel 608-263-1110; Fax: 608-263-1132
E-mail: uwiscpress@uwpress.wisc.edu
Web site: http://www.wisc.edu/wisconsinpress/.

Univ. Pr. of Florida, *(978-0-8130; 978-0-942084; 978-0-9760555; 978-1-61610; 978-1-942852; 978-1-68340)* Orders Addr.: 15 NW 15th St., Gainesville, FL 32611-0279 USA (SAN 207-9275) Tel 352-392-1351; Fax: 352-392-7302; Toll Free Fax: 800-680-1955; Toll Free: 800-226-3822
E-mail: press@upf.com; orders@upf.com
Web site: http://www.upf.com.

Univ. Pr. of Mississippi, *(978-0-87805; 978-1-57806; 978-1-934110; 978-1-60473; 978-1-61703; 978-1-62103; 978-1-62674; 978-1-62846; 978-1-4968)* 3825 Ridgewood Rd., Jackson, MS 39211-6492 USA (SAN 203-1914) Tel 601-432-6205; Fax: 601-432-6217; Toll Free: 800-737-7788 (orders only)
E-mail: kburgess@ihl.state.ms.us; press@mississippi.edu
Web site: http://www.upress.state.ms.us.

Univ. Pr. of New England, *(978-0-87451; 978-0-915032; 978-1-58465; 978-1-61168; 978-1-5126)* Orders Addr.: One Court St., Suite 250, Lebanon, NH 03755 USA Tel 603-448-1533 (ext. 255); Fax: 603-448-9429; Toll Free: 800-421-1561
E-mail: University.Press@Dartmouth.edu
Web site: http://www.upne.com.

Univelt, Inc., *(978-0-87703; 978-0-912183)* Orders Addr.: P.O. Box 28130, San Diego, CA 92198 USA; Edit Addr.: 740 Metcalf St., Suite 13, Escondido, CA 92025-1671 USA (SAN 658-2095)
E-mail: sales@univelt.com
Web site: http://www.univelt.com.

Universal Subscription Service, P.O. Box 35445, Houston, TX 77035 USA (SAN 287-4768).

Universe Publishing, *(978-0-7893; 978-0-87663; 978-1-55550)* Div. of Rizzoli International Pubns., Inc., 300 Park Ave. S., 3rd Flr., New York, NY 10010 USA (SAN 202-537X) Tel 212-387-3400; Fax: 212-387-3444 Do not confuse with similar names in North Hollywood, CA, Englewood, NJ, Mendocino, CA.

University Book Service, Orders Addr.: P.O. Box 608, Grove City, OH 43123 USA (SAN 169-6912); Edit Addr.: P.O. Box 607, Grove City, OH 43123-0607 USA (SAN 282-4841) Toll Free: 800-634-4272.

University of Arizona Pr., *(978-0-8165; 978-1-941451)* 355 S. Euclid Ave., Suite 103, Tucson, AZ 85719 USA (SAN 205-468X) Tel 520-621-1441; Fax: 520-621-8899; Toll Free: 800-426-3797 (orders)
E-mail: orders@uapress.arizona.edu
Web site: http://www.uapress.arizona.edu.

University of Nevada Pr., *(978-0-87417; 978-1-943859)* Orders Addr.: Mail Stop 166, Reno, NV 89557 USA (SAN 203-316X) Tel 775-784-6573; Fax: 775-784-6200; Toll Free: 877-682-6657 (orders only)
E-mail: vfontana@unpress.nevada.edu
Web site: http://www.unpress.nevada.edu.

University of Virginia Pr., *(978-0-8139; 978-0-912759; 978-1-57814)* Orders Addr.: P.O. Box 400318, Charlottesville, VA 22904-4318 USA (SAN 202-5361) Tel 804-924-3468; Fax: 804-982-2655
E-mail: upress@virginia.edu
Web site: http://www.upress.virginia.edu.

University Publishing Associates, Incorporated, *See* **National Film Network LLC**

Untreed Reads Publishing, LLC, *(978-1-61187; 978-1-945447)* 506 Kansas St., San Francisco, CA 94107 USA Tel 415-621-0465; Toll Free Fax: 800-318-6037
E-mail: jhartman@untreedreads.com; kdsullivan@untreedreads.com
Web site: http://www.untreedreads.com.

Upper Access, Inc., *(978-0-942679)* Orders Addr.: 87 Upper Access Rd., Hinesburg, VT 05461 USA (SAN 667-1195) Tel 802-482-2988 main office; Fax: 802-417-3002; Toll Free: 800-310-8320 (orders only)
E-mail: info@upperaccess.com
Web site: http://www.upperaccess.com.

Urban Land Institute, *(978-0-87420)* 1025 Thomas Jefferson St., NW, Suite 500 W., Washington, DC 20007-5201 USA (SAN 203-3399) Tel 202-624-7000; Fax: 202-624-7140; Toll Free: 800-321-5011
E-mail: bookstore@uli.org
Web site: http://www.uli.org/.

U.S. Games Systems, Inc., *(978-0-88079; 978-0-913866; 978-1-57281)* 179 Ludlow St., Stamford, CT 06902 USA (SAN 158-6483) Tel 203-353-8400; Fax: 203-353-8431; Toll Free: 800-544-2637
E-mail: usgames@aol.com
Web site: http://www.usgamesinc.com.

US PubRep, Inc., 5000 Jasmine Dr., Rockville, MD 20853 USA Tel 301-838-9276; Fax: 301-838-9278
E-mail: craigfalk@aya.yale.edu.

Val Publishing, 16 S. Terrace Ave., Mount Vernon, NY 10551 USA (SAN 107-6876) Tel 914-664-7077.

Valiant International Multi-Media Corp., 55 Ruta Ct., South Hackensack, NJ 07606 USA (SAN 652-8813) Tel 201-229-9800; Fax: 201-814-0418.

Valjean Pr., 721 Shadowlawn Ct., Franklin, TN 37069 USA
E-mail: pastorforthemoment@gmail.com.

Valkyrie Distribution, 43 New Hope Ct., Florissant, MO 63033 USA Tel 314-623-6639
E-mail: valkpub@yahoo.com.

Valley Distributors, Inc., 2947 Felton Rd., Norristown, PA 19401 USA (SAN 169-7498) Tel 610-279-7650; Fax: 610-279-9093; Toll Free: 800-355-2665 (orders only).

Valley Media, Inc., 1276 Santa Anita Ct., Woodland, CA 95776 USA Tel 530-661-6600; Fax: 530-661-5472
E-mail: valley@valley-media.com
Web site: http://www.valsat.com.

Valley Record Distributors, *See* **Valley Media, Inc.**

Van Dyke News Agency, 2238 W. Pinedale Ave., Fresno, CA 93711-0453 USA (SAN 168-9630) Tel 209-291-7768; Fax: 209-291-7770.

Van Khoa Bks., 14601 Moran St., Westminster, CA 92683-5629 USA (SAN 110-7534)
E-mail: vankhoa@vinet.com.

Verham News Corp., 75 Main St., West Lebanon, NH 03784 USA (SAN 169-4561) Fax: 603-298-8843.

VHPS Distribution Center, *See* **MPS**

Victory Multimedia, *(978-0-9661850)* Div. of Victory Audio Video Services, Inc., 460 Hindry Ave., Suite D, Inglewood, CA 90301-2045 USA (SAN 631-4112)
E-mail: sbvictory@juno.com.

Vida Life Publishers International, *See* **Vida Pubs.**

Vida Pubs., *(978-0-8297)* 8410 NW 53rd Ter. Ste. 103, Miami, FL 33166-4510 USA Toll Free: 800-843-2548
E-mail: vidapubsales@harpercollins.com
Web site: http://www.editorialvida.com.

Video Project, The, 200 Estates Dr., Ben Lomond, CA 95005-9444 USA Toll Free: 800-475-2638
E-mail: videoproject@videoproject.org
Web site: http://www.videoproject.org.

Vigilante, Richard Bks., *(978-0-9800763; 978-0-9827163)* 7400 Metro Blvd. Suite 217, Minneapolis, MN 55439 USA.

Village Marketing, 145 W. 400 N., Richfield, UT 84701 USA (SAN 631-6751) Toll Free: 800-982-6683.

Vinabind, P.O. Box 340, Steelville, MO 65565 USA (SAN 159-9828).

Vincennes News Agency, P.O. Box 1110, Evansville, IN 47706-1110 USA (SAN 169-2518).

Virginia Periodical Distributors, *See* **Aramark Magazine & Bk. Services, Inc.**

Virginia Pubns., 16 W. Washington St., Lexington, VA 24450 USA Tel 540-462-3993
E-mail: vapublications@rockbridge.net.

Visible Ink Pr., *(978-0-7876; 978-0-8103; 978-1-57859)* Orders Addr.: 1094 Flex Dr., Jackson, TN 38301-5070 USA Toll Free Fax: 800-351-5073; Toll Free: 800-343-4499; Edit Addr.: 43311 Joy Rd., Canton, MI 48187-2075 USA (SAN 860-2271) Tel 734-667-3211; Fax: 734-667-4311
E-mail: inquiries@visibleink.com
Web site: http://www.visibleink.com.

Vision Distributors, *(978-0-9626732)* Div. of Infinite Creations, Inc., Orders Addr.: P.O. Box 9839, Santa Fe, NM 87504 USA Tel 505-986-8221.

Vision Press, *See* **Vision Distributors**

Vision Video, *(978-1-56364)* Orders Addr.: P.O. Box 540, Worcester, PA 19490 USA Tel 610-584-3500; Fax: 610-584-4610; Toll Free: 800-523-0226; Edit Addr.: 2030 Wentz Church Rd., Worcester, PA 19490 USA (SAN 298-7392)
E-mail: info@gatewayfilms.com; info@visionvideo.com
Web site: http://www.gatewayfilms.com.

Vistabooks, *(978-0-89646)* Orders Addr.: 637 Blue Ridge Rd., Silverthorne, CO 80498-8931 USA (SAN 211-0849) Tel 970-468-7673 (phone/fax)
E-mail: vistabooks@compuserve.com
Web site: http://www.vistabooks.com.

Vital Source Technologies, Inc., *(978-0-9651916; 978-1-59377)* 227 Fayetteville St., Suite 400, Raleigh, NC 27601 USA Tel 919-755-8110
E-mail: hayesbarton@vitalbook.com.

Vitality Distributors, 940 NW 51st Pl., Fort Lauderdale, FL 33309 USA (SAN 169-0973) Toll Free: 800-226-8482.

VNU, Div. of Prestel Publishing, 575 Prospect Ave., Lakewood, NJ 08701 USA (SAN 631-7758) Tel 732-363-5679; Fax: 732-363-0338; Toll Free: 888-463-6110.

volcano pr., *(978-0-912078; 978-1-884244)* Orders Addr.: P.O. Box 270, Volcano, CA 95689 USA (SAN 220-0015) Tel 209-296-4991; Fax: 209-296-4995; Toll Free: 800-879-9636; Edit Addr.: 21496 National St., Volcano, CA 95689 USA
E-mail: info@volcanopress.com; sales@volcanopress.com; adam@volcanopress.com
Web site: http://www.volcanopress.com.

VPD, Inc., 150 Parkshore Dr., Folsom, CA 95630-4710 USA (SAN 631-287X) Toll Free: 800-366-2111
Web site: http://www.vpdinc.com/.

Vroman's, A. C., *(978-0-9639197)* 695 E. Colorado Blvd., Pasadena, CA 91101 USA (SAN 169-0027) Tel 626-449-5320; Fax: 626-792-7308.

W5YI Group, Inc., P.O. Box 565101, Dallas, TX 75356 USA.

WA Bk. Service, P.O. Box 514, East Islip, NY 11730-0514 USA (SAN 107-2943).

Wabash Valley News Agency, 2200 N. Curry Pike, No. 2, Bloomington, IN 47404-1486 USA (SAN 169-250X).

Waffle, O. G. Bk. Co. (The Bookhouse), P.O. Box 586, Marion, IA 52302 USA (SAN 112-8817) Tel 319-373-1832.

Waldenbooks Company, Incorporated, *See* **Waldenbooks, Inc.**

Waldenbooks, Inc., *(978-0-681)* Div. of Borders Group, Inc., a/o Calendar Orders, 455 Industrial Blvd., Suite C, LaVergne, TN 37086 USA (SAN 179-3373); Orders Addr.: One Waldenbooks Dr., LaVergne, TN 37096 USA; 11625 Venture, Mira Loma, CA 91752 Tel 951-361-4025; Edit Addr.: 100 Phoenix Dr., Ann Arbor, MI 48108-2202 USA (SAN 200-8858) Tel 734-477-1100
E-mail: customerservice@waldenbooks.com
Web site: http://www.waldenbooks.com; http://www.preferredreader.com.

Walker Art Ctr., *(978-0-935640; 978-1-935963)* Orders Addr.: 1750 Hennepin Ave., Minneapolis, MN 55403 USA (SAN 206-1880) Tel 612-375-7638; Fax: 612-375-7565
E-mail: paul.schumacher@walkerart.org; lisa.middag@walkerart.org.

Wallace's College Bk. Co., P.O. Box 689, Nicholasville, KY 40340-0689 USA (SAN 169-2844) Tel 606-255-0886; Fax: 606-259-9892; Toll Free Fax: 800-433-9329 (orders only); Toll Free: 800-354-9590 (orders only); 800-354-9500
E-mail: orders@wallaces.com.

Walthers, William K. Inc., *(978-0-941952)* 5601 W. Florist Ave., Milwaukee, WI 53201-3039 USA (SAN 238-4868) Tel 414-527-0770; Fax: 414-527-4423; Toll Free: 800-877-7171.

Ware-Pak, Inc., Orders Addr.: 2427 Bond St., University Park, IL 60466 USA Tel 708-534-2600; Fax: 708-534-7803
E-mail: kshay@ware-pak.com
Web site: http://www.ware-pak.com.

Warner Books, Incorporated, *See* **Grand Central Publishing**

Warner Bros. Pubns., *(978-0-7604; 978-0-7692; 978-0-87487; 978-0-89724; 978-0-89898; 978-0-910957; 978-1-55122; 978-1-57623; 978-0-7579)* Div. of AOL Time Warner, 15800 NW 48th Ave., Miami, FL 33014-6422 USA (SAN 203-0586).

Warner Pr., Inc., *(978-0-87162; 978-1-59317; 978-1-68434)* Orders Addr.: P.O. Box 2499, Anderson, IN 46018-2499 USA (SAN 691-4241) Tel 765-648-2116; Fax: 765-622-9511; Toll Free: 800-848-2464; Edit Addr.: 2902 Enterprise Dr., Anderson, IN 46013 USA (SAN 111-8110) Tel 765-644-7721; Fax: 765-640-8005; Toll Free: 800-741-7721 (orders only)
E-mail: jallison@warnerpress.org; wporders@warnerpress.org; rjackson@warnerpress.org
Web site: http://www.warnerpress.org; http://www.francisasburypress.org.

Warner Press Publishers, *See* **Warner Pr., Inc.**

Washington Bk. Distributors, 4930A Eisenhower Ave., Alexandria, VA 22304 USA (SAN 631-0095) Tel 703-212-9113; Fax: 703-212-9114; Toll Free: 800-699-9113
E-mail: zacwbd@prodigy.net
Web site: http://www.washingtonbk.com.

Washington Toy Co., 2163 28th Ave., San Francisco, CA 94116-1732 USA (SAN 107-1718).

Watson, W. R. & Staff, 150 Mariner Green Ct., Corte Madera, CA 94925 USA (SAN 286-0155) Tel 510-524-6156; Fax: 510-526-5023.

Watson-Guptill Pubns., Inc., *(978-0-8230; 978-1-60569)* Div. of Crown Publishing Grp., 575 Prospect St., Lakewood, NJ 08701 USA Tel 732-363-5679; Toll Free Fax: 877-227-6564; Edit Addr.: 1745 Broadway # 124, New York, NY 10019-4305 USA (SAN 282-5384)
E-mail: aalexander@watsonguptill.com
Web site: http://www.watsonguptill.com.

Waverly News Co., 17 State St., Newburyport, MA 01950 USA (SAN 169-3522).

Wayland Audio-Visual, 210 E. 86th St., Suite 405, New York, NY 10028 USA Toll Free: 800-813-1271
E-mail: jm@waylandav.com.

Waymont Bk. Co., 136 Steuben St., Jersey City, NJ 07302 USA (SAN 630-768X) Tel 201-434-4268; Fax: 201-432-1293
E-mail: waymont@worldnet.att.net.

Wayne State Univ. Pr., *(978-0-8143)* Leonard N. Simons Bldg., 4809 Woodward Ave., Detroit, MI 48201-1309 USA (SAN 202-5221) Tel 313-577-6120; Fax: 313-577-6131; Toll Free: 800-978-7323 (customer orders)
E-mail: theresa.martinelli@wayne.edu; Kristina.Stonehill@wayne.edu
Web site: http://wsupress.wayne.edu.

Weiner News Co., 1011 N. Frio, P.O. Box 7608, San Antonio, TX 78207 USA (SAN 169-8427) Tel 210-226-9333; Fax: 210-226-8679.

Weiser, Samuel Incorporated, *See* **Red Wheel/Weiser**

WellSpring Bks., P.O. Box 2765, Woburn, MA 01888-1465 USA (SAN 111-3399) Do not confuse with companies with the same or similar names in Albuquerque, NM, Ukiah, CA, Adelphia, NJ, Woburn, MA, Groton, VT.

Wenatchee News Agency, 434 Rock Island Rd., East Wenatchee, WA 98802-5360 USA (SAN 169-8885) Tel 509-662-3511.

Wesscott Marketing, Inc., *(978-0-9764077)* P.O. Box 26144, Saint Louis Park, MN 55426 USA Fax: 952-541-4905; Toll Free: 800-375-3702.

West, *(978-0-314; 978-0-7620; 978-0-8321; 978-0-8366; 978-0-87632)* Orders Addr.: 610 Opperman Dr., Eagan, MN 55123-1396 USA Tel 651-687-6849; Fax: 651-687-6857; Toll Free: 800-328-2209; 800-328-9378 (Editorial) Do not confuse with The West Group in Prairie Village, KS
E-mail: west.bookstore@thomson.com; customer.service@westgroup.com; janet.linkert@thompson.com
Web site: http://west.thomson.com; http://westacademic.com.

West Music Co., 1212 Fifth St., Coralville, IA 52241 USA Toll Free: 800-397-9378.

West Texas News Co., Orders Addr.: 1214 Barranca, El Paso, TX 79935 USA; Edit Addr.: P.O. Box 26488, El Paso, TX 79926 USA (SAN 169-8184) Tel 915-594-7586; Fax: 915-594-7589.

West Virginia Book Co., The, 1125 Central Ave., Charleston, WV 25302 USA (SAN 920-9956) Tel 304-342-1848; Fax: 304-343-0594; Toll Free: 888-982-7472
E-mail: wvbooks@wvbookco.com.

Western Book Distributors/Booksource, *See* **Western Booksource, Inc.**

Western Booksource, Inc., 4935 Metart Shwayn, Tillamook, OR 97141 USA (SAN 158-4332) Toll Free: 800-825-0100; 230 Fifth Ave., No. 1104, New York, NY 10001 Tel 212-889-9339; Fax: 212-889-9572.

Western International, Inc., *(978-0-9665194)* 2220 Delaware St., Lawrence, KS 66046-3150 USA (SAN 631-1695) Toll Free: 800-634-6737.

Western Library Bks., 560 S. San Vicente Blvd., Los Angeles, CA 90048 USA (SAN 168-9878) Tel 213-653-8880.

Western Merchandisers, 2900 Airport Rd., Denton, TX 76207-2102 USA (SAN 156-4633).

Western Michigan News, *See* **Readmor**

Western Pubns. Service, 2128 Sun Valley Rd., San Marcos, CA 92069 USA (SAN 630-6241) Tel 760-295-2231; Fax: 760-295-3978.

Western Record Sales, 2991 Saint Andrews Rd., Fairfield, CA 94533-7839 USA (SAN 630-6667).

Western Reserve Historical Society, *(978-0-911704; 978-0-9967844)* 10825 East Blvd., Cleveland, OH 44106 USA (SAN 110-8387) Tel 216-721-5722; Fax: 216-721-0645.

Westminster John Knox Pr., *(978-0-664; 978-0-8042; 978-1-61164; 978-1-947888)* Div. of Presbyterian Publishing Corp., Orders Addr.: 100 Witherspoon St., Louisville, KY 40202 USA (SAN 202-9669) Tel 502-569-5052 (outside U.S. for ordering); Fax: 502-569-5113 (outside U.S. for faxed orders); Toll Free Fax: 800-541-5113 (toll-free U.S. faxed orders); Toll Free: 800-227-2872 (customer service)
E-mail: orders@wjkbooks.com
Web site: http://www.wjkbooks.com.

Weston, Edward Fine Arts, P.O. Box 3098, Chatsworth, CA 91313-3098 USA (SAN 168-9967) Tel 818-885-1044; Fax: 818-885-1021.

Weston Woods Studios, Inc., *(978-0-7882; 978-0-89719; 978-1-55592; 978-1-56008)* Div. of Scholastic, Inc., 143 Main St., Norwalk, CT 06851 USA (SAN 630-3838) Tel 203-845-0197; Fax: 203-845-0498; Toll Free: 800-243-5020
E-mail: questions@Scholastic.com
Web site: http://www.scholastic.com/westonwoods.

Westwater Bks., *(978-0-916370; 978-1-941406)* Div. of Belknap Photographic Services, Inc., P.O. Box 2560, Evergreen, CO 80437 USA (SAN 208-3698) Tel 303-674-5410; Fax: 303-670-0586; Toll Free: 800-628-1326.

WFiveYI Group, Inc., The, 7101 N. Ridgeway Ave., Lincolnwood, IL 60712 USA Tel 847-763-0916; Fax: 847-763-0918.

Whatever Publishing, Incorporated, *See* **New World Library**

Whitaker Distributors, *See* **Anchor Distributors**

Whitaker Hse., *(978-0-88368; 978-1-60374; 978-1-62911; 978-1-64123)* Div. of Whitaker Corp., 1030 Hunt Valley Cir., New Kensington, PA 15068 USA (SAN 203-2104) Tel 724-334-7000 Whitaker House/Anchor Distributors; Fax: 724-334-1200 Anchor Distributors; Toll Free Fax: 866-773-7001 Whitaker House; 800-765-1960 Anchor Distributors; Toll Free: 877-793-9800 Whitaker House; 800-444-4484 Whitaker House/Anchor Distributors
E-mail: sales@whitakerhouse.com
Web site: http://www.whitakerhouse.com/; http://www.anchordistributors.com/; http://www.amazon.com/.

Whitewing Pr., P.O. Box 1561, Hemphill, TX 75948 USA Tel 409-787-1526
E-mail: books@whitewingpress.com.

Whiting News Co., 1011 Azalea Dr., Munster, IN 46321-3501 USA (SAN 169-2542).

Whitlock & Co., 10001 Roosevelt Rd., Westchester, IL 60153 USA (SAN 285-9645).

Whitman Distribution Co., Orders Addr.: P.O. Box 513, Lebanon, NH 03766 USA (SAN 631-0540) Fax: 603-448-2576; Toll Free: 800-353-3730; Edit Addr.: 10 Water St., Lebanon, NH 03766 USA
E-mail: distribution@whitmancommunications.com.

Whitman Publishing & Distribution Company, *See* **Whitman Distribution Co.**

Wholesale Distributors, P.O. Box 126, Burlington, IA 52601 USA (SAN 145-8051) Tel 319-753-1683; Fax: 319-753-5988; Toll Free: 800-272-1556.

Wickel, W. W. Co., Inc., 520 N. Exchange Ct., Aurora, IL 60504 USA (SAN 135-1230) Tel 630-820-0044; Fax: 630-820-0057; Toll Free: 800-728-0708.

Wicker Park Pr., Ltd., *(978-0-9789676; 978-1-936679)* 334 Hawthorn Ave,, Glencoe, IL 60022 USA Tel 773-391-1199
E-mail: eric@3ibooks.com
Web site: http://www.wickerparkpress.us.

Wilcor International Bk. Dept., 161 Drive In Rd., Frankfort, NY 13340-5238 USA (SAN 107-7023).

Wild Dog Bks., Orders Addr.: Seven Balsa Ct., Sante Fe, NM 87508 USA
E-mail: WildDogBooks@att.net.

Wiley, John & Sons, Inc., *(978-0-470; 978-0-471; 978-0-7645; 978-0-7821; 978-0-8260; 978-0-87605; 978-0-88422; 978-0-937721; 978-0-939246; 978-1-55828; 978-1-56561; 978-1-56884; 978-1-57313; 978-1-58245; 978-1-878058; 978-1-118; 978-1-119)* Orders Addr.: c/o John Wiley & Sons, Inc., United States Distribution Ctr., 1 Wiley Dr., Somerset, NJ 08875-1272 USA Tel 732-469-4400; Fax: 732-302-2300; Toll Free Fax: 800-597-3299; Toll Free: 800-225-5945 (orders); Edit Addr.: 111 River St., Hoboken, NJ 07030 USA (SAN 200-2272) Tel 201-748-6000; 201-748-6276 (Retail and Wholesale); Fax: 201-748-6088; 201-748-6641 (Retail and Wholesale)
E-mail: compbks@wiley.com; bookinfo@wiley.com; custserv@wiley.com
Web site: http://www.wiley.com/compbooks; http://www.interscience.wiley.com; http://www.wiley.com.

William Thomson, *See* **Thomson, Linda**

Williamson, Darcy, *See* **Southern Cross Pubns.**

Willman Productions, P.O. Box 272345, Fort Collins, CO 80527 USA Tel 970-224-5911; Toll Free: 800-816-7566.

Wilshire Bk. Co., *(978-0-87980)* 9731 Variel Ave., Chatsworth, CA 91311-4315 USA (SAN 168-9932)
E-mail: mpowers@mpowers.com
Web site: http://www.mpowers.com.

Wilson & Assocs., *(978-0-9710427)* P.O. Box 2569, Alvin, TX 77512 USA Tel 281-388-0196; Fax: 413-683-8503 Do not confuse with Wilson & Associates, Gig Harbor, WA
E-mail: john@wilsonpublishing.com; pwilson@wilsonpublishing.com
Web site: http://www.orsapress.com; http://www.thebookdistributor.com; http://www.wilsonpublishing.com.

Wilson & Sons, P.O. Box 996, Bellevue, WA 98009 USA (SAN 129-0010) Tel 425-392-1965
E-mail: dchief@seanst.com.

Wimmer Companies, The, *See* **Wimmer Cookbooks**

Wimmer Cookbooks, *(978-0-918544; 978-0-939114; 978-1-879958)* 4650 Shelby Air Dr., Memphis, TN 38118 USA Tel 901-362-8900; 800-727-1034; Fax: 901-795-9806; Toll Free Fax: 800-794-9806; Toll Free: 800-727-1034 Do not confuse with Wimmer Cooksbooks in Atlanta, GA
E-mail: wimmer@wimmerco.com
Web site: http://www.wimmerco.com.

Windham County News Co., P.O. Box 8127, Brattleboro, VT 05304 USA (SAN 159-9917) Tel 802-254-2373.

Windhover Performing Arts Ctr., 257 Granite St., Rockport, MA 01966 USA Tel 978-546-3611
Web site: http://www.windhover.org.

Wine Appreciation Guild, Ltd., *(978-0-932664; 978-1-891267; 978-1-934259; 978-1-935879)* 360 Swift Ave., Unit 30, South San Francisco, CA 94080-6220 USA (SAN 169-0264) Tel 650-866-3020; Fax: 650-866-3513; Toll Free: 800-242-9462 (orders only)
E-mail: Jim@wineappreciation.com; bryan@wineappreciation.com
Web site: http://www.wineappreciation.com.

Winebaum News, Inc., P.O. Box 1620, Raymond, NH 03077-3620 USA (SAN 169-4529).

Wipf & Stock Pubs., *(978-0-9653517; 978-1-55635; 978-1-57910; 978-1-59244; 978-1-59752; 978-1-60608; 978-1-60899; 978-1-61097; 978-1-62032; 978-1-62189; 978-1-62564; 978-1-63087; 978-1-4982; 978-1-5326)* Orders Addr.: 199 W 8th Ave Ste 3, Eugene, OR 97401 USA (SAN 990-3038) Tel 541-344-1528; Fax: 541-344-1506; Edit Addr.: 199 W 8th Ave Ste 3, Eugene, OR 97401 USA Tel 541-344-1528; Fax: 541-344-1506
Web site: http://wipfandstock.com/; http://slantbooks.com.

WIPRO, 2 Christie Heights St., Leonia, NJ 07605 USA Tel 201-840-4755.

Wisdom Pubns., *(978-0-86171; 978-1-61429)* 199 Elm St., Somerville, MA 02144 USA (SAN 246-022X) Tel 617-776-7416 ext 24; Fax: 617-776-7841; Toll Free Fax: 800-338-4550 (orders only); Toll Free: 800-462-6420 (orders only)
E-mail: marketing@wisdompubs.org
Web site: http://www.wisdompubs.org.

Wittenborn Art Bks., *(978-0-8150; 978-0-89648)* Div. of Alan Wofsy Fine Arts, Orders Addr.: 1109 Geary Blvd., San Francisco, CA 94109 USA Tel 415-292-6500; Fax: 415-292-6594; Edit Addr.: P.O. Box 2210, San Francisco, CA 94126 USA Tel 510-482-3677; Toll Free: 800-660-6403
E-mail: art-books.com@jps.net
Web site: http://www.art-books.com.

Wizard Works, *(978-0-9621543; 978-1-890692)* Orders Addr.: P.O. Box 1125, Homer, AK 99603-1125 USA Toll Free: 877-210-2665
E-mail: wizard@xyz.net
Web site: http://www.xyz.net/~wizard.

Wolper Sales Agency, Inc., 6 Centre Sq., Suite 302A, Easton, PA 18042-3606 USA (SAN 285-9785) Tel 610-559-9550; Fax: 610-559-9898.

Wolverine Distributing, Inc., *(978-0-941875)* P.O. Box 503, Powell, WY 82435 USA (SAN 666-1211) Tel 307-754-2948; Fax: 307-754-2968; Toll Free: 800-967-1633
E-mail: wolverine@tctwest.net.

Wolverine Gallery, *See* **Wolverine Distributing, Inc.**

Women Ink, 777 United Nations Plaza, New York, NY 10017 USA (SAN 630-8309) Tel 212-687-8633; Fax: 212-661-2704
E-mail: wink@womenink.org
Web site: http://www.womenink.org.

Woodbine Publishing Co., The, 15621 Chemical Ln., No. B, Huntington Beach, CA 92649 USA (SAN 114-4243) Tel 714-894-9080; Fax: 714-894-4949; Toll Free: 800-451-4788
Web site: http://www.safaripress.com.

Woodcrafters Lumber Sales, Inc., 212 NE Sixth Ave., Portland, OR 97232 USA (SAN 112-6075) Tel 503-231-0226; Toll Free: 800-777-3709.

Woodland Distribution, Orders Addr.: 118 Woodland Dr., Chapmanville, WV 25508 USA Tel 304-752-7152; Fax: 304-752-9002.

Woodstocker Books/Arthur Schwartz & Company, *(978-1-879504)* 15 Meads Mountain Rd., Woodstock, NY 12498-1016 USA (SAN 630-0464) Tel 845-679-4024; Fax: 845-679-4093; Toll Free: 800-669-9080 (orders only)
E-mail: woodstockerbooks@woodstockerbooks.com
Web site: http://www.aschwartzbooks.com.

Word Distribution, *See* **Word Entertainment**

Word Entertainment, *(978-0-9644619; 978-1-933876)* 25 Music Sq. W., Nashville, TN 37203 USA Tel 615-726-7900; Toll Free Fax: 800-671-6601; Toll Free: 800-876-9673
E-mail: matt.taylor@wordentertainment.com
Web site: http://www.wordentertainment.com.

Word For Today, The, *See* **Calvary Chapel Resources**

Word of Life Distributors, 2707 W. Olympic Blvd. Ste. 100, Los Angeles, CA 90006-2850 USA (SAN 108-433X) Toll Free: 800-347-7057.

WordWorks Publishing, *(978-1-887913)* Orders Addr.: 207 E. Pine Ridge Dr., Westfield, IN 46074 USA Tel 317-867-1879 (phone/fax) Do not confuse with Wordworks Publishing, Austin, TX
E-mail: joanetta.hendel@comcast.net.

Workamper Bookstore, 201 Hiram Rd., Heber Springs, AR 72543-8747 USA (SAN 631-547X) Tel 501-362-2637; Toll Free: 800-446-5627 (orders only)
Web site: http://www.workamper.com.

Workman Publishing Co., Inc., *(978-0-7611; 978-0-89480; 978-0-911104; 978-1-56305; 978-1-5235)* Orders Addr.: 225 Varick St., New York, NY 10014-4381 USA (SAN 203-2821) Tel 212-254-5900; Fax: 212-254-8098; Toll Free: 800-722-7202
E-mail: info@workman.com
Web site: http://www.workman.com.

World Bank Pubns., *(978-0-8213; 978-1-4648)* Orders Addr.: P.O. Box 960, Herndon, VA 20172-0960 USA Toll Free: 800-645-7247; Edit Addr.: 1818 H St., NW, Mail Stop: U11-1104, Washington, DC 20433 USA (SAN 219-0648) Tel 703-661-1580; 202-473-1000 (Head Office); Fax: 202-614-1237
E-mail: books@worldbank.org
Web site: http://www.worldbank.org/publications.

World of Reading, Ltd., P.O. Box 13092, Atlanta, GA 30324-0092 USA Tel 404-233-4042; Fax: 404-237-5511; Toll Free: 800-729-3703.

World Publications, Incorporated, *See* **World Pubns. Group, Inc.**

World Pubns. Group, Inc., *(978-0-7669; 978-0-9640034; 978-1-57215; 978-0-7429; 978-1-4132; 978-1-4279; 978-1-4376; 978-1-4513; 978-1-4643; 978-1-4785)* Orders Addr.: P.O. Box 509, East Bridgewater, MA 02333 USA (SAN 631-7014)
E-mail: sales@wrldpub.net
Web site: http://www.wrldpub.com.

World Univ., *(978-0-941902)* P.O. Box 2470, Benson, AZ 85602 USA (SAN 239-7943) Tel 520-586-2985; Fax: 520-586-4764
E-mail: desertsanctuary@theriver.com
Web site: http://worlduniversity.org.

World Wide Distributors, Limited, *See* **Island Heritage Publishing**

World Wide Hunting Books, *See* **Woodbine Publishing Co., The**

World Wide Pubns., *(978-0-89066)* P.O. Box 668089, Charlotte, NC 28266-8089 USA (SAN 159-9941) Toll Free: 800-788-0442.

World Wisdom, Inc., *(978-0-941532; 978-1-933316; 978-1-935493; 978-1-936597; 978-1-937786)* Orders Addr.: P.O. Box 2682, Bloomington, IN 47402-2682 USA (SAN 239-1406) Tel 812-330-3232; Fax: 812-333-1642; Toll Free: 888-992-6651; Edit Addr.: 1501 E. Hillside Dr., Bloomington, IN 47401 USA
Web site: http://www.worldwisdom.com.

Worldwide Media Service, Inc., Affil. of Hudson County News Agency, 30 Montgomery St., Jersey City, NJ 07302-3821 USA (SAN 630-4826) Tel 201-332-7100; Fax: 201-332-0265; Toll Free: 800-345-6478
Web site: http://www.americanmagazine.com.

Wright Bk./Educational, 2195 Owendale Dr., Dayton, OH 45439 USA (SAN 159-9968).

Wright Group/McGraw-Hill, *(978-0-322; 978-0-7802; 978-0-940156; 978-1-55624; 978-1-55911; 978-1-4045)* Div. of Mcgraw-Hill School Education Group, Orders Addr.: P.O. Box 545, Blacklick, OH 43004-0545 USA Tel 614-755-5645; Toll Free: 800-722-4726; 800-442-9685 (customer service)
Web site: http://www.wrightgroup.com/.

Writers & Bks., *(978-0-9618487; 978-0-9863305)* 740 University Ave., Rochester, NY 14607-1259 USA (SAN 156-9678).

Wybel Marketing Group, Orders Addr.: 213 W. Main St., Barrington, IL 60010 USA Tel 847-382-0384.

Wyoming Periodical Distributor, P.O. Box 2340, Casper, WY 82601 USA (SAN 169-9245).

Xlibris Corp., *(978-0-7388; 978-0-9663501; 978-1-4010; 978-1-4134; 978-1-59926; 978-1-4257; 978-1-4363; 978-1-4415; 978-1-4500; 978-1-4535; 978-1-4568; 978-1-4628; 978-1-4653; 978-1-4691; 978-1-4771; 978-1-4797; 978-1-4836; 978-1-4931; 978-1-4990; 978-1-5035;-1-5144; 978-1-5245; 978-1-4990-9726-9; 978-1-4990-9725-2; 978-1-4990-9724-5; 978-1-5434) Orders Addr.: 1663 S. Liberty Dr. Suite 200, Bloomington, IN 47403 USA (SAN 299-5522) Tel 812-334-5223; Fax: 812-334-5223; Toll Free: 888-795-4274*
E-mail: info@xlibris.com; orders@xlibris.com; dave.weinman@xlibris.com; customersupport@xlibris.com; digitalcontent@authorsolutions.com
Web site: http://www2.xlibris.com.

Xlibris Corporation, *See* **Xlibris Corp.**

X-S Bks., Inc., 81 Brookside Ave., Amsterdam, NY 12010-0740 USA (SAN 169-4634).

Yale Univ., Far Eastern Pubns., *(978-0-88710)* 340 Edwards St., Box 208252, New Haven, CT 06520-8252 USA (SAN 219-0710) Tel 203-432-3109; Fax: 203-432-3111
Web site: http://www.yale.edu/fep.

Yale Univ. Pr., *(978-0-300)* Orders Addr.: c/o Triliteral LLC, 100 Maple Ridge Dr., Cumberland, RI 02864 USA Tel 401-531-2800; Fax: 401-531-2801; Toll Free Fax: 800-406-9145; Toll Free: 800-405-1619; Edit Addr.: 302 Temple St., New Haven, CT 06511 USA (SAN 203-2740) Tel 203-432-0960; Fax: 203-432-0948
E-mail: yupmkt@yale.edu
Web site: http://www.yale.edu/yup/; http://www.yale.edu/yup/index.html.

Yankee Bk. Peddler, Inc., 999 Maple St., Contoocook, NH 03229 USA (SAN 169-4510) Tel 603-746-3102; Fax: 603-746-5628; Toll Free: 800-258-3774
E-mail: ybp@office.ybp.com
Web site: http://www.ybp.com.

Yankee Paperback & Textbook Co., P.O. Box 18880, Tucson, AZ 85731 USA (SAN 112-1073) Tel 520-325-7229 (phone/fax); Toll Free: 800-340-2665 (in Arizona, California, Nevada, Colorado, New Mexico and Utah only).

Yankee Paperback Distributors, *See* **Yankee Paperback & Textbook Co.**

Yankee Peddler Bookshop, *(978-0-918426)* 4299 Lake Rd., Williamson, NY 14589-9615 USA (SAN 209-925X)
E-mail: byankeep@rochester.rr.com
Web site:
http://www.shoprochester.com/yankeepeddler-abc.

YBP Library Services, *See* **GOBI Library Solutionis from EBSCO**

Ye Olde Genealogie Shoppe, *(978-0-932924; 978-1-878311)* Orders Addr.: P.O. Box 39128, Indianapolis, IN 46239 USA (SAN 200-7010) Tel 317-862-3330; Toll Free: 800-419-0200 (orders)
E-mail: yogs@iquest.net
Web site: http://www.yogs.com.

Yosemite Assn., *(978-0-939666; 978-1-930238)* Orders Addr.: P.O. Box 230, El Portal, CA 95318 USA (SAN 662-197X) Tel 209-379-2648; Fax: 209-379-2486; Edit Addr.: 5020 El Portal Rd., El Portal, CA 95318 USA
E-mail: dguy@yosemite.org
Web site: http://www.yosemite.org.

Young News, Inc., 1600 E. Grand Blvd., Detroit, MI 48211-3144 USA (SAN 169-3999) Fax: 517-753-7774.

Youthlight, Inc., *(978-1-889636; 978-1-59850)* Orders Addr.: P.O. Box 115, Chapin, SC 29036 USA (SAN 256-6400) Tel 803-345-1070; Fax: 803-345-0888; Toll Free: 800-209-9774; Edit Addr.: 105 Fairway Pond Dr., Chapin, SC 29036 USA
E-mail: yl@sc.rr.com; yl@youthlightbooks.com
Web site: http://www.youthlight.com; http://www.youthlightbooks.com.

Yuma News, Incorporated, *See* **Arizona Periodicals, Inc.**

YWAM Publishing, *(978-0-927545; 978-0-9615534; 978-1-57658)* Div. of Youth With A Mission International, P.O. Box 55787, Seattle, WA 98155 USA (SAN 248-4021)
E-mail: customerservice@ywampublishing.com
Web site: http://www.ywampublishing.com.

Zabel, C. & W. Co., Orders Addr.: P.O. Box 953, East Brunswick, NJ 08816-0953 USA (SAN 169-4731) Tel 732-254-1000; Fax: 732-254-0121; Edit Addr.: 76 Pennsbury Way, E Brunswick, NJ 08816-5278 USA (SAN 241-6441).

Zagat Survey, *(978-0-943421; 978-0-9612574; 978-1-57006; 978-1-60478)* 4 Columbus Cir., New York, NY 10019 USA (SAN 289-4777) Tel 212-977-6000; Fax: 212-765-9438; Toll Free: 866-999-0991
E-mail: tradesales@justzagat.com; theinz@zagat.com
Web site: http://www.zagat.com.

Zeitlin Periodicals Co., Inc., 7917 Lark Meadow Ave., Las Vegas, NV 89131-4710 USA (SAN 160-8088).

Zondervan, *(978-0-00; 978-0-310; 978-0-937336)* Div. of HarperCollins Christian Publishing, Orders Addr.: c/o Zondervan XNET Ordering Dept., 5249 Corporate Grove, Grand Rapids, MI 49512 USA (SAN 298-9107); Edit Addr.: 5300 Patterson Ave., SE, Grand Rapids, MI 49530 USA (SAN 203-2694) Tel 616-698-6900; Fax: 616-698-3439
Web site: http://www.zondervan.com.

Zondervan Publishing House, *See* **Zondervan**

Zubal, John T. Inc., *(978-0-939738)* 2969 W. 25th St., Cleveland, OH 44113 USA (SAN 165-5841) Tel 216-241-7640; Fax: 216-241-6966.